Beringer® Vineyards, St. Helena, Napa Valley, California

CRESO

King Croesus ruled the ancient nation of Lydia more than 2500 years ago.

And yet the legend of Croesus' vast wealth lives with us today. His name still represents that which is rich, exquisite and perfect.

Now, the legend lives in Creso. A proprietary wine which rightfully takes its name from that illustrious sovereign.

Bolla's most commanding creation, Creso, has been honored with gold medals at the 1989 VinExpo at Bordeaux and the 1989 Banco d'Assaggio di Torgiano, Italy's most prestigious wine competition.

Rich in color. Exquisite in taste. Perfectly balanced. Live the legend that has been masterfully captured in Creso – the only wine worthy to bear the name of one of history's greatest kings.

THE
WINE SPECTATOR

Ultimate Guide To Buying Wine

1993 EDITION

WINE SPECTATOR PRESS
San Francisco, California

Nothing compares to the smell of real flowers.

Compromise never feels right.

The Wines From The  House of Santa Margherita

Luna Dei Feldi — Pinot Grigio — Chardonnay — Cuvée Margherita — Cabernet Sauvignon — Merlot

For your complimentary Guide to Fine Wines, call 1-800-395-5478.

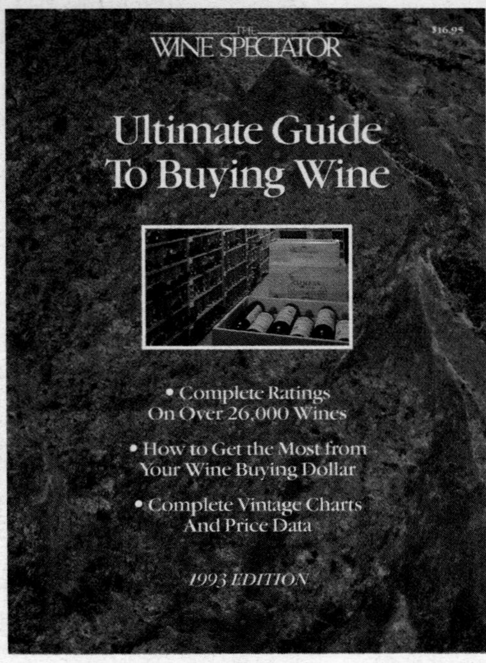

The Wine Spectator's Ultimate Guide to Buying Wine
1993 Edition

ISBN 1-881659-00-3
ISSN 1058-5729

Published by Wine Spectator Press, a division of M. Shanken Communications, Inc./West, Opera Plaza Suite 2014, 601 Van Ness Ave., San Francisco, CA 94102, (415) 673-2040, (415) 673-0103 (fax).

M. Shanken Communications, Inc. also publishes *The Wine Spectator, Impact, Impact International, Market Watch, Food Arts, Cigar Aficionado, Impact Research Reports, Leaders, Impact Yearbook, Impact International Directory, The Wine Spectator's Wine Country Guide, The Wine Spectator's Great Restaurant Wine Lists* and sponsors the *Impact* Marketing Seminars and the California and New York Wine Experiences. Headquarters offices are at 387 Park Avenue South, New York, NY 10016, (212) 684-4224, (212) 684-5424 (fax).

Manufactured in the United States

Contents

SECTION A: SPECIAL REPORT ON BUYING WINE

SECTION B: ALL WINES LISTED BY COUNTRY, TYPE, PRODUCER

SECTION C: ALL WINES LISTED ALPHABETICALLY BY PRODUCER

SECTION D: SELECTED RED WINES LISTED BY VINTAGE, SCORE, PRODUCER

SECTION E: SPECIAL RATINGS

He knew that he was behaving like a schoolboy, but no matter how hard he tried he couldn't stop looking at her. So after a while he simply gave up and stared

TATION

Imported by Seagram Chateau & Estate Wines Company, New York, N.Y. Photograph: Robert Whitman Agency: Frankfurt Gips Balkind N.Y./L.A.

Perrier-Jouët *fleur* de Champagne

FOREWORD

Welcome to the second edition of *The Wine Spectator*'s Ultimate Guide to Buying Wine.

Last year, we asked you to send us your comments regarding the first edition of this guide. You responded with many thoughtful and interesting letters. By far the majority of you told us that there were three main ways to improve the guide: 1) Include tasting notes for the wines listed; 2) Add an alphabetical listing of wine producers; 3) Expand the vintage charts to include more regions.

This new edition of the *Ultimate Guide to Buying Wine* delivers all of these improvements and more.

This 500-page volume is packed with ratings and price data on more the than 26,000 wines from the pages of *The Wine Spectator*. We have added more than 13,000 tasting notes for wines reviewed after January 1989. These tasting notes, as our readers suggested, make the guide even more useful. Every major wine-producing region is included with reviews of wines from 21 countries. More than 132 vintages are represented, ranging from 1991 back to 1771.

Wine ratings are listed in three separate indexes for easy access. The first index is by country of origin and wine type. The second index is new—the wines are listed alphabetically by producer regardless of country of origin. The third index lists selected collectible red wines by vintage and score. But wine-rating data is only part of our *Ultimate Guide to Buying Wine*. You will also find our comprehensive vintage charts (completely revised and expanded) and other useful features on buying and enjoying wine.

Our original goal in producing *The Wine Spectator's Ultimate Guide to Buying Wine* was to create a reference especially valuable to wine lovers and collectors as well as to members of the wine trade—so valuable that you would refer to it constantly. We wanted to play a helpful role in your wine decisions—to buy, sell, drink or hold. We think that this second edition brings us even closer to achieving that goal.

The efforts of the entire *Wine Spectator* team have made this book possible. Special thanks go to associate editor Liza Gross for her thorough and methodical project coordination, and to Mark Norris and Dave Budai for their various acts of computer wizardry. Thanks to Kathy McGilvery and Kim Viniconis for their design efforts, and to Donna Marianno Morris and her production staff: Kevin Mulligan, Jane Van Ginkel, Shawn Wilson, Larry Hughes and Jennifer Salazar. Thanks also to *Wine Spectator* editors Jim Gordon, Harvey Steiman, James Laube and Thomas Matthews, tasting coordinator Ray Bush, and free-lance contributors Steve Heimoff and J. Patrick Forden.

This book is, we believe, the largest and most complete collection of wine ratings and price data anywhere. We hope this guide provides you with a comprehensive reference for all of your wine needs. Again, we would like to ask for your help to make this guide the best it can be. Please take the time to write us about your observations and suggestions.

Marvin R. Shanken
Editor and Publisher

Gregory S. Walter
President

How to Use This Book

The pages that follow contain a lot of data—more than 500 pages of wine ratings, vintage charts, price analyses and useful "how to" feature articles. This book is designed as an easy-to-use reference to the wine ratings published in *The Wine Spectator*. This section will help you best apply the information contained here. Below is a detailed look at each of the five sections that make up this "ultimate guide."

SECTION A: A SPECIAL REPORT ON BUYING WINE—This section begins with "The Tasters," a personal look at the senior editors who taste the wines, their credentials and qualifications, plus background on the tasting program at *The Wine Spectator*. Several other useful features on buying and enjoying wines follow.

SECTION B: ALL WINES LISTED BY COUNTRY, TYPE AND PRODUCER—This section, beginning on page B-1, contains wine ratings and tasting notes organized in alphabetical order by country, type and producer.

SECTION C: ALL WINES LISTED BY PRODUCER—This section, beginning on page C-1, contains wine ratings organized in alphabetical order by producer. Use this section to find a wine when you are not sure of its region, or if you want a quick snapshot of a producer's full range of wines.

SECTION D: SELECTED RED WINES LISTED BY VINTAGE, SCORE AND PRODUCER—This section, beginning on page D-1, contains wine ratings organized by vintage and score. The wines selected for this section are the more collectible red wines available. Use these listings to compare wines from a particular vintage.

SECTION E:* THE WINE SPECTATOR'S *SPECIAL RATINGS—This section, beginning on page E-1, lists wines earning ratings of "Spectator Selection," "Cellar Selection" or "Best Buy."

THE WINE RATINGS

The wine ratings contained in this guide are taken from the tasting results that have been published in *The Wine Spectator* over the past decade. Therefore, while the majority of the ratings in this book are quite recent, some ratings are not as current.

While we feel that these older ratings can be very useful in presenting, in many cases, a nearly complete vertical representation of a particular wine, we also feel the need to caution you to pay particular attention to the date on each of the ratings. This will tell you how current the rating is.

You may also find, in some cases, two ratings for the same vintage of the same wine. This occurs when, in addition to a recent rating of a particular wine, we have included an earlier rating where that wine has earned one of our "Special Ratings." In this case, you will see the most recent rating followed on the next line by the earlier rating with one of the following special-ratings designations: "SS," "CS" or "BB."

In general, ratings and tasting notes included here are from *The Wine Spectator*'s tasting panel. Other sources for the ratings are: individual tasting reports by our senior editors or tastings conducted by a senior editor as part of the research for one of our Wine Spectator Press books currently on the market.

There is one other type of rating you will see in this book, primarily in the sections for red Bordeaux, red Burgundy and California Cabernet. These are ratings based on barrel tastings. Barrel tastings are tastings conducted on wines before they are bottled and released for sale. These are, by definition, very preliminary ratings and should be treated as such. Many things can happen to a wine between the time it is tasted in barrel and the time that you purchase it at your local store. Wines can improve or decline during that period, and can even show signs of poor shipping or storage conditions. We have included these barrel tasting results because we feel it gives you a better picture of our complete evolutionary experience with a particular wine. We have used the initials "BT" in parentheses to indicate a barrel-tasting review. In addition, these wines will have a plus (+) next to the score to indicate a preliminary range.

THE RATINGS: PIECE BY PIECE

Because of the very large number of ratings presented here, each wine listing must be as brief as possible. Therefore, we have used abbreviations and shortcuts throughout this book. For your convenience, we have included a key to these abbreviations called ''Key to Symbols'' in the lower left-hand corner of every other page in sections B through D. Below are two typical wine listings, and explanations for each of the key pieces.

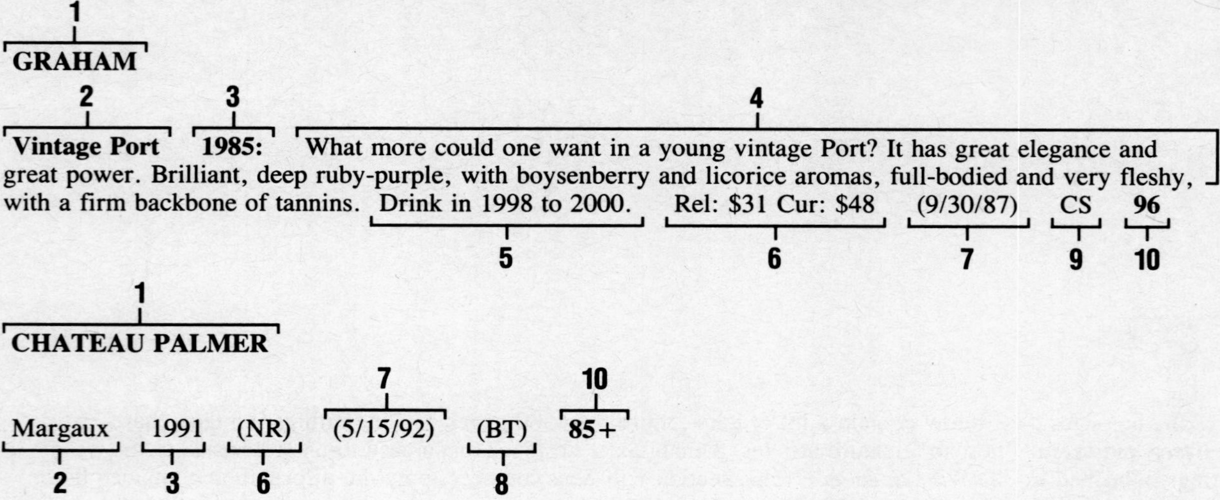

1. PRODUCER'S NAME—This is the name of the winery or producer. It is in all capital letters to set it off from the rest of the wine's information.

2. WINE TYPE/DESCRIPTION—This contains the wine type and any varietal name, appellation, or other vineyard or special designation, such as Sonoma Valley or Martha's Vineyard or Cask 23.

3. VINTAGE—This is the year the wine was harvested and vinified.

4. TASTING NOTE—This is the tasting note for the wine as published. These notes give a more complete picture of the wine than the score alone.

5. DRINKABILITY—In those ratings where we have included a tasting note, we have also included our estimate as to when a wine will be at its best.

6. PRICE DATA—This is the wine's price information and can come in four distinct forms: (NR) means that at the time of the tasting, the wine had not been released and no official price had been set. ($NA) means that no price data was available, and occurs typically with older wines. A single price, such as $37, signifies that the only price available was the suggested retail price on release. Two prices, Rel: $31 Cur: $47, show the price on release, and the current market price for the wine. A word on the current market prices in this book. *The Wine Spectator* maintains a price-tracking department to track wine prices from many sources, including auctions, retailer advertisements and catalogs and wholesale price books. The current market prices represent a weighted average of all price sources, and as such are our ''best educated guess.'' Prices may—and will—vary.

7. DATE TASTED—This date represents the tasting date as well as the issue of *The Wine Spectator* in which the rating was first published. For ratings included from one of the three Wine Spectator Press books, the following format is used: (CA-date) for *California's Great Cabernets* by James Laube, (CH-date) for *California's Great Chardonnays* by James Laube, and (VP-date) for *Vintage Port* by James Suckling.

8. TASTER'S INITIALS—Unless noted with one of the initials here, all wine ratings in this book are the results of blind tastings conducted by *The Wine Spectator* tasting panel. The initials used are: (JG) for Jim Gordon, (HS) for Harvey Steiman, (JL) for James Laube, (JS) for James Suckling, (TM) for Thomas Matthews, (PM) for Per-Henrik Mansson, (TR) for Terry Robards, and (BT) indicating a barrel tasting.

9. SPECIAL RATINGS—These are used to indicate special ratings given by the tasting panel. For a separate listing of all of these special ratings, see Section E. The special designations used here are: SS for Spectator Selection, CS for Cellar Selection and BB for Best Buy.

10. SCORE—This is the number, from *The Wine Spectator*'s 100-point scale, that represents the taster's evaluation of the wine's quality. A plus (+) next to the wine's score indicates a preliminary rating. If the plus is used in conjunction with (BT) then the rating is from a barrel tasting.

Impeccable Burgundies

Since 1859

The Tasters

The wine ratings and other data contained in this book are the result of hundreds of tastings by the senior editors of *The Wine Spectator*. There are two types of tastings used to review wines for the magazine and for this book. First are the regular, twice-weekly blind tastings of new-release wines by *The Wine Spectator*'s tasting panel. Second are the special tastings conducted by our senior editors of a particular type or vintage of wine, frequently conducted on location around the world.

HOW WE TASTE WINE

Wines selected for review in *The Wine Spectator* (and for inclusion in this book) are tasted blind. The tastings are arranged by our tasting coordinator and his staff, who bag and code the wine bottles. Neither the tasting coordinator nor his staff participate in any official tastings. All capsules and corks are removed from the bottles prior to tasting, and corks are substituted to ensure that the wines remain anonymous. Tasters are told only the general type of wine (varietal or region) and the vintage. Price is not taken into account in scoring. Wines are sampled one at a time, but tasters will often compare several close-scoring wines of a similar type before removing the bags.

Wines are chosen for tasting from those sent to our office for review and from wines purchased at retail. Since *The Wine Spectator* serves a national audience, we prefer to review wines that are widely available, which are of wider interest to our readers.

Wines scoring below 60 are automatically retasted. We also retaste wines that score lower than their reputations or our tasting experience suggests. The higher score prevails. All retastings are conducted blind, under the same conditions as our normal tastings.

ABOUT OUR WINE RATINGS

Tasters for *The Wine Spectator* score wines using our 100-point scale. Ratings reflect how highly our tasting panel regards each wine relative to other wines.

Ratings are based on immediate quality, as well as on how good the wines will be when they are at their peaks, regardless of how soon that will be.

THE WINE SPECTATOR *100-POINT SCALE*

95-100 — Classic, a great wine.
90-94 — Outstanding, superior character and style.
80-89 — Good to very good, a wine with special qualities.
70-79 — Average, drinkable wine that may have minor flaws.
60-69 — Below average, drinkable but not recommended.
50-59 — Poor, undrinkable, not recommended.

"+"—With a score indicates a range, and is used primarily to indicate a preliminary score.

Unless otherwise indicated, the wine ratings in this book are from our tasting panel. Reviews from individual tasters are signed with their initials. A key to these initials, and other abbreviations used in the book appears on every other page in the listings section.

A brief look at the backgrounds and credentials of our senior tasters begins on the next page.

The Wine Spectator

Marvin R. Shanken

Editor and Publisher

Marvin Shanken, 48, has been involved in beverage-industry publishing for nearly 20 years, but his involvement in wine goes back much further.

In the early 1970s, while he was a partner in a Wall Street investment firm, Shanken bought *Impact*, then a little-known beverage-industry newsletter. In 1975, he left Wall Street to enter the world of publishing and run *Impact* full-time. His interest in wine led him to purchase *The Wine Spectator* in 1979. Today, *The Wine Spectator* is the largest and most influential wine publication in the world. Shanken continues to shape the editorial direction of *The Wine Spectator* through his work with the magazine's editors and also writes his column "From the Editor" in each issue.

In addition to his editorial duties, Shanken is chairman of M. Shanken Communications Inc., publisher of *Impact, Impact International, Market Watch, Food Arts* and his newest magazine, *Cigar Aficionado*, and event chairman of the New York and California Wine Experiences.

Shanken earned a bachelor's degree in business and finance from the University of Miami, and an M.B.A. in real estate and finance from American University in Washington, D.C.

He lives with his wife, Hazel, and his daughter, Jessica, in New York. He has two daughters, Samantha and Allison, from a previous marriage.

Jim Gordon

Managing Editor

Jim Gordon, 39, is a career journalist with 17 years of experience writing and editing for newspapers and magazines. He joined *The Wine Spectator* in 1984 as associate editor, later became news editor and was named managing editor in 1987.

Gordon manages a staff of editors, writers and photographers from the editorial offices in San Francisco. His writing and wine-tasting assignments have included reports from Bordeaux, Burgundy, the Rhône Valley, Italy, California and Germany. He has been a member of *The Wine Spectator*'s tasting panel since 1984.

Before joining *The Wine Spectator*, Gordon was managing editor of the *St. Helena Star* newspaper for five years in Napa Valley. He began his professional journalism career in 1977 as a reporter and photographer with the *Madison Press* (London, Ohio). Gordon earned a bachelor's degree in English from Denison University in Ohio.

He, his wife, Catherine, and their son, Lucas, live in Novato, Calif.

Harvey Steiman

Editor at Large

Harvey Steiman, 45, has been with *The Wine Spectator* since 1984, first as managing editor and later as executive editor. His columns, features and extensive tasting reports have covered the wines from many diverse regions, including California, France, Italy and the Pacific Northwest. Steiman also creates a regular monthly menu matching food and wine. He has been a member of the tasting panel since 1984.

Steiman is also the host of "In the Kitchen With Harvey" on radio station KNBR in San Francisco. He was host of a similar program on KCBS in San Francisco from 1982 to 1990. A book of recipes from that program, *Harvey Steiman's California Kitchen,* was published in 1990 by Chronicle Books. He is the author of two previous cookbooks, *Great Recipes From San Francisco,* (Tarcher 1979) and, with chef Ken Hom, *Chinese Technique,* (Simon and Schuster 1980).

A music major at the University of California at Los Angeles, he began a career in journalism in 1968 as the sports editor of the *Inglewood Daily News* (in California). He joined *The Miami Herald* in 1969, and in 1973 became its food editor. In 1977, he was named food-and-wine editor of the *San Francisco Examiner*.

He lives in San Francisco with his wife, Carol, and his daughter, Katherine.

James Laube

Senior Editor

James Laube, 41, has spent the last decade traveling, tasting and writing about the wines of the world.

Laube began writing for *The Wine Spectator* in 1980. In 1983, he joined the staff full-time as its first senior editor. He has written regularly on assignment about the wines of Bordeaux, Burgundy, the Loire, the Rhône Valley, Germany, Italy, Spain, Australia, Oregon, Washington, Long Island and California.

In 1989, Laube finished his first book, *California's Great Cabernets* (Wine Spectator Press), which was an immediate success. His second book, *California's Great Chardonnays* (Wine Spectator Press), followed one year later. Prior to joining *The Wine Spectator*, Laube was the Napa bureau chief of the *Vallejo Times-Herald* (in California) for four years, and earlier worked at the *Anaheim Bulletin* (in California) and the Colorado Springs *Gazette-Telegraph*. He earned a bachelor's and master's degree in history from San Diego State University.

He lives with his wife, Cheryl, and their two children, Dwight and Margaux, in Napa, Calif.

Tasting Panel

James Suckling

Senior Editor/European Bureau Chief

James Suckling, 33, joined *The Wine Spectator* in 1981 after spending three years as a reporter for daily newspapers in Madison, Wis., and Washington, D.C. He attended Utah State University, earning a bachelor's degree in journalism and political science and finished course work for a master's degree at the University of Wisconsin-Madison School of Journalism.

In 1984, Suckling was transferred to Paris to cover the European wine scene. In 1986, he was promoted to European bureau chief in London, where he now lives in Greenwich with his wife, Catherine.

In 1990, Suckling finished his first book, *Vintage Port* (Wine Spectator Press), which has been well received on both sides of the Atlantic.

Per-Henrik Mansson

Senior Editor

Per-Henrik Mansson, 41, was born in Sweden and grew up in French-speaking Switzerland near vineyards that overlook Lake Geneva.

In 1987, Mansson joined *The Wine Spectator* as news editor in San Francisco. He was promoted to senior editor and transferred to the London bureau to report on the European wine scene in 1989. In 1991, he moved to Geneva, Switzerland to be more centrally located in Europe.

Mansson attended college in Sweden, where he earned a bachelor's degree in economics. He came to the United States in 1974 and earned a master's degree in international relations at Johns Hopkins University's School of Advanced International Studies in Washington, D.C. Mansson was admitted to the Columbia University School of Journalism in New York where he earned a master's degree in 1978. He moved to Northern California where he worked as a journalist for the San Francisco *Examiner, Wall Street Journal Europe* and other publications.

Mansson lives outside Geneva with his wife, Lynda, and sons, Nicholas and Matthew.

Thomas Matthews

Senior Editor/New York Bureau Chief

Thomas Matthews, 39, began writing for *The Wine Spectator* in 1987, while living in a village in the vineyards near Bordeaux. In 1988, he joined the magazine's staff as a reporter in the London bureau, moving back to the United States in 1989 to become *The Wine Spectator*'s New York bureau chief.

Matthews got his start in the wine business in 1979 picking grapes in Bordeaux and Cognac. From 1982 to 1986, he worked in New York City as the wine buyer for Odeon Restaurant and Café Luxembourg. He has a bachelor's degree in literature and philosophy from Bennington College in Vermont and a master's degree in political science from Yale University in Connecticut.

Matthews lives in New York with his wife, Sara.

Ray Bush

Tasting Coordinator

Ray Bush, 38, has been *The Wine Spectator*'s tasting coordinator since 1985. He is responsible for all the behind-the-scenes duties and research to compile each issue's Buying Guide plus the many special tastings.

Prior to joining *The Wine Spectator*, Bush worked in retail wine sales in San Francisco from 1983 to 1986, and was the cellar master for the 1984, 1985 and 1986 San Francisco Fair and Exposition Wine Competitions.

Bush has been a member of the following tasting panels: the San Francisco *Examiner*'s 1983 "California Living" panel, the 1986 University of San Francisco Alumni Association, the 1986 Foothill Counties Wine Show (Calaveras County) and the San Francisco Symphony (1986 to 1991). He also came in third in the First Annual California Wine Tasting Olympics in 1983.

In 1978, Bush earned a bachelor's degree from Georgia State University. Bush was born in East Point, Ga., and lives in San Francisco.

Wine-Buying Strategies

REGARDLESS OF YOUR LEVEL OF INTEREST IN WINE, YOU'RE IN FOR FUN AND CHALLENGES

BY JAMES LAUBE

10 Tips to Better Wine Buying

1. Always taste before you buy. Don't get trapped buying what your friends or critics call the best. Trust your own palate. Taste a bottle before you buy six bottles or a case.
2. Diversify your collection. You may have passions for one kind of wine or another, but variety is the spice of life with wine, so shop around for different styles of wines.
3. Shop for values. Go out of your way to look for best buys to get the most mileage out of your wine dollar.
4. Drink your wines before they get too old. Even the most age-worthy reds from Bordeaux or California reach drinkability in 10 years. You've paid good money for your wines; don't let them slide over the hill.
5. Keep costs in perspective. A few fine wines are expensive, but far too many well-made, reasonably prices wines are ignored because they lack the image and prestige of higher-priced wines.
6. Buy wine by the case. Most retailers give you a 10 percent discount—or one bottle free.
7. Beware of last year's superstar. Last year's hero could be this year's goat.
8. Stockpile wines you like so that you don't run out or hesitate to open the last bottle.
9. Investing in futures can be risky business.
10. Assemble your wines with rhyme and reason. Think about your needs before parting with your cash.

RULE NO. 1 OF BUYING WINE IS TO TRUST YOUR OWN TASTE

If you're new to wine, you're in for an adventure. Devising a buying strategy can be as simple as choosing a few brands you like and sticking with them, or it can be as complex as collecting verticals of the world's greatest wines or buying wine futures.

For many wine drinkers, maintaining brand loyalty is a tried-and-true way to keep your cellar stocked with reliable wines that suit your taste and budget. More daring collectors expand their hobby of wine collecting into a more sophisticated enterprise. They keep tabs on new wines and vintages from old-guard producers in Bordeaux, Burgundy, Italy, Spain or Germany, and a watchful eye on up-and-coming producers from the New World, such as California, Oregon, Washington, Australia, New Zealand and Chile.

Regardless of your level of interest in wine, you're in for some fun and challenges. Wine is a living thing and is constantly changing. Every year you'll be presented with a seemingly endless stream of new wines, producers, appellations and vintages. Even when you find a winery or style of wine that appeals to you, your tastes will likely change over time, and you'll discover new things that appeal to your taste. The combination of possibilities is endless:

Rule No. 1 of buying wine is to trust your own taste. No one knows your taste preferences better than you, so it's important to be comfortable deciding which wines appeal to you and which don't. The best advice is to taste a wine by buying a single bottle before you commit to several bottles or a case. The importance of this rule is further magnified for expensive wines. It makes no sense to pay $20, $30 or $40 for a wine you've never tried and might not like. You'll be far happier with your buying decisions if you taste a wine and decide you like it before committing to more bottles. There's a big wine world to choose from, with literally thousands of different wines. Even if your friends or wine critics rave about a wine, there's no guarantee that you'll like it.

Gaining experience with the world's fine wines takes time, but it is a fascinating journey. You're likely to learn as much from your buying mistakes as you will from your triumphs. Part of the fun of wine is learning where and how it's grown and vinified, which food types match well with different wines, and which wine types and vintages improve with cellaring and bottle age.

Before you start buying wine, it's a good idea to assess your needs. How much wine do you drink and on what occasions? Do you want to cellar young wines for drinking in a few years? You may also decide to budget money for your wine hobby so you can determine how much you can realistically afford to spend on wine. For some people it's easy to identify their wine needs. For others it's wiser to plan a strategy before heading to the wine shop. Remember, it's easier to buy a case of wine than it is to drink it.

It's also easy to buy more wine than you realistically need. Buying wine on a whim can be fun, particularly when you spot a special bottle you've been looking for. But fanciful buying also increases the odds that you'll return home with a wine you may not need for which you may have paid too much. Planning ahead allows you to set aside a specific amount of money for buying wine by the case. Many retailers and wineries offer a 10 percent discount for case purchases. Discount stores, however, usually pass along the 10 percent discount on all purchases.

Once you've outlined your needs, you'll need a place to shop. Years ago, about the only source to buy fine wine was the traditional fine-wine merchant. Today your options abound. You see fine wine in scores of discount chain stores and upscale supermarkets, some of which present a dazzling selection. Retailers have also become more aggressive with sales promotions, selling wine through ads in newspapers and magazines via telephone and toll-free "800" numbers. A growing list of retailers publish catalogs, especially during the holiday season, offering hundreds of wines and special gift packages. There are even wine-of-the-month clubs. Once you join, the club selects wines for you and ships them to your home for you to sample. Most of the time, though, you'll be purchasing wine at a retail store, so it helps to get to know your local wine stores and merchants, including what kinds of wines they stock and their pricing strategies.

A well-informed retailer is an excellent source of sound buying advice and tips about what's new and interesting in his store. Retailers can also help find special wines that may be hard to find. Some retail stores even do the shopping for their customers. When a special wine comes in, they set aside a few bottles or a case and bill the customer, holding the wine until it's picked up.

While you're visiting wine shops, take special notice of how the wines are stored and if the temperature is cool. Light and heat are enemies of wine. Wine shops that are warm or hot in summer months may not be the best place to buy your wines. It's also wise to examine wine bottles to make sure the fill level is good—up to the neck of the bottle—and that wine hasn't leaked through the cork. If wine leaks out, that means air is getting into the bottle and oxidizing the wine. Avoid bottles with low fills or leaks.

As wine gets costlier, it makes greater sense to develop a buying strategy. One fun way to defray costs and taste a broad selection of wines is to join a club or group that tastes wines regularly. This way you can spread out some of the costs and taste expensive wines such as Château Lafite-Rothschild, Romanée-Conti, Gaja or Château d'Yquem. Each member brings a bottle of wine to the tasting and shares it among six, eight or 12 people. Some wine syndicates even order cases of wines together, which is another way to cut costs (with a 10 percent discount) and broaden your exposure to the world of fine wines.

For those who like to take risks, buying wine futures, where you pay a discounted price in advance of a wine's delivery, is one way to obtain hard-to-get wines, presumably at reduced prices. Buying futures works this way. Young, unbottled wines are sold at discounted prices through retailers or wineries. Once the wine is bottled and ready for sale, it is delivered to the consumer. Most of the time, consumers pay less for futures and futures can be a good way to obtain hard-to-get wines or larger bottles.

Others buy wine futures for speculation purposes. They hope that the price they pay for futures is sufficiently lower than the price will be when the wine is released. If that's true, they can resell the wine at a profit. But there are risks in buying futures. The major danger is that you're buying a wine you haven't tried. Unless you're intimately familiar with the producer, vintage or style of wine, you're gambling. You could also pay more for a wine than is necessary. If the economy sours, the price on release may be far less than anticipated, reducing the savings you hoped to achieve. Finally, in buying futures you may tie up your money with one or two producers and miss out on some of the other bargains once that vintage is released. There's also the possibility that your retailer may go out of business before the wine is released, making your wine and your money difficult to recover.

When you're on the road touring wine country, you'll also discover that many wineries have specialty wines or older vintages no longer on the market that they sell only at the winery. Be on the lookout for some of those rarities, but don't necessarily expect to find great bargains. Most wineries give a 10 percent discount on sales, but they mark their wines up to full retail price. You can often find them less expensive at your local retail outlet. □

WHAT'S IN THAT BOTTLE?

Ever since the Benzigers started messing around with time-honored methods and stuffy tradition, a lot of people have learned to stop asking silly questions and start enjoying wine again.

We're talking significant enjoyment.

But some of you out there still need to know *why* the Benzigers use four different trellis systems instead of the conventional one, and why they ferment their Chardonnay five degrees cooler and for several days longer than everyone else does.

Because they crush to a different drummer. They rack to a different pinion. It's just something that runs in the family.

Our advice is to ignore the Benzigers altogether, and do what this man is doing. Reaching for another glass of Benziger.

BENZIGER
A TASTE OF UNCONVENTIONAL WISDOM.

The Ups and Downs of Buying Wine at Auction

DESPITE COMPLICATED BIDDING PROCEDURES, AUCTION NEWCOMERS ENJOY THE THRILL OF THE CHASE

BY THOMAS MATTHEWS

In 1992, wine auctions continued to grow in popularity and volume, despite an overall decline in total wine sales in America, because auction buyers can find wines that are ready to drink at prices that are easy to swallow.

Sterling Vineyards Merlot 1979 for $9 a bottle. Léoville-Barton 1979 for $18. Léoville-Poyferré 1970 for $25. These may look like prices from some dusty archive, but they are all recent auction figures. While rare, old bottles may sell for thousands of dollars, most auctions concentrate on mature wines from reputable producers—the wines most wine lovers want to drink.

In 1991, the total U.S. wine market declined 2.6 percent—according to *Impact*, a drinks-industry newsletter—the seventh straight year of falling sales. Yet in the same period, wine auctions grew rapidly as commercial houses scheduled more sales and charity auctions mushroomed across the country. One primary reason is that, unlike the sticker shock consumers experience with many new releases, prices for many wines have actually fallen in auction sales since 1989.

Buying wine at auction is unfamiliar and complicated for many wine consumers, compared with shopping in a retail store. Prices can vary widely. It only takes two determined bidders to drive a wine far beyond its nominal worth. Yet auctions are the archetype of the free market: no one is forced to pay more than he thinks an object is worth. Besides offering scarce wines at fair prices, auctions provide another benefit—the thrill of the chase. That's why, according to the auctioneers, new bidders are constantly raising paddles at American wine auctions.

Wine auctions have a short track record in America. Regularly scheduled live auctions by established auction houses date back only to the mid-1980s. Only two states, California and Illinois, make it legal and practical to hold commercial wine auctions. Currently there are two main players in the United States: Christie's, which offers six wine auctions per year in Chicago and Los Angeles, and Butterfield & Butterfield, which holds six main sales per year in San Francisco. Together, they add up to more than 10,000 lots annually. It's

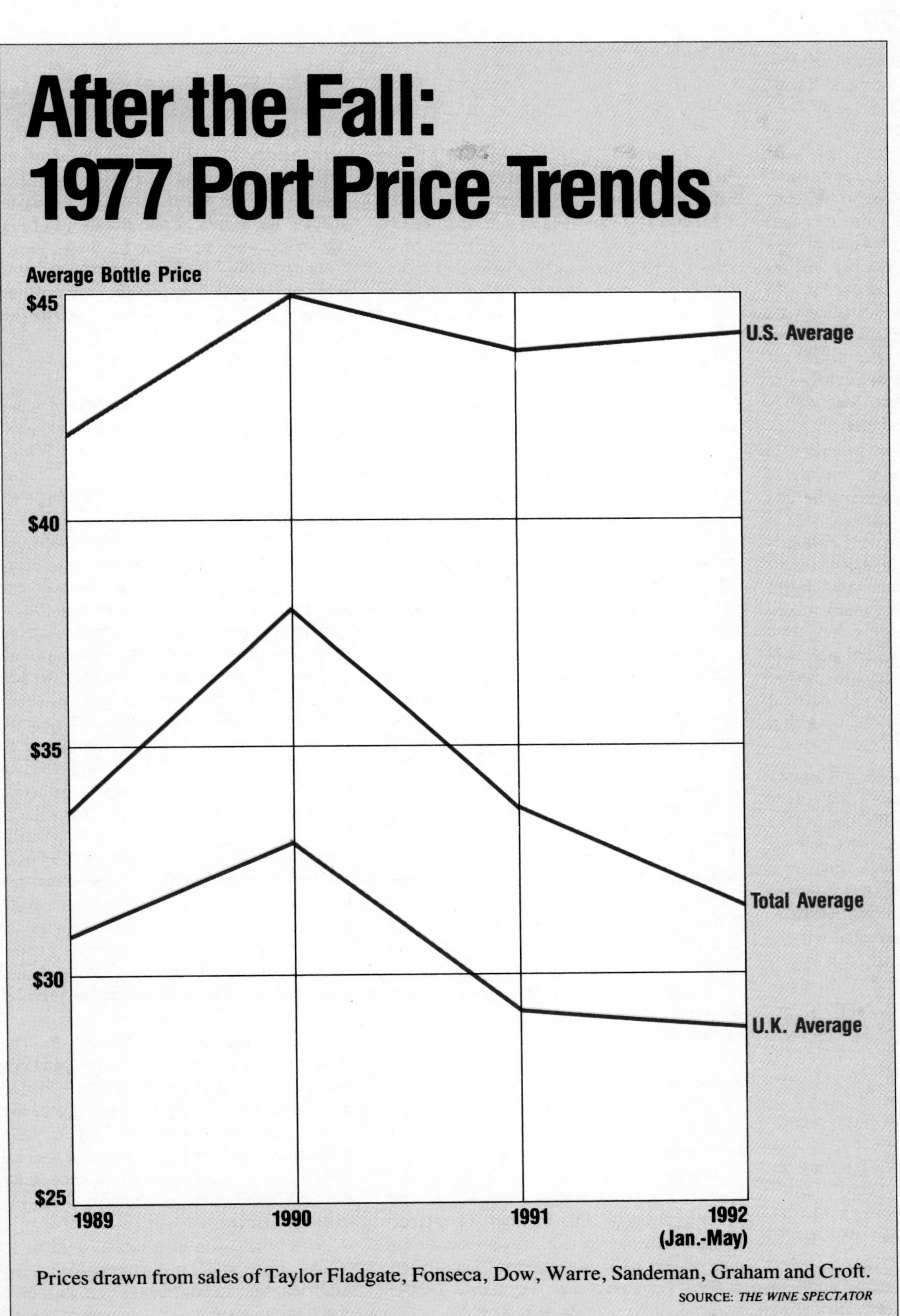

Prices drawn from sales of Taylor Fladgate, Fonseca, Dow, Warre, Sandeman, Graham and Croft.

SOURCE: *THE WINE SPECTATOR*

enough to turn growing numbers of wine lovers into auction bidders.

Wine Auction Houses and How They Work

London has always been the center of the wine-auction market, and Christie's has long been its headquarters. James Christie included wine in his first auction in 1766, and it remained an important element in English sales through the 19th century. After a pause due to the World Wars, Christie's revived wine auctions in 1966 with a separate wine department headed by J. Michael Broadbent, who remains firmly in charge.

Christie's holds a variety of regularly scheduled wine auctions in London. The most important venue is King Street, where twice-monthly sales serve as the stock market of wine, establishing what amounts to commodity prices for the most widely traded wines. Many wine merchants buy and sell there, reducing the changes of getting a great bargain to slim. The traditional auction season runs from September through July. In 1991-1992, King Street sold almost 12,500 lots, each an average of about 15 bottles, for a total of nearly $8 million.

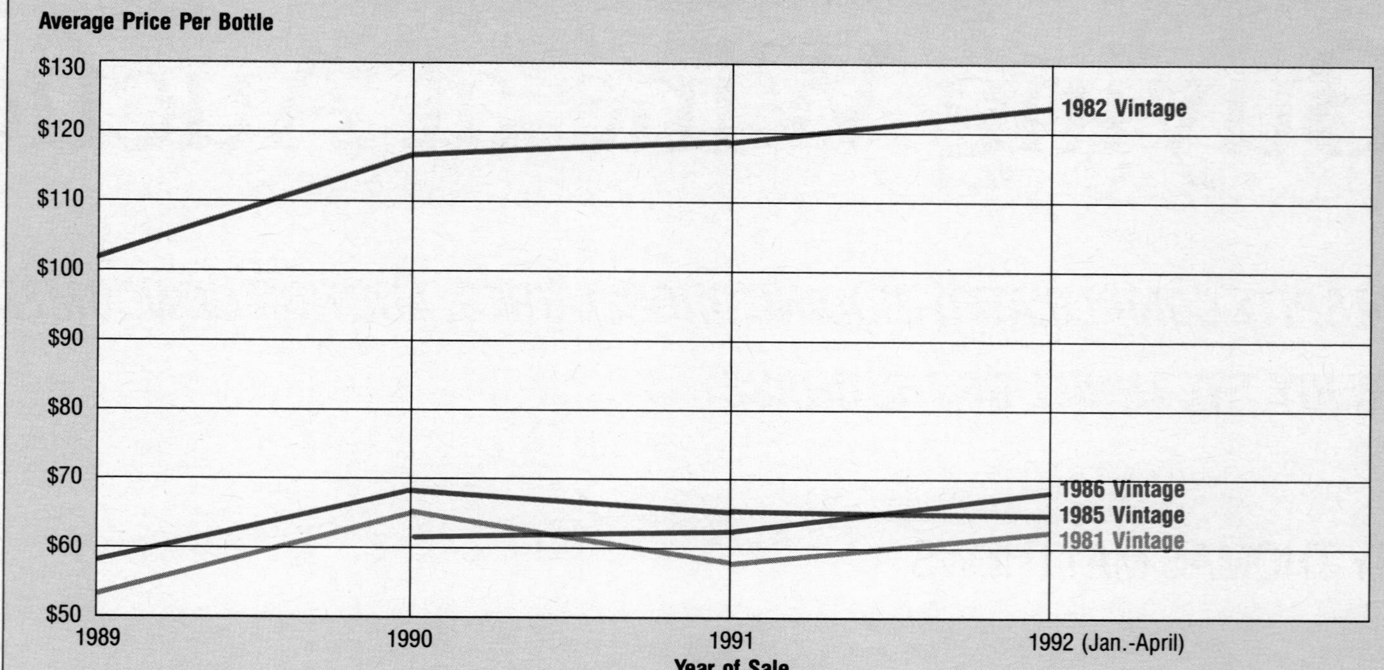

Christie's covers both the high and low end of the market. Their Finest and Rarest sales may include such rarities as the 1787 Lafite-Rothschild which may have once belonged to Thomas Jefferson. It sold for $156,450 in 1985—a world record for a single bottle. Regular sales in South Kensington, London, cater to a more casual crowd and feature smaller lots of everyday wines. This more accessible market continues to grow, and, according to Christie's, seems to be an indication that the consumer base for wine auctions is increasing steadily. In addition, sales of wines from celebrity cellars, such as the recent disposal of Robert Maxwell's wines, draw many new bidders.

Christie's main U.K. competitor is Sotheby's wine department, which is supervised by author and merchant Serena Sutcliffe. Sutcliffe joined Sotheby's late in 1990 after the wine department had suffered a period of turmoil and lack of direction. She has oriented the sales more toward consumers by offering many mixed and small lots and by adding her own tasting notes to many wines. The policy is working; sales volume for the period January-April, 1992, was up 58 percent over 1991, according to Sutcliffe, with a high proportion of new buyers.

There are other, smaller auction houses based in the United Kingdom that offer periodic wine sales, such as Phillips in Oxford, England. Wine auctions are also held in many European countries; Christie's organizes regular sales in Geneva, Switzerland, and Amsterdam, Netherlands.

Prices for certain categories of wines, such as vintage Port, generally run lower in European markets than in U.S. auctions. But the logistics and expenses of transporting wine overseas are daunting. Shipping adds $50 or more to each case of wine, and there is much obligatory and confusing paperwork. When the dollar is exceptionally strong against foreign currencies, however, Americans may find it worthwhile to bid abroad. If so, it may be advisable to store the wine where it is purchased until it is either resold or can be consolidated into larger, less expensive shipments.

For the most part, however, and especially for beginners, U.S. sales probably offer the best introduction to wine auctions.

Christie's U.S. wine operation is based in Chicago and run by Michael Davis. Its six sales a year generally alternate between Chicago and Los Angeles. The sales are large, often running over 1,200 lots. Most of the stock comes from private collectors, though retailers and restaurateurs are other sources. Most of the buyers are consumers, according to Davis. In the 1991-1992 season, Christie's Chicago sold 5,400 lots for nearly $4 million.

Butterfield & Butterfield, a smaller auction house based in San Francisco, offers six to seven wine auctions a year. Bruce Kaiser is director of the wine department, which had its best year in 1991-1992, with sales around $2.5 million. Butterfield's also holds regular auctions of more affordable wines at its Butterfield's West location. The sales are held in San Francisco, with major auctions simulcast in Los Angeles.

Few other options are open to Americans who want to buy or sell wine at auction. The Chicago Wine Co., which specializes in silent auctions and also operates as a retail outlet, holds several live auctions a year. Since 1990, it has staged occasional live commercial auctions in Boston, which may lead to other such sales in Massachusetts.

The procedures for buying or selling wine at auction are simple in concept but more complicated in detail. The auction houses themselves are the best sources of information for interested wine buffs, but here is an outline of the process.

Collectors who want to sell will generally contact the auction houses directly, usually with a list of the wines they want to auction. If the auction house is interested, a more formal inventory and appraisal will be made. The auction house may assist with packing and transportation, but most costs are generally borne by the vendor. A reserve price is set, below which the auction house will not sell the wines, and a description with an estimate is entered in the catalog. The seller agrees to pay the auction house a commission, usually 15 percent but sometimes negotiable, on the hammer price of any wines sold.

Catalogs are sent worldwide to collectors and trade members. Several hundred people may actually attend the auction, while others will bid over the telephone or send in bids by mail. Absentee buyers specify lot numbers and maximum bids, which the auctioneers bid for them, promising not to bid higher than necessary to win the lot or to drop out if the maximum is reached. Successful bidders agree to pay a buyer's premium, usually 10 percent of the hammer price, to the auction house as a commission.

The wines are then collected or shipped to the purchaser. Buyers who live close enough to the auction houses to pick up their own wines have few problems. Those who require shipping will find the logistics more difficult.

The laws regulating the sale and transport of alcoholic beverages are complicated, and, while auction houses can help make arrangements for transportation and legal paperwork, the buyer is responsible for final legal clearance and all charges. Charges range from $25 to $50 or more per case, depending on distance and the method and speed of shipment. About half the buyers at any given U.S. auction are from out-of-state, and many of those are from out of the country, so while barriers exist, they can be overcome.

Charity wine auctions are increasing even more rapidly than commercial auctions. More and more organizations are turning to wine auctions, often accompanied by tastings and gala dinners, to raise money for such causes as cancer research, special schools and cultural organizations. Some have become premier social events in their communities and raise hundreds of thousands of dollars. Others are more low-key. Charity auctions permit donors and buyers to take limited tax deductions related to the value of the wines. Prices are generally higher than normal market value, but some special bottles, such as large-format, specially etched limited editions, are only available in such settings.

The wine-auction scene is relatively young and still underdeveloped in America, but, in contrast to many aspects of the wine market, it continues to grow. *The Wine Spectator* provides full coverage of this dynamic area in its Auction News section, which includes regular reports of both commercial and charity auctions, in-depth market analyses and a full calendar of events. Wine auctions can't satisfy all the needs of most wine buffs, but they offer an alternative market that can supply fine wines at reasonable prices and spice the purchase with the thrill of the chase.

Buying and Selling at Auction

Auctions are poor sources for many wines, but excellent places to buy some of the wines connoisseurs want most.

Variety is not an auction strong suit. The only white wines regularly offered at auction are top Burgundies, vintage Champagnes, dessert wines and California Chardonnays. Red wines from entire countries, such as Australia and Spain, rarely appear at auction. Country wines, "fighting varietals," and wines made for early drinking are also uncommon in most auction catalogs.

Auctions concentrate on the wines that make up the heart of most wine cellars: Bordeaux, vintage Port, red Burgundy and California Cabernet Sauvignon. These wines make up 80 percent to 90 percent of an average sale. The rest will be red Rhônes, other red California varietals, old Madeira and an occasional surprise such as vintage Tokay.

But within these few red- and white-wine categories, there is plenty of variety and depth. A recent sale offered 22 vintages of Lafite, from 1874 to 1982. Another included 35 different Bordeaux from the outstanding 1970 vintage, which is now rare in retail stores. Prices for Robert Mondavi's Cabernet Sauvignon Reserve tend to drop from retail release to auction sales, so collectors with patience can save significantly; a sale in June, 1992,

Rare wines bring high prices and wide publicity. The 1874 Lafite sold for $1,265, almost double the $638 that another bottle from the vintage fetched earlier in the year. The Lafite probably made a tidy profit for the vendor and filled a difficult hole for some collector.

Most prices, however, are more accessible. The average lot at Butterfield & Butterfield sells for around $350 for about 10 bottles, or roughly $35 per bottle. Many wines sell for less. Sterling Cabernet 1979 for $9 per bottle, Ravenswood Zinfandel 1980 for $18, and 1976 Cos d'Estournel at $24 are all near or below the release price for current vintages. In effect, the auction buyer gets a wine's tasting track record and the carrying cost of maturing it for free.

There are risks in buying at auction. The condition of older wines is crucial to quality; poor storage can ruin the best wine. Without a physical inspection—which is rarely possible for auction stock—the buyer is gambling on the purchase. Most retailers will take back a bad bottle, but auction-house policy is "buyer beware." Most catalogs are conscientious in listing any visible problems with ullage, or fill level, label quality or other defects, and will trumpet an impeccable provenance. But the older the wine, the more fragile it is. Buyers should make every effort to learn as much about the wine's condition as possible.

Of course there are no buyers without sellers. In general, U.S. law doesn't make it easy for a wine collector to change his mind; once he's bought the wine, he's stuck with it. Only a handful of states permit a private individual to sell his wines to a local retailer, and it is technically illegal to sell wines directly to friends or other collectors. Bottles donated to charity are eligible for tax write-offs to some degree. But in general wine is hardly a liquid asset.

Auction houses will accept wine from anywhere if they think the bottles will attract bidders. Auctioneers say more and more collectors are looking to auctions to sell excess stock. Some make serious money selling their old wines. Others are just happy to have room in their cellars and cash in hand.

Average Bottle Prices for Selected 1977 Vintage Ports

	1991 All	1991 U.S.	1991 U.K.	1989 All	1989 U.S.	1989 U.K.
Taylor	$43	$56	$38	$43	$49	$42
Fonseca	41	52	33	37	50	34
Dow	30	43	26	32	42	28
Warre	28	39	25	30	36	27
Sandeman	27	31	26	28	31	27
Graham	38	51	33	34	44	32
Croft	28	34	27	30	44	27

SOURCE: *THE WINE SPECTATOR*

BEFORE A BIDDER EVER RAISES HIS PADDLE, HE SHOULD STUDY THE STATE OF THE WINE MARKET AND BECOME FAMILIAR WITH CURRENT AUCTION AND RETAIL PRICES FOR THE WINES HE WANTS TO BUY

The Current Market

Before a bidder ever raises his paddle, he should study the state of the wine market and become familiar with current auction and retail prices for the wines he wants to buy.

The bulk of the wine on offer—and the most consistent prices—will be claret, the red wines of Bordeaux. While prewar and even prephylloxera wines are not uncommon at auction, the majority of claret comes from good vintages over the past 20 years. In England, wines as young as 1988 and 1989 are occasionally offered, but legal restrictions in the United States generally keep younger wines off the auction market.

This year has seen little increase in most Bordeaux prices, and many vintages have lost value. For example, comparing auction prices from 1990 and 1991 for vintages from 1945 to 1986, Château Latour, one of wine's true blue-chip stocks, saw average prices decrease for 17 vintages and increase for only three. Margaux slipped in 17 out of 21 years, and Pichon-Lalande in 11 of 17. This is bad news for impatient speculators banking on rapid returns, but good news for wine lovers who plan to drink what they buy.

The highest-priced recent vintages for Bordeaux are currently 1982, 1975 and 1970, and even these are trading near the prices for 1989s from the same châteaux. Because of the phenomenal succession of high-quality, high-quantity harvests since 1979, the prices for other vintages have tended to flatten out. Even though their original release prices varied considerably, the 1979, '81, '83, '85 and '86 vintages of any given estate are all trading for roughly similar prices. For example, 1992 average auction prices for Ducru-Beaucaillou run like this: '79-$36, '81-$29, '83-$25, '85-$33, '86-$34 and '88-$29.

Vintage Port, however, is a puzzle. It represents only a tiny fraction of total Port production—the very best of the best. It's offered at prices that compare favorably to equivalent Bordeaux, and lives for decades, yet its market has all but collapsed. Prices have not moved, except downward, for three years in England. Tighter supplies in the United States result in higher prices, but appreciation is still slow and chancy.

According to *The Wine Spectator* auction database, no widely traded Port vintage rose in price from 1990 to 1991. The 1963 Ports, from one of the top vintages of the century and now at their peaks, dropped an average of 18 percent on the year. The 1977s, from another classic vintage with decades of life left, slipped 11 percent last year and continue their slide in 1992. The only Port brand showing consistent appreciation is Nacional from Quinta do Noval. Only about 200 cases are produced in any declared vintage from a tiny plot of old, ungrafted vines. Nacional rarely comes up at auction, but could be considered an investment-grade wine. Few others, despite their undoubted quality, can make the same claim.

California Cabernet Sauvignons present the least predictable market of all the major auction categories. Their track record is too short and their buyer base is too small to keep prices in consistent patterns. The wines are almost never traded in London, the heart of the auction market, but appear frequently in the U.S. auction catalogs.

Among the best-known Cabernet producers, Heitz has shown the strongest growth. Its Martha's Vineyard bottlings command prices ranging from $50 per bottle for the 1980 to more than $300 for the fully mature 1968. Most vintages trade for significantly higher prices now than they did in 1989.

Prices for other producers have been more erratic. Even big, reliable wineries such as Beaulieu and Mondavi have not achieved consistent appreciation at auction. On the other hand, smaller, newer estates sometimes catch fire, and their prices skyrocket. Forman 1985 shot from $32 per bottle in 1990 to $60 this year. Dunn and Spotteswoode have also achieved impressive growth. It's too early, however, to know if these levels can be sustained, or if they are the result of speculative fever.

No summary can do justice to the wide range of other wines and spirits offered at auction. A wine buff devoted to Vega Sicilia or Vosne-Romanée or Veuve Clicquot should follow the sales, taste as many wines as possible and submit conservative bids hoping that lightning will strike. These wines may show rapid appreciation, but a timely bid may stock the cellar at very tasty prices.

Does it make sense to approach wine as an investment? Can auctions serve buyers who are looking principally for financial return on resale, hoping cases will outperform other collectibles or the consumer index?

No one can guarantee that prices will rise. Wine is particularly risky because it varies so much. In any given vintage, some producers will outperform others, and these variations may not become apparent for some time. Every vintage follows its own pattern of development; only the longest-lived have a real chance for significant appreciation. Even a great wine in a great vintage will vary from bottle to bottle, depending primarily on storage conditions and on chance factors such as the condition of the original cork. The structure of the wine market also works against the speculator, because the laws regarding trade are so complex that the market is kept relatively limited and static.

Despite these obstacles, however, many wines have outperformed the inflation rate. Some have shown stronger appreciation than other collectibles such as coins or even gold, over specific periods. A few have even been bonanzas for early buyers. A case of Château Latour 1961 could have been purchased for about $100 as a futures offering in 1963. Today, the average case price is $5,250. Château Mouton-Rothschild 1982 was initially offered at around $60 per bottle; it now sells for $140.

The Wine Spectator believes wine's primary purpose is for drinking. A careful buyer can realize significant savings by buying at auction, either by purchasing wines relatively young and cellaring them, or by finding undervalued older wines for current consumption. If prices subsequently rise, the satisfaction of financial growth can intensify the pleasure of the palate.

It's time for a change to the wines of Ernest and Julio Gallo.

NORTHERN SONOMA
RESERVE CELLARS
1985
VINTAGE

Wine

A FEW EASY RULES TO MAKE CHOOSING A BOTTLE TO ACCOMPANY YOUR MEAL A LABOR OF LOVE— NOT A TASK FRAUGHT WITH PERIL

BY HARVEY STEIMAN

PHOTOGRAPHY BY RICK MARIANI
STYLING BY ROBERT SKOTNICKI

Who decided that wine-and-food matching should be a chore? Read enough books and articles on the subject, sift through enough rules and helpful advice, and you might think it's better to forget the whole thing and drink a beer. So before this wine-and-food thing gets out of hand, let's put everything in perspective.

Choosing a bottle to drink with dinner should not be an occasion for nail chewing. It should be a joy, a pleasant pastime like playing tennis, taking a walk and listening to classical music. But all those tennis videos showing you how to refine your backstroke, all those ads for the perfect $100 walking shoes and all those lectures on what Mozart really meant, perfect as they are for the serious aficionado, do little more for many of us than raise the intimidation factor.

It is the same with this wine-and-food game. Just as the rule mongers and lesson-givers can actually take the joy out of those activities, too much information on choosing the right wine can form a black cloud over dinner.

So let's clear the air. In my book, there is one overriding criterion for matching food and wine. Engrave it on your wine cellar wall. Copies suitable for framing are available upon request. Steiman's Central Premise of wine-and-food matching reads:

"*The object of the game is to enjoy the meal. Therefore, drink the wine you like with the food you like.*

and Food Made Simple

All the rest is fine-tuning."

Those who wish to delve into it will find plenty of opportunity for fine-tuning. The possibilities for flawless matches are endless, and we shall explore some of them in this article. But those who just want to wash down dinner with a compatible glass of wine can relax. Just follow the Central Premise. What's the worst that can happen? In the rare circumstance when the wine clashes with the food—and it is rare—you might need a sip of water or a bite of bread in between bites and sips. The point is, you will enjoy dinner.

And that brings us to the First Principle: "*Always drink a better wine and sacrifice the food match rather than settle for a mediocre wine to make a good match.*"

Much has been written recently about one of the minor miracles of the dining table, in which faulty wines taste better when they match up with food. Textures and flavors of food can change the way we perceive a wine we drink with it, a phenomenon that is at the very core of big-league wine-and-food matching. Experienced wine-and-food matchers know how to tweak the food to bring out the best in a wine. Or they can find just the right wine to be tweaked by the elements in the food to bring out the best in both the wine and the food.

This is advanced stuff, like learning how to place your lob in tennis. The important thing to remember is that it is fine-tuning. Most of us are happy to place our tennis lobs so they fall inbounds. Rest assured, any good wine will fall inbounds. All it has to do is land on the table.

A bad wine destroys dinner like a lob that lands out of bounds. A bad match will not destroy dinner because of a reason so obvious: *Most of us drink most of our wine without food.*

Consider the usual scenario. You sit down to a plate of—let's pick a typical example here—lamb chops with red wine sauce. You have carefully selected a 10-year-old Cabernet because Cabernet matches up well with lamb. You pour the wine. You take a few sips, admiring the way it has aged. You take a bite of food and a sip of wine. And another sip, because the wine is so good. And so on. How many bites in an average serving of lamb chops? Eight? Ten? How many sips of wine in the 8 ounces of Cabernet in the two glasses you might consume with the lamb? Allowing two teaspoons per sip (a generous gulp, actually), that's about 24 sips.

How many people do you know who take a sip of wine after every bite? Observe people enjoying themselves at dinner, as I have, and you cannot help but notice the typical pattern: several bites of food followed by a sip or two of wine. The actual number of sips of wine taken immediately after a bite of food? Usually no more than five or six per course.

That argues strongly for the Central Premise: First drink a wine you like. Do not make the mistake of drinking a mediocre wine because it will taste better with your food. Do not stock your cellar with "food-friendly" wines that have no special character of their own. Remember: *Most of us drink most of our wine without food.*

How can we create a successful wine-and-food match without compromising on the quality of the wine? One way is to follow "The Rules," the most famous of which demands white wine with fish and red wine with meat. Other rules command us to drink white wines before red, dry wines before sweet, young wines before old. (One of the new rules that keeps popping up in articles and books is that tart, acidic wines go best with food. Not always. A squeeze of lemon is nice on many things, too, but you can have too much of a good thing.)

What it comes down to, after all, is that following the rules reduces the odds of making a bad match. It does not guarantee success, but at least you know dinner won't be awful. The most exciting wine-and-food experiences, however, are the ones that go beyond washing down the food acceptably to create tastes and textures that are new and wonderful.

The real keys to a successful food-and-wine match are (1) the size and weight of the wine, and (2) the richness and intensity of the food. The old rule about white wine with fish and red wine with meat comes down to us from the days when white wines were light and red wines were weighty. Today, when most Chardonnays and white Burgundies are heavier and fuller-bodied than most Pinot Noirs and even some Cabernets, color coding does not work consistently.

With a hearty beef stew, most of us instinctively pass up a delicate white wine for a flavorful red. Why? We're trying to balance the body and intensity of the wine with the same elements in the food. These instincts are right, but the important factor is not the color of the wine but the delicacy or heartiness of the wine and food.

So the Second Principle is this: "*For a comfortable wine-and-food match, the wine should be at least as full-bodied as the food it accompanies.*"

Hearty food needs a hearty wine, because a lighter wine will fade into the background. With lighter food, you have more leeway. Lighter wines will balance nicely, of course, but heartier wines will still show you all they have. Purists may complain that full-bodied wines "overwhelm" less hearty foods, but the truth is that anything but the blandest food still tastes fine after a sip of a heavyweight wine. Not true the other way around.

Body balancing is the secret behind some of the classic wine-and-food matches. Muscadet washes down a plate of oysters because it's just weighty enough to match the delicacy of a raw bivalve. Cabernet complements grilled lamb chops or roast lamb because they're equally vigorous. Pinot Noir or Burgundy makes a better match with roast beef because the richness of texture is the same in both.

One way to make your own classic matches is to follow the same path as the first person who tried Muscadet with oysters. Find a similarly light-bodied wine, such as dry Champagne or a dry Riesling. Don't get stuck on Cabernet with lamb. Try Zinfandel or Côtes du Rhône, which are built along similar lines. Instead of Burgundy or Pinot Noir with roast beef, sample a little St.-Emilion or Barbera. That's one way to put a little variety into your wine life without straying too far from the original purpose.

Unfortunately, wines do not carry labels listing their weightiness on some widely accepted scale. We can get some idea from the label, however. Most Cabernets are rich and weighty, and most Beaujolais are not. Likewise, most Chardonnays are bigger wines than most Champagnes. But not all. Some Burgundies are as delicate as some Beaujolais. Some Chardonnays are steelier and lighter than certain Rieslings.

For this reason, a taste of the wine is worth 10 times more than a look at the label. Nothing beats personal experience, but well-written tasting notes in publications such as *The Wine Spectator* should provide a pretty good idea of where a wine stands on the light-to-heavy scale. Consult the charts on this page for a quick read on how typical examples of the world's better-known wines fit into this range.

Consulting the chart, you can choose a red wine with fish or a white wine with beef stew, if you are so inclined, and make a good match. The red wine for fish need only balance the richness and intensity of the dish. Broiled salmon steak or fresh tuna taste fine with red wines of modest to medium tannins. Rich, full-bodied Chardonnays handle a beef stew with aplomb.

Weighing Red Wines

It's important to match the wine's body to the heartiness of the food it accompanies

Lighter Body

Beaujolais
Valpolicella
Dolcetto
Burgundy Côte de Beaune
Rioja
Italian, U.S. Barbera
Chianti Classico
California Pinot Noir
St.-Emilion, Pomerol
Burgundy Côte de Nuits
Médoc classified growths
Washington Merlot
California Merlot
Zinfandel
California, Washington Cabernet
Rhône, U.S. Syrah
Brunello di Montalcino
Barbaresco
Barolo

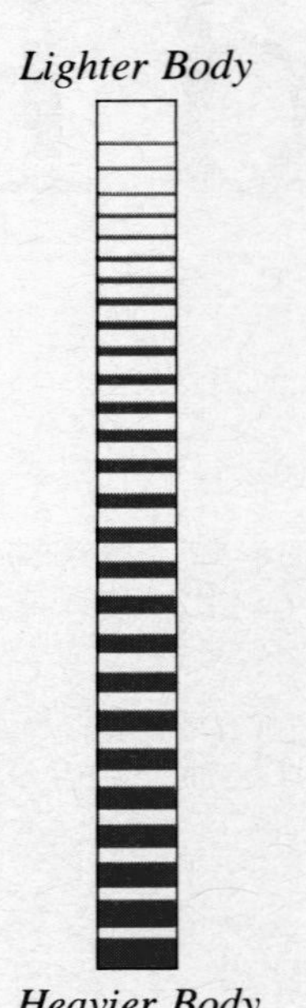

Heavier Body

Aside from body, several other attributes of wine affect the way it matches up with a particular dish. None is as important as size and weight, but each one can help build a bridge or set up a roadblock to the food.

• Sweetness: The mere presence of sugar is not enough to affect a match, so long as the wine tastes balanced and not cloying. Anyone who prefers sugared iced tea should not insist on bone-dry wines. Frankly sweet wines, however, like to find some sweetness in the dish you drink them with. It could be fruit, could be a touch of honey, could be almonds. Peppery or spicy foods like a little sweetness, too.

• Tannin: Many red wines have noticeable tannin, which affects the way a wine feels in the mouth. The astringent burr of tannin reacts to certain components in the food. Fats and oils in the food tend to neutralize harshness in the wine. So does salt. Think of rich, creamy foods for tannic wines. A chunk of Parmigiano Reggiano cheese is perfect.

• Alcohol: Full-bodied wines tend to be high in alcohol, light-bodied wines low. When alcohol is high enough to be noticeable, it can taste a little sweet, which matches well with slightly sweet foods, such as onion-sauced chicken. Very salty food, such as ham, can make high-alcohol wine taste bitter.

• Temperature: A much bigger factor than most people realize. Cold temperature tends to mask sweetness and mute flavor. Also, cold emphasizes tannin in red wine. Cold food, muted by temperature, does better with lighter wines, especially if they are also chilled. Think of cold cuts with Beaujolais or Alsace Gewürztraminer. Spicy food calls for the refreshing texture of a chilled beverage, so if you want to serve wine with spicy food, lean toward chillable ones. If they're a little sweet, so much the better.

• Acidity: As a rule, very tart wines taste less acidic when you drink them with food, especially food that has an acidic bite itself. Sweet food tends to make acidic wines taste even worse. Very soft wines have trouble matching up to any food, because they tend to wimp out. Drink them by themselves. But as long as the acidity (or lack of it) is not the most prominent aspect of the wine, it helps liven the match. After all, most dishes taste fine with a squeeze of lemon.

Finally, we come to flavor, for most of us the most enjoyable aspect of the food-and-wine game. Flavors in wine can enhance a dish, such as adding seasoning or extra ingredients. Once the other aspects of the wine-and-food match are functioning well, the flavor nuances can lift the experience onto a loftier plane.

Other than tannin, this is where a wine's color makes the biggest difference, because red wines often do have a flavor profile different from whites. All wines share many common flavors; reds, whites and rosés can all be spicy, buttery, leathery, earthy, floral. But the apple, pear and citrus flavors in many white wines seldom show up in reds, and the currant, cherry and stone flavors of red grapes usually do not appear in whites.

These flavors in the wine can *echo* those in the food or *complement* them. An example of echoing the flavors would be a Zinfandel with distinct raspberry flavors served with a duck breast in raspberry sauce. An example of complementing the flavors would be a Chablis with citrus flavors served with shrimp sautéed with olive oil and garlic. A particularly exciting match can do both at the same time. For example, add a healthy pinch of chopped dill to that shrimp with olive oil and garlic, and serve it with a crisp, citrusy Sauvignon Blanc that has an herbal flavor of its own.

When you echo a flavor in the food with the wine, the flavor in the food tends to cancel out the same flavor in the wine. At the very least, it will mute the flavor in the wine. I first noticed this phenomenon when drinking an earthy 10-year-old red Burgundy with duck and turnips. The earthy flavor of the turnips muted the earthiness in the wine. The unexpected result was that the Burgundy tasted richer in fruit and more youthful, without losing its wonderful sense of maturity. That made for a memorable match.

Savvy wine-and-food matchers can use this information to great advantage. Let's say you want to serve a wine you like except for one flavor component. Try to echo that flavor component in the food, and they will tend to cancel each other out.

Weighing White Wines

It's important to match the wine's body to the heartiness of the food it accompanies

Lighter Body

Soave, Orvieto
Off-dry German wines (other than Riesling)
Off-dry Riesling (U.S., Australian, German)
Muscadet
Dry Riesling (Alsace, U.S.)
Chenin Blanc (including Vouvray)
Champagne
U.S. Sauvignon Blanc
Bordeaux white
U.S. Gewürztraminer
Pouilly-Fumé, Sancerre
French Chablis (and other unoaked Chardonnays)
Gavi
Mâcon (including Pouilly-Fuissé)
Alsace Gewürztraminer
California barrel-fermented or barrel-aged Chardonnay
Meursault, Puligny-Montrachet, Chassagne-Montrachet
Rhône whites

Heavier Body

If you're serving a Cabernet Sauvignon with a touch more olive flavor than you care for, you can add a few sliced olives to the sauce, or make the sauce with olive oil instead of butter. Or, at the table, you can drizzle a little olive oil over the dish. Either way, the olive flavors achieve two ends: They make a bridge between the food and the wine, and they soften the impact of the olive flavor in the wine. Net result: You like the wine even more.

The trick to making these flavor bridges is to identify the dominant flavor in the food. That is not necessarily the main ingredient. Often the key flavor is an ingredient added to give the dish its own character. A good example is chicken sauté. Finish the dish with white wine and olives, and the best flavor bridge might be with a Sauvignon Blanc or a Sémillon. But finish it with red wine and mushrooms, and you might think first of Pinot Noir or red Burgundy.

Here is a helpful hint: When you see the word "with" in a menu title, chances are the key flavor ingredients come after the conjunction, not before, as in "monkfish medallions with lemon cream," or "veal chops with wild mushrooms." For a fine-tuned match, the wine's flavors need to address the lemon in the first dish, the wild mushrooms in the second.

Cooking methods can affect the flavor bridge drastically, too. The smoky flavors of grilling or barbecuing tilt the balance in a totally different direction from neutral cooking processes, such as boiling or steaming.

Two things to remember about these flavor bridges: They come into play only if the basic structure of the wine matches well with the food, and it's dangerous to generalize about them. They are wine-specific, so they don't necessarily work perfectly with every wine of a given type. Not all Chardonnays have the pearlike fruit that tastes so good with broiled scallops. But because most good Chardonnays share certain flavor characteristics that match up well with certain food flavors, they work often enough to be useful.

With these caveats in mind, let's live dangerously and look at some flavor bridges that connect more often than not:

• Chardonnay and mustard.

Type: Complement
Why it works: Apple flavor in the wine against the distinctive flavor of the mustard.
Dishes to try: Chicken or rabbit in mustard sauce.

• Sauvignon Blanc and goat cheese.

Type: Complement
Why it works: Herbal-vegetal flavors in the wine against earthy flavors of the cheese.
Dishes to try: Goat cheese spreads, goat cheese stuffings for chicken.

• Champagne and blue cheese.

Type: Echo
Why it works: Earthy flavors in the wine with earthiness and gaminess of the cheese.
Dishes to try: Blue cheese appetizers.

• White Rhône and nutmeg.

Type: Echo
Why it works: Spicy flavors of the wine against the aromatic spice.
Dishes to try: Custard-based first courses (such as poultry or vegetable mousses), which are often flavored with nutmeg.

• Red Rhône and Beef

Type: Complement or echo
Why it works: Black pepper flavor in the wine complements the meaty flavors, echoes any peppery seasonings.
Dishes to try: Simple roast beef, broiled or pan-fried steaks, with or without peppery coating.

• Cabernet Sauvignon and lamb.

Type: Complement
Why it works: Currant, berry and herbal flavors of the wine against gaminess of the meat.
Dishes to try: Roast leg of lamb, broiled lamb chops with neutral sauces.

• Pinot Noir and mushrooms.

Type: Complement or echo
Why it works: Earthy flavor of mushrooms can *complement* berrylike flavors in the wine, or *echo* earthy flavors in an older wine.
Dishes to try: Chicken in mushroom sauce, mushroom risotto.

• Riesling and almonds.

Type: Echo
Why it works: Slight nutty flavor in the wine balances almond flavor, emphasizing wine's fruit.
Dishes to try: Trout amandine (for drier wines), almond tart (for sweet dessert wines).

• Sauternes and caramel.

Type: Complement
Why it works: The honey flavor in the wine becomes more complex with caramel overtones.
Dishes to try: Baked apples, caramelized fruit tart.

• Cream sherry and mocha.

Type: Echo
Why it works: Coffeelike flavors in the wine against coffee-chocolate flavors of mocha.
Dishes to try: Mocha mousse, mocha soufflé.

Remember, these flavor bridges work both ways. You can use them to select a wine for foods that have these characteristics. Or, if you have some control over the food preparation itself, you can tweak the food to match with the wine. Serving Chardonnay with salmon? Try adding a little mustard to the sauce. Serving a white Rhône instead? Try a little nutmeg in the sauce.

Another way to fine-tune a wine-and-food match, detailed in "Cooking With Kamman at Napa Valley's School for Chefs," (*The Wine Spectator*, Nov. 15, 1991), involves tinkering with the food to match the basic components of the actual wine being served with it. Madeleine Kamman, who teaches the pros the finer points of cooking for wine at the Beringer School for American Chefs in Napa Valley, always tastes the wine in the kitchen with a little sample of the food. Then she adjusts the seasoning or adds something to the sauce to bring everything into balance.

Fascinating as that process is, I see an inherent danger in making too much of it. A person could get the impression that good food-and-wine matches are impossible without all this fussing around. Someone who just wants to drink a good glass of wine with dinner might feel guilty about not bothering to match flavors with echoes and complements, and that might prompt a reasonable person to chuck the whole thing and drink beer or iced tea. Sometimes I fear that we food-and-wine specialists can do more harm than good by delving too deeply into these finer points.

That is why the First Principle is to drink a wine you like to drink by itself, rather than sacrifice wine quality to the food match. Then, if you want to take it another step, move on to the Second Principle, which is to select a wine that is at least as full-bodied as the food. Finally, if the search for a perfectly fine-tuned wine-and-food match appeals to you, consider details such as flavor matches. This is the fun part, but it can become an obsession.

Along the way, never lose sight of the Central Premise: *The object of the game is to enjoy the meal.* Don't be afraid to try a little fine-tuning if the spirit is willing. Who knows? Dinner might taste better than ever. □

So-Called Wine Enemies

Certain foods have a reputation, greatly exaggerated in most cases, for ruining the wine served with them. The important thing to remember about most of these foods is that they are a problem only if they dominate the dish. Just because a sauce contains one of these ingredients doesn't render it an enemy of wine.

Sooner or later, if you read about matching food and wine, you will encounter a list of "wine enemies" that includes foods such as anchovies, artichokes, garlic and tomatoes as wine-killing culprits.

Here is a typical enemies list, and some comments:

Artichokes: Artichokes do contain a chemical that tends to make anything—including water—consumed with them taste sweet. Their effect depends, however, on how much artichoke there is in the dish. If artichoke is the main ingredient, watch out for softer, more flavorful wines, which can clash. If artichoke is part of the mixture, such as chicken with mushrooms and artichokes or lamb stew with artichokes and other vegetables, just drink a wine with sufficient acidity to compensate for the slight sweetening effect.

Garlic: Who came up with this one? Most cuisines from wine-drinking regions use garlic lavishly. Raw garlic has such a strong, harsh flavor that it can rob a complex wine of its subtleties, but a lively, fruity wine can handle it. What do you think Italians drink with pesto, water? No, a simple red.

Tomatoes: Another mystery. Yes, raw tomatoes make a definite flavor statement and nudge the balance of a dish toward acidity, but that's no problem for well-balanced wines. Tomatoes, mozzarella, basil and olive oil make a classic first-course salad. Try it with a crisp white.

Anchovies: Every hear of *bagna caôda*? It's a northern Italian dip made mostly of garlic, anchovies and hot olive oil. The Piedmontese dip vegetables into it and drink a fruity red, such as their Freisa. Complex wines lose their subtlety, of course, but simple, refreshing wines make the grade.

Hot peppers: A light nip of heat from chili peppers bothers few wines of any substance. As the burn quotient rises, however, the best wine choices become increasingly fruitier and sweeter. Try a sweet Chenin Blanc or Vouvray with peppery fish stews, or sweet sherry with a hot curry.

Geographical Hocus-Pocus

Sooner or later, anyone interested in matching wine and food will hear one piece of advice: Match the food of a region to a wine of the region. Having beef Burgundy? Drink red Burgundy. Eating spaghetti with tomato ragù? Drink Chianti. Enjoying choucroute garni? Drink Alsace Gewürztraminer.

The reasoning is unimpeachable. Cooks in a region tend to prepare foods that taste good with the wines of their region. And winemakers tend to tailor their wines to the foods they eat most of the time. Therefore, a natural affinity emerges between the wine and the food.

These gastronomic partners came about in times when the only wines available to the cooks of a region were the wines their neighbors made. Today, communication and travel make more things possible. In the United States, we can mix and match cuisines and wines if we choose.

With that in mind, use these regional wine-and-food partnerships as stylistic models rather than following them slavishly. Take the beef Burgundy and red Burgundy match, for example. The best Burgundies for this match are rich, flavorful and full-bodied, to stand up to the hearty beef, mushroom and onion stew. Certain California Zinfandels match that wine description, and, it turns out, match the food better than a fancy-priced Burgundy. The Burgundy shows better with simpler, less-assertive food, such as roasts, and the Zinfandel comes into its own with the stew.

Using the Chianti as a model, try lighter reds from the Rhône or a California Merlot for similar structure but a different flavor profile to match with the spaghetti sauce. Instead of Gewürz with that choucroute and sausage, why not try a white Rioja or Washington Sémillon for a change of pace?

Sampling a variety of wines with a classic northern Italian osso buco (veal shanks in broth with lemon and parsley), a group of us discovered that a rich-textured, flavorful California Chardonnay made a much better match than the Valpolicella usually suggested with it. This is one of the finest wine-and-food combinations I know.

All it takes to find your own similar matches is a little curiosity.

A Simple Dinner for Wine

ROQUEFORT-SCENTED SHRIMP
CHAMPAGNE

•••••••••

MUSHROOM-SMOTHERED SALMON STEAKS
PINOT NOIR OR BURGUNDY

•••••••••

ALMOND TART
SWEET RIESLING

•••••••••

... SHRIMP WITH ... ROQUEFORT-SCENTED .. BUTTER ..

1 pound large or jumbo shrimp
1/2 cup dry white wine
1 shallot, chopped
1 sprig parsley
4 tablespoons mayonnaise
1 tablespoon Roquefort cheese
Dash Tabasco

Place the shrimp, the wine, the shallots and the parsley in a saucepan. Add 1/2 cup water and bring to a boil. Simmer the shrimp until they are done, about five minutes. Remove the shrimp and boil the liquid until it reduces to about 1/4 cup. Strain the liquid and set it aside.

Meanwhile, peel the shrimp and arrange them on six appetizer plates.

Add the mayonnaise, cheese and Tabasco to the reduced and strained shrimp-cooking liquid. Spoon this sauce over the shrimp and garnish the plates with parsley, chervil or chives. Serve at room temperature. Serves six.

... MUSHROOM-SMOTHERED ... .. SALMON STEAKS ..

6 salmon steaks, 6 to 8 ounces each
5 tablespoons butter
1 pound white mushrooms, sliced
1/2 pound shiitake mushrooms, sliced
1/2 medium onion, finely chopped
1 clove garlic, finely chopped
1 tablespoon cassis liqueur
1 tablespoon flour
1/2 cup red wine
1/2 cup beef broth
1 tablespoon chopped fresh thyme

In a large non-stick skillet, with 1 tablespoon butter, lightly brown the salmon steaks about two minutes on each side. Arrange them in a baking pan. Preheat the oven to 400 degrees Fahrenheit.

Add the remaining butter to the skillet and sauté the mushrooms, stirring or tossing them occasionally, until they brown. Add the cassis and let them simmer in their own juices about six to eight minutes. As they start to dry up, add the flour, stir once or twice, and add the remaining ingredients to the pan and boil the mixture for 10 minutes. Spoon this over the salmon steaks and bake seven to eight minutes, or until the salmon is barely cooked through.

Serve with rice or noodles and a green vegetable. Serves six.

... CHEZ PANISSE ... .. ALMOND TART ..

9-inch prebaked tart shell
3/4 cup whipping cream
3/4 cup sugar
1 teaspoon orange liqueur
2 or 3 drops almond extract
1 cup sliced almonds

In a 2-1/2- or 3-quart saucepan, combine the cream, sugar, liqueur and almond extract. Boil the mixture, stirring it occasionally. It should bubble up and thicken slightly. Remove from heat and stir in the almonds. Let the mixture stand 15 minutes.

Line the bottom of an oven with aluminum foil (the tart can boil over). Preheat the oven to 400 degrees.

Fill the tart shell with the mixture, which should still be liquid. Bake the tart 30 to 35 minutes, or until the top browns lightly. Allow the tart to cool slightly before removing the pan's ring. Cool the tart on a rack. (Note: To remove the tart from the bottom of the pan—not necessary unless you want to display it on a platter—slide a knife between the crust and the pan about 20 minutes after it comes from the oven to loosen it before lifting it off with a very wide spatula.)

—Harvey Steiman

PHOTOGRAPHY BY RICK MARIANI/STYLING BY ROBERT SKOTNICKI

This straightforward, three-course dinner is a tasty exercise in wine-and-food pairing

MERIDIAN™

SANTA BARBARA COUNTY

CHARDONNAY

Great Chardonnay comes from Santa Barbara County. For the second year in a row, a wine from this county has won the annual Vintners Club Chardonnay Taste-Off.”

Steve Pitcher, S.F. CHRONICLE, March 1991

“The combination of Santa Barbara's cool climate fruit and veteran winemaker Chuck Ortman's sure touch combine to make the most show stopping $9.75 Chardonnay in California.”

Richard Nalley, COPLEY NEWS SERVICE, Sept. 1991

'Mr. Chardonnay', himself. Charles Ortman...”

THE WINE SPECTATOR, April 1989

“Best Buy. Meridian 1990 Santa Barbara County Chardonnay. A bold, rich, ripe style, with exotic honey, pineapple, orange and nutmeg flavors. Pretty oak shadings add to its depth and richness.” Rated 87.

THE WINE SPECTATOR, January 1992

...the next superstar winery...But unlike the other superstar wineries that offer you glitz and charge you plenty...Meridian offers excellent wine at a very moderate price.”

Dan Berger, L.A. TIMES, January 1990

THE SANTA BARBARA COAST.
CHARLES ORTMAN.
MERIDIAN'S UNBEATABLE COMBINATION.

MERIDIAN VINEYARDS, PASO ROBLES, CA

Shapes, Sizes and Degrees

A BIT OF FINE TUNING CAN ENHANCE YOUR ENJOYMENT OF CERTAIN WINE TYPES

BY JIM GORDON

Different wine glasses are traditionally used to augment the special qualities of different wines

Knowing a few basic terms and standards can aid your appreciation of wine. In this section you will find an explanation of several popular types of wine glasses, the traditional terminology for wine bottles of varying sizes and tips on the preferred temperatures at which to serve different wines.

Wine Glasses

There is no right or wrong glass for wine. But certain shapes and sizes have become traditional over the years, and often for practical reasons. In general, wine is best appreciated when drunk from a clear, smooth-surfaced, stemmed glass. Colored or faceted wine glasses don't afford the best view of a wine's color and clarity. Holding a wine glass by its stem gets your hand out of the way so you can see the wine, and it enables you to give the wine a slight swirl to release more aromas into the air.

Sherry and Port glasses traditionally are small. This is because Port and sherry are fortified wines, usually drunk in small quantities.

You can drink Champagne out of the stemmed, flat saucer that was popular in the past, but the tall Champagne glasses, called flutes, are now in vogue. They make it less likely your Champagne will spill out of the glass during a wild party.

The white wine glass pictured on this page is probably the best all-around wine glass to have. Glasses much like this are used by many professional wine tasters when they analyze wines. Remember that it's wise not to fill a wine glass more than half full. That will leave enough air space to let the aromas come out. The standard white wine glass's narrow opening concentrates the bouquet.

Generally, glasses for red table wines are wider than those for white, but beyond that it's really up to your personal preference. Don't spend much time worrying about the choices; try one style and see if it suits you.

Bottle Sizes

A great majority of the world's premium wines are sold in a standard bottle that holds 750 milliliters. Standard-bottle heights, shapes and colors vary from region to region and wine variety to wine variety, but they all hold 750 milliliters, or about 25 ounces. That equals five to six good-sized pours. Some people still call this size a fifth, recalling the days when bottles about this size held one fifth of a gallon.

The other two sizes most frequently found in wine shops and on restaurant wine lists are the half-bottle and the magnum. Half-bottles, sometimes called tenths, hold 375 milliliters. Even smaller than a half-bottle is a split, or quarter-bottle, used mostly for sparkling wines. Magnums hold as much wine as two standard bottles, or 1.5 liters. Double magnums hold the equivalent of four bottles, or 3 liters.

You rarely encounter a bottle larger than a double magnum. These behemoths carry Biblical-sounding names. They start with the jeroboam, holding the equivalent of about six bottles, or 5 liters. (In Champagne, however, a jeroboam is a 3-liter bottle.) Imperials and methuselahs are both eight-bottle sizes, and a salmanazar holds the equivalent of an entire 12-bottle case. A balthazar holds the same as 16 bottles. And the king of wine bottles, holding the equivalent of 15 to 20 bottles, is named nebuchadnezzar.

Wine-bottle designations include, from left, half-bottle, bottle, magnum and double magnum and imperial

Serving Temperatures

The best temperature at which to serve wines is another topic, like choosing the proper wine glass, where the rules can get confusing. In general, sparkling wines should be served as cold as you can get them. It takes at least an hour in the refrigerator to bring one down from room temperature. Most white wines are also best when served cold, at refrigerator temperature or a bit warmer, to preserve their freshness and fruitiness and to make their impression on the palate more refreshing. For most red wines, connoisseurs prefer to serve them at cellar temperature, about 55 to 65 degrees Fahrenheit.

With that said, there's a bit of fine tuning that can enhance your enjoyment of certain wine types. In the whites, rich, full-bodied wines such as white Burgundy, Chardonnay and Sémillon often show more of their complexity when served warmer than other whites. Cellar temperature is good. If you don't have a really cool cellar, about 40 minutes in the fridge should do it. Most sweet dessert wines will be at their best using the same rule.

Pouring a red wine at room temperature can be a mistake, especially in the summer when rooms are quite warm. A warm red wine seems to lose some of its flavor, and the tannins tend to feel rough. The idea of room temperature was appropriate in drafty, damp English manors in the 19th century, but not in most homes today.

Light, fresh-tasting red wines such as Beaujolais and many Pinot Noirs can be good when moderately chilled. Half an hour in the refrigerator should be plenty of time. Most rosés and blush wines are best when served at refrigerator temperature like the majority of white wines. □

Keeping Track of Inventory

KEEPING RECORDS IS ONE WAY THAT AVID WINE COLLECTORS AVOID LOSING BOTTLES IN THE SHUFFLE

VINOUS MEMORY IS NOTED BY MANY WINE LOVERS, EVEN THOSE WHO CAN'T REMEMBER WHERE THEY PUT THEIR CAR KEYS

BY STEVE HEIMOFF

JOYCE OUDKERKPOOL

Collectors with large collections say that keeping track becomes necessary simply to know where things are

Losing, and years later finding, three bottles of Château Pétrus in one's own cellar may not be the sort of thing that happens to most of us, but that may be because we do not have wine collections the size of Marvin Overton's.

The Fort Worth, Texas, neurosurgeon-rancher has so many bottles (he won't say how many) that it's quite understandable how a few of them could occasionally get lost in the shuffle. These things happen. Stacy Childs, a Birmingham, Ala., physician, recently rediscovered four bottles of 1974 Heitz Martha's Vineyard in his 6,000-bottle cellar years after he thought he'd run out of it, and Sid Cross, a Vancouver, Wash., attorney, has friends who found some 1961 Château Palmer lurking in the shadows long after they thought it was history.

All three were serendipitous finds; the wines were fantastic when opened. The ending might not have been so happy had the wines not been methuselahs. It makes you wonder if there's a foolproof way of keeping track of your goodies down in the cellar so this sort of thing won't happen.

Right up front, let's admit there isn't. If you have 1,000 bottles, that's 1,000 more things to stay on top of, added to all the other minutiae of existence, and human nature rebels against keeping track of every sparrow that falls to earth. Besides, one could argue that keeping statistics on wine isn't the point; enjoying it is.

But keeping track of your inventory can be a good idea, and not just to avoid having good wines go bad on you. There are other reasons for keeping a log, particularly if you include some kind of tasting notes in addition to the number crunching. Collectors with particularly large collections say that, starting at about 1,000 bottles, keeping track becomes necessary simply to know where things are. Others, with personalities that tend to be organized (such as lawyers), find that record keeping is just something they gravitate toward naturally. Still others say that record keeping enables them to record their drinking patterns. And collectors who go so far as to record their tasting observations say notes help them understand what styles of wine they like, and how their taste evolves over time.

There seem to be three basic schools of thought on keeping records: the do-it-by-handers, the techies and the to-hell-with-its. Eugene Wong, a Honolulu physician, is a do-it-by-hander. He keeps a looseleaf binder that's divided into different sections, such as white Burgundy and Sauternes. Whenever something goes into or out of his 3,500-bottle cellar, a notation goes into the binder, just like a ledger book.

Childs used to have a manual system, but went high tech a few years ago when he transferred his inventory to Lotus 1-2-3, a popular computer spreadsheet program. That has its advantages; you can get up-to-the-minute printouts on the state of the cellar, and computer users are particularly enamored of the various "sort" options by which they can arrange the contents of their collections. Moreover, pecking away at a personal computer feels great, if you enjoy that sort of thing (but that's a different story).

But there's one huge disadvantage to computers. "It's cumbersome to boot the computer up every time you want to enter something. In the middle of a dinner party, you go down and get two more bottles and you don't want to take the time to put it in the computer," Childs says.

Childs found a solution for that. "I print out a copy of my wine list every six months, keep it in the cellar and pencil in every time I do something. Then, once or twice a year, I take the marked-up list and enter it into the computer. That makes it really easy."

Maybe so, but in actuality, points out Cross, you're then keeping two separate systems, and that doesn't make much sense. Cross prefers to keep his inventory in a looseleaf binder because "it's more personal and hands on, rather than a distant, computer-type feel." He has another, more practical reason for his hands-on approach. "It takes more discipline, which makes you reflect on your inventory as to which [wines] are coming into drinkability and which are drinking up now."

Andy Lawlor, a Dexter, Mich., collector with 7,000 bottles, also attempts to keep inventory on his PC, but runs into the same kind of problem Childs does. "I must say it doesn't get updated too often. New purchases, everyday drinking and giving to charity often don't get listed, so it's always out of date." Lawlor keeps purchase receipts in a manila folder in the cellar and usually gets around to entering them in the computer at some point, but consumption rarely gets recorded as a debit. But Lawlor claims he possesses a vinous memory "that keeps things from getting too far out of kilter."

Vinous memory is a phenomenon noted by many wine lovers who shun record keeping. Even those who can't remember where they put the car keys last night say they have an uncanny knack for recalling the whereabouts of each bottle, or the taste of a Zinfandel they had back in 1979. Wong doesn't bother to keep tasting notes, he says, "because I have a good memory to keep track of tastings in my head." Jeff Zell, a Potomac, Md., collector with 2,000 bottles, says, "I pick sections of my cellar and memorize them pretty easily, so I have a visual of the entire cellar. I can give you a rough estimate of 90 percent of it from memory." Zell does put neck tags on his bottles.

Back to Overton. He admits he's tried computers, cellar logs, scratch pads and everything else you can think of to keep track of his collection, "but nothing works. In fact," he adds, "I think it's impossible to keep track. I don't know how it happens, but you don't really completely know how many bottles you have at any one time." It might be possible, he speculates, but not without putting in more time and effort than is worth the candle.

Maybe that's true when you start getting up to collections the size of Overton's. Those of us with more modest cellars will no doubt find the going easier, but it's a trade-off—we're not likely to experience the thrill of finding long-lost bottles of Pétrus at the bottom of the trove. □

Steve Heimoff is a free-lance writer in Oakland, Calif.

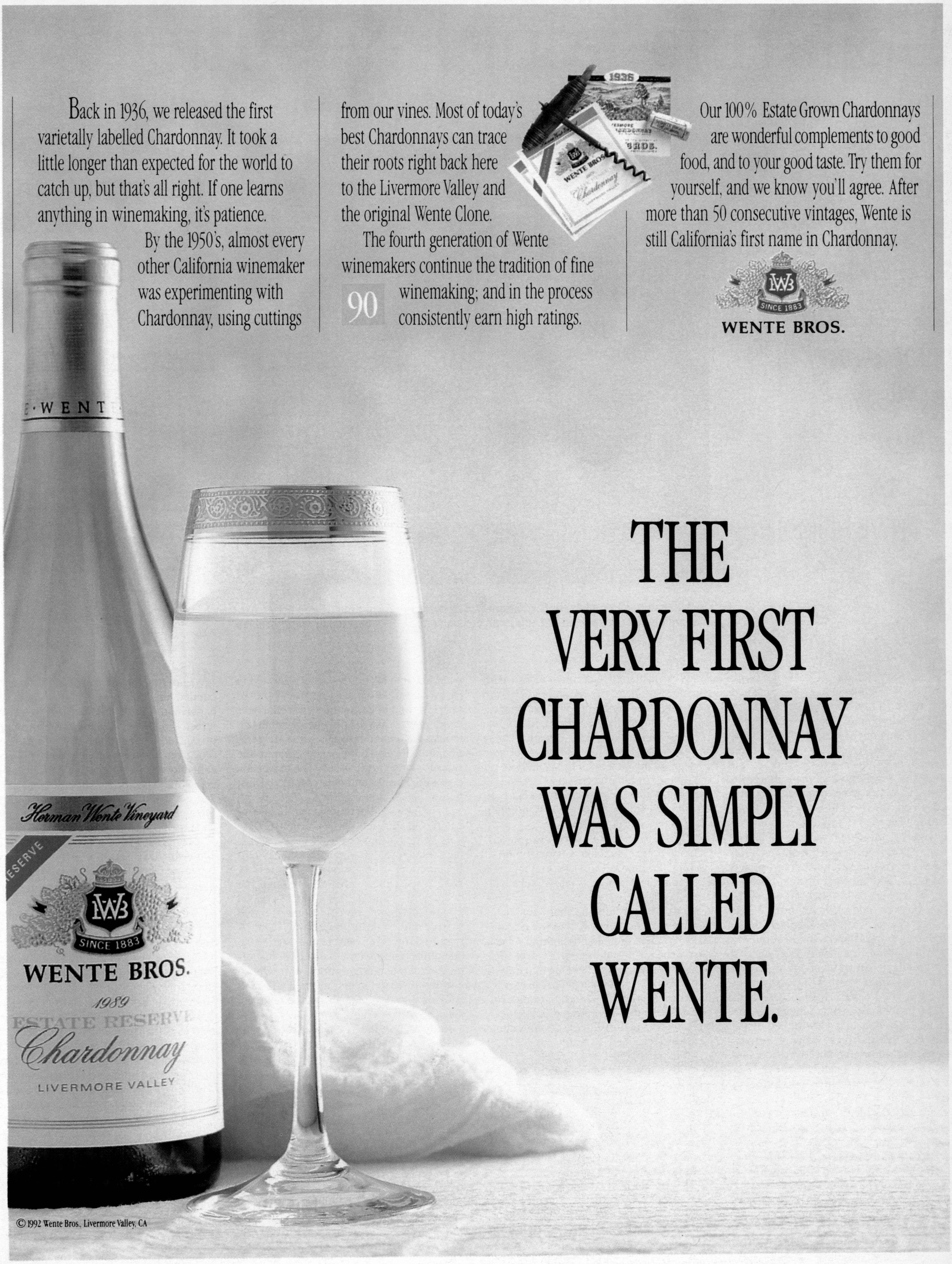

Back in 1936, we released the first varietally labelled Chardonnay. It took a little longer than expected for the world to catch up, but that's all right. If one learns anything in winemaking, it's patience.

By the 1950's, almost every other California winemaker was experimenting with Chardonnay, using cuttings from our vines. Most of today's best Chardonnays can trace their roots right back here to the Livermore Valley and the original Wente Clone.

The fourth generation of Wente winemakers continue the tradition of fine winemaking; and in the process consistently earn high ratings.

90

Our 100% Estate Grown Chardonnays are wonderful complements to good food, and to your good taste. Try them for yourself, and we know you'll agree. After more than 50 consecutive vintages, Wente is still California's first name in Chardonnay.

WB SINCE 1883
WENTE BROS.

THE VERY FIRST CHARDONNAY WAS SIMPLY CALLED WENTE.

Herman Wente Vineyard
RESERVE
WB SINCE 1883
WENTE BROS.
1989
ESTATE RESERVE
Chardonnay
LIVERMORE VALLEY

Cellaring Your Investments

THE BIGGEST CHANGE A NEW CELLAR MADE FOR SCHEICH HAS BEEN IN HIS LEVEL OF INVOLVEMENT IN THE WINE WORLD

SCHEICH RECALLS, 'IF I WERE GOING TO BUY GOOD WINES, I'D BE WASTING MY INVESTMENT WITHOUT A GOOD CELLAR'

BY STEVE HEIMOFF

TOM SOBOLIK/BLACK STAR

Jack Scheich, a Long Island, N.Y., attorney, discovered that building a wine cellar had profoundly unexpected but enjoyable consequences. He's now much more involved in the wine world

Jack Scheich, a 49-year-old Long Island, N.Y., attorney, knew the time had come to build himself a real wine cellar when his burgeoning Bordeaux collection started getting out of hand. Up until then, he'd kept a few cases in a corner of the basement below his ranch-style home. But as Scheich began buying more and more of his favorite wine around 1986, it became obvious to him that his storage conditions needed to match the quality of the classified growths he was accumulating.

He'd been attending wine-appreciation classes and reading Lichine, Johnson and Broadbent, who all went on and on about how a proper cellar should be dark, vibration-free and climate controlled. Scheich's cellar wasn't particularly dark, and during Long Island's torrid summers it certainly didn't qualify as cool.

"I realized that, if I were going to buy good wines, I'd be wasting my investment without a good cellar," Scheich recalls.

The problem was that Scheich had no idea where or how to get a wine cellar. He mentioned this one day to his wine instructor, who told him about a local firm that built cellars. Scheich called them up, and the company's contractor visited Scheich to determine his needs and budget. Together, they decided to wall off a portion of the basement, which Scheich, who's single, used as a game room. The contractor took measurements, drew chalk lines on the floor and worked up a schematic drawing for an 8-foot-by-8-foot cellar that would hold 1,000 bottles, four times what Scheich then owned, at a projected cost of $5,700.

The contractor built the cellar with four stud walls made of wood paneling and stained walnut. The walls and ceiling were heavily insulated and lined inside with plastic sheeting to prevent humidity from escaping. The builders installed fluorescent lighting and gave Scheich his choice of a wooden or glass door. Scheich chose the glass one, "because I wanted to be able to snap on my basement lights and see inside, and show my friends." A single through-wall refrigeration unit kept conditions at a steady 57 degrees Fahrenheit and 70 percent humidity.

Once the cellar was completed, Scheich's next decision was what kind of racking to choose. He was aesthetically partial to the diamond-shaped racks he'd seen in magazine photos, but the contractor convinced him he could double his storage capacity if he went to square bins, so he did. The walnut-and-aluminum racks cost Scheich an additional $1,500. The contractor also talked Scheich into buying two small tables for the cellar, useful for things such as opening cases, writing in his cellar book and so on. The entire project, from start to finish, took only about one week.

What happened next is almost predictable. "Then my buying frenzy started," Scheich laughs. The heavily hyped 1982 and '83 Bordeaux were on the market, and Scheich—now that he had a fine place to mature his wine—bought in quantity. He snapped up 15 cases of the '85. When they arrived on his doorstep, Scheich realized it was building time again.

He called the same company, and the contractor came out for a second time. They decided to expand the cellar to 12 feet by 12 feet, which would increase its capacity to almost 4,000 bottles. Scheich postponed the work for a few months because summer was coming and he didn't want to leave his bottles unrefrigerated in case a heat wave came along. Work started that fall, and because the new cellar was much bigger than the old one, Scheich had to install a second through-wall refrigeration unit. He also put in a new ceramic-tile floor for esthetic purposes. The expansion cost him $5,000 and was completed just before Thanksgiving 1989.

The new cellar might have been finished, but Scheich wasn't. Right off the bat, he began buying what he calls "all these little toys," things such as fancy bottle openers, thermometers, humidity gauges and clocks. This past summer, he decided to upgrade his climate-control system. At night, he could hear the two refrigeration units humming, and it bothered him. The double units were also unsightly, so this fall, Scheich is installing a "remote refrigeration" unit, whose motor will be out in his yard and will feed cool air into the cellar through a vent. Its cost: $2,700.

But the biggest change the cellar wrought has been in Scheich's level of involvement in the world of wine. As he puts it, "Since I put the cellar in, collecting has become a hobby, an avocation, something that keeps me off the streets. I've learned more about wine, because now it's not just having a few bottles in the corner. Now there's a commitment to wine collecting. I've expanded my going to blind tastings and component tastings, and going to courses and lectures and becoming more knowledgeable. Much more of my free time is devoted to wine, and I'm more involved with people who are involved with wine. And an awful lot of that is due to the cellar."

It's a simple formula, Scheich says. "Without the cellar, I wouldn't have expanded my collection, and without the expansion, I wouldn't have the greater interest." So the cellar has had profoundly unexpected, but enjoyable, consequences.

Scheich enjoys showing off his new cellar to friends. "I'm very proud of it, and when people visit, I'll take them down and we'll stand around and talk about it. Most of my friends and business associates have never seen a wine cellar."

He admits that some of his friends don't care too much about wine and "don't appear to have the enthusiasm I do for the cellar," but that's OK. He's met many new friends at wine functions who are fellow collectors, and gets great enjoyment in bringing them over and comparing cellar notes.

Scheich's rate of buying has continued to increase, because having thousands of empty bins in the cellar motivates him to fill them. "I bought a lot of '89 Bordeaux futures, and because of the bad crop there in 1991, I'll probably buy '90 futures," he says. From the Bordeaux-only bias he started with a few years ago, Scheich has now expanded his interest to include wines from Burgundy, Alsace, Sauternes and the Rhône Valley, and the cellar is filling up quickly. "I can see where it [the cellar] will continue to grow out of all proportion to my ability to drink," Scheich muses.

That will probably lead to—you guessed it—another cellar expansion. In fact, Scheich recently brought the contractor out to his home for a third visit, and they figured out another area of the basement the cellar can grow into. He has no plans to begin construction soon, Scheich says, "but if I absolutely have to expand, at least I know I have the room." □

Vintage Charts

The best guarantee of satisfaction in evaluating a wine for purchase is the quality behind a producer's name. Once you've picked a producer with a track record for quality, in many cases, the next question is "which vintage should I buy?"

Knowing the relative merits of each vintage can help you make more informed buying decisions. This section will present our qualitative ratings of vintages in the world's major wine regions for the last 10-20 years.

The ratings presented here are updated periodically based solely on the ongoing wine evaluations of our senior editors. The vintages in this section are rated on *The Wine Spectator*'s 100-point scale. For each vintage you will find the score, our rating, a comment on the characteristics of the vintage or the wines from that vintage, and our drinkability recommendation.

Vintage charts are by necessity general in nature. Ratings listed are averages for the years and regions. Many good wines are produced in "bad" years, just as bad wines are produced in "good" years. Use our vintage charts as a general guide to overall quality.

THE WINE SPECTATOR 100-POINT SCALE

100-95 — Classic, a great wine.

90-94 — Outstanding, superior character and style.

80-89 — Good to very good, a wine with special qualities.

70-79 — Average, drinkable wine that may have minor flaws.

60-69 — Below average, drinkable but not recommended.

50-59 — Poor, undrinkable, not recommended.

"+"—With a score indicates a range; used primarily to indicate a preliminary score.

FRANCE/*ALSACE*

Vintage	Score	Rating	Comment	Drinkability
1990	95	Classic	Exceptionally ripe year; stunning Rieslings and Pinot Blancs; some fine late-harvest wines	Hold
1989	96	Classic	Super dessert wines, rich and round	Drink or Hold
1988	95	Classic	Excellent balance, firm and opulent	Drink or Hold
1987	85	Very Good	Steely, lean and fresh	Drink
1986	84	Good	Light, elegant and delicious	Drink
1985	90	Outstanding	Concentrated, intensely fruity with good backbone	Drink or Hold
1984	74	Average	Slightly unripe, thin and simple	Drink
1983	93	Outstanding	Very rich, superbly structured; many dessert wines	Drink
1982	80	Good	Large production; fruity and simple	Drink
1981	89	Very Good	Racy, classy and elegant; some great sweet wines	Drink
1980	72	Average	Unripe, meager; most past their primes	Drink

FRANCE/*BORDEAUX RED*

Vintage	Score	Rating	Comment	Drinkability
1991	76	Average	Uneven quality, delicate, fruity and firm; forget most of St.-Emilion and Pomerol	Not Released
1990	95	Classic	Firm structure with opulent fruit and intense flavors; massive crop diluted some; best estates most successful	Not Released
1989	98	Classic	Bold, dramatic, rich, tannic and long-aging; applies only to top estates	Hold
1988	92	Outstanding	Rich and concentrated with classic structure	Hold
1987	73	Average	Light, simple and quick maturing	Drink
1986	95	Classic	Powerful, intense and tannic; best in Médoc	Hold
1985	95	Classic	Ripe, supple and balanced; consistently fine quality	Hold
1984	70	Average	Unripe, tough and tannic; mediocre quality	Drink
1983	86	Very Good	Balanced, rich and fruity; some are simple	Drink or Hold
1982	96	Classic	Extremely ripe, opulent and concentrated; many are stunning	Drink or Hold
1981	82	Good	Classic claret; elegant, balanced and charming	Drink or Hold
1980	78	Average	Light, pleasant wine for early drinking	Drink
1979	83	Good	Supple, fruity and delicate; perfect now	Drink
1978	86	Very Good	Structured, fleshy and complex; best are improving	Drink or Hold
1977	60	Below Average	Poor, unripe and acidic; well past their primes	Drink
1976	80	Good	Early promise unfulfilled; fully mature now	Drink
1975	85	Very Good	Hard, tannic and slowly evolving; time will tell	Drink
1974	58	Poor	Unripe and diluted; never worth much	Drink
1973	68	Below Average	Early maturing, luncheon wines; mostly faded	Drink
1972	60	Below Average	Acidic, light wines; never very interesting	Drink
1971	80	Good	Uneven quality; Pomerol and St.-Emilion still good, but Médoc and Graves fading quickly	Drink
1970	91	Outstanding	Excellent all-around vintage; structured with plenty of fruit	Drink or Hold
1966	89	Very Good	Classic but hard wines; best are still improving	Drink
1964	80	Good	Uneven quality; outstanding Pomerol and St.-Emilion; rain in Médoc	Drink
1961	99	Classic	Best since 1945; great concentration, structure and longevity; best are still youthful	Drink or Hold

FRANCE/*BURGUNDY RED*

Vintage	Score	Rating	Comment	Drinkability
1989	94	Outstanding	Seductive, harmonious and brimming with fruit	Hold
1988	93	Outstanding	Solid tannins and great concentration	Hold
1987	85	Very Good	Flavorful, delicious and early drinking	Drink
1986	81	Good	Aromatic, tannic and lean	Hold
1985	97	Classic	Plush, complex and seductive	Drink or Hold
1984	73	Average	Many thin, watery wines	Drink
1983	85	Very Good	Inconsistent; rot spoiled some wines	Drink or Hold
1982	80	Good	Overproduction diluted some wines	Drink
1981	74	Average	Light and thin wines	Drink
1980	79	Average	Was good, now past its peak	Drink
1979	84	Good	Supple, silky and balanced	Drink
1978	92	Outstanding	Big, flavorful wines	Drink or Hold
1977	65	Below Average	Never a good year	Drink
1976	87	Very Good	Tough wines; still coming around	Drink or Hold
1975	65	Below Average	Past its peak	Drink
1974	65	Below Average	Past its peak	Drink
1973	75	Average	Light style but charming	Drink
1972	81	Good	Lean wines with style	Drink
1971	89	Very Good	Best wines are still evolving	Drink
1970	81	Good	Forgotten vintage that's holding up	Drink
1969	93	Outstanding	Classic structure; flavorful	Drink

FRANCE/*BURGUNDY WHITE*

Vintage	Score	Rating	Comment	Drinkability
1989	94	Outstanding	Rich and opulent, with masses of fruit and flavor; should age well	Hold
1988	86	Very Good	Firm and fruity with good concentration and balance	Drink or Hold
1987	84	Good	Fresh and simple with medium-term aging potential	Drink

FRANCE/*BURGUNDY WHITE (continued)*

Vintage	Score	Rating	Comment	Drinkability
1986	92	Outstanding	Excellent acidity and focused fruit; many marked by botrytis; best are classic	Drink
1985	96	Classic	Bold and powerful; exuberant fruit with firm acidity and great aging potential	Drink or Hold
1984	78	Average	Light and very simple; very high in green acidity	Drink
1983	85	Very Good	Uneven quality; some outstanding and powerful wines	Drink or Hold
1982	83	Good	Some surprises but generally light, slightly diluted wines; most past their primes	Drink
1981	82	Good	Difficult vintage; high acidity but top producers very good	Drink
1980	73	Average	Mostly unripe and diluted wines produced	Drink

FRANCE/*CHAMPAGNE*

Vintage	Score	Rating	Comment	Drinkability
1986	86	Very Good	Good quality; lean and firm	Drink
1985	96	Classic	Superb balance with great structure and ripe fruit	Drink or Hold
1984	83	Good	Large harvest; pleasant and early drinking	Drink
1983	83	Good	Large harvest; pleasant	Drink
1982	94	Oustanding	Rich and complex with abundant fruit	Drink or Hold
1981	84	Good	Angular and hard with clean fruit; some surprises	Drink or Hold
1980	82	Good	Generous and very fruity with average structure	Drink
1979	91	Outstanding	Classy, elegant and firm; aging well	Drink

FRANCE/*RHONE RED/CHATEAUNEUF-DU-PAPE*

Vintage	Score	Rating	Comment	Drinkability
1989	96	Classic	Hot year with an average crop; powerful, concentrated reds built for aging	Hold
1988	90	Outstanding	Dry, temperate year; balanced wines with focused fruit and firm backbones	Hold
1987	75	Average	Wet weather with rot prevalent and light, fruity wines; some lacking character	Drink
1986	88	Very Good	Racy wines with plenty of steely tannins and super-clean fruit; underrated	Hold
1985	86	Very Good	Ripe and exuberant with loads of fruit that's evolving quickly	Drink or Hold
1984	78	Average	Another difficult growing season; many unripe wines but a few surprises	Drink
1983	89	Very Good	Small crop of Grenache; tannic, powerful wines now coming into their own	Drink or Hold
1982	84	Good	Variable year but many wines still fresh; balanced with an abundance of fruit	Drink
1981	97	Classic	Best of the decade; small crop in a drought year; striking, vibrant wines with superb structure	Drink or Hold

FRANCE/*SAUTERNES*

Vintage	Score	Rating	Comment	Drinkability
1989	98	Classic	Incredibly rich with lots of botrytis; built for aging	Hold
1988	95	Outstanding	Concentrated and well balanced; extremely fine and firm	Hold
1987	75	Average	Light, simple, sweet wines; many taste diluted	Drink
1986	90	Outstanding	Intense, focused and honeyed with lively acidity	Hold
1985	79	Average	Little botrytis; clean and sweet	Drink or Hold
1984	68	Below Average	Few good wines; a wet, difficult harvest	Drink
1983	95	Classic	Thick and powerful with abundant botrytis; a classic year	Hold
1982	77	Average	Mostly sweet, fat and alcoholic; Suduiraut an exception	Drink or Hold
1981	83	Good	Medium richness with fine balance	Drink
1980	82	Good	Good year; balanced and lightly botrytised	Drink

GERMANY/*RIESLING*

Vintage	Score	Rating	Comment	Drinkability
1990	97	Classic	Powerful with high acidity and extract yet great harmony	Hold
1989	96	Classic	Super-botrytised, massive, rich, round	Hold
1988	94	Outstanding	Classic, balanced and firm; best in Middle Mosel	Drink or Hold
1987	82	Good	Fresh, light and surprisingly good	Drink or Hold
1986	86	Very Good	Aromatic, elegant and fruity	Drink
1985	83	Good	Racy and well structured; problems in Rheingau and Rheinpflaz	Drink or Hold
1984	74	Average	Unripe with aggressive acidity; only top producers drinkable	Drink
1983	93	Outstanding	Super-fruity, ripe and round; little botrytis	Drink or Hold
1982	78	Average	Overproduction; diluted and soft; very good ausleses	Drink

GERMANY/*RIESLING (continued)*

Vintage	Score	Rating	Comment	Drinkability
1981	81	Good	Clean, lean and light	Drink
1980	65	Below Average	Very green, unripe and thin	Drink
1979	88	Very Good	Small crop; fresh and well structured	Drink
1978	70	Average	Green and thin but drinkable	Drink
1977	75	Average	Difficult, light and elegant; most already consumed	Drink
1976	97	Classic	Huge, ripe and powerful; plenty of botrytis	Drink
1975	94	Outstanding	Superb class, great balance and firm structure	Drink
1974	66	Below Average	Mean with no harmony and little fruit	Drink
1973	82	Good	Better than expected with ripe acidity and good fruit	Drink
1972	70	Average	Lean with high acidity; most past their primes	Drink
1971	98	Classic	Powerful and elegant with superb structure; long-lived	Drink

ITALY/*PIEDMONT*

Vintage	Score	Rating	Comment	Drinkability
1989	94	Outstanding	Ripe, concentrated, supple wines	Hold
1988	90	Outstanding	Firm, focused, generous wines	Hold
1987	85	Good	Light style but pretty fruit	Hold
1986	87	Very Good	Soft, generous wines	Hold
1985	95	Classic	Rich, ripe, concentrated and elegant	Hold
1984	80	Good	Light style; spicy and fruity	Drink or Hold
1983	75	Average	Very light, sometimes thin	Drink or Hold
1982	90	Outstanding	Powerful, tannic and long-lived	Hold
1981	75	Average	Light, fruity and mature	Drink
1980	70	Average	Very light; some wines are thin	Drink
1979	86	Very Good	Less tannic that most vintages	Drink or Hold
1978	90	Outstanding	Firm and classically structured	Drink or Hold

ITALY/*TUSCANY*

Vintage	Score	Rating	Comment	Drinkability
1990	98	Classic	Concentrated and highly extracted with firm tannins and fresh acidity	Drink or Hold
1989	79	Average	Some light pleasant wines; others very diluted	Drink or Hold
1988	96	Classic	Balanced with excellent concentration, firm acidity and fine tannins	Drink or Hold
1987	82	Good	Variable quality but some good surprises; medium structure	Drink or Hold
1986	86	Very Good	Slightly lean but solid wines with good fruit	Drink or Hold
1985	95	Outstanding	Hot, super-ripe year; big, rich wines with tons of fruit	Drink or Hold
1984	75	Average	Light, difficult vintage, most wines insipid	Drink
1983	86	Very Good	Pretty wines with good intensity and backbone	Drink or Hold
1982	90	Outstanding	Very ripe fruit with plenty of tannin; rich, round wines	Drink or Hold
1981	85	Good	Focused fruit with firm tannins; some exceptional	Drink
1980	77	Average	Tricky weather for most; uneven quality with some unripe	Drink
1979	80	Good	Best wines still rich and supple	Drink
1978	87	Very Good	Tough and tannic; starting to come around	Drink or Hold

PORTUGAL/*VINTAGE PORT*

Vintage	Score	Rating	Comment	Drinkability
1987	88	Very Good	Balanced and elegant with good finesse	Hold
1986	80	Good	Firm, gutsy and a little simple	Hold
1985	96	Classic	Opulent and intense with a solid backbone	Hold
1984	81	Good	Lean and linear; one-dimensional	Drink or Hold
1983	92	Outstanding	Powerful, tannic and age-worthy	Hold
1982	84	Good	Sweet and raisiny; unbalanced	Drink or Hold
1980	87	Very Good	Solid and well structured with focused fruit	Drink or Hold
1979	74	Average	Light, sweet and insipid	Drink
1978	84	Good	Fruity, soft and ready	Drink
1977	97	Classic	Tough, tannic and complex; ageless	Hold
1976	76	Average	Simple and variable; short	Drink
1975	80	Good	Light and one-dimensional but fruity	Drink
1974	74	Average	Aromatic and angular; small production	Drink
1972	79	Average	Light, fragrant and easy to drink	Drink
1970	95	Classic	Harmonious and well structured with intense fruit	Drink or Hold
1969	72	Average	Light and simple; tiny production	Drink
1968	77	Average	One-dimensional and fruity; small crop	Drink
1967	88	Very Good	Focused fruit; angular and elegant	Drink

PORTUGAL/*VINTAGE PORT* (continued)

Vintage	Score	Rating	Comment	Drinkability
1966	93	Outstanding	Iron backbone with good concentration and fresh flavors	Drink or Hold
1965	80	Good	Rich, focused fruit; tiny production	Drink
1964	81	Good	Appealing fruit; stylish, soft and round	Drink
1963	98	Classic	Copious fruit; forceful and extremely age-worthy	Drink or Hold
1962	82	Good	Pleasant, fruity and soft	Drink
1961	80	Good	Very ripe, roasted flavors; sweet	Drink
1960	87	Very Good	Balanced, sweet and elegant; at its peak	Drink
1958	84	Good	Fragrant, fragile and fruity	Drink
1957	85	Very Good	Angular, tannic and lively; tiny production	Drink
1955	94	Outstanding	Harmonious, refined, fruity and solid	Drink or Hold
1954	85	Very Good	Fragrant, balanced, fresh and fruity	Drink
1952	80	Good	Fruity, simple and sweet; tiny production	Drink
1950	86	Very Good	Subtle, sweet and soft	Drink
1948	99	Classic	Massive, super-ripe and powerful	Drink or Hold
1947	93	Outstanding	Balanced, integrated and attractive	Drink
1945	98	Classic	Youthful and concentrated; super quality	Drink or Hold
1935	95	Classic	Aromatic, refined and firmly structured	Drink
1934	93	Outstanding	Ripe, powerful and concentrated	Drink
1931	95	Classic	Luscious, rich and complete	Drink
1927	100	Classic	Superb concentration, balance and breeding; large production	Drink
1912	98	Classic	Concentrated, powerful and superbly structured	Drink

SPAIN/*RIOJA*

Vintage	Score	Rating	Comment	Drinkability
1990	88	Very Good	Well concentrated with rich fruit and plenty of tannins	Hold
1989	85	Very Good	Balanced, fruity and ripe	Hold
1988	81	Good	Medium-bodied and focused with clean fruit	Drink or Hold
1987	87	Very Good	Elegant and refined, with ripe fruit flavors and strong backbone	Drink or Hold
1986	83	Good	Pleasant, fruity and early maturing	Drink
1985	89	Very Good	Better than expected; rich, balanced and delicious	Drink or Hold
1984	75	Average	Difficult, weak and underripe	Drink
1983	84	Good	Uneven quality but plenty of surprises	Drink
1982	88	Very Good	Slightly overrated; maturing quickly and very ripe	Drink
1981	91	Outstanding	Underrated, polished, rich and firm	Drink or Hold
1980	78	Average	Light and early maturing	Drink
1978	86	Very Good	Plenty of fruit, tannins and acidity	Drink or Hold
1976	84	Good	Solid, rich wines with classy structure	Drink
1975	92	Outstanding	Underrated; well built, tannic and fruity	Drink
1973	88	Very Good	Fruity and balanced with fine tannins	Drink
1970	89	Very Good	Excellent harmony of fruit and tannins	Drink
1964	96	Classic	Monumental, powerful and opulent; many still excellent	Drink or Hold

UNITED STATES/*CALIFORNIA CABERNET SAUVIGNON*

Vintage	Score	Rating	Comment	Drinkability
1991	88+	Very Good	Ripe, supple and balanced	Not Released
1990	90+	Outstanding	Rich, deep, supple and complex	Not Released
1989	85	Very Good	Uneven quality; a few are great	Hold
1988	86	Very Good	Ripe, elegant and balanced	Drink or Hold
1987	90	Outstanding	Deep, rich, complex and tannic	Hold
1986	95	Classic	Classic structure;, age-worthy	Hold
1985	97	Classic	California's finest; elegant and stylish	Hold
1984	94	Outstanding	Rich, fruity and opulent	Drink or Hold
1983	81	Good	Lean and tannic; uneven quality	Hold
1982	78	Average	Austere and structured; uneven quality	Drink
1981	85	Very Good	Supple, charming and balanced	Drink
1980	84	Good	Ripe, opulent and balanced	Drink
1979	88	Very Good	Austere but age-worthy	Drink
1978	93	Outstanding	Ripe, flavorful and age-worthy	Drink

UNITED STATES/*CALIFORNIA CABERNET SAUVIGNON* (continued)

Vintage	Score	Rating	Comment	Drinkability
1977	82	Good	Elegant and charming	Drink
1976	75	Average	Ripe but awkward	Drink
1975	86	Very Good	Elegant and well balanced	Drink
1974	91	Outstanding	Bold, rich, opulent and dramatic	Drink
1973	87	Very Good	Elegant, charming, subtle and balanced	Drink
1972	67	Below Average	Rainy; simple, watery and uninspired	Drink
1971	68	Below Average	Rainy harvest and poor quality; mediocre	Drink
1970	95	Classic	Deep, complex, elegant and age-worthy	Drink
1969	92	Outstanding	Elegant, supple, balanced and charming	Drink
1968	96	Classic	Rich, concentrated, powerful and tannic	Drink
1967	82	Good	Elegant, supple and balanced; early charm	Drink
1966	91	Outstanding	Rich, complex, balanced and delightful	Drink
1965	83	Good	Ripe, balanced and charming; serviceable	Drink
1964	91	Outstanding	Ripe, complex and balanced; enduring	Drink
1963	69	Below Average	Frost; short crop with uneven quality; not memorable	Drink
1962	69	Below Average	Frost damage; mediocre and uninspiring	Drink
1961	71	Average	Severe frosts; decent quality but past their primes	Drink
1960	84	Good	Fruity, elegant and balanced; commendable	Drink
1959	87	Very Good	Elegant, balanced and complex; enduring	Drink
1958	95	Classic	Amazingly youthful, complex, elegant and age-worthy	Drink

UNITED STATES/*CALIFORNIA CHARDONNAY*

Vintage	Score	Rating	Comment	Drinkability
1991	88+	Very Good	Ripe, complex and age-worthy; should be excellent	Not Released
1990	91	Outstanding	Ripe, rich, concentrated and age-worthy	Drink or Hold
1989	85	Very Good	Uneven quality but some are superb	Drink
1988	89	Very Good	Ripe, balanced and delicate; forward	Drink or Hold
1987	85	Very Good	Hard and austere; uneven quality but some are fine	Drink
1986	91	Outstanding	Deep, rich, concentrated and complex	Drink
1985	92	Outstanding	Ripe, elegant, concentrated and harmonious	Drink
1984	87	Very Good	Very ripe and fleshy; early maturing	Drink
1983	81	Good	Austere with uneven quality; most have faded	Drink
1982	79	Average	Huge crop; very ripe but unbalanced	Drink
1981	87	Very Good	Ripe and forward; charming when young	Drink
1980	86	Very Good	Very rich, ripe and full-bodied	Drink
1979	89	Very Good	Austere, elegant, balanced and age-worthy	Drink
1978	85	Very Good	Ripe, intense and powerful	Drink
1977	84	Good	Drought year; elegant, balanced and charming	Drink
1976	77	Average	Drought year, very ripe and unbalanced	Drink
1975	85	Very Good	Ripe, elegant, balanced and charming	Drink
1974	88	Very Good	Ripe, rich, bold and balanced	Drink
1973	85	Very Good	Elegant, subtle, balanced and charming	Drink
1972	67	Below Average	Rainy; simple, watery and uninspired	Drink
1971	68	Average	Rainy harvest; poor quality	Drink
1970	89	Very Good	Complex, elegant and balanced	Drink

UNITED STATES/*CALIFORNIA MERLOT*

Vintage	Score	Rating	Comment	Drinkability
1990	88+	Very Good	Ripe and complex; best since 1987	Not Released
1989	83	Good	Large crop but uneven quality	Hold
1988	85	Very Good	Small crop; fruity and balanced	Drink or Hold
1987	91	Outstanding	Rich and complex; best of the decade	Drink or Hold
1986	87	Very Good	Huge crop; ripe and powerful	Drink or Hold
1985	88	Very Good	Ripe and balanced but variable	Drink or Hold
1984	86	Very Good	Fleshy, ripe and forward	Drink
1983	87	Very Good	Intense and tannic; better than Cabernet	Drink
1982	86	Very Good	Uneven quality; diluted wines	Drink
1981	84	Good	Ripe and fruity	Drink
1980	83	Good	Large crop of ripe, early drinking wines	Drink

SOURCE: *THE WINE SPECTATOR, VINTAGE PORT, CALIFORNIA'S GREAT CABERNETS, CALIFORNIA'S GREAT CHARDONNAYS*

At $165.00 each we don't sell many bottles. But we don't make many, either.

ROYAL
LOCHNAGAR

Selected Reserve Single Highland Malt

"THE MOST EXCLUSIVE WHISKY IN THE WORLD"

Royal Lochnagar Selected Reserve, Imported by Schieffelin & Somerset Co., New York, N.Y., Single Highland Malt 43% alc/vol, 86 proof.

The Benefits of Blind Tasting

BLIND TASTINGS ALLOW WINE DRINKERS TO AVOID 'LABEL DRINKING,' WHICH CAN MAR CRITICAL JUDGMENT

BY STEVE HEIMOFF

JOYCE OUDKERKPOOL

Blind tastings can dispell preconceived notions about wine, as well as sharpen a taster's expertise

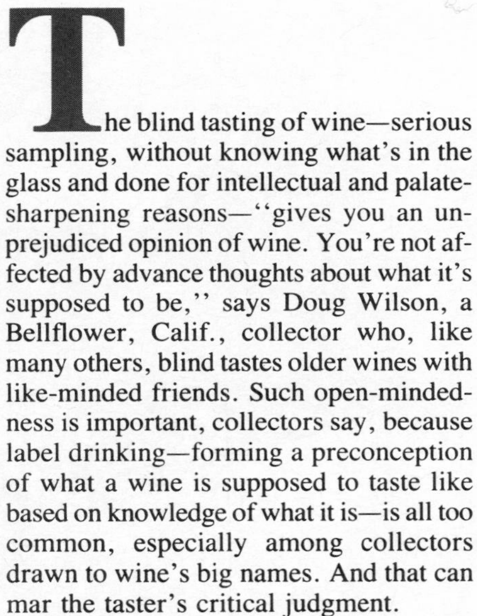

The blind tasting of wine—serious sampling, without knowing what's in the glass and done for intellectual and palate-sharpening reasons—"gives you an unprejudiced opinion of wine. You're not affected by advance thoughts about what it's supposed to be," says Doug Wilson, a Bellflower, Calif., collector who, like many others, blind tastes older wines with like-minded friends. Such open-mindedness is important, collectors say, because label drinking—forming a preconception of what a wine is supposed to taste like based on knowledge of what it is—is all too common, especially among collectors drawn to wine's big names. And that can mar the taster's critical judgment.

That this is true is testified to by almost everyone who's seriously blind tasted wines for any length of time. Riverside, Calif., collector Bipin Desai, who has sponsored some of the nation's most spectacular blind (and non-blind) tastings, tells the funny but revealing story of a famous collector at a blind tasting of Bordeaux. This collector scored Lynch-Bages, a fifth growth, ahead of Mouton-Rothschild, a first growth. "When the results were revealed, he very quietly changed his score" on the scoring sheet, says Desai, who was seated near him. The collector had the notion that a fifth growth cannot possibly be better than a first, so much so that he chose to deny the evidence of his own palate. Yet that's exactly the kind of myth that blind tasting can dispel.

There are actually many different reasons to blind taste. Desai likes to include little-known wines in his blind tastings so that others who would normally turn their noses up at them can discover how exciting they can be. He recently served a Château Musar, the Lebanese red wine, at a blind tasting, and "when it was revealed, it was a revelation to everyone." Half the group thought it was a great Bordeaux, the other half a top-notch Burgundy. The results, says Desai, showed the tasters (all of whom were well-known collectors) "that just because they don't know a wine doesn't mean it doesn't deserve a high score."

Birmingham, Ala., collector Wimberly Miree likes to blind taste wines "because of the challenge. It's a measure of your accumulated knowledge and experience." Miree and his group prefer so-called double-blind tastings, in which the tasters know nothing at all about the wines they're tasting, not vintage or varietal or even what continent they're from. The absence of such knowledge "forces you to concentrate, to really think" about the wines, Miree says. In fact, the amount of concentration that's needed—bringing together all the facts, trivia and accumulated knowledge in the taster's memory—is so great that Miree's tastings always begin with a period of silent meditation.

Not all tasters like the open-endedness of double-blind tastings. Wilson calls them "pretty hairy" and says his group makes so many mistakes in identifying the wines that double blinds seem to defeat the whole purpose of tasting, that of gaining knowledge. Instead, says Wilson, he prefers regular, or single, blind tastings (the word "single" is generally not used).

Single blind tastings are often based on a theme, such as a vertical of a particular California Cabernet Sauvignon (Beaulieu Vineyards Private Reserve, for example), in which the tasters know in advance what the wines are, but don't know what's in their glasses. That provides just enough knowledge for a mental framework for the tasting and enables tasters to apprehend individual differences in a family of wines while avoiding total chaos. As Desai puts it, a single-blind tasting "is more interesting [than a double blind], because then you can concentrate on the right kind of characteristics you're looking for."

Some people blind taste because it helps them do their jobs better, and it is perhaps they who approach blind tastings with the most perspicacity. Peter Granoff, sommelier at San Francisco's Square One restaurant, who double-blind tastes newly released wines with sommeliers from other local restaurants, calls his group's tastings deductive. He explains, "The object isn't simply to guess the wine. It's to do a thorough, deductive analysis of the wine. And as you're going through the analysis, you're narrowing the range of possibilities of what it could be." The most difficult part of such analysis, Granoff says, is the mind's tendency to categorize the unknown. "It's hard to avoid coming to a conclusion about what the wine is, and then you start finding things that support your conclusion, whether they're there or not." The only way around that danger, Granoff stresses, is an almost Zen-like emptying of the mind.

From Granoff's point of view, then, guessing the wine wrong is not considered failure at all, as long as the guess was based on sound enological principles. Desai agrees. "It's the *logic* that counts," not successfully guessing the wine. "If I'm wrong, I'm not terribly concerned," he says. Desai recently confused a fairly young Australian Chardonnay for a mature Montrachet; the Down Under wine had the nose and aftertaste he had learned to associate with the *grand cru* Burgundy. But the error "didn't embarrass me," Desai explains, "because if you have accurately determined the wine's qualities based on logic, that is all that really counts."

Yet the pressure to correctly identify a blind-tasted wine always seems to be there, and that's one reason some collectors shy away from blind tastings. Desai (who says he once correctly guessed all 21 wines in a tasting of 1979 classified-growth Bordeaux), says that blind tastings, especially double-blind ones, "can make people uneasy because of the risk of embarrassment."

Blind tasting can indeed take a taster down a few pegs, says Granoff, who has made his share of mistakes. Once he was waxing poetic over the intensely citrusy aromas of some Mâcons he was blind tasting, "when all of a sudden, I realized that the housekeeper had polished the tasting glasses with Lemon Pledge." But far from being embarrassed, Granoff found the incident amusing. He explains, "You need that kind of humbling experience at least once a month to keep you in check."

Some collectors dislike blind tastings of any kind because they feel they undermine the intellectual pleasure of tasting, particularly of old, rare wines. Ann Arbor, Mich., collector Ron Weiser says that, while he can understand the idea of "not being influenced by what you know about the wine," certain kinds of wines don't lend themselves to blind tasting, such as a 90-vintage tasting of Château Lafite he attended. "It was a comparative tasting, where you could try the '45 against the '53 and the '59 and get some feeling for the differences in style and maturation process," Weiser says. "And knowing what the vintages were made it more fun." Miree agrees. "There are some special wines you don't want to waste your time guessing, like '45 Mouton or '29 Bordeaux. I'd rather know up front what they are and concentrate my brain power into dissecting what I'm tasting, and form memory-bank connections with that name and vintage."

Blind tasting can be fun and can sharpen a taster's expertise. But a word of warning: No matter how educated your palate is, you're going to fail sometimes when you blind taste and occasionally you'll flop badly. "We all have days when we're right on the money, and other days when we can't divine anything to save our souls," Granoff says about his blind tastings. "It's a mystery to me why it happens that way." □

Bistro
SYLVAIN FESSY
BEAUJOLAIS-VILLAGES
There's a new name in Beaujolais.
Sylvain Fessy. A young man whose Beaujolais roots go back five generations.
His wines are fun and fresh, the way Beaujolais was always meant to be. They bring the true spirit of "the Beaujolais" to wherever friends get together.
It's fun. It's fresh. It's Fessy.
· SYLVAIN FESSY ·
PATERNO IMPORTS

The Top 100

Each year the editors of *The Wine Spectator* choose 100 of the most exciting wines from the thousands reviewed to present our Top 100 wines of the year. All of the wines considered for our Top 100 come from blind tastings by two or more tasters in our San Francisco editorial offices and on location in Europe. The result each year is 100 wine choices that would make splendid drinking for even the toughest wine critic.

We could have simply given you a list of the highest-scoring wines, but that would only be part of the story. Many of the most exciting wines we review set our pulses racing because they represent a special style or make a real contribution to the great diversity that makes wine so much fun. We call this the "excitement factor."

It is for this reason that "The Top 100" is not simply a list of the highest-scoring wines from a particular year. A wine's score only reflects how good it is, regardless of price or where it comes from. Absolute quality is only one factor. We also consider:

Overall Value—We expect more of higher-priced wines. In other words, a $50 Cabernet had better deliver. It makes our spines tingle when a wine strikes us as just as impressive as those that cost several times its price. That's why, for example, we ranked the 1985 Château Lynch-Bages No. 1 in our 1988 ranking. It rates right up there with first-growth Bordeaux at a fraction of the price.

Relative Value Within Its Type—The Top 100 favors highly rated wines that are priced below average for the type. In other words, a $35 Chassagne-Montrachet is a *relatively* good value. A $35 Italian Chardonnay is not.

Availability—The Top 100 favors wines that are not in extremely limited supply. Some wines made in tiny quantities, however, such as *cru* Burgundies, were so highly rated and reasonably priced in their categories that we decided they are well worth searching for. We made exceptions to the rule for these.

Rarity of Excellence Within Its Type—We like to find outstanding wines in categories that don't usually produce good-quality wines. For example, the best Sauvignon Blanc may make the list ahead of the 15th-best Chardonnay, even if both wines have the same rating.

On the following pages are the Top 100 lists for 1991, 1990, 1989 and 1988. Over the years, the editors have found it difficult to narrow each of these lists to only 100 wines and decide their order. For example, how do you differentiate between similarly priced wines with the same high scores? (One may rank ahead of another because it has broader appeal.) We shuffled the wines around several different ways until we agreed on the lists you see. There are a lot of terrific wines on these lists.

The Top 100: 1991's Best Wines

Rank	Score	Wine
1	97	CHATEAU DE BEAUCASTEL Châteauneuf-du-Pape 1989 $35 (10/15/91) CS
2	100	CHATEAU MOUTON-ROTHSCHILD Pauillac 1988 $105 (4/30/91)
3	98	CAYMUS Cabernet Sauvignon Napa Valley Special Selection 1987 Rel: $60 Cur: $82 (10/31/91) CS
4	96	CHATEAU LAGRANGE St.-Julien 1988 $26 (4/30/91)
5	98	SASSICAIA 1988 Rel: $60 Cur: $66 (9/15/91)
6	97	CHATEAU MARGAUX Margaux 1988 Rel: $75 Cur: $80 (3/31/91) CS
7	98	CHATEAU HAUT-BRION Pessac-Léognan 1988 $95 (4/30/91)
8	95	CHATEAU MONTELENA Cabernet Sauvignon Napa Valley 1987 Rel: $30 Cur: $37 (10/31/91) SS
9	95	CHATEAU PICHON-BARON Pauillac 1988 Rel: $30 Cur: $33 (3/31/91) SS
10	95	CHATEAU LYNCH-BAGES Pauillac 1988 $35 (3/15/91) CS
11	95	DR. BURKLIN-WOLF Riesling Auslese Rheinpfalz Wachenheimer Gerümpel 1989 $34 (12/15/90)
12	96	THE HESS COLLECTION Cabernet Sauvignon Napa Valley Reserve 1987 Rel: $34 Cur: $55 (10/15/91)
13	96	DOMAINE D'AUVENAY Meursault Les Narvaux 1989 $60 (8/31/91)
14	96	CHATEAU PALMER Margaux 1988 $65 (2/28/91) CS
15	97	JOSEPH DROUHIN Corton-Charlemagne 1989 $92 (8/31/91)
16	97	DOMAINE D'AUVENAY Puligny-Montrachet Les Folatières 1989 $95 (8/31/91)
17	96	LOUIS JADOT Chambertin Clos de Bèze 1988 $97 (3/15/91)
18	95	DOMAINE DE MARCOUX Châteauneuf-du-Pape Vieilles Vignes 1989 $30 (10/15/91)
19	95	WOODWARD CANYON Charbonneau Walla Walla County 1988 $26 (10/15/91)
20	94	THE HESS COLLECTION Cabernet Sauvignon Napa Valley 1987 Rel: $17 Cur: $22 (4/15/91) SS
21	94	CHAPPELLET Cabernet Sauvignon Napa Valley Reserve 1987 Rel: $18 Cur: $21 (10/15/91)
22	94	DR. BURKLIN-WOLF Riesling Auslese Rheinpfalz Forster Pechstein 1989 $25 (12/15/90)
23	93	FONTODI Chianti Classico Riserva 1985 $16 (9/15/91)
24	93	QUAIL RIDGE Cabernet Sauvignon Napa Valley 1987 $16 (9/30/91)
25	92	MERIDIAN Cabernet Sauvignon Paso Robles 1988 $12 (9/30/91) SS
26	92	HOGUE Merlot Washington 1989 $12 (10/15/91) SS
27	93	LEONETTI Merlot Washington 1989 $18 (5/31/91)
28	93	LES CAILLOUX Châteauneuf-du-Pape 1989 $19 (10/15/91)
29	94	EGON MULLER Riesling Spätlese Mosel-Saar-Ruwer Scharzhofberger 1989 $31 (12/15/90)
30	94	CHATEAU LARRIVET-HAUT-BRION Pessac-Léognan 1988 $25 (4/30/91)
31	94	CHATEAU CLERC-MILON Pauillac 1988 $26 (4/30/91) SS
32	94	CHATEAU HAUT-BAILLY Pessac-Léognan 1988 $30 (4/30/91)
33	94	CHATEAU PAVIE-DECESSE St.-Emilion 1988 $27 (3/31/91)
34	93	DOMAINE DANIEL RION Nuits-St.-Georges Les Lavières 1988 $33 (2/15/91)
35	94	JEAN GROS Vosne-Romanée Clos des Réas 1988 $50 (2/28/91)
36	93	GEYSER PEAK Johannisberg Riesling Late Harvest Mendocino County Selected Dried Berries 1990 $13/375ml (8/31/91)
37	94	F. CHAUVENET Meursault Genevrières 1989 $42 (8/31/91)
38	95	CHATEAU COS D'ESTOURNEL St.-Estèphe 1988 Rel: $30 Cur: $36 (7/15/91) CS
39	95	HEITZ Cabernet Sauvignon Napa Valley Martha's Vineyard 1986 Rel: $60 Cur: $70 (4/15/91) CS
40	95	JOSEPH DROUHIN Montrachet Marquis de Laguiche 1988 Rel: $180 Cur: $230 (2/28/91)
41	94	DUNN Cabernet Sauvignon Howell Mountain 1987 Rel: $36 Cur: $70 (4/15/91)
42	94	BERINGER Cabernet Sauvignon Napa Valley Private Reserve 1987 Rel: $40 Cur: $47 (10/31/91)
43	95	DOMAINE MEO-CAMUZET Vosne-Romanée Au Cros-Parantoux 1989 $91 (11/15/91)
44	93	HOUSE OF NOBILO Chardonnay Gisborne Tietjen Vineyard Reserve 1989 $18 (9/15/91)
45	94	PHILIPPE PICHON Condrieu 1989 $45 (11/15/91)
46	94	ORNELLAIA 1988 $49 (9/15/91)
47	94	CHARTRON & TREBUCHET Chassagne-Montrachet Les Morgeots 1989 $54 (2/15/91)
48	92	CHATEAU DE MARBUZET St.-Estèphe 1988 Rel: $15 Cur: $17 (7/15/91) SS
49	92	MARKHAM Chardonnay Napa Valley 1989 $12 (6/15/91) SS
50	92	LOUIS JADOT Beaune Boucherottes 1988 $33 (3/31/91)
51	92	LES FIEFS DE LAGRANGE St.-Julien 1988 $17 (4/30/91)
52	92	DOMAINE FRANCOIS LEGROS Chambolle-Musigny Les Noirots 1989 $30 (11/15/91)
53	92	CHATEAU DE FRANCE Pessac-Léognan 1988 $18 (2/28/91) SS
54	92	CHATEAU ST. JEAN Cabernet Sauvignon Alexander Valley 1987 $16 (6/30/91) SS
55	93	CA' DEL BOSCO Maurizio Zanella 1988 Rel: $32 Cur: $57 (9/30/91)
56	93	REVERE Chardonnay Napa Valley Reserve 1988 Rel: $18 Cur: $26 (5/15/91)
57	92	ROSSIGNOL-FEVRIER Volnay 1988 $32 (3/31/91)
58	91	LATAH CREEK Cabernet Sauvignon Washington Limited Bottling 1988 $12.50 (10/15/91)
59	92	CHOPIN-GROFFIER Vougeot 1988 $32 (5/15/91)
60	91	LATAH CREEK Merlot Washington Limited Bottling 1989 $11 (9/30/91)
61	92	JOSEPH DROUHIN Morey-St.-Denis Monts-Luisants 1988 $38 (2/28/91)
62	93	POGGIO ANTICO Brunello di Montalcino Riserva 1985 $55 (8/31/91)
63	93	WOODWARD CANYON Chardonnay Columbia Valley 1990 $18.50 (11/15/91)
64	93	ISOLE E OLENA Cepparello 1988 $32 (9/15/91)
65	90	DOMAINE LE PEU DE LA MORIETTE Vouvray 1989 $12 (4/30/91)
66	93	WOODWARD CANYON Cabernet Sauvignon Columbia Valley 1988 $24 (10/15/91)
67	94	CHATEAU DE MEURSAULT Meursault 1986 $55 (7/31/91)
68	93	PAUL JABOULET AINE Hermitage La Chapelle 1989 $45 (8/31/91) CS
69	92	KESSELSTATT Riesling Auslese Mosel-Saar-Ruwer Oberemmeler Karlsberg 1989 $32 (12/15/90)
70	92	JOH. JOS. PRUM Riesling Auslese Mosel-Saar-Ruwer Wehlener Sonnenuhr 1989 $35 (12/15/90)
71	91	FETZER Johannisberg Riesling Late Harvest Sonoma County Reserve 1988 $10/375ml (3/31/91)
72	91	MERIDIAN Syrah Paso Robles 1988 $14 (3/31/91)
73	91	ELIO ALTARE Barbera d'Alba 1989 $13 (3/15/91)
74	92	CLOS DU VAL Cabernet Sauvignon Stags Leap District 1987 Rel: $18.50 Cur: $22 (6/30/91)
75	92	FATTORIA VALTELLINA Chianti Classico Giorgio Regni Riserva 1985 $20 (9/15/91)
76	91	FONTODI Chianti Classico 1988 $13 (9/15/91) SS
77	90	ARTERBERRY Chardonnay Willamette Valley 1988 $10 (1/31/91)
78	91	VILLA CAFAGGIO Chianti Classico Riserva 1985 $13 (9/15/91)
79	92	KENWOOD Cabernet Sauvignon Sonoma Valley Jack London Vineyard 1987 Rel: $18 Cur: $21 (1/31/91)
80	93	GRAHAM Vintage Port Malvedos 1988 Rel: $26 Cur: $29 (1/31/91)
81	93	CHATEAU HAUT-BAGES-AVEROUS Pauillac 1988 $23 (4/30/91)
82	92	MONTICELLO Chardonnay Napa Valley Corley Reserve 1988 Rel: $17.25 Cur: $20 (1/31/91) SS
83	91	ROSEMOUNT Shiraz Hunter Valley 1989 $8 (2/15/91) SS
84	93	CALERA Pinot Noir San Benito County Jensen 1987 $30 (4/30/91)
85	91	PRESTON WINE CELLARS Chardonnay Washington Barrel Fermented 1989 $12 (5/31/91)
86	91	KUNDE Chardonnay Sonoma Valley 1990 $12 (12/15/91) SS
87	92	ROSEMOUNT Chardonnay Hunter Valley Show Reserve 1989 $16 (5/31/91)
88	91	CAYMUS Conundrum California 1990 $18 (11/30/91)
89	92	CHATEAU MONBRISON Margaux 1988 $20 (2/28/91)
90	92	SAN FELICE Brunello di Montalcino Campogiovanni 1986 $28 (11/30/91)
91	90	FLORA SPRINGS Sauvignon Blanc Napa Valley 1990 $9.25 (11/30/91) SS
92	91	IRON HORSE Brut Sonoma County Green Valley Late Disgorged 1986 $24 (11/30/91)
93	90	KESSELSTATT Riesling Spätlese Mosel-Saar-Ruwer Scharzhofberger 1989 $13 (12/15/90)
94	90	ROCCHE COSTAMAGNA Barbera d'Alba 1988 $11.50 (3/15/91)
95	91	R.H. PHILLIPS Syrah California EXP 1988 $15 (11/15/91)
96	90	LAR DE LARES Tierra de Barros Gran Reserva 1982 $14 (6/15/91)
97	91	ACACIA Pinot Noir Carneros Napa Valley St. Clair Vineyard 1988 $20 (2/28/91)
98	92	ANDERSON'S CONN VALLEY Cabernet Sauvignon Napa Valley Estate Reserve 1988 $24 (11/15/91)
99	92	CASTELLO BANFI Brunello di Montalcino Poggio all'Oro 1985 $30 (12/15/91) CS
100	91	SCHARFFENBERGER Blanc de Blancs Mendocino County 1986 $20 (3/15/91)

The Top 100: 1990's Best Wines

Beringer.
1986
NAPA VALLEY
CABERNET SAUVIGNON
Beringer Private Reserve Cabernet Sauvignon is a tribute to the art of winemaking and vineyard selection. Winemaker Edward Sbragia selects only wine of outstanding quality for the Private Reserve wines. For this 1986 Private Reserve Cabernet Sauvignon Edward chose special lots for their complementary, rich varietal flavors and aging potential. Produced and bottled by Beringer Vineyards, St. Helena, Napa Valley, California.

Rank	Score	Wine
1	95	BERINGER Cabernet Sauvignon Napa Valley Private Reserve 1986 Rel: $35 Cur: $39 (9/15/90) CS
2	99	CAYMUS Cabernet Sauvignon Napa Valley Special Selection 1985 Rel: $50 Cur: $127 (4/30/90)
3	96	CHARTRON & TREBUCHET Chassagne-Montrachet Les Morgeots 1988 $34 (2/28/90)
4	95	POGGIO ANTICO Brunello di Montalcino 1985 $36 (11/30/90) CS
5	98	HEITZ Cabernet Sauvignon Napa Valley Martha's Vineyard 1985 Rel: $60 Cur: $118 (4/30/90)
6	97	OPUS ONE Napa Valley 1987 Rel: $68 Cur: $69 (11/15/90) CS
7	95	DOMAINE DANIEL RION Nuits-St.-Georges Les Vignes Rondes 1987 $35 (4/30/90)
8	98	JOH. JOS. PRUM Spätlese Mosel-Saar-Ruwer Wehlener Sonnenuhr (Cask 2) 1988 $24 (9/30/89)
9	96	SPOTTSWOODE Cabernet Sauvignon Napa Valley 1987 Rel: $36 Cur: $56 (9/15/90) SS
10	95	WOODWARD CANYON Cabernet Sauvignon Columbia Valley 1987 $18.50 (12/31/90)
11	95	DUCKHORN Cabernet Sauvignon Napa Valley 1987 Rel: $20 Cur: $27 (6/30/90) CS
12	96	C. VON SCHUBERT Spätlese Mosel-Saar-Ruwer Maximin Grunhauser Abtsberg 1988 $18 (9/30/89)
13	95	WILLIAM HILL Cabernet Sauvignon Napa Valley Reserve 1987 Rel: $24 Cur: $25 (11/15/90) SS
14	95	ZILLIKEN Spätlese Mosel-Saar-Ruwer Saarburger Rausch 1988 $17 (9/30/89)
15	96	SILVERADO Cabernet Sauvignon Napa Valley Limited Reserve 1986 Rel: $35 Cur: $38 (12/15/90) CS
16	95	LA JOTA Cabernet Sauvignon Howell Mountain 1987 Rel: $25 Cur: $28 (7/31/90) SS
17	96	BOLLINGER Brut Champagne Grand Année 1985 $45 (12/31/90)
18	95	DUNN Cabernet Sauvignon Howell Mountain 1986 Rel: $30 Cur: $91 (7/31/90) CS
19	95	GROTH Cabernet Sauvignon Napa Valley Reserve 1985 Rel: $30 Cur: $166 (4/15/90)
20	96	EMMANUEL ROUGET Echézeaux 1988 $81 (11/15/90)
21	95	BODEGAS VEGA SICILIA Ribera del Duero Unico 1979 Rel: $75 Cur: $80 (3/31/90)
22	95	DOPFF AU MOULIN Riesling Alsace Grand Cru Schoenenberg 1988 $19 (10/15/89)
23	94	ST. FRANCIS Merlot Sonoma Valley Reserve 1986 $20 (1/31/90)
24	94	CAYMUS Cabernet Sauvignon Napa Valley 1986 Rel: $22 Cur: $29 (3/15/90) SS
25	94	SANFORD Chardonnay Santa Barbara County Barrel Select 1988 Rel: $25 Cur: $28 (8/31/90)
26	94	KISTLER Chardonnay Sonoma Valley Kistler Estate 1988 $26 (4/30/90)
27	94	GIUSEPPE MASCARELLO & FIGLIO Barolo Santo Stefano di Perno 1985 $35 (10/15/90)
28	94	SIMI Cabernet Sauvignon Alexander Valley Reserve 1985 Rel: $25 Cur: $28 (8/31/90) SS
29	94	SILVER OAK Cabernet Sauvignon Napa Valley 1986 Rel: $26 Cur: $54 (10/31/90) CS
30	93	CHATEAU LA TOUR MARTILLAC Blanc Pessac-Léognan 1987 $15 (1/31/90)
31	93	BENZIGER Cabernet Sauvignon Sonoma County 1987 $10 (9/30/90) SS
32	95	STERLING Reserve Napa Valley 1986 Rel: $35 Cur: $43 (3/15/90) CS
33	94	DOMAINE JEAN CHARTRON Puligny-Montrachet Les Folatières 1988 $38 (3/15/90)
34	92	SILVERADO Cabernet Sauvignon Napa Valley 1987 Rel: $14 Cur: $18 (4/15/90) SS
35	93	LANSON Brut Champagne 1985 $37 (12/31/90)
36	92	SILVERADO Merlot Napa Valley 1987 $14 (4/15/90)
37	92	FRANCISCAN Chardonnay Napa Valley Oakville Estate Reserve 1987 $15 (6/15/90)
38	91	LAR DE BARROS Tierra de Barros Tinto Reserva 1986 $8 (10/15/90) SS
39	90	ROSEMOUNT Shiraz Hunter Valley 1988 $8 (1/31/90) SS
40	93	CAYMUS Cabernet Sauvignon Napa Valley 1987 Rel: $16 Cur: $19 (9/15/90)
41	93	FERRARI-CARANO Chardonnay Alexander Valley 1988 Rel: $18 Cur: $18 (5/31/90) SS
42	93	ARGYLE Chardonnay Oregon Barrel Fermented 1987 $18.50 (12/15/90)
43	93	MERRYVALE Chardonnay Napa Valley 1987 $19 (2/15/90)
44	92	RUTHERFORD RANCH Cabernet Sauvignon Napa Valley 1985 Rel: $11 Cur: $11 (5/15/90) SS
45	92	BYRON Chardonnay Santa Barbara County 1988 $12 (4/30/90) SS
46	93	FATTORIA DI FELSINA Chianti Classico Berardenga Vigneto Rancia Riserva 1985 Rel: $23 Cur: $23 (4/30/90) CS
47	93	LOUIS M. MARTINI Cabernet Sauvignon Sonoma Valley Monte Rosso 1987 Rel: $20 Cur: $23 (11/15/90)
48	93	MAZZOCCO Cabernet Sauvignon Alexander Valley Claret Style 1987 $20 (8/31/90)
49	93	SILVER OAK Cabernet Sauvignon Alexander Valley 1986 Rel: $26 Cur: $37 (10/31/90) SS
50	93	DOMAINE GEOFFROY Gevrey-Chambertin Clos Prieur 1987 $29 (3/31/90)
51	94	CHATEAU MAGDELAINE St.-Emilion 1986 Rel: $48 Cur: $48 (2/15/90)
52	93	CLOS DU BOIS Chardonnay Alexander Valley Winemaker's Reserve 1987 Rel: $24 Cur: $24 (2/28/90)
53	93	OLIVIER LEFLAIVE FRERES Puligny-Montrachet 1987 $33 (6/30/90)
54	93	PODERE IL POGGIOLO Brunello di Montalcino 1985 $34 (11/30/90)
55	93	MICHEL BOUZEREAU Meursault Genevrières 1988 $37 (7/15/90)
56	93	CHATEAU ST. JEAN Chardonnay Alexander Valley Robert Young Vineyards Reserve 1.5L 1985 Rel: $40 Cur: $40 (9/30/90)
57	95	E. GUIGAL Côte-Rôtie La Turque 1986 Rel: $99 Cur: $340 (10/15/90) CS
58	95	JEAN GROS Richebourg 1987 Rel: $99 Cur: $170 (3/31/90)
59	94	GAJA Cabernet Sauvignon Darmagi 1986 Rel: $76 Cur: $76 (1/31/90)
60	96	CHATEAU D'YQUEM Sauternes 1984 Rel: $149 Cur: $151 (3/31/90)
61	92	WILLIAMS SELYEM Pinot Noir Sonoma Coast 1988 $40 (5/31/90)
62	92	VITICCIO Prunaio 1986 $19 (3/31/90) SS
63	91	SNOQUALMIE Merlot Columbia Valley Reserve 1987 $12 (9/30/90)
64	91	CAPEZZANA Ghiaie della Furba 1985 $20 (1/31/90)
65	92	DOMAINE AUFFRAY Chablis Les Clos 1988 $38 (3/31/90)
66	92	DOMAINE DAUVISSAT-CAMUS Chablis Les Clos 1988 $41 (7/31/90)
67	92	BODEGAS VEGA SICILIA Valbuena Ribera del Duero 3.0 1985 $40 (10/15/90)
68	91	SAINTSBURY Pinot Noir Carneros 1988 $15 (12/15/90) SS
69	91	EDMUNDS ST. JOHN Les Fleurs du Chaparral Napa Valley 1987 $15 (8/31/90)
70	91	BROWN BROTHERS Chardonnay King Valley Family Reserve 1987 $15.50 (7/15/90) SS
71	92	FREEMARK ABBEY Johannisberg Riesling Late Harvest Napa Valley Edelwein Gold 1989 $22/375ml (7/15/90)
72	92	LUCIANO SANDRONE Barolo Cannubi Boschis 1985 $30 (1/31/90)
73	92	ELIO ALTARE Barolo 1985 $24 (1/31/90)
74	92	CLERICO Barolo Ciabot Mentin Ginestra 1985 Rel: $27 Cur: $40 (4/15/90) CS
75	92	PESQUERA Ribera del Duero Reserva 1986 $26 (9/30/90)
76	92	VILLA BANFI Brunello di Montalcino 1985 Rel: $30 Cur: $30 (10/15/90)
77	91	BRIDGEHAMPTON Chardonnay Long Island Grand Vineyard Selection 1988 $18 (3/31/90)
78	90	CLINE Oakley Cuvée Contra Costa County 1988 $12 (2/28/90)
79	91	TRIMBACH Riesling Alsace Cuvée Frédéric Emile 1988 $15 (10/15/89)
80	91	SELVAPIANA Chianti Rufina Vigneto Bucerchiale Riserva 1985 $19 (9/15/90)
81	91	PONZI Pinot Noir Willamette Valley Reserve 1987 $20 (2/15/90)
82	91	LEONETTI Cabernet Sauvignon Washington 1987 $22 (6/15/90)
83	91	DOMAINE MUMM Brut Carneros Winery Lake Cuvée Napa 1987 $22 (11/15/90)
84	92	E. GUIGAL Hermitage 1986 Rel: $32 Cur: $32 (2/28/90) CS
85	92	PRINCE FLORENT DE MERODE Corton Renardes 1987 $36 (3/31/90)
86	92	CA'ROME Barbaresco Maria di Brun 1985 $37 (1/31/90)
87	90	SIMI Sauvignon Blanc Sonoma County 1988 $8 (10/31/90)
88	90	SILVERADO Sauvignon Blanc Napa Valley 1988 $8.50 (2/15/90) SS
89	90	KENDALL-JACKSON Sauvignon Blanc Lake County Vintner's Reserve 1989 $9 (10/31/90)
90	90	BODEGAS BERBERANA Rioja Reserva 1985 $10 (2/28/90)
91	90	A. RAFANELLI Zinfandel Dry Creek Valley 1988 $9.75 (9/15/90)
92	90	GRGICH HILLS Fumé Blanc Napa Valley 1988 $10 (3/31/90)
93	90	SNOQUALMIE Cabernet Sauvignon Columbia Valley 1987 $10 (9/30/90)
94	90	DOMAINE DU GOUR DE CHAULE Gigondas 1986 $13 (9/15/90)
95	90	VALFIERI Barolo 1985 $13.50 (10/15/90)
96	90	LYTTON SPRINGS Zinfandel Sonoma County 1988 $12 (7/31/90)
97	90	PRODUTTORI DEL BARBARESCO Barbaresco 1986 $12 (10/31/90)
98	90	J.J. VINCENT Pouilly-Fuissé 1988 $15 (10/31/90)
99	90	DOMAINES SCHLUMBERGER Riesling Alsace Kitterlé 1988 $14 (10/15/89)
100	91	N. JOLY Savennières Clos de la Coulée de Serrant 1989 $33 (11/30/90)

The Top 100: 1989's Best Wines

1 98 CAYMUS Cabernet Sauvignon Napa Valley Special Selection 1984 Rel: $35 Cur: $118 (7/15/89) CS
2 97 CHATEAU CLERC-MILON Pauillac 1986 Rel: $23 Cur: $32 (5/31/89)
3 97 HEITZ Cabernet Sauvignon Napa Valley Martha's Vineyard 1984 Rel: $40 Cur: $77 (3/15/89) SS
4 97 CHATEAU PICHON-BARON Pauillac 1986 Rel: $31 Cur: $58 (5/31/89)
5 97 KENDALL-JACKSON Cabernet Sauvignon California Cardinale 1985 $45 (11/15/89)
6 98 CHATEAU MARGAUX Margaux 1986 Rel: $80 Cur: $100 (6/15/89) CS
7 98 CHATEAU CHEVAL BLANC St.-Emilion 1986 Rel: $80 Cur: $85 (6/30/89) CS
8 98 CHATEAU MOUTON-ROTHSCHILD Pauillac 1986 Rel: $102 Cur: $114 (5/31/89) CS
9 97 CHATEAU PICHON-LALANDE Pauillac 1986 Rel: $50 Cur: $57 (5/31/89)
10 96 PENFOLDS Shiraz South Australia Grange Hermitage Bin 95 1982 Rel: $60 Cur: $68 (9/30/89) CS
11 98 ROMANEE-CONTI Romanée-St.-Vivant 1986 Rel: $195 Cur: $195 (8/31/89)
12 98 ROMANEE-CONTI La Tâche 1986 Rel: $250 Cur: $250 (8/31/89) CS
13 95 JOHNSON TURNBULL Cabernet Sauvignon Napa Valley Vineyard Selection 82 1986 Rel: $14.50 Cur: $25 (8/31/89)
14 96 STERLING Reserve Napa Valley 1985 Rel: $30 Cur: $38 (7/15/89) SS
15 95 SEPPELT Tawny Port Australia Old Trafford NV $15 (3/15/89)
16 95 DOMAINE MEO-CAMUZET Vosne-Romanée Aux Brûlées 1987 $63 (12/15/89)
17 95 DOMAINE MEO-CAMUZET Vosne-Romanée Au Cros-Parantoux 1987 $63 (12/15/89)
18 95 DUNN Cabernet Sauvignon Napa Valley 1986 Rel: $27 Cur: $55 (10/15/89) CS
19 95 CHATEAU LA DOMINIQUE St.-Emilion 1986 Rel: $29 Cur: $29 (6/30/89)
20 95 SPOTTSWOODE Cabernet Sauvignon Napa Valley 1986 Rel: $30 Cur: $71 (9/15/89)
21 95 KENWOOD Cabernet Sauvignon Sonoma Valley Artist Series 1986 Rel: $30 Cur: $31 (11/30/89) CS
22 95 BERINGER Cabernet Sauvignon Napa Valley Private Reserve 1985 Rel: $30 Cur: $42 (12/15/89) SS
23 95 ROBERT MONDAVI Cabernet Sauvignon Napa Valley Reserve 1986 Rel: $35 Cur: $39 (11/15/89)
24 94 LAUREL GLEN Cabernet Sauvignon Sonoma Mountain Counterpoint 1987 $13 (10/31/89)
25 94 SILVERADO Cabernet Sauvignon Napa Valley 1986 Rel: $13.50 Cur: $18 (8/31/89) SS
26 94 CUVAISON Cabernet Sauvignon Napa Valley 1986 Rel: $15 Cur: $20 (7/15/89)
27 94 FROG'S LEAP Cabernet Sauvignon Napa Valley 1987 Rel: $15 Cur: $20 (12/31/89) SS
28 92 ROSEMOUNT Shiraz Hunter Valley 1986 $9 (4/15/89)
29 92 CARNEROS CREEK Pinot Noir Carneros Fleur de Carneros 1987 $9 (2/28/89) SS
30 94 FERRARI-CARANO Chardonnay Alexander Valley 1987 Rel: $16 Cur: $23 (5/31/89)
31 94 B.R. COHN Cabernet Sauvignon Sonoma Valley Olive Hill Vineyard 1986 Rel: $18 Cur: $27 (5/31/89)
32 94 DUCKHORN Cabernet Sauvignon Napa Valley 1986 Rel: $18 Cur: $24 (7/31/89) SS
33 94 BUENA VISTA Cabernet Sauvignon Carneros Private Reserve 1985 Rel: $18 Cur: $23 (10/15/89) SS
34 94 CLOS RENE Pomerol 1986 Rel: $19 Cur: $25 (6/15/89) SS
35 94 BERINGER Cabernet Sauvignon Napa Valley Private Reserve 1984 Rel: $25 Cur: $38 (2/15/89) CS
36 94 CASTELLARE DI CASTELLINA I Sodi di San Niccolo 1986 Rel: $25 Cur: $29 (11/30/89)
37 94 FATTORIA DI AMA Chianti Classico Castello di Ama Vigneto Bellavista 1985 Rel: $30 Cur: $30 (7/31/89)
38 95 ROBERT MONDAVI Cabernet Sauvignon Napa Valley Reserve 1985 Rel: $40 Cur: $43 (11/15/89) SS
39 95 DIAMOND CREEK Cabernet Sauvignon Napa Valley Volcanic Hill 1987 Rel: $40 Cur: $41 (12/15/89)
40 96 STAG'S LEAP WINE CELLARS Cask 23 Napa Valley 1985 Rel: $75 Cur: $141 (11/30/89)
41 95 SASSICAIA 1986 Rel: $50 Cur: $50 (12/15/89)
42 95 OPUS ONE Napa Valley 1985 Rel: $55 Cur: $69 (6/15/89)
43 94 GAJA Cabernet Sauvignon Darmagi 1985 Rel: $70 Cur: $70 (3/15/89) CS
44 90 VALLANA Barbera 1986 $6 (2/15/89) BB
45 90 SAUSAL Zinfandel Alexander Valley 1986 $6.75 (3/31/89) SS
46 90 HOGUE Johannisberg Riesling Yakima Valley 1988 $6 (10/15/89) BB
47 93 STRAUS Merlot Napa Valley 1986 $11 (2/28/89)
48 93 ROSEMOUNT Cabernet Sauvignon Hunter Valley 1986 $11 (1/31/89) SS
49 93 GUNDLACH BUNDSCHU Merlot Sonoma Valley Rhinefarm Vineyards 1987 Rel: $13 Cur: $16 (10/31/89) SS
50 93 MOUNT EDEN Chardonnay Edna Valley MEV MacGregor Vineyard 1987 Rel: $14 Cur: $20 (4/30/89) SS
51 93 CHATEAU OLIVIER Graves 1985 Rel: $15 Cur: $24 (2/15/89) SS
52 93 KEENAN Cabernet Sauvignon Napa Valley 1986 Rel: $16.50 Cur: $17 (8/31/89)
53 93 SHAFER Cabernet Sauvignon Stags Leap District 1986 Rel: $16 Cur: $20 (9/30/89) SS
54 94 DOM RUINART Brut Blanc de Blancs Champagne 1982 Rel: $61 Cur: $70 (12/31/89) CS
55 93 WOODWARD CANYON Cabernet Sauvignon Columbia Valley 1986 $18.50 (10/15/89)
56 93 NAVARRO Gewürztraminer Late Harvest Anderson Valley Vineyard Selection 1986 $18.50 (2/28/89)
57 93 DOMAINE AUFFRAY Chablis Vaillons 1988 $20 (12/15/89)
58 93 ORNELLAIA 1986 Rel: $25 Cur: $41 (12/15/89) CS
59 92 NALLE Zinfandel Dry Creek Valley 1987 Rel: $10 Cur: $10 (5/31/89) SS
60 92 LE MASSE Chianti Classico 1985 $12 (7/15/89)
61 93 CHATEAU MOUTON-BARONNE-PHILIPPE Pauillac 1986 Rel: $23 Cur: $23 (5/31/89)
62 92 WILLIAMS SELYEM Pinot Noir Russian River Valley Allen Vineyard 1987 $20 (5/31/89)
63 93 KUMEU RIVER Chardonnay Kumeu 1987 $29 (3/31/89)
64 93 BERNARD BURGAUD Côte-Rôtie 1986 $31 (1/31/89)
65 93 OLIVIER LEFLAIVE FRERES Puligny-Montrachet Les Chalumeaux 1986 $36 (4/15/89)
66 93 JOSEPH PHELPS Insignia Napa Valley 1985 Rel: $40 Cur: $46 (7/31/89) CS
67 93 DOMAINE DANIEL RION Vosne-Romanée Les Chaumes 1986 Rel: $47 Cur: $54 (4/30/89) CS
68 91 A. RAFANELLI Cabernet Sauvignon Dry Creek Valley 1986 $9.50 (9/30/89)
69 90 HESS Chardonnay California Hess Select 1988 $9 (11/30/89) SS
70 92 DOMAINE RASPAIL-AY Gigondas 1986 $15 (1/31/89)
71 92 CHATEAU DE MARBUZET St.-Estèphe 1986 Rel: $15 Cur: $16 (6/30/89)
72 92 BURGESS Cabernet Sauvignon Napa Valley Vintage Selection 1985 Rel: $18 Cur: $23 (7/15/89)
73 91 KIONA Chardonnay Yakima Valley Barrel Fermented 1987 $10 (10/15/89)
74 92 ROBERT MONDAVI Pinot Noir Napa Valley Reserve 1985 Rel: $19 Cur: $22 (4/15/89) SS
75 92 MATANZAS CREEK Merlot Sonoma County 1986 Rel: $20 Cur: $20 (6/30/89)
76 92 CHATEAU MONTELENA Cabernet Sauvignon Napa Valley 1985 Rel: $25 Cur: $44 (11/15/89) CS
77 92 CHANSON PERE & FILS Beaune Clos des Fèves 1985 Rel: $25 Cur: $33 (1/31/89)
78 92 E. GUIGAL Côte-Rôtie Côtes Brune et Blonde 1985 Rel: $30 Cur: $34 (1/31/89)
79 91 RIDGE Zinfandel Sonoma County Lytton Springs 1987 Rel: $11 Cur: $11 (10/31/89)
80 91 EDMUNDS ST. JOHN Syrah Sonoma County 1986 $12 (4/15/89)
81 92 SEAN H. THACKREY Syrah Napa Valley Orion 1987 $30 (9/30/89)
82 91 MICHEL TRIBAUT Brut Monterey County 1985 $13 (5/31/89)
83 90 RIDGE Zinfandel Sonoma County Geyserville 1987 Rel: $14 Cur: $14 (10/31/89)
84 92 KISTLER Chardonnay Sonoma Valley Kistler Estate Vineyard 1987 Rel: $22 Cur: $55 (7/15/89)
85 92 FERRARI-CARANO Chardonnay California Reserve 1986 Rel: $28 Cur: $42 (5/31/89)
86 90 LATAH CREEK Merlot Washington Limited Bottling 1987 $10 (10/15/89)
87 90 CASTELLO DI VOLPAIA Chianti Classico 1985 $10 (6/30/89) SS
88 91 BUENA VISTA Cabernet Sauvignon Carneros 1986 $11 (10/15/89)
89 91 TUDAL Cabernet Sauvignon Napa Valley 1986 Rel: $14.50 Cur: $20 (12/15/89)
90 91 BERNARD PRADEL Cabernet Sauvignon Napa Valley 1985 $12 (4/30/89)
91 91 CHATEAU LA LOUVIERE Pessac-Léognan 1986 Rel: $15 Cur: $25 (6/15/89)
92 92 CHATEAU ST.-PIERRE St.-Julien 1986 Rel: $17 Cur: $21 (9/15/89) SS
93 91 COLUMBIA Cabernet Sauvignon Yakima Valley Otis Vineyard 1985 $15 (10/15/89)
94 91 PESQUERA Ribera del Duero 1986 $26 (4/30/89)
95 90 GRGICH HILLS Johannisberg Riesling Napa Valley 1987 $7.75 (8/31/89)
96 90 FREEMARK ABBEY Johannisberg Riesling Napa Valley 1988 $8 (8/31/89)
97 91 SIMI Cabernet Sauvignon Sonoma County 1985 Rel: $13 Cur: $18 (9/30/89)
98 91 COSENTINO Chardonnay Napa Valley 1987 $11.50 (3/15/89)
99 91 ROBERT MONDAVI Pinot Noir Napa Valley Reserve 1986 Rel: $22 Cur: $23 (10/15/89)
100 90 KENDALL-JACKSON Syrah Sonoma Valley Durell Vineyard 1987 $17 (12/15/89)

The Top 100: 1988's Best Wines

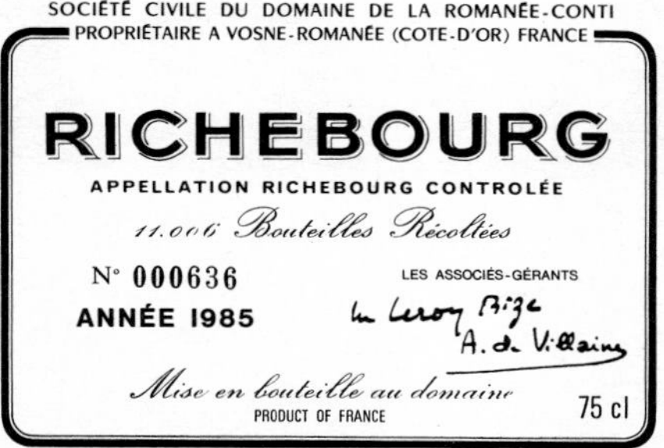

Rank	Score	Wine
1	97	CHATEAU LYNCH-BAGES Pauillac 1985 Rel: $37 Cur: $45 (4/30/88) CS
2	99	CHATEAU MARGAUX Margaux 1985 Rel: $76 Cur: $92 (4/30/88)
3	100	ROMANEE-CONTI Richebourg 1985 Rel: $210 Cur: $310 (2/29/88)
4	97	TOLLOT-BEAUT Corton 1985 Rel: $49 Cur: $49 (3/15/88)
5	97	GAJA Barbaresco Sori Tildin 1985 Rel: $94 Cur: $125 (12/15/88)
6	96	CASTELLARE DI CASTELLINA I Sodi di San Niccolo 1985 Rel: $25 Cur: $31 (5/31/88)
7	95	LOUIS JADOT Beaune Clos des Ursules 1985 Rel: $30 Cur: $30 (3/15/88) SS
8	95	SPOTTSWOODE Cabernet Sauvignon Napa Valley 1985 Rel: $25 Cur: $94 (11/15/88) CS
9	97	CHATEAU D'YQUEM Sauternes 1983 Rel: $180 Cur: $229 (1/31/88)
10	97	JOSEPH DROUHIN Montrachet Marquis de Laguiche 1986 Rel: $200 Cur: $244 (10/31/88) CS
11	98	LOUIS LATOUR Romanée-St.-Vivant Les Quatre Journaux 1985 Rel: $99 Cur: $110 (3/15/88)
12	98	CHATEAU PETRUS Pomerol 1985 Rel: $160 Cur: $350 (5/31/88)
13	96	GAJA Barbaresco Costa Russi 1985 Rel: $83 Cur: $100 (12/15/88)
14	96	GAJA Barbaresco Sori San Lorenzo 1985 Rel: $88 Cur: $102 (12/15/88)
15	95	RIDGE Cabernet Sauvignon Santa Cruz Mountains Monte Bello 1985 Rel: $40 Cur: $89 (7/15/88) CS
16	95	CHATEAU BEYCHEVELLE St.-Julien 1985 Rel: $35 Cur: $39 (8/31/88) CS
17	95	CHATEAU PICHON-LALANDE Pauillac 1985 Rel: $40 Cur: $53 (2/29/88) CS
18	95	CHATEAU DUCRU-BEAUCAILLOU St.-Julien 1985 Rel: $50 Cur: $51 (6/15/88)
19	95	DOMAINE DAUVISSAT-CAMUS Chablis Les Clos 1986 $40 (9/15/88)
20	95	GAJA Barbaresco 1985 Rel: $45 Cur: $58 (12/15/88) CS
21	93	FRESCOBALDI Pomino Tenuta di Pomino 1985 Rel: $12 Cur: $16 (9/15/88) SS
22	92	BONNY DOON Le Cigare Volant California 1986 Rel: $13.50 Cur: $25 (11/15/88)
23	92	KENDALL-JACKSON Syrah Sonoma Valley Durell Vineyard 1986 $14 (11/30/88)
24	92	ANTINORI Chianti Classico Pèppoli 1985 Rel: $16 Cur: $16 (5/31/88)
25	94	TORRES Chardonnay Penedès Milmanda 1987 $35 (12/15/88)
26	93	PENFOLDS Shiraz South Australia Grange Hermitage Bin 95 1981 Rel: $49 Cur: $62 (12/31/88) CS
27	94	PESQUERA Ribera del Duero Janus Reserva Especial 1982 Rel: $75 Cur: $75 (9/15/88)
28	92	SAN FELICE Predicato di Biturica 1982 Rel: $19 Cur: $19 (1/31/88) SS
29	90	BONNY DOON Pinot Noir Oregon Bethel Heights Vineyard 1985 $18 (6/15/88)
30	91	CLERICO Arte 1985 $22 (1/31/88)
31	94	B.R. COHN Cabernet Sauvignon Sonoma Valley Olive Hill Vineyard 1985 Rel: $16 Cur: $35 (11/15/88)
32	94	ARROWOOD Cabernet Sauvignon Sonoma County 1985 Rel: $19 Cur: $25 (12/15/88)
33	97	DOMAINE MEO-CAMUZET Richebourg 1985 Rel: $150 Cur: $235 (3/31/88)
34	97	CHATEAU LAFITE-ROTHSCHILD Pauillac 1985 Rel: $80 Cur: $99 (5/31/88) CS
35	97	CHATEAU LATOUR Pauillac 1985 Rel: $82 Cur: $95 (4/30/88)
36	96	CHATEAU HAUT-BRION Graves 1985 Rel: $70 Cur: $84 (4/30/88)
37	98	ROMANEE-CONTI La Tâche 1985 Rel: $225 Cur: $310 (2/29/88)
38	94	CHATEAU PICHON-BARON Pauillac 1985 Rel: $32 Cur: $36 (4/30/88)
39	91	CHATEAU MUSAR Lebanon 1980 Rel: $11 Cur: $18 (7/31/88)
40	92	CA' DEL BOSCO Maurizio Zanella 1985 Rel: $38 Cur: $38 (9/15/88)
41	95	KENDALL-JACKSON Cabernet Sauvignon California Proprietor's Reserve 1985 $20 (12/15/88)
42	96	LOUIS JADOT Nuits-St.-Georges Clos des Corvées 1985 Rel: $44 Cur: $46 (3/15/88)
43	96	JAFFELIN Clos de Vougeot 1985 $49 (6/15/88)
44	94	FROG'S LEAP Cabernet Sauvignon Napa Valley 1986 Rel: $14 Cur: $20 (12/31/88)
45	94	ROBERT MONDAVI Cabernet Sauvignon Napa Valley 1985 Rel: $15 Cur: $20 (12/15/88) SS
46	94	DUNN Cabernet Sauvignon Napa Valley 1985 Rel: $20 Cur: $64 (9/15/88) CS
47	94	CHATEAU MONTELENA Cabernet Sauvignon Napa Valley 1984 Rel: $20 Cur: $39 (10/15/88)
48	95	LOUIS JADOT Bonnes Mares 1985 Rel: $48 Cur: $78 (3/15/88)
49	95	DOMAINE DANIEL RION Vosne-Romanée Beaux-Monts 1985 Rel: $38 Cur: $55 (2/29/88)
50	95	CHATEAU CLIMENS Barsac 1983 Rel: $50 Cur: $50 (1/31/88) CS
51	95	CHATEAU FIGEAC St.-Emilion 1985 Rel: $37 Cur: $53 (5/15/88)
52	95	CHATEAU LA MISSION HAUT-BRION Graves 1985 Rel: $70 Cur: $73 (4/30/88)
53	94	OPUS ONE Napa Valley 1984 Rel: $50 Cur: $70 (5/31/88)
54	94	BIONDI-SANTI Brunello di Montalcino Riserva 1982 Rel: $80 Cur: $98 (10/15/88) CS
55	93	FERRARI-CARANO Chardonnay Alexander Valley 1986 Rel: $16 Cur: $28 (7/15/88)
56	93	GIRARD Chardonnay Napa Valley 1986 Rel: $13.50 Cur: $28 (8/31/88) SS
57	93	KENDALL-JACKSON Merlot Alexander Valley 1986 $16 (12/31/88)
58	93	CHATEAU DU TERTRE Margaux 1985 Rel: $14 Cur: $23 (6/30/88) SS
59	93	POMMERY Brut Champagne 1982 $24 (2/15/88)
60	93	PIERRE GELIN Gevrey-Chambertin 1985 $25 (4/15/88)
61	93	PAUL JABOULET AINE Côte-Rôtie Les Jumelles 1985 Rel: $35 Cur: $35 (9/30/88)
62	92	CHATEAU MEYNEY St.-Estèphe 1985 Rel: $16 Cur: $17 (8/31/88)
63	92	AVIGNONESI Chardonnay Il Marzocco 1986 $16 (2/15/88)
64	92	CLOS RENE Pomerol 1985 Rel: $17 Cur: $20 (3/15/88)
65	93	CHATEAU LARMANDE St.-Emilion 1985 Rel: $23 Cur: $23 (5/15/88)
66	93	CHATEAU LA CROIX Pomerol 1985 Rel: $25 Cur: $25 (5/15/88)
67	93	CHATEAU L'EGLISE-CLINET Pomerol 1985 Rel: $30 Cur: $57 (2/29/88)
68	93	BOLLINGER Brut Champagne Grand Année 1982 $30 (7/15/88)
69	94	CHATEAU RIEUSSEC Sauternes 1983 Rel: $52 Cur: $57 (1/31/88)
70	94	PRINCE FLORENT DE MERODE Pommard Clos de la Platière 1985 Rel: $45 Cur: $45 (3/15/88)
71	94	MOILLARD Echézeaux 1985 $47 (4/15/88)
72	94	DOMAINE JEAN CHARTRON Puligny-Montrachet Clos de la Pucelle 1986 $50 (5/31/88)
73	93	CHATEAU RAYAS Châteauneuf-du-Pape Réserve 1985 Rel: $41 Cur: $49 (7/31/88)
74	91	TORRES Penedès Gran Sangre de Toro Reserva 1983 $9.50 (6/15/88) SS
75	90	CASTELLO DEI RAMPOLLA Chianti Classico 1985 $8 (9/15/88)
76	93	STERLING Three Palms Vineyard Napa Valley 1985 Rel: $20 Cur: $22 (12/31/88)
77	95	JEAN-NOEL GAGNARD Bâtard-Montrachet 1986 $93 (12/31/88)
78	91	A. RAFANELLI Zinfandel Dry Creek Valley 1986 $7 (9/15/88)
79	92	CAYMUS Cabernet Sauvignon Napa Valley Cuvée 1985 $12 (7/15/88)
80	92	CORBANS Chardonnay Marlborough 1986 $10 (5/15/88)
81	91	INGLENOOK Gravion Napa Valley 1986 $9.50 (4/30/88) SS
82	91	PRESTON Sirah-Syrah Dry Creek Valley 1985 $9.50 (1/31/88)
83	91	INGLENOOK Merlot Napa Valley Reserve 1985 Rel: $10.50 Cur: $14 (10/15/88) SS
84	91	ALSACE WILLM Gewürztraminer Alsace 1985 $11 (7/15/88)
85	92	SILVERADO Chardonnay Napa Valley 1986 Rel: $12 Cur: $16 (4/30/88)
86	92	SAINTSBURY Pinot Noir Carneros 1986 $14 (6/15/88)
87	92	COSENTINO Cabernet Franc North Coast 1986 $14 (7/31/88)
88	90	ANTINORI Chianti Classico Santa Cristina 1985 $6 (10/31/88) BB
89	90	HUSCH Gewürztraminer Anderson Valley 1987 $7 (9/15/88)
90	90	BUENA VISTA Sauvignon Blanc Lake County 1987 $7.50 (6/15/88)
91	90	NAVARRO White Riesling Anderson Valley 1986 $7.50 (4/30/88)
92	90	CHRISTIAN BROTHERS Cabernet Sauvignon Napa Valley 1985 $8 (6/15/88)
93	90	SAN FELICE Chianti Classico Il Grigio Riserva 1982 $11 (5/31/88)
94	92	CHATEAU ST. JEAN Chardonnay Alexander Valley Belle Terre Vineyards 1986 Rel: $16 Cur: $20 (7/15/88)
95	92	KISTLER Chardonnay Russian River Valley Dutton Ranch 1987 Rel: $18 Cur: $45 (12/31/88)
96	91	BERINGER Chardonnay Napa Valley Private Reserve 1986 Rel: $16 Cur: $22 (4/15/88)
97	91	PAUL JABOULET AINE Hermitage La Chapelle 1986 Rel: $35 Cur: $35 (9/30/88)
98	90	NALLE Zinfandel Dry Creek Valley 1986 Rel: $9 Cur: $9 (6/30/88)
99	91	ZACA MESA Pinot Noir Santa Barbara County Reserve 1986 $15 (6/15/88)
100	93	DOM PERIGNON Brut Champagne 1982 Rel: $75 Cur: $84 (10/15/88)

THE WORLD ACCORDING TO

RUFFINO

Bring Tuscany home in a bottle.

Protecting Your Wine Investment

THE PRIME THREAT TO WINE THESE DAYS IS THEFT

Marvin Brownstein, who lost his home and wine collection in the Oakland, Calif., fire, discovered that his insurance did not specifically cover his wine, leaving him unable to replace his valuable, expensive bottles

J. PATRICK FORDEN

BY STEVE HEIMOFF

In last October's disastrous Oakland, Calif., firestorm, which destroyed 2,777 single-family homes in the hills above Oakland and Berkeley, many fine-wine collections were lost, including Marvin Brownstein's. His 1,200-bottle cellar included treasures such as 1961 Pétrus, '62 Bonnes Mares, '66 Palmer and '70 Beaulieu Vineyards Private Reserve. Most of the bottles exploded from the 2,000-degree heat, and those that didn't boiled in the glass.

Brownstein, a pathologist, conservatively estimated the value of his wine collection at $36,000. He had homeowner's insurance that, in theory, covered the wine, but it didn't do him much good. "Our total personal property content value was not as high as our losses," he says, meaning that his insurance settlement wasn't enough to cover everything that went up in flames. Brownstein's wine was included in his policy as "unscheduled personal property," so it was automatically lumped in with everything else that wasn't specifically inventoried. (Unscheduled means simply that the property does not have to be itemized.)

As a result, the check that Brownstein's insurance company sent him for his personal property was enough to buy the things he needed to get started again—furniture, clothes, appliances—but nowhere enough to replace his wine.

Most insurance companies cover wine as unscheduled personal property, which is fine as far as it goes. In general, it protects wine from all the threats your other property is insured against: fire, flood, theft, earthquake. But as Brownstein discovered, such insurance is good only up to a point. If a disaster of some kind brings your losses to their insured limit, you'll have to choose what to replace and what not to.

Even if it's only your wine that's stolen or destroyed, you probably won't be able to recover its full value, particularly if it's collectible. That's because unscheduled personal property is generally insured only for its replacement value, as opposed to its actual, or market, value. Usually (as in the case of appliances and electronic equipment), replacement value is higher than actual value, because such things depreciate with age.

But collectible wine is a weird commodity, one of the few things that increases in value as it gets older. That bottle of '61 Pétrus Brownstein lost is worth as much as $1,900 at auction today—but if he had been able to collect on it, his insurance company would only have reimbursed him for the cost of a current vintage of Pétrus, about $220. (Still, that's a lot more than Brownstein paid when he bought it years ago.)

So what can a collector do who wants to insure his wine for its full value, and collect on it if he loses everything?

To begin with, most homeowner's policies simply won't cover wine as scheduled property, the way they will rare paintings, stamps or jewelry. Bill Kalinyak, Brownstein's insurance agent at Farmers Insurance Group, says that his company, like most other insurers, "considers wine as unscheduled personal property. You can't cover wine under a scheduled policy."

But there is one insurance company known for scheduling one-of-a-kind items that other insurers won't touch: Lloyd's of London. You can't buy insurance directly from Lloyd's; you have to go through an international insurance brokerage firm that does business with Lloyd's, such as Alexander & Alexander or Rollins Burdick Hunter. Marcia O'Kane, a manager in the San Francisco office of Alexander & Alexander, says it's possible to purchase scheduled coverage of wine with Lloyd's through her firm. In general, says O'Kane, such coverage will protect wine against loss from fire, theft, earthquake damage, accidental breakage (remember New York retailer William Sokolin, who inadvertently smashed his Thomas Jefferson bottle of Château Margaux?) and, in some cases, spoilage due to mechanical failure. The typical cost of such a policy, O'Kane says, is $1.50 for each $100 worth of value, but there are minimum premiums—about $500 to $1,000—as well as other fees, which can add up to $750 to the final tab. You should also be prepared to offer details about the wines' provenance and storage conditions.

The Chubb Group of Insurance Companies has also recently decided to insure private collections as scheduled property. They have offices throughout the nation.

Brownstein didn't realize that scheduled coverage for his wine was available (because Kalinyak never told him), but even if he had, he might not have purchased it, for a very human reason. "You think in terms of a partial loss of your property, not a total loss," he says. That's true, but there are stronger reasons to protect your wine collection than fear of a fire that wipes out everything you own. The prime threat to wine these days isn't natural disaster, it's theft.

Theft of fine wines is growing by leaps and bounds, according to Roger Livdahl, a senior wine appraiser. In 1991, Livdahl appraised $1,240,585 worth of wine losses due to criminal activity, mainly theft and arson. Livdahl recommends buying some kind of scheduled insurance for wine, particularly if you have a valuable collection, because insurance companies tend to lowball clients on replacement costs if prices haven't been agreed upon beforehand. Of course, since scheduled items need to be itemized, Livdahl also suggests that wine owners have their collections reappraised every few years to keep track of both depletions and increases in value.

Theft was the last thing Russ Davis, an attorney in Irvine, Calif., was worried about when he stored his wine collection at a commercial storage facility. But thieves picked the store's lock and got away with 109 bottles of Davis' wine, including Caymus Special Selection, Château Lynch-Bages, Calera Pinot Noir and Cabernet Sauvignons from Château Montelena, Silver Oak and Robert Mondavi Reserve.

Davis, like Brownstein, had his wine insured as unscheduled personal property under his homeowner's policy, which covered replacement costs. The final chapter in Davis' story is happier than Brownstein's, though, because Davis was reimbursed for his losses and received, on average, 40 percent more for the wines than he paid for them. (A current vintage of Montelena costs a lot more today than it did in 1982.) Davis didn't get as much money as he would have if the insurance company had paid him the wines' actual cash value, but he still considers himself lucky.

If your wine is uninsured, or you think it's underinsured, the best place to begin remedying the situation is with your agent. Insurance policies tend to be flexible, and you may be able to work something out better than you expected. If your agent flat out says the company can't insure your wine, contact a large insurance broker (or Chubb) and ask to speak with their personal insurance department. If that person acts like he never heard the word wine, ask if the company can place surplus insurance through Lloyd's. Keep on trying until you find someone who understands what you're looking for. Obtaining scheduled insurance for your wine may not be the easiest thing to do, but you'll sleep better knowing your collection is safe. □

THE WINE SPECTATOR
NOV. 15, 1991
Our Annual Cabernet Report
A Massive Study of 400 New California Cabernet Sauvignons
Wines for The Perfect Thanksgiving
Michael Broadbent, Taster Extraordinaire
Napa Valley's Exclusive Cooking School
$2.50
All It Takes Is $40 To Keep The Wine Spectator Flowing All Year Long.
Now you can save 27% off the cover price of The Wine Spectator. The one magazine with a real nose for what's happening in wine. The magazine that talks about wine in a way that's entertaining, accessible and easy to swallow.
Let The Wine Spectator introduce you to fascinating personalities from the world of wine. Take you to great restaurants across the country and around the world – and give you irresistible recipes for food and wine combinations. Plus inside tips on good values, great vintages and even greater collecting.
Best of all, every single issue comes with the famous Wine Spectator Buying Guide – a pull-out section full of lively reviews and ratings of over 100 new wine releases. What's more, you'll also receive our special double issue featuring the Top 100 Wines of the Year.
Call or send in the attached card today. And before long, The Wine Spectator will be flowing your way.
Call 1-800-622-2062
THE WINE SPECTATOR
Full, Rich, Mellow Châteauneuf-du-Pape
Introductory Offer.
❑ Yes! Please send me 1 year (22 issues) of THE WINE SPECTATOR, including the special issue featuring the Top 100 Wines of the Year, for $40.
That's a 27% savings off the cover price. Mail to: The Wine Spectator, P.O. Box 1960, Marion, OH 43305
Name
Company
Address
City/State/Zip
Charge to: ❑ Visa ❑ MasterCard ❑ American Express
❑ Check Enclosed ❑ Bill Me
Card #
Exp.
Signature
Please Check: ❑ Consumer(k) ❑ Food & Beverage Director(r)
❑ Retailer(f) ❑ Importer(b) ❑ Winery(d)
❑ Distributor(e) ❑ Other(s)
Please allow 6-8 weeks for delivery of first issue. Send foreign orders prepaid in U.S. dollars. Canada: $53.50 (including GST); all others $110.
CALIFORNIA RESIDENTS: ADD 7.25% SALES TAX
D2XU-9

SECTION B: Wines Listed by Country/Type/Producer

AUSTRALIA

Cabernet Sauvignon & Blends

BAROSSA VALLEY
Cabernet Sauvignon South Australia 1987: Ripe and toasty, with firm texture, plenty of generous cherry and currant fruit beneath a thin shell of hard tannins. Needs until 1993 to '94 to shed the tannin. $11 (1/31/90) **83**
Shiraz Cabernet Barossa Valley 1985: Flavorful, aromatic and beautifully balanced, the spicy berry flavors emerge gracefully on the firm texture and crisp structure. Drinkable now, but brief cellaring would not be amiss. $8 (9/30/89) BB **86**

BERRI
Cabernet Sauvignon Barossa Valley 1985 $7 (4/30/88) **76**
Cabernet Shiraz Australia 1985 $10 (7/01/87) **89**
Shiraz Cabernet South Australia Vintage Selection 1986 $9.50 (3/15/88) **80**

BLACK OPAL
Cabernet Sauvignon Hunter Valley 1985 $8 (7/15/88) BB **81**
Cabernet Sauvignon South Eastern Australia 1987: Effusively fruity with attractive raspberry, plum and currant flavors that are rich and concentrated with a gentle dose of oak and tannins; well balanced and elegant in style with a fruity aftertaste. Needs time to soften. Start drinking now to 1995. $8 (2/28/90) BB **85**

WOLF BLASS
Cabernet Merlot South Australia Black Label 1983: Extremely minty and assertive with chocolate and cherry flavors underneath, but the mint clearly dominates. Fairly tannic on the finish. Pricey for an exaggerated wine. $25 (4/30/89) **77**
Cabernet Sauvignon South Australia President's Selection 1986: Earthy, barnyardy aromas and flavors hang on through the finish, when modest spice and raisin flavors peek through. Seems soft and unpromising. $18 (3/15/92) **78**
Cabernet Sauvignon South Australia President's Selection 1983 $13.50 (4/30/88) **76**
Cabernet Sauvignon South Australia Yellow Label 1988: Ripe, rich and smooth, with generous currant and plum aromas and flavors and hints of exotic spices and vanilla on the finish. Has finely integrated tannins that should keep it humming through 1995 to '97, when it should be at its best. $10 (3/15/92) **88**
Cabernet Sauvignon South Australia Yellow Label 1984: Mature and spicy, with lean, slightly bitter flavors that keep this from opening up as much as it could. Drinkable now. $10 (4/30/89) **78**
Cabernet Sauvignon South Australia Yellow Label 1983 $9 (12/15/87) **86**
Cabernet Shiraz Australia Black Label 1980 $18 (7/01/87) **89**
Cabernet Shiraz Australia Yellow Label 1983 $8 (7/01/87) **87**
Cabernet Shiraz Clare-Barossa Valleys Black Label 1982 $25 (4/15/88) **88**
Cabernet Shiraz Langhorne Creek 1981 $18 (7/01/87) **90**

BLUE PYRENEES
Cabernet Sauvignon Australia 1982 $20 (5/31/87) **89**

BROWN BROTHERS
Cabernet Sauvignon Victoria Family Reserve 1987: Toasty, smoky Rhône-like aromas are followed by nice plummy, oaky flavors in this deep, concentrated and well-balanced wine. It's fully tannic. Drink now. $11.50 (9/15/90) **83**
Cabernet Sauvignon Victoria Family Selection 1987: Big, tasty and exuberant. Full-bodied and very fruity, with lively acidity and ripe plum, currant and cherry notes. Drink now. $9.50 (7/15/90) **82**
Cabernet Sauvignon Victoria Family Selection 1985: Tart and tannic, astringent, with modest red cherry flavor. Not for current drinking, but may not age gracefully. $7.50 (5/15/89) **76**
Cabernet Sauvignon Victoria St.-George Vineyard 1984 $8 (5/31/87) **86**
Shiraz Mondeuse Cabernet Sauvignon Australia 1983 $10 (7/01/87) **87**

CAPE MENTELLE
Cabernet Sauvignon Margaret River 1988: Has a green, herbaceous edge, with sage, bell pepper and currant flavors that turn murky and tannic. This one's for those who like the veggies in their Cabernet. Drink now. $19 (6/30/92) **79**
Cabernet Sauvignon Western Australia 1987: Lacks flair now, but a serious attempt with Cabernet Sauvignon. Tannic and peppery, with bell pepper flavors and firm currant and tobacco notes, framed by oak on the finish. A tightly structured wine that needs time to mellow; drink in 1993 to '97. $18 (3/31/91) **84**

CASSEGRAIN
Cabernet Sauvignon Pokolbin 1986: Ripe, intense and concentrated, makes no pretense at subtlety. The cherry, raspberry, berry and currant flavors are jammy and lively, with firm tannins. Needs food now to temper the wild flavors, but it could be cellared until 1993 to '97. $18 (3/31/91) **83**
Cabernet Shiraz Merlot South Eastern Australia 1988: Exotic, with prematurely ripe flavors of raspberries and tamarind. A wild, mangy wine that has hints of mothballs on the finish. Tasted twice. $8 (9/30/91) **69**

CHATEAU REYNELLA
Cabernet Sauvignon Coonawarra 1988: Impressive for its supple core of raspberry, currant, anise and plum flavors and subtle oak shadings, this is a ripe, plummy, full-bodied, hedonistic pleasure. Ready to enjoy now, or cellar two to three years. Drink now to 1995. $8.50 (4/30/91) **86**
Cabernet Sauvignon Coonawarra 1984 $7.50 (4/30/88) **80**
Cabernet Sauvignon Coonawarra 1980 $15 (5/31/87) **84**

CHATEAU TAHBILK
Cabernet Sauvignon Goulburn Valley 1988: A Cabernet built to cellar. Ripe, rich and intense, with concentrated cherry, currant, mint and spice notes framed by toasty oak and firm, but not overbearing tannins. The finish is complex and lingering. A château with a track record for gaining in the bottle. Start drinking in 1994 or '95. $12 (3/31/91) **87**
Cabernet Sauvignon Goulburn Valley 1987: One for the cellar. Very firm and tannic, full-bodied and packed with flavor. This wine needs time for its concentrated currant and black cherry flavors to open up, and it seems to have the requisite balance. Try now. $11 (7/31/90) **89**
Cabernet Sauvignon Goulburn Valley 1986: Lush and tasty. Deeply colored, concentrated and fruity, with plum, currant and blackberry flavors, firm tannins but supple in texture. Fruity finish lingers. Drink now. $10 (3/31/89) **88**
Cabernet Sauvignon Goulburn Valley 1984 $7.50 (11/15/87) **81**

CHITTERING
Cabernet Merlot Western Australia 1988: Full-bodied and perhaps a bit heavy, with ripe plum and currant aromas and flavors lurking in the background, ready to emerge if the tannins can subside with cellaring until 1993. $18 (9/30/91) **79**

CLYDE PARK
Cabernet Sauvignon Geelong 1984 $15 (3/15/88) **79**

COCKATOO RIDGE
Cabernet Merlot South Eastern Australia 1990: The fully ripe flavors on a light frame of tannins make this an enjoyable wine to drink now. Offers plum, prune and chocolate flavors shaded by tobacco and berry notes. $7 (6/30/92) BB **82**

COLDSTREAM HILLS
Cabernet Sauvignon Lilydale 1987: Cedary, chocolaty aromas are immediately enticing, but it would be a better bet for the cellar with more generosity of fruit to balance the excellent wood character. With cellaring, it could develop into a spicy, complex wine. Try it in 1993. $20 (1/31/90) **84**

CULLENS
Cabernet Merlot Margaret River 1985 $15 (11/15/87) **87**

DENMAN
Cabernet Sauvignon Hunter Valley 1983 $5 (11/15/87) **76**

ELDERTON
Cabernet Sauvignon Merlot Barossa Valley 1984 $11 (4/30/88) **86**

GOVERNOR PHILLIP
Cabernet Shiraz Barossa Valley 1986: Very earthy aromas, ripe and broad on the palate, opening up beautifully to generous, ripe cherry and blackberry flavors on the finish. Probably best to decant this wine before drinking. $6 (7/31/89) BB **83**

GRANTS
Cabernet Sauvignon Barossa Valley 1984 $8 (11/15/87) **73**

HARDY'S
Cabernet Malbec Reynella McLaren Vale Hardy Collection No. 9 1984 $6.50 (7/15/88) **76**
Cabernet Sauvignon Coonawarra 1987: A tangy, fruity, slightly herbal tasting Cabernet that's direct and pleasing. Drink now. $10.50 (7/15/90) **81**
Cabernet Sauvignon Keppoch 1986: This very straightforward Cabernet is full of cherry and herb flavors, with mild tannins and good balance. Clean and crisp in style; drink now. $7.50 (7/15/90) **79**
Cabernet Sauvignon Keppoch 1985 $7.25 (10/31/88) **80**
Cabernet Sauvignon Keppoch Bird Series 1985 $6 (9/30/88) BB **81**
Cabernet Sauvignon McLaren Vale Captain's Selection 1985 $4.50 (7/15/88) **75**
Cabernet Sauvignon McLaren Vale The Hardy Collection No. 8 1986: Light-bodied yet firm, with cedary aromas, currant, strawberry and pepper flavors and a good amount of wood. Drink now. $10.50 (1/31/89) **76**
Cabernet Sauvignon South Australia Bird Series 1988: Firm and fruity, with generous currant and berry aromas and flavors. Tannic enough to need until 1993 or so to soften. $8 (3/15/92) BB **83**
Cabernet Sauvignon South Australia The Hardy Collection 1988: Nicely balanced and moderate in tone, with appealing herb, oak, mint, currant and cherry aromas and flavors, modest tannins and enough length to savor it all on the finish. A likable wine that will benefit from brief cellaring; try now. $10 (2/15/91) **83**
Shiraz Cabernet South Eastern Australia Captain's Selection 1990: A real mouthful, with very ripe fruit flavors and accents of smoke, herb and eucalyptus on the finish. Full-bodied, moderately tannic and drinkable now, but could be aged through about 1994. $6 (6/30/92) BB **82**

HENSCHKE
Cabernet Sauvignon Barossa Ranges Keyneton Cyril Henschke 1988: A dark, ripe-tasting Cabernet, with plenty of fruit flavor and a generous dose of chocolate and spice from oak aging. Overall, it's rich, smooth and round. Drinkable now, but could be aged through about 1994. $23 (6/30/92) **85**
Cabernet Sauvignon Barossa Valley Cyril Henschke 1986: Plump and plummy, bursting with exquisitely defined ripe fruit flavor. Cinnamon and vanilla nuances lend complexity. A remarkably deep wine; drinkable now, but it can be cellared through 1993 at least. $23 (9/15/89) **91**
Cabernet Sauvignon Barossa Valley Cyril Henschke 1985: Very firm and powerful, with massive plum and cassis flavors and a firm smack of wood on the palate. Framed by plenty of soft tannins, it is a wine that needs cellaring. Try it in 1993. $21 (1/31/89) **90**
Cabernet Sauvignon Barossa Valley Cyril Henschke 1984 $18.50 (12/15/87) **94**
Keyneton Estate Barossa Ranges Keyneton 1988: A rich, distinctive red wine, with a black olive character that overrides the plum and chocolate flavors underneath. A smooth texture and moderate tannins make it drinkable now. Fine if you like a funky, herbal style of Shiraz. A blend of Shiraz, Cabernet Sauvignon and Malbec. $14 (6/30/92) **82**
Keyneton Estate Barossa Valley 1985: Despite the varietal blend, it lacks the complexity you might expect. Instead it is a simple, herbal, earthy wine with a touch of plum on the finish; drinkable now. $11.50 (3/31/89) **79**
Keyneton Estate Barossa Valley 1984 $12 (2/15/88) **85**

HILL-SMITH
Cabernet Sauvignon Barossa Valley 1984 $9.50 (8/31/87) **75**
Cabernet Sauvignon Barossa Valley 1981 $9.50 (7/16/86) **82**

HOLLICK
Cabernet Merlot Coonawarra 1985 $16 (5/31/88) **72**
Cabernet Sauvignon Coonawarra 1988: Soft and almost watery, with a strong gamy edge to the flavors that not everyone will like. Fruit comes through on the finish. $14 (3/15/92) **74**

HOUGHTON
Cabernet Sauvignon Frankland River Wildflower Ridge 1988: Spicy and tannic, with coffee, plum and floral notes that turn a bit murky on the finish. Drinkable, but lacking focus. Ready now or in 1993. $9 (7/15/91) **78**
Cabernet Shiraz McLaren Vale Wildflower Ridge 1985 $9 (12/31/88) **88**

HUNGERFORD HILL
Cabernet Merlot Hunter Valley 1985: A bit heavy-handed with oak, but there are still pretty currant and plum flavors that are attractive, if simple, now. With time the wood may come into balance with the fruit, but now it dominates. Drink now to 1996. $10 (2/28/90) **80**
Cabernet Sauvignon Coonawarra 1984 $11 (3/15/88) **79**

Key to Symbols

The scores reported here are the results of blind tastings conducted by our panel of senior editors. Wines that carry the initials below are results of individual tastings.

THE WINE SPECTATOR 100-POINT SCALE ***95-100***—Classic, a great wine; ***90-94***—Outstanding, superior character and style; ***80-89***—Good to very good, a wine with special qualities; ***70-79***—Average, drinkable wine that may have minor flaws; ***60-69***—Below average, drinkable but not recommended; ***50-59***—Poor, undrinkable, not recommended. "+"—With a score indicates a range; used primarily with barrel tastings to indicate a preliminary score.

SPECIAL DESIGNATIONS SS—Spectator Selection, CS—Cellar Selection, BB—Best Buy, ($NA)—Price not available, (NR)—Not released.

TASTER'S INITIALS (JG)—Jim Gordon, (HS)—Harvey Steiman, (JL)—James Laube, (JS)—James Suckling, (TM)—Thomas Matthews, (TR)—Terry Robards, (PM)—Per-Henrik Mansson, (BT)—Barrel Tasting (these wines were tasted blind from barrel samples), (CA- date)—*California's Great Cabernets* by James Laube, (CH-date)—*California's Great Chardonnays* by James Laube, (VP -date)—*Vintage Port* by James Suckling.

DATE TASTED Dates in parentheses represent the issue in which the rating was published.

AUSTRALIA

Cabernet Sauvignon & Blends

JOHNSTONE

Cabernet Shiraz Hunter Valley 1988: An odd woody character interferes with the Cabernet flavor, but there are enough ripe, plummy notes to recommend it for casual drinking. The finish is soft and elegant. Drink now. $6.50 (7/15/91) **75**

JUD'S HILL

Cabernet Merlot Australia 1985 $13 (4/30/88) **80**

KOALA RIDGE

Cabernet Sauvignon Barossa Valley 1988: Very firm, almost hard-edged and astringent, but it has a solid core of ripe currant and cherry flavor and oak to spare. The tannins could use until 1994 or '95 to soften. $10 (3/15/92) **83**

Cabernet Sauvignon Barossa Valley 1985: Fresh, focused and fruity, with lots of well-modulated peach, pear, vanilla and honey flavors in elegant proportions. It's flavorful without being weighty. A stylish wine; needs until about 1993 to polish the texture. Tasted twice. $9 (1/31/89) **84**

KRONDORF

Cabernet Sauvignon Franc McLaren Vale 1984 $9 (4/15/87) BB **89**

LAKE'S FOLLY

Cabernet Sauvignon Hunter Valley 1985: A nice Cabernet for current drinking. Has a toasty, woody nose, tart cherry and plum flavors and a clean finish. $15.50 (3/31/89) **80**

LEASINGHAM

Cabernet Malbec Australia Bin 56 Winemakers Selection 1984 $7.25 (11/15/87) **84**

Cabernet Sauvignon Australia Bin 49 Winemakers Selection 1982 $7.25 (11/15/87) **83**

Cabernet Shiraz Australia Bin 68 1983 $5.25 (11/15/87) **79**

Shiraz Cabernet Malbec Australia Hutt Creek Claret 1984 $4 (9/30/87) BB **81**

LEEUWIN

Cabernet Sauvignon Margaret River 1983 $18 (5/31/88) **86**

Cabernet Sauvignon Margaret River 1979: Fully mature despite its high level of tannin, the black cherry and currant flavors are true but rather simple, with a metallic aftertaste. Lacks complexity and the fruit may not outlast the tannins. Drink now through 1996. $20 (9/15/89) **79**

PETER LEHMANN

Cabernet Sauvignon Barossa Valley 1987: Plain and simple, with ripe plum, currant, tea and spice flavors that come across as one-dimensional. Still, it's quite drinkable and likely to show more pizzazz when paired with food. $8 (3/31/91) **80**

Cabernet Sauvignon Barossa Valley 1986: Ripe aromas and flavors of plum, bordering on prune and cedar, show generously against a firm structure. Tannins are fine enough to encourage cellaring until 1993 to see what develops. $9 (1/31/90) **85**

Cabernet Sauvignon Barossa Valley 1983 $9 (7/01/87) **81**

Shiraz Cabernet Barossa Valley 1986: Light in color, smooth in texture and fruity in flavor, offering slightly vegetal floral, currant and berry flavors. Not as harmonious as it could be. Drinkable now. $8 (2/28/91) **78**

Shiraz Cabernet Barossa Valley 1985: Ripe, bordering on raisiny, but restrained enough to show gentle cherry and toast flavors that linger appealingly on the finish. Drinkable now. $7 (1/31/90) **83**

LINDEMANS

Cabernet Sauvignon Coonawarra 1986: Rich, smooth and complex, with ripe, intense plum and currant flavors that are flanked by leathery, oaky nuances. Well balanced, deep and intriguing, with firm tannins on the finish. Drink now to '97. Tasted twice. $14 (10/31/90) **83**

Cabernet Sauvignon Coonawarra 1985: Complex and unusual, its leathery, decadent character is balanced artfully against plummy flavors, lending it depth and delicacy. $14 (4/30/89) **86**

Cabernet Sauvignon Coonawarra 1984 $12 (2/15/88) **84**

Cabernet Sauvignon Coonawarra 1982 $8 (9/30/86) **79**

Cabernet Sauvignon Coonawarra St.-George Vineyard 1986: Ripe and spicy, with firm, tannic plum and currant flavors. Seems one-dimensional and lacking finesse, but you get plenty of flavor. Drink now to 1994. $25 (6/30/92) **82**

Cabernet Sauvignon Coonawarra St.-George Vineyard 1985: Broad and lush, with ripe, supple black cherry, currant and plum flavors. Soft and smooth on the palate, picking up tannins on the finish. Drink in the next year or two. $21 (4/30/89) **80**

Cabernet Sauvignon Coonawarra St.-George Vineyard 1984 $15 (1/31/88) **88**

Cabernet Sauvignon Coonawarra St.-George Vineyard NV $15 (5/31/87) **88**

Cabernet Sauvignon South Australia Bin 45 1985 $6 (1/31/88) **79**

Cabernet Shiraz Coonawarra Limestone Ridge 1984 $15 (7/01/87) **87**

Pyrus Coonawarra 1986: Ripe and opulent, with decadent, earthy, barnyardy plum and currant flavors that finish with a strong oaky note. Not for everyone. Drink now. A blend of Cabernet Sauvingon, Malbec and Cabernet Franc. $25 (6/30/92) **77**

Shiraz Cabernet Coonawarra Limestone Ridge Lindemans Classic 1982: Herbal, bay leaf aromas and flavors permeate this soft, supple wine that turns a bit dry and medicinal on the finish. Drinkable now. $38 (7/31/90) **70**

Shiraz Cabernet Coonawarra Limestone Ridge Vineyard 1986: Fruity, delicious and decidedly spicy, as if the Shiraz provides the gamy, peppery character and the Cabernet supplies the clear, ripe cherry and berry core. Distinctive and attractive from the aroma through the finish. Has firm tannins, but is ready to drink now through 1994. $25 (6/30/92) **86**

Shiraz Cabernet Coonawarra Limestone Ridge Vineyard 1986: Flavorful, perhaps straightforward, the aromas and flavors lean toward cherry and plum, with overtones of nutmeg and toast, the texture is silky and smooth. Drinkable now. $25 (7/31/90) **84**

Shiraz Cabernet Coonawarra Limestone Ridge Vineyard 1985: Green olive and pickely flavors override the black cherry and spicy flavors. But firm tannins bring up the rear and it's well balanced. Tasted twice. $21 (7/31/89) **68**

LONGLEAT

Cabernet Sauvignon Goulburn Valley Revi Resco 1986: Deep and rich in color, but a bit woody and curiously flat on the palate, an eccentric wine that seems a bit unbalanced toward somewhat harsh oak. $9 (9/30/89) **73**

MILDARA

Cabernet Merlot Coonawarra 1985 $5.50 (1/31/88) BB **80**

Cabernet Merlot Coonawarra 1984 $5 (6/15/87) BB **82**

Cabernet Merlot Murray River Valley 1986: Light and quaffable. Fresh and fruity, with cherry and plum flavors and a light, floral aftertaste. Try it lightly chilled. $7.50 (3/31/89) **80**

Cabernet Sauvignon Coonawarra 1986: Concentrated and elegant. Pure Cabernet flavor with tones of vanilla and some coffee notes, it has ripe and supple flavors. Graceful and harmonious, medium-bodied with a long finish. $10 (1/31/89) **90**

Cabernet Sauvignon Coonawarra 1985 $8 (4/15/88) BB **89**

Cabernet Sauvignon Coonawarra 1984 $6.50 (4/30/87) **77**

Cabernet Sauvignon McLaren Vale Private Reserve 1985: A rich, smoky wine with deep color, firm tannins and ripe flavors. Tarry aromas and flavors dominate. Built for cellaring, though drinkable now. $13 (1/31/89) **85**

Cabernet Sauvignon Murray River Valley 1986: A velvety wine with delicious fruit flavors. Ripe, plummy, cedary flavors are short on the finish. Drinkable now. $8 (1/31/89) **80**

MITCHELTON

Cabernet Merlot Australia Print Label 1985: Has a ripe, herbal style, showing generous strawberry and cherry flavors, with a heavy overlay of tarragon and bay leaf notes. Tart structure balances the richness. Drink now. $17 (1/31/90) **78**

Cabernet Sauvignon Goulburn Valley 1988: Generous plum, herb, currant and tea flavors are well integrated with fine, rounded tannins in this warm, supple wine. Easy to drink and enjoyable now, but capable of gaining in the bottle. Try now through 1994. $13 (4/15/91) **86**

Cabernet Sauvignon Goulburn Valley 1986: Very minty, bordering on vegetal, with more spice and herb aromas and flavors than fruit; lean and a bit short. $13 (1/31/90) **73**

Cabernet Shiraz Merlot Victoria 1987: Has an herbal style, but there are plenty of generous cherry and currant flavors to make this delicious to drink now. The soft, supple balance and gentle tannins should keep it developing in the cellar through the short term. Drink now to 1994. $9 (1/31/90) **86**

MONTROSE

Cabernet Sauvignon Mudgee 1987: Drier and less fruity than most Aussie Cabs, opting instead for a solid, well-crafted style, with straightforward currant and herb aromas and flavors. Modest in flavor and texture. Drink now through 1994. $10 (2/28/91) **81**

Cabernet Sauvignon Mudgee 1986: A classy Cabernet, firm and elegant, showing fairly well-concentrated cedar aromas and spicy currant flavors, it's very well made, long and focused on the finish. Drink now. $8 (7/31/89) **86**

Cabernet Sauvignon Mudgee 1984 $10 (4/30/88) **88**

Cabernet Sauvignon Mudgee Special Reserve 1985: Firm, tightly structured and still a bit astringent, with plum and herbal aromas and flavors that as yet have not quite pierced the veil of tannin. Needs to soften at least until 1993. $16 (1/31/90) **80**

ORLANDO

Cabernet Sauvignon Coonawarra St.-Hugo 1987: Has lots of vegetal flavors—celery, herbs and carrots—in a medium-bodied wine, with peppery notes that taste more like Shiraz than Cabernet. Dry, earthy and tannic on the finish. Drink now or in 1993. $15 (5/31/91) **78**

Cabernet Sauvignon Coonawarra St.-Hugo 1986: Overtly ripe and generous, with distinctive smoky cherry and tomato aromas and flavors that open up on the palate. The flavor profile won't please everyone, but it's a well-made wine. Drinkable now. Tasted twice. $8 (2/28/91) **81**

Cabernet Sauvignon Coonawarra St.-Hugo 1985: Impressively concentrated and rich, yet there is subtlety and orchestration of flavors in the interplay of plum, cassis and chocolate against hints of vanilla and toast. $15 (4/30/89) **90**

Cabernet Sauvignon South Eastern Australia Jacob's Creek 1989: Herbal, earthy and pruny tasting, with plenty of tobacco and leather aromas and a dry finish. Distinctive, but its rough flavors may not add up to everyone's style of Cabernet. $7 (6/30/92) **77**

Cabernet Sauvignon South Eastern Australia Jacob's Creek 1988: Ripe and plummy, with generous, supple fruit flavor, picking up a spicy, smoky note on the aftertaste. Not very tannic and easy to drink now or in 1993. A fair price. $7 (7/15/91) BB **83**

Cabernet Sauvignon South Eastern Australia Jacob's Creek 1987: An elegant, smooth-textured Aussie Cabernet, with plenty of fruit complexity. Has cherry, currant and spice flavors, good balance and a lingering finish. The moderate tannins make it drinkable now or in 1993. $7 (7/31/90) BB **85**

Cabernet Sauvignon South Eastern Australia Jacob's Creek 1986 $7 (5/15/89) BB **87**

OXFORD LANDING

Cabernet Shiraz South Australia 1988: A nice, clean, medium-bodied Cabernet, with good plum and herbal flavors. Has medium tannins and good balance, with fruit flavors lingering on the finish. $7 (9/15/90) **73**

PENFOLDS

Cabernet Sauvignon South Australia Bin 707 1987: Strong herbal, oak and earthy notes dominate this wine. Has a touch of black cherry and plum flavors, but comes across as simple. Drink now or in 1993. $38 (5/31/91) **83**

Cabernet Sauvignon South Australia Bin 707 1986: Very ripe and generous, a smooth, supple, ebullient wine showing plenty of raspberry, cherry and spice flavors, especially a welcome smack of black pepper. It's the intensity and richness that are so appealing. Drinkable now. $28 (9/30/89) **90**

Cabernet Sauvignon South Australia Bin 707 1981 $18 (7/01/87) **90**

Cabernet Shiraz South Australia Bin 389 1987: Ripe and generous, but nicely reined in, so that the soft-textured chocolate, cherry and berry flavors emerge attractively on the palate and linger on the finish. Fine tannins should hold it well past 1995, but it's soft enough to drink now. $14 (2/28/91) **88**

Cabernet Shiraz South Australia Bin 389 1986: Firmer and tougher in structure than past '89s, a bit lean and hard-edged, drying on the finish, which overshadows the focused raspberry and chocolate aromas and flavors. Needs time in the cellar to soften. Try in 1993. $15 (1/31/90) **83**

Cabernet Shiraz South Australia Bin 389 1985 $14 (12/31/88) **86**

Cabernet Shiraz South Australia Bin 389 1983 $15 (7/01/87) **91**

Cabernet Shiraz South Australia Koonunga Hill 1987: Beautifully articulated cherry, berry and slightly gamy aromas and flavors are molded into a dense, concentrated wine that's drinkable now for its effusive fruit. Has the fine tannins to carry it through at least 1994 or '95 in the cellar. $7.50 (2/28/91) BB **86**

Cabernet Shiraz South Australia Koonunga Hill 1986: Lots of mint gives this wine character. The plum and cherry help balance out the tannins. $7.50 (5/15/89) **78**

Cabernet Shiraz South Australia Koonunga Hill 1984 $7 (7/01/87) **89**

PETALUMA

Cabernet Merlot Coonawarra 1986: Soft, warm, ripe and rich, with bright cherry, plum, anise and berry notes. Gentle, supple tannins and plenty of fruit flavor pours through on the finish. Drink now or in 1993. $25 (5/31/91) **87**

Cabernet Merlot Coonawarra 1984 $18 (5/31/87) **92**

Cabernet Sauvignon Coonawarra 1984 $18 (5/31/87) **91**

Cabernet Shiraz Coonawarra 1982 $16 (7/01/87) **89**

PREECE

Cabernet Sauvignon Goulburn Valley 1989: Tight, ripe and fruity, with black cherry, currant, plum and cedary oak flavors all neatly wrapped together. Finishes with enough tannin to warrant cellaring until 1994 or '95. $13 (3/15/92) **84**

REDBANK

Cabernet Sauvignon South Eastern Australia Long Paddock 1986: Very firm and hard in structure, with earthy aromas and modest Cabernet flavors submerged beneath a wall of tough tannins. If it's going anywhere, it won't be there before 1995. $13 (1/31/90) **74**

Cabernet Sauvignon South Eastern Australia Long Paddock 1985: A bit earthy and leathery, with metallic notes, but modest plum flavor peeks through, making it a decent, if slightly flawed drink. Ready now. $7 (7/15/91) **74**

Key to Symbols

The scores reported here are the results of blind tastings conducted by our panel of senior editors. Wines that carry the initials below are results of individual tastings.

THE WINE SPECTATOR 100-POINT SCALE 95-100—Classic, a great wine; ***90-94***—Outstanding, superior character and style; ***80-89***—Good to very good, a wine with special qualities; ***70-79***—Average, drinkable wine that may have minor flaws; ***60-69***—Below average, drinkable but not recommended; ***50-59***—Poor, undrinkable, not recommended. "+"—With a score indicates a range; used primarily with barrel tastings to indicate a preliminary score.

SPECIAL DESIGNATIONS SS—Spectator Selection, CS—Cellar Selection, BB—Best Buy, ($NA)—Price not available, (NR)—Not released.

TASTER'S INITIALS (JG)—Jim Gordon, (HS)—Harvey Steiman, (JL)—James Laube, (JS)—James Suckling, (TM)—Thomas Matthews, (TR)—Terry Robards, (PM)—Per-Henrik Mansson, (BT)—Barrel Tasting (these wines were tasted blind from barrel samples), (CA-date)—*California's Great Cabernets* by James Laube, (CH-date)—*California's Great Chardonnays* by James Laube, (VP-date)—*Vintage Port* by James Suckling.

DATE TASTED Dates in parentheses represent the issue in which the rating was published.

Cabernet Sauvignon South Eastern Australia Redbank Cabernet 1986: Youthful color, generous currant and spice aromas and broad flavors wrapped in fine tannins add up to a first-rate cellar candidate. Cedar and spice notes add complexity to the flavor. Should be drinkable now and continue to develop through 1995 to '97. $54 (1/31/90) **89**
Sally's Paddock South Eastern Australia 1986: Firm structure and tightly focused flavors of ripe currant, mint and smoke make this a standout, a classically built wine built to grow into itself with cellaring. Tannins need until 1993 to '95 to subside. $32 (1/31/90) **86**

ROO'S LEAP
Cabernet Sauvignon McLaren Vale 1985 $10 (11/30/88) **89**
Cabernet Sauvignon McLaren Vale Limited Edition 1986: Herbal aromas and ripe cherry flavors ride smoothly on a broad frame that artfully folds in notes of toast, vanilla and coffee. Drinkable now with rich food, but should be best after 1993. $9.50 (1/31/90) **85**

ROSEMOUNT
Cabernet Sauvignon Coonawarra Kirri Billi Vineyard 1986: Generous currant, herb and chocolate aromas and flavors waste no effort trying to be subtle or delicate. This is a full-on Cabernet that's plush in texture and flavor. Drink now to 1994. $19.50 (10/31/90) **88**
Cabernet Sauvignon Coonawarra Show Reserve 1988: Dark-colored, with deep, rich, pure Cabernet flavors, layers of weedy black currant, plum and cherry notes and herb and spice nuances. The finish brings out the tannins and oak. A bit rough now, but with time it should smooth out. Drink in 1993 to '96. $16 (5/31/91) **89**
Cabernet Sauvignon Coonawarra Show Reserve 1987: Dense and almost thick in texture, offering a sense of richness without excessive weight. Hints at smoke and chocolate around the solid core of herbal cherry and currant flavors. Balanced, harmonious and long. Drinkable now, but better after 1993. Tasted twice. $15 (2/28/91) **88**
Cabernet Sauvignon Coonawarra Show Reserve 1985: Earthy and grassy but fruity enough to make it interesting, showing some peach aromas and flavors. Drink it soon. $14 (1/31/89) **82**
Cabernet Sauvignon Coonawarra Show Reserve 1984 $13.50 (2/28/87) **86**
Cabernet Sauvignon Hunter Valley 1989: Firm and focused, with generous currant and plum flavors that become tight and somewhat tannic on the finish. Needs to soften, perhaps by 1993 or '94. $10 (9/30/91) **82**
Cabernet Sauvignon Hunter Valley 1988: Jammy on the nose, tart and sharply focused on the palate, showing lots of raspberry and lemon flavors. Not for every palate, but it could broaden with cellaring. A disppointing vintage for this usually very good wine. Drink now. $10 (1/31/90) **76**
Cabernet Sauvignon Hunter Valley 1987: Herbal, toasty aromas and flavors edge out the modest currant flavor in this deeply colored, modestly built, clean and appealing wine. Mature enough to drink now. $10 (7/31/89) **83**
Cabernet Sauvignon Hunter Valley 1986 $11 (1/31/89) SS **93**
Cabernet Sauvignon Hunter Valley 1985 $9 (1/31/88) **85**
Cabernet Sauvignon Hunter Valley 1984 $9.50 (4/30/87) **78**
Cabernet Shiraz South Eastern Australia 1989: Charming, light-bodied and freshly fruity, but with deep enough cherry and plum flavors to last nicely on the finish. Soft and ready to drink. $6 (7/31/90) BB **81**
Shiraz Cabernet South Eastern Australia 1990: Ripe, supple and generous, with tasty plum, spice, cherry and floral notes that are elegant, lively and stay with you on the finish. Not too tannic; ready now to 1994. $7 (7/15/91) BB **84**

ROUGE HOMME
Cabernet Sauvignon Coonawarra 1984: Very attractive and drinkable style with plenty of ripe, clean Cabernet flavors and black cherry, cedar and plum flavors, with enough extract and tannin for aging. A serious wine. $12 (2/15/88) **84**

ST.-HUBERTS
Cabernet Sauvignon Yarra Valley 1984 $13 (11/15/87) **84**

SALTRAM
Cabernet Sauvignon Hazelwood 1985: Very ripe, almost "cooked" aromas and flavors, but the black cherry flavor that comes through on the finish suggests that this will be a rich, if somewhat exotic wine by now. Drink now. $8.50 (7/31/89) **79**
Cabernet Shiraz Barossa Valley 1984: Very smooth, generous and focused, with gentle tannins to support the delicious, ripe cherry, chocolate and spice flavors; a big wine with plenty to offer now. Could develop in the cellar through at least 1993. $12 (1/31/90) **89**

SEAVIEW
Cabernet Sauvignon South Australia 1986: Delicious, lush and complex, with currant, spice, chocolate and plum flavors, a broad, velvety texture and a lasting finish. Tempting now, but firm tannins and good balance indicate it should improve with cellaring. Try it in 1993 to '94. $10 (7/31/90)**88**
Cabernet Shiraz South Australia 1987: Firm and focused, with medium-intense cherry and chocolate aromas and flavors. Finishes fresh and lively. Drinkable now with hearty food, but probably best after 1993 or '94. $8 (9/30/91) BB **82**
Cabernet Shiraz South Australia 1987: Attractive; tastes rich, flavorful and full-bodied, yet not harsh with tannins. Full of currant, plum and berry flavors that last on the finish. $8 (7/31/90) BB **84**

SEPPELT
Cabernet Sauvignon Padthaway Black Label 1988: Tight and austere, with lean cedar, currant, herb and plum flavors that begin to fan out on the finish, but lack depth and richness. Has ample tannins for cellaring two to three years; best in 1993 to '97. $12 (3/31/91) **81**
Cabernet Sauvignon South Eastern Australia Black Label 1985 $11 (4/30/88) **64**
Cabernet Sauvignon South Eastern Australia Black Label 1982 $12.50 (4/01/86) **78**
Cabernet Sauvignon South Eastern Australia Murray River 1987 $5 (4/15/88) **77**
Cabernet Sauvignon South Eastern Australia Reserve Bin 1988: Has some rough edges, but won't shortchange you on flavor. The smoke, plum, currant and anise flavors are tight and firm, finishing with a measure of complexity. A good price. Drink now to 1994. $9 (7/15/91) **82**
Cabernet Shiraz South Eastern Australia 1986: A minty style of Cabernet with some of the broadness of Shiraz, with a lean texture but enough generosity of plum and raisin flavors to make it appealing to drink now. $8 (1/31/90) **82**

STANLEY
Shiraz Cabernet Coonawarra Private Reserve 1985 $4 (12/15/87) **78**

MARK SWANN
Cabernet Sauvignon Coonawarra 1987: A lively wine that's light in color, with aromas and focused flavors of raspberry, cherry and currant that linger into a solid finish. Drinkable now for the generous fruit. $7 (2/28/91) BB **84**
Cabernet Sauvignon Coonawarra 1985 $7 (10/31/88) BB **88**
Cabernet Sauvignon Coonawarra 1984 $8 (8/31/87) **77**
Cabernet Sauvignon Coonawarra 1982 $7.50 (3/16/84) **78**
Cabernet Sauvignon South Australia 1989: Crisp and berrylike, with an odd, salty, peanut-brittle note to the aromas and flavors that fades on the finish. Drinkable now. $8 (3/15/92) **81**
Cabernet Sauvignon South Australia Proprietor's Reserve 1988: So loaded with raspberry and currant flavors it almost seems sweet, echoing cherry and spice on the finish. A firm structure and moderate tannins keep it in bounds. Drinkable now. $5.50 (2/28/91) BB **86**
Cabernet Sauvignon South Australia Proprietor's Reserve 1987: Light and appealing, with exotic spices mingling with the cherry and currant flavors; soft and velvety in texture, it's a bit tannic but drinkable now. $5.50 (7/31/89) BB **81**
Cabernet Sauvignon South Australia Proprietor's Reserve 1986 $5 (10/31/88) **78**

TALTARNI
Cabernet Sauvignon Victoria 1986: Firm and tannic, with a good dose of currant and berry aromas and flavors and hints of cedar and mint on the finish. Needs until 1995 to soften the tannins. $10 (9/30/91) **81**
Cabernet Sauvignon Victoria 1984 $9.25 (11/15/87) **85**
Cabernet Sauvignon Victoria 1982 $9.25 (4/30/87) **84**
Cabernet Sauvignon Victoria 1981 $7.50 (5/16/85) **80**
Cabernet Sauvignon Victoria 1980 $6.75 (3/01/84) **81**

TYRRELL'S
Cabernet Merlot Australia Old Winery 1988: Plump and supple, with ripe plum, currant and spicy anise notes that are generous and well behaved, with flavors and structure more reminiscent of Shiraz than Merlot. Not too tannic and ready to drink now or in 1993. $7.50 (3/31/91) BB **84**
Cabernet Merlot Hunter Valley 1987: A nice, clean, medium-bodied wine, with good plum and herbal flavors. Has medium tannins and good balance, with fruit flavors lingering on the finish. $7 (9/15/90) **79**
Cabernet Merlot Hunter Valley 1986: Smooth, spicy and focused, with generous and persistent vanilla-tinged cherry and cassis flavors. Built to cellar, but you could drink this wine tonight with a steak. Should develop at least through 1993 or '94. $8 (1/31/90) BB **88**
Cabernet Merlot Hunter Valley 1985: Soft, ripe and appealing, a bit light in color but generous with its spicy strawberry and currant flavors; has firm texture and good length. Best to drink now or in 1993. $9 (7/31/89) **84**
Cabernet Merlot Hunter Valley 1984 $9 (7/15/88) **82**
Cabernet Merlot New South Wales Victoria 1983 $8 (3/15/88) **84**
Cabernet Sauvignon Hunter Valley Classic 1984: This refreshing, flavorful wine has vibrant plum and cherry flavors and an overlay of spice and cloves. Firm acidity and tannins give it backbone, and it has beautiful balance and a long finish. $7 (9/15/90) BB **88**
Cabernet Sauvignon Hunter Valley Premier Selection 1983 $8 (4/30/88) BB **87**
Cabernet Sauvignon South Eastern Australia Old Winery 1986: A tough, earthy wine, with a strong core of currant flavors that extend into a long finish. Has little else to qualify as complexity, but should be pleasant after 1993 or '94. $9 (3/15/92) **84**

VIRGIN HILLS
Cabernet Sauvignon Bendigo 1984 $17 (4/30/88) **68**

AUDREY WILKINSON
Cabernet Sauvignon Hunter Valley 1986: A distinctive wine, with a strong streak of red currant and raspberry aromas and flavors running all the way through to the long finish. Tannic, but neither austere nor harsh. Should be best around 1994 or '95. $13.50 (9/30/91) **87**

WIRRA WIRRA
Cabernet Sauvignon McLaren Vale 1984 $14 (1/31/88) **84**
Cabernet Shiraz Merlot McLaren Vale Church Block 1985 $11 (3/15/88) **89**

WOODLEY
Shiraz Cabernet South Eastern Australia Queen Adelaide 1988: A simple, tart red, with pleasant plum and lime aromas and flavors. An unusual style, but should be fine with food. Drinkable now. $7 (2/29/92) BB **82**

WYNDHAM
Cabernet Sauvignon Hunter Valley Bin 444 1983 $6.50 (7/15/88) BB **82**
Cabernet Sauvignon South Eastern Australia Bin 444 1988: Earthy, cedary flavors mark this as a rustic, hearty red, but the lingering finish is a good sign. Medium-bodied and soft enough in tannins to drink now. $7.50 (6/30/92) **80**
Cabernet Shiraz Hunter Valley 1987: Finely concentrated blackberry and boysenberry aromas and flavors make this wine appealing now, but it has the structure and early complexity to mark it as a cellar candidate. A stylish wine with a great future. Drink now through 1995. $7 (1/31/90) BB **91**
Cabernet Shiraz Hunter Valley 1986 $6.50 (12/31/88) BB **87**
Cabernet Shiraz Hunter Valley 1985 $6.50 (3/15/88) BB **87**
Cabernet Shiraz South Eastern Australia 1989: Soft and very earthy, with barnyardy aromas and gamy flavors that don't seem too fresh. It's palatable, though. Tasted twice, with consistent notes. $7.50 (6/30/92) **76**

WYNNS
Cabernet Hermitage Coonawarra 1984 $10 (12/31/88) **79**
Cabernet Sauvignon Coonawarra 1982 $15 (11/30/88) **90**

YALUMBA
Cabernet Shiraz Coonawarra 1984 $6 (1/31/88) **78**
Cabernet Shiraz South Eastern Australia Oxford Landing 1989: This ripe, medium-weight wine has distinctive herbal aromas and flavors, but sweet currant notes come through on the finish. Drinkable now, but could improve through 1994. $7 (2/29/92) BB **82**
Cabernet Shiraz Coonawarra 1985: Aromatic, but lacking in intensity and complexity on the palate, even turning a bit thin and sour on the finish. The spicy, leathery aromas are the only appealing thing about this wine. $6.50 (9/30/89) **67**

YARRA YERING
Cabernet Sauvignon Coldstream Dry Red Wine No. 1 1984 $14 (5/31/88) **73**

CHARDONNAY

ARROWFIELD
Chardonnay South Eastern Australia 1990: Soft and slightly sour, with nice, tart peach and honey aromas and flavors. An unusual style, but seems too sweet-and-sour for our taste. $4 (5/31/92) **77**

BALGOWNIE
Chardonnay Coonawarra Series One Premier Cuvée 1987 $6.50 (9/30/88) **74**

BAROSSA VALLEY
Chardonnay South Australia 1988: Plenty of toasty oak, but there's enough fresh, ripe Chardonnay flavor to stand up to it. The pear, toast, melon and spice flavors are attractive. Drink now to 1994. $11 (3/15/90) **81**

BERRI
Chardonnay Barossa Valley 1986 $12 (5/31/87) **89**
Chardonnay South Australia Vintage Selection 1986 $7.75 (2/15/88) **89**

BLACK OPAL
Chardonnay Hunter Valley 1987: Ripe, round and complex, marked by deliciously sweet oak; balanced and elegant flavors fall a bit short on the finish. The interplay of pear- citrus flavors with spicy oak keeps it interesting. $9 (7/31/89) **85**
Chardonnay Hunter Valley 1986 $8 (12/31/87) **79**
Chardonnay Hunter Valley 1985 $8 (5/15/87) BB **87**

WOLF BLASS
Chardonnay South Australia Première Release 1987: Typically ripe and generous, with appealing green apple and vanilla aromas and flavors, simple and easy to drink. $9 (4/15/89) **82**
Chardonnay South Australia Première Release 1986 $10 (5/15/88) **81**

BROWN BROTHERS
Chardonnay Australia Family Reserve NV $9 (5/31/87) **86**
Chardonnay King Valley 1987: Appealingly earthy, with tangy pear and mineral notes; smoothly balanced, a bit on the soft side, but firm enough to cellar. Drink up now. $11 (7/31/89) **84**

AUSTRALIA

Chardonnay

Chardonnay King Valley Family Reserve 1988: A distinctive style that packs in plenty of flavor. Ripe, rich, bold and buttery, offering layers of concentrated mandarin orange, peach, butterscotch and honey flavors that linger on the aftertaste. Has just the right kiss of oak. Drink now to 1994. $17 (9/15/91) **90**
Chardonnay King Valley Family Reserve 1987: A Chardonnay that's rich, complex, delicious and beautifully balanced, with everything you could ask for. Flavors of fig, pear, butter and spice last from the aroma to the lingering finish. $15.50 (7/15/90) SS **91**
Chardonnay King Valley Family Selection 1988: A well-balanced and smooth-textured wine in a modest style. A mineral note in the medium-rich pear and spice flavors makes it distinctive. $11.50 (7/15/90) **80**
Chardonnay Victoria Estate Selection 1985 $8 (8/31/87) **85**

LEO BURNING
Chardonnay South Australia 1987 $7 (5/31/88) **72**

CAPE MENTELLE
Chardonnay Margaret River 1990: Crisp and focused, with sharply defined peach, pear and spice aromas and flavors, hinting at toast and butter on the long finish. The structure is tight, suggesting this will improve with cellaring through 1993 to '95. 21,000 cases made. $20 (5/31/92) **91**
Chardonnay Margaret River 1989: Tight and crisp, a lean wine, with sappy, modest fruit flavors and a touch of bitterness on the finish. A very spicy style that not everyone will like. Drinkable now. $20 (2/29/92) **80**
Chardonnay Margaret River 1989: Heavily oaked, with distinct pine flavors that add to the straightforward pineapple and grapefruit notes. A simple style, with flavors that trail off. Drink now. 200 cases made. $20 (3/31/91) **80**

CASSEGRAIN
Chardonnay Hastings Valley Fromenteau Vineyard 1989: Rich and concentrated, with ripe pear, pineapple, citrus and spice flavors and sumptuous oak adding butter and toast notes. The complex, well-integrated flavors are long on the finish. Drink now to 1994. $25 (3/31/91) **89**
Chardonnay Hunter Valley Vintage Selection 1989: Tight and focused, with bright pineapple, citrus, toast and butterscotch flavors that keep flowing right through the finish. What it lacks in finesse, it makes up in flavor. Drink now. 1,100 cases made. $20 (2/15/92) **86**
Chardonnay South Eastern Australia 1989: Bold, rich and assertive, with intense, concentrated pear, vanilla, pineapple and citrus flavors flanked by spicy oak. Balanced, concentrated and drinks well now, but can age through 1994. $14.50 (3/31/91) **87**

CEDAR CREEK
Chardonnay South Eastern Australia Bin 33 1990: Ripe and spicy, with a lively feel to the generous apple, honey and butter aromas and flavors. Has a sense of richness without excess weight. Drinkable now. $6 (5/31/92) BB **85**

CHATEAU REYNELLA
Chardonnay McLaren Vale 1990: A buttery, creamy, full-flavored Chardonnay that's ripe, full-bodied and heavily oak-influenced. Might be too toasty for some, but it's surely assertive. $10.50 (11/30/91) **84**
Chardonnay McLaren Vale 1988: A pretty complex wine, with doughy, toasty and nutmeg notes, plenty of butterscotch aromas and flavors from start to finish and good acidity. Reasonably priced. $9 (7/31/90) **85**
Chardonnay McLaren Vale 1987 $11.50 (12/31/88) **82**
Chardonnay McLaren Vale 1985 $7 (5/15/88) BB **89**

CHITTERING
Chardonnay Western Australia 1988: Smells pretty, with ripe fruit and creamy vanilla aromas, and the peach, fig, spice and oak flavors are rich and elegant. The oaky finish picks up a toasty note. Drink now to 1993. $18 (9/15/91) **88**

CLYDE PARK
Chardonnay Geelong 1986 $15 (2/15/88) **90**

COLDSTREAM HILLS
Chardonnay Lilydale Three Vineyards Blend 1987: Tight, lean and crisp but by no means light. It's intense with tart green apple—complete with the skins—finishing with a leafy aftertaste. Give it a year or two to fully develop. $20 (1/31/90) **87**
Chardonnay Lilydale Three Vineyards Blend 1986 $18 (5/31/88) **72**
Chardonnay Lilydale Yarra Ridge Vineyard 1987: Smooth and elegant, gaining complexity as it develops maturity, this wine shows nutmeg, vanilla, peach and pear aromas and flavors that are harmonious and balanced. Drinkable now. $19 (10/15/90) **87**
Chardonnay Lilydale Yarra Ridge Vineyard 1986 $18 (5/31/88) **68**

CULLENS
Chardonnay Western Australia Margaret River 1985 $18 (11/15/87) **83**

DENMAN
Chardonnay Hunter Valley Private Bin 1985 $6 (12/31/87) **80**

EVANS FAMILY
Chardonnay Hunter Valley 1985 $13 (4/15/87) **78**
Chardonnay Hunter Valley Vintage Selection 1986 $14 (2/15/88) **88**

ANDREW GARRETT
Chardonnay South Australia 1986 $9.75 (12/31/87) **80**

GRANTS
Chardonnay McLaren Vale 1986 $8 (12/15/87) **77**

HARDY'S
Chardonnay Australia NV $10 (5/31/87) **86**
Chardonnay Padthaway Clare Valley The Hardy Collection 1988: Tastes rich, ripe, oaky, full-bodied and flavorful, but comes up a bit short on fruit and aftertaste, with buttery, toasty aromas, ripe pear and spice flavors and a tart finish. $10.50 (7/15/90) **80**
Chardonnay Padthaway Hardy Collection No. 1 1987: Very woody aromas and flavors, watery in texture rather than ponderous, so the fruit is submerged and the wine seems one-dimensional. $11.50 (2/15/89) **69**
Chardonnay Padthaway Hardy Collection No. 1 1987 $7 (5/31/88) **72**
Chardonnay South Australia Eileen Hardy 1989: A ripe, buttery wine that's deeply colored and deeply flavorful. The solid core of pineapple and pear flavor is shaded by hints of nutmeg, caramel and vanilla notes. A broad style that already shows finesse; should continue to develop through 1993 or '94. 3,500 cases made. $19 (2/15/92) **91**
Chardonnay South Australia Nottage Hill 1991: Crisp and lively, with bright lemon and peach aromas and flavors. This fruity wine has plenty of zing and finishes with refreshing grapefruit and spice notes. $8 (5/31/92) BB **87**
Chardonnay South Eastern Australia 1987: Drinkable, but not recommended. Smelling oaky and slightly spicy, it tastes dull and coarse. Tasted twice with consistent results. $7.50 (7/15/90) **69**
Chardonnay South Eastern Australia Bird Series 1991: Crisp and fruity, with pleasant apple and pear flavors and a nice touch of spice and vanilla on the finish. Light on its feet; has harmony and balance. Drinkable now. $7.50 (6/30/92) BB **85**
Chardonnay South Eastern Australia Bird Series 1990: A soft wine, with broad-based, buttery, spicy pear flavors that linger on the finish. Easy to drink, if not particularly deep or complex. $7.50 (9/15/91) BB **84**
Chardonnay South Eastern Australia Bird Series 1987 $6 (5/31/88) **75**
Chardonnay Sunraysia 1988: A rich, ripe, full-blown Chardonnay, with tons of tropical notes of sweet pineapple, banana and honey. Soft, smooth and unctuous on the finish. $7 (7/31/90) BB **82**

HEGGIES
Chardonnay Barossa Valley 1987: Deep in color with gold and yellow hues, loaded with pineapple, pear, fig and other exotic fruit flavors and plenty of oak. Altogether well balanced and appealing. $14 (1/31/90) **83**
Chardonnay Barossa Valley 1985 $13 (12/15/87) **69**

HILL-SMITH
Chardonnay Barossa Valley 1986 $8 (11/15/87) **73**
Chardonnay Barossa Valley 1985 $9.50 (5/15/87) **72**

HOLLICK
Chardonnay Coonawarra 1986 $16 (5/15/88) **86**

HOUGHTON
Chardonnay Western Australia Gold Reserve 1987: Extremely earthy, soapy, and somewhat bitter, with bitter almond flavors. Not enticing. $10 (10/31/90) **69**
Chardonnay Western Australia Wildflower Ridge 1990: Full of zingy, lively fruit flavors that linger nicely on the aftertaste. Concentrated pear and pineapple flavors are accented by a bit of spice and toast. Oak is in the background. 10,000 cases made. $9 (11/30/91) BB **84**
Chardonnay Western Australia Wildflower Ridge 1989: Soft and supple, with modest butter, caramel and pear flavors. A bit watery and sweet on the finish. Drinkable, if unexceptional. 10,000 cases made. $9 (9/15/91) **76**

HUNGERFORD HILL
Chardonnay Hunter Valley 1986 $12 (2/15/88) **86**

JOHNSTONE
Chardonnay Hunter River Valley 1989: Floral, butterscotch and vanilla flavors predominate in this perfumed, interesting wine, with a soft texture and pleasant character. Drinkable now. 10,000 cases made. $7 (5/31/92) BB **84**

KOALA RIDGE
Chardonnay Barossa Valley 1990: A straightforward, spicy, floral-tasting Chardonnay, with lively acidity. Has good fruit flavors, but doesn't come together as well as it might on the finish. $10 (11/30/91) **80**
Chardonnay Barossa Valley 1989: Plenty of apple, pear and nutmeg aromas and flavors persist on the long finish, which echoes almond and vanilla notes. Crisp and lively. Packed with flavor; a solid package. Drink now. A good value. 10,000 cases made. $9 (5/31/91) **85**
Chardonnay Barossa Valley 1987: Simple, direct fruity style that is pleasant and easy on the pocketbook. The ripe pear and melon flavors offer modest depth and complexity. Drink now. $7 (3/15/90) **80**
Chardonnay Barossa Valley 1986 $8 (2/15/89) **84**

KRONDORF
Chardonnay Australia 1985 $13 (4/15/87) **85**
Chardonnay Barossa Valley 1986 $8 (3/31/87) BB **87**

LEASINGHAM
Chardonnay Clare Valley Domaine 1989: This ripe, exotic style is very smooth and soft, with effusive tropical fruit, fig and lemon aromas and flavors. Fat and sassy, this is a big wine, with a touch of heat on the finish. Drinkable now. $8.50 (10/15/90) **83**

LEEUWIN
Chardonnay Margaret River Second Release 1983 $24 (5/31/88) **84**

PETER LEHMANN
Chardonnay Barossa Valley 1988: Ripe, broad and buttery, with a fair concentration of pear and orange flavors to round out the oak; a bit astringent. Drink now. $11 (7/31/89) **81**

LINDEMANS
Chardonnay Padthaway 1989: Showing maturity, with generous toast- and honey-scented pear and pineapple aromas and flavors. A big wine, with a smooth texture and a refreshing sense of balance on the finish. Drink soon. $12 (5/31/92) **88**
Chardonnay Padthaway 1988: An exotic wine, with fig, ripe pear, butter and honey aromas and flavors. A good core of fruit dominates this soft, thick and viscous wine. Tasted twice. $15 (7/31/90) **81**
Chardonnay Padthaway 1986 $12 (12/31/87) **87**
Chardonnay Padthaway 1985 $9 (2/28/87) **81**
Chardonnay South Australia Bin 65 1985 $6 (2/28/87) **77**
Chardonnay South Eastern Australia Bin 65 1991: Bright and lively, with generous apple, pear and spice aromas and flavors and hints of smoke and toast on the long finish. A stylish wine, with plenty of flavor and a crisp texture to support it. $7 (5/31/92) BB **87**
Chardonnay South Eastern Australia Bin 65 1990: Crisp and floral, reminiscent of a Riesling, with nice tropical fruit aromas and flavors. Tart, refreshing and flavorful. Drinkable now. $7 (2/28/91) BB **85**
Chardonnay South Eastern Australia Bin 65 1989: Ripe and fruity, with tropical flavors of papaya and pineapple, a smooth texture and gold color. Touches of butter and honey add complexity in the lingering aftertaste. $6 (4/30/90) BB **85**
Chardonnay South Eastern Australia Bin 65 1988 $6 (5/15/89) BB **87**
Chardonnay Victoria Bin 65 1987 $6 (2/15/88) BB **83**

MILDARA
Chardonnay Barossa Valley 1989: Ripe and round in texture, but a bit of mustiness creeps in around the edges of the fig and pineapple flavors, keeping it from being as enjoyable as it could be. $7.50 (2/28/91) **75**
Chardonnay Barossa Valley 1987 $12 (12/31/88) **88**
Chardonnay Coonawarra 1985 $7.50 (4/15/87) **84**
Chardonnay Merbian Church Hill 1987 $5.50 (2/15/88) **79**
Chardonnay Merbian Church Hill 1986 $5 (6/15/87) BB **82**
Chardonnay Murray River Valley 1987: Austere, steely style, with earthy, pineapple aromas and flavors, hard-edged and unfocused. $8 (2/15/89) **70**

Key to Symbols

The scores reported here are the results of blind tastings conducted by our panel of senior editors. Wines that carry the initials below are results of individual tastings.

THE WINE SPECTATOR 100-POINT SCALE ***95-100***—Classic, a great wine; ***90-94***—Outstanding, superior character and style; ***80-89***—Good to very good, a wine with special qualities; ***70-79***—Average, drinkable wine that may have minor flaws; ***60-69***—Below average, drinkable but not recommended; ***50-59***—Poor, undrinkable, not recommended. "+"—With a score indicates a range; used primarily with barrel tastings to indicate a preliminary score.

SPECIAL DESIGNATIONS SS—Spectator Selection, CS—Cellar Selection, BB—Best Buy, ($NA)—Price not available, (NR)—Not released.

TASTER'S INITIALS (JG)—Jim Gordon, (HS)—Harvey Steiman, (JL)—James Laube, (JS)—James Suckling, (TM)—Thomas Matthews, (TR)—Terry Robards, (PM)—Per-Henrik Mansson, (BT)—Barrel Tasting (these wines were tasted blind from barrel samples), (CA-date)—*California's Great Cabernets* by James Laube, (CH-date)—*California's Great Chardonnays* by James Laube, (VP-date)—*Vintage Port* by James Suckling.

DATE TASTED Dates in parentheses represent the issue in which the rating was published.

MITCHELTON
Chardonnay Goulburn Valley Reserve 1988: With each sip this wine reveals more flavor, depth and complexity, with a wonderful interplay of toasty oak, ripe pear, honey, melon and butterscotch flavors that are very well focused and linger on the palate. Very impressive bottling. Drink now to 1994. $14 (3/15/90) **90**
Chardonnay Goulburn Valley Wood Matured 1990: Ripe and fruity, with peach, floral and sappy oak flavors. Simple, but offers plenty of flavor. Drink now. $15 (2/15/92) **82**
Chardonnay Goulburn Valley Wood Matured Reserve 1989: Offers mature, buttery, spicy aromas and flavors, with plenty of fig and pear charactistics at the core. A medium-weight wine with appealing flavors. Drinkable now. $15 (6/30/92) **86**
Chardonnay Goulburn Valley Wood Matured Reserve 1989: Has attractive, ripe, rich pear, pineapple, citrus and oak flavors in a straightforward style. The flavors fan out on the finish. Ready to drink now. $15 (3/31/91) **84**
Chardonnay Victoria 1991: Lively wine with generous pear and saplike aromas and flavors, echoing flavors that remind us of canned pears. Drinkable now. $8 (2/29/92) **77**
Chardonnay Victoria 1989: Intense and spicy, with rich pineapple, tart apple and melon notes. It's balanced, but the wood flavors on the finish aren't a plus. Drink now to 1993. $8 (4/15/91) **80**
Chardonnay Victoria 1988: A bit heavy-handed with the oak, with vegetal flavors creeping into the Chardonnay flavor. The oaky style, though pleasant, lacks complexity; may appeal to some more than others. Drink now. $10 (3/15/90) **79**

MONTROSE
Chardonnay Australia Show Reserve 1986 $14 (5/31/87) **91**
Chardonnay Mudgee 1989: Crisp and brightly focused, with lively grapefruit and pear aromas and flavors, firm acidity and enough length to call for another sip. Not quite as broad as most Aussie Chardonnays, but a step up from most in intensity. $10 (2/28/91) **85**
Chardonnay Mudgee 1988: A balanced wine, with pineapple and rich buttery accents that show well against the firm acidity. Drink now. Tasted twice. $9 (6/15/90) **84**
Chardonnay Mudgee 1987: Sturdy but not outstanding. Toasty and smoky flavors dominate. Modest pear and pineapple flavors on top of a soft structure. Muted aromas except for the oak. $8 (7/31/89)**78**
Chardonnay Mudgee 1986 $10 (2/15/88) **81**
Chardonnay Mudgee Special Reserve 1984 $15 (5/15/87) **89**
Chardonnay Mudgee Stoney Creek Vineyard Special Reserve 1986: Complex style that combines plenty of ripe, full-bodied buttery pear and spice flavors with ample oak. Lots of richness, depth and flavor, a wine to sink your teeth into. Drink now to 1993. $13 (3/15/90) **87**
Chardonnay South Eastern Australia Bin 747 1989: This exotic wine is ripe, spicy, floral and round, with honey-edged pear and fig aromas and flavors. Balanced, smooth and generous. Drinkable now. 2,000 cases made. $8 (2/28/91) BB **83**

MOUNTADAM
Chardonnay Eden Valley 1990: Rich, spicy and full of generous fig, pear and nutmeg aromas and flavors, finishing smooth and creamy. The fruit keeps coming on the finish, but it's nicely balanced and could become elegant with cellaring until 1993 to '94. $20 (2/29/92) **90**
Chardonnay Eden Valley 1989: High in extract, rich, bold and concentrated, with tiers of butter, pineapple, spice and apple-scented flavors. Makes no pretense at subtlety, but packs in plenty of Chardonnay flavor that stays with you. Ready now through 1994. $25 (3/31/91) **90**
Chardonnay Eden Valley High Eden Ridge 1986 $17 (5/15/88) **77**

NORMANS
Chardonnay South Australia Chais Clarendon 1989: A little too broad and spicy, with more oak than fruit and a soft texture that borders on flat. Drinkable, but not as lively as it could be. 500 cases made. $14 (2/15/92) **78**
Chardonnay South Australia Chandlers Hill 1991: Smooth, full-bodied and flavorful, emphasizing peach and pear flavors shaded by spicy oak notes. Drinkable now, but should be best in 1993. 500 cases made. $7 (2/29/92) BB **86**

ORLANDO
Chardonnay McLaren Vale St.-Hugo 1986: Deep yellow color, smells oxidized and tastes rich but rancid, with a cooked pineapple flavor. The style will be too extreme for some. Tasted twice with consistent results. $15 (7/31/90) **68**
Chardonnay McLaren Vale St.-Hugo 1985: Gloriously ripe and deep, first in its color but then with butterscotch woven through the complex pear and vanilla aromas and flavors, finishing long and resonant. Delicious now, but if it's lasted this long you can expect it to be around through 1993. $15 (7/31/89) **91**
Chardonnay South Australia St.-Hugo 1988: Ripe, spicy, fat and rich, with spicy oak notes to balance the generous pear and pineapple flavors. A real mouthful of smooth-textured wine. Drink now. $15 (9/15/91) **89**
Chardonnay South Eastern Australia Jacob's Creek 1991: Focused, flavorful and almost thick on the palate, with generous fig, apple and vanilla aromas and flavors. Has viscosity and a firm enough structure to keep it balanced. Drinkable now. $7 (5/31/92) BB **86**
Chardonnay South Eastern Australia Jacob's Creek 1990: A very spicy style, with a soft texture and piny, floral nuances to the lush fruit flavors. The balance is crisp enough to let the flavors linger on the finish. Drinkable now. $7 (5/15/91) BB **84**
Chardonnay South Eastern Australia Jacob's Creek 1989: Smells more interesting than it tastes, with minty, peachy aromas, followed by pear and banana flavors that seem a bit dull, with a short finish. Drink now. $7 (6/15/90) **76**
Chardonnay South Eastern Australia Jacob's Creek 1988 $7 (1/31/90) **80**
Chardonnay South Eastern Australia Jacob's Creek 1987 $6.50 (3/15/89) BB **83**

OXFORD LANDING
Chardonnay South Australia 1990: Ripe and buttery, with lush pineapple and almond aromas and flavors and a creamy texture. Stylish and generous, if less than elegant. Drinkable now. 4,000 cases made. $7 (2/28/91) BB **85**
Chardonnay South Australia 1989: Richly decadent, with spicy clove flavors and aromas, this wine is lush and fruity and has good intensity. It's a little soft, but cleanly made. 4,000 cases made. $7 (10/15/90) BB **82**

PEACOCK HILL
Chardonnay Hunter Valley 1987 $11 (5/31/88) **73**

PENFOLDS
Chardonnay South Australia 1988: Has smoky aromas but sharp grapefruit and citric flavors are framed by oak. A sense of restaint and elegance characterizes this wine, but it could use a shade more fruit. $9.50 (1/31/90) **83**
Chardonnay South Australia 1987: Fruity and crisp with sunny aromas and flavors of peach and pine; has a lean structure; balanced and tasty. $8 (2/15/89) **80**

PETALUMA
Chardonnay Australia 1989: Vibrant and fruity, with plenty of grapefruit and pineapple flavors at the core; intense, concentrated and shaded by hints of honey and vanilla. Oak notes are well integrated, and emerge on the finish. Balanced and drinkable now, but better in 1993. $30 (11/30/91) **91**
Chardonnay Australia 1987: Ripe and complex, with lots of spicy toastiness balanced against a smooth core of pear and fig flavors. Rich, but not too weighty. Drinkable now. $21 (5/31/91) **88**
Chardonnay Australia 1986 $18 (5/31/87) **90**

PIPERS BROOK
Chardonnay Tasmania 1990: Ripe and smooth, with a generous level of spicy oak layered between the sweet pear and pineapple flavors. Drinkable now, but could use until 1993 to settle down. $25 (2/15/92) **87**
Chardonnay Tasmania 1989: Elegant and perfumed, with spicy pear and apple flavors that aren't intruded upon by oak. A crisp, refreshing style that shows a measure of restraint and finishes with a hint of flint and mineral. Drink now to 1993. $25 (3/31/91) **86**
Chardonnay Tasmania 1988: Firm and spicy, with a good dose of toasty oak, but has plenty of buttery pear and apple flavors underneath that are fresh, rich and complex. Ready now through 1994. $25 (3/31/91) **86**

PREECE
Chardonnay Goulburn Valley 1990: Tight and fruity, with a pretty core of apple, spice and pineapple flavor. An appealing style, with moderate depth and complexity. Drink now. $13 (2/15/92) **83**
Chardonnay Goulburn Valley 1989: Ripe and exotic, with lots of tropical fruit aromas and flavors, broadening on the palate to encompass the leesy flavors of extended maceration, spice, vanilla and butter notes. Fresh and appealing. Should be fine through 1993. $14 (9/15/91) **86**

RICHMOND GROVE
Chardonnay Hunter Valley French Cask 1989: Ripe and juicy, with a round texture and plenty of pineapple and spice aromas and flavors. Hints at oak and vanilla on the finish, but has nice balance for current drinking. $7 (5/15/91) BB **83**

RIDDOCH
Chardonnay Victoria 1987: High-toned and rich with alluring pear, pineapple and buttery flavors. Elegant and decadent, with nice oak overtones. Well-balanced with a good lingering finish. A good value. $9 (10/15/90) **88**
Chardonnay Victoria 1986 $9 (5/31/88) **69**

ROO'S LEAP
Chardonnay Coonawarra Barrel Fermented 1991: Fresh and lively, with refreshing lemon, floral and pear aromas and flavors, turning a bit strongly toward oak on the finish. Drinkable now. $10 (6/30/92) **83**
Chardonnay Coonawarra Barrel Fermented 1990: Ripe and smooth, with generous oak-scented pear and vanilla aromas and flavors that are long and mouth-filling. Appealing to drink soon. $10 (9/15/91) **82**
Chardonnay Hunter Valley Barrel Fermented 1987: Firmly balanced, concentrated and complex, a harmonious wine that plays ripe pear and pineapple flavor against spicy oak; has a sense of richness and power without excess weight. $10 (2/15/89) **88**

ROSEMOUNT
Chardonnay Hunter Valley Giants Creek Vineyard 1987: A new vineyard-designated wine from Rosemount, Giants Creek is leaner and more narrowly focused than most Rosemount Chardonnays, and the leafy green apple flavors are tart and not as opulent as most efforts from this winery. With time it may be more charming, but for now it's hard and sharp. 200 cases made. $20 (3/15/90) **80**
Chardonnay Hunter Valley Matured in Oak Casks 1990: Flavorful and elegant, with spicy grapefruit and pear aromas and flavors and mineral overtones on the finish. Has plenty to offer for immediate drinking, plus the balance for developing in the cellar through 1993 or '94. A good value. $9 (5/15/91) **88**
Chardonnay Hunter Valley Matured in Oak Casks 1989: Rich and buttery tasting, built on ripe fruit. A bit soft and unfocused, but has a nicely lingering finish. Drink now. $9 (4/30/90) **80**
Chardonnay Hunter Valley Matured in Oak Casks 1988: Plenty of fresh ripe tropical fruit flavors, with hints of pear and apple, and subtle oak seasoning. A clean, well-made, balanced Chardonnay that offers good value. Drink now. $10 (3/15/90) **82**
Chardonnay Hunter Valley Matured in Oak Casks 1987 $10.50 (3/15/89) **87**
Chardonnay Hunter Valley Matured in Oak Casks 1986 $9 (5/31/88) **87**
Chardonnay Hunter Valley Matured in Oak Casks 1985 $10 (4/15/87) **83**
Chardonnay Hunter Valley Roxburgh 1986 $25 (5/31/87) **91**
Chardonnay Hunter Valley Roxburgh 1985 $25 (8/31/87) **88**
Chardonnay Hunter Valley Show Reserve 1989: An elegant wine, with lots of depth to the Burgundian flavors, offering honey- and almond-tinged pear and apple flavors that extend into a long finish. Medium weight, ripe and stylish. Smooth enough to drink now, but cellaring until 1993 wouldn't hurt. 4,600 cases made. $16 (5/31/91) **92**
Chardonnay Hunter Valley Show Reserve 1988: More elegant and refined than prevous bottlings, this Show Reserve still has plenty of subtle pear and butterscotch flavors that stay with you from start to finish. Well balanced; drink it now. $16 (3/15/90) **85**
Chardonnay Hunter Valley Show Reserve 1987: Outstanding. Has a smooth, silky texture, delicate balance and subtle flavors of ripe fig, honey and toasty vanilla and oak that are long and full on the finish. Shows great finesse. $16.50 (2/15/89) **92**
Chardonnay Hunter Valley Show Reserve 1986 $16 (12/31/87) **90**
Chardonnay Hunter Valley Show Reserve 1985 $15 (4/15/87) **88**

ROTHBURY
Chardonnay Hunter Valley 1991: Smooth in texture and fresh in flavor, with a nice buttery edge to the basic pear and apple notes. Drinkable now. $9.50 (2/29/92) **83**
Chardonnay Hunter Valley 1984 $8 (7/01/86) **69**
Chardonnay Hunter Valley Brokenback Vineyard 1989: Crisp in structure but generous in flavor and texture. It shows lemon-tinged almond and floral aromas and flavors, silky smoothness and a bit of tension on the finish. Drinkable now. $9 (10/15/90) **84**
Chardonnay Hunter Valley Brokenback Vineyard 1988: Terrifically concentrated fig, honey, nectarine and peach flavors lend this wine its style. Smooth in texture, firm in structure, long and toasty. Drink now. (JL) $10 (3/15/89) **89**
Chardonnay Hunter Valley Brokenback Vineyard 1987 $7.50 (2/15/88) **88**
Chardonnay Hunter Valley Brokenback Vineyard 1986 $9.50 (5/31/87) **90**
Chardonnay Hunter Valley Brokenback Vineyard Barrel Fermented 1990: Rich and unctuous, with a smooth texture and earthy, buttery pear and spice flavors that extend into a solid finish. A bit on the woody side, but generous and appealing. Drinkable now. $15 (5/31/92) **89**
Chardonnay Hunter Valley Reserve 1988: This deep gold wine is not for the faint of heart. Smoky and spicy accents add to the ripe apple, pear and butterscotch flavors. Rich with good length, but it's a little heavy-handed. $18.50 (10/15/90) **85**
Chardonnay Hunter Valley Reserve 1987: Deep gold, with mature flavor; a big, rich, deep, full-bodied wine with flavors of peach, apricot, honey and smoky oak. A big, concentrated Chardonnay for fans of that style. $19 (2/15/89) **89**
Chardonnay Hunter Valley Reserve 1986 $15 (2/15/88) **83**
Chardonnay Hunter Valley Reserve 1985 $25 (5/31/87) **92**

ST.-HUBERTS
Chardonnay Yarra Valley 1985 $13.25 (12/31/87) **66**

SALTRAM
Chardonnay Hazelwood 1987: A ripe, well-rounded Chardonnay with nice tropical flavors balanced by firm acid. Medium-bodied with pear, floral and oak aromas and a pleasant lingering aftertaste. $8.50 (7/31/89) **82**
Chardonnay McLaren Vale Hunter Valley Mamre Brook 1987: A deep gold, oaky, toasty Chardonnay that pulls out all the stops. But where's the fruit to round out the oak? The finish is long and woody tasting. $12 (7/31/89) **82**

SEAVIEW
Chardonnay South Australia 1989: Lively and fruity, with distinctive grapefruit and pineapple aromas and flavors. A bit coarse or rustic in style, but enjoyable to drink now. $10 (9/15/91) **82**
Chardonnay South Australia 1988: Looks rich, but tastes simply fruity. Has straightforward, fruit cocktail flavors and decent balance. $10 (7/15/90) **71**

AUSTRALIA

Chardonnay

SEPPELT

Chardonnay Barooga Padthaway Black Label 1989: Crisp, with bold pineapple, citrus, grapefruit and buttery oak flavors in a rich, concentrated, complex style. Picks up nice smoky butterscotch notes on the finish. Drink now to 1994. $14 (3/31/91) **89**

Chardonnay Barooga Padthaway Black Label Great Western Vineyards 1987: Soft and generous, brimming with buttery pear flavors, turning somewhat earthy and toasty from prominent use of oak; the structure could be firmer. $15 (7/31/89) **79**

Chardonnay South Eastern Australia Reserve Bin 1990: Soft and almost watery, with enough pear and spice aromas and flavors to make it interesting and drinkable. $9 (9/15/91) **78**

Chardonnay South Eastern Australia Reserve Bin 1989: A beautifully fruity wine, with layers of fresh apple, ripe pear, and toasty vanilla nuances that linger on the palate and make you want to go back for another sip. Just delicious. $10 (7/31/90) **88**

Chardonnay South Eastern Australia Reserve Bin 1987 $9 (5/31/88) **80**

Chardonnay South Eastern Australia Reserve Bin 1986 $8 (2/15/88) **87**

Chardonnay South Eastern Australia Reserve Bin 1985 $8 (9/30/86) **74**

Chardonnay South Eastern Australia Reserve Bin 1984 $8.50 (2/01/86) **84**

MARK SWANN

Chardonnay Barossa Valley 1989: A moderate, well-modulated style that's not as big and ripe as most Aussie Chardonnays, offering modest pear, vanilla and spice flavors and a crisp texture. It's a bit short, but enjoyable. $7 (2/28/91) **79**

Chardonnay McLaren Vale 1983 $11 (9/16/84) **81**

Chardonnay South Australia Proprietor's Reserve 1987: Lean and restrained, with delicate peach and pear flavors, a crisp structure and a touch of oak, but a bit shallow. Drink now. $5 (2/15/89) **79**

Chardonnay Victoria 1990: This floral, spicy, grapefruit-flavored style of Chardonnay emphasizes freshness instead of oak. A very charming, crisp wine to enjoy now. 2,345 cases made. $8 (11/30/91) BB **84**

Chardonnay Victoria Proprietor's Reserve 1989: A polished wine that's broad in texture, but a bit shy on flavor. Hints at walnut and spice on the finish. Drinkable now. $7 (5/31/91) **78**

TARRA WARRA

Chardonnay Yarra Glen 1989: Old enough to have mature aromas and flavors, shading the pear and oak core with touches of spicy complexity on the long finish. The flavors stay with you a long time. Delicious now. 2,000 cases made. $28 (2/29/92) **88**

Chardonnay Yarra Glen 1988: Powerful, complex and graceful, with glorious pear, spice, smoke and tangerine peel flavors competing for attention. It's impeccably balanced, long on the finish and elegant. Has enough crisp acidity to match with rich food today or keep in the cellar through 1994 to see what more can develop. 2,800 cases made. $25 (12/31/90) **92**

TUNNEL HILL

Chardonnay Yarra Valley 1990: Crisp and a little astringent, but modest ripe pear and green apple-skin characteristics come through on the palate. Give it until 1993 or '94 to sort itself out. 2,700 cases made. $16 (2/15/92) **83**

TYRRELL'S

Chardonnay Hunter Valley 1989: A rich Australian Chardonnay. Ripe, full pineapple and apple flavors dominate this wine, with butter and spice notes coming out on the finish. Clean and well balanced. $7 (10/15/90) BB **84**

Chardonnay Hunter Valley 1988: Flat, fat, uninspiring, with enough ripe fruit and oak flavor to make it drinkable, but not much else. $9 (7/31/89) **68**

Chardonnay Hunter Valley 1986 $7.50 (5/15/88) **82**

Chardonnay Hunter Valley Vat 47 Pinot Chardonnay 1989: Simply packed with fruit flavors—pineapple, peach and grapefruit—plus ginger, nutmeg and other spices. An intense, lively and vivid wine that tastes fine now, but should age well through at least 1994. Toasty, buttery notes linger on the finish. $16 (11/30/91) **88**

Chardonnay Hunter Valley Vat 47 Pinot Chardonnay 1988: Soft and broad, with unfocused pear and butter aromas and flavors; a bit earthy. Despite a deep gold color, some might call it watery. $16 (7/31/89) **77**

Chardonnay Hunter Valley Vat 47 Pinot Chardonnay 1986 $12 (5/15/88) **85**

Chardonnay South Eastern Australia Old Winery 1990: Mellowed by wood aging and modest in fruit flavor, but has plenty of body and decent spicy apple flavors. $8 (11/30/91) **77**

AUDREY WILKINSON

Chardonnay Hunter Valley 1987: Tart and lively, with modest green apple and chalk aromas and flavors. Not the usual Aussie blockbuster, it's rather restrained, attempting elegance but basically light in flavor. Drinkable now. 3,600 cases made. $14 (9/15/91) **78**

WIRRA WIRRA

Chardonnay McLaren Vale David Paxton's Hillstowe Vineyard 1985 $14 (12/31/87) **64**

WOODLEY

Chardonnay South Eastern Australia Queen Adelaide 1990: Lean and austere, with little generosity of fruit, offering mostly earthy mineral notes and finishing short. $7 (9/15/91) **74**

Chardonnay South Eastern Australia Queen Adelaide 1987 $8 (5/31/88) **78**

WYNDHAM

Chardonnay Hunter Valley 1989: Smooth, ripe and honeyed, with nice vanilla and nutmeg overtones to the core of fig and pear flavors. An attractive wine to drink soon for all its fruit and spice. $11.50 (5/15/91) **85**

Chardonnay Hunter Valley 1987: Deep yellow-gold, extremely toasty and buttery with a leesy flavor that may appeal to others more than us. The label says "Oak Cask Chardonnay," which is fair warning. $7.75 (1/31/90) **71**

Chardonnay Hunter Valley Bin 222 1988: An oaky style, but there's plenty of fresh, ripe, flavor to stand up to it. The fig, lemon and pear flavors play off each other. $7 (1/31/90) **83**

Chardonnay South Eastern Australia Bin 222 1990: Soft and earthy, with a slightly oily texture and a lot of ripe nectarine, earth and spice flavors. Soft enough that some might find it dull. $7.25 (5/31/92)**75**

Chardonnay South Eastern Australia Bin 222 1989: Ripe and smooth, with opulent pear, apricot and pineapple flavors jockeying for position, shaded nicely by oak without being overwhelming. The flavors persist on the finish. Drinkable now. $6.50 (9/15/91) BB **86**

Key to Symbols

The scores reported here are the results of blind tastings conducted by our panel of senior editors. Wines that carry the initials below are results of individual tastings.

THE WINE SPECTATOR 100-POINT SCALE 95-100—Classic, a great wine; ***90-94***—Outstanding, superior character and style; ***80-89***—Good to very good, a wine with special qualities; ***70-79***—Average, drinkable wine that may have minor flaws; ***60-69***—Below average, drinkable but not recommended; ***50-59***—Poor, undrinkable, not recommended. "+"—With a score indicates a range; used primarily with barrel tastings to indicate a preliminary score.

SPECIAL DESIGNATIONS SS—Spectator Selection, CS—Cellar Selection, BB—Best Buy, ($NA)—Price not available, (NR)—Not released.

TASTER'S INITIALS (JG)—Jim Gordon, (HS)—Harvey Steiman, (JL)—James Laube, (JS)—James Suckling, (TM)—Thomas Matthews, (TR)—Terry Robards, (PM)—Per-Henrik Mansson, (BT)—Barrel Tasting (these wines were tasted blind from barrel samples), (CA-date)—*California's Great Cabernets* by James Laube, (CH-date)—*California's Great Chardonnays* by James Laube, (VP-date)—*Vintage Port* by James Suckling.

DATE TASTED Dates in parentheses represent the issue in which the rating was published.

DAVID WYNN

Chardonnay South Eastern Australia 1990: Rich and slightly sweet, with a soft texture and pear and honey flavors. Above average in quality, but pretty fat. $11 (11/30/91) **79**

WYNNS

Chardonnay Coonawarra 1987 $16 (12/31/88) **84**

YALUMBA

Chardonnay Barossa Valley 1987: Ripe and full-bodied but balanced with an underlying lemony acidity; tight and focused on the finish. The flavors need time to develop. Drink now. $8 (3/15/89) **85**

Chardonnay Eden Valley 1986 $7 (12/31/87) **78**

Chardonnay South Eastern Australia Oxford Landing 1991: Ripe and buttery, with a rich texture and pear, vanilla and spice flavors that mingle nicely on the finish. A full-bodied wine to drink now. $7 (2/29/92) BB **83**

Dessert

BROWN BROTHERS

Muscat of Alexandria Victoria Lexia 1986: A fruity dessert wine made from Muscat. Very aromatic and perfumed, with forward apricot aromas and orange flavors; sweet and soft in structure. $8 (5/15/89) **77**

Muscat of Alexandria Victoria Lexia Family Selection 1987: Floral, perfumey aromas and flavors, rather than gobs of fruit, mark this not-too-sweet dessert wine. Not for everyone. $8.50 (7/31/90) **73**

Port Victoria Family Selection 1987: Dense, rich and concentrated, with flavors of ripe cherry, plum and cinnamon echoing on the long finish. A beautifully balanced wine with just enough of a tannin-alcohol grip to make it age-worthy. Drink 1995 and beyond. $12.50 (7/31/90) **84**

CAMPBELLS

Muscat Rutherglen Old NV $15 (7/01/87) **92**

Tokay Rutherglen Old NV $15 (7/01/87) **91**

CHATEAU REYNELLA

Port South Australia 1981: Rich in texture, with a nice balance of mature aromas and flavors, stewed plum and a hint of menthol on the finish. Drinkable now, but should be fine for a decade or more. $11.50 (11/15/91) **85**

Tawny Port South Australia Old Cave Fine Old NV: Smoky, spicy aromas and flavors distinguish this otherwise mild, lighter tawny Port. $12 (11/15/91) **77**

HARDY'S

Port Australia 1982: The distinctive and unusual aroma of beets shoulders past any suggestion of fruit and it seems drier and less lush than a Port should be, making this a stylized wine that is not for everyone. $15 (7/31/90) **72**

Tawny Port Australia Tall Ships NV: Light in color—a classic tawny—with complex spice and orange peel aromas and flavors; a bit sharp on the palate, more like a digestif than a Port in that way, but well made and fascinating to drink. $11 (7/31/90) **83**

HEGGIES

Rhine Riesling Late Harvest Barossa Valley Botrytis Affected 1986 $8/375ml (2/15/88) **92**

HILL-SMITH

Sémillon Late Harvest Barossa Valley Autumn Harvest Botrytis 1986: Ripe and sweet with overtones of brown sugar, toast and fig, smooth and assertive but it could be more refined. Should age well through 1995. $10/375ml (3/15/89) **84**

Sémillon Late Harvest Barossa Valley Autumn Harvest Botrytis 1985 $8/375ml (2/15/88) **88**

Sémillon Late Harvest Barossa Valley Autumn Harvest Botrytis 1983 $8/375ml (8/31/86) **84**

PETER LEHMANN

Sémillon Late Harvest Barossa Valley Botrytis Sauternes 1988: Sweet and rich, with appealing honey, pineapple and ginger aromas and flavors; a firm structure and sufficient length let the flavors echo. Drinkable now. $6/375ml (4/15/91) BB **83**

Sémillon Late Harvest Barossa Valley Botrytis Sauternes 1987: Ripe, sweet and exuberantly fruity, bursting with apricot, butter, honey and nutmeg aromas and flavors, which keep exuding through the long finish. Has the tobacco edge of a fine Sauternes, very long and complex. $8/375ml (10/31/89) **89**

Sémillon Late Harvest Barossa Valley Botrytis Sauternes 1984 $15 (7/01/87) **89**

LINDEMANS

Sémillon Late Harvest Padthaway Botrytis Griffith 1988: Ripe, smooth and generous, sweet and frankly slightly syrupy, but so full of apricot, fig and slightly toasty flavors that it would be hard to resist if a glass were sitting before you. Drink sooner rather than later. $12/375ml (7/31/90) **83**

Sémillon Late Harvest Padthaway Botrytis Griffith 1987: Elegant and unctuously rich, glowing with buttery pear and apricot aromas and flavors, impeccably balanced with just enough acidity. Offers more fruit and honey notes than the tobacco character often associated with Sémillon. A terrific value. $12/375ml (10/31/89) **91**

Tawny Port Australia Macquarie Very Special Wood Matured NV: There is still a bit of ruby in the color and more fruit in the flavor than one might expect from a tawny Port, but the richness and complexity make a winning combination. The wine has plenty of appeal. $11 (7/31/90) **84**

MORRIS

Tokay Australia Show Reserve NV $15 (7/01/87) **92**

PENFOLDS

Rhine Riesling Late Harvest South Australia 1987: Concentrated and rich on the palate, with ripe pineapple and honey aromas and flavors, vibrantly balanced with a zing of lemony acidity, long and flavorful. Delicious now, but it could age well through 1995. $5.50/375ml (3/15/89) BB **88**

Sémillon Late Harvest South Australia 1987: Sweet style, with fairly delicate fig and honey aromas and flavors, a touch of oak and good length. Could be more distinctive, but it's well crafted and smoothly balanced. Drinkable now, but it should develop more nuances with age through 1993. $6.50/375ml (3/15/89) **84**

PEWSEY VALE

Rhine Riesling Late Harvest Barossa Valley Botrytis 1986 $8/375ml (2/15/88) **90**

Rhine Riesling Late Harvest Barossa Valley Botrytis Individual Vineyard Selected 1987: Ripe and honeyed, with oily texture and sappy flavors, plus a touch of volatile acidity that robs it of its fruit and freshness. $9/375ml (10/31/89) **71**

ROSEWOOD

Muscat Australia Liqueur NV $50 (7/01/87) **91**

Muscat Rutherglen Old Liqueur NV $40 (7/01/87) **90**

Muscat Rutherglen Special Liqueur NV $30 (7/01/87) **91**

SEAVIEW

Port Australia Flagship NV: A ruby-style Port, with modest intensity of berry and plum flavors. Shows more spicy oak on the finish than fruit. Drinkable now. $9 (11/15/91) **79**

SEPPELT

Port Australia Para No. 113 NV: Burnished mahogany color and rich sweetness make this attractively spicy wine especially appealing. Maple flavors sneak in on the finish. 1,000 cases made. $25 (11/15/91) **83**

Port Barossa Valley Para Port Bin 109 NV $25 (2/15/88) **92**

Port Barossa Valley Para Port No. 110 NV: Dark and coffee-colored, pours like syrup, with sweet coffee and brown sugar aromas and flavors; a bit hot and harsh on the finish. A tasty drink, but lacks the finesse of some of the others we've tasted. $25 (3/15/89) **79**

Port McLaren Flat Barossa 1978 $15 (2/15/88) **70**
Tawny Port Australia Old Trafford NV: Sensationally complex and rich, a dessert in a glass with sweet flavors of caramel, coffee and many spices, extraordinarily long and dynamic. It just stays with you forever. $15 (3/15/89) **95**
Tawny Port Barossa Valley Mt. Rufus NV $12 (2/15/88) **78**

MARK SWANN
Gold Vintner's Select Rutherglen NV $10/375ml (12/31/88) **92**
Port Australia Vintage 1980 $10 (4/16/84) **78**

YALUMBA
Muscat Rutherglen Museum Show Reserve NV: Ripe, rich and spicy, with remarkably deep fig and honey aromas and flavors and nutmeg, coffee and caramel overtones. Dark in color, but this brightly flavored, hedonistic wine just keeps echoing richness and flavor. Fewer than 300 cases made. $10/375ml (4/15/91) **91**
Port Barossa Valley Galway Pipe NV: A terrific tawny-style Port, with amazing depth and richness. Smells rich and mature then fairly explodes on the palate, with coffee, caramel, walnut and spice flavors that ricochet on the finish for what seems like minutes. $18 (4/15/91) **91**
Port Barossa Valley Galway Pipe NV $10.50 (1/31/87) **95**
Sémillon Late Harvest Barossa Valley Botrytis Affected 1984: Nicely focused pineapple and fig flavors gain depth with overtones of vanilla, nuts and a touch of tobacco; sweet without being cloying. Could be richer and more unctuous, but it's a tasty dessert wine to drink now. $5.50/375ml (3/15/89)**83**
Tawny Port South Australia Clocktower NV: Sweet and smooth, with marvelous almond, walnut, coffee and caramel aromas and flavors that linger enticingly on the finish. Offers profound, harmonious flavors at a reasonable price. Drink soon for dessert. $8.50 (4/15/91) BB **84**
Tawny Port South Australia Clocktower NV $6 (5/31/87) BB **90**

PINOT NOIR

BANNOCKBURN
Pinot Noir Geelong 1986: Spicy, toasty aromas and flavors are reminiscent of a pickle barrel on the finish; it's more earthy and leathery than fruity. Tannic and a bit heavy. Drinkable, within the style, but not exceptional. $26 (1/31/90) **73**
Pinot Noir Geelong 1985 $16.50 (3/15/88) **74**

BROWN BROTHERS
Pinot Noir Victoria 1983 $9 (7/01/87) **83**

CASSEGRAIN
Pinot Noir New South Wales Morrillon Vinyard 1988: Mature color and flavors with leather, mint, spice and stewed plum notes, finishing with dry tannins. Drink now. 680 cases made. $20 (2/29/92)**80**

HUNGERFORD HILL
Pinot Noir Hunter Valley 1986: Has very smoky, almost burnt aromas and flavors that cast a touch of bitterness on the bright cherry flavor. $12 (2/28/90) **74**
Pinot Noir Hunter Valley 1984 $11 (3/15/88) **70**

LINDEMANS
Pinot Noir Padthaway 1986: Simple and decent with black cherry flavors but not what you'd expect, or hope for, with Pinot Noir. Drink now. $12 (9/15/89) **73**
Pinot Noir Padthaway 1984 $12 (2/15/88) **82**

MOUNTADAM
Pinot Noir Eden Valley 1988: An attractive style that strives for complexity and succeeds, with silky cherry, plum and raspberry flavors, firm but refined tannins and subtle oak shadings. A well-balanced wine that finishes with complexity. Its $25 price tag, however, is steep. Drink now to 1994. 1,500 cases made. $25 (3/31/91) **86**

PIPERS BROOK
Pinot Noir Tasmania 1990: Tight, firm and a bit acidic, giving a harsh edge to the basic currant flavor that will need until 1994 or '95 to soften. Finishes with spicy fruit flavors, so may be best then. $25 (2/29/92) **81**

ROO'S LEAP
Pinot Noir McLaren Vale 1988: Ripe and racy, with minty overtones to the firmly supported, classic currant aromas and flavors that are smooth, generous and long. A wine to enjoy now, while it's so lively. $8 (2/28/91) **86**

ROSEMOUNT
Pinot Noir Hunter Valley 1989: Lean and finely focused, with pleasant berry and smoke aromas and flavors that persist into a modest finish. Drinkable now; might be better in 1993. $10 (9/30/91) **81**
Pinot Noir Hunter Valley 1985 $9.50 (4/30/87) **84**
Pinot Noir Hunter Valley NV $9 (7/01/87) **80**
Pinot Noir Hunter Valley Giants Creek Vineyard 1987: Light, aromatic style, with plenty of nutmeg-tinged cherry and berry aromas and flavors, supple texture and good length. Drink now. $20 (2/28/90) **84**

ROTHBURY
Pinot Noir Hunter Valley 1983 $10 (7/01/87) **87**
Pinot Noir Hunter Valley Director's Reserve 1983 $15 (7/01/87) **89**

ST.-HUBERTS
Pinot Noir Yarra Valley 1985 $11.50 (11/15/87) **80**

TARRA WARRA
Pinot Noir Yarra Glen 1989: Ripe and raisiny, with firm, coarse, gritty tannins that turn to dry cherry on the finish. Some may find the flavors intriguing; others may find them murky. Drink now to 1995. Tasted twice, with consistent notes. 390 cases made. $28 (4/15/92) **80**
Pinot Noir Yarra Glen 1988: One of Australia's best Pinot Noirs. A big, rich, tannic style that's packed with flavor, including ripe cherry and plum. It's well balanced and finishes with rich flavors and plenty of oak. Best to drink now to '95. $25 (12/31/90) **86**

TERRACE VALE
Pinot Noir Hunter Valley 1986 $9.25 (3/15/88) **81**

TOLLEY'S
Pinot Noir Barossa Valley Selected Harvest 1983 $5 (11/15/87) **76**

TUNNEL HILL
Pinot Noir Yarra Valley 1990: Soft and fragrant, with generous cherry, plum and spice aromas and flavors and a velvety texture. A little short, but nice while it lasts. 1,200 cases made. $16 (2/29/92) **84**

TYRRELL'S
Pinot Noir Hunter River 1988: Very spicy and minty, austere and tart on the palate, with sharply focused cherry and candied fruit managing to emerge on the finish. $14 (1/31/90) **68**
Pinot Noir Hunter River 1985 $10 (7/01/87) **87**

SAUVIGNON BLANC

BROWN BROTHERS
Sauvignon Blanc Victoria Family Selection Limited Production 1988: A fully mature Sauvignon Blanc, with buttery, nutty flavors and a bright gold color. Modest apple and pear flavors are accented by honey on the finish. Drink now, before it turns the corner toward old age. $15 (6/30/92) **83**

KOALA RIDGE
Sauvignon Blanc Barossa Valley 1987: Herbal and grassy, with candied fruit and slightly sour flavors. An extreme style that won't appeal to everyone. $8 (10/31/89) **68**

LINDEMANS
Sauvignon Blanc South Eastern Australia Bin 95 1990: Modestly flavorful, with simple spice and citrus notes. Tastes as if it had oak aging, but not quite enough fruit intensity to balance it out. Still pleasant, however. $6 (6/30/92) **79**

ORLANDO
Sauvignon Blanc South Eastern Australia Jacob's Creek 1990: A ripe, soft style of Sauvignon Blanc that tastes like pineapple. Simple and straightforward, but could be more crisp and last longer on the aftertaste. $7 (6/30/92) **79**

ROO'S LEAP
Fumé Blanc Barossa Valley 1991: Lively and fresh, packed with grapefruit, lemon and herb flavors. Nicely balanced for drinking now. $8 (6/30/92) **83**

TALTARNI
Sauvignon Blanc Victoria 1989: Citrusy and simple, with lemony acidity but little flavor to bolster it. Drinkable, but nothing special. $10 (10/31/90) **76**
Sauvignon Blanc Victoria 1988: Leans toward the herbaceous side of Sauvignon Blanc, it's very rich and distinctive, with herb, grass, fig and tobacco notes on the finish. Long, full-bodied and complex with just the right touch of oak. $15 (9/15/89) **89**
Sauvignon Blanc Victoria Frenchmans Vineyard 1991: Crisp and lively, offering varietal aromas of fresh grass and grapefruit and tart fruit flavors that fill the mouth and linger on the finish. Has great balance. $11.50 (6/30/92) **84**

SÉMILLON

CASSEGRAIN
Sémillon Hunter Valley Vintage Selection 1989: Round and gentle, offering pleasant spice and toast notes to surround the basic pear and fig flavors. Fresh and straightforward. Drinkable now. 1,050 cases made. $20 (9/30/91) **81**

ROSEMOUNT
Sémillon Hunter Valley Wood Matured 1987: Smooth and round, with welcome restraint to the smoke, tobacco and fig flavors. Its supple texture and honeyed finish make this wine appealing to drink now. $9 (10/31/89) **84**

TYRRELL'S
Sémillon Hunter Valley Classic 1988: An austere style of Sémillon that's tart and crisp, with hints of melon and lots of citrus notes. Balanced, with lively acidity. Drink now or in 1993. 5,000 cases made. $7 (4/15/91) **80**

WOODSTOCK
Sémillon McLaren Vale 1989: A wine with personality and style. Soft and fragrant, with lots of sage, vanilla and fig aromas and flavors. A little short on intensity, but pleasant. 500 cases made. $8 (2/29/92) **83**

SÉMILLON BLENDS

CHITTERING
Western Australia 1988: Fruity and pleasant to drink, but not particularly distinctive, with modest pear and lemon aromas and flavors. Drink soon. $10 (9/30/91) **75**

COLDRIDGE
Sémillon Chardonnay Victoria 1990: Has good intensity and breadth of flavor, with tiers of melon, citrus, fig and spice notes that are rich and full-bodied. Offers plenty of flavor and character for the price. Drink now or in 1993. $6 (4/15/91) BB **82**

HARDY'S
Sémillon Chardonnay Captain's Selection South Eastern Australia 1991: Firm and focused, this balanced wine is a bit austere rather than round, with lemon, fig and mineral aromas and flavors. Drinkable now. $6 (6/30/92) BB **83**

LINDEMANS
Sémillon Chardonnay Bin 77 South Eastern Australia 1990: Soft and round, with almond-tinged melon and pear aromas and flavors, with fig notes echoing on the finish. A pleasant wine to drink now. $6 (6/30/92) BB **81**
Sémillon Chardonnay Bin 77 South Eastern Australia 1988: Light and elegant, with fresh pear, melon, spice and subtle oak shadings. A well-mannered wine, with pleasant flavors; drink now. $6 (4/15/91) BB **81**

PENFOLDS
Sémillon Chardonnay Koonunga Hill South Australia 1989: Ripe and smooth, with a nice tanginess and good balance; this full-bodied wine has beautifully rich apple, fig and butterscotch flavors. A great value for so much fruit flavor. $6 (9/15/90) BB **86**

ROSEMOUNT
Sémillon Chardonnay Hunter Valley 1987: Appealing pear and earthy flavors on a firm structure. Smooth and pleasant in texture, medium-bodied, with nice fruity aromas. An interesting combination of these two varieties of grapes. $9 (7/31/89) **82**
Sémillon Chardonnay South Eastern Australia 1990: Ripe, smooth, full-bodied and ample, with strong fig and honey aromas and flavors. Polished, generous and ready to drink now. $7 (5/31/91) BB **84**
Sémillon Chardonnay South Eastern Australia 1988: Straightfoward, with a likable soft texture, earthy and flinty tones and apple and pear aromas and flavors. Medium finish. Drink now. $6 (6/15/90) BB **78**

SEAVIEW
Shiraz South Australia 1989: Ripe, soft, rich and generous, with plenty of fig and pineapple aromas and flavors shaded by vanilla and spice notes. Enjoyable to drink now. $8 (9/30/91) **83**

SEPPELT
Sémillon Chardonnay Moyston South Australia 1991: Toasty, ripe, and smoky with hints of lemon, pear and butter flavors peeking through. Soft in texture and drinkable now. $7 (6/30/92) **81**

YALUMBA
Sémillon Chardonnay Eden Valley 1987: Smells great but tastes a little flat, though there are some nice fig and vanilla aromas and flavors to give it personality. Drink now. $7.50 (4/15/89) **79**

SHIRAZ

BANNOCKBURN
Shiraz Geelong 1984: Peppery and plush, with mature berry and toast aromas and flavors, velvety tannins and a seasoning of Syrah's black pepper quality. Drinkable now, but could improve with cellaring through 1994. $13 (10/31/89) **81**

BERRI
Shiraz Barossa Valley 1985 $9.25 (2/15/88) **85**

BROWN BROTHERS
Shiraz Australia 1983 $9 (7/15/87) **92**

Shiraz Victoria 1985: Classic peppery, spicy, plummy aromas and flavors rest comfortably on a firm structure; its velvety texture should be smoothed out nicely to make it drinkable now. $7 (5/15/89) BB **83**

Shiraz Victoria Family Selection 1986: A rich, flavorful and distinctive tasting wine, packed with ripe blackberry, cherry and spice flavors and backed up with firm tannins and acidity. The fruit really lasts on the finish, but the oak sneaks in to make its own statement. $8 (7/15/90) **85**

CAPE MENTELLE

Shiraz Margaret River 1989: Very distinctive and full of peppery, meaty, currantlike flavors that fill out a frame of moderate tannins and good acidity. Has a lingering finish, too. $15 (5/31/92) **84**

Shiraz Margaret River 1988: Hale and hearty in flavor, with exotic, incenselike aromas. A very lively, berry-flavored red, with lots of black pepper for accent. Tempting to drink now, but should be better by 1993 to '95. Very small production, only 200 cases made. $15 (2/28/91) **88**

CASSEGRAIN

Shiraz Pokolbin Leonard Select Vineyard 1987: An attempt at a major-league Shiraz that succeeds. Very ripe and spicy, with rich plum, anise and tar notes backed by firm tannins and intense oak. It manages to have the fruit concentration and balance to keep it on track. Needs cellaring until about 1994 for the tannins to soften. 2,500 cases made. $20 (3/15/91) **87**

Shiraz South Eastern Australia 1988: Light and fruity with berry and cherry notes of modest depth and interest. Drink now. Tasted twice. 1,500 cases made. $12.50 (2/15/92) **77**

Shiraz South Eastern Australia 1988: Light and fruity with berry and cherry notes of modest depth and interest. Drink now. Tasted twice. 1,500 cases made. $12.50 (2/15/92) **77**

CHATEAU TAHBILK

Shiraz Goulburn Valley 1988: Solid and plummy, with tarry, peppery, gamy overtones to the basic cherry and plum flavors. A chunky wine that stays generous on the finish. Best after 1994. $10 (2/15/92) **82**

Shiraz Goulburn Valley 1987: A big, ripe, tannic but complex style of Shiraz that packs in plenty of flavor. The ripe plum, currant and minty herb flavors are intense and lively, and the tannins indicate it needs three to five years' cellaring to mellow. Impressive on the finish, where the flavors fan out and linger. Drink in 1993 to '98. $11 (3/15/91) **87**

Shiraz Goulburn Valley 1984 $6 (11/15/87) **77**

Shiraz Victoria 1986: A definition of finesse. So opulent and seductive that the smoothness and delicacy of the texture come almost as a surprise. Explosive blackberry, currant, plum and vanilla aromas are only the beginning, and the subtle echoes of fruit and spice carry over on the feather-light finish. Tannins are beautifully integrated. Should keep improving past 2000. 16,000 cases made. $10 (3/31/89) **88**

ANDREW GARRETT

Shiraz South Australia Clarendon Estate 1982 $8.75 (11/15/87) **80**

HARDY'S

Shiraz McLaren Vale 1989: Ripe and firm, with plenty of black cherry and oak flavors, full tannins and a touch of the gamy Shiraz character on the finish. Very good, if a bit tough at this stage. Has good depth and length; should age well through about 1996. $7.50 (5/31/92) BB **85**

Shiraz McLaren Vale 1987: A seductive red wine with loads of sweet cherry flavor, firm tannins and a lingering finish. Drink now. $7.50 (7/15/90) BB **87**

Shiraz McLaren Vale 1986 $7.50 (12/31/88) BB **89**

Shiraz McLaren Vale Bird Series 1988: A firm, intense, feisty Shiraz, with a solid core of peppery plum and cherry-tinged flavors and a sense of elegance. Picks up a trace of oak on the finish. Drink now to 1994. $7.50 (9/30/91) BB **84**

Shiraz McLaren Vale Padthaway Bird Series 1984 $5.50 (7/15/88) **79**

Shiraz South Australia Eileen Hardy 1988: Ripe, rich, spicy and lavishly oaked, but generous with its ripe cherry and plum flavors, setting up a marvelous tension that resolves itself on the smooth, velvety finish. Delicious to drink now, but should hold through 1995. 3,500 cases made. $19 (2/15/92)**91**

HENSCHKE

Shiraz Australia Keyneton Mount Edelstone 1987: Meaty and rustic, with olive, black pepper and spicy currant flavors. Plenty of flavor builds on the finish. Has soft, supple tannins, lots of character and is fun to drink. Drink now to 1993. $16.50 (5/31/91) **86**

Shiraz Barossa Ranges Keyneton Hill of Grace 1988: What's not to like? Soft and rich, packed with pepper, black cherry and smoke flavors. Soft tannins and easy acidity combine with all the fruit flavor to make it immediately appealing. Ready to enjoy now. 2,500 cases made. $27 (5/31/92) **88**

Shiraz Barossa Ranges Keyneton Hill of Grace 1987: One of Australia's finest red wines. Extremely ripe in flavor and plush in texture, with a great combination of fruit, spice, chocolate and tobacco. Complex, intense and satisfying, showing enough oak. Resembles a Côte-Rôtie. Tempting to drink now, but should improve through 1997. 2,000 cases made. $27 (5/31/92) CS **91**

Shiraz Barossa Ranges Keyneton Mount Edelstone 1989: Offers all the character you'd want in a Shiraz. Has a deep color, effusive plum, smoke and earth aromas and ripe, rich cherry and prune flavors. Muscular and concentrated, with a long finish. Probably best to drink in 1994 to '96. $17 (5/31/92) **88**

Shiraz Barossa Ranges Keyneton Mount Edelstone 1988: This powerful, youthful wine needs time to mature. Firm, concentrated, tannic and tight, with focused black cherry and spice flavors and a long finish that picks up smoky, peppery notes. Delivers flavor and muscle in equal proportions. Try after 1994. $17 (5/31/92) **90**

Shiraz Barossa Valley Hill of Grace 1986: Generous, expansive and glowing with plum and spice aromas and flavors, with that distinctive leathery tobacco tinge on the finish that's typical of Shiraz. Drink now. $26 (9/30/89) **87**

Shiraz Barossa Valley Mount Edelstone 1986: Ripe, rich and concentrated, with defined plum and cherry flavors, turning smoky on the finish. Complex and delicious now, but should improve with age. Drink now to '95. 2,000 cases made. $17 (10/31/89) HR **90**

Shiraz Barossa Valley Mount Edelstone 1985: Leathery and spicy flavors rest comfortably on a smooth, medium- weight structure; it has a velvety texture, with plum and spicy wood flavors. Drink now or in 1993. $14.50 (3/31/89) **81**

Shiraz Barossa Valley Mount Edelstone 1984 $14 (2/15/88) **90**

HILL-SMITH

Shiraz Barossa Valley 1986: Ripe, but reined in, smooth textured, balanced and a bit tannic. Offers attractive cherry and berry flavors shaded by tobacco and leather, turning up the intensity of fruit on the finish. A well-crafted wine that's drinkable now, but it's worth cellaring until 1993 or '94 to soften the tannins. $9 (2/28/91) BB **86**

Shiraz Barossa Valley 1984 $6.25 (5/15/87) **82**

HOUGHTON

Shiraz McLaren Vale Wildflower Ridge 1985 $9 (12/31/88) **88**

HUNGERFORD HILL

Shiraz Hunter Valley 1988: This wine is young, intense, tight and peppery, with a solid core of fruit and tannins and ample oak, but it needs time to soften and open up. Then it should be more accessible. Finish turns dry and oaky. Drink now to '94. $10 (2/28/90) **80**

LEASINGHAM

Shiraz Australia Bin 61 1982 $4.25 (12/15/87) **79**

PETER LEHMANN

Shiraz Barossa Valley 1987: Unmistakably Shiraz from start to finish, this is a rich, ripe and powerful style, packed with strong mint and plum flavors and firm tannins. Ready now, but capable of improving through about 1993. Could use a little finesse. 4,500 cases made. $8 (4/15/91) BB **84**

Shiraz Barossa Valley 1983 $7 (7/01/87) **81**

Shiraz Barossa Valley Dry Red 1985: A spicy, cedary style that's firm and focused, medium-bodied and modulated rather than ebullient. The toasty, cinnamon aromas and flavors are appealing now, but it will probably be better after the modest tannin subsides around 1993. $7.25 (7/31/89) BB **84**

Shiraz Barossa Valley Dry Red 1983 $5 (4/30/87) **79**

LINDEMANS

Shiraz Barossa Valley 1986: Firm and concentrated, with long-lasting, well-focused plum and red cherry flavors, simple and appealing to drink now. $12 (5/15/89) **83**

Shiraz Hunter Valley 1987: The generous cherry and leather aromas and flavors and tannins close in on the finish, making this tart, crisply focused style seem more austere than the usual Aussie Shiraz. Best to cellar until 1993 to soften the tannins. $10 (2/15/91) **81**

Shiraz Hunter Valley Bin 3110 Lindemans Classic 1965: Thick, rich and unctuous, this is a remarkably complex wine with tiers of chocolate, cedar, coffee and herb flavors that are still quite fresh and lively. There is enough depth and tannin to sustain this wine another 15 years. Worth going out of your way to try. Who says Aussie wines don't age? $95 (9/15/89) **96**

Shiraz Hunter Valley Bin 4110 Lindemans Classic 1970: Fully mature with rich, plum, cedar, herb, coffee and spice notes that are still quite tannic and robust. It's ready now but has the depth and tannins to carry it another decade given proper storage. Drink now through 2000. $60 (9/15/89) **89**

Shiraz Hunter Valley Bin 5910 Lindemans Classic 1980: Smells great but lacks a bit of follow-through on the palate, leaving it hard-edged and leathery. Aromas of earth, spice and plum are enticing. Better with a wedge of cheese, to soften the funky flavors. Drinkable now. $30 (7/31/90) **73**

Shiraz South Australia Bin 50 1986: Spicy, leathery aromas and flavors make this one immediately appealing for serving with roasts or grills, although there are some vegetal overtones that would bother some people. $5.50 (5/15/89) **78**

Shiraz South Eastern Australia Bin 50 1989: Tastes so young and fresh that you'd think it's not finished yet, but a great beam of pure currant flavor makes it appealing. Tart and a bit rough with tannin. $6 (5/31/92) **80**

Shiraz South Eastern Australia Bin 50 1987: A very solid Shiraz with the characteristic flavors of the Syrah grape. It has plum and pepper flavors, meaty, earthy aromas, moderate tannins and good balance. Drink now. $5.50 (7/15/90) BB **84**

MILDARA

Shiraz Coonawarra 1986 $9 (12/31/88) **89**

MITCHELL

Shiraz Clare Valley Peppertree Vineyard 1989: Has nice coffee and plum aromas and flavors, but leans toward the sour end of the spectrum on the finish. Drinkable now. 500 cases made. $10.50 (2/15/92) **76**

MITCHELTON

Shiraz Goulburn Valley 1989: Light and fruity, with simple cherry and berry notes. Easy to drink. Best to enjoy now. 7,500 cases made. $8 (2/15/92) **80**

Shiraz Goulburn Valley 1988: This Shiraz offers a nice balance of fruit, oak and tannin, with pretty, lively raspberry, cherry, plum and currant flavors in a warm, supple style. The flavors stay with you from start to finish. Easy to drink now or cellar through 1994. $8 (3/15/91) BB **86**

MONTROSE

Shiraz Mudgee 1988: A simple but correct Shiraz, with light raspberry and spice notes and a strong tannic presence. Could stand a little more flavor and body, but it's drinkable. Some may find the raspberry notes pleasing. Drink now to 1994. Tasted twice. $9 (3/15/91) **78**

Shiraz Mudgee 1984 $10 (7/01/87) **87**

Shiraz Mudgee 1983 $7 (3/15/88) **86**

PENFOLDS

Shiraz South Australia Grange Hermitage Bin 95 1985: Very ripe and tasty, with rich plum flavors that border on Port-like. Very spicy and oaky, too, but concentrated. An exotic style that packs a wallop with flavor. The tannins on the finish suggest it needs cellaring until 1994. Not quite the depth you expect from Grange, but '85 is simply a lesser vintage. $80 (2/29/92) **88**

Shiraz South Australia Grange Hermitage Bin 95 1984 $80 (4/15/91) (TM) **89**

Shiraz South Australia Grange Hermitage Bin 95 1983: A gorgeous wine for people who like 'em full-blown, with tiers and tiers of cherry, plum, coffee and spice flavors. The ripe fruit flavors are accented by plenty of smoky, spicy notes from oak aging. Has firm, fine tannins, deep color and a long, lingering finish. Drink in 1993 to 2000. $80 (3/15/91) **92**

Shiraz South Australia Grange Hermitage Bin 95 1982 $60 (4/15/91) (TM) **94**

Shiraz South Australia Grange Hermitage Bin 95 1981 $49 (4/15/91) (TM) **89**

Shiraz South Australia Grange Hermitage Bin 95 1980 $112 (4/15/91) (TM) **88**

Shiraz South Australia Grange Hermitage Bin 95 1979 $125 (4/15/91) (TM) **89**

Shiraz South Australia Grange Hermitage Bin 95 1978 $129 (4/15/91) (TM) **85**

Shiraz South Australia Grange Hermitage Bin 95 1977 $155 (4/15/91) (TM) **82**

Shiraz South Australia Grange Hermitage Bin 95 1976 $125 (4/15/91) (TM) **86**

Shiraz South Australia Grange Hermitage Bin 95 1974 $45 (4/15/91) (TM) **79**

Shiraz South Australia Grange Hermitage Bin 95 1971 $225 (4/15/91) (TM) **95**

Shiraz South Australia Grange Hermitage Bin 95 1970 $75 (4/15/91) (TM) **85**

Shiraz South Australia Grange Hermitage Bin 95 1968 $55 (4/15/91) (TM) **87**

Shiraz South Australia Grange Hermitage Bin 95 1967 $67 (4/15/91) (TM) **91**

Shiraz South Australia Grange Hermitage Bin 95 1966 $110 (4/15/91) (TM) **96**

Shiraz South Australia Grange Hermitage Bin 95 1965 $120 (4/15/91) (TM) **84**

Shiraz South Australia Grange Hermitage Bin 95 1955 $355 (4/15/91) (TM) **93**

Shiraz South Australia Magill Estate Vineyard 1985: This wine has a beautiful aroma and lots of new oak with pretty cherry and oak flavors of moderate depth, finishing with hints of leather and bacon. $45 (7/31/89) **87**

REDBANK

Shiraz Victoria Mountain Creek 1985: Leans heavily on smoky, charred oak flavors, but may work well with summer barbecues and grilled fare. Could use a little more concentration with the plummy fruit flavor. Drink now to 1994. $9 (9/30/91) **84**

ROSEMOUNT

Shiraz Hunter Valley 1989: An absolutely delicious wine at a terrific price. It's rich, warm, ripe and

Key to Symbols

The scores reported here are the results of blind tastings conducted by our panel of senior editors. Wines that carry the initials below are results of individual tastings.

THE WINE SPECTATOR 100-POINT SCALE 95-100—Classic, a great wine; ***90-94***—Outstanding, superior character and style; ***80-89***—Good to very good, a wine with special qualities; ***70-79***—Average, drinkable wine that may have minor flaws; ***60-69***—Below average, drinkable but not recommended; ***50-59***—Poor, undrinkable, not recommended. "+"—With a score indicates a range; used primarily with barrel tastings to indicate a preliminary score.

SPECIAL DESIGNATIONS SS—Spectator Selection, CS—Cellar Selection, BB—Best Buy, ($NA)—Price not available, (NR)—Not released.

TASTER'S INITIALS (JG)—Jim Gordon, (HS)—Harvey Steiman, (JL)—James Laube, (JS)—James Suckling, (TM)—Thomas Matthews, (TR)—Terry Robards, (PM)—Per-Henrik Mansson, (BT)—Barrel Tasting (these wines were tasted blind from barrel samples), (CA-date)—*California's Great Cabernets* by James Laube, (CH-date)—*California's Great Chardonnays* by James Laube, (VP-date)—*Vintage Port* by James Suckling.

DATE TASTED Dates in parentheses represent the issue in which the rating was published.

generous, with smooth, supple spice, raspberry, blackberry and plum flavors and hints of tobacco, cedar and oak on the finish. Goes down easy. Drink now through 1994. $8 (2/15/91) SS **91**
Shiraz Hunter Valley 1988: An outstanding red wine. Very ripe and rich, with plenty of tension between the plummy, cherrylike Shiraz flavors and the toasty, vanilla aromas of new oak; tightly structured but showing enough generous flavor to warrant cellaring until 1993 and beyond. Drinkable now with a hunk of roast. $8 (1/31/90) SS **90**
Shiraz Hunter Valley 1987: Broad, rich and lush, with blueberry, plum and currant flavors that are plush and satiny yet flanked by firm, gentle tannins. The finish tapers off, but the fruit is very pretty and spicy. Drink now. $9 (7/31/89) **87**
Shiraz Hunter Valley 1986 $9 (4/15/89) **92**
Shiraz Hunter Valley 1985 $8 (2/15/88) **80**
Shiraz Hunter Valley 1984 $7.50 (4/30/87) **83**
Shiraz McLaren Vale Show Reserve 1989: A firm, muscular style that showcases the meaty, nutty plum and black cherry aromas and flavors. A mouth-filling wine that keeps pumping the flavor through a long finish. The tannins are well integrated, but this should benefit from cellaring through 1993 to '95. $15 (2/29/92) **89**
Shiraz South Eastern Australia 1990: A stylish wine, with power and grace in equal portions, offering generous currant, toast and plum flavors shaded by hints of pepper and gaminess. Beautifully balanced from start to finish, with dark cherry flavor holding on through the finish. Almost drinkable now, but best after 1993. A great value. $8.50 (2/15/92) SS **92**

ROTHBURY
Shiraz Hunter Valley Herlstone Vineyard 1987: Rings true for Shiraz, with ripe, dried prune, pepper, cherry and leathery oak flavors. Rough-hewn, it but has plenty of character, and isn't too tannic; drink now. $9.50 (5/31/91) **85**
Shiraz Hunter Valley Herlstone Vineyard 1986: Soft and leathery, almost decadent, with simple, supple flavors and texture; drinkable now. $10.50 (7/31/89) **76**
Shiraz Hunter Valley Herlstone Vineyard 1985:
Light, fruity and simple, soft on the palate, with vaguely cherry or strawberry flavors. Drink now. $10.50 (3/31/89) **78**
Shiraz Hunter Valley Herlstone Vineyard 1984 $9.50 (5/15/87) **90**
Shiraz Hunter Valley Syrah 1989: Firm in texture and somewhat tannic, with a moderate level of plum and spice flavor. Drinkable, but better after 1993. $9.50 (2/29/92) **80**

SALTRAM
Shiraz Hazelwood 1984: Spicy, earthy and a bit leathery, an old-fashioned Aussie Shiraz with the emphasis on earthiness over any notion of concentrated fruit. An appealing wine that ought to fit nicely on any table. $8.50 (7/31/89) **81**

SEAVIEW
Shiraz South Australia 1987: Ripe and chewy, with gobs of plum, cedar and vanilla aromas and flavors that spread across the palate and linger into a finish that hints at spice and chocolate. The tannins are present without interfering with the fruit. Best now through 1994. $10 (9/30/91) **86**

SEPPELT
Shiraz South Eastern Australia Black Label 1984 $12 (12/31/88) **87**
Shiraz South Eastern Australia Black Label 1983 $10 (2/15/88) **74**

MARK SWANN
Shiraz Eden Valley 1980 $6.50 (3/16/84) **80**

TALTARNI
Shiraz Victoria 1988: Super-ripe, concentrated and full-bodied, with the distinctive, gamy flavor of Shiraz. Has deep, deep color, an abundance of tannins and a great finish. The plum, pepper and prune flavors are shaded by the earthy spiciness of the grape. So rich it seems drinkable now, but it will improve if cellared until at least 1996. $14 (5/31/92) **89**
Shiraz Victoria 1987: Very firm and tannic, with a solid core of berry and plum flavor that should emerge from its cocoon of tannin by 1995 or '96. A cellarable wine. $10 (9/30/91) **82**
Shiraz Victoria 1986: Dense, tannic and concentrated, with pretty floral, minty and crushed pepper notes, adding to the ripe plum and currant flavors. Very tannic and powerful on the finish. Best to cellar until 1993 at the earliest. $10 (10/31/90) **84**
Shiraz Victoria 1985 $10 (11/30/88) SS **91**
Shiraz Victoria 1984 $9.25 (2/15/88) **75**
Shiraz Victoria 1982 $9.25 (4/30/87) **86**
Shiraz Victoria 1980 $6.75 (3/16/84) **77**

TERRACE VALE
Shiraz Hunter Valley Bin 6 1986 $9.50 (3/15/88) **73**

TYRRELL'S
Shiraz Hunter Valley 1982 $7 (7/15/88) **75**
Shiraz Hunter Valley Classic 1986: Offers very attractive plum and cherry aromas and flavors with overtones of truffle and toast, a round texture and smooth tannins. All the pieces are there. Drink now or by 1993. $8 (1/31/90) BB **84**

AUDREY WILKINSON
Shiraz Hunter Valley Hermitage 1985: Not as broad and fruity as some Shirazes, but it's well balanced and refined enough to highlight its cherry and berry aromas and flavors. Drinkable now, with hearty food. $13 (9/30/91) **79**

WYNDHAM
Shiraz Hunter Valley Bin 555 1986: Bright and fruity, almost like a Beaujolais, smooth in texture and crisp in structure. A solid drink for now, given its floral and berry aromas and flavors. $7 (1/31/90) BB **85**
Shiraz South Eastern Australia Bin 555 1988: Soft and ready to drink, with smooth, rounded tannins and moderate plum and orange flavors. Graceful and well balanced. $7.50 (6/30/92) **83**

Sparkling

ANGAS
Brut Australia NV $8 (12/31/87) **76**
Brut Rosé Australia NV $8 (12/31/87) **78**

CHATEAU REYNELLA
Brut South Australia NV: An odd duck, but pleasant. Slightly sweet on balance, with hints of licorice and nutmeg to the basic pear and orange flavors. $9 (11/15/91) **79**

HARDY'S
Brut Australia Grand Reserve NV: A fruity, soft and round sparkling wine, with a touch of sweetness. Straightforward and easy to appreciate. $8 (2/29/92) BB **83**

LASSETER
Brut Australia 1985: Very mature, complex and distinctive. Shows fine fruit flavor in a mellow, complex combination of toasty, caramel, smoky flavors. The finish lingers. $17 (10/31/89) **87**
Brut Australia NV $10 (12/31/88) **84**

SEAVIEW
Brut South Australia 1988: Lean and crisp, with a nice mineral edge to the grapefruit and apple flavors. A fruity style that's dry and crisp enough to drink with oysters. $9.75 (11/15/91) BB **83**

SEPPELT
Brut Australia Fleur de Lys 1985 $18 (12/31/88) **85**
Brut South Eastern Australia Imperial NV: Big and assertive. A full-flavored sparkling wine with strong toasty, earthy aromas and buttery flavors. Smooth textured. $10 (1/31/90) **82**

TALTARNI
Brut Australia Taché NV: The pale salmon color and crisp, refreshing flavors add up to a sparkler with class and plenty of appeal. Modest berry and toast aromas and flavors stay with you on the finish. Drink soon. $16 (6/30/92) **83**

TYRRELL'S
Brut Pinot Noir Hunter Valley 1983 $19 (9/30/88) **82**

YALUMBA
Brut South Australia Angas NV: A pleasant but straightforward off-dry sparkler, with very fruity bubble gum aromas, nutty flavors and a rich gold color. $9 (12/31/90) **78**
Brut de Brut Australia 1984 $8.25 (3/15/88) **84**
Brut Rosé South Australia Angas NV: With a smooth, creamy texture and good balance of flavor and acidity, this is a very satisfying rosé, showing focused cherry and cinnamon flavors. A good value. $9 (12/31/90) **84**

Other Australia Red

CASSEGRAIN
Chambourcin South Eastern Australia 1990: The dense purple color is appealing, but gamy flavors obscure the berrylike fruit of this French-American hybrid grape, making it a wine not everyone will like. Best in 1993. $12 (2/15/92) **77**

GOVERNOR PHILLIP
Classic Australian Red Australia NV: Light, silky and graceful, glowing gently with enough spicy strawberry flavor to make this a fine alternative to, say, a youthful Beaujolais. Drink now. $5 (7/31/89) BB **82**

HARDY'S
Premium Classic Dry Red McLaren Vale 1986: Tries for subtlety rather than power and succeeds in a limited way, becoming light and smooth on the palate after showing attractive minty and red cherry aromas. Drink soon. $6 (5/15/89) **75**
Premium Classic Dry Red South Australia 1988: Tastes fresh, light, clean and fruity. Has sufficient berry flavor to make it satisfying, plus light tannins and good balance. $5.25 (7/31/90) BB **78**

KOALA RIDGE
Hermitage Barossa Valley 1985: Showing maturity and smoothness, a gentle, supple wine offering coffee, plum and raisin aromas and flavors, a bit spicy, balanced. Drinkable now. $9 (1/31/90) **80**

ORLANDO
Merlot South Eastern Australia Jacob's Creek 1990: Soft, supple and ultimately simple, but with ample raisin and herb flavors. Not for the cellar; fine to drink tonight. $7 (6/30/92) **79**
Merlot South Eastern Australia Jacob's Creek 1989: More like Shiraz than Merlot, with leathery, smoky overtones to the modest berry aromas and flavors. Smooth and supple. Drinkable, in a distinctive style. 4,600 cases made. $7 (9/30/91) **82**

ROSEMOUNT
Dry Red Diamond Reserve Hunter Valley 1988: Fresh and delicious raspberry and plum flavors in a smooth, supple pleasing and easy-to-drink style. Drink now. $6.50 (2/28/90) BB **83**

TYRRELL'S
Dry Red Winemaker's Selection Vat 9 Hunter River 1984: Complex and decidedly earthy, but has coffee, cedar, walnut and spice overtones that some will find fascinating and others will find strange. Cherry flavor sneaks in on the finish. Drinkable now. $14.50 (2/15/92) **83**
Long Flat Red Hunter Valley 1986: Smooth and supple, with smoky overtones to the basic cherry flavor. A medium-weight wine with simple structure and flavors. Best to drink slightly chilled. $6 (1/31/90) **79**
Long Flat Red Hunter Valley 1985: Dusky, spicy cherry aromas and flavors ride smoothly on a medium-weight frame; simple and easy to drink. $5.25 (7/31/89) BB **81**
Long Flat Red South Eastern Australia 1988: Bright cherry and cinnamon aromas and flavors characterize this medium-weight, stylish red. Drinkable now, and should be fine through 1993 or '94. $7 (2/15/92) BB **84**

WYNDHAM
Merlot Hunter Valley 1986: A deep and vibrant wine, from the first glimpse of the color to the last echoes of berries, chocolate and mint on the finish. Soft and round, with generous fruit and supple texture. Drink now. $8 (1/31/90) BB **85**

Other Australia White

CHATEAU TAHBILK
Marsanne Goulburn Valley 1989: Medium-bodied, a bit astringent and austere, but the exotic lemon and rhubarb flavors persist on the finish. May need until 1993 to smooth out. $10 (7/15/91) **80**

HARDY'S
Premium Classic Dry White South Australia 1988: Likable and exotic, with pineapple aromas and flavors. Soft and ripe, with a pleasant finish. Quaffable and attractive for current drinking. $5.25 (6/15/90) BB **79**
Premium Classic Dry White South Australia 1988: Full and broad in structure, very ripe, almost figgy, on the nose, soft and flavorful. Blend of Trebbiano, Crouchen and Riesling. Drink soon. $6 (5/15/89) **79**

HOUGHTON
White Burgundy Swan Valley 1988: A ripe, broad and generous wine, with fig and tobacco aromas and flavors that turn snappy and a bit leathery on the finish. An appealing wine that needs hearty food to balance it. Drinkable now. $7.50 (9/30/91) BB **84**

MITCHELTON
Marsanne Goulburn Valley 1990: An Australian white wine made from a Rhône grape. Rich, round and mouth-filling, with ripe pear, apricot and honey aromas and flavors and hints of almond on the finish. Drinkable now. $8 (6/30/92) BB **84**

PEWSEY VALE
Rhine Riesling Adelaide Hills Individual Vineyard Selection 1990: Odd minty, herbal aromas and flavors tend to obscure the light fruit, making this a wine not everyone will enjoy. $9.50 (7/15/91) **76**
Rhine Riesling Barossa Valley Individual Vineyard Selection 1987: Ripe and rich, almost figgy, full-bodied and flavorful, not the delicate charmer you might expect. As a Riesling, it's too much like a Chardonnay. Needs food. $5.50 (3/15/89) **79**

ROSEMOUNT
Diamond Reserve Dry White Hunter Valley 1987: A blend of Sémillon and Sauvignon Blanc. Watery and short on flavor. Wood predominates. $6.50 (7/31/89) **68**
Traminer Riesling South Eastern Australia 1991: A broad, flavorful wine with pretty floral and apple flavors and a soft texture. Somewhat sweet. 12,000 cases made. $7 (2/29/92) BB **83**

TYRRELL'S
Long Flat White Hunter Valley 1989: A generous, up-front wine, with concentrated fig, vanilla and orange aromas that are mirrored in the flavors. Exotic floral notes add a bit of intrigue. Has a soft, ripe feel. 90,000 cases made. $5 (10/31/90) BB **86**

CHILE

Cabernet Sauvignon & Blends

ALAMEDA
Cabernet Sauvignon Maipo Valley 1988: Fruity and smooth, with attractive currant and cherry flavors and nice spice and vanilla notes throughout. Attractively supple and very enjoyable. Drink now. $5.50 (6/15/92) BB **84**

CALITERRA
Cabernet Sauvignon Maipo 1989: A stylish wine, with good Cabernet flavor. Concentrated and full-bodied, offering rich plum and currant flavors laced with vanilla and spice notes. Has a lingering, spicy finish. Hold until 1994 or '95. $6 (6/15/92) BB **87**
Cabernet Sauvignon Maipo 1988: Simple and fruity, with firm tannins and tart acidity giving a hard edge to the wild berry and cherry flavors. Drying on the finish, but should be fine by 1994. $6 (10/15/91) **79**
Cabernet Sauvignon Maipo 1987: An international style of Cabernet that's marked by the sweet, spicy smell of new oak barrels. Solid cherry and berry flavors and firm tannins back up the oak, for a clean, complete, tasty package. Drink now or in 1993. $6 (9/15/90) BB **86**
Cabernet Sauvignon Maipo 1986 $6 (7/31/89) BB **85**

CANEPA
Cabernet Sauvignon Maipo Valley 1990: Heavy on the herb and currant flavors that tend to lag on the finish. A little gamy, with a pruny component. Soft and almost sweet, but drinkable. $6 (6/15/92) BB **81**
Cabernet Sauvignon Maipo Valley 1986: Leathery, herbal aromas give way to soft, pleasant plum flavors. Fully mature and ready to drink now. $6 (6/15/90) **75**
Cabernet Sauvignon Maipo Valley 1985 $4 (11/15/87) **75**
Cabernet Sauvignon Maipo Valley Finisismo 1983: Hearty, straightforward and full-bodied, with modest plum and berry flavors and hints of anise and smoke. Drinkable now. $9 (6/30/90) **76**
Cabernet Sauvignon Maipo Valley Reserva 1988: A concentrated, supple-textured, lively, balanced Cabernet with layers of berry, currant and smoke flavors and moderate tannins. Fruit flavors linger on the finish, suggesting it should age well through 1993. $6.50 (6/15/90) BB **84**

CARTA VIEJA
Cabernet Sauvignon Maule Valley 1987: Woody but pleasant, with spicy, toasty aromas and flavors. A bit austere on the palate, but drinkable now. $6 (6/15/91) **78**
Cabernet Sauvignon Maule Valley 1986: A light, spicy style, with hints of strawberry in the nutmeg and vanilla notes. Short but tasty. $4 (6/15/90) **75**
Cabernet Sauvignon Maule Valley 1985: Acceptable but not recommended. Pungently herbal in aroma and lean in flavor with tannins that dry the mouth. $3 (7/31/89) **68**
Cabernet Sauvignon Maule Valley Antiqua Selection 1986: An oaky wine that's extremely herbal, smoky, lean and slightly bitter, with ripe currant flavor lurking in the background. If you don't mind the odd flavors, it's balanced to age through 1993 to '95. $8 (6/15/91) **75**

LOS CATADORES
Cabernet Sauvignon Lontue Selección Especial 1986: Mature and ready to drink, emphasizing menthol aromas, ripe, pruny flavors and a touch of chocolaty richness. The tannins are smooth and the balance is a bit soft. Enjoy now. 5,000 cases made. $5 (6/15/92) BB **84**

CONCHA Y TORO
Cabernet Merlot Rapel 1986: Tastes full-bodied, flavorful and assertive, with moderate tannins. It has cherry, berry and tomato flavors and good balance. Drink up now. $4.25 (9/15/90) BB **80**
Cabernet Sauvignon Maipo 1985: The toasty, sulfury aroma is a turnoff, but there are decent fruit flavors underneath. A simple, straightforward and slightly flawed wine with plum and tomato flavors. $5 (9/15/90) **69**
Cabernet Sauvignon Maipo 1984 $5.50 (4/30/88) BB **89**
Cabernet Sauvignon Maipo Casillero del Diablo Pirque Vineyard 1984: A simple, muddy-tasting Cabernet that's vegetal in flavor and undistinguished. Drinkable, but very average quality. $9 (6/15/92) **74**
Cabernet Sauvignon Maipo Marqués de Casa Concha Puente Alto Vineyard 1987: Extremely smoky, almost bitter flavors persist through the finish. Tasted twice. $9.50 (6/15/92) **67**
Cabernet Sauvignon Maipo Puente Alto Vineyard Private Reserve Don Melchor 1988: Perhaps Chile's best red wine. Powerful and intense, pouring on the spice, with smoke, tobacco and cedar aromas backed by rich, ripe plum, prune and pepper flavors. A real mouthful, graced with chocolate and spice notes. Full-bodied and long on the finish. Best to wait until 1994 or '95 to drink. 4,000 cases made. $14 (5/15/92) SS **91**
Cabernet Sauvignon Maipo Puente Alto Vineyard Private Reserve Don Melchor 1987: Like a Bordeaux in style, with classic cedar, cigar box and mint aromas, full, fruity flavors and firm tannins. A touch of vanilla and smoke on the finish adds complexity. Drink up now. $13 (6/30/90) **85**
Cabernet Sauvignon Maipo Puente Alto Vineyard Special Reserve 1983: Mature, smoky aromas and flavors are distinctive but not ones that everyone will like. A lively wine with plenty of concentration and flavor, drinkable now, if you like the style. $8 (9/15/90) **75**
Cabernet Sauvignon Maipo Puente Alto Vineyard Special Reserve 1983: A wine that lacks balance. Wild and gamy flavors, with pungent herbal smells. Decent oak flavors, with a velvety texture, but not likable. $8 (2/15/90) **65**
Cabernet Sauvignon Maipo Reserva Special Casillero del Diablo 1984 $7 (11/15/87) **85**
Cabernet Sauvignon Maipo Special Reserve 1981 $6.75 (4/30/88) **80**

COUSINO-MACUL
Cabernet Sauvignon Maipo 1988: Well rounded and fairly full-bodied, with plum and cherry flavors, though not particularly lengthy on the finish. A wine to sink your teeth into; good with a hearty meal. $8 (5/15/92) **81**
Cabernet Sauvignon Maipo 1987: A dull, vegetal flavor overrides the fruit in this medium-bodied wine. Average quality. $6 (9/15/90) **71**
Cabernet Sauvignon Maipo 1986: A one-dimensional wine, with fruit intensity that unfortunately is dominated by herbs. Medium-bodied, simple and straightforward, with smoky notes. Tasted twice. $8 (9/15/90) **72**
Cabernet Sauvignon Maipo 1984 $5.50 (2/15/89) BB **86**
Cabernet Sauvignon Maipo 1983 $6 (5/15/88) BB **85**
Cabernet Sauvignon Maipo Antiguas Reservas 1987: Tight, with fairly ripe plum and currant flavors and an earthy tinge on the finish. A tasty wine, but not complex. Should be at its best in 1993 to '95. $10 (6/15/92) **82**
Cabernet Sauvignon Maipo Antiguas Reservas 1986: Lively berry flavors are crisp and focused, and the plum notes are matched by a touch of chocolate in this lean wine. A hint of vinegar emerges on the finish, but it's still quite good. $10 (5/31/92) **83**
Cabernet Sauvignon Maipo Antiguas Reservas 1985: An herbal, earthy wine, with smooth-textured raspberry and currant aromas and flavors and echoes of bay leaf and other herb flavors on the finish. Drinkable now, but will probably evolve through 1993 to '95. $10.50 (10/15/91) **81**
Cabernet Sauvignon Maipo Antiguas Reservas 1984 $9 (9/15/90) **77**
Cabernet Sauvignon Maipo Antiguas Reservas 1981 $9 (2/15/89) **80**
Cabernet Sauvignon Maipo Antiguas Reservas 1980 $8 (5/15/88) **80**

ERRAZURIZ
Cabernet Sauvignon Aconcagua Valley 1987: Good tasting, solid and full of fruit once you get past the overly sulfury, woody smell. It has the rich, very fruity, densely packed flavors of a very good wine, plus a firm structure. $9 (9/15/90) **82**
Cabernet Sauvignon Aconcagua Valley 1985 $5.50 (9/15/88) **82**
Cabernet Sauvignon Aconcagua Valley Antigua Reserva Don Maximiano 1984 $7.50 (9/15/88) BB **87**
Cabernet Sauvignon Aconcagua Valley Antigua Reserva Don Maximiano 1980 $6 (11/15/87) **68**
Cabernet Sauvignon Aconcagua Valley Don Maximiano Estate Reserva 1989: Offers lip-smacking berry flavors and a subtle tea and mineral quality on the finish. Very firm and generous, with significant tannins. Ripe plum and currant flavors also come through. Needs at least until 1994 or '95 to let the tightness open up. $10 (6/15/92) **87**
Cabernet Sauvignon Aconcagua Valley Don Maximiano Estate Reserva 1988: Straightforward and fairly rich, with currant and black cherry aromas and flavors. Refreshing and well rounded, with lengthy fruit flavors and a nice touch of vanilla on the finish. $9 (6/15/92) **85**

LIBERTY SCHOOL
Cabernet Sauvignon Lontue NV $6 (9/15/88) BB **80**

MONTES
Cabernet Sauvignon Curicó 1988: Firm and moderately tannic, with currant and cherry flavors. Well balanced, with a solid core of fruit and good structure. Drink now. $8 (6/15/92) **84**
Cabernet Sauvignon Curicó Montes Alpha Private Selection 1988: Offers appetizing oak accents on top of a good fruit structure dominated by plum and currant flavors. Gamy, with chocolate and spice notes. A stylish, firm, full-bodied wine that's supple and seductive. $14 (5/15/92) **87**
Cabernet Sauvignon Curicó Villa Montes 1989: Firm and juicy, with good plum and chocolate flavors. Well balanced, full-bodied and concentrated, with nice spice and coffee notes on the finish. A solid effort. $6 (6/15/92) BB **84**
Cabernet Sauvignon Curicó Villa Montes 1988: The aggressive herbal aromas and flavors don't appeal to us, though it's well made. Tastes green and a bit coarse, with plum flavor underneath. $4.50 (2/15/90) **73**
Cabernet Sauvignon Curicó Villa Montes 1987: Wonderfully spicy from aging in oak barrels. It tastes soft and supple with ample fruit flavors surrounded by a blanket of nutmeg, cinnamon and cedar notes. Medium-bodied and ready to drink. $7 (2/15/90) BB **84**
Cabernet Sauvignon Curicó Villa Montes Special Selection 1987: Rich, dense, soft fruit flavors make this deep red Cabernet stand out. Has an herbaceous aroma, but the flavors are very fruity and satisfying and the structure is solid. Drink up now. $12 (9/15/90) **84**

ALEJANDRO HERNANDEZ MUNOZ
Cabernet Sauvignon Maipo Cabernet Viña Portal del Alto Gran Vino 1984 $3.50 (3/15/90) **77**
Cabernet Sauvignon Maipo Viña Portal del Alto Gran Reserva Tinto 1983: A smooth, deliciously complex Cabernet that shows the benefits of age in its complex aromas of earth, spice and fruit, followed by cherry and plum flavors in a silky, modestly tannic texture. Fine to drink now, but could be cellared through about 1993. $4 (9/15/90) BB **82**

OAK BLUFFS
Cabernet Sauvignon Colchagua 1990: A well-made wine that emphasizes fruit, with good berry and cherry flavors. Has good balance and moderate tannins. Smooth and ready to drink. 25,000 cases made. $6 (6/15/92) BB **85**

PEREZ-LLANO
Cabernet Sauvignon Rancagua Gran Vino 1988: Lean and crisp, with modest cherry and tea aromas and flavors. $5 (6/15/92) **76**

LA PLAYA
Cabernet Sauvignon Maipo Valley 1988: Good spice and plum flavors make for a fairly intense wine, with a nice smoky, almost peppery quality. A bit like a Shiraz, with firm tannins. Soft, accessible and ready to drink. $5 (6/15/92) BB **83**
Cabernet Sauvignon Maipo Valley 1986: A simple, clean, correct Cabernet of moderate depth and flavor; more cedar flavor from oak aging than fruit comes through. Passable but unexciting. Drink now or in 1993. $4.50 (3/15/90) **74**

PORTAL DEL ALTO
Cabernet Sauvignon Maipo Valley 1987: Smooth and flavorful, with nice touches of herb, currant and spice in a package of moderate tannins and good acidity. A well-balanced Cabernet for drinking now. 25,000 cases made. $3.50 (6/15/92) BB **83**
Cabernet Sauvignon Maipo Valley Gran Reserva 1986: Mature and ready to drink, with leathery, herbal, gamy flavors and soft tannins. Well balanced enough to make it enjoyable. 18,000 cases made. $3.75 (6/15/92) BB **79**

LOS PUMAS
Cabernet Sauvignon Curicó Valley 1988: Barnyardy aromas and bell pepper flavors make it a drinkable but not exciting Cabernet. Tastes soft and ready to drink now. $4 (9/15/90) **69**

ST.-MORILLON
Cabernet Sauvignon Lontue 1986: Light and smooth, with spicy currant and plum aromas and flavors that remain focused through the finish. Drinkable now. $5.50 (10/15/91) BB **83**
Cabernet Sauvignon Lontue 1985: Tastes clean, crisp and fruity, with moderate tannins and smooth texture, yet it remains simple. The plum, carrot and tomato flavors are pretty basic. $4 (9/15/90) **75**

VALLE DE SAN FERNANDO
Cabernet Sauvignon San Fernando 1988: Flavorful, tannic and fairly full-bodied, with nice pepper, spice, cherry and currant flavors. Firm and robust; a hearty, no-nonsense wine. Good now or in 1993. $5 (6/15/92) BB **83**
Cabernet Sauvignon San Fernando 1985: A nicely flavorful, medium-weight Cabernet with black cherry and plum flavors and a clean finish. No need to cellar. $7 (7/31/89) **79**
Cabernet Sauvignon San Fernando 1983 $4 (11/15/88) **77**
Cabernet Sauvignon San Fernando Gran Reserva 1986: Age has ripened and softened this still tannic, straightforward Cabernet, but it has enough mature aromas and solid fruit flavors to keep it lively. Solid cherry and currant flavors and a touch of mint are the key elements. $5 (6/15/92) BB **84**
Cabernet Sauvignon San Fernando Gran Reserva 1984:A fine value. Focused cherry flavors and a firm structure of acid and tannins give it life. Straightforward and satisfying; drink up now. $6 (7/31/89) BB **83**
Cabernet Sauvignon San Fernando Gran Reserva 1982$6 (11/15/88) BB **81**

SAN JOSE DE SANTIAGO
Cabernet Sauvignon Colchagua Valley 1990: This Chilean red has full-blown Cabernet flavors of currant and mint, accented by a bit of spice. Intense in flavor and moderate in tannins, with a lasting, fruity finish. Best to drink now while it's fresh. $5 (5/15/92) BB **85**

SAN MARTIN
Cabernet Sauvignon Maipo Valley International Series 1987: Soft, fruity and pleasant, with

Key to Symbols

The scores reported here are the results of blind tastings conducted by our panel of senior editors. Wines that carry the initials below are results of individual tastings.

THE WINE SPECTATOR 100-POINT SCALE ***95-100***—Classic, a great wine; ***90-94***—Outstanding, superior character and style; ***80-89***—Good to very good, a wine with special qualities; ***70-79***—Average, drinkable wine that may have minor flaws; ***60-69***—Below average, drinkable but not recommended; ***50-59***—Poor, undrinkable, not recommended. "+"—With a score indicates a range; used primarily with barrel tastings to indicate a preliminary score.

SPECIAL DESIGNATIONS SS—Spectator Selection, CS—Cellar Selection, BB—Best Buy, ($NA)—Price not available, (NR)—Not released.

TASTER'S INITIALS (JG)—Jim Gordon, (HS)—Harvey Steiman, (JL)—James Laube, (JS)—James Suckling, (TM)—Thomas Matthews, (TR)—Terry Robards, (PM)—Per-Henrik Mansson, (BT)—Barrel Tasting (these wines were tasted blind from barrel samples), (CA-date)—*California's Great Cabernets* by James Laube, (CH-date)—*California's Great Chardonnays* by James Laube, (VP-date)—*Vintage Port* by James Suckling.

DATE TASTED Dates in parentheses represent the issue in which the rating was published.

slightly herbal, currantlike aromas and flavors. Balanced; modest in scope. Ready to drink. $4.50 (6/15/90) BB **78**

SAN PEDRO

Cabernet Sauvignon Las Encinas Vino Tinto Seco 1987: Medium weight, ripe and smooth, with pleasant currant and plum flavors shaded by tea and smoke notes. Drinkable now. Tasted twice. (NA) (6/15/92) **80**

Cabernet Sauvignon Lontue Castillo de Molina 1982: A clean and simple light- to medium-bodied wine. Soft, with cedar, plum and cherry flavors; drinkable now. $7.50 (2/15/89) **78**

Cabernet Sauvignon Lontue Castillo de Molina 1981 $7.50 (11/15/87) BB **83**

Cabernet Sauvignon Lontue Castillo de Molina 1979 $7.50 (3/15/87) **81**

Cabernet Sauvignon Lontue Gato Negro 1989: Light, lean, simple and a little tired. Drinkable, but hardly remarkable, with a hint of cherry flavor and a somewhat bitter nuance on the finish. $4.75 (6/15/92) **75**

Cabernet Sauvignon Lontue Gato Negro 1985 $4.50 (11/15/88) BB **80**

Cabernet Sauvignon Lontue Gato Negro 1984 $4.50 (5/15/88) BB **83**

Cabernet Sauvignon Lontue Gato Negro 1983 $4.50 (3/15/87) **76**

Cabernet Sauvignon Lontue Gato de Oro 1986: A supple wine at an affordable price that's ready to drink now. It has ripe plum and cherry flavors, once you get by the slightly herbal smells, and it's smooth and medium-bodied, with good vanilla flavors and a fruity aftertaste. $4.50 (2/15/90) BB **85**

SANTA CAROLINA

Cabernet Sauvignon Maipo Valley Estrella de Oro 1982: Dry and oaky with lean, smoky Cabernet flavor of modest proportions. Drink now to 1994. $8 (3/15/90) **76**

Cabernet Sauvignon Maipo Valley Los Toros Vineyard Reserva 1985: Has a ripe fruit and mineral quality that is appealing, but turns simple on the finish. Drink now. $8 (5/15/92) **77**

Cabernet Sauvignon Maipo Valley Santa Rosa Vineyard 1986 $4 (4/30/88) **78**

SANTA MONICA

Cabernet Sauvignon Rancagua 1989: Lean and firm- textured, with nicely focused plum, berry and chocolate aromas and flavors. The tannins are present, but not overwhelming. Give it until 1994 to polish the tannins, but this wine is almost drinkable now. $5 (10/15/91) BB **85**

Cabernet Sauvignon Rancagua 1988: A straightforward and ripe wine. Firm, with lots of plum and sweet berry flavors. Well balanced and flavorful. Good vanilla and oak notes. Drink now. $6 (3/15/90) BB **86**

Cabernet Sauvignon Rancagua Tierra de Sol 1985: Lean and spicy, with strong smoky overtones to the modest plum and cherry flavors. Tasted three times. ($NA) (6/15/92) **74**

SANTA RITA

Cabernet Sauvignon Maipo Valley 120 1988: Tight and tart, with berrylike aromas, currant and vanilla flavors and strawberry notes on the finish. Moderately tannic, with good acidity and balance. A wine with verve and character. May be best in 1994, but tempting now. $6 (5/31/92) BB **86**

Cabernet Sauvignon Maipo Valley 120 1986: Lean, sleek and sharply focused, with distinctively minty and currant flavors plus a nice overlay of chocolaty richness, velvety texture and good length. Drink up now. $5 (5/15/89) BB **83**

Cabernet Sauvignon Maipo Valley 120 Medalla Real 1987: Very fresh and lively tasting, with plenty of cherry, plum and currant flavors and a pleasant aftertaste. Drink now. $11 (6/15/90) **78**

Cabernet Sauvignon Maipo Valley 120 Medalla Real 1984 $9 (11/15/87) **85**

Cabernet Sauvignon Maipo Valley Casa Real 1989: Lean in texture, but ripe and smoky on the palate, with generous fruit and oak flavors that persist into a long finish. Marked strongly by oak; will appeal to those who revel in that character. Drinkable now. (NA) (6/15/92) **81**

Cabernet Sauvignon Maipo Valley Medalla Real 1988: Rich and concentrated despite the full-blown tannins, with good berry and currant flavors and a nice touch of spice and coffee on the finish. Ripe, balanced and tightly focused. The fruit should stand up well to aging; hold until 1994 or '95. 5,000 cases made. $11 (5/15/92) **88**

Cabernet Sauvignon Maipo Valley Medalla Real 1987: Don't let the herbal, piny aromas put you off; the crisp, lively blackberry and currant flavors taste great and linger into a solid finish. Drinkable now. $12 (6/15/91) **82**

Cabernet Sauvignon Maipo Valley Medalla Real 1986: Weedy, herbal, oaky style that's modest in flavor. This wine has limited appeal, though it's a fair price. Drink now or in 1993. $5 (3/15/90) **78**

Cabernet Sauvignon Maipo Valley Medalla Real 1985 $8 (3/31/88) **75**

Cabernet Sauvignon Maipo Valley Reserva 1988: Rough-hewn and tightly wound, with loads of pure raspberry, strawberry and currant flavors. Intense and tart, with a concentration that bodes well for aging. Best in 1994. $8.50 (6/15/92) **86**

Cabernet Sauvignon Maipo Valley Reserva 1987: A youthful, crisp Cabernet, with lively fruit flavors, great balance, firm tannins and a touch of oak to add complexity. Cranberry and cherrylike flavors with an herbal accent linger on the finish. Drink now through 1994. Tasted twice. $11.50 (9/15/90) **85**

Cabernet Sauvignon Maipo Valley Reserva 1986: Supple and fruity, with ripe cherry and black current flavors and a touch of herbs. The beautifully defined Cabernet flavor plays off elegantly against the soft tannins to produce a charming wine that is drinkable now but should last until 1994. $6.25 (5/15/89) BB **87**

STONY HOLLOW

Cabernet Sauvignon San Fernando 1988: Supple and generous, with lots of currant, plum and berry aromas and flavors that remain polished and gentle through the solid finish. Drinkable now. $6 (6/15/92) BB **84**

MIGUEL TORRES

Cabernet Sauvignon Curicó District 1990: Firm and focused, with cherry, currant and cedar flavors and nice hints of chocolate and spice emerging on the finish. Well balanced, though in a lighter style. A solid wine. $7 (6/15/92) BB **85**

Cabernet Sauvignon Curicó District 1989: This red offers plenty of pure Cabernet flavor, with cherry, currant and cedar notes in a medium-bodied style. A pleasant drink at a very fair price. Drink now to 1994. $7 (6/15/91) BB **82**

Cabernet Sauvignon Curicó District 1988: An incredible value. A sturdy, firmly tannic Cabernet, with clean plum and vanilla flavors and a spicy, oaky aroma. Full- bodied, rich and focused fruit. Good now, but should continue to develop through 1993. $4.50 (9/15/90) BB **87**

Cabernet Sauvignon Curicó District 1985 $5 (3/31/88) **73**

Cabernet Sauvignon Curicó District 1984 $4.50 (1/31/87) **79**

UNDURRAGA

Cabernet Sauvignon Maipo Valley 1989: A simple, straightforward red wine, with a bit of strawberry and tomato flavor and firm tannins. Palatable, but nothing special. Tasted twice. $6 (6/15/92) **74**

Cabernet Sauvignon Maipo Valley 1988: A generous, fruity red wine worth trying. It's smooth, plummy and rich tasting, with abundant soft tannins and a great, fruity finish. Try now through 1993. $5.25 (9/15/90) BB **83**

Cabernet Sauvignon Maipo Valley 1987: Its pure fruit flavor shines through. Full of vibrant plum, cherry and berry flavors with smooth, polished texture. Medium-bodied, well balanced, clean and fresh, with mild tannins and a lingering finish. Ready to drink. $5.25 (2/15/90) BB **87**

Cabernet Sauvignon Maipo Valley Reserve Selection 1987: Has plenty of flavor—and tannins. Marked by spicy, cedary aromas and concentrated cherry and berry flavors. Tempting to drink this wine now, but should improve in the cellar through about 1995. $8 (6/15/92) BB **87**

Cabernet Sauvignon Maipo Valley Reserve Selection 1986: Earthy and gamy, with lots of rich, smoky cherry and mature Cabernet aromas and flavors that smooth out, rounding nicely. A distinctive style that might take some getting used to, but it has its rewards. Drinkable now. 3,500 cases made. $8 (6/15/91) BB **83**

Cabernet Sauvignon Maipo Valley Reserve Selection 1985: A soft, supple, fruity Cabernet that's also showing the spicy, leathery aromas of maturity. Well balanced and elegant in texture. Drink up now. $7.75 (3/15/90) BB **85**

Cabernet Sauvignon Maipo Valley Santa Ana 1985 $5 (11/15/87) **78**

VALDIVIESO

Cabernet Sauvignon Maipo Valley 1984: Odd salt and sage flavors make this unappealing. Medium-bodied and moderately tannic, but the fruit flavor is obscure. $8 (6/15/92) **71**

VALLE DE SAN FERNANDO

Cabernet Sauvignon San Fernando Gran Reserva 1984: A pleasant wine, with nice plum and cherry flavors that are carried on a frame of oak. Modest tannins. Fruity and delicious. $6 (9/15/90) BB **81**

Cabernet Sauvignon San Fernando Valley 1988: Clean, bright and crisp, with focused fruit flavors of cherry and plum, a hint of spicy wood-aged flavor, moderate tannins and a fruity, tart finish. Drinkable now. $6 (9/15/90) BB **84**

LOS VASCOS

Cabernet Sauvignon Colchagua 1990: Focused, fruity and pure, with rich spice and berry flavors. If you love fruit, this is your wine; has everything from raspberries to prunes. Not weighty, but fairly concentrated. May need until 1994 to smooth out. $7 (5/31/92) BB **88**

Cabernet Sauvignon Colchagua 1989: Fairly intense and fruity, this wine is firm and focused, with lots of currant flavor. Nothing particularly distinctive, but it's still well made. Probably best after 1994. $7 (6/15/92) BB **83**

Cabernet Sauvignon Colchagua 1988: Lively and pleasant, with ripe currant, plum and berry notes that are fresh and clean. The light tannins make it easy to drink now, and the $7 price tag makes it easy on your bank account. Drink now. $7 (6/15/91) BB **82**

Cabernet Sauvignon Colchagua 1987 $5 (9/15/90) BB **86**

Cabernet Sauvignon Colchagua 1985 $5 (11/15/87) **84**

Cabernet Sauvignon Colchagua 1984 $4.50 (4/30/88) BB **88**

Cabernet Sauvignon Colchagua Reserve 1989: $11 (6/15/92) **84**

VINA DEL MAR

Cabernet Sauvignon Curicó Selección Especial 35 1988: A lively, spicy, generous, medium-weight wine, with appealing nutmeg and chocolate overtones to the basic cherry flavor. A bit earthy on the finish, but it's balanced and drinkable now. $6 (6/15/91) BB **81**

Cabernet Sauvignon Curicó Selección Especial 35 1987: An unusual Cabernet made in a Rhône style that's worth trying. It has broad fruit and herb flavors, soft but firm tannins, and a spicy, earthy finish. Drink up now. $6 (9/15/90) BB **83**

Cabernet Sauvignon Lontue 1988: Shows decent, mature fruit and spice flavors and leathery, gamy notes that are within bounds. Reasonably satisfying. Soft and ready to drink, with mild tannins. $6 (6/15/92) **79**

Cabernet Sauvignon Lontue 1985 $6 (4/30/88) BB **86**

Cabernet Sauvignon Lontue Selección Especial 17 1986: A ready-to-drink Cabernet with plenty of plum and cherry flavors, a spicy, herbal aroma, and supple texture. Medium-bodied and not very tannic. From Viña San Pedro. $6 (2/15/90) BB **80**

Cabernet Sauvignon Maipo Reserve 1986: Still full of raspberry and cherry aromas, but the soft, murky texture is disappointing and the finish falls flat. Acceptable for drinking now but past its prime. $9 (6/15/92) **78**

VINOS EXPOSICION

Cabernet Sauvignon Talca Conde del Maule 1988: Firm in texture, but the flavors seem to hit a wall and fade on the finish. While they last you get cherry and currant and a hint of smoke. Drinkable now, but might be better in 1993 or '94. $6 (6/15/92) **79**

Cabernet Sauvignon Talca Escudo de Talca 1990: An appealing wine, this is lean and tart, with a bright beam of red plum and currant running through the aroma and flavor. Smooths out on the finish and picks up polish. Drinkable now. $5 (6/15/92) BB **82**

Cabernet Sauvignon Talca Molino Viejo 1990: Lively, tart and refreshing, with focused red cherry and berry aromas and flavors and hints of toast and spices on the finish. Drinkable now. $5 (6/15/92) BB **82**

Cabernet Sauvignon Talca Reserva de Talca 1989: Tough in texture and earthy in flavor, with a modest component of ripe fruit to keep it from sliding off the edge. Drinkable now with hearty food. $6 (6/15/92) **77**

VINTERRA

Cabernet Sauvignon Maipo & Napa Valleys NV: An unusual Chile/California non-vintage wine that's a great buy. Big and concentrated with deep plum and berry flavors and notes of cedar and mint. Earthy, leathery accents add complexity. Drink now through 1994. $7 (2/15/90) BB **86**

WALNUT CREST

Cabernet Sauvignon Maipo 1985: Shows true Cabernet flavors of plums, currants and a touch of smoke in a smooth, but firmly structured package of moderate tannins and acidity. Clean, well made and well proportioned. Drink now. $4 (6/30/90) BB **80**

CHARDONNAY

CALITERRA

Chardonnay Curicó 1991: Good pear, apple and spice flavors mix well in this rich wine that's stylish and easy to like. Well rounded and well made, oozing with fruit. Has a nice, buttery, spicy finish. Ready to drink now. $6 (6/15/92) BB **86**

Chardonnay Curicó 1990: A simple but correct style of Chardonnay, with spice, citrus and light fig and melon notes. Elegant and easy to drink now. $6 (6/15/91) **78**

Chardonnay Curicó 1989: Made in a delicate, light style. Has crisp fruit flavors, medium body and a clean finish. $7 (9/15/90) **79**

CANEPA

Chardonnay Maipo Valley 1989: Looks, smells and tastes green and grassy, like a Sauvignon Blanc. It's lean and tart, with a crisp, minerally aftertaste. $6.50 (6/30/90) **72**

CONCHA Y TORO

Chardonnay Maipo 1987: Earthy, sour pineapple flavors are difficult to like. $5 (4/30/90) **67**

Chardonnay Maipo Casillero del Diablo Santa Isabel Vineyard 1989: A well-balanced wine, with lean, simple butter, pear and apple flavors. Has basically the right components, but isn't very lively. $7.50 (6/15/92) **78**

Chardonnay Maipo Marqués de Casa Concha Santa Isabel Vineyard 1990: Has the deep gold color of an Australian Chardonnay. Offers plenty of ripe pear and fig flavors and loads of butterscotch notes in an unctuous, oaky style, with a good, toasty finish. $9.50 (6/15/92) **86**

COUSINO-MACUL

Chardonnay Maipo 1989: A soft, simple, easy-drinking Chardonnay with apple and citrus flavors. Well made and medium-bodied. $7 (9/15/90) **76**

Chardonnay Maipo 1987: A very well-made Chardonnay that's rich and smooth, with attractive pear, fig and melon flavors that go down easy. Drink now. A good value. $6 (3/31/90) BB **85**

Chardonnay Maipo Reserva 1989: If you like spice, this is your wine. Nutmeg and cinnamon dominate the decadent, spicy vanilla flavors, but the fruit is a little thin. Stylish and sumptuous. Spice notes linger on the finish. $10.50 (5/15/92) **84**

Chardonnay Maipo Reserva 1988: A rich, deeply colored Chardonnay that's made in a buttery-oaky style, with modest pear and peach flavors underneath. $7.75 (4/30/90) BB **82**

CHILE

Chardonnay

ERRAZURIZ
Chardonnay Maule Valley 1991: Lively, fresh and crisp, with zingy apple flavors. Well balanced and medium-bodied, with nice citrus notes on the finish. $11 (6/15/92) **84**
Chardonnay Maule Valley Reserva 1989: A stylish, oak-accented Chardonnay that is fruity and buttery in aroma and smooth and fairly rich in flavor. The acidity is well balanced, and the finish lingers. $7 (9/15/90) BB **83**

MONTES
Chardonnay Curicó Oak Barrel Fermented 1991: Crisp and lively but not very rich or flavorful, with lean, lemony, grassy flavors. Tastes green on the finish. Decent, but unexciting. $9 (6/15/92) **78**

SAN MARTIN
Chardonnay Maipo Valley International Series 1988: Very fresh and citrusy in flavor, tangy with acidity, lean in texture but there's plenty of fruit. Clean, straightforward; drink it now. $4.50 (4/30/90) BB **81**

SAN PEDRO
Chardonnay Lontue 1990: Clean, simple and slightly sweet, with fruit cocktail flavors of apple and pineapple and earthiness on the finish. $7 (6/15/92) **76**

SANTA CAROLINA
Chardonnay Maipo Valley Santa Rosa Vineyard Reserva 1990: Earthy and crisp, with toasty, earthy aromas that have plenty of spice and butter notes and delicious fig, pear and apple flavors. Has nice concentration throughout, with mineral undertones, and pulls through on the finish. A wine that delivers what it promises. $8 (6/15/92) BB **89**
Chardonnay Maipo Valley Valle del Maipo NV: An earthy, slightly dirty character overrides the melon-tinged flavor. Decent but unexciting. $5 (3/31/90) **71**

SANTA MONICA
Chardonnay Rancagua 1989: A good middle-of-the-road Chardonnay, with citrus and apple flavors and a nice touch of butter around the edges. Crisp, solid and likable, but not very distinctive. $6 (6/15/92) BB **80**
Chardonnay Rancagua 1988: Earthy, woody flavors detract from the ripe Chardonnay flavor. Decent, but the flavors lack vitality and depth. $6 (3/31/90) **70**
Chardonnay Rancagua Tierra de Sol 1991: Fruity and fresh, with good tropical fruit flavors of banana and pineapple. Full-bodied, well made and attractive, with an emphasis on the fruit component. Nice and buttery on the finish. ($NA) (6/15/92) **85**

SANTA RITA
Chardonnay Maipo Valley 120 1991: A fine example of Chardonnay. Buttery, rich and pleasant, dominated by clean, ripe pear, pineapple and spice flavors. Full-bodied, with beautiful fruit and a nice touch of spiciness on the finish. $7 (5/15/92) BB **89**
Chardonnay Maipo Valley Casa Blanca 1991: Tart and lemony, with simple bell pepper, honey and citrus notes. Simple but pleasant. Drink now. ($NA) (6/15/92) **78**
Chardonnay Maipo Valley Medalla Real 1991: Has plenty of spice and vanilla notes, but not quite enough fruit flavor to balance out the oakiness. Gets earthy on the finish. A one-dimensional wine that accentuates style over substance. 4,000 cases made. $11 (5/15/92) **83**
Chardonnay Maipo Valley Medalla Real 1990: A lively wine, with crisp apple and lemon aromas and flavors that are a bit earthy and musty, turning tart and lemony on the finish. Drinkable now. $11.50 (6/15/91) **82**
Chardonnay Maipo Valley Reserva 1991: Pear, pineapple and spice flavors flow through this wine, and vibrant apricotlike notes just keep pouring on and on. Concentrated, with a rich texture and tons of fruit. Rich and full-bodied, with a great, buttery, spicy finish. Intense, balanced and drinkable now, but it might benefit from a couple more years' aging. ($NA) (6/15/92) **90**
Chardonnay Maipo Valley Reserva 1989: A light, fresh Chardonnay, with apple and fig flavors and a bit of spice. Simple and likable, but it doesn't have much depth. Tasted twice with identical scores. $9.50 (6/30/90) **78**
Chardonnay Maipo Valley Reserva 1987: Perfumed fruit flavors are simple and decent, with hints of melon and pear; well balanced, easy-to-drink style. $7.50 (3/31/90) **79**

STONY HOLLOW
Chardonnay San Fernando 1990: A straightforward Chardonnay, with apple and mineral flavors and a soft, almost sweet texture. Accents of honey and butter on the finish give it modest complexity. $6 (6/15/92) BB **81**

MIGUEL TORRES
Chardonnay Curicó District 1991: A tart, thin, lean wine that's light on the citrus and apple flavors. Palatable, but not distinctive. $8 (6/15/92) **74**
Chardonnay Curicó District 1989: A clean and fruity style that offers ripe melon and apple flavors and crisp acidity on the finish. $7.50 (3/31/90) **75**

UNDURRAGA
Chardonnay Maipo Valley 1991: Thin, with modest grapefruit and grass flavors. Not particularly distinctive as a Chardonnay, but still a good, basic white wine. $7 (6/15/92) **78**

LOS VASCOS
Chardonnay Colchagua 1990: Very pungent and earthy, with extremely resinous sage and herbal notes. Finishes with good toast and cream flavors. A style not everyone will appreciate. 2,000 cases made. $9 (6/15/92) **78**

VINA DEL MAR
Chardonnay Lontue Reserve 1991: An earthy, Burgundian style that pumps through fig, honey and pear flavors. The finish is rounded out by buttery notes, with a touch of spice. $9 (6/15/92) **83**

VINTERRA
Chardonnay Maipo & Napa Valleys NV: Ripe and fruity, with simple pear and apple notes and a touch of spicy oak. More character and depth than most Chardonnays at this price. Drink now. $7 (3/31/90) BB **84**

WALNUT CREST
Chardonnay Maipo 1988: A middle-of-the road wine with lots of floral aromas, and simple apple and melon flavors. $4 (4/30/90) **74**

Key to Symbols

The scores reported here are the results of blind tastings conducted by our panel of senior editors. Wines that carry the initials below are results of individual tastings.

THE WINE SPECTATOR 100-POINT SCALE 95-100—Classic, a great wine; ***90-94***— Outstanding, superior character and style; ***80-89***—Good to very good, a wine with special qualities; ***70-79***—Average, drinkable wine that may have minor flaws; ***60-69*** —Below average, drinkable but not recommended; ***50-59*** —Poor, undrinkable, not recommended. "+"— With a score indicates a range; used primarily with barrel tastings to indicate a preliminary score.

SPECIAL DESIGNATIONS SS—Spectator Selection, CS—Cellar Selection, BB—Best Buy, ($NA)—Price not available, (NR)—Not released.

TASTER'S INITIALS (JG)—Jim Gordon, (HS)—Harvey Steiman, (JL)—James Laube, (JS)—James Suckling, (TM)—Thomas Matthews, (TR)—Terry Robards, (PM)—Per-Henrik Mansson, (BT)—Barrel Tasting (these wines were tasted blind from barrel samples), (CA-date)—*California's Great Cabernets* by James Laube, (CH-date)—*California's Great Chardonnays* by James Laube, (VP-date)—*Vintage Port* by James Suckling.

DATE TASTED Dates in parentheses represent the issue in which the rating was published.

Merlot

ALAMEDA
Merlot Maipo Valley Santa Maria Vineyard 1987: Some soft berry flavor and herbs in this basic Merlot. Not particulary dazzling, but flavorful and well rounded. Firm tannins; a good wine to wash down a burger. $5.50 (6/15/92) BB **82**

ROBERT ALLISON
Merlot Maipo Valley 1987: Herbal, tobacco-tinged aromas and flavors show a bit of ripe currant flavor on the finish, balancing the slightly intrusive tannins. Drink now. $5 (6/30/90) **77**

CANEPA
Merlot Maipo Valley 1990: Smells juicy, with nice herbal and cherry flavors and a hint of menthol. Well rounded, balanced, clean and smooth, with a good touch of complexity. Not a powerful wine, but it's delicious. $6 (6/15/92) BB **84**
Merlot Maipo Valley 1988: Easy to like and ready to drink. An elegant, soft, medium-bodied Merlot, with plummy, herbal flavors and good balance. $6 (6/30/90) BB **79**

CONCHA Y TORO
Merlot Rapel 1986: A weedy, vegetal style of Merlot, but it has some attractive if coarse currant plum and pepper notes. A serviceable red of modest distinction. Drink now or in 1993. $4.50 (3/15/90) **76**
Merlot Rapel Marqués de Casa Concha Peumo Vineyard 1989: This plush, almost velvety wine is overflowing with fruit flavors, its chocolaty richness matched by plum, mint and a bit of cedar and berry. Well balanced, rich and smooth. Not very tannic and ready to drink now. $9.50 (5/15/92) **85**

COUSINO-MACUL
Merlot Maipo Limited Release 1989: Well rounded and polished, with a slightly herbal aroma indicative of Merlot, nice, ripe plum and cherry flavors and a hint of chocolate. A full-bodied wine, with a good finish. $11 (5/31/92) **85**
Merlot Maipo Limited Release 1988: More restrained than most Chilean Merlots, with plenty of tannins and body. Shows modest cedary, spicy notes on a backbone of plum flavor. A big, firm wine that will need until 1994 to smooth itself out. $11 (5/31/92) **84**

MONTES
Merlot Curicó Valley Villa Montes 1989: A straightforward, clean Merlot that's flavorful but not complex. Has herbal, bell pepper aromas, good plum and tobacco flavors and modest tannins. Drinkable now. $7 (9/15/90) **79**

LA PLAYA
Merlot Maipo Valley 1988: A little blunt on the palate because of the tannins. Chocolate and plum flavors have a discordant gamy note. A solid wine, but it may taste better in 1993 or 1994. $5 (6/15/92) BB **82**
Merlot Maipo Valley 1987: A simple but correct Merlot, with fairly oaky herb and currant flavors that come across as blunt and one-dimensional; easy on the pocketbook though. Drink now or in 1993. $4.50 (3/15/90) **75**

VALLE DE SAN FERNANDO
Merlot San Fernando 1990: A simple wine, with ripe plum flavors and earthy overtones. Fairly lean, tart and tannic on the finish. Unexciting, though drinkable. $5 (6/15/92) **75**

SAN PEDRO
Merlot Lontue 1989: A supple, smooth wine that integrates fruit and spice. Has plenty of rich, dense plum, cherry and currant flavors and a lingering, spicy, fruity finish. Firm but not harsh, well balanced and full-bodied. Tempting now, but should be better by 1994. $7 (5/31/92) BB **89**
Merlot Lontue 1988: Soft in texture and deep in flavor, with blueberry, blackberry and herb notes. A likable, lush wine that's ready to enjoy right now. $5 (12/31/90) BB **84**
Merlot Lontue Gato de Oro 1987: A delicious, light-bodied, young and supple wine. It's packed with berry and floral aromas and smooth on the palate. Ready to drink now. $6 (2/15/89) BB **81**

SANTA CAROLINA
Merlot Maipo Valley Santa Rosa Vineyard Reserva Especial 1989: Hard-edged and tart, with generous berry flavors and unusual anise and raspberry tones. Clean and well made. May be better after a couple years' aging. An interesting style. $8 (6/15/92) BB **83**

SANTA RITA
Merlot Maipo Valley 120 1989: Tart, powerful and focused, with lots of currant and cherry flavors and firm tannins. Full-bodied, but in a tight style that may loosen up by 1993 or '94. Has plenty of fruit and potential. $6 (6/15/92) BB **85**
Merlot Maipo Valley 120 1989: This soft, velvety red has a modest intensity of currant and herbal aromas and flavors. Fresh and drinkable. $7 (6/15/91) BB **80**

VALDIVIESO
Merlot Maipo Valley 1989: Soft and light, with generous plum and currant aromas and flavors, turning slightly bitter and smoky on the finish. Drinkable now. Tasted twice. $8 (6/15/92) **79**

VINA DEL MAR
Merlot Curicó Selección Especial 12 1989: Light and spicy, with herbal overtones to the charming raspberry and strawberry aromas and flavors. A bit soft on the finish, but it's a pleasant drink. $6 (6/15/91) BB **80**
Merlot Curicó Selección Especial 12 1988: Smooth, soft and pleasant with nice berry flavors. Despite its turning pruny on the finish this is an easy-to-drink Beaujolais style of Merlot. Clean and well-made. $6 (9/15/90) BB **82**
Merlot Lontue 1990: Soft and supple, emphasizing bright cherry and berry flavors, light tannins and nice touches of vanilla and spice. Clean, simple and ready to drink. Tasted twice. $6 (6/15/92) BB **83**
Merlot Lontue 1988: Ripe, smooth and deliciously fruity at a good price. A wine to enjoy now for its freshness and rich plummy flavors. Balanced toward the soft side. $6 (7/31/89) BB **80**
Merlot Maipo Reserve 1989: Decent plum and cherry flavors are slightly marred by apparent oxidation. Port-like in richness, with off-putting nuttiness. Fairly tannic. An odd bird. Tasted twice. $9 (5/15/92) **78**

WALNUT CREST
Merlot Rapel 1989: An exuberantly fruity wine, with lush, well-rounded raspberry, blackberry and sage flavors. Smells like a young Beaujolais, though it tastes like a Dolcetto from Italy. Has a light texture and a nice grapey finish. $4.50 (5/15/92) BB **83**
Merlot Rapel 1987: A remarkable new value, with beautiful fruit flavors in a well-proportioned package. Has deep berry, floral and tobacco accents, moderate tannins and good balance. Drinkable now. $4 (6/30/90) BB **85**

Sauvignon Blanc

ALAMEDA
Sauvignon Blanc Maipo Valley 1989: A light, fruity style that turns a bit simple and watery. Serve well chilled to give the melon and pear flavors an edge. $7 (10/15/91) **75**

CALITERRA
Sauvignon Blanc Curicó 1991: Crisp and lively, with pleasant grapefruit and lime aromas and flavors, hinting at herbs on the light finish. Drink it cold and soon. $5 (6/15/92) **79**
Sauvignon Blanc Curicó 1990: Toasty and flinty, with a flash of sulfur to the herb, melon and spice notes. Drink now. $5 (10/15/91) **78**

CANEPA
Sauvignon Blanc Maipo Valley 1991: A truly great value. Intense, clean and fresh, exhibiting all the

zesty fruit of the Sauvignon Blanc grape in its grapefruit, apple and grass flavors. Has great balance, crisp acidity and a lingering, fruity finish. Very focused and appealing. $5 (5/15/92) BB **88**

CARTA VIEJA
Sauvignon Blanc Maule Valley 1989: Tart and biting with flinty, herbal and citrus notes. For fans of sharp, austere flavors. Drink now. 15,000 cases made. $6 (10/15/91) **75**

LOS CATADORES
Sauvignon Blanc Lontue Selección Especial 1990: A full-blown style, with plenty of butterscotch notes that tend to suppress the fruit flavors. Has heavy-handed though somewhat interesting fig flavors. An attempt at something distinctive that went awry. Drinkable. 5,000 cases made. $5 (6/15/92) **79**

CONCHA Y TORO
Sauvignon Blanc Maipo Casillero del Diablo Santa Isabel Vineyard Special Release 1989: A pleasant, medium-bodied Sauvignon Blanc, with earthy, spicy flavors and a touch of honey. Appealing in a rustic style. $7.50 (5/15/92) **80**

COUSINO-MACUL
Sauvignon Blanc Maipo 1991: Smells and tastes swampy and musty. Has texture and fruitiness, but the off flavors keep it from getting off the ground. Tasted three times. $7 (6/15/92) **70**

ERRAZURIZ
Sauvignon Blanc Maule Valley Reserva 1991: A nicely balanced, clean Sauvignon Blanc that marries ripe pear and apple flavors with smooth spice and vanilla accents from oak aging. Complex, concentrated and long on the finish. $7 (6/15/92) BB **87**

MONTES
Sauvignon Blanc Curicó Villa Montes 1991: Clean, crisp and simple in flavor. Its freshness and lightness are virtues; should be a versatile wine with dinner. $6 (6/15/92) BB **80**
Sauvignon Blanc Curicó Villa Montes 1990: A touch earthy, but the flavors ring true for Sauvignon Blanc, with herbs and spice. Drink now. $4.50 (10/15/91) **78**

OAK BLUFFS
Sauvignon Blanc Colchagua 1990: Tastes dry and appley, but an earthy, dirty streak takes the fun out of it. Marginal quality. $6 (6/15/92) **70**

LA PLAYA
Sauvignon Blanc Maipo Valley 1990: Tart, gamy and simple, with very limited appeal. Drink now. $5 (10/15/91) **71**

PORTAL DEL ALTO
Sauvignon Blanc Maipo Valley 1991: Floral aromas and a decent core of fruit flavor give this soft, simple wine a measure of appeal. $3.50 (6/15/92) **76**

ST.-MORILLON
Sauvignon Blanc Lontue 1991: An extreme style, showing deep color and featuring more buttery, oaky aromas and flavors than fruit. Gets earthy on the finish, too. Not for everyone, but it has its own appeal. $5.50 (6/15/92) **79**

VALLE DE SAN FERNANDO
Sauvignon Blanc San Fernando 1990: Doesn't have much zing despite the nice floral aromas and simple Muscat-like flavors. An average white wine; not very distinctive. $4 (6/15/92) **77**

SAN JOSE DE SANTIAGO
Sauvignon Blanc Colchagua Valley 1990: Tart and lean, with the main flavors being citrus and spice. Simple but drinkable. Serve well chilled. $3 (10/15/91) **75**

SAN PEDRO
Sauvignon Blanc Lontue 1991: A simple but refreshing white wine, with anise and floral aromas and herbal, lemony flavors. Very crisp in balance. Try with oysters. $7 (6/15/92) **79**
Sauvignon Blanc Lontue Gato Blanco 1991: Tastes simple and fruity, like canned fruit cocktail. Has good acidity, but it offers nothing special in the flavors. Average quality. Tasted twice. $4.75 (6/15/92)**75**

SANTA CAROLINA
Sauvignon Blanc Maipo Valley Santa Rosa Vineyard Reserva 1990: Green and tart, with appley, grassy aromas and lemony flavors. Thin and simple but palatable. Tasted twice. $8 (6/15/92) **73**

SANTA MONICA
Sauvignon Blanc Rancagua 1991: A focused and flavorful wine, with a nice zip of citrus and herb flavors and pleasant vanilla notes on the finish. Lively, clean, well made and refreshing. Would do well on its own or paired with fish. 5,000 cases made. $6 (5/15/92) BB **85**
Sauvignon Blanc Rancagua 1989: Fresh and clean, with pleasant melon, spice and citrus flavors that are well focused and lively. A terrific value. Serve chilled. 2,000 cases made. $5 (10/15/91) BB **80**
Sauvignon Blanc Rancagua 1988: Crisp and refreshing, with attractive melon, lemon and citric notes. Elegantly balanced; simple but pleasant. Drink now. $6 (3/31/90) BB **85**

SANTA RITA
Sauvignon Blanc Maipo Valley 120 1991: Grapefruit flavors dominate this well-made, balanced wine. Has interesting earthy notes and a restrained character, making it a good quaff. $6 (6/15/92) BB **84**
Sauvignon Blanc Maipo Valley 120 1990: Attractive floral, pear, spice and hazelnut flavors are ripe, rich and supple, finishing with a long aftertaste. Drink now or in 1993. $7 (10/15/91) BB **86**
Sauvignon Blanc Maipo Valley Medalla Real 1991: Fresh and lively, with focused citrus and herb flavors and smooth vanilla notes on the finish. Nicely concentrated. A good, well-balanced example of Sauvignon Blanc. ($NA) (6/15/92) **84**
Sauvignon Blanc Maipo Valley Reserva 1991: Textbook Sauvignon Blanc. Crisp and juicy, with grassy aromas and pear and citrus flavors. The fruit echoes on the long finish. Well made and concentrated; compares to the best of France and California. 5,000 cases made. $7.50 (6/15/92) BB**88**
Sauvignon Blanc Maipo Valley Reserva 1990: A classy wine that's intense, rich and flavorful. Pretty fig, melon, pear and spice notes finish with a splash of herbs and toast. Drink now. $8.50 (10/15/91) BB **85**

MIGUEL TORRES
Sauvignon Blanc Curicó District 1991: Elegant and perfumed, with light melon, litchi nut, citrus, fig and spice notes. A graceful and refined white wine. Drinks well now. $7 (4/15/92) BB **84**
Sauvignon Blanc Curicó District 1990: A touch earthy and gamy, but it has decent citrus and pear-tinged flavors. $7 (10/15/91) **74**
Sauvignon Blanc Curicó District Bellaterra 1990: Aromatic and spicy tasting, but very thin on fruit. Almost like a spice tea rather than a wine. Nutmeg, cinnamon and vanilla flavors from oak aging obscure the taste of the grape. Tasted twice, with consistent notes. ($NA) (6/15/92) **77**

UNDURRAGA
Sauvignon Blanc Maipo Valley 1991: A basic, unrefined Sauvignon Blanc, with plenty of grassy aromas, grapefruit flavors and crisp acidity. Nothing fancy, but solid in quality. $6 (5/15/92) **79**
Sauvignon Blanc Maipo Valley 1989: Very ripe, oily and vegetal, with garlic and onion flavors to match the melon and pear. Best with food. Drink now. $5.25 (3/31/90) **75**

LOS VASCOS
Sauvignon Blanc Colchagua 1990: Rich and flavorful, with a spicy hazelnut flavor that adds to the pear and citrus notes. Shows uncommon complexity and finesse for a wine in this price range. From one of Chile's best wineries. $7 (10/15/91) BB **86**
Sauvignon Blanc Colchagua 1988: Clean and fruity, with generous melon, apple, pear and spice flavors that gain a touch of lemon and spice on the finish. Nice fruit complexity. Terrific price. Drink now. $4.75 (3/31/90) BB **83**

VINA DEL MAR
Fumé Blanc Lontue 1991: A rich, flavorful, unusual style of Sauvignon Blanc, with fig, honey and pear flavors reminiscent of a late-harvest wine. May not be everyone's style, but it sure is unctuous and distinctive. $6 (6/15/92) BB **85**

VINOS EXPOSICION
Sauvignon Blanc Talca Conde del Maule 1991: A lean white wine, with funky, herbal, chalky flavors and a little bit of lemon and peach on the finish. Acceptable quality, but not much fun to drink. 12,000 cases made. $6 (6/15/92) **75**

Other Chile Red

ALEJANDRO HERNANDEZ MUNOZ
Pinot Noir Maipo Viña Portal del Alto Gran Vino 1984: Big, full, ripe and fruity, with straightforward plum and currant notes and a good dose of oak that gets dry and heavy-handed on the finish. Won't remind you much of Pinot Noir; but at this price it's a decent value in red table wine. Drink now to 1994. $3.50 (3/15/90) **74**

Other Chile White

SANTA MONICA
Sémillon Rancagua Seaborne 1989: A vibrant, herbaceous style that offers plenty of character, with layers of melon, spice, citrus and pear flavors that stay with you. The finish is long and intense. A great buy at $4. 2,000 cases made. $4 (10/15/91) BB **84**
Sémillon Rancagua Seaborne 1988: Light, fruity, floral and delicate, with melon and pear flavors. Well balanced; goes down easy. $5 (3/31/90) BB **81**

FRANCE
ALSACE/*GEWÜRZTRAMINER*

J.B. ADAM
Gewürztraminer Alsace Vendange Tardive 1990: Lacks personality. Earthy and rather sweet, with ripe fruit aromas. Medium-bodied and lightly sweet, with spice and earth notes on the finish. Drink now. $40 (2/15/92) (BT) **80+**

DOMAINE LUCIEN ALBRECHT
Gewürztraminer Alsace Cuvée Martine Albrecht 1990: Easy to drink; a lovely aperitif. Has ripe pear and lemon aromas, medium-bodied, with lightly sweet pear and apple flavors and a medium finish. Drink now. ($NA) (2/15/92) **85**
Gewürztraminer Alsace Sélection de Grains Nobles 1989 ($NA) (11/15/90) **93**
Gewürztraminer Alsace Vendange Tardive 1989 ($NA) (11/15/90) **85**

LEON BEYER
Gewürztraminer Alsace 1990: Balanced, with ripe pear and spice aromas, medium-bodied, with slightly off-dry lemon, butter and pear flavors and a light, spicy finish. Drink now. $17 (2/15/92) **84**
Gewürztraminer Alsace 1989 $16 (11/15/90) **90**
Gewürztraminer Alsace 1988 $11.50 (10/15/89) **85**
Gewürztraminer Alsace Cuvée des Comtes d'Eguisheim 1990: A powerful wine, with an extremely long finish. One of the few Gewürztraminers that's a food wine in this vintage. Brilliant aromas of spice, honey and ripe pear lead to spice and almond flavors. Full-bodied and slightly off-dry, with firm acidity and a long burnt almond finish. Better in 1993 to '95. $38 (2/15/92) **91**
Gewürztraminer Alsace Cuvée des Comtes d'Eguisheim 1989 $33 (11/15/90) **91**
Gewürztraminer Alsace Cuvée des Comtes d'Eguisheim 1988 $25 (10/15/89) **89**
Gewürztraminer Alsace Sélection de Grains Nobles 1990: Overripe and burnt, with an earthy, barnyardy character detracting too much for us. (NR) (2/15/92) (BT) **70+**
Gewürztraminer Alsace Sélection de Grains Nobles 1989 ($NA) (11/15/90) **96**
Gewürztraminer Alsace Vendange Tardive 1990: A little light for a vendange tardive and a little sweet for regular. Medium-bodied and off-dry, with fresh lemon and honey aromas, spicy, light honey flavors and hints of orange on the finish. Drink now. (NR) (2/15/92) (BT) **80+**
Gewürztraminer Alsace Vendange Tardive 1989 ($NA) (11/15/90) **75**

DOMAINE PAUL BLANCK
Gewürztraminer Alsace 1990: Round and attractive, with spice, nutmeg and cinnamon aromas. Full-bodied and slightly off-dry, with a round, soft mouth-feel and a spicy pear finish. Drink now. ($NA) (2/15/92) **84**
Gewürztraminer Alsace Altenbourg 1990: Big and fat; a bit tiring to taste. Full-bodied and off-dry, with almond and spice aromas, very ripe, almost overripe, pear and lemon flavors and a light finish. Drink now. ($NA) (2/15/92) **83**
Gewürztraminer Alsace Altenbourg Vieilles Vignes 1990: A serious wine for a Sylvaner; drink before dinner. Medium-bodied and slightly off-dry, with intense lemon rind and floral aromas, lemon and cream flavors and a spicy finish. Drink now. ($NA) (2/15/92) **84**
Gewürztraminer Alsace Furstentum Vieilles Vignes 1990: A simple aperitif-style Sylvaner, with lime and spice aromas. Medium-bodied and lightly sweet, with lime and spice flavors and a simple finish. Drink now. ($NA) (2/15/92) **79**

E. BOECKEL
Gewürztraminer Alsace 1990: Balanced and lively, with lots of focused fruit. Has grapefruit, pear and spice aromas. Medium-bodied and slightly off-dry, with ripe grapefruit and spice flavors and a long, flavorful finish. Drink now to 1994. $14.50 (2/15/92) **84**
Gewürztraminer Alsace Vendange Tardive 1990: A drier-style vendange tardive, with an impressive concentration of fruit. Should go well with rich food. Big and powerful, with honey, spice, beeswax and orange peel notes, lots of spicy fruit flavors and a clean finish. Can age for decades. Try in 1994 to '97. $36 (2/15/92) (BT) **90+**

BOTT FRERES
Gewürztraminer Alsace Cuvée Exceptionnelle 1990: Refreshing and rich, with lime, honey and spice aromas. Medium-bodied and off-dry, with citrus, almond, lime and spice flavors and a medium finish. Drink or hold. $15 (2/15/92) **87**
Gewürztraminer Alsace Cuvée Exceptionnelle 1989: Beautifully articulated spice and fruit flavors make this an almost textbook example of an Alsace Gewürztraminer, echoing apple, caramel, cinnamon and ginger. Dry and firm in structure; could make a fine aperitif or companion to sausage dishes. $13.50 (6/30/91) **87**
Gewürztraminer Alsace Réserve Personnelle 1990: Round and easy to drink. Very spicy, with burnt almond aromas and spice, almond and lemon flavors. Full-bodied and off-dry, with a simple finish. Drink now. $18 (2/15/92) **84**
Gewürztraminer Alsace Réserve Personnelle 1989: Soft and generous, with a round texture and vanilla overtones to the grapefruit and rose petal aromas and flavors, turning toward apple and honey notes on the finish. A wine with finesse and complexity. $17 (6/30/91) **88**
Gewürztraminer Alsace Vendange Tardive 1990: A gentler late-harvest Gewürz, but a bit one-dimensional. Has spice and tropical fruit aromas, almond, spice and smoke flavors and a medium finish. Medium-bodied and sweet. Drink now. $38 (2/15/92) (BT) **80+**
Gewürztraminer Alsace Vendange Tardive 1988: Extremely earthy and sweet, but not enough to overpower the bitter dirtiness in this wine. Not recommended. Tasted twice. $40 (7/31/91) **63**

DOMAINE MARCEL DEISS
Gewürztraminer Alsace Altenberg de Bergheim Vendange Tardive 1990: A lovely, balanced Gewürz, with chewy fruit and spicy apricot flavors. Delicious now, but hold back. Better in 1994 to '96. (NR) (2/15/92) (BT) **90+**
Gewürztraminer Alsace Bergheim 1990: Sweet and delicious, with succulent honey and apricot flavors and a fresh finish. Serve with dessert. Drink on release. $12 (2/15/92) **87**
Gewürztraminer Alsace St.-Hippolyte 1990: Sweet and flavorful, with tons of pineapple and almond flavors. Serve as an aperitif. Drink on release. ($NA) (2/15/92) **85**

DOPFF AU MOULIN
Gewürztraminer Alsace 1989 $14 (11/15/90) **82**
Gewürztraminer Alsace 1988 ($NA) (10/15/89) **84**
Gewürztraminer Alsace Brand 1988 ($NA) (10/15/89) **82**
Gewürztraminer Alsace Brand de Turckheim 1990: Lots of fruit and power in this wine. Has wet hay, honey and fruit aromas, with lemon and vanilla flavors and a dry finish. Drink now. ($NA) (2/15/92) **87**

Key to Symbols

The scores reported here are the results of blind tastings conducted by our panel of senior editors. Wines that carry the initials below are results of individual tastings.

THE WINE SPECTATOR 100-POINT SCALE ***95-100***—Classic, a great wine; ***90-94***—Outstanding, superior character and style; ***80-89***—Good to very good, a wine with special qualities; ***70-79***—Average, drinkable wine that may have minor flaws; ***60-69***—Below average, drinkable but not recommended; ***50-59***—Poor, undrinkable, not recommended. "+"—With a score indicates a range; used primarily with barrel tastings to indicate a preliminary score.

SPECIAL DESIGNATIONS SS—Spectator Selection, CS—Cellar Selection, BB—Best Buy, ($NA)—Price not available, (NR)—Not released.

TASTER'S INITIALS (JG)—Jim Gordon, (HS)—Harvey Steiman, (JL)—James Laube, (JS)—James Suckling, (TM)—Thomas Matthews, (TR)—Terry Robards, (PM)—Per-Henrik Mansson, (BT)—Barrel Tasting (these wines were tasted blind from barrel samples), (CA-date)—*California's Great Cabernets* by James Laube, (CH-date)—*California's Great Chardonnays* by James Laube, (VP-date)—*Vintage Port* by James Suckling.

DATE TASTED Dates in parentheses represent the issue in which the rating was published.

Gewürztraminer Alsace Réserve 1990: Very tropical, with exotic aromas of almond, butter and orange peel. Medium-bodied and lightly off-dry, with butter, almond and honey flavors and a light finish. Drink now. ($NA) (2/15/92) **84**
Gewürztraminer Alsace Réserve 1989 $13 (11/15/90) **87**
Gewürztraminer Alsace de Riquewihr 1990: A lovely aperitif wine, with pretty spice and honey aromas. Medium-bodied, off-dry and spicy, with pear flavor. Drink now. ($NA) (2/15/92) **84**
Gewürztraminer Alsace Sélection de Grains Nobles 1990: Shows lots of character, but is quite closed and firm. The aromas are very pungent, but the subdued flavors need time to develop. Better after 1994. (NR) (2/15/92) (BT) **90+**
Gewürztraminer Alsace Sélection de Grains Nobles 1989 ($NA) (11/15/90) **94**
Gewürztraminer Alsace Vendange Tardive 1989 ($NA) (11/15/90) **81**
Gewürztraminer Alsace Vendange Tardive 1988 ($NA) (10/15/89) **90**

DOPFF & IRION
Gewürztraminer Alsace 1989 ($NA) (11/15/90) **81**
Gewürztraminer Alsace 1988 $11 (10/15/89) **82**
Gewürztraminer Alsace Cuvée La René Dopff 1990: A restrained wine, with good concentration of fruit. Medium-bodied, with almond, honey and spice aromas, almond, cream and pear flavors and an elegant finish. Better in 1993. ($NA) (2/15/92) **84**
Gewürztraminer Alsace Cuvée La René Dopff 1989 ($NA) (11/15/90) **80**
Gewürztraminer Alsace Les Sorcières 1990: Tight, firm, full-bodied and dry, with ripe pineapple and spice aromas, very ripe fruit flavors and a long, powerful, spicy finish. Drink now. ($NA) (2/15/92) **85**
Gewürztraminer Alsace Sporen 1990: This extremely accessible, drier wine has elegant aromas of blanched almond and pear. Medium-bodied and dry, with pear, spice and almond flavors and a round, soft finish. Drink now. ($NA) (2/15/92) **86**
Gewürztraminer Alsace Vendange Tardive 1990: Powerful and brooding, with intense aromas of pear, spice and petrol. Medium-bodied and sweet, with strong lemon, honey, burnt almond and white pepper flavors and a muscular structure. Try in 1994 to '97. (NR) (2/15/92) (BT) **90+**

HUGEL
Gewürztraminer Alsace 1990: A very pretty wine, with pear and honey aromas. Medium-bodied and spicy, with vanilla, banana and spice flavors and a round mouth-feel. Drink now. ($NA) (2/15/92) **84**
Gewürztraminer Alsace 1989 $16 (11/15/90) **85**
Gewürztraminer Alsace 1988 $14.25 (10/15/89) **83**
Gewürztraminer Alsace "R" Sélection de Grains Nobles 1989 ($NA) (11/15/90) **89**
Gewürztraminer Alsace "S" Sélection de Grains Nobles 1989 ($NA) (11/15/90) **96**
Gewürztraminer Alsace "T" Sélection de Grains Nobles 1989 ($NA) (11/15/90) **91**
Gewürztraminer Alsace Réserve Personnelle Jubilée 1990: Lovely and elegant, with extremely fresh fruit flavors. There's good power lurking underneath. Quite exotic, with very youthful pear and freshly crushed grape aromas. Medium- bodied and slightly off-dry, with lots of cream and pear flavors and a light, spicy finish. Has excellent acidity. Drink now or hold. ($NA) (2/15/92) **92**
Gewürztraminer Alsace Vendange Tardive 1990: A compact vendange tardive, with an excellent depth of fruit. Full-bodied and medium sweet, showing classy aromas of mango, grass and spice. Has a viscous structure, with deep spice, lemon and honey flavors and a long, honeyed finish. Better in 1994 to '96. (NR) (2/15/92) (BT) **90+**
Gewürztraminer Alsace Vendange Tardive 1989 ($NA) (11/15/90) **90**

JOSMEYER
Gewürztraminer Alsace Les Archenets 1990: A very delicate Gewürz, with lovely aromas and flavors, but it's a little short on the finish. Medium-bodied and dry, with almond and meat aromas and a velvety mouth-feel of tropical fruit and lemon flavors. Drink now. $28 (2/15/92) **85**
Gewürztraminer Alsace Les Folastries 1990: Excellent balance in a dry-style Gewürz, with very good finesse. Medium-bodied and dry, with delicate aromas of honey, pear and spice, elegant almond, spice and pear flavors and a medium finish. Better in 1993 or '94. $20 (2/15/92) **89**
Gewürztraminer Alsace Cuvée des Folastries 1989 $16 (11/15/90) **83**
Gewürztraminer Alsace Hengst 1989 ($NA) (11/15/90) **90**
Gewürztraminer Alsace Sélection de Grains Nobles 1990: Classic Gewürz character, with spice, exotic fruit and almond flavors. Very firm and delicious. Better after 1994. (NR) (2/15/92) (BT) **90+**
Gewürztraminer Alsace Sélection de Grains Nobles 1989 ($NA) (11/15/90) **85**
Gewürztraminer Alsace Vendange Tardive 1990: Subtle, yet rich, with cream and peach aromas and flavors and a medium finish. Drink on release. (NR) (2/15/92) (BT) **85+**
Gewürztraminer Alsace Vendange Tardive 1989 ($NA) (11/15/90) **88**

KIENTZHEIM-KAYSERBERG
Gewürztraminer Alsace 1990: Offers light, elegant fruit, Has almond and citrus aromas and melts like butter in the mouth. Medium-bodied and slightly off-dry, with medium-rich lemon, spice and tropical fruit flavors and a fresh finish. Drink now. ($NA) (2/15/92) **84**
Gewürztraminer Alsace Altenberg 1990: A distinctive, off-dry Gewürztraminer, with dried apricot and spice aromas. Medium-bodied and lightly sweet, with earthy, grassy, dried apricot flavors and a long, spicy finish. Drink now or hold. ($NA) (2/15/92) **87**
Gewürztraminer Alsace Furstentum 1990: A full-blown vendange tardive-style wine, with lots of fruit and acidity. Big and rich; perfect with fruit or as an aperitif. Drink now. ($NA) (2/15/92) **87**

MARC KREYDENWEISS
Gewürztraminer Alsace Kritt 1990: Verges on a vendange tardive style, with intense aromas of pears and cream, lovely pear and cream flavors and a very fruity finish. Medium-bodied and off-dry. Drink now. $20 (2/15/92) **85**
Gewürztraminer Alsace Kritt 1989 $19 (11/15/90) **79**
Gewürztraminer Alsace Kritt 1988 $19 (10/15/89) **86**
Gewürztraminer Alsace Kritt Sélection de Grains Nobles 1990: An extremely perfumed, floral style of Gewürz, with intense anise, violet and rose aromas and flavors. Sweet and exotic. Better in 1994 or '95. (NR) (2/15/92) (BT) **90+**
Gewürztraminer Alsace Kritt Vendange Tardive 1989 ($NA) (11/15/90) **83**

KUENTZ-BAS
Gewürztraminer Alsace 1989 ($NA) (11/15/90) **86**
Gewürztraminer Alsace Cuvée Tradition 1988 ($NA) (10/15/89) **84**
Gewürztraminer Alsace Eichberg 1990: Quite thick and syrupy; could use a little more acidity on the finish. Full-bodied and sweet, with very fresh lemon and honey aromas, full honey and lemon flavors and a syrupy finish. Better in 1994 to '96. $30 (2/15/92) (BT) **80+**
Gewürztraminer Alsace Eichberg 1989 ($NA) (11/15/90) **93**
Gewürztraminer Alsace Eichberg Cask 2 1990: A pleasant aperitif style. Has lovely tropical fruit and almond aromas, ripe banana and apple flavors and a round finish. Medium-bodied and off-dry. Drink now or hold. $30 (2/15/92) **83**
Gewürztraminer Alsace Eichberg Vendange Tardive 1989 ($NA) (11/15/90) **86**
Gewürztraminer Alsace Pfersigberg Vendange Tardive 1990: Another very good vendange tardive. Has lemon, lime, spice, apple and honey aromas and flavors and a fresh finish. Medium-bodied and sweet. Drink in 1993 to '95. $45 (2/15/92) (BT) **85+**
Gewürztraminer Alsace Réserve Personnelle 1990: A pretty wine for sipping. Medium-bodied and off- dry, with lovely pear, spice and honey aromas. Dances on the palate, with elegant pear and marzipan flavors and a light, sweet finish. Drink now or hold. $22 (2/15/92) **84**
Gewürztraminer Alsace Réserve Personnelle 1989 ($NA) (11/15/90) **84**

CUVEE LEON
Gewürztraminer Alsace 1988: True spicy aromas say Gewürz, but the flavors are a little bitter, with almond and vanilla notes. $11 (3/31/91) **80**

GUSTAVE LORENTZ
Gewürztraminer Alsace 1989 ($NA) (11/15/90) **85**
Gewürztraminer Alsace 1988 ($NA) (10/15/89) **89**
Gewürztraminer Alsace 1986: Just what you look for in Gewürztraminer, an effusive aroma of flowers, spices and cheese, a lively and dry texture with flavors that echo the aroma and a twinge of bitterness to give it tension. $11 (7/31/89) **86**
Gewürztraminer Alsace Altenberg 1990: Very sweet for this category, but a delicious sipping wine. Has exotic aromas of mango, spice and pear. Medium-bodied and medium-sweet, with honey and spice flavors and a sweet finish. Drink now. $39 (2/15/92) **86**
Gewürztraminer Alsace Altenberg 1989 ($NA) (11/15/90) **85**
Gewürztraminer Alsace du Domaine 1990: Simple, with slightly odd aromas of spice, bacon and rubber, but good fruit flavors. Medium-bodied, with light spice and cream flavors, but a rather short finish. Drink now. $20 (2/15/92) **76**
Gewürztraminer Alsace Réserve 1990: Silky, with a lovely balance of fresh fruit and acidity. Shows beautiful aromas of petrol, spice and citrus. Medium-bodied and dry, with lots of pear flavors and a lovely, balanced finish. Drink now. ($NA) (2/15/92) **87**
Gewürztraminer Alsace Réserve 1989 ($NA) (11/15/90) **79**
Gewürztraminer Alsace Sélection de Grains Nobles 1988 ($NA) (10/15/89) **91**
Gewürztraminer Alsace Vendange Tardive 1990: Has overripe fruit, with a rather earthy, barnyardy character and a bitter aftertaste. Just too much for us. Lacks grace. $49 (2/15/92) (BT) **75+**

MADER
Gewürztraminer Alsace 1990: Round and delicious, with delicate spice and pear aromas. Medium-bodied and slightly off-dry, with lovely lemon, spice and pear flavors and a round, light finish. Drink now. $14 (2/15/92) **85**
Gewürztraminer Alsace Vendange Tardive 1990: Very silky, but a little out of balance for the moment. Shows lemon, light tropical fruit and cream aromas. Medium-bodied and medium sweet, with lemon and vanilla flavors and a rather hot finish. Better in 1994 to '96. $48 (2/15/92) (BT) **80+**

ALBERT MANN
Gewürztraminer Alsace Furstentum Vendange Tardive 1990: A little heavy-handed, but shows quite an amazing concentration of fruit. If you want a massively fat, sweet wine, go for this. Has super-ripe honey, apricot and pineapple aromas. Full-bodied and sweet, with buttery, lemony, oily fruit flavors and a thick finish. Drink now, but it will age. (NR) (2/15/92) (BT) **85+**
Gewürztraminer Alsace Hengst Vendange Tardive 1990: Very sweet and rich, with perfumed aromas of dried apricot and spice. Full-bodied and sweet, with thick, nutty dried apricot flavors and a long finish. Better in 1994 to '98. (NR) (2/15/92) (BT) **90+**
Gewürztraminer Alsace Steingrubler Vendange Tardive 1990: Elegant and fresh, with intense lemon, cream and tropical fruit aromas. Medium-bodied and lightly sweet, with concentrated toasty almond and spice flavors and a crisp finish. Better in 1993 to '95. (NR) (2/15/92) (BT) **85+**
Gewürztraminer Alsace Steingrubler Vieilles Vignes 1990: Like a vendange tardive. Better as an aperitif or with fresh fruit. Full-bodied and slightly sweet, with intense pineapple, spice and almond aromas, a thick fruit structure and a rich pear and spice finish. Drinkable now, but better in 1993 or '94. ($NA) (2/15/92) **87**

MURE
Gewürztraminer Alsace Clos St.-Landelin Vorbourg Vendange Tardive 1990: Lovely as an aperitif, with creamy lemon and peach flavors and a soft finish. Drink in 1993 to '95. $28 (2/15/92) (BT) **85+**
Gewürztraminer Alsace Clos St.-Landelin Vorbourg Sélection de Grains Nobles 1989: Sweet, rich and beautifully focused, offering delicate shades of rose petal, grapefruit, apricot and pear aromas and flavors that keep taking turns with nutmeg and cinnamon nuances as they persist through a long finish. A great dessert wine. Drinkable now, but probably best in 1997 to 2000. Limited availability. 180 cases made. $56 (9/15/91) **93**
Gewürztraminer Alsace Clos St.-Landelin Vorbourg Vendanges Tardives 1989: Soft, flavorful, complex and a little sweet, with pleasant ginger and apricot aromas and flavors. Sweet enough to balance a tinge of bitterness nicely. Drinkable now, but probably better in 1993 or '94. 1,635 cases made. $29 (9/15/91) **90**
Gewürztraminer Alsace Zinnkoepflé 1990: Fresh, balanced and dry, with a lovely pine, floral and fruit character. Refreshing on the finish. A very good dry wine for this overripe vintage. Drink on release. $15 (2/15/92) **86**
Gewürztraminer Alsace Zinnkoepflé 1989 ($NA) (11/15/90) **84**

DOMAINE OSTERTAG
Gewürztraminer Alsace 1988 ($NA) (10/15/89) **86**
Gewürztraminer Alsace Fronholz Sélection de Grains Nobles 1990: A classy wine, with lots of petrol, spice and honey aromas and fresh flavors of cream, honey and spice. Sweet and fruity, with great elegance and excellent acidity. Better in 1993 to '95. (NR) (2/15/92) (BT) **90+**
Gewürztraminer Alsace Vignoble d'Epfig 1989 $14 (11/15/90) **90**
Gewürztraminer Alsace Vignoble d'Epfig Vendange Tardive 1990: Offers plenty of nutty, spicy flavors and sweet fruit but lacks a little on the finish. Drink on release. $50 (2/15/92) (BT) **85+**

PREISS-HENNY
Gewürztraminer Alsace 1990: Shows an exciting balance of fresh, dry fruit. A refined Gewürz, with subdued, pretty aromas of pear and spice. Medium-bodied and dry, with balanced pear and spice flavors and crisp acidity. Drink now. ($NA) (2/15/92) **86**
Gewürztraminer Alsace Cuvée Marcel Preiss Vendange Tardive 1990: Powerful, with tons of fruit and an iron backbone. The petrol, almond and spice aromas have hints of orange peel. Medium-bodied and sweet, with incredibly spicy honey flavors and a super-long, flavorful finish. Try in 1994 to '97. (NR) (2/15/92) (BT) **85+**

DOMAINES SCHLUMBERGER
Gewürztraminer Alsace 1989 ($NA) (11/15/90) **73**
Gewürztraminer Alsace 1988 ($NA) (10/15/89) **78**
Gewürztraminer Alsace Fleur de Guebwiller 1990: Made from raisiny grapes. Like sucking on a piece of caramel; has rather burnt flavors and is thick and fat. ($NA) (2/15/92) **81**
Gewürztraminer Alsace Kessler 1989 ($NA) (11/15/90) **90**
Gewürztraminer Alsace Kitterlé 1989 ($NA) (11/15/90) **78**
Gewürztraminer Alsace Sélection de Grains Nobles 1989 ($NA) (11/15/90) **79**
Gewürztraminer Alsace Sélection de Grains Nobles 1988 ($NA) (10/15/89) **78**

LOUIS SIPP
Gewürztraminer Alsace 1990: Elegant, with excellent, focused flavors. Medium-bodied and dry, with orange peel and spice aromas, elegant spice, almond and apple skin flavors and a light finish. Drink now. ($NA) (2/15/92) **87**
Gewürztraminer Alsace Osterberg Cuvée Particulière de Nos Vignobles 1990: A blockbuster of a wine in the classic dry style. Wonderfully balanced, full-bodied and dry, with lemon, almond and pecan aromas and masses of spicy fruit flavors. Better in 1993 to '96. ($NA) (2/15/92) **92**
Gewürztraminer Alsace Sélection de Grains Nobles 1990: Racy and spicy, with buttery pecan and honey flavors and a lively finish. Very balanced for such a sweet wine. Better in 1994 to '96. (NR) (2/15/92) (BT) **90+**
Gewürztraminer Alsace Vendange Tardive 1990: Has great concentration of fruit and great balance. Full-bodied and medium sweet, with pure grapefruit and nut extract, concentrated grapefruit and lemon flavors and a long, fresh finish. Better in 1993 to '97. (NR) (2/15/92) (BT) **90+**

PIERRE SPARR
Gewürztraminer Alsace 1989 ($NA) (11/15/90) **79**
Gewürztraminer Alsace Brand 1990: Another vendange tardive-style Gewürz, with very good concentration. Brilliant spice, pie crust and pineapple aromas lead to medium-bodied, lightly sweet pineapple and pear flavors and a fresh, medium-spicy almond finish. Better in 1993 or '94. $22 (2/15/92) **87**
Gewürztraminer Alsace Brand 1989 ($NA) (11/15/90) **88**
Gewürztraminer Alsace Carte d'Or 1990: A pleasant, balanced wine that's clean and elegant. Medium-bodied and dry, with almond and spice aromas, spicy, creamy flavors and a fresh finish. Drink on release. $10 (2/15/92) **82**
Gewürztraminer Alsace Cuvée Centenaire Mambourg 1990: Oily, ripe, distinctive and full-bodied. Gold in color, with ripe pineapple and spice aromas and lightly sweet, rich honey, spice, burnt almond and caramel flavors. Sweet but fresh on the finish. Drink now or hold. $18 (2/15/92) **86**
Gewürztraminer Alsace Cuvée Centenaire Mambourg Sélection de Grains Nobles 1989 ($NA) (11/15/90) **87**
Gewürztraminer Alsace Cuvée Centenaire Mambourg Vendange Tardive 1989 ($NA) (11/15/90) **68**
Gewürztraminer Alsace Mambourg Vendange Tardive 1990: Medium-bodied and sweet, with a rather odd sunflower oil and butter flavor. Fat and hard to drink. $37 (2/15/92) (BT) **70+**
Gewürztraminer Alsace Réserve 1990: Rather restrained, with excellent acidity for this group. Offers lemon meringue and almond aromas. Medium-bodied and lightly off-dry, with spicy citrus flavors and a dry finish. Drink now or hold. $14 (2/15/92) **89**

TRIMBACH
Gewürztraminer Alsace 1990: Delicious. Medium- bodied and slightly off-dry, with lemony, spicy pear aromas, plenty of pear and almond flavors and a light finish. Drink now. $13 (2/15/92) **86**
Gewürztraminer Alsace 1989 $11 (11/15/90) **86**
Gewürztraminer Alsace 1988 $8.50 (10/15/89) **83**
Gewürztraminer Alsace Carte d'Or 1989 ($NA) (11/15/90) **85**
Gewürztraminer Alsace Cuvée des Seigneurs de Ribeauvillé 1990: A blowtorch of a wine; like drinking pear eau-de-vie. Has amazingly fresh aromas of flowers, almonds and pears. Medium-bodied and off-dry, with peach and pear flavors and a light, spicy, white pepper finish. High in alcohol. Drink now. ($NA) (2/15/92) **90**
Gewürztraminer Alsace Hors Choix Sélection de Grains Nobles 1989 ($NA) (11/15/90) **97**
Gewürztraminer Alsace Réserve 1989 ($NA) (11/15/90) **92**
Gewürztraminer Alsace Vendange Tardive 1990: Super-focused and exciting, with lively spice, lemon and grapefruit flavors, a long finish and excellent acidity. Better after 1995. $77 (2/15/92) (BT) **90+**
Gewürztraminer Alsace Vendange Tardive 1989 ($NA) (11/15/90) **97**
Gewürztraminer Alsace Vendange Tardive 1988 ($NA) (10/15/89) **87**

TURCKHEIM
Gewürztraminer Alsace Cuvée Réserve 1989: Textbook Alsace Gewürztraminer, from its heady floral aromas to its smooth, rich texture and spicy flavors. Leaves a great taste in your mouth. $16.50 (10/31/91) **87**

DOMAINE WEINBACH
Gewürztraminer Alsace Clos des Capucins (Cask 21) 1989 ($NA) (11/15/90) **79**
Gewürztraminer Alsace Clos des Capucins Cuvée Laurence (Cask 8) 1989 $50 (11/15/90) **79**
Gewürztraminer Alsace Clos des Capucins Cuvée Laurence (Cask 17) 1989 $50 (11/15/90) **80**
Gewürztraminer Alsace Clos des Capucins Quintes Sélection de Grains Nobles 1989 $275 (11/15/90) **87**
Gewürztraminer Alsace Clos des Capucins Réserve Personnelle 1988: Soft, fruity and spicy, a gentle example of balancing the nutmeg and rose petal overtones of Gewürz against ripe, generous orange and pear flavors. $21 (6/30/91) **84**
Gewürztraminer Alsace Cuvée Laurence 1990: An attractive aperitif, with lots of sweet fruit. Full-bodied and slightly sweet, with burnt almond, dried date, honey and spice aromas, spicy honey and pear flavors and a flavorful finish. Drink now. $29 (2/15/92) **87**
Gewürztraminer Alsace Cuvée Laurence 1988 $34 (10/15/89) **83**
Gewürztraminer Alsace Cuvée Théo 1990: Sweet and elegant, but what do you serve it with? Has fresh honey, quince jam and spice aromas and a lightly sweet palate of spice and honey. Long and sweet on the finish. Drink now. $20 (2/15/92) **85**
Gewürztraminer Alsace Cuvée Théo 1988 ($NA) (10/15/89) **85**
Gewürztraminer Alsace Vendange Tardive 1990: Not the normal style, but an understated wine, with excellent concentration of fruit. The fresh honey and spice aromas have hints of lemon peel. Medium-bodied and sweet, with a thick fruit structure, racy acidity and a smoky finish. Try in 1994 to '96. $57 (2/15/92) (BT) **90+**
Gewürztraminer Alsace Vendange Tardive 1988 $67.50 (10/15/89) **92**

ALSACE WILLM
Gewürztraminer Alsace 1990: A lovely, rich wine, with light honey, spice and earth aromas. Medium-bodied and slightly off-dry, with plenty of spicy, lemony flavors and a fresh finish. Drink now. $13 (2/15/92) **85**
Gewürztraminer Alsace 1989: Broad and ripe, yet still elegant, with effusive apricot, spice and rose petal aromas and flavors that lighten up and echo on the finish, with hints of hazelnut and macadamia. Appealing to drink now. Much better than a bottle tasted earlier. $12.50 (9/15/91) **86**
Gewürztraminer Alsace Clos Gaensbroennel 1990: A true vendange tardive wine. A great value. Has complex aromas of peach, apricot, spice and botrytis. Medium-bodied and sweet, with spicy almond and botrytis flavors, good acidity and a long finish. Better in 1993 to '95. $24 (2/15/92) **89**
Gewürztraminer Alsace Clos Gaensbroennel Kirchberg de Barr 1989 ($NA) (11/15/90) **83**
Gewürztraminer Alsace Clos Gaensbroennel Vendange Tardive 1990: A seamless wine, with intense grapefruit aromas. Medium-bodied and sweet, with tangerine peel, orange and honey flavors and a fresh, creamy finish. Better in 1993 to '95. $50 (2/15/92) (BT) **85+**
Gewürztraminer Alsace Gaensbroennel Vendange Tardive 1989 ($NA) (11/15/90) **80**
Gewürztraminer Alsace Sélection de Grains Nobles 1990: Less sweet, but shows very intense varietal character of fruit, cloves and other spices. A little light on the finish. Drink on release. (NR) (2/15/92) (BT) **80+**
Gewürztraminer Alsace Sélection de Grains Nobles 1989 ($NA) (11/15/90) **86**

DOMAINE ZIND-HUMBRECHT
Gewürztraminer Alsace 1988 ($NA) (10/15/89) **83**
Gewürztraminer Alsace Clos Windsbuhl 1989 $36 (11/15/90) **83**
Gewürztraminer Alsace Clos Windsbuhl Vendange Tardive 1990: Intense and classic, with lots of spice, almond and hay flavors and a strong backbone. A drier style that should be paired with food. Drink in 1993 to '95. $70 (2/15/92) (BT) **90+**
Gewürztraminer Alsace Goldert Vendange Tardive 1990: Another excellent, nutty, spicy Gewürz made to go with rich food, but can also work with desserts. Try in 1993 to '95. $60 (2/15/92) (BT) **90+**
Gewürztraminer Alsace Heimbourg Vendange Tardive 1990: Subtle, but has plenty of spicy almond and fruit characteristics. Medium and rich. Better in 1993. $45 (2/15/92) (BT) **85+**
Gewürztraminer Alsace Hengst Vendange Tardive 1990: A wine with endless flavor. Has intense almond, spice, honey and fruit aromas and flavors and a wonderful finish. Better in 1994. $65 (2/15/92) (BT) **95+**
Gewürztraminer Alsace Herrenweg 1990: Has slightly odd burnt rubber aromas, but also an impressive concentration of fruit flavor. Slightly sweet on the finish. Lacks class. $23 (2/15/92) **82**
Gewürztraminer Alsace Herrenweg Turckheim 1989 $25 (11/15/90) **84**
Gewürztraminer Alsace Rangen de Thann Clos St.-Urbain 1990: Tastes more like Pinot Gris to us. Extremely ripe and intense with fig, smoky, butter aromas and flavors; off-dry, fat and rich. Drink on release or cellar it. $50 (2/15/92) **91**
Gewürztraminer Alsace Rangen Vendange Tardive 1988 ($NA) (10/15/89) **85**

FRANCE

Alsace/Pinot Blanc

J.B. ADAM
Pinot Blanc Alsace 1990: A voluptuous wine that will be delicious to sip chilled before dinner. Offers intense honey, apple, leaf and almond aromas and flavors. Off-dry, full- bodied and round, with white pepper notes and a smoky finish. Drink now. ($NA) (2/15/92) **87**

DOMAINE LUCIEN ALBRECHT
Pinot Blanc Alsace 1989: An interesting, earthy, nutty white wine, with lots of aroma but very restrained fruit flavors. $7 (11/15/90) **75**
Pinot Blanc Alsace Vieilles Vignes Barrel Fermented 1990: Fat and overripe; lacks class. Has extremely ripe vanilla and hot honey aromas and flavors. Full-bodied and dry, with a spicy almond finish. Drink now. ($NA) (2/15/92) **72**

LEON BEYER
Pinot Blanc Alsace 1989 $12 (11/15/90) **78**
Pinot Blanc Alsace Blanc de Blancs 1990: Has a very smoky hazelnut character and very good balance. Medium-bodied and dry, with almond, spice and apple aromas, lots of almond flavors and a creamy texture. Drink now. $12.50 (2/15/92) **88**
Pinot Blanc Alsace Blanc de Blancs 1988 $8.75 (10/15/89) **79**
Pinot Blanc Alsace Blanc de Blancs 1987: Has the distinctive, spicy Alsace aroma and long finish. Clean, fresh and dry in the mouth, with almost floral flavors and a good spicy finish. $9 (7/31/89) **84**

DOMAiNE PAUL BLANCK
Pinot Blanc Alsace Kientzheim Klevner 1990: An exotic, ripe style of Pinot Blanc, with papaya, pear and cream aromas and apple and almond flavors. Medium-bodied and dry, with crisp acidity on the finish. Drink now. ($NA) (2/15/92) **88**
Pinot Blanc Alsace Klevner 1990: Steely and impressive for a Pinot Blanc. Very refreshing. Medium-bodied and dry, with stone, leaf and fig aromas, tons of fruit and a very crisp finish. Could use another year or two to round out. ($NA) (2/15/92) **87**
Pinot Blanc Alsace Riquewihr Klevner 1990: An explosion of fruit, with a zingy finish. Has pretty aromas of apple and cream. Medium-bodied, with lovely floral and cream flavors and firm acidity on the finish. Drink now or hold. ($NA) (2/15/92) **90**

E. BOECKEL
Pinot Blanc Alsace Réserve 1990: Somewhat simple, with grapefruit, apple and vanilla aromas, apple and vanilla flavors and a slightly short, dry finish. Medium-bodied and dry. Needs time to develop; better in 1993. $9 (2/15/92) **82**

DOMAINE MARCEL DEISS
Pinot Blanc Alsace Bennwihr 1990: Extremely focused and restrained, with laser-guided, intense apple and mango flavors and crisp acidity. Very long finish. Delicious now, but better in 1993. $13 (2/15/92) **89**
Pinot Blanc Alsace Bergheim 1990: A very refreshing Pinot Blanc, with enticing aromas and flavors of mango and lemon and a crisp finish. Try on release. ($NA) (2/15/92) **87**

DOPFF & IRION
Pinot Blanc Alsace 1989 ($NA) (11/15/90) **84**
Pinot Blanc Alsace Cuvée René Dopff 1990: A dense wine, with intense mineral flavors. A little rough; could use a year or two to mellow. Medium-bodied, with almond, stone and pear aromas, pear and stone flavors and a smoky, almost spicy finish. Drink now. ($NA) (2/15/92) **85**
Pinot Blanc Alsace Cuvée René Dopff 1988 ($NA) (10/15/89) **82**

HUGEL
Pinot Blanc Alsace 1990: Has beautiful aromas and a delicate mouth-feel. Medium-bodied, with floral, fruity aromas and flavors and a light finish. Drink now. ($NA) (2/15/92) **85**
Pinot Blanc Alsace 1989 ($NA) (11/15/90) **86**
Pinot Blanc Alsace 1988 $9 (10/15/89) **83**

JOSMEYER
Pinot Blanc Alsace Les Lutins 1990: A fragrant wine in a lovely, round, rich style. Medium-bodied, with floral, very creamy aromas, rich floral, almond and stone flavors and a round finish. Drink now. $16 (2/15/92) **86**
Pinot Blanc Alsace Les Lutins 1989 $15 (11/15/90) **85**
Pinot Blanc Alsace Pinot Auxerrois "H" Vieilles Vignes 1990: Amazing concentration for a Pinot Blanc. Why buy Chardonnay? Round, harmonious and medium-bodied, with smoked almond and apple aromas and succulent, smoky almond and apple flavors. Drink now or hold. $24 (2/15/92) **91**
Pinot Blanc Alsace Pinot Auxerrois "H" Vieilles Vignes 1989 ($NA) (11/15/90) **89**

KIENTZHEIM-KAYSERBERG
Pinot Blanc Alsace 1990: Packed with fruit. Full-bodied and lightly sweet, with dense fruit structure and lots of tropical fruit aromas and flavors and a peppery finish. Drink now. ($NA) (2/15/92) **86**

MARC KREYDENWEISS
Pinot Blanc Alsace Kritt 1989 $14 (11/15/90) **83**
Pinot Blanc Alsace Kritt 1988 $13 (10/15/89) **87**
Pinot Blanc Alsace Kritt Klevner 1990: Really fun to drink; like drinking liquid banana ice cream. Excellent as an aperitif wine or with dessert. Full-bodied and sweet, with amazing aromas of banana cream pie and overflowing with banana, coconut and cream flavors. Drink now. ($NA) (2/15/92) **89**
Pinot Blanc Alsace Kritt Klevner 1989 $17 (11/15/90) **86**

KUENTZ-BAS
Pinot Blanc Alsace 1989 ($NA) (11/15/90) **73**
Pinot Blanc Alsace Cuvée Tradition 1990: A lovely Pinot Blanc for sipping, with mineral, stone and apple aromas and flavors. Off-dry and smoky on the finish. Drink now. $12.50 (2/15/92) **84**
Pinot Blanc Alsace Cuvée Tradition 1989: Short and simple, with earthy citrus and spice aromas and flavors that make it drinkable. $14 (9/15/91) **79**
Pinot Blanc Alsace Cuvée Tradition 1988 ($NA) (10/15/89) **84**

CUVEE LEON
Pinot Blanc Alsace 1988: Pretty and approachable, although sweeter than Alsace normally is, with apple and floral aromas and delicate fruit flavors. Easy to drink. $10 (3/31/91) **83**

GUSTAVE LORENTZ
Pinot Blanc Alsace 1990: More like a young Chardonnay. Has freshly sliced apple and cream aromas and apple and hazelnut flavors. Medium-bodied and dry, with a crisp finish. Needs time; better in 1993. ($NA) (2/15/92) **85**
Pinot Blanc Alsace 1989 $11 (11/15/90) **83**
Pinot Blanc Alsace 1988 $12 (10/15/89) **79**
Pinot Blanc Alsace Réserve 1986: A smooth-drinking, middle-of-the-road white wine with earthy, vanilla aromas and modest fruit flavors. Resembles a white Burgundy more than many Alsace wines. $7 (7/31/89) **78**

MADER
Pinot Blanc Alsace 1990: Shows plenty of character on the nose, but a little less on the palate. Full-bodied and dry, with light hay, cream and pear aromas, smoky almond and cream flavors and a flavorful finish. Drink now. $9 (2/15/92) **85**

ALBERT MANN
Pinot Blanc Alsace Pinot Auxerrois Non Filtré 1990: Shows very good fruit concentration, but a butterscotch character dominates. Medium-bodied, with vanilla and apple aromas, apple and toasted vanilla flavors and a woody finish. Unfiltered. Try now to 1994. $9.50 (2/15/92) **84**

DOMAINE OSTERTAG
Pinot Blanc Alsace Barriques 1990: A lively wine that will give many top-notch Chardonnays competition. Has delicate floral, pear and rose petal aromas. Medium-bodied, with lovely apple and cream flavors and a creamy finish. Drinkable now, but will improve with age. $15 (2/15/92) **89**
Pinot Blanc Alsace Barriques 1989: A dry, sturdy white wine, with lean apple and almond flavors and a lingering finish that picks up a bit of vanilla and honey. $14 (7/31/91) **81**

PREISS-HENNY
Pinot Blanc Alsace 1990: Attractive, with smoked almond and apple aromas. Full-bodied and round, with a creamy texture and a spicy, tropical fruit finish. Drink now. ($NA) (2/15/92) **86**

DOMAINES SCHLUMBERGER
Pinot Blanc Alsace 1990: Wonderful Pinot Blanc, with rich tropical fruit, apple and cream flavors and refreshing finish. Oily, without being too fat. Drink on release. ($NA) (2/15/92) **89**
Pinot Blanc Alsace 1988 ($NA) (10/15/89) **84**

LOUIS SIPP
Pinot Blanc Alsace 1990: Can't get much more youthful. Has freshly crushed grape and almond aromas and flavors. Medium-bodied, with lots of fruit. Drink now or hold. ($NA) (2/15/92) **85**

PIERRE SPARR
Pinot Blanc Alsace Diamant d'Alsace 1990: Brimming with fruit for a Pinot Blanc. Has lovely honey, cream and apple aromas. Medium-bodied, with a soft, round fruit structure and lots of apple and cream flavors. Drink now. $10 (2/15/92) **87**

TRIMBACH
Pinot Blanc Alsace 1990: Super clean and fresh. A more delicate style, but has plenty of pear and apple flavors. Drink on release. $9 (2/15/92) **84**
Pinot Blanc Alsace 1989 $9.50 (11/15/90) **86**
Pinot Blanc Alsace 1988: Broad, deep flavors of melon, peach, toast and earth develop slowly on the palate and on the finish in this rich wine. Has an elegant texture and a sense of finesse in the balance. $8 (11/15/90) BB **87**
Pinot Blanc Alsace Sélection 1989 ($NA) (11/15/90) **86**

DOMAINE WEINBACH
Pinot Blanc Alsace 1989 $18 (11/15/90) **88**
Pinot Blanc Alsace Clos des Capucins 1988 ($NA) (10/15/89) **80**
Pinot Blanc Alsace Clos des Capucins Réserve Particulière 1988 $19 (10/15/89) **74**
Pinot Blanc Alsace Réserve 1990: Wild and exciting for a Pinot Blanc. Sip and enjoy. Has exotic cream, smoke and tropical fruit aromas. Medium-bodied and slightly off-dry, overflowing with smoky almond, white pepper and banana flavors and a rich finish. Drink now. $11 (2/15/92) **88**

ALSACE WILLM
Pinot Blanc Alsace 1990: Another very good Pinot Blanc. Has creamy vanilla and honey aromas; medium-bodied and off-dry, with lovely stone and apple flavors and an almond finish. Drink now. $9 (2/15/92) **84**
Pinot Blanc Alsace 1989 ($NA) (11/15/90) **83**

DOMAINE ZIND-HUMBRECHT
Pinot Blanc Alsace 1989 ($NA) (11/15/90) **76**
Pinot Blanc Alsace 1988 ($NA) (10/15/89) **87**

Riesling

J.B. ADAM
Riesling Alsace Cuvée Jean-Baptiste Kaefferkopf 1990: Has an iron backbone of fruit and acidity. Very traditional in style; great for aging. Medium-bodied and dry, with lemon, pine and sand aromas, a compact, spicy fruit character and iron acidity. Needs time; try in 1993 to '95. $19 (2/15/92) **87**
Riesling Alsace Réserve 1990: Rich, with a delicate grassy character. Use with food as you would a Sauvignon Blanc. Has intense lemon, bread crust and light grass aromas and gooseberry and slightly grassy flavors. Full-bodied and off-dry, with medium acidity. Drink now. $11.50 (2/15/92) **85**
Riesling Alsace Vendange Tardive 1990: Spicy, with a lovely, round mouth-feel. Medium-bodied and medium sweet, with apricot, orange peel and pear aromas, a silky texture and lovely, sweet lemon and cream flavors. Try now to 1993. $40 (2/15/92) (BT) **90+**

DOMAINE LUCIEN ALBRECHT
Riesling Alsace Pfingstberg Sélection de Grains Nobles 1989 ($NA) (11/15/90) **87**

LEON BEYER
Riesling Alsace 1989 ($NA) (11/15/90) **84**
Riesling Alsace 1988 $10.50 (10/15/89) **80**
Riesling Alsace Cuvée Particulière 1990: An up-front, ready-to-drink Riesling, with enticing pie crust, almond and lemon aromas and flavors. Medium-bodied and dry, with a light, dry, honey-tinged finish. Drink now or hold. ($NA) (2/15/92) **88**
Riesling Alsace Cuvée Particulière 1989 $29 (11/15/90) **92**
Riesling Alsace Réserve 1987: Refreshing and well-made, if not a standout. Has good acidity, floral aromas and modest fruit flavor. $13 (7/31/89) **76**
Riesling Alsace Sélection de Grains Nobles 1989 ($NA) (11/15/90) **80**
Riesling Alsace Sélection de Grains Nobles 1988 $25 (10/15/89) **87**
Riesling Alsace Vendange Tardive 1989 ($NA) (11/15/90) **79**

DOMAINE PAUL BLANCK
Riesling Alsace Furstentum Jeunes Vignes 1990: Rather developed, with slightly mature flavors. An old style of Riesling, but delicious now. Medium-bodied and dry, with floral and honey aromas, light honey flavors and a tart, developed honey finish. Drink now. ($NA) (2/15/92) **83**
Riesling Alsace Furstentum Vieilles Vignes 1990: Another deliciously rich and silky Riesling. Offers beautiful aromas of apple, juniper and cream. Medium-bodied and dry, with rich apple, cream and spice flavors and a fruity finish. Try now to 1993. ($NA) (2/15/92) **89**
Riesling Alsace Kientzheim 1990: Firm and hard, but one-dimensional. Medium-bodied and dry, with very lemony aromas, straightforward lemon flavors and a medium finish. Try now to 1993. ($NA) (2/15/92) **82**
Riesling Alsace Patergarten 1990: Focused, with very attractive dried fruit flavors. Has peaches-and-cream aromas, medium-bodied, dry, light dried apricot flavors and a crisp finish. Try now to 1993. ($NA) (2/15/92) **87**

Key to Symbols

The scores reported here are the results of blind tastings conducted by our panel of senior editors. Wines that carry the initials below are results of individual tastings.

THE WINE SPECTATOR 100-POINT SCALE *95-100*—Classic, a great wine; *90-94*—Outstanding, superior character and style; *80-89*—Good to very good, a wine with special qualities; *70-79*—Average, drinkable wine that may have minor flaws; *60-69*—Below average, drinkable but not recommended; *50-59*—Poor, undrinkable, not recommended. "+"—With a score indicates a range; used primarily with barrel tastings to indicate a preliminary score.

SPECIAL DESIGNATIONS SS—Spectator Selection, CS—Cellar Selection, BB—Best Buy, ($NA)—Price not available, (NR)—Not released.

TASTER'S INITIALS (JG)—Jim Gordon, (HS)—Harvey Steiman, (JL)—James Laube, (JS)—James Suckling, (TM)—Thomas Matthews, (TR)—Terry Robards, (PM)—Per-Henrik Mansson, (BT)—Barrel Tasting (these wines were tasted blind from barrel samples), (CA-date)—*California's Great Cabernets* by James Laube, (CH-date)—*California's Great Chardonnays* by James Laube, (VP-date)—*Vintage Port* by James Suckling.

DATE TASTED Dates in parentheses represent the issue in which the rating was published.

Riesling Alsace Riquewihr 1990: Starts slowly, but builds on the finish. Very focused and balanced, offering fresh lemon, apple and fruit aromas and lots of medium-bodied green apple and cream flavors. Try now to 1994. ($NA) (2/15/92) **88**
Riesling Alsace Sand 1990: A focused, classic Alsace Riesling, with banana and pineapple aromas. Medium-bodied, with pineapple and spice flavors. Try now to 1994. ($NA) (2/15/92) **86**
Riesling Alsace Schlossberg Jeunes Vignes 1990: A very crisp, focused and fruity wine. Medium-bodied and dry, with subtle cream and apple aromas, apple and papaya flavors, firm acidity and a spicy finish. Try in 1993 or '94. ($NA) (2/15/92) **86**
Riesling Alsace Schlossberg Vieilles Vignes 1990: Fresh and spicy, with wonderful balance and lots of juicy fruit flavor. Has intense honey, cream and peach aromas. Medium-bodied and dry, with spicy honey and cream flavors and a fresh finish. Try now to 1994. ($NA) (2/15/92) **88**

E. BOECKEL
Riesling Alsace Vendange Tardive 1990: A little on the heavy side. Full-bodied and lightly sweet, with orange peel, almond and smoke aromas, light honey, smoke and almond flavors and a slightly bitter finish. Somewhat high in alcohol. Needs time; try in 1993 to '95. (NR) (2/15/92) (BT) **80+**
Riesling Alsace Wiebelsberg 1990: Very distinctive in style, multidimensional and rich, yet firm. A real mouthful, with honey, cream and dried apricot aromas and flavors. Full-bodied and dry, with honey, smoke and spice flavors and medium acidity. Packed with fruit on the finish. Try now to 1994. $17 (2/15/92) **92**

BOTT FRERES
Riesling Alsace Cuvée Exceptionnelle 1989: Simple and fruity, with slightly earthy apple and floral aromas and flavors and a firm structure. $13 (7/31/91) **81**
Riesling Alsace Réserve 1990: Gives lots of pleasure now, with intense almond and peach aromas. Medium-bodied and dry, with almond and peach flavors and a round mouth-feel that's almost oily. Drink now. $14 (2/15/92) **88**
Riesling Alsace Vendange Tardive 1990: An opulent wine, with super-fresh crushed grape, mineral and almond aromas. Full-bodied and slightly off-dry, with dried apricot and spice flavors and a very long finish. Better in 1993 to '95. $35 (2/15/92) (BT) **90+**
Riesling Alsace Vin de Prestige des Vignobles Réserve Personnelle 1990: A real charmer. Alluring, with intense spice and almond aromas and flavors. Medium-bodied and almost off-dry, with tons of fruit and a very long finish. Very drinkable now, but might be better in 1993. $16 (2/15/92) **91**

DOMAINE MARCEL DEISS
Riesling Alsace Altenberg de Bergheim Vendange Tardive 1990: Like a burning fuse on the palate; explodes with flavor on the finish. Firm and well structured, with plenty of medium-sweet lemon, cream, lime and spice flavors. Better in 1994 to '96. (NR) (2/15/92) (BT) **90+**
Riesling Alsace Bennwihr 1990: This striking wine has lovely cream, apple and lemon flavors and a fresh, firm finish. Better after 1993. ($NA) (2/15/92) **88**
Riesling Alsace Bergheim Engelgarten 1990: A spellbinding Riesling, with extremely opulent fruit. Shows cream, lemon, lime and grapefruit character and focused, ripe fruit flavors. Better in 1994. ($NA) (2/15/92) **90**
Riesling Alsace Bergheim Engelgarten Vieilles Vignes 1990: A rock-solid wine built of rich fruit and firm acidity. Has impressive petrol, grapefruit and lemon flavors. Bone dry. Better after 1994. ($NA) (2/15/92) **93**
Riesling Alsace Graberg 1990: A beautiful, creamy, lemony, perfumed wine, with a fresh finish. Drink on release. ($NA) (2/15/92) **90**
Riesling Alsace St.-Hippolyte 1990: Like eating a bunch of freshly picked Riesling grapes. Offers masses of fruit and fresh acidity. Try in 1993 to '95. ($NA) (2/15/92) **92**
Riesling Alsace Schoenenbourg Vendange Tardive 1990: A drier style of vendange tardive, with an excellent concentration of spicy fruit flavors and a firm structure. Better in 1993 to '95. (NR) (2/15/92) (BT) **85+**

DOPFF AU MOULIN
Riesling Alsace 1988 ($NA) (10/15/89) **84**
Riesling Alsace Propre Récolte 1989 ($NA) (11/15/90) **79**
Riesling Alsace Réserve 1990: Another big, oily wine. Somewhat too old-style for us; could use a little more finesse. Full-bodied and dry, with pungent tropical fruit aromas, lemon, almond and spice flavors and a rather thick, tart finish. Try now to 1993. ($NA) (2/15/92) **85**
Riesling Alsace Réserve 1989: Lean and lively, with somewhat greenish peach and apple aromas and flavors. Seems tart, but it has the potential to grow into itself by 1993 or '94. $12 (9/15/91) **82**
Riesling Alsace de Riquewihr 1990: A charged-up Riesling, with plenty of fruit and flavor. Medium-bodied, with attractive pineapple and lime aromas, rich lemon and pineapple flavors and lively acidity on the finish. Try now to 1993. ($NA) (2/15/92) **87**
Riesling Alsace Schoenenbourg 1990: This generous style of Riesling has almond, thyme, lemon and spice aromas. Full-bodied and off-dry, with super-rich honey, spice and almond flavors and a long, long finish. Try now to 1993. ($NA) (2/15/92) **90**
Riesling Alsace Schoenenbourg 1989 ($NA) (11/15/90) **78**
Riesling Alsace Sélection de Grains Nobles 1989 ($NA) (11/15/90) **95**
Riesling Alsace Vendange Tardive 1989 ($NA) (11/15/90) **86**
Riesling Alsace Vendange Tardive 1988 ($NA) (10/15/89) **83**

DOPFF & IRION
Riesling Alsace 1989 ($NA) (11/15/90) **81**
Riesling Alsace Cuvée René Dopff 1990: A little rough, but shows good fruit concentration. Has pine, canned pear and light vanilla aromas. Medium-bodied, with pine and apple skin flavors and a slightly astringent finish. Needs time; try now to 1993. ($NA) (2/15/92) **82**
Riesling Alsace Cuvée René Dopff 1988 $9.25 (10/15/89) **85**
Riesling Alsace Les Murailles 1990: Quite forward, but it's slightly awkward. Has mature almond, honey, grass and spice aromas. Medium-bodied and off-dry, with almond and spice flavors, but a little candied and tart on the finish. Drink now. ($NA) (2/15/92) **83**
Riesling Alsace Les Murailles 1988 ($NA) (10/15/89) **79**
Riesling Alsace Les Murailles Château de Riquewihr 1989 ($NA) (11/15/90) **80**
Riesling Alsace Schoenenbourg 1990: A compact wine, with focused fruit flavors, light honey, dried apricot and flint aromas and dried apricot and spice flavors. Medium-bodied and dry. Shows plenty of fruit on the finish, but it's slightly tart and grassy. Try now to 1993. ($NA) (2/15/92) **87**
Riesling Alsace Schoenenbourg 1989 ($NA) (11/15/90) **81**
Riesling Alsace Vendange Tardive 1990: Has excellent weight and concentration, dense without being heavy. Full-bodied and lightly sweet, with spice, lemon, botrytis and almond aromas, spice, almond, lemon and cream flavors and a long finish. Better in 1993 or '94. (NR) (2/15/92) (BT) **90+**
Riesling Alsace Vendange Tardive 1988 ($NA) (10/15/89) **87**

HUGEL
Riesling Alsace 1990: A blockbuster Riesling overflowing with classy fruit structure and refined aromas of honey, apricot and spice. Medium-bodied and dry, with masses of apricot, spice and fruit flavors and a long, long finish. Built for aging; try now to 1994. $14 (2/15/92) **91**
Riesling Alsace 1989 ($NA) (11/15/90) **87**
Riesling Alsace 1988 $12.50 (10/15/89) **87**
Riesling Alsace Cuvée Tradition 1989 ($NA) (11/15/90) **86**
Riesling Alsace Cuvée Tradition 1988 ($NA) (10/15/89) **89**
Riesling Alsace Jubilée Réserve Personnelle 1990: A wine of tremendous balance and excellent finesse, with elegant mineral, lime and fruit aromas and flavors. Medium-bodied and dry, with lovely, integrated, ripe acidity. Needs time; try now to 1994. ($NA) (2/15/92) **91**
Riesling Alsace Jubilée Réserve Personnelle 1989 ($NA) (11/15/90) **90**
Riesling Alsace Vendange Tardive 1990: Thick and powerful in a drier style of wine. Has beautiful cream, green apple and lime aromas. Full-bodied and off-dry, with lemon, lime and spice flavors and a long, flavorful finish. Excellent potential for aging. Try in 1993 to '96. (NR) (2/15/92) (BT) **90+**
Riesling Alsace Vendange Tardive 1989 ($NA) (11/15/90) **90**

JOSMEYER
Riesling Alsace Brand Vendange Tardive 1990: This more elegant style of vendange tardive has a rather short finish, but lovely aromas of petrol and spice. Medium-bodied and sweet, with lemony fruit flavors and a light finish. Try now to 1993. (NR) (2/15/92) (BT) **85+**
Riesling Alsace Grand Cru Hengst Cuvée de la St.-Martin 1990: An early drinking Riesling, with lots of fruit. Medium-bodied and off-dry, with honey and lime aromas and flavors and a light finish. Drink now. $45 (2/15/92) **88**
Riesling Alsace Grand Cru Hengst Vendange Tardive 1990: A vibrant wine, with gooseberry and honey aromas. Medium- to full-bodied and off-dry, with very good concentration, lots of lemon, lime and spice flavors and a long, crisp finish. Better in 1993 to '95. (NR) (2/15/92) (BT) **90+**
Riesling Alsace Hengst 1990: Ripe fruit shows well in this well-proportioned Riesling. Medium-bodied and dry, with lovely lime and pear aromas, lots of spicy cream and fruit flavors and a silky finish. Try now to 1993. ($NA) (2/15/92) **89**
Riesling Alsace Hengst 1989 ($NA) (11/15/90) **90**
Riesling Alsace La Kottabe 1990: Juicy and succulent, with earthy tropical fruit aromas. A medium- to full-bodied, dry wine, with earthy, grassy lemon flavors, a spicy finish and crisp acidity. Try now to 1993. $17 (2/15/92) **86**
Riesling Alsace La Kottabe 1989 ($NA) (11/15/90) **86**
Riesling Alsace Les Pierrets 1990: Extremely well balanced, with lots of finesse. Has lemon and tropical fruit aromas, lemon and spice flavors and a fine, minty finish. Medium-bodied and dry. Needs time; try now to 1993. ($NA) (2/15/92) **89**

KIENTZHEIM-KAYSERBERG
Riesling Alsace 1990: Attractive and flamboyant, with lots of fruit; great as an aperitif. Offers intense tropical fruit and pie crust aromas. Full-bodied, with a slightly off-dry, rich, fat yet elegant fruit structure and a very powerful finish. Drink now or hold. ($NA) (2/15/92) **85**
Riesling Alsace Schlossberg 1990: Ripe and powerful, albeit a bit one-dimensional. Has honey, peach and cream aromas. Medium-bodied and dry, with ripe pineapple flavor and a lingering finish. Try now to 1993. ($NA) (2/15/92) **86**

MARC KREYDENWEISS
Riesling Alsace 1988 $15.50 (10/15/89) **86**
Riesling Alsace Andlau 1990: A really showy Riesling, with opulent fruit and subtle yet intense apple and cream aromas. Full-bodied and super-fruity, with rich apple and pie crust flavors that go on and on, but it could use a little more acidity on the finish. Drink now or hold. ($NA) (2/15/92) **88**
Riesling Alsace Andlau 1989 $18 (11/15/90) **83**
Riesling Alsace Kastelberg 1990: A real beauty. Has gorgeous aromas and flavors of spice and apple pie. Medium-bodied and dry, with a beautiful balance of acidity and ripe fruit. Perfect now, but will improve with age. ($NA) (2/15/92) **91**
Riesling Alsace Kastelberg 1989 ($NA) (11/15/90) **82**
Riesling Alsace Kastelberg Vendange Tardive 1988 $26 (10/15/89) **90**
Riesling Alsace Weibelsberg Vendange Tardive 1989 ($NA) (11/15/90) **79**
Riesling Alsace Weibelsberg 1990: A blockbuster, with lots of fruit and zest. Offers radiant aromas of honey, cream and pear. Full-bodied and lightly off-dry, with a superb concentration of spicy apple and melon flavors and a long, long finish. A giant wine. Try now to 1994. ($NA) (2/15/92) **93**
Riesling Alsace Weibelsberg 1989 ($NA) (11/15/90) **84**
Riesling Alsace Weibelsberg 1988 $23 (10/15/89) **84**
Riesling Alsace Weibelsberg Sélection de Grains Nobles 1988 ($NA) (10/15/89) **95**

KUENTZ-BAS
Riesling Alsace 1989 ($NA) (11/15/90) **69**
Riesling Alsace Cuvée Tradition 1988 ($NA) (10/15/89) **84**
Riesling Alsace Eichberg 1990: Dense and thick, teeming with fruit. Has modest honey and tropical fruit aromas, oily, rich lemon and tropical fruit flavors and a long finish. Full-bodied and almost off-dry. Try now to 1994. $25 (2/15/92) **87**
Riesling Alsace Pfersigberg 1989 ($NA) (11/15/90) **83**
Riesling Alsace Pfersigberg Vendange Tardive 1990: Delicious, with lovely aromas of almond, spice and apple. Medium-bodied and sweet, with vanilla, apricot and spice flavors and a long, silky finish. Drink now or hold. $45 (2/15/92) (BT) **85+**
Riesling Alsace Réserve Personnelle 1989 ($NA) (11/15/90) **79**
Riesling Alsace Réserve Personnelle 1988 ($NA) (10/15/89) **84**
Riesling Alsace Réserve Personnelle (Cask 1) 1990: Very classy, elegant and understated. Has beautiful cream and peach aromas, a balance of honey, apple and spice flavors and a very spicy finish. Medium-bodied and dry. A seamless wine that needs some time. Try now to 1994. $20 (2/15/92) **88**
Riesling Alsace Réserve Personnelle (Cask 2) 1990: Somewhat simple, but a pleasant, sweeter style of Riesling. Drink as an aperitif. Very rich and ripe, verging on overripe. Full-bodied and off-dry, with ripe tropical fruit flavors and a long, flavorful finish. Drink now. $20 (2/15/92) **83**

GUSTAVE LORENTZ
Riesling Alsace 1990: A pretty, medium-strength wine that's easy and accessible. Medium-bodied and dry, with lovely pineapple and coconut aromas, light citrus flavors and a clean finish. Try now to 1993. $11 (2/15/92) **84**
Riesling Alsace 1989 $15 (11/15/90) **74**
Riesling Alsace 1988 $15 (10/15/89) **85**
Riesling Alsace Altenberg 1990: Full-bodied and almost off-dry, with enticing almond, tropical fruit and cream flavors, banana, cream and spice aromas, a round mouth-feel and a slightly tart finish. Drink on release or hold. $35 (2/15/92) **88**
Riesling Alsace Altenberg 1989 ($NA) (11/15/90) **88**
Riesling Alsace Altenberg de Bergheim 1988 ($NA) (10/15/89) **84**
Riesling Alsace Réserve 1990: Clean, crisp and fresh, exploding with lime and lemon characteristics. Has beautiful lime and lemon tart aromas. Medium-bodied and dry, with elegant lime and honey flavors and a light finish. Drink now or hold. $13 (2/15/92) **89**
Riesling Alsace Réserve 1989 ($NA) (11/15/90) **75**
Riesling Alsace Réserve 1986: Dry, flavorful and assertive, with floral, almost kerosenelike aromas that are nevertheless attractive and not unusual for Riesling. Has crisp acidity. $9.50 (7/31/89) **79**
Riesling Alsace Vendange Tardive 1990: A wine with excellent weight and fine acidity. Medium-bodied and off-dry, with lemon, lime and spice aromas and flavors and a crisp finish. Better in 1993 to '96. $59 (2/15/92) (BT) **90+**
Riesling Alsace du Domaine 1990: Fat and concentrated, with an earthy lemon character, but lacks class. Light gold in color. Full-bodied and rich, with almond and wet hay aromas, earthy lemon flavors and a short finish. Drink now. $15 (2/15/92) **82**

MADER
Riesling Alsace 1990: A beautiful and complex Riesling, with plenty of subtlety. Medium-bodied, with fig, cream and apple aromas, whipped cream and apple flavors and a rich finish. Try now to 1993. $12 (2/15/92) **90**
Riesling Alsace Rosacker 1990: Offers great depth and complexity. Has enticing coconut, honey, apple and spice aromas. Medium-bodied and dry, with super-ripe apple and coconut flavors and an intensely rich finish. Better in 1994. $22 (2/15/92) **94**
Riesling Alsace Vendange Tardive 1990: Another powerful, racy wine, with fresh grapefruit and citrus aromas. Full-bodied and lightly sweet, with concentrated lemon and grapefruit flavors and a long, spicy finish. Better in 1993 to '96. $48 (2/15/92) (BT) **90+**

ALBERT MANN
Riesling Alsace Grand Cru Schlossberg 1990: A live wire, with super-fresh fruit flavors; like freshly

crushed grapes macerated in lime juice. Medium-bodied, with rich lemon, spice and grapefruit flavors and super-fresh acidity. Better in 1993 or '94. $16 (2/15/92) **90**
Riesling Alsace Hardt 1990: Voluptuous yet elegant, with plenty of fruit. Medium-bodied and dry, with fresh apricot and almond aromas, honey and lemon flavors and a silky finish. Drink on release or hold. $12 (2/15/92) **90**
Riesling Alsace Pfleck Vendange Tardive 1990: As elegant as an acrobat, with classy lemon, honey and cream aromas and tons of lemon and pear flavors. Delicious now but will age. Full-bodied and medium sweet, with great power of acidity and fruit. Goes on and on. Better in 1994 to '97. (NR) (2/15/92) (BT) **90+**

MURE
Riesling Alsace Clos St.-Landelin Vorbourg 1990: More mature in style, with anise, earth and smoke aromas and flavors. Big and round; serve with food. Drink on release. ($NA) (2/15/92) **85**
Riesling Alsace Clos St.-Landelin Vorbourg 1989 ($NA) (11/15/90) **87**
Riesling Alsace Clos St.-Landelin Vorbourg Sélection de Grains Nobles 1990: Not as sweet as some wines in this category, but has delicate apple, lemon and white pepper aromas and flavors. More like a vendange tardive. Better in 1994 to '97. $67 (2/15/92) (BT) **85+**
Riesling Alsace Clos St.-Landelin Vorbourg Sélection de Grains Nobles 1989: Smooth and ripe, with rich peach, pear and honey aromas and flavors. Not too sugary or sweet, but definitely balanced for after-dinner sipping. Best after 1994 or '95. 120 cases made. $69 (9/15/91) **87**
Riesling Alsace Clos St.-Landelin Vorbourg Vendange Tardive 1989: A big, focused wine, with more floral, tobacco and sappy flavors than fruit; hints at green apple. Tart and resiny. Drinkable now, but may be better in 1993. 1,400 cases made. $37 (9/15/91) **80**
Riesling Alsace Grand Cru Clos St.-Landelin Vorbourg Vendange Tardive 1990: Has intensely rich cream and almond aromas, vanilla flavors and a round, thick, fat structure. Drink in 1993 or '94. (NR) (2/15/92) (BT) **85+**

DOMAINE OSTERTAG
Riesling Alsace 1988 ($NA) (10/15/89) **89**
Riesling Alsace en Barriques Heissenberg 1989: Supple, flavorful and generous, with more of the mineral, floral side of Riesling to the flavor profile than fruit, finishing with a solid mineral character. Best after 1993. $24 (7/31/91) **85**
Riesling Alsace Fronholz 1989: Crisp and zingy in structure, with tempting apple, floral and pine flavors that are concentrated and long lasting on the finish. Very classy. Drinkable now, but should age nicely through 1995. $24 (7/31/91) **87**
Riesling Alsace Fronholz Elevée en Barrique Vendange Tardive 1990: An elegant, racy wine built for aging. Offers honey, lemon and hints of spice on the nose. Medium-bodied and off-dry, with rich lemon and spice flavors, a long lemon finish and excellent acidity. Try in 1993 to '95. (NR) (2/15/92) (BT) **85+**
Riesling Alsace Fronholz Sélection de Grains Nobles 1990: Has an intense character of dried apricots, figs and honey. As sweet as syrup and just as concentrated. Drink in 1994 to '96. (NR) (2/15/92) (BT) **90+**
Riesling Alsace Heissenberg Elevée en Barriques Vendange Tardive 1990: Elegant and silky, with lemon, honey and spice aromas. Medium-bodied and sweet, with lemon meringue and pie crust flavors and a lovely, silky finish. Try in 1994. $50 (2/15/92) (BT) **85+**
Riesling Alsace Muenchberg 1989: Not sweet, but rich in fruit intensity, packed with peach, apricot and pineapple flavors. Turns a bit dry and austere on the finish, but that should improve with time in the cellar. Drinkable now, but should be better after 1993. $33 (7/31/91) **88**
Riesling Alsace Muenchberg 1988 ($NA) (10/15/89) **81**
Riesling Alsace Muenchberg Sélection de Grains Nobles 1990: Super-sweet, with creamy lime and lemon flavors and a nectarlike finish. Better in 1994 to '96. (NR) (2/15/92) (BT) **90+**
Riesling Alsace Muenchberg Vendange Tardive 1990: Has excellent concentration of honeydew melon and honey characteristics. Intense lemon, honey and lanolin aromas. Full-bodied and sweet, with honey, clove and spice flavors and a long, sweet honeydew melon finish. Better in 1993 to '95. $50 (2/15/92) (BT) **90+**
Riesling Alsace Vignoble d'Epfig 1990: Big and oily. Could use a little more finesse. Shows intense almond, spice and earth aromas, lots of oily apple and spice flavors and a long finish. Full-bodied and dry. Try now to 1993. $16 (2/15/92) **85**
Riesling Alsace Vignoble d'Epfig 1989: Full-bodied, focused and flavorful, with well-defined peach and apple aromas and flavors, floral nuances and a long finish. Has vanilla richness on the aftertaste. Drinkable now, but better after 1993. $14 (7/31/91) **87**

PREISS-HENNY
Riesling Alsace 1990: Another fairly rustic and disjointed wine, with toffee, caramel and apple aromas, green apple-skin flavors and a slightly astringent finish. Better in 1993? $11 (2/15/92) **80**
Riesling Alsace Château de Mittelwihr 1989: The piny aroma and crisp, spicy flavors of Riesling really come through. An aggressive, tart wine that's coarse now, but may benefit from cellaring until about 1993. $13 (10/31/91) **78**
Riesling Alsace Cuvée Marcel Preiss 1990: Rather subdued at first. Has light cream and honey aromas. Full-bodied and dry, with apple, cream and grass flavors and a creamy finish. Should improve with another year or two of bottle age. ($NA) (2/15/92) **85**

DOMAINES SCHLUMBERGER
Riesling Alsace 1989 ($NA) (11/15/90) **86**
Riesling Alsace 1988 ($NA) (10/15/89) **85**
Riesling Alsace Kitterlé 1989 ($NA) (11/15/90) **89**
Riesling Alsace Kitterlé 1988 $14 (10/15/89) **90**
Riesling Alsace des Prince Abbés 1990: Ripe and pretty, with apricot and fruity tart flavors and a creamy finish. Drink on release. ($NA) (2/15/92) **87**
Riesling Alsace Saering 1988 ($NA) (10/15/89) **82**

LOUIS SIPP
Riesling Alsace 1990: Shows little on the nose, but has lots of lively flavors. Medium-bodied, with lemon and lime aromas, a good concentration of lemon and lime flavors, medium acidity and a tasty finish. Try now to 1993. ($NA) (2/15/92) **87**
Riesling Alsace Kirchberg de Barr Cuvée Particulière de Nos Vigno 1990: Bowls you over with fruit. A big, fat wine, with lovely apricot and pineapple aromas, intense, spicy mineral and pepper flavors and a crisp finish. Medium-bodied and off-dry. Drink now or hold. ($NA) (2/15/92) **89**

Key to Symbols

The scores reported here are the results of blind tastings conducted by our panel of senior editors. Wines that carry the initials below are results of individual tastings.

THE WINE SPECTATOR 100-POINT SCALE *95-100*—Classic, a great wine; *90-94*—Outstanding, superior character and style; *80-89*—Good to very good, a wine with special qualities; *70-79*—Average, drinkable wine that may have minor flaws; *60-69*—Below average, drinkable but not recommended; *50-59*—Poor, undrinkable, not recommended. "+"—With a score indicates a range; used primarily with barrel tastings to indicate a preliminary score.

SPECIAL DESIGNATIONS SS—Spectator Selection, CS—Cellar Selection, BB—Best Buy, ($NA)—Price not available, (NR)—Not released.

TASTER'S INITIALS (JG)—Jim Gordon, (HS)—Harvey Steiman, (JL)—James Laube, (JS)—James Suckling, (TM)—Thomas Matthews, (TR)—Terry Robards, (PM)—Per-Henrik Mansson, (BT)—Barrel Tasting (these wines were tasted blind from barrel samples), (CA-date)—*California's Great Cabernets* by James Laube, (CH-date)—*California's Great Chardonnays* by James Laube, (VP-date)—*Vintage Port* by James Suckling.

DATE TASTED Dates in parentheses represent the issue in which the rating was published.

PIERRE SPARR
Riesling Alsace Altenbourg Cuvée Centenaire 1989 ($NA) (11/15/90) **79**
Riesling Alsace Carte d'Or 1990: Shows good fruit, but could use more elegance. The pineapple and tropical fruit aromas and flavors have a hint of earthiness. Medium-bodied and rather fat and oily. Drink now. $10 (2/15/92) **81**
Riesling Alsace Carte d'Or Réserve 1990: A racy wine that grabs your attention. Seductive and elegant, with beautiful cream, apple and peach aromas and flavors. Medium-bodied, dry and crisp despite the very rich finish; needs food. Try now to 1993. $12 (2/15/92) **90**
Riesling Alsace Schlossberg Cuvée Réserve 1989 ($NA) (11/15/90) **86**

TRIMBACH
Riesling Alsace 1990: A tight Riesling in a focused package; needs bottle age. Has lovely floral aromas, floral, spicy flavors and a light vanilla finish. Medium-bodied, with medium acidity. Try now to 1994. $14 (2/15/92) **87**
Riesling Alsace 1989 $10 (11/15/90) **86**
Riesling Alsace 1988 $7.50 (10/15/89) **86**
Riesling Alsace Clos Ste.-Hune 1986 ($NA) (5/15/89) **91**
Riesling Alsace Clos Ste.-Hune 1985 $50 (5/15/89) **90**
Riesling Alsace Clos Ste.-Hune 1983 ($NA) (5/15/89) **95**
Riesling Alsace Clos Ste.-Hune 1982 $24 (5/15/89) **85**
Riesling Alsace Clos Ste.-Hune 1981 ($NA) (5/15/89) **91**
Riesling Alsace Clos Ste.-Hune 1979 ($NA) (5/15/89) **87**
Riesling Alsace Clos Ste.-Hune 1976 ($NA) (5/15/89) **91**
Riesling Alsace Clos Ste.-Hune 1975 ($NA) (5/15/89) **95**
Riesling Alsace Clos Ste.-Hune 1973 ($NA) (5/15/89) **82**
Riesling Alsace Clos Ste.-Hune 1971 ($NA) (5/15/89) **94**
Riesling Alsace Clos Ste.-Hune 1967 ($NA) (5/15/89) **85**
Riesling Alsace Clos Ste.-Hune 1966 ($NA) (5/15/89) **94**
Riesling Alsace Clos Ste.-Hune Hors Choix Vendange Tardive 1989 ($NA) (11/15/90) **97**
Riesling Alsace Clos Ste.-Hune Vendange Tardive 1989 ($NA) (11/15/90) **96**
Riesling Alsace Cuvée Frédéric Emile 1990: Compact, with a seductive, elegant fruit structure and super-firm acidity. Another wine with the essence of Riesling. Try after 1994. ($NA) (2/15/92) **91**
Riesling Alsace Cuvée Frédéric Emile 1989 ($NA) (11/15/90) **92**
Riesling Alsace Cuvée Frédéric Emile 1988 $15 (10/15/89) **91**
Riesling Alsace Cuvée Frédéric Emile Sélection de Grains Nobles 1990: Very dry for this category; medium sweet, with a unique herbal, earthy, spicy character. A little too lean for us. May be better with time. Drink in 1994 or '95. $100 (2/15/92) (BT) **85+**
Riesling Alsace Frédéric Emile Sélection de Grains Nobles 1989 ($NA) (11/15/90) **90**
Riesling Alsace Cuvée Frédéric Emile Vendange Tardive 1990: A superb, classic vendange tardive, with racy acidity and intense lime, lemon and dried apricot flavors. Off-dry, so serve with an array of dishes. Drink in 1993 to '97. $75 (2/15/92) (BT) **95+**
Riesling Alsace Cuvée Frédéric Emile Vendange Tardive 1989 ($NA) (11/15/90) **95**
Riesling Alsace Réserve 1989 ($NA) (11/15/90) **90**

TURCKHEIM
Riesling Alsace Cuvée Réserve 1989: A good, solid Riesling that showcases the variety's fruit flavors. Crisp in balance, with floral aromas and full grapefruit and spice flavors. Should be fine with a wide range of foods. $14 (10/31/91) **84**

DOMAINE WEINBACH
Riesling Alsace Clos des Capucins Cuvée Ste.-Catherine 1989 $43 (11/15/90) **80**
Riesling Alsace Clos des Capucins Cuvée Théo 1989 $31 (11/15/90) **88**
Riesling Alsace Clos des Capucins Réserve Personnelle 1989: Lean and crisp, this firmly focused white wine offers modest lemon and floral aromas and flavors, making it a good match for fish. 175 cases made. $23 (7/31/91) **81**
Riesling Alsace Clos des Capucins Réserve Personnelle 1988: The earthy, piny aromas and flavors turn this lean, light-textured, dry white wine in a non-fruity direction, which won't please everyone. $18 (7/31/91) **78**
Riesling Alsace Clos des Capucins Schlossberg 1989 $31 (11/15/90) **84**
Riesling Alsace Clos des Capucins Sélection de Grains Nobles 1990: Shows great polish, with a sweet but wonderful balance of acidity and rich marzipan, apple and spice flavors. Better in 1995 to '98. (NR) (2/15/92) (BT) **95+**
Riesling Alsace Clos des Capucins Sélection de Grains Nobles 1989 ($NA) (11/15/90) **96**
Riesling Alsace Cuvée Ste.-Catherine 1988 $30 (10/15/89) **87**
Riesling Alsace Cuvée Ste.-Catherine (Cask 1) 1990: So rich it verges on vendange tardive. A crowd pleaser, built in a seductive style. Offers wet hay, vanilla and lemon aromas, lemon, honey and pie crust flavors and a very fruity finish. Medium-bodied and off-dry. Drink on release. $25 (2/15/92) **88**
Riesling Alsace Cuvée Ste.-Catherine (Cask 2) 1990: Good as an aperitif or with a rich cream sauce. Has intense spice, apple and almond aromas. Medium-bodied and off- dry, with honey, spice and almond flavors and a mile-long finish. Try now to 1994. $25 (2/15/92) **91**
Riesling Alsace Cuvée Ste.-Catherine (Cask 3) 1990: Delicious to sip on its own. Shows lots of fruit flavors, with wet hay, earth and hazelnut aromas, ripe fruit, hazelnut and earth flavors and a flavorful finish. Medium-bodied and dry. Drink now or hold. $25 (2/15/92) **87**
Riesling Alsace Cuvée Ste.-Catherine (Cask 17) 1990: A lovely aperitif style of Riesling, with aromas of petrol, pine and lemon. Medium-bodied and off-dry, with ripe lemon and spice flavors and a flavorful finish. Try now to 1993. $25 (2/15/92) **88**
Riesling Alsace Cuvée Théo 1990: A delicate style, with all the fruit you could want. Offers apple, cream and tropical fruit aromas, loads of creamy, spicy almond and apple flavors and a long finish. Medium-bodied and almost off-dry. Try now to 1993. $18 (2/15/92) **88**
Riesling Alsace Cuvée Théo 1988 ($NA) (10/15/89) **80**
Riesling Alsace Schlossberg 1990: A distinctive Riesling, with a spicy, earthy character. Medium-bodied and off- dry, with almond, spice and ripe tropical fruit aromas, spice, anise and earth flavors and a silky finish. Should gain complexity with age. Try now to 1993. $18 (2/15/92) **90**
Riesling Alsace Vendange Tardive 1990: A rich, sweet vendange tardive, with spice, almond and lemon aromas, a velvety mouth-feel and rich botrytis spice, honey and apple flavors. Full-bodied and lightly sweet. Better in 1994 to '97. $57 (2/15/92) (BT) **90+**

ALSACE WILLM
Riesling Alsace 1990: Clean, crisp and classy. Has peach and dried fruit aromas, intense, medium-bodied peach and cream flavors and high acidity on the finish. Better in 1993 or '94. $11 (2/15/92) **87**
Riesling Alsace 1989 $12.50 (11/15/90) **85**
Riesling Alsace Cuvée Emile Willm 1990: Fruity and juicy, with fresh honey and cream aromas and rich, wonderful flavors of intense dried apricot and cream. Medium-bodied and dry, with lots of pear character on the finish. Try now to 1993. $23 (2/15/92) **90**
Riesling Alsace Cuvée Emile Willm 1989 ($NA) (11/15/90) **80**
Riesling Alsace Kirchberg de Barr 1990: Has a lovely, elegant fruit structure; sings in the glass. Medium-bodied and dry, with beautiful aromas of honeydew melon and cream, intense lemon and melon flavors and a crisp finish. Try now to 1993. $23 (2/15/92) **89**
Riesling Alsace Kirchberg de Barr 1989 ($NA) (11/15/90) **82**

WOLFBERGER
Riesling Alsace 1987: Smooth, soft Riesling with a strong perfumey aroma and simple fruit flavors. $8 (7/31/89) **71**

DOMAINE ZIND-HUMBRECHT
Riesling Alsace 1988 ($NA) (10/15/89) **87**
Riesling Alsace Brand 1990: An electrifying wine, with super-charged flavors. Smooth and superb, with great acidity and ripe fruit flavors. Drinkable now, but can age. $35 (2/15/92) **93**

Riesling Alsace Brand Vendange Tardive 1990: Shows superb concentration, with masses of lemon and honey flavors. Sweet and thick, like syrup. Wonderful now, but better in 1994 to '97. $55 (2/15/92) (BT) **90+**
Riesling Alsace Brand Vendange Tardive 1989 ($NA) (11/15/90) **87**
Riesling Alsace Clos St.-Urbain Rangen 1989 $45 (11/15/90) **86**
Riesling Alsace Clos Windsbuhl Vendange Tardive 1990: Very well focused, with great elegance. Offers lovely aromas and flavors of hazelnut, peach and white pepper and a medium-sweet finish. Better in 1995 or '96. $75 (2/15/92) (BT) **90+**
Riesling Alsace Herrenweg 1990: Delicious and refreshing, with creamy lemon and lime flavors and a silky mouth-feel. Delicious now, but better in 1993. $25 (2/15/92) **90**
Riesling Alsace Herrenweg 1989 $24 (11/15/90) **89**
Riesling Alsace Herrenweg Vendange Tardive 1990: A magical wine. Tastes like freshly crushed grapes. Off-dry, with super-intense lime, grape, apple and many other flavors and a great, firm structure. Try in 1994 to '97. $40 (2/15/92) (BT) **95+**
Riesling Alsace Rangen 1988 ($NA) (10/15/89) **86**
Riesling Alsace Turckheim 1990: Has amazingly ripe fruit flavor, but still maintains plenty of lively acidity. Long and refreshing. Try after 1994. $20 (2/15/92) **90**
Riesling Alsace Wintzenheim 1989: Flavorful and elegant, with complex spice and honey notes accenting the basic fruit flavor in a subtle but satisfying way. Concentrated and smooth in texture. A step up from the ordinary. $21 (10/31/91) **87**

Tokay Pinot Gris

J.B. ADAM
Tokay Pinot Gris Alsace Cuvée Jean-Baptiste 1990: A mouthful of fruit. Full-bodied and slightly off-dry, with smoky burnt almond and spice aromas, tons of intense fruit flavors and crisp acidity. Better in 1993 to '95. $16 (2/15/92) **87**
Tokay Pinot Gris Alsace Réserve 1990: Sip this one on its own. Has spicy almond and smoke aromas and tastes like a fruit cocktail with pineapple flavors. Medium-bodied and off-dry, with a light finish. Drink now. $13 (2/15/92) **83**
Tokay Pinot Gris Alsace Sélection de Grains Nobles 1990: Shows interesting aromas and flavors of dried apricot and oranges, but is slightly fat on the finish. Nonetheless, it's a very good dessert wine. Try after 1993. (NR) (2/15/92) (BT) **85+**
Tokay Pinot Gris Alsace Vendange Tardive 1990: Has a juicy fruit structure, with plenty of earthy flavors and a slightly bitter finish. Lightly sweet, with very fresh honey, spice, almond and apple aromas, melon and apple flavors and a short finish. Drink now. $40 (2/15/92) (BT) **85+**

DOMAINE LUCIEN ALBRECHT
Tokay Pinot Gris Alsace Pfingstberg 1990: A pleasant aperitif-style Tokay Pinot Gris, with fresh grapefruit and almond aromas. Medium-bodied and off-dry, with slightly spicy honey and almond flavors and a light, crisp finish. Drink now. (NR) (2/15/92) **84**
Tokay Pinot Gris Alsace Pfingstberg 1989 ($NA) (11/15/90) **80**
Tokay Pinot Gris Alsace Réserve du Domaine 1989 ($NA) (11/15/90) **80**
Tokay Pinot Gris Alsace Sélection de Grains Nobles 1990: Somewhat overdone, with an impressively ripe, burnt fruit and apple character, but a little tiring on the palate. Drink on release or age. (NR) (2/15/92) (BT) **80+**
Tokay Pinot Gris Alsace Vendange Tardive 1990: A viscous monster of a wine in a round, oily style. Full-bodied, lightly sweet and massive, with fig, honey, spice and nectarine aromas, dense smoke, tobacco and fruit flavors and a rich finish. Better in 1993 or '94. (NR) (2/15/92) (BT) **90+**
Tokay Pinot Gris Alsace Vendange Tardive 1989 ($NA) (11/15/90) **88**

LEON BEYER
Tokay Pinot Gris Alsace Cuvée Particulière 1988 $12 (10/15/89) **78**
Tokay Pinot Gris Alsace Réserve 1990: A full-blown Tokay Pinot Gris that needs food. Full-bodied and dry, with ripe fruit and smoky almond aromas, extremely ripe tropical fruit and nutty almond flavors and a long finish. Shows lots of alcohol. Drink now. (NR) (2/15/92) **88**
Tokay Pinot Gris Alsace Réserve 1989 ($NA) (11/15/90) **84**
Tokay Pinot Gris Alsace Sélection de Grains Nobles 1989 ($NA) (11/15/90) **93**
Tokay Pinot Gris Alsace Vendange Tardive 1990: A very distinctive wine with smoky pineapple and cigar aromas, medium-bodied and lightly sweet, with very smoky earth and fruit flavors and a long finish. Drink now or hold. (NR) (2/15/92) (BT) **85+**
Tokay Pinot Gris Alsace Vendange Tardive 1989 ($NA) (11/15/90) **77**

DOMAINE PAUL BLANCK
Tokay Pinot Gris Alsace 1990: An impressive dry wine for the vintage. Very smoky, with plenty of almond and fruit character on the nose and palate. Medium-bodied and bone dry, with fresh apple and smoke flavors and a crisp finish. Better in 1993 to '95. (NR) (2/15/92) **87**
Tokay Pinot Gris Alsace Altenberg 1990: More like a vendange tardive wine. A boring, sweet Tokay Pinot Gris, with almond and light pineapple aromas. Medium-bodied and lightly sweet, with almond and pineapple flavors and a sweet finish. Drink now. (NR) (2/15/92) **79**
Tokay Pinot Gris Alsace Furstentum 1990: A little off-dry, but nicely balanced to go with food. Has coconut, smoke and spice aromas, tropical fruit and coconut flavors and a long finish. Medium-bodied and slightly off-dry. Better in 1993 or '94. (NR) (2/15/92) **85**
Tokay Pinot Gris Alsace Graffreben 1990: A very simple, fruity Tokay Pinot Gris. Medium-bodied, with high, slightly green acidity and rich banana and light tropical fruit aromas and flavors. Drink now. (NR) (2/15/92) **83**
Tokay Pinot Gris Alsace Patergarten 1990: Well balanced, fresh and youthful, with fresh cream, vanilla and apple aromas. Medium-bodied and dry, with apple and tropical fruit flavors and a very creamy mouth-feel on the finish. Drink now or hold. (NR) (2/15/92) **87**

BOTT FRERES
Tokay Pinot Gris Alsace Réserve Personnelle 1990: A beauty, with a lovely balance of fresh acidity and fruit. Medium-bodied and dry, with cream, almond and fruit aromas, whipped cream and pear flavors and a touch of smokiness on the finish. Drink now. $18 (2/15/92) **89**
Tokay Pinot Gris Alsace Vendange Tardive 1990: Another blockbuster vendange tardive, showing very ripe fruit aromas with hints of almond and smoke. Medium-bodied and medium sweet, with smoky pineapple and honey flavors and a long, smoky caramel finish. Better in 1993 or '94. $38 (2/15/92) (BT) **85+**

DOMAINE MARCEL DEISS
Tokay Pinot Gris Alsace Bergheim 1990: Super-concentrated, with chewy mango, banana, almond and smoke flavors that last for minutes on the finish. Drink or hold. $23 (2/15/92) **90**

DOPFF AU MOULIN
Tokay Pinot Gris Alsace 1988 ($NA) (10/15/89) **86**
Tokay Pinot Gris Alsace Sélection de Grains Nobles 1989 ($NA) (11/15/90) **87**
Tokay Pinot Gris Alsace Sélection de Grains Nobles 1988 ($NA) (10/15/89) **87**

DOPFF & IRION
Tokay Pinot Gris Alsace La Cuvée René Dopff 1990: A standout in this vintage, with spice, smoke, almond and apple aromas and flavors. Full-bodied and dry, with excellent acidity a long, racy finish. Better in 1993 to '95. (NR) (2/15/92) **91**
Tokay Pinot Gris Alsace La Cuvée René Dopff 1989 ($NA) (11/15/90) **85**
Tokay Pinot Gris Alsace La Cuvée René Dopff 1988 $10 (10/15/89) **79**
Tokay Pinot Gris Alsace Les Maquisards 1990: Shows lovely fruit, with powerful tropical fruit and green apple character and a hint of smoke. Medium-bodied and dry, with spicy apple and nut flavors and a crisp, clean finish. Better in 1993 or '94. (NR) (2/15/92) **86**
Tokay Pinot Gris Alsace Les Maquisards 1989 ($NA) (11/15/90) **87**

Tokay Pinot Gris Alsace Sporen 1990: Super-clean and steely, with vivid fruit flavors. Medium-bodied and dry, with moderate melon and cream aromas, melon and apple flavors and a crisp finish. Drink now or hold. (NR) (2/15/92) **86**
Tokay Pinot Gris Alsace Vendange Tardive 1990: A delicious, true dessert-style vendange tardive. Has lovely honey, spice and apricot aromas, delicious lime and spice flavors and a fresh finish. Medium-bodied and sweet. Drink now or hold. (NR) (2/15/92) (BT) **85+**

HUGEL
Tokay Pinot Gris Alsace Cuvée Tradition 1990: A big Tokay Pinot Gris, with a creamy texture and firm acidity. Has dried fruit and melon aromas. Full-bodied and dry, with a powerful concentration of fruit flavor and firm acidity. Better in 1993 to '95. (NR) (2/15/92) **88**
Tokay Pinot Gris Alsace Jubilée 1990: An exotic wine, with the power of a top white Burgundy. Concentrated aromas of tangerine and coconut; full-bodied and dry, with super-rich fruit flavors and a long, balanced finish of acidity. Very harmonious. Better in 1993 to '95. (NR) (2/15/92) **92**
Tokay Pinot Gris Alsace Sélection de Grains Nobles 1990: Elegant and exotic, with almond, spice, floral and tropical fruit aromas and flavors and lively acidity. Built for aging. Drink after 1995. (NR) (2/15/92) (BT) **90+**
Tokay Pinot Gris Alsace Sélection de Grains Nobles 1989 ($NA) (11/15/90) **94**
Tokay Pinot Gris Alsace Tradition 1988 ($NA) (10/15/89) **86**
Tokay Pinot Gris Alsace Vendange Tardive 1990: Like a slow-burning fuse, ready to explode with fruit. Offers focused, super-clean mango, pear and lemon aromas. Medium-bodied and medium sweet, with a compact fruit structure, super-ripe lemon and tropical fruit flavors and a long finish. Better in 1994 to '96. (NR) (2/15/92) (BT) **90+**
Tokay Pinot Gris Alsace Vendange Tardive 1989 ($NA) (11/15/90) **90**

JOSMEYER
Tokay Pinot Gris Alsace 1990: Has excellent, crisp acidity. Refreshing, with fresh grapefruit and apple aromas, grapefruit and peach flavors and a crisp finish. Medium-bodied and dry. Drinkable now, but better in 1993 or '94. $18 (2/15/92) **86**
Tokay Pinot Gris Alsace 1989 ($NA) (11/15/90) **86**
Tokay Pinot Gris Alsace Cuvée de Centennaire 1990: Excellent, with smoky almond and bark aromas. Medium-bodied and dry, with almond, spice and tropical fruit flavors and a long, powerful finish. Better in 1993 or '94. $30 (2/15/92) **91**
Tokay Pinot Gris Alsace Hengst Sélection de Grains Nobles 1989 ($NA) (11/15/90) **86**
Tokay Pinot Gris Alsace Vendange Tardive 1990: A real bombshell; exploding with fruit, yet it retains great elegance. Medium-bodied and lightly sweet, with beautiful, focused melon and honey aromas, intense honey, smoke, almond and melon flavors and a mile-long finish. Better in 1994 to '96. (NR) (2/15/92) (BT) **90+**

KIENTZHEIM-KAYSERBERG
Tokay Pinot Gris Alsace 1990: Elegant and ripe, with smoky, spicy fruit aromas and flavors. Medium-bodied and lightly off-dry, with ripe peach and coconut flavors and a fresh finish. Drink now or hold. (NR) (2/15/92) **85**

MARC KREYDENWEISS
Tokay Pinot Gris Alsace 1988 $23 (10/15/89) **86**
Tokay Pinot Gris Alsace Grand Cru Moenchberg 1990: Well made and enticing for sipping on its own. Offers ripe pineapple, coconut and fruit aromas, rich banana and pineapple flavors, fresh acidity and a long finish. Medium-bodied and off-dry. Drink now. (NR) (2/15/92) **87**
Tokay Pinot Gris Alsace Grand Cru Moenchberg Sélection de Grains Nobles 1990: Incredibly ripe; like drinking crème brûlée. Has tons of butterscotch, caramel and impressive sweet flavors. Better after 1995. (NR) (2/15/92) (BT) **90+**
Tokay Pinot Gris Alsace Moenchberg Sélection de Grains Nobles 1989 ($NA) (11/15/90) **90**
Tokay Pinot Gris Alsace Vendange Tardive Grand Cru Moenchberg 1989 ($NA) (11/15/90) **88**

KUENTZ-BAS
Tokay Pinot Gris Alsace Cuvée Jeremy Sélection de Grains Nobles 1989 ($NA) (11/15/90) **90**
Tokay Pinot Gris Alsace Cuvée Tradition 1989 ($NA) (11/15/90) **86**
Tokay Pinot Gris Alsace Cuvée Tradition 1988 ($NA) (10/15/89) **81**
Tokay Pinot Gris Alsace Pfersigberg Vendange Tardive 1990: Like drinking freshly crushed grapes. Very harmonious, with ripe apricot, pineapple and spice aromas, lively acidity and extremely well-focused flavors of lime, honey and fruit. Medium-bodied and lightly sweet. Better in 1993 to '96. $60 (2/15/92) (BT) **90+**
Tokay Pinot Gris Alsace Réserve Personnelle 1990: Offers exotic fruit character in a slightly off-dry package. Medium-bodied, with apple, banana and spice aromas, apple and banana flavors and a smoky, buttery finish. Drink now or in 1993. $22 (2/15/92) **84**
Tokay Pinot Gris Alsace Réserve Personnelle 1989 ($NA) (11/15/90) **81**
Tokay Pinot Gris Alsace Réserve Personnelle 1988 ($NA) (10/15/89) **86**
Tokay Pinot Gris Alsace Vendange Tardive 1990: A youthful wine, with exceedingly fresh apple, melon and cream aromas and ripe pineapple and cream flavors. Medium-bodied and sweet, with excellent acidity and a crisp finish. Drink now or hold. $45 (2/15/92) (BT) **85+**

GUSTAVE LORENTZ
Tokay Pinot Gris Alsace 1989 $15 (11/15/90) **82**
Tokay Pinot Gris Alsace 1988 $14 (10/15/89) **87**
Tokay Pinot Gris Alsace Altenberg 1990: A surprisingly sweet wine that lacks definition. Medium-bodied and sweet, with wet earth, grass and fruit aromas, wet hay and tangerine flavors and a cloying finish. Drink now. $39 (2/15/92) **79**
Tokay Pinot Gris Alsace Altenberg de Bergheim 1988 ($NA) (10/15/89) **83**
Tokay Pinot Gris Alsace Réserve 1989 ($NA) (11/15/90) **82**
Tokay Pinot Gris Alsace Sélection de Grains Nobles 1989 ($NA) (11/15/90) **86**
Tokay Pinot Gris Alsace Vendange Tardive 1990: Has very grapey aromas, with hints of grapefruit and smoke. Full-bodied and sweet, with fantastic grapefruit and smoke flavors. The finish seems to go on forever, and keeps evolving into smoky cedar and tobacco flavors. Better in 1994 to '98. $59 (2/15/92) (BT) **90+**

MADER
Tokay Pinot Gris Alsace 1990: Super-clean, with concentrated, extremely fresh fruit flavors. Medium-bodied and off-dry, with apple and cream aromas, intense cream and tropical fruit flavors and a refreshing finish. Better in 1993 or '94. $14 (2/15/92) **85**
Tokay Pinot Gris Alsace Vendange Tardive 1990: Firm and focused, with very ripe fruit and smoke aromas. Full-bodied and off-dry, with thick, powerful peach, apricot and spice flavors and a long, flavorful finish. Better in 1993 to '96. $48 (2/15/92) (BT) **85+**

ALBERT MANN
Tokay Pinot Gris Alsace 1990: Has lots of tropical fruit: banana and coconut aromas, banana and dried coconut flavors and a crisp finish. Medium-bodied and off-dry. Drink now. $11 (2/15/92) **84**
Tokay Pinot Gris Alsace Grand Cru Hengst Vendange Tardive 1990: Ripe and rich, but remains elegant, with lovely, creamy mango and melon aromas. Medium-bodied and off-dry, with lemon and tropical fruit flavors and a fresh honey finish. Drink in 1993 or '94. (NR) (2/15/92) (BT) **85+**
Tokay Pinot Gris Alsace Sélection de Grains Nobles 1990: Perfectly balanced, with lots of spice and ripe fruit flavors. Firm and delicious. Better in 1994 to '96. (NR) (2/15/92) (BT) **90+**
Tokay Pinot Gris Alsace Vieilles Vignes 1990: A very delicate wine, with beautiful, exotic aromas of orchids. Medium-bodied and dry, with lovely floral flavors and a fresh, delicate, slightly chalky finish. Drink now. $15 (2/15/92) **86**

MURE
Tokay Pinot Gris Alsace Clos St.-Landelin Vorbourg 1990: Thick and rich, with a balance of

acidity and supercharged blanched almond, apple and pear flavors. Rich and wonderful. Better after 1993. $57 (2/15/92) **88**
Tokay Pinot Gris Alsace Clos St.-Landelin Vorbourg 1989 ($NA) (11/15/90) **82**
Tokay Pinot Gris Alsace Clos St.-Landelin Vorbourg Sélection de Grains Nobles 1990: An impressive dessert wine, with alluring tangerine, orange and violet aromas and flavors. A real charmer. Better in 1995. (NR) (2/15/92) (BT) **90+**
Tokay Pinot Gris Alsace Clos St.-Landelin Vorbourg Sélection de Grains Nobles 1989: Simple and sweet, with pleasant peach and honey aromas and flavors that linger into the ripe finish. Drinkable now, but best after 1994 or '95. 105 cases made. $60 (9/15/91) **85**
Tokay Pinot Gris Alsace Clos St.-Landelin Vorbourg Vendange Tardive 1989: Sweet, with a sugary, cakelike flavor that tends to cover whatever fruit there might be. Hints at peach, with a touch of spice. Drinkable now. 280 cases made. $33 (9/15/91) **81**

DOMAINE OSTERTAG
Tokay Pinot Gris Alsace Barriques 1990: Incredibly impressive, with an array of aromas and flavors. This sensual wine has tropical fruit, vanilla and cream aromas, freshly crushed grape flavors and a crisp finish. Medium-bodied and dry, with lovely richness and excellent aging potential. Better in 1993 to '95. $26 (2/15/92) **91**
Tokay Pinot Gris Alsace Muenchberg Vendange Tardive 1990: Tastes like a light Sauternes, with butter, pine, almond and cream aromas and vanilla, honey and apple flavors. Medium-bodied and lightly sweet, with a light, fresh finish. Better in 1994 to '96. $50 (2/15/92) (BT) **85+**
Tokay Pinot Gris Alsace Muenchberg 1988 $28 (10/15/89) **84**

DOMAINES SCHLUMBERGER
Tokay Pinot Gris Alsace 1988 ($NA) (10/15/89) **81**
Tokay Pinot Gris Alsace Vendange Tardive 1989 ($NA) (11/15/90) **78**

LOUIS SIPP
Tokay Pinot Gris Alsace Barrique 1990: Seems woody, but has interesting vanilla, almond and pine aromas and intense new wood flavors. Medium-bodied and dry, with a light, woody, smoky finish. Try in 1993 or '94. (NR) (2/15/92) **85**
Tokay Pinot Gris Alsace Vendange Tardive 1990: Has amazing concentration of fruit, but it's a little heavy-handed. Perhaps better in a few years. Very thick, fat and very ripe. Gold in color, with super-ripe smoke, cedar and botrytis spice aromas. Full-bodied and lightly sweet, with smoky tobacco and apricot flavors and a dense finish. Drink now or hold. (NR) (2/15/92) (BT) **85+**

PIERRE SPARR
Tokay Pinot Gris Alsace Carte d'Or 1990: This juicy, delicious dry white wine has wonderful lemon, apple and cream aromas and cream, apple and grapefruit flavors. Medium- bodied and dry, with firm acidity and a long litchi finish. Drinkable now, but better in 1993 or '94. $9.50 (2/15/92) **85**
Tokay Pinot Gris Alsace Carte d'Or 1989 ($NA) (11/15/90) **88**
Tokay Pinot Gris Alsace Cuvée Centenaire Vendange Tardive 1989 ($NA) (11/15/90) **78**
Tokay Pinot Gris Alsace Cuvée Réserve 1990: An excellent Tokay Pinot Gris; like a great white Burgundy. Rich, yet delicate and refined. Full-bodied and dry, with vanilla ice cream and fruit aromas. Overflowing with tropical fruit, vanilla, almond and cream flavors and a smoky finish that goes on and on. Better in 1993 to '96. $11 (2/15/92) **92**
Tokay Pinot Gris Alsace Prestige Tête de Cuvée 1989 ($NA) (11/15/90) **89**

TRIMBACH
Tokay Pinot Gris Alsace 1988 $9 (10/15/89) **83**
Tokay Pinot Gris Alsace Hors Choix Sélection de Grains Nobles 1989 ($NA) (11/15/90) **99**
Tokay Pinot Gris Alsace Réserve 1990: A striking wine, with fresh peach and fruit aromas. Medium-bodied and steely, with fresh peach flavors and a very youthful finish. Better in 1993 or '94. $16 (2/15/92) **88**
Tokay Pinot Gris Alsace Réserve Sélection de Grains Nobles 1989 ($NA) (11/15/90) **90**
Tokay Pinot Gris Alsace Réserve Tradition 1989 ($NA) (11/15/90) **85**
Tokay Pinot Gris Alsace Réserve Tradition 1988 ($NA) (10/15/89) **86**
Tokay Pinot Gris Alsace Sélection de Grains Nobles 1990: Offers plenty of finesse and class, with sweet, intense orange peel, mango and other tropical fruit flavors and a supercharged finish. Better after 1994. (NR) (2/15/92) (BT) **90+**
Tokay Pinot Gris Alsace Vendange Tardive 1990: Sings like Pavarotti. Vibrant and refreshing, with elegant fresh grape, melon and cream aromas. Medium-bodied and sweet, with a creamy texture of pineapple and ripe pear flavors and a long, crisp finish. Better in 1993 to '96. (NR) (2/15/92) (BT) **90+**

TURCKHEIM
Tokay Pinot Gris Alsace Cuvée Réserve 1989: A smooth, rich texture and modest fruity, nutty flavors make for a full-bodied, but not particularly flavorful wine. $15 (10/31/91) **79**

DOMAINE WEINBACH
Tokay Pinot Gris Alsace Clos des Capucins Cuvée Ste.-Catherine 1989 $43 (11/15/90) **90**
Tokay Pinot Gris Alsace Clos des Capucins Cuvée Ste.-Catherine 1988: Ripe and earthy, with generous orange, pear and caramel aromas and flavors and a smooth texture. Simple and solid on the finish. $35 (7/31/91) **79**
Tokay Pinot Gris Alsace Clos des Capucins Sélection de Grains Nobles 1990: Extremely refined and elegant, with subtle aromas and flavors of apricot, bark, almond and fruit. Better after 1994. (NR) (2/15/92) (BT) **90+**
Tokay Pinot Gris Alsace Clos des Capucins Sélection de Grains Nobles 1989 ($NA) (11/15/90) **95**
Tokay Pinot Gris Alsace Clos des Capucins Vendange Tardive 1989 ($NA) (11/15/90) **86**
Tokay Pinot Gris Alsace Cuvée Ste.-Catherine 1990: Another aperitif-style Tokay Pinot Gris. Offers tropical fruit and coconut aromas, almond and marzipan flavors and a sweet finish. A medium-bodied, sweet wine to drink now. $25 (2/15/92) **83**
Tokay Pinot Gris Alsace Vendange Tardive 1990: A little rough and disjointed. Medium-bodied and lightly sweet, with banana and coconut aromas, smoky, meaty, earthy flavors and a long, smoky finish. Better in 1993 to '96. $57 (2/15/92) (BT) **85+**

ALSACE WILLM
Tokay Pinot Gris Alsace 1990: Firm and well crafted, with orange peel, peach and apple aromas. Medium-bodied and dry, with concentrated peach and grapefruit flavors and a firm acid backbone. Better in 1993 or '94. $13 (2/15/92) **84**
Tokay Pinot Gris Alsace 1989 ($NA) (11/15/90) **87**

Key to Symbols

The scores reported here are the results of blind tastings conducted by our panel of senior editors. Wines that carry the initials below are results of individual tastings.

THE WINE SPECTATOR 100-POINT SCALE ***95-100***—Classic, a great wine; ***90-94***—Outstanding, superior character and style; ***80-89***—Good to very good, a wine with special qualities; ***70-79***—Average, drinkable wine that may have minor flaws; ***60-69***—Below average, drinkable but not recommended; ***50-59***—Poor, undrinkable, not recommended. "+"—With a score indicates a range; used primarily with barrel tastings to indicate a preliminary score.

SPECIAL DESIGNATIONS SS—Spectator Selection, CS—Cellar Selection, BB—Best Buy, ($NA)—Price not available, (NR)—Not released.

TASTER'S INITIALS (JG)—Jim Gordon, (HS)—Harvey Steiman, (JL)—James Laube, (JS)—James Suckling, (TM)—Thomas Matthews, (TR)—Terry Robards, (PM)—Per-Henrik Mansson, (BT)—Barrel Tasting (these wines were tasted blind from barrel samples), (CA-date)—*California's Great Cabernets* by James Laube, (CH-date)—*California's Great Chardonnays* by James Laube, (VP-date)—*Vintage Port* by James Suckling.

DATE TASTED Dates in parentheses represent the issue in which the rating was published.

Tokay Pinot Gris Alsace Cuvée Emile Willm 1990: A classic, well-proportioned Tokay Pinot Gris. Has tropical fruit and cream aromas, plenty of mango and grapefruit flavors and a smoky finish. Medium-bodied and dry, with a seamless fruit structure. Drink now or hold. $25 (2/15/92) **89**
Tokay Pinot Gris Alsace Cuvée Emile Willm Vendange Tardive 1990: Elegant and rather delicate, with pretty aromas of cream and melon. Medium-bodied and lightly sweet, with honey, cream and grapefruit flavors and a fresh finish. Drink now. $51 (2/15/92) (BT) **85+**
Tokay Pinot Gris Alsace Sélection de Grains Nobles 1990: A medium-bodied wine that can go with food. Has lovely almond, fruit and marzipan character on the nose and palate, with a slightly bitter finish. Better after 1994. (NR) (2/15/92) (BT) **85+**
Tokay Pinot Gris Alsace Sélection de Grains Nobles 1989 ($NA) (11/15/90) **90**

DOMAINE ZIND-HUMBRECHT
Tokay Pinot Gris Alsace 1988 ($NA) (10/15/89) **82**
Tokay Pinot Gris Alsace Clos Jebsal 1988 ($NA) (10/15/89) **90**
Tokay Pinot Gris Alsace Clos Jebsal Vendange Tardive 1990: Ripe and very sweet, with smoky, honeyed dried apricot notes. Great as dessert. Better in 1994 to '96. $70 (2/15/92) (BT) **90+**
Tokay Pinot Gris Alsace Clos St.-Urbain Rangen Sélection de Grains Nobles 1989 ($NA) (11/15/90) **85**
Tokay Pinot Gris Alsace Clos Windsbuhl Vendange Tardive 1990: Very overripe and sweet; slightly overdone. Has caramel and butterscotch flavors and lots of dried apricot character. A pure dessert wine that's more like a sélection de grains nobles. Try now to 1994. $75 (2/15/92) (BT) **85+**
Tokay Pinot Gris Alsace Clos Windsbuhl Vendange Tardive 1989 ($NA) (11/15/90) **91**
Tokay Pinot Gris Alsace Rangen de Thann Clos St.-Urbain 1990: Has an amazing concentration of fruit, but it's a little too alcoholic for us. Very ripe, with tons of raisin and tropical fruit character and a slightly off-dry finish. Drink on release. $50 (2/15/92) **87**
Tokay Pinot Gris Alsace Vieilles Vignes 1990: Like eating a crème brûlée dessert; made from overripe grapes. Has masses of smoky raisin and tropical fruit flavors. A wine for those looking for tons of ripe fruit. Drink on release. $30 (2/15/92) **90**

OTHER ALSACE

J.B. ADAM
Muscat Alsace 1990: A firm, dry Muscat, with delicate fruit and excellent balance. Offers perfumed aromas of tangerines and oranges. Medium-bodied and dry, with dried orange and floral flavors and a crisp finish. Drink now or hold. (NR) (2/15/92) **87**

LEON BEYER
Muscat Alsace Cuvée Particulière 1990: Has good fruit flavors, but it's a little odd on the finish. Medium-bodied and slightly off-dry, with orange peel and honey aromas, orange peel and earth flavors and a slightly rubbery finish. Drink now. (NR) (2/15/92) **79**
Pinot Gris Alsace 1989: Fairly generous and fruity, with melon and honey notes that linger nicely on the finish. A medium-bodied white that should be versatile with food. $16.50 (10/31/91) **82**
Pinot Gris Alsace Sélection de Grains Nobles 1983: A rare late-harvest wine with intriguing earthy aromas, concentrated almond and honeylike flavors, a silky texture and long finish. $48/375ml (7/31/89) **87**

DOMAINE PAUL BLANCK
Muscat d'Alsace Alsace 1990: Big and powerful, with earthy, grassy, light honey aromas and flavors. Dry and full-bodied, with rich fruit and a chalky finish. Drink now. (NR) (2/15/92) **86**
Pinot d'Alsace Alsace 1990: Near perfection in a Pinot Blanc. A great value. Has beautiful aromas of banana, pineapple and flowers. Medium-bodied and dry, with succulent flavors of banana, pineapple and melon and a lovely almond finish. Drink now or hold. (NR) (2/15/92) **89**

BOTT FRERES
Pinot d'Alsace Alsace Sélection 1990: Not our idea of a good Pinot Blanc. Has rather odd earthy, dusty rubber and apple aromas. Medium-bodied and off-dry, with earthy hay and ripe apple flavors and a mushroomy finish. Drink now. $13 (2/15/92) **78**
Tokay d'Alsace Alsace Cuvée Exceptionnelle 1989: The simple, slightly earthy aromas and flavors turn a bit more generous on the finish, echoing orange and rose petal notes. $13.50 (7/31/91) **80**

DOPFF & IRION
Muscat Alsace Les Amandiers 1990: An odd, green Muscat, with rather sour, green, orange peel aromas. Medium-bodied and dry, with grassy, minty flavors and a sour finish. Drink now. (NR) (2/15/92) **73**

HUGEL
Muscat Alsace Cuvée Tradition 1990: Somewhat disjointed, but shows good fruit flavors. Has almond, apple and honey aromas. Medium-bodied and dry, with almond and chalk flavors and a short finish. Drink now. (NR) (2/15/92) **80**

JOSMEYER
Muscat Alsace 1990: Perfectly balanced in a slightly off-dry style. Delicious as an aperitif. Medium-bodied, with orange blossom and fruit aromas, lovely peach, apricot and orange peel flavors and a lovely finish. Drink now. $28 (2/15/92) **89**

KUENTZ-BAS
Sylvaner Alsace Cuvée Tradition 1990: This no-nonsense, light-bodied dry white has lemon and light spice aromas and flavors and crisp acidity. Drink now. $11 (2/15/92) **81**

MADER
Muscat Alsace d'Alsace 1990: Like a garden in bloom. Beautiful aromas of flowers and cream lead to orange, floral and cream flavors and a lovely, creamy finish. Medium-bodied and dry. Drink now. $11 (2/15/92) **89**

MURE
Muscat Alsace Clos St.-Landelin Vorbourg Vendanges Tardives 1989: Lemony, floral aromas and flavors are fresh and appealing and persist into a long finish. Seems soft and generous, with well-defined Muscat character and charm. Drinkable now. 136 cases made. $29 (9/15/91) **87**

DOMAINE OSTERTAG
Muscat Alsace Fronholz 1990: An excellent Muscat to go with food. Medium-bodied and bone dry, with honey and lilac aromas, vanilla bean, floral and cantaloupe flavors and a crisp finish. Drink now. $18 (2/15/92) **87**
Pinot Gris Alsace Barriques 1989: Apple, pear and peach flavors are rounded out by a touch of spice and butter in this crisp, fruity wine. The flavors linger nicely on the finish. $24 (7/31/91) **84**
Pinot Gris Alsace Muenchberg Sélection de Grains Nobles 1990: Tastes like a wild top-class Sauternes. Very sweet, with lemon and exotic fruit flavors and tons of smoky vanilla and wood notes. Try after 1994. (NR) (2/15/92) (BT) **90+**
Sylvaner Alsace Vieilles Vignes 1990: A nice, everyday wine. Has lovely apple and cream aromas, cream, grapefruit and spice flavors and a round, delicate finish. Medium-bodied and dry. Drink now. $13 (2/15/92) **83**
Sylvaner Alsace Vieilles Vignes 1989: A neutral-tasting white wine that doesn't go beyond a simple piny flavor. Crisp and clean, though. $12 (7/31/91) **77**

PREISS-HENNY
Sylvaner Alsace Château de Mittelwihr 1989: Drinkable but dull, with simple apple flavors that turn stale on the finish. Tasted twice. $10 (10/31/91) **68**

DOMAINES SCHLUMBERGER
Muscat Alsace 1990: Offers tons of peach and floral notes, with a dried orange peel character. Dry and delicious on the finish. Perfect with food. (NR) (2/15/92) **86**

Sylvaner Alsace 1990: Earthy and decadent, with meaty asparagus flavors and a short finish. Drink on release. (NR) (2/15/92) **79**

TRIMBACH
Sylvaner Alsace Sélection 1989 ($NA) (11/15/90) **81**

TURCKHEIM
Chasselas Alsace 1989: A decent, sturdy, dry white wine, with modest fruit flavors. Average quality. $11.50 (10/31/91) **75**
Pinot Noir Alsace Cuvée à l'Ancienne 1988: Crisp and focused, with plenty of Pinot Noir character, especially the bright plum and cherry flavors. Drinkable now, but it could use until 1993 or '94 to soften. $25 (10/31/91) **82**
Pinot Noir Alsace Cuvée Réserve 1989: Light and pleasantly floral and fruity, with charming hints of raspberry, strawberry and rose petal. A good wine to serve slightly chilled. Drinkable now. $15 (10/31/91) **80**
Pinot Noir Alsace Rouge de Turckheim 1988: Solidly built, but not particularly graceful. A stubby wine, with modest earth and berry flavors and hints of spice on the finish. Drinkable now, with hearty food. $40 (10/31/91) **77**
Sylvaner Alsace Cuvée Réserve 1989: Modest apple and lemon flavors give it a bit of life. Tastes clean, but simple. $11.50 (10/31/91) **77**

DOMAINE WEINBACH
Muscat Alsace Clos des Capucins 1988: Light and crisp, with modest apple and spice aromas and flavors. A bit soft on the finish. $23 (7/31/91) **78**
Sylvaner Alsace Réserve 1990: A round, easy- drinking Sylvaner. Medium-bodied and dry, with very lemony almond aromas, round, light cream and spice flavors and a soft finish. Drink now. $9.50 (2/15/92) **83**

DOMAINE ZIND-HUMBRECHT
Muscat d'Alsace Alsace 1990: Ripe and rich, with juniper, pine nut and fruit characteristics and an off-dry, fruity finish. A bit heavy-handed. Drink on release. $14 (2/15/92) **83**
Pinot d'Alsace Alsace 1990: A solid wine, with impressive apple, pineapple and lemon flavors and a concentrated finish. Drink on release. $15 (2/15/92) **86**
Sylvaner Alsace 1990: A real blockbuster; the best Sylvaner we've ever had. Starts with subtle floral and lime aromas, but the flavors blast off in your mouth with intense lemon and honey. Thick and rich on the finish. Drink on release. $12.50 (2/15/92) **92**

BEAUJOLAIS RED

PHILIPPE ANTOINE
Beaujolais-Villages 1988 $5.50 (5/31/89) **77**
Brouilly 1988 $11.50 (5/31/89) **82**
Fleurie 1988 $11.50 (5/31/89) **84**
Juliénas 1988 $11.50 (5/31/89) **85**
Moulin-à-Vent 1988 $11.50 (5/31/89) **88**
Régnié 1988 $11.50 (5/31/89) **81**

BARTON & GUESTIER
Beaujolais-Villages 1988 $9 (5/31/89) **77**
Beaujolais-Villages St.-Louis 1988 $7.50 (5/31/89) **75**
Brouilly 1988 $11 (5/31/89) **82**
Moulin-à-Vent 1988 $13 (5/31/89) **84**

DOMAINE PAUL BERNARD
Fleurie 1990: Rich and flavorful, packed with cherry and strawberry flavors on a firm structure of moderate tannins and good acidity. Could pass as a Burgundy, at half the price. $13 (10/31/91) **87**

JEAN CLAUDE BOISSET
Beaujolais 1988: A good, straightforward Beaujolais, with modest cherry and spice flavors, medium body and a clean finish. $6.75 (11/15/90) **77**
Beaujolais-Villages 1988: Earthy, funky aromas overshadow the modest, mature fruit flavors. Drink it soon before the fruit fades more. $7.50 (11/15/90) **76**

GEORGES DUBOEUF
Beaujolais 1990: Light and fruity, with a nice balance of plum and cherry flavors against a soft background of velvety texture. Drinkable now. $6.50 (9/30/91) BB **84**
Beaujolais 1989: Fresh, light and lively, with generous berry and cherry flavors, crisp balance and a clean, fruity finish. Just what you want from Beaujolais. $7 (11/15/90) BB **86**
Beaujolais Château de la Plume 1990: A good Beaujolais. Crisp, fruity and clean, with peppery notes adding complexity to the cherry flavor. Moderately tannic. Drink now through 1993. $6.50 (10/31/91) BB **84**
Beaujolais-Villages 1990: Rich and supple, with concentrated, well-focused plum, black cherry, watermelon and strawberry flavors. Delicious to drink now. $7 (9/15/91) BB **87**
Beaujolais-Villages 1989: Exuberantly fruity and fresh, with spicy, floral aromas and gobs of ripe cherry and berry flavors supported by firm acidity and light tannins. The spiciness and fruit complexity make it special. $8 (11/15/90) BB **87**
Beaujolais-Villages 1988 $8 (5/31/89) **83**
Beaujolais-Villages Château de la Grande Grange 1990: An herbal, earthy edge adds dimension to the light, fruity berry notes. Hints of flowers and strawberries on the finish. $7 (9/15/91) BB **82**
Beaujolais-Villages Château des Vierres 1990: Spicy and solidly built; not as light and friendly as most Beaujolais. A bit tannic and bitter on the finish. Drink it cool. $7 (11/15/91) **79**
Brouilly 1990: Crisp and sharply focused, with herbal, stalky flavors that get in the way of the pleasant watermelon and berry flavors. Drinkable now, but could improve through 1993. $9.50 (9/15/91) **81**
Brouilly 1988 $11 (5/31/89) **83**
Brouilly Château de Nervers 1990: An earthy wine, with a strong undercurrent of wild strawberry and berry flavors to balance the slightly barnyardy flavors. Drinkable now. $9.50 (9/15/91) **82**
Brouilly Château de Nervers 1988 $11 (5/31/89) **89**
Brouilly Domaine des Nazins 1990: A gutsy wine, with strong wild plum and berry flavors that fill the mouth and persist on the finish. Should gain from cellaring until 1993. Drinkable now. $9.50 (9/15/91) **87**
Chénas 1990: Ripe, concentrated and extremely well made, with pretty floral and berry aromas and layers of plum, black cherry and currant flavors. The finish lingers. Drink now. $8.50 (9/15/91) **88**
Chénas 1988 $10 (5/31/89) **85**
Chiroubles 1990: Fresh and snappy, with crisp berry, plum, raspberry and spice notes that hang with you. Delicious from start to finish. Ready now. $9.50 (9/15/91) **88**
Chiroubles 1988 $11 (5/31/89) **84**
Chiroubles Domaine Desmures Père et Fils 1990: A full-bodied, full-flavored Beaujolais whose piny, stemmy flavors may be too strong for some. May just need time in the cellar; try in 1993. Tasted twice. 5,000 cases made. $9.50 (10/31/91) **79**
Côte-de-Brouilly 1990: An earthy style, with a core of bright, plummy strawberry flavor at the center and strongly earthy, mushroomy flavors around it. Drinkable now. Tasted twice. $9.50 (11/15/91) **76**
Côte-de-Brouilly Domaine de la Madone 1990: Very light and crisp, with earthy, green fruit aromas and flavors that are not appealing. Drinkable now. 2,500 cases made. $9.50 (9/15/91) **77**
Fleurie 1990: Crisp and lively, with sharply focused raspberry, cherry, strawberry and watermelon flavors that are clean and refreshing. Enjoy now. $11 (9/15/91) **89**
Fleurie 1988 $14.50 (5/31/89) **89**
Fleurie Château des Déduits 1990: Ripe and almost jammy in flavor, with stiff tannins and firm acidity that will need until 1993 or later to soften. The structure is so solid and the flavors so good that the wait should be worth it. $11 (10/31/91) **87**

Juliénas 1990: Supple and generous, with pretty plum, cherry and spice flavors that linger. Well proportioned and tasty to drink now. $9.50 (9/15/91) **86**
Juliénas Domaine de la Seigneurie 1990: Dense and tart, with lots of cherry and spice aromas and flavors, a firm texture and a finish that echoes the spice. Needs until 1993 to soften. 5,000 cases made. $9.50 (10/31/91) **84**
Morgon 1990: Fruity, with an earthy edge, hinting at iron as well as cherries and spice. Concentrated and sharply focused, with interesting flavors. $9 (9/15/91) **80**
Morgon 1988 $10.75 (5/31/89) **87**
Morgon Jean Descombes 1990: Firm and fruity, with focused cherry, boysenberry and meat aromas and flavors that keep on giving through the long finish. A solid wine that could use until 1993 to reach its best. $9 (9/30/91) BB **87**
Morgon Jean Descombes 1988 $11.25 (5/31/89) **90**
Moulin-à-Vent 1990: Firm and focused, with a good concentration of blackberry and currant aromas and flavors shaded by a nice floral edge. At its best in 1993. $11 (9/15/91) **84**
Moulin-à-Vent 1988 $12.25 (5/31/89) **87**
Moulin-à-Vent Domaine des Rosiers 1990: Ripe and rich, with a round texture that plays the generous plum, raspberry and strawberry flavors against grace notes of spice and vanilla. Probably at its best now. $11 (9/15/91) **85**
Moulin-à-Vent New Barrel Aged 1988 $12.25 (5/31/89) **93**
Régnié 1990: Has a herbaceous, greenish edge to the flavors, but plenty of pretty berry and raspberry flavors to hang on to. Drink now. $8 (9/15/91) **81**
Régnié 1988 $8 (5/31/89) **83**
Régnié Domaine du Potet 1990: Crisp, light and full of bright strawberry and raspberry aromas and flavors. A delicate wine that keeps you coming back for another sip. Better served slightly chilled. 5,000 cases made. $8 (9/30/91) BB **85**
St.-Amour 1990: Firm and tight, with ripe berry, cherry and strawberry flavors that show more depth on the finish than up front. Plenty of fruit concentration and crisp acidity carry the flavors. Drink now. $11 (9/15/91) **87**
St.-Amour Domaine des Pins 1990: Firm and tight, with a rough, stemmy finish, but also offers plenty of ripe berry flavors. Drink now. 4,000 cases made. $11 (9/15/91) **82**

PIERRE & PAUL DURDILLY
Beaujolais Les Grandes Coasses 1990: Tart and fruity, with slightly sour, stemmy accents that take away from the plum and berry flavors. $7 (9/30/91) **74**

PIERRE FERRAUD & FILS
Beaujolais-Villages Cuvée Ensorceleuse 1988 $10 (5/31/89) **81**
Brouilly Domaine Rolland 1988 $16 (5/31/89) **84**
Chénas Cuvée Jean-Michel 1988 $10 (5/31/89) **89**
Chiroubles Domaine de la Chapelle du Bois 1988 $12 (5/31/89) **79**
Côte-de-Brouilly 1988 $16 (5/31/89) **83**
Fleurie 1988 $15 (5/31/89) **87**
Fleurie Château de Grand Pre 1988 $16 (5/31/89) **86**
Juliénas 1988 $12 (5/31/89) **73**
Morgon Domaine de l'Eveque 1988 $16 (5/31/89) **89**
Moulin-à-Vent 1988 $16 (5/31/89) **83**
Régnié 1988 $10 (5/31/89) **81**
St.-Amour 1988 $12 (5/31/89) **85**

DOMAINE JEAN GAUDET
Morgon 1988 $10 (5/31/89) **87**

GERARD GELIN
Beaujolais-Villages Domaine des Nugues 1989: Takes all the fresh fruit flavor of Beaujolais and wraps it in a light, stylish cloak of oak seasoning. Very clean and easy to like. $8 (11/15/90) BB **86**

DOMAINE DE L'INSTITUT PASTEUR
Côte-de-Brouilly 1988 $10 (5/31/89) **84**

LOUIS JADOT
Beaujolais Jadot 1990: Crisp, light, focused and fruity, with plenty of strawberry and raspberry flavors that keep kicking in on the finish. Drinkable now; best slightly chilled. $9.25 (9/30/91) BB **85**
Beaujolais Jadot 1989: Has a light, crisp texture and modest strawberry and raspberry aromas and flavors, but it's clean and fresh. Drink soon. $6 (11/15/90) **79**
Morgon 1990: A tart, woody style, with plenty of focused blackberry and spice aromas and flavors that persist on the finish. Needs until 1993 to soften. $12 (9/30/91) **83**
Moulin-à-Vent 1990: Simple and chunky, with a nice beam of leafy, strawberry aromas and flavors that keep on coming on the finish. Drink chilled. $15 (9/30/91) **79**

JAFFELIN
Beaujolais-Villages Domaine de Riberolles 1987: Light and snappy, with earthy aromas and a lean streak of ripe strawberry flavor that lasts through the finish. Drink soon. $7 (4/15/89) **79**

KERMIT LYNCH
Beaujolais 1990: Lush and fruity, with pretty black cherry, pepper, plum and spice flavors. Forward and attractive to drink now. $10 (9/15/91) **83**

MOILLARD
Brouilly Château Belliard 1990: Light in color, but firmly tannic and not as rich in flavor as it could be. The nice floral and nutty aromas and flavors could be livelier. $13 (9/15/91) **82**
Chiroubles 1990: A touch earthy, with hints of juniper, but it also has a silky texture, with plenty of berry and plum flavors. Ready now. $13 (9/15/91) **84**
Fleurie Château du Vivier 1990: Packed with flavor; its deep, concentrated, rich black currant, cherry, anise and spice flavors are intense and lively. The finish echoes fruit on and on, plus there's a good dose of tannin. Drink now through 1993. 1,660 cases made. $17 (9/15/91) **91**
Juliénas Bois de la Salle 1990: Strives for power, with intense fruit, but turns a bit sour and biting on the finish, where it picks up a gamy, drying edge. $13 (9/15/91) **81**
Morgon Domaine du Crêt de Ruyère 1990: Very firm and concentrated, with lots of plum and cherry flavors shaded by a hint of earthiness. Has enough tannin to want until 1993. $13 (9/15/91) **86**
Moulin-à-Vent Château du Vivier 1990: Very firm and tight, and more tannic than most Beaujolais, with medium-intense cherry and plum aromas and flavors that need until 1993 or '94 to emerge. $16 (9/30/91) **82**
Régnié Domaine de Reyssiers 1990: Dull, earthy, mature flavors make this out of sync for the '90 vintage. It should be fresh and fruity. Drinkable, but marginal. Tasted twice. $12 (9/30/91) **66**
St.-Amour Domaine des Pins 1990: Has a pleasant, buttery, nutmeg edge to the core of currant, plum and cherry flavors, and a nice measure of subtlety and finesse that adds grace and intrigue to the fruit. Drink up now. $16 (9/15/91) **86**

MOMMESSIN
Beaujolais-Villages Château de Montmelas 1988 $9.50 (5/31/89) **78**
Brouilly Château de Briante 1988 $11.50 (5/31/89) **81**
Chiroubles Château de Rasset 1988 $11.25 (5/31/89) **83**
Fleurie 1988 $13.50 (5/31/89) **87**
Juliénas Domaine de la Conseillere 1988 $10.50 (5/31/89) **81**
Morgon 1988 $10 (5/31/89) **86**
Morgon Domaine de Lathevalle 1988 $10 (5/31/89) **88**
Moulin-à-Vent Domaine de Champ de Cour 1988 $12.50 (5/31/89) **91**
Régnié 1988 $10.50 (5/31/89) **85**
St.-Amour Domaine de Monreve 1988 $12 (5/31/89) **84**

FRANCE
Beaujolais Red

DOMAINE DU MONT VERRIER
Beaujolais-Villages 1988 $10 (5/31/89) **76**

NICOLAS
Beaujolais-Villages 1989: Pretty deep and flavorful, with ripe cherry and plum notes following the earthy, almost barnyardy aromas. A gutsy, ripe dinner wine. $8 (11/15/90) BB **82**

PELLERIN
Brouilly 1987: Very light and delicate, with subtle strawberry and earthy aromas and flavors; smooth and refined. $8.50 (4/15/89) **83**

DOMAINE DE PETIT-CHENE
Moulin-à-Vent 1988 $10 (5/31/89) **88**

CHATEAU DES RAVATYS
Brouilly 1988 $10 (5/31/89) **78**

DOMAINE DE LA ROCHELLE
Moulin-à-Vent 1988 $10 (5/31/89) **91**

ANTONIN RODET
Beaujolais-Villages Rodet 1988: Lacks the generous fruit one expects from a Beaujolais, leaning more toward herbal, slightly toasty aromas and flavors on a lean frame. A dull wine. Tasted twice. $8 (11/15/90) **75**

DOMAINE ST.-CHARLES
Beaujolais-Villages Château du Bluizard 1988: Sturdy and robust for a Beaujolais, with tart cherry and plum flavors, deep color and some depth of flavor. Substantial and flavorful rather than light and charming. $8 (11/15/90) BB **82**

THORIN
Beaujolais-Villages 1988 $7 (5/31/89) **79**
Moulin-à-Vent Château des Jacques 1988 $16 (5/31/89) **88**

TRENEL & FILS
Beaujolais-Villages 1990: Has a pleasant core of supple plum flavor but also a leafy edge. Drink now. $10 (9/15/91) **81**
Beaujolais-Villages 1988 $9 (5/31/89) **78**
Chénas 1988 $14 (5/31/89) **86**
Chiroubles 1988 $12 (5/31/89) **83**
Côte-de-Brouilly 1990: Crisp and lively, with firmly supported berry and currant aromas and flavors, plus enough tannin to need until 1993 to be at its best. $15 (9/15/91) **82**
Fleurie 1988 $14 (5/31/89) **86**
Morgon Côte de Py 1988 $17 (5/31/89) **92**
Moulin-à-Vent La Rochelle 1988 $17 (5/31/89) **90**
Régnié 1988 $12 (5/31/89) **83**
St.-Amour 1988 $15 (5/31/89) **87**

GEORGES VIORNERY
Côte-de-Brouilly 1990: A full-flavored, full-bodied Beaujolais, with plenty of black cherry and strawberry flavors, firm tannins and a lingering finish. Not a light charmer, but a serious red wine to drink now through 1994. $13 (10/31/91) **88**

Beaujolais White

GEORGES DUBOEUF
Beaujolais Blanc 1989: A modest wine, with attractive earth and spice flavors and a lingering finish. Simple, but interesting enough to recommend for current drinking. $9 (11/30/90) **80**

Bordeaux Red/*Bordeaux*

CHATEAU LES ALOUETTES
Bordeaux Kosher 1986: An herbal, pickley aroma and simple fruit flavors add up to an acceptable but uninteresting wine. $10 (3/31/90) **70**

BARTON & GUESTIER
Bordeaux Cabernet Sauvignon 1988: An acceptable wine with decent plum and berry flavors. Tannic and dried-out. Coated with a lot of woody flavors. Drink up now. $6 (2/15/90) **73**
Bordeaux Fondation Rouge 1989: The soft, watery texture is not encouraging, but it has ripe berry aromas and flavors that persist into a modest finish. Drinkable now. $9 (7/31/91) **75**
Bordeaux Merlot 1988: A nice, medium-bodied Merlot that's crisp with moderate tannins. It's fresh, with a good core of plum and berry flavors, smooth and well-balanced, with a pleasant, fruity finish. Drink now. $6 (2/15/90) BB **84**

CHATEAU BAULOS
Bordeaux Prince Albert Poniatowski 1988: Thin and harsh, with a lot more tannin than the fruit can sustain. Has berry flavor, but leans toward smoke and earthiness on the finish. $8.75 (8/31/91) **69**

BEAU MAYNE
Bordeaux 1983 $5 (3/31/87) BB **81**

CHATEAU BOIS-VERT
Bordeaux 1983 $3.75 (11/16/85) **53**

CHATEAU BONNET
Bordeaux 1989 (NR) (4/30/91) (BT) **80+**
Bordeaux 1988: Light and austere, with strong herbal overtones to the modest berry aromas and flavors. A simple, drinkable wine. $7.50 (4/30/91) **77**
Bordeaux 1987: Has an herbal style, with enough appealing strawberry flavors to keep it in balance; light, clean and refreshing. Drink soon. $7 (4/15/90) **79**
Bordeaux 1986 $6 (5/15/89) **73**
Bordeaux 1983 $4.75 (5/01/86) **72**
Bordeaux 1982 $4.50 (4/16/85) **73**
Bordeaux Reserve 1988: An earthy wine, with a velvety texture, good intensity of flavor and a crisp finish that echoes anise and tar notes. Drink soon. Tasted twice. $11 (7/15/91) **78**

LE BORDEAUX PRESTIGE
Bordeaux 1985 $9.50 (9/30/88) **80**

CHATEAU BRIOT
Bordeaux 1985 $4 (5/15/87) **75**

LA CAVE TROISGROS
Bordeaux Rouge 1989: Fresh and lively, with a crisp texture and lots of blackberry and currant aromas and flavors, soft tannins and a smooth finish. Good for current drinking. 2,000 cases made. $9.50 (5/15/91) **82**

CHATEAU DU CHALET
Bordeaux 1987: It's a bit lean but carries enough bright strawberry and cherry flavor to be appealing to drink now. $6 (4/15/90) **78**

CHARTRON LA FLEUR
Bordeaux 1986: A very dry but concentrated wine, with a mask of tannins hiding potentially good fruit flavor underneath. Drink up now. $4.50 (5/15/89) **74**

DOMAINE DE CHEVAL BLANC
Bordeaux 1985 $5 (5/15/88) **78**

CHEVALIER DUCLA
Bordeaux 1986: Very attractively put together. Clean, nicely fruity and fresh in flavor, with good balance and firm structure. Drink it up. $5.50 (5/15/89) BB **80**

CHEVALIER VEDRINES
Bordeaux 1985 $6 (6/30/88) **77**

LA COMBE DES DAMES
Bordeaux 1985 $6.50 (3/15/88) **74**

CHATEAU LES CONFRERIES
Bordeaux 1985 $3.50 (2/15/88) **75**

LA COUR PAVILLON
Bordeaux 1986: Light and smooth, with herbal, cedary overtones to the modest currant aromas and flavors. A bit short, but drinkable. $7.25 (2/28/91) **77**
Bordeaux 1985 $6.75 (7/15/88) **67**
Bordeaux 1983 $7 (8/31/87) **68**

CHATEAU DAVRIL
Bordeaux 1987: Light and pleasantly spicy, its velvety texture carrying the bright cherry and strawberry flavor amiably. Drinkable now, and it's fairly priced. $5 (9/30/89) **79**

LUCIEN DESCHAUX
Bordeaux Rouge 1990: A bit tough around the edges, its astringency puts the brakes on otherwise good herb and currant Bordeaux flavors. Drink with hearty food, or wait until 1993 or '94. Tasted twice. $6 (1/31/92) **75**

LES DOUELLES
Bordeaux 1982 $3 (10/01/85) BB **79**

CHATEAU DUCLA
Bordeaux 1988: Light in texture and flavor, with modest currant and toast character that becomes crisp and citrusy on the finish. $7 (8/31/91) **74**

CHATEAU L'ESPERANCE
Bordeaux 1986: Light, cedary Bordeaux for current drinking, a bit spicy with a touch of cherry flavor on the finish. $7 (9/30/89) **77**

CHATEAU FAURIE-PASCAUD
Bordeaux 1986 $5 (6/30/88) **79**

CHATEAU GOFFRETEAU
Bordeaux Rouge 1989: Offers lots of flavor and interest for a youthful, drinkable style of Bordeaux, hinting at chocolate and toast against a solid core of currant and berry flavors. Drink now and enjoy. $8 (5/15/91) BB **84**

CHATEAU LAGRAVE PARAN
Bordeaux 1989: Very fruity, light and lively, with well-defined currant and berry aromas and flavors and a velvety texture. A bit light on the finish. Drinkable now, but it could shed more tannin by 1993. $8 (2/28/91) **79**
Bordeaux 1988: Great value for an '88 Bordeaux. Hardy, fruity and pretty tannic, with rather simple—if ripe—jammy, cherry and berry aromas and flavors. May come together nicely with cellaring; try it again in 1993. $6 (7/15/90) BB **82**
Bordeaux 1987: Firm and slightly tannic but offering enough cherry and currant flavor to keep it in balance. It also gets some nice complexity from hints of cedar and toast. Start drinking now through 1993. $7 (5/15/90) BB **80**

CHATEAU LAMARTINE
Bordeaux 1989 (NR) (4/30/91) (BT) **75+**

CHATEAU LAURETAN
Bordeaux 1986: A hearty but very basic Bordeaux, with nicely fruity and herbal flavors and a hint of earthiness. $5 (5/15/89) **79**

MICHEL LYNCH
Bordeaux 1988: A hard, woody, lean style that's not showing much fruit. Offers a hint of plum and spice, but turns vegetal and herbal on the aftertaste. Drink now to 1993. $8 (10/31/91) **76**
Bordeaux 1983 $6.75 (10/15/87) **75**

MAITRE D'ESTOURNEL
Bordeaux 1985 $7.25 (5/31/88) **84**

CHATEAU MAROTTE
Bordeaux 1986 $3.50 (4/30/88) **70**

MARQUIS DES TOURS
Bordeaux 1988: Light but surprisingly tannic, offering pleasant but modest currant and strawberry aromas and flavors. Worth waiting until 1993 or '94 to see what develops. $5 (2/28/91) **78**

YVON MAU
Bordeaux Officiel du Bicentenaire de la Revolution Française 1986: Basic Bordeaux. Tastes generally fruity and clean, if a bit too harsh. Ultimately simple. Showed better than a bottle reviewed earlier. $4.50 (6/30/89) **72**

MAISON MOUEIX
Bordeaux Rouge 1988: Lean, crisp and focused, with medium-weight cherry, currant and toast aromas and flavors and hints of tobacco. Balanced for current drinking. $6 (1/31/92) BB **81**

CHATEAU DU MOULIN DE PEYRONIN
Bordeaux 1986: A very herbal, vegetal-tasting Bordeaux that's tannic and concentrated but offers little in the way of rich fruit flavor. Good, but not distinctive or complex. $10 (3/31/90) **73**

MOUTON-CADET
Bordeaux 1988: Smooth and generous, with pleasant plum, currant and beet aromas and flavors. Easy to drink now. $9 (4/30/91) BB **81**
Bordeaux 1987: A light wine that shows its toasty oak a bit more than one might expect for this vintage,

Key to Symbols

The scores reported here are the results of blind tastings conducted by our panel of senior editors. Wines that carry the initials below are results of individual tastings.

THE WINE SPECTATOR 100-POINT SCALE 95-100—Classic, a great wine; ***90-94***—Outstanding, superior character and style; ***80-89***—Good to very good, a wine with special qualities; ***70-79***—Average, drinkable wine that may have minor flaws; ***60-69***—Below average, drinkable but not recommended; ***50-59***—Poor, undrinkable, not recommended. "+"—With a score indicates a range; used primarily with barrel tastings to indicate a preliminary score.

SPECIAL DESIGNATIONS SS—Spectator Selection, CS—Cellar Selection, BB—Best Buy, ($NA)—Price not available, (NR)—Not released.

TASTER'S INITIALS (JG)—Jim Gordon, (HS)—Harvey Steiman, (JL)—James Laube, (JS)—James Suckling, (TM)—Thomas Matthews, (TR)—Terry Robards, (PM)—Per-Henrik Mansson, (BT)—Barrel Tasting (these wines were tasted blind from barrel samples), (CA-date)—*California's Great Cabernets* by James Laube, (CH-date)—*California's Great Chardonnays* by James Laube, (VP-date)—*Vintage Port* by James Suckling.

DATE TASTED Dates in parentheses represent the issue in which the rating was published.

not quite generous enough with its cherry flavor to balance the oak, but it's pleasant enough. Drink now to 1993. $7.50 (4/15/90) **79**
Bordeaux 1986: Light and brightly fruity, with enough herbal flavor and velvety texture to keep the strawberry flavor interesting. Drink it now for its youthful charm. $7.25 (2/15/89) BB **81**
Bordeaux 1985 $6.50 (5/15/88) BB **80**

PONTALLIER JOHNSON
Bordeaux Merlot 1982 $8 (10/15/87) **77**

CHATEAU RAUZAN DESPAGNE
Bordeaux 1985 $5.75 (2/15/88) **72**

ARMAND ROUX
Bordeaux Verdillac 1989: A simple, solid wine, with vegetal, slightly bitter flavors and rough tannins. Not appealing, but it's drinkable. $7 (1/31/92) **71**
Bordeaux Verdillac 1988: A solid, fresh, straightforward Bordeaux that displays attractive berry aromas and flavors. Drink up now. $6.25 (7/15/90) BB **79**

ST.-JOVIAN
Bordeaux 1985 $4.50 (5/15/88) **75**
Bordeaux Cabernet Sauvignon 1986 $4.50 (7/31/88) **78**
Bordeaux Merlot 1986: A good, middle-of-the-road red with plummy flavors and medium body. A bit of tannin helps add firmness. $5 (5/15/89) **76**

CHATEAU ST.-SULPICE
Bordeaux 1988: Firm and flavorful, with a definite herbal edge to the currant and smoke aromas and flavors. Medium intensity makes it drinkable now, but it should be fine through 1993 to '95. $7.50 (8/31/91) BB **81**
Bordeaux 1982 $6 (5/15/87) **73**

DOMAINE SAINTE-ANNE
Bordeaux 1987: Soft, light and fruity, with herbal notes in the berry and cedar flavors. Simple and pleasant for current drinking. $5 (5/15/90) **77**

SIRIUS
Bordeaux 1988: A lightweight, with vegetal aromas and modest currant and chocolate flavors, austere and tough for its style. Maybe better after 1993. $15 (8/31/91) **77**

CHATEAU TALMONT
Bordeaux 1989: Light and a bit watery in texture, with pleasant strawberry and currant aromas and flavors that fade quickly. Drinkable now. $8 (2/28/91) **74**

BORDEAUX SUPÉRIEUR

BEAUCLAIRE
Bordeaux Supérieur 1988: Straightforward, ripe and firmly structured, with herbal, plummy aromas, modest fruit flavors and decent balance. A touch of cassis adds interest. Drink now. $6 (12/31/90) **79**

CHATEAU BELLERIVE
Bordeaux Supérieur 1985 $7 (11/15/87) **70**
Bordeaux Supérieur 1982 $8 (12/16/85) **72**

CHATEAU BRASSAC
Bordeaux Supérieur 1986 $5.50 (8/31/88) BB **80**

CHATEAU CANDELAY
Bordeaux Supérieur 1986: A good value, and nice as far as it goes. Has clean, simple plum flavors, medium body and a bit of tannin. Drink up now. $5 (6/15/89) **78**

CHATEAU LES CHARMILLES
Bordeaux Supérieur 1985 $8 (2/15/88) **71**

CHATEAU LA CROIX DE GIRON
Bordeaux Supérieur 1986: A decent quaff. Light, simple and basically herbal in flavor with modest fruit underneath. $5.25 (5/15/89) **76**

CHATEAU LA CROIX ST.-JEAN
Bordeaux Supérieur 1986 $6 (11/30/88) BB **81**

CHATEAU GOFFRETEAU
Bordeaux Supérieur 1988: Lean, firm and fruity, with a decidedly herbal edge to the pleasant strawberry and currant aromas and flavors. Drinkable now, but cellaring until 1993 wouldn't hurt. 3,000 cases made. $6 (2/28/91) BB **81**
Bordeaux Supérieur 1986: Soft, fruity and appealing. Light but well-balanced with firm acidity and modest tannins and the plum and cherry flavors linger on the finish. $6 (6/15/89) BB **82**

CHATEAU LE GRAND VERDUS
Bordeaux Supérieur 1988: Tannic, but it has nicely focused plum and currant flavors. A full-bodied wine, with good Merlot characteristics. Almost drinkable now, but it may be best to wait until 1993 to '95. $7.50 (10/31/91) BB **80**

CHATEAU LES GRANDS JAYS
Bordeaux Supérieur 1986: A sturdy, well-made Bordeaux with firm tannins and good fruit flavors. Drink up now. $6 (5/15/89) **77**

CHATEAU DE LA GRAVE
Bordeaux Supérieur 1988: Bursting with bright cherry and strawberry aromas and flavors, with overtones of toast and smoke, this is a straightforward, fruity wine with enough tannin to carry it through 1994. Drink soon. $8 (7/15/90) BB **82**

CHATEAU HAUT MALLET
Bordeaux Supérieur 1987: An earthy, simple wine, with pleasant red cherry and cedar aromas and flavors to make it interesting. Drink soon. $7.50 (4/15/90) **76**

CHATEAU HAUT-COLAS NOUET
Bordeaux Supérieur 1985 $4 (11/15/87) **71**

CHATEAU JALOUSIE-BEAULIEU
Bordeaux Supérieur 1985 $7 (12/31/88) **70**

CHATEAU JONQUEYRES
Bordeaux Supérieur Cuvée Vieilles Vignes 1988: A real melange of unpopular flavors—green bean, gamy, barnyardy—and not our style at all. Tasted twice. 4,000 cases made. $12 (3/31/91) **65**

CHATEAU LAGARENNE
Bordeaux Supérieur 1988: A stylish Bordeaux Supérieur, with ripe, sweet fruit and interesting tobacco, cedar, vanilla, and classic berry aromas and flavors. The firm tannins may need a few years to soften; try in 1993. $8 (7/31/90) BB **82**

CHATEAU LAMARTINE
Bordeaux Supérieur 1991: Surprisingly ripe and intense for the vintage, but it seems a bit disjointed. (NR) (5/15/92) (BT) **80+**
Bordeaux Supérieur 1984 $9 (5/15/87) **76**

CHATEAU LANDEREAU
Bordeaux Supérieur 1985 $6.75 (2/15/88) BB **81**

CHATEAU LESCALLE
Bordeaux Supérieur 1986: Quite satisfying. Robust and direct in flavor, with ripe plum and spice notes on a firm, moderately tannic framework. $8 (6/30/89) **81**

CHATEAU DE LUCAT
Bordeaux Supérieur 1982 $4 (10/01/85) **71**

G. MICHELOT
Bordeaux Supérieur 1982 $5 (1/01/86) BB **74**

CHATEAU DE PARENCHERE
Bordeaux Supérieur 1986: Toasty, cedary wine, ripe and generous on the palate, lean and somewhat austere and tannic in texture. Give it until 1993 or '94 and it should be fine. $9 (6/30/89) **81**

PIERRE JEAN
Bordeaux Supérieur 1988: Tough and tannic, with more herb and floral aromas and flavors than fruit, making it lean and uninviting. Needs until 1995 to '97 to soften, but it's a gamble. 700 cases made. $8 (7/31/91) **75**

CHATEAU DU PINTEY
Bordeaux Supérieur 1988: Light and lean, with a somewhat tannic texture for the modest berry and herbal aromas and flavors. Drink with something roasted. $11 (8/31/91) **75**

CHATEAU REYNIER
Bordeaux Supérieur 1983 $3.50 (10/16/85) BB **83**

CHATEAU ROC MIGNON D'ADRIEN
Bordeaux Supérieur 1989: Has a lot more character than the price would suggest. Vibrant in color, with a dense texture and concentrated flavors of currant, vanilla and plum tightly wrapped in firm tannins that will need until 1993 to '95 to settle down. $6 (2/28/91) BB **82**

ST.-JOVIAN
Bordeaux Supérieur Premium 1988: Firm in texture, more than a little tannic and especially aromatic, with lots of ripe currant aroma and flavor and just a little toasty and warm on the finish. Drinkable now, but it will probably better around 1993. $5.50 (7/31/91) BB **80**

CHATEAU DE SOURS
Bordeaux Supérieur 1986: Very firm texture, but the currant and cedar aromas and flavors make their presence felt. Should be good to drink now. $7 (9/30/89) **78**

CHATEAU LA TERRASSE
Bordeaux Supérieur 1989: A firm, fruity, soft wine that has nice peppery overtones to the basic currant flavor, turning a bit spicy on the finish. Drink now. $8 (3/31/91) **79**
Bordeaux Supérieur 1986: Tart and herbal in style. Has good acidity, but the flavors are green, vegetal and smoky; not much fruit showing. $8 (6/30/89) **76**
Bordeaux Supérieur 1985 $6 (11/15/87) **78**
Bordeaux Supérieur 1982 $4.50 (11/16/85) **74**

CHATEAU TOUR DE BELLEGARDE
Bordeaux Supérieur 1986: Very easy to like in a simple but flavorful style. Has fresh, grapey, black cherry flavors and good structure. Drink now. $4.75 (5/15/89) **77**

CHATEAU TRINITE VALROSE
Bordeaux Supérieur Ile de Patiras 1988: Earthy, barklike aromas and flavors tend to obscure the ripe berry and cherry flavors that emerge on the finish. Drinkable but awkward. $7 (8/31/91) **78**

CHATEAU TROCARD
Bordeaux Supérieur 1988: Cedary tobacco aromas and flavors characterize this medium-weight wine. Shows impressive density of flavor, including enough black cherry and currant flavors to be worth cellaring. Hints at chocolate on the finish. Try in 1994 or '95. $8.50 (1/31/92) BB **83**

CHATEAU VIEUX GABRIAN
Bordeaux Supérieur 1988: Firm and focused, with herb- and mint-tinged cherry, currant and berry flavors that carry through on the finish. The tannins are well integrated. Drinkable now, but possibly better around 1993. $11 (4/30/91) **84**

CÔTES DE FRANCS

CHATEAU LES CHARMES-GODARD
Côtes de Francs 1989: Shows lots of berry, herbal, Cabernet Sauvignon character, with medium-full tannins and a clean finish. Not complex, but it's well made. Drink after 1995. (NR) (3/15/92) **86**

CHATEAU LA CLAVERIE
Côtes de Francs 1989: A gorgeous wine on the verge of entering the major leagues. Has wonderfully deep vanilla, smoke and cassis aromas and flavors held together with tons of velvety tannins. Try after 1995. $21 (3/15/92) **88**
Côtes de Francs 1988 $18 (8/31/90) (BT) **80+**

CHATEAU DE FRANCS
Côtes de Francs 1989 (NR) (4/30/90) (BT) **75+**
Côtes de Francs 1988 (NR) (8/31/90) (BT) **80+**

LAURIOL
Côtes de Francs 1986: Has attractive earthy aromas, smooth but lean plummy flavors, and perhaps a bit too much tannin for its fruit content. Still, it's good for current drinking. $8 (6/15/89) **73**
Côtes de Francs 1985 $6.50 (6/30/88) **78**

CHATEAU LA PRADE
Côtes de Francs 1988 (NR) (6/30/89) (BT) **70+**

CHATEAU PUYGUERAUD
Côtes de Francs 1989: Offers lots of mint and blackberry nuances, thick fruit flavors and a chewy finish. Almost drinkable now, but better in 1994. $18 (3/15/92) **83**
Côtes de Francs 1988 $15 (8/31/90) (BT) **80+**
Côtes de Francs 1986: Tastes like fresh Cabernet with a bit of oak aging for extra structure. Flavors are clean, ripe cherry and plum. Slightly tannic upon release, but it should be good to drink now. $12 (6/15/89) **84**
Côtes de Francs 1985 $9 (6/30/88) **83**
Côtes de Francs 1983 $7.50 (10/16/85) **82**

FRONSAC/CANON-FRONSAC

CHATEAU BARRABAQUE
Canon-Fronsac Cuvée Prestige 1991: Offers lots of ripe berry and plum aromas and flavors and medium tannins. Good, but it has a light finish. (NR) (5/15/92) (BT) **80+**

CHATEAU CANON DE BREM
Canon-Fronsac 1990: Another clean, ripe '90, with lots of tannins that give it a firm backbone. (NR) (5/15/92) (BT) **80+**
Canon-Fronsac 1989: Lively berry, mint and fruit aromas give this soft, silky wine a polished character. Try after 1994. $23 (3/15/92) **84**
Canon-Fronsac 1988 $13 (6/30/89) (BT) **80+**
Canon-Fronsac 1987 $14 (6/30/89) (BT) **80+**
Canon-Fronsac 1986 $15 (3/31/90) **86**
Canon-Fronsac 1985 $19 (5/15/87) (BT) **80+**

FRANCE
Bordeaux Red/Fronsac/Canon-Fronsac

CHATEAU CANON-FRONSAC
Canon-Fronsac 1990: Has extremely focused, ripe fruit aromas and flavors and well-integrated tannins. Excellent for the vintage. (NR) (5/15/92) (BT) **85+**
Canon-Fronsac 1989: A tough little wine, with herbal and boysenberry flavors and very firm tannins. Should improve with age. Try after 1994. (NR) (3/15/92) **82**

CHATEAU CANON MOUEIX
Canon-Fronsac 1990: A very accessible wine, with a soft texture and ripe fruit flavor. (NR) (5/15/92) (BT) **80+**
Canon-Fronsac 1989: We underscored this wine when it was in barrel. This '89 Bordeaux is round and attractive, with lots of vanilla, plum and black cherry aromas and flavors that linger on the finish. The medium tannin structure makes it quite approachable now, but it will be better in 1994. $22 (3/15/92) **86**
Canon-Fronsac 1988 $16 (8/31/90) (BT) **85+**
Canon-Fronsac 1987 $14 (6/30/89) (BT) **75+**
Canon-Fronsac 1986 Rel: $15 Cur: $18 (6/30/88) (BT) **80+**
Canon-Fronsac 1985 Rel: $15 Cur: $19 (5/15/87) (BT) **80+**

CHATEAU DE CARLES
Fronsac 1990: Shows plenty of lovely berry and cherry aromas and flavors, with a hint of earthiness on the finish and medium-fine tannins. (NR) (5/15/92) (BT) **85+**
Fronsac 1989 (NR) (4/30/91) (BT) **80+**

CHATEAU DALEM
Fronsac 1990: Big and polished, with all the fruit and tannin structure you could hope for from a Fronsac at this stage. (NR) (5/15/92) (BT) **90+**

CHATEAU DE LA DAUPHINE
Fronsac 1990: A lighter and more elegant style of '90, with silky tannins and lovely fruit. (NR) (5/15/92) (BT) **80+**
Fronsac 1989: Has lots of chocolate and roasted coffee bean flavors, firm tannins and a medium finish. Somewhat one-dimensional. Better in 1993. $20 (3/15/92) **80**
Fronsac 1988 $12 (8/31/90) (BT) **80+**
Fronsac 1987 $17 (6/30/89) (BT) **75+**
Fronsac 1986 $20 (6/30/88) (BT) **75+**
Fronsac 1985 $20 (9/30/88) **84**

CHATEAU FONTENIL
Fronsac 1990: Shows lots of new wood, but has the structure of ripe tannins and fruit to take it. A classy wine. (NR) (5/15/92) (BT) **90+**
Fronsac 1989 (NR) (4/30/91) (BT) **85+**
Fronsac 1986: Pleasantly fruity before the tannins kick in, leaving a thin, somewhat watery texture on the palate. Does not appear to have the richness to stand up to the tannins. Past its prime. $14 (2/15/90) **76**
Fronsac 1985 Rel: $14 Cur: $17 (9/30/88) **87**

CHATEAU HAUT-CANON-LA TRUFFIERE
Canon-Fronsac 1991: Has good blueberry and other fruit aromas and flavors, but it's quite diluted on the finish. (NR) (5/15/92) (BT) **75+**

CHATEAU MAZERIS
Canon-Fronsac 1990: With lots of plum and ripe fruit aromas, this has mouth-coating tannins and excellent fruit flavors. (NR) (5/15/92) (BT) **85+**
Canon-Fronsac 1989 (NR) (4/30/91) (BT) **85+**
Canon-Fronsac 1988 $18 (6/30/89) (BT) **75+**
Canon-Fronsac 1987 $12 (6/30/89) (BT) **75+**
Canon-Fronsac 1986 $12 (6/30/88) (BT) **80+**
Canon-Fronsac 1985 Rel: $12 Cur: $16 (5/15/87) (BT) **80+**

CHATEAU MAZERIS-BELLEVUE
Canon-Fronsac 1991: Shows good wild berry character, but it's slightly diluted on the center palate. (NR) (5/15/92) (BT) **80+**

A. MOUEIX
Fronsac 1985 $9.50 (9/30/88) **83**

CHATEAU MOULIN HAUT-LAROQUE
Fronsac 1991: Good for the vintage, with a deep color and ripe berry aromas, but it just lacks length on the finish. (NR) (5/15/92) (BT) **80+**
Fronsac 1986: Hard and tannic, with oak, anise and a touch of rubber in the aromas, blunt and a little funky tasting. Drink now. $11 (11/15/89) **78**

CHATEAU MOULIN-PEY LABRIE
Canon-Fronsac 1991: Deep in color, with lovely aromas, it lacks a middle palate, but does show sweet fruit flavors and a firm tannin backbone. (NR) (5/15/92) (BT) **80+**

CHATEAU ROUSSELLE
Fronsac 1991: Another very pleasant wine, with attractive fruit and medium tannins, but it just doesn't make it on the palate. (NR) (5/15/92) (BT) **75+**

CHATEAU LA VALADE
Fronsac 1986: Firm, flavorful and well-balanced, with a unique licorice aroma, clean fruit flavors and a lingering finish. $5.25 (5/15/89) BB **81**

CHATEAU LA VIEILLE CURE
Fronsac 1990: Extremely focused, with elegant fruit flavors and fine tannins that cleanse the palate. (NR) (5/15/92) (BT) **85+**
Fronsac 1989: Enticing and well polished, with lots of ripe plum and berry aromas and flavors and plenty of silky tannins, too. This producer is really improving in quality. Better after 1996. $16 (3/15/92) **88**
Fronsac 1988: Oaky and tannic, but this hard-edged style has a solid core of black cherry and currant flavors, too. Picks up herb and vegetal notes on the aftertaste. Drink now to 1994. $19 (10/31/91) **81**
Fronsac 1987 $14 (5/15/90) **82**
Fronsac 1986 $15 (5/15/91) **81**
Fronsac 1985 $15 (12/31/88) **88**

CHATEAU VILLARS
Fronsac 1991: Very aromatic, with a lovely perfumed berry nose, light black licorice flavors and a very watery finish. (NR) (5/15/92) (BT) **75+**

Graves/Pessac-Léognan

CHATEAU BAHANS-HAUT-BRION
Pessac-Léognan 1991: Not the most powerful wine, but it's very balanced, with plenty of tobacco and earth flavors and a fine backbone of tannins. (NR) (5/15/92) (BT) **85+**
Pessac-Léognan 1990: Rich and smoky, with an earthy berry character and a lovely backbone of ripe tannins. Second wine of Haut-Brion. (NR) (5/15/92) (BT) **90+**
Pessac-Léognan 1989: Along with very firm tannins, this wine shows fresh blackberry and stone aromas and flavors and a velvety mouth-feel. Quite dense on the palate. The second wine of Haut-Brion. Try after 1997. $32 (3/15/92) **90**
Pessac-Léognan 1988 $20 (8/31/90) (BT) **80+**
Pessac-Léognan 1987 $19 (6/30/89) (BT) **75+**
Pessac-Léognan 1986 Rel: $22 Cur: $26 (9/15/89) **86**
Graves 1985 $20 (5/15/87) (BT) **80+**

CHATEAU BARET
Pessac-Léognan 1989: A big wine, with fantastic aromas and flavors of chocolate, fruit, nutmeg and berry. Has a tight tannin structure; needs lots of time. A great value. Try after 1998. $18 (3/15/92) **93**
Pessac-Léognan 1988 $15 (6/30/89) (BT) **70+**
Pessac-Léognan 1987 $14 (6/30/89) (BT) **75+**
Pessac-Léognan 1986 $16 (5/15/87) (BT) **70+**

CHATEAU LE BONNAT
Graves 1989: Lean and leathery, with floral and currant notes that are tightly wrapped in tannin. Needs time to soften and evolve. Try after 1996. $18 (4/30/92) **81**
Graves 1988: Beautifully focused berry and cherry aromas and flavors glide smoothly across the palate, making this drinkable now, but it has the concentration and balance to keep maturing through 1994 or '95. A juicy wine that should appeal to Bordeaux enthusiasts for its pure flavors. $18 (12/31/88) **87**
Graves 1987: Has better color and more focused flavors than most '87s, showing dark cherry, chocolate and toast flavors on a sturdy structure worth cellaring through 1993, but it's drinkable now. $12 (4/15/90) **83**

CHATEAU BONNET
Graves 1985 $5.50 (4/15/88) BB **84**

CHATEAU BOUSCAUT
Pessac-Léognan 1991: An astringent wine. Despite good fruit flavors, it seems very disjointed and lacking in concentration. (NR) (5/15/92) (BT) **75+**
Pessac-Léognan 1990 (NR) (4/30/91) (BT) **90+**
Pessac-Léognan 1989: The fruit jumps out of the glass, with masses of cassis, berry and earth aromas and flavors and a bounty of velvety tannins to back them up. Try after 1997. $22 (3/15/92) **93**
Pessac-Léognan 1988 $20 (4/30/91) **87**
Pessac-Léognan 1987 $10 (6/30/89) (BT) **80+**
Pessac-Léognan 1986 Rel: $9 Cur: $14 (2/15/89) **78**
Graves 1985 $15 (12/31/88) **90**
Graves 1981 $12 (5/01/84) **86**

CHATEAU BROWN
Pessac-Léognan 1988 $17 (6/30/89) (BT) **80+**
Pessac-Léognan 1987 $15 (6/30/89) (BT) **75+**
Pessac-Léognan 1986 $19 (5/15/87) (BT) **80+**

CHATEAU CARBONNIEUX
Pessac-Léognan 1991: Doesn't offer much in the mouth. Has pretty aromas and modest flavors, but it's just too diluted to be good. (NR) (5/15/92) (BT) **75+**
Pessac-Léognan 1990: Not a huge wine, but round and soft, with sweet floral and fruit aromas and flavors and a good backbone of tannins. (NR) (5/15/92) (BT) **85+**
Pessac-Léognan 1989: A delicate wine, with sweet berry and coffee flavors and medium, round tannins. Lacks a bit of intensity on the palate, but it shows class. Try after 1995. $22 (3/15/92) **85**
Pessac-Léognan 1988 $20 (2/28/91) **86**
Pessac-Léognan 1987 $15 (5/15/90) **80**
Pessac-Léognan 1986 $18 (9/15/89) **87**
Graves 1985 $16 (11/30/88) **87**

CHATEAU CARMES-HAUT-BRION
Pessac-Léognan 1988 $22 (6/30/89) (BT) **75+**
Pessac-Léognan 1987 $20 (6/30/89) (BT) **75+**
Pessac-Léognan 1986 $26 (6/30/88) (BT) **80+**

CHATEAU DE CHANTEGRIVE
Pessac-Léognan 1989: A pretty wine, with cherry, herb and berry aromas and flavors wrapped in medium, silky tannins. Not as big and powerful as some, but very attractive. Much better than from the barrel. Try after 1996. (NR) (3/15/92) **88**
Pessac-Léognan Cuvée Edouard 1989: Has plenty of cassis and berry aromas and flavors and a highly extracted tannin character, but it's a little flat on the finish, with too much wood. Tasted twice. Drink after 1995. (NR) (3/15/92) **85**

CHATEAU CHENE VERT
Pessac-Léognan 1987 (NR) (6/30/89) (BT) **65+**

DOMAINE DE CHEVALIER
Pessac-Léognan 1989: We underrated this from the barrel. A captivating wine, with masses of rich fruit and super-fine tannins. The vanilla, smoke, earth and fruit flavors go on and on. This is classic. Try after 1999. $59 (3/15/92) **96**
Graves 1961: Deep garnet. Sweet and fruity in aroma, with vanilla extract and beefy notes emerging. Has elegant, ripe fruit and sweet cassis flavors and a tannic structure. Close to its peak. ($NA) (4/30/92) (TR) **91**

DOMAINE DE CHEVALIER
Pessac-Léognan 1991: An alluring wine, with attractive berry, vanilla and cedar aromas and flavors and medium tannins on the finish. (NR) (5/15/92) (BT) **85+**
Pessac-Léognan 1990: Has amazing tar, plum and ripe fruit aromas that follow through on the palate. A great backbone of tannins makes it a complete knockout. (NR) (5/15/92) (BT) **95+**
Pessac-Léognan 1988: Much subtlety and grace despite a high dose of fine tannins. The creamy vanilla overtones add richness and depth to the focused plum, currant and blackberry flavors. Almost drinkable now, but better after 1995 to '98. 5,000 cases made. $37 (7/15/91) **91**
Pessac-Léognan 1987 $29 (6/30/89) (BT) **80+**
Pessac-Léognan 1986 Rel: $33 Cur: $38 (6/15/89) **89**
Graves 1985 Rel: $43 Cur: $62 (9/30/88) CS **92**
Graves 1984 Rel: $20 Cur: $35 (8/31/87) **90**
Graves 1979 $47 (10/15/89) (JS) **87**
Graves 1961 $180 (3/16/86) (TR) **76**
Graves 1959 $100 (10/15/90) (JS) **97**
Graves 1945 $180 (3/16/86) (JS) **59**

Key to Symbols

The scores reported here are the results of blind tastings conducted by our panel of senior editors. Wines that carry the initials below are results of individual tastings.

THE WINE SPECTATOR 100-POINT SCALE 95-100—Classic, a great wine; ***90-94***—Outstanding, superior character and style; ***80-89***—Good to very good, a wine with special qualities; ***70-79***—Average, drinkable wine that may have minor flaws; ***60-69***—Below average, drinkable but not recommended; ***50-59***—Poor, undrinkable, not recommended. "+"—With a score indicates a range; used primarily with barrel tastings to indicate a preliminary score.

SPECIAL DESIGNATIONS SS—Spectator Selection, CS—Cellar Selection, BB—Best Buy, ($NA)—Price not available, (NR)—Not released.

TASTER'S INITIALS (JG)—Jim Gordon, (HS)—Harvey Steiman, (JL)—James Laube, (JS)—James Suckling, (TM)—Thomas Matthews, (TR)—Terry Robards, (PM)—Per-Henrik Mansson, (BT)—Barrel Tasting (these wines were tasted blind from barrel samples), (CA-date)—*California's Great Cabernets* by James Laube, (CH-date)—*California's Great Chardonnays* by James Laube, (VP-date)—*Vintage Port* by James Suckling.

DATE TASTED Dates in parentheses represent the issue in which the rating was published.

CHATEAU DE CRUZEAU
Pessac-Léognan 1990: Plenty of pretty raspberry and other fruit character in this wine. Extremely polished, with lots of fine tannins on the finish. From the same family that brings you La Louvière. (NR) (5/15/92) (BT) **90+**
Pessac-Léognan 1989: Offers excellent fruit flavors and tobacco, berry and vanilla notes, as well as plenty of tannins, but seems a little dry on the finish. Drink after 1996. $14 (3/15/92) **86**
Pessac-Léognan 1988: A solid effort, displaying the distinctive herb and mineral aromas and flavors of the appellation against a modest core of currant flavor. The lean framework shows plenty of tannin for the long haul. Drink after 1994 or '95. $14 (2/28/91) **87**
Pessac-Léognan 1987 $12 (6/30/89) (BT) **75+**
Pessac-Léognan 1986 $10 (6/30/89) **87**
Graves 1985 $9 (6/15/88) BB **85**
Graves 1982 $7 (12/16/85) **84**

CHATEAU FERRANDE
Graves 1981 $7.50 (3/16/85) **75**

CHATEAU DE FIEUZAL
Pessac-Léognan 1991: Very pleasant, with tar, tobacco and game flavors and supple tannins. (NR) (5/15/92) (BT) **80+**
Pessac-Léognan 1990: A solid wine, with an iron backbone of tannins and super-condensed fruit. Doesn't give much now, but appears to have great depth. (NR) (5/15/92) (BT) **90+**
Pessac-Léognan 1989: A big Bordeaux, with great presence on the palate and a stylish character of black pepper, raisin, earth, game and fruit flavors. Has a full tannin structure, but it's ripe and firm. Try after 1998. $32 (3/15/92) **95**
Pessac-Léognan 1988 $32 (4/30/91) **91**
Pessac-Léognan 1987 $18 (5/15/90) **81**
Pessac-Léognan 1986 Rel: $21 Cur: $25 (6/30/89) **90**
Graves 1985 $24 (6/15/88) **90**
Graves 1982 Rel: $12 Cur: $22 (5/01/85) **81**
Graves 1982 Rel: $12 Cur: $22 (2/01/85) **81**
Graves 1979 $25 (10/15/89) (JS) **83**

CHATEAU DE FRANCE
Pessac-Léognan 1991: A subtle wine, with lovely, light, delicate berry and tobacco flavors and silky tannins. (NR) (5/15/92) (BT) **80+**
Pessac-Léognan 1989: Extremely elegant and long, with chocolate and cherry aromas and flavors and a fine tannin structure. Shows class. Try after 1996. $22 (3/15/92) **89**
Pessac-Léognan 1988: A pleasant surprise. Lots of bright, lively cherry, raspberry and currant aromas and flavors pervade this beautifully balanced, harmonious wine. The tannins are integrated into the whole structure, turning smooth and elegant on the finish. Tempting now, but cellaring until 1993 to '97 should bring out its best. $18 (2/28/91) SS **92**
Pessac-Léognan 1987 $15 (6/30/89) (BT) **80+**
Pessac-Léognan 1986 $15 (6/30/88) (BT) **80+**

CHATEAU LA GARDE
Pessac-Léognan 1988 $15 (6/30/89) (BT) **75+**
Pessac-Léognan 1987 $13 (6/30/89) (BT) **70+**
Pessac-Léognan 1986 $14 (5/15/87) (BT) **70+**

DOMAINE DE GRAND MAISON
Pessac-Léognan 1986: Earthy, a bit stinky, but firm and generous with enough dark cherry flavors to be appealing in a more or less typical Graves style. Firm enough to indicate cellaring until 1993. $8.50 (4/15/90) **80**

CHATEAU HAUT-BAILLY
Pessac-Léognan 1990 (NR) (4/30/91) (BT) **85+**
Pessac-Léognan 1989: Highly extracted, with tons of grape and blackberry nuances on the nose and palate. Shows great intensity of fruit and tannins. Try after 1997. $32 (3/15/92) **92**
Pessac-Léognan 1988: Enormously thick, dense and tannic, this is rich, intense and deeply concentrated, with layers of currant, cedar, spice and vanilla flavors that gently unfold on the palate. Despite the tannins, it's gentle and subtle. Needs cellaring until 2000. $30 (4/30/91) **94**
Pessac-Léognan 1987 $20 (6/30/88) (BT) **85+**
Pessac-Léognan 1986 $23 (6/15/89) **91**
Graves 1985 $28 (6/15/88) **89**
Graves 1984 $15 (6/15/87) **87**
Graves 1983 $21 (4/16/86) **86**
Graves 1981 Rel: $13 Cur: $21 (6/01/84) **87**
Graves 1979 $28 (10/15/89) (JS) **84**
Graves 1945 $200 (3/16/86) (JL) **94**

CHATEAU HAUT-BERGEY
Pessac-Léognan 1989 (NR) (4/30/91) (BT) **85+**
Pessac-Léognan 1988 $12 (6/30/89) (BT) **80+**
Pessac-Léognan 1987 (NR) (6/30/89) (BT) **65+**
Pessac-Léognan 1986 (NR) (6/30/88) (BT) **80+**

CHATEAU HAUT-BRION
Pessac-Léognan 1991: Delicious, with more fruit than La Mission, showing a firm backbone and a surprising amount of concentration for this vintage. Close to outstanding in quality. (NR) (5/15/92) (BT) **85+**
Pessac-Léognan 1990: Shows wonderful ripeness, and everything is in near-perfect proportion. A dense, balanced wine, with great, ripe tannins and fruit aromas and flavors. (NR) (5/15/92) (BT) **95+**
Pessac-Léognan 1989: Big and meaty, with lots of fruit and full tannins, but shows a sweetness and silkiness on the finish. A wine for aging. Try after 1998. $150 (3/15/92) **97**
Pessac-Léognan 1988: Amazingly harmonious, complex and supple, with intense, generous plum, currant, spice, cedar, cherry and anise flavors that have a wonderful sense of finesse and grace. The tannins are intense, yet graceful, allowing the flavors to pour through on the finish. Best to cellar until 2001 to 2009. $95 (4/30/91) **98**
Pessac-Léognan 1987: Distinctive for its rich, earthy, leathery flavors of ripe, smooth currant, herb, tea and spice. The flavors are broad and complex, particularly for an '87. Smooth, mellow tannins are a big plus. Not a long ager, but it's beautifully proportioned. Drink now to '97. $70 (10/15/90) **90**
Pessac-Léognan 1986 $88 (6/30/89) **92**
Graves 1985 Rel: $70 Cur: $83 (4/30/88) **96**
Graves 1984 Rel: $36 Cur: $44 (7/31/87) **80**
Graves 1983 $86 (9/30/86) SS **95**
Graves 1982 Rel: $60 Cur: $120 (7/01/85) **92**
Graves 1981 Rel: $56 Cur: $73 (5/01/89) **92**
Graves 1979 $90 (11/15/91) (JS) **92**
Graves 1978 $105 (11/15/91) (JS) **96**
Graves 1975 $125 (11/15/91) (JS) **92**
Graves 1974 $33 (11/15/91) (JS) **74**
Graves 1971 $110 (11/15/91) (JS) **85**
Graves 1970 $140 (11/15/91) (JS) **94**
Graves 1966 $310 (11/15/91) (JS) **94**
Graves 1962 $170 (11/15/91) (JS) **93**
Graves 1961 $430 (11/15/91) (JS) **100**
Graves 1959 $340 (11/15/91) (JS) **98**
Graves 1949 $370 (11/15/91) (JS) **95**
Graves 1945 $840 (11/15/91) (JS) **99**

CHATEAU HAUT-GARDERE
Pessac-Léognan 1986: Hard as nails—tastes a bit metallic, too—its tightly wound raspberry and plum fruit is buried beneath a sheet of prickly tannin. Needs cellaring at least until 1994, then see what develops. It could turn out to be quite a graceful wine. $11 (9/30/89) **81**
Graves 1985 $15 (7/31/88) **77**

CHATEAU HAUT-LAGRANGE
Pessac-Léognan 1991: A relatively smooth, soft style of wine, with a lot of currant character. Surprisingly good. (NR) (5/15/92) (BT) **85+**

CHATEAU LES HAUTS DE SMITH
Pessac-Léognan 1988 (NR) (6/30/89) (BT) **75+**
Pessac-Léognan 1987 (NR) (6/30/89) (BT) **70+**

L DE LA LOUVIERE
Pessac-Léognan 1990: A monster of a wine, with mouth-puckering tannins that seem coarse, but it also has plenty of fruit. (NR) (5/15/92) (BT) **85+**

CHATEAU LARRIVET-HAUT-BRION
Pessac-Léognan 1991: Has attractive cherry and earth aromas and flavors, but it's quite diluted and really isn't giving much at the moment. (NR) (5/15/92) (BT) **75+**
Pessac-Léognan 1990: Very sturdy, with firm tannins and focused berry, dark chocolate and tar flavors. (NR) (5/15/92) (BT) **90+**
Pessac-Léognan 1989: A decadent wine, with smoky, gamy earth and berry aromas and flavors and a full, round tannin structure. It's not giving much now, making it somewhat difficult to taste. Has perhaps a little too much oak on the palate. Not as good as the '88. Try after 1997. $33 (3/15/92) **89**
Pessac-Léognan 1988 $25 (4/30/91) **94**
Pessac-Léognan 1987 $17 (6/30/89) (BT) **75+**
Pessac-Léognan 1986 $17 (6/15/89) **82**

CHATEAU LA LOUVIERE
Pessac-Léognan 1990: What a beauty. Offers lovely, sweet berry and raspberry aromas and flavors and fine tannins. Keeps you coming back for more. (NR) (5/15/92) (BT) **90+**
Pessac-Léognan 1989: A perennial *Wine Spectator* favorite. Like crushed grapes; this stylish wine has very concentrated mint and berry flavors and compact, silky tannins. A little tough now, but it should round with age. Try after 1998. $22 (3/15/92) **91**
Pessac-Léognan 1988: Rich, ripe and supple, with pretty currant, plum, cherry and smoky oak flavors that are deep and complex. The tannins are fine and soft, but firm. A seductive wine, with length and persistence; the finish lingers on and on. A stylish '88. Cellar until 1997. $20 (8/31/91) SS **92**
Pessac-Léognan 1987 $20 (6/30/89) (BT) **80+**
Pessac-Léognan 1986: Rich and elegant with a firm, tannic structure, but the fruit comes rolling through on the finish. The Cabernet flavor is matched with more austere earth, cedar, mineral and plum flavors. Can stand until 1994 to 1996 in the cellar. $25 (6/15/89) **91**
Graves 1985 $16 (6/30/88) **87**
Graves 1983 Rel: $11 Cur: $17 (11/30/86) **78**
Graves 1982 Rel: $11 Cur: $25 (10/16/85) SS **94**

CHATEAU MAGNEAU
Graves 1987: Aromatic with a leathery, floral character, but the tannins clamp down on the palate and the wine does not have the intensity to stand up to it. $12 (5/15/90) **78**

CHATEAU MALARTIC-LAGRAVIERE
Pessac-Léognan 1989: Shows ripe fruit, with cherry and raspberry flavors and silky tannins, but it seems to lack a bit of intensity. Try after 1996. $24 (3/15/92) **85**
Pessac-Léognan 1988: Ripe and focused, with lots of smoky, toasty overtones to the currant and cherry flavors, turning supple on the finish, despite firm support from well- integrated tannins. A well-crafted wine that should be at its best after 1994 or '95. $20 (7/15/91) **84**
Pessac-Léognan 1987 $18 (6/30/89) (BT) **80+**
Pessac-Léognan 1986 Rel: $18 Cur: $27 (6/15/89) **90**
Graves 1985 $22 (5/15/87) (BT) **90+**

CHATEAU MERIC
Graves 1988: Simple, ripe and straightforward, with modest currant, cedar and tobacco aromas and flavors. Has a firm texture and turns a bit tough on the finish. Best around 1993. $17 (4/30/91) **76**

CHATEAU LA MISSION-HAUT-BRION
Pessac-Léognan 1991: Elegant and balanced, with fine tannins, fresh acidity and a flavorful finish. (NR) (5/15/92) (BT) **85+**
Pessac-Léognan 1990: A powerful, muscular wine, with loads of ripe tannins and full fruit flavors that go on and on. (NR) (5/15/92) (BT) **95+**
Pessac-Léognan 1989: Rich and firm, with lots of pepper, game and earth notes on the nose and palate and plenty of velvety tannins. The mixture of new oak and fruit makes this exceedingly attractive. Try after 1997. $120 (3/15/92) **96**
Pessac-Léognan 1988 $90 (11/15/91) (JS) **90**
Pessac-Léognan 1987 $39 (11/15/91) (JS) **84**
Pessac-Léognan 1986 Rel: $50 Cur: $60 (11/15/91) (JS) **97**
Graves 1985 $70 (11/15/91) (JS) **95**
Graves 1984 $55 (11/15/91) (JS) **85**
Graves 1983 $63 (11/15/91) (JS) **87**
Graves 1982 $95 (11/15/91) (JS) **93**
Graves 1981 $60 (11/15/91) (JS) **87**
Graves 1980 $35 (11/15/91) (JS) **86**
Graves 1979 Rel: $48 Cur: $75 (11/15/91) (JS) **86**
Graves 1978 $135 (11/15/91) (JS) **94**
Graves 1975 $280 (11/15/91) (JS) **90**
Graves 1974 $60 (11/15/91) (JS) **87**
Graves 1973 $36 (11/15/91) (JS) **80**
Graves 1972 $50 (11/15/91) (JS) **77**
Graves 1971 $90 (11/15/91) (JS) **91**
Graves 1970 $145 (11/15/91) (JS) **83**
Graves 1969 $38 (11/15/91) (JS) **84**
Graves 1968 $50 (11/15/91) (JS) **67**
Graves 1967 $85 (11/15/91) (JS) **89**
Graves 1966 $185 (11/15/91) (JS) **93**
Graves 1965 $60 (11/15/91) (JS) **76**
Graves 1964 $200 (11/15/91) (JS) **91**
Graves 1963 $165 (11/15/91) (JS) **78**
Graves 1962 $161 (11/15/91) (JS) **90**
Graves 1961 $520 (11/15/91) (JS) **98**
Graves 1960 $200 (11/15/91) (JS) **84**
Graves 1959 $310 (11/15/91) (JS) **94**
Graves 1958 $130 (11/15/91) (JS) **83**
Graves 1957 $165 (11/15/91) (JS) **85**
Graves 1956 ($NA) (11/15/91) (JS) **87**
Graves 1955 $400 (11/15/91) (JS) **89**
Graves 1954 ($NA) (11/15/91) (JS) **86**
Graves 1953 $400 (11/15/91) (JS) **93**
Graves 1952 $190 (11/15/91) (JS) **98**

Graves 1950 $350 (11/15/91) (JS) **79**
Graves 1949 $600 (11/15/91) (JS) **95**
Graves 1948 ($NA) (11/15/91) (JS) **98**
Graves 1947 $680 (11/15/91) (JS) **100**
Graves 1946 $700 (11/15/91) (JS) **85**
Graves 1945 $800 (11/15/91) (JS) **94**
Graves 1944 $175 (11/15/91) (JS) **78**
Graves 1943 $300 (11/15/91) (JS) **88**
Graves 1942 $260 (11/15/91) (JS) **83**
Graves 1941 $450 (11/15/91) (JS) **81**
Graves 1940 $330 (11/15/91) (JS) **82**
Graves 1939 $190 (11/15/91) (JS) **87**
Graves 1938 $128 (11/15/91) (JS) **81**
Graves 1937 $195 (11/15/91) (JS) **88**
Graves 1936 $200 (11/15/91) (JS) **62**
Graves 1935 $580 (11/15/91) (JS) **85**
Graves 1934 $350 (11/15/91) (JS) **86**
Graves 1933 $480 (11/15/91) (JS) **74**
Graves 1931 $380 (11/15/91) (JS) **70**
Graves 1929 $780 (11/15/91) (JS) **100**
Graves 1928 $470 (11/15/91) (JS) **84**
Graves 1926 $380 (11/15/91) (JS) **59**
Graves 1924 $450 (11/15/91) (JS) **89**
Graves 1921 $650 (11/15/91) (JS) **85**
Graves 1919 $300 (11/15/91) (JS) **85**
Graves 1918 $350 (11/15/91) (JS) **83**
Graves 1916 $350 (11/15/91) (JS) **82**
Graves 1914 $780 (11/15/91) (JS) **65**
Graves 1904 $600 (11/15/91) (JS) **85**
Graves 1899 ($NA) (11/15/91) (JS) **92**
Graves 1895 $750 (11/15/91) (JS) **99**
Graves 1888 ($NA) (11/15/91) (JS) **95**
Graves 1877 ($NA) (11/15/91) (JS) **93**

CHATEAU OLIVIER
Pessac-Léognan 1991: A succulent wine, with lovely cherry flavors and fine tannins, although it's light in the center. (NR) (5/15/92) (BT) **80+**
Pessac-Léognan 1990: Excellent flavor intensity on the finish fills your taste buds; shows excellent tannin and fruit structure. (NR) (5/15/92) (BT) **90+**
Pessac-Léognan 1989: A wine rated "classic" at less than $20 is extremely rare. This is a heavyweight boxer of a Bordeaux, with tons of fruit and lots of tannins giving it great muscle tone. The coffee, earth, spice and berry aromas and flavors go on and on. This estate has improved in quality by leaps and bounds. Try after 1999. $19 (3/15/92) SS **95**
Pessac-Léognan 1988 Rel: $23 Cur: $31 (2/15/91) **91**
Pessac-Léognan 1987 Rel: $20 Cur: $24 (6/30/89) (BT) **80+**
Pessac-Léognan 1986 Rel: $16 Cur: $20 (6/30/88) (BT) **85+**
Graves 1985 Rel: $15 Cur: $25 (2/15/89) SS **93**
Graves 1983 Rel: $15 Cur: $23 (5/01/89) **92**
Graves 1982 Rel: $17 Cur: $26 (3/15/87) **89**
Graves 1981 $14 (10/16/85) **86**

CHATEAU LE PAPE
Pessac-Léognan 1988 (NR) (6/30/89) (BT) **60+**
Pessac-Léognan 1987 (NR) (6/30/89) (BT) **75+**

CHATEAU PAPE-CLEMENT
Pessac-Léognan 1990: A decadent wine, with gamy berry aromas, rich fruit flavors and a firm backbone of tannins. Very close to being outstanding. (NR) (5/15/92) (BT) **85+**
Pessac-Léognan 1989: A lovely wine, with ripe plum and tobacco aromas and flavors and firm tannins. Try after 1997. $43 (3/15/92) **88**
Pessac-Léognan 1988: Rich and elegant, with classic Bordeaux aromas of cedar, tar, currant and spice held in check by firm, polished tannins and lively acidity. The earthy, flinty flavors add dimension and depth to the fruit, which was tightly wrapped up when tasted. Drink now to 1998. $40 (12/31/90) **93**
Pessac-Léognan 1987 Rel: $24 Cur: $27 (5/15/90) **84**
Pessac-Léognan 1986 $36 (6/30/89) **92**
Graves 1985 $44 (6/30/88) **83**
Graves 1983 Rel: $20 Cur: $30 (3/31/87) **89**
Graves 1982 Rel: $24 Cur: $34 (2/01/85) **84**
Graves 1981 Rel: $17 Cur: $20 (6/01/84) **77**
Graves 1979 $40 (10/15/89) (JS) **84**
Graves 1962 $120 (11/30/87) (JS) **90**
Graves 1961 $140 (3/16/86) (TR) **77**
Graves 1959 $100 (10/15/90) (JS) **80**

CHATEAU PIQUE-CAILLOU
Pessac-Léognan 1991: Watery and weedy, with a metallic note and drying tannins; it's very diluted. (NR) (5/15/92) (BT) **65+**
Pessac-Léognan 1988 (NR) (6/30/89) (BT) **75+**
Pessac-Léognan 1987 (NR) (6/30/89) (BT) **70+**
Pessac-Léognan 1986 (NR) (6/30/88) (BT) **80+**

CHATEAU RAHOUL
Graves 1988: Light in color and lean and woody in aroma and flavor, offering modest fruit and hints of toast in the background. Possibly a bit watery in texture. Misses the mark for this vintage. Tasted twice. $18 (8/31/91) **80**
Graves 1986: Firm in texture and gently flavorful, with a supple core of cranberry and cherry flavors overlaid with meaty, more mature overtones. Seems to be developing well and should continue through 1993 to '95. Could stand to lose some tannin. $18 (12/31/90) **83**

Key to Symbols

The scores reported here are the results of blind tastings conducted by our panel of senior editors. Wines that carry the initials below are results of individual tastings.

THE WINE SPECTATOR 100-POINT SCALE 95-100—Classic, a great wine; *90-94*—Outstanding, superior character and style; *80-89*—Good to very good, a wine with special qualities; *70-79*—Average, drinkable wine that may have minor flaws; *60-69*—Below average, drinkable but not recommended; *50-59*—Poor, undrinkable, not recommended. "+"—With a score indicates a range; used primarily with barrel tastings to indicate a preliminary score.

SPECIAL DESIGNATIONS SS—Spectator Selection, CS—Cellar Selection, BB—Best Buy, ($NA)—Price not available, (NR)—Not released.

TASTER'S INITIALS (JG)—Jim Gordon, (HS)—Harvey Steiman, (JL)—James Laube, (JS)—James Suckling, (TM)—Thomas Matthews, (TR)—Terry Robards, (PM)—Per-Henrik Mansson, (BT)—Barrel Tasting (these wines were tasted blind from barrel samples), (CA-date)—*California's Great Cabernets* by James Laube, (CH-date)—*California's Great Chardonnays* by James Laube, (VP-date)—*Vintage Port* by James Suckling.

DATE TASTED Dates in parentheses represent the issue in which the rating was published.

CHATEAU RESPIDE-MEDEVILLE
Graves 1985 $12 (2/29/88) **85**

CHATEAU DE ROCHEMORIN
Pessac-Léognan 1990: A well-articulated wine, with lovely proportions of ripe fruit and round tannins. Has plenty of everything. (NR) (5/15/92) (BT) **90+**
Pessac-Léognan 1989: Shows lovely, rich, earthy nutmeg and berry aromas and flavors coupled with chunky, velvety tannins. Try after 1997. $14 (3/15/92) **88**
Pessac-Léognan 1988 $13 (6/30/89) (BT) **75+**
Pessac-Léognan 1987 (NR) (6/30/89) (BT) **75+**
Pessac-Léognan 1986 Rel: $10 Cur: $15 (6/15/89) **84**
Graves 1985 Rel: $9 Cur: $14 (6/15/88) **85**

CHATEAU LE SARTRE
Pessac-Léognan 1991: A straightforward wine, with berry flavors and tannins, but it's quite light on the finish. (NR) (5/15/92) (BT) **75+**
Pessac-Léognan 1990: A balanced wine, with an ample amount of ripe tannins and fruit, but it seems slightly lean. (NR) (5/15/92) (BT) **80+**
Pessac-Léognan 1987 (NR) (6/30/89) (BT) **75+**

CHATEAU SMITH-HAUT-LAFITTE
Pessac-Léognan 1991: Well made, packed with berry and earth flavors and round, ripe tannins. A firm, supple wine. (NR) (5/15/92) (BT) **85+**
Pessac-Léognan 1990 (NR) (4/30/91) (BT) **85+**
Pessac-Léognan 1989: A vivid wine, with exciting black cherry and earth aromas and flavors and medium-hard tannins. A mean, tough wine that needs time. Try after 1997. $19 (3/15/92) **91**
Pessac-Léognan 1988 $15 (6/30/89) (BT) **80+**
Pessac-Léognan 1987 $15 (5/15/90) **84**
Pessac-Léognan 1986 $15 (6/30/88) (BT) **85+**
Graves 1985 Rel: $15 Cur: $23 (11/30/88) **89**
Graves 1981 Rel: $12 Cur: $18 (6/01/84) **79**
Graves 1979 $20 (10/15/89) (JS) **69**

CHATEAU LA TOUR-HAUT-BRION
Pessac-Léognan 1991: Fresh and flavorful, with plenty of tobacco, berry and cherry flavors and fine tannins. (NR) (5/15/92) (BT) **80+**
Pessac-Léognan 1990: Has lovely, rich coconut and tobacco flavors, fine tannins and a firm backbone. (NR) (5/15/92) (BT) **85+**
Pessac-Léognan 1989: Unbelievable for a second wine. Shows enormous class, with tobacco, chocolate, berry and vanilla aromas and flavors and full, yet fine tannins. Truly outstanding. The second wine of La Mission. Try after 1998. $52 (3/15/92) **95**
Pessac-Léognan 1988 $37 (6/15/91) CS **91**
Pessac-Léognan 1987 $22 (5/15/90) **87**
Pessac-Léognan 1986 $33 (6/30/88) (BT) **85+**
Graves 1985 $42 (2/15/89) **86**
Graves 1983 Rel: $25 Cur: $31 (3/15/87) **90**
Graves 1979 $30 (11/15/91) (JS) **85**
Graves 1975 $115 (11/15/91) (JS) **84**
Graves 1970 $150 (11/15/91) (JS) **84**
Graves 1966 $175 (11/15/91) (JS) **84**
Graves 1964 ($NA) (11/15/91) (JS) **83**
Graves 1962 $40 (11/30/87) (JS) **85**
Graves 1961 $200 (11/15/91) (JS) **89**
Graves 1959 $190 (11/15/91) (JS) **84**
Graves 1958 $120 (11/15/91) (JS) **85**
Graves 1957 ($NA) (11/15/91) (JS) **86**
Graves 1955 ($NA) (11/15/91) (JS) **87**
Graves 1953 ($NA) (11/15/91) (JS) **86**
Graves 1950 ($NA) (11/15/91) (JS) **50**
Graves 1947 $580 (11/15/91) (JS) **91**
Graves 1945 $520 (11/15/91) (JS) **87**
Graves 1943 ($NA) (11/15/91) (JS) **85**
Graves 1940 ($NA) (11/15/91) (JS) **83**
Graves 1929 $550 (11/15/91) (JS) **85**
Graves 1928 ($NA) (11/15/91) (JS) **68**

CHATEAU LA TOUR-LEOGNAN
Pessac-Léognan 1987 (NR) (6/30/89) (BT) **70+**
Pessac-Léognan 1986: Firm and hard now, but beneath the tough surface beats a heart of graceful cherry and currant flavor, cedary and slightly smoky. Has real Graves character that should emerge with short-term cellaring. Drink now through 1997. $11 (2/15/89) **85**

CHATEAU LA TOUR-MARTILLAC
Pessac-Léognan 1991: There's plenty going on in the glass, with very attractive berry, tobacco and tar characteristics and supple tannins. (NR) (5/15/92) (BT) **85+**
Pessac-Léognan 1990: Starts out slowly, but takes off on the palate, with tar, berry and earth flavors and full tannins. A big wine for aging. (NR) (5/15/92) (BT) **90+**
Pessac-Léognan 1989 $20 (4/30/91) (BT) **85+**
Pessac-Léognan 1988 $24 (2/28/91) **88**
Pessac-Léognan 1987 $15 (6/30/88) (BT) **75+**
Pessac-Léognan 1986 $15 (2/15/90) **90**
Graves 1985 $19 (8/31/88) **87**

HAUT-MÉDOC

CHATEAU D'AGASSAC
Haut-Médoc 1989: Very silky and balanced, with ripe blackberry and raspberry aromas and flavors and excellent, ultrafine tannins. Better after 1995. (NR) (3/15/92) **88**

CHATEAU ARNAULD
Haut-Médoc 1991: Shows interesting, earthy ash aromas, modest, decent fruit flavors and medium tannins. (NR) (5/15/92) (BT) **75+**
Haut-Médoc 1990: This earthy style has a herbaceous character, medium fruit concentration and medium-light tannins. (NR) (5/15/92) (BT) **80+**
Haut-Médoc 1989: Sweetly perfumed, with lots of ripe berry character to keep you coming back for more. The silky tannins are well integrated. Try after 1995. $14 (3/15/92) **88**
Haut-Médoc 1988 $15 (4/30/91) **84**
Haut-Médoc 1987 $13 (11/30/89) (JS) **79**
Haut-Médoc 1986 $18 (11/30/89) (JS) **82**
Haut-Médoc 1985 $15 (2/15/88) **82**
Haut-Médoc 1983 $8 (1/01/86) **75**
Haut-Médoc 1982 $17 (11/30/89) (JS) **71**

CHATEAU D'ARSAC
Haut-Médoc 1989: A little light for the vintage, with gamy, earthy berry aromas and flavors and medium-silky tannins on the finish. Almost drinkable now, but better after 1994. $9 (3/15/92) **82**
Haut-Médoc 1988 $7 (6/30/89) (BT) **70+**
Haut-Médoc 1987 $6 (6/30/89) (BT) **70+**
Haut-Médoc 1985 $5.75 (2/15/89) **75**

CHATEAU BARREYRES
Haut-Médoc 1986: Ripe earth and herb flavors on a light-to-medium frame, smooth but tannic enough to need until almost 1993 to be ready. $8.25 (6/30/89) **78**

CHATEAU LA BATISSE
Haut-Médoc 1985 $10 (6/30/88) **82**

CHATEAU BEAUMONT
Haut-Médoc 1991: Lovely and delicate, with a palate full of flavors that include licorice, chocolate and vanilla. Has light tannins and a fine finish. (NR) (5/15/92) (BT) **80+**
Haut-Médoc 1990: Very sweet and soft, with interesting wild berry aromas and flavors. (NR) (5/15/92) (BT) **85+**
Haut-Médoc 1989: A simple, straightforward Cabernet-based wine, with clean fruit and medium tannins. Better in 1994. $14 (3/15/92) **82**
Haut-Médoc 1988 $15 (7/15/91) **82**
Haut-Médoc 1987 $13 (6/30/89) (BT) **75+**
Haut-Médoc 1986 $9 (6/30/89) **84**
Haut-Médoc 1985 $8.50 (4/30/88) **74**

CHATEAU BEL-AIR
Haut-Médoc 1988: Leans toward the weedy black currant and herbal spectrum of Bordeaux, with firm fruit and tannins that fan out on the finish. Balanced, with a racy edge to the flavors. Drink in 1994 to '97. $15 (4/30/91) **85**
Haut-Médoc 1986: A lithe, supple wine, glowing with plum, berry and currant aromas and flavors, generous and concentrated. A touch of herbal aroma lends complexity to this harmonious, restrained red. Drink now. A fine value. $9 (11/15/89) BB **88**
Haut-Médoc 1985 $5 (3/15/88) BB **80**
Haut-Médoc 1983 $6 (12/31/86) **83**
Haut-Médoc 1981 $6 (5/01/84) **72**

CHATEAU BELGRAVE
Haut-Médoc 1988: An earthy, herbal edge takes the freshness off this wine, and its flavors lean more toward dill and cedar than fruit. Could be fine after 1993 or '94. $28 (7/31/91) **79**
Haut-Médoc 1986: A clean, well-made wine to drink now. The cedar and chocolate flavors add dimension to the faint cherry notes, but the finish get watery. Drink now or in 1993. $16 (3/31/90) **81**

CHATEAU BREUIL
Haut-Médoc 1991: Light and fruity, but very diluted. There just isn't much there. Second wine of Cissac. (NR) (5/15/92) (BT) **70+**

CHATEAU DE CAMENSAC
Haut-Médoc 1989: Not quite as good as the '88, but it's very well made, with a fine balance of coffee, tobacco and vanilla aromas and flavors and medium tannins. Not a wine to age long, but very pretty and approachable now. Better after 1995. $22 (3/15/92) **86**
Haut-Médoc 1988: Smells and tastes moldy, perhaps corky. Tasted three times, with consistent notes. $16 (7/15/91) **55**
Haut-Médoc 1987 $12 (6/30/89) (BT) **75+**
Haut-Médoc 1986 $14 (6/30/89) **83**
Haut-Médoc 1985 $16 (5/15/87) (BT) **90+**
Haut-Médoc 1979 $22 (10/15/89) (JS) **82**

CHATEAU CANTELAUDE
Haut-Médoc 1986: Fairly rich, but not with the classic fruit of the Médoc. Has herbal aromas, plum and chocolaty flavors and a faintly fruity finish. $17 (6/30/89) **78**

CHATEAU CANTEMERLE
Haut-Médoc 1991: Offers plenty of pretty raspberry and berry flavors, but it's very light, with weediness on the finish. (NR) (5/15/92) (BT) **75+**
Haut-Médoc 1990: Rather exotic, with blueberry and game aromas and flavors and firm tannins. Not showing very well; might get a higher score once the wine's in bottle. (NR) (5/15/92) (BT) **85+**
Haut-Médoc 1989: As solid as a rock, with rich plum and chocolate flavors and super-firm tannins. A wine clearly showing it's worthy of the 1855 classification. Try after 1996. $35 (3/15/92) **91**
Haut-Médoc 1988 $25 (3/15/91) **85**
Haut-Médoc 1987 $21 (5/15/90) **87**
Haut-Médoc 1986 $30 (6/30/89) **89**
Haut-Médoc 1985 $30 (8/31/88) **88**
Haut-Médoc 1984 $17 (6/15/87) **85**
Haut-Médoc 1982 $30 (5/01/89) **92**
Haut-Médoc 1981 Rel: $13 Cur: $17 (5/01/84) **70**
Haut-Médoc 1979 $20 (10/15/89) (JS) **78**
Haut-Médoc 1962 $113 (11/30/87) (JS) **90**
Haut-Médoc 1961 $150 (3/16/86) (TR) **78**
Haut-Médoc 1945 $300 (3/16/86) (JL) **92**

CHATEAU CARONNE STE.-GEMME
Haut-Médoc 1989 (NR) (4/30/91) (BT) **80+**
Haut-Médoc 1988 (NR) (6/30/89) (BT) **75+**
Haut-Médoc 1987 (NR) (6/30/89) (BT) **75+**

CHATEAU CISSAC
Haut-Médoc 1991: Rather crisp and smoky, with berry flavors and medium tannins. (NR) (5/15/92) (BT) **80+**
Haut-Médoc 1989: Tight and closed up for now, but very ripe, with black cherry and tobacco flavors and tons of tannins. Has a very good backbone, so it needs time to come around. Not as good as we remembered last year. Try after 1995. $19 (3/15/92) **85**
Haut-Médoc 1987 $14 (11/30/89) (JS) **81**
Haut-Médoc 1986 $20 (11/30/89) (JS) **79**
Haut-Médoc 1985 $16 (7/31/88) **79**
Haut-Médoc 1982 $20 (11/30/89) (JS) **81**

CHATEAU CITRAN
Haut-Médoc 1991: Very well made, with perfumed aromas and lovely, sweet fruit flavors. Slightly diluted, but it's still very pretty. (NR) (5/15/92) (BT) **85+**
Haut-Médoc 1990: Silky and concentrated, with lots of sweet berry flavor and well-integrated tannins. (NR) (5/15/92) (BT) **90+**
Haut-Médoc 1989: Blasts off like a rocket on your palate. Deep and dark in color, with ripe cassis and mint aromas and flavors and super-powerful tannins. Extremely impressive and well balanced. Try after 1997. $20 (3/15/92) **93**
Haut-Médoc 1988 Rel: $15 Cur: $20 (4/30/91) **91**
Haut-Médoc 1987 $14 (6/30/89) (BT) **75+**
Haut-Médoc 1983 $10 (4/01/86) **82**
Haut-Médoc 1982 Rel: $6 Cur: $12 (4/01/85) **78**

CHATEAU CLEMENT-PICHON
Haut-Médoc 1988: Earthy, leathery aromas and flavors characterize this wine, which echoes currant and plum flavors on the finish. Drinkable, but it's unexceptional. Tasted twice. $15 (8/31/91) **78**
Haut-Médoc 1987 $14 (11/30/89) (JS) **73**
Haut-Médoc 1986: An earthy, gamy wine with all its hard edges intact. It might have come around by now, but it will always be an austere wine. $11 (9/30/89) **76**

LES CLOCHERS DU HAUT-MEDOC
Haut-Médoc 1983 $7 (6/15/87) **60**

CHATEAU COUFRAN
Haut-Médoc 1990 (NR) (4/30/91) (BT) **85+**
Haut-Médoc 1989: A wine with an exceedingly deep fruit and tannin structure, showing tons of tobacco and cassis character. Hold back from drinking until at least 1996. $14 (3/15/92) **89**
Haut-Médoc 1988: Firmly tannic, with a good concentration of basic currant and cedar aromas and flavors. Seems tough and simple now, but cellaring should bring it around. This chunky wine will need at least until 1998 to show its true colors. $15 (4/30/91) **84**
Haut-Médoc 1987 $12 (11/30/89) (JS) **81**
Haut-Médoc 1986 $13 (11/30/89) (JS) **82**
Haut-Médoc 1985 Rel: $11 Cur: $17 (6/30/88) **85**
Haut-Médoc 1982 Rel: $9 Cur: $18 (11/30/89) (JS) **83**

CHATEAU DECORDE
Haut-Médoc 1989: A very ripe style, with an almost raisiny character on the nose and palate, plenty of firm tannins and a clean finish. Better after 1994. (NR) (3/15/92) **83**

DEMOISELLE DE SOCIANDO-MALLET
Haut-Médoc 1989: Firm and tightly structured, with silky tannins and sweet cherry, herb and fruit flavors. The second wine of the excellent *crus bourgeois* Sociando-Mallet. Better after 1994 or '95. $21 (3/15/92) **84**

CHATEAU LA FLEUR BECADE
Haut-Médoc 1988 (NR) (6/30/89) (BT) **70+**

CHATEAU FONTESTEAU
Haut-Médoc 1988 (NR) (6/30/89) (BT) **70+**
Haut-Médoc 1987 (NR) (6/30/89) (BT) **70+**

CHATEAU FOURNAS BERNADOTTE
Haut-Médoc 1988: Woody notes dominate the modest plum flavors in this medium-bodied, simple and tannic wine. Harsh to drink, but gamblers may want to cellar it until 1995. $18 (6/15/91) **76**
Haut-Médoc 1987 $13 (6/30/89) (BT) **65+**

CHATEAU GRAND MOULIN
Haut-Médoc 1983 $6.75 (4/16/86) **63**

CHATEAU GREYSAC
Haut-Médoc 1991: Has decent fruit and tannins, but it falls too much on the finish for us. (NR) (5/15/92) (BT) **75+**

CHATEAU HANTEILLAN
Haut-Médoc 1991: Good for the vintage, with attractive raspberry and cherry aromas, modest, good fruit flavors and a chocolaty, toasty finish. (NR) (5/15/92) (BT) **80+**
Haut-Médoc 1989: Rather light-bodied, weedy and earthy for the vintage, with slightly odd vanilla and margarine flavors and a bitter finish. Drink on release. $14 (3/15/92) **77**
Haut-Médoc 1988 $17 (6/30/89) (BT) **75+**
Haut-Médoc 1987 $13 (11/30/89) (JS) **75**
Haut-Médoc 1986 $15 (11/30/89) (JS) **81**
Haut-Médoc 1982 $18 (11/30/89) (JS) **81**

CHATEAU LABAT
Haut-Médoc 1981 $7 (4/01/85) **72**

CHATEAU LACHESNAYE
Haut-Médoc 1991: Light and pleasant; should make for nice drinking near release. (NR) (5/15/92) (BT) **75+**
Haut-Médoc 1988 $24 (6/30/89) (BT) **75+**
Haut-Médoc 1987 $19 (6/30/89) (BT) **75+**

CHATEAU LA LAGUNE
Haut-Médoc 1989: Not as good as the '88 La Lagune. Tastes like a delicious chocolate-covered raisin. Full-bodied and silky, with plenty of tannins and ripe fruit flavors. A little overdone for us. Better in 1996. $35 (3/15/92) **86**
Haut-Médoc 1988: Wonderfully rich and delicious, with intense, concentrated black cherry, currant, plum and spicy oak flavors that add up to a remarkably stylish, complex wine. The finish is elegant, long and fruity, with fine tannins. Drink in 1995 to 2000. $24 (4/30/91) **91**
Haut-Médoc 1987: Delicious, elegant and harmonious, packed with sweet fruit, vanilla and chocolate flavors, with layers of cedar and smoke. It has a soft, supple finish of plum and cherry. Terrific to drink now, but it probably will age gracefully through 1995. $20 (5/15/90) **89**
Haut-Médoc 1986 Rel: $22 Cur: $26 (6/30/89) **89**
Haut-Médoc 1985 Rel: $22 Cur: $29 (5/15/88) **89**
Haut-Médoc 1984 Rel: $13 Cur: $16 (3/31/87) **86**
Haut-Médoc 1983 Rel: $20 Cur: $30 (4/16/86) **85**
Haut-Médoc 1982 Rel: $28 Cur: $46 (5/01/89) **97**
Haut-Médoc 1981 Rel: $25 Cur: $30 (5/01/89) **82**
Haut-Médoc 1979 $29 (10/15/89) (JS) **86**
Haut-Médoc 1962 $65 (11/30/87) (JS) **80**
Haut-Médoc 1945 $200 (3/16/86) (JL) **87**

CHATEAU DE LAMARQUE
Haut-Médoc 1991: Shows really delicious berry and raspberry flavors and velvety tannins. (NR) (5/15/92) (BT) **85+**
Haut-Médoc 1989: Understated, with very ripe raspberry, chocolate and cherry aromas and flavors and silky tannins. Needs time to open up. Try after 1995. $26 (3/15/92) **89**
Haut-Médoc 1988: Elegant and subtle, with pretty currant, black cherry and plum flavors, but then the tannins begin to take hold. The fruit pours through on the finish, with a touch of smokiness. Cellar until 1995. $20 (4/30/91) **86**
Haut-Médoc 1987 ($NA) (11/30/89) (JS) **74**
Haut-Médoc 1986 $12 (11/30/89) (JS) **75**
Haut-Médoc 1982 ($NA) (11/30/89) (JS) **79**

CHATEAU LAMOTHE-BERGERON
Haut-Médoc 1988 (NR) (6/30/89) (BT) **80+**
Haut-Médoc 1987 (NR) (6/30/89) (BT) **70+**

CHATEAU LAMOTHE-CISSAC
Haut-Médoc 1987 $10 (11/30/89) (JS) **74**
Haut-Médoc 1986 $12 (11/30/89) (JS) **69**

CHATEAU LANDAT
Haut-Médoc 1987 $7 (11/30/89) (JS) **73**

CHATEAU LANDAY
Haut-Médoc 1982 $6.75 (2/16/85) **77**
Haut-Médoc 1981 $6.50 (2/16/85) **72**

CHATEAU LANESSAN
Haut-Médoc 1991: Has an amazing amount of fruit for the vintage, with sweet fruit flavors and integrated tannins. Very good for this year. (NR) (5/15/92) (BT) **85+**
Haut-Médoc 1990 (NR) (4/30/91) (BT) **80+**

Haut-Médoc 1989: A wine with plenty of ripe fruit, full, firm tannins and vanilla, berry and herb aromas that follow through on the palate. Drink after 1995. $29 (3/15/92) **85**
Haut-Médoc 1988 $25 (7/31/91) **80**
Haut-Médoc 1987 $14 (6/30/89) (BT) **70+**
Haut-Médoc 1986 $16 (6/30/88) (BT) **80+**
Haut-Médoc 1985 $16 (4/30/88) **87**

CHATEAU LAROSE-TRINTAUDON
Haut-Médoc 1991: Has delicate, perfumed aromas and medium-light, good fruit flavors, but it's a little diluted. (NR) (5/15/92) (BT) **75+**
Haut-Médoc 1990: One of the better vintages from this estate, showing very good richness, supple tannins and interesting black cherry, mint, licorice and game flavors. (NR) (5/15/92) (BT) **85+**
Haut-Médoc 1989: An excellent value, and one of the best wines ever from this large producer. Has potential for aging, showing plenty of black cherry and earth flavors and well-integrated tannins. Very clean and focused. Try after 1995. $12 (3/15/92) **87**
Haut-Médoc 1988 $12 (4/30/91) **84**
Haut-Médoc 1987 $9 (11/30/89) (JS) **71**
Haut-Médoc 1986 $10 (11/30/89) (JS) **78**
Haut-Médoc 1985 $8.50 (11/30/88) BB **84**
Haut-Médoc 1983 Rel: $7 Cur: $13 (10/15/86) **73**
Haut-Médoc 1982 Rel: $6 Cur: $15 (11/30/89) (JS) **79**
Haut-Médoc 1979 Rel: $5 Cur: $15 (10/15/89) (JS) **76**

CHATEAU LESTAGE-SIMON
Haut-Médoc 1991: Shows very good fruit concentration for the year, with berry and plum characteristics and medium tannins. (NR) (5/15/92) (BT) **80+**
Haut-Médoc 1990: Rich and concentrated, with loads of flavor and silky tannins. Shows class. (NR) (5/15/92) (BT) **85+**
Haut-Médoc 1987 $13 (11/30/89) (JS) **74**
Haut-Médoc 1986 $13 (11/30/89) (JS) **85**
Haut-Médoc 1982 Rel: $10 Cur: $15 (11/30/89) (JS) **84**

CHATEAU LIVERSAN
Haut-Médoc 1990: A refined style, with delicious fruit flavors and silky tannins. Understated, but very good. (NR) (5/15/92) (BT) **85+**
Haut-Médoc 1989: A pretty wine, with an elegant structure of silky tannins and focused berry, cherry and vanilla flavors. Almost as good as the barrel sample last year. Better in 1995. $18 (3/15/92) **87**
Haut-Médoc 1988: Stylish and flavorful, with harmonious currant, plum and oak aromas and flavors, nicely integrated tannins and a soft, fleshy texture. Approachable now, but it should be better by 1994 to '96. $14 (7/31/91) **87**
Haut-Médoc 1987 $13 (6/30/89) (BT) **75+**
Haut-Médoc 1985 $16 (4/30/88) **90**

CHATEAU MAGNOL
Haut-Médoc 1988 (NR) (6/30/89) (BT) **80+**
Haut-Médoc 1987 (NR) (6/30/89) (BT) **75+**
Haut-Médoc 1983 $9.50 (7/31/87) **77**
Haut-Médoc 1981 $8.75 (8/31/87) **69**

CHATEAU MALESCASSE
Haut-Médoc 1991: A pretty little wine, with pleasant vanilla and berry aromas and flavors and a light, fruity finish. (NR) (5/15/92) (BT) **75+**
Haut-Médoc 1990: From a consistently good producer, this is an elegant and fruity wine, with medium-light tannins and fresh fruit flavors. (NR) (5/15/92) (BT) **80+**
Haut-Médoc 1989: A no-nonsense wine, with bright berry and cherry aromas and flavors, medium tannins and a light, earthy finish. Drinkable on release, but better after 1993. $16 (3/15/92) **84**
Haut-Médoc 1988 Rel: $14 Cur: $22 (6/30/89) (BT) **85+**
Haut-Médoc 1987 $9 (11/30/89) (JS) **74**
Haut-Médoc 1986 $9 (11/30/89) (JS) **88**
Haut-Médoc 1982 Rel: $7 Cur: $18 (11/30/89) (JS) **82**

CHATEAU DE MALLERET
Haut-Médoc 1989: A big, burly wine, with lots of velvety tannins and a firm backbone. Offers lovely, sweet blackberry flavor on the finish. Better after 1996. (NR) (3/15/92) **90**
Haut-Médoc 1981 $6 (3/01/85) **77**

CHATEAU MOULIN DE CITRAN
Haut-Médoc 1989: Perfumed, with lovely strawberry and berry aromas, but it's rather light and simple for the vintage. The second wine of Citran. Drink on release. $14 (3/15/92) **80**

CHATEAU MOULIN ROUGE
Haut-Médoc 1987 $12 (11/30/89) (JS) **74**
Haut-Médoc 1986 $14 (11/30/89) (JS) **87**
Haut-Médoc 1983 $10 (7/31/87) **83**
Haut-Médoc 1982 ($NA) (11/30/89) (JS) **80**

CHATEAU PICHON
Haut-Médoc 1985 $13 (8/31/88) **85**

CHATEAU PROCHE PONTET
Haut-Médoc 1988 (NR) (6/30/89) (BT) **60+**

CHATEAU RAMAGE LA BATISSE
Haut-Médoc 1991: Has supple fruit and tannins, but it's just too light on the finish to be anything more than average. (NR) (5/15/92) (BT) **75+**
Haut-Médoc 1989: Extremely well concentrated, with masses of chewy fruit flavors, velvety tannins and tobacco, cherry and vanilla notes on the long finish. Try after 1995. $15 (3/15/92) **88**
Haut-Médoc 1987 $12 (11/30/89) (JS) **82**
Haut-Médoc 1986 $14 (11/30/89) (JS) **82**
Haut-Médoc 1982 $11 (11/30/89) (JS) **68**

Key to Symbols

The scores reported here are the results of blind tastings conducted by our panel of senior editors. Wines that carry the initials below are results of individual tastings.

THE WINE SPECTATOR 100-POINT SCALE 95-100—Classic, a great wine; ***90-94***—Outstanding, superior character and style; ***80-89***—Good to very good, a wine with special qualities; ***70-79***—Average, drinkable wine that may have minor flaws; ***60-69***—Below average, drinkable but not recommended; ***50-59***—Poor, undrinkable, not recommended. "+"—With a score indicates a range; used primarily with barrel tastings to indicate a preliminary score.

SPECIAL DESIGNATIONS SS—Spectator Selection, CS—Cellar Selection, BB—Best Buy, ($NA)—Price not available, (NR)—Not released.

TASTER'S INITIALS (JG)—Jim Gordon, (HS)—Harvey Steiman, (JL)—James Laube, (JS)—James Suckling, (TM)—Thomas Matthews, (TR)—Terry Robards, (PM)—Per-Henrik Mansson, (BT)—Barrel Tasting (these wines were tasted blind from barrel samples), (CA-date)—*California's Great Cabernets* by James Laube, (CH-date)—*California's Great Chardonnays* by James Laube, (VP-date)—*Vintage Port* by James Suckling.

DATE TASTED Dates in parentheses represent the issue in which the rating was published.

BARONS EDMOND & BENJAMIN ROTHSCHILD
Haut-Médoc 1987: A pleasant cherry aroma raises hopes, but on the palate it's light and simple. A pleasant, simple wine for drinking now. $24 (3/31/91) **75**
Haut-Médoc 1986: A whiff of sulfur on the nose blew off as the wine breathed, revealing a medium-weight wine, with modest cherry flavor and a rather hot finish. Tasted twice. $48 (3/31/91) **76**

CHATEAU SEGUR
Haut-Médoc 1988: Flavorful and concentrated, with ripe fruit and leather overtones, turning chocolaty and somewhat bittersweet on the finish. A gutsy wine, with earthy overtones. Distinctive; drinkable now, but better around 1993. $15 (12/31/90) **82**
Haut-Médoc 1982 $6 (4/16/85) **75**

CHATEAU SENEJAC
Haut-Médoc 1989 $11 (4/30/91) (BT) **85+**
Haut-Médoc 1988: A distinctively earthy style that may be too extreme for some. The plum and cherry flavors have to fight through the earthiness; will have limited appeal. Cellar until 1995 to '97. Rel: $11 Cur: $14 (4/30/91) **78**
Haut-Médoc 1987 $9 (6/30/89) (BT) **70+**

CHATEAU SOCIANDO-MALLET
Haut-Médoc 1991: This estate does it again in a light year. A pretty wine, with very good, fruity aromas and a good backbone, but it's slightly hollow on the center palate. (NR) (5/15/92) (BT) **85+**
Haut-Médoc 1990 (NR) (4/30/91) (BT) **85+**
Haut-Médoc 1989: Beautifully crafted, with subdued blueberry, mint and toasted vanilla aromas, equally fine fruit flavors and full, silky tannins. Better after 1995. $32 (3/15/92) **90**
Haut-Médoc 1988 $26 (3/31/91) **87**
Haut-Médoc 1987 $15 (5/15/90) **88**
Haut-Médoc 1986 $25 (11/30/89) (JS) **94**
Haut-Médoc 1985 Rel: $17 Cur: $24 (4/30/88) **85**
Haut-Médoc 1984 Rel: $11 Cur: $17 (3/31/87) **84**
Haut-Médoc 1983 Rel: $15 Cur: $26 (4/16/86) **77**
Haut-Médoc 1982 $43 (11/30/89) (JS) **92**

CHATEAU SOUDARS
Haut-Médoc 1991: Elegant, with cherry and floral aromas and flavors, medium tannins and a light finish. (NR) (5/15/92) (BT) **80+**
Haut-Médoc 1990 (NR) (4/30/91) (BT) **85+**
Haut-Médoc 1989: Rather earthy, with herbal, tobacco and berry aromas and flavors, full tannins and a firm finish. A little rustic. Needs time; try after 1996. $18 (3/15/92) **85**
Haut-Médoc 1988 $15 (4/30/91) **88**
Haut-Médoc 1987 $12 (11/30/89) (JS) **77**
Haut-Médoc 1986 $13 (11/30/89) (JS) **79**

CHATEAU LA TONNELLE
Haut-Médoc 1987 ($NA) (11/30/89) (JS) **76**
Haut-Médoc 1986 $11 (11/30/89) (JS) **70**
Haut-Médoc 1985: Distinctive, intense and smoky, perhaps a bit austere from lack of fruit on the finish, but there are some nice berryish aroma and flavor to start with and lots of toasty tartness, too. Drink now. $10 (2/15/89) **77**

CHATEAU LA TOUR CARNET
Haut-Médoc 1991: Round and smooth, but it's a little diluted on the finish. Smooth and fruity. (NR) (5/15/92) (BT) **75+**
Haut-Médoc 1990 (NR) (4/30/91) (BT) **75+**
Haut-Médoc 1989: A great improvement for this estate. It jumps out of the glass and grabs you by the throat, with tons of ripe fruit, tar and berry aromas and flavors and chewy tannins. A wine for aging. Try after 1997. $24 (3/15/92) **92**
Haut-Médoc 1988 $15 (8/31/91) **82**
Haut-Médoc 1986 $22 (5/15/87) (BT) **80+**
Haut-Médoc 1985 $22 (12/31/88) **71**
Haut-Médoc 1983 $13 (2/29/88) **69**
Haut-Médoc 1945 $130 (3/16/86) (JL) **88**

CHATEAU LA TOUR-HAUT-CAUSSAN
Haut-Médoc 1991: Quite a chewy wine, with chocolate and berry aromas and flavors and a medium tannin structure. (NR) (5/15/92) (BT) **80+**

CHATEAU TOUR DU HAUT-MOULIN
Haut-Médoc 1988: Alluring, with plenty of fruity black cherry and currant flavors that build on the palate. The tannins are supple and polished. A pleasant wine that should reach maturity by 1995 or so. $20 (4/30/91) **88**
Haut-Médoc 1987 $15 (11/30/89) (JS) **80**
Haut-Médoc 1986 $16 (11/30/89) (JS) **90**
Haut-Médoc 1985 $15 (2/15/89) **84**
Haut-Médoc 1982 $16 (11/30/89) (JS) **84**

CHATEAU TOUR-DU-MIRAIL
Haut-Médoc 1987 $10 (11/30/89) (JS) **83**
Haut-Médoc 1986 $12 (11/30/89) (JS) **79**
Haut-Médoc 1982 ($NA) (11/30/89) (JS) **79**

CHATEAU TOUR-DU-ROC
Haut-Médoc 1987 $10 (11/30/89) (JS) **74**
Haut-Médoc 1986 $11 (11/30/89) (JS) **76**
Haut-Médoc 1982 ($NA) (11/30/89) (JS) **84**

CHATEAU TROUPIAN
Haut-Médoc 1991: Has good ripeness, but it's too watery and light. (NR) (5/15/92) (BT) **75+**
Haut-Médoc 1990: A straightforward wine, with sweet fruit and light tannins; seems a bit diluted on the finish. (NR) (5/15/92) (BT) **80+**

CHATEAU VERDIGNAN
Haut-Médoc 1991: Very aromatic, with herb and earth aromas and good, round fruit flavors and tannins. Quite good for this appellation in this vintage, but it's a bit rustic. (NR) (5/15/92) (BT) **80+**
Haut-Médoc 1990 (NR) (4/30/91) (BT) **85+**
Haut-Médoc 1989: This beautifully sculptured wine has luscious blackberry and tobacco flavors and full tannins, all shaped into a beautiful bottle. A great improvement. Tasted twice. Hold until after 1997. $17 (3/15/92) **90**
Haut-Médoc 1988 $15 (4/30/91) **86**
Haut-Médoc 1987 $15 (11/30/89) (JS) **78**
Haut-Médoc 1986 $15 (11/30/89) (JS) **76**
Haut-Médoc 1985 $13 (2/15/88) **81**
Haut-Médoc 1983 Rel: $8 Cur: $18 (4/01/86) **69**
Haut-Médoc 1982 Rel: $7.50 Cur: $16 (11/30/89) (JS) **76**

CHATEAU VILLEGEORGE
Haut-Médoc 1989: Straightforward, with a good berry and earth character and medium tannins, but a strange stewed character emerges on the finish. Perhaps better after 1994. $14 (3/15/92) **79**
Haut-Médoc 1988 $15 (6/30/89) (BT) **80+**
Haut-Médoc 1987 $12 (6/30/89) (BT) **75+**

Haut-Médoc 1986 $13 (5/15/87) (BT) **70+**
Haut-Médoc 1985 $13 (5/15/87) (BT) **80+**

LISTRAC

CHATEAU CLARKE
Listrac 1991: A modest wine, with plum and other fruit flavors, but it's very watery on the finish. (NR) (5/15/92) (BT) **70+**
Listrac 1989: Tannic, with a gamy, earthy, almost raisiny character and a tough finish. Chewy and closed. Needs time; try after 1996. $16 (3/15/92) **85**
Listrac 1988: Ripe, tannic and rougher than one might expect for such a simple, fruity wine. Blueberry, anise and currant flavors dominate. Needs until 1993 to '95 to settle down. $18 (4/30/91) **81**
Listrac 1987 Rel: $15 Cur: $24 (6/30/89) (BT) **75+**
Listrac 1986 $17 (11/15/89) **90**
Listrac 1982 $13 (10/15/86) **68**

CHATEAU DUCLUZEAU
Listrac 1987 $7 (11/30/89) (JS) **79**
Listrac 1986 $11 (11/30/89) (JS) **83**
Listrac 1982 ($NA) (11/30/89) (JS) **80**

CHATEAU FONREAUD
Listrac 1991: Attractive on the nose, but a little too diluted. Has a minty, fruity character, but also drying tannins and a watery sensation on the finish. (NR) (5/15/92) (BT) **75+**
Listrac 1989 (NR) (4/30/91) (BT) **85+**
Listrac 1988: Flavorful, but a bit rustic and simple, with solid currant, anise and smoke aromas and flavors. Chunky on the finish. Drink after 1993. $15 (4/30/91) **82**
Listrac 1987 $10 (6/30/89) (BT) **65+**
Listrac 1986 $10 (6/30/88) (BT) **70+**

CHATEAU FOURCAS-DUPRE
Listrac 1991: Extremely light, with cherry aromas and flavors and medium tannins, but the finish is watery. (NR) (5/15/92) (BT) **70+**
Listrac 1989: A little rustic, but built like a brick house, with hard tannins and a fruity blackberry and mint finish. Try after 1996. $25 (3/15/92) **86**
Listrac 1988: A simple wine, with a tough veneer, turning tannic and drying on the finish. Barely has enough currant flavor to prevail; a tough call. Try in 1995. $22 (4/30/91) **83**
Listrac 1987 $15 (6/30/89) (BT) **75+**
Listrac 1986 $15 (6/30/88) (BT) **75+**
Listrac 1983 Rel: $9 Cur: $15 (10/31/86) **89**

CHATEAU FOURCAS-HOSTEN
Listrac 1990 (NR) (4/30/91) (BT) **85+**
Listrac 1989: This schizophrenic wine shows luscious blackberry aromas and flavors but also hard, full tannins. Needs time to calm down. Better after 1997. $19 (3/15/92) **87**
Listrac 1988: Medium-bodied, with more herbal and cedar aromas and flavors than fruit, which leans toward modest plum and berry. Best to drink after 1993. $13 (7/15/91) **82**
Listrac 1987 $11 (6/30/89) (BT) **70+**
Listrac 1986 $13 (11/15/89) **79**
Listrac 1983 Rel: $11 Cur: $16 (10/15/86) **83**

CHATEAU FOURCAS-LOUBANEY
Listrac 1988: This very firm, well-balanced Bordeaux has finesse, but only modest fruit flavors. Firmly tannic, a bit dry on the finish and austere in flavor, but it also has the structure and cedary, spicy notes that Bordeaux does best. $17 (2/28/91) **83**

CHATEAU LESTAGE
Listrac 1988: Firm and tannic, with enough concentration of orange-tinged cherry flavor to balance the tannins, echoing cedar and spice on the finish. Best after 1995. $20 (8/31/91) **82**

MARGAUX

CHATEAU D'ANGLUDET
Margaux 1991: Firm and tight, with silky tannins and attractive berry and raspberry flavors. (NR) (5/15/92) (BT) **85+**
Margaux 1990: Exceptionally polished, with ultrafine tannins and ripe fruit. An excellent example of the appellation. (NR) (5/15/92) (BT) **90+**
Margaux 1989: A vivid wine, with bright blackberry, cherry and chocolate aromas and flavors, firm tannins and a rich finish. Better after 1995. $33 (3/15/92) **87**
Margaux 1988 $22 (2/28/91) **85**
Margaux 1987 Rel: $13 Cur: $16 (5/15/90) **78**
Margaux 1986 Rel: $17 Cur: $25 (11/30/89) (JS) **90**
Margaux 1985 Rel: $17 Cur: $23 (4/15/88) **90**
Margaux 1983 Rel: $17 Cur: $38 (10/15/86) **93**
Margaux 1982 Rel: $15 Cur: $25 (11/30/89) (JS) **90**

CHATEAU BARON DE BRANE
Margaux 1989: Throws a long bomb, but doesn't quite make it to the goal line. Offers an impressive concentration of ripe fruit and tannins and a very firm finish. Better in 1996. (NR) (3/15/92) **89**

BARTON & GUESTIER
Margaux 1985 $12 (4/30/88) **75**

CHATEAU BOYD-CANTENAC
Margaux 1988 $20 (6/30/89) (BT) **85+**
Margaux 1987 $15 (6/30/89) (BT) **75+**
Margaux 1986 $15 (5/15/87) (BT) **80+**
Margaux 1985 $22 (4/15/88) **90**
Margaux 1983 $19 (4/16/86) **86**
Margaux 1982 Rel: $15 Cur: $25 (5/01/85) **91**
Margaux 1961 $120 (3/16/86) (TR) **65**

CHATEAU BRANE-CANTENAC
Margaux 1989: Lives up to its classification; a great improvement in quality. Like a Rodin sculpture, this wine is dense and solid, with extremely extracted fruit and tannins, but it remains racy and balanced. Better in 1998. $42 (3/15/92) **94**
Margaux 1988: Earthy, leathery aromas and flavors tend to obscure the modest raspberry and currant notes. A lean wine, with little concentration. Tasted twice. $42 (8/31/91) **76**
Margaux 1987 $25 (6/30/89) (BT) **80+**
Margaux 1986 Rel: $26 Cur: $30 (6/15/89) **87**
Margaux 1985 Rel: $24 Cur: $30 (6/30/88) **89**
Margaux 1983 Rel: $19 Cur: $28 (4/16/86) **94**
Margaux 1982 Rel: $22 Cur: $33 (5/01/85) **88**
Margaux 1979 $23 (10/15/89) (JS) **80**
Margaux 1962 $65 (11/30/87) (JS) **60**
Margaux 1961 $115 (3/16/86) (TR) **64**
Margaux 1945 $200 (3/16/86) (JL) **87**

CHATEAU CANTENAC-BROWN
Margaux 1991: Has good concentration backed by an intensely herbaceous character and velvety tannins, but the somewhat metallic finish distracts. (NR) (5/15/92) (BT) **80+**
Margaux 1990: Highly extracted, with lots of ripe fruit flavors and smoky, toasty vanilla characteristics. Shows excellent winemaking. (NR) (5/15/92) (BT) **90+**
Margaux 1989: A voluptuous wine, with a round, rich fruit and tannin structure, lots of velvety tannins and a smooth finish. Not as good as from the barrel. Better in 1996. $32 (3/15/92) **89**
Margaux 1988 $25 (4/30/91) **89**
Margaux 1987 Rel: $18 Cur: $22 (2/15/90) **78**
Margaux 1986 $24 (6/30/88) (BT) **85+**
Margaux 1984 $19 (5/15/87) **85**
Margaux 1982 Rel: $12 Cur: $21 (5/01/85) **91**
Margaux 1981 Rel: $12 Cur: $18 (3/01/85) **91**
Margaux 1959 $100 (10/15/90) (JS) **89**
Margaux 1945 $150 (3/16/86) (JL) **75**

CHATEAU CANUET
Margaux 1991: Another herbaceous-style wine, with berry and leaf aromas and flavors and medium tannins. (NR) (5/15/92) (BT) **80+**
Margaux 1990: A dense wine, with tons of ripe fruit and a very silky texture. Extremely impressive. (NR) (5/15/92) (BT) **90+**
Margaux 1989: A smoky, fruity wine, with extremely ripe fruit that verges on overripe. Full-bodied, with lots of alcohol and a rather burnt fruit finish. A little overdone, but it's still good. Drink after 1995. $18 (3/15/92) **82**
Margaux 1988 $15 (8/31/90) (BT) **85+**
Margaux 1987 $12.50 (5/15/90) **74**
Margaux 1986 $15 (11/30/89) (JS) **88**

CHATEAU DE CLAIREFONT
Margaux 1985 $9.25 (4/30/88) **79**

CHATEAU DE LA DAME
Margaux 1988: Very tight and tannic for a second-label wine from Malescot-St.-Exupéry, with a modest concentration of cherry, currant and leather flavors. It's sturdy in structure, with years ahead of it before it softens up enough to enjoy. Try in 1995 to '98. $15 (2/15/91) **86**

CHATEAU LA DAME DE MALESCOT
Margaux 1989: Well built for aging, but it's not giving much at the moment. Aromas of game, earth and tobacco follow through on the palate. Full-bodied, with a velvety mouth-feel. Better after 1994. Also produced by Malescot-St.- Exupéry. (NR) (3/15/92) **86**

CHATEAU DAUZAC
Margaux 1989: From an overlooked estate, the '89 Dauzac has plenty of luscious blackberry aromas and flavors, super-firm tannins and solid, compact fruit on the finish. The tannins melt in your mouth. Better in 1996. $26 (3/15/92) **90**
Margaux 1988: A supple, flavorful Margaux that's easy to like, with plenty of cherry, chocolate and spice flavors on a moderately tannic structure. The fruity, oaky notes linger nicely on the aftertaste. $20 (6/30/91) **90**
Margaux 1987 $15 (6/30/89) (BT) **70+**
Margaux 1986 $20 (6/30/88) (BT) **70+**
Margaux 1985 $21 (9/30/88) **87**

CHATEAU DESMIRAIL
Margaux 1989: Already accessible at an early age, this wine shows plenty of plum and chocolate flavors and soft, silky tannins. Drinkable now, but better in 1994. $27 (3/15/92) **86**
Margaux 1988 $25 (6/30/89) (BT) **80+**
Margaux 1987 $18 (6/30/89) (BT) **70+**
Margaux 1986 $22 (6/30/89) **90**
Margaux 1985 $20 (5/15/87) (BT) **80+**

CHATEAU DURFORT-VIVENS
Margaux 1989: Almost like a fluffy chocolate mousse in the mouth, with loads of blackberry, coffee and dark chocolate character and super-velvety tannins. Try in 1996. $28 (3/15/92) **92**
Margaux 1988: Earthy and leathery, with light fruit up front, but it turns to barnyardy flavors on the finish. Not our style. Tasted twice. $40 (8/31/91) **73**
Margaux 1987 $24 (6/30/89) (BT) **75+**
Margaux 1986 $25 (6/15/89) **90**
Margaux 1985 $20 (5/15/87) (BT) **80+**

CHATEAU GISCOURS
Margaux 1991: Light and delicate, with berry and tar flavors, hints of chocolate and light tannins. (NR) (5/15/92) (BT) **85+**
Margaux 1990: Classy, with perfumed aromas, lovely, sweet fruit flavors and a fine backbone of tannins and acidity. (NR) (5/15/92) (BT) **90+**
Margaux 1989: Like biting into a rich raspberry tart, this wine is bursting with ripe fruit and smoky vanilla character, ultrafine tannins and a long finish. Clearly better than the '88. Try in 1997. $41 (3/15/92) **92**
Margaux 1988 $30 (4/30/91) **89**
Margaux 1987 $20 (6/30/89) (BT) **75+**
Margaux 1986 $30 (6/15/89) **83**
Margaux 1985 $35 (9/30/88) **86**
Margaux 1983 $30 (5/01/89) **78**
Margaux 1982 Rel: $26 Cur: $34 (12/01/85) **88**
Margaux 1981 Rel: $12 Cur: $44 (6/01/84) **82**
Margaux 1980 $23 (2/16/84) **80**
Margaux 1979 $36 (10/15/89) (JS) **87**
Margaux 1978 $46 (2/16/84) **87**
Margaux 1976 $45 (2/16/84) **83**
Margaux 1970 $90 (2/16/84) **81**
Margaux 1964 $120/1.5L (2/16/84) **89**
Margaux 1962 $33 (11/30/87) (JS) **68**
Margaux 1961 $125 (3/16/86) (TR) **78**

CHATEAU LA GURGUE
Margaux 1991: A nice, pretty wine that displays a crowd-pleasing texture, elegant fruit flavors and fine tannins. (NR) (5/15/92) (BT) **85+**
Margaux 1989: A real beauty, with blackberry and raspberry aromas and flavors and a tannin structure that tickles your palate. Extremely fine. Try after 1997. $30 (3/15/92) **92**
Margaux 1988: A stylish, young wine that needs time to develop. The spicy, toasty oak notes dominate the lean fruit flavors, but it comes around on the finish, with ripe plum and currant notes. Intriguing and complex; it develops as you sip. Try in 1996 or later. Rel: $29 Cur: $32 (4/30/91) **90**
Margaux 1987 $13 (5/15/90) **81**
Margaux 1986 $22 (11/30/89) (JS) **85**
Margaux 1985 $17 (2/15/88) **90**
Margaux 1983 $9.75 (1/01/86) **90**
Margaux 1982 $24 (11/30/89) (JS) **85**

CHATEAU HAUT-BRETON-LARIGAUDIERE
Margaux 1985 $16 (2/15/88) **82**

CHATEAU D'ISSAN
Margaux 1991: Elegant and ripe, with sweet fruit flavors and silky tannins. Very delicate and flavorful. (NR) (5/15/92) (BT) **85+**
Margaux 1990: Extremely ripe, with an almost raisiny, tarry character and lots of tannins. Perhaps just slightly overdone, but it may show better in bottle. (NR) (5/15/92) (BT) **85+**
Margaux 1989: Quite meaty and smoky, with rich chocolate and fruit flavors and medium, velvety tannins. The '88 is better. Try after 1996. $27 (3/15/92) **84**
Margaux 1988 $30 (4/30/91) **88**
Margaux 1987 $20 (5/15/90) **76**
Margaux 1986 Rel: $22 Cur: $27 (6/15/89) **83**
Margaux 1985 Rel: $23 Cur: $26 (4/15/88) **88**
Margaux 1984 Rel: $10 Cur: $19 (3/31/87) **86**
Margaux 1983 Rel: $24 Cur: $32 (4/16/86) **91**

CHATEAU KIRWAN
Margaux 1991: Not much here; has an earthy berry character, but it's very light and diluted. (NR) (5/15/92) (BT) **75+**
Margaux 1990: A very pretty wine, well knit with raspberry and other fruit flavors and fine tannins. (NR) (5/15/92) (BT) **85+**
Margaux 1989: In addition to wild fruit, this wine also shows excellent polish, with plum, wild raspberry, tobacco and vanilla aromas and flavors, medium-full tannins and a long finish. Much better than the barrel sample. Drink after 1995. $32 (3/15/92) **87**
Margaux 1988 $28 (4/30/91) **87**
Margaux 1987 $22 (6/30/89) (BT) **70+**
Margaux 1986 $25 (6/30/89) **82**
Margaux 1985 Rel: $29 Cur: $33 (2/15/89) **90**
Margaux 1983 Rel: $16 Cur: $22 (7/16/86) **86**
Margaux 1945 $150 (3/16/86) (JL) **88**

CHATEAU LABEGORCE
Margaux 1991: Rather light and diluted, with the modest fruit flavors marred by metallic-tasting tannins on the finish. (NR) (5/15/92) (BT) **75+**
Margaux 1987: $30 (3/31/91) **77**
Margaux 1986: A pretty blend of fruit and oak, with well-balanced and integrated currant, cherry and toasty wood flavors. The balance is delicate despite firm tannins. Appears to have the ingredients for a full decade of cellaring. Drink 1993 to '97. $15 (2/15/90) **86**

CHATEAU LABEGORCE-ZEDE
Margaux 1991: Not a big wine, but it's very pleasant, with a good backbone and a good amount of delicate, minty berry flavors. (NR) (5/15/92) (BT) **80+**
Margaux 1990: A very concentrated wine that also shows finesse. Goes on and on, with complex, fruity aromas and flavors and an excellent tannin structure. (NR) (5/15/92) (BT) **90+**
Margaux 1989: What happened here? Although the quality is very good, it's disappointing after the great sample we tasted from the barrel last year. Offers vibrant plum and blackberry aromas and flavors and silky tannins. Not a blockbuster, but it's very good just the same. Better in 1994. $24 (3/15/92) **86**
Margaux 1988 $20 (4/30/91) **83**
Margaux 1987 $16 (11/30/89) (JS) **84**
Margaux 1986 Rel: $18 Cur: $22 (11/30/89) (JS) **91**
Margaux 1985 $13 (2/29/88) **84**
Margaux 1983 $15 (10/15/86) **88**
Margaux 1982 $21 (11/30/89) (JS) **87**

CHATEAU LAMOUROUX
Margaux 1988 (NR) (6/30/89) (BT) **75+**
Margaux 1987 (NR) (6/30/89) (BT) **70+**

CHATEAU LASCOMBES
Margaux 1989 $23 (4/30/90) (BT) **80+**
Margaux 1988: Smooth and generous, with simple raspberry, currant, smoke and spice aromas and flavors that persist into a finish that points toward cedar and fruit. Should be best after 1994. $25 (8/31/91) **82**
Margaux 1987 $24 (6/30/89) (BT) **80+**
Margaux 1986 $24 (6/30/88) (BT) **80+**
Margaux 1985 Rel: $20 Cur: $31 (5/15/87) (BT) **80+**
Margaux 1983 $32 (2/15/88) **84**
Margaux 1981 Rel: $19 Cur: $31 (5/16/85) **85**
Margaux 1979 $15 (10/15/89) (JS) **84**

CHATEAU MALESCOT-ST.-EXUPERY
Margaux 1989: Impressive, with lots of blackberry character and firm tannins, but it's a little hot on the finish. Try in 1995. $28 (3/15/92) **87**
Margaux 1988: Extremely intense in fruit flavor, with firm tannins and acidity, a mouth-filling texture and enough oak for accents. Chunky and rough at this stage, but it has the sheer intensity for cellaring until at least 1997. $23 (4/30/91) **89**
Margaux 1987 $20 (6/30/89) (BT) **70+**
Margaux 1986 Rel: $26 Cur: $29 (6/15/89) **88**
Margaux 1985 Rel: $24 Cur: $27 (9/30/88) **87**
Margaux 1983 Rel: $16 Cur: $22 (9/30/86) **82**
Margaux 1981 Rel: $13 Cur: $22 (5/01/89) **87**
Margaux 1962 $80 (11/30/87) (JS) **65**
Margaux 1961 $105 (3/16/86) (TR) **66**
Margaux 1959 $150 (10/15/90) (JS) **87**
Margaux 1945 $200 (3/16/86) (JL) **81**

CHATEAU MARGAUX
Margaux 1991: An elegant, well-crafted wine, showing fine concentration and depth, with vanilla-scented, well-articulated black currant and tobacco aromas and flavors and impressive length. (NR) (5/15/92) (BT) **90+**

Key to Symbols

The scores reported here are the results of blind tastings conducted by our panel of senior editors. Wines that carry the initials below are results of individual tastings.

THE WINE SPECTATOR 100-POINT SCALE 95-100—Classic, a great wine; ***90-94***—Outstanding, superior character and style; ***80-89***—Good to very good, a wine with special qualities; ***70-79***—Average, drinkable wine that may have minor flaws; ***60-69***—Below average, drinkable but not recommended; ***50-59***—Poor, undrinkable, not recommended. "+"—With a score indicates a range; used primarily with barrel tastings to indicate a preliminary score.

SPECIAL DESIGNATIONS SS—Spectator Selection, CS—Cellar Selection, BB—Best Buy, ($NA)—Price not available, (NR)—Not released.

TASTER'S INITIALS (JG)—Jim Gordon, (HS)—Harvey Steiman, (JL)—James Laube, (JS)—James Suckling, (TM)—Thomas Matthews, (TR)—Terry Robards, (PM)—Per-Henrik Mansson, (BT)—Barrel Tasting (these wines were tasted blind from barrel samples), (CA-date)—*California's Great Cabernets* by James Laube, (CH-date)—*California's Great Chardonnays* by James Laube, (VP-date)—*Vintage Port* by James Suckling.

DATE TASTED Dates in parentheses represent the issue in which the rating was published.

Margaux 1990: May be equal to or better than '89. Graceful and powerful, this is dense and closed in now, but it also shows tons of sweet currant flavor. (NR) (5/15/92) (BT) **95+**
Margaux 1989: A great Bordeaux that only needs time to develop. Seductive, with a superb concentration of vanilla, spice, blackberry and cherry aromas and flavors. Has an iron backbone of tannins, but it still shows class and finesse. Seems to last forever on the palate. Try after 1999. $145 (3/15/92) CS **99**
Margaux 1988 Rel: $75 Cur: $80 (3/31/91) CS **97**
Margaux 1987 $55 (5/15/90) **87**
Margaux 1986 Rel: $80 Cur: $110 (6/15/89) CS **98**
Margaux 1985 Rel: $76 Cur: $98 (12/15/89) (JS) **97**
Margaux 1984 Rel: $35 Cur: $60 (2/28/87) CS **93**
Margaux 1983 Rel: $70 Cur: $103 (12/15/89) (JS) **92**
Margaux 1982 Rel: $60 Cur: $135 (12/15/89) (JS) **98**
Margaux 1981 $95 (7/15/87) (HS) **97**
Margaux 1980 Rel: $30 Cur: $66 (7/15/87) (HS) **80**
Margaux 1979 $116 (12/15/89) (JS) **91**
Margaux 1978 $165 (12/15/89) (JS) **92**
Margaux 1977 $40 (7/15/87) (HS) **75**
Margaux 1976 $89 (7/15/87) (HS) **81**
Margaux 1975 $110 (7/15/87) (HS) **88**
Margaux 1971 $88 (7/15/87) (HS) **77**
Margaux 1970 $135 (7/15/87) (HS) **70**
Margaux 1967 $60 (7/15/87) (HS) **84**
Margaux 1966 $170 (7/15/87) (HS) **90**
Margaux 1964 $85 (7/15/87) (HS) **86**
Margaux 1962 $275/1.5L (12/15/89) (JS) **86**
Margaux 1961 $1,050/1.5L (12/15/89) (JS) **98**
Margaux 1959 $330 (10/15/90) (JS) **93**
Margaux 1957 $150 (7/15/87) (HS) **90**
Margaux 1955 $150 (7/15/87) (HS) **79**
Margaux 1953 $430 (12/15/89) (JS) **84**
Margaux 1952 $575/1.5L (7/15/87) (HS) **85**
Margaux 1950 $600/1.5L (7/15/87) (HS) **89**
Margaux 1949 $300 (7/15/87) (HS) **95**
Margaux 1947 $380 (7/15/87) (HS) **96**
Margaux 1945 $700 (3/16/86) (JL) **90**
Margaux 1943 $320 (7/15/87) (HS) **78**
Margaux 1937 $400 (7/15/87) (HS) **82**
Margaux 1934 $300 (7/15/87) (HS) **88**
Margaux 1929 $750 (7/15/87) (HS) **83**
Margaux 1928 $700 (7/15/87) (HS) **73**
Margaux 1928 $1,600/1.5L (7/15/87) (HS) **84**
Margaux 1926 $450 (7/15/87) (HS) **77**
Margaux 1924 $173 (7/15/87) (HS) **73**
Margaux 1923 $300 (7/15/87) (HS) **81**
Margaux 1920 $420 (7/15/87) (HS) **79**
Margaux 1918 $440 (7/15/87) (HS) **80**
Margaux 1917 $300 (7/15/87) (HS) **62**
Margaux 1909 $480 (7/15/87) (HS) **65**
Margaux 1908 $530 (7/15/87) (HS) **85**
Margaux 1905 $800 (7/15/87) (HS) **64**
Margaux 1900 $2,400 (7/15/87) (HS) **93**
Margaux 1899 $1,700 (7/15/87) (HS) **94**
Margaux 1898 $2,000 (7/15/87) (HS) **75**
Margaux 1893 $1,500 (7/15/87) (HS) **95**
Margaux 1892 $1,000 (7/15/87) (HS) **80**
Margaux 1887 $850 (7/15/87) (HS) **81**
Margaux 1875 $15,000/3L (12/15/88) (JS) **100**
Margaux 1870 $3,300 (7/15/87) (HS) **89**
Margaux 1868 $1,900 (7/15/87) (HS) **69**
Margaux 1865 $5,000 (7/15/87) (HS) **97**
Margaux 1864 $3,500 (7/15/87) (HS) **98**
Margaux 1848 $10,000 (7/15/87) (HS) **95**
Margaux 1847 $50,000/1.5L (7/15/87) (HS) **96**
Margaux 1791 $75,000 (7/15/87) (HS) **97**
Margaux 1771 $75,000 (7/15/87) (HS) **99**

CHATEAU MARQUIS-D'ALESME-BECKER
Margaux 1988 $20 (6/30/89) (BT) **75+**
Margaux 1987 $15 (6/30/89) (BT) **70+**
Margaux 1985 Rel: $19 Cur: $30 (6/30/88) **84**
Margaux 1984 $16 (6/15/87) **69**
Margaux 1983 $15 (12/31/86) **84**

CHATEAU MARQUIS DE TERME
Margaux 1988: Rich, concentrated and lavishly oaked, with a texture that is almost thick, supporting generous chocolate, toast and black cherry and currant flavors that seem plush on the finish. Has well-integrated tannins, but give it until 1998 to 2000. Rel: $23 Cur: $30 (4/30/91) **92**
Margaux 1987 $20 (6/30/89) (BT) **75+**
Margaux 1986: Rather heavily oaked and barky, which outplays the ripe currant and cassis flavors, leaving a wood-dominated wine. Drink 1993 to 1996. Rel: $23 Cur: $30 (6/30/89) **79**

CHATEAU MARSAC-SEGUINEAU
Margaux 1988 (NR) (6/30/89) (BT) **75+**
Margaux 1987 (NR) (6/30/89) (BT) **65+**
Margaux 1983 $9 (9/30/86) **68**

CHATEAU MONBRISON
Margaux 1990: Lovely and luscious, with rich berry, raspberry and smoke aromas and flavors and an elegant backbone of tannins. (NR) (5/15/92) (BT) **90+**
Margaux 1989: Always one of our favorites from Margaux, the '89 Monbrison is loaded with fruit that defines purity. Compact and fine, with silky tannins. Even better than the '88. Drink in 1996. $40 (3/15/92) **93**
Margaux 1988: A fine value for a premium Bordeaux. Very flavorful, firm and fruity, with concentrated cassis, herb, cherry and tobacco flavors. The juicy, generous fruit flavors are accented with cedar and cinnamon notes from oak aging. Very elegant and delicious; drink now through 1996. $20 (2/28/91) **92**
Margaux 1987 $20 (5/15/90) **85**
Margaux 1986 $20 (11/30/89) (JS) **92**
Margaux 1984 $15 (5/15/87) **78**
Margaux 1982 Rel: $14 Cur: $22 (11/30/89) (JS) **90**

CHATEAU PALMER
Margaux 1991: Extremely elegant and polished, but it has understated berry and raspberry aromas and flavors and silky tannins. (NR) (5/15/92) (BT) **85+**
Margaux 1990: Gorgeous, offering lots of currant and berry aromas and flavors and delicate tannins. Very long on the finish. (NR) (5/15/92) (BT) **90+**

Margaux 1989: A brooding giant of a wine, with tons of fruit buried under a massive tannin structure. Extremely well integrated. Needs time to open; try in 1997. $60 (3/15/92) **95**
Margaux 1988 $65 (2/28/91) CS **96**
Margaux 1987 Rel: $28 Cur: $32 (5/15/90) **84**
Margaux 1986 Rel: $40 Cur: $54 (6/15/89) **94**
Margaux 1985 Rel: $40 Cur: $50 (4/15/88) **90**
Margaux 1984 $41 (10/15/87) **84**
Margaux 1983 Rel: $45 Cur: $81 (7/16/86) CS **90**
Margaux 1982 $78 (5/01/85) **95**
Margaux 1981 Rel: $24 Cur: $52 (5/01/85) **90**
Margaux 1980 $28 (5/01/85) **86**
Margaux 1979 $67 (10/15/89) (JS) **90**
Margaux 1978 Rel: $35 Cur: $92 (5/01/85) **81**
Margaux 1962 $190 (11/30/87) (JS) **80**
Margaux 1961 $500 (3/16/86) (TR) **93**
Margaux 1959 $300 (10/15/90) (JS) **98**
Margaux 1945 $430 (3/16/86) (JL) **90**

PAVILLON ROUGE DU CHATEAU MARGAUX
Margaux 1991: Raspberry and currant aromas and flavors are echoed by sweet, ripe fruit notes on the delicious finish. The second label of Château Margaux. (NR) (5/15/92) (BT) **85+**
Margaux 1990: This second wine of Château Margaux is not as good as the first, but it offers the same explosion of fruit, bursting with complex red berry and vanilla-scented complexity. (NR) (5/15/92) (BT) **90+**
Margaux 1989: Intriguing oak and fruit aromas give way to ripe, smooth, polished, complex cherry, prune, chocolate and smoke flavors. There's no shortage of tannins on the finish. Tight and compact; best to cellar until 1996 or '97. $32 (4/30/92) **87**
Margaux 1988 $30 (4/30/91) **88**
Margaux 1987 Rel: $19 Cur: $23 (5/15/90) **79**
Margaux 1986 Rel: $24 Cur: $29 (6/30/89) **84**
Margaux 1985 Rel: $23 Cur: $35 (4/15/88) SS **93**
Margaux 1983 Rel: $25 Cur: $34 (6/30/87) **80**
Margaux 1982 $38 (7/15/87) (HS) **85**
Margaux 1981 $26 (7/15/87) (HS) **87**
Margaux 1980 $20 (7/15/87) (HS) **76**
Margaux 1979 $33 (7/15/87) (HS) **78**
Margaux 1916 ($NA) (7/15/87) (HS) **63**

CHATEAU POUGET
Margaux 1988 $18 (6/30/89) (BT) **85+**
Margaux 1987 $15 (6/30/89) (BT) **70+**
Margaux 1986 $16 (5/15/87) (BT) **70+**
Margaux 1985 $14 (5/15/87) (BT) **70+**
Margaux 1983 Rel: $11 Cur: $19 (2/15/87) **86**

CHATEAU PRIEURE-LICHINE
Margaux 1991: Another pretty wine, with ripe, delicious fruit flavors, but it's a little light on the finish. (NR) (5/15/92) (BT) **80+**
Margaux 1990: Ripe and aromatic, with tons of sweet, plummy flavors and silky tannins. A very fine wine indeed. (NR) (5/15/92) (BT) **90+**
Margaux 1989: Shows plenty of crushed cherry and toasted oak character on the nose and palate, but it's quite tough and tannic. The '88 is better. Needs time to mellow; try in 1995. $31 (3/15/92) **86**
Margaux 1988 $30 (4/30/91) **90**
Margaux 1987 Rel: $13 Cur: $16 (2/15/90) **78**
Margaux 1986 Rel: $21 Cur: $25 (6/15/89) **92**
Margaux 1985 $24 (2/15/88) **82**
Margaux 1984 $14 (11/30/86) **80**
Margaux 1983 Rel: $18 Cur: $30 (4/16/86) **96**
Margaux 1982 Rel: $15 Cur: $32 (5/01/85) **89**
Margaux 1981 Rel: $12 Cur: $22 (11/01/84) **86**
Margaux 1959 $50 (10/15/90) (JS) **80**

CHATEAU RAUSAN-SEGLA
Margaux 1991: Lovely and fruity, with mint and berry flavors and medium-light tannins. Shows class. (NR) (5/15/92) (BT) **80+**
Margaux 1990: Shows good intensity of black cherry flavors and firm tannins. Not a blockbuster, but well made. (NR) (5/15/92) (BT) **85+**
Margaux 1989: This beautiful wine has plenty of delicious blackberry and chocolate flavors, firm tannins and a silky finish. Not as outstanding as last year from the barrel. Drink after 1995. $44 (3/15/92) **88**
Margaux 1988 $40 (3/15/91) **92**
Margaux 1986 Rel: $28 Cur: $40 (9/15/89) **87**
Margaux 1985 Rel: $24 Cur: $33 (5/31/88) **92**
Margaux 1981 Rel: $16 Cur: $23 (10/16/84) **86**
Margaux 1979 $34 (10/15/89) (JS) **69**
Margaux 1961 $125 (3/16/86) (TR) **63**
Margaux 1945 $150 (3/16/86) (JL) **73**

CHATEAU RAUZAN-GASSIES
Margaux 1991: Doesn't offer much, although sweet strawberry-accented flavors emerge on the finish. (NR) (5/15/92) (BT) **75+**
Margaux 1990 (NR) (4/30/91) (BT) **80+**
Margaux 1989 $24 (4/30/91) (BT) **80+**
Margaux 1988 $35 (8/31/91) **85**
Margaux 1987 $20 (6/30/88) (BT) **70+**
Margaux 1986 $24 (6/30/89) **88**
Margaux 1959 $93 (10/15/90) (JS) **73**
Margaux 1945 $300 (3/16/86) (JL) **91**

CHATEAU RICHETERRE
Margaux 1986: Light and perfumey, with soft texture, subtle cherry and apple flavors; a simple, delicate wine to drink up now. $12.50 (2/15/89) **78**

CHATEAU SEGONNES
Margaux 1988 $18 (6/30/89) (BT) **75+**
Margaux 1987 (NR) (6/30/89) (BT) **70+**

CHATEAU SIRAN
Margaux 1991: Elegant and refined, with light raspberry flavors and a succulent texture. (NR) (5/15/92) (BT) **80+**
Margaux 1990 (NR) (4/30/91) (BT) **85+**
Margaux 1989: Ripe, almost jammy, and very well balanced, with silky, almost refreshing tannins. Not as outstanding as from the barrel. Better in 1994. $25 (3/15/92) **88**
Margaux 1988 Rel: $19 Cur: $22 (6/30/91) **88**
Margaux 1987 $14 (6/30/89) (BT) **75+**
Margaux 1985 $15 (9/30/88) **90**

CHATEAU DU TERTRE
Margaux 1991: Lovely and polished, with pleasant fruit flavors and medium tannins. (NR) (5/15/92) (BT) **80+**
Margaux 1990 (NR) (4/30/91) (BT) **85+**
Margaux 1989: A sensationally perfumed wine, with wonderful raspberry and toasty oak aromas. Rich and succulent, with tons of grip from the silky tannins. Try after 1996. $29 (3/15/92) **90**
Margaux 1988 $40 (6/30/91) **86**
Margaux 1987 $18 (6/30/89) (BT) **70+**
Margaux 1986 $22 (6/15/89) **89**
Margaux 1985 Rel: $14 Cur: $29 (6/30/88) SS **93**
Margaux 1983 Rel: $14 Cur: $30 (7/16/86) **91**

CHATEAU LA TOUR-DE-BESSAN
Margaux 1989: Exceedingly ripe, with an almost pruny character on the nose that follows through on the palate. A little dumb right now, but it may mellow later. Better in 1996. (NR) (3/15/92) **87**

CHATEAU LA TOUR-DE-MONS
Margaux 1991: Shows very good, vivid fruit flavors, fine tannins and a medium finish. (NR) (5/15/92) (BT) **85+**
Margaux 1989: Thick and chewy, with lots of velvety tannins and plenty of chocolate and blackberry flavors. Another overlooked estate. Try after 1996. $25 (3/15/92) **88**
Margaux 1986 $19 (11/30/89) (JS) **90**
Margaux 1986 $17 (6/15/89) **90**
Margaux 1982 $17 (11/30/89) (JS) **90**
Margaux 1945 $200 (3/16/86) (JL) **89**

MÉDOC

CHATEAU BELLERIVE
Médoc 1986: Firm and more than a bit tannic, medium-bodied and clean, with bright red cherry and berry flavor. Give it a short time for the tannin to resolve, and drink now through 1994. Good value. $4.50 (2/15/89) **79**

CHATEAU LE BOSCQ
Médoc 1988: A firm, fruity, taut wine, with cedar and plum aromas and flavors that persist into a long, generous finish. Doesn't have a lot of style or grace, but all the pieces are there to age well through 1995 to '98. $20 (4/30/91) **84**
Médoc 1986: Good for weekday drinking. It's simple, but has a nice ripe plum and cherry streak running through it. Moderately tannic and firmly structured. $10 (6/30/89) **75**
Médoc 1983 $8 (1/01/86) **70**
Médoc 1982 $6 (10/01/85) BB **76**

CHATEAU LA CARDONNE
Médoc 1991: A light wine, with chocolate and tobacco aromas and flavors and light tannins. Early developing, but it has lovely fruit. (NR) (5/15/92) (BT) **75+**
Médoc 1990: Ripe and inviting, with plenty of fruit and balanced tannins. A lovely wine and a good value. (NR) (5/15/92) (BT) **80+**
Médoc 1989 $11 (4/30/91) (BT) **80+**
Médoc 1987 $10 (6/30/88) (BT) **70+**
Médoc 1986 $10 (2/15/90) **84**
Médoc 1985 $9 (12/31/88) **83**
Médoc 1983 $7 (10/15/86) **79**

CHATEAU LA CROIX LANDON
Médoc 1988 (NR) (6/30/89) (BT) **75+**

LUCIEN DESCHAUX
Médoc 1990: A simple, sturdy red, with pruny aromas and flavors that turn toward cherry and toast on the finish. Drinkable now, but better in 1993. 3,500 cases made. $8 (1/31/92) BB **80**

CHATEAU GREYSAC
Médoc 1990 (NR) (4/30/91) (BT) **80+**
Médoc 1989: Lighter in style for a wine from this vintage, but it shows pretty herb and berry flavors and a clean finish. Not as good as we had hoped after an excellent barrel sample. Drink on release. $12 (3/15/92) **79**
Médoc 1988: Spicy, cedary and fragrant, with plum and apple aromas and flavors. Nicely focused and elegant, with lots of room to grow. Try to hold off until 1996 to '98. $15 (4/30/91) **87**
Médoc 1987 $9 (6/30/89) (BT) **75+**
Médoc 1986 $10 (11/30/89) (JS) **85**
Médoc 1985 $9 (12/31/88) **77**
Médoc 1983 Rel: $8.50 Cur: $12 (7/31/87) **65**
Médoc 1982 Rel: $8 Cur: $16 (11/30/89) (JS) **80**
Médoc 1981 $8 (6/01/84) **77**

CHATEAU LOUDENNE
Médoc 1989: An early-drinking, ripe wine, with pleasant berry and tar aromas and flavors and a medium finish. Better in 1993. $13 (3/15/92) **81**
Médoc 1988: Tannic and tight, marked by oak, but offers enough plum and cherry aromas and flavors to promise that it will develop with cellaring until 1993 to '95. Seems awkward now. $10 (8/31/91) **82**
Médoc 1987 Rel: $10 Cur: $16 (11/30/89) (JS) **75**
Médoc 1986 $12 (11/30/89) (JS) **74**
Médoc 1985 $13 (11/30/88) **75**
Médoc 1982 $10 (11/30/89) (JS) **74**
Médoc 1981 $11 (9/01/84) **84**

CHATEAU MOULIN DE BEL-AIR
Médoc 1989: Surprisingly light for the vintage, with clean green bean and cassis flavors and a light finish. Drink on release. (NR) (3/15/92) **77**

CHATEAU LES ORMES-SORBET
Médoc 1988: Fragrant, with spice and cherry aromas, but a bit lean and light on the palate, offering cherry, currant and anise flavors that are almost reminiscent of Burgundy. Should be ready to drink by now. $20 (4/30/91) **84**
Médoc 1987 $14 (6/30/89) (BT) **75+**

CHATEAU PATACHE D'AUX
Médoc 1988: Lean and tight, with spice and cedar aromas and flavors, but it has the potential to be a pleasant drink when the tight tannins subside around 1995 to '97. Rel: $10 Cur: $17 (4/30/91) **80**
Médoc 1982 Rel: $5 Cur: $18 (5/01/85) **83**

CHATEAU PLAGNAC
Médoc 1991: The aromas are a little too weedy and herbaceous, but the sweet fruit flavors and well-knit tannins are decent. (NR) (5/15/92) (BT) **75+**
Médoc 1990: A bit austere and lean, but it shows lovely cherry and berry aromas and flavors and medium tannins. (NR) (5/15/92) (BT) **80+**
Médoc 1989: Much better than in barrel. Very traditional in style, with tobacco, tar, earth and fruit flavors that bombard your taste buds. A little rustic, but it shows very impressive fruit concentration. Better after 1998. $11.50 (3/15/92) **88**
Médoc 1988 $8.50 (4/30/91) **79**
Médoc 1987 $8 (11/30/89) (JS) **77**
Médoc 1986 $9 (11/30/89) (JS) **82**
Médoc 1985 $9 (8/31/88) **68**

CHATEAU POTENSAC

Médoc 1988: Dark in color and tightly packed with black cherry, currant, herb and olive notes. Has a green edge to the tannins and finish. Will require cellaring until 1994 to soften. Tasted twice. $14 (10/31/91) **80**

Médoc 1987: Herbal, rough and simple, with a short finish. Not very enjoyable at this stage, but maybe it will improve with a couple years' aging. Tasted twice. $9.50 (5/15/90) **72**

Médoc 1986 $15 (11/30/89) (JS) **86**

Médoc 1985 Rel: $11 Cur: $21 (5/15/87) (BT) **80+**

Médoc 1983 Rel: $9 Cur: $28 (10/15/86) **75**

CHATEAU ROQUEGRAVE

Médoc 1983 $6 (4/01/86) **63**

CHATEAU ST.-BONNET

Médoc 1985 $6 (4/15/88) **79**

CHATEAU ST.-CHRISTOPHE

Médoc 1985 $6.50 (7/31/88) BB **82**

CHATEAU ST.-SEVE

Médoc 1985 $6 (11/15/87) **70**

ALFRED SCHYLER

Médoc 1985 $8.50 (6/30/88) **72**

CHATEAU LA TOUR DE BY

Médoc 1991: A refreshing wine, with pleasant fruit flavors and medium tannins, but it's slightly watery on the finish. (NR) (5/15/92) (BT) **75+**

Médoc 1989: Alluring and well crafted, with black cherry and smoke aromas that follow through on the palate, very well-integrated tannins and a chewy finish. Lots of fruit for the money; better than what we tasted in barrel. Better after 1993. $15 (3/15/92) **85**

Médoc 1988: Elegant, smooth and balanced. Not a real blockbuster, but it offers nice cherry and currant flavors, with earthy, cedary notes that give it complexity. A supple and easy-to-drink wine. Drink now to 1994. $12.50 (6/15/91) **86**

Médoc 1987 $10 (11/30/89) (JS) **79**

Médoc 1986 $12 (11/30/89) (JS) **80**

Médoc 1983 $7 (10/16/85) **78**

Médoc 1982 Rel: $5.50 Cur: $15 (11/30/89) (JS) **80**

CHATEAU LA TOUR-HAUT-CAUSSAN

Médoc 1989: A beautiful wine, with impressive plum, berry and smoke aromas and deliciously ripe fruit flavors. Silky and succulent on the finish. Better after 1994. $15 (3/15/92) **87**

Médoc 1988: Tannic and austere, with little enough flavor to compete with the moderate but hard-edged tannins. Needs until 1995 to soften. $12.50 (7/15/91) **79**

Médoc 1987 $13 (11/30/89) (JS) **80**

Médoc 1986 $14 (11/30/89) (JS) **88**

Médoc 1984 $10 (2/15/88) **80**

Médoc 1982 $16 (11/30/89) (JS) **83**

CHATEAU LA TOUR-ST.-BONNET

Médoc 1985 $9 (6/30/88) **83**

Moulis

CHATEAU BRILLETTE

Moulis 1991: More like a Gamay than a Cab. Light, simple and easy to drink. (NR) (5/15/92) (BT) **70+**

Moulis 1989: Shows more promise on the nose, with extremely concentrated vanilla, blackberry and tar aromas, than on the palate, where it's rather simple. Try after 1995. $17 (3/15/92) **86**

Moulis 1988: A medium-weight wine, on the tart side, but it offers plenty of ripe currant and cherry flavors. A bit oaky and tannic on the finish, but should be fine after 1993 or '94. $15 (8/31/91) **81**

Moulis 1987 $15 (11/30/89) (JS) **72**

Moulis 1986 $14 (11/30/89) (JS) **78**

Moulis 1982 $23 (11/30/89) (JS) **85**

CHATEAU CHASSE-SPLEEN

Moulis 1991: The terrific balance between the fruit and delicate tannins in this wine caresses your palate. (NR) (5/15/92) (BT) **85+**

Moulis 1990 (NR) (4/30/91) (BT) **85+**

Moulis 1989: Luscious, with all the gorgeous raspberry and berry flavors you could want. Shows lovely, rich, ripe fruit. Perhaps the best wine ever produced at this underrated estate. A superb value. Try after 1996. $35 (3/15/92) **95**

Moulis 1988 $26 (3/31/91) **89**

Moulis 1987 $15 (2/15/90) **78**

Moulis 1986 $26 (11/30/89) (JS) **90**

Moulis 1985 Rel: $22 Cur: $30 (5/15/88) **86**

Moulis 1984 $13 (6/15/87) **74**

Moulis 1983 Rel: $16.50 Cur: $24 (4/16/86) **87**

Moulis 1982 Rel: $15 Cur: $36 (11/30/89) (JS) **90**

CHATEAU DUPLESSIS-FABRE

Moulis 1989: Has a tightly packed fruit and tannin structure and plenty of everything to keep it going for years. Don't drink until after 1996. $9 (3/15/92) **88**

Moulis 1987 $7 (11/30/89) (JS) **71**

Moulis 1986 $7 (11/30/89) (JS) **74**

Moulis 1982 ($NA) (11/30/89) (JS) **79**

CHATEAU MALMAISON

Moulis 1991: Offers berry and cherry flavors and medium tannins. Has good fruit concentration for the year. (NR) (5/15/92) (BT) **80+**

Moulis 1989: A gorgeous, ripe berry and blackberry character emerges in this wine that shows lots of fruit on the front of the palate and firm tannins on the back. From Baronne Nadine de Rothschild. Better in 1995 or '96. (NR) (3/15/92) **85**

Key to Symbols

The scores reported here are the results of blind tastings conducted by our panel of senior editors. Wines that carry the initials below are results of individual tastings.

THE WINE SPECTATOR 100-POINT SCALE 95-100—Classic, a great wine; ***90-94***—Outstanding, superior character and style; ***80-89***—Good to very good, a wine with special qualities; ***70-79***—Average, drinkable wine that may have minor flaws; ***60-69***—Below average, drinkable but not recommended; ***50-59***—Poor, undrinkable, not recommended. "+"—With a score indicates a range; used primarily with barrel tastings to indicate a preliminary score.

SPECIAL DESIGNATIONS SS—Spectator Selection, CS—Cellar Selection, BB—Best Buy, ($NA)—Price not available, (NR)—Not released.

TASTER'S INITIALS (JG)—Jim Gordon, (HS)—Harvey Steiman, (JL)—James Laube, (JS)—James Suckling, (TM)—Thomas Matthews, (TR)—Terry Robards, (PM)—Per-Henrik Mansson, (BT)—Barrel Tasting (these wines were tasted blind from barrel samples), (CA-date)—*California's Great Cabernets* by James Laube, (CH-date)—*California's Great Chardonnays* by James Laube, (VP-date)—*Vintage Port* by James Suckling.

DATE TASTED Dates in parentheses represent the issue in which the rating was published.

CHATEAU MAUCAILLOU

Moulis 1988: Ripe, fairly oaky and a bit awkward, but it has plenty of stylish nutmeg, chocolate and vanilla overtones to the ripe but modest plum and currant flavors. Needs time to settle down; try in 1993 to '95. $14 (7/31/91) **82**

Moulis 1987 $14 (6/30/89) (BT) **70+**

Moulis 1986 $18 (6/30/88) (BT) **85+**

Moulis 1985 $18 (8/31/88) **88**

Moulis 1983 $16 (3/15/87) **87**

Moulis 1982 Rel: $15 Cur: $25 (11/30/89) (JS) **90**

Moulis 1981 $12 (10/01/85) **88**

CHATEAU LA MOULINE

Moulis 1988: An austere wine, with a mild core of plum and currant flavors packed into a tannic frame, and enough cedary overtones to add spice as it matures. Best after 1993. $20 (2/15/91) **81**

CHATEAU POUJEAUX

Moulis 1991: A pretty wine, with delicate, fresh fruit aromas and flavors and caressing tannins. (NR) (5/15/92) (BT) **80+**

Moulis 1990: A serious wine, with well-integrated, ripe fruit and oak flavors and ultravelvety tannins. Will age for a long time, but will also give great pleasure in its youth. Just short of outstanding. (NR) (5/15/92) (BT) **85+**

Moulis 1989: A beautiful wine, with pretty blackberry and cherry aromas that open to sweet, almost jammy fruit flavors. Plenty of velvety tannins hold it together. Better after 1995. $21 (3/15/92) **90**

Moulis 1988 $15 (2/28/91) **88**

Moulis 1987 $15 (5/15/90) **74**

Moulis 1986 $22 (11/30/89) (JS) **88**

Moulis 1985 $18 (9/30/88) **87**

Moulis 1983 Rel: $13 Cur: $19 (10/31/86) **79**

Moulis 1982 $27 (11/30/89) (JS) **88**

CHATEAU LA SALLE DE POUJEAUX

Moulis 1989: Starts off well but finishes slowly. Offers beautiful mint and blackberry aromas, sweet fruit flavors and round tannins, but seems to fall a bit on the finish. The second wine of Poujeaux. Try after 1995. $15 (3/15/92) **85**

Pauillac

CHATEAU ARMAILHAC

Pauillac 1991: Firm and lively, with plenty of berry, chocolate, earth and tobacco flavors and a good tannin backbone. (NR) (5/15/92) (BT) **85+**

Pauillac 1990: Ripe and minty, with fresh fruit flavors and well-integrated tannins. Not a big wine, but very well balanced. (NR) (5/15/92) (BT) **85+**

Pauillac 1989: Hard as a rock right now, this is a tough wine, with tons of tannins holding down whatever is underneath, which appears to be rich fruit. Needs time; try after 1998. $26 (3/15/92) **94**

DOMAINES BARONS DE ROTHSCHILD

Pauillac Réserve Spéciale 1987: Tries hard to be fruity, but it's mostly herbal, light in texture, supple and velvety, with appealing plum and smoke flavors. Finishes short. Enjoy soon. $12 (12/31/90) **81**

Pauillac Réserve Spéciale NV: A delicious sample from a famous Bordeaux district. Well structured with supple texture and ripe plum and cherry flavors. Nice spicy and smoky aromas. Moderate tannins with a clean, chocolate flavor on the finish. An unusual non-vintage bottling from the Lafite group. A good value. $12 (2/15/90) **85**

CHATEAU BATAILLEY

Pauillac 1990 (NR) (4/30/91) (BT) **85+**

Pauillac 1989: Offers pleasant berry and tomato flavors and round tannins, but it's rather light and easy to drink. Not as good as the '88. Tasted twice. Drink on release. $28 (3/15/92) **81**

Pauillac 1988: An elegant wine, with a wonderful concentration of currant, tobacco and blackberry flavors that join up with hints of pepper and cedar on the finish. The tannins are present without intruding. Strikingly well balanced and should be ready to drink around 1995 to '98. Rel: $23 Cur: $27 (4/30/91) **90**

Pauillac 1987 $18 (6/30/89) (BT) **75+**

Pauillac 1986 $34 (6/30/88) (BT) **80+**

Pauillac 1961 $100 (3/16/86) (TR) **84**

Pauillac 1945 $300 (3/16/86) (JL) **87**

CHATEAU BELLEGRAVE-VAN DER VOORT

Pauillac 1988: Tough and tannic, with a metallic edge that not everyone will like, but it's concentrated and ripe and could develop into a good wine with cellaring until about 2000. $20 (8/31/91) **83**

Pauillac 1986: Despite its deep color, it's rather light and uncomplicated, with smoky black cherry and currant notes and soft tannins. Maturing. Drink now to 1994. $19 (10/31/91) **80**

CHATEAU BERNADOTTE

Pauillac 1988 $20 (6/30/89) (BT) **80+**

Pauillac 1987 $20 (11/30/89) (JS) **79**

Pauillac 1986 $20 (11/30/89) (JS) **92**

Pauillac 1985 $19 (3/31/88) **89**

Pauillac 1983 $14 (2/15/87) **90**

CARRUADES DE LAFITE

Pauillac 1991: Extremely attractive, with lovely spice and fruit flavors, a hint of vanilla and firm tannins. Second label of Lafite-Rothschild. (NR) (5/15/92) (BT) **80+**

Pauillac 1990: Beautiful and very refined, with berry, tobacco and cherry aromas and flavors and very fine tannins. (NR) (5/15/92) (BT) **85+**

Pauillac 1989: Clean and fresh, with lovely spice and blackberry aromas and flavors and medium tannins. A real charmer. Try after 1994. Rel: $24 Cur: $27 (3/15/92) **89**

Pauillac 1988 Rel: $19 Cur: $25 (8/31/90) (BT) **80+**

Pauillac 1987 $19 (6/30/89) (BT) **75+**

Pauillac 1986 $30 (5/15/87) (BT) **70+**

Pauillac 1967 $29 (11/30/87) **82**

Pauillac 1964 $49 (11/30/87) **81**

Pauillac 1962 $68 (11/30/87) (JS) **75**

Pauillac 1961 $80 (11/30/91) (JG) **90**

Pauillac 1959 $100 (11/30/91) (JG) **90**

Pauillac 1937 $125 (11/30/87) **77**

Pauillac 1934 $145 (11/30/87) **84**

Pauillac 1902 $280 (11/30/87) **80**

CHATEAU CLERC-MILON

Pauillac 1991: Supple and rather delicate, with cigar box and blackberry characteristics and medium tannins. (NR) (5/15/92) (BT) **80+**

Pauillac 1990: Incredibly rich and concentrated; a super-powerful, impressive wine, with all the ripe fruit flavors you could hope for. (NR) (5/15/92) (BT) **95+**

Pauillac 1989: Superbly made Bordeaux, giving the essence of Cabernet Sauvignon. Has lots of cassis and earth aromas and flavors, spiced with excellent new wood, and an outstanding backbone of well-integrated tannins. Try after 1999. $32 (3/15/92) **96**

Pauillac 1988 $26 (4/30/91) SS **94**

Pauillac 1987 $19 (6/30/89) (BT) **80+**

Pauillac 1986 Rel: $23 Cur: $37 (5/31/89) **97**

Pauillac 1985 Rel: $18 Cur: $28 (5/15/88) **91**
Pauillac 1984 $18 (6/15/87) **78**
Pauillac 1983 $16 (4/01/86) **91**
Pauillac 1982 Rel: $15 Cur: $29 (4/01/85) **86**

CHATEAU COLOMBIER-MONPELOU
Pauillac 1988: Earthy, leathery aromas and flavors overwhelm the basic cherry flavor. A tough wine to like. Tasted twice. $15 (10/31/91) **75**

CHATEAU CORDEILLAN-BAGES
Pauillac 1991: An elegant wine, with vivid tobacco, chocolate and cassis flavors coupled with a firm tannin backbone. (NR) (5/15/92) (BT) **85+**
Pauillac 1990: Showing wonderful finesse in an understated style, this ravishing wine has beautiful fruit and cassis aromas and sweet, succulent fruit flavors. Another winner from Jean-Michel Cazes; very tiny production. (NR) (5/15/92) (BT) **90+**
Pauillac 1989: Deep and dark, with extraordinarily intense blackberry, smoke and vanilla flavors, super-velvety tannins and a fine finish. Yet another superbly ripe '89. A tiny-production wine from the producers of Lynch-Bages. What a debut vintage. Try after 1998. $24 (3/15/92) **96**

CHATEAU CROIZET-BAGES
Pauillac 1991: A pleasant, fruity wine, with light currant and milk chocolate flavors and medium tannins. (NR) (5/15/92) (BT) **80+**
Pauillac 1990 (NR) (4/30/91) (BT) **85+**
Pauillac 1989 $17 (4/30/91) (BT) **80+**
Pauillac 1988 $28 (8/31/91) **73**
Pauillac 1987 $15 (6/30/88) (BT) **60+**
Pauillac 1986 $15 (6/30/89) **78**
Pauillac 1962 $60 (11/30/87) (JS) **83**

CHATEAU DUHART-MILON
Pauillac 1991: Lovely plummy aromas and flavors bring you back for more. A wine with an elegant backbone of tannins and plenty of fruit. (NR) (5/15/92) (BT) **85+**
Pauillac 1990: A joy to taste; makes you yearn for more, with its rich tobacco and vanilla aromas and flavors and silky tannins. Gets better and better. (NR) (5/15/92) (BT) **90+**
Pauillac 1989: Extremely well balanced, with cassis, berry and smoke characteristics and medium tannins. Not a blockbuster, but very well made. Drink after 1996. $30 (3/15/92) **90**
Pauillac 1988 Rel: $20 Cur: $29 (8/31/91) **88**
Pauillac 1987 $22 (5/15/90) **79**
Pauillac 1986 $30 (5/31/89) **90**
Pauillac 1985 $34 (6/30/88) **87**
Pauillac 1979 $31 (10/15/89) (JS) **86**

CHATEAU FONBADET
Pauillac 1988: Tight, focused and concentrated, with nicely articulated plum and currant aromas and flavors and hints of chocolate and cedar on the long finish. A good wine that has the richness and length to warrant cellaring until 1996 to '98. $16 (8/31/91) **89**
Pauillac 1987 $15 (6/30/89) (BT) **75+**
Pauillac 1982 $16 (8/01/85) **86**

LES FORTS DE LATOUR
Pauillac 1991: Has a surprising backbone of firm tannins and good, fleshy fruit flavors. A little herbaceous in the aromas, but overall it's a very good wine. The second label of Latour. (NR) (5/15/92) (BT) **85+**
Pauillac 1990: Super-hard and firm, with an excellent backbone of tannin, yet showing plenty of ripe fruit. (NR) (5/15/92) (BT) **90+**
Pauillac 1989: Big and hard, with compact plum, tobacco and cedar flavors and full, silky tannins. Try after 1999. (NR) (3/15/92) **91**
Pauillac 1987 (NR) (6/30/89) (BT) **75+**
Pauillac 1986 $38 (5/15/87) (BT) **70+**
Pauillac 1985 Rel: $40 Cur: $51 (8/31/91) **87**
Pauillac 1983 $32 (10/15/90) **85**
Pauillac 1982 $55 (10/15/90) **86**
Pauillac 1979 $33 (10/15/89) (JS) **87**

CHATEAU GRAND-PUY-DUCASSE
Pauillac 1989: Firm and focused, with ripe, intense plum- and cherry-tinged flavors that fan out on the finish, picking up a touch of anise and oak. Because of the intensity of the tannins, it needs cellaring until 1996. $23 (4/30/92) **86**
Pauillac 1988: Spicy, exotic aromas and flavors run through this massively concentrated but still elegant wine. Has plenty of tannin, but the jammy currant, spice and cedar flavors make their presence felt. Will need until 1997 to 2001 to soften. $21 (4/30/91) **89**
Pauillac 1987 $18 (6/30/89) (BT) **75+**
Pauillac 1986 Rel: $22 Cur: $26 (6/30/89) **85**
Pauillac 1985 Rel: $19 Cur: $24 (2/29/88) **90**

CHATEAU GRAND-PUY-LACOSTE
Pauillac 1991: Shows pleasant fruit flavors, but lacks a bit of definition to be more than simply good. (NR) (5/15/92) (BT) **80+**
Pauillac 1990: Extremely well crafted, with fine, focused plum and cherry flavors and compact tannins. (NR) (5/15/92) (BT) **90+**
Pauillac 1989: A polished wine, with pretty vanilla and cassis flavors and a fine tannin structure. Just lacks a bit of depth to be classic. Drink after 1996. $36 (3/15/92) **91**
Pauillac 1988 $33 (4/30/91) **90**
Pauillac 1987 $22 (5/15/90) **77**
Pauillac 1986 $25 (5/31/89) **88**
Pauillac 1985 Rel: $23 Cur: $30 (6/30/88) **91**
Pauillac 1984 $24 (10/15/87) **83**
Pauillac 1979 $37 (10/15/89) (JS) **88**
Pauillac 1961 $150 (3/16/86) (TR) **96**
Pauillac 1945 $380 (3/16/86) (JL) **80**

CHATEAU HAUT-BAGES-AVEROUS
Pauillac 1991: A bit diluted, with decent berry and cherry flavors and herbaceous tones, but not very impressive. The second label of Lynch-Bages. (NR) (5/15/92) (BT) **75+**
Pauillac 1990: An elegant, well-structured wine, showing pretty cassis and berry characteristics and well-integrated tannins. (NR) (5/15/92) (BT) **90+**
Pauillac 1989: Shows excellent harmony, with powerful tar, blackberry and fruit aromas and a super-rich palate. The ample tannins are fully integrated, giving it excellent balance. Try after 1997. $26 (3/15/92) **90**
Pauillac 1988 $23 (4/30/91) **93**
Pauillac 1987 $15 (11/30/89) (JS) **85**
Pauillac 1986 Rel: $15 Cur: $19 (11/30/89) (JS) **90**
Pauillac 1985 $17 (4/30/88) **82**
Pauillac 1982 $25 (11/30/89) (JS) **89**
Pauillac 1979 $18 (10/15/89) (JS) **84**

CHATEAU HAUT-BAGES-LIBERAL
Pauillac 1991: A very aromatic '91, with sweet, ripe fruit flavors and silky tannins. Firm and extremely well made. (NR) (5/15/92) (BT) **85+**
Pauillac 1990: Superbly concentrated, with masses of vanilla, chocolate and berry characteristics and full, velvety tannins. Truly outstanding. (NR) (5/15/92) (BT) **85+**
Pauillac 1989: Smoky and earthy, with good fruit and velvety tannins. Not a blockbuster, but very appealing. Try after 1997. $24 (3/15/92) **89**
Pauillac 1988 $17 (3/15/91) **88**
Pauillac 1987 $14 (6/30/89) (BT) **75+**
Pauillac 1986 Rel: $17 Cur: $21 (5/31/89) **91**
Pauillac 1985 Rel: $16 Cur: $24 (4/30/88) **88**
Pauillac 1984 $19 (6/15/87) **67**
Pauillac 1983 $18 (5/01/86) **67**
Pauillac (Belgian Bottled) 1959 $55 (10/15/90) (JS) **85**

CHATEAU HAUT-BAGES-MONPELOU
Pauillac 1989 (NR) (4/30/90) (BT) **85+**

CHATEAU HAUT-BATAILLEY
Pauillac 1991: Very silky, with complex milk chocolate and tobacco flavors and a tannic structure that melts in your mouth. (NR) (5/15/92) (BT) **85+**
Pauillac 1990: Rather light and slightly diluted, but it has clean berry and tea leaf characteristics and light tannins. Must have been recently racked. (NR) (5/15/92) (BT) **80+**
Pauillac 1989: Another charming wine, with pleasant licorice, berry and fruit flavors and a medium-silky tannin structure. Tasted twice. Try after 1994. $30 (3/15/92) **87**
Pauillac 1988 $26 (8/31/91) **87**
Pauillac 1987 $17 (5/15/90) **86**
Pauillac 1986 $23 (5/31/89) **85**
Pauillac 1985 Rel: $17 Cur: $21 (11/30/88) **81**
Pauillac 1979 $30 (10/15/89) (JS) **82**
Pauillac 1961 $95 (3/16/86) (TR) **91**

CHATEAU LACOSTE-BORIE
Pauillac 1989: Beautifully sculpted, with luscious cassis and herb aromas and flavors and fine, elegant tannins. A wine that pinpoints its fruit on your palate. The second wine of Grand-Puy-Lacoste. Try after 1996. $18 (3/15/92) **89**
Pauillac 1988: Lovely fruit, cedar and herb aromas and flavors run through this polished, elegant wine from start to finish. It's just delicious, with finely integrated tannins, lively acidity and opulent fruit flavors that linger on and on. Tempting to drink soon, but best after 1994 or '95. $19 (4/30/91) **89**
Pauillac 1986: Heavily vegetal and herbal with some berry and cassis flavors, lighter than most Pauillacs from this vintage, but it comes across as simple. Ready now through 1994. $15 (6/30/89) **84**
Pauillac 1983 $7.50 (6/15/87) **75**

CHATEAU LAFITE-ROTHSCHILD
Pauillac 1991: Starts out tough and powerful, turning smooth and pleasant in the mouth, with pretty chocolate and black cherry flavors, but it seems short on the finish. (NR) (5/15/92) (BT) **85+**
Pauillac 1990: Surprisingly closed for the moment, but lots of fruit and tannins are hiding underneath. The tobacco, berry and vanilla character really draws you into the wine. (NR) (5/15/92) (BT) **95+**
Pauillac 1989: This famous first growth never comes out on top in blind tastings when its wines are young, but everything is in the bottle to make it a classic Lafite. An enticing wine, with rich berry, cassis and herb aromas and flavors and well-integrated tannins. Very classy, as always. Better after 1997. $145 (3/15/92) **95**
Pauillac 1988 $100 (4/30/91) CS **96**
Pauillac 1987 $60 (11/30/91) (JG) **88**
Pauillac 1986 $102 (11/30/91) (JG) **96**
Pauillac 1985 Rel: $80 Cur: $101 (11/30/91) (JG) **95**
Pauillac 1985 Rel: $80 Cur: $101 (5/31/88) CS **97**
Pauillac 1984 Rel: $51 Cur: $62 (11/30/91) (JG) **87**
Pauillac 1983 Rel: $60 Cur: $100 (11/30/91) (JG) **90**
Pauillac 1982 Rel: $85 Cur: $180 (11/30/91) (JG) **96**
Pauillac 1981 Rel: $70 Cur: $150 (11/30/91) (JG) **91**
Pauillac 1980 $60 (11/30/91) (JG) **86**
Pauillac 1979 $115 (11/30/91) (JG) **92**
Pauillac 1978 $155 (11/30/91) (JG) **94**
Pauillac 1977 $40 (11/30/91) (JG) **87**
Pauillac 1976 $150 (11/30/91) (JG) **88**
Pauillac 1975 $190 (11/30/91) (JG) **71**
Pauillac 1974 $62 (11/30/91) (JG) **89**
Pauillac 1973 $55 (11/30/91) (JG) **87**
Pauillac 1972 $47 (11/30/91) (JG) **82**
Pauillac 1971 $105 (11/30/91) (JG) **87**
Pauillac 1970 $210 (11/30/91) (JG) **92**
Pauillac 1969 $45 (11/30/91) (JG) **80**
Pauillac 1968 $125 (11/30/91) (JG) **61**
Pauillac 1967 $80 (11/30/91) (JG) **80**
Pauillac 1966 $180 (11/30/91) (JG) **84**
Pauillac 1965 $120 (11/30/91) (JG) **73**
Pauillac 1964 $90 (11/30/91) (JG) **87**
Pauillac 1963 $200 (11/30/91) (JG) **69**
Pauillac 1962 $190 (11/30/91) (JG) **93**
Pauillac 1961 $520 (11/30/91) (JG) **91**
Pauillac 1961 $1,250/1.5L (11/30/91) (JG) **93**
Pauillac 1960 $105 (11/30/91) (JG) **92**
Pauillac 1959 $580 (11/30/91) (JG) **94**
Pauillac 1959 $1,250/1.5L (11/30/91) (JG) **98**
Pauillac 1958 $100 (11/30/91) (JG) **77**
Pauillac 1957 $110 (11/30/91) (JG) **87**
Pauillac 1956 $230 (11/30/91) (JG) **85**
Pauillac 1955 $350 (11/30/91) (JG) **94**
Pauillac 1954 $290 (11/30/91) (JG) **82**
Pauillac 1953 $500 (11/30/91) (JG) **94**
Pauillac 1953 $1,100/1.5L (11/30/91) (JG) **96**
Pauillac 1952 $240 (11/30/91) (JG) **90**
Pauillac 1951 $150 (11/30/91) (JG) **78**
Pauillac 1950 $300 (11/30/91) (JG) **91**
Pauillac 1949 $750 (11/30/91) (JG) **87**
Pauillac 1949 $1,000/1.5L (11/30/91) (JG) **90**
Pauillac 1948 $675 (11/30/91) (JG) **61**
Pauillac 1947 $450 (11/30/91) (JG) **74**
Pauillac 1946 $450 (11/30/91) (JG) **79**
Pauillac 1946 $450 (12/15/88) (TR) **90**
Pauillac 1945 $950 (11/30/91) (JG) **96**
Pauillac 1944 $380 (11/30/91) (JG) **63**
Pauillac 1943 $290 (11/30/91) (JG) **87**
Pauillac 1943 $700/1.5L (11/30/91) (JG) **85**
Pauillac 1942 $320 (11/30/91) (JG) **80**
Pauillac 1941 $500 (11/30/91) (JG) **69**
Pauillac 1940 $700 (11/30/91) (JG) **85**
Pauillac 1939 $320 (12/15/88) (TR) **78**

Pauillac 1938 $230 (11/30/91) (JG) **83**
Pauillac 1937 $250 (11/30/91) (JG) **81**
Pauillac 1934 $450 (11/30/91) (JG) **90**
Pauillac 1933 $200 (11/30/91) (JG) **80**
Pauillac 1931 $550 (11/30/91) (JG) **77**
Pauillac 1929 $950 (11/30/91) (JG) **87**
Pauillac 1929 $1,700/1.5L (11/30/91) (JG) **88**
Pauillac 1928 $700 (11/30/91) (JG) **66**
Pauillac 1926 $550 (11/30/91) (JG) **89**
Pauillac 1926 $900/1.5L (11/30/91) (JG) **69**
Pauillac 1925 $195 (11/30/91) (JG) **56**
Pauillac 1924 $450 (11/30/91) (JG) **88**
Pauillac 1923 $300 (11/30/91) (JG) **75**
Pauillac 1922 $325 (11/30/91) (JG) **64**
Pauillac 1921 $500 (12/15/88) (TR) **77**
Pauillac 1920 $575 (11/30/91) (JG) **94**
Pauillac 1919 $600 (11/30/91) (JG) **76**
Pauillac 1918 $525 (11/30/91) (JG) **80**
Pauillac 1917 $500 (11/30/91) (JG) **75**
Pauillac 1916 $375 (11/30/91) (JG) **71**
Pauillac 1916 $900/1.5L (11/30/91) (JG) **89**
Pauillac 1914 $550 (11/30/91) (JG) **58**
Pauillac 1913 $500 (11/30/91) (JG) **82**
Pauillac 1912 $675 (11/30/91) (JG) **69**
Pauillac 1911 $400 (11/30/91) (JG) **83**
Pauillac 1910 $575 (11/30/91) (JG) **69**
Pauillac 1909 $500 (11/30/91) (JG) **73**
Pauillac 1908 $900 (11/30/91) (JG) **86**
Pauillac 1907 $700 (11/30/91) (JG) **64**
Pauillac 1906 $350 (11/30/91) (JG) **90**
Pauillac 1905 $550 (11/30/91) (JG) **88**
Pauillac 1904 $660 (11/30/91) (JG) **84**
Pauillac 1903 $650 (11/30/91) (JG) **68**
Pauillac 1902 $850 (11/30/91) (JG) **80**
Pauillac 1901 $700 (11/30/91) (JG) **74**
Pauillac 1900 $1,900 (11/30/91) (JG) **79**
Pauillac 1900 $5,500/1.5L (11/30/91) (JG) **70**
Pauillac 1899 $2,200 (12/15/88) (TR) **78**
Pauillac 1898 $1,000 (12/15/88) (TR) **79**
Pauillac 1897 $1,200 (12/15/88) (TR) **81**
Pauillac 1896 $1,100 (12/15/88) (TR) **79**
Pauillac 1895 $2,100 (12/15/88) (TR) **89**
Pauillac 1894 $1,000 (11/30/91) (JG) **71**
Pauillac 1893 $1,200 (12/15/88) (TR) **84**
Pauillac 1892 $1,200 (11/30/91) (JG) **72**
Pauillac 1891 $1,100 (11/30/91) (JG) **70**
Pauillac 1890 $1,100 (12/15/88) (TR) **83**
Pauillac 1889 $850 (12/15/88) (TR) **85**
Pauillac 1888 $900 (12/15/88) (TR) **82**
Pauillac 1887 $1,000 (11/30/91) (JG) **67**
Pauillac 1886 $1,100 (12/15/88) (TR) **88**
Pauillac 1882 $800 (12/15/88) (TR) **82**
Pauillac 1881 $750 (11/30/91) (JG) **66**
Pauillac 1880 $1,400 (12/15/88) (TR) **82**
Pauillac 1879 $2,800 (12/15/88) (TR) **83**
Pauillac 1878 $2,200 (12/15/88) (TR) **83**
Pauillac 1877 $2,500 (12/15/88) (TR) **88**
Pauillac 1876 $1,800 (12/15/88) (TR) **84**
Pauillac 1875 $3,000 (12/15/88) (TR) **91**
Pauillac 1875 $8,000/1.5L (12/15/88) (TR) **97**
Pauillac 1874 $2,200 (12/15/88) (TR) **84**
Pauillac 1870 $3,500 (11/30/91) (JG) **92**
Pauillac 1870 $8,500/1.5L (11/30/91) (JG) **62**
Pauillac 1869 $4,000 (11/30/91) (JG) **87**
Pauillac 1868 $4,000 (11/30/91) (JG) **91**
Pauillac 1865 $6,500 (11/30/91) (JG) **50**
Pauillac 1864 $5,000 (12/15/88) (TR) **84**
Pauillac 1858 $4,000 (12/15/88) (TR) **96**
Pauillac 1848 $10,000 (12/15/88) (TR) **92**
Pauillac 1846 $8,000 (12/15/88) (TR) **83**
Pauillac 1844 $6,000 (12/15/88) (TR) **84**
Pauillac 1832 $9,000 (11/30/91) (JG) **78**
Pauillac 1806 $5,000 (12/15/88) (TR) **83**

CHATEAU LATOUR

Pauillac 1991: This illustrates Latour's greatness in less-than-good years. A solid wine, with very firm tannins and well-focused currant and berry flavors. (NR) (5/15/92) (BT) **90+**
Pauillac 1990: Takes your breath away; quintessential Latour, with a giant tannin structure, deep fruit flavors and an amazingly long finish. (NR) (5/15/92) (BT) **95+**
Pauillac 1989: We underrated Latour when we tasted it from the barrel. A gorgeous wine, with a captivating mixture of ripe berry and tobacco flavors and new wood notes. Has excellent concentration and a balance of fine tannins. Try after 1998. $145 (3/15/92) **97**
Pauillac 1988 $90 (4/30/91) **93**
Pauillac 1987 $60 (10/15/90) **80**
Pauillac 1986 $90 (3/31/90) (HS) **93**
Pauillac 1985 Rel: $82 Cur: $91 (3/31/90) (HS) **96**
Pauillac 1984 Rel: $40 Cur: $56 (3/31/87) **92**
Pauillac 1983 Rel: $72 Cur: $85 (3/31/90) (HS) **93**
Pauillac 1982 $151 (3/31/90) (HS) **99**
Pauillac 1981 $90 (3/31/90) (HS) **90**
Pauillac 1979 $100 (3/31/90) (HS) **90**
Pauillac 1978 $145 (3/31/90) (HS) **94**
Pauillac 1976 $90 (3/31/90) (HS) **87**
Pauillac 1975 $150 (3/31/90) (HS) **93**
Pauillac 1971 $120 (3/31/90) (HS) **84**
Pauillac 1970 $220 (3/31/90) (HS) **97**
Pauillac 1967 $110 (3/31/90) (HS) **79**
Pauillac 1966 $210 (3/31/90) (HS) **93**
Pauillac 1965 $135 (3/31/90) (HS) **74**
Pauillac 1964 $190 (3/31/90) (HS) **86**
Pauillac 1964 $400/1.5L (3/31/90) (HS) **88**
Pauillac 1963 $100 (3/31/90) (HS) **77**
Pauillac 1962 $525/1.5L (3/31/90) (HS) **92**
Pauillac 1961 $700 (3/31/90) (HS) **99**
Pauillac 1960 $200 (3/31/90) (HS) **88**
Pauillac 1959 $450 (10/15/90) (JS) **98**
Pauillac 1959 $1,000/1.5L (3/31/90) (HS) **95**
Pauillac 1958 $130 (3/31/90) (HS) **81**
Pauillac 1956 $250 (3/31/90) (HS) **62**
Pauillac 1955 $320 (3/31/90) (HS) **90**
Pauillac 1953 $290 (3/31/90) (HS) **80**
Pauillac 1952 $250 (3/31/90) (HS) **91**
Pauillac 1950 $330 (3/31/90) (HS) **79**
Pauillac 1949 $630 (3/31/90) (HS) **94**
Pauillac 1948 $380 (3/31/90) (HS) **84**
Pauillac 1947 $400 (3/31/90) (HS) **91**
Pauillac 1945 $1,200 (3/31/90) (HS) **98**
Pauillac 1944 $500 (3/31/90) (HS) **70**
Pauillac 1943 $330 (3/31/90) (HS) **67**
Pauillac 1942 $330 (3/31/90) (HS) **59**
Pauillac 1940 $370 (3/31/90) (HS) **64**
Pauillac 1937 $430 (3/31/90) (HS) **89**
Pauillac 1936 $400 (3/31/90) (HS) **75**
Pauillac 1934 $410 (3/31/90) (HS) **83**
Pauillac 1929 $2,300/1.5L (3/31/90) (HS) **95**
Pauillac 1928 $2,500/1.5L (3/31/90) (HS) **91**
Pauillac 1926 $775 (3/31/90) (HS) **87**
Pauillac 1924 $700 (3/31/90) (HS) **91**
Pauillac 1920 $550 (3/31/90) (HS) **50**
Pauillac 1918 $575 (3/31/90) (HS) **75**
Pauillac 1900 $1,900 (3/31/90) (HS) **90**
Pauillac 1899 $1,900 (3/31/90) (HS) **94**
Pauillac 1899 $4,000/1.5L (3/31/90) (HS) **50**
Pauillac 1893 $4,500 (3/31/90) (HS) **67**
Pauillac 1892 $1,200 (3/31/90) (HS) **63**
Pauillac 1875 $1,800 (3/31/90) (HS) **77**
Pauillac 1875 $3,800/1.5L (12/15/88) **95**
Pauillac 1874 $3,200 (3/31/90) (HS) **97**
Pauillac 1870 $4,000 (3/31/90) (HS) **94**
Pauillac 1865 $15,000/1.5L (3/31/90) (HS) **94**
Pauillac 1864 $10,000/1.5L (3/31/90) (HS) **59**
Pauillac 1847 $18,000/1.5L (3/31/90) (HS) **93**

CHATEAU LYNCH-BAGES

Pauillac 1991: Extremely well crafted, with integrated blackberry and currant flavors and silky tannins. (NR) (5/15/92) (BT) **85+**
Pauillac 1990: This gripping wine has a superb concentration of fruit and tannins, but still retains an amazing amount of class and finesse. (NR) (5/15/92) (BT) **95+**
Pauillac 1989: A wine with great mass, this is a complete fruit bomb, with blueberry, cassis and mint flavors and tons of silky tannins. Truly amazing; better than the superb '85. Try after 1998. $53 (3/15/92) **98**
Pauillac 1988 $35 (3/15/91) CS **95**
Pauillac 1987 $27 (2/15/90) **86**
Pauillac 1986 $37 (10/31/89) (JS) **94**
Pauillac 1985 Rel: $37 Cur: $50 (10/31/89) (JS) **93**
Pauillac 1985 Rel: $37 Cur: $50 (4/30/88) CS **97**
Pauillac 1984 Rel: $19 Cur: $22 (10/31/89) (JS) **87**
Pauillac 1983 Rel: $25 Cur: $45 (10/31/89) (JS) **88**
Pauillac 1982 Rel: $27 Cur: $61 (10/31/89) (JS) **90**
Pauillac 1982 Rel: $27 Cur: $61 (3/01/85) CS **94**
Pauillac 1981 Rel: $15 Cur: $40 (10/31/89) (JS) **90**
Pauillac 1981 Rel: $15 Cur: $40 (6/01/84) **92**
Pauillac 1980 $24 (10/31/89) (JS) **88**
Pauillac 1979 $38 (10/31/89) (JS) **87**
Pauillac 1978 $53 (10/31/89) (JS) **92**
Pauillac 1977 $25 (10/31/89) (JS) **78**
Pauillac 1976 $52 (10/31/89) (JS) **70**
Pauillac 1975 $65 (10/31/89) (JS) **90**
Pauillac 1973 $30 (10/31/89) (JS) **82**
Pauillac 1971 $65 (10/31/89) (JS) **67**
Pauillac 1970 $125 (10/31/89) (JS) **90**
Pauillac 1967 $45 (10/31/89) (JS) **79**
Pauillac 1966 $102 (10/31/89) (JS) **90**
Pauillac 1964 $90 (10/31/89) (JS) **76**
Pauillac 1962 $139 (10/31/89) (JS) **94**
Pauillac 1962 $139 (11/30/87) (JS) **80**
Pauillac 1961 $220 (10/31/89) (JS) **86**
Pauillac 1960 $55 (10/31/89) (JS) **76**
Pauillac 1959 $250 (10/15/90) (JS) **95**
Pauillac 1958 $60 (10/31/89) (JS) **79**
Pauillac 1957 $85 (10/31/89) (JS) **88**
Pauillac 1955 $250 (10/31/89) (JS) **92**
Pauillac 1954 $75 (10/31/89) (JS) **74**
Pauillac 1953 $320 (10/31/89) (JS) **77**
Pauillac 1952 $100 (10/31/89) (JS) **83**
Pauillac 1949 $175 (10/31/89) (JS) **84**
Pauillac 1947 $350 (10/31/89) (JS) **90**
Pauillac (Danish Bottled) 1945 $350 (10/31/89) (JS) **80**
Pauillac 1945 $350 (3/16/86) (JL) **65**

CHATEAU LYNCH-MOUSSAS

Pauillac 1991: Slightly herbal and earthy, with good, sweet fruit flavors on the middle palate, but it ends a bit short. (NR) (5/15/92) (BT) **75+**

Key to Symbols

The scores reported here are the results of blind tastings conducted by our panel of senior editors. Wines that carry the initials below are results of individual tastings.

THE WINE SPECTATOR 100-POINT SCALE 95-100—Classic, a great wine; ***90-94***—Outstanding, superior character and style; ***80-89***—Good to very good, a wine with special qualities; ***70-79***—Average, drinkable wine that may have minor flaws; ***60-69***—Below average, drinkable but not recommended; ***50-59***—Poor, undrinkable, not recommended. "+"—With a score indicates a range; used primarily with barrel tastings to indicate a preliminary score.

SPECIAL DESIGNATIONS SS—Spectator Selection, CS—Cellar Selection, BB—Best Buy, ($NA)—Price not available, (NR)—Not released.

TASTER'S INITIALS (JG)—Jim Gordon, (HS)—Harvey Steiman, (JL)—James Laube, (JS)—James Suckling, (TM)—Thomas Matthews, (TR)—Terry Robards, (PM)—Per-Henrik Mansson, (BT)—Barrel Tasting (these wines were tasted blind from barrel samples), (CA-date)—*California's Great Cabernets* by James Laube, (CH-date)—*California's Great Chardonnays* by James Laube, (VP-date)—*Vintage Port* by James Suckling.

DATE TASTED Dates in parentheses represent the issue in which the rating was published.

Pauillac 1990 (NR) (4/30/91) (BT) **85+**
Pauillac 1989: There's plenty of fruit in this rather idiosyncratic wine, along with an intense tobacco, herbal and berry character and full, well-integrated tannins. Yet another super '89. Try after 1997. $21 (3/15/92) **90**
Pauillac 1988 $25 (8/31/91) **85**
Pauillac 1987 $17 (6/30/89) (BT) **70+**
Pauillac 1986 $18 (6/30/89) **86**
Pauillac 1959 $115 (10/15/90) (JS) **86**

MOULIN DES CARRUADES
Pauillac 1983 $14 (10/31/86) **88**

MOULIN DE DUHART
Pauillac 1989 (NR) (4/30/90) (BT) **80+**
Pauillac 1987 (NR) (6/30/89) (BT) **70+**

CHATEAU MOUTON-BARONNE-PHILIPPE
Pauillac 1990 (NR) (4/30/91) (BT) **85+**
Pauillac 1988: This big, powerful wine crams plenty of ripe currant, prune and chocolate aromas and flavors into a solid frame that coats the mouth with tannin. Needs until 1996 to '98 to soften. $25 (4/30/91) **90**
Pauillac 1987 Rel: $16 Cur: $20 (6/30/89) (BT) **80+**
Pauillac 1986 $23 (5/31/89) **93**
Pauillac 1985 Rel: $18 Cur: $29 (5/15/88) SS **91**
Pauillac 1984 $17 (6/15/87) **64**
Pauillac 1983 $16 (3/01/86) **88**
Pauillac 1982 Rel: $15 Cur: $28 (4/01/85) **86**
Pauillac 1981 Rel: $12 Cur: $16 (6/01/84) **81**
Pauillac 1961 $123 (3/16/86) (TR) **62**
Pauillac 1945 $390 (3/16/86) (JL) **80**

CHATEAU MOUTON-ROTHSCHILD
Pauillac 1991: Round and flavorful, displaying excellent balance and grace, with good fruit, a great tannic structure and bitter dark chocolate, cedar and berry flavors. (NR) (5/15/92) (BT) **90+**
Pauillac 1990: A decadent wine, with a superb concentration of earthy, gamy currant flavors and full tannins. (NR) (5/15/92) (BT) **95+**
Pauillac 1989: One of the stars in every vintage, the '89 Mouton defines class and concentration. An exciting wine, with thick, chewy cassis, mint and berry flavors, full, silky tannins and great harmony. Try after 2000. $150 (3/15/92) **99**
Pauillac 1988 $105 (4/30/91) **100**
Pauillac 1987 Rel: $56 Cur: $78 (5/15/90) **89**
Pauillac 1986 Rel: $102 Cur: $140 (5/15/91) (PM) **97**
Pauillac 1986 Rel: $102 Cur: $140 (5/31/89) CS **98**
Pauillac 1985 Rel: $90 Cur: $96 (4/30/88) **94**
Pauillac 1984 Rel: $40 Cur: $59 (3/31/87) **92**
Pauillac 1983 Rel: $57 Cur: $90 (3/01/86) **96**
Pauillac 1982 $210 (5/15/91) (PM) **93**
Pauillac 1981 Rel: $40 Cur: $100 (6/16/86) (TR) **86**
Pauillac 1980 $85 (6/16/86) (TR) **67**
Pauillac 1979 $110 (10/15/89) (JS) **96**
Pauillac 1978 $140 (5/15/91) (PM) **92**
Pauillac 1977 $78 (6/16/86) (TR) **68**
Pauillac 1976 $88 (6/16/86) (TR) **85**
Pauillac 1975 $160 (5/15/91) (PM) **89**
Pauillac 1974 $145 (6/16/86) (TR) **67**
Pauillac 1973 $120 (6/16/86) (TR) **75**
Pauillac 1972 $100 (6/16/86) (TR) **55**
Pauillac 1971 $95 (6/16/86) (TR) **78**
Pauillac 1970 $195 (5/15/91) (PM) **84**
Pauillac 1969 $220 (6/16/86) (TR) **78**
Pauillac 1968 $420 (6/16/86) (TR) **64**
Pauillac 1967 $90 (6/16/86) (TR) **87**
Pauillac 1966 $220 (5/15/91) (PM) **88**
Pauillac 1965 $850 (6/16/86) (TR) **61**
Pauillac 1964 $120 (6/16/86) (TR) **84**
Pauillac 1963 $1,150 (6/16/86) (TR) **77**
Pauillac 1962 $230 (5/15/91) (PM) **93**
Pauillac 1961 $620 (5/15/91) (PM) **90**
Pauillac 1960 $550 (6/16/86) (TR) **84**
Pauillac 1959 $500 (5/15/91) (PM) **98**
Pauillac 1958 $850 (6/16/86) (TR) **68**
Pauillac 1957 $575 (6/16/86) (TR) **86**
Pauillac 1956 $2,500 (6/16/86) (TR) **85**
Pauillac 1955 $400 (5/15/91) (PM) **95**
Pauillac 1954 $3,000 (6/16/86) (TR) **81**
Pauillac 1953 $680 (5/15/91) (PM) **94**
Pauillac 1952 $400 (6/16/86) (TR) **90**
Pauillac 1951 $1,600 (6/16/86) (TR) **84**
Pauillac 1950 $800 (6/16/86) (TR) **83**
Pauillac 1949 $1,250 (5/15/91) (PM) **87**
Pauillac 1948 $1,650 (6/16/86) (TR) **87**
Pauillac 1947 $1,350 (5/15/91) (PM) **75**
Pauillac 1947 $1,350 (6/16/86) (TR) **95**
Pauillac 1946 $7,000 (6/16/86) (TR) **77**
Pauillac 1945 $2,000 (5/15/91) (PM) **100**
Pauillac 1945 $2,000 (3/16/86) (JL) **95**
Pauillac 1944 $950 (6/16/86) (TR) **86**
Pauillac 1943 $500 (6/16/86) (TR) **78**
Pauillac 1940 $525 (6/16/86) (TR) **77**
Pauillac 1939 $500 (6/16/86) (TR) **55**
Pauillac 1938 $500 (6/16/86) (TR) **73**
Pauillac 1937 $440 (5/15/91) (PM) **91**
Pauillac 1936 $250 (6/16/86) (TR) **63**
Pauillac 1934 $450 (5/15/91) (PM) **90**
Pauillac 1933 $300/375ml (6/16/86) (TR) **78**
Pauillac 1929 $1,000 (5/15/91) (PM) **75**
Pauillac 1928 $950 (5/15/91) (PM) **89**
Pauillac 1926 $800 (6/16/86) (TR) **65**
Pauillac 1925 $1,100 (6/16/86) (TR) **40**
Pauillac 1924 $1,900 (6/16/86) (TR) **69**
Pauillac 1921 $500 (5/15/91) (PM) **80**
Pauillac 1920 $700 (6/16/86) (TR) **75**
Pauillac 1919 $600 (5/15/91) (PM) **79**
Pauillac 1918 $1,600 (5/15/91) (PM) **83**
Pauillac 1916 $400 (6/16/86) (TR) **67**
Pauillac 1914 $400 (6/16/86) (TR) **65**
Pauillac 1912 $400 (6/16/86) (TR) **62**
Pauillac 1910 $400 (5/15/91) (PM) **76**
Pauillac 1909 $750 (6/16/86) (TR) **65**
Pauillac 1908 $700 (6/16/86) (TR) **50**
Pauillac 1907 $600 (6/16/86) (TR) **50**
Pauillac 1906 $800 (6/16/86) (TR) **66**
Pauillac 1905 $950 (5/15/91) (PM) **88**
Pauillac 1900 $1,800 (5/15/91) (PM) **90**
Pauillac 1899 $1,800 (6/16/86) (TR) **82**
Pauillac 1888 $1,100 (6/16/86) (TR) **60**
Pauillac 1886 $1,200 (6/16/86) (TR) **60**
Pauillac 1881 $1,400 (6/16/86) (TR) **74**
Pauillac 1878 $3,200 (5/15/91) (PM) **99**
Pauillac 1874 $2,100 (5/15/91) (PM) **95**
Pauillac 1870 $3,500 (5/15/91) (PM) **87**
Pauillac 1869 $1,700 (6/16/86) (TR) **40**
Pauillac 1867 $2,100 (6/16/86) (TR) **40**

PAUILLAC DE LATOUR
Pauillac 1991: Forward and nice now, with lovely, sweet fruit flavors and light tannins. The third label of Latour. (NR) (5/15/92) (BT) **80+**
Pauillac 1990: Offers a good amount of tannins, ripe fruit and a lovely, spicy vanilla and berry character. (NR) (5/15/92) (BT) **85+**

CHATEAU PEDESCLAUX
Pauillac 1988 $20 (6/30/89) (BT) **80+**
Pauillac 1986: Pleasant with fresh cedar, currant and cherry notes, elegant balance, but it's lacking in depth and concentration. Drink now through 1994. $18 (2/15/90) **79**

CHATEAU PIBRAN
Pauillac 1991: A strongly herbaceous, bell pepper-flavored wine. Feels a bit metallic on the palate, with full tannins. A little too coarse for us. (NR) (5/15/92) (BT) **75+**
Pauillac 1990: Offers lots of cassis and berry aromas and flavors, but the tannins slowly but surely build on the finish. Excellent for a *crus bourgeois*. (NR) (5/15/92) (BT) **90+**
Pauillac 1989: Graceful yet powerful, with a lovely harmony of berry, cassis and smoke flavors and well-knit, silky tannins. One of the best values in the vintage. Try after 1997. $25 (3/15/92) **95**
Pauillac 1988 $27 (8/31/90) (BT) **85+**
Pauillac 1987 $20 (11/30/89) (JS) **85**
Pauillac 1986 $18 (11/30/89) (JS) **88**
Pauillac 1982 $18 (11/30/89) (JS) **90**

CHATEAU PICHON-BARON
Pauillac 1991: Shows excellent structure, oozing with focused, sweet blackberry flavors backed up by chocolate notes and steely tannins. (NR) (5/15/92) (BT) **90+**
Pauillac 1990: Spellbinding, with masses of cassis, tobacco and fruit aromas and flavors and full, silky tannins. (NR) (5/15/92) (BT) **95+**
Pauillac 1989: Defines purity and intensity. Shows unbelievable concentration of fruit, with amazing blackberry, cassis, dark chocolate and vanilla flavors and a great tannin structure. A breathtaking wine. Try after 1998. $60 (3/15/92) **98**
Pauillac 1988 $30 (3/31/91) SS **95**
Pauillac 1987 Rel: $20 $25 (10/15/90) **88**
Pauillac 1986 Rel: $31 $41 (5/31/89) **97**
Pauillac 1985 $32 (4/30/88) **94**
Pauillac 1984 $23 (9/30/88) **78**
Pauillac 1983 Rel: $18 Cur: $36 (3/01/86) **94**
Pauillac 1982 Rel: $12 Cur: $43 (9/30/88) **78**
Pauillac 1981 Rel: $13 Cur: $32 (9/30/88) **84**
Pauillac 1980 $17 (9/30/88) **79**
Pauillac 1979 $38 (10/15/89) (JS) **88**
Pauillac 1978 $51 (9/30/88) **80**
Pauillac 1977 $13 (9/30/88) **76**
Pauillac 1976 $30 (9/30/88) **73**
Pauillac 1975 $46 (9/30/88) **74**
Pauillac 1974 $4 (9/30/88) **78**
Pauillac 1973 $13 (9/30/88) **78**
Pauillac 1972 $13 (9/30/88) **68**
Pauillac 1971 $31 (9/30/88) **71**
Pauillac 1970 $70 (9/30/88) **83**
Pauillac 1969 $21 (9/30/88) **78**
Pauillac 1967 $65 (9/30/88) **80**
Pauillac 1966 $62 (9/30/88) **80**
Pauillac 1964 $85 (9/30/88) **88**
Pauillac 1962 $85 (9/30/88) **88**
Pauillac 1961 $165 (9/30/88) **84**
Pauillac 1960 $50 (9/30/88) **81**
Pauillac 1959 $135 (10/15/90) (JS) **94**
Pauillac 1958 $95 (9/30/88) **79**
Pauillac 1957 $110 (9/30/88) **76**
Pauillac 1955 $100 (9/30/88) **81**
Pauillac 1954 $95 (9/30/88) **80**
Pauillac 1953 $150 (9/30/88) **80**
Pauillac 1952 $105 (9/30/88) **84**
Pauillac 1950 $150 (9/30/88) **83**
Pauillac 1949 $175 (9/30/88) **87**
Pauillac 1947 $175 (9/30/88) **80**
Pauillac 1945 $290 (9/30/88) **75**

CHATEAU PICHON-LALANDE
Pauillac 1991: Wonderfully generous for the vintage, with a dense, supple texture shaded by round, rich fruit flavors and lovely, silky tannins. Almost outstanding. (NR) (5/15/92) (BT) **85+**
Pauillac 1990: A pretty wine, with elegant blackberry aromas and flavors and medium tannins. Very good, but perhaps not showing as well as it should right now. Tasted twice. (NR) (5/15/92) (BT) **85+**
Pauillac 1989: Hard as nails and not giving much now, but it has a dense fruit and tannin structure. Will most likely receive higher scores as it evolves. Try after 1998. $71 (3/15/92) **92**
Pauillac 1988 $50 (4/30/91) **91**
Pauillac 1987 $30 (2/15/90) **87**
Pauillac 1986 Rel: $50 Cur: $59 (5/31/89) **97**
Pauillac 1985 Rel: $40 Cur: $52 (2/29/88) CS **95**
Pauillac 1984 $27 (1/31/87) CS **94**
Pauillac 1983 Rel: $44 Cur: $54 (3/01/86) SS **97**
Pauillac 1982 Rel: $29 Cur: $100 (2/01/85) SS **94**
Pauillac 1981 Rel: $21 Cur: $56 (5/01/85) **93**
Pauillac 1980 Rel: $14 Cur: $33 (5/01/85) **92**
Pauillac 1980 Rel: $14 Cur: $33 (3/01/84) CS **90**
Pauillac 1979 $65 (5/01/85) **90**
Pauillac 1978 $90 (5/01/85) **91**
Pauillac 1962 $138 (11/30/87) (JS) **85**

Pauillac 1961 $230 (3/16/86) (TR) **79**
Pauillac 1959 $200 (10/15/90) (JS) **97**
Pauillac 1945 $400 (3/16/86) (JL) **80**

CHATEAU PLANTEY
Pauillac 1989: Very ripe, with stewed tomato and prune characteristics and medium-dry tannins. Lacks a bit of grace. Try after 1994. (NR) (3/15/92) **78**

CHATEAU PONTET-CANET
Pauillac 1991: Firm and steely, with focused currant and tar flavors and a very good tannin backbone. (NR) (5/15/92) (BT) **85+**
Pauillac 1990: A big, burly wine that's thick and rich, with tons of tar, mint and tobacco flavors and full tannins. This estate gets better every vintage. (NR) (5/15/92) (BT) **90+**
Pauillac 1989: Pretty mint, spice and cassis aromas follow through to the palate in this very balanced wine. Has plenty of everything to keep it going for years. Somewhat rustic now; try after 1995. $27 (3/15/92) **89**
Pauillac 1988 $24 (6/30/89) (BT) **80+**
Pauillac 1987 $14 (6/30/89) (BT) **75+**
Pauillac 1986 $21 (5/31/89) **89**
Pauillac 1985 $22 (5/15/87) (BT) **80+**
Pauillac 1961 $95 (3/16/86) (TR) **66**
Pauillac 1945 $250 (3/16/86) (JL) **60**

RESERVE DE LA COMTESSE
Pauillac 1988: Has classic Bordeaux cigar box aromas, but a subtle horsey, barnyardy quality detracts from the solid core of currant and plum flavors. Firmly tannic and well balanced, with ample oak. Biting tannins emerge on the finish. Needs cellaring until 1994 to 2000. $23 (3/15/91) **88**
Pauillac 1987: There are pretty currant, mint and plum flavors of moderate depth and intensity, but the wood dominates now. Lacks complexity and turns bitter on the finish. Drink now. Tasted twice. $14 (5/15/90) **82**
Pauillac 1986 $20 (5/31/89) **90**
Pauillac 1983 Rel: $18 Cur: $21 (3/01/86) **82**

LES TOURELLS DE LONGUEVILLE
Pauillac 1991: Lots of currant and tar flavors and well-extracted tannins give excellent focus to this wine. The second wine of Pichon-Baron. (NR) (5/15/92) (BT) **85+**
Pauillac 1990: Pumped up and muscular, with tons of extracted berry flavors and velvety tannins. (NR) (5/15/92) (BT) **90+**
Pauillac 1989: For a second wine, this is superb. Mammoth, with an outstanding concentration of fruit and tannins and impressive cassis, tobacco and cedar flavors. Tightly wound and in need of time. Try after 1999. $27 (3/15/92) **94**
Pauillac 1988 $25 (8/31/90) (BT) **85+**
Pauillac 1987 $17 (6/30/89) (BT) **75+**

POMEROL

CHATEAU BEAUREGARD
Pomerol 1991: Pleasant and light, with straightforward red berry flavors and silky tannins. (NR) (5/15/92) (BT) **75+**
Pomerol 1990: Round and rich, with a bounty of chocolate, truffle and berry flavors and velvety tannins. A delicious wine. (NR) (5/15/92) (BT) **90+**
Pomerol 1988: A lush wine, packed with generous plum, herb, currant and spice flavors that are concentrated and well focused. Gains a firm, tannic edge on the finish, but the black cherry flavor comes through. Balanced, attractive and gusty; best to cellar until 1996 to 2000. $36 (7/31/91) **90**
Pomerol 1986 $22 (6/15/89) **87**
Pomerol 1982 Rel: $16 Cur: $20 (5/15/89) (TR) **89**

CHATEAU LE BON-PASTEUR
Pomerol 1990: Big and concentrated, with an explosion of plum and menthol flavors and mouth-coating tannins. A monster of a wine; shows much better than last year. (NR) (5/15/92) (BT) **90+**
Pomerol 1989: Tight and tannic, with a core of ripe, fleshy plum, black cherry, chocolate and oak flavors. A young, unevolved wine that needs until 1996 for the tannins to soften. 3,500 cases made. $35 (4/30/92) **88**
Pomerol 1988: A broad-structured, full-bodied wine, with plenty of soft tannins and modest currant and herb flavors. Too tough and tannic to enjoy now; drink in 1993 to '96. $23 (2/28/91) **85**
Pomerol 1987 $22 (5/15/90) **81**
Pomerol 1986 Rel: $22 Cur: $25 (6/15/89) **92**
Pomerol 1985 Rel: $20 Cur: $29 (5/15/88) **92**
Pomerol 1984 Rel: $12 Cur: $23 (6/15/87) **86**
Pomerol 1983 Rel: $22 $28 (6/16/86) **86**
Pomerol 1982 $54 (5/15/89) (TR) **91**
Pomerol 1979 $28 (10/15/89) (JS) **91**

CHATEAU BONALGUE
Pomerol 1989 (NR) (4/30/91) (BT) **85+**
Pomerol 1988 (NR) (6/30/89) (BT) **85+**
Pomerol 1987 $18 (6/30/89) (BT) **80+**
Pomerol 1986 $27 (6/30/88) (BT) **85+**

CHATEAU BOURGNEUF-VAYRON
Pomerol 1990: Full-bodied, but it still has lovely finesse, with ripe plum, blackberry and olive flavors and full, fine tannins. (NR) (5/15/92) (BT) **90+**
Pomerol 1989: We underrated this from the barrel. Shows serious winemaking, with a classy mixture of raspberry, licorice and new-wood flavors and super-silky tannins. Has great balance and restraint. Try after 1996. $32 (3/15/92) **90**
Pomerol 1988: Distinctive for its red cherry and currant flavors, this elegant and well-defined wine has hints of plum and spice to add dimension. Structured with firm tannins and a long, fruity aftertaste. Drink in 1996 to 2000. 5,000 cases made. $19 (6/30/91) **90**
Pomerol 1987 $13 (6/30/89) (BT) **75+**
Pomerol 1986 Rel: $22 Cur: $26 (6/30/88) (BT) **80+**
Pomerol 1985 $28 (11/30/88) **86**

Key to Symbols

The scores reported here are the results of blind tastings conducted by our panel of senior editors. Wines that carry the initials below are results of individual tastings.

THE WINE SPECTATOR 100-POINT SCALE ***95-100***—Classic, a great wine; ***90-94***—Outstanding, superior character and style; ***80-89***—Good to very good, a wine with special qualities; ***70-79***—Average, drinkable wine that may have minor flaws; ***60-69***—Below average, drinkable but not recommended; ***50-59***—Poor, undrinkable, not recommended. "+"—With a score indicates a range; used primarily with barrel tastings to indicate a preliminary score.

SPECIAL DESIGNATIONS SS—Spectator Selection, CS—Cellar Selection, BB—Best Buy, ($NA)—Price not available, (NR)—Not released.

TASTER'S INITIALS (JG)—Jim Gordon, (HS)—Harvey Steiman, (JL)—James Laube, (JS)—James Suckling, (TM)—Thomas Matthews, (TR)—Terry Robards, (PM)—Per-Henrik Mansson, (BT)—Barrel Tasting (these wines were tasted blind from barrel samples), (CA-date)—*California's Great Cabernets* by James Laube, (CH-date)—*California's Great Chardonnays* by James Laube, (VP-date)—*Vintage Port* by James Suckling.

DATE TASTED Dates in parentheses represent the issue in which the rating was published.

Pomerol 1982 $23 (5/15/89) (TR) **83**

CHATEAU LA CABANNE
Pomerol 1991: Shows firm tannins and earthy berry flavors in a pretty but light package. (NR) (5/15/92) (BT) **80+**
Pomerol 1990: A traditionally styled Pomerol, with rich, decadent, earthy aromas and flavors and full, velvety tannins. A super wine from an up-and-coming estate in the region. (NR) (5/15/92) (BT) **90+**
Pomerol 1989: Extremely extracted, with ripe fruit, almost burnt aromas and flavors and masses of big tannins. A wine to lay away for quite a while; seems a little coarse. This producer continues to improve and really hit it right in 1989. Try after 1998. $30 (3/15/92) **92**
Pomerol 1987 $20 (6/30/89) (BT) **80+**
Pomerol 1986 (NR) (6/30/88) (BT) **85+**
Pomerol 1985 (NR) (5/15/87) (BT) **80+**
Pomerol 1961 ($NA) (4/30/92) (TR) **77**

CHATEAU CERTAN DE MAY
Pomerol 1990: Like a good, young vintage Port; shows wonderfully sweet, ripe fruit flavors and rich, silky tannins. A wonderful wine. (NR) (5/15/92) (BT) **95+**
Pomerol 1989 $75 (4/30/91) (BT) **90+**
Pomerol 1988: An earthy, tannic, gripping wine that's bold and full-bodied, with mineral, spice, currant and plum flavors that are chunky and chalky. This rough-hewn style needs time to soften and mellow; start drinking in 1997. 2,000 cases made. $66 (6/30/91) **90**
Pomerol 1987 $50 (6/30/89) (BT) **85+**
Pomerol 1986 Rel: $53 Cur: $71 (9/15/89) **93**
Pomerol 1985 Rel: $70 Cur: $84 (4/30/88) **86**
Pomerol 1982 $150 (5/15/89) (TR) **92**
Pomerol 1979 $76 (10/15/89) (JS) **90**

CHATEAU CERTAN-GIRAUD
Pomerol 1988: Very elegant and earthy in style, firm in structure and filled with ample cherry, currant, cedar and toast flavors that signify a complex, sophisticated wine. Beautifully balanced, long and spicy on the finish. The tannins are soft and supple; drink it now through 1996. $23 (2/28/91) **89**
Pomerol 1987 $18 (6/30/89) (BT) **75+**
Pomerol 1986: Smooth and supple, with earthy, almost gamy aromas and flavors, meaty in texture, but long and elegant at the same time. Tannins should subside by 1993 or '94. $22 (6/30/89) **86**
Pomerol 1985 $25 (4/30/88) **85**
Pomerol 1982 $39 (5/15/89) (TR) **90**

CHATEAU CLINET
Pomerol 1991: Attractive, with chocolate and licorice flavors, elegant tannins and a focused finish. (NR) (5/15/92) (BT) **85+**
Pomerol 1990: Like chocolate mousse, with magnificent aromas and masses of flavor and tannins. Has it all. (NR) (5/15/92) (BT) **95+**
Pomerol 1989 $56 (4/30/91) (BT) **90+**
Pomerol 1988 $31 (2/28/91) **92**
Pomerol 1987 $25 (6/30/89) (BT) **90+**
Pomerol 1986 Rel: $25 Cur: $29 (9/15/89) **78**
Pomerol 1985 $34 (4/30/88) **91**
Pomerol 1982 $38 (5/15/89) (TR) **78**

CLOS DU CLOCHER
Pomerol 1989 (NR) (4/30/91) (BT) **85+**
Pomerol 1988 $22 (6/30/89) (BT) **80+**
Pomerol 1987 $18 (6/30/89) (BT) **80+**
Pomerol 1986 $20 (6/30/88) (BT) **80+**
Pomerol 1985 Rel: $17 Cur: $20 (2/29/88) **88**
Pomerol 1982 $33 (5/15/89) (TR) **83**

CLOS L'EGLISE
Pomerol 1990: Extremely rich, with plum and grape skin characteristics and full, velvety tannins. Very impressive. (NR) (5/15/92) (BT) **90+**
Pomerol 1989 $24 (4/30/91) (BT) **95+**
Pomerol 1988: Medium in weight and intensity, with elegant, supple black cherry, herb, tea and spice flavors. Not too tannic; enjoy 1993 to '96. 2,800 cases made. $24 (6/30/91) **83**
Pomerol 1987 $20 (6/30/89) (BT) **75+**
Pomerol 1986 $28 (2/15/90) **86**
Pomerol 1985 Rel: $21 Cur: $25 (5/15/87) (BT) **80+**
Pomerol 1982 $27 (5/15/89) (TR) **88**
Pomerol 1961 $75 (3/16/86) (TR) **63**
Pomerol 1945 $230 (3/16/86) (JL) **87**

CLOS DES LITANIES
Pomerol 1982 ($NA) (5/15/89) (TR) **83**

CLOS RENE
Pomerol 1988: Tight raspberry, currant, cedar and plum flavors are sharply focused, with firm tannins and a rich core of fruit. Has excellent balance and depth, but it's going to need time to mellow. Drink in 1998. $24 (4/30/91) **88**
Pomerol 1987 $20 (6/30/89) (BT) **75+**
Pomerol 1986 Rel: $19 Cur: $24 (6/15/89) SS **94**
Pomerol 1985 Rel: $17 Cur: $20 (3/15/88) **92**
Pomerol 1983 Rel: $17 Cur: $23 (3/16/86) **91**
Pomerol 1982 $27 (5/15/89) (TR) **87**
Pomerol 1962 $35 (11/30/87) (JS) **60**
Pomerol 1959 $50 (10/15/90) (JS) **88**
Pomerol 1945 $100 (3/16/86) (JL) **79**

CHATEAU LA CONSEILLANTE
Pomerol 1991: Offers plenty of vanilla, plum and tobacco flavors and a light, silky finish, but in the end it doesn't give as much as it should. (NR) (5/15/92) (BT) **80+**
Pomerol 1990: Very ripe and raisiny, with ripe fruit and smoke flavors. Almost Port-like in structure, with plenty of tannins. Could use a bit more grace, but it's very impressive. (NR) (5/15/92) (BT) **90+**
Pomerol 1989: Tastes like melted milk chocolate, with a bit of spice. A big, fleshy wine, with rich, forward fruit flavor and full, round tannins. It will age, but it will be ready before some '89s. Try after 1996. $107 (3/15/92) **92**
Pomerol 1988 $56 (3/31/91) **90**
Pomerol 1987 $35 (5/15/90) **86**
Pomerol 1986 Rel: $40 Cur: $54 (6/15/89) **93**
Pomerol 1985 Rel: $50 Cur: $60 (2/29/88) **93**
Pomerol 1984 Rel: $26 Cur: $37 (3/31/87) **93**
Pomerol 1983 Rel: $33 Cur: $40 (11/15/86) **84**
Pomerol 1982 Rel: $29 Cur: $72 (5/15/89) (TR) **96**
Pomerol 1962 $55 (11/30/87) (JS) **60**
Pomerol 1959 $150 (10/15/90) (JS) **88**

CHATEAU LA CROIX
Pomerol 1990 (NR) (4/30/91) (BT) **90+**
Pomerol 1989 (NR) (4/30/91) (BT) **90+**
Pomerol 1988: Firm and chunky, with modest currant and plum aromas and flavors overlaid with smoke and spice notes. A modest wine. 5,000 cases made. $19 (7/31/91) **82**

Pomerol 1987 $15 (6/30/89) (BT) **75+**
Pomerol 1986 $25 (6/30/88) (BT) **80+**
Pomerol 1985 $25 (5/15/88) **93**
Pomerol 1983 Rel: $14 Cur: $20 (11/30/86) **84**
Pomerol 1982 $23 (5/15/89) (TR) **89**
Pomerol 1981 $14 (5/01/89) **72**
Pomerol 1979 Rel: $11 Cur: $22 (4/01/84) **60**

CHATEAU LA CROIX DE GAY
Pomerol 1991: An interesting wine, with tar, coffee and vanilla characteristics, supple tannins and a smoky finish. (NR) (5/15/92) (BT) **85+**
Pomerol 1990: A big, fat wine, with lots of ripe fruit, an oily, thick mouth-feel and meaty tannins. (NR) (5/15/92) (BT) **90+**
Pomerol 1989: A lovely wine, with delicious berry and raspberry aromas and flavors, firm tannins and no-nonsense fruit. Try after 1995. Rel: $19 Cur: $25 (3/15/92) **88**
Pomerol 1988 $26 (6/30/91) **89**
Pomerol 1987 $20 (6/30/89) (BT) **80+**
Pomerol 1986 Rel: $20 Cur: $25 (6/30/88) (BT) **90+**
Pomerol 1985 $33 (3/15/88) CS **91**
Pomerol 1983 Rel: $16 Cur: $23 (7/01/86) CS **94**
Pomerol 1982 Rel: $16 Cur: $23 (5/15/89) (TR) **91**
Pomerol 1945 $360 (3/16/86) (JL) **70**

CHATEAU LA CROIX DU CASSE
Pomerol 1989 (NR) (4/30/91) (BT) **90+**
Pomerol 1988 $20 (6/30/89) (BT) **85+**
Pomerol 1987 $17 (6/30/88) (BT) **75+**
Pomerol 1985 $25 (5/15/88) **82**

CHATEAU LA CROIX-TOULIFAUT
Pomerol 1982 ($NA) (5/15/89) (TR) **80**

CHATEAU L'EGLISE-CLINET
Pomerol 1988: Engagingly complex, rich and distinctive, with layers of berry, currant, smoke and spice flavors that are broad, ripe and tarry. Plenty of leathery tannins show through on the finish, but altogether it's very well proportioned. Can use cellaring until 1998 to 2002. $47 (12/31/90) **91**
Pomerol 1987: Attractive for its ripe rich currant and plum flavors and then the tannins grab on. A bit awkward now, but the flavors are pleasing. Could use a little more concentration. $22 (2/15/90) **83**
Pomerol 1986 Rel: $29 Cur: $44 (6/15/89) **91**
Pomerol 1985 Rel: $30 Cur: $57 (2/29/88) **93**
Pomerol 1983 Rel: $19 Cur: $24 (3/16/86) **88**
Pomerol 1982 Rel: $18 Cur: $42 (5/15/89) (TR) **87**

DOMAINE DE L'EGLISE
Pomerol 1990 (NR) (4/30/91) (BT) **90+**
Pomerol 1989: Beautifully perfumed, with blueberry and spice aromas and flavors. Full-bodied, with a balance of full, silky tannins. Shows great harmony. Try after 1998. $33 (3/15/92) **93**

CHATEAU L'ENCLOS
Pomerol 1989: Tight and gutsy, with a dark color and intense currant and plum flavors. An earthy edge to the fruit is distracting, and it's quite tannic. Cellar until 1996. 5,000 cases made. $30 (4/30/92) **82**
Pomerol 1988: Herbal and cedary, with tight plum and currant flavors. A tightly reined-in style, with firm tannins and moderate depth. Doesn't quite have the opulence for greatness. Drink in 1994 to 2000. Tasted twice. $17 (3/15/91) **85**
Pomerol 1987 $15 (6/30/89) (BT) **80+**
Pomerol 1986 $20 (6/15/89) **92**
Pomerol 1984 Rel: $16 Cur: $20 (3/31/87) **83**
Pomerol 1982 Rel: $20 Cur: $32 (5/15/89) (TR) **86**
Pomerol 1945 $100 (3/16/86) (JL) **78**

CHATEAU ENCLOS-HAUT-MAZEYRES
Pomerol 1982 ($NA) (5/15/89) (TR) **84**

CHATEAU L'EVANGILE
Pomerol 1991: A bit herbaceous and green, this is made in a traditional style, showing funky, earthy berry aromas and flavors and a good tannic backbone. (NR) (5/15/92) (BT) **75+**
Pomerol 1990: Quite traditional and rustic, with tomato, earth and herbal aromas and flavors, velvety tannins and excellent concentration. (NR) (5/15/92) (BT) **90+**
Pomerol 1989: An expansive wine that draws you in, covering your taste buds with black olive, berry and chocolate flavors, backing it all up with plenty of rich tannins. Hold until at least 1997. $70 (3/15/92) **92**
Pomerol 1988 Rel: $38 Cur: $48 (6/30/91) **87**
Pomerol 1987 Rel: $25 Cur: $31 (6/30/89) (BT) **80+**
Pomerol 1986 $62 (9/15/89) **88**
Pomerol 1985 Rel: $55 Cur: $78 (2/29/88) **92**
Pomerol 1984 Rel: $31 Cur: $40 (2/15/87) **79**
Pomerol 1983 Rel: $42 Cur: $52 (3/16/86) **92**
Pomerol 1982 Rel: $55 Cur: $105 (5/01/89) **90**
Pomerol 1961 $260 (3/16/86) (TR) **77**

CHATEAU FEYTIT-CLINET
Pomerol 1990: Superbly made, with a lovely balance of vanilla, toast, berry and earth aromas and flavors and ultrafine tannins. (NR) (5/15/92) (BT) **90+**
Pomerol 1989 (NR) (4/30/91) (BT) **90+**
Pomerol 1985 $30 (4/30/88) **88**
Pomerol 1983 Rel: $13 Cur: $19 (7/16/86) **70**
Pomerol 1982 Rel: $15 Cur: $20 (5/15/89) (TR) **91**

CHATEAU LA FLEUR-PETRUS
Pomerol 1990: Extremely polished and elegant, with compact fruit flavors and silky tannins; closed in at this early stage. (NR) (5/15/92) (BT) **90+**
Pomerol 1989: Has wonderful tobacco and black olive flavors, but is a little austere on the finish from the masses of tannins. It just doesn't quite seem together at the moment, but it's still very good. Tasted twice. May improve in the bottle. Try after 1997. Rel: $57 Cur: $66 (3/15/92) **88**
Pomerol 1988 $63 (6/30/89) (BT) **85+**
Pomerol 1987 $36 (6/30/89) (BT) **80+**
Pomerol 1986 Rel: $52 Cur: $57 (2/15/90) CS **93**
Pomerol 1985 Rel: $50 Cur: $62 (6/30/88) **86**
Pomerol 1982 $85 (5/15/89) (TR) **88**
Pomerol (English Bottled) 1959 $150 (10/15/90) (JS) **92**
Pomerol 1945 $300 (3/16/86) (JL) **63**

CHATEAU LA FLEUR DE GAY
Pomerol 1991: This is so good in such a difficult year that it's almost shocking. A firm wine, with lots of fruit flavors and silky tannins. (NR) (5/15/92) (BT) **90+**
Pomerol 1990: A stunning wine, with seductive vanilla, chocolate, berry and other fruit aromas and flavors plus an ultrasolid tannin structure. Superbly made. (NR) (5/15/92) (BT) **95+**
Pomerol 1989: Stellar in quality, with great concentration, but also great finesse. Exuberant blackberry and tobacco aromas, with hints of cedar, follow through to masses of fruit on the palate and full, silky tannins. A wine for the next century. $88 (3/15/92) **98**
Pomerol 1988 $57 (6/30/91) **94**
Pomerol 1987 $38 (6/30/89) (BT) **85+**
Pomerol 1986 Rel: $43 Cur: $63 (10/31/89) CS **95**
Pomerol 1982 $45 (5/15/89) (TR) **88**

CHATEAU LE GAY
Pomerol 1990: This is superb, with amazing black truffle, earth and fruit aromas and flavors and masses of well-defined tannins. (NR) (5/15/92) (BT) **95+**
Pomerol 1989: Impressively concentrated, with herbal and ripe cassis aromas and super-ripe fruit flavors. A big wine, with great concentration of fruit and round tannins. Try after 1997. Rel: $70 Cur: $110 (3/15/92) **91**
Pomerol 1988: Hard and woody, with hard-edged tannins dominating the plum and herb-laced fruit flavors. A young, undeveloped, tough wine that needs time to round out. Drink in 1995 or so, but it may always be rough-edged. Tasted three times. $30 (4/30/91) **83**
Pomerol 1985 $25 (4/16/86) (BT) **60+**
Pomerol 1982 $44 (5/15/89) (TR) **89**

CHATEAU GAZIN
Pomerol 1991: Smooth, round and impressive, with tobacco, berry and chocolate flavors. (NR) (5/15/92) (BT) **85+**
Pomerol 1990: Absolutely wonderful, with super-ripe plum and truffle aromas and flavors and full yet velvety tannins. This estate is a rising star in the region. (NR) (5/15/92) (BT) **95+**
Pomerol 1989: Super-sweet and ripe, with coffee, tobacco, chocolate and berry aromas and flavors and silky, firm tannins. Balanced yet concentrated. Better after 1998. $45 (3/15/92) **91**
Pomerol 1988 $30 (6/30/91) **87**
Pomerol 1987 $22 (6/30/89) (BT) **80+**
Pomerol 1986 $21 (5/15/87) (BT) **80+**
Pomerol 1985 Rel: $21 Cur: $31 (9/30/88) **90**
Pomerol 1982 $30 (5/15/89) (TR) **88**
Pomerol 1961 $120 (3/16/86) (TR) **83**

CHATEAU GOMBAUDE-GUILLOT
Pomerol 1987 (NR) (6/30/89) (BT) **70+**
Pomerol 1982 ($NA) (5/15/89) (TR) **83**

CHATEAU LA GRAVE-TRIGANT DE BOISSET
Pomerol 1990: Gorgeous and polished, with a bounty of plum, berry and smoke aromas and flavors and full, round tannins. (NR) (5/15/92) (BT) **90+**
Pomerol 1989: Very elegant, well balanced and silky, with delicious chocolate, cherry and oak aromas and flavors. As powerful as we remembered, but it may evolve in the bottle. Try after 1997. $35 (3/15/92) **88**
Pomerol 1988 $24 (8/31/90) (BT) **90+**
Pomerol 1987 $21 (6/30/89) (BT) **80+**
Pomerol 1986 $35 (3/31/90) **89**
Pomerol 1985 $24 (5/15/87) (BT) **80+**
Pomerol 1982 $43 (5/15/89) (TR) **91**
Pomerol 1979 $23 (10/15/89) (JS) **90**

CHATEAU HAUT-MAILLET
Pomerol 1989 (NR) (4/30/91) (BT) **85+**

CHATEAU HERMITAGE
Pomerol 1982 ($NA) (5/15/89) (TR) **83**

CHATEAU LAFLEUR
Pomerol 1990: Huge and powerful, a giant of a wine, with so much fruit and extract that it's almost hard to believe at this point. (NR) (5/15/92) (BT) **95+**
Pomerol 1989: A compact wine, with rich fruit squeezed into the bottle. Shows tons of black olive and berry flavors and an impressive amount of round tannins. Better after 1998. $225 (3/15/92) **96**
Pomerol 1988: A young, unevolved wine that combines a fine balance between toasty, spicy oak notes and pretty ripe currant and black cherry flavors. A gentle style that offers finesse and grace, but it's deceptively concentrated and well focused. Best to cellar until at least 1995. 1,500 cases made. Rel: $95 Cur: $125 (10/31/91) **90**
Pomerol 1986 Rel: $100 Cur: $160 (10/31/89) **90**
Pomerol 1985 $170 (5/01/89) **95**
Pomerol 1982 $250 (5/01/89) **91**
Pomerol 1981 Rel: $22 Cur: $100 (6/01/84) **80**
Pomerol 1979 $220 (10/15/89) (JS) **96**
Pomerol 1945 $400 (3/16/86) (JL) **64**

PENSEES DE LAFLEUR
Pomerol 1990: A monster of a wine. Heavily extracted, with moss, earth, berry and rich fruit characteristics and an atom bomb of tannins. Built for the next century. (NR) (5/15/92) (BT) **95+**

CHATEAU LAFLEUR-GAZIN
Pomerol 1989: A sturdy wine, with full tannins and fruit. Shows plenty of herb and berry flavors and ripe, silky tannins. Try after 1995. (NR) (3/15/92) **87**
Pomerol 1945 ($NA) (3/16/86) (JL) **58**

CHATEAU LAFLEUR DU ROY
Pomerol 1982 ($NA) (5/15/89) (TR) **83**

CHATEAU LAGRANGE
Pomerol 1990: A big, chewy wine, with lots of tobacco, earth and chocolate flavors and full tannins. (NR) (5/15/92) (BT) **90+**
Pomerol 1989: Luscious, with beautiful chocolate and cherry aromas and flavors and succulent, silky tannins. The juicy finish keeps you coming back for more. Try after 1995. $29 (3/15/92) **87**
Pomerol 1988 $25 (6/30/89) (BT) **85+**
Pomerol 1985 $21 (4/16/86) (BT) **80+**
Pomerol 1982 $30 (5/15/89) (TR) **84**

CHATEAU LATOUR A POMEROL
Pomerol 1990: Not showing as well as it should, but it has lovely, ripe fruit flavors and round tannins. (NR) (5/15/92) (BT) **85+**
Pomerol 1989: A rich wine, with plenty of tobacco, game and herbal, almost meaty aromas and flavors and full tannins. A traditional, big-style Pomerol that's perhaps a little too traditional for some, but we find it outstanding. Try after 1997. $39 (3/15/92) **90**
Pomerol 1988 $55 (6/30/89) (BT) **95+**
Pomerol 1987 $35 (6/30/89) (BT) **80+**
Pomerol 1986 $35 (5/15/87) (BT) **90+**
Pomerol 1985 $50 (5/15/87) (BT) **90+**
Pomerol 1982 $77 (5/15/89) (TR) **92**
Pomerol 1961 $1,700 (3/16/86) (TR) **94**
Pomerol 1959 $580 (10/15/90) (JS) **90**

CHATEAU LA LOUBIERE
Pomerol 1983 $15 (6/16/86) **77**
Pomerol 1982 $13 (5/15/89) (TR) **88**

CHATEAU LA MADELEINE
Pomerol 1985 $10 (3/15/88) **56**

FRANCE

Bordeaux Red/*Pomerol*

CHATEAU MAZEYRES
Pomerol 1989 (NR) (4/30/91) (BT) **90+**
Pomerol 1986 (NR) (6/30/88) (BT) **70+**

CHATEAU MONTVIEL
Pomerol 1989 (NR) (4/30/91) (BT) **85+**
Pomerol 1987 $20 (6/30/89) (BT) **80+**
Pomerol 1986 $29 (6/30/88) (BT) **80+**

CHATEAU MOULINET
Pomerol 1989 (NR) (4/30/91) (BT) **90+**
Pomerol 1988: Austere and closed in, with tightly concentrated plum, currant and spice flavors framed by hard, toasty oak. Quite tannic and definitely needs six to 10 years to soften. Best to try after 1996. $17 (7/31/91) **88**
Pomerol 1987 $15 (6/30/89) (BT) **75+**
Pomerol 1986 $15 (6/30/88) (BT) **80+**
Pomerol 1982 $9.75 (5/15/89) (TR) **87**

CHATEAU NENIN
Pomerol 1987 $20 (6/30/88) (BT) **75+**
Pomerol 1986: Very light in color and body, with rose-tinged red cherry and plum flavors making it attractive and almost drinkable on release. Drink now. $22 (6/30/89) **84**
Pomerol 1982 $26 (5/15/89) (TR) **89**
Pomerol 1959 $100 (10/15/90) (JS) **88**
Pomerol 1945 $250 (3/16/86) (JL) **74**

CHATEAU PETIT-VILLAGE
Pomerol 1991: Has good concentration, with olive and herbal flavors, but it finishes a little coarse. (NR) (5/15/92) (BT) **80+**
Pomerol 1990: Very refined, with rich fruit flavors and elegant, silky tannins. Very firm and well sculpted. (NR) (5/15/92) (BT) **85+**
Pomerol 1989: Big and pumped up, with lots of fruit flavors and full tannins. A little rustic, but impressively concentrated. Try after 1995. Rel: $46 Cur: $52 (3/15/92) **88**
Pomerol 1988 Rel: $26 Cur: $33 (8/31/90) (BT) **90+**
Pomerol 1987 $22 (6/30/89) (BT) **80+**
Pomerol 1986 $24 (6/30/88) (BT) **90+**
Pomerol 1982 $58 (5/15/89) (TR) **92**
Pomerol 1959 $90 (10/15/90) (JS) **86**

LA PETITE EGLISE
Pomerol 1986: Lots of hard edges to this medium-weight, densely textured wine, its tobacco, tar and oaky flavors surrounding the modest fruit. Should become complex in the earthy style with time. Try again in 1993. $15 (9/15/89) **78**

CHATEAU PETRUS
Pomerol 1990: Like an old master painting, this shows a palette full of aromas and flavors that include truffle, berry, earth and chocolate, ultrafine tannins and a long, sweet finish. Could be as glorious as the '89. (NR) (5/15/92) (BT) **95+**
Pomerol 1989: A Rolls Royce of a wine. Explosive and opulent; perhaps as great as the 1961. Big and powerful, with super-rich berry, tobacco and olive flavors and full, round, ripe tannins. Will go on for decades; try after 1999. $390 (3/15/92) **100**
Pomerol 1988: An aristocratic wine, with a deep, dense color and rich, concentrated currant, plum, herb and spice flavors that are sharply focused, intense and lively, with uncommon depth and richness. A muscular style that's young and backward. It's going to need until 1997 to open up and may age well into the next decade. 3,500 cases made. Rel: $221 Cur: $300 (8/31/91) **94**
Pomerol 1987 $175 (2/15/91) (JS) **85**
Pomerol 1986 Rel: $200 Cur: $350 (2/15/91) (JS) **96**
Pomerol 1985 Rel: $160 Cur: $390 (2/15/91) (JS) **97**
Pomerol 1984 Rel: $125 Cur: $250 (2/15/91) (JS) **83**
Pomerol 1983 Rel: $125 Cur: $300 (2/15/91) (JS) **91**
Pomerol 1982 $550 (2/15/91) (JS) **96**
Pomerol 1981 $290 (2/15/91) (JS) **90**
Pomerol 1980 $180 (2/15/91) (JS) **86**
Pomerol 1979 $310 (2/15/91) (JS) **90**
Pomerol 1978 $350 (2/15/91) (JS) **89**
Pomerol 1976 $280 (2/15/91) (JS) **86**
Pomerol 1975 $500 (2/15/91) (JS) **93**
Pomerol 1973 $290 (2/15/91) (JS) **78**
Pomerol 1971 $470 (2/15/91) (JS) **94**
Pomerol 1970 $510 (2/15/91) (JS) **92**
Pomerol 1968 $200 (2/15/91) (JS) **79**
Pomerol 1967 $360 (2/15/91) (JS) **87**
Pomerol 1966 $450 (2/15/91) (JS) **93**
Pomerol 1964 $580 (2/15/91) (JS) **94**
Pomerol 1962 $470 (2/15/91) (JS) **94**
Pomerol 1961 $2,100 (2/15/91) (JS) **100**
Pomerol 1959 $820 (2/15/91) (JS) **96**
Pomerol 1958 $420 (2/15/91) (JS) **85**
Pomerol 1955 $580 (2/15/91) (JS) **91**
Pomerol 1953 $740 (2/15/91) (JS) **92**
Pomerol 1952 $650 (2/15/91) (JS) **89**
Pomerol 1950 $1,100 (2/15/91) (JS) **99**
Pomerol 1949 $1,550 (2/15/91) (JS) **98**
Pomerol 1948 $1,200 (2/15/91) (JS) **91**
Pomerol 1947 $1,900 (2/15/91) (JS) **97**
Pomerol 1945 $2,700 (2/15/91) (JS) **100**

CHATEAU LE PIN
Pomerol 1989 $163 (4/30/90) (BT) **95+**
Pomerol 1988: Delicious, complex and enticing from the first whiff. Plush and deep, with gentle, elegant black cherry, currant, plum, spice and nutmeg flavors that linger on the finish. Has substantial tannins, but they're smooth and rounded, making this wine tempting to drink now. Should peak between 1996 to 2004. 500 cases made. $65 (6/30/91) CS **95**
Pomerol 1987 Rel: $45 Cur: $90 (6/30/89) (BT) **85+**
Pomerol 1986 Rel: $55 Cur: $140 (6/15/89) **95**
Pomerol 1982 $280 (5/15/89) (TR) **95**

CHATEAU PLINCE
Pomerol 1990: A young wine in a refreshing style; very perfumed and elegant, with vanilla and berry flavors. (NR) (5/15/92) (BT) **85+**
Pomerol 1989 $15 (4/30/91) (BT) **80+**
Pomerol 1987 Rel: $16 Cur: $19 (6/30/89) (BT) **75+**
Pomerol 1985 $17 (5/15/87) (BT) **70+**
Pomerol 1982 $25 (5/15/89) (TR) **92**

CHATEAU LA POINTE
Pomerol 1990: Ripe, with lots of fruity flavors that recall a raspberry tart. Has medium-full tannins and a long finish. (NR) (5/15/92) (BT) **85+**
Pomerol 1989: Great winemaking from an underrated producer. Has a wonderful combination of tobacco, berry and smoke aromas and flavors and great balance of full tannins. A major-league wine. Try after 1998. $28 (3/15/92) **95**
Pomerol 1988: Simple and polished, with pleasant, modest cherry and spice flavors that taper off on the finish. Best after 1993. 3,000 cases made. $35 (7/31/91) **83**
Pomerol 1987 $21 (6/30/88) (BT) **70+**
Pomerol 1986 $21 (6/15/89) **90**
Pomerol 1982 $22 (5/15/89) (TR) **85**
Pomerol 1962 $35 (11/30/87) (JS) **80**
Pomerol 1945 $250 (3/16/86) (JL) **78**

CHATEAU PRIEURS DE LA COMMANDERIE
Pomerol 1989 (NR) (4/30/91) (BT) **90+**
Pomerol 1987 (NR) (6/30/88) (BT) **70+**
Pomerol 1986 (NR) (6/30/88) (BT) **75+**
Pomerol 1985 $27 (9/30/88) **93**
Pomerol 1983 $25 (9/30/86) **79**

CHATEAU LA ROSE FIGEAC
Pomerol 1982 ($NA) (5/15/89) (TR) **85**

CHATEAU ROUGET
Pomerol 1990: Sweet and succulent, with silky tannins and rich, almost sweet, intensely fruity flavors. (NR) (5/15/92) (BT) **85+**
Pomerol 1989 $21 (4/30/91) (BT) **85+**
Pomerol 1982 $21 (5/15/89) (TR) **86**

CHATEAU DE SALES
Pomerol 1990: Very extracted, with grilled meat and fruit aromas and flavors and an abundance of tannins. Very traditional in style. (NR) (5/15/92) (BT) **85+**
Pomerol 1989 $18 (4/30/91) (BT) **90+**
Pomerol 1988 $17 (6/30/89) (BT) **70+**
Pomerol 1986 $20 (6/30/89) **86**
Pomerol 1985 Rel: $14 Cur: $18 (6/30/88) **87**
Pomerol 1982 $32 (5/15/89) (TR) **88**

CHATEAU TAILHAS
Pomerol 1988: Has wonderful depth, with a tight core of cherry, currant, spice and stalky, cedary flavors. It's also tightly tannic, with excellent intensity and length. Needs cellaring until 2000 or so. $20 (4/30/91) **91**
Pomerol 1982 $15 (5/15/89) (TR) **82**

CHATEAU TAILLEFER
Pomerol 1989 (NR) (4/30/91) (BT) **90+**
Pomerol 1988: Tight and tannic, leaving a dry flavor impression, but concentrated, with meaty currant, black cherry, herb and tea flavors. The tannins are green and stalky on the finish. Will need until 1995 or '96 to mellow. $22 (6/30/91) **87**
Pomerol 1987 $18 (6/30/89) (BT) **75+**
Pomerol 1986 $20 (6/30/88) (BT) **80+**
Pomerol 1985 Rel: $19 Cur: $24 (6/30/88) **81**
Pomerol 1982 $24 (5/15/89) (TR) **85**

CHATEAU TROTANOY
Pomerol 1990: Rich and powerful, but it shows great finesse; the afterburners come on at the finish. (NR) (5/15/92) (BT) **95+**
Pomerol 1989: Not as powerful as we expected, but a classy wine just the same. Firm and rich, with an excellent fruit and tannin structure. Keeps your attention with a rich tobacco and pepper character. Try after 1996. $87 (3/15/92) **90**
Pomerol 1988: Packs in plenty of flavor, with tiers of plum, black cherry, anise and toasty, smoky oak notes that are a bit rough and tough now, but nothing out of the ordinary. The flavors are persistent and lingering. Best to cellar until 1995 or '96. Tasted twice. Rel: $48 Cur: $59 (8/31/91) **89**
Pomerol 1987 $45 (6/30/89) (BT) **85+**
Pomerol 1986 $68 (10/31/89) **83**
Pomerol 1985 Rel: $70 Cur: $76 (4/30/88) **93**
Pomerol 1983 $54 (10/15/88) (JS) **88**
Pomerol 1982 $155 (5/15/89) (TR) **90**
Pomerol 1981 $64 (10/15/88) (JS) **95**
Pomerol 1980 $42 (10/15/88) (JS) **83**
Pomerol 1979 $62 (10/15/89) (JS) **88**
Pomerol 1978 $89 (10/15/88) (JS) **83**
Pomerol 1976 $71 (10/15/88) (JS) **86**
Pomerol 1975 $130 (10/15/88) (JS) **84**
Pomerol 1971 $195 (10/15/88) (JS) **90**
Pomerol 1970 $175 (10/15/88) (JS) **95**
Pomerol 1967 $95 (10/15/88) (JS) **84**
Pomerol 1966 $140 (10/15/88) (JS) **92**
Pomerol 1962 $139 (10/15/88) (JS) **88**
Pomerol 1961 $610 (10/15/88) (JS) **96**
Pomerol 1959 $360 (10/15/90) (JS) **90**
Pomerol 1955 $200 (10/15/88) (JS) **94**
Pomerol 1953 $300 (10/15/88) (JS) **86**
Pomerol 1952 $140 (10/15/88) (JS) **83**
Pomerol 1947 $550 (10/15/88) (JS) **80**
Pomerol 1945 $1,050 (10/15/88) (JS) **98**
Pomerol 1934 $350 (10/15/88) (JS) **60**
Pomerol 1928 $600 (10/15/88) (JS) **95**
Pomerol 1924 $650 (10/15/88) (JS) **89**

VIEUX CHATEAU CERTAN
Pomerol 1989: An impressive wine, with beautiful plum, blackberry, meat and earth flavors and full, silky tannins. Well balanced and rather understated for the moment. Try after 1996. $89 (3/15/92) **91**
Pomerol 1988: Ripe, earthy aromas and flavors spread out nicely on a supple, broad-textured

Key to Symbols

The scores reported here are the results of blind tastings conducted by our panel of senior editors. Wines that carry the initials below are results of individual tastings.

THE WINE SPECTATOR 100-POINT SCALE ***95-100***—Classic, a great wine; ***90-94***—Outstanding, superior character and style; ***80-89***—Good to very good, a wine with special qualities; ***70-79***—Average, drinkable wine that may have minor flaws; ***60-69***—Below average, drinkable but not recommended; ***50-59***—Poor, undrinkable, not recommended. "+"—With a score indicates a range; used primarily with barrel tastings to indicate a preliminary score.

SPECIAL DESIGNATIONS SS—Spectator Selection, CS—Cellar Selection, BB—Best Buy, ($NA)—Price not available, (NR)—Not released.

TASTER'S INITIALS (JG)—Jim Gordon, (HS)—Harvey Steiman, (JL)—James Laube, (JS)—James Suckling, (TM)—Thomas Matthews, (TR)—Terry Robards, (PM)—Per-Henrik Mansson, (BT)—Barrel Tasting (these wines were tasted blind from barrel samples), (CA-date)—*California's Great Cabernets* by James Laube, (CH-date)—*California's Great Chardonnays* by James Laube, (VP-date)—*Vintage Port* by James Suckling.

DATE TASTED Dates in parentheses represent the issue in which the rating was published.

structure, offering lots of plum and spice notes through the long finish. Hints at herbs and minerals, too. Drink after 1994. $60 (3/31/91) **91**
Pomerol 1987: Attractive for its suppleness and drinkability. The elegant plum and tobacco notes show a shade of richness and depth. Not much in the way of tannin. Drink now to 1993. Tasted twice. $30 (5/15/90) **84**
Pomerol 1986 Rel: $40 $55 (6/15/89) **93**
Pomerol 1985 Rel: $38 Cur: $49 (6/30/88) **90**
Pomerol 1983 Rel: $33 Cur: $42 (3/16/86) **83**
Pomerol 1982 Rel: $29 Cur: $59 (5/15/89) (TR) **89**
Pomerol 1979 $40 (10/15/89) (JS) **87**
Pomerol 1962 $65 (11/30/87) (JS) **60**
Pomerol 1961 $180 (3/16/86) (TR) **90**
Pomerol 1959 $165 (10/15/90) (JS) **91**
Pomerol 1945 $700 (3/16/86) (JL) **50**

CHATEAU VIEUX-FERRAND
Pomerol 1982 ($NA) (5/15/89) (TR) **82**

CHATEAU LA VIOLETTE
Pomerol 1982 $25 (5/15/89) (TR) **88**
Pomerol 1979 $35 (10/15/89) (JS) **79**

ST.-EMILION

CHATEAU L'ANGELUS
St.-Emilion 1990: This concentrated, rich wine feels round and ripe in the mouth, with chewy tannins and earthy, smoky flavors. (NR) (5/15/92) (BT) **90+**
St.-Emilion 1990 (NR) (4/30/91) (BT) **85+**
St.-Emilion 1989: A pumped-up wine that flexes its muscles, with superbly intense tobacco, plum and chocolate aromas following through on the palate. Has a deep, luscious mouth-feel and thick, velvety tannins. A rising star of St.-Emilion. Try after 1996. $53 (3/15/92) **94**
St.-Emilion 1988: Big and powerful, with a definite smack of oak, offering plenty of concentrated earthy, smoky and slightly bitter notes around a focused core of currant and berry flavors. The firm tannins don't get in the way. Should be a humdinger by 1998 to 2000. $41 (3/31/91) **93**
St.-Emilion 1987 $30 (5/15/90) **85**
St.-Emilion 1986 Rel: $26 Cur: $30 (6/30/89) **94**
St.-Emilion 1985 Rel: $26 Cur: $32 (3/31/88) CS **94**
St.-Emilion 1983 Rel: $22 Cur: $30 (3/16/86) **92**
St.-Emilion 1982 Rel: $20 Cur: $32 (5/15/89) (TR) **88**
St.-Emilion 1979 $27 (10/15/89) (JS) **82**
St.-Emilion 1962 $45 (11/30/87) (JS) **68**

CHATEAU L'ARROSEE
St.-Emilion 1989: Rich, smooth, deep and complex, with layers of plum, currant, spice and vanilla flavors all woven together with a measure of subtlety and finesse. Firmly tannic and oaky, too, but it comes across as soft and fleshy. Tempting now, but probably better around 1995 to 2000. 5,000 cases made. $40 (4/30/92) **93**
St.-Emilion 1988: An ultrasmoky wine, with richness, elegance and finesse, graced with complex and intriguing tiers of plum, currant, raspberry, cedar and smoke. You don't get much better in the way of style or finesse. The finish keeps repeating the flavors. Drink in 1995 to 2002. 5,000 cases made. $34 (3/15/91) **94**
St.-Emilion 1987: Soft and spicy, with intriguing cinnamon, nutmeg and cherry aromas and flavors that linger on the finish. Balanced, harmonious and already drinkable. Tasted twice. $25 (5/15/90) **82**
St.-Emilion 1986 Rel: $31 Cur: $36 (2/15/89) **87**
St.-Emilion 1985 Rel: $24 Cur: $47 (2/29/88) **85**
St.-Emilion 1983 Rel: $20 Cur: $34 (5/16/86) **87**
St.-Emilion 1982 $45 (5/15/89) (TR) **91**

CHATEAU AUSONE
St.-Emilion 1990: A mighty and powerful wine, with a ton of tannins and ripe, rich fruit flavors. Made for aging a very long time. (NR) (5/15/92) (BT) **95+**
St.-Emilion 1989: A real beauty, with plum, vanilla and chocolate aromas and flavors followed by a silky, fine tannin structure. Very fine on the finish. Try after 1997. $180 (3/15/92) **93**
St.-Emilion 1988 Rel: $76 Cur: $98 (8/31/90) (BT) **95+**
St.-Emilion 1987 Rel: $55 Cur: $68 (6/30/89) (BT) **85+**
St.-Emilion 1986 Rel: $90 Cur: $115 (6/30/89) **85**
St.-Emilion 1985 $100 (5/31/88) **87**
St.-Emilion 1983 $130 (11/30/87) (TR) **96**
St.-Emilion 1982 $170 (5/15/89) (TR) **93**
St.-Emilion 1981 $86 (11/30/87) (TR) **90**
St.-Emilion 1980 $40 (11/30/87) (TR) **86**
St.-Emilion 1979 $100 (10/15/89) (JS) **92**
St.-Emilion 1978 $90 (11/30/87) (TR) **93**
St.-Emilion 1977 $29 (11/30/87) (TR) **83**
St.-Emilion 1976 $130 (11/30/87) (TR) **89**
St.-Emilion 1974 $28 (11/30/87) (TR) **76**
St.-Emilion 1973 $45 (11/30/87) (TR) **77**
St.-Emilion 1972 $30 (11/30/87) (TR) **75**
St.-Emilion 1971 $105 (11/30/87) (TR) **83**
St.-Emilion 1970 $130 (11/30/87) (TR) **82**
St.-Emilion 1969 $27 (11/30/87) (TR) **76**
St.-Emilion 1967 $64 (11/30/87) (TR) **79**
St.-Emilion 1966 $125 (11/30/87) (TR) **85**
St.-Emilion 1964 $87 (11/30/87) (TR) **78**
St.-Emilion 1962 $170 (11/30/87) (JS) **85**
St.-Emilion 1961 $300 (11/30/87) (TR) **82**
St.-Emilion 1959 $230 (10/15/90) (JS) **79**
St.-Emilion 1958 $95 (11/30/87) (TR) **79**
St.-Emilion 1957 $250 (11/30/87) (TR) **74**
St.-Emilion 1956 $175 (11/30/87) (TR) **86**
St.-Emilion 1955 $230 (11/30/87) (TR) **91**
St.-Emilion 1954 $180 (11/30/87) (TR) **87**
St.-Emilion 1953 $280 (11/30/87) (TR) **78**
St.-Emilion 1952 $150 (11/30/87) (TR) **85**
St.-Emilion 1950 $230 (11/30/87) (TR) **78**
St.-Emilion 1949 $500 (11/30/87) (TR) **91**
St.-Emilion 1947 $220 (11/30/87) (TR) **83**
St.-Emilion 1945 $320 (3/16/86) (JL) **75**
St.-Emilion 1943 $350 (11/30/87) (TR) **84**
St.-Emilion 1942 $250 (11/30/87) (TR) **81**
St.-Emilion 1937 $175 (11/30/87) (TR) **83**
St.-Emilion 1936 $300 (11/30/87) (TR) **82**
St.-Emilion 1929 $330 (11/30/87) (TR) **83**
St.-Emilion 1928 $600 (11/30/87) (TR) **83**
St.-Emilion 1926 $620 (11/30/87) (TR) **82**
St.-Emilion 1925 $175 (11/30/87) (TR) **75**
St.-Emilion 1924 $250 (11/30/87) (TR) **95**
St.-Emilion 1923 $200 (11/30/87) (TR) **76**
St.-Emilion 1921 $250 (11/30/87) (TR) **94**
St.-Emilion 1918 $480 (11/30/87) (TR) **87**
St.-Emilion 1916 $430 (11/30/87) (TR) **86**
St.-Emilion 1914 $380 (11/30/87) (TR) **79**
St.-Emilion 1913 $380 (11/30/87) (TR) **81**
St.-Emilion 1912 $380 (11/30/87) (TR) **79**
St.-Emilion 1905 $600 (11/30/87) (TR) **82**
St.-Emilion 1902 $300 (11/30/87) (TR) **83**
St.-Emilion 1900 $1,000 (11/30/87) (TR) **78**
St.-Emilion 1899 $1,200 (11/30/87) (TR) **77**
St.-Emilion 1894 $800 (11/30/87) (TR) **85**
St.-Emilion 1879 $700 (11/30/87) (TR) **93**
St.-Emilion 1877 $2,200 (11/30/87) (TR) **92**

CHATEAU BALESTARD LA TONNELLE
St.-Emilion 1990 (NR) (4/30/91) (BT) **80+**
St.-Emilion 1989: Like drinking *framboise*; has lots of fresh raspberry character and silky tannins. Not a blockbuster, but it's very pleasant. Should be coming around after 1994. $28 (3/15/92) **85**
St.-Emilion 1988: Refined and elegant, with rich currant, blueberry, black cherry and plum flavors that are supple, silky, deep and concentrated. The flavors are long and persistent. Drink in 1998. $25 (4/30/91) **91**
St.-Emilion 1987 $20 (6/30/89) (BT) **75+**
St.-Emilion 1986 $22 (6/30/88) (BT) **80+**
St.-Emilion 1982 $25 (5/15/89) (TR) **83**

CHATEAU BEAU-SEJOUR BECOT
St.-Emilion 1988: Firm and juicy, with lots of anise- and cedar-scented raspberry and currant aromas and flavors up front, turning tannic and tight on the finish. Drink after 1998. $21 (6/30/91) **87**
St.-Emilion 1986 $22 (7/31/89) **79**
St.-Emilion 1982 $25 (5/15/89) (TR) **85**

CHATEAU DU BEAU-VALLON
St.-Emilion 1987: Nicely defined plum and toast aromas and flavors ride gently on a tough and tannic texture, making this wine appealing. Cellaring until 1993 should polish the tannins, but will the fruit flavors survive? $10 (5/15/90) **81**
St.-Emilion 1986: Very soft and supple, but the generous raspberry and cherry fruit practically jumps out of the glass, making this pleasant to drink now and worth cellaring through 1993 to see what develops. $10 (9/30/89) **84**
St.-Emilion 1985 $8.50 (9/30/88) **82**

CHATEAU BEAUSEJOUR-DUFFAU-LAGARROSSE
St.-Emilion 1990: Wild and exciting, with super-ripe, dense, deep fruit flavors that almost jump out of the glass. A superb wine. (NR) (5/15/92) (BT) **95+**
St.-Emilion 1989: The fruit jumps out of the glass, offering a bounty of raspberry, plum and smoky fruit characteristics and full, soft tannins. Very ripe and concentrated. Better after 1997. $44 (3/15/92) **91**
St.-Emilion 1988: Has plenty of rustic flavors, with earth, mineral, toasty oak and subtle black cherry flavors that build on the palate. The tannins are fine and the finish picks up a cedary quality. Drink in 1996 to 2000. $32 (4/30/91) **87**
St.-Emilion 1987 $20 (6/30/89) (BT) **85+**
St.-Emilion 1986 Rel: $27 Cur: $34 (6/30/89) **91**
St.-Emilion 1982 $30 (5/15/89) (TR) **90**

CHATEAU BELAIR
St.-Emilion 1990: One of the best Belairs ever made. Rich and smoky, with lovely, rich fruit aromas and flavors and super tannins. (NR) (5/15/92) (BT) **90+**
St.-Emilion 1989: Caresses your palate with fine tannins and a flavorful blackberry character. Not a massive wine, but it's very complete. Better after 1995. $34 (3/15/92) **89**
St.-Emilion 1988 $28 (8/31/90) (BT) **80+**
St.-Emilion 1987 $25 (6/30/89) (BT) **85+**
St.-Emilion 1986 Rel: $26 Cur: $35 (3/31/90) **82**
St.-Emilion 1985 $29 (4/16/86) (BT) **80+**
St.-Emilion 1982 $36 (5/15/89) (TR) **90**
St.-Emilion 1961 $125 (3/16/86) (TR) **75**

CHATEAU BERGAT
St.-Emilion 1989 (NR) (4/30/90) (BT) **80+**

CHATEAU BERLIQUET
St.-Emilion 1983 $12 (12/31/86) **90**

CHATEAU CADET-PIOLA
St.-Emilion 1989 $24 (4/30/91) (BT) **80+**
St.-Emilion 1988: Firm and concentrated, with nicely articulated cherry and anise aromas and flavors that open and broaden on the long finish. The tannins are present, but not intrusive, and the flavors have plenty of depth and personality. Best to drink after 1997. 3,000 cases made. $20 (7/15/91) **89**
St.-Emilion 1987 $16 (6/30/89) (BT) **70+**
St.-Emilion 1982 $23 (5/15/89) (TR) **88**

CHATEAU CANON
St.-Emilion 1990: Has the grace of a ballerina, with well-integrated, ultrafine tannins and ripe fruit flavors. (NR) (5/15/92) (BT) **90+**
St.-Emilion 1989: A little low-key right now, but it shows plenty of ripe berry and raspberry aromas and flavors coupled with round, rich tannins. Long and flavorful on the finish. Try after 1996. $53 (3/15/92) **90**
St.-Emilion 1988: Ripe, rich and balanced, rolling out a long line of plum, currant, anise, vanilla, cedar and cherry flavors as it plays itself out across the palate. Elegant and concentrated, with well-harmonized tannins that need until 1997 to 2000 to soften. $40 (6/30/91) **90**
St.-Emilion 1987 $32 (5/15/90) **79**
St.-Emilion 1986 $45 (6/30/89) **93**
St.-Emilion 1985 Rel: $34 Cur: $47 (5/15/89) (TM) **91**
St.-Emilion 1983 Rel: $31 Cur: $42 (5/15/89) (TM) **88**
St.-Emilion 1982 $64 (5/15/89) (TM) **91**
St.-Emilion 1981 $28 (5/15/89) (TM) **82**
St.-Emilion 1980 $19 (5/15/89) (TM) **80**
St.-Emilion 1979 $40 (5/15/89) (TM) **89**
St.-Emilion 1978 $50 (5/15/89) (TM) **84**
St.-Emilion 1975 $38 (5/15/89) (TM) **84**
St.-Emilion 1971 $45 (5/15/89) (TM) **85**
St.-Emilion 1970 $60 (5/15/89) (TM) **93**
St.-Emilion 1966 $75 (5/15/89) (TM) **91**
St.-Emilion 1964 $75 (5/15/89) (TM) **89**
St.-Emilion 1962 $100 (5/15/89) (TM) **93**
St.-Emilion 1961 $100 (5/15/89) (TM) **88**
St.-Emilion 1959 $125 (5/15/89) (TM) **95**
St.-Emilion 1955 $110 (5/15/89) (TM) **88**
St.-Emilion 1953 $125 (5/15/89) (TM) **88**
St.-Emilion 1947 $250 (5/15/89) (TM) **91**

FRANCE
Bordeaux Red/*St.-Emilion*

CHATEAU CANON-LA-GAFFELIERE
St.-Emilion 1990 (NR) (4/30/91) (BT) **90+**
St.-Emilion 1989: A concentrated wine, with lots of herb and vanilla aromas and flavors, medium tannins and a long finish. Shows very good potential. Better after 1995. $29 (3/15/92) **88**
St.-Emilion 1988: Soft and earthy, with anise and plum notes making themselves felt through the overlay of cedar and fresh soil aromas and flavors. Approaching drinkability; should be fine around 1995 to '98. $30 (6/30/91) **86**
St.-Emilion 1986 Rel: $21 Cur: $28 (6/30/89) **91**
St.-Emilion 1985 Rel: $20 Cur: $37 (5/15/87) (BT) **90+**

CHATEAU CAP DE MOURLIN
St.-Emilion 1989: Like raspberry jam, this is a thick, chunky wine, with gorgeous fruit. Offers rich, fruity aromas, thick, rich berry flavors and a smoky finish. Better after 1995. $23 (3/15/92) **87**
St.-Emilion 1988: Tough, chewy and tannic, this hard-edged wine packs in plenty of blackberry, currant, strawberry and plum flavors. It only needs time, as the tannic finish reminds you. Drink in 1996 to '98. $20 (4/30/91) **84**
St.-Emilion 1987 $15 (6/30/89) (BT) **70+**
St.-Emilion 1986 $18 (6/30/89) **87**
St.-Emilion 1985 $15 (5/15/87) (BT) **80+**

CHATEAU CAP DE MOURLIN (JACQUES)
St.-Emilion 1982 ($NA) (5/15/89) (TR) **86**

CHATEAU CAP DE MOURLIN (JEAN)
St.-Emilion 1982 ($NA) (5/15/89) (TR) **81**

CHATEAU CARTEYRON
St.-Emilion 1982 $7.25 (9/01/85) **79**

CHATEAU DU CAUZE
St.-Emilion 1986: Nicely complex and full-flavored in a supple, medium-bodied package. Smells slightly smoky, tastes ripe and plummy, with cedar and spice accents and moderate tannins. Drink up now. $15 (6/30/89) **84**

CHATEAU CHAUVIN
St.-Emilion 1988: Soft and generous, with modestly intense berry and currant aromas and flavors and hints of cedar and anise on the finish. The tannins are well integrated. Almost drinkable now, but it should be best after 1995. 3,800 cases made. $20 (6/30/91) **84**
St.-Emilion 1986: An odd buttery-earthy component robs this of its charm; coming off thick and heavy at first, it thins out on the finish. $15 (6/30/89) **75**

CHATEAU CHEVAL BLANC
St.-Emilion 1990: Better than the '89. Shows super fruit and great finesse, plus an iron backbone of tannins. (NR) (5/15/92) (BT) **95+**
St.-Emilion 1989: An outstanding Cheval, but it certainly doesn't reach the expectations we had when it was a barrel sample. A zingy wine, with good intensity of pretty berry, licorice and vanilla flavors and silky tannins. Another well-balanced wine for earlier drinking. Tasted twice. Try after 1996. $150 (3/15/92) **90**
St.-Emilion 1988: Has wonderful amplitude and finesse, with rich, intense currant, plum, cherry and spice flavors that are absolutely delicious and toasty oak flavors that come through on the finish. A tempting wine to drink now, but it's built for the long haul. Hold until at least 1995 or '96 for the tannins to mellow. $105 (12/31/90) CS **93**
St.-Emilion 1987 $57 (2/15/91) (JS) **82**
St.-Emilion 1986 Rel: $80 Cur: $85 (2/15/91) (JS) **93**
St.-Emilion 1986 Rel: $80 Cur: $85 (6/30/89) CS **98**
St.-Emilion 1985 Rel: $80 Cur: $91 (2/15/91) (JS) **98**
St.-Emilion 1984 $69 (2/15/91) (HS) **85**
St.-Emilion 1983 Rel: $63 Cur: $80 (2/15/91) (JS) **96**
St.-Emilion 1982 Rel: $69 Cur: $150 (2/15/91) (JS) **97**
St.-Emilion 1982 Rel: $69 Cur: $150 (2/16/85) CS **96**
St.-Emilion 1981 Rel: $46 Cur: $80 (2/15/91) (JS) **90**
St.-Emilion 1980 $46 (2/15/91) (JS) **84**
St.-Emilion 1979 $78 (2/15/91) (JS) **88**
St.-Emilion 1978 $115 (2/15/91) (JS) **94**
St.-Emilion 1977 $32 (2/15/91) (JS) **74**
St.-Emilion 1976 $80 (2/15/91) (JS) **88**
St.-Emilion 1975 $140 (2/15/91) (JS) **91**
St.-Emilion 1974 $46 (2/15/91) (JS) **83**
St.-Emilion 1973 $60 (2/15/91) (JS) **83**
St.-Emilion 1972 $40 (2/15/91) (JS) **82**
St.-Emilion 1971 $120 (2/15/91) (JS) **89**
St.-Emilion 1970 $165 (2/15/91) (JS) **88**
St.-Emilion 1969 $41 (2/15/91) (JS) **75**
St.-Emilion 1967 $90 (2/15/91) (JS) **85**
St.-Emilion 1966 $160 (2/15/91) (JS) **87**
St.-Emilion 1964 $220 (2/15/91) (JS) **85**
St.-Emilion 1962 $125 (2/15/91) (JS) **85**
St.-Emilion 1961 $480 (2/15/91) (JS) **96**
St.-Emilion 1960 $125 (2/15/91) (JS) **81**
St.-Emilion 1959 $270 (2/15/91) (JS) **90**
St.-Emilion 1958 $180 (2/15/91) (JS) **86**
St.-Emilion 1955 $280 (2/15/91) (JS) **94**
St.-Emilion 1953 $430 (2/15/91) (JS) **87**
St.-Emilion 1952 $270 (2/15/91) (JS) **91**
St.-Emilion 1951 $150 (2/15/91) (JS) **76**
St.-Emilion 1949 $570 (2/15/91) (JS) **84**
St.-Emilion 1948 $300 (2/15/91) (JS) **97**
St.-Emilion 1947 $1,150 (2/15/91) (JS) **100**
St.-Emilion 1946 $340 (2/15/91) (JS) **87**
St.-Emilion 1945 $580 (3/16/86) (JL) **95**
St.-Emilion 1943 $185 (2/15/91) (JS) **85**
St.-Emilion 1941 $175 (2/15/91) (JS) **71**
St.-Emilion 1940 $520 (2/15/91) (JS) **83**
St.-Emilion 1938 $125 (2/15/91) (JS) **75**
St.-Emilion 1937 $400 (2/15/91) (JS) **93**
St.-Emilion 1936 $280 (2/15/91) (JS) **81**
St.-Emilion 1934 $330 (2/15/91) (JS) **93**
St.-Emilion 1933 $280 (2/15/91) (JS) **88**
St.-Emilion 1931 $230 (2/15/91) (JS) **72**
St.-Emilion 1930 $280 (2/15/91) (JS) **82**
St.-Emilion 1929 $450 (2/15/91) (JS) **90**
St.-Emilion 1928 $480 (2/15/91) (JS) **92**
St.-Emilion 1926 $400 (2/15/91) (JS) **85**
St.-Emilion 1924 $380 (2/15/91) (JS) **69**
St.-Emilion 1923 $200 (2/15/91) (JS) **65**
St.-Emilion 1921 $2,000 (2/15/91) (JS) **100**
St.-Emilion 1919 $500 (2/15/91) (JS) **70**
St.-Emilion 1917 $500 (2/15/91) (JS) **70**
St.-Emilion 1916 $400 (2/15/91) (JS) **71**
St.-Emilion 1915 $500 (2/15/91) (JS) **72**
St.-Emilion 1908 $500 (2/15/91) (JS) **71**
St.-Emilion 1905 $600 (2/15/91) (JS) **70**
St.-Emilion 1899 $1,200 (2/15/91) (JS) **90**

CLOS FOURTET
St.-Emilion 1990 (NR) (4/30/91) (BT) **85+**
St.-Emilion 1989: Solid as a rock, with deep plum and tar aromas and flavors held down by a firm tannin structure. Not giving much now, but should reward patience. Try after 1996. Rel: $26 Cur: $31 (3/15/92) **89**
St.-Emilion 1988: Ripe and fruity in aroma, with black cherry, currant and rose petal notes. The fruit is developing a smooth, soft texture, then the tannins clamp down, making it austere and tight. Best to hold until 1995. $23 (10/31/91) **86**
St.-Emilion 1987 $20 (6/30/89) (BT) **80+**
St.-Emilion 1986 Rel: $29 Cur: $41 (6/30/89) **80**
St.-Emilion 1982 Rel: $20 Cur: $31 (5/15/89) (TR) **87**
St.-Emilion 1961 $120 (3/16/86) (TR) **66**
St.-Emilion 1945 $280 (3/16/86) (JL) **68**

CLOS J. KANON
St.-Emilion 1987: An earthy style, with leathery, gamy aromas and generous currant flavor, turning simple and soft on the finish. Drinkable now. Second label of Canon. $10 (5/15/90) **77**
St.-Emilion 1986: The first thing that strikes you is the layer upon layer of complex flavor, including plum, currant, anise, nutmeg and vanilla, all wrapped in a focused and beautifully balanced package. Supple enough to drink now, but cellaring until at least 1993-'95 will not harm it. $17 (11/15/89) **91**

CHATEAU CLOS DES JACOBINS
St.-Emilion 1991: The cedar and tobacco aromas and flavors are attractive, but slightly weedy. Still, this wine shows good fruit and tannins. (NR) (5/15/92) (BT) **80+**
St.-Emilion 1990: Not showing its best right now, but it has lots of focused fruit on the palate and firm tannins. (NR) (5/15/92) (BT) **85+**
St.-Emilion 1989: A good, straightforward wine, with plum and berry flavors and a balance of ripe tannins. More accessible than others. Try after 1994. $45 (3/15/92) **85**
St.-Emilion 1988 $26 (4/15/91) **90**
St.-Emilion 1987 $23 (5/15/90) **73**
St.-Emilion 1986 $34 (6/30/89) **94**
St.-Emilion 1985 $31 (9/30/88) **89**
St.-Emilion 1984 $20 (5/15/87) **83**
St.-Emilion 1982 $39 (5/15/89) (TR) **83**
St.-Emilion 1981 Rel: $16 Cur: $31 (6/01/84) **81**

CLOS LABARDE
St.-Emilion 1986: Distinctive, with earthy, meaty aromas lending it complexity and ripe currant flavors giving it a bit of depth. Firmly structured and a bit tannic. Drink up now. $15 (6/30/89) **82**

CLOS LARCIS
St.-Emilion 1991: Has an earthy vanilla character, but it's very watery on the finish. (NR) (5/15/92) (BT) **70+**
St.-Emilion 1989: Big and burly, with jammy blackberry and black licorice aromas that evolve on the palate to tobacco and olive flavors. A rich, decadent wine, with tons of soft tannins. Better after 1996. $28 (3/15/92) **92**

CHATEAU CLOS LA MADELAINE
St.-Emilion 1982 ($NA) (5/15/89) (TR) **83**

CLOS DE L'ORATOIRE
St.-Emilion 1989 (NR) (4/30/91) (BT) **80+**
St.-Emilion 1988 (NR) (6/30/89) (BT) **75+**
St.-Emilion 1987 (NR) (6/30/89) (BT) **75+**
St.-Emilion 1982 ($NA) (5/15/89) (TR) **78**

CHATEAU CLOS ST.-MARTIN
St.-Emilion 1991: Almost like wine cut with water; has light, earthy strawberry flavors and faint tannins. (NR) (5/15/92) (BT) **65+**
St.-Emilion 1989: Very approachable and pretty. Smells like cappuccino with chocolate, and tastes like ripe, wild berries with an earthy element. Has medium tannins and a silky finish. Better after 1994. (NR) (3/15/92) **86**
St.-Emilion 1988 (NR) (6/30/89) (BT) **90+**
St.-Emilion 1987 (NR) (6/30/89) (BT) **80+**

CHATEAU LA CLOTTE
St.-Emilion 1985 Rel: $27 Cur: $32 (5/15/88) **87**
St.-Emilion 1983 $12 (5/16/86) **68**

CHATEAU LA CLUSIERE
St.-Emilion 1989 (NR) (4/30/91) (BT) **80+**
St.-Emilion 1988 $20 (6/30/89) (BT) **65+**
St.-Emilion 1982 ($NA) (5/15/89) (TR) **88**

CHATEAU LA COMMANDERIE
St.-Emilion 1991: Extremely light and fruity, with a watery texture in the middle of the palate and a light, fruity finish. (NR) (5/15/92) (BT) **70+**
St.-Emilion 1990: A generous wine, with rich chocolate and nutmeg aromas and flavors, full, round tannins and excellent concentration. (NR) (5/15/92) (BT) **90+**
St.-Emilion 1989: Why bother buying black truffles? Just buy this wine. Captivating, with rich black truffle aromas and super-fruity flavors. A real mouthful, with tons of velvety tannins. Try after 1999. $19 (3/15/92) **92**
St.-Emilion 1988 $15 (10/31/91) **79**
St.-Emilion 1983 $10.50 (1/01/86) **79**

Key to Symbols

The scores reported here are the results of blind tastings conducted by our panel of senior editors. Wines that carry the initials below are results of individual tastings.

THE WINE SPECTATOR 100-POINT SCALE 95-100—Classic, a great wine; ***90-94***—Outstanding, superior character and style; ***80-89***—Good to very good, a wine with special qualities; ***70-79***—Average, drinkable wine that may have minor flaws; ***60-69***—Below average, drinkable but not recommended; ***50-59***—Poor, undrinkable, not recommended. "+"—With a score indicates a range; used primarily with barrel tastings to indicate a preliminary score.

SPECIAL DESIGNATIONS SS—Spectator Selection, CS—Cellar Selection, BB—Best Buy, ($NA)—Price not available, (NR)—Not released.

TASTER'S INITIALS (JG)—Jim Gordon, (HS)—Harvey Steiman, (JL)—James Laube, (JS)—James Suckling, (TM)—Thomas Matthews, (TR)—Terry Robards, (PM)—Per-Henrik Mansson, (BT)—Barrel Tasting (these wines were tasted blind from barrel samples), (CA-date)—*California's Great Cabernets* by James Laube, (CH-date)—*California's Great Chardonnays* by James Laube, (VP-date)—*Vintage Port* by James Suckling.

DATE TASTED Dates in parentheses represent the issue in which the rating was published.

CHATEAU CORBIN
St.-Emilion 1986: Complex and seductive. Aromas of fully ripe currants and spicy oak are followed by supple plum and black currant flavors and a moderately tannic, lingering finish. $15 (6/30/89) **88**
St.-Emilion 1985 $15 (5/31/88) **86**

CHATEAU CORBIN-MICHOTTE
St.-Emilion 1988: Vegetal, barklike aromas and flavors obscure what little fruit there is. Could be OK after 1994 or '95, but it's a risky call. Tasted twice. 3,000 cases made. $15 (7/15/91) **72**

CHATEAU CORMEIL-FIGEAC
St.-Emilion 1988: A tough wine, with smoky overtones. Light on the intensity scale, but not shy in the tannin department. Maybe cellaring until 1995 to '98 will soften it up and make it pretty. $20 (4/30/91) **85**
St.-Emilion 1986: Very tannic for its fruit component, yet there are subdued cherry flavors underneath. Rough-hewn and straightforward. $12 (6/30/89) **75**

CHATEAU COTE DE BALEAU
St.-Emilion 1991: Round, ripe and easy, with rather tart cherry and berry flavors and light, supple tannins. (NR) (5/15/92) (BT) **80+**
St.-Emilion 1989: Surprisingly light and simple, with weedy berry flavors and a light tannin structure. Good, but nothing to write home about. Second wine of Grandes-Murailles. Drink after 1993. (NR) (3/15/92) **81**

CHATEAU LE COUVENT
St.-Emilion 1982 $13 (6/16/86) **78**

COUVENT DES JACOBINS
St.-Emilion 1989: Intense, ripe and focused, with rich, lively berry, cherry and currant flavors that glide across the palate. The tannins come through on the finish, but they're silky and round. Almost drinkable now, but better in 1996. $28 (4/30/92) **89**
St.-Emilion 1988: Lean and oaky, with more spice and toast from oak than fruit at this point, although nice raspberry and currant flavors sneak in on the finish. A bit harsh now, but perhaps it will settle down by 1996 to '98. $28 (3/31/91) **81**
St.-Emilion 1985 $27 (3/31/88) **84**
St.-Emilion 1983 Rel: $18 Cur: $27 (3/16/86) **95**

CHATEAU LA CROIX DU CASSE
St.-Emilion 1991: Like an overblown, raisiny, late-harvest California Zinfandel, but lacking the fruit and backbone of a fine wine. (NR) (5/15/92) (BT) **65+**

CHATEAU CROQUE-MICHOTTE
St.-Emilion 1982 $25 (5/15/89) (TR) **83**

CHATEAU CURE-BON-LA-MADELAINE
St.-Emilion 1982 ($NA) (5/15/89) (TR) **84**

CHATEAU DASSAULT
St.-Emilion 1989 (NR) (4/30/91) (BT) **85+**
St.-Emilion 1988: Firm and tannic, with modest black cherry, coffee and spice aromas and flavors that emerge unscathed on the finish. Has the stuff to develop with cellaring through at least 1994 or '95. $16 (7/15/91) **83**
St.-Emilion 1987 $14 (6/30/89) (BT) **75+**
St.-Emilion 1982 $20 (5/15/89) (TR) **90**

CHATEAU DESTIEUX
St.-Emilion 1988: Lean and taut, with a tannic structure and modest cherry and spice aromas and flavors. Offers little of the currant flavor that characterizes the vintage in many other wines. Balanced and built for long aging; try around 2000. $19 (6/30/91) **81**
St.-Emilion 1985 $14 (3/31/88) **84**

CHATEAU LA DOMINIQUE
St.-Emilion 1990 (NR) (4/30/91) (BT) **90+**
St.-Emilion 1989: A big wine that's built for aging. Prune, raspberry and smoke aromas explode from the glass, while the palate is fortified with tons of fruit, new oak and velvety tannins. Try after 1998. $32 (3/15/92) **91**
St.-Emilion 1988: Soft and pleasant, with nice violet-tinged currant and plum aromas and flavors that persist into a long, elegant finish. Has all the pieces to come together and be lovely by around 1995 to '98. $25 (6/30/91) **86**
St.-Emilion 1987 $20 (6/30/89) (BT) **80+**
St.-Emilion 1986 $29 (6/30/89) **95**
St.-Emilion 1985 $30 (3/31/88) **83**
St.-Emilion 1983 Rel: $18 Cur: $32 (5/16/86) **88**
St.-Emilion 1979 $27 (10/15/89) (JS) **81**

CHATEAU DURAND-LAPLAGNE
St.-Emilion 1982 $7.50 (9/16/85) **79**

CHATEAU JEAN FAURE
St.-Emilion 1983 $17 (3/31/87) **87**
St.-Emilion 1982 $14 (11/16/85) **85**

CHATEAU FAURIE-DE-SOUCHARD
St.-Emilion 1989 (NR) (4/30/91) (BT) **80+**
St.-Emilion 1988 $22 (6/30/89) (BT) **75+**
St.-Emilion 1987 $19 (6/30/89) (BT) **70+**

CHATEAU FIGEAC
St.-Emilion 1990: Rich and decadent, with earthy fruit aromas and flavors, full tannins and a long finish. (NR) (5/15/92) (BT) **90+**
St.-Emilion 1989: As always, a unique wine in a decadent style, with amazingly ripe berry and black truffle aromas and flavors and a long finish of sweet fruit. Has tons of tannins, but they're soft and rich. Better after 1998. $69 (3/15/92) **93**
St.-Emilion 1988: Rich and generous, but distinctively earthy and spicy, with a gentle core of ripe cherry and currant flavors and more authoritative cedar and clove overtones. Has tremendous character, depth and personality. The flavor profile won't please everyone, but it will enchant some. Best after 2000. $45 (6/30/91) **93**
St.-Emilion 1987 $35 (10/31/91) (JS) **83**
St.-Emilion 1986 $45 (10/31/91) (JS) **87**
St.-Emilion 1985 Rel: $37 Cur: $50 (10/31/91) (JS) **95**
St.-Emilion 1984 Rel: $26 Cur: $29 (3/31/87) **83**
St.-Emilion 1983 Rel: $37 Cur: $42 (10/31/91) (JS) **85**
St.-Emilion 1982 $67 (10/31/91) (JS) **93**
St.-Emilion 1981 $39 (10/31/91) (JS) **73**
St.-Emilion 1980 $30 (5/01/85) **90**
St.-Emilion 1979 $43 (10/31/91) (JS) **88**
St.-Emilion 1978 $51 (10/31/91) (JS) **89**
St.-Emilion 1976 $36 (10/31/91) (JS) **87**
St.-Emilion 1975 $60 (10/31/91) (JS) **78**
St.-Emilion 1971 $75 (10/31/91) (JS) **84**
St.-Emilion 1970 $75 (10/31/91) (JS) **92**
St.-Emilion 1966 $125 (10/31/91) (JS) **85**
St.-Emilion 1964 $110 (10/31/91) (JS) **93**
St.-Emilion 1962 $66 (10/31/91) (JS) **85**
St.-Emilion 1961 $139 (10/31/91) (JS) **97**
St.-Emilion 1955 ($NA) (10/31/91) (JS) **96**
St.-Emilion 1953 ($NA) (10/31/91) (JS) **86**
St.-Emilion 1952 $100 (10/31/91) (JS) **85**
St.-Emilion 1950 $165 (10/31/91) (JS) **91**
St.-Emilion 1949 $220 (10/31/91) (JS) **99**
St.-Emilion 1947 $620 (10/31/91) (JS) **93**
St.-Emilion 1945 $300 (10/31/91) (JS) **96**
St.-Emilion 1943 $150 (10/31/91) (JS) **90**
St.-Emilion 1942 $125 (10/31/91) (JS) **85**
St.-Emilion 1939 $125 (10/31/91) (JS) **83**
St.-Emilion 1937 $125 (10/31/91) (JS) **69**
St.-Emilion 1934 $160 (10/31/91) (JS) **79**
St.-Emilion 1929 $400 (10/31/91) (JS) **98**
St.-Emilion 1926 $300 (10/31/91) (JS) **87**
St.-Emilion 1924 $350 (10/31/91) (JS) **88**
St.-Emilion 1911 $400 (10/31/91) (JS) **78**
St.-Emilion 1906 $350 (10/31/91) (JS) **78**
St.-Emilion 1905 $430 (10/31/91) (JS) **95**

CHATEAU LA FLEUR
St.-Emilion 1990: Another elegant, pretty wine, with fine tannins and lovely plum and berry flavors. (NR) (5/15/92) (BT) **85+**
St.-Emilion 1989: A delicate wine for early drinking, offering pretty tobacco and vanilla aromas and flavors and medium tannins. Better after 1994. $18 (3/15/92) **84**
St.-Emilion 1986: Soft and velvety, already showing mature tobacco and earth overtones to the solid core of plum and cassis flavors. Tannins need until 1993 to soften. $13.50 (2/15/90) **82**

CHATEAU LA FLEUR-POURRET
St.-Emilion 1991: Why bother? Very watery and light. (NR) (5/15/92) (BT) **65+**
St.-Emilion 1990: A well-proportioned wine, with fine tannins and focused berry and earth flavors. A real smoothy. (NR) (5/15/92) (BT) **85+**
St.-Emilion 1989: A little light for the vintage, but shows delicious raspberry and blackberry aromas and flavors. A wine for early drinking, but hold back until 1993. (NR) (3/15/92) **82**
St.-Emilion 1988 (NR) (8/31/90) (BT) **75+**
St.-Emilion 1987 (NR) (6/30/88) (BT) **75+**

CHATEAU FOMBRAUGE
St.-Emilion 1986: Rugged but flavorful, definitely in need of cellaring before it's ready. Dusky cedar and currant flavors. Gutsy and tannic, so drink in 1995 or beyond. $19 (6/30/89) **86**
St.-Emilion 1985 Rel: $15 Cur: $22 (5/15/88) **87**

CHATEAU FONPLEGADE
St.-Emilion 1989 (NR) (4/30/91) (BT) **85+**
St.-Emilion 1988: Firm and concentrated, with a nice core of currant and cedar aromas and flavors that are balanced and graceful right through the long finish. A hint of mint adds class. Needs until 1995 to settle down. $18 (6/30/91) **85**
St.-Emilion 1987 $15 (6/30/89) (BT) **70+**
St.-Emilion 1986 $15 (6/30/88) (BT) **80+**
St.-Emilion 1985 $15 (5/15/87) (BT) **70+**
St.-Emilion 1982 $25 (5/15/89) (TR) **77**

CHATEAU FONROQUE
St.-Emilion 1990: Very elegant, with plum and black cherry flavors, firm tannins and a hint of earth on the finish. (NR) (5/15/92) (BT) **85+**
St.-Emilion 1989: This exuberant wine has rather exotic raspberry and berry aromas and flavors, very firm tannins and a rich finish. Better after 1996. $24 (3/15/92) **88**
St.-Emilion 1988 $18 (8/31/90) (BT) **90+**
St.-Emilion 1987 $15 (6/30/89) (BT)**75+**
St.-Emilion 1986 $19 (6/30/88) (BT) **80+**
St.-Emilion 1985 $23 (5/15/87) (BT) **80+**
St.-Emilion 1982 $21 (5/15/89) (TR) **78**

CHATEAU FRANC BIGAROUX
St.-Emilion 1988: A real surprise. Firm and focused, with lots of currant, plum and cedar aromas and flavors that linger through the slightly drying finish. Has plenty of style and personality; should turn into a terrific wine around 1997 to 2000. $24 (7/31/91) **91**

CHATEAU DE FRANC-MAYNE
St.-Emilion 1991: Surprisingly good, with very focused blackberry flavors and firm tannins, but slightly diluted. (NR) (5/15/92) (BT) **80+**
St.-Emilion 1990: Very ripe, with blackberry and earth flavors and full, silky tannins, but showing great restraint and finesse. (NR) (5/15/92) (BT) **90+**
St.-Emilion 1989: Built like a blacksmith's anvil; really solid, with tons of tannins and superb fruit concentration. Stays on your palate for days. Made by Jean-Michel Cazes. Try after 2000. $28 (3/15/92) **94**
St.-Emilion 1988 Rel: $15 Cur: $20 (7/15/91) **83**
St.-Emilion 1987 (NR) (6/30/88) (BT) **75+**
St.-Emilion 1986 $16 (6/30/88) (BT) **65+**

CHATEAU FUMET-PEYROUTAS
St.-Emilion 1985 $7.25 (7/31/88) BB **84**

CHATEAU LA GAFFELIERE
St.-Emilion 1990 (NR) (4/30/91) (BT) **60+**
St.-Emilion 1989 $33 (4/30/91) (BT) **90+**
St.-Emilion 1988: An earthy style, with aromas and flavors reminiscent of freshly turned wet soil, but it has a beam of black cherry and currant flavor that manages to make it worth cellaring until 1998 to 2004 to see what develops. $36 (4/30/91) **84**
St.-Emilion 1987 $20 (6/30/89) (BT) **75+**
St.-Emilion 1986 $28 (5/15/87) (BT) **80+**
St.-Emilion 1985 $31 (5/15/87) (BT) **80+**
St.-Emilion 1982 $29 (5/15/89) (TR) **88**
St.-Emilion 1979 $28 (10/15/89) (JS) **81**
St.-Emilion 1962 $60 (11/30/87) (JS) **88**
St.-Emilion 1961 $102 (3/16/86) (TR) **76**
St.-Emilion 1959 $93 (10/15/90) (JS) **82**
St.-Emilion 1945 $140 (3/16/86) (JL) **85**

CHATEAU GRAND-BARRAIL-LAMARZELLE-FIGEAC
St.-Emilion 1986: Not our style. Smells tarry and tastes slightly bitter, although the chocolaty flavors linger on the finish. May improve with age. Gamblers should try it now. $15 (6/30/89) **72**
St.-Emilion 1982 ($NA) (5/15/89) (TR) **85**

CHATEAU GRAND-CORBIN-DESPAGNE
St.-Emilion 1945 $100 (3/16/86) (JL) **70**

CHATEAU GRAND-MAYNE
St.-Emilion 1989: Shows great polish, with lovely fruit balanced by firm tannins. The finish goes on and on. Try after 1996. $22 (3/15/92) **93**
St.-Emilion 1988: Firm and flavorful, with artfully balanced plum, currant, chocolate and bay leaf

aromas and flavors, well-integrated tannins and a long finish. Best if cellared until 1994 to '97. Rel: $15 Cur: $19 (7/15/91) **87**
St.-Emilion 1986: Herbal, leathery, earthy style, velvety on the palate. The flavors lean away from the generous fruit typical of St.-Emilion, although the plum and cherry character slips in on the finish. Drink in 1993. $16 (6/30/89) **87**

CHATEAU GRAND PONTET
St.-Emilion 1988: Firmly tannic, with modestly concentrated plum and currant flavors trying to work free from a net of astringency. Needs to develop finesse with time, perhaps by 1998 to 2000. $21 (7/15/91) **86**
St.-Emilion 1982 ($NA) (5/15/89) (TR) **83**

CHATEAU GRANDES-MURAILLES
St.-Emilion 1989: An attractive wine that lures you in with toasted oak, giving it a coffee and milk chocolate character. Full tannins follow through on the finish. Try after 1996. (NR) (3/15/92) **88**
St.-Emilion 1982 ($NA) (5/15/89) (TR) **81**

CHATEAU GUADET-ST.-JULIEN
St.-Emilion 1989 (NR) (4/30/91) (BT) **75+**
St.-Emilion 1988 (NR) (6/30/89) (BT) **75+**
St.-Emilion 1987 (NR) (6/30/89) (BT) **70+**

CHATEAU HAUT-CADET
St.-Emilion 1981 $6.50 (4/01/85) **73**

CHATEAU HAUT-CORBIN
St.-Emilion 1991: Very distinctive, with barnyardy berry aromas and flavors and fine, integrated tannins. (NR) (5/15/92) (BT) **85+**
St.-Emilion 1990: Quite hard and closed, but shows a very good, firm backbone, with intense cherry and cedar aromas and flavors. (NR) (5/15/92) (BT) **85+**
St.-Emilion 1989: A substantial wine, with masses of fruit and tannins. The minty berry character keeps you coming back for more, but it's a little dry on the finish. Better in 1996. $26 (3/15/92) **89**
St.-Emilion 1986 $14 (5/15/87) (BT) **70+**

CHATEAU HAUT-FAUGERES
St.-Emilion 1988: Firm, ripe and supple, with earthy plum and cherry flavors and nice oak seasoning. Drinkable now, but it should improve through 1994. $17 (4/30/92) **84**

CHATEAU HAUT-SARPE
St.-Emilion 1989 (NR) (4/30/91) (BT) **85+**
St.-Emilion 1988: Rough and tannic now, but it has plenty of cranberry, cherry and currant aromas and flavors that persist into a fairly long finish. A chunky wine that needs until 1998 to 2003 to soften. $16 (6/30/91) **83**
St.-Emilion 1987 $14 (6/30/89) (BT) **75+**
St.-Emilion 1982 $20 (5/15/89) (TR) **87**
St.-Emilion 1979 Rel: $11 Cur: $14 (4/01/84) **78**

CHATEAU JACQUES-BLANC
St.-Emilion Cuvée du Maitre 1988: Lean and austere, with somewhat earthy flavors dominating the modest cedar and currant notes. Comes off as thin despite a fair amount of tannin. May well become a charming wine by 1993 or '94. $23 (4/30/91) **78**

PIERRE JEAN
St.-Emilion 1988: Firm and spicy, with nicely focused currant, cedar and nutmeg aromas and flavors. Has a smooth texture and tannins that should only need until 1994 to '96 to sort themselves out. $10 (6/30/91) BB **85**

CHATEAU LE JURAT
St.-Emilion 1986 (NR) (5/15/87) (BT) **70+**

CHATEAU LAFLEUR-POURRET
St.-Emilion 1989 (NR) (4/30/91) (BT) **70+**

CHATEAU LAFLEUR-ST.-EMILION
St.-Emilion 1990 (NR) (4/30/91) (BT) **95+**
St.-Emilion 1989 (NR) (4/30/91) (BT) **85+**

CHATEAU LARCIS-DUCASSE
St.-Emilion 1991: A little diluted, but very pretty, with lovely, fruity, earthy aromas and ripe berry flavors. (NR) (5/15/92) (BT) **80+**
St.-Emilion 1989: A wine with an ironlike coating of tannins. Tight and closed, with compact fruit. Built like a weight lifter. Wait until after 1998 to try. $28 (3/15/92) **91**
St.-Emilion 1988: A hard, tough-edged style that's not showing much generosity. The fruit is ripe, with hints of plum and black cherry, but it's only moderately concentrated and the tannins tend to dominate. Drink in 1995 and beyond. $20 (4/30/91) **82**
St.-Emilion 1987 $17 (6/30/89) (BT) **75+**
St.-Emilion 1987 $17 (6/30/88) (BT) **70+**
St.-Emilion 1986 Rel: $20 Cur: $25 (6/30/88) (BT) **80+**
St.-Emilion 1982 $25 (5/15/89) (TR) **85**

CHATEAU LARMANDE
St.-Emilion 1991: A very light package, with strange orange peel aromas and flavors and a short finish. (NR) (5/15/92) (BT) **75+**
St.-Emilion 1990 (NR) (4/30/91) (BT) **85+**
St.-Emilion 1989: Classically well made and sophisticated, with impressive blackberry, mint and chocolate aromas and flavors and very firm tannins on the finish. Almost like a Médoc in structure. Drink after 1997. $26 (3/15/92) **95**
St.-Emilion 1988 $23 (4/30/91) **86**
St.-Emilion 1987 $17 (6/30/89) (BT) **80+**
St.-Emilion 1986 Rel: $19 Cur: $24 (6/30/89) **91**
St.-Emilion 1985 $23 (5/15/88) **93**
St.-Emilion 1983 Rel: $13 Cur: $16 (3/16/86) **87**
St.-Emilion 1982 $28 (5/15/89) (TR) **91**
St.-Emilion 1981 $10 (8/01/84) **76**

CHATEAU LAROQUE
St.-Emilion 1983 $13 (2/15/88) **64**

CHATEAU LEYDET-FIGEAC
St.-Emilion 1985 $18 (9/30/88) **84**

CHATEAU MAGDELAINE
St.-Emilion 1990: Classy, with plenty of rich, mouth-coating fruit flavors and tannins. Defines elegance. One of the best Magdelaines we've ever tasted. (NR) (5/15/92) (BT) **90+**
St.-Emilion 1989: Starts off slowly, but quickly builds up, with impressive raspberry, plum, licorice and smoke flavors. Plenty of silky tannins hold the whole thing together. Better after 1996. $44 (3/15/92) **88**
St.-Emilion 1988: Has a supple texture and simple currant, herb and spice flavors that are soft and supple, with firm tannins. Nearing maturity; best to cellar until 1994. $50 (10/31/91) **81**
St.-Emilion 1987 $34 (6/30/89) (BT) **80+**
St.-Emilion 1986 $48 (2/15/90) **94**
St.-Emilion 1985 $40 (6/30/88) **90**
St.-Emilion 1982 $51 (5/15/89) (TR) **95**
St.-Emilion 1979 $38 (10/15/89) (JS) **89**
St.-Emilion 1961 $250 (3/16/86) (TR) **86**
St.-Emilion 1959 $125 (10/15/90) (JS) **89**

CHATEAU MATRAS
St.-Emilion 1982 ($NA) (5/15/89) (TR) **80**

CHATEAU MAUVINON
St.-Emilion 1983 $10 (11/30/86) **87**

CHATEAU MONT BELAIR
St.-Emilion 1989: Shows a smoky, toasty overlay of oak up front, but also has ripe raspberry, tar and black cherry flavors that turn to roasty coffee notes. Has ample tannins for an '89. Drink in 1994. $12 (11/15/91) **81**

A. MOUEIX
St.-Emilion 1981 $7.50 (9/01/85) **78**

JEAN-PIERRE MOUEIX
St.-Emilion 1988: Firm and tight, with a smoky currant and spice edge and a touch of earthiness on the aftertaste. One-dimensional at this stage, but perhaps with cellaring it will be more interesting. Drink after 1995. $12.50 (4/30/92) **82**

CHATEAU MOULIN DU CADET
St.-Emilion 1990: Has plenty of lovely fruit, with vanilla, plum and berry aromas and flavors and a good backbone of tannins. (NR) (5/15/92) è(BT) **85+**
St.-Emilion 1989: A delicious wine, with lots of jammy raspberry flavors and soft, round tannins. A little simple; quite approachable. Better after 1994. (NR) (3/15/92) **86**
St.-Emilion 1988 (NR) (6/30/89) (BT) **80+**
St.-Emilion 1987 (NR) (6/30/89) (BT) **75+**

CHATEAU PAVIE
St.-Emilion 1991: Offers lovely fruit aromas and flavors, a racy texture and elegant tannins. (NR) (5/15/92) (BT) **80+**
St.-Emilion 1990: Impressively concentrated, but perhaps a little overdone, with tons of straightforward fruit flavors and masses of tannins. Some may like it better than we did; may show better after bottling. (NR) (5/15/92) (BT) **85+**
St.-Emilion 1989: A lovely, balanced wine, with elegant berry, coffee and fruit aromas and flavors and very silky tannins. Shows an extremely firm structure. Try after 1997. $45 (3/15/92) **90**
St.-Emilion 1988 $46 (3/31/91) **89**
St.-Emilion 1987 $30 (5/15/90) **82**
St.-Emilion 1986 $35 (6/30/89) **93**
St.-Emilion 1985 $38 (5/15/88) **92**
St.-Emilion 1983 Rel: $23 Cur: $28 (3/16/86) **92**
St.-Emilion 1982 Rel: $23 Cur: $45 (5/15/89) (TR) **89**
St.-Emilion 1981 Rel: $15 Cur: $21 (6/01/84) **84**
St.-Emilion 1979 $34 (10/15/89) (JS) **86**
St.-Emilion 1961 $125 (3/16/86) (TR) **62**

CHATEAU PAVIE-DECESSE
St.-Emilion 1991: Supple and pleasant, with fruity vanilla flavors and light, delicate tannins. (NR) (5/15/92) (BT) **80+**
St.-Emilion 1990: Extremely extracted and rich, with masses of ripe fruit flavors and velvety tannins. Very impressive. (NR) (5/15/92) (BT) **90+**
St.-Emilion 1989: Well crafted in a tight, firm style, with lovely chocolate and fruit aromas and flavors, an excellent tannin structure and a very silky mouth-feel. Better after 1995. $29 (3/15/92) **90**
St.-Emilion 1988 $27 (3/31/91) **94**
St.-Emilion 1987 $21 (6/30/89) (BT) **75+**
St.-Emilion 1986 $33 (6/30/89) **93**
St.-Emilion 1985 $27 (3/31/88) **89**
St.-Emilion 1983 Rel: $17 Cur: $25 (3/16/86) **92**
St.-Emilion 1982 $30 (5/15/89) (TR) **89**

CHATEAU PAVIE-MACQUIN
St.-Emilion 1982 ($NA) (5/15/89) (TR) **89**

LE PETIT CHEVAL
St.-Emilion 1987: An understated wine, with currant and strawberry aromas and flavors lightly accented by cedar and spice and smoothly integrated tannins. Balanced and elegant; the second wine of Cheval Blanc. Drink in 1994 to '96. Tasted twice. $35 (3/31/91) **89**

CHATEAU PETIT-FAURIE-DE-SOUTARD
St.-Emilion 1989 (NR) (4/30/91) (BT) **75+**
St.-Emilion 1988: Pleasant, with a nice touch of herb and spice adding to the plum and currant flavors. Picks up a slight metallic note on the finish. Not too tannic; drink in 1996. $20 (4/30/91) **82**
St.-Emilion 1987 $15 (6/30/89) (BT) **75+**
St.-Emilion 1986 $15 (6/30/89) **80**

CHATEAU PETIT-FIGEAC
St.-Emilion 1991: Like a pleasant Loire Cabernet Franc, but not a serious Bordeaux. Drink young and chilled. (NR) (5/15/92) (BT) **70+**
St.-Emilion 1990: Seamless in style, with lovely, smoky berry aromas and flavors and round, ripe tannins. Great improvement for this estate. (NR) (5/15/92) (BT) **90+**
St.-Emilion 1989: Excellent quality from a little-known estate. Ripe and big, offering a wealth of blackberry, chocolate and smoke aromas and flavors and very sweet, well-integrated tannins. Drink after 1996. $21 (3/15/92) **90**
St.-Emilion 1988 $17 (8/31/90) (BT) **85+**

CHATEAU PUY-BLANQUET
St.-Emilion 1990: A pretty wine, with beautiful blackberry aromas, ripe fruit flavors and a fine tannin structure. (NR) (5/15/92) (BT) **85+**
St.-Emilion 1989: An excellent value. Dark and massive, with prune, coffee and grape must aromas and flavors; highly extracted and rich. A little rough for the moment, but it should mellow into a real beauty with time. Better after 1997. $16 (3/15/92) **90**

Key to Symbols

The scores reported here are the results of blind tastings conducted by our panel of senior editors. Wines that carry the initials below are results of individual tastings.

THE WINE SPECTATOR 100-POINT SCALE 95-100—Classic, a great wine; ***90-94***—Outstanding, superior character and style; ***80-89***—Good to very good, a wine with special qualities; ***70-79***—Average, drinkable wine that may have minor flaws; ***60-69***—Below average, drinkable but not recommended; ***50-59***—Poor, undrinkable, not recommended. "+"—With a score indicates a range; used primarily with barrel tastings to indicate a preliminary score.

SPECIAL DESIGNATIONS SS—Spectator Selection, CS—Cellar Selection, BB—Best Buy, ($NA)—Price not available, (NR)—Not released.

TASTER'S INITIALS (JG)—Jim Gordon, (HS)—Harvey Steiman, (JL)—James Laube, (JS)—James Suckling, (TM)—Thomas Matthews, (TR)—Terry Robards, (PM)—Per-Henrik Mansson, (BT)—Barrel Tasting (these wines were tasted blind from barrel samples), (CA-date)—*California's Great Cabernets* by James Laube, (CH-date)—*California's Great Chardonnays* by James Laube, (VP-date)—*Vintage Port* by James Suckling.

DATE TASTED Dates in parentheses represent the issue in which the rating was published.

St.-Emilion 1988 $15 (6/30/89) (BT) **75+**
St.-Emilion 1987 $14 (6/30/88) (BT) **75+**
St.-Emilion 1986 $16 (6/30/88) (BT) **80+**
St.-Emilion 1985 $13 (4/16/86) (BT) **60+**
St.-Emilion 1983 $9.50 (12/31/86) **76**

CHATEAU RIPEAU
St.-Emilion 1982 ($NA) (5/15/89) (TR) **88**

CHATEAU DU ROCHER
St.-Emilion 1983 $11 (5/15/87) **73**

CHATEAU DU ROCHER-BELLEVUE-FIGEAC
St.-Emilion 1991: A pretty wine, with wild berry and cherry characteristics, light, supple tannins and a delicate finish. (NR) (5/15/92) (BT) **80+**
St.-Emilion 1990: Elegant and fruity, with plenty of strawberry and cherry flavors and silky tannins. Almost Burgundian in texture. (NR) (5/15/92) (BT) **80+**
St.-Emilion 1989 $15 (4/30/90) (BT) **80+**
St.-Emilion 1988 $13 (4/30/91) **87**
St.-Emilion 1986 Rel: $12 Cur: $17 (5/15/87) (BT) **80+**

CHATEAU ROLAND
St.-Emilion 1986: Light and cranberrylike in flavor. A touch of earthy, leathery flavor makes it seem more mature than it is. $11.25 (6/30/89) **79**

BARON PHILIPPE DE ROTHSCHILD
St.-Emilion 1985 $10.50 (9/30/88) **85**

CHATEAU DE ROUFFLIAC
St.-Emilion 1985 $15 (9/30/88) **89**

CHATEAU ST.-ANDRE-CORBIN
St.-Emilion 1990: Slightly one-dimensional, showing attractive grape jam and ripe tomato characteristics and medium tannins. (NR) (5/15/92) (BT) **80+**

CHATEAU LA SERRE
St.-Emilion 1989 $17 (4/30/91) (BT) **85+**
St.-Emilion 1988: Offers tart cranberry flavors, but it's somewhat awkward, with an almost sweet aftertaste. Medium-bodied. Drink now. $18 (6/15/91) **80**
St.-Emilion 1987 $15 (6/30/89) (BT) **75+**
St.-Emilion 1985 $15 (5/15/88) **91**

CHATEAU SOUTARD
St.-Emilion 1985 $20 (5/15/88) **85**
St.-Emilion 1982 $30 (5/15/89) (TR) **84**

CHATEAU TERTRE-DAUGAY
St.-Emilion 1989: Tough, tight and tannic, with crisp, intense, cedary currant and plum flavors. So compact and hard that it's difficult to judge, except to say it will require cellaring, probably until 1998. $29 (4/30/92) **83**
St.-Emilion 1988: Pretty black cherry, plum and currant flavors gain velocity and tannins toward the finish. Needs cellaring until 1995 or so. $20 (4/30/91) **85**
St.-Emilion 1985 Rel: $15 Cur: $18 (5/15/87) (BT) **80+**

CHATEAU TERTRE-ROTEBOEUF
St.-Emilion 1991: Shows lots of new wood and pretty fruit flavors. Medium-bodied and supple, with a light finish. (NR) (5/15/92) (BT) **85+**
St.-Emilion 1990: Offers brilliant, bright cherry, blackberry and vanilla flavors wrapped up with super-elegant tannins. Superbly made; may make it to 1995 or more after bottling. (NR) (5/15/92) (BT) **90+**
St.-Emilion 1989: Extremely robust in style, with captivating wild raspberry, eucalyptus and smoke aromas, rich tobacco, fruit and toast flavors and full, hard tannins. Needs a long time to come around. Try after 1998. $45 (3/15/92) **93**
St.-Emilion 1988 $40 (6/15/91) **90**
St.-Emilion 1987 Rel: $15 Cur: $22 (2/15/90) **83**
St.-Emilion 1986 Rel: $25 Cur: $34 (6/30/89) **90**
St.-Emilion 1985 Rel: $23 Cur: $27 (6/30/88) **89**
St.-Emilion 1983 Rel: $11 Cur: $20 (5/16/86) **81**
St.-Emilion 1982 Rel: $10 Cur: $25 (9/16/85) **85**

CHATEAU TOUR-BALADOZ
St.-Emilion 1985 $11.50 (2/29/88) **82**

CHATEAU LA TOUR-FIGEAC
St.-Emilion 1989 (NR) (4/30/91) (BT) **85+**
St.-Emilion 1988 $17 (6/30/89) (BT) **70+**
St.-Emilion 1987 $14 (6/30/89) (BT) **75+**
St.-Emilion 1982 $22 (5/15/89) (TR) **89**

CHATEAU TOUR-GRAND-FAURIE
St.-Emilion 1985: Herbal style, with soft black cherry and slightly vegetal flavors, but the fruit dominates and the tarry finish lends a hard touch. Drink now through 1993. $9.75 (2/15/89) **79**

CHATEAU LA TOUR DU PIN
St.-Emilion 1982 $12 (5/01/85) **81**

CHATEAU LA TOUR-DU-PIN-FIGEAC
St.-Emilion 1988: Tough and somewhat tannic, with modest currant and blackberry flavors that turn tannic and earthy on the finish. Best after 1994. Tasted twice. $24 (7/15/91) **77**
St.-Emilion 1987 $17 (6/30/89) (BT) **80+**
St.-Emilion 1982 $21 (5/15/89) (TR) **88**

CHATEAU LA TOUR-DU-PIN-FIGEAC-BELIEVIER
St.-Emilion 1989: Firm and intense, with gripping tannins that hold the cherry, currant and spice flavors tightly in check. Picks up toasty, buttery oak notes on the finish, but requires patience. Drink after 1996 or '97. From Giraud-Belivier. 4,000 cases made. $24 (4/30/92) **83**
St.-Emilion 1982 ($NA) (5/15/89) (TR) **82**

CHATEAU TRIMOULET
St.-Emilion 1988: Supple and stylish, with a nice spiciness and layers of currant and cassis flavors. Beautifully rounded, with a pretty, earthy aftertaste and a hint of chocolate. Concentrated and elegant; drink in 1994 to '98. 2,000 cases made. $16 (6/15/91) **91**
St.-Emilion 1982 $15 (5/15/89) (TR) **81**

CHATEAU TROPLONG-MONDOT
St.-Emilion 1991: A wine with firm tannins and a good dose of clean berry, earth and cedar aromas and flavors. (NR) (5/15/92) (BT) **80+**
St.-Emilion 1990: Dense and ripe, with intense aromas and flavors of prunes and plums and velvety tannins. Always a winner in good years. (NR) (5/15/92) (BT) **90+**
St.-Emilion 1989: Very firm, with plenty of grape, vanilla and black cherry flavors and medium, velvety tannins. Well crafted and showing promise. Better after 1996. $26 (3/15/92) **89**
St.-Emilion 1988 $21 (7/15/91) **85**
St.-Emilion 1987 $16 (6/30/89) (BT) **80+**
St.-Emilion 1986 Rel: $20 Cur: $23 (6/30/89) **88**
St.-Emilion 1985 $21 (6/30/88) **88**

CHATEAU TROTTE VIEILLE
St.-Emilion 1990 (NR) (4/30/91) (BT) **90+**
St.-Emilion 1989: An absolutely delicious wine. Powerful wild raspberry aromas and sweet fruit flavors turn to milk chocolate notes on the finish. The tannins are firm, but very soft. Try in 1995. Rel: $32 Cur: $46 (3/15/92) **90**
St.-Emilion 1988: Elegant and balanced, with a pretty core of currant, plum and cherry-tinged flavors. Not too tannic, with lively acidity. The finish gets simple. Developing a smooth texture. Drink in 1995 to '98. Rel: $20 Cur: $36 (4/30/91) **85**
St.-Emilion 1987 $15 (6/30/89) (BT) **80+**
St.-Emilion 1982 $35 (5/15/89) (TR) **87**
St.-Emilion 1962 $30 (11/30/87) (JS) **75**

VIEUX CHATEAU GUIBEAU
St.-Emilion 1982 $8 (9/16/85) **80**

CHATEAU VIEUX SARPE
St.-Emilion 1982 ($NA) (5/15/89) (TR) **83**

CHATEAU VILLADIERE
St.-Emilion 1982 $8 (9/01/85) **75**

CHATEAU VILLEMAURINE
St.-Emilion 1991: Balanced and fruity, with lovely currant and berry flavors and silky tannins. Very good for such a difficult year. (NR) (5/15/92) (BT) **85+**
St.-Emilion 1989: A real beauty, with luscious mint, black cherry and berry aromas. The flavors are understated but fine, with ultrarefined tannins. A truly well-balanced wine. Approachable, but better after 1997. (NR) (3/15/92) **93**
St.-Emilion 1987 (NR) (6/30/88) (BT) **75+**
St.-Emilion 1986 $39 (6/30/88) (BT) **80+**
St.-Emilion 1982 $40 (5/15/89) (TR) **83**

CHATEAU YON-FIGEAC
St.-Emilion 1982 ($NA) (5/15/89) (TR) **87**

ST.-EMILION SATELLITES

CHATEAU DU CHEVALIER
Montagne-St.-Emilion 1986: $19 (3/31/91) **71**

CHATEAU FAIZEAU
Montagne-St.-Emilion 1983 $9 (11/15/87) **75**

CHATEAU DE LUSSAC
Lussac-St.-Emilion 1982 $6.75 (5/01/84) **73**

CHATEAU MAISON-BLANCHE
Montagne-St.-Emilion 1985: Light and fairly smooth already, a velvety wine with some concentration of berry fruit, distinctively spicy and herbal. Drink up now. $13 (2/15/89) **80**

CHATEAU MAISON-NEUVE
Montagne-St.-Emilion 1985 $7 (3/15/88) **78**

CHATEAU LE MAYNE
Puisseguin-St.-Emilion 1982 $7.50 (12/01/85) **64**

CHATEAU ST.-ANDRE-CORBIN
St.-Georges-St.-Emilion 1990 (NR) (4/30/91) (BT) **80+**
St.-Georges-St.-Emilion 1989: Incredibly ripe wine with plum and berry aromas and compacted fruit structure; full tannins but they remain soft. This wine needs time to open. Hold until after 1997. $15 (4/30/92) **91**
St.-Georges-St.-Emilion 1988 (NR) (6/30/89) (BT) **80+**
St.-Georges-St.-Emilion 1987 (NR) (6/30/89) (BT) **75+**
St.-Georges-St.-Emilion 1986 $22 (3/31/90) **77**
St.-Georges-St.-Emilion 1985 (NR) (5/15/87) (BT) **80+**

CHATEAU ST.-GEORGES
St.-Georges-St.-Emilion 1988: Simple earth, plum and currant notes are intense and metallic. Not much fun, but drinkable. $18 (4/30/92) **73**
St.-Georges-St.-Emilion 1986: Bold, generous, rich and elegant, this ripe, medium-bodied and flavorful wine, has smoked bacon, spice and berry aromas and flavors. Not very tannic, it's drinkable now. $14 (7/15/90) **87**
St.-Georges-St.-Emilion 1985: A good value in Bordeaux. Supple and delicious, full of soft cherry and plum flavors accented by a touch of spice. Nicely balanced and medium-bodied. Drink up now. $11 (7/31/89) **87**

CHATEAU TOUR CALON
Montagne-St.-Emilion 1986: Light and delicate, with pleasant cedar and tobacco aromas and flavors plus a hint of currant, turning a bit tight and tannic on the finish. Drink now. $10 (9/30/89) **81**

ST.-ESTÈPHE

CHATEAU ANDRON BLANQUET
St.-Estèphe 1990: Not giving much at the moment and it's rather astringent, but has decent, ripe fruit flavors underneath the tannins. (NR) (5/15/92) (BT) **80+**

CHATEAU BEAU-SITE
St.-Estèphe 1991: Rather angular in style, but offers good fruit flavors and a solid tannin backbone. (NR) (5/15/92) (BT) **80+**
St.-Estèphe 1990: A muscular wine, with excellent depth of fruit and tannins, which is just the tip of the iceberg of quality. A great value. (NR) (5/15/92) (BT) **90+**
St.-Estèphe 1989: A great value. Cassis and earth characteristics dominate, along with a fresh, silky tannin structure. A little hard at the moment; drink after 1996. Rel: $17 Cur: $20 (3/15/92) **90**
St.-Estèphe 1988 $14 (6/30/89) (BT) **80+**
St.-Estèphe 1987 $12 (11/30/89) (JS) **81**
St.-Estèphe 1986 Rel: $15 Cur: $18 (11/30/89) (JS) **86**
St.-Estèphe 1982 $18 (11/30/89) (JS) **86**

CHATEAU CALON-SEGUR
St.-Estèphe 1991: Lightly fruity, with tar and black cherry flavors and light tannins on the finish. (NR) (5/15/92) (BT) **80+**
St.-Estèphe 1990 (NR) (4/30/91) (BT) **85+**
St.-Estèphe 1989: What a surprise. Big and powerful, but very elegant at the same time, with lots of spice, juniper, vanilla and berry flavors and a super tannin structure. Try after 1998. $41 (3/15/92) **95**
St.-Estèphe 1988 $30 (7/15/91) **85**
St.-Estèphe 1987 $25 (6/30/89) (BT) **75+**
St.-Estèphe 1986 $32 (5/31/89) **86**
St.-Estèphe 1985 $30 (5/31/88) **88**
St.-Estèphe 1983 Rel: $16 Cur: $28 (10/31/86) **83**
St.-Estèphe 1962 $69 (11/30/87) (JS) **70**
St.-Estèphe 1961 $110 (3/16/86) (TR) **84**
St.-Estèphe 1959 $110 (10/15/90) (JS) **82**
St.-Estèphe 1945 $420 (3/16/86) (JL) **94**

CHATEAU CAPBERN-GASQUETON
St.-Estèphe 1991: Light and fresh, with strawberry and cherry flavors and light tannins, but it's just too diluted to be good. Second wine of Calon-Ségur. (NR) (5/15/92) (BT) **75+**
St.-Estèphe 1989: A pleasant wine, with herbal and cherry aromas and flavors and medium fruit and tannins. Somewhat unfocused. A wine for early drinking. Try after 1994. $27 (3/15/92) **84**
St.-Estèphe 1988 (NR) (6/30/89) (BT) **75+**
St.-Estèphe 1986 $20 (11/30/89) (JS) **76**
St.-Estèphe 1985 Rel: $18 Cur: $23 (8/31/88) **85**
St.-Estèphe 1983 $19 (2/15/88) **66**
St.-Estèphe 1982 Rel: $11 Cur: $24 (11/30/89) (JS) **83**

CHATEAU CHAMBERT-MARBUZET
St.-Estèphe 1991: Very attractive, with violet, berry and vanilla aromas and supple tannins. Light on the finish, but delicious nonetheless. The second wine of Haut-Marbuzet. (NR) (5/15/92) (BT) **80+**
St.-Estèphe 1990: Doesn't show much on the nose at the moment, but the palate shows a great depth of ripe fruit and solid tannins. Has terrific potential. (NR) (5/15/92) (BT) **90+**
St.-Estèphe 1989 $21 (4/30/91) (BT) **85+**
St.-Estèphe 1988 $26 (8/31/90) (BT) **75+**
St.-Estèphe 1987 $18 (11/30/89) (JS) **79**
St.-Estèphe 1986 Rel: $25 Cur: $28 (11/30/89) (JS) **89**
St.-Estèphe 1985 Rel: $28 Cur: $32 (6/30/88) **87**
St.-Estèphe 1983 $15 (9/30/86) **77**
St.-Estèphe 1982 $30 (11/30/89) (JS) **88**

CHATEAU LA COMMANDERIE
St.-Estèphe 1988 (NR) (6/30/89) (BT) **75+**

CHATEAU COS D'ESTOURNEL
St.-Estèphe 1991: Super-elegant and focused, showing more concentration than most in this difficult vintage, with cassis and other red berry flavors that blend nicely with vanilla and spice notes. Ends with supple tannins. (NR) (5/15/92) (BT) **90+**
St.-Estèphe 1990 (NR) (4/30/91) (BT) **90+**
St.-Estèphe 1989: A designer wine that wears its oak like an Armani suit. Shows an impressive concentration of spice, berry and vanilla aromas and flavors and an excellent tannin structure. Try after 1997. $60 (3/15/92) **95**
St.-Estèphe 1988 Rel: $30 Cur: $36 (7/15/91) CS **95**
St.-Estèphe 1987 $30 (5/15/90) **81**
St.-Estèphe 1986 Rel: $40 Cur: $45 (5/15/90) (HS) **92**
St.-Estèphe 1985 Rel: $33 Cur: $54 (5/15/90) (HS) **95**
St.-Estèphe 1984 $29 (5/15/90) (HS) **81**
St.-Estèphe 1983 Rel: $29 Cur: $61 (5/15/90) (HS) **85**
St.-Estèphe 1983 Rel: $29 Cur: $61 (5/16/86) SS **95**
St.-Estèphe 1982 Rel: $23 Cur: $95 (5/15/90) (HS) **92**
St.-Estèphe 1982 Rel: $23 Cur: $95 (7/16/85) CS **93**
St.-Estèphe 1981 Rel: $23 Cur: $41 (5/15/90) (HS) **87**
St.-Estèphe 1980 $38 (5/15/90) (HS) **83**
St.-Estèphe 1979 $45 (5/15/90) (HS) **92**
St.-Estèphe 1978 $54 (5/15/90) (HS) **93**
St.-Estèphe 1977 $30 (5/15/90) (HS) **85**
St.-Estèphe 1976 $46 (5/15/90) (HS) **84**
St.-Estèphe 1975 $69 (5/15/90) (HS) **88**
St.-Estèphe 1973 $31 (5/15/90) (HS) **82**
St.-Estèphe 1971 $50 (5/15/90) (HS) **91**
St.-Estèphe 1970 $95 (5/15/90) (HS) **89**
St.-Estèphe 1969 $21 (5/15/90) (HS) **58**
St.-Estèphe 1967 $34 (5/15/90) (HS) **82**
St.-Estèphe 1966 $120 (5/15/90) (HS) **74**
St.-Estèphe 1964 $75 (5/15/90) (HS) **84**
St.-Estèphe 1962 $124 (5/15/90) (HS) **79**
St.-Estèphe 1961 $190 (5/15/90) (HS) **87**
St.-Estèphe 1960 $85 (5/15/90) (HS) **79**
St.-Estèphe 1959 $200 (10/15/90) (JS) **90**
St.-Estèphe 1958 $95 (5/15/90) (HS) **89**
St.-Estèphe 1956 $60 (5/15/90) (HS) **79**
St.-Estèphe 1955 $140 (5/15/90) (HS) **90**
St.-Estèphe 1954 $80 (5/15/90) (HS) **81**
St.-Estèphe 1953 $240 (5/15/90) (HS) **91**
St.-Estèphe 1952 $100 (5/15/90) (HS) **95**
St.-Estèphe 1950 $100 (5/15/90) (HS) **86**
St.-Estèphe 1949 $195 (5/15/90) (HS) **80**
St.-Estèphe 1947 $220 (5/15/90) (HS) **91**
St.-Estèphe 1945 $300 (5/15/90) (HS) **77**
St.-Estèphe 1943 $220 (5/15/90) (HS) **85**
St.-Estèphe 1942 $110 (5/15/90) (HS) **78**
St.-Estèphe 1937 $260 (5/15/90) (HS) **64**
St.-Estèphe 1934 $220 (5/15/90) (HS) **88**
St.-Estèphe 1929 $450 (5/15/90) (HS) **92**
St.-Estèphe 1928 $500 (5/15/90) (HS) **90**
St.-Estèphe 1926 $300 (5/15/90) (HS) **77**
St.-Estèphe 1924 $300 (5/15/90) (HS) **82**
St.-Estèphe 1921 $200 (5/15/90) (HS) **65**
St.-Estèphe 1920 $350 (5/15/90) (HS) **93**
St.-Estèphe 1917 $250 (5/15/90) (HS) **73**
St.-Estèphe 1905 $250 (5/15/90) (HS) **65**
St.-Estèphe 1904 $210 (5/15/90) (HS) **63**
St.-Estèphe 1899 $850 (5/15/90) (HS) **87**
St.-Estèphe 1898 $500 (5/15/90) (HS) **72**
St.-Estèphe 1890 $330 (5/15/90) (HS) **69**
St.-Estèphe 1870 $1,240 (5/15/90) (HS) **90**
St.-Estèphe 1869 $1,200 (5/15/90) (HS) **82**

CHATEAU COS-LABORY
St.-Estèphe 1991: Shows interesting citrus and berry aromas and velvety tannins, but it's rather diluted. (NR) (5/15/92) (BT) **75+**
St.-Estèphe 1990: Has excellent texture, with lots of velvety tannins and rich smoke, tar and berry flavors. (NR) (5/15/92) (BT) **90+**
St.-Estèphe 1989: Quite subtle on the nose, with minty spice and berry aromas, but very intense on the palate, with lots of fruit and silky tannins. Try after 1997. $18 (3/15/92) **93**
St.-Estèphe 1988 $20 (4/30/91) **85**
St.-Estèphe 1987 $15 (6/30/88) (BT) **65+**
St.-Estèphe 1986 $16 (6/30/88) (BT) **75+**
St.-Estèphe 1985 $16 (4/30/88) **87**
St.-Estèphe 1984 $12 (6/15/87) **73**
St.-Estèphe 1983 Rel: $9.50 Cur: $20 (5/16/86) **86**
St.-Estèphe 1961 ($NA) (4/30/92) (TR) **83**

CHATEAU LE CROCK
St.-Estèphe 1987 $16 (11/30/89) (JS) **79**
St.-Estèphe 1986 Rel: $18 Cur: $21 (11/30/89) (JS) **92**
St.-Estèphe 1985 $16 (2/15/88) **79**
St.-Estèphe 1983 $9.50 (12/16/85) **81**
St.-Estèphe 1982 $20 (11/30/89) (JS) **80**

CHATEAU DEMERAULMONT
St.-Estèphe 1988: Firm in texture and spicy and ripe in flavor, with appealing blackberry, currant, nutmeg and vanilla aromas and flavors. Dark in color and flavor. With its lavish tannins, this could use a bit more intensity, but it should be fine after cellaring until 1995. $10 (8/31/91) BB **82**

CHATEAU HAUT-COUTELIN
St.-Estèphe 1982 $13 (2/15/88) **81**

CHATEAU HAUT-MARBUZET
St.-Estèphe 1991: A seductive wine, with gorgeous, fresh, ripe fruit flavors and racy tannins. Very refreshing and well made; almost outstanding. (NR) (5/15/92) (BT) **85+**
St.-Estèphe 1990: Voluptuous and seductive, with incredibly rich fruit and loads of tannins. The spicy berry and earth flavors are wonderful. (NR) (5/15/92) (BT) **95+**
St.-Estèphe 1989: Seductive, with vanilla, spice, nutmeg and licorice flavors all wrapped in a velvety tannin package. A real beauty. Try after 1997. $32 (3/15/92) **90**
St.-Estèphe 1988 Rel: $25 Cur: $28 (12/31/90) SS **91**
St.-Estèphe 1987 $20 (5/15/90) **85**
St.-Estèphe 1986 $30 (11/30/89) (JS) **92**
St.-Estèphe 1985 Rel: $25 Cur: $47 (6/30/88) **91**
St.-Estèphe 1982 $57 (11/30/89) (JS) **92**
St.-Estèphe 1979 $30 (10/15/89) (JS) **85**
St.-Estèphe 1962 $50 (11/30/87) (JS) **70**
St.-Estèphe (English Bottled) 1959 $60 (10/15/90) (JS) **83**

CHATEAU LES HAUTS DE BRAME
St.-Estèphe 1986: Lean, clean and spicy, with pleasant cedary overtones to the crisp cherry flavors, nicely focused and long. Almost drinkable now, but cellaring until 1993 will rub the edges off the slightly scratchy tannins. A kosher wine. $22 (10/31/89) **82**

CHATEAU LAFFITTE-CARCASSET
St.-Estèphe 1981 $7 (3/16/85) **74**

CHATEAU LAFON-ROCHET
St.-Estèphe 1991: Very pretty and aromatic, with a good amount of wild berry and tar aromas and flavors and a medium finish. (NR) (5/15/92) (BT) **80+**
St.-Estèphe 1990: A complex wine, with an array of aromas and flavors including violets, chocolate and berries; shows lovely structure in a smooth package. This property continues to improve each vintage. (NR) (5/15/92) (BT) **90+**
St.-Estèphe 1989: A chewy wine, with tons of plum, fruit and tobacco flavors and full tannins. Fat and muscular. Try after 1998. $18 (3/15/92) **92**
St.-Estèphe 1988 $17 (6/30/89) (BT) **85+**
St.-Estèphe 1987 $14 (6/30/89) (BT) **80+**
St.-Estèphe 1986 $20 (6/30/88) (BT) **85+**
St.-Estèphe 1985 $16 (5/15/87) (BT) **70+**
St.-Estèphe 1961 $80 (3/16/86) (TR) **58**
St.-Estèphe 1945 $100 (3/16/86) (JL) **75**

CHATEAU LILIAN-LADOUYS
St.-Estèphe 1991: Has lots of vanilla, toast and fruit aromas and flavors plus a delicious, velvety texture, although slightly diluted on the finish. (NR) (5/15/92) (BT) **80+**
St.-Estèphe 1990: For a relative newcomer, this is a very good effort. A big, concentrated wine, with tannins that coat your mouth. (NR) (5/15/92) (BT) **90+**
St.-Estèphe 1989 (NR) (4/30/91) (BT) **85+**

CHATEAU DE MARBUZET
St.-Estèphe 1991: Lovely and elegant, with cigar box and berry aromas and flavors and silky tannins. Lacks concentration, but it's good. Second wine of Cos d'Estournel. (NR) (5/15/92) (BT) **80+**
St.-Estèphe 1989: Pretty smoke, licorice and berry flavors are highlighted with firm tannins and a crisp finish. Very well balanced. Try after 1995. $21 (3/15/92) **89**
St.-Estèphe 1988: Full-bodied and flavorful, with generous, concentrated plum, currant, cedar and anise aromas and flavors shaded by classy oak notes and fine tannins. Can develop well through 1995 to '99 at least. $15 (7/15/91) SS **92**
St.-Estèphe 1987 $14 (11/30/89) (JS) **80**
St.-Estèphe 1986 $15 (11/30/89) (JS) **86**
St.-Estèphe 1985 Rel: $11 Cur: $21 (6/30/88) **87**
St.-Estèphe 1983 Rel: $9 Cur: $22 (10/15/86) **91**
St.-Estèphe 1982 $19 (11/30/89) (JS) **86**

CHATEAU MEYNEY
St.-Estèphe 1991: A polished wine, with good fruit and earth aromas and flavors, finishing with medium-firm tannins. (NR) (5/15/92) (BT) **80+**
St.-Estèphe 1990: Shows very focused, medium-rich fruit flavors and balanced tannins. Not as great as we hoped for this estate. (NR) (5/15/92) (BT) **85+**
St.-Estèphe 1989: This beautifully balanced Bordeaux has rich berry, plum and spice flavors and silky tannins on the finish. Try after 1996. $22 (3/15/92) **93**
St.-Estèphe 1988 $17 (3/15/91) **88**
St.-Estèphe 1987 $14 (5/15/90) **87**
St.-Estèphe 1986 $19 (11/30/89) (JS) **88**
St.-Estèphe 1985 Rel: $16 Cur: $20 (8/31/88) **92**
St.-Estèphe 1984 Rel: $10 Cur: $14 (5/15/87) **79**
St.-Estèphe 1983 Rel: $11 Cur: $21 (10/15/86) **92**
St.-Estèphe 1982 $25 (11/30/89) (JS) **86**
St.-Estèphe 1979 $18 (10/15/89) (JS) **87**

Key to Symbols

The scores reported here are the results of blind tastings conducted by our panel of senior editors. Wines that carry the initials below are results of individual tastings.

THE WINE SPECTATOR 100-POINT SCALE 95-100—Classic, a great wine; ***90-94***—Outstanding, superior character and style; ***80-89***—Good to very good, a wine with special qualities; ***70-79***—Average, drinkable wine that may have minor flaws; ***60-69***—Below average, drinkable but not recommended; ***50-59***—Poor, undrinkable, not recommended. "+"—With a score indicates a range; used primarily with barrel tastings to indicate a preliminary score.

SPECIAL DESIGNATIONS SS—Spectator Selection, CS—Cellar Selection, BB—Best Buy, ($NA)—Price not available, (NR)—Not released.

TASTER'S INITIALS (JG)—Jim Gordon, (HS)—Harvey Steiman, (JL)—James Laube, (JS)—James Suckling, (TM)—Thomas Matthews, (TR)—Terry Robards, (PM)—Per-Henrik Mansson, (BT)—Barrel Tasting (these wines were tasted blind from barrel samples), (CA-date)—*California's Great Cabernets* by James Laube, (CH-date)—*California's Great Chardonnays* by James Laube, (VP-date)—*Vintage Port* by James Suckling.

DATE TASTED Dates in parentheses represent the issue in which the rating was published.

CHATEAU MONTROSE
St.-Estèphe 1991: This sound wine has focused fruit flavors and firm tannins, although it's slightly short on the finish. (NR) (5/15/92) (BT) **80+**
St.-Estèphe 1990: A delicious wine, with wonderful, sweet fruit flavors and an abundance of spicy berry and chocolate notes on the finish. (NR) (5/15/92) (BT) **90+**
St.-Estèphe 1989: A beast of a wine that's reverting to its old style. Giant in structure, ripping your palate with jammy tar and plump, overripe fruit flavors and masses of tannins. Still, one of the most concentrated Bordeaux we have tasted in recent memory. Really needs time. Try after 1997. $47 (3/15/92) **95**
St.-Estèphe 1988 $41 (3/31/91) **87**
St.-Estèphe 1987 $17 (2/15/90) **80**
St.-Estèphe 1986 $31 (5/15/89) SS **96**
St.-Estèphe 1985 $33 (4/30/88) **90**
St.-Estèphe 1984 Rel: $14 Cur: $19 (3/31/87) **88**
St.-Estèphe 1983 Rel: $18.50 Cur: $35 (5/16/86) **87**
St.-Estèphe 1982 Rel: $18 Cur: $42 (5/01/85) **92**
St.-Estèphe 1981 Rel: $14 Cur: $32 (12/01/84) **90**
St.-Estèphe 1979 $30 (10/15/89) (JS) **81**
St.-Estèphe 1970 $102 (4/01/86) **80**
St.-Estèphe 1962 $98 (11/30/87) (JS) **90**
St.-Estèphe 1961 $185 (3/16/86) (TR) **87**
St.-Estèphe 1959 $125 (10/15/90) (JS) **90**
St.-Estèphe 1945 $300 (3/16/86) (JL) **88**

CHATEAU LES ORMES DE PEZ
St.-Estèphe 1991: Offers pleasant, polished fruit flavors and medium tannins, but it's slightly diluted on the finish. (NR) (5/15/92) (BT) **80+**
St.-Estèphe 1990: Not giving much at the moment, but it has very good fruit and firm tannins. (NR) (5/15/92) (BT) **85+**
St.-Estèphe 1989: Offers lots of delicious black licorice and fruit aromas and flavors. Medium-bodied, with medium tannins. Should be drinking earlier than many; try after 1995. $24 (3/15/92) **86**
St.-Estèphe 1988 $21 (4/30/91) **88**
St.-Estèphe 1987 $15 (5/15/90) **83**
St.-Estèphe 1986 $21 (11/30/89) (JS) **87**
St.-Estèphe 1985 $16 (4/30/88) **89**
St.-Estèphe 1983 $17 (10/15/86) **86**
St.-Estèphe 1982 $25 (11/30/89) (JS) **87**

CHATEAU DE PEZ
St.-Estèphe 1989: The fruit and vanilla notes in this wine dance across your palate, with medium-silky tannins following through on the finish. Not one to age for a long time, but very attractive nonetheless. Try after 1994. $21 (3/15/92) **89**
St.-Estèphe 1988: Smooth and straightforward, with a touch of buttery aroma and lean plum and cherry flavors. A workmanlike Bordeaux. Doesn't echo much on the finish. $19 (6/15/91) **83**
St.-Estèphe 1986: A good-value wine that's gushing with ripe cherry and plum and cranberry flavors, yet tightly held by very firm acidity and tannins. Beautifully balanced and bound to improve with cellaring. Drink 1994 to 2000. $17 (6/30/89) **90**
St.-Estèphe 1985 Rel: $15 $20 (6/30/88) **90**
St.-Estèphe 1982 Rel: $12 Cur: $21 (4/01/86) **90**

CHATEAU PHELAN-SEGUR
St.-Estèphe 1991: Fruity and direct, with berry flavors and medium tannins, but it's a little short. (NR) (5/15/92) (BT) **80+**
St.-Estèphe 1990: A wine with plenty of tar and fruit characteristics and medium tannins; shouldn't disappoint. (NR) (5/15/92) (BT) **85+**
St.-Estèphe 1989: Quite closed up for the moment, but shows good berry and spice flavors and medium tannins. Try after 1995. $23 (3/15/92) **85**
St.-Estèphe 1988 $20 (7/15/91) **87**
St.-Estèphe 1987 $16 (11/30/89) (JS) **82**
St.-Estèphe 1986 $19 (11/30/89) (JS) **86**
St.-Estèphe 1982 $26 (11/30/89) (JS) **88**
St.-Estèphe 1961 $43 (3/16/86) (TR) **67**

CHATEAU TRONQUOY-LALANDE
St.-Estèphe 1991: Very strange; doesn't taste completely fermented. Tasted from two samples. (NR) (5/15/92) (BT) **65+**
St.-Estèphe 1989 $14 (4/30/90) (BT) **90+**
St.-Estèphe 1988: A roasted, tobacco quality pervades this firmly tannic, full-bodied wine, but decent plum and prune flavors fill it out. $14 (7/15/91) **84**
St.-Estèphe 1987 $13 (11/30/89) (JS) **84**
St.-Estèphe 1986 $15 (11/30/89) (JS) **92**
St.-Estèphe 1982 $18 (11/30/89) (JS) **86**

ST.-JULIEN

BARTON & GUESTIER
St.-Julien 1985 $13 (2/15/88) **83**

CHATEAU BEYCHEVELLE
St.-Julien 1991: Quite light and straightforward, with medium tannins and earthy berry flavors. (NR) (5/15/92) (BT) **80+**
St.-Julien 1990: Seductive, with understated floral, fruity aromas and flavors and a refined tannin structure. Should develop beautifully. (NR) (5/15/92) (BT) **90+**
St.-Julien 1989: One of the best wines ever produced from this estate. Intense ripe cherry aromas and flavors come through in this wine that's big and alcoholic, with full, silky tannins. Built more like Port than wine. Try after 1998. $48 (3/15/92) **95**
St.-Julien 1988 $40 (4/30/91) **93**
St.-Julien 1987 $28 (5/15/90) **79**
St.-Julien 1986 $37 (5/31/89) **93**
St.-Julien 1985 $35 (8/31/88) CS **95**
St.-Julien 1984 $32 (5/15/87) **78**
St.-Julien 1983 Rel: $25 Cur: $30 (3/01/86) **88**
St.-Julien 1982 Rel: $25 Cur: $47 (12/31/89) (TM) **89**
St.-Julien 1981 Rel: $17 Cur: $26 (5/01/84) **81**
St.-Julien 1979 $47 (10/15/89) (JS) **92**
St.-Julien 1978 $44 (12/31/89) (TM) **86**
St.-Julien 1971 $44 (12/31/89) (TM) **85**
St.-Julien 1967 $37 (12/31/89) (TM) **83**
St.-Julien 1962 $89 (11/30/87) (JS) **95**
St.-Julien 1961 $155 (3/16/86) (TR) **68**
St.-Julien 1959 $130 (10/15/90) (JS) **80**
St.-Julien 1948 $175 (12/31/89) (TM) **92**
St.-Julien 1945 $410 (3/16/86) (JL) **88**
St.-Julien 1929 $500 (12/31/89) (TM) **95**

CHATEAU BRANAIRE-DUCRU
St.-Julien 1991: Offers good, ripe fruit flavors, but seems a little muddled on the palate. (NR) (5/15/92) (BT) **80+**
St.-Julien 1990: Pretty and elegant, with an up-front floral and fruity character, ultrafine, ripe tannins and lovely balance. (NR) (5/15/92) (BT) **90+**
St.-Julien 1989: Handsome, with elegant black cherry and licorice aromas and flavors and well-balanced tannins. An elegant, well-crafted wine to drink after 1997. $35 (3/15/92) **90**
St.-Julien 1988 Rel: $16 Cur: $22 (8/31/90) (BT) **85+**
St.-Julien 1987 $15 (6/30/89) (BT) **80+**
St.-Julien 1986 Rel: $16 Cur: $27 (6/30/88) (BT) **85+**
St.-Julien 1985 Rel: $25 Cur: $29 (6/30/88) **89**
St.-Julien 1983 $24 (3/01/86) **88**
St.-Julien 1961 $125 (3/16/86) (TR) **79**
St.-Julien 1959 $140 (10/15/90) (JS) **86**
St.-Julien 1945 $175 (3/16/86) (JL) **67**

CLOS DU MARQUIS
St.-Julien 1988: A second wine of Léoville-Las Cases. A strong earthy note dominates the black cherry and currant flavors. A rustic style that won't appeal to everyone. Needs cellaring until 1995 for the tannins to soften. Tasted twice, with consistent notes. $19 (10/31/91) **80**
St.-Julien 1987: The herb and tobacco flavors are balanced against modest cherry flavor; light and appealing but not particularly deep. Drink now. $12 (5/15/90) **79**
St.-Julien 1986: Appealing cherry and currant flavors almost make up for unfortunate overtones of horsiness and mossiness that get in the way. Lean and a bit awkward, it should have come around by now. Rel: $17 Cur: $20 (9/15/89) **84**
St.-Julien 1985 Rel: $14 Cur: $20 (9/30/88) **84**

CHATEAU DUCRU-BEAUCAILLOU
St.-Julien 1991: Very well made, showing complex tobacco, chocolate, cedar and fruit aromas and flavors and firm tannins. (NR) (5/15/92) (BT) **85+**
St.-Julien 1990: An earthy wine, with blackberry and smoke aromas and flavors and a fine backbone of tannins, but lacks a bit on the finish. Perhaps it was recently racked and will show much better later. (NR) (5/15/92) (BT) **85+**
St.-Julien 1989: A rich wine, with plum and earth aromas and flavors, a velvety mouth-feel and an excellent, ripe tannin structure. The '88 may be a tiny bit better. Try after 1997. $65 (3/15/92) **91**
St.-Julien 1988 $48 (4/30/91) **92**
St.-Julien 1987 $35 (5/15/90) **86**
St.-Julien 1986 $52 (6/30/89) **91**
St.-Julien 1985 $50 (6/15/88) **95**
St.-Julien 1984 Rel: $24 Cur: $31 (8/31/87) **87**
St.-Julien 1983 Rel: $27 Cur: $43 (6/16/86) **90**
St.-Julien 1982 Rel: $28 Cur: $74 (5/01/85) **92**
St.-Julien 1981 Rel: $25 Cur: $45 (5/01/85) **93**
St.-Julien 1980 Rel: $13 Cur: $25 (5/01/84) CS **88**
St.-Julien 1979 $51 (10/15/89) (JS) **87**
St.-Julien 1978 $74 (5/01/85) **91**
St.-Julien 1962 $120 (11/30/87) (JS) **80**
St.-Julien 1961 $290 (3/16/86) (TR) **94**
St.-Julien 1959 $220 (10/15/90) (JS) **90**
St.-Julien 1945 $540 (3/16/86) (JL) **79**

CHATEAU DULUC
St.-Julien 1989 (NR) (3/15/92) **84**

LES FIEFS DE LAGRANGE
St.-Julien 1991: A very pretty wine, with raspberry and fruit characteristics and medium tannins. Shows class; very good for being the second wine of Lagrange. (NR) (5/15/92) (BT) **85+**
St.-Julien 1990: Extremely well crafted, offering vivid berry and raspberry aromas and flavors and well-defined tannins. Great for a second wine. (NR) (5/15/92) (BT) **90+**
St.-Julien 1989 (NR) (4/30/91) (BT) **85+**
St.-Julien 1988 $17 (4/30/91) **92**
St.-Julien 1987 $14 (6/30/88) (BT) **70+**
St.-Julien 1986 $17 (6/30/88) (BT) **80+**
St.-Julien 1985 Rel: $17 Cur: $20 (5/15/87) (BT) **70+**
St.-Julien 1983 Rel: $10 Cur: $13 (5/01/86) **85**

CHATEAU DU GLANA
St.-Julien 1989: Has an impressive amount of roasted coffee bean and tobacco aromas and flavors and full tannins, but seems a little dry on the finish. (NR) (3/15/92) **87**
St.-Julien 1988 (NR) (6/30/89) (BT) **75+**
St.-Julien 1987 ($NA) (11/30/89) (JS) **81**
St.-Julien 1986 $17 (11/30/89) (JS) **84**
St.-Julien 1982 ($NA) (11/30/89) (JS) **85**

CHATEAU GLORIA
St.-Julien 1991: Lovely and delicate, with cassis and mint flavors and medium tannins. (NR) (5/15/92) (BT) **80+**
St.-Julien 1990: A beautiful wine, with wonderful raspberry and earth aromas and ultrafine tannins. (NR) (5/15/92) (BT) **90+**
St.-Julien 1989: Offers vivid aromas and flavors of crushed raspberries and earth, with full, silky tannins and a long, tasty finish. Very well made. Try after 1997. $29 (3/15/92) **92**
St.-Julien 1988 $23 (3/31/91) **90**
St.-Julien 1987 $14 (5/15/90) **80**
St.-Julien 1986 $18 (5/31/89) **89**
St.-Julien 1985 Rel: $14 Cur: $22 (4/15/88) **89**
St.-Julien 1984 Rel: $8 Cur: $15 (3/15/87) BB **87**
St.-Julien 1983 Rel: $10 Cur: $20 (10/15/86) **83**
St.-Julien 1982 Rel: $13 Cur: $34 (11/30/89) (JS) **83**
St.-Julien 1981 Rel: $10 Cur: $24 (6/01/84) **82**
St.-Julien 1979 $18 (10/15/89) (JS) **83**

CHATEAU GRUAUD-LAROSE
St.-Julien 1991: A ripe, earthy style of wine, with sweet fruit flavors, medium tannins and a pretty finish. (NR) (5/15/92) (BT) **85+**
St.-Julien 1990: Thick and chewy, with tons of ripe fruit flavors and tannins. Has excellent depth of fruit and wonderful structure. (NR) (5/15/92) (BT) **90+**
St.-Julien 1989: An exceedingly well-made, classy wine, with very focused blackberry, cedar and fruit flavors and a compact fruit and tannin structure. Try after 1997. $49 (3/15/92) **93**
St.-Julien 1988 $31 (3/31/91) **84**
St.-Julien 1987 $22 (2/28/91) (TR) **83**
St.-Julien 1986 $34 (2/28/91) (TR) **89**
St.-Julien 1985 $31 (2/28/91) (TR) **93**
St.-Julien 1984 $21 (2/28/91) (TR) **83**
St.-Julien 1983 Rel: $19 Cur: $41 (2/28/91) (TR) **85**
St.-Julien 1982 Rel: $40 Cur: $55 (2/28/91) (TR) **89**
St.-Julien 1981 Rel: $18 Cur: $36 (2/28/91) (TR) **90**
St.-Julien 1980 $25 (2/28/91) (TR) **83**
St.-Julien 1979 $34 (2/28/91) (TR) **89**
St.-Julien 1978 $47 (2/28/91) (TR) **91**
St.-Julien 1977 $33 (2/28/91) (TR) **71**
St.-Julien 1976 $30 (2/28/91) (TR) **85**

St.-Julien 1975 $55 (2/28/91) (TR) **89**
St.-Julien 1974 $28 (2/28/91) (TR) **63**
St.-Julien 1973 $28 (2/28/91) (TR) **76**
St.-Julien 1971 $31 (2/28/91) (TR) **85**
St.-Julien 1970 $70 (2/28/91) (TR) **89**
St.-Julien 1969 $15 (2/28/91) (TR) **50**
St.-Julien 1968 $15 (2/28/91) (TR) **65**
St.-Julien 1967 $33 (2/28/91) (TR) **78**
St.-Julien 1966 $115 (2/28/91) (TR) **87**
St.-Julien 1964 $70 (2/28/91) (TR) **88**
St.-Julien 1962 $90 (2/28/91) (TR) **94**
St.-Julien 1961 $240 (2/28/91) (TR) **95**
St.-Julien 1959 $140 (2/28/91) (TR) **85**
St.-Julien 1957 $65 (2/28/91) (TR) **78**
St.-Julien 1955 $150 (2/28/91) (TR) **87**
St.-Julien 1953 $150 (2/28/91) (TR) **88**
St.-Julien 1952 $185 (2/28/91) (TR) **85**
St.-Julien 1950 $250 (2/28/91) (TR) **83**
St.-Julien 1949 $270 (2/28/91) (TR) **85**
St.-Julien 1947 $400 (2/28/91) (TR) **88**
St.-Julien 1945 $300 (2/28/91) (TR) **96**
St.-Julien 1943 $200 (2/28/91) (TR) **83**
St.-Julien 1937 $150 (2/28/91) (TR) **87**
St.-Julien 1934 $182 (2/28/91) (TR) **83**
St.-Julien 1929 $550 (2/28/91) (TR) **85**
St.-Julien 1928 $500 (2/28/91) (TR) **94**
St.-Julien 1926 $230 (2/28/91) (TR) **95**
St.-Julien 1924 $400 (2/28/91) (TR) **89**
St.-Julien 1921 $250 (2/28/91) (TR) **87**
St.-Julien 1920 $300 (2/28/91) (TR) **85**
St.-Julien 1918 $300 (2/28/91) (TR) **78**
St.-Julien 1907 $260 (2/28/91) (TR) **72**
St.-Julien 1906 $300 (2/28/91) (TR) **85**
St.-Julien 1899 $600 (2/28/91) (TR) **83**
St.-Julien 1893 $500 (2/28/91) (TR) **78**
St.-Julien 1887 $400 (2/28/91) (TR) **71**
St.-Julien 1878 $500 (2/28/91) (TR) **83**
St.-Julien 1870 $2,300 (2/28/91) (TR) **87**
St.-Julien 1865 $1,800 (2/28/91) (TR) **65**
St.-Julien 1844 ($NA) (2/28/91) (TR) **85**
St.-Julien 1834 ($NA) (2/28/91) (TR) **83**
St.-Julien 1819 ($NA) (2/28/91) (TR) **89**

CHATEAU LAGRANGE
St.-Julien 1991: Extremely impressive for the vintage, with vivid, delicate fruit flavors and firm tannins. (NR) (5/15/92) (BT) **85+**
St.-Julien 1990: Stunning vanilla, berry and chocolate aromas and flavors are held together with super-firm tannins. A complex, complete wine. This estate continues to amaze us with its great wines. (NR) (5/15/92) (BT) **95+**
St.-Julien 1989: Like the '88, this is superbly crafted, with berry, licorice and cassis aromas and flavors and a huge alcohol and tannin structure, but it's not overpowering. Shows great balance. Try after 1998. $29 (3/15/92) **95**
St.-Julien 1988 $26 (4/30/91) **96**
St.-Julien 1987 $25 (6/30/88) (BT) **75+**
St.-Julien 1986 Rel: $20 Cur: $28 (2/15/90) **86**
St.-Julien 1985 $23 (9/30/88) **83**
St.-Julien 1961 $90 (3/16/86) (TR) **67**

CHATEAU LALANDE-BORIE
St.-Julien 1989: Shows attractive blackberry jam, tobacco and earth flavors and well-integrated tannins. Not a huge wine, but very good for the vintage. Drink after 1995. $22 (3/15/92) **88**
St.-Julien 1988: A medium-weight, smoothly balanced and flavorful wine that's fruity and focused, with straightforward currant and raspberry aromas and flavors. Turns a bit tough on the finish as the tannins emerge. Drink after 1995 or '96. $17 (4/30/91) **87**
St.-Julien 1987 $15 (11/30/89) (JS) **81**
St.-Julien 1986 $17 (11/30/89) (JS) **91**
St.-Julien 1982 $15 (11/30/89) (JS) **92**

CHATEAU LANGOA BARTON
St.-Julien 1991: A solid wine, with medium-ripe fruit and smoke aromas and flavors and a firm tannin backbone. (NR) (5/15/92) (BT) **80+**
St.-Julien 1990: Shows great restraint, but still coats your palate with a kaleidoscope of wonderful, ripe fruit flavors and integrated tannins. (NR) (5/15/92) (BT) **90+**
St.-Julien 1989: Has an extremely impressive, velvety mouth-feel, with rich chocolate, berry and cedar aromas and flavors and a long, almost sweet finish. Try after 1997. $28 (3/15/92) **94**
St.-Julien 1988 $25 (7/15/91) **86**
St.-Julien 1987 $17 (6/30/89) (BT) **75+**
St.-Julien 1986 Rel: $22 Cur: $26 (6/30/88) (BT) **85+**
St.-Julien 1985 $20 (6/15/88) **91**
St.-Julien 1961 $113 (3/16/86) (TR) **63**
St.-Julien 1945 $250 (3/16/86) (JL) **71**

LADY LANGOA
St.-Julien 1989 (NR) (4/30/91) (BT) **80+**

CHATEAU LEOVILLE-BARTON
St.-Julien 1991: Another fruity, firm wine, with berry, herb and olive flavors, licorice notes and a medium finish. (NR) (5/15/92) (BT) **80+**

Key to Symbols

The scores reported here are the results of blind tastings conducted by our panel of senior editors. Wines that carry the initials below are results of individual tastings.

THE WINE SPECTATOR 100-POINT SCALE 95-100—Classic, a great wine; ***90-94***—Outstanding, superior character and style; ***80-89***—Good to very good, a wine with special qualities; ***70-79***—Average, drinkable wine that may have minor flaws; ***60-69***—Below average, drinkable but not recommended; ***50-59***—Poor, undrinkable, not recommended. "+"—With a score indicates a range; used primarily with barrel tastings to indicate a preliminary score.

SPECIAL DESIGNATIONS SS—Spectator Selection, CS—Cellar Selection, BB—Best Buy, ($NA)—Price not available, (NR)—Not released.

TASTER'S INITIALS (JG)—Jim Gordon, (HS)—Harvey Steiman, (JL)—James Laube, (JS)—James Suckling, (TM)—Thomas Matthews, (TR)—Terry Robards, (PM)—Per-Henrik Mansson, (BT)—Barrel Tasting (these wines were tasted blind from barrel samples), (CA-date)—*California's Great Cabernets* by James Laube, (CH-date)—*California's Great Chardonnays* by James Laube, (VP-date)—*Vintage Port* by James Suckling.

DATE TASTED Dates in parentheses represent the issue in which the rating was published.

St.-Julien 1990: Another great St.-Julien, with masses of tannins coated with super-ripe fruit flavors. A real beauty. (NR) (5/15/92) (BT) **90+**
St.-Julien 1989: A luscious wine, with full, round tannins and rich tobacco, blackberry and chocolate flavors. Try after 1997. $41 (3/15/92) **94**
St.-Julien 1988 Rel: $20 Cur: $24 (3/31/91) **91**
St.-Julien 1987 $20 (5/15/90) **80**
St.-Julien 1986 Rel: $24 Cur: $28 (5/31/89) **90**
St.-Julien 1985 Rel: $24 Cur: $33 (4/15/88) **92**
St.-Julien 1983 Rel: $24 Cur: $27 (3/01/86) **92**
St.-Julien 1962 $80 (11/30/87) (JS) **70**
St.-Julien 1961 $100 (3/16/86) (TR) **76**
St.-Julien 1959 $125 (10/15/90) (JS) **85**
St.-Julien 1945 $340 (3/16/86) (JL) **73**

CHATEAU LEOVILLE-LAS CASES
St.-Julien 1988 $45 (2/15/92) (HS) **95**
St.-Julien 1987 $32 (2/15/92) (HS) **88**
St.-Julien 1986 Rel: $44 Cur: $61 (2/15/92) (HS) **95**
St.-Julien 1986 Rel: $44 Cur: $61 (9/15/89) CS **96**
St.-Julien 1985 Rel: $45 Cur: $56 (2/15/92) (HS) **92**
St.-Julien 1984 $33 (2/15/92) (HS) **85**
St.-Julien 1983 Rel: $26 Cur: $45 (2/15/92) (HS) **88**
St.-Julien 1982 Rel: $30 Cur: $120 (2/15/92) (HS) **95**
St.-Julien 1981 Rel: $23 Cur: $45 (2/15/92) (HS) **90**
St.-Julien 1980 $29/1.5L (2/15/92) (HS) **82**
St.-Julien 1979 $53 (2/15/92) (HS) **89**
St.-Julien 1978 $75 (2/15/92) (HS) **87**
St.-Julien 1977 $20 (2/15/92) (HS) **78**
St.-Julien 1976 $64 (2/15/92) (HS) **83**
St.-Julien 1975 $75 (2/15/92) (HS) **88**
St.-Julien 1971 $75 (4/01/86) **76**
St.-Julien 1970 $90 (2/15/92) (HS) **77**
St.-Julien 1966 $110 (2/15/92) (HS) **86**
St.-Julien 1964 $71 (2/15/92) (HS) **88**
St.-Julien 1962 $93 (2/15/92) (HS) **81**
St.-Julien 1961 $200 (2/15/92) (HS) **92**
St.-Julien 1959 $210 (2/15/92) (HS) **80**
St.-Julien 1955 $125 (2/15/92) (HS) **81**
St.-Julien 1953 $300 (2/15/92) (HS) **87**
St.-Julien 1952 $165 (2/15/92) (HS) **73**
St.-Julien 1950 $230 (2/15/92) (HS) **73**
St.-Julien 1949 $195 (2/15/92) (HS) **89**
St.-Julien 1948 $150 (2/15/92) (HS) **65**
St.-Julien 1947 $380 (2/15/92) (HS) **86**
St.-Julien 1945 $430 (2/15/92) (HS) **94**
St.-Julien 1928 $600 (2/15/92) (HS) **90**

CHATEAU LEOVILLE-POYFERRE
St.-Julien 1991: Round and easy, with good raspberry flavors and medium tannins. A little dry on the finish. (NR) (5/15/92) (BT) **80+**
St.-Julien 1990: A real blockbuster, bursting with ripe currant and berry flavors and full tannins, but with an incredible amount of harmony. (NR) (5/15/92) (BT) **95+**
St.-Julien 1989: This beautiful wine has perfumed raspberry and other fruit aromas and medium, silky tannins. A seductive wine. Try after 1996. $42 (3/15/92) **90**
St.-Julien 1988 $23 (7/15/91) **81**
St.-Julien 1987 $24 (5/15/90) **86**
St.-Julien 1986 $24 (5/31/89) **86**
St.-Julien 1985 Rel: $19 Cur: $29 (4/30/88) **92**
St.-Julien 1984 $24 (10/15/87) **85**
St.-Julien 1983 Rel: $20 Cur: $28 (3/01/86) **83**
St.-Julien 1982 Rel: $20 Cur: $40 (6/01/85) **89**
St.-Julien 1981 Rel: $12 Cur: $20 (6/01/84) **88**
St.-Julien 1961 $97 (3/16/86) (TR) **77**
St.-Julien 1945 $210 (3/16/86) (JL) **80**

CHATEAU DU MOULIN DE LA BRIDAN
St.-Julien 1983 $11 (4/01/86) **76**

CHATEAU MOULIN-RICHE
St.-Julien 1987 ($NA) (11/30/89) (JS) **79**
St.-Julien 1986 $20 (11/30/89) (JS) **88**
St.-Julien 1985 $20 (6/15/88) **83**
St.-Julien 1982 ($NA) (11/30/89) (JS) **90**

CHATEAU ST.-PIERRE
St.-Julien 1991: A pretty wine, with a soft fruit and tannin structure and lovely smoke and berry flavors on the finish. (NR) (5/15/92) (BT) **80+**
St.-Julien 1990: Extremely well crafted and fine, this '90 is super-ripe but beautifully balanced, with lovely aromas and flavors. (NR) (5/15/92) (BT) **90+**
St.-Julien 1989: A wine with everything. Has a superb, velvety tannin structure, with rich blackberry, nutmeg and other spice aromas that follow through on the palate. Drink after 1998. $39 (3/15/92) **94**
St.-Julien 1988 $32 (4/30/91) **85**
St.-Julien 1987 $17 (5/15/90) **89**
St.-Julien 1986 Rel: $17 Cur: $22 (9/15/89) SS **92**
St.-Julien 1985 $19 (4/16/86) (BT) **70+**
St.-Julien 1982 Rel: $15 Cur: $22 (12/16/85) CS **93**
St.-Julien 1979 $24 (10/15/89) (JS) **84**
St.-Julien 1962 $55 (11/30/87) (JS) **68**

CHATEAU TALBOT
St.-Julien 1991: Shows modest concentration, with berry and plum flavors, velvety tannins and a light, delicate finish. (NR) (5/15/92) (BT) **85+**
St.-Julien 1990: The essence of fresh cassis; very reduced, with rich fruit flavors that coat the tannins. Very impressive. (NR) (5/15/92) (BT) **90+**
St.-Julien 1989: Big and rustic, with lots of raisin and berry aromas and flavors and full, velvety tannins. Not classy, but has an impressive concentration of fruit. Try after 1997. $43 (3/15/92) **90**
St.-Julien 1988 $25 (3/15/91) **90**
St.-Julien 1987 $23 (5/15/90) **85**
St.-Julien 1986 $32 (5/31/89) **91**
St.-Julien 1985 $26 (4/30/88) **87**
St.-Julien 1984 $19 (5/15/87) **80**
St.-Julien 1983 Rel: $22 Cur: $28 (9/30/86) **89**
St.-Julien 1982 Rel: $26 Cur: $45 (5/01/89) **88**
St.-Julien 1981 Rel: $17 Cur: $34 (6/01/84) **83**
St.-Julien 1979 $31 (10/15/89) (JS) **84**
St.-Julien 1962 $55 (11/30/87) (JS) **55**
St.-Julien 1959 $100 (10/15/90) (JS) **86**
St.-Julien 1945 $310 (3/16/86) (JL) **81**

CHATEAU TERREY-GROS-CAILLOUX
St.-Julien 1991: Light and weedy, with strawberry flavors and a light finish. (NR) (5/15/92) (BT) **65+**
St.-Julien 1989 Cur: $16 (4/30/91) (BT) **85+**
St.-Julien 1988 $14 (6/30/89) (BT) **80+**
St.-Julien 1987 $12 (11/30/89) (JS) **85**
St.-Julien 1986 $12 (11/30/89) (JS) **87**

Other Bordeaux Red

CHATEAU BEAUSEJOUR
Côtes de Castillon 1986: Simple but beautifully balanced. Tastes smooth and fruity with enough liveliness and fresh flavor to make it interesting. $5 (6/15/89) BB **80**

CHATEAU DE BEL-AIR
Lalande-de-Pomerol 1985 $18 (9/30/88) **85**

CHATEAU DE BELCIER
Côtes de Castillon 1985 $5 (6/30/88) **76**

CHATEAU BERTINERIE
Premières Côtes de Blaye 1988: A very interesting wine that's meaty and rich, with smoky, oaky undertones that catch your attention immediately. It has firm tannins, but the ripe plummy aromas and flavors make it accessible now. $10 (7/15/90) **85**

CHATEAU CAYLA
Premières Côtes de Bordeaux 1986: Simple jug-wine style. Solid, fruity aromas aren't quite backed up in flavor, which turns simple and a bit harsh on the finish. $7 (6/30/89) **76**
Premières Côtes de Bordeaux 1985 $4 (5/31/88) **73**

CHATEAU CHANGROLLE
Lalande-de-Pomerol 1982 $6 (12/16/84) **78**

CHATEAU CLAIRAC
Premières Côtes de Blaye 1985 $4.50 (4/15/88) **76**

CHATEAU LA CROIX DE MILLORIT
Côtes de Bourg 1986: Light and spicy, with leathery overtones to the strawberry aromas and flavors, hinting at plum on the finish. Showing maturity; drink soon. $9/375ml (5/15/91) **79**

CHATEAU DUPLESSY
Premières Côtes de Bordeaux 1985 $6 (5/31/88) **75**

CHATEAU GRAND-CHEMIN
Côtes de Bourg 1985: The label is a dead ringer for Lynch-Bages but the wine isn't. Soft, supple and aromatic. Easy to enjoy now for its smoothness and lean, leathery flavors. $8 (6/15/89) **76**

CHATEAU GRAND-CLARET
Premières Côtes de Bordeaux 1988: Firm and ripe, this somewhat tough-textured wine has enough black cherry and plum flavors to suggest that cellaring until 1993 or '94 could bring it around. $7 (7/31/91) **78**

CHATEAU GRAND-ORMEAU
Lalande-de-Pomerol 1985 $16 (5/31/88) **88**

CHATEAU DE LA GRAVE
Côtes de Bourg 1982 $5.25 (2/16/85) **70**
Côtes de Bourg 1981 $4.99 (2/16/85) **74**

CHATEAU LA GROLET
Côtes de Bourg 1989: Soft and fragrant, with a velvety texture and nicely articulated currant and herb aromas and flavors. Medium-weight tannins give it a firm texture that could soften with cellaring until 1993 or '94. $9 (8/31/91) BB **82**
Côtes de Bourg 1985 $7 (5/15/88) **69**

CHATEAU HAUT-RIAN
Premières Côtes de Bordeaux 1988: Flavorful, generous and nicely balanced, offering appealing strawberry and currant flavors and a light touch of oak. Generally simple, but delicious to drink now. $7 (5/15/90) BB **81**

CHATEAU LEON
Côtes de Bordeaux 1983 $5.50 (11/15/86) **79**

CHATEAU LEZONGARS
Premières Côtes de Bordeaux 1985 $7 (11/15/87) **72**

CHATEAU MAYNE-DAVID
Côtes de Castillon 1985 $6 (2/28/87) BB **81**

CHATEAU DE LA MEULIERE
Premières Côtes de Bordeaux 1988: Very light in color, aroma and texture, offering modest strawberry aromas and flavors on a tannic framework. A bit short. Try after 1993. $9 (2/28/91) **76**

CHATEAU PERENNE
Premières Côtes de Blaye 1989: Light and flavorful, with modest currant and tobacco aromas and flavors and light tannins. Easy to drink. $9 (3/31/91) **78**
Premières Côtes de Blaye 1986: A good dinner wine that's light, but fruity and refreshing. Has spicy, fruity aromas, clean cherry and cranberry aromas and a clean finish. $7 (6/30/89) **82**
Premières Côtes de Blaye 1985 $7 (2/15/88) **80**
Premières Côtes de Blaye 1982 $5 (11/16/85) BB **79**

CHATEAU PEYRAUD
Premières Côtes de Blaye 1989: Firm in texture and nicely fruity, offering plum and currant flavors that linger through the finish. Drinkable now. $8 (3/31/91) **80**

CHATEAU LA PIERRIERE
Côtes de Castillon 1986 $6 (12/31/88) **77**

CHATEAU PITRAY
Côtes de Castillon 1988: Light but flavorful, with attractive cherry, strawberry and floral aromas and flavors. Has a smooth texture, a firm backbone of tannin and a hint of caramel on the finish. Well crafted for drinking by 1993 or '94. $7 (2/28/91) BB **83**
Côtes de Castillon 1986: Light and lively, with attractive cherry and strawberry flavors on a firm, crisp framework, plus a touch of toastiness. Drink now. $6 (9/30/89) BB **81**

CHATEAU PLAISANCE
Premières Côtes de Blaye Cuvée Spéciale 1989: Spicy, lively aromas and flavors of cinnamon, cherry, vanilla and cedar mark this as a cut above most out-of-the-way Bordeaux. A well-crafted wine for drinking now or cellaring until about 1993. $9 (2/28/91) BB **85**
Premières Côtes de Bordeaux Cuvée Spéciale 1989: A generous, supple wine, with nicely articulated plum, currant and berry aromas and flavors shaded by a nice hint of oak. The tannins are present, but not overwhelming. Should be at its best after 1994. 2,000 cases made. $13 (1/31/92) **86**

CHATEAU DE PRIEURE
Premières Côtes de Bordeaux 1985 $4.50 (5/31/88) **71**

CHATEAU ROC DE CAMBES
Côtes de Bourg 1991: Rather strange, with a slightly cooked, raisiny character and tar aromas and flavors, but it shows decent structure. (NR) (5/15/92) (BT) **75+**
Côtes de Bourg 1990: A big, ripe wine, with smoky coffee flavors and full tannins. Strong and muscular. (NR) (5/15/92) (BT) **90+**

CHATEAU ST.-ANDRE-CORBIN
1990: Slightly one-dimensional, showing attractive grape and ripe tomato characteristics and medium tannins. (NR) (5/15/92) (BT) **80+**

CHATEAU SAUVAGE
Premières Côtes de Bordeaux 1986: Delicious fruit overlaid with just the right touch of oak, characterizes this firm-textured, lean and finely focused wine. Drink now or by 1993. $9 (4/15/90) **81**

CHATEAU SEGONZAC
Premières Côtes de Blaye 1986: Fine for its style. Clean and light, with tart cherry and plum flavors, medium body and a crisp finish. $9 (6/30/89) **79**
Premières Côtes de Blaye 1985 $9 (2/15/88) **85**

CHATEAU SIAURAC
Lalande-de-Pomerol 1990: A little rustic, but shows lots of character, with a good concentration of berry and earth flavors and tons of tannins. (NR) (5/15/92) (BT) **85+**
Lalande-de-Pomerol 1989 (NR) (4/30/91) (BT) **80+**
Lalande-de-Pomerol 1988 $20 (6/30/89) (BT) **75+**
Lalande-de-Pomerol 1987 $17 (6/30/89) (BT) **75+**

CHATEAU TAYAC
Côtes de Bourg 1988: Simple and straightforward, with modest currant and vanilla flavors, a solid dose of tannin and enough balance to be drinkable now. $10 (1/31/92) **78**

DOMAINE LA TUQUE BEL-AIR
Côtes de Castillon 1985 $8.50 (9/30/88) **72**

Bordeaux White/*Graves/Pessac-Léognan*

CHATEAU BARET
Pessac-Léognan 1990: Harmonious and elegant, it offers restrained pear and vanilla flavors and bright acidity. Not huge, but it's well structured. (NR) (9/30/91) (BT) **80+**
Pessac-Léognan 1988 $19 (6/30/89) (BT) **80+**
Pessac-Léognan 1987 $15 (6/30/89) (BT) **75+**

CHATEAU LE BONNAT
Graves 1988: Has smoky aromas and sweet vanilla flavors from oak aging, but the fruit flavor remains in the background. Stylish and long-lasting on the finish. One could ask only for more fruit intensity. $17 (3/31/90) **84**

CHATEAU BOUSCAUT
Pessac-Léognan 1990: A simple wine for a pleasant aperitif on a summer's evening. Light and clean, with crisp apple flavors and a fresh, lemony finish. (NR) (9/30/91) (BT) **80+**
Pessac-Léognan 1989: Intense vanilla and coconut aromas and rich but somewhat flabby flavors suggest overripe grapes; the wine is oily and rich, with earthy, poached pear flavors. $17 (9/30/91) **79**
Pessac-Léognan 1988 $15 (6/30/89) (BT) **80+**
Pessac-Léognan 1987 $13 (6/30/89) (BT) **85+**

CHATEAU CARBONNIEUX
Pessac-Léognan 1990: Much better than the 1989, with delicate vanilla and lemony, floral aromas and bright fruit flavors, crisp acidity and good intensity. Cur: $18 (9/30/91) (BT) **85+**
Pessac-Léognan 1989: Ripe and balanced, with pretty herb, pear, oak and fig flavors that are round and smooth. The finish is short. Drink now. $22 (2/28/91) **81**
Pessac-Léognan 1988 $20 (6/30/89) (BT) **80+**
Pessac-Léognan 1987 $15 (6/30/89) (BT) **80+**
Graves 1985 Rel: $13 Cur: $19 (3/31/87) **81**
Graves 1982 Rel: $11 Cur: $26 (2/15/84) **81**

CHATEAU DE CHANTEGRIVE
Graves Cuvée Caroline 1990: This château's new-oak selection offers rich butter and coconut aromas and full-bodied, earthy pear and toasty flavors. The wood isn't excessive, and the Sauvignon character comes out. (NR) (9/30/91) (BT) **85+**
Graves Cuvée Caroline 1989: This reserve wine sees some new wood, which adds a touch of vanilla to the pleasant pear and apple flavors. $12 (9/30/91) **83**

CHATEAU CHERCHY
Graves 1986 $6.50 (5/31/88) **77**
Graves 1985 $5 (6/30/87) BB **80**

DOMAINE DE CHEVALIER
Pessac-Léognan 1990: A very pretty wine, with finesse and elegance. Toasty oak and earthy aromas lead to a silky palate of sweet vanilla, coconut and lemon cream flavors. (NR) (9/30/91) (BT) **90+**
Pessac-Léognan 1989: Graceful and even delicate, a sign of deft winemaking in this very ripe harvest. The wine's lemon and vanilla aromas marry nicely, and the oak and fruit elements are in perfect balance. Rel: $60 Cur: $93 (9/30/91) **90**
Pessac-Léognan 1988 Cur: $62 (6/30/89) (BT) **90+**
Pessac-Léognan 1987 $49 (6/30/89) (BT) **95+**
Graves 1985 $99 (5/15/87) (BT) **90+**
Graves 1983 Rel: $65 Cur: $96 (11/15/87) **86**

CHATEAU COUCHEROY
Pessac-Léognan 1990: Crisp and clean, with ripe pear, fig and honey flavors that finish with a touch of walnut. Drink now. $8 (3/31/92) BB **81**

CHATEAU COUHINS-LURTON
Pessac-Léognan 1990: Lovely butter and vanilla flavors from barrel fermentation combine with rich, earthy pear flavors in a balanced and concentrated wine. Should age well. (NR) (9/30/91) (BT) **90+**
Pessac-Léognan 1989: Razor-edged acidity and good depth make this a wine for the dinner table. The earthy apple aromas are intense; the lemon and kiwi flavors promise to develop well with a year or two in the bottle. From André Lurton. $25 (9/30/91) **88**
Pessac-Léognan 1988: Has more intensity and richness than many white Bordeaux, showing distinct grapefruit and herbal aromas and flavors, full body and a long, silky finish. Pleasant and solid, but needs cellaring. Try now through 1994. $28 (5/31/90) **83**
Pessac-Léognan 1987 $25 (6/30/89) (BT) **90+**
Pessac-Léognan 1986 $22 (8/31/88) **88**
Graves 1983 $12 (7/16/86) **74**

CHATEAU DE CRUZEAU
Pessac-Léognan 1990: Clean and floral, with grassy herb, grapefruit and spice flavors that are refreshing and lively. Drinks well now. 5,000 cases made. $14 (3/31/92) **83**
Pessac-Léognan 1989: An intense, ripe, unusual white Bordeaux that really stands out in a crowd. Very fresh, fruity, concentrated and delicious, with peachy, honeyed, almost sweet flavors that linger a long time on the finish. 2,000 cases made. $16 (6/15/91) **90**
Pessac-Léognan 1988: Light and lively, with crisp grapefruit aromas and flavors scented with a touch of toasty vanilla oak, silky and smooth on the finish. Drinkable now. $13 (5/31/90) **82**
Pessac-Léognan 1987 $9 (7/31/89) **82**
Pessac-Léognan 1986 $8 (4/30/88) **82**

CHATEAU DOMS
Graves 1985 $7 (4/30/87) **70**

FRANCE

Bordeaux White/*Graves*/*Pessac-Léognan*

CHATEAU DE FIEUZAL
Pessac-Léognan 1990: Quite closed now, but the balance and elegance promise outstanding development. The lemon and herbal aromas follow through with toasty marmalade flavors. (NR) (9/30/91) (BT) **90+**
Pessac-Léognan 1988 $45 (6/30/89) (BT) **95+**
Pessac-Léognan 1987 $40 (6/30/89) (BT) **90+**
Graves 1985 $39 (11/15/87) **90**

CHATEAU LA GARDE
Pessac-Léognan 1988 $15 (6/30/89) (BT) **85+**
Pessac-Léognan 1987 $13 (6/30/89) (BT) **80+**

CHATEAU DU GRAND-ABORD
Graves 1984 $4 (6/01/86) **57**

CHATEAU GRAVILLE-LACOSTE
Graves Dry 1990: Nutty, foxy and lemony aromas persist through the finish, echoing sour lemon candy flavors on the finish. A stylish wine, with flavors not everyone will warm up to. Drinkable now. $13 (9/15/91) **75**

CHATEAU HAUT-BRION
Pessac-Léognan 1990: This wine aims for elegance rather than power, with a lively, lemony aroma and fresh, pleasantly sharp fruit flavors just softened by toasty oak and lots of finesse. (NR) (9/30/91) (BT) **90+**
Pessac-Léognan 1989: Very fresh and long, it makes you want to take another sip. This balanced, elegant wine offers round, buttery aromas and enticing flavors of peaches, apricots and oranges. $90 (9/30/91) **94**
Pessac-Léognan 1988: Firm and tight, with lemony flavors, lively acidity, and spicy oak aromas. Start drinking now. $84 (12/15/90) **87**
Pessac-Léognan 1987 Rel: $70 Cur: $75 (1/31/90) **78**
Graves 1985 Rel: $81 Cur: $105 (11/15/87) **79**

CHATEAU LARRIVET-HAUT-BRION
Pessac-Léognan 1990: Subtle, complex aromas of apples, lemons, earth and vanilla don't quite carry through on the light palate, but the structure and balance are good. (NR) (9/30/91) (BT) **85+**
Pessac-Léognan 1989: A creamy texture and round vanilla flavors over lemony acidity make it taste like lemon meringue pie; it's intense but could be from anywhere. ($NA) (9/30/91) **82**
Pessac-Léognan 1987 (NR) (7/15/88) (BT) **80+**

CHATEAU LAVILLE-HAUT-BRION
Pessac-Léognan 1990: A rich, round wine, with the concentration typical of this château. The nose is dominated by oak now, with aromas of vanilla and butter; it's full-bodied and soft on the palate, with melon, pear and earth flavors. (NR) (9/30/91) (BT) **90+**
Pessac-Léognan 1989: The vivid, exotic coconut and orange aromas are entrancing. The vanilla and pear flavors carry through to the finish in this fresh, clean wine. Rel: $70 Cur: $109 (9/30/91) **94**
Pessac-Léognan 1988: Has appealing aromas of fruit and wood, but the oaky flavors dominate the citrus, fig and pear notes. It's balanced, with good length. Drink up now. $64 (12/15/90) **85**
Pessac-Léognan 1987 $50 (11/15/91) (JS) **93**
Graves 1985 $66 (11/15/91) (JS) **95**
Graves 1983 Rel: $57 Cur: $72 (11/15/91) (JS) **89**
Graves 1982 $99 (11/15/91) (JS) **83**
Graves 1981 $87 (11/15/91) (JS) **83**
Graves 1980 $61 (11/15/91) (JS) **65**
Graves 1979 $56 (11/15/91) (JS) **87**
Graves 1975 $130 (11/15/91) (JS) **89**
Graves 1972 $90 (11/15/91) (JS) **86**
Graves 1971 $151 (11/15/91) (JS) **91**
Graves 1970 $137 (11/15/91) (JS) **88**
Graves 1969 $125 (11/15/91) (JS) **86**
Graves 1968 $80 (11/15/91) (JS) **78**
Graves 1967 $135 (11/15/91) (JS) **90**
Graves 1966 $135 (11/15/91) (JS) **73**
Graves 1965 $70 (11/15/91) (JS) **78**
Graves 1962 $135 (11/15/91) (JS) **89**
Graves 1961 $230 (11/15/91) (JS) **77**
Graves 1960 $125 (11/15/91) (JS) **50**
Graves 1959 $300 (11/15/91) (JS) **96**
Graves 1958 $190 (11/15/91) (JS) **85**
Graves 1957 $125 (11/15/91) (JS) **83**
Graves 1955 $300 (11/15/91) (JS) **65**
Graves 1954 $240 (11/15/91) (JS) **78**
Graves 1953 $380 (11/15/91) (JS) **69**
Graves 1952 $250 (11/15/91) (JS) **84**
Graves 1950 $350 (11/15/91) (JS) **92**
Graves 1949 $350 (11/15/91) (JS) **99**
Graves 1948 $300 (11/15/91) (JS) **94**
Graves 1947 $300 (11/15/91) (JS) **95**
Graves 1946 $200 (11/15/91) (JS) **84**
Graves 1945 $580 (11/15/91) (JS) **98**
Graves 1943 $280 (11/15/91) (JS) **87**
Graves 1942 $250 (11/15/91) (JS) **85**
Graves 1941 $175 (11/15/91) (JS) **78**
Graves 1940 $175 (11/15/91) (JS) **83**
Graves 1939 $330 (11/15/91) (JS) **84**
Graves 1938 $200 (11/15/91) (JS) **77**
Graves 1936 $200 (11/15/91) (JS) **80**
Graves 1935 $200 (11/15/91) (JS) **79**
Graves 1934 $300 (11/15/91) (JS) **87**
Graves 1933 $200 (11/15/91) (JS) **76**
Graves 1929 $750 (11/15/91) (JS) **94**
Graves 1928 $500 (11/15/91) (JS) **83**
Graves Crême de Tête 1964 $200 (11/15/91) (JS) **93**

CHATEAU LA LOUVIERE
Pessac-Léognan 1990: Broad, rich and complex, with layers of pear, peach, honey and spice flavors framed by toasty, buttery oak notes. Deep and complex, with a long, full finish. Drinks well now, but can be cellared through 1995. $25 (3/31/92) **89**
Pessac-Léognan 1989: Intense fruit flavors give this wine focus and life, and the wood doesn't get in the way. There are grassy gooseberry aromas and earth and pear flavors, with a touch of honey. $30 (9/30/91) **87**
Pessac-Léognan 1988: Lean and silky, with delicate grapefruit, almond and mineral flavors that are pleasant, focused and lingering on the finish. Drinkable now. Rel: $15 Cur: $22 (5/31/90) **83**
Pessac-Léognan 1987: Shows real style. A buttery white Graves with spicy touches from oak aging, clean but light fruit flavors and a pleasantly dry finish. Good for current drinking. $15 (7/31/89) **85**
Pessac-Léognan 1986 $20 (8/31/88) **87**
Graves 1983 $9.75 (9/16/85) **88**

CHATEAU MALARTIC-LAGRAVIERE
Pessac-Léognan 1988: Extremely buttery and spicy, with the effects of oak aging overpowering the modest intensity of fruit. An exaggerated style that almost seems candied; not for all tastes. Tasted twice with consistent notes. $31 (7/31/91) **79**
Pessac-Léognan 1987 $30 (6/30/89) (BT) **90+**
Graves 1985 $23 (11/15/87) **84**

CHATEAU DU MAYNE
Graves 1983 $6 (9/16/85) **78**

CHATEAU LE MERLE
Graves 1984 $6 (12/01/85) **74**

CHATEAU OLIVIER
Pessac-Léognan 1990: Intense, almost aggressive, this wine offers the earthy, grassy aromas characteristic of Sauvignon Blanc. Crisp acidity and tannins give definition to ripe fruit and brighten apple and kiwi flavors. (NR) (9/30/91) (BT) **80+**
Pessac-Léognan 1989: A simple, straightforward dry white, with candied flavors and hints of grapefruit and apple. Picks up caramel and vanilla notes on the finish. Drinkable now. Tasted twice. $19 (5/15/92) **79**
Pessac-Léognan 1988: An overtly earthy wine, with appley, earthy aromas, a tart, astringent texture and chalky, gamy flavors. Not for everyone, but it stays within bounds for a white Pessac-Léognan. $23 (3/31/91) **82**
Pessac-Léognan 1987 Rel: $20 Cur: $25 (6/30/89) (BT) **75+**
Pessac-Léognan 1986 Rel: $16 Cur: $19 (3/31/89) **88**
Graves 1984 $15 (3/31/87) **73**

CHATEAU PIRON
Graves 1984 $7.50 (7/16/86) **80**
Graves 1983 $6.50 (5/16/85) **73**
Graves 1982 $6.75 (3/01/84) **71**

LES PLANTIERS DU HAUT-BRION
Graves 1974: Where has this been since 1974? In oak? It's very woody and deep golden in color, but it's also rich and honeyed, with some pineapple fruit and good length. A curiosity, but it's sound. $24 (3/31/89) **80**

CHATEAU R
Graves Dry 1983 $6 (2/01/85) **78**

CHATEAU RAHOUL
Graves 1988: Dominated by spicy, buttery accents of oak aging, with modest pear and grapefruit flavors underneath. Tight with acidity, it should be best to drink now through 1993. $20 (3/31/91) **84**

CHATEAU RESPIDE-MEDEVILLE
Graves 1984 $7.50 (7/16/86) **84**

CHATEAU DE ROCHEMORIN
Pessac-Léognan 1990: A tart, earthy wine, with lots of grapefruit aromas turning toasty and mulchlike on the palate. Has lots of intensity, but the flavor profile will not appeal to everyone. Drink after 1993. 4,000 cases made. $16 (5/15/92) **80**
Pessac-Léognan 1989: A very attractive, stylish white Bordeaux. Full-flavored, concentrated and intense, with smooth, rich lemon, pear, herb and mineral flavors overlain with toasty, oaky aromas. 2,000 cases made. $17 (6/15/91) **90**
Pessac-Léognan 1988: Lean in texture but showing plenty of peach and vanilla flavors, plus enough restraint to qualify as delicate. Drink soon. $15 (5/31/90) **82**
Pessac-Léognan 1987 $9 (7/31/89) **80**
Pessac-Léognan 1986 $10 (8/31/88) **86**

CHATEAU LE SARTRE
Pessac-Léognan 1990: It's a little clumsy now, but the grassy, earthy aromas have good varietal character, and the earth and pear flavors have concentration. (NR) (9/30/91) (BT) **80+**
Pessac-Léognan 1989: Delicious, elegant white Bordeaux. Cleanly made, smooth and fruity, full of fig, almond, pineapple and melon flavors. Crisp and fruity on the finish. $13.50 (3/31/91) **88**
Pessac-Léognan 1988 $12 (6/30/89) (BT) **80+**

CHATEAU SMITH-HAUT-LAFITTE
Pessac-Léognan 1990: Lacks the power of the 1989. The clean, grassy aromas lead to crisp, fresh apple and herbal flavors; it's a well-knit, refreshing wine. (NR) (9/30/91) (BT) **80+**
Pessac-Léognan 1989: Rich fruit gets an added dimension from toasty oak. Full aromas of vanilla, butter and melon give way to toast, orange and slightly minty flavors, backed by good acidity. $30 (9/30/91) **88**
Pessac-Léognan 1988 $30 (6/30/89) (BT) **80+**
Pessac-Léognan 1987 $17 (6/30/89) (BT) **85+**

CHATEAU LA TOUR-LEOGNAN
Pessac-Léognan 1990: Rich and round, with smooth texture and appealing buttery, figgy aromas and flavors that persist into a polished and elegant finish. A graceful wine that kicks in with a touch of honey and vanilla on the finish. $19 (6/30/92) **86**
Pessac-Léognan 1988 ($NA) (6/30/89) (BT) **80+**

CHATEAU LA TOUR-MARTILLAC
Pessac-Léognan 1989: Well-focused herb, fig, melon and weedy notes in a complex but simple style. Should go down easy in the next year. 2,500 cases made. $28 (2/28/91) **86**
Pessac-Léognan 1987: One of the best Bordeaux whites we've tasted in a while, deliciously rich and complex with tiers of citric, earth, stone and fig flavors that are intense and lively. The finish goes on and on. Definitive style. Drink now through 1995. 3,500 cases made. $15 (1/31/90) **93**

CHATEAU LA TOUR-MARTILLAC
Pessac-Léognan 1990: Well defined, with good intensity and pretty aromas of vanilla and ripe fruit, with orange, pineapple and toast flavors; it's concentrated and lively. (NR) (9/30/91) (BT) **90+**

Other Bordeaux White

ALPHA
Bordeaux 1990: An experiment from three notable red-wine producers, Michel Rolland, Alain Raymond and Jean-Michel Arcaute. The aromas promise a chocolate milkshake, while the flavors are

Key to Symbols

The scores reported here are the results of blind tastings conducted by our panel of senior editors. Wines that carry the initials below are results of individual tastings.

THE WINE SPECTATOR 100-POINT SCALE 95-100—Classic, a great wine; ***90-94***—Outstanding, superior character and style; ***80-89***—Good to very good, a wine with special qualities; ***70-79***—Average, drinkable wine that may have minor flaws; ***60-69***—Below average, drinkable but not recommended; ***50-59***—Poor, undrinkable, not recommended. "+"—With a score indicates a range; used primarily with barrel tastings to indicate a preliminary score.

SPECIAL DESIGNATIONS SS—Spectator Selection, CS—Cellar Selection, BB—Best Buy, ($NA)—Price not available, (NR)—Not released.

TASTER'S INITIALS (JG)—Jim Gordon, (HS)—Harvey Steiman, (JL)—James Laube, (JS)—James Suckling, (TM)—Thomas Matthews, (TR)—Terry Robards, (PM)—Per-Henrik Mansson, (BT)—Barrel Tasting (these wines were tasted blind from barrel samples), (CA-date)—*California's Great Cabernets* by James Laube, (CH-date)—*California's Great Chardonnays* by James Laube, (VP-date)—*Vintage Port* by James Suckling.

DATE TASTED Dates in parentheses represent the issue in which the rating was published.

all butter and earth; the fruit gets lost in the wood. Will it come into balance? (NR) (9/30/91) (BT) **75+**
Bordeaux 1989: Earthy and oily, with ripe, rich, broad pear, spice and citrus notes in a round, smooth, complex style. Weakens a bit on the finish. Drink now. 5,000 cases made. $16 (2/28/91) **84**

AUGEY
Bordeaux 1984 $4.50 (10/15/86) **75**

CHATEAU BALLUE-MONDON
Bordeaux Sauvignon Blanc Sec 1988: A very simple white wine with straightforward floral and herbal flavors but little concentration or length. $8 (3/31/90) **71**

BARTON & GUESTIER
Bordeaux Blanc Fondation 1725 1990: Soft and fresh, with pleasant pear and spice aromas and flavors shaded by herb notes. Drinkable now. Better than when reviewed earlier. $9 (9/15/91) **81**
Bordeaux Sauvignon Blanc 1988: Has Sauvignon character in spades, from the pungently grassy aromas to its straightforward sweet-pea flavors. The balance is good but the flavors are one-dimensional. $6 (3/31/90) **78**

BEAU MAYNE
Bordeaux 1985 $5 (4/30/87) **80**

CHATEAU BERGEY
Entre-Deux-Mers 1990: A crisp, correct white Bordeaux, with modest melon, lemon and mineral flavors. Fresh and lively. $6 (11/15/91) BB **82**

CHATEAU BONNET
Entre-Deux-Mers 1990: Fresh and fruity, with lots of citrus, fig and melon aromas and flavors and hints of herbs on the finish. A broad, generous white Bordeaux, with a light touch. Drinkable now. From André Lurton. $9 (7/31/91) BB **85**
Entre-Deux-Mers Oak Aged 1989: Always reliable, Bonnet takes a step forward in quality with this wood-fermented bottling. Pear and apple aromas mingle with the grassiness of Sauvignon Blanc in this lively wine. $13 (9/30/91) **85**
Entre-Deux-Mers 1988: Fresh, light and refreshing, a white Bordeaux with pleasing almond and orange blossom aromas and a soft finish with a touch of peach. Drink soon. $7 (5/31/90) BB **80**
Entre-Deux-Mers 1987 $6 (8/31/88) **79**
Entre-Deux-Mers 1986 $4.50 (4/30/88) **79**

LA CAVE TROISGROS
Bordeaux Blanc 1990: Grassy, grapefruity flavors dominate this soft white Bordeaux that has flavor, but is almost too vegetal to really enjoy. $9 (6/15/91) **75**

CHATEAU CHEVAL BLANC
Bordeaux 1989: Floral, perfumed aromas and flavors seem a bit stale in the context of this stolid, firm-textured wine. $5 (7/31/91) **76**

CHEVALIER VEDRINES
Bordeaux Sauvignon Blanc 1986 $6 (5/31/88) **77**

CHATEAU COTES DES CHARIS
Bordeaux Sauvignon Blanc Sec 1990: Grassy and grapefruity at first, but it turns stale and earthy on the finish. $10 (6/15/91) **70**

LA COUR PAVILLON
Bordeaux Sec 1989: With pleasant almond and floral-scented pear flavors, this is light, simple and drinkable now. $7.25 (3/31/91) **78**
Bordeaux Sec 1986: Decent quality white wine with hints of fruit and a mature, slightly nutty aftertaste. $7 (3/31/89) **71**
Bordeaux Sec 1984 $7 (7/15/87) **63**

PIERRE DOURTHE
Bordeaux Sémillon 1990: A soft, simple white wine, with grassy, appley flavors. Drinkable, but not much to get excited about. $4 (6/15/91) **75**
Bordeaux 1987 $10 (9/30/88) **83**

CHATEAU DUCLA
Entre-Deux-Mers 1990: Has Sauvignon Blanc character in spades. Offers pungent, powerful sweet pea, onion and grass aromas followed by pear and herb flavors suspended in a smooth texture, with a lingering, fruity finish. A blend of Sauvignon Blanc, Sémillion and 10 percent Muscadelle. 4,000 cases made. $7 (6/15/91) BB **84**
Entre-Deux-Mers 1987 $5 (9/30/88) BB **81**

CHATEAU DE FRANCS
Côtes de Francs 1990: All the components are magnified—intense aromas of earth and pear, bright citrus flavors, with strong, grassy fruit—but they're not totally in harmony. Give it time in the bottle. (NR) (9/30/91) (BT) **80+**

CHATEAU GODARD
Côtes de Francs Les Charmes 1990: A well-made wine without pretensions, it has lively apple, pear and earth flavors and fresh acidity. (NR) (9/30/91) (BT) **80+**

CHATEAU LE GORRE
Bordeaux Blanc Sec 1988: A basic, fruity, pleasant-tasting white wine with fruit cocktail flavors. $9 (3/31/90) **72**

CHATEAU GUIBON
Entre-Deux-Mers 1990: Light, supple and refreshing, this white Bordeaux has pretty grapefruit, almond, pear and floral notes that gain a touch of vanilla on the finish. Drink now. $5.50 (3/31/92) BB **82**

PIERRE JEAN
Bordeaux Blanc de Blancs 1990: A textbook white Bordeaux that's fairly concentrated and round in texture, with melon and almond flavors and a lingering, mineral finish. $7 (6/15/91) BB **81**

CHATEAU LAMOTHE
Bordeaux 1985 $5 (10/15/87) **71**

CHATEAU LARROQUE
Bordeaux Sec 1987: Crisply fruity and medium-bodied. Has grapefruit and apple flavors and good acid balance. $5 (3/31/89) **78**
Bordeaux 1985 $3.75 (10/15/87) BB **79**
Bordeaux 1984 $3.75 (12/15/86) BB **85**

CHATEAU LAUNAY
Bordeaux Blanc Sec 1990: Light and lively, with strong, appealing Bartlett pear and pineapple aromas and flavors that linger gently on the finish. A balanced, smooth wine that should be fun to drink through 1993 to '95. $9 (9/15/91) **84**

CHATEAU LAURETAN
Bordeaux 1986 $5.50 (8/31/88) **78**

ALEXIS LICHINE
Bordeaux Blanc 1986: An earthy, mature style. Has a bit of fruit flavor and nutty, smoky touches. $4.50 (3/31/89) **70**

CHATEAU LOUDENNE
Bordeaux 1986: A clean, simple, innocuous wine with hints of apple in the aroma and a smooth feel in the mouth. $12 (3/31/89) **72**
Bordeaux 1985 $10.50 (7/15/87) **73**

MICHEL LYNCH
Bordeaux 1990: An engaging, herb-scented white wine, with grapefruit and melon flavors and a lingering, fruity finish. A cut above average. $8 (10/15/91) BB **85**
Bordeaux 1986 $6 (10/15/87) **77**

BLANC DE LYNCH-BAGES
Bordeaux 1990: A new white wine from the famous Pauillac estate. Flavorful, soft and generous, with herbal, earthy aromas turning toward spice and vanilla on the palate. Plush and strongly oak-accented, with solid pear and cream flavors at the center. Should improve through 1994 or '95. 2,400 cases made. $29 (5/15/92) **92**

MAITRE D'ESTOURNEL
Bordeaux 1987 $7 (8/31/88) BB **83**
Bordeaux 1985 $5 (12/31/86) BB **84**

M. DE MALLE
Bordeaux 1983 $6.25 (7/01/86) **54**

CHATEAU MAROTTE
Bordeaux 1986 $3.50 (3/31/88) **73**

YVON MAU
Bordeaux Officiel du Bicentenaire de la Revolution Française 1988: A white wine that is very floral and fruity in aroma, but it tastes simple and straightforward, with subdued grassy, lemony flavors. $4.50 (7/31/89) **77**

A. MOUEIX
Bordeaux 1984 $2.50 (4/16/86) BB **86**

MOUTON-CADET
Bordeaux Blanc 1987: Simple and watery in character. Has a touch of stony, earthy flavor, but not much else. $7.25 (7/31/89) **70**
Bordeaux 1986 $5.50 (5/31/88) **75**

CHATEAU NICOT
Haut-Benauge 1984 $4 (11/16/85) **69**

PAVILLON BLANC DU CHATEAU MARGAUX
Bordeaux 1983 $93 (7/15/87) (HS) **86**
Bordeaux 1979 $49 (7/15/87) (HS) **91**
Bordeaux 1978 $50 (7/15/87) (HS) **80**
Bordeaux 1961 $65 (7/15/87) (HS) **84**
Bordeaux 1928 $300 (7/15/87) (HS) **86**
Bordeaux 1926 $300 (7/15/87) (HS) **92**

CHATEAU LE REY
Bordeaux 1986 $4 (9/30/88) **76**

CHATEAU REYNIER
Entre-Deux-Mers 1984 $3.25 (12/16/85) **62**

ST.-JOVIAN
Bordeaux Premium 1990: A touch of almond and vanilla from oak aging gives this soft white wine a bit more interest than the simple apple and floral flavors warrant by themselves. $5.50 (6/15/91) **76**

SIRIUS
Bordeaux 1988: An earthy, herbal wine, with strong onion and garlic overtones up front, turning smooth and buttery on the finish. Unusual, but pleasant to drink. $15 (9/15/91) **79**
Bordeaux Sauvignon Blanc 1987 $4 (8/31/88) **69**

CHATEAU TALBOT
Bordeaux 1985 $9 (4/30/87) **75**

CHATEAU TAREY DU CASTEL
Bordeaux NV $3.25 (5/31/88) **77**

CHATEAU THIEULEY
Bordeaux 1985 $4 (5/31/88) **78**

LE SEC DE LA TOUR-BLANCHE
Bordeaux Sauvignon 1989: Light and earthy, with almond and toast accents, but it's basically a simple white wine. Drinkable now. $9 (3/31/91) **78**

VALMAISON
Bordeaux 1986 $4 (11/15/87) BB **78**

BURGUNDY RED/*CÔTE DE BEAUNE*/ALOXE-CORTON

BERTRAND AMBROISE
Corton Le Rognet 1989: A supercharged Corton, with the deep color and richness of Syrah. Very closed in now, with ultraripe fruit flavors and velvety tannins. Try in 1996 to see how it's developing. $45 (1/31/92) **93**
Corton Le Rognet 1988: Rich, thick and plummy, with a firm texture and spicy, supple but firm tannins. This is a well-proportioned wine that gains amplitude, depth and complexity on the finish. A good candidate for cellaring until 1995 to 2000. $43 (11/30/90) **92**
Corton Le Rognet 1987: Young and intense, with sharply focused cherry, spice, leather and oak flavors that fan out on the palate, leaving a broad array of flavors that linger on the finish. Too young to drink now; it has the power and depth for a decade of drinking. Start in 1993. $38 (3/31/90) **90**

PIERRE ANDRE
Corton Clos du Roi 1985 $45 (7/15/88) **88**
Corton Pougets 1985 $45 (7/15/88) **90**

DR. BAROLET
Aloxe-Corton Villamont 1952 $75 (8/31/90) **92**

ADRIEN BELLAND
Corton Grèves 1982 $16.50 (9/01/85) **87**

BICHOT
Aloxe-Corton 1983 $18 (11/30/86) **68**
Corton Hospices de Beaune Cuvée Docteur-Peste 1989: Ripe, plummy and full-bodied, with firm tannins, good intensity of flavor and stewed plum, dark cherry and anise flavors lingering on the finish. Probably best from 1993 to '96. $100 (1/31/92) **88**

PIERRE BITOUZET
Aloxe-Corton Valozières 1986: Earthy cherry and spice aromas and flavors, which turn a bit austere and astringent on the finish, make this a lean and distinctive syle. Drink now. Tasted twice. $19 (8/31/90) **78**

BONNEAU DU MARTRAY
Corton 1985 $62 (10/15/88) **91**

BOUCHARD PERE & FILS
Aloxe-Corton 1989: Solid, with lots of earthy plum and strawberry aromas and flavors, a velvety mouth-feel and a very good tannin structure. Try in 1994. $36 (1/31/92) **87**
Corton Le Corton Domaines du Château de Beaune 1989: Multidimensional, with violet and

smoke characteristics that keep changing in the glass. Has plenty of backbone to hold it together. Try in 1995. $79 (1/31/92) **92**
Corton Le Corton Domaines du Château de Beaune 1988: Dense, tannic and chewy, packed with ripe cherry, chocolate, toast and vanilla flavors. This big, full-blown, powerful style needs cellaring until 1995 or '96 to mellow, but by then the texture should be silky smooth. Very complete. 1,400 cases made. $77 (3/31/91) **91**
Corton Le Corton Domaines du Château de Beaune 1986 $47 (7/31/88) **85**
Corton Le Corton Domaines du Château de Beaune 1983 $37 (9/15/86) **83**

CAPTAIN-GAGNEROT
Corton Les Renardes 1985 $70 (12/31/88) **92**

JEANNE-MARIE DE CHAMPS
Corton Hospices de Beaune Cuvée Charlotte-Dumay 1985 $76 (10/15/88) **87**

DOMAINE CHANDON DE BRIAILLES
Aloxe-Corton 1983 $25 (9/15/86) **84**
Corton Bressandes 1988: Generous and supple up front before the tannins kick in. The plum, cherry, spice and cedar flavors are concentrated and very rich, finishing with good length. Drink in 1995 and beyond. $75 (2/28/91) **89**
Corton Bressandes 1986: Has plenty of cherry, spice and berry flavors, but it's also quite tannic and firmly structured with a touch of stemminess on the finish. As such, it should be a bit softer and more complex in two to five years. Drink now through 1995. $43 (2/28/90) **88**
Corton Clos du Roi 1986: Big and chewy, firmly tannic and toasty with ample berry and cherry flavor that's a bit coarse and powerful now. Drink now through 1996. $47 (2/28/90) **85**

CHANSON PERE & FILS
Corton 1986: Don't let the light color fool you; this is rich and generous beyond what you would expect from this vintage. It's smoky, chocolaty and succulent in flavor. Very well made, it's a good candidate to develop in the cellar through the mid-1990s. One of the better values among Grand Cru 1986s. $30 (4/30/89) **90**

F. CHAUVENET
Corton 1989: Splendid, with lovely toasted raspberry and cherry flavors and velvety tannins. A joy to taste. Try in 1995. $50 (1/31/92) **93**
Corton 1986 $50 (7/31/88) **87**
Corton 1985 $53 (7/31/87) **96**
Corton Bressandes 1988 $58 (7/15/90) (BT) **90+**
Corton Hospices de Beaune Docteur-Peste 1985 $133 (7/15/88) **97**

CHEVALIER PERE & FILS
Aloxe-Corton 1983 $19 (9/15/86) **85**

DOMAINE DU CLOS FRANTIN
Corton 1989: Extremely closed in, with earthy strawberry flavors, firm acidity and full tannins. From Bichot. Try in 1994. (NR) (1/31/92) **86**
Corton 1988 $52 (7/15/90) (BT) **75+**

EDMOND CORNU
Aloxe-Corton Les Moutottes 1987: Earthy and gamy, with a lean, silky texture and spicy, gamy aromas and flavors that shoulder past the cherry notes. Light and polished enough to drink now, but it's not for everyone's taste. $35 (12/31/90) **83**
Corton Les Bressandes 1987: Toasty, spicy and deep, with sharply focused flavors including a solid core of cherry, layered with earthiness and spices through the long finish. Remarkably full and rich for the vintage. Should develop well through 1994 or '95. 225 cases made. $53 (12/31/90) **90**

DOUDET-NAUDIN
Corton Renardes 1945 ($NA) (8/31/90) **86**

JOSEPH DROUHIN
Aloxe-Corton 1989: A pretty wine, with layers of ripe cherry, berry and earth aromas and flavors and a good tannin structure. Try in 1994. $27 (1/31/92) **89**
Aloxe-Corton 1988 $37 (7/15/90) (BT) **75+**
Aloxe-Corton 1986: Nicely ripe and generous, it's seductive and spicy in aroma, then turns leaner on the palate, where this moderately tannic wine tastes clean, smooth and almost sweet with fruit. $25 (4/30/89) **83**
Aloxe-Corton 1985 $23 (11/15/87) **90**
Corton 1988 $64 (7/15/90) (BT) **85+**
Corton 1985 $48 (11/15/87) **92**
Corton Bressandes 1988: Wonderfully harmonious, with smooth, elegant plum, cassis, cherry, vanilla and toasty flavors that are rich and deep, finishing with a subtle burst of flavor. The tannins sneak in on the finish to support all the fruit. Drink in 1995 to 2005. $60 (11/15/90) **92**
Corton Bressandes 1986: Very hard and tannic, with just enough cherryish flavor peeking through to make it worth cellaring at least through 1992 to see what develops. Silky texture and excellent length are just covered with tannin now. $45 (4/30/89) **90**

DUBREUIL-FONTAINE
Aloxe-Corton 1988 (NR) (7/15/90) (BT) **75+**
Corton Bressandes 1989 (NR) (7/15/90) (BT) **85+**
Corton Bressandes 1985: Not as big or focused as other '85 Cortons, this one is medium-bodied, fairly rich in flavor, but overall it seems muted. There are some generous cherry and plum flavors that are fairly subtle on the finish. Drink now through 1995. $50 (1/31/89) **86**
Corton Bressandes 1982 $24 (10/16/85) **85**
Corton Clos du Roi 1989: A well-crafted wine, packed with cherry and strawberry aromas and flavors, lovely hints of oak and very round tannins. Try in 1995. (NR) (1/31/92) **92**
Corton Clos du Roi 1987: Lots of earthy, gamy and spicy flavors make this distinctive, and it has enough tannin to require aging through 1994 to polish the texture. Not for every taste, but well made in an earthy style. Rel: $34 Cur: $55 (12/31/90) **85**
Corton Clos du Roi 1985 Rel: $49 Cur: $63 (7/15/88) **90**
Corton Clos du Roi 1982 $25 (9/16/85) **86**

Key to Symbols

The scores reported here are the results of blind tastings conducted by our panel of senior editors. Wines that carry the initials below are results of individual tastings.

THE WINE SPECTATOR 100-POINT SCALE 95-100—Classic, a great wine; ***90-94***—Outstanding, superior character and style; ***80-89***—Good to very good, a wine with special qualities; ***70-79***—Average, drinkable wine that may have minor flaws; ***60-69***—Below average, drinkable but not recommended; ***50-59***—Poor, undrinkable, not recommended. "+"—With a score indicates a range; used primarily with barrel tastings to indicate a preliminary score.

SPECIAL DESIGNATIONS SS—Spectator Selection, CS—Cellar Selection, BB—Best Buy, ($NA)—Price not available, (NR)—Not released.

TASTER'S INITIALS (JG)—Jim Gordon, (HS)—Harvey Steiman, (JL)—James Laube, (JS)—James Suckling, (TM)—Thomas Matthews, (TR)—Terry Robards, (PM)—Per-Henrik Mansson, (BT)—Barrel Tasting (these wines were tasted blind from barrel samples), (CA-date)—*California's Great Cabernets* by James Laube, (CH-date)—*California's Great Chardonnays* by James Laube, (VP-date)—*Vintage Port* by James Suckling.

DATE TASTED Dates in parentheses represent the issue in which the rating was published.

FAIVELEY
Corton Clos des Cortons 1989: Muscular, with a solid tannin and fruit structure, yet it shows very succulent fruit on the finish. Try in 1995. Rel: $68 Cur: $74 (1/31/92) **91**
Corton Clos des Cortons 1988: Elegant and lively, with fresh, ripe cherry and raspberry flavors, spicy oak notes and crisp acidity. The fine, supple tannins are in check and the finish is long and lingering. Deceptively rich on the aftertaste. Cellar until 1995. $120 (3/31/91) **90**
Corton Clos des Cortons 1987: Rich, meaty flavors are tight and complex, needing time to develop. Has accents of ripe cherry, currant and spicy oak that are well defined, with firm tannins on the aftertaste. Drink now to 1994. $50 (3/31/90) **92**
Corton Clos des Cortons 1985 $80 (3/15/88) **79**

MARIE-PIERRE GERMAIN
Aloxe-Corton Les Vercots 1989: This attractive wine has ripe fruit character and well-integrated tannins. Very supple. Try in 1993. (NR) (1/31/92) **88**

MACHARD DE GRAMONT
Aloxe-Corton Les Morais 1985 $34 (7/15/88) **80**

LOUIS JADOT
Corton Pougets 1989: A monster wine, packed to the brim with black cherry and vanilla aromas and flavors and full, round tannins. Built for long-term aging; try in 1995. $64 (1/31/92) **93**
Corton Pougets 1988: Deep, ripe, rich and intense, with beautiful black cherry, currant and strawberry flavors that are sharply focused and well defined, spreading out on the palate and finishing with good length, intensity and complexity. Drink in 1995 to 2000. 550 cases made. $61 (3/31/91) **93**
Corton Pougets 1987: Not the big, rich wine we have come to expect, but it's aromatic, with spicy cherry running through to the zingy finish. Crisp, even a bit tart in texture, a lighter-styled Beaune that should be at its best now to 1994. Rel: $39 Cur: $45 (6/15/90) **87**
Corton Pougets 1986 $42 (4/30/89) **86**
Corton Pougets 1985 $47 (3/15/88) **89**

JAFFELIN
Aloxe-Corton 1989: A wine with plenty of luscious cherry, plum and other fruit flavors and firm tannins; almost steely. Try in 1994. $27 (1/31/92) **89**
Corton 1989: This focused wine has refined cherry and smoke flavors, elegant tannins and a long berry finish. Try in 1994. $54 (1/31/92) **91**
Corton 1986 $45 (12/31/88) **87**
Corton 1983 Rel: $33 Cur: $45 (4/01/86) CS **91**

LOUIS LATOUR
Aloxe-Corton 1955 ($NA) (8/31/90) (**85**
Aloxe-Corton Les Chaillots 1985 $37 (4/15/88) **76**
Aloxe-Corton Domaine Latour 1989: Light and refreshing, with plenty of strawberry and earth aromas and flavors and light tannins. Better in 1992. (NR) (1/31/92) **84**
Corton Château Corton Grancey 1989: Soft and round for a Corton, with lovely chestnut and creamy berry flavors and soft tannins. Delicious. Try in 1993. (NR) (1/31/92) **89**
Corton Château Corton Grancey 1985 Rel: $46 Cur: $60 (3/15/88) **89**
Corton Château Corton Grancey 1959 $130 (8/31/90) **89**
Corton Château Corton Grancey 1953 $195 (8/31/90) **91**
Corton Château Corton Grancey 1947 $96 (8/31/90) **85**
Corton Clos de la Vigne au Saint 1985 $43 (3/15/88) **89**
Corton Domaine Latour 1985 $38 (3/15/88) **90**

OLIVIER LEFLAIVE FRERES
Corton Bressandes 1986 $45 (7/31/88) **88**

DOMAINE LEQUIN-ROUSSOT
Corton Les Languettes 1985 $39 (7/15/88) **86**

DOMAINE LEROY
Corton Renardes 1989: A gorgeous Corton, with great class. Has complex toast, cherry and violet aromas and flavors and ultrafine tannins. Try in 1995. $117 (1/31/92) **95**

LUPE-CHOLET
Aloxe-Corton 1985 $18 (3/15/88) **84**

PROSPER MAUFOUX
Aloxe-Corton 1982: A fully mature, light-colored Burgundy with an amber edge. Shows pleasant tea, nut and vanilla flavors, but not much fruit; past its prime. $27 (6/15/92) **79**

DOMAINE MEO-CAMUZET
Corton 1989: A sizable wine, not huge like most Cortons, but balanced toward oak, especially on the finish. Fruit comes through like gangbusters up front, offering currant and cherry for starters, turning toward plum as the finish kicks in. Should improve through 1995. $76 (11/15/91) **93**
Corton 1986 $50 (10/31/88) **89**

PRINCE FLORENT DE MERODE
Aloxe-Corton 1987: Ripe, rich, smooth and velvety, with pretty anise, cherry, tar and spice flavors that are complex and deep. The flavors keep building, finishing with attractive smoke and spice notes and firm tannins. Best between 1993 to '95. $30 (2/28/91) **87**
Corton Bressandes 1987: Earthy, spicy and elegant, with tiers of pretty cherry, raspberry and strawberry flavors and hints of earth, nutmeg, toast and vanilla all neatly knit together. A beautifully crafted wine that finishes with subtle nuances and grace. Drink in 1994 to 2000. $42 (3/31/91) **92**
Corton Bressandes 1986: Surprisingly light in color and texture, but the round texture and flavors of cherry, spice and toast emerge nicely on the finish. A medium-weight wine with a good future. Drink now through 1994. $38 (8/31/89) **84**
Corton Bressandes 1985 $52 (2/15/88) **93**
Corton Clos du Roi 1987: Heavily oaked, with an array of coffee, vanilla, chocolate and berry notes that are rich and full, with full tannins and plenty of flavor on the aftertaste. Drink now through 1994. $44 (3/31/90) **87**
Corton Clos du Roi 1986: Has lovely berry and strawberry aromas, but the flavors seem buried beneath a layer of smoky astringency, making this a bit of a gamble to cellar. It is not as astringent as many '86s, and could develop into a lovely wine. Drink now through 1994. $49 (8/31/89) **80**
Corton Maréchaudes 1987: Beautifully articulated Pinot Noir aromas and flavors are enhanced by the smooth, elegant structure, harmonious balance and complex finish. Almost drinkable now, but better in 1993. $36 (8/31/90) **88**
Corton Maréchaudes 1986: Tough and astringent, with enough richness of toast and ripe cherry flavors to warrant cellaring to see what develops. It needs until 1992 to '95 to show what it has. It needs to put some meat on its bones. $33 (8/31/89) **82**
Corton Maréchaudes 1985 $49 (3/15/88) **81**
Corton Renardes 1987: An earthy, woody and tannic red Burgundy in a reined-in style, with a beautiful core of rich, supple, concentrated strawberry, cherry and spice flavors. Wonderfully balanced; should age a decade with ease. Begin drinking now. 250 cases made. $36 (3/31/90) **92**
Corton Renardes 1986: Has the power and tannins, but the earthy, barklike aromas and flavors obscure what fruit is apparent. The firm structure is impressive for those who like the style. $38 (8/31/89) **76**

MOILLARD
Aloxe-Corton Les Affouages 1989: Rather astringent, with slightly drying tannins and an earthy strawberry character. Try in 1994. (NR) (1/31/92) **83**
Corton Clos des Vergennes 1989: A beautiful wine, with an elegant structure of black cherry and

chocolate flavors and firm, silky tannins. From Domaine Chachat-Ocquidant & Fils. Better in 1994. $40 (1/31/92) **89**
Corton Clos des Vergennes 1985 $36 (5/31/87) **92**
Corton Clos des Vergennes 1983 $19 (10/01/85) **88**
Corton Clos du Roi 1984 $24 (5/31/87) **87**
Corton Clos du Roi Domaine Thomas-Moillard 1989: Has rather earthy cherry flavors in a one-dimensional package. Slightly astringent on the finish. From the négociants of Moillard. Try in 1995. $41 (1/31/92) **85**

MOMMESSIN
Aloxe-Corton Les Valzoières 1989: Beautiful, with refined chocolate and raspberry flavors and a firm finish. Deep and concentrated. Try in 1994. $28 (1/31/92) **88**
Corton 1985 $28 (2/15/88) **91**
Corton Bressandes 1988 $30 (7/15/90) (BT) **90+**
Corton Les Grèves 1989: Rich, like chocolate mousse, with extremely firm tannins and a rich, smoky finish. Try in 1995. $45 (1/31/92) **91**

GASTON & PIERRE RAVAUT
Aloxe-Corton 1985 $35 (7/31/88) **88**
Corton Hautes-Mourottes 1985 $46 (7/31/88) **92**

TOLLOT-BEAUT
Aloxe-Corton 1989: This sturdy wine has an excellent backbone of fresh fruit and supple tannins. Shows plenty of cedar, violet and earth notes. Try in 1994. (NR) (1/31/92) **90**
Aloxe-Corton 1988 $35 (7/15/90) (BT) **85+**
Aloxe-Corton 1985 $35 (3/15/88) **89**
Corton 1989: Very ripe and succulent, offering vivid blackberry and raspberry flavors and supple tannins. Try in 1994. $67 (1/31/92) **90**
Corton 1988 $55 (7/15/90) (BT) **80+**
Corton 1986: Despite the light color, the rich, smoky aromas and firm-textured, spicy plum flavors are framed by fine tannins, so it comes off as elegant. Has impressive length, but it lacks the power associated with most Cortons. Drink now through 1993. $45 (8/31/89) **87**
Corton 1985 $49 (3/15/88) **97**
Corton Bressandes 1989: Seductive, with luscious violet and wild raspberry flavors and full, silky tannins. Try in 1994. $67 (1/31/92) **92**
Corton Bressandes 1988 $55 (7/15/90) (BT) **90+**

CHARLES VIENOT
Corton Maréchaude 1985 $57 (7/15/88) **84**

BEAUNE

BICHOT
Beaune 1988: Charming strawberry and cherry flavors, with overtones of toast and vanilla, make this wine crisp, zingy and lighter in style. Balanced and already drinkable. $15 (8/31/90) **82**
Beaune Bressandes 1986 $24 (7/31/88) **80**
Beaune Hospices de Beaune Cuvée Guigone-de-Salins 1989: Overpriced, but it's a generous, fruity, ripe-tasting Burgundy, with spicy, buttery accents that keep it interesting. Well balanced and flavorful. Drink now to 1994. $68 (1/31/92) **83**

JEAN-MARC BOILLOT
Beaune Montrevenots 1988: A tight, muscular Beaune, with firm plum, black cherry and currant flavors framed by tight tannins. Has plenty of fruit on the finish, but it will take until 1995 or so before it begins to soften. $37 (5/15/91) **88**

BOUCHARD PERE & FILS
Beaune Clos de la Mousse Domaines du Château de Beaune 1989 $36 (7/15/90) (BT) **85+**
Beaune Clos de la Mousse Domaines du Château de Beaune 1986 $33 (7/31/88) **78**
Beaune Grèves Vigne de l'Enfant Jésus 1989 $59 (7/15/90) (BT) **95+**
Beaune Grèves Vigne de l'Enfant Jésus 1988: This classy wine is firm, deep and concentrated, with a delicious core of black cherry, currant, cedar and toasty earth flavors. Picks up subtle tea, tobacco and spice notes on the long, long finish. Tight now; needs cellaring until 1994 or '95, and then it should last for another five to 10 years. Tasted three times. 1,500 cases made. $59 (4/30/91) **91**
Beaune Grèves Vigne de l'Enfant Jésus 1986 $47 (7/31/88) **82**
Beaune Grèves Vigne de l'Enfant Jésus 1985 $61 (1/31/89) **91**
Beaune Grèves Vigne de l'Enfant Jésus 1983 $30 (9/15/86) **85**
Beaune Marconnets Domaines du Château de Beaune 1989: Has good concentration of berry flavor, with red licorice, cedar and smoke notes and a chewy finish. Try from 1994. $39 (1/31/92) **90**
Beaune Marconnets Domaines du Château de Beaune 1986 $24 (7/31/88) **83**
Beaune Marconnets Domaines du Château de Beaune 1985: Smooth, rich and flavorful, showing focused black cherry and berry flavors with smoky overtones, seemingly richer on the finish than at the start. Drink now. $35 (1/31/89) **89**
Beaune Teurons Domaines du Château de Beaune 1988 $36 (7/15/90) (BT) **70+**
Beaune Teurons Domaines du Château de Beaune 1986 $32 (7/31/88) **81**
Beaune Teurons Domaines du Château de Beaune 1985: Firm and slightly tannic, with ripe berry flavors and more than a touch of oak, it's toasty and sweet on the finish. By now the tannin should be softened; it should be fine to drink now. $35 (1/31/89) **85**
Beaune Teurons Domaines du Château de Beaune 1983 $21 (9/15/86) **71**

PIERRE BOUREE FILS
Beaune Epenottes 1989: Has beautiful, restrained aromas of wet earth and leaves, and it's packed with smooth black cherry and chestnut flavors. Already very silky. Try from 1994. $30 (1/31/92) **91**
Beaune Epenottes 1987: Focused flavors of sun-dried cherry, cinnamon and nutmeg are concentrated and long, making this a delicious wine to drink now but it's also worth cellaring to see how much more complexity it can achieve. Drink 1993 to '95. $35 (6/15/90) **88**

CHANSON PERE & FILS
Beaune Clos des Fèves 1988: A pleasantly fresh and fruity wine, with ripe cherry and raspberry flavors, moderate tannins and the right touch of acidity and oak. Drink now to 1993. $35 (8/31/90) **84**
Beaune Clos des Fèves 1987: Firm and generous with ripe plum and cherry flavors that are supple with enough tannin for three to five years' cellaring. Try now. Rel: $23 Cur: $27 (7/31/89) **85**
Beaune Clos des Fèves 1985: Rich, almost chocolaty on the nose, turning bright, berryish and satiny on the palate, with a lean texture but deep flavors; it's focused and long. Drink now to 1994. Rel: $25 Cur: $33 (1/31/89) **92**
Beaune Clos des Marconnets 1986: Pungently earthy, tart and somewhat tannic, but there's enough concentration of raspberry flavor to suggest it might soften and be more likable after 1993 or '94. $20 (5/31/89) **81**

DOMAINE JEAN CHARTRON
Beaune Hospices de Beaune Cuvée Cyrot-Chaudron 1988: Lean and focused, with a shining core of black cherry and plum flavors, hints of toast and plenty of crisp acidity to carry it through a solid finish. Has enough tannin to keep developing through 1993 to '95. $40 (2/15/91) **88**

F. CHAUVENET
Beaune Clos des Mouches 1986 $27 (12/31/88) **82**
Beaune Grèves 1989: A seductive Burgundy, with toasty, smoky aromas laced with black cherry and chocolate flavors. The tannins need time to smooth out; try in 1995 and beyond. $30 (1/31/92) **91**
Beaune Grèves 1988 $25 (7/15/90) (BT) **85+**
Beaune Grèves 1986 $25 (12/31/88) **79**
Beaune Hospices de Beaune Rousseau-Deslandes 1980 $36 (6/16/86) **91**
Beaune Teurons 1988 $25 (7/15/90) (BT) **70+**

A.R. CHOPPIN
Beaune Bressandes 1985 $32 (9/30/87) **90**
Beaune Cent-Vignes 1985 $32 (10/31/87) **81**
Beaune Grèves 1985 $32 (9/30/87) **79**
Beaune Teurons 1987: Ripe and generous in flavor, lean and firm in texture with spicy berry, plum and vanilla aromas and flavors that fill the mouth and linger nicely. Drinkable now, but it's well balanced for short-term aging; best now through 1994. $30 (2/28/90) **87**
Beaune Teurons 1985 $32 (10/31/87) **87**
Beaune Toussaints 1987: Very firm in structure and texture, with vivid cherry and strawberry flavors, spicy and generous. A simple, likable wine. Drinkable now. $30 (2/28/90) **83**

DOMAINE HENRI CLERC & FILS
Beaune Chaume Gaufriot 1985 $29 (11/15/88) **81**

JOSEPH DROUHIN
Beaune Clos des Mouches 1989: A classy red Burgundy that grows on you with each sip. The black cherry, earth and spice notes are subtle, elegant and sharply focused, with just the right touch of tannin. Should improve until 1995. 800 cases made. Rel: $40 Cur: $46 (2/29/92) **92**
Beaune Clos des Mouches 1988: Beautifully aromatic, showing plenty of cherry, strawberry and spice aromas and flavors and firm tannins that will need at least until 1994 to settle down. Has plenty of flavor to carry it through. $50 (2/15/91) **88**
Beaune Clos des Mouches 1987: Lean and tart, with mouthpuckering spice and cherry flavors that are elegant but lack the concentration necessary for long aging. Has a long enough finish to warrant cellaring until 1993. 4,000 cases made. $47 (6/15/90) **83**
Beaune Clos des Mouches 1986 $38 (11/15/87) (BT) **95+**
Beaune Grèves 1989: Pure Pinot Noir, with clean, bright cherry, cinnamon and toast notes and a firm finish. Try from 1994. $47 (1/31/92) **88**
Beaune Grèves 1959 $90 (8/31/90) **80**

DOMAINE DUCHET
Beaune Cent-Vignes 1985 $27 (3/15/88) **85**

FAIVELEY
Beaune Champs-Pimont 1989: A crowd pleaser, with intense strawberry-tinged aromas, ripe, almost sweet flavors and a silky finish. Try from 1994. $34 (1/31/92) **90**
Beaune Champs-Pimont 1985 $36 (3/15/88) **86**

JEAN GARAUDET
Beaune Clos des Mouches 1989: Deep and concentrated, with a blast of sharply focused currant and raspberry flavors that pick up a touch of boysenberry. Nicely balanced, with a pleasant touch of oak. The finish is long and full. Drink in 1993 to '99. $32 (11/15/91) **91**
Beaune Clos des Mouches 1988: Young and fragrant, with rich berry, strawberry and boysenberry flavors and firm acidity backed by ample oak. A bit tough and tannic, too, but a few years' cellaring should dissolve the wrapper of tannin. Drink now to 1995. $40 (11/15/90) **86**

JACQUES GERMAIN
Beaune Les Boucherottes 1989 $45 (7/15/90) (BT) **85+**
Beaune Cent-Vignes 1989 $45 (7/15/90) (BT) **85+**
Beaune Cent-Vignes 1988 $45 (7/15/90) (BT) **90+**
Beaune Les Crâs 1989: A real beauty that shows lots of class, with nice berry flavors and supple tannins. Try from 1994. (NR) (1/31/92) **90**
Beaune Les Crâs 1988 (NR) (7/15/90) (BT) **90+**
Beaune Les Teurons 1989: An elegant wine, with violet and black cherry aromas that jump out of the glass and flavors that become seductive. Try from 1994. $50 (1/31/92) **92**
Beaune Les Teurons 1988: Smooth, ripe and polished, with plum, raspberry and spice aromas and flavors that are long and elegant. It's youthful and concentrated enough to keep developing through at least 1994. 300 cases made. $42 (2/15/91) **90**
Beaune Les Teurons 1986 $33 (7/31/88) **70**
Beaune Vignes-Franches 1989: Gorgeous, with mellow violet, black cherry and smoke aromas and flavors that turn to silk on the finish. Try from 1993. $45 (1/31/92) **91**
Beaune Vignes-Franches 1988 $42 (7/15/90) (BT) **90+**

DOMAINE ALETH GIRARDIN
Beaune Clos des Mouches 1988: Hard and tannic, with a strong earthy, musty flavor that creeps into the finish, shouldering past what light fruit is present. Possibly better after 1995. Tasted twice. $36 (7/15/91) **71**

MACHARD DE GRAMONT
Beaune Les Chouacheux 1985 $34 (5/31/88) **89**

DOMAINE JEAN GUITTON
Beaune Les Sizies 1986: Very tart, tannic and earthy, it's astringent, with little of the concentration or balance that would suggest ageability. $19 (5/31/89) **69**

LOUIS JADOT
Beaune Boucherottes 1989: A sensual wine, with lovely, caressing strawberry and violet aromas and flavors and tender tannins. Try from 1994. $38 (1/31/92) **90**
Beaune Boucherottes 1988: Remarkably charming and elegant, with ripe, rich cherry, tea, raspberry and spicy oak flavors that spread out on the palate. The tannins are very fine and well integrated, and the crisp acidity lends life to the flavors on the finish. Persistent from start to finish. Start drinking in 1995. 625 cases made. $33 (3/31/91) **92**
Beaune Boucherottes 1985 $30 (3/15/88) **91**
Beaune Bressandes 1989 $42 (7/15/90) (BT) **80+**
Beaune Bressandes 1988 Rel: $26 Cur: $30 (7/15/90) (BT) **80+**
Beaune Bressandes 1986: Very well balanced for a 1986, with good concentration of black cherry, spice and nutmeg flavors that are rich and delicate. Has the structure and tannins to develop for another five years, but it should be ready to drink by now. Rel: $24 Cur: $28 (5/31/89) **90**
Beaune Bressandes 1985 $30 (3/15/88) **87**
Beaune Les Chouacheux 1989 $42 (7/15/90) (BT) **85+**
Beaune Les Chouacheux 1988 $25 (7/15/90) (BT) **90+**
Beaune Les Chouacheux 1986: Ripe and even-handed with generous black cherry and spicy oak flavors, soft tannins and an abrupt finish. Drinkable now. $24 (5/31/89) **85**
Beaune Les Chouacheux 1985 $30 (3/15/88) **91**
Beaune Clos des Couchereaux 1989 $42 (7/15/90) (BT) **85+**
Beaune Clos des Couchereaux 1988: Delicate and seductive, with graceful ripe cherry, currant, strawberry and spicy oak flavors that are elegant and well integrated. A silky style that's elegant, subtle and gains firmness with tannins on the finish. Drink in 1994 to '98. 875 cases made. $33 (3/31/91) **90**
Beaune Clos des Couchereaux 1985 Rel: $30 Cur: $39 (3/15/88) **91**
Beaune Clos des Ursules 1989: This Burgundy has a distinctive personality. It smells like a forest after rain, with a wet earth, leaf and dark character and plenty of tannins on the vanilla and cherry-tinged finish. Try in 1995. 1,100 cases made. $43 (2/29/92) **91**
Beaune Clos des Ursules 1988: Tight and tannic, with a firm concentration of rich currant, cherry, raspberry and spice flavors that are firmly wrapped in tannins now and in need of cellaring until 1994 or '95. 1,000 cases made. $40 (3/31/91) **91**
Beaune Clos des Ursules 1987: Complex and delicate on the nose, but brawny enough on the palate to justify cellaring until 1993 to '95 to bring out the spicy, smoky, chocolaty richness. A keeper. $27 (6/15/90) **81**
Beaune Clos des Ursules 1986 Rel: $27 Cur: $33 (3/15/89) **88**

Beaune Clos des Ursules 1985 Rel: $30 Cur: $48 (3/15/89) **91**
Beaune Clos des Ursules 1985 Rel: $30 Cur: $48 (3/15/88) SS **95**
Beaune Clos des Ursules 1983 $25 (3/15/89) **93**
Beaune Clos des Ursules 1980 $26 (3/15/89) **83**
Beaune Clos des Ursules 1978 $47 (3/15/89) **89**
Beaune Clos des Ursules 1976 $40 (3/15/89) **85**
Beaune Clos des Ursules 1973 ($NA) (3/15/89) **86**
Beaune Clos des Ursules 1971 $60 (3/15/89) **78**
Beaune Clos des Ursules 1969 $120 (3/15/89) **90**
Beaune Clos des Ursules 1966 $130 (3/15/89) **90**
Beaune Clos des Ursules 1964 ($NA) (3/15/89) **86**
Beaune Clos des Ursules 1962 ($NA) (3/15/89) **79**
Beaune Clos des Ursules 1961 ($NA) (3/15/89) **88**
Beaune Clos des Ursules 1959 ($NA) (3/15/89) **98**
Beaune Clos des Ursules 1957 ($NA) (3/15/89) **89**
Beaune Clos des Ursules 1954 ($NA) (3/15/89) **81**
Beaune Clos des Ursules 1952 ($NA) (3/15/89) **87**
Beaune Clos des Ursules 1949 ($NA) (3/15/89) **86**
Beaune Clos des Ursules 1947 ($NA) (3/15/89) **95**
Beaune Clos des Ursules 1945 ($NA) (3/15/89) **84**
Beaune Clos des Ursules 1937 ($NA) (3/15/89) **92**
Beaune Clos des Ursules 1933 ($NA) (3/15/89) **80**
Beaune Clos des Ursules 1928 ($NA) (3/15/89) **97**
Beaune Clos des Ursules 1926 ($NA) (3/15/89) **88**
Beaune Clos des Ursules 1923 ($NA) (3/15/89) **78**
Beaune Clos des Ursules 1919 ($NA) (3/15/89) **90**
Beaune Clos des Ursules 1915 ($NA) (3/15/89) **95**
Beaune Clos des Ursules 1911 ($NA) (3/15/89) **81**
Beaune Clos des Ursules 1906 ($NA) (3/15/89) **92**
Beaune Clos des Ursules 1904 ($NA) (3/15/89) **88**
Beaune Clos des Ursules 1895 ($NA) (3/15/89) **80**
Beaune Clos des Ursules 1887 ($NA) (3/15/89) **90**
Beaune Hospices de Beaune Cuvée Dames-Hospitalier 1985 $85 (3/15/88) **90**
Beaune Hospices de Beaune Cuvée Nicolas-Rolin 1985 $85 (3/15/88) **92**

JAFFELIN
Beaune Les Bressandes 1989: Elegant and focused, with subtle berry aromas and flavors. Try from 1993. $28 (1/31/92) **85**
Beaune Les Champimonts 1989: Like cassis jam. Black currant aromas and cherry flavors dominate this balanced, pretty wine. Try from 1993. $27 (1/31/92) **89**
Beaune Les Champimonts 1988 $30 (7/15/90) (BT) **75+**
Beaune Les Champimonts 1983 $18 (9/15/86) **68**
Beaune du Châpitre 1986 $18 (12/31/88) **77**
Beaune Hospices de Beaune Cuvée Clos des Avaux 1986 $65 (12/31/88) **85**

DOMAINE PIERRE LABET
Beaune Coucherias 1989 (NR) (7/15/90) (BT) **90+**

LOUIS LATOUR
Beaune Domaine Latour 1989: Juicy and flavorful, smelling of freshly crushed berries, with fruit flavors that are almost sweet. Medium-long on the finish. Try from 1994. (NR) (1/31/92) **91**
Beaune Vignes Franches 1985 Rel: $31 Cur: $42 (3/15/88) **90**

LIGER-BELAIR
Beaune Les Avaux 1947 ($NA) (8/31/90) **87**

LUPE-CHOLET
Beaune Avaux 1986 ($NA) (7/31/88) **89**

CHATEAU DE MEURSAULT
Beaune Cent-Vignes 1985: Smells wonderful with cherry and toasty oak aromas. On the palate it's more supple, with pretty smoke and spice box flavors, not quite as opulent or concentrated as the best '85s, but it's very appealing, nonetheless. Drink now through 1994. $31 (2/28/90) **87**

MOILLARD
Beaune 1983 $10 (10/16/85) **68**
Beaune Grèves 1985 $25 (3/15/87) **89**
Beaune Grèves 1984 $11.50 (2/15/87) **87**
Beaune Grèves Domaine Thomas-Moillard 1989: Shows lots of character, but it's a little overdone. Has brooding depth and a silky finish, delivering tons of berry, wild mushroom and smoke flavors. Try from 1995. $28 (1/31/92) **89**
Beaune Grèves Domaine Thomas-Moillard 1986 $14 (12/31/88) **80**
Beaune Hospices de Beaune Cuvée Clos des Avaux 1988: Crisp and focused, with lots of distinctive raspberry flavor shaded by plum and anise notes. A tasty wine that needs until 1993 to '95 to smooth out the edges. Should be a beauty. $80 (8/31/91) **88**

MOMMESSIN
Beaune 1989: Rather wild, with wild mushroom, rose petal, black cherry and juniper notes playing against a silky background of polished tannins. Try from 1994. $18 (1/31/92) **90**
Beaune Les Cent-Vignes 1989: Has lots of character, with subtle, pretty earth, chalk and cedar nuances, but it lacks a bit of concentration on the palate. Try from 1994. $23 (1/31/92) **86**
Beaune Les Epenottes 1989 $23 (7/15/90) (BT) **90+**

DOMAINE RENE MONNIER
Beaune Cent-Vignes 1985 $25 (10/31/87) **89**

DOMAINE MARC MOREY
Beaune Les Paules 1988: Light, smooth and fruity, with pleasant blackberry and cherry aromas and flavors and richness on the finish. Drinkable now. $24 (8/31/90) **85**
Beaune Les Paules 1985 $15 (12/31/88) **84**

Key to Symbols

The scores reported here are the results of blind tastings conducted by our panel of senior editors. Wines that carry the initials below are results of individual tastings.

THE WINE SPECTATOR 100-POINT SCALE ***95-100***—Classic, a great wine; ***90-94***—Outstanding, superior character and style; ***80-89***—Good to very good, a wine with special qualities; ***70-79***—Average, drinkable wine that may have minor flaws; ***60-69***—Below average, drinkable but not recommended; ***50-59***—Poor, undrinkable, not recommended. "+"—With a score indicates a range; used primarily with barrel tastings to indicate a preliminary score.

SPECIAL DESIGNATIONS SS—Spectator Selection, CS—Cellar Selection, BB—Best Buy, ($NA)—Price not available, (NR)—Not released.

TASTER'S INITIALS (JG)—Jim Gordon, (HS)—Harvey Steiman, (JL)—James Laube, (JS)—James Suckling, (TM)—Thomas Matthews, (TR)—Terry Robards, (PM)—Per-Henrik Mansson, (BT)—Barrel Tasting (these wines were tasted blind from barrel samples), (CA-date)—*California's Great Cabernets* by James Laube, (CH-date)—*California's Great Chardonnays* by James Laube, (VP-date)—*Vintage Port* by James Suckling.

DATE TASTED Dates in parentheses represent the issue in which the rating was published.

ALBERT MOROT
Beaune Bressandes 1988: Ripe and berrylike in flavor and very fruity, but delicate in texture for an '88. Warm, generous, light in tannins and ready to drink now through 1993. Tasted twice. $30 (3/31/91) **87**
Beaune Cent-Vignes 1988: Very smooth, elegant and enjoyable, with lots of plush, generous plum and cherry flavors and hints of spice. Beautifully balanced and crisp, it lingers on the aftertaste. Drink now through 1995. Tasted three times. 225 cases made. $30 (4/30/91) **91**
Beaune Grèves 1988: Attractive currant and plum flavors are lively, focused and rich, with a crisp texture and intense tannins. Still a bit rough around the edges, but well crafted. This sturdy style should age well for the next decade; drink in 1993 to '99. $32 (7/15/91) **86**
Beaune Teurons 1988: Intense and hard-edged. Has pretty aromas, but turns green and metallic on the palate, with a flash of currant and earthiness on the finish. Drink in 1993 to '96. Tasted twice. $33 (7/15/91) **80**

DOMAINE MUSSY
Beaune Epenottes 1986: Lighter, softer and more accessible than most '86s, actually generous in spicy aromas and strawberry flavor despite its light color, a bit tannic but within reasonable limits. Drink now. $28 (5/31/89) **86**
Beaune Montremenots 1986: Crisp and firmly built, with a lean texture, finely focused berry and spice aromas and flavors, and a pleasing echo of plum on the finish. It should develop into a lovely wine by 1993. $28 (5/31/89) **86**

PARIGOT PERE & FILS
Beaune Grèves 1987: A brilliant purple color indicates the ripeness and freshness of this sturdy wine, with violet-tinged plum and toast flavors echoing nicely on the palate. Drinkable now, but it should develop through 1994. $26 (2/28/90) **88**

PAUL PERNOT
Beaune Teurons 1990: Crisp and focused, with bright, vibrant black cherry, wild berry and toast aromas and flavors that remain intense and elegant right through the long finish. Has the raw material to develop well through 1995 to 2000. 85 cases made. $33 (4/30/92) **90**
Beaune Teurons 1988: Bright and lively, with exotic berry flavors and layers of cherry, plum and spice. Has plenty of finesse and elegance. The flavors fan out on the aftertaste, with spicy, herbal-tinged notes. Drink in 1994 to '98. Tasted twice. $33 (3/31/91) **86**

POTHIER-RIEUSSET
Beaune Boucherottes 1988: Tart, rich, dark cherry, plum and spice notes add dimension to the toasty oak flavors in a wine that's well balanced, rich and deep yet elegant and polished. Tempting now, but it should reach its peak around 1995. $35 (11/30/90) **88**
Beaune Boucherottes 1986: With an attractive richness, including a prominent component of vanilla from oak, this wine has good mouth-feel and a long finish. Drink now. $19 (5/31/89) **88**

DOMAINE PRIEUR-BRUNET
Beaune Clos du Roy 1988: An appealing wine, with a narrow band of tight cherry and spice flavors that is simple but pleasing, and tannins that are a bit green and tealike. Best to cellar until 1993 to see what happens. $30 (12/31/90) **82**

REMOISSENET
Beaune Grèves 1988: Warm, rich and meaty, with generous, ripe, supple cherry, plum, strawberry and spice notes that are moderately complex and intriguing. Gentle enough to drink now, but it has enough concentration to last for eight to 10 years. Start drinking in 1995. 500 cases made. Rel: $30 Cur: $38 (11/30/90) **90**

TOLLOT-BEAUT
Beaune Clos du Roi 1988: Intense and sharply focused, showing plenty of strawberry and plum aromas and flavors, firm tannins and a long, lively finish. Not particularly complex, and not as woody as some previous vintages, but well made. Should be at its best in 1994 to '98. $53 (2/28/91) **86**
Beaune Clos du Roi Premier Cru 1989: So satiny and polished it melts on the palate, with ripe plum and cherry notes and a long, memorable finish. Try from 1995. (NR) (1/31/92) **91**
Beaune Grèves 1989: Round, sweet and delicate, with plenty of raspberry aromas and flavors. Try from 1994. (NR) (1/31/92) **90**
Beaune Grèves 1988 $35 (7/15/90) (BT) **85+**

LEON VOILLAND
Beaune Clos du Roy 1945 ($NA) (8/31/90) **90**

CHASSAGNE-MONTRACHET

BOUCHARD PERE & FILS
Chassagne-Montrachet 1988: Lean and tight, with a vegetal note and firm cedar, black cherry and spice flavors that turn earthy and simple on the finish. Seems to have the fruit; perhaps it's just closed up tight now. Needs until 1993 or '94 to open. $22 (4/30/91) **85**

JOSEPH DROUHIN
Chassagne-Montrachet 1989: Very solid, with a deep character of black cherry and earth and integrated tannins. Closed on the finish, but it shows potential; try in 1994. $23 (1/31/92) **87**

FONTAINE-GAGNARD
Chassagne-Montrachet 1985 $16 (12/31/88) **85**

JEAN-CHARLES FORNEROT
Chassagne-Montrachet Les Champs-Gain 1985: Nicely earthy in aroma and firm in structure, not a carbon copy of anything. Tastes ripe and round; the finish lingers. $19 (7/31/89) **83**
Chassagne-Montrachet La Maltroie 1985: A ripe, spicy Burgundy that's generous in flavor, firm in structure and fairly complex in aroma. Nicely balanced. Drink now. $19 (7/31/89) **86**

JEAN-NOEL GAGNARD
Chassagne-Montrachet Morgeot 1989: Very light and very red in color, with pretty cinnamon-tinged strawberry flavors and hints of toast and vanilla on the finish. Drinkable now, but should improve through 1993 or '94. $25 (11/15/91) **87**
Chassagne-Montrachet Morgeot 1988: Elegant and understated, with lovely herb, currant, cherry and strawberry flavors that are tart and refreshing. Has a supple seam of velvety tannins that allows the flavors to glide across the palate. Start drinking now. $20 (12/31/90) **86**
Chassagne-Montrachet Morgeot 1985 $18 (11/30/87) **79**

LOUIS JADOT
Chassagne-Montrachet Morgeot Clos de la Chapelle Domaine Duc de Magenta 1989 (NR) (7/15/90) (BT) **80+**
Chassagne-Montrachet Morgeot Clos de la Chapelle Domaine du Duc de Magenta 1988: Intense, concentrated, and well focused, with tiers of rich cherry, berry, chocolate and toasty oak flavors that are framed by firm, chewy tannins. Best to cellar until 1994 or '95. $20 (3/31/91) **85**
Chassagne-Montrachet Morgeot Clos de la Chapelle Domaine du Duc de Magenta 1986: Earthy, toasty aromas and flavors compete with a light but tannic structure, obscuring what youthful fruit is there is in this red wine. Try now. $18 (10/31/89) **77**
Chassagne-Montrachet Morgeot Clos de la Chapelle Domaine du Duc de Magenta 1985 $19 (4/15/88) **83**

JAFFELIN
Chassagne-Montrachet 1989: A refreshing Burgundy, with lots of chewy fruit, medium tannins and plenty of strawberry and earth flavors. Try in 1993. $18 (1/31/92) **86**
Chassagne-Montrachet 1988 $20 (7/15/90) (BT) **80+**

OLIVIER LEFLAIVE FRERES
Chassagne-Montrachet 1989 (NR) (7/15/90) (BT) **80+**
Chassagne-Montrachet 1986 $26 (2/29/88) **89**
Chassagne-Montrachet 1985 $32 (10/31/88) **83**

DOMAINE LEQUIN-ROUSSOT
Chassagne-Montrachet Morgeot 1985 $24 (5/31/88) **86**

CHATEAU DE LA MALTROYE
Chassagne-Montrachet Boudriottes 1985 $17 (10/15/88) **86**
Chassagne-Montrachet Clos St.-Jean 1985 $19 (10/15/88) **89**
Chassagne-Montrachet Clos St.-Jean 1983 $12.50 (11/16/85) **65**

HENRI MEURGEY
Chassagne-Montrachet Clos de la Boudriotte 1985 $40 (10/31/88) **88**

MOILLARD
Chassagne-Montrachet Morgeot 1985 $15 (5/31/87) **84**

MOMMESSIN
Chassagne-Montrachet 1989 (NR) (7/15/90) (BT) **75+**

BERNARD MOREAU
Chassagne-Montrachet Morgeot La Cardeuse 1986 $16 (12/31/88) **61**

BERNARD MOREY
Chassagne-Montrachet 1987: The earthy aromas and flavors, with a hint of sauerkraut, seem out of place in this light, smooth-textured red wine. Drinkable, but funky. $20 (10/31/89) **75**

PAUL PILLOT
Chassagne-Montrachet Clos St.-Jean 1986: A firm, light red wine with delicate nutmeg and strawberry aromas and flavors, fine tannins, good concentration and length. Drinkable now, but better in 1993 after the tannins subside. $23 (2/28/90) **84**
Chassagne-Montrachet Clos St.-Jean 1985 $24 (11/15/88) **86**

DOMAINE PRIEUR-BRUNET
Chassagne-Montrachet Morgeot 1988: Spicy, earthy, firmly tannic and not showing great generosity, but ripe berry, vanilla and nutmeg aromas and flavors manage to emerge, suggesting that aging until 1993 will polish it. $17 (11/15/90) **83**

DOMAINE ROUX PERE & FILS
Chassagne-Montrachet Clos St.-Jean 1983 $13 (9/16/85) **86**

Pernand-Vergelesses

DOMAINE CHANDON DE BRIAILLES
Pernand-Vergelesses Ile des Vergelesses 1988: Firm, tight and tannic, with clean cherry and plum flavors that are young and somewhat one-dimensional now. With time it should be more supple; try in 1994. $35 (2/28/91) **83**

CHANSON PERE & FILS
Pernand-Vergelesses Les Vergelesses 1988: Lush and fruity on the nose, with aromas of berries; modest and somewhat reserved on the palate, but smooth and growing in intensity on the finish. Not a complex wine, but flavorful and appealing. $24 (8/31/90) **85**

DOMAINE DELARCHE
Pernand-Vergelesses 1989: A decent-tasting wine, with good pear and spice flavors in a narrow spectrum, modest citrus notes and a fairly short finish. On the dry, austere side, but enjoyable. $15/375ml (4/30/91) **82**
Pernand-Vergelesses Ile des Vergelesses 1985 $23 (10/15/88) **89**

JOSEPH DROUHIN
Pernand-Vergelesses 1985 $17 (11/15/87) **91**

DUBREUIL-FONTAINE
Pernand-Vergelesses Ile des Vergelesses 1989: Very perfumed, with raspberry, cherry and earth characters and very firm tannins. Slightly aggressive on the finish. Better in 1993. (NR) (1/31/92) **84**
Pernand-Vergelesses Ile des Vergelesses 1982 $18 (10/16/85) **78**

LOUIS JADOT
Pernand-Vergelesses 1989 (NR) (7/15/90) (BT) **80+**
Pernand-Vergelesses 1988 $16 (7/15/90) (BT) **80+**
Pernand-Vergelesses 1985 $18 (4/15/88) **85**
Pernand-Vergelesses Clos de la Croix de Pierre 1989: Extremely fruity, with intense raspberry aromas and flavors and a hint of cedar. Has a rather juicy finish. Better in 1993. $21 (1/31/92) **86**
Pernand-Vergelesses Clos de la Croix de Pierre 1988: Rich, fruity and attractive, with pretty aromas and ripe plum, black cherry and nutmeg-tinged oak flavors that stay with you on the finish. A charming style that renders both elegance and grace. Drink now to 1994. $17 (3/31/91) **86**
Pernand-Vergelesses Clos de la Croix de Pierre 1987: The earthy, herbal, funky aromas and flavors aren't for everyone, but the generous cherry and toast notes that come through on the finish suggest it will improve with cellaring until 1993. For fans of eccentric Burgundies. $15 (11/15/90) **79**
Pernand-Vergelesses Clos de la Croix de Pierre 1986 $17 (7/31/89) **85**
Pernand-Vergelesses Clos de la Croix de Pierre 1985 $18 (4/15/88) **83**

JAFFELIN
Pernand-Vergelesses 1989: Has lots of juicy strawberry flavor, smoke notes and light tannins. Delicious now. $19 (1/31/92) **86**

DOMAINE RAPET
Pernand-Vergelesses 1988: Ripe and fleshy, with attractive plum, cherry, currant and spice flavors that turn gamy and woody. Tannins on the finish suggest this should be cellared until 1994 or so. $31 (2/28/91) **79**

Pommard

COMTE ARMAND
Pommard Clos des Epeneaux 1988: Very rough and youthful, but sharply focused, intense and bursting with berry and cherry flavors, hinting at smoke and spice on the long finish. Needs until 1994 or '95 to settle down, but it should be great. $46 (2/28/91) **90**
Pommard Clos des Epeneaux 1987: An austere wine that's firmly acidic, with hard oak and berry flavors and hard drying tannins on the finish. Needs a year or two to mellow, but it may not have the fruit concentration to outlast the tannins. Drink in 1991 to '93. $41 (8/31/90) **81**
Pommard Clos des Epeneaux 1985 $44 (3/15/88) **91**

BARTON & GUESTIER
Pommard 1985 $21 (11/30/87) **81**

BICHOT
Pommard 1988: Tight and intense, with firm tannnins and ample oak, but beneath that is a wonderful array of fresh, ripe, rich cherry, berry and raspberry flavors that are young and lively. Needs a couple of years to soften and gain more complexity. Drink now to 1995. $25 (8/31/90) **87**
Pommard 1986: Enticing smoke and cherry flavors with a touch of damp earth, rendering a wine of delicacy, elegance and moderate depth. Drink now through 1993. $20 (9/15/89) **79**
Pommard 1983 $19 (9/15/86) **83**
Pommard Hospices de Beaune Cuvée Cyrot-Chaudron 1989: Very fruity, ripe and generous, with firm tannins and a bit of spice flavor for complexity. Tempting now, but should be best from 1993 to '95. $70 (1/31/92) **86**
Pommard Hospices de Beaune Cuvée Cyrot-Chaudron 1985 $60 (10/31/88) **91**
Pommard Rugiens 1988 $40 (7/15/90) (BT) **80+**

JEAN-MARC BOILLOT
Pommard Saucilles 1988: Tart, lean and tannic, with sharp, earthy cherry and currant flavors that turn harsh and austere on the finish. Lacks charm and finesse; who knows what will happen with cellaring, but it looks like a gamble. Drink 1994. $47 (5/15/91) **77**

JEAN CLAUDE BOISSET
Pommard 1985 $28 (4/30/88) **78**
Pommard Rugiens 1985 $33 (3/15/88) **76**

BOUCHARD PERE & FILS
Pommard 1989 $38 (7/15/90) (BT) **80+**
Pommard 1988: A lovely display of rich, opulent fruit flavor, with black cherry, plum, anise and leathery cedar notes from oak. A complex wine that picks up an earthy, coffeelike nuance on the finish. The tannins are dry and firm; best to cellar until 1995 or '96. 3,500 cases made. $37 (4/30/91) **90**
Pommard 1983 $23 (9/15/86) **74**
Pommard Clos du Pavillon 1989: Super-ripe and massive, with a beautiful, silky mouth-feel and firm tannins. Has wonderful mushroom and fruit flavors and fine balance. Try in 1995. (NR) (1/31/92) **92**
Pommard Premier Cru Domaines du Château de Beaune 1988: A complex, flavorful style where the interplay between fruit and oak is well integrated. The cassis, cherry, plum and spice flavors are elegant and supple, with fine tannins and just the right touch of oak on the finish. Tempting now, but best in 1994 to 2000. $53 (3/31/91) **89**
Pommard Premier Cru Domaines du Château de Beaune 1986 $41 (7/31/88) **87**

DOMAINE JEAN-MARC BOULEY
Pommard Les Rugiens 1987: Overly mature, earthy, sweaty and somewhat sour; it's musty on the finish. $34 (11/15/90) **63**
Pommard Les Rugiens 1985 $30 (10/31/88) **92**

DOMAINE F. BUFFET
Pommard Rugiens 1985 $40 (10/15/88) **88**

ROGER CAILLOT
Pommard 1987: Pretty peppery aromas are followed by ripe, supple, gentle plum and cherry flavors that gets simple on the finish; pleasant overall. Drink up now. $35 (9/15/89) **79**

CHARTRON & TREBUCHET
Pommard Les Epenottes 1988: Tannic in structure, but it's also developing a smooth, silky texture that complements the herb, plum and cherry flavors. Spicy on the finish, but it has good length. Cellar until 1994. $45 (2/28/91) **87**

F. CHAUVENET
Pommard Les Chanlins 1989: Tough to compare to others in this group; offers ripe strawberry aromas and flavors and full tannins, but it's slightly dry on the finish. Try in 1995. $45 (1/31/92) **86**
Pommard Les Chanlins 1988 $55 (7/15/90) (BT) **85+**
Pommard Les Chanlins 1986 $40 (7/31/88) **90**
Pommard Epenottes 1989: A brutish wine that knocks you off your feet, with concentrated fruit and full tannins. It has great balance. Try in 1997. $45 (1/31/92) **94**
Pommard Epenottes 1985 $48 (7/31/87) **95**
Pommard Hospices de Beaune Cuvée Dames de la Charite 1982 Rel: $36 Cur: $55 (2/01/85) CS **91**

MAURICE CHENU
Pommard 1989 (NR) (7/15/90) (BT) **70+**
Pommard 1988 (NR) (7/15/90) (BT) **75+**

DOMAINE COSTE-CAUMARTIN
Pommard 1987: Herbal and bordering on vegetal, with aromas of rotting earth and leaves, but it's not terribly unpleasant. Those who prefer funky Burgundies will appreciate the smooth texture and complexity. Try in 1993. $21 (11/15/90) **76**
Pommard Clos de Boucherottes 1989: Opulent, with polished raspberry, earth and smoke flavors, a long, long finish and an excellent backbone of elegant tannins. Try in 1995. $38 (1/31/92) **92**
Pommard Les Fremiers 1989: An intriguing, muscular wine, with concentrated dried cherry, berry and earth aromas and flavors and a great backbone of tannins. Try in 1995. $35 (1/31/92) **92**
Pommard Les Fremiers 1987: Light in texture, with somewhat leafy, herbal overtones to the fragile strawberry and cherry flavors. The finish suggests Burgundian sweetness and complexity will develop with age; try now. $26 (11/15/90) **79**

DOMAINE DE COURCEL
Pommard Clos des Epeneaux 1985 $37 (4/30/88) **89**
Pommard Rugiens 1985 $40 (4/30/88) **92**

JOSEPH DROUHIN
Pommard 1989: Offers delicious raspberry and earth flavors and firm tannins, but it's a little too earthy on the finish. Try in 1994. $43 (1/31/92) **85**
Pommard 1988 $40 (7/15/90) (BT) **85+**
Pommard 1986: Beneath the tough exterior beats the heart of a very charming wine, wrapped around a core of ripe cherry flavor and velvety texture; then comes the long, spicy finish. Should be drinkable by now. $27 (4/30/89) **87**
Pommard 1985 $33 (11/15/87) **93**
Pommard 1981 $28 (9/01/84) **83**
Pommard Epenottes 1989: A more delicate style of a Pommard from this vintage, but well proportioned, with lots of fruit and tannins and a succulent finish. Try in 1995. $56 (1/31/92) **89**
Pommard Epenottes 1988 $55 (7/15/90) (BT) **85+**
Pommard Epenottes 1986 $40 (7/31/88) **83**
Pommard Epenottes 1985 $41 (11/15/87) **95**
Pommard Rugiens 1989: A no-nonsense Pommard, with fresh strawberry, cinnamon and berry flavors. Has medium concentration and tannins. Try in 1994. $56 (1/31/92) **87**

FAIVELEY
Pommard Les Chaponnières 1989: Built for aging, with extremely concentrated berry, tar and earth characteristics and full tannins. Tough and chewy. Try in 1996. $50 (1/31/92) **90**

JEAN GARAUDET
Pommard 1988: Richly concentrated cherry and plum flavors need a few years to soften and loosen up in this firm, tight wine. Has plenty of cherry and spice on the finish, as well as a dash of oak. Best to cellar until 1993 to '96. $37 (11/15/90) **88**
Pommard 1987: Ripe, fleshy and supple with smooth, silky cherry and plum flavors that are very appetizing. Wonderful depth and balance allow the full impact of the fruit to come through with finesse. Lengthy aftertaste. Drink now through 1994. $25 (9/15/89) **88**
Pommard Les Charmots 1988: Deep, rich and intense, with ripe plum, cassis, cherry and subtle game flavors that smell and taste terrific. Firmly tannic, thick and concentrated, with all the ingredients for greatness, but it needs a few years to mellow. Best to hold until 1994 or '95 at the earliest. $46 (11/15/90) **90**
Pommard Les Charmots 1987: Rich and elegant, it's firm with a steely tannic backbone but there are also plenty of fleshy black cherry and spicy flavors that are long and generous on the palate. Delicious to drink now through 1994. $30 (9/15/89) **88**
Pommard Noizons 1989: Ripe, smooth and elegant, with gorgeous currant, blackberry and cherry

flavors shaded by vanilla and spice notes on the long, generous finish. Tempting now, but should continue to develop through 1994. $34 (11/15/91) **91**

DOMAINE ALETH GIRARDIN
Pommard Charmots 1988: Rich, deep and intense, with a streak of earthiness that adds dimension to the ripe, focused currant, plum and black cherry flavors. A rustic style, with plenty of flavor; tight and tough now, finishing firm and tannic. Drink in 1993 to '98. $44 (7/15/91) **87**

LOUIS JADOT
Pommard 1988: Hard-edged and herbal, with tight currant and berry notes that turn rough and tannic. Tough going from start to finish. Seems to be missing the middle core of fruit, leaving a hollow center. Drink in 1994. $36 (3/31/91) **83**
Pommard Chaponnières 1985 $39 (3/15/88) **91**
Pommard Grands Epenottes 1989: Very firm and focused, with floral, violet and berry flavors and medium-hard tannins. Try in 1995. $50 (1/31/92) **88**
Pommard Grands Epenottes 1988: Solid up front, with ripe, intense cherry, currant and berry flavors framed by toasty oak and spice notes, but it turns simple at mid-palate before gaining a complex finish. Drink in 1994 to '99. $38 (3/31/91) **86**

JAFFELIN
Pommard 1989: Intense, with black cherry, tar and toast flavors and rather hard tannins in a rustic style. Try in 1994. $33 (1/31/92) **85**
Pommard 1986: Tough and austere, with a wide streak of chalky flavors that keep the cherry flavor from blossoming. Give it time and it should develop nicely. $26 (4/30/89) **79**
Pommard 1985 $38 (3/15/88) **89**
Pommard 1983 $19 (9/15/86) **81**

LABOURE-ROI
Pommard Les Bertins 1985 $29 (3/15/88) **79**

LOUIS LATOUR
Pommard Epenottes 1985 $46 (3/15/88) **89**

OLIVIER LEFLAIVE FRERES
Pommard 1989: Has wild mushroom and berry aromas and flavors in a medium-bodied package, with medium, slightly dry tannins. Try in 1994. $32 (1/31/92) **84**
Pommard 1988 $31 (7/15/90) (BT) **75+**
Pommard Epenottes 1989: Shows toasted, roasted coffee and berry flavors and a silky mouth-feel, but it has a full tannin finish. Try in 1995. $40 (1/31/92) **88**

DOMAINE LEROY
Pommard Les Vignots 1989: A gorilla of a wine; needs to be caged and not let out for 10 years. We might consider killing for a bottle of this. Has full tannins and full fruit, yet it's wonderfully balanced. Try in 1998. $75 (1/31/92) **96**
Pommard Les Vignots 1988: Lean, dry and tannic, with a good dose of spicy oak. Has plenty of peppery cherry and plum flavors, too, but the finish turns very dry and tannic. Cellar until 1994. 209 cases made. $84 (4/30/91) **88**

DOMAINE CHANTAL LESCURE
Pommard Les Bertins 1988: A big, sturdy Pommard, with depth and concentration, that manages to maintain elegance and grace. The black cherry, plum and currant flavors are flanked by thick, firm but supple tannins that bode well for cellaring until 1993 or '94. 500 cases made. $40 (11/30/90) **88**

LUPE-CHOLET
Pommard Les Boucherottes 1983 $19 (6/16/86) **86**

ROBERT MAX
Pommard 1982 $16 (12/16/84) **82**

PRINCE FLORENT DE MERODE
Pommard Clos de la Platière 1987: This earthy style is soft and sweet on the palate, but the barnyardy character is too strong and the structure too weak to please most Burgundy fanciers. Drink now or cellar through 1994. $36 (8/31/90) **76**
Pommard Clos de la Platière 1986: Austere style like most 1986s, with a rich aroma followed by a mouthful of tannin and lean, structured black cherry and spicy oak flavors. The fruit comes through on the aftertaste. Drink in three years. $35 (7/31/89) **86**
Pommard Clos de la Platière 1985 $45 (3/15/88) **94**
Pommard Clos de la Platière 1984 $23 (2/15/88) **71**

JEAN MICHELOT
Pommard 1987: Dry, tannic and leathery despite some pretty aromas of rose petal and berries. A hint of fruit comes through, with oak and spice seasonings, but right now it's tightly wrapped up. Drink now through 1994. $33 (8/31/90) **78**
Pommard 1985 $29 (4/30/88) **87**
Pommard 1983 $21 (6/16/86) **78**

MOILLARD
Pommard Clos des Epeneaux 1985 Rel: $40 Cur: $45 (6/30/88) CS **92**
Pommard Rugiens 1985 $40 (6/30/88) **85**

MOMMESSIN
Pommard 1989: Rather chewy, with meaty chestnut and blackberry flavors, medium tannins and a fresh finish. Try from 1994. $28 (1/31/92) **88**

DOMAINE RENE MONNIER
Pommard Les Vignots 1985 $30 (11/15/88) **89**
Pommard Les Vignots 1982 $17 (7/01/85) **81**

DOMAINE MUSSY
Pommard 1986: Lean and simple, and more than a bit dull. Flat and uninspiring. $32 (4/30/89) **66**
Pommard 1985 $35 (10/15/88) **86**
Pommard Premier Cru 1986: Ripe and generous for an '86, wrapped in plenty of tannin but showing spicy cherry and vanilla aromas and flavors, velvety texture and good length. Real potential here. $35 (4/30/89) **86**

Key to Symbols

The scores reported here are the results of blind tastings conducted by our panel of senior editors. Wines that carry the initials below are results of individual tastings.

THE WINE SPECTATOR 100-POINT SCALE ***95-100***—Classic, a great wine; ***90-94***—Outstanding, superior character and style; ***80-89***—Good to very good, a wine with special qualities; ***70-79***—Average, drinkable wine that may have minor flaws; ***60-69***—Below average, drinkable but not recommended; ***50-59***—Poor, undrinkable, not recommended. "+"—With a score indicates a range; used primarily with barrel tastings to indicate a preliminary score.

SPECIAL DESIGNATIONS SS—Spectator Selection, CS—Cellar Selection, BB—Best Buy, ($NA)—Price not available, (NR)—Not released.

TASTER'S INITIALS (JG)—Jim Gordon, (HS)—Harvey Steiman, (JL)—James Laube, (JS)—James Suckling, (TM)—Thomas Matthews, (TR)—Terry Robards, (PM)—Per-Henrik Mansson, (BT)—Barrel Tasting (these wines were tasted blind from barrel samples), (CA-date)—*California's Great Cabernets* by James Laube, (CH-date)—*California's Great Chardonnays* by James Laube, (VP-date)—*Vintage Port* by James Suckling.

DATE TASTED Dates in parentheses represent the issue in which the rating was published.

DOMAINE PARENT
Pommard 1982 $18 (11/01/85) **83**
Pommard Les Epenottes 1959 ($NA) (8/31/90) **94**

PARIGOT PERE & FILS
Pommard Les Charmots 1987: Plenty of concentrated raspberry and cherry flavors with firm tannins and structure. Rough and tough on the finish, lacking a velvety texture. Drink 1993 and beyond. $28 (7/31/89) **87**
Pommard Les Charmots 1985 Rel: $24 Cur: $34 (6/15/87) CS **93**

DOMAINE JEAN PASCAL
Pommard La Chanière 1986 $30 (10/15/88) **78**

CHATEAU DE POMMARD
Pommard 1989: This succulent wine creeps up on you, with a leafy, earthy berry character and medium tannins. Try in 1994. (NR) (1/31/92) **86**
Pommard 1979 Rel: $33 Cur: $38 (9/01/85) **88**

POTHIER-RIEUSSET
Pommard 1986: Simple and decent with earthy cherry flavors that are very ripe and gamy. Drink now through 1994. $25 (9/15/89) **76**
Pommard Clos de Verger 1986: A remarkably attractive '86 with pretty toast, cherry, spice and cinnamon notes that are supple and elegant yet backed by firm tannins. Drink now through 1993. $33 (9/15/89) **87**
Pommard Rugiens 1986: Light, simple, and decent with beetlike flavors but not much in the way of depth; little to captivate the imagination. Drink up now. $35 (9/15/89) **72**

LA POUSSE D'OR
Pommard Les Jarollières 1988: Crisp and firm in texture, but loaded with expressive raspberry, strawberry and plum flavors shaded by oak on the finish. Tightly wrapped and ready for the cellar; should emerge around 1996 to 2000 as a beauty. $57 (8/31/91) **88**
Pommard Les Jarollières 1986: Another tough, austere '86 Burgundy, with some earthy flavors and enough velvety texture to make it worth taking a chance on cellaring. Try it now. $45 (4/30/89) **70**
Pommard Les Jarollières 1985 $39 (3/15/88) **87**

CHATEAU DE PULIGNY-MONTRACHET
Pommard 1988: Crisp and flavorful, with lively raspberry and cherry aromas and flavors and notes of toast and vanilla. A bit tart and tannic, built to grow with age. Try in 1993 to '95. $34 (8/31/90) **83**

THORIN
Pommard 1986: Thin and tannic without much fruit or charm. Best to drink it now while there's still a faint hint of wild berry fruit remaining. Tasted twice. $24 (2/28/90) **75**

CHARLES VIENOT
Pommard 1985 $33 (4/30/88) **81**

SANTENAY

ADRIEN BELLAND
Santenay Comme 1987: Very crisp and lemony, but the strawberry aromas manage to echo on the finish of this lean, lighter-weight wine. Try now. $22 (11/15/90) **78**
Santenay Comme 1982 Rel: $12 Cur: $25 (8/01/85) CS **91**

BICHOT
Santenay 1986: Lean, crisp and tannic, with green flavors that never quite penetrate the restrictive structure. Might be more generous by now. $12 (10/15/89) **78**
Santenay Clos Rousseau 1988 $20 (7/15/90) (BT) **70+**
Santenay Les Gravières 1985 $15 (3/15/88) **66**

PIERRE BOUREE FILS
Santenay Gravières 1985 $30 (5/31/88) **88**

F. CHAUVENET
Santenay 1985 $18 (7/31/87) **84**

FRANCOISE & DENIS CLAIR
Santenay Clos de la Comme 1988: A very firm, flavorful Burgundy, with lively strawberry and cherry flavors backed by solid tannins and accented with spicy, earthy notes. Tempting to drink now, but should improve if cellared until about 1994. $25 (6/15/92) **85**

LOUIS CLAIR
Santenay Gravières Domaine de L'Abbaye 1985 $17 (10/15/87) **88**

JOSEPH DROUHIN
Santenay 1989: Very lively, with beautiful, fresh raspberry, cherry and other fruit aromas and flavors and medium tannins. Try in 1993. $44 (1/31/92) **87**
Santenay 1985 $17 (11/15/87) **88**

JEAN-NOEL GAGNARD
Santenay Clos de Tavannes 1989: Crisp in texture, with flavors that lean toward strawberry and leather, finishing with a nice echo of spice and anise notes. Needs until 1993 or '94 to open up. $25 (11/15/91) **85**
Santenay Clos de Tavannes 1988: Has a light color, but the spice, berry and red cherry aromas and flavors have plenty of snap, lingering through a lively finish. It's drinkable now, but cellaring through 1994 can only add some welcome nuances. $25 (11/15/90) **84**

DOMAINE JEAN GIRARDIN
Santenay Clos Rousseau Château de la Charrière 1987: Elegant and stylish, with pretty cherry, raspberry and hints of strawberry flavors that are fresh, rich and clean. Finishes with a slight bite, but nothing serious. An easy-drinking style that's ready to drink now through 1993. $25 (2/28/91) **87**
Santenay La Comme Château de la Charrière 1987: Simple and pleasant, with attractive cherry and raspberry flavors and moderate tannins. Ready to drink now. $25 (2/28/91) **83**
Santenay La Comme Château de la Charrière 1986: Typical '86, generous in aroma and flavor but the scratchy tannins clamp down and fight the not quite intense enough flavors to a draw. Cellaring until 1993 could help. $23 (10/15/89) **80**

LOUIS JADOT
Santenay Clos de Malte 1989 (NR) (7/15/90) (BT) **80+**

JAFFELIN
Santenay 1989: Nothing ambitious, but it's very pretty, with smoky cherry and berry character and fine tannins. Try in 1993. $17 (1/31/92) **85**
Santenay La Maladière 1989: Pleasant and easy to drink, this red Burgundy has lovely red licorice and berry flavors and a light finish. Try in 1993. $20 (1/31/92) **82**
Santenay La Maladière 1988: Smells attractive, with smoke and plum aromas, but it doesn't quite follow through on the palate. The flavors thin out a bit and it's a touch tannic, but this is a pleasant drink. Drink now through 1995. $21 (8/31/91) **84**
Santenay La Maladière 1985 $22 (3/15/88) **84**

JESSIAUME PERE & FILS
Santenay Les Gravières 1988: Elegant and fruity, with pretty plum, strawberry and cherry flavors that are ripe and attractive. The finish has firm tannins, good length and a touch of oak. Drink in 1994 to 2000. $21 (3/31/91) **86**

LOUIS LATOUR
Santenay 1989: Light, like a Beaujolais, with fresh Pinot character and light tannins, but not much beyond. Drink with pizza or burgers on release. (NR) (1/31/92) **80**

OLIVIER LEFLAIVE FRERES
Santenay 1986 $17 (7/31/88) **81**

DOMAINE LEQUIN-ROUSSOT
Santenay 1987: Light and earthy, with hints of strawberry and spice, but shows very little in the way of aroma at this point. Should benefit from cellaring until late 1992. $15 (11/15/90) **76**
Santenay 1985 $18 (5/31/88) **78**
Santenay La Comme 1985 $24 (5/31/88) **85**

PROSPER MAUFOUX
Santenay Les Gravières 1985: Round and velvety, with long-lasting spicy cherry and toast flavors, a bit herbal on the nose but it has generous flavors on a fairly light frame. Drinkable now. $17 (10/15/89) **85**
Santenay Les Gravières 1985 $18 (10/15/88) **87**

MOMMESSIN
Santenay Grand Clos Rousseau 1989 (NR) (7/15/90) (BT) **80+**
Santenay Grand Clos Rousseau 1988 $23 (7/15/90) (BT) **75+**

BERNARD MOREY
Santenay Grand Clos Rousseau 1987: Ripe, generous and velvety, with lovely Bing cherry and toast aromas and flavors that carry through the long finish. Short-term cellaring could contribute more finesse, but it's already delicious and has more depth than you would expect from this modest appellation. $24 (10/15/89) **87**

LA POUSSE D'OR
Santenay Clos Tavannes 1989: A blockbuster for this appellation. Packed to the brim with vanilla, berry and fruit flavors, as well as full tannins. Try in 1994. $29 (1/31/92) **91**
Santenay Clos Tavannes 1988: Tough, tannic and earthy, with a plum and tobacco edge to the aroma. A hard wine, with enough flavor packed into it to last until the tannins subside, perhaps around 1997 or '98. $28 (8/31/91) **83**
Santenay Clos Tavannes 1986 $27 (6/15/89) **78**
Santenay Clos Tavannes 1985 $22 (3/15/88) **67**

DOMAINE PRIEUR-BRUNET
Santenay Maladière 1988: Tannic in structure but generous in flavor, offering plum, raspberry and spice aromas and flavors that are concentrated enough to balance the formidable tannins. Still needs until at least 1995 to soften and open up on the finish. $20 (11/15/90) **80**

DOMAINE ROUX PERE & FILS
Santenay 1985 $21 (10/31/87) **83**

Savigny-lès-Beaune

PIERRE ANDRE
Savigny-lès-Beaune Clos des Guettes 1985 $20 (7/31/88) **85**

BICHOT
Savigny-lès-Beaune 1988 $17 (7/15/90) (BT) **80+**
Savigny-lès-Beaune 1986: Appealingly aromatic, it's a bit austere and astringent on the palate, but the spicy strawberry flavors peek through on the finish. Should develop fine and be drinkable now. $10 (10/15/89) **81**
Savigny-lès-Beaune Hospices de Beaune Cuvée Fouquerand 1988: A smoky, almost cooked character marks this red Burgundy. Its good cherry and spice flavors are overrun by a burnt character, and the end result isn't very appealing. $39 (1/31/92) **78**

PIERRE BITOUZET
Savigny-lès-Beaune Les Lavières 1986: Tight and concentrated, with cherry, spice and wood flavors that are young and intense. Needs time to soften and develop a smoother texture. Drink now to 1995. $15 (3/31/90) **87**
Savigny-lès-Beaune Les Lavières 1985 $19 (3/15/88) **67**

SIMON BIZE & FILS
Savigny-lès-Beaune Les Bourgeots 1989: Very aromatic, with beautiful cedar, violet, mushroom and berry aromas that echo on the chewy palate. Perhaps a bit dry on the finish. Try from 1994. $19 (1/31/92) **85**
Savigny-lès-Beaune Aux Vergelesses 1989: Gentle yet complex, with lovely leafy cherry and strawberry aromas and flavors and firm, polished tannins. Try from 1994. $27 (1/31/92) **87**

BOUCHARD PERE & FILS
Savigny-lès-Beaune 1989: A simple, straightforward Savigny-lès-Beaune, with herbal notes. May be better in 1993. $29 (1/31/92) **82**
Savigny-lès-Beaune Les Lavières Domaines du Château de Beaune 1989 $29 (7/15/90) (BT) **80+**
Savigny-lès-Beaune Les Lavières Domaines du Château de Beaune 1988: Full-bodied, dense and flavorful, with earthy, herbal notes shading the berry flavor and very firm tannins. Probably best to cellar until 1993 to '95. Tasted twice. 1,230 cases made. $29 (4/30/91) **83**
Savigny-lès-Beaune Les Lavières Domaines du Château de Beaune 1986 $25 (7/31/88) **78**

VALENTIN BOUCHOTTE
Savigny-lès-Beaune Hauts-Jarrons 1988: Tight and concentrated, with firm spice, cinnamon, cherry, plum and smoky oak flavors, finishing with a meaty oak aftertaste and ample tannins for cellaring until 1993 or '94. $31 (2/28/91) **83**

DOMAINE CHANDON DE BRIAILLES
Savigny-lès-Beaune Les Lavières 1988: Ripe and plummy, with pretty floral aromas, tight, compact cherry and currant flavors and firm tannins that keep them in check. The flavors need time to mellow and expand; hold until 1993 to '95. $31 (2/28/91) **86**

MAURICE CHENU
Savigny-lès-Beaune 1989 (NR) (7/15/90) (BT) **75+**
Savigny-lès-Beaune 1988 (NR) (7/15/90) (BT) **75+**

A.R. CHOPPIN
Savigny-lès-Beaune Vergelesses 1987: Youthful, violet-tinged cherry and raspberry aromas and flavors pierce through a thin veil of velvety tannin in this well-balanced but somewhat short-finished wine. Drinkable now. $32 (2/28/90) **79**
Savigny-lès-Beaune Vergelesses 1985 $25 (10/31/87) **87**

DOMAINE BRUNO CLAIR
Savigny-lès-Beaune La Dominode 1989: Classy Savigny-lès-Beaune, made in a clean, focused style, full of vanilla and raspberry flavors. Has a balanced, supple finish. Try from 1994. (NR) (1/31/92) **89**
Savigny-lès-Beaune La Dominode 1985 $24 (3/15/88) **80**

JOSEPH DROUHIN
Savigny-lès-Beaune 1989: Flavorful and quite rich for this group, with red licorice and berry notes and a fresh, juicy finish. Try from 1993. $23 (1/31/92) **87**
Savigny-lès-Beaune 1988 $22 (7/15/90) (BT) **80+**
Savigny-lès-Beaune 1985 $21 (11/15/87) SS **91**
Savigny-lès-Beaune 1981 $16 (9/01/84) **79**

DUBREUIL-FONTAINE
Savigny-lès-Beaune Les Vergelesses 1989 (NR) (7/15/90) (BT) **80+**
Savigny-lès-Beaune Les Vergelesses 1988 (NR) (7/15/90) (BT) **75+**
Savigny-lès-Beaune Les Vergelesses 1985: Lean and crisp, with sharply focused cherry and strawberry fruit, overtones of cinnamon and toast, smooth and silky on the finish. Drink now. $24 (1/31/89) **88**

MAURICE ECARD
Savigny-lès-Beaune Les Peuillets 1989: Light and charming, with very pretty strawberry and watermelon aromas and flavors, turning tight and tannic on the palate. Has the polish and style to be worth cellaring until 1994 or '95. $25 (11/15/91) **87**
Savigny-lès-Beaune Les Serpentières 1989: A ripe, rangy style, with plenty of strawberry and plum flavors intertwined with spice and leather overtones. Not a lightweight by any means; needs until 1994 or '95 to settle down. $25 (11/15/91) **88**
Savigny-lès-Beaune Les Serpentières 1987: Firm and somewhat tannic for such a light, soft wine, but the ripe cherry fruit tinged with toast is appealing. The tannins should have subsided by now, making it fine for current drinking. $17 (10/15/89) **80**

MACHARD DE GRAMONT
Savigny-lès-Beaune Les Guettes 1985 $25 (7/31/88) **89**

JAFFELIN
Savigny-lès-Beaune 1989: Offers fresh, lively cherry and berry aromas and flavors and medium tannins. Easy to like. Try from 1993. $18 (1/31/92) **85**

LOUIS LATOUR
Savigny-lès-Beaune 1989: Has pretty, modest smoky strawberry and vanilla notes in a light style. Try on release. (NR) (1/31/92) **84**

DOMAINE LEROY
Savigny-lès-Beaune Les Narbantons 1989: Offers very attractive vanilla, berry and licorice aromas and flavors in a smooth yet fresh package. Try from 1994. $65 (1/31/92) **91**

LUPE-CHOLET
Savigny-lès-Beaune Les Serpentières 1985 $17 (3/15/88) **83**

MOMMESSIN
Savigny-lès-Beaune 1985 $17 (7/31/88) **80**

MONGEARD-MUGNERET
Savigny-lès-Beaune Les Narbantons 1989: Light, with rather appealing earthy stewed tomato and plum flavors. Try now. $28 (1/31/92) **78**

ALBERT MOROT
Savigny-lès-Beaune Vergelesses La Bataillère 1988: Ripe and earthy, with spicy, cedary aromas from oak and rich cherry and leather flavors that turn dry and tannic on the finish. Balanced and intense; needs cellaring until 1995 to soften. $26 (3/31/91) **86**

JEAN-MARC PAVELOT
Savigny-lès-Beaune 1986: Generous aromas and flavors of wild strawberry and cinnamon manage to maintain their integrity over fairly insistent tannins, suggesting that cellaring until 1993 will soften it to sure drinkability. $18 (10/15/89) **84**
Savigny-lès-Beaune Les Guettes 1985 $20 (2/15/88) **89**

TOLLOT-BEAUT
Savigny-lès-Beaune Lavières 1989: A serious wine, with gorgeous toasty vanilla and violet notes that ripple through the palate. Long and delicious on the finish. Try from 1994. (NR) (1/31/92) **90**
Savigny-lès-Beaune Lavières 1988 $28 (7/15/90) (BT) **85+**

HENRI DE VILLAMONT
Savigny-lès-Beaune Le Village 1988: Compact in scale, with firm tannins and modest flavors that need time to soften up in the cellar, but by 1993 or '94 the strawberry, nutmeg, clove and vanilla flavors should emerge nicely. $18 (3/31/91) **80**

Volnay

BICHOT
Volnay 1988: This spicy, racy style has distinctive cranberry, berry and cinnamon aromas and flavors, very firm tannins and a tight structure. The good length suggests that cellaring until 1993 to '95 will serve it well. $25 (8/31/90) **84**
Volnay 1983 $18 (9/15/86) **68**
Volnay Hospices de Beaune Cuvée Blondeau 1988: Spicy oak notes are amply balanced by concentrated plum and cherry flavors in this deep-colored, fully tannic Burgundy. Has good depth and complexity of flavor and a lingering, fruity finish. Stylish and attractive. Best to drink after 1993. Tasted twice. $60 (6/15/92) **87**
Volnay Hospices de Beaune Cuvée Blondeau 1985: Firm and concentrated, with ripe cherry and vanilla flavors that extend to a lingering finish, smooth and flavorful, but already showing some delicious harmony. $53 (4/30/89) **88**
Volnay Hospices de Beaune Cuvée Blondeau 1982 Rel: $26 Cur: $38 (8/01/84) SS **92**
Volnay Premier Cru 1986 $25 (7/31/88) **84**
Volnay-Santenots 1986: Tart, lean and tannic, with citrus flavors. Hard to like now, though it might be better around 1993 to '95. $22 (10/31/89) **77**

BITOUZET-PRIEUR
Volnay Clos des Chênes 1987: A hard, tannic, gamy style that's difficult to warm up to. Like many '87s it lacks generosity and depth, but it's pleasant enough to drink. Some may find the style appealing. Drink now through 1994. $36 (12/31/90) **80**
Volnay Pitures 1985 $36 (7/31/88) **91**

DOMAINE LUCIEN BOILLOT
Volnay Les Angles 1985 $33 (7/15/88) **86**

PIERRE BOILLOT
Volnay-Santenots 1988: A lively, flavorful wine, with lots of berry, plum and spice aromas and flavors. Drink now through 1995. $37 (8/31/90) **85**
Volnay-Santenots 1987: Smooth, aromatic and generous with cinnamon and rose-tinged cherry flavors, plus a touch of earthiness. Attractive now, but cellaring through 1994 should help. $37 (6/15/90) **86**

JEAN CLAUDE BOISSET
Volnay Clos des Chênes 1985 $28 (4/15/88) **86**

BOUCHARD PERE & FILS
Volnay-Caillerets Ancienne Cuvée Carnot Château de Beaune 1989: Fantastic concoction of rich, focused Pinot Noir flavor that takes on a racy edge. With its ultrafine tannins, the texture is smooth and polished but the fruit is deep, complex and persistent. An outstanding wine from a highly rated year. Should get even better if aged until about 1996. 1,500 cases made. $52 (2/29/92) CS **94**
Volnay-Caillerets Ancienne Cuvée Carnot Château de Beaune 1988: Has fruity, perfumed aromas, ripe cherry, plum and raspberry flavors that are tight and lean, crisp acidity, supple tannins and pretty flavors on the aftertaste. Balanced and complex; try between 1995 and 2000. $47 (3/31/91) **87**
Volnay-Caillerets Ancienne Cuvée Carnot Château de Beaune 1986 $34 (7/31/88) **83**
Volnay-Caillerets Ancienne Cuvée Carnot Château de Beaune 1985 $44 (1/31/89) **87**
Volnay Frémiets Clos de la Rougeotte Domaines du Château 1985: Lean and concentrated, with

leathery, herbal undertones to the cherry and strawberry flavor, long and elegant on the finish. A bit tannic on release; time in the cellar should have made it drinkable by now. $35 (1/31/89) **88**
Volnay Taillepieds Domaines du Château de Beaune 1989: A decadent style, with leaf, mushroom, berry and cherry aromas and flavors and silky tannins. Try in 1995. $48 (1/31/92) **88**
Volnay Taillepieds Domaines du Château de Beaune 1988: Earthy, chalky aromas and flavors marked this one for the cellar, where it should have developed into a fuller, more generous wine than the tough, tight wine it was on release. Drink now. $50 (3/31/91) **88**

DOMAINE JEAN-MARC BOULEY
Volnay-Caillerets 1985 $27 (10/15/88) **90**
Volnay Clos des Chênes 1985 $27 (10/15/88) **87**

DOMAINE F. BUFFET
Volnay Champans 1985 $35 (10/15/88) **91**
Volnay Clos de la Rougeotte 1985 $35 (10/15/88) **91**

F. CHAUVENET
Volnay Clos des Chênes 1989: A kinder, gentler Volnay, with lovely mushroom, white chocolate and fruit flavors and silky tannins. Try in 1994. $40 (1/31/92) **90**
Volnay Premier Cru 1989: This more elegant style of Volnay has earth and berry flavors and medium tannins. Try in 1994. $36 (1/31/92) **88**

JOSEPH DROUHIN
Volnay 1989 $43 (7/15/90) (BT) **80+**
Volnay 1988 $36 (7/15/90) (BT) **80+**
Volnay 1985 $29 (11/15/87) **88**
Volnay Chevret 1989: A very fruity style of Volnay, with lots of plum and earth characters and medium-full tannins. Try in 1995. (NR) (1/31/92) **90**
Volnay Clos des Chênes 1989: This seductive wine offers lovely earthy berry and other fruit aromas and flavors and excellent tannins. Try in 1994. $50 (1/31/92) **91**
Volnay Clos des Chênes 1988: Extremely tannic, tight and more astringent than most '88s, but without the rich fruit flavor for balance. Hints of cherry and spice sneak through on the finish, but it's a gamble. Will need until 1995 to settle down. $45 (2/15/91) **85**
Volnay Clos des Chênes 1987: Minty aromas and flavors dominate this light, slightly tannic wine, but its red cherry flavor peeks through on the finish. By now it should have softened up and become a lovely drink. $30 (6/15/90) **85**
Volnay Clos des Chênes 1986 $31 (4/30/89) **80**

REMY GAUTHIER
Volnay-Santenots 1985 $27 (3/15/88) **87**

CHATEAU DES HERBEUX
Volnay-Santenots 1988: Firm tannins and austere cherry, plum and spice flavors fill the mouth, but also leave a long, tough, tannic finish. A hard, tight wine for the cellar; best to wait until 1995 to 2000 to drink. $36 (11/30/90) **88**

JAFFELIN
Volnay 1989: Succulent, with juicy cherry, berry and earth flavors and a round mouth-feel. Very sweet fruit emerges on the finish. Try in 1994. $29 (1/31/92) **89**
Volnay 1988: Ripe and generous, with elegant plum, black cherry, wild berry and spice flavors that are bright and lively. Not too tannic. Drink now or hold through 1994. $30 (8/31/91) **88**
Volnay 1986: Has all the classic smoky raspberry and vanilla aromas and flavors, and it's a bit more generous on the palate than most '86s. Finishes well, too. $27 (4/30/89) **86**
Volnay 1985 $30 (3/15/88) **88**
Volnay 1983 $17 (10/16/85) **92**

DOMAINE MICHEL LAFARGE
Volnay 1989: Rich and opulent, with plenty of intense chocolate, earth, berry and meat aromas and flavors and a long, velvety finish. Try in 1994. $41 (1/31/92) **88**
Volnay Clos des Chênes 1989: Monumentally rich, with wonderfully opulent berry, chestnut and cherry flavors, an earthy note, silky tannins and a long, full finish. Try in 1995. $67 (1/31/92) **95**
Volnay Clos des Chênes 1988: Ripe, rich raspberry, strawberry and cherry flavors are deep and concentrated, staying with you from start to finish. Tightens up on the finish, where the tannins show their strength, but there's plenty of flavor to like. Best to cellar until 1995. $65 (7/15/91) **90**
Volnay Clos du Château des Ducs 1989: An outstanding wine, with opulent, meaty, earthy currant aromas and flavors. The afterburners kick in on the finish, with tannins and ripe fruit. Try in 1996. $67 (1/31/92) **94**
Volnay Clos du Château des Ducs 1988: A pretty core of elegant, rich black cherry and currant flavors is fresh and lively, with lots of depth and intrigue. The fruit lingers long on the finish, echoing plum and cherry notes. Has plenty of tannins for cellaring through 1994. $65 (7/15/91) **90**
Volnay Premier Cru 1988: Tight and compact, with pretty, ripe plum, currant and spice notes that are firmly wrapped in thick tannins. A nice touch of cranberry and anise comes through on the finish. Best to cellar until 1996. $44 (7/15/91) **87**

PIERRE LATOUR
Volnay-Caillerets 1953 ($NA) (8/31/90) **86**
Volnay-Caillerets 1952 ($NA) (8/31/90) **90**

OLIVIER LEFLAIVE FRERES
Volnay 1987: Stemmy, thin, shallow and tannic, with barely enough peppery cherry flavor to stand up to it. Tasted twice, with consistent notes. Drink now to 1993. $27 (8/31/90) **78**
Volnay Clos de la Barre 1989: Exuberant, with wonderful cherry, berry and mushroom nuances and a round, velvety mouth-feel. Try in 1995. $38 (1/31/92) **92**
Volnay Clos de la Barre 1988 $40 (7/15/90) (BT) **85+**
Volnay Clos de la Barre 1986 $28 (7/31/88) **89**

LUPE-CHOLET
Volnay Hospices de Beaune Cuvée Blondeau 1986 ($NA) (7/31/88) **91**

MARQUIS D'ANGERVILLE
Volnay Clos des Ducs 1985 $35 (3/15/88) **80**

CHATEAU DE MEURSAULT
Volnay Clos des Chênes 1988: Despite fine, delicate tannins, the texture is soft and supple, with generous oak, plum, cherry and vanilla flavors that are complex and well balanced and linger on the finish. Drink in 1994 or '95. $47 (7/15/91) **87**

MOILLARD
Volnay Clos des Chênes 1985 $32 (7/15/88) **89**
Volnay Clos des Chênes 1983 $15 (12/01/85) **75**

MOMMESSIN
Volnay Clos des Chênes 1988 $38 (7/15/90) (BT) **85+**
Volnay Hospices de Beaune Cuvée General-Muteau 1985 $80 (3/15/88) **91**

DOMAINE MONTHELIE-DOUHAIRET
Volnay Champans 1985 $25 (7/15/88) **87**

POTHIER-EMONIN
Volnay 1986: Pretty fruit and florals aromas with tart, lean, compact fruit on the palate. Leans toward the austere style, but it opens up with cherry and berry flavors on the finish. Drink up now. $24 (4/30/89) **85**

POTHIER-RIEUSSET
Volnay 1985 $21 (2/15/88) **93**

LA POUSSE D'OR
Volnay Les Caillerets 1988: Very firm and tannic, but it has a bright beam of raspberry and plum flavor that turns into earthiness on the finish. A hard-edged wine that needs until 1995 to show what it has. $49 (8/31/91) **85**
Volnay Les Caillerets 1985 $35 (3/15/88) **90**
Volnay Les Caillerets Clos des 60 Ouvrées 1988: Ripe and a bit alcoholic, but sharply focused, with solid raspberry and smoke flavors that extend into the finish. The tannins need until 1995 to '98 to smooth out. $53 (8/31/91) **82**
Volnay Les Caillerets Clos des 60 Ouvrées 1987: Fresh, firm and crisp, a lighter wine with pleasant cherry and spice aromas and flavors that are a bit short and simple. Try it now. $29 (6/15/90) **82**
Volnay Les Caillerets Clos des 60 Ouvrées 1986: Lean and austere with simple but pretty berry, toast and tart cherry fruit that gets more generous and tannic on the finish. Needs cellaring, drink in 1993. $41 (4/30/89) **83**
Volnay Les Caillerets Clos des 60 Ouvrées 1985 Rel: $39 Cur: $49 (3/15/88) **86**
Volnay Clos d'Audignac 1989: Like sniffing black truffles; shows beautiful autumnal aromas, with an extremely firm, tannic backbone. Built for aging. Try in 1996. $45 (1/31/92) **92**
Volnay Clos de la Bousse d'Or 1989: More delicate in style, with smashing aromas and flavors of violet, berry, earth—the descriptors go on—as does the fine finish. Try in 1994. $60 (1/31/92) **90**
Volnay Clos de la Bousse d'Or 1986: Hard and tannic, but it shows a thin beam of berry fruit; it's pretty austere, decadent stuff. Try it now. $46 (4/30/89) **75**

DOMAINE PRIEUR-BRUNET
Volnay-Santenots 1988: Tight and compact, with sharply focused cherry and spice flavors that don't reveal much now, but with time and maturity it should show more generosity. Start drinking in 1994 or '95. $35 (11/30/90) **85**

ROSSIGNOL-FEVRIER
Volnay 1988: Tight, lean, intense and concentrated, with pretty aromas and a solid core of black cherry, currant, berry and raspberry flavors tightly wrapped in firm tannins. A keeper; will probably reach maturity in 1995 or '96. 185 cases made. $32 (3/31/91) **92**

ARMAND ROUX
Volnay Hospices de Beaune Général Muteau 1959 $115 (8/31/90) **91**

DOMAINE ROUX PERE & FILS
Volnay en Champans 1988: Has wonderful aromas, but it's not quite as flavorful on the palate. A rich, smoky wine, with pretty currant and berry flavors that are concentrated and thick. Drink now through 1995. $35 (3/31/90) **86**
Volnay en Champans 1985 $25 (3/15/87) **92**

JACQUES THEVENOT-MACHAL
Volnay-Santenots 1988: Rich, deep, concentrated and tannic, with a wealth of ripe cherry, currant, plum and earthy oak flavors on a rather lean framework, with a pretty toasty oak overlay. Youthful and in need of cellaring; hold off drinking until 1994 at the earliest. $36 (11/15/90) **89**

OTHER CÔTE DE BEAUNE RED

DOMAINE D'AUVENAY
Auxey-Duresses 1989: This beautiful wine shows serious winemaking, with fresh cherry, berry and toasty oak notes and fine tannins. From Domaine Leroy. Try in 1993. $42 (1/31/92) **88**

BICHOT
Monthélie Hospices de Beaune Cuvée Lebelin 1985 $52 (10/15/87) **86**

JEAN CLAUDE BOISSET
Côte de Beaune-Villages 1982 $5 (7/01/85) BB **86**

BOUCHARD PERE & FILS
Côte de Beaune-Villages 1982 $19 (5/16/84) SS **88**
Côte de Beaune-Villages Clos des Topes Bizot 1983 $22 (9/15/86) **82**

DOMAINE JEAN CHARTRON
Puligny-Montrachet Clos du Caillerets 1989 (NR) (7/15/90) (BT) **85+**
Puligny-Montrachet Clos du Caillerets 1988 (NR) (7/15/90) (BT) **85+**

CHARTRON & TREBUCHET
Côte de Beaune-Villages 1988: Sturdy and straightforward for a red Burgundy, with good cherry flavors, firm tannins and a short finish. $16 (2/28/91) **79**

F. CHAUVENET
Auxey-Duresses Le Val 1989: Starts out nicely on the nose, but falls apart on the palate. Very diluted. Drink on release. (NR) (1/31/92) **79**
Côte de Beaune-Villages 1985 $16 (7/31/87) **84**
Monthélie Champs-Fulliot 1989: Light and straightforward, but it has lovely strawberry and dark chocolate nuances and a light finish. Drink on release. $20 (1/31/92) **81**
Puligny-Montrachet 1985 $16 (6/15/87) **81**

MAURICE CHENU
Côte de Beaune-Villages 1989 (NR) (7/15/90) (BT) **85+**
Côte de Beaune-Villages 1988 (NR) (7/15/90) (BT) **80+**

J.-F. COCHE-DURY
Auxey-Duresses 1987: Beautifully articulated strawberry, raspberry and cherry aromas and flavors carry right on through to the long, elegant finish in this well-focused, supple wine. Tannins can use cellaring until 1993. $30 (2/28/90) **87**
Meursault 1987: Light, supple style of red wine, with plenty of strawberry and cherry aromas and flavors to trip lightly over the palate, but with enough tannin to require cellaring until 1993. $30 (2/28/90) **80**

EDMOND CORNU
Ladoix 1987: An austere style that's tight, tart and herbal, with lime and metallic notes on the finish. Drink up now. $18 (2/28/91) **78**

Key to Symbols

The scores reported here are the results of blind tastings conducted by our panel of senior editors. Wines that carry the initials below are results of individual tastings.

THE WINE SPECTATOR 100-POINT SCALE ***95-100***—Classic, a great wine; ***90-94***—Outstanding, superior character and style; ***80-89***—Good to very good, a wine with special qualities; ***70-79***—Average, drinkable wine that may have minor flaws; ***60-69***—Below average, drinkable but not recommended; ***50-59***—Poor, undrinkable, not recommended. "+"—With a score indicates a range; used primarily with barrel tastings to indicate a preliminary score.

SPECIAL DESIGNATIONS SS—Spectator Selection, CS—Cellar Selection, BB—Best Buy, ($NA)—Price not available, (NR)—Not released.

TASTER'S INITIALS (JG)—Jim Gordon, (HS)—Harvey Steiman, (JL)—James Laube, (JS)—James Suckling, (TM)—Thomas Matthews, (TR)—Terry Robards, (PM)—Per-Henrik Mansson, (BT)—Barrel Tasting (these wines were tasted blind from barrel samples), (CA-date)—*California's Great Cabernets* by James Laube, (CH-date)—*California's Great Chardonnays* by James Laube, (VP-date)—*Vintage Port* by James Suckling.

DATE TASTED Dates in parentheses represent the issue in which the rating was published.

JOSEPH DROUHIN
Côte de Beaune-Villages 1986 $13 (6/15/89) **78**
Côte de Beaune-Villages 1985 $14 (11/15/87) **85**
Maranges Première Cru 1989: A refreshing wine, with nice polish. Very plummy, with firm tannins and a fresh finish. Better in 1993. $20 (1/31/92) **85**

JEAN-CHARLES FORNEROT
St.-Aubin Les Perrières 1985: An inviting, reasonably affordable Burgundy. Distinct meaty, earthy aromas and flavors plus an almost fruity component. $15 (7/31/89) **82**

JEAN GARAUDET
Monthélie 1989: Ripe, smooth and generous, with a sense of richness that lets the currant, berry and anise flavors roll smoothly over the palate. Has enough tannin and roughness to need until 1994 or '95 to hit its stride. $22 (11/15/91) **86**
Monthélie 1988: A generous wine, offering spicy strawberry aromas that deepen and strengthen as the flavors develop, extending into a long, smoky, cherry-tinged finish. A very classy Burgundy, with more dimensions than many big-name appellation wines. Drinkable now, but should keep improving through 1993 to '95. $23 (11/15/90) **88**

JACQUES GERMAIN
Chorey-lès- Beaune Château de Chorey 1989: Fresh and lively, with cherry and other fruit aromas and flavors, good acidity and light tannins. Drink on release. $24 (1/31/92) **84**
Chorey-lès-Beaune Château de Chorey 1986: Lean, but has a nice touch of complexity, showing herbal, spicy and fruity notes, with moderate tannins. Ready to drink. $16 (7/31/89) **80**

MACHARD DE GRAMONT
Chorey-lès-Beaune Les Beaumonts 1985 $22 (7/31/88) **84**

LOUIS JADOT
Côte de Beaune-Villages 1989: A wine with an attractive character of olives, cherries and berries and a hint of earth. Medium-bodied, with medium tannins. Try in 1993. $18 (1/31/92) **84**
Côte de Beaune-Villages 1988 $14 (7/15/90) (BT) **75+**
Côte de Beaune-Villages 1986 $15 (6/15/89) **78**
Côte de Beaune-Villages 1985 $17 (4/15/88) **79**
Monthélie 1989: This intense little wine has lots of chocolate and walnut aromas and flavors, firm tannins and a chewy finish. Try in 1993. $21 (1/31/92) **87**

JAFFELIN
Auxey-Duresses 1989: Very focused and fresh, with pretty cherry and chestnut flavors and a fresh finish. Perfect to drink now. $16 (1/31/92) **85**
Chorey-Côte-de-Beaune 1989: Very light and stemmy, with weedy flavors and light tannins. Drink on release. $13 (1/31/92) **75**
Côte de Beaune-Villages 1989: Light but lively, with minty cherry and earth nuances and light, silky tannins. Somewhat simple on the finish. Try in 1993. $14 (1/31/92) **82**
Ladoix Côte de Beaune 1989: Fun to drink now, with pretty licorice, strawberry and cherry character, light, silky tannins and a very fresh finish. $13 (1/31/92) **85**
Monthélie 1989: Has loads of finesse and elegance, offering enticing cedar, cherry and berry aromas and flavors and fine tannins. Better in 1993. $19 (1/31/92) **87**
Monthélie 1988 $21 (7/15/90) (BT) **80+**
Monthélie 1986 $15 (6/15/89) **79**
St.-Aubin 1989: A ripe red Burgundy, with cherry and smoke aromas and flavors and a fresh finish. Somewhat one-dimensional. Try in 1993. $14 (1/31/92) **84**

JAYER-GILLES
Bourgogne Hautes Côtes de Beaune 1989: Has masses of new wood, wonderful vanilla and plum aromas and full fruit flavor, but it's a little dry on the finish. Perhaps somewhat overdone. Better in 1993. $24 (1/31/92) **84**
Bourgogne Hautes Côtes de Beaune 1988: Highly aromatic and rich in aroma and flavor, featuring spicy oak-tinged raspberry, cherry and plum aromas and flavors. Much richer and more generous than most Hautes Côtes. Drinkable now. $26 (5/15/91) **88**

LEROY
Auxey-Duresses Les Clous 1988: Tight and lean, with hard-edged tannins, but it also has pretty, ripe raspberry and black cherry-tinged flavors that turn earthy and smoky on the finish. An exotic style, with a wide range of flavor. Drink in 1994 or '95. $52 (5/15/91) **85**

LUPE-CHOLET
Monthélie 1983 $9 (9/15/86) **69**

M & G
Côte de Beaune-Villages 1987 $20 (3/31/91) **73**

DOMAINE RENE MANUEL
Meursault Clos de La Baronne 1988: Pungent and earthy, with a strong leafy, tarry component that strays from the ripe berry and cherry flavors. An odd-ball style, with some off-the-mark flavors; drink it now. 300 cases made. $18 (3/31/91) **79**

PRINCE FLORENT DE MERODE
Ladoix Les Chaillots 1987: Very light in color, with a mature, spicy, crisp texture and modest strawberry and lemon flavors on the finish. A tart style that's drinkable now. $18 (11/15/90) **77**
Ladoix Les Chaillots 1986: Smells fine, but the bitter, metallic flavors make it difficult to warm up to. Simple fruit makes it drinkable. $18 (8/31/89) **74**

CHATEAU DE MEURSAULT
Bourgogne Pinot Noir du Château 1988: Light and refreshing, with ripe cherry and strawberry flavors. Simple but pleasant, with firm tannins. Drink now to 1993. $16 (1/31/92) **82**

MOILLARD
Bourgogne Hautes Côtes de Beaune Les Alouettes 1989: Shows straightforward strawberry and earth flavors and a fresh, round mouth-feel. Drink on release. $17 (1/31/92) **83**
Bourgogne Hautes Côtes de Beaune Les Alouettes 1988: Light and crisp in structure, but the nicely focused berry, currant and vanilla aromas and flavors show the sort of intensity that pairs well with light summer main dishes. $15 (7/15/91) **83**
Ladoix Côte de Beaune 1989: A serious little wine, with spicy plum and berry aromas and flavors and silky tannins. Better in 1993. (NR) (1/31/92) **85**

MOMMESSIN
Auxey-Duresses 1989: Soft and easy, with pretty chestnut and cherry flavors and a light finish. Drink on release. $13 (1/31/92) **82**
Côte de Beaune-Villages 1985 $13 (2/15/88) **85**
Maranges 1989: A wild little wine, with tons of black cherry and berry flavors and a lively finish. Wonderful to drink now. $13 (1/31/92) **87**

DOMAINE MONTHELIE-DOUHAIRET
Monthélie 1985 $16 (6/30/88) **81**

DOMAINE JEAN MORETEAUX
Côte de Beaune-Villages 1983 $8.50 (3/16/86) **63**

DOMAINE DU MOULIN AUX MOINES
Auxey-Duresses 1983 $10 (3/15/87) **76**

PAUL PERNOT
Blagny La Pièce Sous Le Bois 1990: Tart, thin and woody, with a spurt of fruit at the very end that lifts it into the respectable range. $33 (4/30/92) **79**

DOMAINE PONNELLE
Côte de Beaune Les Pierres Blanches 1987: Smells and tastes more like a Rhône than a Burgundy, with spicy, tarry, peppery flavors. The lighter body and elegance, however, give it away as a Burgundy, albeit a light one. Drink now. $14 (3/31/91) **83**

PRUNIER
Auxey-Duresses Clos du Val 1987 $25 (11/15/89) **84**

CHATEAU DE PULIGNY-MONTRACHET
Monthélie 1988: Earth, smoke and mint aromas and flavors hang awkwardly on a medium frame, but a little cellaring could bring it around. Try now through 1994. $16 (11/15/90) **77**

GASTON & PIERRE RAVAUT
Ladoix Les Corvées 1985 $26 (7/31/88) **88**

TOLLOT-BEAUT
Chorey-Côte-de-Beaune 1989: Extremely well focused for an undervalued wine type, with light vanilla, raspberry and berry flavors and a classy tannin structure. Better in 1993. (NR) (1/31/92) **87**
Chorey-Côte-de-Beaune 1985 $18 (4/15/88) **83**
Chorey-lès-Beaune 1988: Has lovely floral, plum, cherry and strawberry aromas and flavors that are elegant and lively, finishing with a firm, modestly tannic structure. Beautifully balanced, with deliciously delicate proportions. Start drinking now, or cellar through 1994. $25 (12/31/90) **88**

CÔTE DE NUITS/CHAMBOLLE-MUSIGNY

ARLAUD
Bonnes Mares 1983 $30 (12/01/85) **91**

GHISLAINE BARTHOD
Chambolle-Musigny 1988: Sturdy and a bit more rugged than one expects from this appellation, but showing some seductive currant, cherry and vanilla aromas and flavors. Tough now, but has the potential to evolve well beyond 1995. Tasted twice. $50 (3/15/91) **88**
Chambolle-Musigny Les Beaux-Bruns 1988: This elegant, subtle style has spicy cherry, plum and cedar flavors, but it's not overly generous, finishing with tartness and firm tannins. Best to cellar until about 1994. $45 (2/28/91) **83**
Chambolle-Musigny Les Crâs 1988: Lots of cherry and currant aromas and flavors make a fine impression, and the firm tannins bode well for long-term cellaring. A wine with plenty of personality. Best to drink after 1993. $45 (2/28/91) **87**
Chambolle-Musigny Les Véroilles 1988: An austere, tannic and sharp style, with hard-edged cherry, plum and cedar flavors framed by drying tannins. Doesn't have much in the way of fruit or charm now, but perhaps with time it will reveal more depth. Cellar until 1994. $45 (2/28/91) **81**

G. BARTHOD-NOELLAT
Chambolle-Musigny Charmes 1984 $27 (10/31/87) **82**
Chambolle-Musigny Les Crâs 1985 $37 (7/31/88) **88**

DOMAINE BERTHEAU
Bonnes Mares 1987: Spicy and elegant, with smoky, cinnamon and cherry aromas and flavors that are lean, delicate and focused, echoing the spice and cherry flavors on the long finish. Lots of style and class. Drink after 1993. $55 (6/15/90) **89**
Chambolle-Musigny 1987: Light and delicate, with woodsy mushroom aromas and flavors. Not unpleasant, but those who prefer more fruit should try something else. Has a future. Drink now to 1993. $25 (6/15/90) **80**
Chambolle-Musigny Les Amoureuses 1987: Lean and crisp, but the earthy aromas and flavors obscure the fruit. An unimpressive wine now, but it has enough cherry and strawberry flavors to let it evolve with cellaring until 1993 to '94. $50 (6/15/90) **84**
Chambolle-Musigny Les Charmes 1987: Light and delicate, with subtle red cherry and cinnamon aromas and flavors, and a lean texture, clean and appealing. Drinkable now, but cellaring until 1993 would not hurt. $35 (6/15/90) **81**

BOUCHARD PERE & FILS
Chambolle-Musigny 1989 (NR) (7/15/90) (BT) **85+**
Chambolle-Musigny 1986 $29 (7/31/88) **73**

PIERRE BOUREE FILS
Bonnes Mares 1985 $85 (5/31/88) **91**
Chambolle-Musigny 1987: Looks and smells older than it is, but the cinnamon and floral aromas and flavors complement the red cherry and plum flavors nicely. A lighter, delicate style that's drinkable now but best around 1993. $44 (6/15/90) **82**
Chambolle-Musigny Charmes 1987: Light but tannic, with cherry, cinnamon and chocolate aromas and flavors. Needs cellaring until 1993 to '95 to soften the tannin, but then it should be lovely. $56 (6/15/90) **82**

GUY CASTAGNIER
Bonnes Mares 1989: Intense, with plenty of cherry, licorice and hazelnut flavors and an abundance of fine tannins and chewy fruit. Slightly short on the finish. Try after 1994. $67 (1/31/92) **91**
Bonnes Mares 1988: Ripe, rich and smooth textured, with forward black cherry, currant and floral aromas and flavors that taper off a bit on the finish. There's plenty to enjoy. Best after 1994. $67 (7/15/91) **87**
Bonnes Mares 1986: Remarkably concentrated, tannic too, but delicate overall. Flavors run toward cherry, blackberry and earthy spice, with firm tannins and exceptional length. $50 (4/15/89) **91**
Chambolle-Musigny 1989: Showy, with lots of fruit on the nose, but firm and focused on the palate. Try in 1994. $39 (1/31/92) **88**
Chambolle-Musigny 1986: Very light color, surprisingly mature aromas, but lively strawberry and cinnamon flavors bode well for this to develop in the cellar through at least 1993. $31 (7/15/89) **84**

DOMAINE CECI
Chambolle-Musigny Les Echanges 1988: Firm and concentrated, with ripe currant and cherry flavors buried under fine-textured tannins, echoing fruit and spice on the long finish. A harmonious wine that should only keep improving through 1996 to '98. 425 cases made. $33 (7/15/91) **91**
Chambolle-Musigny Les Echanges 1987: Light, metallic flavors detract from hints of cherry flavor in this earthy, gamy, somewhat astringent wine. Could improve with cellaring through 1994. $20 (3/31/90) **72**

F. CHAUVENET
Chambolle-Musigny Les Charmes 1982 $33 (4/30/87) **83**

DOMAINE DES CHEZEAUX
Chambolle-Musigny Les Charmes 1985 $75 (6/15/88) **91**

CHOPIN-GROFFIER
Chambolle-Musigny 1989: A pleasure to taste, with smoky, toasty black cherry aromas and flavors, silky tannins and a long finish. Try after 1993. $32 (1/31/92) **90**

MICHEL CLERGET
Chambolle-Musigny 1986: Light and lean, with delicate plum and rose petal aromas and flavors that peek through the astringency on the finish. Could be more generous. $23 (8/31/89) **78**
Chambolle-Musigny 1985 $38 (5/15/88) **73**
Chambolle-Musigny Les Charmes 1986: Earthy style, lean and flavorful, but not exactly bursting

with fruit. The flavors run toward smoke, mushrooms and wet earth, and there is a bitterness on the finish that may or may not resolve with aging. Try it now. $33 (8/31/89) **76**
Chambolle-Musigny Les Charmes 1985 $56 (5/15/88) **83**

JOSEPH DROUHIN
Bonnes Mares 1989: A real mouthful, with layers of plum, berry and other fruit flavors and a sweet, ripe fruit and tannin structure. Try in 1994. $99 (1/31/92) **93**
Chambolle-Musigny 1989: Like eating fudge; big and rich, with licorice and black cherry flavors, firm tannins and a very long finish. Try in 1994. $41 (1/31/92) **91**
Chambolle-Musigny 1988 $38 (7/15/90) (BT) **85+**
Chambolle-Musigny 1986 $27 (7/31/88) **88**
Chambolle-Musigny 1985 $33 (11/15/87) **93**
Chambolle-Musigny Les Amoureuses 1988: Very firm and focused, showing more now on the palate than on the nose, offering a tannic structure, modest plum and black cherry flavors and a touch of toast on the finish. Drink after 1994. $76 (12/31/90) **87**
Chambolle-Musigny Les Amoureuses 1955 $250 (8/31/90) (TR) **65**
Chambolle-Musigny Les Baudes 1989: Subtle and pretty, with focused, sweet fruit flavors and very fine tannins. Try after 1993. $52 (1/31/92) **89**
Chambolle-Musigny Feusselottes 1989: Big and focused, full of lovely pepper, spice and berry nuances wrapped up with firm tannins and very ripe fruit. Better after 1994. (NR) (1/31/92) **92**
Chambolle-Musigny Premier Cru 1989: Shows good power, but it's understated, wrapped in a beautiful package of ripe fruit, firm tannins and a silky finish. Try after 1994. (NR) (1/31/92) **89**
Chambolle-Musigny Les Sentiers 1989: Very stylish and ripe, with masses of truffle and berry flavors and tons of mouth-coating tannins. Needs time; try from 1994 to '97. (NR) (1/31/92) **92**

DROUHIN-LAROZE
Bonnes Mares 1988: Tannic and tight, with lots of compact, focused cherry, currant and plum flavors. Beautifully proportioned and potentially elegant once the tannins subside and the solid core of flavor emerges. Give it until 1994 or '95. $81 (12/31/90) **93**
Bonnes Mares 1987: Lively and appealing, with crisp structure and generous blackberry and strawberry aromas and flavors, revealing its pedigree with a long and elegant finish. Drinkable now, but better to hold onto it until 1993 to '95 to see how it develops. $38 (3/31/90) **89**

DOMAINE DUJAC
Bonnes Mares 1989 $80 (7/15/90) (BT) **75+**
Bonnes Mares 1988 $86 (7/15/90) (BT) **90+**
Bonnes Mares 1987: Very light in color, almost delicate, but wrapped in enough oak and tannin to make it worth cellaring at least until 1993 to '95, though you could try it now. The strawberry and wild raspberry flavors are extremely appealing. $62 (3/31/90) **91**
Bonnes Mares 1986 $60 (4/15/89) **85**
Chambolle-Musigny Les Gruenchers 1987: Beautifully focused cherry, toast and vanilla aromas and flavors sail easily over the palate on a supple structure. Complex, concentrated and elegant. Delicious to drink now, but the firm tannins can use cellaring until 1993 to '95. $47 (3/31/90) **93**
Chambolle-Musigny Les Gruenchers 1986 $48 (7/31/88) **76**
Chambolle-Musigny Les Gruenchers 1985 $43 (3/31/88) **74**

FAIVELEY
Chambolle-Musigny 1989: A straightforward Chambolle, with clean cherry and berry flavors and medium tannins. Try in 1993. $34 (1/31/92) **85**
Chambolle-Musigny 1985 $45 (5/15/88) **89**
Chambolle-Musigny 1981 $24 (5/01/86) **88**
Musigny Le Musigny 1949 $250 (8/31/90) (TR) **92**

JEAN GRIVOT
Chambolle-Musigny La Combe d'Orvaux 1987: Beguilingly aromatic, but tannic enough to need more cellaring than most '87s. Has spicy, toasty, cedary strawberry aromas and flavors, delicate and complex on the finish. Drink 1994 to '96. $47 (6/15/90) **85**

DOMAINE ROBERT GROFFIER
Bonnes Mares 1989: Decidedly earthy, with flavors that run more toward barnyardy and bacony than fruity, but it has a meaty texture and enough depth to warrant cellaring until 1995 for fans of the style. Tasted twice. $79 (1/31/92) **81**
Bonnes Mares 1988: Has great smoke, chocolate, floral and ripe aromas, but the smoke seems to take over on the palate and it finishes a bit harsh. Still, there's plenty to like, especially the ripe cherry flavor. Cellar until 1995 to '98. $80 (11/15/90) **90**
Bonnes Mares 1987: Depth and complexity on the nose, with toasty cherry and spicy aromas followed by spicy strawberry and cherry flavors. Elegant but tannic. Drink now. $67 (7/31/89) **89**
Chambolle-Musigny Amoureuses 1988: Aromatically pleasing, with plenty of fruit and oak, this is rich and complex, with elegant black cherry, cassis, berry and spice flavors and hints of nutmeg and toast. Beautifully focused, tight and concentrated, with the fruit and oak beaming through the finish. Drink in 1993 to '95 and beyond. $66 (11/15/90) **93**
Chambolle-Musigny Amoureuses 1987: Ripe, round and supple, with delicate nuances that add grace notes to the basically cherry and sweet oak aromas and flavors. Hints of nutmeg and rose petal suggest this could age into a beauty. Try it now. $51 (8/31/89) **86**
Chambolle-Musigny Amoureuses 1986: Pretty color and aromas, but the flavors don't ring as true, with pretty Pinot Noir flavor and supple plum and cherry flavors. A touch of mossiness on the finish also detracts. Drink now. $50 (2/28/89) **84**
Chambolle-Musigny Les Sentiers 1988: Elegant and well proportioned, with a pretty core of spicy cherry, wild berry and smoky vanilla and oak flavors that are subtle and understated but deeply concentrated and long on the finish. Should be near its peak in 1993 to '95. $45 (11/15/90) **89**
Chambolle-Musigny Les Sentiers 1987: Ripe and supple, but it shows admirable restraint and finesse in balancing the tart cherry and nutmeg aromas and flavors against the toasty vanilla character of the oak. Understated and elegant. Try around 1993. $37 (8/31/89) **87**
Chambolle-Musigny Les Sentiers 1986: A deep colored wine offering richness, depth and concentration, packed with ripe plum, cherry and a touch of gamy earthiness. Very complex, full and lasting on the palate. Drink 1993 to '95. $36 (2/28/89) **90**

HAEGELEN-JAYER
Chambolle-Musigny 1988: Earthy and funky, with lots of gamy overtones to the somewhat tart, vinegary fruit flavors. Not our style. $39 (5/15/91) **73**

Key to Symbols

The scores reported here are the results of blind tastings conducted by our panel of senior editors. Wines that carry the initials below are results of individual tastings.

THE WINE SPECTATOR 100-POINT SCALE 95-100—Classic, a great wine; *90-94*—Outstanding, superior character and style; *80-89*—Good to very good, a wine with special qualities; *70-79*—Average, drinkable wine that may have minor flaws; *60-69*—Below average, drinkable but not recommended; *50-59*—Poor, undrinkable, not recommended. "+"—With a score indicates a range; used primarily with barrel tastings to indicate a preliminary score.

SPECIAL DESIGNATIONS SS—Spectator Selection, CS—Cellar Selection, BB—Best Buy, ($NA)—Price not available, (NR)—Not released.

TASTER'S INITIALS (JG)—Jim Gordon, (HS)—Harvey Steiman, (JL)—James Laube, (JS)—James Suckling, (TM)—Thomas Matthews, (TR)—Terry Robards, (PM)—Per-Henrik Mansson, (BT)—Barrel Tasting (these wines were tasted blind from barrel samples), (CA-date)—*California's Great Cabernets* by James Laube, (CH-date)—*California's Great Chardonnays* by James Laube, (VP-date)—*Vintage Port* by James Suckling.

DATE TASTED Dates in parentheses represent the issue in which the rating was published.

CHATEAU DES HERBEUX
Musigny 1988: Lovely strawberry and raspberry flavors float in this light, almost ethereal wine, but, if anything, it errs on the side of simplicity in its effort to be delicate. Doesn't quite capture the intensity of the vintage, but it's a nice wine. $75 (12/31/90) **83**

LOUIS JADOT
Bonnes Mares 1988: Firm and concentrated, with nicely focused berry, currant and vanilla aromas and flavors. Has a silky texture underneath the solid tannins, but it's a good bet to keep developing beyond 1994 or '95. $65 (3/15/91) **88**
Bonnes Mares 1987: There are beautiful cinnamon, nutmeg, rose petal and berry aromas through the flavors and the long finish of this restrained, elegant, harmonious red Burgundy. A step above most '87s in concentration and length. Drink 1994 and beyond. 250 cases made. $52 (6/15/90) **91**
Bonnes Mares 1986: Very firm texture, but delicate overall, with good concentration of strawberry and anise aromas and flavors, overlaid with rose petal and a hint of toast. Very fine. Drink 1993. $57 (4/15/89) **89**
Bonnes Mares 1985 Rel: $48 Cur: $68 (3/15/88) **95**
Chambolle-Musigny 1986: Lean and light, with some strawberry and brown sugar aromas and flavors to make it interesting, but it seems prematurely old and the acidity sticks out on the finish. May be better by now. $30 (7/15/89) **78**
Chambolle-Musigny 1985 Rel: $33 Cur: $39 (5/15/88) **91**
Musigny Le Musigny 1989 $100 (7/15/90) (BT) **85+**
Musigny Le Musigny 1988 Rel: $82 Cur: $100 (7/15/90) (BT) **85+**
Musigny Le Musigny 1986: Very tough and tannic, with not enough to like on the aroma or the finish to outlast the astringency. A touch of cherry on the finish is the only bright spot for those looking for cellar material. $70 (4/15/89) **77**
Musigny Le Musigny 1985 $74 (3/31/88) **88**

JAFFELIN
Chambolle-Musigny 1989: Firm and forceful, with plenty of acidity and tannins and good fruit. Try in 1993. $28 (1/31/92) **89**
Chambolle-Musigny 1988: With very pretty aromas and flavors on a supple, delicate frame, this harmonious wine keeps you coming back for another sip to see what develops. Almost drinkable now, but holding enough in reserve to want cellaring until 1993 to '95. $32 (12/31/90) **88**
Chambolle-Musigny 1983 $21 (3/16/86) **81**

LABOURE-ROI
Chambolle-Musigny 1988: Despite a firm, tannic edge, there's plenty of flavor behind this wine. With time, the cherry, plum, spice and nutmeg flavors should be more complex and alluring. Needs cellaring until 1994 or '95. 1,000 cases made. $35 (2/28/91) **86**
Chambolle-Musigny Domaine Cottin 1989: A very herbal, atypical Chambolle that tastesgreen and unripe. The tea and vegetal flavors don't add up to much enjoyment. Bitter on the finish, too. Tasted twice. 400 cases made. $30 (3/31/92) **76**

LOUIS LATOUR
Bonnes Mares 1989: Gorgeous, with beautiful toast, vanilla and raspberry aromas, masses of fruit flavors, plenty of new wood and silky tannins. Needs time; try in 1995. (NR) (1/31/92) **93**

OLIVIER LEFLAIVE FRERES
Bonnes Mares 1987: A nice marriage of toasty oak and ripe, appealing cherry and plummy Pinot Noir flavors. Has firm structure and tannins and very good balance, and it finishes with a complexity of tasty earth, fruit and oak flavors. Drink now to 1995. Tasted twice. $50 (9/30/90) **88**

DOMAINE FRANCOIS LEGROS
Chambolle-Musigny Les Noirots 1989: A seductive style, with deep, rich, complex raspberry, strawberry, anise and toasty oak flavors that are engagingly silky and long on the finish. Tempting now, but should improve through 1996. 200 cases made. $30 (11/15/91) **92**

DOMAINE LEROY
Chambolle-Musigny Les Fremières 1989: An explosion of fruit, with pure violet and fruit extract and toasty tannins. Try after 1994. $80 (1/31/92) **94**

GEORGES LIGNIER
Bonnes Mares 1987: Very firm and concentrated, with toasty, smoky aromas and flavors centered around a solid core of cherry flavor. Complex and powerful with a long finish. Needs cellaring until 1993 to '94 to settle down. $75 (3/31/90) **92**
Chambolle-Musigny 1987: An earthy style, with mushroom and cherry aromas and flavors, light, subtle and tart. Simpler than one would expect. Drink now. Tasted twice. $32 (6/15/90) **77**

LUPE-CHOLET
Bonnes Mares 1988 (NR) (7/15/90) (BT) **90+**
Chambolle-Musigny 1986 $20 (7/31/88) **81**

CLAUDE MARCHAND
Chambolle-Musigny 1986: Light in color, leathery in scent, starting out lean and tannic but opening out into a fairly generous, if earthy, finish. Cinnamon, strawberry and red cherry flavors are amply supported by firm tannins and crisp acidity. Should develop at least until 1994. $32 (7/15/89) **85**

MOILLARD
Bonnes Mares 1984 $35 (5/31/87) **92**
Bonnes Mares Domaine Thomas-Moillard 1986 $45 (11/15/88) **86**
Chambolle-Musigny 1984 $15 (11/30/86) **89**
Musigny 1984 $38 (5/31/87) **92**

MOMMESSIN
Chambolle-Musigny Les Charmes 1988 $42 (7/15/90) (BT) **90+**

CHARLES MORTET
Chambolle-Musigny Les Beaux Bruns 1989: Packs in plenty of flavor with layers of buttery oak and ripe wild berry, strawberry, cherry and plum flavors that are all bright. Silky texture with fine tannins. Tempting now but can age through 1995. 225 cases made. $34 (1/31/92) **89**

GEORGES MUGNERET
Chambolle-Musigny Les Feusselottes 1989: Crisp and lively, this light-colored wine has well-focused currant and plum aromas and flavors that are tight and focused on the long finish. Needs until 1995 to '98 to show what it has. $47 (4/30/92) **87**
Chambolle-Musigny Les Feusselottes 1988: Shows delicious, rich cherry, cassis and wild berry flavor up front, but then the tannins kick in, reminding you how young, intense and concentrated it is. The finish is hard and firm; best to cellar until 1994. $54 (11/15/90) **86**
Chambolle-Musigny Les Feusselottes 1987: Spicy, rich and utterly delicious, the cinnamon- and vanilla-tinged cherry, strawberry and plum aromas and flavors are framed elegantly with sweet oak, long and firm and satisfying. Drinkable now, but try to hold off at least until 1993 to '94 to see it develop. 175 cases made. $41 (10/15/89) **92**
Chambolle-Musigny Les Feusselottes 1986 $45 (11/15/88) **90**

JACQUES-FREDERIC MUGNIER
Chambolle-Musigny 1989: Has excellent concentration for this group. Like a barrel sample or fermenting grape juice, with pure cherry and strawberry flavors and firm tannins. Try in 1994. $41 (1/31/92) **91**
Chambolle-Musigny 1988: Light and elegant, with pretty raspberry and strawberry aromas and flavors and hints of butter and spice on the finish. Almost approachable now, but best after 1993 or '94. $48 (5/15/91) **86**
Chambolle-Musigny Les Amoureuses 1989: A chameleon of a wine. Has beautiful, elegant aromas, but is massive and tannic on the palate. Try from 1995. $62 (1/31/92) **90**

Chambolle-Musigny Les Amoureuses 1988: Light in texture and flavor, but has nice earthy strawberry aromas and flavors that persist into a delicate finish. Has enough tannin to need until 1993 to '95 to be at its best. $80 (5/15/91) **86**
Chambolle-Musigny Les Fuées 1988: Lean and crisp, with sharply focused raspberry, nutmeg and vanilla aromas and flavors. Long and lively on the finish. Should be best after 1994. $60 (5/15/91) **89**
Musigny 1989: A lovely wine, but lacks a bit of power for a Musigny. Very user-friendly except for the price. Try in 1994. $125 (1/31/92) **88**

NICOLAS
Bonnes Mares 1959 ($NA) (8/31/90) (TR) **75**

DOMAINE PONSOT
Chambolle-Musigny Les Charmes 1988: Ample and generous without being weighty, with dusky, spicy black cherry and currant aromas and flavors, a polished texture and a long finish, hinting at vanilla and fruit. Offers plenty of pleasure already, and promises plenty of development through 1995 to '98. $58 (4/30/91) **92**
Chambolle-Musigny Les Charmes 1985 $75 (6/15/88) **94**

REMOISSENET
Bonnes Mares 1988: Very earthy and decadent, with lots of leathery, gamy flavors that shoulder past the otherwise ripe fruit flavors and supple textures. You have to like funk to like this one, but there is a lot to like. Tasted twice. $80 (12/31/90) **84**
Bonnes Mares 1985 $88 (3/15/88) **82**

DOMAINE DANIEL RION
Chambolle-Musigny Les Beaux Bruns 1989: Very pretty, with a grapey, earthy character and an excellent concentration of fresh fruit and tannins. Try after 1994. $45 (1/31/92) **89**
Chambolle-Musigny Les Beaux Bruns 1988: Intense and lively, but not weighty, with cassis, plum, currant and spice notes that are elegantly structured, with hints of nutmeg and toast. A young, vibrant, balanced wine that could use a little more flavor on the finish. Best to cellar until 1994 or '95. $37 (1/31/91) **87**
Chambolle-Musigny Les Beaux Bruns 1986: Smells sensational, with generous raspberry, cherry and rose petal aromas, a bit lean and astringent on the palate, but more generous than most '86s. The fruit flavors barely prevail over the tannins, which should recede by 1994. $39 (4/15/89) **86**
Chambolle-Musigny Les Beaux Bruns 1985 $33 (3/31/88) **88**

DOMAINE G. ROUMIER
Bonnes Mares 1989: Big and complex, with masses of fruit and tannins and a long, almost tough finish. A traditional, big wine that needs time. Try in 1994. $70 (1/31/92) **93**
Chambolle-Musigny 1989: A pretty wine, with everything in the right place, from the tannins to the black cherry flavor and good acidity. Try after 1993. $38 (1/31/92) **90**
Chambolle-Musigny 1988: Very focused, nicely tart and fairly tannic, packed with delicious raspberry and cherry flavors. A toasty, earthy quality lends it complexity. Supple but firm in texture and lingering on the finish. Start drinking in 1995. $30 (7/15/91) **89**
Chambolle-Musigny 1985 $26 (2/15/88) **87**
Chambolle-Musigny Amoureuses 1989: Traditional, with lots of power, showing rich plum and ripe fruit flavors and slightly coarse tannins. Try from 1994. $62 (1/31/92) **88**
Musigny 1989: Like a vintage Port; still closed in, but it has masses of chocolate flavor and a tannic structure. A gigantic wine. Try in 1996. $95 (1/31/92) **96**

HERVE ROUMIER
Chambolle-Musigny 1986: Lean and a bit astringent, but there are generous toast, vanilla and cherry flavors lurking beneath the slightly scratchy surface. When the tannins resolve, surely by 1993, this should be a lovely, rich and warm wine. $29 (8/31/89) **82**
Chambolle-Musigny Les Amoureuses 1985 $65 (3/31/88) **89**

DOMAINE B. SERVEAU
Chambolle-Musigny 1989: Has good fruit, but it's a little simple, with berry and earth aromas and flavors and a medium finish. Try in 1993. (NR) (1/31/92) **83**
Chambolle-Musigny Les Amoureuses 1989: Elegant and attractive, with pretty cherry and berry flavors and a firm backbone. Try in 1993. $50 (1/31/92) **85**
Chambolle-Musigny Les Amoureuses 1988: Dry and tannic, holding down the fresh cherry, anise and plum flavors. Will require patience, but it will probably always be tannic. Acidity sustains the flavors. Drink in 1994 or '95. $66 (2/28/91) **84**
Chambolle-Musigny Les Amoureuses 1985 $75 (6/15/88) **91**
Chambolle-Musigny Les Chabiots 1989: Rather light for a *premier cru*, with simple, fresh berry aromas and flavors. Drink now. $30 (1/31/92) **79**
Chambolle-Musigny Les Chabiots 1988: An elegant style, with intense strawberry, cherry and raspberry flavors framed by firm tannins. Has good length and crisp acidity. Best to cellar until 1994. $39 (2/28/91) **86**
Chambolle-Musigny Les Chabiots 1987: A strong whiff of nail polish detracts from an otherwise rich and full-bodied wine, with strong black cherry and toast flavors on the finish. A complex but flawed wine. Tasted twice. $30 (6/15/90) **78**
Chambolle-Musigny Les Chabiots 1985 $39 (6/15/88) **90**
Chambolle-Musigny Les Chabiots 1984 $23 (4/15/87) **91**
Chambolle-Musigny Les Sentiers 1989: Wonderful; a classy, polished wine, with beautiful berry, strawberry and vanilla aromas and flavors and a long finish. Try from 1994 to '97. $30 (1/31/92) **93**
Chambolle-Musigny Les Sentiers 1988: Borders on sourness, with tart, blunt cherry and plum flavors. Lacks focus, although it's drinkable. Ready now through 1994. $39 (2/28/91) **79**

HENRI DE VILLAMONT
Chambolle-Musigny 1988: Very ripe, with stewed plum flavors, but also very sharp and intense, with firm tannins and good intensity, but lacking in charm and finesse. Perhaps with time it will gain those latter attributes, but for now it's rather intense and one-dimensional. Needs until 1993 or '94. $39 (2/15/91) **83**

COMTE DE VOGUE
Bonnes Mares 1989: An intensely ripe, well-crafted wine, with plenty of flavor. Has lovely, velvety fruit and firm tannins. Try after 1994. $93 (1/31/92) **94**
Bonnes Mares 1988: Very spicy earth and tobacco aromas and flavors add a nice background to the solid plum and berry notes in a chewy wine that has plenty to offer. Best to cellar until at least 1994. $93 (3/31/91) **89**
Bonnes Mares 1987: A light, delicate wine, with pleasant cinnamon, anise and smoke flavors around a lean core of raspberry and strawberry. Complex and drinkable now. $69 (7/15/90) **87**
Bonnes Mares 1979 $60 (11/16/84) (HS) **88**
Bonnes Mares 1976 $55 (11/16/84) (HS) **90**
Bonnes Mares 1972 $115 (11/16/84) (HS) **79**
Bonnes Mares 1971 $175 (11/16/84) (HS) **88**
Bonnes Mares Avery Bottling 1959 $172 (11/16/84) (HS) **87**
Bonnes Mares 1959 $172 (11/16/84) (HS) **83**
Bonnes Mares 1955 $290 (11/16/84) (HS) **91**
Bonnes Mares 1949 $1,100/1.5L (11/16/84) (HS) **90**
Bonnes Mares Grivolet 1934 $400 (11/16/84) (HS) **82**
Chambolle-Musigny 1989: Very harmonious, with pure fruit and plenty of smoky, earthy berry character. Has excellent tannins and crisp acidity. Try after 1993. $44 (1/31/92) **89**
Chambolle-Musigny Les Amoureuses 1989: Polished and flashy, displaying a seamless structure of ripe fruit, supple tannins and a long finish. Made for aging. Try from 1994. $93 (1/31/92) **93**
Chambolle-Musigny Les Amoureuses 1988: Lively, fruity and elegant, with spicy cinnamon and rich cherry flavors. With lovely balance, firm tannins and lingering flavors on the finish, this has all the pieces to develop beautifully by 1994 or '95. $93 (2/28/91) **89**
Chambolle-Musigny Les Amoureuses 1987: An elegant, delicate style, with carefully articulated strawberry, cherry and cinnamon aromas and flavors. Very tasty, nicely balanced and subtle. Drinkable now, but should improve through 1993 to '94. $74 (3/31/90) **87**
Chambolle-Musigny Les Amoureuses 1971 $95 (11/16/84) (HS) **86**
Chambolle-Musigny Les Amoureuses 1970 $55 (11/16/84) (HS) **78**
Musigny Cuvée Vieilles Vignes 1989: Superbly concentrated, with tons of chocolate, vanilla and mushroom flavors. Powerful, but extremely elegant. Try in 1995. $134 (1/31/92) **96**
Musigny Cuvée Vieilles Vignes 1988: Big, chewy tannins almost obscure the delicate, complex cherry, tea and cinnamon flavors lingering in the background, but those flavors are ready to emerge with cellaring until 1998 to 2000. A classy wine with a great future. Rel: $134 Cur: $149 (2/28/91) **90**
Musigny Cuvée Vieilles Vignes 1987: Light and appealing, with attractive strawberry, cherry and floral aromas and flavors. Beautifully balanced, smooth and drinkable now, but aging through 1993 to '94 would probably bring out more complexity. $100 (3/31/90) **87**
Musigny Cuvée Vieilles Vignes 1985 Rel: $125 Cur: $150 (3/31/88) **92**
Musigny Cuvée Vieilles Vignes 1979 $114 (11/16/84) (HS) **87**
Musigny Cuvée Vieilles Vignes 1976 $87 (11/16/84) (HS) **86**
Musigny Cuvée Vieilles Vignes 1972 $130 (11/16/84) (HS) **80**
Musigny Cuvée Vieilles Vignes 1971 $240 (11/16/84) (HS) **90**
Musigny Cuvée Vieilles Vignes 1969 $210 (11/16/84) (HS) **65**
Musigny Cuvée Vieilles Vignes 1966 $210 (11/16/84) (HS) **92**
Musigny Cuvée Vieilles Vignes 1962 $500/1.5L (11/16/84) (HS) **90**
Musigny Cuvée Vieilles Vignes 1961 $300 (11/16/84) (HS) **93**
Musigny Cuvée Vieilles Vignes 1959 $350 (11/16/84) (HS) **89**
Musigny Cuvée Vieilles Vignes 1957 $160 (8/31/90) (HS) **95**
Musigny 1953 $200 (11/16/84) (HS) **81**
Musigny 1952 $200 (11/16/84) (HS) **85**
Musigny 1949 $480 (11/16/84) (HS) **98**
Musigny 1945 $1,210/1.5L (11/16/84) (HS) **96**
Musigny 1937 $650 (11/16/84) (HS) **93**
Musigny 1934 $600 (11/16/84) (HS) **95**

VOLPATO-COSTAILLE
Chambolle-Musigny 1988: Earthy, spicy aromas and flavors in a lightweight, somewhat drying and tannic wine. Tasted twice. $34 (2/28/91) **78**

Fixin

CLEMANCEY FRERES
Fixin Les-Hervelets 1985 $21 (4/30/88) **71**

FAIVELEY
Fixin 1989: Certainly captures your attention, with smoky chestnut and berry aromas and earthy flavors framed by medium tannins and a fresh finish. Better from 1993. $21 (1/31/92) **85**

GELIN & MOLIN
Fixin Clos du Châpitre Domaine Marion 1985 $25 (4/30/88) **82**

PIERRE GELIN
Fixin Clos Napoléon 1985 $25 (4/30/88) **76**

LOUIS JADOT
Fixin 1989: A real fruit bomb, with focused raspberry, violet and earth aromas, intense flavors and a long, flavorful finish. Better from 1993. $21 (1/31/92) **88**

JAFFELIN
Fixin 1989: Has loads of grapey, earthy strawberry aromas and flavors, medium tannins and a light finish. Try from 1993. $18 (1/31/92) **85**

JEHAN JOLIET
Fixin Clos de la Perrière 1985 $25 (7/31/88) **90**

MOILLARD
Fixin 1989: An ambitious wine in this category, with intense berry and earth flavors and super-firm tannins. Shows very good potential. Try from 1993. (NR) (1/31/92) **88**
Fixin Clos d'Entre Deux Velles 1989: Well crafted, with refreshing cherry aromas and impressive fruit concentration. The tannins are well integrated and the finish is delicious. From M. Lamblin. Try after 1993. (NR) (1/31/92) **86**
Fixin Clos d'Entre Deux Velles 1985 $16 (5/31/87) **79**
Fixin Clos d'Entre Deux Velles 1984 $11 (11/30/86) **78**
Fixin Clos de la Perrière 1986: Firm and fairly well concentrated for an '86, definitely tannic but showing a velvety texture and more focused flavors than most '86s. Probably best to drink now. $18 (2/28/89) **85**
Fixin Clos de la Perrière 1983 $12 (10/16/85) **78**
Fixin Confrérie des Chevaliers du Tastevin 1988: Lean and crisp, with sharply focused berry and lemon aromas and flavors that re-emerge on the finish after hiding behind a swell of tannin. Has the intensity to develop with cellaring until 1995 or so. $19 (8/31/91) **84**

MOMMESSIN
Fixin 1989: Has plenty of everything, displaying a rich, silky mouth-feel and lovely cherry, bark and watermelon aromas and flavors. Better starting in 1993. $15 (1/31/92) **87**
Fixin 1988 $19 (7/15/90) (BT) **75+**

MONGEARD-MUGNERET
Fixin 1989: A simple Fixin, with chestnut and berry aromas and flavors, light tannins and a chewy finish. Try from 1993. $25 (1/31/92) **83**
Fixin 1986: Light and aromatic, with spicy cherry and caramel aromas and flavors on a lean frame. A bit astringent on release, but it should have softened up by now. $19 (10/15/89) **84**

PIERRE PONNELLE
Fixin Hervelets 1959 ($NA) (8/31/90) (TR) **94**

Gevrey-Chambertin

DOMAINE PIERRE AMIOT
Gevrey-Chambertin Les Combottes 1988: A tart but elegant Burgundy, with generous cherry, cassis and spice flavors that carry through the long finish. Has the opulent flavors balanced with firm acidity that we look for. Try in 1993. $64 (3/15/91) **89**
Gevrey-Chambertin Les Combottes 1987: Has a velvety texture and it's lean and compact, with pretty spice, cherry and toast notes and a measure of subtlety and finesse, finishing with a pretty, smoky aftertaste. Drink now through 1994. $42 (12/15/89) **88**

DOMAINE BACHELET
Charmes-Chambertin Vieilles Vignes 1986: Plenty of bright, attractive cherry and plum flavor that gets hard and tight on the palate, finishing on the tannic side. Simply needs time to soften. Drink 1993 to 1995. $43 (7/15/89) **87**
Gevrey-Chambertin Les Corbeaux Vieilles Vignes 1986: Fresh and lively, with clean berry and herbal flavors, slightly rough tannins and a good finish. Good fruit flavors but not exactly deep or complex. Drink now. $30 (7/15/89) **83**
Gevrey-Chambertin Vieilles Vignes 1986: Full of fresh, ripe, lively berry and cherry flavors with

bright, clean aromas to bring you in. Very forward, well-balanced and delicious on release. Drink up now. $24 (7/15/89) **88**

BARTON & GUESTIER
Gevrey-Chambertin 1985 $21 (4/30/88) **89**

BEAULT-FORGEOT
Mazis-Chambertin Hospice de Beaune Cuvée Madeleine-Collignon 1980 $56 (7/01/84) **91**

BICHOT
Gevrey-Chambertin 1983 $13 (2/01/86) **58**

DOMAINE LUCIEN BOILLOT
Gevrey-Chambertin Les Cherbaudes 1987: Has oodles of fruit flavor, ranging from raspberry to red plum, that lingers on the finish, but it's lean and firm in mid-palate, with tannins reining it in. Try in 1993. $25 (5/31/90) **85**

JEAN CLAUDE BOISSET
Gevrey-Chambertin 1982 $9 (6/01/85) **74**

BOUCHARD AINE
Chambertin Clos de Bèze 1959 $90 (8/31/90) (TR) **84**
Chambertin Clos de Bèze Domaine Marion 1989: A very extracted and rustic style. Fleshy and beefy, with rich berry flavor and chewy tannins. Try after 1994. (NR) (1/31/92) **88**

BOUCHARD PERE & FILS
Chambertin 1989 (NR) (7/15/90) (BT) **90+**
Chambertin 1986 $78 (7/31/88) **81**
Chambertin Clos de Bèze 1989: Seamless, with terrific black cherry, berry and earth aromas and flavors. Try after 1994. $92 (1/31/92) **92**
Chambertin Clos de Bèze 1988: Beautifully aromatic and generous on the nose, offering lots of spicy, vanilla-scented plum and berry flavors that turn a bit lean and tough on the palate, echoing spice and mint notes on the long finish. This muscular wine has years to go before it gains finesse. Try in 1997 or '98. $82 (4/30/91) **89**
Gevrey-Chambertin 1982 $18 (6/16/84) **80**

PIERRE BOUREE FILS
Chambertin 1987: Tastes beautifully elegant, complex and complete. Has hints of tea, leather, anise, cherry and earth. So delicious and subtle that it's tempting to drink on release, but it should have developed more focus and distinction and the fine-textured tannins smoothed out. Try now. $100 (5/31/90) **90**
Chambertin 1985 $113 (5/31/88) **92**
Charmes-Chambertin 1988: A silky textured, spicy flavored Burgundy, with flair, concentration and a long finish. Beautiful oaky notes accent the firm cherry and strawberry flavors. The outline is there, it just needs until 1993 to '97 to fill in. $75 (3/31/91) **89**
Charmes-Chambertin 1987: Big and flavorful, with smoky, tarry accents on the plum and black cherry flavors. Concentrated and rich, with firm, fine tannins. Try it now to 1994. $66 (5/31/90) **87**
Charmes-Chambertin 1985 Rel: $68 Cur: $85 (5/31/88) **88**
Gevrey-Chambertin 1989: Not giving much now, with a hard finish, but should improve after the intense cherry and earth aromas and flavors and hard tannins sort themselves out. Try from 1994. $35 (1/31/92) **85**
Gevrey-Chambertin Les Cazetiers 1987: Light in fruit flavor, but it has an elegant texture, good complexity and a lingering finish. Aromas of tea and smoke give way to an almost sweet tea and brown sugar flavor. Drink now or through 1993. $66 (5/31/90) **80**
Gevrey-Chambertin Les Cazetiers 1985 $67 (5/31/88) **91**
Gevrey-Chambertin Clos de la Justice 1988: An earthy, gamy wine, with cooked rhubarb and berry flavors. Not the freshest or most appealing at this stage. Might be better after 1994, but finishes with a definite earthy twinge. Tasted twice. $54 (3/31/92) **78**
Gevrey-Chambertin Clos de la Justice 1985 $51 (5/31/88) **85**
Gevrey-Chambertin Clos St.-Jacques 1987: Very ripe and tasty, with delicious, chocolaty oak accents blending into the cherry and plum flavors. Tannins keep it from being great right now, but the oak and fruit should come into better balance by about 1993. $56 (5/31/90) **86**
Latricières-Chambertin 1959 $150 (8/31/90) (TR) **98**

ALAIN BURGUET
Gevrey-Chambertin Vieilles Vignes 1988: Beautiful in color, with deep, ripe plum, currant and black cherry flavors. Has a fleshy texture and plenty of depth. The tannins are firm and well proportioned, and the finish extends the flavors. Drink in 1993 to '95. $45 (12/31/90) **88**
Gevrey-Chambertin Vieilles Vignes 1986: Very attractive and well made in a medium-bodied style. Offers leather, herb and plum aromas and is well balanced with ripe fruit and firm tannins. Drink now. $33 (7/15/89) **84**

GUY CASTAGNIER
Charmes-Chambertin 1989: A stocky wine, with raspberry, cherry and smoke aromas and flavors, chewy tannins and a thick texture. Try after 1994. $62 (1/31/92) **90**
Latricières-Chambertin 1989: Excellent, with pure cherry extract, masses of mouth-puckering fruit and firm tannins. Long and delicious. Try after 1994. $62 (1/31/92) **93**
Latricières-Chambertin 1988: Tart, lean and crisp, with a beam of deeply concentrated cherry, cassis and raspberry flavors that are bright and intense. Beautifully focused, long and persistent on the finish, this is a classy wine, with plenty of tannin for cellaring until 1997 and beyond. $63 (7/15/91) **93**
Mazis-Chambertin Mazy-Chambertin 1989: A masterpiece, with wonderfully concentrated black cherry, berry and smoke flavors and a long, silky finish. Try after 1995. $62 (1/31/92) **93**
Mazis-Chambertin Mazy-Chambertin 1988: Has a pretty core of ripe, firm, focused strawberry, cherry, raspberry and spice flavors that are neatly woven together. Firm tannins on the finish let the fruit shine through. A solid wine that needs cellaring until 1996. $63 (7/15/91) **91**

PHILLIPE CHARLOPIN
Chambertin 1989: Firmly tannic, but not overbearing, with delicious ripe plum and currant-scented flavors. Offers wonderful rose petal and plum aromas and is developing a silky texture. Needs time to evolve; try around 1995 and beyond. 250 cases made. $35 (11/15/91) **91**

CHARLOPIN-PARIZOT
Gevrey-Chambertin 1985 $22 (11/30/87) **64**

Key to Symbols

The scores reported here are the results of blind tastings conducted by our panel of senior editors. Wines that carry the initials below are results of individual tastings.

THE WINE SPECTATOR 100-POINT SCALE ***95-100***—Classic, a great wine; ***90-94***—Outstanding, superior character and style; ***80-89***—Good to very good, a wine with special qualities; ***70-79***—Average, drinkable wine that may have minor flaws; ***60-69***—Below average, drinkable but not recommended; ***50-59***—Poor, undrinkable, not recommended. "+"—With a score indicates a range; used primarily with barrel tastings to indicate a preliminary score.

SPECIAL DESIGNATIONS SS—Spectator Selection, CS—Cellar Selection, BB—Best Buy, ($NA)—Price not available, (NR)—Not released.

TASTER'S INITIALS (JG)—Jim Gordon, (HS)—Harvey Steiman, (JL)—James Laube, (JS)—James Suckling, (TM)—Thomas Matthews, (TR)—Terry Robards, (PM)—Per-Henrik Mansson, (BT)—Barrel Tasting (these wines were tasted blind from barrel samples), (CA-date)—*California's Great Cabernets* by James Laube, (CH-date)—*California's Great Chardonnays* by James Laube, (VP-date)—*Vintage Port* by James Suckling.

DATE TASTED Dates in parentheses represent the issue in which the rating was published.

Gevrey-Chambertin Cuvée Vieilles Vignes 1990: Ripe, plush and generous, with a velvety smooth texture and beautifully articulated raspberry, black cherry and anise aromas and flavors intertwining through the long finish. Tempting to drink now, but should be at its best after 1996. 150 cases made. $40 (4/30/92) **90**
Gevrey-Chambertin Cuvée Vieilles Vignes 1989: Smoky and elegant, with firm, concentrated plum, currant and spice flavors and buttery, toasty oak notes. Balanced, rich and complex. Tempting now, but probably best around 1995. $75 (11/15/91) **88**
Gevrey-Chambertin Cuvée Vieilles Vignes 1988: Tough and tart, offering decent black cherry and earth aromas and flavors, but lacking the intensity and grace to promise a lot for the cellar. Try in 1995, but don't expect great things. $31 (12/31/90) **79**

F. CHAUVENET
Charmes-Chambertin 1988 $78 (7/15/90) (BT) **90+**
Charmes-Chambertin 1986 $65 (7/31/88) **90**
Charmes-Chambertin 1985 $72 (7/31/87) **97**
Charmes-Chambertin 1983 $24 (9/15/86) **88**
Gevrey-Chambertin Charreux 1985 $33 (10/15/87) **88**
Gevrey-Chambertin Clos St.-Jacques 1989: Sneaks up and grabs you, with hard-to-define, exotic notes complemented by lovely truffle and wild berry aromas and flavors, all presented against an excellent tannic background. Try after 1994. $45 (1/31/92) **89**
Gevrey-Chambertin Clos St.-Jacques 1986 $35 (7/31/88) **85**
Gevrey-Chambertin Estournelles St.-Jacques 1989: Wonderfully proportioned, with a superb concentration of fruit. Has layers of earth, berry and smoke flavors and super-integrated tannins. Try from 1994. $40 (1/31/92) **91**
Gevrey-Chambertin Estournelles St.-Jacques 1986 $35 (7/31/88) **89**
Gevrey-Chambertin Lavaux St.-Jacques 1989: A beautiful wine, with enticing black cherry and cedar aromas and flavors, firm tannins and a fresh, smoky finish. Try after 1993. $45 (1/31/92) **88**
Gevrey-Chambertin Lavaux St.-Jacques 1988 $48 (7/15/90) (BT) **70+**
Gevrey-Chambertin Lavaux St.-Jacques 1986 $35 (7/31/88) **86**
Gevrey-Chambertin Petite Chapelle 1988 $40 (7/15/90) (BT) **70+**
Mazis-Chambertin 1983 $27 (6/30/87) **72**

DOMAINE DES CHEZEAUX
Griotte-Chambertin 1988: Ripe and concentrated, turning a bit tarry and coffeelike on the finish, which tends to overshadow the plum and currant flavors. Still, it's a distinctive wine that needs until 1995 to show what it has. 450 cases made. $110 (5/15/91) **90**
Griotte-Chambertin 1985 $100 (6/15/88) **91**

DOMAINE BRUNO CLAIR
Gevrey-Chambertin Les Cazetiers 1989: A captivating wine built in a muscular style, with glorious cherry, berry and smoke aromas and flavors and excellent tannins. Try in 1994. $61 (1/31/92) **89**

DOMAINE DU CLOS FRANTIN
Chambertin 1989: A caressing style, with intense black cherry, berry and earth aromas and flavors presented in a silky texture and framed by super-firm tannins. Try after 1994. $73 (1/31/92) **88**
Chambertin 1986: Delicate but amazingly flavorful, echoing cherry, leather and vanilla flavors at great length, a bit tannic at this point, but time in the cellar should polish it beautifully. Drink 1993. $63 (2/28/89) **90**
Gevrey-Chambertin 1989: A big, fat Gevrey, but it lacks grace; verges on being too jammy and tannic. From Bichot. Try from 1994 to '96. $29 (1/31/92) **84**
Gevrey-Chambertin 1988: Concentrated fruit aromas and flavors balanced against firm tannins and a supple texture make this an immediately likable wine, but it's worth cellaring to see what develops. Berry, cherry and plum flavors dominate. $37 (7/15/90) **87**
Gevrey-Chambertin 1987: A firm, straightforward style, with accurate Gevrey aromas and flavors, leaning toward strawberry and a touch of spice. Gentle tannins. Drink now. $20 (3/31/90) **82**

DOMAINE CLAUDINE DESCHAMPS
Gevrey-Chambertin Bel-Air 1985 $28 (3/31/88) **87**

JOSEPH DROUHIN
Chambertin 1989: Silky, subtle and elegant, with lovely currant and violet aromas and flavors and a long finish. Try after 1994. $114 (1/31/92) **90**
Chambertin 1988: Polished, elegant and generous, brimming with sharply focused raspberry, cherry and plum flavors that keep echoing in the long finish. So flavorful you hardly notice the well-integrated tannins. Beautifully crafted to mine all the flavors possible from this vineyard. You could drink it now, but try to wait until at least 1995 to 2000. $112 (2/15/91) **94**
Chambertin 1986: Supple and subtle, smooth with layers of plum, cherry, spice and toast, elegant and medium-bodied with a dry, slightly tannic finish. Drink 1993. $80 (2/28/89) **90**
Chambertin 1985 Rel: $75 Cur: $102 (11/15/87) **95**
Charmes-Chambertin 1989: Rich and opulent, with concentrated raspberry and smoke aromas and flavors and silky tannins. Try after 1994. $80 (1/31/92) **92**
Charmes-Chambertin 1988: Despite firm, drying tannins, this has a wealth of rich, concentrated fruit flavor, echoing black cherry, plum, spice and nutmeg, and a long, complex finish, but it needs time to come together. Cellar until 1995 or '96 to see what happens. 50 cases made. $65 (11/15/90) **93**
Charmes-Chambertin 1986: Deep, rich and delicate with focused black cherry, plum, spice and floral flavors that offer elegance and finesse with depth and complexity. Tannins are in proportion. Drink now. In an "off" year for Burgundy, this is one of the shining stars. Rel: $56 Cur: $60 (2/28/89) CS **91**
Charmes-Chambertin 1985 $60 (11/15/87) **89**
Gevrey-Chambertin 1988 $41 (7/15/90) (BT) **75+**
Gevrey-Chambertin 1986: Rich, toasty and earthy with ripe raspberry, cherry and spicy flavors, backed with firm, tight tannins on the finish. Lacks charm and finesse. Drink now. $27 (2/28/89) **83**
Gevrey-Chambertin 1985 $33 (11/15/87) **91**
Gevrey-Chambertin Les Cazetiers 1989: Has lots of fruit extract, with wonderfully seductive, fruity aromas and flavors backed up by silky tannins. Try after 1993. $70 (1/31/92) **91**
Gevrey-Chambertin Lavaux St.-Jacques 1989: This pretty wine has lovely raspberry and smoke aromas and flavors and silky tannins. Try after 1993. $70 (1/31/92) **86**
Griotte-Chambertin 1989: A subtle yet powerful wine, with lovely, concentrated cherry and violet flavors, a touch of spice and firm tannins. Try after 1995. $90 (1/31/92) **91**
Griotte-Chambertin 1988: Enticing, with game and rose petal aromas, it delivers plenty of rich, complex, elegant fruit flavor on the palate. Tiers of cherry, berry, spice and oak have a tough edge, but it's nothing a little time in the bottle won't resolve. Oaky and tannic on the finish; try in 1995 to 2000. $81 (11/15/90) **91**
Griotte-Chambertin 1986 $81 (7/31/88) **92**
Griotte-Chambertin 1985 $68 (11/15/87) **95**
Latricières-Chambertin 1988: Lots of wild berry aromas and flavors keep coming back with every sip in this generous, if inelegant wine. Once the moderate tannins subside, it ought to be enjoyable. Try after 1994. $72 (2/15/91) **87**
Mazis-Chambertin 1989: Beautiful blackberry and cherry aromas follow through on the palate in a wine that's overflowing with supple fruit and tannins. Try after 1995. $86 (1/31/92) **92**

DROUHIN-LAROZE
Chambertin Clos de Bèze 1988: Beautifully defined flavors wrap themselves around a supple, smoothly polished frame in this undeniably elegant wine. Cherry, currant, plum, cinnamon and vanilla only begin to describe the flavors. Has the tannin to last beyond 1995. $88 (12/31/90) **92**
Chambertin Clos de Bèze 1987: Spicy strawberry and cherry aromas hang elegantly on a firm structure. The velvety texture and delicate flavors are immediately appealing. Drink 1993 to '95. $40 (3/31/90) **90**

Chambertin Clos de Bèze 1985 Rel: $70 Cur: $110 (10/15/88) **92**
Chapelle-Chambertin 1988: Lean and a little tough, but the cherry, currant, nutmeg and vanilla flavors ring true. It finishes clean and long. Needs until 1993 to '95 to polish the considerable tannins. $68 (12/31/90) **88**
Gevrey-Chambertin Clos Prieur 1988: Very light in color, with lovely cinnamon and strawberry aromas and flavors and hints at rhubarb pie on the finish. A lean, lovely wine that grows in depth with every sip. Drink now or in 1993. $44 (12/31/90) **88**
Gevrey-Chambertin Lavaux-St.-Jacques 1988: Very light in color, with a slightly bitter edge to the modest strawberry and anise flavors that keeps it from being appealling. Perhaps better after cellaring until 1993. $44 (12/31/90) **80**
Latricières-Chambertin 1988: You can feel the backbone in this beautifully proportioned wine, but the overall effect is one of delicacy and complexity. Subtle cherry, currant and spice flavors intertwine gracefully through the long finish. Cellar until 1993 to '95. $68 (12/31/90) **91**
Latricières-Chambertin 1987: Seems light and delicate at first, but then the concentration of berry and cherry flavors kicks in on the finish, holds on for length and promises a long life as a result. Drink 1994. $36 (3/31/90) **88**
Latricières-Chambertin 1987: Lean, tart and fruity, with spice, pear, melon and vanilla notes that are a bit coarse, but with time it should round out. Delicate on the finish. Drink now to 1994. $36 (3/31/90) **88**
Mazis-Chambertin 1985 $47 (10/15/88) **90**

DOMAINE DUJAC
Charmes-Chambertin 1989: Like the name says, it's charming, with super-velvety tannins and voluptuous strawberry and berry aromas and flavors. Try after 1993. $72 (1/31/92) **90**
Charmes-Chambertin 1988: A rustic style of Burgundy, with woody, earthy aromas, stiff tannins and earthy, plummy flavors. Very likable in its style. Fruit and spice notes linger on the finish, promising improvement if aged through 1995 to '98. $60 (3/31/91) **85**
Charmes-Chambertin 1986 $50 (7/31/88) **85**
Charmes-Chambertin 1985 $100 (3/15/88) **95**
Gevrey-Chambertin Aux Combottes 1989: Offers immediate gratification, with its round, wonderful texture and strawberry notes. Try after 1993. $65 (1/31/92) **86**
Gevrey-Chambertin Aux Combottes 1988: Very fruity, fresh and charming, but has nice, firm acidity and adequate tannins to balance it out. Has sour cherry and strawberrylike aromas, ripe, spicy flavors and a lingering, fruity finish. $54 (3/31/91) **86**
Gevrey-Chambertin Aux Combottes 1987: Light, but elegant and complex. Smells and tastes spicy, with tea, smoke, anise and wild strawberries. Mild tannins make it enjoyable now. Tasted twice. $42 (5/31/90) **80**

FREDERIC ESMONIN
Gevrey-Chambertin Les Corbeaux 1989: Full of bright flavors and intense character, bursting with blueberry, wild raspberry and rhubarb; a real mouthful of fruit. Needs to tame its tannins, however, so lay off until 1995 to '98. $42 (3/31/92) **88**
Gevrey-Chambertin Estournelles St.-Jacques 1989: Tight and tannic, with a bright beam of raspberry and red cherry flavor shining through it all. Has intensity and length, but needs until 1995 to '97 to soften the tannins. $42 (3/31/92) **86**
Gevrey-Chambertin Lavaux St.-Jacques 1989: Firm and lively, with polished tannins and a nice array of chocolate-tinged currant, plum and earth flavors. Approaching drinkability, but can use until 1995 to settle down. $42 (3/31/92) **88**
Griotte-Chambertin 1989: Smooth, polished and generous, with a tightly focused beam of raspberry, blackberry and cherry flavor shining through the frame of spicy oak, vanilla and anise. A beautifully proportioned wine that can use until 1997 to 2000 to show what it has. $80 (3/31/92) **92**
Mazis-Chambertin Mazy-Chambertin 1989: Ripe and generous, with a polished, silky texture and plenty of currant, plum and spice aromas and flavors. Has a solid tannin component that needs until 1996 or '97 to soften. $80 (3/31/92) **89**
Ruchottes-Chambertin 1989: Aromatic and remarkably deep, offering plenty of ripe blackberry, currant and plum flavors shaded by herbs and smoke. Decidedly tannic, but concentrated enough to warrant cellaring until 1997 to 2000. Has real elegance despite the tannins. $80 (3/31/92) **91**

DOMAINE MICHEL ESMONIN
Gevrey-Chambertin Clos-St.-Jacques 1987: Round and aromatic, with the vanilla, toast and spice aromas and flavors of delicious new oak, and enough concentration of berry and currant flavors to balance the wine on the finish. Needs cellaring until 1993 to absorb the oak. $44 (3/31/90) **87**
Gevrey-Chambertin Estournelles St.-Jacques 1988: Lean, firm and tannic, with tart, concentrated, well-integrated black cherry, blackberry and oak flavors. Balanced, with firm acidity and tannins, but needs until 1994 or '95 to chisel away the tannins. $40 (3/31/91) **84**

FAIVELEY
Chambertin Clos de Bèze 1989: A broad-shouldered wine, with distinctive chestnut, berry and smoke aromas and flavors and firm tannins. Try after 1994. $99 (1/31/92) **90**
Chambertin Clos de Bèze 1988 $114 (7/15/90) (BT) **95+**
Chambertin Clos de Bèze 1987: Lean in texture and flavor, with faint red cherry and cinnamon aromas and flavors; has firm tannins but it's gentle enough to drink today. Best from now to 1995. $70 (3/31/90) **83**
Chambertin Clos de Bèze 1986 $66 (7/15/89) **88**
Chambertin Clos de Bèze 1985 $105 (3/15/88) **96**
Gevrey-Chambertin 1989: An elegant style, with lovely perfumed cherry aromas and flavors, medium tannins and a silky mouth-feel. Try from 1993. $34 (1/31/92) **87**
Gevrey-Chambertin 1985 $38 (4/15/88) **90**
Gevrey-Chambertin Les Cazetiers 1989: Smoky and earthy, with vanilla aromas and flavors. Quite chewy and firm. Better in 1994. $47 (1/31/92) **89**
Gevrey-Chambertin Les Cazetiers 1988: Intense and deeply concentrated, with rich, sweet black cherry, currant, cedar and spice flavors that are well integrated and complex. Still tight and in need of cellaring until 1995 or '96. $57 (3/31/91) **89**
Gevrey-Chambertin Les Cazetiers 1985 $53 (3/31/88) **92**
Gevrey-Chambertin La Combe Aux Moines 1989: A pretty, rustic style, with chestnut, berry and cherry aromas and flavors, ending with round, silky tannins. Try after 1993. $47 (1/31/92) **87**
Latricières-Chambertin 1989: An earthy style, with barnyard, violet and berry aromas and flavors, a very silky finish and firm tannins. Try after 1993. $81 (1/31/92) **89**
Latricières-Chambertin 1985 $77 (3/15/88) **88**
Mazis-Chambertin 1989: A monumental wine, with opulent smoke, berry and raspberry flavors that go on and on, with a super-long finish. Try after 1994. $79 (1/31/92) **95**
Mazis-Chambertin 1985 $81 (3/15/88) **92**

FORTNUM & MASON
Charmes-Chambertin (English Bottled) 1947 ($NA) (8/31/90) (TR) **94**

PIERRE GELIN
Chambertin Clos de Bèze 1985 $77 (3/15/88) **84**
Gevrey-Chambertin 1985 $25 (4/15/88) **93**
Gevrey-Chambertin 1982 $19 (3/16/85) **80**
Mazis-Chambertin 1985 $25 (3/15/88) **90**

DOMAINE GEOFFROY
Gevrey-Chambertin Les Champeaux 1986: A Burgundy of substance, with concentrated berry and earthy aromas, full, almost sweet fruit and the firm structure characteristic of '86. Tannic on the finish. Drink now. $36 (7/15/89) **85**
Gevrey-Chambertin Clos Prieur 1987: Beautifully concentrated, focused, harmonious and artfully balanced between the generous blackberry and cherry flavors and the vanilla, toast and spice of oak. Full-bodied, bursting with fruit and already graceful. Has the stuffing to age well into the late '90s. 150 cases made. $29 (3/31/90) **93**
Gevrey-Chambertin Clos Prieur 1986: Concentrated, focused, almost chewy in texture, with salty, earthy aromas, fine cherry and currant flavors and a fruity, crisp finish. Firm tannins and acid indicate cellaring until 1992 to '93. $29 (7/15/89) **89**
Gevrey-Chambertin Les Escorvées 1986: Fresh and quaffable, but a very bizarre Burgundy. Effusively grapey and berrylike in flavor, with a purple color, and very ripe, almost Port-like aromas. $26 (7/15/89) **79**
Mazis-Chambertin 1987: Very firm and focused, with sharply defined cherry and berry aromas and flavors that cut through the ample, velvety tannins like a bright beam to a luscious finish. Already complex and delicious, but it needs cellaring until 1994 to bring the tannin into line. $48 (3/31/90) **92**

DOMAINE ROBERT GROFFIER
Chambertin Clos de Bèze 1987: Rough and tannic now but there's plenty of fruit to like in this wine with toasty, ripe cherry and earthy, slightly vegetal notes on the finish. Drink 1994 to 1998. $45 (7/31/89) **88**
Gevrey-Chambertin 1986: Has pretty cherry and strawberry aromas with a nice toasty overlay of oak, but on the palate the flavors are concentrated and delicate. Drink now. $27 (2/28/89) **85**

CHATEAU DES HERBEUX
Chambertin 1988: Lighter and more delicate than most, offering fragile strawberry and plum aromas and flavors held in check by a firm structure. Should evolve very nicely in the cellar, gaining complexity and richness until 1994 to '96. $75 (12/31/90) **87**

BERNARD HERESZTYN
Gevrey-Chambertin Les Goulots 1988: The flavors are bright, deep, rich and complex; wonderful black cherry, currant, raspberry and spice flavors keep pouring out. Finishes with a nice dose of tannin, suggesting it needs cellaring until 1996 or so. $44 (7/15/91) **90**

STANISLAS HERESZTYN
Gevrey-Chambertin 1987: Very well made in a lighter style. Shows good complexity and concentration of berry and toast aromas and flavors, held in check with slightly gritty tannins that need until 1993 to soften. $25 (3/31/90) **83**
Gevrey-Chambertin Les Champonnets 1988: Tough, tannic and lean, with herb-scented blackberry flavors, but doesn't quite have the intensity to promise great things when the tannin subsides in 1995 to '97. $37 (12/31/90) **82**

R. HERESZTYN-BAILLY
Gevrey-Chambertin 1986: Like most '86s, ripe and wonderful on the nose and austere and tannic on the palate, but this one has the generosity of pure Burgundian flavor to make it worth waiting until 1994 to smooth out. $20 (7/15/89) **86**
Gevrey-Chambertin Les Goulots 1986: Lean, crisp and tannic with a modest core of ripe cherry and plum flavors that fight the tannin to a standstill, but should be softened enough to drink now through 1994. $28 (10/15/89) **82**

LOUIS JADOT
Chambertin Clos de Bèze 1989: Offers gorgeous blackberry and cherry aromas and a glorious backbone of fine tannins and concentrated fruit flavor. Try after 1994. $105 (1/31/92) **93**
Chambertin Clos de Bèze 1988: An elegant, dynamic wine, with beautifully focused black cherry, currant and toast aromas and flavors that sail across the palate on a smooth structure, echoing on the long finish. A harmonious, gloriously flavorful wine that should be at its best after 1995. 350 cases made. $97 (3/15/91) **96**
Chambertin Clos de Bèze 1987: An elegant, almost delicate wine, with charming spice, cherry, raspberry and smoke aromas and flavors blending harmoniously with the light texture. It has enough tannin to hold it while it grows in the cellar. Should be best around 1994 to '96. $65 (7/15/90) **89**
Chambertin Clos de Bèze 1986 $63 (7/15/89) **90**
Chambertin Clos de Bèze 1985 Rel: $66 Cur: $79 (3/15/88) **89**
Chapelle-Chambertin 1989 (NR) (7/15/90) (BT) **85+**
Chapelle-Chambertin 1988: Tightly structured, focused and plush, with currant, plum and spice aromas and flavors hinting at tea on the long finish. The firm tannins need until 1996 to '98 to soften. 175 cases made. $75 (3/15/91) **93**
Chapelle-Chambertin 1985 $54 (3/15/88) **90**
Gevrey-Chambertin 1986: A good if not exciting Pinot with cherry and spice flavors and a touch of dryness or woodiness that robs it of luster. $25 (7/15/89) **77**
Gevrey-Chambertin Clos St.-Jacques 1989: Charming, with focused cherry and smoke flavors and super-firm tannins. Tempting to drink now, but should be better in 1994. $65 (1/31/92) **90**
Gevrey-Chambertin Clos St.-Jacques 1988: Solid but chunky in texture, offering slightly gamy berry and currant aromas and flavors. Tannic and tight on the finish. Should be at its best after 1994. 175 cases made. $52 (3/15/91) **88**
Gevrey-Chambertin Clos St.-Jacques 1986: Ripe and well-built, full-bodied, shows tasty oak, solid fruit flavors and a long finish that echoes fruit and vanilla. Drink now. $44 (7/15/89) **84**
Gevrey-Chambertin Clos St.-Jacques 1985 $45 (3/31/88) **94**
Gevrey-Chambertin Estournelles St.-Jacques 1988: Solidly built, but generous and elegant, with complex raspberry, plum and cherry aromas and flavors darting in and out. A very well-crafted wine that should keep developing well through 1995 and beyond. 175 cases made. $50 (3/15/91) **91**
Gevrey-Chambertin Estournelles St.-Jacques 1986: Ripe, fruity and elegant, too. Has sophisticated cedar and cinnamon aromas to accent the ripe currant and plum flavors, good acid and firm tannins. $40 (7/15/89) **87**
Gevrey-Chambertin Estournelles St.-Jacques 1985 $41 (3/31/88) **86**
Griotte-Chambertin 1988: Balanced, elegant and harmonious, offering a beautiful interplay of plum, currant and berry aromas and flavors shaded by sweet vanilla and spice notes. The tannins are smoothly integrated. Finishes lean and muscular, hinting at chocolate and tea. Approaching drinkability, but try to hold off until at least 1995. 100 cases made. $75 (3/15/91) **94**
Griotte-Chambertin 1987: Elegant, spicy and complex aromas and flavors make this wine immediately appealling, although the lean, austere structure does not allow it to show all that it could. Cellaring until 1993 to '94 should soften it up at least a bit. $50 (7/15/90) **80**
Mazis-Chambertin 1987: A deliciously harmonious and complete red Burgundy from the spicy-oaky aroma to the pure beam of cherry and strawberry flavors, to the lingering, almost sweet finish. Fine but firm tannins are well integrated, and everything falls into place. Tempting now, but it should develop through 1995. $50 (5/31/90) **92**
Ruchottes-Chambertin 1988: Tough, hard-edged and firmly tannic, but it has a solid core of currant and berry flavors on its compact structure. Needs lots of time to soften and broaden; should be best after 1995 to '98. 175 cases made. $75 (3/15/91) **91**

JAFFELIN
Chambertin Le Chambertin 1986 $65 (12/31/88) **89**
Chambertin Le Chambertin 1983 $48 (4/16/86) **93**
Charmes-Chambertin 1989: Refreshing but light, with floral, cherry and berry notes. Has a light finish supported by light tannins. Try after 1993. $66 (1/31/92) **87**
Charmes-Chambertin 1988 $68 (7/15/90) (BT) **90+**
Charmes-Chambertin 1986 $45 (12/31/88) **77**
Gevrey-Chambertin 1989: Packed with rich, round fruit, this wine has plenty of wild raspberry and strawberry aromas and flavors and full, supple tannins. Try from 1993. $30 (1/31/92) **88**
Gevrey-Chambertin 1988: Ripe and tight, with a solid core of black cherry, boysenberry, anise and subtle oak seasoning. A well-rounded wine that's rich and concentrated. Gritty tannins make it best to cellar until 1996. $25 (8/31/91) **88**
Gevrey-Chambertin 1986: Tight and tough, with tannin to burn, but a pretty good component of plummy cherry flavor should develop well over time. Drink now. $49 (2/28/89) **85**

Gevrey-Chambertin 1983 $17 (10/01/85) **77**
Gevrey-Chambertin Lavaux St.-Jacques 1989: Fresh and fruity, but seems a little diluted for a *premier cru.* Drink now. $40 (1/31/92) **81**

LABOURE-ROI
Gevrey-Chambertin 1988: Tart, peppery, leafy, very tight and tannic, more like a very lean Rhône than a generous Burgundy. With cellaring until 1994 to '98 it could emerge as a complex, enjoyable wine. 1,000 cases made. $35 (12/31/90) **81**

LOUIS LATOUR
Chambertin Cuvée Hèritiers Latour 1989: Not what you expect in Chambertin. Much too light and very diluted. Drink now. (NR) (1/31/92) **78**
Chambertin Cuvée Hèritiers Latour 1985 Rel: $76 Cur: $90 (3/15/88) **95**
Charmes-Chambertin 1985 Rel: $50 Cur: $68 (3/15/88) **85**
Gevrey-Chambertin 1989: A ripe, round wine, with ground coffee and berry aromas and flavors and a velvety finish. Should improve with cellaring until 1994. (NR) (1/31/92) **87**
Gevrey-Chambertin 1985 $36 (10/15/88) **77**

LEBEGUE-BICHOT
Chambertin Clos de Bèze 1945 $310 (8/31/90) (TR) **96**

PHILIPPE LECLERC
Gevrey-Chambertin 1984 $26 (7/15/87) **90**
Gevrey-Chambertin Les Cazetiers 1988: Heavily oaked, with mature coffee, currant and cherry notes that turn earthy and tannic on the finish. A rustic style that has pleasant flavors. Drink in 1995. $80 (7/15/91) **82**
Gevrey-Chambertin Les Cazetiers 1987: The ripe fruit aromas and flavors are held in check by substantial drying tannins that will take till 1994 to '95 to ease their grip. Worth a gamble because the fruit concentration is there. $63 (5/31/90) **85**
Gevrey-Chambertin Les Cazetiers 1985 Rel: $64 Cur: $70 (10/15/88) **89**
Gevrey-Chambertin Les Cazetiers 1984 $38 (8/31/87) **83**
Gevrey-Chambertin Les Cazetiers 1982 Rel: $21 Cur: $45 (11/16/85) **68**
Gevrey-Chambertin Les Champeaux 1985 $55 (10/31/88) **79**
Gevrey-Chambertin La Combe aux Moines 1988: Offers pleasant, ripe cherry, plum and spice notes, but the tannins are scratchy and the flavors turn a bit simple on the finish. Hold until 1994. $80 (7/15/91) **82**
Gevrey-Chambertin La Combe aux Moines 1987: Good quality, but nothing special. Has reasonably ripe plum and earth flavors, with firm tannins and spicy, smoky aromas. $68 (5/31/90) **76**
Gevrey-Chambertin Combe aux Moines 1985 $70 (10/15/88) **92**
Gevrey-Chambertin Combe aux Moines 1984 $42 (8/31/87) **82**
Gevrey-Chambertin Les Platières 1988: Light in color, with mature plum and cherry flavors that turn murky and earthy. The tannins are strong, too. Cellar until 1994. $45 (7/15/91) **74**
Gevrey-Chambertin Les Platières 1987: Distinctive. Made in a big, spicy style with full body, heady aromas of vanilla and spice, but coarse tannins and not quite enough plum flavor to balance the woody component. Try it 1993 to '95. $35 (5/31/90) **81**
Gevrey-Chambertin Les Platières 1985 Rel: $38 Cur: $45 (10/15/88) **90**

DOMAINE RENE LECLERC
Gevrey-Chambertin Combes aux Moines 1985 Rel: $55 Cur: $61 (10/31/88) **82**

OLIVIER LEFLAIVE FRERES
Charmes-Chambertin 1989: Lovely, with tanned leather and berry aromas and flavors, very firm tannins and a silky mouth-feel. Try after 1993. $60 (1/31/92) **88**
Charmes-Chambertin 1986 $50 (7/31/88) **88**
Gevrey-Chambertin 1989 (NR) (7/15/90) (BT) **75+**
Gevrey-Chambertin 1988 $35 (7/15/90) (BT) **80+**

DOMAINE LEROY
Chambertin 1989: Intense and velvety, with beautiful blackberry, smoke and ripe currant aromas and flavors. Kicks in at the end, with refined tannins. Try from 1994. $306 (1/31/92) **93**
Gevrey-Chambertin Les Combottes 1989: Shows superb breeding and class, with superlative cherry, coffee, vanilla and cedar aromas and flavors and a finish of super-fine tannins. Try from 1994. $117 (1/31/92) **93**
Latricières-Chambertin 1989: Truly superb, with gorgeous toast, cherry and berry aromas and flavors and an incredibly seductive finish. Try after 1994. $250 (1/31/92) **93**

GEORGES LIGNIER
Gevrey-Chambertin 1987: Not deep or powerful, but there's a lot to enjoy in this wine, now or through 1993. Very complex and well-balanced, playing spice, tea and tobacco aromas off sweet-seeming plum and cherry flavors. $29 (5/31/90) **84**
Gevrey-Chambertin Les Combottes 1987: Ripe, welcoming fruit flavor lasts from first whiff to the finish. Smoothly textured and elegantly balanced, it needs till 1993 to '95 for a slightly rough edge of tannin to round out. $34 (5/31/90) **87**

LUPE-CHOLET
Gevrey-Chambertin Lavaux St.-Jacques 1983 $27 (11/30/86) **59**

M & G
Gevrey-Chambertin 1987: $40 (3/31/91) **73**

HENRI MAGNIEN
Gevrey-Chambertin 1985 $25 (10/15/87) **81**
Gevrey-Chambertin 1983 $13 (2/01/86) **68**
Gevrey-Chambertin 1982 $12 (7/01/85) **89**
Gevrey-Chambertin Les Cazetiers 1985 $35 (10/15/87) **88**
Gevrey-Chambertin Les Cazetiers 1983 $18 (12/16/85) **72**
Gevrey-Chambertin Les Cazetiers 1982 $16 (5/01/84) **80**
Gevrey-Chambertin Premier Cru 1985 $29 (10/15/87) **80**

CLAUDE MARCHAND
Charmes-Chambertin 1986: Deep and intense with focused, concentrated cherry, plum, spice and oak, layered with firm, tight tannins and acidity. This one's built for the cellar. The fruit stays with you on the finish. Drink 1995 and beyond. $50 (7/15/89) **92**

Key to Symbols

The scores reported here are the results of blind tastings conducted by our panel of senior editors. Wines that carry the initials below are results of individual tastings.

THE WINE SPECTATOR 100-POINT SCALE 95-100—Classic, a great wine; *90-94*—Outstanding, superior character and style; *80-89*—Good to very good, a wine with special qualities; *70-79*—Average, drinkable wine that may have minor flaws; *60-69*—Below average, drinkable but not recommended; *50-59*—Poor, undrinkable, not recommended. "+"—With a score indicates a range; used primarily with barrel tastings to indicate a preliminary score.

SPECIAL DESIGNATIONS SS—Spectator Selection, CS—Cellar Selection, BB—Best Buy, ($NA)—Price not available, (NR)—Not released.

TASTER'S INITIALS (JG)—Jim Gordon, (HS)—Harvey Steiman, (JL)—James Laube, (JS)—James Suckling, (TM)—Thomas Matthews, (TR)—Terry Robards, (PM)—Per-Henrik Mansson, (BT)—Barrel Tasting (these wines were tasted blind from barrel samples), (CA-date)—*California's Great Cabernets* by James Laube, (CH-date)—*California's Great Chardonnays* by James Laube, (VP-date)—*Vintage Port* by James Suckling.

DATE TASTED Dates in parentheses represent the issue in which the rating was published.

Gevrey-Chambertin 1987: A wine with earthy, spicy aromas and flavors, but the coarse, somewhat austere texture will need until 1993 to '94 to soften. $22 (7/15/90) **81**
Gevrey-Chambertin 1986: Has full fruit, but with conplexity and structure for aging. Very concentrated cherry and berry flavors, firm tannins and crisp acidity. Flavors really linger on the finish. Drink now. $28 (7/15/89) **89**

DOMAINE JEAN-PHILIPPE MARCHAND
Charmes-Chambertin 1987: Lighter than most, with decadent earth, mushroom and spice aromas and flavors that tend to obscure the fruit. Seems stale and old before its time. $60 (12/31/90) **76**
Gevrey-Chambertin Les Combottes 1987: A bit firm and tannic, but plenty of smoke and cherry flavors balance the austerity. This wine should grow into its spicy finish with cellaring until 1993. $30 (7/15/90) **82**

DOMAINE MARCHAND-GRILLOT
Gevrey-Chambertin Petite Chapelle 1986: Pleasant, lean and crisp with fresh peach and cherry flavor of moderate depth. Drink by 1993. $30 (10/15/89) **76**

DOMAINE MAUME
Charmes-Chambertin 1988: Tough and toasty, with hard-edged tannins, but also has a solid core of cherry, currant, spice and vanilla flavors. The finish showcases the tannins now; try cellaring until 1996. $60 (7/15/91) **86**
Gevrey-Chambertin 1987: Smells fine, but it turns tight and tough on the palate, which overshadows the light, strawberry-spice flavors. Maybe better in 1993. $25 (3/31/90) **77**
Gevrey-Chambertin en Pallud 1987: Light and aromatic, with floral, spicy aromas and a hint of red cherry flavor. Well-crafted, but not designed to impress. Drink now. $36 (3/31/90) **80**
Mazis-Chambertin 1987: Terribly tannic, tough and drying on the palate, but it smells attractively spicy and floral. Maybe cellaring until 1995 will bring it around, but for now it's a tough go. $56 (3/31/90) **74**

MOILLARD
Chambertin 1984 $42 (5/31/87) **76**
Chambertin Clos de Bèze 1984 $42 (5/31/87) **80**
Chambertin Clos de Bèze 1983 Rel: $37 Cur: $60 (9/16/85) CS **93**
Charmes-Chambertin 1985 $55 (5/31/88) **94**
Gevrey-Chambertin 1987: Smells overly earthy and woody, tastes thin and bitter. Tasted twice. $20 (3/31/90) **66**

MOMMESSIN
Charmes-Chambertin 1985 $45 (2/15/88) **83**
Gevrey-Chambertin 1985 $25 (2/15/88) **90**
Gevrey-Chambertin Estournelles St.-Jacques 1989 (NR) (7/15/90) (BT) **80+**
Gevrey-Chambertin Lavaux St.-Jacques 1989: Lovely, with strawberry and earth notes, finishing with extremely supple tannins. Better after 1993. $45 (1/31/92) **85**

CHARLES MORTET
Chambertin 1989: Has superb concentration of ultrafine fruit and tannins, overflowing with concentrated blackberry, raspberry and licorice flavors. Try after 1994. $68 (1/31/92) **94**
Chambertin 1987: Lighter and less assertive than some, but glowing with spicy, floral complexity. Elegant, balanced and harmonious, almost drinkable. But there is enough tannin to indicate cellaring until 1993 to soften it. $69 (3/31/90) **87**
Chambertin 1986: Plenty of flavor, with fresh, lively plum, cherry and spice flavors that are elegant and focused, finishing with elegance and finesse and a long, pretty aftertaste. Drink 1993. $62 (2/28/89) **91**
Chambertin 1985 $64 (6/15/88) **90**
Gevrey-Chambertin 1989: Tight, crisp and firm with fine tannins and plenty of currant and cherry-tinged flavor. Needs time to unfold and soften, but this wine has very good potential. Needs until 1994 or '95. $25 (1/31/92) **88**
Gevrey-Chambertin 1988: Ripe and opulent, with brilliantly focused raspberry aromas and flavors, bracing acidity and rich tannins, all nicely integrated in a harmonious, elegant package. Give it until 1994 or '95 to open up. $35 (2/15/91) **89**
Gevrey-Chambertin 1987: Light in texture but fairly generous in flavor, with good concentration of cherry and spice flavors that expand on the finish. Cellaring this one until 1993 to '94 should bring out all its qualites. $28 (3/31/90) **86**
Gevrey-Chambertin 1986 $24 (2/28/89) **87**
Gevrey-Chambertin Les Champeaux 1989: Crisply focused, with delicate cherry, plum and toasty oak aromas and flavors, lean texture and impressive length. Built on a small frame, this has the capacity to become quite a wine. Drink after 1994. $34 (1/31/92) **90**
Gevrey-Chambertin Les Champeaux 1988: A square-jawed, straightforward, fruity wine, with firm tannins and acidity, clean cherry and strawberry flavors and good balance. Not yet elegant or long lasting, but solid and delicious. Drink now to 1995. $46 (3/15/91) **87**
Gevrey-Chambertin Les Champeaux 1987: Tight and tannic, with persistent cherry and vanilla flavors trapped beneath the astringency, plus some meaty complexity on the nose. Desperately needs cellaring to soften the tannins, perhaps until 1993 to '95. $36 (3/31/90) **81**
Gevrey-Chambertin Les Champeaux 1986 $33 (2/28/89) **86**
Gevrey-Chambertin Clos Prieur 1989: Ripe, spicy and peppery, with fleshy currant, cherry and plum flavors. Complex and lively, with smoky notes on the aftertaste. Best between 1993 and '96. $30 (1/31/92) **88**
Gevrey-Chambertin Clos Prieur 1988: Generous, sharply focused raspberry, cherry and vanilla aromas and flavors carry through from the first whiff to the final echo of the long finish in this lean but flavorful wine. The well-integrated tannins will need until 1994 or '95 to soften. $41 (2/15/91) **91**
Gevrey-Chambertin Clos Prieur 1987: Lean style, fairly tart and tannic, but endowed with enough spicy red cherry flavor to make it worth cellaring on a gamble. Drink 1993 to '95. $32 (3/31/90) **83**
Gevrey-Chambertin Clos Prieur 1986 $30 (2/28/89) **84**
Gevrey-Chambertin Clos Prieur 1985 $29 (7/31/88) **92**

GEORGES MUGNERET
Ruchottes-Chambertin 1989: Crisp, lively and tightly packed with cherry, black raspberry and currant flavors bursting to get out from behind a forward wall of tannin. Once the roughness subsides—around 1998—this should show all its depth and richness. 300 cases made. $66 (4/30/92) **91**
Ruchottes-Chambertin 1988: Firm and tight, with a rich core of strawberry, cinnamon, nutmeg and oak flavors that is deep, complex and concentrated, but also tightly bound by tannins. This wine will benefit from cellaring; try in 1996 or so to see how it's developing. $80 (11/15/90) **92**
Ruchottes-Chambertin 1987: Impeccably balanced and elegant with wonderful dimensions of toasty oak, spicy cherry and smoky raspberry flavors that are intense yet subtle, finishing with great length and complexity. Tempting now, but best 1993 to '98. 250 cases made. $56 (10/15/89) **93**
Ruchottes-Chambertin 1986 $55 (11/15/88) **91**
Ruchottes-Chambertin 1985 $63 (2/15/88) **92**
Ruchottes-Chambertin 1984 $34 (3/15/87) **83**
Ruchottes-Chambertin 1982 $26 (9/01/85) SS **92**

PHILIPPE NADDEF
Gevrey-Chambertin 1988: Lean and sharply focused, with a sharp streak of vinegar running through the berry and toast flavors. A flavorful wine, with a distinctive character that may not please everyone. Drink after 1993. $25 (7/15/91) **80**
Gevrey-Chambertin 1987: Has richness and depth, starting with the purple color, berry-filled aromas and round, generous berry, currant and vanilla flavors. Missing a bit of concentration, but the ripe flavors are balanced with gentle tannins, making this a good short-term cellar candidate. Drink now to 1993. $19 (3/31/90) **86**
Gevrey-Chambertin 1985 $25 (4/15/88) **94**

Gevrey-Chambertin Les Cazetiers 1987: Generous in flavor, soft in structure and supported with just enough tannin to indicate cellaring until 1993 to '94 to see what develops. Shows plenty of berry, currant and dusky spice flavors that are persistent on the finish. $35 (3/31/90) **88**
Gevrey-Chambertin Les Champeaux 1987: Very firm and tannic, but it has ample richness and full flavors of cherry, anise and vanilla to carry it through its aging cycle. The generous fruit rides smoothly over the fine tannins, making this almost drinkable now, but it should be better around 1994. $28 (3/31/90) **90**
Gevrey-Chambertin Les Champeaux 1985 $29 (3/31/88) **80**
Mazis-Chambertin 1988: Hard, earthy and tart, with vinegary flavors that turn vegetal and sour. Not our style. Tasted twice. $60 (7/15/91) **69**
Mazis-Chambertin 1987: Very ripe, spicy and generous, with plenty of cherry, cinnamon and vanilla aromas and flavors, all echoing on the long finish. It rests gently on a supple, velvety structure. Drinkable now, best around 1994. $50 (3/31/90) **89**

DOMAINE PONSOT
Griotte-Chambertin 1988: Floral, plum and currant aromas and flavors burst from every sip of this rich, concentrated wine that echoes fruit and spice on the long finish. Has plenty of tannin that will need until 1996 to 2000 to settle down. $150 (5/15/91) **89**
Latricières-Chambertin 1988: Ripe and concentrated, with beautifully articulated currant, plum and cinnamon aromas and flavors that extend well into a long finish. Has the intensity and structure to develop through at least 1998 to 2000. 200 cases made. $150 (5/15/91) **91**

REMOISSENET
Chambertin 1985 $100 (3/15/88) **91**

ANTONIN RODET
Gevrey-Chambertin 1986: This wine has the austerity and hard tannins typical of '86, but generous anise-scented cherry and berry flavors balance it nicely. Has hints of caramel on the finish. Wants cellaring until 1993. $25 (7/15/90) **86**
Gevrey-Chambertin Lavaux St.-Jacques 1982 $35 (6/30/87) **92**

PHILIPPE ROSSIGNOL
Gevrey-Chambertin 1987: Enticingly toasty and spicy in aroma, but it tastes overly woody, thin and slightly bitter. Disjointed at this age, and there are not enough cherry and plum flavors to balance it out. $23 (5/31/90) **69**

CHRISTOPHE ROUMIER
Ruchottes-Chambertin 1989: Breathtaking, with seductive chocolate, cherry, vanilla and berry aromas and flavors. A truly superb wine that ends with firm tannins. Try after 1995. $70 (1/31/92) **94**

ARMAND ROUSSEAU
Chambertin 1988: Smooth and elegant, with generous, complex currant, chocolate, raspberry and nutmeg aromas and flavors that persist well into a very long finish. The silky texture makes it tempting now, but give it until 1997 to 2000. 132 cases made. $201 (5/15/91) **93**
Chambertin 1985 Rel: $100 Cur: $120 (3/15/88) **97**
Chambertin Clos de Bèze 1989: Impressive, with wonderful vanilla, blackberry and cherry aromas and flavors. Has outstanding potential. Try after 1995. $135 (1/31/92) **93**
Chambertin Clos de Bèze 1988: Ripe, generous, spicy, elegant and polished, with an opulent texture and flavors that are very long and complex. It just keeps giving and giving as it rolls out its plum, vanilla, raspberry and chocolate flavors. Delicious now, but just wait until 1995 to 2000. 328 cases made. $188 (5/15/91) **95**
Charmes-Chambertin 1985 $63 (10/15/88) **86**
Gevrey-Chambertin 1989: A seductive, super-focused Gevrey that's packed to the brim with fruit, showing an impressive violet, vanilla and spice character. Try from 1993. (NR) (1/31/92) **88**
Gevrey-Chambertin Clos St.-Jacques 1989: Fat and comfortable, with intense raspberry, berry and earth aromas and flavors and a silky finish. Better after 1993. $93 (1/31/92) **90**
Gevrey-Chambertin Clos St.-Jacques 1985 $80 (10/15/88) **92**
Mazis-Chambertin Mazy-Chambertin 1989: Has an excellent concentration of cherry, berry, strawberry and chestnut flavors and firm tannins. Better from 1994 to '97. (NR) (1/31/92) **90**
Mazis-Chambertin Mazy-Chambertin 1985 $61 (10/15/88) **85**
Ruchottes-Chambertin Clos des Ruchottes 1989: An attractive wine, with plenty of chestnut, white chocolate and berry aromas and flavors and firm tannins. Try after 1994. (NR) (1/31/92) **90**

DOMAINE ROY PERE & FILS
Gevrey-Chambertin Clos Prieur 1988: Earthy, austere, papery aromas and flavors make this an unwelcome wine, lacking grace and fruit. $35 (12/31/90) **68**
Gevrey-Chambertin Vieilles Vignes 1988: Tough, smoky, austere and tannic, with little grace or fruit to save it. Might come around with cellaring, but the odds aren't good. $30 (12/31/90) **72**

LEONARD DE ST.-AUBIN
Gevrey-Chambertin 1985 $25 (11/30/87) **66**

SERAFIN PERE & FILS
Charmes-Chambertin 1989: A pristine style of wine, with beautiful cherry-tartlike notes, a smoky character, luscious fruit flavors and firm tannins. Try after 1994. $65 (1/31/92) **92**
Gevrey-Chambertin 1988: Rich and complex, with tiers of spice, currant, cherry and pretty smoky oak notes that fan out on the palate. The flavors are deep and intriguing, the texture is smooth and supple and the tannins are firm, but not astringent. Best to cellar until 1996. 75 cases made. $35 (3/31/91) **92**
Gevrey-Chambertin Les Cazetiers 1989: A seductive wine, with a wonderful toasty character and silky fruit flavor. Try after 1993. $54 (1/31/92) **89**
Gevrey-Chambertin Les Cazetiers 1988: Very ripe and concentrated, with a laser beam of focused raspberry and plum flavors framed by tough tannins and firm acidity on the long finish. Needs time to settle down. Try after 1996. 125 cases made. $53 (5/15/91) **91**
Gevrey-Chambertin Le Fonteny 1989: Beautiful and enticing, with lovely spice, berry and cherry aromas and flavors. Fresh and firm on the finish. Try after 1993. $50 (1/31/92) **86**
Gevrey-Chambertin Le Fonteny 1988: Smooth and beautifully integrated, with a real sense of elegance and finesse. Has a strong backbone, but delicate features. The flavors run toward plum, spice and earth. Drink around 1996 to '98. 150 cases made. $50 (5/15/91) **92**
Gevrey-Chambertin Vieilles Vignes 1989: A big, velvety Gevrey, with plenty of vanilla, smoke, violet and cherry flavors. Long, firm tannins emerge on the finish. Try from 1994. $45 (1/31/92) **92**
Gevrey-Chambertin Vieilles Vignes 1987: Has the concentration, structure and balance to age nicely, balancing sweet oak with anise, spice and berry aromas and flavors. Firmly tannic, but the flavors seem to float as they persist on the finish. Drink around 1993 to '95. $35 (3/31/90) **91**

DOMAINE TORTOCHOT
Chambertin 1985 $90 (12/31/88) **94**

LOUIS TRAPET
Chambertin 1988: Ripe and elegant, with good intensity of black cherry and currant aromas and flavors, crisp acidity to support it and nice nutmeg and smoke shadings to give it depth. Best after 1997. 25 cases made. $133 (7/15/91) **92**
Chambertin 1987: Concentrated, focused, deep black cherry flavor lasts from first sniff to the lingering aftertaste, while hints of earth, leather and spice add complexity. The balance is fine, and the tannins are smooth but solid. Try it in 1994 to '97. $75 (5/31/90) **91**
Chambertin 1985 $80 (3/15/88) **88**
Chambertin Cuvée Vieilles Vignes 1988: An earthy style, with lots of barklike overtones to the basic cherry flavor, hinting at tar and nutmeg on the finish. A flavorful wine that needs until 1995 to '98 to sort itself out. 15 cases made. $133 (7/15/91) **89**
Chapelle-Chambertin 1988: Firm and concentrated, with generous currant and cherry aromas and flavors and nicely integrated, coarse-textured tannins. Harmonious and balanced, but needs until 1994 to '96 for the tannins to settle down. 15 cases made. $84 (7/15/91) **89**
Chapelle-Chambertin 1985 Rel: $64 Cur: $73 (3/15/88) **84**
Chapelle-Chambertin Réserve Jean Trapet 1987: Earthy, mossy and lean in texture, with gamy flavors that overpower any fruit. Drinkable, if not quite our style. Tasted twice. $62 (3/15/91) **79**
Gevrey-Chambertin 1988: Firm and chunky in texture and not very concentrated, with mildly berrylike, gamy flavors that finish a bit tired and tannic. Try after 1993 or '94. 50 cases made. $40 (7/15/91) **81**
Gevrey-Chambertin 1987: Earthy, mushroomy aromas and flavors rest on a dry, tannic foundation that lacks the fruit to give it much charm. Tasted twice with consistent notes. $30 (7/15/90) **74**
Gevrey-Chambertin 1985 $40 (5/31/88) **79**
Latricières-Chambertin 1988: Firm, tannic and reined in, with nice, ripe plum and currant aromas and flavors that manage to peek through the tannic, tight structure. Needs time to develop; try after 1994 or '95. 20 cases made. $84 (7/15/91) **84**
Latricières-Chambertin 1987: Exotic and complex in flavor, with aromas ranging from smoke to ripe plum and tea. Tannins have a fine texture, and a core flavor of fruit and spice lingers on the finish. Nicely balanced and flavorful. Try now through 1994. $62 (5/31/90) **88**

G. VACHET-ROUSSEAU
Gevrey-Chambertin 1988: Ripe and flavorful, but tough at the edges, corraling the black cherry and currant flavors with rather coarse tannins. It has enough concentration and length to warrant cellaring until 1994 to '97. $30 (12/31/90) **85**
Gevrey-Chambertin 1983 $16 (5/01/86) **64**

CHARLES VIENOT
Gevrey-Chambertin 1985 $32 (4/30/88) **87**

Morey-St.-Denis

DOMAINE PIERRE AMIOT
Clos de la Roche 1988: Fruity and plush, with ample cherry and cassis flavors, turning soft and peppery on the finish. Of good quality, with well-integrated tannins and luscious fruit flavor. Needs until 1993 or beyond to mature. $75 (3/15/91) **86**
Clos de la Roche 1987: After a bit of earthiness on the nose, the wild berry and spice flavors emerge on the palate against a background of moderate tannin. Drink now. $49 (12/15/89) **86**
Clos de la Roche 1982 $28 (6/16/85) SS **93**
Morey-St.-Denis Aux Charmes 1982 $18 (7/01/85) **88**
Morey-St.-Denis Les Ruchots 1988: Has ripe, generous fruit and pepper flavors, but the tannins clamp down on the finish and the fruit doesn't linger. Should be cellared until at least 1993. $57 (2/28/91) **80**

BOUCHARD PERE & FILS
Clos de la Roche 1989: Quite muscular, with wild blueberry aromas and flavors enveloped in an iron backbone of tannin and acidity. Try after 1995. (NR) (1/31/92) **89**

PIERRE BOUREE FILS
Clos de la Roche 1989: A splendid wine, with outstanding toast, berry and cherry aromas and flavors. Has superb finesse and super-firm tannins. Try from 1995. $65 (1/31/92) **94**
Clos de la Roche 1988: Tough and tannic, with tightly reined-in, concentrated plum and berry aromas and flavors, crisp acidity and impressive length. Not a powerful wine, but the nuances of herb, tea and cola sneak in on the long finish. Drink after 1995. 150 cases made. $85 (3/31/91) **91**
Clos de la Roche 1987: A more sturdy, straightforward style than this wine usually offers, but the finish hints at the cinnamon, strawberry and rose petal complexity this can attain with cellaring until 1993 to '95. $86 (6/15/90) **85**
Morey-St.-Denis 1987: Tastes leathery, woody and slightly spicy, but where's the fruit? Comes out thin and too mature for its age. Decent quality but lacks pizzazz. $35 (5/15/90) **74**

GUY CASTAGNIER
Clos de la Roche 1989: Extremely well crafted, with whistle-clean raspberry and strawberry flavors, a creamy texture and firm tannins. Try after 1994. $62 (1/31/92) **90**
Clos de la Roche 1988: Tightly focused, with reined-in plum, cherry and spice flavors that emerge on the third or fourth sip, then spread through a generous finish. Lots of spice echoes on the aftertaste. Give it until 1995 to open up. $63 (7/15/91) **91**
Clos de la Roche 1986: Tough and tannic, with woody, oxidized aromas and flavors. This will be a while coming around, if it ever arrives. Try 1994. $43 (7/15/89) **75**
Clos St.-Denis 1989: Offers superbly focused black cherry and strawberry aromas and flavors and a silky texture of fine tannins. Try after 1994. $62 (1/31/92) **91**
Clos St.-Denis 1988: Very pretty floral and berry aromas and flavors rest comfortably on a light, supple frame, offering generous flavors that persist through the crisp finish. Elegant and tasty, with echoes of black cherry and spice. Should be best after 1994 or '95. $63 (7/15/91) **89**
Clos St.-Denis 1986: Lean and austere wine, sweet and berryish on the nose, but tight and tough on the palate, very tannic on release but balanced enough to be delicate by now. $43 (7/15/89) **84**
Morey-St.-Denis 1989: Very fresh and clean, with floral, cherry and vanilla aromas and flavors, supple tannins and a fresh finish. Drink on release. (NR) (1/31/92) **86**
Morey-St.-Denis 1986: Very light, just a shade darker than a rosé, very shy on the nose and sharply acidic and drying on the finish. $28 (7/15/89) **66**

F. CHAUVENET
Clos St.-Denis 1989: A bit coarse, but shows good potential, with smoky berry, stewed tomato and vanilla characters and hard tannins. Try after 1994. $60 (1/31/92) **87**
Clos St.-Denis 1988 $48 (7/15/90) (BT) **85+**
Clos St.-Denis 1986: Lean and concentrated with ripe plum, cherry and spicy flavors, followed by an ample dose of tannin. Needs time for development in the next few years. Drink now through 1995. $50 (2/28/89) **90**
Clos St.-Denis 1985 $67 (7/31/87) **94**

DOMAINE BRUNO CLAIR
Morey-St.-Denis 1985 $20 (5/15/88) **73**
Morey-St.-Denis en la rue de Vergy 1989: Rich and powerful for the appellation, with plenty of cherry, herb and plum flavors and excellent backbone. Try after 1994. $36 (1/31/92) **90**

JOSEPH DROUHIN
Clos de la Roche 1989: Traditionally styled, with distinctive, smoky, earthy berry aromas and flavors and a very velvety texture. Try from 1994 to '96. $77 (1/31/92) **88**
Clos de la Roche 1988: Has a tannic structure, but plenty of flavor to carry past the roughness, bursting with black cherry and raspberry flavors and a touch of herb and smoke to make it more interesting. Long and generous; worth cellaring until 1995 to 2000. $73 (2/15/91) **93**
Clos de la Roche 1986: Hard and austere, but there is some concentration of plummy, raspberry flavor that shows signs that it should develop into a real charming with some cellaring. Try now. $53 (7/15/89) **83**
Clos de la Roche 1985 $60 (11/15/87) **97**
Clos St.-Denis 1989: Extremely aromatic, with a delicious, smoky plum and berry character and sweet, supple tannins on the finish. Try after 1994. $76 (1/31/92) **91**
Morey-St.-Denis Clos Sorbé 1989: A very good Morey-St.-Denis, with plum and earth aromas and flavors and firm tannins on the long, flavorful finish. Try after 1993. (NR) (1/31/92) **86**
Morey-St.-Denis Monts-Luisants 1988: This lively, beautifully focused wine is bursting with delicious plum, raspberry and blackberry aromas and flavors, with a slight meaty edge that adds depth and richness. The flavors echo on a long finish. Approaching drinkability, but try to hold off until 1994 or '95. $38 (2/28/91) **92**

DOMAINE DUJAC
Clos de la Roche Clos la Roche 1989: An attractive, rustic style, with chestnut and berry aromas and flavors, firm tannins and an earthy finish. Try after 1994. $80 (1/31/92) **89**
Clos de la Roche Clos la Roche 1988: Has nice currant and raspberry flavors, with pretty toasty oak and earth notes, but it's also very dry and tannic on the finish. Needs time to come together; start drinking in 1995. 275 cases made. $75 (3/31/91) **90**
Clos de la Roche Clos la Roche 1987: A very firm and tightly reined-in wine, with generous plum and toast aromas and flavors, taut structure and a hint of green olive on the somewhat tannic finish. Needs to be cellared until 1994 to '95 at least. $53 (3/31/90) **86**
Clos de la Roche Clos la Roche 1986 $56 (7/31/88) **79**
Clos de la Roche Clos la Roche 1985 $85 (3/15/88) **95**
Clos St.-Denis 1989: A delicate style, with subtle smoke, vanilla, cherry, berry and tobacco aromas and flavors and fine tannins. Try after 1993. $80 (1/31/92) **91**
Clos St.-Denis 1987: Has the fragrance and depth of flavor many of the wines of this vintage missed, showing plum, toast and brown sugar flavors, and, despite a touch of gaminess, enough complexity to make it worth cellaring until 1993 to '95 at least. $58 (3/31/90) **85**
Clos St.-Denis 1986 $56 (7/31/88) **89**
Clos St.-Denis 1985 $89 (3/15/88) **91**
Morey-St.-Denis 1989: This pleasant wine has an earthy strawberry character and fresh fruit flavors, but it's a bit light and diluted on the finish. Try after 1993. $40 (1/31/92) **84**

FAIVELEY
Clos de la Roche 1986: Tough and tannic, showing some cherry flavor but it's so thoroughly wrapped in tannin it's hard to tell where it will go. Try in 1993. $55 (7/15/89) **82**
Clos de la Roche 1985 $88 (3/15/88) **78**
Morey-St.-Denis Clos des Ormes 1989: Lovely and silky, with a very good intensity of cream and cherry flavors and fine tannins. Try after 1993. $44 (1/31/92) **88**

JAFFELIN
Clos St.-Denis 1989: This laser-guided wine zeros in on the palate, packed tightly with lots of fruit and tannins. Try after 1995. $53 (1/31/92) **94**
Morey-St.-Denis Les Ruchots 1989: Big and fleshy, with plenty of berry and cherry flavors and a silky finish. Try after 1993. $30 (1/31/92) **86**
Morey-St.-Denis Les Ruchots 1988 $31 (7/15/90) (BT) **80+**

OLIVIER LEFLAIVE FRERES
Clos de la Roche 1988 $60 (7/15/90) (BT) **90+**
Clos St.-Denis 1989: A real beauty, with classy vanilla, smoke and strawberry aromas and flavors and a succulent finish of fine tannins and sweet fruit. Try after 1994. $56 (1/31/92) **93**
Morey-St.-Denis 1989: Extremely ripe and round, with masses of plum and other fruit flavors and firm tannins. Better after 1994. $30 (1/31/92) **87**

DOMAINE LEROY
Clos de la Roche 1989: This great wine is bursting at the seams with layers of luscious fruit flavors, wood notes and fine tannins. Try from 1995. $230 (1/31/92) **94**

GEORGES LIGNIER
Clos de la Roche 1987: Spicy and velvety and beautifully balanced. Elegant and firm of texture, showing subtle plum, nutmeg and vanilla aromas and flavors that are long and elegant. Cellar until 1993 to '95. $55 (3/31/90) **90**
Clos de la Roche 1985 $63 (3/15/88) **85**
Clos St.-Denis 1987: Shows the flavor and elegant structure of a *grand cru*. Complex aromas, full fruit flavors and a generous dash of toast and vanilla from oak aging. A bit harsh with tannin on release. Probably best from now to 1996. $49 (5/15/90) **89**
Clos St.-Denis 1985 $54 (3/15/88) **91**
Morey-St.-Denis 1987: Fruity and fairly intense, but it's tight in structure, with firm acidity and tannins. Smells herbal and aniselike, tastes like raspberries and strawberries. May be smoothed out by now. $25 (5/15/90) **82**
Morey-St.-Denis 1985 $23 (3/15/88) **82**
Morey-St.-Denis Clos des Ormes 1987: Tasty and tightly focused. Tastes fruity and intense, with a great, lingering finish. Smooth textured, full of cherry, vanilla and spice flavors, moderately tannic. Drink 1993 to '95. $32 (5/15/90) **88**
Morey-St.-Denis Clos des Ormes 1985 $28 (3/15/88) **86**

CLAUDE MARCHAND
Morey-St.-Denis 1987: Earthy, complex and intriguingly Burgundian in aroma, this is like many '87s. Tasty cherry and mineral flavors dry up on the finish. Best now to 1994. $30 (9/30/90) **80**
Morey-St.-Denis Clos des Ormes 1987: With funky Burgundian aromas and flavors, mature cherry and spice notes, and barnyardy character, this is of marginal quality. Best to drink soon, if at all. $30 (9/30/90) **69**
Morey-St.-Denis Clos des Ormes 1986: Lean and sharply focused, with characteristic strawberry and spice aromas and flavors, with a nice hint of chocolate on the long and well-defined finish. Drink now through 1994. $33 (7/15/89) **85**

MOILLARD
Morey-St.-Denis Monts Luisants 1989: Excellent for this group, with intense plum, vanilla and ripe fruit aromas that follow through on the palate. Smooth and powerful. From Madame Prevot. Try after 1994. $28 (1/31/92) **89**
Morey-St.-Denis Monts Luisants 1988: Dense and concentrated, with overtones of herbs and seemingly tropical fruit flavors adding interesting nuances to the basic cherry core, tightly built around fine tannins. Should need until 1994 or '95 for polish. 500 cases made. $30 (12/15/90) **91**
Morey-St.-Denis Monts Luisants 1985 $21 (5/31/87) **87**

MOMMESSIN
Clos de Tart 1989: Extremely polished and rich, with an impressive, peppery berry character and tons of ultrafine tannins. Try after 1994. $52 (1/31/92) **92**
Clos de Tart 1988 $112 (7/15/90) (BT) **95+**
Clos de Tart 1985 $95 (2/15/88) **91**
Clos de Tart 1950 $125 (8/31/90) (TR) **78**

Key to Symbols

The scores reported here are the results of blind tastings conducted by our panel of senior editors. Wines that carry the initials below are results of individual tastings.

THE WINE SPECTATOR 100-POINT SCALE ***95-100***—Classic, a great wine; ***90-94***—Outstanding, superior character and style; ***80-89***—Good to very good, a wine with special qualities; ***70-79***—Average, drinkable wine that may have minor flaws; ***60-69***—Below average, drinkable but not recommended; ***50-59***—Poor, undrinkable, not recommended. "+"—With a score indicates a range; used primarily with barrel tastings to indicate a preliminary score.

SPECIAL DESIGNATIONS SS—Spectator Selection, CS—Cellar Selection, BB—Best Buy, ($NA)—Price not available, (NR)—Not released.

TASTER'S INITIALS (JG)—Jim Gordon, (HS)—Harvey Steiman, (JL)—James Laube, (JS)—James Suckling, (TM)—Thomas Matthews, (TR)—Terry Robards, (PM)—Per-Henrik Mansson, (BT)—Barrel Tasting (these wines were tasted blind from barrel samples), (CA-date)—*California's Great Cabernets* by James Laube, (CH-date)—*California's Great Chardonnays* by James Laube, (VP-date)—*Vintage Port* by James Suckling.

DATE TASTED Dates in parentheses represent the issue in which the rating was published.

DOMAINE PONSOT
Clos de la Roche 1984 Rel: $29 Cur: $48 (2/15/88) **73**
Clos de la Roche Cuvée Vieilles Vignes 1988: Lean and austere, but shows plenty of rose petal and plum flavors and hints of earthiness on the finish. Smooth and elegant; should be fine after 1993 to '95. $185 (5/15/91) **88**
Clos de la Roche Cuvée Vieilles Vignes 1985 $200 (6/15/88) **90**
Clos de la Roche Cuvée William 1988: Lean and graceful, with a fine intensity of rose petal, tar and currant aromas and flavors. Concentrated enough to ward off the well-integrated tannins. Tempting now, but best after 1994. $150 (5/15/91) **89**
Clos St.-Denis Cuvée Vieilles Vignes 1988: A smooth, elegant wine, with unfortunate earthy, dirty, burnt coffee aromas, but the ripe cherry and chocolate flavors end up being more appealing to us. Try after 1995. Tasted twice. $165 (7/15/91) **85**
Morey-St.-Denis Monts-Luisants 1988: An intensely earthy style, with concentrated pear, citrus, mineral and spice flavors that offer a distinct personality. It's a bit coarse around the edges, but the flavors stay with you. Drink now to 1993. $40 (4/30/91) **85**

REMOISSENET
Clos de la Roche 1985 $72 (3/15/88) **91**

DOMAINE G. ROUMIER
Morey-St.-Denis Clos de la Bussière 1989: Starts strong, with focused blackberry notes, but finishes a little short, with stemmy watermelon aromas and flavors and a very light finish. Try after 1993. $38 (1/31/92) **85**
Morey-St.-Denis Clos de la Bussière 1988: Tough in structure and earthy tasting, with biting tannins and a plummy, pruney flavor. Very tart and tannic on the finish. Should improve if aged until 1995, but it will always be earthy. $30 (7/15/91) **83**
Morey-St.-Denis Clos de la Bussière 1985 $27 (4/30/88) **92**

ARMAND ROUSSEAU
Clos de la Roche 1988: Fragrant and generous, with beautiful rose petal-scented raspberry and red cherry aromas and flavors that linger enticingly on the long finish. A graceful wine that should be at its best after 1994 or '95. 200 cases made. $75 (5/15/91) **91**

DOMAINE F. & L. SAIER
Clos des Lambrays 1989: An unusually peppery wine, more like a Côtes du Rhône than a Burgundy. Solidly built, offering pleasant black cherry and pepper flavors on the finish. Drinkable after 1993. $68 (11/15/91) **85**
Clos des Lambrays 1988: Tough, compact and sharply focused, with plenty of ripe berry and plum aromas and flavors, firm tannins and a hard edge that will need until 1997 to 2001 to soften. A powerful wine, with a fine future. 2,775 cases made. $75 (3/31/91) **91**
Clos des Lambrays Domaine des Lambrays 1985 $55 (2/15/88) **78**

DOMAINE B. SERVEAU
Morey-St.-Denis Les Sorbets 1989: A vivid wine, with fresh strawberry and earth aromas and flavors, firm tannins and fresh acidity. Try after 1993. $30 (1/31/92) **86**
Morey-St.-Denis Les Sorbets 1988: Broad in structure, light in texture and exotic in flavor, offering strawberry, guava and plum aromas and flavors. Has ample tannins without being aggressive. Long, elegant and approaching drinkability. Try in 1993. $35 (2/28/91) **88**
Morey-St.-Denis Les Sorbets 1987: Crisp, well-balanced and reasonably fruity, with cherry, spice and slightly herbal flavors. Moderately tannic, but ready to drink now through 1994. $30 (5/15/90) **83**
Morey-St.-Denis Les Sorbets 1985 $39 (6/15/88) **88**
Morey-St.-Denis Les Sorbets 1984 $22 (3/15/87) **87**

NUITS ST.-GEORGES

BERTRAND AMBROISE
Nuits-St.-Georges 1989: Excellent for a simple Nuits-St.-Georges, this is a rugged wine, with effusive fruit that gives way to full tannins. Try from 1994 to '97. $30 (1/31/92) **90**
Nuits-St.-Georges en rue de Chaux 1989: A blockbuster village Nuits that blasts holes in your palate with fruit and tannins; a real mouthful. Better in 1994. $38 (1/31/92) **91**
Nuits-St.-Georges en rue de Chaux 1988: Brilliantly ripe and lively, with bright raspberry and black cherry aromas and flavors, nicely integrated oak notes and a velvety texture that supports a long, flavorful finish. Tempting to drink soon, but try to wait until 1997. 200 cases made. $40 (5/15/91) **93**
Nuits-St.-Georges Les Vaucrains 1989: Exotic and powerful, with masses of raspberry and berry flavors and velvety tannins. Try in 1995. $38 (1/31/92) **94**

DOMAINE DE L'ARLOT
Nuits-St.-Georges Clos de l'Arlot 1989: Young vines or overproduction? Very light and verging on diluted, but it has pleasant cherry and strawberry flavors and light tannins. Drink on release. (NR) (1/31/92) **78**
Nuits-St.-Georges Clos de l'Arlot 1988: Light in color, but the smooth, creamy spice, rose petal and berry aromas and flavors win the day, offering plenty of flavor in a style that's lighter than most 1988s. The tannins are already well resolved. Drinkable now. $43 (3/31/91) **87**
Nuits-St.-Georges Clos des Forêts St.-Georges 1989: Truly delicious, emphasizing ripe fruit and a firm tannin structure. Try after 1994. (NR) (1/31/92) **90**
Nuits-St.-Georges Clos des Forêts St.-Georges 1988: Very firm and flavorful, with nicely focused black cherry, tar and rose petal aromas and flavors. A bit tart and tannic, but balanced and harmonious. Needs until 1993 to settle down. $53 (3/31/91) **85**
Nuits-St.-Georges Clos des Forêts St.-Georges 1987: A bit too stemmy to be immediately appealing, but it has spicy nutmeg and juniper notes to add to the plum flavors, and enough tannin to require cellaring until 1993 to '95. $43 (3/31/90) **83**

BEAULT-FORGEOT
Nuits-St.-Georges Les Plateaux 1981 $17 (7/01/84) **83**

JULES BELIN
Nuits-St.-Georges Les St.-Georges 1943 ($NA) (8/31/90) (TR) **91**

DOMAINE BERTAGNA
Nuits-St.-Georges Aux Murgers 1985: Earthy and lean, with modest cherry and berry fruit, balanced and clean, with hints of leather, spice and toast. Drink now. $41 (2/28/89) **85**

BICHOT
Nuits-St.-Georges Les Boudots Hospices de Nuits Cuvée Mesny de Boissea 1986: Firm, dense, even a bit tough, with meat and cherry aromas and flavors tightly wrapped in firm tannins. Will need until 1993 to '95 to soften. $36 (3/31/90) **77**
Nuits-St.-Georges Les Maladières Hospices de Nuits 1986: Earthy, drying and sour, with a mossy flavor that covers the plum fruit. $33 (2/28/89) **75**
Nuits-St.-Georges Les Maladières Hospices de Nuits Cuvée Grangier 1986: Earthy, tealike aromas and flavors characterize this light, complex wine. Not for those looking for a fruity style, but a well-made Burgundy nonetheless. $30 (3/31/90) **80**
Nuits-St.-Georges Les Vignerondes Hospices de Nuits Cuvée Richard de Bligny 1986: Firm and concentrated, with velvety texture and ample flavors of cherry, leather and toast; complex and long. Drink now through 1994. $40 (2/28/89) **85**

DOMAINE LUCIEN BOILLOT
Nuits-St.-Georges Les Pruliers 1987: The beautifully articulated berry, cassis and tea aromas and flavors make an immediately attractive wine, and the firm but unobstrusive tannins mark it as a good cellar candidate. Try now or in 1993. $25 (7/15/90) **88**

JEAN CLAUDE BOISSET
Nuits-St.-Georges 1985 $25 (4/30/88) **79**

BOUCHARD PERE & FILS
Nuits-St.-Georges 1983 $21 (9/15/86) **68**
Nuits-St.-Georges Les Cailles 1959 $90 (8/31/90) (TR) **87**
Nuits-St.-Georges Clos-St.-Marc 1989: Intensely fruity and rich, with tons of plum and leather aromas and flavors and firm tannins. Try in 1994. $59 (1/31/92) **89**
Nuits-St.-Georges Clos-St.-Marc 1988 $52 (7/15/90) (BT) **75+**
Nuits-St.-Georges Clos-St.-Marc 1985: Pretty peach, nut and honey flavors are delicate and elegant on the palate. The texture is silky, and the concentrated finish is long and full. $53 (2/28/89) **87**
Nuits-St.-Georges Clos-St.-Marc 1983 $33 (9/15/86) **74**
Nuits-St.-Georges La Richemone 1989: A textbook Nuits-St.-Georges, with spicy, earthy berry flavors and an intense, spicy, tannic finish. Try from 1994 to '97. (NR) (1/31/92) **89**

PIERRE BOUREE FILS
Nuits-St.-Georges Les Vaucrains 1985 $68 (5/31/88) **93**

CATHIARD-MOLINIER
Nuits-St.-Georges Les Meurgers 1986: Dense, tannic and lacking focus. The ripe plum and strawberry flavors are astrigent and tannic. Needs some time to come together. Drink now or in 1993. $22 (2/28/89) **77**

JEANNE-MARIE DE CHAMPS
Nuits-St.-Georges Les Didiers Hospices de Nuits Cuvée Cabet 1988: The wood in this wine is rough and harsh, overshadowing the ripe fruit notes, leaving clean, plummy Pinot Noir flavors that aren't too tannic, just woody. Best to cellar a year or so. Drink now to '94. $49 (9/30/90) **83**
Nuits-St.-Georges Les Didiers Hospices de Nuits Cuvée Cabet 1985 $53 (3/15/88) **96**
Nuits-St.-Georges Les Didiers Hospices de Nuits Cuvée Jacques Duret 1988: Has plenty of roasty, toasty aromas and flavors, but with a rich core of cherry-tinged Pinot Noir flavor to match. The combination of cherry, plum and vanilla-flavored oak gives it a classy, elegant style. Drink now to 1995 and beyond. $49 (9/30/90) **89**
Nuits-St.-Georges Les Terres Blanches 1988: Ripe and generous, with a strong accent of new oak aromas and a fine concentration of currant, berry and vanilla flavors that extend into a long, intense finish. Needs until 1993 to '95 to settle down. 73 cases made. $39 (7/15/91) **90**

F. CHAUVENET
Nuits-St.-Georges Les Chaignots 1989: This pungent wine has loads of tobacco, berry and chocolate characteristics, velvety tannins and a long finish. Try in 1994. $45 (1/31/92) **91**
Nuits-St.-Georges Les Chaignots 1988 $38 (7/15/90) (BT) **80+**
Nuits-St.-Georges Les Chaignots 1986 $40 (7/31/88) **87**
Nuits-St.-Georges Les Perrières 1985 $48 (7/31/87) **80**
Nuits-St.-Georges Les Plateaux 1982 $16 (1/01/85) **78**
Nuits-St.-Georges Les Pruliers 1989: Shows an alluring character of chocolate, coffee and plum and velvety tannins. Better in 1994. $45 (1/31/92) **88**

JEAN CHAUVENET
Nuits-St.-Georges Les Bousselots 1985 $49 (5/31/88) **88**

CHEVALIER DE BEAUBASSIN
Nuits-St.-Georges 1985 $31 (4/30/88) **84**

DENIS CHEVILLON
Nuits-St.-Georges Les Chaignots 1987: This firm, fruity and sturdy wine has concentrated, jammy cassis, grape and cherry flavors and hints of smoke and tea, but mostly solid structure and intensity. Drink in 1993. $33 (7/15/90) **87**
Nuits-St.-Georges Les Pruliers 1987: The firm texture and straightforward flavors of cassis and berry make this an attractive wine that needs cellaring until 1993. $38 (7/15/90) **84**

ROBERT CHEVILLON
Nuits-St.-Georges 1989: Lovely and focused, with a classic spicy strawberry character and silky tannins. Better after 1993. $36 (1/31/92) **89**
Nuits-St.-Georges 1986: Smells pretty but on the palate it's tough and thin with cherry and berry flavors that lack richness and depth. $37 (12/15/89) **74**
Nuits-St.-Georges 1985 $40 (4/30/88) **85**
Nuits-St.-Georges Les Vaucrains 1989: Elegant and focused, with plenty of plum, earth and berry flavors and satinlike tannins. Try after 1993. $65 (1/31/92) **89**

A. CHOPIN
Nuits-St.-Georges Aux Murgers 1988: Ripe, opulent and complex, this smoothly burnished wine is glowing with plush, toasty berry and cherry flavors that hint at vanilla and nutmeg on the long, polished finished. Seductive now, but should be at its best after 1993 to '94. 200 cases made. $28 (7/15/90) **91**
Nuits-St.-Georges Aux Murgers 1987: Thick, tarry flavors carry a few pleasant hints of violets or cherries, but this wine leans toward the earthy, barnyardy style that not everyone will love at first sip. But it has character and depth, and should develop well through at least 1993. $26 (12/15/89) **85**
Nuits-St.-Georges Aux Murgers 1986 $29 (10/15/88) **78**

CHOPIN-GROFFIER
Nuits-St.-Georges 1989: Rich and velvety, with loads of spicy cherry and berry flavors and a luscious finish. Try from 1994 to '96. $32 (1/31/92) **91**
Nuits-St.-Georges Les Chaignots 1989: Dazzling, with plum, cedar and smoke aromas and flavors and wonderfully integrated tannins. Try in 1994. $40 (1/31/92) **93**

DOMAINE DU CLOS FRANTIN
Nuits-St.-Georges 1989: An extremely concentrated and impressive red Burgundy, with layers of cedar, spice and fruit flavors and a long silky finish. From Bichot. Better after 1994. 800 cases made. $29 (2/29/92) **91**
Nuits-St.-Georges 1988 $37 (7/15/90) (BT) **80+**
Nuits-St.-Georges 1986 $20 (11/15/88) **82**
Nuits-St.-Georges 1983 $18 (2/01/86) **83**

JOSEPH DROUHIN
Nuits-St.-Georges 1989 $43 (7/15/90) (BT) **85+**
Nuits-St.-Georges 1986: Pretty aromas and unusually accessible tannins for a 1986 Burgundy. Packed with cherry and anise aromas along with spicy, supple and long flavors. Drink now. $25 (4/30/89) **86**
Nuits-St.-Georges 1985 $29 (11/15/87) **92**
Nuits-St.-Georges Les Boudots 1989: An earthy, slightly dry style, with berry and chocolate flavors and drying tannins. Try after 1994. $70 (1/31/92) **80**
Nuits-St.-Georges Les Roncières 1986: Aromatic but lean on the palate, it shows concentrated anise and cherry aromas, with some rather tough tannins that will need at least till 1993 to come around. $38 (4/30/89) **85**
Nuits-St.-Georges Les Roncières 1985 $38 (11/15/87) **93**

FAIVELEY
Nuits-St.-Georges 1989: Straightforward, with pleasant plum and earth aromas and flavors and rustic tannins. Try from 1994 to '96. $33 (1/31/92) **83**
Nuits-St.-Georges 1985 $40 (3/15/88) **90**
Nuits-St.-Georges Clos de la Maréchale 1989: Very traditional, with an opulent wild mushroom, earthy, barnyardy character and full tannins. Try after 1994. $42 (1/31/92) **85**
Nuits-St.-Georges Clos de la Maréchale 1988: Gamy, herbal aromas and flavors tend to obscure the modest core of cherry; comes off as stemmy and unyielding. Tasted twice. $50 (3/15/91) **76**
Nuits-St.-Georges Clos de la Maréchale 1985 $51 (3/15/88) **85**
Nuits-St.-Georges Clos de la Maréchale 1982 $20 (5/01/86) **84**
Nuits-St.-Georges Les Damodes 1989: Another textbook Nuits, with licorice, spice, cedar and fruit flavors. Succulent, with firm tannins. Better in 1994. $45 (1/31/92) **90**
Nuits-St.-Georges Les Damodes 1988: A tightly wound, firm style, with a solid core of cherry, currant, oak and spice flavor that is a bit closed and backward now. Definitely needs cellaring, probably until 1996 or '97. Tasted twice. $52 (3/31/91) **85**
Nuits-St.-Georges Les Porêts St.-Georges 1989: A rather old-styled wine, with earthy berry flavors and silky tannins. Try after 1993. $42 (1/31/92) **84**
Nuits-St.-Georges Les Porêts St.-Georges 1988 $54 (7/15/90) (BT) **90+**
Nuits-St.-Georges Les Porêts St.-Georges 1985 $47 (3/15/88) **76**
Nuits-St.-Georges Les St.-Georges 1989: A classy wine, with a succulent, silky mouth-feel, gamy, smoky berry flavors and fine tannins. Try after 1993. $54 (1/31/92) **92**

DOMAINE FOREY PERE & FILS
Nuits-St.-Georges Les Perrières 1989: An elegant wine, with lovely, spicy, gamy earth and berry aromas and flavors, silky tannins and good acidity. Try after 1994. (NR) (1/31/92) **89**

DOMAINE HENRI GOUGES
Nuits-St.-Georges 1986 $30 (7/31/88) **84**
Nuits-St.-Georges Les Chaignots 1986 $40 (7/31/88) **90**
Nuits-St.-Georges Clos des Porrets-St.-Georges 1989: A fighter of a wine, with tough tannins and chewy fruit. Slightly unbalanced now, but built for aging. Try in 1995. $45 (1/31/92) **87**
Nuits-St.-Georges Clos des Porrets-St.-Georges 1988 $50 (7/15/90) (BT) **80+**
Nuits-St.-Georges Les Pruliers 1989: A very refined style of Nuits, with beautiful spice and berry aromas, good fruit flavor and silky tannins. Try in 1993. $45 (1/31/92) **86**
Nuits-St.-Georges Les St.-Georges 1989: Subtle and not showing much now, but the stuffing of fruit and tannin is there. Try in 1994. $49 (1/31/92) **89**
Nuits-St.-Georges Les St.-Georges 1988 $54 (7/15/90) (BT) **75+**
Nuits-St.-Georges Les St.-Georges 1985 $45 (2/15/88) **68**
Nuits-St.-Georges Les Vaucrains 1989: Beautiful vanilla, spice and raspberry aromas and flavors are held up by solid tannins and acidity. Try in 1994. $49 (1/31/92) **90**

MACHARD DE GRAMONT
Nuits-St.-Georges Les Allots 1985 $35 (5/31/88) **86**
Nuits-St.-Georges Les Hauts Poirets 1985 $41 (6/15/88) **84**
Nuits-St.-Georges Les Hauts Pruliers 1985 $36 (2/15/88) **90**
Nuits-St.-Georges en la Perrière Noblot 1985 $41 (5/31/88) **89**
Nuits-St.-Georges Les Vallerots 1985 $47 (5/31/88) **78**

JEAN GRIVOT
Nuits-St.-Georges Les Boudots 1989: Has slightly bizarre, barnyardy vegetable and fruit aromas and flavors and medium tannins. Try after 1994. (NR) (1/31/92) **77**
Nuits-St.-Georges Les Boudots 1988: Firm and concentrated, with sufficient tannins to carry the wild berry and currant flavors without overwhelming them. A flavorful wine that needs cellaring until 1993 or '94 to polish the texture. $54 (4/30/91) **87**
Nuits-St.-Georges Les Charmois 1987: This lean and spicy wine has more tea and toast aromas and flavors than fruit, but it's nicely balanced, elegant and smooth despite a relatively high level of tannin. Drink 1993 to '94. $47 (7/15/90) **81**
Nuits-St.-Georges Les Pruliers 1988: Smooth and polished. This charming wine has lots of appealing plum and black cherry aromas and flavors and a touch of spice, all on a medium-weight frame. Long on the finish. Drink now or in 1993. Rel: $53 Cur: $57 (4/30/91) **89**
Nuits-St.-Georges Les Pruliers 1987: A tough, tannic and not very generous wine, with flavors that lean more toward leaves than fruit. It seems flat and uninspired. $55 (7/15/90) **71**
Nuits-St.-Georges Les Roncières 1987: Firm, concentrated and balanced, with forward strawberry, cherry and vanilla aromas and flavors, hints of caramel on the finish, velvety tannins and ripe, sweet fruit. A wine worth cellaring until 1993 to '94 to see what develops. Drinkable now. $55 (7/15/90) **88**

JEAN GROS
Nuits-St.-Georges 1989: A pretty wine, with attractive spice and blueberry flavors, silky tannins and an earthy finish. Try from 1994 to '97. $39 (1/31/92) **87**
Nuits-St.-Georges 1988: Tightly wound, tannic and a bit drying on the finish, with modest mushroom-tinged cherry flavors that turn toward lemon-lime on the finish. Needs time to smooth out. Try in 1994. $42 (2/28/91) **81**
Nuits-St.-Georges 1985 $36 (7/31/88) **85**

HAEGELEN-JAYER
Nuits-St.-Georges Les Damodes 1988: Lean, firm and tannic, with a solid beam of currant, plum and strawberry flavors shaded by spice and a touch of earthiness on the long finish. Needs until at least 1996 to shed the tannin. $39 (5/15/91) **89**

LOUIS JADOT
Nuits-St.-Georges 1989 (NR) (7/15/90) (BT) **80+**
Nuits-St.-Georges 1988 $27 (7/15/90) (BT) **75+**
Nuits-St.-Georges 1985 $30 (4/15/88) **91**
Nuits-St.-Georges Les Boudots 1988: Ripe and focused, with vibrant cherry, currant and toast aromas and flavors. Bigger and more boisterous that most Burgundies, but holding enough in reserve to be best around 1995 to '98. $49 (2/28/91) **88**
Nuits-St.-Georges Les Boudots 1986: A harmonious and pretty wine, made in a lighter style, with cinnamon and strawberry aromas and flavors. Beautifully focused on the finish. Drink now. $38 (4/30/89) **85**
Nuits-St.-Georges Les Boudots 1985 $42 (3/15/88) **75**
Nuits-St.-Georges Clos des Corvées 1989: Silky, with lovely cherry and earth flavors and a medium finish. Offers a little less than you might expect. Try after 1993. $56 (1/31/92) **85**
Nuits-St.-Georges Clos des Corvées 1988: Hard and tannic, but stylish and flavorful, offering cherry, chocolate and toast aromas and flavors that are rich, round and long. Needs until 1997 to 2000 to shed its tannins. $49 (2/28/91) **89**
Nuits-St.-Georges Clos des Corvées 1987: Lean, firm and tannic, with smoky, earthy cherry aromas and flavors, that are astringent enough to require cellaring until 1993 to '95. $35 (4/30/90) **84**
Nuits-St.-Georges Clos des Corvées 1986 $37 (4/30/89) **83**
Nuits-St.-Georges Clos des Corvées 1985 $44 (3/15/88) **96**

JAFFELIN
Nuits-St.-Georges 1989: Very ripe in style, verging on raisins, with full tannins and an earthy finish. Try from 1994 to '96. $27 (1/31/92) **83**
Nuits-St.-Georges 1986: Lean and tart, with plummy strawberry flavor, turning toasty on the long finish. Could be more substantial. $28 (2/28/89) **80**
Nuits-St.-Georges 1983 $19 (9/15/86) **72**
Nuits-St.-Georges Les Damodes 1989: Has a lot of finesse for a ripe, rich wine. Still holding back, but shows plenty of polished tannins. Try in 1995. $36 (1/31/92) **90**

J. JAYER
Nuits-St.-Georges Les Lavières 1985 $38 (3/15/88) **88**

LAROCHE
Nuits-St.-Georges 1988: Lean and elegant, but with plenty of pretty flavors. Ripe cherry, spice, cola and toasty oak notes are smooth up front but finish with firmness and just the right touch of tannin. Tempting now to 1994. $28 (11/15/90) **87**

DOMAINE FRANCOIS LEGROS
Nuits-St.-Georges Les Perrières 1989: Charming, light and fruity, with pretty raspberry and cherry flavors and spicy oak shadings that make it quite attractive already. Crisp and balanced, with a smoky, stewed plum note on the finish. Ready now, but can age through 1995. $29 (11/15/91) **87**

DOMAINE LEQUIN-ROUSSOT
Nuits-St.-Georges 1985 $39 (4/15/88) **75**

DOMAINE LEROY
Nuits-St.-Georges Aux Allots 1989: Truly excellent for a village wine. An explosion of fruit, with fine tannins and tons of licorice character. Try from 1994 to '96. $75 (1/31/92) **92**
Nuits-St.-Georges Aux Allots 1988: Firm, tannic and concentrated, with beautifully defined black cherry, currant and spice aromas and flavors. Rich in texture, powerful and elegant at the same time; a wine with great potential. Needs until 1994 to '96 to begin to soften the tannins. 186 cases made. $84 (4/30/91) **89**
Nuits-St.-Georges Aux Boudots 1989: A benchmark for Nuits-St.-Georges, with hedonistic coffee, chocolate, tobacco and berry aromas and flavors and superbly fine tannins. Try after 1994. $117 (1/31/92) **95**
Nuits-St.-Georges Aux Boudots 1988: A very intense, flavorful, stylishly oaky Burgundy, with firm tannins and acidity, effusive fruit and spice flavors and a long finish. Assertive and fruity, with tart cherry and berry notes and great structure, giving it plenty of potential for aging. Try in 1994 and beyond. 311 cases made. $230 (4/30/91) **93**
Nuits-St.-Georges Aux Lavières 1989: Has a beautiful violet and grape character, with supple, full tannins and a long, focused finish. Try after 1994. $75 (1/31/92) **89**
Nuits-St.-Georges Aux Lavières 1988: Big, tart and dense, with cherry, cedar and meat flavors and an unfortunate hint of sauerkraut, hinting at stemminess on the tannic finish. Definitely harsh at this point; needs at least until 1994 or '95 to settle down. Tough to judge, but it might come through in the end. 194 cases made. $84 (4/30/91) **82**
Nuits-St.-Georges Les Vignerondes 1989: Pure satin in the mouth, with delicious, spicy, peppery berry flavors and elegant, silky tannins. Try after 1994. $117 (1/31/92) **92**

LUPE-CHOLET
Nuits-St.-Georges Château Gris 1989 $48 (7/15/90) (BT) **85+**
Nuits-St.-Georges Château Gris 1988 $50 (7/15/90) (BT) **90+**
Nuits-St.-Georges Château Gris 1987: Soft and redolent of berries, cherries and brown sugar, more aromatic than flavorful. Its astringency takes a back seat to the fruit on the finish. Drink now to '93. $38 (3/31/90) **84**
Nuits-St.-Georges Château Gris 1986 $33 (7/31/88) **86**
Nuits-St.-Georges Château Gris 1985 $39 (2/15/88) **88**
Nuits-St.-Georges Château Gris 1983 $24 (6/16/86) **77**
Nuits-St.-Georges Les Vignes Rondex Hospice de Nuits 1986 ($NA) (7/31/88) **91**

BERTRAND MACHARD DE GRAMONT
Nuits-St.-Georges Les Allots 1987: A lighter wine, with pleasantly spicy strawberry and cherry flavors on a firmly tannic backbone. It needs only short-term cellaring to show all it has, so it should be drinkable now. Tasted twice. $30 (7/15/90) **82**
Nuits-St.-Georges Les Hauts Pruliers 1988: Firm and tight, with an elegant core of currant, plum and black cherry flavors that pick up a touch of cedar and spice on the aftertaste. The tannins are rich and concentrated, suggesting cellaring until 1996. $37 (7/15/91) **88**
Nuits-St.-Georges Les Hauts Pruliers 1987: Lean, firm and tight, with tannin-wrapped black cherry and toast flavors, and very light aromas. But it all comes together with some intensity on the finish. Cellar until at least 1993 to '94. $32 (4/30/90) **85**
Nuits-St.-Georges Les Hauts Pruliers 1986: Pretty strawberry jam aromas and flavors are flanked by firm, dry tannins. Overall it's balanced, but it needs time to open. Drink now. $22 (12/15/89) **77**

DOMAINE MEO-CAMUZET
Nuits-St.-Georges 1989: Seductive, with toasty, buttery oak, but the wood blends beautifully with the ripe, elegant cherry and plum flavors. A delicious young Burgundy that should only get better through 1995. Finishes long and complex. $52 (11/15/91) **92**
Nuits-St.-Georges 1988: Rich, glorious fruit cascades over the palate, echoing black cherry and plum flavors through the long finish. An elegant wine, with lively balance and marvelous intensity. Drinkable now, but it should gain by aging until 1993. $50 (11/30/90) **91**
Nuits-St.-Georges 1987: Lean, firm and concentrated with delicate cherry, plum and spicy oak flavors that are nicley balanced. Needs a year or two to soften and mature. Drink now through 1994. $42 (12/15/89) **86**
Nuits-St.-Georges 1986 $32 (11/15/88) **90**
Nuits-St.-Georges Aux Boudots 1989: A nice display of toasty, buttery oak, but it has pretty currant, plum and cherry-tinged flavors, too. Elegant but concentrated, with deft balance and fine structure. Needs until 1995 to pull together. $81 (11/15/91) **90**
Nuits-St.-Georges Aux Boudots 1988: Very firm and tightly wound, with sharply focused black cherry and toast aromas and flavors that last on the long finish. Tannic and almost thick, but so packed with character it should turn into a great wine with cellaring until 1994 to '96. $80 (11/30/90) **92**
Nuits-St.-Georges Aux Boudots 1987: Firm and tannic with compact cherry, plum and spicy oak flavors that are intense and assertive. A lively wine that is drinkable now but could be cellared until 1996. $56 (12/15/89) **88**
Nuits-St.-Georges Aux Boudots 1986 $46 (11/15/88) **92**
Nuits-St.-Georges Aux Murgers 1989: Offers beautiful oak and fruit complexities, with deep, intense, rich cherry and currant flavors. The toasty, buttery oak notes add dimension and texture to the flavors. The finish is long and beguiling. Drinkable now, or cellar through 1997. $81 (11/15/91) **94**
Nuits-St.-Georges Aux Murgers 1988: Concentrated and elegant, with harmonious black cherry and toast aromas and flavors beautifully knit with hints of nutmeg and rose petal. A bit tough right now, keeping it from showing all it has, but cellaring until 1993 should polish it. $80 (11/30/90) **91**
Nuits-St.-Georges Aux Murgers 1987: Remarkably deep and complex with seductive toasty oak, black cherry and spice flavors of great intensity and balance; the flavors keep lingering long and full on the palate. Fruit echoes long on the aftertaste. Drink now through 1998. $56 (12/15/89) **93**
Nuits-St.-Georges Aux Murgers 1986 $48 (11/15/88) **90**
Nuits-St.-Georges Aux Murgers 1985 $50 (4/15/88) **90**

ALAIN MICHELOT
Nuits-St.-Georges 1988: Aromatic, elegant and fine in texture, with appealing cherry, currant, nutmeg and vanilla aromas and flavors that are long and intense without being heavy. A subtle wine, with many facets. Best after 1994. $39 (7/15/91) **91**
Nuits-St.-Georges 1982 $17 (5/01/84) **86**
Nuits-St.-Georges Les Cailles 1988: Light and spicy, with leathery red cherry and strawberry aromas and flavors, turning crisp and fresh on the finish. Best after 1993. $54 (5/15/91) **83**
Nuits-St.-Georges Les Cailles 1982 $19 (7/16/85) **90**
Nuits-St.-Georges Les Chaignots 1988: Rich and concentrated, with an earthy edge to the ripe currant and berry flavors that are generous and long on the finish. Has all the pieces to age well through at least 1995. 400 cases made. $56 (5/15/91) **90**
Nuits-St.-Georges Les Champs-Perdrix 1986: A heavy dose of wood dominates the black cherry flavors, so it's intense and tannic. Could use a shade more richness and a touch of finesse. Should be softened by now. $30 (12/15/89) **81**
Nuits-St.-Georges Les Porets-St.-Georges 1988: A distinct earthy, muddy edge tends to obscure the generous berry and cherry flavors. A tough wine now; should need until 1994 to '96 to settle down. $56 (5/15/91) **83**
Nuits-St.-Georges Les Richemone 1988: Crisp, flavorful and generous, with ripe raspberry and currant aromas and flavors that persist through a strong finish. A bit tannic and tight, but it has a lot of flavor to develop. Try in 1994 to '96. $54 (5/15/91) **89**
Nuits-St.-Georges Les Vaucrains 1988: Tight and focused, with light, appealing cherry and currant aromas and flavors that persist through the finish, where hints of toast and nutmeg emerge. Needs until 1993 to '95 to shed the tannins. $56 (5/15/91) **87**
Nuits-St.-Georges Les Vaucrains 1986: Pretty black cherry, toast and smoky oak flavors are soft, rich and velvety, with a tug of tannin on the finish. But it's all in balance. Drink now through 1994. $30 (12/15/89) **88**

MOILLARD
Nuits-St.-Georges Clos de Thorey 1985 $38 (5/31/87) **89**
Nuits-St.-Georges Clos de Thorey 1984 $24 (5/31/87) **84**
Nuits-St.-Georges Clos de Thorey 1983 $19 (9/16/85) **84**
Nuits-St.-Georges Clos de Thorey Domaine Thomas-Moillard 1989: Pristine, with focused chocolate, smoke and fruit aromas and flavors and firm tannins. Try after 1994. $35 (1/31/92) **89**
Nuits-St.-Georges Clos de Thorey Domaine Thomas-Moillard 1988: Lean and lovely, with generous raspberry, strawberry, vanilla and nutmeg aromas and flavors that keep slipping in and out of the spotlight. A long, brightly flavorful wine that's balanced toward elegance. Tempting now, but better around 1993. $50 (12/31/90) **89**
Nuits-St.-Georges Clos de Thorey Domaine Thomas-Moillard 1987: Firm, concentrated and a bit on the tannic side, but the ripe cherry and plum flavors emerge nicely through it all and linger effectively. Give it until 1993 to smooth out the scratchy tannins, and it should be wonderful. $27 (12/15/89) **88**
Nuits-St.-Georges Clos de Thorey Domaine Thomas-Moillard 1986 $28 (11/15/88) **78**
Nuits-St.-Georges Hospices de Nuits Cuvée Jacques Duret 1988: The focal point is a strong toasty oak flavor, but ripe currant, black cherry, anise and meat notes balance it nicely. Elegant and focused, with silky-smooth tannins and plenty of length. Ready now, but capable of improving through 1994. $68 (8/31/91) **89**

MOMMESSIN
Nuits-St.-Georges Les Vaucrains 1989: An individualistic wine, with an interesting, rich, earthy berry character and fine tannins. Try in 1994. $45 (1/31/92) **90**

CHARLES MONCAUT
Nuits-St.-Georges Les Argillières 1984 $32 (6/15/87) **90**

MONGEARD-MUGNERET
Nuits-St.-Georges Les Boudots 1989: If you like old-fashioned wines with lots of barnyardy, earthy nuances, this is for you. Try after 1993. $49 (1/31/92) **84**
Nuits-St.-Georges Les Boudots 1987: Despite the light color, this is a very smoky, earthy, tannic wine with just barely enough raspberry and chocolate aroma and flavor to keep it in balance. Could have more intensity. Drink now to '94. $32 (4/30/90) **81**
Nuits-St.-Georges Les Boudots 1984 $23 (2/15/88) **78**

GEORGES MUGNERET
Nuits-St.-Georges Les Chaignots 1989: Smooth and generous, with a definite smoky, earthy edge to the modest cherry and currant flavors. Softens and fades a bit on the finish. Almost drinkable now. $43 (4/30/92) **86**
Nuits-St.-Georges Les Chaignots 1988: Lean, tart and tannic, with spicy oak flavors dominating the ripe cherry and other fruit flavors that turn stemmy and "green" on the finish. A difficult style to warm up to; drink in 1993 to '95. $47 (11/15/90) **80**
Nuits-St.-Georges Les Chaignots 1987: Firm, tannic and a bit oaky and lean in texture, but there are enough pretty strawberry, cherry and spice aromas to warrant holding on to it to see what develops. Drink now to '94. 500 cases made. $41 (10/15/89) **87**
Nuits-St.-Georges Les Chaignots 1986 $40 (11/15/88) **89**
Nuits-St.-Georges Les Chaignots 1984 $26 (3/15/87) **89**

GERARD MUGNERET
Nuits-St.-Georges Les Boudots 1988: An earthy-styled Burgundy, with toasty, barnyardy aromas and flavors. Good, but only for fans of earthy wines. $48 (2/28/91) **76**
Nuits-St.-Georges Les Boudots 1987: Smooth, elegant and complex, this medium-weight wine has generous tobacco- and nutmeg-tinged plum and cassis aromas and flavors. The nicely integrated tannins will need until 1993 to soften. $40 (7/15/90) **88**

REMOISSENET
Nuits-St.-Georges Aux Argillats 1985 $34 (10/15/88) **87**

GILLES REMORIQUET
Nuits-St.-Georges 1982 $19 (7/16/85) **84**

HENRI & GILLES REMORIQUET
Nuits-St.-Georges Rue de Chaux 1985 $22 (7/31/88) **81**

DOMAINE DANIEL RION
Nuits-St.-Georges 1986: Ripe and plummy, with good depth and intensity of flavors. A rather robust wine, showing smoky and cherry character. Maybe time in the cellar will bring it more harmony. $31 (4/30/89) **85**
Nuits-St.-Georges 1985 $28 (3/15/88) **85**
Nuits-St.-Georges Clos des Argillières 1989: Like eating black cherries and currants with fudge. Coats your mouth with succulent fruit and firm tannins. Try after 1993. $63 (1/31/92) **91**
Nuits-St.-Georges Clos des Argillières 1988: Supple and elegant for an '88, but still intense and concentrated, with plenty of currant, cherry, nutmeg and spice flavors all beginning to come together, flanked by firm, austere tannins. Plenty of fruit pours through on the finish. Well balanced, but hold off until 1994 or '95. 600 cases made. $54 (1/31/91) **91**
Nuits-St.-Georges Clos des Argillières 1987: The marvelous concentration of cherry, vanilla and toast carries through from the first whiff to the last echo of the long, long finish in this jam-packed, elegant wine. Worth cellaring until 1993 to see what happens as it develops more finesse. Rel: $30 Cur: $36 (4/30/90) **92**
Nuits-St.-Georges Clos des Argillières 1986 $47 (4/30/89) **90**
Nuits-St.-Georges Clos des Argillières 1985 Rel: $44 Cur: $55 (3/15/88) **94**
Nuits-St.-Georges Grandes Vignes 1989: Clean and straightforward, with lots of juicy fruit flavors and firm tannins. Try after 1994. $38 (1/31/92) **88**
Nuits-St.-Georges Grandes Vignes 1988 $33 (7/15/90) (BT) **85+**

Key to Symbols

The scores reported here are the results of blind tastings conducted by our panel of senior editors. Wines that carry the initials below are results of individual tastings.

THE WINE SPECTATOR 100-POINT SCALE *95-100*—Classic, a great wine; *90-94*—Outstanding, superior character and style; *80-89*—Good to very good, a wine with special qualities; *70-79*—Average, drinkable wine that may have minor flaws; *60-69*—Below average, drinkable but not recommended; *50-59*—Poor, undrinkable, not recommended. "+"—With a score indicates a range; used primarily with barrel tastings to indicate a preliminary score.

SPECIAL DESIGNATIONS SS—Spectator Selection, CS—Cellar Selection, BB—Best Buy, ($NA)—Price not available, (NR)—Not released.

TASTER'S INITIALS (JG)—Jim Gordon, (HS)—Harvey Steiman, (JL)—James Laube, (JS)—James Suckling, (TM)—Thomas Matthews, (TR)—Terry Robards, (PM)—Per-Henrik Mansson, (BT)—Barrel Tasting (these wines were tasted blind from barrel samples), (CA-date)—*California's Great Cabernets* by James Laube, (CH-date)—*California's Great Chardonnays* by James Laube, (VP-date)—*Vintage Port* by James Suckling.

DATE TASTED Dates in parentheses represent the issue in which the rating was published.

Nuits-St.-Georges Hauts Pruliers 1989: The essence of a great Nuits. Spice, berry and fruit flavors jump out of the glass along with plenty of silky tannins. Try in 1994. $63 (1/31/92) **92**
Nuits-St.-Georges Hauts Pruliers 1988: Intense and lively, with pretty floral aromas and ripe plum, cassis, currant and cherry flavors that are elegantly structured and packed with fruit. Best to cellar until 1995 or '96 at the earliest. 300 cases made. $54 (1/31/91) **91**
Nuits-St.-Georges Hauts Pruliers 1987: Very ripe and generous, with sharply focused, beautifully defined black cherry, toast and nutmeg aromas and flavors, concentrated and long. Cellar until at least 1993 to '94. $35 (4/30/90) **91**
Nuits-St.-Georges Hauts Pruliers 1986 $45 (4/30/89) **91**
Nuits-St.-Georges Hauts Pruliers 1985 Rel: $43 Cur: $50 (3/15/88) **88**
Nuits-St.-Georges Les Lavières 1988: Powerful, rich aromas and flavors of plum, raspberry and nutmeg carry through this mouthfilling, dramatic wine. The broad range of flavors persists on the long finish, and it has a modest level of well-integrated tannins to shed in the cellar, perhaps by 1995. Should be a great one. 750 cases made. $33 (2/15/91) **93**
Nuits-St.-Georges Les Lavières 1987: Smooth, fruity and focused, with beautifully defined cherry and raspberry aromas and flavors, a velvety texture and a smoky, lively finish. Drink now to 1994. $21 (4/30/90) **87**
Nuits-St.-Georges Les Vignes Rondes 1989: A super-classy Nuits, with gorgeous white truffle, violet and berry aromas and flavors and super-fine tannins. Try after 1994. $63 (1/31/92) **93**
Nuits-St.-Georges Les Vignes Rondes 1988: Rich, tight and forward, with intense cassis, currant and plum nuances that are tightly concentrated and firmly tannic. The finish brings out the toasty nutmeg and oak elements and the finish is long and lingering, but this wine needs until 1995 or '96 to soften and mellow. 244 cases made. $54 (1/31/91) **92**
Nuits-St.-Georges Les Vignes Rondes 1987: Immediately attractive, with opulent cherry and plum flavors framed by sweet, toasty oak. The flavors unfold with complexity on the long finish. Intense and concentrated, but elegant enough to keep you coming back for another sip. Drink 1993 to '95. 300 cases made. $35 (4/30/90) **95**
Nuits-St.-Georges Les Vignes Rondes 1986 $43 (4/30/89) **88**
Nuits-St.-Georges Les Vignes Rondes 1985 $40 (3/15/88) **91**

RION PERE & FILS
Nuits-St.-Georges Les Murgers 1987: Firm, tannic and concentrated, with enough appealing and slightly floral cherry and strawberry flavors to balance the bite of astringency on the finish. Drink 1993 to '96. $31 (3/31/90) **79**

EMMANUEL ROUGET
Nuits-St.-Georges 1989: An earthy style, with bright, elegant, fresh cherry and spice-tinged flavors. Balanced with soft but ample tannins. Drink now, or cellar through 1994. $48 (11/15/91) **86**
Nuits-St.-Georges 1987: Crisp and snappy, with lots of finely focused plum, raspberry and strawberry flavors to make it smooth and inviting enough to drink now, although cellaring until 1993 or '94 would bring out more depth. $32 (3/31/90) **86**

LEONARD DE ST.-AUBIN
Nuits-St.-Georges 1985 $25 (11/30/87) **71**

DOMAINE B. SERVEAU
Nuits-St.-Georges Chaines Carteaux 1988: A mean, hard, tough wine, with the wood and tannin dominating the cherry and raspberry notes. Needs time to soften, but it may always be a shade woody. Drink in 1994 or '95. Tasted three times. $39 (3/31/91) **84**
Nuits-St.-Georges Chaines Carteaux 1985 $39 (6/15/88) **86**

Vosne-Romanée

ROBERT ARNOUX
Romanée-St.-Vivant 1988: Beautifully focused strawberry, rose petal and nutmeg aromas and flavors mark this lean, lively, complex wine as a winner. Just as the tannins threaten to take over, the fruit emerges again. Drink in 1993 to '95. $250 (11/15/90) **91**
Vosne-Romanée Les Chaumes 1988: Fans of the earthy, barnyardy style will find a lot to like here, finishing with spicy chocolate and smoke flavors that are clean and refreshing. An unusual style that should evolve with cellaring until 1994 to '98. Much better than two bottles tasted earlier from a different source. $45 (2/28/91) **80**
Vosne-Romanée Les Suchots 1988: Tannic and earthy, finishing with enough raspberry and currant flavors to bring it into balance. Has plenty of flavor to keep it going and balance to age through at least 1994. Will appeal to fans of the rustic style. Much better than two bottles tasted earlier from a different source. $60 (2/28/91) **86**
Vosne-Romanée Les Suchots 1985 $52 (7/31/88) **90**

DOMAINE BERTAGNA
Vosne-Romanée Les Beaux Monts Bas 1985 $35 (10/15/88) **82**

BICHOT
Vosne-Romanée Les Beaux Monts 1988: Light, smooth and elegant, with lots of cinnamon and nutmeg notes in the generous black cherry and plum flavors; this is a supple wine that shows lovely finesse. Almost drinkable now, but try to hold off until 1993 or '94. $34 (7/15/90) **87**

BOUCHARD PERE & FILS
Echézeaux 1989: Starts out beautifully, with gorgeous black cherry, chocolate and cedar aromas, but finishes a bit short. Try after 1994. $62 (1/31/92) **88**
La Romanée Château de Vosne-Romanée 1989 $298 (7/15/90) (BT) **90+**
La Romanée Château de Vosne-Romanée 1988 $238 (7/15/90) (BT) **90+**
La Romanée Château de Vosne-Romanée 1986 $200 (7/31/88) **91**
Vosne-Romanée Aux Reignots Château de Vosne-Romanée 1989: Gorgeous, with massive fruit and tannins and complex red licorice, blackberry, cherry and smoke aromas and flavors. From Domaine de la SCI du Château de Vosne-Romanée. An ager; try after 1996. (NR) (1/31/92) **93**
Vosne-Romanée Aux Reignots Château de Vosne-Romanée 1988 $50 (7/15/90) (BT) **70+**
Vosne-Romanée Aux Reignots Château de Vosne-Romanée 1986 $50 (7/31/88) **89**
Vosne-Romanée Aux Reignots Château de Vosne-Romanée 1985 $51 (2/28/89) **90**

PIERRE BOUREE FILS
Vosne-Romanée 1987: Although trying to be elegant, this comes off as sour and thin, with a hint of bitterness and a touch of plum flavor to save it from disaster. Tasted twice with consistent results. $44 (7/15/90) **68**

CHANSON PERE & FILS
Vosne-Romanée Suchots 1988: True to form, with lively, well-defined plum, cherry and toast aromas and flavors, this is appealing from start to finish. It's easy to drink and ready now, but should hold on through 1993 to '94. $55 (9/30/90) **87**

F. CHAUVENET
Echézeaux 1989: A complex Burgundy, with earthy cedar and smoke notes, mouth-filling flavors and a silky finish. Try after 1994. $56 (1/31/92) **92**
Echézeaux 1988 $50 (7/15/90) (BT) **90+**
Echézeaux 1985 $47 (7/31/87) **89**
Vosne-Romanée Les Suchots 1985 $46 (7/31/87) **92**

DOMAINE BRUNO CLAIR
Vosne-Romanée Les Champs Pedrix 1989: Offers beautiful black cherry and concentrated raspberry flavors and extremely well-integrated tannins. A mouthful that should be better after 1994. (NR) (1/31/92) **91**

GEORGES CLERGET
Vosne-Romanée Les Violettes 1986: Thin, astringent and tart, with barklike flavors that try but never quite do open up on the finish. Maybe with time it can soften up. Try 1994. $23 (8/31/89) **71**

MICHEL CLERGET
Echézeaux 1986: Firm and slightly astringent, but it has generous flavors, with an herbal edge clouding the cherry flavor. It finishes lean and a bit muddled, but it should be a drinkable wine by now. $31 (8/31/89) **85**
Echézeaux 1985 $51 (7/31/88) **82**

DOMAINE DU CLOS FRANTIN
Echézeaux 1989: Packed with fruit and tannins. Very powerful, but manages to remain balanced. From Bichot. Try after 1995. $45 (1/31/92) **93**
Echézeaux 1988 $56 (7/15/90) (BT) **95+**
Echézeaux 1986 $30 (11/30/88) **90**
Echézeaux 1985 $37 (9/15/87) **96**
Grands Echézeaux 1989: A sturdy wine, with intense blackberry, cherry and chocolate flavors and strong acidity and tannins. From Bichot. Try from 1995 to '97. $56 (1/31/92) **90**
Grands Echézeaux 1987: Spicy, peppery, almost herbal flavors make the first impression, but the smooth textured finish yields a suggestion of vanilla, raspberry and currant flavor that should develop well through 1993 to '95. A subtle wine. $56 (7/15/90) **86**
Grands Echézeaux 1986: Tannic and tough, but the delicate strawberry flavor and spicy overtones ride over the rough texture, suggesting that time in the cellar will be rewarded. Drink 1993. $60 (2/28/89) **87**
Richebourg 1989: A kaleidoscope of aromas and flavors, from chocolate and coffee to strawberry and plum. Has super-firm tannins and an explosive finish. From Bichot. Try from 1995 to '98. $117 (1/31/92) **95**
Richebourg 1986: Unusually herbal aromas and flavors resolve into well-focused cherry and berry flavor on the finish, but the bay leaf overtones pervade this wine from the first tannic sip to the firm aftertaste. Cellar at least until 1993. $100 (8/31/89) **88**
Vosne-Romanée 1989: Ripe, rich and succulent, with lots of plum, cedar and black cherry aromas and flavors and an opulent finish. From Bichot. Try after 1993. $30 (1/31/92) **89**
Vosne-Romanée 1986 $19 (12/31/88) **80**
Vosne-Romanée 1985 $29 (10/15/87) **91**
Vosne-Romanée Les Malconsorts 1989 $32 (7/15/90) (BT) **85+**
Vosne-Romanée Les Malconsorts 1988 $58 (7/15/90) (BT) **85+**
Vosne-Romanée Les Malconsorts 1987: A smooth, subtle and velvety wine showing lots of charming plum and berry aromas and flavors with overtones of toast, vanilla and spice. Very fine and elegant, drinkable now to '95. $30 (7/15/90) **88**
Vosne-Romanée Les Malconsorts 1986 $30 (10/31/88) **79**
Vosne-Romanée Les Malconsorts 1985 $40 (9/30/87) **95**

JOSEPH DROUHIN
Echézeaux 1988: Delicate, focused and fragrant, with lots of spice, chocolate and smoke overtones to the plum and cassis flavors. Has a supple texture and superb length, but needs until 1993 to '95 to open up the tannin currently holding it in. 250 cases made. $60 (11/15/90) **93**
Echézeaux 1986 $60 (7/31/88) **92**
Grands Echézeaux 1989: Refined and powerful, with concentrated blackberry aromas and flavors and rich tannins. Has an excellent acid backbone. Try from 1995 to '97. $114 (1/31/92) **91**
Grands Echézeaux 1985 $75 (11/15/87) **93**
Romanée-St.-Vivant 1989: Tight and solid, with a concentrated, fruity, earthy character and full tannins. Try from 1994 to '98. (NR) (1/31/92) **92**
Vosne-Romanée Les Beaumonts 1989: Pretty, subtle and polished, with lovely cherry, vanilla and strawberry notes. Try after 1994. $70 (1/31/92) **91**
Vosne-Romanée Les Beaumonts 1988: Tight, lean and focused, with pretty black cherry, currant and spicy, toasty oak flavors that emerge before the drying tannins dominate the finish. Needs cellaring until 1997 or '98 at the earliest. Tasted three times. $56 (3/31/91) **80**
Vosne-Romanée Les Beaumonts 1985 Rel: $42 Cur: $53 (11/15/87) **93**
Vosne-Romanée Les Suchots 1989: Earthy and flavorful, made in a chewy, muscular style, with a good concentration of black cherry and cedar flavors. Try in 1993. $70 (1/31/92) **89**
Vosne-Romanée Les Suchots 1988: Lively and elegant, with lots of raspberry and wild strawberry flavors packed into a firm framework. The tannins are held in check, adding to the tension that should resolve itself with cellaring until 1995. $57 (2/28/91) **90**
Vosne-Romanée Les Suchots 1985 $42 (11/15/87) **94**

DOMAINE DUJAC
Echézeaux 1988: Packed with rich, ripe, gorgeous flavors of black cherry, raspberry, minerals and spicy oak. The texture is supple and smooth before the tannins kick in on the finish. Concentrated and peppery on the aftertaste, picking up a touch of anise. Cellar until 1997 or '98. $70 (3/31/91) **90**
Echézeaux 1987: Except for a dose of tannin, it tastes mature and ready to drink now. Has brown sugar, cinnamon and prune flavors that linger on the finish. Enjoyable, but seems to be ahead of its time. Tasted twice. $56 (5/15/90) **82**
Echézeaux 1986: Lean, toasty and peppery, with remarkably generous berry and spice on the finish, suggesting that this is an excellent cellar candidate. Beautifully knit, long and elegant. Drink 1993. $52 (4/30/89) **89**

RENE ENGEL
Echézeaux 1989: Rich, earthy and spicy, with concentrated cherry, strawberry and red currant flavors that persist on the finish. Nearing drinkability, but will improve through 1998. $47 (11/15/91) **89**
Echézeaux 1988: Deep, rich, complex and firmly tannic, but offering a wealth of cherry, plum and currant aromas and flavors. Hints of earth and chalk emerge on the finish, but that should fade with the tannins. Try in 1995. 200 cases made. $56 (3/31/91) **92**
Echézeaux 1986 $38 (11/30/88) **78**
Echézeaux 1985 $32 (10/15/87) **90**
Grands Echézeaux 1989: Elegant and spicy, with pure cherry and cinnamon notes that dance on the palate. Mildly tannic, but the crisp acidity keeps the flavors lively and refreshing. Best to hold through 1994. 150 cases made. $75 (11/15/91) **90**
Grands Echézeaux 1986 $50 (11/30/88) **71**
Grands Echézeaux 1985 $43 (10/15/87) **86**
Vosne-Romanée 1989: Intense and firmly tannic, but with a tight core of plum and currant flavors. Years away from drinking, with its hard, austere shell; cellar until 1997. $34 (11/15/91) **85**
Vosne-Romanée 1988: Smells opulent and rich, but the tannin and acidity shoulder past the plum and cherry flavors. Those who like vibrant, tart wines will love it, while others may find it hard to warm up to. Try in 1994 to '95. $30 (7/15/90) **81**
Vosne-Romanée 1986: Smells great but it's very lean and short on the palate, its spicy cherry flavor turning astringent on the finish. Might develop with time. Try now. $29 (2/28/89) **75**
Vosne-Romanée 1985 $24 (10/15/87) **77**
Vosne-Romanée 1983 $19 (2/16/86) **67**
Vosne-Romanée Les Brûlées 1989: Crisp and focused, this tough-edged wine shows ample tannins and a solid core of raspberry and red cherry flavor that needs until 1998 to 2000 to break through the wall of tannin. $35 (11/15/91) **87**
Vosne-Romanée Les Brûlées 1988: A lovely interplay of berry, plum, violet and rose petal aromas and flavors, all on a lean frame, marks this as a special wine. Modestly tannic, but flavorful and generous on the finish. Drink after 1994 or '95. 400 cases made. $45 (2/28/91) **89**
Vosne-Romanée Les Brûlées 1986 $32 (10/31/88) **68**
Vosne-Romanée Les Brûlées 1985 $28 (10/15/87) **85**
Vosne-Romanée Les Brûlées 1983 $22 (3/16/86) **78**

FAIVELEY
Echézeaux 1989: Subdued at first, but builds into a rich wine, with cherry and mint flavors and mouth-coating, supple tannins. Needs cellaring until at least 1995. $68 (1/31/92) **89**
Echézeaux 1987: Not opulent, but flavorful and firmly supported by fine tannins and generous fruit. Lavishly oaked. Needs cellaring until 1993 to soften the somewhat brittle tannins. $53 (3/31/90) **80**
Echézeaux 1985 $74 (3/31/88) **89**
Echézeaux 1981 $40 (5/01/86) **68**
Vosne-Romanée 1989: Ripe black cherry aromas are echoed on the palate, with smoky notes. Has plenty of fruit in reserve. Try in 1994. $35 (1/31/92) **88**

DOMAINE FOREY PERE & FILS
Echézeaux 1989: Ripe and rich, with lovely violet, cherry and blackberry aromas and flavors and a chewy finish. Try from 1994 to '96. (NR) (1/31/92) **90**
Vosne-Romanée 1989: Harder than most from this appellation. Chewy and big, with strawberry notes and plenty of firm tannins. Try in 1995. (NR) (1/31/92) **85**

JEAN GRIVOT
Richebourg 1989: An extremely elegant Richebourg, with a stylish floral, cinnamon and fruit character. Velvety and sweet on the finish. Try from 1994 to '97. (NR) (1/31/92) **93**
Vosne-Romanée 1985 $31 (4/30/88) **87**
Vosne-Romanée Les Beaumonts 1989: A bit too earthy for us, with barnyardy aromas dominating the otherwise nice cherry, bark and chestnut flavors underneath. Try in 1993. (NR) (1/31/92) **75**

A.-F. GROS
Echézeaux 1988: Youthful, tight and tannic, but supple enough to let the cherry, currant and nutmeg flavors emerge in an elegant, beautifully crafted wine. The tannins will need until 1994 to '96 to become polished. $84 (2/15/91) **91**
Richebourg 1989: Decadent, with intense, gamy, smoky, fruity flavors, velvety tannins and an ultralong, flavorful finish. Try from 1994 to '98. $130 (1/31/92) **97**
Richebourg 1988: Absolutely sensational, very rich and concentrated, with magnificently articulated plum, currant and berry flavors and lovely hints of wildflowers, anise and chocolate on the nose. A plush, generous, elegant wine that should keep developing into the 21st century. $190 (2/15/91) **97**
Vosne-Romanée Aux Réas 1988: Earthy, leathery flavors dominate the cherry and plum flavors. A bit too much wood for us. Of marginal quality. Tasted twice. $41 (2/28/91) **71**

JEAN GROS
Richebourg 1989: A monster of a wine, with an amazing concentration of fruit and violet aromas. Like a young Taylor vintage Port, but still full of finesse. Try from 1996 to '98. $180 (1/31/92) **98**
Richebourg 1988: A sensational wine, with a magnificent interplay of plum, currant, nutmeg and vanilla flavors, a supple texture and vibrant acidity. It's long and almost sweet on the finish and beautifully balanced, echoing all the flavors for many minutes. Can only become richer and more complex with cellaring past 1995 to 2000. 125 cases made. $190 (2/28/91) **98**
Richebourg 1987: The class shows clearly in this wine, sending out waves of vanilla, cherry and toast aromas, reining in the flavors to a delicate, finely proportioned finish marked by richness of oak and a touch of gaminess. A gorgeous wine, drinkable now, but cellar it until 1994 to '95 at least. 900 cases made. Rel: $99 Cur: $175 (3/31/90) **95**
Vosne-Romanée 1989: A village Vosne of great quality and concentration, with an intriguing smoky, toasty character and red licorice and plum aromas and flavors. Try after 1993. $39 (1/31/92) **90**
Vosne-Romanée 1988: Earthy, toasty aromas and flavors tend to shoulder past the ripe blackberry and plum flavors in this lean, tough wine. Needs until 1995 to '98 to lose the tannins, but has enough richness to warrant patience. $38 (2/28/91) **90**
Vosne-Romanée 1987: Aromatically seductive, with hints of violet, spice and vanilla surrounding a delicate core of raspberry and red cherry flavors. Smooth and elegant, a caress rather than a punch. Drinkable now, but better around 1993 to '95. $32 (4/30/90) **89**
Vosne-Romanée Clos des Réas 1989: A multidimensional Burgundy, with plummy, earthy, toasty notes and a rich mouth-feel. Try from 1993. $70 (1/31/92) **92**
Vosne-Romanée Clos des Réas 1988: Flavorful, graceful and elegant, this beautifully proportioned wine balances plum, raspberry and strawberry flavors against nuances of oak, offering depth and power at the same time. Stash away until 1995 and watch it develop into a beauty. 1,100 cases made. $50 (2/28/91) **94**
Vosne-Romanée Clos des Réas 1987: Deep, rich and opulent, with marvelous tension between the fruit and the oak, leather and cinnamon notes, from the first whiff to the last echo of the long, long finish. A generous, delicious wine, supple and seductive. Drink 1993 to '95, if you can wait that long. Rel: $37 Cur: $50 (4/30/90) **93**
Vosne-Romanée Clos des Réas 1986 $36 (2/28/89) **90**
Vosne-Romanée Clos des Réas 1985 $55 (7/31/88) **87**

DOMAINE GROS FRERE & SOEUR
Grands Echézeaux 1989: An extremely aromatic, fresh style of Grands Echézeaux, with clean berry and fruit flavors and compact, hard tannins. Built for aging. Try from 1994 to '97. $80 (1/31/92) **92**
Grands Echézeaux 1988: Silky, supple textures and opulent currant and vanilla flavors make this immediately appealing, but the sufficient tannins mark it for the cellar until at least 1995 to '98. Has great structure, flavor and future. $110 (3/15/91) **94**
Grands Echézeaux 1985 $75 (3/31/88) **71**
Richebourg 1989: Another brooding monster, with Port-like aromas and concentration, tons of black cherry, chocolate and cedar flavors and a big tannic grip. Try from 1995 to '99. $130 (1/31/92) **95**
Richebourg 1988: Ripe, rich and thick, with currant and plum aromas and flavors and a hard edge of tannin that will need until 1995 to 2000 to soften. Not as graceful as some, but that may come with age. $192 (2/28/91) **91**
Vosne-Romanée 1989: Aromatic and concentrated, with full-throttle plum and strawberry aromas and flavors. Try after 1994. $39 (1/31/92) **91**
Vosne-Romanée 1988: Has pretty aromas of currant, strawberry, vanilla and spice, with flavors to match. Smooth, polished and elegant, with firm, fine tannins on the finish, echoing fruit and oak. Cellar until 1995 or '96. $46 (3/31/91) **89**
Vosne-Romanée 1985 $35 (4/15/88) **70**

ALAIN GUYARD
Vosne-Romanée Aux Réas 1987: Tight and somewhat tannic for the narrow range of smoky, herbal aromas and flavors, this wine seems green and drying on the palate. $29 (7/15/90) **71**

Key to Symbols

The scores reported here are the results of blind tastings conducted by our panel of senior editors. Wines that carry the initials below are results of individual tastings.

THE WINE SPECTATOR 100-POINT SCALE ***95-100***—Classic, a great wine; ***90-94***—Outstanding, superior character and style; ***80-89***—Good to very good, a wine with special qualities; ***70-79***—Average, drinkable wine that may have minor flaws; ***60-69***—Below average, drinkable but not recommended; ***50-59***—Poor, undrinkable, not recommended. "+"—With a score indicates a range; used primarily with barrel tastings to indicate a preliminary score.

SPECIAL DESIGNATIONS SS—Spectator Selection, CS—Cellar Selection, BB—Best Buy, ($NA)—Price not available, (NR)—Not released.

TASTER'S INITIALS (JG)—Jim Gordon, (HS)—Harvey Steiman, (JL)—James Laube, (JS)—James Suckling, (TM)—Thomas Matthews, (TR)—Terry Robards, (PM)—Per-Henrik Mansson, (BT)—Barrel Tasting (these wines were tasted blind from barrel samples), (CA-date)—*California's Great Cabernets* by James Laube, (CH-date)—*California's Great Chardonnays* by James Laube, (VP-date)—*Vintage Port* by James Suckling.

DATE TASTED Dates in parentheses represent the issue in which the rating was published.

HAEGELEN-JAYER
Echézeaux 1988: Leathery, barnyardy aromas and flavors overwhelm everything else in this wine. Tasted twice. $61 (8/31/91) **67**

LOUIS JADOT
Vosne-Romanée 1989: Quite intense on the palate, with plenty of strawberry notes, but seems delicate on the finish and lacking in generosity. Try in 1993. $40 (1/31/92) **89**
Vosne-Romanée 1985 $33 (3/31/88) **86**
Vosne-Romanée Les Suchots 1988: The toasty oak notes dominate the currant, plum and cherry flavors. A tough wine to judge now because of the strong oak and tannin qualities; perhaps with time more fruit will show through. Drink in 1995 and beyond. $63 (8/31/91) **82**

JAFFELIN
Echézeaux 1989: This elegant, refined wine also shows great firmness and backbone, with pretty currant and wild raspberry flavors. Try from 1994 to '96. $60 (1/31/92) **91**
Echézeaux 1986 $45 (12/31/88) **86**
Echézeaux 1983 $30 (5/01/86) **90**
Romanée-St.-Vivant 1989: Like a springtime shower. Fresh and beautiful, with lots of floral and strawberry aromas and flavors, a ripe, fruity finish and silky tannins. Try from 1994 to '96. $80 (1/31/92) **91**
Vosne-Romanée 1989: Not a blockbuster, but lively nonetheless, with fresh, moderate amounts of cherry, red licorice and plum flavors. Try after 1993. $29 (1/31/92) **86**
Vosne-Romanée 1986: Light, fruity and slightly spicy, a bit rough with tannin, but the strawberry flavor seems simple for the price. Try now. $30 (2/28/89) **79**

HENRI JAYER
Echézeaux 1988 $140 (5/15/91) (HS) **94**
Echézeaux 1987 ($NA) (5/15/91) (HS) **87**
Echézeaux 1986 $120 (5/15/91) (HS) **88**
Echézeaux 1985 $330 (5/15/91) (HS) **96**
Echézeaux 1982 Rel: $41 Cur: $160 (6/16/86) CS **94**
Echézeaux 1981 $130 (5/15/91) (HS) **82**
Echézeaux 1980 $220 (5/15/91) (HS) **89**
Echézeaux 1979 $200 (5/15/91) (HS) **92**
Echézeaux 1978 $380 (5/15/91) (HS) **91**
Echézeaux 1976 ($NA) (5/15/91) (HS) **90**
Echézeaux 1972 ($NA) (5/15/91) (HS) **81**
Echézeaux 1970 ($NA) (5/15/91) (HS) **80**
Echézeaux 1969 ($NA) (5/15/91) (HS) **91**
Richebourg 1987 ($NA) (5/15/91) (HS) **87**
Richebourg 1986 $330 (5/15/91) (HS) **93**
Richebourg 1985 $510 (5/15/91) (HS) **99**
Richebourg 1980 $290 (5/15/91) (HS) **88**
Richebourg 1979 $300 (5/15/91) (HS) **93**
Vosne-Romanée Les Beaumonts 1988 ($NA) (5/15/91) (HS) **89**
Vosne-Romanée Les Brûlées 1987 ($NA) (5/15/91) (HS) **85**
Vosne-Romanée Les Brûlées 1986 $105 (5/15/91) (HS) **90**
Vosne-Romanée Les Brûlées 1985 $240 (5/15/91) (HS) **93**
Vosne-Romanée Les Brûlées 1980 $185 (5/15/91) (HS) **88**
Vosne-Romanée Les Brûlées 1979 $150 (5/15/91) (HS) **88**
Vosne-Romanée Les Brûlées 1978 $280 (5/15/91) (HS) **92**
Vosne-Romanée Les Brûlées 1976 ($NA) (5/15/91) (HS) **81**
Vosne-Romanée Les Brûlées 1972 ($NA) (5/15/91) (HS) **87**
Vosne-Romanée Cros Parantoux 1988 ($NA) (5/15/91) (HS) **93**
Vosne-Romanée Cros Parantoux 1987 ($NA) (5/15/91) (HS) **86**
Vosne-Romanée Cros Parantoux 1986 $100 (5/15/91) (HS) **87**
Vosne-Romanée Cros Parantoux 1985 $240 (5/15/91) (HS) **95**
Vosne-Romanée Cros Parantoux 1980 $175 (5/15/91) (HS) **89**
Vosne-Romanée Cros Parantoux 1978 $200 (5/15/91) (HS) **94**

J. JAYER
Echézeaux 1988: Deep, rich and complex, with lots of spice- and leather-scented currant, plum and smoke aromas and flavors and a round, generous finish. Has the intensity and richness to develop well beyond 1994 or '95. $100 (3/15/91) **91**
Vosne-Romanée Les Rouges 1985 $44 (3/15/88) **80**

JAYER-GILLES
Echézeaux 1989: A monumental Echézeaux that will need time to come around. Inky purple, it's hugely concentrated, overflowing with fruit and tannins. Try after 1995. $101 (1/31/92) **94**
Echézeaux 1982 $23 (11/01/85) **58**

DOMAINE FRANCOIS LAMARCHE
Echézeaux 1987: Ripe, supple, toasty flavors peek through, but it's also fairly dry, firm and tannic. Balanced toward the tannic side, but probably worth cellaring until 1993. Earthy cherry flavors come through on the finish. $48 (9/30/90) **87**
Vosne-Romanée La Grande Rue 1987: Deliciously rich, deep and complex, with a wealth of ripe plum, cherry and spicy tea notes that give it uncommon depth and flavor, especially for an '87. The buttery oak flavors add finesse and texture to the finish, where the fruit powers through. Tempting now, but best in 1993 to '97. $68 (9/30/90) **91**
Vosne-Romanée La Grande Rue 1985 $60 (10/15/88) **89**
Vosne-Romanée Malconsorts 1985 $44 (10/15/88) **84**
Vosne-Romanée Suchots 1985 $36 (10/15/88) **91**

LOUIS LATOUR
Echézeaux 1985 $49 (3/15/88) **87**
Romanée-St.-Vivant Les Quatre Journaux 1989: Multidimensional, with beautiful chestnut, smoke, plum and cherry aromas and flavors, fine tannins and a satin mouth-feel. Try from 1994 to '98. (NR) (1/31/92) **93**
Romanée-St.-Vivant Les Quatre Journaux 1985 $99 (3/15/88) **98**
Romanée-St.-Vivant Les Quatre Journaux 1953 $230 (8/31/90) (TR) **94**
Vosne-Romanée Beaumonts 1985 $36 (3/15/88) **86**

LEROY
Richebourg 1988: Lean in texture, but remarkably generous in flavor. A harmonious, seamless wine, bursting with remarkably complex spice, currant, plum and berry flavors that linger on and on in an extraordinary finish. A classic Burgundy for the cellar that's already a paragon of balance and complexity. Likely best around 2000. 191 cases made. $325 (4/30/91) **96**
Romanée-St.-Vivant 1988: Despite a tightly wound, richly tannic, tart structure, this has remarkably generous flavors, including raspberry, cranberry and currant shaded by the merest hint of oak to round it out. Every sip brings out another dimension. Keep until at least 1998 to 2000. 244 cases made. $325 (4/30/91) **95**
Vosne-Romanée Les Beaux Monts 1988: A deep, concentrated wine that's richly tannic, but generous with its wild berry, spice and maple aromas and flavors. Very well constructed, finishing tart and focused. Built to keep developing through 1996 to 2000. 560 cases made. $180 (4/30/91) **93**

DOMAINE LEROY
Richebourg 1989: A captivating wine, with power and polish. Shows great concentration of fruit, yet has an incredibly silky texture and near perfect balance. Try from 1995 to '98. $306 (1/31/92) **96**

Romanée-St.-Vivant 1989: A super wine. Powerful and tannic, yet elegant and rich, with plenty of violet nuances and a superb finish. Try from 1995 to '98. $306 (1/31/92) **95**
Vosne-Romanée Les Beaux-Monts 1989: So velvety it melts in the mouth, with chestnut, pepper, vanilla and raspberry aromas and flavors. Try after 1993. $117 (1/31/92) **92**
Vosne-Romanée Les Brûlées 1989: An exquisite wine, with exuberant violet, blackberry and vanilla aromas and flavors backed by ultrafine, supple tannins. Try from 1994 to '96. $117 (1/31/92) **94**
Vosne-Romanée Les Genevrières 1989: Ripe yet subtle, with almost sweet fruit flavor and an explosive, peppery finish. Try in 1995. $75 (1/31/92) **91**

BERTRAND MACHARD DE GRAMONT
Vosne-Romanée Les Réas 1988: Pretty spice, cedar and floral notes turn to tart, tannic flavors of cherry and plum that linger and expand on the finish. Intense, tight and flavorful, but rough around the edges. Will need until at least 1995 to soften up; should repay cellaring. $32 (7/15/91) **89**

DOMAINE MEO-CAMUZET
Richebourg 1989: Smooth, seductive and profound, a gorgeous expression of Burgundian fruit flavor—currant, blackberry, black cherry and plum—shaded by vanilla, smoke and nutmeg nuances. Round and concentrated, this one just explodes across the palate, but stays light and elegant through it all. Try to wait until 1997, if you can. $270 (11/15/91) **97**
Richebourg 1988: Elegant and delicate, despite its enormous richness and concentration of flavor. The currant, cherry, plum and spice flavors gently unfold on the palate, offering one flavor after another. Has great harmony and finesse, with acidity to sustain the flavors. Drink in 1997 to 2007. $253 (11/30/90) **96**
Richebourg 1987: Very rich, round and succulent, intense as a Pinot Noir can be, yet smooth and polished enough to show off the wild berry, cherry and spice aromas and flavors to the best advantage. Worth cellaring until at least 1995, to allow the tannins to soften and allow the smoke and oak character to integrate. $165 (12/15/89) **96**
Richebourg 1986 $160 (7/31/88) **97**
Richebourg 1985 Rel: $150 Cur: $280 (3/31/88) **97**
Vosne-Romanée 1989: Ripe, supple and generous, with beautifully articulated currant, plum and blackberry aromas and flavors that dissolve into a crisp spiciness on the finish. Long and smooth; tempting to drink now, but should improve through 1996 to '99. $47 (11/15/91) **91**
Vosne-Romanée 1988: Tight and crisp, with ripe, elegant cherry, blackberry and spice notes shaded by toasty oak. Should open up nicely with time in the bottle; has plenty of tannin to cellar until 1994. $50 (12/31/90) **87**
Vosne-Romanée 1987: Offers a lot of subtlety in a beautifully fashioned, smooth-textured package radiating spicy strawberry and raspberry flavors and an overlay of toast and vanilla. Flavors echo seductively on the finish. Almost drinkable now, it has the stuff to age gracefully through at least 1994. $35 (12/15/89) **90**
Vosne-Romanée 1986 $30 (10/31/88) **88**
Vosne-Romanée Aux Brûlées 1989: Rich and supple, with the sort of lacy acidity that carries the raspberry, currant and plum flavors through the long finish in style. The sweet oak overtones never mask the fruit, and the tannins are beautifully integrated. Best after 1995. $91 (11/15/91) **94**
Vosne-Romanée Aux Brûlées 1988: Seductive with its alluring herb, tea and cherry notes, it turns very tannic and austere on the palate. There appears to be enough concentration to cellar another five years, but it may not have the depth to be outstanding. $84 (11/30/90) **89**
Vosne-Romanée Aux Brûlées 1987: Stunningly beautiful berry and spice aromas and flavors capture your attention from the first sniff right through to the velvety finish, growing richer and more elegant with every sip. Has a bit of tannin to lose on the finish, so cellaring until 1994 is called for. Delicious already. $63 (12/15/89) **95**
Vosne-Romanée Les Chaumes 1989: Ripe and smoky, with a distinct butterscotch note on the finish that adds depth to the cherry, currant and toast aromas and flavors. A full-bodied wine, with a rich texture and well-integrated tannins. Needs until 1995 to '98 to gain polish. 100 cases made. $62 (1/31/92) **91**
Vosne-Romanée Les Chaumes 1988: Extremely tight and tannic, with a solid core of smoky, chocolaty plum flavor underneath, but it will need five to seven years to begin to open and reveal its full potential. Give it until 1996 to 2000. $60 (11/30/90) **88**
Vosne-Romanée Les Chaumes 1986 $38 (12/31/88) **83**
Vosne-Romanée Les Chaumes 1985 $80 (3/31/88) **92**
Vosne-Romanée Au Cros-Parantoux 1989: Polished, elegant and beautifully spicy, a seductive wine, with a satiny texture and oodles of currant, plum and strawberry flavors that fan out across the palate and keep harmonizing on the finish. Well-integrated oak and tannin components should keep this developing through 1995 to '97. $91 (11/15/91) **95**
Vosne-Romanée Au Cros-Parantoux 1988: With great tension between the bright, vivid, cherry, currant and blackberry flavors, this is intense, richly concentrated and beautifully proportioned, with lovely toasty oak nuances. The tannins are firm but well integrated. Best to hold off until 1995. $84 (11/30/90) **94**
Vosne-Romanée Au Cros-Parantoux 1987: A powerful Burgundy with a raw edge that needs cellaring to smooth the bristly texture, but it has gorgeous cherry, spice and chocolate-toast flavors that become deeper and deeper with every sip. Drink 1995 to 2000. $63 (12/15/89) **95**
Vosne-Romanée Au Cros-Parantoux 1986 $60 (7/31/88) **93**

MOILLARD
Echézeaux 1985 $47 (4/15/88) **94**
Echézeaux 1984 Rel: $22 Cur: $30 (11/15/86) SS **96**
Grands Echézeaux 1984 $39 (5/31/87) **90**
Romanée-St.-Vivant 1984 $42 (5/31/87) **87**
Vosne-Romanée Malconsorts 1984 Rel: $21 Cur: $28 (12/15/86) CS **95**
Vosne-Romanée Malconsorts Domaine Thomas-Moillard 1989: Heady perfumes are followed by great concentration of black cherry, cedar and rose petal notes. The seductive, elegant, firm finish goes on and on. Try in 1995. (NR) (1/31/92) **93**
Vosne-Romanée Malconsorts Domaine Thomas-Moillard 1988: Ultratight and hard-edged, with firm, dry tannins and rich, concentrated berry, cherry and weedy anise flavors that are going to need years to evolve and soften. Best to cellar until 1997 or '98. $50 (3/31/91) **88**
Vosne-Romanée Malconsorts Domaine Thomas-Moillard 1987: Richly perfumed, ripe and elegant, with concentration and power to spare, balanced and flavorful. The black cherry, plum and toast flavors just sail on and on, making it delicious to drink now, but it has the tannin to keep developing through 1995 at least. 1,000 cases made. $30 (8/31/89) **91**
Vosne-Romanée Malconsorts Domaine Thomas-Moillard 1986 $29 (10/31/88) **88**
Vosne-Romanée Malconsorts Domaine Thomas-Moillard 1985 $38 (7/31/88) **95**

MOMMESSIN
Echézeaux 1989 (NR) (7/15/90) (BT) **80+**
Echézeaux 1979 $18 (2/16/86) **86**
Vosne-Romanée Aux Brûlées 1989: A textbook Burgundy, with all the wild raspberry, black cherry and smoke character you could want. Try in 1993. $38 (1/31/92) **89**

CHARLES MONCAUT
Vosne-Romanée Cuvée Particulière 1983 $16 (9/15/86) **62**

MONGEARD-MUGNERET
Echézeaux 1984 $28 (2/15/88) **68**
Echézeaux Vieille Vigne 1989: A benchmark Burgundy, with sweet fruit flavors and smoky notes that gain complexity in the mouth and on the supple finish. Try after 1995. $59 (1/31/92) **93**
Echézeaux Vieille Vigne 1988: Ripe, round and definitely oaky, offering plenty of toast- and chocolate-tinged dark cherry aromas and flavors. Tight and tannic enough to need until 1994 to '97 to shed excess astringency. The high level of oak could be bothersome. $61 (2/15/91) **88**
Echézeaux Vieille Vigne 1987: Smoky, toasty aromas are concentrated and there is good cherry flavor, in an intense but light and lively style. Has fine structure for short-term aging. Drink now to '95. $42 (5/15/90) **86**
Echézeaux Vieille Vigne 1986 $44 (8/31/89) **90**
Grands Echézeaux 1989: This exquisite style has layers of vanilla, smoke and plum, silky tannins and fresh acidity on the finish. Try from 1994 to '98. $95 (1/31/92) **93**
Grands Echézeaux 1987: Stiffly structured, built for aging till 1993 to '97, with concentrated cherry, toast and spice flavors. Somewhat complex already, it should develop more with time in the cellar. $65 (5/15/90) **85**
Grands Echézeaux 1986: Ripe and generous on the nose, lean and balanced on the palate, showing typical black cherry and toast aromas and flavors, long and complex on the finish. It has a sense of restraint that just adds to the finesse. Cellar at least until 1993. $73 (8/31/89) **92**
Richebourg 1989: Approachable, with a textbook Richebourg satin character. Offers plenty of earth, chocolate and fruit flavors. Try from 1994 to '96. $95 (1/31/92) **92**
Richebourg 1985 $123 (3/15/88) **92**
Vosne-Romanée 1989: Pretty and aromatic, with strawberry and cherry aromas and flavors and just enough supple tannins to make it nice to try around 1993. $34 (1/31/92) **85**
Vosne-Romanée 1986: Meaty in flavor and texture, with a hard edge of tannin that ought to keep the wine developing well at least through 1993. Generous, spicy and a bit earthy, despite its light color. $26 (8/31/89) **79**
Vosne-Romanée Les Orveaux 1989: Well crafted and velvety, with everything in the right place, packed with black cherry and berry flavors, modest smoke and licorice notes and a long finish. Try in 1995. $43 (1/31/92) **94**
Vosne-Romanée Les Orveaux 1987: Very light color, with animallike aromas and flavors that shoulder past the candied strawberry flavors. Not very likable. Tasted twice with consistent results. $35 (7/15/90) **62**
Vosne-Romanée Les Orveaux 1986: Lean and tart, but there is a generous beam of raspberry fruit with overtones of rhubarb and nutmeg that keep it interesting. Needs time to soften up, perhaps until 1993. $34 (8/31/89) **82**
Vosne-Romanée Les Orveaux 1985 $32 (3/15/88) **82**
Vosne-Romanée Les Orveaux 1984 $18 (2/15/88) **68**
Vosne-Romanée Les Petits Monts 1987: Tarry, anise and smoky aromas obscure what little cherry aromas and flavors are present. Light in color and texture; best to drink after 1993. $35 (4/30/90) **74**
Vosne-Romanée Les Suchots 1987: A tart style, but very spicy and complex, from the first whiff of toast and cinnamon to the last echo of strawberry and nutmeg. A lean wine that will need until 1993 to '94 to soften up. $35 (6/15/90) **82**

GERARD MUGNERET
Vosne-Romanée 1988: Austere and tannic, with a solid core of cherry and strawberry flavor. The tannins and structure are firm and drying; this will need until 1994 or '95 to soften. $37 (2/28/91) **86**
Vosne-Romanée 1987: A pleasant, simple wine, offering attractive berry and cassis aromas and flavors, a lean, firm structure and fairly impressive length. Drink now to '93. $32 (7/15/90) **79**
Vosne-Romanée Les Suchots 1988: Very dry and tannic, with austere cherry and spice flavors. The finish gets too dry for us. With time the fruit may show through; hold until 1994. $57 (2/28/91) **84**
Vosne-Romanée Les Suchots 1987: A light and attractive wine, with spicy cranberry and cassis aromas and flavors. Drink now. $42 (7/15/90) **82**

RENE MUGNERET
Vosne-Romanée 1985 $27 (4/30/88) **90**
Vosne-Romanée 1983 $16 (11/16/85) **73**
Vosne-Romanée 1982 $17 (7/16/85) **86**

MUGNERET-GIBOURG
Echézeaux 1989: Tight and slightly tannic for its modest size, with nice raspberry and currant aromas and flavors winding through the long finish. Has the goods to improve with cellaring through 1995 to '97, and needs the time to soften. $62 (4/30/92) **88**
Echézeaux 1988: Lean and sharply focused, with a beam of raspberry flavor shining right through the long-lasting finish. Needs time to flesh out the texture, but for now the tart acidity and hard-edged tannins prevail. Try after 1993 to '95. $70 (11/15/90) **89**
Echézeaux 1987: Gorgeous fruit and toasty oak flavors make this one especially attractive. The cherry, plum and spicy flavors are rich, deep, long and full on the palate with a measure of elegance and finesse. Tannic finish, but the fruit fights through. Drink 1993 to '98. 500 cases made. $50 (10/15/89) **93**
Echézeaux 1986 $55 (11/30/88) **83**
Echézeaux 1985 $57 (2/29/88) **93**
Echézeaux 1984 $32 (3/15/87) **85**
Vosne-Romanée 1989: Very light in color and extremely tart, offering tightly packed raspberry and strawberry flavors that never quite take off. Seems too harsh and thin to improve, but cellaring until 1996 to '98 could help. $34 (4/30/92) **81**
Vosne-Romanée 1988: Tough, hard and austere, like a highly filtered, overly acidic wine that lacks fruit and charm. May have very limited appeal. Tasted twice. $34 (12/31/90) **64**
Vosne-Romanée 1987: Tight, firm and concentrated with firm tannins framing the rich, complex cherry and plum flavors. This wine has fine cellaring potential. It needs time for the tannins to soften. Best around 1993 to '98. 1,400 cases made. $30 (10/15/89) **90**
Vosne-Romanée 1986 $33 (12/31/88) **81**
Vosne-Romanée 1985 $33 (2/29/88) **85**

B. MUGNERET-GOUACHON
Echézeaux 1985 $29 (12/31/88) **91**

A. PERNIN-ROSSIN
Vosne-Romanée 1986 $31 (2/28/89) **61**

REMOISSENET
Echézeaux 1985 $73 (3/15/88) **75**
Richebourg 1985 $138 (3/15/88) **91**
Vosne-Romanée Clos de Réas 1949 $138 (8/31/90) (TR) **95**
Vosne-Romanée Les Suchots 1985 $75 (3/15/88) **91**

DOMAINE DANIEL RION
Vosne-Romanée 1989: Quite complex, with plenty of smoky plum, cedar and berry aromas and flavors and supple tannins. Try from 1993. $37 (1/31/92) **89**
Vosne-Romanée 1987: Beautifully focused and elegant, with generous herb-scented raspberry and vanilla aromas and flavors that are immediately likable. Drink now or by 1993. $21 (4/30/90) **89**
Vosne-Romanée 1986: Very fragrant, lean and somewhat tannic, but the gentle strawberry, floral and spicy flavors push their way through the tannin. Should develop well at least through 1994. $31 (4/30/89) **87**
Vosne-Romanée 1985 $28 (2/29/88) **78**
Vosne-Romanée 1983 $19 (2/01/86) **63**
Vosne-Romanée Beaux-Monts 1989: Very distinctive, with earthy black cherry, mushroom and leaf aromas and flavors. Try in 1993. $63 (1/31/92) **90**
Vosne-Romanée Beaux-Monts 1988: Fruit aromas and flavors jump out of the glass, then carry through the long finish of this crisp-structured, brightly flavorful wine. The tannins are integrated enough to show off the raspberry and red cherry flavors. Drink after 1994. 275 cases made. $53 (2/15/91) **92**
Vosne-Romanée Beaux-Monts 1986: Plummy and generous, velvety, remarkably concentrated and long and artfully balanced with sweet new oak. The fruit wins in the end, and it should develop well at least through 1994. $43 (4/30/89) **91**
Vosne-Romanée Beaux-Monts 1985 Rel: $38 Cur: $55 (2/29/88) **95**

FRANCE

Burgundy Red/*Côte de Nuits*/Vosne-Romanée

Vosne-Romanée Les Chaumes 1989: Silky and classy, with strawberry, cherry and smoke aromas and flavors and firm, yet seamless tannins. Try after 1993. $63 (1/31/92) **92**

Vosne-Romanée Les Chaumes 1988: Sharply focused, with intense cassis, black cherry, currant and spice flavors and plenty of tannin for cellaring. The acidity is firm and austere, giving this wine excellent structure, and on the finish the fruit spills over. Hold until 1995 or '96. 225 cases made. $54 (1/31/91) **93**

Vosne-Romanée Les Chaumes 1987: In the lighter style, firm, tart and tight, with sharply focused cherry and toast aromas and flavors, clean and very long. Drink now to 1993. $35 (4/30/90) **88**

Vosne-Romanée Les Chaumes 1986 Rel: $47 Cur: $54 (4/30/89) CS **93**

DOMAINE DE LA ROMANEE-CONTI

Echézeaux 1988: Tannic and flavorful, if not quite as focused as some of the other *grands crus*, hinting at plum and cherry flavors with echoes of vanilla, tea and cedar notes on the finish. Has the depth and dimension to age gracefully. Needs until 1995 to '98 to soften. 1,730 cases made. $225 (4/30/91) **92**

Echézeaux 1987: Most forward of the DRCs, with beautiful aromas of currant, berries and spices that fairly leap out of the glass then hang on to the long finish. Tannic, tart and tightly wound, but so focused and concentrated that it has to be great after cellaring until 1993 to '97. $98 (9/30/90) **92**

Echézeaux 1986: A complete, elegant wine, playing ripe cherry and berry flavor against the toasty vanilla overtones of oak, it's round and smooth, opening out into a lovely finish. Persistent and harmonious. Almost drinkable now, but better after 1993. Rel: $110 Cur: $171 (8/31/89) **92**

Echézeaux 1985 Rel: $95 Cur: $140 (2/29/88) **96**

Echézeaux 1984 Rel: $52 Cur: $82 (2/28/87) **90**

Echézeaux 1983 Rel: $75 Cur: $88 (11/30/86) **63**

Echézeaux 1952 $125 (8/31/90) (TR) **97**

Grands Echézeaux 1988: Deep and concentrated, with lots of smoky nutmeg and tea overtones to the core of plum and cherry flavor, hinting at violet on the nose. Very firm and tannic; will need until 2000 to soften. Should age well. 1,000 cases made. $315 (4/30/91) **92**

Grands Echézeaux 1987: Tannins keep the sharply focused raspberry and cherry flavors in check, but the meaty currant flavors that emerge on the finish bode well. Cellar until at least 1994 to '96. $145 (9/30/90) **89**

Grands Echézeaux 1986: Tight and concentrated, built around firm tannins and acidity that frame beautifully focused and complex cherry, raspberry and plum fruit against sweet vanilla and toast. Tastes as if it can develop at least through 1999, which ought to take the edge of tannin off enough to let the complete character emerge. $160 (8/31/89) **94**

Grands Echézeaux 1985 Rel: $140 Cur: $183 (2/29/88) **94**

Grands Echézeaux 1984 Rel: $64 Cur: $85 (2/28/87) **88**

Grands Echézeaux 1983 $100 (11/30/86) **64**

Grands Echézeaux 1942 $230 (8/31/90) (TR) **93**

Richebourg 1988: Tight and beautifully focused, with a laser beam of plum, raspberry and tart cherry flavor, hinting at cola and spice around the edges, nailed in place by lavish tannins and sharp acidity. It's an age-worthy package, already showing a glimmer of silky texture, but definitely not to be touched before 1998 to 2000. 1,000 cases made. $400 (4/30/91) **94**

Richebourg 1987: A firm, rich and tannic style, with very complex and enticing flavors of smoked bacon, cherry, spice and earth that are tightly concentrated and in need of another five to seven years' cellaring. The tannins on the finish are very firm but not biting. Should be a classic after 1997 to 2001. $190 (9/30/90) **93**

Richebourg 1986: Very firm and deeply concentrated, but wrapped in enough tannin to need at least until 1995 to begin emerging from its shell. Already has great finesse and structure, echoing ripe cherry and sweet spices on the long but tannic finish. $230 (8/31/89) **94**

Richebourg 1985 Rel: $210 Cur: $320 (2/29/88) **100**

Richebourg 1984 $102 (2/28/87) **91**

Richebourg 1983 $150 (11/30/86) **52**

Richebourg 1954 $175 (8/31/90) (TR) **88**

Richebourg 1947 $750 (8/31/90) (TR) **65**

Romanée-Conti 1988: A seductive wine, with a firm backbone of tannin and acidity, this offers tremendously generous spice, floral and plum aromas and a fleshy texture that allows the finish to echo fruit, tea and spice flavors on the extraordinarily long finish. Already displays tremendous depth, and can only gain with cellaring through at least 1998. 536 cases made. $600 (4/30/91) **98**

Romanée-Conti 1987: So tough and tannic that you almost don't notice the currant and cranberry flavors. Very tightly wound and marked by new oak, this wine will need until 1995 to 2000 to show what it can be. Worth betting on because of the track record, but it's so backward it's hard to tell now. Rel: $350 Cur: $580 (9/30/90) **89**

Romanée-Conti 1986: Incredibly subtle, lean and tart, the gorgeous red cherry, plum and cedar flavors already emerging from behind a screen of tannin that will need until 1993 to begin to soften toward drinkability. Has the generosity to warrant the cellaring, and the grace and harmony to become a lovely wine. Rel: $400 Cur: $600 (8/31/89) **95**

Romanée-Conti 1985 Rel: $375 Cur: $1,100 (1/31/90) (JS) **99**

Romanée-Conti 1984 $640 (1/31/90) (JS) **94**

Romanée-Conti 1983 Rel: $250 Cur: $650 (1/31/90) (JS) **78**

Romanée-Conti 1982 $450 (1/31/90) (JS) **85**

Romanée-Conti 1979 $790 (1/31/90) (JS) **90**

Romanée-Conti 1978 $1,330 (1/31/90) (JS) **95**

Romanée-Conti 1975 $680 (1/31/90) (JS) **82**

Romanée-Conti 1964 $950 (1/31/90) (JS) **98**

Romanée-Conti 1963 $1,100 (1/31/90) (JS) **50**

Romanée-Conti 1959 $1,600 (1/31/90) (JS) **68**

Romanée-Conti 1953 $2,000 (1/31/90) (JS) **93**

Romanée-Conti 1937 $1,950 (12/15/88) **94**

Romanée-Conti 1935 $700 (1/31/90) (JS) **50**

Romanée-Conti 1934 $1,800 (1/31/90) (JS) **66**

Romanée-Conti 1929 $2,100 (1/31/90) (JS) **50**

Romanée-St.-Vivant 1988: A magical wine that's rich and amazingly complex in aroma and flavor. Firmly tannic, but so generous that it seems smooth and silky, with aromas and flavors that lean toward plum, berry, spice and vanilla. It's a classic in every way. Will need until 2000 to 2005 to show all it has. 1,600 cases made. $360 (4/30/91) **97**

Romanée-St.-Vivant 1987: Very firm and tight, but spicy plum, cinnamon, currant and other fruit flavors emerge from the tart, somewhat tannic package. Not a big wine, but it needs until 1994 to '96 at the earliest to show what it has. $175 (9/30/90) **89**

Romanée-St.-Vivant 1986: Indescribably concentrated and elegant at the same time, starting off deceptively smooth and gentle, then building up the intensity and vibrancy until it climaxes to a sensational finish that echoes cherry, tobacco, berry and vanilla seemingly forever. Tannic enough to need until at least 1995 to soften. $195 (8/31/89) **98**

Romanée-St.-Vivant 1985 $175 (2/29/88) **88**

Romanée-St.-Vivant 1984 Rel: $70 Cur: $89 (2/28/87) **96**

Romanée-St.-Vivant 1983 $125 (11/30/86) **66**

La Tâche 1988: Particularly flavorful, focused and generous, with a smooth texture and beautifully integrated tannins to support the well-defined cherry, raspberry, nutmeg, vanilla and smoke flavors. Nothing sticks out in this harmonious, vibrant wine. Needs until 1995 to '99 to grow into itself. 1,680 cases made. $450 (4/30/91) **98**

La Tâche 1987: Tannins are the most prevalent characteristic now, but the meaty coffee and chocolate nuances indicate this has the potential to emerge as a complex, subtle, spicy, almost delicate wine. Has a sense of weightless concentration. Cellar until at least 1995 to '97. $225 (9/30/90) **92**

La Tâche 1986: A magical wine, as elegant as we have tasted, loaded with complex aromas and flavors of cherry, currant, blackberry and cedar, all of which mesh together with subtlety. A triumph in every way. Try to wait until 1995 or 2000 to drink it. 2,000 cases made. $250 (8/31/89) CS **98**

La Tâche 1985 Rel: $225 Cur: $360 (2/29/88) **98**

La Tâche 1984 Rel: $105 Cur: $160 (2/28/87) **95**

La Tâche 1983 Rel: $150 Cur: $195 (11/30/86) **61**

EMMANUEL ROUGET

Echézeaux 1989: Ripe, rich and effusively fruity, with layers of plum, currant, and black cherry flavors that are intense and concentrated. Finishes with a long aftertaste and hints of vanilla and toasty oak. Has plenty of tannin for cellaring through 1998. $98 (11/15/91) **93**

Echézeaux 1988: A plush texture and expansive berry and cassis aromas and flavors make this immediately appealing. The complexity develops on the long finish in layer after layer; it's obvious this is going to be a great wine. The length is stunning and it's tempting already, but give it until at least 1995 to mature. 200 cases made. $81 (11/15/90) **96**

Echézeaux 1987: Light in color, but packed with cherry and strawberry flavors framed by sweet oak and enough tannin to require until 1993 to '94 to subside. It is the fruit that is so appealing in this wine. $55 (3/31/90) **88**

Echézeaux 1986 $55 (12/31/88) **87**

Vosne-Romanée 1989: Smooth and generous, with lovely currant, plum and black cherry aromas and flavors that keep giving on the long finish. A supple, elegant wine, with tannins that are well integrated enough to drink now, but should continue to improve through 1995 to '98. $48 (11/15/91) **91**

Vosne-Romanée 1987: One of the sleepers of this vintage. Lovely strawberry, plum, and black cherry flavors hang elegantly on a supple structure, ample and generous yet held in restraint by just the right touch of tannin. Well made and concentrated. Cellar until 1993 to '94. $32 (3/31/90) **91**

Vosne-Romanée Les Beaumonts 1986 $40 (12/31/88) **89**

Vosne-Romanée Cros Parantoux 1989: This crisp, lively wine bursts onto the palate, with juicy currant, cherry and blackberry flavors that keep pumping through the long, fairly tart finish. Balanced for the long haul, with the tannins pretty well submerged. Best after 1995. $83 (11/15/91) **94**

ARMAND ROUX

Echézeaux 1959 $110 (8/31/90) (TR) **94**

Richebourg 1959 $130 (8/31/90) (TR) **91**

Vougeot

ROBERT ARNOUX

Clos Vougeot 1988: Earthy, aromatic, flavorful and a bit drying on the finish, with gamy flavors tending to overshadow the ripe cherry and berry notes. Turns tough on the aftertaste and doesn't seem to have the richness to balance the tannins. Try after 1995. Tasted twice. $70 (3/15/91) **78**

THOMAS BASSOT

Clos de Vougeot 1942 ($NA) (8/31/90) (TR) **84**

DOMAINE BERTAGNA

Vougeot Clos de la Perrière 1985: Bursting with spicy plum and cherry flavor on a lean and elegant frame, already smoothing out to a velvety texture. A bit short compared to others, but very tasty and pleasant. Drink now through 1995. $40 (4/15/89) **87**

Vougeot Les Crâs 1985 $30 (3/31/88) **85**

BOUCHARD PERE & FILS

Clos de Vougeot 1959 $120 (8/31/90) (TR) **85**

CAPTAIN-GAGNEROT

Clos Vougeot 1985 $67 (12/31/88) **86**

GUY CASTAGNIER

Clos de Vougeot 1989: Tightly structured, with vivid strawberry and berry aromas, but a little light on fruit. Needs time; try after 1994. $64 (1/31/92) **85**

Clos de Vougeot 1988: Good and fruity, with berry and cherry flavors accented by earthy, brown sugar notes. Has a firm structure. Solid and enjoyable; try in about 1994. $65 (8/31/91) **86**

DOMAINE CECI

Clos de Vougeot 1988: Ripe and spicy, with opulent vanilla-, cedar- and nutmeg-scented plum and currant aromas and flavors. Smooth and elegant, with subtle rose petal and chocolate hints on the finish. Tasty now, but should be at its best after 1996 to '98. 212 cases made. $48 (7/15/91) **93**

Clos de Vougeot 1987: Concentrated, focused cherry and toast aromas and flavors are carried home over a firm-textured, solid structure. Lots of flavor and structure, but it needs cellaring to soften its edges. Drink now or hold. $40 (3/31/90) **82**

F. CHAUVENET

Clos de Vougeot 1989: Ripe in a seductive way, with strawberry, spice and earth aromas and flavors and medium-firm tannins. Try after 1994. $60 (1/31/92) **90**

Clos de Vougeot 1986 $57 (12/31/88) **79**

CHOPIN-GROFFIER

Clos Vougeot 1989: This wine shows how Clos Vougeot should be. Multidimensional, with masses of chocolate, spice and fruit flavors and lots of supple tannins. Try after 1994. $72 (1/31/92) **94**

Clos Vougeot 1988: Spicy, with lots of nutmeg and anise aromas and flavors to go along with a tough core of currant and cherry flavors. Could be more generous. Needs until 1995 to '98 to become polished. $70 (5/15/91) **87**

Vougeot 1989: Polished and seductive, with plenty of violet, cherry, cedar and fruit aromas and flavors and ultrafine tannins on the finish. Try after 1993. $32 (1/31/92) **93**

Vougeot 1988: Ripe and generous, with lots of blackberry and black cherry aromas and flavors shaded by smoke, nutmeg and a delicate touch of earthiness. Has the intensity and complexity to age well; keep until 1995 to '97. Reasonably priced; not the *grand cru*. 200 cases made. $32 (5/15/91) **92**

DOMAINE DU CLOS FRANTIN

Clos de Vougeot 1989: Has great class, with wonderful blackberry and cherry flavors and silky, super-firm tannins. Extremely well crafted. Try after 1994. $56 (1/31/92) **91**

Clos de Vougeot 1987: A smoky, earthy and complex wine that's a bit austere on the palate, but the butter, nut and vanilla aromas and flavors have an immediate appeal. The length and complexity indicate that it should be fine after 1993 to '95. $56 (7/15/90) **85**

Clos de Vougeot 1986 $37 (11/30/88) **87**

Key to Symbols

The scores reported here are the results of blind tastings conducted by our panel of senior editors. Wines that carry the initials below are results of individual tastings.

THE WINE SPECTATOR 100-POINT SCALE 95-100—Classic, a great wine; ***90-94***—Outstanding, superior character and style; ***80-89***—Good to very good, a wine with special qualities; ***70-79***—Average, drinkable wine that may have minor flaws; ***60-69***—Below average, drinkable but not recommended; ***50-59***—Poor, undrinkable, not recommended. "+"—With a score indicates a range; used primarily with barrel tastings to indicate a preliminary score.

SPECIAL DESIGNATIONS SS—Spectator Selection, CS—Cellar Selection, BB—Best Buy, ($NA)—Price not available, (NR)—Not released.

TASTER'S INITIALS (JG)—Jim Gordon, (HS)—Harvey Steiman, (JL)—James Laube, (JS)—James Suckling, (TM)—Thomas Matthews, (TR)—Terry Robards, (PM)—Per-Henrik Mansson, (BT)—Barrel Tasting (these wines were tasted blind from barrel samples), (CA-date)—*California's Great Cabernets* by James Laube, (CH-date)—*California's Great Chardonnays* by James Laube, (VP-date)—*Vintage Port* by James Suckling.

DATE TASTED Dates in parentheses represent the issue in which the rating was published.

JOSEPH DROUHIN
Clos de Vougeot 1988: Ripe cherry and smoke aromas and flavors promise a wine of richness and depth once the tough tannins soften, perhaps after 1995. Has sharply defined flavors, elegance and the intensity to age well. $85 (2/15/91) **90**
Clos de Vougeot 1986: An impressive '86 for its richness and depth and tannin, but there's a rich core of black cherry flavor with spice and toast on the finish. Begin drinking now. $55 (4/15/89) **86**
Clos de Vougeot 1985 $57 (11/15/87) **94**

ROBERT DROUHIN
Clos de Vougeot 1989: Has plenty of richness in a traditional style, with plummy, lightly stemmy aromas and flavors and mouth-coating tannins. Try from 1994. $88 (1/31/92) **89**

DROUHIN-LAROZE
Clos de Vougeot 1988: Ripe and aromatic on the nose, with lots of spicy oak aromas to round it out. Turns a bit tough and tannic on the palate, perhaps from an overdose of oak, but plenty of ripe cherry and plum flavors come through on the finish. Give it until at least 1994. $81 (12/31/90) **89**
Clos de Vougeot 1987: A pleasant wine, with charming plum and cherry aromas and flavors, simple structure and enough backbone to permit cellaring until 1993 to '94. $38 (3/31/90) **79**
Clos de Vougeot 1985 $60 (10/15/88) **88**

RENE ENGEL
Clos Vougeot 1989: Firm in texture, but generous in flavor, with a ripe currant and blackberry character that manages to make its presence felt despite a formidable frame of hard tannins. Definitely a wine for the cellar; try after 1997. $66 (11/15/91) **85**
Clos Vougeot 1988: Rich, full-bodied and tannic, yet elegant underneath it all, showing lots of violet- and smoke-tinged plum and berry flavors that persist into the long finish. A bit tart and closed-in; will need until 1995 to '98 to soften. 500 cases made. $75 (3/15/91) **91**
Clos Vougeot 1986 $50 (11/30/88) **81**
Clos Vougeot 1985 $43 (10/15/87) **85**
Clos Vougeot 1983 $30 (2/16/86) **80**

FAIVELEY
Clos de Vougeot 1989: Good and straightforward, with nice plum and earth flavors and firm tannins. Try after 1993. $78 (1/31/92) **85**
Clos de Vougeot 1988 $92 (7/15/90) (BT) **90+**

JEAN GRIVOT
Clos de Vougeot 1988: Tart, firm and spicy, this well-structured wine should smooth out nicely if cellared until 1994 or later. Tasted twice. $70 (4/30/91) **85**
Clos de Vougeot 1985 $62 (4/30/88) **81**

DOMAINE GROS FRERE & SOEUR
Clos Vougeot Musigny 1989: Offers an impressive concentration of fruit and tannins. The smoke, berry and violet aromas and flavors are superb, and very classy. Try in 1993. $60 (1/31/92) **91**
Clos Vougeot Musigny 1988: With pretty aromas of rose petal, plum and cherry and similar flavors, this rich, complex, well-integrated wine oozes with flavor. The toasty oak notes add dimension, the acidity is crisp and lively and the tannins are firm, but fine. Start drinking in 1996 or '97. Tasted twice. 100 cases made. $95 (3/31/91) **92**
Clos Vougeot Musigny 1985 $70 (3/31/88) **75**

A.-F. GROS
Clos Vougeot Le Grand Maupertuis 1989: Excellent and understated, with toasty berry and plum flavors and silky tannins. Try in 1993. (NR) (1/31/92) **90**

HAEGELEN-JAYER
Clos Vougeot 1988: Gamy, animal aromas and flavors are not for us, although modest plum and cherry flavors peek through. Turns a bit tough and stemmy on the finish. $69 (5/15/91) **73**
Clos Vougeot 1985 $64 (4/15/88) **90**

CHATEAU DES HERBEUX
Clos Vougeot 1988: Firm and concentrated, with flavors that lean more toward smoke and spice than fruit, although the black cherry character makes its presence felt against the tannic finish. Needs cellaring to tame the tannins. Try in 1994 to '96. $65 (11/30/90) **86**

LOUIS JADOT
Clos Vougeot 1989: Refined and aromatic, with an iron backbone of tannins, but a little light on fruit. Try in 1993. $74 (1/31/92) **87**
Clos Vougeot 1988: Extremely earthy and tannic, with a rustic, barnyardy character overriding the modest cherry flavors. Acceptable in quality, but some may find it too earthy. Tasted twice. $68 (11/15/91) **73**
Clos Vougeot 1986: Has pretty black cherry and berry flavor, good intensity and depth for an '86, and enough tannin for three to five years' cellaring. Drink now or hold. $50 (4/15/89) **87**
Clos Vougeot 1985 Rel: $53 Cur: $85 (3/31/88) **82**

JAFFELIN
Clos de Vougeot 1989: Distinctive, with chestnut, berry and cherry flavors and a rich structure of fruit and tannins. Try in 1993. $60 (1/31/92) **89**
Clos de Vougeot 1986 $45 (12/31/88) **77**
Clos de Vougeot 1985 $49 (6/15/88) **96**

J. LABET & N. DECHELETTE
Clos Vougeot Château de la Tour 1989 $77 (7/15/90) (BT) **85+**
Clos Vougeot Château de la Tour 1988: Smells sensational, offering bouquets of roses, truffles and cherry all tightly wrapped in tannin. Has the power and grace to age beautifully, but give it at least until 1995 to 2000 to soften the hardness. $50 (11/30/90) **91**
Clos Vougeot Château de la Tour 1987: Aromatic in a decadent sort of way, leaning toward tea, herb and orange peel aromas and flavors. Tannic and flavorful, with a polished texture, but not for fans of fruity Burgundy. Should be drinkable in 1993. Tasted twice. $50 (2/15/91) **84**
Clos Vougeot Château de la Tour 1985 $53 (6/15/88) **90**
Clos Vougeot Château de la Tour 1979 $40 (9/01/84) **66**

DOMAINE FRANCOIS LAMARCHE
Clos de Vougeot 1987: Plenty of barnyardy Burgundian aromas add to the light cherry, tea and spice notes in this elegant wine. Like many '87s, it lacks a core of rich concentrated fruit flavors, but it still has plenty of flavor and intrigue. Drink now to '95. $55 (9/30/90) **86**
Clos de Vougeot 1985 $48 (10/15/88) **90**

LEROY
Clos de Vougeot 1988: Lean and tough, with tart balance, firm tannins and good concentration of wild cherry and plum flavors that persist through a long finish. Has a hint of volatile acidity, but generally is just rough enough to need until 1996 to 2000 to soften. 500 cases made. $260 (4/30/91) **89**

DOMAINE LEROY
Clos de Vougeot 1989: Clos Vougeot at its best; a massive wine that has everything, including incredible finesse and class. Try from 1994. $193 (1/31/92) **95**

DOMAINE MEO-CAMUZET
Clos de Vougeot 1989: Tough in texture, but ripe and generous, with currant and cherry flavors persisting into a long finish. The fruit wins over the tannins at the end. Should continue to develop well through 1996. 650 cases made. $91 (11/15/91) CS **94**
Clos de Vougeot 1988: Offers opulent black cherry, blackberry, spice and toast aromas and flavors, tightly wrapped in firm tannins, that are graceful to the last echo. Give it until 1994 to '97 to open up. $95 (11/30/90) **92**
Clos de Vougeot 1986 $55 (11/30/88) **91**
Clos de Vougeot 1985 Rel: $65 Cur: $101 (3/31/88) **93**

MOILLARD
Clos de Vougeot 1984 $32 (5/31/87) **90**
Clos de Vougeot 1983 Rel: $26 Cur: $45 (10/16/85) CS **95**

MONGEARD-MUGNERET
Clos de Vougeot 1989: A delicate wine, with lovely, toasty berry and earth flavors and gentle tannins. Try in 1993. $77 (1/31/92) **87**
Clos de Vougeot 1987: Smooth and elegant, with modest raspberry, chocolate and vanilla aromas and flavors, touched by hints of cinnamon. A pleasant wine, with firm tannins to keep it in the cellar at least through 1993 to '95. $53 (5/15/90) **81**
Clos de Vougeot 1986: An abundance of smoke, tannin and spice dominates now but with enough fruit concentration for balance. The fruit fights through on the finish, matching the tannin stride for stride. $56 (7/31/89) **87**
Vougeot Les Crâs 1989: A delicate wine, with understated fruit and supple tannins that build and build on the finish. Try after 1994. (NR) (1/31/92) **93**

CHARLES MORTET
Clos de Vougeot 1989: Firm and fruity, with pleasant berry and spice aromas and flavors and a hard edge of tannin that needs until 1997 to '99 to soften. Has style and intensity. $47 (1/31/92) **86**
Clos Vougeot 1986: A wine with pretty cherry and spice flavors that are lean and astringent, showing signs of complexity and depth. Drink now to '94. $43 (4/15/89) **84**

GEORGES MUGNERET
Clos Vougeot 1988: Tart, chewy, tannic and drying on the finish, but showing enough strawberry, lime and clay aromas and flavors to suggest that cellaring until 1996 to '98 will chisel away at the tannins and let the flavors come through. For now, it's awfully tough. $90 (11/15/90) **84**
Clos Vougeot 1987: Supple and concentrated with rich, ripe cherry and spice flavors that are framed with firm tannins and a smoky aftertaste that lingers. Can stand cellaring. Drink 1994 to '98. 135 cases made. $68 (10/15/89) **91**
Clos Vougeot 1986 $73 (11/30/88) **90**

HENRI REBOURSEAU
Clos de Vougeot 1983 $25 (11/16/85) **49**

DOMAINE DANIEL RION
Clos Vougeot 1989: Subtle yet powerful, with focused cherry, berry and cedar aromas and flavors and a bounty of silky tannins. Try after 1994. $94 (1/31/92) **92**
Clos Vougeot 1988: Young and intense, with tightly compact fruit. The cassis, blackberry, currant and spice flavors are so tightly wound that it may take another five to seven years to reach maturity. Start drinking in 1996 to '98, but even then it may be too young. 175 cases made. $75 (1/31/91) **92**
Clos Vougeot 1986 $70 (4/15/89) **90**

RION PERE & FILS
Clos Vougeot 1987: Hard, firm, tannic and oaky, this is a wine that will require patience for the fruit to emerge. Hints of cherry, spice and plum come through, but they're dominated by the wood and tannins. Balanced and well made on the finish. Best to cellar until 1993. $48 (11/15/90) **86**

DOMAINE G. ROUMIER
Clos Vougeot 1989: Sneaks up on you, with freshly picked cherry and berry flavors, silky tannins and a medium finish. Try after 1994. $62 (1/31/92) **87**

JEAN TARDY
Clos de Vougeot 1987: A hard, astringent wine, tart and thin on the palate, although the red cherry flavor manages to sneak through, suggesting it may get better with cellaring until 1993 to '95. $49 (3/31/90) **70**

Other Côte de Nuits Red

BERTRAND AMBROISE
Côte de Nuits-Villages 1989: A wine with pure fruit, framed by lovely blackberry, strawberry and cedar aromas and flavors and firm tannins. Better from 1994. $20 (1/31/92) **86**

MAISON AMBROISE
Côte de Nuits-Villages 1987: Very firm and ripe, with a stiff backbone of tannin and generous black cherry and smoke aromas and flavors. Has the depth to develop with cellaring until 1993 to '94. $15 (2/28/90) **82**

DOMAINE DE L'ARLOT
Côte de Nuits-Villages Clos du Châpeau 1989: Straightforward, with focused strawberry and cherry flavors and light tannins. Drink now. (NR) (1/31/92) **83**
Côte de Nuits-Villages Clos du Châpeau 1988: Smells funky, with more tea leaf and herb overtones than we care for, but it tastes fine, with a lean texture, nicely focused strawberry flavors and hints of vanilla on the finish. Drinkable now. $21 (3/31/91) **80**

JEAN CLAUDE BOISSET
Côte de Nuits-Villages 1983 $13 (2/01/86) **78**

CHARLOPIN-PARIZOT
Marsannay en Montchenovoy 1990: Crisp and berrylike, but with enough flesh to bring out the smooth, polished texture. Balanced and appealing, with simple, refreshing flavors that are more like Beaujolais than Burgundy. Drinkable now, but better around 1993. $19 (4/30/92) **84**

A. CHOPIN
Côte de Nuits-Villages 1985 $9 (10/31/87) BB **83**

DOMAINE BRUNO CLAIR
Marsannay 1988: Crisp and spicy, with pleasant strawberry and nutmeg flavors and slightly earthy overtones. A lean wine that should be charming by 1993 or '94. $16 (11/15/91) **80**
Marsannay Les Longeroies 1989: Very focused, with fresh raspberry and strawberry aromas and a very firm structure. Shows great potential. Try from 1993. $18 (1/31/92) **87**
Marsannay Les Vaudenelles 1989: Floral and citric, with refreshing aromas and flavors, but simple and ready to drink. $18 (1/31/92) **81**

JOSEPH DROUHIN
Côte de Nuits-Villages 1985 $19 (11/15/87) **86**

A.-F. GROS
Bourgogne Hautes Côtes de Nuits 1988: A sturdy, herb-flavored wine, with open aromas of cherry and pine and similar flavors. A little green tasting, but well balanced and clean. $22 (3/31/91) **80**
Bourgogne Hautes Côtes de Nuits 1989: Lean and ungenerous, with leafy, green fruit flavors making it tighter and leaner than we would prefer. Drinkable, but simple. $19 (6/15/92) **78**

MICHEL GROS
Bourgogne Hautes Côtes de Nuits 1989: A wine with lovely aromas and fresh flavors. Not structured for the long term, but delicious now. (NR) (1/31/92) **82**
Bourgogne Hautes Côtes de Nuits 1987: Soft and velvety, with light but attractive cherry and toast aromas and flavors; a bit short. Drinkable now. $14 (2/28/90) **78**

FRANCE

Burgundy Red/*Côte de Nuits*/Other Côte de Nuits Red

DOMAINE GROS FRERE & SOEUR
Bourgogne Hautes Côtes de Nuits 1989: Relatively light and easy drinking, with clean berry flavors and a fresh finish. Drink now. (NR) (1/31/92) **82**

LOUIS JADOT
Marsannay 1986 $11 (6/15/89) **77**

JAFFELIN
Côte de Nuits-Villages 1989: Traditionally styled, with lovely smoke and berry aromas and flavors and silky tannins. Delicious and round. Drink now. $15 (1/31/92) **84**

JAYER-GILLES
Bourgogne Hautes Côtes de Nuits 1989: A hefty Hautes Côtes de Nuits, with plenty of new wood and loads of raspberry flavor and tannins. Try from 1993. $24 (1/31/92) **86**
Côte de Nuits-Villages 1989: New oak masks everything now, but has masses of fruit and soft tannins. Very impressive for this category. Try from 1993. $32 (1/31/92) **87**

MOILLARD
Bourgogne Hautes Côtes de Nuits Les Vignes Hautes 1989: Chewy, with medium tannins, plenty of berry and earth flavors and an almost peppery finish. Try now or hold. (NR) (1/31/92) **84**
Bourgogne Hautes Côtes de Nuits 1983 $6.50 (11/01/85) **76**

MOMMESSIN
Côte de Nuits-Villages 1985 $17 (7/31/88) **85**

MONGEARD-MUGNERET
Bourgogne Hautes Côtes de Nuits 1989: Light and easy to drink, but lacks depth on the palate; it seems diluted. Drink now. $16 (1/31/92) **77**

PATRIARCHE
Bourgogne Hautes Côtes de Nuits Cuvée Varache 1989: Lean and tight, with austere plum and cherry-scented fruit flavors. A low-profile wine that lacks richness and depth. Drink now. $11 (1/31/92) **81**

CHATEAU DE PULIGNY-MONTRACHET
Côte de Nuits-Villages 1988: A lightly flavored, but spicy and interesting Pinot Noir, with oaky accents in the aroma, modest cherry flavors and very firm tannins. Needs cellaring until 1993 to '94 for the tannins to soften. $17 (3/31/91) **82**

DOMAINE DANIEL RION
Côte de Nuits-Villages 1986 $15 (7/31/88) **81**

PHILIPPE ROSSIGNOL
Côte de Nuits-Villages 1985 $24 (7/31/88) **89**

DOMAINE SIRUGUE
Côte de Nuits-Villages Clos de la Belle Marguerite 1988: A very nice Burgundy that's clean, fruity, balanced and aromatic, with currant, berry and vanilla. A bit tannic, but already drinkable. Should be fine through 1993 or '94. $16 (3/31/91) **83**

LOUIS TRAPET
Marsannay 1987: The earthy tea and leather flavors ride roughshod over the strawberry and plum notes. Not too tannic, but the finish is short. A simple wine; drink now to 1993. $17 (3/31/91) **78**

Chalonnaise

MICHEL BRIDAY
Rully Champ Clou 1987: Earthy, slightly sour and stemmy overtones take the edge off this otherwise flavorful, modest-scale wine. $16 (12/31/90) **68**

CHANSON PERE & FILS
Givry 1988: Light, crisp and brightly fruity, with modest strawberry and spice flavors and hints of lemon and lime on the finish. Should be drinkable now. $13 (12/31/90) **78**

JEAN CHOFFLET
Givry 1985 $12 (11/15/87) **70**

JOSEPH DROUHIN
Mercurey 1985 $17 (11/15/87) **83**

DUVERNAY
Rully Les Cloux 1988: Ripe and spicy, with a firm texture, nicely focused black cherry and slightly herbal aromas and flavors. Its soft tannins will need until nearly 1993 to smooth out. Has more complexity on the nose than on the palate now. $18 (12/31/90) **82**

FAIVELEY
Mercurey Clos des Myglands 1985 $20 (4/30/88) **75**
Mercurey Clos des Myglands 1981 $11 (6/16/86) **68**
Mercurey Clos du Roy 1988: Firm and tannic, but it has lots of generous currant and plum aromas and flavors shaded by toast and vanilla notes. Concentrated and spicy on the long finish. Best to cellar until 1993. $22 (3/31/91) **84**
Mercurey Clos du Roy 1985 $23 (4/30/88) **81**
Mercurey Domaine de la Croix Jacquelet 1988: Firm and tannic, with an open texture that needs time to bring the modest currant and berry aromas and flavors together. Should be best after 1993 or '94. $18 (3/31/91) **81**
Rully 1986 $18 (6/15/89) **83**

JAFFELIN
Rully 1986 $13 (6/15/89) **77**

DOMAINE JOBLOT
Givry Clos du Cellier aux Moines 1989: A distinctive wine, with fascinating smoked meat, earth and fruit flavors and full, supple tannins. Try in 1993. $25 (1/31/92) **90**
Givry Clos du Cellier aux Moines 1988: Ripe and generous, with plump black cherry and vanilla aromas and flavors that are toasty, spicy, supple and round. The modest tannins need until 1993 to become smooth and polished. $19 (12/31/90) **84**

Key to Symbols

The scores reported here are the results of blind tastings conducted by our panel of senior editors. Wines that carry the initials below are results of individual tastings.

THE WINE SPECTATOR 100-POINT SCALE 95-100—Classic, a great wine; ***90-94***—Outstanding, superior character and style; ***80-89***—Good to very good, a wine with special qualities; ***70-79***—Average, drinkable wine that may have minor flaws; ***60-69*** —Below average, drinkable but not recommended; ***50-59***—Poor, undrinkable, not recommended. "+"—With a score indicates a range; used primarily with barrel tastings to indicate a preliminary score.

SPECIAL DESIGNATIONS SS—Spectator Selection, CS—Cellar Selection, BB—Best Buy, ($NA)—Price not available, (NR)—Not released.

TASTER'S INITIALS (JG)—Jim Gordon, (HS)—Harvey Steiman, (JL)—James Laube, (JS)—James Suckling, (TM)—Thomas Matthews, (TR)—Terry Robards, (PM)—Per-Henrik Mansson, (BT)—Barrel Tasting (these wines were tasted blind from barrel samples), (CA-date)—*California's Great Cabernets* by James Laube, (CH-date)—*California's Great Chardonnays* by James Laube, (VP-date)—*Vintage Port* by James Suckling.

DATE TASTED Dates in parentheses represent the issue in which the rating was published.

Givry Clos de la Servoisine 1989: Shows plenty of earthy aromas and flavors, hints of cinnamon, chocolate and berry and supple tannins. Try in 1993. $25 (1/31/92) **88**

DOMAINE DU CHATEAU DE MERCEY
Mercurey 1983 $10 (5/01/86) **56**

MOILLARD
Rully 1989: Don't let the light color fool you. This has plenty of strawberry and cherry flavor to balance the toasty, tealike edge, and enough firm tannins to need until 1993 to '95 to soften. $14 (8/31/91) **82**

REMOISSENET
Givry du Domaine Thénard 1988: Very earthy aromas and flavors obscure what little fruit this wine has. Tasted twice. $19 (3/31/91) **68**
Givry du Domaine Thénard 1985 $18 (4/30/88) **77**
Mercurey Clos Fortoul 1988: Enticing ripe fruit flavors and a smooth texture make this very enjoyable for drinking now through 1994. Has good structure, but moderate tannins. $17 (3/31/91) **83**

DOMAINE F. & L. SAIER
Mercurey Les Champs Martins 1988: Smells wonderful, with generous, deep cherry, berry and tea aromas and flavors, but turns hard and tannic on the palate. Flavors come up short, but this is worth cellaring until 1994 to '95 to see what develops. 300 cases made. $17 (8/31/91) **80**
Mercurey Les Champs Martins 1985 $20 (3/31/88) **83**
Mercurey Les Chenelots 1988: Very lean, excessively tannic and earthy, with little discernible fruit flavor. Tasted twice. $17 (4/30/91) **67**

CHARLES VIENOT
Mercurey 1985 $12 (4/30/88) **85**

Other Burgundy Red

GHISLAINE BARTHOD
Bourgogne 1988: Smooth and generous, with ample if simple currant, smoke and slightly gamy aromas and flavors. Firm-textured and ready to drink. $20 (3/31/91) **82**

BICHOT
Bourgogne Le Bourgogne Bichot Pinot Noir 1985 $8 (11/15/87) **81**
Bourgogne Château de Dracy Pinot Noir 1989: A smooth, easy-to-drink red wine, with light tannins and good fruit flavors. Straightforward and attractive. Doesn't need aging; drink now. Tasted twice. $9 (6/15/92) **82**
Bourgogne Château de Dracy Pinot Noir 1986 $6.50 (12/31/88) **76**
Bourgogne Château de Montpatey Pinot Noir 1989: It'd be difficult to find a more enjoyable Pinot Noir at this price. This smooth wine offers solid plum and berry flavors accented by pepper and spice. Medium-bodied, well balanced and ready to drink now. Tasted twice. $10 (6/15/92) BB **85**
Bourgogne Croix St.-Louis 1989: Pleasant, satisfying Burgundy for the price, with ample cherry and spice flavors and a smooth, modestly tannic texture. Ready to drink now. $9 (6/15/92) BB **83**
Bourgogne Croix St.-Louis 1986 $6 (10/31/88) **77**

HENRI BOILLOT
Bourgogne 1985 $13 (12/31/88) **76**

JEAN CLAUDE BOISSET
Bourgogne Conférie des Chevaliers du Tastevin 1989: A tannic, earthy style of red Burgundy whose flavors are less fruity and more funky than we would prefer. Drinkable, if a bit coarse in texture. $7 (6/15/92) **76**
Bourgogne Rouge Tastevinage 1988: Earthy, barnyardy flavors are mercifully modest in scope, making this drinkable, if not terribly appealing. $11 (8/31/91) **72**

PIERRE BOUREE FILS
Bourgogne 1988: Hard-edged and tannic, with an overabundance of oak and murky fruit flavors. The result is a simple, hard-to-like, tough and tannic wine. Tasted twice, with consistent notes. $15 (3/31/92) **73**

LIONEL J. BRUCK
Bourgogne St.-Vincent Pinot Noir 1983 $10 (2/15/87) **78**

CAVE DES VIGNERONS DE BUXY
Bourgogne Pinot Noir Grande Réserve 1985 $7 (6/30/88) **75**
Bourgogne Pinot Noir Grande Réserve 1983 $5 (2/01/86) **73**

DOMAINE JEAN CHARTRON
Bourgogne Clos de la Combe 1990: Intense and firmly tannic, with ripe plum and currant flavors underneath. A bold, concentrated wine that needs until 1994 to mellow, when it should be more appealing. $11 (3/31/92) **85**
Bourgogne Pinot Noir L'Orme 1988 (NR) (7/15/90) (BT) **75+**

CHARTRON & TREBUCHET
Bourgogne 1989 (NR) (7/15/90) (BT) **75+**

F. CHAUVENET
Bourgogne Pinot Noir Château Marguerite de Bourgogne 1985 $10 (6/30/88) **80**

ROBERT CHEVILLON
Bourgogne 1989: Astringent and mouth-puckering, with good black cherry flavor, but very high acidity on the finish. Try in 1993. $16 (1/31/92) **77**

J.-F. COCHE-DURY
Bourgogne Pinot Noir 1987: Lean and lithe, with brightly focused raspberry aromas and flavors, plus a touch of vinegar that will not appeal to some. Drinkable now. $25 (2/28/90) **79**

DOMAINE COSTE-CAUMARTIN
Bourgogne 1989: Big, rich and powerful for this category, offering plenty of berry and earth flavors and muscular tannins. Try in 1993. $15 (1/31/92) **87**

CHATEAU DE DRACY
Bourgogne Pinot Noir 1988: Tannic and tough, with subdued aromas and flavors hinting at ripe cherry, but it lacks grace or concentration. $8 (2/28/90) **68**

JOSEPH DROUHIN
Bourgogne Pinot Noir Laforet 1989: Pretty floral and fruit aromas turn tight and firm on the palate, with light raspberry, cherry and spicy nutmeg notes. Not too tannic. Ready to drink now through 1993. 5,000 cases made. $9 (4/30/91) BB **85**
Bourgogne Pinot Noir Laforet 1988: There aren't many Pinots this good for less money. Tastes firm, tart and fresh, with ample strawberry and cherry flavors that linger nicely on the aftertaste. A light red for drinking now through 1993. $10 (3/31/91) BB **84**
Bourgogne Pinot Noir Laforet 1987 $8.75 (6/15/89) **78**
Bourgogne Pinot Noir Laforet 1985 $8.50 (11/15/87) **78**
Bourgogne Pinot Noir Laforet 1983 $7.50 (11/01/85) **71**

FAIVELEY
Bourgogne Joseph Faiveley 1989: Has complex aromas and flavors for a Bourgogne, showing pepper, chocolate and berry, but it's rather light on the finish. Drink on release. $12 (1/31/92) **84**
Bourgogne Joseph Faiveley 1979 $8 (4/16/86) BB **75**

JEAN GARAUDET
Bourgogne Passetoutgrains 1990: A very reasonably priced Burgundy that includes Gamay grapes.

A strong beam of currant flavor runs through this fruity-smelling, tightly textured wine. Firm tannins indicate it may need until 1994 to soften up. $10 (6/15/92) **84**

MACHARD DE GRAMONT
Bourgogne Pinot Noir Domaine de la Vierge Romaine 1985 $13 (6/30/88) **81**

DOMAINE ROBERT GROFFIER
Bourgogne 1989: An earthy style, with currant and cherry flavors that are crisp, but the earthy flavors return on the finish. Drink now to 1993. Tasted twice. $14 (1/31/92) **78**

LOUIS JADOT
Bourgogne 1989 (NR) (7/15/90) (BT) **70+**
Bourgogne Pinot Noir 1989: A good, mellow sipping wine, with cherry, berry and truffle flavors and light, round tannins. Drink on release. (NR) (1/31/92) **83**
Bourgogne Pinot Noir 1988 (NR) (7/15/90) (BT) **70+**
Bourgogne Pinot Noir Jadot 1985 $11 (4/30/88) **78**

JAFFELIN
Bourgogne Pinot Noir 1989: Light and simple, with cherry and cinnamon aromas and flavors and a very fresh finish. Drink on release. $10 (1/31/92) **83**

JEAN-LUC JOILLOT
Bourgogne Tastevinage 1985 $15 (6/30/88) **84**

LABOURE-ROI
Bourgogne 1988: Very generous, fruity and lively aromas and flavors make this an unusually well-crafted, simple Burgundy, offering plenty of strawberry, cherry and currant flavors and hints of spice on the finish. Drinkable now. 2,000 cases made. $12 (3/31/91) **83**

DOMAINE MICHEL LAFARGE
Bourgogne 1989: Well structured, with lovely blackberry flavors, firm tannins and a flavorful finish. Try in 1993. $19 (1/31/92) **85**

LOUIS LATOUR
Bourgogne Cuvée Latour 1989: A light wine, with fresh pine, berry and strawberry flavors and a fresh finish. Serve slightly chilled. Drink on release. (NR) (1/31/92) **80**

PHILIPPE LECLERC
Bourgogne Les Bons Bâtons 1988: Thin and hard-edged, with ugly burnt orange peel and tobacco flavors. $22 (8/31/91) **64**

LEROY
Bourgogne 1989: Intriguingly firm, with earth, black truffle and berry flavors and good tannins. The oak may dominate a bit, but this is a beautiful wine. Try in 1993. $18 (1/31/92) **85**
Bourgogne d'Auvenay 1988: Rich yet elegant, with intense, complex black cherry, raspberry, currant and earth notes that add dimension and character to the flavor. A balanced wine, with crisp acidity and firm tannins. Best in 1993 to '96. 5,000 cases made. $15 (4/30/91) **87**
Bourgogne d'Auvenay 1985 $12 (3/31/88) **73**

LUPE-CHOLET
Bourgogne Clos de Lupé 1985 $15 (3/31/88) **79**
Bourgogne Clos de la Roche 1986 $10 (7/31/88) **78**
Bourgogne Pinot Noir Comte de Lupé 1989: Flavorful and aromatic, with delicious violet, cherry and cedar aromas and flavors. Drink on release. $7.50 (1/31/92) **86**
Bourgogne Pinot Noir Comte de Lupé 1988: Light and crisp, with delicate strawberry and cinnamon aromas and flavors, well focused and long. Drinkable now, but cellaring until 1993 wouldn't hurt. $9 (2/28/90) BB **83**
Bourgogne Hautes Côtes de Beaune 1987: A very light and delicate red, with charming vanilla-scented cherry and cinnamon aromas and flavors, simple and attractive. Drink now. $10 (4/15/90) **78**

DOMAINE MEO-CAMUZET
Bourgogne 1989: Ripe, chewy and firm textured, with spicy black cherry aromas and flavors. Has more style than most basic Burgundies. Dry and moderately tannic; needs until 1993 or '94 to soften. $23 (11/15/91) **83**
Bourgogne Passetoutgrains 1990: A ripe, bold style that gushes with raspberry, cherry and currant flavors framed by smoky oak and firm, drying tannins. Still, on the finish you taste a rich core of fruit. Best to cellar until 1994. $17 (3/31/92) **86**
Bourgogne Passetoutgrains 1989: Light and crisp, with sharply focused raspberry and blackberry aromas and flavors that persist into a long finish. An early-drinking alternative to full-fledged red Burgundy. $17 (7/15/91) **84**

MOILLARD
Bourgogne Pinot Noir 1985 $7 (3/31/88) **78**
Bourgogne Hautes Côtes de Nuits Les Hameaux 1986 $11 (12/31/88) **81**
Bourgogne Passetoutgrains Notre Dame des Ceps 1990: Light and simple, with modest cherry and tobacco aromas and flavors, hinting at stemminess on the finish. $9.50 (8/31/91) **75**

MOMMESSIN
Bourgogne Pinot Noir 1983 $5 (2/16/86) **61**

MONGEARD-MUGNERET
Bourgogne 1989: Delicious, with round, fruity chestnut, strawberry and earth aromas and flavors and a long, silky finish. Drink on release. $9.50 (1/31/92) **85**

DOMAINE JEAN MORETEAUX
Bourgogne Pinot Noir Les Clous 1985 $9 (11/15/87) **77**

CHARLES MORTET
Bourgogne 1989: Rough going now, with burnt coffee flavors and tough tannins, but it also shows pretty currant and plum-scented fruit flavors. Stalky and green on the finish. Drink now through 1995. $14 (1/31/92) **87**
Bourgogne 1986: Thick and earthy, with an undertone of ripe fruit, broad and simple. A sturdy red wine to drink soon with hearty food. $15 (6/15/89) **79**

MUGNERET-GIBOURG
Bourgogne 1989: The beautiful currant and berry component in the aromas tightens up on the palate and turns tannic and austere. Should grow softer and rounder by about 1994. $17 (6/15/92) **82**

POTHIER-RIEUSSET
Bourgogne Rouge 1986 $10 (6/15/89) **79**
Bourgogne Rouge 1985 $7.50 (6/30/88) BB **83**

DOMAINE RAPET
Bourgogne en Bully 1988: Generous berry and cherry aromas are the nicest aspect of this otherwise modest, tough-textured wine. $19 (3/31/91) **80**

DOMAINE B. SERVEAU
Bourgogne 1989: A traditionally styled red, with bark, earth and berry aromas and flavors and medium-hard tannins. Try in 1993. $10 (1/31/92) **83**
Bourgogne Rouge 1985 $13 (11/15/87) **76**

CHARLES VIENOT
Bourgogne 1985 $9 (6/15/89) **78**
Bourgogne 1983 $6.50 (12/16/85) **75**
Bourgogne 1982 $6 (11/01/85) **52**

A. & P. DE VILLAINE
Bourgogne La Digoine Bouzeron 1989: Crisp, fruity and focused, with a bright beam of cherry and plum flavor shaded by cream and nutmeg notes around the edges. Drinkable now, but it has room to grow through 1993 or '94. $17 (11/15/91) **84**

HENRI DE VILLAMONT
Bourgogne Pinot Noir 1989: Light, fruity and very modest, with some Pinot Noir character and a pleasant hint of tobacco on the finish. Drinkable now. $11 (3/31/91) **78**

JEAN-CLAUDE VOLPATO
Bourgogne Passetoutgrain 1988: This average wine is tough, tannic and stemmy, with just a touch of plum and cherry flavors. Drinkable, but not very likable. $13 (3/31/91) **73**

BURGUNDY WHITE/*CÔTE DE BEAUNE*/ALOXE-CORTON

JEAN-CLAUDE BELLAND
Corton-Charlemagne 1986: Lean yet concentrated, with spicy, earthy, flinty pear and lemon flavors, great structure and firm intensity, along with a long, full finish. $58 (3/31/89) **89**

BICHOT
Corton-Charlemagne 1985 $63 (3/15/88) **87**

PIERRE BITOUZET
Corton-Charlemagne 1988: A big, powerful wine, with marvelously spicy, earthy aromas and flavors and hard-edged mineral and chalk notes that won't appeal to everyone, but it shows every sign of developing beautifully with cellaring until 1993 to '95. 500 cases made. $75 (12/31/90) **91**
Corton-Charlemagne 1987: Gloriously ripe and spicy, its pear and honey-apple flavors balance beautifully against the nutmeg and toasty oak, but the fruit emerges on the finish as complex and generous. Drinkable now, but oh what a gorgeous wine this can be with cellaring until 1993 to '95. $68 (11/15/89) **92**
Corton-Charlemagne 1986 $72 (9/30/88) **95**

BONNEAU DU MARTRAY
Corton-Charlemagne 1989: Extraordinary potential, with outstanding structure. Full-bodied and massively proportioned, with striking lemon, cream and pineapple aromas, tons of lemon and earth flavors and an iron backbone of acidity. Drink in 1995 to '98. $80 (8/31/91) **95**
Corton-Charlemagne 1988: Offers a broad array of ripe fruit, with layers of apple, pear, melon and spice notes in a crisp, tight, focused package. The texture is beginning to round out, with a smooth, creamy feeling. May be best in 1993 to '95; best to try a bottle to see for yourself. 3,500 cases made. $78 (9/15/91) **92**
Corton-Charlemagne 1986: A full-throttle white Burgundy, what some might consider overdone, full-bodied, toasty, oaky and powerful. The crisp acidity suggests that cellaring could tame it by 1994 to '96. Rel: $60 Cur: $73 (2/28/90) **88**
Corton-Charlemagne 1985 Rel: $65 Cur: $77 (5/31/88) **84**

BOUCHARD PERE & FILS
Corton-Charlemagne 1989: Has an interesting dried fruit character, but it's more advanced than some Corton-Charlemagnes. Has coconut and dried apricot aromas, apricot and dried fruit flavors, an iron backbone of acidity and a super finish. Full-bodied. Drink in 1993 to '95. $77 (8/31/91) **87**

DOMAINE CHANDON DE BRIAILLES
Corton 1988: Shows subdued character, offering a little bit of spice, pepper and butterscotch, mostly as nuances to the ripe pear flavor. A nice wine, but not as deep as it could be. $88 (2/28/91) **84**

CHARTRON & TREBUCHET
Corton-Charlemagne 1989: Not as big and flavorful as Corton can be, but a well-modulated, ripe, fruity wine. The ripe pear, citrus, toast and vanilla flavors don't quite merge into something harmonious yet, but perhaps cellaring until 1993 or '94 will do it. Tasted twice. $105 (2/28/91) **85**
Corton-Charlemagne 1988: Big and powerful from the first sip, turning rich, spicy and nutty, with overtones of brown sugar and vanilla on the long, long finish. The flavors just keep coming in waves on the finish, which marks this as a great cellar candidate for drinking sometime after 1994. $70 (2/28/90) **95**
Corton-Charlemagne 1987: A bit understated for Corton, but there's an underlying sense of power and concentration of fresh, ripe fruit that builds gently on the palate. The smoky pear, peach and pineapple flavors grow on the finish. $79 (3/31/89) **91**
Corton-Charlemagne 1986 $92 (5/31/88) **95**

F. CHAUVENET
Corton-Charlemagne 1985 $70 (4/30/87) **96**
Corton-Charlemagne Hospices de Beaune Cuvée François de Salins 1985 $140 (7/31/87) **96**
Corton Vergennes Hospices de Beaune Cuvée Paul Chanson 1982 $83 (8/01/85) **95**

DOMAINE DU CLOS FRANTIN
Corton-Charlemagne 1989: The nose gives more than the palate; too forward to be great. Full-bodied, with extravagant vanilla, apple and pineapple aromas, apple, pineapple and vanilla flavors and a forward finish. From Bichot. Drink now. ($NA) (8/31/91) **85**
Corton-Charlemagne 1988: Has too many cider, pear and wood flavors; it lumbers rather than dances. Of marginal quality for a wine of this pedigree, but some may find its funkiness appealing. Tasted twice. $66 (4/30/91) **71**
Corton-Charlemagne 1986: Smooth and rich, full of extract, showing tart apple and peach flavor and bracing acidity. Try now. $55 (3/31/89) **87**

J.-F. COCHE-DURY
Corton-Charlemagne 1987: Has a pull-out-the-stops style, with powerful, concentrated smoky, oaky pear and fig aromas and flavors, but a serious gamy component as well that appeals to some and offends others. Best to drink starting 1993. $122 (2/28/90) **88**

DOMAINE DELARCHE
Corton-Charlemagne 1986 $65 (9/30/88) **85**

MARIUS DELARCHE PERE & FILS
Corton-Charlemagne 1989: Not easy to evaluate now; the center is closed in. Pie crust, lemon and dried fruit aromas lead to lemony straw and chalk flavors and a superbly long finish. Full-bodied. Drink in 1994 to '96. $60 (8/31/91) **89**
Corton-Charlemagne 1988: This wine embodies power and grace. Beautifully complex, with pear, apple, honeycomb, lemon and lots of butter aromas and flavors. Has a very long and sharply focused finish. Save for a special occasion sometime after 1993, but if you can't wait, enjoy it now. 1,000 cases made. $60 (7/31/90) **94**

JOSEPH DROUHIN
Corton-Charlemagne 1990: Ripe, intense and powerful, with striking pear, spice and vanilla aromas and flavors. Tight and controlled, but flings delicious flavors at you on the long finish. Tempting to drink now, but probably best around 1995 or '96. $75 (5/15/92) **92**
Corton-Charlemagne 1989: A masterpiece, with magnificent flavors and structure. Full-bodied, with subtle yet intense straw, earth, lemon and apple aromas. Has superbly balanced, intense flavors and a sublime backbone of acidity. Drink in 1995 to '98. $92 (8/31/91) **97**
Corton-Charlemagne 1987: Powerful, full-bodied, rich and flavorful, bursting with ripe apple, orange, toast and vanilla flavors, long and harmonious. Very tasty on release; best to drink now. $90 (3/31/89) **90**
Corton-Charlemagne 1986 $98 (12/15/88) **90**
Corton-Charlemagne 1985 $78 (4/30/87) **94**

FRANCE

BURGUNDY WHITE/*CÔTE DE BEAUNE*/ALOXE-CORTON

DUBREUIL-FONTAINE
Corton-Charlemagne 1989: Solid and focused, with generous pear and hazelnut aromas and flavors, but a tannic edge robs it of its smoothness. Give it until 1995 to smooth out. $71 (3/31/92) **84**

FAIVELEY
Corton-Charlemagne 1989: A monumental white wine, built like a great red, with multidimensional aromas of almonds, minerals, apples and green olives. Full-bodied, with apple and earth flavors, but it has a super backbone and a concentration seldom seen in a white wine. Drink in 1995 to '98. ($NA) (8/31/91) **98**

LOUIS JADOT
Corton-Charlemagne 1989: A more forward style compared to the others in this group, but impressive nonetheless, with vanilla, tropical fruit and cream aromas. Full-bodied, with ripe apple and tropical fruit flavors and a hint of coconut on the flavorful finish. Drink now through 1994. $114 (8/31/91) **89**
Corton-Charlemagne 1988: This grandly proportioned wine has crisp, vibrant fruit flavors ably supported by orange, pear, lemon and fig notes, with accents of spice, honey and butter from oak aging. Beautifully focused, silky in texture and long on the finish. Tempting now, but should be better from 1993 to '98. 725 cases made. $98 (4/30/91) **93**
Corton-Charlemagne 1986: A powerful, earthy wine, balancing pear and honey flavors with toasty oak and a fantail of butterscotch on the finish, which is long and rich. Impressive already, but cellaring through 1993 can't hurt. $92 (5/31/89) **92**

JAFFELIN
Corton-Charlemagne 1990: Big and flavorful, with lots of spicy honey, almond and pear aromas and flavors and hints of mineral and chalk on the finish. The flavors are strong, but it needs until 1995 to '98 to soften the edges. $55 (4/15/92) **84**
Corton-Charlemagne 1989: So concentrated it verges on being overly tannic; rips your palate out. A full-bodied wine, with super-concentrated apple, dried fruit and mineral aromas, masses of apple and mineral flavors and a powerful finish. Drink in 1994 to '96. $75 (8/31/91) **94**
Corton-Charlemagne 1984 $60 (5/01/86) **86**

MICHEL JUILLOT
Corton-Charlemagne 1987: Tough and broad, not very subtle, but offering powerful green apple, spice and earth aromas and flavors, good concentration and length. Give it until 1993 or '94 to smooth out a bit. $77 (2/28/90) **84**

LABOURE-ROI
Corton-Charlemagne 1989: Bold, intense and sharply focused, with well-articulated, smoky, spicy pear and apple aromas and flavors. Has style, but seems a little awkward. Packed with enough flavor to warrant cellaring until at least 1995 to '97. $59 (4/15/92) **88**
Corton-Charlemagne 1988: Smells as if it's going to be big and powerful. Ripe, rich, buttery and honeyed, but remarkably smooth and elegant, it's long but not terribly concentrated. Echoes honey and pear on the finish. Drink now. 300 cases made. $50 (10/15/90) **90**

LOUIS LATOUR
Corton-Charlemagne 1989: A highly extracted wine, with masses of fruit. Has a decadent white truffle and barnyardy character, with white pepper, mineral, toast and apple aromas. Full-bodied, with intense earth and spice flavors. Has lots of everything on the long finish. Drink in 1994 to '98. $93 (8/31/91) **93**
Corton-Charlemagne 1988: This great, full-bodied wine has power with grace. Tons of apricot, pear and apple flavors are rounded out by loads of ginger, almond and butter, yet it stays balanced and elegant in texture. The finish is long and lingering. Tempting now, but it has a long life ahead and should easily age through 2000. 250 cases made. $85 (10/15/90) **95**
Corton-Charlemagne 1985 Rel: $88 Cur: $95 (11/15/87) **96**
Corton-Charlemagne 1982 Rel: $65 Cur: $78 (12/01/85) **82**

OLIVIER LEFLAIVE FRERES
Corton-Charlemagne 1989: A ripe wine, layered with tons of fruit and acidity, with buttery vanilla aromas and masses of buttery apple and cream flavors. Full-bodied, with super acidity. Drink in 1993 to '95. ($NA) (8/31/91) **92**
Corton-Charlemagne 1988: Big, deep and intense, with a rough texture at first, offering powerful pear, lemon, butter and cream aromas and flavors. Smooths out on the finish. Impressive now, but should be best around 1994 to '96. 1,200 cases made. $78 (8/31/91) **91**
Corton-Charlemagne 1986: Big and full-bodied, with lots of sulfur apparent on the nose and palate. Ripe pear and toast aromas and flavors are buried, and this wine will probably last for decades, but right now it's not very likable. Probably best to drink after 1996 to '97. Tasted twice. $67 (7/31/90) **83**

A. LIGERET
Corton-Charlemagne 1987: A rich, deep, spicy white Burgundy from one of the best appellations. One of the best of the '87 vintage. Has nice structure of acid and tannins, plus ripe, pearlike, almost meaty flavors and a lingering aftertaste. 390 cases made. $83 (10/15/90) **90**

PROSPER MAUFOUX
Corton-Charlemagne 1989: Wood dominates now, but there's good fruit flavor underneath. Offers tropical fruit, coconut and mineral aromas and lots of vanilla and wood flavors. Full-bodied, with modest fruit, but it's a little tough on the finish. Try again in 1993 to '94. $70 (8/31/91) **88**

MOILLARD
Corton-Charlemagne 1986 $70 (5/31/88) **90**
Corton-Charlemagne 1984 $51 (5/31/87) **90**
Corton-Charlemagne 1983 $34 (10/01/85) **92**

REINE PEDAUQUE
Corton-Charlemagne 1989: Shows a good concentration of fruit, but new wood dominates this full-bodied wine. Has vanilla, custard and apple aromas and lots of new wood and ripe fruit flavors, but it's very woody on the finish. Drink now through 1994. $78 (8/31/91) **85**
Corton-Charlemagne 1985: A healthy young Corton that still needs time to evolve. The ripe pear, spice and oak flavors ring true but they're a bit coarse and alcoholic. The finish, however, is long and flavorful with hints of honey and spice coming through. $60 (11/15/89) **92**
Corton-Charlemagne 1982 $33 (8/01/85) **73**

Key to Symbols

The scores reported here are the results of blind tastings conducted by our panel of senior editors. Wines that carry the initials below are results of individual tastings.

THE WINE SPECTATOR 100-POINT SCALE ***95-100***—Classic, a great wine; ***90-94***—Outstanding, superior character and style; ***80-89***—Good to very good, a wine with special qualities; ***70-79***—Average, drinkable wine that may have minor flaws; ***60-69***—Below average, drinkable but not recommended; ***50-59***—Poor, undrinkable, not recommended. "+"—With a score indicates a range; used primarily with barrel tastings to indicate a preliminary score.

SPECIAL DESIGNATIONS SS—Spectator Selection, CS—Cellar Selection, BB—Best Buy, ($NA)—Price not available, (NR)—Not released.

TASTER'S INITIALS (JG)—Jim Gordon, (HS)—Harvey Steiman, (JL)—James Laube, (JS)—James Suckling, (TM)—Thomas Matthews, (TR)—Terry Robards, (PM)—Per-Henrik Mansson, (BT)—Barrel Tasting (these wines were tasted blind from barrel samples), (CA-date)—*California's Great Cabernets* by James Laube, (CH-date)—*California's Great Chardonnays* by James Laube, (VP-date)—*Vintage Port* by James Suckling.

DATE TASTED Dates in parentheses represent the issue in which the rating was published.

PIERRE PONNELLE
Corton-Charlemagne 1989: Hard, but it has very good concentration, offering perfumed lemon and vanilla aromas and intense vanilla, freshly cut wood and apple flavors. Full-bodied, with firm acidity and a long finish. Drink in 1994 to '96. $85 (8/31/91) **88**

REMOISSENET
Corton-Charlemagne Diamond Jubilee 1986 $82 (12/15/88) **82**
Corton-Charlemagne Diamond Jubilee 1985 Rel: $100 Cur: $110 (3/15/88) **90**

ANTONIN RODET
Corton-Charlemagne 1989: This will take years to come around; be patient. Has earthy, ripe fruit and coconut aromas and a huge amount of grapefruit, hazelnut and mineral flavors. A full-bodied wine, with a great backbone. Drink in 1995 to '98. $65 (8/31/91) **92**

CHASSAGNE-MONTRACHET

AMIOT-BONFILS
Chassagne-Montrachet Les Caillerets 1988: Weedy, floral, woolly aromas and flavors shoulder past the other flavors in an otherwise smooth-textured, round, ripe wine. Starts bad, finishes well. Tasted twice. $27 (5/15/90) **70**
Chassagne-Montrachet Les Champs-Gains 1988: Has earthy pear aromas and flavors that are broad and deep, with citrus, toast and spice nuances that add dimension and flavor. Drink now to 1994. $27 (3/31/90) **86**

AMIOT-PONSOT
Chassagne-Montrachet Les Champs-Gains 1987: Young and coarse with spicy vanilla and butterscotch flavors that are well structured, tight and compact, but in the end the Chassagne character comes through. Drink now. $42 (5/31/89) **86**

BACHELET-RAMONET
Chassagne-Montrachet 1988: The overall impression is funky, but interesting. A salty, toasty aroma makes it stand out, and the modest lemon and spice flavors give it substance. For fans of earthy wines. Tasted twice. $37 (4/30/91) **80**
Chassagne-Montrachet 1987: Earthy and elegant, with light, delicate pear, spice and vanilla notes and a touch of butterscotch and pineapple. Well balanced, but a little coarse on the finish. $36 (11/15/89) **87**
Chassagne-Montrachet Caillerets 1987: Rich and tangy, with pretty earth, pear, lemon and spicy oak flavors that are young and intense, finishing with a rich, smoky bacon flavor that stays with you. Just a touch of coarseness on the finish. Drink now to 1994. $35 (5/15/90) **87**
Chassagne-Montrachet Caillerets 1985 $41 (2/29/88) **91**

C. BERGERET
Chassagne-Montrachet 1985 $31 (8/31/87) **69**
Chassagne-Montrachet Morgeot 1985 $35 (8/31/87) **71**

BICHOT
Chassagne-Montrachet Morgeot-Vignes-Blanches 1988: Shows a wide range of flavors from apple and pear to floral and candied, with butter and nutmeg accents. Crisp and direct in structure. $40 (2/15/91) **82**
Chassagne-Montrachet La Romanée 1986 $32 (4/30/88) **90**

BLAIN-GAGNARD
Chassagne-Montrachet Caillerets 1985 $45 (5/31/88) **88**

JEAN CLAUDE BOISSET
Chassagne-Montrachet 1988: A sturdy, solid style of Chassagne, showing plenty of apple and pear flavors. Finishes dry, somewhat austere and a bit earthy. Has plenty of room to develop through 1994. Tasted twice. $28 (2/15/91) **86**
Chassagne-Montrachet Les Vergers 1989: Slightly more evolved than some, but it has interesting character. Offers unusual aromas of gooseberries and hazelnuts, hazelnut and apple flavors and a slight vanilla, chalk and lilac character. Full-bodied. Drink now or in 1993. $38 (8/31/91) **86**

BOUCHARD PERE & FILS
Chassagne-Montrachet 1989: Very fruity and firm, with tempting spice, honey, pear and orange flavors that are pleasant, focused and wrapped in an elegant texture. Has a clean, fruity finish, with hints of vanilla. Reasonably priced for this appellation. $17 (4/30/91) **88**
Chassagne-Montrachet 1982 $17 (7/01/84) **80**

HUBERT BOUZEREAU
Chassagne-Montrachet 1985 $35 (8/31/87) **93**

PHILIPPE BOUZEREAU
Chassagne-Montrachet Les Meix Goudard 1986 $29 (11/15/88) **77**

CHANSON PERE & FILS
Chassagne-Montrachet Les Embazées 1989: A quite traditionally styled Chassagne, with lots of earthy character. Wet hay, earth and cream aromas in a full-bodied style, with earthy flavors and a slightly chalky finish. Drink now. $37 (8/31/91) **85**

CHARTRON & TREBUCHET
Chassagne-Montrachet 1989: Spicy and toasty, with intense pear, lemon, smoke and vanilla flavors all neatly balanced, with subtlety and finesse. An understated style that still manages to pack in plenty of flavor. Drink now through 1995. Tasted twice. $46 (2/15/91) **88**
Chassagne-Montrachet 1988: Pretty, well-defined honey, smoke and spicy flavors combine to give this wine elegance and depth. There's a touch of astringency that will likely disappear with time, but what a honeyed aftertaste. Drink now through 1994. 1,000 cases made. $26 (2/28/90) **91**
Chassagne-Montrachet Les Morgeots 1990: Young and tight, with focused pear, vanilla, hazelnut and spice flavors that are concentrated and lively. Echoes toast and butter notes on the finish, but needs a year or two to open up. Drink after 1993. $40 (3/31/92) **86**
Chassagne-Montrachet Les Morgeots 1989: Elegant and stylish, with intense butter, spice and pear flavors and hints of orange and vanilla. Has great depth and amplitude, revealing layers of flavor and texture with each sip. Amazingly subtle and fruity, with beautifully defined flavors. Delicious; drink now through 1996. 500 cases made. $54 (2/15/91) **94**
Chassagne-Montrachet Les Morgeots 1988: Incredible depth and concentration with layers of fresh, ripe, rich honey, pear, spice and toasty vanilla flavors on the finish that echo on and on. You rarely see wines of this kind of depth, concentration and complexity anywhere. Drink now through 1995. 200 cases made. $34 (2/28/90) **96**
Chassagne-Montrachet Les Morgeots 1987 $40 (3/15/89) **90**

F. CHAUVENET
Chassagne-Montrachet 1985 Rel: $35 Cur: $43 (3/15/87) SS **96**
Chassagne-Montrachet 1982 $13 (3/16/85) **86**
Chassagne-Montrachet Les Caillerets 1989: Opulent, but a bit clumsy now. It's packed with fruit and has rich, ripe pineapple, vanilla and toast aromas, full-bodied pineapple and mint flavors and a long, slightly chalky, toasty finish. Drink now through 1994. ($NA) (8/31/91) **87**
Chassagne-Montrachet Clos St.-Marc 1986 $38 (6/30/88) **87**
Chassagne-Montrachet Clos St.-Marc 1985 $43 (6/15/87) **91**
Chassagne-Montrachet Morgeot 1986 $45 (5/31/88) **93**
Chassagne-Montrachet Morgeot 1985 Rel: $37 Cur: $52 (5/15/87) CS **96**

FERNAND COFFINET
Chassagne-Montrachet 1989: Crisp and focused, with a strong earthy component to the basic pear

and floral flavors. Hints at peanuts on the long finish, which takes away from its grandeur. Best to drink after 1993. $34 (3/31/92) **80**
Chassagne-Montrachet 1985 $25 (5/15/87) **94**
Chassagne-Montrachet Blanchot-Dessus 1989: Crisp and tightly focused, this spicy wine has buttery pear and apple flavors that extend into a solid finish. Needs to soften; probably best after 1993. $36 (3/31/92) **85**

MARC COLIN
Chassagne-Montrachet 1989: Sharp and focused, with razor-sharp acidity paving the way to butterscotch, grapefruit and honey flavors. A crisp, long finish bodes well for the patient collector. Drink in 1994 to '96. ($NA) (8/31/91) **90**
Chassagne-Montrachet Les Caillerets 1989: A straightforward wine with refined fruit structure. Subtle aromas of minerals, vegetables and fruit follow through on the palate, with vanilla notes on the finish. Drink now through 1994. ($NA) (8/31/91) **86**
Chassagne-Montrachet Les Champs-Gains 1989: Has subtle aromas and flavors; very drinkable now. Hay and apricot aromas follow through on the palate, with an appley finish. ($NA) (8/31/91) **86**

MADAME FRANCOIS COLIN
Chassagne-Montrachet Clos Devant 1988: Smoky, earthy and decadent, a generous wine with more toast and pine aromas and flavors than fruit; smooth in texture and well balanced. 175 cases made. $26 (5/15/90) **83**

MICHEL COLIN-DELEGER
Chassagne-Montrachet 1989: Fresh, crisp, firm and focused, with chalky hay and lemon aromas and flavors that are round and full. Citrus, butter and banana notes emerge on the medium-long finish. Drink now through 1994. $32 (8/31/91) **86**
Chassagne-Montrachet 1988: Extremely earthy and intense, with a pretty core of spice, pear, lemon and citrus notes that fit together nicely on the palate. The concentration and structure are firm, and it's a touch tannic. Probably not for everyone, but if you like a hint of earthiness in your white Burgundy, this wine should appeal. Drink now through 1993. $40 (2/28/91) **86**
Chassagne-Montrachet Les Chaumées 1989: An exuberant wine, with an abundance of fresh fruit. Full-bodied, it has lemon peel aromas, with a mineral element and very rich earth and apple flavors and wonderful acidity. Packed with fruit. Drink now through 1995. $38 (8/31/91) **91**
Chassagne-Montrachet Les Chaumées 1988: Ripe, smooth and elegant, with creamy pear and silky spice flavors that are remarkably well integrated and sophisticated, finishing with a measure of delicacy and finesse. Delicious now, but it should age well through 1993. 400 cases made. $48 (2/28/91) **90**
Chassagne-Montrachet Les Chênevottes 1989: Rich, rustic and almost decadent, with rustic aromas of earth and fruit. Full-bodied, with an oily mouth-feel and rich flavors. Drink now through 1994. $66 (8/31/91) **89**
Chassagne-Montrachet Morgeot 1989: Has a rather odd, slightly oxidized character, with earthy aromas of ripe fruit and toasted wood. Full-bodied, with odd fruit and wood flavors. A slightly "off" bottle? Drink now. $40 (8/31/91) **79**
Chassagne-Montrachet Morgeot 1987: Missing the finesse of '85 and '86, but the flavors are true, offering concentrated pear and spice and picking up earthy, pineapple flavors on the finish. Very good; drink now. $43 (5/31/89) **88**
Chassagne-Montrachet Les Remilly 1989: Grows on you; offers wonderfully focused fruit. Full-bodied, with slight mushroom, toast, hazelnut and fruit aromas, with ripe fruit, toast and lemon flavors and a focused finish. Drink now through 1994. $38 (8/31/91) **91**
Chassagne-Montrachet Les Remilly 1988: Very smooth, silky and delicious, with gentle pear, pineapple, almond and honey aromas and flavors melding smoothly on the long finish. It seems to open up nicely at the end. Drinkable now, probably best around 1993. 200 cases made. $30 (5/15/90) **90**
Chassagne-Montrachet Les Remilly 1986 $38 (10/31/88) **93**
Chassagne-Montrachet Les Vergers 1989: Silky and classy, with lively fruit. Full-bodied, with vibrant honey, lemon tart and earth aromas, intense lemon, apple and cream flavors, lovely acidity and a wonderful finish. Drink now through 1995. $57 (8/31/91) **93**
Chassagne-Montrachet Les Vergers 1988: Very ripe and tangy, with intense pear, pineapple and nutmeg aromas and flavors that linger on the finish. With all its intensity, it could be smoother and more integrated. Perhaps cellaring until 1993 will accomplish that. 300 cases made. $33 (5/15/90) **88**
Chassagne-Montrachet Les Vergers 1987: Ripe and flavorful with layers of honey, spice, pear and tobacco notes that need a year or two to come together. Fruit and oak flavors echo on the finish. Complete and satisfying. Drink up now. $42 (11/15/89) **90**

CORON PERE
Chassagne-Montrachet 1985 $20 (8/31/87) **83**

GEORGES DELEGER
Chassagne-Montrachet 1986 $82 (12/15/88) **89**

JOSEPH DROUHIN
Chassagne-Montrachet 1990: Lean and crisp, with tart pear and citrus notes that fan out, gaining a touch of honey and oak. Drinks well now. $36 (5/15/92) **85**
Chassagne-Montrachet 1989: A firm wine, with an abundance of butterscotch, vanilla, pear and apple flavors. Quite hard at this stage, but promising given the concentration of fruit to support the wood. Subtle despite all its stuffing. Drink in 1993 to '95. $50 (8/31/91) **88**
Chassagne-Montrachet 1988: Rich, round and flavorful, with intense pear, spice, melon and honey notes that are complex and subtle, gaining intensity and depth on the finish. Should get better in a year or two. Drink now through 1994. $39 (3/31/90) **87**
Chassagne-Montrachet 1987 $39 (3/15/89) **82**
Chassagne-Montrachet 1986 $35 (6/30/88) **84**
Chassagne-Montrachet 1982 $22 (10/01/84) **87**
Chassagne-Montrachet Clos St.-Jean 1989: Big, oily and quite delicious, with vanilla and butterscotch aromas followed by roasted almond, banana and pear flavors. Try in 1993 to '95. ($NA) (8/31/91) **88**
Chassagne-Montrachet Marquis de Laguiche 1989: Aromatically pleasing, rich, smoky and perfumed, with intense, vivid and elegant aromas of pear, spice, toast and cream. Has wonderful balance between the fruit and oak, with flavors that linger on and on. Tempting now, but best in 1993 to '96. $58 (2/15/91) **90**
Chassagne-Montrachet Marquis de Laguiche 1987: Lean and crisp, with muted flavors of toast and hints of pear or peach. Maybe in time it will develop greater depth and flavor. Drink now through 1994. Rel: $48 Cur: $61 (3/15/89) **84**
Chassagne-Montrachet Marquis de Laguiche 1986 $43 (5/31/88) **91**
Chassagne-Montrachet Marquis de Laguiche 1985 $40 (2/29/88) **93**
Chassagne-Montrachet Marquis de Laguiche 1983 $35 (2/29/88) **91**

FAIVELEY
Chassagne-Montrachet 1989: A rather straightforward wine in this otherwise classy crowd. Has simple butterscotch aromas and flavors and good acidity on the finish. Drink now or in 1993. $70 (8/31/91) **83**
Chassagne-Montrachet Les Vergers 1989: A lavish wine, with plenty of fruit and oak. Wonderful vanilla bean, honey and citrus aromas lead to intense vanilla and lemon flavors. Full-bodied, with a fine finish of vanilla and oak. Drink now through 1995. $83 (8/31/91) **90**

FONTAINE-GAGNARD
Chassagne-Montrachet Morgeot 1985 $45 (5/31/88) **71**

JEAN-NOEL GAGNARD
Chassagne-Montrachet 1989: Succulent and quite exotic, with fascinating earth and white truffle flavors and delicate, yet intense apple, pear and citrus notes on the finish. Drink in 1993 to '96. $55 (8/31/91) **88**
Chassagne-Montrachet 1986: Restrained and seemingly simple, but there is quite a bit of earthy pineapple and citric fruit just waiting to come together with some time in the cellar. Drink now or in 1993. $36 (3/15/89) **83**
Chassagne-Montrachet 1985 $40 (9/15/87) **92**
Chassagne-Montrachet 1984 $32 (4/30/87) **96**
Chassagne-Montrachet 1983 $25 (10/01/85) **87**
Chassagne-Montrachet Les Caillerets 1989: A well-made wine, with classy concentration. Has fresh wet stone, honey and lemon aromas, focused lemon, stone and pine nut flavors and a long, toasted vanilla finish. Full-bodied. Drink now through 1995. $64 (8/31/91) **91**
Chassagne-Montrachet Les Caillerets 1985 $45 (9/15/87) **94**
Chassagne-Montrachet Morgeot 1989: An exciting wine, with wonderfully rich fruit and balanced acidity. Full-bodied, with floral, honey and apricot aromas, focused ripe fruit and honey flavors, exciting acidity and light vanilla notes on the finish. Drink now through 1994. $63 (8/31/91) **90**
Chassagne-Montrachet Morgeot 1988: Very crisp and tart, with lemon, strawberry and spice aromas and flavors and a tight structure that will need until 1993 or '94 to soften and become more appealing. $54 (11/15/90) **80**
Chassagne-Montrachet Morgeot 1986 $54 (11/15/88) **89**
Chassagne-Montrachet Morgeot 1985 $45 (9/15/87) **86**
Chassagne-Montrachet Première Cru 1989: Has a pleasant balance of fruit, wood and fresh acidity, with hay and grapefruit aromas and flavors. Drink now through 1994. $60 (8/31/91) **89**
Chassagne-Montrachet Première Cru 1988: Spicy, fruity, ripe, round and complex, a beautifully focused wine with appealing nutmeg-tinged pear, apple and floral aromas and flavors. Long and concentrated, it's balanced enough to age well through 1993 to '95, but you could drink it now. 500 cases made. $50 (10/15/90) **91**
Chassagne-Montrachet Première Cru 1986 $47 (12/15/88) **74**

HENRI GERMAIN
Chassagne-Montrachet Morgeot 1989: Rich and smoky, with an impressive amount of fruit. Has toast, bacon, earth and fruit aromas, with a velvety mouth-feel of ripe lemon and cream flavors and a good finish. Full-bodied. Drink now through 1994. ($NA) (8/31/91) **91**
Chassagne-Montrachet Morgeot 1988: Has attractive but simple honey, pear and spice flavors, with moderate intensity and depth and a buttery oak note on the finish. Drink now. $43 (4/30/91) **83**
Chassagne-Montrachet Morgeot 1986: Soft, smooth and spicy, shining with fresh peach, pear and toast aromas and flavors, leading toward a nice touch of butter on the finish. Balanced and flavorful. $39 (3/15/89) **86**

JEAN GERMAIN
Chassagne-Montrachet 1985 $35 (9/15/87) **89**
Chassagne-Montrachet 1983 $18 (9/01/85) **93**

LOUIS JADOT
Chassagne-Montrachet 1989: Ripe, rich and lush, yet restrained, with a creamy texture. Has fig, baked apple, pear and plenty of honey flavors, with mineral touches that make it interesting and quite classy. Drink in 1994 to '96. $39 (8/31/91) **89**
Chassagne-Montrachet 1986: Smooth, round and subtly scented, already showing marvelous complexity, as well as appealing peach and pear flavors and nice hints of toasty oak. Long and rich, but reined in. $32 (5/31/89) **91**
Chassagne-Montrachet 1985 $32 (2/29/88) **91**
Chassagne-Montrachet 1984 $30 (2/29/88) **81**
Chassagne-Montrachet 1983 $28 (2/29/88) **89**
Chassagne-Montrachet Morgeot 1984 $38 (2/29/88) **88**
Chassagne-Montrachet Morgeot 1983 $34 (2/29/88) **86**
Chassagne-Montrachet Morgeot Clos de la Chapelle Domaine du Duc de Magenta 1989: Affluent and rich in style, with a silky mouth-feel. This full-bodied wine shows delicate tropical fruit and mineral aromas, tropical fruit, pineapple and hazelnut flavors and a vanilla finish. Drink now through 1994. $50 (8/31/91) **90**
Chassagne-Montrachet Morgeot Clos de la Chapelle Domaine du Duc de Magenta 1988: Very toasty and oaky in flavor, but supported by generous honey, pear and lemon flavors that make it true to type. Focused, harmonious and well balanced with acidity. A white Burgundy worth looking for. Drink now through 1994. $43 (4/30/91) **89**
Chassagne-Montrachet Morgeot Clos de la Chapelle Domaine du Duc de Magenta 1986: Woody, perfumey and intensely spicy, long and focused. Very well made, but will the pear and apple flavor ever come into balance? If it does, it will be a doozy. $41 (5/31/89) **85**
Chassagne-Montrachet Morgeot Clos de la Chapelle Domaine du Duc de Magenta 1985 $38 (2/29/88) **89**

JAFFELIN
Chassagne-Montrachet 1990: Tart and earthy, showing lean lemon and pear notes. A simple wine, with sound flavors, but lacking in richness and depth. Drink now to 1995. $28 (4/15/92) **81**
Chassagne-Montrachet 1989: A classy Chassagne-Montrachet, with full-throttle tropical fruit character. Smooth and rounded, with pineapple, mango and banana aromas and flavors backed by good acidity and a mineral touch. Drink in 1993 to '95. $40 (8/31/91) **87**
Chassagne-Montrachet 1987: Lean and austere with tight, citris, pear, spice and oaky flavors that are a bit harsh and tannic. Needs some time to come around. $30 (3/15/89) **83**
Chassagne-Montrachet Les Caillerets 1989: More forward in style, with evolved flavors. Has good aromas and flavors of butterscotch, lemon and apple, with a firm mouth-feel and a toasty finish. Drink now or in 1993. $30 (8/31/91) **86**
Chassagne-Montrachet Les Caillerets 1983 $20 (6/01/85) **91**
Chassagne-Montrachet Les Vergers 1990: Crisp, ripe and appley, with hints of butter and spice. Full-bodied, well proportioned and drinkable now. $32 (4/15/92) **85**
Chassagne-Montrachet Les Vergers 1989: Beautifully crafted and very pretty, with ripe fruit aromas and hints of pineapple and vanilla. Full-bodied, with extremely attractive pineapple and vanilla flavors and a toasty finish. Drink now through 1994. $30 (8/31/91) **87**

LABOURE-ROI
Chassagne-Montrachet 1989: Big and a bit rough, with a deep golden color, toasted hazelnut aromas and pineapple and roasted almond flavors. Drink in 1993 to '95. $42 (8/31/91) **88**
Chassagne-Montrachet 1985 $32 (8/31/87) **91**

LAROCHE
Chassagne-Montrachet 1989: Silky and elegant, with intense, spicy butter and pear flavors framed by subtle, but pleasing smoky oak nuances. A pinch of nutmeg on the finish adds dimension. A seductive style, with compelling fruit, wonderful balance and plenty of length on the finish. Drink now through 1995. 1,000 cases made. $45 (2/28/91) **90**
Chassagne-Montrachet 1988: Crisp, pure and fruity, more like a Chablis than a Montrachet, with green apple flavors and a mineral, austere finish. $33 (2/15/91) **83**
Chassagne-Montrachet Première Cru 1988: Combines richness with an elegant, light feel on the palate, starting with apple aromas and finishing with lingering notes of pear and vanilla. Has good, crisp structure. Try now or hold. 350 cases made. $39 (2/15/91) **90**

LOUIS LATOUR
Chassagne-Montrachet 1989: Focused and well presented. A distinctive wine, with hay, apple and wet straw dominating the aromas and plenty of rich, ripe honey flavors. Has a crisp finish. Drink now through 1994. $42 (8/31/91) **88**
Chassagne-Montrachet 1986 $38 (9/30/88) **90**
Chassagne-Montrachet 1985 $33 (2/29/88) **88**

Chassagne-Montrachet 1984 $33 (2/29/88) **78**
Chassagne-Montrachet 1982 $33 (2/29/88) **88**
Chassagne-Montrachet Première Cru 1986 $43 (2/29/88) **92**

OLIVIER LEFLAIVE FRERES
Chassagne-Montrachet 1989: Clean and subtle, with apple and cream aromas and plenty of lemon and citrus flavors on the finish. Drink in 1993 to '95. $41 (8/31/91) **85**
Chassagne-Montrachet 1988: Crisp and focused, with tightly reined-in pear and apple flavors and hints of citrus and toast on the finish. Needs until 1993 to '95 to soften. $37 (8/31/91) **86**
Chassagne-Montrachet Les Baudines 1986: A firm, crisp texture and earth, butter and citrus aromas and flavors make this a complex wine. Mineral flavors echo on the finish. A well-made, medium-bodied wine that lacks pizzazz. $38 (10/15/90) **85**
Chassagne-Montrachet Les Chaumées 1989: Deliciously balanced, with alluring fruit flavors and butter and pear aromas that follow through on the palate. Has a silky, creamy mouth-feel and a long finish. Drink now through 1994. ($NA) (8/31/91) **90**

LEROY
Chassagne-Montrachet Les Chênevottes 1988: Full flavored and full-bodied, with chalky butterscotch flavors and a rich, lingering aftertaste. Not greatly appealing right now, but seems to have what it needs to age into a very nice wine by 1994 to '96. 170 cases made. $116 (4/30/91) **86**
Chassagne-Montrachet Les Ruchottes 1988: Extremely full flavored and complex, with generous pear, pineapple, butter, cream and spice flavors. Has fine depth, good acidic structure and a lingering aftertaste that echoes honey and spice. Tempting to drink now, but should improve in the cellar through 1996. 125 cases made. $116 (4/30/91) **90**

A. LIGERET
Chassagne-Montrachet Réserve Antonin Toursier 1988: Elegant and well proportioned, with ripe pear, honey, spice and pepper notes followed by toasty French oak. Tightly wound and a bit tannic now, but it has all the ingredients for a fine wine. Best to drink now through 1994. $45 (2/15/91) **84**

LUPE-CHOLET
Chassagne-Montrachet Morgeot Vignes Blanches 1987: Smells and tastes earthy, woody and gamy. Has redeeming fruit and spice flavors on the finish, but an earthy, oxidized character dominates. $45 (11/15/89) **73**
Chassagne-Montrachet La Romanée 1986 $26 (2/29/88) **85**

CHATEAU DE LA MALTROYE
Chassagne-Montrachet Clos de la Maltroye 1983 $21 (6/01/86) **80**
Chassagne-Montrachet Grandes Ruchottes 1989: Fresh and fruity, with subtle flavors of citrus, pear, peach and toast. Medium-bodied, with moderate depth. Not as full-blown as the best from this appellation, but well balanced. Drink now or in 1993. $40 (2/28/91) **86**
Chassagne-Montrachet Maltroie-Crets 1986 $27 (10/31/88) **74**
Chassagne-Montrachet Morgeot-Fairendes 1986 $26 (9/30/88) **86**
Chassagne-Montrachet Morgeot-Fairendes 1983 $19 (11/16/85) **79**
Chassagne-Montrachet Morgeot Vigne Blanche 1989: This subtle style has tightly reined-in fruit that's elegant and concentrated. The complex honey, pear, citrus and toasty oak flavors are woven together in a stylish package. Flavorful and lively on the finish. Drink now through 1995. $40 (2/28/91) **87**
Chassagne-Montrachet Morgeot Vigne Blanche 1986 $29 (9/30/88) **90**
Chassagne-Montrachet Morgeot Vigne Blanche 1983 $17 (6/16/85) **88**
Chassagne-Montrachet La Romanée Première Cuvée 1988: A modestly proportioned Chassagne that's lean in fruit flavor, but nicely spiced up with cedar and butterscotch aromas. Its basic flavor is earthy. Good to drink now through 1994. $31 (8/31/91) **83**

PROSPER MAUFOUX
Chassagne-Montrachet 1985 $31 (4/30/88) **89**
Chassagne-Montrachet Les Chênevottes 1989: Rather elegant for a Chassagne, with delicate aromas of hay, cream and apple. Medium- to full-bodied, with coconut and apple flavors and a round, silky mouth-feel. Drink now or in 1993. $37 (8/31/91) **88**
Chassagne-Montrachet Les Chênevottes 1987: A clumsy, disjointed effort that's pungently earthy, with hints of botrytis and a touch of sulfur that tastes dirty. Drink now if you must. $37 (2/28/91) **71**

MOILLARD
Chassagne-Montrachet La Romanée 1987: Concentrated and thick. Woody flavors dominate, leaving a buttery, honey flavor that may not appeal to everyone. Definitely on the oaky side. $31 (11/15/89) **74**
Chassagne-Montrachet La Romanée 1986 $40 (4/30/88) **88**

MOMMESSIN
Chassagne-Montrachet 1989: Rather forward in style, but delicious, with a stony, chalky apple character on the nose and palate and hazelnut notes on the finish. Drink now. ($NA) (8/31/91) **83**
Chassagne-Montrachet Première Cru 1989: Seems very woody, but it has pleasant fruit. Offers vanilla, almond, honey and bark aromas, bark and lemon flavors and a toasted finish. Medium-bodied. Drink now. ($NA) (8/31/91) **85**

BERNARD MOREAU
Chassagne-Montrachet Grandes Ruchottes 1986 $38 (9/30/88) **91**

BERNARD MOREY
Chassagne-Montrachet 1982 $11 (3/01/85) **86**
Chassagne-Montrachet Les Baudines 1986 $41 (12/15/88) **88**
Chassagne-Montrachet Les Embrazées 1986 $40 (12/15/88) **91**
Chassagne-Montrachet Morgeot 1987: Smells exotic and spicy, but the flavors are reined in and it's austere in structure. Should be drinkable by now. $42 (5/31/89) **88**
Chassagne-Montrachet Morgeot 1986 $35 (12/15/88) **88**

JEAN-MARC MOREY
Chassagne-Montrachet Les Caillerets 1989: Focused and fresh, showing generous pear, lemon and anise aromas and flavors, slipping in mineral notes on the finish. A refreshing wine, finishing with depth and focus. Drinkable now, but better after 1993. $54 (3/31/92) **88**
Chassagne-Montrachet Les Caillerets 1986 $39 (12/15/88) **85**
Chassagne-Montrachet Champs-Gains 1989: Fresh and tightly wound, with a firm texture and subtle pear, butter and nutmeg aromas and flavors, turning silky and generous on the finish. Has the potential to be an outstanding wine. Needs until 1993 to '95 to show what it has. $54 (3/31/92) **90**
Chassagne-Montrachet Champs-Gains 1986 $38 (12/15/88) **88**
Chassagne-Montrachet Champs-Gains 1985 $30 (10/31/87) **75**
Chassagne-Montrachet Les Chaumées 1986 $38 (12/15/88) **90**
Chassagne-Montrachet Les Chênevottes 1989: Focused and elegant, with complex pear, lemon, spice and oak aromas and flavors. Beautifully balanced and delicate on the finish without losing any of its richness. Drinkable now, but has the stuff to age through 1995 and beyond. $54 (3/31/92) **91**
Chassagne-Montrachet Les Chênevottes 1986 $34 (12/15/88) **86**

DOMAINE MARC MOREY
Chassagne-Montrachet 1986 $34 (9/30/88) **83**
Chassagne-Montrachet Morgeot 1986 $37 (9/30/88) **94**
Chassagne-Montrachet Virondot 1986 $42 (12/15/88) **91**

MICHEL NIELLON
Chassagne-Montrachet Les Vergers 1988: An earthy wine, with strong lemon and apple aromas and flavors shaded by spice, toast and earth notes. The crisp texture keeps it in line. Drinkable now through 1994. $38 (8/31/91) **87**

REINE PEDAUQUE
Chassagne-Montrachet 1989: This ready-to-drink Chassagne-Montrachet has juicy flavors, with a complex lemon, grapefruit and hazelnut character. A nice hazelnut-mineral touch adds complexity. $35 (8/31/91) **88**

FERNAND PILLOT
Chassagne-Montrachet Grandes Ruchottes 1988: Intense and concentrated, smooth and focused with ripe pear, peach and tangerine flavors and a pretty touch of buttery oak that adds dimension and complexity to the flavors. Tempting now, but can be cellared until 1994. $43 (5/15/90) **90**
Chassagne-Montrachet Morgeot 1988: A gentle, elegant style that unfolds gracefully, offering pretty honey, citrus, pear and melon flavors, framed by toasty oak; young and still developing. Drink now through 1994. $35 (5/15/90) **91**
Chassagne-Montrachet Les Vergers 1988: Made in a subtle, delicate style, but with plenty of rich vanilla, pear, lemon and butter flavors that combine to give it depth and dimension. A touch of honey comes through on the finish. Drink now through 1994. $35 (5/15/90) **87**
Chassagne-Montrachet Les Vergers 1985: Redolent of butterscotch, this distinctively earthy wine has impressive depth, but the one character tends to overpower whatever else is there, right through to the finish. Drink soon. $28 (5/31/89) **85**

JEAN PILLOT
Chassagne-Montrachet Les Caillerets 1988: Young and intense, yet elegant and well defined, with complex pear, lemon, butter and spice flavors that are tightly packed together. Picks up mineral and lemon notes on the finish. Has plenty of finesse, but cellar until 1993. $39 (2/28/91) **88**

PAUL PILLOT
Chassagne-Montrachet Les Caillerets 1985 $30 (10/31/87) **84**
Chassagne-Montrachet Les Grandes Ruchottes 1987: A delicious wine, big, rich and oaky with buttery spice, honey, smoke and pear flavors that are deep and concentrated, finishing with a lovely smoky aftertaste that defines elegance and finesse. Drink now through 1995. $38 (2/28/90) **91**
Chassagne-Montrachet Les Grandes Ruchottes 1986 $30 (11/15/88) **91**
Chassagne-Montrachet Les Grandes Ruchottes 1985 $30 (10/31/87) **88**
Chassagne-Montrachet La Romanée 1987: Smooth and rich, with lots of vanilla-tinged pear and toast aromas and flavors that are sharply focused, long and elegant. A powerful wine with grace. Drinkable now, but cellaring until 1993 or '94 shouldn't harm it. $48 (2/28/90) **91**

DOMAINE PONAVOY
Chassagne-Montrachet 1988: Spicy, rich and buttery, but well supported, with crisp, appley acidity and a touch of astringency that keeps it from being as smooth and elegant as it could be. Has lots of intensity, but it should be in better balance by now. 300 cases made. $40 (2/15/91) **86**

DOMAINE PRIEUR-BRUNET
Chassagne-Montrachet Les Embazées 1989: An expressive wine, with lots of interesting ripe fruit flavor. The lemon peel aromas have earthy nuances. A full-bodied wine, with ripe peach and cream flavors and an intense fruit finish. Drink now through 1994. $54 (8/31/91) **88**

DOMAINE RAMONET
Chassagne-Montrachet 1989 $45 (9/30/91) (HS) **87**
Chassagne-Montrachet 1988: Ripe, spicy and buttery, with layers of rich pear, lemon, nutmeg and citrus notes that are full-bodied and assertive. Could use a little more finesse, but altogether it's a pleasant drink. Start drinking now to 1993. $43 (2/28/91) **86**
Chassagne-Montrachet Les Caillerets 1989 $60 (9/30/91) (HS) **92**
Chassagne-Montrachet Les Caillerets 1988 $61 (9/30/91) (HS) **93**
Chassagne-Montrachet Les Caillerets 1987 $40 (9/30/91) (HS) **88**
Chassagne-Montrachet Les Caillerets 1985 $65 (9/30/91) (HS) **90**
Chassagne-Montrachet Morgeot 1988: Intense, rich, ripe and earthy, with crisp acidity and tightly wound pear, toast, apple and melon flavors that are sharply focused and powerful. A big, dramatic style, with a long, full finish. Drink now to '95 and beyond. 250 cases made. $59 (2/28/91) **92**
Chassagne-Montrachet Morgeot 1987: Overripe, earthy style, with a solid core of pear and apple flavor that emerges nicely on the finish, but it is tempered by a somewhat scratchy texture that should have softened by now. $49 (2/28/90) **79**
Chassagne-Montrachet Morgeot 1986 $55 (9/30/91) (HS) **90**
Chassagne-Montrachet Morgeot 1985 $60 (9/30/91) (HS) **88**
Chassagne-Montrachet Morgeot 1983 $60 (9/30/91) (HS) **87**
Chassagne-Montrachet Morgeot 1970 $75 (9/30/91) (HS) **92**
Chassagne-Montrachet Les Ruchottes 1988 $45 (9/30/91) (HS) **92**
Chassagne-Montrachet Les Ruchottes 1987: Earthy style, with good concentration of green apple and pineapple aromas and flavors shaded by a touch of vanilla and toast. Drinkable now but probably better after 1991. $52 (2/28/90) **86**
Chassagne-Montrachet Les Ruchottes 1986 $83 (9/30/91) (HS) **90**
Chassagne-Montrachet Les Ruchottes 1985 $70 (9/30/91) (HS) **87**
Chassagne-Montrachet Les Ruchottes 1984 $40 (9/30/91) (HS) **86**
Chassagne-Montrachet Les Ruchottes 1983 $70 (9/30/91) (HS) **89**
Chassagne-Montrachet Les Ruchottes 1982 $60 (9/30/91) (HS) **91**
Chassagne-Montrachet Les Ruchottes 1981 $40 (9/30/91) (HS) **87**
Chassagne-Montrachet Les Ruchottes 1978 $70 (9/30/91) (HS) **86**
Chassagne-Montrachet Les Ruchottes 1974 $50 (9/30/91) (HS) **81**
Chassagne-Montrachet Les Ruchottes 1973 $60 (9/30/91) (HS) **89**
Chassagne-Montrachet Les Ruchottes 1972 $60 (9/30/91) (HS) **93**
Chassagne-Montrachet Les Ruchottes 1969 $100 (9/30/91) (HS) **89**
Chassagne-Montrachet Les Ruchottes 1966 $100 (9/30/91) (HS) **86**
Chassagne-Montrachet Les Ruchottes 1959 $200 (9/30/91) (HS) **84**

REMOISSENET
Chassagne-Montrachet Les Caillerets 1985 $63 (2/29/88) **90**

ANTONIN RODET
Chassagne-Montrachet 1981 $14 (12/01/84) **58**
Chassagne-Montrachet Morgeot 1989: An extremely appealing balance of fruit and oak. Has very perfumed, floral, clove, honey and light pineapple aromas; it's full-bodied, with honey, mineral and fruit flavors and a long finish of cloves and honey. Drink now to 1994. $40 (8/31/91) **91**

Key to Symbols

The scores reported here are the results of blind tastings conducted by our panel of senior editors. Wines that carry the initials below are results of individual tastings.

THE WINE SPECTATOR 100-POINT SCALE ***95-100***—Classic, a great wine; ***90-94***—Outstanding, superior character and style; ***80-89***—Good to very good, a wine with special qualities; ***70-79***—Average, drinkable wine that may have minor flaws; ***60-69***—Below average, drinkable but not recommended; ***50-59***—Poor, undrinkable, not recommended. "+"—With a score indicates a range; used primarily with barrel tastings to indicate a preliminary score.

SPECIAL DESIGNATIONS SS—Spectator Selection, CS—Cellar Selection, BB—Best Buy, ($NA)—Price not available, (NR)—Not released.

TASTER'S INITIALS (JG)—Jim Gordon, (HS)—Harvey Steiman, (JL)—James Laube, (JS)—James Suckling, (TM)—Thomas Matthews, (TR)—Terry Robards, (PM)—Per-Henrik Mansson, (BT)—Barrel Tasting (these wines were tasted blind from barrel samples), (CA-date)—*California's Great Cabernets* by James Laube, (CH-date)—*California's Great Chardonnays* by James Laube, (VP-date)—*Vintage Port* by James Suckling.

DATE TASTED Dates in parentheses represent the issue in which the rating was published.

DOMAINE ROUX PERE & FILS
Chassagne-Montrachet 1989: Extremely ripe, with captivating, heavy-duty tropical fruit aromas and flavors coated with honey, pear and banana notes. Nicely balanced, with sharp lemon and grapefruit-dominated acidity. Drink now through 1994. $45 (8/31/91) **89**
Chassagne-Montrachet 1988: Refreshingly crisp and concentrated with a narrow beam of grapefruit, honey and pear flavors that gain depth and complexity on the finish. Delicious now but can be cellared. Drink now to 1994. $35 (2/28/90) **88**
Chassagne-Montrachet 1986 $34 (2/29/88) **90**
Chassagne-Montrachet 1985 $32 (8/31/87) **86**
Chassagne-Montrachet Morgeot 1989: A wine with outstanding intensity of fruit and wonderful balance. Has honey, clove and pineapple aromas, electrifying butter, honey and cream flavors, refreshing acidity and a lingering finish. Drink now through 1995. $55 (8/31/91) **92**
Chassagne-Montrachet Morgeot 1988: Attractive for its honey and spice flavors, but there's a touch of astringency and oakiness that needs time to mellow. Drink now to 1993. $39 (2/28/90) **86**
Chassagne-Montrachet Morgeot 1987: Light and mildly appealing, with floral and somewhat honey and peachlike aromas more reminiscent of Riesling than Chardonnay. Probably best to drink soon. $43 (5/31/89) **79**
Chassagne-Montrachet Morgeot 1986 $36 (2/29/88) **91**

LEONARD DE ST.-AUBIN
Chassagne-Montrachet 1986 $25 (12/31/87) **76**

DOMAINE ETIENNE SAUZET
Chassagne-Montrachet 1989: Firm and exciting, full of honey, coconut, apple and modest mineral notes. Built for aging; drink in 1993 to '95. $60 (8/31/91) **90**
Chassagne-Montrachet 1988: Lovely honey, pear, spice and earthy mineral flavors are rich, complex, deep and enticing, with a silky-smooth texture and hints of nutmeg and citrus on the finish. Tight, firm and ready to drink now through 1994. $38 (2/15/91) **91**

HENRI DE VILLAMONT
Chassagne-Montrachet Les Vergers 1986 $29 (12/15/88) **81**

MEURSAULT

PIERRE ANDRE
Meursault 1989: Lively and crisp, with excellent acidity, offering plenty of grapefruit and apple aromas. Full-bodied, with intense grapefruit flavors and lively acidity. Drink in 1993 to '95. $23 (8/31/91) **84**

DOMAINE D'AUVENAY
Meursault Les Narvaux 1989: This is to beg or kill for. Tastes like nectar, with captivating aromas of lilacs, honey, butter and melon. Full-bodied, with multidimensional flavors and toasty notes. Superbly long on the finish. From Lalou Bize-Leroy. Drink in 1994 to '96. Rel: $60 Cur: $68 (8/31/91) **96**

R. BALLOT-MILLOT & FILS
Meursault Charmes 1987: Spicy and generous in flavor and aroma, but lacking the silkiness and concentration of the best wines. The honey and pear flavors are pleasant, but a chalkiness intrudes on the finish. Drink soon; tasted twice. $34 (8/31/90) **77**
Meursault Les Criots 1985 $34 (4/30/88) **88**

BICHOT
Meursault 1989: Has good flavors, but it's a little simple, with apple tart aromas and similar flavors, fresh acidity and a tasty finish. Drink in 1993 or '94. $26 (8/31/91) **84**
Meursault 1987: Crisp, tart and balanced with simple, correct, slightly underripe fruit. Drinkable but uninspired. $24 (9/30/89) **75**
Meursault Charmes 1988: A big, showy wine that has so much flavor you almost have to chew it. Full-bodied, toasty and figgy in aroma, it's rich with vanilla, pear and honey flavors that linger nicely on the finish. Impressive now, but needs time to soften around the edges. Try it in 1993 or later. $40 (7/15/90) **92**
Meursault Charmes 1986 $37 (3/15/88) **82**
Meursault Charmes 1985 $30 (2/15/88) **93**
Meursault Genevrières 1989: Rather subdued now; could become even better. Shows great class, with many layers of fruit. Has toasted bread, hazelnut and apple pie aromas, full-bodied apple pie and cream flavors and a medium finish. Drink in 1993 to '95. $33 (8/31/91) **90**
Meursault Goutte-d'Or 1988: Rich and round, with definite earthy overtones to the pear, butter and vanilla aromas and flavors. Seems a little hard-edged, with a touch of volatility that will appeal to some and turn others off. Drink in 1993 to '96. $35 (1/31/92) **82**
Meursault Hospices de Beaune Cuvée Goureau 1986 $55 (2/15/88) **92**
Meursault Poruzots 1989: A more restrained style, with an excellent backbone of acidity. A full-bodied wine, with restrained white truffle, vanilla, honey and apple aromas, lively acidity, lemon and cream flavors and a fresh finish. Drink in 1992 or '93. $31 (8/31/91) **90**
Meursault Poruzots 1988: A sturdy Meursault with long-lasting flavors. Unusually peppery and woody in aroma, and rather rough and choppy in texture, but with attractive toast and spice flavors on the finish. $36 (7/15/90) **85**

BITOUZET-PRIEUR
Meursault 1987: A very pleasant and long-lasting wine that tastes well balanced and moderately flavorful, with spice, apple and butter notes. Smells slightly earthy, but has good fruit flavor. $28 (7/15/90) **86**
Meursault Charmes 1987: A well-built wine, with intriguing flavors that aren't for everyone. Earthy and spicy, with lots of mineral and hazelnut aromas and flavors. Pear and butterscotch echo on the solid finish. $41 (2/28/91) **87**
Meursault Clos du Cromin 1987: Rich and ripe for this lean vintage. It has plenty of pear, vanilla, spice and honey flavors. Well balanced and smooth textured. $34 (8/31/90) **87**

GUY BOCARD
Meursault Charmes 1985 $32 (4/30/87) **91**
Meursault Les Grands Charrons 1986 $27 (10/15/88) **69**
Meursault Limozin 1986 $28 (10/15/88) **84**
Meursault Limozin 1985 $28 (4/30/87) **85**

JEAN-MARC BOILLOT
Meursault 1989: Offers superb richness and power, with impressively ripe aromas of pineapple, apple and tropical fruit, lots of pear and coconut flavors and a long, lively finish. Full-bodied. As good as any *premier cru* Meursault. Drink now through 1994. ($NA) (8/31/91) **91**

PIERRE BOILLOT
Meursault 1988: Ripe and generous, offering well-modulated pear, vanilla and nutmeg aromas and flavors that, together with butterscotch, echo on the long finish. Not a big wine, but it's flavorful and worth keeping until 1993 to gain complexity. $37 (8/31/90) **87**
Meursault Charmes 1988: Well made and well balanced, with plenty of spicy complexity. The spice, toast, floral and fruit aromas and flavors continue through the aftertaste. Drink now. 600 cases made. $47 (8/31/90) **90**
Meursault Charmes 1987: The dull and flat pear, citrus and spice flavors could use a little more richness and depth, but some may find it subtle and more appealing. Drink now. $44 (8/31/90) **79**

JEAN CLAUDE BOISSET
Meursault 1988: Ripe and round, but decidedly earthy and perhaps even oxidized, with spicy pear flavor and a touch of honey. Distinctive, but not as balanced as it could be. Drinkable now. $28 (5/31/91) **83**
Meursault 1988: Clean, floral and fresh, a lighter style Meursault with more delicacy than heft, showing apple flavor and a bit of honey on the short finish. $28 (5/15/90) **81**

BOUCHARD PERE & FILS
Meursault 1989: A good, but atypical wine for its region. Aromas of salted peanuts and grapefruit lead to lively but unusual fruit flavors for a Meursault. Smooth in texture and slightly herbal in flavor. $37 (4/30/91) **83**
Meursault 1983 $20 (4/30/87) **75**
Meursault Clos des Corvées de Citeaux 1986: Hard-edged, modest in scope, but tasty in an earthy-pineapple way. For those who want understatement, this is the one. Drink now. $26 (3/15/89) **83**
Meursault Genevrières Domaines du Château de Beaune 1989: Offers very good, straightforward flavors and character. Has floral, honey, asparagus and orange aromas and apple tart and honey flavors. Full-bodied; medium in acidity and on the finish. Drink now through 1994. $63 (8/31/91) **85**
Meursault Genevrières Domaines du Château de Beaune 1986: The honey and pineapple flavors offer complexity and depth but it's a little dull and lacks vitality. Not a quintessential Mersault but it does have character. $44 (3/15/89) **77**

HUBERT BOUZEREAU
Meursault Limozin 1985 $27 (8/31/87) **88**
Meursault Les Narvaux 1985 $25 (4/30/87) **73**

MICHEL BOUZEREAU
Meursault Genevrières 1989: Polished, round and silky, with lots of generous pear, pineapple, nutmeg and vanilla aromas and flavors playing against each other, echoing honey and a touch of butter on the finish. A lovely wine to drink now, but cellaring until 1993 to '95 couldn't hurt. 400 cases made. $46 (5/31/91) **93**
Meursault Genevrières 1988: It's wound up tight, but this is a very polished and elegant wine underneath. A toasty, nutty, oaky quality accents the intense, tight grapefruit, apple and pineapple flavors that linger beautifully on the tangy finish. Won't show its best until 1993 to '96. 400 cases made. $37 (7/15/90) **93**
Meursault Les Grands Charrons 1989: Very focused and elegant, with generous pineapple, apple and honey aromas and flavors. Built with some reserve, it holds the flavors in check and adds a layer of mineral on the aftertaste that is pleasant and bodes well for the future. Drink in 1993 or '94. 2,000 cases made. $33 (5/31/91) **90**
Meursault Les Grands Charrons 1988: Smooth and spicy, this harmonious wine has beautifully integrated fruit and oak right through the long finish. Flavors of peach, toast and vanilla compete with the core of pear that lingers on the aftertaste. Drinkable now, but should be better in 1993 or '94. 1,000 cases made. $25 (8/31/90) **91**
Meursault Les Tessons 1989: Fresh and generous, with pear and apple aromas and flavors framed by a definite smack of oak. A bit hard around the edges, but should become a nice one by 1993 or '94. $35 (5/31/91) **87**
Meursault Les Tessons 1988: Beautifully fruity, with intense lemon, apple, pear, vanilla and spice flavors that linger on the finish. Has great balance, but the lean structure and firm acidity need time to broaden out; best to cellar until 1993 to '95. 600 cases made. $28 (8/31/90) **90**
Meursault Les Tessons 1985 $25 (5/31/88) **70**

PHILIPPE BOUZEREAU
Meursault Charmes 1987: Has plenty of toasty, buttery aromas and basically ripe flavors, but finishes a bit too sour for us. Good, but not as well-balanced as it might be. $37 (11/15/89) **75**
Meursault Genevrières 1987: Pear, citrus and spice notes are ripe and forward up-front, but lack intensity and depth. A rather one-dimensional wine. Drink now. Tasted twice. $37 (7/15/90) **80**
Meursault Les Narvaux 1989: Austere, tart and earthy, with astringent, closed-in flavors that turn chalky. Hints of honey and green apple come through on the finish. May be better with bottle time. Drink now to 1994. $37 (11/30/91) **74**
Meursault Les Narvaux 1986: Ripe and butterscotchy on the nose, broad and soft on the palate, this one pulls back on the throttle without showing a lot of grace. Slightly bitter finish. Try now. $31 (3/15/89) **81**
Meursault Poruzots 1987: A bit too tannic and tart to enjoy on release, but it should have developed by now. Has attractive pear aromas, good acidity for aging, appley flavors and a lingering finish. $36 (11/15/89) **83**

BOYER-MARTENOT
Meursault Les Narvaux 1983 $15 (2/16/86) **60**

JEANNE-MARIE DE CHAMPS
Meursault Charmes Hospices de Beaune Cuvée de Bahèzre-de-Lanlay 1989: Spicy and rich in aroma and elegant in structure, but undertones of leafy, metallic notes robs a bit of fruit flavor. Good, but overall on the rustic, earthy side. $75 (8/31/91) **82**

CHANSON PERE & FILS
Meursault 1989: Very simple and light; picked too early. Has light apple and chalk aromas, with medium-bodied flavors of apples and honey. Light on the finish. Drink now. $30 (8/31/91) **78**

CHARTRON & TREBUCHET
Meursault 1989: Exotic ginger, vanilla, pear and spice flavors are rich and full-bodied, adding up to a complex and pleasing wine. The flavors stay with you from start to finish. Can stand cellaring, too. Best to drink now through 1994. Tasted twice. $41 (2/28/91) **88**
Meursault Les Charmes 1990: Packs in plenty of flavor, with honey, citrus and pear notes, and it's a bit rough around the edges, finishing with toasty oak. Drink now to 1994. $44 (3/31/92) **87**
Meursault Les Charmes 1989: Beautifully articulated pear, apple and vanilla aromas and flavors make this immediately likable, and beneath the fruit lies a solid underpinning of acidity. Has length, echoing spice and fruit. Wonderful now, but better after 1993. 200 cases made. $57 (2/28/91) **91**
Meursault Les Charmes 1986 $45 (5/31/88) **87**
Meursault Genevrières Hospices de Beaune Cuvée Baudot 1987: A crisp, lean, concentrated Mersault with honey, pear and spicy flavors that are focused, subtle and complex. The finish is firm and rich with good length and a pretty aftertaste. $87 (3/15/89) **91**

F. CHAUVENET
Meursault Les Boucheres 1986 $40 (6/30/88) **77**
Meursault Les Casse Têtes 1989: Somewhat one-dimensional, but extremely well made. A full-bodied wine, with clean tropical fruit and apple aromas, lush pineapple and apple flavors and fresh acidity. Drink now through 1994. $26 (8/31/91) **85**
Meursault Les Casse Têtes 1985 $32 (8/31/87) **84**
Meursault Les Casse Têtes 1984 $19 (7/16/86) **71**
Meursault Les Casse Têtes 1982 $11 (3/01/85) **82**
Meursault Charmes Hospices de Beaune Cuvée de Bahèzre-de-Lanlay 1985: Rich and elegant, with concentrated fruit, hints of melon, fig, spice and toasty oak; clean and well balanced, finishing with a touch of citrus and nuttiness. $141 (3/15/89) **86**
Meursault Les Genevrières 1989: An explosion of aromas and flavors. Has mango, tropical fruit and stone aromas and electrifying apple, mineral and juniper flavors; incredibly lively on the finish. Full-bodied. Drink in 1993 to '96. $42 (8/31/91) **94**
Meursault Les Genevrières 1986 $40 (4/30/88) **85**
Meursault Les Genevrières Hospices de Beaune Cuvée Baudot 1983 $55 (11/01/85) **88**
Meursault Les Gouttes d'Or 1989: Somewhat disappointing. Ripe and fruity, but slightly astringent, with apple pie and cream aromas and flavors that seem very ripe. Lots of vanilla notes and new wood emerge on the finish. Drink now. ($NA) (8/31/91) **86**
Meursault Hospices de Beaune Cuvée Jehan-Humblot 1985 $90 (7/31/87) **91**
Meursault Hospices de Beaune Cuvée Loppin 1982 Rel: $33 Cur: $65 (1/01/85) CS **92**
Meursault Les Perrières 1989: Wonderfully balanced, with amazingly intense flavors. Full-bodied,

with pineapple and other tropical fruit aromas, pure cream, apricot and vanilla flavors and a firm backbone. Long on the finish. Drink in 1993 to '96. $41 (8/31/91) **91**
Meursault Les Perrières 1986 $40 (4/30/88) **86**
Meursault Les Poruzots 1989: Amazingly concentrated, with superb fruit flavors. Has wet hay, smoke, mineral and apple aromas, rich, round flavors of hay, truffles and vanilla beans and a long finish. Drink in 1993 or '94. $53 (8/31/91) **94**
Meursault Les Poruzots 1986 $40 (4/30/88) **92**

CHEVALIER DE BEAUBASSIN
Meursault 1985 $24 (4/30/88) **81**

DENIS CHEVILLON
Meursault Charmes 1959 ($NA) (8/31/90) (TR) **86**

J.-F. COCHE-DURY
Meursault 1987: A tart, crisp style, with sharply focused green apple and vanilla flavors and a touch of earthiness for nuance. But snappy acidity carries the finish a long way. Drink now to 1994. $33 (2/28/90) **86**
Meursault Les Chevalières 1987: Very full, ripe and round, yet graceful and elegant, with focused buttery pineapple aromas and flavors and a welcome touch of honey on the finish. Delicious now, but should remain drinkable through at least 1993 or '94. $36 (2/28/90) **91**
Meursault Perrières 1987: Crisply structured, tasty and artfully balanced between green apple, honey and vanilla flavors, all of which come together beautifully on the finish with elegance and finesse. Delicious to drink now. $50 (2/28/90) **90**
Meursault Les Rougeots 1987: Ripe and generous, with lots of pear, nutmeg and vanilla aromas and flavors that rest gently on a firm structure. Not a big, powerful wine, but the flavors are bold and well-defined. Drink now. $33 (2/28/90) **90**

CORON PERE
Meursault 1985 $18 (8/31/87) **64**

JEAN-PIERRE DICONNE
Meursault Clos des Luchets 1989: A lively, elegant style of Meursault, with vanilla bean and dried fruit aromas. Medium-bodied, with lively acidity and fresh vanilla and apple flavors. Drink in 1993 or '94. ($NA) (8/31/91) **87**
Meursault Les Narvaux 1989: This firm, full-bodied wine draws you in, with somewhat floral, buttery, creamy aromas and floral, apple flavors. Has an iron backbone of acidity. Drink in 1993 to '96. ($NA) (8/31/91) **89**

JOSEPH DROUHIN
Meursault 1990: Crisp and clean, with sharply focused pear, citrus, hazelnut and apple flavors that turn smooth, complex and creamy on the finish. Has delicacy and character. Drinks well now, but can hold through 1995. 2,000 cases made. $32 (5/15/92) **91**
Meursault 1989: Stuffed with fruit, but a wonderful backbone of acidity gives it elegance. Full-bodied, with very lively acidity, mango and butter aromas, focused, earthy lemon flavors and a long finish. Drink in 1993 to '96. $45 (8/31/91) **90**
Meursault 1988: Rich and earthy, with deep pear, spice, lemon and citrus notes that are very attractive. Has fine balance and a long finish with plenty of flavor. Drink now to 1994. $34 (3/31/90) **89**
Meursault 1986 $29 (5/31/88) **83**
Meursault Charmes 1990: Smooth and silky, with layers of pear, hazelnut, spice and toasty oak flavors, all combining to give this wine extra depth, richness and complexity. The finish is long and lingering. Drink now to 1996. $48 (5/15/92) **90**
Meursault Charmes 1989: A rich, up-front style. Intense aromas of chalk, cream and apples follow through on the palate and on the long finish. Drink in 1993 or '94. $65 (8/31/91) **91**
Meursault Genevrières 1989: More forward than some and almost candied, but very concentrated, with butter, toast and tropical fruit aromas and flavors. Round and rich, with full-blown flavors. Drink now through 1994. $60 (8/31/91) **86**
Meursault Perrières 1990: Tight and spicy, with a broad array of ripe pear, peach, almond and citrus notes before gaining a touch of honey. Has lots of flavor, but it's missing the extra finesse to rate outstanding. Drink now to 1995. $48 (5/15/92) **87**
Meursault Perrières 1989: Has delightful aromas and flavors; hard to resist now. Fresh apple, with hints of cream and tropical fruit notes, shows on the nose and palate. Medium on the finish. Drink now through 1994. (2/28/91) $60 (8/31/91) **87**
Meursault Perrières 1988: Rich and earthy, with deep pear, spice, lemon and citrus notes that are very attractive. Has fine balance and a long finish. Drink now to 1994. $48 (3/31/90) **88**
Meursault Perrières 1987 $44 (4/30/89) **80**
Meursault Perrières 1986 $41 (5/31/88) **88**
Meursault Perrières 1985 $40 (4/30/87) **87**

FAIVELEY
Meursault 1989: Focused, with an excellent backbone of acidity. This full-bodied wine has light pineapple, pine nut and vanilla aromas, intense new wood, lemon and pineapple flavors, firm acidity and a long finish. Drink in 1993 or '94. $68 (8/31/91) **87**
Meursault Les Bouchères 1989: Very ripe, with dried apricot aromas and flavors; verges on a late-harvest wine. Very juicy and lemony. Drink now. $82 (8/31/91) **88**

JEAN-PHILIPPE FICHET
Meursault 1989: Fruity, direct and well structured, with plenty of pear and pineapple flavors, hints of earthiness and oak and a lingering finish. Best to cellar until 1993 or later, when it should be more open and complex. $28 (8/31/91) **88**
Meursault Perrières 1989: Toasty smelling, creamy textured and rich tasting, this is a soft, generous Meursault, with plenty of baby fat. Drink now through 1995. 200 cases made. $43 (8/31/91) **91**

HENRI GERMAIN
Meursault 1988: Concentrated and sharply focused lemon, pear and vanilla aromas and flavors leap right out to grab you, then hold on through a long, elegant finish. Give it until 1993 or so, when it should be even more beautiful. 300 cases made. $35 (2/28/91) **91**
Meursault 1986: A big, fat, rich wine with plenty of concentrated flavors of ripe pear, spice and a touch of honey and oak on the finish. $27 (4/30/89) **88**
Meursault Charmes 1989: Mind blowing, with super-rich aromas and flavors. Has caramel, butterscotch and cream aromas and flavors, with an intensity and finish that can't be beat. Truly decadent. $55 (8/31/91) **93**
Meursault Charmes 1988: Complex and elegant with pretty smoky oak flavors blended with honey, vanilla and apple flavors that are silky smooth and creamy on the finish. Delicious from start to finish. Drink now to 1993. $42 (5/15/90) **89**
Meursault Charmes 1986: Lean and firm with concentrated earth, pear, honey and oak flavors that are dry and firm on the finish. $39 (4/30/89) **86**
Meursault Clos du Cromin 1989: Offers very good concentration. Has buttery, roasted coconut and floral aromas, with concentrated apple and vanilla flavors and a long, fresh finish. Drink in 1993 to '95. $55 (8/31/91) **88**
Meursault Limozin 1989: Tough and hard now, but has very good concentration, with steely apple and straw aromas and steely apple flavors. Full-bodied and very concentrated, but rather hard on the finish. Drink in 1993 to '96. $50 (8/31/91) **88**

JEAN GERMAIN
Meursault 1989: A rather heady, rich wine, with floral, tropical fruit and spice aromas, pineapple and spice flavors, firm acidity and a long finish. Full-bodied; drink in 1993 to '95. $40 (8/31/91) **86**
Meursault Bouchères 1989: Creamy and smooth, with attractive character. Coconut and apple aromas follow through on the palate, with pleasant honey flavors. Has good acidity and a medium finish. Better in 1993 or '94. ($NA) (8/31/91) **87**
Meursault Clos des Meix-Chavaux 1989: Starts off with a bang. Has intense honey, almond, coconut and tropical fruit aromas and coconut, vanilla and honey flavors. Full-bodied, with medium acidity and a focused finish. Drink in 1993 to '95. ($NA) (8/31/91) **89**
Meursault Goutte d'Or 1989: Focused, with excellent fruit. Has pie crust, apple and honey aromas, focused mineral, apple and hay flavors and a super finish. Full-bodied. Drink in 1993 to '95. ($NA) (8/31/91) **91**

ALBERT GRIVAULT
Meursault 1989: This racy, steely style of Meursault is refreshing and powerful. Has rich straw, mineral, apple and tropical fruit aromas, full-bodied, with mineral and apple flavors and a very firm acid backbone. Drink in 1993 to '95. $48 (8/31/91) **88**
Meursault Clos des Perrières 1989: Not as generous as some, but has excellent freshness. Medium-bodied, with apple and light apricot aromas, fresh apple and apricot flavors and lively acidity on the finish. Drink now through 1994. $80 (8/31/91) **87**
Meursault Clos des Perrières 1984 $50 (8/31/87) **90**

CHATEAU DES HERBEUX
Meursault Perrières 1988: Luscious and ripe, with loads of brilliantly focused nutmeg, pear, honey, butter and caramel flavors. Toasty aromas show the oak influence, and the sweet spiciness lingers on the finish. Tempting to drink now, but it may not peak until 1994. $42 (7/15/90) **92**

LOUIS JADOT
Meursault 1989: A super-charged style of Meursault that needs time in the bottle to develop. Has ripe tropical fruit and dough aromas and toasted vanilla and apple flavors. Full-bodied, with good acidity and a closed finish. Drink in 1993 to '95. $35 (8/31/91) **89**
Meursault Perrières 1989: Starts off slowly, but takes off like a rocket on the finish. Has subtle aromas of honey, stones and apples and delicate, closed-in apple and mineral flavors, but this full-bodied wine explodes on the finish. Drink in 1994 to '98. ($NA) (8/31/91) **91**
Meursault Perrières 1988: A classy, solid, focused wine, distinguished by buttery, spicy, honeyed fruit flavors that are ripe and fairly broad, yet supported by firm acidity. Lingers beautifully on the finish. Best to cellar until at least 1993. 225 cases made. $57 (4/30/91) **90**

JAFFELIN
Meursault 1990: Spicy and generous in a bold, ripe style. Packs in plenty of honey, pear and hazelnut flavors that lose some of their zip on the finish, picking up a trace of oxidation. $24 (5/15/92) **84**
Meursault 1989: Straightforward and flavorful. Smells like a freshly baked apple pie. Full-bodied, with apple flavors and a round, smooth mouth-feel. Apple notes echo on the finish. Drink now through 1994. $25 (8/31/91) **85**
Meursault 1987: Ripe and mature with nutty honey, pear and spicy apple flavors that are full and round on the palate, finishing with complex flavors and decent length. $25 (3/15/89) **83**
Meursault 1983 $17 (6/01/85) **86**
Meursault Les Bouchères 1989: A little too ripe for us, but interesting nonetheless. Deep yellow, verging on gold, with overripe apple aromas. Full-bodied, with lemon, very ripe apple and hazelnut flavors. Drink now. $27 (8/31/91) **81**

FRANCOIS JOBARD
Meursault 1987: Fairly basic for Meursault, with spice and apple aromas and tart, metallic flavors, but not a lot of concentration or length on the finish. $25 (7/15/90) **76**
Meursault 1986: Intense and perfumed, lean and earthy with decent fruit, a touch of oiliness and a simple, rather plain aftertaste. $30 (9/30/89) **82**
Meursault Blagny 1987: Concentrated and rich, yet supple in texture, with ripe pear, citrus, butterscotch and earth notes that are well balanced and integrated. Finishes with good acidity and length. Drink now. $37 (7/15/90) **85**
Meursault Charmes 1987: With crisp, fresh apple, pear and citrus notes and a trace of honey on the finish, this appealing wine has good balance and moderate depth. It's not what you'd expect from this appellation. Drink now. $34 (8/31/90) **80**
Meursault Genevrières 1987: A bit heavy-handed with pine resin flavor, this is an unbalanced wine that does not have the fruit concentration to stand up to the oak. The light pear and citrus notes don't stand a chance. $34 (8/31/90) **75**
Meursault Poruzots 1987: A bit earthy, with light citrus and pear notes. It's uninspired, especially at this price, but drinkable now. $40 (7/15/90) **76**
Meursault Poruzots 1985 $28 (11/15/87) **73**

LABOURE-ROI
Meursault 1989: A big, full-blown style, with very toasted, ripe apple aromas. Full-bodied, with a liberal use of new wood and ripe, smoky apple flavors. Has a long finish. Drink in 1993 to '95. $38 (8/31/91) **89**
Meursault 1988: Full-bodied and concentrated, with lots of mineral overtones to the pear and spice aromas and flavors, and hints of peach and smoke on the long finish. A bit disjointed now, but cellaring until 1993 should smooth it out. $35 (8/31/90) **87**
Meursault 1986 $28 (4/30/88) **86**
Meursault 1985 $32 (11/15/86) **70**

LAROCHE
Meursault 1988: Has delicate apple and pear flavors along with nutmeg and butter nuances. Lean, sharp and a bit rough on the finish. Should be better by now. $28 (8/31/90) **82**
Meursault Perrières 1986 $20 (10/31/88) **82**

DOMAINE LAROCHE
Meursault Poruzots 1986 $27 (10/31/88) **89**

LOUIS LATOUR
Meursault 1989: A traditional style of Meursault, with very good finesse, showing wet hay and apple aromas, citrus and mineral flavors and fresh acidity. A full-bodied wine to drink now through 1994. $38 (8/31/91) **89**
Meursault 1985 $25 (11/15/87) **86**
Meursault 1984 $28 (4/30/87) **83**
Meursault Château de Blagny 1989: Rather forward and simple, but delicious. Has lemony, appley aromas and flavors, with a round mouth-feel and an earthy, grassy, honey finish. Drink now. $93 (8/31/91) **86**

Key to Symbols

The scores reported here are the results of blind tastings conducted by our panel of senior editors. Wines that carry the initials below are results of individual tastings.

THE WINE SPECTATOR 100-POINT SCALE ***95-100***—Classic, a great wine; ***90-94***—Outstanding, superior character and style; ***80-89***—Good to very good, a wine with special qualities; ***70-79***—Average, drinkable wine that may have minor flaws; ***60-69***—Below average, drinkable but not recommended; ***50-59***—Poor, undrinkable, not recommended. "+"—With a score indicates a range; used primarily with barrel tastings to indicate a preliminary score.

SPECIAL DESIGNATIONS SS—Spectator Selection, CS—Cellar Selection, BB—Best Buy, ($NA)—Price not available, (NR)—Not released.

TASTER'S INITIALS (JG)—Jim Gordon, (HS)—Harvey Steiman, (JL)—James Laube, (JS)—James Suckling, (TM)—Thomas Matthews, (TR)—Terry Robards, (PM)—Per-Henrik Mansson, (BT)—Barrel Tasting (these wines were tasted blind from barrel samples), (CA-date)—*California's Great Cabernets* by James Laube, (CH-date)—*California's Great Chardonnays* by James Laube, (VP-date)—*Vintage Port* by James Suckling.

DATE TASTED Dates in parentheses represent the issue in which the rating was published.

Meursault Château de Blagny 1982 Rel: $65 Cur: $78 (12/01/85) **45**
Meursault Première Cru 1983 $24 (11/16/85) **83**

OLIVIER LEFLAIVE FRERES
Meursault 1989: This tight, finely focused Meursault has elegant aromas of apples and tropical fruit. Full-bodied, with tight apple and mineral flavors, steely acidity and a lemony finish. Better in 1993 or '94. $39 (8/31/91) **88**
Meursault 1988: Broad and spicy, with well-defined pear, toast and almond aromas and flavors. Slightly astringent on the finish; will need until 1994 or '95. $37 (8/31/91) **86**
Meursault 1984 $22 (7/16/86) **80**
Meursault Charmes 1989: Absolutely delicious, like home-baked apple pie and vanilla ice cream. Has apple and triple-cream aromas and flavors, with a lovely roundness but fresh acidity. Drink now. ($NA) (8/31/91) **90**
Meursault Genevrières 1988: Rich and generous, with a broad texture and lots of spicy pear and toast aromas and flavors. Very toasty on the finish. A graceful wine, with well-defined Meursault character. Best after 1993. 300 cases made. $40 (8/31/91) **90**
Meursault Les Poruzots 1989: Shows very good fruit and a vanilla finish. Honey, cream and white truffle aromas lead to rich, full vanilla, wet straw and earth flavors. Has a medium, milky finish. Drink now. ($NA) (8/31/91) **86**

LEROY
Meursault Les Narvaux 1988: Tart and austere at this young age, but offers plenty of fruit flavors, including apricot and pineapple. Has a sturdy structure that should make it age well. The fruit lingers on the aftertaste. Drink in 1993 to '95. 400 cases made. $100 (4/30/91) **87**
Meursault Perrières 1988: Has all the honey, butterscotch and richness one looks for in a Meursault, with lively, focused fruit flavors and a long, lingering finish. Full-bodied, creamy in texture and built for drinking now through 1995. 200 cases made. $150 (4/30/91) **89**

A. LIGERET
Meursault Les Narvaux 1988: Correct but not exciting. A straightforward, full-bodied Chardonnay with some pear and apple flavors, and touches of butter, but it could be more focused and complex. 1,400 cases made. $45 (10/15/90) **83**

LUPE-CHOLET
Meursault 1986 $26 (2/15/88) **80**
Meursault 1984 $20 (10/31/86) **90**
Meursault Charmes 1988: Swampy, fishy aromas and flavors are unpleasant, detracting from some otherwise excellent honey and caramel flavors on the finish. Tasted twice. $40 (2/28/90) **69**
Meursault Hospices de Beaune Cuvée Goureau 1986 $45 (2/15/88) **89**

M & G
Meursault Les Forges 1987: $42 (3/31/91) **75**

DOMAINE RENE MANUEL
Meursault Clos de la Baronne 1989: Bright and focused, with lots of toast, butter and honey overtones to the sharply defined pear and apple flavors, turning toward smoky, toasty notes on the finish. An impressive wine that would be fine to drink now, but should come together nicely around 1994. 300 cases made. $29 (1/31/92) **89**
Meursault Clos des Bouches Chères 1989: Has interesting aromas, but the new wood is slightly overdone on the finish. Has ripe pineapple and tropical fruit aromas, with tropical fruit and banana flavors and a roasted coconut finish. Drink on release. From Labouré-Roi. $68 (8/31/91) **84**
Meursault Clos des Bouches Chères 1988: Very rich, spicy, concentrated and focused, with lots of complex smoky pear and nutmeg aromas and flavors. It's so intense that it will need cellaring until 1993 to '94 to soften the edges. 500 cases made. $50 (8/31/90) **86**
Meursault Clos des Bouches Chères 1985 $39 (8/31/87) **93**
Meursault Poruzots 1985 $37 (8/31/87) **85**

DOMAINE JOSEPH MATROT
Meursault 1989: Slightly simple and forward, but pleasant in flavor. Aromas of coconut and bananas open to almond, banana and vanilla flavors that are slightly short. Drink on release. $42 (8/31/91) **82**
Meursault 1987: Ripe and buttery with straightforward honey, butter, pineapple and oak flavors that are blunt and uncomplicated. Drink now. $25 (5/15/90) **81**
Meursault Blagny 1989: For the patient collector. Outlandishly fresh, with aromas of freshly crushed grapes, apples and perfume. Full-bodied, with tons of fresh apple and crushed grape flavors and superb acidity. Drink in 1994 to '97. $63 (8/31/91) **93**
Meursault Charmes 1989: Very subtle and firm; more evolved than some. Has understated lemon, apple and cream aromas and flavors, with tons of honey notes on the finish. Drink in 1993 to '95. $65 (8/31/91) **89**
Meursault Les Chevalières 1989: An opulent wine, with a strong backbone. Offers ripe apple, coconut and toast aromas, lots of pear and toasted vanilla flavors, good acidity and a long finish. Full-bodied. Drink now through 1994. $48 (8/31/91) **87**
Meursault Les Chevalières 1986 $36 (12/15/88) **65**

PIERRE MATROT
Meursault 1985 $28 (12/31/87) **75**
Meursault Perrières 1989: A very backward style, but it shows great potential. The essence of freshly crushed Chardonnay grapes, offering apple skin, honey and cream on the nose and palate. Has great concentration. Drink in 1994 to '97. ($NA) (8/31/91) **91**

PROSPER MAUFOUX
Meursault 1989: Tight, lean and crisp, with lemon and pear flavors that are tightly wound and a bit earthy on the finish. Decent to drink now. $32 (4/15/92) **77**
Meursault 1987: Elegant yet earthy with ripe pear, green apple, spice and lemon flavors that are well balanced and fan out on the finish. Drink now. $27 (5/15/90) **86**

MAZILLY PERE
Meursault 1984 $18 (4/30/87) **64**

MESTRE-MICHELOT
Meursault Charmes 1987: Has rich, figgy, toasty oak flavors and citrus notes on the finish, but the flavors are one-dimensional and lack complexity and depth. Drink now. $50 (8/31/90) **79**
Meursault Le Limozin 1986: Rich and smoky, bursting with tropical fruit, vanilla and toasty aromas and flavors, long and honeyed without being heavy. There is a hard and stony edge to the flavor that by now should have developed into smooth complexity. $39 (3/15/89) **86**
Meursault Sous la Velle 1988: Not as smooth and elegant as some '88s, but the solid pear, honey and spice aromas and flavors could become polished by 1993 or '94. $40 (2/28/91) **83**

CHATEAU DE MEURSAULT
Meursault 1986: Rich, bold and flavorful, showing lots of concentration, but maintaining smoothness and elegance, too. Earthy, creamy butterscotch notes accent the ripe pear and apple flavors. Mature and delicious now, but could be aged until at least 1996. 2,500 cases made. $55 (7/31/91) **94**
Meursault 1985 $50 (12/31/87) **95**

C. MICHELOT
Meursault Charmes 1988: Concentrated and flavorful, but not especially lively, offering correct pear, pineapple and butterscotch flavors. Has a somewhat coarse texture that makes it inelegant now. Cellaring until 1993 could soften it up. $55 (2/28/91) **84**
Meursault Grands Charrons 1987: A bit earthy in aroma, but tastes smooth, lush and flavorful. Has more roundness and appeal than most '87s. $41 (8/31/90) **82**
Meursault Les Tillets 1987: An unusually rich style reminiscent of Sauternes, with figgy, tobacco-like flavors and a sweet texture. It's different, but still likable. $32 (8/31/90) **78**

G. MICHELOT
Meursault Clos du Cromin 1986: Beautifully focused pear, floral and vanilla aromas remain controlled and elegant on the palate, with plenty of power in reserve to carry it for years. It's just beginning to develop the characteristic honeyed aftertaste, and should be drinkable now. $39 (3/15/89) **91**

JEAN MICHELOT
Meursault 1988: Beautifully smooth, sculpted and generous, with flavors that echo hazelnuts and nutmeg against a backdrop of gentle pear flavor. May be a bit woody, but balanced and elegant. Drinkable now, better in 1993. $33 (5/15/90) **88**
Meursault 1986 $27 (12/15/88) **90**

MICHELOT-BUISSON
Meursault 1987: An extremely earthy, full-bodied wine. Has barnyardy aromas, buttery, earthy flavors, hints of pear and a spicy, earthy finish. Drink now through 1993. $37 (8/31/90) **81**
Meursault Charmes 1986: A woody style, but it's attractive wood, full of vanilla and toasty aromas and flavors. The lemony fruit is submerged, but if you like the style, drink it now. $50 (3/15/89) **85**
Meursault Genevrières 1988: Earthy, but wrapped around a solid core of ripe pear and melon flavors. It's rich and full on the palate, opening out into a lingering, spicy butterscotch finish. Drinkable now, but should keep improving through 1993. 385 cases made. $55 (2/28/91) **93**
Meursault Genevrières 1987: Despite appealing pear, honey and butter notes, it does not have enough fruit concentration. It strives for boldness and richness, but it misses the mark. Drink now. $50 (8/31/90) **78**
Meursault Genevrières 1986: An earthy style, with chalky, stony, cheesy flavors competing with vestiges of pear and grapefruit flavor, turning muddy on the finish. $50 (3/15/89) **72**
Meursault Le Limozin 1985 $37 (8/31/87) **93**

MOILLARD
Meursault 1987: Tastes sour, flat and boring, a clumsily composed awkward-tasting wine that is palatable, but should be avoided. Tasted twice. $24 (11/15/89) **63**
Meursault Charmes 1987: Big and oaky with supple fruit flavors of ripe pear and spice, but it's soft and simple on the finish. $33 (9/30/89) **74**
Meursault Charmes 1986 $37 (5/31/88) **74**
Meursault Charmes 1985 $30 (11/30/86) **95**
Meursault Clos du Cromin 1986 $28 (10/15/88) **88**
Meursault Poruzots 1986 $37 (5/31/88) **82**

MOMMESSIN
Meursault 1989: Forward and drinkable now, with lots of flavor. Has melted butter, biscuit and apple aromas and apple and dough flavors. A full-bodied wine that's medium in acidity, but slightly short on the finish. Drink now. ($NA) (8/31/91) **84**
Meursault Première Cru 1989: A rich, opulent style, with coconut, honey and vanilla aromas and flavors, plenty of coconut and almond nuances and a very long finish. Drink now through 1994. ($NA) (8/31/91) **86**

CHARLES MONCAUT
Meursault 1983 $16 (6/01/86) **66**

DOMAINE RENE MONNIER
Meursault Charmes 1985 $39 (12/15/88) **87**
Meursault Les Chevalires 1986 $34 (10/15/88) **89**
Meursault Le Limozin 1986 $32 (12/15/88) **89**

DOMAINE MONTHELIE-DOUHAIRET
Meursault 1989: Has delicious flavors, but it's rather advanced in its evolution, with butterscotch and ripe apple aromas, caramel, vanilla and apple flavors and a nutty finish. Full-bodied. Drink now. $25 (8/31/91) **85**
Meursault Les Santenots 1989: This no-nonsense wine has ripe must, grapefruit and vanilla aromas and flavors, an elegant, creamy mouth-feel and a silky finish. Drink now. ($NA) (8/31/91) **87**

PIERRE MOREY
Meursault Charmes 1989: The strong earth, nut and honey flavors are concentrated and complex, but it's also a bit dirty. Not for everyone, but an intriguing drink. $64 (11/30/91) **84**
Meursault Charmes 1987: Rich with honey and butterscotch flavors and a touch of oak. The finish is attractive with good length and plenty of flavor to hang on to. Drink now. $41 (2/28/90) **87**
Meursault Charmes 1986 $47 (12/15/88) **89**
Meursault Genevrières 1987: Rich and full, with ample fruit, vanilla and spice flavors and a very long finish that echoes honey, apple and spice. Smooth and elegant in texture, complex in flavor. Drinkable now but should improve through 1994. $41 (11/15/89) **91**
Meursault Perrières 1989: So subtle it's hard to describe. A superb wine, with fresh grape and green apple aromas and compact apple, butterscotch and cream flavors. Full-bodied, with a super-long finish. Drink in 1994 to '97. $64 (8/31/91) **94**
Meursault Perrières 1986 $47 (12/15/88) **92**
Meursault Les Tessons 1989: Spicy pear and lemon flavors get earthy on the finish, but this crisp, flavorful wine has a long finish and should be best around 1993 or '94. $44 (3/31/92) **82**
Meursault Les Tessons 1986 $35 (12/15/88) **90**
Meursault Les Tessons 1983 $17 (10/16/85) **76**

NOIROT-CARRIERE
Meursault Perrières 1986: Meursault in spades, with more caramel, butter and earthy aromas and flavors than one would ask for, it's a deliberate style that strikes us as awkward. Drinkable now. $39 (2/28/90) **77**

PATRIARCHE
Meursault Réserve Ste.-Anne 1986: Mature, tight, oaky flavors dominate the ripe pear, earth and spice notes. Balanced with good depth of flavors, finishing with hints of ginger and oatmeal. Drink now to 1994. $29 (12/15/91) **85**
Meursault Réserve Ste.-Anne 1985: Thick and intense with layers of butterscotch, honey, pear and spice flavors that fan out on the palate, finishing with delicacy and finesse. $23 (9/30/89) **88**

REINE PEDAUQUE
Meursault Genevrières 1989: Surprisingly excellent, with impressive freshness and focused fruit. Has delicate straw and juniper aromas. Full-bodied, with pine and honey flavors and a sublimely refreshing finish. Drink in 1993 to '96. $48 (8/31/91) **91**

MICHEL POUHIN-SEURRE
Meursault Le Limosin 1989: Intense and lively, with creamy almond, pear, spice and hazelnut flavors that are well focused and in need of cellaring perhaps a year or two. Balanced, with good length. Drink now to 1994. $44 (11/15/91) **89**
Meursault Le Limosin 1986 $25 (2/15/88) **88**
Meursault Poruzots 1989: An earthier style that manages to corral enough fruit to keep it balanced and interesting. The oak, pear, spice and citrus notes are well integrated, finishing with a sharp focus on the fruit. Drink now to 1994. 150 cases made. $64 (11/15/91) **90**

DOMAINE JACQUES PRIEUR
Meursault Clos de Mazeray 1989: Big and ripe, with toasted coconut and tropical fruit aromas and coconut and pineapple flavors. Full-bodied, with lively acidity. Drink now through 1995. $25 (8/31/91) **86**
Meursault Perrières 1989: This opulent yet firm wine has great fruit and structure. Intensely aromatic, with tons of cream, pineapple and tropical fruit aromas. Full-bodied, with intense pineapple and cream flavors. Has an impressively long finish. Drink in 1993 to '96. $30 (8/31/91) **89**

FRANCE
Burgundy White/*Côte de Beaune*/ Meursault

DOMAINE PRIEUR-BRUNET
Meursault 1989: A seamless, well-balanced wine, with mineral, straw and ripe apple aromas and coconut, lemon and vanilla flavors. Has excellent acidity and balance. Drink now through 1994. ($NA) (8/31/91) **88**
Meursault Charmes 1989: A well-integrated, user-friendly wine. Offers hay, melon and apple aromas, succulent fruit and honey flavors and fresh acidity. Drink now. $54 (8/31/91) **89**
Meursault Charmes 1988: Well made, flavorful and correct, with appley, clovelike aromas and flavors, a smooth texture and a pleasant, spicy finish. $35 (8/31/90) **85**
Meursault Charmes 1986: A pretty, complex wine with silky texture, elegant structure and fresh, ripe, spicy pear and honey flavors that get complex and tasty on the finish. $30 (4/30/89) **90**
Meursault Chevalières 1989: Needs a few years of bottle age, but has great class, with intense aromas of pineapple, mint, tropical fruit and vanilla and intense flavors of mint and tropical fruit. Full-bodied, with super-firm acidity. Drink in 1993 to '95. $45 (8/31/91) **90**
Meursault Chevalières 1988: Crisp and sharply focused, offering plenty of intense anise- and smoke-tinged pear and pineapple flavors that will need until 1993 to soften, although you could drink it now. $30 (2/28/91) **89**
Meursault Les Forges Dessus 1989: A seamless, big wine. Full-bodied, with grapefruit, straw and butter aromas, intense butter and grapefruit flavors, excellent acidity and finish. Drink in 1993 to '95. ($NA) (8/31/91) **89**

CHATEAU DE PULIGNY-MONTRACHET
Meursault 1989: Firm and concentrated, but the smoke-tinged pear aromas and flavors also seem metallic and won't be for everyone. Give it until 1993 to see if it softens. $42 (2/28/91) **82**
Meursault Les Perrières 1989: A flinty, austere style of Meursault that's tight and sharply focused at the first sip, but broadens on the palate to display lovely spice, pear, vanilla and mineral flavors on the long finish. Tempting now, but try to hold onto it until 1993 to see what develops. 980 cases made. $57 (2/28/91) **91**
Meursault Les Poruzots 1989: Focused and well built, offering generous apple, honey and nutmeg flavors that linger on the palate. An elegant, beautifully shaped wine that keeps echoing spice and vanilla flavors. Drinkable, but should be better around 1993 to '95. 375 cases made. $55 (2/28/91) **90**
Meursault Les Poruzots 1988: A modest but well-built Meursault, with apple, spice and straightforward fruity aromas and a clean finish. $52 (7/15/90) **79**

REMOISSENET
Meursault Charmes 1986 $49 (12/15/88) **68**
Meursault Cuvée Maurice Chevalier 1986: Has an overload of *terroir*. Not our style. Very earthy and chalky in flavor, with butter and a hint of pineapple. Tasted twice. $35 (3/15/89) **65**
Meursault Cuvée Maurice Chevalier 1985 $42 (3/15/88) **75**
Meursault Genevrières 1986 $49 (12/15/88) **91**
Meursault Genevrières 1985 $60 (3/15/88) **89**

ANTONIN RODET
Meursault Perrières 1989: Strikingly rich and flavorful, with vanilla, ripe apple and apricot aromas and intense cream, honey and apricot flavors. Full-bodied, with impressive acidity on the finish. Drink in 1993 to '95. ($NA) (8/31/91) **88**

DOMAINE ROUGEOT-LATOUR
Meursault Charmes 1986 $38 (6/30/88) **90**
Meursault Les Pellans 1986 $25 (10/15/88) **69**

DOMAINE GUY ROULOT
Meursault Charmes 1989: A seductive, creamy wine, with delicious fruit. Has toasty hazelnut and apple aromas, with rich apple, pie crust and vanilla flavors and super-fresh acidity. Drink now or in 1993. $65 (8/31/91) **91**
Meursault Les Luchets 1989: Wonderful extract of flavors. Has plenty of everything, with butterscotch, straw and honey aromas, super-fresh apple, coconut and vanilla flavors and lively acidity. Full-bodied. Drink now through 1994. $39 (8/31/91) **91**
Meursault Les Meix Chavaux 1988: Spicy, earthy and full-flavored, with a flinty touch of grapefruit peel on the dry, somewhat austere finish. A generally medium-weight, complex wine. Perhaps only needs cellaring until 1993 to settle down. $33 (5/15/90) **87**
Meursault Perrières 1989: Big and oaky, but has excellent concentration. Offers oaky, toasted, roasted almond aromas, butter and apple flavors and a hint of smoke, but it still retains its freshness. Full-bodied. Drink in 1994 to '96. $65 (8/31/91) **90**
Meursault Les Tessons Clos de Mon Plaisir 1989: Captivating, with all the character of Meursault you could ask for. Has roasted pine nut, ripe apple and coconut aromas and super-intense apple, pineapple and vanilla flavors. Full-bodied, with great backbone and finish. Drink in 1993 or '94. $50 (8/31/91) **93**
Meursault Les Tessons Clos de Mon Plaisir 1988: Ripe, round and inviting, with delicious aromas and flavors of butterscotch, cream, pear and vanilla. The tangy finish lingers, hinting at lemon and grapefruit. Stylish and complex. Drink now. 3,000 cases made. $35 (5/15/90) **91**

DOMAINE ROUX PERE & FILS
Meursault 1985 $27.50 (2/28/87) **82**
Meursault Clos des Poruzots 1989: Slightly forward, but offers rich truffle character. Try with white meats in cream sauce. Has perfumed, white truffle, butterscotch and mineral aromas. Full-bodied, with white pepper and apple flavors and racy acidity. Drink in 1993 or '94. $45 (8/31/91) **89**

ROLAND THEVENIN
Meursault Les Casse Têtes 1985 $20 (4/30/87) **87**

JACQUES THEVENOT-MACHAL
Meursault Porusot 1987: A good wine from a light vintage. A lean style for Meursault, with appley, spicy aromas, modest fruit flavors and firm structure. $38 (7/31/89) **81**
Meursault Poruzots 1986 $38 (3/15/88) **86**

THORIN
Meursault 1987 $25 (12/15/88) **84**

VINCENT VIAL
Meursault 1947 ($NA) (8/31/90) (TR) **90**

Key to Symbols

The scores reported here are the results of blind tastings conducted by our panel of senior editors. Wines that carry the initials below are results of individual tastings.

THE WINE SPECTATOR 100-POINT SCALE 95-100—Classic, a great wine; ***90-94***—Outstanding, superior character and style; ***80-89***—Good to very good, a wine with special qualities; ***70-79***—Average, drinkable wine that may have minor flaws; ***60-69***—Below average, drinkable but not recommended; ***50-59***—Poor, undrinkable, not recommended. "+"—With a score indicates a range; used primarily with barrel tastings to indicate a preliminary score.

SPECIAL DESIGNATIONS SS—Spectator Selection, CS—Cellar Selection, BB—Best Buy, ($NA)—Price not available, (NR)—Not released.

TASTER'S INITIALS (JG)—Jim Gordon, (HS)—Harvey Steiman, (JL)—James Laube, (JS)—James Suckling, (TM)—Thomas Matthews, (TR)—Terry Robards, (PM)—Per-Henrik Mansson, (BT)—Barrel Tasting (these wines were tasted blind from barrel samples), (CA-date)—*California's Great Cabernets* by James Laube, (CH-date)—*California's Great Chardonnays* by James Laube, (VP-date)—*Vintage Port* by James Suckling.

DATE TASTED Dates in parentheses represent the issue in which the rating was published.

CHARLES VIENOT
Meursault 1989: Starts off very well, but finishes rather short and dull. Medium-bodied, with toasted mineral and apple aromas, vanilla and apple flavors and decent acidity, but slightly dull on the finish. Drink now through 1994. $35 (8/31/91) **84**

HENRI DE VILLAMONT
Meursault Les Genevrières 1986 $29 (12/15/88) **71**

Montrachet

AMIOT-BONFILS
Montrachet 1988: Lean and powerful, with caramel- and butterscotch-tinged pear and orange aromas and flavors, tightly fit into a concentrated package. Needs cellaring until 1993 or' 95 to soften. $135 (2/28/90) **90**

BACHELET-RAMONET
Bienvenues-Bâtard-Montrachet 1979 ($NA) (2/29/88) **93**

BICHOT
Bâtard-Montrachet 1983 $60 (2/29/88) **90**
Bienvenues-Bâtard-Montrachet 1989: A little forward and simple. Has wonderful toast and apple pie aromas and vanilla and apple flavors. Full-bodied, with medium acidity and a fresh finish. Drink in 1993 or '94. $84 (8/31/91) **84**
Montrachet 1989: Doesn't do very well in this group. A little rustic, with roasted almond, vanilla and ripe fruit aromas, apple and almond flavors and a slightly oxidized, woody finish. Full-bodied. Drink in 1993 to '95. $170 (8/31/91) **85**

JEAN-MARC BOILLOT
Bâtard-Montrachet 1989: Another full-blown, take-no-prisoners wine. Fantastic, with dried apricot verging on raisin aromas and masses of super-ripe, full-bodied toast, earth, tropical fruit and butterscotch flavors. Offers tons of flavor on the finish. Drink in 1993 to '96. ($NA) (8/31/91) **93**

BOUCHARD PERE & FILS
Chevalier-Montrachet Domaines du Château de Beaune 1989: This delicious wine melts in your mouth. Has truffle, apple and earth aromas, with a hint of butter, intensely buttery mineral flavors and an appley finish. Full-bodied, with crisp acidity. Drink in 1993 to '96. $148 (8/31/91) **92**
Chevalier-Montrachet Domaines du Château de Beaune 1986: Earthy and a bit sulfury, ultimately simple, finishing with tart, coarse, astringent flavors. Tasted twice. $92 (2/28/89) **68**
Montrachet Domaines du Château de Beaune 1989: A sublime balance and integration of rich fruit and acidity; a glass of class. Has honey, lemon, truffle and earth aromas. Full-bodied; the superbly ripe fruit flavors have great elegance, class and power. Drink in 1994 to '96. $230 (8/31/91) **94**

ROGER CAILLOT
Bâtard-Montrachet 1985 $90 (5/31/88) **93**

DOMAINE JEAN CHARTRON
Chevalier-Montrachet 1990: Lean and young, with attractive oak, pear, spice and citrus notes that lack focus and follow-through. Succeeds with flavor, but lacks that extra dimension for greatness. Drink after 1993. $120 (3/31/92) **86**
Chevalier-Montrachet 1989: Elegant, beautifully focused and rich in flavor; the honey-shaded pear, apple and nutmeg aromas and flavors linger for minutes on the finish and get prettier with every sip. A beautiful wine, with no exaggeration of flavors. Tempting to drink now, but best after 1993 or '94. 250 cases made. $125 (2/28/91) **94**
Chevalier-Montrachet 1988: An absolutely delicious white Burgundy, with layers of rich, ripe, apple, smoke, vanilla and pear that are amazingly deep and concentrated. Mouthfilling butter and nutmeg flavors on the plush and silky aftertaste. Rel: $95 Cur: $117 (2/28/90) **97**
Chevalier-Montrachet 1987 $100 (2/28/89) **92**
Chevalier-Montrachet 1986 $125 (5/31/88) **95**
Chevalier-Montrachet 1985 $75 (10/31/87) **91**

CHARTRON & TREBUCHET
Bâtard-Montrachet 1990: Bold and ripe, with solid pear, spice, butter and hazelnut flavors that are a bit rough around the edges now, but with bottle aging it should be richer and smoother. Has a complex, smoky aftertaste. Drink after 1993. 225 cases made. $108 (3/31/92) **91**
Bâtard-Montrachet 1989: Big, rich and firmly supported, with bright apple, spice and toast flavors. This luscious wine has great depth of flavor, length and power, and finishes with an overlay of butter and spice. Should be drinkable by now, but best to cellar until 1993 to '95. Tasted twice. 250 cases made. $120 (2/28/91) **92**
Bâtard-Montrachet 1988: With sharply focused lemon, citrus, pear and honey flavors, this is a concentrated, amazingly complex wine with intensity that builds to the finish. A remarkable wine that should only improve with three to five years' aging. Drink now through 1995. Rel: $90 Cur: $100 (2/28/90) **95**
Bâtard-Montrachet 1987 $100 (3/31/89) **92**
Montrachet Le Montrachet 1987: A very woody style, but it's beautiful wood, resulting in a toasty, honeyed wine of smoky richness. Hints of pear, grapefruit and tropical fruit flavors peek through, suggesting that time in the cellar will polish it beautifully. Drink 1993 to '98. $240 (2/28/89) **93**

F. CHAUVENET
Criots-Bâtard-Montrachet 1989: Tight as a drum right now, but it has great potential. Offers very ripe aromas of honey, apricot and butterscotch and masses of honey and butterscotch flavors. Full-bodied, with a superb backbone. Needs time; drink in 1993 to '95. ($NA) (8/31/91) **94**

DOMAINE HENRI CLERC & FILS
Bâtard-Montrachet 1986: Smells great, but it needs time for the structure to smooth out. Toasty lemon, pear and spice aromas and flavors power through to a rich finish. Time should polish it and provide some depth. Drink now to 1995. $104 (3/31/89) **90**
Bienvenues-Bâtard-Montrachet 1989: Powerful, rich and opulent, with ripe tropical fruit flavors and butter and honey aromas. A full-bodied wine, with rich, intense grapefruit flavors and a long, rich, toasty finish. Drink in 1993 to '96. $113 (8/31/91) **89**
Bienvenues-Bâtard-Montrachet 1986 $69 (2/29/88) **90**

FERNAND COFFINET
Bâtard-Montrachet 1988: Smells great, but turns woody and less than generous on the palate, finally opening up with modest richness and complexity on the finish. The aromas are magnificent, dressing up a core of pineapple and pear with a lot of oak, which tends to overpower the fruit on the palate. May be better after 1994. $95 (3/31/92) **85**

MARC COLIN
Montrachet 1989: Has a wonderful earthy character, like white truffles. Multidimensional, with exceedingly ripe fruit aromas that show hints of earth and wood. Full-bodied, with white truffle, earth and apple flavors, a balance of acidity and a long finish. Drink in 1994 to '98. ($NA) (8/31/91) **90**

JOSEPH DROUHIN
Bâtard-Montrachet 1990: A real mouthful of flavor that seems unfocused at this stage. Waves of pear, apple, nutmeg and peach flavors crash across the palate in this powerful, tightly controlled wine. Let it have until 1996 to settle down. $128 (5/15/92) **90**
Bâtard-Montrachet 1989: Linear and elegant in style, with wet hay, earth, stone and honey aromas and flavors. Full-bodied, with medium acidity and finish. Drink in 1993 to '95. $155 (8/31/91) **90**
Bâtard-Montrachet 1987: Emphasizes delicacy over intense flavor. Very firm and elegant, but the peach and pineapple flavors seem to be lurking far in the background. The structure is impeccable. $98 (3/31/89) **90**
Bâtard-Montrachet 1986 $113 (12/31/88) **94**

Bâtard-Montrachet 1985 $95 (2/29/88) **95**
Bâtard-Montrachet 1984 $65 (2/29/88) **92**
Chevalier-Montrachet 1989: Keeps coming at you with the aromas and flavors. A complete wine, with subtle cream, toast and honey aromas and honey, apple, white truffle and cream flavors. Full-bodied, with great intensity of fruit and wood on the finish. Drink in 1993 to '96. $110 (8/31/91) **95**
Chevalier-Montrachet 1985 $100 (4/30/87) **84**
Montrachet Marquis de Laguiche 1989: This is a wine to age into the next century; a collector's wine. Like a slowly burning fuse to a stick of dynamite, with an explosion of fruit at the finish. Has understated cream, apple and earth aromas, a lovely balance of supremely intense lemon, cream and earth flavors, wonderful acidity and a lingering finish. Full-bodied. Drink in 1996 to '98. $360 (8/31/91) **98**
Montrachet Marquis de Laguiche 1988: Has wonderful aromas and intense, concentrated almond, honey, pear and butter flavors that are tightly reined in now and in need of cellaring. Picks up toast, butter and layers of fruit on the powerful aftertaste. Drink now to 1996 and perhaps beyond. Rel: $180 Cur: $230 (2/28/91) **95**
Montrachet Marquis de Laguiche 1987 Rel: $180 Cur: $200 (10/15/90) **95**
Montrachet Marquis de Laguiche 1986 Rel: $200 Cur: $240 (10/31/88) CS **97**
Montrachet Marquis de Laguiche 1985 Rel: $142 Cur: $300 (2/29/88) **100**
Montrachet Marquis de Laguiche 1979 $250 (2/29/88) **97**

JEAN-NOEL GAGNARD
Bâtard-Montrachet 1989: Amazingly well sculptured, with everything in the right place. Has zesty lemon, apple and earth aromas. Full-bodied, with very tightly structured, compact fruit flavors. Shows honey, vanilla and lemon notes on the finish. Built for aging; drink in 1994 to '96. $140 (8/31/91) **97**
Bâtard-Montrachet 1986 $93 (12/31/88) **95**

CHATEAU DES HERBEUX
Chevalier-Montrachet 1988: Complex, restrained and exotic. Nutmeg, spices, pear and honeydew melon flavors make this a delicious wine to drink now but will reward the patient collector. Long, supple finish. Could be cellared until 1993. $100 (7/31/90) **90**
Montrachet 1988: More wood than fruit, with vanilla, pear and some sulfur notes. Tart on the finish. May get better by 1993. $165 (7/31/90) **78**

LOUIS JADOT
Bâtard-Montrachet 1989: A blockbuster, but it has great finesse. Butterscotch, anise and apple aromas in a full-bodied wine, with superb concentration of fruit and a massive backbone. Big and toasty. Drink in 1993 to '96. Rel: $110 Cur: $135 (8/31/91) **93**
Bâtard-Montrachet 1986: Impressively rich and concentrated, its honeyed pear, apple and toasty flavors extend on and on through a full and expansive finish. As powerful as it is, it still remains elegant. Delicious now, but try to keep your hands off it until at least 1994. $99 (5/31/89) **93**
Bâtard-Montrachet 1985 $88 (2/29/88) **94**
Bâtard-Montrachet 1983 $80 (2/29/88) **92**
Chevalier-Montrachet Les Demoiselles 1988: Rich, concentrated and very tight in structure, with firmly reined-in pear, vanilla and wood aromas and flavors. Has a nice tension between the fruit and the oak. Seems woody now, but should turn out to be a complex, spicy wine after 1994 or '95. 225 cases made. $127 (5/31/91) **92**
Chevalier-Montrachet Les Demoiselles 1985 Rel: $150 Cur: $168 (2/29/88) **94**
Chevalier-Montrachet Les Demoiselles 1984 $95 (2/29/88) **92**
Montrachet 1973 $300 (2/29/88) **98**

JAFFELIN
Bâtard-Montrachet 1990: Big and powerful, with tightly packed pear, melon, honey and butterscotch aromas and flavors. Remains tight and unyielding through the smoky finish, suggesting it will need until 1995 to '98 to be at its best. $75 (4/15/92) **85**
Bâtard-Montrachet 1989: Jolts your palate; big and fat, with a huge amount of fruit. Has pure honey, apricot and apple aromas and flavors, a thick mouth-feel, like honey, and a closed finish. Slightly diluted on the finish. Needs time; drink in 1993 to '96. $110 (8/31/91) **90**
Bâtard-Montrachet 1984 $77 (6/01/86) **84**
Bienvenues-Bâtard-Montrachet 1989: Not giving much now, but could get better. Full-bodied, herbal and slightly spicy, with apple aromas and firm, compact fruit flavors, apple notes, excellent acidity and a hard finish. Closed up now; drink in 1993 to '96. $75 (8/31/91) **91**
Montrachet Le Montrachet 1989: A very flashy wine now. Has a symphony of aromas: coconut, almond, lemon, apples and earth. Full-bodied, with great complexity and concentration of flavors. Drink in 1993 to '96. $150 (8/31/91) **96**

LAROCHE
Criots-Bâtard-Montrachet 1986 $63 (10/31/88) **87**

LOUIS LATOUR
Bâtard-Montrachet 1987: Rich, earthy and oily, but with plenty of spice, pear and honey flavors that come across as somewhat astringent now, but with plenty of concentration. The aftertaste of honey and spice lingers. Drink now through 1994. $82 (2/28/90) **89**
Bâtard-Montrachet 1985 $93 (11/15/87) **93**
Chevalier-Montrachet Les Demoiselles 1989: Very big, bold and chewy, offering very ripe apple, honey and earth aromas and vanilla, apple and mango flavors. Full-bodied, with good acidity and a chewy finish. Drink in 1993 to '95. $122 (8/31/91) **90**
Chevalier-Montrachet Les Demoiselles 1986 Rel: $150 Cur: $170 (10/31/88) **94**
Montrachet 1988: One for the cellar. An extremely intense, focused, flavorful Montrachet, with pure apricot, pear and honey flavors tightly bound by acidity. This has great potential, but needs until 1993 to '96 to show its best stuff. $200 (10/15/90) **93**
Montrachet 1986 Rel: $125 Cur: $188 (10/31/88) **95**
Montrachet 1979 $176 (2/29/88) **88**

DOMAINE LEFLAIVE
Bâtard-Montrachet 1989: A wild wine, with full-throttle, ripe flavors. Very exotic, with perfumed crushed grape, toast and honey aromas. Full-bodied, with lots of fruit and a hint of orange peel on the finish. Drink in 1993 to '95. $119 (8/31/91) **93**
Bienvenues-Bâtard-Montrachet 1987: A very unusual style of Montrachet that's enjoyable but atypical. Its Riesling-like flavors and piney finish are unexpected, but the rich, honeyed nuances are pleasant. $79 (12/31/90) **83**
Bienvenues-Bâtard-Montrachet 1979 $130 (2/29/88) **95**
Chevalier-Montrachet 1989: Really closed up now, but still shows great potential. Superbly balanced, with everything in the right place. Has multidimensional mineral, lemon and earth aromas, full-bodied, yet restrained cream, vanilla, honey and earth flavors, super acidity and a super-long finish. $132 (8/31/91) **96**
Chevalier-Montrachet 1987: Ripe, buttery and almost unctuous in richness, with vanilla, pear, honey and brown sugar flavors and a spicy, floral overtone giving it complexity. Has a rich texture and a long finish. Drink now to 1997. $99 (12/31/90) **94**
Chevalier-Montrachet 1983 $175 (2/29/88) **97**

OLIVIER LEFLAIVE FRERES
Bâtard-Montrachet 1989: Offers an incredible amount of richness, with layers of fruit and body. Full-bodied, with nectarine, honey and lime aromas, a dense, thick mouth-feel and a toasty, long finish. Drink in 1993 to '95. $137 (8/31/91) **91**

DOMAINE LEQUIN-ROUSSOT
Bâtard-Montrachet 1987: A woody style, with smooth texture and vanilla bean aromas and flavors. But does it have the concentration of fruit to balance the oak? Not for everyone, but the pear and lemon flavors marry pretty well with the vanilla. Try now. $79 (7/31/90) **85**

PROSPER MAUFOUX
Bâtard-Montrachet 1989: Velvety, with an impressive amount of wood. The aromas show a rich combination of wood and honey. Full-bodied, with ripe pear, honey and vanilla flavors. Pear notes linger on the very long finish. Drink in 1993 to '96. $88 (8/31/91) **91**
Criots-Bâtard-Montrachet 1989: A classy, subtle wine that's caressing on the palate. Has exciting aromas of vanilla, apple, melon and fruit, a rather restrained structure of creamy apple and butter flavors and a long finish. A full-bodied wine that needs time. Drink in 1993 to '96. $87 (8/31/91) **91**
Montrachet 1989: Very classy, with power and elegance. Offers light almond tart, juniper and honey aromas and full-bodied, intensely focused flavors that go on forever. Drink in 1994 to '98. $172 (8/31/91) **89**

MOILLARD
Bâtard-Montrachet 1986 $70 (5/31/88) **94**

MICHEL NIELLON
Chevalier-Montrachet 1988: Tight and crisp, with none of the expansiveness you might expect from a *grand cru*, but has lovely lemon and spice aromas and flavors. Might be better after 1994. $92 (8/31/91) **86**

REINE PEDAUQUE
Bâtard-Montrachet 1989: Refreshing and elegant, but could use a little more concentration to make it outstanding. Full-bodied, with grapefruit, peach and cream aromas, medium intensity of peach and apple flavors and a medium finish. Drink now through 1994. $100 (8/31/91) **86**

PAUL PERNOD
Bâtard-Montrachet 1989: A seductive wine that's elegant and creamy, with buttery pear flavors, a plush texture and complex nuances adding flavor and dimension with each sip. The finish lingers on and on, each time offering a new flavor. Drink now to 1996. 100 cases made. $160 (2/28/91) **93**

DOMAINE JACQUES PRIEUR
Montrachet 1989: Tight and closed in, with excellent fruit. Needs bottle age to open. Full-bodied and holding back plenty, with vivid lemon, orange and floral aromas and modestly concentrated flavors wrapped in firm acidity. Has a long finish. Drink in 1996 to '98. $100 (8/31/91) **92**
Montrachet 1986: Rich and extraordinarily well balanced on the palate, smooth and focused, scented with the right touch of sweet oak, with peach and pear flavor that finishes long and delicious. An ager. Drink 1993 to '97. $165 (2/28/89) **92**

DOMAINE PRIEUR-BRUNET
Bâtard-Montrachet 1988: An austere, tart and sharply focused wine. Good concentration of green apple and pear flavors, with a rather restrained finish at this point that will probably be better by 1993. Should be a treat with oysters. $75 (7/31/90) **87**

DOMAINE RAMONET
Bâtard-Montrachet 1988: Has fabulous aromas of complex pear, toast, butter and earth, with flavors to match. Deep, complex, rich and engaging, picking up smoky toast, mineral and butterscotch flavors that are lively and seductive. Drink now to 1998. 140 cases made. $190 (2/28/91) **95**
Bâtard-Montrachet 1987: Smells ripe, opulent and earthy, turning tight and slightly astringent on the palate, offering subtle lemon-tinged pear and smoke aromas and flavors. Has subtlety and grace, just needs cellaring until 1994 to soften. Rel: $119 Cur: $280 (2/28/90) **87**
Bâtard-Montrachet 1986 $154 (9/30/91) (HS) **94**
Bâtard-Montrachet 1985 $141 (9/30/91) (HS) **92**
Bâtard-Montrachet 1984 $95 (9/30/91) (HS) **84**
Bâtard-Montrachet 1983 $85 (9/30/91) (HS) **93**
Bâtard-Montrachet 1982 $125 (9/30/91) (HS) **92**
Bâtard-Montrachet 1979 $120 (9/30/91) (HS) **88**
Bâtard-Montrachet 1978 $230 (9/30/91) (HS) **95**
Bâtard-Montrachet 1976 $120 (9/30/91) (HS) **85**
Bâtard-Montrachet 1974 $60 (9/30/91) (HS) **86**
Bâtard-Montrachet 1973 $125 (9/30/91) (HS) **94**
Bâtard-Montrachet 1971 $250 (9/30/91) (HS) **94**
Bâtard-Montrachet 1970 $250 (9/30/91) (HS) **87**
Bâtard-Montrachet 1969 $300 (9/30/91) (HS) **96**
Bâtard-Montrachet 1966 $300 (9/30/91) (HS) **91**
Bâtard-Montrachet 1964 $300 (9/30/91) (HS) **88**
Bienvenues-Bâtard-Montrachet 1988 $100 (9/30/91) (HS) **95**
Bienvenues-Bâtard-Montrachet 1987 $91 (9/30/91) (HS) **91**
Bienvenues-Bâtard-Montrachet 1986 $123 (9/30/91) (HS) **93**
Bienvenues-Bâtard-Montrachet 1985 $137 (9/30/91) (HS) **92**
Bienvenues-Bâtard-Montrachet 1984 $90 (9/30/91) (HS) **87**
Bienvenues-Bâtard-Montrachet 1983 $135 (9/30/91) (HS) **88**
Bienvenues-Bâtard-Montrachet 1982 $110 (9/30/91) (HS) **93**
Bienvenues-Bâtard-Montrachet 1979 $100 (9/30/91) (HS) **92**
Bienvenues-Bâtard-Montrachet 1978 $150 (9/30/91) (HS) **90**
Montrachet 1988: Deep, rich and amazingly concentrated, with tiers of fresh, ripe, complex pear, honey, toast, spice, cream and butter flavors. Has a wonderful sense of harmony and finesse, with elegance and grace. The texture is still a bit tannic, but a couple of years' cellaring should smooth it out. White Burgundies don't get much better. Drink 1993 to '99. 100 cases made. Rel: $590 Cur: $680 (2/28/91) **96**
Montrachet 1987 $330 (9/30/91) (HS) **93**
Montrachet 1986 $710 (9/30/91) (HS) **93**
Montrachet 1985 $720 (9/30/91) (HS) **96**
Montrachet 1984 $330 (9/30/91) (HS) **89**
Montrachet 1983 $550 (9/30/91) (HS) **94**
Montrachet 1982 $680 (9/30/91) (HS) **96**
Montrachet 1981 $320 (9/30/91) (HS) **92**
Montrachet 1980 $250 (9/30/91) (HS) **90**
Montrachet 1979 $460 (9/30/91) (HS) **93**
Montrachet 1978 $820 (9/30/91) (HS) **97**

REMOISSENET
Bâtard-Montrachet 1986 $87 (2/29/88) **81**
Bienvenues-Bâtard-Montrachet 1986 $100 (11/15/88) **95**
Montrachet Le Montrachet du Domaine Thénard 1986 Rel: $125 Cur: $137 (12/31/88) **85**
Montrachet Le Montrachet du Domaine Thénard 1985 $145 (2/29/88) **91**

ANTONIN RODET
Bâtard-Montrachet 1989: Has glorious aromas and character. Double cream, stone and fruit aromas follow through to the palate in a refined style. Wonderful on the finish. Drink in 1994 to '96. ($NA) (8/31/91) **92**
Montrachet 1989: Not as action-packed as some, but it's a pretty wine. Has beautiful earth, smoke, wild flower and fruit aromas. Full-bodied, with ripe fruit and lemon flavors, but a lovely elegance. Drink in 1993 to '95. $195 (8/31/91) **89**

DOMAINE DE LA ROMANEE-CONTI
Montrachet 1988: An outstanding, multidimensional wine, with great fruit complexity, depth and length on the aftertaste. Toasty, salty aromas lead to rich pineapple, butterscotch, mineral, pear and spice flavors. A very firm structure and a long finish promises fine potential for aging. Drink in 1993 to '98. 288 cases made. Rel: $600 Cur: $640 (4/30/91) **94**
Montrachet 1987: The deep gold color and rich aromas of toast and earth lead to concentrated flavors of pineapple, almond, pear and honey, backed by firm acidity and a measure of tannin that supports

it wonderfully. A wine with a great pedigree from a not-so-great vintage. Still, it's stunning. Rel: $525 Cur: $700 (12/31/90) **94**
Montrachet 1985 $720 (2/28/87) (HS) **96**
Montrachet 1984 $450 (2/28/87) (HS) **93**
Montrachet 1983 $690 (2/28/87) (HS) **95**
Montrachet 1982 $560 (2/28/87) (HS) **93**
Montrachet 1981 $470 (2/28/87) (HS) **91**
Montrachet 1980 $400 (2/28/87) (HS) **88**
Montrachet 1979 $500 (2/28/87) (HS) **89**
Montrachet 1978 $730 (2/28/87) (HS) **98**
Montrachet 1977 $300 (2/28/87) (HS) **90**
Montrachet 1976 $510 (2/28/87) (HS) **94**
Montrachet 1975 $430 (2/28/87) (HS) **89**
Montrachet 1974 $430 (2/28/87) (HS) **87**
Montrachet 1973 $560 (2/28/87) (HS) **99**
Montrachet 1972 $600 (HS) **92**
Montrachet 1971 $750 (HS) **94**
Montrachet 1970 $680 (HS) **86**
Montrachet 1969 $990 (HS) **88**
Montrachet 1968 $830 (HS) **85**
Montrachet 1967 $1,280 (HS) **85**
Montrachet 1966 $1,200 (HS) **95**
Montrachet 1964 $800 (HS) **82**

DOMAINE ETIENNE SAUZET
Bâtard-Montrachet 1989: A gigantic wine, with a fantastic concentration of fruit and wood. Has butter, butterscotch and masses of fruit aromas. Full-bodied, with superb, ripe tropical fruit flavors and a superlative finish. Drink in 1993 to '96. $156 (8/31/91) **97**
Bâtard-Montrachet 1988: Intense and lively, with creamy butterscotch, toast, honey and pear flavors that are rich and complex, finishing with great length and echoing the flavors. Delicious from start to finish. Ready to drink now through 1995. 60 cases made. Rel: $92 Cur: $195 (2/28/91) **93**
Bâtard-Montrachet 1986 $85 (2/29/88) **90**

DOMAINE BARON THENARD
Montrachet 1988: Flavorful, well balanced and rich in texture, this is a finely tuned white Burgundy, with grace and finesse. Layers of vanilla, honey, pear and spice linger through the finish, indicating a wine with a long life in the cellar. Tempting now, but so tight it needs until 1993 to '98 to be ready to drink. $180 (12/31/90) **93**

Puligny-Montrachet

AMIOT-BONFILS
Puligny-Montrachet Les Demoiselles 1988: Spicy, floral, woody aromas and flavors tend to obscure the gentle fruit, but this is a solid wine that should have developed nicely by now. Has subtleties to offer. $33 (3/15/90) **87**

PIERRE ANDRE
Puligny-Montrachet 1989: A live wire of a wine, offering apple and cream aromas and intense earth, apple and lemon flavors. Has a lively finish, with fresh acidity. Full-bodied. Drink in 1993 to '95. $32 (8/31/91) **87**

DOMAINE D'AUVENAY
Puligny-Montrachet Les Folatières 1989: There isn't much more you could want in white Burgundy; lemon, butter, toast, hazelnut, ripe apple—the list of characteristics goes on and on. Massive, yet superbly balanced, with great finesse. From Lalou Bize-Leroy. Drink in 1994 to '98. $95 (8/31/91) **97**

ADRIEN BELLAND
Puligny-Montrachet 1985 $35 (9/15/87) **89**
Puligny-Montrachet 1984 $27 (1/31/87) **75**
Puligny-Montrachet 1983 $20 (9/16/85) **88**

BICHOT
Puligny-Montrachet 1989: A subtle yet concentrated wine in need of bottle age. Full-bodied, with intriguing honey and clove aromas, intense sunflower and lemon flavors and lively acidity. Drink in 1993 to '96. $30 (8/31/91) **88**
Puligny-Montrachet 1987: Lacks pizzazz, but otherwise clean and decent with tart, crisp pear and melon flavors that fade on the finish. $28 (9/30/89) **77**
Puligny-Montrachet Les Chalumeaux 1989: Balanced, yet it has a good dose of wood. Still fresh, with lemon, butter and toasted aromas; full-bodied, with balanced lemon and lightly toasted flavors and firm acidity. Drink now to 1994. $39 (8/31/91) **88**
Puligny-Montrachet Les Chalumeaux 1988: Very oaky in character, with woody aromas, rough and buttery flavors and a sense of tightness. Fruit comes through only on the finish. Difficult to like. $39 (6/30/90) **76**
Puligny-Montrachet Hameau de Blagny 1989: Ripe, focused and solid, with great structure and undeveloped flavors. What's there shows pear, smoke and vanilla flavors and a nice sense of urgency. Drinkable now, but should be much better around 1993 to '95. $38 (1/31/92) **87**

HENRI BOILLOT
Puligny-Montrachet Clos de la Moushere 1986 $36 (9/30/88) **75**

JEAN-MARC BOILLOT
Puligny-Montrachet 1989: Super-concentrated, with an underlying elegance. Has wonderfully ripe aromas of coconut, honey and vanilla; full-bodied, with intense honey and lemon flavors, superb acidity and a long finish. Drink in 1993 to '96. ($NA) (8/31/91) **91**
Puligny-Montrachet Les Pucelles 1986 $43 (9/30/88) **92**

JEAN CLAUDE BOISSET
Puligny-Montrachet 1988: Lean, earthy and sharply focused, with flavors leaning toward citrus and floral, plus a strong wood component. Needs time to soften. Drink now. $29 (6/30/90) **81**
Puligny-Montrachet 1987: Light and earthy-chalky tasting without much punch on the palate. $33 (7/31/89) **70**

Key to Symbols

The scores reported here are the results of blind tastings conducted by our panel of senior editors. Wines that carry the initials below are results of individual tastings.

THE WINE SPECTATOR 100-POINT SCALE 95-100—Classic, a great wine; ***90-94***—Outstanding, superior character and style; ***80-89***—Good to very good, a wine with special qualities; ***70-79***—Average, drinkable wine that may have minor flaws; ***60-69***—Below average, drinkable but not recommended; ***50-59***—Poor, undrinkable, not recommended. "+"—With a score indicates a range; used primarily with barrel tastings to indicate a preliminary score.

SPECIAL DESIGNATIONS SS—Spectator Selection, CS—Cellar Selection, BB—Best Buy, ($NA)—Price not available, (NR)—Not released.

TASTER'S INITIALS (JG)—Jim Gordon, (HS)—Harvey Steiman, (JL)—James Laube, (JS)—James Suckling, (TM)—Thomas Matthews, (TR)—Terry Robards, (PM)—Per-Henrik Mansson, (BT)—Barrel Tasting (these wines were tasted blind from barrel samples), (CA-date)—*California's Great Cabernets* by James Laube, (CH-date)—*California's Great Chardonnays* by James Laube, (VP-date)—*Vintage Port* by James Suckling.

DATE TASTED Dates in parentheses represent the issue in which the rating was published.

Puligny-Montrachet Les Folatières 1989: Shows lots of character, with many subtleties. Offers autumnal aromas of leaves, tea and hints of apple. Full-bodied, with reserved hay, apple and grapefruit flavors and a firm, long finish. Drink in 1993 to '95. $38 (8/31/91) **88**

BOUCHARD PERE & FILS
Puligny-Montrachet 1986: Spicy and rather gentle for an '85, a complete, harmonious wine, showing some black cherry flavor and nutmeg-tinged toasty oak aromas and flavors, smooth and modestly proportioned. Drink now. $31 (2/28/89) **87**
Puligny-Montrachet 1982 $18 (6/16/84) **87**
Puligny-Montrachet Les Champs-Gains 1989: A straightforward wine, with very good fruit. Has aromas of peaches and honey, with dried apricot nuances, similar flavors and a chalky, toasted component on the finish. Full-bodied. Drink now to 1994. ($NA) (8/31/91) **85**
Puligny-Montrachet Les Folatières 1986: Lively and well focused with fresh, rich, ripe honey, pear and spicy flavors that have depth and concentration. Strong finish with depth and vitality. Outstanding white Burgundy. $33 (2/28/89) **90**
Puligny-Montrachet Les Folatières 1985 $33 (2/29/88) **85**
Puligny-Montrachet Les Pucelles 1989: A delicious, understated style of wine. Offers lemon tart and cream aromas, with nuances of hay. Full-bodied, with lovely cream, hazelnut and lemon flavors. Has a toasty finish. Drink in 1993 or '94. $50 (8/31/91) **90**

MICHEL BOUZEREAU
Puligny-Montrachet 1985 $30 (5/31/88) **88**
Puligny-Montrachet Les Champs-Gains 1989: Ripe and polished, with lots of generous butter, spice and rich pear aromas and flavors. Has a lovely array of flavors that fit nicely into an elegant package. Smooth and complex on the finish. Drinkable now, but should only get better through 1993 or '94. 1,000 cases made. $42 (5/31/91) **91**
Puligny-Montrachet Les Champs-Gains 1988: An immediately attractive wine that's soft, ripe and generous with pear and nutmeg aromas and flavors, yet light enough to be lively and stylish. Drink now to 1995. 500 cases made. $32 (7/31/90) **90**

PHILIPPE BOUZEREAU
Puligny-Montrachet Les Champs-Gains 1986 $38 (11/15/88) **86**
Puligny-Montrachet Les Champs-Gains 1985 $34 (4/15/87) **94**

ROGER CAILLOT
Puligny-Montrachet Les Folatières 1988: Smells floral and simple and tastes muddled, with a drying sensation on the finish. Nothing to distinguish it. $40 (6/30/90) **73**

LOUIS CARILLON
Puligny-Montrachet 1989: Intense, ripe and full-bodied, with ripe apple and tangerine aromas, intense apple, earth and honey flavors and a very long finish. Drink in 1993 to '95. $50 (8/31/91) **88**
Puligny-Montrachet 1988: A tight, austere, flinty style, with reined-in chalk, mineral, pear and nutmeg flavors that need time to soften and mellow. Has potential, but needs cellaring until 1993 to reveal its rewards. $36 (2/28/91) **85**
Puligny-Montrachet 1987: Tart, rich, compact but not concentrated with whiffs of smoke, pear and citric flavors that finish with a bite. $36 (9/30/89) **82**
Puligny-Montrachet Les Champs-Gains 1989: An earthy, slightly rustic style, but has enticing fruit. Has light asparagus, hay and lime aromas, lemon, hay and honey flavors and a chalky, earthy finish. Full-bodied. Drink now to 1995. $50 (8/31/91) **87**
Puligny-Montrachet Les Perrières 1989: Slightly earthy, but very fresh and interesting. Has lemon peel and fruit aromas and flavors, a very creamy mouth-feel and grapefruit notes and fresh acidity on the finish. Drink now to 1994. $50 (8/31/91) **89**
Puligny-Montrachet Les Perrières 1988: Austere and intense, with tightly reined-in pear, lemon and spice flavors that are appealing. Drink now or in 1993. $39 (2/28/91) **88**

CHANSON PERE & FILS
Puligny-Montrachet 1989: A clean wine, with decent fruit. Offers fresh aromas of bananas, minerals and apples and focused mineral, bark and apple flavors. Full-bodied, with very good acidity and a long finish. Drink in 1993 to '95. $37 (8/31/91) **84**
Puligny-Montrachet 1988: Tight, tough, earthy and hard-edged, with mineral and mulch flavors overshadowing any fruit or spice. Doesn't have much intensity. $44 (10/15/90) **71**

DOMAINE JEAN CHARTRON
Puligny-Montrachet Clos du Cailleret 1990: Intense and sharply focused, with tight pear, oak, spice and citrus flavors. A big, concentrated, young and backward wine that needs cellaring until 1993 to blossom. $57 (3/31/92) **88**
Puligny-Montrachet Clos du Cailleret 1989: Spicy, fresh and lively, with a soft texture and generous flavors, offering plenty of peach, pear and nutmeg aromas and flavors. Echoes caramel and honey on the focused, lingering finish. Lovely to drink now through 1995. Tasted twice. $79 (2/28/91) **89**
Puligny-Montrachet Clos de la Pucelle 1990: Complex and appealing, with intense pear, spice, butter and vanilla flavors that are broad, mouth-filling, smooth and generous. A real mouthful of Puligny-Montrachet that keeps you coming back for more. Drink now, or cellar through 1995. 1,000 cases made. $53 (3/31/92) **91**
Puligny-Montrachet Clos de la Pucelle 1989: Soft, elegant and tasty, with hints of hazelnut and pear aromas and flavors. Doesn't quite have the intensity it should until the finish, when it echoes spice and honey. Drinkable now, but should keep evolving until 1993 to '95. Tasted twice. $69 (2/28/91) **88**
Puligny-Montrachet Clos de la Pucelle 1988: Very earthy style, tart and tough in texture, with tightly reined-in fresh pear and spice aromas and flavors, softening on the finish. Drink now through 1993. Rel: $40 Cur: $48 (3/15/90) **85**
Puligny-Montrachet Clos de la Pucelle 1987 $45 (2/28/89) **81**
Puligny-Montrachet Clos de la Pucelle 1986 $50 (5/31/88) **94**
Puligny-Montrachet Clos de la Pucelle 1985 $39 (11/15/87) **74**
Puligny-Montrachet Les Folatières 1990: Tight and reined in, yet delicate in style, with pretty pear, spice, floral and lemon notes that are appealing and complex. The flavors linger on the finish. Drink after 1993. $48 (3/31/92) **89**
Puligny-Montrachet Les Folatières 1989: Fresh, focused and fruity, with lots of well-modulated peach, pear, vanilla and honey flavors in elegant proportions. It's flavorful without being weighty. A stylish wine; needs until 1993 to polish the texture. Tasted twice. $62 (2/28/91) **88**
Puligny-Montrachet Les Folatières 1988: Pear, honey and spice aromas and flavors merge effortlessly on an elegant, supple structure, becoming smooth and harmonious. A classy wine from first whiff to last echo of the aftertaste. Drink now. 1,000 cases made. $38 (3/15/90) **94**
Puligny-Montrachet Les Folatières 1987 $45 (2/28/89) **88**
Puligny-Montrachet Les Folatières 1986 $50 (5/31/88) **88**

CHARTRON & TREBUCHET
Puligny-Montrachet 1988: It's the finish that marks this as a great cellar candidate, as the pear, pineapple, toast and caramel flavors come together with grace and subtlety. Starts off a bit rough, but cellaring until 1993 should smooth it nicely. $30 (3/15/90) **90**
Puligny-Montrachet Les Garennes 1988: Lean, sharply focused grapefruit and pear flavors carry through to a long and elegant finish, very smooth and packed with flavor. Getting to be delicious now, but just wait to see what develops with cellaring until 1993 or '94. $38 (3/15/90) **91**
Puligny-Montrachet Les Garennes 1987: Beautifully defined Puligny, classic pear, honey and toasty buttery flavors that are tightly knit and impeccably well balanced. The aftertaste is long and flavorful. $40 (2/28/89) **90**
Puligny-Montrachet Les Garennes 1986 $49 (5/31/88) **93**
Puligny-Montrachet Les Referts 1988: Concentrated and sharply focused, with elegant structure and appealing apple and spice aromas and flavors. A touch of buttery richness on the finish made this drinkable on release, but it should be even better now. $35 (3/15/90) **89**

Puligny-Montrachet Les Referts 1987: Thin and austere, lacking depth of flavor, but what's there—the pear, spice and toasty oak flavors—are nice and true, though maybe a bit green. $40 (2/28/89) **79**
Puligny-Montrachet Les Referts 1986 $46 (5/31/88) **91**

F. CHAUVENET
Puligny-Montrachet Champs-Gain 1989: Subdued, with elegant fruit and a toasty finish. Medium- to full-bodied, with delicate honey and apple aromas, a velvety mouth-feel and toast and apple flavors. Drink now to 1994. $30 (8/31/91) **87**
Puligny-Montrachet Champs-Gains 1984 $40 (4/30/87) **88**
Puligny-Montrachet Champs-Gains 1982 $17 (3/16/85) **88**
Puligny-Montrachet La Garenne 1989: A linear wine, with compact fruit character. Offers lemon and cream puff aromas, creamy lemon flavors and firm acidity. Medium-bodied; drink in 1993 or '94. ($NA) (8/31/91) **86**
Puligny-Montrachet Reuchaux 1985 $35 (2/28/87) **66**
Puligny-Montrachet Reuchaux 1982 $20 (9/16/85) **85**

GERARD CHAVY
Puligny-Montrachet 1985 $28 (12/31/87) **82**
Puligny-Montrachet 1984 $22 (11/15/87) **69**
Puligny-Montrachet Les Pucelles 1986 $30 (12/15/88) **91**

DOMAINE HENRI CLERC & FILS
Puligny-Montrachet Les Combettes 1987: Not for everyone. Extremely deep in color. Smells and tastes intriguingly smoky and oaky, but there's not much fruit to balance it and it lacks a smooth follow-through. $41 (7/31/89) **75**
Puligny-Montrachet Les Folatières 1989: Very forward and mature in color, with fig, tropical fruit and butter aromas. Full-bodied, with buttery apple and slight cardboard flavors. Tasted twice. Drink now. $64 (8/31/91) **76**
Puligny-Montrachet Les Folatières 1987: Heavy with oak and smoke flavors and deep gold in color. A bit of orange flavor gives it fruit and the structure is good, but it's styled for oak enthusiasts only. $41 (7/31/89) **79**
Puligny-Montrachet Les Folatières 1986 $44 (11/15/88) **93**

MADAME FRANCOIS COLIN
Puligny-Montrachet Les Demoiselles 1988: Spicy and complex, with a welcome sense of richness and depth without weight. Flavors focus on pear and nutmeg, with hints of vanilla on the long finish. Drinkable now. $47 (6/30/90) **89**

JOSEPH DROUHIN
Puligny-Montrachet 1990: Tight, tart and crisp in texture, with a chalky edge to the moderate level of pear and apple flavors. Drinkable now, but should be best around 1994. $36 (5/15/92) **81**
Puligny-Montrachet 1989: Has good flavors, but is rather simple. Full-bodied, with apple aromas and an abundance of apple and vanilla flavors, but short on the finish. Drink now. $50 (8/31/91) **83**
Puligny-Montrachet 1988: An awkward style that combines intense pear and spice flavors that turn oaky and muted on the finish. Drink now. $39 (3/15/90) **78**
Puligny-Montrachet 1987 $38 (4/15/89) **87**
Puligny-Montrachet 1986 $34 (2/29/88) **88**
Puligny-Montrachet 1984 $27 (2/29/88) **83**
Puligny-Montrachet Clos de la Garenne 1989: Impressive; very concentrated, yet still wonderfully balanced. Full-bodied, showing freshly cut apple, pie crust and earth aromas and similar flavors. Drink in 1993 to '96. $67 (8/31/91) **90**
Puligny-Montrachet Clos de la Garenne 1987: Light and elegant with tart pear, spice and lemony flavors of medium depth. Smokiness comes through on the finish. $44 (4/15/89) **81**
Puligny-Montrachet Clos de la Garenne 1986 $40 (6/15/88) **89**
Puligny-Montrachet Les Folatières 1990: A smooth, polished, smoky, pear-flavored wine, with a strong earthy edge. Remains spicy and earthy through the finish. Best after 1993. $60 (5/15/92) **85**
Puligny-Montrachet Les Folatières 1989: Absolutely delicious. Melts in your mouth, with béarnaise sauce aromas and light, buttery apple flavors. Full-bodied, with an incredibly creamy mouth-feel and a very long finish. Drink now to 1995. $67 (8/31/91) **94**
Puligny-Montrachet Les Folatières 1987: Leans toward the woody side, but there's some pretty lemon, pear and spicy flavors of moderate depth. $44 (4/15/89) **78**
Puligny-Montrachet Les Folatières 1986 Rel: $40 Cur: $48 (5/31/88) **91**
Puligny-Montrachet Les Folatières 1985 $35 (2/29/88) **88**
Puligny-Montrachet Les Pucelles 1990: Firm in texture, with sharply focused pear, spice and nutmeg aromas and flavors, hinting at smoke on the finish. Drinkable now, but better after 1993. $64 (5/15/92) **86**
Puligny-Montrachet Les Pucelles 1989: Offers pleasant fruit, but it's a little short on the finish. Medium gold in color, with ripe honey and light tropical fruit aromas and full-bodied honey, earth and toast flavors. Light, almost diluted melon and honey notes emerge on the finish. Drink now. $68 (8/31/91) **84**
Puligny-Montrachet Les Pucelles 1986 $50 (2/29/88) **90**
Puligny-Montrachet Les Pucelles 1985 $50 (4/30/87) **92**

FAIVELEY
Puligny-Montrachet 1989: A full-blown, full-bodied style, but still has finesse. Offers honey, apple tart and butterscotch aromas, a bounty of ripe fruit flavor and excellent acidity and finish. Drink in 1993 to '96. $72 (8/31/91) **88**
Puligny-Montrachet Les Combettes 1989: Has good intensity and fresh acidity, but it's a little simple now, with rich lemon aromas, lemon, chalk and vanilla flavors, firm acidity and a chalky finish. Full-bodied. Drink now to 1995. $89 (8/31/91) **87**

JEAN GERMAIN
Puligny-Montrachet 1989: An intriguing wine, with plenty of character. Offers blanched almond and apple aromas and hazelnut and honey flavors. Full-bodied, with refreshing acidity and a balanced finish. Drink in 1993 to '95. ($NA) (8/31/91) **86**
Puligny-Montrachet 1983 $12 (9/01/85) **90**
Puligny-Montrachet Les Champs-Gains 1989: Superlative winemaking; a wonderful use of fruit and wood. Has lovely apple, cream and butterscotch aromas, with pear, apple and vanilla notes on the long finish. Full-bodied. Drink now to 1995. $54 (8/31/91) **91**
Puligny-Montrachet Les Champs-Gains 1983 $27 (3/01/86) **96**
Puligny-Montrachet Les Grands Champs 1989: Clean and fresh, with lemon and apple aromas, fresh, crisp acidity and clean apple and vanilla flavors. Drink now to 1994. $48 (8/31/91) **85**

MACHARD DE GRAMONT
Puligny-Montrachet Les Houillères 1985 $47 (5/31/88) **73**

CHATEAU DES HERBEUX
Puligny-Montrachet Les Combettes 1986: Buttery, toasty, smooth and spicy, beautifully focused and long, elegant and balanced. Flavors run toward pear and vanilla, with a hint of smoke on the finish. Delicious on release, better by now. $21 (2/28/89) **89**

LOUIS JADOT
Puligny-Montrachet 1989: Pleasant and flavorful, with nicely defined pear and vanilla aromas and flavors. Turns slightly buttery on the finish, but seems sturdy rather than elegant. Drinkable now. $36 (1/31/92) **86**
Puligny-Montrachet 1988: Lean and crisp, with vague apple and lemon aromas and flavors and a touch of toast on the tart, spicy finish. Needs until 1993 or '94 to grow into itself. $36 (5/31/91) **87**
Puligny-Montrachet 1985 $33 (2/29/88) **90**
Puligny-Montrachet 1984 $30 (2/29/88) **89**
Puligny-Montrachet 1983 $25 (2/29/88) **66**

Puligny-Montrachet Clos de la Garenne Domaine du Duc de Magenta 1989: Well crafted and elegant, with a future for aging. Strikingly rich aromas of minerals and lemons in a full-bodied wine, with an abundance of mineral, honey and lemon flavors and a slightly toasted finish. Drink in 1993 to '96. $61 (8/31/91) **93**
Puligny-Montrachet Clos de la Garenne Domaine du Duc de Magenta 1988: Beautifully complex and complete, with a host of attractive aromas blending into rich fruit, spice and vanilla flavors that last and last on the finish. Young and firm in structure; should age well through about 1994. 725 cases made. $52 (4/30/91) **91**
Puligny-Montrachet Clos de la Garenne Domaine du Duc de Magenta 1986: Beautifully defined Puligny Montrachet with rich toast, spice, pear and vanilla flavors in harmony with an elegant structure. Long-tasting on the finish. Drink now. $57 (5/31/89) **91**
Puligny-Montrachet Clos de la Garenne Domaine du Duc de Magenta 1985 $50 (2/29/88) **92**
Puligny-Montrachet Les Combettes 1989: Rich and velvety, with a slightly bitter finish; needs time. Has creamy, freshly cut pear tart aromas, subtle stone, vanilla and almond flavors and a long finish. Full-bodied. Drink in 1993 to '95. $67 (8/31/91) **90**
Puligny-Montrachet Les Combettes 1985 $45 (2/29/88) **93**
Puligny-Montrachet Les Combettes 1984 $37 (2/29/88) **89**
Puligny-Montrachet Les Combettes 1983 $34 (2/29/88) **87**

JAFFELIN
Puligny-Montrachet 1990: A spicy, floral, generous white Burgundy, with distinctive rose petal and nutmeg nuances to the ripe pear and apple flavors. Buttery rich, but stays light enough to remain lively through the finish. Drinkable now. $28 (5/15/92) **87**
Puligny-Montrachet 1989: Almost too liberal use of wood in the maturation. Has toasted coconut, apple and mineral aromas, with a full-bodied palate of toast, butterscotch and fruit flavors. Slightly harsh on the finish. Drink on release. $42 (8/31/91) **83**
Puligny-Montrachet 1985 $33 (4/15/87) **92**
Puligny-Montrachet 1983 $21 (2/01/86) **92**
Puligny-Montrachet Champ Canet 1986 $40 (12/15/88) **85**
Puligny-Montrachet Les Folatières 1983 $20 (6/16/85) **90**
Puligny-Montrachet La Garenne 1990: Crisp and lively, with simple but pleasing lemon, pear and apple notes. A dusty flavor emerges on the aftertaste. Drink now to 1995. $34 (4/15/92) **85**
Puligny-Montrachet La Garenne 1989: Wonderfully concentrated, with rich butter and fig aromas, hazelnut and butter flavors and a finish that goes on and on. Full-bodied. Drink in 1993 to '96. $30 (8/31/91) **91**

LABOURE-ROI
Puligny-Montrachet 1989: A very overripe style, with overripe fruit. Has musty apple aromas and musty, wet cellar and honey flavors. Full-bodied, with a medium finish. Drink now. $45 (8/31/91) **80**
Puligny-Montrachet 1985 $23 (11/15/86) **81**

LAROCHE
Puligny-Montrachet 1989: Hard, tight and somewhat bitter, with hints of Muscat and spice showing on the finish, but altogether a tough wine to cuddle up to. Drink now. $47 (2/28/91) **80**

DOMAINE LAROCHE
Puligny-Montrachet Château de Puligny-Montrachet 1986 $60 (9/30/88) **92**
Puligny-Montrachet Folatières 1988: Made in a lean, tight style, with pear and apple flavors, a touch of vanilla and a tart finish. Good and crisp. Drink now. $39 (6/30/90) **84**

LOUIS LATOUR
Puligny-Montrachet 1989: Traditionally styled, with good fruit flavor and acidity. Full-bodied, with apple, mineral and earth aromas, straw, apple and mineral flavors and crisp acidity. Drink in 1993 to '95. $43 (8/31/91) **87**
Puligny-Montrachet 1986 $41 (9/30/88) **82**
Puligny-Montrachet 1985 $30 (2/29/88) **89**
Puligny-Montrachet 1983 $35 (2/29/88) **90**
Puligny-Montrachet Les Folatières 1989: Wonderful now, but better in a few years. A full-bodied wine, with apple, cream and modest lemon aromas and flavors. Butterscotch notes emerge on the finish. Drink now to 1994. $52 (8/31/91) **90**
Puligny-Montrachet Les Folatières 1982 $38 (2/29/88) **86**

DOMAINE LEFLAIVE
Puligny-Montrachet 1989: Very fresh and exciting, with clean, creamy, floral aromas, flinty vanilla bean flavors and wonderful acidity. Tasted twice. Drink in 1993 to '96. $49 (8/31/91) **86**
Puligny-Montrachet 1985 $40 (2/29/88) **88**
Puligny-Montrachet Clavoillon 1989: Fresh and elegant, with wonderful structure and finesse, yet great richness. Has stony mineral and pear aromas and similar flavors. Very creamy, with fresh acidity. Drink now to 1995. $62 (8/31/91) **94**
Puligny-Montrachet Clavoillon 1985 $65 (2/29/88) **90**
Puligny-Montrachet Les Folatières 1985 $49 (2/29/88) **91**
Puligny-Montrachet Les Pucelles 1989: This compact style of wine needs time; not as great as expected. Has grapefruit and lemon aromas and flavors, lovely mineral, apple and chalk notes, a long pear finish and firm acidity. Tasted twice. Drink in 1993 to '95. $79 (8/31/91) **88**
Puligny-Montrachet Les Pucelles 1986 Rel: $65 Cur: $77 (9/30/88) **93**
Puligny-Montrachet Les Pucelles 1985 $80 (2/29/88) **92**
Puligny-Montrachet Les Pucelles 1982 $71 (2/29/88) **94**
Puligny-Montrachet Les Pucelles 1979 $100 (2/29/88) **95**

OLIVIER LEFLAIVE FRERES
Puligny-Montrachet 1989: A surprisingly good wine, with fig, apple and tropical fruit aromas and rich yet restrained tropical fruit and vanilla flavors. Full-bodied, with a long finish. Drink in 1993 to '95. $43 (8/31/91) **90**
Puligny-Montrachet 1988: Soft and spicy, with a strong earthy undercurrent to the lemon and toast aromas and flavors. Seems tight and ungenerous despite the soft texture. $38 (8/31/91) **83**
Puligny-Montrachet 1987: Incredibly rich and toasty, with butterscotch and oak, but has the fruit integrity to stand up to the flavors imparted by heavily toasted barrels. It's big and full-bodied, with pear and tangerine notes and generous acidity. Try now to 1994. 3,000 cases made. $33 (6/30/90) **93**
Puligny-Montrachet 1986 $30 (7/31/89) **88**
Puligny-Montrachet 1984 $25 (6/01/86) **83**
Puligny-Montrachet Les Chalumeaux 1986: Gorgeous Puligny with richness and complexity, well-honed honey, toast, pear and spicy nutmeg flavors and a silky-smooth texture and a pretty aftertaste that lingers. $36 (4/15/89) **93**
Puligny-Montrachet Les Champs-Gains 1989: Compact, firm, focused and intensely ripe. Very tightly structured, with perfumed, floral and apple aromas, full-bodied stone and honey flavors and firm acidity. Drink in 1993 to '95. $53 (8/31/91) **91**
Puligny-Montrachet Les Champs-Gains 1986 $36 (2/29/88) **87**
Puligny-Montrachet Les Combettes 1986 $46 (2/29/88) **90**
Puligny-Montrachet Les Folatières 1986 $36 (2/29/88) **91**
Puligny-Montrachet Les Garennes 1989: Intensely earthy, with rich fruit. Distinctive lemon, vanilla and fig aromas follow through on the palate. Has lively acidity and a chalky finish. Drink now to 1994. ($NA) (8/31/91) **86**

A. LIGERET
Puligny-Montrachet Les Referts 1988: Very perfumed and stylish, with toasty, buttery aromas and full peach, orange and apricot flavors. The finish is rich but dry, with great layers of fruit and mineral flavors. Drink now to 1996. 350 cases made. $51 (12/31/90) **92**

LUPE-CHOLET
Puligny-Montrachet Les Chalumeaux 1987: Very good. Has rich flavors of pear and spice that are more mature than you'd expect, but it's well-balanced and has a long aftertaste. $46 (11/15/89) **82**

DOMAINE MAROSLAVAC
Puligny-Montrachet Clos du Vieux Château 1988: Smells great, but this wine gets a little hard-edged and austere on the palate offering tart apple and hints of butter and vanilla on the finish. With age, it could smooth out nicely. Drink 1993 to '94. 500 cases made. $40 (7/31/90) **83**

DOMAINE JOSEPH MATROT
Puligny-Montrachet Les Chalumeaux 1989: Not a blockbuster, but very fine. Full-bodied, tasting of freshly crushed grapes with a few stems, and fresh apple and pear flavors. Has refreshing acidity. Drink in 1993 to '95. $66 (8/31/91) **89**

PIERRE MATROT
Puligny-Montrachet Les Combettes 1989: Has the essence of fresh grapes, with perfumed fresh apple and grape aromas. Full-bodied, with super-intense fruit flavor, excellent acidity and a very long finish. Built for aging; drink in 1993 to '95. $45 (8/31/91) **93**
Puligny-Montrachet Les Combettes 1986 $37 (12/15/88) **88**

PROSPER MAUFOUX
Puligny-Montrachet 1989: Tight and tart, with flavors that emerge and blossom on the finish, echoing nutmeg, pear, vanilla and cream notes. Lacks the immediate fruit flavors up front, but makes up for it with a long finish. Drink in 1993 and beyond. $36 (8/31/91) **87**
Puligny-Montrachet 1988: Deliciously round and smooth with pretty honey, pear and smoky oak flavors that are deceptively complex and glide across the palate. Fine tension between fruit and oak; the finish lingers on and on. Drink now to 1994. $31 (4/30/90) **90**
Puligny-Montrachet 1986: Tartness and bitter flavors detract from the ripe apple and spicy oak flavors. Unbalanced and lacking charm and finesse. $36 (5/31/89) **68**
Puligny-Montrachet Folatières 1989: A lovely concentration of butter, vanilla and grapefruit aromas and flavors. Grapefruit and banana notes come through on the finish of this full-bodied wine. Drink now to 1994. $43 (8/31/91) **85**
Puligny-Montrachet Hameau de Blagny 1989: The wood in this wine is not very well integrated. Has lemon tart, toasted almond and freshly cut wood aromas. Full-bodied, with plenty of lemon flavors, but very woody on the finish. Drink in 1993 or '94. $39 (8/31/91) **81**

C. MICHELOT
Puligny-Montrachet 1987: Big and powerful, with rich texture and nice honey and caramel notes on the finish. A bit shy of fruit and a bit too generous with the alcohol. $41 (6/30/90) **80**

MOILLARD
Puligny-Montrachet 1986 $33 (5/31/88) **88**

MOMMESSIN
Puligny-Montrachet 1989: Concentrated in flavor, but it has a little too much wood on the finish. Has tropical fruit, vanilla and apple aromas and intense vanilla, honey and apple flavors. Nuances of freshly cut wood echo on the long finish. Full-bodied. Drink now to 1994. ($NA) (8/31/91) **84**

DOMAINE RENE MONNIER
Puligny-Montrachet Les Folatières 1986 $44 (11/15/88) **81**

DOMAINE JEAN PASCAL
Puligny-Montrachet Les Chalumeaux 1986 $40 (6/15/88) **91**
Puligny-Montrachet Les Champs-Gains 1985 $31 (9/15/87) **92**
Puligny-Montrachet Hameau de Blagny 1986 $40 (6/15/88) **93**

PATRIARCHE
Puligny-Montrachet 1985: Rich, crisp, tart and clean with lovely honey, pear, spice and toast flavors that are deep and complex, smooth and concentrated, long and full on the finish. $30 (9/30/89) **90**

REINE PEDAUQUE
Puligny-Montrachet Les Folatières 1989: Exciting, with a lively character. Ripe grapefruit and green hazelnut aromas open to intense apricot, hazelnut and grapefruit flavors and super-intense acidity. Full-bodied. Drink in 1994 to '96. $42 (8/31/91) **90**

PAUL PERNOT
Puligny-Montrachet 1990: A clumsy style that offers plenty of flavor, with ripe tropical fruit notes and a hint of lemon sherbet. Pleasant to drink now. $45 (4/15/92) **81**
Puligny-Montrachet 1989: A tight, tart style that's not very generous, with barely ripe peach, apple and pear flavors that lack dimension. Has concentration, but not much complexity. Very austere for a Puligny-Montrachet. Drink now to 1994. $52 (2/28/91) **80**
Puligny-Montrachet 1988: Leans toward the sour, bitter spectrum of flavor. It's tart and rustic, and perhaps a bit off. Tasted twice, with consistent results. $40 (2/28/91) **72**
Puligny-Montrachet Folatières 1990: Ripe, rich and harmonious, with elegant pear, hazelnut, vanilla and spice flavors that are sharply focused and well integrated. A trace of smokiness emerges on the long, complex finish. Drink now through 1995. 400 cases made. $60 (4/15/92) **91**
Puligny-Montrachet Folatières 1989: Sharply focused, elegant, complex and concentrated, with attractive pear, butter, toast and spice notes on a silky-smooth texture. The finish turns a bit coarse; perhaps a year or two of cellaring will help. Drink now to 1995. $70 (2/28/91) **89**
Puligny-Montrachet Folatières 1988: An assertive, very powerful Puligny, with ample floral, spice and earth aromas, solid fruit flavors and a tough structure of acidity and tannin. Intense, vibrant and stylish, with the earthy complexity and slight decadence that many connoisseurs prize in white Burgundy. Drink now to 1997. $74 (12/31/90) **93**
Puligny-Montrachet Folatières 1986 $50 (2/28/89) **89**
Puligny-Montrachet Les Pucelles 1988: A classy, complex wine from the toasty aromas of oak aging to the focused, tight pear flavors to the lingering, buttery aftertaste. Young and evolving. Drinkable now, but should be better by 1993 or '94. $60 (12/31/90) **90**

JEAN PILLOT
Puligny-Montrachet 1989: Made in a very funky, woody style. A heady, piny aroma and sulfury, piny flavors mar its overall quality, but it does have a nice, rich texture and honey and pear notes on the finish. Tasted twice. 450 cases made. $42 (4/30/91) **76**

MICHEL POUHIN-SEURRE
Puligny-Montrachet 1989: A strong earthy, barnyardy flavor dominates, but there's fruit here, too. Not for everyone; the flavors are a bit hollow. Drink now. $52 (11/15/91) **78**

DOMAINE JACQUES PRIEUR
Puligny-Montrachet Les Combettes 1989: A thick, oily wine, with a long finish. Has lemon, toast and vanilla aromas and full-bodied lemon, toast, blanched almond and hazelnut flavors. Very dense. Drink in 1993 to '95. $33 (8/31/91) **90**

CHATEAU DE PULIGNY-MONTRACHET
Puligny-Montrachet 1989: An elegant, understated style, with honey, pear and nutmeg flavors that are decent, but lacking in sophistication. Finishes tart and watery. $66 (2/28/91) **74**
Puligny-Montrachet 1986 $60 (2/29/88) **81**
Puligny-Montrachet 1985 $55 (2/29/88) **79**

REMOISSENET
Puligny-Montrachet Les Combettes 1986 $57 (11/15/88) **92**
Puligny-Montrachet Les Folatières 1986 $50 (11/15/88) **85**
Puligny-Montrachet Les Folatières 1985 $56 (2/29/88) **79**

J. RIGER-BRISET
Puligny-Montrachet 1987: Starts off smelling and tasting very attractive, with lots of toasty oak and butterscotch character, but it turns lean and a bit tough on the palate before the butterscotch echoes on the finish. Drink now. $35 (3/15/90) **82**

ANTONIN RODET
Puligny-Montrachet Les Clavoillons 1989: A little simple and nutty, with poached pear and caramel aromas. Full-bodied, with pear, caramel and mineral flavors and a rather short finish. Drink now. $43 (8/31/91) **82**

DOMAINE ROUX PERE & FILS
Puligny-Montrachet Champs-Gains 1989: Lively and tart, with earthy apricot, pear and grapefruit flavors that are intense but not vivid. The finish turns chalky and dull. Drink now to 1994. $55 (2/28/91) **83**
Puligny-Montrachet Champs-Gains 1988: Broad-textured, flavorful and even a bit blunt, a powerful wine that might develop finesse with cellaring until 1993. But for now the ripe apple and honey flavors just keep building and building through the long finish. $40 (3/15/90) **92**
Puligny-Montrachet Les Enseignères 1989: Sneaks up on you and grabs your palate, with a symphony of floral, honey and tropical fruit aromas and flavors. Full-bodied, but very balanced, with superb acidity and a flavorful, honeyed finish. Drink now to 1995. $45 (8/31/91) **89**
Puligny-Montrachet Les Enseignères 1986 $36 (2/29/88) **92**
Puligny-Montrachet Les Enseignères 1985 $34 (9/15/87) **88**
Puligny-Montrachet La Garenne 1989: Subdued now, but very rich and firm. Has graceful aromas of kiwi and light tropical fruits. Full-bodied, with a restrained, firm structure and mineral and fig flavors. Very long on the finish. Drink in 1993 to '95. $55 (8/31/91) **90**
Puligny-Montrachet La Garenne 1987: A well-made, but simple wine that emphasizes the fruit with crisp pear, citrus and vanilla notes and a slightly tannic finish. $44 (4/15/89) **83**
Puligny-Montrachet La Garenne 1986 $38 (12/31/87) **89**
Puligny-Montrachet La Garenne 1985 $30 (4/15/87) **92**

LEONARD DE ST.-AUBIN
Puligny-Montrachet 1989: A strong, pungent, earthy gardenia character dominates the ripe pear and vanilla flavors. Of marginal quality; turns bitter and coarse on the aftertaste. Drink now, if ever. $28 (8/31/91) **73**
Puligny-Montrachet 1986 $25 (11/15/87) **87**

DOMAINE ETIENNE SAUZET
Puligny-Montrachet 1989: Offers wonderful elegance and finesse. A full-bodied wine, with subtle aromas of pineapple, apple and vanilla, ripe apple and grapefruit flavors and very crisp acidity. Drink in 1994 to '96. $63 (8/31/91) **90**
Puligny-Montrachet 1986 $40 (4/30/88) **92**
Puligny-Montrachet Champ Canet 1989: More forward in style, with very ripe fruit character. Has a rather advanced gold color, with overripe aromas of fruit and honey. Full-bodied, with a fat mouth-feel, cream and apple flavors and a light, toasty finish. Drink now. $85 (8/31/91) **87**
Puligny-Montrachet Champ Canet 1988: Tight and austere, with flinty pear, fig, vanilla and spice flavors that are concentrated and tannic, finishing with a touch of coarseness. It should have smoothed out by now. Drink now to 1995. 200 cases imported. $50 (12/31/90) **91**
Puligny-Montrachet Champ Canet 1986 $50 (4/30/88) **91**
Puligny-Montrachet Champ Canet 1985 $37 (10/15/87) **90**
Puligny-Montrachet Les Combettes 1989: Well-crafted, with impressive use of new wood. Full-bodied, with intense tropical fruit, pineapple and butterscotch aromas, vanilla bean flavors and a lovely, long, flavorful, toasty finish. Drink now to 1994. $84 (8/31/91) **90**
Puligny-Montrachet Les Combettes 1988: Complex and engaging, with intense pear, spice, citrus, vanilla and butterscotch flavors in delicate layers. Has a sense of richness, and the flavors linger on a smooth, silky finish. Drink now or cellar through 1994. Rel: $56 Cur: $61 (12/31/90) **93**
Puligny-Montrachet Les Combettes 1986 $50 (4/30/88) **93**
Puligny-Montrachet Les Combettes 1985 $50 (2/29/88) **90**
Puligny-Montrachet Les Perrières 1989: A more forward style of wine that's rich and toasty in flavor and on the finish. Very buttery, with caramel and apple aromas and flavors. Round and buttery on the finish. Drink now. $84 (8/31/91) **88**
Puligny-Montrachet Les Perrières 1988: Ripe and generous, with pretty pear, toast, lemon and spice flavors that are well focused and integrated, picking up a trace of mineral on the finish. Complex and intriguing, with lovely butterscotch notes. Drink now to 1995. 287 cases made. $70 (2/28/91) **90**
Puligny-Montrachet Les Perrières 1985 $39 (10/15/87) **93**
Puligny-Montrachet Les Referts 1989: Big and rich, but it shows restraint. Strong lemon tart, toast and ripe apple aromas follow through on the palate. Full and firm on the finish. Drink in 1993 to '95. Rel: $81 Cur: $87 (8/31/91) **91**
Puligny-Montrachet Les Referts 1988: A rich, packed-in style that's tight, flinty, concentrated and complex, with intense pear, citrus, melon and toasty vanilla and oak shadings. It's well balanced and delicate, and has probably mellowed and softened by now. $47 (12/31/90) **92**
Puligny-Montrachet Les Referts 1986 $45 (2/29/88) **87**
Puligny-Montrachet Les Truffières 1986 $45 (2/29/88) **93**
Puligny-Montrachet Les Truffières 1985 $42 (2/29/88) **91**

BERNARD THEVENOT
Puligny-Montrachet 1982 $15 (10/16/84) **84**

JACQUES THEVENOT-MACHAL
Puligny-Montrachet Les Charmes 1986 $35 (2/29/88) **82**
Puligny-Montrachet Les Folatières au Chaniot 1988: Shows real restraint and elegance, holding in its pear and spice flavors until the long finish. Try now or in 1993. $40 (12/31/90) **88**
Puligny-Montrachet Les Folatières au Chaniot 1987: Decent but unexciting Puligny, with spice, wool and pear flavors that are unfocused. $43 (4/15/89) **78**
Puligny-Montrachet Les Folatières au Chaniot 1986 $38 (2/29/88) **81**

THORIN
Puligny-Montrachet 1987: Tight and drawn in but with fine potential. The honey, toast, and earthy flavors should be opening by now, and the finish is pretty. $32 (11/15/89) **87**

CHARLES VIENOT
Puligny-Montrachet 1984 $31 (2/28/87) **63**

Key to Symbols

The scores reported here are the results of blind tastings conducted by our panel of senior editors. Wines that carry the initials below are results of individual tastings.

THE WINE SPECTATOR 100-POINT SCALE ***95-100***—Classic, a great wine; ***90-94***—Outstanding, superior character and style; ***80-89***—Good to very good, a wine with special qualities; ***70-79***—Average, drinkable wine that may have minor flaws; ***60-69***—Below average, drinkable but not recommended; ***50-59***—Poor, undrinkable, not recommended. "+"—With a score indicates a range; used primarily with barrel tastings to indicate a preliminary score.

SPECIAL DESIGNATIONS SS—Spectator Selection, CS—Cellar Selection, BB—Best Buy, ($NA)—Price not available, (NR)—Not released.

TASTER'S INITIALS (JG)—Jim Gordon, (HS)—Harvey Steiman, (JL)—James Laube, (JS)—James Suckling, (TM)—Thomas Matthews, (TR)—Terry Robards, (PM)—Per-Henrik Mansson, (BT)—Barrel Tasting (these wines were tasted blind from barrel samples), (CA-date)—*California's Great Cabernets* by James Laube, (CH-date)—*California's Great Chardonnays* by James Laube, (VP-date)—*Vintage Port* by James Suckling.

DATE TASTED Dates in parentheses represent the issue in which the rating was published.

Puligny-Montrachet Champs-Gain 1989: Wonderful in the aroma, offering multidimensional honey, hazelnut and vanilla, but a letdown on the palate. Medium-bodied and very woody on the finish. Drink now. $42 (8/31/91) **83**

Puligny-Montrachet Champs-Gain 1987: Clean and well-made but light in flavor, with floral aromas and modest apple and pear notes on the palate. $38 (7/31/89) **79**

HENRI DE VILLAMONT

Puligny-Montrachet Les Folatières 1986 $30 (12/15/88) **85**

St.-Aubin

JEAN CLAUDE BOISSET

St.-Aubin Les Charmois 1989: A little too much wood for us. Has vanilla and light asparagus aromas and medium-bodied lemon flavor, but it's very woody on the finish. Drink now. $19 (8/31/91) **78**

CHARTRON & TREBUCHET

St.-Aubin La Chatenière 1989: An elegant style, balanced with pure pear, spice, nectarine and vanilla notes that are well mannered and not overly rich. The finish fans out, picking up the pear and spice notes. Drink up now. $24 (2/28/91) **86**

St.-Aubin La Chatenière 1988: Surprisingly rich and full-bodied, its ripe pineapple and pear aromas and flavors are marked by sweet oak. Broad and flavorful. Delicious on release; the wood should be more integrated into the wine by now. $18 (3/15/90) **85**

St.-Aubin La Chatenière 1987: Distinctive and reasonably complex. Toasty and earthy in aroma, with modest fruit and butterscotch flavors and a lingering finish. Drink up now. $20 (4/15/89) **83**

St.-Aubin Les Combes 1990: Rich, smooth and complete, with fresh, lively pear, apple, spice and lemon notes that are well focused and enticing. Balanced and ready to drink now through 1994. $23 (3/31/92) **84**

MARC COLIN

St.-Aubin La Chatenière 1989: Fresh and delicious, with very good intensity. Aromas of melons, butter and lemons follow through on the palate. Medium in intensity, with a fresh finish. Drink now. ($NA) (8/31/91) **85**

St.-Aubin Les Combes 1989: Has a round mouth-feel, vanilla and apple pie aromas and interesting lemon meringue pie flavors. Medium-bodied, with a long finish. Drink now. ($NA) (8/31/91) **83**

JOSEPH DROUHIN

St.-Aubin 1987: Clean and nicely balanced, medium-bodied, with modest peach and apple flavors and a touch of complexity. Drink now. $21 (4/15/89) **81**

St.-Aubin 1986 $20 (10/15/88) **82**

JAFFELIN

St.-Aubin 1989: A medium-rich, soft wine, with yogurt, light butter and lemon aromas and flavors and a round mouth-feel. Drink now. $16 (8/31/91) **83**

St.-Aubin 1985 $13 (3/31/87) **84**

OLIVIER LEFLAIVE FRERES

St.-Aubin Premier Cru 1989: A well-crafted wine, with good intensity. Lemon, cream and butter aromas and flavors. Has good concentration and finish. Drink now. $31 (8/31/91) **84**

REINE PEDAUQUE

St.-Aubin 1989: Quite lively, with a pleasant character and honey and lemon aromas. Medium-bodied, with fresh acidity and an earthy-lemon finish. Drink now. $18 (8/31/91) **82**

DOMAINE ROUX PERE & FILS

St.-Aubin La Chatenière 1989: Round and approachable, with clean flavors. Lemon, honey and melon aromas lead to a creamy lemon flavor. Full-bodied, with a velvety mouth-feel. Drink now. $26 (8/31/91) **81**

St.-Aubin La Pucelle 1989: A lean, easy-to-drink white, with straw and honey aromas, honey and floral flavors and a simple finish. Medium-bodied. Drink now. $26 (8/31/91) **80**

St.-Aubin La Pucelle 1988: Light and crisp, with delicate, sharply focused green apple and spice flavors that are tightly wound. Drink now. $19 (3/15/90) **85**

GERARD THOMAS

St.-Aubin La Chatenière 1989: Has lots going for it in this group. A full-bodied wine, with ripe fruit, honey, toast and bark aromas, rich lemon, honey and toasted vanilla flavors and a long, smooth finish. Drink now. $28 (8/31/91) **87**

St.-Aubin Murgers des Dents Chien 1989: Fresh and floral, with floral and honey aromas, fresh honey flavors and crisp acidity. Drink now. $25 (8/31/91) **83**

CHARLES VIENOT

St.-Aubin 1984 $13 (3/31/87) **78**

Other Côte de Beaune White

DOMAINE D'AUVENAY

Auxey-Duresses 1989: An intense, focused white wine, with wonderful fruit. Very ripe, with mineral, apple and lemon aromas and flavors and a hint of toast and vanilla notes. Has excellent acidity. From Lalou Bize-Leroy. Drink now to 1994. $37 (8/31/91) **89**

BICHOT

Savigny-lès-Beaune Savigny Blanc 1989: A very ripe style, with interesting flavors of ripe dried apricots. The orange aromas are tinged with coconut and vanilla notes. Full-bodied, with medium acidity and a long finish. Drink now. $19 (8/31/91) **83**

SIMON BIZE & FILS

Savigny-lès-Beaune 1989: Deliciously intense, with plenty of character. Has tangerine, pear and vanilla aromas, a firm mouth-feel, lovely pear and vanilla flavors and a pretty finish. Full-bodied. Drink now to 1994. $22 (8/31/91) **88**

BOUCHARD PERE & FILS

Beaune Clos St.-Landry Domaines du Château de Beaune 1989: A little too overripe and overly woody. A full-bodied style, with very ripe butter, apple and hazelnut aromas and hazelnut flavors, but a little dull in the mouth. Drink now. $50 (8/31/91) **79**

Beaune Clos St.-Landry Domaines du Château de Beaune 1986: Bitterness on the finish detracts from the racy, stony, honey and pear flavors, but the length on the finish is encouraging. Drink now. $33 (2/28/89) **81**

CHANSON PERE & FILS

Beaune Clos des Mouches 1989: Clean and fruity, but disappointing for this appellation. Shows fresh pear and citrus aromas and flavors, with a clean finish. Drink now. $15 (8/31/91) **79**

Bourgogne Hautes Côtes de Beaune 1989: Offers decent fruit in an earthy style. Has lemon and earth aromas, slightly oxidized flavors and a dull finish. Drink now. $12 (8/31/91) **75**

Pernand-Vergelesses 1989: Offers lovely fresh fruit, but it's a little short on the finish. Has fresh apple and stone aromas and fresh apple and mineral flavors. Medium-bodied, with a slightly chalky finish. Drink now. $18 (8/31/91) **80**

Pernand-Vergelesses 1986: An attractive, earthy tasting, lean-structured Chardonnay with light to medium body, fig and mineral flavors and good balance. Flavors linger a bit on the finish. Drink now. $16 (7/31/89) **79**

Pernand-Vergelesses Les Caradeux 1988: Lean and hard-edged, with woody, gluey flavors obscuring what little fruit there is. $25 (8/31/90) **72**

DOMAINE CHANTEL-LESCURE

Côte de Beaune Les Grande Chatelaine 1989: Very well crafted, with a nice use of wood. Full-bodied, with lemon and light toasted oak aromas and plenty of vanilla, toast and lemon flavors. Has a medium finish. From Labouré-Roi. Drink now to 1994. $38 (8/31/91) **84**

CHARTRON & TREBUCHET

Beaune 1987: Big and fat, with nutmeg and honey flavors but there's a hole in the middle, and the finish tapers off. What's missing is finesse. $30 (2/28/89) **83**

Pernand-Vergelesses 1988: Broad and generous, with soft, supple texture and earthy pear and honey flavors. Approachable now. $18 (3/15/90) **83**

St.-Romain 1990: Ripe and floral, with spice, hazelnut, honey and pear notes that are complex and well proportioned. Picks up a trace of almond and earth flavor on the finish. Ready now through 1994. $20 (3/31/92) **86**

St.-Romain 1989: Simple but correct, with pretty perfumed pear, vanilla and honey flavors that are attractive, but not especially complex. Won't shortchange you on flavor. Drink now. $20 (2/28/91) **85**

Santenay Sous la Fée 1988: Elegant style, with ripe pear, spice and vanilla flavors of moderate depth and concentration. The flavors stay with you on the long finish. Drink now to 1994. $18 (3/15/90) **87**

Santenay Sous la Fée 1987: Austere in flavor, very dry, but with hints of clove and peach. Lean and straightforward, with good acidity. $23 (4/30/89) **79**

F. CHAUVENET

St.-Romain 1989: Rather dull and forward, with celery, grapefruit and apple aromas, celery and apple flavors and a slightly candied, oxidized finish. Medium-bodied. Drink now. ($NA) (8/31/91) **77**

DOMAINE BRUNO CLAIR

Marsannay Rosé 1989: A very dry, crisp, beautifully balanced rosé that should be excellent with a wide variety of foods. Its vibrant acidity and tangy finish carry the light cherry and melon flavors. $13 (11/15/91) **86**

DOMAINE HENRI CLERC & FILS

Beaune Chaume Gaufriot 1989: A super-ripe, almost overdone style, but it has lots of character. Deep gold, with intense lemon tart aromas. Full-bodied, with lots of lemon and toast flavors and a long finish. Drink now. $30 (8/31/91) **81**

MARIUS DELARCHE PERE & FILS

Pernand-Vergelesses Ile des Vergelesses 1989: Simple and traditional. The lemon aromas have a hint of sage. Medium- to full-bodied, with lemon and wet earth flavors and a light finish. Drink now. ($NA) (8/31/91) **80**

DOMAINE CLAUDINE DESCHAMPS

Côte de Beaune 1989: Very simple and clean, with clean lime and pear aromas, green apple flavors and a tart finish. Medium-bodied. Drink now. From Labouré-Roi. ($NA) (8/31/91) **78**

JEAN-PIERRE DICONNE

Auxey-Duresses 1989: Clean and pretty, with floral, rose petal aromas, clean, crisp flavors and a long finish. Medium-bodied. Drink now. ($NA) (8/31/91) **84**

JOSEPH DROUHIN

Auxey-Duresses 1989: Crisp and flavorful, with vanilla, orange peel and apple aromas and flavors. A lovely concentration of lemon. Drink now. $22 (8/31/91) **84**

Beaune Clos des Mouches 1990: A white Burgundy with a good pedigree. Lean and lively, with generous honey- and toast-accented pear and peach flavors that ramble on through the finish. Has plenty of room to grow. Drink after 1994. 800 cases made. $64 (5/15/92) CS **92**

Beaune Clos des Mouches 1988: Elegant and nicely proportioned, showing delicious complexity of apple, spice and floral flavors on the long finish. Crisp acidity maintains balance, and the flavors seem to grow with each sip. A harmonious wine that's drinkable now, but better after 1993. 2,000 cases made. $64 (7/31/90) **90**

Beaune Clos des Mouches 1987: A solid, chunky Chardonnay, medium-bodied, firm and well balanced, showing some appealingly honeyed flavors. A bit drying on the finish. Rel: $48 Cur: $53 (4/30/89) **81**

Beaune Clos des Mouches 1986 $56 (12/15/88) **87**

Pernand-Vergelesses 1989: Has smoky, toasty aromas, firm earth and fig flavors that turn slightly bitter and touches of honey and oak on the finish, but some may find the earthiness a put-off. Drink now to 1993. $23 (2/28/91) **86**

St.-Romain 1989: A very good concentration of apple and pie crust character, with vanilla and apple aromas, fresh lemony flavors and wonderful freshness on the finish. Drink now. $22 (8/31/91) **84**

DUBREUIL-FONTAINE

Pernand-Vergelesses Ile des Vergelesses 1985: Not for the faint of palate. A mature wine that's strongly earthy in aroma and chalky and nutty in flavor. $22 (2/28/89) **73**

JACQUES GERMAIN

Pernand-Vergelesses 1989: Holds back a little on the finish, but has good fruit and ripe apple, pear and coconut aromas. Full-bodied, with butterscotch and apple flavors and an earthy finish. Drink now or in 1993. ($NA) (8/31/91) **84**

JEAN GERMAIN

St.-Romain Clos Sous le Château 1989: A lively wine; drink with food that marries well with Sauvignon Blanc. Offers buttery celery and grapefruit aromas and flavors, with a refreshing amount of acidity. Drink now. $24 (8/31/91) **85**

St.-Romain Clos Sous le Château 1984 $15 (7/16/86) **77**

St.-Romain Clos Sous le Château 1983 $12 (9/16/85) **83**

ALAIN GRAS

St.-Romain 1989: Stylish, with a distinctive, earthy, grassy, fruity character. Has celery, wet hay and tropical fruit aromas in a medium-bodied style, with intense grapefruit and wet hay flavors and a fresh finish. Drink now. $20 (8/31/91) **84**

LOUIS JADOT

Auxey-Duresses Domaine du Duc de Magenta 1989: Forward and delicious, with very good richness. Shows vanilla, cream and apple character, with very rich flavors and very good concentration. Drink now. $25 (8/31/91) **88**

Auxey-Duresses Domaine du Duc de Magenta 1988: Complex and intriguing, with rich, polished, concentrated honey, pear, spice and toasty oak flavors and a long, full finish that keeps you coming back for another sip. Delicious. Drink now to 1994. Tasted twice. $23 (4/30/91) **88**

Pernand-Vergelesses 1989: No pretensions, but delicious. Offers focused, light lemon, stone and vanilla aromas, lovely focused fruit flavors and a crisp finish. Medium-bodied. Drink now. ($NA) (8/31/91) **87**

Pernand-Vergelesses 1988: Has lots of flavor—butter, pear, custard—even though it lacks great complexity. Broad, mouth-filling and well balanced, with plenty of spicy accents and a lingering finish. $21 (4/30/91) **85**

Savigny-lès-Beaune Blanc 1988: Earthy, oaky aromas lead to tight, austere flavors of apple skin and lemon. It's dominated by oak at this stage, but should be more generous by 1993. $24 (4/30/91) **80**

JAFFELIN

Auxey-Duresses 1989: An apple-and-cream wine. Full-bodied, with rich apple pie, vanilla and flowers on the nose. Has apple and pie crust flavors and a lovely vanilla-bean finish. Drink now. $16 (8/31/91) **85**

Auxey-Duresses 1985 $13 (3/31/87) **79**

Auxey-Duresses 1983 $11 (11/01/85) **79**

St.-Romain 1989: The flavors kick in on the finish of this medium-bodied wine. Has lemon, hay and honey aromas, honey and light butter flavors and a fresh finish. Drink now. $18 (8/31/91) **82**

Santenay Les Graviéres 1989: Big and full, with lots of character. Offers ripe apple and light apricot aromas and rich apple, tropical fruit and vanilla flavors. Full-bodied, with medium acidity and a long, flavorful finish. Drink now to 1994. $25 (8/31/91) **88**

JAYER-GILLES
Bourgogne Hautes Côtes de Beaune 1989: If you like nice toasted wood and fruit, this is for you. Has plenty of toasty wood, with lovely pear aromas. Full-bodied, with oaky apple flavors, medium acidity and a long vanilla finish. Drink now. $24 (8/31/91) **86**
Bourgogne Hautes Côtes de Beaune 1988: A fresh, clean white Burgundy that emphasizes its apple, spice and vanilla aromas and flavors. Lean and lithe in structure, with flavors that are generous enough to persist into a better-than-average finish. $22 (6/15/91) **84**

JEAN LAFOUGE
Auxey-Duresses 1985 $19 (6/15/87) **75**

LUPE-CHOLET
Bourgogne Hautes Côtes de Beaune 1988 $10 (4/30/90) **80**
Pernand-Vergelesses 1988: Tart, lean and flavorful with pretty apple, lemon, fig and spice flavors in a subtle, elegant style that finishes with crisp, mouthwatering acidity. Drink now to 1993. $15 (3/15/90) **83**
Savigny-lès-Beaune 1985 $10 (11/15/86) **78**

PROSPER MAUFOUX
Auxey-Duresses 1988: Woody aromas and flavors tend to dominate this modestly structured wine, offering only some pleasant honey and spice flavors on the finish. Tasted twice. $18 (4/30/91) **75**

MOILLARD
Bourgogne Hautes Côtes de Beaune Les Alouettes 1989: Distinctly earthy aromas and flavors manage to hint at lemon and vanilla on the palate. A simple wine to drink soon. 1,330 cases made. $15 (6/15/91) **78**

DOMAINE MONTHELIE-DOUHAIRET
Monthélie 1989: Already quite forward and slightly tired, offering nutty earth and apple aromas and oxidized, candied, ripe flavors. Medium-bodied. Drink now. ($NA) (8/31/91) **71**
Monthélie Premier Cru 1989: More evolved than some '89s, but rich in fruit. Has opulent butterscotch and apple aromas, baked apple and caramel flavors and a flavorful finish. Full-bodied. Drink now. ($NA) (8/31/91) **82**

REINE PEDAUQUE
Auxey-Duresses 1989: Light and forward, but it has good vanilla and lemon flavors. Slightly candied aromas follow through on the finish. Drink now. $22 (8/31/91) **79**
Savigny-lès-Beaune 1989: Has odd, slightly candied honey and vanilla aromas and blanched almond flavors. Medium-bodied, with a slight astringency and honey notes, but rather dull on the finish. Drink now. $22 (8/31/91) **71**

DOMAINE PONNELLE
Côte de Beaune Les Pierres Blanches 1988: Extremely earthy, chalky and dirty flavors override the peach and nectarine notes. Not for everyone. $18 (2/28/91) **68**

PRUNIER
Auxey-Duresses 1986: Distinct for its ginger, honey and earthy flavors, it is a bit coarse and ripe. Drink now. $25 (11/15/89) **84**

CHATEAU DE PULIGNY-MONTRACHET
Monthélie Chardonnay 1989: Firm textured, generous in flavor, spicy, buttery and ripe. Fig, earth and mineral flavors predominate. Not as fresh as you might expect from an '89, but it's a decent drink. $26 (2/28/91) **82**

ROLAND THEVENIN
Auxey-Duresses Chanterelle 1984 $10 (3/31/87) **69**

CHARLES VIENOT
Savigny-lès-Beaune 1989: Rather simple, but showing good, focused fruit flavor. Medium-bodied, with honey and slightly grassy aromas, grassy flavors and a light finish. Drink now. $24 (8/31/91) **82**

Chalonnaise

BICHOT
Rully 1984 $8 (6/01/86) **50**

JEAN-MARC BOILLOT
Montagny Premier Cru 1988: The spicy butterscotch and caramel aromas and flavors make this a very distinctive wine. You could ask for more fruit flavor, but it's attractive as is. $22 (8/31/90) **79**

CHATEAU DE CHAMIREY
Mercurey 1985 $14 (1/31/87) **85**

CHARTRON & TREBUCHET
Mercurey 1986 $20 (5/31/88) **69**
Rully La Chaume 1990: Ripe and full-bodied, with bold pear, citrus and melon notes. A rough-hewn style that's ready to drink now. $20 (3/31/92) **82**
Rully La Chaume 1989: Lean and crisp, with sharply focused grapefruit and peach aromas and flavors. Simple, lively and drinkable now. Tasted twice. $18 (4/30/91) **78**
Rully La Chaume 1988: Firm and toasty, with lush nutmeg-tinged apple and pineapple aromas and flavors touched by honey on the long, focused finish. Delicious to drink on release, but should show all it has by now. Excellent value. $14 (3/15/90) **88**
Rully La Chaume 1987 $15 (4/30/89) **74**

JOSEPH DROUHIN
Montagny 1986 $15 (6/15/88) **83**
Rully 1989: Has oaky aromas of spice, vanilla and butter, with ample fruit to stand up to it. Pear, honey and vanilla notes are fresh and intriguing. Very well made. Drink now or in 1993. $18 (2/28/91) **86**
Rully 1987: Crisp, light and nicely balanced for drinking now. Has lively citrus flavors with hints of peach and butter. $15 (4/30/89) **81**
Rully 1986 $14 (6/15/88) **88**

Key to Symbols

The scores reported here are the results of blind tastings conducted by our panel of senior editors. Wines that carry the initials below are results of individual tastings.

THE WINE SPECTATOR 100-POINT SCALE 95-100—Classic, a great wine; ***90-94***—Outstanding, superior character and style; ***80-89***—Good to very good, a wine with special qualities; ***70-79***—Average, drinkable wine that may have minor flaws; ***60-69***—Below average, drinkable but not recommended; ***50-59***—Poor, undrinkable, not recommended. "+"—With a score indicates a range; used primarily with barrel tastings to indicate a preliminary score.

SPECIAL DESIGNATIONS SS—Spectator Selection, CS—Cellar Selection, BB—Best Buy, ($NA)—Price not available, (NR)—Not released.

TASTER'S INITIALS (JG)—Jim Gordon, (HS)—Harvey Steiman, (JL)—James Laube, (JS)—James Suckling, (TM)—Thomas Matthews, (TR)—Terry Robards, (PM)—Per-Henrik Mansson, (BT)—Barrel Tasting (these wines were tasted blind from barrel samples), (CA-date)—*California's Great Cabernets* by James Laube, (CH-date)—*California's Great Chardonnays* by James Laube, (VP-date)—*Vintage Port* by James Suckling.

DATE TASTED Dates in parentheses represent the issue in which the rating was published.

DUVERNAY
Mercurey La Chiquette 1988: Earthy, but flavorful, with a smooth texture and pear and fig flavors that turn to honey and almond on the long finish. Has more depth and interest than most Mercureys. Drinkable now. $17 (4/30/91) **87**

FAIVELEY
Mercurey Clos Rochette 1988: Ripe, round and generous, within the confines of the modest Mercurey structure, offering plenty of appealing pear, grapefruit and orange peel aromas and flavors. Drinkable now. $22 (4/30/91) **86**
Mercurey Blanc Clos de la Rochette 1983 $14 (3/31/87) **62**
Rully 1983 $10 (8/31/86) **74**

JAFFELIN
Rully Barrel Fermented 1989: A woody style, with plenty of spice and vanilla notes to accompany the solid core of pear and apple flavors. An aromatic wine that needs to soften and polish its texture. Try in 1993. $16 (8/31/91) **82**
Rully Barrel Fermented 1988: A finely crafted wine, smooth in texture and generous, offering ripe pear, toast and vanilla aromas and flavors. Harmonious; drink now. $13 (3/15/90) **86**
Rully Blanc 1987: A solid, reserved wine showing subdued spice and charming pear flavors and a full feeling on the palate. Drink now. $13 (3/15/89) **82**
Rully Blanc 1986 $12 (2/15/88) **87**
Rully Blanc 1985 $11 (3/31/87) **88**

OLIVIER LEFLAIVE FRERES
Montagny Premier Cru 1987: Very toasty and earthy in aroma, yet lean and tight in structure, with modest lemon and apple flavors. Drink now. $16 (8/31/90) **80**
Rully Premier Cru 1989: A well put-together white wine, with plenty of pear and grapefruit flavors, a touch of astringency and a clean, dry finish. $20 (7/31/91) **81**

LUPE-CHOLET
Rully Marissou 1988: Exotic tropical fruit aromas and flavors provide much of the appeal in the soft, broad-textured, easy-to-drink wine. $16 (3/15/90) **80**

PROSPER MAUFOUX
Montagny 1984 $11 (3/31/87) **56**
Montagny Première Cru 1989: Simple but attractive honey, pear and spice flavors turn a bit earthy on the aftertaste. Cleans up on the finish. Drink now to 1993. $20 (8/31/91) **84**

ANTONIN RODET
Montagny Les Chagnots 1985 $10 (11/15/86) **65**

ALAIN ROY-THEVENIN
Montagny Château de la Saule 1988: Crisp, fruity and fresh, with distinctive apple flavors and a lingering aftertaste. It's clean, well balanced and well made. $12 (8/31/90) **83**

DOMAINE F. & L. SAIER
Mercurey Blanc Les Chenelots 1988: A spicy, crisp wine, with lots of lively grapefruit, vanilla and nutmeg aromas and flavors. Generous and not too complex, but well made and drinkable now. $17 (4/30/91) **83**

JEAN VACHET
Montagny Les Coeres 1986: Spicy, crisp and well-proportioned, a medium-scale wine with attractive floral, nutmeg and citrus-apple aromas and flavors, likable now and probably worth keeping for the short term. Drink now. $16 (1/31/89) **83**

Mâconnais/ Mâcon

LES ACACIAS
Mâcon-Villages Cave de Viré 1989: Firm, but not entirely clean tasting. It's full-bodied and earthy in flavor, but a muddy aftertaste holds it back. $11 (2/28/91) **71**
Mâcon-Viré Vieilles Vignes 1988: With vague hints of grapey flavors, this lean, earthy wine is a bit on the funky side, but it's balanced and drinkable. Tasted twice. $9 (8/31/90) **76**

DOMAINE D'AZENAY
Mâcon-Azé 1990: Thin, green and earthy, with light, stripped celery notes that are simple and uninteresting. $12 (3/31/92) **70**

BARTON & GUESTIER
Mâcon St.-Louis Chardonnay 1990: Dull and unfocused, with pear and lemon notes that turn simple on the finish. Marginal quality. $8 (3/31/92) **72**
Mâcon-Villages 1988: Smoky, earthy aromas and flavors pervade the wine, almost turning to black pepper on the finish, overshadowing the modest grapefruit flavors. It seems balanced and attractive for drinking now. $9 (9/30/89) **81**

BICHOT
Mâcon-Villages 1989: A fresh, spicy and floral wine, with lively structure and clean, fruity aromas and flavors that echo nicely on the finish. Drink now. $9 (7/15/90) **83**
Mâcon-Villages 1987: Ripe but not heavy, clean, fruity and rich enough to last awhile on the palate. Flavors lean toward fig and toast. $6 (1/31/89) BB **82**

JEAN CLAUDE BOISSET
Mâcon-Blanc-Villages 1988: Shows nice maturity, with spicy butterscotch aromas, but the flavors are slightly tired and the finish is dry and earthy. $9 (12/31/90) **76**
Mâcon-Blanc-Villages 1987: Good but one-dimensional. Its flavor is simple butterscotch and its balance is soft. $8.50 (9/15/89) **76**

CAVE DE CHARDONNAY
Mâcon-Chardonnay Chardonnay de Chardonnay 1988: A bargain for Burgundy, this nicely balanced, medium-bodied wine, with vanilla, apple and spice flavors, tastes clean, fresh, well made and even a bit complex. $9 (7/15/90) BB **81**

GEORGES DUBOEUF
Mâcon-Lugny Fête des Fleurs 1989: An earthy, appealing, well-balanced Mâcon, with spicy, buttery accents and subtle pear flavors. Drink now. $9 (10/31/90) **84**
Mâcon-Villages 1989: A generous, fruity style offering peach, nectarine and pear flavors. It's balanced toward the soft side, but fine for drinking now. $8.50 (10/31/90) **81**
Mâcon-Villages 1988: A light, smooth wine with subdued fruit flavors and just enough honey on the finish to keep it interesting. $8 (9/30/89) **79**
Mâcon-Villages La Coupe Perration 1988: Light, fresh and crisp, with a pleasant grassy edge to the delicate pear and peach aromas and flavors. $8 (9/30/89) **77**

DOMAINE EMILIAN GILLET
Mâcon-Clessé Quintaine 1988: Has nice flavors on a medium frame, offering good concentration of grapefruit, apple and a touch of herb. It's smooth and balanced, but ultimately simple. Drink now. $17 (8/31/90) **80**

LOUIS JADOT
Mâcon-Villages La Fontaine 1988: A bit austere, but has good pear and spice flavors, a feeling of roundness and a dry, slightly honeyed finish. $9 (9/15/89) **84**

PIERRE JANNY
Mâcon-Villages Domaine du Prieuré 1987: Simple and straightforward both in the nose and on the palate. Herbal and lemon aromas and flavors dominate in this unexciting wine. $7 (1/31/89) **74**

MAURICE JOSSERAND
Mâcon-Péronne Domaine du Mortier 1988: A spicy, butterscotch-flavored Mâcon that dances lightly across the palate and lingers on the finish. Distinctive and satisfying to drink. 500 cases made. $8 (12/31/90) BB **84**

LABOURE-ROI
Mâcon-Villages 1989: An earthy style that's a bit less lively than its young age would suggest, but it's flavorful, with rustic apple, earth and spice notes on the finish. Drinkable now. 5,000 cases made. $10 (4/30/91) **80**

LAROCHE
Mâcon-Villages 1988: Earthy and slightly tired at first, the pleasant, delicate spice and vanilla aromas and flavors emerge on the finish. Drink now. $8.50 (7/15/90) **79**

M & G
Mâcon-Villages 1988: $14 (3/31/91) **78**

PROSPER MAUFOUX
Mâcon-Villages 1989: Despite an earthy edge to the flavors, this wine has plenty of ripe, rich fruit. The pear, melon, spice and honeyed flavors linger on the finish. Drink now or in 1993. $11 (8/31/91) **81**
Mâcon-Villages 1988: Light and simple, with appealing grapefruit and vanilla aromas and flavors that linger nicely on the finish. Drink now. $10.50 (7/15/90) **82**

MOILLARD
Mâcon-Villages Domaine de Montbellet 1989: Simple, fruity and pleasant, with distinctive earth and grass overtones; drinkable now. $10.50 (4/30/91) **77**

MOREAU
Mâcon-Villages 1990: Coarse and bitter, with strong sulfury flavors that interrupt the flow of fruit. Marginal quality. Tasted twice. $9 (3/31/92) **68**

REINE PEDAUQUE
Mâcon-Villages Coupées 1988: Somewhat broader than most Mâcons, leaning more toward the honey-caramel end of the flavor spectrum than the fruit end. Austere. $9.50 (9/30/89) **76**

CAVE DE PRISSE
Mâcon-Prissé Les Clochettes 1986: Well-balanced and pretty. This wine shows nice complexity, with vanilla and some butterscotch aromas and flavors. $8.50 (1/31/89) **84**

DOMAINE DES ROCHES
Mâcon-Igé 1989: Enjoyable but controversial. Very toasty and earthy in aroma and buttery in flavor, with the earthy character so pronounced that it verges on barnyardy. $9 (10/31/90) **76**
Mâcon-Igé 1987: Very nicely structured, and the flavors hang together well; it's earthy, buttery and slightly honeyed on the finish, harmonious and subtle. $7 (5/15/89) BB **84**

ROBERT SARRAU
Mâcon-Villages 1989: Crisp, tight and restrained, but with enough apple and citrus flavors to make it satisfying. Sound and well made. Drink now. $8 (10/31/90) **81**

DOMAINE TALMARD
Mâcon-Chardonnay 1989: A reasonably fruity but straightforward Chardonnay without much aroma, but it has decent herb and lemon flavors. $10 (10/31/90) **78**
Mâcon-Chardonnay 1988: A fresh, crisp and flavorful wine, with a round texture and vanilla overtones to the lively grapefruit and green apple flavors. Could use more finesse. $9 (7/15/90) **80**

JEAN-CLAUDE THEVENET
Mâcon-Pierreclos 1988: Earthy and toasty, with hints of butterscotch and vanilla lending richness to the moderate concentration of apple and peach flavors. This is a Chardonnay with modest finesse and style that's drinkable now. $6.25 (7/15/90) BB **84**

THORIN
Mâcon-Villages 1987: Chalky, flinty, spicy style, with enough apple flavor to carry it. Austere rather than generous. $8.50 (1/31/89) **74**

CHATEAU DE LA TOUR DE L'ANGE
Mâcon-Villages Chardonnay 1989: Promises butter and spice in the aromas, but delivers very light, watery apple flavors. An average, drinkable wine without much excitement. $9 (8/31/91) **72**

DOMAINE DU VIEUX ST.-SORLIN
Mâcon-La Roche Vineuse 1989: A clean, fruity-tasting wine that's firmly structured and spicy in flavor. Hints of vanilla and nutmeg add interest to the basic pear flavors. Drink now. A fine value for white Burgundy. $13.50 (2/28/91) **82**
Mâcon-La Roche Vineuse Eleve en futs de Chêne 1988: A Mâcon with a lot of style, and relatively high-profile oak components. It's ripe, round and focused, with nutmeg, vanilla, toast and peach flavors competing for attention. A wine with plenty of personality. Drinkable now. $11 (7/15/90) **86**

J.J. VINCENT
Mâcon-Villages 1988: A sound, acceptable-quality Mâcon, with modest pear flavors and a buttery, nearly mature taste on the finish. $7 (10/31/90) **79**
Mâcon-Villages Pièce d'Or 1990: Crisp and clean with layers of honey, pear, melon and pineapple flavor. Balanced and refreshing. Drink now. A good value. $9.50 (8/31/91) **81**
Mâcon-Villages Pièce d'Or 1987: An earthy, herbal style, straightforward, toasty and a bit on the blunt side. $7 (5/15/89) **77**

POUILLY

PHILIPPE ANTOINE
Pouilly-Fuissé 1986 $15 (4/30/88) **79**

CHATEAU DE BEAUREGARD
Pouilly-Fuissé 1983 $15 (3/16/85) **78**

ANDRE BESSON
Pouilly-Fuissé Domaine de Pouilly 1988: A good, even complex Pouilly-Fuissé that has aromas of spice and butterscotch, plus ample flavors of apple and pear. Well-balanced and clean tasting. Drink now. $15 (7/31/90) **86**

BICHOT
Pouilly-Fuissé 1988: Earth, butterscotch and chalk flavors make up this aggressive, rather blunt wine that lacks solid fruit in the middle and is overly dry on the finish. Better than bottles tasted earlier. $13 (12/31/90) **73**
Pouilly-Fuissé 1987 $10 (4/30/89) **84**
Pouilly-Fuissé 1986 $11 (3/15/88) **79**
Pouilly-Fuissé 1985 $16 (3/31/87) **85**

JEAN CLAUDE BOISSET
Pouilly-Fuissé 1986 $10 (9/30/87) **90**
Pouilly-Fuissé 1985 $16 (3/31/87) **77**

BOUCHARD AINE
Pouilly-Fuissé Réserve 1985 $18 (3/31/87) **87**

BOUCHARD PERE & FILS
Pouilly-Fuissé 1989: Fresh, lively and generous, offering appealing apple, honey and spice aromas and flavors. Medium in weight, with a firm texture. A bit astringent on release; perhaps better by now. $25 (4/30/91) **85**
Pouilly-Fuissé 1984 $20 (3/31/87) **87**
Pouilly-Vinzelles 1984 $13 (3/31/87) **79**

F. CHAUVENET
Pouilly-Fuissé Clos de France 1987: Crisp, lean and simple, with some earthiness and chalkiness on the palate that will not appeal to everyone. $13 (4/30/89) **78**
Pouilly-Fuissé Clos de France 1986 $14 (10/15/87) **79**

RAOUL CLERGET
Pouilly-Fuissé 1986 $10 (10/15/88) **67**

LOUIS CURVEUX
Pouilly-Fuissé Les Menestrières 1988: Stylishly oaky and elegant. Has plenty of vanilla and spice flavors, with a modest fruit component of apple and peach. The flavors linger nicely on the finish. $23 (7/31/90) **86**

DOMAINE DELACOUR
Pouilly-Fuissé 1984 $18 (3/31/87) **84**

LUCIEN DESCHAUX
Pouilly-Fuissé La Cuvée du Maitre 1990: Dull, oily, rubbery flavors further ruin an otherwise light, simple wine. Tasted twice. $14 (3/31/92) **64**

JOSEPH DROUHIN
Pouilly-Fuissé 1987 $18 (4/30/89) **83**
Pouilly-Fuissé 1986 $18 (6/30/88) **76**

GEORGES DUBOEUF
Pouilly-Fuissé 1989: Straightforward, well balanced, lean, focused and tasty, emphasizing crisp lemon and grapefruit flavors. Should be a versatile wine at the table. $15 (10/31/90) **86**
Pouilly-Fuissé 1988: Crisp and light, with somewhat grassy peach and lemon aromas and flavors that linger appealingly on the finish. Drink it while it's fresh and lively. $12 (9/30/89) **84**
Pouilly-Fuissé 1987 $12 (6/15/88) **81**
Pouilly-Fuissé 1986 $14 (7/31/87) **82**
Pouilly-Fuissé 1985 $15 (3/31/87) **80**

J.A. FERRET
Pouilly-Fuissé Les Perrières Cuvée Spéciale 1986: Extra aging has made it rich and mature, with buttery, earthy, slightly oxidized aromas and flavors. Has pear, honey and butterscotch, plus a lingering finish. Drink now. $30 (7/31/90) **82**

HENRY FESSY
Pouilly-Fuissé 1986 $10 (10/15/88) **82**

SYLVAIN FESSY
Pouilly-Fuissé Cuvée Gilles Guérrin 1986 $12 (12/31/87) **86**

THIERRY GUERIN
Pouilly-Fuissé 1985 $19 (3/31/87) **81**
Pouilly-Fuissé Clos de France 1988: Elegant and flavorful, offering classic toasty, earthy aromas plus ripe apple and pear flavors with hints of vanilla and honey for complexity. Well-balanced and lasting on the finish. $23 (7/31/90) **89**

RENE GUERIN
Pouilly-Fuissé La Roche 1988: An earthy, almost decadent wine, with toasty aromas, nutty, honeyed flavors and a crisp finish. Enjoyable if you like the funky, mature style. $22 (9/30/91) **84**

LOUIS JADOT
Pouilly-Fuissé 1988: Crisp-textured and focused, a bright beam of citrus and mineral flavors carrying through to a long finish, seasoned with a touch of toast in the aroma. Drink now. $16 (9/30/89) **85**
Pouilly-Fuissé 1985 $19 (3/31/87) **90**
Pouilly-Fuissé Cuvée Réserve Spéciale 1989: Spicy and stylish, with a polished mouth-feel and lively butter and spice notes surrounding a core of pear and apple flavors. Very harmonious and well balanced in a flavorful, but not heavy style. $21 (7/31/91) **87**

JAFFELIN
Pouilly-Fuissé 1990: Tightly wound fruit and firm acidity characterize this medium-bodied, rather lean wine, with grapefruit and apple flavors. Clean and well made. $18 (7/31/91) **83**
Pouilly-Fuissé 1985 $19 (4/15/87) **89**
Pouilly-Fuissé 1984 $19 (3/31/87) **89**

LABOURE-ROI
Pouilly-Fuissé 1988: Deliciously fruity and spicy, with orange and nutmeg aromas and full flavors of pear, tangerine and honey that keep developing as you sip. Shows the stylish flavors and round texture of oak aging. 3,000 cases made. $18 (10/31/90) **89**
Pouilly-Fuissé 1985 $18 (3/31/87) **92**

DOMAINE LAPIERRE
Pouilly-Fuissé 1985 $13 (3/31/87) **90**

ROGER LASSARAT
Pouilly-Fuissé Clos de France 1986 $26 (4/30/88) **90**
Pouilly-Fuissé Clos de France 1985 $23 (12/31/87) **88**

LOUIS LATOUR
Pouilly-Fuissé Latour 1984 $25 (4/30/87) **68**

CHATEAU DE LAYE
Pouilly-Vinzelles 1983 $8 (12/01/85) **55**

A. LIGERET
Pouilly-Fuissé 1988: Has decent pear and butter flavors, but smells musty and earthy, turning dry and bitter on the finish. Tasted twice. $21 (2/15/91) **70**

LUPE-CHOLET
Pouilly-Fuissé 1987: Lean and herbal, perhaps a bit stemmy, crisp and firm in structure but not very generous with flavor. $13 (4/30/89) **70**
Pouilly-Fuissé 1984 $19 (8/31/86) **64**

MANCIAT-PONCET
Pouilly-Fuissé La Roche 1985 $20 (2/15/88) **88**

PROSPER MAUFOUX
Pouilly-Fuissé 1989: Smells attractive, but the flavors are a bit flat on the palate. The pear, melon and citrus flavors are decent. Gets better with each sip. Drink now. $23 (8/31/91) **83**
Pouilly-Fuissé 1984 $17 (3/31/87) **78**

CHARLES MONCAUT
Pouilly-Fuissé 1985 $18 (6/15/87) **62**

REINE PEDAUQUE
Pouilly-Fuissé Griselles 1988: Earthy, muddy aromas and flavors take away the refreshing element of this wine, which is otherwise balanced and well made. $16 (9/30/89) **76**

PELLERIN
Pouilly-Fuissé 1987 $12 (4/30/89) **75**

ANTONIN RODET
Pouilly-Fuissé Rodet 1985 $19 (10/15/87) **80**

LEONARD DE ST.-AUBIN
Pouilly-Fuissé 1990: A wine with an earthy, foxy quality that interferes with the ripe pear and melon flavor. It's drinkable but may be a bit too swampy for some. Drink now. $15 (8/31/91) **75**

ROGER SAUMAIZE
Pouilly-Fuissé Clos de la Roche 1989: A very sturdy, tightly structured wine that needs time in the cellar to show the full effects of its spicy, toasty apple and vanilla flavors that are wrapped in firm acidity and tannins. Very long on the finish. Drink now to 1995. $28 (7/31/91) **91**
Pouilly-Fuissé Les Ronchevats 1989: Very generous and complex, with lots of apple, pear, vanilla and spice flavors that are fairly deep and long lasting on the finish. Has enough style and finesse to keep you coming back for another sip. $31 (7/31/91) **89**

ROLAND THEVENIN
Pouilly-Fuissé Les Moulins 1985 $19 (3/31/87) **84**

ROGER VERGE
Pouilly-Fuissé 1986 $15 (3/15/88) **79**

CHARLES VIENOT
Pouilly-Fuissé 1987: Clean and simple but not very flavorful, hints of green apple and chalk on the palate keep it interesting. $14 (4/30/89) **75**
Pouilly-Fuissé 1984 $19 (3/31/87) **80**
Pouilly-Vinzelles 1985 $16 (3/31/87) **70**

J.J. VINCENT
Pouilly-Fuissé 1990: Fresh, clean and crisp with hints of honey, melon, citrus and spice. Elegant and balanced with pretty floral notes on the aftertaste. Drink now to 1993. $18 (8/31/91) **82**
Pouilly-Fuissé 1989: Simple, straightforward and fruity, with generous pineapple flavors. Drinkable now. $15 (4/30/91) **79**
Pouilly-Fuissé 1988: A great value in white Burgundy. Spicy, full-bodied, clean and packed with youthful fruit flavors that should develop with time. Layers of nutmeg, vanilla, pear and apple give it complexity. Tempting now, but should improve through 1993. 5,000 cases made. $15 (10/31/90) **90**
Pouilly-Fuissé 1984 $17 (2/16/86) **71**

M. VINCENT
Pouilly-Fuissé Château Fuissé 1989: Concentrated and fruity, showing plenty of honey and spice aromas, ripe apricot and pear flavors, a crisp texture and a lingering, pleasantly bitter finish. Tasted twice. $38 (8/31/91) **85**
Pouilly-Fuissé Château Fuissé 1987: An earthy style, with lots of mineral and candied aromas and flavors that turn slightly buttery on the finish. Seems tired before its time, but still drinkable. Tasted twice. $23 (11/30/90) **77**
Pouilly-Fuissé Château Fuissé 1986: Quite a treat. Very aromatic and effusive, with lots of spice, fruit and butter aromas and spicy, appley, full-fledged flavors. It's long lasting and complex on the finish. $29 (10/31/90) **89**

ST.-VÉRAN

ANCIEN DOMAINE DU CHAPITRE DE MACON
St.-Véran Les Colombière 1988: Earthy aromas and flavors shoulder past a light core of peach and apple, diminishing the freshness and liveliness. Drink now. $12 (8/31/90) **75**

PHILIPPE ANTOINE
St.-Véran 1986 $10 (4/30/88) **83**

JEAN CLAUDE BOISSET
St.-Véran 1989: A simple wine that's dull and tired, with unusual cardboard and wilted flower flavors that persist into the slightly bitter finish. $12 (7/31/91) **68**
St.-Véran 1988: A medium-weight wine with spicy, vaguely pearlike aromas and flavors on a supple frame. Balanced and harmonious; drink now. $9.50 (7/31/90) **81**
St.-Véran 1984 $10 (3/31/87) **68**

F. CHAUVENET
St.-Véran 1985 $12 (3/31/87) **81**

JOSEPH DROUHIN
St.-Véran 1989: An amply fruity, smooth-textured white Burgundy that has the polish, if not the depth and complexity, of the great ones. Its lemon and pineapple flavors are rounded off nicely by touches of honey and vanilla. A good value in white Burgundy. $16 (2/28/91) **85**

GEORGES DUBOEUF
St.-Véran 1989: Full flavored and ripe, with pear, pineapple, spice and peach notes, good acidity and a lingering finish. A solid value that's interesting and complex enough to keep you coming back for another sip. $10 (10/31/90) **85**
St.-Véran 1988: Light, crisp and fresh, with lively peach, pear and lemon aromas and flavors, zingy acidity and a touch of pleasant grassiness. $9 (9/30/89) **82**
St.-Véran 1987 $9 (10/15/88) **77**
St.-Véran 1986 $9 (7/31/87) **79**
St.-Véran 1985 $10 (3/31/87) **87**
St.-Véran Coupe Louis Dailly 1988: Balanced and nicely focused, but not particualarly intense, its light pear and lemon flavors turning crisp and tangy. $9 (9/30/89) **80**
St.-Véran Coupe Louis Dailly 1987 $9 (10/15/88) **80**

SYLVAIN FESSY
St.-Véran Cuvée Prissé 1986 $8 (2/15/88) **75**

GEORGES BLANC
St.-Véran 1986 $10 (12/31/87) **72**

THIERRY GUERIN
St.-Véran 1989: Despite some earthy aromas, this light, fresh and fruity wine offers some nice touches of pineapple and fig. Drink soon. $9 (3/31/91) **79**
St.-Véran La Côte Rôtie 1987 $8.50 (4/30/89) **80**
St.-Véran La Côte Rôtie 1986 $11 (10/15/88) **79**
St.-Véran La Côte Rôtie 1985 $10 (3/31/87) **72**

LOUIS JADOT
St.-Véran 1984 $9 (3/31/87) **81**
St.-Véran La Chapelle 1989: Simple and a bit earthy, with modest apple and spice flavors and a firm texture; a wine with modest ambitions. Drink soon. Tasted twice. $14 (8/31/91) **78**

JAFFELIN
St.-Véran 1989: Fresh and simple, with modest apple notes. Drink soon. $14 (7/31/91) **80**
St.-Véran 1985 $9.25 (3/31/87) **88**

LAROCHE
St.-Véran 1988: A well-crafted wine of medium weight and medium intensity of lively pear, spice and vanilla aromas and flavors, balanced and fairly long. Drink now. $10 (7/31/90) **81**

ROGER LASSARAT
St.-Véran La Côte Rôtie 1986 $13 (4/30/88) **73**
St.-Véran Cuvée Prestige 1988: Light and crisp, with herbal, grassy aromas and flavors, this is a wine for those who don't care about fruit. Has good length and structure. Drink now. $15 (8/31/90) **77**

PROSPER MAUFOUX
St.-Véran 1989: A spicy style with tart nutmeg, citrus, vanilla and pear notes that echo on the finish. Medium-bodied, it's ready to drink now. $14 (8/31/91) **82**
St.-Véran 1988: A medium-weight wine, soft, round and tasty, with delicate apple, nutmeg and slightly earthy aromas and flavors that linger on the generous finish. Drink now. $12 (7/31/90) **82**
St.-Véran 1985 $12 (3/31/87) **67**

MOMMESSIN
St.-Véran Domaine de l'Evèque 1985 $11 (3/31/87) **76**

CHARLES MONCAUT
St.-Véran 1985 $10 (6/15/87) **75**

CAVE DE PRISSE
St.-Véran Les Blanchettes 1985 $10 (3/31/87) **92**

VIGNERONS
St.-Véran 1983 $7 (10/16/85) BB **82**

J.J. VINCENT
St.-Véran 1988: Butterscotch and earth aromas and ripe fruit and mineral flavors make this a fairly rich, interesting wine. The flavors are well balanced with acidity, and the texture is broad and full. $10 (10/31/90) **85**
St.-Véran 1985 $12 (3/31/87) **87**

OTHER BURGUNDY WHITE

BERTRAND AMBROISE
Bourgogne Chardonnay Blanc 1989: Rich yet subdued, well crafted, with intense aromas of lemons and pie crust. Medium-bodied, with fresh flavors and acidity. Drink now. $15 (8/31/91) **86**

DOMAINE DE L'ARLOT
Nuits-St.-Georges Clos de L'Arlot 1988: Fresh, fruity and lively, with lots of well-crafted orange, peach and almond aromas and flavors, a smooth texture and respectable length. Drinkable now. $27/375ml (4/30/91) **84**

BICHOT
Bourgogne Le Bourgogne Bichot 1988: Pleasant and lightly fruity, with earthy, appley aromas and a touch of anise. Not a lot of depth, but it has straightforward apple and lemon flavors. Affordable. $8 (4/30/90) **76**
Bourgogne Le Bourgogne Bichot 1987: Smooth, light and tasty, with lots of sweet oak aromas and flavos to lend some depth to the simple, appley flavor. $8 (5/15/89) **79**

SIMON BIZE & FILS
Bourgogne Chardonnay Les Champlains 1989: Has a delicious honey and fruit character, offering honey, cream and apple aromas and honey and butter flavors. Medium-bodied; medium in acidity and on the finish. Drink now. ($NA) (8/31/91) **84**

PIERRE BOILLOT
Bourgogne Aligoté 1987: Austere, crisp and lean. Has earthy aromas and a buttery feel on the palate, but the flavors are sparse and tart. Try with oysters. $13 (7/31/90) **75**

LIONEL J. BRUCK
Bourgogne St.-Vincent Pinot Chardonnay 1984 $10 (3/31/87) **79**

CALVET
Bourgogne Chardonnay Première 1987: Has more richness, roundness and depth of flavor than most generic Bourgogne Blancs, smooth and flavorful. Plenty of oak aromas and flavors and good structure set this apart. $10 (4/30/89) **83**

CHANSON PERE & FILS
Bourgogne Chardonnay 1989: A good, clean white, with hay and dried fruit aromas and almond and apple flavors. Medium in body, acidity and on the finish. Drink now. $10 (8/31/91) **81**

MAURICE CHAPUIS
Bourgogne Chardonnay 1989: An accessible, smooth wine, with aromas of freshly cut pears and similar characteristics on the palate. Clean and refreshing. Drink now. ($NA) (8/31/91) **82**

CHARTRON & TREBUCHET
Bourgogne Aligoté Les Equinces 1985 $9 (4/30/87) **70**
Bourgogne Blanc Hommage à Victor Hugo 1988: Medium weight, soft and supple, with charming melon and spice aromas and flavors. Appealing for current drinking. $10 (3/31/90) **83**
Bourgogne Blanc Hommage à Victor Hugo 1987: Has satisfying citrus flavors and an unusual touch of black pepper. Lively balance, spicy finish. $13 (3/15/89) **78**
Bourgogne Blanc Hommage à Victor Hugo 1986 $13 (5/31/88) **70**
Bourgogne Chardonnay 1990: The pear, honey and spice flavors turn earthy, coarse and a touch sour on the finish. Drink now. Tasted twice. $11 (3/31/92) **74**
Bourgogne Chardonnay 1989: Light, simple and fruity; a cleanly made Chardonnay for current drinking. $10 (2/28/91) **78**

DOMAINE BRUNO CLAIR
Morey-St.-Denis en la rue de Vergy 1989: A medium-bodied wine, with delicious fruit flavors and roundness. Has lemon, light mango and tropical fruit aromas, a velvety mouth-feel, creamy, tropical fruit flavors and a long finish. Tasted twice. Drink now. $30 (8/31/91) **86**
Bourgogne Blanc 1989: Round and well crafted, with cream, melon and apple aromas. Medium-bodied, with lovely, creamy apple flavors and a smooth mouth-feel. Drink now. $13 (8/31/91) **82**

DOMAINE HENRI CLERC & FILS
Bourgogne Blanc 1984 $10 (3/31/87) **68**
Bourgogne Chardonnay Blanc Les Champs Perriers 1989: This chewy wine is more like a top-flight Alsatian white. Very stylistic, with almond, spice and floral aromas. Medium-bodied, with spice and floral flavors and an impressive, spicy finish. Drink now. $20 (8/31/91) **86**

JOSEPH DROUHIN
Bourgogne Chardonnay Laforet 1989: Crisp, light and floral, almost like a Riesling, but it has delicacy and charm. The flavors persist, suggesting apples and roses. Drink soon. $9 (4/30/91) BB **82**
Bourgogne Chardonnay Laforet 1988: Generous pear, butter and pleasantly earthy aromas and flavors stay with you through the finish of this medium-bodied, balanced wine. $8.75 (9/30/89) **79**

Key to Symbols

The scores reported here are the results of blind tastings conducted by our panel of senior editors. Wines that carry the initials below are results of individual tastings.

THE WINE SPECTATOR 100-POINT SCALE 95-100—Classic, a great wine; ***90-94***—Outstanding, superior character and style; ***80-89***—Good to very good, a wine with special qualities; ***70-79***—Average, drinkable wine that may have minor flaws; ***60-69***—Below average, drinkable but not recommended; ***50-59***—Poor, undrinkable, not recommended. "+"—With a score indicates a range; used primarily with barrel tastings to indicate a preliminary score.

SPECIAL DESIGNATIONS SS—Spectator Selection, CS—Cellar Selection, BB—Best Buy, ($NA)—Price not available, (NR)—Not released.

TASTER'S INITIALS (JG)—Jim Gordon, (HS)—Harvey Steiman, (JL)—James Laube, (JS)—James Suckling, (TM)—Thomas Matthews, (TR)—Terry Robards, (PM)—Per-Henrik Mansson, (BT)—Barrel Tasting (these wines were tasted blind from barrel samples), (CA-date)—*California's Great Cabernets* by James Laube, (CH-date)—*California's Great Chardonnays* by James Laube, (VP-date)—*Vintage Port* by James Suckling.

DATE TASTED Dates in parentheses represent the issue in which the rating was published.

Bourgogne Chardonnay Laforet 1986 $8.50 (1/31/88) **81**
Bourgogne Chardonnay Laforet 1985 $8.25 (3/31/87) **85**
Bourgogne Chardonnay Laforet 1985 $8.25 (8/31/86) BB **84**
Bourgogne Chardonnay Laforet 1983 $7.50 (6/01/86) **61**

DOMAINE DUJAC
Morey-St.-Denis Vin Gris de Pinot Noir 1986 $13 (4/15/89) **80**

FAIVELEY
Bourgogne Chardonnay 1988: Stylishly smoky on the nose, but it turns flat and simple on the palate. An average wine that lacks fruit and depth. $14 (7/31/90) **74**
Bourgogne Chardonnay Cuvée Joseph Faively 1989: Closed up, but it has very good potential. A medium-bodied wine, with floral, smoked bacon and green apple aromas, very firm acidity, green apple flavors and a long finish. Drink now to 1994. $21 (8/31/91) **85**
Bourgogne Chardonnay Cuvée Joseph Faiveley 1985 $14 (3/31/87) **71**

JEAN GERMAIN
Bourgogne Clos de la Fortune 1989: Quite forward. Has refined honey, earth and lemon aromas in a medium-bodied style, with simple apple flavors and a light finish. Quite woody. Drink now. ($NA) (8/31/91) **81**

L'HERITIER-GUYOT
Vougeot Clos Blanc de Vougeot 1988: A bizarre wine that tastes like apple cider in a plastic cup. Avoid. Tasted twice. 1,041 cases made. $52 (4/15/92) **68**

LOUIS JADOT
Bourgogne Chardonnay 1988: Light and fresh, with a modicum of attractive peach flavors plus a pleasant hint of grass and comfortably round texture. $9.50 (9/30/89) **81**
Bourgogne Chardonnay 1986 $10 (10/15/88) **78**
Bourgogne Chardonnay 1985 $9 (3/31/87) **65**

JAFFELIN
Bourgogne Blanc 1988: A refreshing wine, beautifully balanced for current drinking. Fragrant and generous, with floral aromas and full-bodied fig flavors, supported by firm acidity. A great value. $9 (3/31/90) **85**
Bourgogne Chardonnay 1990: Light and refreshing in style, with clean pear and spice flavors and a firm enough structure to balance against a plate of fish. $9 (7/31/91) BB **81**
Bourgogne Chardonnay du Châpitre 1989: Straightforward and flavorful. Straw, apple and banana aromas open to apple and vanilla flavors. Drink now. $9 (8/31/91) **80**
Bourgogne Chardonnay du Châpitre 1987: Tastes lean and tart, with fig flavors and a nice overlay of cedar and butter aromas. Dry and tart on the finish. $9.50 (3/15/89) **76**
Bourgogne Chardonnay du Châpitre 1985 $9.50 (3/31/87) **80**
Bourgogne Chardonnay du Châpitre 1983 $6.25 (1/01/85) **74**

JAYER-GILLES
Bourgogne Hautes Côtes de Nuits 1989: An interesting wine, with refined, stylistic flavors. Aromas of evergreen, mint and fruit lead to light mineral and earth flavors, with a delicate, refined finish. Medium-bodied. Drink now. $18 (8/31/91) **85**

DOMAINE LAROCHE
Bourgogne Clos du Château 1986: A clean, modest wine with good structure and attractive flavors; it's spicy, toasty, nicely balanced and has a touch of honey on the finish. $16 (1/31/89) **80**

LOUIS LATOUR
Bourgogne Chardonnay Latour 1985 $11 (3/31/87) **79**

DOMAINE LATOUR GIRAUD
Bourgogne Chardonnay 1985 $11 (3/31/87) **79**

OLIVIER LEFLAIVE FRERES
Bourgogne Les Sétilles 1989: Offers lovely aromas for a straightforward wine, with surprisingly focused hay and apple aromas. Medium-bodied, with focused mineral and apple flavors and a light finish. Drink now. $15 (8/31/91) **81**
Bourgogne Les Sétilles 1987: Lean, smooth and crisp in structure, a decent wine with a burnt toast aroma and flavor that cut down on the fruit character. $8.50 (3/31/90) **79**
Bourgogne Les Sétilles 1985 $12 (3/31/87) **87**

LEROY
Bourgogne d'Auvenay 1988: An earthy white Burgundy, with tart lemon and almond flavors and hints of honey and orange on the finish. Some will like it, but it's not our style. 3,000 cases made. $15 (4/30/91) **76**
Bourgogne d'Auvenay 1986 $17 (9/15/89) **84**
Bourgogne d'Auvenay 1983 $15 (12/31/87) **79**

LUPE-CHOLET
Bourgogne Chardonnay Comtesse de Lupé 1988: Not super-ripe or rich, but it has a nice intensity. A well-balanced, nicely fruity Chardonnay that's crisp yet rich enough with honey and pineapple flavors. Drink now. $9 (4/30/90) BB **84**
Bourgogne Chardonnay Comtesse de Lupé 1987: A good value in a white Burgundy. Has nice aromas of pineapple and perfume, tart fruit flavors and a lean structure. $8.25 (3/15/89) BB **80**

DOMAINE RENE MANUEL
Bourgogne Blanc 1989: A good Bourgogne Blanc, with no-nonsense flavors and delicate aromas of apple, butter and lemons. Medium-bodied, with light apple and chalk flavors, medium acidity and a clean finish. From Labouré-Roi. Drink now. ($NA) (8/31/91) **80**

CHATEAU MARQUERITE DE BOURGOGNE
Bourgogne Chardonnay 1985 $14 (6/30/87) **72**

DOMAINE JOSEPH MATROT
Bourgogne Chardonnay 1989: A traditional style of white Burgundy, with aromas of lemons, minerals and hay, lemon and mineral flavors and a chewy finish. Medium-bodied. Drink now. $15 (8/31/91) **81**
Bourgogne Chardonnay 1988: Lean and lemony, with slightly earthy, herbal overtones. Drinkable now. $15 (4/30/91) **76**
Bourgogne Chardonnay 1987: A tart lean wine with buttery aromas, lemony, herbal flavors and a hint of spiciness mixed in. Simple but clean. $14 (4/15/90) **78**

PROSPER MAUFOUX
Bourgogne Aligoté 1989: A straightforward, almost rustic white wine, with broad, earthy grapefruit flavors and a bit of fat in the structure. $12 (7/31/91) **78**
Bourgogne Chardonnay 1989: Simple and clean. Medium-bodied, with fresh citrus aromas, clean, fresh apple flavor and a light finish. Drink now. $12 (8/31/91) **81**

DOMAINE DU CHATEAU DE MERCEY
Bourgogne Blanc Côtes de Beaune 1985 $8.50 (3/31/87) **71**

CHATEAU DE MEURSAULT
Bourgogne Chardonnay Clos du Château 1988: A solid attempt to make something special out of a basic white Burgundy. Fresh, lively and spicy, with vivid honey, pear and vanilla flavors and a dry, clean finish. Has enough oaky accents to give it style. $23 (4/30/91) **83**
Bourgogne Chardonnay Clos du Château 1985: Ripe and round, with lots of butterscotch aromas and flavors, hints of toast and a touch of pineapple that comes through on the finish. Offers more mature flavors than most French Chardonnays—and lots of oak. $20 (3/31/90) **82**

JEAN MICHELOT
Bourgogne Aligoté 1988: Very attractive. A broad-textured, spicy and fruity style that's round and rich. Has apple, pear, vanilla and butter flavors that linger nicely on the aftertaste. $12 (7/31/90) **84**

MOILLARD
Bourgogne Aligoté Long du Bois 1990: An earthy style with a musty note, which masks the fruit up front. A trace of honey and pear sneaks through on the finish. Drink now. $12 (8/31/91) **74**
Bourgogne Blanc Chante Fluté 1988: This wine has a grapey edge to the flavors that's simple and straightforward. Pleasant for everyday drinking. Ready now. $13 (8/31/91) **79**
Hautes Côtes de Nuits 1986: Firm and chunky, with a chalky texture and apple cider flavor, turning a bit honeyed on the finish. Nothing fresh about it, but it's a good drink for tonight. $12 (1/31/89) **78**

MOREAU
Bourgogne Chardonnay 1988: Lightly spicy, with a silky texture and butterscotch overtones to the light pear and pineapple flavors. Balanced and likable. $8 (4/30/91) BB **84**
Bourgogne Chardonnay 1983 $6.50 (6/01/86) **64**

PIERRE MOREY
Bourgogne Aligoté 1985 $9.75 (2/15/88) **74**
Bourgogne Chardonnay 1989: Starts out slowly, but finishes well. This medium-bodied wine has aromas and flavors of straw and freshly cut apples, with fresh acidity. Vanilla and lemon notes emerge on the finish. Drink now. $20 (8/31/91) **81**

REINE PEDAUQUE
Bourgogne Chardonnay Buchère 1989: Light, delicate and refreshing, with fresh aromas of apples and pears, fresh floral flavor and crisp acidity. Has a light, delicate finish. A medium-bodied wine to drink now. $12 (8/31/91) **81**

PAUL PERNOT
Bourgogne Chardonnay Champerrier 1989: Sort of a scaled-down version of a fine Burgundy, with lively flavors on a firm structure. The pear, apple and caramel aromas and flavors linger nicely. Drinkable now. $16 (4/30/91) **83**

PIERRE PONNELLE
Bourgogne Hautes Côtes de Nuits 1989: Astringent, slightly oxidized and candied, with light asparagus and candied fruit aromas. Medium-bodied, with candied fruit flavor and a light finish. Drink now, if ever. $15 (8/31/91) **69**
Vougeot Le Village 1989: Tight and closed in now; could get better than this. Has light pear aromas, plenty of medium-bodied vanilla flavors and a medium lemon finish. Drink now to 1994. $32 (8/31/91) **82**

DOMAINE PONSOT
Morey-St.-Denis Monts-Luisants 1988: Tart and lemony, with lots of subtle mineral notes, earthy and complex fruit aromas and flavors and a real zing of lemon and lime on the finish. Needs time to sort itself out; try in 1993 to '95. $50 (5/31/91) **87**

DOMAINE PRIEUR-BRUNET
Bourgogne Chardonnay Prieur 1989: Firm and clean, with lemon and vanilla aromas, with apple and vanilla flavors, firm acidity and a flavorful finish. Drink now. ($NA) (8/31/91) **83**

CHATEAU DE PULIGNY-MONTRACHET
Bourgogne Clos du Château 1988: Fresh, lively and youthful, it's tasty to drink now. A spunky white Burgundy with ample floral aromas and dry peachy, nutty flavors. $19 (7/31/90) **81**
Côte de Nuits-Villages 1989: A light but stylish white Burgundy, with clean fruit flavors and the spicy vanilla accent of new oak barrels. Drink now. $27 (2/28/91) **83**

DOMAINE ROUGEOT-LATOUR
Bourgogne Chardonnay Clos des Six Ouvrées 1986 $15 (10/15/88) **80**

DOMAINE ROUX PERE & FILS
Bourgogne Chardonnay 1989: Advanced and not showing well, with floral, apple and slightly candied aromas, apple, candied and almost caramel flavors and a light finish. Medium-bodied. Drink now. $18 (8/31/91) **74**

DOMAINE ETIENNE SAUZET
Bourgogne Chardonnay Blanc 1989: Another standout in this category, with ripe apple, vanilla and fresh lemon aromas and apple and vanilla flavors. Full-bodied, with good intensity and a long finish. Drink now to 1993. $31 (8/31/91) **86**

DOMAINE B. SERVEAU
Bourgogne Chardonnay 1989: With a lean texture and herbal aromas and flavors, this strikes us as more like a Sauvignon than a Chardonnay, but it might make a decent companion to rich food. $16 (4/30/91) **73**

ROLAND THEVENIN
Bourgogne Chardonnay Réserve Roland Thévenin 1985 $8 (3/31/87) **76**

THEVENOT-LE-BRUN
Bourgogne Aligoté 1988: Tight and lemony tasting, so it's not for everyone. Grassy and earthy in aroma, lean and tart in flavor. $12 (7/31/90) **72**

TOLLOT-BEAUT
Bourgogne Chardonnay 1989: An ambitious Bourgogne Blanc; a serious white. Toasted, smoky apple aromas; full-bodied, with masses of fruit, firm acidity and a long vanilla and apple finish. Drink now to 1994. ($NA) (8/31/91) **87**

A. & P. DE VILLAINE
Bourgogne Les Clous Bouzeron 1986: Extremely earthy, tart and lemony, crisp and lean enough on the palate, but the nose is too stinky for us. $16 (1/31/89) **65**

CHABLIS

DOMAINE AUFFRAY
Chablis 1986 $13 (11/15/87) **66**
Chablis Champs Royaux 1989: A difficult style to warm up to, with creamy, brassy pear flavors and a certain austerity that takes time to adjust to. The pear and spice flavors peek through on the finish. Not quite as rich as the best '88s. Drink now. $19 (1/31/91) **86**
Chablis Champs Royaux 1988: An elegant, earthy style, with tart pear and subtle vanilla accents. Well balanced; drink now. $12 (3/31/90) **79**
Chablis Champs Royaux 1986 $17 (9/15/88) **88**
Chablis Les Clos 1989: Smells promising, but the flavors are tightly wound, opening up on the finish in a burst of pineapple, pear and spice that's impressively long and concentrated. Drinkable now, but give it until 1993 to let the flavors grow. 1,800 cases made. $50 (1/31/91) **92**
Chablis Les Clos 1988: Remarkably complex, with delicious lemon, pear, toast and apple flavors that are sharply focused, supple, silky smooth and complex. The flavors build on the finish, echoing pear and toast. Drink now to 1994. 1,100 cases made. $38 (3/31/90) **92**
Chablis Les Clos 1986 $36 (10/15/88) **70**
Chablis Fourchaume 1986 $24 (9/15/88) **85**
Chablis Montée de Tonnerre 1989: Frank apple cider aromas and flavors keep this from being as good as it could be, but the floral, spicy flavors on the finish make it somewhat appealing. Drinkable now. $25 (2/28/91) **74**
Chablis Montée de Tonnerre 1988: Tastes better than it smells, gaining buttery pear, honey and butterscotch flavors along the way. Has a good balance that builds fruit velocity on the finish. Drink now. $21 (3/31/90) **87**

FRANCE
CHABLIS

Chablis Montée de Tonnerre 1986 $24 (10/15/88) **75**
Chablis Les Preuses 1986 $36 (9/15/88) **88**
Chablis Les Preuses 1984 $30 (4/15/87) **92**
Chablis Vaillon 1989: Fairly intense and concentrated, showing a broad range of grapefruit, pear and nutmeg aromas and flavors that are nicely balanced and focused on the finish. Drinkable now, but could use until 1993 or '94 to settle down. $27 (1/31/91) **88**
Chablis Vaillon 1988: Ripe and generous, oozing butterscotch aromas and flavors to go with a core of lemon and pear flavor, all of it resting on a firm texture that allows some lovely honey and toast nuances to emerge on the finish. Drinkable now, but this one has a long future. Try 1993 to '96. $20 (12/15/89) **93**
Chablis Valmur 1988: Broad and generous for a Chablis, with generous pear and celery aromas and flavors that are long and intense through the finish. Smoky, woolly overtones detract a bit, but there is a lot to like here. Start drinking now. $32 (12/15/89) **80**

BICHOT
Chablis 1988: Tart and flinty, with earth, pear, apple and melon notes that are lean and elegant, finishing with of wood and citrus. Tempting now but should age through 1995. $17 (3/31/90) **84**
Chablis 1987: A crisp, fruity style with plenty of peach and apple aromas and flavors, silky texture and good length. Very tasty. $11 (3/31/89) **85**
Chablis 1984 $9 (2/16/86) **65**
Chablis Les Vaillons 1988: Lean and green, with celery and herbal nuances to the lemon and apple flavors; tart and a bit coarse in texture. Cellaring until 1993 should help. $17 (12/15/89) **82**

J. BILLAUD-SIMON
Chablis Montée de Tonnerre 1985 $19 (9/30/87) **72**

JEAN CLAUDE BOISSET
Chablis 1985 $14 (1/31/87) **75**
Chablis Grenouille 1982 $15 (6/16/85) **85**

DOMAINE PASCAL BOUCHARD
Chablis 1989: Earthy and chalky, with tight pear and spice flavors, but could be a little more generous. Mineral and grapefruit notes emerge on the aftertaste. Drink now to 1996. $15 (11/30/91) **84**
Chablis Les Clos 1989: Crisp and tart, with green apple, pineapple, citrus and spice flavors that are rich and intense. Has a long, full finish. Drink now to 1996. $36 (11/30/91) **89**

BOUCHARD PERE & FILS
Chablis 1985 $15 (10/15/87) **83**

JEAN-MARC BROCARD
Chablis Domaine Ste.-Claire 1989: The vivid, focused aromas and flavors of melon, apple, mineral and lemon are all Chablis, but a bit riper and a bit less tart than most. A polished, fine-grained texture makes it drinkable now, but it should improve through at least 1993. A good value. $13 (1/31/91) **86**

LA CHABLISIENNE
Chablis 1987 $13 (3/31/89) **82**
Chablis Beauroy 1986 ($NA) (3/31/89) **84**
Chablis Les Clos 1986 ($NA) (3/31/89) **88**
Chablis Fourchaume 1987 $18 (3/31/89) **85**
Chablis Grande Cuvée 1987 ($NA) (3/31/89) **87**
Chablis Grande Cuvée 1986 ($NA) (3/31/89) **90**
Chablis Grenouille 1986 ($NA) (3/31/89) **88**
Chablis Montée de Tonnerre 1986 ($NA) (3/31/89) **86**
Chablis Vaudésir 1986 ($NA) (3/31/89) **90**
Petit Chablis 1987 ($NA) (3/31/89) **77**

DOMAINE ANTOINE CHAPUIS
Chablis Montée de Tonnerre 1985 $21 (8/31/87) **90**

F. CHAUVENET
Chablis Montmain 1982 $10 (7/01/85) **82**

JEAN DAUVISSAT
Chablis Les Preuses 1986: Rich and flavorful, but "off" notes of gaminess and earth take the edge off the honey- and flower-tinged pear and herb aromas and flavors. A mature wine that's drinkable now. $30 (7/15/90) **82**
Chablis Vaillon 1987: Complex flavors and an elegant balance mark this as something special, showing sharply focused pear, honey and butterscotch flavors that carry through a long finish. Charming and forceful at the same time. Relatively fair price, too. Drinkable now. 500 cases made. $22 (1/31/91) **91**
Chablis Vaillon 1986: Mouth-puckering and tart, but very fragrant, hinting at orange blossom aromas and butter and earth flavors. Shows a great deal of maturity, but one wonders if that acidity will ever smooth itself out. Comes together on the finish. $19 (7/15/90) **82**
Chablis Vaillon Vieilles Vignes 1986: Crisp and lemony, with overtones of toast and honey to make it smoother. This classic style of Chablis is quite a mouthful, offering hints of almond and butter on the finish. Drinkable now. $24 (7/15/90) **85**

RENE DAUVISSAT
Chablis Les Clos 1987 $40 (3/31/89) **95**
Chablis La Forêt 1987 $25 (3/31/89) **92**
Chablis Premier Cru La Forêt 1986 $25 (3/31/89) **91**
Chablis Les Preuses 1987 $43 (3/31/89) **97**
Chablis Séchet 1987 $24 (3/31/89) **90**
Chablis Tribaut 1987 $24 (3/31/89) **88**
Chablis Vaillon 1987 $24 (3/31/89) **92**

DOMAINE DAUVISSAT-CAMUS
Chablis Les Clos 1988: Elegant and rich, with more vanilla than you would normally expect from a Chablis. But there are plenty of pear, melon and lemon flavors. Chablis doesn't get much more complex than this. Drinkable now, but should be better by 1993. 500 cases made. $41 (7/31/90) **92**
Chablis Les Clos 1987: Artfully balanced with ripe pear and apple flavor, toasty oak and zingy acidity, complex, lean, crisp and delicious. Needs cellaring to soften the impact, perhaps until 1993 or '94. $37 (10/15/89) **88**

Key to Symbols

The scores reported here are the results of blind tastings conducted by our panel of senior editors. Wines that carry the initials below are results of individual tastings.

THE WINE SPECTATOR 100-POINT SCALE ***95-100***—Classic, a great wine; ***90-94***—Outstanding, superior character and style; ***80-89***—Good to very good, a wine with special qualities; ***70-79***—Average, drinkable wine that may have minor flaws; ***60-69***—Below average, drinkable but not recommended; ***50-59***—Poor, undrinkable, not recommended. "+"—With a score indicates a range; used primarily with barrel tastings to indicate a preliminary score.

SPECIAL DESIGNATIONS SS—Spectator Selection, CS—Cellar Selection, BB—Best Buy, ($NA)—Price not available, (NR)—Not released.

TASTER'S INITIALS (JG)—Jim Gordon, (HS)—Harvey Steiman, (JL)—James Laube, (JS)—James Suckling, (TM)—Thomas Matthews, (TR)—Terry Robards, (PM)—Per-Henrik Mansson, (BT)—Barrel Tasting (these wines were tasted blind from barrel samples), (CA-date)—*California's Great Cabernets* by James Laube, (CH-date)—*California's Great Chardonnays* by James Laube, (VP-date)—*Vintage Port* by James Suckling.

DATE TASTED Dates in parentheses represent the issue in which the rating was published.

Chablis Les Clos 1986 $40 (9/15/88) **95**
Chablis La Forest 1989: Clean and pure, with silky pear, spice, citrus and honey notes that are rich and elegant. The flavors dance across the palate. Drink now to 1994. $24 (12/15/91) **87**
Chablis La Forest 1988: Tart, earthy and slightly musty despite richly concentrated fruit that echoes pear, spice and flint flavors. Drink now; tasted twice. $25 (7/31/90) **74**
Chablis La Forest 1987: Tangy orange-lemon acidity laces through the mineral and apple aromas of this wine, leaving it crisp and refreshing but not very complex. Maybe it will benefit from cellaring. Drink now. $22 (10/15/89) **83**
Chablis La Forest 1986 $25 (9/15/88) **85**
Chablis La Forest 1985 $28 (11/15/87) **74**
Chablis Les Preuses 1988: Tart and lemony, with a pretty hint of butterscotch. It's well balanced, with a smooth texture and lively acidity. Has fine depth of flavor, and finishes with a flash of butterscotch. Drink now to 1993. Tasted twice. $41 (7/31/90) **86**
Chablis Les Preuses 1987: Fairly ripe and full-bodied for a Chablis, with a splash of oak aromas and flavors to lend complexity to the pear and spice at the core. Drinkable now. $37 (10/15/89) **87**
Chablis Les Preuses 1986 $40 (9/15/88) **94**
Chablis Vaillon 1989: Broad and spicy, with a distinct earthy note that pairs well with the honey and pear-scented fruit flavors. Picks up a trace of mustiness on the finish. Drink now to 1993. Tasted twice. $24 (12/15/91) **80**
Chablis Vaillon 1988: Crisp in texture and sharply focused, with lively apple and spice aromas and flavors that turn toward butterscotch and toast on the long finish. Has marvelous intensity of flavor but a welcome sense of restraint as well. Should age well through 1993 to '95. 700 cases made. $25 (7/15/90) **91**
Chablis Vaillon 1987: Simple, clean and decent but uninspired. The tart, crisp lemon and pear fruit could use a little more oomph. Tasted twice. $22 (10/15/89) **78**
Chablis Vaillon 1986 $25 (9/15/88) **84**
Chablis Vaillon 1985 $28 (11/15/87) **88**

M. DEOLIVEIRA
Chablis Les Clos 1985 $34 (8/31/87) **67**

JEAN-PAUL DROIN
Chablis 1987 ($NA) (3/31/89) **80**
Chablis Les Clos 1987 $38 (3/31/89) **93**
Chablis Les Clos 1986 $32 (5/15/88) **87**
Chablis Fourchaume 1987 $24 (3/31/89) **87**
Chablis Fourchaume 1986 $17 (7/15/88) **85**
Chablis Grenouille 1987 $40 (3/31/89) **82**
Chablis Montain 1987 $24 (3/31/89) **89**
Chablis Montée de Tonnerre 1987 $24 (3/31/89) **90**
Chablis Montée de Tonnerre 1986 $21 (5/15/88) **90**
Chablis Vaillon 1987 $24 (3/31/89) **91**
Chablis Valmur 1987 $38 (3/31/89) **86**
Chablis Vaudésir 1987 $38 (3/31/89) **90**
Chablis Vosgros 1987 $24 (3/31/89) **81**

JOSEPH DROUHIN
Chablis 1988: Tinny, tart, sour and simple, with grapefruit and oxidized flavors. Not up to the usual standards. Drink now. $18 (3/31/90) **72**
Chablis 1987: Rich and earthy, with peachy aromas and flavors draped on a steely backbone of lemony acidity, well balanced and fairly subtle. $14 (3/31/89) **84**
Chablis 1986 $14 (5/15/88) **83**
Chablis Bougros 1986 $33 (5/15/88) **87**
Chablis Les Clos 1986 $31 (3/31/89) **95**
Chablis Domaine de Vaudon 1989: Ripe and soft, with more spice than fruit aromas and flavors and more wood than most Chablis, but it does offer nice peach notes. Not typical, but a pleasant white wine. $30 (8/31/91) **84**
Chablis Montmain 1989: Tight and austere, but fans of that style will appreciate the firm mineral, lemon, apricot, earth and toast notes. Balanced, with pretty flavors that linger. Drink now or in 1993. $23 (2/28/91) **86**
Chablis Montmain 1987: Lean and lively, a straightforward wine with floral, almond and peach flavors that stay with you; needs time to develop some shape. Drink now. $22 (3/31/89) **83**
Chablis Premier Cru 1987: An earthy, buttery style, with firm structure; showing some honey and vanilla on the finish, it's smooth and subtle, fleshier than most Chablis. $20 (3/31/89) **87**
Chablis Premier Cru 1986 $20 (5/15/88) **85**
Chablis Les Roncières 1987 $23 (3/31/89) **91**
Chablis Les Suchots 1987 $20 (3/31/89) **89**
Chablis Vaudésir 1989: Lean in style, but packed with flavor. Has intense orange, pear, nutmeg and vanilla notes that are compact and elegant, with a burst of fruit pouring through on the finish. Drink now to 1993. $54 (2/28/91) **89**
Chablis Vaudésir 1988: Distinctive for its citrus and spice flavors, it's well balanced, round and full, with pretty pear, lemon and nutmeg flavors. Drink now or in 1993. $38 (3/31/90) **87**
Chablis Vaudésir 1986 $34 (3/31/89) **92**

JEAN DURUP
Chablis 1987 ($NA) (3/31/89) **86**
Chablis Fourchaume 1987 ($NA) (3/31/89) **88**
Chablis Vaudevey 1987 ($NA) (3/31/89) **90**

DOMAINE DE L'EGLANTIERE
Chablis 1985 $14 (1/31/87) **88**

YVONNE FEBVRE
Chablis Blanchot 1988: Bright, crisply focused aromas and flavors of apple, pineapple and minerals are tightly wrapped in a sturdy frame. It needs time to lose its austerity and start picking up texture. Drinkable now with oysters, and maybe around 1993 with fish. $23 (1/31/91) **85**
Chablis Montée de Tonnerre 1984 $15 (1/31/87) **73**

CHATEAU GRENOUILLES
Chablis Grenouille 1985 $34 (8/31/87) **89**

JAFFELIN
Chablis Fourchaume 1983 $14 (10/16/85) **86**

LABOURE-ROI
Chablis Fourchaume 1988: This wine is earthy and tart, bordering on sour, without much richness or charm. It's a steely, austere style that is hard to warm up to. 2,000 cases made. $22 (7/31/90) **70**

LAROCHE
Chablis 1986 $12 (5/15/88) **88**
Chablis Fourchaume 1988: Light, delicate and earthy, with a touch of mineral flavor identifying it as Chablis, and modifying the basic pear flavor. Drink now or in 1993. $23 (7/31/90) **80**

DOMAINE LAROCHE
Chablis 1990: A fresh and fruity wine, with lively pear, spice, citrus and apple flavors. Subtle, but beautifully balanced, finishing with long fruity notes. Drinkable now, or cellar through 1995. $16 (11/30/91) **90**
Chablis 1988: Fresh and crisp, with tart peach, mineral, pear and spice notes that are rich and delicate. Has pretty floral aromas. Ready now to 1993. $16 (7/31/90) **87**
Chablis 1987: $26 (3/31/91) **74**

Chablis 1983 $13 (11/15/86) **91**

Chablis Les Beauroys 1984 $19 (10/31/87) **79**

Chablis Les Blanchots 1989: An earthy style, with lots of lively mineral, lemon and pear flavors to back it up. Long and stylish, echoing pear on the finish. Elegant and drinkable now, but should repay cellaring through 1993 or '94. 2,300 cases made. $47 (8/31/91) **89**

Chablis Les Blanchots 1987 $40 (3/31/89) **95**

Chablis Les Blanchots 1984 $27 (2/28/87) **93**

Chablis Les Blanchots Vieilles Vignes 1989: Spicy, toasty flavors lend appeal to the basic lemon and apple character in this full-bodied, round-textured Chablis. It's smooth and subtle on the finish. Drinkable now. $72 (1/31/91) **88**

Chablis Les Blanchots Vieilles Vignes 1988: A flinty Chablis, with pear and mineral aromas and flavors, good intensity, lemon notes and a supple finish. Drink now. $58 (7/31/90) **86**

Chablis Les Blanchots Vieilles Vignes 1987 $50 (3/31/89) **94**

Chablis Les Bouguerots 1985 $33 (6/15/87) **86**

Chablis Les Clos 1988: Has a floral style, with very pretty, perfumed aromas and flavors surrounding a core of peach and lemon flavors. Has restraint—perhaps too much, because the finish seems shy—and balance. Drink now. $49 (12/15/89) **83**

Chablis Les Clos 1987 $50 (3/31/89) **90**

Chablis Les Clos 1986 $50 (12/31/88) **89**

Chablis Cuvée Première 1989: Crisp and fruity, with a subtle harmony of pear, apple, mineral and floral aromas and flavors. Holding something in reserve to develop with cellaring, but it's drinkable now. $25 (1/31/91) **87**

Chablis Les Fourchaumes 1988: Crisp and concentrated, its apple flavors zing across the palate on a lean and racy structure. A classic style of Chablis, this should develop well in the cellar through at least 1994. $23 (12/15/89) **88**

Chablis Les Fourchaumes 1987 $26 (3/31/89) **90**

Chablis Les Fourchaumes 1986 $29 (5/15/88) **86**

Chablis Les Fourchaumes 1984 $18 (1/31/87) **85**

Chablis Les Fourchaumes Vieilles Vignes 1987 $45 (3/31/89) **93**

Chablis Les Montmains 1988: This wine offers floral, perfumed aromas and flavors on a lean, smooth structure, echoing citrus and apple on the long, subtle finish. Has more style and complexity than most, and should develop nicely through 1993 to '94. $25 (7/31/90) **84**

Chablis Laroche Cuvée Première 1988: Lean and tightly reined in, with slate and mineral notes to add complexity to the basic apple and toast aromas and flavors. Drinkable now. $16 (12/15/89) **83**

Chablis St.-Martin 1990: Complex and tightly wound, with layers of peach, pear, apple and herb flavors that are focused and woven together. Finishes with a long, full aftertaste of honey and vanilla. Drink now to 1995. $18 (11/30/91) **90**

Chablis St.-Martin 1989: This smooth, tasty wine is short on texture and length, but its spicy pear, almond and mineral aromas and flavors emerge pleasantly on a soft background. $21 (2/28/91) **82**

Chablis St.-Martin 1988: Lean and sharply focused, with generous honey-tinged floral and pear aromas and flavors; smooth and impeccably balanced. Already complex, but it has the richness and length to indicate cellaring until 1993 to '95. $15 (12/15/89) **90**

Chablis St.-Martin 1987 $17 (3/31/89) **82**

Chablis St.-Martin 1986 $16 (12/31/88) **86**

Chablis St.-Martin 1985 $16 (6/30/87) **83**

Chablis Les Vaillons 1989: Crisp, delicate and beautifully aromatic, showing plenty of floral, almond and pear aromas, a silky texture and a nice echo of honey and spice on the long finish. Drinkable now, but probably better around 1993. $33 (1/31/91) **86**

Chablis Les Vaillons 1988: Flinty, earthy, classic Chablis with enough pear flavor to keep it attractive, concentrated and well balanced. Where are the oysters? This wine is ready. $22 (12/15/89) **88**

Chablis Les Vaillons 1987 $25 (3/31/89) **87**

Chablis Les Vaillons 1986 $23 (12/31/88) **86**

Chablis Les Vaillons 1983 $15 (2/16/86) **66**

Chablis Les Vaudevey 1990: A subtle, but understated style, with toasty earth, pear, citrus and apple flavors. Balanced, but the flavors seem a bit muted. Drink now to 1993. $25 (11/30/91) **87**

Chablis Les Vaudevey 1988: Ripe and tart, with intense yet elegant lemon, citrus and grapefruit flavors along with a dash of spicy pear. It's well balanced and has good depth of flavor. Drink now to 1993. $24 (7/31/90) **87**

Chablis Les Vaudevey 1987 $23 (3/31/89) **85**

Chablis Les Vaudevey 1985 $19 (6/15/87) **80**

Chablis Les Vaudevey 1984 $17 (1/31/87) **75**

Chablis Les Vaudevey 1983 $15 (12/01/85) **77**

ROLAND LAVANTUREUX

Chablis 1986: Unfocused Chablis that lacks finesse. There is nothing wrong with the stony aromas, hints of lemon and flinty flavors, but the wine seems fat and flabby. $16 (1/31/89) **68**

Chablis 1985 $17 (5/15/88) **80**

Petit Chablis 1986 $11 (5/15/88) **75**

DOMAINE LONG-DEPAQUIT

Chablis 1990: The earthy seashore aromas and flavors aren't immediately appealing, and they persist on the finish, but it has nice honey and citrus notes. $14 (1/31/92) **79**

Chablis 1987: Lean and crisp, with lemon and grapefruit flavors and a touch of nectarine to make things interesting. Very clean and straightforward. $12 (3/31/89) **83**

Chablis 1986 $15 (5/15/88) **71**

Chablis 1985 $14 (11/15/87) **80**

Chablis Les Beugnons 1984 $12 (7/16/86) **67**

Chablis Les Blanchots 1989: A sturdy, buttery Chablis, with more richness than most, offering plenty of spice and character on the palate. Still seems fresh and able to improve with cellaring until 1993 or '94, but it's drinkable now. $36 (1/31/92) **83**

Chablis Les Blanchots 1988: Elegantly balanced, with fresh, ripe pear, toast and butter tones that are rich and complex. Has a tightness to the structure that should allow it to continue to develop in the bottle for several years. Drink now to 1994. $38 (1/31/91) **88**

Chablis Les Blanchots 1987: Fresh and crisp, with flinty apple and pear aromas and flavors, very firm and lemony on the palate with a touch of spice or toast on the finish. Excellent length. Drink now to 1994. $29 (3/31/89) **88**

Chablis Les Blanchots 1986 $28 (3/31/88) **87**

Chablis Les Blanchots 1984 $20 (9/15/86) **76**

Chablis Les Clos 1988: Terrific from start to finish, with butterscotch, pear, honey and lemon aromas and flavors that all come together nicely in a long finish. Has a great texture, with lots of concentration. Try now, but will probably improve until 1993. 900 cases made. $42 (7/15/90) **90**

Chablis Les Clos 1986 $32 (3/31/88) **90**

Chablis Les Clos 1985 $32 (8/31/87) **88**

Chablis Les Lys 1987 $15 (12/31/88) **85**

Chablis Moutonne 1989: Smooth and spicy, with vanilla overtones to the concentrated pear and apple-tinged flavors, finishing with a hint of mineral. Balanced, supple and ready to drink now through 1995. $40 (3/31/92) **85**

Chablis Moutonne 1988: A complex wine, with earth, mineral, herb, nectarine and peach notes. The beauty of this Chablis is that each element complements the others. The lovely finish makes you want another sip. Try now. 1,380 cases made. $47 (7/31/90) **92**

Chablis Moutonne 1987: Lean and subdued, with crisp apple and slightly smoky aromas and flavors, fairly long, harmonious and nicely balanced. $36 (3/31/89) **85**

Chablis Moutonne 1986 $35 (3/31/88) **88**

Chablis Moutonne 1985 $35 (11/15/87) **87**

Chablis Moutonne 1983 $20 (12/16/85) **87**

Chablis Les Preuses 1987: Riper, fleshier and lusher than most Chablis, with honey-tinged pineapple and pear aromas and flavors focused into a lean beam of brilliant flavor. Long and elegant. $30 (3/31/89) **90**

Chablis Les Vaillons 1988: A subtle, delicate wine. The spice, toast, pear and vanilla flavors unfold slowly over the long finish, hinting at grapefruit and butterscotch at the very end. Give it until 1993 or '94. 2,100 cases made. $20 (7/31/90) **87**

Chablis Les Vaillons 1987 $15 (12/31/88) **86**

Chablis Les Vaillons 1986 $18 (5/15/88) **77**

Chablis Les Vaillons 1985 $21 (6/30/87) **80**

Chablis Les Vaucopins 1989: Earthy, mildewy, sour aromas and flavors put us off. A dirty wine. Tasted twice. $18 (3/31/92) **66**

Chablis Les Vaucopins 1986 $18 (5/15/88) **67**

Chablis Les Vaudésirs 1988: Lovely, balanced, focused and surprisingly soft and ripe for a Chablis, with melon and citrus notes, and a touch of butter and flint. $40 (7/31/90) **87**

Chablis Les Vaudésirs 1987: Very firm and concentrated, a lean wine with direct pineapple and lemon flavors, long and slightly honeyed. Drinkable now, but better around 1993. $30 (3/31/89) **86**

Chablis Les Vaudésirs 1986 $28 (3/31/88) **85**

Chablis Les Vaudésirs 1985 $30 (6/30/87) **86**

Chablis Les Vaudésirs 1984 Rel: $20 Cur: $30 (10/15/86) CS **91**

LUPE-CHOLET

Chablis Château de Viviers 1988: A generous style, with intense fruit, pear, apple, lemon and nutmeg notes that offer a measure of complexity. Well balanced and slightly tannic. Best now or in 1993. $15 (3/31/90) **82**

DOMAINE DE LA MALADIERE

Chablis 1988: Has more buttery ripeness than many Chablis, but it's soft in structure, with butterscotch aromas and chalk and butter flavors. Candied flavors and a chalky texture emerge on the finish. $13 (2/28/91) **81**

CHATEAU DE MALIGNY

Chablis 1988: The candied, perfumed aromas and flavors are not immediately appealing, but it does turn honeyed and smooth on the finish. It won't please everyone, but should develop with cellaring through 1993. $15 (7/31/90) **76**

Chablis Fourchaume 1990: Full of vim and vigor, accented by grapefruit and lemon flavors. Tight in structure and austere on the finish. Should be better by now. $20 (8/31/91) **84**

Chablis Fourchaume 1988: Extremely earthy aromas and woolly flavors tend to overshadow the otherwise delicate lemon and spice aromas and flavors. Not for everyone. $22 (7/31/90) **71**

Chablis Fourchaume 1986: Earthy, chalky aromas and flavors mark this one, but by now it should have developed into a fuller, more generous wine than the tough, tight wine it was on release. $18 (3/31/89) **85**

PROSPER MAUFOUX

Chablis Mont de Milieu 1989: A sturdy, well-structured Chablis, with a lively texture, modest pear and grapefruit flavors and a touch of mineral to add complexity. $24 (8/31/91) **84**

LOUIS MICHEL & FILS

Chablis 1989: Fresh and lively, with very pretty pear, lime and mineral aromas and flavors. Rounder and richer than most Chablis. Drinkable now. 1,000 cases made. $22 (8/31/91) **86**

Chablis 1988: Crisp and concentrated, but oxidized apple aromas and flavors detract from the otherwise lively lemon and pineapple character. The odd flavors won't please everyone. Drink now or in 1993. $17 (7/15/90) **77**

Chablis Montée de Tonnerre 1988: Lean, crisp and spicy, with lively green apple, nutmeg and pineapple aromas and flavors. The good concentration lasts right through the long finish. Could use cellaring until 1993 or '94 to settle it down. $26 (7/31/90) **86**

Chablis Montée de Tonnerre 1987: Crisp, light and spicy at first, turning smooth and creamy on the finish. The butterscotch and honey flavors round out the nutmeg and apple character. Long and tasty; drinkable now. $20 (7/15/90) **87**

Chablis Montmain 1987: Modest aromas and flavors taper off rapidly on the finish in this medium-weight, low-intensity, but lightly spicy and pleasant wine. $20 (7/15/90) **80**

Chablis Vaudésir 1987: Crisp and spicy, with complex green apple, nutmeg, toast and vanilla aromas and flavors on a lean, racy structure. Built to last, but drinkable now when you want that zingy character. Drink now to 1994. $31 (7/15/90) **89**

MOILLARD

Chablis 1989: Nicely focused earth, apple and nutmeg aromas and flavors carry through the long finish, but it seems less lively and youthful than a one-year-old Chablis should be. Drinkable now. $26 (2/28/91) **81**

Chablis 1987: Taut and somewhat tannic, with a bracing zip of lemony acidity to support the fantail of butterscotch flavors that emerges on the finish. Classic mineral aromas mark this as a cellar-worthy Chablis. Drink now. $17 (10/15/89) **86**

Chablis 1985 $14 (5/31/87) **68**

Chablis Vaillon 1985 $16 (5/31/87) **89**

MOREAU

Chablis 1987 ($NA) (3/31/89) **83**

Chablis 1986 ($NA) (3/31/89) **85**

Chablis 1983 $9.50 (12/01/85) **62**

Chablis Beauroy 1986 ($NA) (3/31/89) **90**

Chablis Bougros 1987 ($NA) (3/31/89) **89**

Chablis Bougros 1986 ($NA) (3/31/89) **89**

Chablis Les Clos 1987: Somewhat clumsy, with ripe fruit flavor but not much complexity. The lemon, pear and spice flavors are attractive, but a shade alcoholic. A big, round style from a so-so vintage. Drink now to 1993. $38 (2/28/91) **84**

Chablis Les Clos 1986 $36 (3/31/89) **96**

Chablis Les Clos Clos des Hospices 1987: Elegant and delicate, with pretty ripe fruit flavors that echo floral, honey and pear notes, with a touch of citrus and spice carrying through on the finish. Balanced, complex and well integrated; drink now to 1994. $60 (2/28/91) **89**

Chablis Les Clos Clos des Hospices 1986 $35 (10/15/88) **78**

Chablis Côte de Lechet 1987 $11 (3/31/89) **85**

Chablis Côte de Lechet 1986 $11 (3/31/89) **85**

Chablis Domaine de Bieville 1988: Tight, lean and elegant, with sharply focused, tart lemon, earth and mineral flavors that gradually fan out on the finish, gaining pear and fig notes and a touch of vanilla. Drink now to 1995. $15 (2/28/91) **88**

Chablis Domaine de Bieville 1985 $14 (4/15/87) **84**

Chablis Fourchaume 1987 $24 (3/31/89) **90**

Chablis Fourchaume 1986 $21 (3/31/89) **81**

Chablis Mont de Milieu 1986 $30 (3/31/89) **90**

Chablis Montmain 1987 $21 (3/31/89) **87**

Chablis Montmain 1986: Has a seductive, tart earthiness, but it's complemented by rich, ripe, buttery butterscotch, pear and lemon flavors. A balanced wine that rings true for Chablis. Drink now to 1994. $21 (2/28/91) **87**

Chablis Les Preuses 1987 ($NA) (3/31/89) **90**

Chablis Les Preuses 1986 ($NA) (3/31/89) **95**

Chablis Vaillon 1989: Ripe and full-bodied, with plenty of power. Packs peach, pear and guava flavors in a generous style that offers immediate appeal. Drink now or in 1993. $20 (2/28/91) **87**

Chablis Vaillon 1987 $20 (3/31/89) **91**

FRANCE
CHABLIS

Chablis Vaillon 1986 $21 (3/31/89) **92**
Chablis Valmur 1987 ($NA) (3/31/89) **91**
Chablis Valmur 1986: Distinctive for its rich, creamy butterscotch, lemon, pear and vanilla flavors that are complex, deep and enduring. A beautifully balanced, intense and lively wine that's long and full on the finish. Drink now to 1994. 1,000 cases made. $38 (2/28/91) **90**
Chablis Vaudésir 1987 ($NA) (3/31/89) **90**
Chablis Vaudésir 1986 $36 (3/31/89) **91**
Chablis Vaudevey 1987 ($NA) (3/31/89) **88**
Chablis Vaudevey 1986 ($NA) (3/31/89) **87**
Chablis Voucoupin 1987 ($NA) (3/31/89) **84**
Chablis Voucoupin 1986 ($NA) (3/31/89) **86**

PATRIARCHE
Chablis Cuvée des Quatre Vents 1986: Light and elegant with pretty earth, spice and melon flavors that are simple and delicate, finishing with a trace of oxidation. $13 (10/15/89) **79**

BARON PATRICK
Chablis 1987 $17 (3/31/89) **82**
Chablis 1986 $17 (3/31/89) **84**
Chablis 1979 $13 (6/16/84) **87**
Chablis Les Clos 1987 $30 (3/31/89) **86**
Chablis Les Clos 1986 $30 (3/31/89) **89**
Chablis Premier Cru 1987 $22 (3/31/89) **85**
Chablis Premier Cru 1986 $22 (3/31/89) **85**
Chablis Valmur 1987 $30 (3/31/89) **88**
Chablis Valmur 1986 $30 (3/31/89) **91**

ALBERT PIC & FILS
Chablis 1987 $16 (3/31/89) **82**
Chablis 1986 $16 (3/31/89) **83**
Chablis Blanchot 1987 $40 (3/31/89) **87**
Chablis Blanchot 1986 $40 (3/31/89) **87**
Chablis Bougros 1987 $38 (3/31/89) **85**
Chablis Bougros 1986 $38 (3/31/89) **85**
Chablis Les Clos 1987 $40 (3/31/89) **91**
Chablis Les Clos 1986 $40 (3/31/89) **92**
Chablis Grenouille 1987 $40 (3/31/89) **89**
Chablis Grenouille 1986 $40 (3/31/89) **92**
Chablis Les Preuses 1987 $38 (3/31/89) **84**
Chablis Les Preuses 1986 $37 (9/15/88) **88**
Chablis Valmur 1987 $40 (3/31/89) **86**
Chablis Valmur 1986 $40 (3/31/89) **93**
Chablis Vaudésir 1987 $40 (3/31/89) **89**
Chablis Vaudésir 1986 $40 (3/31/89) **91**

FRANCOIS RAVENEAU
Chablis Blanchot 1987: Beautifully focused, with lemon, pear, spicy oak and flint flavors all in wonderful harmony. Great finesse, balance and delicate flavors on the aftertaste. Simply delicious Chablis; drink now or cellar through 1995. $40 (3/31/90) **92**
Chablis Les Clos 1987: A classically proportioned Chablis that's rich, smooth and elegant, with toasty pear, earth and butterscotch flavors that are framed by crisp, lemony notes. Complex and well balanced. Drink now to 1993. $50 (3/31/90) **90**
Chablis Montée de Tonnerre 1987: Lean, crisp and elegant, with buttery pear, ginger and spice notes that are elegant and lively, finishing with crisp acidity and earthy, toasty flavors. Very well balanced. Drink now to 1995. $35 (3/31/90) **90**
Chablis Valmur 1986 $35 (3/31/89) **93**

JEAN-MARIE RAVENEAU
Chablis Chapelot 1987: Tight, tart and flinty, with subtle pear, apple, vanilla and spice notes that are elegant and very well balanced. The pretty, complex finish picks up some citrus and lemony notes. Drink now to 1993. $25 (3/31/90) **90**
Chablis Vaillon 1987: Stony, flinty, and earthy, with crisp lemon and grass notes. Well balanced, slightly sulfury, but it has delicious buttery notes on the finish. Drink now. $25 (3/31/90) **88**
Chablis Valmur 1987: Has wonderfully toasty pear aromas, rich, intense fruit with power, finesse, breadth and depth, and layers of tart apple, pear, and butterscotch that are enlivened by crisp acidity and a touch of flintiness. Drink now to 1995. $40 (3/31/90) **92**

A. REGNARD & FILS
Chablis Fourchaume 1987 $22 (3/31/89) **89**
Chablis Fourchaume 1986 $22 (3/31/89) **90**
Chablis Fourchaume 1983 $11 (11/01/84) **79**
Chablis Mont de Milieu 1987 $20 (3/31/89) **85**
Chablis Mont de Milieu 1986 $20 (3/31/89) **85**
Chablis Montée de Tonnerre 1987 $20 (3/31/89) **83**
Chablis Montée de Tonnerre 1986 $20 (3/31/89) **90**
Chablis Montmain 1987 $20 (3/31/89) **84**
Chablis Montmain 1986 $20 (9/15/88) **70**
Chablis Vaillon 1987 $20 (3/31/89) **88**
Chablis Vaillon 1986 $20 (3/31/89) **87**

GUY ROBIN
Chablis Vaudésir 1986: Extremely tart and lemony, with hints of pear and earth. This is only for fans of ultratart, tightly reined-in wines. Still needs time; try in 1993. $37 (2/28/91) **83**

DOMAINE MICHEL ROBIN
Chablis Blanchot 1985 $34 (8/31/87) **74**
Chablis Vaillon 1985 $22 (8/31/87) **79**

ANTONIN RODET
Chablis Montmain 1985 $20 (4/15/87) **88**

Key to Symbols

The scores reported here are the results of blind tastings conducted by our panel of senior editors. Wines that carry the initials below are results of individual tastings.

THE WINE SPECTATOR 100-POINT SCALE ***95-100***—Classic, a great wine; ***90-94***—Outstanding, superior character and style; ***80-89***—Good to very good, a wine with special qualities; ***70-79***—Average, drinkable wine that may have minor flaws; ***60-69***—Below average, drinkable but not recommended; ***50-59***—Poor, undrinkable, not recommended. "+"—With a score indicates a range; used primarily with barrel tastings to indicate a preliminary score.

SPECIAL DESIGNATIONS SS—Spectator Selection, CS—Cellar Selection, BB—Best Buy, ($NA)—Price not available, (NR)—Not released.

TASTER'S INITIALS (JG)—Jim Gordon, (HS)—Harvey Steiman, (JL)—James Laube, (JS)—James Suckling, (TM)—Thomas Matthews, (TR)—Terry Robards, (PM)—Per-Henrik Mansson, (BT)—Barrel Tasting (these wines were tasted blind from barrel samples), (CA-date)—*California's Great Cabernets* by James Laube, (CH-date)—*California's Great Chardonnays* by James Laube, (VP-date)—*Vintage Port* by James Suckling.

DATE TASTED Dates in parentheses represent the issue in which the rating was published.

DOMAINE SEGUINOT
Chablis 1988: A middle-of-the-road Chablis marked by earthy, gamy flavors. A touch of pear and spice flavors on the finish saves it from being dull. 1,000 cases made. $16 (2/28/91) **79**

SIMONNET-FEBVRE
Chablis 1986 $12 (5/15/88) **68**
Chablis Les Clos 1986 $29 (7/15/88) **55**
Chablis Vaillon 1986 $17 (5/15/88) **76**

PHILIPPE TESTUT
Chablis 1984 $12 (4/15/87) **90**

THORIN
Chablis Fourchaume 1987: Remarkably elegant and complex with toast, pear, honey and spice flavors with a touch of mineral on the finish. Rich and full-bodied, it's fresh, crisp and lively on the palate. A peasure to drink. $24 (10/15/89) **91**
Chablis Fourchaume 1986: A complex wine with lovely balance. Made in a ripe, fruity style that may surprise fans of more austere, flinty Chablis. Good acidity shows up in the lemony, tart and rather long finish. $23 (2/15/89) **86**

JACQUES TREMBLAY
Chablis Fourchaume 1986 ($NA) (3/31/89) **88**

LAURENT TRIBUT
Chablis 1988: Lean and racy, this wine has delicate Chablis mineral aromas and flavors and a welcome touch of butterscotch and honey sneaking in on the smooth, long finish. Drinkable now, but probably better if cellared until 1993. Tasted twice. $17 (7/31/90) **87**
Chablis Beauroy 1988: Beautifully complex and flavorful without being at all heavy, the spicy apple, lemon and toast flavors ride lightly over the palate in a crisp, lively wine. Drinkable now, but cellaring until 1993 should bring out more nuance. Tasted twice. $17 (7/15/90) **89**

DOMAINE TRIBUT-DAUVISSAT
Chablis 1988: Fresh and lively, stressing citrus aromas and flavors, but with a touch of butter and vanilla to make it interesting. Nicely dry and crisp on the finish. $18 (1/31/91) **84**
Chablis 1987: Too tart, almost sour tasting. Drinkable but not recommended. Tasted twice. $15 (10/15/89) **68**

ANDRE VANNIER
Chablis Les Clos 1986 $32 (9/15/88) **62**
Chablis Les Clos 1983 $18 (3/16/85) **63**
Chablis Les Preuses 1986 $33 (5/15/88) **87**
Chablis Les Preuses 1983 $18 (3/01/85) **90**

CHARLES VIENOT
Chablis Vauignot 1987: A very pretty wine with peach and grapefruit aromas and flavors, with rich honey and caramel character on the aftertaste. Very fine now, but it could improve with time in the cellar. Drink now to 1995. $20 (3/31/89) **89**

CHATEAU DE VIVIERS
Chablis 1984 $12 (7/16/86) **72**

CHAMPAGNE/*BLANC DE BLANCS*

AYALA
Brut Blanc de Blancs Champagne 1985 $33 (12/31/90) **90**
Brut Blanc de Blancs Champagne 1982 $29 (4/15/88) **85**

BARANCOURT
Brut Blanc de Blancs Champagne Cramant NV $20 (5/31/87) **71**
Brut Blanc de Blancs Champagne Cramant Grand Cru NV $30 (12/31/90) **85**

BEAUMET
Brut Blanc de Blancs Champagne NV $30 (12/31/90) **85**
Brut Blanc de Blancs Champagne Cuvée Malakoff 1982 $41 (12/31/90) **91**
Brut Blanc de Blancs Champagne Cuvée Malakoff 1979 $30 (5/31/87) **89**

BILLECART-SALMON
Brut Blanc de Blancs Champagne 1983: Tart, lean, crisp and well balanced, very intense and concentrated, sharp around the edges, and perhaps better with a year or two in the cellar to round out the edges. The toast, vanilla and lemon flavors are lively and well defined. Drink now to 1994. $50 (12/31/89) **88**
Brut Blanc de Blancs Champagne 1982 $43 (5/31/87) **86**

BONNAIRE
Brut Blanc de Blancs Champagne Cramant 1985: Attractive in a fresh, pleasant style. Tastes fruity and delicate, with direct flavors of pear and lemon. $42 (12/31/89) **83**
Brut Blanc de Blancs Champagne Cramant 1983 $38 (2/29/88) **87**
Brut Blanc de Blancs Champagne Cramant 1979 $40 (5/31/87) **86**
Brut Blanc de Blancs Champagne Cramant NV $30 (12/31/89) **90**

BRICOUT
Brut Blanc de Blancs Champagne NV $21 (12/31/87) **85**

DE CASTELLANE
Brut Blanc de Blancs Champagne 1981 $33 (4/15/88) **84**
Brut Blanc de Blancs Champagne 1980 $22 (5/31/87) **91**
Brut Blanc de Blancs Champagne Chardonnay 1983 ($NA) (12/31/90) **90**
Brut Blanc de Blancs Champagne Chardonnay NV: A distinctive and mature style of brut with rich ripe apple, cream, and vanilla flavors and a silky mouth-feel. $30 (12/31/91) **84**

A. CHARBAUT
Brut Blanc de Blancs Champagne 1982: Deliciously rich and vivid, with layers of creamy cherry, toast, vanilla and spice flavors that are deep and concentrated. Plenty of pretty flavors on the aftertaste, too. Drink now to 1994. $43 (4/15/90) **90**
Brut Blanc de Blancs Champagne 1979 $34 (5/31/87) **96**
Brut Blanc de Blancs Champagne NV $40 (12/31/90) **83**
Brut Blanc de Blancs Champagne Certificate 1982: Broad, rich, well-defined pear, vanilla, apple and spice notes, a full-bodied style that's attractive; with time it may display more complexity and finesse, but for now those are modest shortcomings. $82 (12/31/89) **87**
Brut Blanc de Blancs Champagne Certificate 1979 $80 (7/15/88) **92**
Brut Blanc de Blancs Champagne Certificate 1976 Rel: $63 Cur: $82 (2/01/86) SS **97**

DELAMOTTE
Blanc de Blancs Champagne 1985: Crisp and refreshing, a seamless wine, with a nice balance of delicate green apple flavor and toasty, nutty overtones of maturity. The flavors persist into a well-modulated finish. $43 (12/31/91) **87**
Blanc de Blancs Champagne 1982 $28 (4/15/88) **84**
Blanc de Blancs Champagne NV $24 (12/31/87) **79**

DEUTZ
Brut Blanc de Blancs Champagne 1985 $42 (12/31/90) **83**
Brut Blanc de Blancs Champagne 1982 $39 (5/31/87) **90**

ANDRE DRAPPIER
Brut Blanc de Blancs Champagne NV $30 (5/31/87) **76**

Brut Blanc de Blancs Champagne Signature NV $23 (2/01/86) **86**

DUVAL-LEROY
Brut Blanc de Blancs Champagne Chardonnay NV: Very firm and classy, with great balance of dough, coconut, spice and apple aromas and flavors. Has a fine finish. $30 (12/31/91) **88**

ELLNER
Brut Blanc de Blancs Champagne NV: Creamy, rich and complex, with layers of butterscotch, vanilla and honey, in a structured, hardy, sturdy Champagne. Lovely from start to end, with a clean, lingering, vibrant finish. $32 (7/31/89) **90**

GEORGE GOULET
Brut Blanc de Blancs Champagne Cuvée "G" NV $26 (7/31/88) **74**

CHARLES HEIDSIECK
Brut Blanc de Blancs Champagne NV $33 (12/31/90) **84**
Brut Blanc de Blancs Champagne Brut de Chardonnay 1981 $30 (5/31/87) **78**

HENRIOT
Brut Blanc de Blancs Champagne de Chardonnay NV (NR) (12/31/90) **85**

JACQUART
Brut Blanc de Blancs Champagne NV $25 (12/31/90) **85**

JACQUESSON
Blanc de Blancs Champagne NV: An elegant, spicy brut, with white pepper and strawberry flavors and a frothy mouth-feel. Good acidity. $45 (12/31/91) **87**

JEAN-MARIE
Brut Blanc de Blancs Champagne NV (NR) (12/31/90) **77**

KRUG
Brut Blanc de Blancs Champagne Clos du Mesnil 1982 Rel: $120 Cur: $195 (12/31/90) **84**
Brut Blanc de Blancs Champagne Clos du Mesnil 1981: Sophisticated and lean, made for cellaring. Very crisp in style, with tart, lemony flavors and a beautifully creamy texture. Very good now, but collectors value it for its aging potential. Drink now through 1995. Tasted twice. Rel: $120 Cur: $155 (12/31/89) **87**
Brut Blanc de Blancs Champagne Clos du Mesnil 1980 Rel: $100 Cur: $160 (5/31/87) **80**

GUY LARMANDIER
Brut Blanc de Blancs Champagne Cramant NV $27 (5/31/87) **92**

LECHERE
Brut Blanc de Blancs Champagne 1985: Intense and earthy, with ripe pear and fruit cocktail flavors that turn slightly bitter on the finish. Drink now. Tasted twice. $44 (5/15/92) **78**
Brut Blanc de Blancs Champagne NV $25 (12/31/87) **89**
Brut Blanc de Blancs Champagne Cuvée Orient Express NV $45 (12/31/90) **86**
Brut Blanc de Blancs Champagne Grand Cru 1983: A complex, focused wine, with more style than charm. Firm and concentrated, featuring earthy lemon, nutmeg and cedar flavors that extend into a long finish. An austere style, with character and complexity. 500 cases made. $90 (5/15/92) **92**
Brut Blanc de Blancs Champagne Première Cru NV: Better than many vintage Champagnes, with intense, complex apple, malt and vanilla flavors and a fresh, elegant finish. $42 (12/31/91) **91**

R & L LEGRAS
Brut Blanc de Blancs Champagne NV: Clean and delicious with apple and grapefruit flavors and a refreshing finish. $32 (12/31/91) **85**
Brut Blanc de Blancs Champagne Cuvée St.-Vincent 1976 $33 (5/31/87) **85**
Brut Blanc de Blancs Champagne Présidence 1982 $29 (5/31/87) **85**

MARQUIS DE SADE
Brut Blanc de Blancs Champagne Grand Cru NV: Rich in texture, but surprisingly light in flavor, featuring modest pear and toast aromas and flavors. A bit on the simple side, but it's well made. $35 (3/31/92) **85**

G.H. MUMM
Brut Blanc de Blancs Champagne Mumm de Cramant NV $43 (12/31/90) **91**
Brut Blanc de Blancs Champagne Mumm de Cramant NV $40 (5/31/87) **83**

OUDINOT
Brut Blanc de Blancs Champagne NV $25 (12/31/90) **74**

BRUNO PAILLARD
Brut Blanc de Blancs Champagne 1983 $40 (5/31/87) **94**
Brut Blanc de Blancs Champagne 1975 $42 (5/31/87) **70**

JOSEPH PERRIER
Brut Blanc de Blancs Champagne Cuvée Royale NV $37 (12/31/90) **88**
Brut Blanc de Blancs Champagne Cuvée Royale NV $34 (5/31/87) **86**

BATISTE PERTOIS
Brut Blanc de Blancs Champagne Cramant Cuvée de Réserve NV: Has wonderful delicacy in texture and a slight sweetness that will make it fine to drink as an aperitif or with dessert. Subtle lemony, doughy flavors are complex and lingering. $24 (12/31/89) **88**

PHILIPPONNAT
Brut Blanc de Blancs Champagne 1980 $26 (5/31/87) **92**
Brut Blanc de Blancs Champagne Cuvée Première 1980 $39 (12/31/88) **89**
Brut Blanc de Blancs Champagne Grand Blanc 1985 $40 (12/31/90) **87**

LOUIS ROEDERER
Brut Blanc de Blancs Champagne 1983 $45 (12/31/90) **83**
Brut Blanc de Blancs Champagne 1979 $39 (5/31/87) **94**

POL ROGER
Brut Blanc de Blancs Champagne Blanc de Chardonnay 1985: A toasty, complex bubbly, with plenty of winy character, showing buttery, smoky overtones to the crisp apple and lemon flavors. Has layers of flavor wrapped in a tight package. A stylish wine that's drinkable now. $62 (1/31/92) **89**
Brut Blanc de Blancs Champagne Blanc de Chardonnay 1982 $50 (12/31/90) **91**
Brut Blanc de Blancs Champagne Blanc de Chardonnay 1979 $41 (12/31/90) **84**

DOM RUINART
Brut Blanc de Blancs Champagne 1985: Crisp, assertive and packed with flavors—mostly pear, walnut and almond—hinting at toast and honey on the finish. Not as creamy as some Champagnes, but balanced and flavorful. Tasted twice. $88 (12/31/91) **87**
Brut Blanc de Blancs Champagne 1983 $60 (12/31/90) **87**
Brut Blanc de Blancs Champagne 1982: Outstanding Champagne. Very rich, complex and mature, with a fascinating array of nutty, spicy aromas and ripe, satisfying fruit and smoke flavors. Rel: $61 Cur: $70 (12/31/90) **90**
Brut Blanc de Blancs Champagne 1982: Extremely rich and toasty, deep and concentrated; intriguing, with layers of tightly wound vanilla, pear and spicy smoke notes in a very deliberate style. Its deep concentration of fruit makes it a good bet to improve until 1994. Rel: $61 Cur: $70 (12/31/89) CS **94**
Brut Blanc de Blancs Champagne 1981 $61 (12/31/89) **90**
Brut Blanc de Blancs Champagne 1979 Rel: $39 Cur: $52 (10/31/86) **91**
Brut Blanc de Blancs Champagne 1978 Rel: $40 Cur: $50 (5/16/86) **87**
Brut Blanc de Blancs Champagne 1976 Rel: $30 Cur: $45 (10/01/84) **84**

SALON
Brut Blanc de Blancs Champagne Le Mesnil 1982: Very crisp and lemony, with sharply focused citrus, toast and spice aromas and flavors. Picks up impressively developed nutty, buttery flavors on the lively finish. A tight, vibrant wine that offers more complexity than most. Should get better as it ages. $119 (12/31/91) CS **91**
Brut Blanc de Blancs Champagne Le Mesnil 1979 (Disgorged Summer 1988): Crisp, fresh, young and alive with pretty toasty, yeasty aromas and delicate lemon, pear and vanilla notes that are still tightly wound; the finish is clean and dry. Impressive for its vitality; can stand further cellaring. $119 (12/31/89) **93**
Brut Blanc de Blancs Champagne Le Mesnil 1976 $225/1.5L (12/31/88) **91**
Brut Blanc de Blancs Champagne Le Mesnil 1976 Rel: $71 Cur: $105 (5/31/87) **89**

MARIE STUART
Brut Blanc de Blancs Champagne 1979 $25 (12/31/87) **87**
Brut Blanc de Blancs Champagne NV $19 (12/31/87) **85**

TAILLEVENT
Brut Blanc de Blancs Champagne 1985: Floral and earthy, with a touch of bitterness on the finish. The pear, vanilla and spice flavors are elegant and balanced. Ready to drink now. $49 (11/15/91) **84**
Brut Blanc de Blancs Champagne 1983: Lean and compact, it has lemon and spice flavors along with a coarse, metallic quality that detracts a bit. Despite that, there's good intensity and concentration of flavor. $33 (12/31/89) **82**

TAITTINGER
Brut Blanc de Blancs Champagne Comtes de Champagne 1985 $96 (12/31/90) **92**
Brut Blanc de Blancs Champagne Comtes de Champagne 1983 $92 (12/31/90) **93**
Brut Blanc de Blancs Champagne Comtes de Champagne 1982: Amazing for its depth and elegance, a wonderful bottle of bubbly, with sharply defined anise, vanilla and spicy pear notes. Richly concentrated and complex, the fine length on the aftertaste keeps you coming back for another glass. Drink now to 1994. Rel: $83 Cur: $99 (12/31/89) **95**
Brut Blanc de Blancs Champagne Comtes de Champagne 1981 Rel: $69 Cur: $75 (4/15/88) **93**
Brut Blanc de Blancs Champagne Comtes de Champagne 1979 Rel: $65 Cur: $110 (5/31/87) **92**
Brut Blanc de Blancs Champagne Comtes de Champagne 1976 Rel: $66 Cur: $121 (5/16/86) **83**

DE VENOGE
Brut Blanc de Blancs Champagne NV $38 (12/31/90) **86**

BRUT

HENRI ABELE
Brut Champagne NV: Refreshing, yet quite complex, full of black cherry, strawberry and bread dough flavors. A lovely brut that's worth seeking out. $24 (12/31/91) **89**
Brut Champagne Grande Marque Impériale 1982 $29 (7/31/87) **90**
Brut Champagne Le Sourire de Reims NV $24 (7/31/87) **79**

AYALA
Brut Champagne 1985 $59 (12/31/90) **89**
Brut Champagne 1983: Simple, straightforward and uncomplicated, with dough, spice and vanilla flavors that are somewhat ponderous on the palate. A touch of caramel on the finish makes it more interesting. $30 (12/31/89) **80**
Brut Champagne 1982 $27 (4/15/88) **86**
Brut Champagne NV $30 (12/31/91) **86**
Brut Champagne Extra Quality NV $28 (12/31/87) **78**
Brut Champagne Grand Cuvée 1985: A slightly herbal style of Champagne, with earthy aromas and full, lemony flavors. Crisp but round in texture. $57 (12/31/89) **84**
Brut Champagne Grand Cuvée 1982 $52 (4/15/88) **87**

PAUL BARA
Brut Champagne 1982 $34 (12/31/88) **89**

BARANCOURT
Cuvée de Fondateurs Champagne 1985 ($NA) (12/31/90) **90**

BEAUMET
Brut Champagne NV: Pie crust and strawberry character dominates, with a hint of exotic fruit flavor and a very fruity finish. $26 (12/31/91) **86**
Brut Champagne NV: Very smooth and delicate, with gentle flavors of apricot and lemon plus a refreshing zip of pepper on the finish. $22 (12/31/89) **84**

BEAUMONT DES CRAYERES
Brut Champagne Cuvée Prestige NV: It's simple, fruity and slightly sweet, with lots of appley, earthy flavors and medium acidity. (NR) (12/31/91) **82**
Brut Champagne Cuvée Réserve NV: A concentrated wine, with tons of dough, apple and white chocolate flavors and a long, rich finish. (NR) (12/31/91) **91**

BILLECART-SALMON
Brut Champagne 1983: Tart, crisp, lean and concentrated with sharply focused, well-balanced lemon, spice, cherry and vanilla-coconut notes that are quite pleasing. Full-bodied, with a sense of finesse. Ready now or in 1993. $47 (12/31/89) **89**
Brut Champagne NV: A very flavorful wine, with apple and cream flavors and a creamy finish. $28 (12/31/91) **86**

H. BLIN
Brut Champagne NV: This rich, velvety Champagne has lots of flavor and character, but seems a little heavy-handed after a few minutes in the glass. $18 (12/31/91) **85**

BOIZEL
Brut Champagne Réserve NV: A well-proportioned brut, with subtle creamy, doughy, lemony aromas and flavors that make an attractive package. $30 (12/31/91) **86**

BOLLINGER
Brut Champagne Extra RD 1982: Roasted almond and toast aromas turn tight and austere on the palate, where the mature grapefruit and citrus flavors turn to hints of sherry. Drink up. Tasted three times, with consistent notes. $100 (11/15/91) **87**
Brut Champagne Extra RD 1979: Outstanding for its depth, robust flavor and mature winy style, yet it retains finesse. Smells and tastes toasty, slightly earthy and buttery, with complex hints of almonds, butterscotch and spice. Rel: $79 Cur: $87 (12/31/89) **94**
Brut Champagne Extra RD 1976 Rel: $59 Cur: $73 (4/15/88) **88**
Brut Champagne Extra RD 1975 Rel: $64 Cur: $90 (5/16/86) **89**
Brut Champagne Grand Année 1985 Rel: $45 Cur: $50 (12/31/90) **96**
Brut Champagne Grand Année 1983: Floral and grapefruit aromas and flavors make this crisp, medium-bodied wine lively and agreeable, but it's simple. A touch of ginger on the finish is especially appealing. $43 (12/31/89) **86**
Brut Champagne Grand Année 1982 $30 (7/15/88) **93**
Brut Champagne Spécial Cuvée NV: A subtle wine, with wonderfully rich aromas and flavors and plenty of dough, coconut and fruit character. Always a class act. $38 (12/31/91) **92**

BOUCHE PERE & FILS
Brut Champagne Cuvée Réserve NV: A smooth, broad, flavorful wine, with toasty, figgy flavors and a lingering finish. Fine balance and good intensity add up to a Champagne worth buying. $20 (1/31/92) **87**

BRICOUT
Brut Champagne 1985 ($NA) (12/31/90) **81**
Brut Champagne Carte d'Or Prestige 1986: Tart and lemony, this lean, crisp style zings across the palate, but may be too lean for some. Picks up pretty honey and vanilla notes on the finish. Drink now to 1994. $40 (12/31/91) **86**
Brut Champagne Carte d'Or Prestige 1983: Very dry, with floral, nutty aromas and flavors, it's crisp and austere on the finish, not at all generous, deep or smooth. $25 (12/31/89) **75**
Brut Champagne Carte d'Or Prestige NV: A butterball of a brut that smells and tastes like melted butter, but ends on a zesty, lemony note. $30 (12/31/91) **83**
Brut Champagne Carte Noire Réserve NV: A serious non-vintage Champagne, with intense strawberry and earth aromas and flavors. Has a fine bead, a rich mouth-feel and a lovely, classy texture. 3,500 cases made. $30 (12/31/91) **90**
Brut Champagne Elegance de Bricout 1985 ($NA) (12/31/90) **85**
Brut Champagne Elegance de Bricout 1982 $50 (12/31/88) **90**

CANARD-DUCHENE
Brut Champagne Cuvée Bicentenaire NV: A bold, ripe, full-bodied style, with citrus, toast, pear and earth notes that are complex and rich. Good length on the finish carries the fruit and vanilla flavors. Drink now. $29 (11/15/91) **87**
Brut Champagne Cuvée Spéciale de Charles VII NV: A floral, spicy style, with pleasant aromas of honey on the nose and crisp, lemony tartness on the palate, finishing fresh and lively. $75 (12/31/89) **85**
Brut Champagne Patrimoine 1983: Ripe and intense, somewhat alcoholic and soft in a style that manages to correct itself and find a modest equilibrium. After a glass or so the style begins to wear on you. $42 (12/31/89) **80**
Brut Champagne Patrimoine NV: Like drinking poached pears; a firm and tight style, but it has fresh flavors. $34 (12/31/91) **85**

DE CASTELLANE
Brut Champagne 1985 $27 (12/31/90) **84**
Brut Champagne NV: A little coarse, but there are plenty of strawberry and cherry flavors, with an earthy overtone and fresh acidity on the finish. $38 (12/31/91) **83**
Brut Champagne Cuvée Florens de Castellane 1982: A tightly reined-in style. It's austere, with crisp lemony flavors that turn spicy and elegant and a subtle intensity that grows on you after the second and third sip. A tough astringency on the finish turns very dry. Drink now to 1993. $59 (12/31/90) **88**
Champagne Cuvée Commodore 1981 $50 (4/15/88) **87**

CATTIER
Brut Champagne NV: Clean and simple, with light dough and spice aromas and good acidity; crisp and a bit austere on the finish. $17 (12/31/89) **82**
Brut Champagne Chigny-les-Roses Première Cru NV: A real standout; makes you pay attention. Offers tons of dough, pear and apple character. $30 (12/31/91) **92**
Brut Champagne Clos du Moulin NV: This one has it all in good proportions: creamy texture, freshly cut ripe apples and a touch of bread dough on the finish. A rare Champagne produced from a single vineyard. $65 (12/31/91) **89**

CHARLES DE CAZANOVE
Brut Champagne NV: A little simple, with fresh apple and floral character and crisp acidity. $28 (12/31/91) **84**
Brut Champagne Ruban Azur NV: Full-bodied and thick, with cherry and strawberry flavors and a fruity finish. $32 (12/31/91) **87**

A. CHARBAUT
Brut Champagne 1985 $49 (12/31/90) **94**
Brut Champagne 1979 $23 (2/01/86) **74**
Brut Champagne NV: Smells and tastes almost like a Pinot Noir, with floral and strawberry notes, a firm backbone and a clean if somewhat simple finish. $30 (12/31/91) **84**
Brut Champagne Cuvée de Réserve NV: Seductive and delicate, with a super-fine bead and a creamy texture. $35 (12/31/91) **90**
Brut Champagne Extra Quality NV: A fun, light Champagne, with delicious apple and dough flavors and crisp acidity. $30 (12/31/91) **86**

VEUVE CLICQUOT
Brut Champagne 1982 Rel: $32 Cur: $40 (5/31/87) SS **93**
Brut Champagne 1979 Rel: $50 Cur: $75 (12/16/85) **88**
Brut Champagne NV: You can't lose with this classy wine. The refined apple, grapefruit and dough aromas follow through on the palate. Creamy and lively on the finish. $40 (12/31/91) **91**
Brut Champagne Gold Label 1983: Attractive fig, peach, toast and vanilla flavors are rich, deep and complex, with a smooth texture and a long, full finish that keeps echoing the fruitiness. Drink now to 1994. $42 (12/31/90) **90**
Brut Champagne Gold Label 1982 $37 (12/31/88) **85**
Brut Champagne La Grande Dame 1985 Rel: $72 Cur: $80 (12/31/90) **91**
Brut Champagne La Grande Dame 1983: Smooth and elegant, with intense ginger, pear and toast aromas and flavors and a velvety texture; long and fragrant on the finish. A complex wine that gets better with every sip. Much better than a bottle tasted earlier. $79 (12/31/89) **92**
Brut Champagne La Grande Dame 1979 Rel: $61 Cur: $74 (5/16/86) **96**

COMTE AUDOIN DE DAMPIERRE
Brut Champagne Grande Année 1983: A very complete and enjoyable Champagne. Tastes dry, it's almost delicate in texture, with mature flavors of toast, vanilla and honey. Rich in spice and fruit flavors, with a lingering finish. $32 (12/31/90) **89**

DEHOURS
Brut Champagne Réserve NV: A super-fresh wine, with white chocolate, apple and dough aromas and fresh, clean flavors; excellent crisp acidity on finish. (NR) (12/31/91) **87**

DELAMOTTE
Brut Champagne NV: A toasty Champagne that's soft and broad, with grapefruit and ginger flavors and hints of walnut on the finish. Round, generous and easy to drink. $30 (12/31/91) **85**

Key to Symbols

The scores reported here are the results of blind tastings conducted by our panel of senior editors. Wines that carry the initials below are results of individual tastings.

THE WINE SPECTATOR 100-POINT SCALE ***95-100***—Classic, a great wine; ***90-94***—Outstanding, superior character and style; ***80-89***—Good to very good, a wine with special qualities; ***70-79***—Average, drinkable wine that may have minor flaws; ***60-69***—Below average, drinkable but not recommended; ***50-59***—Poor, undrinkable, not recommended. "+"—With a score indicates a range; used primarily with barrel tastings to indicate a preliminary score.

SPECIAL DESIGNATIONS SS—Spectator Selection, CS—Cellar Selection, BB—Best Buy, ($NA)—Price not available, (NR)—Not released.

TASTER'S INITIALS (JG)—Jim Gordon, (HS)—Harvey Steiman, (JL)—James Laube, (JS)—James Suckling, (TM)—Thomas Matthews, (TR)—Terry Robards, (PM)—Per-Henrik Mansson, (BT)—Barrel Tasting (these wines were tasted blind from barrel samples), (CA-date)—*California's Great Cabernets* by James Laube, (CH-date)—*California's Great Chardonnays* by James Laube, (VP-date)—*Vintage Port* by James Suckling.

DATE TASTED Dates in parentheses represent the issue in which the rating was published.

DELBECK
Brut Champagne Heritage NV: A very fruity style, with intense white pepper, apple skin flavors and a crisp finish. (NR) (12/31/91) **84**

DEUTZ
Brut Champagne 1985 $40 (12/31/90) **83**
Brut Champagne NV: Candy, strawberry and fruit cocktail aromas and flavors dominate in this middle-of-the-road brut. $25 (12/31/91) **82**
Brut Champagne 150 Anniversaire NV $50 (12/31/88) **89**
Brut Champagne Cuvée Lallier Gold Lack NV: Crisp, fruity and straightforward, with cherry and vanilla flavors. Tastes correct and clean. $33 (12/31/90) **80**
Brut Champagne Cuvée William Deutz 1982: Elegant and yeasty, with lemon, spice and toast flavors and a slightly coarse texture on the finish. Rel: $61 Cur: $72 (12/31/89) **85**
Brut Champagne Cuvée William Deutz 1979 Rel: $35 Cur: $47 (7/16/85) **90**
Brut Champagne Georges Mathieu 1982: Attractive for its pretty pear, cherry and vanilla notes; well balanced, deep and full-bodied, with plenty of richness and concentration and a full, fruity aftertaste. Ready now to 1993. $40 (12/31/89) **89**
Brut Champagne Georges Mathieu Réserve 1985: Very firm and well-balanced, offering just enough crisp fruit flavor to back up the firmness. It has touches of earthy complexity, but stays basically straightforward in style. $46 (12/31/90) **86**

VVE. A. DEVAUX
Brut Champagne Grande Réserve NV: Round and creamy with a frothy mouth-feel and fresh apple and white pepper flavors and a toasty finish. (NR) (12/31/91) **88**

FRANCOIS DILIGENT
Brut Champagne Carte Blanche NV: Light and delicate, with extremely floral aromas, like a Gewürztraminer; mildly buttery, spicy, white pepper notes follow through on the palate. (NR) (12/31/91) **83**

ANDRE DRAPPIER
Brut Champagne Carte D'Or NV: Rich yet balanced, with an abundance of hazelnut, dough, apple and strawberry flavors. Has a great, silky finish. $39 (12/31/91) **89**

DUVAL-LEROY
Cuvée des Roys Champagne 1985 ($NA) (12/31/90) **84**
Brut Champagne NV: A fresh, clean style of Champagne, with plenty of appley, dough character and a creamy texture. A classic brut. (NR) (12/31/91) **89**
Brut Champagne Fleur de Champagne NV: There's lots of flavor in this one, with plenty of appley, white pepper character and a crisp finish. $25 (12/31/91) **87**

ELLNER
Brut Champagne 1982: An earthy, perfumey style, with a rich, intense, fleshy texture and peach-tinged toast and almond flavors; smooth and elegant. $38 (7/31/89) **91**
Brut Champagne Réserve NV: Ripe, almost sweet, it's bursting with flavor. A showy, buttery Champagne that's immediately likable. $30 (7/31/89) **87**

SERGE FAUST
Brut Champagne Cuvée de Réserve à Vandières NV: Tastes smooth, elegant and full-bodied, from the doughy aroma and the butter, vanilla and slightly sweet pear flavors to the creamy, lingering finish. 1,000 cases made. $33 (12/31/90) **86**

NICHOLAS FEUILLATTE
Brut Champagne Réserve Particulière NV: Lots of grapefruit and fruit cocktail flavors, it's a little coarse. Serve very chilled. $22 (12/31/91) **82**
Brut Champagne Réserve Particulière NV $17 (12/31/87) **73**

HENRI GERMAIN
Brut Champagne NV: A harmonious non-vintage, with subtle strawberry and fresh fruit flavors, hints of dough and crisp acidity. $28 (12/31/91) **88**

GOSSET
Brut Champagne Grande Millésime 1985: Mature in flavor, with rich, nutty spice, cherry and plum flavors and a creamy texture. Has good depth, richness and concentration, with lemony flavors that linger. Ready to drink now. $72 (4/30/91) **89**
Brut Champagne Grande Millésime 1983: Crisp and refreshing, with a lemon-lime thread of zingy acidity running through the long finish. Has a sense of delicacy and pleasant pear and berry notes to make it more interesting. $75 (5/15/92) **90**
Brut Champagne Grande Millésime 1982: Layers of toast, pear, citrus, nutmeg and creamy vanilla nuances are right on the mark for this vintage Champagne that's rich and complex. The finish brings all the flavors together for a complex encore. Drink now to 1993. 4,200 cases made. Rel: $60 Cur: $70 (12/31/90) **90**
Brut Champagne Grande Millésime 1979 Rel: $45 Cur: $112 (7/15/87) **96**
Brut Champagne Grande Réserve NV: A focused, concentrated and beautifully structured brut, with a silky mouth-feel underneath the zesty grapefruit, lemon and strawberry flavors. Shows great breeding for a non-vintage. $35 (12/31/91) **91**
Brut Champagne Réserve NV: A mouth-watering style that verges on being a rosé, with lovely, delicate fruit flavors and a fine finish. Offers lots of strawberry character. $27 (12/31/91) **88**

GEORGE GOULET
Brut Champagne 1982 $30 (7/31/88) **90**
Brut Champagne NV $21 (7/31/88) **83**
Brut Champagne Cuvée du Centenaire 1982 $47 (7/31/88) **87**

ALFRED GRATIEN
Brut Champagne 1979 $28 (9/16/85) **92**
Brut Champagne NV $23 (11/01/85) **93**

MAISON HAMM
Brut Champagne Réserve Première Cru NV: Rich and sexy, this has tons of flavor, with dough, apple and lemon flavors and a velvety mouth-feel. $22 (12/31/91) **90**

CHARLES HEIDSIECK
Brut Champagne 1985 $50 (12/31/90) **93**
Brut Champagne 1983: A Champagne with uncommon character, this mature wine is round, creamy and generous on the palate, with all sorts of honey, toast and earth aromas and flavors. A rich, full-bodied, heady style of Champagne. $41 (3/31/91) **90**
Brut Champagne 1982 Rel: $33 Cur: $40 (12/31/88) SS **93**
Brut Champagne Blanc des Millénaires 1983: Round and elegant in texture, with delicate pear, hazelnut and grapefruit flavors that extend into a long finish. Has style and grace, with plenty of flavor to enjoy. $65 (3/31/92) **90**
Brut Champagne Millésime 1983: Beautiful flavors of rich, toasty, pear, apple and spice, with a fine structure that keeps the flavors lingering on the finish. An impressive package that's ready to drink now. $38 (12/31/89) **87**
Brut Champagne Réserve NV: Fresh and full-bodied, this brut tastes like an apple tart glazed with caramel and sprinkled with almonds. $34 (12/31/91) **90**

HEIDSIECK MONOPOLE
Brut Champagne Diamant Bleu 1982 Rel: $40 Cur: $56 (11/30/87) **89**
Brut Champagne Diamant Bleu 1979 $39 (5/16/86) **93**
Brut Champagne Diamant Rosé 1982 Rel: $55 Cur: $68 (11/30/87) **90**
Brut Champagne Dry Monopole 1985 ($NA) (12/31/90) **90**
Brut Champagne Dry Monopole 1982 $37.50 (12/31/88) **88**

Brut Champagne Dry Monopole NV: Smooth and silky with good pie crust and apple flavors and a fresh finish. $31 (12/31/91) **82**

HENRIOT
Brut Champagne NV $21 (7/01/86) **86**
Brut Champagne Cuvée du Soleil NV $27 (12/31/87) **70**
Brut Champagne Souverain NV: A lively wine that cleans your palate; very bubbly and crisp, with clean flavors. Try it with sushi. $40 (12/31/91) **86**

JACQUART
Brut Champagne 1983: Charming flavor and finesse, with toast, ginger, pear and spice flavors and a long, lingering aftertaste. Drink now to 1993. $43 (4/15/90) **88**
Brut Champagne 1982 $39 (12/31/88) **90**
Brut Champagne NV $24 (12/31/88) **83**
Brut Champagne La Cuvée Renommée 1982 $64 (12/31/88) **90**

JACQUESSON
Brut Champagne Perfection 1985 ($NA) (12/31/90) **84**
Brut Champagne Perfection NV: An extremely fresh wine, with delicious apple and banana flavors, a very silky mouth-feel and a clean, crisp finish. $28 (12/31/91) **87**
Brut Champagne Signature 1979 $34 (7/31/87) **93**

JEAN-MARIE
Brut Champagne 1985 ($NA) (12/31/90) **75**
Brut Champagne NV: Tastes like a red wine with all its cherry, raspberry, earthy character; very full, thick and fat. (NR) (12/31/91) **83**

KRUG
Brut Champagne 1982: Toasty and elegant, with rich, complex, pear, vanilla and spicy notes that are crisp and lively, with a long aftertaste that's slighly coarse. $135 (12/31/89) **92**
Brut Champagne 1981 Rel: $85 Cur: $103 (12/31/88) **91**
Brut Champagne 1976 Rel: $70 Cur: $132 (5/16/86) **93**
Brut Champagne Grande Cuvée NV: A blockbuster in a mature, decadent style. Shows vanilla, apple, truffle and slight cream aromas and flavors, good acidity and a rich, earthy finish. Not everyone's glass of Champagne, but it's impressive to us. $80 (12/31/91) **90**

CHARLES LAFITTE
Brut Champagne Tête de Cuvée NV: A perfumey, fruity wine, with plenty of rose petal and strawberry notes. (NR) (12/31/91) **84**

LANSON
225th Anniversary Spécial Cuvée Champagne 1981 $43 (10/15/88) **89**
225th Anniversary Spécial Cuvée Champagne 1980 $43 (11/30/86) **95**
Brut Champagne 1985: A super Champagne. Wonderfully focused and well balanced, with focused lemon and apple aromas, sweet, ripe lemon flavor and hints of dough. Medium-bodied, with a creamy mouth-feel. $37 (12/31/90) **93**
Brut Champagne 1983: Young, intense, rich and lively, with good depth of flavor and lemon, spice and ginger nuances in an agressive style that needs food to offset some of the coarseness. Drink now. $30 (12/31/89) **85**
Brut Champagne 1982 $27 (10/15/88) **92**
Brut Champagne Black Label NV: Extremely appley and grapey, with lots of acidity and lime notes on the finish. Almost tannic. A young, lively style that needs food. $35 (12/31/91) **87**
Brut Champagne Black Label Cuvée NV $24 (12/31/88) **88**

LAURENT-PERRIER
Brut Champagne 1985 $40 (12/31/90) **87**
Brut Champagne 1982 Rel: $36 Cur: $95 (12/31/88) **93**
Brut Champagne NV $23 (12/31/87) **90**
Brut Champagne Cuvée Grand Siècle 1982 $70 (12/31/88) **92**
Brut Champagne Cuvée Grand Siècle 1979 Rel: $45 Cur: $87 (2/15/88) **90**
Brut Champagne L.P. NV: Focused and interesting, with spicy white pepper and fruit flavors and a flavorful finish. $36 (12/31/91) **87**
Brut Champagne Ultra Cuvée Sans Dosage NV $27 (1/31/88) **73**

LECHERE
Brut Champagne Première Cru NV: An explosive, rich, full-bodied style, with nutty, smoky apple flavors and a super-rich finish. $37 (12/31/91) **90**
Brut Champagne Première Cru Orient Express NV: Crisp and spicy, with pleasant gingersnap and grapefruit aromas and flavors, a delicate texture and plenty of intensity right through the long finish. A stylish wine that finishes a little sweet, but it's balanced and refreshing. $49 (3/31/92) **88**

LECLERC-BRIANT
Brut Champagne 1979 $31 (3/15/88) **85**
Brut Champagne Cuvée Wolfgang Mozart 1983: Has nice, mature nutty, spicy and toasty aromas and similar flavors that dance around a central thread of lemon and vanilla, making this an interesting wine, but it could show a little more finesse. $60 (12/31/91) **85**
Brut Champagne Divine 1985: Crisp and elegant, with lively lemon, vanilla and butter aromas and flavors with hints of pear, all held together in a neat package that focuses the flavors on the finish. $45 (12/31/91) **89**
Brut Champagne Réserve NV $23 (3/15/88) **80**
Brut Champagne Spécial Club 1983: Full-bodied, goes down easy, with plenty of fruit and a touch of coarseness. But overall it's balanced, with lemon, apple and toast notes. Young and lively, ready to drink. 1,800 cases made. $35 (12/31/89) **83**

MARQUIS DE SADE
Brut Champagne Private Reserve 1985: The simple, lemony aromas and flavors have intensity, but little finesse. There's rosemary on the finish, making the wine a little odd. $48 (3/31/92) **79**
Brut Champagne Private Reserve 1985 $50 (12/31/90) **88**
Brut Champagne Private Reserve 1981 $56 (12/31/90) **89**

MAXIM'S
Brut Champagne NV: Interesting and distinctive. Like a light rosé Champagne, with its cherry and strawberry aromas and flavors; the flavors also hint at smoked salmon. From Union Champenoise. (NR) (12/31/91) **85**

MOET & CHANDON
Brut Champagne Impérial 1986: Earthy, grassy aromas and flavors lack depth, but the structure is crisp and refreshing. Drinkable now. $40 (3/31/92) **77**
Brut Champagne Impérial 1985: Not for everyone, but it will more than satisfy lovers of this style. Distinctively earthy with complex aromas, it's lemony and almost peppery in flavor. $57 (12/31/89) **86**
Brut Champagne Impérial 1983: Earthy, bitter, somewhat dirty, overall unbalanced and unpleasant, with a flabby finish. Hard to warm up to. Tasted twice. $40 (12/31/89) **69**
Brut Champagne Impérial 1982 Rel: $33 Cur: $39 (4/15/88) **84**
Brut Champagne Impérial 1980 Rel: $30 Cur: $58 (3/16/85) **91**
Brut Champagne Impérial NV $35 (12/31/91) **85**

MONTAUDON
Brut Champagne M NV: Showy, with bread dough, toast, strawberry and apple flavors, crisp acidity and a flavorful finish. $25 (12/31/91) **90**

G.H. MUMM
Brut Champagne Cordon Rouge 1985 $34 (12/31/90) **86**
Brut Champagne Cordon Rouge 1982 Rel: $37 Cur: $42 (12/31/88) **85**
Brut Champagne Cordon Rouge 1979 Rel: $24 Cur: $40 (2/16/86) **93**
Brut Champagne Cordon Rouge NV $25 (12/31/91) **88**
Brut Champagne Grand Cordon 1985: Earthy, spicy aromas and flavors hint at lemon and cream, but barely manage to make themselves felt through a tight structure that seems dry and austere on the finish. Tasted twice, with consistent notes. $100 (11/15/91) **85**
Brut Champagne René Lalou 1985: Very dry, crisp and austere, fine for its style but not for everyone. Has nutty, smoky aromas, dry, slightly astringent apple flavors and a lingering, dry finish. Rel: $58 Cur: $70 (12/31/90) **86**
Brut Champagne René Lalou 1982 Rel: $55 Cur: $61 (9/30/88) **90**
Brut Champagne René Lalou 1979 Rel: $56 Cur: $68 (5/16/86) **95**

OUDINOT
Brut Champagne 1985 $28 (12/31/90) **90**

BRUNO PAILLARD
Brut Champagne 1985 $40 (12/31/90) **90**
Brut Champagne Première Cuvée NV: A fruity wine, with fruit cocktail and almond character and a clean, simple finish. $40 (12/31/91) **85**

DOM PERIGNON
Brut Champagne 1983: Has oodles of Champagne complexity in a creamy smooth package. Rich, toasty, creamy and elegant, with delicious nutty flavors that linger on the finish. An enormously concentrated wine that shows the full benefit of long-term aging on the yeast. $97 (5/15/92) **95**
Brut Champagne 1982 Rel: $75 Cur: $91 (10/15/88) **93**
Brut Champagne 1980 Rel: $60 Cur: $95 (9/15/86) SS **94**
Brut Champagne 1978 Rel: $61 Cur: $149 (5/16/86) **88**

PERRIER-JOUET
Brut Champagne 1955 ($NA)/1.5L (10/15/87) (JS) **90**
Brut Champagne 1947 ($NA)/1.5L (10/15/87) (JS) **85**
Brut Champagne 1928 ($NA) (10/15/87) (JS) **97**
Brut Champagne 1914 ($NA) (10/15/87) (JS) **55**
Brut Champagne 1911 ($NA) (10/15/87) (JS) **95**
Brut Champagne 1900 ($NA) (10/15/87) (JS) **97**
Brut Champagne 1893 ($NA) (10/15/87) (JS) **80**
Brut Champagne 1825 ($NA) (10/15/87) (JS) **95**
Brut Champagne Fleur de Champagne 1985 $75 (12/31/90) **86**
Brut Champagne Fleur de Champagne 1983: A fresh, crisp wine in a light, somewhat austere style that turns more generous on the palate with bright, lemon-apple flavor and a pleasant touch of spice on the finish. $65 (12/31/89) **88**
Brut Champagne Fleur de Champagne 1982 Rel: $65 Cur: $87 (12/31/88) **88**
Brut Champagne Fleur de Champagne 1979 Rel: $50 Cur: $90 (2/01/86) **93**
Brut Champagne Grand Brut NV: A reined-in style but quite creamy, with vanilla, lemon and apple flavors that blend into a seductive finish. $25 (12/31/91) **88**

JOSEPH PERRIER
Brut Champagne 1985 $37 (12/31/90) **82**
Brut Champagne 1979 $22 (10/01/85) **87**
Brut Champagne NV $19 (11/16/85) **92**
Brut Champagne Cuvée Josephine 1982: Rich and gingery, with toasty vanilla, cherry and lemony flavors that are intense, complex, lively and enticing. Packed with flavor and full of finesse, this is a wonderful 1982 that goes well beyond the average. Drink now to 1994. $100 (12/31/90) **93**
Brut Champagne Cuvée Royale 1985: $37 (12/31/90) **82**
Brut Champagne Cuvée Royale 1982: Very attractive. Extremely flavorful, fruity and figgy tasting, yet light in body and lively on the palate. Creamy and supple in texture. $35 (12/31/89) **89**
Brut Champagne Cuvée Royale NV: Fresh and simple, with lots of fresh cut apple and apple skin flavors and a lively finish. $32 (12/31/91) **84**

PHILIPPONNAT
Brut Champagne Clos des Goisses 1985 $118 (12/31/90) **85**
Brut Champagne Clos des Goisses 1982 $89 (12/31/88) **84**
Brut Champagne Grand Blanc 1982 $38 (12/31/88) **84**
Brut Champagne Royale Réserve NV: Very fizzy, with clean white pepper and apple aromas and flavors and a long, crisp finish. $32 (12/31/91) **85**

PIPER-HEIDSIECK
Brut Champagne 1985 $43 (12/31/90) **88**
Brut Champagne 1982 $32 (12/31/88) **86**
Brut Champagne Cuvée Brut NV: Round and rich, with white pepper, apple and dough aromas and flavors and a long finish. $28 (12/31/91) **88**
Brut Champagne Extra NV $26 (12/31/87) **78**
Brut Champagne Sauvage 1982: Crisp, light and refreshing, with slightly honeyed lemon, apple and toast aromas and flavors. Long and elegant, with mouthwatering acidity. $30 (12/31/89) **89**
Champagne Rare 1985 ($NA) (12/31/90) **80**
Champagne Rare 1979 $65 (3/15/87) **89**
Champagne Rare 1976 $66 (8/01/85) **88**

POMMERY
Brut Champagne 1985 $40 (12/31/90) **87**
Brut Champagne 1982 $24 (2/15/88) **93**
Brut Champagne NV $23 (12/31/87) **79**
Brut Champagne Royale NV: A rich, appley Champagne, with crisp acidity and a clean finish. Very balanced. $30 (12/31/91) **87**

LOUIS ROEDERER
Brut Champagne 1985 $50 (12/31/90) **85**
Brut Champagne 1982 $45 (12/31/88) **93**
Brut Champagne NV $25 (5/16/86) **82**
Brut Champagne Cristal 1985: Smooth and creamy, with decidedly earthy pear and toast aromas and flavors that hint at butter on the finish. A nicely made, stylish wine that's full of character. $132 (5/15/92) **85**
Brut Champagne Cristal 1983: Crisp and full-bodied, with coconut-tinged ginger, spice and lemon aromas and flavors that unfold generously on the palate. This refreshing wine turns crisp and clean on the finish. $120 (12/31/89) **88**
Brut Champagne Cristal 1982 Rel: $106 Cur: $119 (9/30/87) **92**
Brut Champagne Cristal 1981 Rel: $85 Cur: $100 (5/16/86) **91**
Brut Champagne Première NV: A fine style, with strawberry and pie crust flavors, a creamy mouth-feel and lovely balance. $30 (12/31/91) **88**

POL ROGER
Brut Champagne 1979 $41 (9/01/85) **90**
Brut Champagne NV: Delicate and fresh, with lots of apple and dough flavors and crisp acidity. Very long and flavorful on the finish. $37 (12/31/91) **92**
Brut Champagne Cuvée Sir Winston Churchill 1982: Has uncommon depth, complexity and delicacy, with layers of honey, pear, toast and vanilla flavors that take on a rich, creamy texture and then glide across the palate. Long and full on the finish. Drink now to 1994. $50 (4/15/90) **92**
Brut Champagne Extra Cuvée de Réserve 1982: Toasty, buttery and perfumed aromas turn smoky and earthy on the palate, picking up complex mineral and pear flavors and a tannic texture, but it finishes OK. Not for everyone, but the style grows on you. Drink now. $50 (12/31/90) **82**

Brut Champagne Réserve 1985 $62 (12/31/90) **86**
Brut Champagne Réserve NV: Tart and lemony, with fascinating toast and spicy vanilla overtones. Straightforward and charming rather than complex. Drinkable now. $32 (11/15/91) **87**

CHARLES ROYER
Brut Champagne Sélections de Proprietaires NV: (NR) (12/31/91) **84**

RUINART
Brut Champagne NV: This full, rich brut coats the palate with a symphony of flavors, including apple, almond, cinnamon and cream. The first non-vintage from Ruinart. $26 (12/31/91) **89**

MARIE STUART
Brut Champagne NV $22 (12/31/87) **82**
Brut Champagne Cuvée de la Reine NV $26 (12/31/87) **84**

TAILLEVENT
Brut Champagne Grande Réserve NV: Tart, crisp and flavorful, with tiers of peach, pear, vanilla and papaya flavors all neatly woven together, giving it a sense of complexity and finesse. From the owners of Taillevent restaurant in Paris. $43 (11/15/91) **88**

TAITTINGER
Brut Champagne 1985 $50 (12/31/90) **89**
Brut Champagne 1983: Ripe and full-bodied, with a creamy, subtle, delicate texture and pretty ginger, lemon and vanilla notes that echo long and full on the finish. Well crafted with a touch of apple on the finish. $35 (12/31/89) **84**
Brut Champagne NV $26 (12/31/87) **89**
Brut Champagne Collection Lichtenstein 1985: A wine with style and personality, characterized by spicy, toasty, pear-accented flavors. Medium-bodied, offering persistent, harmonious flavors on the finish. $150 (5/15/92) **89**
Brut Champagne Collection Masson 1982: A mature wine, with impressive depth, offering plenty of toasty, spicy notes around a core of pear and hazelnut flavors that keeps unfolding through the long finish. Despite all the flavor intensity, it has delicacy and creamy smoothness. $96 (5/15/92) **94**
Brut Champagne Collection Vieira da Silva 1983: They don't get a whole lot better than this. Extremely flavorful and rich, packed with pear, hazelnut, toast and butter notes that linger on the finish. The powerful fruit flavor and firm acidity give it great strength on the palate. $95 (5/15/92) **94**
Brut Champagne Collection Arman 1981 Rel: $80 Cur: $85 (5/31/87) CS **92**
Brut Champagne La Française NV: Clean and crisp, with medium intensity of pear and apple aromas and flavors and a creamy finish. $35 (12/31/91) **86**
Brut Champagne Millésime 1982 $38 (12/31/88) **89**
Brut Champagne Réserve NV $24 (5/16/86) **73**

JULIEN TARIN
Brut Champagne NV $25 (2/15/87) **78**

ALAIN THIENOT
Brut Champagne NV: With lots of zest from beginning to finish, this one is packed with doughy, lemony aromas and flavors and has a delicious, long finish. (NR) (12/31/91) **89**

DE VENOGE
Brut Champagne 1985 $38 (12/31/90) **86**
Brut Champagne Cordon Bleu NV: The mouth-watering acidity is dominated by grapefruit; this wine could use a little more complexity. $22 (12/31/91) **84**

GEORGES VESSELLE
Brut Champagne Grand Cru NV: A very fruity style with strawberry, cherry and earthy aromas and flavors and a medium-crisp finish. (NR) (12/31/91) **86**

DEMOISELLE VRANKEN
Brut Champagne Grande Cuvée NV: An elegant brut, with a delicate floral and strawberry character and a light finish. (NR) (12/31/91) **86**

ROSÉ

HENRI ABELE
Brut Rosé Champagne NV $29 (7/31/87) **77**
Brut Rosé Champagne Cuvée Réserve 1983: Crisp and fruity, with intensely focused apple and spice aromas and flavors that hint at nutmeg and almond on the finish. Drinkable now, but feels as if it could improve in the bottle through 1994. $50 (3/31/92) **88**
Brut Rosé Champagne Grande Marque Impériale 1982: Rich and creamy, with lots of almond and smoke notes to the basic pear and grapefruit flavors that linger through the finish, modifying themselves and becoming more complex on the aftertaste. A fine Champagne for drinking now. $25 (3/31/92) **88**

AYALA
Brut Rosé Champagne NV $26 (4/15/88) **85**
Brut Rosé Champagne Extra Quality NV $20 (5/31/87) **80**

BEAUMET
Brut Rosé Champagne 1983: Firm and elegant, with spice and cherry aromas and flavors, a touch of smoke and a lively texture to make it interesting. One of the best of the vintage. $30 (12/31/89) **90**
Brut Rosé Champagne 1979 $16 (12/16/85) **79**

BILLECART-SALMON
Brut Rosé Champagne NV $28 (12/16/85) **80**

BOLLINGER
Brut Rosé Champagne Grand Année 1985: Pale copper in color and delicate through and through, with modest cherry and bread dough aromas and flavors. Perhaps a bit metallic on the finish, but it would be enjoyable with food that isn't too rich. Drinkable now. $60 (11/15/91) **85**
Brut Rosé Champagne Grand Année 1983: Rich, toasty and round, with a gentle structure, smooth texture, subtle flavors of strawberry, smoke and a touch of cherry. A nip of crisp lime on the finish keeps it lively. $50 (12/31/89) **89**
Brut Rosé Champagne Grand Année 1982 $35 (7/15/88) **80**
Brut Rosé Champagne Grand Année 1979 $40 (12/16/85) **94**

Key to Symbols

The scores reported here are the results of blind tastings conducted by our panel of senior editors. Wines that carry the initials below are results of individual tastings.

THE WINE SPECTATOR 100-POINT SCALE 95-100— Classic, a great wine; ***90-94***— Outstanding, superior character and style; ***80-89***—Good to very good, a wine with special qualities; ***70-79***—Average, drinkable wine that may have minor flaws; ***60-69***—Below average, drinkable but not recommended; ***50-59***—Poor, undrinkable, not recommended. "+"—With a score indicates a range; used primarily with barrel tastings to indicate a preliminary score.

SPECIAL DESIGNATIONS SS—Spectator Selection, CS—Cellar Selection, BB—Best Buy, ($NA)—Price not available, (NR)—Not released.

TASTER'S INITIALS (JG)—Jim Gordon, (HS)—Harvey Steiman, (JL)—James Laube, (JS)—James Suckling, (TM)—Thomas Matthews, (TR)—Terry Robards, (PM)—Per-Henrik Mansson, (BT)—Barrel Tasting (these wines were tasted blind from barrel samples), (CA-date)—*California's Great Cabernets* by James Laube, (CH-date)—*California's Great Chardonnays* by James Laube, (VP-date)—*Vintage Port* by James Suckling.

DATE TASTED Dates in parentheses represent the issue in which the rating was published.

BRICOUT
Brut Rosé Champagne NV $28 (12/31/88) **90**

DE CASTELLANE
Brut Rosé Champagne NV: Rich and full-bodied, with cherry and strawberry flavors of some depth and complexity, plus a hint of litchi flavor. Tart and rich at the same time, with a creamy, toasty finish. $29 (12/31/90) **88**

A. CHARBAUT
Brut Rosé Champagne NV $32 (12/31/88) **86**
Brut Rosé Champagne Certificate 1982: Pretty orange salmon color, with plenty of Pinot Noir, strawberry and cherry flavors that are beginning to show signs of complexity and nuance. Ready in 1993. $82 (12/31/89) **88**
Brut Rosé Champagne Certificate 1979 $80 (7/15/88) **89**

VEUVE CLICQUOT
Brut Rosé Champagne 1983: Focused strawberry and ginger cookie aromas and flavors hang nicely on a medium-weight, generous frame. Focused flavors turn broad and expansive on the finish. $47 (12/31/89) **86**
Brut Rosé Champagne 1979 $35 (7/16/86) **89**
Brut Rosé Champagne 1978 $60 (12/16/85) **82**

DELAMOTTE
Brut Rosé Champagne NV: A pretty wine. Copper in color, with subtle watermelon, strawberry and cherry aromas and flavors woven through a carpet of toast, mineral and floral flavors, all of which persist into the elegant finish. Not dramatic, but its subtlety is its charm. $38 (12/31/91) **88**
Rosé Champagne Spécial NV $28 (12/31/87) **91**

DEUTZ
Brut Rosé Champagne 1985: A rosé that's delicious and assertive. Firm, well structured and showing good Pinot Noir flavors of cherry and strawberry, with hints of spice for seasoning. $46 (12/31/90) **88**
Brut Rosé Champagne 1982 $35 (12/31/87) **86**
Brut Rosé Champagne 1981 $27 (12/16/85) **67**

DIEBOLT-VALLOIS
Brut Rosé Champagne Cramant NV $21 (10/31/87) **89**

ANDRE DRAPPIER
Brut Rosé Champagne Val des Demoiselles 1981 $23 (12/16/85) **72**

MICHEL GONET
Brut Rosé Champagne NV $21 (12/16/85) **89**

GOSSET
Brut Rosé Champagne 1982 $75 (12/31/88) **88**
Brut Rosé Champagne NV: A copper-colored rosé that has a complex array of flavors, including cherry, orange peel, strawberry, toast and spice. Velvety in texture, flavorful on the finish. Well-balanced and easy to drink. $37 (12/31/90) **85**

GEORGE GOULET
Brut Rosé Champagne 1982 $31 (7/31/88) **85**

ALFRED GRATIEN
Rosé Champagne NV $24 (10/01/85) **81**

CHARLES HEIDSIECK
Brut Rosé Champagne 1983: Pale, delicate and creamy in texture, with lots of toasty overtones to the modest berry and vanilla aromas and flavors. Smooth and flavorful without sacrificing delicacy. $49 (3/31/91) **89**
Brut Rosé Champagne 1982 $40 (12/31/88) **91**
Brut Rosé Champagne 1976 $25 (12/16/85) **61**

HEIDSIECK MONOPOLE
Brut Rosé Champagne 1983: Dry and cherryish, but lacks the richness and texture one expects from a rosé Champagne, leaving it coarse and simple. $40 (12/31/89) **75**
Brut Rosé Champagne 1982 $43 (12/31/88) **84**
Brut Rosé Champagne 1979 $27 (12/16/85) **72**

HENRIOT
Brut Rosé Champagne 1981 $28 (7/01/86) **93**

JACQUART
Brut Rosé Champagne NV $38 (12/31/88) **90**
Brut Rosé Champagne La Cuvée Renommée 1982 $74 (12/31/88) **88**

JACQUESSON
Brut Rosé Champagne Perfection NV $27 (12/31/88) **84**

KRUG
Brut Rosé Champagne NV: A real wine lover's Champagne. Pale in color, but very rich and full-bodied, accented by mature Pinor Noir character that goes deep and lasts long on the finish. $115 (12/31/89) **93**

LANSON
Brut Rosé Champagne 1982 $35 (12/31/88) **88**
Brut Rosé Champagne NV $24 (12/31/86) **73**

GUY LARMANDIER
Brut Rosé Champagne NV: Straightforward, clean and fruity at a reasonable price. Has a fresh pink color, with vibrant flavors of strawberry and cherry. Nearly dry. $20 (12/31/89) **84**

LAURENT-PERRIER
Brut Rosé Champagne Cuvée NV $28 (3/15/88) **92**
Brut Rosé Champagne Grand Siècle Cuvée Alexandra 1982: Pretty salmon color, with rich, toasty, elegant and complex spice, cherry, toast and nutmeg flavors that are broad and expansive, finishing with a cherry and spice aftertaste. $125 (12/31/89) **91**

LECHERE
Brut Rosé Champagne Première Cru Orient Express NV: Smooth and elegant, this pink wine has lovely grapefruit, spice, pear and smoke aromas and flavors wrapped neatly in a polished package, which lets the flavors shine through the long finish. 500 cases made. $54 (3/31/92) **90**

LECLERC-BRIANT
Brut Rosé Champagne NV $28 (3/15/88) **84**

MOET & CHANDON
Brut Rosé Champagne Impériale 1986: Tart and clean, with a cherry edge to the crisp flavors. Dry and a bit rough in texture, but charming and agreeable. Drinkable now. $43 (3/31/92) **83**
Brut Rosé Champagne Impériale 1983: Very smooth and silky, with delicate, subtle cherry, vanilla and spice aromas and flavors and a round texture. $40 (12/31/89) **88**
Brut Rosé Champagne Impériale 1982 $36 (4/15/88) **90**
Brut Rosé Champagne Impériale 1978 $55 (12/16/85) **70**

G.H. MUMM
Brut Rosé Champagne Cordon Rosé 1985: A colorful wine, both literally and in the flavor department, with hints of walnut, toast, orange peel, cherry and earth. A bit tart on the finish. $45 (1/31/92) **86**
Brut Rosé Champagne Cordon Rosé 1983: Earthy, tart and tangy, with lime-tinged cherry aromas

and flavors and earthy overtones that keep it from being delicious; but essentially it's correct and drinkable. $30 (12/31/89) **81**

Brut Rosé Champagne Cordon Rosé 1982 $30 (12/31/88) **83**

OUDINOT

Brut Rosé Champagne 1983: Floral cherry and strawberry aromas and flavors are especially appealing in this simple, elegant wine. The fruit and toast balance neatly for easy sipping. $25 (12/31/89) **88**

DOM PERIGNON

Brut Rosé Champagne 1978 Rel: $89 Cur: $200 (10/15/86) **90**

Brut Rosé Champagne 1975 Rel: $85 Cur: $290 (12/16/85) **93**

PERRIER-JOUET

Brut Rosé Champagne Fleur de Champagne 1985: Distinctive for its mature, smoke and earth notes that complement the spicy cherry and Pinot Noir flavors that are crisp, rich and deep. Flavors linger on the finish. Ready now to 1993. Rel: $70 Cur: $77 (12/31/89) **88**

Brut Rosé Champagne Fleur de Champagne 1982 Rel: $57 Cur: $70 (11/15/87) **89**

Brut Rosé Champagne Fleur de Champagne 1978 Rel: $55 Cur: $100 (12/16/85) **90**

JOSEPH PERRIER

Brut Rosé Champagne Cuvée Royale NV: Tight and tart, with elegant black cherry and cola notes that are crisp and refreshing, but it could use a little more flavor and finesse. Perhaps with time it will gain those attributes; it's pretty but one-dimensional. Drink now to 1993. $40 (12/31/90) **86**

PHILIPPONNAT

Brut Rosé Champagne NV $26 (12/16/85) **72**

Brut Rosé Champagne Royale Réserve NV $38 (12/31/88) **89**

PIPER-HEIDSIECK

Brut Rosé Champagne 1982 $38 (12/31/88) **84**

POMMERY

Brut Rosé Champagne NV $27 (12/16/85) **86**

LOUIS ROEDERER

Brut Rosé Champagne NV $37 (12/16/85) **79**

Brut Rosé Champagne Cristal 1979 $87 (12/16/85) **69**

POL ROGER

Brut Rosé Champagne 1985: A pale copper color and modest bread-dough aromas and flavors characterize this crisp, modestly intense bubbly. A lively wine that has some grace and elegance. Finishes with a touch of cherry. $62 (1/31/92) **89**

Rosé Champagne 1982 $50 (12/31/88) **80**

Rosé Champagne 1979 $41 (12/16/85) **88**

Rosé Champagne 1975 Rel: $33 Cur: $95 (12/16/85) **67**

DOM RUINART

Brut Rosé Champagne 1979 Rel: $55 Cur: $80 (9/30/88) **92**

Brut Rosé Champagne 1978 Rel: $40 Cur: $52 (9/30/86) **91**

Brut Rosé Champagne 1976 Rel: $35 Cur: $60 (12/16/85) **61**

MARIE STUART

Brut Rosé Champagne NV $23 (12/31/87) **80**

TAILLEVENT

Brut Rosé Champagne Phantom of the Opera NV: A pale-colored rosé that's also light in flavor. Wears a delicate mask of nutmeg, vanilla and cherry flavors. $32 (12/31/89) **82**

Rosé Champagne Grande Réserve NV: Rich and creamy, with fresh strawberry, cranberry, cherry and spice notes and a vanilla edge on the finish. Dances lightly on the palate, with a smooth, soft texture and a lingering finish. Drink now. $56 (11/15/91) **88**

TAITTINGER

Brut Rosé Champagne Comtes de Champagne 1985: A full-flavored, dry rosé with bracing acidity, great Pinot Noir flavors and a clean, crisp finish. Its red-wine flavor and slightly rough texture would make it a better choice with dinner rather than before. $110 (5/15/92) **88**

Brut Rosé Champagne Comtes de Champagne 1982: Rich, complex and delicate, pretty to look at, and even better to sip. The fruit is fresh and enticing with spicy cherry, Pinot Noir, nutmeg and spice flavors, all wrapped up in a pretty package. Long satisfying aftertaste. Drink now or in 1993. Rel: $100 Cur: $120 (12/31/89) **92**

Brut Rosé Champagne Comtes de Champagne 1981 Rel: $88 Cur: $100 (4/15/88) **94**

Brut Rosé Champagne Comtes de Champagne 1976 Rel: $70 Cur: $112 (12/16/85) **90**

DE VENOGE

Rosé Champagne Crémant NV $26 (12/31/88) **88**

GEORGES VESSELLE

Brut Rosé Champagne de Noirs NV $30 (12/16/85) **53**

Other Champagne

BEAUMET

Brut Blanc de Noirs Champagne 1985 $30 (12/31/90) **90**

Brut Blanc de Noirs Champagne 1983: Firm, crisp and elegant, a flavorful wine centered around lemon and toast aromas and flavors, sharply focused, long and lively. White pepper and apple flavors are particularly appealing. A classy wine. $30 (12/31/89) **89**

CHARLES DE CAZANOVE

Champagne Stradivarius 1985: Tart, crisp and lemony, with intense grapefruit and vanilla flavors. It's balanced, but lean. Can be enjoyed now or cellared through 1994. 2,000 cases made. $48 (12/31/91) **85**

A. CHARBAUT

Extra Dry Champagne NV $22 (12/31/88) **87**

DEHOURS

Demi-Sec Champagne NV: An off-dry style of non-vintage with vanilla, praline and strawberry flavors and a fruity finish. $30 (12/31/91) **84**

H. GERMAINE

Blanc de Blancs Crémant Champagne 1983 $24 (12/31/90) **89**

Blanc de Blancs Crémant Champagne 1982 $53 (5/31/87) **77**

GEORGE GOULET

Blanc de Blancs Crémant Champagne 1982 $30 (7/31/88) **86**

HEIDSIECK MONOPOLE

Extra Dry Champagne NV $35 (12/31/88) **86**

JACQUART

Extra Dry Champagne NV $23 (12/31/88) **89**

LANSON

Extra Dry Champagne Ivory Label NV $19 (12/31/88) **86**

Extra Dry Champagne White Label NV $19 (12/31/88) **70**

MOET & CHANDON

Extra Dry Champagne White Star NV: Has that salty, nutty something in the aroma that distinguishes real Champagne, following through with mature, complex flavors of dried fruit, spice and vanilla. Soft, a bit sweet and mature. $33 (5/15/92) **85**

G.H. MUMM

Extra Dry Champagne NV: Nice aperitif with fun, slightly sweet fruit flavors and a light almond finish. $20 (12/31/91) **84**

Extra Dry Champagne Cordon Vert NV: Smooth and sweet, but not syrupy, with a honey and caramel edge to the modest apple and spice flavors. A simple wine, with plenty of flavor and a balanced finish. $31 (1/31/92) **86**

BRUNO PAILLARD

Blanc de Blancs Crémant Champagne NV $36 (12/31/90) **85**

PIPER-HEIDSIECK

Extra Dry Champagne NV: A straightforward, fruity Champagne with lots of cherry and strawberry flavors and a crisp finish. $24 (12/31/91) **85**

MARIE STUART

Extra Dry Champagne NV $19 (12/31/87) **74**

Loire Red

CLOS DE L'ABBAYE

Bourgueil 1986: Velvety and fruity, with good concentration of appealing plum and currant aromas and flavors and moderate tannins on release; drinkable now. $16 (8/31/89) **86**

CHATEAU DE LA GRILLE

Chinon 1987: Soft and generous, with more than a hint of leather to go with the core of berry flavor. Drink soon. $18 (8/31/91) **77**

LOGIS DE LA GIRAUDIERE

Anjou Rouge de Cépage Cabernet 1989: Ripe and flavorful, with lots of generous black cherry and smoke aromas and flavors. Rustic in style, but its liveliness makes it appealing for current drinking. $8.50 (8/31/91) **80**

DOMAINE HENRY PELLE

Menetou-Salon Morogues 1987: Lean, herbal and austere, with pungent grassy herbal aromas, bracing acidity and impressive intensity. Real personality here. $11 (7/15/89) **85**

PREYS

Touraine Côte Cuvée Prestige 1989: Light in texture, with ripe currant flavor and a strong undercurrent of gaminess. Not as pleasant as it could be. Drinkable now. $9 (1/31/92) **75**

Loire White/*Muscadet de Sèvre et Maine*

DOMAINE DE L'ALOUETTE

Muscadet de Sèvre et Maine Sur Lie 1989: Very lean and austere, with strong earth, mineral and slightly leesy aromas and flavors. Not for all tastes. $7 (11/30/90) **74**

DOMAINE BARRE

Muscadet de Sèvre et Maine 1990: Very crisp, lean and bracing, as a Muscadet should be. The lemon and green apple flavors are light, but refreshing. $9.50 (9/30/91) **83**

ANDRE-MICHEL BREGEON

Muscadet de Sèvre et Maine Sur Lie 1988: Light, tart and lemony in flavor, with a dry, crisp feel and a hint of pear to help the minerallike character. $6.75 (11/15/90) **77**

CLOS DE BEAUREGARD

Muscadet de Sèvre et Maine Sur Lie 1988: Steely, lean and crisp, with tart, bracing acidity and sharply focused flavors that echo lemon, lime and crisp pear. Excellent value for pairing with oysters. Drink now. $6.75 (4/15/90) BB **84**

LES FRERES COUILLAUD

Muscadet de Sèvre et Maine Château de la Ragotière Sur Lie 1987: Light and lean, with ripe apple and spice aromas and flavors that make it somewhat pleasant and easy to drink. $10 (7/15/89) **77**

LOUIS METAIREAU

Muscadet de Sèvre et Maine Sur Lie Carte Noire 1989: Crisp, lively and light, with modest lemon and mineral flavors giving it substance. Clean and easy to drink. $13 (9/30/91) **80**

Muscadet de Sèvre et Maine Sur Lie Carte Noire 1988: A gentle, spicy style of Muscadet that's light on the palate, but steely enough in the backbone to carry the delicate ginger and mineral flavors through the finish. Drink it soon. $8 (11/30/90) BB **85**

Muscadet de Sèvre et Maine Sur Lie Carte Noire 1986: A crisp, pleasant wine with some decent depth. Lemony and nicely rounded. What you expect from a good Muscadet. $8.75 (2/28/89) **80**

Muscadet de Sèvre et Maine Sur Lie Cuvée One 1989: Very tart and lively, with green apple flavors and a crisp finish. Fine for washing down raw oysters. $18 (9/30/91) **82**

Muscadet de Sèvre et Maine Sur Lie Cuvée One 1987: Light and pleasantly earthy, with distinctive minerallike aromas and flavors, finishing with a tang of lemony acidity. $11 (7/15/89) **81**

DOMAINE DE LA QUILLA

Muscadet de Sèvre et Maine Sur Lie 1989: With its silky texture, vivid grapefruit, almond and floral aromas and flavors and taut backbone of acidity, this is a very dry, perfect oyster or aperitif wine—as Muscadet should be. Drink it soon, while it's fresh. 2,400 cases made. $7 (11/30/90) BB **88**

CHATEAU DE LA RAGOTIERE

Muscadet de Sèvre et Maine Sur Lie 1990: Crisp, flavorful and snappy on the palate, with slightly earthy apple and pine aromas and flavors. $14.50 (6/15/91) **84**

Muscadet de Sèvre et Maine Sur Lie 1988: Tart, lean and correct, with lemon, lime and tart citrus flavors of moderate depth and good intensity, but the finish gets watery. Drink now. $10 (4/15/90) **78**

Pouilly-Fumé

FRANCIS BLANCHET

Pouilly-Fumé Vieilles Vignes 1990: Crisp and fruity, with distinctive earth, juniper, peach and lemon aromas and flavors. Needs time to soften, perhaps until 1993. $13 (9/30/91) **85**

HENRI BOURGEOIS

Pouilly-Fumé Le Demoiselle de Bourgeois 1990: An earthy style, with strong dill pickle and juniper aromas and flavors that persist on the palate. Unusual, but should be fine with fried or sauteed fish. $20 (9/30/91) **84**

JEAN-CLAUDE CHATELAIN

Pouilly-Fumé Domaine des Chailloux 1989: Fresh and fruity, with lots of pear, almond and grapefruit aromas and flavors, plus a nice floral, vanilla touch on the finish. Drinkable now. $18 (3/31/91) **87**

Pouilly-Fumé Domaine des Chailloux 1988: Beautifully crisp and straightforward, this is fruity and well balanced, with clean, fresh grapefruit and citrus flavors, and a ripe, full finish. Would go great with fish. $17.50 (9/15/90) **87**

PAUL FIGEAT

Pouilly-Fumé 1989: An earthy style, with strong gamy aromas and flavors that detract from the modest lemon and spice notes. Not our style. 400 cases made. $20 (11/15/91) **74**

Pouilly-Fumé 1988: Tart, clean, fresh and lively, with well-defined lemon, pear, earth and melon flavors that are elegant and smooth, finishing with fine length and crisp acidity. Drink now. $14 (4/15/90) **88**

DOMAINE DENIS GAUDRY
Pouilly-Fumé Côteaux du Petit Boisgibault 1989: Crisp and lively, with well-focused lemon, pear and vanilla aromas and flavors and a nice touch of herbs. Balanced and fresh on the finish. Drinkable now. $15 (3/31/91) **85**

JEAN-CLAUDE GUYOT
Pouilly-Fumé Les Loges 1988: Crisp, lemony and fresh, with modest pear and honey overtones. A straightforward wine, with appealing flavors. Drinkable now. $11 (3/31/91) **84**

PASCAL JOLIVET
Pouilly-Fumé Cuvée Pascal Jolivet 1987: Spicy, rich and exotic, with pleasant menthol and mint flavors. Ripe and full-bodied, with well-balanced astrigency and a fruity finish. Drink now. $29 (9/15/90) **88**

DE LADOUCETTE
Pouilly-Fumé 1989: Light, tart and flavorful, with an odd jalapeño pepper note that we like, but others may find too odd. Distinctive and ready to drink. $22 (4/30/91) **86**
Pouilly-Fumé Baron de L 1988: Ripe apricot, butter and toast aromas and flavors are held in check by a medium-weight structure that keeps everything in proportion. Has a sense of freshness to balance the buttery creaminess on the long finish. Drinkable now. $49 (5/31/91) **88**
Pouilly-Fumé Baron de L 1985: Flinty, vaguely oysterlike aromas and flavors lend sophistication to this elegant, balanced yet intense and flavorful wine. Distinctive as its wide-lipped bottle. $40 (7/15/89) **90**
Pouilly-Fumé La Ladoucette 1988: A simple wine, with earthy aromas giving way to apple and citrus flavors. It's crisp and well balanced and has a tart finish. $18 (9/15/90) **82**

DOMAINE J.-M. MASSON-BLONDELET
Pouilly-Fumé Les Angelots 1989: Fresh, flinty and smoky aromas and flavors add a nice earthiness to the basic grapefruit and lemon notes in this balanced wine. Hints at almond on the finish. $20 (3/31/91) **84**
Pouilly-Fumé Les Bascoins 1989: Has lots of fruit complexity in a light, lively package, showing a lovely balance of grapefruit, peach and apple aromas and flavors tinged by a touch of herbs. An elegant wine that's drinkable now, but has the balance and style to develop with cellaring until 1993 or '94. $20 (3/31/91) **90**

ROGER MINET
Pouilly-Fumé Cuvée Spécial Vieilles Vignes 1989: Crisp and citrusy, with generous grapefruit and vanilla aromas and flavors that open on the finish. Stays tart and lively throughout. Tasty now, but should keep improving through 1993 or '94. $18 (9/30/91) **88**

F. TINEL-BLONDELET
Pouilly-Fumé 1987: A nicely balanced, unpretentious and accessible wine. Herbal, tropical aromas and spicy flavors give way to a tart, slightly bitter finish. $12 (2/28/89) **78**
Pouilly-Fumé L'Arret Buffatte 1987: Flavorful and attractive, this Pouilly-Fumé displays lovely smokiness and rich, classic Sauvignon Blanc flavors. Nicely structured, with a long, smooth finish. $15 (2/28/89) **86**

SANCERRE

DOMAINE DES BAUMARD
Sancerre 1990: Fresh and lively, with complex apple, spice and melon flavors. Dry and plump, with flavors that keep developing. Ready to drink now. $17 (3/31/92) **88**

HENRI BOURGEOIS
Sancerre Les Baronnes 1990: Crisp and fruity, with pretty grapefruit, pear and lemon aromas and flavors that keep livening up the finish. Spicy, fresh ginger notes add a nice touch. Drinkable now. $18 (9/30/91) **87**
Sancerre Etienne Henri 1989: Tart and herbal, with a lean texture and bright lemon and green pear aromas and flavors. A crisp, refreshing wine, with zippy flavors. Drinkable now. $30 (9/30/91) **83**
Sancerre Le MD de Bourgeois 1990: Crisp and focused, with lovely pear, apple and herb aromas and flavors that persist into a long, lively finish. The marvelous fruit and structure makes this delicious now, but it should develop through 1993 or '94. 3,300 cases made. $22.50 (9/30/91) **90**

CHERRIER PERE
Sancerre Domaine des Chasseignes 1989: Dry and pungently aromatic, with a strong core of grapefruit and lemon flavors. Herbal and toasty around the edges, this lively wine has plenty of character and flavor. Drinkable now. $16 (3/31/91) **86**

COMTE LAFOND
Sancerre 1988: Herbal, floral, toasty and austere, with more mineral than fruit flavors, but hints of peach and lemon peek through on the finish. Probably best to cellar until 1993 to soften the edges. $16 (11/15/90) **84**
Sancerre Omina Pro Petri Sede 1989: Not as pungent as some Sancerre wines, but it has wonderful grapefruit and pear aromas and flavors delicately shaded by herb, grass and other typical Sancerre characteristics. A very well-made wine that should keep developing through at least 1993. $21 (4/30/91) **88**

PAUL COTAT
Sancerre Chavignol Les Culs de Beaujeu 1989: Rich and ripe, with full-bodied honey, pear and herbal notes that are deep and satisfying. Finishes with honeyed notes and a touch of spice. A balanced wine to drink now. $22 (2/28/91) **85**
Sancerre Chavignol Les Culs de Beaujeu 1988: Tart, lean and smoky, this wine is clean, crisp and well balanced, with simple grapefruit and pear flavors. Drink now. $15 (4/15/90) **77**
Sancerre Chavignol La Grande Côte 1989: Intense and concentrated, with rich, ripe pear, lemon, peach and spice flavors framed by subtle vanilla notes. Full-bodied and a bit coarse, but still very well made. May benefit from a year or two in the cellar. Drink now. $25 (2/28/91) **86**
Sancerre Chavignol La Grande Côte 1988: Intense and very tart, with sharply defined flavors and hints of smoke, lemon, herb and spice that are quite attractive. $18 (4/15/90) **85**
Sancerre Chavignol Réserve des Monts Damnés 1989: Has floral, perfumed aromas, with spicy Muscat notes and a coarse, biting texture. Has plenty of flavor and not much finesse, but there's enough richness to add depth to the flavors. Drink now. $19 (2/28/91) **82**

ETIENNE HENRI
Sancerre 1988: A bizarre lemon-lime edge makes this difficult to warm up to. It's very tart, earthy and a bit funky, but some may enjoy the extreme flavors. Drink now. $35 (2/28/91) **75**

PASCAL JOLIVET
Sancerre 1988: Crisp grapefruit and green apple flavors dominate this lean wine, but don't be put off by the herbaceous aromas. This is a real thirst-quencher on a warm day. $15.50 (9/15/90) **84**
Sancerre Domaine du Colombier 1988: Grapefruit flavors are overwhelmed by an assertive herbaceousness in this extreme style, with huge flavors following through to a finish accented by mint and floral notes. $18 (9/15/90) **82**

DOMAINE LAPORTE
Sancerre Domaine du Rochoy 1988: Tart, lean and leafy with hints of lemon and lime flavors. Average quality. Drink now. $16 (4/15/90) **76**
Sancerre Domaine du Rochoy 1987: Lean but elegant. The wine's stony, grassy, lemony flavors grow on you. It ends with a refreshing, tangy finish. $14 (2/28/89) **85**

PROSPER MAUFOUX
Sancerre 1989: Crisp and tangy, with lively herbal, pineapple and grapefruit aromas and flavors that persist on the finish. Seems a bit sulfury now, but should be fine after 1993 or '94. $19 (11/15/91) **78**
Sancerre 1988: An earthy, gamy style that could use a shade more fruit and vitality. The tart grapefruit flavors seem a bit muted. Drink now. $15 (4/15/90) **76**

DOMAINE ALPHONSE MELLOT
Sancerre 1987: $16 (3/31/91) **68**

JEAN PAUL PICARD
Sancerre 1989: Pungent aromas and flavors lean toward an herbal, grassy character, typical of Sauvignon Blanc, the varietal of Sancerre, and the crisp texture and apple flavors echo on the finish. Not for everyone, but definitely has personality. Drinkable now. $14.50 (4/30/91) **82**

HIPPOLYTE REVERDY
Sancerre Les Perriers 1987: Rich and delicious. The appealing tropical fruit and smoky aromas and flavors make this a lovely wine to drink. A textbook Sancerre, with a long finish. $13 (2/28/89) **88**

DOMAINE JEAN-MAX ROGER
Sancerre Le Chêne Marchand 1988: The beautiful, crisp citrus and apple flavors come together and linger on the finish. It's full-bodied and fairly rich, with good balance and slightly herbaceous aromas. $17.50 (9/15/90) **85**

SAVENNIÈRES

DOMAINE DES BAUMARD
Savennières 1988: Hard, firm and tart, with intense grapefruit and lemon flavors that may need a year or two to soften. Plenty of acidity carries the flavor. Drink now. $8.75 (4/15/90) **78**
Savennières Clos du Papillon 1988: Lean and floral with tart, firm grapefruit flavors that are correct and attractive, although the finish tapers off. $9.50 (4/15/90) **85**
Savennières Clos de St.-Yves 1981: Mature and ready to drink with earth, honey, spice and citrus notes that are complex and refreshing. Flavors stay with you on the aftertaste. $18 (3/31/92) **87**
Savennières Trie Spéciale 1990: Complex and lively, with tiers of mineral, herb, citrus and apple flavor. Finishes a bit earthy. Ready now. $23 (3/31/92) **82**

A. JOLY
Savennières Clos de la Coulée de Serrant 1987 $36 (2/15/89) (TM) **86**
Savennières Clos de la Coulée de Serrant 1986 $38 (7/15/89) **87**
Savennières Clos de la Coulée de Serrant 1982 ($NA) (2/15/89) (TM) **87**
Savennières Clos de la Coulée de Serrant 1976 ($NA) (2/15/89) (TM) **93**

N. JOLY
Savennières Clos de la Coulée de Serrant 1989: Distinctive, unusually ripe and complex, offering loads of apricot, pineapple and almost plummy aromas and flavors that just sail on and on through the long finish. Not steely and austere, like Savennières, but almost silky and honeyed. Tempting now, but who knows how good it can become by 1993 to '95. $33 (11/30/90) **91**

PIERRE & YVES SOULEZ
Savennières Château de Chamboureau 1986: A well-made, nicely structured wine, with honey, spice and grassy aromas and flavors and a rounded, attractive finish. $12 (2/28/89) **83**
Savennières Clos du Papillon 1989: Ripe, focused and more than a little sweet, with pleasant lemon custard, mineral and pineapple aromas and flavors. Tastes more like a Vouvray than a dry Savennières, but it's a fine sipper. $22.50 (9/30/91) **85**
Savennières Clos du Papillon 1986: Sweet and quite attractive. The ripe peach flavor is balanced by the wine's crisp acidity and clean flavor. Has a long, appealing finish. $15 (2/28/89) **84**
Savennières Roche aux Moines Château de Chamboureau 1986: Crisp, fruity and slightly funky. Grassy aromas and flavors dominate this decent but ordinary wine. $19 (2/28/89) **77**

OTHER LOIRE WHITE

DOMAINE DES BAUMARD
Côteaux du Layon 1990: Sweet, fruity and spicy, with lively pear, caramel and nutmeg aromas and flavors, echoing orange on the finish. Reminds us of a lighter form of Beaumes de Venise. Drinkable now. $20 (3/31/92) **87**
Côteaux du Layon Clos de Ste.-Catherine 1988: Sweet, with rich, elegant, ripe, almost sugary pear, lemon and lime flavors. Well balanced, with lively acidity. Easy to drink now. $10.50 (4/15/90) **81**
Quarts de Chaume 1990: Sweet and spicy, with honeyed, buttery orange and pear aromas and flavors, hinting at caramel on the finish. A pleasant wine to drink now. $45 (3/31/92) **89**
Quarts de Chaume 1988: Off-dry style, earthy but intriguing with peach, nectarine and oil flavors that are complex, but may not appeal to everyone. Drink now. $20 (4/15/90) **82**

MARC BREDIF
Vouvray 1988: Lively, fruity and delicately sweet, with focused green apple and honey flavors and a hint of mineral on the palette. Balanced and relatively complex. Worth cellaring until 1993 or '94, but it's appealing already. $11 (4/30/91) **87**

CHAMPALOU
Vouvray 1990: A fresh-tasting, sweet Vouvray, with ample flavors of apple, orange and vanilla. Should be fine as an aperitif, with cheeses or with not-so-sweet desserts. Drink now through 1993. $13 (9/30/91) **84**

DOMAINE CHAVET
Menetou-Salon 1987: Fresh and lively, with crisply defined, somewhat grassy aromas and flavors, well balanced, turning slightly appley on the finish. $9.50 (7/15/89) **84**

DOMAINE DU CLOS NAUDIN
Vouvray Demi-Sec 1989: Lovely honey and sage aromas and flavors add plenty of interest to this beautifully balanced, slightly sweet wine. Drinkable now, but cellaring through 1993 couldn't hurt. $19.50 (3/31/91) **88**
Vouvray Sec 1989: Light and delicate, with very pretty melon and vanilla aromas and flavors. Pleasantly soft and hinting at honey on the finish. $17 (3/31/91) **83**

ROBERT MICHELE
Vouvray Les Trois Fils 1989: Tastes better than it smells, with aromas that recall a wet basement, but the flavors are sweet, appley and rather delicate, hinting at minerals on the finish. Not for everyone. $9 (4/30/91) **77**

Key to Symbols

The scores reported here are the results of blind tastings conducted by our panel of senior editors. Wines that carry the initials below are results of individual tastings.

THE WINE SPECTATOR 100-POINT SCALE ***95-100***—Classic, a great wine; ***90-94***—Outstanding, superior character and style; ***80-89***—Good to very good, a wine with special qualities; ***70-79***—Average, drinkable wine that may have minor flaws; ***60-69***—Below average, drinkable but not recommended; ***50-59***—Poor, undrinkable, not recommended. "+"—With a score indicates a range; used primarily with barrel tastings to indicate a preliminary score.

SPECIAL DESIGNATIONS SS—Spectator Selection, CS—Cellar Selection, BB—Best Buy, ($NA)—Price not available, (NR)—Not released.

TASTER'S INITIALS (JG)—Jim Gordon, (HS)—Harvey Steiman, (JL)—James Laube, (JS)—James Suckling, (TM)—Thomas Matthews, (TR)—Terry Robards, (PM)—Per-Henrik Mansson, (BT)—Barrel Tasting (these wines were tasted blind from barrel samples), (CA-date)—*California's Great Cabernets* by James Laube, (CH-date)—*California's Great Chardonnays* by James Laube, (VP-date)—*Vintage Port* by James Suckling.

DATE TASTED Dates in parentheses represent the issue in which the rating was published.

PATRIARCHE
Vin de Pays du Jardin de la France Chardonnay Patriarche 1989: A smooth but modest Chardonnay, with light almond and pear flavors. Clean, correct and unassuming. $7 (8/31/91) **78**

DOMAINE LE PEU DE LA MORIETTE
Vouvray 1989: Strikingly fruity and grassy, with rich, concentrated flavors of apple, custard and vanilla. Off-dry, but balanced, with remarkably lively, complex flavors that hint at grapefruit and honey on the finish. Drinkable now, but should improve through 1993 or '94. 5,000 cases made. $12 (4/30/91) **90**
Vouvray 1987: Flavorful but heavy-handed, with tons of pineapple flavor. Sweet and drinkable, but lacking the fresh, lively characteristics one might expect from a Vouvray. $10 (2/28/89) **69**

PIERRE & YVES SOULEZ
Quarts de Chaume L'Amandier 1988: Honey, peach and earth aromas and flavors give this a lot of the character of a good Barsac, but it's not quite as sweet. Hints of pear and spice on the finish are tasty. Drinkable now; should only get funkier as it ages. $28 (11/30/90) **84**

J. TOUCHAIS
Anjou Moulin Doué La Fontaine 1979: Fully mature and earthy in flavor, with ripe pear and apple notes lingering on the finish. Round and smooth in texture, full-bodied and well balanced with acidity. $28 (11/15/91) **90**

RHÔNE RED/*CHÂTEAUNEUF-DU-PAPE*

PIERRE ANDRE
Châteauneuf-du-Pape 1988: A power-packed wine in need of aging. Concentrated and full-bodied, with spice, tobacco and earth aromas and ripe plum, chocolate and black pepper flavors. Full and Port-like on the finish. Drink in 1994 to '96. Three other bottles tasted "off." $23 (3/31/91) **84**

PERE ANSELME
Châteauneuf-du-Pape 1986: Big and fat, but lacks charm and refinement. Extremely thick and oily, with jam and prune aromas and flavors, rustic tannins and a long finish. Try in 1993 to '96. $14 (10/15/91) **84**
Châteauneuf-du-Pape 1985: A silky-textured wine, with an alluring, earthy character. Medium-bodied, with smoke, berry and light barnyardy aromas leading to earth, berry and meat flavors. Slightly dry on the finish. $14 (10/15/91) **86**
Châteauneuf-du-Pape 1983: Still needs time, but shows very impressive, youthful fruit and vanilla, ripe plum and cherry aromas. Full-bodied, but tightly structured, with plenty of tannins and a long, focused finish. Try in 1993 to '96. Rel: $12 Cur: $23 (10/15/91) **89**
Châteauneuf-du-Pape 1981 $25 (10/15/91) **88**
Châteauneuf-du-Pape Clos Bimard 1989: Slightly one-dimensional, but shows decent fruit. The gamy berry aromas and flavors have a smoky character. Has silky tannins. Try now or in 1993. (NR) (10/15/91) **84**
Châteauneuf-du-Pape Cuvée Prestige Clos Bimard 1988: Tight and firm; needs time. Full-bodied, with enticing cherry, blackberry and slightly earthy aromas, currant, herb and earth flavors and lots of tannins. One to cellar; try in 1994 to '96. $20 (10/15/91) **88**
Châteauneuf-du-Pape La Fiole 1984 $12 (10/31/87) **88**
Châteauneuf-du-Pape La Fiole Grand Cuvée 1984 $13 (10/31/87) **74**
Châteauneuf-du-Pape La Fiole du Pape NV: Tastes mature and enticing. Ready to drink, with smooth tannins, plenty of coffee, spice and almost caramellike flavors. $14 (9/30/89) **86**
Châteauneuf-du-Pape La Fiole du Pape Uno Bono Fiolo NV $13 (1/31/88) **82**

DOMAINE LUCIEN BARROT
Châteauneuf-du-Pape 1989: Not as concentrated as some, but very well balanced. Perfumed raw meat and earth aromas lead to smoky, peppery flavors. Medium-bodied, with full tannins and a long, peppery finish. Try in 1993 or '94. $20 (10/15/91) **88**
Châteauneuf-du-Pape 1988: Silky and delicious, with lovely balance. Has black pepper and cherry aromas and spicy, toasty berry flavors. Medium-bodied, with medium-fine tannins. Try now through 1994. $18 (10/15/91) **87**
Châteauneuf-du-Pape 1986: Another beautiful wine, with wonderful fruit and texture. Offers truffle, thyme and berry aromas, similarly rich flavors, very firm tannins and a finely focused, fruity finish. Better in 1993 or '94. $18 (10/15/91) **89**
Châteauneuf-du-Pape 1981 $16 (9/30/87) **87**

BARTON & GUESTIER
Châteauneuf-du-Pape 1983 $11 (9/30/87) **74**

CHATEAU DE BEAUCASTEL
Châteauneuf-du-Pape 1989: Perhaps the greatest Beaucastel ever produced. This has the class and structure of a great vintage of Mouton-Rothschild. Inky color, with intense aromas of herbs, plum, game and spice; full-bodied, with an explosion of fruit and an iron backbone. Try in 2000. $35 (10/15/91) CS **97**
Châteauneuf-du-Pape 1988: Elegant and understated, with lovely fruit and structure. Has an excellent deep color, with focused black cherry and refined spice aromas, a full body of refined tannins and spice and berry flavors. Needs time to develop; try in 1993 to '95. $28 (10/15/91) **90**
Châteauneuf-du-Pape 1987: Has ripe, clean plum and berry flavors in a rounded, softly tannic texture. Leather and nutmeg aromas and a lingering, soft and spicy finish give it extra complexity. Rel: $17 Cur: $20 (9/30/89) **86**
Châteauneuf-du-Pape 1986 Rel: $25 Cur: $30 (10/15/91) **91**
Châteauneuf-du-Pape 1985 Rel: $16 Cur: $37 (10/15/91) **91**
Châteauneuf-du-Pape 1984 Rel: $12 Cur: $23 (11/30/89) (HS) **89**
Châteauneuf-du-Pape 1983 Rel: $17 Cur: $35 (10/15/91) **90**
Châteauneuf-du-Pape 1982 $30 (11/30/89) (HS) **92**
Châteauneuf-du-Pape 1981 $47 (10/15/91) **96**
Châteauneuf-du-Pape 1980 $30 (11/30/89) (HS) **83**

DOMAINE DE BEAURENARD
Châteauneuf-du-Pape 1989: Pretty and seductive, with lovely plum and berry aromas. Full- to medium-bodied, with pretty fruit flavors and a silky mouth-feel. Try now through 1994. $21 (10/15/91) **86**
Châteauneuf-du-Pape 1988: Very claretlike, with fine tannins and a tight structure. Full-bodied, but very tight and closed in, with cassis and cherry aromas, cassis flavors and ultrafine tannins. Try in 1993 to '95. $20 (10/15/91) **89**
Châteauneuf-du-Pape 1986: A sophisticated wine, with understated fruit and tannins. Enticing aromas of thyme, berry and cherry lead to classy fruit flavors. Full-bodied, with full, silky tannins and a long finish. Try in 1995 to '98. $24 (10/15/91) **88**
Châteauneuf-du-Pape 1985 Rel: $16 Cur: $20 (10/15/91) **87**
Châteauneuf-du-Pape 1983 $20 (10/15/91) **87**
Châteauneuf-du-Pape 1982 $9 (4/01/85) BB **85**
Châteauneuf-du-Pape 1981 $20 (10/15/91) **88**

BICHOT
Châteauneuf-du-Pape 1988: This big, rich, tannic style has intense ripe cherry and spice flavors that are a bit one-dimensional now, but the flavors should broaden with time. Best now to 1995. $13 (9/30/90) **84**
Châteauneuf-du-Pape 1987: Spicy, cedary aromas and flavors make this immediately appealing, although firm tannins will need until 1993 or '94 to soften. A touch of gaminess is pleasant now. $10 (3/15/90) **82**
Châteauneuf-du-Pape 1986 $9 (11/30/88) **86**
Châteauneuf-du-Pape 1985 $12 (11/15/87) **86**

HENRI BOIRON
Châteauneuf-du-Pape 1983 $11 (8/31/86) **79**
Châteauneuf-du-Pape Les Relagnes 1984 $13 (11/15/87) **76**

DOMAINE DU BOIS DAUPHIN
Châteauneuf-du-Pape 1983 $12 (11/15/87) **62**

JEAN CLAUDE BOISSET
Châteauneuf-du-Pape 1986 $12 (11/30/88) **80**

HENRI BONNEAU
Châteauneuf-du-Pape Réserve des Celestins 1986: A very distinctive wine, earthy, ripe and decadent, matching every touch of concentrated plummy, jammy fruit with barky, herbal overtones. Not for everyone. $19 (5/31/89) **82**

BOSQUET DES PAPES
Châteauneuf-du-Pape 1989: A linear wine, with very pretty fruit, this has black cherry and chocolate aromas and ripe chocolate and spice flavors. Full-bodied, with medium-firm tannins and a meaty-flavored finish. Try in 1993 to '95. $18 (10/15/91) **85**
Châteauneuf-du-Pape 1988: A balanced, easy wine, with good fruit. Quite light, offering beautiful cherry, berry and earth aromas, refined fruit flavors and a long finish. Medium-bodied, with elegant tannins. Drink now. $18 (10/15/91) **83**
Châteauneuf-du-Pape 1986: Big and concentrated, showing excellent concentration of meaty, earthy berry flavors. Full-bodied, with full tannins. Still needs time; better in 1993 to '95. $18 (10/15/91) **90**
Châteauneuf-du-Pape 1985 $18 (10/15/91) **86**
Châteauneuf-du-Pape 1984 $17 (11/15/87) **91**
Châteauneuf-du-Pape 1983 $20 (10/15/91) **86**
Châteauneuf-du-Pape 1981 $30 (10/15/91) **93**

BOUCHARD PERE & FILS
Châteauneuf-du-Pape 1985 $11 (9/30/87) **82**

BOURGOGNE ST.-VINCENT
Châteauneuf-du-Pape 1983 $8.50 (7/16/85) **81**

DOMAINE DU PERE CABOCHE
Châteauneuf-du-Pape 1989: Very fat and jammy. Has raisin, pine and plum aromas, full-bodied, jammy plum flavors and a smoky finish. Try in 1993 or '94. $20 (10/15/91) **84**
Châteauneuf-du-Pape 1988: Has an impressive texture of velvety tannins and fruit, but it's slightly one-dimensional. Full-bodied, with deep raspberry and black cherry aromas and very ripe, rich fruit flavor. Thick and rich, with a velvety texture. Try in 1993 to '95. $20 (10/15/91) **87**
Châteauneuf-du-Pape 1986: Quite evolved, with a soft structure and very earthy flavors. Has plum and earth aromas and similar flavors, well-integrated tannins and a medium finish. Drink now. $20 (10/15/91) **81**
Châteauneuf-du-Pape 1985 $20 (10/15/91) **85**
Châteauneuf-du-Pape 1983 $18 (10/15/91) **77**
Châteauneuf-du-Pape 1981 $30 (10/15/91) **87**

CHATEAU CABRIERES
Châteauneuf-du-Pape 1988: Tough, tannic and austere, lacking the bright fruit and generosity one associates with this appellation. A full-bodied, powerful wine, with more toast and black cherry flavor emerging on the finish. Give it until 1993 to scrape away the tannic veneer. $17 (11/30/90) **82**

DOMAINE DU CAILLOU
Châteauneuf-du-Pape 1988: A delicious cherry-raspberry flavor runs deep in this lively, well-balanced wine. Nicely proportioned and long lasting on the palate, with hints of spice and vanilla for complexity. Tempting now, but better in 1993 to '96. $22 (3/31/91) **86**

LES CAILLOUX
Châteauneuf-du-Pape 1989: An impressively well-crafted and subtle wine. Like Cheval Blanc; great finesse. Pure fruit. Grapey, raisiny and earthy on the nose and palate, with well-integrated tannins and a focused grapey, gamy finish. Try in 1994 to '96. 5,000 cases made. $19 (10/15/91) **93**
Châteauneuf-du-Pape 1988: It's more mature than some at this point, with delicious aromas and flavors. Offers basil, light tomato and berry aromas, full-bodied black pepper, spice, meat and berry flavors and silky tannins. Not one to lay away for long. $18 (10/15/91) **88**
Châteauneuf-du-Pape 1986: Round and fruity, with a pleasant earthy, barnyardy character. Has earthy cigar aromas and similar flavors, as well as a hint of tomato. Light finish. $18 (10/15/91) **79**
Châteauneuf-du-Pape 1985 $20 (10/15/91) **82**
Châteauneuf-du-Pape 1983 $25 (10/15/91) **88**
Châteauneuf-du-Pape 1981 $30 (10/15/91) **76**
Châteauneuf-du-Pape Sélection Reflets 1986: Broad and bursting with plum, spice and cherry aromas and flavors, it's a bit tannic, but the fruit persists and carries through on the finish beautifully. Drink now. $14 (5/31/89) **89**

LES CAVES ST.-PIERRE
Châteauneuf-du-Pape Clefs des Prelats 1988: Attractive for its cherry, earth, spice and leather flavors that are supple, generous and framed by smooth tannins. The flavors stay with you on the long, flavorful finish. Ready to drink now through 1995. $13 (1/31/91) **87**

CHANTE CIGALE
Châteauneuf-du-Pape 1989: Firm and moderately tannic, with very good, full-bodied pepper, earth and fruit flavors. Has black cherry, plum and prune aromas, very firm tannins and a peppery finish. Try in 1993 to '95. $14 (10/15/91) **84**
Châteauneuf-du-Pape 1988: A strong wine, with a fairly muscular structure and a good concentration of fruit. Smoky berry and bacon aromas lead to smoky black pepper, meat and cherry flavors. Full-bodied, with medium tannins. Better in 1993 to '96. $18 (10/15/91) **89**
Châteauneuf-du-Pape 1986: Well balanced, with a classy fruit-and-tannin structure. Has attractive chocolate, smoke and cherry aromas and similar flavors, as well as very silky tannins and a long finish. Try in 1993 to '95. $18 (10/15/91) **89**

DOMAINE CHANTE PERDRIX
Châteauneuf-du-Pape 1988: A straight-shooting wine that's plummy, spicy, ripe and focused. Has a slightly gamy quality, with cherry and blackberry flavors and hints of nutmeg and cinnamon hiding around the edge. Drink now through 1995. $17 (5/31/91) **82**

M. CHAPOUTIER
Châteauneuf-du-Pape La Bernardine 1989: A light style, with leather and plum flavors that turn dry and tannic. It's an austere wine that needs a year or so, but it's not a long ager. Drink soon with hearty food. $20 (8/31/91) **84**
Châteauneuf-du-Pape La Bernardine 1988: Despite a musty edge, there's a wall of cherry, plum and spice flavor that is intense, tart and lively. Finishes dry and woody. Drink now to 1994. Tasted twice. $17 (12/31/91) **81**
Châteauneuf-du-Pape La Bernardine 1985: The most appealing aspect is this wine's restraint, with its raspberry, plum and spice flavors coursing elegantly through to a long finish without excess weight. A lot of flavor for such a light-colored, light-bodied wine. Drinkable now. $25 (3/15/90) **89**
Châteauneuf-du-Pape La Bernardine 1983 Rel: $15 Cur: $26 (9/30/87) **89**

CLOS DU MONT-OLIVET
Châteauneuf-du-Pape 1989: An expressive wine, with an abundance of smoky raisin notes and a baked character. Has gamy black truffle and grape aromas in a full- to medium-bodied wine, with

peppery truffle and earth flavors, medium tannins and a medium finish. Quite drinkable. Try now to 1994. $29 (10/15/91) **85**
Châteauneuf-du-Pape 1988: Classy and savory, with plenty of character. Has lots of cassis, herb and berry aromas. Full-bodied, with cassis, earth and berry flavors, tight, integrated tannins and a fresh finish. Better in 1993 or '94. $19 (10/15/91) **88**
Châteauneuf-du-Pape 1986: A little dumb now, but should be better in a few years. Quite sophisticated, with beautiful cherry, chocolate and plum aromas, ripe cassis and berry flavors and firm tannins. Needs a little more time; try in 1993 or '94. $17 (10/15/91) **87**
Châteauneuf-du-Pape 1985 Rel: $15 Cur: $20 (10/15/91) **92**
Châteauneuf-du-Pape 1983 Rel: $14 Cur: $28 (10/15/91) **86**
Châteauneuf-du-Pape 1982 $12 (3/16/86) **91**
Châteauneuf-du-Pape 1981 $30 (10/15/91) **87**

CLOS DE L'ORATOIRE DES PAPES
Châteauneuf-du-Pape 1985 $10 (7/31/88) **87**

CLOS DES PAPES
Châteauneuf-du-Pape 1989: Gracious, delicious and fruity, with a good balance of freshness and tannins. Full-bodied, with strawberry, prune and licorice aromas and ripe berry, slight earth and black licorice flavors. Medium tannins and finish. Try now to 1994. $20 (10/15/91) **86**
Châteauneuf-du-Pape 1988: Not a wine for long-term aging, but elegant and delicious nonetheless. Has very fresh cherry and berry aromas and a nice balance of medium tannins and black pepper flavors. Full-bodied, with a long finish. $19 (10/15/91) **86**
Châteauneuf-du-Pape 1986: Evolving quickly. Rather advanced in color, with light leather and cherry aromas. Medium-bodied, offering light berry and cedar flavors and a light, almost metallic finish. Tasted twice. $18 (10/15/91) **74**
Châteauneuf-du-Pape 1985 $17 (10/15/91) **89**
Châteauneuf-du-Pape 1983 $25 (10/15/91) **88**
Châteauneuf-du-Pape 1981 $30 (10/15/91) **87**

JACQUES CORTENAY
Châteauneuf-du-Pape 1985 $8 (9/30/87) BB **85**

CUVEE DU BELVEDERE
Châteauneuf-du-Pape Le Boucou 1986: This wine offers some pretty cherry and spice flavors and a good dose of firm, lean tannins that bodes well for aging. Could be more generous on the palate. Drink now through 1996. $16 (1/31/89) **86**
Châteauneuf-du-Pape Le Boucou 1985 $18 (2/15/88) **93**
Châteauneuf-du-Pape Le Boucou 1983 $16 (11/15/87) **62**

DELAS
Châteauneuf-du-Pape 1985 $17 (10/31/87) **91**
Châteauneuf-du-Pape 1983: Barely holding on now, but still drinkable. Has smoky, barnyardy, stinky aromas, with leathery, earthy berry flavors and a dry finish. Drink now. $18 (10/15/91) **72**
Châteauneuf-du-Pape Cuvée de Haute Pierre 1989: Power and grace in a bottle, with ripe berry, cedar and spice aromas. Full- to medium-bodied, with an elegant structure of gamy berry flavors and silky tannins. Has a long finish. Try in 1995 to '97. $16 (10/15/91) **90**
Châteauneuf-du-Pape Cuvée de Haute Pierre 1988: Very elegant and refined, with fresh aromas of berries and wet earth. Medium-bodied, with wonderfully elegant berry and earth flavors, fine tannins and a silky finish. Try in 1993 to '96. $17 (10/15/91) **86**
Châteauneuf-du-Pape Cuvée de Haute Pierre 1986: A lovely, silky wine, with appetizing aromas and flavors. Offers herb, chocolate and spice aromas and a velvety texture of berry and leather flavors. Drink now, but it will improve with age. $20 (10/15/91) **86**
Châteauneuf-du-Pape Cuvée de Haute Pierre 1985 $20 (10/15/91) **86**

LUCIEN DESCHAUX
Châteauneuf-du-Pape Le Vieux Abbe 1987: Smooth and mouth-filling. A mature red wine, with pleasant tea and chocolate overtones to the submerged black cherry and berry flavors. Drinkable now. $10 (12/31/91) **82**

DOMAINE JEAN DEYDIER & FILS
Châteauneuf-du-Pape Les Clefs D'Or 1983 $16 (10/31/87) **78**

GEORGES DUBOEUF
Châteauneuf-du-Pape 1989: Tight, lean and crisp, with oaky currant, tea, cherry and spice flavors of modest proportions. Drinks well now, but has enough tannin to hold for another two to five years. Best around 1994. Tasted twice. $14 (5/31/92) **83**

DOMAINE DURIEU
Châteauneuf-du-Pape 1989: Not for long-term cellaring, but has very clean fruit and a pleasant structure. Very ripe, almost raisiny grape and berry aromas lead to full-bodied, firm, peppery fruit flavors, medium tannins and a lively finish. Try now or in 1993. $17 (10/15/91) **85**
Châteauneuf-du-Pape 1988: Fresh, fruity and ripe, with firm, medium tannins. Offers smoky cedar and cherry aromas and full-bodied black pepper and berry flavors. Medium on the finish. Try now to 1994. $16 (10/15/91) **86**
Châteauneuf-du-Pape 1986: The best of the '80s for this producer. Very classy and well structured, with excellent balance and fruit. This full-bodied wine has cherry and fresh herb aromas, classy cassis, herb and berry flavors, fine, integrated tannins and a long, firm finish. Drink now through 1994. $16 (10/15/91) **89**
Châteauneuf-du-Pape 1985 $14 (10/15/91) **79**
Châteauneuf-du-Pape 1984 $13 (11/15/87) **78**
Châteauneuf-du-Pape 1983 $14 (10/15/91) **82**
Châteauneuf-du-Pape 1981 $25 (10/15/91) **90**

CHATEAU DES FINES ROCHES
Châteauneuf-du-Pape 1989: A medium-weight red, with decidedly gamy overtones to the modest red cherry flavor. Hints at pepper and leather on the finish, but gently. Drinkable now. Tasted twice, with consistent notes. $20 (5/31/92) **81**
Châteauneuf-du-Pape 1986: Well proportioned, elegant and balanced, with spicy cherry, leather and earth tones that are complex and enticing without being heavy. Dry and peppery on the finish. Drink now to 1994. $14 (9/30/90) **85**
Châteauneuf-du-Pape 1985 $12 (10/31/87) **80**

Key to Symbols

The scores reported here are the results of blind tastings conducted by our panel of senior editors. Wines that carry the initials below are results of individual tastings.

THE WINE SPECTATOR 100-POINT SCALE ***95-100***—Classic, a great wine; ***90-94***—Outstanding, superior character and style; ***80-89***—Good to very good, a wine with special qualities; ***70-79***—Average, drinkable wine that may have minor flaws; ***60-69***—Below average, drinkable but not recommended; ***50-59***—Poor, undrinkable, not recommended. "+"—With a score indicates a range; used primarily with barrel tastings to indicate a preliminary score.

SPECIAL DESIGNATIONS SS—Spectator Selection, CS—Cellar Selection, BB—Best Buy, ($NA)—Price not available, (NR)—Not released.

TASTER'S INITIALS (JG)—Jim Gordon, (HS)—Harvey Steiman, (JL)—James Laube, (JS)—James Suckling, (TM)—Thomas Matthews, (TR)—Terry Robards, (PM)—Per-Henrik Mansson, (BT)—Barrel Tasting (these wines were tasted blind from barrel samples), (CA-date)—*California's Great Cabernets* by James Laube, (CH-date)—*California's Great Chardonnays* by James Laube, (VP-date)—*Vintage Port* by James Suckling.

DATE TASTED Dates in parentheses represent the issue in which the rating was published.

Châteauneuf-du-Pape 1984 $12 (9/30/87) **89**

DOMAINE FONT DE MICHELLE
Châteauneuf-du-Pape 1989: A ripe, old style of wine. Slightly rustic, with raisin, baked bean and berry aromas. Full-bodied, with ripe raisin flavors, masses of tannins and a slightly dry finish. Try in 1993 to '95. $18 (10/15/91) **83**
Châteauneuf-du-Pape 1988: Silky and balanced, with delicious, elegant black cherry, berry and chocolate aromas and cherry and earth flavors. Medium-bodied, with silky tannins. Try now or in 1993. $21 (10/15/91) **86**
Châteauneuf-du-Pape 1986: Delicious and just about ready to drink, with new tanned leather, chocolate and berry aromas. Medium-bodied, with gamy berry flavors. Has a ripe sweetness and a velvety finish. Better in 1993 or '94. $20 (10/15/91) **89**
Châteauneuf-du-Pape 1985 Rel: $13 Cur: $20 (10/15/91) **84**
Châteauneuf-du-Pape 1983 $25 (10/15/91) **85**
Châteauneuf-du-Pape 1981 $20 (10/15/91) **88**

CHATEAU FORTIA
Châteauneuf-du-Pape 1983 Rel: $14 Cur: $24 (12/31/87) **87**
Châteauneuf-du-Pape Tête de Cru 1985: This earthy, gamy style has smoky cherry and plum flavors that are ultimately simple, but pleasant. Drink now to 1995. Tasted twice. $22 (5/31/92) **81**

DOMAINE LOU FREJAU
Châteauneuf-du-Pape 1988: Spicy and full of cherry flavor, but the overall impact is earthy, cedary and tobaccolike. Very enjoyable, but won't be everyone's style. Drink now through 1995. $17 (3/31/91) **82**
Châteauneuf-du-Pape 1986: There's an elegant concentration of fresh, ripe, tannic fruit but the raspberry, cherry, earth and spice flavors offer depth and complexity. The finish is coarse and tannic, but balanced. Drink in 1994 to '98. $15.50 (1/31/89) **87**

CHATEAU DE LA GARDINE
Châteauneuf-du-Pape 1989: The Latour of Châteauneuf-du-Pape. A giant wine, with great reserve and restraint. Inky color with a red rim. Overflowing with plum and pepper aromas and flavors, it has a super-firm structure and masses of fruit and tannins. A wine for the patient; try in 1995 to '98, but it will improve for decades. $25 (10/15/91) **95**
Châteauneuf-du-Pape 1988: Delicate and fresh, with modestly firm tannins. Has black cherry and berry aromas, plum, berry and cherry flavors and a fresh finish. Medium in body and tannins. Drink now to 1993. $33 (10/15/91) **85**
Châteauneuf-du-Pape 1986: Built for aging, it has an iron backbone of tannins. Ripe and tight, showing blackberry, spice and wet earth aromas, full-bodied fruit flavors and firm tannins. Try in 1995 to '98. Rel: $17 Cur: $23 (10/15/91) **90**
Châteauneuf-du-Pape 1985 Rel: $15 Cur: $18 (12/31/87) **87**
Châteauneuf-du-Pape 1984 $15 (12/31/87) **78**
Châteauneuf-du-Pape 1983 Rel: $12 Cur: $20 (10/15/91) **89**
Châteauneuf-du-Pape 1981 $30 (10/15/91) **86**
Châteauneuf-du-Pape Cuvée des Générations 1985: Tastes more like a great Bordeaux, but still maintains that wonderful Châteauneuf character. Surprisingly youthful. Has a deep, inky color and fresh rosemary, spice and berry aromas that follow through on the palate. Shows intense fruit on the finish, with silky tannins. Start drinking 1995. $25 (10/15/91) **92**

DOMAINE DU GRAND TINEL
Châteauneuf-du-Pape 1989: Softer than some, but extremely delicious and generous, with aromatic grape and plum aromas and plush fruit on the palate. Has smoky, spicy chocolate flavors and a licorice finish. Try in 1993 to '95. $15 (10/15/91) **88**
Châteauneuf-du-Pape 1988: An alluring, aromatic wine, with slightly barnyardy, roasted meat and berry aromas. Full-bodied, with well-integrated, medium tannins and fresh fruit flavors. Slightly short at the moment; better in 1993 or '94. $17 (10/15/91) **87**
Châteauneuf-du-Pape 1986: Not a heavyweight, but it's delicious to drink. Pretty violet and plum aromas open to a silky palate of black cherry, earth and berry. Has medium tannins and a fresh finish. Perfect now. $20 (10/15/91) **86**
Châteauneuf-du-Pape 1985 $23 (10/15/91) **75**
Châteauneuf-du-Pape 1983 $25 (10/15/91) **87**
Châteauneuf-du-Pape 1981 $27 (10/15/91) **89**

DOMAINE ALAIN GRANGEON
Châteauneuf-du-Pape 1986: A bit flat and stripped, but there's some black cherry and spicy flavors that come through. Simple and decent but unexciting. $16 (1/31/89) **77**

E. GUIGAL
Châteauneuf-du-Pape 1988: Rough and tannic, but so powerful and generous that it's almost sure to develop beautifully with cellaring until 1993 to '95. The ripe black cherry and black pepper flavors just pop out of the glass, hinting at plum and berry on the finish, with overtones of cedar and chocolate. 5,000 cases made. Rel: $20 Cur: $23 (11/30/90) **90**
Châteauneuf-du-Pape 1986: Ripe, broad and appealing, with flavors that lean toward the gamy end of the spectrum, complex and persistent. Chocolate and raspberry flavors linger on the long finish. Drinkable now, perhaps better around 1993 or '94. $19 (3/15/90) **87**
Châteauneuf-du-Pape 1985 Rel: $18 Cur: $24 (10/15/88) **87**
Châteauneuf-du-Pape 1983 Rel: $18 Cur: $30 (11/30/87) **87**

DOMAINE DU HAUT DES TERRES BLANCHES
Châteauneuf-du-Pape 1989: Firm and tannic, but well within bounds, offering enough plum and pepper flavors to keep it sailing into the finish. Best after 1993. $16 (5/31/92) **84**
Châteauneuf-du-Pape 1988: Light in color, with lots of nutmeg and other spice notes to go with the modest strawberry flavors, echoing pepper and mineral on the long finish. Should require until 1997 to 2000 to soften the tannins. $16 (7/15/91) **85**
Châteauneuf-du-Pape Réserve du Vatican 1983 $12 (9/30/87) **88**

PAUL JABOULET AINE
Châteauneuf-du-Pape 1983: Evolved and ready to serve; perfect with game dishes. Has chestnut, toast and berry aromas and licorice, berry and cedar flavors. Full-bodied, with medium tannins and a smoky, slightly dry finish. Drink now. Rel: $10 Cur: $20 (10/15/91) **85**
Châteauneuf-du-Pape Les Cèdres 1989: Rich and ripe, with lots of berry and black cherry aromas and flavors that make quite an entrance on the palate and just keep going and going, echoing anise and fruit on the solid finish. Approachable now, but the tannins will be smoother by 1994 or '95. $23 (7/15/91) **91**
Châteauneuf-du-Pape Les Cèdres 1988: A broad wine, with good fruit and tannins. The black cherry, herb and spice aromas lead to full-bodied, rich pepper and spice flavors. Has full tannins and a long finish. Try in 1993 to '95. $23 (10/15/91) **86**
Châteauneuf-du-Pape Les Cèdres 1986: Smooth and delectable, with gamy, slightly cheesy berry aromas. Full-bodied, with creamy berry and game flavors and very silky tannins. Drink now, but it will improve with age. $20 (10/15/91) **87**
Châteauneuf-du-Pape Les Cèdres 1985 Rel: $20 Cur: $23 (10/15/91) **88**
Châteauneuf-du-Pape Les Cèdres 1981 $30 (10/15/91) **86**

DOMAINE FRANCOIS LAGET
Châteauneuf-du-Pape 1985 $14 (9/30/87) **71**
Châteauneuf-du-Pape 1984 $14 (12/31/87) **76**
Châteauneuf-du-Pape 1983 $12 (9/30/87) **89**

LANCON PERE & FILS
Châteauneuf-du-Pape Domaine de la Solitude 1983 $14 (12/31/87) **58**

DOMAINE DE MARCOUX
Châteauneuf-du-Pape 1988: Light and drinkable. Medium-red color, medium-bodied, with fresh, perfumed cherry aromas, cherry and berry flavors, light tannins and a light finish. $24 (10/15/91) **82**
Châteauneuf-du-Pape 1986: Rather light and simple, with dusty cherry and spice aromas, fresh peppery flavors and a light, almost dry finish. Drink now. $20 (10/15/91) **84**
Châteauneuf-du-Pape 1983: At its peak, with beautiful aromas and flavors. Has very attractive cherry, herb and spice aromas, with a hint of leather, elegant fruit and earth flavors and a soft, round mouth-feel. Medium-bodied. Drink now. $25 (10/15/91) **87**
Châteauneuf-du-Pape 1981 $30 (10/15/91) **85**
Châteauneuf-du-Pape Vieilles Vignes 1989: A huge wine. Inky color, with chocolate-covered cherry aromas and bitter chocolate and cassis flavors. Full-bodied and amazingly concentrated, like crushed grapes. Still like a barrel sample; drink next century. $30 (10/15/91) **95**

CHATEAU MAUCOIL
Châteauneuf-du-Pape Réserve Suzeraine 1985 $13 (11/15/87) **86**

PROSPER MAUFOUX
Châteauneuf-du-Pape 1988: Ripe and generous on the nose, but earthy and tough on the palate, especially on the finish, where it gets a little bitter. Distinctively Châteauneuf, but not immediately appealing. Try in 1994. $16 (5/31/92) **81**

DOMAINE DE MONPERTUIS
Châteauneuf-du-Pape 1987: A lively style, it has pretty raspberry and peppery notes that are austere and tight, with hints of herbs and spice. A true-to-form Châteauneuf-du-Pape that's quite satisfying. Drink now to 1994. $14 (6/30/90) **83**
Châteauneuf-du-Pape 1986: Has pungent herbal, peppery aromas and soft, rich flavors of chocolate and leather. Full tannins give it texture, but also tend to dry it out. $18 (9/30/89) **73**

CHATEAU MONT-REDON
Châteauneuf-du-Pape 1989: Classy, powerful and dense, with beautiful structure. Deep dark purple color, with ripe fruit, plum and vanilla aromas; full-bodied, with focused plum and violet flavors, full, super-fine tannins and a long finish. Try 1994 to '97. 1,000 cases made. $21 (10/15/91) **91**
Châteauneuf-du-Pape 1988: A delicious, early drinking red. Ruby-magenta color, with very fresh cherry and banana aromas, very ripe berry and cherry flavors and light tannins. Medium-bodied, with a round mouth-feel. Rel: $21 Cur: $25 (10/15/91) **83**
Châteauneuf-du-Pape 1986: A velvety wine, with good structure. Full-bodied, with fresh cherry and toasted chestnut aromas, juicy berry and cherry flavors and firm, velvety tannins. Needs time; try in 1993 to '96. $17 (10/15/91) **85**
Châteauneuf-du-Pape 1985 Rel: $12 Cur: $25 (10/15/91) **90**
Châteauneuf-du-Pape 1984 $11 (9/30/87) **92**
Châteauneuf-du-Pape 1983 $25 (10/15/91) **88**
Châteauneuf-du-Pape 1981 $30 (10/15/91) **90**

LOUIS MOUSSET
Châteauneuf-du-Pape 1982 $6 (12/16/84) **75**

CHATEAU DE LA NERTHE
Châteauneuf-du-Pape 1989: Attractively crafted, with appealing fruit and balance. Has jam, berry and redwood aromas and lots of jam, berry and strawberry flavors. Full-bodied, with velvety tannins and a medium finish. Has a touch of new wood. Try in 1994 to '97. $25 (10/15/91) **87**
Châteauneuf-du-Pape 1988: Classy, with a restrained, refined structure. Has lovely balance and fine tannins, with ripe berry and chestnut aromas and cherry, berry and spice flavors. Needs time; try in 1993 to '96. $25 (10/15/91) **88**
Châteauneuf-du-Pape 1986: Quite lush and rich, with a velvety mouth-feel. Offers cherry, black cherry and chocolate aromas and flavors, a hint of chestnut and firm tannins. Better in 1993 or '94. $18 (10/15/91) **87**
Châteauneuf-du-Pape 1985 $17 (10/15/91) **86**
Châteauneuf-du-Pape 1983 $25 (10/15/91) **88**
Châteauneuf-du-Pape 1981 $30 (10/15/91) **94**
Châteauneuf-du-Pape Cuvée des Cadettes 1989: A stylish wine, with an impressive amount of new wood. Full-bodied, with classy plum and earth aromas, vanilla, earth and chocolate flavors and an oaky finish. Try in 1994 to '96. $30 (10/15/91) **88**
Châteauneuf-du-Pape Cuvée des Cadettes 1988: A superbly well-crafted wine, with excellent character and structure. More elegant than most '89s, showing mint, herb, rosemary and berry aromas and spicy vanilla, berry, cherry and herb flavors. Full-bodied, with super-integrated tannins and a long, flavorful finish. Try in 1994 to '96. $30 (10/15/91) **89**

DOMAINE DU PEGAU
Châteauneuf-du-Pape Cuvée Réserve 1988: Ripe and jammy, offering intense pepper, plum, spice and earth notes that are supple and elegant, with a fine interplay of flavors. Long and hot on the finish and not too tannic, but plenty of fruit comes through on the aftertaste. Drinkable now, but probably at its peak around 1994. $17 (11/15/91) **88**

DU PELOUX
Châteauneuf-du-Pape 1986: A rather mature wine for an '86, with ripe cherry and plum aromas and flavors, peppery overtones and a smooth, velvety texture. Drink now. $12 (4/15/89) **85**

PIGNAN
Châteauneuf-du-Pape Réserve 1988: Light and delicious; still shows its class. Medium-red color, with light cherry and vegetable aromas, black pepper and berry flavors, light tannins and a light finish. Drink now. Rel: $25 Cur: $30 (10/15/91) **82**
Châteauneuf-du-Pape Réserve 1986: A wine for everyday drinking, with light, fresh cherry and berry aromas, light, fruity pepper flavors and silky tannins. Drink now. $23 (10/15/91) **83**
Châteauneuf-du-Pape Réserve 1985 Rel: $14 Cur: $38 (8/31/87) SS **95**
Châteauneuf-du-Pape Réserve 1983 $38 (10/15/91) **85**
Châteauneuf-du-Pape Réserve 1981 $35 (10/15/91) **94**
Châteauneuf-du-Pape Réserve 1980 Rel: $13 Cur: $30 (10/15/86) **87**

CHATEAU RAYAS
Châteauneuf-du-Pape Réserve 1988: Classy and well structured, not giving much at the moment. Has fresh, fruity cherry and blackberry aromas, an intensely fruity palate, full, firm tannins and a closed finish. Needs time; try in 1993 to '95. $71 (10/15/91) **90**
Châteauneuf-du-Pape Réserve 1986: Firm and concentrated, with generous pepper- and spice-tinged cherry and berry aromas and flavors, turning a bit austere on the finish. A classic style, if a bit on the earthy side. $48 (12/15/89) **88**
Châteauneuf-du-Pape Réserve 1985 $41 (7/31/88) **93**
Châteauneuf-du-Pape Réserve 1983 Rel: $30 Cur: $43 (10/15/91) **89**

DOMAINE DE LA ROQUETTE
Châteauneuf-du-Pape 1989: A little tough, but should evolve into a very good wine. Elegantly complex aromas of spice, cedar and plum lead to full-bodied, superbly focused cedar, berry and earth flavors. Has a super-long finish. Try in 1994 to '96. $17 (10/15/91) **86**
Châteauneuf-du-Pape 1988: A solid wine, with interesting barnyardy, fruity characteristics. Has perfumed aromas of plums and cherries. Full- to medium-bodied, with firm tannins and a medium finish. Better in 1993 or '94. $17 (10/15/91) **86**
Châteauneuf-du-Pape 1986: Somewhat evolved in character, but very delicious now, with cedar, tobacco and berry aromas and berry and earth flavors. Full-bodied, with a velvety mouth-feel. $18 (10/15/91) **85**
Châteauneuf-du-Pape 1985 $13 (7/31/88) SS **90**

DOMAINE ROGER SABON & FILS
Châteauneuf-du-Pape 1988: A ripe, flavorful wine, with layers of cherry, toast, spice, pepper and subtle oak shadings. It's intense and complex, but the tannins are soft and round. It's drinkable now, but has the intensity and depth to cellar. Drink now to 1997. $20 (9/30/90) **88**
Châteauneuf-du-Pape Cuvée Prestige 1988: Broad and fruity, with ripe cherry flavor and hints of berry, chocolate, spice and leather. Has firm, slightly dry tannins, but it's altogether balanced and offers a modest degree of complexity. Drink now to 1994. $23 (9/30/90) **85**
Châteauneuf-du-Pape Cuvée Réserve 1988: Big and full-bodied, with hard cherry and plum flavors and spicy, peppery seasoning. A rather blunt style; drink now or hold. $20 (9/30/90) **80**

DOMAINE DES SENECHAUX
Châteauneuf-du-Pape 1985 $17 (10/15/88) **85**

CHATEAU SIMIAN
Châteauneuf-du-Pape 1988: Earthy and spicy, with a lean core of plum and cherry flavors, echoing pepper and smoke notes. A bit tannic and alcoholic, but almost drinkable now. Best after 1993. 1,700 cases made. $20 (7/15/91) **86**

DOMAINE DE LA SOLITUDE
Châteauneuf-du-Pape 1989: Attractive for its ripe, fruity plum and leathery flavors and balance. Drinks well now, but has tannin to shed, so cellaring it until 1995 should make it more approachable. 1,000 cases made. $19 (5/31/92) **86**

CHATEAU ST.-ANDRE
Châteauneuf-du-Pape 1988: Sturdy and fruity, with a solid core of ripe berry, cassis and plum flavors framed by a modest tannic structure, firm balance and solid power. Hints of coffee and cedar on the finish add complexity. Drinkable now with a roast, but cellaring until 1993 to '95 shouldn't hurt. $16 (11/30/90) **87**

THORIN
Châteauneuf-du-Pape 1986 $13 (11/30/88) **87**

L. DE VALLOUIT
Châteauneuf-du-Pape 1989: Extremely earthy, with musty tobacco notes that overwhelm the modest plum and cherry flavors. A rugged wine that needs until 1995 to '97 to smooth out. $16 (12/31/91) **77**

CHATEAU DE VAUDIEU
Châteauneuf-du-Pape 1984 $13 (11/15/87) **72**

DOMAINE DE LA VIEILLE JULIENNE
Châteauneuf-du-Pape 1978 $20 (11/15/87) **67**
Châteauneuf-du-Pape 1972 $20 (11/15/87) **73**

LE VIEUX DONJON
Châteauneuf-du-Pape 1989: Slightly one-dimensional, but has a very pleasant grapey character, with extremely peppery, grapey aromas and flavors, velvety tannins and a grapey finish. Try in 1993 or '94. $17 (10/15/91) **85**
Châteauneuf-du-Pape 1988: Tightly knit, with firm tannins, this full-bodied wine has raspberry, raisin and light cedar aromas, plum and raisin flavors and a medium finish. Try in 1993 to '96. $16 (10/15/91) **85**
Châteauneuf-du-Pape 1986: This savory wine is overflowing with earthy, spicy flavors. Has plum and cherry aromas, lovely cherry, pepper and fruit flavors, well-integrated tannins and a flavorful finish. Better in 1993 to '96. $15 (10/15/91) **88**
Châteauneuf-du-Pape 1985 $16 (2/15/88) **79**
Châteauneuf-du-Pape 1984 $14 (10/31/87) **79**
Châteauneuf-du-Pape 1981 $30 (10/15/91) **89**

DOMAINE DU VIEUX LAZARET
Châteauneuf-du-Pape 1989: Slightly one-dimensional, with an earthy, meaty character. Medium red color, with vibrant raisin and spice aromas, fresh fruit, plum and smoke flavors and refreshing acidity. Medium-bodied. Try now to 1994. $16 (10/15/91) **85**
Châteauneuf-du-Pape 1986: Graceful and elegant, with rich, ripe raspberry, plum, cherry, earth and spicy flavors that are well defined and lively on the palate. Fine, well-balanced tannins lead to a delicate, subtle finish. Drink in 1993 to '96. $14 (1/31/89) **89**
Châteauneuf-du-Pape 1985: Wonderfully decadent, but losing a bit on the palate. Red color with a brick edge. Has attractive leather, spice, berry and earth aromas and gamy earth and berry flavors. Medium-bodied, turning slightly dry on the finish. Rel: $12 Cur: $20 (10/15/91) **82**

DOMAINE DU VIEUX TELEGRAPHE
Châteauneuf-du-Pape 1989: Closed in and not giving much now. Not quite as concentrated as we would have expected, but has a lovely balance and elegance in a medium-bodied style. Offers cedar, earth and plum aromas, rustic tannins and cedar, berry and earth flavors. Try in 1993 or '94. $24 (10/15/91) **87**
Châteauneuf-du-Pape 1988: A fresh, up-front style, with raisin and plum aromas and fresh flavors of black licorice and cherry. Has medium tannins and a black pepper finish. Slightly short. Better in 1993. Rel: $20 Cur: $23 (10/15/91) **85**
Châteauneuf-du-Pape 1987: This pleasant wine has correct and simple ripe cherry, leather and spice flavors and drying tannins, but it could use a little more velocity and concentration. Balanced to drink now or in 1993. $17 (9/30/90) **81**
Châteauneuf-du-Pape 1986 Rel: $17 Cur: $20 (10/15/91) **90**
Châteauneuf-du-Pape 1985 Rel: $17 Cur: $34 (10/15/91) **82**
Châteauneuf-du-Pape 1984 Rel: $12 Cur: $25 (9/30/87) **89**
Châteauneuf-du-Pape 1983 Rel: $17 Cur: $35 (10/15/91) **85**
Châteauneuf-du-Pape 1981 Rel: $35 Cur: $40 (10/15/91) **80**

CORNAS

GUY DE BARJAC
Cornas 1985 $17 (10/15/88) **81**

A. CLAPE
Cornas 1986: Generous fruit, with ripe plum and pepper flavors backed by firm tannins, but the structure's a bit soft and fleshy. The fruit flavors are pretty and the tannins are dry. Drink now to 1994. $22 (1/31/89) **88**
Cornas 1984 $12.50 (8/31/87) **78**

JEAN-LUC COLOMBO
Cornas Les Ruchets 1989: Rich and full-bodied, with generous black cherry and tobacco aromas and flavors, a smooth texture and well-camouflaged tannins. Soft enough to drink now with hearty food, but worthy of cellaring until 1995 or '96 to see what that can bring out. $45 (11/15/91) **89**
Cornas Les Ruchets 1988: A bit tough around the edges, but it offers plenty of rich cherry, chocolate, spice and pepper notes that have very good depth. The tannins are firm but rounded, and the fruit comes through on the finish. Drink in 1994. $45 (10/15/91) **87**
Cornas Les Ruchets 1987: Very firm and tannic, with a modest core of black cherry and spice flavors, but it doesn't have as much breadth and richness as you could want. Try in 1995. Tasted twice. $50 (11/15/91) **75**

MARCEL JUGE
Cornas 1986: Tart, lean and spicy, with cherry, earth and leathery notes that are austere and firm but build on the palate. Balanced with fine length. Drink now to 1994. Tasted twice. $23 (11/30/90) **83**
Cornas Cuvée C 1986 $25 (6/15/89) **85**
Cornas Cuvée S C 1986 $30 (6/15/89) **87**

JEAN LIONNET
Cornas 1987: A dense, delicious wine that's inky in color, with concentrated violet, blackberry and plum aromas and flavors that fill the mouth without excess tannin. Drinkable now, but there's enough tannin to indicate cellaring until 1993 to '95. 4,000 cases made. $23 (3/31/90) **90**
Cornas 1986: An earthy style, with lean cracked pepper and plum flavors that are long and full on the finish. Tannins suggest you give it some time to round out. Drink now and beyond. $23 (1/31/89) **87**
Cornas Cuvée Rochepertuis 1988: Has good, clean, well-defined tart cherry and currant notes and a firm texture, but it's ultimately simple. Well balanced, with a hint of spice on the finish. Best now to 1994. $28 (1/31/91) **83**

CAVE DE TAIN L'HERMITAGE
Cornas Michel Courtial 1986: Concentrated, intense, spicy and stylish, with black pepper-scented plum and cherry aromas, gaining some berry flavors on the finish. Tannic, with a sense of roundness from aging in small oak barrels. Delicious on release, better now. $11 (7/31/89) **89**

NOEL VERSET
Cornas 1987: Vibrant, rich and delicious, with exuberant violet, blueberry and plum aromas. But the flavors are not quite so generous or appealing, hinting at gaminess on the firm, slightly astringent finish. Needs cellaring until 1993 or '94. $23 (3/31/90) **88**
Cornas 1986: The cracked pepper and plum aromas are very pretty, but the palate is much leaner, and it finishes with plenty of tannin. Needs time to smooth out and grow into its flavors. Drink in 1994. $25 (1/31/89) **86**

J. VIDAL-FLEURY
Cornas 1988: Hard and tight, with intense, firm, black cherry flavors and spicy, leathery notes. Has plenty of concentration and flavor, with good length and depth. Drink now to 1994. $20 (1/31/91) **85**

CÔTE-RÔTIE

PERE ANSELME
Côte-Rôtie Tête de Cuvée 1982 $13 (10/15/87) **68**

PIERRE BARGE
Côte-Rôtie 1988: Hard and tight, with roasted coffee, cherry and plum notes that turn murky and tannic on the finish. Will never be a beauty, but it may be more accessible with time, once the tannins soften. Drink in 1994 and beyond. $42 (7/31/91) **84**

GUY BERNARD
Côte-Rôtie 1988: A strong smoky, roasted, vegetal character dominates, but if you like those flavors this wine's for you. It's balanced, firmly tannic and drying on the finish. Some may wish for more fruit. Drink 1991 to '94. Tasted twice. $30 (10/15/90) **78**

BERNARD BURGAUD
Côte-Rôtie 1989: Big, tough and concentrated, its ample plum and currant flavors fighting against a strong earthy, barnyardy, toasty oak component. Could develop into a wonderful wine, but isn't giving much up yet. Try in 1995. Tasted twice. $32 (1/31/92) **84**
Côte-Rôtie 1988: Has all the traditional flavors in abundance—currant, cherry, leather and game—wrapped in a firm, tannic package, but it's long and generous enough to be a good bet for developing until 1994 to '96. Very youthful in color and flavor. $40 (3/31/91) **87**
Côte-Rôtie 1987: Very powerful and intense, from its deep, inky purple color and pungent, leathery aromas to its thick, gamy, currant and cherry flavors and tannic finish. Not for the timid. Try in 1993. $29 (2/28/90) **85**
Côte-Rôtie 1986 $31 (1/31/89) **93**
Côte-Rôtie 1984 $22 (10/15/87) **90**
Côte-Rôtie 1983 $18 (5/01/86) **92**

M. CHAPOUTIER
Côte-Rôtie 1989: A big, earthy wine, with enough plum, pepper and butter notes to keep it in line. Fully tannic and rustic in its balance, but likable if this is your style. $30 (7/31/91) **86**
Côte-Rôtie 1988: A mild-mannered wine, with a firm texture and modest red cherry, black pepper and slightly gamy aromas and flavors. Approaching drinkability, but probably best after 1993. $27 (11/15/91) **84**

DOMAINE CLUSEL
Côte-Rôtie 1988: Bold black cherry, plum and blackberry flavors burst through on the palate and build on a solid support of firm, chewy tannins. Hints of black pepper on the finish suggest this will have excellent character after it ages through 1994 to '96. $36 (11/15/91) **87**

GILBERT CLUSEL
Côte-Rôtie La Viallière 1986: Brawny, powerful and oaky, with barely enough spicy black cherry aromas and flavors to compete with the slightly drying wood at this point. But it's still very tasty and full of the classic black pepper seasoning; it just needs to round out. Try it now. $23 (4/15/89) **85**

A. DERVIEUX-THAIZE
Côte-Rôtie Côte Blonde la Garde Cuvée Réserve 1988: Hard-edged, tannic and tight, with austere plum and currant flavors that are tightly reined in. Finish gets oaky too. Perhaps with time this wine will show more generosity. Hold until 1993. $42 (8/31/91) **79**

GEORGES DUBOEUF
Côte-Rôtie Domaine de la Rousse 1988: Tight and firm, with ripe currant, plum and roasted oak notes. Balanced and harmonious, with lively acidity and firm tannins. Best to cellar until 1994 or '95. $18 (7/31/91) **87**

PIERRE GAILLARD
Côte-Rôtie Côte Brune et Blonde 1989: Smooth, rich and balanced, with layers of currant, cherry and plum flavors that are framed by buttery, toasty oak. The flavors are long and lingering on the aftertaste. Hold until 1993. $28 (10/15/91) **89**
Côte-Rôtie Côte Brune et Blonde 1988: Ripe, round and generous, bursting with anise- and black-pepper tinged black cherry and plum flavors that are plush and long. Has enough tannin to carry it for years in the cellar, but it's so fruity you can drink it tonight with a grilled steak. Probably best in 1995 to 2005. $30 (11/30/90) **90**
Côte-Rôtie Côte Brune et Blonde 1987: Smooth and well balanced, with ripe fruit flavors, a touch of smoke, leafy, minty aromas and firm, full tannins. $24 (8/31/89) **82**

Key to Symbols

The scores reported here are the results of blind tastings conducted by our panel of senior editors. Wines that carry the initials below are results of individual tastings.

THE WINE SPECTATOR 100-POINT SCALE 95-100—Classic, a great wine; ***90-94***—Outstanding, superior character and style; ***80-89***—Good to very good, a wine with special qualities; ***70-79***—Average, drinkable wine that may have minor flaws; ***60-69***—Below average, drinkable but not recommended; ***50-59***—Poor, undrinkable, not recommended. "+"—With a score indicates a range; used primarily with barrel tastings to indicate a preliminary score.

SPECIAL DESIGNATIONS SS—Spectator Selection, CS—Cellar Selection, BB—Best Buy, (\$NA)—Price not available, (NR)—Not released.

TASTER'S INITIALS (JG)—Jim Gordon, (HS)—Harvey Steiman, (JL)—James Laube, (JS)—James Suckling, (TM)—Thomas Matthews, (TR)—Terry Robards, (PM)—Per-Henrik Mansson, (BT)—Barrel Tasting (these wines were tasted blind from barrel samples), (CA-date)—*California's Great Cabernets* by James Laube, (CH-date)—*California's Great Chardonnays* by James Laube, (VP-date)—*Vintage Port* by James Suckling.

DATE TASTED Dates in parentheses represent the issue in which the rating was published.

Côte-Rôtie Côte Brune et Blonde 1986 $25 (11/30/88) **86**

GENTAZ-DERVIEUX
Côte-Rôtie Côte Brune Cuvée Réserve 1987: Extremely barnyardy and dry, a style that's not for everyone. The finish gets very dry and tannic. Drink now. $40 (6/30/90) **73**

FRANCOIS GERARD
Côte-Rôtie 1988: A rustic style, with a healthy dose of animal aromas and flavors that are extremely leathery. Does have solid cherry flavor. Not for everyone. Try around 1996. $36 (7/31/91) **70**
Côte-Rôtie 1987: Has a tough shell and watery flavors, but also some decent fruit flavor, with hints of cherry and berry. Tannins dominate. Pleasant but unexciting. Drink now or in 1993. $30 (10/15/90) **77**

E. GUIGAL
Côte-Rôtie Côtes Brune et Blonde 1987 Rel: $25 Cur: $34 (1/31/91) **90**
Côte-Rôtie Côtes Brune et Blonde 1986: Well balanced and very appealing. Peppery in aroma and flavor, with supple texture, ripe raspberry and blueberry flavors and modest tannins to balance it out. Drink now through 1994. Rel: $28 Cur: $36 (2/28/90) **90**
Côte-Rôtie Côtes Brune et Blonde 1985: Full and generous, a peppery, spicy wine that's sweet with the scents of vanilla and black cherry. Long, silky and rich, with the structure and tannic bite to age. Should improve even more in the bottle. Drink in 1993 to 2000. Rel: $30 Cur: $34 (1/31/89) **92**
Côte-Rôtie Côtes Brune et Blonde 1984 Rel: $25 Cur: $28 (11/30/87) **83**
Côte-Rôtie Côtes Brune et Blonde 1983 Rel: $21 Cur: $34 (4/30/87) CS **92**
Côte-Rôtie Côtes Brune et Blonde 1982 $40 (3/15/90) (HS) **89**
Côte-Rôtie Côtes Brune et Blonde 1980 Rel: $13 Cur: $30 (9/16/84) **89**
Côte-Rôtie Côtes Brune et Blonde 1978 $83 (3/15/90) (HS) **95**
Côte-Rôtie Côtes Brune et Blonde 1976 $55 (3/15/90) (HS) **88**
Côte-Rôtie Côtes Brune et Blonde 1969 $100 (3/15/90) (HS) **93**
Côte-Rôtie Côtes Brune et Blonde 1966 $125 (3/15/90) (HS) **88**
Côte-Rôtie Côtes Brune et Blonde 1964 $100 (3/15/90) (HS) **92**
Côte-Rôtie Côtes Brune et Blonde 1962 $85 (3/15/90) (HS) **89**
Côte-Rôtie Côtes Brune et Blonde 1961 $100 (3/15/90) (HS) **82**
Côte-Rôtie La Landonne 1987: Very classy, jam-packed with coffee, cedar, plum and blackberry flavors and wrapped in a velvety smooth robe of cedary, spicy oak notes. Tempting now for its opulence, but should be cellared until at least 1995 for all the flavors to develop. 300 cases made. Rel: $125 Cur: $135 (7/31/91) CS **93**
Côte-Rôtie La Landonne 1986: Tight and tannic, but beautifully proportioned, with leather, currant, herb and mineral aromas and flavors wrapped in a hard-edged package that will take years to soften. Could try it in 1995, but probably best to wait until 2000. 250 cases made. Rel: $99 Cur: $135 (10/15/90) **91**
Côte-Rôtie La Landonne 1985 $350 (3/15/90) (HS) **90**
Côte-Rôtie La Landonne 1984 $100 (3/15/90) (HS) **86**
Côte-Rôtie La Landonne 1983 $290 (3/15/90) (HS) **94**
Côte-Rôtie La Landonne 1982 $180 (3/15/90) (HS) **90**
Côte-Rôtie La Landonne 1981 $150 (3/15/90) (HS) **82**
Côte-Rôtie La Landonne 1980 $150 (3/15/90) (HS) **84**
Côte-Rôtie La Landonne 1979 $195 (3/15/90) (HS) **91**
Côte-Rôtie La Landonne 1978 $430 (3/15/90) (HS) **95**
Côte-Rôtie La Mouline 1987: Enticingly accented by oak and full and rich in flavor, with everything in the right proportions. Ripe plum and black cherry notes are broadened by nutmeg, cedar and vanilla flavors, all bundled in an elegant, supple package. Enticing to drink now, but should be cellared until at least 1997 to show its best stuff. 300 cases made. Rel: $115 Cur: $125 (7/31/91) **92**
Côte-Rôtie La Mouline 1986: Warm, generous and packed with fruit flavor, this fleshy wine has broad black cherry, black pepper and mineral aromas and flavors that open up and extend on the finish. Almost drinkable now, but should benefit from cellaring until at least 1993 to soften the tannins. Rel: $99 Cur: $150 (10/15/90) **93**
Côte-Rôtie La Mouline 1985 $350 (3/15/90) (HS) **98**
Côte-Rôtie La Mouline 1983 $310 (3/15/90) (HS) **94**
Côte-Rôtie La Mouline 1982 $200 (3/15/90) (HS) **92**
Côte-Rôtie La Mouline 1981 $150 (3/15/90) (HS) **90**
Côte-Rôtie La Mouline 1979 $185 (3/15/90) (HS) **85**
Côte-Rôtie La Mouline 1978 $450 (3/15/90) (HS) **96**
Côte-Rôtie La Mouline 1977 $250 (3/15/90) (HS) **75**
Côte-Rôtie La Mouline 1976 $350 (3/15/90) (HS) **87**
Côte-Rôtie La Mouline 1975 $110 (3/15/90) (HS) **75**
Côte-Rôtie La Mouline 1974 $300 (3/15/90) (HS) **89**
Côte-Rôtie La Mouline 1973 $130 (3/15/90) (HS) **84**
Côte-Rôtie La Mouline 1971 $300 (3/15/90) (HS) **88**
Côte-Rôtie La Mouline 1970 $300 (3/15/90) (HS) **74**
Côte-Rôtie La Mouline 1969 $900 (3/15/90) (HS) **90**
Côte-Rôtie La Mouline 1968 $300 (3/15/90) (HS) **82**
Côte-Rôtie La Mouline 1967 $510 (3/15/90) (HS) **86**
Côte-Rôtie La Mouline 1966 $370 (3/15/90) (HS) **88**
Côte-Rôtie La Turque 1987: A stunning wine that's rich, ripe and round, with great depth of cherry, plum, leather, chocolate and spice flavors that persist into an explosive finish. Tannins are well integrated but present. Should continue to improve through 2000. 300 cases made. Rel: $145 Cur: $165 (7/31/91) **95**
Côte-Rôtie La Turque 1986: A concentrated, powerful, flavorful wine, just oozing with plum, berry and spice aromas and flavors that are long and sweet on the finish. There 's lots of complexity here already, but it's so tight that it could keep developing well into the next century. 250 cases made. Rel: $99 Cur: $350 (10/15/90) CS **95**
Côte-Rôtie La Turque 1985 $570 (3/15/90) (HS) **98**

BERNARD GUY
Côte-Rôtie 1987: Fine if you like this roasted style. It's pungently smoky and peppery on the nose and soft but tannic on the palate, with modest fruit underneath. The smoky flavor lingers on the finish. $25 (8/31/89) **87**
Côte-Rôtie 1986 $29 (9/30/88) **89**

PAUL JABOULET AINE
Côte-Rôtie Les Jumelles 1985 $35 (9/30/88) **93**

JOSEPH JAMET
Côte-Rôtie 1985: A powerful, beefy wine, with full-throated black cherry and black pepper aromas and flavors, intense and complex without being overly heavy. Not for the faint of heart, but it should be drinking beautifully now. $33 (4/15/89) **88**

JASMIN
Côte-Rôtie 1988: An elegant style that manages to combine its muscle with soft, polished edges. Has classic flavors of black pepper, cherry and earth, and the structure is firmly tannic without being heavy or bitter. Cellar at least until 1993 to '95. $32 (12/31/90) **89**
Côte-Rôtie 1987: Offers wonderful smoked bacon, spice, herb and raspberry aromas and flavors tightly wound together and framed by firm but not overpowering tannins. A complete and flavorful wine that keeps you coming back for more. Drink now to 1995. 900 cases made. $30 (6/30/90) **90**

MICHEL OGIER
Côte-Rôtie 1988: An aggressive wine, with wild berry flavors and an edge of burnt toast and black pepper that gives it quite a bite on the finish. Needs cellaring until 1995 or '96 to polish the roughness. $38 (11/15/91) **87**

ANDRE PASSAT
Côte-Rôtie 1985 $25 (10/15/87) **88**

R. ROSTAING
Côte-Rôtie Côte Blonde 1987: Loaded with ripe, rich raspberry, cherry and currant flavors that pick up a touch of mint and spice. Full-bodied, firmly tannic and hot on the finish. Best to cellar till 1993 to '95. $40 (6/30/90) **86**

LES CAVES ST.-PIERRE
Côte-Rôtie Marquis de Tournelles 1987: A straightforward style, with a solid core of ripe cherry and currant flavors firmly wrapped in tannins and hints of coffee, tea and spice. Balanced, but in need of cellaring until 1993 to '96. $23 (1/31/91) **84**

L. DE VALLOUIT
Côte-Rôtie 1989: A solid wine, with a concentrated beam of plum and currant flavors shaded by a touch of spice and earthiness. The tannins are well integrated, with a refreshingly tart, crisp edge. Finishes smooth and generous. Almost drinkable already, but best after 1993. $30 (1/31/92) **89**
Côte-Rôtie 1985 $20 (10/15/87) **75**

J. VIDAL-FLEURY
Côte-Rôtie Côte Blonde La Chatillonne 1984 $26 (10/31/87) **73**
Côte-Rôtie Côtes Brune et Blonde 1988: Deep, ripe, rich and intense with layers of currant, cherry, leather and spice, with smooth, supple tannins that are firm and structured, finishing with lots of oak and spice. Excellent length. Drink now to 1995. $30 (10/15/90) **88**
Côte-Rôtie Côtes Brune et Blonde 1985 $25 (3/15/90) (HS) **90**
Côte-Rôtie Côtes Brune et Blonde 1945 $175 (3/15/90) (HS) **85**
Côte-Rôtie Côtes Brune et Blonde 1934 $280 (3/15/90) (HS) **85**

Côtes du Rhône

CHATEAU D'AIGUEVILLE
Côtes du Rhône 1987: Earthy, almost stinky, but the structure is fine and it finishes clean. May have improved by now. $5 (1/31/89) **73**
Côtes du Rhône 1984 $4.50 (10/15/87) **68**

ALIGNE
Côtes du Rhône 1985 $6 (2/28/87) **74**

DOMAINE DE L'AMEILLAUD
Côtes du Rhône 1984 $4.50 (6/01/86) **72**

PERE ANSELME
Côtes du Rhône-Villages Marescal 1985 $5.25 (12/31/87) **75**
Côtes du Rhône-Villages Seguret 1986: Very tart and tangy, tannic enough to cover all but a peek at its sour cherry flavor. Short and undistinguished. $5.25 (5/15/89) **72**

DOMAINE LES AUSSELONS
Côtes du Rhône Vinsobres 1987: Simple red wine with some pleasantly earthy strawberry flavors that last on the finish. Drinkable now. $8 (6/30/90) **75**

G. BAROUX
Côtes du Rhône Château de Bourdines 1988: A straightforward wine, with the sort of tobacco, leather and cherry aromas and flavors you would expect. It's spicy, but a bit simple and not distinctive. Highly drinkable, however, through 1993. $8 (12/15/90) **79**

DOMAINE MICHEL BERNARD
Côtes du Rhône Domaine de la Serrière 1987: A light style, leaning toward leather in the aroma and cherry on the palate. Not particularly dense, but balanced and drinkable. $7 (3/15/91) **77**

BICHOT
Côtes du Rhône 1987 $3.50 (11/15/88) **72**
Côtes du Rhône 1985 $5.75 (12/15/87) **75**
Côtes du Rhône Château d'Orsan 1989: A light, fruity wine, with a bitter edge that takes away some of the charm. Drinkable now. $7 (6/15/92) **74**

CHATEAU DU BOIS DE LA GARDE
Côtes du Rhône 1989: Fruity, generous and smooth textured, with nice pepper aromas, a firm backbone of ripe plum and chocolate flavors and spice notes that linger on the finish. $8 (5/31/91) **83**
Côtes du Rhône 1988: Light in color, but lively and crisp on the palate, with bright cherry and strawberry aromas and flavors and a touch of nutmeg. It's drinkable now, but worth saving until 1993 to see what develops. 3,000 cases made. $7 (10/31/90) BB **82**

JEAN CLAUDE BOISSET
Côtes du Rhône 1987: Fruity, straightforward and medium-bodied, with good but modest cherry and pepper flavors. Nicely balanced. Fine for current consumption. $4.50 (7/31/89) **78**
Côtes du Rhône 1986 $4 (10/31/87) **73**
Côtes du Rhône 1985 $3.75 (11/30/86) BB **77**

BOKOBSA
Côtes du Rhône Cuvée du Centenaire 1986: An innocuous and very simple wine. Has woody aromas and flavors and not much fruit. $6.50 (2/28/90) **68**

CHATEAU LA BORIE
Côtes du Rhône Cuvée de Prestige 1985 $6 (7/15/87) **74**
Côtes du Rhône Cuvée de Prestige 1983 $4 (3/16/85) BB **87**

BOUCHARD PERE & FILS
Côtes du Rhône 1989: Fruity and lively, with berry and cherry aromas and flavors that are smoothly focused and hint at toast and smoke around the edges. Drinkable now. $8.50 (7/15/91) BB **82**

LAURENT CHARLES BROTTE
Côtes du Rhône-Villages Seguret 1986: A spicy style, emphasizing the black pepper zing over the cherry flavor, light and fairly graceful. Drink now. $6 (9/30/89) BB **80**

DOMAINE BRUSSET
Côtes du Rhône-Villages Côteaux des Trabers 1988: Nicely balanced, focused and flavorful; a very good wine. Shows elegantly textured currant and plum flavors, accented by black pepper and vanilla for a complete package. 2,000 cases made. $7.75 (12/15/90) BB **86**
Côtes du Rhône-Villages Cairanne Côteaux des Trabers 1986: Harsh and unpleasant, with a Port-like aroma and grapey, harsh wood flavors. Medicinal and very tannic. $7 (6/15/89) **61**

CAVE DES COTEAUX CAIRANNE
Côtes du Rhône 1986 $7.25 (7/31/88) **86**
Côtes du Rhône Domaine le Château 1985 $6.25 (8/31/87) BB **85**
Côtes du Rhône Le Château a Cairanne 1987: Light and refreshing, with attractive black pepper and toast overtones to the strawberry aromas and flavors. Drink now. $7 (12/15/89) **77**
Côtes du Rhône Le Château a Cairanne 1986 $6 (7/31/88) BB **82**
Côtes du Rhône-Villages 1988: A wine you can sink your teeth into that's a good buy, too. Full-bodied, with firm tannins, deep plum and spice flavors with nice peppery overtones, but not much of a finish. $6.50 (2/28/90) BB **81**
Côtes du Rhône-Villages Cairanne 1988: Has the distinctive berry and pepper aromas and flavors of a young Rhône, but turns a bit tight on the palate. Drink now to 1993. $6.25 (6/30/90) **76**

DOMAINE DES CEDRES
Côtes du Rhône Pons Dominique 1986: Just what you want from a Côtes du Rhône. It's flavorful, with plenty of berry and spice, good balance and a clean finish. $10 (3/31/90) **82**

M. CHAPOUTIER
Côtes du Rhône 1987: Light and mature, with nice chocolate and game overtones to the modest cherry and berry flavors. The tannins are soft enough to drink this now. Tasted twice. $9 (12/31/91) **79**
Côtes du Rhône Cuvée de Belleruche 1989: A concentrated, tannic, robust wine, with spicy aromas, blackberry flavors and a pleasant, lingering finish. Has distinctive character and good balance. Tasted twice. $13 (6/15/92) **82**
Côtes du Rhône Cuvée de Belleruche 1986: What a pretty wine! With its generous blueberry and vanilla flavors, satiny texture and marvelous concentration, this is drinkable now and more intense in flavor than the light color would suggest. $12 (12/15/89) **87**

CAVE DES VIGNERONS A CHUSCLAN
Côtes du Rhône Prieure St.-Julien 1985 $4.25 (12/31/87) BB **79**

ABEL CLEMENT
Côtes du Rhône 1988: A good-value quaffing wine. Jammy flavors dominate, with pepper and spice, medium-bodied, with mild tannins and blackberry flavors on the finish. $6 (2/28/90) BB **80**
Côtes du Rhône 1985 $5 (1/31/87) BB **78**

PIERRE COMBE
Côtes du Rhône-Villages Domaine des Richards 1990: Deliciously fruity and fresh, with blackberry, plum and vanilla flavors that are deep and long on the finish. Smooth, full-bodied and rich in texture. Drink now through 1994. 1,200 cases made. $7.50 (10/15/91) BB **89**
Côtes du Rhône-Villages Domaine des Richards 1987: Smooth and tasty, a simple, light Rhône, with attractive fruit flavors, a silky texture and pepper aromas. Drink now. $4 (1/31/89) **78**

CRU DE COUDELET
Côtes du Rhône 1987: A pleasant, drinkable wine, with generous, grapey aromas and flavors marked by a touch of leather and earthiness. Drinkable now. From Château de Beaucastel. $12 (12/15/89) **76**
Côtes du Rhône 1986 $15 (9/30/88) **84**
Côtes du Rhône 1985 $12 (4/30/88) **85**

DELAS
Côtes du Rhône St.-Esprit 1988: Straightforward, but flavorful and well crafted, offering characteristic black pepper-scented cherry and sweet tomato aromas and flavors and firm but not excessively tannic texture. It's just the thing to match with a meat loaf or steak. Drinkable now. 3,000 cases made. $6.75 (12/15/90) BB **84**
Côtes du Rhône St.-Esprit 1985 $5.50 (12/15/87) BB **80**

GEORGES DUBOEUF
Côtes du Rhône 1990: Crisp, fruity and lively, with generous black cherry and berry flavors and a touch of smokiness adding interest on the finish. A bit on the light side, but it has enough guts to get by. $8 (12/31/91) BB **84**
Côtes du Rhône 1989: One of the first Rhônes from this great Beaujolais producer, this is fresh, floral and fruity, like a Beaujolais but with more backbone. It's full of berry flavors, with a hint of vanilla, and backed by solid tannins. Simple but enjoyable. $6 (10/15/90) BB **80**

DOMAINE DURIEU
Côtes du Rhône-Villages 1988: Spicy, earthy, woody aromas and flavors are unique, but may not be to everyone's taste, and they carry through on the long finish. A well-made, if quirky wine. Drinkable now. $6 (3/15/91) **78**

CHATEAU DE FONSALETTE
Côtes du Rhône Réserve 1985 $15.50 (9/30/88) **87**

DOMAINE LOU FREJAU
Côtes du Rhône 1986: Earthy, tannic and vaguely berryish, it lacks the intensity to suggest that cellaring will let it develop. Maybe try it now. $8 (5/31/89) **73**

DOMAINE LES GOUBERT
Côtes du Rhône 1986 $6.75 (3/31/88) **78**
Côtes du Rhône-Villages Beaumes de Venise 1987: Very peppery, smoky and tart, with some jammy, strawberry flavors. A tough middleweight of a wine that needs perhaps until now to show all it has. $9 (7/31/89) **81**
Côtes du Rhône-Villages Beaumes de Venise 1985 $9.25 (4/30/88) **80**
Côtes du Rhône-Villages Sablet 1985 $8.25 (4/30/88) **76**

DOMAINE DE LA GUICHARDE
Côtes du Rhône 1988: This spicy, generous wine is hearty without being rough. Especially aromatic, with spice, cedar and leather overtones to the core of cherry flavor, which carries through on the somewhat tannic finish. Drinkable now, but best after 1993. $7 (3/15/91) BB **84**

E. GUIGAL
Côtes du Rhône 1988: Firm and flavorful, with lots of black pepper and leather overtones to the basic currant flavor. A solid wine without a lot of flair; a bit of a disappointment from this usually reliable producer. Drink soon. $11.50 (7/15/91) **81**
Côtes du Rhône 1986: A stylish wine that packs a punch and delivers deep plum and berry flavors. Full-bodied, with tasty vanilla accents, spicy aromas and firm tannins. $9 (2/28/90) **84**
Côtes du Rhône 1985 $8 (9/30/88) **85**
Côtes du Rhône 1984 $7 (12/15/87) BB **84**
Côtes du Rhône 1982 $6 (5/01/86) BB **85**
Côtes du Rhône 1981 $5 (5/01/84) BB **86**
Côtes du Rhône 1980 $4.50 (5/01/84) BB **85**

PAUL JABOULET AINE
Côtes du Rhône Parallele 45 1988: Bubbling over with grapey, berrylike flavors, it's soft and appealing from the first whiff to the velvety finish. Drink now for the attractive fruit flavors. $6.50 (12/15/89) BB **84**
Côtes du Rhône Parallele 45 1985 $6.50 (4/30/88) **73**

JEAN LIONNET
Côtes du Rhône Cépage Syrah 1986 $10 (9/30/88) **79**

KERMIT LYNCH
Côtes du Rhône 1985: Lean and firm, with impressive concentration of cherry and berry aromas and flavors, velvety texture and good length. Needs to shed some tannin. Try now. $9 (1/31/89) **83**

PROSPER MAUFOUX
Côtes du Rhône 1990: An intensely flavored, jammy, peppery wine that's deep in color, firm in tannins and very fruity. Solid, tempting to drink now, but it could be cellared through 1995. $8 (6/15/92) BB **84**
Côtes du Rhône 1989: Effusively fruity, with attractive cherry and berry flavors and a touch of earthiness. Round and a little soft on the palate, with raspberry on the finish. $9 (5/31/91) **84**
Côtes du Rhône 1988: A modestly proportioned wine with plenty of strawberry and black pepper aromas and flavors and firm tannins. Drink now. $6.50 (6/30/90) **79**
Côtes du Rhône 1987 $6.25 (6/15/89) **74**

MOILLARD
Côtes du Rhône Les Violettes 1990: Sturdy and fruity, with plum, spice and cherry flavors in a medium-bodied, ready-to-drink package. $7 (10/15/91) BB **82**
Côtes du Rhône Les Violettes 1989: Straightforward, harmonious and full-bodied, with plum, berry and chocolate aromas and flavors that persist on the finish, along with nice nutmeg and spice notes. A well-crafted wine. $7.50 (5/31/91) BB **85**
Côtes du Rhône Les Violettes 1988: Smooth, ripe and soft, with abundant aromas and flavors of

grape, wild berry and, yes, violets. A very appealing wine to drink on release, but it has enough substance to last at least through this year. $6 (8/31/89) BB **84**
Côtes du Rhône Les Violettes 1985 $4.50 (11/15/86) BB **85**

MOMMESSIN
Côtes du Rhône 1986 $4.75 (4/30/88) BB **82**

DOMAINE DE LA MORDOREE
Côtes du Rhône 1988: An odd mix of earthy and floral aromas, with thin flavors, showing some plum and spice. Simple and boring, with a coarse finish. $5.50 (2/28/90) **68**

LOUIS MOUSSET
Côtes du Rhône 1983 $2.50 (12/16/84) BB **81**

J.Y. MULTIER
Côtes du Rhône Cépage Syrah 1990: Spicy, peppery aromas and flavors add appealing shadings to the basic cherry flavor. Has lots of flavor and style, and the flavors linger on the finish. Drinkable now, but should last through 1994. $15 (6/15/92) **85**
Côtes du Rhône Cépage Syrah 1988: You don't expect a Côtes du Rhône to be herbal, but rosemary and bay leaf aromas pervade this wine that you'll either love or hate. Good as a marinade, but too shy of fruit for us to want to drink. $10 (12/15/90) **74**

CHATEAU D'ORSAN
Côtes du Rhône 1987 $4 (11/15/88) **77**
Côtes du Rhône 1986 $4 (2/29/88) BB **81**
Côtes du Rhône 1985 $6.75 (12/15/87) **79**

PATRIARCHE
Côtes du Rhône-Villages Cuvée Leblanc-Vatel 1985: A mature, spicy wine, with light texture and an undertone of astringency that keeps it from being as smooth and graceful as it could be. $5.50 (8/31/89) **77**

DU PELOUX
Côtes du Rhône 1986: Very light color and appealing strawberry aromas and flavors compete with a bit more tannin than you might expect. Probably better now. $4.50 (5/15/89) **75**
Côtes du Rhône-Villages 1986: Firm textured and medium-bodied, with spicy cherry flavor and balanced tannins. Drink now. $5.50 (5/15/89) **78**

DOMAINE RABASSE CHARAVIN
Côtes du Rhône 1985 $6 (8/31/87) BB **81**

LA RAMILLADE
Côtes du Rhône 1982 $5 (11/01/85) BB **84**

DOMAINE DE LA RENJARDIERE
Côtes du Rhône 1983 $4.50 (3/16/86) BB **84**

PAR E. REYNAUD
Côtes du Rhône Château des Tours 1989: A solid wine, with fine tannins, firm structure and modestly intense cherry and spice flavors. A bit rough to drink now, but it should be ready around 1993. $12 (3/15/91) **80**

ARMAND ROUX
Côtes du Rhône La Berberine 1988: Straightforward and attractive, with smoky aromas, very peppery flavors, crisp raspberry and cherry notes and a clean finish. 1,000 cases made. $7.50 (10/31/90) BB **81**

CHARLES ROUX
Côtes du Rhône-Villages Rasteau 1985: Firm in structure, velvety in texture and generous in flavor, with peppery cherry character balanced artfully with a touch of smoke. Drinkable now, but it should hold through 1995. Gets better with every sip. $10 (2/28/90) **89**

DOMAINE ROGER SABON & FILS
Côtes du Rhône 1989: A leathery, gamy wine, with plenty of tannin. Not likable. $12 (11/15/91) **70**
Côtes du Rhône 1988: Solid, spicy and medium-bodied, with modest tannins, good balance and enough cherry and berry flavor to keep you interested. $11 (10/31/90) **79**

CHATEAU ST.-ESTEVE D'UCHAUX
Côtes du Rhône 1989: Spicy and firm, with cherry flavor chiming in on the palate and hanging on as the finish turns crisp and a little tannic. Drinkable now, with hearty food. Best after 1993. $9 (11/15/91) **80**
Côtes du Rhône Grand Réserve 1989: Firm and flavorful, with basic cherry and blackberry flavors rounded out by vanilla-scented oak and a welcome earthy mineral touch on the finish. The tannins could use until 1993 or '94 to settle down. $11.50 (11/15/91) **83**
Côtes du Rhône-Villages 1989: Firm and flavorful, with good, basic Rhône flavors of cherry and blueberry and a nice hint of black pepper on the finish. The smooth texture makes this tempting to drink now, but it has enough to want until 1993 to '95 to gain polish. $10 (11/15/91) **84**

DOMAINE ST.-GAYAN
Côtes du Rhône 1988: Tannic and tight, with ungenerous flavors. It hints at wild berries and leather on the nose, but doesn't offer much on the palate. Perhaps it has improved. $8 (10/31/90) **75**
Côtes du Rhône 1985 $6 (4/30/88) **75**

LES CAVES ST.-PIERRE
Côtes du Rhône-Villages Les Lissandres 1988: Firm and ripe, with nicely focused cherry and blackberry aromas and flavors, hinting at black pepper and nutmeg on the generous finish. A supple, easy-to-drink wine that should be enjoyable for current drinking. $7.25 (12/15/90) BB **84**

DOMAINE STE.-ANNE
Côtes du Rhône-Villages Cuvée Notre-Dame des Cellettes 1987: Very youthful, with berrylike flavors, sturdy, full-bodied, bursting with fruit, it's built to develop with some time in the bottle. Drink now. $7.50 (1/31/89) **80**

SERRE DE LAUZIERE
Côtes du Rhône-Villages 1988: Firm textured, flavorful but ultimately simple, with nice grape and raspberry flavors echoing on the finish. Should be fine to drink now. $7 (10/31/90) **78**

DOMAINE LA SOUMADE
Côtes du Rhône-Villages Rasteau 1986: Lush flavors on a firm structure make this appealing to pop open with a roast chicken now. The grapey cherry flavor carries through nicely. $11 (2/28/90) **82**
Côtes du Rhône-Villages Rasteau Cuvée Réserve 1982 $5.50 (10/31/87) **69**

THORIN
Côtes du Rhône L'Escalou 1987: An austere style, modest in flavor and structure, not very interesting. $6 (1/31/89) **67**

CHATEAU DU TRIGNON
Côtes du Rhône-Villages Rasteau 1986: Tough with drying tannins and earthy aromas, but the generous cherry and plum flavors are appealing and the fruit emerges from a tannic background with a hint of tomato on the finish to make it an interesting wine. $9 (12/15/90) **80**

CHATEAU DES VALLONNIERES
Côtes du Rhône 1990: This hearty, medium-bodied wine shows plenty of good, smooth plum and pepper flavors. Moderately tannic; ready to drink now through 1994. 4,000 cases made. $8.75 (6/15/92) **83**

L. DE VALLOUIT
Côtes du Rhône St.-Vincent 1990: A ripe, fruity style, with a gamy edge that makes it seem more serious than it is. A good, straightforward wine that's drinkable now. $7 (6/15/92) BB **82**

J. VIDAL-FLEURY
Côtes du Rhône 1989: A straightforward Rhône, with modest fruit flavors, plenty of pepper accents and strong tannins. $10 (6/15/92) **81**
Côtes du Rhône 1988: A cut above the average Côtes du Rhône. Full of ripe, clean fruit flavor, with firm acid and tannin structure and a lingering fruity finish. Drink now. $9 (12/15/90) **85**
Côtes du Rhône 1985 $7.50 (10/31/87) BB **88**

LA VIEILLE FERME
Côtes du Rhône Réserve 1989: A big, full-bodied, fruity wine that's rich, with plenty of flavor and depth. Has toasty plum, cherry and earthy berry flavors and picks up peppery notes on the finish, where it also gets tannic. Best to drink now to 1996. $9 (3/15/91) BB **87**
Côtes du Rhône Réserve 1988: You can't go wrong at this price. Ripe and full-bodied, with mild tannins, a slightly rough texture and plenty of black cherry and pepper flavors in a square-shouldered style. $7.50 (12/15/90) BB **84**
Côtes du Rhône Réserve 1987 $6.50 (6/15/89) BB **80**
Côtes du Rhône Réserve 1985 $7 (11/15/88) BB **85**

VIGNOBLE DE LA JASSE
Côtes du Rhône 1986: Mossy, earthy aromas and astringent, austere flavors can be off-putting, but ripe berry emerges on the finish. For fans of the old style. From Daniel Combe. $8 (12/15/89) **79**

Crozes-Hermitage

PERE ANSELME
Crozes-Hermitage 1986: A good wine with hamburgers. Broad, ripe and fruity. Plum and cherry flavors are soft and supple, but tannins kick in on the finish. Drink now. $7.75 (7/31/89) **80**
Crozes-Hermitage 1983 $7.50 (10/15/87) BB **84**

BERNARD CHAVE
Crozes-Hermitage 1988: Tough, with spice, pepper, berry, pickle and vinegar flavors supported by firm tannins. Drink now to 1994. Tasted twice. $14 (2/15/91) **78**
Crozes-Hermitage 1985 $12 (11/30/88) **86**

CHATEAU CURSON
Crozes-Hermitage 1989: Ripe and supple, with generous blackberry, black cherry and plum aromas and flavors, hinting at vanilla and chocolate around the edges. Seems polished and almost elegant. Drinkable by 1993 or '94. $17 (7/15/91) **89**

DELAS
Crozes-Hermitage 1985 $7.50 (12/15/87) **78**

DESMEURE
Crozes-Hermitage Domaine des Remizières Cuvée Particulaire 1986: Very fruity and elegant, with appealing strawberry, raspberry and spicy aromas, turning tough and tight on the palate, it's dry and more austere than the fragrance would suggest. Drink now to 1995. $8 (5/31/89) BB **84**

GEORGES DUBOEUF
Crozes-Hermitage 1989: Earthy and elegant, with ripe, supple, polished currant, cherry, anise and smoky oak flavors that are rich and lively. Finishes with tart cherry and currant notes and smooth tannins. Drink in 1993 to '99. $10 (6/15/92) **87**
Crozes-Hermitage 1988: A rich, complex, firmly structured and reasonably priced wine, with smoke, leather and pepper aromas and smooth, spicy, crisp berry flavors. Tastes good now, but it could be cellared through 1993. A good value. $9 (1/31/91) **85**

FERRATON PERE
Crozes-Hermitage La Matinière 1988: Fresh, clean and lively, with soft berry, strawberry and pepper notes, supple tannins and a clean, fruity aftertaste. Delicious on release, but can develop in the cellar. Drink now to 1993. $14 (6/30/90) **85**

ALAIN GRAILLOT
Crozes-Hermitage 1989: Packed with blackberry flavor, accented by pepper notes and virtually oozing with fresh, jammy flavors. Firm tannins lurk beneath the fruit. Appears soft and approachable, but should improve with time; drink now through 1996. $14 (3/31/91) **88**
Crozes-Hermitage 1986: Dense in color, aroma and structure, with concentrated but reined-in cherry, anise and toasty aromas and flavors. Tightly framed with somewhat austere tannin, but the fruit shines through at the finish. Drink now through 1995. $9.75 (4/15/89) **88**

PAUL JABOULET AINE
Crozes-Hermitage Domaine de Thalabert 1989: Exuberantly fruity and dense in flavor, with blackberry jam and pepper notes gushing out in the aromas and continuing through the long finish. Hints of spice, butter and vanilla from oak aging lend it complexity. Has firm tannins and is well balanced overall. Tempting to drink now, but should be better after 1994. $18 (7/15/91) **90**
Crozes-Hermitage Domaine de Thalabert 1988: Earthy, barnyardy style, with tart cherry and berry flavors that are rich and deep, but dry and tannic on the finish. Best now to 1995. $13 (10/15/90) **83**
Crozes-Hermitage Domaine de Thalabert 1987: A soft, supple style, with harmonious aromas and flavors of cherry, berry and earth, plus a hint of violet on the finish. Well made, lingering on the finish. $10 (3/31/90) **83**
Crozes-Hermitage Domaine de Thalabert 1986 $13.50 (9/30/88) **88**
Crozes-Hermitage Domaine de Thalabert 1985 Rel: $13 Cur: $20 (9/30/88) **85**

LUPE-CHOLET
Crozes-Hermitage 1987: A soft, generous style, with plenty of blackberry and black pepper aromas and flavors. Simple and appealing to drink now. $8 (3/31/90) BB **83**

CAVE DE TAIN L'HERMITAGE
Crozes-Hermitage Michel Courtial 1986: Very earthy aromas, but showing good cherry flavor and the tart, slightly tannic structure earns it a place with hearty food. $6 (5/15/89) **77**

J. VIDAL-FLEURY
Crozes-Hermitage 1988: A complex style, with intriguing smoky, toasty aromas and pure, elegant,

Key to Symbols

The scores reported here are the results of blind tastings conducted by our panel of senior editors. Wines that carry the initials below are results of individual tastings.

THE WINE SPECTATOR 100-POINT SCALE ***95-100***—Classic, a great wine; ***90-94***—Outstanding, superior character and style; ***80-89***—Good to very good, a wine with special qualities; ***70-79***—Average, drinkable wine that may have minor flaws; ***60-69***—Below average, drinkable but not recommended; ***50-59***—Poor, undrinkable, not recommended. "+"—With a score indicates a range; used primarily with barrel tastings to indicate a preliminary score.

SPECIAL DESIGNATIONS SS—Spectator Selection, CS—Cellar Selection, BB—Best Buy, ($NA)—Price not available, (NR)—Not released.

TASTER'S INITIALS (JG)—Jim Gordon, (HS)—Harvey Steiman, (JL)—James Laube, (JS)—James Suckling, (TM)—Thomas Matthews, (TR)—Terry Robards, (PM)—Per-Henrik Mansson, (BT)—Barrel Tasting (these wines were tasted blind from barrel samples), (CA-date)—*California's Great Cabernets* by James Laube, (CH-date)—*California's Great Chardonnays* by James Laube, (VP-date)—*Vintage Port* by James Suckling.

DATE TASTED Dates in parentheses represent the issue in which the rating was published.

rich cherry, currant and spice flavors that are well proportioned. Has a full, rich flavor on the finish. Needs a year or two to mellow. Drink now to 1996. $13 (12/31/90) **86**
Crozes-Hermitage 1986 $10 (5/31/88) **78**
Crozes-Hermitage 1985 Rel: $11 Cur: $15 (10/31/87) CS **92**

WILLI'S WINE BAR
Crozes-Hermitage Cuvée Anniversaire 1988: An extremely vegetal style that's thin on the finish. Smells and tastes like green beans and onions; not what we look for in a Rhône, but it's drinkable. 500 cases made. $11 (3/31/91) **70**

GIGONDAS

DANIEL BRUSSET
Gigondas Les Hauts de Montmirail 1989: Ripe, smooth and generous, offering a tempting balance of black cherry, plum and blackberry flavors against a background of spicy, toasty oak. Has enough tannin to want until 1995 to attain its full polish. 800 cases made. $22 (11/15/91) **91**
Gigondas Les Hauts de Montmirail 1988: Uncommonly deep in color, with rich aromas. The well-defined, rich currant, cherry, plum, spice and mineral flavors are amazingly complex and elegant. The finish is full and assertive, but wonderfully balanced. Drink now to 1994 and beyond. 800 cases made. $17 (9/30/90) **90**

GEORGES DUBOEUF
Gigondas 1989: Ripe and peppery, with a strong tobacco streak running through the basic black cherry flavor. A sturdy wine, with generous flavors. OK to drink now, but probably better after 1994. $12 (1/31/92) **84**
Gigondas 1988: A straightforward wine that's fruity and focused, with plum and cherry flavors, a slightly floral aroma, moderate tannins and a dry finish. $10 (9/30/90) **79**

MICHEL FARAUD
Gigondas Domaine du Cayron 1988: Bold, rich and concentrated, jam-packed with currant, black cherry, plum and anise notes that are firm and tightly wound. Hints of black pepper and spicy oak round out the flavors on the aftertaste. Enticing now, but will probably benefit from cellaring so the tannins can soften. Best around 1993 to '95. $14 (10/15/91) **89**
Gigondas Domaine du Cayron 1985 $16 (11/30/88) **93**

DOMAINE DE FONT-SANE
Gigondas 1985: Very ripe and supple, with rich plum, cherry, and black pepper flavors in a full-bodied yet elegant style. Despite the deep color, it's not too tannic. Finish gets woody; give it some time. Drink now to 1996. $13 (1/31/89) **86**

DOMAINE LES GOUBERT
Gigondas 1986: A ripe, woody style, with lots of cedar and spice aromas. A bit astringent and thin on the finish, but well made and nearing drinkability. Best to drink now or in 1993. $13 (3/15/90) **81**
Gigondas 1985 $11 (4/30/88) **89**
Gigondas Cuvée Florence 1986 $24 (4/30/88) **92**

DOMAINE DU GOUR DE CHAULE
Gigondas 1986: Exotic aromas of raisins, spice and leather give way to rich, mature fruit flavors and firm tannins. The flavors are complex and intriguing and it's drinkable now, but it could be cellared through 1993 or beyond. Great quality for the price. 2,000 cases made. $13 (9/15/90) **90**

DOMAINE GRAND-ROMAINE
Gigondas 1989: Firm in texture and gloriously aromatic, with floral and berry aromas and flavors that echo on the finish. The tannins are present without being overpowering. Best after 1993 or '94. 1,300 cases made. $16 (8/31/91) **87**
Gigondas Medaille d'Argent 1990: The tannins are a little tough, but it has so many floral, plummy and spicy aromas and flavors that it's almost drinkable now. Best after 1993. $16 (1/31/92) **85**
Gigondas Medaille d'Or 1990: Firm and full-bodied, with generous currant, plum and spicy floral aromas and flavors, plus tough-edged tannins that need until 1994 to '96 to soften. 1,300 cases made. $16 (1/31/92) **87**

E. GUIGAL
Gigondas 1988: A big, ripe, bold and tannic style, with intense, concentrated cherry, currant, leather and toast flavors. Very peppery and tannic on the finish. Best to cellar until 1993 or '94 for it to soften. Rel: $13 Cur: $16 (3/31/91) **85**
Gigondas 1986: Has classic, earthy northern Rhône aromas and flavors, offering plenty of black pepper and black cherry aromas that turn leathery and spicy on the tight, tannic finish. Put this away until 1993 to let the tannins subside. Rel: $15 Cur: $18 (11/30/90) **87**
Gigondas 1985 Rel: $12 Cur: $17 (9/30/88) SS **91**
Gigondas 1984 Rel: $12 Cur: $15 (11/30/87) **86**
Gigondas 1983 Rel: $12 Cur: $19 (7/31/87) **91**

PAUL JABOULET AINE
Gigondas 1989: The deep color, powerful aromas and strong tannic grip almost don't let the rich grape and berry flavors emerge. Hard to tell when to drink; try around 1995 to '97. $18 (7/15/91) **84**

PROSPER MAUFOUX
Gigondas 1985 $11 (4/30/88) **65**

CHATEAU DE MONTMIRAIL
Gigondas Cuvée de Beauchamp 1985 $14 (9/30/88) **78**
Gigondas Cuvée de Beauchamp 1983 $11 (11/30/86) **90**

LOUIS MOUSSET
Gigondas 1983 $6 (12/01/84) **75**

DOMAINE LES PALLIERES
Gigondas 1986: A maturing, medium-weight wine that has gently peppery, spicy fruit flavors to make it interesting. Drinkable now, but should hold at least through 1993. $21 (11/15/91) **79**
Gigondas 1984: Full of tobacco, coffee and leather aromas and ripe, peppery flavors. A full but smooth and rich wine, with full but soft tannins. Drinkable now through 1995. $14 (9/30/89) **86**
Gigondas 1983: Has plenty of spice, pepper and ripe plummy flavors that are lean and muscular with firm, fine, elegantly balanced tannins, finishing with a smoky quality and hints of bacon. Drink now to 1995. $15 (1/31/89) **88**
Gigondas 1982 $11 (5/31/87) **89**
Gigondas 1981 $10.25 (3/15/87) **90**

CHATEAU RASPAIL-AY
Gigondas 1988: An earthy, funky style, with a strong barklike edge to the modest cherry flavors. Tannic enough to need until 1998 to 2000, but it doesn't have the intensity to go the distance. $19 (11/15/91) **79**
Gigondas 1986: Has beautifully defined plum, black cherry and raspberry flavor that's rich, ripe and deep. The vibrant fruit echoes long and full on the palate. Tannins are fine and integraged. Gigondas doesn't get much better. Drink now to 1997. $15 (1/31/89) **92**

L. DE VALLOUIT
Gigondas 1989: Fruity and generous, with wild berry, wild plum and spice aromas and flavors, peppery overtones and floral notes on the finish. The tannins are firm but not excessive. Approaching drinkability, but should be at its best after 1993. $13 (1/31/92) **89**

J. VIDAL-FLEURY
Gigondas 1985 $13 (10/31/87) **86**

HERMITAGE

M. CHAPOUTIER
Hermitage Monier de la Sizeranne 1989: Dense and concentrated, with opulent prune and blackberry aromas and flavors that persist into a long, powerful finish. Tannins are present, but not overwhelming. Has a sense of elegance that cellaring until 1995 to 2000 should polish nicely. Rel: $23 Cur: $31 (8/31/91) **89**
Hermitage Monier de la Sizeranne 1988: Firm and focused, with nicely balanced cherry, pepper and tobacco aromas and flavors that are harmonious, intense and full of character. Seems a little tough and perhaps woody on the finish, but it has plenty of room to grow. Try in 1995 to '98. Tasted twice. $25 (12/31/91) **85**
Hermitage Monier de la Sizeranne 1983 Rel: $19 Cur: $28 (5/01/86) **83**
Hermitage Monier de la Sizeranne 1981 Rel: $10 Cur: $25 (11/01/84) **88**
Hermitage Monier de la Sizeranne Grande Cuvée NV $14 (5/01/86) **83**
Hermitage Le Pavillon NV: Meaty, smoky, baconlike aromas and flavors permeate this velvety, complex wine. Full-bodied, long and powerful, with some tannin to shed. Drink now to 1995. $60 (1/31/89) **88**

BERNARD CHAVE
Hermitage 1989: Rich and concentrated, with abundant smoky, toasty plum and currant aromas and flavors that are wrapped, for now, in a blanket of tannin, but it's thick and generous enough to warrant cellaring until 1995 to '99. Should be a wonderful wine. 83 cases made. $40 (12/31/91) **91**
Hermitage 1986 $32 (11/30/88) **86**

J.L. CHAVE
Hermitage 1987: Earthy, with herb and spice flavors, but it also has a core of meaty currant and raspberry flavors. A complex wine that manages to balance the fruit flavors with the earthy ones. Not too tannic to drink tonight, but probably best between 1993 and '95. $48 (6/30/90) **89**
Hermitage 1984 Rel: $25 Cur: $30 (8/31/87) **89**
Hermitage 1980 Rel: $25 Cur: $37 (5/01/86) **83**

DESMEURE
Hermitage Domaine des Remizières 1986: Harsh and unrelenting on the nose at this point, but surprisingly pretty on the palate, with strawberry and raspberry flavors and a fairly smooth finish. Problematical whether the harshness will age out. Try it now. $19 (4/15/89) **68**

E. GUIGAL
Hermitage 1988: Ripe and generous, with a strong gamy quality that sneaks in on the finish. A style not everyone will love, but it has intensity and balance. Drink around 1993. Rel: $30 Cur: $35 (12/31/91) **83**
Hermitage 1987: An austere, tightly reined-in style, with more fruit on the nose than on the palate. The leather, berry, pepper, spice and subtle oak shadings are well proportioned and well defined, but in need of a few years' cellaring for the tannins to soften and the flavors to evolve. Drink in 1993 to '97. Rel: $29 Cur: $36 (1/31/91) **86**
Hermitage 1986: Very firm and elegant, with a burst of raspberry and black pepper flavors that just go on forever on the finish. Soft tannins and a touch of new oak frame the wine beautifully, and with time it ought to emerge gorgeously. Drink starting 1993. Rel: $32 Cur: $41 (2/28/90) CS **92**
Hermitage 1985 Rel: $33 Cur: $39 (4/15/89) CS **92**
Hermitage 1983 Rel: $21 Cur: $33 (4/30/87) **87**
Hermitage 1982 Rel: $18 Cur: $27 (5/01/86) **91**
Hermitage 1980 Rel: $13 Cur: $42 (9/01/84) CS **91**
Hermitage 1978 $65 (3/15/90) (HS) **91**
Hermitage 1976 $75 (3/15/90) (HS) **80**
Hermitage 1969 $100 (3/15/90) (HS) **84**
Hermitage 1966 $100 (3/15/90) (HS) **90**
Hermitage 1964 $100 (3/15/90) (HS) **93**

DOMAINE DE L'HERMITE
Hermitage 1983 $9.50 (5/01/86) **88**
Hermitage 1980 $12.25 (5/01/86) **84**

PAUL JABOULET AINE
Hermitage La Chapelle 1989: Jam-packed with ripe, rich plum, currant, black cherry and anise flavors that turn to chocolate and toast on the finish. A beautifully focused, deeply concentrated wine that combines power with finesse. Approachable now, but probably at its best between 1994 and 2000. $45 (8/31/91) CS **93**
Hermitage La Chapelle 1988: A pure expression of Hermitage that's intense, ripe and flavorful, with pepper, cherry, berry and smoke aromas and flavors and a rich structure. Long and vibrant, with well-integrated tannins. Best to drink after 1994. $40 (3/31/91) **92**
Hermitage La Chapelle 1986 $35 (11/15/89) (JS) **89**
Hermitage La Chapelle 1985 $50 (11/15/89) (JS) **93**
Hermitage La Chapelle 1984 $25 (11/15/89) (JS) **80**
Hermitage La Chapelle 1983 $72 (11/15/89) (JS) **94**
Hermitage La Chapelle 1982 Rel: $17 Cur: $55 (11/15/89) (JS) **89**
Hermitage La Chapelle 1981 $40 (11/15/89) (JS) **83**
Hermitage La Chapelle 1980 $38 (11/15/89) (JS) **79**
Hermitage La Chapelle 1979 $50 (11/15/89) (JS) **86**
Hermitage La Chapelle 1978 $180 (11/15/89) (JS) **98**
Hermitage La Chapelle 1976 $100 (11/15/89) (JS) **87**
Hermitage La Chapelle 1975 $45 (11/15/89) (JS) **81**
Hermitage La Chapelle 1974 $105 (11/15/89) (JS) **85**
Hermitage La Chapelle 1973 $70 (11/15/89) (JS) **89**
Hermitage La Chapelle 1972 $125 (11/15/89) (JS) **90**
Hermitage La Chapelle 1971 $155 (11/15/89) (JS) **85**
Hermitage La Chapelle 1970 $155 (11/15/89) (JS) **93**
Hermitage La Chapelle 1969 $210 (11/15/89) (JS) **92**
Hermitage La Chapelle 1967 $71 (11/15/89) (JS) **83**
Hermitage La Chapelle 1966 $270 (11/15/89) (JS) **95**
Hermitage La Chapelle 1964 $250 (11/15/89) (JS) **93**
Hermitage La Chapelle 1962 $250 (11/15/89) (JS) **91**
Hermitage La Chapelle 1961 $600 (11/15/89) (JS) **100**
Hermitage La Chapelle 1959 $500 (11/15/89) (JS) **77**
Hermitage La Chapelle 1955 $330 (11/15/89) (JS) **88**
Hermitage La Chapelle 1953 $550 (11/15/89) (JS) **90**
Hermitage La Chapelle 1952 $480 (11/15/89) (JS) **77**
Hermitage La Chapelle 1949 $680 (11/15/89) (JS) **77**
Hermitage La Chapelle 1944 $800 (11/15/89) (JS) **93**
Hermitage La Chapelle 1937 $800 (11/15/89) (JS) **50**

H. SORREL
Hermitage 1985 $29 (7/31/88) **87**
Hermitage Le Gréal 1988: Behind the hard, tough, tannic shell beats the heart of a rich, smooth, generous wine. Blackberry, black cherry and spice aromas and flavors come through, especially on the long finish. Cellar until at least 1997 to 2000. $49 (11/15/91) **88**
Hermitage Le Gréal 1983 $19 (5/01/86) **84**
Hermitage Le Gréal 1980 $25 (5/01/86) **74**
Hermitage Le Vignon 1988: Barnyardy flavors are austere and a bit vinegary, but there's some currant and berry flavor, too. Funky style. Drink 1993 to 1995. $36 (8/31/91) **77**

FRANCE
RHÔNE RED/ *HERMITAGE*

CAVE DE TAIN L'HERMITAGE
Hermitage 1986: An earthy, buttery, spicy wine, the sort you'll love or hate, very distinctive and elegant on the palate, bordering on decadent, with hints of anise on the finish. $15 (7/15/89) **82**
Hermitage Michel Courtial 1986: A supple style, with nicely focused berry and plum flavors marked by vanilla and toast accents and an attractive gaminess. A complex wine that is soft enough to drink now, although cellaring until 1993 to '95 wouldn't hurt. $15 (3/31/90) **89**

LES CAVES ST.-PIERRE
Hermitage Tertre des Carmes 1988: Distinctive for its elegance and grace notes, very spicy and peppery on the nose and palate, but the ripe cherry and leather flavors come through and add a dimension of complexity and finesse. Clean and balanced. Drink now to 1994. $23 (12/31/90) **88**

L. DE VALLOUIT
Hermitage 1983 $12 (5/01/86) **79**

J. VIDAL-FLEURY
Hermitage 1985 $22 (10/31/87) **89**
Hermitage 1945 $175 (3/15/90) (HS) **80**
Hermitage 1937 $135 (3/15/90) (HS) **91**

OTHER RHÔNE RED

JEAN CLAUDE BOISSET
Côtes du Ventoux 1988: Sturdy and straightforward, with salt and pepper flavors, a modest fruit component and plenty of tannin. $4 (10/15/90) **75**

LA BOUVERIE
Costières de Nimes 1989: Earthy, leathery aromas and flavors team with modest cherry notes to make this wine rather like a medium-weight Châteauneuf-du-Pape. $6 (7/15/91) **79**

DOMAINE LE CLOS DES CAZAUX
Vacqueyras Cuvée des Templiers 1983 $11 (1/31/87) **83**

PIERRE COMBE
Vacqueyras Domaine des Richards 1989: A fresh-tasting, exuberant young wine, with strawberry and cherry flavors and firm acidity and tannins. Almost drinkable now, but should improve through 1993. 1,500 cases made. $9.50 (10/15/91) **86**

DOMAINE LE COUROULU
Vacqueyras 1985: Ripe and characteristically peppery, with lots of berry flavor and a lean structure, but also some nice buttery, smoky intensity on the finish. Drink now. $8 (1/31/89) BB **83**

CUILLERON
St.-Joseph 1983 $12.50 (2/16/86) **76**
St.-Joseph Cuvée de la Côte 1987: Broad and soft in texture, with good plum flavors and hints of pepper and smoke for complexity. It's well-balanced and firmly tannic. Try it now. $16 (11/30/90) **80**

LUCIEN DESCHAUX
Côtes du Ventoux La Cuvée du Chanoine 1990: A simple, straightforward wine, with broad, grapey flavors and a tomato edge that will not appeal to some. Drinkable now. $5.50 (1/31/92) **75**
Côtes du Ventoux Le Vieux Presbytere 1989: A light, spicy wine, with a solid core of berry flavor surrounded by hints of pepper, nutmeg and tomato. Needs to lose some tannin. Try in 1993 or '94. 5,000 cases made. $6 (12/31/91) BB **80**

GEORGES DUBOEUF
St.-Joseph 1988: Soft, deeply flavored and marked by vegetal and smoky flavors. The firm tannins outweigh the soft acidity. $11 (11/30/90) **76**

LA FORGE
Côtes du Lubéron 1989: Simple and fruity, with pleasant wild berry and cherry flavors. Drink soon. $7 (11/15/91) **79**

PIERRE GAILLARD
St.-Joseph Clos de Cuminaille 1988: Distinctly peppery, aromatic and flavorful, with black pepper, cherry and raspberry flavors. A solid wine, with enough rounding of its tannic edge to be drinkable with hearty food. Better around 1993. $15 (12/31/90) **87**
St.-Joseph Clos de Cuminaille 1987: Ripe, generous and supple, bursting with black pepper and violet-tinged blackberry and cherry flavors that turn firm and a bit earthy on the finish. An easy wine to warm up to. Drinkable now. $14 (3/15/90) **87**

PAUL JABOULET AINE
St.-Joseph Le Grand Pompée 1985 $11.25 (10/15/88) **86**

DOMAINE DES LONES
Côteaux du Tricastin 1988: Lean and focused, bordering on elegant. Spicy, peppery aromas follow through to flavors of nutmeg, cherry and cinnamon. Drinkable now. $11 (5/31/91) **84**
Côteaux du Tricastin 1988: Light and lively, with spicy cherry flavors, a touch of earthiness and a simple structure. Drinkable now. $7.50 (10/15/90) **78**
Côteaux du Tricastin 1986 $7.25 (10/15/88) **82**

CHATEAU DE MILLE
Côtes du Lubéron 1985 $8.50 (12/15/88) **83**

MOILLARD
St.-Joseph 1988: Lots of spice and fruit with tiers of black cherry, pepper, plum and cedar notes. Firm and elegantly textured, not too tannic so you can drink it soon. Picks up leathery notes on the finish. Drink now through 1995. 940 cases made. $15 (8/31/91) **85**
Vacqueyras 1989: Smooth, medium-bodied, with earthy aromas and slightly muddy flavors. Of average quality. $9.50 (10/15/91) **77**

DOMAINE DE LA MORDOREE
Lirac 1986 $11 (9/30/88) **88**

PHILIPPE PICHON
St.-Joseph 1988: Firm and fruity, with simple cherry, game and smoke aromas and flavors. A modest wine, with hints of tobacco and herbs on the finish. Should be best after 1993. $21.50 (11/15/91) **76**

PAR E. REYNAUD
Vacqueyras Château des Tours Réserve 1989: Deep in color, intense in aroma, tannic in structure and packed with deep menthol and black cherry flavors. It's a rough young wine that will need until about 1995 to soften; by then it should be very good. $14.50 (10/15/91) **85**

CHATEAU DES ROQUES
Vacqueyras Cuvée de Noe 1986: Spicy and distinctive flavors on a smooth, generous frame, with an unusual cardamom edge to the black pepper and berry aromas and flavors, supple and velvety. Drinkable now, but could age through 1993. From E. Dusser. $7.50 (12/15/89) BB **88**

DOMAINE ST.-SAUVEUR
Côtes du Ventoux 1988: Fruity, floral aromas and flavors make this medium-weight, blackberry-flavored, rich wine appealing. Shy enough in tannin to be drinkable now. $4.50 (10/15/91) BB **83**

CAVE DE TAIN L'HERMITAGE
St.-Joseph Michel Courtial 1986: Hearty, sturdy and flavorful, if not complex. Has ripe, plummy flavors, firm acid and tannins and an astringent but lingering finish that suggests it will improve through until 1993. $8 (7/31/89) **79**

CHATEAU VAL JOANIS
Côtes du Lubéron 1988: Distinctive for its smoky, baconlike aromas, concentrated raspberry and blueberry flavors and very firm tannins. Drinkable now, but should improve through 1993. $7 (6/30/90) BB **82**

L. DE VALLOUIT
St.-Joseph Rouge 1989: A hard-edged wine, with harsh tannins and ripe but interesting plum flavors, with overtones of sesame and soy sauce. Drink with Chinese food? $13 (1/31/92) **76**
Vin de Pays des Collines Rhodanienn Les Sables 1989: Crisp and spicy, with modest berry flavors and hints of toast and pepper. A nicely made, balanced wine for current drinking. 100 percent Syrah. $6.25 (12/31/91) BB **81**
Vin de Pays des Collines Rhodanienn Les Sables 1988: Fresh, firm and lively, with modest strawberry, raspberry and spice aromas and flavors to make it interesting. Drinkable now. 100 percent Syrah. $4.75 (6/30/90) BB **78**

J. VIDAL-FLEURY
St.-Joseph 1988: Deep and concentrated in flavor, showing peppery aromas, intense black cherry and plum flavors and a broad, smooth texture. It's firmly tannic, but should be drinkable now through 1993. $14 (1/31/91) **84**
Vacqueyras 1988: Generous, ripe and powerful, with toast-accented black cherry, plum and spice aromas and flavors hinting at cedar and nutmeg on the finish, this big wine is polished and sculpted to be drinkable already. Serve with something hearty. Tempting now, but could use until 1993 or '94 to polish up. $13.50 (12/15/90) **89**

LA VIEILLE FERME
Côtes du Ventoux 1988: Ripe fruit flavors plus distinctive overtones of leather make this immediately appealing, the soft texture allowing the grapey-plum flavor to show though a moderate veil of tannin. Drink now or in 1993. $8 (6/30/90) **78**
Côtes du Ventoux 1987 $5.75 (6/15/89) BB **81**
Côtes du Ventoux 1986 $6 (10/15/88) BB **83**

RHÔNE WHITE/ *CHÂTEAUNEUF-DU-PAPE*

PIERRE ANDRE
Châteauneuf-du-Pape 1984 $17 (10/01/85) **84**
Châteauneuf-du-Pape Blanc 1990: Crisp, fruity and charming, with a firm texture and plenty of grapefruit, peach and spice aromas and flavors. A straightforward wine that should be best before 1993. $19 (11/15/91) **83**

PERE ANSELME
Châteauneuf-du-Pape 1990: A rather modest, clean and refreshing wine to drink now. Offers fresh lemon and cream aromas, lemon, hazelnut, cream and melon flavors and firm acidity. Medium-bodied. Gains on the finish, with mineral notes. $20 (10/15/91) **82**

CHATEAU DE BEAUCASTEL
Châteauneuf-du-Pape 1989: Wild and exotic, with excellent concentration and distinction. Offers ripe peach, almond and Mandarin orange aromas, lively peach and spice flavors and a long, earthy finish. Try in 1993 to '95. $35 (10/15/91) **91**
Châteauneuf-du-Pape 1986 $29 (2/29/88) **84**
Châteauneuf-du-Pape 1985 $27 (11/15/87) **82**
Châteauneuf-du-Pape Blanc 1989: A wild and exotic wine, with excellent concentration and distinction, ripe peach, almond and Mandarin orange aromas, lively peach and spice flavors and a long, earthy finish. Try in 1993 to '95. 2,000 cases made. $35 (10/15/91) **91**
Châteauneuf-du-Pape Roussanne Vieille Vigne 1988: Rich and intense, with ripe honey, butterscotch, spice and custard notes and hints of nutmeg and clove on the finish. Altogether very spicy, big and ripe, with a lingering finish. Can stand a year or two to settle down; drink now to 1994. $46 (12/31/90) **87**

DOMAINE DE BEAURENARD
Châteauneuf-du-Pape 1990: A well-crafted wine with appealing suppleness. Has creamy aromas, a creamy texture, vanilla and apple flavors, a firm structure and a long finish. $25 (10/15/91) **86**
Châteauneuf-du-Pape 1989: A bit on the weird side, medium-bodied, with strange onion, garlic and earth aromas and lemon, mineral and apple flavors. $25 (10/15/91) **75**

BOSQUET DES PAPES
Châteauneuf-du-Pape 1990: An early drinking, fresh style, though lean and steely. The melon and grape aromas follow through on the palate. Medium in acidity, with a lively finish. $22 (10/15/91) **82**
Châteauneuf-du-Pape 1989: Round and buttery, with well-focused fruit, this has fine lemon meringue, apple and earth aromas and apple, vanilla, earth and hazelnut flavors. Full-bodied, with a long finish. $18 (10/15/91) **87**

LAURENT CHARLES BROTTE
Châteauneuf-du-Pape 1987: Seems hard and ungenerous, not the ripe, open wine one expects from this region. Good, but lacks depth and richness. $14 (10/31/89) **74**

DOMAINE DU PERE CABOCHE
Châteauneuf-du-Pape 1990: Lively, fruity and interesting, with freshly sliced peach aromas and hints of almond. Medium-bodied, round and delicious, with a strawberries-and-cream flavor and an almond finish. $20 (10/15/91) **85**

LES CAILLOUX
Châteauneuf-du-Pape 1990: A serious wine, with good concentration, full-bodied, with honeydew melon and green apple aromas, ripe honey and melon flavors, an excellent backbone and a very rich finish. Better in 1993 or '94. $18 (10/15/91) **88**
Châteauneuf-du-Pape 1989: Wonderfully focused, with a refreshing quality. Has apple, banana and honey aromas, super-clean, intense apple, banana, butter and honey flavors and a long finish. $17 (10/15/91) **89**

CHANTE CIGALE
Châteauneuf-du-Pape 1990: Ripe and flavorful, but needs a little bottle age. Has perfumed crushed grape and honey aromas, almond, honey and ripe fruit flavors, very good acidity and a long, flavorful finish. Full-bodied. Better in 1993 to '95. $25 (10/15/91) **90**
Châteauneuf-du-Pape 1989: Not a blockbuster, but very pleasant, with fresh apple and pear aromas, tart, lively fruit and mineral flavors and a crisp finish. $15 (10/15/91) **85**

Key to Symbols

The scores reported here are the results of blind tastings conducted by our panel of senior editors. Wines that carry the initials below are results of individual tastings.

THE WINE SPECTATOR 100-POINT SCALE ***95-100***—Classic, a great wine; ***90-94***—Outstanding, superior character and style; ***80-89***—Good to very good, a wine with special qualities; ***70-79***—Average, drinkable wine that may have minor flaws; ***60-69***—Below average, drinkable but not recommended; ***50-59***—Poor, undrinkable, not recommended. "+"—With a score indicates a range; used primarily with barrel tastings to indicate a preliminary score.

SPECIAL DESIGNATIONS SS—Spectator Selection, CS—Cellar Selection, BB—Best Buy, ($NA)—Price not available, (NR)—Not released.

TASTER'S INITIALS (JG)—Jim Gordon, (HS)—Harvey Steiman, (JL)—James Laube, (JS)—James Suckling, (TM)—Thomas Matthews, (TR)—Terry Robards, (PM)—Per-Henrik Mansson, (BT)—Barrel Tasting (these wines were tasted blind from barrel samples), (CA-date)—*California's Great Cabernets* by James Laube, (CH-date)—*California's Great Chardonnays* by James Laube, (VP-date)—*Vintage Port* by James Suckling.

DATE TASTED Dates in parentheses represent the issue in which the rating was published.

CLOS DU MONT-OLIVET
Châteauneuf-du-Pape 1990: Has an impressive fruit and earth character, with pear, almond and melon aromas, rich, fruity flavors, a mineral, earthy character and a fresh finish. $20 (10/15/91) **86**
Châteauneuf-du-Pape 1989: Decent, but rather boring among this group, with candied apple aromas, almond and spice flavors and a light, almost dull finish. $20 (10/15/91) **78**

CLOS DES PAPES
Châteauneuf-du-Pape 1990: A good, classic Châteauneuf blanc. Fresh mineral, spice and apple aromas open to medium-bodied, blanched almond and mineral flavors. Has nice concentration and a smooth finish. $25 (10/15/91) **85**
Châteauneuf-du-Pape 1989: Shows good fruit and a clean, ripe character, with peaches-and-cream aromas and hints of almond, full-bodied almond, spice and mineral flavors and a simple finish. $25 (10/15/91) **85**

DELAS
Châteauneuf-du-Pape 1985 $18 (11/15/87) **73**
Châteauneuf-du-Pape Cuvée de Haute Pierre 1990: A rather traditional style, with earthy almond flavors. Full-bodied, with almond and honey aromas, very ripe flavors verging on raisins and a spicy almond finish. $21 (10/15/91) **80**
Châteauneuf-du-Pape Cuvée de Haute Pierre 1989: Simple and fruity, but nothing more. Full-bodied, with fruit cocktail aromas and similar flavors. Has clean, fresh acidity on the finish. $20 (10/15/91) **79**

DOMAINE JEAN DEYDIER & FILS
Châteauneuf-du-Pape Les Clefs d'Or 1986 $17 (11/15/87) **74**

DOMAINE FONT DE MICHELLE
Châteauneuf-du-Pape 1990: A fruit bomb, with freshly crushed grape and melon aromas that explode on the palate. Has a lovely concentration and balance of fruit. Better in 1993 to '94; should age well. $20 (10/15/91) **89**
Châteauneuf-du-Pape 1985 $15 (11/15/87) **81**

CHATEAU DE LA GARDINE
Châteauneuf-du-Pape 1990: Somewhat atypical, but well made. It's difficult to tell if the fruit will emerge from the new wood. Shows blanched almond, vanilla and fruit aromas. Full-bodied, with lots of new wood flavor, a firm backbone and a toasty finish. Very tight and closed in; better in 1993 or '94. $20 (10/15/91) **86**
Châteauneuf-du-Pape Blanc Vielles Vignes 1989: Superbly crafted with beautiful fruit and new wood, almost like a Burgundy. Has classy apple, earth and mineral aromas, with intense toasty, tropical fruit flavor and a long, elegant finish. Better in 1993 to '96. Limited supply. $25 (10/15/91) **90**

DOMAINE DU GRAND TINEL
Châteauneuf-du-Pape 1990: A fat, soft wine made from very ripe fruit; somewhat tiring to drink. Shows typical fig, pineapple and tropical fruit aromas and very ripe, tropical fruit flavors, and has a full-bodied, thick, oily texture. $18 (10/15/91) **81**

PAUL JABOULET AINE
Châteauneuf-du-Pape Les Cèdres 1989: Jaboulet's red Châteauneuf is much better. Straightforward and fruity, with modestly interesting mineral, lemon and onion aromas and mineral, earth and spice flavors. Full-bodied, with medium acidity and a medium finish. $22 (10/15/91) **80**

DOMAINE DE LA JANASSE
Châteauneuf-du-Pape 1989: Ripe, full-bodied and spicy, with pleasant floral and honey overtones to the basic pear flavor, hinting at orange on the finish. Pleasant and drinkable now; not as heavy as some white Rhônes. $20 (10/15/91) **85**

DOMAINE DE MARCOUX
Châteauneuf-du-Pape 1990: Tightly structured, with plenty of rather exotic flavors and cantaloupe, almond and spice aromas. Full-bodied, with very good concentration and a firm structure. Will improve with age. $20 (10/15/91) **88**

DOMAINE DE MONPERTUIS
Châteauneuf-du-Pape 1988: Attractive for its fresh honey, almond, floral and pear notes, this rich, full-bodied style offers plenty of flavor and depth. Doesn't have much finesse, but you don't expect that from a rambunctious young white Rhône. Drink now or in 1993. $29 (3/31/91) **87**

CHATEAU MONT-REDON
Châteauneuf-du-Pape 1990: Exotic and exciting, with plenty of banana and apple aromas. Full-bodied, with lots of banana and ripe melon flavors and an attractive mineral finish. $20 (10/15/91) **85**
Châteauneuf-du-Pape 1987: Has an earthy, gamy style with enough floral aromas and flavors to make it attractive and nice hints of honey and almond on the finish. Drink now. $20 (10/31/89) **79**

CHATEAU DE LA NERTHE
Châteauneuf-du-Pape 1990: This firm wine has focused, rich, super-fresh banana, vanilla and melon aromas and flavors, a chalky, silky mouth-feel and a fresh finish. $30 (10/15/91) **87**
Châteauneuf-du-Pape 1989: A classy, gracious style, the beautiful cream, peach and pineapple aromas follow through on the palate. Very creamy in texture and flavor, with a delicious finish. $20 (10/15/91) **87**
Châteauneuf-du-Pape Clos de Beavenir 1990: A very clever wine, with excellent use of new-wood maturation. Super-ripe, full-bodied, with complex almond and fruit aromas, wonderfully focused vanilla, almond, nutmeg and apple flavors and a very long, rich, toasty finish. Better in 1993 or '94. $30 (10/15/91) **87**

CHATEAU RAYAS
Châteauneuf-du-Pape Réserve 1989: An extremely flavorful, classy wine, with super-focused tangerine and melon aromas, vivid pineapple, melon and blanched almond flavors and a long, lively finish. Rel: $30 Cur: $59 (10/15/91) **90**
Châteauneuf-du-Pape Réserve 1986: Very woody at first, with heady vanilla aromas, but it opens up to piny, earthy flavors plus suggestions of peach and pear. An acceptably bitter edge keeps it in check, and the finish is long and rich. $44 (3/15/89) **85**

DOMAINE DE LA ROQUETTE
Châteauneuf-du-Pape 1990: Fat and rich, with an almost overripe character. Has fresh melon and peach aromas. Full-bodied, with an oily mouth-feel, an abundance of ripe fruit flavors and honey and spice notes on the finish. $25 (10/15/91) **84**

DOMAINE DU VIEUX LAZARET
Châteauneuf-du-Pape 1990: Light and refreshing; an early-drinking wine that's good, but nothing special. Clean, fresh aromas of peach and apple follow through to a light, refreshing palate and a fresh finish. $16 (10/15/91) **81**
Châteauneuf-du-Pape 1986: Has *terroir* by the spadeful, but is otherwise austere. An earthy, claylike aroma is followed by oily, slightly austere, earthy flavors of honey and a bit of pear. Try now. $14.50 (3/15/89) **81**

DOMAINE DU VIEUX TELEGRAPHE
Châteauneuf-du-Pape 1990: A round, caressing style that's fatter and oiler than some, with pungent banana and melon aromas, a round mouth-feel and tropical fruit flavors. Spicy and fruity on the finish. $20 (10/15/91) **86**
Châteauneuf-du-Pape 1986 $15 (11/15/87) **77**

OTHER RHÔNE WHITE

JEAN CLAUDE BOISSET
Côtes du Rhône 1986 $4.50 (11/15/87) **70**

LA BOUVERIE
Costières de Nimes 1989: Simple and fruity, with hints of almond and walnut around the core of pear flavor. Round on the finish. $6 (7/15/91) **79**

DOMAINE DE LA CAVALE
Côtes du Lubéron 1987: Lean and crisp, with tart melon and herbal flavors. Well made but not generous in flavor. $7 (2/15/89) **77**

M. CHAPOUTIER
Côtes du Rhône Blanc 1988: A supple, mature white wine, with generous spice, honey and pear aromas and flavors that expand on the finish. Drinkable now. Tasted twice. $13 (12/31/91) **83**
Hermitage Chante-Alouette Blanc 1989: Clean and somewhat blunt, with pretty honey and floral aromas and flavors. Simple and pleasant. Tasted twice. $26 (12/31/91) **79**
Hermitage Chante-Alouette Blanc 1988: Big and flavorful, with lots of spice and honey aromas and flavors that blossom on the finish. A buttery style that shies away from fruit and keeps a firm structure. Probably best to drink after 1993. Tasted twice. $20 (12/31/91) **84**
Hermitage Chante-Alouette Blanc 1985: A powerfully flavored wine that's not for everyone, but packs plenty of punch. Has a deep, brassy color, pungent, musty, candylike aromas, and mature nutty, lemony flavors. $23 (3/15/90) **80**
Hermitage Chante-Alouette Blanc 1983 $16 (5/01/86) **70**
Hermitage Spécial Cuvée 180th Anniversary 1986: Spicy, with hints of orange blossom, honey and peach in an earthy, oxidized style. It's not for everyone. Drink now or in 1993. $24 (12/31/90) **83**

J.L. CHAVE
Hermitage 1983 Rel: $20 Cur: $48 (5/01/86) **81**

CUILLERON
Condrieu 1988: Elegant, rich and floral, with pretty spice, pear and citrus flavors that are lively and perfumed. The flavors dance across the palate and last on the finish. Try it now, but it should improve until 1994 or so. 100 cases made. $34 (12/31/90) **91**
St.-Joseph Blanc 1988: Ripe, luscious and alcoholic, with pretty floral, almond, spice, orange and citrus nunaces. A true-to-form Rhône made in a deliberate style that will appeal to some more than others. Drink now to 1994. $17 (12/31/90) **81**

CHATEAU CURSON
Crozes-Hermitage 1990: Lean and silky in texture, with earthy, nutty, slightly floral and pear aromas and flavors. Ever-so-slightly bitter on the finish. Drinkable now, but could gain from cellaring until 1993. $18 (10/15/91) **82**

VINCENT L. DARNAT
Côtes du Rhône Blanc 1985 $5.50 (2/29/88) BB **81**

DEZORMEAUX
Condrieu Viognier Côteaux du Colombier 1987: Big and rich, with a bouquet of floral fruit on the nose and rich tropical fruit, spice and vanilla on the palate, long and full-bodied. Delicious on release, probably best now. $37 (3/15/89) **87**

CHATEAU DE FONSALETTE
Côtes du Rhône 1986: Packs a lot of punch but the flavors are subdued. Full-bodied, with pear flavors and a touch of nutty maturity on the palate and sweet vanilla on the finish. $18.50 (3/15/89) **80**

LA FORGE
Côtes du Lubéron 1990: Lean, crisp and gently fruity, with modest apple and spice flavors that finish clean and fresh. Drinkable now. $7 (11/15/91) BB **81**

PIERRE GAILLARD
Côtes du Rhône Viognier Clos de Cuminaille 1990: A lavish wine that's ripe and fruity, with generous butter, pear, orange and peach aromas and flavors extending into a long finish. Keeps pumping out the flavor without turning heavy. Beautifully aromatic, as well. Drinkable now. 20 cases made. $30 (10/15/91) **92**
Côtes du Rhône Viognier Clos de Cuminaille 1986: Fascinating. Bright and fruity but with enough restraint on the palate to keep it balanced. Has an overlay of honey and butterscotch flavors and spicy, orange aromas. $25 (3/15/89) **87**

DOMAINE LES GOUBERT
Côtes du Rhône-Villages Sablet 1986 $7 (3/31/88) **68**

CHATEAU GRILLET
Château-Grillet 1986: An intense style, with earthy, lemony flavors that turn a bit bizarre on the finish before picking up some nutty, buttery notes. Drink now or in 1993. $75 (11/30/90) **80**

E. GUIGAL
Condrieu Viognier 1990: Rich and seductive, a creamy-textured wine, with beautifully articulated pear, melon, honey and orange blossom aromas and flavors that continue to echo on the long finish. Hints of vanilla and spice add depth and character. Drinkable now, but should be better around 1993 to '95. 5,000 cases made. Rel: $40 Cur: $45 (12/31/91) **90**
Condrieu Viognier 1987: Big and flavorful, but it holds something in reserve, allowing its elegant grapefruit, peach, vanilla and spice aromas and flavors to unfold gracefully. Tasty now, but it has the stuff to age through the late 1990s. $48 (3/15/89) **89**
Côtes du Rhône Blanc 1990: A pleasant wine that's ripe in flavor, but firm in texture, offering pear and nutmeg aromas and flavors that persist into a solid finish. Drinkable now. $9 (12/31/91) **81**
Côtes du Rhône Blanc 1989: An attractive white Rhône, with a variety of interesting fruit and spice flavors and a broad, smooth texture. Hints of pear and honey linger on the finish to give it extra appeal. $10 (3/31/91) **83**
Côtes du Rhône Blanc 1988: One of the most generous white Rhônes we've ever tasted. Ripe and fruity in flavor, marked by tropical fruit and almond notes in a soft, round texture. $9 (3/15/90) **83**
Hermitage 1989: Rich, earthy and smooth, with distinct apple cider, spice and honey flavors on the finish, plus a little bitterness. Drinkable now. Rel: $25 Cur: $31 (1/31/92) **81**
Hermitage 1988: Floral and earthy, with a core of pear, honey, apricot and spice notes. Ripe, rich and full-bodied, but finishes on the rough side. Drink now or in 1993. Rel: $23 Cur: $30 (3/31/91) **87**
Hermitage 1986 $27 (3/15/90) (HS) **88**
Hermitage 1985 $23 (12/15/87) **76**
Hermitage 1981 $15 (5/01/86) **64**
Tavel 1989: Very light orange-amber, with distinctive Rhône-like black pepper and cherry aromas and flavors. Dry and full-bodied for a rosé. Not for all tastes, but it's well crafted. $15 (3/31/91) **80**

PAUL JABOULET AINE
Crozes-Hermitage Moute Blanche 1987 $11.50 (10/15/88) **70**
Hermitage Le Chevalier de Sterimberg 1983 $11 (5/01/86) **78**

PROSPER MAUFOUX
Côtes du Rhône 1989: An earthy aroma and chalky, minerallike flavors don't leave much to like. Unpleasantly dry on the finish. $8 (3/31/91) **67**
Côtes du Rhône 1987: Ripe and exotic, with floral, spicy aromas and rich, vanilla- and honey-scented pear flavors. Soft and mellow. A good value. $6 (7/15/89) **81**

CHATEAU MONT-REDON
Côtes du Rhône 1987: Rich and full-bodied, with pear, spice, almond and apple flavors that show more finesse, grace and balance than most white Rhônes. It's not alcoholic. $8 (10/31/89) BB **86**

PHILIPPE PICHON
Condrieu 1989: Ripe, rich and seductive, a plush pillow of a wine, with all sorts of apricot, honey, hazelnut, vanilla and floral aromas and flavors that keep taking turns as it extends into a long, long finish. An exotic, substantial wine that offers plenty of pleasure now, but should keep improving through 1993 to '95. $45 (11/15/91) **94**

CHATEAU DES ROQUES
Côtes du Rhône-Villages Cuvée Bethleem 1988: An aggressive, overripe white that tastes like cooked apricots and almonds. Drinkable but coarse. $7.50 (3/31/90) **68**

CHATEAU ST.-ESTEVE D'UCHAUX
Côtes du Rhône Blanc de Viognier 1990: Rich and spicy through and through, with marvelous floral, honey and pear aromas and flavors. Tightens up and throws in grapefruit flavor on the finish. Has a pleasant mineral edge that hints at bitterness, but it's drinkable and fresh. $24 (11/15/91) **87**

CHATEAU DE SEGRIES
Lirac 1985: Soft and generous, a velvety wine with carefully balanced berry and plum aromas and flavors plus a nice touch of tobacco. Drinkable now. $10 (12/15/89) **81**

H. SORREL
Hermitage Les Rocoules 1984 $20 (5/01/86) **83**

CAVE DE TAIN L'HERMITAGE
Crozes-Hermitage Michel Courtial 1986: Tastes lively, tangy and concentrated, with floral, pearlike aromas and pineappley, spicy flavors. Has great balance. Drink it up now. A good value. $8.50 (3/15/90) **84**

L. DE VALLOUIT
Crozes-Hermitage Blanc 1990: Strikes an interesting balance between earthiness and fruitiness, playing its chalky mineral nuances against a core of ripe pear and Muscat-like flavors. Drinkable now. $11 (12/31/91) **81**
St.-Joseph Blanc 1990: Smooth and round, with generous pear, spice and pineapple aromas and flavors. Has restraint to frame the flavors nicely. Drinkable now. $15 (12/31/91) **85**

GEORGES VERNAY
Condrieu 1990: Firm and concentrated, a big wine that needs time to fill in its structure. For now, it shows lovely floral, almond and pear aromas and flavors backed by lively acidity. Probably better now than on release. $43 (10/15/91) **88**
Condrieu 1988: Wonderfully perfumed and aromatic with thick, rich, concentrated pineapple, guava and spicy fruit flavors that are young and powerful with an alcoholic aftertaste. $40 (10/31/89) **81**
Condrieu 1987: Earthy and exotic, with grapefruit, orange peel and smoky aromas and flavors, but smooth and soft in texture for a wine with so many citrus flavors. Less powerful than it is persistent. Drink now. $36 (3/15/89) **85**
Condrieu Côteau de Vernon 1987: Thick, dense, heavy and alcoholic, lacking grace and finesse. Some may admire the rich concentration and honey flavors, but it lacks charm. $43 (10/31/89) **77**

LA VIEILLE FERME
Côtes du Lubéron 1989: This sturdy wine offers a firm texture and attractive fig and honey flavors, with a nice hint of spice on the finish. Drinkable now. $7 (4/30/91) BB **80**
Côtes du Lubéron 1988: An austere style wine that emphazizes earthy, chalky, honeylike aromas and flavors over straight fruit, but a hint of orange emerges on the finish. Its balance is good and its subtlety is appealing. $6.50 (3/15/90) **78**
Côtes du Lubéron 1986 $6 (4/15/88) **71**
Côtes du Rhône Réserve 1988: Plenty of flavor, depth and intensity with spicy lemon, pear and nectarine flavors that are quite pleasant. Stays in bounds. A good value. $8 (10/31/89) **85**

SAUTERNES

CHATEAU D'ARCHE
Sauternes 1988: Intense, rich and supple, with generous, buttery pear, spice and fig flavors that are uncommonly thick and lush. Picks up a nice note of tobacco on the aftertaste. Drink now to 1995. $20/375ml (4/30/91) **87**
Sauternes 1987 ($NA) (6/15/90) **85**
Sauternes 1986: Spicy, gingery aromas and flavors add zing to the ripe pear and honey character. Smooth and generous right through the long finish, but not as opulent and rich as it could be. Drink now. $32 (12/31/89) **85**
Sauternes 1983 Rel: $23 Cur: $39 (1/31/88) **93**

CHATEAU D'ARCHE-PUGNEAU
Sauternes 1989 (NR) (6/15/90) (BT) **75+**
Sauternes 1988 (NR) (6/15/90) (BT) **75+**
Sauternes 1987 ($NA) (6/15/90) **71**

CHATEAU D'ARMAJAN-DES-ORMES
Sauternes 1989 (NR) (6/15/90) (BT) **90+**
Sauternes 1987 ($NA) (6/15/90) **72**

DOMAINE DE BARJUNEAU-CHAUVIN
Sauternes 1989 (NR) (6/15/90) (BT) **85+**
Sauternes 1987 ($NA) (6/15/90) **74**

BARTON & GUESTIER
Sauternes 1985 $12 (5/31/88) **75**

CHATEAU BASTOR-LAMONTAGNE
Sauternes 1989 (NR) (6/15/90) (BT) **95+**
Sauternes 1988: Extremely sweet, ripe and earthy, with sugar, fig and tobacco flavors. Starts out great, but lacks acidity, botrytis character and pure fruit flavor. Good, but not great for Sauternes. $18 (2/15/91) **82**
Sauternes 1987 $17 (6/15/90) **67**
Sauternes 1985 $20 (5/31/88) **82**
Sauternes 1983 $20 (1/31/88) **82**

Key to Symbols

The scores reported here are the results of blind tastings conducted by our panel of senior editors. Wines that carry the initials below are results of individual tastings.

THE WINE SPECTATOR 100-POINT SCALE ***95-100***—Classic, a great wine; ***90-94***—Outstanding, superior character and style; ***80-89***—Good to very good, a wine with special qualities; ***70-79***—Average, drinkable wine that may have minor flaws; ***60-69***—Below average, drinkable but not recommended; ***50-59***—Poor, undrinkable, not recommended. "+"—With a score indicates a range; used primarily with barrel tastings to indicate a preliminary score.

SPECIAL DESIGNATIONS SS—Spectator Selection, CS—Cellar Selection, BB—Best Buy, ($NA)—Price not available, (NR)—Not released.

TASTER'S INITIALS (JG)—Jim Gordon, (HS)—Harvey Steiman, (JL)—James Laube, (JS)—James Suckling, (TM)—Thomas Matthews, (TR)—Terry Robards, (PM)—Per-Henrik Mansson, (BT)—Barrel Tasting (these wines were tasted blind from barrel samples), (CA-date)—*California's Great Cabernets* by James Laube, (CH-date)—*California's Great Chardonnays* by James Laube, (VP-date)—*Vintage Port* by James Suckling.

DATE TASTED Dates in parentheses represent the issue in which the rating was published.

CHATEAU BECHEREAU
Sauternes 1989 (NR) (6/15/90) (BT) **80+**

CHATEAU BOUYOT
Barsac 1988 (NR) (6/15/90) (BT) **70+**
Barsac 1987 ($NA) (6/15/90) **74**

CHATEAU BROUSTET
Barsac 1989 (NR) (6/15/90) (BT) **90+**
Barsac 1988: Ripe and rich, with lots of almond, honey and vanilla aromas and flavors that are sweet and concentrated without being cloying. A bit earthy or moldy on the finish. Drinkable, but probably better after it settles down around 1995 to '98. $19/375ml (3/31/91) **83**
Barsac 1986 $20 (6/30/88) (BT) **75+**

CHATEAU CAILLOU
Barsac 1989 $24 (6/15/90) (BT) **95+**
Barsac 1988 Rel: $37 Cur: $41 (6/15/90) (BT) **85+**
Barsac 1987 ($NA) (6/15/90) **85**
Barsac 1986 $30 (6/30/88) (BT) **75+**
Barsac 1983 Rel: $22 Cur: $28 (1/31/88) **76**

CHATEAU CAMERON
Sauternes 1989 (NR) (6/15/90) (BT) **85+**
Sauternes 1988 (NR) (6/15/90) (BT) **85+**
Sauternes 1987 ($NA) (6/15/90) **82**

CHATEAU CANTEGRIL
Barsac 1989 (NR) (6/15/90) (BT) **85+**

DOMAINE DE CAPLANE
Sauternes 1985 $11 (9/30/88) **81**

CHATEAU DE LA CHARTREUSE
Sauternes 1988 (NR) (6/15/90) (BT) **80+**
Sauternes 1987 ($NA) (6/15/90) **77**
Sauternes 1983 Rel: $10 Cur: $26 (1/31/88) **90**

CHATEAU CLIMENS
Barsac 1989 $60 (6/15/90) (BT) **90+**
Barsac 1988 $48 (6/15/90) (BT) **90+**
Barsac 1986: Despite the high level of volatile acidity, the intense tobacco, butter and tarry notes are more appealing than most '86s we've seen. Pretty flavors on the aftertaste, but it could use more concentration and richness. $48 (12/31/89) **84**
Barsac 1983 Rel: $50 Cur: $55 (1/31/88) CS **95**

CHATEAU CLOS HAUT-PEYRAGUEY
Sauternes 1989 (NR) (6/15/90) (BT) **80+**
Sauternes 1988 $26 (6/15/90) (BT) **85+**
Sauternes 1987 ($NA) (6/15/90) **83**
Sauternes 1986 $23 (6/30/88) (BT) **80+**

CHATEAU COUTET
Barsac 1989 (NR) (6/15/90) (BT) **95+**
Barsac 1988 $47 (6/15/90) (BT) **90+**
Barsac 1987 $27 (6/15/90) **80**
Barsac 1986 $32 (6/30/88) (BT) **80+**
Barsac 1983 $30 (1/31/88) **86**

CHATEAU DOISY DAENE
Sauternes 1989 $27 (6/15/90) (BT) **85+**
Sauternes 1988: Fat, rich and ripe, with lots of fig, floral and tobacco aromas and flavors that turn a bit earthy and smoky on the sweet finish. A solid Sauternes that should be best after 1996 to '98. $34/375ml (11/15/91) **87**
Sauternes 1986: Earthy, matchstick aromas and flavors cut through whatever fruit and richness might be present. Hard to expect this to develop. Tasted twice. $35 (12/31/89) **68**
Sauternes 1985 $24 (5/31/88) **73**
Sauternes 1983 Rel: $21 Cur: $30 (1/31/88) **87**

CHATEAU DOISY-DUBROCA
Barsac 1989 (NR) (6/15/90) (BT) **90+**
Barsac 1988 $30 (6/15/90) (BT) **85+**

CHATEAU DOISY-VEDRINES
Sauternes 1989 $46 (6/15/90) (BT) **90+**
Sauternes 1988 $31 (6/15/90) (BT) **90+**
Sauternes 1986: Ripe, round and honeyed, with a welcome touch of botrytis adding complexity, spicy and toasty on the long finish. Drink now to 1996. $19 (12/31/89) **86**
Sauternes 1983 Rel: $18 Cur: $29 (1/31/88) **73**

CHATEAU DUDON
Barsac 1989 (NR) (6/15/90) (BT) **60+**

CHATEAU FARLURET
Barsac 1988 (NR) (6/15/90) (BT) **85+**

CHATEAU FILHOT
Sauternes 1989 (NR) (6/15/90) (BT) **85+**
Sauternes 1988 $25 (6/15/90) (BT) **85+**
Sauternes 1987 $19 (6/15/90) **68**
Sauternes 1986 $19 (12/31/89) **83**
Sauternes 1983 Rel: $21 Cur: $34 (1/31/88) **86**
Sauternes 1980 Rel: $11.50 Cur: $25 (5/01/84) **80**

CHATEAU GRAVES
Barsac 1989 (NR) (6/15/90) (BT) **90+**

CHATEAU GUIRAUD
Sauternes 1989 (NR) (6/15/90) (BT) **85+**
Sauternes 1988 $38 (6/15/90) (BT) **85+**
Sauternes 1987 ($NA) (6/15/90) **72**
Sauternes 1986 $48 (12/31/89) **89**
Sauternes 1983 $30 (1/31/88) **76**
Sauternes Le Dauphin 1987: Wimpy, lacking fruit and character. Simple ripe apricot flavors are shallow and thin. Château Guiraud's second wine. $11 (12/31/89) **72**

CHATEAU HAUT-BERGERON
Sauternes 1989 (NR) (6/15/90) (BT) **90+**
Sauternes 1988 (NR) (6/15/90) (BT) **90+**
Sauternes 1987 ($NA) (6/15/90) **81**

CHATEAU HAUT-BOMMES
Sauternes 1989 (NR) (6/15/90) (BT) **85+**
Sauternes 1988 (NR) (6/15/90) (BT) **75+**
Sauternes 1987 ($NA) (6/15/90) **74**

CHATEAU HAUT-CLAVERIE
Sauternes 1988 (NR) (6/15/90) (BT) **85+**

CHATEAU LES JUSTICES
Sauternes 1989 (NR) (6/15/90) (BT) **85+**
Sauternes 1988: Plenty of ripe pear and pineapple flavors and hints of tobacco and almond. This bold, sweet dessert wine should be cellared until about 1996 or beyond. $38 (11/15/91) **87**
Sauternes 1987 ($NA) (6/15/90) **75**
Sauternes 1986 $16 (12/31/89) **85**
Sauternes 1983 $15 (1/31/88) **67**

CHATEAU LAFAURIE-PEYRAGUEY
Sauternes 1989 (NR) (6/15/90) (BT) **95+**
Sauternes 1988: A bit thin, but the rich honey, pear, peach and fig flavors are attractive, if a bit sugary. The finish turns simple. Very good, but not all one hopes for in such a fine vintage. 4,500 cases made. Rel: $35 Cur: $40 (4/30/91) **85**
Sauternes 1987 $27 (6/15/90) **87**
Sauternes 1986 Rel: $27 Cur: $38 (12/31/89) **86**
Sauternes 1985 Rel: $32 Cur: $38 (9/30/88) **92**
Sauternes 1983 Rel: $24 Cur: $70 (1/31/88) **91**

CHATEAU LAMOTHE
Sauternes 1988: Light and fruity, with appealing nectarine and earth aromas and flavors that are a bit grassy, smoothing out on the finish. Drinkable now. $16/375ml (3/31/91) **84**
Sauternes 1986: Has complexity and subtlety in a medium-weight framework, ripe and round without being overblown. Smooth and well balanced for drinking now or through 1994. $29 (12/31/89) **85**

CHATEAU LAMOTHE-DESPUJOLS
Sauternes 1989 (NR) (6/15/90) (BT) **85+**
Sauternes 1987 ($NA) (6/15/90) **84**

CHATEAU LAMOTHE-GUIGNARD
Sauternes 1989 (NR) (6/15/90) (BT) **85+**
Sauternes 1988 $35 (6/15/90) (BT) **85+**
Sauternes 1987 ($NA) (6/15/90) **77**
Sauternes 1986 $30 (6/30/88) (BT) **75+**

CHATEAU LANGE
Sauternes 1988 (NR) (6/15/90) (BT) **80+**
Sauternes 1987 ($NA) (6/15/90) **78**

CHATEAU LIOT
Barsac 1989 $28 (6/15/90) (BT) **85+**
Barsac 1988: Sweet, clean and modestly flavorful, with pear, pineapple and peach notes. Tempting now, but should gain complexity if aged until at least 1994. $25/375ml (11/15/91) **84**
Barsac 1986: Rich and fairly concentrated, showing lots of toast and spice notes gracing the pear and honey aromas and flavors, long and elegant on a medium-weight frame. A bit tannic, it needs until 1993 to '95 to show what it has. $22 (12/31/89) **87**
Barsac 1985 $9.25 (5/31/88) **84**
Barsac 1983 Rel: $11 Cur: $17 (4/01/86) **56**

CHATEAU DE MALLE
Sauternes 1989 (NR) (6/15/90) (BT) **85+**
Sauternes 1988 $15 (6/15/90) (BT) **85+**
Sauternes 1987 $15 (6/15/90) **81**
Sauternes 1986 $15 (6/30/88) (BT) **85+**
Sauternes 1981 $13 (8/31/86) **84**

CHATEAU MAYNE DES CARMES
Sauternes 1989: An earthy character influences the fig, honey and walnut flavors in this medium-weight wine. Good if you don't mind a little funkiness. The finish is modest and slightly bitter. $20 (6/30/92) **83**

CHATEAU MENOTA
Barsac 1988 (NR) (6/15/90) (BT) **80+**
Barsac 1987 ($NA) (6/15/90) **78**

CHATEAU MONT-JOYE
Barsac 1989 (NR) (6/15/90) (BT) **75+**
Barsac 1987 ($NA) (6/15/90) **63**

DOMAINE DE MONTEILS
Sauternes 1988 (NR) (6/15/90) (BT) **80+**
Sauternes 1987 ($NA) (6/15/90) **72**

CHATEAU NAIRAC
Barsac 1989 (NR) (6/15/90) (BT) **85+**
Barsac 1988 $30 (6/15/90) (BT) **85+**
Barsac 1987 $31 (6/15/90) **81**
Barsac 1986 $31 (12/31/89) **77**
Barsac 1983 Rel: $15 Cur: $29 (4/15/87) **92**

CHATEAU PAJOT
Sauternes 1983 $8 (1/31/88) **62**

CHATEAU PASCAUD-VILLEFRANCHE
Sauternes 1986: Tobacco and toasty aromas and flavors frame the fairly ripe but not-too-concentrated fruit. Sweet and simple. $24 (12/31/89) **78**
Sauternes 1983 $10 (1/31/88) **65**

CHATEAU PIADA
Barsac 1983 $11 (1/31/88) **70**
Sauternes 1989 (NR) (6/15/90) (BT) **85+**
Sauternes 1988 (NR) (6/15/90) (BT) **90+**
Sauternes 1987: There's true Sauternes character in this kosher wine. Has toasty, ripe aromas marked by botrytis and rich, nutty flavors. Full-bodied and sweet, with a long, full finish. $35 (3/31/91) **86**

CHATEAU PIOT-DAVID
Barsac 1989 (NR) (6/15/90) (BT) **85+**

CHATEAU PROST
Barsac 1989 (NR) (6/15/90) (BT) **70+**

CHATEAU RABAUD-PROMIS
Sauternes 1989 (NR) (6/15/90) (BT) **85+**
Sauternes 1988 $35 (6/15/90) (BT) **95+**
Sauternes 1987 ($NA) (6/15/90) **83**
Sauternes 1986 $28 (6/30/88) (BT) **95+**
Sauternes 1983 $54 (1/31/88) **90**

CHATEAU RAYMOND-LAFON
Sauternes 1983 Rel: $38 Cur: $54 (1/31/88) **93**

CHATEAU DE RAYNE-VIGNEAU
Sauternes 1989 $41 (6/15/90) (BT) **80+**
Sauternes 1988: Smooth, flavorful and modest in scope, with nice pineapple and vanilla aromas and flavors and hints of butterscotch on the finish. Drinkable now, but should be better after 1993 to '95. $24/375ml (11/15/91) **86**
Sauternes 1987 ($NA) (6/15/90) **77**
Sauternes 1986 $49 (12/31/89) **86**
Sauternes 1983 Rel: $17 Cur: $20 (1/31/88) **77**

CHATEAU RIEUSSEC
Sauternes 1989 $66 (6/15/90) (BT) **90+**
Sauternes 1988: Light and sweet, it's more sugary than honeylike, offering nice apricot, caramel and spice flavors that stick around on the finish. Drink in 1994 or '95. Rel: $50 Cur: $69 (11/15/91) **84**
Sauternes 1987 $31 (6/15/90) **89**
Sauternes 1986 Rel: $50 Cur: $62 (12/31/89) **80**
Sauternes 1985 $38 (5/31/88) **86**
Sauternes 1983 Rel: $52 Cur: $74 (1/31/88) **94**
Sauternes 1982 Rel: $13 Cur: $45 (2/01/85) **86**
Sauternes 1981 Rel: $14 Cur: $38 (12/01/84) **90**

CHATEAU ROLLAND
Barsac 1988 (NR) (6/15/90) (BT) **80+**
Barsac 1987 ($NA) (6/15/90) **77**

CHATEAU ROMER DU HAYOT
Sauternes 1989 (NR) (6/15/90) (BT) **80+**
Sauternes 1988: Drinkable, but flawed and flat tasting. Tasted twice. $17/375ml (4/30/91) **72**
Sauternes 1986: Pleasant and showing some attractive fruit, but it finishes sugary and plain. Drinkable now. $22 (12/31/89) **78**
Sauternes 1983 $19 (1/31/88) **72**
Sauternes 1982 $13 (10/16/85) **82**

CHATEAU ROUMIEU-LACOSTE
Barsac 1989 (NR) (6/15/90) (BT) **85+**

CHATEAU ST.-MARC
Barsac 1989 (NR) (6/15/90) (BT) **85+**
Barsac 1987 ($NA) (6/15/90) **69**

CHATEAU SIGALAS-RABAUD
Sauternes 1989 (NR) (6/15/90) (BT) **90+**
Sauternes 1986: Simple, sweet and fruity, with a touch of oxidation that takes away from the quality. $42 (12/31/89) **77**
Sauternes 1985 $41 (7/15/88) **82**
Sauternes 1983 $24 (1/31/88) **88**

CHATEAU SUAU
Barsac 1989 (NR) (6/15/90) (BT) **85+**
Barsac 1988 (NR) (6/15/90) (BT) **80+**
Sauternes 1986 (NR) (6/30/88) (BT) **85+**

CHATEAU SUDUIRAUT
Sauternes 1989 $60 (6/15/90) (BT) **90+**
Sauternes 1988 $45 (6/15/90) (BT) **85+**
Sauternes 1986: Ripe and golden, with buttered pear and pineapple aromas and long, honeyed fruit flavors. Lacks the roundness that should come with age. Drink now to 1995. $35 (12/31/89) **85**
Sauternes 1985 ($NA) (11/30/88) (JS) **81**
Sauternes 1984 $22 (11/30/88) (JS) **81**
Sauternes 1983 Rel: $30 Cur: $40 (11/30/88) (JS) **85**
Sauternes 1982 $42 (11/30/88) (JS) **83**
Sauternes 1979 Rel: $19 Cur: $40 (11/30/88) (JS) **86**
Sauternes 1978 $22 (11/30/88) (JS) **78**
Sauternes 1976 $65 (11/30/88) (JS) **77**
Sauternes 1975 $66 (11/30/88) (JS) **84**
Sauternes 1972 $25 (11/30/88) (JS) **77**
Sauternes 1970 $52 (11/30/88) (JS) **81**
Sauternes 1969 $70 (11/30/88) (JS) **88**
Sauternes 1959 $240 (11/30/88) (JS) **93**
Sauternes 1928 $300 (11/30/88) (JS) **90**
Sauternes Cuvée Madame 1982 $150 (11/30/88) (JS) **90**

CHATEAU LA TOUR BLANCHE
Sauternes 1989 (NR) (6/15/90) (BT) **85+**
Sauternes 1988 $29 (6/15/90) (BT) **85+**
Sauternes 1987 ($NA) (6/15/90) **82**
Sauternes 1986 $26 (12/31/89) **79**
Sauternes 1985 $25 (7/15/88) **85**
Sauternes 1983 $32 (1/31/88) **87**

CHATEAU VIOLET
Sauternes 1987 ($NA) (6/15/90) **79**

CHATEAU D'YQUEM
Sauternes 1986: Very ripe, flavorful, sweet and straightforward, offering more caramel and pear flavors than the expected richness and depth. Lively and worth drinking for its sweetness and balance, but it's not the profound, complex wine that the reputation and vintage would suggest. Tasted twice. $310 (2/28/91) **87**
Sauternes 1985: Very sweet and spicy, with rich melon, apricot and fig aromas and flavors. Lacks the caramel, molasses and spice overtones of other vintages. This wine is young and somewhat sugary, but the intensity and richness win out in the end. Hold until 1995. $225 (3/31/90) **94**
Sauternes 1984: Smooth and polished, with generous fig, caramel and molasses aromas and flavors. Sweet but elegant, echoing apricot and ginger on the finish. A very well-made wine from an unheralded vintage. Drink now or cellar through at least 1994. Rel: $149 Cur: $175 (3/31/90) **96**
Sauternes 1983 Rel: $180 Cur: $240 (1/31/88) **97**
Sauternes 1976 $370 (12/15/88) **94**
Sauternes 1937 $2,640/1.5L (12/15/88) **93**

OTHER FRANCE DESSERT

CHATEAU LE BARRADIS
Monbazillac 1988: Light and not very sweet, this dessert wine has modest melon, nutmeg and earthy aromas and flavors, but it's a bit short and simple. $20 (7/15/91) **76**

MARC BREDIF
Vouvray Vin Moelleux Nectar 1985: By the bottle, this wine looks as if it should be sweet, but it's off-dry, with earthy, green apple aromas and flavors that are distinctive, but won't appeal to everyone. $9/375ml (6/15/91) **75**

DOMAINE DU CLOS NAUDIN
Vouvray Moelleux 1989: Frankly sweet and fruity, with lots of spice and honey overtones to the melon and apricot flavors. Smooth and rich on the finish. Drinkable, but this sort of wine gets better as it dries out. Try in 1993 or '94. $34 (4/30/91) **83**
Vouvray Moelleux Réserve 1989: Ripe, sweet and honeyed, with lovely hazelnut, floral and spice

aromas and flavors, richly textured, smooth and elegant. A touch of vinegar on the palate is not out of bounds. Delicious to drink now, but cellaring until 1993 to '95 couldn't hurt. $54 (3/31/91) **89**

DOMAINE DE DURBAN
Muscat de Beaumes-de-Venise 1988: Moderately sweet, offering generous orange, litchi and pear aromas and flavors shaded by nutmeg and cinnamon. Very fruity and generous, but not too terribly sweet. Drinkable now. $15 (3/31/91) **86**

LEYRAT
Pineau des Charentes Grande Réserve Sélection Robert Haas NV: This sweet Cognac-laced aperitif smells a bit strange, what with all the estery Cognac overtones, but the smooth, spicy almond and caramel flavors are immediately appealing and linger nicely. $23 (3/31/91) **82**

M & G
Vouvray Moelleux 1988: $10 (3/31/91) **81**

DOMAINE DU MAS BLANC
Banyuls Vendanges Tardives 1982: Sweet, very spicy, mature and earthy, with coffeelike aromas and flavors. It's slightly tannic, but echoes cherry and nutmeg on the finish. $26 (2/28/91) **80**
Banyuls Vieilles Vignes 1982: Dark amber in color and sweet, with lots of ripe cherry, coffee and nutmeg aromas and flavors. Flavorful in a straightforward sort of way. $27 (2/28/91) **82**
Banyuls Vieilles Vignes 1976: Appealing coffee, nutmeg and prune aromas and flavors are overlaid with a nice touch of oak in this sweet but not unctuous wine. Dark amber in color and obviously mature, but still lively and tasty, if a bit short. $40 (2/28/91) **85**

PROSPER MAUFOUX
Muscat de Beaumes-de-Venise NV: Fruity, spicy, sweet and generous, this golden wine has apricot and nutmeg aromas and flavors, turning very spicy on the finish. $18 (7/15/91) **85**
Muscat de Beaumes-de-Venise NV: Ripe, sweet and buttery, with racy, spicy overtones to the apricot and litchi fruit, thick in texture but balanced and lively. $16 (8/31/89) **88**

DOMAINE DE LA MELOTERIE
Vouvray Demi-Sec 1989: An impressive, light dessert wine. Soft, gently sweet and fragrant, with lovely melon, honey and floral aromas and flavors that persist into a long finish. $9 (6/15/91) **87**

DOMAINE LE PEU DE LA MORIETTE
Vouvray Moelleux Cuvée Exceptionelle 1989: Earthy, floral aromas and apple flavors characterize this frankly off-dry wine. Not particularly rich, but the flavors persist on the finish. $19 (6/15/91) **80**

CHATEAU DE RICAUD
Loupiac 1986: Sweet and sugary, with fig and vanilla aromas and flavors, hinting at tobacco on the finish. Drink soon. $17/375ml (12/31/89) **80**

DOMAINE ST.-SAUVEUR
Muscat de Beaumes-de-Venise Vin Doux Naturel 1988: Dark gold color, with lots of honey, maple and caramel notes around the modest pear flavor, but it smells rough, with aromas approximating brandy instead of wine. Enjoyable to drink, but not especially characteristic. $17 (3/31/91) **80**

OTHER FRANCE RED

ABBAYE DE VALMAGNE
Côteaux du Languedoc 1988: Ripe and firm, with lots of sweet plum, berry and pepper aromas and flavors, hinting at raisin on the finish. Medium in weight and balanced enough to drink now. 425 cases made. $12 (8/31/91) **80**

PERE ANSELME
Merlot Vin de Pays des Côteaux d'Enserune NV: Uncomplicated but good. Nicely fruity and fresh tasting, medium-bodied, with reasonably concentrated flavors. $5.50 (7/15/89) **78**

VIGNERONS ARDECHOIS
Vin de Pays des Côteaux de l'Ardeche 1988: Firm textured, with straightforward but lively black cherry and woodsy aromas and flavors and more than enough complexity and length to justify the price. Drink soon. $4.50 (4/30/90) BB **79**

CHATEAU DE BEAUREGARD
Côteaux du Languedoc 1989: Soft and fruity, reminiscent of Beaujolais, with attractive strawberry, raspberry and spice aromas and flavors. Smooth and drinkable now. $5 (12/15/91) BB **81**

DANIEL BESSIERE
Côteaux du Languedoc 1987: Smooth and spicy, with lively cherry and toast aromas and flavors, bright and refreshingly concentrated flavors and a silky texture. Drink now. $5 (9/30/89) BB **83**
Faugères 1987: An earthy, leathery wine, with hints of brown sugar and cherry flavors, but it's not for those who look for fruit in their wines. $6 (9/15/89) **73**
Minervois 1986: Ripe and generous, with the kind of concentration of plum and cherry flavors on a supple structure that you'd expect to find in much more expensive wines. Drink up now. $6 (9/15/89) BB **81**
St.-Chinian 1987: Solid, with intriguing wild berry flavors that carry through to the finish. A good wine to drink now. $6 (8/31/89) **79**

BICHOT
Côtes de Duras 1989: A light, clean fruity red, with hints of anise and cherry flavors. An enjoyable quaff, offering more character than you might expect at the low price. Drinks well now. $6 (3/31/92) BB **81**
Vin Rouge NV: Earthy, slightly leathery flavors tend to overbalance the modest cherry flavor, but this is a drinkable, everyday wine with some character. $3 (8/31/89) **75**

CHATEAU DE BLOMAC
Minervois Cuvée Tradition 1988: Effusively fruity aromas turn very firm and almost austere on the palate, but the soft cherry and plum flavors sneak through on the finish. Drinkable now, but the tannins could use until 1993 or '94 to soften. $6 (12/31/91) BB **82**

BOUCHARD AINE
Merlot Vin de Pays de l'Aude NV: Mature spice and cedar aromas dominate the palate, overshadowing any fruit that may be present. For those who want an older taste in a nonvintage wine, although there are still some tannins to lose. $5 (6/30/90) **72**

Key to Symbols

The scores reported here are the results of blind tastings conducted by our panel of senior editors. Wines that carry the initials below are results of individual tastings.

THE WINE SPECTATOR 100-POINT SCALE ***95-100***—Classic, a great wine; ***90-94***—Outstanding, superior character and style; ***80-89***—Good to very good, a wine with special qualities; ***70-79***—Average, drinkable wine that may have minor flaws; ***60-69***—Below average, drinkable but not recommended; ***50-59***—Poor, undrinkable, not recommended. "+"—With a score indicates a range; used primarily with barrel tastings to indicate a preliminary score.

SPECIAL DESIGNATIONS SS—Spectator Selection, CS—Cellar Selection, BB—Best Buy, ($NA)—Price not available, (NR)—Not released.

TASTER'S INITIALS (JG)—Jim Gordon, (HS)—Harvey Steiman, (JL)—James Laube, (JS)—James Suckling, (TM)—Thomas Matthews, (TR)—Terry Robards, (PM)—Per-Henrik Mansson, (BT)—Barrel Tasting (these wines were tasted blind from barrel samples), (CA-date)—*California's Great Cabernets* by James Laube, (CH-date)—*California's Great Chardonnays* by James Laube, (VP-date)—*Vintage Port* by James Suckling.

DATE TASTED Dates in parentheses represent the issue in which the rating was published.

DOMAINE DE LA BOUSQUETTE
St.-Chinian 1986: A very rich, concentrated and plummy-tasting wine, with full, soft texture, abundant tannins and a fruity finish. $8 (3/31/90) **82**

CHATEAU DE CALISSANNE
Côteaux d'Aix en Provence Cuvée Prestige 1988: Very firm and tannic, with aromas and flavors that call to mind a Provence garden—herbal, smoky, vegetal and overripe. A distinctive wine that not everyone will love. $12 (8/31/91) **78**

CHATEAU CANET
Minervois Cuvée Elevée en Futs Grande Réserve 1988: A light, earthy style with strawberry flavor. A metallic edge to the flavor, however, diminishes its appeal. $6 (5/31/90) **69**

CHATEAU CAPENDU
Corbières Cuvée Elevée en Futs Grande Réserve 1988: Firm and fruity, but a bit coarse in texture, with generous berry and leather aromas and flavors. Drink soon. $6 (5/31/90) **77**

DOMAINE CAPION
Cabernet Sauvignon Merlot Vin de Pays d'Oc 1989: This straightforward wine has plenty of tannin and modest currant and tobacco flavors. Drink with hearty food. $9 (1/31/92) **77**
Syrah Vin de Pays d'Oc 1989: Solid, fruity and moderately spicy, with chewy tannins and a nice streak of cherry and peach flavors carrying through the finish. Drinkable now, but could improve through 1993. A good value. $9 (12/15/91) **82**

CHATEAU DU CEDRE
Cahors Le Prestige 1988: A full-bodied, fruity wine, with ripe, plummy aromas and flavors, firm tannins and a nice peppery quality. Pop this open at your next barbecue. 3,300 cases made. $14 (8/31/91) **84**

DOMAINE DU CEDRE
Cahors 1988: Soft, ripe and generous, with abundant currant and cherry aromas and flavors. Like a Beaujolais, but firmer and more substantial. Medium-bodied, charming and ready to drink. $10 (8/31/91) **83**
Cahors 1987: Firm and flavorful, with peppery cherry and berry aromas and flavors that manage to make themselves heard over a steady hum of tannin. Drink with something hearty. $11 (8/31/91) **81**
Cahors Le Prestige 1987: Stiff, tannic and lumbering. Very woody in smell and taste, nearly covering the plum and cherry flavors underneath. May soften up if cellared till 1994, but it's a gamble. $14 (3/15/90) **75**

CELLIER DE LA DONA
Côtes du Roussillon-Villages 1988: Fruity, lively and crisp, with an interesting spicy aroma and strawberry and boysenberry flavors that linger on the aftertaste. Ripe and inviting; easy to enjoy now. 2,700 cases made. $8.50 (10/15/90) BB **85**

CHATEAU DE CHAMBERT
Cahors 1986: Deep, concentrated, plummy and cedary, this could easily be mistaken for a good Bordeaux, yet it has the gentleness, suppleness and sunny quality of this warm region. Excellent finish. Drink now. Rel: $12 Cur: $28 (8/31/89) **87**

CHANTEFLEUR
Cabernet Sauvignon Vin de Pays de l'Ardèche 1988: A very sturdy, flavorful and reasonably priced wine for current drinking, with firm and well-structured tannins, crisp acidity, currant and plum flavors and a lingering finish. $6 (5/31/90) BB **80**
Merlot Vin de Pays d'Oc 1988: Tastes light, but it has firm acidity and tannins. A decent mealtime drink. $6 (5/31/90) **75**

CHANTOVENT
Cabernet Sauvignon Vin de Pays d'Oc Prestige 1988: Earthy smelling and fruity tasting, with soft, supple plum and blackberry flavors and a lingering finish. Fresh. Enjoy it while it is young. $6 (3/15/90) BB **81**
Cabernet Sauvignon Vin de Pays d'Oc Prestige 1987: Light, simple and refreshing, with pleasant cherry and vanilla aromas and a touch of earthiness on the finish. A fine value. $5 (10/31/89) **78**
Cabernet Sauvignon Vin de Pays d'Oc Prestige 1986: Smooth and grapey tasting, soft and very agreeable in a simple style, with clean aromas and black cherry flavors. $6.50 (5/15/89) **79**
Merlot Vin de Pays d'Oc Prestige 1988: A simple and rough-cut wine. Tannic, with floral, fruity menthol aromas. Oak flavors dominate, with berry sneaking through. Drink now. $6 (3/15/90) **73**
Merlot Vin de Pays d'Oc Prestige 1986: Acceptable quality. Smells too herbal and stale, but tastes reasonably fruity. $6.50 (5/15/89) **69**

GUY CHEVALIER
Cabernet Syrah Vin de Pays de l'Aude 1990: Light, tough and somewhat harsh, with an underlying streak of generous currant and berry flavor that might come out with cellaring until 1993. $8.50 (12/31/91) **79**
Corbières La Coste 1989: A tough, stemmy structure and flavor tend to obscure what little ripe berry flavor there is. A hard wine to warm up to. $9 (8/31/91) **72**
Vin de Pays de l'Aude Le Texas 1989: Smells good, but it's tannic and tough, with little generosity of fruit to overcome the rough texture. Too tough to be graceful and too weak to be powerful. Hard to like. $9 (7/15/91) **74**

CLOS DE L'EGLISE
Madiran 1988: Sturdy and simple, with slightly herbal and berry aromas and nice cherry flavors. Drink now, with hearty beef. $12.50 (8/31/91) **79**

CLOS STE. NICOLE
Cabernet Sauvignon French-California Cuvée NV: A light, herbal, toasty wine with harmonious structure; simple and drinkable now. 75 percent Cabernet Sauvignon from France and 25 percent red from California. $5 (10/31/89) **77**
Merlot French-California Cuvée NV: Light in texture but generous in flavor, with berry and cherry aromas and flavors touched by nutmeg and cedar. A bit on the austere side, but smooth and tasty. Drinkable now. 95 percent Merlot from France and 5 percent California Cabernet Sauvignon. $5 (10/31/89) **79**

CLOS TRIGUEDINA
Cahors 1983: Lean and fruity, with lots of vibrant currant and berry aromas and flavors and hints of bay leaf and herbs. Has firm tannins and a solid structure. Drinkable now, but should hold through 1993 or '94. $11 (2/28/91) **80**
Cahors Prince Probus 1985: Broad, solid and flavorful, with attractive cherry and currant aromas and flavors, well-integrated tannins and a solid structure. Drinkable now, but should develop well though 1993. $17 (2/28/91) **82**

JEAN CORDIER
Rouge NV: A dry, simple wine with a bit of berry flavor. Clean but boring. $3 (12/31/90) **75**

CUVEE DES ERMITES
NV: Light and simple, with a distinct earthy, gamy edge to the modest strawberry flavor. Fruit comes through on the finish. Drinkable now. $7.50 (1/31/92) **78**

CUVEE PIERRE ROUGE
1990: A hearty, simple, fruity, robust red, with direct herb, plum and pepper flavors. Basic refreshment. Tasted twice. 850 cases made. $7 (6/30/92) **78**

CHATEAU LA DECELLE
Côteaux du Tricastin 1989: Clean and well balanced, offering characteristic peppery aromas and nice plum and berry flavors. A simple, drinkable style that's a good value. $7.50 (7/15/91) BB **82**

CHATEAU DONA BAISSAS
Côtes du Roussillon-Villages 1990: A ripe wine, with spicy currant and cherry flavors that are well proportioned. Drink now. $8 (3/31/92) **79**
Côtes du Roussillon-Villages 1988: Soft and appealing, with wild cherry and berry flavors, this has a modicum of tannin but it's not designed to age. Drink up now, with grilled chicken or pork. $7 (10/15/90) **77**

CHATEAU ETANG DES COLOMBES
Corbières Cuvée du Bicentenaire 1986: Earthy, with more currant and strawberry flavors than aroma—it smells a bit weedy—but has good balance, fine tannins and enough character to make a second sip interesting. Drinkable, but better starting in 1993. $9 (3/31/91) **77**

CHATEAU FABAS
Minervois 1986: Lots of wild berry and slightly bitter flavors make this an awkward wine, drinkable but wild and woolly. $5.50 (9/15/89) **72**

DOMAINE DE FONTSAINTE
Corbières Réserve la Demoiselle 1986: A slightly spicy, slightly fruity, generally low-key wine. Drinkable, but tries to be so subtle that it hides its character. Maybe aging will bring it out. $7 (8/31/89) **77**

FORTANT
Cabernet Sauvignon Vin de Pays d'Oc 1988: Earthy, with hints of green bean and pepper, this is a tough wine to warm up to, but with food it might taste tamer. $6 (4/30/91) **70**
Merlot Vin de Pays d'Oc 1988: An intense little wine, with strong plum and earth flavors that turn metallic on the finish. Needs food to soften the blow of the finish. Drink now. $6 (5/31/91) **70**

DOMAINES GAVOTY
Côtes de Provence Cuvée Clarendon 1987: A rustic, herbal and meaty tasting red that's tannic and medium-bodied but short on flavor. $8.50 (3/31/90) **72**

HERZOG
Cabernet Sauvignon Vin de Pays d'Oc 1988: A disjointed kosher wine, with strange salty, vegetal aromas. Hearty and tannic, with faint berry flavors. A bitter finish doesn't help. $6 (3/15/90) **67**
Cabernet Sauvignon Vin de Pays d'Oc NV: A real surprise. The nice plum and toasty vanilla aromas follow through in this balanced, harmonious wine. 2,500 cases made. $7 (3/31/91) BB **88**
Merlot Vin de Pays d'Oc NV: $7 (3/31/91) **75**

CHATEAU DE JAU
Côtes du Roussillon 1988: Earthy, barnyardy aromas and flavors take this out of the running for us, although the plum notes that persist on the finish will appeal to those more tolerant of these characteristics. $6 (8/31/91) **75**

DOMAINE DES JOUGLA
St.-Chinian 1986: Soft and pleasant tasting, showing herbal and plummy flavors. Simple in structure, ready to drink. $6.75 (5/15/89) **76**

CHATEAU LAVILLE BERTROU
Minervois 1988: An austere style, with a firm structure and modest aromas and flavors of cherry and mineral earthiness. Best after 1993. $8 (8/31/91) **76**

ROGER MARES
Cabernet Syrah Mas des Bressad 1988: A balanced, harmonious, medium-bodied wine, with gentle, ripe berry flavor and plenty of spicy, toasty overtones. Velvety and smooth on the finish. Ideal for drinking now with roast chicken. $10.50 (10/31/90) **81**

CHATEAU MAROT
Bergerac 1988: A solid red wine, offering appealing berry, plum and spice aromas and flavors. Modest in scope, but drinkable with meat or poultry. $7 (8/31/91) **79**

DOMAINE DU MAS BLANC
Collioure Cuvée Cosprons Levants 1988: A solid, flavorful red, with a distinctive flavor profile that centers around currant, black cherry and tomato. Has modest intensity, but enough to warrant a drinker's attention. Drinkable now. $21 (3/31/91) **82**

MAS DE DAUMAS GASSAC
Vin de Pays de l'Herault 1989: Firm and fruity, with an appealing concentration of currant and plum aromas and flavors that linger on the finish. Smells fine, but the flavors aren't as developed as could be hoped for. Has well-integrated tannins. Drinkable now, and should be fine through 1994. $25 (12/15/91) **83**
Vin de Pays de l'Herault 1987: Thick, supple and loaded with fresh ripe berry and spice flavors, with a firm texture that gives it body without being heavy. Youthful, refreshing and fairly tannic; drink or hold. Drink now to 1998. $23 (10/31/89) **85**
Vin de Pays de l'Herault 1986 $25 (12/15/88) **81**

MAS DE GOURGONNIER
Côteaux des Baux en Provence Les Baux de Provence 1988: Spicy, earthy aromas and flavors have enough of a solid core of strawberry and cherry character to make this balanced, if a little rough around the edges. Cellar until 1993. $8.50 (4/30/91) **79**

MARILYN MERLOT
Merlot Vin de Pays de l'Aude 1987: Marilyn's from France this time, and she's not quite as appealing as she was as a Californian. Light, soft and simple, with fresh berry aromas and flavors and an overlay of tobacco. Easy to drink, but do so soon. $6 (3/15/90) **77**

LA METAIRIE
Corbières 1989: A solid, chunky wine, with nice plum and cherry flavors, somewhat reined-in tannins and enough flavor to be worth pouring with a hearty roast. Drink around 1993. $7 (12/15/91) **78**

CHATEAU MILLEGRAND
Minervois 1988: Generous and fruity, with enough earthy undertones to lend richness to the simple, straightforward strawberry aromas and flavors. Drink soon. $5 (4/30/90) **77**

MOCERI
Cabernet Sauvignon Vin de Pays de l'Aude 1987: Straightforward and ready to drink, with black cherry flavor and medium body. Won't disappoint at this price. $4 (6/30/90) BB **77**
Merlot Vin de Pays de l'Aude 1987: A likable French wine, especially at this price, with solid cherry and plum flavors and hints of tobacco in a medium-bodied, basically soft style. $4 (6/30/90) BB **78**

LES PRODUCTEURS DU MONT TAUCH
Fitou 1985: Reminiscent of some Chiantis, this has modest berry and slightly chalky flavors, firm structure and enough tannins to cut through rich meats. Drink now. $6 (4/15/89) **79**

CHATEAU MONTUS
Madiran 1985 $10 (4/15/89) **79**

CHATEAUX DE MOUJAN
Côteaux du Languedoc 1987: Light and pleasant, with ripe, sunny flavors of plum and brown sugar, all of which carries through to a good finish. A good choice for an everyday wine. $4 (8/31/89) **80**

DOMAINE LA NOBLE
Merlot Vin de Pays de l'Aude 1990: Leans toward the herbal, vegetal end of the taste spectrum, with cooked plum and spice flavors. Decent but unexciting. Drink now. $7 (3/31/92) **73**

CHATEAU LES OLLIEUX
Corbières 1988: Robust and flavorful, with plenty of bang for the buck. Smells fresh and tastes full, lively and peppery, almost like a Côtes du Rhône. $5.25 (11/30/90) BB **80**

DOMAINE D'ORMESSON
Vin de Pays d'Oc 1985: Soft and fruity, with enough smoky aromas and flavors with the bright cherry flavor to lend interest. Good for everyday quaffing. Drink now. $4 (4/15/89) **77**
DOMAINES OTT
Côtes de Provence Société Civile des Domaines 1987: Clean and firm textured, with ripe aromas, this simple, mature wine offers spicy plum and meaty flavors. Drinkable now. $22 (5/31/91) **78**

CHATEAU LA PALME
Côtes du Frontonnais 1988: Looks and smells 10 years older than it is; tired, oxidized, funky and altogether unpleasant. Tasted twice. $7 (7/31/91) **63**

CHATEAU DE PARAZA
Minervois Cuvée Spéciale 1988: Tannic in texture and light in flavor; an unbalanced wine that doesn't seem to be going anywhere. Tasted twice. $7 (5/31/91) **67**

CHATEAU PECH DE JAMMES
Cahors 1987: A hearty country wine with firm tannins, concentrated, ripe flavors of blackberry and anise, and a tannic but lingering finish. $9 (6/30/90) **78**

CHATEAU DE PENNAUTIER
Cabardès 1989: Simple and cherrylike, with friendly fruit and not much depth. Drink soon. $7 (12/15/91) **75**

DOMAINE PERRIERE
Vin de Pays de l'Aude Les Amandiers 1988: On the earthy side, this has a modicum of currant flavor, firm structure and a modest finish. Drink soon. $4.50 (4/15/90) **77**

CHATEAU DE PIBARNON
Bandol 1987: A very tough, tannic wine that smells cedary and tastes woody and rough, but has enough blackberry flavor underneath to make it worth cellaring till about 1994 to see what develops. $17 (3/15/90) **75**

PLACE D'ARGENT
Cabernet Sauvignon Vin de Pays de l'Aude 1985: With lightly herbal, smoky aromas and delicate cherry flavors, this one has the earthy appeal and light texture to make a good value as a low-priced dinner companion. Drink now. $5.50 (4/15/89) **78**
Merlot Vin de Pays de l'Aude 1987: Simple and fruity, with sturdy texture, light to medium body and hints of fresh strawberry and black cherry flavors. A modest wine, easy to drink. $5 (4/30/90) **77**

CHATEAU PRADEAUX
Bandol 1986: Woody, vegetal aromas and flavors overpower whatever fruit might be there, and it's rough and tannic for such a light wine. $18 (10/31/90) **83**

PRIEURE DE ST.-JEAN DE BEBIAN
Côteaux du Languedoc 1989: Tight and tannic, with chewy plum and wood flavors that turn bitter on the finish. A hearty style that needs food to soften the edges. Drink now to 1994. 150 cases made. $23 (6/30/92) **77**

DOMAINE DU PUGET
Cabernet Sauvignon Vin de Pays de l'Aude 1989: Simple in flavor and coarse in texture, this earthy, tomato-flavored red has little to offer in the way of enjoyment. Tasted twice. $5 (6/30/92) **72**
Merlot Vin de Pays de l'Aude 1989: Simple and herbal in flavor, medium-bodied, with moderate tannins. Decent to drink now, but nothing to get excited about. Tasted twice. $5 (6/30/92) **77**
Merlot Vin de Pays de l'Aude 1988: Light, herbal style, with smoky notes that shoulder past the delicate currant and cherry flavors. Simple and straightforward, for drinking soon. A decent value. $4 (6/30/90) **76**

RESERVE ST.-MARTIN
Minervois Mourvèdre 1989: Ripe, smooth and simple, with earthy, gamy undertones to the basic black cherry flavor. Drinkable now. Tasted twice. $8 (12/31/91) BB **80**

RESPLANDY
Merlot Vin de Pays d'Oc 1989: An earthy, very herbal Merlot with peppery overtones. Fairly tannic and full-bodied. Best to drink now, while the flavors are fresh. $6 (6/30/92) **79**

PAR E. REYNAUD
Vin de Pays de Vaucluse Domaine des Tours 1989: A very well-made wine that seems a bit tannic for its light texture and modest cherry and berry aromas and flavors. Give it until 1993 to see what happens. $8 (3/31/91) **78**

DOMAINE RICHEAUME
Cabernet Sauvignon Côtes de Provence 1988: Tough and tannic, with appealing game, pepper and currant aromas and flavors. Needs until 1993 to '95 for the tannins to soften, but the relatively short finish does not suggest long aging will make it much better. $15 (10/31/90) **75**
Syrah Côtes de Provence 1988: Leather, spice and game flavors tend to obscure the fruit in this wine that's not altogether unappealing, but not impressive either. $15 (10/31/90) **73**

LA ROGUE
Bandol 1987: Leather and smoke nuances add to the basic berry flavor in a smooth, harmonious, medium-bodied and thoroughly drinkable wine. Drink soon. $10.50 (11/30/90) **83**

DOMAINE LA ROSIERE
Syrah Côteaux des Baronnies 1988: Soft-textured and well-balanced, with fairly concentrated, jammy, blackberry flavors and smoky aromas. $6.50 (2/28/90) **78**

ST.-CESAIRE
Vin de Pays des Bouches du Rhône NV: Wild berry aromas and flavors are appealing, but the coarse texture and unexpectedly harsh tannins are not. $4.25 (6/30/90) **72**

DOMAINE DE ST.-LUC
Côteaux du Tricastin 1989: Light and fruity, with generous raspberry and strawberry flavors wrapped in a light blanket of tannin. Drinkable now with food, but probably best around 1993. $7 (12/31/91) BB **83**
Côteaux du Tricastin 1988: Very tannic and lean. The berry and cherry flavors and aromas don't linger long enough in this austere, unbalanced wine. $11 (8/31/91) **77**

DOMAINE SARDA-MALET
Côtes du Roussillon 1986: Earthy, bitter, slightly moldy and sour. This is not a friendly wine. Tasted twice. $7.50 (10/15/90) **60**

DOMAINE DU SAULT
Corbières 1988: Lean and astringent, offering earthy, leathery aromas and flavors instead of generous fruit, but the berry flavors come through on the finish. Drink soon. $5 (6/30/90) **74**

DOMAINE TEMPIER
Bandol Cuvée Spéciale Cabassaou 1987: Very firm, generous, well balanced, harmonious and focused, offering appealing plum, blackberry and black pepper aromas and flavors held tightly in check by fine tannins and crisp acidity. Cellar until at least 1993 or '94 to let the flavors meld. $23 (10/31/90) **88**
Bandol Cuvée Spéciale La Migoua 1987: Generous in texture and flavor, offering slightly gamy, smoky plum and blackberry notes. It's round and ripe on the finish, with hints of earth and brown sugar that are especially nice. Drink now. $22 (10/31/90) **86**
Bandol Cuvée Spéciale La Tourti 1987: Smells terrific, with raspberry, game and smoke aromas competing for attention, but it's a bit shy on the palate and turns lean and tart on the finish. Raspberry flavor comes through lightly on the finish, making for a charming wine to drink now or by 1993. $22 (10/31/90) **82**

FRANCE

Other France Red

DOMAINE DE TREVALLON
Côteaux d'Aix en Provence Les Baux 1987: A very tannic, young wine with plenty of meaty, peppery aromas, and berry and black cherry flavor wrapped in a dense coat of woody tannins. Very dry on the finish. Undrinkable now; should develop more smoothness by 1994. $18 (3/31/90) **78**
Côteaux d'Aix en Provence Les Baux 1986: Has lots of personality. Warm, ripe and broad on the palate, with plummy, concentrated flavors and peppery aromas with a distinct earthy overtone. Drink up now. $21 (4/15/89) **87**

TROUBADOUR
Merlot Vin de Pays de l'Aude 1987: An herbal, slightly minty wine, light enough on the palate that it requires no further aging, simple and easy to drink. $5 (8/31/89) **76**

CHATEAU DE VALLONGUE
Côteaux d'Aix en Provence Les Baux 1988: Very bitter and tannic, saved only by a late spark of berry flavor and a smattering of peppercorn. The tannins need until 1995 to '97 to soften, but it's probably better to drink it sooner, with something hearty. $11 (12/15/91) **73**

CHATEAU VANNIERES
Bandol 1986: Leathery, animallike aromas and flavors persist through the aftertaste, bringing this otherwise well-made wine down several notches. Not for every taste. $15 (9/15/89) **67**
Côtes de Provence La Provence de Vannières 1986: A mouthful of concentrated, ripe fruit and characteristic Provence spiciness, with overtones of bay leaf. Seems like just the wine for roast chicken or braised beef. Drink now. $15 (8/31/89) **80**

DOMAINE DU VIEUX CHENE
Vin de Pays de Vaucluse 1990: Only slightly darker than a rosé, but it has sufficient tannin and modest berry flavor to warrant cellaring until 1993 or '94 to see what happens as it softens. $7 (1/31/92) **77**

CLOS DE VILLEMAJOU
Corbières 1988: Appealing for its vigorous style, earthy, wild berry and cherry aromas and flavors, leathery overtones and smooth texture. Drink soon. $6 (4/30/90) **78**
Corbières 1985: The extra years have added a few layers of earthy, woodsy aromas and flavors, but the plum and berry flavors barely make their presence felt against a tough texture. $7.50 (5/31/90) **71**

CHATEAU JULIEN VILLERAMBERT
Minervois Cuvée Trianon 1989: Chunky, tannic and tight, with very modest cherry flavor. Not appealing now, but could improve enough by 1994 or '95. $15 (12/15/91) **73**

Other France Sparkling

LES ACACIAS
Brut Crémant de Bourgogne Cépage Chardonnay NV: Dry, crisp and clean, with tart apple flavors and mineral overtones that mimic Chablis. Medium-bodied, with a lemony finish. $11 (6/15/90) **78**

BEAUVOLAGE
Brut Blanc de Blancs Touraine Reserve 1989: Crisp, fresh and engaging, a simple, lively wine, with green apple and spice aromas and flavors. $24 (1/31/92) **83**
Brut Rosé Touraine Reserve NV: A robust rosé, with delicious plum, toast, spice and herb flavors. Very flavorful and assertive; can easily fill in for a red wine with dinner. $29 (1/31/92) **84**
Brut Touraine Reserve 1989: Soft and flavorful, with abundant aromas and nut, honey and apple cider flavors. Rich, ripe and inviting in a soft style. $24 (1/31/92) **84**
Brut Vouvray Suprême Cuvée Comtesse Anne 1985: A dry, earthy style, with a thread of apple and spice flavors running through it, hinting at butter and mineral flavors on the finish. The texture could be finer, but it's a pleasant bubbly to sip. $39 (1/31/92) **80**
Cuvée Rouge et Noir Haut Poitou 1985: An unusual sparkling wine. Deep red, tastes ripe and warm, with raisin and plum flavors. Soft in texture, off-dry in balance and easy to drink. $35 (1/31/92) **81**

DOMAINE DU BICHERON
Blanc de Blancs Crémant de Bourgogne NV: A real gem. Has generous honey, butter and pineapple aromas and flavors on a crisp but smooth structure. The creamy texture and long aftertaste are quite pleasant. $12 (3/31/90) **84**

MAISTRE BLANQUETIER
Brut Blanquette de Limoux Le Berceau NV: A great alternative to Champagne. Dry, clean and restrained, but creamy textured and flavorful enough for a lingering finish. $9 (4/15/90) **81**

BOUVET
Brut Saumur Saphir 1988: Round, ripe and almost sweet, with apple, pear, smoke and honey flavors and a soft texture. Recommended as an aperitif or with dessert. $14 (1/31/92) **82**
Brut Saumur Saphir 1985: A deliciously peachy wine wrapped in a creamy smooth texture, with a slightly sweet finish. Easy to like. $12 (6/15/90) **84**
Brut Saumur Signature NV: An aggresive, rich style that is not for everyone. It has plenty of butter, toast and lemon flavors and a butterscotch candy finish. Tasted three times. $11.50 (6/15/90) **75**
Brut Rosé NV: A rosé that smells spicy and floral, but with strawberry and herbal flavors and a hint of tart cherry. Tastes like a bubbly Cabernet; a little coarse and assertive, but should make a good dinner wine. $10 (6/15/90) **80**
Brut Rosé Excellence NV: Crisp, floral and delicate, with berry and sweet cherry flavors. It's lean, clean, fresh and lively but austere. $12 (6/15/90) **80**
Rubis NV: Simple, unusual and deeper in color than most red wines. Sweet, with plum, cherry and berry flavors and a sweet, cloying finish. Tastes like a sparkling Zinfandel. $10 (6/15/90) **72**

BRUMMELL
Blanc de Blancs Carte Noir NV: An inexpensive, dry, light-bodied sparkler that tastes clean and subtle. Its lightly fruity flavors have a touch of earth or almonds in the aroma and on the finish. $7.25 (6/15/90) **79**

LE CARDINALE
Brut NV: Dry, delicate and refreshing, with modest lemon and apple flavors, a creamy texture and a clean finish. $5.25 (6/15/90) BB **80**

BARON CHAGALE
Brut Blanc de Blancs NV: Acceptable but heavy-handed. Has bubble gum aromas and thick pineapple and banana flavors in a slightly sweet, soft-textured style. $6 (6/15/90) **70**

PAUL CHAMBLAIN
Brut Blanc de Blancs NV: Simple and clean, soft and slightly sweet, with spicy, floral flavors. Tasted twice. $6.75 (6/15/90) **74**

CHARBAUT FRERES
Brut Blanc de Blancs Crémant de Bourgogne 1986: Dry, earthy and austere, with restrained fruit and toasted almond flavors that linger on the finish. A good wine in a lean style. $15 (1/31/92) **80**
Brut Rosé Crémant de Bourgogne 1986: Pale salmon in color, this simple wine has berry aromas and flavors that are firm, crisp and well balanced, with a touch of austerity. $11.50 (12/31/90) **79**

DARGENT
Brut Blanc de Blancs Côtes du Jura Chardonnay 1988: Very dry and austere, with tangy lemon and grapefruit flavors and a tart finish. Fine in its style. $10.50 (6/15/90) **83**

BERNARD DELMAS
Brut Blanquette de Limoux NV: A mature, soft, creamy-textured wine that is subtly fruity, with attractive toasty, lemony flavors. Tastes very clean. $14 (3/31/90) **79**

CHARLES DE FERE
Brut Tradition NV: Soft and gently spicy, with a nice grapefruit tinge to the apple and toast aromas and flavors. A simple wine, with appealing flavors. $12 (11/30/91) **82**
Brut Blanc de Blancs NV: Won't pass as Champagne, but it's a decent-quality bubbly, with spice and apple flavors and an off-dry balance. Simple and drinkable. $10 (1/31/92) **79**
Brut Blanc de Blancs Réserve NV: Smells and tastes like Chenin Blanc, with earthy melon and pear flavors. A straightforward simple wine that is decent to drink. Drink now. $10 (6/15/90) **77**
Brut Rosé NV: Pretty ordinary stuff, with earthy, doughy aromas, dry tomato flavors and a light copper color. Look for this winery's brut or blanc de blancs instead. Tasted twice. $10 (6/15/90) **70**

LA FOLIE
Brut Blanc de Blancs Réserve NV: Smells and tastes tired, with an unpleasant vegetal aftertaste. No fruit flavor to speak of, and very difficult to like. Tasted twice. $5.50 (6/15/90) **63**

GRAND IMPERIAL
Brut NV: Great for the price. A basically dry, clean and straightforward sparkling wine, with doughy, earthy aromas and green apple and mineral flavors. $4.50 (6/15/90) **76**

GRANDIN
Brut Ingrandes-Sur-Loire NV: Light and easy to like. Tastes clean, fruity and almost delicate in style, with hints of apple and melon. Tart fruit flavors linger on the aftertaste. $10 (6/15/90) **82**

GRATIEN
Brut Saumur NV: Full and rich, with apple and butter flavors, toasty aromas and a lingering finish. A bold, assertive sparkler that has depth and complexity. Tasted twice. $9.25 (6/15/90) **83**

PHILIPPE HERARD
Brut Blanc de Blancs NV: Simple but drinkable. A strong nutty, toasty aroma is followed by soft, insipid apple flavors. $9.50 (6/15/90) **74**

DE JESSY
Extra Dry NV: Sweet, with green apple, pear and butterscotch flavors. Hints of honey give this fruity wine a richness and a late-harvest taste. Creamy texture. Nice for its style; serve with dessert. $9 (6/15/90) **81**

KRITER
Blanc de Blancs Brut de Brut 1985: Not recommended. Overly earthy and vegetal tasting, with off-putting aromas and a bitter aftertaste. Tasted three times with consistent results. $9 (6/15/90) **57**
Brut Blanc de Blancs Impérial 1983: Dry and not at all appealing. Floral, rubberlike and vegetal aromas carry over to the palate. The finish is bitter, too. Tasted twice. $12 (6/15/90) **57**
Brut Rosé NV: An unusual dry rosé with red wine flavors. Tastes of strawberry but with off-putting hints of tomato and leather. Medium-bodied, with only a slight finish. Tasted three times, with consistent results. $9 (6/15/90) **71**
Demi-Sec NV: Sweet and almost cloying, with simple, bubble gum aromas and bland sweet flavors. Acceptable but unappealing. Tasted three times, with consistent results. $9 (6/15/90) **71**
Demi-Sec Délicatesse NV: A dessert or aperitif wine, with sweet honey and pineapple flavors. Has an unusual deep gold color and attributes of a late-harvest wine, with nice toasty flavors and a good finish. $12 (6/15/90) **83**

LAURENS
Blanc de Blancs Blanquette de Limoux Clos des Demoiselles 1986: A spicy, earthy wine, with creamy texture and hints of almond and pepper on the finish. $11 (12/31/90) **81**

DOMAINE DE MARTINOLLES
Brut Blanquette de Limoux 1990: Crisp and fruity, with lively grapefruit, pear and toast aromas and flavors that persist on the finish. A pleasant wine with style and verve. $10 (3/31/92) **84**
Brut Blanquette de Limoux 1989: A fruity, lively, generous style of bubbly, offering spicy grapefruit and toast aromas and flavors. Dry and spicy on the finish. This wine has character. 5,000 cases made. $9 (3/31/92) BB **83**
Brut Blanquette de Limoux 1986: Soft and simple, with an earthy edge to the aromas and a spicy edge to the basic pear and honey flavors. $11 (3/31/92) **78**
Brut Blanquette de Limoux NV $8 (4/15/90) BB **84**

MONMOUSSIN
Brut Touraine Etoile 1986: Soft and light, with fresh apple and lemon flavors, good balance and a lingering finish. $13 (12/31/90) **82**
Extra Dry Vouvray 1985: Light, toasty and buttery, with sweet lemon and apple flavors and a soft finish. Very easy to like. $13 (12/31/90) **81**

MURE
Brut Crémant d'Alsace Réserve NV: A dry, tart wine with toast, earth and apple flavors. Austere, as a good Alsace wine should be. Don't be put off by hints of sauerkraut on the aroma. Try it with grilled sausages. $7 (6/15/90) **79**

JEAN PHILIPPE
Brut Blanquette de Limoux 1986: Stylish, flavorful and dry. Very toasty, with butterscotch flavors and a round, creamy texture. Clean but short on the finish. $11 (6/15/90) **80**

DOMAINE ROBERT
Brut Blanc de Blancs Blanquette de Limoux 1986: A simple, fruity style with ripe pear and pineapple flavors that pick up a touch of vanilla on the finish. Lacks finesse and elegance, but it's a serviceable sparkler. $8.75 (6/15/90) **78**

SILVER CLOUD
Brut Blanc de Blancs Blanquette de Limoux 1985: Quite a find at such a low price. It's flavorful and mature, with complex aromas of fruit, smoke and almonds, a creamy texture and fine bubbles. $9 (4/15/90) **85**

VARICHON & CLERC
Blanc de Blancs 1989: This smooth, creamy wine has gentle pear, apple, vanilla and toast flavors intertwining elegantly on the palate. A refreshing wine, with grace and style. $9 (3/31/92) BB **87**
Brut Blanc de Blancs NV: A great value. Easy drinking, soft and dry, with applelike flavors, complex hints of earth and toast in the aromas and solid fruit flavors. $7 (12/31/89) BB **87**
Brut Blanc de Blancs Black Orchid Cuvée Spéciale NV: Earthy grapefruit flavors turn a bit a sour on the finish, but this would make a decent aperitif served chilled. $8 (3/31/92) **77**
Demi-Sec NV: A smooth, easygoing wine that's a great value. Very floral, fruity and honeyed in aroma and flavor, somewhat sweet and soft and silky in texture. $7 (1/31/90) BB **82**

Key to Symbols

The scores reported here are the results of blind tastings conducted by our panel of senior editors. Wines that carry the initials below are results of individual tastings.

THE WINE SPECTATOR 100-POINT SCALE 95-100—Classic, a great wine; ***90-94***—Outstanding, superior character and style; ***80-89***—Good to very good, a wine with special qualities; ***70-79***—Average, drinkable wine that may have minor flaws; ***60-69***—Below average, drinkable but not recommended; ***50-59***—Poor, undrinkable, not recommended. "+"—With a score indicates a range; used primarily with barrel tastings to indicate a preliminary score.

SPECIAL DESIGNATIONS SS—Spectator Selection, CS—Cellar Selection, BB—Best Buy, ($NA)—Price not available, (NR)—Not released.

TASTER'S INITIALS (JG)—Jim Gordon, (HS)—Harvey Steiman, (JL)—James Laube, (JS)—James Suckling, (TM)—Thomas Matthews, (TR)—Terry Robards, (PM)—Per-Henrik Mansson, (BT)—Barrel Tasting (these wines were tasted blind from barrel samples), (CA-date)—*California's Great Cabernets* by James Laube, (CH-date)—*California's Great Chardonnays* by James Laube, (VP-date)—*Vintage Port* by James Suckling.

DATE TASTED Dates in parentheses represent the issue in which the rating was published.

VEUVE DU VERNAY
Brut Blanc de Blancs NV: Simple, soft and fruity, with a nice touch of crisp apple and nectarine flavors on the finish. A clean bubbly for easy sipping. $7 (11/30/91) BB **82**

VEUVE AMIOT
Brut Saumur Cuvée Haute Tradition NV: Very flavorful and direct. An off-dry sparkler, with lively, assertive, fruity herbal flavors riding a full body of alcohol and acid. $13 (3/31/90) **78**

ALSACE WILLM
Brut Crémant d'Alsace NV: If you like Alsatian wines, you'll enjoy this unique, earthy-smelling, soft-textured wine. It has plenty of creamy, meaty flavors and a lingering finish. $10.50 (4/15/90) **83**

WOLFBERGER
Crémant d'Alsace NV: A rare treat from Alsace that has pungent aromas of earth and toast, an off-dry spicy flavor and a clean finish. Don't expect Chardonnay character, but it's very good. $12 (7/31/89) **83**

Other France White

DOMAINE AUFFRAY
Chardonnay Vin de Pays de l'Yonne 1988: Clean, lean and slightly earthy and lemony. A simple lunchtime wine. Light-bodied, with a hint of butter and a tart finish. $8 (4/15/90) **75**

BEAUCLAIRE
Vin de Pays des Côtes de Gascogne 1990: Broad but refreshingly lively, with generous almond, floral and pear aromas and flavors. Soft and appealing to drink now. 2,000 cases made. $5 (6/30/92) BB **83**

BICHOT
Côtes de Duras 1987: Soft, simple and pleasant to drink now, showing enough honeyed pear flavor to make it lively and attractive. Priced right. $4 (5/15/89) **77**

BOUCHARD PERE & FILS
Chardonnay Vin de Pays d'Oc Première 1989: Light, fruity and pleasant, but more reminiscent of canned fruit cocktail than fresh fruit. A bit tart on the finish. Drink soon. $9 (4/30/91) **75**

LAURENT CHARLES BROTTE
Vin de Pays d'Oc Viognier 1991: Probably the world's lowest-priced Viognier. Fruity, with ripe peach and honey flavors that are round and fleshy. Moderately rich and concentrated. A young wine that might benefit from time in the bottle, but it's probably best to drink now. $8 (6/30/92) BB **81**

CHANTEFLEUR
Chardonnay Vin de Pays d'Oc 1988: Light, floral and almond flavored, gentle on the palate. Easy to drink, offering a bit of complexity. $6 (4/30/90) **79**

COLLECTION FOLLE EPOQUE
Blanc de Blancs NV: Crisp and light, with lemony aromas and a touch of almond on the finish. An austere style that needs food to come into its own. $5.50 (6/30/92) **78**

JEAN CORDIER
Vin de Table Blanc Français NV: A simple, drinkable wine, with fruit cocktail flavors and hints of mature, nutty character. Light and innocuous. Tasted twice. $3 (12/31/90) **72**

GEORGES DUBOEUF
Chardonnay Vin de Pays d'Oc 1989: Soft in texture, but the modest pear, toast and vanilla aromas and flavors are easy to like in this simple wine with nice flavors. Has a bit of astringency that isn't bad; drink now. $6.50 (11/15/90) BB **80**

FORTANT
Chardonnay Vin de Pays d'Oc 1989: Oaky, bitter notes blur the fruit flavors in a wine that won't remind most of Chardonnay. Drink now. $6 (5/31/91) **69**

HERZOG
Chardonnay Vin de Pays d'Oc 1989: $9 (3/31/91) **76**

DOMAINE DES JOUGLA
Limoux 1988: Very likable, delicate but flavorful. Light and clean tasting, showing mild orange and almond flavors in a crisp structure. $8 (3/31/90) **80**

LABOURE-ROI
Chardonnay Vin de Pays d'Oc 1989: Crisp and spicy, with an earthy edge to the simple apple flavors. Drinkable now. $6 (6/30/92) BB **81**

LAROCHE
Chardonnay 1987: Soft and somewhat spicy, a simple, delicate wine that may strike some as bland. $7 (10/31/89) **73**

DOMAINE DE MARTINOLLES
Chardonnay Vin de Pays de l'Aude 1990: Simple and well-balanced, with apple and spice flavors and a milky character. 4,000 cases made. $7 (6/30/92) **77**

MAS DE DAUMAS GASSAC
Vin de Pays de l'Herault NV: Very exotic and spicy, with a deep gold color, peach and floral aromas, honey and sweet fruit flavors and a kiss of butter and vanilla from wood aging. Full-bodied. Try it before the meal with pâté. Distinctive and expensive. A blend of Viognier and Chardonnay. $37 (3/31/90) **85**

LES PRODUCTEURS DU MONT TAUCH
Corbières 1987: Acceptable quality. Nicely tart, but tastes somewhat dull and tired. Not much fruit flavor. $5 (2/15/89) **68**

DOMAINE DU MONTMARIN
Vin de Pays des Côtes de Thongue Cépage Marsanne 1987: Simple, clean and inoffensive, with light fruit flavors and adequate balance. $5 (2/15/89) **74**

DOMAINES OTT
Bandol 1989: Crisp and earthy, with strong overtones of almond and vanilla that keep hanging through the finish. Won't please everyone. $22 (6/30/92) **76**
Bandol Cuvée Marine 1989: The light coppery color matches the light cherrylike aromas and flavors. Simple, very modest, dry and balanced toward early drinking. Tasted twice. $19 (7/15/91) **79**
Côtes de Provence Clair de Noirs 1990: A dry rosé that tastes leathery, earthy and a bit plummy, but overall it's tired and dull. You probably have to drink it on the Riviera, where it's produced, to appreciate it. $20 (6/30/92) **73**
Côtes de Provence Clair de Noirs 1987: Orange in color, rather than pink, with smoke- and leather-tinged peach aromas and flavors. Dry, with good structure and fairly impressive length, turning smooth and vanillalike on the finish. $18.50 (7/15/89) **83**
Côtes de Provence Clair de Noirs 1986 $17.50 (7/31/88) **80**

DOMAINE DE PETIT ROUBIE
Sauvignon Blanc Côteaux du Languedoc Picpoul de Pin 1988: Has delicate floral and mineral flavors, a smooth, rich texture and soft balance. Good, but one could ask for more acidity and flavor intensity. $7 (3/31/90) **74**

DOMAINE DE POUY
Vin de Pays des Côtes de Gascogne Cépage Ugni Blanc 1989: Very crisp and lively, with firm acidity framing the light, clean apple and melon flavors. Good but simple. $5 (11/30/90) BB **80**

RESERVE ST.-MARTIN
Corbières Marsanne 1991: Lean and austere, with chalky mineral aromas and flavors and crisp lemon notes on the finish. $7 (6/30/92) **75**

RESPLANDY
Vin de Pays d'Oc Marsanne 1990: Light, smooth and creamy, with floral and citrus overtones to the modest pear flavor. Finishes crisp and clean. $8 (6/30/92) **80**

DOMAINE ST.-MARTIN DE LA GARRIGUE
Chardonnay Vin de Pays des Côteaux de Bessilles 1989: Sturdy, simple and refreshing, with butterscotch and oak overtones to the generous pear and vanilla flavors. Not a heavy wine, but offers lots of flavor for early consumption. $12 (4/30/91) **82**

DOMAINE DU TARIQUET
Vin de Pays des Côtes de Gascogne 1989: A sturdy wine, with great peach, pineapple and almond aromas, full-bodied peach, apricot and pear flavors and a nice, lingering finish. A real mouthful, and a real discovery. $5.75 (11/15/90) BB **86**

BAUM
Riesling Eiswein Mosel-Saar-Ruwer Ockenheimer St. Rochuskapelle 1983 $25 (10/01/84) **86**
Riesling Qualitätswein Mosel-Saar-Ruwer Piesporter Michelsberg 1983 $4 (4/01/84) **79**
Riesling Spätlese Mosel-Saar-Ruwer Piesporter Goldtröpfchen 1983 $11 (10/01/84) **85**
Riesling Spätlese Mosel-Saar-Ruwer Weingartener Trappenberg 1983 $5 (10/01/84) **77**

BISCHOFLICHE WEINGUTER
Riesling Auslese Mosel-Saar-Ruwer Dhroner Hofberger 1988 ($NA) (9/30/89) **78**
Riesling Auslese Mosel-Saar-Ruwer Kaseler Neis'chen 1988 ($NA) (9/30/89) **90**
Riesling Auslese Mosel-Saar-Ruwer Kaseler Neis'chen 1983 $10.50 (4/01/85) **86**
Riesling Kabinett Mosel-Saar-Ruwer Trittenheimer Apotheke 1983 $8 (5/01/85) **79**
Riesling Spätlese Mosel-Saar-Ruwer Ayler Kupp 1988 ($NA) (9/30/89) **84**
Riesling Spätlese Mosel-Saar-Ruwer Kaseler Nies'chen 1983 $8.50 (5/01/85) **76**
Riesling Spätlese Mosel-Saar-Ruwer Trittenheimer Apotheke 1988 ($NA) (9/30/89) **85**

BISCHOFLICHES PRIESTERSEMINAR
Riesling Auslese Mosel-Saar-Ruwer Erdener Treppchen 1985 $14 (11/30/87) **86**

JOH. JOS. CHRISTOFFEL
Riesling Auslese Mosel-Saar-Ruwer Erdener Treppchen 1990: Has pretty, sweet fruit flavors and fresh, floral pineapple and almond aromas. Medium-bodied and sweet, with pineapple flavors, medium acidity and a medium finish. Could use a little more at the end. Drinkable now. (NR) (12/15/91) **87**
Riesling Auslese Mosel-Saar-Ruwer Erdener Treppchen 1988 ($NA) (9/30/89) **92**
Riesling Auslese Mosel-Saar-Ruwer Urziger Würzgarten 1990: Closed in now, but it has good fruit structure. Medium-bodied and medium sweet, with light floral, pie crust and melon aromas, melon and honey flavors and a rather short finish. Better after 1993. $25 (12/15/91) **86**
Riesling Auslese Mosel-Saar-Ruwer Urziger Würzgarten Gold Cap (AP991) 1990: Has plenty of everything, but needs time in the bottle. The aromas are rather closed, but show hints of flint and honey. Medium-bodied and sweet, with focused, spicy honey flavors and firm acidity. Better after 1994. (12/15/91) **90**
Riesling Spätlese Mosel-Saar-Ruwer Erdener Treppchen 1990: An up-front, delicious spätlese, with delicate lemon, spice and earth aromas. Medium-bodied and lightly sweet, with fruity flavors and hints of lemon and mineral on the finish. Drink now. (NR) (12/15/91) **86**
Riesling Spätlese Mosel-Saar-Ruwer Erdener Treppchen 1988 $10 (9/30/89) **84**
Riesling Spätlese Mosel-Saar-Ruwer Urziger Würzgarten 1990: Simple and sweet, not showing much aroma. Medium-bodied and sweet, with plenty of lemon and lime flavors. A little boring. Drink now. $15 (12/15/91) **80**
Riesling Spätlese Mosel-Saar-Ruwer Urziger Würzgarten 1988 ($NA) (9/30/89) **85**

DR. FISCHER
Riesling Auslese Mosel-Saar-Ruwer Ockfener Bockstein 1990: This thick, concentrated wine grows dramatically in the glass. It's more like a beerenauslese, with fresh tropical fruit and honey aromas, tons of fresh honey and melon flavors and a balance of acidity. Full-bodied and sweet, with an endless finish. Better from 1994. $29 (12/15/91) **92**
Riesling Auslese Mosel-Saar-Ruwer Ockfener Bockstein 1983 $12 (3/16/85) **90**
Riesling Auslese Mosel-Saar-Ruwer Wawerner Herrenberg 1990: Electrifying, with incredibly high acidity and concentrated fruit. Medium-bodied and sweet, with perfumed green apple aromas and intense green apple, lime and grapefruit flavors. Super-long and refreshing. Try from 1994. $21 (12/15/91) **91**
Riesling Auslese Mosel-Saar-Ruwer Wawerner Herrenberg 1988 ($NA) (9/30/89) **94**
Riesling Auslese Mosel-Saar-Ruwer Wawerner Herrenberg Gold Cap 1990: A closed, well-structured wine, but light compared to other gold capsules. Rather awkward now. Shows lovely lemon and cream aromas. Medium-bodied and sweet, with concentrated lemon and lime flavors and a touch of honey. Has good acidity and a slightly bitter finish. Better from 1994. $65/375ml (12/15/91) **88**
Riesling Beerenauslese Mosel-Saar-Ruwer Ockfener Bockstein 1990: Not a heavyweight, but very elegant. Somewhat odd in the aromas, but overflowing with mineral, honey, smoke and botrytis character on the nose and palate. Full-bodied and sweet, with a refreshing finish. Slightly awkward in balance. Better from 1993 to '95. (NR) (12/15/91) **88**
Riesling Eiswein Mosel-Saar-Ruwer Wawerner Herrenberg 1990: Really sneaks up on you and finishes strong. Full-bodied and sweet, with intense, lovely lemon, lime and floral aromas and flavors, full acidity and a lively finish. Try from 1996. (NR) (12/15/91) **88**
Riesling Kabinett Mosel-Saar-Ruwer Ockfener Bockstein 1990: Rather simple, with white pepper and herb aromas. Medium-bodied and lightly sweet, with melon and cream flavors and a light finish. Developed. Tasted twice. Drink now. $16 (12/15/91) **82**
Riesling Kabinett Mosel-Saar-Ruwer Ockfener Bockstein 1988 $13 (9/30/89) **85**
Riesling Qualitätswein Mosel-Saar-Ruwer Ockfener Bockstein 1990: Odd; tastes more like canned apple juice than wine. The intense aromas of freshly cut apples develop a metallic note. Light-bodied, with very high acidity and a crisp finish. Tasted twice. Drink now. $14 (12/15/91) **74**
Riesling Qualitätswein Mosel-Saar-Ruwer Ockfener Bockstein 1988 $6 (9/30/89) **81**
Riesling Spätlese Mosel-Saar-Ruwer Ockfener Bockstein 1990: Superbly balanced. Has striking fresh aromas of crushed grapes and lemons. Full-bodied and medium sweet, with masses of mineral and lemon flavors, super well-knit acidity and a long finish. 2,000 cases made. $20 (12/15/91) **90**
Riesling Spätlese Mosel-Saar-Ruwer Ockfener Bockstein 1988 $15 (9/30/89) **83**
Riesling Spätlese Mosel-Saar-Ruwer Ockfener Bockstein 1985 $13 (5/15/87) **88**

FRIEDRICH-WILHELM-GYMNASIUM
Riesling Auslese Mosel-Saar-Ruwer Graacher Domprobst 1990: This very attractive wine has lovely potential. Racy and wild, with beautiful honey and cream aromas. Full-bodied and sweet, with rich honey, cream and peach flavors and a long finish. Better after 1994. $20 (12/15/91) **89**
Riesling Auslese Mosel-Saar-Ruwer Graacher Himmelreich 1988 ($NA) (9/30/89) **81**
Riesling Auslese Mosel-Saar-Ruwer Mehringer Blattenberg 1989 ($NA) (12/15/90) **82**
Riesling Auslese Mosel-Saar-Ruwer Mehringer Gold Kupp 1988 $30 (9/30/89) **95**
Riesling Auslese Mosel-Saar-Ruwer Neumagener Rosengärtchen 1990: Not a showstopper, but pleasant. Offers blanched almond and fruit on the nose and palate, with ample fruit and acidity, but it's slightly light at the end. Drink now or hold. $20 (12/15/91) **85**
Riesling Auslese Mosel-Saar-Ruwer Trittenheimer Apotheke 1990: A zingy wine, with lively fruit and acidity. Medium-bodied and lightly sweet, with cassis, berry and lemon aromas, intense currant and lemon flavors and steely acidity. Has excellent concentration and balance. Try after 1994. $20 (12/15/91) **89**
Riesling Auslese Mosel-Saar-Ruwer Trittenheimer Apotheke 1989 $19 (12/15/90) **82**
Riesling Beerenauslese Mosel-Saar-Ruwer Graacher Himmelreich 1989 $150 (12/15/90) **90**
Riesling Kabinett Mosel-Saar-Ruwer Falkensteiner Hofberg 1990: Round and rich, with ripe fruit flavors. Quite juicy, with plenty of concentrated lemon and melon character on the nose and palate. Medium-bodied and off-dry. Very good to drink now. $11 (12/15/91) **84**
Riesling Kabinett Mosel-Saar-Ruwer Graacher Himmelreich 1989 $10 (12/15/90) **84**
Riesling Kabinett Mosel-Saar-Ruwer Mehringer Zellerberg 1990: Well proportioned, with all the necessary fruit and acidity. Offers perfumed aromas of grapefruit, mineral and apple. Medium-bodied and off-dry, with powerful, fresh fruit flavors. Medium in acidity and on the finish. Drinkable now, but better after 1994. $10 (12/15/91) **87**
Riesling Spätlese Mosel-Saar-Ruwer Falkensteiner Hofberg 1989 ($NA) (12/15/90) **83**
Riesling Spätlese Mosel-Saar-Ruwer Graacher Himmelreich 1990: Has lovely honey, lemon and anise aromas, apple and licorice flavors and a medium finish. Medium-bodied and lightly sweet. Drinkable now. $12 (12/15/91) **86**
Riesling Spätlese Mosel-Saar-Ruwer Oberemmeler Raul 1990: An extreme wine, with excellent concentration and an outrageous amount of acidity. Can age for decades. Slightly hard, but needs time to develop. Medium- to full-bodied and off-dry, with rich anise, tropical fruit and mineral aromas, intense anise and slightly buttery flavors and a short finish. Very high in acidity. Better after 1994. $11 (12/15/91) **91**
Riesling Spätlese Mosel-Saar-Ruwer Oberemmeler Rosenberg 1989 ($NA) (12/15/90) **80**
Riesling Spätlese Mosel-Saar-Ruwer Trittenheimer Apotheke 1990: Has pretty fruit in a classic style, with zingy honey, spice and flint aromas and mineral and lime flavors. Medium-bodied, with medium acidity and a light finish. Drink now or hold. $12 (12/15/91) **86**

GEBERT
Riesling Qualitätswein Mosel-Saar-Ruwer Ockfener Bockstein 1986 $6 (11/30/87) **74**
Riesling Qualitätswein Mosel-Saar-Ruwer Ockfener Bockstein 1985 $6.50 (5/15/87) **82**

GOLDENER OKTOBER
Riesling Qualitätswein Mosel-Saar-Ruwer Piesporter Michelsberg 1987 $7 (11/30/88) **85**

FRITZ HAAG
Riesling Auslese Mosel-Saar-Ruwer Brauneberger Juffer-Sonnenuhr 1990: Not a blockbuster, but truly fine, with great charm. Medium-bodied and lightly sweet, with extremely fine lemon, flint and spice aromas and flavors and a clean finish. Try from 1993. $37 (12/15/91) **89**
Riesling Auslese Mosel-Saar-Ruwer Brauneberger Juffer-Sonnenuhr 1989 $32 (12/15/90) **81**
Riesling Auslese Mosel-Saar-Ruwer Brauneberger Juffer-Sonnenuhr 1988 ($NA) (9/30/89) **86**
Riesling Auslese Mosel-Saar-Ruwer Brauneberger Juffer-Sonnenuhr (AP16) 1988 ($NA) (9/30/89) **85**
Riesling Auslese Mosel-Saar-Ruwer Brauneberger Juffer-Sonnenuhr Gold Cap 1990: A lively wine bubbling with fruit. Medium-bodied and medium sweet, with focused lemon and spice aromas, super-fresh lemon and spice flavors and a long finish. Better from 1993 to '95. $104 (12/15/91) **92**
Riesling Auslese Mosel-Saar-Ruwer Brauneberger Juffer-Sonnenuhr Gold Cap 1989 $60 (12/15/90) **90**
Riesling Auslese Mosel-Saar-Ruwer Brauneberger Juffer-Sonnenuhr Long Gold Cap 1990: Thick and rich, almost overpowering, with turbocharged aromas of lime and honey. Medium-bodied, very opulent and sweet, with thick, syruplike fruit and rich honey flavors. Better from 1993 to '96. $113/375ml (12/15/91) **94**
Riesling Auslese Mosel-Saar-Ruwer Brauneberger Juffer-Sonnenuhr Long Gold Cap 1989 $150 (12/15/90) **92**
Riesling Kabinett Mosel-Saar-Ruwer Brauneberger Juffer-Sonnenuhr 1990: A fruit bomb. Full-bodied and off-dry, with very ripe grapefruit and apple aromas and flavors and a ripe, round mouth-feel. Delicious already, but wait until 1993. $16 (12/15/91) **87**
Riesling Kabinett Mosel-Saar-Ruwer Brauneberger Juffer-Sonnenuhr 1989 $18 (12/15/90) **85**
Riesling Kabinett Mosel-Saar-Ruwer Brauneberger Juffer-Sonnenuhr 1988 ($NA) (9/30/89) **83**
Riesling Kabinett Mosel-Saar-Ruwer Brauneberger Juffer-Sonnenuhr 1985 $9 (6/30/87) **70**
Riesling Spätlese Mosel-Saar-Ruwer Brauneberger Juffer-Sonnenuhr 1990: Shows a wonderful concentration of classy fruit flavors, with aromas of spice and freshly crushed white grapes. Medium-bodied and lightly sweet, with super-sweet grape and honey flavors and a long finish. A serious wine. Better from 1993. $23 (12/15/91) **91**
Riesling Spätlese Mosel-Saar-Ruwer Brauneberger Juffer-Sonnenuhr 1989 $27 (12/15/90) **86**
Riesling Spätlese Mosel-Saar-Ruwer Brauneberger Juffer-Sonnenuhr 1988 ($NA) (9/30/89) **86**
Riesling Spätlese Mosel-Saar-Ruwer Brauneberger Juffer-Sonnenuhr 1986 ($NA) (4/15/89) **91**
Riesling Spätlese Mosel-Saar-Ruwer Brauneberger Juffer-Sonnenuhr 1985 ($NA) (4/15/89) **97**

REINHOLD HAART
Riesling Auslese Mosel-Saar-Ruwer Piesporter Goldtröpfchen 1988 ($NA) (9/30/89) **88**
Riesling Kabinett Mosel-Saar-Ruwer Piesporter Goldtröpfchen 1988 ($NA) (9/30/89) **88**
Riesling Spätlese Mosel-Saar-Ruwer Piesporter Goldtröpfchen 1988 ($NA) (9/30/89) **92**
Riesling Spätlese Mosel-Saar-Ruwer Piesporter Goldtröpfchen (AP6) 1988 ($NA) (9/30/89) **91**
Riesling Spätlese Mosel-Saar-Ruwer Piesporter Goldtröpfchen 1985 ($NA) (4/15/89) **78**

HAVEMEYER
Riesling Spätlese Mosel-Saar-Ruwer Piesporter Goldtröpfchen 1985 $17 (11/30/87) **68**

DR. HEIDEMANNS-BERGWEILER
Riesling Auslese Mosel-Saar-Ruwer Bernkasteler Alte Badstube am Doctorberg 1988 ($NA) (9/30/89) **81**
Riesling Auslese Mosel-Saar-Ruwer Graacher Himmelreich 1988 ($NA) (9/30/89) **79**
Riesling Spätlese Mosel-Saar-Ruwer Bernkasteler Badstube 1988 ($NA) (9/30/89) **85**
Riesling Spätlese Mosel-Saar-Ruwer Bernkasteler Doctor 1986 ($NA) (4/15/89) **85**
Riesling Spätlese Mosel-Saar-Ruwer Wehlener Sonnenuhr 1988 ($NA) (9/30/89) **88**

VON HOVEL
Riesling Auslese Mosel-Saar-Ruwer Oberemmeler Hütte 1989 $27 (12/15/90) **86**
Riesling Auslese Mosel-Saar-Ruwer Oberemmeler Hütte Gold Cap 1989 $45/375ml (12/15/90) **92**
Riesling Auslese Mosel-Saar-Ruwer Oberemmeler Hütte Gold Cap 1988 ($NA) (9/30/89) **81**
Riesling Beerenauslese Mosel-Saar-Ruwer Oberemmeler Hütte 1989 $88/375ml (12/15/90) **93**
Riesling Eiswein Mosel-Saar-Ruwer Oberemmeler Hütte 1989 $147/375ml (12/15/90) **87**
Riesling Kabinett Mosel-Saar-Ruwer Oberemmeler Hütte 1989 $12 (12/15/90) **80**
Riesling Kabinett Mosel-Saar-Ruwer Oberemmeler Hütte 1985 $8 (10/15/87) **80**
Riesling Kabinett Mosel-Saar-Ruwer Scharzhofberger 1989 $12 (12/15/90) **86**
Riesling Kabinett Mosel-Saar-Ruwer Scharzhofberger 1988 $12 (9/30/89) **86**
Riesling Spätlese Mosel-Saar-Ruwer Oberemmeler Hütte 1989 $16 (12/15/90) **90**
Riesling Spätlese Mosel-Saar-Ruwer Oberemmeler Hütte 1988 $15 (9/30/89) **89**
Riesling Spätlese Mosel-Saar-Ruwer Scharzhofberger 1989 $16 (12/15/90) **82**

IMMICH-BATTERIEBERG
Riesling Auslese Mosel-Saar-Ruwer 1988 ($NA) (9/30/89) **96**
Riesling Auslese Halbtrocken Mosel-Saar-Ruwer Enkircher Batterieberg 1990: A delicious wine, showing plenty of refined fruit, with perfumed aromas of melons and strawberries and similar flavors. Light-bodied and off-dry, with a flavorful finish and plenty of fresh acidity. Try in 1994 to '96. (NR) (12/15/91) **87**
Riesling Auslese Mosel-Saar-Ruwer Enkircher Batterieberg 1990: Tightly structured, needs time in the bottle. Has intense aromas of very ripe apricots and fruit and spicy mineral and grapefruit flavors. Medium-bodied, lightly sweet and powerful. Try after 1994. (NR) (12/15/91) **91**

Key to Symbols

The scores reported here are the results of blind tastings conducted by our panel of senior editors. Wines that carry the initials below are results of individual tastings.

THE WINE SPECTATOR 100-POINT SCALE ***95-100***—Classic, a great wine; ***90-94***—Outstanding, superior character and style; ***80-89***—Good to very good, a wine with special qualities; ***70-79***—Average, drinkable wine that may have minor flaws; ***60-69***—Below average, drinkable but not recommended; ***50-59***—Poor, undrinkable, not recommended. "+"—With a score indicates a range; used primarily with barrel tastings to indicate a preliminary score.

SPECIAL DESIGNATIONS SS—Spectator Selection, CS—Cellar Selection, BB—Best Buy, ($NA)—Price not available, (NR)—Not released, ***/**/*—Designations used by German producers to indicate successively higher-quality auslese wines, separating them from the estate's regular lots of auslese. Three stars is the highest rating.

TASTER'S INITIALS (JG)—Jim Gordon, (HS)—Harvey Steiman, (JL)—James Laube, (JS)—James Suckling, (TM)—Thomas Matthews, (TR)—Terry Robards, (PM)—Per-Henrik Mansson, (BT)—Barrel Tasting (these wines were tasted blind from barrel samples), (CA-date)—*California's Great Cabernets* by James Laube, (CH-date)—*California's Great Chardonnays* by James Laube, (VP-date)—*Vintage Port* by James Suckling.

DATE TASTED Dates in parentheses represent the issue in which the rating was published.

Riesling Spätlese Halbtrocken Mosel-Saar-Ruwer Enkircher Batterieberg 1990: A big, oily, off-dry wine to go with food. A wine for Mosel halbtrocken aficionados. Exceedingly balanced, with mineral and lemon rind aromas and rich mineral and spice flavors. Medium-bodied and off-dry. Rather fat for a Mosel wine. Drink now or hold. (NR) (12/15/91) **88**
Riesling Spätlese Mosel-Saar-Ruwer Enkircher Batterieberg 1990: An unconventional, powerful, dry style that needs food; try it with fish in cream sauces. Has creamy tropical fruit aromas. Medium- to full-bodied and off-dry, with white pepper and spice flavors and a dry finish. Better in 1993. (NR) (12/15/91) **90**
Riesling Spätlese Mosel-Saar-Ruwer Enkircher Batterieberg 1988 ($NA) (9/30/89) **96**

KARL JOSTOCK-THUL
Riesling Kabinett Mosel-Saar-Ruwer Piesporter Treppchen 1983 $4.75 (11/01/84) **79**

HERIBERT KERPEN
Riesling Auslese Mosel-Saar-Ruwer Bernkasteler Badstube 1990: Opulent, with extroverted flavors and fresh cream and pineapple aromas. Medium-bodied, sweet and very juicy, with honey, lemon and spice flavors. The acidity and finish are elegant. Drink now or hold. $17 (12/15/91) **89**
Riesling Auslese Mosel-Saar-Ruwer Graacher Himmelreich 1990: A pretty wine, with everything in the right place. Medium-bodied and sweet, offering light pineapple and peach aromas, biscuit and spice flavors, mouth-watering acidity and a medium finish. Better after 1993. $17 (12/15/91) **88**
Riesling Auslese Mosel-Saar-Ruwer Kollektion Kerpen Wehlener Sonnenuhr 1990: Rather hard and closed in still, but it shows an excellent concentration of fruit. Has aromas of pure honey and flowers. Medium-bodied and lightly sweet, with orange peel and honey flavors. Very spicy on the finish. Try after 1994. (NR) (12/15/91) **88**
Riesling Auslese Mosel-Saar-Ruwer Wehlener Sonnenuhr ** 1990: Wonderfully fruity and super-elegant. This seductive wine has pretty, creamy peach aromas and lovely flavors of honey and spice. Medium-bodied and medium sweet, with very high acidity. Try after 1994. $22 (12/15/91) **90**
Riesling Auslese Mosel-Saar-Ruwer Wehlener Sonnenuhr * 1990:** A pretty wine, with an elegant balance of sweet fruit and firm acidity. Medium-bodied, with beautiful lemon and peach aromas, focused sweet honey and apple flavors and lovely acidity on the finish. Better after 1994. $18/375ml (12/15/91) **90**
Riesling Auslese Mosel-Saar-Ruwer Wehlener Sonnenuhr 1990: Delicious, showing very good fruit, but it's rather one-dimensional. A medium-bodied wine, with flinty aromas and flavors and a sweet finish. Drink now or hold. $17 (12/15/91) **87**
Riesling Auslese Mosel-Saar-Ruwer Wehlener Sonnenuhr (AP12) 1988 $15 (9/30/89) **84**
Riesling Beerenauslese Mosel-Saar-Ruwer Wehlener Sonnenuhr 1990: Racy and intense; built like a long-distance runner, with lean, muscular fruit and an acidic structure. Full-bodied and very sweet, with powerful honey, lemon and spice aromas and racy acidity that tones down the huge amount of richness. Try from 1995 to '98. $66/375ml (12/15/91) **91**
Riesling Eiswein Mosel-Saar-Ruwer Wehlener Sonnenuhr 1990: Classy and silky, retaining plenty of Riesling character even though it's extremely sweet. Very flinty, spicy and fruity. Medium-bodied and sweet, with fresh, flinty, spicy fruit flavors, high acidity and a lively finish. Better in 1994. $75/375ml (12/15/91) **89**
Riesling Spätlese Mosel-Saar-Ruwer Wehlener Sonnenuhr 1988 $12 (9/30/89) **90**

KESSELSTATT
Riesling Auslese Mosel-Saar-Ruwer Bernkasteler Doctor 1990: An eye-opener. Quite promising, with rich honey aromas and subtle botrytis spice notes. Medium-bodied and sweet, with super-rich honey and lemon flavors and super-lively acidity. Better in 1994. $50 (12/15/91) **90**
Riesling Auslese Mosel-Saar-Ruwer Josephshöfer 1989 $39 (12/15/90) **86**
Riesling Auslese Mosel-Saar-Ruwer Oberemmeler Karlsberg 1989 $32 (12/15/90) **92**
Riesling Auslese Mosel-Saar-Ruwer Scharzhofberger 1989 $25 (12/15/90) **87**
Riesling Auslese Mosel-Saar-Ruwer Scharzhofberger Gold Cap 1989 $48 (12/15/90) **92**
Riesling Beerenauslese Mosel-Saar-Ruwer Scharzhofberger 1989 $220 (12/15/90) **94**
Riesling Eiswein Mosel-Saar-Ruwer Oberemmeler Karlsberg 1983: Ripe pineapple and peach flavors, with touches of honey and butter, balance elegantly against zingy acidity, keeping the richness from becoming overwhelming. Delicious now, but it should age for a decade. $150 (4/30/89) **90**
Riesling Kabinett Mosel-Saar-Ruwer Graacher Himmelreich 1989 $10 (12/15/90) **77**
Riesling Kabinett Mosel-Saar-Ruwer Josephshöfer 1990: Fresh and pleasant, medium-bodied, with flour and apple aromas, fresh apple, floral and anise flavors and fresh acidity. Better in 1993. $11 (12/15/91) **84**
Riesling Kabinett Mosel-Saar-Ruwer Josephshöfer 1989 $8.50 (12/15/90) **87**
Riesling Kabinett Mosel-Saar-Ruwer Josephshöfer 1988 $14 (9/30/89) **90**
Riesling Kabinett Mosel-Saar-Ruwer Piesporter Goldtröpfchen 1990: Really delicious, with lots of fruit. Has fresh cookie and grape aromas and a mouthfilling texture of silky fruit. Medium-bodied and lightly sweet, with a long, sweet finish. Drink now or hold. $14 (12/15/91) **86**
Riesling Kabinett Mosel-Saar-Ruwer Piesporter Goldtröpfchen 1988 ($NA) (9/30/89) **84**
Riesling Kabinett Mosel-Saar-Ruwer Scharzhofberger 1990: Surprisingly weighty, but a little one-dimensional. Medium-bodied and off-dry, with apple and wet earth aromas, rich, ripe melon flavors and medium acidity. Drink now. $11 (12/15/91) **84**
Riesling Kabinett Mosel-Saar-Ruwer Scharzhofberger 1989 $11 (12/15/90) **84**
Riesling Qualitätswein Mosel-Saar-Ruwer 1990: Refreshing and easy to drink. Medium-bodied and sweet, with ripe apple and melon aromas, lovely melon flavors and a silky finish. Drink now or hold. $10 (12/15/91) **83**
Riesling Qualitätswein Mosel-Saar-Ruwer Berkastler Badstube 1989 $8 (12/15/90) **82**
Riesling Qualitätswein Mosel-Saar-Ruwer Josephshöfer 1989 $7 (12/15/90) **83**
Riesling Spätlese Mosel-Saar-Ruwer Bernkastler Lay 1989 $13 (12/15/90) **85**
Riesling Spätlese Mosel-Saar-Ruwer Josephshöfer 1990: An exotic style that's more like freshly crushed grapes than wine. Medium-bodied and medium sweet, with pineapple and honey aromas, spicy honey flavors, firm acidity and a fresh finish. Better in 1994. $17 (12/15/91) **90**
Riesling Spätlese Mosel-Saar-Ruwer Josephshöfer 1989 $14 (12/15/90) **84**
Riesling Spätlese Mosel-Saar-Ruwer Kaseler Nies'chen 1990: Exceedingly fresh and delicious, with cookie, floral and fruit aromas. Medium-bodied and lightly sweet, with plenty of juicy fruit flavors and well-knit acidity. Drinkable now, but better in 1993. $16 (12/15/91) **88**
Riesling Spätlese Mosel-Saar-Ruwer Kaseler Nies'chen 1988 $20 (9/30/89) **94**
Riesling Spätlese Mosel-Saar-Ruwer Ockfener Bockstein 1989 $16 (12/15/90) **82**
Riesling Spätlese Mosel-Saar-Ruwer Piesporter Goldtröpfchen 1990: Lovely, sweet and graceful, with light aromas of apricot and melon. Medium-bodied and medium sweet, with spicy honey and apple flavors and a long finish. There's real concentration here. Better in 1994. $15 (12/15/91) **90**
Riesling Spätlese Mosel-Saar-Ruwer Piesporter Goldtröpfchen 1989 $15 (12/15/90) **86**
Riesling Spätlese Mosel-Saar-Ruwer Scharzhofberger 1989 $13 (12/15/90) **90**
Riesling Trockenbeerenauslese Mosel-Saar-Ruwer Scharzhofberger 1989 $150 (12/15/90) **94**

LEONARD KREUSCH
Riesling Kabinett Mosel-Saar-Ruwer Bereich Bernkastel 1986 $6 (11/30/88) **84**
Riesling Kabinett Mosel-Saar-Ruwer Zeltinger Himmelreich 1986 $5.75 (11/30/88) **84**

J. LAUERBURG
Riesling Spätlese Mosel-Saar-Ruwer Bernkasteler Doctor 1986 ($NA) (4/15/89) **83**
Riesling Spätlese Mosel-Saar-Ruwer Bernkasteler Doctor 1985 ($NA) (4/15/89) **82**
Riesling Spätlese Mosel-Saar-Ruwer Bernkasteler Lay 1985 ($NA) (4/15/89) **78**

JOSEFINENGRUND LEIWEN
Riesling Auslese Mosel-Saar-Ruwer Leiwener Laurentiuslay 1985 $11 (1/31/87) **83**
Riesling Kabinett Mosel-Saar-Ruwer Leiwener Klostergarten 1985 $6 (1/31/87) **82**

DR. LOOSEN
Riesling Auslese Mosel-Saar-Ruwer Erdener Prälat 1990: A full-blown, super-ripe style, with exotic honey and mango aromas. Medium- to full-bodied, with very ripe pineapple and bread crust flavors. Quite an oily wine, with an outstanding finish. Try from 1994. $31 (12/15/91) **91**
Riesling Auslese Mosel-Saar-Ruwer Erdener Prälat Gold Cap 1990: A gigantic wine, with great radiance and balance. Too young for the moment, but shows great promise. Very reserved, revealing little aroma, but it's full-bodied and sweet, with excellent depth of fruit and superb structure. Better from 1994 to '98. $46 (12/15/91) **95**
Riesling Auslese Mosel-Saar-Ruwer Urziger Würzgarten 1990: Rich and oozing with fruit, this is truly superb. Shows pineapple extract aromas, with super-concentrated pineapple and honey flavors. Medium-bodied and sweet, with firm acidity. Better from 1993 to '96. $27 (12/15/91) **92**
Riesling Auslese Mosel-Saar-Ruwer Urziger Würzgarten Gold Cap 1990: A burly wine, with immense muscles of fruit and acidity. Has intensely rich lemon and spice aromas. Full-bodied and sweet, with great power of fruit and acidity. Needs time; better from 1994 to '98. $46 (12/15/91) **94**
Riesling Auslese Mosel-Saar-Ruwer Wehlener Sonnenuhr Gold Cap 1990: An erotic wine, with ravishing cream, peach, lemon and light botrytis spice aromas. Medium-bodied and sweet, with lovely spice and thick fruit flavors. Has a lively finish. Try from 1993 to '95. $34 (12/15/91) **93**
Riesling Kabinett Mosel-Saar-Ruwer Bernkasteler Lay 1990: Super-fresh and super-fine, with vivid character. Shows very fresh apple and melon aromas and extremely intense, fresh flavors. Like biting into a bunch of fresh grapes. Medium-bodied and off-dry. Better from 1994. $13 (12/15/91) **90**
Riesling Kabinett Mosel-Saar-Ruwer Erdener Treppchen 1990: Oozing with fruit. Almost surreal, it's as great as a kabinett gets. Has incredibly fresh pineapple and melon aromas. Medium-bodied, off-dry and lightly sweet, overflowing with freshly crushed grape flavors, high acidity and a long finish. Better in 1993. $16 (12/15/91) **93**
Riesling Spätlese Mosel-Saar-Ruwer Erdener Treppchen 1990: Enticing, with wonderful elegance and richness, this very racy wine really grows on you. Offers light honey and mineral aromas. Medium-bodied and medium sweet, with rich honey, apple and spice flavors and a very long finish. Better from 1993 to '96. $20 (12/15/91) **93**

DR. MEYER
Riesling Qualitätswein Mosel-Saar-Ruwer Piesporter Michelsberg 1987 $4 (10/15/88) BB **88**

MILZ
Riesling Auslese Mosel-Saar-Ruwer Dhroner Hofberger 1988 ($NA) (9/30/89) **91**
Riesling Auslese Mosel-Saar-Ruwer Piesporter Hofberger 1990: A bit simple, but shows good fruit. Has very rich lemon aromas, lemon and honey flavors and a light finish. Medium-bodied and medium sweet. Try after 1993. $20 (12/15/91) **86**
Riesling Auslese Mosel-Saar-Ruwer Trittenheimer Altärchen 1990: A little backward, but has impressive concentration. Extremely youthful, with excellent potential. Medium-bodied and medium sweet, with lemon, apple and peach aromas and delicious peach and spice flavors. Very flinty. Better in 1994. $20 (12/15/91) **90**
Riesling Auslese Mosel-Saar-Ruwer Trittenheimer Felsenkopf 1988 ($NA) (9/30/89) **78**
Riesling Auslese Mosel-Saar-Ruwer Trittenheimer Felsenkopf Gold Cap 1990: A delicate auslese, with attractive peach and anise aromas and flavors and a sweet, elegant fruit structure. Tasted twice; the first bottle was flawed. Drink now or hold. $23 (12/15/91) **87**
Riesling Auslese Mosel-Saar-Ruwer Trittenheimer Leiterchen Gold Cap 1990: Full and rich, with an earthy apricot character on the nose and palate. Shows lots of fruit and firm acidity. Tasted twice; the first bottle was a dud. Try in 1994. $23 (12/15/91) **88**
Riesling Eiswein Mosel-Saar-Ruwer Trittenheimer Apotheke 1990: A formidable wine, with great class. Has intense lime, spice and flint aromas, medium-bodied, super-sweet, smashing flint and lime flavors and electrifying acidity on the finish. Better after 1995. $42/375ml (12/15/91) **91**
Riesling Spätlese Mosel-Saar-Ruwer 1990: Rather hard and awkward now; difficult to assess. The muted aromas reveal modest cassis and green apple. Medium-bodied and sweet, with green apple flavors, rather hard acidity and a buttery tone on the finish. Tasted twice. Better in 1993? $9.25 (12/15/91) **78**
Riesling Spätlese Mosel-Saar-Ruwer Piesporter Hofberg 1988 ($NA) (9/30/89) **83**
Riesling Spätlese Mosel-Saar-Ruwer Trittenheimer Altärchen 1990: Too prematurely developed for us at this stage; an old-fashioned style. Has light floral, peach and caramel aromas. Medium-bodied and sweet, with cream and apple flavors, medium acidity and a buttery finish. Drink now. $14 (12/15/91) **81**
Riesling Spätlese Mosel-Saar-Ruwer Trittenheimer Altärchen 1988 ($NA) (9/30/89) **83**
Riesling Spätlese Mosel-Saar-Ruwer Trittenheimer Apotheke 1990: Good, with clean fruit, but it's a little simple. Medium-bodied and lightly sweet, with melon, honey, almond and black licorice aromas, straightforward melon flavors and a slightly buttery finish. Drink now. $14 (12/15/91) **84**

MONCHHOF
Riesling Kabinett Mosel-Saar-Ruwer Urziger Würzgarten 1988 $15 (9/30/89) **90**
Riesling Spätlese Mosel-Saar-Ruwer Erdener Treppchen 1988 ($NA) (9/30/89) **86**
Riesling Spätlese Mosel-Saar-Ruwer Urziger Würzgarten 1988 ($NA) (9/30/89) **84**
Riesling Spätlese Mosel-Saar-Ruwer Wehlener Klosterberg 1988 ($NA) (9/30/89) **83**

EGON MULLER
Riesling Auslese Mosel-Saar-Ruwer Le Gallais Wiltingener Braune Kupp 1989 ($NA) (12/15/90) **89**
Riesling Auslese Mosel-Saar-Ruwer Scharzhofberger 1990: Very zingy, like drinking a fresh fruit salad. Medium-bodied and sweet, with potent lemon and tropical fruit aromas, super-ripe lemon, lime and tropical fruit flavors, high acidity and a very long, flavorful finish. Better from 1995. (NR) (12/15/91) **90**
Riesling Auslese Mosel-Saar-Ruwer Scharzhofberger 1989 ($NA) (12/15/90) **93**
Riesling Auslese Mosel-Saar-Ruwer Scharzhofberger Gold Cap 1990: Superb, with great concentration and balance. Yellow in color, with ripe apricot, lemon and botrytis aromas. Medium-bodied and sweet, with exquisitely rich apricot and orange blossom flavors and super-crisp acidity. Better from 1995. (NR) (12/15/91) **95**
Riesling Auslese Mosel-Saar-Ruwer Scharzhofberger Gold Cap 1989 $385 (12/15/90) **97**
Riesling Beerenauslese Mosel-Saar-Ruwer Le Gallais Wiltinger Braune Kupp 1990: Built for aging, with great finesse. Superlative winemaking. Has refined mineral, lemon, cream, peach and floral aromas. Full-bodied and super-sweet, but with an amazing amount of finesse and freshness. Try from 1995. (NR) (12/15/91) **96**
Riesling Beerenauslese Mosel-Saar-Ruwer Le Gallais Wiltingener Braune Kupp 1989 ($NA) (12/15/90) **91**
Riesling Beerenauslese Mosel-Saar-Ruwer Scharzhofberger 1990: Thick, massive and mind-blowing. Light amber-gold in color, with concentrated raisin and dried apricot aromas and tons of dried fruit flavors. It's like syrup, but the high acidity refreshes the palate. The finish goes on and on. Better in 1994, but will age for decades. (NR) (12/15/91) **97**
Riesling Beerenauslese Mosel-Saar-Ruwer Scharzhofberger 1989 ($NA) (12/15/90) **95**
Riesling Beerenauslese Mosel-Saar-Ruwer Scharzhofberger 1988 $70 (9/30/89) **99**
Riesling Eiswein Mosel-Saar-Ruwer Scharzhofberger 1989 ($NA) (12/15/90) **97**
Riesling Eiswein Mosel-Saar-Ruwer Scharzhofberger 1988 ($NA) (9/30/89) **92**
Riesling Kabinett Mosel-Saar-Ruwer Le Gallais Wiltinger Braune Kupp 1990: The lovely mineral, spice and apple aromas are wonderful, but the palate needs to develop. Medium-bodied and off-dry, with spicy white pepper flavors and a medium finish. Tasted twice. Better in 1994. $17 (12/15/91) **85**
Riesling Kabinett Mosel-Saar-Ruwer Scharzhofberger 1990: A fine wine, with a gentle character. Aromas of flowers and lemons follow through on the palate. Slightly off-dry, with a crisp, refreshing finish. Try from 1993. $22 (12/15/91) **84**
Riesling Kabinett Mosel-Saar-Ruwer Scharzhofberger 1989 $25 (12/15/90) **86**

GERMANY

Riesling/*Mosel-Saar-Ruwer*

Riesling Kabinett Mosel-Saar-Ruwer Scharzhofberger 1988 $13 (9/30/89) **92**
Riesling Spätlese Mosel-Saar-Ruwer Le Gallais Wiltingener Braune Kupp 1989 $29 (12/15/90) **85**
Riesling Spätlese Mosel-Saar-Ruwer Scharzhofberger 1990: Like biting into an apple just picked from the tree. Has attractive floral and peach aromas, lovely, fresh apple and pear flavors, plenty of acidity and a crisp finish. Medium-bodied and lightly sweet. Try from 1994. $29 (12/15/91) **88**
Riesling Spätlese Mosel-Saar-Ruwer Scharzhofberger 1989 $31 (12/15/90) **94**
Riesling Trockenbeerenauslese Mosel-Saar-Ruwer Le Gallais Wiltingener Braune Kupp 1989 ($NA) (12/15/90) **95**
Riesling Trockenbeerenauslese Mosel-Saar-Ruwer Scharzhofberger 1990: A masterpiece, an absolute giant. Brilliant gold in color, with hints of orange. The dried apricot and fruit aromas have hints of smoke and cedar. Thick like maple syrup and many times sweeter, with pure dried fruit extract flavor and lively acidity. Drink tomorrow or next century. (NR) (12/15/91) **99**
Riesling Trockenbeerenauslese Mosel-Saar-Ruwer Scharzhofberger 1989 ($NA) (12/15/90) **100**

RUDOLF MULLER

Riesling Kabinett Mosel-Saar-Ruwer Ockfener Bockstein 1985 $7 (4/15/87) **83**
Riesling Kabinett Mosel-Saar-Ruwer Piesporter Goldtröpfchen 1985 $9.50 (4/15/87) **90**
Riesling Kabinett Mosel-Saar-Ruwer Piesporter Goldtröpfchen 1983 $7.50 (6/16/85) **90**
Riesling Kabinett Mosel-Saar-Ruwer Piesporter Treppchen 1986 $6.75 (1/31/88) **78**
Riesling Kabinett Mosel-Saar-Ruwer Piesporter Treppchen 1985 $6 (4/15/87) **79**
Riesling Kabinett Mosel-Saar-Ruwer Reiler Mullay-Hofberg 1986 $7.25 (1/31/88) **76**
Riesling Kabinett Mosel-Saar-Ruwer Scharzhofberger 1985 $8 (4/15/87) **74**
Riesling Qualitätswein Mosel-Saar-Ruwer Scharzhofberger 1985 $6.50 (5/15/87) **84**
Riesling Spätlese Mosel-Saar-Ruwer Ockfener Bockstein 1983 $9.25 (5/15/87) **72**
Riesling Spätlese Mosel-Saar-Ruwer Piesporter Treppchen 1986 $8.25 (11/30/87) **80**
Riesling Spätlese Mosel-Saar-Ruwer Wehlener Sonnenuhr 1986 $8.25 (11/30/87) **83**
Riesling Spätlese Mosel-Saar-Ruwer Wehlener Sonnenuhr 1985 $7.50 (3/31/87) **92**

MULLER-BURGGRAEF

Riesling Auslese Mosel-Saar-Ruwer Kanzemer Sonnenberg 1990: Very forward, delicious to drink now. Light lemon and honeysuckle aromas lead to light fruit flavors. Medium-bodied and medium sweet, with firm acidity. $15 (12/15/91) **84**
Riesling Auslese Mosel-Saar-Ruwer Ockfener Bockstein 1990: Not giving much now, but should show more with age. Elegantly balanced, with subtle aromas of lemon rind and flowers. Medium-bodied and medium sweet, with pronounced acidity and a crisp finish. Better from 1993 to '96 $14 (12/15/91) **86**
Riesling Auslese Mosel-Saar-Ruwer Ockfener Geisberg 1990: Not as concentrated as some, but very attractive nonetheless, with elegant peach, ripe apple and cream aromas. Full-bodied and sweet, with lovely honey and tropical fruit flavors. Medium in acidity and on the finish. Better after 1993. $13 (12/15/91) **85**
Riesling Auslese Mosel-Saar-Ruwer Reiler Mullay-Hofberg 1990: A drink-now wine that should be a little fresher. Offers pretty honey and lemon aromas, lemon rind and almond paste flavors and a rather forward finish. Medium-bodied and sweet. Drink now. $13 (12/15/91) **81**
Riesling Kabinett Mosel-Saar-Ruwer Ockfener Bockstein 1990: A tasty wine, with plenty of fruit to keep your attention. Moderate in depth and class. Medium-bodied and lightly sweet, with fresh peach aromas, peach and apple flavors, good acidity and a very flavorful finish. Drink now or hold. $9.50 (12/15/91) **84**
Riesling Kabinett Mosel-Saar-Ruwer Scharzhofberger 1990: Quite full and easy to drink. A straightforward Riesling, with lots of cream and apple aromas. Medium-bodied and off-dry, with apple flavors and a fresh finish. Drink now or hold. $13 (12/15/91) **83**
Riesling Spätlese Mosel-Saar-Ruwer Kanzemer Sonnenberg 1990: A little too forward for us, with candied apple aromas and developed apple flavors. Medium-bodied and lightly sweet, with a light finish. Drink now. $11 (12/15/91) **80**
Riesling Spätlese Mosel-Saar-Ruwer Reiler Mullay-Hofberg 1990: Very good, with all the concentration you'd expect. Has light green-apple skin and melon aromas. Medium-bodied and medium sweet, with light honey and melon flavors and a light, spicy finish. Better after 1993. $10 (12/15/91) **85**

PETER NICOLAY

Riesling Auslese Mosel-Saar-Ruwer Erdener Prälat 1986 $21 (1/31/88) **83**
Riesling Auslese Mosel-Saar-Ruwer Erdener Treppchen 1990: Elegant, intense, complex and racy all at the same time, with marvelous nectarine, apricot, vanilla and floral aromas and flavors. Finishes with a delicate touch of honey, and a fine vein of acidity runs through it all. Delicious now, but probably best around 1995 to '98. 350 cases made. $22 (1/31/92) **91**
Riesling Auslese Mosel-Saar-Ruwer Urziger Goldwingert 1990: Crisp and citrusy, with juicy grapefruit, apple and honey aromas and flavors that stay with you on the lively finish. Beautifully proportioned, sweet without being cloying and crisp without being harsh. Drinkable now, but better after 1993. $35 (1/31/92) **88**
Riesling Auslese Mosel-Saar-Ruwer Urziger Goldwingert 1989 $30 (12/15/90) **89**
Riesling Auslese Mosel-Saar-Ruwer Urziger Goldwingert 1985 $10 (1/31/87) **79**
Riesling Auslese Mosel-Saar-Ruwer Urziger Würzgarten 1989 $30 (12/15/90) **83**
Riesling Auslese Trocken Mosel-Saar-Ruwer Urziger Würzgarten 1990: Dry and extremely tart, with strong earthy aromas and lemony, kerosene-scented flavors that persist on the finish. Not immediately appealing. Tasted twice, with consistent notes. $35 (1/31/92) **65**
Riesling Beerenauslese Mosel-Saar-Ruwer Erdener Prälat 1990: Very sweet, rich and honeyed, with layers of apricot, honey and spice flavors that have firm support from acidity. Has the flavor and intensity to develop with age, although it seems a little simple now. Drink after 1995. 25 cases made. $90 (1/31/92) **92**
Riesling Eiswein Mosel-Saar-Ruwer Urziger Würzgarten 1985 $66 (11/30/87) **94**
Riesling Kabinett Mosel-Saar-Ruwer Erdener Treppchen Artist 1986 $40/1.5L (9/15/88) **77**
Riesling Kabinett Mosel-Saar-Ruwer Urziger Goldwinger 1988 ($NA) (9/30/89) **85**
Riesling Kabinett Mosel-Saar-Ruwer Urziger Würzgarten 1986 $10 (11/30/87) **90**
Riesling Kabinett Mosel-Saar-Ruwer Urziger Würzgarten 1985 $7 (11/15/86) **85**
Riesling Spätlese Mosel-Saar-Ruwer Erdener Treppchen 1985 $8 (11/15/86) **68**
Riesling Spätlese Mosel-Saar-Ruwer Urziger Goldwingert 1990: A purely fruity, sweet wine, with dense, ripe apricot, peach and pear flavors, rich body and good balance. A very good wine for fans of pure fruit. $22 (1/31/92) **87**
Riesling Spätlese Mosel-Saar-Ruwer Urziger Goldwingert 1986 ($NA) (4/15/89) **86**
Riesling Spätlese Mosel-Saar-Ruwer Urziger Goldwingert 1985 ($NA) (4/15/89) **84**
Riesling Trockenbeerenauslese Mosel-Saar-Ruwer Urziger Goldwingert 1990: Sweet and rich, but a lively acidity weaves seamlessly through, keeping it refreshing and lithe. The flavors don't shortchange, with apricot, nectarine, flower and spice notes running through the long finish. Tempting to drink now, but probably better after 1995 to '97. 35 cases made. $350 (1/31/92) **94**
Riesling Trockenbeerenauslese Mosel-Saar-Ruwer Urziger Würzgarten 1989 $325 (12/15/90) **91**

DR. PAULY-BERGWEILER

Riesling Auslese Mosel-Saar-Ruwer Bernkasteler Alte Badstube am Doctorberg 1990: Smooth and generous, with distinctive nectarine and spice aromas and flavors that become richer and deeper on the long finish. The texture is soft and gentle, although a streak of acidity keeps it fresh. Drink now to 1994. 100 cases made. $45 (1/31/92) **90**
Riesling Auslese Mosel-Saar-Ruwer Bernkasteler Alte Badstube am Doctorberg 1989 $45 (12/15/90) **80**
Riesling Auslese Mosel-Saar-Ruwer Bernkasteler Alte Badstube am Doctorberg 1985 $30 (1/31/88) **91**
Riesling Auslese Mosel-Saar-Ruwer Bernkasteler Lay 1985 $14 (1/31/87) **85**
Riesling Auslese Mosel-Saar-Ruwer Graacher Himmelreich 1988 ($NA) (9/30/89) **80**
Riesling Auslese Mosel-Saar-Ruwer Wehlener Sonnenuhr 1990: Crisp and firm in texture, with a sense of reserve about the apple, lemon and melon aromas and flavors. The flavors seem coiled and ready to emerge with cellaring until 1993 to '95. Finishes delicate and fresh. $35 (1/31/92) **87**
Riesling Auslese Mosel-Saar-Ruwer Wehlener Sonnenuhr 1983 $15.50 (9/01/85) **82**
Riesling Beerenauslese Mosel-Saar-Ruwer Bernkasteler Alte Badstube am Doctorberg 1990: Sweet but focused and sharply balanced, with refreshing acidity and complex peach, honey, spice, grapefruit and floral aromas and flavors. Seductive to drink now, but probably better after 1995 to '97. 40 cases made. $86 (1/31/92) **95**
Riesling Beerenauslese Mosel-Saar-Ruwer Bernkasteler Badstube 1989 $60 (12/15/90) **86**
Riesling Beerenauslese Mosel-Saar-Ruwer Wehlener Sonnenuhr 1989 $70 (12/15/90) **83**
Riesling Eiswein Mosel-Saar-Ruwer Bernkasteler Badstube 1985 $100 (9/15/88) **87**
Riesling Eiswein Mosel-Saar-Ruwer Graacher Himmelreich 1990: Tangy, complex and elegant, with intense pineapple, apricot and lemon aromas and flavors that are sweet, but neither unctuous nor syrupy. Acidity races through this one, keeping it refreshing and lively. Very flavorful. Better to drink after 1996 to '98. 60 cases made. $90 (1/31/92) **96**
Riesling Eiswein Mosel-Saar-Ruwer Graacher Himmelreich 1989 $100 (12/15/90) **81**
Riesling Eiswein Mosel-Saar-Ruwer Graacher Himmelreich 1983 $90 (9/16/85) **87**
Riesling Kabinett Mosel-Saar-Ruwer Bernkasteler Alte Badstube am Doctorberg 1988 ($NA) (9/30/89) **76**
Riesling Kabinett Mosel-Saar-Ruwer Graacher Himmelreich 1985 $8 (11/15/86) **82**
Riesling Kabinett Mosel-Saar-Ruwer Wehlener Sonnenuhr 1989 $18 (12/15/90) **84**
Riesling Spätlese Mosel-Saar-Ruwer Bernkasteler Alte Badstube am Doctorberg 1990: Fruity and flavorful, with crisp, lively acidity and charm. The peach and melon flavors are sweet and concentrated. Should develop complexity with age; try to cellar until at least 1993. $35 (1/31/92) **89**
Riesling Spätlese Mosel-Saar-Ruwer Bernkasteler Alte Badstube am Doctorberg 1989 $30 (12/15/90) **80**
Riesling Spätlese Mosel-Saar-Ruwer Bernkasteler Alte Badstube am Doctorberg 1986 $24 (4/15/89) **82**
Riesling Spätlese Mosel-Saar-Ruwer Bernkasteler Alte Badstube am Doctorberg 1985 ($NA) (4/15/89) **86**
Riesling Spätlese Mosel-Saar-Ruwer Bernkasteler Badstube 1985 $10 (9/30/86) **90**
Riesling Spätlese Mosel-Saar-Ruwer Bernkasteler Badstube 1983 $9.50 (10/01/85) **78**
Riesling Spätlese Mosel-Saar-Ruwer Bernkasteler Lay 1988 ($NA) (9/30/89) **86**
Riesling Spätlese Mosel-Saar-Ruwer Brauneberger Juffer 1983 $9.50 (10/01/85) **70**
Riesling Spätlese Mosel-Saar-Ruwer Wehlener Sonnenuhr 1986 $13 (11/30/87) **86**
Riesling Trockenbeerenauslese Mosel-Saar-Ruwer Bernkasteler Alte Badstube am Doctorberg 1990: A magnificent wine that's rich, smooth, complex and layered with flavors and textures that echo for minutes on the finish. Starts with honey, apricot and grapefruit and evolves into something altogether new and seductive. Has just enough acidity to keep everything in extraordinary balance. Drinkable now. 20 cases made. $350 (1/31/92) **98**

WEINGUT HERBERT PAZEN

Riesling Spätlese Mosel-Saar-Ruwer Zeltinger Himmelreich 1990: Ripe and flavorful, with ample apple and peach flavors backed by bracing acidity that balances the sweetness. Floral accents lend it complexity, and the fruit lingers nicely on the finish. $11.50 (12/15/91) **87**

DR. F. PRUM

Riesling Spätlese Mosel-Saar-Ruwer Graacher Domprobst 1985 $12 (10/15/87) **74**

JOH. JOS. PRUM

Riesling Auslese Mosel-Saar-Ruwer Graacher Himmelreich 1990: Has an extremely impressive balance of fine, sweet fruit and elegant acidity. Medium-bodied and medium sweet, with lovely tropical fruit and lemon aromas, a wonderful interplay of luscious tropical fruit and lemon flavors and a steely finish. Better from 1994. $24 (12/15/91) **92**
Riesling Auslese Mosel-Saar-Ruwer Wehlener Sonnenuhr 1989 $35 (12/15/90) **92**
Riesling Auslese Mosel-Saar-Ruwer Wehlener Sonnenuhr 1988 $33 (9/30/89) **90**
Riesling Auslese Mosel-Saar-Ruwer Wehlener Sonnenuhr 1985 $20 (5/31/87) **90**
Riesling Auslese Mosel-Saar-Ruwer Wehlener Sonnenuhr (AP1191) 1990: An absolute joy to taste. Has wonderful aromas of freshly crushed grapes, flowers and peaches. Medium-bodied and sweet, with impressive fresh grape, honey and melon flavors and a balance of fine acidity. Better after 1994. $29 (12/15/91) **93**
Riesling Auslese Mosel-Saar-Ruwer Wehlener Sonnenuhr (Cask 27) 1990: Has impressive fruit, but lacks a bit of concentration on the finish. Shows ripe grapefruit aromas, medium-bodied and medium sweet honey and crushed grape flavors and a fresh, racy finish. Try after 1994. (NR) (12/15/91) (BT) **86+**
Riesling Auslese Mosel-Saar-Ruwer Wehlener Sonnenuhr Gold Cap 1990: Rich and silky, a vivid wine. Offers extremely fresh sliced-apple and grape aromas, fresh grape and apple flavors and a long finish. Medium-bodied and sweet. Better after 1995. (12/15/91) (BT) **96+**
Riesling Auslese Mosel-Saar-Ruwer Wehlener Sonnenuhr Gold Cap 1988 $80 (9/30/89) **98**
Riesling Auslese Mosel-Saar-Ruwer Wehlener Sonnenuhr Long Gold Cap 1990: Fast and furious in the mouth. Has masses of everything, with intense pineapple aromas. Full-bodied and sweet, with dense fruit structure and brilliant flavors, but the acidity balances everything out. Try after 1995. $250 (12/15/91) (BT) **96+**
Riesling Auslese Mosel-Saar-Ruwer Wehlener Sonnenuhr Long Gold Cap 1989 $249 (12/15/90) **94**
Riesling Beerenauslese Mosel-Saar-Ruwer Wehlener Sonnenuhr 1989 ($NA) (12/15/90) **95**
Riesling Eiswein Mosel-Saar-Ruwer Bernkasteler Johannisbrünchen 1990: Big and burly, a giant of a wine that smashes your palate with sweet fruit and nearly tears it apart. Full-bodied and very sweet, with ripe honey, spice and dried apricot aromas, spice, honey and smoke flavors and a very sweet finish. Better after 1996. (NR) (12/15/91) **96**
Riesling Kabinett Mosel-Saar-Ruwer Wehlener Klosterberg 1990: A brilliant wine from a rather pedestrian site. Like smelling and drinking fresh grape must. Has perfumed apple, floral and melon aromas and a palate full of sweet apple flavor and crisp acidity. Better in 1994. $15 (12/15/91) **91**
Riesling Kabinett Mosel-Saar-Ruwer Wehlener Klosterberg 1983 $9 (11/16/84) SS **91**

Key to Symbols

The scores reported here are the results of blind tastings conducted by our panel of senior editors. Wines that carry the initials below are results of individual tastings.

THE WINE SPECTATOR 100-POINT SCALE *95-100*—Classic, a great wine; *90-94*—Outstanding, superior character and style; *80-89*—Good to very good, a wine with special qualities; *70-79*—Average, drinkable wine that may have minor flaws; *60-69*—Below average, drinkable but not recommended; *50-59*—Poor, undrinkable, not recommended. "+"—With a score indicates a range; used primarily with barrel tastings to indicate a preliminary score.

SPECIAL DESIGNATIONS SS—Spectator Selection, CS—Cellar Selection, BB—Best Buy, ($NA)—Price not available, (NR)—Not released, ***/**/*—Designations used by German producers to indicate successively higher-quality auslese wines, separating them from the estates's regular lots of auslese. Three stars is the highest rating.

TASTER'S INITIALS (JG)—Jim Gordon, (HS)—Harvey Steiman, (JL)—James Laube, (JS)—James Suckling, (TM)—Thomas Matthews, (TR)—Terry Robards, (PM)—Per-Henrik Mansson, (BT)—Barrel Tasting (these wines were tasted blind from barrel samples), (CA-date)—*California's Great Cabernets* by James Laube, (CH-date)—*California's Great Chardonnays* by James Laube, (VP-date)—*Vintage Port* by James Suckling.

DATE TASTED Dates in parentheses represent the issue in which the rating was published.

Riesling Kabinett Mosel-Saar-Ruwer Wehlener Nonnenberg 1983 $9 (5/01/85) **87**
Riesling Kabinett Mosel-Saar-Ruwer Wehlener Sonnenuhr 1989 $21 (12/15/90) **91**
Riesling Kabinett Mosel-Saar-Ruwer Wehlener Sonnenuhr 1985 $11.50 (4/15/87) **76**
Riesling Spätlese Mosel-Saar-Ruwer Bernkasteler Badstube 1983 $11 (11/16/85) **50**
Riesling Spätlese Mosel-Saar-Ruwer Graacher Himmelreich 1985 $15.50 (4/15/89) **91**
Riesling Spätlese Mosel-Saar-Ruwer Wehlener Sonnenuhr 1990: Filled to the brim with fresh fruit. Truly exciting, bubbling with fresh peach and honey suckle aromas. Medium-bodied and sweet, overflowing with apple and peach flavors and a long, fresh finish. Try from 1994. $24 (12/15/91) **93**
Riesling Spätlese Mosel-Saar-Ruwer Wehlener Sonnenuhr 1989 $29 (12/15/90) **91**
Riesling Spätlese Mosel-Saar-Ruwer Wehlener Sonnenuhr 1986 ($NA) (4/15/89) **92**
Riesling Spätlese Mosel-Saar-Ruwer Wehlener Sonnenuhr 1985 ($NA) (4/15/89) **88**
Riesling Spätlese Mosel-Saar-Ruwer Wehlener Sonnenuhr 1983 $13 (5/01/85) SS **91**
Riesling Spätlese Mosel-Saar-Ruwer Wehlener Sonnenuhr (Cask 1) 1988 $20 (9/30/89) **97**
Riesling Spätlese Mosel-Saar-Ruwer Wehlener Sonnenuhr (Cask 2) 1988 $24 (9/30/89) **98**

S.A. PRUM
Riesling Auslese Mosel-Saar-Ruwer Graacher Himmelreich 1988 $25 (9/30/89) **94**
Riesling Auslese Mosel-Saar-Ruwer Wehlener Sonnenuhr 1988 $25 (9/30/89) **85**
Riesling Kabinett Mosel-Saar-Ruwer Graacher Himmelreich 1988 ($NA) (9/30/89) **81**
Riesling Spätlese Mosel-Saar-Ruwer Bernkasteler Graben 1988 $17.50 (9/30/89) **88**
Riesling Spätlese Mosel-Saar-Ruwer Graacher Himmelreich 1988 $18 (9/30/89) **81**
Riesling Spätlese Mosel-Saar-Ruwer Wehlener Sonnenuhr 1988 $18 (9/30/89) **83**

ZACH. BERGWEILER PRUM-ERBEN
Riesling Qualitätswein Mosel-Saar-Ruwer Bernkasteler Badstube Dr. Heidemanns Bergweiler 1987: A light, refreshing drink. Has delicate peach and floral flavors in a nearly dry style. Clean and well balanced. $11 (4/30/89) **81**

MAX FERD. RICHTER
Riesling Auslese Mosel-Saar-Ruwer Brauneberger Juffer 1989 $17 (12/15/90) **80**
Riesling Auslese Mosel-Saar-Ruwer Brauneberger Juffer-Sonnenuhr 1990: Very young and rambunctious, with fresh pineapple and tropical fruit flavors. Medium-bodied and sweet, with licorice and lemon rind flavors and a lingering finish. Try from 1994. $25 (12/15/91) **90**
Riesling Auslese Mosel-Saar-Ruwer Brauneberger Juffer-Sonnenuhr 1988 ($NA) (9/30/89) **87**
Riesling Auslese Mosel-Saar-Ruwer Graacher Himmelreich 1990: A lovely, racy wine. Exceedingly fresh, with lemon, apple and pear aromas and pear and apple flavors. Medium-bodied and medium sweet, with lively acidity. Better after 1993. $25 (12/15/91) **87**
Riesling Auslese Mosel-Saar-Ruwer Mülheimer Helenenkloster 1990: Starts with very fresh lemon aromas and the flavors dance across the palate. Medium-bodied and medium sweet, with incredibly powerful acidity. Better from 1994. $22 (12/15/91) **90**
Riesling Auslese Mosel-Saar-Ruwer Mülheimer Helenenkloster 1989 $20 (12/15/90) **87**
Riesling Auslese Mosel-Saar-Ruwer Veldenzer Elisenberg 1989 $16 (12/15/90) **80**
Riesling Eiswein Mosel-Saar-Ruwer Mülheimer Helenenkloster 1990: A supersonic wine, with racy acidity and fruit. Classic, with an incredible concentration of exotic lime, flint and fruit aromas. Medium-bodied and very sweet, with exquisite honey, lime and spice flavors and a long, long finish. Try from 1994 to '98. $100 (12/15/91) **93**
Riesling Eiswein Mosel-Saar-Ruwer Mülheimer Helenenkloster 1989 $50/375ml (12/15/90) **82**
Riesling Kabinett Mosel-Saar-Ruwer Brauneberger Juffer 1989 $11 (12/15/90) **84**
Riesling Kabinett Mosel-Saar-Ruwer Graacher Himmelreich 1989 $11 (12/15/90) **85**
Riesling Kabinett Mosel-Saar-Ruwer Wehlener Sonnenuhr 1990: This pretty wine has lots of style and develops quickly. Like a bouquet of freshly cut flowers on the nose. Medium-bodied, with intense mineral and lime flavors, super-fresh acidity and a long finish. Better after 1993. $12 (12/15/91) **84**
Riesling Kabinett Mosel-Saar-Ruwer Wehlener Sonnenuhr 1989 $11 (12/15/90) **85**
Riesling Qualitätswein Halbtrocken Mosel-Saar-Ruwer Dr. Richter 1990: A firm, well-structured wine, with no-nonsense fruit; still a little backward. Medium-bodied and off-dry, with mineral and fruit aromas, firm acidity and a citrus, melon-flavored finish. Better after 1993. $9 (12/15/91) **84**
Riesling Qualitätswein Halbtrocken Mosel-Saar-Ruwer Dr. Richter 1989 $8 (12/15/90) **83**
Riesling Spätlese Mosel-Saar-Ruwer Brauneberger Juffer 1989 $13 (12/15/90) **84**
Riesling Spätlese Mosel-Saar-Ruwer Brauneberger Juffer-Sonnenuhr 1990: Quite a mouthful, with intense lime, anise and mineral aromas. Medium-bodied, medium sweet and very concentrated, with lots of honey, lime and spice flavors and a long finish. Has excellent potential; better after 1993. $15 (12/15/91) **90**
Riesling Spätlese Mosel-Saar-Ruwer Brauneberger Juffer-Sonnenuhr 1988 ($NA) (9/30/89) **94**
Riesling Spätlese Mosel-Saar-Ruwer Veldenzer Elisenberg 1990: A live wire that needs time to develop in the bottle. Offers delicate aromas of mineral and fruit. Medium-bodied and medium sweet, with electrified anise, spice and grape flavors, excellent acidity and a long, powerful finish. Better after 1994. $14 (12/15/91) **90**
Riesling Spätlese Mosel-Saar-Ruwer Veldenzer Elisenberg 1988 ($NA) (9/30/89) **94**
Riesling Spätlese Mosel-Saar-Ruwer Wehlener Sonnenuhr 1989 $13 (12/15/90) **81**
Riesling Spätlese Mosel-Saar-Ruwer Wehlener Sonnenuhr 1988 ($NA) (9/30/89) **88**
Riesling Trockenbeerenauslese Mosel-Saar-Ruwer Mülheimer Sonnenlay 1989 $100/375ml (12/15/90) **92**

SCHLOSS SAARSTEIN (EBERT)
Riesling Auslese Mosel-Saar-Ruwer Serriger Schloss Saarstein 1990: A bit simple, but very attractive, with fresh lemon aromas and a pleasant balance of fresh fruit and acidity. Medium-bodied and medium sweet. Better from 1993. $23 (12/15/91) **85**
Riesling Auslese Mosel-Saar-Ruwer Serriger Schloss Saarstein Gold Cap 1988 $25 (9/30/89) **88**
Riesling Beerenauslese Mosel-Saar-Ruwer Serriger Schloss Saarstein 1990: This racy wine is brilliant yellow in color, with ripe lime, honey and botrytis aromas. Full-bodied and super-sweet, with concentrated fruit, cream, lime and lemon flavors and a massive amount of acidity. Gets better and better in the glass. Try from 1996. (NR) (12/15/91) **94**
Riesling Beerenauslese Mosel-Saar-Ruwer Serriger Schloss Saarstein Gold Cap 1990: Powerful yet refined. Truly outstanding, with amazing pineapple, tropical fruit and dried apricot aromas. Full-bodied and very sweet, with dried apricot, peach and botrytis flavors, firm acidity and a mile-long finish. Try from 1994 to '96. $47 (12/15/91) **93**
Riesling Eiswein Mosel-Saar-Ruwer Serriger Schloss Saarstein 1990: Has outstanding concentration, but isn't overwhelming. Opens slowly in the glass. Classic, with impressive aromas of honey and grapefruit. Full-bodied and very sweet, with refreshing tropical fruit and lemon flavors and a crisp finish. Better from 1994 to '96. (NR) (12/15/91) **92**
Riesling Kabinett Mosel-Saar-Ruwer Serriger Schloss Saarstein 1990: Extremely accessible for a young Saar wine. Very fresh and aromatic, with an impressive bouquet of lemon, pineapple and melon aromas. Medium-bodied, with fresh lemon and apple flavors, very crisp acidity and a long finish. Better from 1993. $11 (12/15/91) **86**
Riesling Kabinett Mosel-Saar-Ruwer Serriger Schloss Saarstein (AP10) 1988 ($NA) (9/30/89) **83**
Riesling Kabinett Mosel-Saar-Ruwer Serriger Schloss Saarstein (AP15) 1988 ($NA) (9/30/89) **90**
Riesling Qualitätswein Mosel-Saar-Ruwer 1990: Very crisp, refreshing and attractive, but slightly simple. Has creamy lemon and fruit aromas. Medium-bodied and dry, with very crisp acidity and a super-clean finish. Try now. $9 (12/15/91) **82**
Riesling Spätlese Mosel-Saar-Ruwer Serriger Schloss Saarstein 1990: Shows excellent balance of super-ripe fruit and great acidity. Very elegant and classic. Medium-bodied, with fresh lemon and apple aromas, lots of pineapple and melon flavors and super-refreshing acidity. Better from 1994. $15 (12/15/91) **90**
Riesling Spätlese Mosel-Saar-Ruwer Serriger Schloss Saarstein 1988 ($NA) (9/30/89) **85**

DR. LOOSEN ST. JOHANNISHOF
Riesling Auslese Mosel-Saar-Ruwer Erdener Prälat 1985 $20 (11/15/86) **92**
Riesling Auslese Mosel-Saar-Ruwer Erdener Prälat Gold Cap 1988 ($NA) (9/30/89) **90**
Riesling Auslese Mosel-Saar-Ruwer Wehlener Sonnenuhr Gold Cap 1988 ($NA) (9/30/89) **93**
Riesling Kabinett Mosel-Saar-Ruwer Bernkasteler Badstube 1983 $6.50 (4/01/85) **78**
Riesling Kabinett Mosel-Saar-Ruwer Erdener Treppchen 1983 $7 (3/16/85) **85**
Riesling Kabinett Mosel-Saar-Ruwer Wehlener Sonnenuhr 1988 ($NA) (9/30/89) **84**
Riesling Kabinett Mosel-Saar-Ruwer Wehlener Sonnenuhr 1985 $8 (1/31/87) **81**
Riesling Kabinett Mosel-Saar-Ruwer Wehlener Sonnenuhr 1983 $6 (4/01/85) **78**
Riesling Spätlese Mosel-Saar-Ruwer Bernkasteler Doctor 1986 ($NA) (4/15/89) **82**
Riesling Spätlese Mosel-Saar-Ruwer Erdener Prälat 1988 ($NA) (9/30/89) **90**
Riesling Spätlese Mosel-Saar-Ruwer Erdener Prälat 1986 ($NA) (4/15/89) **85**
Riesling Spätlese Mosel-Saar-Ruwer Erdener Treppchen 1985 $11 (1/31/87) **85**
Riesling Spätlese Mosel-Saar-Ruwer Erdener Treppchen 1983 $9 (3/01/85) **87**

WILLI SCHAEFER
Riesling Auslese Mosel-Saar-Ruwer Graacher Domprobst 1988 $13 (9/30/89) **80**
Riesling Kabinett Mosel-Saar-Ruwer Graacher Himmelreich 1988 $8 (9/30/89) **81**
Riesling Spätlese Mosel-Saar-Ruwer Graacher Domprobst 1988 $10 (9/30/89) **80**
Riesling Spätlese Mosel-Saar-Ruwer Wehlener Sonnenuhr 1988 $10 (9/30/89) **87**

C. VON SCHUBERT MAXIMIN GRUNHAUS
Riesling Auslese Mosel-Saar-Ruwer Abtsberg 1990: Very underdeveloped, it needs time. Packed with plenty of exotic fruit. Full-bodied and sweet, with intense aromas of lemons and freshly crushed grapes, focused lemon and honey flavors and a lively, steely finish. Better from 1994. $48 (12/15/91) **90**
Riesling Auslese Mosel-Saar-Ruwer Abtsberg 1989 $40 (12/15/90) **85**
Riesling Auslese Mosel-Saar-Ruwer Abtsberg (Cask 96) 1989 ($NA) (12/15/90) **95**
Riesling Auslese Mosel-Saar-Ruwer Abtsberg (Cask 98) 1989 $45 (12/15/90) **90**
Riesling Auslese Mosel-Saar-Ruwer Abtsberg (Cask 133) 1989 $70 (12/15/90) **90**
Riesling Auslese Mosel-Saar-Ruwer Herrenberg 1990: A real fruit bomb. Perfect for aging. Extremely perfumed, with lots of lemon and ripe fruit aromas. Full-bodied and medium sweet, with masses of lemon and tropical fruit flavors, plenty of acidity and a long finish. Better from 1993. $55 (12/15/91) **90**
Riesling Auslese Mosel-Saar-Ruwer Herrenberg 1989 $40 (12/15/90) **86**
Riesling Auslese Mosel-Saar-Ruwer Herrenberg (Cask 92) 1990: Has wonderful balance and freshness, perhaps more in the style of a normal auslese than a gold capsule, but it's lovely. Medium-weight, with vivid fruit. Extremely flowery, fresh aromas lead to ripe apple and apricot flavors, full steely acidity and a tasty finish. Medium-bodied and medium sweet. Terribly young; better from 1993 to '95. (NR) (12/15/91) **90**
Riesling Auslese Mosel-Saar-Ruwer Herrenberg (Cask 93) 1989 $80 (12/15/90) **91**
Riesling Auslese Mosel-Saar-Ruwer Herrenberg (AP153) 1988 $30 (9/30/89) **95**
Riesling Beerenauslese Mosel-Saar-Ruwer Abtsberg 1989 ($NA) (12/15/90) **99**
Riesling Eiswein Mosel-Saar-Ruwer Abtsberg 1990: Superlative balance and concentration. Enormously powerful and deep, with classy botrytis spice, cream, apple and lemon aromas and a great balance of mineral, floral and apple flavors. Full-bodied and super-sweet, with a super-long finish that goes on and on. Drink forever. (NR) (12/15/91) **96**
Riesling Kabinett Mosel-Saar-Ruwer Abtsberg 1990: Wonderfully fresh and lively, packed with exotic fruit. Has lovely pineapple, peach and cream aromas, medium-bodied, off-dry, focused lemon and pineapple flavors, lots of acidity and a clean finish. Better from 1993. $25 (12/15/91) **91**
Riesling Kabinett Mosel-Saar-Ruwer Abtsberg 1989 $20 (12/15/90) **90**
Riesling Kabinett Mosel-Saar-Ruwer Brüderberg 1989 $9.50 (12/15/90) **78**
Riesling Kabinett Mosel-Saar-Ruwer Herrenberg 1990: A symphony of flavors. Smells and tastes like freshly crushed grapes. Medium-bodied and medium sweet, with lively acidity and an excellent fruit structure that dances across your palate. Dry on the finish. Drinkable now, but better in 1993. $23 (12/15/91) **90**
Riesling Kabinett Mosel-Saar-Ruwer Herrenberg 1988 $10 (9/30/89) **89**
Riesling Kabinett Mosel-Saar-Ruwer Herrenberg 1987: A good example of a Mosel, showing fairly ripe orange aromas and grapefruit flavors that carry through to the finish. Clean and crisp. $12 (4/30/89) **82**
Riesling Qualitätswein Mosel-Saar-Ruwer Abtsberg 1988 $10 (9/30/89) **80**
Riesling Qualitätswein Mosel-Saar-Ruwer Abtsberg 1987: Vibrantly crisp but delicate, with sharply focused flavors of peach and tangerine, racy acidity and a lingering finish. There's an intriguing hint of pepper in the aroma. $13 (4/30/89) **87**
Riesling Qualitätswein Mosel-Saar-Ruwer Herrenberg 1989 $13 (12/15/90) **80**
Riesling Spätlese Mosel-Saar-Ruwer Abtsberg 1990: Tastes like a wine that just finished its fermentation, as youthful as they get. Medium-bodied, with freshly crushed grape aromas, super-charged apple, honey and grape flavors and excellent acidity. Built for aging; better from 1995. $30 (12/15/91) **92**
Riesling Spätlese Mosel-Saar-Ruwer Abtsberg 1989 $28 (12/15/90) **90**
Riesling Spätlese Mosel-Saar-Ruwer Abtsberg (Cask 96) 1990: This concentrated yet reserved style is undeveloped now, but it's top class. Gets better in the glass, with very fresh melon and lime aromas and flavors. Full-bodied and medium sweet, with excellent acidity. Better from 1994. (NR) (12/15/91) **91**
Riesling Spätlese Mosel-Saar-Ruwer Abtsberg 1988 $18 (9/30/89) **96**
Riesling Trockenbeerenauslese Mosel-Saar-Ruwer Herrenberg 1989 ($NA) (12/15/90) **96**

J. & H. SELBACH
Riesling Hochgewächs Mosel-Saar-Ruwer 1987 $7 (10/15/88) **78**
Riesling Kabinett Mosel-Saar-Ruwer Brauneberger Mandelgraben 1983 $4.50 (11/16/84) BB **84**
Riesling Kabinett Mosel-Saar-Ruwer Zeltinger Himmelreich 1985 $7.50 (10/15/88) **86**
Riesling Spätlese Mosel-Saar-Ruwer Bernkasteler Kurfürstlay 1990: Very tart acidity and a strong sulfur scent add up to a raw, aggressive wine. Age should improve it, since there is a decent amount of apple and pineapple flavor underneath the acidity. Try cellaring until about 1993. $9 (12/15/91) **78**
Riesling Spätlese Mosel-Saar-Ruwer Piesporter Goldtröpfchen 1985 $14 (9/15/88) **89**

SELBACH-OSTER
Riesling Auslese Mosel-Saar-Ruwer Zeltinger Himmelreich 1990: Soothing and relaxing, like listening to a symphony. Has fresh honey and grape skin aromas, medium-bodied, sweet, super-fresh lemon and grape flavors and a fresh finish. Better after 1994. (NR) (12/15/91) **90**
Riesling Auslese Mosel-Saar-Ruwer Zeltinger Sonnenuhr * 1990:** Shows great finesse. Extremely fresh and flowery, with delicate honey, floral and fruit aromas. Medium-bodied and medium sweet, with a lovely balance of honey and cookie flavors and a sweet finish. Better from 1994 to '96. $21/375ml (12/15/91) **90**
Riesling Auslese Mosel-Saar-Ruwer Zeltinger Sonnenuhr 1990: A serious wine, with a majestic structure that is extremely concentrated and compact, with intense mineral, flint and fruit aromas and flavors and a superb balance of acidity. Better after 1994. (NR) (12/15/91) **91**
Riesling Auslese Mosel-Saar-Ruwer Zeltinger Sonnenuhr (AP5) 1988 $22 (9/30/89) **91**
Riesling Beerenauslese Mosel-Saar-Ruwer Zeltingen-Rachtiger Sonnenuhr 1989 $56/375ml (12/15/90) **91**
Riesling Beerenauslese Mosel-Saar-Ruwer Zeltinger Sonnenuhr 1990: A thick, opulent wine, with masses of fruit. Full-bodied and super-sweet, with a thick honey structure, superb intense spice

and honey aromas and intense honey and syrup flavors. Almost drinkable now, but better in 1994 to '96. $75/375ml (12/15/91) **91**

Riesling Eiswein Mosel-Saar-Ruwer Bernkasteler Badstube 1990: Very fruity, with intense honey, apricot and sweet-and-sour aromas. Giant on the palate, with superb concentration of super-sweet fruit flavors. Very high in acidity. Try after 1997. $87/375ml (12/15/91) **95**

Riesling Eiswein Mosel-Saar-Ruwer Zeltinger Himmelreich 1986: Very pretty aromas of spicy peach and wildflowers turn bitter and green on the palate, calling into question the aging potential of this wine. $40/375ml (4/30/89) **76**

Riesling Eiswein Mosel-Saar-Ruwer Zeltinger Himmelreich 1985: Once you get past the heavy dose of sulfur on the nose, it has very pretty peach and honey flavors with a touch of almond. This needs till the turn of the century to reach maturity. $35/375ml (4/30/89) **83**

Riesling Hochgewächs Mosel-Saar-Ruwer Graacher Himmelreich 1986 $6 (10/15/88) **81**

Riesling Kabinett Mosel-Saar-Ruwer Bernkasteler Badstube 1989 $10 (12/15/90) **84**

Riesling Kabinett Mosel-Saar-Ruwer Graacher Himmelreich 1985 $10 (10/15/88) **80**

Riesling Kabinett Mosel-Saar-Ruwer Wehlener Klosterberg 1986 $8 (11/30/88) **86**

Riesling Kabinett Mosel-Saar-Ruwer Wehlener Sonnenuhr 1989 $10 (12/15/90) **81**

Riesling Kabinett Mosel-Saar-Ruwer Zeltingen-Rachtiger Sonnenuhr 1989 $10.50 (12/15/90) **85**

Riesling Kabinett Mosel-Saar-Ruwer Zeltinger Himmelreich 1988 $8.50 (9/30/89) **81**

Riesling Spätlese Mosel-Saar-Ruwer Bernkasteler Badstube 1989 $11.50 (12/15/90) **87**

Riesling Spätlese Mosel-Saar-Ruwer Bernkasteler Badstube 1985 $9.50 (9/15/88) **90**

Riesling Spätlese Mosel-Saar-Ruwer Graacher Himmelreich 1985 $8 (9/15/88) **82**

Riesling Spätlese Mosel-Saar-Ruwer Wehlener Klosterberg 1988 $11 (9/30/89) **84**

Riesling Spätlese Mosel-Saar-Ruwer Wehlener Sonnenuhr 1989 $10 (12/15/90) **87**

Riesling Spätlese Mosel-Saar-Ruwer Zeltingen-Rachtiger Himmelreich 1989 $11.50 (12/15/90) **86**

Riesling Spätlese Mosel-Saar-Ruwer Zeltinger Schlossberg 1990: Lively, with plenty of sweet fruit and minerals on the nose and palate. Medium-bodied and medium sweet, with honey and melon aromas, lively acidity and a long pineapple and spice finish. Better after 1994. $13 (12/15/91) **89**

Riesling Spätlese Mosel-Saar-Ruwer Zeltinger Sonnenuhr 1990: An impressive, spicy wine that needs a few years to show its fullest. Has lovely, fresh honey and spice aromas, ripe pineapple and spice flavors, firm acidity and a clean finish. Medium-bodied. Better after 1994. (NR) (12/15/91) **88**

Riesling Spätlese Mosel-Saar-Ruwer Zeltinger Sonnenuhr 1988 $12.50 (9/30/89) **93**

Riesling Trockenbeerenauslese Mosel-Saar-Ruwer Zeltingen-Rachtiger Sonnenuhr 1989 $100/375ml (12/15/90) **97**

Riesling Trockenbeerenauslese Mosel-Saar-Ruwer Zeltinger Sonnenuhr 1990: Dense and smoky, with an incredibly spicy, honeyed character on the nose and palate. Super-sweet, with burnt toast and botrytis spice character. Long and sticky on the finish, with stunning depth and power and enormous structure. Better after 1997. (NR) (12/15/91) **93**

BERT SIMON

Riesling Auslese Mosel-Saar-Ruwer Kaseler Gold Cap 1989 $32 (12/15/90) **84**

Riesling Auslese Mosel-Saar-Ruwer Patheiger Kaseler Kehrnagel Long Gold Cap 1989 $24/375ml (12/15/90) **86**

Riesling Auslese Mosel-Saar-Ruwer Serriger Herrenberg 1990: Steely sweet, with tons of fruit, but a bit aggressive now. Offers lots of melon and lime aromas and flavors. Medium-bodied and medium sweet, with very steely acidity and a long, tart finish. Better from 1994. $21 (12/15/91) **84**

Riesling Auslese Mosel-Saar-Ruwer Serriger Herrenberg 1989 $21 (12/15/90) **85**

Riesling Auslese Mosel-Saar-Ruwer Serriger Würtzberg 1990: Shows a lovely balance of high-wire acidity and fruit, with exquisite floral and honey aromas. Medium-bodied and sweet, with full acidity and intense honey and lemon aromas. Try from 1994. $21 (12/15/91) **88**

Riesling Auslese Mosel-Saar-Ruwer Serriger Würtzberg 1988 ($NA) (9/30/89) **87**

Riesling Auslese Mosel-Saar-Ruwer Serriger Würtzberg Gold Cap 1990: Racy and exciting, with huge depth and power. Medium-bodied and sweet, with intense lemon, spice and botrytis aromas, focused lemon, lime and spice flavors and steely acidity. Try from 1995. $30 (12/15/91) **91**

Riesling Auslese Mosel-Saar-Ruwer Serriger Würtzberg Gold Cap 1989 $31 (12/15/90) **86**

Riesling Beerenauslese Mosel-Saar-Ruwer Serriger Würtzberg 1989 $53/375ml (12/15/90) **93**

Riesling Kabinett Halbtrocken Mosel-Saar-Ruwer Mertesdorfer Herrenberg 1989 $13 (12/15/90) **79**

Riesling Kabinett Mosel-Saar-Ruwer Eitelsbacher Marienholz 1990: Subtle, with a nice balance of acidity and fruit, but a little short. Has classy cream and peach aromas. Medium-bodied and off-dry, with fresh, clean apple and vanilla flavors, well-integrated acidity and very good balance. Drink now or hold. $11 (12/15/91) **85**

Riesling Kabinett Mosel-Saar-Ruwer Eitelsbacher Marienholz 1989 $13 (12/15/90) **87**

Riesling Kabinett Mosel-Saar-Ruwer Serriger Herrenberg 1990: Medium-bodied and off-dry, with ripe peach and tropical fruit aromas, creamy apple flavors, medium acidity and a clean finish. A pleasant wine to drink now. $11 (12/15/91) **84**

Riesling Kabinett Mosel-Saar-Ruwer Serringer Herrenberg 1989 $11.50 (12/15/90) **85**

Riesling Kabinett Mosel-Saar-Ruwer Serriger Würtzberg 1990: Lovely, with creamy apple aromas and flavors. Very juicy and off-dry, with all the fruit you could want in a kabinett. Drink now or hold. $11 (12/15/91) **84**

Riesling Kabinett Mosel-Saar-Ruwer Serriger Würtzberg 1989 $13 (12/15/90) **84**

Riesling Kabinett Mosel-Saar-Ruwer Serriger Würtzberg 1988 ($NA) (9/30/89) **82**

Riesling Qualitätswein Mosel-Saar-Ruwer 1988 $6 (9/30/89) **84**

Riesling Spätlese Mosel-Saar-Ruwer Kastel-Staadt Maximiner Prälat 1989 $13 (12/15/90) **85**

Riesling Spätlese Mosel-Saar-Ruwer Patheiger Kaseler Kehrnagel 1990: Extremely well balanced, with everything to offer. Creamy peach aromas lead to an abundance of fruit flavor, lovely acidity and a refreshing but slightly simple finish. Better from 1993. $13 (12/15/91) **86**

Riesling Spätlese Mosel-Saar-Ruwer Patheiger Kaseler Kehrnagel 1989 $15 (12/15/90) **78**

Riesling Spätlese Mosel-Saar-Ruwer Serriger Würtzberg 1990: Squeaky clean and discreet, with mineral, cookie and fruit aromas and anise, mineral and fruit flavors. Medium-bodied and medium sweet, with balanced acidity. Better from 1993. $13 (12/15/91) **87**

Riesling Spätlese Mosel-Saar-Ruwer Serriger Würtzberg 1989 $15 (12/15/90) **87**

Riesling Spätlese Mosel-Saar-Ruwer Serriger Würtzberg 1988 ($NA) (9/30/89) **90**

Key to Symbols

The scores reported here are the results of blind tastings conducted by our panel of senior editors. Wines that carry the initials below are results of individual tastings.

THE WINE SPECTATOR 100-POINT SCALE *95-100*—Classic, a great wine; *90-94*—Outstanding, superior character and style; *80-89*—Good to very good, a wine with special qualities; *70-79*—Average, drinkable wine that may have minor flaws; *60-69* —Below average, drinkable but not recommended; *50-59* —Poor, undrinkable, not recommended. "+"—With a score indicates a range; used primarily with barrel tastings to indicate a preliminary score.

SPECIAL DESIGNATIONS SS—Spectator Selection, CS—Cellar Selection, BB—Best Buy, ($NA)—Price not available, (NR)—Not released, ***/**/*—Designations used by German producers to indicate successively higher-quality auslese wines, separating them from the estates's regular lots of auslese. Three stars is the highest rating.

TASTER'S INITIALS (JG)—Jim Gordon, (HS)—Harvey Steiman, (JL)—James Laube, (JS)—James Suckling, (TM)—Thomas Matthews, (TR)—Terry Robards, (PM)—Per-Henrik Mansson, (BT)—Barrel Tasting (these wines were tasted blind from barrel samples), (CA-date)—*California's Great Cabernets* by James Laube, (CH-date)—*California's Great Chardonnays* by James Laube, (VP-date)—*Vintage Port* by James Suckling.

DATE TASTED Dates in parentheses represent the issue in which the rating was published.

Riesling Trockenbeerenauslese Mosel-Saar-Ruwer Serriger Würtzberg 1989 $96/375ml (12/15/90) **95**

STUDERT-PRUM

Riesling Auslese Mosel-Saar-Ruwer Wehlener Sonnenuhr 1988 ($NA) (9/30/89) **86**

THANISCH (KNABBEN-SPIER)

Riesling Auslese Mosel-Saar-Ruwer Bernkasteler Badstube 1988 $25 (9/30/89) **82**

Riesling Auslese Mosel-Saar-Ruwer Bernkasteler Lay 1988 ($NA) (9/30/89) **92**

Riesling Spätlese Mosel-Saar-Ruwer Bernkasteler Doctor 1988 $15 (9/30/89) **90**

Riesling Spätlese Mosel-Saar-Ruwer Bernkasteler Doctor 1986 ($NA) (4/15/89) **79**

Riesling Spätlese Mosel-Saar-Ruwer Bernkasteler Lay 1988 $12 (9/30/89) **89**

Riesling Spätlese Mosel-Saar-Ruwer Bernkasteler Lay 1985 ($NA) (4/15/89) **82**

Riesling Spätlese Mosel-Saar-Ruwer Graacher Himmelreich 1985 ($NA) (4/15/89) **85**

DR. H. THANISCH (MULLER-BURGGRAEFF)

Riesling Auslese Mosel-Saar-Ruwer Bernkasteler Doctor 1990: Somewhat one-dimensional, but it has beautiful pineapple and honey aromas and spice and floral flavors. Medium-bodied and sweet, with firm acidity and a fresh finish. Try in 1993 or '94. $55 (12/15/91) **86**

Riesling Auslese Mosel-Saar-Ruwer Bernkasteler Doctor 1988 ($NA) (9/30/89) **90**

Riesling Auslese Mosel-Saar-Ruwer Brauneberger Juffer-Sonnenuhr 1989 $25 (12/15/90) **85**

Riesling Auslese Mosel-Saar-Ruwer Brauneberger Juffer-Sonnenuhr 1988 ($NA) (9/30/89) **85**

Riesling Beerenauslese Mosel-Saar-Ruwer Bernkasteler Doctor 1989 $240 (12/15/90) **91**

Riesling Eiswein Mosel-Saar-Ruwer Bernkasteler Doctor 1989 $190 (12/15/90) **88**

Riesling Kabinett Halbtrocken Mosel-Saar-Ruwer Bernkasteler Doctor 1989 ($NA) (12/15/90) **74**

Riesling Kabinett Mosel-Saar-Ruwer Bernkasteler Badstube 1990: A very good wine for this appellation, with wonderfully fresh fruit. Medium-bodied and off-dry, with refreshing floral and mineral aromas, attractive lemon-lime and apple flavors, fresh acidity and a super-long finish. Better after 1994. (NR) (12/15/91) **87**

Riesling Kabinett Mosel-Saar-Ruwer Bernkasteler Badstube 1986 $11 (11/30/87) **72**

Riesling Kabinett Mosel-Saar-Ruwer Bernkasteler Badstube 1985 $11 (4/15/87) **88**

Riesling Kabinett Mosel-Saar-Ruwer Bernkasteler Doctor 1986 $29 (11/30/87) **84**

Riesling Kabinett Mosel-Saar-Ruwer Bernkastler Lay 1989 $13.50 (12/15/90) **81**

Riesling Kabinett Mosel-Saar-Ruwer Graacher Himmelreich 1989 $14 (12/15/90) **79**

Riesling Kabinett Mosel-Saar-Ruwer Lieserer Niederberg-Helden 1990: Absolutely brutal acidity slaps you in the face; needs time. Has dried apricot and tropical fruit aromas. Medium-bodied and medium sweet, with honey and dried apricot flavors and scorching acidity. A little simple. Try in 1995. (NR) (12/15/91) **81**

Riesling Kabinett Mosel-Saar-Ruwer Lieserer Niederberg-Heldenberg 1989 $14 (12/15/90) **87**

Riesling Kabinett Mosel-Saar-Ruwer Lieserer Niederberg-Heldenberg 1988 ($NA) (9/30/89) **86**

Riesling Spätlese Mosel-Saar-Ruwer Bernkasteler Doctor 1990: A sweet, fresh style that would make an excellent aperitif. Medium-bodied and medium sweet, with lemon and mineral aromas, opulent, freshly crushed grape and honey flavors, good acidity and a lovely finish. Better after 1993. (NR) (12/15/91) **87**

Riesling Spätlese Mosel-Saar-Ruwer Bernkasteler Doctor 1989 ($NA) (12/15/90) **71**

Riesling Spätlese Mosel-Saar-Ruwer Bernkasteler Doctor 1986 ($NA) (4/15/89) **64**

Riesling Spätlese Mosel-Saar-Ruwer Bernkasteler Doctor 1985 ($NA) (4/15/89) **77**

Riesling Spätlese Mosel-Saar-Ruwer Bernkasteler Graben 1990: A simple wine to drink now. It has light apple and mineral aromas and is lightly sweet, with apple and caramel flavors and a light finish. Medium-bodied. (NR) (12/15/91) **82**

Riesling Spätlese Mosel-Saar-Ruwer Bernkasteler Kurfürstlay 1986 $12 (11/30/87) **88**

Riesling Spätlese Mosel-Saar-Ruwer Bernkasteler Kurfürstlay 1985 $9.50 (4/15/89) **72**

Riesling Spätlese Mosel-Saar-Ruwer Brauneberger-Juffer-Sonnenuhr 1990: Pristine, with pretty aromas of apple and cream and a supercharged palate of fruit. Medium-bodied and lightly sweet, with a fresh finish. Drink now or hold. (NR) (12/15/91) **86**

Riesling Spätlese Mosel-Saar-Ruwer Brauneberger-Juffer-Sonnenuhr 1989 $19 (12/15/90) **78**

Riesling Spätlese Mosel-Saar-Ruwer Graacher Himmelreich 1990: Forward in style, but has excellent fruit. Quite classy, with delicate lime, mineral and melon aromas. Medium-bodied and medium sweet, with rich lime and honey flavors and a rich, racy finish. Drink now or hold. (NR) (12/15/91) **87**

Riesling Spätlese Mosel-Saar-Ruwer Lieserer Niederberg-Helden 1990: Medium-bodied and lightly sweet, fresh and delicious. Offers lemon and modest peach aromas and fresh apple and honey flavors. Drink now or hold. (NR) (12/15/91) **85**

Riesling Spätlese Mosel-Saar-Ruwer Lieserer Niederberg-Helden 1989 $15 (12/15/90) **81**

Riesling Spätlese Mosel-Saar-Ruwer Lieserer Niederberg-Helden 1988 ($NA) (9/30/89) **70**

DR. H. THANISCH (VDP)

Riesling Beerenauslese Mosel-Saar-Ruwer Bernkasteler Doctor 1990: Shows all the class and glory of this legendary vineyard; a must-have for collectors. Stunning almond, lemon, spice, honey and mineral aromas lead to super-focused, full-bodied dried apricot and spice flavors. Has an incredible amount of acidity and a super-long finish. Try after 1996. (NR) (12/15/91) **95**

Riesling Qualitätswein Mosel-Saar-Ruwer 1990: Very lively and intriguing, with pine, apple and lemon aromas, fresh apple and lemon flavors, crisp acidity and a lively finish. Medium-bodied and off-dry. Better after 1994. $11 (12/15/91) (BT) **80+**

Riesling Spätlese Mosel-Saar-Ruwer Bernkasteler Doctor 1990: Very good and very refined, with ripe lemon, peach and cream aromas. Medium-bodied and lightly sweet, with lemon and cream flavors and light honey notes on the finish. Tasted twice. Drink now or hold. $51 (12/15/91) **87**

Riesling Spätlese Mosel-Saar-Ruwer Bernkasteler Lay 1990: Rich and honeyed, with excellent fruit, this lively wine shows excellent balance. Has extremely attractive honey, coconut and fruit aromas. Medium-bodied and medium sweet, with excellent concentration, firm acidity and a racy finish. Better after 1994. $22 (12/15/91) **88**

Riesling Spätlese Mosel-Saar-Ruwer Bernkasteler Schlossberg 1990: Deliciously enticing, very fruity and juicy. Medium-bodied and lightly sweet, with fresh melon and honey aromas, very fresh grape and honey flavors and a sweet, flavorful finish. An excellent value. Try after 1994. $20 (12/15/91) **90**

H. THAPRICH

Riesling Spätlese Mosel-Saar-Ruwer Bernkasteler Badstube 1983 $8.50 (4/01/85) **80**

Riesling Spätlese Mosel-Saar-Ruwer Bernkasteler Lay 1983 $8.25 (3/16/85) **78**

TYRELL

Riesling Auslese Mosel-Saar-Ruwer Eitelsbacher Karthäuserhofberg 1990: A fruit explosion; extremely vibrant, with freshly cut green apple and melon aromas and lots of fresh fruit flavor. Full-bodied and medium sweet, with high acidity. Better from 1994. $21 (12/15/91) **90**

Riesling Auslese Mosel-Saar-Ruwer Eitelsbacher Karthäuserhofberg (Cask 4) 1990: Understated in the aromas and elegant on the palate. Could move up a few points in a few years. Medium-bodied and sweet, offering fresh melon and apple aromas, creamy apple flavors, very high acidity and a long, zingy finish. Better from 1994. (NR) (12/15/91) **88**

Riesling Auslese Mosel-Saar-Ruwer Eitelsbacher Karthäuserhofberg (Cask 6) 1990: Steely and lively, with plenty of concentration. Has powerful mineral, pine and sweet fruit aromas, intense lemon and lime flavors and steely acidity. Full-bodied and sweet. Better from 1993 to '96. (NR) (12/15/91) **91**

Riesling Auslese Mosel-Saar-Ruwer Eitelsbacher Karthäuserhofberg (Cask 16) 1990: Needs time to develop in the bottle, it's a little awkward now. Could move up a few notches. Medium-bodied and sweet, with discreet lemon and fruit aromas, steely acidity and a rather lean fruit structure. Try from 1994. (NR) (12/15/91) **88**

Riesling Kabinett Mosel-Saar-Ruwer Eitelsbacher Karthäuserhofberg 1990: Extremely classy, with excellent concentration. A serious wine, with delicate yet intense aromas of minerals, limes and lemons. Medium-bodied and off-dry, packed to the brim with fruit and excellent acidity. Shows lots of flavor on the crisp finish. Better in 1993 or '94. $16 (12/15/91) **88**

Riesling Kabinett Mosel-Saar-Ruwer Eitelsbacher Karthäuserhofberg (AP3) 1988 ($NA) (9/30/89) **85**

Riesling Kabinett Mosel-Saar-Ruwer Eitelsbacher Karthäuserhofberg (AP9) 1988 ($NA) (9/30/89) **85**

Riesling Qualitätswein Mosel-Saar-Ruwer Eitelsbacher Karthäuserhofberg 1990: Delicious and packed with fruit, perfect for sipping in warm weather. Shows intense lemon and grapefruit aromas, a round yet crisp texture and loads of lemony apple flavors. Medium-bodied and medium sweet. Drink now or hold. $14 (12/15/91) **88**

Riesling Spätlese Mosel-Saar-Ruwer Eitelsbacher Karthäuserhofberg 1990: The super-focused fruit in this wine zeros in on your palate. Delightfully perfumed, with plenty of cantaloupe and apple aromas. Medium-bodied and sweet, with intensely focused apple flavors and super-crisp acidity. Gains a lot in the glass. Better from 1994. (NR) (12/15/91) **90**

Riesling Spätlese Mosel-Saar-Ruwer Eitelsbacher Karthäuserhofberg 1988 ($NA) (9/30/89) **86**

Riesling Spätlese Mosel-Saar-Ruwer Eitelsbacher Karthäuserhofberg (AP8) 1988 ($NA) (9/30/89) **85**

Riesling Spätlese Mosel-Saar-Ruwer Eitelsbacher Karthäuserhofberg (AP10) 1988 ($NA) (9/30/89) **95**

VEREINIGTE HOSPITIEN

Riesling Auslese Mosel-Saar-Ruwer Piesporter Schubertslay 1988 ($NA) (9/30/89) **90**

Riesling Auslese Mosel-Saar-Ruwer Wehlener Sonnenuhr 1988 ($NA) (9/30/89) **90**

Riesling Kabinett Mosel-Saar-Ruwer Serriger Schloss Saarfelser Schlossberger 1988 ($NA) (9/30/89) **79**

Riesling Spätlese Mosel-Saar-Ruwer Wiltinger Hölle 1988 ($NA) (9/30/89) **83**

WEGELER-DEINHARD

Riesling Auslese Mosel-Saar-Ruwer Bernkasteler Graben 1989 $22 (12/15/90) **85**

Riesling Auslese Mosel-Saar-Ruwer Wehlener Sonnenuhr 1990: Very approachable and easy to drink. Medium-bodied and sweet, with almond and apricot aromas, blanched almond and peach flavors and a light finish. Better after 1994. $18 (12/15/91) **85**

Riesling Auslese Mosel-Saar-Ruwer Wehlener Sonnenuhr 1988 $17.50 (9/30/89) **85**

Riesling Kabinett Mosel-Saar-Ruwer 1990: A weighty wine with plenty of fruit. Lovely apple, pear and lemon aromas follow through to the palate. Medium-bodied, with good acidity and plenty of weight. Better after 1994. (NR) (12/15/91) **86**

Riesling Kabinett Mosel-Saar-Ruwer Bernkasteler Badstube 1989 $10.50 (12/15/90) **83**

Riesling Kabinett Mosel-Saar-Ruwer Bernkasteler Badstube 1988 $9 (9/30/89) **79**

Riesling Kabinett Mosel-Saar-Ruwer Wehlener Sonnenuhr 1989 $13.50 (12/15/90) **86**

Riesling Kabinett Mosel-Saar-Ruwer Wehlener Sonnenuhr 1985 $10 (10/15/87) **73**

Riesling Spätlese Mosel-Saar-Ruwer 1990: A lovely, delicate wine that should go well with food. Light-bodied and off-dry, with aromas of freshly cut melons and peaches, plenty of melon flavors and a fresh finish. Better after 1993. $16 (12/15/91) **85**

Riesling Spätlese Mosel-Saar-Ruwer Bernkasteler Doctor 1990: Refined, with subtle aromas of mineral and apple. Medium-bodied and lightly sweet, with anise and spice flavors and a medium finish. Better after 1993. $46 (12/15/91) **86**

Riesling Spätlese Mosel-Saar-Ruwer Bernkasteler Doctor 1986 ($NA) (4/15/89) **91**

Riesling Spätlese Mosel-Saar-Ruwer Bernkasteler Graben 1989 $17 (12/15/90) **81**

Riesling Spätlese Mosel-Saar-Ruwer Bernkasteler Graben 1988 $14.50 (9/30/89) **84**

Riesling Spätlese Mosel-Saar-Ruwer Graacher Himmelreich 1989 $17 (12/15/90) **83**

Riesling Spätlese Mosel-Saar-Ruwer Wehlener Sonnenuhr 1990: Fresh and exciting, offering delicate aromas of mineral, peach and apricot. Medium-bodied and lightly sweet, with lovely mineral and biscuit flavors and a clean finish. Quite a serious wine to drink now or hold. $18 (12/15/91) **87**

Riesling Spätlese Mosel-Saar-Ruwer Wehlener Sonnenuhr 1989 $17 (12/15/90) **87**

Riesling Spätlese Mosel-Saar-Ruwer Wehlener Sonnenuhr 1988 $15 (9/30/89) **88**

Riesling Spätlese Mosel-Saar-Ruwer Wehlener Sonnenuhr 1986 ($NA) (4/15/89) **88**

Riesling Spätlese Mosel-Saar-Ruwer Wehlener Sonnenuhr 1985 ($NA) (4/15/89) **84**

DR. WEINS-PRUM

Riesling Auslese Mosel-Saar-Ruwer Erdener Prälat 1988 ($NA) (9/30/89) **86**

Riesling Auslese Mosel-Saar-Ruwer Graacher Domprobst 1990: A punchy wine, with intense honey and apricot aromas and lovely apple and honey flavors. Medium-bodied and lightly sweet, with good acidity. Try from 1993. $22 (12/15/91) **90**

Riesling Auslese Mosel-Saar-Ruwer Urziger Würzgarten 1990: A fine style, with refined mineral, flint and fruit aromas. Medium-bodied and medium sweet, with honey, lime and spice flavors and steely acidity. Better from 1993 to '95. $22 (12/15/91) **88**

Riesling Auslese Mosel-Saar-Ruwer Wehlener Sonnenuhr Gold Cap 1990: Showy, with lots of fruit and character. Has vivid apple and other fruit aromas. Medium-bodied and sweet, with developed apple and peach flavors. Drinkable now, but better in a few years. $34 (12/15/91) **89**

Riesling Kabinett Mosel-Saar-Ruwer Bernkasteler Badstube 1990: A great value. This beautiful wine is bursting with ripe green apple aromas and flavors. Medium-bodied and off-dry, with lively acidity and a long, flavorful finish. Drink from 1993. $11 (12/15/91) **90**

Riesling Kabinett Mosel-Saar-Ruwer Wehlener Sonnenuhr 1988 ($NA) (9/30/89) **84**

Riesling Spätlese Mosel-Saar-Ruwer Urziger Würzgarten 1988 ($NA) (9/30/89) **82**

Riesling Spätlese Mosel-Saar-Ruwer Waldracher Sonnenberg 1990: Surprisingly delicious in spite of the high acidity. Has light apple, lemon and anise aromas. Medium-bodied and lightly sweet, with anise and apple flavors and a good finish. Tasted twice. Drink now. $15 (12/15/91) **86**

Riesling Spätlese Mosel-Saar-Ruwer Wehlener Sonnenuhr 1990: Starts off strong, but slows just slightly on the finish. Medium-bodied and medium sweet, with opulent peach, guava and honey aromas, honey and lemon flavors and a light finish. Better from 1993 to '95. $16 (12/15/91) **89**

Riesling Spätlese Mosel-Saar-Ruwer Wehlener Sonnenuhr 1988 ($NA) (9/30/89) **84**

WELLER-LEHNERT

Riesling Auslese Mosel-Saar-Ruwer Piesporter Goldtröpfchen 1988 ($NA) (9/30/89) **86**

WINZERGENOSSENSCHAFT

Riesling Auslese Mosel-Saar-Ruwer Piesporter Goldtröpfchen 1990: Tart, taut and lemony, an austere wine that goes for structure rather than charm. Drinkable, but should be better in 1993 or '94. $14.50 (1/31/92) **80**

Riesling Auslese Mosel-Saar-Ruwer Piesporter Michelsberg 1990: Aromatic, crisp, flavorful and delicately sweet, but balanced with lively acidity and plenty of peach, pine and apple aromas and flavors. Has enough balance to drink before or during a meal. $11 (1/31/92) **87**

Riesling Spätlese Mosel-Saar-Ruwer Graacher Himmelreich 1990: Overtly earthy flavors override the basic peach and apricot component. Simple but good. $9 (12/15/91) **80**

Riesling Spätlese Mosel-Saar-Ruwer Piesporter Goldtröpfchen 1990: Delicate but rich in flavor, developing complexity as you sip it. Blends peach, floral and melon flavors in a sweet but well-balanced package. Has charming flavors and a steely backbone. $11.50 (1/31/92) **88**

Riesling Spätlese Mosel-Saar-Ruwer Piesporter Michelsberg 1990: Peachy, grapey and sweet, with a soft texture and a light body. Simple and pleasant. $9.50 (12/15/91) **80**

Riesling Spätlese Mosel-Saar-Ruwer Zeltinger Himmelreich 1990: Blends the classic Riesling flavors of peach, pine and mineral together in a crisp, straightforward, off-dry package. Charming and true to type. $9 (12/15/91) **85**

WOLFGANG ZAHN

Riesling Spätlese Mosel-Saar-Ruwer Piesporter Goldtröpfchen 1983 $10 (5/16/85) **86**

DR. ZENZEN

Riesling Beerenauslese Mosel-Saar-Ruwer Erdener Treppchen 1976 $90 (2/01/86) **90**

Riesling Kabinett Mosel-Saar-Ruwer Erdener Treppchen 1981 $8 (4/01/86) **70**

Riesling Spätlese Mosel-Saar-Ruwer Valwiger Herrenberg 1982 $12 (2/01/86) **74**

ZILLIKEN

Riesling Auslese Mosel-Saar-Ruwer Ockfener Bockstein 1990: Lively and racy, with concentrated, pure honey and melon aromas and flavors. Full-bodied and sweet, with very high acidity and a very long finish. Try from 1995. $25 (12/15/91) **89**

Riesling Auslese Mosel-Saar-Ruwer Saarburger Rausch 1990: A little dumb still, it needs more time in the bottle but should age well. Shows creamy honey and apple aromas, anise, honey and flint flavors and excellent acidity, although it's a little short on the finish. Full-bodied and sweet. Better from 1994. $31 (12/15/91) **89**

Riesling Auslese Mosel-Saar-Ruwer Saarburger Rausch 1989 $35 (12/15/90) **88**

Riesling Auslese Mosel-Saar-Ruwer Saarburger Rausch Gold Cap 1990: A hidden monster. Compact and thick, with loads of fruit, but closed in. Needs time to develop in the glass. Full-bodied and sweet, with subdued mineral, lime and lemon aromas and flavors, extremely steely acidity and a compact fruit structure. A wine for the cellar. Try from 1995. $110 (12/15/91) **93**

Riesling Auslese Mosel-Saar-Ruwer Saarburger Rausch Long Gold Cap 1989 $64 (12/15/90) **95**

Riesling Eiswein Mosel-Saar-Ruwer Saarburger Rausch 1990: Has electrifying acidity. Medium-bodied and very sweet, with powerful honey, passion fruit and lemon rind aromas, very high acidity and a sweet-and-sour finish. Better from 1994 to '96. (NR) (12/15/91) **91**

Riesling Eiswein Mosel-Saar-Ruwer Saarburger Rausch 1989 ($NA) (12/15/90) **96**

Riesling Eiswein Mosel-Saar-Ruwer Saarburger Rausch 1988 ($NA) (9/30/89) **97**

Riesling Kabinett Mosel-Saar-Ruwer Ockfener Bockstein 1990: This very attractive, drink-now wine has honey, apple and wet earth aromas and juicy fruit flavors. Medium-bodied and off-dry, with a round texture and racy acidity. Should improve with age. $12 (12/15/91) **86**

Riesling Kabinett Mosel-Saar-Ruwer Ockfener Bockstein 1989 $14 (12/15/90) **81**

Riesling Kabinett Mosel-Saar-Ruwer Saarburger Rausch 1990: Very tightly structured, but has very good concentration of attractive fruit. Medium-bodied and off-dry, with creamy vanilla, pineapple and peach aromas, mature flavors, medium acidity and a long finish. Better from 1994. $13 (12/15/91) **86**

Riesling Kabinett Mosel-Saar-Ruwer Saarburger Rausch (AP5) 1989 $14 (12/15/90) **77**

Riesling Kabinett Mosel-Saar-Ruwer Saarburger Rausch (AP12) 1989 $14 (12/15/90) **85**

Riesling Kabinett Mosel-Saar-Ruwer Saarburger Rausch (AP5) 1988 $9 (9/30/89) **78**

Riesling Kabinett Mosel-Saar-Ruwer Saarburger Rausch (AP7) 1988 $9 (9/30/89) **79**

Riesling Qualitätswein Mosel-Saar-Ruwer Zilliken 1990: Refined, with subtle apple, lemon and melon aromas that open to an off-dry palate full of apple skin and grape flavors. Has very high acidity and a crisp finish. Better from 1993. $9.25 (12/15/91) **84**

Riesling Spätlese Mosel-Saar-Ruwer Ockfener Bockstein 1989 $18 (12/15/90) **79**

Riesling Spätlese Mosel-Saar-Ruwer Saarburger Rausch 1990: Surprisingly mature for a young wine, but delicious all the same. Has oily, very ripe fruit and mineral aromas that follow through on the palate, medium-firm acidity and a spicy finish. Drink now. $17 (12/15/91) **85**

Riesling Spätlese Mosel-Saar-Ruwer Saarburger Rausch 1989 $19 (12/15/90) **85**

Riesling Spätlese Mosel-Saar-Ruwer Saarburger Rausch 1988 $17 (9/30/89) **95**

Riesling Spätlese Mosel-Saar-Ruwer Saarburger Rausch 1985 $9.25 (5/15/87) **78**

Riesling Spätlese Mosel-Saar-Ruwer Saarburger Rausch (AP6) 1989 $19 (12/15/90) **84**

NAHE

HANS CRUSIUS & SOHN

Riesling Auslese Nahe Niederhäusener Felsensteyer 1990 ($26/500ml) (12/15/91) **87**

Riesling Auslese Halbtrocken Nahe Schlossböckelheimer Felsenberg 1990 $25 (12/15/91) **89**

Riesling Auslese Nahe Schlossböckelheimer Felsenberg Gold Cap 1989 $35 (12/15/90) **91**

Riesling Auslese Nahe Traisener Rotenfels 1989 $24 (12/15/90) **88**

Riesling Kabinett Nahe Traisener Rotenfels 1990 $15 (12/15/91) **86**

Riesling Kabinett Nahe Traisener Rotenfels 1989 $14 (12/15/90) **85**

Riesling Qualitätswein Halbtrocken Nahe 1989 $11 (12/15/90) **82**

Riesling Qualitätswein Halbtrocken Nahe Crusius Riesling 1990 $12 (12/15/91) **80**

Riesling Spätlese Halbtrocken Nahe Schlossböckelheimer Felsenberg 1990 (NR) (12/15/91) **88**

Riesling Spätlese Nahe Traisener Rotenfels 1990 $18 (12/15/91) **84**

Riesling Spätlese Nahe Traisener Rotenfels 1989 $17 (12/15/90) **78**

SCHLOSSGUT DIEL

Riesling Auslese Nahe Dorsheimer Goldloch 1990: Unconventional, almost dry, but keeps you coming back for more. Full-bodied, with pie crust, peach and cream aromas, peach, citrus and spice flavors and high acidity, but it has a lovely, balanced finish. Drink now to 1994. $33 (12/15/91) **88**

Riesling Auslese Nahe Gold Cap 1990: A lovely, aromatic wine, with an elegant structure. Has an undeveloped botrytis character, with honeysuckle, beeswax and melon aromas. Full-bodied and sweet, with intense honey flavors and high acidity on the finish. Better in 1993. $52 (12/15/91) **91**

Riesling Eiswein Nahe 1990: Great class and excitement in a glass. Full-bodied, with wonderful acidity and balance. Super-sweet, but not cloying, with focused sweet-and-sour spice and botrytis aromas and rich, wonderful melon and honey flavors. Perfect to drink now, but it will age very well through 1994. (NR) (12/15/91) **94**

Riesling Kabinett Nahe 1990: Slightly developed and round, with good fruit. Medium-bodied and medium sweet, with ripe apple and cookie aromas, spicy melon flavors, fresh acidity and a crisp finish. Drink now or in 1993. $17 (12/15/91) **85**

Riesling Spätlese Nahe 1990: Takes a few minutes to develop in the glass. The ripe apricot aromas have hints of earth. Medium-bodied and medium sweet, with plenty of apricot flavors, medium acidity and a mineral finish. Drink now or hold. Tasted twice. $18 (12/15/91) **86**

Riesling Spätlese Nahe Dorsheimer Pittermännchen 1990: Unique character in this wine; try with white meat. Full-bodied, with baked apple and spice aromas, spicy, peppery, fruity flavors, good acidity and a long finish. Try now through 1994. $24 (12/15/91) **89**

STAATLICHEN WEINBAUDOMANEN

Riesling Auslese Nahe Münsterer Dautenpflänzer 1989 $14 (12/15/90) **86**

Riesling Auslese Nahe Niederhäusener Hermannshöhle 1989 $25 (12/15/90) **86**

Riesling Beerenauslese Nahe Münsterer Pittersberg 1989 $41 (12/15/90) **91**

Riesling Beerenauslese Nahe Niederhäusener Hermannsberg 1989 $65 (12/15/90) **87**

Riesling Kabinett Nahe Altenbamberger Rothenberg 1989 $10 (12/15/90) **78**

Riesling Kabinett Nahe Niederhäusener Steinberg 1989 $9 (12/15/90) **80**

Riesling Kabinett Nahe Schlossböckelheimer Kupfergrube 1990: Like freshly crushed grapes. A rich wine, offering lemon curd and tropical fruit aromas, medium-bodied, fresh apple, honeysuckle and melon flavors, fresh acidity and a clean finish. Better in 1993. $10 (12/15/91) **87**

Riesling Auslese Nahe Schlossböckelheimer Kupfergrube 1989 $19 (12/15/90) **90**

Riesling Qualitätswein Nahe Münsterer Pittersberg 1990: Rather exotic and exciting to taste. Has apricot, mineral and melon aromas, ripe apricot and orange flavors and firm acidity. Full-bodied, but a little short on the finish. Better in 1993 or '94. $7 (12/15/91) **84**

Riesling Qualitätswein Nahe Niederhäusener Steinberg 1990: A light, easy-drinking wine; quite developed. Has melon and biscuit aromas, medium-bodied, lightly sweet melon flavors, light acidity and a tart finish. Drink now. $8 (12/15/91) **79**

Riesling Qualitätswein Nahe Schlossböckelheimer Kupfergrube 1990: Young and wild; still tastes like a barrel sample. Has aromas of freshly sliced peaches and melons. Full-bodied, with lots of substance, very rich, ripe fruit and a super-firm backbone of acidity. Try from 1993 to '96. $8 (12/15/91) **87**

Riesling Qualitätswein Nahe Schlossböckelheimer Kupfergrube 1989 $9 (12/15/90) **85**

Riesling Spätlese Halbtrocken Nahe Niederhäusener Hermannshöhle 1990: A little dull, but it has decent fruit. Full-bodied, with honeycomb and earth aromas and honey, mineral and spice flavors, but it's slightly diluted on the finish. Drink now. $14 (12/15/91) **79**

Riesling Spätlese Nahe Niederhäusener Hermannsberg 1990: Vivid and elegant, almost top class. Full-bodied, with concentrated peach, wet earth and fruit aromas, intense spice and peach flavors, lively acidity and a refreshing finish. Better from now to '94. $14 (12/15/91) **89**

Riesling Spätlese Nahe Niederhäusener Kertz 1989 $14 (12/15/90) **86**

Riesling Spätlese Nahe Schlossböckelheimer Kupfergrube 1989 ($NA) (12/15/90) **90**

Riesling Spätlese Nahe Serriger Vogelsang 1983 $7 (11/01/84) **80**

Riesling Trockenbeerenauslese Nahe Schlossböckelheimer Kupfergrub 1989 $150 (12/15/90) **88**

Riesling Trockenbeerenauslese Nahe Schlossböckelheimer Kupfergrube 1990: Refined and elegant, showing great class and restraint. Gorgeous perfumed lemon and cream aromas lead to plenty of spice, lemon and honey flavors. Full-bodied and severely sweet, with a super amount of acidity. Better from 1995 to '98. $250 (12/15/91) **92**

RHEINGAU

GEHEIMRAT ASCHROTT

Riesling Kabinett Rheingau Hochheimer Kirchenstüch 1988 ($NA) (9/30/89) **79**

Riesling Kabinett Rheingau Hochheimer Stielweg 1988 ($NA) (9/30/89) **87**

Riesling Spätlese Halbtrocken Rheingau Hochheimer Hölle 1988 ($NA) (9/30/89) **92**

Riesling Spätlese Rheingau Hochheimer Hölle 1988 ($NA) (9/30/89) **85**

GEORG BREUER

Riesling Auslese Rheingau Charta 1990: A dry style with good fruit. Needs food. Medium-bodied and dry, with perfumed lemon and spice aromas, spice flavors and very tart acidity on the finish. Better from 1993. $10 (12/15/91) **83**

Riesling Auslese Rheingau Rüdesheimer Bischofsberg 1990: Elegant and nicely balanced but rather simple. Has honey and freshly crushed grape aromas, medium-bodied, medium sweet, lovely lemon and apple flavors and fresh acidity on the finish. Drink now. $25 (12/15/91) **86**

Riesling Beerenauslese Rheingau Rüdesheimer Bischofsberg 1990: A monster with a huge concentration of fruit. Deep gold in color, with amazingly rich aromas of roasted almonds, honey, apricots and fruit. Full-bodied and super-sweet, this is as thick as molasses and even sweeter. Can age as long as you like. $100 (12/15/91) **97**

Riesling Kabinett Halbtrocken Rheingau Rüdesheimer Berg Schlossberg Charta 1988 $22 (9/30/89) **83**

Riesling Kabinett Halbtrocken Rheingau Rüdesheimer Bischofsberg Charta 1988 $16 (9/30/89) **82**

Riesling Kabinett Rheingau Rüdesheimer Berg Schlossberg Charta 1990: Impressive on the nose, but a little undeveloped and rough on the palate. Needs pairing with food for drinking now. Shows beautiful cream, coconut and peach aromas. Medium-bodied and off-dry, with spicy lemon flavors and a very tart finish. Better from 1994. $12 (12/15/91) **82**

Riesling Qualitätswein Rheingau Charta 1988 $14 (9/30/89) **81**

Riesling Qualitätswein Rheingau Rüdesheimer Berg Roseneck Charta 1988 $14 (9/30/89) **85**

Riesling Qualitätswein Rheingau Rüdesheimer Berg Rottland Charta 1988 $14 (9/30/89) **85**

Riesling Spätlese Rheingau Rauenthaler Nonnenberg Charta 1990: Balanced and classy, with very focused fruit flavors. A lively, fresh wine, with almond, lemon and orange peel aromas and powerful spice, lemon and almond flavors. Medium-bodied. Drink in 1993 to '94. $15 (12/15/91) **88**

FREIHERR ZU KNYPHAUSEN

Riesling Kabinett Halbtrocken Rheingau Erbacher Marcobrunn Charta 1988 ($NA) (9/30/89) **82**

Riesling Kabinett Halbtrocken Rheingau Erbacher Steinmorgen 1988 ($NA) (9/30/89) **86**

Riesling Kabinett Rheingau Erbacher Steinmorgen 1988 ($NA) (9/30/89) **87**

Riesling Kabinett Rheingau Kiedricher Sandgrub 1988 ($NA) (9/30/89) **84**

FURST LOWENSTEIN

Riesling Kabinett Halbtrocken Rheingau Blausilber 1990: Not for everyone. Lacks elegance and grace. Almost like cooked fruit. Medium-bodied, off-dry and quite fat, with spicy canned fruit aromas and an unusual canned orange flavor. Medium in acidity and on the finish. Better from 1993? (NR) (12/15/91) **81**

Riesling Kabinett Rheingau Charta 1990: Very disjointed, needs time. Medium-bodied and off-dry, with smoky almond and fruit aromas, intense mandarin orange flavors and firm acidity. Try again after 1994. (NR) (12/15/91) **82**

Riesling Spätlese Halbtrocken Rheingau Rosasilber 1990: A middle-of-the-road, good-quality Rheingau, with almond, honey and orange peel aromas, medium-bodied spice, almond and orange peel flavors and a simple finish. Juicy and appealing. Drink now. (NR) (12/15/91) **85**

Riesling Spätlese Rheingau Charta 1990: Like freshly cut grapefruit, tart and a little raw. Somewhat one-dimensional and rather boring. Has grapefruit and spice aromas, tart orange peel and grapefruit flavors and a fresh finish. Medium-bodied and off-dry. Try from 1993. (NR) (12/15/91) **83**

FURST VON METTERNICH

Riesling Kabinett Halbtrocken Rheingau Schloss Johannisberg 1988 $15 (9/30/89) **85**

Riesling Qualitätswein Rheingau Schloss Johannisberg 1988 $15 (9/30/89) **75**

SCHLOSS GROENESTEYN

Riesling Auslese Rheingau Rüdesheimer Berg Rottland 1989 $40 (12/15/90) **85**

Riesling Kabinett Halbtrocken Rheingau Kiedricher Wasseros 1990: A little rough on the palate, but it shows excellent fruit concentration. Needs time. Medium-bodied and off-dry, with ripe fruit and lemon aromas and lemon and spice flavors. Very high in acidity but balanced. Has a fresh finish. Better from 1993. $12 (12/15/91) **85**

Riesling Kabinett Rheingau Kiedricher Gräfenberg 1989 $12 (12/15/90) **83**

Riesling Kabinett Rheingau Kiedricher Gräfenberg 1988 ($NA) (9/30/89) **91**

Riesling Kabinett Rheingau Kiedricher Sandgrub 1990: Has decent fruit, but it's a little simple, with lemon, earth and slightly candied aromas and earthy lemon flavors. Medium-bodied and lightly sweet, with a light finish. Drink now. $12 (12/15/91) **80**

Riesling Kabinett Rheingau Kiedricher Sandgrub 1989 $12 (12/15/90) **81**

Riesling Kabinett Rheingau Kiedricher Sandgrub 1988 ($NA) (9/30/89) **89**

Key to Symbols

The scores reported here are the results of blind tastings conducted by our panel of senior editors. Wines that carry the initials below are results of individual tastings.

THE WINE SPECTATOR 100-POINT SCALE 95-100— Classic, a great wine; ***90-94***— Outstanding, superior character and style; ***80-89***—Good to very good, a wine with special qualities; ***70-79***—Average, drinkable wine that may have minor flaws; ***60-69***—Below average, drinkable but not recommended; ***50-59***—Poor, undrinkable, not recommended. "+"—With a score indicates a range; used primarily with barrel tastings to indicate a preliminary score.

SPECIAL DESIGNATIONS SS—Spectator Selection, CS—Cellar Selection, BB—Best Buy, ($NA)—Price not available, (NR)—Not released, ***/**/*—Designations used by German producers to indicate successively higher-quality auslese wines, separating them from the estates's regular lots of auslese. Three stars is the highest rating.

TASTER'S INITIALS (JG)—Jim Gordon, (HS)—Harvey Steiman, (JL)—James Laube, (JS)—James Suckling, (TM)—Thomas Matthews, (TR)—Terry Robards, (PM)—Per-Henrik Mansson, (BT)—Barrel Tasting (these wines were tasted blind from barrel samples), (CA-date)—*California's Great Cabernets* by James Laube, (CH-date)—*California's Great Chardonnays* by James Laube, (VP-date)—*Vintage Port* by James Suckling.

DATE TASTED Dates in parentheses represent the issue in which the rating was published.

Riesling Kabinett Rheingau Rüdesheimer Berg Rottland 1990: Quite developed for a '90. Lacks a bit of freshness. Medium-bodied and medium sweet, with muted aromas of lemon drops and cream, slightly candied anise flavors and a lemony finish. Drink now. $12 (12/15/91) **79**

Riesling Kabinett Rheingau Rüdesheimer Berg Rottland 1988 ($NA) (9/30/89) **74**

Riesling Kabinett Rheingau Rüdesheimer Berg Rottland 1985 $9 (10/15/87) **78**

Riesling Kabinett Rheingau Rüdesheimer Berg Rottland 1983 $5.75 (1/01/85) BB **86**

Riesling Kabinett Rheingau Rüdesheimer Klosterlay 1988 ($NA) (9/30/89) **82**

Riesling Spätlese Rheingau Kiedricher Gräfenberg 1989 $16 (12/15/90) **78**

Riesling Spätlese Rheingau Kiedricher Sandgrub 1989 $16 (12/15/90) **83**

Riesling Spätlese Rheingau Rüdesheimer Berg Rottland 1990: A rather lean wine, with an unripe fruit character. A pitiful showing for this estate. Slightly confected, with overwhelming green apple aromas. Medium-bodied and quite dry, the result of the scorchingly high acidity. Does have modest cream and lime flavors, but it's rather short on the finish. Drink on release. $18 (12/15/91) **75**

Riesling Spätlese Rheingau Rüdesheimer Berg Rottland 1989 $15 (12/15/90) **80**

Riesling Spätlese Rheingau Rüdesheimer Berg Schlossberg 1990: A silky sweet wine, but a little dull on the finish. Shows very fresh lemon, tropical fruit and floral aromas. Medium-bodied and medium sweet, with straightforward lemon and floral flavors and a slightly metallic finish. Drink now. $18 (12/15/91) **82**

WEINGUT HUPFELD

Riesling Kabinett Rheingau Hochheimer Königin Victoria Berg 1990: A little hard and closed now, but it shows promise, with refined peach and clove honey aromas. Medium-bodied and lightly sweet, almost dry, with full acidity and a spicy finish. Better after 1993. $13 (12/15/91) **84**

Riesling Spätlese Rheingau Hochheimer Königin Victoria Berg 1990: Has pretty flavors, medium-bodied and lightly sweet, with lemon and cream aromas, delicate almond and spice flavors and lightly crisp acidity. Drink now. $17 (12/15/91) **85**

SCHLOSS JOHANNISBERG

Riesling Auslese Rheingau 1990: Shows excellent botrytis influence, a seductive wine. Medium-bodied and sweet, with subtle honey and tropical fruit aromas, reserved lemon and honey flavors and a super level of acidity. Extremely lively on the finish. Better from 1994. $40 (12/15/91) **90**

Riesling Kabinett Rheingau 1990: Lively and fresh, with plenty of clean fruit. Could move up a few points. Has a lovely, creamy, fruity nose. Medium-bodied and off-dry, with lemon meringue and spice flavors and firm acidity, but finishes a little short. Better from 1994. $18 (12/15/91) **83**

Riesling Kabinett Rheingau 1989 ($NA) (12/15/90) **86**

Riesling Kabinett Rheingau Rotlack 1983 $12 (8/01/85) **88**

Riesling Qualitätswein Rheingau 1990: Deliciously elegant, with plenty of character; a classic. Light-bodied and off-dry, with intense peach and cream aromas, a silky mouth-feel and plenty of lemon and cream flavors. Drink now. $12 (12/15/91) **86**

Riesling Qualitätswein Rheingau 1989 ($NA) (12/15/90) **84**

Riesling Spätlese Rheingau 1990: A deceptive wine that starts out meekly, but finishes with a bang. Shows more and more character all the time. Has powerful lemon, lime and floral aromas, lemon, spice and licorice flavors, firm acidity and a zingy finish. Full-bodied and sweet. Better from 1993. $25 (12/15/91) **88**

Riesling Spätlese Rheingau Grünlack 1983 $20 (8/01/85) **90**

Riesling Spätlese Trocken Rheingau 1990: A little lean and mean, but should improve with age. Medium-bodied and very dry, with lemon and spice aromas and flavors, a lean fruit structure and slightly astringent acidity. Needs time to mellow. Try from 1995. $25 (12/15/91) **83**

FRANZ KUNSTLER

Riesling Auslese Rheingau Hochheimer Herrenberg 1990: Oozing with honey, with an explosive mouthful of dried exotic fruit flavors, great concentration and firm acidity. Try after 1994. $25 (12/15/91) **94**

Riesling Auslese Rheingau Hochheimer Hölle 1990: A bombshell, packed to the casing with fruit. Has lovely honey and earth aromas and flavors in a medium-sweet package and a super-long finish. Better in 1994. $30 (12/15/91) **92**

Riesling Kabinett Rheingau Hochheimer Kirchenstück Charta 1990: A deceptive wine. Seems delicate at first, but reveals more depth and power each time you go back to it. Offers impressive peach and floral aromas and flavors and a lovely balance of fresh acidity. Better in 1993. $14 (12/15/91) **89**

Riesling Spätlese Rheingau Hochheimer Herrenberg 1990: Delicate and refined, yet vividly fruity. A real beauty, offering honey and rose petal aromas and beautiful melon and strawberry flavors. Medium-bodied and sweet, with a fresh finish. Better from 1993. $15 (12/15/91) **92**

Riesling Spätlese Rheingau Hochheimer Hölle Charta 1990: A concentrated, rich wine for the dinner table. Hangs on for a long time. Full-bodied and off-dry, with intense honey, almond and peach aromas, loads of spicy peach flavors and a long, rich, almond-flavored finish. Drink now to 1994. $20 (12/15/91) **91**

LANDGRAF VON HESSEN

Riesling Kabinett Halbtrocken Rheingau Winkeler Jesuitengarten 1988 ($NA) (9/30/89) **80**

Riesling Kabinett Rheingau Johannisberger Klaus 1988 ($NA) (9/30/89) **81**

Riesling Kabinett Rheingau Prinz von Hessen 1988 ($NA) (9/30/89) **80**

Riesling Spätlese Rheingau Eltville Sonnenberg 1988 ($NA) (9/30/89) **89**

LANGWERTH VON SIMMERN

Riesling Auslese Rheingau Hattenheimer Mannberg 1989 $50 (12/15/90) **94**

Riesling Auslese Rheingau Hattenheimer Nussbrunnen 1990: Has good botrytis character, but it needs time to develop in the bottle. Medium-bodied, with burnt toast, almond and spice aromas, sweet, slightly burnt toast, botrytis and honey flavors and a medium finish. Better from 1993. $30 (12/15/91) **87**

Riesling Auslese Rheingau Hattenheimer Nussbrunnen 1989 $57 (12/15/90) **91**

Riesling Beerenauslese Rheingau Erbacher Marcobrunn 1990: Delicate, with refined cream and lemon aromas. Medium-bodied and very sweet, with a lovely, creamy caramel finish. Good acidity. Drinkable now, but better from 1994. $300 (12/15/91) **91**

Riesling Beerenauslese Rheingau Hattenheimer Nussbrunnen 1990: Wonderfully elegant, overflowing with sweet, rich fruit. Shows subtle aromas of ripe pears and cream. Full-bodied and super-sweet, with honey and tropical fruit flavors and a lovely, creamy, honeyed finish. The richness grows in the glass. Drinkable now, but better from 1994 to '96. $300 (12/15/91) **90**

Riesling Kabinett Rheingau Eltviller Sonnenberg 1990: A well-made, standard spätlese in a good vintage, but too tart and simple to be top class. Has delicate lemon and floral aromas, good concentration of fruit and a lightly spicy finish. Medium sweet. Drink now. $10 (12/15/91) **84**

Riesling Kabinett Rheingau Eltviller Sonnenberg 1989 $11 (12/15/90) **80**

Riesling Kabinett Rheingau Erbacher Marcobrunn 1989 $16 (12/15/90) **83**

Riesling Kabinett Rheingau Hattenheimer Mannberg 1989 $25 (12/15/90) **84**

Riesling Kabinett Rheingau Hattenheimer Mannberg 1985 $8.50 (1/31/87) **83**

Riesling Kabinett Rheingau Hattenheimer Nussbrunnen 1990: Very good, offering attractive almond, lemon and cream aromas. Medium-bodied and off-dry, with almond and lemon flavors and a light finish. Drink now. $10 (12/15/91) **86**

Riesling Kabinett Rheingau Hattenheimer Nussbrunnen 1989 $13.50 (12/15/90) **88**

Riesling Kabinett Rheingau Kiedricher Sandgrub 1990: Tasty, with a good amount of fruit and character. Quite developed, offering egg yolk, cream and apple aromas, lemon, pie crust and almond flavors and a long finish. Medium-bodied and lightly sweet. Drink now. $13 (12/15/91) **86**

Riesling Kabinett Rheingau Kiedricher Sandgrub 1988 ($NA) (9/30/89) **80**

Riesling Spätlese Rheingau Erbacher Marcobrunn 1989 $25 (12/15/90) **87**

Riesling Spätlese Rheingau Hattenheimer Nussbrunnen 1990: Classy and focused with excellent fruit. One of the better spätleses from the region. Full-bodied and medium sweet, with powerful spice, mineral and almond aromas, spicy mineral flavors and a long, racy finish. Drinkable, but better in 1993. $22 (12/15/91) **89**

Riesling Spätlese Rheingau Hattenheimer Nussbrunnen 1989 $25 (12/15/90) **84**
Riesling Spätlese Rheingau Hattenheimer Nussbrunnen 1988 ($NA) (9/30/89) **84**
Riesling Spätlese Rheingau Hattenheimer Nussbrunnen 1983 $12 (4/01/85) **76**
Riesling Spätlese Rheingau Rauenthaler Baiken 1989 $25 (12/15/90) **87**
Riesling Spätlese Rheingau Rauenthaler Baiken 1988 ($NA) (9/30/89) **90**
Riesling Trockenbeerenauslese Rheingau Erbacher Marcobrunn 1989 ($NA) (12/15/90) **99**
Riesling Trockenbeerenauslese Rheingau Hattenheimer Nussbrunnen 1990: A blockbuster of a wine that blasts your palate with sweetness. Seems more like a big beerenauslese than a trockenbeerenauslese. Full-bodied and very, very sweet. Has tons of lime, peach and honey aromas, intense, smoky burnt almond and honey flavors and extremely high acidity. Better from 1996. $500 (12/15/91) **94**

SCHLOSS REINHARTSHAUSEN
Riesling Auslese Rheingau Erbacher Schlossberg 1990: An elegant style that gets better and better in the glass. Has an aromatic nose of lemons and apples. Medium-bodied and sweet, with a creamy texture, lemon and tropical fruit flavors and a long finish. Better after 1993. $25 (12/15/91) **90**
Riesling Auslese Rheingau Erbacher Siegelsberg 1989 ($NA) (12/15/90) **92**
Riesling Beerenauslese Rheingau Hattenheimer Wisselbrunnen 1990: A strange wine that's thick like a dessert wine, but on the dry side. Lacks a bit of finesse. Has spicy, earthy aromas and flavors and is thick and syrupy, with medium-sweet, spicy flavors. Drink now or hold. $100 (12/15/91) **87**
Riesling Kabinett Halbtrocken Rheingau Rüdesheimer Bischofsberg 1990: Very young, but with very good richness. Quite developed, but still awkward. Has petrol, almond and grapefruit aromas and medium-bodied, off-dry, rather oily fruit flavors. Rich and flavorful, with a long finish. Better from 1993. $18 (12/15/91) **85**
Riesling Qualitätswein Rheingau Erbacher Schlossberg 1989 ($NA) (12/15/90) **86**
Riesling Spätlese Rheingau Erbacher Marcobrunn 1990: Explodes with fruit in your mouth, but needs time to show its best. Has potent aromas of peaches and almonds. Medium-bodied and very sweet, with supercharged acidity bringing to life peach, cream and almond flavors. A delicious wine; start drinking in 1994. $25 (12/15/91) **91**
Riesling Spätlese Rheingau Erbacher Siegelsberg 1989 ($NA) (12/15/90) **89**
Riesling Spätlese Rheingau Hattenheimer Nussbrunnen 1990: A lively wine, with eye-opening fruit. A little more power at the finish would make it truly outstanding. Has focused honey and peach aromas with a hint of botrytis. Medium-bodied and medium sweet, with intense honey, coconut and peach flavors, lively acidity and a crisp finish. Drink now or hold. $25 (12/15/91) **89**
Riesling Trockenbeerenauslese Rheingau Erbacher Marcobrunn 1937 ($NA) (12/15/88) **95**

BALTHASAR RESS
Riesling Auslese Rheingau Rüdesheimer Berg Rottland 1990: Extremely well-balanced, with refined, understated power. Has dried peach aromas and honey, almond and peach flavors. Full-bodied and sweet, with a lively finish. Better from 1993. $33 (12/15/91) **90**
Riesling Kabinett Halbtrocken Rheingau Geisenheimer Kläuserweg Charta 1988 $9.50 (9/30/89) **89**
Riesling Kabinett Halbtrocken Rheingau Hattenheimer Nussbrunnen Charta 1988 $9.50 (9/30/89) **78**
Riesling Kabinett Rheingau Hattenheimer Charta 1990: Extremely well balanced, with delicious fruit. Perfect for serving with fish. Complex aromas of lemon, spice and anise lead succulent fruit flavors. Medium-bodied and off-dry, with balanced, racy acidity. A juicy wine to drink now or hold. $14 (12/15/91) **86**
Riesling Kabinett Rheingau Johannisberger Erntebringer 1990: Could use a little more freshness on the nose and palate, but it's decent for a regional wine. Medium-bodied and lightly sweet, offering slightly candied peach and cream aromas, peach, cream and almond flavors and a light finish. Drink now. $12 (12/15/91) **84**
Riesling Spätlese Halbtrocken Rheingau Rüdesheimer Berg Rottland 1988 $14 (9/30/89) **89**
Riesling Spätlese Rheingau Charta Hochheimer 1990: Somewhat one-dimensional, but has very good fruit flavors. Has attractive lemon, almond and peach aromas and spicy fruit flavors. Medium-bodied and off-dry, with firm acidity. A little short on the finish. Drink now. $19 (12/15/91) **85**
Riesling Spätlese Rheingau Rüdesheimer Berg Schlossberg 1990: Very light and short for a spätlese. Medium-bodied and lightly sweet, with gardenia and melon aromas and pleasant melon flavors, but fades quickly on the finish. Drink now. $20 (12/15/91) **80**
Riesling Spätlese Rheingau Rüdesheimer Berg Schlossberg 1988 $13.50 (9/30/89) **84**
Riesling Spätlese Rheingau Rüdesheimer Klosterlay 1990: Simple, more like a kabinett in style. Has refined mineral and grapefruit aromas and fresh flavors. Medium-bodied and lightly sweet, with a light finish. Drink now. $19 (12/15/91) **81**
Riesling Spätlese Rheingau Schloss Reichartshausen 1990: Round and easy going, a no-nonsense wine. Offers lemon, banana, almond and apple aromas and tropical fruit flavors. Medium-bodied, medium sweet and medium in acidity. Drink now. $18 (12/15/91) **84**

SCHLOSS SCHONBORN
Riesling Auslese Rheingau 1990: Exquisitely crafted, with superb finesse and great elegance. The aromas are reminiscent of walking through a field of flowers. Medium-bodied and medium sweet, with a smooth, refined fruit structure, intense lemon and spice flavors and lively acidity on the finish. Better from 1993 to '96. (NR) (12/15/91) **91**
Riesling Auslese Rheingau Hattenheimer Nussbrunnen 1989 ($NA) (12/15/90) **87**
Riesling Auslese Rheingau Rüdeshemier Berg Schlossberg 1989 ($NA) (12/15/90) **90**
Riesling Kabinett Halbtrocken Rheingau Geisenheimer Schlossberg 1988 ($NA) (9/30/89) **81**
Riesling Kabinett Rheingau Bereich Johannisberg 1985 $10.50 (1/31/88) **81**
Riesling Kabinett Rheingau Johannisberger Klaus 1989 $10 (12/15/90) **83**
Riesling Kabinett Rheingau Winkeler Gutenberg 1989 ($NA) (12/15/90) **92**
Riesling Spätlese Halbtrocken Rheingau Hochheimer Hölle 1988 ($NA) (9/30/89) **89**
Riesling Spätlese Halbtrocken Rheingau Hochheimer Kirchenstück 1989 ($NA) (12/15/90) **87**
Riesling Spätlese Halbtrocken Rheingau Johannisberger Klaus 1990: Rich and powerful, with great character. Great to serve with white meat or pork. Medium-bodied and off-dry, with strong almond and currant aromas, rich strawberry and fresh fruit flavors and firm acidity. Better from 1993. (NR) (12/15/91) **90**
Riesling Spätlese Halbtrocken Rheingau Rüdesheimer Bischofsberg 1988 ($NA) (9/30/89) **88**
Riesling Spätlese Rheingau 1989 ($NA) (12/15/90) **86**
Riesling Spätlese Rheingau Erbacher Marcobrunn 1990: Elegant and understated, with a balance of alluring fruit character. The lovely lemon, cream and earth aromas have light coconut notes. Medium-bodied and lightly sweet, with decadently rich honey, tropical fruit and earth flavors and a fresh finish. Drink now or hold. $41 (12/15/91) **91**
Riesling Spätlese Rheingau Erbacher Marcobrunn 1989 ($NA) (12/15/90) **93**
Riesling Spätlese Rheingau Hattenheimer Nussbrunnen 1989 ($NA) (12/15/90) **90**
Riesling Spätlese Rheingau Hattenheimer Nussbrunnen 1988 $21 (9/30/89) **86**
Riesling Spätlese Rheingau Hattenheimer Pfaffenberg 1990: Has good concentration of fruit, with lemon, bread crust and almond aromas. Medium-bodied and medium sweet, with honey and almond flavors and an interesting, creamy finish. Drink now or hold. (NR) (12/15/91) **87**
Riesling Spätlese Rheingau Hattenheimer Pfaffenberg 1989 ($NA) (12/15/90) **91**
Riesling Spätlese Rheingau Hochheimer Kirchenstück 1990: Very good, medium-bodied and medium sweet, with floral, creamy aromas, mineral and cream flavors, good acidity and a long finish. Drink now. (NR) (12/15/91) **87**
Riesling Spätlese Rheingau Hochheimer Kirchenstück 1989 ($NA) (12/15/90) **84**
Riesling Spätlese Trocken Rheingau Hattenheimer Pfaffenberg 1990: As dry as a desert, but with fresh, spicy fruit. Only for true lovers of trocken wines. Offers lovely cream, honey and spice aromas, modest spice flavors and lots of acidity. Medium-bodied and bone dry, lean and tart on the finish. Better from 1993. (NR) (12/15/91) **81**
Riesling Trockenbeerenauslese Rheingau Hochheimer 1990: A compact wine that squeezes in all the fruit and flavor you could want, but retains a great amount of finesse. It has the aromas of a young wine, with botrytis characteristics of almond, smoke and flint. Full-bodied and thickly sweet, with an oily texture, compact fruit flavors and lively acidity. Somewhat short. Try from 1994 to '98. (NR) (12/15/91) **92**

STAATSWEINGUTER
Riesling Kabinett Halbtrocken Rheingau Eltville Hochheimer Kirchenstüch 1988 $8 (9/30/89) **88**
Riesling Kabinett Rheingau Eltville Rauenthaler Baiken 1988 $7.50 (9/30/89) **79**
Riesling Kabinett Rheingau Eltville Rauenthaler Gehrn 1988 $8 (9/30/89) **78**
Riesling Spätlese Rheingau Eltville Rauenthaler Baiken 1988 $25 (9/30/89) **89**

SCHLOSS VOLLRADS
Riesling Kabinett Halbtrocken Rheingau Blausilber 1990: A clean wine, with plenty of spicy Riesling character. Spicy, fresh, flinty apricot aromas give way to spicy flavors, hints of minerals and a long finish. Medium-bodied, steely fresh and off-dry. Better from 1994. (NR) (12/15/91) **86**
Riesling Kabinett Rheingau 1983 $8 (3/01/85) **80**
Riesling Kabinett Rheingau Blaugold 1985 $12 (5/15/87) **78**
Riesling Kabinett Rheingau Charta 1990: Needs time to come around, but has very good potential. Medium-bodied, off-dry and very flavorful, with fresh lemon and apricot aromas, rich, spicy fruit flavors and a crisp finish. Try from 1993 to '95. (NR) (12/15/91) **85**
Riesling Qualitätswein Rheingau Grüngold 1985 $8.50 (5/15/87) **89**
Riesling Spätlese Halbtrocken Rheingau Rosasilber 1990: Has beautiful balance and elegance. Medium-bodied and off-dry, with almond, lemon and apricot aromas, orange blossom, spice and almond flavors and a clean, crisp finish. Drink now or hold. (NR) (12/15/91) **86**
Riesling Spätlese Rheingau Charta 1990: A strange artificial fruit character detracts. Nothing to stage a coup for. Has canned fruit cocktail and ripe fruit aromas and flavors. Very young and awkward, with a tart finish. Perhaps will develop better with time. Try after 1993? (NR) (12/15/91) **83**

WEGELER-DEINHARD
Riesling Auslese Rheingau Rüdesheimer Berg Rottland 1990: On the light side, but has a good balance of fruit, acidity and sweetness. Has delicate lemon tart and tropical fruit aromas. Medium-bodied, with medium sweetness and plenty of lemon, spice and tropical fruit flavors. Has good acidity and a medium finish. Better after 1993. $25 (12/15/91) **85**
Riesling Auslese Rheingau Winkler Hasensprung 1990: Light overall, with lemon, peach, spice and melon aromas and flavors. Medium sweet and balanced, with a light finish. Drink now. $23 (12/15/91) **83**
Riesling Kabinett Halbtrocken Rheingau Winkeler Hasensprung Charta 1988 $15 (9/30/89) **92**
Riesling Kabinett Rheingau 1990: This no-nonsense wine is well made, but rather modest in size. Shows floral, lemon, almond and green apple aromas. Medium-bodied and lightly sweet, with floral and spice flavors and hints of grass. Drink now. (NR) (12/15/91) **85**
Riesling Kabinett Rheingau Rüdesheimer Berg Rottland 1990: A lively wine that refreshes your palate. Slightly one-dimensional, with light almond and rich tropical fruit aromas. Medium-bodied, with rich, spicy almond flavors and very firm acidity. A live wire to drink now or hold. $12 (12/15/91) **85**
Riesling Kabinett Rheingau Rüdesheimer Berg Rottland 1988 ($NA) (9/30/89) **88**
Riesling Spätlese Rheingau 1990: Gives more on the nose than on the palate. Medium-bodied and off-dry, with almond, peach, pie crust and lemon-lime aromas and lovely pie crust and spice flavors but finishes dull. Better after 1993. (NR) (12/15/91) **85**
Riesling Spätlese Rheingau Mittelheimer St. Nikolaus 1988 ($NA) (9/30/89) **89**
Riesling Spätlese Rheingau Rüdesheimer Berg Rottland 1988 ($NA) (9/30/89) **81**

DR. WEIL
Riesling Auslese Rheingau Kiedricher Gräfenberg 1989 ($NA) (12/15/90) **83**
Riesling Beerenauslese Rheingau 1989 ($NA) (12/15/90) **98**
Riesling Kabinett Halbtrocken Rheingau Kiedricher Wasseros Charta 1988 ($NA) (9/30/89) **84**
Riesling Kabinett Rheingau Kiedricher Gräfenberg 1989 ($NA) (12/15/90) **83**
Riesling Spätlese Halbtrocken Rheingau 1989 ($NA) (12/15/90) **91**
Riesling Spätlese Rheingau 1989 ($NA) (12/15/90) **78**
Riesling Spätlese Rheingau Kiedricher Gräfenberg 1988 ($NA) (9/30/89) **84**
Riesling Trockenbeerenauslese Rheingau 1989 ($NA) (12/15/90) **93**

DOMDECHANT WERNER'SCHES
Riesling Auslese Rheingau Hochheimer 1989 ($NA) (12/15/90) **88**
Riesling Auslese Rheingau Hochheimer Domdechaney 1990: A wine with attractive aromas and flavors that's ready to drink. Offers earthy biscuit, spice and fruit aromas and flavors. Medium-bodied and medium sweet, with mouthfilling peach and spice flavors and a light finish. Drink now. (NR) (12/15/91) **85**
Riesling Beerenauslese Rheingau Hochheimer 1989 ($NA) (12/15/90) **79**
Riesling Eiswein Rheingau Hochheimer Domdechaney 1990: An understated, refined eiswein that's as well crafted as a Porsche 911 and just as racy. Medium-bodied and very sweet, with beautiful honey, lime and kiwi fruit aromas, rich honey, melon and lime flavors and a sizzling level of acidity. Better from 1994 to '98. (NR) (12/15/91) **93**
Riesling Kabinett Halbtrocken Rheingau Hochheimer Stein 1989 ($NA) (12/15/90) **84**
Riesling Kabinett Halbtrocken Rheingau Werner Hochheimer Stein 1988 $10.50 (9/30/89) **87**
Riesling Kabinett Rheingau Hochheimer Domdechaney 1989 ($NA) (12/15/90) **88**
Riesling Kabinett Rheingau Hochheimer Hölle 1990: A joy to drink, with deliciously fresh fruit flavors. Fruity and elegant, with clean, perfumed aromas of banana, tropical fruit and spice. Medium-bodied and lightly sweet, with fresh lemon, peach and spice flavors, refreshing, ripe acidity and a long finish. Drink now. (NR) (12/15/91) **88**
Riesling Kabinett Rheingau Hochheimer Hölle 1988 $10.50 (9/30/89) **87**
Riesling Kabinett Rheingau Hochheimer Hölle (AP989) 1989 ($NA) (12/15/90) **86**
Riesling Kabinett Rheingau Hochheimer Hölle (AP1490) 1989 ($NA) (12/15/90) **83**
Riesling Qualitätswein Rheingau Hochheimer 1989 ($NA) (12/15/90) **77**
Riesling Spätlese Rheingau Hochheimer Domdechaney 1990: An early-drinking style that doesn't have much sophistication or power. Medium-bodied, with lovely floral and honey aromas, honey and cream flavors, medium acidity and a light finish. Drink now. (NR) (12/15/91) **85**
Riesling Spätlese Rheingau Hochheimer Domdechaney 1989 $16 (12/15/90) **83**
Riesling Spätlese Rheingau Hochheimer Domdechaney 1988 $12.50 (9/30/89) **93**
Riesling Spätlese Rheingau Hochheimer Hölle 1990: This solid wine has intense grapefruit and lemon aromas. Medium-bodied and sweet, with a velvety mouth-feel and a honeyed, creamy, spicy finish. A little short at the end. Drink now. (NR) (12/15/91) **84**
Riesling Spätlese Halbtrocken Rheingau Hochheimer Hölle 1990: A delicious wine, but it fades quickly on the finish. Shows freshly cut lemons and crushed almonds on the nose. Medium-bodied and off-dry, with ripe lemon and clean tropical fruit flavors touched by a bit of spice, but it's light on the finish. Drink now. (NR) (12/15/91) **84**
Riesling Spätlese Halbtrocken Rheingau Hochheimer Hölle 1988 $12.50 (9/30/89) **93**
Riesling Spätlese Trocken Rheingau Hochheimer Kirchenstüch 1990: Very tart, dry and severe in style; only for trocken fanatics. Very dry and lemony, with petrol, lemon and light spice aromas, hints of spice and an extremely tart finish. Medium-bodied. Better after 1993. (NR) (12/15/91) **78**
Riesling Trockenbeerenauslese Rheingau Hochheimer 1989 ($NA) (12/15/90) **84**

RHEINHESSEN

BALBACH
Riesling Auslese Rheinhessen Niersteiner Hipping 1989 ($NA) (12/15/90) **80**
Riesling Auslese Rheinhessen Niersteiner Oelberg 1990: Has lots going on in the glass. Impres-

sively balanced, full-bodied and sweet, with powerful cookie, apple and spice aromas and very opulent apple and spice flavors. Rich and oily, with a long finish. Drink now or hold. (NR) (12/15/91) **90**
Riesling Auslese Rheinhessen Niersteiner Pettenthal 1989 ($NA) (12/15/90) **84**
Riesling Auslese Rheinhessen Niersteiner Pettenthal 1985 $16 (1/31/87) **79**
Riesling Beerenauslese Rheinhessen Niersteiner Pettenthal 1989 ($NA) (12/15/90) **84**
Riesling Kabinett Halbtrocken Rheinhessen Niersteiner Bildstock 1990: Another big wine that needs food. The palate isn't as good as the nose. Full-bodied and dry, with floral, lemony, perfumed aromas, lemon and spice flavors and plenty of alcohol, but it's slightly short on the finish. Drinkable now, but will improve with age. (NR) (12/15/91) **84**
Riesling Kabinett Rheinhessen 1989 ($NA) (12/15/90) **69**
Riesling Kabinett Rheinhessen Niersteiner Bildstock 1983 $7 (3/01/85) **80**
Riesling Kabinett Rheinhessen Niersteiner Klostergarten 1990: A joy to drink now. Medium-bodied and off-dry, with pretty pie crust, floral and cream aromas, zingy, fresh cream and lemon flavors, fresh acidity and a clean finish. Drink now. $17 (12/15/91) **85**
Riesling Kabinett Rheinhessen Niersteiner Klostergarten 1985 $8 (1/31/87) **60**
Riesling Kabinett Rheinhessen Niersteiner Rehbach 1988 $9 (9/30/89) **82**
Riesling Spätlese Rheinhessen Niersteiner Hipping 1990: Slightly advanced, but very good. Yellow in color, with very ripe fruit and spice aromas. Full-bodied, medium sweet and round, with apricot, spice and pie crust flavors and a long finish. Drink now, but will improve. $21 (12/15/91) **86**
Riesling Spätlese Rheinhessen Niersteiner Hipping 1989 ($NA) (12/15/90) **84**
Riesling Spätlese Rheinhessen Niersteiner Hipping 1988 $12 (9/30/89) **85**
Riesling Spätlese Rheinhessen Niersteiner Pettenthal 1990: Overripe in style, but delicious all the same. Has marzipan, earth and apricot aromas, ripe, almost overripe fruit flavors, good acidity and a rich finish. Full-bodied. Drink now. (NR) (12/15/91) **85**
Riesling Spätlese Rheinhessen Niersteiner Pettenthal 1989 ($NA) (12/15/90) **85**
Riesling Spätlese Rheinhessen Niersteiner Pettenthal 1988 $12 (9/30/89) **86**
Riesling Spätlese Rheinhessen Niersteiner Pettenthal 1985 $10 (1/31/87) **61**
Riesling Spätlese Rheinhessen Niersteiner Pettenthal 1983 $9 (4/16/85) **83**
Riesling Spätlese Rheinhessen Niersteiner Rehbach 1989 ($NA) (12/15/90) **88**
Riesling Spätlese Rheinhessen Niersteiner Rehbach 1988 $12 (9/30/89) **88**
Riesling Spätlese Rheinhessen Niersteiner Spiegelberg 1989 ($NA) (12/15/90) **81**
Riesling Spätlese Trocken Rheinhessen Niersteiner Oelberg 1990: Rich and fat, with lots of fruit, but unbalanced and a little high in alcohol. Apricot, honey and syrup aromas lead to nutty honey and burnt toast flavors. A full-bodied, dry wine that's medium in acidity and on the finish. Drink now. (NR) (12/15/91) **79**

BASSERMANN-JORDAN
Riesling Beerenauslese Rheinhessen Deidesheimer Kieselberg 1990: Has extraordinary aging potential. Extremely backward, but superbly concentrated, with heady aromas of freshly crushed grapes, dry peaches and honey. Full-bodied and very sweet, with masses of spicy lemon and honey flavors and tons of steely acidity. Try from 1994 to '98. $150 (12/15/91) **93**

BAUM
Riesling Kabinett Rheinhessen Mainzer Domherr 1985 $5 (10/15/86) BB **82**
Riesling Qualitätswein Rheinhessen Niersteiner Gutes Domtal 1984 $4.50 (5/16/85) **76**

GUNDERLOCH
Riesling Auslese Rheinhessen Nackenheimer Rothenberg 1990: Wonderfully elegant, almost understated and fresh, with subtle lemon, perfume and apple aromas and modest botrytis notes. Full-bodied and medium sweet, with honey, lemon and spice flavors, excellent acidity and a very long, spicy finish. Drinkable now, but better in 1993. $26 (12/15/91) **91**
Riesling Auslese Rheinhessen Nackenheimer Rothenberg Gold Cap 1990: A splendidly exotic wine, with outstanding concentration and class. Has intense gooseberry, grass and lemon aromas, thick, ripe fruit, apricot, botrytis and spice flavors, full acidity and a remarkably balanced finish. Full-bodied and sweet. Drinkable now, but better in 1993. $40 (12/15/91) **93**
Riesling Kabinett Rheinhessen Semi-Dry Nackenheimer Rothenberg 1990: Big, oily and round, somewhat like a Chardonnay. Incredibly rich for a Kabinett, with tropical fruit, banana and lemon aromas. Full-bodied and dry, with ripe peach flavor and an excellent balance of acidity. Perfect for serving with food. Better in 1993. $11 (12/15/91) **89**
Riesling Qualitätswein Trocken Rheinhessen 1990: Very high in acidity and extremely tart. Needs time. Very floral and citric on the nose. Medium-bodied and dry, with steely acidity, intense lemon and biscuit flavors and a fresh finish. Better in 1993 or '94. $10 (12/15/91) **82**
Riesling Spätlese Rheinhessen Nackenheimer Rothenberg 1990: An extremely youthful wine that needs time to develop. Shows beautiful honey, floral and spice aromas. Medium-bodied and sweet, with exciting clove, honey and melon flavors and fresh acidity. Delicious now, but better from 1993. $16 (12/15/91) **87**
Riesling Spätlese Trocken Rheinhessen Nackenheimer Rothenberg 1990: A heady wine, with a wildly earthy character. Needs pairing with food. Has sweaty, grassy, fresh aromas. Full-bodied and dry, with intense grass, lemon and spice flavors, masses of acidity and a tart finish. Needs time. Try from 1994. $21 (12/15/91) **86**

LOUIS GUNTRUM
Riesling Auslese Rheinhessen Oppenheimer Schützenhütte 1989 ($NA) (12/15/90) **91**
Riesling Auslese Trocken Rheinhessen Niersteiner Pettenthal 1989 ($NA) (12/15/90) **84**
Riesling Beerenauslese Rheinhessen Niersteiner Pettenthal 1989 ($NA) (12/15/90) **86**
Riesling Kabinett Halbtrocken Rheinhessen Oppenheimer Herrenberg 1988 ($NA) (9/30/89) **88**
Riesling Kabinett Rheinhessen Niersteiner Bergkirche 1989 ($NA) (12/15/90) **84**
Riesling Kabinett Trocken Rheinhessen Classic Niersteiner Olberg 1989 ($NA) (12/15/90) **86**
Riesling Kabinett Trocken Rheinhessen Classic Oppenheimer Sackträger 1989 ($NA) (12/15/90) **86**
Riesling Spätlese Rheinhessen Heiligenbaum 1988 ($NA) (9/30/89) **91**
Riesling Spätlese Rheinhessen Oppenheimer Herrenberg 1989 ($NA) (12/15/90) **74**
Riesling Spätlese Trocken Rheinhessen Niersteiner Pettenthal 1989 ($NA) (12/15/90) **82**
Riesling Spätlese Trocken Rheinhessen Oppenheimer Kreuz 1989 ($NA) (12/15/90) **79**
Riesling Trockenbeerenauslese Rheinhessen Oppenheimer Sackträger 1989 ($NA) (12/15/90) **85**

Key to Symbols

The scores reported here are the results of blind tastings conducted by our panel of senior editors. Wines that carry the initials below are results of individual tastings.

THE WINE SPECTATOR 100-POINT SCALE ***95-100***—Classic, a great wine; ***90-94***—Outstanding, superior character and style; ***80-89***—Good to very good, a wine with special qualities; ***70-79***—Average, drinkable wine that may have minor flaws; ***60-69***—Below average, drinkable but not recommended; ***50-59***—Poor, undrinkable, not recommended. "+"—With a score indicates a range; used primarily with barrel tastings to indicate a preliminary score.

SPECIAL DESIGNATIONS SS—Spectator Selection, CS—Cellar Selection, BB—Best Buy, ($NA)—Price not available, (NR)—Not released, ***/**/*—Designations used by German producers to indicate successively higher-quality auslese wines, separating them from the estate's regular lots of auslese. Three stars is the highest rating.

TASTER'S INITIALS (JG)—Jim Gordon, (HS)—Harvey Steiman, (JL)—James Laube, (JS)—James Suckling, (TM)—Thomas Matthews, (TR)—Terry Robards, (PM)—Per-Henrik Mansson, (BT)—Barrel Tasting (these wines were tasted blind from barrel samples), (CA-date)—*California's Great Cabernets* by James Laube, (CH-date)—*California's Great Chardonnays* by James Laube, (VP-date)—*Vintage Port* by James Suckling.

DATE TASTED Dates in parentheses represent the issue in which the rating was published.

HEYL ZU HERRNSHEIM
Riesling Auslese Rheinhessen Niersteiner Oelberg 1990: A powerful, traditional wine, with superb concentration of fruit. Offers lovely peach and tropical fruit aromas and flavors, racy acidity and a long, flavorful finish. Better from 1993. $24 (12/15/91) **91**
Riesling Auslese Rheinhessen Niersteiner Olberg 1989 $25 (12/15/90) **88**
Riesling Kabinett Halbtrocken Rheinhessen Niersteiner Pettenthal 1988 ($NA) (9/30/89) **91**
Riesling Kabinett Rheinhessen Niersteiner Olberg 1989 $12 (12/15/90) **85**
Riesling Kabinett Rheinhessen Niersteiner Olberg 1988 ($NA) (9/30/89) **90**
Riesling Kabinett Rheinhessen Niersteiner Pettenthal 1990: A live wire, with everything going for it. Medium-bodied and dry, offering creamy cassis and melon aromas, lively acidity, focused apple and spice flavors and a long, fresh finish. Better in 1993. $9 (12/15/91) **85**
Riesling Kabinett Rheinhessen Niersteiner Pettenthal 1989 $11 (12/15/90) **85**
Riesling Spätlese Halbtrocken Rheinhessen Niersteiner Pettenthal 1990: A wonderfully attractive, creamy wine that needs a tad more concentration to be outstanding. Has rich cream and peach aromas, rich honey, almond and peach flavors and refreshing acidity. Medium-bodied and off-dry. Drinkable now, but better from 1993. $14 (12/15/91) **86**
Riesling Spätlese Halbtrocken Rheinhessen Niersteiner Pettenthal 1988 ($NA) (9/30/89) **95**
Riesling Spätlese Rheinhessen Niersteiner Brudersberg 1990: Excellent concentration of fruit, with vivid flavors. Classical in every way. The lemon curd aromas have a light spicy note. Medium-bodied and sweet, with honey and spice flavors, great acidity and a long finish. Better in 1993 or '94. $15 (12/15/91) **90**
Riesling Spätlese Rheinhessen Niersteiner Brudersberg 1989 $15 (12/15/90) **86**
Riesling Spätlese Rheinhessen Niersteiner Olberg 1990: Not as great as we hoped, but has delicious fruit character. Medium-bodied and medium sweet, with developed ripe apple and pineapple aromas, excellent acidity and very ripe apple flavors. Excellent balance of acidity and fruit. Drink now or hold. $15 (12/15/91) **85**
Riesling Spätlese Rheinhessen Niersteiner Olberg 1989 $15 (12/15/90) **84**
Riesling Spätlese Rheinhessen Niersteiner Olberg 1988 ($NA) (9/30/89) **89**
Riesling Spätlese Rheinhessen Niersteiner Pettenthal 1989 $15 (12/15/90) **84**
Riesling Spätlese Trocken Rheinhessen Niersteiner Brudersberg 1990: Better than most trockens, with rich fruit that takes the sting out of the acidity. Has creamy lemon and tropical fruit aromas. Medium-bodied and dry, with rich lemon and apricot flavors, firm acidity and a fruity finish. Better in 1993. $15 (12/15/91) **85**
Riesling Trockenbeerenauslese Rheinhessen Niersteiner Olberg 1989 $50 (12/15/90) **90**

KURFURSTENHOF
Riesling Spätlese Rheinhessen Bornheimer Adelberg 1983 $4.50 (12/01/85) **51**

DR. MEYER
Riesling Kabinett Rheinhessen Bereich Nierstein 1987 $4 (10/15/88) BB **81**
Riesling Qualitätswein Rheinhessen Zeller Schwarze Katz 1987 $4 (11/30/88) **75**
Riesling Spätlese Rheinhessen Mainzer Domherr 1986 $5 (11/30/88) BB **82**

RUDOLF MULLER
Riesling Kabinett Rheinhessen Niersteiner Spiegelberg 1986 $5.75 (11/30/87) **64**

REINHOLD SENFTER
Riesling Kabinett Rheinhessen Niersteiner Oelberg 1986 $8.25 (1/31/88) **85**

RHEINPFALZ

BASSERMANN-JORDAN
Riesling Auslese Rheinpfalz Deidesheimer Hohenmorgen 1990: A beauty. Shows refined aromas of ripe peaches, almonds and cream. Medium-bodied and medium sweet, with super-clean peach and tropical fruit flavors, firm acidity and a long finish. A delicious wine to drink now, but better from 1994. $38 (12/15/91) **90**
Riesling Auslese Rheinpfalz Deidesheimer Hohenmorgen 1989 ($NA) (12/15/90) **87**
Riesling Kabinett Rheinpfalz Deidesheimer 1989 $9 (12/15/90) **89**
Riesling Kabinett Rheinpfalz Deidesheimer Herrgottsaker 1983 $7 (3/16/85) **74**
Riesling Kabinett Rheinpfalz Deidesheimer Hohenmorgen 1989 $10 (12/15/90) **86**
Riesling Kabinett Rheinpfalz Deidesheimer Leinhöhle 1990: Elegant and racy, overflowing with grapefruit character. Medium-bodied and off-dry, with ginger and grapefruit aromas, masses of grapefruit flavor and a crisp finish. Drink now. $14 (12/15/91) **88**
Riesling Kabinett Rheinpfalz Deidesheimer Paradiesgarten 1990: A rich, full style, more like a spätlese. Medium-bodied and off-dry, with petrol, pine and lemon aromas, oily, fat fruit flavors and a lemony grapefruit finish. Drink now. $15 (12/15/91) **89**
Riesling Spätlese Rheinpfalz Forster Jesuitengarten 1990: Lively, concentrated and extremely fresh, a wine that fills you with fruit and refreshes you with acidity. Has grapefruit and pie crust aromas. Full-bodied and medium sweet, with focused, ripe grapefruit and honey flavors and steely acidity. Drink now or hold. $26 (12/15/91) **91**
Riesling Spätlese Rheinpfalz Forster Kirchenstück 1990: A mouthful of crisp grapefruit and peach flavors, with lively acidity. Magnificently balanced, would be perfect to serve with foods such as fish and white meats. Aromas of mineral, earth and peach give way to rich peach flavors. Medium-bodied and off-dry, with a crisp finish. Drink now or hold. $19 (12/15/91) **92**

DR. BURKLIN-WOLF
Riesling Auslese Rheinpfalz Forster Pechstein 1990: A sweet wine that's difficult not to drink now, but should be aged. Offers strong grapefruit and apricot aromas, full-bodied, sweet, rich apricot and coconut flavors and excellent acidity. Drink now or hold. (NR) (12/15/91) **90**
Riesling Auslese Rheinpfalz Forster Pechstein 1989 $25 (12/15/90) **94**
Riesling Auslese Rheinpfalz Wachenheimer Gerümpel 1989 $34 (12/15/90) **95**
Riesling Beerenauslese Rheinpfalz Wachenheimer Gerümpel 1990: Like eating a spoonful of honey. The longer you wait to drink it the better. Gold in color, with smoky almond and honey aromas. Full-bodied and super-sweet, with exquisite acidity that makes this concentrated bombshell extremely fresh. An astonishing wine. Drinkable, but wait until 1995 to try. $130/375ml (12/15/91) **96**
Riesling Beerenauslese Rheinpfalz Wachenheimer Gerümpel 1989 ($NA) (12/15/90) **95**
Riesling Beerenauslese Rheinpfalz Wachenheimer Goldbächel 1988 $30 (9/30/89) **87**
Riesling Beerenauslese Rheinpfalz Wachenheimer Rechbächel 1989 $95/375ml (12/15/90) **93**
Riesling Kabinett Halbtrocken Rheinpfalz 1988 $8 (9/30/89) **85**
Riesling Kabinett Rheinpfalz Deidesheimer Hohenmorgen 1985 $6.25 (6/30/87) **61**
Riesling Kabinett Rheinpfalz Forster Mariengarten 1990: Wild and exotic, with lovely mineral, spice and peach aromas. Medium-bodied and off-dry, with refreshing, exotic fruit flavors, excellent richness, fresh acidity and a long finish. Drink now or hold. $12 (12/15/91) **89**
Riesling Kabinett Rheinpfalz Ruppertsberger 1990: Rather light in style, with odd peach, spice and sawdust aromas. Medium-bodied and off-dry, with light floral and peach flavors and firm acidity. Drink now or in 1993. $12 (12/15/91) **80**
Riesling Kabinett Rheinpfalz Ruppertsberger Hoheburg 1989 ($NA) (12/15/90) **87**
Riesling Kabinett Rheinpfalz Wachenheimer Gerümpel 1989 $9 (12/15/90) **83**
Riesling Kabinett Rheinpfalz Wachenheimer Rechbächel 1989 ($NA) (12/15/90) **78**
Riesling Spätlese Rheinpfalz Deidesheimer Hohenmorgen 1989 $14 (12/15/90) **84**
Riesling Spätlese Rheinpfalz Forster Jesuitengarten 1990: This lovely, aromatic wine has a classy structure on the finish. Slightly oily yet restrained, with intense pineapple and lemon rind aromas. Medium-bodied and medium sweet, with concentrated lemon and vanilla flavors and firm acidity. Drinkable now, but better in 1994. $23 (12/15/91) **90**
Riesling Spätlese Rheinpfalz Forster Jesuitgartener 1989 $18 (12/15/90) **90**
Riesling Spätlese Rheinpfalz Wachenheimer Gerümpel 1989 $15 (12/15/90) **85**
Riesling Spätlese Rheinpfalz Wachenheimer Rechbächel 1990: A wonderful wine, with ripe fruit

flavors, a round mouth-feel and lovely aromas of lemons and peaches. Medium-bodied and off-dry, with lovely, creamy peach flavors and a balance of ripe acidity. Drink now. $15 (12/15/91) **89**
Riesling Spätlese Trocken Rheinpfalz Geheimrat Dr. Albert Bürklin-Wolf 1990: A lovely, spicy wine that shows good concentration and balance. Weighty and broad, with hazelnut and fruit aromas and grapefruit and spice flavors. Full-bodied and dry, with excellent acidity and a silky mouth-feel. Drink now or hold. (NR) (12/15/91) **85**
Riesling Spätlese Trocken Rheinpfalz Geheimrat Dr. Albert Bürklin-Wolf 1989 ($NA) (12/15/90) **80**
Riesling Spätlese Trocken Rheinpfalz Wachenheimer Gerümpel 1988 $10 (9/30/89) **88**
Riesling Trockenbeerenauslese Rheinpfalz Ehrenfelser Wachenheimer Mandelgarten 1990: An explosive sweet wine. Deep gold in color, with wonderful reduced aromas of caramel, lime, lemon and dried apricot. Absolutely massive and incredibly sweet, with electrifying sweet lemon and honey flavors. Intense acidity. Needs time. A Riesling cross. Try from 1996 to '98. (NR) (12/15/91) **93**
Riesling Trockenbeerenauslese Rheinpfalz Ruppertsberger Linsenbusch 1988 $9 (9/30/89) **79**
Riesling Trockenbeerenauslese Rheinpfalz Wachenheimer Luginsland 1989 $165 (12/15/90) **95**

MESSMER BURRWEILER
Riesling Kabinett Halbtrocken Rheinpfalz Schlossgarten 1988 $8 (9/30/89) **87**
Riesling Kabinett Rheinpfalz Schlossgarten 1988 ($NA) (9/30/89) **90**
Riesling Spätlese Rheinpfalz Schäwer 1988 $9 (9/30/89) **87**
Riesling Spätlese Trocken Rheinpfalz Schlossgarten 1988 $10 (9/30/89) **94**

JAKOB DEMMER
Riesling Spätlese Rheinpfalz Weingartener Trappenberg 1986 $5 (11/30/88) BB **88**

WEINGUT GRAFSCHAFT LEININGEN
Riesling Auslese Rheinpfalz Kirchheimer Römerstrasse 1989: Fresh and fruity, with definite nectarine and peach aromas and flavors. The slight sweetness is balanced with refreshing acidity. Not as lively and crisp as some, but the flavors are charming. $15 (1/31/92) **83**
Riesling Kabinett Halbtrocken Rheinpfalz Kirchheimer Römerstrasse Renommée 1989: Nearly dry, flavorful, with lots of mineral and earth character, but lacking in strong fruit flavor. For fans of the steely, tight style. $10 (1/31/92) **80**
Riesling Kabinett Rheinpfalz Kirchheimer Schwarzerde 1990: What's not to like? Plenty of tangy fruit flavor fills out this crisp, clean, tasty Riesling. Lemon, pineapple and a bit of peach fill the mouth and stay with you on the finish. 3,000 cases made. $9 (12/15/91) BB **88**

LINGENFELDER
Riesling Spätlese Halbtrocken Rheinpfalz Freinsheimer Goldberg 1990: Rich and round, with wonderfully ripe fruit and lovely honey and peach aromas. Full-bodied and off-dry, with spicy honey and smoke flavors and a round mouth-feel. Drink now. $13 (12/15/91) **91**
Riesling Spätlese Rheinpfalz Freinsheimer Goldberg 1990: A stunning wine, with wonderfully ripe, sweet fruit flavors. Gold in color, with rich lemon meringue and peach aromas and layers of lemon, honey and baked cake flavors. Full-bodied and medium sweet, with firm acidity and a long finish. Drink now or hold. $13 (12/15/91) **92**
Riesling Spätlese Rheinpfalz Freinsheimer Goldberg 1989 $15 (12/15/90) **90**
Riesling Spätlese Rheinpfalz Freinsheimer Goldberg 1988 $12 (9/30/89) **89**
Riesling Spätlese Trocken Rheinpfalz Freinsheimer Goldberg 1989 $15 (12/15/90) **88**
Riesling Spätlese Trocken Rheinpfalz Freinsheimer Goldberg 1988 $12 (9/30/89) **91**
Riesling Trockenbeerenauslese Rheinpfalz Freinsheimer Goldberg 1989 $100/375ml (12/15/90) **96**
Riesling Trockenbeerenauslese Rheinpfalz Grosskarlbacher Osterberg 1989 $85/375ml (12/15/90) **92**

MULLER-CATOIR
Riesling Kabinett Halbtrocken Rheinpfalz Haardter Bürgergarten 1990: No way is this a kabinett. It's as powerful as a top spätlese. Has masses of fruit, with ripe apricot aromas and flavors and hints of honey and wax. Full and off-dry, with an extraordinary richness and fatness and a long finish. Drink now. $13 (12/15/91) **89**
Riesling Kabinett Halbtrocken Rheinpfalz Haardter Bürgergarten 1988 $9 (9/30/89) **92**
Riesling Spätlese Rheinpfalz Haardter Herrenletten 1990: A titillating wine that keeps you coming back for more. More like an auslese, it's mind-blowing for a spätlese. Full-bodied and medium sweet, with concentrated dried apricot and coconut aromas, breathtaking honey and dried fruit flavors and a balance of acidity. Drink now or hold. $16 (12/15/91) **95**
Riesling Spätlese Trocken Rheinpfalz Mussbacher Eselshaut 1988 $14 (9/30/89) **92**

K. NECKERAUER
Riesling Kabinett Halbtrocken Rheinpfalz Weisenheimer Hasenzeile 1988 $7 (9/30/89) **72**
Riesling Spätlese Trocken Rheinpfalz Weisenheimer Altenberg 1988 $8 (9/30/89) **81**
Riesling Spätlese Trocken Rheinpfalz Weisenheimer Hahnen 1988 $8 (9/30/89) **82**

PFEFFINGEN
Riesling Auslese Rheinpfalz Ungsteiner Herrenberg 1989 $25 (12/15/90) **85**
Riesling Auslese Rheinpfalz Ungsteiner Weilberg 1989 $25 (12/15/90) **85**
Riesling Kabinett Rheinpfalz Ungsteiner Hönigsäckel 1990: Round and easy to drink, with a lovely peach and pie crust character. The elegant aromas are similar to a peach tart. Medium-bodied and off-dry, with succulent fruit flavors and a peachy finish. Drink now. $12 (12/15/91) **87**
Riesling Kabinett Rheinpfalz Ungsteiner Hönigsäckel 1989 $16 (12/15/90) **81**
Riesling Kabinett Rheinpfalz Ungsteiner Hönigsäckel 1988 $15 (9/30/89) **88**
Riesling Kabinett Halbtrocken Rheinpfalz Ungsteiner Hönigsäckel 1990: Oily like a great Chardonnay, but crisp like a fine German Riesling. Perfect to serve with food. Has lovely lemon, earth and pie crust aromas, succulent lemon, pie crust and fruit flavors and a rich finish. Medium-bodied, medium in acidity and off-dry. Drink now or hold. $12 (12/15/91) **89**
Riesling Kabinett Halbtrocken Rheinpfalz Ungsteiner Hönigsäckel 1988 ($NA) (9/30/89) **92**
Riesling Spätlese Halbtrocken Rheinpfalz Ungsteiner Herrenberg 1990: Ripe and round, with the structure of a top white Burgundy. Has ripe tropical fruit and spice aromas and rich, oily fruit that gives a bounty of flavor. Full-bodied, off-dry and long on the finish. Drinkable now, but better from 1993. $16 (12/15/91) **91**
Riesling Spätlese Halbtrocken Rheinpfalz Ungsteiner Herrenberg 1989 $16 (12/15/90) **85**
Riesling Spätlese Halbtrocken Rheinpfalz Ungsteiner Herrenberg 1988 $16 (9/30/89) **90**
Riesling Spätlese Rheinpfalz Ungsteiner Herrenberg 1990: Fresh and refined, with delicate peach and lemon aromas. Medium-bodied and off-dry, with peach and lemon flavors, medium acidity and a long finish. Drink now or hold. $16 (12/15/91) **87**
Riesling Spätlese Rheinpfalz Ungsteiner Herrenberg 1989 $16 (12/15/90) **90**
Riesling Spätlese Rheinpfalz Ungsteiner Herrenberg 1988 $16 (9/30/89) **94**
Riesling Spätlese Trocken Rheinpfalz Ungsteiner Weilberg 1990: A very good dry wine, with plenty of finesse, fine pie crust and melon aromas, lemon, earth and spice flavors, high acidity and a crisp finish. Medium-bodied and dry. Drink now or hold. $17 (12/15/91) **87**
Riesling Spätlese Trocken Rheinpfalz Ungsteiner Weilberg 1989 $16 (12/15/90) **84**

REICHSRAT VON BUHL
Riesling Auslese Rheinpfalz Forster Freundstück 1990: An elegant, balanced, textbook auslese. Perfect for serving with dessert. Shows plenty of pear, apple and lemon character on the nose and palate. Medium-bodied and sweet, with a velvety texture and a lovely finish. Drink now. $14 (12/15/91) **90**
Riesling Auslese Rheinpfalz Forster Ungeheuer 1990: Vibrant yet subtle, with freshly sliced lemon and honey aromas and intense lemon and tropical fruit flavors that go on and on. Medium-bodied and sweet. Drink now or hold. $28 (12/15/91) **91**
Riesling Beerenauslese Rheinpfalz Forster Pechstein 1990: Very concentrated and sweet, but seems rather high in volatile acidity. Has too much of a buttery character and odd flavors. Medium-bodied and very sweet, with buttery, pungent honey aromas, buttery almond and almost unclean flavors and a sweet, buttery flavor. Drink now. $75 (12/15/91) **78**
Riesling Kabinett Halbtrocken Rheinpfalz Deidesheimer Nonnenstück 1990: A light, fresh wine, with very crisp acidity. Has fresh, floral aromas and light, spicy floral flavors. Medium-bodied and off-dry, with high acidity and a tart finish. Better from 1993. $14 (12/15/91) **83**
Riesling Kabinett Rheinpfalz Forster Freundstück 1990: Lovely and elegant, with wonderful finesse; this has spätlese quality. Offers strong pineapple, cedar and lemon aromas, medium-bodied, medium sweet, focused honey and spice flavors and a lovely balance of acidity. Drink now. $14 (12/15/91) **87**
Riesling Spätlese Rheinpfalz Forster Jesuitengarten 1990: A perfect wine for serving with white meats. Fresh, delicate, floral aromas follow through on the palate. Medium-bodied and off-dry, with crisp acidity and a creamy lemon finish. Gains in the glass. Drink now. $22 (12/15/91) **89**
Riesling Spätlese Trocken Rheinpfalz Forster Ungeheuer 1990: Slightly austere, with delicate fruit flavors, but has seeringly dry, crisp acidity. Has fresh floral, almond and citrus aromas, floral, spice and mineral flavors and high acidity. Medium-bodied and super-dry. Better from 1993. $22 (12/15/91) **83**

SICHEL
Riesling Beerenauslese Rheinpfalz Deidesheimer Hofstück 1988: A remarkable value. Frankly sweet, but zingy acidity balances the ripe apple, pear and peach flavors refreshingly. Made from hand-selected Huxelrebe grapes. Delicious now, but it's worth cellaring until well into the 21st century. 550 cases made. $9.75/375ml (3/15/90) **92**

WEGELER-DEINHARD
Riesling Auslese Rheinpfalz Deidesheimer Herrgottsacker 1989 $17 (12/15/90) **85**
Riesling Kabinett Rheinpfalz 1990: Classic, with intensely floral aromas and ripe fruit flavors. Medium-bodied and off-dry, with racy, crisp acidity and a long finish. A classic food wine. Better from 1993. $11 (12/15/91) **89**
Riesling Kabinett Rheinpfalz Deidesheimer Herrgottsacker 1989 $10 (12/15/90) **82**
Riesling Spätlese Rheinpfalz 1990: A delicate style, with fresh floral and melon aromas. Medium-bodied and off-dry, with spicy, flinty, fruity flavors and fresh acidity. A little short. Drink now. $15 (12/15/91) **86**
Riesling Spätlese Rheinpfalz Deidesheimer Herrgottsacker 1989 $13 (12/15/90) **87**
Riesling Spätlese Rheinpfalz Deidesheimer Herrgottsacker 1988 $11 (9/30/89) **84**
Riesling Spätlese Rheinpfalz Forster Ungeheuer 1990: Somewhat diluted and lacking in fruit. Light-bodied and off-dry, with light grass and lemon aromas. Lacks concentration and flavor. Perhaps made from overcropped grapes. Drink now. $15 (12/15/91) **78**
Riesling Spätlese Rheinpfalz Forster Ungeheuer 1988 $12 (9/30/89) **86**
Riesling Spätlese Trocken Rheinpfalz Deidesheimer Herrgottsacker 1988 ($NA) (9/30/89) **85**
Riesling Trockenbeerenauslese Rheinpfalz Deidesheimer Herrgottsacker 1989 ($NA) (12/15/90) **93**

Other Germany

DEINHARD
Sparkling Riesling Lila Imperial NV: Has the spicy aromas, and floral, fruity flavors of a Riesling. Sweet but well-balanced, almost delicate. $7 (8/31/89) BB **81**

SCHLOSSGUT DIEL
Grauburgunder Tafelwein Nahe 1990: A very good *barrique* (aged in new oak barrels) wine. Elegantly floral, with an almost cut grass character. Medium-bodied, with lively acidity and a focused, floral, grassy flavor. Has a long finish. 100 percent Grauburgunder (Pinot Gris). Drink now or in 1993. (NR) (12/15/91) **85**
Nahe Victor 1990: One of the better examples of a *barrique* wine. Wonderfully fruity, with refreshing structure. Has fresh, almost pungent aromas of peach and vanilla, intense hazelnut and cream flavors and very lively acidity. A blend of Grauburgunder and Weissburgunder (Pinot Blanc). Drink now or in 1993. $33 (12/15/91) **88**

WEINGUT GRAFSCHAFT LEININGEN
Gewürztraminer Spätlese Rheinpfalz Kirchheimer Geibkopf 1989: Flavorful and full-bodied but steely, with generous apple, mineral and floral flavors and a touch of honey on the finish. Very dry and complex; reminds us more of an Alsace than a Mosel, but it's very good. 600 cases made. $14 (1/31/92) **90**
Ruländer Auslese Trocken Rheinpfalz Kirchheimer Kreuz 1989: Dry and almost austere, with spicy, slightly honeyed aromas and flavors and hints of mustard on the finish. Drinkable now, but might be better after 1993. $14 (1/31/92) **80**
Ruländer Beerenauslese Rheinpfalz Kircheimer Kreuz Secundus 1989: Sweet and ripe, with generous pineapple and peach flavors and a hint of honey. A tough streak of acidity tips it away from being cloying. The texture could be smoother and the honey flavors could be more prominent, but it's a good sweet wine. Best after 1995. $45 (1/31/92) **84**
Ruländer Trockenbeerenauslese Rheinpfalz Kircheimer Kreuz Primus 1989: Sweet and cloying, with an unsettling, tough seam of acidity that makes the texture seem rough, despite the heavy hit of sugar. Finishes with pineapple and earth flavors. Could get smoother with age. Try in 1994 or '95. $60 (1/31/92) **85**
Scheurebe Auslese Rheinpfalz Bissersheimer Goldberg 1989: A silky texture and lemony nectarine flavors make this medium-bodied wine immediately likable, although the intensity wanes on the finish. Drinkable now. $13 (1/31/92) **84**
Spätburgunder Rotwein Trocken Rheinpfalz Kleinkarlbacher Herrenberg 1989: Light red in color, with a silky texture and delicate strawberry, cherry and oak aromas and flavors. An oak spiciness runs through the wine, dominating the finish. Drinkable now. $10/500ml (1/31/92) **82**

LINGENFELDER
Scheurebe Auslese Mosel-Saar-Ruwer Grosskarlbacher Burgweg 1989 $20/375ml (12/15/90) **88**
Scheurebe Auslese Rheinpfalz Grosskarlbacher Burgweg 1990: Sublime, with aromas of mangos, bananas and all sorts of tropical fruits. Full-bodied and sweet, with succulent lemon, spice and grapefruit flavors and a velvety mouth-feel. Shows plenty of subtle botrytis character and good acidity. Drink now or hold. $15 (12/15/91) **91**
Scheurebe Beerenauslese Mosel-Saar-Ruwer Grosskarlbacher Burgweg 1989 $65/375ml (12/15/90) **88**
Scheurebe Spätlese Mosel-Saar-Ruwer Grosskarlbacher Burgweg 1989 $14 (12/15/90) **90**
Scheurebe Spätlese Rheinpfalz Freinsheimer Goldberg 1990: Has staggering concentration and complexity. Full-bodied and off-dry, with tropical fruit and spice aromas, an oily mouth-feel, rich pineapple, tropical fruit and spice flavors and soft acidity. Drink now. (NR) (12/15/91) **92**
Scheurebe Spätlese Trocken Rheinpfalz Grosskarlbacher Burgweg 1990: Round and almost fat, with lots of richness. Medium-bodied and almost off-dry, with explosive aromas of grapefruit and perfume, intense grapefruit flavors and medium acidity. Drink now. $14 (12/15/91) **88**
Scheurebe Trockenbeerenauslese Rheinpfalz Grosskarlbacher Burgweg 1990: Has a spellbinding amount of sweetness and concentration. Very undeveloped, but has great balance and finesse at the same time. Amazingly fresh and spicy, with a bounty of Riesling character on the nose. Full-bodied and sweet, with grapefruit extract, thick honey and spice flavors and super-acidity. Better from 1994 to '98. $150 (12/15/91) **96**

MULLER-CATOIR
Muscateller Spätlese Rheinpfalz Haardter Bürgergarten 1990: A real mouthful, with all the concentration and power you could want. Intense aromas of spice, exotic fruit and almond lead to oily

spice and orange peel flavors. Full-bodied and off-dry, with medium acidity and a long, flavorful finish. Drink now. (NR) (12/15/91) **92**

Rieslaner Auslese Rheinpfalz Mussbacher Eselshaut 1990: Has an amazing amount of concentration. A phenomenal dessert wine. Has intense spice, lemon and crème brûlée aromas, spice and tropical fruit flavors, supercharged acidity and a mile-long finish. Full-bodied and super-sweet. Drinkable now, but better from 1993 to '95. $23 (12/15/91) **93**

Rieslaner Beerenauslese Rheinpfalz Mussbacher Eselshaut 1990: A superlative wine with outstanding concentration, but shows an amazing backbone of acidity. Top class. Has enchanting aromas of flowers and sweet tropical fruits. Full-bodied and super-sweet, with honey, lemon and peach flavors, full acidity and a refreshing finish. Drinkable now, but will improve for years. $39 (12/15/91) **96**

Rieslaner Trockenbeerenauslese Rheinpfalz Mussbacher Eselshaut 1990: Exciting is an understatement for this wine. Its concentration of sweet fruit leaves you speechless. Golden colored, with an enticing bouquet of honey and orange peel aromas. Full-bodied and super-sweet, the fruit takes off like a thermonuclear blast of flavors. Has great racy acidity. Can age forever. Better from 1996 to '98. $53/375ml (12/15/91) **97**

Scheurebe Eiswein Rheinpfalz Haardter Mandelring 1990: Rich and fat, supercharged with sweet, honeyed fruit flavors. Needs time to come together. Full-bodied, sweet and rich, with intense honey and tropical fruit flavors, smoky almond and honey notes and an extremely long finish. Drinkable now, but better from 1993 to '96. (NR) (12/15/91) **94**

Scheurebe Spätlese Rheinpfalz Haardter Mandelring 1990: Like freshly squeezed grapefruit juice or grape concentrate, with intense banana, melon and grapefruit aromas. Full-bodied and medium sweet, with concentrated grapefruit flavor and lively acidity. Drink now. $15 (12/15/91) **91**

WEINGUT HERBERT PAZEN

Scheurebe Hochgewächs Mosel-Saar-Ruwer 1990: Fruity, soft, off-dry and simple in flavor, with peach and apple notes that drop off quickly. Pleasant but straightforward. $9 (12/15/91) **79**

PFEFFINGEN

Scheurebe Auslese Rheinpfalz Ungsteiner Herrenberg 1990: Tastes like a banana tart. Exquisite, with stunning balance and refinement. Full-bodied and medium sweet, with super-ripe banana and tropical fruit aromas, lovely banana and pie crust flavors and refreshing acidity. Drink now or age. $28 (12/15/91) **92**

Scheurebe Auslese Trocken Rheinpfalz Ungsteiner Herrenberg 1989 $25 (12/15/90) **85**

Scheurebe Beerenauslese Rheinpfalz Ungsteiner Herrenberg 1990: Big, fat and sweet, with plenty of character, and enormous depth of fruit. Like pure honey. Golden colored, with extremely ripe almond, honey and spice aromas. Full-bodied and super-sweet, with almond and honey flavors and a wonderfully long, sweet finish. Drink now. $30/375ml (12/15/91) **93**

Scheurebe Spätlese Halbtrocken Rheinpfalz Ungsteiner Herrenberg 1989 $16 (12/15/90) **84**

Scheurebe Spätlese Rheinpfalz Ungsteiner Herrenberg 1990: Not a big wine, but it has lovely balance. Very subtle for a Scheurebe. Medium-bodied and off-dry, with fresh floral and melon aromas, orange peel and tropical fruit flavors and a crisp finish. Drink now. $16 (12/15/91) **88**

Scheurebe Spätlese Rheinpfalz Ungsteiner Herrenberg 1989 $16 (12/15/90) **81**

JOH. JOS. PRUM

Scheurebe Kabinett Mosel-Saar-Ruwer Wehlener Klosterberg 1990: A brilliant wine from a rather pedestrian site. Smells and tastes like fresh grape must. Has perfumed apple, floral and melon aromas and a palate full of sweet apple flavor and crisp acidity. Better in 1994. 500 cases made. $15 (1/31/92) **91**

J. & H. SELBACH

Scheurebe Hochgewächs Mosel-Saar-Ruwer 1989: A thin, lean, tart wine without much fruit. Refreshing, but its muddy mineral flavors aren't our cup of tea. $8 (12/15/91) **70**

Scheurebe Qualitätswein Halbtrocken Mosel-Saar-Ruwer Brauneberger Klostergarten 1990: Light and lively, with crisp green apple and grapefruit flavors that linger through the aftertaste. Beautifully balanced and fragrant. 1,500 cases made. $8.50 (12/15/91) BB **85**

SICHEL

Novum 1987 $7.50 (10/15/88) **85**

HEINRICH VOLLMER

Pinot Blanc Kabinett Trocken Rheinpfalz Weisser Burgunder Ellerstadter Kirchenstück 1990: An unusual German wine whose bottle shape, spicy aromas and rich texture stand out from the crowd. Attractive floral and butter flavors and a lingering finish lend it extra class. $9 (1/31/92) **85**

Key to Symbols

The scores reported here are the results of blind tastings conducted by our panel of senior editors. Wines that carry the initials below are results of individual tastings.

THE WINE SPECTATOR 100-POINT SCALE 95-100—Classic, a great wine; ***90-94***—Outstanding, superior character and style; ***80-89***—Good to very good, a wine with special qualities; ***70-79***—Average, drinkable wine that may have minor flaws; ***60-69***—Below average, drinkable but not recommended; ***50-59***—Poor, undrinkable, not recommended. "+"—With a score indicates a range; used primarily with barrel tastings to indicate a preliminary score.

SPECIAL DESIGNATIONS SS—Spectator Selection, CS—Cellar Selection, BB—Best Buy, ($NA)—Price not available, (NR)—Not released, ***/**/*—Designations used by German producers to indicate successively higher-quality auslese wines, separating them from the estates's regular lots of auslese. Three stars is the highest rating.

TASTER'S INITIALS (JG)—Jim Gordon, (HS)—Harvey Steiman, (JL)—James Laube, (JS)—James Suckling, (TM)—Thomas Matthews, (TR)—Terry Robards, (PM)—Per-Henrik Mansson, (BT)—Barrel Tasting (these wines were tasted blind from barrel samples), (CA-date)—*California's Great Cabernets* by James Laube, (CH-date)—*California's Great Chardonnays* by James Laube, (VP-date)—*Vintage Port* by James Suckling.

DATE TASTED Dates in parentheses represent the issue in which the rating was published.

ABBAZIA DI ROSAZZO
Ronco della Abbazia 1988: Dark brass in color, spicy and a bit tired in aroma and flavor, this dessert wine lacks the richness and intensity that could make it better. $11/375ml (7/15/91) **73**

AVIGNONESI
Vin Santo 1977 $18 (10/01/85) **92**

MARCO DE BARTOLI
Marsala Superióre Vigna la Miccia 1985: A real eye-opener, with light, subtle flavors of almond, walnut, maple syrup and lemon. Delicate, clean and tasty. Try this fortified wine the next time you want a lighter style of sherry for a treat. $16 (3/31/90) **87**
Moscato di Pantelleria 1987: Aromas and flavors of almond and dried apricot are distinctive and delicious. Not terribly sweet, but it's definitely a dessert wine. A touch of caramel and orange peel on the finish is also nice. $16 (3/31/90) **87**

BENI DI BATASIOLO
Moscato d'Asti 1989: Soft, sweet and charming, with aromas like a bouquet of flowers and flavors that echo litchi, cinnamon and pear on the long, sweet finish. Light enough to drink a lot of it. $14 (7/15/91) **85**

LA BOATINA
Verduzzo 1989: Sweet and slightly spicy, a golden-colored wine, with a silky texture, a moderate level of sweetness and vague apricot and fig flavors. A nicely balanced dessert wine that tastes fine by itself, or can be matched with less-sweet desserts. $17 (1/31/92) **84**

CASTELLARE DI CASTELLINA
Vin Santo 1984: A sweet style; its almond and hazelnut aromas and flavors give this *vin santo* more of a sherry feel than most. A very attractive, balanced style that relies more on toasty complexity than opulence. $28/375ml (9/30/90) **88**

COLOSI
Malvasia delle Lipari Passito di Salina 1989: With its amber color and pungent tropical fruit aromas, this tastes as if it's a cross between a light sherry and a mango nectar. A strong woody component chokes off the sweetness and fruit. Not for everyone, but it has style. 1,500 cases made. $20/375ml (3/31/92) **81**

FRESCOBALDI
Pomino Tenuta di Pomino Vin Santo 1981 $20 (10/15/88) **87**

CASTELLO DI GABBIANO
Vin Santo 1985: On the dry side, offering plenty of spicy, sherrylike aromas and flavors and echoes of wood and spice on the finish. A little bitter, but fragrant and suitable as an aperitif. Tasted twice. $20 (3/15/91) **78**

ISOLE E OLENA
Vin Santo NV: An opulent dessert wine from a fine Chianti producer. Smooth, rich and subtle, sweet without being cloying. An elegant wine offering delicious almond, hazelnut and tea aromas and flavors that grow and persist on the finish. Harmonious and beautifully balanced. $17/375ml (3/31/90) **93**

JERMANN
Moscato Rosa del FVG Vigna Bellina 1989: A sweet, floral, spicy tasting rosé, with rose petal aromas and Gewürztraminer-like flavors. Charming if served cold as an aperitif. $26 (3/15/91) **81**

LUNGAROTTI
Vin Santo 1985: Not very sweet, but lively and flavorful, balancing a sherrylike character with a honeylike sweetness. A pleasant drink. $7/375ml (3/15/91) **79**
Vin Santo 1983: Amber in color, fragrant with almond and orange peel; this sherrylike wine comes off as moderately sweet and gentle on the palate, not too cloying or rich. $9.50 (3/15/89) **81**

MACULAN
Torcolato 1988: Ripe and rich, with opulent honey, fig and nutmeg aromas and flavors. Very sweet, but slightly—and appealingly—bitter on the long finish. A dramatic wine that's tempting to drink now, but ought to develop more dimension with age. 1,500 cases made. $35 (4/15/91) **91**
Torcolato 1985: With earthy fig and almond aromas reminiscent of Sauternes, this sweet white dessert wine opens with a burst of fig and honey flavor, which carries through to the finish. A bit cloying, but aging should balance it. Drink in the mid-1990s. $15/375ml (3/31/89) **84**
Torcolato 1983 $29 (11/15/87) **82**

MARTINI DI CIGALA
San Giusto a Rentennano Vin Santo 1982 $18/375ml (12/31/88) **96**
San Giusto a Rentennano Vin Santo 1981 $25 (12/31/87) **89**

CASTELLO DI MONTEGROSSI
Vin Santo 1982: Rich and sweet, as if it were a vanilla-nut cookie in a glass, smooth, nutty and opulent. Flavors hint at orange rind and almonds. Very seductive and satisfying. Should be delicious with biscotti. $19/375ml (3/31/90) **92**

BARONE RICASOLI
Brolio Vin Santo 1981: An intense, complex dessert wine, with fascinating almond, butter, caramel, dried pear and vanilla notes. Very long-lasting on the finish. Ideal sipped by itself or with the traditional biscotti. $25 (9/15/91) **90**
Brolio Vin Santo 1977: A drier style that's light and elegant next to some of the sweeter versions, showing distinctive hazelnut and orange peel aromas and flavors. Balanced and refreshing. $13 (3/31/90) **85**

I SELVATICI
Vin Santo 1984: Remarkably complex and intense, with rich, concentrated and delicious flavors, offering loads of lush smoke, spice, anise, nectarine, peach and cinnamon. The flavors are full and long on the finish. Drink now to 1995. $16/375ml (4/30/91) **89**

Italy North Red/*Cabernet DOC*

COLLAVINI
Cabernet Sauvignon Grave del Friuli 1984: A distinctive and delicious wine, with well-articulated but light currant and cherry flavors, toasty chocolate overtones, a firm texture and a long-lasting finish. Drinkable now, but cellaring until 1993 to '95 shouldn't hurt. $8 (4/15/90) BB **85**

ENO-FRIULIA
Cabernet Sauvignon Collio 1988: Vegetal, green bean aromas make it seem coarse, but they give way to pleasant, ripe cherry and spice flavors that finish nicely. Drinkable now. $12 (7/15/91) **76**

LIVIO FELLUGA
Cabernet Franc Collio 1988: Elegant and peppery, with ripe, clean plum and currant-tinged flavors. The moderate tannins make it ideal for drinking now or in 1993. $15 (6/30/91) **84**

MACULAN
Breganze Cabernet Fratta 1986: Beautifully fragrant, with sweet vanilla-tinged oak framing rich cassis flavor, turning rich, chocolaty and opulent on the palate and long and soft on the finish. A major-league wine that should age beautifully through 1995. $29 (3/31/89) **92**

FOSS MARAI
Cabernet Piave 1990: A hard-edged wine, with strong vegetal aromas and flavors. Tart, with currant and berry notes, but not enough to make it over the hump. $8.75 (1/31/92) **76**

TIEFENBRUNNER
Cabernet Alto Adige 1987: Has good concentration of pure Cabernet aroma and flavor on a medium-weight frame, with balanced tannins and a touch of sweet vanilla on the finish. Well made, worth cellaring until 1993. $9 (3/31/89) **84**

Valpolicella DOC

ANSELMI
Recioto della Valpolicella 1985: Ripe and focused, but not especially heavy or alcoholic for an Amarone, with nicely articulated plum, currant and toast aromas and flavors that linger on the finish. Drinkable now with cheese, but the tannins could use until 1993 or '94 to subside. $19 (6/30/91) **86**

BOLLA
Valpolicella 1986: Spicy aromas give way to austere, stemmy flavors. Not easy to like, but it's light enough to be good with a plate of spaghetti. $6 (12/15/89) **71**
Valpolicella Vigneti di Jago Classico 1986: Very ripe and relatively full-bodied, but a bit awkward, offering more flavor intensity on the one hand but more tannin and tarry toastiness on the other. Has more backbone but less harmony than most. $12 (12/31/90) **78**

VILLA BORGHETTI
Valpolicella Classico 1989: An earthy, tart, cherry-flavored wine, with plenty of acidity, but rather lean flavors. $7 (4/30/92) **78**

DAL FORNO ROMANO
Valpolicella Superióre 1986: Full-bodied with full flavors, an aromatic, deeply colored wine, with lots of spicy, leathery overtones to the olive and black cherry flavors. Very ripe and distinctive. Crisp on the finish. Drink now, if this is your style. 400 cases made. $20 (4/30/92) **84**

REMO FARINA
Recioto della Valpolicella Amarone Classico 1983: A light style that's dry, slightly bitter, vegetal and tannic. $12.50 (3/31/90) **70**

LEONARDINI
Valpolicella 1990: Fresh and light, with bright cherry and plum flavors, good balance and a clean finish. Well made in a modest style. 2,300 cases made. $5 (4/30/92) BB **81**

MASI
Valpolicella Classico Superióre 1987: Smooth and mature, with an elegant texture and good balance, but there's nothing special about the flavors. $7.25 (12/31/90) **78**

LUIGI RIGHETTI
Recioto della Valpolicella Amarone Capitel de' Roari 1983 $16 (2/15/89) **90**

GUERRIERI RIZZARDI
Valpolicella Classico Superióre 1987: Light and crisp, with appealing cherry and strawberry aromas. Lively, lean and tart on the palate. Drinkable now. $6.50 (3/31/90) **79**
Valpolicella Poiega Classico 1988: Crisp and peppery, a light, fruity wine with appealing cherry and strawberry flavors plus a hint of black pepper. Has more intensity than most Valpolicellas. Drink now. $9 (12/15/89) **82**

SANTI
Recioto della Valpolicella 1985: Very ripe and distinctively spicy, showing lots of cinnamon, nutmeg and cardamom, with a modest core of ripe black cherry flavor. A wine to enjoy for its fragrance and harmonious balance. Not as alcoholic as some. Drink now to 1995. $20 (6/30/91) **83**

ZENATO
Recioto della Valpolicella Amarone Classico 1981: Not as ripe and fat as most, this is sharply focused with ripe cherry and berry flavors, though hot on the finish. $11 (3/15/89) **81**
Valpolicella Classico Superióre 1988: Smooth, complex and flavorful, combining good cherry and plum flavors with peppery, gamy accents. Drink now through 1994. $8 (4/30/92) BB **83**

Vino da Tavola

ABBAZIA DI ROSAZZO
Pignolo 1987: Jammy, spicy and generous, with a hearty texture and peppery overtones to the plummy, currantlike aromas and flavors. Has enough tannin to want until 1994 or '95 to soften. Made from Pignolo, an ancient grape variety indigenious to Friuli that's very rare and close to extinction. $36 (6/30/91) **85**
Ronco dei Roseti 1987: Ripe, rich, concentrated and marked by new oak, a style reminiscent of a good California Cabernet. The generous, focused plum and cedar flavors are immediately appealing. Drinkable now, but best after 1993. $35 (7/15/91) **87**
Ronco dei Roseti 1986: An impressive concentration of berry and plum aromas and flavors packed into a lean and lively frame. Drink now. $22 (3/15/89) **85**
Ronco dei Roseti 1983 $20 (9/15/88) (TM) **87**

ANTONUTTI
Poggio Alto 1986: Tannic but smooth and concentrated underneath. Lean in texture, showing nice raspberry and vanilla aromas and flavors that hold on through the finish. Cellar until 1993 or '94 for the tannins to subside. 250 cases made. $15 (4/15/90) **86**

BELLAVISTA
Solesine 1986: Another in the new wave of ripe, rich, delicious Italian Cabernets, loaded with plum, cassis and chocolate aromas and flavors on a velvety background, supple and expansive on the finish. Already drinkable, but cellaring to soften the tannins should bring it to its best around 1993. $30 (5/15/89) **92**

BERTANI
Catullo 1984: Distinctive and ripe, with aromas of leather and sandalwood and spicy, woody flavors layered over tart but sweet plum. $9 (2/15/89) **86**

BOLLA
Creso Rosso 1986: Smooth and gentle, beautifully balanced, harmonious and generous of flavor, offering smoky, slightly chocolaty raspberry and black cherry aromas and flavors. Firm tannins and a velvety texture want cellaring until 1993 to '94 to smooth out. Limited availability. 4,500 cases made. $25 (4/15/90) **88**

CA' DEL BOSCO
Maurizio Zanella 1988: Rich, ripe, round and generous, with a marvelous interplay of oak and plum, currant and cherry aromas and flavors. A spicy finish brings it home smoothly, and the tannins are well integrated. Almost drinkable now, but has the structure to age gracefully through at least 1995. 1,400 cases made. Rel: $32 Cur: $57 (9/30/91) **93**
Maurizio Zanella 1987: Lush and opulent, with distinctive earth and currant aromas and flavors, a supple texture, velvety tannins and the sort of leather, spice and plum nuances that add complexity and richness. Long and smooth enough on the finish to drink tonight, but should age well through at least 1994 to '95. 1,200 cases made. Rel: $40 Cur: $45 (4/15/90) **92**
Maurizio Zanella 1985 $38 (9/15/88) **92**
Pinot Nero Pinero 1988: A pungently smoky-smelling wine, with roasty toasted marshmallow flavors and traces of cherry. More fruit and spice nuances pile on the aftertaste. A heavily oaked style that's not for everybody. 250 cases made. $50 (1/31/92) **83**
Pinot Nero Pinero 1987: An elegantly styled wine without much Pinot Noir character. It has ripe, plummy, almost pruny flavors, spicy, leathery aromas and a touch of expensive oak. Drinkable now. Tasted twice, with consistent results. $69 (6/15/90) **82**

FARALTA
Rosso del Friuli-Venezia Giuli 1986: Highly perfumed but tough and overly herbal on the palate,

turning soft and green on the finish. The aromas of black pepper and flowers are appealing, but the wine seems out of balance. $12.50 (4/15/90) **74**

MARCO FELLUGA
Carantan 1988: Deeply colored, with very fruity, rich flavors, a supple texture and moderate oak shadings of chocolate and toast. Has fine concentration and length. Tempting now, but should be better after 1995. 1,000 cases made. $36 (4/30/92) **88**

BARONE FINI
Cabernet Sauvignon Cabernello 1988: Very light, with modest cherrylike flavors that are perfectly drinkable, if not particularly reminiscent of Cabernet Sauvignon. $10 (7/15/91) **76**

LIVON
Schioppettino 1988: Firm and flavorful without being dense, making a strong statement with plum, cherry and spice aromas and flavors. The tannins are well integrated, making this drinkable already. Should improve through 1993 or '94. 275 cases made. $13 (1/31/92) **86**
Schioppettino 1987: A hearty, spicy wine with smoky aromas, tart cherry and black pepper flavors and good balance. Drink it now for its lively, spicy character. $18 (4/15/90) **81**

MACULAN
Cabernet Sauvignon Palazzotto 1987: Light and supple, leaning toward red cherry and spice flavors in a delicate style that is appealing to drink now. Has a leafy edge. $30 (1/31/92) **82**
Cabernet Sauvignon Palazzotto 1986: Lean and woody, with slightly sour and mossy flavors on the finish that detract from an otherwise decent, well-balanced and modestly concentrated wine. $19 (3/31/89) **71**

MASI
Campo Fiorin 1985: A decent wine, with pungent smoky, herbal aromas and tomatolike flavors. Firm tannins and full body give it oomph. $11.50 (9/15/90) **77**
Campo Fiorin 1983: Ripe and surprisingly tannic, not at all the light-style Valpolicella that is so common. It's even a bit hot, but the flavors are true and intense enough to command attention. $7.50 (5/15/89) BB **81**

MASO CANTANGHEL
Pinot Nero Altesino Riserva 1988: A delicate, charming wine, with brilliant color, lovely aromas of cherry, strawberry and oak and flavors that are harmonious and long. Not blessed with great depth, but it's an appealing wine. Drink now. $33 (2/15/91) **84**

RONCHI DI CIALLA
Schiopettino di Cialla 1983: Spicy, dusky aromas and flavors lend interest to this lean and finely focused wine from Friuli that's pleasantly bitter on the finish. Tannic, it needs time to open up, perhaps until 1993. $25 (3/31/89) **84**

RONCO DEL GNEMIZ
Rosso 1986: Tough and tart, with some concentration of herbal cherry flavors opening on the finish. Needs lots of time. If it lasts through 1995, it could be delicious. $15 (3/31/89) **80**

TEDESCHI
Capitel San Rocco 1983: Has plenty of ripe fruit—cherries and plums—and spice that sit evenly on the palate, but it lacks the depth and refinement found in finer wines. Drink now. $11 (2/15/89) **84**

VALLE SELEZIONE ARALDICA
L'Araldo Collina Friulana 1985: A lively wine, with distinctive berry, black cherry, smoke and root beer flavors and a firm texture, but it's generous on the finish, echoing ripe fruit and spices. Enjoyable to drink now, but cellaring until 1993 to '95 might bring out even more. $20 (5/15/91) **84**

VENEGAZZU
Della Casa 1985: Firm and elegant, with Bordeaux-like berry, chocolate and earth aromas and flavors that are generous and long. Has richness and roundness and just the right touch of tannin to carry it through 1993. $25 (3/31/90) **91**
Della Casa 1983: Firm, tannic and concentrated, with chocolaty plum and maturing leather aromas and flavors, and it's slightly raisiny on the palate. Drink now. $25 (2/15/89) **86**

VIGNALTA
Gemola 1988: Medium-bodied, tannic and firmly structured, with herb and cherry flavors. Not generous, but has nice spicy notes and distinctive flavors. $22 (9/30/91) **81**
Merlot 1988: Ripe, soft, generous and not especially complex, but brimming with ripe currant, herb and tar aromas and flavors. Drinkable now. $18 (4/15/91) **80**

ZONIN
Berengario Barrel Aged 1988: Extremely rich and ripe, with distinctive plum and prune aromas and flavors that seem unfocused and covered at the moment by a blanket of tannin. Needs until 1993 to '95 to soften. $30 (1/31/92) **84**
Merlot Cabernet del Friuli Le Vendemmie 1989: Very light and delicate, with modest red currant and tea aromas and flavors. A humble wine that's easy to drink but austere. $6 (1/31/92) **78**

OTHER RED DOC

BOLLA
Bardolino 1990: Light enough to be a rosé, with pleasant strawberry, spice and lemon aromas and flavors. The flavors are subdued but charming. Drink soon. $8 (1/31/92) **79**

CA' DEL BOSCO
Franciacorta 1988: A light, crisp, tart wine, with modest berry flavors. Simple and refreshing. Would be best served slightly chilled. $11 (1/31/92) **81**
Franciacorta 1987: Tight and austere, with mint, herb and currant flavors that are attractive but a bit thin and shallow. Well made, but unexciting. Drink now or in 1993. $16 (12/31/90) **77**

TENUTA IL BOSCO
Pinot Nero Oltrepò Pavese 1988: Simple, clean, grapey aromas and flavors persist pleasantly on the palate. It lacks the depth and complexity of a Burgundy, but it's a respectable red to drink with roast chicken. 2,000 cases made. $9.50 (6/30/91) **81**

Key to Symbols

The scores reported here are the results of blind tastings conducted by our panel of senior editors. Wines that carry the initials below are results of individual tastings.

THE WINE SPECTATOR 100-POINT SCALE ***95-100***—Classic, a great wine; ***90-94***—Outstanding, superior character and style; ***80-89***—Good to very good, a wine with special qualities; ***70-79***—Average, drinkable wine that may have minor flaws; ***60-69***—Below average, drinkable but not recommended; ***50-59***—Poor, undrinkable, not recommended. "+"—With a score indicates a range; used primarily with barrel tastings to indicate a preliminary score.

SPECIAL DESIGNATIONS SS—Spectator Selection, CS—Cellar Selection, BB—Best Buy, (SNA)—Price not available, (NR)—Not released.

TASTER'S INITIALS (JG)—Jim Gordon, (HS)—Harvey Steiman, (JL)—James Laube, (JS)—James Suckling, (TM)—Thomas Matthews, (TR)—Terry Robards, (PM)—Per-Henrik Mansson, (BT)—Barrel Tasting (these wines were tasted blind from barrel samples), (CA-date)—*California's Great Cabernets* by James Laube, (CH-date)—*California's Great Chardonnays* by James Laube, (VP-date)—*Vintage Port* by James Suckling.

DATE TASTED Dates in parentheses represent the issue in which the rating was published.

BORGO CONVENTI
Merlot Collio 1987: Very fruity and floral, yet balanced and smooth, lean and lively but not too sharp or acidic. Drink now. $15 (3/31/89) **84**

GIOVANNI DRI
Refosco Colli Orientali del Friuli 1986: Distinctively tart and peppery with ripe plum flavor that is fresh and lively. Not too tannic; drink now or in the next three to five years. $11 (9/15/89) **82**

ENO-FRIULIA
Merlot Collio 1988: Light and bright, with sharply focused strawberry and cinnamon aromas and flavors shaded by a touch of cedar. Balanced and drinkable, but tastes as though it can benefit from aging until about 1993. $12 (4/30/91) **82**

LIVIO FELLUGA
Merlot Collio 1988: Light and fruity, with elegant black cherry, anise, smoke and cedary notes that linger. Medium-bodied and not too tannic, this versatile style would pair well with a variety of foods. Drink now or in 1993. $16 (7/15/91) **84**

FORADORI
Teroldego Rotaliano Vigneto Morei 1988: Firm in structure, but a little loose in the flavor department, edging toward sour cherry and medicinal flavors on the finish. Tasted twice, with consistent notes. 2,500 cases made. $16 (1/31/92) **69**

GAIERHOF
Teroldego Rotaliano 1988: Has herbal, smoky, tomatolike flavors in a lean structure. Drinkable, but not very fruity or interesting. $11 (9/30/91) **75**

CASA GIRELLI
Pinot Nero Trentino i Mesi 1988: A simple, pleasant wine, with modest wild berry and toast aromas and flavors. Smooth in texture and easy to drink. 1,500 cases made. $10 (2/15/91) **81**

LIVON
Refosco Colli Orientali del Friuli dal Peduncolo Rosso Riul 1988: Tart and fruity, with a sour edge that takes away from the pleasant cherry and berry flavors. Drinkable now, but could develop through 1993 or '94. 250 cases made. $11 (1/31/92) **79**

MACULAN
Breganze Rosso Brentino 1986: Lean and tannic, with enough plush plum and berry flavor poking through to justify aging it a few years to see what develops. Seems very closed now, better around 1993. $9.50 (3/31/89) **85**

MASI
Bardolino Classico Superióre 1988: Light and spicy, and just a shade darker in color than rosé, suggesting that this might be best sipped chilled on a warm day. Has nice hints of orange and strawberry on the long finish. $6 (5/15/91) BB **82**

TENUTA MAZZOLINO
Oltrepò Pavese 1990: Solid and simple, with appealing plum and currant aromas and flavors that ease off on the finish. Drinkable now. $14 (1/31/92) **77**
Oltrepò Pavese Barbera 1990: Ripe and fruity, with generous black currant aromas and flavors. An exuberant wine without a lot of finesse. Drinkable now, but has enough tannin to keep through 1994. $10.50 (4/30/92) **82**
Oltrepò Pavese Barbera 1989: Light and fruity, with pleasant strawberry and watermelon aromas and flavors, hinting at anise on the finish. Drinkable now for its charming freshness. $10 (4/15/91) **82**

PUIATTI
Merlot Collio 1989: Soft and simple, with strong herb and tobacco aromas and a modest core of grapey flavor that comes through on the finish. Drinkable now. $26 (1/31/92) **78**

RONCHI DI CIALLA
Refosco Colli Orientali del Friuli dal Peduncolo Rosso di Cialla 1983: Crisp and flavorful, with berry and cherry flavors interweaving on the finish to bring some added life to an otherwise simple and somewhat tannic wine. $23 (3/31/89) **79**

RUSSIZ SUPERIORE
Merlot Collio 1989: A concentrated, intense young wine, with plenty of herbal richness to balance the youthful tannins. Keeps it all in balance, a good bet to save until about 1995 or later to reach optimum drinkability. $27 (4/30/92) **86**

ZENATO
Bardolino Classico Superióre 1989: This lightweight wine is lightly fruity and gently peppery, with pleasant strawberry flavor. Serve lightly chilled this summer. $7.75 (7/15/91) **78**

ITALY NORTH WHITE/*CHARDONNAY DOC*

BOLLINI
Chardonnay Trentino 1990: Light and fruity, with spicy, floral overtones to the pear flavor. Dry and refreshing on the finish. Drink soon. $9 (1/31/92) **82**
Chardonnay Trentino 1988 $7 (9/15/89) **85**
Chardonnay Trentino 1987 $7.25 (9/15/89) **84**

CA' DEL BOSCO
Chardonnay Franciacorta 1989: Rich and round in texture, with flavors that owe more to the barrel fermentation than to the natural ripeness of the fruit, which seems modest for the scale of the wine. Drinkable now. An attempt to make an interesting wine. Tasted twice. $31 (1/31/92) **85**
Chardonnay Franciacorta 1986 $38 (9/15/89) **85**

JOSEF BRIGL
Chardonnay Alto Adige 1989: A decent wine without much Chardonnay character. Has slightly nutty, appley flavors, but lacks concentration and style. $10 (7/15/91) **77**

CAVIT
Chardonnay Trentino 1988 $6 (9/15/89) **84**

COLTERENZIO
Chardonnay Alto Adige 1989: Light, fruity and fresh, with plenty of attractive peach, apple and pear flavors that linger on the finish. Any oak influence is subdued enough not to be noticed. Drinkable now. 2,000 cases made. $8 (1/31/91) BB **84**

CASA GIRELLI
Chardonnay Trentino i Mesi 1989: Soft in texture, with subtle almond and pear aromas and flavors. Not a wine that reaches out and grabs you, but one that can be consumed comfortably by itself or with dinner. Drinkable now. $8 (2/15/91) BB **81**

HOSTATTER
Chardonnay Alto Adige 1988 (SNA) (9/15/89) **83**

ISTITUTO AGRARIO PROVINCIALE
Chardonnay Trentino 1987 $10 (9/15/89) **80**
Chardonnay Trentino 1982 $10.50 (9/15/89) **80**

KETTMEIR
Chardonnay Alto Adige 1988 $11 (9/15/89) **84**

ALOIS LAGEDER
Chardonnay Alto Adige Buchhoiz 1988 $13 (9/15/89) **88**

Chardonnay Alto Adige Loewengang 1986 $19 (9/15/89) **82**
Chardonnay Alto Adige Loewengang 1985 $19 (9/15/89) **90**

LIVON
Chardonnay Grave del Friuli Vigneto Medeuzza 1988: Not a blockbuster, but a delicate, floral, crisp and lively wine with good intensity of Chardonnay flavor emerging on the long-lasting finish. Drink now. $14 (12/31/90) **82**

MALPAGA
Chardonnay Trentino 1988 $8 (9/15/89) **85**
Chardonnay Trentino 1987 $8 (9/15/89) **75**

MASI
Chardonnay Trentino Rosabel 1987 ($NA) (9/15/89) **79**

PIGHIN
Chardonnay Grave del Friuli 1990: Spicy, piny, herbal aromas and flavors don't remind us much of Chardonnay, but this is a pleasant, light wine for drinking soon. $12 (1/31/92) **77**
Chardonnay Grave del Friuli 1988 $8 (9/15/89) **85**
Chardonnay Grave del Friuli Pighin di Capriva 1988 $9.25 (9/15/89) **80**

PLOZNER
Chardonnay Grave del Friuli 1988 $6 (9/15/89) **78**

POJER E SANDRI
Chardonnay Trentino 1987 $8 (9/15/89) **84**
Chardonnay Trentino 1985 $7.50 (9/15/89) **82**

PUIATTI
Chardonnay Collio 1990: Tight in texture, with modest spice and floral pear flavors. A charming wine. Drink up now. $19 (1/31/92) **81**

SANTA MARGHERITA
Chardonnay Alto Adige 1989: Very light in color, almost like water, with crisp texture but little fruit evident other than aromas and flavors of unripe peach. A totally average wine. $13 (12/31/90) **75**

TIEFENBRUNNER
Chardonnay Alto Adige 1990: A round, spicy style, with plenty of charm. Refreshing, with pear and nutmeg flavors and even a tiny hint of cherry. Drinkable now. $10 (1/31/92) **83**
Chardonnay Alto Adige 1989: A charming wine that's crisp, appley and straightforward, like a lower-level Chablis. Drink now for its freshness and fruit. $10 (7/15/91) **82**
Chardonnay Alto Adige Linticlarus 1989: Has plenty of body, but modest flavor, showing pleasant apple and spice characteristics that persist into the finish. Reminds us of an Alsatian Pinot Blanc. Drinkable now. 750 cases made. $10.50 (1/31/92) **81**

VENICA
Chardonnay Dolegna del Collio 1989: Light in texture, spicy in aroma and in flavor and crisply balanced, with a firm concentration of lemon and apple flavors that linger on the finish. Drinkable now, but has the structure to develop through 1993 or so. $17 (1/31/91) **84**

CA' VESCOVO
Chardonnay Aquileia 1989: Light, soft and uncomplicated, with fruity, floral flavors. Drink now. 5,000 cases made. $8 (7/15/91) **76**

VINATTIERRI
Chardonnay Alto Adige Atesino Vinattieri 1989: Fresh and fruity, decent, with little Chardonnay character, but it does offer interest. $18 (8/31/91) **80**

PETER ZEMMER
Chardonnay Alto Adige 1990: Crisp and fruity, a lean-textured wine, with modest green apple flavor. Drinkable now. $10 (1/31/92) **78**

ZENI
Chardonnay Trentino 1988 $12 (9/15/89) **85**

Chardonnay Vino da Tavola

ABBAZIA DI ROSAZZO
Chardonnay 1990: Modest in flavor, with distinct, earthy, buttery overtones to the simple pear and apple flavors. Has a low flavor profile, but it's pleasant. Drinkable now. $22 (1/31/92) **75**

BELLAVISTA
Chardonnay Uccellanda 1987 $30 (9/15/89) **83**
Chardonnay Uccellanda 1986 $30 (9/15/89) **92**

BORTOLUZZI
Chardonnay 1988 $11 (9/15/89) **87**
Chardonnay 1987: Good but not exceptional. Shows some pear flavors and has a nice smooth texture, but tastes a bit dull and woody. $11 (5/15/89) **72**

LA CADALORA
Chardonnay della Vallagarina 1988 $11.25 (9/15/89) **79**
Chardonnay della Vallagarina 1987: Fruity, medium-bodied and crisply balanced, with pear and orange flavors and a smack of wood. Drink now. $8.25 (3/31/89) **84**

CASTELCOSA
Chardonnay 1987 $12.50 (9/15/89) **82**
Chardonnay 1986 $9.50 (9/15/89) **85**
Chardonnay Pra di Pradis 1986 $13 (9/15/89) **83**

LA CASTELLADA
Chardonnay 1988: Very fruity, clean and fresh, with peach, vanilla and honey flavors that linger on the finish. Well balanced and ready to enjoy now, like an exceptional Mâcon. $14 (3/31/90) **86**

ENO-FRIULIA
Chardonnay 1989: Medium-bodied and modestly flavorful, with hints of fig, almond and melon. A lively, leesy texture adds some interest, and the finish lingers. $12 (3/31/91) **80**

MARCO FELLUGA
Chardonnay 1988 $9 (9/15/89) **82**
Chardonnay 1987 $9 (9/15/89) **80**

FOSSI
Chardonnay dell'Alto Adige 1988: Thick with butter and butterscotch flavors and light on fruit, but it's stylish. Soft, easy to drink and good as far as it goes. 1,000 cases made. $11.50 (7/15/91) **82**

STELIO GALLO
Chardonnay 1987 ($NA) (9/15/89) **83**
Chardonnay 1986 ($NA) (9/15/89) **81**

JERMANN
Chardonnay 1989: Spicy and lively, with lots of earthy, oaky aromas but the fruit flavors are simple and crisp. Decent, but it could be more harmonious, especially at this price. $18 (3/31/91) **80**
Chardonnay 1987 $15 (9/15/89) **85**
Chardonnay 1985 $12 (9/15/89) **91**
Chardonnay Dreams 1988: Intense, concentrated and flavorful, with attractive grapefruit, pear and melon flavors that are framed by toasty dry oak. Well balanced toward the oaky side, drying out on the finish. Drink now. $40 (4/30/90) **86**
Chardonnay Dreams NV: Big and full flavored, with ripe flavors of pear and butterscotch, zingy lemon acidity and the rich texture of a fine white Burgundy. Has everything you want, depth, complexity, length and balance, plus a label from somewhere over the rainbow. $34 (3/31/90) **92**

MACULAN
Chardonnay 1985 $22 (9/15/89) **87**
Chardonnay Ferrata 1987 $22 (9/15/89) **90**
Chardonnay Ferrata 1986 $18 (9/15/89) **87**
Chardonnay Ferrata 1984 $25 (9/15/89) **87**

MASO CANTANGHEL
Chardonnay Altesino Vigna Piccola 1989: Nicely balanced and harmonious, with attractively modulated peach and apple aromas and flavors, nutmeg accents and a floral overtone. An ingratiating wine that should be consumed soon, while it's still fresh. $25 (1/31/91) **89**

VOLPE PASINI
Chardonnay 1987 ($NA) (9/15/89) **82**

PUIATTI
Chardonnay 1989: Very smooth but dry. A harmonious blend of buttery, oaky notes combine with peach, spice and pear flavors in a well-balanced, well-rounded package. $17 (3/31/91) **84**

GUERRIERI RIZZARDI
Chardonnay 1988 ($NA) (9/15/89) **80**

MARIN RONCO FORNAZ
Chardonnay 1988 ($NA) (9/15/89) **84**

RONCO DEL GNEMIZ
Chardonnay 1989: Ripe, generous and beautifully accented with oak nuances of nutmeg and vanilla. Peach and pear flavors fill it out nicely, and it's well balanced with acidity. Polished and harmonious. $27 (7/15/91) **88**
Chardonnay 1987 $18 (9/15/89) **90**

TORRE ROSAZZA
Chardonnay 1989: Fresh, fruity, lively and a bit rough and unpolished, but generally agreeable for its pear and lemon flavors. Drinkable now. $15 (2/15/91) **78**
Chardonnay 1988 $14 (9/15/89) **81**

TORRESELLA
Chardonnay 1988 $6 (9/15/89) **83**
Chardonnay 1986: Well made and refreshing. Light in style, with a spritzy texture, an appealing flavor of almonds and a floral aroma. Reasonably priced. $5.75 (3/31/89) **79**

VENEGAZZU
Chardonnay 1988 $8.50 (9/15/89) **77**

VIGNALTA
Chardonnay 1989: Fresh and fruity, with an appealing nutmeg and vanilla edge to the lively apple and peach aromas and flavors. Tempting to drink now, with lighter meals. $18 (8/31/91) **84**
Chardonnay Seleziòne Vendemmia 1988: Smooth, fruity and floral, medium-bodied, with moderate concentration of pear and apple flavors. Drinkable now. $18 (2/15/91) **80**

VIGNE DAL LEON
Chardonnay Tullio Zamò 1989: Fresh and fruity, with a roundness of texture that comes from a light dose of oak aging. A floral edge keeps it light, but the spice and fruit flavors persist on the long finish. $27 (7/15/91) **84**

Pinot Grigio DOC

BANEAR
Pinot Grigio Grave del Friuli 1990: Crisp and fruity. A simple wine, with orange, grapefruit and melon aromas and flavors that extend into a solid finish. Drink soon. $8 (1/31/92) **80**

LA BOATINA
Pinot Grigio Collio 1990: Stale, cardboard notes intrude on the modest applelike flavors in this dry, simple white wine. Drink soon. $14 (1/31/92) **71**

COLTERENZIO
Pinot Grigio Alto Adige 1989: Light and earthy, with modest flavors hinting at banana and lemon, but basically simple and refreshing. Drinkable now. $10 (3/31/91) **79**

ENO-FRIULIA
Pinot Grigio Collio 1990: Very light and citrusy, with hints of almond and rose petal in the aroma. A pleasant, light, dry white wine. $14 (1/31/92) **77**
Pinot Grigio Collio 1989: Earthy, somewhat vegetal aromas and flavors carry through on the palate, turning nutty and a bit floral on the finish. Drinkable now. $12 (3/31/91) **80**

LIVIO FELLUGA
Pinot Grigio Colli Orientali del Friuli 1989: Slightly candied on the palate, with spicy fruit flavors on the finish. A wine of modest dimensions that's earthy, simple, likable and drinkable now. $18 (3/31/91) **78**

GAIERHOF
Pinot Grigio Trentino 1990: Earthy grapefruit flavors dominate this lean-textured, dry wine. Drink soon. $11 (1/31/92) **75**

LIVON
Pinot Grigio Grave del Friuli Braide Grande 1989: Fruity, spicy and harmonious, with notable intensity but little complexity. Highly drinkable, if not dramatic. 825 cases made. $11 (1/31/92) **81**

PUIATTI
Pinot Grigio Collio 1990: Crisp and flavorful, with lively grapefruit and apple aromas and flavors. There's a hint of earthiness at first, but the finish is long and fruity. Attractive to drink soon. $19 (1/31/92) **82**
Pinot Grigio Collio 1989: Fruity and fresh, with flavors more reminiscent of Muscadet than Italy. Smooth and showing more personality than most. Drinkable now. $17 (3/31/91) **85**

CA' RONESCA
Pinot Grigio Colli Orientali del Friuli 1989: Crisp and fruity, with nicely balanced pear and melon flavors and a smooth texture. Drinkable now. $19 (3/31/91) **81**

SARTORI
Pinot Grigio Grave del Friuli 1990: A simple, fruity wine, with almond overtones to the basic apple and citrus flavors. Drink soon. $8 (1/31/92) **78**

SUBIDA DI MONTE
Pinot Grigio Collio 1989: Fresh, dry and austere, with modest pear and vanilla aromas and flavors and a light texture. Soft and spicy on the finish. $10.50 (7/15/91) **79**

TIEFENBRUNNER
Pinot Grigio Alto Adige 1990: Simple, fruity, soft and dry, with attractive melon and apple aromas and flavors. Seems to have a little more finesse than most Pinot Grigios. Drink soon. $11 (1/31/92) **80**
Pinot Grigio Alto Adige 1989: Fresh, fruity and lively, with generous orange-scented pear and almond aromas and flavors that persist on the finish. $10 (6/30/91) **83**

ITALY

Italy North White/ *Pinot Grigio DOC*

PETER ZEMMER
Pinot Grigio Alto Adige 1990: This solid white wine offers attractive melon and almond aromas and flavors. Drink soon. $10 (1/31/92) **76**

Other Vino da Tavola

ABBAZIA DI ROSAZZO
Ronco delle Acacie 1989: An incredibly spicy, toasty, buttery flavor is backed by concentrated pear and honey notes and wrapped in a silky-smooth texture. Hints of ginger and nutmeg resonate on the finish. Its style is matched only by its price. $36 (7/15/91) **89**
Ronco di Corte 1989: Very fruity and floral, with aromas that remind us of Gewürztraminer and mouthfilling pineapple and grapefruit flavors. Appealing for its direct fruitiness. A blend of 80 percent Sauvignon Blanc and 20 percent Pinot Bianco. $27 (7/15/91) **84**

BERTANI
Catullo 1987: Light and lively, but quite flavorful, with grapefruit, floral and melon flavors on a crisp framework. Drink now. $8 (3/31/89) **86**

FRANCO FURLAN
Tai di Castelcosa NV: Medium-bodied, with fruity aromas and abundant peach and grapefruit flavors. Well balanced with good, crisp acidity. Reminiscent of Riesling. $16 (4/30/90) **81**

JERMANN
Pinot Bianco 1989: Lively and flavorful, with lots of grapefruit, orange and litchi flavors that persist into a long finish. Has just a shade of herbal overtones. Easy to like. $18 (4/15/91) **87**
Pinot Grigio 1989: Fruity and round, with a peppery edge to the peach, pear and melon flavors. Clean and crisp on the finish. A well-made wine to drink now. $18 (3/31/91) **82**
Sauvignon Blanc 1989: Crisp and focused, with generous pear, apple and grapefruit flavors. Very bright and a bit floral on the finish. Drinkable now for the fruit. $18 (4/15/91) **84**
Vinnae da Vinnaioli 1989: Like a straightforward Chablis, it's crisp, lean and firmly structured. Grapefruit is the dominant flavor. The texture is lively and the finish is clean. $18 (4/15/91) **84**
Vintage Tunina 1989: Tart and lively, with vivid orange and grapefruit flavors that make it appealing and distinctive. A peach flavor lingers on the aftertaste. Very flavorful now, but may gain more complexity if aged until 1993 or so. $35 (4/15/91) **88**

MACULAN
Dindarello 1989: Very fresh and lively, not very sweet but generously fruity, offering pleasant fig, apricot and cinnamon aromas and flavors. Balanced and drinkable now. $24 (7/15/91) **84**
Prato di Canzio 1987: Brilliant on the palate, with apple, honey, caramel and toast flavors, round and smooth, only a bit softer than it could be. Tastes terrific. $17 (10/15/89) **83**

MASI
Masianco 1987: Lean and racy, its pear and apple fruit lifted by time in oak. A simple wine that's easy to drink now. $6.75 (5/15/89) **78**

MONTEVINO
Pinot Grigio del Veneto 1989: Simple, fruity and spicy, with pear flavors that taper off a bit on the finish. $6.50 (7/15/91) **74**

RONCO DEL GNEMIZ
Müller Thurgau 1989: Ripe and fruity, with lovely orange-scented pear and apple aromas and flavors that hint at wildflowers on the generous finish. $18 (7/15/91) **82**

SANTA MARGHERITA
Cuvée Margherita del Veneto 1988: Very light in color, with earthy, herbal aromas and flavors and little fruit to speak of on a thin frame. $11 (12/31/90) **73**

ZONIN
Pinot Grigio 1990: A simple, medium-weight wine, with modest melon and apple flavors and decidedly earthy undertones. Drink soon. $7 (1/31/92) **79**

Other White DOC

ABBAZIA DI ROSAZZO
Colli Orientali del Friuli Ribolla Gialla 1990: Simple, with firm texture and modest melon and citrus aromas and flavors. Drink soon. $21 (1/31/92) **76**
Sauvignon Colli Orientali del Friuli 1989: Spicy and floral, with fresh, light apricot and grapefruit flavors and zingy acidity. Crisp and refreshing for current enjoyment. $19 (7/15/91) **83**

ANSELMI
Soave Classico Capitel Foscarino 1989: Simple and earthy, with a nice hint of grapefruit flavor sneaking in on the finish. Pleasant enough. Tasted twice. 940 cases made. $20 (7/15/91) **76**
Soave Classico Superióre 1989: Modestly flavorful, with hints of wood and earth accenting the light floral and lemon flavors. $8 (7/15/91) **81**

BOLLA
Soave Classico Vigneti di Castellaro 1989: Soft and silky, smooth textured, with almond and floral aromas and flavors, balanced and delicate. $12 (12/31/90) **81**

BOSCAINI
Soave Classico Monteleone 1989: Charming, crisp, clean and refreshingly fruity. A good dinner-time wine, with light, floral aromas and zesty apricot and lemon flavors. $8 (6/30/91) BB **82**

CA' DEL BOSCO
Franciacorta 1989: Surprisingly tart, because the aromas and flavors seem so ripe, but a sharp thread of acidity runs through the modest pineapple, pear and honey flavors. Turns toward hazelnut on the finish. Better starting in 1993. $11 (9/15/91) **82**
Franciacorta 1988: A blend of Chardonnay and Pinot Bianco. A tart, lean style, with firm honey and nutmeg flavors and lemony grapefruit notes. Drinkable but unexciting. Drink now. Tasted twice. $17 (4/30/90) **78**

ENO-FRIULIA
Pinot Bianco Collio 1990: Ripe, round and flavorful, with medium-intense peach, spice and almond aromas and flavors and hints of vanilla on the finish. A dry, simple style that could serve as an aperitif, as well as a dinner companion. $14 (1/31/92) **78**
Tocai Friulano Collio 1990: Fresh and lively, with zingy, citrusy flavors and textures. Not especially crisp, but it's a round, friendly wine for drinking soon. $14 (1/31/92) **80**

LIVIO FELLUGA
Tocai Friulano Colli Orientali del Friuli 1989: Has nutty, spicy, earthy flavors, with a crisp texture and nice pear and caramel notes on the finish. Drinkable now. $16 (4/15/91) **81**

MARCO FELLUGA
Sauvignon Collio 1990: Flavorful, but not everyone will warm up to it, with its earthy peach and apple flavors that seem a bit dirty and dull. Drinkable now. $21 (5/15/92) **73**

LIVON
Tocai Friulano Collio Vigneto di Ruttars 1988: Smooth, round and elegant, with generous melon, pear and almond aromas and flavors, a satiny texture and enough concentration to stand up to a plate of grilled fish. $15 (12/31/90) **82**

MACULAN
Breganze Bianco Breganze di Breganze 1987: Much more character than you expect from Tocai and Pinot Grigio, it's fresh and lively, with melon and almond aromas and flavors galore, opening up to honey and apricot on the finish. $7.50 (5/15/89) BB **85**

FOSS MARAI
Prosecco di Valdobbiadene 1989: If you like dry Chenin Blanc, you'll probably like this sprightly, apple- and rose-scented fresh wine. Makes up in brightness what it lacks in depth. Drink soon. $7.50 (12/31/90) **78**

TENUTA MAZZOLINO
Oltrepò Pavese Pinot Guarnazzola 1990: Soft and pleasant, with vague vanilla and toast aromas and flavors, hinting at melon and apple on the finish. Drink soon. $15 (1/31/92) **77**

DORO PRINCIC
Pinot Bianco Collio 1989: Fresh, simple and soft in texture, with ample pear, apple and nutmeg aromas and flavors but no oak. $14 (7/15/91) **78**
Tocai Friulano Collio 1989: Fresh and crisp, like biting into a green apple. Balanced toward liveliness. A straightforward wine, with plenty of flavor. $14 (8/31/91) **82**

PUIATTI
Pinot Bianco Collio 1989: A well-made wine, with a personality of its own. Smooth and flavorful, with a nice beam of orange, cream, spice and vanilla aromas and flavors that are dry and harmonious. Drinkable now. $17 (4/15/91) **85**

RONCO DEL GNEMIZ
Tocai Friulano Colli Orientali del Friuli 1989: Smooth and fruity, with pleasant apple and pear aromas and flavors and hints of spice on the finish. $18 (8/31/91) **83**

CA' RONESCA
Sauvignon Colli Orientali del Friuli del Podere 1989: Smooth, soft and flavorful, with pleasant peach, grapefruit and almond aromas and flavors, good concentration and length. A bit herbal on the nose. Drinkable now. $19 (4/15/91) **84**

RUSSIZ SUPERIORE
Sauvignon Collio 1990: Distinct varietal characteristics, offering pungent herb aromas and a bit of delicacy on the palate, finishing strong and grassy. Drinkable now. $27 (5/15/92) **80**

SANTA SOFIA
Soave Classico Superióre 1990: Pale, fresh and slightly spicy, light textured, with pleasant almond and peach aromas and flavors. Refreshing to drink soon. A good value. $8.75 (5/15/92) **83**

SANTI
Bianco di Custoza I Frari 1990: Crisp and fruity, this lightweight wine has pleasant floral overtones and simple grapefruit and pear flavors. Drinkable now. $10 (9/15/91) **83**

SUBIDA DI MONTE
Sauvignon Collio 1989: A Danish pastry of a wine, with aromas that include lots of butter, cinnamon, hazelnut and almond. Very unusual for a Sauvignon Blanc and light on fruit flavor, but one of the most distinctive white wines we've tasted in years. $11 (7/15/91) **87**

TIEFENBRUNNER
Pinot Bianco Alto Adige 1989: Crisp and fruity, with strong floral overtones, hinting at orange blossom and shoe polish and finishing with lime and pear notes. Not for everyone, but it has intensity and character. Tasted twice. $9 (8/31/91) **78**

VENICA
Tocai Friulano Collio 1989: Very dry, but surprisingly soft, with toasty, ever-so-slightly bitter flavors that need a good plate of fish to bring them into balance. Drink soon. $15 (2/15/91) **82**

CA' VESCOVO
Aquieleia 1989: Light and simple, with modest melon and earth aromas and flavors. Drink soon. 3,500 cases made. $9 (1/31/92) **75**

LA VIARTE
Colli Orientali del Friuli Ribolla 1988: Smooth and delicately fruity, offering fresh melon, peach and grapefruit aromas and flavors and a touch of vanilla. Has good length, turning steely and refreshing on the finish. Drinkable now. $18 (12/31/90) **85**
Sauvignon Colli Orientali del Friuli 1989: Classic varietal characteristics, from the grassy, sweet pea aromas to the grapefruit and herb flavors, with crisp acidity and good sense of concentration. A serious, assertive wine that may benefit from aging until 1993. $19 (7/15/91) **83**

VIGNE DAL LEON
Tocai Friulano Colli Orientali del Friuli 1989: An odd minty edge keeps getting in the way of the fruit in this light, simple wine. Not for everyone. $18 (7/15/91) **77**

ZENATO
Bianco di Custoza Sole del Benaco 1989: Light and fresh, with appealing pear and vanilla aromas and flavors. $9 (6/30/91) **80**
Lugana San Benedetto 1989: Light, simple and fresh, with hints of almond and pear flavors. $9.25 (7/15/91) **77**

Piedmont Red/*Barbaresco DOCG*

BAVA
Barbaresco 1982: Ripe, spicy and generous, with plenty of cherry, currant and anise aromas and flavors and hints of smoke and nutmeg on the long finish. The ample tannins still need until 1995 to '98 to resolve themselves. 2,500 cases made. $23 (4/30/91) **83**

BERSANO
Barbaresco 1983: Lighter than you'd expect from Barbaresco. Mature with a range of aromas and flavors that compete for your attention—bay leaf, tea, leather, raspberries and anise. Very smooth. Drink now. $7.75 (1/31/89) **79**
Barbaresco 1975 ($NA) (9/15/88) (HS) **76**
Barbaresco 1971 ($NA) (9/15/88) (HS) **78**
Barbaresco 1964 ($NA) (9/15/88) (HS) **85**

Key to Symbols

The scores reported here are the results of blind tastings conducted by our panel of senior editors. Wines that carry the initials below are results of individual tastings.

THE WINE SPECTATOR 100-POINT SCALE ***95-100***—Classic, a great wine; ***90-94***—Outstanding, superior character and style; ***80-89***—Good to very good, a wine with special qualities; ***70-79***—Average, drinkable wine that may have minor flaws; ***60-69***—Below average, drinkable but not recommended; ***50-59***—Poor, undrinkable, not recommended. "+"—With a score indicates a range; used primarily with barrel tastings to indicate a preliminary score.

SPECIAL DESIGNATIONS SS—Spectator Selection, CS—Cellar Selection, BB—Best Buy, ($NA)—Price not available, (NR)—Not released.

TASTER'S INITIALS (JG)—Jim Gordon, (HS)—Harvey Steiman, (JL)—James Laube, (JS)—James Suckling, (TM)—Thomas Matthews, (TR)—Terry Robards, (PM)—Per-Henrik Mansson, (BT)—Barrel Tasting (these wines were tasted blind from barrel samples), (CA-date)—*California's Great Cabernets* by James Laube, (CH-date)—*California's Great Chardonnays* by James Laube, (VP-date)—*Vintage Port* by James Suckling.

DATE TASTED Dates in parentheses represent the issue in which the rating was published.

LA CA' NOVA
Barbaresco 1986: Complex and fascinating, with plenty of tannins but good balance that shows off the anise, floral and raspberry aromas and flavors. Long and complex, packing plenty of punch now. Give it until 1994 to '98 to absorb the tannins. $14.50 (10/31/90) **87**

CA' ROME
Barbaresco 1985: Powerful, focused, concentrated and massive, loaded with ripe raspberry, anise and smoke aromas and flavors; spicy and complex. Not for the faint of heart but with cellaring until at least 1993 to 1995, this should be a beauty. 292 cases made. $28 (1/31/90) **88**
Barbaresco Maria di Brun 1985: Very firm, tannic and austere, with hints of spice and earthiness on the reined-in raspberry and anise aromas and flavors that grow more complex on the finish. Drink in 1993. $37 (1/31/90) **92**

CANTINA DEL GLICINE
Barbaresco 1985: Tight, light, tannic and not very generous in flavor, but boasts plenty of rough tannins. Seems thin and drying on the palate. An old-style wine that could repay cellaring until 1995 to 2000, but we're skeptical. $27 (8/31/91) **75**

CAVALOTTO
Barbaresco Vigna San Giuseppe Riserva 1985: Ripe and generous, but not a huge wine. Classic raspberry and anise aromas and flavors are balanced with hints of orange peel and brown sugar that emerge on the finish. A bit hot on the finish, but the alcohol and tannin should carry it well past 1995 to '98. 1,000 cases made. $22 (2/28/91) **90**

CERETTO
Barbaresco Asij 1987: Earthy and spicy, with hard, drying tannins, but it also has plenty of ripe raspberry, anise, herb and spice notes. A rich and complex wine that needs until about 1996 before it's ready. Tasted twice. $22 (7/15/91) **86**
Barbaresco Asij 1985: Earthy, swampy, gamy, harsh and tannic. Tasted three times. $15 (1/31/90) **64**
Barbaresco Bricco Asili Bricco Asili 1987: A smooth, polished style that allows the generous plum, raspberry and currant aromas and flavors to emerge, echoing plum and vanilla on the finish. You can feel the roundness and balance contributed by aging in small oak barrels. Almost drinkable, but better after 1994 or '95. Rel: $40 Cur: $50 (4/30/91) **89**
Barbaresco Bricco Asili Bricco Asili 1986: Very firm and tannic, but showing generous cherry and raspberry aromas and flavors with hints of anise and toast. An complex, earthy style that needs cellaring until at least 1995, but it will always be tannic. $35 (4/15/90) **85**
Barbaresco Bricco Asili Bricco Asili 1985: Thick and concentrated with lush anise, black cherry, raspberry and spice flavor that is already showing signs of complexity and depth. The roundness of the tannins suggests it should be ready in three to five years but could probably age up to 20. A full nelson tannic finish. Drink 1995 to 2005. 603 cases made. Rel: $35 Cur: $41 (8/31/89) **89**
Barbaresco Bricco Asili Bricco Asili 1984 Rel: $15 Cur: $20 (9/15/88) (HS) **80**
Barbaresco Bricco Asili Bricco Asili 1982 Rel: $19 Cur: $63 (9/15/88) (HS) **87**
Barbaresco Bricco Asili Bricco Asili 1978 $55 (3/01/86) (JS) **90**
Barbaresco Bricco Asili Bricco Asili 1976 ($NA) (9/15/88) (HS) **89**
Barbaresco Bricco Asili Bricco Asili 1974 ($NA) (3/01/86) (JS) **90**
Barbaresco Bricco Asili Faset 1987: Firm, concentrated and tannic, with a rich core of anise, raspberry, currant and vanilla flavors. A distinct earthiness comes through on the palate and finish. This gutsy wine needs cellaring until 1995 or '96. $31 (7/15/91) **89**
Barbaresco Bricco Asili Faset 1985: Very spicy and rich in fruit, held in check by prominent tannins, but the beautifully defined anise and raspberry aromas and flavors emerge through the tannin. Needs until 1997 to 2000 to soften. $31 (1/31/90) **87**

MICHELE CHIARLO
Barbaresco Rabajà 1988: Rich and seductive, with a tight, tannic core of currant, cherry, anise and raspberry flavors. Doesn't overpower, but comes at you with a full chorus of fruit that's smooth and supple—for a young Barbaresco. Try after 1996. 400 cases made. $47 (1/31/92) **90**

FRATELLI CIGLIUTI
Barbaresco Serraboella 1986: Firmly tannic and thick with tightly reined-in black cherry and spice flavors that are closed and dense on the palate. Best to lay this one down for five to seven years. Try in 1994. $20 (8/31/89) **86**

GUASTI CLEMENTE & FIGLI
Barbaresco 1978: Mature and complex, with smoke, raspberry, anise and tar flavors, but still a bit rough around the edges. From an excellent vintage. Near its peak. Drink now to 1998. 4,500 cases made. $20 (1/31/92) **84**

LE COLLINE
Barbaresco Riserva Spéciale 1979 $15 (7/31/87) **79**

GIUSEPPE CORTESE
Barbaresco 1982 $19 (12/15/88) **85**
Barbaresco Rabajà 1986: The remarkably rich, complex and concentrated cherry, tar, leather, spice and cola flavors are very well structured, with good acidity and firm but not overpowering tannins. A well-proportioned Barbaresco that's complex and enticing. Drink 1993 to 2000. $19 (9/15/90) **89**
Barbaresco Rabajà 1983: Hard-edged structure, medicinal flavors and a high level of earthiness make this a hard wine to get excited about, although the core of raspberry flavor makes it worth cellaring until 1993 to see what develops. $18 (1/31/90) **75**
Barbaresco Rabajà 1981: Tired and extremely earthy; the barnyard and spicy anise flavors are very mature and tarry on the finish. It's drinkable and may appeal to some more than others. Try with a wedge of cheese. $12 (8/31/89) **72**
Barbaresco Spéciale 1983: Very ripe and fully mature; the ripe plum and spice flavors are rich and attractive, and the tannins have softened. Drink now through 1995. $13 (8/31/89) **79**

FONTANAFREDDA
Barbaresco 1983 $11.50 (9/15/88) (HS) **80**
Barbaresco 1982 ($NA) (9/15/88) (HS) **81**
Barbaresco 1978 ($NA) (9/15/88) (HS) **86**

DE FORVILLE
Barbaresco 1981 $14 (2/16/86) **63**

GAJA
Barbaresco 1988: Firm, tight and earthy, with intense raspberry, plum, berry and anise flavors that gain a touch of tea and spice. Complex and long; needs cellaring until 1998. $65 (4/30/92) **91**
Barbaresco 1986: Complex and aromatic, with spice, anise and toast aromas mingling with generous Nebbiolo flavor. Plenty of tannin, too; the sort that clamps down after two or three seconds on the palate and doesn't let go. Cellaring until 1995 should bring it into balance, and then it should have a long life. Rel: $47 Cur: $54 (1/31/90) CS **92**
Barbaresco 1985 Rel: $45 Cur: $77 (12/15/88) CS **95**
Barbaresco 1983 Rel: $35 Cur: $50 (9/15/89) (HS) **93**
Barbaresco 1982 $95 (9/15/89) (HS) **93**
Barbaresco 1981 $95 (9/15/89) (HS) **90**
Barbaresco 1980 Rel: $14 Cur: $75 (7/01/85) **88**
Barbaresco 1979 $110 (9/15/89) (HS) **89**
Barbaresco 1978 $130 (9/15/89) (HS) **93**
Barbaresco 1976 $115 (9/15/89) (HS) **91**
Barbaresco 1974 $125 (9/15/89) (HS) **89**
Barbaresco 1971 $135 (9/15/89) (HS) **86**
Barbaresco 1967 $88 (9/15/89) (HS) **83**
Barbaresco 1964 $100 (9/15/89) (HS) **87**
Barbaresco 1961 $210 (9/15/89) (HS) **92**
Barbaresco Costa Russi 1988: A tannic, powerful young wine, offering a deep core of plum, raspberry, anise, spice and floral notes that are broad and complex. Not quite as deep as the other Gaja single-vineyard wines, but it shows a measure of elegance and finesse. Needs until 1999 at the earliest. 737 cases made. $100 (4/30/92) **92**
Barbaresco Costa Russi 1986: Thick, concentrated and closed in, with an earthy edge to the ripe cherry and raspberry flavors and a hard veneer to the somewhat coarse tannins. Will need cellaring until 1993 to '95 to resolve the tannins. Rel: $85 Cur: $109 (1/31/90) **89**
Barbaresco Costa Russi 1985 Rel: $83 Cur: $108 (12/15/88) **96**
Barbaresco Costa Russi 1982 $95 (9/15/88) (HS) **91**
Barbaresco Sorì San Lorenzo 1988: Deep, concentrated and powerful, with bare-knuckle tannins that stand up to the ripe, rich, earthy currant, chocolate, vanilla and raspberry flavors. Dense and complex, a real mouthful, with a fantastic finish. Will need until 2000 at the earliest. 877 cases made. $125 (4/30/92) CS **96**
Barbaresco Sorì San Lorenzo 1986: Ripe, generous and round, wrapped in a blanket of fine but abundant tannins, the basic raspberry flavor gaining interest from overtones of anise and earthiness. Sharply focused and elegant. Needs cellaring until at least 1994. Rel: $89 Cur: $109 (1/31/90) **91**
Barbaresco Sorì San Lorenzo 1985 Rel: $88 Cur: $150 (12/15/88) **96**
Barbaresco Sorì San Lorenzo 1983 $95 (9/15/88) (HS) **90**
Barbaresco Sorì Tildin 1988: A ripe, intense, deeply concentrated wine that has a seam of elegance and finesse. The rich raspberry, anise, plum and spice flavors are braced by crisp acidity and firm, fine tannins. Has all the ingredients for greatness, but needs until 1998 to soften. 832 cases made. $125 (4/30/92) **92**
Barbaresco Sorì Tildin 1986: Very rich, smooth and opulent, with generous raspberry and cherry aromas and flavors that carry through the long finish. Very fine tannins and firm acidity are folded neatly into a silky, polished wine that is bordering on drinkability already. Probably best after 1993. Rel: $94 Cur: $105 (1/31/90) **93**
Barbaresco Sorì Tildin 1985 Rel: $94 Cur: $120 (9/15/89) (HS) **98**
Barbaresco Sorì Tildin 1983 $95 (9/15/89) (HS) **88**
Barbaresco Sorì Tildin 1982 $130 (9/15/89) (HS) **94**
Barbaresco Sorì Tildin 1981 $140 (9/15/89) (HS) **87**
Barbaresco Sorì Tildin 1979 $195 (9/15/89) (HS) **89**
Barbaresco Sorì Tildin 1978 $200 (9/15/89) (HS) **90**
Barbaresco Sorì Tildin 1973 $150 (9/15/89) (HS) **88**
Barbaresco Sorì Tildin 1971 $180 (9/15/89) (HS) **91**
Barbaresco Sorì Tildin 1970 $220 (9/15/89) (HS) **78**

BRUNO GIACOSA
Barbaresco 1985: Not very friendly now, rough and tannic, but with time it should blossom into something more attractive. The fruit is rich and dense, with anise, currant and raspberry notes. The tannins are something else. Drink 1996 to 2004. $42 (8/31/89) **84**
Barbaresco 1983 $24 (7/31/87) **88**
Barbaresco Gallina di Neive 1986: Has the classic raspberry and anise aromas and flavors of Barbaresco, with spicy strawberry and floral nuances on the finish. A craftily balanced, graceful wine that needs until 1995 to '98 to begin to show what it has. $40 (8/31/91) **88**
Barbaresco Santo Stefano 1982 $57 (9/15/88) **92**
Barbaresco Santo Stefano di Neive 1986: Ripe and fragrant, with hard tannins that keep the flavors firmly in check. The anise, smoke and raspberry flavors are pleasant enough and should come through with cellaring through 1994 to '96. $62 (8/31/91) **83**
Barbaresco Santo Stefano di Neive Riserva 1985: Tannic, bitter overtones tend to overshadow the modest level of flavor, which focuses on anise, making this a difficult wine to appreciate. Seems too rough ever to be balanced. Try in 1995. $60 (8/31/91) **77**
Barbaresco Santo Stefano di Neive Riserva 1982 $60 (9/15/88) (HS) **90**

GIACOSA FRATELLI
Barbaresco 1986: With intense, complex tar, rose petal, raspberry and spice notes, this has plenty of flavor and a sense of elegance and finesse. The tannins are firm and crisp, but held in check, and the finish is long and lingering. Drink in 1993 to '99. 2,500 cases made. $17 (7/15/91) **87**
Barbaresco Sorì Secondine 1986: A thick veil of tannins obscure the modest flavor intensity, burying the relatively delicate berry and earthy flavors before they have a chance to emerge. 2,000 cases made. $11.50 (10/31/90) **72**

MARCHESI DI BAROLO
Barbaresco Rio Sordo 1988: Rich and intense, with deeply concentrated plum, currant, raspberry and anise flavors that have razor-sharp acidity and firm, gritty tannins. Best to be patient. Drink after 1997. $18 (1/31/92) **86**

MARCHESI DI GRESY
Barbaresco Camp Gros Martinenga 1985: Very tannic, but the flavors are sensational—ripe raspberry, plum and anise keep tripping over each other in their exuberance—beautifully concentrated and showing some elegance already. Drink in 1994 to 1999. 1,030 cases made. Rel: $58 Cur: $70 (1/31/89) **92**
Barbaresco Camp Gros Martinenga 1983 Rel: $30 Cur: $76 (9/15/88) (HS) **88**
Barbaresco Camp Gros Martinenga 1982 $26 (9/15/88) (HS) **89**
Barbaresco Camp Gros Martinenga 1979 $40 (9/15/88) (HS) **88**
Barbaresco Gaiun Martinenga 1986: Attractive aromas of vanilla, spice and cherry are elegant and well proportioned, and the supple, smooth fruit flavors verge on sweetness. Chocolate and vanilla notes emerge on the finish. The tannins are there to carry it through the decade, but you can uncork a bottle around 1994 to catch it on its way up. $64 (9/15/90) **90**
Barbaresco Gaiun Martinenga 1985: Deep, rich and full-bodied, with ripe cherry, plum and raspberry flavor. With its satiny texture beneath a veil of tannin, it's a very impressive wine now. It's also very long and elegant. Probably at its best from 1995 to 2000. 1,030 cases made. Rel: $55 Cur: $72 (1/31/89) CS **95**
Barbaresco Gaiun Martinenga 1983 Rel: $30 Cur: $76 (9/15/88) (HS) **84**
Barbaresco Gaiun Martinenga 1982 $26 (9/15/88) (HS) **87**
Barbaresco Martinenga 1986: Has lots of fresh, ripe fruit flavor. The intense cherry, strawberry, anise and spice notes are elegant and well balanced, with crisp acidity and smooth tannins. It picks up vanilla and brown sugar notes on the aftertaste. Drink in 1993 to '98. $56 (9/15/90) **88**
Barbaresco Martinenga 1985: Rich and earthy, with overtones of mint and anise, very tannic, full-bodied and concentrated. Needs lots of cellar time for the raspberry flavor to emerge. Drink in 1995 to 2000. Rel: $39 Cur: $52 (1/31/89) **90**
Barbaresco Martinenga 1984 Rel: $20 Cur: $38 (9/15/88) (HS) **84**
Barbaresco Martinenga 1983 Rel: $20 Cur: $62 (9/15/88) (HS) **87**
Barbaresco Martinenga 1982 Rel: $20 Cur: $70 (9/15/88) (HS) **86**
Barbaresco Martinenga 1979 $30 (9/15/88) (HS) **81**
Barbaresco Martinenga 1978 $40 (9/15/88) (HS) **89**

GIUSEPPE MASCARELLO & FIGLIO
Barbaresco Marcarini 1985: Impressive for its intensity and flavor; this 1985 is rich with plum, anise, tar and raspberry flavors and firm, drying tannins. Will need three to five years to develop fully, but it should be worth the wait. Drink 1994 to 2000. $30 (8/31/89) **85**

MOCCAGATTA
Barbaresco Bric Balin 1987: Rich and firm, with tight anise, raspberry, chocolate and rose petal notes and very crisp tannins. Has good depth and intensity, and the fruit comes through on the finish. Drink in 1996 to 2002. $28 (7/15/91) **89**
Barbaresco Vigneto Basarin 1987: Spice, anise, raspberry and toast flavors are ripe and concen-

trated, and hints of chocolate and vanilla emerge before the tannins take hold and dry out the finish. Will require patience. Best between 1996 and 2001. $23 (7/15/91) **86**

CASTELLO DI NEIVE
Barbaresco Vigneto Santo Stefano 1987: Hard and tight, with austere tea, orange peel and nut flavors, but without much depth or generosity. Perhaps it will fill out with time, but for now it could use some flavor. Start drinking in 1993 to '95. Tasted twice. $20 (12/31/90) **79**
Barbaresco Vigneto Santo Stefano 1982 $27 (9/15/88) (HS) **86**

ODDERO
Barbaresco 1982 $15 (9/15/88) **84**

ELIA PASQUERO
Barbaresco Sorì Paitin 1985: Tough in texture but explosive in flavor, shining a bright beam of raspberry, coffee and vanilla flavors through the somewhat tannic structure. Already has impressive complexity and length, it just needs softening from cellaring until 1993 to '95. $14 (3/31/90) **88**

PRODUTTORI DEL BARBARESCO
Barbaresco 1988: Tart, tight, crisp and full of flavor, with intense raspberry, cherry, anise and tea notes. Firmly tannic, but has a nice sense of proportion. Best around 1996. $16 (4/30/92) **86**
Barbaresco 1986: Relatively light and elegant, but marvelously focused and concentrated, with brilliant raspberry, anise, earth and nutmeg aromas and flavors playing across the tongue. Needs until 1995 to shed its excess tannin. $12 (10/31/90) **90**
Barbaresco 1984 $12 (9/15/88) (HS) **80**
Barbaresco 1983 $17 (9/15/88) (HS) **85**
Barbaresco 1982 $16 (9/15/88) (HS) **87**
Barbaresco 1979 $17 (9/15/88) (HS) **90**
Barbaresco Asili Riserva 1985: Earthy aromas and flavors add depth and complexity to the concentrated cherry and raspberry flavors in this broad, chewy, firmly tannic wine. It's beautifully proportioned, but needs until at least 1995 to develop fully. $27 (10/31/90) **92**
Barbaresco Asili Riserva 1982 $22 (9/15/88) (HS) **89**
Barbaresco Moccagatta Riserva 1982 $22 (9/15/88) (HS) **89**
Barbaresco Montefico Riserva 1982 $22 (9/15/88) (HS) **85**
Barbaresco Montefico Riserva 1978 $22 (9/15/88) (HS) **92**
Barbaresco Montestefano Riserva 1985: A lighter style, but it's still tannic and firm in structure, offering a nice burst of raspberry and anise flavors before the tannins sweep in to keep it under wraps. Worth holding until 1995 to '98. $25 (10/31/90) **82**
Barbaresco Montestefano Riserva 1982 Rel: $18 Cur: $22 (9/15/88) (HS) **88**
Barbaresco Ovello Riserva 1985: Earthy, raspberry and tar aromas and flavors are classic—so are the tannins, which swarm over the fruit on the long finish. A big wine that needs until 1998 to 2000 to show what it has. $25 (10/31/90) **86**
Barbaresco Ovello Riserva 1982 $22 (9/15/88) (HS) **86**
Barbaresco Paje Riserva 1982 $22 (9/15/88) (HS) **91**
Barbaresco Pora Riserva 1982 $18 (9/15/88) (HS) **91**
Barbaresco Pora Riserva 1979 $24 (9/15/88) (HS) **91**
Barbaresco Rabajà Riserva 1982 $22 (9/15/88) (HS) **89**
Barbaresco Rio Sordo Riserva 1982 $22 (9/15/88) (HS) **87**
Barbaresco Seleziòne del Trentennio "30" 1988: Intense and concentrated, with sharply focused cherry, raspberry, anise and rose petal flavors that are deep and complex. The tannins and acidity taste raw. Very tightly wound. Cellar until 1999 for best results. 2,000 cases made. $28 (4/30/92) **91**

PRUNOTTO
Barbaresco 1987: Earthy and dirty with mushroomy flavors overriding the raspberry and cherry notes that turn bitter on the finish. Tasted twice, with consistent notes. $27 (3/31/92) **70**
Barbaresco Montestefano 1987: Leathery, earthy and tannic, a tough wine to warm up to. If you can taste past the tannins, there's a core of dense tar, anise and raspberry flavor. But it needs time. Try after 1998. Tasted twice, with consistent notes. 820 cases made. $37 (3/31/92) **76**
Barbaresco Montestefano 1986: Focused and balanced, with earth, smoke, toast, plum and tea notes and tannins that are firm, but not as overbearing as a Barbaresco can be. Has an elegant style that should allow it to be approachable by 1993 to '95. $37 (12/31/90) **86**
Barbaresco Montestefano 1985: A big departure in style for Prunotto—much smoother and less tannic—with sharply focused raspberry, vanilla and anise aromas and flavors that are firmly supported by fine tannins and a velvety texture. Drink now to 1994. $29 (3/31/90) **87**
Barbaresco Rabajà Riserva 1982 $19 (7/31/87) **81**

FRANCESCO RINALDI & FIGLI
Barbaresco 1985: A very firm and tannic wine, with raspberry, tea, anise and tar aromas and flavors that are focused and distinctive. Will need cellaring until 1998 to 2000 to bring out all the subtlety and cinnamon notes and subdue the tannins. $23 (9/15/90) **87**
Barbaresco 1983: Briny, oysterlike aromas detract from a generally smooth and subtle wine that's light for a Barbaresco. Simple and tasty, once you get past the odd aromas. $16 (1/31/89) **79**

ALFREDO & GIOVANNI ROAGNA
Barbaresco 1986: Firm and tight, with hard-edged cherry, earth, tar and spice notes that don't bend much now. With time the tannins should be less powerful, but this needs cellaring until about 1995, and then it should age well through the decade and beyond. $26 (7/15/91) **86**
Barbaresco 1985: Very tasty and beautifully balanced, but hidden in a shell of tannins that should need until 1995 to break apart. The raspberry and plum flavor could be a bit more concentrated, but this is a classic that should reward cellaring. $27 (2/28/89) **89**

SCARPA
Barbaresco 1981 $20 (9/15/88) (HS) **84**
Barbaresco 1979 $20 (9/15/88) (HS) **90**
Barbaresco 1978 $27 (9/15/88) (HS) **90**
Barbaresco 1974 $30 (9/15/88) (HS) **89**
Barbaresco I Tetti di Neive 1978 $27 (3/15/87) **83**

LE TERRE FORTI
Barbaresco 1982: Made in the old style, with mature, smoky aromas and flavors and hints of vanilla and elegant cherry fading on the finish. It's nearing its peak and should be consumed between now and 1995. $19 (9/15/90) **77**

Key to Symbols

The scores reported here are the results of blind tastings conducted by our panel of senior editors. Wines that carry the initials below are results of individual tastings.

THE WINE SPECTATOR 100-POINT SCALE 95-100—Classic, a great wine; ***90-94***—Outstanding, superior character and style; ***80-89***—Good to very good, a wine with special qualities; ***70-79***—Average, drinkable wine that may have minor flaws; ***60-69***—Below average, drinkable but not recommended; ***50-59***—Poor, undrinkable, not recommended. "+"—With a score indicates a range; used primarily with barrel tastings to indicate a preliminary score.

SPECIAL DESIGNATIONS SS—Spectator Selection, CS—Cellar Selection, BB—Best Buy, ($NA)—Price not available, (NR)—Not released.

TASTER'S INITIALS (JG)—Jim Gordon, (HS)—Harvey Steiman; (JL)—James Laube, (JS)—James Suckling, (TM)—Thomas Matthews, (TR)—Terry Robards, (PM)—Per-Henrik Mansson, (BT)—Barrel Tasting (these wines were tasted blind from barrel samples), (CA-date)—*California's Great Cabernets* by James Laube, (CH-date)—*California's Great Chardonnays* by James Laube, (VP-date)—*Vintage Port* by James Suckling.

DATE TASTED Dates in parentheses represent the issue in which the rating was published.

TRAVERSA
Barbaresco Sorì Ciabot 1985: Still rough and tough, with intense and concentrated smoke, tar, rose petal and plum flavors, it's firmly tannic and well balanced with toasty oak. Best to try in 1994 to '96. $23 (9/15/90) **86**

VALFIERI
Barbaresco 1986: Tough, intense and tannic, with spice and earth notes adding to the ripe cherry and anise flavors. The tannins and acidity dominate. Best to cellar until 1994 or '95 at the earliest. $12 (9/15/90) **82**
Barbaresco 1985: Light in color but tough and tannic, it's already mature. Old-fashioned, without enough concentration and texture to mature gracefully. $8.25 (7/31/89) **70**

VIETTI
Barbaresco 1985: Powerful, concentrated and ferociously tannic, showing very clean raspberry and anise aromas and flavors. Rough rather than refined. By 1995 it should be tame enough to approach cautiously, but it will never be elegant. $28 (7/31/89) **81**
Barbaresco 1982 $15 (7/31/87) **84**
Barbaresco della Località Rabajà 1986: Ripe and generous, with heavy-duty tannins keeping the sweet raspberry and toast flavors in check. Needs time to shed the tannins, but there is plenty of flavor to emerge in 1995 to '98. $18 (10/31/90) **87**

Barbera DOC

ELIO ALTARE
Barbera d'Alba 1989: Exuberantly fruity and flavorful, supported by crisp acidity and rich tannins, and bursting with blackberry, raspberry and currant flavors that echo on the long finish. Beautifully balanced and built to keep developing well beyond 1995. 250 cases made. $13 (3/15/91) **91**
Barbera d'Alba 1988: With beautifully defined cherry and raspberry aromas and flavors, firm texture and fair concentration and length, this wine announces itself as a cut above the usual Barbera. Has finesse and grace. Drink now. $10 (3/31/90) **84**
Barbera d'Alba 1987: Amazingly rich, smooth and supple, a first-rate wine that's lush with seductive vanilla, plum, currant and cherry flavors that are enticing to drink now, but it has the depth and concentration to last more than a decade. Barbera doesn't get much better. 1,000 cases made. $12 (8/31/89) **92**

BENI DI BATASIOLO
Barbera d'Alba 1989: Round in texture and generous in flavor, with fine plum, wild berry and vanilla aromas and flavors, hinting at anise on the finish. Fruit flavors are appealing. Drinkable now. $11.50 (2/15/92) **84**
Barbera d'Alba 1988: Lean and crisply focused, with a bright beam of raspberry and strawberry flavors shaded by vanilla and rose petal notes, all supported by tingly acidity. Nicely balanced and flavorful, and drinkable now for its lively fruit. Tasted twice. $10.50 (4/15/91) **88**

BAVA
Barbera d'Asti 1985: Lean and focused, with lots of berry aromas and flavors. Smooth and very fine in texture and a bit tart, but rounded at the edges. Drinkable now, but feels like it can develop through 1994. $13 (3/15/91) **87**

BERSANO
Barbera d'Asti 1987: Very light and lean, with mature flavors hinting at caramel and dried fruit. A bit simple and grapey on the palate, but drinkable now. $9 (3/15/91) **80**

LUIGI CALDI
Barbera d'Asti 1985: A pretty nice drink, with the characteristic smoky, plummy, spicy aromas and flavors. The tart finish may not be for everyone, but it shows an earthy character that makes it interesting. $7 (7/31/89) **78**

CASETTA
Barbera d'Alba Vigna Lazaretto 1987: A lively, fruity and generous wine, with concentrated ripe raspberry and blackberry aromas and flavors and hints of anise and toast on the long finish. Reaching drinkability. 3,000 cases made. $9 (3/15/91) BB **89**

PIO CESARE
Barbera d'Alba 1987: Tart and tannic, with sharply focused blackberry and raspberry flavors. Will need until 1994 or '95 to grow into its acidity. $12 (4/15/91) **81**
Barbera d'Alba 1985 $11.50 (11/15/88) **78**

MICHELE CHIARLO
Barbera d'Asti Granduca Superióre 1989: A crisp, tart style, with generous raspberry and blackberry aromas and flavors that persist on the lively finish. Drinkable now, but it may be best around 1994. $10 (2/15/92) **84**
Barbera d'Asti Superióre 1986: Smooth, mature and mellow, with enough lively acidity to balance the medium-weight, ripe fruit and game flavors. Long and cedary on the finish. Reaching full maturity; drink now. $18 (3/15/91) **86**
Barbera d'Asti Superióre Valle del Sole 1987: Firm and spicy, with lots of anise-tinged plum and toast aromas and flavors, moderate tannins and a definite thwack of limy acidity on the finish. Approaching drinkability. $19 (2/15/92) **84**

FRATELLI CIGLIUTI
Barbera d'Alba Serraboella 1989: Deeply colored and deeply flavored, with ripe cherry and berry flavors, firm tannins and good acidity. A bit tart to drink now, best to cellar until about 1993. $15 (11/30/91) **87**

CLERICO
Barbera d'Alba 1988: Light, lively and deftly balanced, with a crisp texture, lots of raspberry and spice aromas and flavors and well-integrated tannins. Easy to like; drinkable now. $12 (3/15/91) **84**
Barbera d'Alba 1987: A Dolcetto style that's fresh, crisp and lively with pretty raspberry, plum and smoky notes, finishing with spice and cedar. Drink now slightly chilled. $8 (8/31/89) **85**
Barbera d'Alba 1985 $8.25 (11/30/87) **84**

CONTERNO FANTINO
Barbera d'Alba Vignota 1989: A dense wine, bursting at the seams with raspberry and blackberry flavors that are lean and sharply focused. Brilliant magenta in color, intense, but not especially deep. Drink now through 1993 or '94. $20 (3/15/91) **86**

LUIGI COPPO
Barbera d'Asti Camp du Rouss 1988: Typically very spicy and lean in texture, but spicy, cedary overtones add extra dimension to the ripe berry and cherry flavors. Drinkable now, but should improve through 1993 or '94. $21 (3/15/91) **88**
Barbera d'Asti Camp du Rouss 1986: Beautifully crafted, with polished texture, persistent raspberry and cherry flavors, framed with the toast and vanilla aromas and flavors of oak. Fine tannins could use until 1993 to soften, but the wine is delicious now. $19 (3/31/90) **87**
Barbera d'Asti Pomorosso 1987: Finely focused, with a smooth texture and wonderful, concentrated anise-tinged raspberry, plum and cola aromas and flavors. A stylish, complex wine that's built to continue evolving at least through 1994. Drinkable now. 271 cases made. $41 (3/15/91) **90**
Barbera d'Asti Pomorosso 1986: Light in color, with cedary, spicy flavors, this mature, earthy wine tries to be elegant rather than weighty—and succeeds. Light on fruit, but tasty and long on the finish. Drinkable now. $41 (3/15/91) **84**

CORINO
Barbera d'Alba Vigna Giachini 1989: Unusually deep, rich and complex, with focused, concen-

trated blackberry, spice and chocolate flavors that linger on the finish. The right touch of oak adds an extra dimension. Graceful and delicious. Try now to 1994. 300 cases made. $14 (11/30/91) **91**

GIUSEPPE CORTESE

Barbera d'Alba 1990: Extremely tart, unripe berries mixed with gamy smells that are not appealing. $12 (2/15/92) **71**

Barbera d'Alba 1989: Lively, generous and exuberantly fruity, offering plenty of blackberry, raspberry and plum flavors against the support of juicy acidity. The flavors linger nicely. Drinkable now, but should be fine through 1995. $11 (7/15/91) **86**

Barbera d'Alba 1988: Ripe, rich and concentrated, brimming over with cherry, raspberry and currant aromas and flavors, shaded by spicy oak and supported by crisp acidity and well-integrated tannins. Enjoy now for its brilliant aromas. $9 (3/15/91) **86**

RICCARDO FENOCCHIO

Barbera d'Alba Pianpolvere Soprano 1988: A bit on the oaky side, with a strong scent of pine and oak adding spice to the cherry and raspberry aromas and flavors. Tart and lively on the finish and drinkable now, but it wouldn't hurt to give it until 1993 or '94 to let the oak settle in. 829 cases made. $10 (3/15/91) **84**

Barbera d'Alba Pianpolvere Soprano 1987: Very light in color and mature on the nose, but still light and fruity on the palate. A lean wine, with a narrow band of flavors. Drinkable now. 772 cases made. $10 (3/15/91) **75**

Barbera d'Alba Pianpolvere Soprano 1986: Lean and firm, but filled smoothly with delicate leather and wild strawberry flavors; it's a bit spicy on the nose, finishing long and flavorful. Firm acidity, but not out of balance. $8.50 (3/15/89) **83**

Barbera d'Alba Pianpolvere Soprano 1985 $15 (3/15/91) **86**

GAJA

Barbera d'Alba Vignarey 1987: Dominated by oak, but sweet and spicy. A rich, round wine that keeps pumping flavor on the long finish. Has jammy blackberry and plum flavors shaded by cedar and chocolate that squeeze between the tannin and crisp acidity. Cellar until 1994. 780 cases made. $35 (4/15/91) **88**

Barbera d'Alba Vignarey 1986: Ripe raspberry, plum and cedar aromas and flavors play off each other in this crisp-textured, firm, flavor-packed wine. Seems expansive and broad as the flavors develop. Approachable, but can use until 1993 or '94 to further soften the tannins. 1,100 cases made. $27 (3/15/91) **88**

Barbera d'Alba Vignarey 1984 $13 (2/15/87) **82**

BRUNO GIACOSA

Barbera d'Alba Altavilla d'Alba 1987: Focused, concentrated raspberry and cranberry aromas clash a bit with a strong earthy undercurrent, turning somewhat metallic on the finish. A tough wine that may or may not come around after cellaring until 1994 or '95. 900 cases made. $12 (3/15/91) **73**

Barbera d'Alba Altavilla d'Alba 1986: Very mature, tart, leathery and slightly medicinal, but it still has acceptable balance and flavor, turning gamy on the finish. Drink now. 816 cases made. $12 (3/15/91) **77**

GIACOSA FRATELLI

Barbera d'Alba Maria Gioana 1986: Not a big wine, but harmonious and attractive in flavor, offering pleasant raspberry and cherry flavors at the core, with firm, well-integrated tannins and a smooth texture on the finish. Could use time to soften. 2,000 cases made. $22 (3/15/91) **86**

MARCARINI

Barbera d'Alba Ciabot Camerano 1988: Seductive, very ripe, generous and round, with concentrated, supple berry and plum flavors, lovely overtones of spice and vanilla and a long, smooth, elegant finish. Tempting to drink now, but probably better after 1993. $18 (3/15/91) **90**

MARCHESI DI BAROLO

Barbera del Monferrato 1985 $5 (9/15/87) BB **82**

Barbera del Monferrato Le Lune 1988: Earthy aromas and flavors surround a solid core of black cherry in this medium-weight, chunky wine. Drinkable now. $6 (7/15/91) **78**

GIUSEPPE MASCARELLO & FIGLIO

Barbera d'Alba Fasana 1987: Light and earthy, with hints of raspberry and spice, but it's mostly tart, tannic and not too generous. Drinkable now. $10 (3/15/91) **80**

Barbera d'Alba Fasana 1985 $9 (11/30/87) **85**

Barbera d'Alba Superióre Ginestra 1987: Spicy, peppery nuances add interest to the ripe plum and raspberry aromas and flavors in a harmonious, supple wine that's smooth enough to drink right away. Could use until 1993 to soften the finish. $11 (3/15/91) **85**

Barbera d'Alba Superióre Santo Stefano di Perno 1987: Showing lots of raspberry and anise aromas and flavors, crisp and direct, with a tart structure and an overlay of toast and vanilla. Rounder and longer than many Barberas; it's just the thing for washing down a hearty dinner. $13 (9/15/90) **83**

FATTORIA MASSARA

Barbera d'Alba 1987: Ripe and flavorful, with plenty of smoky berry and prune aromas and flavors. It's a bit on the acidic side, but tries to balance it with flavor. Not immediately welcoming. $7.75 (9/15/90) **74**

MIRAFIORE

Barbera d'Alba 1987: Ripe and more than a touch raisiny, but soft and balanced, with some nicely integrated tannins. Hints at leather on the finish. Drinkable now. $12 (4/15/91) **83**

MOCCAGATTA

Barbera d'Alba 1989: Ripe, lively and concentrated, with generous, jammy blackberry and raspberry aromas and flavors shaded lightly by oak, but mostly explosive fruit that lingers on the finish. $14 (3/15/91) **89**

NEGRO

Barbera d'Alba Nicolon 1989: Lively enough on the palate, showing lots of concentrated berry and plum flavors. Ripe, dense, dark and flavorful, marked by enough sharp acidity to want until 1994 or '95 to soften around the edges. $11.50 (3/15/91) **88**

CASTELLO DI NEIVE

Barbera d'Alba Vigneto Messoirano 1988: Firm in texture, with focused, tart berry and vanilla aromas and flavors that are modest in intensity. Could use until 1993 or '94 to settle the moderate tannins. $11 (7/15/91) **83**

Barbera d'Alba Vigneto Messoirano 1987: Earthy, stinky, barely hinting at fruit and a bit metallic. Not pleasant. Tasted twice. $11 (4/15/91) **69**

ODDERO

Barbera d'Alba 1985 $9 (7/15/88) **77**

PARUSSO

Barbera d'Alba 1988: Zinfandel fans should go for this. With herb, berry and spice aromas and flavors, a firm texture and concentrated fruit on the finish, it could be mistaken for a Zinfandel. A well-crafted wine, with plenty of personality. Best starting now. $12 (3/15/91) **85**

ELIA PASQUERO

Barbera d'Alba Sorì Paitin 1989: Very good. Emphasizes the fruit. Bright and lively, with great currant, raspberry and cherry flavors that linger on a long finish. Tempting to drink now for its freshness, but balanced to improve with aging until 1995 or later. 1,000 cases made. $10 (11/30/91) BB **88**

Barbera d'Alba Sorì Paitin 1988: Lighter than most, with nicely focused raspberry, cherry and currant aromas and flavors, crisp acidity and lively balance. Drinkable now. $8 (3/15/91) **83**

LIVIO PAVESE

Barbera d'Asti Superióre 1986: An earthy, leathery style, with lots more spice than fruit flavor, hinting at plum or raisin on the finish. Drinkable, but not exciting. Drink up. $9 (3/15/91) **76**

CASTELLO POGGIO

Barbera d'Asti 1988: Crisp and fruity, with lively, tart berry flavors that jazz up the finish. Drinkable now. 5,000 cases made. $9 (10/31/91) BB **85**

PRUNOTTO

Barbera d'Alba 1989: Crisp and lively, with sharply focused plum, blackberry and lemon aromas and flavors. Hints of anise and tobacco stay with you on the finish. Drinkable now, but best after 1993. $11 (2/15/92) **83**

Barbera d'Alba 1987: Flavorful and subtle, it unfolds its ripe berry and cherry flavors gracefully on a velvety texture. Tasty to drink now. $9.50 (3/31/90) **85**

Barbera d'Alba 1985 $8 (7/15/88) **81**

Barbera d'Alba 1983 $6 (7/15/87) BB **89**

Barbera d'Alba Pian Romualdo 1987: Full-flavored, assertive and full-bodied, there's plenty of life in this one, with intense cherry and smoke flavors and a crisp finish. Tasted twice. $14 (9/15/90) **81**

FRANCESCO RINALDI & FIGLI

Barbera d'Alba 1987: Firmly tannic but generous, with ripe plum and wild raspberry aromas and flavors polished by the scent and texture of oak. The finish is smooth and generous. Drink now. $10 (3/15/91) **87**

Barbera d'Alba 1986: Charming and very likable. A blast of vanilla on the nose preceeds the lush plum on the palate. Drink now. $9 (2/15/89) **88**

ROCCHE COSTAMAGNA

Barbera d'Alba 1988: Beautifully articulated raspberry and cherry aromas and flavors are carried on a crisp background of lively acidity, rounded out with a hint of vanilla and cedar on the nose and finish, along with a lovely echo of blackberry. Tempting to drink now, but has plenty of room to grow. Drink after 1993. 350 cases made. $11.50 (3/15/91) **90**

SCARPA

Barbera d'Asti 1985: Rich, with pretty raspberry and spice flavors and a touch of cherry, too. Lush and firm on the palate with fine balance of flavor and fruit complexity that ripples on the finish. Tasty now but probably better once the tannins settle down. Drink now to 1996. $12 (8/31/89) **88**

RENZO SEGHESIO

Barbera d'Alba 1989: Fruity, simple and crisp in texture, with firm tannins and lively acidity framing the low-profile berry and grape flavors. Drinkable now. 1,500 cases made. $12 (11/30/91) **81**

G.D. VAJRA

Barbera d'Alba Bricco delle Viole Riserva 1985: Lean and firmly tannic, but the wild blackberry aromas and flavors triumph over the tannins and this somewhat tart wine finishes lively and smooth. Drink now. $22 (7/31/89) **83**

VALFIERI

Barbera d'Alba 1987: Tart and simple, with currant and cherry flavors and slightly swampy aromas. Drinkable, but difficult to like. $7 (9/15/90) **69**

VIETTI

Barbera d'Alba della Località Scarrone 1987: Well proportioned, with spice, lemon and rich plum and raspberry notes that are smooth and thick on the palate. Not too tannic, you can drink it now or hold it up to five years. Drink now to 1995. $11 (8/31/89) **86**

Barbera d'Alba Pian Romualdo 1989: Ripe and rich but unusually flavored, with concentrated chocolate, earth and herb flavors. Drink now to 1993. $19 (11/30/91) **83**

Barbera d'Alba Pian Romualdo 1988: Well balanced, with distinctive earthy, gamy aromas and flavors, but not typical of the grape variety, making this a wine for those more tolerant of gaminess than we are. Tasted twice. $15 (3/15/91) **79**

Barbera d'Alba Scarrone 1989: Very fresh and grapey, with exuberant raspberry and grape jam flavors and a crisp, lively texture. Drink now. $13 (3/15/91) **85**

BAROLO DOCG

GIOVANNI ACCOMASSO & FIGLIO

Barolo Vigneto Rocchette 1985: Extremely earthy and bordering on sour, with more spice and tobacco flavors than fruit. Not our style, but finishes solid enough. $24 (1/31/92) **75**

ELIO ALTARE

Barolo 1985: Rich and elegant, with generous floral and berry aromas and flavors supported by—rather than hidden by—the tannins. One of the most elegant Barolos we've tried, long and pure. Drink 1995 to 2000. 606 cases made. $24 (1/31/90) **92**

Barolo 1982 $13 (6/30/87) **88**

Barolo Vigneto Arborina 1982 $15 (9/15/87) **87**

AZELIA

Barolo Bricco Fiasco 1985: A tough, chewy, earthy style, with gritty tannins that overshadow the ripe anise and raspberry-tinged fruit flavors. The earthiness may be too overpowering for some. Drink in 1996 or '97. $30 (7/15/91) **81**

Barolo Bricco Punta 1982 $23 (11/15/88) **92**

BENI DI BATASIOLO

Barolo 1985: Powerful, tannic, hard as nails, but showing generous, ripe plum, prune and anise flavors that persist through the finish. Not for the faint of heart. Cellar until 1995 at least. $15 (3/31/90) **84**

Barolo La Corda della Briccolina 1987: Lavishly oaked in small French barrels, with strong vanilla and toast flavors, but it also has a tight core of currant, raspberry, cherry and anise. Packs a wallop with tannins, too. May be too heavy-handed with oak for some. Drink after 1996. $35 (1/31/92) **84**

Barolo Riserva 1982: Firm and tannic, with lots of spicy anise, raspberry and toast aromas and flavors and plenty of grip on the finish. Needs more time in the bottle to soften the tannins. Do not approach before 1998. $17 (3/31/90) **79**

BAVA

Barolo 1985: Light in color, but firm and tannic on the palate, with nicely shaded tar, anise, earth and brown sugar aromas and flavors. Has nice plum and raspberry flavors, but will need until 1995 to '98 to settle down. 2,000 cases made. $19 (4/30/91) **83**

BEL COLLE

Barolo Riserva 1982: An earthy, funky style, with tough tannins that still need to be resolved and anise and berry flavors that emerge on the finish. Almost drinkable now, but it has enough character to indicate cellaring until 1995. $15 (3/31/90) **85**

Barolo Vigna Monvigliero 1985: Tough and tannic, with a lean line of raspberry fruit and overtones of nutmeg and anise plus a touch of earthiness to add depth and complexity. Flavors last on the finish. Aim to drink 1995 to 2000. $20 (10/15/90) **87**

BERSANO

Barolo 1985: Restrained tannins allow the relatively modest and simple raspberry, anise and nutmeg aromas and flavors to emerge on the palate. Could be more generous, but it's balanced and ready to drink now. $10 (10/15/90) **79**

Barolo 1983 $9 (11/15/88) **81**

Barolo 1974 ($NA) (9/15/88) (HS) **79**

Barolo 1971 ($NA) (9/15/88) (HS) **77**

Barolo 1964 ($NA) (9/15/88) (HS) **80**

ITALY
Piedmont Red/ *Barolo DOCG*

CA' ROME

Barolo 1985: Extremely fragrant, but a real monster on the palate, offering a powerful, tannic structure, with lovely rose petal and tar aromas and flavors and dense cherry and berry flavors hovering way in the background. Needs at least until 1998 to 2005 to shed the tannins. $35 (10/15/90) **89**

CARRETTA

Barolo Poderi Cannubi 1985: Has nice flavors—the typical anise-scented raspberry and floral character—but lacks intensity for such a celebrated vintage. The tannins need until 1995 to '97 to soften. $26 (1/31/92) **82**

Barolo Poderi Cannubi 1980 $14 (9/15/87) **62**

CEREQUIO

Barolo 1982 $19 (11/15/88) **91**

Barolo 1979: Mature but still tannic, showing lovely orange peel and floral overtones on the nose and earthy, leathery, chocolate flavors that overwhelm the fruit on the finish. If you drink it now, serve with hearty food. $13 (7/31/89) **69**

Barolo Riserva 1980: Firm, lean and lively, with enough concentration of leathery, spicy raspberry flavors to balance the hard edge of tannin that remains. A mature Barolo that still has some oomph left. Drinkable now. $13 (7/31/89) **80**

CERETTO

Barolo Bricco Rocche Bricco Rocche 1986: Firm, focused and elegant, with lots of anise, nutmeg, raspberry and plum aromas and flavors. Has more spice than fruit, but still has plenty of style and grace. Needs until 1995 to 2000 to settle the tannins, but there is enough intense flavor to survive the trip. Tasted three times. 632 cases made. $119 (4/30/91) **89**

Barolo Bricco Rocche Bricco Rocche 1985: Toasty and herbal, with slightly oxidized aromas and flavors. A woody style that is structured well enough to gain complexity with age, but the flavors aren't as pure as we would like. Tasted twice. 410 cases made. Rel: $56 Cur: $98 (3/31/90) **86**

Barolo Bricco Rocche Bricco Rocche 1982 $95 (9/15/88) (HS) **91**

Barolo Bricco Rocche Bricco Rocche 1980 $60 (3/01/86) (JS) **90**

Barolo Bricco Rocche Brunate 1986: Rich in texture, but very leathery and metallic in flavor, with perhaps a touch of raspberry. Mostly an earthy wine that is about as good as it will get. Tasted three times. 1,590 cases made. $40 (4/30/91) **80**

Barolo Bricco Rocche Brunate 1985: Despite the light color, there is plenty of concentration and complexity, a fine layer of tannin and many layers of plum, vanilla, raspberry, toast and anise flavors. A middle-of-the-road style that leans toward the traditional but has plenty of class. Drink after 1994. 2,190 cases made. $41 (1/31/90) **92**

Barolo Bricco Rocche Brunate 1983: Relatively light, fragrant and graceful, with beautiful anise-tinged raspberry aromas and flavors, plus enough tannin to keep it honest. Very attractive to drink now or in 1993. Rel: $27 Cur: $37 (7/31/89) **85**

Barolo Bricco Rocche Brunate 1979 $42 (3/01/86) (JS) **86**

Barolo Bricco Rocche Brunate 1978 $92 (9/15/88) (HS) **86**

Barolo Bricco Rocche Brunate 1967 ($NA) (10/20/87) **90**

Barolo Bricco Rocche Prapò 1986: Very lively, concentrated and complex, offering a solid core of raspberry, black cherry and spice aromas and flavors. A harmonious wine, with elegance, fine tannins and plenty of flavor to develop with cellaring until 1995 to '98. 929 cases made. $50 (2/28/91) **91**

Barolo Bricco Rocche Prapò 1985: Tight, tough and concentrated, with ripe plum and berry flavors emerging from behind a blanket of scratchy tannins. The color looks paler and older than it should for an '85, making this a difficult wine to recommend for the cellar. Drink now. Tasted twice. $50 (3/31/90) **78**

Barolo Bricco Rocche Prapò 1983: Firm and remarkably concentrated for an '83; a bit raw, but the velvety texture, cedary aromas, ripe fruit, anise spiciness and depth of flavor lift it well above the ordinary. Has the sort of richness that should allow it to age well through 1996. $31 (7/31/89) **86**

Barolo Bricco Rocche Prapò 1978 $95 (3/01/86) (JS) **95**

Barolo Bricco Rocche Prapò 1976 ($NA) (9/15/88) (HS) **82**

Barolo Bricco Rocche Prapò 1971 ($NA) (10/30/87) **88**

Barolo Cannubi 1971 ($NA) (3/01/86) (JS) **85**

Barolo Zonchera 1987: Broad and generous, with flavors that lean more toward toast and smoke than the raspberry and vanilla that emerge on the tannic finish. Gets better on the third or fourth sip. Tannic enough to need until 1996 to '98 to soften. $23 (8/31/91) **86**

Barolo Zonchera 1985: Has distinct stewed plum and cherry flavors, but it's dry and tannic, with mature, leathery flavors. Drink in 1993 to '97. $16 (6/15/90) **82**

Barolo Zonchera 1984 $16 (9/15/88) (HS) **83**

Barolo Zonchera 1982 $16 (6/30/87) **90**

Barolo Zonchera 1980 Rel: $9.50 Cur: $16 (2/16/86) SS **96**

PIO CESARE

Barolo 1985: Behind the wall of tannin lurks a heart of pure, shining cherry and berry flavor that should develop as time chisels away at the tannins. The tannins are fine and soft, but this wine isn't for anyone looking for softness or charm. Try in 2000. $38 (5/15/91) **89**

Barolo 1983 $34 (9/15/88) (HS) **88**

Barolo 1982 $36 (9/15/88) (HS) **91**

Barolo 1981 $25 (9/15/88) (HS) **87**

Barolo 1978 Rel: $19 Cur: $28 (9/15/88) (HS) **85**

Barolo 1974 $40 (9/15/88) (HS) **77**

Barolo 1971 $38 (9/15/88) (HS) **80**

Barolo Ornato Riserva 1985: Ripe, rich and supple, with a sense of sweetness and roundness that makes the strong tannins recede into the background and shows off the cherry, raspberry and coffee flavors. Hints of tar and anise are especially intriguing. Should be ready to try around 1995. 500 cases made. $48 (5/15/91) **91**

Barolo Riserva 1982 $31 (11/15/88) **86**

Barolo Riserva 1980 $19 (2/15/87) **72**

Barolo Riserva 1978 Rel: $19 Cur: $28 (10/01/84) SS **89**

MICHELE CHIARLO

Barolo Granduca 1985: Elegant, spicy and almost drinkable, this approachable style of '85 Barolo offers lovely raspberry aromas and flavors, a long finish and manageable tannins. Best to let it develop in the cellar until 1993 to '97 to bring out the spice. $20 (2/28/91) **89**

Barolo Rocche di Castiglione Riserva 1985: A dense, young, compact '85 that still needs lots of time, but you can taste the rich core of cedar, chocolate, anise and raspberry flavors. A solid wine, with deep, concentrated flavors. Needs until 1998. $43 (1/31/92) **88**

Barolo Rocche di Castiglione Riserva 1983: Tannic, earthy and not very generous, turning tough and scratchy on the finish. Should taste just fine with rich food. Drink soon. $30 (2/28/91) **78**

Barolo Vigna Rionda di Serralunga Riserva 1985: Lean and sharply focused, with a tough, tannic edge and a core of raspberry, apple and anise flavor. Turns weedy on the finish. Needs until 1995 to 2000 to shed enough of its tannins to make for happy drinking. $39 (2/28/91) **81**

Barolo Vigna Rionda di Serralunga Riserva 1983: Smooth and elegant, with hints of tar, rose petal, anise and caramel. Already developed, it's a mature wine that is balanced and relatively light on its feet. Drink soon, and serve with mushrooms or game. $36 (2/28/91) **87**

Barolo Vigna Rionda di Serralunga Riserva 1982: Powerful, tough and concentrated, with engaging tension between the tannins and the plum, anise and chocolate flavors. Massive, with the sort of concentration that should outlast the tannins. Try in 1994. 3,500 cases made. $32 (1/31/90) **89**

GUASTI CLEMENTE & FIGLI

Barolo 1985: Still pretty tight and austere, but beginning to open, with hints of rose petal and anise aromas and steely raspberry and currant-tinged flavors. Needs until 1997 to reach maturity. $27 (1/31/92) **81**

CLERICO

Barolo 1984 $13 (8/31/88) **85**

Barolo Ciabot Mentin Ginestra 1985: Smells like anise-flavored grappa at first, turning tannic and powerful on the palate, but the raspberry and vanilla flavors emerge forcefully from the grip of tannin. Big enough to need until the turn of the century, but it has the power and complexity to win in the end. Needs cellaring until 1998 to 2000. 800 cases made. Rel: $27 Cur: $40 (4/15/90) CS **92**

Barolo Ciabot Mentin Ginestra 1983 $19 (12/15/87) **88**

Barolo Vigna Bricotto della Bussia 1980 $8.25 (9/01/85) BB **86**

ALDO CONTERNO

Barolo Bricco Bussia Vigna Cicala 1985: Firm and concentrated, packed with intense cherry, plum and smoke aromas and flavors and wrapped in tannin without being weighted down. Has the structure and concentration to develop beautifully with age. Try it in 1995 to 2000. $40 (6/15/90) **90**

Barolo Bricco Bussia Vigna Cicala 1982 $20 (9/15/87) **86**

Barolo Bricco Bussia Vigna Colonnello 1985: Very spicy and complex, with narrowly focused flavors of raspberry, anise and cherry; it's tough, tannic and lean. The fruit and tannin play a balancing act, but the finish ends in a tie. Needs cellaring until at least 1996. $40 (6/15/90) **84**

Barolo Bussia Soprana 1985: With a lean texture and complex, generous anise-tinged raspberry jam aromas and flavors, this massively tannic wine has enough fruit concentration to cellar until 2000 to subdue the tannins. The smoky plum flavors evident on the finish should stay with it through the years. $40 (9/15/90) **87**

Barolo Bussia Soprana 1983 $25 (9/15/88) (HS) **85**

Barolo Bussia Soprana 1982 Rel: $17.50 Cur: $30 (9/15/87) **85**

Barolo Bussia Soprana 1980 $35 (9/15/88) (HS) **86**

Barolo Bussia Soprana 1978 $70 (9/15/88) (HS) **92**

Barolo Bussia Soprana 1974 $60 (9/15/88) (HS) **90**

Barolo Bussia Soprana 1971 $50 (9/15/88) (HS) **87**

Barolo Granbussia 1982 ($NA) (9/15/88) (HS) **93**

GIACOMO CONTERNO

Barolo 1985: Firm and tannic, with excellent richness of flavor to balance. Flavors lean toward raspberry with anise, tar and smoke overtones. Needs cellaring through 1994 to '95 to begin to soften the tannins. $23 (4/15/90) **87**

Barolo 1983 $23 (9/15/88) (HS) **88**

Barolo 1982 $25 (9/15/88) (HS) **90**

Barolo Monfortino Reserva 1982 $57 (6/30/87) **91**

Barolo Riserva Spéciale 1978 $40 (9/15/88) (HS) **83**

Barolo Riserva Spéciale 1970 ($NA) (9/15/88) (HS) **88**

CONTERNO FANTINO

Barolo Sorì Ginestra Riserva 1982: Big and tough, with berry and chocolate flavors just beginning to emerge behind a wall of tannin. Give it until 1994 to '98 to see if the leather and truffle aromas integrate into the wine. A traditional style that's well made. $24 (1/31/90) **84**

CONTRATTO

Barolo 1983: Smoky, herbal, decadent style that's fairly smooth and mellow on the palate; drinkable if somewhat eccentric. Drink soon. $10 (3/31/90) **75**

Barolo 1979 $9 (9/30/86) **76**

Barolo del Centenario Riserva 1978 $18 (5/16/86) **86**

PAOLO CORDERO DI MONTEZEMOLO

Barolo 1980 Rel: $16 Cur: $20 (12/15/87) CS **91**

Barolo Enrico VI 1983 $20 (9/15/88) (HS) **86**

Barolo Enrico VI 1982 $20 (9/15/88) (HS) **88**

Barolo Enrico VI 1981 $25 (9/15/88) (HS) **88**

Barolo Enrico VI 1980 ($NA) (9/15/88) (HS) **85**

Barolo Monfalletto 1984 ($NA) (9/15/88) (HS) **88**

Barolo Monfalletto 1983: Woody, vegetal aromas and flavors overpower whatever fruit might be there, and it's rough and tannic for such a light wine. $17 (2/28/89) **85**

Barolo Monfalletto 1980 Rel: $11 Cur: $20 (1/31/87) **91**

Barolo Monfalletto 1979 $35 (9/15/88) (HS) **82**

Barolo Monfalletto 1978 $25 (9/15/88) (HS) **84**

Barolo Monfalletto 1977 ($NA) (9/15/88) (HS) **69**

Barolo Monfalletto 1975 ($NA) (9/15/88) (HS) **77**

Barolo Monfalletto 1973 ($NA) (9/15/88) (HS) **65**

Barolo Monfalletto 1971 ($NA) (9/15/88) (HS) **85**

LUIGI EINAUDI

Barolo 1982 $23 (6/30/87) **81**

RICCARDO FENOCCHIO

Barolo Pianpolvere Soprano 1984: Tannic texture and swampy flavors overwhelm the light, thin fruit in this awkward, unbalanced wine. $15 (7/31/89) **62**

Barolo Pianpolvero Soprano 1982: Very tannic and concentrated, but the flavors run more toward toast, coffee and anise than fruit, echoing enough very ripe raspberry and cherry on the finish to suggest that cellaring until 1994 to '96 could be beneficial. Made in the old style. $26 (7/31/89) **74**

EREDI VIRGINIA FERRERO

Barolo S. Rocco 1982 $22 (7/15/88) **92**

Barolo S. Rocco Riserva 1979: Smells lovely, with tea, bay leaf and chocolate aromas, but it's drying up fast on the palate. It tastes old, tired and tannic. $19 (7/31/89) **67**

FONTANAFREDDA

Barolo 1983 $16 (9/15/88) (HS) **83**

Barolo 1982 $16 (9/15/88) (HS) **84**

Barolo 1978 $13 (2/15/84) **80**

Barolo Lazarito 1982 $42 (9/15/88) (HS) **90**

Barolo San Pietro 1982 $42 (9/15/88) (HS) **85**

Barolo Vigna la Rosa 1982 Rel: $40 Cur: $45 (2/15/88) CS **90**

FRANCO-FIORINA

Barolo 1982 $22 (5/31/88) **79**

Key to Symbols

The scores reported here are the results of blind tastings conducted by our panel of senior editors. Wines that carry the initials below are results of individual tastings.

THE WINE SPECTATOR 100-POINT SCALE ***95-100***—Classic, a great wine; ***90-94***—Outstanding, superior character and style; ***80-89***—Good to very good, a wine with special qualities; ***70-79***—Average, drinkable wine that may have minor flaws; ***60-69***—Below average, drinkable but not recommended; ***50-59***—Poor, undrinkable, not recommended. "+"—With a score indicates a range; used primarily with barrel tastings to indicate a preliminary score.

SPECIAL DESIGNATIONS SS—Spectator Selection, CS—Cellar Selection, BB—Best Buy, ($NA)—Price not available, (NR)—Not released.

TASTER'S INITIALS (JG)—Jim Gordon, (HS)—Harvey Steiman, (JL)—James Laube, (JS)—James Suckling, (TM)—Thomas Matthews, (TR)—Terry Robards, (PM)—Per-Henrik Mansson, (BT)—Barrel Tasting (these wines were tasted blind from barrel samples), (CA-date)—*California's Great Cabernets* by James Laube, (CH-date)—*California's Great Chardonnays* by James Laube, (VP-date)—*Vintage Port* by James Suckling.

DATE TASTED Dates in parentheses represent the issue in which the rating was published.

BRUNO GIACOSA
Barolo 1980 $19 (9/15/87) **78**
Barolo 1978 $31 (9/16/84) **88**
Barolo Collina Rionda di Serralunga 1985: Mature and earthy, it's very tight, firm and tannic, with concentrated anise, tar and raisin flavors on the finish; this is built to need until 1998 to 2000 to soften enough to tell where it's going. Doesn't show the richness one expects at this point. $50 (4/30/91) **86**
Barolo Le Rocche di Castiglione Falletto 1982: Very tannic, but there is a powerful thread of raspberry, leather and anise flavor that cuts through. Will it balance out in time? You'd better like tannic wine to cellar this one, and give it at least until 2000. $38 (7/31/89) **80**
Barolo Riserva 1982: Mature and earthy, with agressive tannins that are sharp and harsh. Hard to predict where this one will end up. If you cellar it, there won't be much fruit, but to drink it now you need to fight the tannins. Try now to 1995. $65 (1/31/90) **72**
Barolo Rocche 1982 $41 (9/15/88) **90**
Barolo Villero di Castiglione 1983: Lean and earthy, but fairly elegant with its hints of plummy flavor, sweet anise and some chocolaty concentration on the finish. Try now. $29 (1/31/89) **85**

GIACOSA FRATELLI
Barolo 1985: Smells ugly, with more than a hint of ammonia, adding earthiness and musk on the finish. Not a friendly wine. Tasted twice, with consistent notes. 3,000 cases made. $20 (8/31/91) **59**

ELIO GRASSO
Barolo Gavarini Vigna Rüncot 1985: Made in the old style, but it's bitterly tannic, with green, stemmy flavors that obliterate whatever fruit exists underneath. Hard to predict if this will come around. Tasted twice, with identical scores. $42 (8/31/91) **59**

MARCARINI
Barolo Brunate 1985: Attractive for its rich, supple texture and pretty plum, cherry, tar and rose petal flavors; this is a well-balanced, complex, flavorful wine with just the right amount of tannin. The fruit powers through on the finish. Drink in 1995 to 2002. $35 (3/31/90) **90**
Barolo Brunate 1983 $23 (9/15/88) (HS) **89**
Barolo Brunate 1982 $18 (9/15/88) (HS) **90**
Barolo Brunate 1979 $29 (9/15/88) (HS) **88**
Barolo Brunate 1978 $50 (9/15/88) (HS) **80**
Barolo Brunate 1971 $60 (9/15/88) (HS) **89**
Barolo Brunate 1964 ($NA) (9/15/88) (HS) **96**
Barolo La Serra 1983 $17 (9/15/88) (HS) **87**
Barolo La Serra 1982 $18 (9/15/88) (HS) **91**
Barolo La Serra 1980 $9.50 (4/16/86) **89**
Barolo La Serra 1978 $18 (9/16/84) **79**

MARCHESI DI BAROLO
Barolo Brunate 1985: Big, tough, chunky and chewy, with huge, drying tannins and intense coffee, cherry, currant and anise flavors. This is a bold, assertive, powerful style. Don't drink this one alone; it needs food. Best to cellar until 1995 to '96. 514 cases made. $29 (10/15/90) **85**
Barolo Brunate 1982: Firm, tannic and lively, with some anise-tinged raspberry flavor vibrantly showing through. One of the more supple examples from a tough but excellent vintage. Drink in 1994. $14 (2/15/89) **89**
Barolo Cannubi 1985: Packed with tight cherry, currant, toasty and spicy earthy flavors that are very tightly wound, intense and tannic but balanced, with hints of prunes and leather coming through on the finish. Best to cellar until 1995 or '96, but then it should age until 2005. 2,165 cases made. $29 (10/15/90) **88**
Barolo Castel la Volta 1987: Aromatic and rich in flavor, with lots of anise and tar notes woven into the basic raspberry and plum aromas and flavors. Has firm tannins and a round texture. Hints at the spice and vanilla of oak on the finish. Drink after 1996 or '97. $20 (1/31/92) **89**
Barolo Coste di Rosé 1985: Brutally tannic; a big, powerful wine that's packed with cherry, anise and leathery earthy flavors, but then the tannins overwhelm. Should have the fruit concentration to last until 2000, but you might want to take a sip around 1996 or so. 579 cases made. $29 (10/15/90) **86**
Barolo Riserva 1982: Tannic and tight, but there are some pleasant raspberry flavors and hints of sandalwood and spice underneath. Needs time for the tannin to resolve. Drink in 1995. $14 (2/15/89) **87**
Barolo Riserva 1978: Looking for a mature Barolo for dinner this weekend? Try this. Its spice, anise and leather flavors are supported by a firm structure. The slightly powdery tannins should carry it at least until 1999. $20 (2/28/89) **86**
Barolo Valletta 1985: Intense and concentrated, with smoky plum, anise and cherry flavors that pick up some earthy leathery flavors along the way. Packed with fruit and framed by firm tannins. Typical of the '85s, it's well focused, complete and in need of extended cellaring. Wait until 1997. 1,120 cases made. $29 (10/15/90) **88**

BARTOLO MASCARELLO
Barolo 1983 $27 (5/31/88) **88**

GIUSEPPE MASCARELLO & FIGLIO
Barolo 1982 $28 (6/30/87) **81**
Barolo 1978 $19 (9/16/84) **91**
Barolo Belvedere 1985: Enormously complex and concentrated, with its sharply focused core of cherry, plum, smoke and currant flavors already showing nuances of rose petal and tar, wrapped lightly in a tannic veil that will need cellaring until 1995 to 2000 to let all the complexities emerge. A wonderful '85 that's full of potential. 500 cases made. Rel: $35 Cur: $42 (6/15/90) CS **93**
Barolo Dardi 1982 $18 (9/15/87) **87**
Barolo Monprivato 1986: Smells ripe and fruity, with black cherry, raspberry and anise flavors that are rich and complex. The tannins are also quite substantial, but held in check. The fruit wins on the finish. Cellar until 1995. $47 (7/15/91) **88**
Barolo Monprivato 1985: Ripe, spicy and concentrated, with generous blackberry, raspberry and pepper aromas and flavors and tough tannins that trample through on the finish. Lots of wood aromas and flavors, too. A classic structure that needs at least until 1998 to 2000 to soften. $53 (6/15/90) **86**
Barolo Monprivato 1983 Rel: $28 Cur: $40 (9/15/88) (HS) **86**
Barolo Monprivato 1982 Rel: $22 Cur: $30 (9/15/88) (HS) **89**
Barolo Monprivato 1981 $23 (9/15/88) (HS) **84**
Barolo Monprivato 1980 $23 (9/15/88) (HS) **76**
Barolo Monprivato 1979 $23 (9/15/88) (HS) **83**
Barolo Monprivato 1978 $42 (9/15/88) (HS) **86**
Barolo Monprivato 1974 $80 (9/15/88) (HS) **91**
Barolo Monprivato 1971 $73 (9/15/88) (HS) **81**
Barolo Monprivato 1970 $60 (9/15/88) (HS) **80**
Barolo Monprivato Falletto 1983: Unusually lively and tart, with crisp raspberry flavor shooting through the leathery flavors and a modicum of tannins. Drinkable now, with the right kind of rich and spicy food. $23 (7/31/89) **80**
Barolo Santo Stefano di Perno 1985: Powerful, complex and elegant, with blackberry, plum, cedar, smoke and gamy aromas and flavors that carry through the long finish. Tannic but balanced. Cellar until 2000. A better showing than two previous tastings. 800 cases made. $35 (10/15/90) **94**
Barolo Villero 1983 $17 (10/15/88) **77**

FATTORIA MASSARA
Barolo 1985: Earthy, drying, tannic and not very concentrated, showing a pretty raspberry flavor that quickly gets lost among the tannins. The nose has appeal, with its spice- and tar-tinged berry aromas. Drink in 1995. $20 (6/15/90) **80**

MAURO MOLINO
Barolo Vigna Conca 1986: Intensely fruity and round from aging in small oak barrels; it's rich and flavorful without being tough or terribly tannic. Spicy raspberry and anise flavors dominate. Tempting now, but aging until 1995 to 2000 should bring it to its best. $29 (2/28/91) **87**
Barolo Vigna Conca 1985: An intense, tannic style that's hard and unyielding now, but there's a decent core of peppery, ripe Zinfandel flavor. Dry finish. Drink now. $25 (3/31/90) **82**

COLLI MONFORTESI
Barolo 1982 $15 (4/30/87) SS **92**

ODDERO
Barolo 1983 $15 (9/15/88) (HS) **85**
Barolo 1982 $14 (9/15/88) (HS) **92**
Barolo 1980 $7 (5/16/86) **73**
Barolo Rocche di Bussia 1985: Extremely earthy and barnyardy, with scratchy tannins that take away any fun this wine could provide. Despite pleasant strawberry and spice flavors, the ugly flavors knock it out of contention for us. Tasted twice. $21 (8/31/91) **65**

PARUSSO
Barolo 1985: A tough wine, but the focused cherry and raspberry flavors manage to make themselves heard above the tannic din. A bit metallic on the finish, but the anise and tar overtones give it good possibilities with cellaring until 1996 to '98. $27 (4/30/91) **84**
Barolo Mariondino 1986: Firm and tannic, with earthy anise flavors dominating the lean core of raspberry. Chewy and a bit tough on the finish. Drink after 1996. $23 (4/30/91) **83**

LIVIO PAVESE
Barolo Riserva Spéciale 1978 $12 (9/16/84) **90**

CANTINA DELLA PORTA ROSSA
Barolo Riserva 1985: Firm and focused, with generous raspberry, currant and smoke aromas and flavors that hint at anise and tar on the finish. A beautifully balanced, graceful package that should keep evolving well through 1995 to 2000. $26 (1/31/92) **87**
Barolo Vigna Delizia Riserva 1982: Firm and focused, with pleasantly intense cherry, anise and tar flavors, hinting at smoke on the long finish. Tannic, but not as tough as some '82s, and it has grace and elegance. Best to drink after 1994 to '96. $25 (8/31/91) **87**

PRUNOTTO
Barolo 1987: Firm and tight but showing pretty anise and berry flavors that take on hints of anise and herbs. Tannins are evident, but not dominant. Best to cellar until 1995. $27 (3/31/92) **85**
Barolo 1985: A tough, smoky style that is loaded with dense flavors and dense tannins; a real mouthful of anise and tar-tinged character. Needs cellaring until at least 1994 to '95. $31 (3/31/90) **82**
Barolo Bussia 1986: A tough, earthy style, with a strong barnyard component and lots of anise shouldering past the modest berry flavors. Has intensity, but the flavors need time to develop. Try in 1997 to 2000. Tasted twice, with consistant notes. 2,400 cases made. Rel: $39 Cur: $44 (3/31/92) **78**
Barolo Bussia 1985: A big, generous, chewy wine, with ripe plum, cherry and anise aromas and flavors. It's already harmonious and complex, but there's plenty behind it to develop over the years. Shows raspberry on the long and somewhat tannic finish. Drink after 1996 or '98. 200 cases made. $38 (9/15/90) **92**
Barolo Bussia 1983 $23 (9/15/88) (HS) **88**
Barolo Bussia 1982 Rel: $25 Cur: $30 (9/15/88) (HS) **91**
Barolo Bussia 1978 $50 (9/15/88) (HS) **86**
Barolo Bussia 1974 $65 (9/15/88) (HS) **80**
Barolo Bussia 1971 $75 (9/15/88) (HS) **90**
Barolo Bussia 1967 $49 (9/15/88) (HS) **82**
Barolo Bussia 1964 $85 (9/15/88) (HS) **80**
Barolo Bussia 1961 $110 (9/15/88) (HS) **91**
Barolo Cannubi 1985: Extremely ripe and tannic, with powerful currant, chocolate, tar and coffee flavors that are intense and concentrated. Patience is required, though, because the tannins will need another eight to 10 years to soften. Drink in 1996 and beyond. $32 (3/31/90) **85**
Barolo Cannubi 1983 $26 (9/15/88) (HS) **85**
Barolo Cannubi 1982 $25 (9/15/88) (HS) **75**
Barolo Cannubi 1978 $21 (9/15/88) (HS) **78**
Barolo Ginestra di Monforte d'Alba Riserva 1980 $13 (6/30/87) **78**
Barolo Riserva 1980 $12 (6/30/87) **65**

RENATO RATTI
Barolo 1985: This heavily tannic style tends to overwhelm at first, but if you wade through the tannins you'll find a pretty core of fruit that echos earth, spice and cherry. It's a long way from maturity. Try in 1996. Rel: $23 Cur: $26 (9/15/90) **85**
Barolo 1983 $20 (10/15/88) **87**
Barolo 1982 Rel: $17 Cur: $27 (6/30/87) CS **93**
Barolo 1980 Rel: $10 Cur: $13 (2/15/87) **83**
Barolo 1979 $8.50 (1/01/86) **89**
Barolo Marcenasco 1985: Light in color, but tough and leathery on the palate. Fragrant with juniper and floral aromas and a touch of raspberry, but not much flavor. Try after 1994. Rel: $37 Cur: $43 (10/15/90) **82**
Barolo Marcenasco 1982 Rel: $23 Cur: $36 (6/30/87) **90**
Barolo Marcenasco 1981 $15 (6/30/87) **84**
Barolo Marcenasco Rocche 1983: Smooth and rather light, but there are some attractive raspberry flavors, hints of anise and leather, finely integrated tannins, and it's flavorful and balanced on the finish. $30 (1/31/89) **86**
Barolo Marcenasco Rocche 1981 $19 (6/30/87) **88**

GIOVANNI & BATTISTA RINALDI
Barolo 1983 ($NA) (9/15/88) (HS) **86**
Barolo 1982 ($NA) (9/15/88) (HS) **84**

FRANCESCO RINALDI & FIGLI
Barolo 1986: Ripe and aromatic, but on the palate it gets very tart and tannic, with a good blast of alcohol. The raspberry, anise and earth flavors seem to lose intensity, and the finish is very tannic. Cellar until 1997. Rel: $22 Cur: $30 (7/15/91) **83**
Barolo 1983 $20 (9/15/88) (HS) **84**
Barolo 1982 Rel: $16 Cur: $50 (9/15/88) (HS) **83**
Barolo 1978 Rel: $12 Cur: $70 (9/16/84) **89**
Barolo Cannubbio 1985: Ripe, spicy, hot and tannic, offering lots of plum and raspberry aromas and flavors, but the high-alcohol profile becomes searing on the finish. Not for the faint of heart. Drink in 1995 to 2000. $25 (6/15/90) **78**
Barolo Cannubbio 1982 $16 (10/31/87) **75**
Barolo La Brunata Riserva 1985: Intense and lively, with fresh spice, nutmeg, caramel and raspberry flavors that have a velvety texture and a sense of elegance. There's plenty of richness and depth, and the fruit fights through on the finish. Drink in 1995 to '97. $24 (7/15/91) **89**
Barolo La Brunata Riserva 1982 $27 (6/30/87) **79**

ROCCHE COSTAMAGNA
Barolo Rocche di la Morra 1985: Hot and sharp on the palate, this smells and tastes more like black pepper and anise than fruit. Heavy-handed and severe, not to be touched before 2000—and then what? $25 (2/28/91) **72**

LUCIANO SANDRONE
Barolo 1984 $13.50 (8/31/88) **82**
Barolo 1983 $20 (12/15/87) **90**
Barolo 1982 $15 (6/30/87) **94**

ITALY

Piedmont Red/ *Barolo DOCG*

Barolo Cannubi Boschis 1986: A big, mature rustic style, with intense, rich fruit flavor and hints of caramel, chocolate, cherry and spice, and then the tannins kick in. Altogether well balanced and complex, but needs cellaring until 1995 to 2000. $34 (12/31/90) **89**

Barolo Cannubi Boschis 1985: Ripe, round and generous and smooth and spicy from aging in new oak barrels, but bursting with Barolo flavors that echo forever on the finish. With its layers of berry, cherry and anise flavors, it can only devlop more depth with cellaring through at least 1995. $30 (1/31/90) **92**

SCARPA

Barolo 1985 ($NA) (9/15/88) (HS) **90**
Barolo 1982 ($NA) (9/15/88) (HS) **88**
Barolo 1978 $27 (9/15/88) (HS) **89**
Barolo Le Coste di Monforte 1978 $27 (3/15/87) **81**

PAOLO SCAVINO

Barolo 1985: A sinewy wine, with ripe, spicy flavors extending through a long finish, promising long life and great things when the tannins subside, around 1998 or so. Its massive concentration of raspberry, anise and toast flavors just won't quit. $21 (10/15/90) **88**
Barolo 1983 ($NA) (9/15/88) (HS) **85**
Barolo 1982 ($NA) (9/15/88) (HS) **88**
Barolo Brico dell Fiasco 1985: Dense, concentrated and opulent; a massive wine, with explosive aromas of ripe cherry, plum and anise, flecked with vanilla and toast. Showing the roundness from new small oak barrels, yet a sense of finesse and polish that can only develop beautifully with cellaring until 2000 or beyond. $39 (6/15/90) **90**
Barolo Cannubi 1985: A wine that will leave you speechless with the enormous level of wood and tannins. The fruit doesn't stand a chance. Drink in 1995 to 2001. $30 (1/31/90) **74**

SEBASTE

Barolo 1985 ($NA) (9/15/88) (HS) **90**
Barolo 1984 ($NA) (9/15/88) (HS) **85**
Barolo 1983 ($NA) (9/15/88) (HS) **86**
Barolo 1982 ($NA) (9/15/88) (HS) **91**
Barolo 1979 ($NA) (9/15/88) (HS) **85**
Barolo Bussia Riserva 1984: Light and elegant, with a sharp enough shot of tannin and acidity to support the spicy, toasty raspberry flavors. A vibrant wine that's drinkable now, but best around 1993. $17 (7/31/89) **84**
Barolo Bussia Riserva 1982 $15 (11/15/87) **90**

RENZO SEGHESIO

Barolo Bussia-Pianpolvere 1986: Firm in texture, with crisp raspberry, anise and spice aromas and flavors that show nicely against a backdrop of fine tannins. A solid wine that should improve through 1995 or '96. 1,200 cases made. $28 (1/31/92) **84**

AURELIO SETTIMO

Barolo Vigna Rocche 1982 $19 (5/31/88) **83**
Barolo Vigna Rocche 1980 $17 (5/31/88) **73**
Barolo Vigna Rocche 1979 $25 (5/31/88) **67**

G.D. VAJRA

Barolo 1982 $14 (3/15/87) **91**
Barolo Bricco delle Viole 1982 $19 (8/31/88) **91**
Barolo Fossati Vineyard 1985: Classic tar and anise aromas are followed by deep, ripe, rich and concentrated flavors, with layers of herb, chocolate, tea, nut and cherry, all packed and built with tannins to last 25 years. It's best to give this one until 1998 to 2005 before starting to drink. 333 cases made. $34 (12/31/90) **91**

VALFIERI

Barolo 1985: Earthy and tannic but beautifully balanced; this is dense and concentrated, with cedar, spice, smoke, prune and anise aromas and flavors. Fragrant and appealing on the nose, it needs time to absorb its tannin. Best after 1996. 2,000 cases made. $13 (10/15/90) **90**

VIETTI

Barolo 1978 $12 (9/16/84) **84**
Barolo Bussia 1982 $20 (9/15/87) **89**
Barolo Rocche 1982: Big, tough and powerful, with anise-tinged raspberry flavors touched with tar aromas and flavors. It's as tannic as any but backed with the fruit (and alcohol) to match. Don't touch before 1997. Rel: $45 Cur: $60 (7/31/89) **85**
Barolo Rocche 1980 $30 (9/15/88) (HS) **87**
Barolo Rocche 1979 ($NA) (9/15/88) (HS) **79**
Barolo Rocche 1978 $75 (9/15/88) (HS) **92**
Barolo Rocche 1971 $70 (9/15/88) (HS) **86**
Barolo Rocche 1961 $100 (9/15/88) (HS) **93**
Barolo Villero Riserva 1982 $45 (9/15/88) (HS) **89**

VILLADORIA

Barolo Riserva Spéciale 1978 $14 (8/31/86) **73**

ROBERTO VOERZIO

Barolo 1985: Not lacking in tannin, but gentle compared to many '85s, spicy and elegant with raspberry, cherry and anise flavors that are rich and intense without being overbearing. Drink in 1993 to 2000. $18 (1/31/90) **87**
Barolo 1983 $15 (9/15/88) (HS) **88**
Barolo 1982 $12 (9/15/88) (HS) **90**
Barolo La Serra di La Morra 1982 $12 (7/31/87) **91**

Dolcetto DOC

ABBAZIA DI VALLE CHIARA

Dolcetto d'Ovada 1989: Light, fruity and simple, with fresh currant and berry aromas and flavors. $13 (7/15/91) **79**

ELIO ALTARE

Dolcetto d'Alba 1989: Firm and fruity, this medium-weight wine has a modest intensity of berry flavor and a bit of astringency. Drink with food. $12 (7/15/91) **81**
Dolcetto d'Alba 1988: Has generous, ripe aromas of wild berries and plum, marked by a touch of oak on the palate and a round and firm texture. Easy to drink now. $10 (3/31/90) **82**
Dolcetto d'Alba 1987: A delicious wine for drinking young. Effusively fruity, almost purple in color, with a hint of pepper and ripe, broad blackberry and blueberry flavors that last through the finish. Full-bodied and moderately tannic. $9 (2/28/89) **90**

AZELIA

Dolcetto d'Alba 1987: Alive with berry aromas and flavors, dry and concentrated on the palate, long and refreshing. A well-crafted wine with excellent balance. $7 (3/15/89) **85**
Dolcetto d'Alba Bricco dell'Oriolo 1989: Firm and more than a little tannic, with medium-weight cherry and toast aromas and flavors. Best to drink with food. $9.25 (7/15/91) **79**

BENI DI BATASIOLO

Dolcetto d'Alba 1989: A fragrant wine, with berry and spice aromas, a light texture and modest tannins, but enough fruit flavor to overcome them. Drink with food. $12 (7/15/91) **82**
Dolcetto d'Alba 1988: Firm in style, offering more oak and tannin than most Dolcettos, but plenty of ripe, intense raspberry flavors extend into the long finish and keep it remarkably fresh. A bit austere for a Dolcetto, but clearly a fine meal-time wine. Drinkable now. $10.50 (12/31/90) **85**

CANTINA DEL GLICINE

Dolcetto d'Alba 1989: Firm and flavorful, with an earthy, barnyardy edge to the basic berry flavors. Drinkable now. Tasted twice. $12.50 (11/30/91) **79**

CASCINA BORDINO

Dolcetto d'Alba 1988: Deep, dense and concentrated, yet it retains a sense of lightness and silkiness on the palate. Plum and earth aromas are immediately attractive, as is the distinctive toastiness and firmness of texture. Drink now. $9.50 (3/31/90) **84**

CAVALOTTO

Dolcetto d'Alba Mallera 1987 $10 (3/15/89) **83**

CERETTO

Dolcetto d'Alba Rossana 1989: Youthful and slightly astringent, but fruity and generous, with berry and currant aromas and flavors. Could be smoother. Try now or in 1993. $16 (4/30/91) **79**
Dolcetto d'Alba Rossana 1987 $12 (3/15/89) **86**
Dolcetto d'Alba Vigna 1985 $11 (3/15/89) **77**

CHIONETTI

Dolcetto di Dogliani Briccolero 1989: Very firm and generous, with concentrated currant, berry and plum aromas and flavors rounded out by a touch of oak. Built to stand up to whatever food one might introduce to it. Drink now or in 1993. $16 (4/30/91) **87**

ALDO CONTERNO

Dolcetto d'Alba 1987: Generous and velvety, with gently unfolding cherry and raspberry flavors, this is easy to drink and already attractive. Has just enough of a tannin bite to make it interesting. Drink now. $12 (9/15/90) **84**

LUIGI COPPO

Dolcetto d'Alba 1989: A light style, with simple berry and cherry aromas and flavors, a soft texture and modest intensity on the finish. $10.50 (7/15/91) **81**

GIUSEPPE CORTESE

Dolcetto d'Alba 1990: Light and tart, with modest beet root and berry flavors. Drink now. $13 (1/31/92) **79**
Dolcetto d'Alba 1989: Fresh and light, like a Beajolais, offering lively strawberry and raspberry aromas and flavors that are dry and clean on the finish. Drink now, perhaps slightly chilled. $9.75 (12/31/90) **83**
Dolcetto d'Alba 1988: Fine example of a Rioja and reasonably priced. Very complex and rich in flavor, with cedar and vanilla aromas, smooth, spicy raspberry and cherry flavors and a crisp, fruity finish. Drink now. $8 (3/31/90) **78**

DE FORVILLE

Dolcetto d'Alba Vigneto Loreto 1989: Fruity and soft in texture, with a toasty edge to the lively cherry, strawberry and black pepper aromas and flavors. A bit coarse and hearty, but likable. Drinkable now. $12 (2/28/91) **81**

FRANCO-FIORINA

Dolcetto d'Alba 1989: Smooth and gentle, with nice blackberry and cherry aromas and flavors, a silky texture and a hint of vanilla on the finish. $13 (4/30/91) **83**
Dolcetto d'Alba 1987: Beguiling aromas of wild berries and flowers turn drying and surprisingly tannic on the palate, making this a wine for drinking only with very rich or flavorful food. $8.75 (7/31/89) **76**

BRUNO GIACOSA

Dolcetto d'Alba 1989: Brilliantly focused raspberry and cherry flavors, shaded by vanilla and black pepper notes, make this instantly appealing, and the flavors persist through a long, generous finish. Craftily balanced and polished. Drink now or hold until 1993 to '95. $12 (2/28/91) **88**

ELIO GRASSO

Dolcetto d'Alba Gavarini Vigna dei Grassi 1989: Shows more tannin and has a tougher texture than one would expect, and offers precious little fruit flavor. $18 (7/15/91) **76**

MARCARINI

Dolcetto d'Alba Boschi di Berri 1989: Wonderfully rich and concentrated, bursting with ripe cherry, berry and chocolate aromas and flavors that are harmonious and balanced. Spicy notes sneak in on the finish. Drinkable now, but should improve in 1993. $23 (4/30/91) **89**
Dolcetto d'Alba Boschi di Berri 1988: Tart and earthy, without much zip on the palate, this is a decent but uninspiring wine that will survive with food. Drink now. $17 (3/31/90) **86**
Dolcetto d'Alba Boschi di Berri 1987: Beautifully focused floral-tinged berry aromas and flavors carry through to a zingy finish; this crisp, racy, flavorful wine cries out for a plate of antipasto. The concentration of flavor without excessive weight is impressive. $13 (3/15/89) **89**
Dolcetto d'Alba Fontanazza 1989: Fruity, spicy, generous and lively, offering lots of plum, berry and cola aromas and flavors and a velvety texture. Long enough to keep you coming back for another sip. $13 (4/30/91) **84**
Dolcetto d'Alba Fontanazza 1988: Lively, generous and ripe, with lots of berry and cherry aromas and flavors. Soft and succulent, reined in with just enough tannin to make it velvety. Drink now. $11 (3/31/90) **87**
Dolcetto d'Alba Fontanazza 1987: Earthy, slightly sour, not at all the clean, fruity quaff you expect from Dolcetto, but a good wine to accompany a simple dinner nonetheless. $9.75 (3/15/89) **78**

MARCHESI DI BAROLO

Dolcetto d'Alba Madonna di Como 1990: A simple style, with tart, thin beet and currant flavors that fade. Drink now. $10 (1/31/92) **77**
Dolcetto d'Alba Madonna di Como 1989: Firm and finely focused, offering ebullient raspberry, red cherry and spice aromas and flavors that linger on the long finish. Not a complex wine, but extremely appealing and likable. Drink soon, while it's fresh. 2,656 cases made. $9 (12/31/90) BB **88**
Dolcetto d'Alba Madonna di Como 1987: Lively, delicious and interesting. It's young and brash, but packed with layers of plum and raspberry flavors that linger on the palate. Drink up now. $8 (2/15/89) **87**

Key to Symbols

The scores reported here are the results of blind tastings conducted by our panel of senior editors. Wines that carry the initials below are results of individual tastings.

THE WINE SPECTATOR 100-POINT SCALE ***95-100***—Classic, a great wine; ***90-94***—Outstanding, superior character and style; ***80-89***—Good to very good, a wine with special qualities; ***70-79***—Average, drinkable wine that may have minor flaws; ***60-69***—Below average, drinkable but not recommended; ***50-59***—Poor, undrinkable, not recommended. "+"—With a score indicates a range; used primarily with barrel tastings to indicate a preliminary score.

SPECIAL DESIGNATIONS SS—Spectator Selection, CS—Cellar Selection, BB—Best Buy, ($NA)—Price not available, (NR)—Not released.

TASTER'S INITIALS (JG)—Jim Gordon, (HS)—Harvey Steiman, (JL)—James Laube, (JS)—James Suckling, (TM)—Thomas Matthews, (TR)—Terry Robards, (PM)—Per-Henrik Mansson, (BT)—Barrel Tasting (these wines were tasted blind from barrel samples), (CA-date)—*California's Great Cabernets* by James Laube, (CH-date)—*California's Great Chardonnays* by James Laube, (VP-date)—*Vintage Port* by James Suckling.

DATE TASTED Dates in parentheses represent the issue in which the rating was published.

PODERI E MARENGO-MARENDA
Dolcetto d'Alba Le Terre Forti 1990: Tannic and chewy, with intense, tight currant and earthy plum flavors. Drinkable now, but might improve with cellaring through 1993. $12 (1/31/92) **84**

GIUSEPPE MASCARELLO & FIGLIO
Dolcetto d'Alba Bricco Falletto 1987: Smooth, rich and velvety, with dazzling berryish, plummy aromas and flavors, balanced with a touch of earthiness on the nose. Very fine. $9 (3/15/89) **88**
Dolcetto d'Alba Bricco Ravera 1988: Lovely berry and rose petal aromas and flavors make this medium-bodied, balanced and generous wine enjoyable to sip. Drinkable now. $10 (9/15/90) **82**
Dolcetto d'Alba Gagliassi 1989: Brilliant in color and flavor, offering mainly berries, with more than a light touch of astringency, though some thought it soft and supple. Needs food to soften it enough to be at its best. $13 (7/15/91) **85**
Dolcetto d'Alba Gagliassi 1987: Surprisingly tannic and tart, but bursting with berry aromas and raw flavors, enough to suggest that cellaring until 1993 will soften it up and keep the fruit alive. $10 (3/31/90) **80**
Dolcetto d'Alba Gagliassi Monforte 1987 $9 (3/15/89) **82**

FATTORIA MASSARA
Dolcetto d'Alba 1990: Fruity and smooth, with ripe, rich currant, blackberry and anise flavors that are quite pleasing. Has a nip of tannin on the finish, but the fruit pours through. Drink now. 1,000 cases made. $9.50 (1/31/92) **86**

MAURO MOLINO
Dolcetto d'Alba 1989: Fresh, lively and brightly focused, with buoyant raspberry, strawberry and plum flavors that persist appealingly on the long finish. Not a complex or profound wine, but one that provides plenty of pleasure for immediate drinking. $14 (2/28/91) **87**
Dolcetto d'Alba 1988: Light and deft, brilliant ruby in color, with delicate berry and vanilla flavors. A classic style of Dolcetto for current drinking. $12 (3/31/90) **82**

CASTELLO DI NEIVE
Dolcetto d'Alba Vigneto Basarin 1989: Crisp, tart and earthy, with modest ripe berry and cherry flavors. It's a bit rough around the edges. Drink now. $12 (2/28/91) **80**
Dolcetto d'Alba Vigneto Basarin 1987 $11 (3/15/89) **80**
Dolcetto d'Alba Vigneto Valtorta 1986 $12 (3/15/89) **73**

LUIGI OBERTO
Dolcetto d'Alba 1990: Fruity, berrylike aromas and flavors ride nicely on a smooth-textured structure, leaving a generous aftertaste of berries and plums. Drinkable now. $14 (3/31/92) **87**

ODDERO
Dolcetto d'Alba 1989: Earthy aromas and flavors tend to get in the way of the ripe plum and berry notes, but it's drinkable and friendly. $8.75 (4/30/91) **78**
Dolcetto d'Alba 1987 $9.50 (3/15/89) **78**
Dolcetto d'Alba 1986 $9.50 (3/15/89) **85**

PRUNOTTO
Dolcetto d'Alba 1985 $10 (3/15/89) **84**
Dolcetto d'Alba Gagliassi di Monforte Riserva 1985 $11.50 (3/15/89) **88**

FRANCESCO RINALDI & FIGLI
Dolcetto d'Alba 1989: Deep color and concentrated berry flavors make this an attractive wine to drink now, but it seems to have enough depth and sense of reserve to benefit from short-term aging. Try now or in 1993. $12 (7/15/91) **80**
Dolcetto d'Alba Roussot 1988: Could be fresher, but the light-textured touch of astringency allows the berry flavors to show through. $10 (7/15/91) **78**
Dolcetto d'Alba Roussot Alto 1987: Light and ebulliently fruity, all cherries and raspberries, with enough tannin to keep it from getting too exuberant. Velvety enough to drink now. $9 (3/31/90) **86**

ROCCHE COSTAMAGNA
Dolcetto d'Alba 1989: Fresh and lively, with plenty of blackberry and plum aromas and flavors and hints of currant on the finish. A zingy wine that's enjoyable to quaff. Drink now. $12 (4/30/91) **83**

LUCIANO SANDRONE
Dolcetto d'Alba 1990: Exuberantly fruity, with gobs of berry, cherry and plum aromas and flavors, a bit tannic but soft enough to drink now. Probably best in 1993. $14 (3/31/92) **87**
Dolcetto d'Alba 1989: Brilliantly fruity, bursting with blackberry and raspberry aromas and flavors. With its polished texture and generosity, this could make an enjoyable sipper, as well as a good companion to food. Some tasters thought it was hard and tannic. $12 (7/15/91) **87**

RENZO SEGHESIO
Dolcetto d'Alba 1989: Strong earthy, barnyardy aromas and flavors overwhelm the wild berry notes in this firm, medium-bodied wine. Drinkable, but not exciting. Tasted twice. 1,100 cases made. $12 (11/30/91) **77**

VALFIERI
Dolcetto d'Alba 1988: Generous and open, with pleasant leather and spice overtones to the ripe raspberry and cherry aromas and flavors. Has a velvety texture and the flavors extend into a long, tasty finish. Drinkable now. $8.50 (12/31/90) **81**
Dolcetto d'Alba 1987: Simple and fresh, but not effusively fruity. It has pleasant, smooth berry flavors, a velvety texture and a clean, persistent finish. $5.75 (3/15/89) **78**

VIETTI
Dolcetto d'Alba Bussia 1990: There's a mouthful of fruit in each sip. Ripe and flavorful, with firm tannins and lively currant, berry and plum flavors that linger on the finish. $11 (11/30/91) **85**
Dolcetto d'Alba Bussia 1989: Youthful, jammy and concentrated, with a crisp texture and generous floral berry and young-wine flavors that are reminiscent of Beaujolais Nouveau. A bracing wine that begs to be drunk soon. $12 (2/28/91) **85**
Dolcetto d'Alba della Località Disa 1988: The first thing you notice is the floral rose petal complexity of the aroma, then the raspberry and strawberry flavors come through on the palate. Could be longer on the finish, but it's immediately appealing. $12 (9/15/90) **87**

VILLADORIA
Dolcetto d'Alba 1987 $6 (3/15/89) **65**

ROBERTO VOERZIO
Dolcetto d'Alba 1990: Attractive for its currant and berry flavors, and picks up a nice touch of anise on the finish. Drink now. $12 (1/31/92) **82**
Dolcetto d'Alba Priavino 1988: Spicy, with lots of black pepper and nutmeg overtones to the generous raspberry flavors. Has a smooth, velvety texture that should match up beautifully with roast chicken. Drinkable now, but has the concentration to last through at least 1993. $11 (12/31/90) **87**

VINO DA TAVOLA

ABBAZIA DI VALLE CHIARA
Torre Albarola 1988: Lively, fruity and jazzed up with what tastes like French oak barrels. A concentrated, spicy, rich wine whose fruit flavors linger on the finish. $24 (1/31/92) **87**

GIOVANNI ACCOMASSO & FIGLIO
Nebbiolo delle Langhe 1982: Mature but still tannic, light and leathery in flavor but far too astringent for the intensity of flavor. $14 (7/31/89) **65**

ELIO ALTARE
1989: Firm and concentrated, packing in plenty of concentrated raspberry and anise aromas and flavors and hints of plum on the finish. A solid wine. Drink in 1993 to '96. $11.50 (7/15/91) **85**
Nebbiolo Vigna Arborina 1987: Very stylish, oaky and full-bodied, with plum and cherry flavors and plenty of butter and toast from the barrel aging. Try from now to 1994. $32 (9/15/90) **84**
Nebbiolo Vigna Arborina 1986: Ebulliently fruity, with intense raspberry flavor, supported by jaw-stunning acidity and relatively modest tannin. Drink it with rich food now, or save it till 1995. $20 (2/28/89) **90**
Nebbiolo delle Langhe 1988: Aromatic and complex, light on the palate but marked by tough tannins and plenty of fruit aromas and flavors. Raspberry and anise are especially pleasant. Best drunk soon with richly textured foods. $10 (3/31/90) **81**
Nebbiolo delle Langhe 1987: Grapey and berryish like a Beaujolais, but a tad more tannic, yet still in balance for drinking soon. The light texture and ebullient fruit are revelations for this usually tough wine type. $9 (7/31/89) **85**
Nebbiolo Vigna Larigi 1987: Brilliant fruit, smooth texture and a lovely touch of oak add up to a stylish wine that's rich enough to be drinkable now and tough enough to benefit from cellaring until 1993. Cherry, blackberry and vanilla aromas and flavors compete for attention. 100 percent Barbera. 166 cases made. $28 (5/31/90) **89**

BERSANO
Castellengo 1986: Has ripe, slightly raisiny aromas and flavors, but it's balanced and mature, with hints of tar and anise on the finish. A medium-weight wine that's a bit tannic, but drinkable now through 1993. $16 (4/15/91) **88**

GIACOMO BOLOGNA
Barbera Bricco dell' Uccellone 1988: Dense, ripe and concentrated, but the crisp acidity pierces through the thicket of flavors to keep it in balance, extending the raspberry, cherry and spice flavors long into the finish. Although the tannins aren't too obtrusive, it needs until 1994 or '95 to settle down. 1,400 cases made. $45 (3/15/91) **91**
Barbera Bricco dell' Uccellone 1987: Focused, concentrated flavors of raspberry, spice and cedar are nicely wrapped in a velvety structure that's long and spicy. Well-integrated tannins can use until 1994 or '95 to settle down, but this one can be enjoyed already. $45 (3/15/91) **88**
Barbera Bricco dell' Uccellone 1986: Ripe, generous and sharply focused, with a lean line of bracing acidity to balance the ripe, almost dried cherry and plum flavors shaded by spice and attractive earth notes on the finish. Long, elegant and drinkable now, but cellaring until 1993 could soften the acidity a bit. $38 (3/15/91) **89**
Barbera Bricco dell' Uccellone 1985 $33 (8/31/89) **88**
Barbera Bricco della Bigotta 1988: Ripe, rich and round, with a concentrated mouthful of smoky, toasty currant, plum and raspberry flavors that linger on the finish, echoing spice and chocolate. A great example of the new style of intense, oak-aged Barbera. Tempting to drink now, but should keep improving through 1995. 1,200 cases made. $40 (3/15/91) **92**
Barbera Bricco della Bigotta 1987: Vibrant, balanced and sharply focused, with concentrated raspberry and blackberry aromas and flavors shaded attractively with anise, vanilla and toast notes. Round and smooth on the finish. Drinkable now, but can use until 1993 to '95 to settle down. $34 (3/15/91) **88**
Barbera Bricco della Bigotta 1986: Ripe, firm and focused, with a bright beam of raspberry and cherry flavor, crisp acidity and nice touches of spice and vanilla on the long, supple finish. Well made and drinkable now. $34 (3/15/91) **88**

CARRETTA
Quercia Bric 1989: Lean and crisp, with a narrow bead of anise-scented currant and plum flavors. Finishes with a strong whiff of raspberry. Needs food to balance the tartness. $20 (1/31/92) **84**

CASAL THAULERO
Abbazia di Propezzano 1986: Very ripe and spicy, with plum and berry aromas and deep flavors that linger on the long finish, which echoes chocolate and ripe fruit. A smooth-textured, mildly tannic wine that has plenty of room to grow. Drink now or hold until 1993 or '94. $19 (7/15/91) **89**

CASCINACASTLE'T
Passum 1984 $25 (12/31/88) **61**

PIO CESARE
Nebbiolo 1983 $8 (2/16/86) **88**
Ornato 1983 $16 (3/31/88) **82**
Rosso del Piemonte 1989: Hearty and aromatic, with spice and chocolate aromas, modest plum and berry flavors and a good finish. Good for everyday drinking. Drink now. $12 (1/31/92) **83**

MICHELE CHIARLO
Barilot 1986: An earthy, chocolaty, spicy wine, with a solid core of ripe cherry flavor to balance the drying tannins. Interesting and on the gamy side, hinting at brown sugar on the finish. Drink soon. A blend of 60 percent Barbera and 40 percent Nebbiolo. 1,108 cases made. $27 (2/28/91) **80**

CLERICO
Arte 1988: Firm, focused and wonderfully harmonious, balancing generous, spicy raspberry, cherry and chocolate aromas and flavors against lively acidity and well-integrated tannins. Has a long finish. Marvelous balance and a smooth texture make this drinkable now, but it should develop well with cellaring through 1995. 516 cases made. $26 (2/28/91) **90**
Arte 1987: Uncommonly light for a Piemontese red, with plenty of berry flavors and enough tannin to qualify as a Nebbiolo. Definitely needs food. Drink now or in 1993. $22 (1/31/90) **78**
Arte 1986: A juicy, lively wine, with focused raspberry flavor, a hint of anise and firm tannins. It's crisply balanced and true to the character of Nebbiolo. $22 (2/15/89) **88**
Arte 1985 $22 (1/31/88) **91**

ALDO CONTERNO
Nebbiolo Il Favot Monforte Bussia 1983: Very spicy and complex, a wine with real character; it has the aroma and flavor of new oak barrels against a kirschlike cherry and raspberry core, hinting at chocolate and nutmeg on the finish. Firm tannins recede on the finish, making this drinkable now. $12.50 (5/31/90) **84**
Nebbiolo Il Favot Monforte Bussia NV: Lots of fruit and concentration make this one of the more accessible examples of Nebbiolo that you are likely to find. Rich raspberry and cherry aromas and flavors linger on the finish and seem almost plush on the palate. Drink now. $10 (5/31/90) **83**
Nebbiolo delle Langhe Bussia Conca Tre Pile 1985 $13 (11/15/88) **85**

CONTERNO FANTINO
Monprá 1988: Powerful, dense and fruity, with ripe cherry and raspberry flavors shaded by anise, spice and vanilla notes. Firmly tannic and rounded out by new oak. Everything is well integrated and harmonious. Best to drink after 1994. $27 (3/15/91) **91**

LUIGI COPPO
Mondaccione 1988: Drinkable but awkward, with herb and tea flavors and a thin finish. $34 (1/31/92) **73**
Mondaccione 1987: Unusually deep and rich for Freisa, which is usually light and fizzy. Delicious strawberry, raspberry, cinnamon and anise aromas and flavors float lightly on a supple structure. Has firm tannins but gentle structure, making it drinkable now, although it could be cellared until 1994. $13.50 (3/31/90) **87**

GIUSEPPE CORTESE
Nebbiolo delle Langhe Vigna in Rabajà 1988: Earthy, leathery aromas and flavors may be too much for some, but this well-balanced, drinkable wine should wash down a roast or steak nicely enough. $12.50 (2/28/91) **80**

DESSILANI
Barbera del Piemonte 1986: Supple and generous, with firm acidity to support the polished plum and

raspberry flavors. Smooth and lively on the finish. A terrific value that's drinkable now. $7 (3/15/91) BB **87**

Caramino Riserva 1985: Tart and spicy, with firm and tannic herb, cherry and anise flavors that are tight and austere. The finish is very dry and tannic. Will need until 1993 to soften and mature. $13 (9/15/90) **79**

CASCINO DRAGO

Bricco del Drago 1987: A tough, slightly musty wine, with a hard shell of tannin surrounding a modest core of raspberry flavor. Could be drinkable by 1995. $17 (1/31/92) **75**

Bricco del Drago Vigna delle Mace 1986: Tough and tannic, with a solid core of currant and plum flavors that seem, for the moment, to be locked into a shell of tannic astringency. Give it until 1997 to 2000 to see what develops. $22 (1/31/92) **81**

Bricco del Drago Vigna delle Mace 1985: Smells and tastes like a bowl full of berries, but there's a pretty good shot of tannin, which will keep it in the cellar for at least five years. An experimental wine that may or may not develop into something worthwhile. Try in 1993. $22 (1/31/89) **79**

Bricco del Drago Vigna delle Mace 1982 $14 (11/30/87) **84**

Campo Romano 1990: Very crisp and tannic, a tough wine, with little flavor at the core. Hints at berry and anise. May be better after 1994 or '95. $14 (1/31/92) **73**

LUIGI EINAUDI

Nebbiolo delle Langhe 1983 $8 (7/01/86) **70**

GAJA

Cabernet Sauvignon Darmagi 1986: A powerful, generous wine from the first whiff of cedar-tinged Cabernet flavor to the last echo of plum, vanilla and toast on the finish. Rich in flavor, showing concentration and depth to spare; delicious to drink now but cellaring until 1993 or '94 can only add polish. 900 cases made. $76 (1/31/90) **94**

Cabernet Sauvignon Darmagi 1985: Dense and concentrated, starting out very firm and tannic but opening up magically on the finish with a burst of plum, berry, leather and toast flavors that echo forever. May be best around 1995 to 2000. Best Cabernet yet from Gaja, but whoa, the price. Rel: $70 Cur: $75 (3/15/89) CS **94**

Cabernet Sauvignon Darmagi 1983 $51 (7/15/88) **91**

ELIO GRASSO

Gavarini 1989: Ripe and flavorful, with generous plum, blackberry and anise aromas and flavors. The tannins are firm, but not excessive. Drink now with rich food, or wait until 1993 or '94 for the tannins to settle. $20 (7/15/91) **83**

MARCARINI

Lasarin Nebbiolo delle Langhe 1989: Firm and concentrated, with overtones of black pepper lending interest to the ripe plum and berry aromas and flavors. Tannic enough to need until 1993 to be smooth. $9.50 (4/30/91) **84**

Nebbiolo delle Langhe 1988: Very light and especially fragrant, shining a bright beam of raspberry from the first whiff to the long finish. Not especially rich or complex, but well crafted and tasty. Drinkable now. $10 (3/31/90) **84**

MARCHESI DI GRESY

Nebbiolo Martinenga 1986 $11 (10/15/88) **82**

MAURO MOLINO

Acanzio 1989: Tight and firm, with a core of currant and cherry flavor that takes on an earthy edge. Also a bit woody, but should be more generous with time. Start drinking in 1995. $15 (1/31/92) **85**

Nebbiolo delle Langhe 1989: Brilliant cherry, raspberry and anise flavors express the Nebbiolo character clearly and forcefully in this medium-weight wine, with tannins nicely reined in making it drinkable now. Feels like it should keep improving through 1993. $14 (2/28/91) **86**

Nebbiolo delle Langhe 1988: Fresh and fragrant, but with a richness, firmness and roundness reminiscent of new oak that makes this a more complex and serious wine than most varietal Nebbiolos. Drink now or in 1993. $12 (3/31/90) **84**

Pinotu 1989: Firm and tannic, with a tight core of oak, cherry and currant flavors that are tightly bound in tannins and oak. Not too accessible now, but with time it should be more approachable. Drink in 1993. 125 cases made. $20 (8/31/91) **84**

LUIGI & ITALO NERVI

Spanna 1988: Firm, flavorful and a bit tannic, but balanced for early drinkability. The modest intensity of berry and spice flavors is appealing. $9 (7/15/91) **80**

PRODUTTORI DEL BARBARESCO

Nebbioio delle Langhe 1988: A light color, slightly earthy, bright raspberry aromas and flavors and modest tannins make this a serviceable wine that only hints at its Nebbiolo origins, with a bit more tannin than one might expect. Drinkable now. $9 (2/28/91) **82**

ALFREDO & GIOVANNI ROAGNA

Opera Prima IV NV: A tough wine that manages to keep the muscle of Nebbiolo without going overboard, but it's woody, dry and bitter on the finish with tea notes. Try in 1993. Tasted twice. $23 (7/31/89) **76**

Opera Prima Imbottigliato il 15 Novembre 1986 NV $17 (12/31/87) **82**

ROCCHE COSTAMAGNA

Roccardo Nebbiolo delle Langhe 1989: Firm and fruity, with jammy cherry and currant aromas and flavors that persist on a long, only slightly tannic finish. Drinkable now with food, but best around 1993. $13 (4/30/91) **85**

SEBASTE

Bricco Viole 1986: Very smooth and elegant, absolutely delicious, showing many layers of plum and cherry flavors and hints of spice and leather. On the light side, and not really for long-term aging. Drink up now. $16 (1/31/89) **89**

Bricco Viole 1985 $13 (10/31/87) **91**

RENZO SEGHESIO

Ruri Nebbiolo 1989: Firm and flavorful, with concentrated berry and plum aromas and flavors, a solid structure and enough tannin to keep it going at least through 1994 or '95. 1,500 cases made. $14 (1/31/92) **84**

Key to Symbols

The scores reported here are the results of blind tastings conducted by our panel of senior editors. Wines that carry the initials below are results of individual tastings.

THE WINE SPECTATOR 100-POINT SCALE ***95-100***—Classic, a great wine; ***90-94***—Outstanding, superior character and style; ***80-89***—Good to very good, a wine with special qualities; ***70-79***—Average, drinkable wine that may have minor flaws; ***60-69***—Below average, drinkable but not recommended; ***50-59***—Poor, undrinkable, not recommended. "+"—With a score indicates a range; used primarily with barrel tastings to indicate a preliminary score.

SPECIAL DESIGNATIONS SS—Spectator Selection, CS—Cellar Selection, BB—Best Buy, ($NA)—Price not available, (NR)—Not released.

TASTER'S INITIALS (JG)—Jim Gordon, (HS)—Harvey Steiman, (JL)—James Laube, (JS)—James Suckling, (TM)—Thomas Matthews, (TR)—Terry Robards, (PM)—Per-Henrik Mansson, (BT)—Barrel Tasting (these wines were tasted blind from barrel samples), (CA-date)—*California's Great Cabernets* by James Laube, (CH-date)—*California's Great Chardonnays* by James Laube, (VP-date)—*Vintage Port* by James Suckling.

DATE TASTED Dates in parentheses represent the issue in which the rating was published.

TRAVAGLINI

Spanna 1988: Nicely articulated raspberry and anise aromas and flavors run through this balanced, fresh and lively wine. The tannins are present, but not intrusive, and the flavors linger well. Not deep or complex, but appealing and drinkable. $10 (7/15/91) **83**

VALLANA

Barbera 1988: A spicy, light but flavorful style, balancing fresh raspberry aromas and flavors against nice nutmeg and pepper accents. Drink now. $7 (3/31/90) **80**

Barbera 1986 $6 (2/15/89) BB **90**

Barbera del Piemonte 1988: Crisp and sharply focused, with lots of spice, oak and raspberry aromas and flavors. Stylish, with supple texture and plenty of flavor. It's ripe and cedary on the long finish. Drinkable now but could keep developing through 1993. $8 (3/15/91) **88**

VIETTI

Fioretto 1987: Smells opulent and wonderful, with plum, smoke, leather and anise, but the flavors are not as concentrated and complex as the aromas promise. Soft and very tasty. Drinkable now, but worth cellaring until at least 1993. $17 (6/15/90) **85**

ROBERTO VOERZIO

Vignaserra 1988: An elegant, flavorful blend of Nebbiolo and Barbera that has the berry flavors and well-integrated tannins to be drinkable now, but the balance and intensity bode well for aging through 1995 or later. $24 (3/31/92) **85**

Vignaserra 1987: A tough wine to warm up to, with a tart style that dominates the ripe plum, raspberry, cherry and spice flavors. Might be too tart for many, but it's lively and firm, with plenty of tannins for cellaring. Drink in 1993. $18 (8/31/91) **85**

OTHER PIEDMONT RED DOC

GIACOMO BOLOGNA

Brachetto d'Acqui 1987: Light, sweet and *frizzante*, a rosé-colored wine that bursts with spicy berry aromas and flavors. It's just the thing to sip chilled on a warm afternoon. A beguiling wine. $16 (3/31/90) **84**

LUIGI CALDI

Gattinara 1982: Offers mature, spicy aromas and flavors on a lightweight, very austere frame that finishes tight and astringent. Not very generous. $12 (1/31/90) **69**

ANTICHI VIGNETI DI CANTALUPO

Ghemme Collis Breclemae 1985: A light wine, with surprising depth of flavor, offering black cherry, orange peel, tobacco and spice in modest proportions, but persisting nicely on the finish. Drinkable now, although the tannins could soften more by 1994 or '95. $25 (1/31/92) **81**

CANTINA DELLA PORTA ROSSA

Diano d'Alba Vigna Bruni 1990: Ripe and generous, with distinctive anise-scented raspberry and tar aromas and flavors, a smooth texture and a kiss of oak on the finish that adds a pleasant vanilla scent and round texture. Drinkable now, despite it smooth complement of tannins. May be best around 1993 to '94. 522 cases made. $14 (3/31/92) **84**

Diano d'Alba Vigna Bruni 1988: Brilliantly fruity, offering bright cherry and berry aromas and flavors balanced artfully with vanilla and chocolate overtones from oak. Well crafted, distinctive and appealing. Drinkable now, but the tannins could use until 1993 to soften. $25 (2/15/91) **85**

CERETTO

Nebbiolo d'Alba Lantasco 1988: Offers maturity and elegance, with caramel and brown sugar overtones to the modest raspberry and orange peel flavors. Needs to shed some tannin. Try in 1993. $18 (4/30/91) **81**

FRANCO-FIORINA

Freisa delle Langhe 1989: Still fruity and slightly fizzy, a sort of crackling Beaujolais, even a year and a half after the vintage. Serve chilled with appetizers. $16 (7/15/91) **78**

GAJA

Nebbiolo d'Alba Vignaveja 1985: Delicious but tannic, with appealing anise- and olive-tinged raspberry flavor, generous and open. Needs time for the tannin to subside. Drink now to 1996. $30 (2/15/89) **87**

Nebbiolo d'Alba Vignaveja 1983 Rel: $16 Cur: $28 (2/15/87) SS **94**

MARCHISIO

Roero Vigneti Mongalletto 1987: Light in color, with delicate strawberry and cinnamon aromas and flavors. Soft, appealing and simple. Drink now, slightly chilled. $10 (3/31/90) **78**

GIUSEPPE MASCARELLO & FIGLIO

Grignolino del Monferrato Casalese Besso 1988: Light, almost rosé in color, but if you expect fruit aromas and flavors, you've got the wrong wine. This is a dry, austere wine with the merest hint of berry flavor in the background. $9.50 (1/31/90) **75**

Nebbiolo d'Alba San Rocco 1986: Fresh, lively blackberry and raspberry flavors run through this wine from the first whiff to the last echo of the long finish, with floral and cedar overtones. Has enough tannin to want cellaring until 1993. A real discovery. $15 (9/15/90) **85**

MORBELLI

Carema 1982: Mature, but artfully balanced, meaty, smoky and peppery, with plenty of ripe cherry flavor to anchor it at the center, tannic but not harsh for a Nebbiolo. Has more going for it than many Barolos and Barbarescos we have tasted from this vintage. Drink now to 1995. $21 (11/30/89) **87**

LUIGI & ITALO NERVI

Gattinara 1983: Tough, tannic, earthy and coarse, a leathery wine with little grace or complexity. $11 (5/31/90) **63**

Gattinara Vigneto Molsino 1983: A lighter style, but still fairly tannic, with its faint fruit losing a battle with a wall of tannins. $15 (5/31/90) **68**

Gattinara Vigneto Valferana 1983: A toasty, spicy style, with hints of raspberry. A bit austere on the finish but generally well balanced. $15 (5/31/90) **77**

GIUSEPPE POGGIO

Bricco Trionzo 1985 $10 (3/15/89) **72**

TRAVAGLINI

Gattinara 1986: A tough, tannic wine, with a modest intensity of anise-tinged raspberry flavor. Finishes a little hot, but it could be a good drink by 1996. $18 (1/31/92) **82**

Gattinara Numerata 1985: Firm and focused, a mouthful of concentrated berry, tobacco and anise aromas and flavors that run the tannins to a dead heat on the finish. Best after 1995. $26 (1/31/92) **84**

VALLANA

Gattinara 1983: Very mature and earthy, from the first whiff to the last echo of the finish, distinguished only by a pleasant spicy pruny flavor on the aftertaste. Drink soon. $10 (1/31/90) **76**

PIEDMONT WHITE/VINO DA TAVOLA

BENI DI BATASIOLO

Chardonnay delle Langhe 1990: Firm in texture and modest in character and intensity, with pleasant pear and toast aromas and flavors. A bit on the austere side. Might benefit from cellaring until 1993 or '94. $12 (1/31/92) **79**

Chardonnay delle Langhe 1989: Lean and tart, with green apple flavors and plenty of acidity. As a crisp white wine it's fine, but it lacks Chardonnay character. $14 (7/15/91) **79**

Chardonnay delle Langhe Vigneto Morino 1989: An overtly oaky style, with heavy butter and spice

aromas and thick, buttery caramel and honey flavors, but there's not much fruit to support it. Still a good wine, but leans heavily toward oak. $27 (7/15/91) **82**
Chardonnay delle Langhe Vigneto Morino 1988 $25 (12/31/90) **87**

BOLLA
Chardonnay 1989: Light and earthy tasting with a nutty finish. Unusual for a Chardonnay, but interesting and fairly complex if you like a light style. $6 (4/30/90) **76**
Chardonnay 1988 $6 (9/15/89) (JS) **82**

TENUTA CA DU RUSS
Arneis del Piemonte 1989: Fresh, fruity and generous, brimming with citrus and pear aromas and flavors. Soft and round in texture. Drinkable now. $16 (1/31/92) **84**

CARRETTA
Bianco del Poggio 1990: Very light in color, aroma and flavor, showing a pleasant fruity, nutty flavor that leans toward apple and almond. Drink soon. $14 (1/31/92) **78**

CERETTO
Arneis Blangé 1990: Soft and flavorful, with floral, apricot and orange flavors that persist into a long finish. Not a dramatic wine, but balanced and drinkable now. $19 (8/31/91) **83**
Arneis Blangé 1989: Light, fresh and nicely soft, with floral, pear and almond flavors. Good but very straightforward. $19 (7/15/91) **82**

PIO CESARE
Bianco del Piemonte 1990: Round in texture and focused in flavor, with pleasant peach, pear and almond aromas and flavors. Clean and refreshing, with enough body to stand up to a piece of grilled fish. Drinkable now. $12 (9/15/91) **81**
Chardonnay 1988: An austere style, with reined-in flavors that echo vanilla, citrus, pear and oak. Has a smooth, elegant texture. A sound, well-made, somewhat shy wine from an area not known for Chardonnay. Drink now to 1993. 400 cases made. $37 (9/15/91) **86**
Chardonnay 1987 $29 (9/15/89) **92**
Chardonnay 1986 $29 (9/15/89) **88**

DE FORVILLE
Chardonnay 1989: Not very inviting, with flavors that lean toward toast and spice at the expense of fruit and a smooth texture. $12 (2/15/91) **75**

FRANCO-FIORINA
Chardonnay 1989: Stylish, very ripe and buttery, with nicely focused pear and melon flavors shaded by butterscotch on the nose and finish. Austere despite all the flavors. Drink now. $21 (3/31/91) **83**
Favorita delle Langhe 1988: A light, simple wine with just enough flavor to keep it going. Spicy and floral on the nose, with soft, cedary flavors. $12 (4/30/90) **75**
Freisa delle Langhe 1989: Lacks the freshness and liveliness this quaffable wine can have. Seems herbal and woody, rather than fruity. 1,166 cases made. $15 (4/15/91) **70**

GAJA
Chardonnay Gaia & Rey 1988: An assertive, aggressive wine that's not for everyone. The woody, toasty aromas give way to ripe but oak-tinged flavors of pear and melon, with a strong note of spice and oak on the finish. Tasted twice. $68 (12/31/90) **86**
Chardonnay Gaia & Rey 1987 $43 (9/15/89) **95**
Chardonnay Gaia & Rey 1985 Rel: $45 Cur: $58 (9/15/89) **98**
Chardonnay Rossj-Bass 1988: Notable for its expensive wood flavors, it is an attractive wine with honey, wood and butterscotch flavors. But the fruit lacks the richness and concentration for greatness. Drink now. $45 (3/31/90) **85**

MARCHESI DI GRESY
Chardonnay 1987 $37 (9/15/89) (HS) **85**

MOCCAGATTA
Chardonnay Bric Buschet 1987 ($NA) (9/15/89) **75**
Chardonnay Vigneto Buschet 1988 ($NA) (9/15/89) **74**

ODDERO
Chardonnay delle Langhe 1990: Greenish fruit flavors mark this as a modest white wine, with little Chardonnay verve or character. A pleasant wine to drink soon. $11 (1/31/92) **77**

ALFREDO & GIOVANNI ROAGNA
Chardonnay 1987 $20 (9/15/89) **89**

SAN STEFANO
1990: Ebulliently fruity and delicate, with a hint of crackly texture to set off the luscious pear, litchi and peach flavors. Turns slightly spicy on the barely sweet finish. $17 (1/31/92) **88**

VIETTI
Arneis 1990: Ebulliently fruity, soft and pleasant, with nice apricot, pear and vanilla aromas and flavors, hinting at sweet spices on the finish. Drinkable now. $17 (9/15/91) **85**

ROBERTO VOERZIO
Piccoli Vigneti di Langhe 1990: The citrusy aromas are appealing, but the flavors turn a bit sour on the finish. A hearty, rough-textured wine, with simple, fruity flavors. $16 (5/15/92) **74**

WHITE DOC

MARZIANO & ENRICO ABBONA
Roero Arneis 1990: Crisp and fruity, with sharply focused apple and orange flavors and a hint of cherry on the solid finish. Has a fine structure and a hint of astringency that should be softened by 1993. A stylish package and a stylish wine. $13/375ml (5/15/92) **85**

CASTELLO BANFI
Gavi Principessa 1989: Round and full of bright fruit, but it's crisp and dry on the palate, offering lots of fresh nectarine, grapefruit and spice flavors. Drink now. $12 (12/31/90) **83**

BENI DI BATASIOLO
Gavi 1989: Fresh and crisp, with lively lemon, peach and fig aromas and flavors all tightly wrapped in bracing acidity. Drinkable now, but probably better in 1993. $10.50 (8/31/91) **82**

LA BATTISTINA
Gavi 1987: A supple, smooth-textured wine. Rich, with luscious vanilla and nutmeg aromas, high-class oak and pear flavors and a lingering finish. Lacking only in fruit concentration. $18 (4/30/90) **83**

BAVA
Gavi 1989: Extremely dry and somewhat rough in texture, but it comes through with apricot and grapefruit flavors. Not for sipping by itself, but should be good with pasta. 2,500 cases made. $13 (7/15/91) **78**

BOLLA
Gavi di Gavi 1987: Delicate fig and date aromas grow to full-bodied richness on the palate, turning to almond, honey and spice on the finish. A well-made wine with flavors that will not appeal to everyone. $8 (10/15/89) **81**

MICHELE CHIARLO
Gavi Granduca 1989: Light in texture but nicely concentrated in flavor, offering peach, honey and spice characters. Appealing to drink now, and should hold through 1993. $12 (1/31/91) **84**

CORTE VECCHIA
Bianco di Custoza 1989: Full-bodied, dry and distinctive—not for everyone—but offers floral, smoky apple aromas and flavors in abundance. A bit bitter on the finish. $7 (7/15/91) **77**

GIACOSA FRATELLI
Gavi 1989: A solid wine that's not very lively, with perfumed pear and walnut aromas and flavors that fade quickly. Drink soon. Tasted twice. 1,200 cases made. $14 (7/15/91) **71**
Roero Arneis 1989: Light, crisp and spritzy, with simple pear and mineral flavors and decent balance. A good quaffing wine. 1,200 cases made. $17 (7/15/91) **77**

CANTINA DELLA PORTA ROSSA
Roero Arneis 1990: Fruity aromas and flavors run into a chalky streak on the palate that cuts them short. Don't chill too much, and it'll be fine. $17 (1/31/92) **78**

LA ROCCA
Gavi 1989: Earthy from start to finish, this simple wine has little to recommend it. $19.50 (8/31/91) **70**

VALFIERI
Gavi 1987: Despite a minty, earthy edge, this has attractive flavors of peach and apple and the firm structure to develop nicely over the next year or two. Drink up now. $5.75 (7/31/89) **79**
Gavi Villa Montersino Vigneti Borghero 1989: Fairly stylish and rich, dominated by spicy, woody aromas and flavors, modest fruit concentration and a round, buttery texture. Hints of caramel and honey linger on the finish. 2,200 cases made. $16 (7/15/91) **83**

SPARKLING

CASTELLO BANFI
Brut 1986: A coarse, simple bubbly, with modest almond and floral aromas and flavors. Attractive, simple and soft. $20 (3/31/92) **83**
Brut 1985: A tasty sparkling wine that shows good fruit flavor and a bit of complexity from aging. Has doughy, appley, buttery aromas, crisp appley flavors and a dry finish. $15.50 (6/30/90) **81**

BERA
Asti Spumante NV: Light, sweet and fruity, with charming pear and litchi aromas and flavors, turning soft and perfumed on the finish. Light in alcohol (7 percent), good for after-dinner sipping. $15 (7/15/91) **83**
Moscato d'Asti NV: The floral, perfumed aromas turn rich and fruity in this sweet, *frizzante*-style dessert wine that's very light in alcohol (7 percent), making it a perfect after-dinner wine for the summer. $14 (7/15/91) **84**

GUIDO BERLUCCHI
Cuvée Impériale NV: Delicate and light, with doughy aromas, apple and lemon flavors and a smooth texture. $12.50 (9/15/89) **81**

BONARDI
Moscato d'Asti NV: Light, fresh and appealing, slightly sparkling, with aromas of grapefruit and flavors of peach and litchi. Soft and sweet on the finish. $12 (3/31/90) **81**

CA' DEL BOSCO
Franciacorta Brut NV: Fresh ginger, citrus and honey flavors are clean and attractive in a crisp, ready-to-drink style. The finish echoes the flavors. Drink now. $41 (12/31/91) **86**
Franciacorta Crémant NV: A rich, dark, yeasty bubbly, with plenty of character, offering a range of toast, vanilla and pear aromas and flavors that weave in and out through the finish. Has substance and complexity. 1,667 cases made. $46 (12/31/91) **90**
Franciacorta Dosage Zero NV: A complex style, with toasty, buttery hazelnut, ginger and spice flavors that are rich and full blown. Picks up honey-cake flavors on the finish. Ready now through 1995. $35 (12/31/91) **89**
Franciacorta Rosé NV: An unusual style, where the flavors stray from pure fruit to more exotic flavors such as tea, spice and toasty, buttery oaklike nuances. Not for everyone, but a distinctive style nonetheless. Drink now. $42 (12/31/91) **83**

BURATI
Asti Spumante NV: Very sweet and assertively fruity. Has apricot and honey flavors and a creamy texture. $6.50 (3/15/89) **75**

CASCINETTA
Moscato d'Asti 1987: A little older than most sweet Moscato on the market, but it has a richness of flavor that makes up for any lack of freshness and fruitiness. $9 (12/31/90) **80**

COLLAVINI
Brut Spumante il Grigio NV: Soft and fleshy, with hints of spice, pear, strawberry and vanilla flavors that stay clean through the finish. Picks up toasty notes on the aftertaste. Drink now. $11 (5/15/92) **83**

CONTRATTO
Brut Classico Disgorged Winter 1989 NV: Tastes clean, crisp and dry. Modest lemon and almond flavors are well supported by acidity. $10 (6/15/90) **82**

FERRARI
Brut NV: Dry and crisp, an elegant wine with creamy texture, appealing bread dough, lemon, pear and spice aromas and flavors, all harmoniously assembled into a smooth and attractive package. $20 (12/31/90) **88**
Brut Perlé 1985: Has maturity and elegance, a smooth, tasty wine offering subtle peach, nutmeg, toast and vanilla aromas and flavors that linger attractively on the palate. $30 (12/31/90) **88**

GIULIO FERRARI
Riserva del Fondatore 1982: Extremely earthy, nutty and buttery, a mature sparkler with little fruit or youthful edge to balance the old-wine flavors. For those who like mature bubblies, the balance is fine. 400 cases made. $50 (12/31/90) **86**

NINO FRANCO
Prosecco di Valdobbiadene Rustico 1987: Spicy, floral flavors distinguish this crisp, dry wine. Earthy and dry on the finish. Good quality. $12 (12/31/91) **79**

FRESCOBALDI
Brut 1985: Complex spice, toast and yeast aromas and flavors are well integrated, harmonious and balanced, with a crisp texture and a creamy, almost gingery finish. $12 (12/31/90) **86**

GANCIA
Asti Spumante NV: Light, sweet and charming, with ebullient litchi, nutmeg and floral aromas and flavors, this smooth, creamy and immediately likable style is light enough to encourage a second glass. $12.50 (8/31/90) **84**
Brut Chardonnay NV: Very crisp and dry, showing modest melon and mineral flavors and a bracing acidity. The lingering finish offers a bit of complexity. Tasted twice. $11 (12/31/90) **82**
Brut Chardonnay NV: Light, elegant and sophisticated, showing clean, zesty floral aromas, delicate fruit and spice flavors, a smooth texture and a lingering finish. Not sweet; it's a great value from Italy. $7 (12/31/89) BB **86**

LUNGAROTTI
Brut NV: Smooth in texture but assertive, with its toasty walnut flavors. Soft on the palate with slow, tiny bubbles. $23 (3/15/89) **82**

FOSS MARAI
Brut Chardonnay NV: A charmer at a reasonable price. Very smooth and creamy, with good, subtle flavors of pear and almond and fine effervescence. $8 (3/15/89) BB **84**
Prosecco di Valdobbiadene NV: Soft and fruity, a pleasant wine. It's simple and unpretentious and slightly off-dry, with hints of lemon and vanilla to make it interesting. $11 (12/31/90) **78**

ITALY

Piedmont White/*Sparkling*

MARTINI & ROSSI
Brut Riserva Montelera NV: Unfocused lemon, earth and toast aromas and flavors make for a simple wine with a soft, slightly sweet structure. Drink cold. $15 (12/31/90) **72**

ZONIN
Brut Blanc de Blancs Chardonnay NV: Light and crisp, with delicate peach and vanilla notes that develop more oomph on the finish. Starts off like it's going to be light and fresh, and picks up steam as the flavors develop. Very nicely made, even though it's not *méthode champenoise*. A good value. 5,000 cases made. $12 (12/31/91) **88**
Pinot Grigio del Veneto 1989: Soft and generous, with flavors leaning toward the almond and walnut end of the spectrum rather than toward fruit. $7 (7/15/91) **75**

Tuscany Red/*Brunello di Montalcino DOCG*

ALTESINO
Brunello di Montalcino 1982 $22 (9/15/86) **85**
Brunello di Montalcino 1981 $22 (9/15/86) **80**
Brunello di Montalcino 1980 $18 (9/15/86) **91**
Brunello di Montalcino 1979 $20 (9/15/86) **82**
Brunello di Montalcino Riserva 1983: Soft and velvety, with generous raspberry flavors and an unsual overtone of petroleum. Appealing and already drinkable. Short-term cellaring through 1993 to '94, won't hurt, however. $29 (11/30/89) **86**
Brunello di Montalcino Vigna Altesino 1985: Very ripe, concentrated and tannic, with raisin and prune aromas and flavors managing to step out from behind a wall of hard-edged tannins. Needs at least until 1998 to 2005 to shake the tannins loose, but there is enough concentration to warrant cellaring. A solid wine. $32 (9/30/90) **91**
Brunello di Montalcino Vigna Altesino 1983: Tough and tannic, but elegant enough to make you focus on the meaty plum and raspberry flavors. The tannins seem drying on the finish, but it's anyone's guess how this will age. Try it in 1993 to see how it's developing. Tasted much better than the bottle tasted earlier. $26 (1/31/90) **84**

ARGIANO
Brunello di Montalcino 1979 $11 (9/15/86) **77**
Brunello di Montalcino Riserva 1978 $12 (9/15/86) **68**
Brunello di Montalcino Riserva 1977 $13 (9/15/86) **67**

CASTELLO BANFI
Brunello di Montalcino 1985: A classic wine from a classic vintage. Very ripe and concentrated, with cherry, coffee and nutmeg flavors that carry through to the long finish. Beautifully proportioned, but veiled in tannins that will need until at least the turn of the century to recede. $30 (10/15/90) **92**
Brunello di Montalcino 1982 Rel: $28 Cur: $35 (12/15/87) **89**
Brunello di Montalcino 1981 Rel: $23 Cur: $32 (3/31/87) CS **92**
Brunello di Montalcino 1980 Rel: $20 Cur: $33 (9/15/86) **90**
Brunello di Montalcino 1979 $18 (4/16/85) SS **90**
Brunello di Montalcino Poggio all'Oro 1985: Has all the ripeness, richness and complexity one could ask for in a beautifully modulated, elegant package. The aromas and flavors run toward plum, spice, coffee and anise, turning toward prune on the finish. Maintains its elegance through the long, complex finish. Drink after 1997. 1,200 cases made. $30 (12/15/91) CS **92**

FATTORIA DEI BARBI
Brunello di Montalcino 1982: Lean and astringent, with some spicy vanilla and leathery flavors around a core of berry flavor. Attractive, but a bit disappointing in its lack of subtlety and generosity. Rel: $20 Cur: $25 (3/15/89) **78**
Brunello di Montalcino 1981 Rel: $20 Cur: $24 (9/15/86) **85**
Brunello di Montalcino Blue Label 1986: Focused flavors and a velvety texture add up to a classy wine that offers plenty of black cherry, raspberry, anise and floral aromas and flavors. The tannins close it down on the finish, although they aren't excessive. Best after 1993 or '94. Rel: $28 Cur: $34 (8/31/91) **84**
Brunello di Montalcino Blue Label 1981: Despite classic aromas of raspberry, anise and tar, this is tough and drying on the palate. Overwhelming tannins wipe out any subtlety on the finish, but the ripe cherry flavors manage to sneak through. An outside shot for the cellar. Try in 1996 to '98. Tasted twice. Rel: $20 Cur: $24 (1/31/91) **81**
Brunello di Montalcino Riserva 1985: Lean and focused, this elegant wine has a strong thread of raspberry, plum and spice aromas and flavors that persist into a tight finish. Needs until 1995 to 2000 to start spreading out. The fruit prevails. $46 (11/30/91) **87**
Brunello di Montalcino Riserva 1977 $20 (9/15/86) **86**
Brunello di Montalcino Vigna del Fiore 1982: Thin, metallic, hard and excessively earthy, very tough and sour. $22 (3/15/89) **64**

BIONDI-SANTI
Brunello di Montalcino Il Greppo 1983: It's tough and tannic, but there is remarkable concentration of raspberry and anise to ride over the tannin and suggest that cellaring until at least 1995 will soften the edges and bring out more nuances. The focused flavors and depth of fruit are especially impressive. Rel: $66 Cur: $75 (11/30/89) **91**
Brunello di Montalcino Il Greppo 1982 Rel: $45 Cur: $62 (10/15/88) **92**
Brunello di Montalcino Il Greppo 1981 Rel: $40 Cur: $53 (9/15/86) **93**
Brunello di Montalcino Il Greppo 1980 $40 (9/15/86) **88**
Brunello di Montalcino Il Greppo 1978 Rel: $45 Cur: $55 (9/15/86) **70**
Brunello di Montalcino Riserva 1985: Firm, tannic and metallic tasting, with a cedary edge to the plum and raspberry flavors. Not a big wine, but focused and balanced. Should be fine in 1995 to '97. In three tastings there was considerable bottle variation. $180 (3/31/92) **82**
Brunello di Montalcino Riserva 1982 Rel: $80 Cur: $97 (10/15/88) CS **94**

CAMIGLIANO
Brunello di Montalcino 1980 $8.50 (9/15/86) **72**
Brunello di Montalcino Riserva 1977 $11 (8/01/85) **85**

CAPARZO
Brunello di Montalcino 1985: A controversial style, with earthy, mulchy, herbal notes and hints of cherry and spice. Has a firm texture and firm tannins, too. Best to cellar until 1995. $34 (7/15/91) **83**

Key to Symbols

The scores reported here are the results of blind tastings conducted by our panel of senior editors. Wines that carry the initials below are results of individual tastings.

THE WINE SPECTATOR 100-POINT SCALE 95-100—Classic, a great wine; ***90-94***—Outstanding, superior character and style; ***80-89***—Good to very good, a wine with special qualities; ***70-79***—Average, drinkable wine that may have minor flaws; ***60-69***—Below average, drinkable but not recommended; ***50-59***—Poor, undrinkable, not recommended. "+"—With a score indicates a range; used primarily with barrel tastings to indicate a preliminary score.

SPECIAL DESIGNATIONS SS—Spectator Selection, CS—Cellar Selection, BB—Best Buy, ($NA)—Price not available, (NR)—Not released.

TASTER'S INITIALS (JG)—Jim Gordon, (HS)—Harvey Steiman, (JL)—James Laube, (JS)—James Suckling, (TM)—Thomas Matthews, (TR)—Terry Robards, (PM)—Per-Henrik Mansson, (BT)—Barrel Tasting (these wines were tasted blind from barrel samples), (CA-date)—*California's Great Cabernets* by James Laube, (CH-date)—*California's Great Chardonnays* by James Laube, (VP-date)—*Vintage Port* by James Suckling.

DATE TASTED Dates in parentheses represent the issue in which the rating was published.

Brunello di Montalcino 1982 $31 (9/15/86) **95**
Brunello di Montalcino 1981 $18 (9/15/86) **90**
Brunello di Montalcino 1980 $23 (9/15/86) **88**
Brunello di Montalcino La Casa 1985: Very ripe and spicy, with hints of raisin, cherry and raspberry notes and a touch of anise. The texture is a bit chewy, but there's a suppleness to the tannins and it's beginning to round out on the palate. Best to cellar until 1996 or so. $53 (7/15/91) **88**
Brunello di Montalcino La Casa 1982: Smells barnyardy and tastes decayed. Not what you'd hope for with Brunello. Tasted twice. $50 (11/30/89) **67**
Brunello di Montalcino La Casa 1981: A mature, complex-tasting Brunello that shows some benefits of age. Smells spicy, earthy and slightly oxidized, but it has solid cherry, coffee and cola flavors. Very enjoyable now, but can be cellared until about 1995. $50 (6/15/90) **83**
Brunello di Montalcino La Casa 1979 $27 (9/15/86) **89**
Brunello di Montalcino Riserva 1981: Has lost its freshness and fruit without gaining complexity or depth. The mature flavors don't agree with us. Smells leathery and earthy, appears brown in color and tastes austere and nutty. $23 (6/15/90) **70**

S. CARLO
Brunello di Montalcino 1983: A beautifully perfumed, youthful wine, with full tannins, moderate fruit flavors and a sense of richness. What it lacks in finesse, it makes up for in exuberance. $23 (6/15/90) **86**

IL CASELLO
Brunello di Montalcino 1982 $18 (7/31/88) **84**
Brunello di Montalcino 1981 $15 (10/31/87) **84**

CASTIGLIONE DEL BOSCO
Brunello di Montalcino 1979 $14 (4/30/87) **93**

CERBAIONA
Brunello di Montalcino 1985: Very tough and tannic, with a modest level of fruit and lots of earthiness riding on the tough astringency. Not for us. $60 (11/30/91) **71**

LA CHIESA DI S. RESTITUTA
Brunello di Montalcino 1982: Earthy and sour, with moldy flavors and a harsh finish. Very earthy, musty, woody and dried out. Dull and bitter. Tasted twice. $23 (3/15/89) **56**

CIACCI PICCOLOMINI D'ARAGONA
Brunello di Montalcino 1984: Incredibly elegant and sophisticated, with its layering of rich new oak over solid ripe cherry, raspberry and floral flavors. Delicious and long-lasting on the finish and tempting to drink now, but it should be better by about 1993. 850 cases made. $25 (6/15/90) **91**

COL D'ORCIA
Brunello di Montalcino 1985: Very firm and elegant, offering excellent balance between the solid core of cherry and raspberry flavors and the spicy overlay of coffee and anise. A tightly wound, compact wine that's already beginning to soften around the edges. Should be approachable by 1995 or so. $23 (11/30/90) **88**
Brunello di Montalcino 1981 $22 (9/15/86) **70**
Brunello di Montalcino 1979 Rel: $15 Cur: $24 (9/15/86) CS **94**
Brunello di Montalcino Poggio al Vento Riserva 1982: Deep, dark, rich and spicy, especially on the nose, which is already expansive. On the palate, it's still tight and tannic enough to put the brakes on the focused plum, cherry and anise flavors. Lively acidity adds to the equation. Cellar until at least 2000. Tasted three times. 500 cases made. $40 (4/15/91) **89**
Brunello di Montalcino Riserva 1981 $22 (7/31/88) **89**
Brunello di Montalcino Riserva 1978 $18 (9/15/86) **65**

CONTI D'ATTIMIS
Brunello di Montalcino Ferrante 1983: Mature and complex, with nice raspberry, anise, earth and toast aromas and flavors and a smooth texture. This is an elegant wine, with a fairly long finish. Drinkable now, but it has the balance to age through at least 1993 to '96, when the firm tannins should subside. $35 (9/30/90) **88**

EMILIO COSTANTI
Brunello di Montalcino 1982 $32 (7/31/88) **81**
Brunello di Montalcino 1981 $20 (9/15/86) **80**
Brunello di Montalcino 1980 $17 (9/15/86) **89**

GEOGRAFICO
Brunello di Montalcino 1985: Very dry, with smoky, bitter coffee and stale, tired flavors. The finish shows ripe prune flavor, but this wine lacks focus and amplitude. Start drinking in 1994 to '96. $30 (7/15/91) **80**

GREPPONE MAZZI
Brunello di Montalcino 1982 ($NA) (9/15/86) **90**
Brunello di Montalcino 1981 ($NA) (9/15/86) **70**

LISINI
Brunello di Montalcino 1985: A tough wine, with burnt aromas and flavors that hint at raspberry and rose petal on the finish. Smells generous, but the flavors could be more intense. Should be better after 1995. Tasted twice. $33 (8/31/91) **81**
Brunello di Montalcino 1983: Firm and leathery, with enough ripe cherry and raspberry flavor to give the tannic toughness a run for its money. Not much generosity or elegance. $22 (7/31/89) **73**
Brunello di Montalcino 1982: The structure may be austere, but the ripe plum and cherry flavor comes through loud and clear. May seem dry on the finish, but the fruit says it could outlast the tannin. Try now. $25 (1/31/89) **84**
Brunello di Montalcino 1975 $30 (9/15/86) **78**

MASTROIANNI
Brunello di Montalcino 1982: A complex-tasting, lively, balanced wine that's approaching maturity but still has a way to go. Has aromas of spice, dried fruit and cedar, with flavors of cherry and raspberry that linger on the aftertaste. Best to cellar it until at least 1993. $17 (6/15/90) **87**
Brunello di Montalcino 1979 $17 (9/15/86) **72**

VILLA NICOLA
Brunello di Montalcino 1985: This wine from Lee Iaccoca's estate in Italy is generous, exotic and almost opulent, but the tough tannins hold it back. Ripe raspberry, chocolate, anise and nutmeg aromas and flavors carry through the long finish. Easily needs until 2000 to tame the tannins. 1,000 cases made. $32 (11/30/90) **91**
Brunello di Montalcino Riserva 1981 $14 (9/15/88) **75**

PERTIMALI
Brunello di Montalcino 1982 $25 (1/31/88) **77**
Brunello di Montalcino Riserva 1985: Ripe, tannic and redolent of smoke, coffee, plum and raspberry flavors, but the high tannin level waves a caution flag for aging. Will the flavors outlast the tannin? Try in 1998. $41 (11/30/90) **83**

PIAN DI CONTE
Brunello di Montalcino 1982 ($NA) (9/15/86) **90**
Brunello di Montalcino 1981 ($NA) (9/15/86) **88**

PODERE IL POGGIOLO
Brunello di Montalcino 1985: Spicy, elegant and plush in texture, with supple tannins supporting beautifully focused raspberry, anise and toast aromas and flavors. A hint of tamarind adds an exotic note to this A-1 wine that ought to keep improving through at least the rest of the century. 480 cases made. $34 (11/30/90) **93**

LA PODERINA
Brunello di Montalcino 1979 $13 (2/16/86) **69**

IL PODERUCCIO
Brunello di Montalcino 1986: Slightly bitter aromas and flavors give way to a rich core of anise, plum and tar aromas and flavors, all wrapped in a tough package that needs until 1995 to '97 to approach drinkability. Tasted twice. $21 (3/31/92) **83**
Brunello di Montalcino I Due Cipressi 1985: Very focused, concentrated and spicy, with all sorts of exotic accents to the basic raspberry and plum flavors. Hints of anise, nutmeg, tar and vanilla make this a lively, elegant wine that has the balance and firm tannins to keep developing well past 1995. 1,500 cases made. $22 (4/15/91) **91**

POGGIO ANTICO
Brunello di Montalcino 1986: Elegant and harmonious, with a marvelous interplay of raspberry, anise, tar and smoke aromas and flavors, all sliding smoothly across the palate on a lean, lithe structure. Hints at cherry and flowers on the long finish. Has a great future. Try after 1996. 5,000 cases made. $40 (8/31/91) **91**
Brunello di Montalcino 1985: Rich and opulent, with generous cherry, raspberry and anise aromas and flavors flecked by touches of chocolate, coffee, nutmeg and other exotic spices. The tannins are there but not domineering, making for a seductive wine that ought to start being presentable around 1994 to '98. Rel: $36 Cur: $42 (11/30/90) CS **95**
Brunello di Montalcino 1982: A rare treat in a Brunello, this wine is impeccably balanced and complex, showing a solid core of raspberry flavor surrounded by overtones of smoke, tar, anise and spice. An elegant, appealing wine that is already drinkable, but should age well into the 21st century. $25 (11/30/89) **92**
Brunello di Montalcino 1979 $12.50 (9/15/86) **72**
Brunello di Montalcino Riserva 1985: Intense and lively, with layers of rich raspberry, cedar, anise, plum and coffee flavors that are well integrated, with complexity and finesse. Not overly tannic, and it has a long, lingering finish. Best to cellar until 1996. 900 cases made. $55 (8/31/91) **93**

POGGIO SALVI
Brunello di Montalcino 1985: A tough, concentrated, powerfully built, chunky wine, with raspberry, anise and nutmeg aromas and flavors and more than a little heat and tannin on the finish. Keep it away from polite company until at least 1995 to '98. 1,500 cases made. $30 (11/30/90) **83**
Brunello di Montalcino 1981 $20 (10/15/88) **88**
Brunello di Montalcino 1979 $15 (3/15/87) **88**
Brunello di Montalcino Riserva 1981: Smells terrific, but the volatile acidity may be too dominant for many. A traditional style, with rich, complex cherry, anise, tar and wood flavors that are long and full on the finish. Nearing full maturity. Try in 1993 to '95. 1,000 cases made. $35 (11/30/90) **85**

IL POGGIONE
Brunello di Montalcino 1982 $30 (9/15/88) **88**
Brunello di Montalcino 1981 $28 (9/15/86) **93**
Brunello di Montalcino Riserva 1979 $35 (9/15/86) **79**
Brunello di Montalcino Riserva 1978 $35 (7/01/84) SS **92**

DEI ROSETI
Brunello di Montalcino 1982: Firm and elegant, with a lively interplay of raspberry, cherry, anise and cedary aromas and flavors, generous and concentrated on the palate. It should age well at least through the turn of the century. $20 (7/31/89) **89**
Brunello di Montalcino 1979 $10 (8/31/86) **88**

SAN FELICE
Brunello di Montalcino Campogiovanni 1986: Lean, firm and bursting with fruit, with a strong thread of raspberry, cherry, plum and anise flavor running through it, hinting at vanilla and spice on the finish. A beautifully balanced wine, with elegance and charm, not to mention impressive length. Almost drinkable now, but should be at its best after 1995. 4,700 cases made. $28 (11/30/91) **92**
Brunello di Montalcino Campogiovanni 1985: This tough, well-proportioned young wine has rich coffee, cedar, chocolate and currant flavors that are nicely balanced and firmly supported by a wallop of tannin. The fruit is fresh and clean, and there's a sense of grace and harmony. Needs until 1996 to 2000 to reach maturity. $24 (9/30/90) **85**
Brunello di Montalcino Campogiovanni 1982 Rel: $22 Cur: $27 (7/31/88) CS **92**

SOLDERA
Brunello di Montalcino 1985: Has a solid core of intensely concentrated fruit, with tiers of rich, ripe raisin, black cherry, raspberry and anise flavors that fan out on the palate and stay with you through the finish. It's going to need time, though; best around 1996 or '97. $90 (7/15/91) **89**

LA TORRE
Brunello di Montalcino 1985: Tough, tannic and focused, with concentrated raspberry, red cherry and nutmeg aromas and flavors. It's a bit sharp on the finish, but cellaring should bring it around by 1996 to 2000. $30 (4/15/91) **78**

VAL DI SUGA
Brunello di Montalcino 1985: A hard edge of cedar and toast flavors holds back the otherwise concentrated chocolate, raspberry and vanilla notes in this tough and tannic wine. Needs cellaring until at least 1995. $23 (9/30/90) **88**
Brunello di Montalcino Riserva 1982: Soft and supple, with generous raspberry, tea and leather flavors darting in and out of focus as the wine rides gently to a subtle, smoky finish. Has elegance and pizzazz. Drink now or in 1993. $20 (11/30/89) **89**
Brunello di Montalcino Riserva 1978 $13.50 (3/15/87) **67**
Brunello di Montalcino Vigna del Lago 1985: Hard and tannic, with drying fruit that echoes cherry, anise and chocolate, but packs in plenty of flavor despite the powerful tannins. Has lots of complexity, but it requires patience. Start drinking in 1995 to '98. 615 cases made. $52 (7/15/91) **90**

CHIANTI DOCG

CASTELLO D'ALBOLA
Chianti Classico 1988: Like a classified-growth Bordeaux. Offers vanilla, plum and berry aromas, round, delicious fruit, pepper, vanilla and spice flavors, firm tannins and a long finish. Full-bodied. Tasted twice. Drink now to 1994. $10 (9/15/91) **89**
Chianti Classico 1986: Rich and round, with a sharp edge of scratchy tannins that will need cellaring to soften, perhaps until 1993. The cedary, chocolaty overtones to the ripe cherry and berry flavors make it appealing already. $7.50 (11/30/89) **85**
Chianti Classico Riserva 1985: A tough, austere wine, bristling with tannin but not bursting with flavor, which is actually fairly modest and not distinctive, offering some berry and spice. Try now. $12 (11/30/89) **76**

FATTORIA DI AMA
Chianti Classico Castello di Ama 1988: Tannic in structure, but generous in flavor, offering plum, raspberry and spice aromas and flavors that are concentrated enough to balance the formidable tannins. Still needs until at least 1995 to soften and open up on the finish. $18 (4/15/91) **87**
Chianti Classico Castello di Ama 1987 $9 (11/30/89) (HS) **87**
Chianti Classico Castello di Ama 1986: A serious, concentrated wine, with deep, rich color, ripe fruit and firm tannins and acidity. Hasn't bloomed yet. $8 (1/31/89) **87**
Chianti Classico Castello di Ama Vigneto Bellavista 1986 $36 (11/30/89) (HS) **90**
Chianti Classico Castello di Ama Vigneto Bellavista 1985: Very spicy, opulent and ripe, almost exotic in its heady fruit intensity both in aroma and flavor, round and rich on the palate, firmly supported by fine tannins. The fruit flavors seem to echo for hours. A great cellar candidate, perhaps best around 1993 to '95. 1,000 cases made. $30 (7/31/89) **94**
Chianti Classico Castello di Ama Vigneto Bellavista 1983 $25 (12/15/87) **90**
Chianti Classico Castello di Ama Vigneto La Casuccia Riserva 1986 $40 (11/30/89) (HS) **87**
Chianti Classico Castello di Ama Vigneto La Casuccia Riserva 1985: A very extracted, full-bodied style. Smoked bacon, meat and almost jamlike aromas lead to full-bodied berry, grape and chocolate flavors. Better in 1993 or '94. $40 (9/15/91) **89**
Chianti Classico Castello di Ama Vigneto San Lorenzo 1986 $36 (11/30/89) (HS) **84**
Chianti Classico Castello di Ama Vigneto San Lorenzo 1985 $32 (11/30/89) (HS) **86**

ANTINORI
Chianti Classico 1988: Needs time to come together, but it has very good potential. Shows lovely plum and vanilla aromas, full-bodied plum, cedar and berry flavors, velvety tannins and a fruity finish. Better in 1993 to '95. $11 (9/15/91) **86**
Chianti Classico Pèppoli 1988: Defines elegance and finesse. Offers delicate plum, berry and mint aromas, lovely ripe mint, berry and tobacco flavors and a fine tannin structure. Drinkable now, but it will improve. $19 (9/15/91) **88**
Chianti Classico Pèppoli 1987: Doesn't have the depth of flavor that we liked so much in the '85 and '86. Vibrant ruby in color and grapey, jammy berry aromas are immediately likable, and the simple, straightforward flavors are ready to go right now. Reminds us of a good Beaujolais-Villages. Rel: $17 Cur: $22 (5/15/90) **83**
Chianti Classico Pèppoli 1986: Very smooth and harmonious, with chocolate- and vanilla-tinged raspberry and cherry aromas and flavors, deep, complex and very well integrated. Drink now. Rel: $17 Cur: $22 (7/15/89) **90**
Chianti Classico Pèppoli 1985 Rel: $16 Cur: $22 (5/31/88) **92**
Chianti Classico Riserva 1985: Rich and complex, a wine of depth and elegance, showing well-modulated cherry, anise, toast and vanilla aromas and flavors, beautifully structured, long and fine. Drinkable now, but cellaring until 1993 to '95 wouldn't hurt. $9 (10/15/89) **89**
Chianti Classico Riserva 1982 $10 (11/30/89) (HS) **87**
Chianti Classico Santa Cristina 1985 $6 (10/31/88) BB **90**
Chianti Classico Tenute Marchese Riserva 1987 ($NA) (11/30/89) (HS) **88**
Chianti Classico Tenute Marchese Riserva 1985: Tastes like there's a good amount of Cabernet Sauvignon here. Supple and classy, offering intense eucalyptus, mint and berry aromas and a medium-ripe, smoky finish. Drinkable now, but better in 1993 to '95. $21 (9/15/91) **91**
Chianti Classico Tenute Marchese Riserva 1983 $16 (11/30/89) (HS) **90**
Chianti Classico Tenute Marchese Riserva 1982: Firm and concentrated, turning supple and elegant as the ripe cherry and blackberry flavors develop on the palate, becoming rich and generous on the finish. A gentle grip of tannin gives it backbone, and the wherewithal to age through 1993 to '95. Rel: $16 Cur: $19 (5/31/89) **90**
Chianti Classico Tenute Marchese Riserva 1980 $16 (9/15/87) **90**
Chianti Classico Villa Antinori Riserva 1987: A little rough around the edges, but the plum and blackberry flavors manage to make their presence felt against a background of tough tannins. Better after 1993. $11 (11/30/91) **82**
Chianti Classico Villa Antinori Riserva 1983: Austere and somewhat tannic, but it also has some ripe prune and raspberry flavor. Simple, but a pleasant choice for roast chicken. $9.25 (3/31/89) **79**

B. ARRIGONI
Chianti Putto 1987: Simple, clean fruity aromas and flavors, crisp texture and a modest price add up to a good buy to slosh down a plate of spaghetti. $4.50 (11/30/89) **78**

BADIA A COLTIBUONO
Chianti Cetamura 1988: A good, old-fashioned Chianti that's firm and tight on the palate, but spicy, smoky and fruity enough to drink now with a hearty meal. $7 (12/15/90) BB **82**
Chianti Classico 1987 $8 (11/30/89) (HS) **85**
Chianti Classico Riserva 1985: Hard to hold yourself back from this one. Has a delicious concentration of fruit, with deep, rich plum and earth aromas. Full-bodied. Better in 1993 or '94. $16 (9/15/91) **90**
Chianti Classico Riserva 1983 $15 (11/30/89) (HS) **78**
Chianti Classico Riserva 1982 $13 (7/31/88) **88**

CASTELLO BANFI
Chianti 1987: Don't let the raffia bottle put you off. The wine inside is ripe and spicy, with generous cherry and cinnamon aromas and flavors, firm texture and more richness on the finish than wines twice the price. Drink now. $7.50/1L (11/30/89) BB **85**
Chianti Classico Riserva 1985: Beneath its tough, tannic exterior beats a heart of focused spice and cherry plushness, turning smooth and echoing anise on the finish. Could use cellaring until 1993 or '94 to whittle away some of the tannin. $9 (5/15/90) **86**
Chianti Classico Riserva 1982 $7 (12/15/87) **83**
Chianti Classico Riserva 1981 $7 (8/31/86) **80**

FEDERICO BONFIO
Chianti Le Poggiolo Riserva 1985: Lean and spicy, with firm tannins and modest cinnamon and red cherry aromas and flavors, hinting at wood on the finish. Drinkable now, but the tannins could use until 1993 to soften. $10.50 (3/31/90) **76**
Chianti Le Poggiolo Riserva 1982 $7 (11/15/87) **73**
Chianti Le Portine Riserva 1985: Smooth and flavorful, with spicy, cedary accents to the light cherry aromas and flavors. Velvety in texture, becoming even more generous on the finish without extra weight. Drinkable now, but supported with enough gentle tannin to justify cellaring until 1993 or '94. $9.50 (3/31/90) **85**
Chianti Le Portine Riserva 1982 $9 (11/15/87) **79**
Chianti Proprietor's Reserve 1985: Lean and spicy, with firm tannins and modest cinnamon and red cherry aromas and flavors, hinting at wood on the finish. Drinkable now, but the tannins can use until 1993 to soften. $15 (3/31/90) **85**

BORGIANNI
Chianti Classico 1982 $3.50 (4/01/85) **71**

BOSCARELLI
Chianti Colli Senesi 1986: Earthy and softly tannic, but there's a lushness and generosity of flavor and texture that makes it likable. Drink now. $8 (1/31/89) **78**
Chianti Colli Senesi 1984 $6 (9/15/87) **72**

VILLA BROTINI
Chianti Classico Villa Brotini 1984 $5.75 (12/31/87) **77**

BRUGNANO
Chianti Colli Fiorentini 1986: Fine now for everyday drinking. Smooth and fruity, showing plenty of ripe cherry and plum flavors, with touches of leather and wood on a soft but firm structure. $5 (1/31/89) BB **85**

CASTELLO DI CACCHIANO
Chianti Classico 1988: Packed with fruit and tannins. Perfumed plum, cherry and blackberry aromas lead to lots of full-bodied mint and berry flavors, full tannins and a long finish. From E. Ricasoli-Firidolfi. Built for aging; try in 1993 to '96. ($NA) (9/15/91) **90**
Chianti Classico 1986: Ripe and generous, with plenty of black cherry and raspberry flavor, well-knit tannins; smooth and supple enough to drink already, but cellaring for another year or two would not hurt. $8 (5/15/90) **86**
Chianti Classico 1985 $10 (10/31/88) **87**
Chianti Classico 1983 $6 (9/15/87) **73**
Chianti Classico Millennio Riserva 1985: Spicy and slightly chocolaty, but still very tannic and tight; this wine lacks the generosity to guarantee that it will develop well with age. Try it in 1993 to '94. $18 (9/15/90) **80**

VILLA CAFAGGIO
Chianti Classico 1988: Has lots of lively strawberry and cherry flavors in a medium-weight but fairly tannic frame. A well-balanced wine that needs cellaring until 1993 or a fairly rich dish served with it. $10 (11/30/90) **83**
Chianti Classico 1987: A fine, sharp style. Ripe and round with clear cherry flavors but also a good underpinning of crisp acidity. The fruit is strong. Drink now or in 1993. $9 (9/15/89) **86**
Chianti Classico 1986: Ripe and round, with spicy aromas and generous black cherry flavors firmly supported by gentle tannins, wrapped in a nice overlay of sweet oak. Well made and already likable. Drink now or in 1993. $9 (3/31/90) **89**
Chianti Classico 1985 $8 (5/31/88) **84**
Chianti Classico 1983 $10.50 (9/15/87) **91**
Chianti Classico 1982 $4 (10/16/85) **66**
Chianti Classico Riserva 1986: Fragrant and appealing, with generous cherry, raspberry and anise aromas and flavors, a supple texture and enough tannin to carry it at least through 1993. Drinkable now. $18 (12/15/90) **86**
Chianti Classico Riserva 1985: Has great concentration, built like a great Bordeaux. Deep ruby in color, with vanilla, plum, mint and berry aromas and masses of fruit. Built for aging. Try in 1993 to '95. $13 (9/15/91) **91**
Chianti Classico Riserva 1983 $10 (5/31/88) **80**

VILLA CALCINAIA
Chianti Classico 1988: An extremely well-crafted, delicious wine. Has plummy aromas and a good amount of wood, with plenty of plum and fruit flavors enhanced by the vanilla, wood character. Medium-bodied, with fine tannins and a velvety finish. From Conti Capponi. Try in 1993 to '96. $11.50 (9/15/91) **89**
Chianti Classico Riserva 1985: Slightly one-dimensional. A very traditional and well-made wine, with plum, chestnut and slight tomato aromas and plum and cherry flavors. Drink now. ($NA) (9/15/91) **84**

CAMIGLIANO
Chianti Colli Senesi 1985 $3.50 (12/15/87) **77**
Chianti Colli Senesi 1983 $2.75 (5/16/85) BB **82**

PODERE CAPACCIA
Chianti Classico 1988: Rich and delicious, a well-crafted wine, with nice wood components on the palate. Has surprisingly complex chocolate, cedar and tobacco aromas, with a hint of plums. Medium-bodied, with refined tobacco, chocolate and vanilla flavors, medium tannins and a long, velvety finish. ($NA) (9/15/91) **89+**
Chianti Classico Riserva 1985: Classy in structure, with well-focused fruit and silky tannins. Full-bodied, with black truffle, wet earth and fresh raspberry aromas. Needs time, but it's delicious. Try in 1993 to '94. ($NA) (9/15/91) **88**

CAPEZZANA
Chianti Montalbano 1983 $6 (9/15/86) BB **83**
Chianti Montalbano Conte Contini Bonacossi 1988: Firm and fruity, with interesting herbal, leather and earth flavors that keep it a bit rough. Has firm tannins and a dry finish. $8 (10/31/91) **79**

CARATELLO
Chianti Classico 1988: Very light and mature in color, with mature aromas and flavors, offering leather, spice and herb flavors rather than fruit. A modest, drinkable style. $9 (12/15/90) **77**
Chianti Classico 1986: Lean and spicy but not quite clean; it's slightly astringent, and the fruit doesn't come through as well as it should. $6.75 (1/31/89) **68**
Chianti Classico 1983 $4 (8/31/86) **70**
Chianti Classico 1982 $3.50 (3/01/86) BB **85**

CARPINETO
Chianti Classico 1988: Rich and chewy, with tobacco and berry aromas and plenty of delicious fruit, cedar and tobacco flavors. Medium-bodied, with medium tannins and a chewy finish. Drink now. $12 (9/15/91) **87**
Chianti Classico Riserva 1985: A wonderful glass of perfectly balanced wine. Has rich plum and berry aromas, with a hint of chocolate that carries through to the palate. Drink now. $19 (9/15/91) **89**

CASA FRANCESCO
Chianti Classico 1982: Mature, spicy and earthy, with floral overtones and enough fruit to make it appealing in a lighter style. Drink soon. $6 (11/30/89) **81**

CASTELL'IN VILLA
Chianti Classico 1988: A serious wine, showing lots of fruit and tannins. Has mint, herb and berry aromas, plenty of fresh fruit flavor, medium-firm tannins and a long finish. Try now or in 1993. $13 (9/15/91) **88**
Chianti Classico 1986: The spicy, floral aromas and flavors sit on a lean, light frame, making this a drinkable, if unexceptional wine. It's slightly tannic, but drinkable now. $13 (9/15/90) **79**
Chianti Classico 1985: Deep and rich in flavor, packed with plum, cherry, spice and other complexities. Very firm in acid and tannins, built to cellar till 1993. $11.50 (6/30/89) **86**
Chianti Classico 1983 $7 (9/15/87) **87**
Chianti Classico Riserva 1985: More mature than some, but very rich and delicious. Medium-bodied, with black licorice, chocolate and berry aromas and sweet berry and licorice flavors. Drink now. ($NA) (9/15/91) **83**
Chianti Classico Riserva 1982: At its peak, with lightly smoky, elegant, black cherry aromas. Velvety, not particularly big or generous, but the restraint is welcome. Should be great with a roast. Drink soon. $18 (11/30/90) **86**

CASTELLARE DI CASTELLINA
Chianti Classico 1988: A nice herbal edge makes the modest raspberry and cherry flavors a bit more interesting in this medium-weight, fairly tannic wine. Give it until 1993 to settle down. $12.50 (11/30/90) **82**
Chianti Classico 1987: With tobacco and cedar overtones to the modest cherry aromas and flavors, this offers more complexity than most young Chiantis. Tannins are a bit tough. Cellaring until 1993 should soften them. $11 (11/30/89) **81**
Chianti Classico 1986: Generously aromatic, but crisp and lean on the palate, offering cedary, spicy cherry aromas and tightly reined-in flavors. Drinkable now. $11 (10/15/89) **82**

Key to Symbols

The scores reported here are the results of blind tastings conducted by our panel of senior editors. Wines that carry the initials below are results of individual tastings.

THE WINE SPECTATOR 100-POINT SCALE ***95-100***—Classic, a great wine; ***90-94***—Outstanding, superior character and style; ***80-89***—Good to very good, a wine with special qualities; ***70-79***—Average, drinkable wine that may have minor flaws; ***60-69***—Below average, drinkable but not recommended; ***50-59***—Poor, undrinkable, not recommended. "+"—With a score indicates a range; used primarily with barrel tastings to indicate a preliminary score.

SPECIAL DESIGNATIONS SS—Spectator Selection, CS—Cellar Selection, BB—Best Buy, ($NA)—Price not available, (NR)—Not released.

TASTER'S INITIALS (JG)—Jim Gordon, (HS)—Harvey Steiman, (JL)—James Laube, (JS)—James Suckling, (TM)—Thomas Matthews, (TR)—Terry Robards, (PM)—Per-Henrik Mansson, (BT)—Barrel Tasting (these wines were tasted blind from barrel samples), (CA-date)—*California's Great Cabernets* by James Laube, (CH-date)—*California's Great Chardonnays* by James Laube, (VP-date)—*Vintage Port* by James Suckling.

DATE TASTED Dates in parentheses represent the issue in which the rating was published.

Chianti Classico 1985 $11 (3/31/88) **85**
Chianti Classico Riserva 1986 $11 (11/30/89) (HS) **86**
Chianti Classico Riserva 1985: Shows good fruit flavor, but it's somewhat astringent, with coffee, chocolate and plum aromas and flavors. Medium-bodied. $17 (9/15/91) **77**

CASTELVECCHI
Chianti Classico Riserva 1982: Smooth, mature and quite complex, a subtle wine, showing nutmeg, tea and brown sugar aromas and flavors around a delicate core of raspberry flavor. Probably as good as it's going to get. $13 (5/15/90) **85**

CECCHI
Chianti 1986: Light and spicy in style, with modest, tart fruit flavors. Berrylike flavors turn earthy on the finish. $5 (1/31/89) **80**
Chianti Classico 1986: Spicy and generous all the way through, from the effusively cinnamon- and cherry-spiked aromas to the finish that echoes cherry and chocolate. Has a tannic grip that warrants cellaring until 1993, although it's drinkable now with hearty food. $7 (7/15/89) **86**

VILLA CERNA
Chianti Classico 1988: A flavorful, graceful glass of wine, with mushroom, pepper, floral, violet and berry aromas. Full-bodied, with an excellent depth of classy vanilla, chocolate and berry flavors. Has medium tannins and a long finish. Delicious now, but better in 1993. $9.50 (9/15/91) **89**
Chianti Classico Riserva 1985: Shows plenty of fruit and tannins, but it's well balanced, with chocolate, plum and black cherry aromas and lots of chocolate, berry and mint flavors. Drinkable now, but needs a little more time. $16 (9/15/91) **87**
Chianti Classico Riserva 1983: Aromatic and elegant, developing complexity and depth, a bit tannic, but that should disappear next to a good roast. Spicy, leathery and toasty flavors blend nicely with the fruit. $8.25 (3/31/89) BB **84**

FATTORIA DEL CERRO
Chianti Colli Senesi 1987: Light, tart and simple, with fresh but very light strawberry flavor. $5 (7/31/89) **74**

VILLA CILNIA
Chianti Colli Aretini 1990: Crisp and focused, with bright raspberry, anise and earth aromas and flavors that stick around on the finish. Has the fruit, character and structure to drink well through 1994. $10 (1/31/92) **86**
Chianti Colli Aretini 1989: Bursting with cherry, strawberry and raspberry aromas and flavors, this is a medium-weight wine but very lively, fruity and flavorful. Drinkable now. $10 (4/30/91) **85**
Chianti Colli Aretini 1988: Ripe and lively, with beautifully defined cherry, raspberry and currant aromas and flavors that linger impressively. With its chewy texture and intensity on the finish, this should keep developing well past 1994 or '95. 1,900 cases made. $10 (4/15/91) **89**
Chianti Colli Aretini 1987 $8.25 (10/15/89) **76**
Chianti Colli Aretini 1986 $9 (5/31/89) BB **87**
Chianti Colli Aretini Riserva 1986: Earthy flavors tend to overshadow the mild but pleasant plum and spice flavors. A firm-textured wine that's drinkable, if unexciting. $18 (10/31/91) **76**

COLI
Chianti 1987: Simple, ripe, clean and spicy, a generous if slightly tannic wine for early drinking. $6 (11/30/89) **76**

CONTI D'ATTIMIS
Chianti Classico Ermanno 1987: Firm and slightly tannic, but with enough intensity of spice, raspberry and anise aromas and flavors to be a welcome companion with roast chicken or beef. Drink now. $11 (9/15/90) **82**
Chianti Classico Ermanno Riserva 1985: A ripe and complex wine. It still has plenty of tannin, but the generous cherry and toast aromas and flavors persisting on the long finish suggest that cellaring until 1993 will soften it enough to make it more appealing. $13 (9/15/90) **84**
Chianti Classico Odorico 1988: Tannic but not very intense, this is a simple wine, with leathery, slightly gamy flavors that are tough and ungenerous on the finish. Drink now. $10 (11/30/90) **78**

VILLA DIEVOLE
Chianti Classico 1988: Crisp, spicy and fruity, with nicely articulated cherry and raspberry flavors that linger on the finish, echoing cinnamon and iris. Has the ripeness and intensity to develop well through 1993 to '95. $13 (9/15/91) **85**
Chianti Classico 1987: With gentle cherry, strawberry and nutmeg aromas and flavors, this soft, light style is pleasant and ready to drink now. $8 (12/15/90) **83**
Chianti Classico Dieulele 1988: Rich and elegant, with a silky texture and aromas that add hints of flowers and spice to the solid core of raspberry and cherry flavors. Crisp acidity and well-modulated tannins make this a good candidate for cellaring until 1993 to '95. 2,000 cases made. $22 (4/15/91) **91**
Chianti Classico Vigna Campi Nuovi 1988: Firm and focused, with appealing raspberry and spice aromas and flavors. Lean; approaching drinkability. Could finish stronger. $15 (4/15/91) **82**
Chianti Classico Vigna Campi Nuovi 1987: Lean and tart, with spicy anise and pepper aromas and silky-textured cherry and berry flavors emerging on the long finish. A well-modulated wine that ought to pair well with many different kinds of food. Drinkable now. $10 (11/30/90) **84**
Chianti Classico Vigna Petrignano 1988: A light, soft style, with generous plum, spice and toasty oak aromas and flavors and hints of hazelnut and vanilla on the finish. Drinkable now. Tasted twice. $12 (1/31/92) **84**
Chianti Classico Vigna Sessina 1988: Smooth, soft and generous, this clean wine has fragrant plum and spice aromas and flavors, but isn't as intense and concentrated as it could be. Drinkable now. Tasted twice. $12 (1/31/92) **84**

TENUTA FARNETA
Chianti di Collalto 1989: Shows a bit of complexity, but still a modest wine, with appealing, earthy flavors. Smooth and ready to drink. 3,000 cases made. $7.50 (10/31/91) BB **81**
Chianti di Collalto 1988: Cedary, spicy aromas and flavors are immediately appealing in a taut, lithe structure that focuses the flavors, spreading them on the finish. Has plenty of tannin that needs until 1993 or '95 to subside, but the concentration should carry it. A terrific value. $6 (12/15/90) BB **88**
Chianti Villa Farneta 1988: Starts with a good shot of super-ripe plum flavor, but trails off quickly on the finish. Basically simple but flavorful. $13.50 (10/31/91) **79**

FATTORIA DI FELSINA
Chianti Classico 1988 $13 (11/30/89) (BT) (HS) **86**
Chianti Classico 1987 $10 (11/30/89) (HS) **83**
Chianti Classico 1986 $7.50 (11/30/89) (HS) **78**
Chianti Classico Berardenga 1988: A gorgeous wine, with super-fresh fruit. Has beautiful black cherry, bark and smoke aromas. Medium-bodied, with smoky, spicy berry flavors, silky tannins and a crisp finish. Needs to be decanted an hour in advance. Drink now or in 1993. $13 (9/15/91) **89**
Chianti Classico Berardenga 1987: Big and intense, but a bit tart as well, with lots of ripe berry flavor, earthy, spicy overtones and a long finish. A bit heavy-handed, but cellaring could straighten out the clumsiness. Try it in 1993. $8 (5/15/90) **83**
Chianti Classico Berardenga 1986 $7.50 (12/15/88) **72**
Chianti Classico Berardenga Riserva 1985: A tightly knit wine, with an extremely firm structure. Offers mint, bark, chocolate and berry aromas. Medium-bodied, with a silky mouth-feel. Drink now to 1994. $15 (9/15/91) **86**
Chianti Classico Berardenga Riserva 1983 $12 (11/30/89) (HS) **87**
Chianti Classico Berardenga Vigneto Rancia Riserva 1985: Outstanding. Very rich and concentrated, almost chocolaty in flavor and full-bodied, with supple texture and plenty of cherry and ripe plum flavors, firm tannins and hints of smoke and spice. Drink now through 1994. 900 cases made. $23 (4/30/90) CS **93**

Chianti Classico Berardenga Vigneto Rancia Riserva 1983 $17 (12/15/88) **91**

LE FILIGARE

Chianti Classico 1988: Superbly elegant, with delicate flavors and a gracious structure. Medium-bodied, with fresh plum, blackberry and cherry aromas, licorice, blackberry and chocolate flavors, medium tannins and a silky finish. Drink now. ($NA) (9/15/91) **91**

FATTORIA DI FOGNANO

Chianti Colli Senesi 1985: Very ripe, but a bit short and flat, overbalanced toward tannin. The cherry flavor doesn't come through on the finish as well as it starts. Somewhat bitter, and it smells of bark. $6.50 (5/15/89) **67**

CASTELLO DI FONTERUTOLI

Chianti Classico 1988: Very firm and concentrated, offering beautifully focused black cherry and raspberry aromas and flavors that carry through the long finish. A bit tannic and rough-hewn, but a few years in the cellar should add a bit of polish. Drink starting in 1993. $14 (11/30/90) **85**

Chianti Classico 1987: Ripe, round and generous, with an appealing touch of new oak to the spicy plum and berry aromas and flavors, all of it supported with firm texture and enough tannin to keep it from being totally smooth until 1993, but it's drinkable now. 1,500 cases made. $11 (11/30/89) **90**

Chianti Classico 1986: Well-balanced and quite lovely, with lush, plummy flavor and good, soft texture. Drink now. $11 (1/31/89) **85**

Chianti Classico 1985 $11 (11/30/89) (HS) **88**

Chianti Classico Riserva 1983 $15 (11/30/89) (HS) **88**

Chianti Classico Ser Lapo Riserva 1986: Concentrated, vivid tart cherry, raspberry and floral flavors compete for attention against a somewhat austere background of firm tannins and juicy acidity. Needs cellaring until 1993 to '95 to polish all the textures. $25 (11/30/90) **88**

Chianti Classico Ser Lapo Riserva 1985: Super-fresh and exciting, with a very elegant structure. Medium-bodied, with plum, wet earth and berry aromas, focused tomato and berry flavors, firm tannins and a lingering, crisp finish. Drink now. $18 (9/15/91) **87**

Chianti Classico Ser Lapo Riserva 1983: A serious, mature and lovely wine, with violets and a touch of vanilla on the nose, plum and leather on the palate and an agreeable finish. Drinkable now, and for several years. $15 (1/31/89) **88**

FONTODI

Chianti Classico 1989: The flavors are bright and generous in this solidly built, tightly packed wine. Raspberry, plum and rhubarb flavors race across the palate, but this is wrapped up smartly in fine tannins and will need until 1994 or '95 to show all it has. $13 (11/30/91) **89**

Chianti Classico 1988: Classy, elegant and harmonious, with a wonderful balance of fruit. Has very fresh blackberry, tar, freshly cut mushroom, mint and fruit aromas and ripe plum and berry flavors. Full-bodied, with fine tannins and a fine finish. Drink now or in 1993. 3,333 cases made. $13 (9/15/91) SS **91**

Chianti Classico 1987: Has the complexity and richness on the nose, but the tough tannins wrestle the smoky cherry flavors to the mat on the finish. Needs until 1994 to soften the tannins, but then what? $8 (11/30/89) **81**

Chianti Classico 1986 $9 (1/31/89) **74**

Chianti Classico Riserva 1985: A wine supercharged with fine fruit and an excellent backbone of tannins and acidity. Has stunning aromas of blackberry, cedar, cassis and mint, and a crisp finish. Ready to drink now, but it will improve. $16 (9/15/91) **93**

Chianti Classico Riserva 1983 $8.75 (9/15/87) **87**

Chianti Classico Riserva 1982 $7.50 (9/15/87) **87**

Chianti Classico Vigna del Sorbo Riserva 1985: Full and flavorful, with a firm backbone of acidity and tannins. Has fresh blackberry, cedar and meat aromas and intense blackberry and licorice flavors and acidity. Ready to drink now, but better in 1993. $25 (9/15/91) **88**

FOSSI

Chianti 1990: Very firm, flavorful and fairly tannic, a robust Chianti, with plum and black pepper flavors and plenty of body. Probably best to drink after 1993. $8.50 (4/30/92) **83**

Chianti 1988: An earthy, distinctive style that doesn't hide its tannins. Offers plum and sun-dried tomato flavors. Best to wait a year or two to smooth out the rough texture. 4,500 cases made. $8 (10/31/91) BB **84**

Chianti Classico Riserva 1985: Earthy, with more woodsy, minerallike aromas and flavors than fruit, but it's firm-textured and has enough plum and cherry notes lurking in the background to warrant cellaring until 1993 to '95 to see what develops. 2,500 cases made. $18 (9/15/91) **82**

CASA FRANCESCO

Chianti Riserva 1985: A light style, with a real sense of elegance and grace, plus fairly persistent raspberry, vanilla and nutmeg flavors. The tannins are present without overwhelming the fruit. Drinkable now. $8.50 (9/15/91) **88**

FRESCOBALDI

Chianti 1989: Earthy animal aromas and flavors won't be to everyone's taste, but the soft structure and ripe fruit flavor make this a decent drink. Tasted twice. $5.50 (4/15/91) **70**

Chianti 1988: Soft and luscious, offering a bright beam of cherry and strawberry flavors, supple texture and a generous, supple finish. Drink soon. $5 (11/30/89) BB **85**

Chianti 1987: Lean and somewhat austere, its cherry flavor shortened by a metallic edge. Drinkable now. $4.50 (5/15/89) **75**

Chianti 1986 $3.50 (12/15/87) **75**

Chianti Rufina Castello di Nipozzano Riserva 1988 ($NA) (11/30/89) (BT) (HS) **90**

Chianti Rufina Castello di Nipozzano Riserva 1986: Very lively and fruity, with cranberry and pepper flavors, good balance and a hint of chocolaty richness on the finish. Easy to enjoy with meals. $11 (9/15/90) **82**

Chianti Rufina Castello di Nipozzano Riserva 1985: Very well made, offering dusky cherry and berry flavors, supple texture and a firm structure. Drinkable now, but it should age gracefully for years to come. $11 (11/30/89) **88**

Chianti Rufina Castello di Nipozzano Riserva 1983 $10 (11/30/89) (HS) **89**

Chianti Rufina Montesodi 1988 $19 (11/30/89) (BT) (HS) **87**

Chianti Rufina Montesodi 1985: Since this is from Rufina and not Classico, it's a ringer, but it's excellent. Has a generous amount of French wood, but it works in aromas, finely tuned berry, mint and vanilla flavors, silky tannins and a fine finish. Full-bodied. Try in 1993 to '95. $35 (9/15/91) **90**

Chianti Rufina Montesodi 1982 Rel: $28 Cur: $34 (12/15/88) **86**

CASTELLO DI GABBIANO

Chianti Classico 1987: A core of concentrated cherry and strawberry flavor is surrounded by somewhat coarse tannins and an overlay of earthy flavors, but it's approachable now if you drink it with cheese. $7 (11/30/89) **81**

Chianti Classico 1986: Lean and racy, with sharply focused cherry, berry and cedar aromas and flavors, it's fairly long and a bit tannic. Drink soon. $7.75 (5/31/89) BB **82**

Chianti Classico 1985 $7 (2/15/88) **72**

Chianti Classico 1983 $6 (5/31/87) BB **85**

Chianti Classico 1982 $6.25 (1/01/86) **68**

Chianti Classico Riserva 1982 $10.50 (7/31/88) **84**

Chianti Classico Riserva Gold Label 1982: Spicy, toasty, remarkably concentrated, but also tannic and tough on the finish. An austere style, but generous enough at the end to warrant cellaring until at least 1993 to see what develops. $21 (11/30/89) **79**

Chianti Classico Riserva Gold Label 1981 $18 (2/15/88) **81**

CANTINA GATTAVECCHI

Chianti Colli Senesi 1990: Tastes very young and fresh, with raspberry and pepper notes, but the stiff tannins and firm acidity indicate it should be cellared until at least 1993 before drinking. $7.75 (4/30/92) **80**

GEOGRAFICO

Chianti Classico 1988: Tough and tannic, with interesting, bright cherry and spice flavors, but somewhat awkward, with a drying, leathery finish. Drink in 1993. $9.75 (11/30/91) **78**

Chianti Classico Castello di Fagnano 1989: Light, tart and slightly off, with muddy flavors that overwhelm the modest berry flavor. $9.75 (1/31/92) **70**

Chianti Classico Castello di Fagnano 1988: Supple and smooth textured, with great balance and a sense of elegance. Rich and fairly concentrated, with ripe plum and black cherry flavors that linger nicely on the finish. $9.75 (10/31/91) **86**

Chianti Classico Contessa di Radda 1987: Soft and tasty, with pleasant ripe berry and floral aromas and flavors. A bit tannic on the finish, but drinkable now. $11 (10/31/91) **80**

Chianti Classico Tenuta Montegiachi Riserva 1986: An aromatic wine that turns a bit too tough and tannic on the palate, with attractive spice and cherry aromas that don't quite come through on the palate. Tannic enough to need until 1993 to '95. $14.50 (10/31/91) **79**

PODERI DI GRETOLE

Chianti Classico 1988: Full-blown, with exuberant, fruity flavors dominated by cherry and ripe plum notes. A touch of earthiness adds complexity. Balanced for drinking now. $8 (10/31/91) BB **82**

Chianti Classico Riserva 1986: Complex aromas are the hallmark of this mature, ready-to-drink wine, with attractive minty, earthy aromas followed by decent cherry and plum flavors. A bit dry on the finish, but fine overall. $11 (10/31/91) **83**

CASTELLI DEL GREVEPESA

Chianti Classico Sant'Angiolo Vico Labate 1988: A monster of a wine that needs time to develop; it's like a barrel sample. Cigar box, tobacco, berry and cherry aromas lead to full-bodied flavors of tar, berries and bitter chocolate and full tannins, but it's slightly short on the finish. Don't drink now, try in 1994 to '96. ($NA) (9/15/91) **88**

VITTORIO INNOCENTI

Chianti 1987: Soft, ripe and generous, with plenty of spicy, toasty cherry aromas and flavors overlaid with definite hints of black pepper and oak. Drinkable now. $7 (5/15/90) BB **83**

Chianti 1986: A bit on the astringent side, but the black pepper-scented grape aromas and flavors manage to make their presence felt in this sturdy, simple wine. Drinkable now with hearty food, but probably better around 1993. $7 (3/31/90) **77**

ISOLE E OLENA

Chianti Classico 1988: A bit tough and tannic, but with plenty of concentrated cherry, currant and floral flavors and hints of spice and oak on the finish. Needs until 1993 to '96 to let the tannins subside, but it should be a beauty. A great value. $9 (11/30/90) BB **89**

Chianti Classico 1987: A very sophisticated Chianti. Full-flavored, spicy and berrylike with hints of coffee and vanilla and a cherry aftertaste. Crisp with tannins and acid on release, but should be drinkable now. Rel: $9 Cur: $12 (9/15/89) **88**

Chianti Classico 1986 $7.50 (7/31/88) **86**

Chianti Classico 1985 Rel: $7.50 Cur: $14 (5/31/88) BB **89**

Chianti Classico 1983 Rel: $5 Cur: $9 (12/15/86) BB **85**

LAMOLE DI LAMOLE

Chianti Classico 1988: Classy, with elegant mint, berry and fruit aromas and focused fruit flavors. New wood used in the maturation has come together on the palate. Full-bodied, but extremely balanced, with mint, earth and excellent fruit flavors, fine tannins and a long finish. From Fattoria Pile e Lamole. Drink now. $12 (9/15/91) **90**

Chianti Classico Vigneto di Campolungo 1985: Spicy, herbal aromas mark this as distinctive from the start, with generous, sharply focused black cherry and raspberry flavors emerging on the palate. Tannic, like most '85 riservas, but concentrated enough to age gracefully through at least 1993 to '94. $20 (4/30/90) **90**

LANCIOLA II

Chianti Colli Fiorentini 1987: A disappointing wine from a good vintage. Lots of wood, and it's hard and mossy. A wine of inferior quality. $7.75 (5/15/89) **68**

LILLIANO

Chianti Classico 1988: Equal parts of ripe blackberry flavor and gravelly tannins, marked by more than a touch of earthy flavors, make this a wine not everyone will love. Must be consumed with hearty food. $10 (11/30/90) **81**

Chianti Classico 1987: Has a ripe, intense style, bursting with plummy, berrylike Sangiovese flavor and more than a touch of the earthy, gamy aspects of traditional Chianti. Raw on release, but it should have come around by now. $8.50 (11/30/89) **86**

Chianti Classico 1986: Thin and bitter, with anise and plum notes, but not much to rave about. Tasted twice. $7.75 (5/15/89) **70**

Chianti Classico 1985 $6 (10/31/87) **74**

Chianti Classico Riserva 1985: Still tough and tannic, but you can feel the intensity of complex cherry and toast flavors straining to get through. Worth cellaring until 1993 to '95 to see what develops. $14 (11/30/89) **89**

FATTORIA DI LUCIGNANO

Chianti Colli Fiorentini 1990: This concentrated, stylish wine has plenty of oak-accented fruit flavor to stand up to the tannins. Tempting to drink now, but it should be better in 1993 and beyond. $7.50 (4/30/92) BB **85**

Chianti Colli Fiorentini 1987: Straightforward and solidly oaky, with spicy, leathery aromas and modest fruit flavors. $6 (6/30/89) **76**

LUIANO

Chianti Classico Riserva 1978 $6 (8/31/86) **71**

MACHIAVELLI

Chianti Classico Riserva 1986: Lean and firm in texture, with focused cherry and spice aromas and flavors that persist into a long, somewhat tannic finish. Drinkable now with rich food, but probably best after 1993. $16 (10/31/91) **84**

Chianti Classico Vigna di Fontalle Riserva 1985: An outstanding wine, with great class and structure. Very dark ruby in color. Has powerful berry and cassis aromas and masses of structure, but it's very velvety. Needs time to develop. Try in 1994 to '97. ($NA) (9/15/91) **91**

LA MADONNINA

Chianti Classico 1988: Middle-of-the-road. Medium in body and tannins, with wild blackberry and earthy chestnut aromas and earthy berry flavors. Drink now. ($NA) (9/15/91) **84**

VILLA MARCIALLA

Chianti Colli Fiorentini 1986: Soft and velvety, with ripe cherry and toast aromas and flavors, it's a bit short and simple. $6 (10/15/89) **79**

MARTINI DI CIGALA

Chianti Classico San Giusto a Rentennano 1987: A basic, decent Chianti, with clean, fruity aromas and flavors, but little depth or ripeness. Tasted twice. $9 (3/31/90) **74**

Chianti Classico San Giusto a Rentennano 1986: Crisp cherry and currant flavors are dominated by young tannins. Has an earthy, smoky component and good, ripe fruit. $8 (1/31/89) **79**

Chianti Classico San Giusto a Rentennano 1985 $8 (11/30/87) **87**

Chianti Classico San Giusto a Rentennano 1983 $6.25 (9/15/87) **80**

Chianti Classico San Giusto a Rentennano Riserva 1985: Opulent aromas and flavors of spicy plum and cherry cascade appealingly over the palate in this nicely packaged, medium-bodied wine.

Drinkable now, but it has the spice-box intensity, complexity and tannin to stand cellaring until 1995. $17 (11/30/89) **91**
Chianti Classico San Giusto a Rentennano Riserva 1983 $11 (11/15/87) **87**

LE MASSE
Chianti Classico 1988: Generous, flavorful, ripe and balanced, with lots of raspberry, plum and floral aromas and flavors, a tight structure and firm acidity. A bit rough around the edges now, and probably best after 1993. $12.50 (4/30/91) **87**
Chianti Classico 1985: A triumph of modern winemaking, ripe, rich and complex, with a firm grip of tannin to keep it in line, with sweet oak, blackberry and cherry flavors competing for attention on the broad finish. Has elegance and roundness, and impressive length. Drink now. $12 (7/15/89) **92**
Chianti Classico Riserva 1985: Well crafted, with elegant fruit and structure, no rough edges here. Has wonderful blackberry and black licorice aromas and razor-sharp berry flavors. Drink now or hold. $20 (9/15/91) **89**

MELINI
Chianti Borghi d'Elsa 1989: Light in texture but generous in flavor, offering lots of black cherry and raspberry notes plus a nice hint of smoke. Drinkable now. $6.50 (10/31/91) **81**
Chianti Classico 1987: Very fresh, clean and jammy tasting, with raspberry and bright cherry flavors, simple structure and soft tannins. Drink now. $7 (4/30/90) **80**
Chianti Classico 1986 $6 (10/31/88) BB **83**
Chianti Classico 1985 $5 (7/31/88) BB **82**
Chianti Classico Isassi 1988: A full-bodied wine that's extremely fresh and enticing, with lots of fruit. Has complex violet, tomato and rose petal aromas and very lively fruit flavor and acidity, like freshly crushed grapes. Drink now or in 1993. BB $8.50 (9/15/91) **89**
Chianti Classico Laborel Riserva 1986: Lean and tannic, but a streak of lively plum and cherry flavors persist into the crisp finish. Needs to soften with cellaring until 1994 or '95. $10 (10/31/91) **83**
Chianti Classico Vigneti la Selvanella Riserva 1985: Harmonious and refined, with attractive violet, mint and berry aromas. Full-bodied, with a silky texture and plenty of berry, cherry and mint flavors. Has lovely balance. Drink now. $7 (9/15/91) BB **87**

CASTELLO DI MONSANTO
Chianti Classico Il Poggio Vineyard Riserva 1985: Tough and tannic, but the spicy, cedary raspberry aromas and flavors manage to make themselves felt. Needs cellaring to tame the tannins, perhaps until 1994 to '95. Rel: $25 Cur: $30 (3/31/90) **80**
Chianti Classico Il Poggio Vineyard Riserva 1983 $23 (11/30/89) (HS) **86**
Chianti Classico Il Poggio Vineyard Riserva 1982 $23 (11/30/89) (HS) **93**
Chianti Classico Il Poggio Vineyard Riserva 1981 $17 (11/30/89) (HS) **82**
Chianti Classico Il Poggio Vineyard Riserva 1979 $16 (9/15/87) **93**
Chianti Classico Riserva 1986: Tough, tannic and lean, but it has a nice concentration of cherry and anise flavors. Drinkable now with rich food, but better around 1994. $15 (4/15/91) **85**
Chianti Classico Riserva 1985 $10 (11/30/89) (HS) **89**
Chianti Classico Riserva 1982 $10 (2/15/88) **72**
Chianti Classico Riserva 1981 $10 (12/15/87) **67**
Chianti Classico Riserva 1979 $9.50 (11/01/84) **83**

FATTORIA MONTAGLIARI
Chianti Classico Riserva 1985: Very pleasing, with generous, mature fruit. Strong cherry, chocolate and blackberry aromas lead to medium-bodied cherry, chocolate and berry flavors. Drink now. ($NA) (9/15/91) **83**

VILLA DE MONTE
Chianti Rufina Riserva 1985: Has more leather, mineral and earth flavors than fruit, but it's nicely rounded from aging. Smooth, mature and simple. 1,400 cases made. $13 (4/30/92) **80**
Chianti Rufina Riserva 1979: Complex, interesting and showing its age in the leathery aromas and smooth, spicy, woody flavors. May have had more fruit a few years earlier, but it's still a good bottle of wine. 950 cases made. $16 (4/30/92) **81**

CASTELLO DI MONTEGROSSI
Chianti Classico 1988: Incredibly packed with fruit, yet it shows great class, with mint, green tobacco and cherry aromas and tons of strawberry, tobacco and cherry flavors. Full-bodied, with full yet soft tannins and a long finish. From E. Ricasoli-Firidolfi. Better in 1994. $15 (9/15/91) **91**
Chianti Classico 1986: Very firm and generous of flavor, rounding out the Chianti cherry flavor with hints of toast and vanilla, showing depth of flavor, complexity and excellent length. Delicious now, but should hold through 1993. $8 (7/15/89) **89**
Chianti Classico 1985 $5.50 (9/15/88) **86**

FATTORIA MONTELLORI
Chianti Putto 1988: Ripe, grapey, generous and smooth, a delicious wine to drink now for its exuberance and suppleness. $6 (11/30/89) **83**

NICCOLINI
Chianti 1990: Nicely fruity and focused, with bright cherry and plum flavors accented by a bit of black pepper and herbs. Well balanced, with moderate tannins and a fruity finish. Drink now through 1994. $6 (4/30/92) BB **84**

NOZZOLE
Chianti Classico Riserva 1986: Firmly tannic, with tart cherry and nutmeg aromas and flavors. A lean and lively style that should be fine with grilled meat or poultry. Drinkable now. $9.50 (10/31/91) **83**
Chianti Classico Riserva 1985: A little mean now, but it shows promise, with an abundance of focused fruit, full tannins, elegant aromas of violets, strawberries and cherries and an elegant finish. Try in 1995 to '97. $13 (9/15/91) **88**
Chianti Classico Riserva 1981 $7 (10/31/87) **72**
Chianti Classico Vigneto la Forra 1982: Smells and tastes very mature, with all the earthy, dried tomato flavors associated with age, but it's still more than a little tight and tannic. Drink with rich pasta sauces, but it's nothing special. $20 (10/31/91) **77**

PAGLIARESE
Chianti Classico 1985 $6 (3/31/88) **76**
Chianti Classico Boscardini Riserva 1981 $9.25 (5/31/88) **82**
Chianti Classico Boscardini Riserva 1980 $9.50 (3/15/87) **85**

Key to Symbols

The scores reported here are the results of blind tastings conducted by our panel of senior editors. Wines that carry the initials below are results of individual tastings.

THE WINE SPECTATOR 100-POINT SCALE ***95-100***—Classic, a great wine; ***90-94***—Outstanding, superior character and style; ***80-89***—Good to very good, a wine with special qualities; ***70-79***—Average, drinkable wine that may have minor flaws; ***60-69***—Below average, drinkable but not recommended; ***50-59***—Poor, undrinkable, not recommended. "+"—With a score indicates a range; used primarily with barrel tastings to indicate a preliminary score.

SPECIAL DESIGNATIONS SS—Spectator Selection, CS—Cellar Selection, BB—Best Buy, ($NA)—Price not available, (NR)—Not released.

TASTER'S INITIALS (JG)—Jim Gordon, (HS)—Harvey Steiman, (JL)—James Laube, (JS)—James Suckling, (TM)—Thomas Matthews, (TR)—Terry Robards, (PM)—Per-Henrik Mansson, (BT)—Barrel Tasting (these wines were tasted blind from barrel samples), (CA-date)—*California's Great Cabernets* by James Laube, (CH-date)—*California's Great Chardonnays* by James Laube, (VP-date)—*Vintage Port* by James Suckling.

DATE TASTED Dates in parentheses represent the issue in which the rating was published.

PODERE IL PALAZZINO
Chianti Classico 1988: Bursting with fruit, but it still has great balance. Offers lovely perfumed aromas of violet, mint and plum and full-bodied, intensely focused mint, raspberry and blackberry flavors. Medium in tannins and finish. Drinkable now, but it will improve. $16 (9/15/91) **90**
Chianti Classico 1987: Has extremely earthy, swampy aromas that put us off. Tastes OK, but it's difficult to get past the aromas. Tasted twice. $12 (3/31/90) **67**
Chianti Classico 1986: For consumers who want an assertive, woody character. Very distinctive in style, with effusive earthy, toasty aromas, and a meaty, chocolaty flavor. Ripe fruit is underneath. $9 (1/31/89) **86**
Chianti Classico 1985 $11 (11/30/87) SS **93**
Chianti Classico 1983 $5 (9/16/85) **78**
Chianti Classico Riserva 1985: Packed to the brim with ripe fruit and earth flavors. Not for everyone, it's decadent, offering barnyardy berry and ripe fruit aromas, ripe blackberry and chocolate flavors and a velvety mouth-feel. A full-bodied wine to drink now. $22 (9/15/91) **88**
Chianti Classico Riserva 1983 $21 (11/15/87) **80**
Chianti Classico Riserva 1981 $6.25 (4/16/86) **69**

CASTELLO DELLA PANERETTA
Chianti Classico 1988: Rustic and short, with decent fruit. Offers dark chocolate aromas, with floral hints and a slight musty note, and medium-bodied chocolate flavors. Drink now. ($NA) (9/15/91) **79**
Chianti Classico Riserva 1985: A standout, with super-rich, opulent fruit. Has cherry, green tobacco, cedar and spice aromas and cedar, berry and chocolate flavors. Full-bodied. Drinkable now, but it will improve with age. ($NA) (9/15/91) **92**

PANZANO
Chianti Classico Riserva 1985: Refreshing and easy to drink. Fresh blackberry and bitter chocolate aromas lead to medium-bodied fresh fruit flavors. Has silky tannins, fine acidity and a firm finish. Tasted twice. Drink now. ($NA) (9/15/91) **86**

PASOLINI
Chianti 1986: A smooth, mature Chianti that's ready to drink now. Tastes plummy, has soft tannins and medium body. $6.50 (12/15/90) **78**
Chianti 1985 $5 (9/15/88) **79**

PODERE PETROIO
Chianti Classico 1988: Very crisp and drinkable, but a little high in acidity. Picked too early? Elegant and subtle, with mint, berry and chocolate aromas. Medium-bodied, with peppery cherry flavors, medium tannins and a crisp finish. Drinkable now, but better in 1993 or '94. ($NA) (9/15/91) **83**
Chianti Classico Cru Montetondo 1988: Flavorful and wonderful, with all the character you could want. Has perfumed aromas of wet earth and berries, and the palate blasts off. Full-bodied, with great balance, super-fine tannins and a symphony of flavors. Drink now to 1994. ($NA) (9/15/91) **90**

PLACIDO
Chianti 1989: Has pretty currant and cherry-tinged flavors in a straight-ahead style. At $6, it won't shortchange you on fruit, but you don't get a whole lot more. Drink now. $6 (7/15/91) **76**

POGGERINO
Chianti Classico 1988: Ripe but simple, a little *frizzante*. Cherry and prune flavors dominate. Full-bodied, with decent balance and little on the finish. $12.50 (11/30/91) **78**

POGGIARELLO
Chianti Classico De Rham i Riservati 4 1985 $6 (10/31/88) BB **83**

POGGIO A FRATI
Chianti Classico Riserva 1985: Still seems a little disjointed, needs time to soften the rough edges. Shows basil, tomato and berry aromas and straightforward fruit flavors. From Rocca di Castagnoli. Better in 1993 or '94. ($NA) (9/15/91) **84**

POGGIO AL SOLE
Chianti Classico 1988: A blockbuster. Full-bodied, with meaty, ripe berry aromas and masses of fruit and chocolate flavors. Has a huge tannin structure, but it's supple and focused on the finish. Try in 1993 to '95. ($NA) (9/15/91) **91**
Chianti Classico Riserva 1985: Decadent and earthy, but it has an abundance of fruit, with freshly cut mushroom, earth, berry and very sweet fruit aromas and flavors, silky tannins and a delicious finish. Drink now to 1994. ($NA) (9/15/91) **88**

IL POGGIOLINO
Chianti Classico Riserva 1985: The lovely aromas of violets, roses, truffles and fruit are impressive, but it's rather simple and almost too crisp on the palate. Medium-bodied, with lots of violet flavors, but it's rather high in acidity. Drink now. ($NA) (9/15/91) **84**

FATTORIA LA QUERCE
Chianti 1985 $9.50 (11/30/87) **83**
Chianti Classico 1988 $9 (11/30/89) (BT) (HS) **86**
Chianti Classico 1987 $7 (11/30/89) (HS) **80**
Chianti Classico 1986 $7 (11/30/89) (HS) **81**

CASTELLO DI QUERCETO
Chianti Classico 1988: Refreshing, with plenty going on in the glass. Vanilla, tar and cherry aromas open to a palate full of cherry and tar flavors. Has medium tannins and a juicy finish. Can improve. From Alessandro François. Drink now or in 1993. $14 (9/15/91) **86**
Chianti Classico Riserva 1985: Gloriously rich and round, with opulent plum, cherry and raspberry aromas and flavors that seem to open up as they linger on the palate. The tannins are firm enough to support the generous flavors but do not intrude. Drinkable, but why not wait to see what develops, at least through 1995. 1,800 cases made. $16 (11/30/89) **91**

LA QUERCIA
Chianti Classico 1988: Very fruity and exciting in a super-fresh style, with exotic rose petal, cherry and floral aromas. Medium-bodied, with intense cherry flavors, medium tannins and a focused finish. From Giovanni Cappelli. Drink now. ($NA) (9/15/91) **86**

FATTORIA QUERCIABELLA
Chianti Classico 1988: Wonderfully fragrant, with overpowering fruit. Has enticing mint, raspberry and fruit aromas, with smoky berry and raspberry flavors, medium tannins and a velvety finish. Full-bodied. Better in 1993 to '95. $13 (9/15/91) **90**
Chianti Classico Riserva 1985: A well-crafted wine, with lovely tobacco and chocolate character. The plum, cherry and tomato aromas are elegant. Medium-bodied, with plum, cedar and berry flavors, fine tannins and a rich finish. Drink now. $17 (9/15/91) **89**

CASTELLO DEI RAMPOLLA
Chianti Classico 1987: Ripe and tannic, with well-focused cherry, plum and floral aromas and flavors. Medium weight and soft in texture, but has enough astringency to need until 1993 to '95 to settle down. $15 (4/15/91) **84**
Chianti Classico 1985 $8 (9/15/88) **90**
Chianti Classico 1983 $6.50 (7/31/87) BB **84**
Chianti Classico 1982 $6 (10/16/85) **64**
Chianti Classico Riserva 1985: A problematic wine, loaded with rich chocolate, raisin and cherry flavors, but smothered with fairly tough tannins that will need until 1994 or '95 to soften. Tasted three times. $16 (4/30/90) **81**

BARONE RICASOLI
Chianti 1989: Woody, vegetal aromas and flavors overpower whatever fruit might be there, and it's rough and tannic for such a light wine. $7 (4/15/91) BB **83**

Chianti Classico Brolio 1988: A big style, with lots of earthy fruit character. Shows plum and leather aromas, with a hint of mint, and juicy tobacco and meat flavors. Full-bodied, with medium tannins and a slightly dry finish. Drink now or hold. $9.50 (9/15/91) **84**
Chianti Classico Brolio 1987: Firm and flavorful, with generous black cherry and plum aromas and flavors and hints of smoke and spice on the finish. A bit tannic, but drinkable now. $12 (10/31/91) **84**
Chianti Classico Brolio 1986: Has spicy, appealing aromas, but it turns tart and unyielding on the palate, with little underlying fruit or intensity of flavor to warrant longer aging. Drink with something rich. Tasted twice. $8 (11/30/90) **77**
Chianti Classico Brolio 1985 $7 (11/30/89) (HS) **85**
Chianti Classico Brolio 1984 $4 (9/15/87) **73**
Chianti Classico Brolio Riserva 1985: A subtle wine with plenty of character. Has fresh blackberry and cherry aromas, lush, generous berry flavors and a hint of smoke, with silky tannins and a crisp finish. Medium-bodied. Drink now. $12 (9/15/91) **86**
Chianti Classico Brolio Riserva 1983: Soft, supple and spicy, a big wine that lacks the backbone to really take off. Tasty and easy to drink. $10 (5/15/90) **80**
Chianti Classico Brolio Riserva 1983: Mature and rich, with velvety texture, complex flavors of cedar, spice, dark cherry and toast. An intriguing wine that would be better if it had a bit more concentration. $8 (3/31/89) BB **83**
Chianti Classico Brolio Riserva del Barone 1983 $11 (11/30/89) (HS) **85**
Chianti Classico Brolio Riserva del Barone 1978 $10.50 (6/01/85) **90**
Chianti Ricasoli 1990: Fruity and hearty, with fresh, straightforward berry and cherry flavors. Full-bodied, but without a lot of tannins. Ready to drink now. $6 (11/30/91) BB **81**
Chianti Ricasoli 1986: Vivid aromas and flavors of cherry, plum and leather lend character to this medium-weight, artfully balanced, likable wine. Drink soon. $5.50 (5/15/89) BB **84**
Chianti Classico Ricasoli 1987 $6 (11/30/89) (HS) **79**
Chianti Classico Ricasoli Riserva 1983 $8 (11/30/89) (HS) **83**
Chianti Classico San Ripolo 1988: Attractive berry and cedar flavors make this a wine on the wild side. Has good concentration and balance, with a nice touch of ripe plum. 1,000 cases made. $9.50 (10/31/91) BB **84**
Chianti Classico San Ripolo 1987: Medium weight and flavorful, with odd rhubarb and other vegetal aromas and flavors that not everyone will like, but it's otherwise balanced and well made. $10 (4/15/91) **79**

RIECINE
Chianti Classico 1988: Ripe, rich and concentrated, with plum and raspberry aromas echoing on the palate with hints of chocolate and cedar on the finish. The tannins are firm but integrated. A well-crafted wine that should be at its best after 1993. $22 (4/30/91) **89**
Chianti Classico 1987: Aromatic, with wild berries and herbs that turn tough and tannic on the palate; the fruit comes through on the finish. Needs until 1995 to shed some tannin. $20 (4/30/91) **83**
Chianti Classico Riserva 1985: A rich, luscious wine, with lots of spicy berry character. Has rich, ripe aromas of black cherries, chocolate and berries. Medium-bodied, with plum, pepper, tar and spice flavors, medium tannins and a long finish. From John and Palmina Abbagnano Dunkley. Drink now to 1994. $19 (9/15/91) **87**

ROCCA DELLE MACIE
Chianti Classico 1987 ($NA) (11/30/89) (HS) **82**
Chianti Classico 1986 ($NA) (11/30/89) (HS) **80**
Chianti Classico Riserva 1985: Has decent fruit, but it's rather tired, with wet earth, berry and musty aromas. Medium-bodied, with plum, leather and berry flavors, light tannins and a short finish. Drink now. $14 (9/15/91) **77**
Chianti Classico Riserva di Fizzano 1987 ($NA) (11/30/89) (HS) **89**
Chianti Classico Riserva di Fizzano 1985 ($NA) (11/30/89) (HS) **88**
Chianti Classico Riserva di Fizzano 1982: With mature color and complex aromas, this should be terrific once the somewhat chalky tannins resolve. Reminiscent of a Brunello di Montalcino, it has firm structure, earthy raspberry flavors and excellent length. Drink now. $15.50 (3/31/89) **87**
Chianti Classico Tenuta Sant'Alfonso 1988: Perfect with just about any dish. Sit back and enjoy. The intense aromas of ripe plums and berries have a hint of tobacco. Full-bodied, with ripe plum and tobacco flavors, velvety tannins and a crisp finish. Drink now. ($NA) (9/15/91) **89**

RUBENTINO
Chianti 1990: A light, non-tannic wine, with hints of spice in the cherry and plum flavors. Smooth, pleasant and ready to drink. $6.50 (4/30/92) **78**
Chianti Classico 1989: Light, crisp cherry and raspberry flavors keep this wine lively, simple and refreshing. 4,500 cases made. $8.50 (4/30/92) **81**

RUFFINO
Chianti 1990: Crisp and light, with very little fruit to balance the tobacco-tinged earthiness. $8 (1/31/92) **77**
Chianti Classico 1987: Firmly structured, young and tannic, but it shows inviting spicy, leathery aromas and ripe cherry flavor. Drink now. $7 (4/30/90) BB **83**
Chianti Classico 1984 $5 (11/30/86) **78**
Chianti Classico Aziano 1989: Pleasant and light for everyday drinking, with a few accents of earth and spice over the cherry flavor. $10 (4/30/92) **79**
Chianti Classico Aziano 1988: Like drinking chocolate-covered cherries. Has chocolate, cherry and tobacco aromas, medium-bodied, with lots of ripe fruit, almost verging on being sweet, round tannins and a flavorful finish. Drinkable now, but it will improve. $11 (9/15/91) **83**
Chianti Classico Aziano 1986: Very light in color, earthy on the nose, but the flavors really open up on the palate, singing a tune of strawberry, cherry and leather that comes out charming. $8 (5/31/89) BB **85**
Chianti Classico Aziano 1985 $8.75 (8/31/88) **80**
Chianti Classico Ducale Riserva 1986: Classic. It's firm in texture and spicy in aroma and flavor, with nice hints of raspberry, anise and vanilla extending into a smooth, supple finish. Elegantly balanced and focused. Worth holding until 1993 to '95. $16 (10/31/91) **89**
Chianti Classico Ducale Riserva 1985: Super-opulent, with plenty of everything. Thick, but harmonious, with leather, plum and mushroom aromas, full-bodied, with chocolate fudge and plum flavors. Drinkable now, but better in 1993 to '95. Rel: $13 Cur: $22 (9/15/91) **90**
Chianti Classico Ducale Riserva 1983 Rel: $17 Cur: $21 (11/30/89) (HS) **84**
Chianti Classico Ducale Riserva 1982: Very light in color, spicy and leathery, but not very long or rich. Quite drinkable, but it's not going anywhere. Rel: $20 Cur: $24 (5/31/89) **80**
Chianti Classico Ducale Riserva 1981 $9 (10/31/86) **66**
Chianti Classico Ducale Riserva 1979 Rel: $16 Cur: $23 (9/16/85) **80**
Chianti Classico Ducale Riserva 1978 $16 (11/30/89) (HS) **82**
Chianti Classico Ducale Riserva 1977 $28 (9/16/85) (JS) **89**
Chianti Classico Ducale Riserva 1975 $57 (9/16/85) (JS) **86**
Chianti Classico Ducale Riserva 1971 $61 (9/16/85) (JS) **85**
Chianti Classico Ducale Riserva 1962 ($NA) (9/16/85) (JS) **68**
Chianti Classico Ducale Riserva 1958 $144 (9/16/85) (JS) **82**
Chianti Classico Nozzole Vigneto la Forra 1985 ($NA) (11/30/89) (HS) **90**
Chianti Classico Tenuta Santedame 1988: Big and powerful, with plenty of flavor. Has mint, berry, rich vanilla and meat aromas. Full-bodied, with ripe berry, plum and tar flavors, medium tannins and a velvety finish. Try now to 1994. ($NA) (9/15/91) **88**

CASTEL RUGGERO
Chianti Classico 1988: A very good, new style, but it could use some bottle age. Full-bodied, with mint, earth and berry aromas, lots of cherry and berry flavors and medium tannins, but turns slightly astringent on the finish. Tasted twice. Try now to 1994. ($NA) (9/15/91) **86**

SACCARDI
Chianti Classico 1987: Light in color, aroma and flavor, an innocuous, inoffensive wine that's drinkable but unexciting. $10 (5/15/90) **75**
Chianti Classico 1985 $6 (11/30/87) BB **89**
Chianti Classico Riserva 1983: Firm in texture, but rich in flavor, showing plenty of toasty, woodsy notes to the well-focused cherry and anise flavors. Long and distinctive, a muscular wine. Ready to drink now. $12 (5/15/90) **87**
Chianti Classico Riserva 1981 $9 (11/30/87) **81**

SAN FABIANO
Chianti Classico 1988: Traditionally styled, with a good concentration of fruit. Aromas of cedar, plum and slightly musty wood open to concentrated, almost sweet fruit flavors. Medium-bodied, with medium tannins and a velvety finish. Drink now. $11.25 (9/15/91) **84**
Chianti Classico Cellole 1988: A no-nonsense, straightforward wine, with rather simple cherry and berry aromas. Medium-bodied, with one-dimensional cherry and leather flavors, light tannins and a crisp finish. Drink now. $14.25 (9/15/91) **83**
Chianti Classico Cellole Riserva 1985: Fragrant and generous, offering complex floral, berry and plum aromas and flavors. Tough tannins mark this for the cellar until at least 1993 to '95. The intensity of fruit and flavor keeps it balanced enough to drink now with rich food. $13 (11/30/89) **91**

SAN FELICE
Chianti Classico Campo del Civettino 1988: Sweet and juicy, with lots of fruit, offering wet earth and berry aromas and similar flavors. Very ripe and rich. Drink now. ($NA) (9/15/91) **84**
Chianti Classico Il Grigio Riserva 1987: Soft and pleasant, with modest plum and berry aromas and flavors, hinting at chocolate and leather on the finish. Drinkable now. $13 (1/31/92) **83**
Chianti Classico Il Grigio Riserva 1985: The exotic, spicy aromas are immediately appealing, but the high level of tannin requires cellaring until at least 1993 or '94 to loosen up this tightly packed, distinctively Tuscan wine. Cherry and raspberry flavors manage to poke through the tannin. $10 (9/15/90) **86**
Chianti Classico Il Grigio Riserva 1983 $12 (11/30/89) (HS) **85**
Chianti Classico Il Grigio Riserva 1982 $11 (11/30/89) (HS) **90**
Chianti Classico Poggio Rosso Riserva 1986: Ripe, focused and tasty, with juicy currant, blackberry and floral aromas and flavors. Firm tannins support the long finish. Tasty now, but better after the tannins subside around 1993 to '95. $24 (1/31/92) **86**
Chianti Classico Poggio Rosso Riserva 1985: A lively yet elegant wine, with savory flavors. Has earthy tea and strawberry aromas, medium-bodied, round, luscious fruit flavor, firm tannins and crisp acidity. Drink now. ($NA) (9/15/91) **85**
Chianti Classico Poggio Rosso Riserva 1983 ($NA) (11/30/89) (HS) **87**
Chianti Classico Poggio Rosso Riserva 1982: A mature wine, with appealing tea, strawberry and brown sugar aromas and flavors and a modest structure. It's smooth, but still tannic enough to warrant cellaring until 1993. Interesting for its maturity, but otherwise not special. $15 (9/15/90) **81**
Chianti Classico Poggio Rosso Riserva 1981 $15 (11/30/89) (HS) **87**
Chianti Classico Poggio Rosso Riserva 1978 $14 (3/15/87) **73**

SAN LEONINO
Chianti Classico 1988: Ripe and round, with a firm structure and a strong current of raspberry and cherry flavors wrapped tightly in a blanket of oak, echoing spices, chocolate and fruit on the long finish. Definitely needs cellaring until at least 1993 to '95 to begin to soften the tannins. $10 (12/15/90) **87**

CASTELLO DI SAN POLO IN ROSSO
Chianti Classico 1985: Earthy aromas and flavors dominate this austere, tannic, hard-edged wine. Not likable or likely to develop much with age. Tasted twice. $10 (11/30/89) **67**
Chianti Classico Riserva 1985: Spicy, somewhat gamy, with wild berry aromas and flavors on a tough, tannic structure that tends to obscure some lovely fruit aromas and flavors. Needs cellaring to be approachable, perhaps until 1993 or '94. Tasted twice. $14 (11/30/89) **78**

SAN QUIRICO
Chianti Vecchione 1988: Light and pleasant, with earthy, barnyardy overtones to the modest berry flavors. Drinkable now. $9 (1/31/92) **79**

SANTA TRINITA
Chianti Classico 1988: Intriguingly fresh and focused, with perfumed aromas of roses, cut grass and wet earth. Medium-bodied, with spicy tobacco and plum flavors, medium tannins and a fresh finish. From Le Chiantigiane. Drink now. ($NA) (9/15/91) **86**

VILLA SANTINA
Chianti 1987: Smells fine, but the austere structure and flavors come as a shock after the generous cherry and chocolate aromas. $5 (11/30/89) BB **80**
Chianti Classico 1984 $5 (11/15/87) **72**

A. SARDELLI
Chianti Classico Bartenura 1987: $9 (3/31/91) **70**

SELVAPIANA
Chianti Classico 1986 $5 (11/30/89) (HS) **82**
Chianti Classico Riserva 1985 $11 (11/30/89) (HS) **89**
Chianti Classico Riserva 1983 $10 (11/30/89) (HS) **86**
Chianti Classico Riserva 1982 $10 (11/30/89) (HS) **87**
Chianti Rufina Bucerchiale Riserva 1985: A great wine. It's beautifully focused, complex and deep in flavor, with notes of cherry, spice and chocolate and tannins that are firm but soft. The fruit complexity lingers a long time on the finish. Drink now to 1994. 500 cases made. $19 (9/15/90) **91**

FATTORIA DI SELVOLE
Chianti Classico 1988: Has clean fruit but lacks concentration. Light garnet in color, with mint, cherry and herb aromas and similar flavors, light-bodied. Drink now. ($NA) (9/15/91) **78**
Chianti Classico Lanfredini Riserva 1985: A confusing wine that gives very little on the nose or palate. Has tobacco, cedar and varnish aromas, a medium-bodied, hard, linear structure and a short finish. Drink now. ($NA) (9/15/91) **77**

TALOSA
Chianti Colli Senesi 1988: Ripe, rich and full, bursting with currant, blackberry and vanilla aromas and flavors, this supple wine has a gentle feel despite the intensity of flavor. It's soft enough to drink now, but cellaring until 1993 or '94 should polish it even more. Another fine value. 4,800 cases made. $8 (11/30/90) BB **88**

TERRABIANCA
Chianti Classico Vigna della Croce Riserva 1985: An attractive, graceful wine, with toffee, teak and cherry aromas and mint, berry and chocolate flavors. Medium- to full-bodied, with a velvety mouth-feel and a fine finish. Drink now. ($NA) (9/15/91) **87**

CASTELLO DI TIZZANO
Chianti Classico Riserva 1982: Light, tart and graceful, with hints of plum, cherry and cinnamon to make it interesting. Fine to wash down dinner, but it still has some tannin to lose. $18 (7/15/89) **78**

VIGNE TOSCANE
Chianti Terre Toscane 1989: Light and crisp, with modest cherry and currant aromas and flavors, this is a bit tart, but balanced and drinkable. $5 (11/30/90) BB **80**

TRACOLLE
Chianti Classico 1988: Has very ripe fruit, but the odd aromas—spice, raisin, berry and nail polish—make us suspicious. Full-bodied, with mint and berry flavors. Tasted twice. ($NA) (9/15/91) **69**

CASTELLO DI UZZANO
Chianti Classico 1988: Needs aging, but should be very good. An old style, with delicate raspberry and cherry aromas, very ripe plum and chocolate flavors and super-firm tannins. Full-bodied. Built for aging. Try in 1993 to '95. ($NA) (9/15/91) **87**
Chianti Classico Riserva 1985: Traditionally styled, with elegant fruit and fine tannins. Has perfumed aromas of cedar, leather, plum and tea. Medium-bodied, with light toffee, coffee, plum and berry flavors, light tannins and a crisp finish. Drink now. ($NA) (9/15/91) **85**

S. VALERIA
Chianti Classico Riserva 1985: Simple and fruity, with light, simple plum and cherry aromas. Medium- to light-bodied, with plum, berry and chestnut flavors. Light in tannins and on the finish. Drink now. ($NA) (9/15/91) **78**

FATTORIA VALTELLINA
Chianti Classico Giorgio Regni 1988: An appealing, early-drinking wine, with lots of leathery, earthy nuances. The black cherry aromas have hints of tomato and earth. Medium-bodied, with earthy berry flavors and a fresh finish. Drink now. $19 (9/15/91) **83**
Chianti Classico Giorgio Regni Riserva 1985: A joy to drink, with exuberant fruit and a lovely texture. Superbly balanced, with intense cassis, violet and berry aromas and an excellent balance of intense cherry, cassis and black cherry flavors. Medium-bodied, with a silky texture. Drink now. $20 (9/15/91) **92**

VIGNA VECCHIA
Chianti Classico 1988: Concentrated and flavorful, but the woody, menthol notes won't please everyone. Ripe, plummy and cedary, with plenty of acidity and firm tannins. Drink now or in 1993. $10.50 (10/31/91) **83**

VECCHIE TERRE DI MONTEFILI
Chianti Classico 1988: A seamless wine, with wonderful balance, a classic. Has freshly cut mushroom, chocolate and blackberry aromas and full-bodied, concentrated fruit flavors, but has great elegance and balance of fine tannins. Try now to 1994. $20 (9/15/91) **90**
Chianti Classico 1986: A tough style, firm, lean and sharply focused, with enough concentration of cherry and raspberry flavors to indicate cellaring until 1993 or '94. $14 (4/30/90) **85**
Chianti Classico Riserva 1985: Decadently rich and powerful, but it has a lovely suppleness. Offers intense mint, eucalyptus and black cherry aromas and loads of berry, chocolate and meat flavors. Full-bodied, with a rich, velvety mouth-feel, supple tannins and a super-long finish. Can improve, but it's enjoyable now. ($NA) (9/15/91) **90**

CASTELLO DI VERRAZZANO
Chianti Classico 1988: This subtle wine grows on you. Has aromas of sage and fruit, fresh, medium-bodied herb, berry and smoke flavors, silky tannins and a crisp finish. Drink now or in 1993. $8 (9/15/91) **85**
Chianti Classico Cinquecentenario di Verrazzano Riserva 1985: A good wine, with plenty of mature spice, plum and berry flavors. Has plum, spice and tobacco aromas. Medium-bodied, with silky tannins and a medium finish. Drink now. ($NA) (9/15/91) **83**

VESCOVADO DI MURLO
Chianti 1990: Charming and quaffable, with fruity aromas and bright cherry flavors. Straightforward and clean, with nice spiciness on the finish. $6 (10/31/91) BB **83**

CASTELLO VICCHIOMAGGIO
Chianti Classico Prima Vigna Riserva 1985: Sleek and refined, with a smooth mouth-feel. Offers black olive and berry aromas, delicious, medium-bodied berry flavors and finely tuned tannins. Drink now. $20 (9/15/91) **86**

FATTORIA VIGNALE
Chianti Classico 1988: Slightly one-dimensional, but delicious. Has subtle cherry, cedar and truffle aromas. Medium-bodied, with cherry flavor, medium tannins and a medium finish. Drink now or in 1993. ($NA) (9/15/91) **85**
Chianti Classico Riserva 1985: Powerful and rich, with a bounty of fruit. Perfect for serving with grilled steak. Has lovely licorice, berry and coffee bean aromas and berry, cherry and coffee flavors. Medium-bodied, with a velvety texture, full tannins and a long finish. Drinkable now, but it will improve with time. ($NA) (9/15/91) **88**

VIGNAMAGGIO
Chianti Classico 1988: Very refreshing, with plenty of fruit and acidity. Has focused black cherry and chocolate aromas, full-bodied cherry and berry flavors, medium tannins and mouth-puckering acidity. Try now or in 1993. $16.50 (9/15/91) **85**
Chianti Classico 1986: Ripe and plummy, with lots of enjoyable fruit wrapped in smooth tannins, jammy and stylish and a bit spicy on the finish. Drinkable now, but cellaring until 1993 wouldn't hurt. $12 (5/15/90) **85**
Chianti Classico 1985 $11 (8/31/88) **86**
Chianti Classico Mona Lisa Riserva 1986: Crisp and tart, with plenty of focused plum and berry aromas and flavors that persist on the long, zingy finish. A tasty wine, with lots of interest. Gets spicier and more complex with each sip as the shades of new oak emerge. Drinkable now. 4,000 cases made. $20 (10/31/91) **88**
Chianti Classico Mona Lisa Riserva 1985: Classy and balanced, with lovely structure. Herbal, smoky plum aromas follow through on the palate. Medium-bodied, with fine tannins and a concentrated finish. Drink now. $17 (9/15/91) **89**
Chianti Classico Riserva 1985: A middle-of-the-road wine, with mint, tobacco and plum aromas, tobacco and cedar flavors, medium tannins and a flavorful finish. A medium-bodied wine to drink now. $17 (9/15/91) **81**
Chianti Classico Riserva 1983: Spicy, cedary aromas and flavors dominate this medium-weight, somewhat austere wine. Fairly intense raspberry and cinnamon flavors on the finish. A bit tannic, but very drinkable. $14 (5/15/90) **85**

VIGNOLE
Chianti Classico 1988: Outstanding concentration of fruit and flavor. Excitingly fruity, with crisp acidity. Full-bodied, with intense vanilla, raspberry and chocolate aromas, a great concentration of freshly crushed fruit flavor, velvety tannins and a long finish. Drink now to 1994. ($NA) (9/15/91) **90**

VISTARENNI
Chianti Classico 1988: A wine with lovely balance that melts in your mouth. Has complex aromas of tar, leather and tea and fresh berry and tea flavors. Medium-bodied, with medium-silky tannins and fresh acidity. Drink now. $11 (9/15/91) **86**
Chianti Classico 1987: Intense spicy cherry aromas and flavors roll over the palate in waves in this medium-weight, artfully balanced wine. Toasty vanilla notes add roundness and complexity. Drink now. $10 (10/15/89) **89**
Chianti Classico 1986: Woody, earthy, lean and tart, a rough go because of the wood and tartness, but some pleasant cherry flavor manages to emerge on the palate and on the finish. $18 (7/31/89) **78**
Chianti Classico Riserva 1985: A simple, no-nonsense wine that offers stewed tomato, cherry and tobacco aromas and flavors, lots of fruit and medium intensity. Drink now. ($NA) (9/15/91) **81**
Chianti Classico Vigneto Assòlo 1988: More like a rosé than a red wine, with chestnut, berry and cherry aromas, light-bodied, fresh fruit flavor, light tannins and a light finish. Drink now. $16 (9/15/91) **78**

VITICCIO
Chianti Classico 1988: This rich wine has more on the palate than on the nose, with light black cherry and cedar aromas. Medium-bodied, with focused chocolate, cedar and berry flavors and plenty of velvety tannins. Try now or in 1993. $10 (9/15/91) **87**
Chianti Classico 1987: A robust, hearty wine that's full-bodied and tannic, but only modestly fruity. Drinkable now, with pizza or spaghetti. $9 (4/30/90) **78**
Chianti Classico 1986: Lean and sharply focused, with smoke-tinged berry flavor and excellent concentration through a fine finish. Drink now. $8 (3/31/89) BB **88**
Chianti Classico 1984 $5.75 (11/15/87) **74**
Chianti Classico Riserva 1985: Tough and tannic, with woody, barky overtones to the ripe cherry flavors, it's hard in texture because the wood seems to dominate. Needs until 1993 or '94 for the tannin to resolve. $11 (11/30/89) **85**
Chianti Classico Riserva 1983: Marture, complex and a bit tannic, with hints of orange peel and spices to make the flavors more interesting. Drinkable now. $12 (11/30/89) **80**
Chianti Classico Viticcio Riserva 1983 $8 (11/15/87) **77**
Chianti Classico Viticcio Riserva 1982 $8.75 (11/15/87) **84**
Chianti Classico Viticcio Riserva 1978 $12.50 (11/30/87) **78**
Chianti Classico Viticcio Riserva 1975 $13.50 (11/15/87) **71**

CASTELLO DI VOLPAIA
Chianti Classico 1988: Clean and quaffable, with simple cherry, berry and chocolate aromas and medium-bodied cherry and earth flavors. Light in tannins and on the finish. Tasted twice. Drink now. $13.50 (9/15/91) **85**
Chianti Classico 1987 $16 (11/30/89) (HS) **85**
Chianti Classico 1986: A solid wine, with decent fruit and spice flavors, but it's basically simple. A good wine for drinking but not thinking about. Tasted twice. $10 (3/31/90) **75**
Chianti Classico 1985 $10 (6/30/89) SS **90**
Chianti Classico 1983 $8 (9/15/87) (HS) **88**
Chianti Classico Riserva 1985: A pretty, middle-of-the-road wine, with truffle, earth and berry aromas and flavors, medium-fine tannins and balanced acidity and finish. $13 (9/15/91) **84**
Chianti Classico Riserva 1983: Firm and tannic, with well-developed, harmonious aromas and flavors, hinting at dried tomato, plum and leather, very smooth but still a bit tannic. Drink now. $11.50 (5/31/89) **87**
Chianti Classico Riserva 1982 $11 (9/15/87) (HS) **84**
Chianti Classico Riserva 1981 ($NA) (9/15/87) (HS) **86**
Chianti Classico Riserva 1977 ($NA) (9/15/87) (HS) **81**
Chianti Classico Riserva 1970 ($NA) (9/15/87) (HS) **85**

VILLA ZINGALE
Chianti Riserva 1988: Simple, soft and drinkable, offering light cherry and berry flavors. 2,000 cases made. $8.50 (4/30/92) **77**

ROSSO DI MONTALCINO DOC

ALTESINO
Rosso di Montalcino 1988: The earthy, rubbery aromas and flavors are too much for the modest cherry flavor lurking in the background. Tasted twice. $14.50 (7/15/91) **73**
Rosso di Montalcino 1986: Light in color and flavor, but tight enough on the palate to think that brief cellaring will open up the reined-in berry and spice flavors. Try now. $10 (7/15/89) **80**

CASTELLO BANFI
Rosso di Montalcino Centine 1988: Has pretty strawberry and raspberry aromas and flavors that are held together on a frame of modest tannins. Approachable now with a plate of beef or chicken. $8 (12/15/91) BB **81**
Rosso di Montalcino Centine 1987: Tastes tight with tannins and acidity, but has intense fruit flavors and spicy complexity lurking underneath. Flavors linger on the finish, indicating it should loosen up by 1993. $8 (6/15/90) BB **85**
Rosso di Montalcino Centine 1986: Very likable in a lean and crisp sort of way, but there are also plenty of lively cherry and spice aromas and flavors. It's clean and firm with tannins on the finish. Drinkable now. $7 (11/30/89) BB **87**
Rosso di Montalcino Centine 1985 $7 (11/30/87) BB **88**
Rosso di Montalcino Centine 1983 $7 (4/30/87) BB **89**

BIONDI-SANTI
Rosso di Montalcino Il Greppo 1984: Soft and ripe, almost effusive in its fruitiness, with prune and cherry flavors, plus just enough tannin to give it grip. Drinkable now. $22 (1/31/90) **82**

CASTIGLIONE DEL BOSCO
Rosso di Montalcino 1988: Aromatic and a bit austere, but the flavors are complex and inviting, with orange peel, nutmeg and anise notes to the basic red cherry flavor. Drinkable now with hearty food, or cellar until 1993 or '94. $11 (7/15/91) **82**

CAPARZO
Rosso di Montalcino 1988: Spicy, earthy aromas and flavors make this medium-weight, easy-to-drink wine a good match for hearty food. Drinkable now. $14 (4/30/91) **81**
Rosso di Montalcino 1986: Old-style meaty, gamy aromas and flavors shoulder past the gentle raspberry and anise character, but it finishes very tasty and smooth, except for a snap of tannic grip on the finish. $10 (9/30/89) **86**

CAPRILI
Rosso di Montalcino 1986: Drink it now. Light but firm, with a jammy, brown sugar flavor and a slightly smoky finish. $10 (1/31/89) **78**

S. CARLO
Rosso di Montalcino 1986: Vibrant with toasty cherry aromas and flavors, a bit earthy, but attractively silky in texture and slightly tart and lively on the finish. $10 (7/15/89) **82**

CERBAIONA
Rosso di Montalcino 1988: A ripe, generous wine, with appealing currant and plum aromas and flavors, but a pretty stiff whack of tannin makes it seem rustic in style. Drinkable with hearty food, but best to wait until 1993 or '94. $21 (1/31/92) **82**

CIACCI PICCOLOMINI D'ARAGONA
Rosso di Montalcino 1988: As tannic as many Brunellos, but offering distinct raspberry and cherry aromas and flavors balanced with a touch of oak. A bit shy on flavor for so much tannin, but it may be worth waiting until 1993 to '95 to see what develops. $16 (4/30/91) **82**

Key to Symbols

The scores reported here are the results of blind tastings conducted by our panel of senior editors. Wines that carry the initials below are results of individual tastings.

THE WINE SPECTATOR 100-POINT SCALE 95-100— Classic, a great wine; ***90-94***— Outstanding, superior character and style; ***80-89***—Good to very good, a wine with special qualities; ***70-79***—Average, drinkable wine that may have minor flaws; ***60-69***—Below average, drinkable but not recommended; ***50-59***—Poor, undrinkable, not recommended. "+"— With a score indicates a range; used primarily with barrel tastings to indicate a preliminary score.

SPECIAL DESIGNATIONS SS—Spectator Selection, CS—Cellar Selection, BB—Best Buy, ($NA)—Price not available, (NR)—Not released.

TASTER'S INITIALS (JG)—Jim Gordon, (HS)—Harvey Steiman, (JL)—James Laube, (JS)—James Suckling, (TM)—Thomas Matthews, (TR)—Terry Robards, (PM)—Per-Henrik Mansson, (BT)—Barrel Tasting (these wines were tasted blind from barrel samples), (CA-date)—*California's Great Cabernets* by James Laube, (CH-date)—*California's Great Chardonnays* by James Laube, (VP-date)—*Vintage Port* by James Suckling.

DATE TASTED Dates in parentheses represent the issue in which the rating was published.

COL D'ORCIA
Rosso di Montalcino 1988: A very attractive, medium-bodied wine. Soft and pleasant, showing moderate tannins, nice plummy flavors, good balance and a fruity, spicy finish. A good value, too. $9 (4/30/91) **84**

LISINI
Rosso di Montalcino 1988: Tart and tannic, but generous, with a bright beam of fresh and dried cherry flavors. A bit rough around the edges, but worth cellaring until 1993 or '94 to see what happens. $14 (4/30/91) **79**

MASTROIANNI
Rosso di Montalcino 1987: Firm and somewhat austere, but it has the berry and spice flavors of Sangiovese lingering on the finish and the tannins to cut through a rich roast. Drink now to 1994. $10 (7/15/91) **79**

VILLA NICOLA
Rosso di Montalcino 1988: A stylish, deeply fruity wine, with serious concentration and depth. Has brilliant black cherry and berry flavors accented by spice, toast and vanilla notes from aging in small oak barrels. Round and elegant in texture. Drinkable now, but best to cellar until 1993 to '95. $15 (1/31/91) **89**

VIGNETI PACENTI SIRO
Rosso di Montalcino 1989: A tasty overlay of new oak gives style to the solid cherry and raspberry flavors, making a well-rounded, appealing wine for drinking now through 1995. $14 (4/30/92) **87**

PERTIMALI
Rosso di Montalcino 1987: Should be great at the dinner table. An aromatic but lean-tasting wine, with attractive berry, floral and spice aromas, a tight core of fruit flavor and firm tannins and acidity. $12.50 (1/31/91) **84**

IL PODERUCCIO
Rosso di Montalcino 1989: A medium-weight wine, with a satisfying combination of cherry, raspberry, chocolate and spice flavors. Moderate tannins and good balance make it fine to drink now. $9 (4/30/92) **83**
Rosso di Montalcino I Due Cipressi 1988: Big in structure, it needs time for the boisterousness of youth to quiet down. Has plenty of tart cherry and berry flavors, but an earthy aroma is difficult to get past at this young age. Tasted twice. $9.50 (4/30/91) **83**

POGGIO ANTICO
Rosso di Montalcino 1989: Lean and lively, with appealing strawberry, raspberry, cinnamon and rose petal flavors on a medium-weight frame. The flavors linger. Drinkable now. $21 (8/31/91) **85**

DEI ROSETI
Rosso di Montalcino 1988: Elegant, fruity and focused, showing ripe raspberry, smoke and pepper aromas, elegant flavors of cherry and berry, moderate tannins, firm acidity and a lingering finish. Drink up now. $13 (1/31/91) **87**
Rosso di Montalcino 1985: Mature and surprisingly tannic, a tough wine that needs cellaring but may not have the concentration to develop well. A gamble, but the winery and vintage have good reputations. $9 (7/15/89) **78**

SAN FILIPPO
Rosso di Montalcino 1987: A very earthy, tannic, rustic style that's difficult to like. Only for fans of the old-style, rough-and-tumble Italian reds. $11 (4/30/91) **68**

VAL DI SUGA
Rosso di Montalcino 1988: Smooth and elegant with a polished texture, offering generous raspberry and currant aromas and flavors and spice and toast notes on the finish. Drinkable now, but you could hold it until 1993 or '94. $10 (4/30/91) **87**
Rosso di Montalcino 1986: Appealing in an earthy style, with lively spice and cherry aromas and flavors, it's supple and already drinkable. $9 (11/30/89) **81**

VINO NOBILE DI MONTEPULCIANO DOCG

AVIGNONESI
Vino Nobile di Montepulciano 1985 $12 (2/15/88) **86**
Vino Nobile di Montepulciano 1981 $7.25 (10/01/85) **86**
Vino Nobile di Montepulciano 1980 $6.75 (7/01/85) **85**

CANTINE BAIOCCHI
Vino Nobile di Montepulciano 1986: Lean, focused and spicy, with a sharp beam of cherry and raspberry flavors adorned with nutmeg, chocolate and smoke overtones. A harmonious, well-crafted wine that ought to be at its best around 1993 to '95. $15 (3/15/91) **87**
Vino Nobile di Montepulciano Riserva 1985: Offers a firm texture with a velvety sheen and concentrated plum and raspberry flavors that turn spicy and toasty on the finish. Drinkable now. $10 (11/30/89) **85**

BIGI
Vino Nobile di Montepulciano 1985: A smooth, mature wine, with cherry, spice and earth aromas, tomato and plum flavors and somewhat drying tannins. The structure is a bit too tough for the modest fruit flavors, but it's still enjoyable to drink now. $11.50 (11/30/90) **81**
Vino Nobile di Montepulciano Riserva 1982 $9 (1/31/88) **77**
Vino Nobile di Montepulciano Riserva 1980 $8 (9/01/85) **84**

BINDELLA
Vino Nobile di Montepulciano Riserva 1985: Extremely austere and overripe at the same time. This is a hard-edged, tannic and woody wine that is unbalanced, leaving what fruit there is to fend for itself. Try if you must around 1994. $27 (10/31/90) **68**

BOSCARELLI
Vino Nobile di Montepulciano 1981 $10 (7/01/86) **71**
Vino Nobile di Montepulciano Riserva 1985: Lean and tannic, a stiff wine with tough structure and not much fruit aroma or flavor. Flavors lean toward tobacco and coffee. Perhaps cellaring until 1993 to '94 will soften it. $15 (6/15/90) **76**
Vino Nobile di Montepulciano Riserva 1981 $11 (10/31/86) **70**

E. CASASLTE
Vino Nobile di Montepulciano 1983 $9 (11/30/87) **86**

CECCHI
Vino Nobile di Montepulciano 1987: Light in color, tasting rather mature, loaded with anise aromas and flavors and just a hint of berry to keep it in balance. Drinkable now. $13 (3/31/92) **77**
Vino Nobile di Montepulciano 1983: Tannic enough to cover the remaining whiffs of spicy, leathery aromas and flavors, which lack the concentration to match the tannin. Drinkable, but only with rich food. $9 (5/15/89) **77**

CONTI D'ATTIMIS
Vino Nobile di Montepulciano Varnero 1987: Floral aromas give way to hard, astringent woody flavors that mask the ripe plum and currant notes. It needs time to soften. Best between 1993 to '95, but it will always be firm. $14 (9/15/90) **75**

DEI
Vino Nobile di Montepulciano Riserva 1985: Fairly powerful but flavorful. Very spicy and full-bodied, with cedary, oaky aromas, and dense plum, cassis and chocolate flavors covered with lots of fine tannins. Wait till 1993 to '96 to drink. $13 (4/15/90) **85**

FASSATI
Vino Nobile di Montepulciano Riserva 1985: Generous, ripe cherry and floral aromas and flavors run smack into a hard edge of raw tannin, but then it seems to balance out on the finish. Try now or age until 1994, and it should soften up to let the flavors emerge. $22 (11/30/89) **86**
Vino Nobile di Montepulciano Riserva 1978 $8.50 (7/01/86) **73**

FATTORIA DI FOGNANO
Vino Nobile di Montepulciano Riserva Talosa 1983: Tannic, but the plum, leather and vanilla aromas and flavors are so beautifully integrated, concentrated and persistent that it should develop well in the cellar. Drinkable now in a chewy sort of way, but best around 1993 or '94. A good value. $7 (5/15/89) BB **85**
Vino Nobile di Montepulciano Riserva Talosa 1981: Despite the attractive spice and raspberry character on the nose, it turns short and drying, almost papery on the finish. $8.50 (5/15/89) **76**

CANTINA GATTAVECCHI
Vino Nobile di Montepulciano Riserva 1985: Ripe, almost raisiny, with a gamy undertone to the cherry aromas and flavors that will please fans of the old-style Tuscan wines. Drinkable now. $11 (11/30/89) **81**

GEOGRAFICO
Vino Nobile di Montepulciano Vigneti alla Cerràia 1986: Light in texture, with spicy vanilla, strawberry and cinnamon aromas and flavors that remain lively and delicate through a long finish. Drinkable now, but has enough tannin to want until 1993 or '94, if you can wait. $15 (7/15/91) **85**

MELINI
Vino Nobile di Montepulciano 1985: A concentrated, dense, almost chewy wine, with smoky, herbal aromas, cherry and plum flavors and firm but fine tannins. Almost drinkable now, but should improve through 1993. $10 (4/15/90) **82**
Vino Nobile di Montepulciano Riserva 1983 $7.50 (6/30/88) **74**

POLIZIANO
Vino Nobile di Montepulciano 1988: A very ripe, hearty, flavorful wine, with a simple, direct structure. Uncomplicated but satisfying. Fine to drink now with pastas and meats. $12 (12/15/91) **81**
Vino Nobile di Montepulciano 1987: Ripe and plummy, with generous fruit aromas and flavors, firm tannins and hints of cherry and herbs on the finish. A distinctive wine that's soft and drinkable, although it has enough tannin to last until 1993 or '94. $12 (3/15/91) **84**
Vino Nobile di Montepulciano 1985 $13 (9/15/88) **89**

SANGUINETO
Vino Nobile di Montepulciano Riserva 1980 $9 (10/31/86) **86**

TALOSA
Vino Nobile di Montepulciano Riserva 1986: Particularly aromatic, offering herbal, tarry cherry and berry aromas and flavors, firm tannins and a chewy enough texture to need until 1993 to '95. $15 (7/15/91) **84**
Vino Nobile di Montepulciano Riserva 1982 $8.50 (4/15/88) **72**

TENUTA TREROSE
Vino Nobile di Montepulciano 1986: Firm and tannic in texture, with nice smoky plum aromas and flavors that seem to slump in the middle. Could be better by 1993 or '94. $16 (7/15/91) **80**
Vino Nobile di Montepulciano 1985 $11 (11/15/88) **90**
Vino Nobile di Montepulciano Riserva 1985: Hearty, ripe, full-bodied and generous, with an earthy edge to the mature cherry and berry flavors. Still tannic enough to require cellaring until perhaps 1993 or '94. $19 (7/15/91) **85**

VINO DA TAVOLA

CASTELLO D'ALBOLA
Acciaiolo 1988: Harmonious and supple, a joy to drink. Offers tomato, vanilla and plum aromas and a refined structure of lovely, smoky fruit flavor and medium tannins. Has a refreshing finish. Try now to 1995. $40 (9/15/91) **88**

ALTESINO
Alte d'Altesi 1988: Decadent, like a wild Fellini film. Has licorice, cigar box, tobacco and ripe fruit aromas, very ripe tobacco, chocolate, filet mignon and earth flavors and full tannins, but it's round and rich on the finish. Full-bodied. Made from Sangiovese and Cabernet Sauvignon. Try in 1994 to '96. $35 (9/15/91) **92**
Alte d'Altesi 1987: Stinky, muddy and murky, with dry, tannic, plum-scented fruit flavor. Of marginal quality. Tasted three times, with consistent notes. $35 (1/31/92) **69**
Alte d'Altesi 1986: Classic plum, cherry and cassis aromas of Cabernet Sauvignon get a gentle lift from the strawberry freshness of Sangiovese in this elegantly balanced, harmonious wine. Drink now. $32 (7/15/89) **85**
Palazzo Altesi 1988: The flavor afterburners ignite with mint and fruit on the finish. Offers floral, mint, berry and cedar aromas and flavors. Full-bodied, with super-focused fruit, medium tannins and an incredibly long finish. Made from Sangiovese. Try in 1993 to '95. $26 (9/15/91) **90**
Palazzo Altesi 1987: The earthy, leathery aromas and flavors are not for everyone, but it has a supple, velvety texture that allows the black cherry and mineral flavors to emerge on the finish. Drinkable now. Tasted twice. $25 (1/31/92) **78**
Palazzo Altesi 1985: Tough and tannic with chocolate, earth and leathery flavors that are interesting, but it could use a little more fruit. As it is, the plum and anise flavors are attractive, but the finish turns dry and tannic. Drink now to 1995. $23 (10/31/90) **82**
Palazzo Altesi 1983 $17 (2/15/88) **88**
Rosso di Altesino 1989: Velvety in texture, aromatic and flavorful, with nicely articulated berry, spice and tobacco character that persists on the finish. Drinkable now with flavorful food, but probably better after 1994. 2,100 cases made. $8 (1/31/92) BB **86**

FATTORIA DI AMA
Castello di Ama Vigna il Chiuso 1988: Extremely Burgundian in style, with plenty of fresh acidity and silky tannins. A full-bodied wine, with classy tea, tanned leather and strawberry aromas, tea, vanilla, spice and fruit flavors, silky tannins and a crisp finish. Made from Pinot Noir. Drink now to 1995. ($NA) (9/15/91) **90**
Colline di Ama 1986 $9 (11/15/87) **82**
Vigna l'Apparita Merlot 1988: ($NA) (9/15/91) **93**
Vigna l'Apparita Merlot 1986 ($NA) (11/30/89) (HS) **87**
Vigna l'Apparita Merlot 1985 ($NA) (11/30/89) (HS) **92**

AMBRA
Barco Reale 1985 $7 (4/15/88) **76**

ANTINORI
Santa Cristina 1989: Ripe and soft, this medium-weight wine has gentle plum and toast aromas and flavors and hints of anise on the finish. Drink soon. Tasted twice. $7 (7/15/91) **80**
Santa Cristina 1988: Fresh, fruity and firm in structure, with spicy aromas, nice raspberry, plum and spice flavors and moderate tannins. Well mannered, well balanced and ready to drink now. $6.50 (1/31/91) BB **85**
Santa Cristina 1987: Light and velvety, with well-tuned Sangiovese aromas and flavors plus a bit of leathery spiciness for interest. A good wine, but not quite the wonder that the '86 was. A major disappointment after the great 1985 vintage. $6 (4/30/89) BB **81**
Solàia 1988: Defines elegance, like a top St.-Emilion. A full-bodied wine, with exceedingly subtle herb, tobacco, mint and berry aromas and subtle tobacco, herb, berry and cigar box-cedar flavors. The

tannins and the finish are refined and silky. Made from Cabernet Sauvignon and Cabernet Franc. Try in 1993 to '95. $65 (9/15/91) **92**

Solàia 1985: Rich, ripe, generous and complex, balancing its concentrated plum and cherry flavors against a backdrop of spicy, vanilla-scented oak. Firmly supported by a framework of fine tannin, this should age through at least 1993 to '95, but you could drink it tonight with something hearty. Rel: $62 Cur: $110 (12/15/89) **92**

Solàia 1982 $62 (7/31/87) **81**

Tignanello 1988: Subtle and focused, with a very refined structure. Has blackberry, currant and cherry aromas, focused cherry and other fruit flavors, refined tannins and a medium finish. Full-bodied. Made from Sangiovese, Cabernet Sauvignon and Cabernet Franc. Drink now to 1994. Rel: $33 Cur: $41 (9/15/91) **91**

Tignanello 1985: Very firm and reserved, with subtle chocolate, caramel and smoke nuances that add to the ripe but gentle raspberry and currant flavors. Avoids the blockbuster style in favor of elegance and subtlety. Drink in 1993 to '95. A blend of 80 percent Sangiovese and 20 percent Cabernet Sauvignon. Rel: $30 Cur: $40 (4/15/90) **87**

Tignanello 1983: Smooth and mature, with spicy, anise-scented plum and cherry aromas and flavors, a velvety texture and resolved tannins. Ready to drink now, but it has the richness and subtlety to gain more in the cellar through at least 1993. Rel: $25 Cur: $41 (12/15/89) **88**

Tignanello 1982 Rel: $37 Cur: $43 (7/15/87) CS **91**

AVIGNONESI

1988: A volcano of a wine waiting to explode with fruit. Black in color, with mint, cassis and grape aromas, full-bodied, incredibly concentrated berry, grape and mint-tinged fruit flavors, huge, supple tannins and a long finish. Made from Merlot. Try in 1998 to 2000. $45 (9/15/91) **93**

Grifi 1988: A muscular wine, with tons of fruit and tannins. Offers subtle mint, herb and fresh cherry aromas. Full-bodied, with compact fruit flavor and full, refined tannins. Very long on the finish. Made from Sangiovese and Cabernet Franc. Try in 1994 to '96. $25 (9/15/91) **91**

Grifi 1987: A bit on the earthy side, but well crafted. Deep, rich aromas and flavors of tea-scented black cherry, raspberry and smoke are carried by a solid frame and sufficient tannin to need until 1994 or '95 to soften. $21 (4/15/91) **86**

Grifi 1986: Crisp and spicy, with a velvety smoothness that nicely sets off the raspberry flavor; it's lean and sharply focused. Drink now. $18 (1/31/89) **86**

Grifi 1985 Rel: $16 Cur: $36 (2/15/88) **85**

Grifi 1983 Rel: $12 Cur: $30 (6/01/86) **91**

Grifi 1982 Rel: $10 Cur: $30 (6/16/85) **87**

BADIA A COLTIBUONO

Coltibuono Rosso 1986 $6.75 (7/31/88) **81**

Sangioveto 1985 ($NA) (11/30/89) (HS) **85**

Sangioveto 1983 $20 (11/30/89) (HS) **84**

Sangioveto 1982 $20 (11/30/89) (HS) **87**

Sangioveto 1981 $21 (9/15/87) (HS) **87**

FATTORIA BAGGIOLINO

Poggio Brandi 1986: Attractive anise, cherry, raspberry and chocolate flavors give way to hard, scratchy tannins, making this tough to drink now. Perhaps with cellaring those rough edges will smooth out. Drink in 1994 or '95. $19 (8/31/91) **86**

Poggio Brandi 1985: A blend of 95 percent Sangioveto and 5 percent Fragolino. Smoky, woody and leathery, with hints of earth and plum, a bit tannic, yet it remains elegant and tasty. Drink now to 1994. $19 (9/15/89) **84**

CASTELLO BANFI

Cabernet Sauvignon Tavernelle 1988: Not a heavyweight wine, but it's delicious to drink. Has chocolate, mint and red berry aromas. Medium-bodied, with a silky texture, fresh tobacco, cedar and berry flavors and a refreshing finish. Made from Cabernet Sauvignon. Drink now. ($NA) (9/15/91) **87**

Cabernet Sauvignon Tavernelle 1984 $18 (1/31/88) **89**

Cabernet Sauvignon Tavernelle 1982 $15 (8/01/85) **88**

PNE 1988: Harmonious and supple, with pretty fruit flavors, this medium-bodied wine has tea, light earth and sweet strawberry aromas, ripe strawberry and earth flavors, silky tannins and a fresh finish. Made from Pinot Noir. Try now to 1994. ($NA) (9/15/91) **86**

Summus 1988: Very good concentration of fruit and tannins, extremely well made. Full-bodied, with fresh strawberry and raspberry aromas, plenty of licorice, strawberry and light vanilla flavors, firm tannins and a long, slightly smoky finish. A unique blend of Sangiovese, Pinot Noir and Cabernet Sauvignon. Better in 1993 to '95. ($NA) (9/15/91) **87**

FATTORIA DEI BARBI

Brusco dei Barbi 1988: Offers rather exotic aromas and flavors in an accessible style. Has light tomato, litchi, sweet cherry and tobacco aromas and tobacco, spice and cherry flavors. A medium-bodied wine, with medium tannins and a crisp finish. Made from Sangiovese by F. Colombini Cinelli. Try now to 1994. $12 (9/15/91) **86**

Brusco dei Barbi 1986: A tough wine at this age. Tightly structured and tannic, but the fruit flavors seem overshadowed. Tastes woody with a bit of cherry and spice. May improve. Drink now. $9 (4/30/89) **79**

Brusco dei Barbi 1985 $9 (10/15/88) **85**

Bruscone dei Barbi 1988: Rather simple but fresh and fruity, with perfumed spearmint aromas and blackberry and cherry flavors. Medium-bodied, with light tannins and a light finish. Made from Sangiovese by F. Colombini Cinelli. Drink now. ($NA) (9/15/91) **84**

CASE BASSE

Soldera Intistiei 1987: Firm, ripe and spicy, with generous currant and plum flavors wrapped tightly with tannins, shaded by a definite overlay of spicy oak notes. A warm, generous wine, with plenty of room to grow. Berry flavors persist on the finish. Drink after 1994. $68 (1/31/92) **87**

BOSCARELLI

1985: Firm and aromatic, its beautifully focused black cherry and anise aromas and flavors soaring over the crisp and powerful structure; if the wood tends to protrude a bit, the heady flavors make up for it. Try now. This wine is 100 percent Sangiovese. $30 (2/15/89) **92**

1983 $29 (6/30/88) **85**

Key to Symbols

The scores reported here are the results of blind tastings conducted by our panel of senior editors. Wines that carry the initials below are results of individual tastings.

THE WINE SPECTATOR 100-POINT SCALE 95-100—Classic, a great wine; ***90-94***—Outstanding, superior character and style; ***80-89***—Good to very good, a wine with special qualities; ***70-79***—Average, drinkable wine that may have minor flaws; ***60-69***—Below average, drinkable but not recommended; ***50-59***—Poor, undrinkable, not recommended. "+"—With a score indicates a range; used primarily with barrel tastings to indicate a preliminary score.

SPECIAL DESIGNATIONS SS—Spectator Selection, CS—Cellar Selection, BB—Best Buy, ($NA)—Price not available, (NR)—Not released.

TASTER'S INITIALS (JG)—Jim Gordon, (HS)—Harvey Steiman, (JL)—James Laube, (JS)—James Suckling, (TM)—Thomas Matthews, (TR)—Terry Robards, (PM)—Per-Henrik Mansson, (BT)—Barrel Tasting (these wines were tasted blind from barrel samples), (CA-date)—*California's Great Cabernets* by James Laube, (CH-date)—*California's Great Chardonnays* by James Laube, (VP-date)—*Vintage Port* by James Suckling.

DATE TASTED Dates in parentheses represent the issue in which the rating was published.

CASTELLO DI CACCHIANO

RF 1988: This very rich wine starts out slowly, but finishes very well. Deep ruby in color, with wild blackberry and mushroom aromas and charmingly rich berry, chocolate and earth flavors, fine tannins and an intense finish. Full-bodied. From E. Ricasoli-Firidolfi. Better in 1993 or '94. $20 (9/15/91) **90**

RF 1986: Firm and lively, with lots of berry and anise aromas and flavors, toasty and round, showing the effects of aging in small oak barrels. Tannic enough to indicate cellaring until 1993, but there is still plenty of flavor. $16 (6/15/90) **85**

RF 1985 $15 (8/31/88) **91**

VILLA CAFAGGIO

San Martino 1985: Has distinctive Sangiovese flavors but they're very tart and it's extremely dry and tannic. Not for everyone, needs time for at least some of the tannins to soften. Drink starting now through 1995. 1,000 cases made. $20 (9/30/89) **79**

Solatio Basilica 1985: Ripe and bordering on pruny, with dry cherry, plum and berry notes. The tannins are substantial and drying on the aftertaste. Cellar until 1994 or '95. $20 (8/31/91) **83**

VILLA CALCINAIA

Cerviolo 1986: Ripe and round, with spicy aromas and generous black cherry flavors firmly supported by gentle tannins, wrapped in a nice overlay of sweet oak. Well made, already likable. Could cellar until 1993. $18.50 (3/31/90) **82**

CAPARZO

Ca' del Pazzo 1987: Ripe and velvety, with generous plum and cherry aromas and flavors shaded by floral and bay leaf notes. Has elegance and grace, but also enough backbone to warrant cellaring through 1995. $24 (8/31/91) **85**

Ca' del Pazzo 1985: Firm textured, a bit tannic and aromatic with the anise- and tar-tinged raspberry and currant character of the grape, turning a bit leathery and tough on the palate. May develop well with cellaring until 1993 to '95, but it's a gamble. Tasted three times. $28 (5/15/90) **77**

CAPEZZANA

Barco Reale 1987: Light and spicy, with a nice hint of vanilla on the persistent finish. A bit tannic and tight, it needs until 1993. $11.50 (7/15/91) **78**

Ghiaie della Furba 1987: Very soft and herbal, with plum, tomato and vegetal flavors that suggest Cabernet. Simple and ready to drink now. Tasted twice. $30 (12/15/91) **79**

Ghiaie della Furba 1985: Ripe and deep, with tightly furled raspberry, plum and cassis flavors beneath a veneer of minerally, earthy character. Not very tannic, but tight enough and powerful enough to require cellaring until 1993 to '94 before it opens up. A Cabernet Sauvignon, Cabernet Franc, Merlot blend. 1,295 cases made. $20 (1/31/90) **91**

CASTELLARE DI CASTELLINA

Coniale di Castellare 1988: As racy and well crafted as a Ferrari, with super-fresh berry, black cherry and vanilla aromas and full-bodied, focused black cherry, mint and vanilla flavors. Has super-fine tannins and a great backbone of acidity. A blend of Cabernet Sauvignon and Sangiovese. Try in 1993 to '96. $35 (9/15/91) **92**

Coniale di Castellare 1987: A dense, tight, chewy style with intense currant, cherry and oaky flavors that are young and tight. Best to let this one rest a while. Start drinking in 1994 to '96. 100 percent Cabernet Sauvignon. $31 (10/31/90) **87**

I Sodi di San Niccolò 1988: A fresh, lively wine, with modest complexity. Has perfumed aromas of cedar, berry, wet earth and cigar box and ripe cherry and green tobacco flavors. Full-bodied, with medium tannins and very crisp acidity on the finish. Made from Sangiovese. Try now to 1994. $35 (9/15/91) **88**

I Sodi di San Niccolò 1987: Strong aromas and flavors of new oak tend to overpower the rather gentle cherry and berry character, but modest anise and tar overtones come through. A stylish, smooth-textured wine that should be drinkable now. 1,612 cases made. $32 (4/15/91) **86**

I Sodi di San Niccolò 1986: Dark, dense and concentrated, with opulent berry and cherry aromas and flavors balanced against rich, toasty oak and vanilla. A powerful wine that remains graceful from first sip to the last kiss of oak on the finish. Drinkable now, but it should gain complexity at least through 1998. 1,000 cases made. $25 (11/30/89) **94**

I Sodi di San Niccolò 1985 $25 (5/31/88) **96**

I Sodi di San Niccolò 1983 $18 (5/31/88) **87**

I Sodi di San Niccolò 1982 ($NA) (9/15/87) (HS) **89**

I Sodi di San Niccolò 1981 ($NA) (9/15/87) (HS) **87**

CECCHI

Spargolo Predicato di Cardisco 1988: Difficult to judge with so much wood, but it has lovely fruit underneath the French oak. Shows beautiful violet, vanilla and berry aromas in a full-bodied style, with freshly cut wood, berry and smoke flavors, medium tannins and a light finish. Made from Sangiovese. Try in 1993 to '96. $16 (9/15/91) **84**

Spargolo Predicato di Cardisco 1985: Earthy and spicy, with tar and forest aromas, but not much in the way of fresh, ripe, concentrated fruit. Tired on the finish, but still packs in plenty of tannin. Drink in 1993 to '96. $36 (1/31/92) **78**

Spargolo Predicato di Cardisco 1983: Tough in texture and earthy in flavor, lacking the smoothness or intensity to overcome the moderate but coarse tannins. It's hard to imagine it evolving further. Drinkable with hearty food. Tasted twice. $25 (3/15/91) **75**

Spargolo Predicato di Cardisco 1982 $12 (9/30/89) **68**

VILLA CERNA

Vigneto La Gavina 1988: Oozing with fruit and vanilla flavor, this is an extremely well-crafted wine that needs time. Dark purple in color, with mint, cassis and berry aromas. Full-bodied, with berry and vanilla flavors, full, silky tannins and a flavorful finish. Made from Cabernet Sauvignon. Try in 1993 to '95. ($NA) (9/15/91) **91**

VILLA CILNIA

Le Vignacce 1988: Well made, with all the necessary components in place. Has cherry, blackberry and currant aromas, full tannins and plenty of mint and berry flavors. Full-bodied. Made from Sangiovese. Try in 1993 to '96. $24 (9/15/91) **89**

Le Vignacce 1986: Ripe and concentrated, framed with sweet oak, showing generous berry, currant and slightly herbal aromas and flavors, full and velvety. Drink now to 1994. $19 (11/30/89) **90**

Le Vignacce 1985: Ripe, soft and generous, glowing with cherry, spice and berry flavors that expand on the finish. Delicious to drink now, but short-term cellaring could soften the tannic bite on the finish and develop more complexity on the palate. $20 (7/15/89) **88**

Vocato 1986: Light, smooth and attractively fruity, with spicy berry flavors glowing on the finish; focused, harmonious and almost delicate. Drinkable now, because of its finesse. $10.50 (5/15/89) **86**

FATTORIA LE CORTI

Masso Tondo 1985: Highly aromatic—leather, spice, raspberry—but a bit hard-edged and subdued on the palate, although peppery and velvety. Needs time to soften. 100 percent Sangiovese. Drink now. $20 (4/30/89) **86**

EMILIO COSTANTI

Vermiglio 1981 $7.50 (10/31/86) **79**

VILLA DIEVOLE

Broccato 1987: Soft, round and nicely balanced, with very pretty strawberry, plum, chocolate and cedar aromas and flavors. Shows polish from aging in small oak barrels. Drinkable now. $19 (12/15/91) **86**

TENUTA FARNETA

Bongoverno 1986: Marked by peppery oak notes, with earthy coffee, cedar and plum flavors that are tight but generous. Distinctive, with firm tannins on the finish. Needs cellaring until 1994 or '95. 500 cases made. $30 (9/30/91) **87**

FATTORIA DI FELSINA
Fontalloro 1986: A solid core of currant, black cherry, plum and anise flavor is ripe and rich, but the tannins and acidity dominate the aftertaste, making it lean and crisp with a hard edge. Cellar until 1994. $25 (8/31/91) **84**
Fontalloro 1985 $24 (9/15/88) **91**

MARSILIO FICINO
Poggio Il Pino 1986: Tea and leather aromas obscure any fruit that may be present, but it remains light and uncomplicated in an earthy way through to the finish. $6 (7/31/89) **70**

CASTELLO DI FONTERUTOLI
Concerto di Fonterutoli 1986: Seems to meld the best of both Cabernet Sauvignon and Sangiovese, offering raspberry, currant and anise aromas and flavors. Fairly rich in texture, and balanced with enough tannin to carry it past 1995. $35 (3/15/91) **87**
Concerto di Fonterutoli 1985: Firm and tannic, with good concentration of fruit, but earthy walnutlike flavors intrude and it seems unbalanced, awkward and hard-edged. Hard to tell where it's going. Try now. $25 (2/15/89) **84**
Concerto di Fonterutoli 1983 $15 (11/30/89) (HS) **86**

FONTODI
Flaccianello 1987: Soft and generous, this is a large-dimension wine with small-dimension tannins and flavors, but they persist nicely into the finish, offering berry, citrus and spice notes. Drinkable now, but the tannins could use until 1993 or '94 to smooth out completely. Tasted twice. $35 (12/15/91) **83**
Flaccianello 1986: Aromatic and tangy, with focused cherry and plum flavor and an undertone of smoke, vanilla and mushrooms. Soft enough to drink tonight, but you could hold onto it until 1993 or '94 to see what develops. 1,750 cases made. $29 (1/31/90) **88**
Flaccianello 1985: Beautiful expression of Sangiovese; it's smooth, rich and delicious, with anise-tinged raspberry flavor, slightly leathery and complex. Drink now. Rel: $23 Cur: $35 (1/31/89) **91**
Flaccianello 1983 $18 (7/15/87) **95**

FRESCOBALDI
Mormoreto Predicato de Bitùrica 1988: Big and powerful, with lots of concentration, yet balanced, with freshly crushed blackberry and cedar aromas and vanilla, chocolate and cherry flavors. Full-bodied, with full, velvety tannins and a long finish. Needs time. Made from Sangiovese and Cabernet Sauvignon. Try in 1994 to '96. $30 (9/15/91) **91**
Mormoreto Predicato di Bitùrica 1983: Silky and supple up front, then it turns austere. The spicy plum and raspberry flavor is attractive, but then the tannins kick in. Needs until 1993 to soften. A blend of Sangiovese and Cabernet Sauvignon. $34 (2/15/89) **88**

CASTELLO DI GABBIANO
Ania 1985: Amazingly concentrated and elegant, bursting with plum, cassis and cherry aromas and flavors, touched by sweet oak and a nip of earthiness to add complexity. Tannins are there, but submerged under the flavors. Start drinking now to 1993. 1,630 cases made. $30 (1/31/90) **93**
Ania 1983 $25 (7/15/87) **83**
Merlot 1988: Smells ripe and meaty, but it's more elegant and refined on the palate, with taut currant, earth, spice and plum flavors and racy oak notes. The fruit persists though the tannins, suggesting it needs two to three years to soften. Drink in 1993 and beyond. $55 (7/15/91) **86**
R & R 1986: Intense and concentrated, but almost delicate, with lovely overtones of green olive and herbs to the solid core of currant and blackberry flavors. Not particularly intense, but beautifully proportioned and elegant. Drinkable now, but could be cellared through 1995. 600 cases made. $38 (1/31/91) **90**
R & R 1985: A blend of Sangiovese, Cabernet Sauvignon and Merlot, with smoky, chocolaty, leathery aromas offering complexity and richness. The tough tannins will need years to soften, perhaps until at least 1995. Lots of currant and cherry flavors lurk beneath the surface, and the spicy flavors are already appealing. $30 (3/31/90) **91**

GEOGRAFICO
Predicato di Bitùrica 1986: Has a nice herb and bay leaf edge, but the currant, plum and cherry flavors come through in style on the finish. An elegant wine, with firm tannins. Needs cellaring until 1994. $21 (8/31/91) **85**

GRATTAMACCO
1988: An accessible and intriguing wine, with cedar, chestnut, earth and barnyardy aromas and sweet fruit, tobacco, and earth flavors. Medium-bodied, with medium-silky tannins and a lively finish. Made from Sangiovese and Cabernet Sauvignon. Drink now. ($NA) (9/15/91) **87**

VITTORIO INNOCENTI
Acerone 1988: Firmly tannic, with spicy berry aromas and flavors that turn somewhat earthy and herbal on the finish. Seems too tannic for the modest concentration of flavors. Try in 1994 or '95. $13 (7/15/91) **80**
Acerone 1985: Smoke and anise flavors give way to ripe plum and cherry flavor and tannins with a metallic touch on the finish. Could use a little more richness and concentration to stand up to the tannins. Drink now or in 1993. $9 (9/15/89) **78**

ISOLE E OLENA
Antiche Tenute 1989: Light, fresh, fruity and spicy, this easy-to-quaff wine is reminiscent of Beaujolais in style, but has its own strawberry and raspberry flavor profile. Drink soon. $6 (10/31/90) BB **82**
Antiche Tenute 1988: A fine alternative to a Beaujolais, it's a light, fruity wine for quaffing. Has strawberry and spice flavors, decent structure and a short, clean finish. $6 (9/15/89) BB **83**
Antiche Tenute 1987: Fresh and charming. It's light in color with soft tannins and focused and persistent strawberry and spice flavors. Nice finish. You could drink this wine everyday and not get tired of it. Drink up now. $4.50 (1/31/89) BB **81**
Antiche Tenute 1986 $5 (11/15/88) **78**
Cepparello 1988: Subtle on the nose, with elegant blackberry, cherry and licorice aromas, but chewy and powerful on the palate. Excellent potential for cellaring. Full-bodied, with ripe, rich fruit and highly concentrated tannins, but it shows great elegance. Made from Sangiovese. Hold until 1994 to '98. $32 (9/15/91) **93**
Cepparello 1986: Fairly rich and supple with plum and chocolaty flavors, but it won't shortchange you on tannin. Pretty pepper and cherry notes echo on the finish. Persistent flavors. Drink now to 1995. $20 (9/30/89) **86**
Cepparello 1985 $15 (11/15/88) **87**
Collezióne de Marchi Cabernet Sauvignon 1988: An exciting and sensual wine to taste. Has thrilling aromas of sweet red licorice, tobacco and olive and chocolate, tobacco and berry flavors. Full-bodied and very supple, with velvety tannins and a long tobacco and berry finish. Try in 1995 to '97. ($NA) (9/15/91) **94**
Collezióne de Marchi l'Ermo 1988: Wonderfully chewy and round, with delicious fruit, like an excellent Crozes-Hermitage. Purple in color, with gamy blueberry, pepper and spice aromas. Full-bodied, with berry and grape flavors, full tannins and a long, soft finish. Made from Syrah. Better in 1993 to '95. ($NA) (9/15/91) **90**

LILLIANO
Anagallis 1985: A Sangiovese blend with very firm texture, woody aromas and flavors and a tight concentration of ripe berry and leather flavors. Already shows depth of flavor and complexity, but it's not likely to outlive its tannins. Drink in 1993 to '95. 667 cases made. $34 (3/31/90) **86**

MARTINI DI CIGALA
San Giusto a Rentennano Percarlo 1986: Strives for elegance and suppleness with ripe cherry, plum and spice flavors finishing with firm, drying tannins that don't stop the fruit from beaming through on the finish. Drink now to 1994. $24 (11/30/89) **88**
San Giusto a Rentennano Percarlo 1985: Chewy, concentrated and harmonious, a big wine with ripe berry and plum aromas and flavors, firm structure and plenty of tannin, but the fruit wins on the finish. Needs time to shed some of that tannin. Try now. $25 (2/15/89) **92**
San Giusto a Rentennano Percarlo 1983 $13 (9/15/87) **77**

CASTELLO DI MONSANTO
Fabrizio Bianchi Vigneto Scanni 1988: Starts out in a charming way, but ends slightly harsh and aggressive. Needs time. Plenty of berry, white chocolate and fruit aromas and flavors. Very refined mouth-feel, with silky tannins and a caressing texture, yet slightly alcoholic and raisinlike on the finish. Made from Sangiovese. Try in 1994 to '96. $30 (9/15/91) **82**
Nemo 1988: Multi-dimensional, with wonderful character and grace. Lovely aromas of freshly cut cedar, violets and flowers lead to full-bodied floral, tobacco and bitter chocolate flavors. Has silky tannins and a lingering finish. Made from Cabernet Sauvignon. Try in 1993 to '95. $30 (9/15/91) **91**
Nemo 1983: A smoky, chewy, tannic style with pepper, earth, anise and plum flavors that gain a touch of herb and spice. The finish is strong, tannic and fruity. It's not a style for everyone, but it's balanced. Drink in 1993 to '99. $28 (9/15/90) **87**
Tinscvil 1985: Ripe, spicy and complex, this is opulent on the nose and tough on the palate, with concentrated dried cherry, raisin and berry flavors lingering on the long finish. Hints of cedar and chocolate make this a fascinating wine, but the level of tannin is scary. Don't drink before 1994. $22 (9/15/90) **88**

CASTELLO DI MONTE ANTICO
1985 $6.75 (6/30/88) **85**
1982 $3.75 (4/01/86) BB **82**

MONTE VERTINE
1983 Rel: $15 Cur: $18 (2/15/87) **85**
Il Sodaccio 1988: Has an impressive raspberry character, with the structure of a fine Burgundy. Offers beautiful aromas of crushed raspberries and cherries. Full-bodied, with intense raspberry flavors, refined tannins and a long finish. Made from Sangiovese. Better in 1993 to '95. $35 (9/15/91) **91**
Il Sodaccio 1987: Very tough and tannic, with lots of interesting aromas and hints of spice on the finish, but the hard tannins make it difficult to warm up to. The tar-tinged cherry and raspberry flavors are likable. It's a toss-up whether the flavors will outlast the tannins; if they do, it will be around 1995 before we know. $32 (1/31/91) **87**
Il Sodaccio 1986: Despite the tannins, this wine is remarkably elegant and fine with rich, ripe violet, plum, cherry and anise flavors that offer harmony and finesse, persisting through the long finish. Drink now to 1996. Rel: $30 Cur: $35 (9/30/89) **90**
Il Sodaccio 1985 $25 (3/15/89) **91**
Il Sodaccio 1983 Rel: $19.50 Cur: $23 (2/15/87) **93**
Le Pergole Torte 1988: Has great class, beckons you to taste it. Splendid black cherry, tobacco, cedar and berry aromas, full-bodied, with cassis, tobacco and cherry flavors, super-refined tannins and a long finish. Made from Sangiovese. Try in 1993 to '95. $44 (9/15/91) **93**
Le Pergole Torte 1987: A bit tough and tannic, but lots of ripe raspberry, cherry and plum flavors come through on the finish in this beautifully proportioned, age-worthy wine. Needs until 1993 to '95 to tame the tannins, but the promise is exceptional. 1,200 cases made. Rel: $41 Cur: $45 (1/31/91) **90**
Le Pergole Torte 1986: An outstanding wine with major-league tannins overriding the pretty ripe cherry and spice flavors. Echoes anise and plum on the finish. Drink now to 1996. Rel: $36 Cur: $42 (9/30/89) **90**
Le Pergole Torte 1985 Rel: $33 Cur: $42 (4/30/89) **88**
Le Pergole Torte 1983 $24.50 (2/15/87) **90**
Le Pergole Torte 1982 $16.50 (7/16/86) **90**
Le Pergole Torte 1981 $11.25 (7/16/85) **87**
Riserva 1988: Ripe and extracted, but very well balanced. The ripe plum aromas have hints of spice and herbs. Full-bodied, with a big concentration of black olive, herb and cherry flavors and full tannins. Try in 1993 to '95. 1991. $30 (9/15/91) **90**
Riserva 1987: Balanced, elegant and powerful, with beautifully reined-in raspberry, black pepper and floral aromas and flavors and hints of tea and meat adding extra dimensions. Stunning in its balance, harmony and elegance. Tempting to drink now, but cellaring until 1993 to '97 should show all it has. 1,200 cases made. Rel: $30 Cur: $36 (3/15/91) **91**
Riserva 1986: Plenty of grape, raspberry and berry flavors in a lean, tannic style that could be consumed now, but it needs rich food to ward off the tannins. Fruit fights through on the finish. Start drinking now to 1995. Rel: $26 Cur: $35 (9/30/89) **86**
Riserva 1982 $18 (2/15/87) **84**
Riserva 1981 $15 (8/31/86) **90**
Sangioveto 1985 $17 (8/31/88) **89**

NOZZOLE
Il Pareto 1988: Extremely rich, with an almost overripe character. Broad and voluptuous, full-bodied, with deep tar, earth and soft raisin aromas, very ripe berry, tar and slight raisin flavors and a short finish. Made from Cabernet Sauvignon. Try in 1994 to '96. ($NA) (9/15/91) **89**

ORNELLAIA
1988: Silky and refined, like a fine Italian silk scarf. This full-bodied wine is deeply colored, with tar, mint and blackberry aromas, mint and blackberry flavors and a wonderful balance of exquisite tannins and firm acidity. Made from Cabernet Sauvignon, Merlot and Cabernet Franc. Try in 1994 to '97. $49 (9/15/91) **94**
1987: Deep in color, rich and complex, with plush currant, cherry and anise flavors well framed by soft tannins and generous oak shadings. Has a long, full finish. Best to cellar until at least 1995 or '96, and then it should last until the next century. $46 (11/30/90) **89**
1986: An outstanding discovery. Ripe and tannic, with lots of tobacco flavor to add depth to the raisin and cherry flavors. Supple, harmonious and complex, a bit tough, built like a claret for long-term aging. Try it in 1993 to see how it is developing. A blend of Cabernet Sauvignon and Merlot. 1,000 cases made. Rel: $25 Cur: $44 (12/15/89) CS **93**
Masseto 1988: Round and velvety, offering plenty of fruit. Deep, dark ruby in color, with super aromas of blackberries, cassis and mint. Full-bodied and overflowing with blackberry and cassis flavors. Has full, velvety tannins and a long, minty finish. Made from Merlot. Try in 1993 to '95. $49 (9/15/91) **90**

PODERE IL PALAZZINO
Grosso Sanese 1988: Very firm, concentrated and full of raspberry, cherry and floral aromas and flavors shaded by hints of nutmeg and vanilla. Long and focused, and tannic enough to cellar until 1993 or '94. $29 (3/15/91) **88**
Grosso Sanese 1987 Enormously rich and complex, with earth, cedar, tar, plum, cherry and spice flavors that are framed by thick tannins and cedary oak. Amazingly complex, assertive and concentrated. Drink in 1993 to '98. $25 (11/30/89) **90**
Grosso Sanese 1986: Ripe and rich, with powerful raspberry flavors framed in smoky, chocolaty aromas and flavors and plenty of tannin, which makes it seems austere on the finish. If the fruit survives, it could be great. Try now. $22 (2/15/89) **87**
Grosso Sanese 1985 $13 (12/15/87) **94**

FATTORIA PETRIOLO
Merlot 1988: Has a green, leafy edge to the cherry and chocolate flavors. The tannins are fine yet strong, leaving a crisp, firm finish, but there's not much fruit. Cellar until 1993. $24 (8/31/91) **83**

LANZA GINORI PONTI
Vigna di Bugialla Poggerino 1988: A very ripe, broad-textured, bold wine, with firm acidity and tannins and a tart, fruity finish. Flavorful and full-bodied, but not particularly complex. 600 cases made. $17 (1/31/92) **84**

CASTELLO DI QUERCETO
La Corte 1988: Slightly rough, but it has very good concentration of fruit and tannins, with smoky cedar, earth and berry aromas and tomato, berry, earth and black truffle flavors. Full-bodied, with full tannins and refreshing acidity. Made from Sangiovese. Needs time, so try it in 1993 to '95. $35 (9/15/91) **87**
La Corte 1985: Gloriously rich and round, with opulent plum, cherry and raspberry aromas and flavors that seem to open up even more as they linger on the palate. The tannins are firm enough to support the generous flavors, but they don't intrude. Drinkable, but why not wait to see what develops, at least through 1993. $20 (11/30/89) **93**
La Corte 1983 $17 (11/30/89) (HS) **83**
Il Querciolàia 1988: Racy and firm, with an excellent backbone of tannin and acidity. Has cigar tobacco and black cherry aromas and rich tobacco, chocolate and berry flavors. Full-bodied, with very firm tannins and a strong acid backbone. Made from Sangiovese and Cabernet Sauvignon. Try in 1993 to '96. $40 (9/15/91) **88**
Il Querciolàia 1986 $35 (11/30/89) (HS) **85**
Il Querciolàia 1985: A bright beam of red cherry and berry flavor shines through a frame of wood-based toast and chocolate that needs time to resolve. The aromas are gorgeous, but it's tannic on the palate, which hides an appealing softness underneath. Drink now. $30 (2/15/89) **85**

CASTELLO DEI RAMPOLLA
Sammarco 1986: Earthy, peppery and leathery, this soft, mature wine sacrifices fruit and the possibility of developing spicy complexity with time for texture. Tasted twice. $46 (3/15/91) **76**
Sammarco 1985 $42 (11/30/89) (HS) **90**
Sammarco 1983 $28 (9/15/88) **88**

BARONE RICASOLI
Tremalvo 1987: Definitive Cabernet, with its herb-tinged cherry and currant flavors, firm structure and generous balance. Supple, well put together and full of satisfying fruit flavors. Drink now through 1994. 1,100 cases made. $18 (12/15/91) **87**

RIECINE
La Gioia di Riecine 1988: A big, burly wine, with lots of fruit and tannins. Has freshly sliced plums, flowers and berries on the nose. Full-bodied, with an excellent concentration of cassis, berry and cherry flavors and a bit of new wood. Very tannic and long on the finish, it needs time to round out. A Sangiovese-based wine from John and Palmina Abbagnano-Dunkley. Try in 1994. $65 (9/15/91) **91**
La Gioia di Riecine 1987: Soft and flavorful, with plenty of appealing raspberry, chocolate and cedar aromas and flavors that fade a bit on the finish, but are well balanced and drinkable despite a moderate level of tannin. Best around 1993 or '94. $45 (4/30/91) **82**

ROCCA DELLE MACIE
Roccato 1988: Extremely concentrated, with tons of fruit and tannins, it needs time. Shows powerful black truffle, smoke, meat and fruit aromas, full-bodied berry, mint and ripe fruit flavors and full tannins, but it has a velvety finish. Made from Sangiovese and Cabernet Sauvignon. Try in 1994 to '96. ($NA) (9/15/91) **90**
Ser Gioveto 1987 ($NA) (11/30/89) (HS) **90**
Ser Gioveto 1986: Lean and elegant, with sharply delineated raspberry, earthy and woodsy aromas and flavors, crisp structure and good length. A bit tannic, but it has the intensity to come through in the end. Try now. $15 (2/15/89) **84**
Ser Gioveto 1985 $15 (11/30/89) (HS) **88**

DEI ROSETI
Belconvento 1987: A medium-weight, rustic wine, with earthy, leathery aromas and flavors that hint at cherry and anise but settle on spice and earthiness. Drinkable now. Tasted twice. $24 (3/15/91) **85**
Belconvento 1985: Full-bodied, rich and spicy, already showing mature leather and chocolate overtones to the plummy flavor on the finish. Drink now or in 1993. $23 (7/15/89) **86**

RUFFINO
Cabreo Il Borgo Predicato di Bitùrica 1988: A big wine, with plenty of fruit and tannins, but it maintains a lovely suppleness. Has ripe chocolate, vanilla, cherry and berry aromas, full-bodied, with plenty of chocolate, berry and nut flavors and round, rich tannins. Made from Sangiovese and Cabernet Sauvignon. Try in 1993 to '95. ($NA) (9/15/91) **90**
Cabreo Il Borgo Predicato di Bitùrica 1985 $21 (9/30/89) **90**
Nero del Tondo 1988: A rich wine that shows a firm backbone of acidity and tannins. Medium- to full-bodied, with tobacco, tar and spice aromas, tobacco and berry flavors and a round, rich mouth-feel. Made from Pinot Noir. Better in 1993. $18 (9/15/91) **88**

SAN FELICE
Predicato di Bitùrica 1985: A tough, earthy wine, with modest intensity of fruit. Offers more spice and toast flavors than currant and berry, which seem to be buried under tannins at the moment. May be better after 1995. $28 (12/15/91) **82**
Predicato di Bitùrica 1983 ($NA) (11/30/89) (HS) **87**
Predicato di Bitùrica 1982 Rel: $19 Cur: $25 (1/31/88) SS **92**
Vigorello 1986: Smells appealing, with generous coffee- and cedar-scented plum and anise aromas. The flavors follow suit, with a hard, bitter edge of tannin on the palate. Try in 1995 to '97. Tasted twice. $19 (12/15/91) **84**
Vigorello 1985: Concentrated and elegant underneath its shell of tough tannins, it offers focused raspberry and currant flavors, with hints of chocolate and toast. Give it until 1993 or '94 to soften the edges, but the finish is long and appealing. $18 (9/15/90) **89**
Vigorello 1983 $17 (11/30/89) (HS) **90**
Vigorello 1982 $15 (11/30/89) (HS) **87**
Vigorello 1981 Rel: $13 Cur: $18 (1/31/88) **84**
Vigorello 1980 Rel: $12 Cur: $18 (2/28/87) SS **95**

SASSICAIA
1988: The stuff that dreams are made of—the greatest Sassicàia ever produced. Has laser-guided flavors and structure. The pure cassis aromas have hints of mint and berries. Full-bodied, with a monumental structure of cassis, mint and vanilla flavors, full, supple tannins and a super-long finish. A blend of Cabernet Sauvignon and Cabernet Franc. Try in 1997. Rel: $60 Cur: $66 (9/15/91) **98**
1987: A weak vintage. Richly aromatic, with lots of classic cassis and plum, but it turns tannic and a bit lean on the palate. Could be more generous, offering pleasant berry flavors, but turns drying on the finish. Drinkable now. $45 (3/15/91) **82**
1986: Remarkably flavorful and complex for such a lean wine. It's beautifully balanced, harmonious, seamless. Hints of plum, spice, anise, tobacco and toasty oak compete for attention, but the whole is greater than the sum of its parts. Drinkable now, but better to cellar it until at least 1994. $50 (12/15/89) **95**
1985 Rel: $48 Cur: $120 (5/15/89) CS **92**
1984 $57 (3/15/89) **85**
1982 Rel: $45 Cur: $110 (7/31/87) **84**

I SELVATICI
Claresco 1990: Dry and lean, with clean cherry flavors and a slightly tannic finish. A bit rough in style, but should be serviceable at the table. Drink now. 4,000 cases made. $6 (9/30/91) **79**
Predicato di Cardisco 1985: Sharp tannins and acidity carve up the palate. Has ripe fruit flavor and anise, chocolate, smoke and currant notes, but wow, the tannins are tough on the finish. Best to cellar until 1995. 1,000 cases made. $25 (8/31/91) **81**

TERRABIANCA
Campaccio Barriques 1988: Approachable and exotic, offering fresh violet, cherry and mint aromas, balanced rose and cherry flavors and elegant tannins. Medium-bodied. Made from Sangiovese. Drinkable now, but better in 1993 or '94. $31 (9/15/91) **87**
Piano del Cipresso 1988: A bit disjointed now, lacking concentration on the finish. Has plum and tobacco aromas and flavors, medium-bodied, with peppery tomato and berry flavors and full tannins. Tasted twice. Made from Sangiovese. Try in 1993 to '95. $29 (9/15/91) **83**

TERRICCI
Antiche Terre de'Ricci 1986: Lean and tough, with plenty of tannin but good concentration of raspberry, strawberry and smoky flavors coming through. A meaty wine with room to grow. Drink now to 1995. Tasted three times. 950 cases made. $23 (5/15/90) **83**
Antiche Terre de'Ricci 1985: Big, plush and elegant, with beautifully focused raspberry and plum flavors shaded by toast and vanilla. Complex and supple on the palate, echoing sage and honey on the finish. Drinkable now. $22 (3/15/89) **91**
Terricci 1986: Goes too far for our tastes. Drinkable, but seems tired and off-base. Overly mature for its age, with rubbery aromas and murky flavors. Tasted twice. $20 (9/30/91) **67**

TERUZZI & PUTHOD
Vigna Peperino 1986: A full-bodied, unusual-tasting wine, with heavy tobacco aromas and slightly cedary and peppery flavors but little fruit. Not much to like. Tasted twice. $11 (1/31/90) **68**
Vigna Peperino 1985 $10.50 (10/31/88) **92**

TOSCOLO
Red Tuscan Table Wine 1986: Simple, light and tasty, with lots of raspberry flavor, fresh and appealing. Drink now. $4.25 (1/31/89) **79**

VIGNAMAGGIO
Gerardino 1985: A solid, firmly structured wine that shows the benefits of aging in its minty, spicy aromas. A supple texture and generous plum and cherry flavors give it substance, and a lingering finish adds extra appeal. Drink now through 1994. $18 (1/31/92) **87**
Gerardino 1987 ($NA) (11/30/89) (HS) **92**
Gerardino 1986 ($NA) (11/30/89) (HS) **91**
Gerardino 1985 ($NA) (11/30/89) (HS) **91**

VINATTIERRI
Rosso 1986: Hard, drying tannins clamp down on the mature currant, anise, cherry and herb flavors. There's a lot to like in this wine, but it would be even more attractive if the tannins weren't so severe. Drink in 1995 or '96. $18 (8/31/91) **83**
Rosso 1985 ($NA) (9/15/87) (HS) **91**
Rosso 1983 $14 (9/15/87) (HS) **84**
Rosso II 1986: Tough and tannic, with a hard core of plum, anise, earth, tar and cherry flavors that turn tannic and sharp on the finish. Cellaring until 1994 may soften it a bit. $18 (8/31/91) **84**

VISTARENNI
Codirosso 1986 $22 (11/30/89) **90**

VITICCIO
Prunaio 1988: Tough and tannic, gangs up on the finish, but underneath the layers of astringency beats a heart of pure Sangiovese flavor that just needs time. Raspberry and plum flavors manage to peek through, especially on the finish. Drink after 1995. $28 (3/31/92) **88**
Prunaio 1986: A Sangiovese blend with lots of complexity on a tight, elegant frame. Shows anise and smoke aromas and cherry, strawberry and blackberry flavors wrapped in a veil of tannin that will need until 1993 to '95 to soften. Offers plenty of style and finesse. 2,820 cases made. $19 (3/31/90) SS **92**
Prunaio 1985: Firm and fruity, with charming plum and vanilla aromas and flavors, wafting subtly across the palate as well, long and delicate on the finish. Velvety texture and delicious to drink on release, probably better by now. $18 (4/30/89) **88**

CASTELLO DI VOLPAIA
Balifico 1987 ($NA) (11/30/89) (HS) **89**
Balifico 1986: Lean and tight, with sharply focused plum and raspberry flavors, very firm and long. Drink now. $19 (4/30/89) **83**
Balifico 1985 $21 (11/30/89) (HS) **91**
Coltassala 1986 ($NA) (11/30/89) (HS) **86**
Coltassala 1985 $19 (11/30/89) (HS) **88**
Coltassala 1983 $22 (9/15/88) **86**
Coltassala 1982 ($NA) (9/15/87) (HS) **87**
Coltassala 1981 ($NA) (9/15/87) (HS) **90**

Other Tuscany Red DOC

AMBRA
Carmignano 1986: Lean and a bit tight, but the reined-in flavors of berries and leather finish harmoniously and smoothly. Drinkable now. $12.50 (5/15/89) **80**

AVIGNONESI
Rosso di Montepulciano 1989: Firm and focused, with a generous component of black cherry and dusky spice flavors, a smooth texture and pretty fair length. Drinkable now. Tasted twice. $12 (4/30/91) **83**

CAPEZZANA
Carmignano 1986: Ripe and spicy, but light in texture, with moderately intense berry, cinnamon and nutmeg aromas and flavors. Tannic and tight on the finish, needs until 1993 to '95. $15 (7/15/91) **81**
Carmignano Riserva 1985: Light in color, but particularly fragrant, spicy and complex. A bit more tannic than the moderately intense raspberry and currant flavors can support, so drink it with something rich. $25 (7/15/91) **83**

IL COLLE
Rosso delle Colline Lucchesi 1986: Aromatic and flavorful, with the smokiness and spiciness of new oak. Has ripe cherry flavors and firm tannins, and it's slightly bitter on the finish. Obviously a serious wine, but one that needs to develop some grace. Drink 1993 to '94. $7.50 (3/31/90) **81**

FRESCOBALDI
Pomino Tenuta di Pomino 1986: Very firm and generous, with a sense of elegance and attractive

Key to Symbols

The scores reported here are the results of blind tastings conducted by our panel of senior editors. Wines that carry the initials below are results of individual tastings.

THE WINE SPECTATOR 100-POINT SCALE *95-100*—Classic, a great wine; *90-94*—Outstanding, superior character and style; *80-89*—Good to very good, a wine with special qualities; *70-79*—Average, drinkable wine that may have minor flaws; *60-69*—Below average, drinkable but not recommended; *50-59*—Poor, undrinkable, not recommended. "+"—With a score indicates a range; used primarily with barrel tastings to indicate a preliminary score.

SPECIAL DESIGNATIONS SS—Spectator Selection, CS—Cellar Selection, BB—Best Buy, ($NA)—Price not available, (NR)—Not released.

TASTER'S INITIALS (JG)—Jim Gordon, (HS)—Harvey Steiman, (JL)—James Laube, (JS)—James Suckling, (TM)—Thomas Matthews, (TR)—Terry Robards, (PM)—Per-Henrik Mansson, (BT)—Barrel Tasting (these wines were tasted blind from barrel samples), (CA-date)—*California's Great Cabernets* by James Laube, (CH-date)—*California's Great Chardonnays* by James Laube, (VP-date)—*Vintage Port* by James Suckling.

DATE TASTED Dates in parentheses represent the issue in which the rating was published.

cherry, raspberry and smoke flavors. There could be more depth, but the anise-tinged fruit is especially appealing. Drink now or in 1993. $14 (1/31/90) **87**
Pomino Tenuta di Pomino 1985 Rel: $12 Cur: $17 (9/15/88) SS **93**

VILLA IL POGGIOLO
Carmignano Riserva 1985: Lean and taut, with lots of spicy, leathery aromas and flavors, it's tart and sharply focused. What it lacks is any apparent fruit. Not for every taste, but a well made wine in the style. $16 (5/15/90) **80**

LE PUPILLE
Morellino di Scansano Riserva 1986: Ripe, smooth and polished, with focused, elegant berry, red cherry and cinnamon aromas and flavors, this 100 percent Sangiovese is ever so slightly tannic as the flavors echo on the long finish. Drinkable now, but probably best after 1993. $16 (6/30/91) **86**

SORBAIANO
Montescudaio Rosso delle Minière 1988: Has grace and finesse, with subtle anise, plum, chocolate and spice notes that are well focused. Has enough tannin to cellar until 1994. $24 (8/31/91) **86**

TALOSA
Rosso di Montepulciano 1989: Simple, lean and somewhat tannic, this hard-edged wine has a core of grape flavor that hangs on through the finish. Best after 1993. $11 (1/31/92) **79**

TUSCANY WHITE/*VINO DA TAVOLA*

CASTELLO D'ALBOLA
Chardonnay 1989: Remarkably delicate in balance for such a lively, fruity wine, offering plenty of lemon-laced pear and apple flavors shaded by oak. The oak is more prominent on the nose than on the palate. Very long and inviting. Drinkable now, but should improve through 1993. 1,667 cases made. $50 (2/15/91) **90**

FATTORIA DI AMA
Chardonnay Colline di Ama 1988 $17 (9/15/89) **82**
Chardonnay Colline di Ama 1987 $17 (9/15/89) **82**
Chardonnay Colline di Ama 1986 $17 (9/15/89) **79**

ANTINORI
Bianco Toscano 1988: Crisp and elegant, rather like a good Sauvignon Blanc, showing pleasant sweet pea and fig aromas and flavors, plus a touch of oak. Lean, juicy and tasty. Drink now. $6.50 (10/15/89) BB **85**
Galestro 1990: Simple and light, with pleasant apple and almond aromas and flavors. Refreshing. $7 (8/31/91) **75**
Galestro 1989: Light, fresh and floral, a simple wine of delicate texture, with hints of melon and lemon and a crisp finish. Drink on a warm day. $7 (12/31/90) **79**

AVIGNONESI
Chardonnay Il Marzocco 1987 Rel: $18 Cur: $23 (9/15/89) **90**
Chardonnay Il Marzocco 1987: Soft, round, gentle and supple with spicy pear and oaky flavors, not a lot of pizzazz, but it's nice and simple. Rel: $18 Cur: $23 (3/31/89) **82**
Chardonnay Il Marzocco 1986 $16 (2/15/88) **92**
Sauvignon Blanc Il Vignola 1988: Silky-smooth, ripe and generous with its peach and melon flavor, plus hints of toast and vanilla to lend complexity. Smells great and tastes smooth and inviting, but the price is daunting. $20 (10/15/89) **87**
Terre di Cortona 1987: Distinctive in flavor and long on the finish, though it's flavors are pretty straightforward. Has an attractive vanillalike, new oak aroma and mostly appley flavors. Rel: $12 Cur: $23 (3/31/89) **83**
Terre di Cortona 1986 $9.50 (2/15/88) **87**

CASTELLO BANFI
Chardonnay Centine 1988: Light, crisp and refreshing, with a touch of almond on the finish and a bit of spritz in the texture. $8 (4/30/90) **78**
Chardonnay Centine 1987: Light in texture but rich in flavor, showing ripe fig, vanilla and almond aromas and flavors, mouthfilling and smooth. Drink now. $8 (3/31/89) **84**
Chardonnay Fontanelle 1988: Smooth, silky and light-textured, with plenty of flavor lingering intensely on the long finish. Pear, fig and butterscotch notes dominate. Drinkable now, but aging until 1993 should add some welcome nuances. $11 (12/31/90) **86**
Chardonnay Fontanelle 1987 $16 (9/15/89) **80**
Chardonnay Fontanelle 1986 $16 (9/15/89) **86**

VILLA CALCINAIA
Cerviolo 1987: A soft and simple white with more wood than fruit and light butterscotch and apple flavors. Drink now. $18 (3/31/90) **79**

CAPEZZANA
Chardonnay 1988 $14 (9/15/89) **84**
Chardonnay 1987 $14 (9/15/89) **82**

CASTELLARE DI CASTELLINA
Canonico di Castellare 1988: Toasty, spicy aromas of new oak pervade this wine, clearly designed to be Burgundian. Its soft, almost subtle pear and butterscotch flavors try to emerge on the finish. If you like 'em oaky, this one's for you. $18 (12/31/90) **79**

VILLA CILNIA
Campo del Sasso 1988: Soft, flabby and not particularly flavorful, offering little fruit or spice. An ordinary wine. Tasted twice. 1,100 cases made. $14 (8/31/91) **76**
Poggio Garbato 1989: Soft, round and generous, with decent apple flavors, but not a lot of complexity. A touch of bitterness on the finish tightens it up. $9.25 (7/15/91) **80**

COL D'ORCIA
Ghiaie Bianche 1989: Smooth, polished and fragrant, with spicy, floral aromas and flavors that turn buttery and rich on the finish. A rather delicate wine that still manages to evolve on the palate, becoming more complex and interesting with each sip. Terrific with seafood. $12 (12/31/90) **87**

FATTORIA DI FELSINA
Berardenga I Sistri 1988: The first Chardonnay release from Felsina. A distinctive, complex and fruity Chardonnay that's packed with orange, banana and spice flavors, then finishes with a smoky, honeyed touch. Smooth texture, fine balance. $24 (3/31/90) **86**

FONTODI
Meriggio 1987: A Sauvignon Blanc made in a rich, buttery style, with fresh grapefruit flavors coming through. Tastes ripe and nicely oaky, with a hint of earthiness, but seems weighty on the finish. $17 (3/31/90) **82**

CASTELLO DI GABBIANO
Bianco del Castello 1987: Simple, round, slightly buttery and floral, with a touch of spicy earthiness on the finish. Drinkable, but not exceptional. $8 (12/31/90) **78**
Chardonnay Ariella 1988: Ripe and concentrated, with very spicy butterscotch flavors, but a bit rough in texture. Cellaring until 1993 could soften it up properly. $23 (1/31/91) **83**
Chardonnay Ariella 1987: Don't let the initial smell put you off. Barnyard aromas give way to rich, ripe flavors of peach, pear, butter and honey. Round in texture, long on the finish, focused and deep in flavor. A new wine from a respected Chianti estate. $23 (3/31/90) **87**

VITTORIO INNOCENTI
Vino Nobile di Montepulciano 1985: Has attractive perfumed aromas, with faint toasty, butterscotch flavors underneath and a soft lush texture. Decent Chardonnay. $10 (3/31/90) **77**

ISOLE E OLENA
Chardonnay Collezióne de Marchi 1989: Rich, oaky and assertive, this strives for power and succeeds. From the deep gold color to the toasty aromas and nutty fruit flavors, it's very stylish and spicy. Hints of nutmeg, cinnamon and vanilla linger on the finish. $23 (7/15/91) **87**
Chardonnay Collezióne de Marchi 1988 $16 (9/15/89) **87**

NOZZOLE
Chardonnay Vigneto le Bruniche 1988: Delicate, with simple, lean mint, lemon and quince flavors that linger on the palate. Well focused and balanced, ready to drink now. $9.25 (3/31/90) **86**

PLACIDO
1989: A middle-of-the-road Chardonnay, with modest butter, pear and apple flavors, a soft structure and not much intensity. $6 (7/15/91) **74**

POGGIO ALLE GAZZE
1989: Simple and refreshing, with pleasant grapefruit and pear aromas and flavors that lie gently on the palate. Drinkable now. $18 (9/15/91) **79**

RUFFINO
Cabreo la Pietra Predicato del Muschio 1986 $18 (9/15/89) **90**
Cabreo la Pietra Predicato del Muschio 1985 $17 (9/15/89) **83**
Cabreo la Pietra Predicato del Muschio 1983 $17 (3/31/87) **90**
Libaio 1990: An austere style of Chardonnay, but has enough pear and fig flavors coming through on the finish to shoulder past the earthy, floral aromas and flavors. Drinkable now. $10 (1/31/92) **81**
Libaio 1987: Lemony, mineral aromas and flavors are reminiscent of Chablis, and so is the light, crisp texture. Clean, refreshing and simple. $8.50 (9/15/89) **78**

SAN FELICE
Belcaro 1990: Fruity, fresh and lively, with vanilla and peach-accented grapefruit aromas and flavors. Shows roundness on the palate, possibly from a touch of new oak. Has personality. Drink soon. $10 (1/31/92) **83**

WHITE DOC

CECCHI
Vernaccia di San Gimignano 1987: A Vernaccia made for the cellar? This one needs a year or two to shed some astringency and austerity, but the structure and definite overlay of oak aromas and flavors show promise. Drink now. $6 (5/15/89) BB **82**

RICCARDO FALCHINI
Vernaccia di San Gimignano 1990: Fresh and floral, with a touch of almond to the basic apple and orange flavors extending into a long, delicate finish. Drinkable now. $9 (5/15/92) **84**

FRESCOBALDI
Pomino Tenuta di Pomino Il Benefizio 1986: Aromatic and spicy, with cinnamon and perfumed flavors, gentle and soft, with honey and spice notes coming through on the finish. $20 (3/31/90) **85**

MELINI
Vernaccia di San Gimignano Lydia 1989: A light, smooth, soft wine, with modest almond and floral aromas and flavors. Drink soon. $8 (7/15/91) **78**

TONI PAOLA
Vernaccia di San Gimignano Ambra delle Torri 1989: Fresh and a little spicy, with simple pear and almond flavors. $9.75 (7/15/91) **75**

BARONE RICASOLI
Vernaccia di San Gimignano 1990: Earthy floral and almond aromas and flavors lean toward honey on the soft, mature finish. Could be fresher, but the nutty, buttery characteristics prevail. Drink soon. $9 (5/15/92) **79**
Vernaccia di San Gimignano 1989: Floral aromas and flavors make this light, lively wine appealing, especially as it echoes peach and apple on the finish. Drink now. $9 (4/15/91) **82**

SALVUCCI
Vernaccia di San Gimignano 1987: Dry and somewhat austere, showing enough floral character to make it interesting in the short term. Drink soon. $5.50 (5/15/89) **77**

SAN QUIRICO
Vernaccia di San Gimignano 1989: Fruity and simple, with modest pear and walnut aromas and flavors. $8.50 (7/15/91) **78**

TERUZZI & PUTHOD
Vernaccia di San Gimignano Terre di Tufo 1989: Soft and generous, with lots of apricot, lemon and honey flavors on a relatively light frame, making for a rich wine with seemingly no weight. A touch of oak adds spice, but it could use more depth. Drinkable now. $20 (12/31/90) **84**

ANGELO DEL TUFO
Vernaccia di San Gimignano 1988: Crisp and lively, with nicely tangy grapefruit flavors. A medium-bodied wine, with almond and spice notes. Refreshing. $7.50 (4/30/90) **81**

OTHER ITALY RED/*RED DOC*

D'ANGELO
Aglianico del Vulture 1985: Heavy-handed with cedar, bark and leathery flavors. There's a touch of fruit here, but it can't stand up to the other flavors. $18 (9/15/89) **70**

CASAL THAULERO
Montepulciano d'Abruzzo 1989: Ripe, almost jammy aromas and flavors turn soft and spicy, making it drinkable and appealing. Flavorful enough to drink with hearty food. $6 (6/30/91) BB **81**
Montepulciano d'Abruzzo 1988: Light and velvety but flavorful, with appealing cherry, strawberry and nutmeg aromas and flavors that are clean, crisp and refreshing. Drink now. $5 (5/31/90) BB **80**

BARONE CORNACCHIA
Montepulciano d'Abruzzo 1988: Hearty, with earthy aromas, peppery, ripe flavors and a snap of tannin. Of decent quality. $5 (12/31/90) **78**

LUNGAROTTI
Torgiano Rubesco 1987: Light and velvety, with gentle tar, raspberry and olive aromas and flavors making it pleasant to drink soon with a savory roast. $11 (5/15/91) **83**
Torgiano Rubesco 1985: Tannic and earthy without the richness and concentration to fill out the frame. Barnyardy aromas may appeal to some. Drink now to 1995. $11 (9/15/89) **74**
Torgiano Rubesco Monticchio Riserva 1980: Has mature aromas and flavors on a medium frame, with well-integrated tannins and smoky, peppery nuances on the finish. The caramel, tar and rose petal overtones are especially nice. Drinkable now. $27 (7/15/91) **84**
Torgiano Rubesco Monticchio Riserva 1978: Rich, toasty and earthy, it's fully mature but still wearing a tannic vest. The flavors are complex and appealing, but the finish turns dry and biting. Drink now to 1998. $23 (9/15/89) **82**
Torgiano Torre di Giano 1989: Dry and clean, with light apple and mineral flavors and a clean, dry finish. Pleasant for sipping with dinner. $11 (7/15/91) **83**

MASTROBERARDINO
Lacryma Christi del Vesùvio 1989: Big and classy, bursting with concentrated berry aroma and flavor—it could be a terrific Zinfandel. The ripe, rich blackberry, plum and cherry flavors are shaded by a touch of black pepper and a hint of oak. Beautifully balanced for the long haul. Drinkable now, but may be better after 1993 or '94. $14 (7/15/91) **89**

Taurasi 1986: Very ripe and focused, with the concentrated blackberry and raspberry aromas and flavors reminiscent of a fine Zinfandel, even down to the hints of black pepper on the nose and finish. The well-integrated tannins may need until 1994 to '97 to soften. A vibrant style. $18 (7/15/91) **87**
Taurasi Riserva 1985: Tarry, smoky aromas and flavors permeate this distinctive wine. Has firm acidity and tannins that will need until 1995 to '98 to let the raspberry flavor come through. $22 (6/30/91) **84**
Taurasi Riserva 1981: Firm and toasty, with earthy, chalky overtones to the basic pear and melon flavor. Medium-bodied and crisp on the finish, with a bit more character than the regular bottling. Rel: $21 Cur: $30 (2/15/89) **78**
Taurasi Riserva 1980: The flavors are fully mature with spice, herb, tea and anise dominating, but the tannins are as hard and firm as a newly bottled wine. The finish gets awfully dry and tannic. Hard to predict when this wine will peak. Try now to 1998. Rel: $15 Cur: $24 (9/15/89) **75**
Taurasi Riserva 1977 Rel: $28 Cur: $54 (10/16/84) CS **92**

ANTONIO & ELIO MONTI
Montepulciano d'Abruzzo 1989: Soft and fruity, but a streak of astringency on the finish and a decadent character in the aroma bring it down a bit for us. $7 (9/30/91) **75**
Montepulciano d'Abruzzo 1988: Deep color, ripe fruit aromas and flavors, a hint of leather and generous intensity make this immediately likable, if not particularly profound. Drink it up. 3,000 cases made. $6.25 (2/15/91) BB **83**

CAMILLO MONTORI
Montepulciano d'Abruzzo 1987: Ripe, supple and focused, with good concentration, modest depth and persistent flavors that lean toward cherry and anise. Drinkable now. $8 (3/31/90) **80**

FATTORIA PARADISO
Sangiovese di Romagna Riserva Superióre Vigna delle Lepri 1987: Flavorful, concentrated and full-bodied, with enjoyable ripe cherry, berry and spice aromas and flavors and an almost thick texture. This is a wine to enjoy with hearty food. Probably best to drink before 1994. $16 (7/15/91) **85**

PATERNOSTER
Aglianico del Vulture 1987: Has the black pepper and cherry flavors familiar to Rhône drinkers, with a sense of lightness under a veil of tannin. Seems astringent now, better after 1994. $16 (1/31/92) **82**

RIVERA
Castel del Monte Il Falcone Riserva 1985: Tight and tannic, but aromatic and concentrated enough to suggest that cellaring until 1993 or '94 will soften the edges and allow the ripe cherry and spice flavors to emerge. $16.50 (12/31/90) **83**

UMANI RONCHI
Montepulciano d'Abruzzo 1989: Simple and fruity, with a light texture and modest flavors. Drinkable. $5 (2/15/91) **75**

CASTELLO DI SALLE
Montepulciano d'Abruzzo 1985: Generous, fruity and flavorful, with lots of plum, cherry, smoke and herb aromas and flavors on a soft supple frame. Modest tannins make it drinkable now. Fresh for its age. $15 (6/15/90) BB **84**

SASSO
Aglianico del Vulture 1985: Unusual and impressive, firm and somewhat tannic, but it's concentrated cherry, plum and anise flavors grow in intensity on the finish. A smoky character pervades the wine, which should be at its best around 1993 to '95. $11 (3/15/89) **83**

STRUZZIERO
Taurasi Riserva 1977 Rel: $22 Cur: $26 (8/31/86) CS **93**

DR. COSIMO TAURINO
Brindisi Patriglione 1981: Big, ripe, smooth and somewhat alcoholic, with raisin, smoke and tar aromas and flavors, but it comes off as a robust, almost sweet wine that could stand in for your favorite Amarone. Drinkable now. $14 (12/31/90) **85**
Brindisi Patriglione Riserva 1979: Smoky and ripe, rough-and-ready, with impressive concentration of cherry flavor on a sturdy frame. Not much nuance, but the flavors are tasty. $12 (3/31/89) **82**
Salice Salentino Riserva 1986: Ripe and earthy, with gobs of black cherry, plum and smoke aromas and flavors that spread onto the finish. A wonderful wine for drinking with flavorful food. Ready to drink, but should be fine through 1995. $8 (1/31/92) BB **84**
Salice Salentino Riserva 1985: A good wine in an earthy style, offering toasty, leathery aromas and flavors overlaid with a lively dose of cherry and berry. Distinctive and easy to drink, with enough depth to enjoy with a roast. $8 (2/15/91) BB **85**
Salice Salentino Riserva 1983: Youthful color and lots of fruit for its age, offering wild berry and mushroom flavors throughout the long finish. Very earthy aromas. Enough tannin to age until 1994. $6.50 (12/15/89) BB **81**
Salice Salentino Riserva 1982 $6 (3/31/89) BB **82**
Salice Salentino Riserva 1980 $5 (12/15/87) BB **84**
Salice Salentino Rosato 1988: Shows lots of personality. Leathery aromas and spicy strawberry flavors give this rosé plenty of oomph. It's crisp, full-bodied and has a lingering finish. $7.25 (3/15/91) BB **84**
Salice Salentino Rosato 1987: Offers the best of white and red wines. Dry and crisp, but with plenty of strawberry and watermelon flavors and a smooth, buttery feel. $6.50 (12/31/89) BB **84**

VALENTINI
Montepulciano d'Abruzzo 1979: A good wine if you're not too fastidious. Full flavored and mature, marked by a very earthy, leathery aroma and coffeelike flavors. $28 (2/15/89) **80**

VALLANIA
Cabernet Sauvignon Colli Bolognesi Terre Rosse 1986: Extremely earthy and smoky, a bitter wine, with little fruit or liveliness. Tasted twice, with consistent notes. $18 (9/30/91) **66**

ZONIN
Montepulciano d'Abruzzo 1988: Light, simple and fruity, with pleasant smoke and anise notes to the basic cherry flavor. A welcoming wine worth drinking with comforting food. $6 (6/30/91) BB **80**
Montepulciano d'Abruzzo 1987: Earthy, with vibrant strawberry and cherry flavors to the earth and mushroom overtones. Light, straightforward and appealing. Drink now. $4.50 (3/31/90) **78**

Key to Symbols

The scores reported here are the results of blind tastings conducted by our panel of senior editors. Wines that carry the initials below are results of individual tastings.

THE WINE SPECTATOR 100-POINT SCALE ***95-100***—Classic, a great wine; ***90-94***—Outstanding, superior character and style; ***80-89***—Good to very good, a wine with special qualities; ***70-79***—Average, drinkable wine that may have minor flaws; ***60-69***—Below average, drinkable but not recommended; ***50-59***—Poor, undrinkable, not recommended. "+"—With a score indicates a range; used primarily with barrel tastings to indicate a preliminary score.

SPECIAL DESIGNATIONS SS—Spectator Selection, CS—Cellar Selection, BB—Best Buy, ($NA)—Price not available, (NR)—Not released.

TASTER'S INITIALS (JG)—Jim Gordon, (HS)—Harvey Steiman, (JL)—James Laube, (JS)—James Suckling, (TM)—Thomas Matthews, (TR)—Terry Robards, (PM)—Per-Henrik Mansson, (BT)—Barrel Tasting (these wines were tasted blind from barrel samples), (CA-date)—*California's Great Cabernets* by James Laube, (CH-date)—*California's Great Chardonnays* by James Laube, (VP-date)—*Vintage Port* by James Suckling.

DATE TASTED Dates in parentheses represent the issue in which the rating was published.

Vino da Tavola

A. BERTELLI
I Fossaretti 1985: Beautifully balanced, sharply focused and supple in texture, an elegant Cabernet that plays its spicy oak against a motherlode of currant and blackberry flavors. Tempting to try soon, but cellaring until 1993 to '95 should only benefit it. 125 cases made. $34 (12/31/90) **92**

CORVO
Duca di Salaparuta Duca Enrico 1984: Amazingly rich, smooth and elegant with complex cherry, cedar, spice and plum flavors that reverberate on the palate. Deftly balanced, with just enough tannin to sustain it until 1997 or 1999. Start drinking now. 4,000 cases made. $27 (9/15/89) **92**

GIROLAMO DORIGO
Montsclapade 1987: Simple, fruity and appealing, offering well-crafted Cabernet aromas and flavors on a medium frame. Has good length. Drinkable now. $25 (2/15/91) **84**

FORADORI
Granato di Mezzolombardo 1988: A mouthful of currant, plum and anise flavors, hinting at chocolate on the finish. A rich wine, with enough tough tannins to need until 1995 to soften. Has the punch to carry it through. 1,000 cases made. $33 (1/31/92) **86**

LUNGAROTTI
Cabernet Sauvignon 1983: Rich and fruity, with firm tannins and plenty of bright raspberry, cherry, currant and plum flavors. The tannins on the finish are beginning to soften, but it can still age. Try now to 1995. $18 (5/15/91) **85**
San Giorgio 1982: Dry tannins tend to rob this wine of its texture, but the herbal, earthy aromas and flavors are definitely mature, hinting at sweet plum on the finish. Seems a bit muddy. It may be better after 1994. $34 (7/15/91) **77**

MASTROBERARDINO
Avellanio 1989: Ripe and rich, with generous blackberry and currant aromas and flavors that persist onto the long finish. Has nice vanilla and spice notes from oak aging. Smooth tannins make it almost drinkable now, but cellaring until 1993 to '94 might not hurt. $10.50 (7/15/91) **87**

PAOLA DI MAURO
Colle Picchioni 1986: A Merlot and Sangiovese blend made in an earthy style, but there are also generous aromas and flavors of spice, cherry and toast on a supple structure and velvety background of tannin. Borders on funky, but it's drinkable now, if you don't mind a small bite of tannin. $15 (3/31/90) **80**
Vigna del Vassalle 1986: A serious wine, with very smoky, herbal aromas, firm texture and floral, raspberry flavors. A blend of Merlot, Montepulciano and Sangiovese, this has distinctive character and persistent flavors. Drinkable now, but cellaring until 1993 or '94 should soften the edges a bit. $12 (3/31/90) **83**

TENUTA MAZZOLINO
Noir 1987: Bold, rich, deep and complex, with tiers of raspberry, chocolate, cherry and vanilla flavors and plenty of tannin and oak shadings. A gutsy wine that won't remind you of Pinot Noir, but it's still delicious. Drink in 1993 to '96. $45 (9/30/91) **86**

FATTORIA PARADISO
Barbarossa 1983: A unique wine from a rare grape variety made in an earthy style, mature and sharply focused, with a firm backbone of acidity and a touch of tannin that almost obscures the fine strand of plummy flavor that pokes through on the finish. At its best now. $13.50 (3/15/89) **80**

REGALEALI
Rosso 1987: Warm, ripe and effusive strawberry and berry aromas and flavor are buried by a layer of scratchy tannin that will need until 1993 to '95 to wear away. There seems to be just enough intensity to outlast the tannin. A gamble. $11 (12/15/89) **77**
Rosso del Conte 1984: Deep, dark and concentrated, quite tannic, but the ripe cherry and dark plum flavors peek through on the finish and the nose is just starting to develop some nice complexity. Drink now. $19 (7/31/89) **84**

RIUNITE
Lambrusco Reggiano NV: A light, slightly sweet, very fruity wine, with a bit of effervescence. Well made for the type. Drink now, chilled. $4.50 (9/30/91) BB **81**

SOLICHIATA
Torrepalino 1987: Very light in color and character, with pleasant strawberry, earth and nutmeg aromas and flavors and more tannin than flavors. Drink soon. $5.75 (4/15/90) **73**

DR. COSIMO TAURINO
Notarpanaro 1981: A distinctive, mature wine, balancing smoky, toasty notes against an undercurrent of ripe black cherry and plum flavors that extend into a long, focused finish. A wine with personality. $9 (5/15/91) **86**
Notarpanaro 1978: A spicy, toasty, slightly thick wine, mature but not yet smooth or elegant. A sturdy, ripe wine for hearty food. $8 (3/31/89) **80**

VALLANIA
Terre Rosse 1985: Spicy, pruny aromas and flavors give this character, but it's so soft it borders on flabby. Drink soon. $9 (3/31/90) **70**

VASELLI
Santa Giulia 1988: Spicy, oaky aromas and flavors turn soft and slightly raisiny on the palate. Simple and easy to drink. $10 (1/31/92) **83**
Santa Giulia Rosso NV: A hard-edged wine, with firm tannins and sharp acidity, but also has a sense of elegance. The spice, herb, cedar and berry flavors turn dry and tannic on the finish. Drink now or in 1993. $19 (1/31/92) **80**

LA VIARTE
Roi 1986: A tough, tannic, earthy style, with little charm. Chocolate, berry and tar notes are rough-and-tumble on the palate. Needs time to mellow, but may always be rough around the edges. Drink in 1993 or '94. $24 (1/31/92) **78**

Other Italy White/*Vino da Tavola*

ANTINORI
Castello della Sala Borro della Sala 1990: Pungent, vegetal aromas turn dry and austere on the palate, with a little grapefruit flavor to relieve the intense varietal character. Could show more balance. Drink with cheese, especially chèvre. $13 (1/31/92) **79**
Castello della Sala Borro della Sala 1989: A flavorful but light style, balancing its slightly herbal, grassy flavors with pear and vanilla. Immediately attractive and easy to drink. Drink soon. $11.50 (1/31/91) **86**
Castello della Sala Borro della Sala 1987: Pineapple and almond aromas and flavors rest on a medium-weight, simple structure; drinkable now. $10 (10/15/89) **77**
Castello della Sala Cervaro della Sala 1989: A tasty wine, with definite apple and apricot Chardonnay character, a twang of oak and a harmonious melding of the two as the flavors combine on the finish. Well made and flavorful, but not heavy. Drinkable now, but it may be better in 1993 or '94. $23 (1/31/92) **85**
Castello della Sala Cervaro della Sala 1988 $21 (1/31/91) **89**
Castello della Sala Cervaro della Sala 1987: A blend of Chardonnay and Gechetto. A woody, style with plenty of vanilla, toast and butterscotch flavors that play off the ripe grapefruit, pear and honey flavors. Wood creeps through on the finish, but altogether it's attractive. Drink now. $20 (4/30/90) **83**

CORVO
Duca di Salaparuta Bianca di Valguarnera 1987: Earthy, toasty, butterscotch aromas and flavors make this a high-profile wine. It seems overripe and a bit flabby on balance, but it also has plenty of complexity and distinctive character. $34 (12/31/90) **81**

FOLONARI
Chardonnay 1987: Spicy, vaguely fruity, soft and simple. $5 (9/15/89) **76**

CARLO HAUNER
Salina Bianco 1989: Light in structure and round in texture, with pear and almond flavors wrapped in sweet oak notes. Soft and fragrant on the finish. Best with food. $11.50 (7/15/91) **81**

LUNGAROTTI
Chardonnay 1989: Simple and refreshing, with clean floral and lightly fruity flavors and a watery finish. A very dry wine for everyday quaffing. $11 (3/31/91) **77**
Chardonnay 1988 $10 (9/15/89) **82**
Chardonnay 1987 $10.50 (9/15/89) **83**
Chardonnay I Palazzi 1985 $16 (9/15/89) **87**
Pinot Grigio 1989: Simple and fruity, with pleasant orange and pear aromas and flavors and hints of butterscotch on the finish. Drinkable now. $11 (3/31/91) **81**

MASTROBERARDINO
Plinius 1990: Very firm and focused, with generous apple, peach and slightly oaky aromas and flavors, echoing citrus and butter on the long finish. Beautifully balanced and a bit austere now. Built to develop a richer texture by 1993 to '95. A blend of Aglianico and Coda di Volpa. 5,000 cases made. $19 (5/15/92) **88**
Plinius d'Irpinia Bianco 1989: Crisp, dry and lemony, with a zesty mouth-feel, pear and lemon flavors and hints of spice. Not generous, but quite enjoyable in an austere style. $17 (7/15/91) **84**

FATTORIA PARADISO
Chardonnay 1988 $10 (9/15/89) **83**
Pagadebit di Romagna Secco Vigna dello Spungone 1989: Very unusual, full flavored, soft and dry, with pungent floral and spice aromas, spicy orangelike flavors and a dry finish. Not for the faint of heart, but it's plenty flavorful. $13 (7/15/91) **79**

PRATOSCURO
1989: Very pretty, light, dry and floral, rounding out on the finish to reveal peach and apricot nuances. Not complex or elegant, but direct and a bit earthy. $18 (12/31/90) **79**

REGALEALI
Chardonnay 1989: Rich, spicy and buttery. A smooth-textured wine, with definite oak aromas and flavors that meld nicely with ripe pineapple and melon notes. Drinkable now. 260 cases made. $45 (1/31/92) **86**
Nozze d'Oro 1989: Dry, lightly fruity and a bit austere, with reserved apple and herbal aromas and flavors, a touch of sparkle from dissolved carbon dioxide and a finish that echoes the fruit. $20 (7/15/91) **82**

SETTESOLI
Bianco 1990: Fruity, fresh, soft and round textured, with appealing peach and pear aromas and flavors that turn floral on the finish. $7 (7/15/91) **79**
Bianco Feudo dei Fiori 1990: Dry and almost austere, with lots of fresh Bartlett pear aromas and flavors that persist into a solid finish. Not a big wine, but it has vitality and style. $9 (6/30/91) **80**

DR. COSIMO TAURINO
Chardonnay 1990: A standard wine, with few distinguishing characteristics. Fairly light, floral and figgy tasting. $7 (5/15/92) **75**

TORREBIANCO
Chardonnay 1987: Has distinctive and appealing floral, honey and almond aromas and flavors, but a hint of grassiness and a soft texture detract from the crispness and liveliness one might expect from Chardonnay. Drinkable now. Tasted twice. $11 (12/31/90) **78**

VALLANIA
Chardonnay 1989: Simple *vino bianco*, without much character to define it as Chardonnay. Drinkable now. Tasted twice. $16.50 (1/31/92) **73**
Chardonnay Cuvée Terre Rosse 1985: A gentle, plush-textured wine, with fascinating almond, orange, nutmeg and pear aromas and flavors that persist on the finish. Mature, but it has plenty of life and a real sense of elegance. Drinkable now. 1,900 cases made. $20 (8/31/91) **85**

LA VIARTE
Liende 1989: Tart in texture and thin in flavor, with a little nutmeg and lemon to lend interest to the modest intensity. Drink with light fish dishes. 100 cases made. $22 (8/31/91) **79**

WHITE DOC

ANTINORI
Orvieto Classico 1987: An earthy, grassy style, smooth in texture but ultimately very light, almost thin. $5 (5/15/89) **78**
Orvieto Classico Campogrande Secco 1990: Simple, light and almost austere, with mineral overtones to the modest pear and apple flavors. Drink soon. $7.25 (3/31/92) **78**
Orvieto Classico Campogrande Secco 1989: Clean and basic, with mild peach flavors and a hint of almond. Refreshing and straightforward. A good value. $7.25 (7/15/91) **80**
Orvieto Classico Castello della Sala 1990: A light, lean wine, with more depth than most Orvietos, showing appealing apricot, pear and mineral character that grows on the finish. $13 (3/31/92) **83**

VILLA BIANCHI
Verdicchio dei Castelli di Jesi Classico 1989: A hearty, straightforward, clean wine, with basic lemon flavors accented by a nutty, buttery note that comes through on the finish. Won't disappoint, especially at this price. From Umani Ronchi. $7 (6/30/91) BB **83**

BUCCI
Verdicchio dei Castelli di Jesi Classico 1988: Earthy, toasty aromas and flavors dominate this medium-weight wine. Only a little fruit, reminiscent of apples cut hours ago, makes it somewhat appealing. $14 (12/31/90) **73**

COLLE DEI BARDELLINI
Vermentino Riviera Ligure di Ponent Vigna "U Munte" 1989: Ripe and exotic, this flowery, fruity, fresh and full-bodied wine bursts with flavor and charms. Has a graceful balance and a smooth texture. Distinctive and appealing. Drink soon. $18 (1/31/91) **89**

FALESCO
Est! Est!! Est!!! di Montefiascone 1989: Tart and grassy, with a strong earthy edge to the lemon flavor that skews it away from the middle ground. Tasted twice. $5.75 (8/31/91) **74**
Est! Est!! Est!!! di Montefiascone Poggio dei Gelsi 1989: Fresh and simple, with nice melon and pear aromas and flavors. $12 (7/15/91) **77**

MASTROBERARDINO
Fiano di Avellino Apianum Vigna d'Oro 1988: Not generous but a nice medium-bodied wine, with lean, austere flavors and earthy aromas. Lively and crisp, with a little spritz. $25 (4/30/90) **79**
Fiano di Avellino Vignadora 1989: Very dry and austere, but subtle pear and spice flavors build up on the finish for a pleasing package overall. 1,500 cases made. $30 (7/15/91) **84**
Fiano di Avellino Vignadora 1986: A disappointing vintage for this usually great producer. Dry and austere, it's getting mature, with some pleasant spicy aromas and flavors; perhaps modest, but it's a pretty good drink. $22.50 (10/15/89) **78**
Greco di Tufo Vignadangelo 1986: Has typically lemony mushroom aromas and flavors on a big structure that seems to float effortlessly across the palate. Earthy flavors take getting used to. $15 (10/15/89) **79**
Lacryma Christi del Vesùvio 1989: This unusual wine has earthy, floral aromas and flavors that turn soft and dry on the finish. Shows a hint of oak, too. Drink soon. Tasted twice. $13 (7/15/91) **76**
Lacryma Christi del Vesùvio 1987: Smooth and elegant, packed with character, with concentrated almond-tinged pear and vanilla aromas and flavors, plus an earthy style that drives the point home beautifully. Drink now. $9 (3/31/89) **89**

FATTORIA PARADISO
Albana di Romagna Secco Vigna dell'Olivo 1989: Floral, fruity, nutty aromas and flavors combine for a smooth, assertive, fairly rich wine. Has a lingering, buttery finish. Not elegant, but good in its style. $13 (7/15/91) **81**

TENUTA POGGIO DEL LUPO
Orvieto 1989: Fresh, lively and light, with simple apple and spice aromas and flavors that echo on the finish. $9 (8/31/91) **80**

BARONE RICASOLI
Orvieto Classico Secco 1990: This light, refreshing wine has pleasant almond overtones to the basic pear flavor. Not flashy, but it's a pleasant drink at a good price. 5,000 cases made. $8 (3/31/92) BB **82**
Orvieto Classico Secco 1989: Light and refreshing, with very pretty almond and floral aromas and flavors and a silky texture. Drink now. 5,000 cases made. $8 (4/15/91) BB **81**

RUFFINO
Orvieto Classico 1990: Earthy nectarine aromas and flavors are pleasant. Best served chilled, as the fruit manages to make a statement on the finish. Drink soon. $8.50 (3/31/92) **82**
Orvieto Classico 1987: Earthy and grassy but fruity enough to make it interesting, showing some peach aromas and flavors. Drink it soon. $6.25 (5/15/89) **78**

DR. COSIMO TAURINO
Salice Salentino Rosato 1989: Light pink in color, dry and spicy, with pleasant watermelon, cherry and nutmeg flavors that persist on the finish. Refreshing to drink soon. $9 (3/31/92) **82**

VALENTINI
Trebbiano d'Abruzzo 1984: Distinctively earthy, toasty and buttery, with some spicy flavors and a chalky edge, long and intense. For fans of earthy, mature white wines. $20 (3/31/89) **80**

VASELLI
Orvieto Classico Secco 1989: Simple, fruity and slightly smoky. Light and dry. Drink soon. $7.75 (7/15/91) **75**
Orvieto Classico Torre Sant'Andrea 1989: Fresh, pearlike aromas and flavors add appeal to this medium-bodied, well-crafted wine, simple and easy to drink but firm enough to stand up to a plate of sautéed fish. $11 (12/31/90) **83**

PORTUGAL
Vintage Port

BARROS

Vintage Port 1987: Marks a return to the major leagues for Barros. Good purple color, with a very fresh, grapey, aromatic nose, medium- to full-bodied, with medium tannins and a balance of elegant fruit. Not a showstopper, but has some class. $28 (VP-1/90) **81**

Vintage Port 1985: This is an early-drinking '85, but it is nicely crafted all the same. Medium purple with a ruby hue, a very fresh and grapey nose, medium-bodied, with clean, fresh fruit flavors, medium tannins and a long finish. Rel: $24 Cur: $29 (VP-1/90) **80**

Vintage Port 1983: A decent early-drinking wine showing simple, fresh fruit flavors but not a lot of complexity or structure. Medium ruby, with a fresh, simple, fruity nose, medium-bodied, with clean fruit flavors, good balance and a medium finish. Rel: $8 Cur: $30 (VP-1/90) **76**

Vintage Port 1978: Sweet and simple. Medium to light ruby, with fresh, floral grape and licorice aromas, light-bodied, with light tannins, and a sweet, short finish. Rel: $7 Cur: $30 (VP-1/90) **75**

Vintage Port 1974 $40 (VP-1/90) **74**

Vintage Port 1970 $60 (VP-1/90) **82**

BORGES

Vintage Port 1985: This is so light and ready to drink that it is more like a ruby or a late-bottled vintage. Medium to light red, with simple aromas of cherries and chocolate, light-bodied and clean, with sweet cherry flavors and light tannins on the finish. $15 (VP-5/90) **70**

Vintage Port 1983: Amazingly sugary; most 1983s are relatively dry. Medium red, with a redwood and mature cherry nose, medium-bodied, with simple, syrupy cherry flavors, medium tannins and a long finish. Too sweet for me but drinkable nonetheless. Rel: $12 Cur: $26 (VP-5/90) **70**

Vintage Port 1982: The best Borges vintage I have tasted. It is not overly roasted and raisiny like many other 1982s and it shows some interesting fruit. Medium to deep ruby, with a chocolate and roasted nut nose, medium-bodied, with sweet, ripe fruit flavors, medium tannins and a silky finish. Rel: $12 Cur: $30 (VP-5/90) **79**

Vintage Port 1980: Another lightweight vintage that is much more like a good ruby or late-bottled vintage. Red with a light ruby center, spicy black cherry aromas, medium- to light-bodied, with light tannins and a sweet fruit finish. Rel: $11 Cur: $23 (VP-5/90) **70**

Vintage Port 1979: Remarkably light and forward. The alcohol is showing now, indicating that it is on its way down. Light red with an almost garnet hue, aromas of cherries and nuts, light-bodied, with simple, sweet cherry flavors and a hot, unbalanced finish. Fading. Rel: $11 Cur: $22 (VP-5/90) **65**

Vintage Port 1970 $86 (VP-5/90) **59**

BURMESTER

Vintage Port 1985: This is a great achievement for a 1985, perhaps one of the best wines of the vintage. Inky color, with berry and grape must aromas, full-bodied, with tons of fruit and tannin, very concentrated. Finish is extremely long. Outstanding. $25 (VP-1/90) **93**

Vintage Port 1984: Very good for an unheralded vintage, if a little lean. Deep ruby, with a concentrated earthy, grapey nose, medium-bodied, with very good fruit flavors, medium tannins and a simple, youthful, fruity finish. ($NA) (VP-1/90) **84**

Vintage Port 1980: This is an enchanting, stylish wine with plenty of exotic, ripe fruit flavors. Deep ruby, with an excellent, earthy, black truffle nose, full-bodied, with ripe fruit flavors and well-integrated tannins. Rel: $18 Cur: $35 (VP-1/90) **88**

Vintage Port 1977: Starts out rather slow on the palate, but it opens into a classy glass of Port. Medium to deep ruby, with a perfumed floral and currant nose, medium-bodied, with medium tannins and a very balanced, clean fruit finish. Not a blockbuster, but very good. Rel: $11 Cur: $35 (VP-1/90) **82**

Vintage Port 1970 $50 (VP-1/90) **86**

Vintage Port 1963 $120 (VP-1/90) **83**

CALEM

Vintage Port 1985: The first vintage that brought Cálem attention. Deep purple, with an intense floral and licorice nose, full-bodied, good grip, a medium concentration of fruit flavors and a long finish. Very good potential. Rel: $25 Cur: $40 (VP-6/90) **88**

Vintage Port 1983: A racy wine with very good structure. It puts Cálem back in the driver's seat for quality. Purple-ruby, with a ripe blackberry nose, full-bodied, with a good concentration of sweet fruit flavors, full tannins and a balanced finish. Rel: $18 Cur: $44 (VP-6/90) **84**

Vintage Port 1980: Extremely sweet and short on body and backbone. Medium ruby, with chocolate, cherry and spice on the nose, medium-bodied, with sweet cherry and tomato flavors, medium tannins and a short finish. Rel: $14 Cur: $42 (VP-6/90) **78**

Vintage Port 1977: It is hard to say what happened here but this is very forward and weak for a 1977. Medium ruby with a garnet edge and slightly burnt vanilla aromas, medium-bodied, with burnt vanilla and fruit flavors, light tannins and a short finish. Rel: $11 Cur: $58 (VP-11/89) **69**

Vintage Port 1975 $45 (VP-2/90) **86**

Vintage Port 1970 $50 (VP-11/89) **80**

Vintage Port 1966 $65 (VP-11/89) **82**

Vintage Port 1963 $85 (VP-12/89) **82**

Vintage Port Quinta do Foz 1987: Made entirely from Cálem's Quinta da Foz, this wine shows lots of fruit, with a rich and velvety mouth-feel. Purple, with ripe fruit and orange peel aromas, full-bodied, with lots of fruit flavors and a velvety finish. $28 (VP-6/90) **84**

Vintage Port Quinta do Foz 1982: A sweet and simple wine with plenty of attractive flavors. Medium ruby, with a plum and roasted nut nose, full-bodied with velvety ripe fruit and a medium finish. Rel: $16 Cur: $37 (VP-6/90) **82**

CHAMPALIMAUD

Vintage Port 1982: For a 1982, this has tons of sweet, almost cloying fruit. Its black color is impressive and its extremely fruity nose stands out. Lacks the class to be considered truly outstanding. Dark purple-ruby, with a jammy nose, full-bodied, with very sweet fruit flavors, medium tannins and a lingering finish. $20 (VP-2/90) **86**

CHURCHILL

Vintage Port 1985: This is an impressive wine on the palate, but I tasted it blind four times in early 1990 and a slightly odd, acetic nose showed three times. It doesn't seem to be getting any worse, however. Deep ruby-purple, with earthy berry and slightly volatile aromas, full-bodied, with lovely, velvety fruit flavors, medium tannins and a sweet, round finish. Rel: $22 Cur: $51 (VP-2/90) **81**

Vintage Port 1982: Delicious, sweet and opulent, but an acetic, varnish aroma detracts from the overall quality. Some people may not mind this "off" characteristic, but it will probably get worse with time. Medium ruby with a purple center, a grapey, earthy, slightly "off" nose, medium-bodied, with silky, well-integrated tannins and a sweet, long finish. $24 (VP-6/90) **78**

Key to Symbols

The scores reported here are the results of blind tastings conducted by our panel of senior editors. Wines that carry the initials below are results of individual tastings.

THE WINE SPECTATOR 100-POINT SCALE 95-100— Classic, a great wine; ***90-94***— Outstanding, superior character and style; ***80-89***—Good to very good, a wine with special qualities; ***70-79***—Average, drinkable wine that may have minor flaws; ***60-69***—Below average, drinkable but not recommended; ***50-59***—Poor, undrinkable, not recommended. "+"—With a score indicates a range; used primarily with barrel tastings to indicate a preliminary score.

SPECIAL DESIGNATIONS SS—Spectator Selection, CS—Cellar Selection, BB—Best Buy, ($NA)—Price not available, (NR)—Not released.

TASTER'S INITIALS (JG)—Jim Gordon, (HS)—Harvey Steiman, (JL)—James Laube, (JS)—James Suckling, (TM)—Thomas Matthews, (TR)—Terry Robards, (PM)—Per-Henrik Mansson, (BT)—Barrel Tasting (these wines were tasted blind from barrel samples), (CA-date)—*California's Great Cabernets* by James Laube, (CH-date)—*California's Great Chardonnays* by James Laube, (VP-date)—*Vintage Port* by James Suckling.

DATE TASTED Dates in parentheses represent the issue in which the rating was published.

Vintage Port Agua Alta 1987: Dense, fruity and backed by a solid grip of tannin and alcohol. The flavors lean toward berry and cherry, and taper off on the finish. Not a very sweet style. Should be best around 2000 to 2005. Rel: $37 Cur: $41 (4/15/91) **83**

Vintage Port Agua Alta 1983: The strange acetic character of this wine overpowers everything else. Medium ruby with a red edge, intense nail polish aroma, medium-bodied, with grapey, varnish flavors and a short hard finish. Best to avoid. Rel: $22 Cur: $40 (VP-7/90) **69**

Vintage Port Fojo 1986: There are some attractive floral fruit flavors, but the nose has a slightly odd component. Medium purple, with a floral, perfumed, slight varnish nose, medium-bodied, with floral, earthy flavors, medium tannins and a good finish. Drink in 1994. ($NA) (VP-2/90) **78**

Vintage Port Fojo 1984: For the rather lean 1984 vintage, this is very ripe, with an abundance of attractive, roasted, ripe fruit flavors. When I tasted this wine blind, some other tasters found it slightly acetic on the nose, but I didn't. Medium ruby-purple, with perfumed black currant aromas, full-bodied, with rich, sweet fruit flavors and medium tannins that firmly hold the wine together. Drink now or in 1993. ($NA) (VP-2/90) **79**

COCKBURN

Vintage Port 1985: Shows an abundance of thick, rich fruit and plenty of backbone. Very inky, dense color, with a rich, floral nose of berries and cherries, full-bodied, medium sweet, with massive anise and cherry flavors and extremely well-integrated tannins and acidity. Drink in 1996 to '98. Rel: $33 Cur: $45 (VP-6/90) **90**

Vintage Port 1983: A delicious wine with richness and intensity. Dessert in a glass. It's ripe and full with spicy, tart cherry, cassis and plum flavors that are remarkably well balanced and showing signs of elegance. Some heat on the finish. Drink starting 1998. Rel: $22 Cur: $45 (8/31/87) CS **92**

Vintage Port 1975 $40 (VP-1/90) **77**

Vintage Port 1970 $63 (VP-12/89) **86**

Vintage Port 1967 $61 (VP-12/89) **85**

Vintage Port 1966 $90 (10/31/88) **91**

Vintage Port 1963 $99 (VP-12/89) **88**

Vintage Port 1960 $74 (10/31/88) **82**

Vintage Port 1958 ($NA) (VP-11/89) **84**

Vintage Port 1955 $132 (VP-11/89) **90**

Vintage Port 1950 $112 (VP-11/89) **76**

Vintage Port 1947 $162 (VP-11/89) **90**

Vintage Port 1935 $350 (VP-2/90) **92**

Vintage Port 1931 $500 (VP-1/90) **89**

Vintage Port 1927 $360 (VP-12/89) **91**

Vintage Port 1912 $350 (VP-10/87) **91**

Vintage Port 1908 $380 (VP-10/87) **89**

Vintage Port 1904 $500 (VP-10/87) **75**

Vintage Port 1896 $400 (VP-2/90) **82**

CROFT

Vintage Port 1985: This is evolving more quickly than I expected, but there are still plenty of clean cherry notes on the nose and palate. Medium to deep ruby, with a slightly roasted nut, cherry nose, medium-bodied, with a well-defined backbone, medium tannins and a sweet finish. Drink in 1995 to 1997. Rel: $30 Cur: $43 (VP-6/90) **81**

Vintage Port 1982: I tasted this at least six times in 1990, and I am amazed by its poor quality. It is light, forward and diluted and has nothing in common with the excellent Ports of this house. Light ruby, with roasted coffee, spice, vanilla and plum on the nose, light-bodied, with light tannins and a dry finish. The alcohol is showing. Best to avoid. Rel: $22 Cur: $42 (VP-4/90) **69**

Vintage Port 1977: When I tasted this in 1988, I thought it was extremely well structured, but the wine has lost some of its body. Deep ruby, with a raisin and chocolate nose, medium-bodied, with medium-hard tannins and a rather austere finish. Slightly out of balance. Perhaps it needs more time. Drink now to 1994. Rel: $14 Cur: $53 (VP-4/90) **85**

Vintage Port 1975 $38 (10/31/88) **80**

Vintage Port 1970 $69 (VP-12/89) **89**

Vintage Port 1966 $91 (VP-12/89) **90**

Vintage Port 1963 $116 (VP-12/89) **91**

Vintage Port 1960 $94 (VP-9/89) **90**

Vintage Port 1955 $170 (VP-11/89) **84**

Vintage Port 1950 $145 (VP-4/90) **77**

Vintage Port 1945 $410 (VP-11/89) **99**

Vintage Port 1935 $270 (VP-2/90) **93**

Vintage Port 1927 $420 (VP-12/89) **87**

Vintage Port Quinta da Roêda 1987: I tasted this Port just after it was blended and it was very impressive. But the last time I tasted it, it had an odd, "off" character on the nose and palate. Medium purple, with a closed, slightly smoky nose, full-bodied, with grapey, earthy fruit flavors, medium tannins and an odd, slightly volatile finish. Final decision pending. Drink 1997 to 2000. ($NA) (VP-2/90) **79**

Vintage Port Quinta da Roêda 1983: Much better than the 1982 Croft, this is rich and well structured with lovely fruit. Medium to deep ruby, with a youthful grape and berry nose, full-bodied, with well-knit medium tannins and more than enough rich raspberry and black cherry flavors to keep it going for years. Drink in 1995 to 1997. $22 (VP-2/90) **85**

Vintage Port Quinta da Roêda 1980: Evolving quickly; should be drunk very soon. Medium red with a brown edge, with chocolate and roasted nut aromas, medium-bodied, with medium tannins and a rather hollow center on the palate. A simple wine. Drink now. Rel: $25 Cur: $30 (VP-2/90) **75**

Vintage Port Quinta da Roêda 1978: Ripe and tough; needs more time. Forward medium to deep ruby with a garnet rim, ripe bitter chocolate, roasted nut and blackberry aromas, full-bodied, with medium tannins and ripe fruit flavors. Drink now to 1994. Rel: $22 Cur: $27 (VP-2/90) **83**

Vintage Port Quinta da Roêda 1967 $50 (VP-1/90) **85**

C. DA SILVA

Vintage Port Presidential 1987: This is a solid 1987 with ample fruit and tannin to give it longevity. Medium purple, with a ripe raisin and tar nose, full-bodied, with full tannins and ripe fruit flavors. A little one-dimensional. Drink in 1996 to 1998. ($NA) (VP-2/90) **80**

Vintage Port Presidential 1985: Seems short on grip and flesh for a 1985, but it's nonetheless a pleasant wine. Medium purple, with a perfumed cranberry nose, medium-bodied, with medium fruit flavors, rather delicate tannins and a light finish. Drink now or in 1993. $30 (VP-2/90) **78**

Vintage Port Presidential 1978: Simple, with clean fruit flavors, but it lacks guts. Medium ruby-purple, with aromas of fresh plums and grapes, medium-bodied, with black cherry flavors and a light finish. Very drinkable, yet simple. Drink now or in 1993. $37 (VP-2/90) **77**

Vintage Port Presidential 1977: This is not up to the standards of a good 1977. It is too forward and light. Medium red, with fresh plum aromas, medium-bodied, with simple plum flavors and a round tannic structure. Drink now or in 1993. $39 (VP-2/90) **72**

Vintage Port Presidential 1970 $54 (VP-2/90) **75**

DELAFORCE

Vintage Port 1985: A ripe and roasted style. Medium ruby, with a raisiny, slightly burnt nose, medium-bodied, with silky, sweet fruit flavors and medium tannins. Drink in 1995 or 1996. Rel: $24 Cur: $35 (VP-6/90) **81**

Vintage Port 1982: Surprisingly forward and light, like a poor ruby. Medium red-ruby, with a burnt chocolate and coffee nose, light-bodied, with coffee and fruit flavors, light tannins and a hot, dry finish; unbalanced. Best to avoid. Rel: $20 Cur: $27 (VP-6/90) **69**

Vintage Port 1977: More forward than many wines from this vintage. Medium red-ruby, with coffee and roasted nut aromas, medium-bodied, with medium tannins and a silky, roasted character. Sweet finish. Drink now or in 1993. Rel: $11 Cur: $54 (VP-2/90) **80**

Vintage Port 1975 $43 (VP-2/90) **76**
Vintage Port 1970 $53 (VP-2/90) **89**
Vintage Port 1966 $75 (VP-2/90) **85**
Vintage Port 1963 $90 (VP-2/90) **93**
Vintage Port Quinta da Corte 1987: Classy and silky in the mouth, showing plenty of elegance and power. Deep purple, with a fresh black olive nose, full-bodied, with medium tannins and balanced tar and blackberry flavors. Drink in 1997. ($NA) (VP-2/90) **87**
Vintage Port Quinta da Corte 1984: Slightly lean and hard, like many other 1984s, but very well balanced. Medium ruby-purple, with aromas of tar, olives and fruit, full-bodied, with plenty of tannins and a medium depth of fruit flavors. Linear in structure but classy. Drink in 1994 to 1996. ($NA) (VP-2/90) **84**
Vintage Port Quinta da Corte 1980: Simple and fruity, but still interesting to drink. Medium to deep ruby with a red hue, milk chocolate and raspberry aromas, medium-bodied and quite tannic and hard, with sweet fruit flavors and a medium finish. Drink now or in 1993. ($NA) (VP-2/90) **81**
Vintage Port Quinta da Corte 1978: Another simple wine, perfectly ready to drink. Medium red, with a fruity, black olive nose, medium-bodied, with sweet fruit flavors, medium tannins and a short finish. $24 (VP-2/90) **80**

DIEZ HERMANOS
Vintage Port 1977: This is a good all-around 1977, although slightly more forward and ready to drink than the very best. Medium brick red, with a very ripe fruit, toffee and chocolate nose, medium- to full-bodied, with medium sweet toffee and fruit flavors, medium tannins and a ripe finish. Slightly simple but very enjoyable. Drink now. ($NA) (VP-4/90) **82**

DOW
Vintage Port 1985: Fleshy and raw, bursting with fruit on the palate but starting to close up. Deep, dark ruby-purple, with intense tar and berry aromas, full-bodied, with ripe berry flavors, full tannins and a long finish. Drink in 1996 to '98. Rel: $30 Cur: $36 (VP-6/90) **89**
Vintage Port 1983: Very stylish and big, with a classy balance of fruit and tannin. Deep ruby-purple, with a multidimensional nose of perfume and grapes, full-bodied, tannic and tightly knit. Drink in 1996 to '98. Rel: $20 Cur: $34 (VP-6/90) **94**
Vintage Port 1980: A good example of Dow's attractively dry Ports. Medium to deep ruby, with a nose of tar and fresh grapes, full-bodied, with peppery fruit flavors, medium tannins and a silky finish. Will improve. Drink now or in 1993. Rel: $15 Cur: $41 (VP-6/90) **90**
Vintage Port 1977: Impressively hard and powerful, but very closed for the moment. Dark ruby, with rich raspberry and earth aromas, full-bodied, with an excellent balance of full tannins and generous berry flavors. Drink in 1995 to '97. Rel: $12 Cur: $57 (VP-4/90) **94**
Vintage Port 1975 $44 (VP-4/89) **80**
Vintage Port 1972 $36 (VP-1/90) **79**
Vintage Port 1970 $70 (VP-12/89) **94**
Vintage Port 1966 $85 (VP-12/89) **94**
Vintage Port 1963 $112 (VP-2/90) **92**
Vintage Port 1960 $96 (VP-2/90) **88**
Vintage Port 1955 $190 (VP-4/90) **91**
Vintage Port 1950 $110 (VP-11/89) **86**
Vintage Port 1947 $340 (VP-11/89) **88**
Vintage Port 1945 $340 (VP-11/89) **89**
Vintage Port 1935 $330 (VP-6/90) **79**
Vintage Port 1934 $260 (VP-6/90) **84**
Vintage Port 1927 $480 (VP-4/90) **87**
Vintage Port Quinta do Bomfim 1989: Powerful, full of marvelous fruit flavors, yet graceful enough to let them roll across the palate gently. Has the intensity and grip to age well. Expect it to keep developing through at least 2004 to 2010. 2,785 cases made. Rel: $24 Cur: $29 (11/30/91) CS **90**
Vintage Port Quinta do Bomfim 1987: Extremely impressive, with generous, rich black cherry notes. Deep inky purple, with ripe black cherry aromas, full-bodied, with full tannins and a great concentration of fruit flavors. Very well structured. Drink in 1998 to 2000. ($NA) (VP-2/90) **86**
Vintage Port Quinta do Bomfim 1986: Very hard and closed at the moment, but still shows good fruit flavors and potential. Very dark ruby with a black center, a grape and licorice nose, medium-bodied, with full, hard tannins, blackberry flavors and a closed finish. Drink in 1996 or '97. ($NA) (VP-2/90) **82**
Vintage Port Quinta do Bomfim 1984: Powerful and hard, with a classy dryness, one of the best wines I have tried from this property. Dark ruby-purple, with a lovely grape and raspberry nose, full-bodied, with tons of tannins and lots of medium-sweet fruit flavors. Very solid. Drink in 1995 or '96. ($NA) (VP-2/90) **86**
Vintage Port Quinta do Bomfim 1982: Very smooth and fruity, lacking the disagreeable roasted, raisiny character of many of the wines from this vintage. Medium ruby with a red hue, delicate grape, cherry and raspberry aromas, medium-bodied, with round cherry flavors and medium tannins. Drink now or in 1993. ($NA) (VP-2/90) **82**
Vintage Port Quinta do Bomfim 1979: One of of the better 1979s I have tasted. Most are rather watery and diluted, with little interesting fruit. This is fairly exciting, with plenty of fruit and tannin. Medium ruby, with a perfumed black cherry nose, medium-bodied, with medium tannins and lovely floral fruit flavors. Drink now. $28 (VP-2/90) **81**
Vintage Port Quinta do Bomfim 1978: All the components, from the rich fruit flavors to the hard tannins, are well integrated. Medium ruby, with a black cherry nose, full-bodied, with medium tannins and very good focused blackberry flavors. Quite dry with a long finish. Drink now. Rel: $27 Cur: $33 (VP-2/90) **85**
Vintage Port Quinta do Bomfim 1965 ($NA) (VP-6/90) **87**

FEIST
Vintage Port 1985: Light for a 1985, but the fruit is clean and pleasant on the palate. Light purple with some ruby, a nose of grapes and spices, medium-bodied, with sweet grape and watermelon flavors, light tannins and finish. Drink now. Rel: $20 Cur: $28 (VP-1/90) **72**
Vintage Port 1982: A well-made wine that lacks concentration of fruit. Medium ruby, with a clean grape and black cherry nose, medium-bodied, with good fruit flavors, medium tannins and a long finish. Drink now. ($NA) (VP-1/90) **78**
Vintage Port 1978: A good, clean, peppery wine for short-term drinking. Light brilliant ruby, with an extremely fresh cherry nose, medium-bodied, with peppery fruit flavors, light tannins and a medium finish. One-dimensional. Drink now. ($NA) (VP-1/90) **78**

FERREIRA
Vintage Port 1987: Well balanced, with delicious sweet fruit and a firm backbone. Inky color, with a very ripe raisin and grape nose, full-bodied, with sweet fruit flavors, medium tannins and a long finish. Drink in 1997 to '99. ($NA) (VP-11/89) **88**
Vintage Port 1985: Rich and sweet; it grows in intensity on the palate. Medium to deep purple, with perfumed, earthy raspberry aromas, full-bodied, with very sweet, syrupy fruit flavors and medium tannins. Very round and luscious. Drink in 1996 to '98. Rel: $20 Cur: $30 (VP-11/89) **87**
Vintage Port 1982: Very ripe and sweet. Deep ruby, with a nose of berries, anise and black pepper, full-bodied, with very ripe fruit flavors, full tannins and a rather short finish. It needs time but will be drinking well soon. Rel: $14 Cur: $28 (VP-11/89) **81**
Vintage Port 1980: A soft, round and deliciously drinkable vintage Port. Medium red, with mature spicy fruit aromas, medium-bodied, with sweet plum flavors, round tannins and a long, fruity finish. Well balanced. Rel: $13 Cur: $27 (VP-11/89) **80**
Vintage Port 1978: There were not many excellent 1978s, but this is one of them. Deep ruby, with a very rich raspberry and black cherry nose, full-bodied, with an excellent concentration of berry flavors and medium tannins. Lovely ripe fruit on the finish. Rel: $11 Cur: $33 (VP-11/89) **89**
Vintage Port 1977: Not a blockbuster for a truly great vintage, but enjoyable all the same. Medium ruby, with rich raspberry aromas, full-bodied, with plenty of grape and plum flavors, medium tannins and a ripe, long finish. Rel: $11 Cur: $45 (VP-11/89) **86**
Vintage Port 1975 $47 (VP-11/89) **81**
Vintage Port 1970 $50 (VP-4/89) **86**
Vintage Port 1966 $81 (VP-11/89) **85**
Vintage Port 1963 $105 (10/31/88) **90**
Vintage Port 1960 $83 (10/31/88) **86**
Vintage Port 1955 $120 (VP-11/89) **85**
Vintage Port 1950 $85 (VP-11/89) **79**
Vintage Port 1945 $250 (VP-11/89) **81**
Vintage Port 1935 $200 (VP-2/90) **93**
Vintage Port Quinta do Seixo 1983: This is one of the best Ferreira vintage Ports ever. It was made entirely from a single property, Quinta do Seixo. It is much drier than most Ferreira vintages, with more punch and stuffing than the 1982. Deep ruby-purple, showing a perfumed, ripe raspberry nose, full-bodied, with lovely raspberry flavors, full tannins and a medium finish. Drink in 1996 to '98. Rel: $14 Cur: $26 (VP-11/89) **91**

FEUERHEERD
Vintage Port 1985: There is some fruit here but it still seems extremely light. Barely passable as a vintage. Medium ruby, with a light grape skin nose, medium-bodied, with round, light tannins, clean fruit flavors and a very simple finish. Drink now. ($NA) (VP-1/90) **72**
Vintage Port 1980: Sweet, simple and aromatic. Medium ruby, almost red, with a fresh black cherry nose, medium-bodied, with pleasant licorice and fruit flavors, quite sweet and round, medium finish. Drink now. ($NA) (VP-1/90) **76**
Vintage Port 1977: This is too mature for such a well-regarded vintage. Medium red with a garnet edge, light black cherry aromas, light-bodied, with round cherry flavors and a simple finish. Best to avoid. $17 (VP-1/90) **69**
Vintage Port 1970 $45 (VP-1/90) **80**

FONSECA
Vintage Port 1985: A hard, take-no-prisoners Port; extremely closed for the moment. Deep inky color, with concentrated blackberry and raisin aromas, full-bodied, with massive raisin flavors, a superb backbone and a very long finish. Drink in 1998 to 2000. Rel: $32 Cur: $39 (VP-6/90) **95**
Vintage Port 1983: This is a rough, tough wine for laying away. Deep, dark purple-ruby, with an intense, ripe raisin and mint nose, full-bodied, with raisin flavors, full tannins and a long finish. Drink in 1996 to '98. Rel: $24 Cur: $38 (VP-6/90) **90**
Vintage Port 1980: I have tasted this numerous times and it just isn't up to par for Fonseca. Medium red with a garnet edge, light plum and brown sugar nose, medium-bodied, with soft, silky chocolate flavors and not much backbone. Drink now. Rel: $22 Cur: $40 (VP-6/90) **74**
Vintage Port 1977: Until recently this wine was understated and closed. Now it has opened into a mammoth wine with so much fruit that it crushes your palate. Deep ruby, with ripe raspberry and cherry aromas, full-bodied, with layers of concentrated, sweet raspberry flavors, tons of tannin and an incredibly long finish. Perhaps as great as the 1948. Drink in 1998 to 2000. Rel: $16 Cur: $62 (VP-4/90) **100**
Vintage Port 1975 $47 (10/31/88) **81**
Vintage Port 1970 $68 (VP-12/89) **96**
Vintage Port 1966 $80 (VP-2/90) **97**
Vintage Port 1963 $164 (VP-12/89) **98**
Vintage Port 1960 $88 (10/31/88) **81**
Vintage Port 1955 $210 (VP-8/88) **96**
Vintage Port 1948 $310 (VP-11/89) **100**
Vintage Port 1945 $580 (VP-11/89) **91**
Vintage Port 1934 $350 (VP-2/90) **91**
Vintage Port 1927 $500 (VP-12/89) **100**
Vintage Port Guimaraens 1987: Extremely racy and classy, well made, with an impressive fruit character and plenty of tannin. Deep purple, with a very ripe, grapey nose, full-bodied, with well-integrated tannins and excellent berry and violet flavors. Long finish. Drink after 2000. ($NA) (VP-2/90) **90**
Vintage Port Guimaraens 1986: Tight, hard and closed at this stage, but it has very good potential. Inky black-purple, with aromas of perfume and grapes, full-bodied, with tons of tannins and medium berry flavors. Drink in 1996 to '98. ($NA) (VP-2/90) **86**
Vintage Port Guimaraens 1984: Lean and tough, a little like a mini-1966. Deep ruby-purple, with licorice and berry aromas, full-bodied, with tough tannins and more than enough black pepper, anise and fruit flavors. Drink in 1994 to '96. ($NA) (VP-2/90) **85**
Vintage Port Guimaraens 1982: A very good 1982 with plenty of chewy fruit and a firm backbone holding everything together. Medium ruby with a purple hue, very a ripe cherry and grape nose, full-bodied, with medium tannins and a long, sweet finish. Drink now to 1994. ($NA) (VP-2/90) **82**
Vintage Port Guimaraens 1978: Very fruity but simple on the palate. Medium ruby with a slight purple hue, fresh mint and cherry nose, medium-bodied, with sweet cassis and cherry flavors, medium tannins and a decent finish. Drink now or in 1993. Rel: $32 Cur: $35 (VP-2/90) **80**
Vintage Port Guimaraens 1976 Rel: $32 Cur: $38 (VP-2/90) **89**
Vintage Port Guimaraens 1974 $42 (VP-1/90) **84**
Vintage Port Guimaraens 1972 $37 (VP-2/90) **75**
Vintage Port Guimaraens 1968 $44 (VP-2/90) **84**
Vintage Port Guimaraens 1967 $55 (VP-2/90) **90**
Vintage Port Guimaraens 1965 $54 (VP-2/90) **89**
Vintage Port Guimaraens 1964 $85 (VP-2/90) **90**
Vintage Port Guimaraens 1962 $70 (VP-2/90) **88**
Vintage Port Guimaraens 1961 $70 (VP-2/90) **85**
Vintage Port Guimaraens 1958 $90 (VP-2/90) **88**
Vintage Port Quinta do Panascal 1987: A typical velvety example of the vintage. Medium purple, with cassis and tomato aromas, medium-bodied, with cassis flavors, medium tannins and a long finish. Well balanced. Drink in 1996 to '98. ($NA) (VP-2/90) **82**
Vintage Port Quinta do Panascal 1986: Very sweet, well-focused fruit flavors and a decent backbone. Medium purple, with earthy, wet leaf aromas, medium-bodied, with medium tannins and a slightly flabby finish. Drink in 1994 or '95. ($NA) (VP-2/90) **79**
Vintage Port Quinta do Panascal 1985: This was an improvement over the weak 1984. Deep ruby, with aromas of grapes and tar, full-bodied, with very hard, slightly harsh tannins and a lean, hard finish. Lacks balance. Drink in 1995 to '98. ($NA) (VP-2/90) **78**
Vintage Port Quinta do Panascal 1984: A weak, borderline wine. Medium red, with a floral plum nose, medium-bodied, with sweet, mature, slightly diluted flavors and a medium roasted finish. Drink now. ($NA) (VP-2/90) **70**
Vintage Port Quinta do Panascal 1983: A little coarse, but it shows very ripe fruit flavors and powerful tannins. Needs time. Medium ruby with a slightly red hue, roasted coffee and berry aromas, full-bodied, with a very tannic backbone, roasted vanilla and berry flavors and an aggressive finish. Drink in 1993 to '95. ($NA) (VP-2/90) **79**

GOULD CAMPBELL
Vintage Port 1985: A good, standard 1985, quite lean and angular. Deep purple, with very grapey raspberry aromas, full-bodied, with medium tannins, sweet fruit and a slightly short finish. Drink in 1995 to '97. Rel: $23 Cur: $32 (VP-6/90) **85**
Vintage Port 1983: This is right up with the major-league 1983s. It is extremely full and concentrated, with a massive fruit structure. Inky color, very concentrated black currant nose, full-bodied, with tons of tannin, velvety fruit flavors and a closed finish. Truly excellent. Drink in 1996 to '98. Rel: $22 Cur: $38 (VP-6/90) **90**
Vintage Port 1980: Balanced, with lots of potential for aging. Deep ruby, with a cassis and tomato

nose, full-bodied, with full tannins and rich, velvety, sweet cassis flavors on the finish. Drink now to 1994. Rel: $15 Cur: $42 (VP-2/90) **86**

Vintage Port 1977: This monumental wine proves how underrated this house is. Dark inky color, with very ripe grapey, floral aromas, full-bodied, with plenty of tannins, tons of fruit and a very long finish. Drink in 1994 to '98. Rel: $11 Cur: $54 (VP-2/90) **93**

Vintage Port 1975 Rel: $44 Cur: $51 (VP-2/90) **76**

Vintage Port 1970 $65 (VP-2/90) **88**

Vintage Port 1966 $75 (VP-2/90) **84**

GRAHAM

Vintage Port 1985: What more could one want in a young vintage Port? It has great elegance and great power. Brilliant deep ruby-purple, with boysenberry and licorice aromas, full-bodied, very fleshy, with a firm backbone of tannins. Drink in 1998 to 2000. Rel: $31 Cur: $48 (VP-6/90) **96**

Vintage Port 1985 Rel: $31 Cur: $48 (9/30/87) CS **91**

Vintage Port 1983: A superb achievement from a very underrated year. Deep, dark ruby-purple, with rich floral and violet aromas, full-bodied, with masses of strawberry flavors, full tannins and a long finish. Drink in 1996 to '98. Rel: $30 Cur: $43 (VP-6/90) **93**

Vintage Port 1980: This is very impressive, with loads of fruit and tannins. Deep ruby, with a floral, cherry and plum nose, full-bodied, with medium tannins and sweet plum flavors on the finish. Drink now or in 1993. Rel: $18 Cur: $42 (VP-6/90) **90**

Vintage Port 1980 Rel: $18 Cur: $42 (4/16/85) CS **88**

Vintage Port 1977: This wine is going through a dumb period at the moment. It is closed and not giving much on the palate. It is still a big, hard and tightly knit wine. Deep purple-ruby, with intense floral, cassis and prune aromas, full-bodied, with plenty of fruit and extremely hard tannins. Built for aging. Drink in 1996 to '98. Rel: $15 Cur: $66 (VP-4/90) **90**

Vintage Port 1977 Rel: $15 Cur: $66 (3/16/84) CS **91**

Vintage Port 1975 $51 (VP-2/89) **78**

Vintage Port 1970 $76 (VP-12/89) **94**

Vintage Port 1966 $75 (VP-12/89) **93**

Vintage Port 1963 $145 (VP-12/89) **97**

Vintage Port 1960 $92 (10/31/88) **88**

Vintage Port 1955 $210 (VP-11/89) **94**

Vintage Port 1954 $155 (VP-2/90) **91**

Vintage Port 1948 $300 (VP-11/89) **95**

Vintage Port 1945 $480 (VP-11/89) **95**

Vintage Port 1942 $420 (VP-4/90) **89**

Vintage Port 1935 $350 (VP-4/90) **94**

Vintage Port 1927 $510 (VP-2/90) **94**

Vintage Port Malvedos 1988: Ripe, opulent and delicious. Beautifully peppery and fruity in flavor, with a silky smooth texture that belies its high alcohol and young age. A very long finish echoes black pepper and chocolate. Tempting to drink now for its fruitiness, but probably best after 2000. Rel: $26 Cur: $29 (1/31/91) **93**

Vintage Port Malvedos 1987: Amazing richness and depth of sweet, chewy fruit flavors. Dark inky color, with intense blackberry and cherry aromas, full-bodied, with sweet grape and cherry flavors and an excellent balance of round, ripe tannins. A great density of ripe fruit. Drink in 2002 to '05. ($NA) (VP-2/90) **91**

Vintage Port Malvedos 1986: Very well structured, showing attractive, balanced, firm tannins and pleasant fruit flavors. Deep ruby, ripe blackberry aromas, full-bodied, with medium tannins and excellent sweet berry flavors. Drink in 1996 to '98. $35 (VP-2/90) **85**

Vintage Port Malvedos 1984: Rather one-dimensional, but it's packed to the brim with fruit. Deep purple, with cassis, tomato and berry aromas, full-bodied, with tough tannins and an abundance of sweet cassis flavors. Drink in 1993 to '95. ($NA) (VP-2/90) **83**

Vintage Port Malvedos 1982: A big, chewy wine, one of the major-league Malvedos vintages. Deep, dark purple, very ripe cassis aromas, full-bodied, with full tannins and very clean, fresh raspberry flavors. Drink in 1994 to '98. ($NA) (VP-2/90) **90**

Vintage Port Malvedos 1979: Too light and too dull. Medium ruby, fresh berry aromas, medium-bodied, with silky, simple fruit flavors and light tannins. Drink now. $34 (VP-2/90) **74**

Vintage Port Malvedos 1978: A difficult wine to assess. It seems closed and not ready but there is also a dryness on the finish. Medium ruby-purple, with a very perfumed berry nose, medium-bodied, with sweet, simple berry flavors, medium tannins and a short finish. Drink now or in 1993. Rel: $30 Cur: $35 (VP-2/90) **82**

Vintage Port Malvedos 1978: Soft and fruity, with a zip of cinnamon on the finish, plus a nice touch of chocolate and raspberry; tasty but not an ager. Drink now. Rel: $30 Cur: $35 (11/30/88) **81**

Vintage Port Malvedos 1976 Rel: $17 Cur: $28 (VP-2/90) **74**

Vintage Port Malvedos 1968 $50 (VP-2/90) **70**

Vintage Port Malvedos 1965 $58 (VP-2/90) **79**

Vintage Port Malvedos 1964 $54 (VP-2/90) **82**

Vintage Port Malvedos 1962 $52 (VP-2/90) **89**

Vintage Port Malvedos 1961 $65 (VP-2/90) **87**

Vintage Port Malvedos 1958 $65 (VP-2/90) **79**

Vintage Port Malvedos 1957 $70 (VP-2/90) **84**

Vintage Port Malvedos 1952 $125 (VP-11/89) **85**

HOOPER

Vintage Port 1985: Not a blockbuster but shows some very pretty fresh fruit character. Medium purple-ruby, with fresh raspberry and chocolate aromas, full-bodied, with plenty of raspberry flavors, silky medium tannins and a fresh finish. Drink in 1994 to '96. Rel: $15 Cur: $19 (VP-6/90) **80**

Vintage Port 1983: Some wines fall apart due to poor handling. This could be one of them. Brick red, with acetic, volatile aromas, medium-bodied, with varnish flavors. Best to avoid. $20 (VP-3/90) **60**

Vintage Port 1982: It is not surprising that this comes from the same lot as the regular 1982 Royal Oporto, another brand produced by Real Companhia Velha. I tasted it blind with a group of 1982s and 1983s and it was hot and out of balance. Medium ruby with a light red rim, aromas of chocolate, cherry and earth, medium-bodied, with very sweet earth and berry flavors and medium tannins. Best to avoid. $18 (VP-5/90) **68**

Vintage Port 1980: Another poor wine. Light brick red, with cherry and cough syrup aromas, medium-bodied, with extremely sweet, cloying fruit flavors and a very sweet finish. Too sugary. Best to avoid. $22 (VP-5/90) **67**

Key to Symbols

The scores reported here are the results of blind tastings conducted by our panel of senior editors. Wines that carry the initials below are results of individual tastings.

THE WINE SPECTATOR 100-POINT SCALE ***95-100***—Classic, a great wine; ***90-94***—Outstanding, superior character and style; ***80-89***—Good to very good, a wine with special qualities; ***70-79***—Average, drinkable wine that may have minor flaws; ***60-69***—Below average, drinkable but not recommended; ***50-59***—Poor, undrinkable, not recommended. "+"—With a score indicates a range; used primarily with barrel tastings to indicate a preliminary score.

SPECIAL DESIGNATIONS SS—Spectator Selection, CS—Cellar Selection, BB—Best Buy, ($NA)—Price not available, (NR)—Not released.

TASTER'S INITIALS (JG)—Jim Gordon, (HS)—Harvey Steiman, (JL)—James Laube, (JS)—James Suckling, (TM)—Thomas Matthews, (TR)—Terry Robards, (PM)—Per-Henrik Mansson, (BT)—Barrel Tasting (these wines were tasted blind from barrel samples), (CA-date)—*California's Great Cabernets* by James Laube, (CH-date)—*California's Great Chardonnays* by James Laube, (VP-date)—*Vintage Port* by James Suckling.

DATE TASTED Dates in parentheses represent the issue in which the rating was published.

HUTCHESON

Vintage Port 1979: Probably should not have been declared. It's too light. Ruby-garnet, with an earthy chocolate nose, light-bodied, with slightly nutty chocolate and fruit flavors. Very simple. Best to avoid. $35 (VP-1/90) **69**

Vintage Port 1970 $50 (VP-1/90) **79**

KOPKE

Vintage Port 1987: This is an elegant wine with good fruit and structure. Deep purple, with a rich, floral, grapey nose, full-bodied, with a good balance of medium tannins and sweet fruit flavors. Drink in 1995 to '97. $24 (VP-1/90) **86**

Vintage Port 1985: A dark horse that should finish among the top 1985s in years to come. Deep purple, with fresh blackberries and raspberries on the nose, full-bodied, with balanced tannins, a firm structure and a lovely finish. Drink in 1996 to '98. Rel: $18 Cur: $20 (VP-1/90) **90**

Vintage Port 1983: A bit one-dimensional but wonderfully rich and fruity. Deep purple, with a dense blackberry nose, full-bodied, with intense grapey flavors, medium tannins and a firm backbone. Drink in 1993 or '94. Rel: $18 Cur: $23 (VP-1/90) **85**

Vintage Port 1982: A very well-made 1982 with lots of finesse. Medium to deep ruby, with a rich strawberry nose, full-bodied, with medium tannins, very good fruit flavors and a medium finish. Slightly one-dimensional. Drink now. Rel: $16 Cur: $26 (VP-1/90) **83**

Vintage Port 1980: Quite hot and unbalanced, it is evolving too quickly. Medium ruby-red, with forward alcohol and vanilla aromas, medium-bodied, with decent peppery, spicy fruit flavors, but a little hot on the finish. Drink now. Rel: $16 Cur: $29 (VP-1/90) **71**

Vintage Port 1979: Very weak and simple. Medium red, with a sweet cherry nose, light-bodied, with very sweet fruit flavors and a short finish. Drinkable but too simple. ($NA) (VP-1/90) **69**

Vintage Port 1978: Past its prime, quite weak. Light to medium red, with spicy berry aromas, light-bodied, light tannins and simple cough syrup flavors. $29 (VP-1/90) **70**

Vintage Port 1977: Too far off the mark for such an excellent vintage. It's simply too mature. Medium red with a garnet edge, slightly nutty cassis aromas, light-bodied, with cassis flavors, light tannins and a very short finish. Best to avoid. ($NA) (VP-1/90) **68**

Vintage Port 1975 $28 (VP-1/90) **82**

Vintage Port 1974 ($NA) (VP-1/90) **74**

Vintage Port 1970 $41 (VP-1/90) **82**

Vintage Port 1966 $65 (VP-1/90) **81**

Vintage Port 1960 $65 (VP-1/90) **87**

MARTINEZ

Vintage Port 1987: Still very closed, but round, ripe and rich, with extremely attractive fruit flavors and plenty of grip on the finish. Deep ruby with a purple center, aromas of flowers, milk chocolate and earth, full-bodied, with round tannins and a long finish. Should be drinkable sooner than the 1985. Drink in 1996 or '97. ($NA) (VP-5/90) **84**

Vintage Port 1985: A burly wine with muscles. Deep, dark ruby, with concentrated cherry aromas, full-bodied and tightly structured, with ripe tannins and rich cherry and earth flavors. Drink in 1996 or '97. Rel: $21 Cur: $27 (VP-6/90) **89**

Vintage Port 1982: Nicely balanced and sweet, holding together well. Medium to deep ruby, with a plum, earth and spice nose, full-bodied, with round, ripe tannins, licorice and fruit flavors and a long finish. Drink now to 1994. Rel: $17 Cur: $28 (VP-6/90) **82**

Vintage Port 1975 $40 (VP-2/90) **75**

Vintage Port 1970 $30 (VP-2/90) **89**

Vintage Port 1967 $56 (VP-2/90) **93**

Vintage Port 1963 $108 (VP-2/90) **82**

Vintage Port 1955 $110 (VP-11/89) **86**

MESSIAS

Vintage Port 1985: An odd, slightly volatile, varnish nose detracts. Medium ruby with a light edge, violet and varnish aromas, medium-bodied, with simple fruit flavors and a short finish. Best to avoid. Rel: $12 Cur: $16 (VP-2/90) **67**

Vintage Port 1984: Much better than the 1985. Medium ruby with a purple hue, roasted nut and fresh black currant aromas, medium-bodied, with clean, fresh, sweet fruit flavors, medium tannins and a long finish. Quite chewy. Drink in 1994 or '95. Rel: $11 Cur: $15 (VP-2/90) **78**

Vintage Port 1982: This is light and quick-maturing, definitely not a wine for the cellar. Medium to light ruby, with a very ripe raisin and earth nose, medium-bodied, with sweet, velvety fruit flavors and an extremely simple finish. Drink now. Rel: $7 Cur: $13 (VP-2/90) **72**

Vintage Port 1963 $40 (VP-2/90) **71**

Vintage Port Quinta do Cachão 1983: One-dimensional but clean, without the depth of fruit to be a major-league 1983. Medium ruby with a purple hue, cassis and strawberry aromas with a smoky character, medium-bodied, with medium tannins and a short finish. Needs a little more time. Drink in 1993. Rel: $8 Cur: $11 (VP-2/90) **77**

Vintage Port Quinta do Cachão 1977: The winemaker says that most bottles of this wine are high in volatile acidity. Medium ruby center turning red, stewed tomato and varnish aromas, medium-bodied, with sweet fruit flavors and very high acidity. Best to avoid. Rel: $7 Cur: $22 (VP-2/90) **60**

Vintage Port Quinta do Cachão 1970 $55 (VP-2/90) **87**

Vintage Port Quinta do Cachão 1966 $30 (VP-2/90) **84**

MORGAN

Vintage Port 1985: Lacks class but it's a good, rough, tough vintage to lay away. Deep purple-red, with ripe, almost raisiny aromas, full-bodied, with velvety, sweet plum flavors, full tannins and a long finish. Drink in 1996 to '98. ($NA) (VP-2/90) **85**

Vintage Port 1977: Ready to drink, with plenty of roasted vanilla and fruit flavors. Not a top-notch 1977, but pleasant nonetheless. Deep red, with coffee, roasted nut and vanilla aromas, full-bodied, with velvety fruit flavors, medium tannins and a very sweet finish. Drink now. ($NA) (VP-1/90) **78**

Vintage Port 1970 ($NA) (VP-2/90) **88**

Vintage Port 1966 ($NA) (VP-2/90) **80**

Vintage Port 1963 ($NA) (VP-2/90) **86**

NIEPOORT

Vintage Port 1987: An impressive example of the vintage, with lots of power and backbone. Inky color, with a very intense, grapey, Syrah-like nose, full-bodied, with full, ripe tannins and plenty of sweet fruit flavors. Extremely long on the finish. Drink in 2000. Rel: $27 Cur: $29 (VP-11/89) **91**

Vintage Port 1985: I have tasted some inspiring bottles of the 1985, but there may be some bottle variation. Nonetheless, it is a massive wine at its best. Deep purple, with a very jammy, grapey nose, full-bodied, with lots of velvety, sweet fruit flavors, medium tannins and a long finish. Drink in 1998 to 2000. Rel: $25 Cur: $39 (VP-6/90) **92**

Vintage Port 1983: There is an abundance of fruit, but it finishes a little short. Medium to deep ruby, with very ripe berry and raspberry aromas, medium-bodied, with fresh, sweet fruit flavors, medium tannins and a decent finish. Drink in 1994 to '96. Rel: $14 Cur: $41 (VP-6/90) **84**

Vintage Port 1982: One of the best 1982s produced. Very deep ruby with an inky center, extremely ripe berry and grape aromas, full-bodied, with focused, ripe raspberry flavors, full tannins and a long, long finish. Not too sweet. Drink in 1994 to '96. Rel: $13 Cur: $39 (VP-6/90) **90**

Vintage Port 1980: Lovely, sweet and balanced, a joy to drink. Deep ruby, with a rich raspberry nose, full-bodied, with soft, velvety, sweet fruit flavors, light tannins and a lingering finish. Lovely now but will improve. Drink now or in 1993. Rel: $12 Cur: $41 (VP-6/90) **87**

Vintage Port 1978: Quite good for the vintage but a little forward. Medium to deep ruby, with simple fruit aromas, medium-bodied, with integrated tannins, very sweet raspberry flavors and a simple finish. Drink now. Rel: $11 Cur: $32 (VP-11/89) **81**

Vintage Port 1977: Powerful, yet maintains a round, rich fruit structure than underscores Niepoort's brilliance. Deep ruby, with an intense raspberry nose, full-bodied, with elegant tannins and masses of sweet fruit flavors. Excellent finish. Drink in 1994 to '96. Rel: $11 Cur: $50 (VP-4/90) **89**

Vintage Port 1975 $37 (VP-11/89) **79**
Vintage Port 1970 $55 (VP-1/90) **93**
Vintage Port 1966 $70 (VP-11/89) **89**
Vintage Port 1963 $90 (VP-11/89) **90**
Vintage Port 1955 $175 (VP-8/90) **98**
Vintage Port 1945 $250 (VP-2/90) **97**
Vintage Port 1942 $240 (VP-4/90) **93**
Vintage Port 1927 $300 (VP-4/90) **97**

OFFLEY

Vintage Port 1987: Simple, but has very good fruit structure. Dark purple, with grapey, floral aromas, full-bodied, with round, chewy fruit flavors, medium tannins and a long finish. Drink in 1995 or '96. ($NA) (VP-1/90) **84**

Vintage Port Boa Vista 1987: Very classy and well crafted. Deep inky color, very ripe black currant aromas, full-bodied, with plenty of racy fruit flavors, a tough backbone and a long finish. Drink in 1997 or '98. ($NA) (VP-1/90) **88**

Vintage Port Boa Vista 1985: Polished, with good fruit and backbone. Deep inky color, elegant perfumed nose, full-bodied, with silky, elegant fruit flavors, medium tannins and a long finish. Drink in 1996 to '98. Rel: $22 Cur: $35 (VP-6/90) **89**

Vintage Port Boa Vista 1983: This 1983 is one of the best. Black-purple, with very intense grape must aromas, full-bodied, with grapey and peppery flavors, full tannins, good backbone and a long finish. Has good grip. Drink in 1994 to '98. Rel: $22 Cur: $33 (VP-1/90) **91**

Vintage Port Boa Vista 1982: This wine suffers from the 1982 syndrome—too ripe, almost burnt fruit. Very deep ruby, with plum and raisin aromas, full-bodied, with velvety fruit flavors, medium tannins and a long finish. Drink now to 1998. Rel: $18 Cur: $29 (VP-6/90) **84**

Vintage Port Boa Vista 1980: This vintage continues to impress, and this is a very good 1980 indeed. Deep ruby, with a ripe plum and blackberry nose, full-bodied, with tons of fruit flavors, good balance, medium tannins and a long finish. Drink now to 1994. Rel: $14 Cur: $29 (VP-6/90) **90**

Vintage Port Boa Vista 1977: Medium ruby, with ripe plum and raisin aromas, full-bodied and ripe, with medium tannins and a long finish. Drink in 1993 or '94. Rel: $11 Cur: $40 (VP-1/90) **88**

Vintage Port Boa Vista 1975 $27 (VP-2/89) **75**
Vintage Port Boa Vista 1972 $30 (VP-2/89) **79**
Vintage Port Boa Vista 1970 $56 (VP-2/89) **81**
Vintage Port Boa Vista 1966 $80 (VP-2/89) **90**
Vintage Port Boa Vista 1963 $106 (VP-2/89) **80**
Vintage Port Boa Vista 1960 $60 (VP-2/89) **78**

OSBORNE

Vintage Port 1985: Well made, but much too light for such an excellent vintage. Medium ruby with a red hue, peppery aromas, medium-bodied, with elegant medium tannins and a light finish. Drink in 1993 or '94. Rel: $20 Cur: $26 (VP-2/89) **76**

Vintage Port 1982: Sweet and simple, even a little boring. Medium ruby-red, with earthy, slightly vegetal, coffee-ground aromas, medium-bodied, with sweet fruit flavors, medium tannins and a short finish. Drink now or in 1993. Rel: $13 Cur: $26 (VP-1/90) **72**

Vintage Port 1970 $50 (VP-1/90) **77**
Vintage Port 1960 $60 (VP-1/90) **82**

A. PINTOS DOS SANTOS

Vintage Port 1985: Maturing too quickly in color and flavor. Medium ruby-red, with a spicy cherry nose, medium-bodied, with round, silky fruit flavors, light tannins and a light finish. Best to avoid. ($NA) (VP-1/90) **69**

Vintage Port 1982: Very light and forward. Medium red, with a black cherry nose, light- to medium-bodied, with clean berry flavors and a light finish. Maturing quickly. Drink now. ($NA) (VP-1/90) **70**

Vintage Port 1980: Slightly out of balance and hot, but there are still some decent fruit flavors. Medium ruby going red, with peppery, grapey aromas and flavors, medium-bodied, with medium tannins and a short finish. Too alcoholic. Drink now. ($NA) (VP-1/90) **70**

Vintage Port 1970 ($NA) (VP-1/90) **70**

POCAS JUNIOR

Vintage Port 1985: Hard and quite tough, with lots of grapey, peppery flavors and a firm backbone. It's still rather lean though. Purple with an inky center, a black pepper nose, medium-bodied, with black pepper and fruit flavors, medium tannins and a hard finish. Rel: $17 Cur: $19 (VP-2/90) **85**

Vintage Port 1975 $38 (VP-2/90) **74**
Vintage Port 1970 $52 (VP-2/90) **84**
Vintage Port 1963 $100 (VP-2/90) **82**
Vintage Port 1960 $80 (VP-2/90) **82**

QUARLES HARRIS

Vintage Port 1985: Firm and well made, with a sufficient structure of fruit and tannin for long-term aging. Medium to deep ruby, with a light tomato and boysenberry nose, medium- to full-bodied, with medium tannins, spicy, peppery fruit flavors and a lingering finish. Drink in 1995 to '97. Rel: $21 Cur: $29 (VP-6/90) **85**

Vintage Port 1983: Has more elegance, power and class than the 1985. Deep purple, with enchanting *crème de framboise* aromas, full-bodied, with an abundance of tannins and concentrated fruit flavors, slightly hard but with a very good, long finish. Drink in 1996 to '98. Rel: $18 Cur: $33 (VP-2/90) **89**

Vintage Port 1980: A well-crafted, firm wine. Medium ruby-red, with focused aromas of violets and perfume, medium-bodied, medium tannins and racy, lean fruit flavors. Drink now or in 1993. Rel: $13 Cur: $29 (VP-2/90) **83**

Vintage Port 1977: Incredibly intense fruit flavors make this exciting and attractive. Ruby-red, with a concentrated nose of tomatoes and cassis, full-bodied, with round tannins and tons of velvety fruit flavors. Drink in 1993 to '96. Rel: $11 Cur: $41 (VP-2/90) **89**

Vintage Port 1975 $38 (VP-4/90) **73**
Vintage Port 1970 $52 (VP-2/90) **89**
Vintage Port 1966 $78 (VP-2/90) **74**
Vintage Port 1963 $110 (VP-2/90) **85**

QUINTA DO CRASTO

Vintage Port 1987: A balanced yet very simple wine. Shows improvement from earlier vintages. Deep purple, with a black pepper nose, medium-bodied, with medium tannins and very grapey, black pepper flavors. One-dimensional. Drink in 1993 to '95. ($NA) (VP-1/90) **80**

Vintage Port 1985: Short, simple and drinkable. Too light for a 1985. Medium ruby, with a light, grapey, Gamay-like nose, medium-bodied, with light tannins and a light, spicy finish. Drink now. $24 (VP-1/90) **71**

Vintage Port 1978: Clean, but it doesn't have the structure of a vintage Port. Medium ruby with a garnet edge, a very strange, perfumed, *crème de cassis* nose, medium- to light-bodied, with very sweet and simple fruit flavors. Lacks structure. Drink now. ($NA) (VP-1/90) **70**

Vintage Port 1958 ($NA) (VP-8/90) **79**

QUINTA DA EIRA VELHA

Vintage Port 1987: A good all-around 1987 with excellent fruit and tannins. Dark ruby with a purple center, aromas of grape skins and bitter chocolate, medium- to full-bodied, with grape skin flavors, medium to full tannins and a long finish. Drink in 1996 to '98. ($NA) (VP-5/90) **86**

Vintage Port 1982: Not as good as the 1978, slightly forward, but still delicious. Medium brick red, with a rich plum nose, medium-bodied, with plenty of sweet cherry flavors, medium tannins and finish. Drink now or in 1993. ($NA) (VP-3/90) **81**

Vintage Port 1978: A delicious 1978. Medium red-ruby, with lovely, perfumed cherry aromas, medium-bodied, with sweet, silky fruit flavors, light tannins and a lovely, long finish. Drink now. Rel: $22 Cur: $30 (VP-3/90) **85**

QUINTA DO INFANTADO

Vintage Port 1985: Pleasant on the palate, this 1985 is quite forward at this point. Deep ruby, with a very ripe and roasted nose, medium-bodied with very sweet fruit flavors and a soft mouth-feel. Drink now or in 1993. $33 (VP-7/90) **76**

Vintage Port 1982: Not much here, it's very simple and sweet, almost cloying. Medium red-ruby, with a roasted nut and beet nose, medium-bodied with sweet fruit flavors and a light finish. Drink now. $35 (VP-7/90) **70**

Vintage Port 1978: There are some lovely aromas and nice fruit on the palate but it's really dry on the finish. Medium red with a garnet hue, and simple fresh cherry aromas, medium-bodied, with sweet berry flavors, light tannins, and a short dry finish. Drink now. ($NA) (VP-7/90) **75**

QUINTA DO NOVAL

Vintage Port 1987: This was not declared officially by Noval but about 1,200 cases were made. It is an exquisite wine with elegant, sweet fruit flavors. It reminds me of a top 1967. Excellent deep inky color, intense nose of blackberries and tar, full-bodied, with very sweet, round fruit flavors, well-integrated tannins and a long finish. Drink in 2000 to '02. ($NA) (VP-1/90) **89**

Vintage Port 1985: Very good, but seems a little stalky. It should come together with time. Medium ruby-purple, with a plum nose, full-bodied, with concentrated plum flavors, full tannins and a long finish. Drink in 1996 to '98. Rel: $22 Cur: $36 (VP-6/90) **86**

Vintage Port 1982: Like many 1982s, this is slightly forward and quite sweet. Deep red, with prunes and vanilla on the nose, medium-bodied, with light raisin flavors, medium tannins and a long finish. Drink now to 1994. Rel: $23 Cur: $42 (VP-6/90) **78**

Vintage Port 1978: Why was this wine declared? It is drinkable but not up to the standards of a top Port shipper. Medium red with a garnet edge, a nose of earth and black pepper, light, sweet plum flavors and an almost untraceable finish. Drink now. Rel: $18 Cur: $39 (VP-11/89) **72**

Vintage Port 1977 $50 (10/31/88) **78**
Vintage Port 1975 $50 (VP-11/89) **81**
Vintage Port 1970 $65 (VP-11/89) **89**
Vintage Port 1967 $75 (VP-12/89) **88**
Vintage Port 1966 $87 (VP-12/89) **91**
Vintage Port 1963 $100 (VP-12/89) **84**
Vintage Port 1960 $86 (VP-11/89) **82**
Vintage Port 1958 $85 (VP-11/89) **82**
Vintage Port 1955 $135 (VP-8/90) **88**
Vintage Port 1950 $230 (VP-11/89) **85**
Vintage Port 1947 $210 (VP-11/89) **93**
Vintage Port 1945 $430 (VP-11/89) **92**
Vintage Port 1942 $200 (VP-4/90) **86**
Vintage Port 1941 $70 (VP-9/85) **50**
Vintage Port 1938 $110 (VP-9/85) **71**
Vintage Port 1934 $310 (VP-2/90) **98**
Vintage Port 1931 $900 (VP-11/89) **99**
Vintage Port 1927 $390 (VP-12/89) **93**

Vintage Port Nacional 1987: This Port shows the essence of freshly crushed grapes. It is as dark as black ink, with a very closed nose, very full-bodied and extremely tannic, with masses of fruit flavors. Drink in 2005 to '10. ($NA) (VP-1/90) **94**

Vintage Port Nacional 1985: After a few rather weak years, this puts Nacional back on top. Very deep ruby-black, with ripe raisiny aromas, an abundance of fruit and tannins and an extremely thick and viscous finish. Drink in 2002 to '07. $200 (VP-11/89) **95**

Vintage Port Nacional 1982: This could have been the best Port made in the often disappointing 1982 vintage, but it seems to have been left in wood too long. Medium ruby, with intense aromas of grape skins and vanilla, full-bodied, with concentrated black cherry flavors and very good structure. Drink in 1995 to '98. $165 (VP-11/89) **86**

Vintage Port Nacional 1980: Good, but not what one expects from Nacional. Medium red, with a bouquet of chocolate and roasted coffee, medium-bodied, with roasted flavors, medium tannins and a silky finish. Drink now or in 1993. $250 (VP-2/90) **80**

Vintage Port Nacional 1978: This should not have been bottled as Nacional. Medium ruby, with chocolate, earth and raisin aromas and flavors, medium-bodied, rather lean and tough and lacking in fruit. Drink now. $250 (VP-11/89) **77**

Vintage Port Nacional 1975 $240 (VP-11/89) **86**
Vintage Port Nacional 1970 $310 (VP-11/89) **98**
Vintage Port Nacional 1967 $400 (VP-11/89) **95**
Vintage Port Nacional 1966 $300 (VP-11/89) **98**
Vintage Port Nacional 1964 $350 (VP-11/89) **84**
Vintage Port Nacional 1963 $780 (VP-11/89) **100**
Vintage Port Nacional 1962 $280 (VP-11/89) **86**
Vintage Port Nacional 1960 $500 (VP-11/89) **84**
Vintage Port Nacional 1950 $800 (VP-11/89) **90**
Vintage Port Nacional 1931 $3,200 (VP-11/89) **100**

QUINTA DA ROMANEIRA

Vintage Port 1987: Earthy and well structured, showing aging potential. Medium to deep purple, with earthy grape aromas, full-bodied, with lots of tannins and a good depth of earthy fruit flavors. Drink in 1996 to '97. ($NA) (VP-1/90) **81**

Vintage Port 1985: Very rustic. Medium ruby, with an earthy licorice nose, medium-bodied, with round tannins, good fruit flavors and some grip on the finish. Drink now to 1994. $29 (VP-1/90) **78**

Vintage Port 1935 ($NA) (VP-2/90) **90**

QUINTA DE LA ROSA

Vintage Port 1988: Ripe and raisiny, with layers of currant, plum and anise flavors. Is also a bit hot, with chewy tannins and a hint of cedar on the aftertaste. Rough-edged now, but better around 1996. $18 (4/15/92) **85**

Vintage Port 1972 ($NA) (VP-10/89) **76**
Vintage Port 1966 ($NA) (VP-10/89) **82**
Vintage Port 1963 ($NA) (VP-10/89) **85**
Vintage Port 1960 ($NA) (VP-10/89) **88**
Vintage Port Feuerheerd Quinta de la Rosa 1927 ($NA) (VP-12/89) **87**

QUINTA DE VAL DA FIGUEIRA

Vintage Port 1987: Extremely well crafted, with a firm structure of medium tannins, fresh strawberry flavors and a floral finish. The fruit and tannins are well integrated and focused on the palate. Great potential here for a new Douro shipper. Drink in 1996. ($NA) (VP-2/90) **83**

RAMOS-PINTO

Vintage Port 1985: Very fine, perhaps a little too elegant for longevity. Deep ruby, with incredibly fresh violet aromas, medium-bodied, with plenty of lovely, elegant, clean raspberry flavors, medium tannins and a balanced finish. Drink in 1994 or '95. Rel: $21 Cur: $36 (VP-11/89) **85**

Vintage Port 1983: Has more grip and power than the 1985, but it's still elegant. Deep ruby with a black center, aromas of licorice, blackberries and earth, full-bodied, with ripe blackberry flavors, full tannins and wonderful elegance and balance. Drink in 1996 to '98. Rel: $17 Cur: $33 (VP-11/89) **89**

Vintage Port 1982: A lovely, silky young Port, but a little short on fruit and tannin. Deep to dark ruby, with very ripe blackberry aromas, medium-bodied, with very sweet fruit flavors, medium tannins and a short finish. Too sweet for me. Drink now or in 1993. Rel: $12 Cur: $35 (VP-11/89) **79**

Vintage Port 1980: This is so sweet it seems almost flabby. Deep ruby, with a very ripe raisin and raspberry nose, medium-bodied, with very sweet, sugary fruit flavors, slightly harsh and out of balance. Drink now. Rel: $11 Cur: $25 (VP-11/89) **74**

Vintage Port 1970 $100 (VP-11/89) **81**
Vintage Port 1963 $80 (VP-11/89) **83**

REBELLO-VALENTE

Vintage Port 1985: Elegant and light for the vintage. Medium ruby, with a light raisin and black pepper nose, medium-bodied, with black pepper and fruit flavors and medium tannins. Lacks punch on the finish. Drink in 1994 to '96. Rel: $23 Cur: $39 (VP-6/90) **81**
Vintage Port 1983: A light wine. Medium ruby-red, with a roasted coffee nose, medium-bodied, with very ripe plum flavors, sweet tannins and a slightly hot and aggressive finish. A bit out of balance. Maybe time in the bottle will help. Drink in 1993 or '94. Rel: $23 Cur: $33 (VP-6/90) **78**
Vintage Port 1980: Starts very slowly on the palate but finishes much better. Medium ruby-red, with a perfumed cherry nose, full-bodied, with sweet fruit flavors, medium tannins and a big, long finish. Drink in 1993 to '95. Rel: $16 Cur: $41 (VP-2/90) **80**
Vintage Port 1977: This is the most recent major-league Rebello-Valente. Medium red with a ruby center, an intense blackberry nose, full-bodied, with an excellent concentration of ripe blackberry flavors, full tannins and a long finish. Drink in 1995 to '98. Rel: $12 Cur: $42 (VP-2/90) **89**
Vintage Port 1975 $55 (VP-2/90) **75**
Vintage Port 1972 $55 (VP-1/90) **83**
Vintage Port 1970 $59 (VP-2/90) **92**
Vintage Port 1967 $82 (VP-2/90) **91**
Vintage Port 1966 $70 (VP-2/90) **82**
Vintage Port 1963 $92 (VP-2/90) **85**
Vintage Port 1960 $55 (VP-11/88) **85**
Vintage Port 1945 $200 (VP-5/90) **92**
Vintage Port 1942 $140 (VP-2/85) **75**

ROCHA

Vintage Port 1985: Beautifully focused cherry, nutmeg and exotic spice aromas and flavors carry through to the long, finely balanced finish, offering just the right hint of toast and spirit. A wine with elegance and grip that should age nicely through at least 2000. $32 (4/15/91) **88**
Vintage Port 1977: Although it presents itself as a vintage Port, this is light-colored, spicy and toasty like a wood Port. A delicate wine, offering finely etched, spicy toast and walnut aromas and flavors, but not much fruit or tannin. Drinkable now. $19 (4/30/91) **81**

ROYAL OPORTO

Vintage Port 1987: A hard-edged, brandy-scented style that comes through with enough plum and cherry flavors on the finish to suggest it should age well through 2001 to '05. Rel: $12 Cur: $15 (11/30/91) **81**
Vintage Port 1985: This has some fruit but it's too evolved for a 1985. Medium ruby, with a grapey, raisiny nose, medium-bodied, with sweet, berry flavors and round tannins. Maturing quickly. Drink now. Rel: $12 Cur: $24 (VP-6/90) **71**
Vintage Port 1984: Why bottle a Port like this? It's light and earthy, with little class. Light ruby, with light, earthy vanilla and smoke aromas, light-bodied, with a light finish. Best to avoid. Rel: $11 Cur: $16 (VP-11/89) **65**
Vintage Port 1983: Some bottles of this are vinegar. Good bottles show some decent fruit and balanced tannins. Deep ruby, with fruit aromas, full-bodied, with raspberry flavors, medium tannins and a long finish. A decent glass of Port. Drink now. Rel: $9 Cur: $17 (VP-6/90) **76**
Vintage Port 1982: Hot and out of balance. Strange flavors. Ruby-red, with an earthy, grassy, raisiny nose, medium-bodied, with very sweet berry flavors and medium tannins, extremely harsh and alcoholic on the finish. Best to avoid. Rel: $9 Cur: $17 (VP-6/90) **60**
Vintage Port 1980: Short, earthy and poor in quality. Light ruby with a garnet rim, light coffee and earth aromas, light-bodied and sweet. Best to avoid. Rel: $8 Cur: $19 (VP-6/90) **60**
Vintage Port 1978: This is just too sweet and simple to be a vintage Port. It's more like a ruby. Light ruby, with an earthy chocolate nose, medium-bodied, with sweet berry flavors and a very dull finish. Best to avoid. Rel: $8 Cur: $24 (VP-11/89) **68**
Vintage Port 1977: Has decent fruit and round tannins, but it's rather light and forward for such a heralded vintage. Medium ruby, with a perfumed raspberry nose, medium- to full-bodied, with clean fruit flavors, light tannins and a long finish. Drink now or in 1993. Rel: $8 Cur: $30 (VP-11/89) **74**
Vintage Port 1970 $28 (VP-11/89) **75**
Vintage Port 1967 $30 (VP-11/89) **72**
Vintage Port 1963 $83 (VP-11/89) **73**
Vintage Port 1871 ($NA) (VP-11/89) **98**

ROZES

Vintage Port 1987: Elegant, lovely flavors, but early maturing. Inky center with a ruby edge, a slight tar and cassis nose, full-bodied, with fresh, sweet, ripe raspberry flavors, firm tannins and a long, elegant, slightly nutty finish. Drink in 1995 or '96. ($NA) (VP-6/90) **86**
Vintage Port 1985: A good, rather chewy 1985 with a solid concentration of flavorful fruit and round tannins. Deep ruby with a red hue, pretty, light cherry aromas, full-bodied, with delicious, round, chewy fruit flavors, medium tannins and a sweet finish. Slightly simple but a good bottle of young Port. Drink in 1995 to '97. Rel: $16 Cur: $21 (VP-5/90) **81**
Vintage Port 1982: Very simple and sugary, with earthy cherry aromas and flavors, but much better than another bottle I tasted in early 1990. Medium ruby center with a lighter rim, earthy cherry and grassy aromas, medium-bodied, with very sweet cherry flavors, sugary tannins and a medium finish. A little hot and unbalanced. Drink now to 1994. ($NA) (VP-6/90) **75**

SANDEMAN

Vintage Port 1985: Elegant and balanced, but a little short on concentration. Medium ruby-purple, with a spicy plum nose, medium-bodied, with clean fruit flavors, medium tannins and finish. Rel: $22 Cur: $38 (VP-6/90) **83**
Vintage Port 1982: Very much like the 1985, although a bottle I tasted in New York had more pronounced roasted, cooked qualities. Perhaps it was poorly stored. The wine is usually an elegant and youthful Port with a lovely balance of fruit and tannin. Deep ruby, with fresh violet and grape aromas, full-bodied with a lovely balance of rich, grapey flavors, medium tannins and finish. Rel: $19 Cur: $41 (VP-6/90) **82**
Vintage Port 1980: Each time I taste this I like it better. It is starting to become an elegant wine. Medium ruby, with fresh berry aromas, plenty of sweet, floral orange flavors, medium ripe tannins and a sweet finish. Rel: $19 Cur: $43 (VP-6/90) **85**

Vintage Port 1977: Extremely well balanced and supple. Medium ruby, with clean berry aromas, full-bodied yet supple, very well balanced, with a long finish. Rel: $15 Cur: $64 (VP-6/90) **85**
Vintage Port 1975 $55 (VP-3/90) **78**
Vintage Port 1970 $74 (VP-3/90) **83**
Vintage Port 1967 $58 (VP-3/90) **90**
Vintage Port 1966 $89 (7/15/90) (JS) **90**
Vintage Port 1963 $125 (7/15/90) (JS) **96**
Vintage Port 1960 $66 (7/15/90) (JS) **79**
Vintage Port 1958 $75 (VP-3/90) **82**
Vintage Port 1957 ($NA) (VP-10/88) **85**
Vintage Port 1955 $135 (VP-3/90) **94**
Vintage Port 1950 $155 (VP-3/90) **87**
Vintage Port 1947 $150 (VP-3/90) **90**
Vintage Port 1945 $280 (VP-3/90) **95**
Vintage Port 1942 $200 (VP-3/90) **88**
Vintage Port 1935 $360 (VP-3/90) **92**
Vintage Port 1934 $240 (VP-3/90) **94**
Vintage Port 1927 $360 (VP-3/90) **92**
Vintage Port 1920 $310 (VP-3/90) **78**
Vintage Port 1917 $250 (VP-3/90) **88**
Vintage Port 1911 $280 (VP-6/90) **82**
Vintage Port 1908 $320 (VP-3/90) **75**
Vintage Port 1904 $420 (VP-3/90) **88**
Vintage Port 1896 $480 (VP-3/90) **81**
Vintage Port 1887 $600 (VP-3/90) **74**
Vintage Port 1870 $700 (VP-3/90) **98**

SMITH WOODHOUSE

Vintage Port 1985: I have tasted this blind with all the other big-name 1985s, and it often holds its own. Medium to deep ruby, with lovely violet aromas, full-bodied, with plenty of grip, full tannins and a powerful finish. Drink in 1996 to '98. Rel: $22 Cur: $37 (VP-6/90) **89**
Vintage Port 1983: Very impressive for its brute strength. Very deep, dark ruby, with a concentrated cassis nose, full-bodied, rich, powerful and overflowing with fruit flavors and hard tannins. Drink in 1997 to '99. Rel: $22 Cur: $37 (VP-6/90) **92**
Vintage Port 1980: Tight, hard and closed, but extremely good for a 1980. Medium to deep ruby, with wonderful perfumed berry aromas, full-bodied, very tannic, with lots of grapey flavors. Still closed. Drink now to 1994. Rel: $15 Cur: $36 (VP-6/90) **90**
Vintage Port 1977: Another hard wine for laying away but not as outstanding as the other great 1977s. Medium ruby with a red hue, intense ripe cherry aromas, full-bodied and very tannic but well knit, with a background of concentrated berry flavors. Drink in 1996 to '98. Rel: $11 Cur: $50 (VP-2/90) **89**
Vintage Port 1975 $40 (VP-2/90) **80**
Vintage Port 1970 $51 (VP-2/90) **86**
Vintage Port 1966 $88 (VP-2/90) **83**
Vintage Port 1963 $100 (VP-2/90) **89**

TAYLOR FLADGATE

Vintage Port 1985: Extremely understated and closed, it starts out slowly but finishes quickly. Deep ruby-purple, with berry and cherry aromas and flavors, full-bodied, very tannic and hard. Great future. Drink in 1997 to 2000. Rel: $32 Cur: $45 (VP-6/90) **90**
Vintage Port 1983: Taylor is always closed and tight when young and this is no exception. Deep ruby-purple, with ripe raisin and violet aromas, full-bodied, with sweet raisin and grape flavors, a lovely balance of full tannins and an explosion of fruit on the finish. Drink in 1996 to '98. Rel: $25 Cur: $42 (VP-6/90) **89**
Vintage Port 1980: Once a little rough, the 1980 Taylor has mellowed. Deep ruby, with cherry and berry aromas, full-bodied, with lots of fruit flavors and hard tannins. Very angular. Drink in 1994. Rel: $21 Cur: $37 (VP-6/90) **88**
Vintage Port 1977: There is an explosion of fruit and tannins in the mouth, but at the same time this wine is in total harmony. Deep, dark ruby, with blackberries and violets on the nose, full-bodied, with masses of blackberry flavors, full, hard tannins and a very long finish. Will age for decades. Drink in 1996 to '98. Rel: $17 Cur: $75 (VP-4/90) **98**
Vintage Port 1977 Rel: $17 Cur: $75 (12/16/83) CS **98**
Vintage Port 1975 $46 (VP-12/89) **78**
Vintage Port 1970 $75 (VP-12/89) **98**
Vintage Port 1966 $86 (VP-12/89) **89**
Vintage Port 1963 $152 (VP-12/89) **97**
Vintage Port 1960 $96 (10/31/88) **84**
Vintage Port 1955 $200 (VP-11/89) **88**
Vintage Port 1948 $290 (VP-11/89) **99**
Vintage Port 1945 $590 (VP-11/89) **97**
Vintage Port 1942 $280 (VP-4/90) **78**
Vintage Port 1938 $270 (VP-4/90) **79**
Vintage Port 1935 $400 (VP-2/90) **88**
Vintage Port 1927 $450 (VP-12/89) **95**
Vintage Port Quinta de Vargellas 1987: Rich, thick and concentrated, like pure *crème de cassis*. Deep purple, with a powerful nose of cassis and perfume, full-bodied, with masses of fruit flavors and plenty of tannins. A monumental wine. Drink in 2000 to '05. ($NA) (VP-2/90) **93**
Vintage Port Quinta de Vargellas 1986: Surprisingly tough and big for a 1986. Deep inky color, with an intense nose of anise and blackberries, full-bodied, with an excellent tannic backbone and long, rich violet and berry flavors on the finish. Drink in 1997 to '99. ($NA) (VP-2/90) **88**
Vintage Port Quinta de Vargellas 1984: Extremely fresh, with plenty of fruit and an attractive, classy hardness on the finish. Deep, inky ruby, with black cherry and anise aromas, full-bodied, with hard tannins and an elegant balance of lovely fruit flavors. Drink in 1994 to '96. ($NA) (VP-2/90) **87**
Vintage Port Quinta de Vargellas 1982: Forward, but still has rich and beautiful fruit flavors. Medium to deep ruby, with licorice and ripe fruit aromas, full-bodied, with round tannins and plenty of blackberry and violet flavors. Drink in 1993 or '94. ($NA) (VP-2/90) **81**
Vintage Port Quinta de Vargellas 1978: I have had this wine numerous times, and there seems to be some bottle variation. I have had boring examples, but the last bottle I had was very good. Medium to deep ruby, with an intense floral and grape nose, full-bodied, with hard tannins and a firm backbone. Very good finesse. Drink now to 1995. Rel: $29 Cur: $36 (VP-2/90) **85**
Vintage Port Quinta de Vargellas 1976 Rel: $29 Cur: $42 (VP-2/90) **81**
Vintage Port Quinta de Vargellas 1974 Rel: $27 Cur: $37 (VP-2/90) **78**
Vintage Port Quinta de Vargellas 1972 $48 (VP-2/90) **84**
Vintage Port Quinta de Vargellas 1969 $50 (VP-2/90) **85**
Vintage Port Quinta de Vargellas 1968 $57 (VP-2/90) **82**
Vintage Port Quinta de Vargellas 1967 $52 (VP-2/90) **82**
Vintage Port Quinta de Vargellas 1965 $53 (VP-2/90) **80**
Vintage Port Quinta de Vargellas 1964 $50 (VP-7/90) **75**
Vintage Port Quinta de Vargellas 1961 $45 (VP-2/90) **68**
Vintage Port Quinta de Vargellas 1958 $55 (VP-2/90) **68**

VAN ZELLER

Vintage Port 1985: Not as good as the 1983, but it shows some power and robust fruit. It should be ready sooner than the 1983. Deep purple with a red hue, a spicy raisin and plum nose, medium-bodied, with sweet raisin flavors that seem slightly burnt. Good tannic backbone. Drink in 1996. ($NA) (VP-1/90) **80**
Vintage Port 1983: This is much better than the 1982 Quinta do Noval. Deep ruby, with a nose full

Key to Symbols

The scores reported here are the results of blind tastings conducted by our panel of senior editors. Wines that carry the initials below are results of individual tastings.

THE WINE SPECTATOR 100-POINT SCALE 95-100—Classic, a great wine; ***90-94***—Outstanding, superior character and style; ***80-89***—Good to very good, a wine with special qualities; ***70-79***—Average, drinkable wine that may have minor flaws; ***60-69***—Below average, drinkable but not recommended; ***50-59***—Poor, undrinkable, not recommended. "+"—With a score indicates a range; used primarily with barrel tastings to indicate a preliminary score.

SPECIAL DESIGNATIONS SS—Spectator Selection, CS—Cellar Selection, BB—Best Buy, ($NA)—Price not available, (NR)—Not released.

TASTER'S INITIALS (JG)—Jim Gordon, (HS)—Harvey Steiman, (JL)—James Laube, (JS)—James Suckling, (TM)—Thomas Matthews, (TR)—Terry Robards, (PM)—Per-Henrik Mansson, (BT)—Barrel Tasting (these wines were tasted blind from barrel samples), (CA-date)—*California's Great Cabernets* by James Laube, (CH-date)—*California's Great Chardonnays* by James Laube, (VP-date)—*Vintage Port* by James Suckling.

DATE TASTED Dates in parentheses represent the issue in which the rating was published.

of violets and perfume, medium-bodied, with elegant, silky fruit flavors, medium tannins and a good finish. Drink in 1996 to '98. Rel: $22 Cur: $36 (VP-1/90) **84**
Vintage Port Quinta do Roriz 1985 ($NA) (VP-7/90) **87**
Vintage Port Quinta do Roriz 1983: This is a good all-around young vintage Port. Deep, dense ruby, with a dark chocolate, fruity nose, full-bodied, fleshy fruit, medium tannins, and tons of ripe fruit on the finish. Drink in 1993 to '95. $22 (VP-7/90) **84**
Vintage Port Quinta do Roriz 1970 ($NA) (VP-7/90) **86**
Vintage Port Quinta do Roriz 1960 ($NA) (VP-7/90) **83**

VASCONCELLOS
Vintage Port Butler & Nephew 1975 $30 (VP-7/90) **74**
Vintage Port Butler & Nephew 1970 $45 (VP-7/90) **76**
Vintage Port Gonzalez Byass 1970 $50 (VP-6/90) **81**
Vintage Port Gonzalez Byass 1963 $82 (VP-7/90) **87**

VIEIRA DE SOUSA
Vintage Port 1985: Has pleasant flavors and aromas, but lacks depth and body. Medium ruby, with a light, earthy beet and berry nose, medium-bodied, with light tannins and advanced flavors. Drink now. ($NA) (VP-1/90) **70**
Vintage Port 1980: Beginning to fade, but still drinkable. Medium ruby-red, with a slightly hot, grapey nose, medium-bodied, with cherry flavors and a very simple finish. Quite out of balance. Drink now. ($NA) (VP-1/90) **70**
Vintage Port 1978: More like a decent, traditional late-bottled vintage with some bottle age. Medium to light ruby, with a simple grapey nose, medium-bodied, with clean, fresh fruit flavors and a short finish. Very easy to drink. Drink now. ($NA) (VP-1/90) **74**
Vintage Port 1970 ($NA) (VP-1/90) **71**

WARRE
Vintage Port 1985: There is plenty of grip and backbone here. Deep purple, with concentrated grape and violet aromas, full-bodied, with huge grapey flavors, excellent backbone and a long finish. Drink in 1993 to 2000. Rel: $28 Cur: $40 (VP-6/90) **91**
Vintage Port 1983: Slightly simple and sweet, but still very good. Deep purple, with fresh violet and berry aromas, full-bodied, with very sweet fruit flavors, full tannins and a medium finish. Drink in 1996 to '98. Rel: $28 Cur: $38 (VP-6/90) **88**
Vintage Port 1983 Rel: $28 Cur: $38 (12/31/86) CS **94**
Vintage Port 1980: A solid vintage Port from an unsung vintage. Medium ruby, with clean perfume and black cherry aromas, full-bodied, with silky, sweet concentrated berry flavors and a medium finish. Drink now. Rel: $16 Cur: $40 (VP-6/90) **88**
Vintage Port 1980 Rel: $16 Cur: $40 (10/01/84) CS **92**
Vintage Port 1977: Rich and highly flavored, starting to open into a superb wine. Deep ruby, with a very perfumed cassis nose, full-bodied, with tons of sweet berry flavors, full, round tannins and a ripe fruit finish. A gentle giant of a wine. Drink in 1995 to '97. Rel: $15 Cur: $61 (VP-4/90) **92**
Vintage Port 1975 $44 (10/31/88) **74**
Vintage Port 1970 $59 (VP-12/89) **88**
Vintage Port 1966 $84 (VP-6/89) **91**
Vintage Port 1963 $121 (VP-12/89) **92**
Vintage Port 1960 $71 (VP-8/88) **82**
Vintage Port 1958 $110 (VP-11/89) **81**
Vintage Port 1955 $185 (VP-11/89) **86**
Vintage Port 1947 $162 (VP-11/89) **88**
Vintage Port 1945 $310 (VP-11/89) **87**
Vintage Port 1934 $250 (VP-2/90) **87**
Vintage Port 1927 $350 (VP-12/89) **93**
Vintage Port 1900 $410 (VP-11/89) **79**
Vintage Port Quinta da Cavadinha 1987: This is quite hard for the normally delicate and fruity wines of Cavadinha. Deep purple, with very grapey, floral aromas, full-bodied, with a hard, tannic backbone and a short finish. Very good level of fruit flavors. Needs time. Drink in 1998 to 2000. ($NA) (VP-2/90) **86**
Vintage Port Quinta da Cavadinha 1986: Very fleshy and elegant for a 1986 and as good as the impressive 1987. It may be one of the best 1986s. Excellent deep inky color, with a nose of tar and berries, full-bodied, with ripe, fleshy fruit flavors, full tannins and a gutsy finish. Good grip. Drink in 1997 to '98. ($NA) (VP-2/90) **85**
Vintage Port Quinta da Cavadinha 1984: A little short, perhaps it's simply closed for the moment. Medium purple-red, with aromas of tar, cassis and tomatoes, medium-bodied, with silky, sweet fruit flavors and medium tannins on the finish. Drink now to 1994. ($NA) (VP-2/90) **81**
Vintage Port Quinta da Cavadinha 1982: Extremely tight and well structured, with a hard backbone and rich fruit flavors. Deep ruby, with a cassis and perfume nose, medium- to full-bodied, with medium tannins and a sweet, balanced, fruity finish. Drink now to 1994. ($NA) (VP-2/90) **86**
Vintage Port Quinta da Cavadinha 1979: A lean, sharply focused style of Port, not too sweet, with slightly medicinal flavors of cherry and toast, firm tannins and a bit of a tough finish for this vintage. Needs until 1996 to 2000 to soften. Rel: $25 Cur: $31 (7/31/90) **82**
Vintage Port Quinta da Cavadinha 1978: Long and silky, with plenty of finesse and mellow fruit flavors. Medium ruby, with a nose of currants and perfume, medium-bodied, with tightly knit tannins, medium sweet currant flavors and a balanced finish. Drink now. $28 (VP-2/90) **83**

WIESE & KROHN
Vintage Port 1985: This has attractive roasted coffee aromas and flavors in a more forward style than many of the top 1985s. Deep ruby with a purple edge, a bitter chocolate and coffee nose, full-bodied, with a velvety mouth-feel, medium tannins and a sweet finish. Drink in 1994 or '95. Rel: $21 Cur: $34 (VP-1/90) **81**
Vintage Port 1984: A wonderfully elegant and well-made wine from an unheralded vintage, like a young 1967 Cockburn. Deep ruby, with a lovely grape and violet nose, medium- to full-bodied, with grapey black pepper flavors, medium tannins and a long finish. Very attractive balance. Drink in 1994 or '95. Rel: $13 Cur: $24 (VP-1/90) **86**
Vintage Port 1982: Very elegant and well-balanced. Medium ruby with a red hue, lovely chocolate, coffee and mahogany aromas, full-bodied, with round, velvety fruit flavors, medium tannins and a long finish. Drink now to 1994. Rel: $23 Cur: $33 (VP-1/90) **83**
Vintage Port 1978: A very good 1978 with excellent aromas. Ruby-red, with rich, ripe, grapey, floral aromas, full-bodied, with lots of ripe fruit and black pepper flavors, very sweet, with plenty of backbone. Drink now to 1994. Rel: $11 Cur: $37 (VP-1/90) **84**
Vintage Port 1975 $55 (VP-1/90) **80**
Vintage Port 1970 $62 (VP-1/90) **74**
Vintage Port 1967 $65 (VP-1/90) **75**
Vintage Port 1965 $100 (VP-1/90) **85**
Vintage Port 1963 $140 (VP-1/90) **87**
Vintage Port 1961 $115 (VP-1/90) **85**
Vintage Port 1960 $115 (VP-1/90) **89**
Vintage Port 1958 $170 (VP-1/90) **87**

OTHER PORT

BARROS
Tawny Port 20 Year Old NV $35 (2/28/90) (JS) **96**

BURMESTER
Tawny Port 20 Year Old NV $40 (2/28/90) (JS) **95**

CALEM
Tawny Port 20 Años NV $35 (4/15/90) (JS) **83**

CHURCHILL
Port Finest Vintage Character NV: Flavorful and somewhat exotic, with tropical fruit, cherry and berry aromas and flavors balanced against somewhat spirity, spicy and toasty components. The flavors linger. $19 (4/15/91) **83**

COCKBURN
Tawny Port 20 Year Old NV $35 (2/28/90) (JS) **86**

CROFT
Tawny Port 20 Year Old NV $38 (2/28/90) (JS) **76**

C. DA SILVA
White Port Presidential NV: Looks like a tawny, but it's rougher and fruitier, with a definite orange character to go along with the brandy and pear flavors. 2,000 cases made. $9 (4/15/92) **80**

DOW
Tawny Port 20 Year Old NV $23 (2/28/90) (JS) **82**

FERREIRA
Tawny Port 20 Year Old Duque de Beaganca NV $38 (2/28/90) (JS) **80**

FONSECA
Tawny Port 20 Year Old NV $40 (2/28/90) (JS) **90**

GOULD CAMPBELL
Late Bottled Port 1985: Smooth and generous, with a suppleness and richness of cherry and spice flavors typical of the vintage. Has its share of grip on the finish, with tannins and alcohol kicking in, but no harshness. Drink after 1998 to 2000. Rel: $23 Cur: $32 (4/15/92) **86**

GRAHAM
Tawny Port 20 Year Old NV $36 (2/28/90) (JS) **84**

HOOPER
Tawny Port 20 Year Old NV $35 (2/28/90) (JS) **78**

KOPKE
Tawny Port 20 Year Old NV $30 (2/28/90) (JS) **88**

MARTINEZ
Tawny Port 20 Year Old Directors NV $25 (2/28/90) (JS) **93**

OFFLEY
Tawny Port 20 Year Old Baron Forrester NV $35 (2/28/90) (JS) **89**

POCAS JUNIOR
Tawny Port 20 Year Old NV $35 (2/28/90) (JS) **89**

QUINTA DO NOVAL
Tawny Port 20 Year Old NV $32 (2/28/90) (JS) **82**
Noval Late Bottled Port NV: Solidly built and easy to enjoy, with generous cherry and berry flavors and a smooth texture. A graceful wine that comes up a bit short on the finish. $14 (11/30/91) **83**

RAMOS-PINTO
Tawny Port 20 Year Old Quinta Bom-Retiro NV $39 (2/28/90) (JS) **84**

ROBERTSON
Tawny Port 20 Year Old Imperial NV $33 (2/28/90) (JS) **81**

ROYAL OPORTO
Tawny Port 20 Year Old NV $25 (2/28/90) (JS) **77**

SANDEMAN
Tawny Port 20 Year Old Imperial NV $29 (2/28/90) (JS) **87**

TAYLOR FLADGATE
Late Bottled Port 1985: Smooth and flavorful, with generous plum, spice and blackberry aromas and flavors and hints of chocolate on the finish. Shows enough grip to balance everything nicely. Drinkable now. $16 (4/15/92) **87**
Tawny Port 20 Year Old NV $38 (2/28/90) (JS) **85**
First Estate Port NV: Sweet, ripe and plummy, with a raisin, cedar and tobacco edge to the flavors. A bit coarse on the finish, but won't shortchange you on flavor. Drinkable now. $13.50 (4/15/92) **81**

WARRE
Tawny Port 20 Year Old Nimrod NV $38 (2/28/90) (JS) **84**
Very Finest Tawny Port Rare Nimrod NV: An amber edge and a delicate core of cherry flavor makes this seem more like a cross between a tawny and a ruby Port than just a simple tawny. Despite a touch of bitterness on the finish, it's smooth, elegant and interesting enough to urge a second glass. $24 (4/15/91) **85**
Port 10 Year Old Sir William NV: On the lighter side and not terribly sweet, aiming more for spice and a delicate balance of nutty caramel flavors. A bit hot and spirity on the finish, but a fine way to end a nice meal. $20 (4/30/91) **83**

WIESE & KROHN
Tawny Port 20 Year Old NV $33 (2/28/90) (JS) **88**

OTHER PORTUGAL

CAVES ALIANCA
Bairrada Colheita 1990: A simple, straightforward white wine, with "juicy fruit" flavors and a coarse texture. Drinkable now. $5 (11/15/91) **74**
Bairrada Garrafeira 1984: An earthy, mature style, clearly from the Old World of winemaking, that tastes like it's been aged for years in old cooperage. The spicy, volatile flavors are best tamed with food. Drink now to 1993. $8 (7/15/91) **78**
Bairrada Reserva 1987: Spicy and peppery, with ripe cherry flavor that turns earthy and gamy. Is also quite tannic, but the style is for short-term drinking. $5 (7/15/91) **77**
Beiras Garrafeira 1982: Has plenty of flavor and character, with complex anise, plum, currant and berry flavors that turn moderately rich on the palate. Has ample tannins for cellaring through 1995. $9 (7/15/91) **84**
Dão Vinho Tinto 1984: A dry, oaky, tannic style, but some may find the mature, cedary plum flavors appealing with the right cuisine. Drink now. $8 (7/15/91) **74**

JOSE MARIA DA FONSECA
Dão Terras Altas 1987: Crisp and light, this tart, slightly tannic wine has modest cedar, tobacco and stalky aromas and flavors. Not appealing now. $7 (11/15/91) **69**
Garrafeira CO 1982: Aromatic and mature, with plenty of tobacco, cedar, cherry, modest raisin and other mature red wine aromas and flavors. Has a smooth texture. A good dinner wine for drinking now. $13.50 (12/31/90) **83**
Garrafeira RA 1982: Very ripe and concentrated, brimming with anise- and chocolate-tinged black cherry, raspberry and smoke aromas and flavors and tannins that are firm without being intrusive. Drinkable now, but cellaring until 1993 should polish the tannins. $13.50 (12/31/90) **88**
Pasmados 1984: Sturdy and robust, with spicy tobacco and ripe cherry aromas and flavors and a round, smooth texture. Drinkable now. $7.25 (4/30/91) BB **83**
Periquita 1987: Dense and a bit tannic, but concentrated enough in its focused boysenberry flavors,

shaded by a touch of herb and vanilla, to drink now with hearty food. Has enough stuffing to cellar through 1994. $5.75 (12/31/90) BB **84**

Periquita Vintage Selection Unfiltered 1987: Solid, somewhat tannic and flavorful, with generous, ripe cherry and spice aromas and flavors. Drinkable, but could use until 1994 or '95 to settle the tannins. $7.25 (11/15/91) **80**

Portalegre Morgado do Reguengo 1987: Firm and focused, with nicely articulated berry, red cherry, vanilla and spice aromas and flavors that persist into a balanced, long finish. Drinkable now. $8.75 (11/15/91) **86**

Tinto Velho Requengos de Monsarax Colheita 1986: Smooth and velvety, with plum and leather aromas and flavors and hints of black pepper on the finish. Smoky overtones suggest drinking with grilled meats. A hearty wine for current drinking. $9.75 (12/31/90) **82**

QUINTA DO CARDO

Douro Castelo Rodrigo 1989: Ebulliently fruity and spicy, with lots of black pepper flavor; like a Rhône, but lighter in texture. Terrifically appealling for its berry flavors and great for short-term quaffing. $7 (12/31/90) BB **84**

QUINTA DO COTTO

Douro Grande Escolha 1987: Deep colored and aromatic, with a toasty, slightly earthy, black cherry and black pepper character that carries through the solid finish. Drink now. $18 (12/31/90) **81**

Douro Vinho Tinto 1987: Herbal and hard-edged, but flavorful, with modest berry and leaf aromas and flavors. Not particularly generous. $9 (4/30/91) **74**

Key to Symbols

The scores reported here are the results of blind tastings conducted by our panel of senior editors. Wines that carry the initials below are results of individual tastings.

THE WINE SPECTATOR 100-POINT SCALE ***95-100***—Classic, a great wine; ***90-94***—Outstanding, superior character and style; ***80-89***—Good to very good, a wine with special qualities; ***70-79***—Average, drinkable wine that may have minor flaws; ***60-69***—Below average, drinkable but not recommended; ***50-59***—Poor, undrinkable, not recommended. "+"—With a score indicates a range; used primarily with barrel tastings to indicate a preliminary score.

SPECIAL DESIGNATIONS SS—Spectator Selection, CS—Cellar Selection, BB—Best Buy, ($NA)—Price not available, (NR)—Not released.

TASTER'S INITIALS (JG)—Jim Gordon, (HS)—Harvey Steiman, (JL)—James Laube, (JS)—James Suckling, (TM)—Thomas Matthews, (TR)—Terry Robards, (PM)—Per-Henrik Mansson, (BT)—Barrel Tasting (these wines were tasted blind from barrel samples), (CA-date)—*California's Great Cabernets* by James Laube, (CH-date)—*California's Great Chardonnays* by James Laube, (VP-date)—*Vintage Port* by James Suckling.

DATE TASTED Dates in parentheses represent the issue in which the rating was published.

BODEGAS BRANAVIEJA
Navarra Pleno 1988: Light, lively and fruity, it's reminiscent of Pinot Noir, with ebullient raspberry and red currant aromas and flavors that are very fresh and polished. The fruit flavors stay with you on the finish. Drink now for its exuberance. $6 (12/15/90) BB **85**

LAS CAMPANAS
Navarra 1984: Lots of concentrated raspberry flavor marks this as a distinctive, full-bodied, focused wine that's balanced, velvety in texture and ready to drink. With nice cedar and nutmeg overtones, this wine has a lot to recommend it. $6 (3/31/90) BB **86**

BODEGAS GUELBENZU
Navarra 1989: Crisp and focused, with a rainbow of plum, blackberry and currant flavors and hints of coffee and caramel on the finish. Has verve. Drinkable now. 3,300 cases made. $11 (4/15/92) **87**
Navarra Evo 1989: Ripe, concentrated and generous with its berry and cherry flavors, accented by smoke and vanilla notes on the finish. Feels as if it can use until 1994 or '95 to smooth the rough edges. 2,250 cases made. $20 (4/15/92) **85**

BODEGAS IRACHE
Navarra Castillo Irache Reserva 1978: Dry and light tasting, almost like a rosé, with plenty of cherry and strawberry flavors, crisp acidity and a lingering fruity aftertaste. $12 (3/31/90) **81**

BODEGAS MAGANA
Navarra 1982: Tart and earthy, without much zip on the palate, this is a decent but uninspiring wine that will survive with food. Drink now. $14 (3/31/90) **73**

MENDIANI
Navarra 1990: Lean and earthy, with strong pepper and barnyardy aromas and flavors. A rough, imposing wine, with little finesse. $4 (4/15/92) **72**

BODEGAS MUGA-VILLFRANCA
Navarra Mendiani 1989: Light and lively, with focused currant, berry and spice aromas and flavors that linger nicely on the finish. A bit oaky, but it's pleasant. $4 (6/15/91) BB **82**

OCHOA
Cabernet Sauvignon Navarra 1987: Strongly herbal, with bay leaf and tarragon dominating the aromas, turning a little fruity on the palate. A lean, somewhat austere wine that could be more generous. 1,980 cases made. $14 (9/30/91) **77**
Navarra 1988: Lively, fruity and smooth, with generous plum, strawberry and spice aromas and flavors and hints of vanilla and nutmeg on the finish. An appealing wine for simple occasions. Drinkable now. 4,200 cases made. $8 (9/30/91) BB **83**
Navarra 1987: Crisp and flavorful, with a generous streak of cherry, beet and leather flavors running through to the finish. Drinkable now. 2,200 cases made. $14 (9/30/91) **79**
Navarra 1986: A simple wine, with ample black cherry and tarry aromas, but little depth or structure on the palate. $5.50 (4/15/89) **73**
Navarra Crianza 1986: Tannic and tough, with little appealing flavor to redeem it. Comes off as coarse and bitter at first, turning spicy and austere on the finish. An unusual wine that not many will like. 3,300 cases made. $10 (11/15/91) **73**
Navarra Crianza 1984: A spicy, medium-bodied, mature-tasting wine for enjoyable current drinking. Smells like leather and spices, tastes plummy. $7.50 (4/15/89) **82**
Navarra Reserva 1982: Smoky bacon and earth aromas and flavors dominate this wine, which seems lean and uninspiring despite its age. 2,000 cases made. $14 (9/30/91) **73**
Navarra Reserva 1980: An aged wine that's lively and ready to drink. Tastes focused, fruity and complex, emphasizing plum and tarry aromas and flavors, with touches of spice and leather and a crisp finish. $10.50 (4/15/89) **85**

BODEGAS PRINCIPE DE VIANA
Cabernet Sauvignon Navarra 1989: Ripe and tasty, with focused currant and berry aromas and flavors turning toward spice and tobacco on the finish. Medium weight, sturdy and well balanced, with well-integrated tannins. Drinkable now. $8 (3/31/91) BB **83**

SENORIO DE SARRIA
Navarra 1985: Distinctively peppery and spicy in flavor with good balance, moderate tannins and cherry and spice flavors that linger on the finish. $5 (7/31/89) **77**
Navarra 1984: Has Pinot Noir-like aromas, with mature cherry, spice, cedar and anise flavors. Firmly tannic, but it's drinkable now or in 1993. Hard to beat at this price. $5 (2/28/90) BB **83**
Navarra Gran Reserva 1981: Showing the benefits of age in the complex aromas, but it's still awfully tannic and drying on the palate. Difficult to like. Tasted twice. $11 (3/31/90) **65**

PENEDÈS

RENE BARBIER
Penedès 1982 $3 (1/31/87) **77**
Cabernet Sauvignon Penedès 1981: A mature, moderately tannic, full-bodied Cabernet, with leathery aromas and herbal flavors. $5 (3/31/90) **74**
Penedès Reserva 1978: Mature, with spicy anise and chocolate aromas, but fairly simple on the palate, with fruit that is drying out. A pleasant, good-value wine to drink now. $4.50 (3/31/90) **77**

GRAN CAUS
Cabernet Sauvignon-Cabernet Franc-Merlot Penedès 1986: Lean and straightforward, with some cherry, berry and leather on the nose, slightly herbal and cheesy hints on the palate and a relatively short finish. $12 (4/30/89) **77**
Cabernet Sauvignon-Cabernet Franc-Merlot Penedès 1985 $12 (10/15/88) **77**
Penedès 1984 $12 (9/15/88) **68**
Penedès Can Ràfols del Caus 1987 $11 (10/15/90) **78**

JEAN LEON
Cabernet Sauvignon Penedès 1984: The mature Cabernet aromas are enticing, but the tight tannins and modest flavor intensity make it come off as lean and mean. Drink it with something rich. $12 (3/31/91) **77**
Cabernet Sauvignon Penedès 1983: Big, rich and fruity, with anise- and wood-tinged berry and currant flavors, concentrated and rather high in alcohol. Well made in the big style. Needs cellaring until 1993 to '95 to tame it. $8.50 (3/31/90) **85**
Cabernet Sauvignon Penedès 1978 $6.50 (4/16/84) **66**

MONT-MARCAL
Penedès Tinto 1988: Has attractive rose petal and cherry aromas and ripe, pure cherry and vanilla-scented flavors. A correct, well-made, engagingly fruity wine, with plenty of flavor. Drink now or in 1993. $8 (3/31/91) **83**

BODEGAS JAUME SERRA
Penedès 1985: Smooth and mature, with nice spicy, leathery accents on top of ripe plum flavors. A pleasant wine, though lacking in concentration. $7.50 (4/15/92) BB **80**
Penedès Tempranillo 1988: Light and pleasant, with ripe raspberry flavors and vanilla notes on the finish. Smooth and easy to drink now. $6 (4/15/92) BB **80**

TORRES
Merlot Penedès Viña Las Torres 1990: A bright, fruity wine for drinking now or in 1993. Smells very ripe and fresh, tastes like blackberries and cherries and has the feel of a Beaujolais. $12 (11/15/91) **86**
Merlot Penedès Viña Las Torres 1989: Very fruity and lively, with crisp texture and ebullient berry aromas and flavors, fresh and appealing for current drinking. $13 (10/15/90) **82**
Merlot Penedès Viña Las Torres 1988: Fresh, clean and fruity, with tart berry and spice flavors and a soft texture. It's the kind of wine you can warm up to now. $10 (3/31/90) **83**
Penedès Coronas 1989: Lean but exuberant, a medium-weight wine, with focused cherry and orange peel aromas and flavors. Modest tannins keep it lively. Drink soon. A good value. $8 (4/15/92) **81**
Penedès Coronas 1988: Light, firm and flavorful, with generous currant and toast aromas and flavors that leave a sweet impression on the finish of this dry wine. Drinkable now. $7 (6/15/91) BB **81**
Penedès Coronas 1987: Lean and slightly tart, with firm tannins and modest cherry, berry and toast aromas and flavors. Straightforward and drinkable now. Made from 100 percent Tempranillo. $6.50 (10/15/90) BB **80**
Penedès Coronas 1986 $6.25 (11/30/89) **78**
Penedès Coronas 1985 $5.50 (11/30/88) BB **86**
Penedès Coronas 1983 $4.50 (6/30/87) BB **84**
Penedès Coronas 1982 $4.50 (2/16/86) (JS) **76**
Penedès Gran Coronas 1985 $11 (11/30/88) **89**
Penedès Gran Coronas 1979 $9 (2/16/86) (JS) **75**
Penedès Gran Coronas Más la Plana Reserva 1985: Tasty and drinkable now. Clean, fruity and slightly spicy, it's medium-bodied with moderate tannins. Has the typical Cabernet spectrum of cherry, plum and maturing herbal flavors. $32 (10/15/90) **85**
Penedès Gran Coronas Más la Plana Reserva 1983: Herbal and tannic, with tobacco and spice notes overshadowing the fruit, but bell pepper and herb flavors complement cherry flavors nicely. Rich and deep; an elegant style that's quite pleasing Drink now. Rel: $26 Cur: $30 (3/31/90) **85**
Penedès Gran Coronas Black Label Reserva 1982 Rel: $27 Cur: $33 (6/15/88) **85**
Penedès Gran Coronas Black Label Reserva 1981 Rel: $18 Cur: $21 (10/15/87) **83**
Penedès Gran Coronas Black Label Reserva 1978 $45 (2/16/86) **85**
Penedès Gran Coronas Reserva 1987: Full, flavorful and solid, with plum and cherry grace notes to the basic currant flavor, hinting at herbs and gaminess on the finish. Tastes good now, but could improve through 1993 or '94. $15 (4/15/92) **84**
Penedès Gran Coronas Reserva 1986: A robust wine, with complex aromas and flavors and firm texture, featuring cinnamon and chocolate nuances to the core of plum and cherry flavors. Drink now. $12 (11/30/89) **86**
Penedès Gran Coronas Reserva 1985: Leans toward the herbal, vegetal spectrum of Cabernet. It's a bit green, but it's pleasant and drinkable. Drink now. $12 (3/31/90) **77**
Penedès Gran Sangre de Toro 1984 $9 (9/15/88) **78**
Penedès Gran Sangre de Toro 1979 $9 (2/16/86) (JS) **79**
Penedès Gran Sangre de Toro Reserva 1987: A ripe, lively, blackberry-flavored wine, with peppery overtones that linger on the finish. Full-bodied, moderately tannic and well balanced. Drink now or in 1993. $10 (11/15/91) **83**
Penedès Gran Sangre de Toro Reserva 1986: Slightly herbal plum and cherry flavors show less subtlety than intensity. A hearty wine that needs time for the tannins to settle down. Drink starting 1993. $10 (10/15/90) **83**
Penedès Gran Sangre de Toro Reserva 1985: Has lots of interesting flavors and a snappy structure. A well-sculpted wine, with generous, complex fruit and spice flavors, a very smooth texture and firm but fine tannins. Drink now or through 1994. $9 (11/30/89) **87**
Penedès Gran Sangre de Toro Reserva 1983 $9.50 (6/15/88) SS **91**
Penedès Gran Sangre de Toro Reserva 1981 $5.50 (6/15/87) **80**
Penedès Más Borras 1989: Light in flavor, medium-bodied, fruity and smoky, with a lingering vanilla taste on the finish. Like an extra-dark rosé. $20 (11/15/91) **79**
Penedès Más Borras 1988: Herbal, leafy aromas and flavors obscure the modest plum and orange peel character in this fairly smooth, medium-bodied wine. Not a great Pinot Noir and not very flavorful, but it's drinkable. 100 cases made. $18 (10/15/90) **79**
Penedès Sangre de Toro 1989: Lean and tart, with focused black currant, herb and spice aromas and flavors that remain firm and crisp on the finish. Best to drink after 1993 or '94. $7 (4/15/92) BB **82**
Penedès Sangre de Toro 1988: Intense, ripe and full-bodied, with plenty of character and flavor, including spicy cherry, vanilla and nutmeg flavors. Not too tannic. Drink now or in 1993. $6.50 (3/31/91) BB **82**
Penedès Sangre de Toro 1987: An attractive wine, with soft texture and spicy, plummy flavors. Smooth and easy to drink; it's for current consumption. $5.25 (11/30/89) BB **82**
Penedès Sangre de Toro 1986 $4.75 (12/15/88) BB **80**
Penedès Sangre de Toro 1985 $5.50 (6/15/88) BB **81**
Penedès Sangre de Toro 1983 $4 (6/15/87) **79**
Penedès Sangre de Toro 1982 ($NA) (2/16/86) (JS) **83**
Penedès Viña Magdala 1986: A medium-bodied, mature, flavorful, elegant wine, with black cherry, toast and vanilla notes that linger on the aftertaste. Mature now, so drink by 1993. $13.50 (11/15/91) **82**
Penedès Viña Magdala 1984: Tastes better than it smells with modest varietal character and ripe, mature plum flavors, with a touch of earthiness on the finish. Drink now. $11 (7/31/89) **76**
Penedès Viña Magdala 1983 $9.50 (6/15/88) **74**
Penedès Viña Magdala 1979 ($NA) (2/16/86) (JS) **72**

VALLFORMOSA
Penedès Vall Fort 1986: Soft and generous, with smoky, tarry cherry aromas and flavors, a smooth texture and not much depth. Drinkable now. $7 (5/31/91) **76**
Penedès Vall Fort 1984: Attractive for its ripe plum and anise notes; it's ripe and full-bodied, with soft, supple tannins. Has plenty of character and style for the price. The fruit echoes on the finish. Drink now or in 1993. $7 (3/31/91) BB **84**
Penedès Vall Reserva Tinto Propia 1980: Fully mature, elegant and smoky, with spicy plum and toasty oak flavors that are well balanced, soft and supple. The tannins are already resolved. Drink now. $10 (3/31/91) **84**

RIBERA DEL DUERO

BODEGAS ISMAEL ARROYO
Ribera del Duero Mesoñeros de Castilla 1986 $6 (4/30/88) **60**

BODEGAS BALBAS
Ribera del Duero 1988: Ripe, fresh, fruity and delicious, with spicy accents of oak and vanilla. A supple, lively, plum- and cherry-flavored wine to drink now through 1995. $15 (9/30/91) **88**
Ribera del Duero 1987: A good, basic wine, with a sweet aroma, cherry and berry flavors, light tannins, and a crisp structure. Ready to drink now. $14 (9/30/90) **81**
Ribera del Duero 1986: Very well balanced and showing well-formed cherry and plum aromas and flavors, layered with hints of toast and vanilla. Harmonious and well made. Drink now. $15 (7/31/89) **87**
Ribera del Duero 1985 $13 (9/15/88) **83**
Ribera del Duero Reserva 1985 ($NA) (3/31/90) (TM) **75**

BODEGAS MAURO
Ribera del Duero 1987: A good, straightforward wine. Tastes crisp and well-structured, with cherry, plum, smoke and vanilla flavors and a lingering finish. Appealing, but it lacks distinction. $17 (10/15/90) **82**
Ribera del Duero 1986: Extremely floral aromas and flavors lend some distinction to this otherwise simple, straightforward, hearty wine. Drinkable now, but it can stand to lose some tannins by cellaring until 1993 or '94. $17 (3/31/90) **76**
Ribera del Duero 1985: Smooth and integrated, with layers of cherry, vanilla, spice and earthy gamy notes that add complexity to the flavors. Not too tannic, but it's long on the finish. Drink now. $15 (3/31/90) **88**
Ribera del Duero 1984 $16 (3/31/90) (TM) **78**

Ribera del Duero 1983 $15 (10/15/87) **82**

VINA MAYOR
Ribera del Duero Crianza 1990: This lively wine with gamy, jammy flavors resembles a southern Rhône, with pepper and tar notes. Effusively fruity, easy to drink and well made. $7 (2/15/92) BB **83**
Ribera del Duero Crianza 1989: Intensely fruity, rich and concentrated, with ripe, complex, well-proportioned cherry, plum and currant flavors that gain a nice spicy edge on the finish. Has plenty of oak and tannin to warrant cellaring until 1994, but you can drink it now, too. $7 (3/31/91) BB **85**
Ribera del Duero Crianza 1987: If you like spicy, aromatic oak, this one's for you. Smoky, toasty accents override the mild plum and cherry flavors. Well balanced and smooth. Oak does the talking, but it's a nice message. $9 (2/15/92) **82**

BODEGA HNOS. PEREZ PASCUAS
Ribera del Duero Viña Pedrosa 1989: Ripe and rich, this smooth-textured wine has layers of plum, prune and game aromas and flavors extending into a solid finish. Has enough tannin to want until 1995 to soften. $18 (4/15/92) **86**
Ribera del Duero Viña Pedrosa 1988: Ripe and generous—not a big wine—but filled with jammy blackberry and raspberry aromas and flavors that turn a bit tough and tannic on the finish. Best starting 1993. $16 (5/31/91) **82**
Ribera del Duero Viña Pedrosa 1987: A hearty, dry and tight wine that's firmly tannic, lean in fruit flavor and dry on the finish. Drink now. $15 (9/30/90) **77**
Ribera del Duero Viña Pedrosa 1986 $14 (3/31/90) **88**
Ribera del Duero Viña Pedrosa 1985 $16 (9/15/88) **83**

PENALBA
Ribera del Duero 1983: An exotic wine, with spicy, anise-tinged cherry and berry aromas and a nice touch of brown sugar on the palate. Subtle, with good character and length. Drinkable now. $12 (2/28/90) **86**
Ribera del Duero Crianza 1985: Firm textured and harmonious, almost elegant, with fine plum, brown sugar and coffee aromas and flavors. It's lively and tannic enough to need cellaring until 1993 to polish it. $9 (2/28/90) **87**
Ribera del Duero Gran Reserva 1980 ($NA) (3/31/90) (TM) **73**
Ribera del Duero Reserva 1982 ($NA) (3/31/90) (TM) **70**

PESQUERA
Ribera del Duero 1989: Firm and fleshy, with generous currant, berry and plum flavors shaded by toasty oak and a nice streak of earthy gaminess that gives it a unique and appealing character. Has style and intensity, plus enough tannin to want until 1996 to '99 in the cellar. $20 (4/15/92) CS **91**
Ribera del Duero 1988: Very fruity, flavorful and well structured, with pretty black cherry and plum notes, lots of spice on the side and a lingering finish. Clean, well made and tempting to drink now, but it should improve through 1995. $17 (9/30/91) **89**
Ribera del Duero 1987: The ripe currant and smoky cherry flavors are well balanced and well proportioned, but ultimately simple and a shade woody. Drink now to 1994. $17 (9/30/90) **84**
Ribera del Duero 1986 Rel: $16 Cur: $20 (4/30/89) **91**
Ribera del Duero 1985 Rel: $16 Cur: $21 (4/30/88) **89**
Ribera del Duero 1984 $14 (10/15/87) **86**
Ribera del Duero 1983 $12 (11/15/87) (JL) **94**
Ribera del Duero 1982 $26 (11/15/87) (JL) **89**
Ribera del Duero 1979 $45 (11/15/87) (JL) **90**
Ribera del Duero 1978 $55 (11/15/87) (JL) **89**
Ribera del Duero 1975 $50 (11/15/87) (JL) **88**
Ribera del Duero Janus Reserva Especial 1982: An elegant wine that unfolds with tiers of smoky bacon, currant and anise flavors that are framed by toasty oak. The finish is impressive for its elegance and finesse. Just the right amount of tannin for drinking now or cellaring. Drink now to 1996. Rel: $75 Cur: $95 (3/31/90) **92**
Ribera del Duero Reserva 1986: Tight, concentrated and oozing with fruit flavor, it has very firm tannins and acidity. Blackberry and raspberry flavors linger on the finish, joined by hints of butter and spice. Tempting to drink now, but better to cellar through at least 1993. 250 cases imported. 2,500 cases made. $26 (9/30/90) **92**
Ribera del Duero Reserva 1985 $30 (3/31/90) (TM) **89**

SENORIO DE NAVA
Ribera del Duero 1986: A very drinkable, crisp, medium-bodied dinner wine, with moderate aspirations. Has cherry and spice aromas, good acidity and a dry finish. $8 (11/15/89) **81**

BODEGAS VEGA SICILIA
Ribera del Duero Unico 1979: Sappy aromas and flavors detract from an otherwise nicely built, smooth and buttery wine. Drinkable now, but don't wait. 1,000 cases made. Rel: $75 Cur: $100 (3/31/90) **95**
Ribera del Duero Unico 1976: Vigorous and spicy, with impressive concentration of cinnamon, anise and plum flavors; it's velvety, smooth and elegant. Already aging gracefully, it's drinkable now, but should only get better. Rel: $60 Cur: $90 (4/30/89) **91**
Ribera del Duero Unico 1973 $97 (3/31/90) (TM) **90**
Ribera del Duero Unico 1962: Still lively, with mellow texture and a core of plum flavor surrounded by clove and vanilla scents. Still veiled by a bit more tannin than even more recent vintages, giving it grip on the finish. Drinkable now. Rel: $106 Cur: $145 (3/31/90) **89**
Ribera del Duero Unico Reserva Especial NV: Ripe and mellow, with a slightly chalky texture but it also has appealing wild berry, clove and earth flavors. Drink now for its mellow appeal, but it doesn't show the depth or vivid character of the vintage wines. $156 (3/31/90) **79**
Ribera del Duero Valbuena 3 Años 1986: A distinctive wine, with beautifully defined currant, nutmeg, cherry and cedar aromas and flavors emerging on the firm palate and lingering on the long finish. A dense but not weighty wine that can easily repay cellaring until 1993 to '95. $47 (12/15/90) **90**
Ribera del Duero Valbuena 3 Años 1985: A vivid, vibrant wine, with focused, concentrated wild berry and plum aromas and flavors framed by sweet oak and a touch of anise. There is so much fruit it's tempting to drink it now, but it has the structure to last through at least 1994 or '95. 1,000 cases made. Rel: $40 Cur: $55 (3/31/90) CS **92**
Ribera del Duero Valbuena 3 Años 1984: Ripe and pleasant, turning tart and spicy on the finish. There's enough concentration to inspire confidence in its ageability. $28 (4/30/89) **79**

Key to Symbols

The scores reported here are the results of blind tastings conducted by our panel of senior editors. Wines that carry the initials below are results of individual tastings.

THE WINE SPECTATOR 100-POINT SCALE 95-100—Classic, a great wine; ***90-94***—Outstanding, superior character and style; ***80-89***—Good to very good, a wine with special qualities; ***70-79***—Average, drinkable wine that may have minor flaws; ***60-69***—Below average, drinkable but not recommended; ***50-59***—Poor, undrinkable, not recommended. "+"—With a score indicates a range; used primarily with barrel tastings to indicate a preliminary score.

SPECIAL DESIGNATIONS SS—Spectator Selection, CS—Cellar Selection, BB—Best Buy, ($NA)—Price not available, (NR)—Not released.

TASTER'S INITIALS (JG)—Jim Gordon, (HS)—Harvey Steiman, (JL)—James Laube, (JS)—James Suckling, (TM)—Thomas Matthews, (TR)—Terry Robards, (PM)—Per-Henrik Mansson, (BT)—Barrel Tasting (these wines were tasted blind from barrel samples), (CA-date)—*California's Great Cabernets* by James Laube, (CH-date)—*California's Great Chardonnays* by James Laube, (VP-date)—*Vintage Port* by James Suckling.

DATE TASTED Dates in parentheses represent the issue in which the rating was published.

Ribera del Duero Valbuena 3 Años 1983 $22 (10/15/88) **88**
Ribera del Duero Valbuena 3 Años 1982 $25 (10/15/88) **90**
Ribera del Duero Valbuena 5 Años 1984: Dark and dusky, with coffee-tinged berry and spice aromas, well-defined flavors and firm, well-integrated tannins. Clearly a classy wine that needs cellaring until 1993 to '94 to soften and open. $49 (3/31/90) **90**
Ribera del Duero Valbuena 5 Años 1982: Very full, ripe, tannic and broad in structure, with focused cherry and currant aromas and flavors. Has impressive depth and length of flavor, hinting at cedar and tar on the generous finish. A big wine, probably best after 1993 or '94. $37 (3/31/90) **91**

RIOJA

MARQUES DE ARIENZO
Rioja 1987: Generous and jammy, with appealing coffee and cherry flavors, but the firm tannins need time to open up. Drink after 1993. $7.50 (3/31/92) **84**
Rioja 1986: Light-bodied but tasty, with clean, ripe cherry flavor and a hint of smoke on the finish. Simple but pretty. Drink now to 1994. $7.50 (3/31/92) **81**
Rioja 1985: Lively and delicious but still young. Has loads of fresh, crisp fruit flavors on a firm structure of acid and tannins. Its long finish is a good indication that it will age. Drinkable now, but better if cellared untill 1993. $8 (7/31/89) BB **84**
Rioja 1983 $5 (6/30/88) BB **81**
Rioja Gran Reserva 1982: Has classic vanilla and tea aromas and follows through with a firm yet lush structure and plum and cedar flavors. It's beginning to dry on the finish. Drink now. $23 (3/31/92) **83**
Rioja Gran Reserva 1981: Vibrant, rich plum and tobacco aromas don't quite carry through on the palate, where strong vanilla flavors dominate, but it has firm tannins. Made in the traditional style. Drink now. $18 (3/31/92) **84**
Rioja Gran Reserva 1978 $18 (3/31/90) (TM) **78**
Rioja Gran Reserva 1976: A very traditional wine, with lots of vanilla and coffee characteristics, but also enough spicy cherry flavor and tannin to keep it lively. Drinkable now, but will hold until 1995. $18 (3/31/92) **87**
Rioja Reserva 1985: Offers enticing smoke, walnut and plum aromas, but lets down slightly on the palate, where it's lean and slightly tough. Needs time, should be better after 1994. $12 (3/31/92) **84**
Rioja Reserva 1983: The cherry and vanilla flavors are true to tradition and easy to drink in this smoky, silky wine. Drinks well now, but will hold through 1995. $12 (3/31/92) **85**
Rioja Reserva 1981: Still showing plenty of life and potential. Has closed-in aromas, tart and plummy flavors and firm tannins and acid. Good now, but probably best by 1994. $12 (7/31/89) **83**
Rioja Reserva 1980 $8 (6/30/88) **76**

ARTADI
Rioja Alavesa 1987 $6 (4/30/88) **80**

BODEGAS BERBERANA
Rioja Carta de Oro 1988: The nutty vanilla and meat aromas and flavors are pleasant, but it lacks fruit. An old-style wine that's drinkable now, but already drying somewhat on the finish. Drink now. ($NA) (3/31/92) **78**
Rioja Carta de Oro 1987: Shows classic aromas of sweet vanilla with cherry notes underneath. A rich, classy wine, with soft coffee and vanilla accents. Drinkable now, but it will improve. ($NA) (3/31/92) **87**
Rioja Carta de Oro 1986: Very firm and tannic, with generous cassis and vanilla aromas and herbal, leafy flavors to go along with the scratchy tannins. Needs to be cellared until at least 1993 to '95 to soften the tannins, and it just might have the depth to make it. $8 (3/31/90) **81**
Rioja Carta de Oro 1985 $6 (7/31/89) **78**
Rioja Carta de Plata 1989: A light wine that's already drinkable, with soft tannins, pleasant cherry flavors and a touch of vanilla. Simple and pleasant. Drink on release. $8.50 (3/31/92) **77**
Rioja Carta de Plata 1988: A firmly structured, spicy smelling, plummy tasting wine, with moderate tannins and hints of oak. Well balanced and attractive for drinking now or in 1993. $7.50 (9/30/91) BB **83**
Rioja Carta de Plata 1987: Lean and spicy, with unusual spice and tomato overtones to the solid berry flavors, showing firm tannins and hints of vanilla and smoke on the finish. An intriguing wine. Best to hold until at least 1993. 1,300 cases made. $7.50 (12/15/90) BB **84**
Rioja Carta de Plata 1986 $6 (5/15/89) BB **88**
Rioja Carta de Plata 1985 $6 (10/31/88) BB **89**
Rioja Gran Reserva 1982: Fresh strawberry and sweet vanilla flavors combine with silky tannins in this well-made wine. Drink now. $20 (3/31/92) **83**
Rioja Gran Reserva 1980 $9 (10/31/88) **82**
Rioja Gran Reserva 1975: A rich, enticing wine that's full-bodied and round, with ripe plum and smoke flavors. Balanced, finishing long and lovely. Delicious now, but it will hold. ($NA) (3/31/92) **88**
Rioja Gran Reserva 1973 ($NA) (3/31/92) **89**
Rioja Reserva 1986: Extremely woody, dominated by vanilla flavors, with modest, sweet cherry notes. A soft, simple wine to drink now. ($NA) (3/31/92) **81**
Rioja Reserva 1985: Lean and rather one-dimensional but pleasant, with nutty, bright cherry flavors. Silky and rather simple on the palate. Not as good as when tasted in 1990. Drink starting in 1993. Rel: $10 Cur: $13 (3/31/92) **82**
Rioja Reserva 1983: Gushes with ripe, almost sweet fruit. Elegant and flavorful, medium-bodied, with firm tannins, woody, plummy aromas and a clean finish. Drink now. $12 (4/30/89) BB **87**
Rioja Reserva 1982 $20 (3/31/92) **85**

VINA BERCEO
Rioja Crianza 1988: Curiously earthy, herbal, and almost vegetal, with simple red cherry flavors; this is drinkable but not necessarily what one expects from a young Rioja. $5 (9/30/90) **70**
Rioja Crianza 1987: Very fresh and almost Pinot Noir-like. Fruity, with aromas of strawberries and flowers, simple flavors of cherry and strawberry and a fruity finish. Enjoy now. $5 (4/15/89) BB **86**
Rioja Crianza 1986: Lean and crisp, with lively wild berry and cherry aromas and flavors that are nicely focused. Beginning to show complexity on the lingering finish. Drink now. $7 (9/30/90) BB **87**
Rioja Crianza 1984 $5.75 (10/15/88) **76**
Rioja Reserva 1985: Straightforward, marked by anise and cherry aromas, spicy fruit flavors, moderate tannins and a lean finish. $10 (3/31/90) **76**
Rioja Reserva 1983: An acceptable wine now, but don't save it any longer. Shows its age with very earthy aromas and flavors and a smooth texture. $10 (11/15/89) **69**
Rioja Reserva 1982 $8.50 (10/15/88) **76**
Rioja Reserva 1980 $8.50 (10/15/88) **77**

BODEGAS BERONIA
Rioja Reserva 1982 $12 (3/31/90) (TM) **82**

BODEGAS BILBAINAS
Rioja Viña Pomal 1983: Has characteristic Rioja smells of brown sugar and leather, with some cherry and plum. Well balanced but lean, with some nutmeg, prune and oaky flavors. Drinkable now, but it's structured to hold until at least 1994. Tasted twice. $8 (6/30/90) **79**
Rioja Viña Pomal Gran Reserva 1978: A rich but restrained Rioja worth searching for. Has very focused flavors of anise and cherry, plus great balance and a lingering aftertaste. Drink now or in 1993. $20 (3/31/90) **88**

BODEGAS BRETON
Rioja Lorinon Crianza 1985: Distinctively smoky and complex, with chocolate, coffee, vanilla and berry flavors, an elegant texture, strong tannins and firm acidity. $9 (3/31/90) **85**

BODEGAS MARTINEZ BUJANDA

Rioja Conde de Valdemar 1987: Elegant and enticing. The flavors are deep and rich, with plum, chocolate and sweet tomato notes over firm tannins. It gives Pesquera a run for its money. Drink after 1995. $8.50 (3/31/92) BB **90**

Rioja Conde de Valdemar 1986: Sweet vanilla is the dominant note in this simple but tasty wine. The cherry flavor is ripe and balanced. Drink now to 1994. $7 (3/31/92) **83**

Rioja Conde de Valdemar 1985 $7 (12/15/88) BB **89**

Rioja Conde de Valdemar Gran Reserva 1982 $20 (11/30/91) (TM) **89**

Rioja Conde de Valdemar Gran Reserva 1981: Attractive smoky berry aromas lead to a rich, seductive wine, with plenty of fruit and life. Well knit and lively, with delicious fruit flavors that should continue to open with age. Drink now through 1995. $20 (3/31/92) **89**

Rioja Conde de Valdemar Gran Reserva 1975: Soft and round, with pretty cherry and chestnut flavors that are luscious and delicate. Still fresh and drinking well now. $25 (3/31/92) **87**

Rioja Conde de Valdemar Gran Reserva 1973: Attractive toasted almond and ripe black cherry flavors run right through this solid, rich wine. Still fresh and young. Drink or hold. $25 (3/31/92) **86**

Rioja Conde de Valdemar Gran Reserva 1970 $30 (3/31/92) **89**

Rioja Conde de Valdemar Reserva 1986: Shows a vivid toast and coffee character, with soft, round tannins and juicy cherry and raspberry flavors. Exuberant and tasty. Drink starting in 1993. $10 (3/31/92) **83**

Rioja Conde de Valdemar Reserva 1985: Very appealing, perfumed and pretty, with bright, exuberant blackberry and boysenberry flavors on a bed of violets and vanilla. Has good concentration. Delicious now, but should improve through 1995. $9 (3/31/92) **91**

Rioja Conde de Valdemar Reserva 1983: Vibrant and lush, made in the classic style, with chocolate, meat and black pepper flavors. Big and solid, but well crafted. Should improve through 1996. ($NA) (3/31/92) **88**

Rioja Conde de Valdemar Reserva 1982 $19 (3/31/92) **89**

Rioja Valdemar Vino Tinto 1989: An interesting wine, but not for everybody. Cherry and plum aromas are backed up with ripe, focused, sweet fruit flavors that linger. Drink now or in 1993. $7 (6/30/90) BB **83**

MARQUES DE CACERES

Rioja 1987: Layers of flavors—chocolate, cherry, plum and smoke—are supported by firm tannins. Rich and well balanced, but needs time in the cellar to open up. Drink after 1993. ($NA) (3/31/92) **88**

Rioja 1986: Earthy and buttery, with astringent tannins on the finish. Sweet American oak dominates the strawberry flavors. $9 (3/31/92) **82**

Rioja 1985: Fresh and pretty, with clean cherry flavors and pleasing tarry notes. Simple but pleasing. Drink now to 1996. $9.50 (3/31/90) **80**

Rioja 1982 $7.50 (11/15/87) (JL) **87**

Rioja 1981 $5.50 (11/01/85) BB **88**

Rioja Gran Reserva 1982: Full-bodied but not overpowering, with attractive, gamy black pepper aromas and loads of ripe cherry flavors. Lush and clean. Drink now or hold. $25 (3/31/92) **89**

Rioja Gran Reserva 1975: Very ripe and quite rich, bearing a resemblance to vintage Port. Still concentrated and tannic, with plenty of plum and peppery raisin flavors. Give it until 1994 to unwind. $26 (3/31/92) **89**

Rioja Gran Reserva 1973: Elegant in a delicate way, with mature aromas of leather and tea lifted by strawberry flavors. Drink now. ($NA) (3/31/92) **83**

Rioja Reserva 1985: The fruit is overripe, almost decadent, like strawberries sweetened with vanilla. Velvety, yet full-bodied, it needs time to pull itself together. Drink in 1994 or later. $18.50 (3/31/92) **87**

Rioja Reserva 1982: Traditional in style and fully mature, with leather and tobacco aromas giving way to brown sugar and jammy strawberry flavors. The sweet fruit matches the tannins in a silky texture. Drink now. $25 (3/31/92) **83**

Rioja Reserva 1981: Cherry and coffee aromas are tempting, and it has some concentration, but the wine is dull and chalky on the palate, with a harsh, dry finish. Tasted twice. $20 (3/31/90) **69**

Rioja Reserva 1975 $9.50 (12/01/85) **67**

BODEGAS CAMPO VIEJO

Rioja 1988: Has oaky aromas of vanilla and toast and is slightly sweet on the palate, like strawberry jam. Not a big wine, but it's harmonious and pretty, with silky tannins. Drink now. ($NA) (3/31/92) **83**

Rioja 1987: Elegant and light on the palate, with delicate tea and strawberry flavors. Not a blockbuster, but it has class. Drink now. $6.50 (3/31/92) BB **83**

Rioja 1986: The coffee aromas of oak give way to pleasant cherry and berry flavors on a soft, balanced frame. Drink now. $6.50 (3/31/92) **81**

Rioja 1985 $6.50 (3/15/90) BB **83**

Rioja 1984 $5.25 (1/31/88) BB **82**

Rioja Gran Reserva 1981: A pleasant wine in the traditional style, with cherry and strawberry flavors wrapped in plenty of sweet vanilla notes. Still fresh. Drink now. ($NA) (3/31/92) **83**

Rioja Gran Reserva 1980: Mature, smooth and complex, with an almost Burgundian profile of spice, smoke and plummy berry flavors that linger on the finish. A polished wine that offers depth of flavor and graceful balance. Drinkable now. $15 (9/30/91) **88**

Rioja Gran Reserva 1978: Nicely balanced, with mature leather and toast nuances in the cherry and plum flavors, but it has plenty of life for a 14-year-old wine. It's velvety, smooth and rather light. $13.50 (9/30/90) **83**

Rioja Marqués de Villamagna Gran Reserva 1982: The sweet cherry and plum flavors are fresh and the texture is round and silky, but the finish is slightly dry. Drink now. $20 (3/31/92) **81**

Rioja Marqués de Villamagna Gran Reserva 1978: Light in color, but the mature red-wine aromas and flavors are distinctive, leaning toward raspberry and mineral. Hints at spice on the finish. Drinkable now. $19 (11/15/91) **84**

Rioja Marqués de Villamagna Gran Reserva 1975: Rich plum flavor and firm tannins give this freshness and verve. More youthful than many 1982s and lovely now, but should improve. $20 (3/31/92) **88**

Rioja Marqués de Villamagna Gran Reserva 1973 ($NA) (3/31/92) **74**

Rioja Marqués de Villamagna Gran Reserva 1970 ($NA) (3/31/92) **87**

Rioja Reserva 1985: Silky and accessible, with attractive cherry, chocolate and nut flavors. Well balanced for current drinking. $9 (3/31/92) **83**

Rioja Reserva 1983: Pretty raspberry flavor doesn't overcome the basic simplicity of this straightforward wine. Silky and compact. Drink now. ($NA) (3/31/92) **81**

Rioja Reserva 1982: Still fresh, offering ripe berry, game and smoke aromas and flavors, firm tannins and enough acidity to give it life. The long finish is silky and clean. Drink now. ($NA) (3/31/92) **84**

Rioja Reserva 1981 $7.25 (11/15/88) **78**

Rioja Viña Alcorta 1985: Light color and ripe flavors mark this as a subtle wine with substance. Has lots of ripe cherry notes and hints of toast and nutmeg and an elegant texture. Drinkable now, but it has enough tannin to carry it through the 1990s. $10 (9/30/90) **85**

Rioja Viña Alcorta 1981 $7.25 (10/31/88) **76**

Rioja Viña Alcorta Reserva 1982 ($NA) (11/15/87) (JL) **87**

Rioja Viña Alcorta Tempranillo 1981: This tired wine has lost its fruit, leaving only chalky, tart flavors. $7 (3/31/90) **64**

CODICE

Rioja 1988: A simple, flavorful wine, with modest black cherry and slightly gamy aromas and flavors and menthol notes on the finish. Drinkable now. $6 (6/15/91) **78**

BODEGAS CORRAL

Rioja Don Jacobo 1985: Very fresh tasting, with strawberry and floral aromas, sweet fruit flavors and a crisp, short finish. $8 (3/31/90) **79**

Rioja Don Jacobo 1982 $7 (11/15/87) (JL) **79**

Rioja Don Jacobo Reserva 1981: A fine example of a Rioja that's reasonably priced. Very complex and rich in flavor, with cedar and vanilla aromas, smooth, spicy raspberry and cherry flavors and a crisp, fruity finish. Drink now. $10.50 (3/31/90) **86**

BODEGAS EL COTO

Rioja Coto de Imaz Gran Reserva 1982 ($NA) (11/30/91) (TM) **85**

Rioja Coto de Imaz Reserva 1981: A good wine that's ripe and chocolaty tasting, though the structure is lean. Has earthy, almost decadent aromas, cherry and spice flavors and a lingering aftertaste. $9 (3/31/90) **81**

Rioja Crianza 1987: Tart and rough in texture, with strong, smoky, rubbery aromas and flavors, resolving into modest plum and berry flavors on the finish, which redeems it. $11 (9/30/91) **79**

Rioja Crianza 1985: Tarry aromas and attractive nectarine and plum flavors combine to make this an appealing wine in a lighter style. Smooth and well mannered. Drinkable now. $5 (3/31/90) BB **81**

Rioja Crianza 1984: Very attractive and easy to drink. Reasonably ripe tasting and smooth, with anise aromas, cherry and berry flavors, moderate tannins and good acid balance. Drink now or in 1993. $7 (3/31/90) BB **81**

CUNE

Rioja Clarete 1987: Light and fragrant, with strongly smoky, tealike aromas and flavors around a lean core of strawberry flavor. Drinkable now. $7 (11/15/91) **78**

Rioja Clarete 1986: Silky in texture, but firmly tannic underneath, with gamy, spicy notes around a core of cherry flavor. Give it until 1993 to loosen up. $7 (3/31/92) BB **84**

Rioja Clarete 1985: Lots of personality here. Attractively earthy, with woody, almost barnyardy aromas, lean berry and cherry flavors and firm tannins. Tastes smoky on the finish. Drink now. $6 (4/15/89) BB **85**

Rioja Clarete 1984 $6 (10/15/88) BB **80**

Rioja Clarete 1982 $4.50 (6/01/85) **83**

Rioja Clarete 1978 $5.50 (6/16/85) **78**

Rioja Contino Reserva 1985: Elegant, dense and concentrated, with lots of cherry, spice and tobacco aromas and flavors and echoes of anise and smoke on the long finish. It's tannic enough to need cellaring until 1993 to '95 to soften all the edges, but it has the concentration to go the distance. $14 (12/15/90) **88**

Rioja Contino Reserva 1984: Reminds us of a good Zinfandel or Côtes du Rhône, with its concentrated berry flavors, hints of black pepper, deep color and firm tannins. Not elegant, but it packs a lot of flavor. 700 cases made. $12 (3/31/90) **84**

Rioja Contino Reserva 1983: Mature but muscular, with chocolate, licorice and earth notes built on a firm, tannic structure. Ripe yet balanced, with enough concentration for further aging. Drink now to 1995. $13 (3/31/92) **89**

Rioja Contino Reserva 1982 $12 (3/31/92) **92**

Rioja Contino Reserva 1980 $10.75 (1/31/87) **83**

Rioja Crianza 1989: Vanilla and strawberry aromas lead to simple berry flavors in this round, very soft wine. Silky and easy to drink. Drink on release. (NR) (3/31/92) (BT) **80+**

Rioja Imperial Gran Reserva 1982: Round and well knit, showing pretty smoke and licorice aromas and chocolate and mint notes over black cherry flavors. Drinks well now, but the tannins are firm enough to hold until at least 1994. $22 (3/31/92) **86**

Rioja Imperial Gran Reserva 1981: Drink this now to enjoy the meaty, earthy flavors while there is still some fruit left. A little dry on the finish and it may toughen up with age. $26 (3/31/92) **82**

Rioja Imperial Gran Reserva 1978: A light wine, with brown sugar, coffee and earth flavors. It's simple and easy to drink, but it's not going to get better. Drink up now. $15 (3/31/90) **70**

Rioja Imperial Gran Reserva 1975 $24 (3/31/92) **84**

Rioja Imperial Gran Reserva 1973 ($NA) (3/31/90) (TM) **85**

Rioja Imperial Reserva 1986: Elegant and refined, with smoky, spicy, earthy aromas leading to balanced, ripe fruit flavors on a lean but muscular frame. Tight now, but it should unwind after 1994. ($NA) (3/31/92) **87**

Rioja Reserva 1985: Very well balanced and flavorful, with ripe, concentrated plum and cherry flavors and a firm structure of acidity and tannins. Hints of cedar, spice and vanilla add complexity. Drinkable now, but better through 1995. $8.50 (3/31/90) **85**

Rioja Viña Real 1988: Full-bodied, with good concentration. The meaty chocolate flavors are supported by firm tannins, giving it a round, rich texture. Made solely from Alavesa grapes. Delicious now, but it will bloom in 1994. $10 (3/31/92) **87**

Rioja Viña Real 1987: Earthy, smoky aromas float from this solid, still closed-in wine. The berry flavor is sweet and ripe and the finish is long and clean. Drink after 1994. $10 (3/31/92) **86**

Rioja Viña Real 1986: Smells great, but the earthy, leathery overtones on the palate need to incorporate themselves into the wine. The raspberry and vanilla aromas are especially appealing. Give it until 1993. 1,500 cases made. $8 (3/31/90) **81**

Rioja Viña Real 1985 $7 (3/31/90) (TM) **85**

Rioja Viña Real 1980 $5.50 (6/01/85) **75**

Rioja Viña Real Gran Reserva 1981: Altogether appealing. Complex and rich in flavor, with ripe, chocolaty, plummy flavors accented by anise and smoke. Firmly tannic, but smooth textured, with a lingering finish. Drink now. 1,000 cases made. $17 (3/31/90) **88**

Rioja Viña Real Gran Reserva 1973: Quite sweet, with vanilla, nut and cherry flavors, and it's still round and soft on the finish. Charming. Drink now. ($NA) (3/31/92) **84**

Rioja Viña Real Gran Reserva 1970: Slightly dry and rather hard, but it has a core of fresh cherry flavor garnished with brown sugar notes. Drink or hold. ($NA) (3/31/92) **85**

BODEGAS FAUSTINO MARTINEZ

Rioja Faustino I Gran Reserva 1982: Smoky, earthy aromas lead to gamy flavors, with modest fruit notes. Has richness on the palate, but finishes rather light. Drink now. $25 (3/31/92) **82**

Rioja Faustino I Gran Reserva 1981 $12 (10/31/88) **88**

Rioja Faustino I Gran Reserva 1978: Gamy, weedy notes dominate in this meager, astringent wine that lacks freshness and fruit. Drink now. ($NA) (3/31/92) **76**

Rioja Faustino I Gran Reserva 1973 ($NA) (3/31/92) **82**

Rioja Faustino I Gran Reserva 1970 ($NA) (3/31/92) **89**

Rioja Faustino V 1985 $7.50 (10/15/88) **83**

Rioja Faustino V Reserva 1987: Big in structure for a Rioja, with firm tannins, deep color and ample chocolate and plum flavors. Very sturdy and flavorful, if not elegant. $13 (1/31/92) **81**

Rioja Faustino V Reserva 1986: Dark and smoky, like roasted meat, with vanilla and cherry flavors as side dishes. Drinkable now, but it has enough tannin to keep it going until 1994 or '95. ($NA) (3/31/92) **86**

Rioja Faustino V Reserva 1985: A silky wine marked by roasted chestnut and chocolate flavors. Agreeable, but it doesn't have much concentration. Drink on release. $18 (3/31/92) **82**

Rioja Faustino VII 1988: A tightly packed, well-balanced Rioja, with ample fruit, firm tannins and acidity and a good finish. Strawberry and raspberry flavors give it depth and substance. Drink now to 1995. $8.50 (1/31/92) BB **85**

GRAN CONDAL

Rioja 1987: Beaujolais-like strawberry and blackberry flavors are pleasant, but dry tannins and earthy notes dominate in this short, simple wine. Drink now or in 1993. $6.50 (3/31/90) **80**

Rioja Gran Reserva 1982 $10 (11/15/87) (JL) **79**

Rioja Gran Reserva 1981 $8 (11/30/87) **80**

Rioja Reserva 1980 $7 (11/30/87) BB **82**

BODEGAS LUIS GURPEGUI MUGA

Rioja Viña Berceo Gran Reserva 1982 $25 (11/30/91) (TM) **87**

Rioja Viña Berceo Reserva 1982 ($NA) (11/15/87) (JL) **85**

R. LOPEZ DE HEREDIA VINA TONDONIA
Rioja Bosconia Gran Reserva 1976: The quality is OK, but it's not our style. Very herbal tasting, with coffee and vegetal aromas, ripe but herbal flavors and plenty of tannins despite its age. $14 (3/31/90) **72**
Rioja Bosconia Gran Reserva 1973: Light, pleasant and mature, showing a distinctive spicy, smoky character. Smells smoky and leathery, with raspberry flavors. $14 (3/31/90) **80**
Rioja Bosconia Reserva 1983: A tart, tannic, tightly packed wine that needs time to smooth out and show its raspberry and cherry flavors. Drink 1995 to '97. $5.50 (3/31/90) **78**
Rioja Bosconia Reserva 1982 $5.50 (11/15/87) (JL) **84**
Rioja Bosconia Reserva 1986: Plump and sweet, but somewhat hollow, with light coffee and nut flavors. Pleasant now, but it won't improve. $13 (3/31/92) **79**
Rioja Bosconia Reserva 1983: Tastes like strawberry jam on toast. Quite simple and sweet, but pleasant. Lacks the structure for further aging. Drink now. $13 (3/31/92) **78**
Rioja Cubillo 1987: Has enough sweet cherry and vanilla flavors for an ice cream sundae, but firm tannins give it structure. In the classic style. Drink after 1993. $9.50 (3/31/92) **84**
Rioja Cubillo 1984: Simple and rough. Tastes lean and tannic, although there are hints of cherry and spice in the spare flavors. $5.50 (3/31/90) **70**
Rioja Tondonia Gran Reserva 1981: Soft and round, with attractive, smoky, earthy aromas, but it's slightly duller on the palate, where the aging fruit flavors suggest it has reached its peak. Drink now. ($NA) (3/31/92) **79**
Rioja Tondonia Gran Reserva 1976: Elegant and sweet in a Burgundian style, with vanilla and raspberry flavors that are smooth and silky. Not big, but stylish. Drink now. $37 (3/31/92) **85**
Rioja Tondonia Gran Reserva 1973: Shows the spice and tea aromas of fine Burgundy and it's elegant on the palate, with cedar and plum notes. A fine, graceful wine to drink now. $44 (3/31/92) **87**
Rioja Tondonia Gran Reserva 1970 $44 (3/31/92) **75**
Rioja Tondonia Reserva 1985: Strikes just the right balance of sweet American oak and rich cherry and plum flavors, with lively acidity and enough tannin to carry it forward. Drinkable now, but better after 1993. $13 (3/31/92) **86**
Rioja Tondonia Reserva 1983: Smooth, fruity, medium-bodied and moderately tannic with straightforward flavors. Value priced. $5.50 (3/31/90) **79**
Rioja Tondonia Reserva 1981 $6 (12/31/87) **78**

LORINON
Rioja Crianza 1988: Light in color, but crisp and flavorful on the palate, with pleasant oak-scented red cherry and raspberry flavors extending into a long, seemingly sweet finish. Best in 1993 to '97. $10 (1/31/92) **83**

MONTE VELAZ
Rioja 1981 $4 (10/15/87) **73**

BODEGAS MONTECILLO
Rioja Crianza 1989: Pretty violet, berry and smoky French oak aromas give way to rich cherry flavors and silky tannins. An elegant wine that will improve with bottle age. (NR) (3/31/92) (BT) **85+**
Rioja Crianza 1988: Could be mistaken for a top Bordeaux. Offers lovely violet, raspberry and spicy French oak aromas and excellent structure. Achieves concentration without losing elegance. Cellar until 1995. ($NA) (3/31/92) **89**
Rioja Crianza 1987: Overripe fruit gives this wine a stewed, jammy character. Fat and simple; the strawberry and vanilla flavors are quite sweet. Drink now. Tasted twice. $6 (3/31/92) **79**
Rioja Especial Gran Reserva 1978: Velvety, smooth and mature, with earthy aromas, plummy, cherrylike flavors and mild tannins. Medium-bodied, mature and ready to drink. $30 (3/31/90) **85**
Rioja Gran Reserva 1975 $29 (12/15/88) **85**
Rioja Viña Cumbrero 1987: A light-textured but flavorful wine that offers a real sense of elegance and plenty of flavor in a delicate frame. Has raspberry and spice aromas and flavors. $6 (8/31/91) BB **85**
Rioja Viña Cumbrero 1986: Has powerful barnyardy smells that carry over to the flavors, overriding what little fruit lies underneath. Not our cup of tea. Tasted twice. $5 (3/31/90) **66**
Rioja Viña Cumbrero 1985: $5 (11/15/88) BB **80**
Rioja Viña Cumbrero 1984 $4 (11/30/87) **69**
Rioja Viña Cumbrero 1982 $4 (12/31/86) BB **89**
Rioja Viña Cumbrero 1981 $4 (6/01/86) BB **73**
Rioja Viña Monty 1978 $7 (9/30/86) **81**
Rioja Viña Monty 1976 $6 (5/16/86) **70**
Rioja Viña Monty Gran Reserva 1982: Big but somewhat tough, showing earthy aromas and flavors and hard tannins. The fruit is shy, but it's a well-knit wine, with class and potential. Drink from 1993. $14 (3/31/92) **87**
Rioja Viña Monty Gran Reserva 1981: Has structure and depth, with ripe, clean black cherry flavors and a little brown sugar nuance for sweetness. Firm and well knit. Better after 1993. $13 (3/31/92) **88**
Rioja Viña Monty Gran Reserva 1980 $7 (11/30/87) **79**
Rioja Viña Monty Gran Reserva 1978: Mature coffee and tobacco flavors are wrapped in silky tannins in a wine that slips down easily and finishes clean. Drink now. $28 (3/31/92) **82**
Rioja Viña Monty Gran Reserva 1975 $28 (3/31/92) **86**
Rioja Viña Monty Gran Reserva 1973 ($NA) (3/31/92) **85**
Rioja Viña Monty Gran Reserva 1970 ($NA) (3/31/92) **87**

BODEGAS MUERZA
Rioja Vega 1989: Light and fruity, with hints of cherry, rose petal and strawberry flavors. A simple style for drinking now. $7 (3/31/91) **77**
Rioja Vega Crianza 1986: A simple wine, with spicy cedar and pepper notes and light cherry-scented flavors. Drink now or in 1993. $10 (3/31/91) **75**

BODEGAS MUGA
Rioja 1986: Ripe and peppery, with black cherry and spice aromas and flavors and a soft texture. Shows quite a bit of maturity. Drinkable now. $12 (5/31/91) **81**
Rioja 1985 $12 (3/31/90) (TM) **83**
Rioja 1984: Approaching maturity, it's toasty and plummy on the aroma, lean and slightly astringent on the palate and has attractive plum and vanilla flavors on the aftertaste. Smells great. Drink now. $8.50 (4/30/89) **82**
Rioja 1982 $7 (11/15/87) (JL) **77**

Key to Symbols

The scores reported here are the results of blind tastings conducted by our panel of senior editors. Wines that carry the initials below are results of individual tastings.

THE WINE SPECTATOR 100-POINT SCALE 95-100—Classic, a great wine; ***90-94***—Outstanding, superior character and style; ***80-89***—Good to very good, a wine with special qualities; ***70-79***—Average, drinkable wine that may have minor flaws; ***60-69***—Below average, drinkable but not recommended; ***50-59***—Poor, undrinkable, not recommended. "+"—With a score indicates a range; used primarily with barrel tastings to indicate a preliminary score.

SPECIAL DESIGNATIONS SS—Spectator Selection, CS—Cellar Selection, BB—Best Buy, ($NA)—Price not available, (NR)—Not released.

TASTER'S INITIALS (JG)—Jim Gordon, (HS)—Harvey Steiman, (JL)—James Laube, (JS)—James Suckling, (TM)—Thomas Matthews, (TR)—Terry Robards, (PM)—Per-Henrik Mansson, (BT)—Barrel Tasting (these wines were tasted blind from barrel samples), (CA-date)—*California's Great Cabernets* by James Laube, (CH-date)—*California's Great Chardonnays* by James Laube, (VP-date)—*Vintage Port* by James Suckling.

DATE TASTED Dates in parentheses represent the issue in which the rating was published.

Rioja Gran Reserva 1976 $20 (3/31/90) (TM) **77**
Rioja Prado Enea Gran Reserva 1982 $40 (11/30/91) (TM) **84**
Rioja Prado Enea Gran Reserva 1981 $35 (3/31/90) (TM) **79**
Rioja Prado Enea Gran Reserva 1976 $24 (3/31/90) (TM) **84**
Rioja Prado Enea Reserva 1981: Firm and elegant, with rich, chocolaty aromas and flavors. Mature, with style and depth, but it's not too weighty. Drink now. $20 (4/30/89) **80**
Rioja Prado Enea Reserva 1978: Fully mature, with aromas and flavors that lean toward the caramel, tar and earthy end of the spectrum rather than the fruit end. For those who like the style, it's a modestly successful wine. $18 (3/31/90) **79**

MARQUES DE MURRIETA
Rioja 1985: Built for aging, it's tart, with currant, orange peel and berry flavors and smoky aromas. Medium-bodied, with full but fine tannins. Drink now to 1996. $17 (2/28/90) **87**
Rioja Castillo Ygay Gran Reserva 1968: A harmonious, rich wine, with ripe plum and cherry flavors. Age has smoothed out the tartness, but it's still crisp and lively, with a deep, full body. Tea and chocolate flavors linger on the finish. Rel: $85 Cur: $96 (3/31/90) **92**
Rioja Castillo Ygay Gran Reserva 1952: A finely polished and beautifully mature wine, with mature vanilla, chocolate, plum, cherry and cedar flavors. Still has a fresh and lively texture. Remarkably well preserved. The flavors have only intensified with age. $150 (3/31/90) **94**
Rioja Gran Reserva 1978: A big wine, with verve and strength. Vivid plum and smoke aromas give way to rich fruit flavors and full tannins. Has good concentration and structure. Drink after 1994. $30 (3/31/92) **87**
Rioja Gran Reserva 1975: A gorgeous wine, brimming with plum, cedar and licorice flavors and young, fresh fruit braced by firm, spicy tannins. Perfectly proportioned, with plenty of time ahead. Drink now or hold. $35 (3/31/92) **93**
Rioja Gran Reserva 1973: Flavorful and exquisitely balanced, with layers of ripe cherry, vanilla and spicy, smoky characteristics. Just at its peak, drink it now and enjoy. ($NA) (3/31/92) **89**
Rioja Gran Reserva 1970 ($NA) (3/31/92) **83**
Rioja Reserva 1986: A real beauty. Perfumed, with dark plum, mint, game and black pepper aromas. Balanced and ripe, with refined tannins that ease into a long, fruity finish. Approachable now, but better after 1994. $20 (3/31/92) **88**
Rioja Reserva 1985: Rich, velvety, generous and ripe, with beautiful plum and smoke flavors that are intense and balanced. The structure is firm, but doesn't get in the way. Echoes plums on the long finish. Drink in 1994 to '96. $20 (3/31/92) **90**
Rioja Reserva 1983: Smoky blackberry flavors and bright acidity give this wine life. Has a soft texture, but enough concentration to make a statement. Drink now to 1994. $13 (3/31/92) **85**
Rioja Reserva 1982 $39 (3/31/92) **84**
Rioja Reserva 1981 $39 (3/31/92) **88**
Rioja Reserva 1980 $27 (3/31/90) **83**

NUESTRA SENORA DE LA ANTIGUA
Rioja 1982 ($NA) (11/15/87) (JL) **84**

BODEGAS OLARRA
Rioja 1982 ($NA) (11/15/87) (JL) **86**
Rioja Añares 1987: A youthful, lively style, with vibrant cherry and raspberry aromas and flavors and smooth texture. Light and pleasant. Drink now for its freshness. $6.50 (3/31/90) BB **83**
Rioja Añares 1985: Very attractive for current drinking. A medium-bodied wine with spicy, fruity, woody aromas and plenty of fruit flavor. Moderately tannic and well balanced. $6 (2/28/89) BB **82**
Rioja Añares 1983: Aging fast, which shows in the color and in the earthy, gamy, peppery aromas and flavors. It's drying a bit on the finish, but drinkable. Get to it fast. $6.50 (2/28/90) **76**
Rioja Añares Gran Reserva 1983: Earthy, barnyardy aromas give way to heavy oaky flavors. The fruit is overripe and hard to find. Quite rich and heavy. Drink now. $19 (3/31/92) **75**
Rioja Añares Gran Reserva 1982 $27 (11/30/91) (TM) **75**
Rioja Añares Gran Reserva 1981: On the downward slope, with overly earthy, gamy flavors and drying tannins. Drink up. $25 (3/31/92) **76**
Rioja Añares Reserva 1985: A straightforward wine, with pretty cherry flavors and an earthy edge over firm tannins. Drinkable now, but it may expand after 1993. $25 (3/31/92) **83**
Rioja Añares Reserva 1983: A soft, supple wine with cherry and coffee flavors, but it lacks concentration and finishes short. Drink now. $12 (2/28/90) **73**
Rioja Añares Reserva 1981 $8 (9/30/86) **88**
Rioja Cerro Añon 1984 $4.50 (12/01/85) **70**
Rioja Cerro Añon 1980 $4.50 (4/01/85) **75**
Rioja Cerro Añon Gran Reserva 1983: A silky, light but balanced wine, with pleasant cherry and chestnut flavors. One-dimensional. Drink now. $19 (3/31/92) **83**
Rioja Cerro Añon Gran Reserva 1982 $27 (11/30/91) (TM) **71**
Rioja Cerro Añon Gran Reserva 1981: A nice mix of raspberry and game aromas and flavors gives this depth and interest. Well structured and still young, with fruit and mint on the finish. Drinkable now, but it will improve. $25 (3/31/92) **87**
Rioja Cerro Añon Gran Reserva 1973: When the weediness blows off, there's a core of fine, delicate cherry flavor that's still fresh and pretty. Fragile, but it has character. Drink now. ($NA) (3/31/92) **81**
Rioja Cerro Añon Gran Reserva 1970 ($NA) (3/31/92) **75**
Rioja Cerro Añon Reserva 1985: Light and simple, with little fruit on a light frame. The earthy, barnyardy notes dominate. Tasted twice. Drink now. ($NA) (3/31/92) **73**
Rioja Cerro Añon Reserva 1983: A very earthy tasting, barnyard smelling, soft-textured wine. You're not missing much if you don't try it. Tasted twice. $10.50 (3/31/90) **61**
Rioja Cerro Añon Reserva 1981 $8 (9/30/86) **78**
Rioja Cerro Añon Reserva 1978 $8 (3/01/85) **83**
Rioja Reserva 1978 $7.50 (3/16/85) **82**
Rioja Tinto 1983 $5 (9/30/86) BB **87**
Rioja Tinto 1980 $4.50 (3/16/85) BB **87**

BODEGAS ONDARRE
Rioja Ondarre 1984 $5 (11/15/88) BB **80**
Rioja Reserva 1981 $7 (12/15/88) BB **84**
Rioja Tidon 1986 $4.50 (12/15/88) **78**

BODEGAS PALACIO
Rioja Cosme Palacio y Hermanos 1987 ($NA) (3/31/90) (TM) **83**
Rioja Cosme Palacio y Hermanos 1986: Beautifully spicy, lush and supple. Has all the freshness of youth, with ample plum and raspberry flavors and a cedary overlay of oak. Drink now. $9 (2/28/89) **88**
Rioja Glorioso 1986 $8 (3/31/90) (TM) **80**
Rioja Glorioso 1985: Fresh and youthful, full of cherry and berry flavors, plus a nice complement of oak. Balanced so well it's drinkable now, but it could be cellared until 1993. $7 (2/28/89) BB **85**
Rioja Glorioso Gran Reserva 1982 $19 (11/30/91) (TM) **84**
Rioja Glorioso Gran Reserva 1981 ($NA) (3/31/90) (TM) **75**
Rioja Glorioso Gran Reserva 1978: A fine example of a mature red wine. Nicely developed from cellaring, with complex, spicy aromas, yet the flavors are quite fresh, showing clean, supple fruit and a measure of oak. Drink up now. $15 (2/28/89) **88**
Rioja Glorioso Reserva 1982 $18 (3/31/90) (TM) **79**
Rioja Glorioso Reserva 1981: Ready to drink now. Mature but still lively in flavor, with complex earth, spice and leather aromas, solid, ripe fruit flavors and a soft finish. $10 (2/28/89) **83**

BODEGAS PALACIOS REMONDO
Rioja Herencia Remondo 1987: Lots of American oak gives a sweet vanilla frame to the peppery, meaty, ripe berry flavors. Jammy, round and rather simple, but very tasty. Drink now. $6 (3/31/92) **84**
Rioja Herencia Remondo 1986: Light and simple, with coffee and earth flavors. Has modest cherry

flavor, but it's slightly bitter on the finish. Drink now. $6 (3/31/92) **76**
Rioja Herencia Remondo 1985 ($NA) (3/31/90) (TM) **81**
Rioja Herencia Remondo 1982 ($NA) (11/15/87) (JL) **90**
Rioja Herencia Remondo Gran Reserva 1982: Silky and light-bodied, with tea and soft vanilla aromas and muted raspberry and caramel flavors. Lacks freshness and verve. Tasted twice. Drink now. $13 (3/31/92) **75**
Rioja Herencia Remondo Gran Reserva 1981: Ruined by volatile acidity. Undrinkable. Tasted twice. ($NA) (3/31/92) **59**
Rioja Herencia Remondo Gran Reserva 1975: Coffee and tobacco aromas give way to sweet vanilla, strawberry jam and brown sugar flavors. A soft, silky wine to drink now. ($NA) (3/31/92) **79**
Rioja Herencia Remondo Gran Reserva 1973 ($NA) (3/31/92) **77**
Rioja Herencia Remondo Gran Reserva 1970 ($NA) (3/31/92) **59**
Rioja Herencia Remondo Reserva 1986: Soft and silky, with vanilla and nut notes wrapped around strawberry flavors. A lighter, more delicate style. Drink now. $9.50 (3/31/92) **79**
Rioja Herencia Remondo Reserva 1985: Dried out and rather dull, with only remnants of cherry flavor, astringent tannins and a short finish. Drink up. ($NA) (3/31/92) **71**

FREDERICO PATERNINA
Rioja Banda Azul 1985: A good, hearty wine at a great price. Broad and soft in texture with nicely plummy flavors, a smoky earthy aroma and moderate tannins. Drink now. $5 (3/15/90) BB **80**

PRIVILEGIO DEL RAY SANCHO
Rioja 1978 $3 (4/01/84) **76**

MARQUES DEL PUERTO
Rioja 1984: A quaffing wine with some complexity, but not much depth or concentration. Mature tasting with earthy, leathery, spicy aromas. Medium-bodied, with cranberry and spice flavors. $7 (2/28/90) **78**
Rioja 1982 $6 (11/15/87) (JL) **78**
Rioja Gran Reserva 1978: Nicely mature, with plenty of plummy flavors and spicy aromas, and a smooth, velvety texture. Medium-bodied and well balanced. Still has lots of lively acidity, but it's ready to drink. $20 (3/31/90) **85**

REMELLURI
Rioja 1990: Vegetal aromas mask attractive cherry and chocolate flavors. Rich, round and still very young. Drink after 1994. (NR) (3/31/92) (BT) **80+**
Rioja 1989: Velvety with full, soft tannins. Has modestly concentrated chocolate and green bean flavors, but it's still quite closed. Give it until 1993 to open up. (NR) (3/31/92) **82**
Rioja 1988: Light and simple, with strawberry and slightly weedy flavors and very soft tannins. Drink now. ($NA) (3/31/92) **75**
Rioja 1986 $11 (12/15/90) **87**
Rioja 1985 $10 (3/31/90) (TM) **88**
Rioja 1984 $9 (3/31/90) (TM) **77**
Rioja 1983 $11.50 (3/31/90) **77**
Rioja 1982 $12 (3/31/90) (TM) **82**
Rioja Alavesa Labastida 1982 $8 (9/30/86) **84**
Rioja Gran Reserva 1985: Silky and pretty, with strawberry and raspberry flavors dominating the oaky vanilla notes. Tasty, but it lacks the structure for long-term aging. Drink now. $40 (3/31/92) **84**
Rioja Gran Reserva 1982 ($NA) (11/30/91) (TM) **87**
Rioja Reserva 1987: Resembles a chocolate malted with a maraschino cherry. Woody, light and slightly drying on the finish. Drink now. $14 (3/31/92) **76**
Rioja Reserva 1986: Vanilla aromas and flavors dominate the light berry character. The structure is light and slightly drying. A simple wine to drink now. ($NA) (3/31/92) **78**

LA RIOJA ALTA
Rioja Reserva 890 Gran Reserva 1973: Deep, round aromas of chocolate, cedar and dried cherry promise more than this light-bodied, dry wine can deliver on the palate. Fading. Drink up. $55 (3/31/92) **77**
Rioja Reserva 904 Gran Reserva 1982: A big wine, with good concentration in the plummy, meaty flavors and full, soft tannins. The smoky finish is long and sweet. Drink now. ($NA) (3/31/92) **84**
Rioja Reserva 904 Gran Reserva 1981: Offers coffee, cedar and brown sugar flavors in a smooth, mature wine. A traditional style that's still fresh. Tasted twice. Drink now. $29 (3/31/92) **82**
Rioja Reserva 904 Gran Reserva 1976 $26 (3/31/90) (TM) **90**
Rioja Reserva 904 Gran Reserva 1975: Quite sweet and fully mature, with coffee and vanilla flavors that dry out on the finish. Showing its age. Drink now. Tasted twice. ($NA) (3/31/92) **82**
Rioja Reserva 904 Gran Reserva 1973 $10 (9/30/86) **84**
Rioja Reserva 904 Gran Reserva 1970 ($NA) (3/31/92) **75**
Rioja Viña Alberdi 1987: Earthy vanilla flavors dominate this traditional-style wine. Has lots of sweet oak, but it's already drying slightly on the finish. Drink now. Tasted twice. $11.50 (3/31/92) **79**
Rioja Viña Alberdi 1986: The smoky roasted aromas are enticing, and lead into cherry and strawberry flavors that are elegant despite the heavy vanilla note. Drink from 1993. $11.50 (3/31/92) **83**
Rioja Viña Alberdi 1985: A silky wine, with lots of oaky vanilla and toast notes layered over black cherry and toffee flavors. Concentrated and well knit. Drink now to 1996. $8 (3/15/90) BB **85**
Rioja Viña Ardanza Reserva 1985: Straightforward but quite tasty, showing cassis and coffee aromas and pretty ripe cherry flavors. Lively and accessible. Drink now to 1995. $18 (3/31/92) **85**
Rioja Viña Ardanza Reserva 1983: Round and accessible, with coffee and nut flavors. Rather simple, but pleasant to drink now. $18 (3/31/92) **81**
Rioja Viña Ardanza Reserva 1982: Marked by gamy black pepper notes, it's round and mature but still has grip. The fruit is subdued. Drink now. $17 (3/31/92) **84**
Rioja Viña Ardanza Reserva 1978 $6 (9/30/86) **65**

BODEGAS RIOJANAS
Rioja Canchales 1987: Simple black cherry and plum flavors are dominated by gamy, tarry flavors and chalky tannins. A simple wine from a weak year. Drink now. $4 (3/15/90) **75**
Rioja Monte Real Gran Reserva 1982: A silky wine, with pretty tea and raspberry flavors. Shows elegance, but seems tame and soft. Tasted twice. Drink now. $19 (3/31/92) **82**
Rioja Monte Real Gran Reserva 1981: A big, firm wine, with lots of black cherry and plum flavors. The tannins are rich, but unobtrusive. Young and muscular, it needs time. Better after 1993. $19 (3/31/92) **89**
Rioja Monte Real Gran Reserva 1975: A decadent style, with meaty flavors softened by a touch of sweetness. An extreme example of the traditional style. Drink up. ($NA) (3/31/92) **78**
Rioja Monte Real Gran Reserva 1973 ($NA) (3/31/92) **85**
Rioja Monte Real Gran Reserva 1970 ($NA) (3/31/92) **72**
Rioja Monte Real Reserva 1985: A rich wine with depth. Smoky, tarry aromas give way to coffee and ripe plum flavors on a muscular frame. Better after 1994. ($NA) (3/31/92) **87**
Rioja Monte Real Reserva 1983: Fruity, spicy and well balanced. A smooth-textured, flavor-packed wine that tastes like black cherries. Fresh and ripe in style. $7.50 (3/31/90) BB **83**
Rioja Puerta Vieja Crianza 1988: A powerful wine, with rich, smoky raspberry aromas and flavors and a long finish. Rich tannins and good acidity give it backbone. A solid wine that will improve with age. Drink in 1993 to '96. ($NA) (3/31/92) **86**
Rioja Viña Albina 1983: Has aromas of dead leaves and tree bark and tastes thin and moldy. Tasted twice. $7.50 (3/31/90) **68**
Rioja Viña Albina Gran Reserva 1982: A big wine that's well crafted and fresh, with attractive berry and game flavors and firm, rich tannins. A good structure promises improvement with age. Start drinking in 1994. $19 (3/31/92) **87**
Rioja Viña Albina Gran Reserva 1981: Blackberry and cream aromas follow through with fresh fruit flavors and firm tannins. Compact and age-worthy. Drink now or hold. $19 (3/31/92) **86**
Rioja Viña Albina Gran Reserva 1975: Quite fresh, with sweet berry, cherry and vanilla flavors complemented by mature, tealike notes and a silky mouth-feel. Drink now. ($NA) (3/31/92) **85**
Rioja Viña Albina Gran Reserva 1973 ($NA) (3/31/92) **81**
Rioja Viña Albina Gran Reserva 1970 ($NA) (3/31/92) **70**
Rioja Viña Albina Reserva 1985: Lean and rather tough, with earthy, gamy flavors and firm tannins. Its character is close to barnyardy. Begin drinking in 1993. ($NA) (3/31/92) **78**

MARQUES DE RISCAL
Rioja 1984: An oddly disjointed wine, with bizarre incense aromas and very little fruit. Tasted twice. $9 (3/31/90) **58**
Rioja 1982 $7 (11/15/87) (JL) **84**
Rioja Gran Reserva 1982 ($NA) (11/30/91) (TM) **84**
Rioja Reserva 1985: Not recommended. Bizarre fruit flavors remind us of Concord grapes, and the finish is bitter and dry. Tasted twice. $9.50 (3/31/90) **62**

BODEGAS SIERRA CANTABRIA
Rioja Codice 1989: Lean and smoky, with caramel and iron overtones to the smoky cherry flavors. Finishes soft and appealing, but may be maturing too quickly. Drink soon. $6 (4/15/92) **77**

OTHER SPAIN RED

RENE BARBIER
Red Table Wine 1983: Fruity and straightforward. Full-flavored, with plenty of plummy, grapey aromas, a round mouth-feel and a fruity aftertaste. $3 (3/31/90) BB **80**

BODEGAS JAIME CARRERAS
Valencia 1985: A light, likable style. Fruity, broad textured and soft. Tastes almost sweet. $4 (3/31/90) BB **80**

CASA DE LA VINA
Valdepeñas Cencibel 1985: A ringer for a Beaujolais. Light and fruity, with bright cherry and plum flavors. Easy to drink now. $6.50 (3/31/90) **82**

CLOS DOFI
Costers del Siurana 1989: Firm, focused and fruity, with generous, jammy plum and cherry aromas and flavors that keep pumping out the fruit through the finish. A graceful wine with a juicy character. Drinkable now, but should improve through 1994 or '95. $40 (1/31/92) **89**

COLEGIATA
Toro Gran Colegiata Tinto de Crianza 1986: Powerful and rustic in flavor, with woody, gamy, smoky aromas and flavors, firm tannins and acidity. Should mellow if cellared until 1995, but it will never be very fruity. $7 (11/30/89) **77**
Toro Tinto 1986: Hearty and satisfying, but a bit rough at this age. Full-bodied, peppery, dark and deep in flavor, with some cherry and smoke accents and full tannins. Drink now to 1994. $5 (11/30/89) BB **82**
Toro Tinto 1985: Very rich and concentrated, deep in color and polished in texture. Has focused flavors of dark cherry, coffee and spice, and a lingering aftertaste. Drink now. $5 (11/30/89) BB **88**

J. DIAZ
Madrid 1985: Has wonderful chocolate, coffee and wild berry aromas and flavors in a rich, smooth, elegant wine. Drink now through 1994. $5.75 (3/31/90) BB **85**

EL DOMINO
Jumilla 1990: Simple and fresh, with nice fruity aromas and lively berry flavors. A sturdy red for everyday drinking, with enough grip to wash down a hearty meal. $7 (4/15/92) BB **80**

BODEGAS C. AUGUSTO EGLI
Utiel-Requena Casa lo Alto 1983: A beautifully balanced but lean-tasting wine. Has spicy cherry flavors on a crisp structure. The finish is long and tasty. Drink now. $9 (7/31/89) **82**

ESTOLA
La Mancha Reserva 1985: A mature red, with dill, herb and leather aromas and modest cherry flavor to back them up. Smooth, medium-bodied and basically light in flavor. $10 (2/15/92) **80**
La Mancha Reserva 1982: A very good wine at a very decent price. Smells toasty and smoky, but the fruit flavor still breaks through. Has a silky texture and generous raspberry and anise flavors that linger. Medium-bodied. Drink now. $6 (11/15/89) BB **87**

FARINA
Tinto Crianzano Tierra del Vino 1986: Rough tasting, but quite flavorful. Smells distinctly salty and tastes woody, wild and berrylike, with slightly rough tannins and good acidity. $7 (11/30/89) **79**

MARQUES DE GRINON
Tinto do Toledo 1985: Has plenty of fresh, ripe cherry and berry flavors framed by toasty oak; a lively, vivid style that is quite attractive, finishing with good length. Ready now to 1995. $12 (2/28/90) **86**

CASTILLO JUMILLA
Jumilla 1985: Simple and sturdy, for everyday drinking. Has good but light flavors of prunes and herbs, moderate tannins and good acid balance. $5 (7/31/89) **75**

LAR DE BARROS
Tierra de Barros Tinto Reserva 1988: Ripe, smoky and mature, with modest tannins and dense, ripe currant, raisin and toast aromas and flavors. Drinkable now, but may improve through 1993 to '95. Tasted twice. $10 (4/15/92) **79**
Tierra de Barros Tinto Reserva 1986: Earthy, ripe, complex and distinctive, with toast, cherry, prune and chocolate flavors intertwined in a soft, velvety package that firms up and gets a little tannic on the finish. Long and concentrated, this complex wine is unlike any other we have tasted from Spain. Should improve through the mid-1990s. $8 (10/15/90) SS **91**

LAR DE LARES
Tierra de Barros Gran Reserva 1982: Distinctive, rich, mature and elegant, with plenty of spicy brown sugar charm around a core of strawberry and raspberry flavors. Hints at leather at first, but echoes fruit on the finish. Refined and elegant. 3,500 cases made. $14 (6/15/91) **90**

MONTE DUCAY
Cariñena Gran Reserva 1982: Definitely worth trying. Shows the benefits of aging, with attractive, developed aromas of anise, fruit and toast, plus good cherry flavors and a smooth texture. $8 (11/30/89) **85**

MONTESIERRA
Somontano 1988: Plenty of fresh, ripe pepper and berry flavors, like a Beaujolais, with crisp acidity and lively cherry and spice notes. Drink now or in 1993. Better than a bottle tasted earlier. $6 (3/31/90) **81**

PADORNINA
El Bierzo 1987: Straightforward and hearty, with vanilla-tinged plum and strawberry aromas and flavors and firm texture. Not terribly dense, but it's balanced and drinkable. 270 cases made. $8 (3/31/90) **81**
El Bierzo 1985: A basic, well-structured wine that tastes tight, tart and plummy, with woody, spicy accents and firm tannins. $7 (6/30/90) **74**

BODEGAS PIQUERAS
Almansa Castillo de Almansa Vino de Crianza 1986: Offers mature flavors dominated by cola, tea and plum and has great balance, with notes of complexity. A fairly elegant wine that's smooth, spicy and ready to drink now. 1,000 cases made. $8.50 (4/15/92) BB **83**
Almansa Castillo de Almansa Vino de Crianza 1985: A different wine, with an appealing texture and flavor. Spicy, mature and flavorful, with sharply focused nutmeg, toast and plum aromas and

flavors. Has a sense of elegance, polish and depth. Drinkable now. 1,000 cases made. $8 (9/30/91) BB **85**

Almansa Castillo de Almansa Vino de Crianza 1983: A very complex, elegant wine that offers aromas of spice, leather and dried fruit, intriguing rich cherry and spice flavors and a long, complex finish. Drinkable now, but it's built for cellaring till 1993. $6.50 (7/31/89) BB **88**

SALVADOR POVEDA

Tinto Gran Reserva Alicante No. 1 1985: Mature, with a meaty texture and leather, prune and beet aromas and flavors. Decent, without a lot of depth. Drinkable now. $9 (11/15/91) **79**

RAIMAT

Cabernet Sauvignon Costers del Segre 1986: Very firm and tannic, with generous cassis and vanilla aromas and herbal, leafy flavors to go along with the scratchy tannins. Needs to be cellared until at least 1993 to '95 to soften the tannins, and it just might have the depth to make it. $10 (3/31/90) **81**

Costers del Segre Abadia 1987: Smooth and harmonious, a gentle wine with high-toned, vanilla, smoke and cassis aromas and flavors that are lithe and artfully balanced between fruit and oak. Appealing now, but cellaring until 1994 shouldn't hurt. $9 (3/31/90) **84**

BODEGA SAN VALERO

Cariñena Don Mendo Tinto Especial 1987: A medium-bodied, light and freshly flavored wine with strawberry, spice and herb accents. Drink it like a young Beaujolais, chilled. $5 (11/30/89) BB **81**

SENORIO DEL MAR

Vino Tinto Seco 1987: A sun-baked wine, with interesting raisin, plum and spice flavors. Medium-bodied, well balanced and light in color. A good change of pace for everyday drinking. $4 (10/31/91) BB **81**

EL SENORIO DE TORO

Toro Etiqueta Blanca 1989: A very hearty, deep-colored, tannic wine, with loads of ripe fruit flavor accented by smoky, tarry notes. Young and rough, but with plenty of flavor. $10 (4/15/92) **82**

TAJA

Jumilla 1987: Lively, hearty and flavorful, with appealing citrus-tinged berry and cherry aromas and flavors that are soft and velvety on the finish. A fun wine that's tasty and easy to drink. $6 (3/31/90) BB **80**

BODEGAS TORRES FILOSO

La Mancha Cosecha Arboles de Castillejo 1986: Light and fruity, with firm tannins supporting pleasant plum, prune and cherry aromas and flavors. Gets a little sharp on the finish, but should accompany dinner well. Drink soon. 3,000 cases made. $7 (4/15/92) **79**

VALDEOBISPO

Bierzo Tinto 1990: Smooth and jammy, light-bodied, with plenty of exuberant cherry and grape flavors and enough tannin to keep it from being cloying. Drinkable now. 2,500 cases made. $7 (4/15/92) **80**

Bierzo Unfiltered 1989: Quite a discovery. A young, intensely flavored wine that will need until about 1994 to mature. Very assertive, from its deep, deep color to its pungent peppery aromas to its ultraripe, dense chocolate and blackberry flavors. 300 cases made. $10 (4/15/92) **87**

VEGA DE MORIZ

Valdepeñas Cencibel 1989: Soft and velvety, with plum and berry flavors. Modest but drinkable now. $5.50 (6/15/91) BB **81**

VINA VERMETA

Tinto 1987: A firm-textured, no-nonsense wine, with grapey, peppery flavors. Sturdy through to the finish. Drinkable now. $6 (11/15/91) **76**

VINOS DE LEON

Tinto Palacio de Leon 1985: Lean, spicy and tannic, but with enough clean cherry, spice and toast flavors to balance. Still, it needs until 1993 to '95 to smooth out. $4.50 (11/15/89) BB **85**

Spain White/*Penedès*

BALADA

Penedès Macabeo Gran Blanc 1988: Light and fresh, with hints of lemon, toast and spice aromas and flavors. Simple and unobtrusive. $8 (3/31/90) **75**

GRAN CAUS

Chardonnay Penedès Chenin Blanc Xarel-lo 1987: Floral and fruity aromas and crisp, slightly herbal flavors make this a pleasant wine for drinking now. Its dryness makes it a good match for many light dishes. $10 (5/15/89) **81**

JEAN LEON

Chardonnay Penedès 1989: As rich as butter pecan ice cream, with fully developed, oaky flavors and a smooth texture. Lush and complex, but owes most of its flavor to wood. For drinking now. $35 (5/31/92) **84**

Chardonnay Penedès 1988: A woody style, but excellent if you like lush honey and spice flavors. Has toast and almond aromas, but the flavors are balanced and the texture is polished and smooth, echoing vanilla and pear on the finish. Drinkable now. $34 (1/31/91) **88**

TORRES

Penedès Fransola 1988: Very attractive in a light, fruity style. Smells like mint and melon and tastes fresh and melony, with a clean finish. $14.50 (3/31/90) **79**

Penedès Fransola Green Label 1990: This light, crisp and austere wine has hints of herb aromas and flavors around a lean core of pear and lemon notes. Best with food. $16 (7/15/91) **81**

Penedès Gran Viña Sol 1989: A good quaffing wine that's floral, spicy, light and crisp, with a touch of honey on the finish. Built like a Sauvignon Blanc, but with more exotic flavors. $10 (12/15/90) **80**

Penedès Gran Viña Sol 1988: Fresh, crisp and melony in flavor, with a hint of spice and enough concentration to lift it above the ordinary. Very clean, dry and attractive. $14 (3/31/90) **83**

Penedès Milmanda 1990: A beautifully crafted wine, spicy, complex and extraordinarily well balanced. Well-defined apple and pear fruit play tug o' war with sweet toasty oak that echoes nutmeg, vanilla and fruit on the long finish. Flavors and rich texture stay with you. 1,500 cases made. $35 (10/31/91) **91**

Penedès Milmanda 1989 $40 (12/15/90) **93**

Key to Symbols

The scores reported here are the results of blind tastings conducted by our panel of senior editors. Wines that carry the initials below are results of individual tastings.

THE WINE SPECTATOR 100-POINT SCALE ***95-100***—Classic, a great wine; ***90-94***—Outstanding, superior character and style; ***80-89***—Good to very good, a wine with special qualities; ***70-79***—Average, drinkable wine that may have minor flaws; ***60-69***—Below average, drinkable but not recommended; ***50-59***—Poor, undrinkable, not recommended. "+"—With a score indicates a range; used primarily with barrel tastings to indicate a preliminary score.

SPECIAL DESIGNATIONS SS—Spectator Selection, CS—Cellar Selection, BB—Best Buy, ($NA)—Price not available, (NR)—Not released.

TASTER'S INITIALS (JG)—Jim Gordon, (HS)—Harvey Steiman, (JL)—James Laube, (JS)—James Suckling, (TM)—Thomas Matthews, (TR)—Terry Robards, (PM)—Per-Henrik Mansson, (BT)—Barrel Tasting (these wines were tasted blind from barrel samples), (CA-date)—*California's Great Cabernets* by James Laube, (CH-date)—*California's Great Chardonnays* by James Laube, (VP-date)—*Vintage Port* by James Suckling.

DATE TASTED Dates in parentheses represent the issue in which the rating was published.

Penedès Milmanda 1988: A fruity, floral style, with simple but pleasant spice, apple and pear notes that glide across the palate. Has moderate depth and intensity, but a clean, lingering finish. Not as good as previous vintages. Tasted twice. $35 (3/31/90) **80**

Penedès Milmanda 1987 $35 (12/15/88) **94**

Penedès Viña Esmeralda 1991: Crisp, floral and very aromatic, with peachy, orangelike flavors and a short finish. Simple, refreshing and a bit sweet. $10 (5/31/92) **80**

Penedès Viña Esmeralda 1990: Frankly fruity and floral in flavor, spilling over with peach and floral aromas followed by off-dry peach and spice notes. A nice touch of tartness keeps it fresh on the finish. Drink up while the weather's warm. $10.50 (7/15/91) **84**

Penedès Viña Esmeralda 1989: Very fresh, light and spicy, with ebullient fruit and floral aromas and flavors, hinting at orange and honeysuckle on the finish. Drink it now, while it's such an appealing quaffer. $9 (3/31/90) **84**

Penedès Viña Sol 1990: Light and dry, with pleasant floral, almond and pear aromas and flavors that persist on the finish. Best by itself. $6 (11/15/91) BB **80**

Penedès Viña Sol 1989: Tart and bordering on sour, with little fruit flavor but plenty of dill and pine notes. Basically thin and difficult to warm up to. Tasted twice. $7 (7/15/91) **73**

Penedès Viña Sol 1988: Musty smelling, but it tastes crisp, light and appley. Simple but good for a weekday quaff. $5.25 (3/31/90) **72**

Rioja

AGE

Rioja Siglo 1988: Round and soft, with plenty of new oak flavor, but it lacks fruit and length. ($NA) (5/31/92) **78**

BODEGAS BERBERANA

Rioja Carta de Oro Crianza 1988: Offers lovely floral, peach and honey aromas and flavors in a rich, clean wine with good balance and length. $7 (5/31/92) **88**

BODEGAS BERONIA

Rioja Crianza 1988: Traditional in style, with plenty of vanilla, nut and honey flavors. $7.50 (5/31/92) **83**

BRETON LORINON

Rioja 1990: Fresh melon and pear flavors, with hints of almond, give this clean, well-made wine interest. Barrel fermented. (NR) (5/31/92) **85**

Rioja Crianza 1989: A well-knit wine with good intensity. The deep melon and almond flavors need time to unfold. Drink starting in 1993. ($NA) (5/31/92) (BT) **85+**

BODEGAS MARTINEZ BUJANDA

Rioja Conde de Valdemar 1990: This barrel-fermented, 100 percent Viura is rich with tropical fruit flavors and honey notes, but it's slightly over-oaked. A worthwhile experiment. $6.50 (5/31/92) **85**

Rioja Valdemar 1990: Tart, bordering on sour, with a watery texture and modest fruit flavors. Picks up a little oak flavor on the finish to make it interesting. Drinkable now. $7 (11/15/91) **72**

MARQUES DE CACERES

Rioja 1988: Floral, grassy aromas and flavors make us think of Sauvignon Blanc, but it's crisp and lively on the palate, even if it's aggressively herbal. Appealing in an austere way. $7.50 (3/31/90) **78**

Rioja Crianza 1989: Fresh and vibrant, with coconut, apple and vanilla flavors. Balanced and well made. $10 (5/31/92) **87**

Rioja Reserva 1987: Fresh and perfumed, but it still has plenty of honey and vanilla. Strikes a balance between the oaky and fruity styles. ($NA) (5/31/92) **85**

BODEGAS CAMPO VIEJO

Rioja Selección José Bezares Crianza 1987: Very perfumed, with butter and apple aromas, becoming round and firm on the palate. The subtle flavors will emerge with time. ($NA) (5/31/92) **85**

CUNE

Rioja Monopole Crianza 1988: Bone dry and almost chalky, it lacks fruit. ($NA) (5/31/92) **78**

FRANCO-ESPANOLAS

Rioja Viña Soledad Gran Reserva 1978: Well focused, with crisp almond and pear flavors that are round and clean. Has body without losing definition, and it's still in excellent condition. ($NA) (5/31/92) **86**

R. LOPEZ DE HEREDIA VINA TONDONIA

Rioja Gravonia 1987: Beyond the honey flavor, there's not much excitement in this traditional wine. ($NA) (5/31/92) **80**

Rioja Tondonia Gran Reserva 1985: Round and full, with clean butter and melon flavors that are balanced and long. Will improve with bottle age. ($NA) (5/31/92) **90**

Rioja Tondonia Gran Reserva 1976: Soft, round and quite rich, with butter, honey and vanilla flavors. Opulent but clean and well balanced. ($NA) (5/31/92) **85**

BODEGAS MONTECILLO

Rioja Viña Cumbrero 1989: A very clean, medium-bodied wine, with light floral and honey aromas, crisp apple and caramel flavors and a pretty good finish. Fresh and light compared to many heavily oaked white Riojas. $6 (7/15/91) BB **80**

Rioja Viña Cumbrero 1988: Dry, austere and simple, with appley, grassy aromas and tart almost bitter flavors that lack depth and richness. Tasted twice. $5 (3/31/90) **72**

BODEGAS MUGA

Rioja Crianza 1988: The honey and lemon flavors are in good balance in this rich, powerful wine. A traditional oaky style. ($NA) (5/31/92) **91**

MARQUES DE MURRIETA

Rioja 1985: Vibrantly aromatic, with spice, nutmeg and apricot, charged with crisp fruit flavors and hints of hazelnut. Nut and fruit flavors linger on the finish. Balanced for aging through 1993, but it's attractive to drink now. $14 (3/31/90) **88**

Rioja 1984: Wild and exotic, with full-blown floral, apricotlike, spicy aromas and nutty, peachy nutmeg flavors. Crisp on the palate and tart and tangy on the finish, indicating it will develop even more with age. Drink now or in 1993. $13 (3/31/90) **85**

Rioja Gran Reserva 1978: A 14-year-old Spanish white? Why not, when it's so distinctive? It has rich, succulent honey and almond aromas and flavors that are lush and generous from start to finish. Some may find the wood aromas intrusive, but the flavor is worth the nose. $29 (3/31/90) **91**

Rioja Reserva 1986: Maturing, but still monumental, rich with honey, vanilla, pear and melon flavors and still has a long life ahead of it. $20 (5/31/92) **92**

BODEGAS OLARRA

Rioja Añares Blanco Seco 1988: Very ripe and flavorful, with flavors that lean toward almond and honey, it's pungently woody and floral on the nose but balanced at the finish. Drink now. $7 (3/31/90) BB **82**

FREDERICO PATERNINA

Rioja Banda Dorada 1987: Drinkable in a pinch. Grassy, grapefruity flavors give this some appeal, although the aroma is unusually earthy. Tasted twice. $5 (3/31/90) **69**

Rioja Reserva 1981: Nut and honey flavors mingle with lemon-lime notes. ($NA) (5/31/92) **83**

LA RIOJA ALTA

Rioja Viña Ardanza Reserva 1988: Flat and flabby, dominated by buttery aromas and flavors. Shows too much wood and not much depth. ($NA) (5/31/92) **77**

Rioja Viña Ardanza Reserva 1985: Smooth and almost oily, with smoky, nutty flavors that have more to do with wood than fruit. Very traditional in style. ($NA) (5/31/92) **82**

BODEGAS RIOJANAS
Rioja Monte Real 1991: Very clean. Slips down easily, with hints of apple and peach flavors. The barrel fermentation hardly shows. $6 (5/31/92) **83**
Rioja Monte Real Crianza 1987: A beauty in the traditional style. Full yet crisp, with honey and peach flavors that are rich and concentrated. Still has a long life ahead of it. ($NA) (5/31/92) **89**
Rioja Viña Albina Gran Reserva 1983: Open, well-defined honey and lemon aromas lead to a rich, honeyed wine. Sweet and almost oily. A good alternative to Sauternes. ($NA) (5/31/92) **87**

Other Spain White

MARQUES DE ALLELLA
Alella 1989 $17 (12/15/90) **80**

HIJOS DE ANTONIO BARCELO
Rueda Vino Blanco Santorcal 1989: This soft, floral and modestly fruity wine is simple, smooth and pleasant, but lacking in flavor. $6 (7/15/91) **77**

CARBALLO DO REI CONDADO
Rias Baixas 1990: An interesting and fairly complex wine that starts out austere and nutty, then opens up to appealing pear, spice and rose petal notes that round out on the finish. Worth a try. 1,200 cases made. $14 (7/15/91) **84**

MARTIN CODAX
Rias Baixas Albariño 1990: A very ripe, buttery, full-bodied wine, with peach underpinnings. Simple and easygoing. $12 (5/31/92) **78**

MORGADIO ALBARINO
Rias Baixas 1990: Full of concentrated fruit flavor in an uncomplicated, well-balanced style. Intense apricot and pear flavors keep this fresh wine very lively, if a bit rough in texture. A good discovery. 2,500 cases made. $22 (7/15/91) **85**
Rias Baixas Albariño 1991: Fresh, tangy and fruity, with ample pear, apricot and caramel flavors. A bit rough, but it's lively and crisp. 3,000 cases made. $20 (5/31/92) **82**

OCHOA
Navarra 1989: An austere, lightweight wine with little flavor to speak of. Would wash down oysters nicely, but it's not much on its own. $8 (11/15/91) **74**

RAIMAT
Chardonnay Costers del Segre 1989: A deep gold-colored, tart and fruity wine, with ample pear and orange flavors and hints of toast and honey to round it out. Flavorful, assertive and well balanced in a bracingly crisp style. $10 (12/15/90) **82**

MARQUES DE RISCAL
Sauvignon Blanc Rueda 1988: A Sauvignon Blanc with a Chardonnay profile. Broad in flavor, with nutty, ripe pear notes and a rich texture. Well balanced. A good value. $7.50 (3/31/90) **81**

EL SENORIO DE TORO
Tarragona Vino Blanco Seco 1988: A simple, light wine, with earthy, spicy aromas and flavors and hints of honey on the finish. Drinkable now. Tasted twice. $4 (5/31/92) **76**

VALDUMIA
Rias Baixas Albariño 1990: Stylish, pleasantly fruity and fresh, with attractive nectarine and vanilla aromas and flavors that stay with you on the finish. A medium-weight wine that's drinkable now. $17.50 (11/15/91) **82**

ANGEL RODRIGUEZ VIDAL
Rueda Martinsancho Verdejo 1990: Crisp and light, this simple white wine has pleasant fruit flavors, hinting at fig on the finish. Drinkable now. 3,000 cases made. $10 (5/31/92) **78**
Rueda Martinsancho Verdejo 1988: Simple, fruity, supple and smooth, with clean, somewhat melonlike flavors. Drink soon. $9 (3/31/90) **77**

Sparkling

CASTELLBLANCH
Brut Cava Extra NV: A fresh and lively sparkling wine, with focused pear, toast and spice aromas and flavors and a lean, almost creamy texture, but pleasant on the palate. $6 (2/29/92) BB **82**

CODORNIU
Brut Blanc de Blancs Cava 1988: Nicely balanced, with subtle Chardonnay aromas and flavors. Very dry, clean and flavorful, hinting at apple, pear and butter on the moderately lengthy finish. $9 (12/31/90) BB **84**
Brut Blanc de Blancs Cava 1986: Light and slightly nutty tasting, it's clean and fresh but doesn't have much fruit flavor. $8 (7/31/89) **77**
Brut Cava Anna de Codorniu 1989: Dry, crisp and clean, with lemon and almond flavors and a tart finish. $8 (5/15/92) **79**
Brut Cava Anna de Codorniu 1988: Light with perfume aromas, it's a bit creamy but not especially complex or rich. Nearly dry and nicely balanced. $8 (12/31/90) **78**
Brut Cava Anna de Codorniu 1987: Made in a simple, straightforward style. The light aromas and flavors are reminiscent of canned fruit cocktail. It's a bit coarse in texture, but not unpleasant. $7 (8/31/90) **75**
Brut Cava Anna de Codorniu 1985 $6.50 (7/31/89) **76**
Brut Cava Chardonnay 1988: Offers plenty of flavor, with rich, full-bodied, creamy toast, pear, earth and vanilla flavors that stay with you. A sparkler with character. Drink now. $15 (5/15/92) **85**
Brut Cava Chardonnay 1986: Refreshing, clean and flavorful. Has figgy aromas and clean, tangy flavors of pear and pineapple, with crisp acidity and lively bubbles. $12 (7/31/89) **84**
Brut Cava Clásico 1989: Simple, ripe and fruity, with spicy pear, vanilla and earth notes that turn bitter on the finish. Drink now. $9 (5/15/92) **75**
Brut Cava Clásico 1986: Fresh and agreeable, it smells clean and fruity, and tastes smooth and creamy. Slightly sweet. $6 (5/15/89) BB **82**

FREIXENET
Brut Cava Carta Nevada NV: This soft, mature, slightly sweet, easy-drinking sparkler has appealing spice and floral flavors, but little depth or structure. $7 (12/31/90) **78**
Brut Cava Cordon Negro NV: Broad, spicy flavors make this a distinctive wine, offering crisp texture and hints of ginger and pepper on the finish. $9 (2/29/92) **80**
Brut Cava Nature 1987: Very smooth and mature tasting, with soft apple and pear flavors accented by spicy, nutty nuances. Could use more zip or intensity, but quite pleasant as it is. $10 (5/15/92) **80**
Brut Cava Nature 1985: A delicate, spicy sparkler with toasty overtones, offering dry, lemony flavors. Clean and easy to drink. $10 (12/31/90) **81**
Extra Dry Cava Cordon Negro NV: Not too sweet for an extra-dry bubbly, with soft texture and yeasty, spicy aromas and flavors, hinting at pear and apple on the finish. $9 (2/29/92) **80**
Seco Cava Carta Nevada NV: Sweet, simple and sugary, with very little flavor; this is drinkable, but of average quality. $7 (12/31/90) **71**

JUVE Y CAMPS
Brut Cava Extra Reserva de la Familia 1986: Decidedly earthy, with distinctive leather aromas and flavors that cast a shadow over the modest lemon and walnut character. Delicate in texture. Has personality and style, but might not be for everyone. $16 (11/15/91) **82**

LEMBEY
Brut Cava 1988: A nutty, floral quality keeps this easy-to-drink wine interesting from the aroma through the finish. Dry, flavorful and seemingly mature, with an agreeably smooth texture. $6 (5/15/92) BB **83**
Brut Cava Pedro Domecq 1986: Not delicate or complex, but full of fruity and floral flavors, with earthy, spicy aromas typical of Spanish sparkling wines. $7.25 (7/15/90) **79**
Sparkling Cava Première Cuvée 1985: Clean, fresh and lively, with a creamy texture, perfumed aromas, peach and apple flavors and nice toasty characteristics. $12 (7/15/91) **85**

MIRO
Brut Cava NV: Crisp, lean and clean, with light, spicy, grassy flavors. Good by itself or with brunch or dinner. $9 (2/29/92) **78**

MONT-MARCAL
Brut Cava NV: This wine won't disappoint. Clean, crisp and only modestly fruity, it has good balance and effervescence. $8 (7/15/90) **78**

PARXET
Brut Nature Chardonnay NV: This nutty, mature-tasting wine finishes very dry, almost bitter. Pretty coarse stuff, and not worth the price. 5,000 cases made. $22 (5/15/92) **76**

ROVELLATS
Brut Cava Imperial NV: Spicy, floral, nutty flavors combine in an almost dry package for a flavorful, distinctively Spanish style of sparkling wine. $13 (12/31/90) **83**
Brut Nature Cava Gran Reserva NV: Dry and almost austere, with earth, nut and apricot flavors. It's not particularly generous as an aperitif, but should be better with meals. $17 (12/31/90) **78**

SEGURA VIUDAS
Brut Cava Aria Estate NV: Despite the bright straw color, it has lovely raspberry and cherry flavors all tightly wrapped in a crisp package, with firm acidity and fine length. Has concentration without weight. A fine value. $10 (11/15/91) **87**
Extra Dry Cava Aria Estate NV: Crisp, clean and spicy, this shoots for delicacy and achieves a nice sense of balance and appealing flavor without weight. Hints of apple and toast are especially likable. Despite being labeled "extra dry," it's not as sweet as most wines so labeled. $10 (11/15/91) **85**

BODEGAS JAUME SERRA
Brut Cava Cristalino NV: Has plenty of flavor, but it's coarse, mature and earthy, with underlying sweet pear notes. Won't be for everyone. Tasted twice, with consistent notes. $8 (2/29/92) **75**
Seco Cava Dry Cristalino NV: A very pleasant little bubbly. Crisp, lemony and nearly dry, with a floral, nutty aroma. $8 (2/29/92) BB **82**

VALLFORMOSA
Brut Cava NV: Smooth, dry and mature, with intriguing toast, spice and almond aromas and light, soft apricot and peach flavors. It's not deep in flavor, but it's light and likable. $7 (12/31/90) BB **80**
Brut Nature Cava NV: On the delicate side, dry, lemony and clean, neutral in flavor but crisp and lively in texture. $9 (12/31/90) **79**

XENIUS
Sparkling Cava NV: A nicely mature, gold-colored, slightly sweet sparkling wine, with great flavors of almond and vanilla and a creamy, rich texture. $7.50 (7/15/90) BB **82**

XIPELLA
Blanc de Blancs Conca de Barberá 1988: Soft and simple, a plain wine with some hints of earthiness to liven it up. $6 (3/31/90) **74**

OTHER INTERNATIONAL

Argentina

VALENTIN BIANCHI
Cabernet Sauvignon Mendoza Elsa's Vineyard 1987: Tight and firm, with cedary plum and spice flavors. Nothing special, but it offers more flavor and character than you might get from a straight red table wine. Drink now. $7 (7/15/91) **77**
Malbec Mendoza Elsa's Vineyard 1985: A rough-and-ready wine, with a texture on the coarse side, wild berry and plum aromas and flavors and hints of tar on the finish. Drinkable now. $6 (7/15/91) **76**

FINCA FLICHMAN
Argenta Mendoza 1988: This Sangiovese blend has characteristic Tuscan aromas and flavors. A bit simple on the palate, but it's easy to drink and balanced. Comparable to a well-made, basic Chianti. $4 (3/15/91) BB **84**
Cabernet Sauvignon Mendoza Caballero de la Cepa 1985: Extremely herbal, vegetal aromas and flavors tend to overpower this oaky, borderline bitter wine. $8 (3/15/91) **68**
Cabernet Sauvignon Mendoza Proprietor's Private Reserve 1987: Firm, flavorful and full of personality, showing hearty cherry, plum and tobacco aromas and flavors, firm tannins, generosity and balance. Drink after 1993 or '94. $6 (3/15/91) BB **81**
Chardonnay Mendoza Caballero de la Cepa 1990: Crisp, tight, clean and balanced, with a narrow band of lemon and citrus flavor. Drink now, with light foods. $8 (7/15/91) **78**
Chardonnay Mendoza Proprietor's Private Reserve 1990: Distinctive for its citrus and orange blossom notes, clean, balanced, moderately rich and flavorful. Crisp and lively. Drink now or in 1993. $6 (4/30/91) BB **83**
Mendoza 1990: Tart and lean, with crisp lemon-lime flavors that are simple, but fresh and clean. Drink up. $4 (7/15/91) **76**
Merlot Proprietor's Private Reserve Mendoza 1988: Weedy, herbal aromas and flavors tend to overwhelm this modest wine and turn it bitter on the finish. $6 (3/15/91) **66**
Selection Flichman Mendoza 1990: Crisp and tart, with lively lemon-lime and racy spicy fruit flavors. A blend of Sémillon and Chenin Blanc, it should be paired with light fair, such as sole. Drink now. $4.50 (7/15/91) **79**
Selection Mendoza 1988: Ripe currant and cherry aromas and flavors are particularly appealing in this broad-textured, generally simple, Malbec-based wine. Drinkable now. $4.50 (3/15/91) BB **79**

FOND DE CAVE
Cabernet Sauvignon Mendoza 1982: A hearty wine that's smoky in aroma, and vegetal and plummy in flavor. Good if you like the style. $7 (2/15/89) **76**

NAVARRO CORREAS
Cabernet Sauvignon Mendoza 1981: A good, everyday wine that's firm and moderately tannic and has plum and cherry flavors. $8.50 (2/15/89) **79**

PASCUAL TOSO
Cabernet Sauvignon Mendoza 1988: Spicy and oaky, with smoky flavors dominating, but plenty of cherry and berry flavors emerge on the palate. A distinctive wine that's drinkable now. $7 (3/15/91) **79**

TRAPICHE
Cabernet Sauvignon Mendoza 1982: Clean and attractive. Has fresh cherry and herbal flavors in a firm but light structure. $4 (2/15/89) BB **81**
Cabernet Sauvignon Mendoza Oak Cask Reserve Vintner's Selection 1986: Sturdy, with pleasant, ripe currant and dusky spice flavors that stick around on the finish. Cellaring until 1993 or '94 could give it polish. Shows better now than when reviewed earlier. $9.75 (10/15/91) **82**
Cabernet Sauvignon Mendoza Reserve 1986: Medium-bodied with straightforward plum and herb flavors. Smooth texture and light tannins make this an easy-to-drink wine. $5.50 (9/15/90) **77**
Cabernet Sauvignon Mendoza Vintner's Selection Oak Cask Reserve 1986: A curiously flavorless wine. Firm and somewhat tannic, but it shows little flavor interest. Innocuous. $8 (7/15/91) **69**
Chardonnay Mendoza Oak Cask Reserve Vintner's Selection 1990: Soft and fruity, not showing much oak at all, with pleasant peach and spice aromas and flavors that lean toward citrus on the finish. Drinkable now. $8 (11/15/91) **81**
Chardonnay Mendoza Reserve 1989: Tastes buttery and woody. Nice fruit aromas, but only modest pineapple and pear flavors. Simple and clean, but nothing to get excited about. $5.50 (9/15/90) **78**
Malbec Mendoza Oak Cask Reserve Vintner's Selection 1988: Soft and fruity against a solid background of tannin, offering pleasant cherry and currant aromas and flavors that stay fruity on the finish. Drinkable now. Better showing than when reviewed earlier. $6.50 (10/15/91) **81**
Malbec Mendoza Reserve 1987: An intense, focused and fruity wine. Smooth, with nice raspberry and plum flavors. Tastes like a Zinfandel, with a hint of spicy oak. Easy to drink now. From Argentina, and one of the few varietal bottlings of this Bordeaux grape. $5 (9/15/90) BB **83**

Brazil

MARCUS JAMES
White Zinfandel Aurora Valley 1987 $4 (6/15/89) **78**

Bulgaria

BALKAN CREST
Cabernet Sauvignon Stara Zagora Oriahovitza Vineyards Reserve 1985: Dirty oak and earth flavors don't remind you much of wine. Of poor quality; avoid. Tasted twice. $6 (7/15/91) **58**
Chardonnay Shoumen Khan Krum Vineyards Reserve 1987: A simple, floral, earthy wine, hinting at apple and fig flavors. Soft and ready to drink. $6 (7/15/91) **79**

Israel

CARMEL
Cabernet Sauvignon Samson 1986: $7.50 (3/31/91) **78**
Chenin Blanc Galil 1989: $6 (3/31/91) **72**

GAMLA
Cabernet Sauvignon Galil 1987: $9.50 (3/31/91) **75**
Cabernet Sauvignon Galil Special Reserve 1986: $12 (3/31/91) **83**
Chardonnay Galil Special Reserve 1988: $11 (3/31/91) **66**
Sauvignon Blanc Galil 1988: $9 (3/31/91) **75**
Sauvignon Blanc Galil Special Reserve 1988: $10 (3/31/91) **74**
Sauvignon Blanc Late Harvest Galil 1988: $14 (3/31/91) **75**

GOLAN
Cabernet Sauvignon Galil 1987: Deeply colored, with ripe plum flavors, menthol notes and refreshingly light tannins. An austere style, with good balance, clean flavors and a nice smokiness. Drink now through 1994. $11.50 (4/15/92) **83**
Cabernet Sauvignon Galil 1986: $11 (3/31/91) **85**
Chardonnay Galil 1990: Pleasant, soft and medium-bodied, with citrus and pineapple flavors and a nice touch of oak and spice. A bit earthy. Drink now, while it's fresh. $11.50 (4/15/92) **81**
Sauvignon Blanc Galil 1988: $8 (3/31/91) **72**

YARDEN
Cabernet Sauvignon Galil 1986: Broad and fat with nice plum and chocolate flavors. Easy to drink, ripe and soft. Nice fruit with spice and earthy notes. Drink now. $14 (6/30/90) **79**
Cabernet Sauvignon Galil 1985: Soft and flavorful. Chocolaty and plummy, with hints of leather in the aromas and sweet fruit flavors. Well-balanced and fairly rich, with just enough tannins to make it last. Drink now. $14 (6/30/90) **82**
Chardonnay Galil 1989: $10 (3/31/91) **84**
Merlot Galil Special Reserve 1988: $14 (3/31/91) **77**
Merlot Galil Special Reserve 1986: Fruity, flavorful and straightforward in style, with ripe cherry and tobacco flavors and a hint of vanilla. Mild tannins make it fine to drink now. 1,000 cases made. $12 (6/30/90) **79**
Mt. Hermon Red Galil 1989: $7 (3/31/91) **70**
Mt. Hermon White Galil 1989: $6 (3/31/91) **77**
Sauvignon Blanc Galil 1989: $9 (3/31/91) **79**

Lebanon

CHATEAU MUSAR
Lebanon 1983: A grown-up wine, though still a little rough in texture. Has harmonious flavors of plum, tar and anise, and displays maturity with vanilla and coffee flavors that persist on the finish. Drink now. Rel: $17 Cur: $20 (7/15/91) **86**
Lebanon 1982: Well rounded, ripe and mature, but it's still fresh, concentrated and generous, offering ripe cherry, nutmeg and anise notes. Attractive caramel flavors underlay firm tannins. Drinkable now, but it might smooth out more by 1993. Rel: $15 Cur: $18 (7/15/91) **87**
Lebanon 1981: Has a sense of richness and elegance, with firm tannins. Very mature and complex on the nose, with somewhat ripe plum and earth flavors. Drink in 1993 to '95. Rel: $18 Cur: $21 (7/15/91) **84**
Lebanon 1980 Rel: $11 Cur: $24 (7/31/88) **91**

Mexico

PINSON
Chardonnay Mexico 1987: Very soft and mature tasting, enjoyable now but don't save it. Has nut and honey flavors on the finish. $4.50 (6/30/90) **73**

SAN MARTIN
Petite Sirah Baja California International Series 1987: Fruity and unctuous, with blackberry and pepper notes, lots of tannins and an almost velvety texture, this wine has good varietal flavors with a soft structure. A great bargain in a disappearing varietal. Drink now. $4 (8/31/90) BB **82**

New Zealand

BABICH
Cabernet Sauvignon Hawke's Bay 1989: The plum-tinged flavors have a tart, green edge, suggesting this is underripe. It's drinkable, but not everyone's cup of Cabernet. Drink now. $10 (7/15/91) **74**
Chardonnay Hawke's Bay 1989: Tart and almost tinny, coming off rather like canned fruit juice. You could drink it, but it's not an elegant or appealing wine. 5,000 cases made. $12 (9/15/91) **71**
Chardonnay Hawke's Bay Irongate 1989: This wine has complex aromas and flavors, with distinct pineapple, citrus, mineral and oak notes that are tight and concentrated. The flavors show more amplitude on the finish, suggesting it may be better with a year or more cellaring. Drink now to 1994. $17 (3/31/91) **88**
Chardonnay Henderson Valley 1986 $10 (5/15/88) **86**

CLOUDY BAY
Sauvignon Blanc Marlborough 1990: Very crisp and tight, with zingy citrus and fig aromas and flavors and hints of honey on the finish. Spicy notes add a nice touch. Drinkable now. $14 (4/15/92) **84**

COOPERS CREEK
Cabernet Sauvignon Huapai Valley 1989: Leans toward the herbal, vegetal spectrum of Cabernet. Offers hints of currant and berry, but it has more tea, herb and spice flavors, with a distinct tobacco note on the aftertaste. Drink after 1994. $10 (4/15/92) **79**

CORBANS
Chardonnay Marlborough 1986 $10 (5/15/88) **92**

HUNTER'S
Chardonnay Marlborough 1986 $13 (2/15/88) **87**

KUMEU RIVER
Chardonnay Kumeu 1990: Pulls out all the stops. Ripe, buttery aromas and rich butterscotch flavors add up to a lush, soft wine that makes a bold style statement. Honey and peach notes are beneath an overlay of oak aging. $28 (4/15/92) **88**
Chardonnay Kumeu 1989 $27 (12/31/90) **91**
Chardonnay Kumeu 1987 $29 (3/31/89) **93**
Merlot Cabernet Kumeu 1987 $18 (12/31/90) **87**

LONGRIDGE
Cabernet Sauvignon Hawke's Bay 1987: A fairly soft wine, but still bizarre. Intensely vegetal, the nice caramel and spice flavors on the finish are its only saving grace. Tasted three times. $10 (9/15/91) **68**
Chardonnay Hawke's Bay 1989: Medium in weight, with plenty of style, but it offers little in the way of fruit flavor. Spicy and oaky, with butter and almond notes on the finish. Drinkable now. $10 (7/15/91) **82**

MORTON
Chardonnay Hawke's Bay 1990: Bright and zingy, with definite pine aromas and flavors that lend an herbal edge to this sharply focused, appley wine. Drinkable now. $10 (7/15/91) **83**
Chardonnay Hawke's Bay White Label 1989: Aggressively tart and grassy in flavor, with a deep color, pungent aromas and grapefruity flavors. Concentrated, but rough in texture. Difficult to say if age will tone it down. $17 (4/15/92) **76**
Chardonnay Hawke's Bay Winemaker's Selection 1988: Very dark and golden in color, but for all its ripe fig, apple and honey aromas and flavors, it's not particularly dense or deep. Seems a bit tired, but the smooth texture and spicy flavors are appealing. Drink it up soon. Tasted twice. $13 (7/15/91) **78**

Key to Symbols

The scores reported here are the results of blind tastings conducted by our panel of senior editors. Wines that carry the initials below are results of individual tastings.

THE WINE SPECTATOR 100-POINT SCALE 95-100— Classic, a great wine; ***90-94***— Outstanding, superior character and style; ***80-89***—Good to very good, a wine with special qualities; ***70-79***—Average, drinkable wine that may have minor flaws; ***60-69***—Below average, drinkable but not recommended; ***50-59***—Poor, undrinkable, not recommended. "+"—With a score indicates a range; used primarily with barrel tastings to indicate a preliminary score.

SPECIAL DESIGNATIONS SS—Spectator Selection, CS—Cellar Selection, BB—Best Buy, ($NA)—Price not available, (NR)—Not released.

TASTER'S INITIALS (JG)—Jim Gordon, (HS)—Harvey Steiman, (JL)—James Laube, (JS)—James Suckling, (TM)—Thomas Matthews, (TR)—Terry Robards, (PM)—Per-Henrik Mansson, (BT)—Barrel Tasting (these wines were tasted blind from barrel samples), (CA-date)—*California's Great Cabernets* by James Laube, (CH-date)—*California's Great Chardonnays* by James Laube, (VP-date)—*Vintage Port* by James Suckling.

DATE TASTED Dates in parentheses represent the issue in which the rating was published.

Chardonnay Hawke's Bay Winemaker's Selection 1986 $12 (2/15/88) **90**
Chardonnay New Zealand Winery Reserve 1986 $38 (5/15/88) **90**

HOUSE OF NOBILO

Chardonnay Gisborne 1990: Crisp and lively, yet rich and almost sappy in texture. The flavors balance grapefruit, pineapple, vanilla and spice on the finish. An intense wine without a great deal of weight. Drinkable now, but should be better after 1993. From New Zealand. $15 (9/15/91) **91**
Chardonnay Gisborne Tietjen Vineyard Reserve 1989: Buttery and flavorful, with a smooth, almost unctuous texture, dripping with honey and butterscotch notes but weighing in with distinctive pear and pineapple flavors that persist into the finish. This wine evolves on the palate, offering different dimensions with each sip. Terrific now, but should improve through 1993. 4,800 cases made. $18 (9/15/91) **93**
Pinotage Huapai Valley 1988: May not remind you of Pinot Noir, but it has a nice character, with ripe, clean, spicy, peppery plum and currant notes and moderate tannins. Drink now through 1994. $15 (7/15/91) **82**

STONELEIGH

Chardonnay Marlborough 1989: Ripe and polished, with a real sense of elegance. This medium-weight wine has well-modulated apple, pear and lemon aromas and flavors and keeps giving on the long finish. Drinkable now. $11 (7/15/91) **86**

South Africa

ROOIBERG

Sauvignon Blanc Robertson 1991: Imagine a Sauvignon Blanc from the Mosel. Crisp, fresh and sappy, like a very dry Riesling. Likable and unusual. Has verve. 550 cases made. $8 (4/15/92) **84**
Syrah Goree 1989: Ripe, plummy and spicy, with generous fruit flavors on a medium-weight frame. Has a claretlike structure and definite Syrah flavors that linger on the finish. Drinkable now. 350 cases made. $11 (4/15/92) **82**

Yugoslavia

AVIA

Chardonnay Yugoslavia Primorska Region 1985: Simple but attractive apple, pear, melon and grapefruit flavors are light and fresh—more like a Chenin Blanc than a Chardonnay—but, then again, it's priced that way, too. Drink up. $3 (3/31/89) **77**
Merlot Yugoslavia Primorska Hrvatska-Istra 1985: Clean and innocuous. Light and fruity, with a smooth texture and spare flavors of plum and herbs. $3 (3/31/89) **75**

CANTERBURY

Cabernet Sauvignon Yugoslavia Istria 1985: Light and aromatic with buoyant cherry and strawberry flavors, a crisp texture and a touch of velvet from soft tannins. The flavors linger nicely. Drinkable now. $5.50 (9/30/89) BB **81**

LE SABLE

Cabernet Sauvignon Primorski Region 1986: Tanky, dirty and gamy. A flawed wine that's best to avoid. $4.50 (3/31/91) **64**
Pinot Noir Oplenac 1987: Despite the French name, there is nothing French about this woody wine that's drinkable, but not identifiable as Pinot Noir. A bit harsh on the finish. $4.50 (3/31/91) **70**

UNITED STATES
California/*Blush*

BANDIERA
White Zinfandel California 1988 $5.25 (6/15/89) **74**

BARON HERZOG
White Zinfandel California 1989: Clean and refreshing, from the pale pink color to the light berry flavors. Fresh, off-dry and simple. $7 (3/31/91) **79**
White Zinfandel California 1988 $6 (6/15/89) **80**

WILLIAM BATES
White Zinfandel California 1988 $4 (6/15/89) **72**

BEL ARBRES
White Zinfandel California 1988 $5.25 (6/15/89) **83**

BELVEDERE
White Zinfandel California Discovery Series 1988 $4 (6/15/89) **78**

BERINGER
White Zinfandel North Coast 1988 $7.50 (6/15/89) **72**

BLOSSOM HILL
White Zinfandel California 1988 $7/1.5L (6/15/89) **79**

BOEGER
White Zinfandel El Dorado 1988 $7.50 (6/15/89) **65**

BONNY DOON
Vin Gris de Cigare California 1990: Vibrant strawberry and spice notes keep this dry rosé interesting. The flavors are concentrated enough to last on the finish. A blend of 70 percent Grenache, 26 percent Mourvèdre and 4 percent Pinot Noir. $7 (7/15/91) BB **84**
Vin Gris de Cigare California 1989: If you could make lemonade out of watermelon, this is what it would taste like. Sweet-and-sour, slightly candied and with a welcome touch of black pepper spiciness, it's an interesting blend of Grenache and Mourvèdre, but not as flavorful as the '88. Drink now. $7.50 (10/31/90) **78**
Vin Gris de Cigare California 1988: A rosé you can drink with pleasure and find more than simple fruit to enjoy. This one has depth of blackberry and subtly earthy flavors that linger on the dry finish. More interesting to drink than most Chardonnay. $6.75 (7/31/89) BB **89**
Vin Gris de Cigare California 1987: Very pale pink, earthy and dry, with distinctive toasty, cherry flavors mingled with earthiness, which reminds us of rosé Champagne. Has more substance than you expect. $6.50 (4/15/89) **84**

BRUTOCAO
White Zinfandel Mendocino 1987 $7 (6/15/89) **69**

BUEHLER
White Zinfandel Napa Valley 1988 $6 (6/15/89) **88**

CALERA
Pinot Noir Blanc California 1990: An off-dry, refreshing, effusive rosé overflowing with fresh cherry and strawberry flavors. Charming, but with enough Pinot Noir flavor to satisfy diehard red-wine drinkers. 1,400 cases made. $7 (10/31/91) BB **84**

CASTORO
White Zinfandel San Luis Obispo 1988 $6 (6/15/89) **67**

CHATEAU SOUVERAIN
White Zinfandel California 1988 $5.75 (6/15/89) **77**

CHRISTIAN BROTHERS
White Zinfandel Napa Valley 1988 $5.50 (6/15/89) **77**

CRESTON
White Zinfandel San Luis Obispo 1988: Lively and attractive. A gentle, supple wine with minty, herbal, currant and cherry flavors that offer nice finesse and a lovely, round almost sweet finish. Drink now. $7 (6/15/89) **86**

DE LOACH
White Zinfandel Russian River Valley 1990: Frankly pink in color, with lots of watermelon and raspberry aromas and flavors. More or less a nice rosé, with little to distinguish it. $7.50 (3/31/91) **77**
White Zinfandel Russian River Valley 1988 $7.50 (6/15/89) **82**

DELICATO
White Zinfandel California 1988 $5.25 (6/15/89) **73**

FENESTRA
White Zinfandel Livermore Valley 1987 $5 (6/15/89) **80**

FETZER
White Zinfandel California 1988 $7 (6/15/89) **85**

E. & J. GALLO
White Grenache California 1987: Pale pink, very fruity, sweet and simple. Watermelon and strawberry aromas become sugary on the palate. A decent quaff served very cold. $3.50 (4/15/89) **72**
White Zinfandel California 1988 $5 (6/15/89) **79**

GARLAND RANCH
White Zinfandel Monterey 1987 $6 (6/15/89) **75**

GLEN ELLEN
Aleatico California Blanc de Noirs Barrel Fermented Imagery Series 1990: A dryish, soft, fragrant rosé, with appealing peach, orange, cream and spice aromas and flavors that linger nicely on the finish. Drink soon. 420 cases made. $12 (3/31/92) **87**
White Zinfandel California Proprietor's Reserve 1989: Somewhat sweet yet crisp and flavorful, with strawberry and apple notes. Good in its style. $5 (12/31/90) **80**
White Zinfandel California Proprietor's Reserve 1988 $5.75 (6/15/89) **84**

GRAND CRU
White Zinfandel California 1988 $5 (6/15/89) **73**

Key to Symbols

The scores reported here are the results of blind tastings conducted by our panel of senior editors. Wines that carry the initials below are results of individual tastings.

THE WINE SPECTATOR 100-POINT SCALE 95-100—Classic, a great wine; ***90-94***—Outstanding, superior character and style; ***80-89***—Good to very good, a wine with special qualities; ***70-79***—Average, drinkable wine that may have minor flaws; ***60-69***—Below average, drinkable but not recommended; ***50-59***—Poor, undrinkable, not recommended. "+"—With a score indicates a range; used primarily with barrel tastings to indicate a preliminary score.

SPECIAL DESIGNATIONS SS—Spectator Selection, CS—Cellar Selection, BB—Best Buy, ($NA)—Price not available, (NR)—Not released.

TASTER'S INITIALS (JG)—Jim Gordon, (HS)—Harvey Steiman, (JL)—James Laube, (JS)—James Suckling, (TM)—Thomas Matthews, (TR)—Terry Robards, (PM)—Per-Henrik Mansson, (BT)—Barrel Tasting (these wines were tasted blind from barrel samples), (CA-date)—*California's Great Cabernets* by James Laube, (CH-date)—*California's Great Chardonnays* by James Laube, (VP-date)—*Vintage Port* by James Suckling.

DATE TASTED Dates in parentheses represent the issue in which the rating was published.

HAGAFEN
Pinot Noir Blanc California 1989: Deep pink in color, it's simple and round, tasting of canned peaches and sugared strawberries. $6 (3/31/91) **74**

HOP KILN
White Zinfandel Russian River Valley 1988 $6.75 (6/15/89) **88**

INGLENOOK-NAVALLE
White Zinfandel California NV $7.50/1.5L (6/15/89) **69**

KARLY
White Zinfandel Amador County 1988 $7 (6/15/89) **76**

KENWOOD
White Zinfandel Sonoma Valley 1988 $6.75 (6/15/89) **86**

CHARLES KRUG
White Zinfandel North Coast 1988 $6 (6/15/89) **72**

LOS HERMANOS
White Zinfandel California 1988 $8/1.5L (6/15/89) **61**

MADRONA
White Zinfandel El Dorado 1988 $5.25 (6/15/89) **76**

MANISCHEWITZ
White Zinfandel Sonoma County 1989: Has an off-putting earthy aroma, but the sweet strawberry flavor is pleasant if simple, and it finishes clean. $6 (3/31/91) **77**

LOUIS M. MARTINI
White Zinfandel Napa Valley 1988 $5.50 (6/15/89) **81**

PAUL MASSON
White Zinfandel California 1988 $7/1.5L (6/15/89) **74**

MCDOWELL VALLEY
Grenache Rosé McDowell Valley Les Vieux Cépages 1990: Dry and lightly fruity, offering pleasant, spicy overtones to the basic watermelon and strawberry aromas and flavors. Hints at leather on the finish. A pleasant drink. $7.50 (6/15/91) BB **82**
Grenache Rosé McDowell Valley Les Vieux Cépages 1989: Off-dry, but it has very clean, rich cherry and strawberry flavors and hints of lemon and pepper making it more interesting. A good California picnic wine—drink it instead of Beaujolais. 3,700 cases made. $6.50 (10/31/90) BB **82**

MIRASSOU
White Zinfandel California 1988 $6.50 (6/15/89) **75**

CK MONDAVI
White Zinfandel California 1988 $5.25 (6/15/89) **85**

ROBERT MONDAVI
White Zinfandel California 1988 $5.50 (6/15/89) **80**

J.W. MORRIS
White Zinfandel California 1988 $5 (6/15/89) **73**

NAPA RIDGE
White Zinfandel Lodi 1988 $6 (6/15/89) **75**

NORTH COAST CELLARS
White Zinfandel North Coast 1987 $6 (6/15/89) **68**

J. PEDRONCELLI
White Zinfandel Sonoma County 1988: Lovely peach and apricot flavors in a fresh, crisp, easy-to-drink, enjoyable style. Very refreshing and well made. Apple nuances come through on the finish. 1,700 cases made. $6 (6/15/89) **87**

JOSEPH PHELPS
Grenache Rosé California Vin du Mistral 1990: Very fruity and fresh, with a brilliant color and lovely pepper-scented blackberry and cherry aromas and flavors that last through the long finish. Dry, lively, refreshing and nicely balanced. 3,000 cases made. $9 (6/15/91) BB **87**
Grenache Rosé California Vin du Mistral 1989: Has lots of red-wine flavors—predominantly peppery cherry and watermelon—in a shocking pink wine. Dry and fruity, with a smooth texture and decent length. Drink now. 1,200 cases made. $9 (11/30/90) **84**

REDWOOD VALLEY
White Zinfandel California 1987 $6/1.5L (6/15/89) **66**

RIVERSIDE FARM
White Zinfandel California 1988 $5.25 (6/15/89) **80**

SANTINO
White Zinfandel Amador County 1988 $5 (6/15/89) **87**

SAUSAL
White Zinfandel Alexander Valley 1988 $6 (6/15/89) **70**

SEBASTIANI
White Zinfandel California 1988 $5 (6/15/89) **69**

AUGUST SEBASTIANI
White Zinfandel California 1988 $7.50/1.5L (6/15/89) **65**

SEGHESIO
White Zinfandel Northern Sonoma 1988 $5.50 (6/15/89) **84**

SHENANDOAH
White Zinfandel Amador County 1988 $6 (6/15/89) **81**

SIMI
Rosé of Cabernet Sauvignon Sonoma County 1990: A raucous combination of sweet red pepper, celery and beet flavors in a slightly sweet rosé. Has plenty of flavor, but lacks harmony. An odd wine that might be great with spicy food. Tasted twice. Not as good as most years. $7 (4/30/92) **77**
Rosé of Cabernet Sauvignon Sonoma County 1988: Crisp, clean and pleasant, with a bright pink color, a bit of sweetness, and spicy, fresh fruit flavors. $7 (11/15/89) **81**

STEVENOT
White Zinfandel Amador County 1989: Crisp, dry and flavorful, with a firm structure and decent flavors of cherry and strawberry giving it substance. $5 (12/31/90) BB **84**

SUTTER HOME
White Zinfandel California 1990: $5.50 (3/31/91) **77**
White Zinfandel California 1989: Sweet and very simple. Tastes like watermelon. Soft, with no crispness. $4.50 (12/31/90) **68**
White Zinfandel California 1988 $5.25 (6/15/89) **77**

IVAN TAMAS
White Zinfandel Mendocino 1988 $5.75 (6/15/89) **85**

WEIBEL
White Zinfandel Mendocino 1988 $5 (6/15/89) **65**

WEINSTOCK
White Zinfandel Sonoma County 1989: The light fragrance of strawberries is promising, but the

acidity can't save the sweet berry flavors from being cloying. $8 (3/31/91) **75**

WILLIAM WHEELER
White Zinfandel Sonoma County Young Vines 1988 $6 (6/15/89) **84**

CABERNET FRANC

AUSTIN
Cabernet Franc Santa Barbara County 1988: Earthy, weedy aromas and flavors dominate the plum and tomato notes in this otherwise well-balanced, almost elegant wine. Not everyone will appreciate the funky aromas, however. Drinkable now. 560 cases made. $12 (11/15/90) **76**

CHATEAU CHEVRE
Cabernet Franc Napa Valley 1985 $16 (7/31/88) **85**

CLOS PEGASE
Cabernet Franc California 1988: Extremely vegetal, with strong, bitter, metallic sulfur flavors. Hard to warm up to. Tasted twice, with identical scores. 318 cases made. $14.50 (10/15/91) **69**

CONGRESS SPRINGS
Cabernet Franc Santa Cruz Mountains 1986: Focused and concentrated like a narrow beam of light, but very woody and toasty on top of the classy raspberry flavors, mouthfilling and very long. A very different style of wine, but one that should develop well with cellaring until at least 1993 to '95. $18 (7/31/89) **88**

COSENTINO
Cabernet Franc Napa County 1987: Firm, woody and tannic, with a simple core of plum- and cherry-scented fruit that lacks concentration. Drink now to 1994. $12.50 (9/30/89) **75**
Cabernet Franc North Coast 1988: Stalky, herbal, vegetal notes interrupt the currant and berry flavors. Has a rich, warm texture, but it's too herbal for some tastes. Ready now through 1994. 500 cases made. $16 (11/15/91) **80**
Cabernet Franc North Coast 1986 $14 (7/31/88) **92**

DEHLINGER
Cabernet Franc Russian River Valley 1989: A lean, tough texture and cooked plum and currant flavors compete with a strong herbal component. The weeds win on the nose, the fruit wins on the finish. Tasted twice. 400 cases made. $12 (3/31/92) **75**
Cabernet Franc Russian River Valley 1988: A soft, ripe, lighter style of wine, featuring pretty plum, cherry, and cedar flavors of moderate depth and intensity. Not too tannic. Drink now, or cellar through 1994. $13 (4/30/91) **84**

GLEN ELLEN
Cabernet Franc Alexander Valley Imagery Series 1988: Firm and somewhat tannic, with ripe blueberry and currant flavors at a modest level of intensity. Soft in the middle and hard around the edges. Needs until 1993 or '94 to crack the tannins. 613 cases made. $16 (3/31/92) **86**

GUENOC
Cabernet Franc Lake County 1985: Weedy and vegetal flavors are intense and pungent, straightforward and blunt. Would probably be better blended with a strong Cabernet. On its own, it's wanting. $12 (2/15/89) **70**

GUNDLACH BUNDSCHU
Cabernet Franc Sonoma Valley Rhinefarm Vineyards 1989: A fresh, fruity, broad wine with blueberry and blackberry flavors and firm tannins. A nice mouthful of flavor. Tempting to drink now, but it should improve through about 1995. 1,560 cases made. $12 (2/29/92) **87**
Cabernet Franc Sonoma Valley Rhinefarm Vineyards 1987: Soft, ripe and generous, with floral nuances in the ripe plum and cherry flavors and substantial tannins that should hold it as it ages through 1994. A supple, engaging wine for short-term drinking. 690 cases made. $12 (9/15/90) **89**

ROBERT KEEBLE
Cabernet Franc Sonoma County 1988: Strongly herbal, almost stalky, a vegetal-tasting wine with just enough currant flavor to keep it honest. Tannic and harsh on the finish. It may be better after 1994, but there's no guarantee. Tasted twice, with consistent notes. 550 cases made. $12 (11/15/91) **79**

KONOCTI
Cabernet Franc Lake County 1988: Grapey and supple, with plum and raspberry notes, this easy-drinking style speaks well but not loudly for Cabernet Franc. Balanced and not too tannic or rich. Drink now. 1,610 cases made. $9.50 (2/28/91) **83**

LA JOTA
Cabernet Franc Howell Mountain 1988: A lovely expression of Cabernet Franc. Layers of currant, plum, vanilla and spice notes are neatly woven together, with a pretty, spicy aftertaste. Demands attention with its elegance, grace and flavors. Has smooth, round tannins. Ready now through 1994. $28 (8/31/91) **89**
Cabernet Franc Howell Mountain 1986: Big, rich, dense and concentrated with a supple texture of fine tannins. Very ripe currant, spice and anise notes are already complex and enticing. Has a touch of bitterness on the finish from tannins. Drink now or hold. $25 (10/15/89) **81**

MADRONA
Cabernet Franc El Dorado 1986: Tastes rough and drying, with lingering astringency and oakiness on the finish. The deep color doesn't help the muffled flavors. 552 cases made. $11 (3/31/92) **73**

NELSON ESTATE
Cabernet Franc Sonoma County 1987: Has pretty oak flavors, but is only moderately deep and intense on the palate, with attractive herb, olive and plum flavors. Not too tannic. 600 cases made. $16 (4/30/91) **82**

NEYERS
Cabernet Franc Napa Valley 1987: Resinous herbal aromas and flavors tend to diminish the otherwise appealing plum and cassis flavors, but the overall effect is lean and woody. Maybe cellaring until 1994 will soften it. $16 (11/15/90) **79**

PARDUCCI
Cabernet Franc Mendocino County 1989: Firm and fruity, with a velvety texture and generous currant and vanilla aromas and flavors that persist into the finish. Drinkable now. $10 (11/15/91) **85**

SEBASTIANI ESTATES
Cabernet Franc California 1988: Earthy, medicinal flavors are hard to look past. The fruit is drying and disjointed, giving way to taut, tight tannins that are green and bitter. Drink now to 1994. $8.50 (7/15/91) **77**

SHENANDOAH
Cabernet Franc Amador County Varietal Adventure Series 1989: Pleasantly fruity, with soft, rich plum, currant and cherry flavors that are mildly tannic, but the flavors persist, finishing with depth and complexity. Drink now, or cellar through 1995. 390 cases made. $10 (8/31/91) **87**

WHITEHALL LANE
Cabernet Franc Napa Valley 1988: Complex and supple with a pretty array of spice, vanilla, currant and chocolate flavors, all wrapped tightly in oak and tannins, but beautifully proportioned. Drink now to 1995. 430 cases made. $18.50 (11/15/90) **88**

CABERNET SAUVIGNON & BLENDS

ABREU
Cabernet Sauvignon Napa Valley Madrona Ranch 1987: Ripe, rich and concentrated, with plenty of flavor. The currant, plum, anise and oak notes are deep and integrated, but also supported by firm, intense tannins. Has a sense of polish and finesse, but it will need until 1996 to soften. 400 cases made. $25 (7/31/91) **89**

ACACIA
Cabernet Sauvignon Napa Valley 1984 $15 (12/15/86) **75**

ADELAIDA
Cabernet Sauvignon Paso Robles 1987: Very flavorful, rich and fruity, with beautifully articulated berry, currant and cherry flavors that emerge with the aromas of wildflowers and continue through the finish. Delicately laced with oak, firmly tannic, well balanced and complex. 1,338 cases made. $14 (2/28/91) **89**
Cabernet Sauvignon Paso Robles 1983: A simple, decent, drinkable, barbecue-style quaffer, certainly nothing special but it has ripe Cabernet flavor and firm tannins. Could stand up to grilled meats. Drink now to 1994. $12 (12/15/89) **75**
Cabernet Sauvignon Paso Robles 1981 $7.25 (3/01/84) **88**

ADLER FELS
Cabernet Sauvignon Napa Valley 1980 $10 (10/01/84) **74**

ALEXANDER VALLEY VINEYARDS
Cabernet Sauvignon Alexander Valley 1991: Young and effusively fruity, with fermentation aromas of ripe grapes, flowers and spice. A toddler of a wine that doesn't appear to have any oak aging yet. Hard to judge. 12 percent Merlot. (NR) (5/15/92) (BT) **86+**
Cabernet Sauvignon Alexander Valley 1990 (NR) (5/15/91) (BT) **90+**
Cabernet Sauvignon Alexander Valley 1989 $14 (5/15/91) (BT) **85+**
Cabernet Sauvignon Alexander Valley 1988: Smooth, velvety and flavorful, with well-defined plum and currant aromas and flavors. A harmonious wine that keeps ladling on the flavor through a long finish. Drinkable now, but should benefit from cellaring through 1994. 10,277 cases made. $12 (9/30/91) **88**
Cabernet Sauvignon Alexander Valley 1987: An elegant style, with herb, cedar and currant aromas and flavors, echoing plum and coffee on the gentle finish. A smooth, subtle wine for early enjoyment, probably best to drink now or in 1993. Rel: $12 Cur: $15 (5/31/90) **87**
Cabernet Sauvignon Alexander Valley 1986 Rel: $11.50 Cur: $16 (CA-3/89) **88**
Cabernet Sauvignon Alexander Valley 1985 Rel: $11 Cur: $18 (CA-3/89) **88**
Cabernet Sauvignon Alexander Valley 1984 Rel: $10.50 Cur: $18 (CA-3/89) **92**
Cabernet Sauvignon Alexander Valley 1984 Rel: $10.50 Cur: $18 (5/15/87) SS **93**
Cabernet Sauvignon Alexander Valley 1983 Rel: $10.50 Cur: $18 (CA-3/89) **90**
Cabernet Sauvignon Alexander Valley 1982 Rel: $10 Cur: $16 (CA-3/89) **90**
Cabernet Sauvignon Alexander Valley 1982 Rel: $10 Cur: $16 (11/01/84) SS **92**
Cabernet Sauvignon Alexander Valley 1981 Rel: $9 Cur: $18 (CA-3/89) **87**
Cabernet Sauvignon Alexander Valley 1980 Rel: $9 Cur: $16 (CA-3/89) **83**
Cabernet Sauvignon Alexander Valley 1979 Rel: $7 Cur: $18 (CA-3/89) **86**
Cabernet Sauvignon Alexander Valley 1978 Rel: $6.50 Cur: $20 (CA-3/89) **80**
Cabernet Sauvignon Alexander Valley 1976 Rel: $5.50 Cur: $18 (CA-3/89) **60**
Cabernet Sauvignon Alexander Valley 1975 Rel: $5.50 Cur: $20 (CA-3/89) **75**

ALMADEN
Cabernet Sauvignon Monterey County 1981 $5.85 (7/01/84) **80**
Cabernet Sauvignon Monterey County Vintage Classic Selection 1983 $5 (10/15/87) **74**

AMIZETTA
Cabernet Sauvignon Napa Valley 1985 $16 (5/31/88) **70**

S. ANDERSON
Cabernet Sauvignon Stags Leap District Richard Chambers Vineyard 1991: Deep, dark, plush and concentrated, a powerful expression of Cabernet Sauvignon, with layers of currant, plum, vanilla and chocolate flavors. Keeps pumping out the flavor. 22 percent Merlot and 3 percent Cabernet Franc. 630 cases made. (NR) (5/15/92) (BT) **92+**
Cabernet Sauvignon Stags Leap District Richard Chambers Vineyard 1990 (NR) (5/15/91) (BT) **90+**
Cabernet Sauvignon Stags Leap District Richard Chambers Vineyard 1989 (NR) (5/15/91) (BT) **90+**

ANDERSON'S CONN VALLEY
Cabernet Sauvignon Napa Valley Estate Reserve 1988: Rich and supple, it's nicely shaded by oak aging, with velvety tannins and warm currant, chocolate, anise, cherry and nutmeg flavors. The fruit and spice linger nicely on the finish. Well balanced, with firm acidity and gentle tannins. Tempting now, but should be better if cellared until about 1995. Second release from this new Napa vineyard. 1,371 cases made. $24 (11/15/91) **92**

ARCIERO
Cabernet Sauvignon Paso Robles 1986: Odd aromas are reminiscent of pepper, raspberry and wood, but berry flavors and soft tannins make this appealing and drinkable now. A decent red with pure fruit flavors. 3,500 cases made. $8.50 (11/15/90) **80**
Cabernet Sauvignon Paso Robles 1985 $6 (12/31/87) **77**

ARROWOOD
Cabernet Sauvignon Sonoma County 1988: Offers plenty of rich, ripe fruit, with layers of raspberry, currant, black cherry and spice flavors flanked by firm tannins. Packs in plenty of flavor and intensity while maintaining balance and harmony. Best around 1994. Rel: $23 Cur: $26 (11/15/91) **88**
Cabernet Sauvignon Sonoma County 1987: Ripe and full, with pretty black cherry and currant flavors and hints of toast and spice. Turns austere and tannic on the finish. Balanced, but needs time to mellow. Try in 1993 to '95. Rel: $22 Cur: $25 (11/15/90) **87**
Cabernet Sauvignon Sonoma County 1986: Plenty of expensive, new oak flavors, it's ripe and supple with currant and plum flavor that grows on you. The toasty and fruity aspects need time to pull together. Ready now. Rel: $20 Cur: $25 (10/15/89) **92**
Cabernet Sauvignon Sonoma County 1985 Rel: $19 Cur: $35 (12/15/88) **94**

VINCENT ARROYO
Cabernet Sauvignon Napa Valley 1987: Extremely tannic but packed with intense, deeply perfumed black cherry, currant, herb and spice flavors that are young and just beginning to evolve. Because of the level of tannin, this wine will need a minimum of six to eight years in the cellar to begin to soften. Not for the faint of heart. Drink 1996 to 2004. 651 cases made. $12 (11/15/90) **91**

AUDUBON
Cabernet Sauvignon Napa Valley 1985 $11 (6/15/88) **77**

AUSTIN
A Genoux Santa Barbara County 1986: The very herbal, woody aromas and flavors won't appeal to everyone, but this is basically a sound wine with full tannins and full body. $15 (12/15/89) **74**

BALDINELLI
Cabernet Sauvignon Shenandoah Valley 1983 $7.75 (11/30/88) **86**

BALVERNE
Cabernet Sauvignon Chalk Hill Laurel Vineyard 1983: A bit raw and coarse but there's some attractive Cabernet flavor, with currant, plum and spicy nuances. Like most '83s this will need some

time to come around, but it's developing some complexity and it has good length. Drink now to 1997 $13 (2/15/89) **86**
Cabernet Sauvignon Sonoma County 1982 $12 (8/31/88) **88**

BANDIERA
Cabernet Sauvignon Napa Valley 1988: Tight and firm, with simple but correct currant, cherry and berry flavors. Finishes a bit tough, but it's ready to drink now. $6.50 (4/15/92) BB **80**
Cabernet Sauvignon Napa Valley 1987: Sharply focused, with deep, rich, concentrated blackberry, plum, currant and mint notes that are woven together. Finishes with firm tannins, but the fruit keeps pouring through on the aftertaste. Best to cellar until 1994. $7 (11/15/91) BB **89**
Cabernet Sauvignon Napa Valley 1986: Firm and tasty, with plenty of cherry, spice and toast aromas and flavors on a sturdy structure. Drink now. $6.50 (10/31/89) BB **85**

LAWRENCE J. BARGETTO
Cabernet Sauvignon Sonoma County Cypress 1985: Firm and tannic for an essentially light wine, with flavors edging toward cranberry and cherry plus hints of tobacco. Drink now; it should be a welcome dinner companion. $8.50 (11/15/89) **79**

BARON HERZOG
Cabernet Sauvignon Sonoma County 1989: $11 (3/31/91) **73**
Cabernet Sauvignon Sonoma County Special Reserve 1986: $16 (3/31/91) **74**

BEAULIEU
Cabernet Sauvignon Napa Valley Beau Tour 1988: A tight, tough, greenish wine, with firm currant and cherry flavors. With cellaring it will soften. Best to start drinking now or in 1993. $7 (9/30/90) **79**
Cabernet Sauvignon Napa Valley Beau Tour 1987: One of the better '89s we've had so far. Smooth and flavorful, with buttery notes that start in the aroma and last through the spicy, long finish. Gets better with each sip. The apple, peach and honey flavors blend harmoniously. Drink now or in 1993. $8 (5/31/89) BB **81**
Cabernet Sauvignon Napa Valley Beau Tour 1986 $7 (10/31/88) **83**
Cabernet Sauvignon Napa Valley Beau Tour 1985 $7 (6/15/88) **83**
Cabernet Sauvignon Napa Valley Beau Tour 1982 $7.50 (10/15/86) **64**
Cabernet Sauvignon Napa Valley Georges de Latour Private Reserve 1990 (NR) (5/15/91) (BT) **85+**
Cabernet Sauvignon Napa Valley Georges de Latour Private Reserve 1989 (NR) (5/15/91) (BT) **85+**
Cabernet Sauvignon Napa Valley Georges de Latour Private Reserve 1987: Sharply focused on the ripe, rich black cherry, plum and currant flavors. Still tart, but very lively, with round, smooth, well-integrated tannins. Has a nice seasoned, spicy oak edge to it, but the fruit pours through on the finish. Try after 1996. Tastes better now than when first reviewed. Rel: $35 Cur: $39 (11/15/91) **92**
Cabernet Sauvignon Napa Valley Georges de Latour Private Reserve 1986 Rel: $31 Cur: $40 (3/31/91) (JL) **93**
Cabernet Sauvignon Napa Valley Georges de Latour Private Reserve 1985 Rel: $25 Cur: $46 (3/31/91) (JL) **95**
Cabernet Sauvignon Napa Valley Georges de Latour Private Reserve 1984 Rel: $25 Cur: $36 (3/31/91) (JL) **92**
Cabernet Sauvignon Napa Valley Georges de Latour Private Reserve 1983 Rel: $24 Cur: $31 (3/31/91) (JL) **82**
Cabernet Sauvignon Napa Valley Georges de Latour Private Reserve 1982 Rel: $24 Cur: $40 (3/31/91) (JL) **90**
Cabernet Sauvignon Napa Valley Georges de Latour Private Reserve 1982 Rel: $24 Cur: $40 (3/15/87) CS **93**
Cabernet Sauvignon Napa Valley Georges de Latour Private Reserve 1981 Rel: $24 Cur: $35 (3/31/91) (JL) **86**
Cabernet Sauvignon Napa Valley Georges de Latour Private Reserve 1980 Rel: $24 Cur: $49 (3/31/91) (JL) **93**
Cabernet Sauvignon Napa Valley Georges de Latour Private Reserve 1980 Rel: $24 Cur: $49 (9/16/85) SS **93**
Cabernet Sauvignon Napa Valley Georges de Latour Private Reserve 1979 Rel: $21 Cur: $55 (3/31/91) (JL) **87**
Cabernet Sauvignon Napa Valley Georges de Latour Private Reserve 1979 Rel: $21 Cur: $55 (3/01/84) SS **93**
Cabernet Sauvignon Napa Valley Georges de Latour Private Reserve 1978 Rel: $19 Cur: $61 (3/31/91) (JL) **90**
Cabernet Sauvignon Napa Valley Georges de Latour Private Reserve 1977 Rel: $16 Cur: $45 (3/31/91) (JL) **79**
Cabernet Sauvignon Napa Valley Georges de Latour Private Reserve 1976 Rel: $19 Cur: $58 (3/31/91) (JL) **88**
Cabernet Sauvignon Napa Valley Georges de Latour Private Reserve 1975 Rel: $16 Cur: $53 (3/31/91) (JL) **83**
Cabernet Sauvignon Napa Valley Georges de Latour Private Reserve 1974 Rel: $12 Cur: $77 (3/31/91) (JL) **79**
Cabernet Sauvignon Napa Valley Georges de Latour Private Reserve 1973 Rel: $9 Cur: $56 (3/31/91) (JL) **75**
Cabernet Sauvignon Napa Valley Georges de Latour Private Reserve 1972 Rel: $6 Cur: $46 (3/31/91) (JL) **71**
Cabernet Sauvignon Napa Valley Georges de Latour Private Reserve 1971 Rel: $8 Cur: $60 (3/31/91) (JL) **79**
Cabernet Sauvignon Napa Valley Georges de Latour Private Reserve 1970 Rel: $8 Cur: $135 (3/31/91) (JL) **93**
Cabernet Sauvignon Napa Valley Georges de Latour Private Reserve 1969 Rel: $6.50 Cur: $110 (3/31/91) (JL) **92**
Cabernet Sauvignon Napa Valley Georges de Latour Private Reserve 1968 Rel: $6 Cur: $170 (3/31/91) (JL) **92**
Cabernet Sauvignon Napa Valley Georges de Latour Private Reserve 1967 Rel: $5.25 Cur: $105 (3/31/91) (JL) **82**
Cabernet Sauvignon Napa Valley Georges de Latour Private Reserve 1966 Rel: $5.25 Cur: $145 (3/31/91) (JL) **87**
Cabernet Sauvignon Napa Valley Georges de Latour Private Reserve 1965 Rel: $5.25 Cur: $115 (3/31/91) (JL) **77**
Cabernet Sauvignon Napa Valley Georges de Latour Private Reserve 1964 Rel: $4.25 Cur: $130 (3/31/91) (JL) **72**
Cabernet Sauvignon Napa Valley Georges de Latour Private Reserve 1963 Rel: $3.50 Cur: $115 (3/31/91) (JL) **74**
Cabernet Sauvignon Napa Valley Georges de Latour Private Reserve 1962 Rel: $3.50 Cur: $120 (3/31/91) (JL) **75**
Cabernet Sauvignon Napa Valley Georges de Latour Private Reserve 1961 Rel: $3.50 Cur: $200 (3/31/91) (JL) **77**
Cabernet Sauvignon Napa Valley Georges de Latour Private Reserve 1960 Rel: $3.50 Cur: $135 (3/31/91) (JL) **85**
Cabernet Sauvignon Napa Valley Georges de Latour Private Reserve 1959 Rel: $3.50 Cur: $330 (3/31/91) (JL) **89**
Cabernet Sauvignon Napa Valley Georges de Latour Private Reserve 1958 Rel: $3 Cur: $510 (3/31/91) (JL) **97**
Cabernet Sauvignon Napa Valley Georges de Latour Private Reserve 1957 Rel: $2.50 Cur: $240 (3/31/91) (JL) **69**
Cabernet Sauvignon Napa Valley Georges de Latour Private Reserve 1956 Rel: $2.50 Cur: $600 (3/31/91) (JL) **88**
Cabernet Sauvignon Napa Valley Georges de Latour Private Reserve 1955 Rel: $2.50 Cur: $550 (3/31/91) (JL) **85**
Cabernet Sauvignon Napa Valley Georges de Latour Private Reserve 1954 Rel: $2.50 Cur: $330 (3/31/91) (JL) **86**
Cabernet Sauvignon Napa Valley Georges de Latour Private Reserve 1953 Rel: $2.50 Cur: $600 (3/31/91) (JL) **91**
Cabernet Sauvignon Napa Valley Georges de Latour Private Reserve 1952 Rel: $2.50 Cur: $600 (3/31/91) (JL) **91**
Cabernet Sauvignon Napa Valley Georges de Latour Private Reserve 1951 Rel: $1.82 Cur: $1,000 (3/31/91) (JL) **92**
Cabernet Sauvignon Napa Valley Georges de Latour Private Reserve 1950 Rel: $1.82 Cur: $760 (3/31/91) (JL) **88**
Cabernet Sauvignon Napa Valley Georges de Latour Private Reserve 1949 Rel: $1.82 Cur: $950 (3/31/91) (JL) **88**
Cabernet Sauvignon Napa Valley Georges de Latour Private Reserve 1948 Rel: $1.82 Cur: $1,040 (3/31/91) (JL) **79**
Cabernet Sauvignon Napa Valley Georges de Latour Private Reserve 1947 Rel: $1.82 Cur: $1,350 (3/31/91) (JL) **89**
Cabernet Sauvignon Napa Valley Georges de Latour Private Reserve 1946 Rel: $1.47 Cur: $1,000 (3/31/91) (JL) **87**
Cabernet Sauvignon Napa Valley Georges de Latour Private Reserve 1945 Rel: $1.47 Cur: $700 (3/31/91) (JL) **70**
Cabernet Sauvignon Napa Valley Georges de Latour Private Reserve 1944 Rel: $1.47 Cur: $680 (3/31/91) (JL) **75**
Cabernet Sauvignon Napa Valley Georges de Latour Private Reserve 1943 Rel: $1.45 Cur: $500 (3/31/91) (JL) **87**
Cabernet Sauvignon Napa Valley Georges de Latour Private Reserve 1942 Rel: $1.45 Cur: $1,300 (3/31/91) (JL) **85**
Cabernet Sauvignon Napa Valley Georges de Latour Private Reserve 1941 Rel: $1.45 Cur: $1,200 (3/31/91) (JL) **89**
Cabernet Sauvignon Napa Valley Georges de Latour Private Reserve 1940 Rel: $1.45 Cur: $1,200 (3/31/91) (JL) **89**
Cabernet Sauvignon Napa Valley Georges de Latour Private Reserve 1939 Rel: $1.45 Cur: $1,500 (3/31/91) (JL) **91**
Cabernet Sauvignon Napa Valley Georges de Latour Private Reserve 1936 Rel: $1.45 Cur: $1,500 (3/31/91) (JL) **86**
Cabernet Sauvignon Napa Valley Rutherford 1990 (NR) (5/15/91) (BT) **85+**
Cabernet Sauvignon Napa Valley Rutherford 1989: Minty, herbal aromas and bright currant flavors make this an appealing wine with a moderate structure that turns gentle and inviting on the finish. Drinkable now. $11 (3/31/92) **81**
Cabernet Sauvignon Napa Valley Rutherford 1988: Hard and tart in texture, with nicely focused cherry and spice aromas and flavors that are fresh and bright up front, echoing fruit and chocolate on the finish. Should be at its best after 1994. Rel: $11 Cur: $13 (7/15/91) **86**
Cabernet Sauvignon Napa Valley Rutherford 1987: Earthy and mushroomy, with pleasant bay leaf, currant and plum flavors that could be brighter and livelier. Tannins are in proportion and the finish fans out. Best to cellar until 1993 to '95. Tasted twice. Rel: $10 Cur: $13 (12/15/90) **85**
Cabernet Sauvignon Napa Valley Rutherford 1986 $11.25 (9/15/89) **85**
Cabernet Sauvignon Napa Valley Rutherford 1985 Rel: $9.50 Cur: $13 (6/15/88) **85**
Cabernet Sauvignon Napa Valley Rutherford 1984 Rel: $9.50 Cur: $15 (8/31/87) **78**
Cabernet Sauvignon Napa Valley Rutherford 1983 Rel: $6.50 Cur: $12 (6/15/87) **80**
Cabernet Sauvignon Napa Valley Rutherford 1982 Rel: $8.50 Cur: $14 (4/16/86) **81**
Cabernet Sauvignon Napa Valley Rutherford 1981 Rel: $9 Cur: $19 (5/16/85) **81**
Cabernet Sauvignon Napa Valley Rutherford 1980 Rel: $9 Cur: $30 (6/01/85) (JL) **88**
Cabernet Sauvignon Napa Valley Rutherford 1979 Rel: $9 Cur: $25 (6/01/85) (JL) **89**
Cabernet Sauvignon Napa Valley Rutherford 1970 $70 (6/01/85) (JL) **90**

BELLEROSE
Cabernet Sauvignon Dry Creek Valley Reserve Cuvée 1987: Very ripe, with prune, plum and black cherry flavors, but it turns sharply tannic and it's a bit hollow in the middle. Has crisp acidity on the finish, but it's an austere style that might be better in 1994. 1,268 cases made. $18 (11/15/91) **83**
Cuvée Bellerose Sonoma County 1986: Soft and velvety, with generous cassis and toast aromas and flavors, and sufficient tannins to need cellaring until 1993 to '94. Has enough restraint to suggest it may be an elegant wine after a few years. $18 (1/31/90) **83**
Cuvée Bellerose Sonoma County 1985 $16 (12/15/88) **82**
Cuvée Bellerose Sonoma County 1984 $14 (11/15/87) **77**
Cuvée Bellerose Sonoma County 1983 $12 (1/31/87) **74**
Cuvée Bellerose Sonoma County 1980 $10.50 (11/01/84) **79**

BELVEDERE
Cabernet Sauvignon Alexander Valley Robert Young Vineyard Gifts of the Land 1985: Very flavorful and serious in structure, with tannins that are still too harsh to make it enjoyable to drink now. The flavors are ripe and pruny, with herbal and pickle accents. It's a toss-up whether the fruit will last until the tannins subside. Probably best to cellar until at least 1993. $16 (1/31/91) **81**
Cabernet Sauvignon Alexander Valley Robert Young Vineyard 1984 $13 (7/15/88) **88**
Cabernet Sauvignon Alexander Valley Robert Young Vineyard 1983 $12 (5/15/87) **88**
Cabernet Sauvignon Alexander Valley Robert Young Vineyard 1982 Rel: $12 Cur: $17 (12/01/85) SS **95**
Cabernet Sauvignon Lake County Discovery Series 1982 $4 (4/01/85) BB **80**
Cabernet Sauvignon Napa Valley Discovery Series 1982 $4 (2/16/86) **71**
Cabernet Sauvignon Napa Valley York Creek Vineyard 1983 $12 (12/31/87) **79**
Cabernet Sauvignon Napa Valley York Creek Vineyard 1982 $12 (9/15/86) **72**
Cabernet Sauvignon Sonoma County Discovery Series 1987: Simple, peppery and balanced, an easy-to-drink style that makes no attempt at pretension. Drink it now. $6 (6/15/90) **75**

BENZIGER
Cabernet Sauvignon Sonoma County 1988: Light in color, as well as in flavor, this well-

Key to Symbols

The scores reported here are the results of blind tastings conducted by our panel of senior editors. Wines that carry the initials below are results of individual tastings.

THE WINE SPECTATOR 100-POINT SCALE *95-100*—Classic, a great wine; *90-94*—Outstanding, superior character and style; *80-89*—Good to very good, a wine with special qualities; *70-79*—Average, drinkable wine that may have minor flaws; *60-69*—Below average, drinkable but not recommended; *50-59*—Poor, undrinkable, not recommended. "+"—With a score indicates a range; used primarily with barrel tastings to indicate a preliminary score.

SPECIAL DESIGNATIONS SS—Spectator Selection, CS—Cellar Selection, BB—Best Buy, ($NA)—Price not available, (NR)—Not released.

TASTER'S INITIALS (JG)—Jim Gordon, (HS)—Harvey Steiman, (JL)—James Laube, (JS)—James Suckling, (TM)—Thomas Matthews, (TR)—Terry Robards, (PM)—Per-Henrik Mansson, (BT)—Barrel Tasting (these wines were tasted blind from barrel samples), (CA-date)—*California's Great Cabernets* by James Laube, (CH-date)—*California's Great Chardonnays* by James Laube, (VP-date)—*Vintage Port* by James Suckling.

DATE TASTED Dates in parentheses represent the issue in which the rating was published.

proportioned wine has pleasant strawberry, spice and vanilla aromas and flavors. Drinkable now. From Glen Ellen. $12 (11/15/91) **84**
Cabernet Sauvignon Sonoma County 1987: A beautiful wine at a great price. Rich, supple and generous, the pretty plum, cherry, spice and nutmeg flavors combine to make a complex, elegant wine. Delicious oak makes it tempting now, but it should improve through 1994 to '95. Rel: $10 Cur: $20 (9/30/90) SS **93**
Cabernet Sauvignon Sonoma County 1986: Supple and medium-bodied, showing fresh berry aromas, smooth flavors and a soft texture. Spice and berry flavors linger on the finish. Drink up now. $10 (7/31/89) **82**
Cabernet Sauvignon Sonoma Mountain 1988: A heavy dose of menthol, herb and bay leaf notes dominate the rich currant and cherry-tinged flavors. More concentrated than most '88s, but it's the herbs, not the fruit, that win out in this one. Drink in 1994. 2,200 cases made. $25 (11/15/91) **85**
Cabernet Sauvignon Sonoma Valley Estate Bottled 1987: Distinctively minty and herbal, with intense, ripe plum and strawberry flavors that are well integrated and balanced, finishing with a touch of tannin. Drink now to 1995. $12 (11/15/90) **85**
Cabernet Sauvignon Sonoma Valley 1986: Has faint hints of herbs and mint on the nose, with currant, plum and vegetal flavors on the palate. Elegantly balanced with attractive flavors. Drink now. 2,000 cases made. $17 (4/30/90) **78**
Cabernet Sauvignon Sonoma Valley 1985 $16 (12/15/88) **83**
A Tribute Sonoma Mountain 1988: A classy Cabernet blend, with supple, generous plum, nutmeg, currant, tobacco and raspberry flavors all woven together. Has a sense of harmony and finesse, and soft, mild tannins. Ready now through 1995. 800 cases made. $26 (1/31/92) **88**
A Tribute Sonoma Mountain 1987: Elegant and intense, with delicate, ripe plum, herb and chocolate flavors giving way to cedar and cherry on the finish. Balanced, rich and not too tannic, but not powerful. Loses intensity on the finish. Drink now. $20 (12/31/90) **85**

BERGFELD
Cabernet Sauvignon Napa Valley 1988: Has nice flavors and texture, offering a welcome balance of currant and berry flavors and spicy oak notes. A bit tannic, but soft at the center. Drinkable now for its classy flavors. $14 (11/15/91) **83**

BERINGER
Cabernet Sauvignon Knights Valley 1989 (NR) (5/15/91) (BT) **85+**
Cabernet Sauvignon Knights Valley 1988: Fresh and lively, with ripe plum, black cherry, spice and tea flavors and tannins that are nicely folded in on the aftertaste. Tempting now, but should smooth out with a few years' cellaring. Try in 1994. $16 (11/15/91) **86**
Cabernet Sauvignon Knights Valley 1987: Ripe and intense, with tightly knit, well-focused flavors of rich cherry, plum, herb and currant. The tannins are thick and strong, but not overbearing. Has a full, powerful finish. Tempting now, but best between 1993 and '98. $15.50 (11/15/90) **90**
Cabernet Sauvignon Knights Valley 1985 $12 (5/31/88) **87**
Cabernet Sauvignon Knights Valley 1983 $9 (4/15/87) **83**
Cabernet Sauvignon Knights Valley 1982 $9 (4/15/87) **90**
Cabernet Sauvignon Knights Valley 1981 $9 (10/01/85) **86**
Cabernet Sauvignon Knights Valley 1980 $8 (2/15/84) **88**
Cabernet Sauvignon Napa Valley Chabot Vineyard 1989 (NR) (5/15/91) (BT) **85+**
Cabernet Sauvignon Napa Valley Chabot Vineyard 1988 (NR) (5/15/90) (BT) **90+**
Cabernet Sauvignon Napa Valley Chabot Vineyard 1987 (NR) (4/15/89) (BT) **90+**
Cabernet Sauvignon Napa Valley Chabot Vineyard 1986 $30 (CA-3/89) **93**
Cabernet Sauvignon Napa Valley Chabot Vineyard 1985: Mature and spicy, with warm, well-focused cedar, plum, currant and cherry notes, firm tannins and a lingering finish. Still a bit rough around the edges, but close to its peak. Hold until 1994. 800 cases made. $30 (11/15/91) **90**
Cabernet Sauvignon Napa Valley Chabot Vineyard 1984: Soft and ripe, but still tannic, with lightly jammy raspberry and cherry aromas and flavors and hints of cedar and spice on the lean finish. The tannins tend to obscure the delicate flavors. Cellar until 1993 to '95. 925 cases made. Rel: $30 Cur: $34 (9/15/90) **85**
Cabernet Sauvignon Napa Valley Chabot Vineyard 1983 Rel: $27 Cur: $34 (CA-3/89) **85**
Cabernet Sauvignon Napa Valley Chabot Vineyard 1982 Rel: $25 Cur: $40 (CA-3/89) **89**
Cabernet Sauvignon Napa Valley Chabot Vineyard 1981 Rel: $23 Cur: $40 (CA-3/89) **87**
Cabernet Sauvignon Napa Valley Private Reserve 1989 (NR) (5/15/91) (BT) **85+**
Cabernet Sauvignon Napa Valley Private Reserve 1988 (NR) (5/15/90) (BT) **95+**
Cabernet Sauvignon Napa Valley Private Reserve 1987: Complex, fascinating and beautifully built. Deep currant, cherry, anise, leather, earth and herbal notes vie for attention. It shows a different facet with every sip. The tannins are firm and powerful without being overwhelming. Best to wait until 1998 to 2000. Rel: $40 Cur: $47 (10/31/91) **94**
Cabernet Sauvignon Napa Valley Private Reserve 1986: Deliciously rich and concentrated, the layers of herb, mint, cherry and plum flavors are tightly wound together and framed by toasty oak and firm tannins. Elegant and stylish, this beautifully proportioned wine echoes fruit and oak. Drink 1994 to 2001. 4,000 cases made. Rel: $35 Cur: $49 (9/15/90) CS **95**
Cabernet Sauvignon Napa Valley Private Reserve 1985: Enormously deep, rich and concentrated with layers of currant, cherry, plum, coffee and spice notes set off by toasty oak. A remarkably complex wine that echoes fruit flavors on the finish. Firm tannins on the finish suggest cellaring until 1994. Rel: $30 Cur: $75 (12/15/89) SS **95**
Cabernet Sauvignon Napa Valley Private Reserve 1984 Rel: $25 Cur: $45 (2/15/89) CS **94**
Cabernet Sauvignon Napa Valley Private Reserve 1983 Rel: $19 Cur: $44 (CA-3/89) **89**
Cabernet Sauvignon Napa Valley Private Reserve 1982 Rel: $19 Cur: $51 (CA-3/89) **92**
Cabernet Sauvignon Napa Valley Private Reserve 1981 Rel: $18 Cur: $31 (6/01/86) CS **92**
Cabernet Sauvignon Napa Valley Private Reserve Lemmon-Chabot Vineyard 1981 Rel: $23 Cur: $40 (4/15/87) **93**
Cabernet Sauvignon Napa Valley Private Reserve Lemmon-Chabot Vineyard 1980 Rel: $20 Cur: $42 (8/01/84) CS **93**
Cabernet Sauvignon Napa Valley Private Reserve Lemmon Ranch Vineyard 1978 Rel: $15 Cur: $36 (4/30/87) **92**
Cabernet Sauvignon Napa Valley Private Reserve Lemmon Ranch Vineyard 1977 Rel: $12 Cur: $75 (CA-3/89) **88**
Cabernet Sauvignon Napa Valley Private Reserve State Lane Vineyard 1980 Rel: $15 Cur: $40 (CA-3/89) **85**
Cabernet Sauvignon Napa Valley Private Reserve State Lane Vineyard 1979 Rel: $15 Cur: $42 (CA-3/89) **89**

BLACK MOUNTAIN
Cabernet Sauvignon Alexander Valley Fat Cat 1986: Wonderfully rich currant, plum and cherry flavors are smooth and lush up-front, but the tannins and oak dominate the finish. The fruit fights through, but this needs until 1995 to mellow. 1,489 cases made. $20 (11/15/91) **86**
Cabernet Sauvignon Alexander Valley Fat Cat 1985: Has plenty of flavor, intensity and depth, but also a sense of elegance and finesse, with well-defined herb, bell pepper, chocolate and currant flavors that are complex and long on the finish. Should improve through 1993. $18 (4/30/90) **87**

BOEGER
Cabernet Sauvignon El Dorado 1987: Very ripe, fruity and generous, with plum, spice and cherry jam notes. Not too tannic and a bit fat around the edges, but it doesn't shortchange you on flavor or pleasure. Picks up attractive smoky oak flavors on the finish. Drink in 1993 to '95. 2,000 cases made. $11 (3/15/91) **85**
Cabernet Sauvignon El Dorado 1985: Mature Cabernet that's ready to drink. A simple style, some decent cherry flavors, but drink up now. $11 (2/15/89) **77**
Cabernet Sauvignon El Dorado 1984 $11 (5/31/88) **81**
Cabernet Sauvignon El Dorado 1983 $10 (8/31/87) **82**
Cabernet Sauvignon El Dorado 1980 $8.50 (4/16/84) **76**

JEAN CLAUDE BOISSET
Cabernet Sauvignon Napa Valley 1984 $7 (12/31/87) **72**
Cabernet Sauvignon Napa Valley 1981 $9 (5/01/85) **80**

BON MARCHE
Cabernet Sauvignon Alexander Valley 1989: This very fruity, supple, easy-to-drink wine offers bell pepper aromas, plum flavors and a lingering finish. Has plenty of flavor and not too much tannin. Drinkable now or in 1993. New from Buehler. 1,960 cases made. $8 (2/28/91) BB **87**

BRANDER
Bouchet Tête de Cuvée Santa Ynez Valley 1989: A flash of smoky oak adds class to the plum and cherry flavors, for a supple, spicy wine that's nearly ready to drink. Medium-bodied, not too tannic. 1,400 cases made. $20 (3/31/92) **84**

BRAREN PAULI
Cabernet Sauvignon Mendocino 1987: Lavishly oaked, with a strong dill and slight pickle flavor, but plenty of ripe currant, plum and berry flavors stand up to it. An exotic style that some may find too oaky, but there's much to admire with the flavors. Reasonably priced. Drink now to 1995. $8.50 (3/31/91) BB **84**

DAVID BRUCE
Cabernet Sauvignon California Vintner's Select 1983 $12.50 (9/30/86) **79**

BRUTOCAO
Cabernet Sauvignon Mendocino 1988: An appealing, straightforward wine with currant and strawberry flavors and moderate tannins. On the light side in texture, and ready to drink now through 1993. 2,000 cases made. $12.50 (3/31/92) **83**
Cabernet Sauvignon Mendocino 1986: Age has mellowed this smoky, cranberry-flavored wine, but it's still stiff on the finish. The spare flavors don't measure up to the nicely developing aromas. Good, but fairly tannic and lean. 1,500 cases made. $12.50 (3/31/92) **82**
Cabernet Sauvignon Mendocino 1982 $9 (11/30/88) **83**

BUEHLER
Cabernet Sauvignon Napa Valley 1988 (NR) (5/15/90) (BT) **80+**
Cabernet Sauvignon Napa Valley 1987: Despite some pretty black currant and cherry aromas, it comes across as disjointed and clumsy on the palate, with the oak flavors out of sorts. Flavors persist on the finish, picking up tobacco and hard oak flavors. Maybe time in the bottle will bring it together. Give it until 1993. 2,950 cases made. Rel: $16 Cur: $19 (7/31/90) **85**
Cabernet Sauvignon Napa Valley 1986: Jam-packed with rich, ripe, concentrated and slightly raw black cherry, currant and spicy oak flavors that are raw and lean on the finish. What's missing is refinement and subtlety. Drink now. Rel: $15 Cur: $18 (4/30/89) **85**
Cabernet Sauvignon Napa Valley 1985 Rel: $14 Cur: $18 (CA-3/89) **93**
Cabernet Sauvignon Napa Valley 1984 Rel: $13 Cur: $23 (CA-3/89) **87**
Cabernet Sauvignon Napa Valley 1983 Rel: $12 Cur: $23 (7/16/86) SS **93**
Cabernet Sauvignon Napa Valley 1982 Rel: $12 Cur: $28 (CA-3/89) **88**
Cabernet Sauvignon Napa Valley 1981 Rel: $11 Cur: $20 (CA-3/89) **85**
Cabernet Sauvignon Napa Valley 1980 Rel: $10 Cur: $25 (CA-3/89) **82**
Cabernet Sauvignon Napa Valley 1978 Rel: $10 Cur: $35 (CA-3/89) **87**

BUENA VISTA
Cabernet Sauvignon Carneros 1988: Crisp and vegetal, with flavors that run more toward rhubarb than currant, but it's smooth and refined enough for another sip. Drink now. $8 (11/15/91) **79**
Cabernet Sauvignon Carneros 1987: Herbal and bell pepper aromas tend to shoulder past the lean berry and cherry flavors in this balanced, graceful and supple wine that's definitely on the herbal side. Drinkable now. $11 (10/15/90) **83**
Cabernet Sauvignon Carneros 1986: Distinct for its richness and complexity, the tart cherry, currant and berry flavors are young and lively but quite enticing. Has smoke, vanilla and chocolate flavors on the finish. Tempting now but capable of aging. Best in 1993 to '1998. $11 (10/15/89) **91**
Cabernet Sauvignon Carneros 1985 $10 (11/15/88) **84**
Cabernet Sauvignon Carneros 1984 $10 (8/31/87) **94**
Cabernet Sauvignon Carneros 1983 $9.75 (6/15/87) **77**
Cabernet Sauvignon Carneros 1982 $11 (9/16/85) **85**
Cabernet Sauvignon Carneros 1981 $11 (2/16/85) **89**
Cabernet Sauvignon Carneros Private Reserve 1986: Has loads of rich, ripe, concentrated fruit flavor, with cherry, currant, herb and toasty oak. The lively acidity amplifies the flavors before the firm tannins kick in. Drink 1994 to 2000. 3,150 cases made. Rel: $25 Cur: $28 (10/15/90) **93**
Cabernet Sauvignon Carneros Private Reserve 1985: Intense yet elegant with firm tannins and lively ripe currant, black cherry and cranberry flavors that are tart and sharply focused. Finishes with a mouthful of berries. Drink 1995 to 2002. 2,900 cases made. Rel: $18 Cur: $26 (10/15/89) SS **94**
Cabernet Sauvignon Carneros Private Reserve 1984 Rel: $18 Cur: $25 (CA-3/89) **90**
Cabernet Sauvignon Carneros Private Reserve 1983 Rel: $18 Cur: $25 (CA-3/89) **87**
Cabernet Sauvignon Carneros Private Reserve 1982 Rel: $18 Cur: $30 (CA-3/89) **85**
Cabernet Sauvignon Carneros Private Reserve Special Selection 1981 Rel: $18 Cur: $30 (CA-3/89) **86**
Cabernet Sauvignon Carneros Special Selection 1980 Rel: $18 Cur: $28 (CA-3/89) **84**
Cabernet Sauvignon Carneros Special Selection 1979 Rel: $18 Cur: $35 (CA-3/89) **92**
Cabernet Sauvignon Carneros Special Selection 1978 Rel: $18 Cur: $50 (CA-3/89) **90**
Cabernet Sauvignon Sonoma County 1986: Plenty of rich, ripe fruit, tiers of plum, cherry, currant and violet flavors and intense tannins, but it's balanced. Needs time to mellow, but it has all the ingredients for greatness. Only patience is required. Drink in 1992 and beyond. $11 (11/15/89) **90**
Cabernet Sauvignon Sonoma Valley 1978 Rel: $12 Cur: $30 (6/01/86) **94**
Cabernet Sauvignon Sonoma Valley 1976 Rel: $12 Cur: $40 (CA-3/89) **66**
Cabernet Sauvignon Sonoma Valley 1975 Rel: $12 Cur: $30 (CA-3/89) **64**
Cabernet Sauvignon Sonoma Valley Cask 34 1977 Rel: $12 Cur: $40 (CA-3/89) **72**
Cabernet Sauvignon Sonoma Valley Cask 25 1974 Rel: $12 Cur: $37 (CA-3/89) **68**
L'Année Carneros 1986: A lean, muscular style, with a narrow band of flavor. Has subtle currant, cherry and berry flavors and aromas, crisp acidity and firm but not overpowering tannins. Well balanced. Start drinking in 1993 to '97. 350 cases made. $35 (2/28/91) **87**
L'Année Carneros 1984 $32/1.5L (2/15/88) **88**

BURGESS
Cabernet Sauvignon Napa Valley Vintage Selection 1987: Has a tough, woody edge to the currant and plum-tinged flavors, leaving a harsh, biting, tannic edge. Seems tart and lean, but perhaps with time it will be more generous. The finish provides a nice touch of fruit. Cellar until 1994 or '95. Rel: $20 Cur: $23 (10/15/91) **85**
Cabernet Sauvignon Napa Valley Vintage Selection 1986: Hard and tannic, with intense currant, coffee and cherry flavors that are tightly wound and in need of cellaring. The core of fruit is here for a fine wine, but it's a few years away from loosening up. Try in 1993 to '94. Tasted twice. Rel: $20 Cur: $23 (7/15/90) **88**
Cabernet Sauvignon Napa Valley Vintage Selection 1985: After showing minty, spicy aromas this settles into rich, mouthfilling currant and cherry flavors, smooth, supple and generous right through the finish. Thick enough to need until 1993 to '95 to develop more grace. Delicious already. Rel: $18 Cur: $22 (7/15/89) **92**
Cabernet Sauvignon Napa Valley Vintage Selection 1984 Rel: $17 Cur: $25 (CA-3/89) **93**
Cabernet Sauvignon Napa Valley Vintage Selection 1983 Rel: $17 Cur: $21 (CA-3/89) **87**
Cabernet Sauvignon Napa Valley Vintage Selection 1982 Rel: $16 Cur: $29 (CA-3/89) **88**
Cabernet Sauvignon Napa Valley Vintage Selection 1981 Rel: $16 Cur: $35 (CA-3/89) **88**

Cabernet Sauvignon Napa Valley Vintage Selection 1980 Rel: $16 Cur: $46 (CA-3/89) **88**
Cabernet Sauvignon Napa Valley Vintage Selection 1980 Rel: $16 Cur: $46 (5/01/84) SS **90**
Cabernet Sauvignon Napa Valley Vintage Selection 1979 Rel: $16 Cur: $43 (CA-3/89) **87**
Cabernet Sauvignon Napa Valley Vintage Selection 1978 Rel: $14 Cur: $47 (CA-3/89) **93**
Cabernet Sauvignon Napa Valley Vintage Selection 1977 Rel: $12 Cur: $38 (CA-3/89) **92**
Cabernet Sauvignon Napa Valley Vintage Selection 1976 Rel: $12 Cur: $40 (CA-3/89) **87**
Cabernet Sauvignon Napa Valley Vintage Selection 1975 Rel: $9 Cur: $37 (CA-3/89) **88**
Cabernet Sauvignon Napa Valley Vintage Selection 1974 Rel: $9 Cur: $65 (CA-3/89) **86**

BYINGTON
Cabernet Sauvignon Napa Valley 1987: Smells rich and fruity, then tightens up and turns tannic on the palate, but the forceful currant and black cherry flavors triumph on the finish. Tannic enough to want until 1994 or '95, but the flavors are well defined already. 1,450 cases made. $16 (11/15/91) **86**

DAVIS BYNUM
Cabernet Sauvignon Napa Valley Reserve Bottling 1984 $7 (12/15/87) **71**
Cabernet Sauvignon Sonoma County 1987: Herbal, toasty flavors dominate in this lean, austere style, offering plenty of tannin and not much fruit concentration to back it up. Try in 1993. 3,175 cases made. $10.50 (11/15/90) **79**
Cabernet Sauvignon Sonoma County 1986: Concentrated and chewy, with a solid core of cherry and currant flavor plus prominent grace notes of oak and bay leaf. Not too tannic, but it has a rough-and-tumble quality that needs cellaring through 1994. $10 (11/15/89) **84**

BYRON
Cabernet Sauvignon Central Coast 1985: Thick tarry and vegetal flavors override the purer cherry notes of Cabernet. Well balanced, it may have limited appeal. Try with spicy tomato-based pastas. Drink now or in 1993. $14 (12/15/89) **76**

CAFARO
Cabernet Sauvignon Napa Valley 1988: Hard and tannic, this lean-textured wine manages to show appealing currant and berry flavors behind a wall of tannin. Echoes cedar and wax notes on the finish. Needs until 1996 to '99. Tasted twice. 423 cases made. Rel: $25 Cur: $27 (11/15/91) **81**
Cabernet Sauvignon Napa Valley 1987: Black cherry, currant and spice notes make this dark, rich and attractive, but it comes up short on the finish, where it gets tight and austere. Drink now to 1994. $20 (11/15/90) **84**
Cabernet Sauvignon Napa Valley 1986: Elegant, with well-defined, supple currant, plum and violet flavors that are quite harmonious. The delicious flavors sneak up on you. Subtle. Drink now. $18 (11/15/89) **93**

CAIN
Cabernet Sauvignon Napa Valley Estate 1987: Herbal and oaky at first, but also very rich and ripe with layers of plum, currant, oak and cherry flavors that are elegantly styled and well proportioned. A very complete and exciting wine that's approachable now. Drink in 1993 to '98. 407 cases made. $25 (10/15/90) **92**
Cabernet Sauvignon Napa Valley 1986: A spicy, herbal style, with plenty of tightly packaged, well-focused, rich currant and cherry flavors. Firm, dry tannins and oak flavors emerge on the finish. Will need two to three years to soften. Start drinking 1993 to '96. $16 (8/31/90) **85**
Cabernet Sauvignon Napa Valley 1985: Fairly lean and tight, but generous in cherry and currant flavor that carries through to the somewhat austere finish. Given time, it should smooth out beautifully. Drink in 1993. $16 (4/15/89) **81**
Cabernet Sauvignon Napa Valley 1984 $14 (5/31/88) **79**
Cabernet Sauvignon Napa Valley 1983 $14 (8/31/87) **75**
Cabernet Sauvignon Napa Valley 1982 $11 (9/30/86) **78**
Five Napa Valley 1991: Tight, deep, rich and concentrated, with sharply focused currant, berry, chocolate and plum flavors that stay with you. The tannins are deep, but very fine, letting the fruit pour through. 4,300 cases made. (NR) (5/15/92) (BT) **92+**
Five Napa Valley 1990 (NR) (5/15/91) (BT) **90+**
Five Napa Valley 1989 (NR) (5/15/91) (BT) **90+**
Five Napa Valley 1987: Rich, smooth and complex, with pretty toasty oak notes and layers of sweet currant, plum, anise and black cherry flavors that are elegant and supple. Has firm tannins, and the flavors linger on the finish. Drink in 1995 to 2000. Tasted twice. $30 (4/30/91) **91**
Five Napa Valley 1986: Remarkably open and generous, a delicious wine with extraordinary balance of plum and cassis with hints of toast and vanilla adding appealing grace notes. A harmonious wine that's smooth enough to enjoy drinking now, but cellaring until 1993 to '95 wouldn't hurt. 4,000 cases made. $30 (2/15/90) **91**
Five Napa Valley 1985 $26 (6/15/89) **87**

CAKEBREAD
Cabernet Sauvignon Napa Valley 1988: Crisp and focused, with a solid core of red currant and plum flavors, tightly reined in with firm tannins. Oak contributes a major share to the flavor. Best after 1995. $24 (11/15/91) **86**
Cabernet Sauvignon Napa Valley 1987: Big, rich and lush with intense, concentrated black cherry, currant and plum flavors that are broad and complex, with a pretty smoky, toasty oak flavor that adds dimension to the flavor and texture package. A youngster; needs time to come together. Fruit echoes on the finish. Best to drink between 1994 and 2001. Rel: $18 Cur: $23 (10/15/90) **90**
Cabernet Sauvignon Napa Valley 1986: Fresh, clean and lively with plenty of black cherry, currant and plum-tinged Cabernet flavor with a note of mintiness. Firm tannins and toasty oak flavors bring up the rear. Drink now to 1998. 5,000 cases made. Rel: $18 Cur: $21 (8/31/89) **90**
Cabernet Sauvignon Napa Valley 1985 Rel: $17 Cur: $20 (CA-3/89) **84**
Cabernet Sauvignon Napa Valley 1984 Rel: $16 Cur: $25 (CA-3/89) **89**
Cabernet Sauvignon Napa Valley 1983 Rel: $16 Cur: $25 (CA-3/89) **77**
Cabernet Sauvignon Napa Valley 1982 Rel: $16 Cur: $28 (CA-3/89) **86**
Cabernet Sauvignon Napa Valley 1981 Rel: $16 Cur: $30 (CA-3/89) **88**
Cabernet Sauvignon Napa Valley 1980 Rel: $14 Cur: $30 (CA-3/89) **84**
Cabernet Sauvignon Napa Valley 1979 Rel: $13 Cur: $30 (CA-3/89) **82**
Cabernet Sauvignon Napa Valley 1978 Rel: $12 Cur: $35 (CA-3/89) **85**
Cabernet Sauvignon Napa Valley Rutherford Reserve 1986: Tight and somewhat tannic, with a real sense of elegance that allows the crisp plum, cherry and currant flavors to skim across the palate, setting off sparks of cedar, spice and tobacco along the way. Should be at its best after 1995. $43 (11/15/91) **89**

Key to Symbols

The scores reported here are the results of blind tastings conducted by our panel of senior editors. Wines that carry the initials below are results of individual tastings.

THE WINE SPECTATOR 100-POINT SCALE ***95-100***—Classic, a great wine; ***90-94***—Outstanding, superior character and style; ***80-89***—Good to very good, a wine with special qualities; ***70-79***—Average, drinkable wine that may have minor flaws; ***60-69***—Below average, drinkable but not recommended; ***50-59***—Poor, undrinkable, not recommended. "+"—With a score indicates a range; used primarily with barrel tastings to indicate a preliminary score.

SPECIAL DESIGNATIONS SS—Spectator Selection, CS—Cellar Selection, BB—Best Buy, ($NA)—Price not available, (NR)—Not released.

TASTER'S INITIALS (JG)—Jim Gordon, (HS)—Harvey Steiman, (JL)—James Laube, (JS)—James Suckling, (TM)—Thomas Matthews, (TR)—Terry Robards, (PM)—Per-Henrik Mansson, (BT)—Barrel Tasting (these wines were tasted blind from barrel samples), (CA-date)—*California's Great Cabernets* by James Laube, (CH-date)—*California's Great Chardonnays* by James Laube, (VP-date)—*Vintage Port* by James Suckling.

DATE TASTED Dates in parentheses represent the issue in which the rating was published.

Cabernet Sauvignon Napa Valley Rutherford Reserve 1985 $40 (CA-3/89) **85**
Cabernet Sauvignon Napa Valley Rutherford Reserve 1984: Generous and supple, with broad cherry and chocolate aromas and flavors, plus firm tannins. Drink now. $35 (2/15/90) **85**
Cabernet Sauvignon Napa Valley Rutherford Reserve 1983 $35 (CA-3/89) **88**
Cabernet Sauvignon Napa Valley Lot 2 1978 Rel: $12 Cur: $50 (CA-3/89) **86**

CALLAWAY
Cabernet Sauvignon California America's Cup 1989: Starts out fresh and lively, with strawberry and cherry flavors, but then the tannins clamp down and it turns tight and dry on the finish. Hard to say if and when it will come into better balance. Try around 1994. $10 (11/15/91) **82**

CAMBIASO
Cabernet Sauvignon Dry Creek Valley 1981 $4.75 (6/16/84) **60**

CANTERBURY
Cabernet Sauvignon California 1989: Simple pepper, herb and olive flavors mark this basic red wine that's best to drink now, while it's fresh. $6 (11/15/91) BB **80**

CAPARONE
Cabernet Sauvignon Santa Maria Valley Tepusquet Vineyard 1981 $10 (3/16/84) **80**

CAREY
Cabernet Sauvignon Santa Ynez Valley 1985: A very well-balanced wine for drinking now. Tastes very clean, it's medium-bodied, spicy and complex, with crisp cherry and plum flavors and moderate tannins. $10 (11/15/89) **83**
Cabernet Sauvignon Santa Ynez Valley 1984 $9 (3/31/88) **72**
Cabernet Sauvignon Santa Ynez Valley Alamo Pintado Vineyard 1981 $9.50 (6/16/84) **76**
Cabernet Sauvignon Santa Ynez Valley La Cuesta Vineyard 1983: A tight, tannic but enjoyable wine that needs until 1994 to taste its best. Tastes youthful and still pretty tannic, but the fruit flavors are up to the challenge, and spice and vanilla add complexity. $9.50 (12/15/89) **83**
Cabernet Sauvignon Santa Ynez Valley La Cuesta Vineyard Reserve 1987: Ripe cherry and currant flavors do battle with green bean and celery overtones that are particularly prominent in the aroma. Has a smooth, velvety texture and shows good length, but the flavors aren't for everyone. 1,100 cases made. $16 (5/31/91) **81**

CARMENET
Sonoma Valley 1989 (NR) (5/15/91) (BT) **85+**
Sonoma Valley 1988: Lavishly oaked, with buttery oak notes dominating the currant and black cherry flavors, but it's a stylish wine, with firm tannins and a sense of harmony and grace. The finish is long and full. Drink in 1995. Rel: $21 Cur: $25 (11/15/91) **87**
Sonoma Valley 1987: Firm and intense, with well-knit cherry, coffee, cedar, herb and currant flavors that are focused and balanced, picking up a touch of tobacco and spice along with gripping tannins. Best to cellar until 1993 to '98. Rel: $20 Cur: $24 (11/15/90) **89**
Sonoma Valley 1986: Rich and supple with good concentration of cassis, cherry, plum and spice and hints of vanilla and clove. Complex and elegant, with a long finish. Drink in 1993 to 1998. Rel: $20 Cur: $27 (7/31/89) **91**
Sonoma Valley 1985 Rel: $18.50 Cur: $28 (CA-3/89) **91**
Sonoma Valley 1984 Rel: $16 Cur: $30 (CA-3/89) **92**
Sonoma Valley 1983 Rel: $18 Cur: $27 (CA-3/89) **85**
Sonoma Valley 1982 Rel: $16 Cur: $33 (CA-3/89) **87**
Sonoma Valley 1982 Rel: $16 Cur: $33 (10/16/85) **93**

CARNEROS CREEK
Cabernet Sauvignon Los Carneros 1985: Lively and attractive, with distinct herb, currant, plum and cherry flavors that are complex and enticing, then the tannins kick in. Lots of flavor concentration and acidity. Drink 1995 to 2001. 1,500 cases made. $15 (10/31/89) **90**
Cabernet Sauvignon Napa Valley 1983 $10.50 (8/31/87) **62**
Cabernet Sauvignon Napa Valley 1982 $11 (2/16/86) **71**
Cabernet Sauvignon Napa Valley 1981 $12 (12/16/84) **77**
Cabernet Sauvignon Napa Valley Fay Vineyard 1982 $13.50 (5/15/87) **70**
Cabernet Sauvignon Napa Valley Reserve 1983 $13.50 (10/15/88) **83**

CASTORO
Cabernet Sauvignon Paso Robles Hope Farms 1986: A pleasant wine with simple yet correct black cherry, anise and currant notes that are balanced with firm tannins. Drink now. $8.50 (12/15/89) **80**

CAYMUS
Cabernet Sauvignon Napa Valley 1988: Smooth and velvety, a medium-weight wine, with complex, subtle tobacco- and chocolate-tinged plum and currant aromas and flavors. Graceful, harmonious and elegant, with plenty of flavor to develop. Best after 1995. $20 (1/31/92) **87**
Cabernet Sauvignon Napa Valley 1987: Cedar, vanilla, spice and currant aromas give way to similar flavors that are full-bodied and rich. The wonderful proportion of oak and tannins balances the solid core of supple fruit. But best between 1994 and 2001. A new wine that blends the Caymus Napa Estate and Napa Cuvée. Rel: $16 Cur: $23 (9/15/90) **93**
Cabernet Sauvignon Napa Valley 1986: Clearly the best regular Cabernet from Caymus yet. Complex, elegant and delicious already, with chocolate- and smoke-tinged plum and cherry aromas and flavors, supple, smooth and amazingly long on the finish. Uncommonly complex and elegant; worth cellaring until 1993 to '95, but you can drink it now. 4,000 cases made. Rel: $22 Cur: $33 (3/15/90) SS **94**
Cabernet Sauvignon Napa Valley 1985 Rel: $18 Cur: $55 (CA-3/89) **92**
Cabernet Sauvignon Napa Valley 1984 Rel: $16 Cur: $50 (CA-3/89) **91**
Cabernet Sauvignon Napa Valley 1983 Rel: $15 Cur: $54 (CA-3/89) **87**
Cabernet Sauvignon Napa Valley 1983 Rel: $15 Cur: $54 (11/30/86) CS **94**
Cabernet Sauvignon Napa Valley 1982 Rel: $14 Cur: $50 (CA-3/89) **90**
Cabernet Sauvignon Napa Valley 1981 Rel: $14 Cur: $52 (CA-3/89) **88**
Cabernet Sauvignon Napa Valley 1980 Rel: $12.50 Cur: $53 (CA-3/89) **90**
Cabernet Sauvignon Napa Valley 1979 Rel: $12 Cur: $63 (CA-3/89) **92**
Cabernet Sauvignon Napa Valley 1978 Rel: $12 Cur: $68 (CA-3/89) **87**
Cabernet Sauvignon Napa Valley 1977 Rel: $10 Cur: $36 (CA-3/89) **77**
Cabernet Sauvignon Napa Valley 1976 Rel: $10 Cur: $60 (CA-3/89) **85**
Cabernet Sauvignon Napa Valley 1975 Rel: $8.50 Cur: $85 (CA-3/89) **89**
Cabernet Sauvignon Napa Valley 1974 Rel: $7 Cur: $105 (2/15/90) (JG) **91**
Cabernet Sauvignon Napa Valley 1973 Rel: $6 Cur: $145 (CA-3/89) **93**
Cabernet Sauvignon Napa Valley 1972 Rel: $4.50 Cur: $110 (CA-3/89) **86**
Cabernet Sauvignon Napa Valley Cuvée 1986 $15 (8/31/89) **90**
Cabernet Sauvignon Napa Valley Cuvée 1985 $12 (7/15/88) **92**
Cabernet Sauvignon Napa Valley Cuvée 1984 $12 (8/31/87) **88**
Cabernet Sauvignon Napa Valley Special Selection 1987: A smashing wine, following in the wake of the great ones in 1984, '85 and '86. Bursting with cherry, plum and prune flavors. Coffee, anise, cedar and tea notes sneak in on the long, complex finish. Intense, but gentle, with tannins rapidly smoothing to a velvety texture. Almost drinkable now, but best in 1996 to 2000. 4,000 cases made. Rel: $60 Cur: $82 (10/31/91) CS **98**
Cabernet Sauvignon Napa Valley Special Selection 1986: A classic from an outstanding vintage. Effusively aromatic. with a complex mix of cedar, wildflower, ripe cherry, plum, chocolate, vanilla and anise flavors on a full-bodied frame. Firm but supple in texture. The finish lingers, indicating greatness. Seductive now, but probably best in 1997 and beyond. 1,350 cases made. Rel: $50 Cur: $122 (1/31/91) CS **98**
Cabernet Sauvignon Napa Valley Special Selection 1985: Has wonderful herb, tea, currant, black cherry and plum aromas, with rich, complex, tightly knit Cabernet flavors wrapped in ginger,

chocolate, vanilla and spice. While the flavors are showy now, they're still years away from reaching full maturity. The tannins are smooth and polished. Start drinking in 1997. 1,000 cases made. Rel: $50 Cur: $190 (4/30/90) **99**
Cabernet Sauvignon Napa Valley Special Selection 1984 Rel: $35 Cur: $185 (7/15/89) CS **98**
Cabernet Sauvignon Napa Valley Special Selection 1983 Rel: $35 Cur: $110 (CA-3/89) **91**
Cabernet Sauvignon Napa Valley Special Selection 1982 Rel: $35 Cur: $140 (CA-3/89) **92**
Cabernet Sauvignon Napa Valley Special Selection 1981 Rel: $35 Cur: $120 (CA-3/89) **93**
Cabernet Sauvignon Napa Valley Special Selection 1980 Rel: $30 Cur: $145 (CA-3/89) **92**
Cabernet Sauvignon Napa Valley Special Selection 1980 Rel: $30 Cur: $145 (3/16/86) SS **96**
Cabernet Sauvignon Napa Valley Special Selection 1979 Rel: $30 Cur: $220 (CA-3/89) **97**
Cabernet Sauvignon Napa Valley Special Selection 1979 Rel: $30 Cur: $220 (6/01/85) SS **93**
Cabernet Sauvignon Napa Valley Special Selection 1978 Rel: $30 Cur: $230 (CA-3/89) **97**
Cabernet Sauvignon Napa Valley Special Selection 1978 Rel: $30 Cur: $230 (6/16/84) CS **95**
Cabernet Sauvignon Napa Valley Special Selection 1976 Rel: $35 Cur: $430 (CA-3/89) **90**
Cabernet Sauvignon Napa Valley Special Selection 1975 Rel: $22 Cur: $250 (CA-3/89) **92**

CECCHETTI SEBASTIANI
Cabernet Sauvignon Alexander Valley 1986: Juicy, fresh and lively at this stage. Young raspberry aromas capture your attention and lead the way to similar flavors. Ripe but not very complex on the palate. Drink now. $8.50 (4/15/89) **83**
Cabernet Sauvignon Sonoma County 1983 $12.50 (9/30/86) **76**

CHALK HILL
Cabernet Sauvignon Chalk Hill 1988: Smooth and silky, with well-modulated cherry and plum aromas and flavors and hints of chocolate and coffee on the well-modulated finish. Drink now to 1995. A good value. $12 (6/15/91) **87**
Cabernet Sauvignon Chalk Hill 1983 $10 (11/15/86) **78**
Cabernet Sauvignon Chalk Hill 1982 $9 (11/01/85) **66**
Cabernet Sauvignon Chalk Hill 1981 $8 (4/01/84) **83**

CHAPPELLET
Cabernet Sauvignon Napa Valley Reserve 1987: The best Chappellet Cabernet in years. Focused and chewy, with powerful currant and berry aromas and flavors shaded by hints of cinnamon, nutmeg and bay leaf, all wrapped neatly in a tightly wound package that should require until 1998 to 2000 to settle all the tannins. 4,900 cases made. Rel: $18 Cur: $21 (10/15/91) **94**
Cabernet Sauvignon Napa Valley Reserve 1986 Rel: $18 Cur: $21 (CA-3/89) **92**
Cabernet Sauvignon Napa Valley Reserve 1985: Big and rich with plenty of attractive mint, vanilla, currant and cherry flavors and fine balance, although the flavors begin to fade on the finish. Still has some rough edges, but it scored much better than a bottle tasted in May 1989. Drink 1994 to '98. Rel: $20 Cur: $25 (2/15/90) **84**
Cabernet Sauvignon Napa Valley Reserve 1984 Rel: $18 Cur: $21 (CA-3/89) **87**
Cabernet Sauvignon Napa Valley 1983 Rel: $12 Cur: $17 (CA-3/89) **77**
Cabernet Sauvignon Napa Valley 1982 Rel: $9.25 Cur: $25 (CA-3/89) **80**
Cabernet Sauvignon Napa Valley 1981 Rel: $11 Cur: $25 (CA-3/89) **79**
Cabernet Sauvignon Napa Valley 1980 Rel: $18 Cur: $31 (CA-3/89) **91**
Cabernet Sauvignon Napa Valley 1979 Rel: $13 Cur: $25 (CA-3/89) **79**
Cabernet Sauvignon Napa Valley 1978 Rel: $13 Cur: $30 (CA-3/89) **88**
Cabernet Sauvignon Napa Valley 1977 Rel: $12 Cur: $24 (CA-3/89) **82**
Cabernet Sauvignon Napa Valley 1976 Rel: $12 Cur: $49 (CA-3/89) **76**
Cabernet Sauvignon Napa Valley 1975 Rel: $10 Cur: $37 (CA-3/89) **78**
Cabernet Sauvignon Napa Valley 1974 Rel: $7.50 Cur: $63 (CA-3/89) **70**
Cabernet Sauvignon Napa Valley 1973 Rel: $7.50 Cur: $65 (CA-3/89) **69**
Cabernet Sauvignon Napa Valley 1972 Rel: $6.50 Cur: $41 (CA-3/89) **67**
Cabernet Sauvignon Napa Valley 1971 Rel: $7.50 Cur: $60 (CA-3/89) **65**
Cabernet Sauvignon Napa Valley 1970 Rel: $7.50 Cur: $95 (CA-3/89) **93**
Cabernet Sauvignon Napa Valley 1969 Rel: $10 Cur: $110 (CA-3/89) **87**
Cabernet Sauvignon Napa Valley 1968 Rel: $5.50 Cur: $90 (CA-3/89) **88**

CHARTRONS
Claret California 1986: Austere and stalky with green tannins and green flavors. The currant, herb and cedary flavors turn vegetal and very dry on the aftertaste. A hint of prune comes through on the finish. A difficult wine to warm up to. Best to cellar until 1994 or '95, but it may always be stalky. $14.50 (11/15/91) **78**

CHATEAU CHEVALIER
Cabernet Sauvignon Napa Valley 1980 $11.25 (1/01/84) **82**

CHATEAU CHEVRE
Chevre Reserve Napa Valley 1986: Rich, full-bodied and ripe, with lavish oak, berry, currant and spice notes in a reserved, understated, austere sytle. Fruit echoes on the finish. Drink in 1994 to 2000. $25 (7/31/89) **88**

CHATEAU DIANA
Cabernet Sauvignon California Limited Edition 1989: Weedy and vegetal, with horsey notes, too. Turns dry and astringent. Even at $5 it's hard to get excited about. $5 (11/15/91) **69**
Cabernet Sauvignon California Limited Edition 1988: Light and simple, with thin, herb-scented currant flavors. Drinkable but uninspired. $5 (10/15/91) **72**
Cabernet Sauvignon California Limited Edition 1986: One of this winery's better efforts, especially at $5. Has structure and attractive flavors, with cedar, currant and plum flavors. It's also quite tannic and oaky, and in need of hearty fare. May always be tannic. Drink now to 1994. 1,000 cases made. $5 (10/15/91) BB **82**
Cabernet Sauvignon Central Coast Limited Edition 1984 $6 (11/30/88) BB **82**

CHATEAU MONTELENA
Cabernet Sauvignon Napa Valley 1991: Tough and gamy, with deeply concentrated currant and plum flavors that are kept alive by crisp acidity and firm, gritty tannins. Young Montelenas often taste this way. Not in oak yet. (NR) (5/15/92) (BT) **83+**
Cabernet Sauvignon Napa Valley 1987: Deep, ripe and powerful, with muscular currant, plum, anise and cherry flavors that are complex and concentrated. This rough-hewn style is focused and intense, with the kind of thick, tight tannins that may require cellaring until 1998. Rel: $30 Cur: $37 (10/31/91) SS **95**
Cabernet Sauvignon Napa Valley 1986: Packed with fruit and tannins, this has a massive concentration of fresh, ripe, rich currant and plum flavors and an edge of leathery, smoky oak. Needs years to approach its peak. Drink 1998 to 2008. Rel: $25 Cur: $35 (10/15/90) **93**
Cabernet Sauvignon Napa Valley 1985 Rel: $25 Cur: $57 (11/15/89) CS **92**
Cabernet Sauvignon Napa Valley 1984 Rel: $20 Cur: $55 (CA-3/89) **94**
Cabernet Sauvignon Napa Valley 1983 Rel: $18 Cur: $34 (CA-3/89) **92**
Cabernet Sauvignon Napa Valley 1983 Rel: $18 Cur: $34 (11/15/87) CS **93**
Cabernet Sauvignon Napa Valley 1982 Rel: $16 Cur: $50 (CA-3/89) **92**
Cabernet Sauvignon Napa Valley 1981 Rel: $16 Cur: $41 (CA-3/89) **80**
Cabernet Sauvignon Napa Valley 1980 Rel: $16 Cur: $56 (CA-3/89) **86**
Cabernet Sauvignon Napa Valley 1979 Rel: $16 Cur: $57 (CA-3/89) **87**
Cabernet Sauvignon Napa Valley 1978 Rel: $16 Cur: $84 (CA-3/89) **93**
Cabernet Sauvignon Napa Valley 1977 Rel: $12 Cur: $75 (CA-3/89) **94**
Cabernet Sauvignon North Coast 1976 Rel: $10 Cur: $75 (CA-3/89) **90**
Cabernet Sauvignon North Coast 1975 Rel: $9 Cur: $38 (CA-3/89) **86**
Cabernet Sauvignon Napa Valley 1974 Rel: $9 Cur: $95 (CA-3/89) **90**
Cabernet Sauvignon Sonoma Alexander Valley 1979 Rel: $14 Cur: $45 (CA-3/89) **88**
Cabernet Sauvignon Sonoma Alexander Valley 1978 Rel: $12 Cur: $68 (CA-3/89) **87**
Cabernet Sauvignon Sonoma Alexander Valley 1977 Rel: $12 Cur: $55 (CA-3/89) **91**
Cabernet Sauvignon Sonoma Alexander Valley 1974 Rel: $9 Cur: $88 (CA-3/89) **87**
Cabernet Sauvignon Sonoma Alexander Valley 1973 Rel: $8 Cur: $100 (CA-3/89) **87**

CHATEAU NAPA-BEAUCANON
Cabernet Sauvignon Napa Valley 1986 $15 (12/31/88) **85**

CHATEAU POTELLE
Cabernet Sauvignon Alexander Valley 1987: Soft and generous, with lots of minty eucalyptus aromas and flavors and a modest level of cherry and currant. Turns soft and drinkable on the finish. Best to drink soon. $16 (8/31/91) **83**
Cabernet Sauvignon Alexander Valley 1986: Ripe and soft, with supple black cherry and currant flavors, round, smooth tannins, good depth, and subtle oak shadings of dill and spice. It's balanced and forward enough to drink now to 1994. $14.50 (10/31/90) **84**
Cabernet Sauvignon Alexander Valley 1984 $13 (12/31/88) **83**

CHATEAU SOUVERAIN
Cabernet Sauvignon Alexander Valley 1990 (NR) (5/15/91) (BT) **85+**
Cabernet Sauvignon Alexander Valley 1989 (NR) (5/15/91) (BT) **90+**
Cabernet Sauvignon Alexander Valley 1988: Rich and full, with well-focused currant, black cherry and spicy oak notes. Well balanced for an '88, with soft tannins. Ready now through 1994. Tasted twice. $10 (11/15/91) **85**
Cabernet Sauvignon Alexander Valley 1987: Has firm tannins, but it's balanced and velvety enough in texture to allow the spicy black cherry and currant flavors to emerge. A stylish wine that needs until 1993 or '94 to resolve its tannins. $9.50 (11/15/90) **87**
Cabernet Sauvignon Alexander Valley 1986: Rich, smooth and seductive with pretty cherry, spice, plum and oak flavors that are quite appealing. Smoke and chocolate flavors battle with the tannins on the finish. $8.50 (11/15/89) BB **85**
Cabernet Sauvignon Alexander Valley Private Reserve 1991: Austere and closed, with hints of currant, berry and spice flavors peeking through. Tart and tannic on the finish, but the flavors and intensity are appealing. 25 percent Cabernet Franc. 2,500 cases made. (NR) (5/15/92) (BT) **87+**
Cabernet Sauvignon Alexander Valley Private Reserve 1987: A big, tannic, young wine that needs time to mellow. Tougher and tighter than most Alexander Valley Cabernets. Built for fans of the hearty, tough style. Try in 1995 if this is your style. 1,700 cases made. $15 (5/15/91) **83**
Cabernet Sauvignon North Coast Vintage Selection 1980 $13 (9/16/85) **83**
Cabernet Sauvignon Sonoma County 1985 $8 (11/30/88) **87**
Cabernet Sauvignon Sonoma County 1984 $8.50 (8/31/87) **83**
Cabernet Sauvignon Sonoma County Vintage Selection 1974 $50 (2/15/90) (JG) **84**

CHATEAU ST. JEAN
Cabernet Sauvignon Alexander Valley 1987: Elegant and lively, with a deep concentration of ripe, rich plum, cherry, currant and spice flavors and pretty oak shadings that echo toast and spice notes. Supple enough to drink now, but it has deceptively firm tannins and crisp acidity that bode well for cellaring. Drink in 1994 to 2000. $16 (6/30/91) SS **92**
Cabernet Sauvignon Alexander Valley 1986: Rich and supple, with good extract, herb, currant and cherry flavors with a halo of toasty vanilla oak and a touch of mineral and spice on the finish. Supple enough to drink now, but should improve through 1995. $19 (10/15/89) **90**
Cabernet Sauvignon Alexander Valley 1985 Rel: $19 Cur: $22.5 (11/15/88) **86**
Cabernet Sauvignon Sonoma County 1981 Rel: $15 Cur: $20 (11/30/86) **72**
Cabernet Sauvignon Sonoma Valley Wildwood Vineyards 1980 $17 (9/01/85) **82**
Cabernet Sauvignon Sonoma Valley Wildwood Vineyards 1979 $17 (7/01/84) **76**

CHESTNUT HILL
Cabernet Sauvignon California 1988: Fruity and lively, with plenty of blackberry and currant aromas and flavors, tart balance and an overlay of dill and smoky oak seasoning. Drinkable now. $7.50 (10/15/91) BB **81**
Cabernet Sauvignon Napa Valley 1983 $7 (10/31/86) BB **91**
Cabernet Sauvignon Sonoma County 1987: Despite the oakiness, there's a good amount of concentrated Cabernet flavor in this wine, as well as a good dose of tannin. Altogether well made for the price. Drink now. $9 (3/31/90) **80**
Cabernet Sauvignon Sonoma County 1985 $7.75 (10/15/88) **77**

CHIMNEY ROCK
Cabernet Sauvignon Stags Leap District 1991: Attractive currant, berry, pepper and cherry flavors are well defined for a wine of this age. Rough and tannic, though—about right for this stage. (NR) (5/15/92) (BT) **86+**
Cabernet Sauvignon Stags Leap District 1988 $18 (5/15/90) (BT) **80+**
Cabernet Sauvignon Stags Leap District 1987: An outstanding wine from a fine vintage. Crisp, with tight currant, plum, spice and oak flavors that fan out on the finish. The tannins are firm, suggesting this wine needs cellaring until 1995 or '96. $18 (7/31/91) SS **90**
Cabernet Sauvignon Stags Leap District 1986: Tart, rich, supple and silky with ripe currant, plum and spicy Cabernet flavors. Has the tannins for aging, but they don't bite back. Well proportioned, ready to drink now or hold through 1999. Rel: $15 Cur: $19 (9/30/89) **87**
Cabernet Sauvignon Stags Leap District 1985 Rel: $15 Cur: $19 (CA-3/89) **87**
Cabernet Sauvignon Stags Leap District 1984 Rel: $15 Cur: $19 (CA-3/89) **82**
Elevage Napa Valley 1991: Offers complex aromas and flavors, with smoky, buttery oak and a core of elegant currant and cherry-tinged flavor. A graceful young wine that's showing well now. 650 cases made. (NR) (5/15/92) (BT) **89+**

CHRISTIAN BROTHERS
Cabernet Sauvignon Napa Valley 1988: Ripe and broad, but with a definite earthy, sour edge to the flavors that persists into the finish. Best after 1993. $6.75 (11/15/91) **76**
Cabernet Sauvignon Napa Valley 1987: Smoky herb and dill flavors dominate the plum and currant notes, but the finish turns dry, harsh, woody and tannic. Hollow in the middle. Drink in 1993 and beyond. $7.50 (10/15/91) **79**
Cabernet Sauvignon Napa Valley 1986: A nicely balanced and polished wine, with modest dimensions and enough complexity to make it interesting. Cherry, coffee and spice flavors linger on the finish. Drink now to 1994. Rel: $9.50 Cur: $12 (11/15/90) **88**
Cabernet Sauvignon Napa Valley 1985 $8 (6/15/88) **90**
Cabernet Sauvignon Napa Valley 1984 $7 (10/15/87) BB **87**
Cabernet Sauvignon Napa Valley 1980 $6.75 (10/01/85) **58**
Montage Première Cuvée Bordeaux-Napa Valley NV $15 (10/15/88) **84**

CHRISTOPHE
Cabernet Sauvignon California 1988: Aims for complexity, with ripe, concentrated plum and currant flavors that build with spicy oak. Attractively balanced, with clean fruit and oak flavors on the finish, but it could use a little more drama. A fair price. Drink now to 1994. $9 (3/31/91) **83**
Cabernet Sauvignon California 1982 $4.50 (12/16/85) BB **85**
Cabernet Sauvignon Napa Valley Reserve 1987: Crisp and fruity, with generous currant, plum and red cherry aromas and flavors that turn spicy on the finish. Drinkable now, but the tannins could use until 1993 or '94 to settle. $12 (11/15/91) **83**
Cabernet Sauvignon Napa Valley Reserve 1986: Mint and eucalyptus aromas and flavors dominate, with just enough dark cherry flavor sneaking in on the finish to make it interesting. Comes off as earthy rather than lively. Drink soon. 2,636 cases made. $12 (11/15/90) **78**
Cabernet Sauvignon Napa Valley Reserve 1985: Earthy, pickle barrel aromas take too much away from the gentle Cabernet flavor, which gains in intensity through the finish. Maybe with cellaring until 1994 to '95 this will meld together, but at this point it's not our style. $12.50 (11/15/89) **74**
Cabernet Sauvignon Napa Valley Reserve 1983 $9.50 (3/31/88) **82**

CINNABAR
Cabernet Sauvignon Santa Cruz Mountains 1987: Dominated by herb, green bean, olive and black currant flavors, framed by hard tannins and oak. A tough, young wine that should be best between 1995 and '99. 714 cases made. $18 (3/31/91) **84**
Cabernet Sauvignon Santa Cruz Mountains 1986: Deliciously fruity with layers of cherry, plum and currant flavors that are refreshingly enticing with crisp acidity and firm tannins that promise further enhancement. Start drinking now, but it should last another decade. Limited availability. $15 (11/15/89) **93**
Cabernet Sauvignon Santa Cruz Mountains Saratoga Vineyard 1988: Firmly tannic and fairly oaky, but underneath are bright plum and cherry-scented fruit flavors. A crisp, hard-edged wine that may always be on the tannic side. Drink in 1994 to '98. 720 cases made. $20 (3/15/92) **82**

CLOS DU BOIS
Cabernet Sauvignon Alexander Valley 1988: Has modestly concentrated ripe black cherry and plum flavors, but the oak creates an odd cedary note that turns vegetal and dull on the aftertaste. Drink in 1994. $14 (7/15/91) **77**
Cabernet Sauvignon Alexander Valley 1987: Elegant, rich, typically Cabernet in style, with plummy, almost sweet fruit flavors and touches of tobacco and bell pepper. Moderate tannins. Drink now to 1994. 17 percent Cabernet Franc. $11 (2/15/90) **86**
Cabernet Sauvignon Alexander Valley 1986: Soft and ripe, with a rich velvety texture and herbal cherry flavors. An on-the-money Alexander Valley style, stylish and smoothly balanced, if a bit hot. Drink soon. $12 (5/31/89) **86**
Cabernet Sauvignon Alexander Valley 1985 $10.50 (4/15/88) **87**
Cabernet Sauvignon Alexander Valley 1984 $10 (6/15/87) **87**
Cabernet Sauvignon Alexander Valley 1981 $9 (3/01/86) **91**
Cabernet Sauvignon Alexander Valley Briarcrest Vineyard 1987: Pretty currant, vanilla, herb and spice flavors take on a chocolate edge. The round, smooth tannins let the fruit wash over on the finish. Still has enough tannins for cellaring until 1995. Rel: $18 Cur: $20 (11/15/91) **88**
Cabernet Sauvignon Alexander Valley Briarcrest Vineyard 1986: Soft, velvety and broad, with appealing herbal and floral aromas and flavors. Lush, ripe currant and cherry flavors linger on the finish. Drinkable now. Rel: $17 Cur: $20 (8/31/90) **87**
Cabernet Sauvignon Alexander Valley Briarcrest Vineyard 1985: Toasty, with herb and cherry flavors. Thick and supple, flanked by firm tannins and oak, and plenty of concentration and flavor that should be ready for drinking now. Rel: $16 Cur: $24 (6/15/89) **86**
Cabernet Sauvignon Alexander Valley Briarcrest Vineyard 1984 Rel: $16 Cur: $24 (CA-3/89) **87**
Cabernet Sauvignon Alexander Valley Briarcrest Vineyard 1983 Rel: $12 Cur: $28 (CA-3/89) **74**
Cabernet Sauvignon Alexander Valley Briarcrest Vineyard 1982 Rel: $12 Cur: $32 (CA-3/89) **66**
Cabernet Sauvignon Alexander Valley Briarcrest Vineyard 1981 Rel: $12 Cur: $30 (CA-3/89) **88**
Cabernet Sauvignon Alexander Valley Briarcrest Vineyard 1980 Rel: $12 Cur: $32 (CA-3/89) **80**
Cabernet Sauvignon Dry Creek Valley Proprietor's Reserve 1982 $19 (9/15/87) **88**
Cabernet Sauvignon Sonoma County 1980 $9 (7/01/84) **81**
Cabernet Sauvignon Sonoma County Dry Creek 1974 $40 (2/15/90) (JG) **74**
Marlstone Vineyard Alexander Valley 1987: A tightly knit, harmonious wine, with rich, intense layers of currant, herb, spice, chocolate and berry flavors that are neatly woven together. Firmly tannic on the finish, but the texture is supple enough to enjoy now. Best after 1996. $20 (7/31/91) **90**
Marlstone Vineyard Alexander Valley 1986: Soft and supple, with modest herb and vanilla-tinged cherry flavors and hints of beets or dill on the finish. This is a tasty wine with distinctive character. Smooth and likable. Drink now. Rel: $20 Cur: $23 (8/31/90) **85**
Marlstone Vineyard Alexander Valley 1985: Ripe and plump, with thick herbal and plum flavors that are soft and velvety on the palate. Tasty but unexciting. Ready soon. Rel: $19.50 Cur: $23 (6/15/89) **81**
Marlstone Vineyard Alexander Valley 1984 Rel: $19.50 Cur: $30 (CA-3/89) **89**
Marlstone Vineyard Alexander Valley 1983 Rel: $20 Cur: $25 (CA-3/89) **70**
Marlstone Vineyard Alexander Valley 1982 Rel: $16 Cur: $30 (CA-3/89) **79**
Marlstone Vineyard Alexander Valley 1981 Rel: $15 Cur: $30 (CA-3/89) **85**
Marlstone Vineyard Alexander Valley 1980 Rel: $15 Cur: $29 (CA-3/89) **77**
Marlstone Vineyard Alexander Valley 1979 Rel: $16 Cur: $38 (CA-3/89) **75**
Marlstone Vineyard Alexander Valley 1978 Rel: $16 Cur: $30 (CA-3/89) **72**

CLOS DU VAL
Cabernet Sauvignon Stags Leap District 1989 (NR) (5/15/91) (BT) **85+**
Cabernet Sauvignon Stags Leap District 1988: Young and tight, with currant, cherry and plum-tinged flavors, none of which dominates. A well-made wine, with more richness than most '88s, but it needs time to evolve and let the tannins soften. Oak adds a nice dimension on the finish. Drink after 1995. Rel: $18 Cur: $20 (3/31/92) **86**
Cabernet Sauvignon Stags Leap District 1987: Ripe and supple, with rich, generous plum, currant, black cherry, chocolate and spicy vanilla notes that are elegant and concentrated, offering finesse and grace. The tannins are smooth and round, and the finish is long and lingering. Best around 1995. Rel: $18.50 Cur: $22 (6/30/91) **92**
Cabernet Sauvignon Stags Leap District 1986: A spicy, exotic wine, with a supple, fleshy texture. Smooth and gentle on the palate, but ultimately generous, bordering on opulent. Plum, currant, chocolate and cedar flavors jostle for attention. Almost drinkable, but best to cellar at least until 1993 to '95. Rel: $17.50 Cur: $21 (5/31/90) **91**
Cabernet Sauvignon Stags Leap District 1985 Rel: $16 Cur: $28 (6/15/89) **90**
Cabernet Sauvignon Stags Leap District 1984 Rel: $15 Cur: $28 (CA-3/89) **92**
Cabernet Sauvignon Stags Leap District 1983 Rel: $15 Cur: $21 (CA-3/89) **86**
Cabernet Sauvignon Stags Leap District 1982 Rel: $13.25 Cur: $28 (CA-3/89) **88**
Cabernet Sauvignon Stags Leap District 1981 Rel: $12.50 Cur: $25 (CA-3/89) **82**
Cabernet Sauvignon Stags Leap District 1980 Rel: $12.50 Cur: $31 (CA-3/89) **88**
Cabernet Sauvignon Stags Leap District 1980 Rel: $12.50 Cur: $31 (2/01/84) CS **88**
Cabernet Sauvignon Stags Leap District 1979 Rel: $12.50 Cur: $35 (CA-3/89) **90**
Cabernet Sauvignon Stags Leap District 1978 Rel: $12 Cur: $37 (CA-3/89) **92**
Cabernet Sauvignon Stags Leap District 1977 Rel: $10 Cur: $28 (CA-3/89) **89**
Cabernet Sauvignon Stags Leap District 1975 Rel: $9 Cur: $40 (CA-3/89) **89**
Cabernet Sauvignon Stags Leap District 1974 Rel: $7.50 Cur: $71 (CA-3/89) **91**
Cabernet Sauvignon Stags Leap District 1973 Rel: $6 Cur: $70 (CA-3/89) **86**
Cabernet Sauvignon Stags Leap District 1972 Rel: $6 Cur: $75 (CA-3/89) **90**

Key to Symbols

The scores reported here are the results of blind tastings conducted by our panel of senior editors. Wines that carry the initials below are results of individual tastings.

THE WINE SPECTATOR 100-POINT SCALE ***95-100***—Classic, a great wine; ***90-94***—Outstanding, superior character and style; ***80-89***—Good to very good, a wine with special qualities; ***70-79***—Average, drinkable wine that may have minor flaws; ***60-69***—Below average, drinkable but not recommended; ***50-59***—Poor, undrinkable, not recommended. "+"—With a score indicates a range; used primarily with barrel tastings to indicate a preliminary score.

SPECIAL DESIGNATIONS SS—Spectator Selection, CS—Cellar Selection, BB—Best Buy, ($NA)—Price not available, (NR)—Not released.

TASTER'S INITIALS (JG)—Jim Gordon, (HS)—Harvey Steiman, (JL)—James Laube, (JS)—James Suckling, (TM)—Thomas Matthews, (TR)—Terry Robards, (PM)—Per-Henrik Mansson, (BT)—Barrel Tasting (these wines were tasted blind from barrel samples), (CA-date)—*California's Great Cabernets* by James Laube, (CH-date)—*California's Great Chardonnays* by James Laube, (VP-date)—*Vintage Port* by James Suckling.

DATE TASTED Dates in parentheses represent the issue in which the rating was published.

Cabernet Sauvignon Napa Valley Gran Val 1985 $8.50 (5/31/88) **88**
Cabernet Sauvignon Napa Valley Gran Val 1984 $8.50 (2/15/87) BB **85**
Cabernet Sauvignon Napa Valley Gran Val 1982 $7.50 (4/16/84) **88**
Cabernet Sauvignon Napa Valley Joli Val 1988: Has bright currant and raspberry flavors and moderate tannins and acidity. Not as concentrated and focused as it could be, but it's fine for everyday drinking. $13 (7/31/91) **82**
Cabernet Sauvignon Napa Valley Joli Val 1986: Has an austere style, lean, firm and compact with earthy tobacco and currant notes that gain depth and complexity on the palate. Needs cellaring until 1994. 5,000 cases made. $12.50 (12/15/89) **87**
Cabernet Sauvignon Napa Valley 1976 Rel: $9 Cur: $55 (CA-3/89) **82**
Reserve Stags Leap District 1985: Rich, complex, balanced and beautifully focused, with tiers of pretty currant, black cherry, smoky, toasty oak and subtle herb seasoning. It's supple, well proportioned and not too tannic, and the flavors linger long and full on the finish. Drink 1993 to '99 and beyond. 750 cases made. Rel: $45 Cur: $53 (11/15/90) **94**
Reserve Stags Leap District 1982 Rel: $28 Cur: $40 (CA-3/89) **90**
Cabernet Sauvignon Stags Leap District Reserve 1979 Rel: $25 Cur: $55 (CA-3/89) **92**
Cabernet Sauvignon Stags Leap District Reserve 1979 Rel: $25 Cur: $55 (9/01/84) SS **91**
Cabernet Sauvignon Stags Leap District Reserve 1978 Rel: $30 Cur: $64 (CA-3/89) **94**
Cabernet Sauvignon Stags Leap District Reserve 1977 Rel: $20 Cur: $53 (CA-3/89) **87**
Cabernet Sauvignon Stags Leap District Reserve 1973 Rel: $10 Cur: $100 (CA-3/89) **90**

CLOS PEGASE
Cabernet Sauvignon Napa Valley 1986: Smells attractive and tastes smooth and fruity, with lots of cherry, plum and herb flavors lingering on the finish, but it's not especially intense or grand. The spice, chocolate and toast nuances on the finish are nice. Drinkable now. $16.50 (9/30/90) **88**
Cabernet Sauvignon Napa Valley 1985 $17 (5/31/88) **86**
Hommage California 1987: Oak gives this wine intense vanilla flavor, but there are also plenty of ripe plum and currant flavors that are elegant and lively. Not too tannic, it's ready to drink now, but probably will be at its peak between 1994 and '98. 1,000 cases made. $20 (8/31/91) **90**

CLOS ROBERT
Cabernet Sauvignon Napa Valley Proprietor's Reserve 1984 $7 (12/31/87) **71**

CLOVERDALE RANCH
Cabernet Sauvignon Alexander Valley Estate Cuvée 1989: Nicely balanced and broad in flavor, with plum, spice and herb notes in a softly tannic texture. Very pleasant, even a bit complex, with a tasty finish. 1,650 cases made. $11 (3/31/92) **84**

B.R. COHN
Cabernet Sauvignon Napa Valley Silver Label 1988: This is a new, less-expensive silver label. Bold and rich, with intense, concentrated plum, currant, black cherry and herb notes that are framed by toasty, buttery oak. Loses power on the finish. Big and chewy now; needs cellaring until 1995 or so. 2,000 cases made. $12 (9/30/91) **87**
Cabernet Sauvignon Sonoma Valley Olive Hill Vineyard 1990 (NR) (5/15/91) (BT) **85+**
Cabernet Sauvignon Sonoma Valley Olive Hill Vineyard 1989 (NR) (5/15/91) (BT) **85+**
Cabernet Sauvignon Sonoma Valley Olive Hill Vineyard 1988: Rich and oaky, but with a pretty seam of smooth, polished currant, herb, plum, chocolate and vanilla flavors that fan out on the finish. The firm tannins suggest cellaring until 1993 to '96. $25 (5/15/91) **89**
Cabernet Sauvignon Sonoma Valley Olive Hill Vineyard 1987: A lavishly oaked wine, with rich, ripe, intense cherry and bold currant flavors. But it's also very elegant, with firm yet integrated tannins. The smoky, meaty flavors play off the fruit, givig it complexity and depth. Delicious now, but it can age through 1994. Rel: $25 Cur: $28 (6/30/90) **92**
Cabernet Sauvignon Sonoma Valley Olive Hill Vineyard 1986: Has great concentration, style, power and grace, with intense ripe black cherry and currant flavors flanked by spice and rich cedar aromas from oak. Should be magnificent by 1994 to '96. Rel: $18 Cur: $26 (5/31/89) **94**
Cabernet Sauvignon Sonoma Valley Olive Hill Vineyard 1985 Rel: $16 Cur: $50 (CA-3/89) **94**
Cabernet Sauvignon Sonoma Valley Olive Hill Vineyard 1984 Rel: $15 Cur: $35 (CA-3/89) **93**

COLONY
Cabernet Sauvignon Sonoma County 1982 $7 (3/16/86) BB **89**

CONCANNON
Cabernet Sauvignon Livermore Valley 1983 $11.50 (6/15/87) **77**
Cabernet Sauvignon Livermore Valley 1981 $12 (12/16/84) **82**
Cabernet Sauvignon Livermore Valley Reserve 1987: Weedy black currant and olive flavors are complemented by plum notes in this balanced wine, and the vegetal notes don't dominate, they blend in. Not too tannic. Drink now to 1994. $16 (7/15/91) **83**
Cabernet Sauvignon Livermore Valley Reserve 1985: A big, deep, rich and flavorful Cabernet with lots of cherry, spice and cedary nuances that add complexity and dimension. Well balanced and supple, yet backed with tannins for aging. Try now to 1994. $13.50 (2/15/89) **87**

CONN CREEK
Cabernet Sauvignon Napa Valley Barrel Select 1987: Tight and tough, with a firmly tannic texture and modest cherry, tobacco and currant aromas and flavors that get richer on the finish, hinting at prune and brown sugar. Best to drink after 1995. $17 (7/15/91) **87**
Cabernet Sauvignon Napa Valley Barrel Select 1986: Four different bottles, tasted blind and on different days, tasted corky. Best to avoid. Rel: $15 Cur: $18 (2/28/91) **55**
Cabernet Sauvignon Napa Valley Barrel Select 1985: A rich, smooth, complex and supple wine, with finely focused, elegant currant, black cherry, spicy oak and mint notes gently woven together. The tannins sneak up on the finish, but it's very well balanced, with harmony and finesse. Start drinking in 1994 to '96. 4,500 cases made. Rel: $15 Cur: $18 (9/15/90) **90**
Cabernet Sauvignon Napa Valley Barrel Select Lot 79 1984 Rel: $13 Cur: $22 (CA-3/89) **86**
Cabernet Sauvignon Napa Valley Barrel Select 1983 Rel: $13 Cur: $25 (CA-3/89) **82**
Cabernet Sauvignon Napa Valley Barrel Select 1982 Rel: $12 Cur: $22 (CA-3/89) **85**
Cabernet Sauvignon Napa Valley 1981 Rel: $14 Cur: $19 (CA-3/89) **85**
Cabernet Sauvignon Napa Valley 1980 Rel: $13 Cur: $35 (CA-3/89) **88**
Cabernet Sauvignon Napa Valley 1979 Rel: $13 Cur: $60 (CA-3/89) **77**
Cabernet Sauvignon Napa Valley 1977 Rel: $12 Cur: $27 (CA-3/89) **90**
Cabernet Sauvignon Napa Valley 1976 Rel: $12 Cur: $26 (CA-3/89) **86**
Cabernet Sauvignon Napa Valley 1974 Rel: $9 Cur: $210 (CA-3/89) **94**
Cabernet Sauvignon Stags Leap District 1973 Rel: $9 Cur: $70 (CA-3/89) **92**
Cabernet Sauvignon Napa Valley Barrel Select Private Reserve 1987 $19 (4/15/89) (BT) **90+**
Cabernet Sauvignon Napa Valley Barrel Select Private Reserve 1986: Elegant, refined and beautifully proportioned, with plum, anise, herb, currant, tea and blackberry flavors that are complex and enticing. Not too tannic. Built to age another decade, but you can start drinking it in 1993. 2,000 cases made. Rel: $37 Cur: $41 (12/15/90) **91**
Cabernet Sauvignon Napa Valley Barrel Select Private Reserve 1985: The intense black cherry, currant, cedar and earth notes offer wonderful harmony and finesse in this rich, complex and supple style. Tannins emerge on the finish, but it's very well made and balanced, with strong fruit flavors. Try in 1995 to '97. 1,000 cases made. Rel: $30 Cur: $33 (9/15/90) **91**
Cabernet Sauvignon Napa Valley Collins Vineyard Private Reserve 1984: A big, rich, beautifully focused wine, with ripe black cherry and plum flavors that are deep and concentrated with layers of complexity. Tightly wound and beautifully balanced. Drink 1995. Rel: $23 Cur: $37 (3/31/89) **94**
Cabernet Sauvignon Napa Valley Collins Vineyard Proprietor's Special Selection 1983 $70 (CA-3/89) **87**
Cabernet Sauvignon Napa Valley Collins Vineyard Proprietor's Special Selection 1982 $70 (CA-3/89) **85**

Cabernet Sauvignon Napa Valley Collins Vineyard Proprietor's Special Selection 1981 $70 (CA-3/89) **86**
Cabernet Sauvignon Napa Valley Collins Vineyard Proprietor's Special Selection 1980 $70 (CA-3/89) **93**
Cabernet Sauvignon Napa Valley Lot 1 1978 Rel: $12 Cur: $55 (CA-3/89) **86**
Cabernet Sauvignon Napa Valley Lot 2 1978 Rel: $12 Cur: $55 (CA-3/89) **92**

CORBETT CANYON
Cabernet Sauvignon California Coastal Classic 1989: Simple, coarse and a little harsh at the edges, with modest cherry and tobacco flavors. Drinkable, but it should be smoother. $7 (11/15/91) **76**
Cabernet Sauvignon Central Coast 1983 $7 (5/16/86) BB **80**
Cabernet Sauvignon Central Coast Coastal Classic 1986: There are cherry, tar and herb flavors in this rich, supple, easy-to-drink, attractively priced wine. Ready now. $6.50/1L (12/15/89) **80**
Cabernet Sauvignon Central Coast Reserve 1987: Despite strong picklelike overtones, this is a pretty approachable wine, with enough cherry flavor to balance the olive and bell pepper notes that hit you first. Drink soon, if the style appeals to you. Tasted twice. $9.50 (11/15/91) **82**
Cabernet Sauvignon Central Coast Select 1984 $8 (2/15/87) **82**
Cabernet Sauvignon Santa Barbara-San Luis Obispo Counties Select 1985 $10 (5/31/88) **79**

CORISON
Cabernet Sauvignon Napa Valley 1990 (NR) (5/15/91) (BT) **90+**
Cabernet Sauvignon Napa Valley 1989 (NR) (5/15/91) (BT) **85+**
Cabernet Sauvignon Napa Valley 1988: Supple, ripe and full-bodied, with more richness and depth than most '88s. Shows pretty currant, plum and black cherry flavors and subtle oak shadings. The flavors are persistent and lingering on the finish, with firm tannins. Drink in 1995. 1,500 cases made. Rel: $22 Cur: $24 (11/15/91) **89**
Cabernet Sauvignon Napa Valley 1987: A seductive wine, with toasty, buttery oak and a solid core of rich, complex black cherry, plum, currant and anise flavors that are young, chunky and firm. Has a full tannic finish, and the flavors are well integrated, intense and powerful. Best to cellar until 1995 or so, but it should last much longer. 1,800 cases made. $20 (11/15/90) **92**

COSENTINO
Cabernet Sauvignon Napa County 1989: Firm and balanced, with an attractive component of plum and currant that softens the tannic edge and makes this drinkable. Better after 1995, when the tannins settle. Tasted twice. 1,800 cases made. $15 (3/31/92) **86**
Cabernet Sauvignon North Coast 1988: Balanced toward tartness, but harmonious and elegant, offering well-focused currant, cherry and coffee aromas and flavors that linger on the lively finish. Approaching drinkability, but best after 1994. 1,800 cases made. $15 (5/31/91) **88**
Cabernet Sauvignon North Coast 1987: Tough and tannic, with rich, ripe cherry and currant flavor and toasty chocolate flavors up-front, but then the tannins take over, drying it out and leaving an herbal aftertaste. Begin drinking in 1993. $16 (6/30/90) **80**
Cabernet Sauvignon North Coast 1985 $10.50 (9/15/88) **84**
Cabernet Sauvignon North Coast Reserve 1987: Despite a tough, tannic edge, this is a ripe, rich, full-bodied wine, with ample currant, cherry and plum flavors and a nice touch of herb. The tannins suggest cellaring until 1995. 505 cases made. $28 (2/28/91) **86**
Cabernet Sauvignon North Coast Reserve 1986: Rich and broad without being heavy, with delicious oak, dill and caraway flavors accenting the concentrated black cherry and currant flavors. A complex wine, but it's already accessible and welcoming. Probably best with cellaring until 1993 to '95. $18 (5/15/90) **90**
Cabernet Sauvignon North Coast Reserve 1985: Has plenty of ripe, supple, generous plum and cherry flavors, but it lacks drama and excitement. Understated and a little dull. Drink now or hold. $18 (4/30/89) **81**
Cabernet Sauvignon North Coast Reserve Edition 1984 $14 (3/31/88) **78**
Cos Meritage Napa Valley 1988: Tight and firm for an '88, with ripe, rich black cherry, currant, raspberry, chocolate and vanilla flavors. Impressive for its concentration and richness. Finishes long and lingering. Try in 1995. $45 (11/15/91) **89**
The Poet California 1989 (NR) (5/15/91) (BT) **85+**
The Poet California 1988: Lean, dry and austere, with firm tannins and modestly intense plum, currant and cherry flavors. Hints at chocolate on the finish. Best to drink after 1993 or '94. 1,000 cases made. $27 (5/31/91) **85**
The Poet California 1987: Firmly textured and tightly wrapped in tannin, this has a solid but not very intense core of nutmeg- and vanilla-tinged currant and plum aromas. Has lots of wood character on the finish. Needs until 1993 to '94 to soften enough to be more appealing. $25 (9/15/90) **85**
The Poet California 1986 $22 (7/31/89) **86**
The Poet California 1985 $18 (8/31/88) **79**

COTES DE SONOMA
Cabernet Sauvignon Sonoma County 1989: Supple and generous, with ripe strawberry, cherry, plum and spice flavors. Quite approachable now, with its soft tannins. Drink now through 1994. $7 (11/15/91) BB **83**

CRESTON
Cabernet Sauvignon Paso Robles 1987: Minty, herbal flavors tend to overshadow the solid core of black cherry and plum, making this seem ripe and a bit overdone. Drinkable now. $10 (11/15/91) **79**
Cabernet Sauvignon Paso Robles Winemaker's Selection 1987: Firm and flavorful, if a bit on the coarse side, with generous wild cherry and plum aromas and flavors that persist into the finish. Could be smoother or more polished, but it's drinkable. $16 (11/15/91) **82**
Cabernet Sauvignon Central Coast Winemaker's Selection 1985: Lean, tart and herbal with faint spice, cherry and cedar notes that are pleasant and clean, with firm oak and tannins on the finish. Drink now to 1994. $16.50 (12/15/89) **75**
Cabernet Sauvignon Central Coast Winemaker's Selection 1984 $16 (12/15/87) **71**
Cabernet Sauvignon San Luis Obispo County 1985: Extremely vegetal and tarry, a style of limited appeal, with green, unripe flavors. Drink now. $12 (12/15/89) **68**

CRONIN
Cabernet Sauvignon Merlot Robinson Vineyard Stags Leap District 1988: There's plenty of fruit in this distinctive cherry and currant-flavored wine. The fruit lingers on the finish. Supple, well-balanced and pleasing to drink now, but it should improve till about 1994. $17 (3/31/92) **88**
Cabernet Sauvignon Merlot Robinson Vineyard 1987: Shows lots of bright, pure fruit flavor in a crisp, well-balanced package. Fresh currant and cherry flavors are accented with nutmeg, cedar and vanilla. A fruity finish marks it as special. Drink now to 1996. $17 (2/28/91) **89**
Cabernet Sauvignon Merlot Robinson Vineyard 1986: Alluring with its wild berry and currant flavors, this wine is very rich, ripe and supple, with fine tannins and plenty of length and fruit echoing on the finish. Drink now to 1994. $16 (2/15/90) **88**
Cabernet Sauvignon Merlot Santa Cruz Mountains 1987: Intense and flavorful, with heaps of spicy currant, herb and sour cherry flavors and a crisp finish. The tannins are under control. Should be best for drinking around 1994. $17 (3/31/92) **84**
Cabernet Sauvignon Merlot Shaw & Cronin Cuvée San Mateo County 1986: Robust in flavor but elegant in texture, with mature cherry, currant, mint and tobacco flavors. The firm, fine tannins are beginning to soften, but it should age beautifully through 1994. $15 (2/28/91) **88**

CRUVINET
Cabernet Sauvignon Alexander Valley 1985 $7 (9/15/88) BB **85**

CRYSTAL VALLEY
Cabernet Sauvignon North Coast 1983 $8.50 (8/31/86) BB **89**
Cabernet Sauvignon North Coast Reserve Edition 1984 $14 (10/15/87) **75**

CUTLER
Cabernet Sauvignon Sonoma Valley Batto Ranch 1987: Lean, lithe and lovely, with generous blackberry, chocolate and herb aromas and flavors that glide smoothly across the palate and stay with you on the long finish. Has plenty of richness and well-submerged tannins to improve through 1995 to '98. 792 cases made. $17 (3/31/92) **90**
Cabernet Sauvignon Sonoma Valley Batto Ranch 1986: Ripe, rich, deep and intense, a big style that's concentrated with currant, cherry and plum flavors, firm tannins and spicy oak that picks up some menthol and toast notes. A wine that needs to gain finesse and complexity and appears to have all the ingredients. Time will tell. Try in 1993 or '94. 1,500 cases made. $17 (11/15/90) **86**
Cabernet Sauvignon Sonoma Valley Batto Ranch 1985: Very firm and rich, with smoky, tarry, currant and black cherry accents, elegantly packed into a generous frame. Already shows remarkable complexity, pretty flavors and a cedary finish that needs until 1993 to smooth out. $20 (7/31/89) **91**
Satyre Sonoma Valley 1986: An opulent wine that's rich, ripe and full-bodied, with herb, currant and cedar flavors, a lush texture, firm tannins and a spicy, woody finish. Drink in 1994 and beyond. Tasted twice. 690 cases made. $20 (2/28/91) **85**

CUVAISON
Cabernet Sauvignon Napa Valley 1988: A hard-edged, tannic style that lacks richness and depth. The plum and currant flavors are austere and one-dimensional, and it drys out on the finish. Drink in 1993. $18 (11/15/91) **82**
Cabernet Sauvignon Napa Valley 1987: Has a great sense of balance and proportion, with layers of rich, intense cherry, chocolate, currant and spice flavors. Has plenty of depth, concentration, length and tannins for cellaring. Hold until at least 1994, but it should age through the decade. Rel: $17.50 Cur: $21 (10/31/90) **92**
Cabernet Sauvignon Napa Valley 1986: Ripe and opulent, with remarkable power on a supple, velvety texture, yet still graceful and elegant, echoing ripe cassis, chocolate and a touch of herb on the long, long finish. Cellaring until 1995 should smooth out the remaining tannins. Rel: $15 Cur: $20 (7/15/89) **94**
Cabernet Sauvignon Napa Valley 1985 Rel: $14 Cur: $25 (3/31/89) **91**
Cabernet Sauvignon Napa Valley 1984 Rel: $14 Cur: $18 (CA-3/89) **89**
Cabernet Sauvignon Napa Valley 1983 Rel: $12 Cur: $15 (CA-3/89) **75**
Cabernet Sauvignon Napa Valley 1982 Rel: $11 Cur: $18 (CA-3/89) **82**
Cabernet Sauvignon Napa Valley 1981 Rel: $11 Cur: $18 (CA-3/89) **74**
Cabernet Sauvignon Napa Valley 1980 Rel: $11 Cur: $19 (CA-3/89) **77**
Cabernet Sauvignon Napa Valley 1979 Rel: $11 Cur: $20 (CA-3/89) **75**
Cabernet Sauvignon Napa Valley 1978 Rel: $10 Cur: $30 (CA-3/89) **72**
Cabernet Sauvignon Napa Valley 1977 Rel: $10 Cur: $30 (CA-3/89) **79**
Cabernet Sauvignon Napa Valley 1976 Rel: $10 Cur: $30 (CA-3/89) **79**
Cabernet Sauvignon Napa Valley 1975 Rel: $10 Cur: $33 (CA-3/89) **79**
Cabernet Sauvignon Napa Valley Philip Togni Signature 1975 Rel: $40 Cur: $60 (CA-3/89) **88**

DALLA VALLE
Cabernet Sauvignon Napa Valley 1988: Shows lots of richness, depth and concentration for an '88, with tight chocolate, currant, berry and spice flavors framed by toasty oak. The tannins are thick and dense, suggesting it needs until at least 1995 to soften. $25 (11/15/91) **85**
Cabernet Sauvignon Napa Valley 1986: Hard, tannic, austere, even stemmy in texture, a tough wine to warm up to, with firm currant, herb and chocolate flavors that turn beefy on the finish. Very dry and tannic on the finish. Patience required until 1994 or '95 at the earliest. $20 (6/30/90) **85**
Maya Napa Valley 1988: Rich and elegant, with tight currant, plum and cherry flavors that hang in there on the finish. Has plenty of tannins, but it's better balanced than many '88s. Needs until about 1995. $45 (11/15/91) **86**

DANIEL
Cabernet Sauvignon Napa Valley 1984 $21 (7/15/88) **89**
Cabernet Sauvignon Napa Valley 1983: Despite a streak of firm tannins, there arepretty plum and spicy currant flavors underneath. Will need time to come around. Drink 1993 and beyond. A notch below Dominus, its sister wine. $20 (4/30/89) **79**

DE LOACH
Cabernet Sauvignon Russian River Valley 1989: An herbal, cedary wine, sporting nice currant, prune and green olive flavors that linger through the finish. Drinkable now, but has enough tannin to carry through at least 1995. $16 (11/15/91) **86**
Cabernet Sauvignon Dry Creek Valley 1984 $11 (12/15/87) **89**
Cabernet Sauvignon Dry Creek Valley 1983 $11 (9/30/86) **85**
Cabernet Sauvignon Dry Creek Valley 1981 $11 (4/01/85) **80**
Cabernet Sauvignon Russian River Valley O.F.S. 1987: A massively proportioned, ultraripe and vegetal style, with high extract of raspberry, cherry and currant flavors that are tannic and rough around the edges. A full-blown style without any pretense toward elegance. Best to cellar until 1995. $22 (10/15/90) **85**

DE LORIMIER
Mosaic Alexander Valley 1987: A well-balanced, well-rounded wine with herbal and plummy flavors in an easy-to-drink style. Drink now through 1994. 1,100 cases made. $18 (3/31/92) **81**
Mosaic Alexander Valley 1986: Starts off extremely vegetal and tarry, although a bit of pleasant fruit comes through on the finish to give it pleasant balance. It has the velvety texture and sense of richness to make it worth holding. Try now. $16 (10/31/89) **84**

DE MOOR
Cabernet Sauvignon Napa Valley 1987: Tough and tannic, with a strong woody edge to the ripe cherry and currant flavors, it's somewhat leathery, too. Not an enticing wine. May be better after 1995, but it's a gamble. $16 (11/15/91) **76**
Cabernet Sauvignon Napa Valley 1985 $14 (CA-3/89) **79**
Cabernet Sauvignon Napa Valley 1984 Rel: $14 Cur: $16 (CA-3/89) **88**
Cabernet Sauvignon Napa Valley 1983 Rel: $12 Cur: $16 (CA-3/89) **86**
Cabernet Sauvignon Napa Valley 1982 Rel: $12 Cur: $18 (CA-3/89) **86**
Cabernet Sauvignon Napa Valley Napa Cellars 1981 Rel: $12 Cur: $25 (CA-3/89) **86**
Cabernet Sauvignon Napa Valley Napa Cellars 1980 Rel: $12 Cur: $20 (CA-3/89) **80**
Cabernet Sauvignon Napa Valley Napa Cellars 1979 Rel: $10 Cur: $25 (CA-3/89) **85**
Cabernet Sauvignon Napa Valley Napa Cellars 1978 Rel: $10 Cur: $28 (CA-3/89) **89**
Cabernet Sauvignon Napa Valley Owners Select 1986: Mature in color and flavor, with muted currant, plum, leather and cherry notes, fine but firm tannins and a drying aftertaste. Standard quality for an '86, lacking in drama. Drink now to 1995. $16 (2/28/91) **78**
Cabernet Sauvignon Napa Valley Owners Select 1982 Rel: $12 Cur: $19 (CA-3/89) **88**

DEER VALLEY
Cabernet Sauvignon Monterey 1985 $5.50 (12/31/87) **72**

DEHLINGER
Cabernet Sauvignon Russian River Valley 1988: Tannic but light, with pleasant greenish plum and currant aromas and flavors. Needs time to soften those tannins. Try after 1996. 650 cases made. $15 (3/31/92) **83**
Cabernet Sauvignon Russian River Valley 1987: An elegant, balanced style, with concentrated cherry, raspberry, currant and earthy herb notes, but they're well proportioned. The tannins, while fine, are very firm, and the finish is drying. Best to cellar until about 1995. $13 (2/28/91) **88**
Cabernet Sauvignon Russian River Valley 1986: A tough but impressively concentrated wine, with delicious currant and plum aromas and flavors that extend well into the long finish. Has a very firm texture and tough tannins that will need cellaring until 1993. The harmonious balance and rich flavors bode well for near-term development. $13 (3/15/90) **90**
Cabernet Sauvignon Russian River Valley 1985 $13 (5/31/89) **74**

Cabernet Sauvignon Russian River Valley 1984 $12 (2/15/88) **76**
Cabernet Sauvignon Russian River Valley 1983 $11 (6/15/87) **85**
Cabernet Sauvignon Russian River Valley 1982 $11 (8/31/86) **73**
Cabernet Sauvignon Sonoma County 1981 $9 (5/16/85) **87**

DELICATO
Cabernet Sauvignon California 1985 $6 (6/30/88) **66**
Cabernet Sauvignon Carneros Napa Valley 1983 $10 (6/15/87) **72**

DEUX AMIS
Cabernet Sauvignon Dry Creek Valley 1987: From a new producer in Dry Creek Valley, this is a firmly tannic wine that's developing a supple texture. The flavors are pure Cabernet, with hints of plum, black cherry and currant. Has a crisp finish. Best to cellar until 1993 or so. 150 cases made. $14 (11/15/91) **83**

DEVLIN
Cabernet Sauvignon Sonoma County 1981 $6 (8/01/85) **83**

DIAMOND CREEK
Cabernet Sauvignon Napa Valley Gravelly Meadow 1991: Massive but elegant, this is a delicious wine. Deep, dark and intense, packed with currant, black cherry, plum and berry flavors. The fruit zips across the palate, finishing with firm tannins. (NR) (5/15/92) (BT) **91+**
Cabernet Sauvignon Napa Valley Gravelly Meadow 1990 (NR) (5/15/91) (BT) **85+**
Cabernet Sauvignon Napa Valley Gravelly Meadow 1989: Earthy, herbal and more tannic than the modest currant and spice flavors seem able to support, but it's smooth and round. Perhaps better after 1995 or '96. Tasted twice. $50 (1/31/92) **83**
Cabernet Sauvignon Napa Valley Gravelly Meadow 1988: Lean and focused, with cedary, spicy aromas and flavors and cranberry and black cherry notes emerging on the firm but not overwhelming finish. Drinkable by 1994 or '95, but you can almost enjoy it today. 465 cases made. Rel: $40 Cur: $45 (11/15/90) **87**
Cabernet Sauvignon Napa Valley Gravelly Meadow 1987 Rel: $40 Cur: $45 (12/15/89) **90**
Cabernet Sauvignon Napa Valley Gravelly Meadow 1986 Rel: $30 Cur: $52 (CA-3/89) **94**
Cabernet Sauvignon Napa Valley Gravelly Meadow 1985 Rel: $30 Cur: $55 (CA-3/89) **92**
Cabernet Sauvignon Napa Valley Gravelly Meadow 1984 Rel: $25 Cur: $62 (CA-3/89) **94**
Cabernet Sauvignon Napa Valley Gravelly Meadow 1983 Rel: $20 Cur: $47 (CA-3/89) **89**
Cabernet Sauvignon Napa Valley Gravelly Meadow 1983 Rel: $20 Cur: $47 (2/01/86) CS **93**
Cabernet Sauvignon Napa Valley Gravelly Meadow 1982 Rel: $20 Cur: $66 (CA-3/89) **89**
Cabernet Sauvignon Napa Valley Gravelly Meadow 1981 Rel: $20 Cur: $67 (CA-3/89) **89**
Cabernet Sauvignon Napa Valley Gravelly Meadow 1980 Rel: $20 Cur: $60 (CA-3/89) **92**
Cabernet Sauvignon Napa Valley Gravelly Meadow 1979 Rel: $15 Cur: $100 (CA-3/89) **91**
Cabernet Sauvignon Napa Valley Gravelly Meadow 1978 Rel: $12.50 Cur: $115 (CA-3/89) **93**
Cabernet Sauvignon Napa Valley Gravelly Meadow 1977 Rel: $10 Cur: $61 (CA-3/89) **89**
Cabernet Sauvignon Napa Valley Gravelly Meadow 1976 Rel: $9 Cur: $90 (CA-3/89) **85**
Cabernet Sauvignon Napa Valley Gravelly Meadow 1975 Rel: $7.50 Cur: $80 (CA-3/89) **85**
Cabernet Sauvignon Napa Valley Gravelly Meadow 1974 Rel: $7.50 Cur: $144 (CA-3/89) **88**
Cabernet Sauvignon Napa Valley Gravelly Meadow Special Selection 1982 Rel: $20 Cur: $45 (CA-3/89) **84**
Cabernet Sauvignon Napa Valley Lake 1987: Extremely tannic and youthful, but full of ripe black currant, black cherry and plum flavors. Cedary and sophisticated in aroma, big in structure and full-bodied, but really too young to size up. Drink in 1998-2008. Rel: $100 Cur: $230 (11/15/90) **91**
Cabernet Sauvignon Napa Valley Lake 1984 Rel: $50 Cur: $250 (CA-3/89) **92**
Cabernet Sauvignon Napa Valley Lake 1978 Rel: $25 Cur: $480 (CA-3/89) **99**
Cabernet Sauvignon Napa Valley Red Rock Terrace 1991: Packs a wallop, with ripe, rich, intense fruit flavors that echo currant, cherry, plum and anise. The tannins are tight and crisp, but the fruit beams through on the finish, with a sense of elegance. (NR) (5/15/92) (BT) **87+**
Cabernet Sauvignon Napa Valley Red Rock Terrace 1990 (NR) (5/15/91) (BT) **85+**
Cabernet Sauvignon Napa Valley Red Rock Terrace 1989: Tough and tannic, with concentrated red cherry, red currant and black pepper aromas and flavors that persist into a long finish. The fruit emerges through the tannins, suggesting that 1998 should find this at its best. Tasted twice. $50 (1/31/92) **89**
Cabernet Sauvignon Napa Valley Red Rock Terrace 1988: Very firm and concentrated, but not as tannic and dense as this wine can often be, featuring black cherry and currant aromas and flavors that extend well into a long, supple finish. A good effort, it's worth cellaring until at least 1995 to see what develops. 588 cases made. Rel: $40 Cur: $45 (11/15/90) **89**
Cabernet Sauvignon Napa Valley Red Rock Terrace 1987 Rel: $40 Cur: $46 (12/15/89) **94**
Cabernet Sauvignon Napa Valley Red Rock Terrace 1986 Rel: $30 Cur: $48 (CA-3/89) **96**
Cabernet Sauvignon Napa Valley Red Rock Terrace 1985 Rel: $30 Cur: $55 (CA-3/89) **93**
Cabernet Sauvignon Napa Valley Red Rock Terrace 1984 Rel: $25 Cur: $65 (CA-3/89) **96**
Cabernet Sauvignon Napa Valley Red Rock Terrace 1984 Rel: $25 Cur: $65 (9/30/86) CS **95**
Cabernet Sauvignon Napa Valley Red Rock Terrace 1983 Rel: $20 Cur: $42 (CA-3/89) **88**
Cabernet Sauvignon Napa Valley Red Rock Terrace 1982 Rel: $20 Cur: $67 (CA-3/89) **87**
Cabernet Sauvignon Napa Valley Red Rock Terrace 1981 Rel: $20 Cur: $66 (CA-3/89) **91**
Cabernet Sauvignon Napa Valley Red Rock Terrace 1980 Rel: $20 Cur: $59 (CA-3/89) **86**
Cabernet Sauvignon Napa Valley Red Rock Terrace 1979 Rel: $15 Cur: $100 (CA-3/89) **92**
Cabernet Sauvignon Napa Valley Red Rock Terrace 1978 Rel: $12.50 Cur: $110 (CA-3/89) **92**
Cabernet Sauvignon Napa Valley Red Rock Terrace First Pick 1977 Rel: $10 Cur: $72 (CA-3/89) **88**
Cabernet Sauvignon Napa Valley Red Rock Terrace Second Pick 1977 Rel: $10 Cur: $45 (CA-3/89) **75**
Cabernet Sauvignon Napa Valley Red Rock Terrace 1976 Rel: $9 Cur: $95 (CA-3/89) **85**
Cabernet Sauvignon Napa Valley Red Rock Terrace 1975 Rel: $7.50 Cur: $88 (CA-3/89) **88**
Cabernet Sauvignon Napa Valley Red Rock Terrace 1972 Rel: $7.50 Cur: $200 (CA-3/89) **74**
Cabernet Sauvignon Napa Valley Red Rock Terrace Special Selection 1982 Rel: $20 Cur: $40 (CA-3/89) **80**
Cabernet Sauvignon Napa Valley Three Vineyard Blend 1985 Rel: $50 Cur: $100 (CA-3/89) **89**
Cabernet Sauvignon Napa Valley Three Vineyard Blend 1984 Rel: $50 Cur: $100 (CA-3/89) **89**
Cabernet Sauvignon Napa Valley Three Vineyard Blend 1981 Rel: $20 Cur: $100 (CA-3/89) **90**
Cabernet Sauvignon Napa Valley Volcanic Hill 1991: Young and backward, with berry and fermentation aromas still showing. A tight core of currant and mulberry flavors peeks through the tannins. (NR) (5/15/92) (BT) **86+**
Cabernet Sauvignon Napa Valley Volcanic Hill 1990 (NR) (5/15/91) (BT) **85+**
Cabernet Sauvignon Napa Valley Volcanic Hill 1989: Hard-edged and solidly built, with tightly wound currant, plum and cherry flavors, well-integrated tannins and nice hints of cedar and chocolate on the finish. Tasted twice. $50 (1/31/92) **86**
Cabernet Sauvignon Napa Valley Volcanic Hill 1988: Tart, tight and steely, this is an austere wine, with tough tannins covering a bright beam of cassis that extends into a long finish. Hints at toast and cedar on the aftertaste. It's balanced toward tartness, but cellaring until 1996 to 2000 should bring it around. 735 cases made. Rel: $40 Cur: $44 (11/15/90) **88**
Cabernet Sauvignon Napa Valley Volcanic Hill 1987 Rel: $40 Cur: $44 (12/15/89) **95**
Cabernet Sauvignon Napa Valley Volcanic Hill 1986 Rel: $30 Cur: $63 (CA-3/89) **96**
Cabernet Sauvignon Napa Valley Volcanic Hill 1985 Rel: $30 Cur: $55 (CA-3/89) **93**
Cabernet Sauvignon Napa Valley Volcanic Hill 1984 Rel: $25 Cur: $60 (CA-3/89) **94**
Cabernet Sauvignon Napa Valley Volcanic Hill 1983 Rel: $20 Cur: $46 (CA-3/89) **89**
Cabernet Sauvignon Napa Valley Volcanic Hill 1982 Rel: $20 Cur: $69 (CA-3/89) **89**
Cabernet Sauvignon Napa Valley Volcanic Hill 1982 Rel: $20 Cur: $69 (12/16/84) CS **92**
Cabernet Sauvignon Napa Valley Volcanic Hill 1981 Rel: $20 Cur: $72 (CA-3/89) **92**
Cabernet Sauvignon Napa Valley Volcanic Hill 1980 Rel: $20 Cur: $67 (CA-3/89) **90**
Cabernet Sauvignon Napa Valley Volcanic Hill First Pick 1979 Rel: $15 Cur: $95 (CA-3/89) **95**
Cabernet Sauvignon Napa Valley Volcanic Hill Second Pick 1979 Rel: $15 Cur: $45 (CA-3/89) **82**
Cabernet Sauvignon Napa Valley Volcanic Hill 1978 Rel: $12.50 Cur: $110 (CA-3/89) **95**
Cabernet Sauvignon Napa Valley Volcanic Hill 1977 Rel: $10 Cur: $63 (CA-3/89) **84**
Cabernet Sauvignon Napa Valley Volcanic Hill 1976 Rel: $9 Cur: $47 (CA-3/89) **87**
Cabernet Sauvignon Napa Valley Volcanic Hill 1975 Rel: $7.50 Cur: $81 (CA-3/89) **93**
Cabernet Sauvignon Napa Valley Volcanic Hill 1974 Rel: $7.50 Cur: $138 (CA-3/89) **87**
Cabernet Sauvignon Napa Valley Volcanic Hill 1973 Rel: $7.50 Cur: $200 (CA-3/89) **80**
Cabernet Sauvignon Napa Valley Volcanic Hill 1972 Rel: $7.50 Cur: $200 (CA-3/89) **85**
Cabernet Sauvignon Napa Valley Volcanic Hill Special Selection 1982 Rel: $20 Cur: $40 (CA-3/89) **79**

DOLAN
Cabernet Sauvignon Mendocino 1984 $12 (5/31/88) **88**
Cabernet Sauvignon Mendocino 1983 $12 (2/29/88) **86**

DOMAINE LAURIER
Cabernet Sauvignon Sonoma County Green Valley 1982 $12 (2/16/85) **82**

DOMAINE MICHEL
Cabernet Sauvignon Sonoma County 1989 (NR) (5/15/91) (BT) **85+**
Cabernet Sauvignon Sonoma County 1987: A tight, tough style that's tannic and hard-edged, but there's ample fruit underneath, with ripe but simple plum, tobacco, herb and oak flavors. It's hard to tell where this one's headed. Best to cellar until 1994 or '95. $19.50 (3/31/91) **84**
Cabernet Sauvignon Sonoma County 1986: The plum and cherry flavors are good but it's hard to say if they'll outlast the intense tannins. Coarse and unbalanced—no fun to drink now. Gamblers could cellar it until 1993. $19 (6/30/90) **75**
Cabernet Sauvignon Sonoma County 1984 $19 (9/15/87) **86**
Cabernet Sauvignon Sonoma County Reserve 1989 (NR) (5/15/91) (BT) **85+**

DOMAINE DE NAPA
Cabernet Sauvignon Napa Valley 1985 $12 (12/15/88) **81**

DOMAINE PHILIPPE
Cabernet Sauvignon Napa Valley Select Cuvée 1984 $6.50 (5/15/88) BB **87**

DOMAINE ST. GEORGE
Cabernet Sauvignon Russian River Valley Select Reserve 1986: A dark, pungent Cabernet that smells of oak and camphor, tastes full of cherry and plum, but finishes harsh with wood tannins. Difficult to tell if aging will tame the woodiness. Cellar till 1993. $9 (5/31/90) **79**
Cabernet Sauvignon Sonoma County 1988: You've heard of claret-style Zinfandel—this is Zinfandel-style claret. Raspberry and briary aromas and flavors are fresh, lively and balanced to accent the fruit. Drink now, with steak or chops. $6 (11/15/90) BB **83**

DOMAINE SAN MARTIN
Cabernet Sauvignon Central Coast 1981 $7.75 (10/01/85) **76**

DOMINUS
Napa Valley 1987: Dense, rich and concentrated, with a solid core of currant, oak, spice and earthy cedar flavors. Picks up a gamy, meaty quality on the finish. Very tannic. Admirable for its power and strength, but will need until 1996 to begin to soften. $45 (11/15/91) **89**
Napa Valley 1986: A big, thick, full-bodied Cabernet that's packed with cherry, currant, chocolate and spice flavors in a tight, tannic shell. Has an earthy, leathery overtone that defines its style. Needs cellaring until 1997 to begin to show its best stuff. $45 (2/28/91) **91**
Napa Valley 1986 $45 (CA-3/89) **93**
Napa Valley 1985: Beneath its hard, tough shell beats a heart of generous, ripe cassis and cherry, overlaid with lots of new oak, tannin and earthiness. Clearly an important wine, but not one that will please everyone. Should be cellared until at least 1995. Tasted twice. Rel: $45 Cur: $55 (2/15/90) **84**
Napa Valley 1984 Rel: $40 Cur: $55 (5/15/88) CS **90**
Napa Valley 1983 Rel: $43 Cur: $52 (4/15/89) **86**

DORE
Cabernet Sauvignon California 1984 $5 (12/31/87) **64**
Cabernet Sauvignon California Limited Release Lot 102 1987: Fairly tannic, with plum and currant flavors struggling to compete. Altogether a pleasant drink, especially for those who desire a crisp, tannic edge to their reds. Drink now. 700 cases made. $8.50 (11/15/91) **80**

DRY CREEK
Cabernet Sauvignon Sonoma County 1989: Tough but focused, with delicious currant, plum and berry aromas and flavors that stay with you through the finish, with the tannins sliding in under the fruit. Drinkable now, but might be better around 1994 to '96. $14 (3/31/92) **86**
Cabernet Sauvignon Sonoma County 1988: Ripe raspberry and currant flavors are framed by tight, stemmy tannins. Has plenty of flavor, but it's a bit awkward now; perhaps with time it will show more finesse. Drink now to 1996. $14 (5/31/91) **81**
Cabernet Sauvignon Sonoma County 1987: Firm, concentrated and packed with jammy currant, cherry and mint aromas and flavors. Has plenty of tannin to lose, so cellar it until at least 1993 to '94. $12.50 (4/15/90) **84**
Cabernet Sauvignon Sonoma County 1986 $11 (3/31/89) **88**
Cabernet Sauvignon Sonoma County 1985 Rel: $11 Cur: $16 (5/31/88) SS **91**
Cabernet Sauvignon Sonoma County 1984 $10 (5/15/87) **85**
Cabernet Sauvignon Sonoma County 1982 $9.50 (2/01/85) **81**
Cabernet Sauvignon Sonoma County 1980 $9.50 (4/16/84) **78**
Cabernet Sauvignon Sonoma County Special Reserve 1980 $13 (5/01/86) **78**
Meritage Dry Creek Valley 1987: Attractive for its balance of ripe currant, plum, anise and cherry flavors and toasty oak shadings. Still tannic, but shows a suppleness on the finish. Best to cellar until 1994. Better than a bottle tasted earlier. 3,021 cases made. $24 (1/31/92) **87**
Meritage Dry Creek Valley 1986: A ripe, jammy, moderately distinctive style that has well-integrated and pleasant soy sauce and cherry flavors and a hint of cedar and coffee. Sauerkraut flavors come through on the finish. Drink now. Tasted twice. $22 (9/15/90) **80**
Meritage Dry Creek Valley 1985: Herb-scented red cherry and strawberry flavor competes with

Key to Symbols

The scores reported here are the results of blind tastings conducted by our panel of senior editors. Wines that carry the initials below are results of individual tastings.

THE WINE SPECTATOR 100-POINT SCALE ***95-100***—Classic, a great wine; ***90-94***—Outstanding, superior character and style; ***80-89***—Good to very good, a wine with special qualities; ***70-79***—Average, drinkable wine that may have minor flaws; ***60-69***—Below average, drinkable but not recommended; ***50-59***—Poor, undrinkable, not recommended. "+"—With a score indicates a range; used primarily with barrel tastings to indicate a preliminary score.

SPECIAL DESIGNATIONS SS—Spectator Selection, CS—Cellar Selection, BB—Best Buy, ($NA)—Price not available, (NR)—Not released.

TASTER'S INITIALS (JG)—Jim Gordon, (HS)—Harvey Steiman, (JL)—James Laube, (JS)—James Suckling, (TM)—Thomas Matthews, (TR)—Terry Robards, (PM)—Per-Henrik Mansson, (BT)—Barrel Tasting (these wines were tasted blind from barrel samples), (CA-date)—*California's Great Cabernets* by James Laube, (CH-date)—*California's Great Chardonnays* by James Laube, (VP-date)—*Vintage Port* by James Suckling.

DATE TASTED Dates in parentheses represent the issue in which the rating was published.

spicy oak for attention in this silky, concentrated, impeccably balanced wine. Flavors linger on a long finish. Just a bit of tannin to resolve; drink now through 1994. 1,000 cases made. $22 (11/15/89) **89**
David S. Stare Vintner's Reserve Sonoma County 1984 $18 (5/31/88) **88**
David S. Stare Vintner's Selection Dry Creek Valley 1983 $15 (12/31/86) **74**

DUCKHORN
Cabernet Sauvignon Napa Valley 1988: Essentially a light wine, with strong tannins on the finish. Lean and crisp, it needs time to soften the astringency so the nicely focused currant and cherry flavors can come through. Drink after 1995. Rel: $20 Cur: $27 (7/31/91) **85**
Cabernet Sauvignon Napa Valley 1987: Delicious, with its intense, concentrated, rich and sharply focused black cherry, currant and chocolate flavors. Despite the abundant flavors and tannins, the texture is still smooth and seductive. Deceptively powerful and amazingly graceful. Best Cabernet yet from Duckhorn. Drink 1993 to 2002. 4,958 cases made. Rel: $20 Cur: $31 (6/30/90) CS **95**
Cabernet Sauvignon Napa Valley 1986: On first sniff, this reveals itself as the complex wine it is, with smooth texture and deep plum, cherry, tar and vanilla flavors, long and perfumed. Almost drinkable, but cellaring until 1995 could bring out its best. 4,000 cases made. Rel: $18 Cur: $30 (7/31/89) SS **94**
Cabernet Sauvignon Napa Valley 1985 Rel: $17.50 Cur: $39 (CA-3/89) **92**
Cabernet Sauvignon Napa Valley 1985 Rel: $17.50 Cur: $39 (6/15/88) CS **91**
Cabernet Sauvignon Napa Valley 1984 Rel: $17 Cur: $32 (CA-3/89) **92**
Cabernet Sauvignon Napa Valley 1983 Rel: $16 Cur: $45 (CA-3/89) **88**
Cabernet Sauvignon Napa Valley 1982 Rel: $15 Cur: $53 (CA-3/89) **90**
Cabernet Sauvignon Napa Valley 1981 Rel: $15 Cur: $68 (CA-3/89) **87**
Cabernet Sauvignon Napa Valley 1980 Rel: $14 Cur: $70 (CA-3/89) **91**
Cabernet Sauvignon Napa Valley 1978 Rel: $10.50 Cur: $82 (CA-3/89) **92**

DUNN
Cabernet Sauvignon Howell Mountain 1990 (NR) (5/15/91) (BT) **90+**
Cabernet Sauvignon Howell Mountain 1989 (NR) (5/15/91) (BT) **90+**
Cabernet Sauvignon Howell Mountain 1988: Quite concentrated for the light '88 vintage, from the deep, deep color to the strong currant and black cherry flavor. Sturdy tannins and firm texture indicate cellaring till about 1996 to bring out its best. Tasted twice. 2,100 cases made. Rel: $39 Cur: $56 (2/29/92) **86**
Cabernet Sauvignon Howell Mountain 1987: Offers a massive concentration of rich currant, cherry, mineral and cedar flavors and finishes with rich, chewy tannins. Uncommonly deep in color, with excellent depth and dimension. Has a long, complex finish, but it's tightly wound and will require cellaring until 1998 to 2004. 2,200 cases made. Rel: $36 Cur: $70 (4/15/91) **94**
Cabernet Sauvignon Howell Mountain 1986: Dense in color and aroma, this wine has a bold, rich, deeply concentrated core of currant, black cherry, plum and toasty, earthy Cabernet flavors. Brace yourself for the intense tannins, but the flavors glide across the palate. It's beautifully balanced and built for cellaring up to a decade or so. 2,000 cases made. Rel: $30 Cur: $100 (7/31/90) CS **95**
Cabernet Sauvignon Howell Mountain 1986 Rel: $30 Cur: $100 (CA-3/89) **94**
Cabernet Sauvignon Howell Mountain 1985 Rel: $30 Cur: $125 (11/30/91) (JL) **88**
Cabernet Sauvignon Howell Mountain 1984 Rel: $25 Cur: $145 (11/30/91) (JL) **96**
Cabernet Sauvignon Howell Mountain 1983 Rel: $18 Cur: $115 (11/30/91) (JL) **91**
Cabernet Sauvignon Howell Mountain 1982 Rel: $15 Cur: $160 (11/30/91) (JL) **94**
Cabernet Sauvignon Howell Mountain 1981 Rel: $14 Cur: $160 (11/30/91) (JL) **93**
Cabernet Sauvignon Howell Mountain 1980 Rel: $13 Cur: $170 (11/30/91) (JL) **95**
Cabernet Sauvignon Howell Mountain 1979 Rel: $12.50 Cur: $210 (11/30/91) (JL) **94**
Cabernet Sauvignon Napa Valley 1990 (NR) (5/15/91) (BT) **90+**
Cabernet Sauvignon Napa Valley 1989 (NR) (5/15/91) (BT) **85+**
Cabernet Sauvignon Napa Valley 1988: An austere style, with a touch of mint and spice, but it has plenty of black cherry, currant, plum and cedar flavors. The tannins are substantial and it could use a little more body in the middle. Cellar until 1996. 2,100 cases made. Rel: $33 Cur: $43 (11/15/91) **87**
Cabernet Sauvignon Napa Valley 1987: Attractive for its deep, rich fruit and spicy aromas, this is very young, intense and complex, with tiers of currant, plum and black cherry flavors and toasty oak notes. Stylish, very complete and firmly tannic on the finish, but it should reward cellaring until 1997 to 2001. 2,300 cases made. Rel: $33 Cur: $52 (11/15/90) **93**
Cabernet Sauvignon Napa Valley 1986: Another stunner from Dunn. Intense and concentrated, with ripe currant, cherry, spice and plum flavors that are remarkably elegant and persistent. Needs aging. Probably best to drink from 1994 to 2004. 2,000 cases made. Rel: $27 Cur: $62 (10/15/89) CS **95**
Cabernet Sauvignon Napa Valley 1985 Rel: $20 Cur: $70 (11/30/91) (JL) **93**
Cabernet Sauvignon Napa Valley 1985 Rel: $20 Cur: $70 (9/15/88) CS **94**
Cabernet Sauvignon Napa Valley 1984 Rel: $18 Cur: $65 (11/30/91) (JL) **97**
Cabernet Sauvignon Napa Valley 1983 Rel: $15 Cur: $90 (11/30/91) (JL) **91**
Cabernet Sauvignon Napa Valley 1983 Rel: $15 Cur: $90 (10/31/86) SS **95**
Cabernet Sauvignon Napa Valley 1982 Rel: $13 Cur: $95 (11/30/91) (JL) **91**
Cabernet Sauvignon Napa Valley 1982 Rel: $13 Cur: $95 (11/01/85) SS **97**

DUNNEWOOD
Cabernet Sauvignon California 1986: A herbaceous style that offers berry-tinged flavor. At its best it's simple and basic, with bell pepper and green bean flavors. Drink now. $7 (6/15/90) **73**
Cabernet Sauvignon Napa Valley Napa Reserve 1986: Attractive currant, cherry and oak flavors are tight and firm and in need of a year or two in the cellar to soften. Best to drink now to 1994. $10.50 (6/15/90) **82**
Cabernet Sauvignon Napa Valley Reserve 1984 $10.50 (12/31/88) **85**

DURNEY
Cabernet Sauvignon Carmel Valley 1981 $12.50 (9/01/84) **82**
Cabernet Sauvignon Carmel Valley Private Reserve 1983: Ripe, aromatic and flavorful, offering plenty of currant and plum flavors and tough tannins, typical of an '83. Dark in color and concentrated, suggesting it could improve with cellaring, perhaps through 1995. $20 (4/30/91) **86**

EBERLE
Cabernet Sauvignon Paso Robles 1988 (NR) (5/15/90) (BT) **80+**
Cabernet Sauvignon Paso Robles 1987: Has a burnt taste that overshadows the ripe currant and berry notes. Lean, tough and tannic, too. Needs time, but may never come around. Hold until 1995 or '96. 3,900 cases made. $16 (11/15/91) **76**
Cabernet Sauvignon Paso Robles 1986: Rich, smooth and complex with cedar, black cherry, spice and currant flavors that are framed by firm, supple tannins and a long, hearty finish. Needs two to three years to round out. Drink now. Rel: $12 Cur: $15 (11/15/89) **85**
Cabernet Sauvignon Paso Robles 1986 Rel: $12 Cur: $15 (CA-3/89) **85**
Cabernet Sauvignon Paso Robles 1985: A very well made if uninspired Cabernet that's firm, tight and closed, offering only hints of spice, oak and plum that come across as simple and direct. With time it should gain some complexity. Drink now to 1994. Rel: $12 Cur: $17 (2/15/89) **82**
Cabernet Sauvignon Paso Robles 1984 Rel: $12 Cur: $17 (CA-3/89) **86**
Cabernet Sauvignon Paso Robles 1983 Rel: $10 Cur: $18 (CA-3/89) **84**
Cabernet Sauvignon Paso Robles 1982 Rel: $10 Cur: $24 (CA-3/89) **72**
Cabernet Sauvignon Paso Robles 1981 Rel: $10 Cur: $24 (CA-3/89) **85**
Cabernet Sauvignon Paso Robles 1980 Rel: $10 Cur: $24 (CA-3/89) **78**
Cabernet Sauvignon San Luis Obispo 1979 Rel: $10 Cur: $25 (CA-3/89) **82**
Cabernet Sauvignon Paso Robles Reserve 1982 Rel: $25 Cur: $30 (CA-3/89) **71**
Cabernet Sauvignon Paso Robles Reserve 1981 Rel: $25 Cur: $35 (CA-3/89) **80**

EDMUNDS ST. JOHN
Les Fleurs du Chaparral Napa Valley 1987: A terrific California novelty. With earthy flavors and aromas reminiscent of a good northern Rhône, it's big and lucious, with a core of plum and blackberry flavors and attractive accents of game and smoke. This is a well-balanced, beautifully structured wine. The tannins are firm but fine. It's tempting now, but it should improve through 1993. 105 cases made. $15 (8/31/90) **91**

EHLERS LANE
Cabernet Sauvignon Napa Valley 1983 $12 (6/15/87) **79**

ELLISTON
Cabernet Sauvignon Central Coast Sunol Valley Vineyard 1985: Mature, smoky and vegetal, with a woody, drying finish. OK, but the extra age hasn't mellowed the structure, it has only dried up most of the fruit flavor. Tasted twice. $16 (11/15/91) **74**

ESTANCIA
Cabernet Sauvignon Alexander Valley 1988: Firm and somewhat tannic for the level of flavor intensity, but generally well put together, offering pleasant currant and black cherry flavors that linger on the finish. Drink in 1993 or '94. $9 (5/31/91) **81**
Cabernet Sauvignon Alexander Valley 1987: Tougher than usual, but it's still good. Fruity and powerful, full-bodied, very flavorful and direct with firm tannins, pungent cherry and herb aromas and a hot finish. $7 (7/15/90) BB **80**
Cabernet Sauvignon Alexander Valley 1986: A well-structured package of a wine for the cellar. The lovely sweet fruit is nicely balanced by firm tannins. Drink now or in 1993. $8 (4/15/89) BB **85**
Cabernet Sauvignon Alexander Valley 1985 $6.50 (6/15/88) BB **87**
Cabernet Sauvignon Alexander Valley 1984 $6.50 (12/31/87) **79**
Cabernet Sauvignon Alexander Valley 1982 $6 (4/15/87) BB **87**
Meritage Alexander Valley 1988: A unique toast and caramel edge to the currant and cherry flavors makes this appealing up-front, but it loses intensity on the finish. A pleasant wine, with character. Ready to drink now through 1995. 2,000 cases made. $14 (11/15/91) **83**
Meritage Alexander Valley 1987: A good value. Has spicy, peppery aromas and a lean texture, broadening into finely focused cherry and currant flavors that persist into a long, elegant finish. Doesn't show everything it has on the first sip, but it reveals marvelous depth and extra dimensions that should develop well with cellaring until 1994. $12 (1/31/91) **88**

ESTRELLA RIVER
Cabernet Sauvignon Paso Robles 1985: Pickle and vegetal flavors are impossible to overlook. Red wine, yes; Cabernet, no. Drink now. Tasted twice. $9 (11/15/89) **67**
Cabernet Sauvignon Paso Robles 1983 $8 (4/15/88) **80**
Cabernet Sauvignon Paso Robles 1982 $10 (6/15/87) **85**
Cabernet Sauvignon Paso Robles 1981 $9 (5/01/85) **88**
Cabernet Sauvignon Paso Robles Founders Epic Collection 1983: Extremely ripe and vegetal, with pungent oaky aromas that are not especially appealing. Barely palatable. Drink now or in 1993. $12 (12/15/89) **65**
Cabernet Sauvignon San Luis Obispo County 1980 $10 (3/16/85) **77**
Cabernet Sauvignon San Luis Obispo County 1979 $6 (3/01/84) BB **84**

ETUDE
Cabernet Sauvignon California 1985 $16 (12/15/88) **92**
Cabernet Sauvignon Napa Valley 1987: Extremely herbal and earthy, this concentrated wine has intensity without grace and sturdiness without suppleness. Perhaps cellaring will soften it. Try in 1994. $24 (10/31/90) **85**
Cabernet Sauvignon Napa Valley 1986: Deep, rich, intense and fruity with layers of cedar, currant, plum and spice flavors that are tightly wound and compact. A heavyweight that needs to shed some of the tannin. Best in 1994 to 1996. 1,250 cases made. $20 (9/30/89) **92**

EYE OF THE SWAN
Cabernet Sauvignon California Limited Edition NV: A rather rough but ripe tasting red with firm tannins. Sturdy, undistinguished stuff. $7 (3/31/92) **77**

FAR NIENTE
Cabernet Sauvignon Napa Valley 1991: Intense and focused, with supple currant, toast, berry and plum flavors. Nicely proportioned, with firm but fine tannins. 15 percent Cabernet Franc and 6 percent Merlot. (NR) (5/15/92) (BT) **87+**
Cabernet Sauvignon Napa Valley 1988: Firm and flavorful, with brightly focused flavors of currant, raspberry, smoke and cedar. More than a touch of wood makes its present felt, but it isn't harsh or difficult. Should smooth out and be at its best after 1994 or '95. Tasted twice. $36 (11/15/91) **85**
Cabernet Sauvignon Napa Valley 1987: Earthy, spicy and supple, with some barnyardy, leathery overtones that the solid core of currant and plum can easily handle. It becomes distinctive on the finish, with a gentle texture and focused fruit flavor. Cellar until 1993 to '95. $33 (11/15/90) **88**
Cabernet Sauvignon Napa Valley 1986 $30 (9/30/89) **91**
Cabernet Sauvignon Napa Valley 1985 Rel: $28 Cur: $31 (CA-3/89) **92**
Cabernet Sauvignon Napa Valley 1984 Rel: $25 Cur: $30 (CA-3/89) **92**
Cabernet Sauvignon Napa Valley 1983 Rel: $25 Cur: $31 (CA-3/89) **87**
Cabernet Sauvignon Napa Valley 1982 Rel: $25 Cur: $36 (CA-3/89) **82**

GARY FARRELL
Cabernet Sauvignon Sonoma County 1987: Green bean and bell pepper notes and an austere edge detract from the currant and cedar flavors in this wine. It needs time to mellow, but the flavors are attractive and balanced. Give it a try in 1993. $16 (10/31/90) **87**
Cabernet Sauvignon Sonoma County Ladi's Vineyard 1988: Lean and focused, with sharp-edged currant aromas and flavors shaded by floral notes. Comes off as austere, but it should be fine after cellaring until 1994. 600 cases made. $18 (8/31/91) **86**

FELTA SPRINGS
Cabernet Sauvignon Sonoma County 1983 $5 (3/31/87) **78**

FENESTRA
Cabernet Sauvignon Livermore Valley 1988: Brilliantly fruity and tannic, with an impressive concentration of currant and plum aromas and flavors, hinting at cedar and tobacco on the finish. The tannins need until 1994 or '95 to settle. $12 (11/15/91) **85**
Cabernet Sauvignon Monterey Smith & Hook Vineyard 1987: Excessively herbal and vegetal aromas and flavors eventually become crisp and spicy on the finish, but where's the fruit? $14 (11/15/91) **75**

FENSALIR
Cabernet Sauvignon Napa Valley 1988: Hard and intense, with firm, drying tannins and a tight core of menthol, currant, plum and spice notes. Some may find the minty menthol notes overbearing and harsh. A young, lively wine that needs time. Drink in 1995 or '96. $14 (11/15/91) **85**

FERRARI-CARANO
Cabernet Sauvignon Alexander Valley 1987: Tightly wound, with ripe plum, cranberry and smoky oak flavors that are a bit disjointed now. Has firm tannins, suggesting it will benefit from cellaring until about 1994. $17.50 (7/15/91) **84**
Cabernet Sauvignon Alexander Valley 1986: A pleasant style, with mint, currant and herb-tinged Cabernet flavor of moderate depth and intensity, but it's lacking on the finish, which is a bit lean and short. Drink now. $17.50 (9/15/90) **80**

FETZER
Cabernet Sauvignon California 1988: Smooth and modestly flavorful, with black cherry and plum flavors, soft tannins and a light, fresh texture. Drink now. $8 (1/31/91) BB **81**
Cabernet Sauvignon California Reserve 1985: Rich and intense with ripe currant, cherry and plum flavors, framed by firm tannins and oak. Fine structure, but it's going to need some time to soften. Drink in 1994 to 1999. $17 (11/15/89) **87**
Cabernet Sauvignon California Valley Oaks 1988: Simple and fruity, with a toasty, tobacco edge

that can strike some tasters as slightly bitter, but it has plenty of currant and plum flavor to last on the finish. Drinkable now. $8 (11/15/91) **82**
Cabernet Sauvignon Lake County 1985 $6.50 (8/31/87) BB **82**
Cabernet Sauvignon Lake County 1984 $8 (5/15/87) **74**
Cabernet Sauvignon Lake County 1983 $5.50 (5/01/86) **83**
Cabernet Sauvignon Lake County 1982 $5.50 (5/16/84) **78**
Cabernet Sauvignon Mendocino County 1981 $7 (12/16/84) **86**
Cabernet Sauvignon Mendocino Barrel Select 1986: Smooth and velvety, with generous black cherry and currant aromas and flavors, plus a leathery undertone that some may love and others may hate. The structure is firm and the flavors are juicy. Drink now. $11 (4/15/90) **90**
Cabernet Sauvignon Mendocino Barrel Select 1985 $10 (12/15/88) **85**
Cabernet Sauvignon Mendocino Barrel Select 1984 $9 (11/30/87) **82**
Cabernet Sauvignon California Barrel Select 1983 $8 (6/15/87) **70**
Cabernet Sauvignon Mendocino Barrel Select 1982 $7 (2/01/85) **73**
Cabernet Sauvignon Mendocino Special Reserve 1987 (NR) (4/15/89) (BT) **85+**
Cabernet Sauvignon Mendocino County 1981 $7 (12/16/84) **86**
Cabernet Sauvignon Sonoma County Reserve 1986: Lean and tight, but packed with plum, currant and smoky oak aromas and flavors that persist into a long finish, where it turns a bit gamy. Should develop complexity with cellaring to 1995 and beyond. $24 (9/30/91) **88**
Cabernet Sauvignon Sonoma County Reserve 1985: A dense, rich, concentrated style, with intense herb, chocolate, currant and black cherry flavors that are tightly fastened down. The tannins are firm yet supple. It's very well balanced, and may show even more depth and complexity. Young and on its way up. Drink 1993 to '96. 3,000 cases made. $24 (8/31/90) **86**
Cabernet Sauvignon Mendocino Special Reserve 1984 $14 (12/31/88) **85**

FIELD STONE
Cabernet Sauvignon Alexander Valley 1987: Has plenty of rich flavors up-front, including olive, cassis and tobacco, with moderate tannins, a velvety texture and a finish that tapers off quickly. Lush tasting and almost ready to drink. Try now to 1995. 4,260 cases made. $14 (2/28/91) **85**
Cabernet Sauvignon Alexander Valley 1983 $11 (10/15/88) **74**
Cabernet Sauvignon Alexander Valley Home Ranch Vineyard 1985: Smells sweet and fruity, then turns austere and a bit harsh on the palate, lacking the softness and generosity this region can produce. $14 (4/15/89) **70**
Cabernet Sauvignon Alexander Valley Hoot Owl Reserve 1986: Supple, fruity, distinctively herbal and less hearty than usual, offering moderate depth of blackberry and currant flavors scented by pleasant herbal accents. The velvety tannins don't get in the way, so it's drinkable now, but it could keep developing through 1993. 4,584 cases made. $20 (12/15/90) **85**
Cabernet Sauvignon Alexander Valley Hoot Owl Creek Vineyards 1985: Has massive tannins and very ripe, full-bodied, jammy black cherry and currant flavor and a very dry finish. Needs time to come around. Drink in 1994. $20 (3/31/89) **87**
Cabernet Sauvignon Alexander Valley Hoot Owl Creek Vineyards 1984 $14 (10/15/88) **82**
Cabernet Sauvignon Alexander Valley Staten Family Reserve 1987: The extremely toasty flavors border on burnt, and turn vegetal and lean. Has a hint of cherry, but not much fruit. An odd style. Tasted twice, with consistent notes. 200 cases made. $25 (11/15/91) **72**
Cabernet Sauvignon Alexander Valley Turkey Hill Vineyard 1985: With attractive, mature Cabernet aromas and flavors on a firm framework of tannin, this is a bit harsh, but it smooths out and echoes spice, chocolate and ripe cherry on the solid finish. Drinkable now, but cellaring until 1993 or '94 should polish the tannins. $18 (2/28/91) **84**
Cabernet Sauvignon Alexander Valley Turkey Hill Vineyard 1984 $16 (12/31/88) **88**
Cabernet Sauvignon Alexander Valley Turkey Hill Vineyard 1982 $12 (3/16/86) **78**

FIRESTONE
Cabernet Sauvignon Santa Ynez Valley 1988: A flavorful but uncomplicated Cabernet, with herb and bell pepper flavors, moderate tannins and a rough finish. $12 (11/15/91) **75**
Cabernet Sauvignon Santa Ynez Valley 1987: Attractive. A crisp, slightly woody-smelling Cabernet that has ample fruit and nice touches of sweet oak on the finish. Well-balanced and deep in flavor, with moderate tannins. $11 (5/31/90) **82**
Cabernet Sauvignon Santa Ynez Valley 1986: Herb and vegetal notes compliment the cherry and currant flavors in this medium-bodied, ready-to-drink wine. $10 (12/15/89) **81**
Cabernet Sauvignon Santa Ynez Valley 1985 $9.50 (8/31/88) **72**
Cabernet Sauvignon Santa Ynez Valley 1984 $9.50 (3/31/88) **72**
Cabernet Sauvignon Santa Ynez Valley 1983 $9 (6/15/87) **77**
Cabernet Sauvignon Santa Ynez Valley 1981 $8 (3/01/85) **89**
Cabernet Sauvignon Santa Ynez Valley Reserve 1988: Strives for complexity, with straightforward currant, toast and herb-tinged plum flavors that are well proportioned, but not especially rich. Successful for its moderation and proportion, but not quite up to reserve caliber or an $18 price tag. Drinks well now through 1994. 1,500 cases made. $18 (2/28/91) **84**
Cabernet Sauvignon Santa Ynez Valley Special Release 1977 $9.50 (4/16/85) **77**
Cabernet Sauvignon Santa Ynez Valley Vintage Reserve 1985: Tarry, vegetal and tannic, with cooked bean flavors that are not particularly appetizing. At $25, it's extremely high priced for what's in the bottle. Not recommended. Tasted twice. $25 (12/15/89) **67**
Cabernet Sauvignon Santa Ynez Valley Vintage Reserve 1979 $12 (3/16/86) **73**

FISHER
Cabernet Sauvignon Napa-Sonoma Counties Coach Insignia 1991: Plush and fruity, with deep, intense, concentrated plum and currant-tinged flavors. There's a wild streak to the flavors and the tannins are rough, but nothing out of line for a barrel sample. 80 percent Cabernet Sauvignon, 10 percent Cabernet Franc and 10 percent Merlot. 2,000 cases made. (NR) (5/15/92) (BT) **85+**
Cabernet Sauvignon Napa-Sonoma Counties Coach Insignia 1990 (NR) (5/15/91) (BT) **90+**
Cabernet Sauvignon Napa-Sonoma Counties Coach Insignia 1989: Hard and tannic, a strapping wine, with a solid core of currant, chocolate and a bit of leather flavor. Needs until 1995 to '97 to break down the tannins. Tasted twice. 1,565 cases made. $18 (3/31/92) **82**
Cabernet Sauvignon Napa-Sonoma Counties Coach Insignia 1988 $15 (5/15/90) (BT) **85+**
Cabernet Sauvignon Napa-Sonoma Counties Coach Insignia 1987: Tight and firm, with tobacco, spice, red cherry and currant flavors. The tannins and oak notes dry out on the finish. Best to cellar until 1995. Rel: $20 Cur: $23 (11/15/91) **84**
Cabernet Sauvignon Sonoma County 1983 $12.50 (6/15/87) **73**
Cabernet Sauvignon Sonoma County 1982 $12.50 (11/01/85) **88**

Key to Symbols

The scores reported here are the results of blind tastings conducted by our panel of senior editors. Wines that carry the initials below are results of individual tastings.

THE WINE SPECTATOR 100-POINT SCALE *95-100*—Classic, a great wine; *90-94*—Outstanding, superior character and style; *80-89*—Good to very good, a wine with special qualities; *70-79*—Average, drinkable wine that may have minor flaws; *60-69*—Below average, drinkable but not recommended; *50-59*—Poor, undrinkable, not recommended. "+"—With a score indicates a range; used primarily with barrel tastings to indicate a preliminary score.

SPECIAL DESIGNATIONS SS—Spectator Selection, CS—Cellar Selection, BB—Best Buy, (SNA)—Price not available, (NR)—Not released.

TASTER'S INITIALS (JG)—Jim Gordon, (HS)—Harvey Steiman, (JL)—James Laube, (JS)—James Suckling, (TM)—Thomas Matthews, (TR)—Terry Robards, (PM)—Per-Henrik Mansson, (BT)—Barrel Tasting (these wines were tasted blind from barrel samples), (CA-date)—*California's Great Cabernets* by James Laube, (CH-date)—*California's Great Chardonnays* by James Laube, (VP-date)—*Vintage Port* by James Suckling.

DATE TASTED Dates in parentheses represent the issue in which the rating was published.

Cabernet Sauvignon Sonoma County 1981 $12 (12/01/84) **85**
Cabernet Sauvignon Sonoma County Coach Insignia 1986: Firm, clean and sharply focused, with nicely defined cherry, plum and chocolate aromas and flavors, medium-bodied and tannic enough to need cellaring until 1994. $20 (1/31/90) **87**
Cabernet Sauvignon Sonoma County Coach Insignia 1985 Rel: $18 Cur: $22 (CA-3/89) **90**
Cabernet Sauvignon Sonoma County Coach Insignia 1984 Rel: $18 Cur: $25 (CA-3/89) **89**

FITCH MOUNTAIN
Cabernet Sauvignon Napa Valley 1985: Juicy but one-dimensional. Attractive at first with ripe, sweet berry aromas and a hint of cedar, but then it feels tart iand almost sour. $9 (4/15/89) **74**

FIVE PALMS
Cabernet Sauvignon Napa Valley 1984 $6 (3/31/87) BB **87**

FLORA SPRINGS
Cabernet Sauvignon Napa Valley Reserve 1991: Ripe and jammy, with cherry, loganberry and currant flavors that turn supple and elegant for a barrel sample. 4 percent Merlot. 1,000 cases made. (NR) (5/15/92) (BT) **86+**
Cabernet Sauvignon Napa Valley 1990 (NR) (5/15/91) (BT) **90+**
Cabernet Sauvignon Napa Valley 1989 (NR) (5/15/91) (BT) **85+**
Cabernet Sauvignon Napa Valley Cellar Select 1988: A medium-bodied, fruity Cabernet, with floral, spicy aromas and ripe plum flavors that tighten up with tannins on the finish. Probably best to try in 1996. Tasted twice, with consistent notes. $24 (2/29/92) **85**
Cabernet Sauvignon Napa Valley Cellar Select 1987: A powerful style that's firm and intense, with black cherry, currant and plum flavors that are very attractive, plush and concentrated until the finish, when the tannins sneak up. Drinkable now, but could use cellaring until at least 1995. 1,200 cases made. $25 (11/15/90) **91**
Cabernet Sauvignon Napa Valley 1986 Rel: $15 Cur: $18 (3/15/90) **85**
Cabernet Sauvignon Napa Valley 1985 Rel: $15 Cur: $18 (7/31/89) **90**
Cabernet Sauvignon Napa Valley 1984 Rel: $13 Cur: $18 (CA-3/89) **85**
Cabernet Sauvignon Napa Valley 1983 Rel: $13 Cur: $17 (12/15/86) **79**
Cabernet Sauvignon Napa Valley 1982 $9 (10/15/86) **78**
Cabernet Sauvignon Napa Valley 1981 $12 (12/16/84) **82**
Cabernet Sauvignon Napa Valley 1980 Rel: $12 Cur: $28 (CA-3/89) **85**
Trilogy Napa Valley 1991: Young, fresh, tight and jammy, offering plum and herb notes. Tannic and concentrated, with a full-blown finish. 40 percent Cabernet Sauvignon, 35 percent Merlot and 25 percent Cabernet Franc. 1,500 cases made. (NR) (5/15/92) (BT) **85+**
Trilogy Napa Valley 1990 (NR) (5/15/91) (BT) **90+**
Trilogy Napa Valley 1989 (NR) (5/15/91) (BT) **90+**
Trilogy Napa Valley 1988: Tough and chewy in texture, with strong anise and smoke aromas and flavors around a submerged core of currant and plum flavors. The tannins need until 1996 to '98 to soften. Tasted twice, with consistent notes. $33 (2/29/92) **86**
Trilogy Napa Valley 1987: Pretty currant, cherry, plum and toast flavors are rich, lively and well integrated, with soft, round tannins and a silky-smooth texture. Has plenty of wood on the finish. Elegant and stylish, with crisp acidity sustaining the flavors. Drink in 1994 to 2000. Much better than bottles reviewed earlier. 2,000 cases made. $35 (5/15/91) **90**
Trilogy Napa Valley 1986 Rel: $33 Cur: $36 (2/15/90) **94**
Trilogy Napa Valley 1985 Rel: $30 Cur: $38 (CA-3/89) **88**
Trilogy Napa Valley 1984 Rel: $30 Cur: $33 (CA-3/89) **84**

THOMAS FOGARTY
Cabernet Sauvignon Napa Valley 1985: An extreme style, with mature barnyardy, leather aromas and flavors against a background of ripe cherry that barely makes its presence felt. Unbalanced toward woody and earthy flavors. 504 cases made. $15 (7/15/91) **70**

FOLIE A DEUX
Cabernet Sauvignon Napa Valley 1987: A generous, supple style that allows the currant, berry and herb flavors to glow, with coffee, cedar and chocolate nuances on the finish. It's firm and smoothly balanced, with flavors bordering on opulent. Drinkable now, but best in the mid-1990s. 1,175 cases made. $18 (11/15/90) **92**
Cabernet Sauvignon Napa Valley 1986: Youthful and lively, with a solid core of blueberry and currant flavors surrounded by overtones of vanilla and toast. An earthiness may detract for some. Drink now or in 1993. $16.50 (4/15/90) **85**
Cabernet Sauvignon Napa Valley 1984 $14.50 (5/31/88) **88**

FOPPIANO
Cabernet Sauvignon Russian River Valley 1985: Mature for its age, but good to drink now. Brownish red in color with tealike aromas and flavors that are soft and mature. $9 (6/30/89) **71**
Cabernet Sauvignon Russian River Valley 1984 $8.50 (4/30/88) **77**
Cabernet Sauvignon Russian River Valley 1981 $7.75 (4/16/85) **81**
Cabernet Sauvignon Sonoma County 1989: A fruity, appealing young Cabernet that's built for drinking now through 1993. Fresh berry and herbal flavors are its hallmark. $9.50 (3/15/92) **82**
Cabernet Sauvignon Sonoma County 1986: Light and spicy, with aromas and flavors that veer off in the direction of tea and herbs, but it manages to rein in enough dark cherry flavor to stay balanced. Already seems mature. $9 (11/15/90) **79**

FOREST LAKE
Cabernet Sauvignon California 1988: Fruity and spicy like a Beaujolais, with candied fruit flavors that persist on the finish. Not a classic style, but a pleasant wine nonetheless. $6.50 (11/15/91) **81**

FORMAN
Cabernet Sauvignon Napa Valley 1988: Has a solid core of tea, black cherry and currant flavor, backed by strong, rich tannins. A young, intense wine that shows more depth and concentration than most '88s. Picks up an herbal, oaky note on the aftertaste. Cellar until 1996. 1,260 cases made. Rel: $32 Cur: $45 (8/31/91) **88**
Cabernet Sauvignon Napa Valley 1987: Concentrated currant, cherry, cedar and spice flavors are tightly wound, firm and tannic in this ripe, intense style. Has a supple, smooth texture before the tannins build up. The fruit flavor shoulders through on the finish. Sure to improve with age. Drink 1994 to 2000. 1,600 cases made. Rel: $26 Cur: $44 (9/30/90) **93**
Cabernet Sauvignon Napa Valley 1986: Austere and very well structured, with firm black cherry, cedar, herb and plum flavors that are tightly wound, deeply concentrated and framed by tannins. Tasty now, but let it be until 1995. Rel: $20 Cur: $51 (6/15/89) **93**
Cabernet Sauvignon Napa Valley 1985 Rel: $18 Cur: $76 (CA-3/89) **93**
Cabernet Sauvignon Napa Valley 1984 Rel: $18 Cur: $70 (CA-3/89) **92**
Cabernet Sauvignon Napa Valley 1983 Rel: $15.50 Cur: $70 (CA-3/89) **90**

FOX MOUNTAIN
Cabernet Sauvignon Russian River Valley Reserve 1985: Dense, earthy and vegetal with some plum flavor, it's also quite tannic. Drink now to 1995. 2,067 cases made. $19 (9/15/89) **75**
Cabernet Sauvignon Russian River Valley Reserve 1984: Firm and concentrated, yet supple enough to display the bright berry and currant flavor in a smooth style. Drink now. $18 (3/15/89) **85**
Cabernet Sauvignon Russian River Valley Reserve 1982 $18 (12/31/87) **77**
Cabernet Sauvignon Russian River Valley Reserve 1981 $16 (12/15/86) **79**

FOXEN
Cabernet Sauvignon Santa Barbara County 1989: Rich and vibrant, jam-packed with ripe currant, black cherry, plum and spice flavors that are sharply focused and backed by smooth tannins and plenty of depth. The tannins are strong enough for cellaring through 1994, but it's tempting to enjoy now for its purity of fruit. 750 cases made. $20 (11/15/91) **91**
Cabernet Sauvignon Santa Barbara County 1988: Deliciously fruity and focused, with generous

blackberry, currant and plum aromas and flavors that extend into a long finish. A wine with personality and plenty of verve. Drinkable now, but could continue to improve through 1994. 350 cases made. $18 (11/15/91) **89**

FRANCISCAN
Cabernet Sauvignon Alexander Valley 1980 $7.50 (10/16/84) **86**
Cabernet Sauvignon Napa Valley 1979 Rel: $8.50 Cur: $18 (CA-3/89) **79**
Cabernet Sauvignon Napa Valley Library Selection 1985 Rel: $17.50 Cur: $20 (CA-3/89) **88**
Cabernet Sauvignon Napa Valley Oakville Estate 1988: An exotic, spicy array of aromas leads to a velvety texture and ripe cherry, cedar and herb flavors. Tempting to drink now, but it could be cellared until 1993 or so. Tasted twice. $12 (11/15/91) **81**
Cabernet Sauvignon Napa Valley Oakville Estate 1987: Tart, herbal and tightly focused, with ripe cherry and bay leaf flavors, turning slightly chocolaty and smooth on the finish. Seems seductive and generous until the crisp acidity and tannins kick in. Needs until 1995 to 2000 to soften the tannins. Tasted twice. $12 (2/15/91) **89**
Cabernet Sauvignon Napa Valley Oakville Estate 1986: Forward and open, this wine has juicy currant, herb and spicy oak flavors that are full-bodied and deceptively tannic. It needs another two to three years to mature fully. Drink now to 1994. $11 (7/15/90) **84**
Cabernet Sauvignon Napa Valley Oakville Estate 1985 $11 (5/15/89) **86**
Cabernet Sauvignon Napa Valley Oakville Estate 1984 $9.50 (9/15/88) **84**
Cabernet Sauvignon Napa Valley Oakville Estate 1983 $9 (4/30/87) **75**
Cabernet Sauvignon Napa Valley Oakville Estate Reserve 1987: Pretty currant, cherry and raspberry flavors are ripe and rich, with good concentration and depth. Finishes with tight, firm tannins, but it's in sync with the '87 vintage. Elegant and stylish, it dances across the palate. 1,600 cases made. $16 (11/15/91) SS **91**
Cabernet Sauvignon Napa Valley Oakville Estate Reserve 1985: Has some generous ripe plum and cherry aromas and flavors, clamped tightly into a firm, tannic framework. The tightness and concentration bode well for this wine with cellaring until at least 1994 to '95. Big and awkward now, but it should grow into itself. 1,400 cases made. Rel: $17.50 Cur: $20 (5/31/90) **88**
Cabernet Sauvignon Napa Valley Private Reserve 1984 Rel: $9 Cur: $15 (CA-3/89) **87**
Cabernet Sauvignon Napa Valley Private Reserve 1983 Rel: $8.50 Cur: $16 (CA-3/89) **85**
Cabernet Sauvignon Napa Valley Reserve 1978 Rel: $15 Cur: $23 (CA-3/89) **78**
Cabernet Sauvignon Napa Valley Reserve 1975 Rel: $12 Cur: $28 (CA-3/89) **82**
Meritage Napa Valley 1988: Flavorful, focused and balanced, with well-defined plum, spice and vanilla aromas and flavors. Not concentrated, but has enough to be drinkable through 1993 to '95. Rel: $16 Cur: $20 (11/15/91) **83**
Meritage Napa Valley 1987: Has plenty of flavor, with layers of herb, plum, cedar and chocolate that are high in extract, but it's a rough-hewn style, with a somewhat coarse texture and firm, drying tannins. Needs cellaring until 1995 or '96 to mellow. A blend of Cabernet Sauvignon and Merlot. 2,900 cases made. Rel: $17 Cur: $21 (4/30/91) **87**
Meritage Napa Valley 1986: Mature and ready to drink, it offers supple currant and cherry flavors along with a touch of herb and oak. Balanced and simple. Drink now. Tasted twice. Rel: $15 Cur: $23 (7/31/90) **79**
Meritage Napa Valley 1985 Rel: $20 Cur: $28 (3/31/90) **90**

FREEMARK ABBEY
Cabernet Sauvignon Napa Valley 1987: Sharply focused, with rich, ripe, tightly wound currant, chocolate, smoke and spicy oak flavors. Dry tannins come through on the finish. Needs cellaring until 1995 to soften. $16 (7/31/91) **86**
Cabernet Sauvignon Napa Valley 1986: Has good Cabernet flavor, with deep currant, herb, cherry and spice notes and an oak overlay adding dimension. Drink now and beyond. Tasted three times. $15 (11/15/90) **83**
Cabernet Sauvignon Napa Valley 1985: Intense and lively with firm, hard tannins and ripe fruit, but lacking finesse and elegance. With time it may gain it, but for now its rather one-dimensional. Tasted three times. $15 (10/31/89) **79**
Cabernet Sauvignon Napa Valley 1984 $14 (2/15/89) **84**
Cabernet Sauvignon Napa Valley 1983 $12 (2/15/88) **68**
Cabernet Sauvignon Napa Valley 1982 Rel: $12 Cur: $17 (2/15/87) **84**
Cabernet Sauvignon Napa Valley 1981 $10.50 (10/01/85) **79**
Cabernet Sauvignon Napa Valley 1980 Rel: $14.50 Cur: $22 (5/16/84) **84**
Cabernet Sauvignon Napa Valley 1979 Rel: $10.50 Cur: $25 (1/01/84) **89**
Cabernet Sauvignon Napa Valley 1969 $52 (4/01/86) **68**
Cabernet Sauvignon Napa Valley Bosché 1987: Laced with herb, olive, currant, mint and spice notes, but it's an austere style where the tannins are still a bit crisp and tight. Best after 1995. Tasted twice. 2,248 cases made. $25 (11/15/91) **87**
Cabernet Sauvignon Napa Valley Bosché 1986: Firm and tannic with a solid core of minty- and herbal-tinged Cabernet flavor that turns earthy and leathery on the finish. A tough style to warm up to. Drink now. Tasted four times, with consistent results. $24 (7/31/90) **76**
Cabernet Sauvignon Napa Valley Bosché 1985: Lean, tight and concentrated with firm black cherry, plum, currant, earth and cedar flavors that are intense and lively with a narrow, focused finish. Plenty of flavor on the aftertaste, but this wine will need cellaring until at least 1994. 3,500 cases made. Rel: $24 Cur: $33 (7/31/89) **90**
Cabernet Sauvignon Napa Valley Bosché 1984 Rel: $20 Cur: $24 (CA-3/89) **88**
Cabernet Sauvignon Napa Valley Bosché 1983 Rel: $18 Cur: $33 (CA-3/89) **86**
Cabernet Sauvignon Napa Valley Bosché 1982 Rel: $15 Cur: $41 (CA-3/89) **88**
Cabernet Sauvignon Napa Valley Bosché 1982 Rel: $15 Cur: $41 (5/16/86) CS **93**
Cabernet Sauvignon Napa Valley Bosché 1981 Rel: $14 Cur: $33 (CA-3/89) **86**
Cabernet Sauvignon Napa Valley Bosché 1980 Rel: $14.50 Cur: $35 (CA-3/89) **88**
Cabernet Sauvignon Napa Valley Bosché 1979 Rel: $12 Cur: $25 (CA-3/89) **93**
Cabernet Sauvignon Napa Valley Bosché 1978 Rel: $12.50 Cur: $56 (CA-3/89) **93**
Cabernet Sauvignon Napa Valley Bosché 1977 Rel: $12.50 Cur: $25 (CA-3/89) **88**
Cabernet Sauvignon Napa Valley Bosché 1976 Rel: $12.50 Cur: $32 (CA-3/89) **85**
Cabernet Sauvignon Napa Valley Bosché 1975 Rel: $10 Cur: $57 (CA-3/89) **90**
Cabernet Sauvignon Napa Valley Bosché 1974 Rel: $7.75 Cur: $70 (CA-3/89) **91**
Cabernet Sauvignon Napa Valley Bosché 1973 Rel: $8 Cur: $70 (CA-3/89) **88**
Cabernet Sauvignon Napa Valley Bosché 1972 Rel: $6 Cur: $30 (CA-3/89) **80**
Cabernet Sauvignon Napa Valley Bosché 1971 Rel: $6.75 Cur: $45 (CA-3/89) **86**
Cabernet Sauvignon Napa Valley Bosché 1970 Rel: $8.75 Cur: $125 (CA-3/89) **91**
Cabernet Sauvignon Napa Valley Sycamore Vineyards 1986: Firm and tight, with a pretty core of black cherry, currant, anise and plum flavors that are rich and concentrated. The tannins are still firm and gritty, like many '86s, but the herb, spice and olive nuances add dimension and complexity. Needs until 1995. 3,000 cases made. $25 (11/15/91) **91**
Cabernet Sauvignon Napa Valley Sycamore Vineyards 1985: A bit awkward now, with crisp acidity and lean, tight, compact fruit, cedar, coffee and currant flavors and hints of cherry that peek through on the finish. Needs time to soften. Drink in 1994 to 2000. $25 (10/31/89) **88**
Cabernet Sauvignon Napa Valley Sycamore Vineyards 1984 Rel: $20 Cur: $23 (12/15/88) **91**

FREMONT CREEK
Cabernet Sauvignon Mendocino-Napa Counties 1986: A ripe, generous style of wine on a smooth, gentle frame, showing plenty of plum and currant aromas and flavors that linger. Hints of maturity on the nose suggest it will be best starting in 1993. $8 (4/30/91) BB **85**
Cabernet Sauvignon Mendocino-Napa Counties 1985 $9.50 (3/31/88) **78**

J. FRITZ
Cabernet Sauvignon Alexander Valley 1985 $10 (12/31/88) **57**

FROG'S LEAP
Cabernet Sauvignon Napa Valley 1991: The tight, compact structure front-loads the fruit, offering plenty of berry and currant flavors up-front. Needs time to round itself out. 8 percent Cabernet Franc. (NR) (5/15/92) (BT) **85+**
Cabernet Sauvignon Napa Valley 1988: Has lovely ripe raspberry, plum and cherry flavors of moderate depth, concentration and intensity. Not too tannic. The pretty black cherry flavors grow on you and fan out on the finish. Drink in 1993 to '95. Rel: $17 Cur: $19 (12/15/90) **88**
Cabernet Sauvignon Napa Valley 1987: Enormous depth and richness, a massively concentrated wine that offers intense currant, plum and cassis flavors framed by toasty oak. For all its tannins, there's a silky texture evolving on the palate and a long aftertaste, both of which bode well for cellaring. Try in 1993 and beyond. 3,900 cases made. Rel: $15 Cur: $25 (12/31/89) SS **94**
Cabernet Sauvignon Napa Valley 1986 Rel: $14 Cur: $41 (CA-3/89) **94**
Cabernet Sauvignon Napa Valley 1985 Rel: $12 Cur: $20 (CA-3/89) **85**
Cabernet Sauvignon Napa Valley 1984 Rel: $10 Cur: $30 (3/31/87) SS **95**
Cabernet Sauvignon Napa Valley 1983 Rel: $10 Cur: $22 (CA-3/89) **80**
Cabernet Sauvignon Napa Valley 1982 Rel: $9 Cur: $25 (CA-3/89) **87**

GAINEY
Cabernet Sauvignon Santa Maria Valley 1988: An earthy tasting wine with leathery aromas and muddled herb and metallic flavors. For fans of the decadent style. Tasted twice. 1,760 cases made. $13 (3/15/92) **77**
Cabernet Sauvignon Santa Barbara County 1987: Earthy and smoky, with olive and currant aromas and flavors, moderate tannins and supple balance. Should be fine in a spicy, earthy style with cellaring until 1993 to '95. 1,695 cases made. $13 (11/15/90) **82**
Cabernet Sauvignon Santa Barbara County Limited Selection 1986: A deliciously complex wine, with aromas of mint, spice, ripe currants and cherries, and mouthfilling flavors. Smooth textured, medium-bodied, well balanced, with flavors that last on the finish. Ready to drink now, but it should improve through 1993. $15 (12/15/89) **89**

E. & J. GALLO
Cabernet Sauvignon California Limited Release Reserve 1980 $8 (11/15/86) **78**
Cabernet Sauvignon Limited Release 1981 $5 (12/31/88) **75**
Cabernet Sauvignon California Reserve NV: Fresh and fruity, with generous currant and berry aromas and flavors that persist on the finish. Drinkable now. $6 (11/15/91) **84**
Cabernet Sauvignon Northern Sonoma Reserve 1984: Ripe, rustic and more than a little earthy, but the plum, cherry and spice flavors win out in the end. A mature, earthy style that's drinkable now. $7 (10/15/91) **80**
Cabernet Sauvignon Northern Sonoma Reserve 1982 $6 (5/31/91) BB **82**

GAN EDEN
Cabernet Sauvignon Alexander Valley 1987: A youngster, still raw, it's big and mouthfilling, with jammy ripe fruit and forceful tannins. Drink in 1994. 2,700 cases made. $18 (3/31/91) **90**
Cabernet Sauvignon Alexander Valley 1986: Plenty of ripe, generous fruit up-front, with layers of spice, currant, plum and cedar in a tight, lean, compact style that's firmer than most Alexander Valley Cabernets. The tannic finish suggests further cellaring before approaching. Drink in 1993 to '97. $15 (2/15/89) **86**

GARLAND RANCH
Cabernet Sauvignon Central Coast 1986: Obviously vegetal, the green bean aromas and cooked, smoky flavors will be unattractive to those who like fruit in their wines. $6.75 (10/31/89) **70**
Cabernet Sauvignon Monterey County 1984 $6.75 (8/31/88) BB **84**

GEYSER PEAK
Cabernet Sauvignon Alexander Valley 1984 $7.50 (3/15/88) **77**
Cabernet Sauvignon Alexander Valley 1983 $7 (3/15/87) BB **87**
Cabernet Sauvignon Alexander Valley 1982 $7 (9/15/86) **68**
Cabernet Sauvignon Alexander Valley 1980 $6.50 (1/01/85) **57**
Cabernet Sauvignon Alexander Valley Estate Reserve 1987: Ripe, rich and focused, with a broad texture, generous black currant, blackberry and chocolate flavors that echo on the long finish and nice spice and vanilla notes from oak. A harmonious wine that should benefit from aging through at least 1993 to '95. 2,200 cases made. $14 (6/15/91) **89**
Cabernet Sauvignon Alexander Valley Estate Reserve 1986: Has the herbal quality often found in Alexander Valley Cabernets but it's balanced by plenty of pretty cherry and currant flavors. The tannins are broad, rich and smooth, making it drinkable now, but it will probably be better in 1994 or '95. 1,200 cases made. $15 (9/30/90) **85**
Cabernet Sauvignon Alexander Valley Estate Reserve 1985 $15 (5/15/89) **77**
Cabernet Sauvignon Sonoma County 1987 $8.50 (11/30/90) BB **88**
Cabernet Sauvignon Sonoma County 1981 $7 (6/16/85) **83**
Réserve Alexandre Alexander Valley 1987 $18 (6/15/91) **90**
Réserve Alexandre Alexander Valley 1986 $20 (9/30/90) **89**
Réserve Alexandre Alexander Valley 1985: Soft, velvety and aromatic, boasting olive- and herb-tinged plum aromas and flavors, spicy and cedary on the finish, complex and artfully balanced. Has the concentration of fruit and balance to warrant cellaring. Probably best now to 1995. 2,100 cases made. $19 (9/30/89) **88**
Réserve Alexandre Alexander Valley 1984 $19 (8/31/88) **89**
Réserve Alexandre Alexander Valley 1983 $15 (4/30/87) **80**

GIRARD
Cabernet Sauvignon Napa Valley 1991: Tough and tight, with a firm core of currant, blackberry, anise and cedar flavors. A rough young wine that has plenty of potential. 8 percent Cabernet Franc. 3,100 cases made. (NR) (5/15/92) (BT) **87+**
Cabernet Sauvignon Napa Valley 1990 (NR) (5/15/91) (BT) **90+**
Cabernet Sauvignon Napa Valley 1989 (NR) (5/15/91) (BT) **85+**
Cabernet Sauvignon Napa Valley 1988: Hard-edged and tannic, with very dry fruit flavors. It takes time to find the currant and berry flavors, but once you do you discover pretty cedar and oak nuances that add dimension. Patience is required—best around 1995. Tasted twice, with consistent notes. 1,360 cases made. $16 (11/15/91) **85**
Cabernet Sauvignon Napa Valley 1987: Intense, concentrated and tannic, with a solid core of austere currant, black cherry and spice flavor that is firm and structured. Needs time to chisel away at the tannins, but it's balanced and well made. Drink 1994 to '99. 1,536 cases made. Rel: $16 Cur: $20 (11/15/90) **86**
Cabernet Sauvignon Napa Valley 1986 Rel: $16 Cur: $19 (11/15/89) **89**
Cabernet Sauvignon Napa Valley 1985 Rel: $15 Cur: $18 (9/15/88) **88**
Cabernet Sauvignon Napa Valley 1984 Rel: $11 Cur: $18 (11/30/87) **88**
Cabernet Sauvignon Napa Valley 1983 Rel: $12 Cur: $15 (12/15/86) **71**
Cabernet Sauvignon Napa Valley 1982 Rel: $12.50 Cur: $32 (CA-3/89) **87**
Cabernet Sauvignon Napa Valley 1981 Rel: $12.50 Cur: $20 (CA-3/89) **86**
Cabernet Sauvignon Napa Valley 1980 Rel: $11 Cur: $25 (CA-3/89) **92**
Cabernet Sauvignon Napa Valley Reserve 1991: Tight and intense, with layers of currant, blackberry and plum flavors. Is also quite tannic and austere at this stage, but the fruit pours through on the aftertaste. 10 percent Cabernet Franc. 822 cases made. (NR) (5/15/92) (BT) **87+**
Cabernet Sauvignon Napa Valley Reserve 1987: Pleasantly fruity, with intense ripe black cherry and currant flavors that have a spicy oak edge. Tannic, but with good depth of flavor. Strong fruit flavors come through on the finish. Best to cellar until 1996. 697 cases made. Rel: $25 Cur: $29 (11/15/91) **88**
Cabernet Sauvignon Napa Valley Reserve 1986: Big and tannic in style, but with concentrated, ripe currant, cherry and spice flavors underneath. At this young age it's rough and raw and needs to develop elegance and smoothness. Try in 1994 or beyond. 560 cases made. Rel: $25 Cur: $39 (11/15/90) **87**

Cabernet Sauvignon Napa Valley Reserve 1985: Has a ripe, effusively fruity style with plenty of depth and tannin. The plum and currant flavors are well focused, but could use a shade more richness and depth. The finish gets tannic. Drink in 1994 to '98. Tasted twice. Rel: $25 Cur: $35 (2/15/90) **86**

Cabernet Sauvignon Napa Valley Reserve 1984 Rel: $25 Cur: $37 (CA-3/89) **92**

Cabernet Sauvignon Napa Valley Reserve 1983 Rel: $18 Cur: $23 (CA-3/89) **87**

GLASS MOUNTAIN QUARRY

Cabernet Sauvignon Napa Valley 1988: Lean and crisp, with pleasant red cherry and spice aromas and flavors on a modest frame. Has charm and grace. Tasty for current drinking. From Markham. 5,448 cases made. $8 (10/15/91) BB **85**

GLEN ELLEN

Cabernet Sauvignon California Proprietor's Reserve 1988: A light, red cherry-flavored wine, with firm tannins and basic flavors. Decent for drinking now through 1993. $6 (11/15/91) BB **79**

Cabernet Sauvignon California Proprietor's Reserve 1987: A spicy, light wine, with almost sweet flavors of strawberry and herbs and light tannins. $6 (1/31/91) **79**

Cabernet Sauvignon California Proprietor's Reserve 1986 $4.50 (7/15/88) BB **82**

Cabernet Sauvignon Sonoma Valley Benziger Family Selection 1984 $14 (10/15/87) **82**

Cabernet Sauvignon Sonoma Valley Benziger Family Selection 1983 $9.75 (5/15/87) **91**

Cabernet Sauvignon Sonoma Valley Glen Ellen Estate 1982 $9.75 (2/01/85) **85**

Cabernet Sauvignon Sonoma Valley Imagery Series 1985 $12.50 (2/15/89) **86**

GRACE FAMILY

Cabernet Sauvignon Napa Valley 1991: Ripe, supple and generous, with rich currant, plum and sage flavors and spicy, toasty oak nuances. The tannins are soft and fleshy and the finish is long and fruity. (NR) (5/15/92) (BT) **90+**

Cabernet Sauvignon Napa Valley 1990 (NR) (5/15/91) (BT) **90+**

Cabernet Sauvignon Napa Valley 1989 (NR) (5/15/91) (BT) **85+**

Cabernet Sauvignon Napa Valley 1988: Dense in color and flavor, this is rich and concentrated, with tiers of ripe black cherry, plum and currant flavors and spicy, toasty oak notes. Has plenty of depth and persistence for an '88. Needs cellaring until 1995 or '96 at the earliest. 178 cases made. Rel: $63 Cur: $160 (6/30/91) **92**

Cabernet Sauvignon Napa Valley 1987: Deep, rich and perfumed with intense layers of concentrated currant, cherry, anise, earth and smoky oak flavors that are amazingly fresh, lively and elegant. A sense of subtlety and finesse keeps you coming back for another sip. Finish echoes fruit and oak. Drink in 1994 to 2002. 106 cases made. Rel: $56 Cur: $200 (6/30/90) **97**

Cabernet Sauvignon Napa Valley 1986 Rel: $40 Cur: $230 (CA-3/89) **93**

Cabernet Sauvignon Napa Valley 1985 Rel: $50 Cur: $290 (CA-3/89) **95**

Cabernet Sauvignon Napa Valley 1984 Rel: $38 Cur: $280 (CA-3/89) **92**

Cabernet Sauvignon Napa Valley 1983 Rel: $38 Cur: $300 (CA-3/89) **91**

Cabernet Sauvignon Napa Valley 1982 Rel: $31 Cur: $250 (CA-3/89) **89**

Cabernet Sauvignon Napa Valley 1981 Rel: $28 Cur: $260 (CA-3/89) **88**

Cabernet Sauvignon Napa Valley 1980 Rel: $25 Cur: $330 (CA-3/89) **92**

Cabernet Sauvignon Napa Valley 1979 Rel: $20 Cur: $380 (CA-3/89) **92**

Cabernet Sauvignon Napa Valley 1978 Rel: $20 Cur: $500 (CA-3/89) **86**

GRAND CRU

Cabernet Sauvignon Alexander Valley Collector's Reserve 1986: A supple and rich style, with pretty ripe cherry, currant, plum and spice flavors and just the right amount of oak and tannin. Deftly balanced, with moderate intensity and depth. Drinkable now, but should peak around 1993. $22 (5/15/90) **85**

Cabernet Sauvignon Alexander Valley Collector's Reserve 1985: Drinkable and attractive. Supple and rich in texture, full-bodied, with ripe, jammy fruit flavors and moderate tannins. Drink up now. $18 (7/15/89) **81**

Cabernet Sauvignon Alexander Valley Collector's Reserve 1982 $15 (9/30/87) **70**

Cabernet Sauvignon Alexander Valley Collector's Reserve 1980 $14.50 (11/01/84) **85**

Cabernet Sauvignon Sonoma County Premium Selection 1988 $12 (3/15/92) **84**

Cabernet Sauvignon Sonoma County Premium Selection 1987 $12 (11/15/91) **85**

Cabernet Sauvignon Sonoma County Premium Selection 1986 $12 (4/30/90) **79**

Cabernet Sauvignon Sonoma County Premium Selection 1985 $9 (6/15/89) **79**

Cabernet Sauvignon Sonoma County 1984 $8.50 (12/31/87) **75**

Cabernet Sauvignon Sonoma County 1983 $8.50 (11/16/85) **68**

GREENWOOD RIDGE

Cabernet Sauvignon Mendocino 1988: A solid wine, with pretty currant, cherry, mint and herb notes. Firmly tannic and well balanced. Drink in 1993 to '97. 407 cases made. $15 (2/29/92) **83**

GRGICH HILLS

Cabernet Sauvignon Napa Valley 1987 (NR) (4/15/89) (BT) **95+**

Cabernet Sauvignon Napa Valley 1986: Firm and tightly structured, but a bit awkward now, with muted black cherry, currant and spice flavors that are concentrated and persistent on the aftertaste. Needs time to come together—try in 1994. Rel: $20 Cur: $26 (11/15/91) **88**

Cabernet Sauvignon Napa Valley 1985: Rich and fruity, with lively raspberry, cherry, currant and anise flavors that are nicely seasoned by spicy, toasty oak notes. Like '85 in general, it's a wonderful balance of ripe fruit and supple, gentle tannins. Delicious now, but it should peak between 1994 and 2000. Rel: $20 Cur: $25 (10/31/90) **90**

Cabernet Sauvignon Napa Valley 1984: Rich and supple, with generous black cherry and currant flavors that are crisp and tart on the finish. Tannins are smooth yet firm. Drink now. Rel: $17 Cur: $37 (4/30/89) **87**

Cabernet Sauvignon Napa Valley 1983 Rel: $17 Cur: $33 (CA-3/89) **88**

Cabernet Sauvignon Napa Valley 1982 Rel: $17 Cur: $29 (CA-3/89) **87**

Cabernet Sauvignon Napa Valley 1981 Rel: $17 Cur: $42 (CA-3/89) **86**

Cabernet Sauvignon Napa-Sonoma Counties 1980 Rel: $16 Cur: $34 (CA-3/89) **90**

GROTH

Cabernet Sauvignon Napa Valley 1991: Rough and intense, but with a beautiful core of currant, herb, spice, wild berry and cherry flavors that all come together on the finish. Sample blend. 15 percent Merlot. (NR) (5/15/92) (BT) **89+**

Cabernet Sauvignon Napa Valley 1990 (NR) (5/15/91) (BT) **90+**

Cabernet Sauvignon Napa Valley 1989 (NR) (5/15/91) (BT) **90+**

Key to Symbols

The scores reported here are the results of blind tastings conducted by our panel of senior editors. Wines that carry the initials below are results of individual tastings.

THE WINE SPECTATOR 100-POINT SCALE 95-100— Classic, a great wine; ***90-94***— Outstanding, superior character and style; ***80-89***—Good to very good, a wine with special qualities; ***70-79***—Average, drinkable wine that may have minor flaws; ***60-69*** —Below average, drinkable but not recommended; ***50-59*** —Poor, undrinkable, not recommended. "+"— With a score indicates a range; used primarily with barrel tastings to indicate a preliminary score.

SPECIAL DESIGNATIONS SS—Spectator Selection, CS—Cellar Selection, BB—Best Buy, ($NA)—Price not available, (NR)—Not released.

TASTER'S INITIALS (JG)—Jim Gordon, (HS)—Harvey Steiman, (JL)—James Laube, (JS)—James Suckling, (TM)—Thomas Matthews, (TR)—Terry Robards, (PM)—Per-Henrik Mansson, (BT)—Barrel Tasting (these wines were tasted blind from barrel samples), (CA-date)—*California's Great Cabernets* by James Laube, (CH-date)—*California's Great Chardonnays* by James Laube, (VP-date)—*Vintage Port* by James Suckling.

DATE TASTED Dates in parentheses represent the issue in which the rating was published.

Cabernet Sauvignon Napa Valley 1988: Earthy in character and tight in texture, with firm tannins surrounding a modest core of pruny flavor. Seems a bit volatile, and it's definitely shaded by herbal, vegetal notes. May be better after 1995. Tasted three times, with consistent notes. $20 (11/15/91) **75**

Cabernet Sauvignon Napa Valley 1987: This leans heavily on bell pepper, olive and herbal aromas and flavors, leaving whatever fruit there is to fend for itself. Seems unbalanced, but it's distinctive. Try in 1993. Rel: $20 Cur: $23 (10/31/90) **81**

Cabernet Sauvignon Napa Valley 1986: Remarkably rich and intense, with delicious toasty oak and tar notes that complement the rich, ripe currant, plum and cherry flavors. Wonderful smoky aftertaste with tannins for aging. Tempting now but best to cellar until 1993. Rel: $18 Cur: $25 (11/15/89) **92**

Cabernet Sauvignon Napa Valley 1985 Rel: $16 Cur: $50 (CA-3/89) **91**

Cabernet Sauvignon Napa Valley 1984 Rel: $14 Cur: $41 (CA-3/89) **92**

Cabernet Sauvignon Napa Valley 1984 Rel: $14 Cur: $41 (2/15/88) **86**

Cabernet Sauvignon Napa Valley 1983 Rel: $13 Cur: $23 (CA-3/89) **88**

Cabernet Sauvignon Napa Valley 1982 Rel: $13 Cur: $40 (CA-3/89) **88**

Cabernet Sauvignon Napa Valley Reserve 1987: Rich and fleshy, with a strong core of black currant and cherry flavors cutting through the hints of tobacco and ash that sneak in on the nose and finish. Has length and intensity, enough to keep it in the cellar through 1997 to see what develops. Tasted twice. 339 cases made. $40 (3/31/92) **88**

Cabernet Sauvignon Napa Valley Reserve 1986: Ripe, mature, warm and generous, with rich, concentrated plum, currant, cedar and spice flavors and hints of anise and tobacco. The tannins are round but firm. Should be cellared until 1996 to 2000. Tasted twice. 500 cases made. Rel: $40 Cur: $78 (4/30/91) **91**

Cabernet Sauvignon Napa Valley Reserve 1985: Ripe, concentrated and powerful, oozing with blackberry, cedar and earth aromas and flavors, enormously complex and distinctive. Not for everyone, but seductive in its way. Drink after 1994. 500 cases made. Rel: $30 Cur: $260 (4/15/90) **95**

Cabernet Sauvignon Napa Valley Reserve 1984 Rel: $25 Cur: $120 (CA-3/89) **94**

Cabernet Sauvignon Napa Valley Reserve 1983 Rel: $25 Cur: $90 (CA-3/89) **92**

GUENOC

Cabernet Sauvignon Guenoc Valley Première Cuvée 1985: Elegant, ripe and supple, with pretty plum and currant flavors of moderate depth and intensity. Clean, well balanced, not too tannic, and it picks up a pretty earthy note on the finish. Drink now to 1996. $17 (10/15/90) **84**

Cabernet Sauvignon Lake County 1987: Lively and well balanced, with pretty plum, cherry, currant and spice flavors that echo fruit from start to finish. It lets the grape sing on through, picking up a nice touch of anise and spicy oak on the aftertaste. Drink in 1993 to '97. $12 (7/15/91) **89**

Cabernet Sauvignon Lake County 1986: Lean, tannic and vegetal, with unfocused fruit and beet flavors. Modest in scope and almost ready to drink. Try it now. $12.50 (4/30/91) **78**

Cabernet Sauvignon Lake County 1983 $9.75 (9/30/86) **89**

Cabernet Sauvignon Lake County 1981 $8.50 (12/16/84) **78**

Cabernet Sauvignon Napa Valley Beckstoffer Reserve 1987: Very fruity and lively, with gorgeous black cherry, currant and plum flavors supported by crisp acidity and firm tannins. More fruit pours through on the finish. Tempting to drink now, but should improve if cellared until around 1995. 1,304 cases made. $24 (6/30/91) **92**

Langtry Meritage Lake-Napa Counties 1988: Fresh, lively and well balanced, with a pretty core of cherry, raspberry, plum and oak flavors that hang together fairly well for an '88. Best to cellar until 1994. $35 (11/15/91) **86**

Langtry Meritage Lake-Napa Counties 1987: Rich, supple, full-bodied and complex, with layers of plum, herb, chocolate and cedar. Balanced, with soft but firm tannins. Tempting now, but it has the intensity, depth and length for cellaring through 1995. $35 (4/15/91) **88**

GUNDLACH BUNDSCHU

Cabernet Sauvignon Sonoma Valley 1986: Deep and lush with pure currant, plum and anise flavor that is quite attractive, with richness and concentration. A touch of bitterness on the finish is a mild detraction. Needs until 1993 to shake off the tannins. 925 cases made. $9.50 (11/15/89) **87**

Cabernet Sauvignon Sonoma Valley 1981 Rel: $7 Cur: $20 (CA-3/89) **84**

Cabernet Sauvignon Sonoma Valley Batto Ranch 1984 Rel: $14 Cur: $17 (CA-3/89) **79**

Cabernet Sauvignon Sonoma Valley Batto Ranch 1983 Rel: $10 Cur: $15 (CA-3/89) **77**

Cabernet Sauvignon Sonoma Valley Batto Ranch 1982 Rel: $10 Cur: $17 (CA-3/89) **70**

Cabernet Sauvignon Sonoma Valley Batto Ranch 1981 Rel: $10 Cur: $18 (CA-3/89) **88**

Cabernet Sauvignon Sonoma Valley Batto Ranch 1980 Rel: $8 Cur: $20 (CA-3/89) **80**

Cabernet Sauvignon Sonoma Valley Batto Ranch 1979 Rel: $8 Cur: $20 (CA-3/89) **80**

Cabernet Sauvignon Sonoma Valley Batto Ranch 1977 Rel: $8 Cur: $20 (CA-3/89) **89**

Cabernet Sauvignon Sonoma Valley Rhinefarm Vineyards 1988 (NR) (5/15/90) (BT) **90+**

Cabernet Sauvignon Sonoma Valley Rhinefarm Vineyards 1987: A herbaceous style, with spice, herb and bell pepper notes, but supple currant, plum and cherry flavors ring through on the finish. Drink in 1993 to '97. $15 (5/15/91) **85**

Cabernet Sauvignon Sonoma Valley Rhinefarm Vineyards 1986 Rel: $12 Cur: $17 (CA-3/89) **89**

Cabernet Sauvignon Sonoma Valley Rhinefarm Vineyards 1985 Rel: $9 Cur: $14 (CA-3/89) **91**

Cabernet Sauvignon Sonoma Valley Rhinefarm Vineyards 1984 Rel: $9 Cur: $15 (CA-3/89) **85**

Cabernet Sauvignon Sonoma Valley Rhinefarm Vineyards 1983 Rel: $9 Cur: $14 (CA-3/89) **73**

Cabernet Sauvignon Sonoma Valley Rhinefarm Vineyards 1982 Rel: $9 Cur: $13 (CA-3/89) **65**

Cabernet Sauvignon Sonoma Valley Rhinefarm Vineyards Reserve 1986: Intense and concentrated, with rich, ripe currant, cherry, plum and spice notes, but also shows a good dose of tannin. Will need until 1995 or '96 to soften from the oak. $25 (8/31/91) **83**

Cabernet Sauvignon Sonoma Valley Rhinefarm Vineyards Reserve 1982 $20 (9/15/87) **71**

Cabernet Sauvignon Sonoma Valley Rhinefarm Vineyards Reserve 1981 Rel: $20 Cur: $26 (CA-3/89) **90**

HACIENDA

Antares Sonoma County 1987: Mint, herb and toast notes shade the nicely focused currant and berry flavors in this concentrated and already complex wine. It has subtlety and length, and enough tannin to suggest cellaring until at least 1994 to '95. $28 (11/15/90) **91**

Antares Sonoma County 1986: Bursting with cherry and berry aromas and flavors, hinting at cinnamon on the finish, all wrapped in a thick blanket of oak. A diamond in the rough. Give it until 1995 to smooth out. $28 (7/31/89) **91**

Cabernet Sauvignon Sonoma County 1986: Tough and chewy, with a bright beam of black cherry flavor that persists into the finish, picking up overtones of anise and tar. Needs time to smooth out the tannins, perhaps until 1995 or '96. $15 (11/15/91) **87**

Cabernet Sauvignon Sonoma County 1985: Smooth and generous, with minty eucalyptus aromas and concentrated menthol-tinged, slightly overripe cherry and plum flavors. It's soft and fairly elegant, but not particularly graceful. Start drinking now. 4,000 cases made. $15 (9/30/90) **83**

Cabernet Sauvignon Sonoma Valley Estate Reserve 1984: Soft, broad, rich and mature, with layers of ripe plum, cherry, currant and smoke flavors and firm but smooth tannins. Ready to drink now, but should also age well through 1998. $18 (5/31/91) **87**

Cabernet Sauvignon Sonoma Valley 1983 $11 (5/31/88) **86**

Cabernet Sauvignon Sonoma Valley 1982 $11 (9/01/85) **63**

Cabernet Sauvignon Sonoma Valley Selected Reserve 1982 $18 (3/31/87) **86**

HAGAFEN

Cabernet Sauvignon Napa Valley 1988 $20 (3/31/91) **88**

Cabernet Sauvignon Napa Valley 1987: Offers lots of yummy, seductive, ripe plum, currant, jam and toasty oak flavors that are rich and complex yet firmly structured with smooth, thick, tannins. It's delicious to drink now but appears to have the depth and concentration for another five to seven years' aging. 1,000 cases made. $20 (4/30/90) **88**

HALLCREST
Cabernet Sauvignon El Dorado County De Cascabel Vineyard 1987: Broad and rich, with broad-based ripe cherry, plum and anise aromas and flavors that expand and persist on the finish. A big wine that needs to acquire some grace. Try cellaring until 1994 to '95. 210 cases made. $13 (11/15/91) **83**

HANNA
Cabernet Sauvignon Sonoma County 1988: Firm in texture, with a nice beam of black cherry and currant flavor running through it, shaded by tar and toast notes to lend personality. Best to drink after 1995. $16 (11/15/91) **86**
Cabernet Sauvignon Sonoma County 1987: Ripe, rich currant flavors blend with a touch of austere tannin and plenty of smoky, toasty oak flavors. It's balanced, but the flavors lack harmony and finesse. Perhaps with time it will be more graceful. Try in 1994 to '96. $16 (8/31/90) **80**
Cabernet Sauvignon Sonoma County 1986: Deeply colored and impressive. Tart but flavorful, with plenty of plum and cherry flavors, a touch of vanilla from oak aging and firm but not harsh tannins. Drinkable now. $16 (7/31/89) **87**
Cabernet Sauvignon Sonoma Valley 1985 $14 (6/30/88) **86**

HANZELL
Cabernet Sauvignon Sonoma Valley 1987: Firmly tannic and tight, with a hard core of currant and earth notes. An unevolved style that's closed and backward, but quite concentrated. Still needs time to soften and open—try around 1996. Rel: $22 Cur: $32 (11/15/91) **84**
Cabernet Sauvignon Sonoma Valley 1986: Big, chewy and complex, with lots of ripe currant, plum and weedy herbal flavors that pack a wallop of tannins on the finish. It's hard, tight, concentrated and well balanced, but best to cellar until 1995 or so. Rel: $22 Cur: $29 (10/31/90) **90**
Cabernet Sauvignon Sonoma Valley 1982 Rel: $20 Cur: $27 (3/31/87) **76**

HARRISON
Cabernet Sauvignon Napa Valley 1991: A dark, tight, intense and tannic wine, with sharply focused currant, plum and tart berry flavors. 690 cases made. (NR) (5/15/92) (BT) **86+**
Cabernet Sauvignon Napa Valley 1989: Bold, dark, ripe and concentrated, with sharply focused currant, black cherry, plum and spice flavors that have just the right touch of tannin and oak. Intense and powerful. Best to cellar until 1998 at the earliest. Tasted twice, with consistent notes. 588 cases made. $30 (4/15/92) **91**

HAWK CREST
Cabernet Sauvignon California 1989: An average, drinkable wine with simple fruit flavors and decent balance, but nothing to lift it out of the ordinary. $9 (3/15/92) **77**
Cabernet Sauvignon Mendocino 1981 $5 (3/16/85) BB **84**
Cabernet Sauvignon North Coast 1987: Leans toward the herbal, vegetal side of Cabernet and has an earthy, tannic bite. Simple and pleasant. Drink now. $8 (3/31/90) **79**
Cabernet Sauvignon North Coast 1986 $7.50 (10/15/88) BB **82**
Cabernet Sauvignon North Coast 1985 $6.50 (7/31/88) **75**
Cabernet Sauvignon North Coast 1984 $7 (10/15/87) **76**
Cabernet Sauvignon North Coast 1981 $5 (2/01/86) **65**

HAYWOOD
Cabernet Sauvignon California Vintner's Select 1989: Basically light and spicy. Owes most of its flavor to wood, but there are some straightforward spice and light cherry flavors to keep it interesting. $8 (3/15/92) **80**
Cabernet Sauvignon Sonoma Valley Los Chamizal Vineyards 1987 $16 (4/15/89) (BT) **80+**
Cabernet Sauvignon Sonoma Valley 1986: Brimming with ripe currant, cherry, berry and plum flavor, framed by firm tannins and woody flavors from oak aging. A young, intense, deliberate wine that is solid from start to finish. Drink in 1996 to 2002. Rel: $16 Cur: $20 (11/15/89) **92**
Cabernet Sauvignon Sonoma Valley 1985 Rel: $14.50 Cur: $20 (CA-3/89) **89**
Cabernet Sauvignon Sonoma Valley 1984 Rel: $12.50 Cur: $20 (CA-3/89) **88**
Cabernet Sauvignon Sonoma Valley 1983 Rel: $12.50 Cur: $20 (CA-3/89) **77**
Cabernet Sauvignon Sonoma Valley 1982 Rel: $11 Cur: $20 (CA-3/89) **79**
Cabernet Sauvignon Sonoma Valley 1981 Rel: $11 Cur: $20 (CA-3/89) **85**
Cabernet Sauvignon Sonoma Valley 1980 Rel: $9.75 Cur: $15 (CA-3/89) **86**
Cabernet Sauvignon Sonoma Valley Los Chamizal Vineyards 1988: Tough and chewy, with hard-edged tannins, but it also has a tight core of herb-tinged currant and black cherry flavors. Dill and spice notes come through on the finish. Cellar through 1995. $16 (11/15/91) **85**

HEITZ
Cabernet Sauvignon Napa Valley 1987: Distinctive, earthy and generous, with a strong beam of mint, spice and currant aromas and flavors. Has subtlety and intensity, but also a streak of earthiness not everyone will love. The fruit comes through on the finish, and should keep coming through for years. Best after 1996 or '97. The first Heitz Cabernet entirely from the former Shown & Sons vineyard. Rel: $20 Cur: $22 (4/15/92) SS **90**
Cabernet Sauvignon Napa Valley 1986: Spicy, with cedar, herb and anise overtones adding a complex cloak to the ripe cherry and currant flavors. The tannins are ample, but rounded off, and the finish is long and full. Drink in 1994 to '98. Rel: $18 Cur: $21 (4/15/91) **88**
Cabernet Sauvignon Napa Valley 1985: An herbal, earthy style, with velvety texture and generous flavors. Broad and flavorful, with more cedar and brown sugar than fruit. Seems early maturing, but it might not have the balance to outlast the 1990s. Drink soon. Rel: $18 Cur: $25 (5/15/90) **80**
Cabernet Sauvignon Napa Valley 1984 Rel: $15 Cur: $30 (1/31/90) (JL) **89**
Cabernet Sauvignon Napa Valley 1983 Rel: $13 Cur: $20 (1/31/90) (JL) **85**
Cabernet Sauvignon Napa Valley 1982 Rel: $13.50 Cur: $26 (1/31/90) (JL) **80**
Cabernet Sauvignon Napa Valley 1981 Rel: $13.25 Cur: $27 (1/31/90) (JL) **86**
Cabernet Sauvignon Napa Valley 1980 Rel: $12 Cur: $24 (1/31/90) (JL) **88**
Cabernet Sauvignon Napa Valley 1979 Rel: $11.25 Cur: $45 (1/31/90) (JL) **86**
Cabernet Sauvignon Napa Valley 1978 Rel: $11 Cur: $30 (1/31/90) (JL) **90**
Cabernet Sauvignon Napa Valley 1977 Rel: $11 Cur: $48 (1/31/90) (JL) **83**
Cabernet Sauvignon Napa Valley 1973 $38 (1/31/90) (JL) **78**
Cabernet Sauvignon Napa Valley 1970 $75 (1/31/90) (JL) **74**
Cabernet Sauvignon Napa Valley MZ-1 NV (NR) (1/31/90) (JL) **75**
Cabernet Sauvignon Napa Valley NV (NR) (1/31/90) (JL) **68**
Cabernet Sauvignon Napa Valley Z-91 NV (NR) (1/31/90) (JL) **90**
Cabernet Sauvignon Napa Valley Bella Oaks Vineyard 1987: Distinctive in its earthy style, with the fruit showing through the cedary, wet wood and tobacco flavors that dominate this medium-weight, elegantly balanced wine. Some may find the flavors too much, but it has class. Best to drink in 1994 or '95. Tasted twice, with consistent notes. 2,360 cases made. Rel: $27 Cur: $31 (6/30/92) **85**
Cabernet Sauvignon Napa Valley Bella Oaks Vineyard 1986: Big and assertive, with intense, concentrated herb, cherry, currant and plum flavors that are firmly tannic and long on the finish. The finish picks up some heat, but overall it's balanced and well made. Drink in 1994 to 2000. 4,974 cases made. Rel: $21.50 Cur: $28 (4/15/91) **89**
Cabernet Sauvignon Napa Valley Bella Oaks Vineyard 1985: Powerful and complex, with lots of ripe cherry, currant and spice aromas and flavors, hinting at chocolate and toast on the long, long finish. A big wine with plenty of grace and elegance. Approaching drinkability, but it has the structure and character to age well into the late 1990s. 3,845 cases made. Rel: $25 Cur: $55 (5/15/90) CS **92**
Cabernet Sauvignon Napa Valley Bella Oaks Vineyard 1984 Rel: $25 Cur: $39 (5/15/89) **86**
Cabernet Sauvignon Napa Valley Bella Oaks Vineyard 1983 Rel: $15 Cur: $33 (CA-3/89) **86**
Cabernet Sauvignon Napa Valley Bella Oaks Vineyard 1982 Rel: $16 Cur: $42 (CA-3/89) **85**
Cabernet Sauvignon Napa Valley Bella Oaks Vineyard 1981 Rel: $16 Cur: $50 (CA-3/89) **90**
Cabernet Sauvignon Napa Valley Bella Oaks Vineyard 1981 Rel: $16 Cur: $50 (4/16/86) **79**
Cabernet Sauvignon Napa Valley Bella Oaks Vineyard 1980 Rel: $20 Cur: $47 (CA-3/89) **93**
Cabernet Sauvignon Napa Valley Bella Oaks Vineyard 1978 Rel: $15 Cur: $60 (CA-3/89) **89**
Cabernet Sauvignon Napa Valley Bella Oaks Vineyard 1977 Rel: $30 Cur: $65 (CA-3/89) **91**
Cabernet Sauvignon Napa Valley Bella Oaks Vineyard 1976 Rel: $30 Cur: $46 (CA-3/89) **85**
Cabernet Sauvignon Napa Valley Fay Vineyard 1978 Rel: $12.75 Cur: $32 (2/16/84) (HS) **80**
Cabernet Sauvignon Napa Valley Fay Vineyard 1977 Rel: $17.50 Cur: $32 (2/16/84) (HS) **78**
Cabernet Sauvignon Napa Valley Martha's Vineyard 1987: Deep, dense, dark and dangerous, this is a powerful wine, with distinctive flavors of currant, mint, eucalyptus and more, cascading and deepening with each sip. Turns gamy and chocolaty on the finish, suggesting this will be a polished, elegant wine by the time it reaches its peak after 1997. 4,740 cases made. Rel: $65 Cur: $75 (3/31/92) CS **95**
Cabernet Sauvignon Napa Valley Martha's Vineyard 1986: Incredibly concentrated, rich and powerful, but still smooth and plush. The flavors of mint, cherry, black currant and spice are deep, long and chewy, with great complexity and polish. Not for everyone, but absolutely full of flavor and beautifully structured, harmonious and complex. Very tempting to drink now, but should improve through 2005 or beyond. Rel: $60 Cur: $70 (4/15/91) CS **95**
Cabernet Sauvignon Napa Valley Martha's Vineyard 1985: Has arrestingly rich, complex currant, black cherry, spice, mint and wild berry flavors that offer uncommon complexity and will only improve with time, despite the firm tannins that surround them now. Minty flavors echo on the finish. Best to cellar until at least 1996 to 2000. 3,800 cases made. Rel: $60 Cur: $140 (4/30/90) **98**
Cabernet Sauvignon Napa Valley Martha's Vineyard 1984 Rel: $40 Cur: $95 (3/15/89) SS **97**
Cabernet Sauvignon Napa Valley Martha's Vineyard 1983 Rel: $32.50 Cur: $61 (CA-3/89) **89**
Cabernet Sauvignon Napa Valley Martha's Vineyard 1982 Rel: $30 Cur: $68 (CA-3/89) **88**
Cabernet Sauvignon Napa Valley Martha's Vineyard 1982 Rel: $30 Cur: $68 (4/15/87) CS **94**
Cabernet Sauvignon Napa Valley Martha's Vineyard 1981 Rel: $30 Cur: $62 (CA-3/89) **89**
Cabernet Sauvignon Napa Valley Martha's Vineyard 1981 Rel: $30 Cur: $62 (4/16/86) CS **91**
Cabernet Sauvignon Napa Valley Martha's Vineyard 1980 Rel: $30 Cur: $68 (CA-3/89) **89**
Cabernet Sauvignon Napa Valley Martha's Vineyard 1980 Rel: $30 Cur: $68 (7/01/85) CS **93**
Cabernet Sauvignon Napa Valley Martha's Vineyard 1979 Rel: $25 Cur: $85 (CA-3/89) **93**
Cabernet Sauvignon Napa Valley Martha's Vineyard 1979 Rel: $25 Cur: $85 (2/15/84) SS **94**
Cabernet Sauvignon Napa Valley Martha's Vineyard 1978 Rel: $22 Cur: $110 (CA-3/89) **91**
Cabernet Sauvignon Napa Valley Martha's Vineyard 1977 Rel: $30 Cur: $81 (1/31/90) (JL) **90**
Cabernet Sauvignon Napa Valley Martha's Vineyard 1976 Rel: $30 Cur: $88 (CA-3/89) **85**
Cabernet Sauvignon Napa Valley Martha's Vineyard 1975 Rel: $25 Cur: $95 (CA-3/89) **92**
Cabernet Sauvignon Napa Valley Martha's Vineyard 1974 Rel: $25 Cur: $290 (CA-3/89) **99**
Cabernet Sauvignon Napa Valley Martha's Vineyard 1973 Rel: $11 Cur: $120 (CA-3/89) **92**
Cabernet Sauvignon Napa Valley Martha's Vineyard 1972 Rel: $12.75 Cur: $140 (CA-3/89) **79**
Cabernet Sauvignon Napa Valley Martha's Vineyard 1970 Rel: $12.75 Cur: $320 (CA-3/89) **98**
Cabernet Sauvignon Napa Valley Martha's Vineyard 1969 Rel: $12.75 Cur: $280 (CA-3/89) **93**
Cabernet Sauvignon Napa Valley Martha's Vineyard 1968 Rel: $9.50 Cur: $430 (CA-3/89) **99**
Cabernet Sauvignon Napa Valley Martha's Vineyard 1967 Rel: $7.50 Cur: $280 (CA-3/89) **86**
Cabernet Sauvignon Napa Valley Martha's Vineyard 1966 Rel: $8 Cur: $440 (CA-3/89) **92**

THE HESS COLLECTION
Cabernet Sauvignon Napa Valley 1991: Bright and crisp, with plenty of minty, herbal plum and currant aromas and flavors that last through a long finish. Not too tannic, but it has plenty of zip. Should make an elegant wine. (NR) (5/15/92) (BT) **85+**
Cabernet Sauvignon Napa Valley 1990 (NR) (5/15/91) (BT) **85+**
Cabernet Sauvignon Napa Valley 1989 (NR) (5/15/91) (BT) **90+**
Cabernet Sauvignon Napa Valley 1988: Ripe and smooth, with intense currant and plum flavors that are broad and generous. Layers of prune and anise notes add dimension to the finish. Complex and appealing. Drink after 1993. Rel: $17.50 Cur: $20 (1/31/92) CS **90**
Cabernet Sauvignon Napa Valley 1987: Strikes a pleasant balance between the opulent, ripe, rich currant and black cherry flavors and the herb and lavish oak notes. Deep, plush and concentrated, with a long, full finish. The firm tannins remind you that it's best to cellar this until 1996 or '97. Rel: $17 Cur: $22 (4/15/91) SS **94**
Cabernet Sauvignon Napa Valley 1986: Firm and well structured with lean, compact cedar, plum and olive flavors that are tight and firm. Well balanced, ready to drink now and beyond. Rel: $14 Cur: $24 (11/15/89) **90**
Cabernet Sauvignon Napa Valley 1985 Rel: $13 Cur: $50 (CA-3/89) **96**
Cabernet Sauvignon Napa Valley 1983 Rel: $13 Cur: $25 (CA-3/89) **84**
Cabernet Sauvignon Napa Valley Reserve 1987: Massively flavorful, with chewy tannins and gobs of currant, plum, blackberry and cedar aromas and flavors, echoing anise and other spices on the long finish. Has an enormous amount of fruit, with the sort of smoothly integrated tannins that should be marvelous around 1996 to '98. 700 cases made. Rel: $34 Cur: $55 (10/15/91) **96**
Cabernet Sauvignon Napa Valley Reserve 1986: Firm, tannic and densely oaky, the tightly reined-in currant, chocolate, mint and plum flavor is deep, intense and concentrated. It has a sense of elegance and grace despite being very young. Drink in 1995 to 2003. 350 cases made. Rel: $33 Cur: $44 (9/15/90) **93**
Cabernet Sauvignon Napa Valley Reserve 1984 Rel: $22 Cur: $100 (CA-3/89) **93**
Cabernet Sauvignon Napa Valley Reserve 1983 Rel: $22 Cur: $75 (CA-3/89) **88**

HESS SELECT
Cabernet Sauvignon California 1988: A ripe, jammy, effusively fruity style, with intense raspberry, cherry, plum and strawberry flavors that are fresh and supple. Not too tannic. A ready-to-drink style that offers plenty of charm. Drink now to 1994. $9.50 (3/31/91) **86**

HIDDEN CELLARS
Cabernet Sauvignon Mendocino County Mountanos Vineyard 1984 $12 (8/31/88) **88**

WILLIAM HILL
Cabernet Sauvignon Napa Valley Gold Label 1983 Rel: $18.25 Cur: $25 (CA-3/89) **85**
Cabernet Sauvignon Napa Valley Gold Label 1982 Rel: $18 Cur: $36 (CA-3/89) **90**
Cabernet Sauvignon Napa Valley Gold Label 1982 Rel: $18 Cur: $36 (6/16/86) SS **94**
Cabernet Sauvignon Napa Valley Gold Label 1981 Rel: $16.25 Cur: $33 (CA-3/89) **85**
Cabernet Sauvignon Napa Valley Gold Label 1980 Rel: $18.25 Cur: $32 (CA-3/89) **87**
Cabernet Sauvignon Napa Valley Gold Label 1979 Rel: $18 Cur: $45 (CA-3/89) **93**
Cabernet Sauvignon Napa Valley Gold Label 1978 Rel: $16.25 Cur: $50 (CA-3/89) **95**
Cabernet Sauvignon Napa Valley Reserve 1990 (NR) (5/15/91) (BT) **80+**
Cabernet Sauvignon Napa Valley Reserve 1989 (NR) (5/15/91) (BT) **85+**
Cabernet Sauvignon Napa Valley Reserve 1988: Has a nice core of tart yet ripe mint and currant-laced fruit flavor, with firm tannins and fine balance for an '88. The flavors stay with you from start to finish, picking up an earthy edge on the aftertaste. Best around 1995. Tasted twice, with consistent notes. $24 (11/15/91) **84**
Cabernet Sauvignon Napa Valley Reserve 1987: A rich core of focused, concentrated currant, black cherry and plum flavors balances beautifully with finely integrated tannins, marking this as a potentially magnificent wine with cellaring until 1995 to 2000. Has the muscle and grace to evolve into a majestic wine, even though it has enough fruit to drink now. Rel: $24 Cur: $27 (11/15/90) SS **95**
Cabernet Sauvignon Napa Valley Reserve 1986: Intense and concentated, a rich but compact Cabernet with crisp acidity and firm tannins. Pretty cassis, toast and vanilla flavors are enticing. Needs three to five years to round out. Start drinking in 1993. Rel: $24.50 Cur: $29 (11/15/89) **91**
Cabernet Sauvignon Napa Valley Reserve 1986 Rel: $24.50 Cur: $29 (CA-3/89) **95**
Cabernet Sauvignon Napa Valley Reserve 1985 Rel: $22.50 Cur: $30 (CA-3/89) **94**
Cabernet Sauvignon Napa Valley Reserve 1984 Rel: $18.25 Cur: $28 (4/15/88) CS **91**
Cabernet Sauvignon Napa Valley Silver Label 1987: Lavishly oaked, with dill and toasty oak nuances and the fruit intensity to stand up to it. The ripe raspberry, strawberry and cherry flavors are a bit rough and chunky. A beam of fruit comes through on the finish. Drink in 1994 to 2000 $14 (11/15/90) **85**
Cabernet Sauvignon Napa Valley Silver Label 1986 $13 (4/15/88) (BT) **85+**

Cabernet Sauvignon Napa Valley Silver Label 1985 $12 (4/30/88) **90**
Cabernet Sauvignon Sonoma County Silver Label 1988 $14 (11/15/91) **82**

HOP KILN
Cabernet Sauvignon Alexander Valley 1984 $10 (3/31/88) **77**
Cabernet Sauvignon Dry Creek Valley 1986: Smells like an herb garden, with mint and spice aromas, but on the palate it's coarse, tannic and drying on the finish. $12 (6/15/89) **69**
Cabernet Sauvignon Dry Creek Valley 1985 $10 (10/15/88) **75**

HOUTZ
Cabernet Sauvignon Santa Ynez Valley 1985 $8 (12/15/89) **63**

HUSCH
Cabernet Sauvignon Mendocino 1986: Supple, soft and very easy to drink, with ripe plum and generous vanilla and spice notes. Smooth all the way through despite modest tannins that will help it improve through 1993. $12 (2/15/90) **84**
Cabernet Sauvignon Mendocino La Ribera 1985 $5 (11/30/87) BB **84**
Cabernet Sauvignon Mendocino La Ribera Vineyards 1988: Firm and lively, with lots of appealing, ripe currant and plum aromas and flavors and hints of black pepper and vanilla. Soft in the tannin department and charming overall. Drinkable now. $12 (6/30/91) **86**
Cabernet Sauvignon Mendocino La Ribera Vineyards 1987: A little shy in the aromas, but the rich, deep, concentrated flavors are highlighted by generous black cherry, nutmeg and chocolate notes that persist into the long finish. A velvety texture shows enough tannin to cellar until 1995 to reveal all the layers. 800 cases made. $12 (11/15/90) **90**
Cabernet Sauvignon Mendocino La Ribera Vineyards 1984 $10 (12/31/87) **73**
Cabernet Sauvignon Mendocino North Field Select 1987 $16 (11/15/90) **87**

INGLENOOK
Cabernet Sauvignon Napa Valley 1987: Firm, tannic and concentrated, with densely packed currant, plum and cedar flavors that persist into a solid finish. Needs time to loosen up. Try after 1996. $10 (11/15/91) **86**
Cabernet Sauvignon Napa Valley 1986: Firm and tough but flavorful, with plum, bell pepper and cherry notes, solid tannins, full body and a rough finish at this age. This hearty, straightforward wine should come around nicely if cellared until at least 1995. Rel: $7.50 Cur: $10 (2/28/91) BB **85**
Cabernet Sauvignon Napa Valley 1985: Austere style, with lean, thin, hard tannins and ripe plum flavors, but it lacks body and depth. Needs time to develop, but the aftertaste is pretty. Drink in 1993. Good value. $9.50 (3/31/89) **83**
Cabernet Sauvignon Napa Valley 1983 $9.50 (3/15/88) **80**
Cabernet Sauvignon Napa Valley 1980 $8 (2/15/84) **87**
Cabernet Sauvignon Napa Valley 1960 $135 (6/01/85) (JL) **89**
Cabernet Sauvignon Napa Valley 1958 $140 (6/01/85) (JL) **88**
Cabernet Sauvignon Napa Valley Reserve Cask 1987 (NR) (4/15/89) (BT) **90+**
Cabernet Sauvignon Napa Valley Reserve Cask 1986: Spicy, generous and complex, with sharply focused currant, plum and nutmeg flavors that zing right through the long finish. A wine with rambunctious flavors that become polished and lively on the finish. Should be at its best after 1996. $25 (10/31/91) **91**
Cabernet Sauvignon Napa Valley Reserve Cask 1985: Smooth and polished, with intense cherry, currant, mint and herb aromas and flavors framed by hints of cedar. A bit tannic, but balanced, and almost elegant right through the finish. A youthful wine that can use until 1996 or '97 to buff the edges. Rel: $16 Cur: $22 (2/15/91) CS **90**
Cabernet Sauvignon Napa Valley Reserve Cask 1984: Ripe and exotic, with lots of coffee, cedar and spice overtones to the gentle core of very ripe cherry and raspberry fruit. A stylish wine with plenty of tannin to support it, but the dominant characteristics are fruit and suppleness. Keep it until 1993 to '94. Tasted twice. $22 (7/31/90) **90**
Cabernet Sauvignon Napa Valley Reserve Cask 1983 Rel: $15.50 Cur: $19 (9/15/87) **88**
Cabernet Sauvignon Napa Valley Reserve Cask 1982 Rel: $22 Cur: $28 (CA-3/89) **91**
Cabernet Sauvignon Napa Valley Reserve Cask 1981 Rel: $15.50 Cur: $25 (CA-3/89) **93**
Cabernet Sauvignon Napa Valley Cask 1980 Rel: $15.50 Cur: $22 (CA-3/89) **88**
Cabernet Sauvignon Napa Valley Cask 1979 Rel: $10.75 Cur: $23 (CA-3/89) **77**
Cabernet Sauvignon Napa Valley Cask 1978 Rel: $9.25 Cur: $23 (CA-3/89) **86**
Cabernet Sauvignon Napa Valley Cask 1977 Rel: $8.75 Cur: $25 (CA-3/89) **84**
Cabernet Sauvignon Napa Valley Cask 1976 Rel: $8.75 Cur: $19 (CA-3/89) **72**
Cabernet Sauvignon Napa Valley Cask A8 1974 Rel: $9 Cur: $47 (2/15/90) (JG) **79**
Cabernet Sauvignon Napa Valley Cask 1974 Rel: $9 Cur: $47 (CA-3/89) **86**
Cabernet Sauvignon Napa Valley Cask 1973 Rel: $8 Cur: $37 (CA-3/89) **67**
Cabernet Sauvignon Napa Valley Cask 1972 Rel: $7 Cur: $42 (CA-3/89) **67**
Cabernet Sauvignon Napa Valley Cask 1971 Rel: $6.50 Cur: $50 (CA-3/89) **73**
Cabernet Sauvignon Napa Valley Cask 1970 Rel: $6.50 Cur: $90 (CA-3/89) **85**
Cabernet Sauvignon Napa Valley Cask 1969 Rel: $6.50 Cur: $75 (CA-3/89) **80**
Cabernet Sauvignon Napa Valley Cask 1968 Rel: $6 Cur: $85 (CA-3/89) **85**
Cabernet Sauvignon Napa Valley Cask 1967 Rel: $6 Cur: $84 (CA-3/89) **73**
Cabernet Sauvignon Napa Valley Cask 1966 Rel: $5.75 Cur: $115 (CA-3/89) **73**
Cabernet Sauvignon Napa Valley Cask 1960 Rel: $2.75 Cur: $125 (CA-3/89) **80**
Cabernet Sauvignon Napa Valley Cask 1958 Rel: $2.50 Cur: $250 (CA-3/89) **94**
Cabernet Sauvignon Napa Valley Cask F-11 1958 Rel: $2.50 Cur: $250 (2/28/87) **79**
Cabernet Sauvignon Napa Valley Cask 1955 Rel: $1.85 Cur: $400 (CA-3/89) **93**
Cabernet Sauvignon Napa Valley Cask 1949 Rel: $1.49 Cur: $750 (CA-3/89) **92**
Cabernet Sauvignon Napa Valley 1946 Rel: $1.49 Cur: $900 (CA-3/89) **87**
Cabernet Sauvignon Napa Valley 1943 Rel: $1.49 Cur: $1,000 (CA-3/89) **91**
Cabernet Sauvignon Napa Valley 1941 Rel: $1.49 Cur: $1,800 (CA-3/89) **100**
Cabernet Sauvignon Napa Valley 1933 Rel: $1.30 Cur: $1,600 (CA-3/89) **95**
Cabernet Sauvignon California Claret-Médoc Type 1897 (NR) (CA-3/89) **87**
Niebaum Claret Napa Valley 1987 (NR) (4/15/89) (BT) **85+**
Niebaum Claret Napa Valley 1986: Mint and cranberry flavors are shaded by plenty of stiff tannins and oaky accents. Tight, lean and rough—not for everybody. Tasted twice. 3,600 cases made. $13 (6/30/91) **74**
Niebaum Claret Napa Valley 1985: Has spicy aromas with cedar, plum and black cherry flavors that are lean and tight on the palate. Finishes with a touch of oakiness and tannin. Drink now or hold. $12 (3/15/89) **82**

Key to Symbols

The scores reported here are the results of blind tastings conducted by our panel of senior editors. Wines that carry the initials below are results of individual tastings.

THE WINE SPECTATOR 100-POINT SCALE 95-100—Classic, a great wine; ***90-94***—Outstanding, superior character and style; ***80-89***—Good to very good, a wine with special qualities; ***70-79***—Average, drinkable wine that may have minor flaws; ***60-69***—Below average, drinkable but not recommended; ***50-59***—Poor, undrinkable, not recommended. "+"—With a score indicates a range; used primarily with barrel tastings to indicate a preliminary score.

SPECIAL DESIGNATIONS SS—Spectator Selection, CS—Cellar Selection, BB—Best Buy, ($NA)—Price not available, (NR)—Not released.

TASTER'S INITIALS (JG)—Jim Gordon, (HS)—Harvey Steiman, (JL)—James Laube, (JS)—James Suckling, (TM)—Thomas Matthews, (TR)—Terry Robards, (PM)—Per-Henrik Mansson, (BT)—Barrel Tasting (these wines were tasted blind from barrel samples), (CA-date)—*California's Great Cabernets* by James Laube, (CH-date)—*California's Great Chardonnays* by James Laube, (VP-date)—*Vintage Port* by James Suckling.

DATE TASTED Dates in parentheses represent the issue in which the rating was published.

Niebaum Claret Napa Valley 1983 $12 (11/30/87) **88**
Reunion Napa Valley 1985: Tight and a bit tough, with well-focused cherry and plum flavors clamped tightly behind firm tannins and pronounced oak character. Like a gorgeous flower in the bud stage, it just needs time to open, perhaps until 1993 to '95. Rel: $35 Cur: $38 (7/15/89) **91**
Reunion Napa Valley 1984 $35 (CA-3/89) **92**
Reunion Napa Valley 1983 Rel: $33 Cur: $38 (11/30/87) CS **95**

INNISFREE
Cabernet Sauvignon Napa Valley 1988: Fresh, fruity and lively, with raspberry and cherry flavors, firm tannins and a fruity finish. A hint of leather and earth in the aroma makes it interesting. Probably best to drink in 1993 to '95. $11 (4/30/91) **84**
Cabernet Sauvignon Napa Valley 1986: An earthy, rustic style that may not be for everyone, with ripe, pruny flavors and barnyardy aromas and firm tannins. Slightly bitter on the finish. A coarse but drinkable wine. $10.50 (6/30/90) **73**
Cabernet Sauvignon Napa Valley 1985: Lean, firm and finely focused; boldly aromatic, with herbal berry and currant flavors; smooth and flavorful at the end. If the wood protrudes a bit, the fruit seems to pack enough punch to carry through. Drink now to 1995. $9 (3/15/89) **86**
Cabernet Sauvignon Napa Valley 1984 $9 (12/15/87) **68**
Cabernet Sauvignon Napa Valley 1983 $9 (11/15/86) **82**
Cabernet Sauvignon Napa Valley 1982 $9 (12/16/85) **80**

IRON HORSE
Cabernets Alexander Valley 1988: A focused, polished wine, with distinctive plum, currant and beet aromas and flavors that glide smoothly across the palate. The flavors are framed by oak but not overwhelmingly so. A balanced effort. Best after 1995. $18.50 (3/31/92) **85**
Cabernets Alexander Valley 1987: Firm and tight, with tannins dominating now, but has generous plum, black cherry and currant flavors underneath. The acidity is fresh and lively, carrying the fruity flavors on the finish. Best to cellar until 1994 to '96. $18.50 (3/15/91) **86**
Cabernets Alexander Valley 1986: Balanced, harmonious and elegant, playing the beautifully articulated currant and plum aromas and flavors against overtones of toast, vanilla and leather. Approaching drinkability now, but it has the complexity and structure to develop through at least 1995. Rel: $17.50 Cur: $22 (4/15/90) **90**
Cabernets Alexander Valley 1985 Rel: $16 Cur: $21 (CA-3/89) **87**
Cabernet Sauvignon Alexander Valley 1984 Rel: $14 Cur: $20 (CA-3/89) **86**
Cabernet Sauvignon Alexander Valley 1983 Rel: $12 Cur: $18 (CA-3/89) **82**
Cabernet Sauvignon Alexander Valley 1982 Rel: $12 Cur: $18 (CA-3/89) **83**
Cabernet Sauvignon Alexander Valley 1981 Rel: $12 Cur: $18 (CA-3/89) **79**
Cabernet Sauvignon Alexander Valley 1980 Rel: $12 Cur: $22 (CA-3/89) **86**
Cabernet Sauvignon Alexander Valley 1979 Rel: $12 Cur: $25 (CA-3/89) **91**
Cabernet Sauvignon Alexander Valley 1978 Rel: $12 Cur: $32 (CA-3/89) **80**

JADE MOUNTAIN
Cabernet Sauvignon Alexander Valley Icaria Creek Vineyard deCarteret 1984 $8.75 (6/30/88) **75**

JEKEL
Cabernet Sauvignon Arroyo Seco 1986: Very vegetal tasting, with olive, bell pepper and onion flavors that not everyone will appreciate, but overall an elegant wine. Moderately tannic, concentrated and well balanced. Try now if this is your style. 2,800 cases made. $13 (11/15/90) **83**
Cabernet Sauvignon Arroyo Seco Home Vineyard 1980 $25 (2/01/86) **63**
Cabernet Sauvignon Monterey 1984: We find this style unpalatable. Not bad in the mid-palate, but it smells vegetal and olivey and finishes the same way. $12 (7/31/89) **63**
Cabernet Sauvignon Monterey 1983: Earthy, pungent and vegetal, with spicy Cabernet flavors. The supple, rich, balanced texture is fine. For fans of this style. Tasted twice. $8 (2/15/89) **67**
Cabernet Sauvignon Monterey 1982 $11 (1/31/87) **71**
Cabernet Sauvignon Monterey Home Vineyard Private Reserve 1982 $20 (2/01/86) **69**
Cabernet Sauvignon Monterey Home Vineyard Private Reserve 1981 $20 (2/01/86) **76**
Cabernet Sauvignon Monterey Home Vineyard Private Reserve 1979 $18 (2/01/86) **77**
Cabernet Sauvignon Monterey Home Vineyard Private Reserve 1978 $16 (2/01/86) **70**

JOHNSON TURNBULL
Cabernet Sauvignon Napa Valley 1988: A minty, herbal wine, with a nice burst of berry and currant flavors keeping it balanced and refreshing to drink. Lively and drinkable now, but should continue to improve through 1994. $16 (11/15/91) **84**
Cabernet Sauvignon Napa Valley 1987: Smooth and creamy, with lots of butter, butterscotch, pear and vanilla flavors that are delicate and elegant, finishing with complexity and finesse. Well proportioned. Drink now to 1994. $16 (11/15/90) **80**
Cabernet Sauvignon Napa Valley Vineyard Selection 82 1986: Incredibly intense and concentrated, with tart black cherry, currant, spice and cedar flavors that are sharply focused and framed by firm tannins and toasty oak. Drink in 1994 to '96. 1,540 cases made. Rel: $14.50 Cur: $25 8/31/89) **95**
Cabernet Sauvignon Napa Valley 1985 Rel: $14.50 Cur: $22 (CA-3/89) **83**
Cabernet Sauvignon Napa Valley 1984 Rel: $14.50 Cur: $23 (CA-3/89) **90**
Cabernet Sauvignon Napa Valley 1983 Rel: $12.50 Cur: $21 (CA-3/89) **88**
Cabernet Sauvignon Napa Valley 1982 Rel: $12.50 Cur: $20 (CA-3/89) **82**
Cabernet Sauvignon Napa Valley 1981 Rel: $12 Cur: $31 (CA-3/89) **87**
Cabernet Sauvignon Napa Valley 1980 Rel: $12 Cur: $29 (CA-3/89) **87**
Cabernet Sauvignon Napa Valley 1979 Rel: $10.50 Cur: $31 (CA-3/89) **85**
Cabernet Sauvignon Napa Valley Vineyard Selection 67 1991: Potently minty and aggressive, with hard-edged currant flavor underneath. Hard to judge at this stage, but has plenty of intensity and flavor. 400 cases made. (NR) (5/15/92) (BT) **85+**
Cabernet Sauvignon Napa Valley Vineyard Selection 67 1990 (NR) (5/15/91) (BT) **90+**
Cabernet Sauvignon Napa Valley Vineyard Selection 67 1989 (NR) (5/15/91) (BT) **85+**
Cabernet Sauvignon Napa Valley Vineyard Selection 67 1988 $15 (5/15/90) (BT) **85+**
Cabernet Sauvignon Napa Valley Vineyard Selection 67 1987: Minty menthol aromas give way to ripe, rich black cherry, plum and currant flavors that stay with you. Well balanced, with crisp acidity, firm tannins and a long fruity aftertaste. Best to cellar until 1996 to 1997. 1,200 cases made. $22 (6/30/91) **89**
Cabernet Sauvignon Napa Valley Vineyard Selection 67 1986: Aromas are so minty they border on camphor, with just enough currant and cherry to make it appealing to those who like the herbal style. Structure is fine, and it should develop well with age. Drink now to 1994. 1,200 cases made. Rel: $20 Cur: $35 (4/15/90) **86**

JORDAN
Cabernet Sauvignon Alexander Valley 1988 (NR) (5/15/90) (BT) **85+**
Cabernet Sauvignon Alexander Valley 1987: Beginning to soften, with generous herb, olive, plum and cherry flavors that are quite inviting. Balanced, with smooth tannins and fine depth and richness. Almost ready to drink, but probably best around 1993 or '94. Rel: $20 Cur: $24 (11/15/91) **90**
Cabernet Sauvignon Alexander Valley 1986: Ripe, smooth, rich, complex and wonderfully proportioned, with currant, plum, nutmeg and cedar flavors that are agile and balanced. Not too tannic and built for drinking now. Rel: $22 Cur: $25 (11/15/90) **88**
Cabernet Sauvignon Alexander Valley 1985: Ripe and floral, with touches of herb, bell pepper, currant and plum flavors that are enticingly supple and complex. Mouthfilling, concentrated, broad and delicious. Drink now to 1999. Rel: $19.50 Cur: $35 (9/15/89) **88**
Cabernet Sauvignon Alexander Valley 1984 Rel: $19 Cur: $45 (CA-3/89) **86**
Cabernet Sauvignon Alexander Valley 1983 Rel: $18 Cur: $31 (CA-3/89) **78**
Cabernet Sauvignon Alexander Valley 1982 Rel: $18 Cur: $39 (CA-3/89) **73**
Cabernet Sauvignon Alexander Valley 1981 Rel: $17 Cur: $46 (CA-3/89) **84**

Cabernet Sauvignon Alexander Valley 1981 Rel: $17 Cur: $46 (5/01/85) CS **90**
Cabernet Sauvignon Alexander Valley 1980 Rel: $17 Cur: $50 (CA-3/89) **80**
Cabernet Sauvignon Alexander Valley 1979 Rel: $16 Cur: $53 (CA-3/89) **79**
Cabernet Sauvignon Alexander Valley 1978 Rel: $16 Cur: $66 (CA-3/89) **81**
Cabernet Sauvignon Alexander Valley 1977 Rel: $14 Cur: $46 (CA-3/89) **77**
Cabernet Sauvignon Alexander Valley 1976 Rel: $10 Cur: $82 (CA-3/89) **79**

JOULLIAN

Cabernet Sauvignon Carmel Valley 1987: Assertive, tannic and flavorful, with weedy dill and slight menthol aromas and flavors that compete with the modest currant note. Needs until 1994 to '96 to settle the tannins. 637 cases made. $14 (7/31/91) **81**

JUDD'S HILL

Cabernet Sauvignon Napa Valley 1991: Big and powerful, packed with rich currant and plum flavors and firm, tight oak and tannins. Finishes with a blast of fruit and chocolate notes. 11 percent Merlot and 3 percent Cabernet Franc. 1,500 cases made. (NR) (5/15/92) (BT) **91+**
Cabernet Sauvignon Napa Valley 1989: Offers a pretty dose of cherry and currant flavors, with coffee, vanilla and cola notes. Intense and tannic; best to give it until 1998 for it to mellow. New from the former owners of Whitehall Lane Winery. $20 (4/15/92) **89**

JUSTIN

Cabernet Sauvignon Paso Robles 1988: Tannic and tough on the palate, with very ripe, almost pruny flavors. Lacks finesse or richness. Try in 1995. $19 (11/15/91) **72**
Reserve Paso Robles 1988: A tough, tight little wine, with snugly wrapped flavors that barely hint at currants and herbs. A slightly burnt edge seems a mite bitter. Try in 1994 or '95. $23 (11/15/91) **75**
Reserve Paso Robles 1987: Very rich and concentrated, with broad cherry, plum and chocolate aromas and flavors that spread across the palate without a great deal of weight. A big wine with finesse. Drink after 1995. A blend of Cabernet Sauvignon, Merlot and Cabernet Franc. 824 cases made. $20 (2/15/91) **90**

KALIN

Cabernet Sauvignon Sonoma County Reserve 1985: A mature style, with a weedy, earthy aroma and flavors of black currant and olive that turn tart on the finish. Drink now through 1994. Tasted twice. $23 (4/15/91) **83**

ROBERT KEEBLE

Cabernet Sauvignon Napa Valley 1987: Rough, definitely tannic but ripe and flavorful, too. The black cherry and plum aromas and flavors are packed into a plush package. Needs to polish the rough edges, which should happen by 1998. 550 cases made. $14 (10/15/91) **89**

KEENAN

Cabernet Sauvignon Napa Valley 1988: Aromatic and flavorful, with more currant and berry flavors than most '88s. Turns a little tannic and tight on the finish, but is a generous wine from start to finish. Drink after 1995 or '96. Tasted twice. $18 (3/31/92) **85**
Cabernet Sauvignon Napa Valley 1987: Very firm and tart, with sharp berry and toast aromas and flavors supported by crisp acidity and a minimum of tannin. Probably best to drink now to 1993. Showed much more richness and complexity from the barrel, before bottling. 2,800 cases made. Rel: $18 Cur: $20 (5/31/90) **86**
Cabernet Sauvignon Napa Valley 1986: Intense, deep, rich and concentrated, with a satiny texture and layers of smoke, plum, black currant and olive flavors that are full-bodied and long on the finish. Drink now to 1994. 3,395 cases made. Rel: $16.50 Cur: $22 (8/31/89) **93**
Cabernet Sauvignon Napa Valley 1985 Rel: $15 Cur: $21 (CA-3/89) **86**
Cabernet Sauvignon Napa Valley 1984 Rel: $13.50 Cur: $27 (CA-3/89) **92**
Cabernet Sauvignon Napa Valley 1984 Rel: $13.50 Cur: $27 (10/15/87) SS **94**
Cabernet Sauvignon Napa Valley 1983 Rel: $11 Cur: $18 (CA-3/89) **87**
Cabernet Sauvignon Napa Valley 1982 Rel: $10 Cur: $28 (CA-3/89) **88**
Cabernet Sauvignon Napa Valley 1981 Rel: $13.50 Cur: $22 (CA-3/89) **84**
Cabernet Sauvignon Napa Valley 1980 Rel: $13.50 Cur: $40 (CA-3/89) **80**
Cabernet Sauvignon Napa Valley 1979 Rel: $12 Cur: $45 (CA-3/89) **74**
Cabernet Sauvignon Napa Valley 1978 Rel: $12 Cur: $35 (CA-3/89) **74**
Cabernet Sauvignon Napa Valley 1977 Rel: $12 Cur: $15 (CA-3/89) **69**

KENDALL-JACKSON

Cardinale Meritage California 1987: Rich, ripe and concentrated, bursting with plum, blueberry and currant aromas and flavors laced with spicy, chocolaty oak that echoes vanilla and cinnamon on the long finish. Keeps pumping out the flavor for minutes on end. A really classy mouthful; should develop and soften through 1997 to 2000. 1,900 cases made. $50 (3/31/92) **95**
Cardinale California 1986: Very different in style from the generous '85 Cardinale. Full-bodied, tart and tannic, with intense, ripe aromas of currant and cherry, loads of youthful tannins and a crisp finish. The focused flavors should match the structure well after time in the cellar. Try in 1993 to '98. 500 cases made. $65 (11/15/90) **91**
Cardinale California 1985 Rel: $45 Cur: $80 (11/15/89) **97**
Cardinale California 1984 $12 (7/31/87) **84**
Cardinale California 1983 $9 (10/16/85) **82**
Cabernet Sauvignon California Proprietor's Grand Reserve 1987: Smooth, spicy and generously fruity, offering currant, berry and vanilla aromas and flavors that keep shining through the finish. The tannins are well submerged, but should keep this developing through 1996. $16 (3/31/92) **87**
Cabernet Sauvignon California The Proprietor's 1986: Not nearly as ripe and opulent as the 1985, this one starts off very smooth and silky, with ripe plum and red cherry aromas and flavors, turning a bit herbal and vegetal on the finish. Drink now. $24 (3/15/90) **85**
Cabernet Sauvignon California Proprietor's Reserve 1985: Sleek and elegant with an overlay of toasty French oak, layers of spice, currant, cassis and cherry flavors that are very attractive, beautifully balanced, supple tannins and a long, satisfying finish. Drink 1993. $20 (12/15/88) **95**
Cabernet Sauvignon California Vintner's Reserve 1989: Lean and crisp, with strong spicy overtones to the raspberry and rhubarb aromas and flavors. Finishes with more than a hint of bell pepper and lots more berry flavors. Drinkable now, and better in 1994. $13 (7/31/92) **84**
Cabernet Sauvignon California Vintner's Reserve 1987 $14 (11/15/91) **82**
Cabernet Sauvignon California Vintner's Reserve 1986 $11 (12/31/88) **85**
Cabernet Sauvignon Lake County 1986 $7.75 (7/31/88) **74**
Cabernet Sauvignon Lake County 1984 $7.50 (11/15/87) BB **81**
Cabernet Sauvignon Lake County 1983 $7 (5/01/86) **69**

KATHRYN KENNEDY

Cabernet Sauvignon Santa Cruz Mountains 1988: Ripe, bold flavors, with tiers of currant, herb, black cherry and oak notes, are tightly packed together, and hints of mint and tea peek through on the finish. Has good intensity and depth of flavor. Best to start drinking in 1995. $45 (11/15/91) **88**
Cabernet Sauvignon Santa Cruz Mountains 1987: Dense, concentrated and tannic, offering explosive cherry, currant and spice aromas and tannins that clamp down on the palate. Tart and tough now; needs until 1995 to 2000 to settle down. 324 cases made. $45 (1/31/91) **89**
Cabernet Sauvignon Santa Cruz Mountains 1986: Lean and tannic, with modest currant aromas and flavors that have strong tobacco and moss overtones. Tasted twice. $30 (3/15/90) **81**
Cabernet Sauvignon Santa Cruz Mountains 1985 $25 (12/15/88) **93**
Lateral California 1989: Oaky, spicy and almost chocolaty, with a velvety texture and modest berry and dill flavors that smooth out on the finish. Drinkable now. 350 cases made. $16.50 (11/15/91) **86**
Lateral California 1988: Deliciously rich and fruity, with layers of ripe plum, cherry, currant and raspberry that have a nice smoky edge. Medium-bodied but not too tannic. Drink now to 1995. 200 cases made. $14.50 (10/15/90) **87**

KENWOOD

Cabernet Sauvignon Sonoma Valley 1987: Dark, rich and intense, but also shows a tight, tannic edge. The chocolate, black cherry, currant and berry flavors shine through, picking up a nice touch of toasty oak on the finish. Intense but delicate. Drink in 1993 to '97. $15 (7/15/91) **90**
Cabernet Sauvignon Sonoma Valley 1986: Aromatic, with mint and meaty aromas, but lean, rich and tannic, with a pretty core of black cherry and currant flavors framed by oak and a coarse, tannic aftertaste. Needs time to develop. Drink now to 2000. $15 (9/30/89) **86**
Cabernet Sauvignon Sonoma Valley 1985: A big, brawny style that's tight, closed and packed with rich, ripe plum, currant and black cherry flavors and a good dose of tannin and oak on the finish. May be ready by 1997. $14.50 (2/15/89) **91**
Cabernet Sauvignon Sonoma Valley 1984 $12 (5/31/88) **83**
Cabernet Sauvignon Sonoma Valley 1983 $10 (2/15/88) **85**
Cabernet Sauvignon Sonoma Valley Artist Series 1988: A very cedary, oaky, minty Cabernet, with big, firm tannins. At this age it's very tough, almost raw, but there seems to be enough fruit underneath to make it worth the gamble of aging until about 1998, when it should open up. Tasted three times. $35 (3/15/92) **83**
Cabernet Sauvignon Sonoma Valley Artist Series 1987: The austerity tends to dominate the ripe currant and cherry flavors, making the tannins seem harsher than they might be. Could use a little more generosity, but perhaps with time it will become more supple. Has the concentration for longer cellaring, but try in 1993. 4,500 cases made. $35 (11/15/90) **88**
Cabernet Sauvignon Sonoma Valley Artist Series 1986: Rich and concentrated, with plenty of elegance and finesse to the currant, plum and tobacco flavors, which are long and harmonious on the finish. The tannins are present without being overwhelming. Give this until 1993 to '95 to soften the edges, then it should be drinkable well into the 21st century. 4,000 cases made. Rel: $30 Cur: $34 (11/30/89) CS **95**
Cabernet Sauvignon Sonoma Valley Artist Series 1985 Rel: $30 Cur: $35 (CA-3/89) **91**
Cabernet Sauvignon Sonoma Valley Artist Series 1984 Rel: $30 Cur: $39 (CA-3/89) **93**
Cabernet Sauvignon Sonoma Valley Artist Series 1983 Rel: $30 Cur: $38 (CA-3/89) **87**
Cabernet Sauvignon Sonoma Valley Artist Series 1983 Rel: $30 Cur: $38 (11/15/86) CS **92**
Cabernet Sauvignon Sonoma Valley Artist Series 1982 Rel: $25 Cur: $40 (CA-3/89) **87**
Cabernet Sauvignon Sonoma Valley Artist Series 1981 Rel: $25 Cur: $52 (CA-3/89) **89**
Cabernet Sauvignon Sonoma Valley Artist Series 1981 Rel: $25 Cur: $52 (9/16/84) SS **89**
Cabernet Sauvignon Sonoma Valley Artist Series 1980 Rel: $20 Cur: $55 (CA-3/89) **80**
Cabernet Sauvignon Sonoma Valley Artist Series 1979 Rel: $20 Cur: $64 (CA-3/89) **91**
Cabernet Sauvignon Sonoma Valley Artist Series 1978 Rel: $20 Cur: $95 (CA-3/89) **90**
Cabernet Sauvignon Sonoma Valley Artist Series 1977 Rel: $15 Cur: $175 (CA-3/89) **82**
Cabernet Sauvignon Sonoma County Artist Series 1976 Rel: $10 Cur: $95 (CA-3/89) **77**
Cabernet Sauvignon Sonoma County Artist Series 1975 Rel: $6.50 Cur: $320 (CA-3/89) **73**
Cabernet Sauvignon Sonoma Valley Jack London Vineyard 1987: Smells great, and packs plenty of ripe cherry and currant flavor into the tannic structure, which bodes well for the future. Hints of spice and vanilla add nuances to the intense flavor. A deep-colored, beautifully balanced, cellar-worthy wine that should start to show all it has around 1997 to 2000. Rel: $18 Cur: $21 (1/31/91) **92**
Cabernet Sauvignon Sonoma Valley Jack London Vineyard 1986: Deep in color and fairly tannic, it's spicy and minty with very intense Cabernet flavor that is firm and sharply focused, allowing the long,full impact of the fruit to come through on the finish. Drink now to 1998. $18 (9/15/89) **90**
Cabernet Sauvignon Sonoma Valley Jack London Vineyard 1985: Very dark, ripe and concentrated, but kept in scale by a ring of soft tannin and a nice touch of mint against a focused core of ripe cherry flavor. Rough now, but a few years in the cellar should make it lovely. Rel: $18 Cur: $21 (10/15/88) **89**
Cabernet Sauvignon Sonoma Valley Jack London Vineyard 1984 Rel: $16 Cur: $21 (11/30/87) **91**
Cabernet Sauvignon Sonoma Valley Jack London Vineyard 1983 Rel: $15 Cur: $21 (2/15/87) **86**
Cabernet Sauvignon Sonoma Valley Jack London Vineyard 1980 Rel: $12.50 Cur: $25 (5/16/84) **80**

KISTLER

Cabernet Sauvignon Sonoma Valley Kistler Estate Vineyard 1987: A weedy, black currant style, with pretty plum and spice notes, but also has a good dose of herb and mint flavors. Balanced, with firm tannins; drink in 1993. Tasted twice. 455 cases made. $25 (2/28/91) **83**
Cabernet Sauvignon Sonoma Valley Kistler Estate Vineyard 1986: Ripe and distinctively peppery—black, bell and chili all in one—turning soft, lush and generous on the palate. There is plenty of tannin to see it through at least 1993, when it should be ready to drink. Tasted three times. Rel: $20 Cur: $28 (9/30/89) **84**
Cabernet Sauvignon Sonoma Valley Kistler Estate Vineyard 1985 Rel: $16 Cur: $28 (CA-3/89) **93**
Cabernet Sauvignon Napa Valley Veeder Hills Vineyard 1983 Rel: $13.50 Cur: $25 (CA-3/89) **78**
Cabernet Sauvignon Napa Valley Veeder Hills Vineyard 1982 Rel: $12 Cur: $26 (CA-3/89) **86**
Cabernet Sauvignon Napa Valley Veeder Hills-Veeder Peak 1981 Rel: $12 Cur: $32 (CA-3/89) **87**
Cabernet Sauvignon Napa Valley Veeder Hills-Veeder Peak 1980 Rel: $16 Cur: $42 (CA-3/89) **85**
Cabernet Sauvignon Sonoma Valley Glen Ellen Vineyard 1980 Rel: $16 Cur: $42 (CA-3/89) **84**

KLEIN

Cabernet Sauvignon Santa Cruz Mountains 1988: Strong smoke and tobacco aromas make this wine taste almost like ash instead of fruit, lending a bitter flavor that nearly obscures a modest core of currant and berry flavors. Best after 1997. Much better than bottles tasted earlier. $25 (1/31/92) **83**
Cabernet Sauvignon Santa Cruz Mountains 1987: Massive, intense and tannic, with rich bell pepper, olive and currant flavors that ring true. It's a deep, powerful, oaky wine that will require years to reach full maturity, but if you're patient this could be a hummer. Check it out in 1995 to see how it's mellowing. $19 (10/15/90) **87**
Cabernet Sauvignon Santa Cruz Mountains 1986: Densely concentrated wine, with smoky, ripe plum aromas and flavors on the finish, yet balanced and supple enough to make it accessible now. Best to cellar it until 1993 to '94 to tame its exuberance. $22 (9/30/89) **89**

KONOCTI

Cabernet Sauvignon Lake County 1986: Elegant and stylish. Has pretty plum and currant flavors, with a touch of bell pepper and herb flavors that add dimension. Not too tannic; ready to drink now. $9 (4/30/90) **80**
Cabernet Sauvignon Lake County 1985: Firm and concentrated, with cherry and blackberry flavors that are tannic enough to need until 1994 to soften up. Very impressive depth and power now, which should develop with age. $7.50 (11/15/89) BB **89**
Cabernet Sauvignon Lake County 1984: A smooth, supple, even-handed Cabernet that lacks vitality and the generous fruit you'd expect from an '84. It's drinkable and pleasant, but lacks pizzazz. Drink now. $7.50 (2/15/89) **76**
Cabernet Sauvignon Lake County 1983 $6 (6/15/87) BB **84**
Cabernet Sauvignon Lake County 1982 $7 (11/15/86) **78**
Meritage Red Clear Lake 1987 $17 (4/15/91) **85**

CHARLES KRUG

Cabernet Sauvignon Napa Valley 1988: A squeaky-clean wine that's tart with biting acidity. An overworked wine that lacks richness and depth, with thin, hollow cherry and plum flavors. Tasted twice. $12 (3/15/92) **73**
Cabernet Sauvignon Napa Valley 1987: Crisp and focused, with berry and spice aromas and flavors hinting at orange peel and caramel on the finish. Could be smoother and fruitier. Tasted twice. $10.50 (11/15/91) **79**

Cabernet Sauvignon Napa Valley 1986: A big, sturdy, flavorful style, packed with herb, currant, cherry and chocolate flavors. Has full tannins and full body, but the fruit component is strong, and it all balances out. A reasonable price, too. $10.50 (2/28/91) **87**
Cabernet Sauvignon Napa Valley 1985 $10.50 (1/31/90) **77**
Cabernet Sauvignon Napa Valley 1982 $7 (10/31/87) **79**
Cabernet Sauvignon Napa Valley 1965 $35 (7/16/85) (JL) **74**
Cabernet Sauvignon Napa Valley 1962 $55 (7/16/85) (JL) **84**
Cabernet Sauvignon Napa Valley 1961 $105 (7/16/85) (JL) **84**
Cabernet Sauvignon Napa Valley 1952 $250 (7/16/85) (JL) **86**
Cabernet Sauvignon Napa Valley 1951 $250 (7/16/85) (JL) **80**
Cabernet Sauvignon Napa Valley 1947 $300 (7/16/85) (JL) **89**
Cabernet Sauvignon Napa Valley Vintage Selection 1986 (NR) (CA-3/89) **87**
Cabernet Sauvignon Napa Valley Vintage Selection 1985: A ripe, supple-textured Cabernet that's just coming into its own. Has spicy, nearly mature aromas and currant and cherry flavors that linger on the finish. Tempting now, but better to cellar until 1995 or so. Rel: $28 Cur: $30 (3/15/92) **89**
Cabernet Sauvignon Napa Valley Vintage Selection 1984: Beautifully balanced, with a solid backbone of acid and ripe, generous, jammy flavors delivered in an elegant package. With berry, currant and minty aromas and flavors. Approachable if tart now, but better perhaps in 1993. Rel: $20 Cur: $28 (6/30/90) **87**
Cabernet Sauvignon Napa Valley Vintage Selection 1983: Tart and tannic but has enough generous cherry, cranberry and currant flavor to appeal to some Cabernet lovers. The aromas are very pretty, but prepare yourself for a tight wine that is not ready to drink. Should soften and become more approachable with age. Try in 1995. Rel: $20 Cur: $26 (6/30/90) **81**
Cabernet Sauvignon Napa Valley Vintage Selection 1981 Rel: $20 Cur: $24 (9/30/90) **90**
Cabernet Sauvignon Napa Valley Vintage Selection 1980 Rel: $15 Cur: $22 (CA-3/89) **79**
Cabernet Sauvignon Napa Valley Vintage Selection 1979 Rel: $12.50 Cur: $26 (CA-3/89) **82**
Cabernet Sauvignon Napa Valley Vintage Selection 1978 Rel: $11 Cur: $26 (CA-3/89) **78**
Cabernet Sauvignon Napa Valley Vintage Selection 1977 Rel: $10 Cur: $30 (CA-3/89) **74**
Cabernet Sauvignon Napa Valley Vintage Selection 1974 Rel: $9 Cur: $50 (2/15/90) (JG) **87**
Cabernet Sauvignon Napa Valley Vintage Selection Lot F-1 1974 Rel: $9 Cur: $50 (CA-3/89) **88**
Cabernet Sauvignon Napa Valley Vintage Selection 1973 Rel: $9 Cur: $40 (CA-3/89) **73**
Cabernet Sauvignon Napa Valley Vintage Selection 1972 Rel: $9 Cur: $37 (CA-3/89) **77**
Cabernet Sauvignon Napa Valley Vintage Selection 1971 Rel: $7.50 Cur: $41 (CA-3/89) **79**
Cabernet Sauvignon Napa Valley Vintage Selection 1970 Rel: $7.50 Cur: $60 (CA-3/89) **75**
Cabernet Sauvignon Napa Valley Vintage Selection 1969 Rel: $6.50 Cur: $55 (CA-3/89) **81**
Cabernet Sauvignon Napa Valley Vintage Selection 1968 Rel: $6.50 Cur: $80 (CA-3/89) **80**
Cabernet Sauvignon Napa Valley Vintage Selection 1966 Rel: $6 Cur: $82 (6/01/85) (JL) **87**
Cabernet Sauvignon Napa Valley Vintage Selection 1965 Rel: $5 Cur: $70 (CA-3/89) **87**
Cabernet Sauvignon Napa Valley Vintage Selection 1964 Rel: $4 Cur: $68 (CA-3/89) **86**
Cabernet Sauvignon Napa Valley Vintage Selection 1963 Rel: $3.50 Cur: $70 (CA-3/89) **74**
Cabernet Sauvignon Napa Valley Vintage Selection 1962 Rel: $3.50 Cur: $100 (CA-3/89) **78**
Cabernet Sauvignon Napa Valley Vintage Selection 1961 Rel: $3.50 Cur: $140 (CA-3/89) **89**
Cabernet Sauvignon Napa Valley Vintage Selection 1960 Rel: $2.25 Cur: $45 (CA-3/89) **79**
Cabernet Sauvignon Napa Valley Vintage Selection 1959 Rel: $2.25 Cur: $140 (CA-3/89) **85**
Cabernet Sauvignon Napa Valley Vintage Selection 1958 Rel: $2 Cur: $280 (CA-3/89) **88**
Cabernet Sauvignon Napa Valley Vintage Selection 1957 Rel: $2 Cur: $240 (7/16/85) (JL) **81**
Cabernet Sauvignon Napa Valley Vintage Selection 1956 Rel: $1.40 Cur: $350 (CA-3/89) **90**
Cabernet Sauvignon Napa Valley Vintage Selection 1952 Rel: $1.26 Cur: $530 (CA-3/89) **92**
Cabernet Sauvignon Napa Valley Vintage Selection 1951 Rel: $1.25 Cur: $400 (CA-3/89) **85**
Cabernet Sauvignon Napa Valley Vintage Selection 1950 Rel: $1.25 Cur: $500 (CA-3/89) **79**
Cabernet Sauvignon Napa Valley Vintage Selection 1946 Rel: $1 Cur: $750 (CA-3/89) **88**
Cabernet Sauvignon Napa Valley 1944 Rel: $0.95 Cur: $420 (CA-3/89) **88**

LA FERRONNIERE
Cabernet Sauvignon Napa Valley 1985: This wine from a new label tastes rich, round and supple, with full-bodied cherry, plum and herb flavors and fairly complex aromas. Moderately tannic. Drink now. $14 (1/31/90) **80**

LA JOTA
Cabernet Sauvignon Howell Mountain 1991: Rich, ripe, bold and concentrated, with sharply focused currant, mulberry, chocolate, spice and coffee flavors. A mouthful of Cabernet, but with a seam of elegance. 2,800 cases made. (NR) (5/15/92) (BT) **90+**
Cabernet Sauvignon Howell Mountain 1990 (NR) (5/15/91) (BT) **90+**
Cabernet Sauvignon Howell Mountain 1989 $24 (5/15/91) (BT) **90+**
Cabernet Sauvignon Howell Mountain 1988: Spicy, peppery aromas and flavors characterize this big, somewhat tannic Cabernet that's marked more by oak than fruit, with modest cherry and plum notes sneaking in on the finish. A rich, gutsy style that may be too powerful for some. Drink after 1995 or '96. Rel: $28 Cur: $32 (8/31/91) **85**
Cabernet Sauvignon Howell Mountain 1987: A beautifully defined wine, with deep, rich, intense and supple black currant flavors. It's pure and complex, with a pretty overlay of toasty oak flavors that blend together, creating a wine of great harmony and finesse. Has enough tannin to last a decade or more. Best to try in 1994 or '95. 2,700 cases made. Rel: $25 Cur: $30 (7/31/90) SS **95**
Cabernet Sauvignon Howell Mountain 1986 Rel: $21 Cur: $30 (10/15/89) **85**
Cabernet Sauvignon Howell Mountain 1985 Rel: $18 Cur: $40 (CA-3/89) **88**
Cabernet Sauvignon Howell Mountain 1984 Rel: $15 Cur: $34 (CA-3/89) **88**
Cabernet Sauvignon Howell Mountain 1983 Rel: $15 Cur: $28 (CA-3/89) **84**
Cabernet Sauvignon Howell Mountain 1982 Rel: $13.50 Cur: $35 (CA-3/89) **84**

LA VIEILLE MONTAGNE
Cabernet Sauvignon Napa Valley 1987: Firm in texture, with focused nutmeg-scented cherry and prune aromas and flavors. Tightly structured, with enough greenish tannin to need until 1995 to '97 to soften. 260 cases made. $14 (6/15/91) **81**
Cabernet Sauvignon Napa Valley 1986: Attractive for its balance of fresh, ripe, rich herb-flavored Cabernet flavor and vanilla-tinged oak. Needs a year or two to mellow. $14 (6/30/90) **84**

LAKESPRING
Cabernet Sauvignon Napa Valley 1987: Firm, focused and decidely minty in aroma, with solid currant and berry flavors that extend into a finish that needs time to resolve the tannins. Try in 1994. Rel: $14 Cur: $18 (10/15/91) **84**

Key to Symbols

The scores reported here are the results of blind tastings conducted by our panel of senior editors. Wines that carry the initials below are results of individual tastings.

THE WINE SPECTATOR 100-POINT SCALE* *95-100—Classic, a great wine; ***90-94***—Outstanding, superior character and style; ***80-89***—Good to very good, a wine with special qualities; ***70-79***—Average, drinkable wine that may have minor flaws; ***60-69***—Below average, drinkable but not recommended; ***50-59***—Poor, undrinkable, not recommended. "+"—With a score indicates a range; used primarily with barrel tastings to indicate a preliminary score.

SPECIAL DESIGNATIONS SS—Spectator Selection, CS—Cellar Selection, BB—Best Buy, ($NA)—Price not available, (NR)—Not released.

TASTER'S INITIALS (JG)—Jim Gordon, (HS)—Harvey Steiman, (JL)—James Laube, (JS)—James Suckling, (TM)—Thomas Matthews, (TR)—Terry Robards, (PM)—Per-Henrik Mansson, (BT)—Barrel Tasting (these wines were tasted blind from barrel samples), (CA-date)—*California's Great Cabernets* by James Laube, (CH-date)—*California's Great Chardonnays* by James Laube, (VP-date)—*Vintage Port* by James Suckling.

DATE TASTED Dates in parentheses represent the issue in which the rating was published.

Cabernet Sauvignon Napa Valley 1986 Rel: $14 Cur: $18 (CA-3/89) **88**
Cabernet Sauvignon Napa Valley 1985 Rel: $12 Cur: $19 (CA-3/89) **88**
Cabernet Sauvignon Napa Valley Reserve Selection 1984 Rel: $15 Cur: $21 (10/31/88) SS **92**
Cabernet Sauvignon Napa Valley 1983 Rel: $11 Cur: $14 (CA-3/89) **85**
Cabernet Sauvignon Napa Valley Vintage Selection 1982 Rel: $14 Cur: $32 (CA-3/89) **88**
Cabernet Sauvignon Napa Valley 1981 Rel: $11 Cur: $22 (CA-3/89) **86**
Cabernet Sauvignon Napa Valley 1980 Rel: $10 Cur: $21 (CA-3/89) **88**

LAMBERT BRIDGE
Cabernet Sauvignon Sonoma County 1984 $10 (4/15/87) **80**
Cabernet Sauvignon Sonoma County 1981 $12 (1/01/85) **75**

LAURA'S
Cabernet Sauvignon Paso Robles 1985: Heavy green bean flavors dominate on the palate, making it a decent, party-style red, but not what you'd expect, much less a wine to lay down. Drink now. $12 (12/15/89) **71**
Cabernet Sauvignon Paso Robles 1983 $8.50 (12/31/87) **80**

LAUREL GLEN
Cabernet Sauvignon Sonoma Mountain 1991: Shows an enormous concentration of complex fruit and oak flavors, even at this early stage. Packed with currant, wild plum, berry, cedar, coffee and more. The tannins are plush yet polished. Delicious already. 5 percent Cabernet Franc. 1,500 cases made. (NR) (5/15/92) (BT) **94+**
Cabernet Sauvignon Sonoma Mountain 1990 (NR) (5/15/91) (BT) **90+**
Cabernet Sauvignon Sonoma Mountain 1989 (NR) (5/15/91) (BT) **90+**
Cabernet Sauvignon Sonoma Mountain 1988: Ripe and concentrated, with dense plum, cherry and currant flavors that are tightly packed and supported by firm, drying tannins. Lacks finesse now, but has enough fruit complexity to be encouraged. Picks up a peppery touch on the finish. Cellar until 1997. 800 cases made. $30 (5/15/91) CS **90**
Cabernet Sauvignon Sonoma Mountain 1987 Rel: $22 Cur: $26 (9/15/90) **90**
Cabernet Sauvignon Sonoma Mountain 1986 Rel: $20 Cur: $30 (5/15/89) **87**
Cabernet Sauvignon Sonoma Mountain 1985 Rel: $18 Cur: $40 (CA-3/89) **93**
Cabernet Sauvignon Sonoma Mountain 1984 Rel: $15 Cur: $45 (CA-3/89) **89**
Cabernet Sauvignon Sonoma Mountain 1983 Rel: $11 Cur: $20 (CA-3/89) **59**
Cabernet Sauvignon Sonoma Mountain 1982 Rel: $12.50 Cur: $35 (CA-3/89) **85**
Cabernet Sauvignon Sonoma Mountain 1981 Rel: $12.50 Cur: $44 (CA-3/89) **92**
Cabernet Sauvignon Sonoma Mountain 1981 Rel: $12.50 Cur: $44 (2/16/85) SS **93**
Cabernet Sauvignon Sonoma Mountain Counterpoint 1989: Ripe and lush, with rangy tannins that make it seem harsh at first, but the generous blackberry, black currant and plum flavors come through strongly on the finish. Has a floral, almost vegetal edge to the flavors, but the fruit prevails. Best after 1995. Tasted three times. $15 (1/31/92) **85**
Cabernet Sauvignon Sonoma County Counterpoint 1988: Simple but pleasant, with pretty plum, cherry, spice and currant flavors of modest depth and concentration. Ready to drink now through 1994. $13 (7/15/91) **83**
Cabernet Sauvignon Sonoma Mountain Counterpoint 1987: Deeply colored and aromatically pleasing. Young, ripe and concentrated with layers of cedar, currant, spice and cherry that linger on the finish. Drink now to 2000. 1,392 cases made. $13 (10/31/89) **94**
Cabernet Sauvignon Sonoma Mountain Counterpoint Cuvée 1985-'86 NV $11 (5/31/88) **89**
Terra Rosa Napa Valley 1988: Attractive, ripe, rich floral, cherry, currant and spicy fruit flavors are more showy up-front than on the finish, where the flavors seem to taper off. Balanced and not too tannic, but not a long ager. Drink now to 1994. $12 (11/15/90) **85**
Terra Rosa Napa Valley 1987: Big and tough but harmonious too, with a wealth of cherry, currant, and berry-scented fruit, along with toasty, coffee-flavored oak, backed by firm tannins that are lightly polished. Plenty of fruit comes through on the finish. Complex. Tasted three times. Two bottles were corky. $14 (7/31/90) **86**

LEEWARD
Cabernet Sauvignon Alexander Valley 1987: Tart and tangy, with sharply focused cherry, raspberry and currant flavors that linger through the long finish. Has odd doughy or volatile aromas, but maybe all it needs is cellaring until 1993 or '94. 1,350 cases made. $13 (11/15/90) **84**
Cabernet Sauvignon Alexander Valley 1986: Sharply focused, intense herbal and berry aromas and flavors are wrapped in an austere wrap of tannin that needs cellaring to soften. Drink now to 1994. $12 (10/15/89) **79**
Cabernet Sauvignon Alexander Valley 1985 $12 (10/31/87) **83**

CHARLES LEFRANC
Cabernet Sauvignon Monterey County 1981 $8.50 (9/16/85) **76**
Cabernet Sauvignon Napa County 1984 $12 (10/15/87) **80**

LIBERTY SCHOOL
Cabernet Sauvignon Alexander Valley Lot 13 NV $6 (1/01/86) **64**
Cabernet Sauvignon California Lot 17 NV $6 (2/29/88) **73**
Cabernet Sauvignon California Lot 18 NV: Solidly and attractively made, with touches of cinnamon, cedar and appealing plum and cherry flavors that linger nicely on the palate. Fairly tannic, but drinkable now. $7.50 (4/30/89) BB **81**
Cabernet Sauvignon California Lot 19 NV: Ripe and herbal, with a very soft structure that seems a bit sweet, but the jammy cherry flavors on the finish manage to fight the herbs to a standstill. $7.50 (11/15/89) **77**
Cabernet Sauvignon California Vintner Select Series Two NV: A firm texture, vibrant fruit flavor and crisp acidity on the finish make this a tasty wine for drinking with dinner. The flavors run toward plum and currant. Drinkable now. $7.50 (11/15/91) BB **82**

LIVINGSTON
Cabernet Sauvignon Napa Valley Moffett Vineyard 1991: Dark and powerful, with a tight, intense core of currant, plum and berry flavors. The fruit is sharply focused, long and concentrated. 1,800 cases made. (NR) (5/15/92) (BT) **88+**
Cabernet Sauvignon Napa Valley Moffett Vineyard 1990 (NR) (5/15/91) (BT) **90+**
Cabernet Sauvignon Napa Valley Moffett Vineyard 1989 (NR) (5/15/91) (BT) **85+**
Cabernet Sauvignon Napa Valley Moffett Vineyard 1988: Ultraripe to the point of being jammy, with rich blackberry flavor and firm tannins, but it's ultimately a bold mouthful of Cabernet. Tempting now, but can stand cellaring through 1994. 1,100 cases made. $30 (11/15/91) **85**
Cabernet Sauvignon Napa Valley Moffett Vineyard 1987: Has great depth and intensity, with ripe, powerful, rich berry, black cherry, currant and plum flavors that linger long and full on the finish. Dark, dense, concentrated and tannic, but impeccably balanced. Built for the next generation—hold off drinking until the mid-1990s. Best in 1998 to 2009. Best yet from Livingston. 987 cases made. Rel: $24 Cur: $28 (11/15/90) **94**
Cabernet Sauvignon Napa Valley Moffett Vineyard 1986 Rel: $24 Cur: $29 (11/30/89) **88**
Cabernet Sauvignon Napa Valley Moffett Vineyard 1985 Rel: $18 Cur: $33 (CA-3/89) **86**
Cabernet Sauvignon Napa Valley Moffett Vineyard 1984 Rel: $18 Cur: $35 (CA-3/89) **87**
Cabernet Sauvignon Napa Valley Stanley's Selection 1990 (NR) (5/15/91) (BT) **85+**
Cabernet Sauvignon Napa Valley Stanley's Selection 1989 $20 (5/15/91) (BT) **85+**

LLORDS & ELWOOD
Cabernet Sauvignon Napa Valley 1982 $8 (12/15/87) **79**

J. LOHR
Cabernet Sauvignon California Cypress 1988: A well-made but basic wine, with the typical plummy, herbal aromas and broad flavors. Medium-bodied, moderately tannic and ready to drink now through 1993. $7 (11/15/91) **80**

Cabernet Sauvignon California 1987: Ripe, generous and concentrated, with ebullient cassis and plum aromas and flavors, and a soft, smooth texture. It's not built for the cellar, but it's delicious right now. $7 (2/15/90) BB **84**
Cabernet Sauvignon California 1986: Fresh and bright fruit livens up this wine. Attractive to drink now for its supple chocolate, cherry and berry aromas and flavors. $6.50 (4/15/89) BB **84**
Cabernet Sauvignon California 1984 $5 (11/30/86) BB **82**
Cabernet Sauvignon Napa Valley Carol's Vineyard Reserve 1985 $14.50 (12/15/88) **89**
Cabernet Sauvignon Napa Valley Carol's Vineyard Reserve Lot 2 1985 $17.50 (9/30/90) **88**
Cabernet Sauvignon Paso Robles Seven Oaks 1988 $13 (3/15/92) **83**
Cabernet Sauvignon Paso Robles Seven Oaks 1987 $12 (4/30/91) **86**

LOLONIS
Cabernet Sauvignon Mendocino County Lolonis Vineyard Private Reserve 1989: An abundantly fruity, flavorful wine, with plenty of fine tannins to back up the ripe currant and black cherry flavors. Firm in structure and well balanced with acidity. A likely candidate for cellaring until about 1995. $15 (11/15/91) **86**
Cabernet Sauvignon Mendocino County Private Reserve 1986: Pretty aromas and flavors of chocolate, vanilla, plum and currant that are elegant and well defined, with moderate depth and intensity. Altogether well balanced and pleasing to drink now through 1994. $15 (5/15/90) **83**

LONG
Cabernet Sauvignon Napa Valley 1990 (NR) (5/15/91) (BT) **90+**
Cabernet Sauvignon Napa Valley 1989 (NR) (5/15/91) (BT) **90+**
Cabernet Sauvignon Napa Valley 1986 Rel: $40 Cur: $48 (CA-3/89) **86**
Cabernet Sauvignon Napa Valley 1985 Rel: $36 Cur: $46 (CA-3/89) **92**
Cabernet Sauvignon Napa Valley 1984 Rel: $32 Cur: $46 (CA-3/89) **88**
Cabernet Sauvignon Napa Valley 1983 Rel: $32 Cur: $41 (CA-3/89) **78**
Cabernet Sauvignon Napa Valley 1980 Rel: $32 Cur: $46 (CA-3/89) **91**
Cabernet Sauvignon Napa Valley 1979 Rel: $32 Cur: $50 (CA-3/89) **90**

LYETH
Red Alexander Valley 1988 (NR) (5/15/90) (BT) **85+**
Red Alexander Valley 1986: Aromatic but lean on the palate, this elegant style features herb- and toast-scented currant aromas and flavors that linger on the focused finish. It's well crafted, subtle and complex, needing until 1993 to show what it has. $23 (11/15/90) **88**
Red Alexander Valley 1985: Rich and supple, with layers of lively plum, currant and cedar flavors that are thick and concentrated, bordered by ample tannins and a soft, smooth texture. Begin drinking now. $22 (5/31/89) **86**
Red Alexander Valley 1984 Rel: $18 Cur: $24 (CA-3/89) **90**
Red Alexander Valley 1983 Rel: $17 Cur: $23 (CA-3/89) **78**
Red Alexander Valley 1982 Rel: $16 Cur: $30 (CA-3/89) **85**
Red Alexander Valley 1981 Rel: $15 Cur: $35 (CA-3/89) **77**

LYTTON SPRINGS
Cabernet Sauvignon Mendocino County Private Reserve 1988: A spicy raspberry flavor reminds us of Zinfandel and it shows a good dose of volatile acidity, but some may find the currant, raspberry and spice notes appealing. Drink in 1993 to '96. $18 (11/15/91) **80**
Cabernet Sauvignon Mendocino County Private Reserve 1987: With a massive concentration of fruit, high extract, and incredibly intense flavors of raisin, currant, black cherry, plum and spicy oak, this is overpowering now and almost like a barrel sample. Could use a warning label: For the next generation. Drink 1995 and beyond. $18 (9/15/90) **88**

MAACAMA CREEK
Cabernet Sauvignon Sonoma County Melim Vineyard 1989: A thick, chewy wine, with ripe, vibrant fruit flavors, ample but soft tannins and a lingering finish. A spicy, peppery accent adds complexity. $8 (11/15/91) BB **86**

MADDALENA
Cabernet Sauvignon Alexander Valley Reserve 1986: Intensely herbal, with pretty black currant flavors, but the herbal flavors dominate and will not appeal to many. Drink now. $10 (3/31/90) **77**
Cabernet Sauvignon Alexander Valley Reserve 1985: Marked by earthy aromas and a broad, juicy texture. Cherry and berry flavors are clean and attractive. Drink now. $11 (6/30/89) **78**
Cabernet Sauvignon Sonoma County 1988: Pleasant and well balanced, with lean cherry and berry flavors and an overlay of oak. Not generous, but very drinkable. $7.50 (3/31/92) **79**
Cabernet Sauvignon Sonoma County 1985 $6 (5/31/88) **74**
Cabernet Sauvignon Sonoma County Vintner's Reserve 1984 $9 (3/31/87) **82**

MADRONA
Cabernet Sauvignon El Dorado 1985: Tough, firm and tannic, but it has a solid core of cedary currant, earth and spice notes. Concentrated, rich and compact, it still needs time. Drink after 1995. 1,620 cases made. $12 (4/15/92) **82**

MARIETTA
Cabernet Sauvignon Sonoma County 1987: Ripe and fruity, with tiers of cherry, currant and plum flavors that are rich and tannic, picking up an attractive, toasty chocolate aftertaste. Gutsy enough to cellar through 1994. 1,250 cases made. $10 (2/28/91) **87**
Cabernet Sauvignon Sonoma County 1985: A clean, crisp, medium-weight wine, with minty, tea-like aromas to add complexity to the solid, lingering plum flavors. Modest tannins and good acidity make it ready to drink now. 1,850 cases made. $10 (6/30/90) **83**
Cabernet Sauvignon Sonoma County 1984 $10 (12/31/87) **78**
Cabernet Sauvignon Sonoma County 1981 $9 (6/16/84) **78**

MARION
Cabernet Sauvignon California 1989: Has plenty of sweet, floral, fruity aromas, but on the palate those flavors turn simple. A pleasant wine that's ready to drink now through 1993. 1,100 cases made. $9 (11/15/91) **83**
Cabernet Sauvignon California 1985 $5.50 (12/31/87) **62**

MARKHAM
Cabernet Sauvignon Napa Valley 1990 (NR) (5/15/91) (BT) **85+**
Cabernet Sauvignon Napa Valley 1989 (NR) (5/15/91) (BT) **85+**
Cabernet Sauvignon Napa Valley 1988 $18 (5/15/90) (BT) **85+**
Cabernet Sauvignon Napa Valley 1987: Offers a solid core of ripe, rich cherry, currant, plum and mint flavors and a slap of oak, too. The tannins are rich and firm, but the fruit fights through on the finish. Like many '87s that are rough and tough. Hold until 1996. $15 (8/31/91) **87**
Cabernet Sauvignon Napa Valley 1986: Beautifully articulated currant and berry aromas and flavors run through this smoothly balanced, harmonious wine that turns elegant and supple on the long finish. Almost drinkable now, but should improve through 1993 to '95. 3,500 cases made. Rel: $13 Cur: $16 (4/30/91) **87**
Cabernet Sauvignon Napa Valley 1985: Lean in structure but bursting with generous blackberry and vanilla flavors, complex and beautifully balanced. Has all the components to age well. Drink after 1994. 3,810 cases made. Rel: $13 Cur: $17 (4/15/90) **91**
Cabernet Sauvignon Napa Valley 1984 Rel: $12 Cur: $18 (CA-3/89) **91**
Cabernet Sauvignon Napa Valley 1983 Rel: $13 Cur: $17 (7/31/89) **90**
Cabernet Sauvignon Napa Valley 1982 Rel: $13 Cur: $20 (CA-3/89) **90**
Cabernet Sauvignon Napa Valley 1981 Rel: $13 Cur: $20 (CA-3/89) **86**
Cabernet Sauvignon Napa Valley 1980 Rel: $13 Cur: $26 (CA-3/89) **89**
Cabernet Sauvignon Napa Valley 1979 Rel: $13 Cur: $31 (CA-3/89) **88**
Cabernet Sauvignon Napa Valley 1978 Rel: $13 Cur: $32 (CA-3/89) **85**

MART IN BROTHERS
Cabernet Sauvignon Paso Robles 1989: Smooth and almost sweet, with buttery chocolate and berry flavors dominating on the palate. Not altogether unappealing, but not classic, either. $12 (11/15/91) **77**

LOUIS M. MARTINI
Cabernet Sauvignon Napa Valley Reserve 1987 $14 (10/15/90) **87**
Cabernet Sauvignon North Coast 1986: Herbal style, redolent of wildflowers, lean and contained on the palate, with good, long berry flavors on the finish. $9.25 (9/15/89) **80**
Cabernet Sauvignon North Coast 1985 $8.25 (10/31/88) **76**
Cabernet Sauvignon North Coast 1983 $7 (3/31/87) **69**
Cabernet Sauvignon North Coast 1981 $6.50 (3/01/85) **83**
Cabernet Sauvignon North Coast Special Selection 1984 (NR) (CA-3/89) **85**
Cabernet Sauvignon North Coast Special Selection 1980 Rel: $12 Cur: $17 (CA-3/89) **84**
Cabernet Sauvignon California Special Selection 1978 Rel: $9 Cur: $25 (CA-3/89) **86**
Cabernet Sauvignon California Special Selection 1977 Rel: $9 Cur: $16 (CA-3/89) **70**
Cabernet Sauvignon California Special Selection 1976 Rel: $9 Cur: $25 (CA-3/89) **86**
Cabernet Sauvignon California Special Selection 1974 Rel: $10 Cur: $40 (CA-3/89) **77**
Cabernet Sauvignon California Special Selection 1972 Rel: $5 Cur: $50 (CA-3/89) **63**
Cabernet Sauvignon California Special Selection 1970 Rel: $8 Cur: $60 (CA-3/89) **88**
Cabernet Sauvignon California Special Selection 1968 Rel: $6 Cur: $70 (CA-3/89) **90**
Cabernet Sauvignon California Special Selection 1966 Rel: $6 Cur: $135 (CA-3/89) **87**
Cabernet Sauvignon California Special Selection 1964 Rel: $6 Cur: $95 (CA-3/89) **85**
Cabernet Sauvignon California Private Reserve 1962 Rel: $3.50 Cur: $80 (CA-3/89) **73**
Cabernet Sauvignon California Special Selection 1961 Rel: $4 Cur: $160 (CA-3/89) **80**
Cabernet Sauvignon California Special Selection 1959 Rel: $4.50 Cur: $140 (CA-3/89) **87**
Cabernet Sauvignon California Special Selection 1958 Rel: $4.50 Cur: $185 (CA-3/89) **88**
Cabernet Sauvignon California Special Selection 1957 Rel: $3.50 Cur: $160 (CA-3/89) **91**
Cabernet Sauvignon California Private Reserve 1956 Rel: $2.50 Cur: $80 (CA-3/89) **77**
Cabernet Sauvignon California Special Selection 1955 Rel: $2.50 Cur: $180 (CA-3/89) **87**
Cabernet Sauvignon California Special Selection 1952 Rel: $2.50 Cur: $300 (CA-3/89) **93**
Cabernet Sauvignon California Special Selection 1951 Rel: $2 Cur: $300 (CA-3/89) **87**
Cabernet Sauvignon California Special Selection 1947 Rel: $1.50 Cur: $550 (CA-3/89) **90**
Cabernet Sauvignon California Special Selection 1945 Rel: $1.50 Cur: $400 (CA-3/89) **75**
Cabernet Sauvignon California Private Reserve Villa del Rey 1943 Rel: $1.50 Cur: $400 (CA-3/89) **70**
Cabernet Sauvignon California Special Reserve 1939 Rel: $1.25 Cur: $1,000 (CA-3/89) **90**
Cabernet Sauvignon Sonoma County 1988: A simple, straightforward wine, with modest concentration of currant flavor and a nice hint of plum on the finish. A modestly built wine. Drinkable now. $9 (4/30/91) BB **81**
Cabernet Sauvignon Sonoma Valley Monte Rosso 1989 (NR) (5/15/91) (BT) **85+**
Cabernet Sauvignon Sonoma Valley Monte Rosso 1988: A crisp, austere, tannic style, with modest proportions of mint and currant flavors. Missing richness and body in the middle. Try after 1994. 1,000 cases made. $25 (11/15/91) **81**
Cabernet Sauvignon Sonoma Valley Monte Rosso 1987 Rel: $20 Cur: $23 (11/15/90) **93**
Cabernet Sauvignon Sonoma Valley Monte Rosso 1986 $20 (CA-3/89) **86**
Cabernet Sauvignon Sonoma Valley Monte Rosso 1985 $22 (CA-3/89) **80**
Cabernet Sauvignon Sonoma Valley Monte Rosso 1984 $22 (CA-3/89) **89**
Cabernet Sauvignon Sonoma Valley Monte Rosso 1983 $22 (CA-3/89) **86**
Cabernet Sauvignon Sonoma Valley Monte Rosso 1982 $22 (CA-3/89) **85**
Cabernet Sauvignon Sonoma Valley Monte Rosso 1981 $25 (12/15/86) **90**
Cabernet Sauvignon Sonoma Valley Monte Rosso Los Niños 1983 $25 (CA-3/89) **83**
Cabernet Sauvignon Sonoma Valley Monte Rosso Los Niños 1982 $25 (CA-3/89) **82**
Cabernet Sauvignon Sonoma Valley Monte Rosso Los Niños 1981 $25 (CA-3/89) **85**
Cabernet Sauvignon Sonoma Valley Monte Rosso Lot 2 1979 Rel: $10 Cur: $19 (CA-3/89) **84**

PAUL MASSON
Cabernet Sauvignon California Vintners Selection 1986: Difficult to find a better California Cabernet at this price. It has the characteristic black cherry and slightly herbal aromas, good, ripe fruit flavors that linger on the finish and a firm structure. Drink now. $6 (6/30/89) **84**
Cabernet Sauvignon Monterey County Vintage Selection Masson 1986: If you don't mind green, vegetal aromas, the juicy fruit flavors that emerge on the palate are lush and smooth. Tannins should be softened by now. $9 (11/15/89) **79**
Cabernet Sauvignon Monterey County Vintage Selection Masson 1985 $8 (9/15/88) **78**

MATANZAS CREEK
Cabernet Sauvignon Sonoma Valley 1983 Rel: $14 Cur: $17.50 (7/16/86) **75**
Cabernet Sauvignon Sonoma Valley 1982 $14 (8/01/85) **88**
Cabernet Sauvignon Sonoma Valley 1981 $16 (4/16/84) **84**

MAYACAMAS
Cabernet Sauvignon Napa Valley 1986: Strongly herbal and vegetal, with garlicky, olivelike aromas and flavors that yield to warm black cherry and black currant notes on the finish. Approaching drinkability now, but the flavors will not woo everyone. Best after 1993. Tasted twice. Rel: $20 Cur: $38 (11/15/91) **82**
Cabernet Sauvignon Napa Valley 1985: A bit tough and tannic, with plenty of artfully defined cherry, cassis and smoke aromas and flavors, plus added dimension of mineral or stony flavors reminiscent of a good Graves. Start drinking 1993 to '95. 2,025 cases made. Rel: $25 Cur: $38 (1/31/90) **92**
Cabernet Sauvignon Napa Valley 1984 Rel: $20 Cur: $28 (CA-3/89) **90**
Cabernet Sauvignon Napa Valley 1983 Rel: $20 Cur: $25 (CA-3/89) **90**
Cabernet Sauvignon Napa Valley 1982 Rel: $20 Cur: $29 (CA-3/89) **77**
Cabernet Sauvignon Napa Valley 1981 Rel: $18 Cur: $41 (CA-3/89) **91**
Cabernet Sauvignon Napa Valley 1980 Rel: $18 Cur: $45 (CA-3/89) **92**
Cabernet Sauvignon Napa Valley 1979 Rel: $18 Cur: $54 (CA-3/89) **95**
Cabernet Sauvignon Napa Valley 1978 Rel: $18 Cur: $80 (CA-3/89) **94**
Cabernet Sauvignon Napa Valley 1977 Rel: $15 Cur: $60 (CA-3/89) **92**
Cabernet Sauvignon Napa Valley 1976 Rel: $15 Cur: $38 (CA-3/89) **84**
Cabernet Sauvignon Napa Valley 1975 Rel: $12 Cur: $63 (CA-3/89) **89**
Cabernet Sauvignon Napa Valley 1974 Rel: $9.50 Cur: $120 (2/15/90) (JG) **97**
Cabernet Sauvignon Napa Valley 1973 Rel: $9 Cur: $80 (CA-3/89) **87**
Cabernet Sauvignon Napa Valley 1972 Rel: $8 Cur: $63 (CA-3/89) **82**
Cabernet Sauvignon Napa Valley 1971 Rel: $8 Cur: $65 (CA-3/89) **86**
Cabernet Sauvignon Napa Valley 1970 Rel: $8 Cur: $110 (CA-3/89) **96**
Cabernet Sauvignon California 1969 Rel: $6.50 Cur: $90 (CA-3/89) **89**
Cabernet Sauvignon California 1968 Rel: $4.50 Cur: $135 (CA-3/89) **88**
Cabernet Sauvignon California 1967 Rel: $4 Cur: $125 (CA-3/89) **65**
Cabernet Sauvignon California 1966 Rel: $3.50 Cur: $125 (CA-3/89) **75**
Cabernet Sauvignon California 1965 Rel: $2.75 Cur: $200 (CA-3/89) **65**
Cabernet Sauvignon California 1963 Rel: $2 Cur: $150 (CA-3/89) **69**
Cabernet Sauvignon California 1962 Rel: $2 Cur: $150 (CA-3/89) **68**

MAZZOCCO
Cabernet Sauvignon Alexander Valley Claret Style 1988: Hard and tight, with smoky, tarry plum, cherry and currant flavors. Shows plenty of tannin on the finish. Best to cellar until 1995. 2,400 cases made. $18 (3/15/92) **85**
Cabernet Sauvignon Alexander Valley Claret Style 1987: Delicious layers of complex, concen-

trated and rich cassis, currant, vanilla and plum flavors abound in this sharply focused, beautifully structured style. It's long and elegant, with just the right balance of tannin, oak and acidity. Tempting now, but should improve to 1993 and beyond. 1,200 cases made. $20 (8/31/90) **93**
Cabernet Sauvignon Alexander Valley Claret Style 1986 $20 (7/31/89) **78**
Matrix Sonoma County 1987: A big, ripe, deep-colored wine that oozes black cherry and currant flavors. Concentrated, firm, well balanced and spiced up with plenty of oak. Tempting now, but should improve in the cellar until at least 1995. A new wine. 430 cases made. $28 (1/31/92) **91**

MCDOWELL VALLEY
Cabernet Sauvignon California 1988: Lean and one-dimensional, with simple herb and plum aromas and flavors. Drinkable now. $10 (11/15/91) **78**
Cabernet Sauvignon California 1987: Straightforward cherry and plum flavors in a blunt, not-so-subtle package add up to a soft, simple, sturdy wine. Drink now or hold until 1993. $9 (11/15/90) **78**
Cabernet Sauvignon McDowell Valley 1986: Earthy, austere, hard and tannic, with no apparent fruit, except for a touch of cherry in the background. Tasted twice. $8 (4/30/90) **70**
Cabernet Sauvignon McDowell Valley 1983 $11 (4/15/88) **76**
Cabernet Sauvignon McDowell Valley 1982 $11 (12/15/86) **89**
Cabernet Sauvignon McDowell Valley 1981 $11 (12/16/84) **78**

MEEKER
Cabernet Sauvignon Dry Creek Valley 1987: Has fine aromas of cassis and chocolate with flavors to match. Tight, tannic, concentrated and dense, but the fruit fights through on the aftertaste. Try after 1996. $14 (10/15/91) **87**
Cabernet Sauvignon Dry Creek Valley 1986: Has nice cherry and currant aromas, but heavy-handed tannins subdue the flavors. Difficult to say whether the fruit will outlast the tannins. Try in 1993 if you're a gambler. $18.50 (2/15/90) **72**
Cabernet Sauvignon Dry Creek Valley 1985: Very tough and tannic, a bluntly aromatic wine with rough-hewn wood aromas and astringent textures that make it hard to drink now. May not soften enough to bring out the modest plum and cherry flavors, but try it now. $18 (4/30/89) **76**
Cabernet Sauvignon Dry Creek Valley 1984 $18 (6/15/88) **78**

MENDOCINO ESTATE
Cabernet Sauvignon Mendocino 1985 $5.50 (2/15/88) **61**
Cabernet Sauvignon Mendocino 1984 $4.75 (6/15/87) **78**
Cabernet Sauvignon Mendocino 1982 $4.25 (10/15/86) BB **87**

MENDOCINO VINEYARDS
Cabernet Sauvignon Mendocino County NV: An everyday wine without much panache. Bell pepper, herbal and some cherry aromas and flavors are followed by a tart, almost sour finish. $6 (4/15/89) **73**

MERIDIAN
Cabernet Sauvignon Paso Robles 1988: A great value. Smooth and generous, this ripe wine has marvelous currant and plum flavors and an overlay of rich chocolate and spice notes. Supple, flavorful and utterly charming, with flavor to burn. Drinkable now, but better around 1993 or '94. 4,000 cases made. $12 (9/30/91) SS **92**

MERLION
Cabernet Sauvignon Napa Valley 1986: Tight, young and leathery, with a solid rich core of currant and peppery Cabernet flavor, but the wood and tannins take over, giving this a hard edge. Best to cellar until 1994 or '95. 550 cases made. $16.50 (11/15/90) **84**
Cabernet Sauvignon Napa Valley 1985 $13.50 (8/31/88) **85**

MERRYVALE
Cabernet Sauvignon Napa Valley 1988: Tough and tannic, with hard-edged currant, plum and black cherry flavors that are also quite oaky. The finish is dry and tannic, but the currant flavor comes through. Needs until 1995 to soften. 3,000 cases made. $18 (7/15/91) **86**
Profile Napa Valley 1990 (NR) (5/15/91) (BT) **90+**
Profile Napa Valley 1989 (NR) (5/15/91) (BT) **85+**
Profile Napa Valley 1988 (NR) (5/15/90) (BT) **85+**
Cabernet Sauvignon Napa Valley Profile 1987: Hard and oaky, with varnishlike aromas and woody notes running roughshod over the currant and plum-tinged flavors. A tough, tannic customer that turns awfully oaky and dry on the finish. May improve by 1995 and beyond. 1,500 cases made. $25 (11/15/91) **83**
Red Table Wine Napa Valley 1986: Very firm tannins dominate this austere style now, overshadowing the cherry and currant flavors underneath. With time the fruit may be more generous and appealing, but for now it's a tight, firm, tannic wine that needs a cool, dark place to mellow out. Drink in 1993 to '94 at the earliest. 1,358 cases made. $25 (10/15/90) **86**
Red Table Wine Napa Valley 1986 $25 (CA-3/89) **89**
Red Table Wine Napa Valley 1985 Rel: $24 Cur: $27 (CA-3/89) **91**
Red Table Wine Napa Valley 1984 Rel: $24 Cur: $28 (CA-3/89) **86**
Red Table Wine Napa Valley 1983 Rel: $18 Cur: $33 (CA-3/89) **88**

PETER MICHAEL
Cabernet Sauvignon Knights Valley Les Pavots 1988: Rich and full-bodied, with layers of plum, currant, coffee and cedar flavors. The tannins clamp down on the finish, but it's balanced with enough rich, concentrated fruit to cellar until 1995. 650 cases made. $25 (11/15/91) **90**

MICHAEL'S
Cabernet Sauvignon Napa Valley Summit Vineyard Reserve 1984 $15 (3/31/88) **75**

RICHARD MICHAELS
Cabernet Sauvignon California 1985 $10 (9/30/88) **78**

MILANO
Cabernet Sauvignon Mendocino County Sanel Valley Vineyard 1985: Deliciously rich plum and cherry flavor emerges on the palate, overriding the velvety tannins and the new oak character. Not harmonious yet, but perhaps cellaring until 1994 will bring it around. $18 (9/30/89) **80**
Cabernet Sauvignon Mendocino County Sanel Valley Vineyard 1982 $12.50 (12/15/87) **83**

MILL CREEK
Cabernet Sauvignon Dry Creek Valley 1988: An oddball, with heavily vegetal flavors wrapped in an appealingly smooth texture. Tastes simple and uninspired. Tasted twice. 1,951 cases made. $12 (11/15/91) **78**
Cabernet Sauvignon Dry Creek Valley 1982 $8.50 (12/31/87) **81**

MIRASSOU
Cabernet Sauvignon California Fifth Generation Family Selection 1986: Ripe and minty, this velvety wine has generous cherry, tobacco and herbal flavors that linger. Drinkable now, but cellaring until 1993 or '94 wouldn't hurt. $9.75 (5/31/91) **83**
Cabernet Sauvignon Monterey County Fifth Generation Harvest Reserve Limited Bottling 1987: An oaky style, with a strong cedary character that overshadows the tart currant and black cherry flavors. Hints of raspberry and anise come through on the finish, but it's tight and firmly tannic. Needs until 1995 to mellow. Tasted twice. 2,235 cases made. $12.50 (11/15/91) **86**
Cabernet Sauvignon Monterey County Fifth Generation Harvest Reserve 1986: Pungent menthol and barnyardy aromas and powerful, tart bay leaf flavors paint an awful caricature of Cabernet. Too wild and woolly for our tastes. Tasted twice with consistent notes. 1,201 cases made. $12.50 (7/31/91) **60**
Cabernet Sauvignon Napa Valley Fifth Generation Harvest Reserve 1985: Ripe and generous, with plummy, almost pruny aromas and flavors balanced nicely with the round texture and vanilla the and tobacco flavors of oak aging. Tannic enough to need until 1993 to settle down. $12 (11/15/89) **81**
Cabernet Sauvignon Napa Valley Fifth Generation Harvest Reserve 1983 $12 (12/15/86) **67**
Cabernet Sauvignon Napa Valley Harvest Reserve 1982 $12 (4/16/86) **82**
Cabernet Sauvignon North Coast 1982 $7 (10/16/85) BB **82**

MISSION VIEW
Cabernet Sauvignon Paso Robles 1986: Tannic, leathery and drying on the palate, this wine has subdued fruit with vegetal and herb notes on the finish. Very tannic. Drink now. $12 (12/15/89) **72**

CK MONDAVI
Cabernet Sauvignon Napa Valley 1983 $4.50 (10/15/87) **65**

ROBERT MONDAVI
Cabernet Sauvignon California Woodbridge 1988: Has modest but true varietal character, with depth and concentration, presenting pure currant, plum, spice and oak flavors in a ready-to-drink style. A solid choice for everyday drinking. $6 (2/28/91) BB **81**
Cabernet Sauvignon California Woodbridge 1987: Leathery, herbal and ripe in equal measure, generous but rough and basic. $6 (9/15/89) **74**
Cabernet Sauvignon California Cabernet 1986 $5.50 (12/15/88) BB **80**
Cabernet Sauvignon California Cabernet 1985 $4.25 (10/31/87) BB **78**
Cabernet Sauvignon Napa Valley 1990 (NR) (5/15/91) (BT) **90+**
Cabernet Sauvignon Napa Valley Unfiltered 1988: Has lots of dark cherry, chocolate, currant, herb and plum flavors, but it's also quite tannic and firm. Not for the faint of heart. Has good potential, but needs cellaring until 1996. $18 (11/15/91) **83**
Cabernet Sauvignon Napa Valley 1987: Crisp structure and fine, generous flavors add up to a wine that should develop well in the cellar. Currant, cherry and plum flavors are shaded with a nice touch of oak. Lacking a bit in complexity, but still worth drinking. $20 (5/31/90) **87**
Cabernet Sauvignon Napa Valley 1986: Classic Cabernet aromas and flavors, a bright beam of currant flavor shining through the toasty, vanilla and brown sugar complexity. Very seductive and elegant, almost drinkable, better perhaps by 1993. Rel: $18 Cur: $21 (7/31/89) **93**
Cabernet Sauvignon Napa Valley 1985 Rel: $15 Cur: $30 (12/15/88) SS **94**
Cabernet Sauvignon Napa Valley 1984 Rel: $13 Cur: $34 (12/31/87) **80**
Cabernet Sauvignon Napa Valley 1983 Rel: $12 Cur: $26 (4/15/87) **94**
Cabernet Sauvignon Napa Valley 1982 Rel: $11 Cur: $24 (7/01/85) **90**
Cabernet Sauvignon Napa Valley 1981 Rel: $11 Cur: $29 (12/16/84) **90**
Cabernet Sauvignon Napa Valley 1979 $25 (7/16/85) (JL) **85**
Cabernet Sauvignon Napa Valley 1978 $34 (6/01/86) **88**
Cabernet Sauvignon Napa Valley 1977 $30 (7/16/85) (JL) **89**
Cabernet Sauvignon Napa Valley 1976 $69 (7/16/85) (JL) **84**
Cabernet Sauvignon Napa Valley 1975 $56 (11/30/91) (JL) **85**
Cabernet Sauvignon Napa Valley 1974 $59 (2/15/90) (JG) **79**
Cabernet Sauvignon Napa Valley 1973 $35 (7/16/85) (JL) **86**
Cabernet Sauvignon Napa Valley 1972 Rel: $6 Cur: $42 (CA-3/89) **75**
Cabernet Sauvignon Napa Valley 1971 Rel: $6 Cur: $60 (7/16/85) (JL) **87**
Cabernet Sauvignon Napa Valley 1970 $93 (11/30/91) (JL) **92**
Cabernet Sauvignon Napa Valley 1969 $80 (11/30/91) (JL) **91**
Cabernet Sauvignon Napa Valley 1968 $100 (11/30/91) (JL) **88**
Cabernet Sauvignon Napa Valley 1967 Rel: $5 Cur: $95 (11/30/91) (JL) **79**
Cabernet Sauvignon Napa Valley 1967 Rel: $5 Cur: $210/1.5L (7/16/85) (JL) **83**
Cabernet Sauvignon Napa Valley 1966 Rel: $5 Cur: $165 (11/30/91) (JL) **88**
Cabernet Sauvignon Napa Valley 1966 Rel: $5 Cur: $370/1.5L (7/16/85) (JL) **79**
Cabernet Sauvignon Napa Valley Reserve 1991: Firm, tight and concentrated, with spice, currant, tobacco and berry flavors and a good dose of oak on the finish. The tannins are firm but fleshy. (NR) (5/15/92) (BT) **87+**
Cabernet Sauvignon Napa Valley Reserve 1990 (NR) (11/30/91) (BT) **92+**
Cabernet Sauvignon Napa Valley Reserve 1989 $18 (11/30/91) (JL) **90**
Cabernet Sauvignon Napa Valley Reserve 1988: Very generous and complex, offering a rich, deep array of plum, vanilla, cinnamon and bay leaf flavors that wash across the palate. Harmonious, balanced and long. Tempting to drink now for its youthful vigor, but worth cellaring until 1994 to '96. $45 (5/31/91) CS **91**
Cabernet Sauvignon Napa Valley Reserve 1987: A rich, smooth, harmonious wine, with smoky cassis and meaty, earthy flavors that are minty and herbal. Altogether very well balanced and complex, with firm tannins and finishes with smoky cassis notes. Best to drink in 1994 to '96, but compared to the barrel sample it comes up short. Rel: $43 Cur: $51 (8/31/90) **90**
Cabernet Sauvignon Napa Valley Reserve 1986: Extremely rich and seductive, complex yet delicate, with layers of cedar, plum, currant and spice flavors that are remarkably rich, supple and concentrated, echoing long and full on the palate. Delicious. Drink 1995 to 2000. Rel: $35 Cur: $42 (11/15/89) **95**
Cabernet Sauvignon Napa Valley Reserve 1985 Rel: $40 Cur: $50 (11/30/91) (JL) **94**
Cabernet Sauvignon Napa Valley Reserve 1985 Rel: $40 Cur: $50 (11/15/89) SS **95**
Cabernet Sauvignon Napa Valley Reserve 1984 Rel: $37 Cur: $42 (11/30/91) (JL) **90**
Cabernet Sauvignon Napa Valley Reserve 1983 Rel: $30 Cur: $37 (11/30/91) (JL) **82**
Cabernet Sauvignon Napa Valley Reserve 1982 Rel: $30 Cur: $43 (11/30/91) (JL) **82**
Cabernet Sauvignon Napa Valley Reserve 1981 Rel: $30 Cur: $36 (11/30/91) (JL) **85**
Cabernet Sauvignon Napa Valley Reserve 1981 Rel: $30 Cur: $36 (2/16/86) CS **94**
Cabernet Sauvignon Napa Valley Reserve 1980 Rel: $30 Cur: $42 (11/30/91) (JL) **86**
Cabernet Sauvignon Napa Valley Reserve 1979 Rel: $25 Cur: $48 (11/30/91) (JL) **91**
Cabernet Sauvignon Napa Valley Reserve 1978 Rel: $40 Cur: $70 (11/30/91) (JL) **91**
Cabernet Sauvignon Napa Valley Reserve 1978 Rel: $40 Cur: $70 (CA-3/89) **92**
Cabernet Sauvignon Napa Valley Reserve 1978 Rel: $40 Cur: $70 (6/01/86) **97**
Cabernet Sauvignon Napa Valley Reserve 1978 Rel: $40 Cur: $70 (8/01/83) CS **92**
Cabernet Sauvignon Napa Valley Reserve 1977 Rel: $35 Cur: $47 (11/30/91) (JL) **89**
Cabernet Sauvignon Napa Valley Reserve 1976 Rel: $25 Cur: $47 (11/30/91) (JL) **84**
Cabernet Sauvignon Napa Valley Reserve 1975 Rel: $30 Cur: $50 (CA-3/89) **86**
Cabernet Sauvignon Napa Valley Reserve 1974 Rel: $30 Cur: $101 (11/30/91) (JL) **89**
Cabernet Sauvignon Napa Valley Reserve 1973 Rel: $12 Cur: $80 (11/30/91) (JL) **92**
Cabernet Sauvignon Napa Valley Reserve 1972 (NR) (11/30/91) (JL) **78**
Cabernet Sauvignon Napa Valley Reserve 1971 Rel: $12 Cur: $130 (11/30/91) (JL) **91**

Key to Symbols

The scores reported here are the results of blind tastings conducted by our panel of senior editors. Wines that carry the initials below are results of individual tastings.

THE WINE SPECTATOR 100-POINT SCALE ***95-100***—Classic, a great wine; ***90-94***—Outstanding, superior character and style; ***80-89***—Good to very good, a wine with special qualities; ***70-79***—Average, drinkable wine that may have minor flaws; ***60-69***—Below average, drinkable but not recommended; ***50-59***—Poor, undrinkable, not recommended. "+"—With a score indicates a range; used primarily with barrel tastings to indicate a preliminary score.

SPECIAL DESIGNATIONS SS—Spectator Selection, CS—Cellar Selection, BB—Best Buy, ($NA)—Price not available, (NR)—Not released.

TASTER'S INITIALS (JG)—Jim Gordon, (HS)—Harvey Steiman, (JL)—James Laube, (JS)—James Suckling, (TM)—Thomas Matthews, (TR)—Terry Robards, (PM)—Per-Henrik Mansson, (BT)—Barrel Tasting (these wines were tasted blind from barrel samples), (CA-date)—*California's Great Cabernets* by James Laube, (CH-date)—*California's Great Chardonnays* by James Laube, (VP-date)—*Vintage Port* by James Suckling.

DATE TASTED Dates in parentheses represent the issue in which the rating was published.

Cabernet Sauvignon Napa Valley Unfiltered 1970 Rel: $12 Cur: $115 (7/16/85) **93**
Cabernet Sauvignon Napa Valley Unfined 1970 Rel: $12 Cur: $115 (CA-3/89) **89**
Cabernet Sauvignon Napa Valley Unfined 1969 Rel: $12 Cur: $135 (CA-3/89) **86**
Cabernet Sauvignon Napa Valley Unfined 1968 Rel: $8.50 Cur: $135 (CA-3/89) **83**

MONT ST. JOHN
Cabernet Sauvignon Napa Valley 1986: Balanced and well proportioned, this '86 is tight and firm, with a good core of currant, plum, cherry and cedar flavors and firm tannins on the finish. The flavors are mild mannered, but this nicely balanced wine should benefit from aging. Drink in 1994 to '96. $14 (4/30/91) **87**
Cabernet Sauvignon Napa Valley 1983: A very tannic wine that tastes rich and spicy from oak aging. Difficult to say if its moderate fruit flavors will outlast the tannins. Drink now. $15 (7/31/89) **78**
Cabernet Sauvignon Napa Valley 1982: Lean and chalky, but the fruit is remarkably well preserved, focused and ripe. Should be at its best now. $15 (3/15/89) **82**
Cabernet Sauvignon Napa Valley Private Reserve 1980 $11.50 (5/16/84) **75**

MONTE VERDE
Cabernet Sauvignon California Proprietor's Reserve 1987: A charming red wine wine that's ready to drink. Has fresh, very fruity and direct flavors of berries and black cherries, intense enough to leave a fruity aftertaste. The texture is supple and soft. $6.50/1L (12/15/89) **80**

MONTEREY PENINSULA
Cabernet Sauvignon Monterey Doctors' Reserve 1984: A tightly wound '84 that still needs time to mellow. The currant, chocolate, herb and plum flavors are young and intense and framed by bold tannins and ample oak. A rough-hewn style for fans of gutsy Cabernets. Drink in 1993 to '96. $16 (2/28/91) **81**
Cabernet Sauvignon Monterey Doctors' Reserve Lot II 1982 $14 (6/15/87) **83**
Cabernet Sauvignon Monterey County 1982 $11 (3/31/87) **74**

MONTEREY VINEYARD
Cabernet Sauvignon Monterey County Classic 1989: A medium-bodied wine, with nice, soft tannins and good plum and spice flavors that linger on the finish. Ready to drink tonight, or could be cellared through 1993. $6 (3/15/92) BB **83**
Cabernet Sauvignon Monterey County Classic 1987: Ripe, flavorful and well balanced, with hearty fruit and bell pepper flavors, firm tannins and a lingering finish. Clean, well made and ready to drink now through 1994. $6 (1/31/91) BB **83**
Cabernet Sauvignon Monterey County Classic 1986: Earthy, smoky, somewhat vegetal-tasting wine, velvety in texture but fairly direct on the flavor scale. $5.50 (10/31/89) **76**
Cabernet Sauvignon Monterey County Limited Release 1986: Crisp, tart and tight, with reined-in herbal overtones to the cherry and tobacco aromas and flavors. Needs cellaring until 1993 to soften the tannin and acidity. Has the balance and subtlety to age gracefully. $10 (11/15/89) **83**
Cabernet Sauvignon Monterey County Limited Release 1985 $10 (8/31/88) **75**
Cabernet Sauvignon Monterey-Sonoma-San Luis Obispo Counties Classic 1985 $5 (2/15/89) **73**

MONTEVINA
Cabernet Sauvignon California 1988: A good everyday wine that's balanced and well-made. Medium-bodied, with moderate tannins and bell pepper and cherry flavors. Ready to drink. $8.50 (2/15/90) **77**
Cabernet Sauvignon Shenandoah Valley Limited Release 1984 $7.50 (8/31/88) BB **86**

MONTICELLO
Cabernet Sauvignon Napa Valley Corley Reserve 1991: Hard, tight and compact, with a core of plum, berry and currant flavors and a touch of oak. Crisp acidity carries the flavors, but it's awkward now. 3,000 cases made. (NR) (5/15/92) (BT) **87+**
Cabernet Sauvignon Napa Valley Corley Reserve 1990 (NR) (5/15/91) (BT) **85+**
Cabernet Sauvignon Napa Valley Corley Reserve 1989 (NR) (5/15/91) (BT) **90+**
Cabernet Sauvignon Napa Valley Corley Reserve 1987: Tough and tannic now, with barely enough currant, cedar and cherry flavor concentration to emerge unscathed on the finish. Cellaring until 1995 should soften the tannins and bring out the full character of this wine. $25 (11/15/90) **90**
Cabernet Sauvignon Napa Valley Corley Reserve 1986: Powerful, tannic and bursting with flavor, this very youthful, exuberant wine shows lots of black cherry, currant and black pepper aromas and flavors framed by toasty oak. Not for early drinking, this needs to be cellared at least until 1994. Rel: $24 Cur: $28 (3/15/90) **92**
Cabernet Sauvignon Napa Valley Corley Reserve 1985 Rel: $22.50 Cur: $35 (7/31/89) **92**
Cabernet Sauvignon Napa Valley Corley Reserve 1984 Rel: $18.50 Cur: $30 (CA-3/89) **91**
Cabernet Sauvignon Napa Valley Corley Reserve 1983 Rel: $24 Cur: $27 (CA-3/89) **88**
Cabernet Sauvignon Napa Valley Corley Reserve 1982 Rel: $15 Cur: $32 (CA-3/89) **90**
Cabernet Sauvignon Napa Valley Jefferson Cuvée 1988: Austere and tight, with bright, firm currant, black cherry and plum flavors. The tannins clamp down on the finish, but with time it should evolve into a fine wine. Best to cellar until 1995. $16 (11/15/91) **85**
Cabernet Sauvignon Napa Valley Jefferson Cuvée 1987: Intense, sharply focused and richly concentrated, the bright black cherry, currant, herb and spice notes are well proportioned and not too tannic in this well-balanced, well-integrated and flavorful wine. It shows great promise. Best to tackle in 1993 to '94, but should age well until 1999. $14 (9/30/90) **90**
Cabernet Sauvignon Napa Valley Jefferson Cuvée 1986: Deep, rich and concentrated, packed with herb, cherry and spicy currant flavors and backed with crisp, firm, tannins. It's developing a soft, satiny texture. Needs time. Drink in 1994. $14 (4/15/89) **89**
Cabernet Sauvignon Napa Valley Jefferson Cuvée 1985 $12 (2/29/88) **87**
Cabernet Sauvignon Napa Valley Jefferson Cuvée 1984 $11 (11/30/87) **90**
Cabernet Sauvignon Napa Valley Jefferson Cuvée 1983 $10 (11/30/86) **77**
Cabernet Sauvignon Napa Valley Jefferson Cuvée 1982 $10 (2/01/86) **91**
Cabernet Sauvignon Napa Valley 1981 $13.50 (7/16/84) **74**

MONTPELLIER
Cabernet Sauvignon California 1988: Ripe, soft and charming, packed full of blackberry flavor on an easy frame of mild tannins and soft acidity. Easy to drink now, but should last through 1993 or so. $7 (7/31/91) BB **83**

MORGAN
Cabernet Sauvignon Carmel Valley 1988: Has plenty of currant, herb and cherry aromas, but turns tight and tart on the palate, with hard tannins that persist into the finish. Tough to drink now, but should improve by about 1994. Tasted twice, with consistent notes. $19 (11/15/91) **81**
Cabernet Sauvignon Carmel Valley 1987: A big, rich, dense and very tannic style is packed with tightly reined-in ripe currant, cherry and plum flavors. It's deep in color, with supple texture emerging before the tannins clamp down. Best to cellar for most of the 1990s. Drink 1997 to about 2004. $16 (9/30/90) **92**
Cabernet Sauvignon Carmel Valley 1986: An elegant, sophisticated wine, showing minty-herbal aromas and polished currant-plum fruit flavors, it's harmonious and beautifully balanced. Drinkable now, but it should develop well through 1993 to '95. $16 (9/15/89) **90**

J.W. MORRIS
Cabernet Sauvignon Alexander Valley 1985: Very simple and straightforward with spicy berry and herbal flavors. Decent but unexciting. $8 (2/15/89) **74**
Cabernet Sauvignon California Private Reserve 1988: A light, fruity wine, with a tarry edge to the flavors. Decent but nothing special, as the label suggests. Drink now. $7 (11/15/91) **74**
Cabernet Sauvignon California Private Reserve 1987: A fine value. Intense in color and flavor and flanked by plenty of oak, but altogether there's a nice sense of balance. Pretty black currant and cherry notes come through on the finish. Drink now to 1994. $8 (3/31/90) **83**

MOUNT EDEN
Cabernet Sauvignon Santa Cruz Mountains 1988 $21 (5/15/90) (BT) **85+**
Cabernet Sauvignon Santa Cruz Mountains 1987: Tough, hard-edged, and tannic, with extra charred, smoked green bean, currant and bizarre ashlike flavors. An anomaly, it's of marginal quality. Needs cellaring until 1996. Tasted twice. Extremely disappointing from this usually reliable Cabernet producer. $28 (4/30/91) **65**
Cabernet Sauvignon Santa Cruz Mountains 1986: Minty, herbal aromas mingle with tart currant and cherry flavors in this lean, firm-textured wine. It's worth cellaring until 1994 to see what happens when it softens up. Rel: $28 Cur: $32 (8/31/90) **83**
Cabernet Sauvignon Santa Cruz Mountains 1985: A big, meaty style, with plenty of intensity, that's ripe and powerful, with no pretensions of finesse. Flavors run toward currant and prune. Tannic and a bit hot on the finish. Tasted twice. 622 cases made. Rel: $28 Cur: $37 (11/15/89) **81**
Cabernet Sauvignon Santa Cruz Mountains 1984 Rel: $22 Cur: $35 (CA-3/89) **84**
Cabernet Sauvignon Santa Cruz Mountains 1983 Rel: $20 Cur: $22 (CA-3/89) **79**
Cabernet Sauvignon Santa Cruz Mountains 1982 Rel: $18 Cur: $27 (CA-3/89) **70**
Cabernet Sauvignon Santa Cruz Mountains 1981 Rel: $18 Cur: $23 (CA-3/89) **86**
Cabernet Sauvignon Santa Cruz Mountains 1980 Rel: $30 Cur: $33 (CA-3/89) **85**
Cabernet Sauvignon Santa Cruz Mountains 1979 Rel: $25 Cur: $35 (CA-3/89) **69**
Cabernet Sauvignon Santa Cruz Mountains 1978 Rel: $25 Cur: $48 (CA-3/89) **88**
Cabernet Sauvignon Santa Cruz Mountains 1977 Rel: $20 Cur: $41 (CA-3/89) **91**
Cabernet Sauvignon Santa Cruz Mountains 1976 Rel: $20 Cur: $81 (CA-3/89) **83**
Cabernet Sauvignon Santa Cruz Mountains 1975 Rel: $20 Cur: $30 (CA-3/89) **90**
Cabernet Sauvignon Santa Cruz Mountains 1974 Rel: $20 Cur: $105 (2/15/90) (JG) **87**
Cabernet Sauvignon Santa Cruz Mountains 1973 Rel: $14 Cur: $110 (CA-3/89) **91**
Cabernet Sauvignon Santa Cruz Mountains 1972 Rel: $20 Cur: $60 (CA-3/89) **84**
Cabernet Sauvignon Santa Cruz Mountains Lathweisen Ridge 1988: Has the firm, stiff structure of a mountain Cabernet, with ripe, complex fruit flavors and a long, lingering finish. The blackberry, black cherry and cedar flavors are concentrated and full. $12 (4/30/91) **87**
Cabernet Sauvignon Santa Cruz Mountains Young Vine Cuvée 1987: Smoky, racy aromas and flavors characterize this hard-edged, somewhat woody wine. The fruit flavors are generous. Finishes toasty. Drink now. $12 (4/15/90) **85**

MOUNT VEEDER
Cabernet Sauvignon Napa Valley 1987: Spicy and focused, showing elegant plum, currant and herb notes before the firm, drying tannins kick in. A big, full-bodied wine that makes no pretense at subtlety or finesse. Needs cellaring—drink in 1995 to 2000. 2,300 cases made. $20 (4/30/91) **85**
Cabernet Sauvignon Napa Valley 1986: A big, blunt style with very ripe fruit and hints of raisins and currants, but after two or three sips the tannins really come on and dry out the palate. Needs time to mellow and gain some finesse. Hold on until 1993 or '94 at the earliest. 2,600 cases made. Rel: $18 Cur: $21 (11/15/90) **83**
Cabernet Sauvignon Napa Valley 1985 Rel: $18 Cur: $22 (CA-3/89) **87**
Cabernet Sauvignon Napa Valley 1984 Rel: $14 Cur: $21 (CA-3/89) **88**
Cabernet Sauvignon Napa Valley 1983 Rel: $14 Cur: $23 (CA-3/89) **84**
Cabernet Sauvignon Napa Valley 1982 Rel: $12.50 Cur: $17 (CA-3/89) **68**
Cabernet Sauvignon Napa Valley 1981 Rel: $12.50 Cur: $21 (7/16/86) **81**
Cabernet Sauvignon Napa Valley Bernstein Vineyards 1980 Rel: $13.50 Cur: $31 (CA-3/89) **87**
Cabernet Sauvignon Napa Valley Bernstein Vineyards 1979 Rel: $13.50 Cur: $42 (CA-3/89) **92**
Cabernet Sauvignon Napa Valley Bernstein Vineyards 1978 Rel: $12.75 Cur: $31 (CA-3/89) **89**
Cabernet Sauvignon Napa Valley Bernstein Vineyards 1977 Rel: $11 Cur: $32 (CA-3/89) **85**
Cabernet Sauvignon Napa Valley Bernstein Vineyards 1976 Rel: $11 Cur: $16 (CA-3/89) **77**
Cabernet Sauvignon Napa Valley Bernstein Vineyards 1975 Rel: $11 Cur: $22 (CA-3/89) **83**
Cabernet Sauvignon Napa Valley 1974 Rel: $8 Cur: $64 (CA-3/89) **80**
Cabernet Sauvignon Napa Valley 1973 Rel: $8 Cur: $65 (CA-3/89) **90**
Cabernet Sauvignon Napa Valley Niebaum-Coppola 1977 Rel: $9.75 Cur: $60 (CA-3/89) **88**
Cabernet Sauvignon Napa Valley Sidehill Ranch 1978 Rel: $13.50 Cur: $40 (CA-3/89) **86**
Meritage Napa Valley 1988: Firm in texture, with crisp plum and berry flavors popping through the curtain of tannins, winding up supple and almost plush on the finish. Needs until 1995 to soften the tannins. 1,290 cases made. Rel: $18 Cur: $24 (7/15/92) **83**
Meritage Napa Valley 1986 Rel: $18 Cur: $24 (CA-3/89) **93**

MOUNTAIN VIEW
Cabernet Sauvignon Mendocino County 1986: Weedy with black currant and herb notes of moderate depth. Won't shortchange you on flavor, and at this price it's a solid value. Drink now. $6.50 (3/31/90) **79**
Cabernet Sauvignon Mendocino County 1985: Earthy and cedary, with firm tannins and herb-tinged fruit and a touch of cherry on the finish. Simple, easy to drink and reasonably priced. $6 (2/15/89) **77**
Cabernet Sauvignon North Coast 1988: Features ripe plum- and herbal-tinged Cabernet flavor of moderate depth and intensity, but the flavors stick with you. Fairly priced and ready to drink now. $6 (4/30/91) BB **80**
Cabernet Sauvignon North Coast 1980 $5 (4/16/84) **62**

MURPHY-GOODE
Cabernet Sauvignon Alexander Valley Estate Vineyard 1988: Offers pretty fruit flavors, with intense berry, jam, currant and black cherry notes. Has plenty of tannins for cellaring, but it's well balanced, with plenty of fruit on the aftertaste. Drink in 1995. $16 (11/15/91) **87**
Cabernet Sauvignon Alexander Valley 1987: Effusively fruity, brimming with currant and raspberry aromas and flavors, nestled into a gentle frame of smooth tannins. Drinkable now. 700 cases made. $16.50 (5/31/90) **89**
Cabernet Sauvignon Alexander Valley Goode-Ready The Second Cabernet 1989 $10 (6/15/91) **80**
Cabernet Sauvignon Alexander Valley Premier Vineyard 1986: Intense and lively, with layers of cedar, spice and ripe cherry and plum flavor, and plenty of crisp acidity and firm tannins to balance things out. Drink now. $16 (11/15/89) **90**

NALLE
Cabernet Sauvignon Dry Creek Valley 1987: Nalle's first Cabernet is tight in structure but profoundly rich in currant, red cherry and raspberry aromas and flavors, with enough supple tannins to keep it going for years in the cellar. Built along the same lines as this winery's excellent Zinfandel, this exuberant young wine should settle down around 1993 to '95. 250 cases made. $18 (1/31/91) **89**

NAPA RIDGE
Cabernet Sauvignon North Coast Coastal 1989: Solidly fruity and firm in texture, with appealing black cherry and currant flavors shaded by herbs. Drinkable now. $6 (11/15/91) **79**
Cabernet Sauvignon North Coast 1987: Has a spicy, dill-like aroma, apparently from oak aging, but the fruit flavor is thin and slightly sour. Drinkable but awkward in style. $7 (11/15/90) **74**
Cabernet Sauvignon North Coast 1982 $5.75 (3/31/87) **72**

NAVARRO
Cabernet Sauvignon Mendocino 1986: An attempt at elegance that mostly succeeds by weaving pleasant plum, cherry and spice flavors through a medium-weight structure, folding in the tannins smoothly. Best after 1993. 830 cases made. $16 (10/15/91) **87**
Cabernet Sauvignon Mendocino 1985: This very good '85 lacks the supple generosity of the best from the vintage, showing more wood and tannin than rich, ripe fruit. The currant and black cherry flavors are appealing, but patience is required for this one to reach full potential. Cellar until 1995 to '99. $14 (11/15/90) **87**

NEVADA CITY
Claret The Director's Reserve Nevada County 1989: Dark in color and deeply flavored, with firm tannins, tight acidity and straightforward fruit. Doesn't have a lot of dimension but is very solidly put together and flavorful. 49 percent Cabernet Sauvignon. 168 cases made. $15 (5/31/92) **83**

NEWLAN
Cabernet Sauvignon Napa Valley 1986: A remarkably elegant and flavorful '86, with a pretty core of black cherry, currant, raspberry and anise flavors and cedary oak notes around the edge. Quite impressive for its richness and depth, and the finish echoes fruit on and on. Best to cellar until 1994 to '96. 1,175 cases made. $15 (4/30/91) **89**
Cabernet Sauvignon Napa Valley 1985: An attractive 1985 that combines ripe, supple, balanced Cabernet flavor with layers of plum and cherry framed by just the right touch of oak. Finishes with pretty fruit flavors that keep you coming back for more. Drink in 1993 to '96. $15 (3/31/90) **87**

NEWTON
Cabernet Sauvignon Napa Valley 1988 (NR) (5/15/90) (BT) **85+**
Cabernet Sauvignon Napa Valley 1987: Offers plenty of spice notes, with herb, anise and dill, but there's a tight core of currant and cherry flavors behind them. Firmly tannic and balanced; needs until 1995 or '96 to mellow. $17 (11/15/91) **87**
Cabernet Sauvignon Napa Valley 1986: Elegant and beautifully balanced, with focused chocolate- and toast-tinged currant and plum flavors, hinting at olives on the long finish, delicious, very fine but not showy. Worth cellaring until at least 1993 to '95. Rel: $16 Cur: $19 (5/31/90) **91**
Cabernet Sauvignon Napa Valley 1985: Firm, slightly tannic, but lithe enough to carry off the ripe berry and currant flavors with some finesse. A bit thick now, it should open up with cellaring. Try it in 1993. Rel: $15.25 Cur: $20 (1/31/89) **89**
Cabernet Sauvignon Napa Valley 1984 Rel: $13.50 Cur: $22 (CA-3/89) **87**
Cabernet Sauvignon Napa Valley 1983 Rel: $12.50 Cur: $36 (CA-3/89) **92**
Cabernet Sauvignon Napa Valley 1983 Rel: $12.50 Cur: $36 (4/15/87) SS **96**
Cabernet Sauvignon Napa Valley 1982 Rel: $12.50 Cur: $21 (CA-3/89) **66**
Cabernet Sauvignon Napa Valley 1981 Rel: $12.50 Cur: $21 (CA-3/89) **83**
Cabernet Sauvignon Napa Valley 1980 Rel: $12 Cur: $30 (CA-3/89) **55**
Cabernet Sauvignon Napa Valley 1979 Rel: $12 Cur: $30 (CA-3/89) **85**
Claret Napa Valley 1988: Subtle and complex, with ripe currant, black cherry and cedar nuances, supple tannins and fine balance. Picks up toasty tobacco, herb and mint notes on the finish. Very successful for an '88. An elegant wine that's tempting to drink now, but should improve through 1996. $11 (3/15/91) **89**

NEYERS
Cabernet Sauvignon Napa Valley 1988: A minty, menthol aroma marks this earthy, medium-bodied, modestly fruity wine. Drinkable now. Tasted twice. $15 (11/15/91) **82**
Cabernet Sauvignon Napa Valley 1987 $15 (4/15/89) (BT) **85+**
Cabernet Sauvignon Napa Valley 1986 $15.50 (4/15/88) (BT) **85+**
Cabernet Sauvignon Napa Valley 1985: Full-flavored, fruity wine, with distinctively minty aromas, deep black cherry flavors and firm tannins. Supple and ready to drink now. $14 (7/15/89) **83**
Cabernet Sauvignon Napa Valley 1984 $12.50 (4/30/88) **75**
Cabernet Sauvignon Napa Valley 1983 $12 (8/31/87) **79**

GUSTAVE NIEBAUM
Cabernet Sauvignon Napa Valley Reference 1985: Ripe and lively, with spice, anise and fresh berry and currant flavors that are intense and complex. The tannins are fine but evident, drying out on the finish. Best to drink in 1993 to '99. 3,400 cases made. $13.50 (10/31/89) **89**
Cabernet Sauvignon Napa Valley Tench Vineyard 1986 $16 (10/15/89) **93**

NIEBAUM-COPPOLA
Rubicon Napa Valley 1991: Dark and ripe, with supple, elegant currant, berry and plum flavors, smooth but firm tannins and good length. (NR) (5/15/92) (BT) **87+**
Rubicon Napa Valley 1989 (NR) (5/15/91) (BT) **85+**
Rubicon Napa Valley 1988 (NR) (5/15/90) (BT) **85+**
Rubicon Napa Valley 1986 (NR) (CA-3/89) **92**
Rubicon Napa Valley 1985: Concentrated and earthy, this is a full-bodied, moderately tannic but complex wine, from the earthy, spicy aromas through the ripe plum and anise flavors and minerallike finish. Try now. 4,464 cases made. Rel: $25 Cur: $35 (11/15/90) **87**
Rubicon Napa Valley 1984 Rel: $30 Cur: $35 (CA-3/89) **85**
Rubicon Napa Valley 1982: Earthy and still tannic for such a long-aged wine, but there is plenty of ripe, spicy currant and cherry flavor and a sense of elegance that warrants waiting until at least 1994 to see what more can develop. $40 (10/15/89) **88**
Rubicon Napa Valley 1981 Rel: $35 Cur: $42 (CA-3/89) **87**
Rubicon Napa Valley 1980 Rel: $30 Cur: $35 (CA-3/89) **87**
Rubicon Napa Valley 1979 Rel: $25 Cur: $44 (CA-3/89) **75**
Rubicon Napa Valley 1978 Rel: $25 Cur: $50 (CA-3/89) **88**
Rubicon Napa Valley 1977 ($NA) (2/28/87) (JG) **93**

OAKFORD
Cabernet Sauvignon Napa Valley 1987: Hard edged and tannic, but showing enough concentration of pepper-tinged black cherry and smoke aromas and flavors to make it interesting. Will need long cellaring to wear away the thick veil of tannin, but has enough balance to age into something elegant by 1995 to '98. 707 cases made. $25 (11/15/90) **91**

OAKVILLE BENCH
Cabernet Sauvignon Napa Valley 1989: Despite a good dose of firm tannins, there's a suppleness to this wine, along with a tight, solid core of ripe cherry, anise and currant-tinged flavors, finishing with toasty, buttery oak notes. A bold wine that's concentrated and complex, but without a track record, it's hard to say how it will age. Try now; gamble if you want to cellar it until 1997. $12 (3/15/92) **87**

OCTOPUS MOUNTAIN
Cabernet Sauvignon Anderson Valley Dennison Vineyards 1989: Pretty plum, currant and cherry flavors are ripe and rich but also tight and hard, with firm tannins that are a bit green. Has good intensity but could use a bit more depth. Drink in 1993 and beyond. $12.50 (7/31/91) **83**

OPTIMA
Cabernet Sauvignon Sonoma County 1987: Intense, complex and elegant, with spicy, minty, herbaceous tones to complement the vanilla, currant, plum and cherry flavors. Lavishly oaked, with the toasty, buttery flavors adding a nice dimension to the finish. Has plenty of tannin; cellar through 1994. 800 cases made. $22 (12/15/90) **92**
Cabernet Sauvignon Sonoma County 1986: Rich, deep and concentrated, packed with ripe currant, cherry and plum flavors that are complex and fairly tannic. The texture is smooth and elegant, with suppleness that gains on the finish. Plenty of flavor on the aftertaste. Drink 1993 to '98. 2,600 cases made. $22 (2/15/90) **91**
Cabernet Sauvignon Sonoma County 1985 $18.50 (12/15/88) **93**
Cabernet Sauvignon Sonoma County 1984 $16.50 (2/29/88) **90**

OPUS ONE
Napa Valley 1988: Not a long-term wine, but should be wonderful over the next few years. Ripe, rich and focused, with a solid core of vanilla- and spice-tinged currant, plum and blackberry flavors that reverberate on the long finish. The well-integrated tannins make it tempting now, but should be at its best after 1994. $62 (10/31/91) **92**
Napa Valley 1987: A great marriage of fruit and oak, with incredibly deep, rich, concentrated flavors. Has lavish oak and ripe, intense currant, black cherry, anise and plum flavors that keep on developing in an amazingly complex wine. It's tannic but supple and beautifully proportioned. Try a bottle now, but cellar a few bottles until the late 1990s. Best Opus yet. 5,000 cases made. Rel: $68 Cur: $74 (11/15/90) CS **97**
Napa Valley 1986: Amazingly rich and concentrated, with tiers of beautiful currant, plum, black cherry, herb and spice flavors that are elegant and sharply defined. Has the tannin and structure for aging but you can sip it now. Best in 1994. A blend of 90 percent Cabernet Sauvignon, 6 percent Merlot and 4 percent Cabernet Franc. Rel: $55 Cur: $85 (11/30/89) **95**
Napa Valley 1985 Rel: $55 Cur: $100 (6/15/89) **95**
Napa Valley 1984 Rel: $50 Cur: $82 (CA-3/89) **94**
Napa Valley 1983 Rel: $50 Cur: $78 (CA-3/89) **89**
Napa Valley 1982 Rel: $50 Cur: $84 (CA-3/89) **90**
Napa Valley 1982 Rel: $50 Cur: $84 (5/01/86) CS **93**
Napa Valley 1981 Rel: $50 Cur: $95 (CA-3/89) **88**
Napa Valley 1981 Rel: $50 Cur: $95 (5/16/85) CS **94**
Napa Valley 1980 Rel: $50 Cur: $135 (CA-3/89) **93**
Napa Valley 1980 Rel: $50 Cur: $135 (4/01/84) CS **91**
Napa Valley 1979 Rel: $50 Cur: $220 (CA-3/89) **90**

PACHECO RANCH
Cabernet Sauvignon Marin County 1985: Strong menthol and eucalyptus overtones make this medium-weight wine taste medicinal, rather than emphasizing its berry and smoke flavors. Off the main drag, but an interesting drink. $10 (11/15/91) **76**

PAHLMEYER
Caldwell Vineyard Napa Valley 1990 (NR) (5/15/91) (BT) **95+**
Caldwell Vineyard Napa Valley 1989 (NR) (5/15/91) (BT) **85+**
Caldwell Vineyard Napa Valley 1988: Fruity and generous, with a cedary edge to the basic currant and blackberry aromas and flavors. A graceful wine, with plenty to like. The tannins are present but well integrated. Best after 1994 to '96. $32 (11/15/91) **89**
Caldwell Vineyard Napa Valley 1987: Big, youthful and consequently awkward, but with a beam of tart currant and plum flavors blazing through the tough tannins and hard-edged oak character. Desperately needs cellaring until at least 1995 to '98. 1,040 cases made. $28 (11/15/90) **91**
Caldwell Vineyard Napa Valley 1986: Distinct, with minty, herbal overtones to the jammy currant and plum flavors, tannic, tough and intense enough to need cellaring until at least 1994 to soften the edges enough to be drinkable. 1,000 cases made. $25 (11/15/89) **89**

PARDUCCI
Cabernet Sauvignon Mendocino County 1984 $8.50 (7/31/88) **74**
Cabernet Sauvignon Mendocino County 1981 $6.50 (2/01/86) **73**
Cabernet Sauvignon Mendocino County 1980 $6.25 (2/01/86) **79**
Cabernet Sauvignon Mendocino County 1979 $8 (2/01/86) **69**
Cabernet Sauvignon Mendocino County 1978 $5.50 (2/01/86) **75**
Cabernet Sauvignon North Coast 1987: Soft in texture, but fairly tannic for the gentle plum and currant flavors. Should be at its best around 1993. $9.50 (4/30/91) **80**
Cabernet Merlot Cellarmaster Selection Mendocino County 1986: With mature aromas and flavors, this medium-weight wine has just enough cherry and beet flavors to balance the modest tannins. Try now. $15 (4/30/91) **79**
Cabernet Merlot Cellarmaster Selection Mendocino County 1978 $12 (2/01/86) **75**

PARSONS CREEK
Cabernet Sauvignon Sonoma County 1986: Light and tannic, with hints of strawberry peeking through on the drying finish, but it's basically a tight, austere wine that may or may not develop with cellaring through 1995. $13 (11/15/89) **75**
Cabernet Sauvignon Sonoma County 1985: Its deep flavors of black currants and cherries are overpowered on the finish by powerful tannins. A rich but raw wine that's drinkable now or could be cellared further. $13 (6/30/89) **76**

PAT PAULSEN
Cabernet Sauvignon Alexander Valley 1984 $11 (4/30/87) **70**
Cabernet Sauvignon Alexander Valley 1983 $11 (7/01/86) **84**
Cabernet Sauvignon Alexander Valley 1982 $10 (3/01/85) BB **85**
Cabernet Sauvignon Sonoma County 1985 $11 (12/31/87) **78**
Cabernet Sauvignon Sonoma County 1981 $8 (1/01/84) **78**

ROBERT PECOTA
Cabernet Sauvignon Napa Valley Kara's Vineyard 1991: Fresh and lively, with ripe currant, berry and spice flavors and fine but firm tannins. Gains complexity on the finish. An elegant wine that should be outstanding. (NR) (5/15/92) (BT) **88+**
Cabernet Sauvignon Napa Valley Kara's Vineyard 1990 (NR) (5/15/91) (BT) **90+**
Cabernet Sauvignon Napa Valley Kara's Vineyard 1989 (NR) (5/15/91) (BT) **90+**
Cabernet Sauvignon Napa Valley Kara's Vineyard 1988: Smooth and generous, with finely proportioned black cherry, currant and plum flavors shaded by herb, bay leaf and chocolate notes. The soft tannins make it approachable. Drinkable now, but should be at its best after 1993 or '94. Rel: $16 Cur: $20 (11/15/91) **89**
Cabernet Sauvignon Napa Valley Kara's Vineyard 1987: Tastes like ripe black cherry with toast and spice notes, but the tannins really clamp down on the flavors, and it's dry and austere on the finish. Once the tannins soften this should be a beauty, but for now it's closed. Drink 1994 to '95. 1,000 cases made. Rel: $16 Cur: $19 (10/15/90) **90**
Cabernet Sauvignon Napa Valley Kara's Vineyard 1986 Rel: $16 Cur: $19 (9/15/89) **86**
Cabernet Sauvignon Napa Valley Kara's Vineyard 1985 Rel: $16 Cur: $20 (CA-3/89) **86**
Cabernet Sauvignon Napa Valley Kara's Vineyard 1984 Rel: $14 Cur: $20 (CA-3/89) **85**
Cabernet Sauvignon Napa Valley 1982 Rel: $12 Cur: $20 (CA-3/89) **85**

J. PEDRONCELLI
Cabernet Sauvignon Sonoma County 1988: Offers lots of nice plum and spice aromas and flavors in a light-textured wine of modest concentration. Charming and graceful; drinkable now. $9.50 (10/15/91) **83**
Cabernet Sauvignon Dry Creek Valley 1987: Tart, lean and concentrated, with sharply focused currant and raspberry flavors, a polished texture and enough tannins to need cellaring until 1994. $8.50 (11/15/90) BB **85**
Cabernet Sauvignon Dry Creek Valley 1986: Lean and astringent, but concentrated enough to make

Key to Symbols

The scores reported here are the results of blind tastings conducted by our panel of senior editors. Wines that carry the initials below are results of individual tastings.

THE WINE SPECTATOR 100-POINT SCALE ***95-100***—Classic, a great wine; ***90-94***—Outstanding, superior character and style; ***80-89***—Good to very good, a wine with special qualities; ***70-79***—Average, drinkable wine that may have minor flaws; ***60-69***—Below average, drinkable but not recommended; ***50-59***—Poor, undrinkable, not recommended. "+"—With a score indicates a range; used primarily with barrel tastings to indicate a preliminary score.

SPECIAL DESIGNATIONS SS—Spectator Selection, CS—Cellar Selection, BB—Best Buy, ($NA)—Price not available, (NR)—Not released.

TASTER'S INITIALS (JG)—Jim Gordon, (HS)—Harvey Steiman, (JL)—James Laube, (JS)—James Suckling, (TM)—Thomas Matthews, (TR)—Terry Robards, (PM)—Per-Henrik Mansson, (BT)—Barrel Tasting (these wines were tasted blind from barrel samples), (CA-date)—*California's Great Cabernets* by James Laube, (CH-date)—*California's Great Chardonnays* by James Laube, (VP-date)—*Vintage Port* by James Suckling.

DATE TASTED Dates in parentheses represent the issue in which the rating was published.

it worth cellaring, and the generous cherry and cassis aromas echo on the finish. Probably best to drink now to 1994. $7 (9/15/89) BB **83**
Cabernet Sauvignon Dry Creek Valley 1985 $7 (10/15/88) **79**
Cabernet Sauvignon Dry Creek Valley 1983 $6.50 (8/31/87) **75**
Cabernet Sauvignon Dry Creek Valley 1981 $6 (12/01/84) BB **80**
Cabernet Sauvignon Dry Creek Valley Reserve 1985: Has deep, dark color and pretty Cabernet aromas. Elegant and well balanced, with currant, plum and cherry-berry flavors, smooth, polished tannins and more extract and concentration than you usually get from Pedroncelli. Drink now to 1996. 1,076 cases made. $14 (3/31/90) **85**
Cabernet Sauvignon Dry Creek Valley Reserve 1982: Extremely ripe and tannic with sizzling alcohol and prune and raisin flavors. The ripe, overblown style may appeal to some more than it did to us. Drink now to 1996. $13 (10/15/89) **73**

PEJU
Cabernet Sauvignon Napa Valley HB Vineyard 1988: A smoky charcoal edge makes this a distinctively tart, tannic and fruity wine that's modest in intensity, with barely enough currant and berry flavors sneaking in on the finish. Harsh, but cellaring until 1995 to '98 could bring it around. 600 cases made. $30 (8/31/91) **82**
Cabernet Sauvignon Napa Valley HB Vineyard 1987: Firm, dry and tannic, but with a solid core of currant, chocolate and cedary oak flavors that are well balanced. It's rather typical of the '87 vintage, with firm, assertive tannins, but there's enough fruit concentration to stand up to them. Drink 1995 to '98. $20 (11/15/90) **87**
Cabernet Sauvignon Napa Valley HB Vineyard 1986: Rich and velvety, a plush wine with layers of cherry, currant, cinnamon and cedar aromas and flavors, concentrated without being heavy, an elegant wine with fine, integrated tannins. It's built for cellaring, but it should be ready to start drinking around 1993 to '94. $20 (11/15/89) **92**

PELLEGRINI FAMILY
Cabernet Sauvignon Alexander Valley Cloverdale Ranch Estate Cuvée 1988: Light in texture, but has a firm backbone to support the modest red cherry and nutmeg aromas and flavors. Already showing maturity, but can use until 1993 to settle the tannins. 800 cases made. $12 (6/15/91) **82**

ROBERT PEPI
Cabernet Sauvignon Napa Valley Vine Hill Ranch 1988 (NR) (5/15/90) (BT) **85+**
Cabernet Sauvignon Napa Valley Vine Hill Ranch 1987: A minty, herbal, camphor-laced wine, with a solid concentration of rich black cherry, currant, cedar and chocolate flavors. Firm, young and tannic; best if cellared until 1996 or '97. 2,400 cases made. $20 (4/30/91) **90**
Cabernet Sauvignon Napa Valley Vine Hill Ranch 1986: A tough, hard-edged, tannic wine. The deeply concentrated currant, earth, mineral and cherry flavors are tightly wound now, and it's in need of cellaring, but the core of fruit is ripe and rich and the oak is strong but balanced. Rel: $18 Cur: $24 (10/31/90) **88**
Cabernet Sauvignon Napa Valley Vine Hill Ranch 1985: Spicy, exotic wine, with dense berry and currant flavors and overtones of mint, eucalyptus and clove, balanced and fairly long. A well-crafted wine, with plenty of style but not much for immediate appeal. Try it in 1993 to '95. Rel: $18 Cur: $23 (7/31/90) **85**
Cabernet Sauvignon Napa Valley Vine Hill Ranch 1984 Rel: $16 Cur: $22 (8/31/89) **80**
Cabernet Sauvignon Napa Valley Vine Hill Ranch 1983 Rel: $16 Cur: $24 (CA-3/89) **80**
Cabernet Sauvignon Napa Valley Vine Hill Ranch 1982 Rel: $14 Cur: $24 (CA-3/89) **88**
Cabernet Sauvignon Napa Valley Vine Hill Ranch 1981 Rel: $14 Cur: $25 (CA-3/89) **86**
Cabernet Sauvignon Napa Valley Vine Hill Ranch 1981 Rel: $14 Cur: $25 (1/01/86) CS **93**

MARIO PERELLI-MINETTI
Cabernet Sauvignon Napa Valley 1987: Lean in texture, but focused, concentrated currant and berry flavors balance nicely against a background of spicy oak notes. A bit rough around the edges. Probably best to drink now to 1993. 1,160 cases made. $12 (4/30/91) **83**

PESENTI
Cabernet Sauvignon San Luis Obispo County Family Reserve 1987: An impressive wine. Has ripe, clean currant and plum flavors, an appealingly deep color and full tannins to stand up to the fruit. Needs a bit more complexity, which cellaring should bring. Drink now to 1995. $8 (12/15/89) **84**
Cabernet Sauvignon San Luis Obispo County Family Reserve 1985: Simple, decent, straightforward wine, with a good dose of tannin that overshadows the cherry-scented Cabernet flavor. Drink now to 1996. $13 (12/15/89) **77**

JOSEPH PHELPS
Cabernet Sauvignon Napa Valley 1990 (NR) (5/15/91) (BT) **85+**
Cabernet Sauvignon Napa Valley 1989: Tight, tannic and leathery, with a thin base of currant and cherry-scented flavors. Needs a shade more richness and depth to stand up to the tannins and oak. Try after 1996, but may always be tannic. Tasted twice, with consistent notes. $17.50 (4/15/92) **78**
Cabernet Sauvignon Napa Valley 1988: Distinctive for its mint and dill aromas, it has a core of rich, tasty currant, plum and berry notes. The tannins are firm, but the fruit fights through on the finish. Best around 1994. Rel: $17.50 Cur: $20 (11/15/91) **86**
Cabernet Sauvignon Napa Valley 1987: Herbal, vegetal, gamy aromas and flavors turn murky and unpleasant on the finish. Tasted twice. $14.50 (7/15/91) **75**
Cabernet Sauvignon Napa Valley 1986 Rel: $15 Cur: $27 (4/15/88) (BT) **85+**
Cabernet Sauvignon Napa Valley 1985 Rel: $14 Cur: $27 (5/15/89) **84**
Cabernet Sauvignon Napa Valley 1984 Rel: $14 Cur: $31 (10/31/88) **91**
Cabernet Sauvignon Napa Valley 1983 Rel: $13 Cur: $31 (8/31/87) **84**
Cabernet Sauvignon Napa Valley 1982 Rel: $12 Cur: $17 (12/15/86) **82**
Cabernet Sauvignon Napa Valley 1981 Rel: $11 Cur: $25 (9/01/85) **86**
Cabernet Sauvignon Napa Valley 1980 Rel: $10.75 Cur: $38 (7/01/84) **89**
Cabernet Sauvignon Napa Valley Backus Vineyard 1991: Bold, ripe and intense, with deeply concentrated herb, currant and cherry flavors. Shows plenty of tannins, too, but it has all the ingredients. (NR) (5/15/92) (BT) **89+**
Cabernet Sauvignon Napa Valley Backus Vineyard 1990 (NR) (5/15/91) (BT) **90+**
Cabernet Sauvignon Napa Valley Backus Vineyard 1989 (NR) (5/15/91) (BT) **90+**
Cabernet Sauvignon Napa Valley Backus Vineyard 1987: An elegant wine, with ripe, supple, generous plum, mint, herb and currant flavors that are framed by toasty oak and dry, rounded tannins. Offers plenty of depth and richness to the flavors. Best to cellar until 1995. $30 (7/15/91) **88**
Cabernet Sauvignon Napa Valley Backus Vineyard 1986: A young and intense wine with deep color and plenty of flavor. Ripe cherry, currant and spice flavors offer a touch of menthol and oak on the finish. Drink now to 1994. Rel: $22 Cur: $37 (1/31/90) **83**
Cabernet Sauvignon Napa Valley Backus Vineyard 1985: A distinct chocolate mint note dominates the black cherry and currant flavors. It's rich and fairly tannic, requiring a few years' cellaring. The finish displays the concentration and structure that bodes well for aging. Drink in 1994. Rel: $27.50 Cur: $45 (12/31/88) **91**
Cabernet Sauvignon Napa Valley Backus Vineyard 1984 Rel: $20 Cur: $42 (CA-3/89) **86**
Cabernet Sauvignon Napa Valley Backus Vineyard 1983 Rel: $16.50 Cur: $28 (CA-3/89) **85**
Cabernet Sauvignon Napa Valley Backus Vineyard 1981 Rel: $15 Cur: $48 (CA-3/89) **91**
Cabernet Sauvignon Napa Valley Backus Vineyard 1978 Rel: $16.50 Cur: $56 (CA-3/89) **89**
Cabernet Sauvignon Napa Valley Backus Vineyard 1977 Rel: $15 Cur: $46 (CA-3/89) **86**
Cabernet Sauvignon Napa Valley Eisele Vineyard 1991: Tight, intense and not well-defined now, with stalky currant flavors. Solid but rough and chewy. Hard to judge. (NR) (5/15/92) (BT) **85+**
Cabernet Sauvignon Napa Valley Eisele Vineyard 1989 (NR) (5/15/91) (BT) **90+**
Cabernet Sauvignon Napa Valley Eisele Vineyard 1987 $40 (4/15/89) (BT) **75+**
Cabernet Sauvignon Napa Valley Eisele Vineyard 1986: An extremely rich and earthy wine, with strong barnyardy, leathery flavors overriding the ripe currant and cherry flavors. It's dry and tannic, with very limited appeal. Drink in 1993. Tasted three times. Rel: $40 Cur: $45 (8/31/90) **77**
Cabernet Sauvignon Napa Valley Eisele Vineyard 1985: Minty, hard, woody and tannic, with lean, firm, hard-as-nails fruit that throws plum and cherry notes, but not much else. Very tight and concentrated, needs a long time in the cellar. Tasted three times. Rel: $40 Cur: $52 (5/31/89) **81**
Cabernet Sauvignon Napa Valley Eisele Vineyard 1984 Rel: $35 Cur: $40 (CA-3/89) **87**
Cabernet Sauvignon Napa Valley Eisele Vineyard 1983 Rel: $25 Cur: $37 (CA-3/89) **86**
Cabernet Sauvignon Napa Valley Eisele Vineyard 1982 Rel: $30 Cur: $47 (CA-3/89) **85**
Cabernet Sauvignon Napa Valley Eisele Vineyard 1981 Rel: $30 Cur: $47 (CA-3/89) **89**
Cabernet Sauvignon Napa Valley Eisele Vineyard 1979 Rel: $30 Cur: $64 (CA-3/89) **92**
Cabernet Sauvignon Napa Valley Eisele Vineyard 1978 Rel: $30 Cur: $106 (CA-3/89) **97**
Cabernet Sauvignon Napa Valley Eisele Vineyard 1977 Rel: $25 Cur: $61 (CA-3/89) **82**
Cabernet Sauvignon Napa Valley Eisele Vineyard 1975 Rel: $15 Cur: $145 (CA-3/89) **97**
Insignia Napa Valley 1991: Has lots of mint and herb notes, but also a tight, tannic core of currant and berry flavor that is intense and long. A stalky edge may disappear with time. A blend of 80 percent Cabernet Sauvignon, 15 percent Merlot and 5 percent Cabernet Franc. (NR) (5/15/92) (BT) **87+**
Insignia Napa Valley 1990 (NR) (5/15/91) (BT) **90+**
Insignia Napa Valley 1989 (NR) (5/15/91) (BT) **85+**
Insignia Napa Valley 1988: Has a strong mint, bay leaf and menthol edge, but also a wealth of rich currant and cedary coffee flavors underneath. Has a strong personality and firm tannins. Best to cellar until 1996. $35 (11/15/91) **86**
Insignia Napa Valley 1986: A smoky, toasty, exotic wine that's rich and smooth, showing lots of currant, plum and mineral flavors right through the long finish. A massive wine, with plenty of future—try in 1996. A blend of 60 percent Cabernet Sauvignon, 30 percent Merlot and 10 percent Cabernet Franc. 4,000 cases made. Rel: $40 Cur: $44 (8/31/90) CS **93**
Insignia Napa Valley 1985: Extremely herbal and earthy, very rich, supple and almost unctuous, but loaded with olive, spice, currant and plum flavors. Long and complex, but so distinctive that not everyone will love it. 4,700 cases made. Rel: $40 Cur: $58 (7/31/89) CS **93**
Insignia Napa Valley 1984 Rel: $30 Cur: $39 (CA-3/89) **89**
Insignia Napa Valley 1983 Rel: $25 Cur: $38 (CA-3/89) **89**
Insignia Napa Valley 1982 Rel: $25 Cur: $36 (CA-3/89) **85**
Insignia Napa Valley 1981 Rel: $25 Cur: $53 (CA-3/89) **92**
Insignia Napa Valley 1980 Rel: $25 Cur: $52 (CA-3/89) **90**
Insignia Napa Valley 1980 Rel: $25 Cur: $52 (7/01/84) CS **90**
Insignia Napa Valley 1979 Rel: $25 Cur: $53 (CA-3/89) **90**
Insignia Napa Valley 1978 Rel: $25 Cur: $77 (CA-3/89) **87**
Insignia Napa Valley 1977 Rel: $25 Cur: $72 (CA-3/89) **91**
Insignia Napa Valley 1976 Rel: $20 Cur: $110 (CA-3/89) **93**
Insignia Napa Valley 1975 Rel: $15 Cur: $110 (CA-3/89) **85**
Insignia Napa Valley 1974 Rel: $12 Cur: $180 (CA-3/89) **90**

R.H. PHILLIPS
Cabernet Sauvignon California 1989: Firm and fruity, with generous currant and spice aromas and flavors. Straightforward and easy to drink, but solid enough to pair with food. $8 (7/31/91) BB **82**
Cabernet Sauvignon California 1985 $6 (11/30/88) **80**
Cabernet Sauvignon California Night Harvest NV $4 (11/30/88) BB **83**

PINE RIDGE
Cabernet Sauvignon Napa Valley Andrus Reserve 1990 (NR) (5/15/91) (BT) **80+**
Cabernet Sauvignon Napa Valley Andrus Reserve 1987 (NR) (4/15/89) (BT) **85+**
Cabernet Sauvignon Napa Valley Andrus Reserve 1986: An extremely oaky wine, with camphor and minty notes that come across as dry and woody on the palate. There are some pretty cherry and plum notes, but they're overpowered by the wood. Drink 1993 to '97. Tasted twice. 802 cases made. Rel: $40 Cur: $44 (5/15/90) **80**
Cabernet Sauvignon Napa Valley Andrus Reserve 1984 Rel: $37 Cur: $40 (CA-3/89) **93**
Cabernet Sauvignon Napa Valley Andrus Reserve 1983 Rel: $35 Cur: $40 (CA-3/89) **88**
Cabernet Sauvignon Napa Valley Andrus Reserve 1980 Rel: $30 Cur: $60 (CA-3/89) **96**
Cabernet Sauvignon Napa Valley Andrus Reserve 1980 Rel: $30 Cur: $60 (12/01/84) CS **93**
Cabernet Sauvignon Napa Valley Andrus Reserve Cuvée Duet 1985 Rel: $40 Cur: $45 (CA-3/89) **92**
Cabernet Sauvignon Napa Valley Diamond Mountain 1989 (NR) (5/15/91) (BT) **85+**
Cabernet Sauvignon Napa Valley Diamond Mountain 1987: Distinctly minty, permeating the currant flavor with powerful herbal overtones. A big, full-bodied wine that does not persist on the finish. Try in 1993. 600 cases made. $35 (11/15/90) **84**
Cabernet Sauvignon Napa Valley Diamond Mountain 1986: Attractive for its ripe currant, cherry and plum flavors, framed by firm tannins and ample oak. Generous, complex and concentrated. Should age well through 1995. Rel: $30 Cur: $33 (11/30/89) **92**
Cabernet Sauvignon Napa Valley Diamond Mountain Andrus Reserve 1988: Tight and perfumed, with bay rum and mint aromas and flavors that overshadow the berry and currant notes. A tight wine that won't show what it has until 1996 to '98, but it's a gamble. $15 (11/15/91) **82**
Cabernet Sauvignon Napa Valley Rutherford Cuvée 1990 (NR) (5/15/91) (BT) **85+**
Cabernet Sauvignon Napa Valley Rutherford Cuvée 1989 (NR) (5/15/91) (BT) **90+**
Cabernet Sauvignon Napa Valley Rutherford Cuvée 1987 $16.50 (3/15/92) **77**
Cabernet Sauvignon Napa Valley Rutherford Cuvée 1986 Rel: $16 Cur: $19 (5/31/90) **90**
Cabernet Sauvignon Napa Valley Rutherford Cuvée 1985 Rel: $16 Cur: $20 (CA-3/89) **93**
Cabernet Sauvignon Napa Valley Rutherford Cuvée 1984 Rel: $14 Cur: $29 (CA-3/89) **90**
Cabernet Sauvignon Napa Valley Rutherford Cuvée 1983 Rel: $14 Cur: $18 (CA-3/89) **84**
Cabernet Sauvignon Napa Valley Rutherford Cuvée 1982 Rel: $13 Cur: $24 (CA-3/89) **90**
Cabernet Sauvignon Napa Valley Rutherford Cuvée 1981 Rel: $13 Cur: $28 (CA-3/89) **88**
Cabernet Sauvignon Napa Valley Rutherford Cuvée Andrus Reserve 1988: Extremely earthy and woody, with strong, harsh, vegetal flavors that are unpleasant to drink. Of marginal quality. Tasted twice, with consistent notes. ($NA) (11/15/91) **65**
Cabernet Sauvignon Napa Valley Rutherford Cuvée 1987: Lean and focused, with lots of mint and menthol notes running through the tart cherry and currant aromas and flavors. A distinctive wine, with generous character and fine balance. Cellar until 1993 to '95. Rel: $16 Cur: $19 (5/31/90) **90**
Cabernet Sauvignon Napa Valley Rutherford District 1980 Rel: $12 Cur: $32 (CA-3/89) **91**
Cabernet Sauvignon Napa Valley Rutherford District 1979 Rel: $9 Cur: $45 (CA-3/89) **85**
Cabernet Sauvignon Napa Valley Rutherford District 1978 Rel: $7.50 Cur: $46 (CA-3/89) **89**
Cabernet Sauvignon Stags Leap District 1987 Rel: $28 Cur: $32 (1/31/92) **85**
Cabernet Sauvignon Stags Leap District Andrus Reserve 1988 Tough in texture and piny in aroma, with solid black cherry and currant flavors lurking beneath the surface of tannins. Needs until 1995 to '97 to soften. Tasted twice, with consistent notes. ($NA) (11/15/91) **82**
Cabernet Sauvignon Stags Leap District Pine Ridge Stags Leap Vineyard 1990 (NR) (5/15/91) (BT) **85+**
Cabernet Sauvignon Stags Leap District Pine Ridge Stags Leap Vineyard 1989 (NR) (5/15/91) (BT) **80+**
Cabernet Sauvignon Stags Leap District Pine Ridge Stags Leap Vineyard 1986 $29 (CA-3/89) **91**
Cabernet Sauvignon Stags Leap District Pine Ridge Stags Leap Vineyard 1985 Rel: $26 Cur: $29 (CA-3/89) **94**
Cabernet Sauvignon Stags Leap District Pine Ridge Stags Leap Vineyard 1984 Rel: $25 Cur: $33 (CA-3/89) **93**
Cabernet Sauvignon Stags Leap District Pine Ridge Stags Leap Vineyard 1983 Rel: $20 Cur: $34 (CA-3/89) **85**
Cabernet Sauvignon Stags Leap District Pine Ridge Stags Leap Vineyard 1982 Rel: $20 Cur: $34 (CA-3/89) **90**

Cabernet Sauvignon Stags Leap District Pine Ridge Stags Leap Vineyard 1982 Rel: $20 Cur: $34 (10/31/86) CS **91**
Cabernet Sauvignon Stags Leap District Pine Ridge Stags Leap Vineyard 1981 Rel: $20 Cur: $46 (CA-3/89) **92**
Cabernet Sauvignon Stags Leap District Stags Leap Cuvée 1981 Rel: $20 Cur: $46 (2/01/85) **88**

PLAM
Cabernet Sauvignon Napa Valley 1988: A strong barnyardy note intrudes on the ripe, rich currant, anise and berry flavors. Not a wine that will appeal to everyone; some will find the barnyardy flavors too dominant. Needs aeration. Drink in 1995 and beyond. Tasted three times, with consistent notes. 1,077 cases made. $28 (9/30/91) **79**
Cabernet Sauvignon Napa Valley 1986: Massive but elegant, brimming with rich, deep, complex currant, plum and black cherry flavors that are elegantly styled, beautifully balanced and finishing with delicious coffee and cedar notes. Long finish. Drink now to 1999. $24 (9/15/89) **92**
Cabernet Sauvignon Napa Valley 1985 $24 (6/30/88) **91**

POPPY HILL
Cabernet Sauvignon California 1987: With a firm texture and flavors than lean more toward oak than fruit, this needs time to settle down even though the tannins are not out of line. Try in 1993. $7.50 (5/31/91) **78**

BERNARD PRADEL
Cabernet Sauvignon Napa Valley 1987: Very ripe and intense, with currant, dill and cherry notes that are well balanced and not too tannic. Ultimately simple but very pleasant. Try in 1993 or '94. 2,200 cases made. $20 (10/15/90) **86**
Cabernet Sauvignon Napa Valley 1986: This big, full-bodied, ripe-tasting and broadly textured wine has touches of spice and chocolate that add complexity on the finish. Drink now through 1993. $12 (1/31/90) **82**
Cabernet Sauvignon Napa Valley 1985 $12 (4/30/89) **91**
Cabernet Sauvignon Napa Valley 1984 $11 (2/29/88) **88**
Cabernet Sauvignon Napa Valley Limited Barrel Selection 1988: Harsh in texture and strongly herbal in flavor, with more vegetal notes than fruit. Could develop into a better wine with cellaring until 1996 or '97. $20 (11/15/91) **80**

PRESTON
Cabernet Sauvignon Dry Creek Valley 1988: A charming, fruity smell leads to simple fruit and oak flavors and a nip of toughness on the finish. Good, but more tannic than the fruit calls for. 3,000 cases made. Rel: $14 Cur: $16 (3/15/92) **80**
Cabernet Sauvignon Dry Creek Valley 1987: Firm and tannic but with a solid core of rich, ripe currant and black cherry that is a bit rough-hewn now. With time it should settle out to a smoother, more elegant style. Hold until 1994. 2,517 cases made. Rel: $14 Cur: $17 (10/31/90) **88**
Cabernet Sauvignon Dry Creek Valley 1986: Firm, concentrated and bursting with ripe cherry and currant flavors, this carefully made wine is defined by elegant oak and fine tannins. It should smooth out nicely with aging until 1993 to '94. 4,027 cases made. Rel: $11 Cur: $17 (3/15/90) **87**
Cabernet Sauvignon Dry Creek Valley 1985 Rel: $11 Cur: $18 (CA-3/89) **89**
Cabernet Sauvignon Dry Creek Valley 1984 Rel: $11 Cur: $17 (CA-3/89) **87**
Cabernet Sauvignon Dry Creek Valley 1983 Rel: $11 Cur: $15 (CA-3/89) **86**
Cabernet Sauvignon Dry Creek Valley 1982 Rel: $11 Cur: $18 (CA-3/89) **87**

QUAIL RIDGE
Cabernet Sauvignon Napa Valley 1987: A big, rich, chewy wine, packed with concentrated cherry, plum, chocolate, cedar and smoke flavors that are tight and complex. Jams in lots of everything, including oak and tannin. Let this one mellow out until 1997. 2,200 cases made. $16 (9/30/91) **93**
Cabernet Sauvignon Napa Valley 1986: A rich, smooth, seductive wine, with pretty, toasty, oaky, ripe currant, cherry, tobacco and anise flavors that are broad and complex before the firm tannins clamp down. Fine structure; long on the finish. Best to cellar until 1993 or '94. $15 (11/15/90) **89**
Cabernet Sauvignon Napa Valley 1985: Tough and tannic, with tobacco- and herb-tinged cherry flavors, masked by a wall of tannin, closed and bitter. With cellaring until 1995, it could smooth out. $15 (7/31/89) **82**
Cabernet Sauvignon Napa Valley 1984 $15 (3/31/89) **88**
Cabernet Sauvignon Napa Valley 1982 $13 (9/16/85) **86**

QUIVIRA
Cabernet Sauvignon Dry Creek Valley 1988: A subtle wine shaped by cedary oak but showing an elegant core of cherry and currant flavors. Not too flashy, but a well-mannered, balanced wine, finishing with firm tannins. Start drinking in 1994. $17.50 (11/15/91) **84**
Cabernet Sauvignon Dry Creek Valley 1987: Ripe, rich and rough-hewn, with chunky cherry, currant and earth flavors that are a bit coarse now but not excessive. Has firm, well-proportioned tannins. Not particularly complex yet, but has all the ingredients. Best to start drinking after 1993. First Cabernet from this producer. 1,500 cases made. $15 (11/15/90) **87**

RABBIT RIDGE
Cabernet Sauvignon Sonoma County 1988: Has a pretty core of currant, black cherry, plum and spice flavors neatly framed by heavy oak. Despite the tannins and wood, the fruit pours through on the aftertaste. Try after 1996. $12 (8/31/91) **89**

A. RAFANELLI
Cabernet Sauvignon Dry Creek Valley 1988: A great value. Firm, concentrated and deep, with a nice tension between the ripe cherry and plum flavors and shades of vanilla- and chocolate-scented oak. A supple wine, with great charm and balance. Almost drinkable now, but cellaring until 1993 to '95 would not hurt. 3,000 cases made. $12.50 (8/31/91) **90**
Cabernet Sauvignon Dry Creek Valley 1987: Pretty cherry, currant, herb and smoky, seasoned oak flavors are well balanced and well proportioned in this complex wine. It has firm but well-structured tannins, with sharply focused currant and oak notes on the finish. Try in 1994 to '95. 2,000 cases made. $12 (8/31/90) **91**
Cabernet Sauvignon Dry Creek Valley 1986: Marvelously concentrated, with cassis and cherry aromas and flavors framed by toasty vanilla overtones that make it harmonious and balanced. Should develop through 2000, but worth trying now. Great price, too. 1,100 cases made. $9.50 (9/30/89) **91**
Cabernet Sauvignon Dry Creek Valley 1985 $8 (9/15/88) **78**

Key to Symbols

The scores reported here are the results of blind tastings conducted by our panel of senior editors. Wines that carry the initials below are results of individual tastings.

THE WINE SPECTATOR 100-POINT SCALE 95-100—Classic, a great wine; ***90-94***—Outstanding, superior character and style; ***80-89***—Good to very good, a wine with special qualities; ***70-79***—Average, drinkable wine that may have minor flaws; ***60-69***—Below average, drinkable but not recommended; ***50-59***—Poor, undrinkable, not recommended. "+"—With a score indicates a range; used primarily with barrel tastings to indicate a preliminary score.

SPECIAL DESIGNATIONS SS—Spectator Selection, CS—Cellar Selection, BB—Best Buy, ($NA)—Price not available, (NR)—Not released.

TASTER'S INITIALS (JG)—Jim Gordon, (HS)—Harvey Steiman, (JL)—James Laube, (JS)—James Suckling, (TM)—Thomas Matthews, (TR)—Terry Robards, (PM)—Per-Henrik Mansson, (BT)—Barrel Tasting (these wines were tasted blind from barrel samples), (CA-date)—*California's Great Cabernets* by James Laube, (CH-date)—*California's Great Chardonnays* by James Laube, (VP-date)—*Vintage Port* by James Suckling.

DATE TASTED Dates in parentheses represent the issue in which the rating was published.

RANCHO SISQUOC
Cabernet Sauvignon Santa Maria Valley 1986: Pronounced vegetal and herbal flavors dominate in a wine that has limited appeal. $10 (12/15/89) **73**

KENT RASMUSSEN
Cabernet Sauvignon Napa Valley 1988: Firm, flavorful and definitely earthy, with a strong core of blackberry and currant flavors shaded by leathery undertones. A bit rough to drink now. Try in 1994 or '95. $20 (11/15/91) **83**
Cabernet Sauvignon Napa Valley 1987 $20 (4/15/89) (BT) **90+**

RAVENSWOOD
Cabernet Sauvignon California 1979 $8 (CA-3/89) **59**
Cabernet Sauvignon California 1978 Rel: $10.50 Cur: $20 (CA-3/89) **81**
Cabernet Sauvignon El Dorado County Madrona Vineyards 1977 $8.50 (CA-3/89) **82**
Cabernet Sauvignon Sonoma County 1986 Rel: $12 Cur: $18 (CA-3/89) **86**
Cabernet Sauvignon Sonoma County 1985 Rel: $12 Cur: $20 (CA-3/89) **85**
Cabernet Sauvignon Sonoma County 1984 Rel: $12 Cur: $25 (CA-3/89) **80**
Cabernet Sauvignon Sonoma County 1983 Rel: $9.50 Cur: $19 (CA-3/89) **76**
Cabernet Sauvignon Sonoma County 1982 Rel: $11 Cur: $24 (4/01/86) SS **95**
Cabernet Sauvignon Sonoma County 1980 Rel: $10.50 Cur: $16 (CA-3/89) **79**
Cabernet Sauvignon Sonoma Valley 1988: Elegant and complex, with intense, concentrated currant, spice, cedar and herb flavors that are well integrated and well defined. Crisp, fine tannins on the finish make it a good candidate to drink in 1994 to '98. Rel: $14 Cur: $17 (3/15/91) **89**
Cabernet Sauvignon Sonoma Valley 1987: Herbal, green olive aromas and flavors forge to the front as this supple, velvety, fairly intense wine rolls over the palate, joining black cherry and currant flavors on the finish. Should be smooth enough to drink now. Rel: $11 Cur: $20 (5/31/90) **84**
Cabernet Sauvignon Sonoma Valley Gregory 1988 $18 (11/15/91) **80**
Cabernet Sauvignon Sonoma Valley Olive Hill 1978 Rel: $10.50 Cur: $26 (CA-3/89) **83**
Pickberry Vineyards Sonoma Mountain 1991: Pretty berry, spice, currant and tobacco flavors are soft, rich and fleshy, with modest tannins. A blend of 75 percent Merlot, 20 percent Cabernet Sauvignon and 5 percent Cabernet Franc. 1,000 cases made. (NR) (5/15/92) (BT) **83+**
Pickberry Vineyards Sonoma Mountain 1989 (NR) (5/15/91) (BT) **80+**
Pickberry Vineyards Sonoma Mountain 1988: Soft and ripe, with jammy plum and cherry flavors that are moderately rich, but not too tannic. Missing the intensity and velocity one expects from Ravenswood. Ready to drink now through 1994. $27 (4/30/91) **82**
Pickberry Vineyards Sonoma Mountain 1986 Rel: $25 Cur: $32 (CA-3/89) **89**

RAYMOND
Cabernet Sauvignon Napa Valley 1988 $17 (5/15/90) (BT) **85+**
Cabernet Sauvignon Napa Valley 1987: Has a core of cherry and currant flavors, but this is distinctive for its mint and bay leaf flavors. It's dominated by the herbal spectrum of Cabernet. Firmly tannic and moderately deep. Doesn't quite have the drama usually found in Raymond wines. Cellar until 1994. $17 (2/28/91) **83**
Cabernet Sauvignon Napa Valley 1986: Has firm texture, somewhat woody aromas and flavors but ultimately rich plum and berry flavors that are beautifully focused, straight through to the elegant finish. Worth cellaring until 1993 to '96 to polish the edges. $16 (5/31/90) **90**
Cabernet Sauvignon Napa Valley 1985: Green bell pepper, olive and tobacco aromas and flavors tend to nudge past the vaguely currantlike flavors in this firm, somewhat coarse-textured wine. With cellaring until 1993 or '94, it should come around. $15 (12/15/89) **84**
Cabernet Sauvignon Napa Valley 1984 Rel: $13 Cur: $17 (2/15/89) **90**
Cabernet Sauvignon Napa Valley 1983 Rel: $13 Cur: $20 (2/15/88) **89**
Cabernet Sauvignon Napa Valley 1982 Rel: $12 Cur: $18 (11/15/86) **91**
Cabernet Sauvignon Napa Valley 1981 Rel: $11 Cur: $16.50 (CA-3/89) **85**
Cabernet Sauvignon Napa Valley 1980 Rel: $12 Cur: $25 (CA-3/89) **82**
Cabernet Sauvignon Napa Valley 1979 Rel: $12 Cur: $20 (CA-3/89) **85**
Cabernet Sauvignon Napa Valley 1978 Rel: $10 Cur: $31 (CA-3/89) **82**
Cabernet Sauvignon Napa Valley 1977 Rel: $8.50 Cur: $25 (CA-3/89) **84**
Cabernet Sauvignon Napa Valley 1976 Rel: $6 Cur: $35 (CA-3/89) **78**
Cabernet Sauvignon Napa Valley 1974 Rel: $5.50 Cur: $60 (CA-3/89) **78**
Cabernet Sauvignon Napa Valley Private Reserve 1988 (NR) (5/15/90) (BT) **90+**
Cabernet Sauvignon Napa Valley Private Reserve 1986: Elegant and polished, with spicy oak notes and juicy Cabernet flavor. The currant, herb, dill and plum flavors are well proportioned and complex, with a lingering aftertaste. Drinking well now, but it has the intensity and depth for further development. Try in 1993. Rel: $26 Cur: $29 (11/15/91) **88**
Cabernet Sauvignon Napa Valley Private Reserve 1985: A rich, bold and complex wine, with intense, concentrated currant, plum, chocolate and spice flavors that are lavishly oaked and very well balanced, finishing with layers of flavor and a sense of elegance that goes on and on. Tempting now, but should peak around 1993. Tasted twice. 2,175 cases made. Rel: $24 Cur: $28 (7/15/90) CS **91**
Cabernet Sauvignon Napa Valley Private Reserve 1984 Ripe and supple with generous cherry, plum, cedar, anise and olive flavors that are rich and tannic yet with enough forward fruit. There's a hard edge to it, indicating it is best to lay it down until 1994. Rel: $20 Cur: $25 (7/15/89) **87**
Cabernet Sauvignon Napa Valley Private Reserve 1983 Rel: $18 Cur: $30 (CA-3/89) **84**
Cabernet Sauvignon Napa Valley Private Reserve 1982 Rel: $16 Cur: $27 (CA-3/89) **85**
Cabernet Sauvignon Napa Valley Private Reserve 1981 Rel: $16 Cur: $35 (CA-3/89) **87**
Cabernet Sauvignon Napa Valley Private Reserve 1980 $34 (CA-3/89) **85**

RENAISSANCE
Cabernet Sauvignon North Yuba 1986: A fragrant wine, with ripe currant and berry aromas and flavors, but sufficiently tannic to need until 1996 to '99 to soften up enough to let those flavors through. A risk to cellar, but probably worth it. $15 (7/15/91) **83**

RICHARDSON
Cabernet Sauvignon Sonoma Valley 1985 $12 (11/30/88) **78**
Cabernet Sauvignon Sonoma Valley Horne 1989: Decidedly minty, with strong menthol flavors that dominate the cherry and berry-scented flavors. Not too tannic and ready to drink now. Tasted twice, with consistent notes. $14 (11/15/91) **78**
Synergy California 1989: Ripe and supple, with smoky, chocolaty flavors held firmly in check by tight tannins. Good, but uncomplicated. Best to cellar until about 1995. $15 (11/15/91) **83**
Synergy Los Carneros 1989: Ripe and fleshy, with sharply focused currant, black cherry and cedar flavors that are complex and firmly tannic. Best to cellar until 1995. 400 cases made. $15 (5/31/92) **84**

RIDGE
Cabernet Sauvignon Howell Mountain 1983 $12 (3/16/86) **83**
Cabernet Sauvignon Howell Mountain 1982 $12 (6/01/85) **88**
Cabernet Sauvignon Napa County 1981 $12 (2/15/84) **63**
Cabernet Sauvignon Napa County York Creek 1986 $18 (CA-3/89) **88**
Cabernet Sauvignon Napa County York Creek 1985 Rel: $16 Cur: $20 (CA-3/89) **92**
Cabernet Sauvignon Napa County York Creek 1984 Rel: $14 Cur: $19 (CA-3/89) **88**
Cabernet Sauvignon Napa County York Creek 1983 Rel: $12 Cur: $20 (CA-3/89) **73**
Cabernet Sauvignon Napa County York Creek 1982 Rel: $12 Cur: $25 (CA-3/89) **73**
Cabernet Sauvignon Napa County York Creek 1981 Rel: $12 Cur: $23 (CA-3/89) **76**
Cabernet Sauvignon Napa County York Creek 1980 Rel: $12 Cur: $30 (CA-3/89) **88**
Cabernet Sauvignon Napa County York Creek 1979 Rel: $12 Cur: $27 (CA-3/89) **88**
Cabernet Sauvignon Napa County York Creek 1978 Rel: $12 Cur: $30 (CA-3/89) **87**
Cabernet Sauvignon Napa County York Creek 1977 Rel: $12 Cur: $35 (CA-3/89) **88**
Cabernet Sauvignon Napa County York Creek 1976 Rel: $10 Cur: $27 (CA-3/89) **68**
Cabernet Sauvignon Napa County York Creek 1975 Rel: $10 Cur: $60 (CA-3/89) **87**

Cabernet Sauvignon Napa County York Creek 1974 Rel: $6.75 Cur: $87 (CA-3/89) **87**

Cabernet Sauvignon Santa Barbara County Tepusquet Vineyard 1981 $9 (4/16/84) **83**

Cabernet Sauvignon Santa Cruz Mountains 1989: Has plenty of complexity in the flavors—chocolate, earth, cedar and bay leaf—but it's light on fruit. Medium-bodied, with firm tannins. Drink in 1993 to '96. 2,850 cases made. $12 (3/31/92) **82**

Cabernet Sauvignon Santa Cruz Mountains 1986: Funky style, with intense oak and barnyardy flavors that dominate the ripe Cabernet flavor. Has limited appeal. Drink now to 1996. Tasted three times. $15 (10/31/89) **68**

Cabernet Sauvignon Santa Cruz Mountains 1985 $12 (6/15/89) **64**

Cabernet Sauvignon Santa Cruz Mountains 1984 $12 (6/15/87) **64**

Cabernet Sauvignon Santa Cruz Mountains 1983 Rel: $12 Cur: $20 (CA-3/89) **84**

Cabernet Sauvignon Santa Cruz Mountains Jimsomare 1985 $16 (2/15/89) **87**

Cabernet Sauvignon Santa Cruz Mountains Jimsomare 1984 $16 (10/31/87) **69**

Cabernet Sauvignon Santa Cruz Mountains Jimsomare 1983 $10 (11/30/86) **78**

Cabernet Sauvignon Santa Cruz Mountains Jimsomare-Monte Bello 1981 $12 (1/01/85) **87**

Cabernet Sauvignon Santa Cruz Mountains Monte Bello 1991: Thick and concentrated, with floral aromas and rich, spicy currant, plum and berry flavors. Elegant despite its power. May be the best Monte Bello since 1985. 10 percent Merlot and 5 percent Petit Verdot. 3,000 cases made. (NR) (5/15/92) (BT) **90+**

Cabernet Sauvignon Santa Cruz Mountains Monte Bello 1990 (NR) (5/15/91) (BT) **90+**

Cabernet Sauvignon Santa Cruz Mountains Monte Bello 1988: Strong meaty, vegetal and smoky aromas and flavors wrap tightly around a modest core of raspberry and currant in this raw, tough-hided wine that needs until 1996 to '99 to shed its tannin and show what it has. Tasted four times. Previous bottles tasted heavy and medicinal. 2,694 cases made. $60 (1/31/92) **84**

Cabernet Sauvignon Santa Cruz Mountains Monte Bello 1987: Powerful and complex but marked by earth, mushroom and leather overtones to the deep, concentrated currant flavor. A good wine for those who like the funkier flavors of Bordeaux. Cellar until 1995 to '98. Tasted twice. 1,117 cases made. Rel: $45 Cur: $52 (11/15/90) **88**

Cabernet Sauvignon Santa Cruz Mountains Monte Bello 1986: Heavy-handed with oak. Leafy, earthy flavors challenge the Cabernet and chocolate flavors. The finish gets woody and tannic. Best to let it sit until 1993 and beyond. Tasted three times. Beware of bottle variation. Rel: $35 Cur: $40 (9/15/89) **82**

Cabernet Sauvignon Santa Cruz Mountains Monte Bello 1985: Rich, tannic, intense and young, but it's packed with concentrated plum, currant, mint, toast and chocolate flavors that unfold with elegance and finesse. Will only get better and more complex with time. Built to last until 2000. Rel: $40 Cur: $89 (7/15/88) CS **95**

Cabernet Sauvignon Santa Cruz Mountains Monte Bello 1984 Rel: $35 Cur: $83 (CA-3/89) **97**

Cabernet Sauvignon Santa Cruz Mountains Monte Bello 1984 Rel: $35 Cur: $83 (9/15/87) CS **95**

Cabernet Sauvignon Santa Cruz Mountains Monte Bello 1982 Rel: $18 Cur: $30 (CA-3/89) **75**

Cabernet Sauvignon Santa Cruz Mountains Monte Bello 1981 Rel: $25 Cur: $64 (CA-3/89) **92**

Cabernet Sauvignon Santa Cruz Mountains Monte Bello 1980 Rel: $30 Cur: $57 (CA-3/89) **80**

Cabernet Sauvignon Santa Cruz Mountains Monte Bello 1978 Rel: $30 Cur: $100 (CA-3/89) **91**

Cabernet Sauvignon Santa Cruz Mountains Monte Bello 1978 Rel: $30 Cur: $100 (10/16/83) CS **91**

Cabernet Sauvignon Santa Cruz Mountains Monte Bello 1977 Rel: $40 Cur: $86 (CA-3/89) **94**

Cabernet Sauvignon Santa Cruz Mountains Monte Bello 1976 Rel: $15 Cur: $57 (CA-3/89) **83**

Cabernet Sauvignon Santa Cruz Mountains Monte Bello 1975 Rel: $10 Cur: $41 (CA-3/89) **88**

Cabernet Sauvignon Santa Cruz Mountains Monte Bello 1974 Rel: $12 Cur: $160 (CA-3/89) **93**

Cabernet Sauvignon Santa Cruz Mountains Monte Bello 1973 Rel: $10 Cur: $110 (CA-3/89) **87**

Cabernet Sauvignon Santa Cruz Mountains Monte Bello 1972 Rel: $10 Cur: $90 (CA-3/89) **84**

Cabernet Sauvignon Santa Cruz Mountains Monte Bello 1971 Rel: $10 Cur: $135 (CA-3/89) **85**

Cabernet Sauvignon Santa Cruz Mountains Monte Bello 1970 Rel: $10 Cur: $220 (CA-3/89) **96**

Cabernet Sauvignon Santa Cruz Mountains Monte Bello 1969 Rel: $7.50 Cur: $200 (CA-3/89) **92**

Cabernet Sauvignon Santa Cruz Mountains Monte Bello 1968 Rel: $7.50 Cur: $200 (CA-3/89) **87**

Cabernet Sauvignon Santa Cruz Mountains Monte Bello 1965 Rel: $6.50 Cur: $260 (CA-3/89) **86**

Cabernet Sauvignon Santa Cruz Mountains Monte Bello 1964 Rel: $6.50 Cur: $300 (CA-3/89) **90**

Cabernet Sauvignon Santa Cruz Mountains Monte Bello 1963 Rel: $5 Cur: $490 (CA-3/89) **70**

RIVER OAKS

Cabernet Sauvignon North Coast 1984 $6 (10/15/87) **75**

Cabernet Sauvignon Sonoma County 1983 $6 (12/15/86) **75**

Cabernet Sauvignon Sonoma County 1982 $6 (4/01/85) BB **82**

Cabernet Sauvignon Sonoma County 1981 $6 (7/01/84) **76**

RIVERSIDE FARM

Cabernet Sauvignon California 1985 $4.50 (5/31/88) **72**

Cabernet Sauvignon North Coast 1983 $3.75 (9/15/86) **77**

ROCKING HORSE

Cabernet Sauvignon Napa Valley Hillside Cuvée 1989: Lively and fruity, with a nice frame of buttery oak shading the rich currant and plum notes. Has plenty of flavor for drinking soon. $17 (3/31/92) **85**

ROLLING HILLS

Cabernet Sauvignon California 1987: Woody tasting at this young age but has great concentration of black cherry and currant flavors plus strong tannins. A deliciously fruity, long finish indicates it may improve nicely if cellared until 1995. $7 (12/15/89) BB **86**

ROMBAUER

Cabernet Sauvignon Napa Valley 1987: A generous, supple wine, with chewy tannins and plenty of herb, currant and black cherry flavors. Picks up a touch of anise on the aftertaste, but probably best to cellar until 1994 for it to soften. 2,400 cases made. $16 (11/15/91) **87**

Cabernet Sauvignon Napa Valley 1986: Firm and tannic, but the underlying texture is smooth and silky, with flavors that are subtle and concentrated. Plum, currant and chocolate flavors slide smoothly into a long and tasty finish. Drinkable now. Rel: $15 Cur: $18 (4/15/90) **88**

Cabernet Sauvignon Napa Valley 1985: Fairly hard and tannic for an 1985, but there's pretty plum and currant flavors underneath all the wood and tannin. Needs time to soften. Drink in 1994 at the earliest. Showed better than in a previous tasting. Rel: $14.75 Cur: $20 (4/30/89) **85**

Cabernet Sauvignon Napa Valley 1984 Rel: $13.50 Cur: $21 (CA-3/89) **84**

Cabernet Sauvignon Napa Valley 1983 Rel: $13.50 Cur: $19 (CA-3/89) **73**

Cabernet Sauvignon Napa Valley 1982 Rel: $12 Cur: $35 (CA-3/89) **83**

Cabernet Sauvignon Napa Valley 1981 Rel: $12 Cur: $24 (CA-3/89) **82**

Cabernet Sauvignon Napa Valley 1980 Rel: $10 Cur: $25 (CA-3/89) **86**

Le Meilleur du Chai Napa Valley 1986: Distinct for its minty dill aromas, this is fairly tight and dry on the palate, lacking richness, although anise and spice flavors fan out on the finish. Drink in 1993 to '98. Tasted twice. 515 cases made. $35 (5/15/91) **84**

Le Meilleur du Chai Napa Valley 1985: Elegant and complex, with layers of currant, cedar and cherry flavors that are supple and intense before the tannins clamp down. Will require patience, but then it should offer rewards. Drink 1995 to 2003. Rel: $37.50 Cur: $43 (10/31/89) **90**

Le Meilleur du Chai Napa Valley 1984: Elegant and focused, with pretty black cherry, currant and spicy tobacco flavors and firm acidity and tannins that give it structure and depth. Oaky on the finish, but the fruit comes through. Drink in 1995. Rel: $32.50 Cur: $40 (3/31/89) **94**

Le Meilleur du Chai Napa Valley 1983 Rel: $30 Cur: $43 (CA-3/89) **90**

ROUDON-SMITH

Cabernet Sauvignon Santa Cruz Mountains 1986: Rough-and-tumble and in need of cellaring, this is tannic, tough and slightly bitter now, with wild berry, currant, oak and cedar flavors. The finish gets awfully dry and doesn't have much fruit. Perhaps with time it will mellow; cellar until 1993. $12 (3/15/91) **81**

Cabernet Sauvignon Santa Cruz Mountains 1984 $12 (6/30/88) **78**

ROUND HILL

Cabernet Sauvignon California House Lot 5 NV $5 (9/30/86) BB **76**

Cabernet Sauvignon California House Lot 6 NV $5 (10/15/87) **72**

Cabernet Sauvignon California House Lot 7 NV: Spicy and peppery on the nose, but thin and tart on the palate, with crisp cherry and cranberry flavors and not much tannin. Drink now. $6.25 (2/15/89) **78**

Cabernet Sauvignon California House Lot 8 NV: A broad wine, with enough maturity to drink now. Cedar, blackberry and herbal flavors are supported by medium tannins and a decent acid balance, but a dusty, tired aroma holds it back. $6.25 (7/31/91) **79**

Cabernet Sauvignon Napa Valley 1988: Soft and simple, offering plenty of pleasant spice notes and a hint of herbs around the edges. Fine to drink now. 4,032 cases made. $9 (11/15/91) **81**

Cabernet Sauvignon Napa Valley 1986 $8 (10/15/88) **82**

Cabernet Sauvignon Napa Valley 1984 $8.50 (5/31/88) **84**

Cabernet Sauvignon Napa Valley 1982 $9 (5/16/86) **88**

Cabernet Sauvignon Napa Valley 1981 $9 (3/16/85) **86**

Cabernet Sauvignon Napa Valley 1980 $7.50 (4/16/84) **81**

Cabernet Sauvignon Napa Valley Reserve 1987: Firm in texture, modest in aroma and solid in flavor, offering a medium level of black cherry, toast and herbal flavors. Drinkable now. $11 (11/15/91) **77**

Cabernet Sauvignon Napa Valley Reserve 1986: Youthful, tannic and medium-bodied, with solid berry flavors and hints of raspberry and plum. Should have enough balance to drink in 1993. $9 (6/30/90) **80**

Cabernet Sauvignon Napa Valley Reserve 1985 $10.50 (5/31/88) **86**

Cabernet Sauvignon Napa Valley Reserve 1984 $10 (10/31/87) **88**

Cabernet Sauvignon Napa Valley Reserve 1983 $9.50 (12/15/86) **92**

RUBISSOW-SARGENT

Cabernet Sauvignon Mt. Veeder 1988: Tough and tannic, with a modest concentration of cedar-tinged currant and berry flavors struggling to get through. Succeeds enough to suggest this should improve through 1996 to '98. Needs every bit of that time to soften its rough edges. 1,007 cases made. $16 (4/15/92) **87**

RUTHERFORD ESTATE

Cabernet Sauvignon Napa Valley 1986: Firm and crisp, with a slightly medicinal edge to the otherwise well-formed currant and plum flavors. Drinkable now, although the tannins could use until 1993 or '94 to soften more. $7 (11/15/91) **80**

Cabernet Sauvignon Napa Valley 1984 $5 (11/15/87) **72**

RUTHERFORD HILL

Cabernet Sauvignon Napa Valley 1986: Musty, muddy aromas and flavors cut through the ripe fruit and make this wine hard to drink pleasurably. Tasted twice, with consistent results. Rel: $14 Cur: $17 (2/28/91) **68**

Cabernet Sauvignon Napa Valley 1985: Extremely herbal, with layers of chocolate, currant, berry and oak flavors that are well balanced. Supple enough to drink now. Rel: $14 Cur: $17 (4/30/90) **82**

Cabernet Sauvignon Napa Valley 1984 Rel: $12.50 Cur: $17 (CA-3/89) **88**

Cabernet Sauvignon Napa Valley 1983 Rel: $12.50 Cur: $22 (CA-3/89) **83**

Cabernet Sauvignon Napa Valley 1982 Rel: $12.50 Cur: $25 (CA-3/89) **83**

Cabernet Sauvignon Napa Valley 1981 Rel: $11.50 Cur: $22 (CA-3/89) **85**

Cabernet Sauvignon Napa Valley 1980 Rel: $11.50 Cur: $21 (CA-3/89) **82**

Cabernet Sauvignon Napa Valley 1979 Rel: $11.50 Cur: $22 (CA-3/89) **87**

Cabernet Sauvignon Napa Valley 1978 Rel: $12 Cur: $25 (CA-3/89) **82**

Cabernet Sauvignon Napa Valley 1977 Rel: $10 Cur: $18 (CA-3/89) **72**

Cabernet Sauvignon Napa Valley 1976 Rel: $9 Cur: $17 (CA-3/89) **73**

Cabernet Sauvignon Napa Valley 1975 Rel: $9 Cur: $18 (CA-3/89) **69**

Cabernet Sauvignon Napa Valley Cask Lot 2 Limited Edition 1980 Rel: $11.50 Cur: $21 (CA-3/89) **88**

Cabernet Sauvignon Napa Valley XVS 1986 $32 (CA-3/89) **88**

Cabernet Sauvignon Napa Valley XVS 1985: Rich and concentrated, packed with toasty oak, ripe black cherry, currant and chocolate notes that finish with a good dose of tannin and coffee and cedar notes. Needs time to soften. Rel: $25 Cur: $29 (4/30/89) **88**

RUTHERFORD RANCH

Cabernet Sauvignon Napa Valley 1987: A hard-edged, tannic wine, with lots of oak that tends to override the fruit flavor. Lacks generosity, but the tough plum and currant flavors are attractive. Needs cellaring until 1996 or '97 to soften. $13 (4/30/91) **83**

Cabernet Sauvignon Napa Valley 1985: A tight, sharply focused, richly flavored wine, with cedary oak, weedy black currant, mint and black cherry flavors that are elegant and graceful despite the veil of tannins. The intensity and concentration of fruit promise more than is showing now. Best to cellar until 1993 at the earliest. 2,200 cases made. Rel: $11 Cur: $15 (5/15/90) SS **92**

Cabernet Sauvignon Napa Valley 1984: Still tight and firm, with ripe berry and cassis aromas and flavors and tart balance, long and sharply focused, with enough flavor and tannin to cellar until at least 1993 or '94. $12.50 (5/31/89) **85**

Cabernet Sauvignon Napa Valley 1983 $10.25 (12/31/87) **83**

Cabernet Sauvignon Napa Valley 1982 $9 (6/15/87) **84**

ST. ANDREW'S WINERY

Cabernet Sauvignon Napa Valley 1986: Impressive for its elegance and balance, this wine manages to provide attractive cherry, currant, herb and spicy oak flavors with supple, elegant, tannins. Flavors carry through on the finish. Drink now to 1995. $14.50 (4/30/90) **87**

Cabernet Sauvignon Napa Valley 1985 $10.50 (5/15/88) **89**

ST. CLEMENT

Cabernet Sauvignon Napa Valley 1988: Supple and generous for an '88, with layers of plum, currant, cherry and spicy oak flavors. Firmly tannic, too, giving it a backbone and strong aftertaste that echoes fruit and oak. Ready now, or cellar until 1994. 1,847 cases made. $20 (3/31/92) **86**

Cabernet Sauvignon Napa Valley 1987: Great cellar candidate from a winery with a fine track record. Offers a wonderful display of ripe, rich currant and plum and blackberry flavors, with subtle oak shadings in the background. The texture is firm and the tannins are round and supple. A complex, concentrated wine. Cellar until at least 1995. 2,248 cases made. Rel: $20 Cur: $23 (9/30/91) CS **90**

Cabernet Sauvignon Napa Valley 1986: With plenty of currant and berry aromas and flavors, touched by herbs and toast on the finish, this intense, concentrated and focused wine is very well made and finely proportioned. It's almost supple enough to drink now, but best to wait until 1993 to '94. 1,872 cases made. Rel: $18 Cur: $21 (9/30/90) **90**

Cabernet Sauvignon Napa Valley 1985 Rel: $17 Cur: $25 (3/15/90) **90**

Cabernet Sauvignon Napa Valley 1984 Rel: $15 Cur: $22 (CA-3/89) **89**

Cabernet Sauvignon Napa Valley 1983 Rel: $14.50 Cur: $20 (CA-3/89) **91**

Cabernet Sauvignon Napa Valley 1982 Rel: $13.50 Cur: $25 (CA-3/89) **91**

Cabernet Sauvignon Napa Valley 1982 Rel: $13.50 Cur: $25 (3/16/85) CS **92**

Cabernet Sauvignon Napa Valley 1981 Rel: $12.50 Cur: $24 (CA-3/89) **85**

Cabernet Sauvignon Napa Valley 1981 Rel: $12.50 Cur: $24 (6/01/84) SS **89**

Cabernet Sauvignon Napa Valley 1980 Rel: $12.50 Cur: $26 (CA-3/89) **82**

Cabernet Sauvignon Napa Valley 1979 Rel: $11 Cur: $38 (CA-3/89) **90**

Cabernet Sauvignon Napa Valley 1978 Rel: $10 Cur: $36 (CA-3/89) **88**

Cabernet Sauvignon Napa Valley 1977 Rel: $10 Cur: $45 (CA-3/89) **90**

Cabernet Sauvignon Napa Valley 1975-'76 Rel: $8 Cur: $50 (CA-3/89) **87**

ST. FRANCIS

Cabernet Sauvignon California 1985 $9 (11/30/87) **88**

Cabernet Sauvignon Sonoma County 1988: Loaded with ripe, rich fruit and an array of herbal scents, this is also lavishly oaked. The fruit pours through, with layers of plum, currant, black cherry and spice notes all combining for a complex wine that has persistence and length. One of the more exciting '88s we've seen. Drink in 1994 to 2000. 1,350 cases made. $14 (8/31/91) **90**

Cabernet Sauvignon Sonoma County 1986: Firm, fruity and generous, full-bodied and robust in style, with focused cassis and cherry flavors and solid tannins. Definitely a wine for the cellar. Try in 1993 to '95. $12 (1/31/90) **89**

Cabernet Sauvignon Sonoma Valley Reserve 1988: Strong earthy, weedy flavors dominate the currant and black cherry flavors. Has good intensity and depth for an '88. The tannins are a bit scratchy—best to cellar until 1995. 1,000 cases made. $24 (8/31/91) **87**

Cabernet Sauvignon Sonoma Valley Reserve (Black Label) 1986 $20 (11/30/89) **94**

Cabernet Sauvignon Sonoma Mountain 1986 (NR) (4/15/88) (BT) **90+**

ST. SUPERY

Cabernet Sauvignon Napa Valley Dollarhide Ranch 1988: An appealing style, with ultraripe plum, jam and spice flavors that are lively and intense up front before the tannins swarm in on the finish. Tempting now, but probably best to cellar until 1994. $13.50 (9/30/91) **85**

Cabernet Sauvignon Napa Valley Dollarhide Ranch 1987: A hard and tannic wine, but with pretty cedar, coffee and currant flavors that rise to the surface. Well balanced, rich and complex, but it needs time to soften. Drink in 1994. $13 (7/15/90) **85**

SANTA BARBARA

Cabernet Sauvignon Santa Ynez Valley 1988: Brightly fruity, a simple wine with concentrated strawberry and raspberry aromas and flavors, shaded toward tea on the finish. Balanced for early drinkability. $12 (11/15/91) **83**

Cabernet Sauvignon Santa Ynez Valley Reserve 1988: A crisp, herbal style, with a nice berry component to the flavors that balances it nicely. A modest wine, with a sense of elegance. Drink now or in 1993. 513 cases made. $18 (11/15/91) **83**

Cabernet Sauvignon Santa Ynez Valley Reserve 1987: The vegetal, herbal aromas and flavors won't be for everyone, and the green bean flavors are an acquired taste, but a streak of raspberry runs through the finish. Drink now to 1994. Tasted twice. 800 cases made. $18 (11/15/90) **77**

Cabernet Sauvignon Santa Ynez Valley Reserve 1984 $13.50 (10/31/87) **81**

Cabernet Sauvignon Santa Ynez Valley Reserve 1974 $16 (12/15/89) **81**

SANTA CRUZ MOUNTAIN

Cabernet Sauvignon Santa Cruz Mountains Bates Ranch 1989 (NR) (5/15/91) (BT) **85+**

Cabernet Sauvignon Santa Cruz Mountains Bates Ranch 1988 (NR) (5/15/90) (BT) **85+**

Cabernet Sauvignon Santa Cruz Mountains Bates Ranch 1987 ($NA) (4/15/89) (BT) **90+**

Cabernet Sauvignon Santa Cruz Mountains Bates Ranch 1986: Thick and rich, with a marvelous density of currant, plum and cedar flavors and hints of herbs on the finish. Already developing a nice bottle bouquet, but needs until at least 1996 to polish the tannins. 994 cases made. Rel: $15 Cur: $18 (11/15/91) **89**

Cabernet Sauvignon Santa Cruz Mountains Bates Ranch 1985 Rel: $15 Cur: $18 (CA-3/89) **92**

Cabernet Sauvignon Santa Cruz Mountains Bates Ranch 1984 Rel: $14 Cur: $18 (CA-3/89) **87**

Cabernet Sauvignon Santa Cruz Mountains Bates Ranch 1983 Rel: $12 Cur: $17 (CA-3/89) **84**

Cabernet Sauvignon Santa Cruz Mountains Bates Ranch 1982 Rel: $12 Cur: $17 (CA-3/89) **72**

Cabernet Sauvignon Santa Cruz Mountains Bates Ranch 1981 Rel: $12 Cur: $20 (CA-3/89) **79**

Cabernet Sauvignon Santa Cruz Mountains Bates Ranch 1980 Rel: $12 Cur: $27 (CA-3/89) **86**

Cabernet Sauvignon Santa Cruz Mountains Bates Ranch 1979 Rel: $12 Cur: $35 (CA-3/89) **79**

Cabernet Sauvignon Santa Cruz Mountains Bates Ranch 1978 Rel: $12 Cur: $30 (CA-3/89) **90**

SANTA YNEZ VALLEY

Cabernet Sauvignon Merlot Santa Barbara County 1987: Light, fruity and very herbal; a style that has limited appeal. Drink now. Tasted twice. $13 (3/31/90) **72**

V. SATTUI

Cabernet Sauvignon Napa Valley Preston Vineyard 1988: Rich, smooth and concentrated, with a solid core of cherry, currant and plum flavors. Picks up a strong leathery note on the aftertaste. Not for everyone, but it has character. Drink in 1994. 2,000 cases made. $20 (11/15/91) **86**

Cabernet Sauvignon Napa Valley Preston Vineyard 1986 Rel: $16.75 Cur: $20 (CA-3/89) **88**

Cabernet Sauvignon Napa Valley Preston Vineyard 1985 Rel: $15.75 Cur: $25 (CA-3/89) **87**

Cabernet Sauvignon Napa Valley Preston Vineyard 1984 Rel: $13.75 Cur: $25 (CA-3/89) **86**

Cabernet Sauvignon Napa Valley Preston Vineyard 1983 Rel: $13.75 Cur: $20 (CA-3/89) **81**

Cabernet Sauvignon Napa Valley Preston Vineyard Reserve 1982 Rel: $22.50 Cur: $45 (CA-3/89) **78**

Cabernet Sauvignon Napa Valley Preston Vineyard Reserve 1980 Rel: $30 Cur: $85 (CA-3/89) **85**

SAUSAL

Cabernet Sauvignon Alexander Valley 1985: Decent flavor, with ripe plum and cherry flavor and hints of herbs. Firm, drying tannins on the finish. Drink now to 1995. $12 (7/31/89) **74**

SBARBORO

Cabernet Sauvignon Sonoma County 1983 $10 (11/15/87) **71**

SEBASTIANI

Cabernet Sauvignon North Coast Proprietor's Reserve 1979 $11 (8/01/84) **58**

Cabernet Sauvignon North Coast Emilia 1986: Earthy, muddy flavors finish tannic and oaky. Too tough and lacking in fruit to go anywhere. Tasted twice. $12.50 (3/31/92) **71**

Cabernet Sauvignon Sonoma County Family Selection 1985 $8 (10/15/88) **80**

Cabernet Sauvignon Sonoma County Reserve 1986: Ripe, rich, lush and concentrated, with lovely plum, currant and black cherry flavors that glide across the palate. Has plenty of tannin and intensity for cellaring, but you can drink it now. Best between 1993 to '97. $13 (1/31/91) **86**

Cabernet Sauvignon Sonoma County Reserve 1985 $12.50 (11/15/90) **86**

Cabernet Sauvignon Sonoma Valley Cherry Block 1985: Ripe, fragrant and complex, with beautifully articulated plum, currant, herb and sweet oak aromas and flavors. Fine tannins click in on the finish, and the length of flavor is impressive. Drink after 1994. $16.50 (3/31/90) **89**

Cabernet Sauvignon Sonoma Valley Eagle Vineyards 1982 $26.50 (9/15/86) **75**

Cabernet Sauvignon Sonoma Valley Eagle Vineyards 1981 $25 (8/01/85) **91**

Cabernet Sauvignon Sonoma Valley Reserve 1982 $11 (12/31/87) **74**

Wildwood Sonoma Valley 1987: A zesty red wine that tries really hard to be graceful. Has plenty of fruit flavor—raspberry, blackberry, tobacco and currant—framed by firm tannins. Well balanced. Start drinking in 1993 or '94. $15 (8/31/91) **86**

SEGHESIO

Cabernet Sauvignon Northern Sonoma 1986: A pleasant everyday wine with clean flavors and good balance. Medium-bodied, with plum and tea flavors. Drink now. Tasted twice. $8 (6/30/90) **76**

Cabernet Sauvignon Northern Sonoma 1985: Balanced and attractive, with enticing herbal aromas that follow through nicely in the mouth with supple, ripe flavors. A nice job; it's drinkable now. $5.50 (4/15/89) BB **84**

Cabernet Sauvignon Northern Sonoma 1983 $6.75 (7/15/88) **69**

Cabernet Sauvignon Northern Sonoma 1982 $5 (4/30/87) **77**

Cabernet Sauvignon Sonoma County 1987 $9 (4/30/91) **85**

SEQUOIA GROVE

Cabernet Sauvignon Napa Valley 1987: Earthy, musty and woody, overshadowing the currant and cherry flavors. An odd wine that's hard to warm up to. Tasted twice, with consistent notes. $18 (11/15/91) **70**

Cabernet Sauvignon Napa County 1986 $16 (CA-3/89) **88**

Cabernet Sauvignon Napa County 1985 Rel: $16 Cur: $21 (CA-3/89) **86**

Cabernet Sauvignon Napa Valley 1984 Rel: $12 Cur: $20 (CA-3/89) **85**

Cabernet Sauvignon Napa Valley Estate 1988 (NR) (5/15/90) (BT) **90+**

Cabernet Sauvignon Napa Valley Estate 1987: A solid wine that's generous with its meaty, smoky notes. Not at all elegant, but the currant and plum flavors emerge on the finish against a background of rustic roughness. Drink after 1996. $26 (11/15/91) **87**

Cabernet Sauvignon Napa Valley Estate 1986: Supple, rich and complex, with chocolate, coffee, mineral, toast and spicy flavors that are clean and correct, but the Cabernet flavor is not as bright and clear as it might be. Drink now to 1999. 1,986 cases made. Rel: $22 Cur: $25 (9/30/89) **84**

Cabernet Sauvignon Napa Valley Estate 1985 Rel: $28 Cur: $34 (CA-3/89) **92**

Cabernet Sauvignon Napa Valley Estate 1982 Rel: $14 Cur: $28 (CA-3/89) **82**

Cabernet Sauvignon Napa-Alexander Valleys 1983 Rel: $12.50 Cur: $18 (CA-3/89) **77**

Cabernet Sauvignon Napa-Alexander Valleys 1982 Rel: $12 Cur: $22 (CA-3/89) **78**

Cabernet Sauvignon Alexander Valley 1981 Rel: $12 Cur: $25 (CA-3/89) **84**

Cabernet Sauvignon Napa Valley 1981 Rel: $12 Cur: $25 (CA-3/89) **80**

Cabernet Sauvignon Napa Valley Cask One 1980 Rel: $12 Cur: $27 (CA-3/89) **85**

Cabernet Sauvignon Napa Valley Cask Two 1980 Rel: $12 Cur: $27 (CA-3/89) **87**

SHADOWBROOK

Cabernet Sauvignon Napa Valley 1985: Despite the extra bottle age, this is still a pretty tough wine, but plenty of generous, mature Cabernet flavors battle the tannins. Should be fine after 1994 or '95. $9.50 (7/15/91) **84**

SHAFER

Cabernet Sauvignon Stags Leap District 1988: Crisp and lively, with some elegance and concentration, offering pleasant plum, berry and coffee aromas and flavors, hinting at cedar on the finish. Balanced for drinking soon or cellaring until 1993 to '95. $19 (8/31/91) **88**

Cabernet Sauvignon Stags Leap District 1987: Has lots of fruit and oak, with ripe currant and cherry flavors framed by toasty, spicy oak that turns chocolaty. Hints of vanilla and berry come through on the finish. Great intensity and depth of fruit. Very complex. 4,900 cases made. Rel: $18 Cur: $21 (7/31/90) **92**

Cabernet Sauvignon Stags Leap District 1986: Elegant and polished, but plenty of tannin to carry the cedary, tobacco-tinged Cabernet flavors of currant and plum through to a long finish. Great depth and finesse now, so imagine what it will be like in 1995. 5,000 cases made. Rel: $16 Cur: $21 (9/30/89) SS **93**

Cabernet Sauvignon Stags Leap District 1985 Rel: $15.50 Cur: $22 (CA-3/89) **91**

Cabernet Sauvignon Stags Leap District 1984 Rel: $14 Cur: $24 (CA-3/89) **91**

Cabernet Sauvignon Stags Leap District 1984 Rel: $14 Cur: $24 (12/15/87) SS **93**

Cabernet Sauvignon Stags Leap District 1983 Rel: $13 Cur: $20 (CA-3/89) **87**

Cabernet Sauvignon Stags Leap District 1982 Rel: $13 Cur: $21 (CA-3/89) **88**

Cabernet Sauvignon Stags Leap District 1980 Rel: $12 Cur: $27 (CA-3/89) **77**

Cabernet Sauvignon Stags Leap District 1979 Rel: $12 Cur: $35 (CA-3/89) **89**

Cabernet Sauvignon Stags Leap District 1978 Rel: $11 Cur: $40 (CA-3/89) **85**

Cabernet Sauvignon Stags Leap District Hillside Select 1991: Tight and compact, with a rich, focused core of currant, plum and cherry flavors. Has plenty of tannins, but they're not out of bounds for this stage. Gaining complexity on the finish. 2,000 cases made. (NR) (5/15/92) (BT) **88+**

Cabernet Sauvignon Stags Leap District Hillside Select 1990 (NR) (5/15/91) (BT) **90+**

Cabernet Sauvignon Stags Leap District Hillside Select 1989 (NR) (5/15/91) (BT) **85+**

Cabernet Sauvignon Stags Leap District Hillside Select 1987 $38 (4/15/89) (BT) **85+**

Cabernet Sauvignon Stags Leap District Hillside Select 1986: Tight, firm and tannic, but it has a solid core of concentrated fruit flavor that echoes cherry, currant, plum and spice, while the texture is developing a smooth, silky quality that lets the fruit and oak glide across the palate. Has plenty of tannin for cellaring. Best in 1995 to 2002. 2,000 cases made. Rel: $32 Cur: $35 (3/15/91) **91**

Cabernet Sauvignon Stags Leap District Hillside Select 1985: Dense in color and flavor, with rich, complex, cedar, herb, currant and cherry flavors that are elegant and stylish, supple tannins and fine balance. Deceptively intense and elegant; the flavors build on the finish. Ready to drink now to 1994. 1,800 cases made. Rel: $24.50 Cur: $30 (5/31/90) CS **91**

Cabernet Sauvignon Stags Leap District Hillside Select 1984 Rel: $24.50 Cur: $33 (4/30/89) **89**

Cabernet Sauvignon Stags Leap District Hillside Select 1983 Rel: $22 Cur: $24 (CA-3/89) **89**

Cabernet Sauvignon Stags Leap District Reserve 1982 Rel: $18 Cur: $35 (CA-3/89) **89**

SHENANDOAH

Cabernet Sauvignon Amador County Artist Series 1987: Full-bodied, thick, ripe and almost chocolaty in flavor, with lots of dense tannins and a very spicy, oaky character. Very flavorful, but will be too heavy-handed for some. Drink after 1995. 985 cases made. $10 (2/28/91) **80**

Cabernet Sauvignon Amador County Artist Series 1986 $12 (10/31/88) **86**

Cabernet Sauvignon Amador County Artist Series 1984 $9 (8/31/87) **89**

SHOWN AND SONS

Cabernet Sauvignon Napa Valley Rutherford 1979 $15 (4/01/84) **63**

SIERRA VISTA

Cabernet Sauvignon El Dorado 1988: Chewy, concentrated and focused, with rough-hewn black cherry and currant-tinged flavors. Has plenty of tannins on the finish, too. Ready now through 1995. 900 cases made. $11 (4/15/92) **84**

Cabernet Sauvignon El Dorado 1984 $9 (3/31/88) **86**

SIGNORELLO

Cabernet Sauvignon Napa Valley Founder's Reserve 1988: Ripe, racy and complex, with rich, deep, tannic, peppery berry-scented flavors, smoky chocolate nuances and a deep plush texture. The flavors on the finish are sharply focused and long. Tempting now, but should improve through 2000. 450 cases made. $25 (5/15/91) **92**

Key to Symbols

The scores reported here are the results of blind tastings conducted by our panel of senior editors. Wines that carry the initials below are results of individual tastings.

THE WINE SPECTATOR 100-POINT SCALE 95-100—Classic, a great wine; ***90-94***—Outstanding, superior character and style; ***80-89***—Good to very good, a wine with special qualities; ***70-79***—Average, drinkable wine that may have minor flaws; ***60-69***—Below average, drinkable but not recommended; ***50-59***—Poor, undrinkable, not recommended. "+"—With a score indicates a range; used primarily with barrel tastings to indicate a preliminary score.

SPECIAL DESIGNATIONS SS—Spectator Selection, CS—Cellar Selection, BB—Best Buy, ($NA)—Price not available, (NR)—Not released.

TASTER'S INITIALS (JG)—Jim Gordon, (HS)—Harvey Steiman, (JL)—James Laube, (JS)—James Suckling, (TM)—Thomas Matthews, (TR)—Terry Robards, (PM)—Per-Henrik Mansson, (BT)—Barrel Tasting (these wines were tasted blind from barrel samples), (CA-date)—*California's Great Cabernets* by James Laube, (CH-date)—*California's Great Chardonnays* by James Laube, (VP-date)—*Vintage Port* by James Suckling.

DATE TASTED Dates in parentheses represent the issue in which the rating was published.

SILVER OAK

Cabernet Sauvignon Alexander Valley 1987: Despite a heavy toast flavor, there's plenty of fruit to admire in this one. The currant, black cherry, plum and herb flavors are neatly wound together and the tannins are supple, but it's best to hold on to this one until at least 1994. Rel: $29 Cur: $31 (10/15/91) **89**

Cabernet Sauvignon Alexander Valley 1986: Smooth, harmonious and distinctive, with well-integrated currant, smoke, herb and meat aromas and flavors marked by lavish oak. A beautifully crafted wine, echoing all the complex flavors on the finish. Almost drinkable now, but better to cellar until 1995. Rel: $26 Cur: $37 (10/31/90) SS **93**

Cabernet Sauvignon Alexander Valley 1985: Extremely rich and oaky with layers of herb, currant and cherry flavors that are very complex and deep. This wine has enormous potential, but needs at least three to five years' cellaring. Drink in 1994 to 2000. Rel: $24 Cur: $61 (10/31/89) **86**

Cabernet Sauvignon Alexander Valley 1984 Rel: $22 Cur: $62 (CA-3/89) **89**

Cabernet Sauvignon Alexander Valley 1983 Rel: $20 Cur: $39 (CA-3/89) **86**

Cabernet Sauvignon Alexander Valley 1982 Rel: $19 Cur: $83 (CA-3/89) **90**

Cabernet Sauvignon Alexander Valley 1982 Rel: $19 Cur: $83 (2/15/87) **90**

Cabernet Sauvignon Alexander Valley 1981 Rel: $19 Cur: $69 (CA-3/89) **86**

Cabernet Sauvignon Alexander Valley 1980 Rel: $18 Cur: $69 (CA-3/89) **88**

Cabernet Sauvignon Alexander Valley 1979 Rel: $16 Cur: $70 (CA-3/89) **85**

Cabernet Sauvignon Alexander Valley 1978 Rel: $16 Cur: $110 (CA-3/89) **93**

Cabernet Sauvignon Alexander Valley 1977 Rel: $14 Cur: $85 (CA-3/89) **88**

Cabernet Sauvignon Alexander Valley 1976 Rel: $12 Cur: $65 (CA-3/89) **86**

Cabernet Sauvignon Alexander Valley 1975 Rel: $10 Cur: $60 (CA-3/89) **88**

Cabernet Sauvignon North Coast 1974 Rel: $8 Cur: $115 (CA-3/89) **93**

Cabernet Sauvignon North Coast 1973 Rel: $7 Cur: $130 (CA-3/89) **81**

Cabernet Sauvignon North Coast 1972 Rel: $6 Cur: $135 (CA-3/89) **86**

Cabernet Sauvignon Napa Valley 1987: Offers a broad array of currant, bay leaf, herb and plum flavors that are austere and compact now, but have good depth and concentration. Young and tight, it needs time for the tannins to soften. Best to cellar until 1995 to '99. Rel: $29 Cur: $34 (10/15/91) **89**

Cabernet Sauvignon Napa Valley 1986: An outstanding wine from an outstanding vintage. Firm in texture and generous in flavor, offering intense currant and dill aromas and flavors that are powerful and long on the finish. This is beautifully made, richly tannic and concentrated. Needs time to shade the flavors—try in 1995 or '96. 3,500 cases made. Rel: $26 Cur: $49 (10/31/90) CS **94**

Cabernet Sauvignon Napa Valley 1985: Remarkably intense and tannic, this 1985 needs years to develop, but the currant, cherry and plum flavors are strong and persistent, long and full on the palate. Young and undeveloped, it should only get better. Drink in 1995 to 2002. Rel: $24 Cur: $68 (10/31/89) **88**

Cabernet Sauvignon Napa Valley 1984 Rel: $22 Cur: $55 (CA-3/89) **86**

Cabernet Sauvignon Napa Valley 1983 Rel: $20 Cur: $37 (CA-3/89) **74**

Cabernet Sauvignon Napa Valley 1982 Rel: $19 Cur: $61 (2/15/87) CS **96**

Cabernet Sauvignon Napa Valley 1981 Rel: $19 Cur: $58 (CA-3/89) **79**

Cabernet Sauvignon Napa Valley 1980 Rel: $18 Cur: $80 (CA-3/89) **73**

Cabernet Sauvignon Napa Valley 1979 Rel: $18 Cur: $75 (CA-3/89) **82**

Cabernet Sauvignon Napa Valley Bonny's Vineyard 1986: A powerful, aromatic wine that's already developing a level of maturity and complexity that suits its nicely focused currant, black cherry and pepper flavors. The fruit holds on against a backdrop of dill and submerged tannins. Best after 1995. Rel: $50 Cur: $60 (10/15/91) **88**

Cabernet Sauvignon Napa Valley Bonny's Vineyard 1985: A distinctive, earthy style, with herb, spice, and mineral flavors that are attractive but thin and uninteresting on the finish. Has limited appeal. Drink now to 1994. Rel: $50 Cur: $74 (11/15/90) **83**

Cabernet Sauvignon Napa Valley Bonny's Vineyard 1984 Rel: $45 Cur: $80 (10/15/89) **84**

Cabernet Sauvignon Napa Valley Bonny's Vineyard 1983 Rel: $40 Cur: $55 (CA-3/89) **82**

Cabernet Sauvignon Napa Valley Bonny's Vineyard 1982 Rel: $35 Cur: $57 (CA-3/89) **78**

Cabernet Sauvignon Napa Valley Bonny's Vineyard 1981 Rel: $35 Cur: $58 (CA-3/89) **77**

Cabernet Sauvignon Napa Valley Bonny's Vineyard 1980 Rel: $30 Cur: $60 (CA-3/89) **70**

Cabernet Sauvignon Napa Valley Bonny's Vineyard 1979 Rel: $30 Cur: $60 (CA-3/89) **72**

SILVERADO

Cabernet Sauvignon Stags Leap District 1988: Young and ripe, with grapey Cabernet flavors that echo cherry and currant. Has medium-bodied, straightforward flavors and moderate tannins. In sync with the '88 vintage, this is more delicate than rich or deep. Ready to drink in 1993 to '97. $16 (3/31/91) **86**

Cabernet Sauvignon Stags Leap District 1987: Another standout from one of California's best wineries. Ripe, round and lovely, bubbling over with spicy strawberry and currant aromas and flavors, long and lively. Should be smooth, elegant and drinkable now. Rel: $14 Cur: $21 (4/15/90) SS **92**

Cabernet Sauvignon Stags Leap District 1986: Deliciously ripe, with rich raspberry, currant and black cherry flavors framed by firm tannins and toasty oak. The firm tannins are typical of the '86 vintage. Best in five to seven years but capable of going 15. At $14, make room for a case. Rel: $14 Cur: $25 (8/31/89) SS **94**

Cabernet Sauvignon Stags Leap District 1985 Rel: $12.50 Cur: $36 (11/15/88) SS **91**

Cabernet Sauvignon Stags Leap District 1984 Rel: $11.50 Cur: $26 (CA-3/89) **91**

Cabernet Sauvignon Stags Leap District 1983 Rel: $11 Cur: $22 (CA-3/89) **88**

Cabernet Sauvignon Stags Leap District 1982 Rel: $11 Cur: $25 (CA-3/89) **88**

Cabernet Sauvignon Stags Leap District 1981 Rel: $11 Cur: $30 (CA-3/89) **90**

Cabernet Sauvignon Stags Leap District Limited Reserve 1987: Dense, concentrated and bursting with plum and currant flavors, with gentle bay leaf and anise overtones and layers of spice and cedar on the long finish. A remarkable wine that is delicious to drink now, but should keep improving through 1996 to '98. 1,526 cases made. Rel: $38 Cur: $43 (10/31/91) **93**

Cabernet Sauvignon Stags Leap District Limited Reserve 1986: The first reserve from Silverado is a classic for the cellar. Plush and generous aromas, with rich and sharply focused flavors, and delicious cherry, plum, currant, oak and spice notes stay with you from start to finish. Tight and concentrated, with a supple texture and firm tannins. Drink in 1996 to 2005. 1,400 cases made. Rel: $35 Cur: $39 (12/15/90) CS **96**

SIMI

Cabernet Sauvignon Sonoma County 1987: Rich, complex and enticing, with intense, well-integrated cherry, toast, currant, plum and chocolate flavors. Broad on the finish, with thick tannins and a touch of leather. Best to cellar until about 1994. $16.50 (5/15/91) **89**

Cabernet Sauvignon Alexander Valley 1986: The sharply focused currant and black cherry flavors in this very ripe, compact and concentrated wine gain intensity toward the finish. A big, complex style with firm tannins, it will require another five to seven years to reach full maturity. Try in 1994 or '95. $15.50 (9/30/90) **88**

Cabernet Sauvignon Sonoma County 1985: Ripe and delicious but elegantly contained in a sharply focused package, playing sweet oak against the beautifully defined Cabernet flavor. Has the finesse and balance to develop in the cellar at least through 1994. Rel: $13 Cur: $21 (9/30/89) **91**

Cabernet Sauvignon Sonoma County 1984 Rel: $11 Cur: $20 (10/31/88) **86**

Cabernet Sauvignon Sonoma County 1982 Rel: $12 Cur: $15 (11/15/86) **90**

Cabernet Sauvignon Alexander Valley 1981 Rel: $11 Cur: $20 (11/01/85) **79**

Cabernet Sauvignon Alexander Valley 1980 Rel: $10 Cur: $28 (7/01/84) **81**

Cabernet Sauvignon Alexander Valley 1979 Rel: $9 Cur: $28 (4/01/84) SS **91**

Cabernet Sauvignon Alexander Valley 1975 Rel: $6 Cur: $32 (CA-3/89) **85**

Cabernet Sauvignon Alexander Valley 1973 Rel: $6 Cur: $25 (CA-3/89) **72**

Cabernet Sauvignon Alexander Valley 1972 Rel: $5 Cur: $25 (CA-3/89) **80**

Cabernet Sauvignon Alexander Valley 1971 Rel: $5 Cur: $30 (CA-3/89) **75**

Cabernet Sauvignon Alexander Valley 1970 Rel: $4.50 Cur: $48 (CA-3/89) **73**

Cabernet Sauvignon Alexander Valley Reserve 1987 $28 (4/15/89) (BT) **90+**

Cabernet Sauvignon Alexander Valley Reserve 1986: Balanced and flavorful, with an elegant feel and plenty of currant, berry and tobacco aromas and flavors that are long and focused on the finish, echoing plum and chocolate. Everything is nicely packed in, so it should come together beautifully with age. The supple texture makes it almost drinkable now, but best after 1994. 1,500 cases made. Rel: $30 Cur: $34 (7/31/91) **89**

Cabernet Sauvignon Alexander Valley Reserve 1985: Dense, rich and complex, this wine keeps unfolding with every sip, offering coffee, cherry, nutmeg, plum, and then herb and currant flavors. It has a velvety texture, with just enough tannin to warrant cellaring through about 1995. Try to resist drinking it before then. 2,300 cases made. Rel: $25 Cur: $29 (8/31/90) SS **94**

Cabernet Sauvignon Alexander Valley Reserve 1984 Rel: $22.50 Cur: $26 (CA-3/89) **92**

Cabernet Sauvignon Sonoma-Napa Counties Reserve 1982 Rel: $20 Cur: $28 (4/15/89) **90**

Cabernet Sauvignon Alexander Valley Reserve 1981 Rel: $25 Cur: $30 (12/15/88) **86**

Cabernet Sauvignon Alexander Valley Reserve 1980 Rel: $20 Cur: $25 (CA-3/89) **84**

Cabernet Sauvignon Alexander Valley Reserve 1979 Rel: $20 Cur: $36 (CA-3/89) **87**

Cabernet Sauvignon Alexander Valley Reserve 1978 Rel: $17 Cur: $42 (CA-3/89) **72**

Cabernet Sauvignon Alexander Valley Reserve 1974 Rel: $20 Cur: $62 (2/15/90) (JG) **85**

Cabernet Sauvignon Alexander Valley Special Reserve 1974 Rel: $20 Cur: $62 (CA-3/89) **83**

Cabernet Sauvignon Alexander Valley Special Selection 1977 Rel: $20 Cur: $23 (CA-3/89) **70**

ROBERT SINSKEY

RSV Carneros Claret 1988: Crisp and tart, with lively, clean black cherry, currant, raspberry and herb notes that are elegantly proportioned and stay with you through the finish. The tannins are well integrated. Tempting now, but should hold through 1995. $28 (11/15/91) **89**

SMITH & HOOK

Cabernet Sauvignon Monterey Santa Lucia Highlands 1988: Strong, almost overbearing herb and bay leaf flavors dominate the currant and berry notes. It's also quite tannic and oaky. May always be oaky. Cellar until 1994. 4,700 cases made. $15 (11/15/91) **80**

Cabernet Sauvignon Monterey 1983 $13.50 (11/15/87) **78**

Cabernet Sauvignon Monterey County 1981 $13.50 (12/16/84) **90**

Cabernet Sauvignon Napa County 1985: Well proportioned, with generous plum and cherry aromas and flavors balanced against cedar and tobacco overtones. Drink now. $12 (9/30/89) **88**

Cabernet Sauvignon Napa County 1982 $17 (6/15/87) **79**

SMITH-MADRONE

Cabernet Sauvignon Napa Valley 1985: Tastes mature, bordering on tired. Tannic and herbal in flavor, with hints of currant flavor coming through on the finish. Tasted twice. Rel: $14 Cur: $19 (4/15/90) **74**

Cabernet Sauvignon Napa Valley 1984 Rel: $14 Cur: $25 (CA-3/89) **91**

Cabernet Sauvignon Napa Valley 1983 Rel: $12.50 Cur: $16 (CA-3/89) **84**

Cabernet Sauvignon Napa Valley 1982 Rel: $12.50 Cur: $16 (CA-3/89) **79**

Cabernet Sauvignon Napa Valley 1981 Rel: $12.50 Cur: $16 (CA-3/89) **78**

Cabernet Sauvignon Napa Valley 1980 Rel: $12.50 Cur: $18 (CA-3/89) **79**

Cabernet Sauvignon Napa Valley 1979 Rel: $14 Cur: $25 (CA-3/89) **86**

Cabernet Sauvignon Napa Valley 1978 Rel: $14 Cur: $25 (CA-3/89) **84**

SOBON ESTATE

Cabernet Sauvignon Shenandoah Valley 1987: A big, ripe, herbal, full-throttle wine, with spicy black cherry intensity but not much held back. Doesn't have the complexity to be great, but it has a rustic appeal. Best to hold until 1993 or '94. 425 cases made. $15 (11/30/90) **83**

SOLARI

Cabernet Sauvignon Napa Valley Larkmead Vineyards 1985: Extra ripe and full-bodied, with a soft structure and tannins that really kick in on the finish, this one needs time in the cellar to tame it, but it's iffy how long the fruit will last. Still, it should be very good now. $10 (3/15/90) **80**

Cabernet Sauvignon Napa Valley Larkmead Vineyards 1984 $12 (4/15/88) **80**

SONOMA CREEK

Cabernet Sauvignon Sonoma Valley 1988: Tight, tough tannins run roughshod over the modest cherry and plum flavors, making it a risk to buy. Tannins should mellow by 1994 or later, but will the fruit still be there? $12 (11/15/91) **74**

SONOMA-LOEB

Cabernet Sauvignon Alexander Valley 1988: Lean and crisp, with good blackberry flavors and moderate tannins. Not a giant, but a good, straightforward glass of wine with a touch of spicy complexity. Probably best to drink now to 1995. 1,000 cases made. $10 (2/29/92) **82**

SPOTTSWOODE

Cabernet Sauvignon Napa Valley 1990 (NR) (5/15/91) (BT) **90+**

Cabernet Sauvignon Napa Valley 1989 (NR) (5/15/91) (BT) **90+**

Cabernet Sauvignon Napa Valley 1988: Flavorful and focused, with well-defined currant, berry and plum aromas and flavors that carry through into a finish distinguished by well-refined tannins. Has the elegance and intensity to develop beautifully with cellaring until 1995 or '96. 2,800 cases made. Rel: $36 Cur: $42 (11/15/91) **90**

Cabernet Sauvignon Napa Valley 1987: Lean and powerful, this has sharply focused blackberry, currant and cherry flavors and lovely touches of vanilla, herb and nutmeg in the aroma and on the long finish. An artistocratic, harmonious wine worth cellaring until at least 1995, but you could drink it tonight. 2,750 cases made. Rel: $36 Cur: $60 (9/15/90) SS **96**

Cabernet Sauvignon Napa Valley 1986: Full-throttle Cabernet: big, rich, deep, intense, concentrated and packed with fruit and tannins. The plum, cherry, currant and spice flavors go on and on. Don't drink this one alone—best left in a cellar until 1994 or longer. 2,400 cases made. Rel: $30 Cur: $100 (9/15/89) **95**

Cabernet Sauvignon Napa Valley 1985 Rel: $25 Cur: $122 (11/15/88) CS **95**

Cabernet Sauvignon Napa Valley 1984 Rel: $25 Cur: $75 (CA-3/89) **90**

Cabernet Sauvignon Napa Valley 1983 Rel: $25 Cur: $95 (CA-3/89) **89**

Cabernet Sauvignon Napa Valley 1982 Rel: $18 Cur: $110 (CA-3/89) **90**

SPRING MOUNTAIN

Cabernet Sauvignon Napa Valley 1988 (NA) (5/15/90) (BT) **85+**

Cabernet Sauvignon Napa Valley 1986 (NA) (CA-3/89) **90**

Cabernet Sauvignon Napa Valley 1985: Correct but unexciting, simple berry, cherry and currant flavors are appealing but it lacks the drama and excitement of the best from the wonderful 1985 vintage. Drink now to 1999. 3,396 cases made. $20 (10/15/89) **85**

Cabernet Sauvignon Napa Valley 1984: A very good wine, one of Spring Mountain's finest, with beautifully focused black cherry, currant, anise and plum flavors that are rich, supple, fleshy and elegant. Has the depth and structure for mid-range aging. Coarse on the finish. Drink in 1994 to 2000. Rel: $15 Cur: $18 (3/15/89) **89**

Cabernet Sauvignon Napa Valley 1983 Rel: $15 Cur: $19 (CA-3/89) **79**

Cabernet Sauvignon Napa Valley 1982 Rel: $15 Cur: $18 (CA-3/89) **66**

Cabernet Sauvignon Napa Valley 1981 Rel: $14 Cur: $16 (CA-3/89) **78**

Cabernet Sauvignon Napa Valley 1980 Rel: $13 Cur: $19 (CA-3/89) **86**

Cabernet Sauvignon Napa Valley 1979 Rel: $13 Cur: $27 (CA-3/89) **87**

Cabernet Sauvignon Napa Valley 1978 Rel: $12 Cur: $25 (CA-3/89) **83**

Cabernet Sauvignon Napa Valley 1977 Rel: $9.50 Cur: $39 (CA-3/89) **85**

STAG'S LEAP WINE CELLARS

Cabernet Sauvignon Napa Valley 1988: Ripe, generous and almost opulent, brimming with berry and currant aromas and flavors that linger on the complex, sophisticated finish. Has a smooth texture and fine tannins. Should keep evolving through at least 1994 or '95. $18 (6/15/91) **90**

Cabernet Sauvignon Napa Valley 1987: Very firm and tart, with strong earthy overtones to the modest cherry flavor, getting a bit barnyardy and funky on the finish. Drinkable now. $18 (8/31/90) **75**

Cabernet Sauvignon Napa Valley 1986: Despite an herbal edge, this has lovely plum and currant flavor at the core and a supple texture. A bit tannic and oaky, but otherwise it's well balanced. Drink now. $18 (6/15/89) **82**

Cabernet Sauvignon Napa Valley 1985 $16 (9/15/88) **90**

Cabernet Sauvignon Napa Valley 1984 $15 (7/15/87) **83**

Cabernet Sauvignon Napa Valley 1981 $15 (12/16/84) **82**

Stags Leap District Stag's Leap Vineyards Cask 23 1987 Intensely herbal and spicy, with dill, currant, bay leaf and spice flavors that are stylish and attractive. Finishes with a good dose of tannin, but also plenty of flavor. Not for everyone, but those who prefer an herbal, earthy edge should find this quite appealing. Drink after 1995. Rel: $55 Cur: $60 (11/15/91) **87**

Stags Leap District Stag's Leap Vineyards Cask 23 1986: Heady aromas of earth, olives and caramel lead to polished, elegant flavors of herbs, black currant and cherry that get deeper and deeper. Very layered and complex, with lots of fine tannins, a long, expansive finish and enough intensity to suggest development through 1995. Rel: $55 Cur: $73 (11/15/90) **93**

Stags Leap District Stag's Leap Vineyards Cask 23 1985: A big, powerful, distinctive wine that balances its intense currant and cherry flavor against an onslaught of earthy, tobacco aromas and flavors. It will not appeal to everyone. Enormously complex, deep and long, this is a wine whose flavors should keep developing through 1995 to 2000. 1,018 cases made. Rel: $75 Cur: $165 (11/30/89) **96**

Cabernet Sauvignon Stags Leap District Stag's Leap Vineyards Cask 23 1984 Rel: $40 Cur: $88 (CA-3/89) **93**

Cabernet Sauvignon Stags Leap District Stag's Leap Vineyards Cask 23 1983 Rel: $35 Cur: $60 (CA-3/89) **88**

Cabernet Sauvignon Stags Leap District Stag's Leap Vineyards Cask 23 1979 Rel: $35 Cur: $85 (CA-3/89) **88**

Cabernet Sauvignon Stags Leap District Stag's Leap Vineyards Cask 23 1978 Rel: $35 Cur: $150 (CA-3/89) **92**

Cabernet Sauvignon Stags Leap District Stag's Leap Vineyards Cask 23 1977 Rel: $30 Cur: $73 (12/01/83) CS **91**

Cabernet Sauvignon Stags Leap District Stag's Leap Vineyards Cask 23 1974 Rel: $12 Cur: $135 (CA-3/89) **88**

Cabernet Sauvignon Stags Leap District Stag's Leap Vineyards-Fay Vineyard Blend 1989 (NR) (5/15/91) (BT) **85+**

Cabernet Sauvignon Stags Leap District Stag's Leap Vineyard 1988: Smooth and supple, with aromas and flavors that lean toward olives and herbs. Shows a modest concentration of currant and berry flavors. An interesting wine that evolves in the glass. Approaching drinkability—best after 1993. Tasted twice. $32 (11/15/91) **85**

Cabernet Sauvignon Stags Leap District Stag's Leap Vineyard 1987: Decidedly herbal, earthy and ripe, with rich plum, cherry, dill and pickle flavors that turn dry and bitter on the finish. Drink now to 1996. $28 (11/15/90) **77**

Cabernet Sauvignon Stags Leap District Stag's Leap Vineyard 1986: Distinctive for its rich, deep, cedar, herb and currant notes and enormous concentration. Elegant and supple with firm tannins, this wine is nearing drinkablity but should age well for another decade or so. Drink in 1993 to 1996. Rel: $28 Cur: $30 (11/30/89) **91**

Cabernet Sauvignon Stags Leap District Stag's Leap Vineyards 1985 Rel: $26 Cur: $42 (CA-3/89) **94**

Cabernet Sauvignon Stags Leap District Stag's Leap Vineyards 1984 Rel: $21 Cur: $28 (CA-3/89) **92**

Cabernet Sauvignon Stags Leap District Stag's Leap Vineyards 1983 Rel: $18 Cur: $33 (CA-3/89) **73**

Cabernet Sauvignon Stags Leap District Stag's Leap Vineyards 1982 Rel: $16.50 Cur: $28 (CA-3/89) **75**

Cabernet Sauvignon Stags Leap District Stag's Leap Vineyards 1981 Rel: $15 Cur: $35 (9/16/84) CS **90**

Cabernet Sauvignon Stags Leap District Stag's Leap Vineyards 1979 Rel: $15 Cur: $40 (CA-3/89) **68**

Cabernet Sauvignon Stags Leap District Stag's Leap Vineyards 1978 Rel: $13.50 Cur: $42 (CA-3/89) **89**

Cabernet Sauvignon Stags Leap District Stag's Leap Vineyards 1977 Rel: $9 Cur: $29 (CA-3/89) **85**

Cabernet Sauvignon Stags Leap District Stag's Leap Vineyards 1976 Rel: $10 Cur: $75 (CA-3/89) **73**

Cabernet Sauvignon Stags Leap District Stag's Leap Vineyards 1975 Rel: $8.50 Cur: $68 (CA-3/89) **74**

Cabernet Sauvignon Stags Leap District Stag's Leap Vineyards 1974 Rel: $8 Cur: $101 (2/15/90) **83**

Cabernet Sauvignon Stags Leap District Stag's Leap Vineyards 1973 Rel: $6 Cur: $150 (CA-3/89) **86**

Cabernet Sauvignon Stags Leap District Stag's Leap Vineyards 1972 Rel: $5.50 Cur: $90 (CA-3/89) **70**

Cabernet Sauvignon Stags Leap District Stag's Leap Vineyards Lot 2 1977 Rel: $10 Cur: $40 (CA-3/89) **90**

Cabernet Sauvignon Stags Leap District Stag's Leap Vineyards Lot 2 1976 Rel: $11 Cur: $23 (CA-3/89) **80**

STAGS' LEAP WINERY

Cabernet Sauvignon Stags Leap District 1987: A strong herbal note dominates the ripe plum and currant flavors, and it's quite oaky, but the flavors are concentrated and persistent, fanning out on the finish. Drink in 1995 to 2000. $18 (6/30/91) **89**

Cabernet Sauvignon Stags Leap District 1986: Leans toward the herbal side of Cabernet, with plenty of currant and plum flavors that are rich, supple and well proportioned, finishing with firm tannins and a touch of earthiness. Cellar until 1994 or so. $17 (10/31/90) **89**

Cabernet Sauvignon Stags Leap District 1985 Rel: $15 Cur: $18 (CA-3/89) **85**

Cabernet Sauvignon Stags Leap District 1984 Rel: $13.50 Cur: $25 (CA-3/89) **87**

Cabernet Sauvignon Stags Leap District 1983 Rel: $12.75 Cur: $20 (CA-3/89) **80**

Cabernet Sauvignon Stags Leap District 1982 Rel: $12 Cur: $20 (CA-3/89) **71**

Cabernet Sauvignon Stags Leap District 1981 Rel: $11 Cur: $22 (CA-3/89) **85**

STAR HILL

Cabernet Sauvignon Napa Valley Doc's Reserve 1987: Very ripe and lavishly oaked, offering a core of black cherry and currant flavor that persists into the finish. Not a graceful wine, but cellaring until 1995 to '97 could polish it nicely. 200 cases made. $24 (11/15/91) **88**

STELTZNER

Cabernet Sauvignon Stags Leap District 1990 (NR) (5/15/91) (BT) **90+**

Cabernet Sauvignon Stags Leap District 1989 (NR) (5/15/91) (BT) **85+**

Cabernet Sauvignon Stags Leap District 1988 $16 (5/15/90) (BT) **85+**

Cabernet Sauvignon Stags Leap District 1987: A stylish wine, with pretty herb, currant, cherry and spice flavors that hang together nicely. The finish is tight and firmly tannic, with hints of cedar and coffee peeking through. Complex. Drink in 1995. Rel: $16 Cur: $20 (11/15/91) **86**

Cabernet Sauvignon Stags Leap District 1986: Ripe, smooth, rich and elegant, a wine with lots of pepper and spice to add to the ripe berry, currant and cherry flavor. The fruit is vibrant and complex and long and full on the finish, with just enough tannin for aging a decade. Drink in 1994 to 1998. Rel: $16 Cur: $19 (12/31/89) **91**

Cabernet Sauvignon Stags Leap District 1985 Rel: $16 Cur: $20 (CA-3/89) **93**

Cabernet Sauvignon Stags Leap District 1984 Rel: $15 Cur: $19 (CA-3/89) **91**

Cabernet Sauvignon Stags Leap District 1983 Rel: $14 Cur: $18 (CA-3/89) **90**

Cabernet Sauvignon Stags Leap District 1982 Rel: $14 Cur: $27 (CA-3/89) **90**

Cabernet Sauvignon Stags Leap District 1982 Rel: $14 Cur: $27 (9/01/85) CS **91**

Cabernet Sauvignon Stags Leap District 1981 Rel: $14 Cur: $33 (CA-3/89) **89**

Cabernet Sauvignon Stags Leap District 1980 Rel: $14 Cur: $30 (CA-3/89) **88**

Cabernet Sauvignon Stags Leap District 1979 Rel: $14 Cur: $42 (CA-3/89) **89**

Cabernet Sauvignon Stags Leap District 1978 Rel: $14 Cur: $45 (CA-3/89) **87**

Cabernet Sauvignon Stags Leap District 1977 Rel: $14 Cur: $45 (CA-3/89) **85**

ROBERT STEMMLER

Cabernet Sauvignon Sonoma County 1982 $15 (4/01/85) **66**

STEPHENS

Cabernet Sauvignon Napa Valley 1981 $8 (2/15/84) **74**

STERLING

Cabernet Sauvignon Napa Valley 1991: Tight, firm and intense, with sharply focused currant, black cherry and wild berry notes that turn tannic on the finish. 11 percent Merlot, 7 percent Petit Verdot and 1 percent Cabernet Franc. (NR) (5/15/92) (BT) **88+**

Cabernet Sauvignon Napa Valley 1990 (NR) (5/15/91) (BT) **85+**

Cabernet Sauvignon Napa Valley 1989 (NR) (5/15/91) (BT) **80+**

Cabernet Sauvignon Napa Valley 1988: Has an herbal, black currant edge to the flavors, and the tannins are soft in the middle, but firm up on the finish. Lacks concentration for the long haul. Drink in 1993. Rel: $15 Cur: $17 (11/15/91) **80**

Cabernet Sauvignon Napa Valley 1987: Broad and generous, offering ebullient blueberry, raspberry and plum aromas and flavors, with its firm tannins lurking just beneath the surface. Balanced and smooth already. Cellaring until 1993 to '95 could bring more complexity. Rel: $13 Cur: $16 (5/15/90) **91**

Cabernet Sauvignon Napa Valley 1986 Rel: $14.50 Cur: $18 (3/31/89) **91**

Cabernet Sauvignon Napa Valley 1985 Rel: $13 Cur: $17 (5/15/88) **89**

Cabernet Sauvignon Napa Valley 1983 Rel: $12.50 Cur: $21 (2/15/87) **81**

Cabernet Sauvignon Napa Valley 1982 Rel: $12.50 Cur: $19 (5/16/86) **66**

Cabernet Sauvignon Napa Valley 1981 Rel: $12 Cur: $16 (8/01/85) **88**

Cabernet Sauvignon Napa Valley 1980 Rel: $12.50 Cur: $35 (2/15/84) **84**

Cabernet Sauvignon Napa Valley 1978 $26 (6/01/86) **95**

Cabernet Sauvignon Napa Valley 1974 $50 (2/15/90) (JG) **90**

Cabernet Sauvignon Napa Valley Diamond Mountain Ranch 1991: A massive young wine that's deep, dark and powerful, with intense, concentrated currant, herb, wild berry and spice notes. The finish provides a long, full burst of fruit flavor. 20 percent Cabernet Franc and 2 percent Merlot. (NR) (5/15/92) (BT) **91+**

Cabernet Sauvignon Napa Valley Diamond Mountain Ranch 1990 (NR) (5/15/91) (BT) **85+**

Cabernet Sauvignon Napa Valley Diamond Mountain Ranch 1989 (NR) (5/15/91) (BT) **85+**

Cabernet Sauvignon Napa Valley Diamond Mountain Ranch 1988 (NR) (5/15/90) (BT) **85+**

Cabernet Sauvignon Napa Valley Diamond Mountain Ranch 1987: A grand, rich wine, with intense, chewy black cherry, plum and currant flavors that unfold on the palate. Good depth and amplitude keep the flavors lively, and they gain intensity on the finish. Has firm tannins on the finish—best to cellar until 1996 to 2002. 3,600 cases made. Rel: $16 Cur: $19 (11/15/90) **91**

Cabernet Sauvignon Napa Valley Diamond Mountain Ranch 1986: Smooth and elegant, with broad cherry and currant aromas and flavors at the core, supple texture and fine tannins to drink after 1993. Very fine and subtle, but it needs the cellaring to settle down. Rel: $14.50 Cur: $18 (3/15/90) **91**

Cabernet Sauvignon Napa Valley Diamond Mountain Ranch 1985 Rel: $16 Cur: $21 (5/31/89) **88**

Cabernet Sauvignon Napa Valley Diamond Mountain Ranch 1984 Rel: $15 Cur: $18 (CA-3/89) **85**

Cabernet Sauvignon Napa Valley Diamond Mountain Ranch 1983 Rel: $15 Cur: $22 (CA-3/89) **87**

Cabernet Sauvignon Napa Valley Diamond Mountain Ranch 1982 Rel: $15 Cur: $37 (CA-3/89) **82**

Cabernet Sauvignon Napa Valley Diamond Mountain Ranch 1982 Rel: $15 Cur: $37 (11/16/85) CS **94**

Napa Valley Reserve 1991: Intense and tight, with firm currant, floral and berry flavors. Has a lot of everything now, from tannins to spice to fruit. Shows length and complexity on the finish. 64 percent Cabernet Sauvignon, 18 percent Merlot, 10 percent Cabernet Franc and 8 percent Petit Verdot. (NR) (5/15/92) (BT) **88+**

Napa Valley Reserve 1990 (NR) (5/15/91) (BT) **85+**

Napa Valley Reserve 1989 (NR) (5/15/91) (BT) **90+**

Napa Valley Reserve 1988 A modestly flavorful, clean wine that's tight and hard in texture due to drying, tough tannins. Has good tart cherry and herbal flavors, but not much on the finish. Needs until about 1996 to soften. $40 (3/31/92) **85**

Napa Valley Reserve 1987 Deep, rich, intense and concentrated, with layers of black cherry, currant, chocolate, coffee and herbal flavors that are a bit austere now but sharply focused, long and full on the finish. It's fairly tannic, but balanced and won't shortchange you on flavor. Drink between 1996 and 2004. 4,400 cases made. Rel: $43 Cur: $48 (11/15/90) **93**

Napa Valley Reserve 1986 Smooth and absolutely delicious, with disarming currant and plum aromas and flavors and an enormous sense of elegance and grace. Polished and very long; clearly a serious wine, already complex but cellar a few bottles until at least 1995. This reserve has a great track record for aging. 3,432 cases made. Rel: $35 Cur: $44 (3/15/90) CS **95**

Cabernet Sauvignon Napa Valley Reserve 1985 Rel: $30 Cur: $46 (7/15/89) SS **96**

Cabernet Sauvignon Napa Valley Reserve 1984 Rel: $25 Cur: $40 (3/31/89) CS **92**

Cabernet Sauvignon Napa Valley Reserve 1983 Rel: $22.50 Cur: $34 (CA-3/89) **82**

Cabernet Sauvignon Napa Valley Reserve 1982 Rel: $22.50 Cur: $36 (CA-3/89) **75**

Cabernet Sauvignon Napa Valley Reserve 1981 Rel: $22.50 Cur: $29 (CA-3/89) **85**

Key to Symbols

The scores reported here are the results of blind tastings conducted by our panel of senior editors. Wines that carry the initials below are results of individual tastings.

THE WINE SPECTATOR 100-POINT SCALE *95-100*—Classic, a great wine; *90-94*—Outstanding, superior character and style; *80-89*—Good to very good, a wine with special qualities; *70-79*—Average, drinkable wine that may have minor flaws; *60-69*—Below average, drinkable but not recommended; *50-59*—Poor, undrinkable, not recommended. "+"—With a score indicates a range; used primarily with barrel tastings to indicate a preliminary score.

SPECIAL DESIGNATIONS SS—Spectator Selection, CS—Cellar Selection, BB—Best Buy, (SNA)—Price not available, (NR)—Not released.

TASTER'S INITIALS (JG)—Jim Gordon, (HS)—Harvey Steiman, (JL)—James Laube, (JS)—James Suckling, (TM)—Thomas Matthews, (TR)—Terry Robards, (PM)—Per-Henrik Mansson, (BT)—Barrel Tasting (these wines were tasted blind from barrel samples), (CA-date)—*California's Great Cabernets* by James Laube, (CH-date)—*California's Great Chardonnays* by James Laube, (VP-date)—*Vintage Port* by James Suckling.

DATE TASTED Dates in parentheses represent the issue in which the rating was published.

Cabernet Sauvignon Napa Valley Reserve 1980 Rel: $27.50 Cur: $44 (CA-3/89) **91**
Cabernet Sauvignon Napa Valley Reserve 1980 Rel: $27.50 Cur: $44 (11/01/84) CS **90**
Cabernet Sauvignon Napa Valley Reserve 1979 Rel: $27.50 Cur: $50 (CA-3/89) **85**
Cabernet Sauvignon Napa Valley Reserve 1978 Rel: $27.50 Cur: $45 (CA-3/89) **90**
Cabernet Sauvignon Napa Valley Reserve 1977 Rel: $27.50 Cur: $48 (CA-3/89) **93**
Cabernet Sauvignon Napa Valley Reserve 1976 Rel: $25 Cur: $34 (CA-3/89) **76**
Cabernet Sauvignon Napa Valley Reserve 1975 Rel: $20 Cur: $49 (CA-3/89) **78**
Cabernet Sauvignon Napa Valley Reserve 1974 Rel: $20 Cur: $80 (CA-3/89) **90**
Cabernet Sauvignon Napa Valley Reserve 1973 Rel: $10 Cur: $70 (CA-3/89) **89**
Napa Valley Three Palms Vineyard 1991: Tight, young and chewy, packing in ripe berry and currant flavors and ample tannins. 91 percent Merlot, 8 percent Cabernet Franc and 1 percent Cabernet Sauvignon. (NR) (5/15/92) (BT) **86+**
Napa Valley Three Palms Vineyard 1989 (NR) (5/15/91) (BT) **85+**
Napa Valley Three Palms Vineyard 1988 Relatively thin and ungenerous, with pleasant enough currant flavor, but it doesn't have much concentration or structure. Might be better after 1994. Tasted twice. $23 (11/15/91) **79**
Napa Valley Three Palms Vineyard 1987: Tastes big, rough, tannic and young, with a core of currant and black cherry, but the tannins really box it in, making it hard and biting. The structure is there, but it needs time in the cellar to develop complexity. Try in 1994 or '95. $23 (11/15/90) **87**
Napa Valley Three Palms Vineyard 1986 $19 (12/31/89) **86**
Napa Valley Three Palms Vineyard 1985 Rel: $20 Cur: $22 (12/31/88) **93**

STEVENOT
Cabernet Sauvignon Calaveras County 1985: Good but unusual in style. Tastes soft and mature for its age, with oaky, herbal aromas and substantial tannins. $7.50 (6/30/89) **76**
Cabernet Sauvignon Calaveras County Grand Reserve 1987: A full-bodied, tannic wine that's sturdy and flavorful if straightforward in its berry flavors. Has a bit of spicy complexity from oak aging. Probably best to drink about 1993 to '95. $9 (3/31/92) **82**
Cabernet Sauvignon Calaveras County Grand Reserve 1984 $15 (12/31/87) **75**

STONE CREEK
Cabernet Sauvignon Napa Valley Limited Bottling 1986: Has plenty of fresh, ripe Cabernet flavor, with layers of cherry, berry and currant and a good dose of oak and tannin. Well balanced and firmly structured, with good concentration of fruit. Drink in 1993. $10 (6/15/90) **85**
Cabernet Sauvignon Napa Valley Special Selection 1986: Lean and firm in texture, with a strong spice and herb component to the focused currant and black cherry flavors. Cherry notes persist on the finish. Approaching drinkability, may be best around 1993 to '95. $10 (11/15/91) **80**
Cabernet Sauvignon Napa Valley Special Selection 1983 $8.75 (5/31/87) BB **91**

STONEGATE
Cabernet Sauvignon Napa Valley 1991: Hard, tight and tannic, a rough-cut wine now, with crisp currant, berry and plum flavors. Concentrated, but tough to judge. 3,000 cases made. (NR) (5/15/92) (BT) **83+**
Cabernet Sauvignon Napa Valley 1990 (NR) (5/15/91) (BT) **85+**
Cabernet Sauvignon Napa Valley 1989 (NR) (5/15/91) (BT) **80+**
Cabernet Sauvignon Napa Valley 1987: Lean and tart, with cedary black currant aromas and flavors that turn green and tart on the finish. Becomes citrusy rather than rich on the finish. May be better after 1995. 2,800 cases made. $14 (3/31/92) **82**
Cabernet Sauvignon Napa Valley 1986: Earthy, ultraripe and coffeelike, a soft but tannic wine that's awkward at this age, but has ripe plum and prune flavors. Drink now to 1995. Tasted twice. Rel: $15 Cur: $17 (2/28/91) **86**
Cabernet Sauvignon Napa Valley 1985 Rel: $16 Cur: $19 (8/31/90) **86**
Cabernet Sauvignon Napa Valley 1984 Rel: $14 Cur: $17 (CA-3/89) **88**
Cabernet Sauvignon Napa Valley 1982 Rel: $12 Cur: $18 (CA-3/89) **80**
Cabernet Sauvignon Napa Valley 1981 Rel: $12 Cur: $17 (CA-3/89) **79**
Cabernet Sauvignon Napa Valley 1980 Rel: $12 Cur: $22 (CA-3/89) **86**
Cabernet Sauvignon Napa Valley 1979 Rel: $12 Cur: $25 (CA-3/89) **84**
Cabernet Sauvignon Napa Valley 1978 Rel: $12 Cur: $27 (CA-3/89) **91**
Cabernet Sauvignon Napa Valley 1977 Rel: $10 Cur: $25 (CA-3/89) **81**

STRATFORD
Cabernet Sauvignon California 1985 $10 (11/30/88) **83**
Cabernet Sauvignon California 1983 $8.50 (2/15/87) **86**
Cabernet Sauvignon Napa Valley 1987: Deep in color and flavor, with rich, supple currant, plum, cherry and toasty oak flavors that combine to give it complexity and finesse. Flavors are concentrated and firmly tannic. Drink now through 1995. $11.50 (4/30/90) **85**
Cabernet Sauvignon Napa Valley Partners' Reserve 1988: Strange earth and iodine flavors mar the cherry and currant-scented flavor in this one. It comes across as hard and tight, with a salty bitter aftertaste. Tasted three times. $16 (3/15/92) **68**
Cabernet Sauvignon Napa Valley Partners' Reserve 1987 $15.50 (4/30/91) **90**

STREBLOW
Cabernet Sauvignon Napa Valley 1987: Green bean and vegetal flavors compete with currant and plum notes, but those who prefer these flavors will warm up to this wine. Firm and tannic. Best around 1993. $16 (10/15/90) **79**
Cabernet Sauvignon Napa Valley 1986: Light and elegant, with fresh, tasty fruit flavors and a lingering finish. Crisp, well balanced and clean. Cedar and spice notes give it extra interest. Drink now through 1994. $16 (7/31/89) **87**
Cabernet Sauvignon Napa Valley 1985 $14.50 (6/15/88) **89**

RODNEY STRONG
Cabernet Sauvignon Alexander Valley Alexander's Crown Vineyard 1987: The best Alexader's Crown in years; this is fresh, clean, elegant and lively, with a ripe black currant edge to the plum and cherry flavors. The tannins are firm but rounded, and the flavors have amplitude, etching fruit on and on. Balanced and supple. Drink in 1994 to 2000. $17 (7/15/91) **89**
Cabernet Sauvignon Alexander Valley Alexander's Crown Vineyard 1985: Elegant and somewhat tannic, with a nice core of plum aroma and flavor. Focused and balanced, but not especially complex. Try in 1993 to '95 to see if it develops complexity. $17 (5/31/91) **87**
Cabernet Sauvignon Alexander Valley Alexander's Crown Vineyard 1984: Herbal, soft and velvety, smooth and ripe, with sage-tinged plum aromas. Drink in 1993. $12 (4/30/89) **80**
Cabernet Sauvignon Alexander Valley Alexander's Crown Vineyard 1982 $12 (10/31/88) **80**
Cabernet Sauvignon Alexander Valley Alexander's Crown Vineyard 1981 $12 (11/30/87) **77**
Cabernet Sauvignon Alexander Valley Alexander's Crown Vineyard 1980 $11 (4/16/85) **86**
Cabernet Sauvignon Alexander Valley Alexander's Crown Vineyard 1979 $12 (4/16/84) **79**
Cabernet Sauvignon Alexander Valley Alexander's Crown Vineyard 1978 $12 (1/01/84) **80**
Cabernet Sauvignon Alexander Valley Reserve 1987: Intensely flavored and chewy, with lots of rich mint and chocolate nuances. The currant, berry and oak flavors remain supple and generous despite all the tannin. The finish echoes currant on and on. Drinkable now, but better by 1996. 1,200 cases made. $28 (9/30/91) **92**
Cabernet Sauvignon Sonoma County 1988: Light and simple, with a tannic edge that requires cellaring until 1993 to '95 to soften, but offering pleasant oak-framed modest plum aromas and flavors. $10 (11/15/91) **80**
Cabernet Sauvignon Sonoma County 1987: Smooth and supple, offering generous currant and blackberry aromas and flavors and a meaty edge. Pleasant to drink now, but has the intensity to carry through at least 1993 to '95. A good value. $10 (6/30/91) **85**
Cabernet Sauvignon Sonoma County 1982 $7 (12/15/86) **69**
Cabernet Sauvignon Sonoma Valley 1981 $7.50 (12/16/84) **86**

STUERMER
Cabernet Sauvignon Lake County 1984: Herbal, woody aromas, an austere structure and a bit of ripe, raisiny flavor does not add up to an attractive wine. Tasted twice. $15 (9/30/89) **66**

SUGARLOAF RIDGE
Cabernet Sauvignon Sonoma Valley 1986: An intense, concentrated, assertive wine that will need another two to three years to settle down. For now the deep mint, currant and oak flavors need time to soften and mellow. Drink now to 1995. 905 cases made. $13 (3/31/90) **82**

SUNNY ST. HELENA
Cabernet Sauvignon California 1989: A generous, reasonably priced wine, with just enough oak seasoning to spice up the currant and black cherry flavors. Has a lively balance, firm but velvety tannins and a nice, lingering finish. Tempting to drink now, but should improve if cellared until 1994 or beyond. $10 (11/15/91) **86**
Cabernet Sauvignon Napa Valley 1985 $9 (10/31/87) **81**
Cabernet Sauvignon North Coast 1988: A rich, elegant, well-balanced wine, with pretty black cherry, currant, plum and spice notes that are well integrated and supported by just the right touch of tannin. Enjoy now for its fresh fruit, or cellar until 1994. 860 cases made. $13 (4/30/91) **85**

SUTTER HOME
Cabernet Sauvignon California 1989: Soft and fruity, with just enough plum, cherry and currant notes to make it interesting. A ready-to-drink wine, with backbone and flavor. $5.50 (10/15/91) BB **83**
Cabernet Sauvignon California 1988: Fragrant and forward, showing plenty of plum and cherry aromas, appealing, straightforward flavors and good structure. Enjoy it now. $5 (11/15/90) BB **81**
Cabernet Sauvignon California 1987: Think of it as a Cabernet Beaujolais. Very fresh, simple and youthful in flavor, with grassy aromas and medium body. $5.50 (6/30/89) **77**
Cabernet Sauvignon California 1986 $5 (11/30/88) **79**

SWANSON
Cabernet Sauvignon Napa Valley 1987: Hard and tight now, with tough, chewy tannins, but it also packs a solid core of currant and black cherry-tinged flavor. An attractive, spicy, minty quality comes through on the aftertaste. Best to cellar until 1996. 300 cases made. $25 (10/15/91) **92**

SYLVAN SPRINGS
Cabernet Sauvignon California Vintner's Reserve 1985 $5 (9/30/88) BB **80**

TAFT STREET
Cabernet Sauvignon California 1985 $7.50 (10/15/88) **78**
Cabernet Sauvignon Napa Valley 1983 $9 (1/31/87) **84**

IVAN TAMAS
Cabernet Sauvignon Mendocino McNab Ranch 1984 $6 (2/15/87) BB **84**
Cabernet Sauvignon North Coast 1985 $7 (12/31/87) **79**

TERRACES
Cabernet Sauvignon Napa Valley 1987: Oodles of luscious oak notes envelop the herb, currant and fruit flavors in this firm but velvety wine. Very deep in color, with plenty of tannin to lose as it ages. Oaky flavors last through the finish. Overall it's big and generous, needing until about 1997 to start showing its best. 300 cases made. $38 (2/29/92) **92**
Cabernet Sauvignon Napa Valley 1986: Incredibly aromatic, rich, deep, complex and concentrated, with toasty currant, spice and herbal aromas and ripe, profound, powerful, intense Cabernet flavors. Well framed by firm tannins and oak, but still showing a silky-smooth texture and a long aftertaste that keeps repeating the fruit and spice themes. Cellar until 1997 to 2000 at the earliest. 150 cases made. $23 (1/31/91) **96**

TIJSSELING
Cabernet Sauvignon Mendocino 1986: A spicy, fruity, well-rounded wine, with good berry and nutmeg flavors and a generous finish. Very clean and crisp, with moderate tannins. Try now. $8 (1/31/90) BB **85**

PHILIP TOGNI
Cabernet Sauvignon Napa Valley 1991: Deep, dark, firm and concentrated, with intense, chewy currant, wild berry, chocolate and spice flavors that turn dense and tannic. 15 percent Merlot and 2 percent Cabernet Franc. 1,200 cases made. (NR) (5/15/92) (BT) **87+**
Cabernet Sauvignon Napa Valley 1990 $24 (5/15/91) (BT) **90+**
Cabernet Sauvignon Napa Valley 1988: Deliciously rich and concentrated, with intense, ripe plum, black cherry, vanilla, sage and spice notes that are long and full on the palate. Tannins are round and smooth with fruit pouring through on the aftertaste. Best to cellar until 1995. 380 cases made. Rel: $26 Cur: $28 (7/15/91) **92**
Cabernet Sauvignon Napa Valley 1987: Plush and generous, with lots of ripe currant, cassis, mint and plum flavors that are rich, deep, supple, wonderfully thick and complex. The firm tannins and acidity carry the flavors. It's beautifully balanced, with a sense of elegance and grace and a hint of mineral. Drink in 1993 to '96. 250 cases made. Rel: $24 Cur: $32 (8/31/90) **94**
Cabernet Sauvignon Napa Valley 1986 Rel: $22 Cur: $30 (CA-3/89) **93**
Cabernet Sauvignon Napa Valley 1985 Rel: $20 Cur: $25 (CA-3/89) **89**
Cabernet Sauvignon Napa Valley 1984 Rel: $18 Cur: $33 (CA-3/89) **86**
Cabernet Sauvignon Napa Valley 1983 Rel: $18 Cur: $40 (CA-3/89) **87**
Cabernet Sauvignon Napa Valley Tanbark Hill Vineyard 1988: Has a nice streak of raspberry-tinged flavor that reminds us of Zinfandel. The fruit has good intensity and depth, and the tannins are firm and ample enough for cellaring through 1994. 250 cases made. $24 (6/30/91) **87**

TOPAZ
Rouge de Trois Napa Valley 1988: Smooth and nicely balanced, with pleasant currant, black cherry and dill aromas and flavors and hints of toast on the finish. Not powerful, but it's well balanced. Drinkable now. 750 cases made. $14.50 (11/15/91) **87**

TOYON
Cabernet Sauvignon Alexander Valley 1982 $10 (11/15/86) **83**

TREFETHEN
Cabernet Sauvignon Napa Valley 1987: Focused, concentrated cherry, strawberry and tobacco flavors are tightly wrapped around a hard core of taut acidity, making for a cedary wine that needs cellaring until 1994 to soften some of the acidity and firm tannins. Rel: $16 Cur: $19 (11/15/90) **86**
Cabernet Sauvignon Napa Valley 1986: Rough with hard edges and lots of tannin. The ripe currant, plum and cherry flavor is attractive, but the tannins may be too much for some. Drink in 1994 to 2002. Rel: $15.25 Cur: $19 (10/31/89) **84**
Cabernet Sauvignon Napa Valley 1985 Rel: $15 Cur: $19 (CA-3/89) **80**
Cabernet Sauvignon Napa Valley 1984 Rel: $14 Cur: $17 (CA-3/89) **84**
Cabernet Sauvignon Napa Valley 1983 Rel: $11.75 Cur: $36 (CA-3/89) **84**
Cabernet Sauvignon Napa Valley 1982 Rel: $11 Cur: $22 (CA-3/89) **58**
Cabernet Sauvignon Napa Valley 1981 Rel: $11 Cur: $35 (CA-3/89) **87**
Cabernet Sauvignon Napa Valley 1981 Rel: $11 Cur: $35 (12/16/84) SS **88**
Cabernet Sauvignon Napa Valley 1980 Rel: $11 Cur: $35 (CA-3/89) **68**
Cabernet Sauvignon Napa Valley 1979 Rel: $11 Cur: $28 (CA-3/89) **86**
Cabernet Sauvignon Napa Valley 1978 Rel: $10 Cur: $38 (CA-3/89) **81**
Cabernet Sauvignon Napa Valley 1977 Rel: $8.50 Cur: $28 (CA-3/89) **86**
Cabernet Sauvignon Napa Valley 1976 Rel: $7.50 Cur: $22 (CA-3/89) **76**
Cabernet Sauvignon Napa Valley 1975 Rel: $7.50 Cur: $55 (CA-3/89) **83**
Cabernet Sauvignon Napa Valley 1974 Rel: $8 Cur: $75 (CA-3/89) **84**
Cabernet Sauvignon Napa Valley Hillside Selection 1987 (NR) (4/15/89) (BT) **90+**

Cabernet Sauvignon Napa Valley Hillside Selection 1986 (NR) (CA-3/89) **90**
Cabernet Sauvignon Napa Valley Hillside Selection 1985: Herbal, with adequate depth and concentration and enough tannins to warrant cellaring until 1993 before beginning to drink. Lacks the great fruit flavors of the best of the vintage. $30 (11/15/90) **80**

TRIONE
Cabernet Sauvignon Alexander Valley 1984 $10 (12/31/87) **74**

TUDAL
Cabernet Sauvignon Napa Valley 1986: Lean, firm and structured, with herb, cherry, cedar and spice notes that are elegant and understated. The tannins are in proportion allowing the flavors to seep through on the palate. Good length on the finish. Drink in 1993 to 1996. 1,800 cases made. Rel: $14.50 Cur: $18 (12/15/89) **91**
Cabernet Sauvignon Napa Valley 1985 Rel: $14.50 Cur: $20 (CA-3/89) **89**
Cabernet Sauvignon Napa Valley 1984 Rel: $12.50 Cur: $27 (CA-3/89) **91**
Cabernet Sauvignon Napa Valley 1983 Rel: $12.50 Cur: $38 (CA-3/89) **86**
Cabernet Sauvignon Napa Valley 1982 Rel: $12 Cur: $39 (CA-3/89) **72**
Cabernet Sauvignon Napa Valley 1981 Rel: $12 Cur: $40 (CA-3/89) **88**
Cabernet Sauvignon Napa Valley 1980 Rel: $11.50 Cur: $55 (CA-3/89) **85**
Cabernet Sauvignon Napa Valley 1979 Rel: $10.75 Cur: $50 (CA-3/89) **90**

TULOCAY
Cabernet Sauvignon Napa Valley 1986: Very ripe, raw and intense, with potent spice box aromas and plenty of heat and alcohol. An overblown, overripe wine that may have limited appeal. Drink with caution in 1993. $12 (6/30/90) **70**
Cabernet Sauvignon Napa Valley Egan Vineyard 1988: Extremely tannic, firm and tight, holding its ample currant and plum flavors in check. Concentrated and flavorful, promising a better drinking experience if aged until about 1997. Difficult to judge now. $15 (11/15/91) **86**
Cabernet Sauvignon Napa Valley Egan Vineyard 1987: Intensely weedy and herbal, with more vegetables than fruit pouring through. For fans of bell pepper, bay leaf and currant flavors, but it misses the mark for Cabernet. The tannins require cellaring until 1994 at the earliest, but the vegetal flavors will be even more pronounced by then. $16.50 (2/15/91) **74**

UNISSENT
Cabernet Sauvignon California 1988: Despite ripe, jammy, peppery aromas, it's rather light and elegant on the palate, with a touch of earthiness and soft tannins. Like many '88s it lacks concentration, so it should drink well in the next few years. Try in 1993 or '94. Tasted twice. $15 (11/15/91) **83**

M.G. VALLEJO
Cabernet Sauvignon California 1986: A simple, fruity style that won't shortchange you on flavor, with rose petal, berry, cherry and currant flavors. Drink now. $5 (6/15/90) BB **82**
Cabernet Sauvignon California 1985: With ripe, generous fruit, hints of herb, black cherry and oak, it's even-handed and well balanced. $4 (2/15/89) **78**
Cabernet Sauvignon California 1983 $4.50 (8/31/87) **67**

VALLEY RIDGE
Cabernet Sauvignon Sonoma County 1989: Light and fruity, with simple, firm currant, plum and black cherry flavors that are elegant and balanced. Has nice character, flavor and style for $9. $9 (11/15/91) **83**

VANINO
Cabernet Sauvignon Sonoma County 1985 $11 (9/30/88) **80**

VENTANA
Magnus Meritage Monterey 1986: Oniony, vegetal aromas and flavors tend to overshadow the ripe cassis flavor in this soft, easily accessible wine. Drink now, while the fruit comes through on the finish. $20 (10/31/89) **79**

VIANSA
Cabernet Sauvignon Napa-Alexander Valleys 1986 (NR) (4/15/88) (BT) **85+**
Cabernet Sauvignon Napa-Sonoma Counties 1986 $15 (7/31/90) **77**
Cabernet Sauvignon Napa-Sonoma Counties 1985 $13 (9/15/89) **72**
Cabernet Sauvignon Napa-Sonoma Counties 1984 $13 (7/31/88) **85**
Cabernet Sauvignon Sonoma-Napa Counties 1983 $15 (11/30/86) **88**
Cabernet Sauvignon Sonoma Valley Grand Reserve 1983 $35 (10/15/88) **88**
Cabernet Sauvignon Sonoma Valley Reserve 1983 $18 (10/15/88) **88**
Obsidian Napa-Sonoma Counties 1987: An austere wine, with crisp raspberry, cherry, herb and spice notes, but has a supple texture before the tannins develop. Moderately rich and complex, but it could use a little more concentration. Drink in 1993 to '98. 202 cases made. $65 (7/15/91) **85**

VICHON
Cabernet Sauvignon Napa Valley 1988: A tight, tough, hard-edged wine, with drying tannins that mask the ripe cherry and berry-tinged flavors. Lacks charm now, but perhaps with cellaring it will smooth out and gain some finesse. Drink in 1996 to 2000. $16 (5/15/91) **84**
Cabernet Sauvignon Napa Valley 1985 Rel: $13 Cur: $19 (CA-3/89) **88**
Cabernet Sauvignon Napa Valley 1984 Rel: $11.25 Cur: $15 (CA-3/89) **88**
Cabernet Sauvignon Napa Valley 1983 Rel: $10 Cur: $14 (CA-3/89) **80**
Cabernet Sauvignon Napa Valley 1982 Rel: $13 Cur: $19 (CA-3/89) **76**
Cabernet Sauvignon Napa Valley 1981 Rel: $13 Cur: $22 (CA-3/89) **80**
Cabernet Sauvignon Napa Valley Volker Eisele Vineyard 1982 Rel: $16 Cur: $19 (CA-3/89) **78**
Cabernet Sauvignon Napa Valley Volker Eisele Vineyard 1980 Rel: $16 Cur: $25 (CA-3/89) **83**
Cabernet Sauvignon Stags Leap District SLD 1988: Beautifully proportioned, with an elegant balance of currant, plum and vanilla aromas and flavors offering subtle hints of spice, tar and chocolate. Has more concentration and flavor than most '88s, and the tannins seem to be well under control. Drinkable now, but best after 1994. 3,300 cases made. $24 (11/15/91) **90**
Cabernet Sauvignon Stags Leap District SLD 1987: Elegant, with subtle but rich currant, cherry, and vanilla flavors that build on the finish. A graceful, harmonious style that is supported by moderate tannins. Best to cellar until 1993. Rel: $17 Cur: $22 (7/31/90) **87**
Cabernet Sauvignon Stags Leap District SLD 1986 Rel: $21 Cur: $25 (10/31/89) **91**
Cabernet Sauvignon Stags Leap District SLD 1985 Rel: $18 Cur: $29 (CA-3/89) **92**
Cabernet Sauvignon Stags Leap District Fay Vineyard 1984 Rel: $14 Cur: $28 (CA-3/89) **85**
Cabernet Sauvignon Stags Leap District Fay Vineyard 1982 Rel: $14 Cur: $23 (CA-3/89) **79**

Key to Symbols

The scores reported here are the results of blind tastings conducted by our panel of senior editors. Wines that carry the initials below are results of individual tastings.

THE WINE SPECTATOR 100-POINT SCALE ***95-100***—Classic, a great wine; ***90-94***—Outstanding, superior character and style; ***80-89***—Good to very good, a wine with special qualities; ***70-79***—Average, drinkable wine that may have minor flaws; ***60-69***—Below average, drinkable but not recommended; ***50-59***—Poor, undrinkable, not recommended. "+"—With a score indicates a range; used primarily with barrel tastings to indicate a preliminary score.

SPECIAL DESIGNATIONS SS—Spectator Selection, CS—Cellar Selection, BB—Best Buy, ($NA)—Price not available, (NR)—Not released.

TASTER'S INITIALS (JG)—Jim Gordon, (HS)—Harvey Steiman, (JL)—James Laube, (JS)—James Suckling, (TM)—Thomas Matthews, (TR)—Terry Robards, (PM)—Per-Henrik Mansson, (BT)—Barrel Tasting (these wines were tasted blind from barrel samples), (CA-date)—*California's Great Cabernets* by James Laube, (CH-date)—*California's Great Chardonnays* by James Laube, (VP-date)—*Vintage Port* by James Suckling.

DATE TASTED Dates in parentheses represent the issue in which the rating was published.

Cabernet Sauvignon Stags Leap District Fay Vineyard 1980 Rel: $16 Cur: $25 (CA-3/89) **85**

VILLA MT. EDEN
Cabernet Sauvignon Napa Valley 1988 (NR) (5/15/90) (BT) **80+**
Cabernet Sauvignon Napa Valley 1987: A soft, plush texture and rich currant and cherry flavors are reminiscent of a St.-Emilion, especially as the flavors come together on the long finish. An appealing style that should repay cellaring until 1993 to '95. Rel: $13 Cur: $15 (2/15/91) **88**
Cabernet Sauvignon Napa Valley 1986: An herb-scented, woody wine that's tight and tannic despite decent varietal flavors of plum and cherry. Rough going now, but should soften up nicely if cellared until 1995 or beyond. Rel: $13 Cur: $15 (2/15/91) **84**
Cabernet Sauvignon Napa Valley 1985 $13 (CA-3/89) **82**
Cabernet Sauvignon Napa Valley 1984 (NR) (CA-3/89) **80**
Cabernet Sauvignon Napa Valley 1983 $10 (CA-3/89) **72**
Cabernet Sauvignon Napa Valley 1982 Rel: $9 Cur: $13 (CA-3/89) **70**
Cabernet Sauvignon Napa Valley 1980 Rel: $11.70 Cur: $16 (CA-3/89) **62**
Cabernet Sauvignon Napa Valley 1979 Rel: $12 Cur: $27 (CA-3/89) **78**
Cabernet Sauvignon Napa Valley 1978 Rel: $8 Cur: $42 (CA-3/89) **78**
Cabernet Sauvignon Napa Valley 1977 Rel: $8 Cur: $22 (CA-3/89) **86**
Cabernet Sauvignon Napa Valley 1976 Rel: $7 Cur: $21 (CA-3/89) **70**
Cabernet Sauvignon Napa Valley 1975 Rel: $7 Cur: $22 (CA-3/89) **89**
Cabernet Sauvignon Napa Valley 1974 Rel: $7 Cur: $95 (CA-3/89) **90**
Cabernet Sauvignon Napa Valley Reserve 1988 $20 (5/15/90) (BT) **85+**
Cabernet Sauvignon Napa Valley Reserve 1982 Rel: $17 Cur: $20 (CA-3/89) **84**
Cabernet Sauvignon Napa Valley Reserve 1981 Rel: $17 Cur: $20 (CA-3/89) **85**
Cabernet Sauvignon Napa Valley Reserve 1980 Rel: $20 Cur: $22 (CA-3/89) **70**
Cabernet Sauvignon Napa Valley Reserve 1979 Rel: $20 Cur: $30 (CA-3/89) **75**
Cabernet Sauvignon Napa Valley Reserve 1978 Rel: $20 Cur: $50 (CA-3/89) **88**

VILLA ZAPU
Cabernet Sauvignon Napa Valley 1988: Firm and flavorful, with pleasant wild berry and smoky oak aromas and flavors that persist on the finish. Unpolished and in need of cellaring to smooth out the rough patches. Drink after 1994. 1,750 cases made. $20 (11/15/91) **86**
Cabernet Sauvignon Napa Valley 1986: Has all the ripe fruit and spice you could want on a modest frame, plus pickle barrel, oaky flavors. Lively and drinkable now. $16 (10/31/89) **79**

VITA NOVA
Reservatum Santa Barbara County 1986: A beautifully fruity, supple, rich wine with ripe currant and chocolate aromas, full flavors, firm tannins and a long finish. Great fruit flavors are framed by oak nuances making a very complete and harmonious package. Drinkable now. $20 (12/15/89) **87**

WEIBEL
Cabernet Sauvignon Mendocino County 1988: Fresh, fruity and easy to drink. Blueberry flavors and light tannins make it appealing to drink now. Reasonably priced, too. 2,800 cases made. $8 (3/15/92) BB **81**
Cabernet Sauvignon Mendocino County 1987: Crisp, light and lively, with generous currant and berry aromas and flavors shaded by a touch of bay leaf and oak coming through on the finish. Very attractive to drink now, but it could be cellared until 1993 or '94. 3,500 cases made. $8 (2/28/91) BB **84**

WENTE BROS.
Cabernet Sauvignon California 1981 $7 (12/16/85) **65**
Cabernet Sauvignon Central Coast 1985: Definitely in the herbal style, with straightforward flavors of cherry, and bay leaf and moderate tannins. Smooth and drinkable now. $8 (11/15/89) **78**
Cabernet Sauvignon Livermore Valley Charles Wetmore Vineyard Estate Reserve 1987: Ripe, supple, flavorful and graceful, with lovely blackberry and currant flavors shaded by herb and mint overtones. Has a velvety texture and tannins that should only need until 1993 to soften up. $18 (4/30/91) **86**
Cabernet Sauvignon Livermore Valley Estate Reserve 1986: Smooth and mature-tasting, with tobacco, herb and leather aromas and modest plum and chocolate flavors. The moderate tannins are well integrated. Drinkable now, but could be cellared through 1993. $12 (10/15/90) **82**

WILLIAM WHEELER
Cabernet Sauvignon Dry Creek Valley 1987: Despite hard-edged tannins, pretty plum, chocolate and currant flavors come through. Needs time to soften and mellow. Try after 1994. 1,440 cases made. $14 (11/15/91) **84**
Cabernet Sauvignon Dry Creek Valley 1986: Very complete and elegant, but the heavy oak tends to dominate the cherry and currant flavors. Not a wine for long-term aging. Drink now or in 1993. 3,045 cases made. $12 (8/31/90) **83**
Cabernet Sauvignon Dry Creek Valley 1985: Plenty of tannins in this black cherry and tobacco-flavored wine. Try it now. $12 (7/15/89) **76**
Cabernet Sauvignon Dry Creek Valley 1984 $11 (4/15/88) **75**
Cabernet Sauvignon Dry Creek Valley Norse Vineyard Private Reserve 1985 $18 (11/15/90) **83**
Cabernet Sauvignon Dry Creek Valley Norse Vineyard Private Reserve 1984 $15 (7/31/89) **60**

WHITE OAK
Cabernet Sauvignon Alexander Valley Myers Limited Reserve 1985: Very tight and tannic in structure, but the ripe, sweet cherry flavors underneath promise a much better wine if it's cellared until 1993 or beyond. $18 (7/31/89) **85**
Cabernet Sauvignon Sonoma County 1987: Very ripe, generous, chunky and a bit awkward now, but it offers plenty of currant and plum aromas and flavors. Has a vegetal edge that should make this more complex as it ages. Best after 1995. $14 (2/29/92) **85**

WHITE ROCK
Claret Napa Valley 1986: Rich and ripe, with generous currant and plum aromas and flavors, but enough oak to panel your wine cellar. With all that fruit, it's too bad the oak sticks out so much. Drink now to 1994. 600 cases made. $18 (10/31/89) **80**

WHITEHALL LANE
Cabernet Sauvignon California NV $7 (10/15/88) **70**
Cabernet Sauvignon California Le Petit NV: This new second wine from Whitehall Lane has plenty of flavor, depth and subtlety, especially at this price. Goes down easy, with pure Cabernet flavor. Drink now. $8.50 (3/31/90) **81**
Cabernet Sauvignon Napa Valley 1989 (NR) (5/15/91) (BT) **85+**
Cabernet Sauvignon Napa Valley 1988: A distinct minty edge dominates the bay leaf, currant and plum-tinged flavors. Balanced, but in need of time to round out the rough edges. Probably best with cellaring until 1995. 4,750 cases made. $18 (11/15/91) **87**
Cabernet Sauvignon Napa Valley 1987: This balanced wine has firm tannins and a supple texture, but mint flavors mask the currant and cherry notes. The mint comes through on the finish, too. Try in 1994. $18 (9/15/90) **84**
Cabernet Sauvignon Napa Valley 1986 $16 (8/31/89) **89**
Cabernet Sauvignon Napa Valley 1985 $16 (11/15/88) **93**
Cabernet Sauvignon Napa Valley 1984 $14 (12/31/87) **84**
Cabernet Sauvignon Napa Valley 1983 $14 (11/30/86) **77**
Cabernet Sauvignon Napa Valley 1982 $12 (2/16/85) **86**
Cabernet Sauvignon Napa Valley NV $6 (12/31/87) **77**
Cabernet Sauvignon Napa Valley Morisoli Vineyard 1991: Grapey and fruity, with intense flavors, but not in the way of finesse or complexity. Hard to judge. 2,500 cases made. (NR) (5/15/92) (BT) **83+**
Cabernet Sauvignon Napa Valley Morisoli Vineyard 1990 (NR) (5/15/91) (BT) **95+**
Cabernet Sauvignon Napa Valley Reserve 1987: Tight and focused, with spice, mint and oak nuances, but there's also ripe, concentrated cherry, currant and raspberry flavors beneath the aromas.

Developing a silky texture now, and it has the tannins for aging through the decade. Try in 1994 or '95. 487 cases made. $28 (11/15/91) **90**
Cabernet Sauvignon Napa Valley Reserve 1986: A powerful, minty, herbal wine where more menthol overrides the ripe currant and cherry flavor. Very intense and assertive. Firm tannins on the finish. Start drinking in 1993. 136 cases made. $30 (11/15/90) **77**
Cabernet Sauvignon Napa Valley Reserve 1985 $30 (11/30/89) **88**

WILD HORSE
Cabernet Sauvignon Paso Robles 1987: Packed with intense fruit flavor reminiscent of cassis liqueur. Ripe and full-bodied, but not too tannic, relying on the concentrated fruit and herb flavors for its power. Tempting to drink now, but better to cellar until 1993 to '96. 2,070 cases made. $13 (4/30/91) **88**
Cabernet Sauvignon Paso Robles Wild Horse Vineyards 1985 $10.50 (6/30/88) **70**

J. WILE & SONS
Cabernet Sauvignon Napa Valley 1987: Aromatic and firm in texture, but a bit short on flavor intensity to match the considerable tannins. A risk to cellar, but it needs until 1995 to '97 to melt down some of the tannins. $10 (5/31/91) **78**
Cabernet Sauvignon Napa Valley 1986 $7 (9/15/88) **75**
Cabernet Sauvignon Napa Valley 1985 $7 (11/15/87) **78**

WILLOW CREEK
Cabernet Sauvignon Napa Valley 1984 $8.50 (3/31/88) **73**
Cabernet Sauvignon Napa-Alexander Valleys 1986: Doesn't disappoint. A full-flavored, broad-textured wine, with plenty of plum and cherry aromas, more modest flavors and moderate tannins. Drink now. $9.50 (7/31/89) **82**

WOLTNER
Cabernet Sauvignon North Coast 1979 $3.50 (3/16/84) **76**

YORK MOUNTAIN
Cabernet Sauvignon San Luis Obispo 1986: Light and somewhat earthy, with enough cherry and berry flavors coming through to make it appealing. Has plenty of spice aromas and a fairly firm texture. Drink now. $15 (11/15/90) **84**
Cabernet Sauvignon San Luis Obispo 1985: Tight and firmly tannic, with ripe plum and cherry notes, it's a well-structured wine that's closed now and in need of time to develop, with a dry, tannic finish. Drink now through 1996. $15 (12/15/89) **83**

ZACA MESA
Cabernet Sauvignon Central Coast 1988: A very tart, cherry-flavored wine with sour, earthy flavors that turn us off. Tasted twice, with consistent notes. 5,000 cases made. $12 (11/15/91) **58**
Cabernet Sauvignon Central Coast Reserve 1987: Soft and ripe, with generous plum and currant aromas and flavors that dovetail nicely with spicy oak and toast nuances on the finish. Drinkable now, but it has the concentration and balance to keep developing through 1993 to '94. $25 (11/15/91) **83**
Cabernet Sauvignon Santa Barbara County 1986: A straightforward, medium-bodied wine, with clean aromas and flavors of plums, bell pepper and cherries. Drink now. $9.50 (12/15/89) **78**
Cabernet Sauvignon Santa Barbara County 1984 $8.50 (10/31/88) **79**
Cabernet Sauvignon Santa Barbara County 1981 $8 (4/01/84) **76**
Cabernet Sauvignon Santa Barbara County American Reserve 1983 $13 (3/31/87) **87**
Cabernet Sauvignon Santa Barbara County Reserve 1986 $15 (12/15/88) **80**
Cabernet Sauvignon Santa Barbara County Reserve 1985 $15 (10/15/88) **79**

ZD
Cabernet Sauvignon California 1982 $12 (7/16/86) **66**
Cabernet Sauvignon Napa Valley 1991: Tight and stalky, with hard currant and berry flavors. Intense, concentrated and rough around the edges, but finishes with pretty berry and floral notes. 300 cases made. (NR) (5/15/92) (BT) **84+**
Cabernet Sauvignon Napa Valley 1990 (NR) (5/15/91) (BT) **85+**
Cabernet Sauvignon Napa Valley 1989 (NR) (5/15/91) (BT) **80+**
Cabernet Sauvignon Napa Valley 1988: This polished, supple wine has spicy oak notes, moderate cherry and plum flavors and firm tannins. Very stylish and seductive, even if it may not have the flavor substance for long aging. Drink now to 1995. $20 (4/30/91) **86**
Cabernet Sauvignon Napa Valley 1987: Herbal, bordering on vegetal, with tomato, herb and celery aromas and flavors that are more prominent than the modest cherry flavor. Tannic and tough on the finish. Perhaps cellaring until 1994 will bring it around. 460 cases made. $16 (2/15/91) **78**
Cabernet Sauvignon Napa Valley 1985 $14 (5/15/89) **81**
Cabernet Sauvignon Napa Valley Estate Bottled 1987: Tough and earthy, with a powerful structure and broad, juicy black cherry and tobacco flavor. There is nothing elegant about it, but time should polish the tannins and make this a complex, enjoyable wine. Start drinking in 1997 to 2000. 316 cases made. $40 (1/31/91) **90**

STEPHEN ZELLERBACH
Cabernet Sauvignon Alexander Valley 1988: Velvety and gentle, with moderate plum, cherry and strawberry aromas and flavors and light tannins. Already drinkable. A good value. $10 (10/31/90) **82**
Cabernet Sauvignon Alexander Valley 1984 $8 (11/30/88) **86**
Cabernet Sauvignon Alexander Valley 1982 $6 (11/30/86) **80**
Cabernet Sauvignon Alexander Valley 1980 $8 (4/01/85) **77**

Chardonnay

ACACIA
Chardonnay Carneros Napa Valley 1990: Crisp and spicy, with ripe pear, melon and oak shadings that are elegant and lively. Drinks well now, but can age through 1994. $16.50 (6/30/92) **85**
Chardonnay Carneros Napa Valley 1989: Tart and austere, with earthy, woody flavors that dominate the ripe pear and melon-tinged fruit flavors. Awkward now—perhaps with time it will mellow. $16 (12/31/90) **84**
Chardonnay Carneros Napa Valley 1988: Along with intense pineapple and grapefruit flavors that are delicious, deep, crisp, rich and concentrated, this wine has a delicte balance, without too much oak flavoring. If you like lots of fruit, this one should be very appealing. $16 (1/31/90) **89**
Chardonnay Carneros Napa Valley 1987 $17 (CH-1/90) **84**
Chardonnay Carneros Napa Valley 1986 Rel: $15 Cur: $18 (CH-1/90) **87**
Chardonnay Carneros Napa Valley 1985 Rel: $15 Cur: $20 (CH-1/90) **80**
Chardonnay Carneros Napa Valley 1984 Rel: $14 Cur: $20 (CH-1/90) **84**
Chardonnay Carneros Napa Valley 1983 Rel: $12 Cur: $19 (12/01/84) **84**
Chardonnay Carneros Napa Valley Marina Vineyard 1990 $18.50 (6/30/92) **82**
Chardonnay Carneros Napa Valley Marina Vineyard 1989 $21 (5/15/92) **85**
Chardonnay Carneros Napa Valley Marina Vineyard 1988 Rel: $20 Cur: $23 (1/31/90) **90**
Chardonnay Carneros Napa Valley Marina Vineyard 1987 Rel: $18 Cur: $21 (CH-1/90) **85**
Chardonnay Carneros Napa Valley Marina Vineyard 1986 Rel: $18 Cur: $22 (CH-1/90) **86**
Chardonnay Carneros Napa Valley Marina Vineyard 1985 Rel: $18 Cur: $22 (CH-1/90) **80**
Chardonnay Carneros Napa Valley Marina Vineyard 1984 Rel: $16 Cur: $22 (CH-1/90) **86**
Chardonnay Carneros Napa Valley Marina Vineyard 1983 Rel: $16 Cur: $22 (CH-1/90) **79**
Chardonnay Carneros Napa Valley Winery Lake Vineyard 1985 Rel: $18 Cur: $25 (CH-1/90) **82**
Chardonnay Carneros Napa Valley Winery Lake Vineyard 1984 Rel: $18 Cur: $30 (CH-1/90) **88**
Chardonnay Carneros Napa Valley Winery Lake Vineyard 1983 Rel: $18 Cur: $25 (CH-1/90) **87**
Chardonnay Carneros Napa Valley Winery Lake Vineyard 1979 Rel: $16 Cur: $26 (CH-1/90) **76**
Chardonnay Napa Valley 1986 Rel: $15 Cur: $17 (CH-1/90) **81**
Chardonnay Napa Valley 1985 Rel: $12.50 Cur: $16 (CH-1/90) **79**
Chardonnay Napa Valley 1984 Rel: $12.50 Cur: $16 (CH-7/90) **89**
Chardonnay Napa Valley 1983 Rel: $12 Cur: $18 (CH-1/90) **80**
Chardonnay Napa Valley 1982 Rel: $12 Cur: $18 (CH-1/90) **80**

ADELAIDA
Chardonnay Paso Robles 1988: Very smooth and complex, offering appealing almond, pear and vanilla aromas and flavors. It's balanced toward crispness, but the flavors linger nicely, echoing spice and fruit on the finish. Delicious now, but should keep improving through 1993. 835 cases made. $14 (2/15/91) **89**
Chardonnay Paso Robles 1987: Very well balanced and flavorful, with ripe pear, nutmeg and lemon notes. Lively with acidity; the fruitiness lingers on the finish. $12.50 (12/15/89) **84**

ADLER FELS
Chardonnay Carneros Sangiacomo Vineyards 1989: Golden in color and very spicy in aroma and flavor, almost like an Alsatian Gewürztraminer. If you're expecting a Chardonnay you might be disappointed, but it's a good, drinkable wine. $12.50 (4/30/91) **80**
Chardonnay Sonoma Valley Sobra Vista Vineyards 1989: Spicy, earthy aromas and flavors hint at peach and grapefruit on the palate. Has a firm, smooth texture. Drinkable now. $12 (4/15/91) **82**

AHERN
Chardonnay Edna Valley Paragon Vineyard 1982 $10 (2/15/84) **84**

ALDERBROOK
Chardonnay Dry Creek Valley 1990: Hard, firm and intense, with oaky pear, honey and melon flavors that stay with you. Drinks well now, and $10 is a fair price. $10 (6/30/92) **82**
Chardonnay Dry Creek Valley 1989: A charming, light, fruity wine, with a crisp texture and a clean finish. Should be great with meals. $10 (3/31/91) **82**
Chardonnay Dry Creek Valley 1988: A winner. Crisp, fruity and well balanced, with apple aromas, fresh pear and apple flavors and a tangy, fruity finish. $10 (2/15/90) **82**
Chardonnay Dry Creek Valley 1987 $9.75 (2/15/89) **90**
Chardonnay Dry Creek Valley 1986 $9.25 (4/15/88) **84**
Chardonnay Dry Creek Valley 1985 $8.75 (2/15/87) **79**
Chardonnay Dry Creek Valley Reserve 1988 $16 (4/15/90) **82**

ALEXANDER VALLEY VINEYARDS
Chardonnay Alexander Valley 1990: Crisp and elegant, with subtle oak, pear and honey notes that stay with you. Shy and undeveloped now, it may show more fruit complexity and depth with time in the bottle. Drink now to 1995. Tasted twice. $11 (7/15/92) **83**
Chardonnay Alexander Valley 1988: Soft, ripe and generous, offering honey, pear and toast aromas and flavors, a silky texture and hints of apple and melon on the finish. Drink now. $12 (6/30/90) **88**
Chardonnay Alexander Valley 1987: Has crisp, sweetish pear and apple flavors with a hint of spicy Gewürztraminer-like flavors that get heavy and weighty on the palate. Tastes clumsy. $11 (1/31/89) **77**
Chardonnay Alexander Valley 1986 $11 (4/30/88) **83**
Chardonnay Alexander Valley 1985 $10.50 (5/31/87) **79**
Chardonnay Alexander Valley 1983 $10 (4/01/85) **87**
Chardonnay Alexander Valley 1982 $10 (3/01/84) **85**

ALTAMURA
Chardonnay Napa Valley 1988: Mature, with lots of oak and butterscotch aromas and flavors, turning toward honey on the finish, where it's ever-so-slightly bitter. A complex wine that's drinkable now. 2,000 cases made. $18 (5/31/92) **86**
Chardonnay Napa Valley 1987: Crisp and intense, with sharply focused lemon, pineapple and pear flavors that are tightly wound and firm. The finish comes through with plenty of flavor. Drink now to 1993. 1,800 cases made. Rel: $16.50 Cur: $21 (6/30/90) **87**
Chardonnay Napa Valley 1986: A complex and full-flavored wine. Crisp, concentrated and youthful, with apple, clove and slightly toasty flavors and a nice, lingering aftertaste. Drink now. Rel: $15 Cur: $21 (4/15/89) **88**
Chardonnay Napa Valley 1985 Rel: $14 Cur: $21 (CH-1/90) **91**

S. ANDERSON
Chardonnay Stags Leap District 1990: Crisp and light, with a decidedly floral edge to the peach and pear aromas and flavors. Turns tart and lean on the finish. May be best after 1993. 1,900 cases made. $19 (7/15/92) **82**
Chardonnay Stags Leap District 1989: Intensely crisp, flavorful and fresh, with no wood flavors interfering with the powerful fruit. Has orange, grapefruit and pine accents. Best to drink now, while it's fresh and lively. $18 (12/31/91) **84**
Chardonnay Stags Leap District 1988: An austere wine, with leafy, minty aromas, fresh grapefruit and herbal flavors and good balance. Straightforward and rather hard-edged. $18 (12/31/90) **79**
Chardonnay Stags Leap District 1987 Rel: $16 Cur: $18 (CH-6/90) **85**
Chardonnay Stags Leap District 1986 Rel: $16 Cur: $18 (CH-3/90) **81**
Chardonnay Stags Leap District 1985 Rel: $14 Cur: $25 (CH-3/90) **92**
Chardonnay Stags Leap District 1984 Rel: $12.50 Cur: $25 (CH-3/90) **89**
Chardonnay Stags Leap District 1983 Rel: $12.50 Cur: $25 (CH-3/90) **86**
Chardonnay Stags Leap District 1982 Rel: $12.50 Cur: $21 (CH-3/90) **72**
Chardonnay Stags Leap District 1981 Rel: $12.50 Cur: $25 (CH-3/90) **80**
Chardonnay Stags Leap District 1980 Rel: $12.50 Cur: $30 (CH-3/90) **83**
Chardonnay Stags Leap District Proprietor's Reserve 1987 $20 (CH-3/90) **89**
Chardonnay Stags Leap District Proprietor's Selection 1983 Rel: $16 Cur: $40 (CH-3/90) **87**

ARCIERO
Chardonnay Paso Robles 1987: A rough-cut wine, with orange and pineapple aromas followed by woody flavors. Not for everyone. $9 (12/15/89) **72**

ARMIDA
Chardonnay Russian River Valley 1990: Soft and generous, with appealing green apple, orange and spice aromas and flavors. Finishes simple and pleasant. Drinkable now. 1,929 cases made. $14 (2/15/92) **81**

ARROWOOD
Chardonnay Sonoma County 1989: Light and fresh, with pleasant peach and nectarine aromas and flavors and hints of mint on the finish. Ends up oakier than it starts, but it's still well balanced. Best starting 1993. Rel: $19 Cur: $21 (7/15/91) **85**
Chardonnay Sonoma County 1988: Rich, smooth, creamy and lively, with intense pineapple, pear, melon, apple and toasty oak flavors that are deeply concentrated and elegantly balanced, offering subtlety and finesse and a long, long, fruity finish. Drink now or in 1993. Rel: $18 Cur: $21 (4/30/90) **92**
Chardonnay Sonoma County 1987 Rel: $18 Cur: $21 (CH-4/90) **89**
Chardonnay Sonoma County 1986 Rel: $18 Cur: $25 (CH-4/90) **89**
Chardonnay Sonoma County Réserve Spéciale 1989 $45 (1/31/92) **92**
Chardonnay Sonoma County Réserve Spéciale 1988 $60 (CH-4/90) **92**

DAVID ARTHUR
Chardonnay Napa Valley 1989: This crisp, earthy wine seems deficient in fruit, making it tart and unfriendly on the finish, but picks up nice grapefruit notes. Try in 1994. $15 (4/15/92) **80**
Chardonnay Napa Valley 1985 $13 (4/15/88) **70**

ASHLY
Chardonnay Monterey 1986 $16.50 (10/31/88) **65**

AU BON CLIMAT
Chardonnay Arroyo Grande Valley 1990: Hard and toasty, with a firm oak edge overshadowing

the taut pear, peach and citrus flavors. A concentrated wine that could use time in the bottle to soften—cellaring until 1993 won't hurt. 275 cases made. $30 (7/15/92) **87**
Chardonnay Santa Barbara County 1990: A young, tight wine that's crisp and clean, with tart green apple and spice flavors that are straightforward and easy to drink. Ready now, but may be more appealing with time. Should hold through 1995. Tasted twice. 3,500 cases made. $16 (7/15/92) **84**
Chardonnay Santa Barbara County 1988: An intense, smoky, oaky wine that's big and a bit rough in structure yet amply fruity, with a touch of earthiness in the aromas. $12.50 (12/15/89) **82**
Chardonnay Santa Barbara County 1987: The pungent sulfury, sour, and bitter flavors are hard to swallow. Unacceptable. Tasted twice. $14 (3/15/89) **58**
Chardonnay Santa Barbara County Reserve 1989 $25 (7/15/91) **86**
Chardonnay Santa Barbara County Reserve 1988 $35 (3/15/91) **91**
Chardonnay Santa Barbara County Reserve 1987 $20 (12/15/89) **87**
Chardonnay Santa Barbara County Reserve 1986 $20 (6/15/88) **84**
Chardonnay Santa Barbara County Reserve Bien Nacido 1990: Broad and rich in texture, with nice butterscotch and earth notes around a core of pear and lemon flavors. Finishes smooth and elegant, with enough intensity to suggest it will improve through 1995. 1,000 cases made. $25 (7/15/92) **90**
Chardonnay Santa Barbara County Reserve Los Alamos Vineyard 1987 $20 (12/15/89) **82**
Chardonnay Santa Ynez Valley Benedict Vineyard 1987 $30 (12/15/89) **80**

BABCOCK
Chardonnay Santa Barbara County 1990: Attractive for its intense pear, citrus and spice flavors and lean focus. Crisp, balanced and ready to drink now through 1994. $13 (7/15/92) **82**
Chardonnay Santa Barbara County 1989: A rich-textured and almost sweet wine, with tinny, tart pineapple and strong earthy aromas and flavors. Drinkable now. Tasted twice. $16 (5/15/92) **77**
Chardonnay Santa Ynez Valley 1987: A very solid, cleanly made wine that seems closed up now. Has very light aromas but good varietal flavors of pear and apple and a smooth, fairly rich texture. Drink now. $12 (12/15/89) **82**
Chardonnay Santa Ynez Valley 1986 $11 (2/15/88) **66**
Chardonnay Santa Ynez Valley Reserve 1986 $14 (2/15/88) **80**
Chardonnay Santa Ynez Valley Selected Barrels Reserve 1987 $20 (12/15/89) **90**

ESTATE WILLIAM BACCALA
Chardonnay Mendocino 1984 $11 (1/31/87) **70**

BALLARD CANYON
Chardonnay Santa Ynez Valley 1988: An earthy, buttery, very stylish wine, with good backbone and body, mostly oaky flavors and a buttery, lingering finish that brings out some fruit. $14 (12/15/89) **86**
Chardonnay Santa Ynez Valley Dr.'s Fun Baby 1988: A crisp, refreshing, picnic-style Chardonnay. Has fresh pine and grapefruit aromas and similar flavors. $10 (12/15/89) **79**

BALVERNE
Chardonnay Chalk Hill Deerfield Vineyard 1984 $11 (11/15/87) **79**

BANCROFT
Chardonnay Howell Mountain 1990: The lively fruit flavors have hints of pear, citrus and vanilla. A crisp, focused style that may benefit from bottle age. Drink now or hold until 1993. $13.50 (5/31/92) **84**
Chardonnay Howell Mountain 1988: Beautiful fruit aromas and flavors are generous and concentrated, layering orange, pear, nutmeg and honey in a focused, opulent package. Has the structure and restraint to develop well through 1993, but it's drinkable now. $14 (12/31/90) **88**

BANDIERA
Chardonnay Napa County 1990: Straightforward and fruity, with ripe pear, spice and honey notes that stay with you. Fairly priced. $6.50 (3/15/92) BB **80**

BANNISTER
Chardonnay Russian River Valley 1990: Smooth and ripe, with layers of broad, rich pear, spice, honey and toast flavors. Offers plenty of flavor and depth, yet it's round, creamy and delicious to drink now. 800 cases made. $16 (3/31/92) **88**
Chardonnay Sonoma County 1989: Fresh and spicy, with a nice overlay of toasty oak notes to the pear and peach flavors. Medium in intensity and ready to drink. 284 cases made. $15 (7/15/91) **85**

LAWRENCE J. BARGETTO
Chardonnay Central Coast Cypress 1990: Forward, fruity and easy drinking, with pleasant, soft apple and pear flavors. $9.50 (7/15/92) **82**
Chardonnay Central Coast Cypress 1989: The decent, tart peach and resin flavors are light, lemony, soft and pleasant, but they turn watery on the aftertaste. Drink now. $9 (7/15/91) **79**
Chardonnay Santa Cruz Mountains 1990: This will appeal to Sauvignon Blanc lovers. Offers plenty of herb, spice and apple notes that are fresh and lively, with hints of grapefruit and melon on the finish. Attractive to drink now. $18 (6/15/92) **85**
Chardonnay Santa Cruz Mountains 1989 $18 (2/28/91) **82**
Chardonnay Santa Cruz Mountains 1988 $18 (6/30/90) **78**
Chardonnay Santa Cruz Mountains Miller Ranch 1987 $15 (4/15/89) **82**
Chardonnay Santa Maria Valley 1985 $10 (11/15/87) **81**

BARON HERZOG
Chardonnay California Selection 1990: Spicy and refreshing, with well-defined peach, pear and nutmeg aromas and flavors. Has a soft texture, but it's flavorful enough to go nicely with a plate of fish or chicken. $10 (9/15/91) **83**
Chardonnay Sonoma County 1989: Light and tart, offering green apple and earthy flavors. Crisp and short. $11 (3/31/91) **75**

BARROW GREEN
Chardonnay California 1988: Tart and lean, with a silky texture and distinctive candied, sour lemon aromas and flavors. Drinkable, but not exciting. Try now. $14.50 (7/15/91) **75**
Chardonnay California 1987: Spicy, generous and toasty, yet it remains elegant and gentle on the palate, with ripe pear and honey flavors that linger appealingly on the finish. Has nice finesse. $16 (11/15/89) **90**

BEAUCANON
Chardonnay Napa Valley 1990: Nice butter and vanilla flavors are wrapped around good grapefruit and citrus components. Smooth, well balanced and easy to enjoy. 5,000 cases made. $9 (7/15/92) BB **83**
Chardonnay Napa Valley 1988: Strives for richness and complexity, with a good dose of smoky, toasty oak notes to support the ripe layers of pear, vanilla, pineapple and citrus flavors. The finish is long and fruity. Drink now or in 1993. 1,800 cases made. $10 (7/15/91) **87**
Chardonnay Napa Valley 1987: Woody, vegetal aromas and flavors overpower whatever fruit might be there, and it's rough and tannic for such a light wine. $12 (1/31/89) **85**

BEAULIEU
Chardonnay Carneros Napa Valley Carneros Reserve 1990: Tight and compact, with subtle toast and pear notes that fan out on the finish, revealing more oak nuances, but it seems to lack focus. Drink now. Tasted twice. $17 (6/30/92) **83**
Chardonnay Carneros Napa Valley Carneros Reserve 1989: Crisp and light with a watery texture, but it has pleasant pineapple, lemon and vanilla aromas and flavors. Drinkable now. $17 (5/31/91) **81**
Chardonnay Carneros Napa Valley Carneros Reserve 1988 $14 (CH-6/90) **89**
Chardonnay Carneros Napa Valley Los Carneros Reserve 1988: Tightly structured, with pretty pear, apple, spice and lemon notes that are well balanced and pleasant on the aftertaste. Drink now. $14 (5/31/90) **84**
Chardonnay Carneros Napa Valley Los Carneros Reserve 1987 Rel: $14 Cur: $16 (CH-5/90) **87**
Chardonnay Carneros Napa Valley Los Carneros Reserve 1986 Rel: $12 Cur: $15 (CH-6/90) **86**
Chardonnay Carneros Napa Valley Los Carneros Reserve 1985 Rel: $12 Cur: $16 (CH-6/90) **84**
Chardonnay Carneros Napa Valley Los Carneros Reserve 1984 Rel: $10 Cur: $16 (CH-4/90) **79**
Chardonnay Carneros Napa Valley Los Carneros Reserve 1983 Rel: $10 Cur: $15 (CH-4/90) **74**
Chardonnay Carneros Napa Valley Los Carneros Reserve 1982 Rel: $10 Cur: $16 (CH-4/90) **72**
Chardonnay Carneros Napa Valley Los Carneros Reserve 1981 Rel: $10 Cur: $18 (CH-4/90) **70**
Chardonnay Napa Valley Beaufort 1990 $9 (3/31/92) **82**
Chardonnay Napa Valley Beaufort 1989 $11 (7/15/91) **81**
Chardonnay Napa Valley Beaufort 1988 $9.50 (4/30/90) **79**
Chardonnay Napa Valley Beaufort 1987 $12.50 (6/15/89) **79**
Chardonnay Napa Valley Beaufort 1986 $9 (7/15/88) **85**
Chardonnay Napa Valley Beaufort 1983 $10.50 (10/01/85) **77**
Chardonnay Napa Valley Beaufort 1979 Rel: $6 Cur: $20 (CH-4/90) **70**
Chardonnay Napa Valley Beaufort 1978 Rel: $6 Cur: $22 (CH-4/90) **70**
Chardonnay Napa Valley Beaufort 1977 Rel: $6 Cur: $22 (CH-4/90) **64**
Chardonnay Napa Valley Beaufort 1976 Rel: $6 Cur: $22 (CH-4/90) **62**
Chardonnay Napa Valley Beaufort 1975 Rel: $5 Cur: $28 (CH-4/90) **61**
Chardonnay Napa Valley Beaufort 1974 Rel: $5 Cur: $25 (CH-4/90) **62**
Chardonnay Napa Valley Beaufort 1973 Rel: $5 Cur: $30 (CH-4/90) **60**
Chardonnay Napa Valley Beaufort 1972 Rel: $5 Cur: $30 (CH-4/90) **60**
Chardonnay Napa Valley Beaufort 1971 Rel: $4 Cur: $30 (CH-4/90) **58**
Chardonnay Napa Valley Beaufort 1970 Rel: $4 Cur: $32 (CH-4/90) **59**
Chardonnay Napa Valley Beaufort 1969 Rel: $2 Cur: $35 (CH-4/90) **57**
Chardonnay Napa Valley Beaufort 1968 Rel: $2 Cur: $35 (CH-4/90) **59**
Chardonnay Napa Valley Beautour 1990 $7.75 (11/15/91) **80**

BEAUREGARD
Chardonnay Napa Valley 1987: Mature and oaky, with earthy butterscotch, pear and honey notes that turn slightly sour and cloying on the finish. Decent but uninspiring; it has a hole in the middle of the flavors. Drink now. 3,500 cases made. $10 (7/15/91) **75**

BELVEDERE
Chardonnay Alexander Valley 1990: A pleasant style, with bold, creamy apple, oak and pear flavors that are decent, but fail to go beyond simplicity. Drink now. $8 (3/31/92) **80**
Chardonnay Carneros 1987: Lean, crisp and very tart, but there is also plenty of lively peach flavor. Give it until 1995. $13 (4/30/89) **84**
Chardonnay Carneros 1986 $13 (7/15/88) **88**
Chardonnay Carneros Winery Lake 1983 $12 (6/01/85) **91**
Chardonnay Carneros Winery Lake 1982 $12 (8/01/84) **60**
Chardonnay Russian River Valley 1990 $11 (7/15/92) **85**
Chardonnay Russian River Valley 1987 $11 (7/15/89) **88**
Chardonnay Russian River Valley Reserve 1989 $9 (3/31/91) **85**
Chardonnay Russian River Valley Reserve 1988 $9 (2/15/90) **85**
Chardonnay Sonoma County 1989 $6 (7/15/91) **71**
Chardonnay Sonoma County Bacigalupi 1986 $13 (7/15/88) **80**
Chardonnay Sonoma County Bacigalupi 1985 $12 (12/15/87) **91**
Chardonnay Sonoma County Bacigalupi 1983 $12 (11/16/85) **73**
Chardonnay Sonoma County Discovery Series 1989 $6 (12/31/90) BB **80**
Chardonnay Sonoma County Discovery Series 1987 $5.25 (7/31/88) **78**
Chardonnay North Coast Discovery Series 1984 $5 (1/01/86) BB **83**
Chardonnay Central Coast Discovery Series 1984 $4.75 (10/16/85) BB **83**
Chardonnay Monterey County Discovery Series 1983 $4.75 (2/01/85) **58**

BENZIGER
Chardonnay Carneros Première Vineyard 1989: Lots of flavor and a delicate texture add up to a wine with finesse and elegance. Floral, pear and hazelnut aromas and flavors are immediately attractive, with richness to burn. Spicy fruit notes emerge on the finish. Drinkable now, but better in 1993 or '94. 1,000 cases made. $14 (2/15/92) **91**
Chardonnay Sonoma County 1990: Simple but pleasant, with spicy pineapple, pear and toast flavors that are straightforward, but flatten out on the finish. Drink now. $12 (5/31/92) **82**
Chardonnay Sonoma County 1989: A ripe, lively style, with intense, sweet pineapple, spice, guava and oak shadings. Rich and concentrated, with a long, full finish. Drink now or in 1993. $12 (11/15/91) **85**
Chardonnay Sonoma County 1988 $10 (6/30/90) **85**
Chardonnay Sonoma County 1987 $9.50 (7/15/89) **87**

BERINGER
Chardonnay Napa Valley 1990: Fresh and fruity, with a nice vanilla edge to the peach and pear aromas and flavors. Finishes smooth and lively. Drinkable now, but it has the goods to grow through 1994. $12 (2/15/92) **88**
Chardonnay Napa Valley 1989: Ripe and earthy, with rich, earthy pineapple and citrus flavors that come across as simple and one-dimensional, turning a touch bitter on the aftertaste. Best to drink soon. $14 (3/15/91) **81**
Chardonnay Napa Valley 1988: Distinctive for its peach, butter and cream flavors, this is a clean, well-made, balanced wine that finishes with traces of apple and pear. It's young and intense, yet it's subtle and delicate on the finish. Drink now. $13 (4/15/90) **87**
Chardonnay Napa Valley 1987 $10 (7/15/89) **80**
Chardonnay Napa Valley 1986 $10.50 (1/31/88) **83**
Chardonnay Napa Valley 1985 $10 (4/30/87) **84**
Chardonnay Napa Valley 1984 $9 (4/15/87) **90**
Chardonnay Napa Valley 1983 $10 (9/01/85) **82**
Chardonnay Napa Valley 1982 $9.75 (4/16/84) **80**
Chardonnay Napa Valley 1981 $10 (6/01/86) **85**
Chardonnay Napa Valley Private Reserve 1990 Rel: $19 Cur: $23 (5/31/92) **90**
Chardonnay Napa Valley Private Reserve 1989 Rel: $19 Cur: $23 (7/15/91) **85**
Chardonnay Napa Valley Private Reserve 1988 Rel: $19 Cur: $21 (6/30/90) **76**
Chardonnay Napa Valley Private Reserve 1987 Rel: $17 Cur: $19 (CH-4/90) **79**
Chardonnay Napa Valley Private Reserve 1986 Rel: $16 Cur: $22 (CH-4/90) **90**

Key to Symbols

The scores reported here are the results of blind tastings conducted by our panel of senior editors. Wines that carry the initials below are results of individual tastings.

THE WINE SPECTATOR 100-POINT SCALE ***95-100***—Classic, a great wine; ***90-94***—Outstanding, superior character and style; ***80-89***—Good to very good, a wine with special qualities; ***70-79***—Average, drinkable wine that may have minor flaws; ***60-69***—Below average, drinkable but not recommended; ***50-59***—Poor, undrinkable, not recommended. "+"—With a score indicates a range; used primarily with barrel tastings to indicate a preliminary score.

SPECIAL DESIGNATIONS SS—Spectator Selection, CS—Cellar Selection, BB—Best Buy, ($NA)—Price not available, (NR)—Not released.

TASTER'S INITIALS (JG)—Jim Gordon, (HS)—Harvey Steiman, (JL)—James Laube, (JS)—James Suckling, (TM)—Thomas Matthews, (TR)—Terry Robards, (PM)—Per-Henrik Mansson, (BT)—Barrel Tasting (these wines were tasted blind from barrel samples), (CA-date)—*California's Great Cabernets* by James Laube, (CH-date)—*California's Great Chardonnays* by James Laube, (VP-date)—*Vintage Port* by James Suckling.

DATE TASTED Dates in parentheses represent the issue in which the rating was published.

Chardonnay Napa Valley Private Reserve 1986 Rel: $16 Cur: $22 (4/15/88) **91**
Chardonnay Napa Valley Private Reserve 1985 Rel: $15 Cur: $24 (CH-4/90) **86**
Chardonnay Napa Valley Private Reserve 1984 Rel: $15 Cur: $24 (CH-4/90) **88**
Chardonnay Napa Valley Private Reserve 1983 Rel: $15 Cur: $24 (CH-4/90) **76**
Chardonnay Napa Valley Private Reserve 1982 Rel: $15 Cur: $22 (CH-4/90) **74**
Chardonnay Napa Valley Private Reserve 1981 Rel: $15 Cur: $26 (CH-4/90) **86**
Chardonnay Napa Valley Private Reserve 1980 Rel: $15 Cur: $25 (CH-4/90) **75**
Chardonnay Napa Valley Private Reserve 1979 Rel: $14 Cur: $25 (CH-4/90) **78**
Chardonnay Napa Valley Private Reserve 1978 Rel: $12 Cur: $15 (CH-4/90) **70**
Chardonnay Napa Valley Centennial Cask Selection 1974 Rel: $5 Cur: $40 (CH-4/90) **70**
Chardonnay Santa Barbara County 1974 $5 (CH-4/90) **88**

BLACK MOUNTAIN
Chardonnay Alexander Valley Douglass Hill 1989: The lovely ripe apple, pear and melon flavor is rich and elegant and gains a nice mineral taste on the finish. Balanced and intense with a subtle aftertaste. Drink now or in 1993. 3,140 cases made. $11 (9/15/91) **88**
Chardonnay Alexander Valley Douglass Hill 1988: Broad and rich, but it's not very heavy or highly concentrated. A likable wine, with pineapple, papaya and nutmeg aromas and flavors. Drink soon. $10 (4/15/90) **88**
Chardonnay Alexander Valley Douglass Hill 1987 $10 (12/31/88) **86**
Chardonnay Alexander Valley Douglass Hill 1985 $10 (8/31/87) **72**
Chardonnay Alexander Valley Gravel Bar 1989 $18 (7/15/92) **74**
Chardonnay Alexander Valley Gravel Bar 1988 $20 (8/31/91) **81**
Chardonnay Alexander Valley Gravel Bar 1987 $18 (4/15/90) **88**

BLUE HERON LAKE
Chardonnay Napa County 1985 $13 (8/31/87) **86**
Chardonnay Wild Horse Valley 1988: Leans toward the earthy end of the spectrum, but it has enough fruit flavor to make it palatable. The ripe pear, nutmeg and spice flavors are a bit cloying on the finish. Drink now. 1,400 cases made. $13 (3/31/91) **76**

BOEGER
Chardonnay El Dorado 1989: Intense and assertive, with ripe pear, melon and apple flavors, but an earthy, spicy, oaky character gives it an added dimension. Drink now. 1,700 cases made. $11.50 (5/31/91) **82**
Chardonnay El Dorado 1986 $10.50 (9/30/88) **89**

JEAN CLAUDE BOISSET
Chardonnay Napa Valley 1983 $9.50 (4/16/86) **86**

BON MARCHE
Chardonnay Alexander Valley 1989: Tastes rich, fruity and velvety, with plenty of melon, pear and spice flavors and a ripe bouquet. Extremely supple and smooth, with a lingering finish. Unusually concentrated for the vintage. 2,435 cases made. $8 (3/31/91) BB **88**
Chardonnay Sonoma County 1990: The aroma is better than the flavor in this soft, soupy wine. Has simple fruit flavors and lacks backbone. Nothing particularly off-putting, it's just dull. $8 (1/31/92) **76**

BONNY DOON
Chardonnay California Grahm Crew 1989: This attractive wine has spice, honey and green apple flavors and a creamy texture. Well balanced and elegant, it echoes peach and apple on the finish. Drink now. 3,000 cases made. $9 (9/30/90) BB **84**
Chardonnay Sonoma County Grahm Crew 1986 $8.50 (10/15/87) **85**
Chardonnay Monterey County La Reina Vineyard Cuvée Fin de Linea 1990: Light and simple, with watery pear and apple notes. Could use more richness and concentration, but it's a decent drink. $12 (3/31/92) **78**
Chardonnay Monterey County La Reina Vineyard 1989: Complex and intriguing, with layers of toasty, buttery oak and ripe, rich, deep and intense pear, peach and spice flavors that are elegant and lingering. A wine with finesse and grace. Drink now to 1995. 3,000 cases made. $14 (3/15/91) **90**
Chardonnay Monterey County La Reina Vineyard 1987 $15 (12/31/88) **88**
Chardonnay Monterey County La Reina Vineyard 1986 $13.25 (3/31/88) **91**
Chardonnay Monterey County La Reina Vineyard 1985 $13 (4/30/87) **73**
Chardonnay Santa Cruz Mountains Estate Bottled 1990 $25 (6/30/92) **83**
Chardonnay Santa Cruz Mountains Estate Bottled 1989 $25 (3/31/92) **83**

BOUCHAINE
Chardonnay Alexander Valley 1982 Rel: $14 Cur: $18 (CH-2/90) **79**
Chardonnay Carneros 1988: Elegant and simple with lemon, pear and melon flavors that lack richness and concentration. The acidity is crisp and carries the flavors, but it's best to drink this one soon. $15 (11/30/90) **82**
Chardonnay Carneros 1987: Beautifully balanced and delicious, with spicy aromas of clove, apple and earth followed by sharply focused pear, apple and nutmeg flavors. An elegant, smoothly textured package. Fruit lingers on the finish. Rel: $14 Cur: $16 (8/31/90) **89**
Chardonnay Carneros 1985 Rel: $15 Cur: $20 (CH-2/90) **87**
Chardonnay Carneros 1984 Rel: $14 Cur: $20 (CH-2/90) **85**
Chardonnay Carneros 1983 Rel: $14 Cur: $23 (CH-2/90) **77**
Chardonnay Carneros Estate Reserve 1988: Round and spicy, with fresh, crisp apple, pear and pineapple flavors that are rich and concentrated and linger on the palate. Balanced, finishing with a touch of citrus and Muscat flavor. Drink now to 1994. 1,500 cases made. $20 (2/29/92) **88**
Chardonnay Carneros Estate Reserve 1987 $19 (5/31/90) **89**
Chardonnay Carneros Estate Reserve 1986 Rel: $19 Cur: $22 (CH-2/90) **88**
Chardonnay Carneros Winery Lake Vineyard 1984 $22 (CH-2/90) **71**
Chardonnay Napa Valley 1990 $15 (7/15/92) **85**
Chardonnay Napa Valley 1989 $15 (2/15/92) **84**
Chardonnay Napa Valley 1986 Rel: $13 Cur: $17 (CH-2/90) **88**
Chardonnay Napa Valley 1985 Rel: $13 Cur: $17 (CH-2/90) **87**
Chardonnay Napa Valley 1984 Rel: $12.50 Cur: $16 (CH-2/90) **66**
Chardonnay Napa Valley 1983 Rel: $12.50 Cur: $18 (CH-2/90) **75**
Chardonnay Napa Valley 1982 Rel: $14.50 Cur: $18 (6/16/84) SS **90**
Chardonnay Napa Valley Cask 85-86 NV $7.50 (7/31/87) BB **81**

BOYER
Chardonnay Monterey County Ventana Vineyard 1990: Lean and simple, with stale citrus and vegetal notes that compete with the pear and melon flavors. The flavors are a bit off the mark, but it's drinkable. Drink now. $12 (7/15/92) **80**
Chardonnay Monterey County Ventana Vineyard 1989: Ripe and fruity, with rich peach, pear, melon and spice flavors that offer good depth and intensity and linger on the finish. Drink now to 1993. $15 (7/15/91) **87**

BRANDER
Chardonnay Santa Ynez Valley 1990: Dirty, stale and earthy, this is a Chardonnay gone bad, with vinegary flavors that are hard to look past. Not recommended. Tasted twice, with consistent notes. 920 cases made. $14 (7/15/92) **64**
Chardonnay Santa Ynez Valley 1987: Delicious fruit flavors in a solid package of crisp acidity and full body. Smells slightly grapefruity and tastes like ripe pear and pineapple. Drink now. $13 (12/15/89) **84**
Chardonnay Santa Ynez Valley Tête de Cuvée 1989: Crisp and lively, with ripe pineapple, grapefruit and spice notes that stay with you. Finishes with good length and echoes of fruit and spice. Drink now to 1993. $22 (7/15/91) **84**

DAVID BRUCE
Chardonnay California 1984 $10 (7/16/86) **79**
Chardonnay Santa Cruz Mountains 1990: Strives for complexity, with its bold, ripe, oaky profile. The buttery pear and spice-tinged Chardonnay flavors come through, but it could use a little more finesse. Perhaps with another year of aging it will be more alluring. Drink after 1993. 691 cases made. $18 (4/30/92) **85**
Chardonnay Santa Cruz Mountains 1987: Has an extreme style that will turn a lot of people off, but it may be your cup of tea. Pungently aromatic, with earthy, smoky, vegetal and buttery notes, followed by buttery flavors and a buttery finish. $18 (2/15/90) **77**
Chardonnay Santa Cruz Mountains 1983 $18 (9/30/86) **69**
Chardonnay Santa Cruz Mountains Estate Reserve 1990: A bold, ripe oaky style that throws a lot of oak and ripe fruit at you. The smoky pear and melon notes are attractive, but it could use time in the bottle to harmonize. Drink after 1993. 181 cases made. $25 (5/31/92) **84**
Chardonnay Santa Cruz Mountains Meyley Vineyard 1990: Grassy, herbal, candied aromas and flavors turn bitter on the finish. Tasted twice, with consistent notes. 229 cases made. $18 (7/15/92) **69**
Chardonnay Santa Cruz Mountains Vineyard Selection 1990: Bitter, earthy and funky, with ripe, peppery pear and oak flavors. An odd-ball style that turns vegetal on the aftertaste. Drink now. Tasted twice, with consistent notes. 662 cases made. $15 (5/31/92) **74**

BRUTOCAO
Chardonnay Mendocino 1988: Ripe, intense and full-bodied, but a touch alcoholic, with pear, spice and citrus notes that thin out on the finish. A fair price. 2,500 cases made. $10 (5/15/92) **81**

BUENA VISTA
Chardonnay Carneros 1990: Delivers a mouthful of flavor. Very forward, with the typical Carneros tropical fruit character. Pineapple and ripe apple notes combine with a hint of herbs and juniper to give it fruit complexity. $12 (11/15/91) **85**
Chardonnay Carneros 1989: Light and fruity, with attractive grapefruit, apple and spice aromas and flavors showing enough racy acidity to keep it lively through the finish. 5,000 cases made. $11 (7/15/91) **85**
Chardonnay Carneros 1987 $10 (10/15/88) **88**
Chardonnay Carneros 1986 $11.50 (6/30/87) **83**
Chardonnay Carneros 1984 $11 (3/01/86) **78**
Chardonnay Carneros Jeanette's Vineyard 1988 $26 (3/31/91) **83**
Chardonnay Carneros Jeanette's Vineyard 1986 $8.50 (2/15/88) **81**
Chardonnay Carneros Jeanette's Vineyard 1985 $13.25 (2/28/87) **83**
Chardonnay Carneros Private Reserve 1988 $16.50 (3/31/91) **82**
Chardonnay Carneros Private Reserve 1987 Rel: $16.50 Cur: $20 (CH-3/90) **82**
Chardonnay Carneros Private Reserve 1986 $16.50 (CH-3/90) **91**
Chardonnay Carneros Private Reserve 1985 $16.50 (CH-3/90) **86**
Chardonnay Carneros Private Reserve 1984 $14.50 (CH-6/90) **75**
Chardonnay Carneros Private Reserve 1983 Rel: $14.50 Cur: $18 (CH-3/90) **84**
Chardonnay Carneros Private Reserve 1982 $16.50 (3/16/86) **70**

BURGESS
Chardonnay Napa Valley Triere Vineyard 1990: A very exotic wine that emphasizes the nutmeg and vanilla flavors of oak aging and backs it up with buttery pear accents. Soft and delicate in texture, but full in flavor, with complexities that develop on the finish. Rel: $15 Cur: $17 (5/31/92) SS **91**
Chardonnay Napa Valley Triere Vineyard 1989: Attractive pear, pineapple and vanilla flavors turn coarse then watery on the aftertaste. Best to drink now. Rel: $16 Cur: $18 (7/15/91) **82**
Chardonnay Napa Valley Triere Vineyard 1988: With its pretty floral and pear aromas, this is immediately appealing, and the slightly astringent texture does not detract from the intense pear and toast flavors, which are both persistent and subtle. Drink now to 1994. $16 (4/30/90) **90**
Chardonnay Napa Valley Triere Vineyard 1987 Rel: $14.50 Cur: $17 (CH-12/89) **85**
Chardonnay Napa Valley Triere Vineyard 1986 Rel: $14 Cur: $19 (CH-12/89) **87**
Chardonnay Napa Valley Vintage Reserve 1985 Rel: $13 Cur: $19 (CH-12/89) **88**
Chardonnay Napa Valley Vintage Reserve 1984 Rel: $13 Cur: $19 (CH-12/89) **79**
Chardonnay Napa Valley Vintage Reserve 1983 Rel: $12 Cur: $20 (CH-12/89) **69**
Chardonnay Napa Valley Vintage Reserve 1982 $12 (CH-12/89) **68**
Chardonnay Napa Valley 1981 Rel: $11 Cur: $16 (CH-12/89) **74**
Chardonnay Napa Valley 1980 Rel: $11 Cur: $18 (CH-12/89) **75**
Chardonnay Napa Valley 1979 Rel: $11 Cur: $18 (CH-12/89) **78**
Chardonnay Napa Valley 1978 Rel: $11 Cur: $18 (CH-12/89) **77**
Chardonnay Napa Valley 1977 Rel: $11 Cur: $23 (CH-12/89) **80**
Chardonnay Carneros Winery Lake Vineyard 1976 Rel: $10 Cur: $20 (CH-12/89) **70**
Chardonnay Carneros Winery Lake Vineyard 1975 Rel: $9 Cur: $40 (CH-12/89) **84**
Chardonnay Carneros Winery Lake Vineyard 1974 Rel: $6 Cur: $25 (CH-12/89) **79**
Chardonnay Napa Valley 1973 Rel: $6 Cur: $30 (CH-12/89) **85**

BYINGTON
Chardonnay Napa Valley 1990: Simple and watery, with ripe pear and melon notes that taste sweet on the finish. Drink now. Tasted twice. 1,961 cases made. $15 (6/30/92) **78**
Chardonnay Napa Valley 1989: A bit woody, with more style than substance. Missing a rich core of concentrated fruit. 3,000 cases made. $15 (12/31/91) **77**

DAVIS BYNUM
Chardonnay Russian River Valley 1988: With apple cider aromas and spicy apple and orange flavors, this is a solid, drinkable wine, with a firm texture and tangy finish. Drinkable now. $10 (4/30/90) **79**
Chardonnay Russian River Valley Limited Release 1989: Crisp and austere, with light grapefruit flavors, medium body and a clean, dry finish. A drinkable wine, but it's not very concentrated. $13 (4/30/91) **79**
Chardonnay Russian River Valley Limited Release 1987: Gentle, peachlike flavors run through this lively, artfully balanced wine. Shows some spicy maturity on the finish. $14 (9/30/89) **80**
Chardonnay Sonoma County Reserve Bottling 1987: Rich and smooth, with buttery, ripe flavors of pear and honey and a soft finish. $9 (7/15/89) **82**

BYRON
Chardonnay Santa Barbara County 1990: Broad and generous, with plenty of spicy, smoky pear and honey aromas and flavors. A bit tannic, but it should be fine through 1994. $14 (6/30/92) **85**
Chardonnay Santa Barbara County 1989: Apple, pear and spice flavors are ripe and appealing, but the fruit struggles to rise above the earthy notes. This wine is definitely not for everyone. $13 (7/15/91) **80**
Chardonnay Santa Barbara County 1988: An outstanding wine that's reasonably priced. Rich, intense and concentrated, with sharply focused honey, apple and pineapple flavors that dance on the palate, framed by just the right amount of oak. Complex and intriguing. Drink now to 1993. $12 (4/30/90) SS **92**
Chardonnay Santa Barbara County 1987 $11 (12/15/89) **91**
Chardonnay Santa Barbara County Reserve 1989 $18 (5/31/92) **82**
Chardonnay Santa Barbara County Reserve 1988 $17 (11/15/90) **86**
Chardonnay Santa Barbara County Barrel Fermented Reserve 1987 $16 (12/15/89) **78**
Chardonnay Santa Barbara County Reserve 1985 $13 (10/31/87) **73**

CAIN
Chardonnay Carneros 1990: Firm and focused, with ripe pear and apple flavors that are straightforward and moderate in intensity and depth. Drink now. 3,000 cases made. $12 (7/15/92) **83**
Chardonnay Carneros 1989: Medium in weight, with ripe, appealing pear, nutmeg and vanilla

flavors, a soft texture and nice hints of spice and citrus on the finish. Drink soon. 2,900 cases made. $16 (7/15/91) **83**
Chardonnay Carneros 1988: Simple and correct, with spicy pear, peach and grapefruit notes that are fresh and zingy with moderate depth. With time it should be more harmonious and complex. Drink now to 1993. $16 (11/30/90) **84**
Chardonnay Carneros 1987 $16 (12/31/89) **86**
Chardonnay Carneros 1986 $16 (9/15/88) **88**
Chardonnay Carneros 1985 $16 (10/31/87) **82**
Chardonnay Napa-Sonoma Counties 1985 $10 (7/31/87) **74**
Chardonnay Napa Valley 1987 $10 (4/30/89) **83**
Chardonnay Napa Valley 1986 $10 (9/30/88) **87**
Chardonnay Napa Valley 1984 $10 (10/31/86) **62**
Chardonnay Napa Valley 1983 $10 (1/01/85) **60**

CAKEBREAD
Chardonnay Napa Valley 1990: Balanced and harmonious, with citrusy aromas and flavors that make it seem young and tight. Has plenty of room to grow. Start drinking now. $21 (1/31/92) **86**
Chardonnay Napa Valley 1989: Simple, fruity and grassy. Not very smooth, but lively enough to want to drink with dinner. Tasted twice. $19.50 (7/15/91) **79**
Chardonnay Napa Valley 1988: Distinctive for its pear, grapefruit and nutmeg flavors, this is a well-balanced, elegant, richly flavored wine with finesse and complexity and a long, pretty aftertaste. Drink now to 1993. $17.50 (3/15/90) **89**
Chardonnay Napa Valley 1987 $21 (6/30/89) **86**
Chardonnay Napa Valley 1986 $20 (2/15/88) **70**
Chardonnay Napa Valley Reserve 1988 $30 (11/30/91) **86**
Chardonnay Napa Valley Reserve 1986 $26 (2/15/90) **88**

CALE
Chardonnay Carneros Sangiacomo Vineyard 1990: Bright and lively, a smooth, complex wine, with focused pear, spice, peach and citrus flavors neatly woven together. Finishes with layers of fruit and oak that linger. Drink now to 1994. 1,000 cases made. $18 (3/31/92) **90**

CALERA
Chardonnay Central Coast 1990: Rich and Burgundian in style, with earthy pear, spice, vanilla and hazelnut flavors that are broad, smooth and complex. Drinks well now, but can age through 1994. $14 (3/31/92) **88**
Chardonnay Central Coast 1989: Has a blazing yellow color, with very ripe apricot and peach aromas and flavors. Fat and smooth, with plenty of butter and caramel notes echoing on the finish. Should match well with hearty food. Drinkable now. $14 (1/31/92) **84**
Chardonnay Central Coast 1988: Very ripe, rich and intense, with plenty of toasty, buttery oak aromas, and ripe pear and pineapple flavor, but the flavors begin to taper off on the finish, bringing a sense of elegance and finesse. Drink now. $14 (11/30/90) **86**
Chardonnay Central Coast 1987 $12 (3/15/90) **82**
Chardonnay Central Coast 1986 $12 (7/31/89) **83**
Chardonnay San Benito County Mount Harlan Vineyard Young Vines 1987 $22 (4/15/89) **86**
Chardonnay Santa Barbara County 1985 $11.75 (7/31/87) **80**
Chardonnay Santa Barbara County 1984 $11.25 (3/16/86) **64**
Chardonnay Santa Barbara County Los Alamos Vineyard 1983 $10.75 (2/01/85) **83**

CALLAWAY
Chardonnay Temecula Calla-Lees 1990: Intense and spicy, with pretty pear, pineapple, earth and oak flavors that are sharply focused, with good richness and depth. Finishes with lots of fruit and echoes long and lingering. Drink now to 1994. $8 (11/30/91) **88**
Chardonnay Temecula Calla-Lees 1989: Has a strong, leesy flavor, like sour pineapple and onion skins. Not very pretty, but drinkable. Tasted three times. $10 (2/28/91) **72**
Chardonnay Temecula Calla-Lees 1988: Elegant, fruity and light in color, with distinct citrus, orange blossoms and honeydew melon flavors that are fresh and clean. Drink now or in 1993. $10 (2/28/90) **86**
Chardonnay Temecula Calla-Lees 1987 $9.75 (12/31/88) **84**
Chardonnay Temecula Calla-Lees 1986 $9.50 (11/15/87) **82**
Chardonnay Temecula Calla-Lees 1985 $9.25 (3/15/87) **86**

CAMBRIA
Chardonnay Santa Barbara County Cambria Vineyard Sur Lie 1988: Fine and straightforward, with clear Chardonnay flavors. Has plenty of bright, fresh pear and pineapple flavors, a crisp texture and a lingering aftertaste. $16 (12/15/89) **84**
Chardonnay Santa Barbara County Reserve 1986: Ripe but delicate tasting, with plenty of pear and pineapple flavors in a smooth, light texture. Its smoothness shows the benefit of aging. 3,000 cases made. $25 (12/15/89) **86**
Chardonnay Santa Maria Valley Katherine's Vineyard 1990 $16 (4/30/92) **90**
Chardonnay Santa Maria Valley Katherine's Vineyard 1989 $16 (12/31/90) **84**
Chardonnay Santa Maria Valley Reserve 1989: Complex and rich, with ripe pear, honey, butterscotch and spice flavors that are deep and compelling. Delicious to drink now, but should continue to age well through 1994. $25 (7/15/92) **89**
Chardonnay Santa Maria Valley Reserve 1988 $25 (12/31/90) **85**

CANTERBURY
Chardonnay California 1990: Ripe and intense, with creamy pear, vanilla and spice flavors that offer more richness and depth than many wines twice its price. Drink now. $8 (7/15/92) BB **83**
Chardonnay California 1989: Soft, supple and fruity, with clean melon, pear and spicy Chardonnay flavors at a very reasonable price. Ready now. $7.50 (7/15/91) BB **82**
Chardonnay California 1985 $6.50 (11/15/86) BB **83**

CAREY
Chardonnay Santa Barbara County 1989: Firmly oaky, but it has plenty of pear, spice and melon flavors. Ripe and clean, with moderate concentration. Drink now. 1,500 cases made. $13 (4/30/91) **82**
Chardonnay Santa Ynez Valley 1988: A fruity, flavorful and light wine, with peach, pear and lemon notes and a hint of honey. Refreshing to drink now. 1,400 cases made. $12 (6/30/90) **83**
Chardonnay Santa Ynez Valley 1987: Very elegant and smooth. Buttery tasting, with pleasing oak and ripe pear flavors, medium body and a lingering finish. $10 (12/15/89) **85**

Key to Symbols

The scores reported here are the results of blind tastings conducted by our panel of senior editors. Wines that carry the initials below are results of individual tastings.

THE WINE SPECTATOR 100-POINT SCALE 95-100—Classic, a great wine; ***90-94***—Outstanding, superior character and style; ***80-89***—Good to very good, a wine with special qualities; ***70-79***—Average, drinkable wine that may have minor flaws; ***60-69***—Below average, drinkable but not recommended; ***50-59***—Poor, undrinkable, not recommended. "+"—With a score indicates a range; used primarily with barrel tastings to indicate a preliminary score.

SPECIAL DESIGNATIONS SS—Spectator Selection, CS—Cellar Selection, BB—Best Buy, ($NA)—Price not available, (NR)—Not released.

TASTER'S INITIALS (JG)—Jim Gordon, (HS)—Harvey Steiman, (JL)—James Laube, (JS)—James Suckling, (TM)—Thomas Matthews, (TR)—Terry Robards, (PM)—Per-Henrik Mansson, (BT)—Barrel Tasting (these wines were tasted blind from barrel samples), (CA-date)—*California's Great Cabernets* by James Laube, (CH-date)—*California's Great Chardonnays* by James Laube, (VP-date)—*Vintage Port* by James Suckling.

DATE TASTED Dates in parentheses represent the issue in which the rating was published.

CARNEROS CREEK
Chardonnay Carneros Fleur de Carneros 1989: A reasonably priced wine that shows class. Pure and fruity, with pineapple and citrus flavors rounded out by touches of vanilla and butter. Balanced, with good acidity, a smooth texture and a lingering aftertaste. 2,000 cases made. $9 (6/30/91) BB **86**
Chardonnay Los Carneros 1990: An outstanding wine, with distinctive character. Smooth and inviting, with lots of peach, pear, hazelnut and vanilla flavors. Has plenty of zing, but it shows subtlety, too. Very pretty, creamy and complex. Tempting to drink now, but it should be better around 1993 or '94. 4,600 cases made. $12.50 (3/31/92) SS **90**
Chardonnay Los Carneros 1989: Flavorful, but not especially harmonious, offering light grapefruit and lemon aromas and flavors that seem watery. Picks up bits of honey and hazelnut on the finish. Try in 1993. Tasted twice. $13 (5/15/91) **78**
Chardonnay Los Carneros 1988 $13 (2/15/90) **85**
Chardonnay Los Carneros 1987 $13 (7/15/89) **81**
Chardonnay Los Carneros 1986 $11.50 (7/15/88) **87**
Chardonnay Los Carneros 1985 $10.50 (11/15/87) **79**
Chardonnay Los Carneros 1984 $10.50 (4/30/87) **86**
Chardonnay Napa Valley 1983 $11 (9/01/85) **80**
Chardonnay Napa Valley 1982 $12 (12/16/84) **71**
Chardonnay Napa Valley 1981 $10 (1/01/84) **81**
Chardonnay Sonoma County 1981 $10 (1/01/84) **79**

MAURICE CARRIE
Chardonnay Temecula 1989: Ample fruit flavors are accented by the nutmeg and vanilla notes of oak aging in this flavorful, well-rounded wine. Well balanced and ready to drink now. A good value, but hard to find outside Southern California. 600 cases made. $7.50 (7/15/92) BB **83**

CARTLIDGE & BROWNE
Chardonnay Napa Valley 1989: With lush melon, toast, pear and spice flavors, this is attractive, rich and full-bodied, with plenty of flavor and character. A fair price, too. Drink now. $9.75 (5/31/91) **84**
Chardonnay Napa Valley 1987: Round, smoky and buttery, with hints of apple and lemon aromas and flavors. A toasty wine, with a bit too much heat on the finish. Chill well for best results. Drink soon. $11 (4/15/90) **81**
Chardonnay Napa Valley 1986 $10 (5/31/88) **83**
Chardonnay Napa Valley 1985 $9.75 (3/31/87) **91**
Chardonnay Napa Valley 1984 $11.50 (1/01/86) **66**
Chardonnay Napa Valley 1983 $11.50 (2/16/85) **78**

CASTORO
Chardonnay San Luis Obispo County 1990: Ripe and fruity, with simple pear and melon-tinged Chardonnay flavors. Drink now. 1,000 cases made. $9.50 (6/30/92) **80**
Chardonnay San Luis Obispo County 1988: A fresh, rather light wine, with piny aromas and good herbal and citrus flavors. $8.50 (12/15/89) **75**

CAYMUS
Chardonnay Napa Valley 1986 $12 (8/31/88) **83**

CECCHETTI SEBASTIANI
Chardonnay Napa Valley 1989: Potent Muscat and spice notes stray from the mainstay Chardonnay flavors, but for some they will hit the spot. Has a nice touch of peach, orange blossom and pear flavor, as well. $6.50 (4/30/91) **80**
Chardonnay Napa Valley Cask Lot 1 1987: Difficult to like. Has some nice peachy aromas, but it tastes tired and dirty and leaves a sour finish. Tasted twice. $9.50 (4/15/89) **64**
Chardonnay Napa Valley Cask Lot 2 1986 $9.50 (12/15/87) **85**

CEDAR MOUNTAIN
Chardonnay Livermore Valley Blanches Vineyard 1990: An earthy, metallic edge detracts from the ripe pear and spice notes. Comes across as awkward. Drink now. Tasted three times. 230 cases made. $13.50 (5/15/92) **79**

CHALK HILL
Chardonnay Chalk Hill 1990: Complex and engaging, with ripe, buttery pear, apple, spice and hazelnut flavors that are rich and deep. The texture is smooth, supple, round and polished, with a long, lingering finish that keeps pumping out the fruit and oak. Drinks well now, or cellar through 1994. $15 (6/15/92) SS **91**
Chardonnay Chalk Hill 1989: Rich and buttery in flavor, creamy in texture and concentrated enough to linger on the finish. Great pear, butterscotch and custard notes give it intensity, and hints of nutmeg and vanilla add spice. $14 (5/15/91) SS **90**
Chardonnay Chalk Hill 1986 $10 (1/31/88) **68**
Chardonnay Chalk Hill 1984 $8 (12/01/85) **82**

CHALONE
Chardonnay Chalone 1990: Crisp and concentrated, with well-defined apple, honey and spice aromas and flavors that fan out on the finish. Each sip offers more complexity and range of flavor. Drinkable now, but better in early 1993. Rel: $22 Cur: $27 (2/15/92) **89**
Chardonnay Chalone 1989: Has very earthy, smoky aromas that border on musty, but the flavors are ripe and the texture is round and supple. Fig and grapefruit flavors come on slowly and gain complexity on the finish, making for a very distinctive, individual wine. Drink now to 1997. Rel: $25 Cur: $27 (11/30/90) **90**
Chardonnay Chalone 1988: Elegant, complex and well balanced, with pretty melon, pear and spice flavors complemented by just the right touch of toasty oak. Altogether pleasing and well made. Drink now to 1993. Rel: $22 Cur: $29 (2/28/90) **89**
Chardonnay Chalone 1987 Rel: $22 Cur: $37 (12/31/88) **90**
Chardonnay Chalone 1986 Rel: $22 Cur: $48 (CH-1/90) **94**
Chardonnay Chalone 1985 Rel: $22 Cur: $68 (CH-4/90) **80**
Chardonnay Chalone 1984 Rel: $18 Cur: $53 (CH-1/90) **88**
Chardonnay Chalone 1983 Rel: $18 Cur: $50 (CH-1/90) **90**
Chardonnay Chalone 1982 Rel: $18 Cur: $65 (CH-1/90) **95**
Chardonnay Chalone 1981 Rel: $17 Cur: $68 (CH-4/90) **93**
Chardonnay Chalone 1980 Rel: $17 Cur: $48 (CH-1/90) **92**
Chardonnay Chalone 1979 Rel: $14 Cur: $55 (CH-1/90) **89**
Chardonnay Chalone Gavilan 1990 $12.50 (6/30/92) **86**
Chardonnay California Gavilan 1989 $12 (12/31/90) **85**
Chardonnay Chalone Gavilan 1988 $12 (4/15/90) **87**
Chardonnay Chalone Reserve 1988 Rel: $40 Cur: $45 (CH-6/90) **89**
Chardonnay Chalone Reserve 1987 Rel: $35 Cur: $85 (CH-5/90) **87**
Chardonnay Chalone Reserve 1986 Rel: $28 Cur: $80 (CH-5/90) **85**
Chardonnay Chalone Reserve 1985 Rel: $28 Cur: $80 (CH-6/90) **94**
Chardonnay Chalone Reserve 1983 Rel: $25 Cur: $53 (CH-5/90) **87**
Chardonnay Chalone Reserve 1982 Rel: $25 Cur: $48 (CH-5/90) **93**
Chardonnay Chalone Reserve 1981 Rel: $20 Cur: $100 (CH-5/90) **86**
Chardonnay Chalone Reserve 1980 Rel: $18 Cur: $125 (CH-5/90) **94**

CHAMISAL
Chardonnay Edna Valley 1989: Distinctively earthy and buttery, with hints of caramel, honey, pear and spice, picking up more of the earthy notes on the finish. Rich, full-bodied and ready to drink now to 1993. 2,865 cases made. $14 (7/15/91) **82**
Chardonnay Edna Valley 1988: An odd leafy flavor takes away from the creamy, buttery and pearlike flavors. Altogether well balanced and attractive. Drink now. 3,000 cases made. $14 (6/30/90) **78**

Chardonnay Edna Valley 1987: Full-blown in style. Rich and buttery, unctuous and ripe, with lots of oak and substantial pear flavors underneath. Fruit echoes on the finish. $14 (7/15/89) **85**
Chardonnay Edna Valley 1986 $13 (5/31/88) **90**
Chardonnay Edna Valley 1985 $10 (11/15/87) **78**
Chardonnay Edna Valley 1984 $10 (6/01/86) **70**
Chardonnay Edna Valley Special Reserve 1989 $18 (11/30/91) **91**
Chardonnay Edna Valley Special Reserve 1988 $18.50 (11/30/90) **90**

CHANSA
Chardonnay Santa Barbara County 1989: Crisp in texture, but the flavors are unfocused, hinting at soy sauce and apple rather than the fresh fruit one would hope for. Drinkable. 1,375 cases made. $10 (4/30/91) **77**

CHAPPELLET
Chardonnay Napa Valley 1989: Has a nice, smooth texture, with modest pear, vanilla, peach and spice flavors, and picks up a touch of toasty oak on the finish. Balanced and ready to drink now. 4,600 cases made. $14 (3/31/92) **83**
Chardonnay Napa Valley 1988: Firm, fruity, focused and concentrated, offering a bright beam of refreshingly tart and lively grapefruit and pineapple flavors. Has length and the sort of structure that could let it improve with aging through 1993 or '94. 3,754 cases made. Rel: $14 Cur: $16 (5/31/91) **88**
Chardonnay Napa Valley 1987: Ripe and full-bodied, with rich apple, pear, lemon and spicy vanilla flavors that are moderately complex and linger on the palate. A pleasant mouthful of Chardonnay. Drink now. 3,800 cases made. Rel: $14 Cur: $17 (6/30/90) **82**
Chardonnay Napa Valley 1986 $14 (CH-3/90) **90**
Chardonnay Napa Valley 1985 Rel: $12.50 Cur: $15 (CH-3/90) **87**
Chardonnay Napa Valley 1984 Rel: $12 Cur: $20 (CH-3/90) **87**
Chardonnay Napa Valley 1983 Rel: $12 Cur: $18 (CH-3/90) **79**
Chardonnay Napa Valley 1982 Rel: $12.50 Cur: $20 (CH-3/90) **85**
Chardonnay Napa Valley 1981 Rel: $14 Cur: $22 (CH-3/90) **80**
Chardonnay Napa Valley 1980 Rel: $14 Cur: $25 (CH-3/90) **84**
Chardonnay Napa Valley 1979 Rel: $12 Cur: $30 (CH-3/90) **79**
Chardonnay Napa Valley 1978 Rel: $11.75 Cur: $40 (CH-3/90) **76**
Chardonnay Napa Valley 1977 Rel: $11.75 Cur: $40 (CH-6/90) **90**
Chardonnay Napa Valley 1976 Rel: $9.75 Cur: $30 (CH-3/90) **71**
Chardonnay Napa Valley 1975 Rel: $6.75 Cur: $40 (CH-3/90) **82**
Chardonnay Napa Valley 1974 Rel: $6.75 Cur: $40 (CH-3/90) **72**
Chardonnay Napa Valley 1973 Rel: $6.75 Cur: $50 (CH-3/90) **91**
Chardonnay Napa Valley 1972 Rel: $6 Cur: $50 (4/16/85) (JG) **90**
Chardonnay Napa Valley 1971 Rel: $6 Cur: $50 (4/16/85) (JG) **78**
Chardonnay Napa Valley 1970 Rel: $6 Cur: $50 (4/16/85) (JG) **86**

CHATEAU DE BAUN
Chardonnay Russian River Valley Barrel Fermented 1990: Pleasantly fruity, with ripe pear, honey, vanilla and spice flavors that are elegant and clean. Drink now. $10 (3/15/92) **82**
Chardonnay Russian River Valley Barrel Fermented 1989: Crisp, tart, and clean, with pear, citrus and apple flavors that offer moderate depth and concentration. Attractive and balanced, but it could use a little more pizzazz. Drink now. Better than a bottle tasted earlier. $10 (6/15/91) **81**

CHATEAU DE LEU
Chardonnay Solano County Green Valley 1989: The wood competes with the fruit in this oaky style, but it's an attractive wine, with toasty cedar, melon and pear flavors. Has good length. Ready to drink now through 1993. $8 (7/15/91) **83**

CHATEAU JULIEN
Chardonnay Monterey County Barrel Fermented 1990: A touch earthy, with a juniper edge to the spicy pear and citrus flavors, but altogether a drinkable wine that's priced right. $8 (6/30/92) **81**
Chardonnay Monterey County Paraiso Springs Vineyard 1984 $12 (2/15/87) **76**
Chardonnay Monterey County Sur Lie Private Reserve 1990: Notably oaky, but also shows a rich core of pear, vanilla and spice flavors. Full-bodied and drinking well now. $15 (6/15/92) **85**

CHATEAU LA GRANDE ROCHE
Chardonnay Napa Valley 1989: Smooth and appealing, with appley, spicy aromas and modest peachy flavors that turn to pear on the finish. Medium-bodied, well-balanced and clean tasting. $13 (11/15/90) **85**

CHATEAU MONTELENA
Chardonnay Alexander Valley 1988: Smooth and creamy, with ripe melon, apple, pineapple and pear-tinged fruit flavors that are soft and generous, echoing vanilla and nutmeg on the finish. Could use a year or so to soften. Drink now to 1993. Rel: $20 Cur: $28 (6/30/90) **85**
Chardonnay Alexander Valley 1987: Bold but harmonious. Rich and fruity, with loads of grapefruit, spice and pineapple flavor, fine structure and balance and a lingering aftertaste. Drink up now. Rel: $20 Cur: $25 (6/30/89) **90**
Chardonnay Alexander Valley 1986 Rel: $18 Cur: $35 (CH-2/90) **91**
Chardonnay Alexander Valley 1985 Rel: $16 Cur: $38 (CH-2/90) **91**
Chardonnay Alexander Valley 1984 Rel: $16 Cur: $35 (CH-2/90) **90**
Chardonnay Alexander Valley 1983 Rel: $14 Cur: $50 (CH-2/90) **84**
Chardonnay Alexander Valley 1982 Rel: $14 Cur: $40 (CH-2/90) **92**
Chardonnay Alexander Valley 1981 Rel: $14 Cur: $42 (CH-2/90) **91**
Chardonnay Napa Valley 1989: Starts out with a burst of apple, pear, melon and toast flavors, then turns light and simple. A pleasant wine that's best drunk soon. Tasted twice. $23 (7/15/91) **83**
Chardonnay Napa Valley 1988: Firm, fruity and straightforward, featuring green apple, melon and slightly toasty aromas and flavors that seem to fan out nicely on the finish. Drink now. Tasted three times. Rel: $20 Cur: $23 (11/30/90) **86**
Chardonnay Napa Valley 1987: Intense, with layers of honey and vegetal flavors and a slightly sour finish. A major disappointment from this winery. Tasted three times. Rel: $20 Cur: $23 (2/15/90) **72**
Chardonnay Napa Valley 1986 Rel: $18 Cur: $28 (CH-2/90) **91**
Chardonnay Napa Valley 1985 Rel: $18 Cur: $38 (CH-2/90) **90**
Chardonnay Napa Valley 1984 Rel: $18 Cur: $40 (CH-2/90) **88**
Chardonnay Napa Valley 1983 Rel: $16 Cur: $50 (CH-2/90) **85**
Chardonnay Napa Valley 1982 Rel: $16 Cur: $40 (CH-2/90) **85**
Chardonnay Napa Valley 1981 Rel: $16 Cur: $42 (CH-2/90) **88**
Chardonnay Napa Valley 1980 Rel: $16 Cur: $39 (CH-2/90) **79**
Chardonnay Napa Valley 1979 Rel: $16 Cur: $40 (CH-2/90) **78**
Chardonnay Napa Valley 1978 Rel: $15 Cur: $45 (CH-2/90) **77**
Chardonnay Napa Valley 1977 Rel: $15 Cur: $60 (CH-2/90) **85**
Chardonnay Napa-Alexander Valleys 1976 Rel: $11 Cur: $50 (CH-2/90) **77**
Chardonnay Napa Valley 1975 Rel: $9 Cur: $75 (CH-2/90) **87**
Chardonnay Napa Valley 1974 Rel: $8 Cur: $75 (CH-2/90) **88**
Chardonnay Napa-Alexander Valleys 1973 Rel: $6.50 Cur: $100 (CH-2/90) **93**
Chardonnay Napa-Alexander Valleys 1972 Rel: $6 Cur: $110 (CH-2/90) **95**

CHATEAU POTELLE
Chardonnay Napa Valley 1989: Nice butterscotch and pear flavors are the focus of this medium-bodied wine. A good, smooth, drinkable wine but not super-concentrated. Fine for drinking now and easy to like. $15 (3/31/92) **84**
Chardonnay Carneros 1988: Smooth, concentrated and well behaved, with lively aromas of anise and pear flavors, and a sense of intensity that lasts through the finish. Delicious to drink now. $13.50 (6/30/90) **88**
Chardonnay Napa Valley 1987: Tart, clean and lively, with subtle toasty oak, pear and vanilla flavors that are young and complex. A delicate style that could use another year of cellaring. Drink now to 1994. $13 (3/31/90) **85**
Chardonnay Napa Valley 1986 $13 (11/15/88) **77**

CHATEAU ST. JEAN
Chardonnay Alexander Valley Belle Terre Vineyards 1989: Crisp, smooth and polished, with plenty of flavor and a sense of harmony and finesse. Honey, nutmeg, orange and pear notes linger on the finish. One of the better '89s. Drink now to 1994. 5,000 cases made. Rel: $18 Cur: $23 (6/30/92) **87**
Chardonnay Alexander Valley Belle Terre Vineyards 1988: Intense and sharply focused, with spice, apple, toast, nutmeg and pear-tinged flavors that are concentrated and rich, and a long, smooth texture. Altogether harmonious and very well balanced. Drink now to 1994. Rel: $16 Cur: $20 (5/31/90) **90**
Chardonnay Alexander Valley Belle Terre Vineyards 1987: Earthy and firm, with lean texture and hints of pear and honey on the finish, subtler than most, with fine balance. Rel: $16 Cur: $21 (5/15/89) **85**
Chardonnay Alexander Valley Belle Terre Vineyards 1986 Rel: $16 Cur: $20 (CH-3/90) **90**
Chardonnay Alexander Valley Belle Terre Vineyards 1985 Rel: $16 Cur: $25 (CH-3/90) **92**
Chardonnay Alexander Valley Belle Terre Vineyards 1984 Rel: $16 Cur: $27 (CH-3/90) **85**
Chardonnay Alexander Valley Belle Terre Vineyards 1983 Rel: $16.75 Cur: $30 (CH-3/90) **89**
Chardonnay Alexander Valley Belle Terre Vineyards 1982 Rel: $15.50 Cur: $20 (CH-3/90) **86**
Chardonnay Alexander Valley Belle Terre Vineyards 1981 Rel: $15 Cur: $18 (CH-3/90) **83**
Chardonnay Alexander Valley Belle Terre Vineyards 1980 Rel: $15 Cur: $24 (CH-3/90) **88**
Chardonnay Alexander Valley Belle Terre Vineyards 1979 Rel: $12 Cur: $22 (CH-3/90) **84**
Chardonnay Alexander Valley Belle Terre Vineyards 1978 Rel: $14 Cur: $20 (CH-3/90) **73**
Chardonnay Alexander Valley Belle Terre Vineyards 1977 Rel: $12 Cur: $22 (CH-3/90) **80**
Chardonnay Alexander Valley Belle Terre Vineyards 1976 Rel: $7.50 Cur: $22 (CH-7/90) **77**
Chardonnay Alexander Valley Belle Terre Vineyards 1975 Rel: $7.50 Cur: $22 (CH-7/90) **88**
Chardonnay Alexander Valley Gauer Ranch 1980 Rel: $14 Cur: $18 (CH-3/90) **74**
Chardonnay Alexander Valley Gauer Ranch 1979 Rel: $14 Cur: $18 (CH-3/90) **70**
Chardonnay Alexander Valley Jimtown Ranch 1989: Crisp and clean, with elegant, refined herb, green apple and spice flavors. For those who prefer delicacy in their Chardonnay. Drink now. $24 (3/31/92) **84**
Chardonnay Alexander Valley Jimtown Ranch 1988 ($NA) (CH-7/90) **88**
Chardonnay Alexander Valley Jimtown Ranch 1987 $15 (CH-3/90) **87**
Chardonnay Alexander Valley Jimtown Ranch 1983 Rel: $16 Cur: $20 (CH-7/90) **87**
Chardonnay Alexander Valley Jimtown Ranch 1981 Rel: $14.75 Cur: $22 (CH-3/90) **87**
Chardonnay Alexander Valley Jimtown Ranch 1980 Rel: $14 Cur: $16 (CH-3/90) **77**
Chardonnay Alexander Valley Riverview Vineyards 1976 Rel: $9.50 Cur: $22 (CH-7/90) **88**
Chardonnay Alexander Valley Robert Young Vineyards 1990: Complex and elegant, with a pretty array of honey, pear, citrus and hazelnut flavors that are neatly woven together. Plush, inviting and drinks well now, but can age through 1995. 5,000 cases made. $22 (6/30/92) **89**
Chardonnay Alexander Valley Robert Young Vineyards 1988: The flavors are mature, ripe and complex enough to go with the creamy texture. Offers aromas and flavors that lean toward pear, butter, vanilla and smoky oak, and hints of mineral and melon emerge on the finish. Soft and drinkable now. Rel: $18 Cur: $25 (6/30/91) **90**
Chardonnay Alexander Valley Robert Young Vineyards 1987 Rel: $18 Cur: $24 (CH-3/90) **91**
Chardonnay Alexander Valley Robert Young Vineyards 1986 Rel: $18 Cur: $30 (CH-3/90) **92**
Chardonnay Alexander Valley Robert Young Vineyards 1985 Rel: $18 Cur: $33 (CH-3/90) **91**
Chardonnay Alexander Valley Robert Young Vineyards 1984 Rel: $20 Cur: $30 (CH-3/90) **88**
Chardonnay Alexander Valley Robert Young Vineyards 1983 Rel: $18 Cur: $33 (CH-3/90) **88**
Chardonnay Alexander Valley Robert Young Vineyards 1982 Rel: $18 Cur: $20 (CH-3/90) **75**
Chardonnay Alexander Valley Robert Young Vineyards 1981 Rel: $18 Cur: $60 (CH-3/90) **86**
Chardonnay Alexander Valley Robert Young Vineyards 1980 Rel: $18 Cur: $30 (CH-3/90) **85**
Chardonnay Alexander Valley Robert Young Vineyards 1979 Rel: $17 Cur: $30 (CH-3/90) **85**
Chardonnay Alexander Valley Robert Young Vineyards 1978 Rel: $17 Cur: $25 (CH-3/90) **84**
Chardonnay Alexander Valley Robert Young Vineyards 1977 Rel: $17 Cur: $22 (CH-3/90) **68**
Chardonnay Alexander Valley Robert Young Vineyards 1976 Rel: $8.75 Cur: $25 (CH-7/90) **92**
Chardonnay Alexander Valley Robert Young Vineyards 1975 Rel: $7.75 Cur: $22 (CH-7/90) **63**
Chardonnay Alexander Valley Robert Young Vineyards Reserve 1987 ($NA/1.5L) (CH-7/90) **96**
Chardonnay Alexander Valley Robert Young Vineyards Reserve 1986 ($NA/1.5L) (CH-7/90) **91**
Chardonnay Alexander Valley Robert Young Vineyards Reserve 1985: Beautifully ripe, fruity and gaining maturity, this is complex in aroma, full and pearlike in flavor and beginning to show the intriguing effects of age in the earthy, buttery notes and creamy, velvety texture. Stays crisp and fruity on the finish. It can be safely cellared through 1995. 978 cases made. Rel: $40/1.5L Cur: $55/1.5L (9/30/90) **93**
Chardonnay Alexander Valley Robert Young Vineyards Reserve 1984 Rel: $40/1.5L Cur: $60/1.5L (CH-3/90) **87**
Chardonnay Alexander Valley Robert Young Vineyards Reserve 1982 Rel: $45 Cur: $50/1.5L (7/01/86) **76**
Chardonnay Dry Creek Valley Frank Johnson Vineyards 1986 Rel: $14 Cur: $19 (CH-7/90) **89**
Chardonnay Dry Creek Valley Frank Johnson Vineyards 1985 $14 (CH-3/90) **87**
Chardonnay Dry Creek Valley Frank Johnson Vineyards 1984 Rel: $14 Cur: $20 (CH-7/90) **88**
Chardonnay Dry Creek Valley Frank Johnson Vineyards 1981 $14.75 (1/01/84) **88**
Chardonnay Dry Creek Valley Frank Johnson Vineyards 1980 Rel: $14 Cur: $16 (CH-3/90) **79**
Chardonnay Dry Creek Valley Frank Johnson Vineyards 1979 $13.50 (CH-3/90) **78**
Chardonnay Sonoma County 1990: Crisp and floral, with a spicy Muscat-like edge to the basic grapefruit and apple flavors. Remains fruity, with little rounding from oak. Drinkable now. $12 (6/30/92) **84**
Chardonnay Sonoma County 1989: Crisp and fruity at first, but turns thin on the finish. Apple and melon flavors give it a bit of life. $12 (6/30/91) **80**
Chardonnay Sonoma County 1988: Distincitve for its fruitiness, with tiers of peach, nectarine, honey and pear flavors that are enlivened by zingy acidity and a pleasant aftertaste. Drink now. $12 (5/31/90) **86**
Chardonnay Sonoma County 1987 $12 (5/15/89) **83**
Chardonnay Sonoma County 1986 $11 (5/31/88) **83**
Chardonnay Sonoma County 1985 $11 (4/30/87) **88**
Chardonnay Sonoma County 1984 $12 (11/16/85) **71**
Chardonnay Sonoma County Bacigalupi 1975 Rel: $10 Cur: $21 (CH-7/90) **86**
Chardonnay Sonoma County Beltane Ranch 1976 Rel: $7.75 Cur: $18 (CH-7/90) **69**
Chardonnay Sonoma County Beltane Ranch 1975 Rel: $12.50 Cur: $21 (CH-7/90) **88**
Chardonnay Sonoma Valley Estate Selection 1990: A ripe, toasty style, with smoky pear, lemon, nutmeg and butter notes that are complex and intense, with a lingering aftertaste. Drink now to 1995. 2,500 cases made. $15 (6/30/92) **85**
Chardonnay Sonoma Valley Estate Selection 1989: A woody, spicy wine, with enticing nutmeg and vanilla aromas and snappy apple, pear and butter flavors that fill it out nicely. 2,021 cases made. $14 (7/15/91) **85**
Chardonnay Sonoma Valley Hunter Farms 1981 Rel: $14.75 Cur: $19 (CH-3/90) **81**
Chardonnay Sonoma Valley Hunter Farms 1980 Rel: $14 Cur: $17 (CH-3/90) **67**
Chardonnay Sonoma Valley Hunter Farms 1979 Rel: $14 Cur: $20 (CH-3/90) **80**
Chardonnay Sonoma Valley Hunter Farms 1978 Rel: $11.25 Cur: $18 (CH-3/90) **65**
Chardonnay Sonoma Valley Hunter Farms 1977 Rel: $10.25 Cur: $25 (CH-3/90) **81**
Chardonnay Sonoma Valley Les Pierres Vineyards 1978 Rel: $13.75 Cur: $22 (CH-3/90) **81**
Chardonnay Sonoma Valley Les Pierres Vineyards 1977 Rel: $13.75 Cur: $21 (CH-3/90) **79**

Chardonnay Sonoma Valley McCrea Vineyards 1987 $15 (CH-3/90) **88**
Chardonnay Sonoma Valley McCrea Vineyards 1986 Rel: $15 Cur: $17 (CH-3/90) **87**
Chardonnay Sonoma Valley McCrea Vineyards 1985 Rel: $14.25 Cur: $18 (CH-7/90) **86**
Chardonnay Sonoma Valley McCrea Vineyards 1984 Rel: $14.25 Cur: $17 (CH-3/90) **87**
Chardonnay Sonoma Valley McCrea Vineyards 1983 Rel: $15.25 Cur: $18 (CH-7/90) **85**
Chardonnay Sonoma Valley McCrea Vineyards 1982 Rel: $13 Cur: $18 (CH-7/90) **88**
Chardonnay Sonoma Valley McCrea Vineyards 1981 Rel: $15 Cur: $18 (CH-3/90) **75**
Chardonnay Sonoma Valley McCrea Vineyards 1980 Rel: $15 Cur: $18 (CH-3/90) **70**
Chardonnay Sonoma Valley McCrea Vineyards 1979 Rel: $14 Cur: $18 (CH-3/90) **70**
Chardonnay Sonoma Valley McCrea Vineyards 1978 Rel: $12 Cur: $20 (CH-3/90) **70**
Chardonnay Sonoma Valley McCrea Vineyards 1977 Rel: $10.25 Cur: $25 (CH-3/90) **85**
Chardonnay Sonoma Valley McCrea Vineyards 1976 Rel: $9.25 Cur: $20 (CH-7/90) **75**
Chardonnay Sonoma Valley McCrea Vineyards 1975 Rel: $8.75 Cur: $20 (CH-7/90) **78**
Chardonnay Sonoma Valley St. Jean Vineyards 1984 $14 (7/31/87) **74**
Chardonnay Sonoma Valley St. Jean Vineyards 1983 $14.75 (3/16/86) **70**
Chardonnay Sonoma Valley St. Jean Vineyards 1982 $14 (2/01/85) **91**
Chardonnay Sonoma Valley Wildwood Vineyards 1980 Rel: $13 Cur: $19 (CH-7/90) **71**
Chardonnay Sonoma Valley Wildwood Vineyards 1978 Rel: $12 Cur: $19 (CH-3/90) **65**
Chardonnay Sonoma Valley Wildwood Vineyards 1977 Rel: $15 Cur: $22 (CH-3/90) **73**
Chardonnay Sonoma Valley Wildwood Vineyards 1976 Rel: $10 Cur: $20 (CH-7/90) **82**
Chardonnay Sonoma Valley Wildwood Vineyards 1975 Rel: $9.50 Cur: $20 (CH-7/90) **70**

CHATEAU SOUVERAIN
Chardonnay Russian River Valley Allen Vineyard 1990: Crisp and flavorful, with lovely peach, nectarine and apple aromas and flavors that turn toward spice and vanilla on the long finish. A lively, graceful wine, with lots of appealing flavor. Drinkable now through 1994. 345 cases made. $13.50 (7/15/92) **88**
Chardonnay Sonoma County 1986 $9 (12/31/87) **83**
Chardonnay Sonoma County Barrel Fermented 1990: Ripe and fresh, with generous pear and vanilla aromas and flavors and hints of melon on the finish. A solid wine that's drinkable now. An especially good value. $10 (12/31/91) BB **88**
Chardonnay Sonoma Valley Carneros Private Reserve 1987: Tastes woody, lemony and crisp, but it's very lean. $12 (4/15/89) **74**
Chardonnay Sonoma Valley Carneros Reserve 1986 $12 (4/30/88) **78**
Chardonnay Sonoma Valley Carneros Sangiacomo Vineyard 1990: Spicy, smoky and complex, with a polished texture and generous pear and apple flavors at the core. Carefully made and appealingly balanced, displaying several dimensions. Should age gracefully through 1993 or '94. 513 cases made. $13.50 (7/15/92) **90**
Chardonnay Sonoma Valley Durell Vineyard 1990: Crisp and focused, with generous, spicy, toasty pear and citrus aromas and flavors. Leans more toward toast and spice on the finish. Drinkable now, but probably better in 1993 or '94. 365 cases made. $13.50 (7/15/92) **85**

CHATEAU WOLTNER
Chardonnay Howell Mountain 1991: Fresh, ripe and fruity, with crisp apple, pear and melon flavors and a pretty, spicy edge. Drink now through 1994. $12 (7/15/92) **84**
Chardonnay Howell Mountain 1989: Pleasant, light and elegant. A crisp, citrus acidity gives it life, and grapefruit and pear flavors lend a little substance. $12 (11/30/90) **83**
Chardonnay Howell Mountain Estate Reserve 1990: A crisp fruit component, showing lemon, pineapple and grapefruit, is nicely accented by spice and vanilla notes from oak aging. Tight, but very flavorful. It will need until about 1993 to start to come into its own. Tasted twice. 3,664 cases made. $26 (7/15/92) **88**
Chardonnay Howell Mountain Estate Reserve 1988 $24 (CH-4/90) **86**
Chardonnay Howell Mountain Estate Reserve 1987 $24 (CH-4/90) **88**
Chardonnay Howell Mountain Estate Reserve 1986 $24 (CH-4/90) **91**
Chardonnay Howell Mountain Estate Vineyards 1989: Tart and simple, with hints of nutmeg to liven up the basic lemon and pineapple aromas and flavors. Finishes well. Drink now. $16 (7/15/91) **82**
Chardonnay Howell Mountain Frederique Vineyard 1990: Crisp, tight, complex and focused, with layers of apple, lemon, pear and smoky vanilla flavors that stay with you from start to finish. While it's appealing now, it has the concentration to age through 1994. 492 cases made. $58 (7/15/92) **89**
Chardonnay Howell Mountain St. Thomas Vineyard 1990: Tight and taut, with crisp lemon, apple, nectarine and pear flavors and subtle oak shadings. Beautifully crafted, but young and unevolved, with a flinty, mineral aftertaste. A distinctive California Chardonnay that's drinkable now, but may be tastier in 1993. 1,097 cases made. $39 (7/15/92) **90**
Chardonnay Howell Mountain St. Thomas Vineyard 1988 $36 (CH-4/90) **86**
Chardonnay Howell Mountain St. Thomas Vineyard 1987 $36 (CH-4/90) **87**
Chardonnay Howell Mountain St. Thomas Vineyard 1986 $36 (CH-4/90) **89**
Chardonnay Howell Mountain St. Thomas Vineyard 1985 $30 (11/15/87) **68**
Chardonnay Howell Mountain Titus Vineyard 1990: Tight and firm, with crisp peach, pear and vanilla flavors that take on a pretty toasty, buttery nuance from the oak. Young and closed—probably best to cellar until 1993. 273 cases made. $58 (7/15/92) **88**
Chardonnay Howell Mountain Titus Vineyard 1988 $54 (CH-4/90) **86**
Chardonnay Howell Mountain Titus Vineyard 1987 $54 (CH-4/90) **85**
Chardonnay Howell Mountain Titus Vineyard 1986 $54 (CH-4/90) **88**
Chardonnay Howell Mountain Titus Vineyard 1985 $40 (11/15/87) **75**
Chardonnay Howell Mountain Woltner Estates 1985 Rel: $18 Cur: $28 (11/15/87) **79**

CHAUFFE-EAU
Chardonnay Carneros Sangiacomo 1990: Crisp and refined, with tart citrus, honey and pineapple notes that are clean and refreshing. Elegant and balanced, with a kiss of oak on the finish. Drink now to 1994. 275 cases made. $16 (6/15/92) **86**

CHESTNUT HILL
Chardonnay California 1988: A highly unusual style, seemingly stale, oxidized and candied, with peanutlike aromas, but no fruit. The finish is smooth, and the structure is elegant. Not for everyone. $8 (4/15/90) **74**
Chardonnay Napa Valley 1984 $7.50 (4/16/86) **72**
Chardonnay Napa Valley Draper Vineyards Reserve 1990: Toasty, spicy aromas and flavors show the effects of oak aging nicely, with the creamy pear and vanilla flavors emerging on the finish. Harmonious, with plenty of flavor to offer. Drinkable now. $12.50 (11/30/91) **87**
Chardonnay Sonoma County 1989: Dull and oxidized, with papery overtones to the very modest nutmeg and pear flavors. Not much life to it. Tasted twice. $7 (7/15/91) **69**
Chardonnay Sonoma County 1986 $8 (12/31/87) **75**

CHIMERE
Chardonnay Edna Valley 1989: Intense and varietal, with plenty of citrus, pear, melon and spice flavors that are rich and well focused. The finish gets a touch coarse, but with a few months' aging the rough edges may round out. Drink now to 1993. 247 cases made. $15 (7/15/91) **83**

CHIMNEY ROCK
Chardonnay Stags Leap District 1989: Tastes stripped, with extremely modest pear and apple flavors lurking in the background. Not exciting. Tasted twice. $16 (7/15/91) **72**
Chardonnay Stags Leap District 1988: This earthy, herbal wine has ripe undertones of peach and pineapple, but a slightly mushroomy component puts us off. Drinkable now. $15 (12/31/90) **77**
Chardonnay Stags Leap District 1987: Attractive for its pretty floral notes and pure Chardonnay fruit. The apple, spice and herb notes combine for complexity. Good length. Drink now. $15 (2/15/90) **81**
Chardonnay Stags Leap District 1986 $14 (10/15/88) **80**

CHRISTIAN BROTHERS
Chardonnay Napa Valley 1989: Fairly crisp and tangy, with apple and grapefruit flavors. A modest wine, with buttery notes. Straightforward, fresh and drinkable now, but it lacks depth. $7 (1/31/92) **79**
Chardonnay Napa Valley 1988: Fresh and floral, with nice rose petal overtones to the apple and slightly celerylike aromas and flavors. A bit earthy on the finish, but it's balanced and drinkable. $7.50 (6/30/91) **78**
Chardonnay Napa Valley 1987: Earthy and gamy, with heavy oak flavors. Clumsy and unappealing, but drinkable. Tasted three times. $10 (11/30/89) **69**
Chardonnay Napa Valley 1984 $8.50 (6/16/86) **76**
Chardonnay Napa Valley Barrel Fermented 1985 $11 (7/31/87) **88**
Chardonnay Napa Valley Barrel Fermented Private Reserve 1987 $11.50 (9/15/89) **83**
Chardonnay Napa Valley Barrel Fermented Private Reserve 1986 $12 (12/31/88) **87**
Chardonnay Napa Valley-Burgundy Montage Première Cuvée NV $15 (10/15/88) **86**

CHRISTOPHE
Chardonnay California 1990: Good fruit flavors and a hint of spice lend a bit of complexity to this otherwise simple, easy-going wine. Has ample pear and apple flavors and a short, clean finish. $7 (7/15/92) BB **81**
Chardonnay California 1989: Fresh and simple, with modest apple and pine aromas and flavors that remain lively on the finish. Drink soon. Tasted twice. $9 (7/15/91) **78**
Chardonnay California 1988: Generally light and lively, with concentration, crisp lemon and floral aromas and flavors that are balanced, turning smooth and delicate on the finish. Drink soon. $7.50 (4/30/90) BB **83**
Chardonnay California 1987 $8.50 (3/31/89) **74**
Chardonnay California 1985 $6.50 (11/15/86) **73**
Chardonnay California 1984 $5.50 (12/01/85) BB **84**
Chardonnay California Reserve 1989 $12 (7/15/91) **80**
Chardonnay California Reserve 1986 $9.50 (4/15/88) **77**

CINNABAR
Chardonnay Santa Cruz Mountains 1990: Broad and rich, with generous pear, honeysuckle and earth aromas and flavors, turning tart and crisply focused on the finish. Needs time to soften. Try in 1994. 1,705 cases made. $20 (3/31/92) **88**
Chardonnay Santa Cruz Mountains 1989: Assertively woody, with buttery, spicy aromas and flavors that don't have enough fruit to back them up. Some will find it attractive, but it favors style over substance. $18 (3/31/91) **79**

CLONINGER
Chardonnay Monterey 1989: This pleasant marriage of ripe fruit and oak offers a measure of elegance and finese. The melon, pear and spicy Chardonnay flavors are nicely balanced, with subtle toasty oak shadings and a lingering finish. Best now to 1993. $15 (7/15/91) **85**

CLOS DU BOIS
Chardonnay Alexander Valley Barrel Fermented 1990: Ripe and fruity, with tiers of pear, apple and citrus flavors that border on sweet. A simple wine that's drinkable now. Tasted twice, with consistent notes. $13 (3/31/92) **81**
Chardonnay Alexander Valley Barrel Fermented 1989: Spicy, earthy, moderately intense and balanced, hinting at olives or grassiness and lacking ripeness and generosity on the finish. Drinkable now. $11 (12/31/90) **80**
Chardonnay Alexander Valley Barrel Fermented 1988: Clean, refreshing and easy to enjoy. A medium-bodied, very fruity, peachy-tasting wine, with good acidity and structure and a lingering aftertaste. $11 (2/15/90) **84**
Chardonnay Alexander Valley Barrel Fermented 1988 $11 (CH-2/90) **85**
Chardonnay Alexander Valley Barrel Fermented 1987 $11 (CH-2/90) **87**
Chardonnay Alexander Valley Barrel Fermented 1986 Rel: $10 Cur: $13 (CH-12/89) **80**
Chardonnay Alexander Valley Barrel Fermented 1985 Rel: $9 Cur: $12 (CH-2/90) **84**
Chardonnay Alexander Valley Barrel Fermented 1984 Rel: $8 Cur: $12 (CH-2/90) **84**
Chardonnay Alexander Valley Barrel Fermented 1982 $9 (4/16/84) **85**
Chardonnay Alexander Valley Barrel Fermented 1980 $15 (4/16/84) **92**
Chardonnay Alexander Valley Calcaire Vineyard 1990: Lean and simple, with earthy, smoky pear flavors, a crisp texture and a bit of astringency on the finish. Should be at its best in 1993 or '94. $18 (7/15/92) **83**
Chardonnay Alexander Valley Calcaire Vineyard 1989: The ripe pear and pineapple flavors are showy at first but fade on the finish, picking up a slight chalky aftertaste. Drink now, while the fruit's still showing. $17 (7/15/91) **82**
Chardonnay Alexander Valley Calcaire Vineyard 1988: Has a beautiful core of ripe, rich pear, apple, spice and nutmeg flavors that hang together in a powerful yet elegant style. The toasty oak adds dimension and depth to the flavors, and the finish lingers on and on. Drink now to 1993. Rel: $17 Cur: $22 (5/15/90) **91**
Chardonnay Alexander Valley Calcaire Vineyard 1987 $20 (CH-2/90) **88**
Chardonnay Alexander Valley Calcaire Vineyard 1986 Rel: $16 Cur: $22 (CH-2/90) **85**
Chardonnay Alexander Valley Calcaire Vineyard 1985 Rel: $18 Cur: $25 (CH-2/90) **83**
Chardonnay Alexander Valley Calcaire Vineyard 1984 Rel: $12 Cur: $30 (CH-2/90) **90**
Chardonnay Alexander Valley Calcaire Vineyard 1984 Rel: $12 Cur: $30 (6/01/86) SS **93**
Chardonnay Alexander Valley Calcaire Vineyard 1983 Rel: $12 Cur: $30 (CH-2/90) **91**
Chardonnay Alexander Valley Calcaire Vineyard 1982 $11.25 (7/01/84) **92**
Chardonnay Dry Creek Valley Flintwood Vineyard 1989: Earthy and bitter with sour, hard-edged pineapple, citrus and spice notes. An exotic, highly manipulated style that misses the mark. Drink now. Tasted three times with consistent notes. Rel: $17 Cur: $22 (3/31/92) **72**
Chardonnay Dry Creek Valley Flintwood Vineyard 1988: Starts out smooth and elegant, offering pretty pear, vanilla, pineapple and spicy oak flavors that fan out on the finish, where the smoky nuances become attractive. Drink now to 1993. $18 (6/30/90) **89**
Chardonnay Dry Creek Valley Flintwood Vineyard 1987 $20 (CH-2/90) **87**
Chardonnay Dry Creek Valley Flintwood Vineyard 1986 Rel: $19.50 Cur: $23 (CH-2/90) **88**
Chardonnay Dry Creek Valley Flintwood Vineyard 1985 Rel: $18 Cur: $28 (3/31/87) **93**
Chardonnay Dry Creek Valley Flintwood Vineyard 1984 Rel: $11.25 Cur: $38 (6/01/86) **92**
Chardonnay Dry Creek Valley Flintwood Vineyard 1983 Rel: $10.50 Cur: $37 (7/01/85) SS **92**

Key to Symbols

The scores reported here are the results of blind tastings conducted by our panel of senior editors. Wines that carry the initials below are results of individual tastings.

THE WINE SPECTATOR 100-POINT SCALE 95-100—Classic, a great wine; *90-94*—Outstanding, superior character and style; *80-89*—Good to very good, a wine with special qualities; *70-79*—Average, drinkable wine that may have minor flaws; *60-69*—Below average, drinkable but not recommended; *50-59*—Poor, undrinkable, not recommended. "+"—With a score indicates a range; used primarily with barrel tastings to indicate a preliminary score.

SPECIAL DESIGNATIONS SS—Spectator Selection, CS—Cellar Selection, BB—Best Buy, (SNA)—Price not available, (NR)—Not released.

TASTER'S INITIALS (JG)—Jim Gordon, (HS)—Harvey Steiman, (JL)—James Laube, (JS)—James Suckling, (TM)—Thomas Matthews, (TR)—Terry Robards, (PM)—Per-Henrik Mansson, (BT)—Barrel Tasting (these wines were tasted blind from barrel samples), (CA-date)—*California's Great Cabernets* by James Laube, (CH-date)—*California's Great Chardonnays* by James Laube, (VP-date)—*Vintage Port* by James Suckling.

DATE TASTED Dates in parentheses represent the issue in which the rating was published.

Chardonnay Dry Creek Valley Flintwood Vineyard 1982 $11.25 (7/01/84) **79**
Chardonnay Dry Creek Valley Flintwood Vineyard 1980 Rel: $17 Cur: $32 (CH-2/90) **87**
Chardonnay Russian River Valley Winemaker's Reserve 1988: Big, ripe and bold, with complex honey, pear, spice and herbal notes. A distinctive style, with plenty of richness and depth. Has a buttery aftertaste. Drink now to 1994. Tasted twice. Rel: $24 Cur: $28 (12/31/91) **86**
Chardonnay Alexander Valley Winemaker's Reserve 1987 $24 (2/28/90) **93**
Chardonnay Alexander Valley Proprietor's Reserve 1986 Rel: $22.50 Cur: $25 (CH-5/90) **78**
Chardonnay Alexander Valley Proprietor's Reserve 1985 Rel: $22 Cur: $25 (CH-5/90) **85**
Chardonnay Alexander Valley Proprietor's Reserve 1984 Rel: $18 Cur: $21 (10/31/86) **87**
Chardonnay Alexander Valley Proprietor's Reserve 1981 Rel: $15 Cur: $22 (CH-5/90) **70**

CLOS PEGASE
Chardonnay Alexander Valley 1985 Rel: $13 Cur: $15 (CH-3/90) **87**
Chardonnay Carneros 1988 $16.50 (5/15/90) **90**
Chardonnay Carneros 1987: Very vibrant and fruity in flavor, with a big structure of acidity. Full-bodied, with intensely ripe peach and pear flavors, hints of vanilla and honey and an almost sweet finish that lasts and lasts. $15.50 (2/15/90) **89**
Chardonnay Carneros 1986 $15.50 (CH-3/90) **89**
Chardonnay Napa Valley 1990: Crisp in texture, with ripe pear and citrus aromas and flavors. Leans toward oak and a slight bitterness on the finish. Tight and unyielding now—should be best around 1993 or '94. $13 (7/15/92) **85**
Chardonnay Napa Valley 1989: Crisp and fruity, with plenty of bold apple and pear aromas and flavors. The texture turns creamy on the finish. Drinkable now, but probably better staring in 1993. Much better than a bottle tasted earlier. $13 (9/15/91) **88**
Chardonnay Napa Valley 1988: There is a lot to like in this wine, with its pure pear and lemon flavors and elegant butterscotch on the finish, but in the middle it's missing the core of concentration for greatness. Drink now. $12 (6/30/90) **86**
Chardonnay Napa Valley 1987 $12 (CH-3/90) **86**
Chardonnay Napa Valley 1986 Rel: $12 Cur: $14 (CH-3/90) **85**
Chardonnay Sonoma County Hommage 1989: Crisp, clean and full-bodied, with distinct pear and grapefruit flavors that are ripe and attractive. The flavors fade on the finish, but this is a young, well-balanced wine that may benefit from a few more months' bottle age. Drink now to 1994. 1,792 cases made. $18.50 (8/31/91) **87**

CLOS ROBERT
Chardonnay Napa Valley 1985 $6 (7/31/87) **68**
Chardonnay Napa Valley Lot 3 1989: Soft and simple, with nice apple and earthy notes. Not rich or concentrated, but it's pleasant to drink now. $9 (7/15/91) **78**

CLOS DU VAL
Chardonnay California 1983 Rel: $11.50 Cur: $15 (2/16/85) **79**
Chardonnay California 1982 Rel: $11.50 Cur: $16 (6/01/90) **78**
Chardonnay California Gran Val 1986 $8.50 (4/15/88) **77**
Chardonnay California Gran Val 1984 $6.50 (4/16/86) **75**
Chardonnay Carneros Napa Valley Carneros Estate 1990: Decent but uninspired, with light pear and spice notes. Lacks its usual rich flavors and depth. Drink now. Tasted twice. $16 (3/31/92) **75**
Chardonnay Carneros Napa Valley Carneros Estate 1989: Intense and elegant, with ripe pear, spice, pineapple and citrus flavors that are woven together with fine balance. The aftertaste keeps echoing the flavors. Drink now. Rel: $15 Cur: $17 (3/31/91) **89**
Chardonnay Carneros Napa Valley Carneros Estate 1988: Rich, smooth and creamy with well-defined pear and apple flavors. The wine is simple and direct but lacks oomph. Drink now. Rel: $16 Cur: $18 (6/30/90) **83**
Chardonnay Carneros Napa Valley Carneros Estate 1987 Rel: $13 Cur: $17 (CH-6/90) **89**
Chardonnay Carneros Napa Valley Carneros Estate 1986 Rel: $12 Cur: $14 (CH-6/90) **84**
Chardonnay Napa Valley 1987 $12 (CH-6/90) **87**
Chardonnay Napa Valley 1985 Rel: $11.50 Cur: $17 (CH-6/90) **87**
Chardonnay Napa Valley 1984 Rel: $11.50 Cur: $15 (CH-6/90) **85**
Chardonnay Napa Valley 1983 Rel: $11.50 Cur: $15 (CH-6/90) **82**
Chardonnay Napa Valley 1981 Rel: $12.50 Cur: $18 (CH-6/90) **78**
Chardonnay Napa Valley 1980 Rel: $12.50 Cur: $18 (CH-6/90) **80**
Chardonnay Napa Valley Joli Val 1989: Has delicate spice, vanilla, melon and mineral notes, but lacks richness and concentration, with the flavors turning watery on the finish. Drink now. $13 (7/15/91) **79**
Chardonnay Napa Valley Joli Val 1988: A wine with plenty of tart peach and apple flavors, it finishes with good length. Ready to drink now. $12.50 (1/31/90) **86**

B.R. COHN
Chardonnay Sonoma Valley Olive Hill Vineyard 1989: A very lean, dry and austere wine, with tart pear, earth and vegetal flavors. Difficult to get excited about. Tasted twice. 4,800 cases made. $14 (5/31/91) **78**
Chardonnay Sonoma Valley Olive Hill Vineyard 1988: Seems closed in and restrained, although there is some vanilla-tinged pear and apple on the finish to remind you it's Chardonnay. A bit astringent. Drink now. $15 (10/31/89) **82**
Chardonnay Sonoma Valley Olive Hill Vineyard 1986 $12 (10/31/88) **87**
Chardonnay Sonoma Valley Olive Hill Vineyard Barrel Reserve 1985 $21 (6/30/87) **88**
Chardonnay Sonoma Valley Olive Hill Vineyard Silver Label 1990: A focused, generous wine that shows appealing apple, citrus and vanilla aromas and flavors and brings on spice and honey notes on the finish. Seems a little tight and ungenerous, should be better after 1993. 3,500 cases made. $14 (7/31/92) **85**

COLBY
Chardonnay Napa Valley 1988: Very crisp in texture and strongly spicy, almost tarry in flavor. A buttery wine, with richness, but not a lot of flavor in the middle. A style that many will like. $15 (9/15/91) **82**
Chardonnay Napa Valley 1986: Has fabulous aromas of complex pear, toast, butter and earth, with flavors to match. Deep, complex, rich and engaging, picking up smoky toast, mineral and butterscotch flavors that are lively and seductive. Drink now to 1998. 140 cases made. $11 (5/31/89) **81**
Chardonnay Napa Valley 1985 $10.75 (11/15/87) **87**

CONCANNON
Chardonnay California Selected Vineyards 1985 $10.50 (6/30/87) **81**
Chardonnay California Selected Vineyards 1984 $9 (4/16/86) **88**
Chardonnay Santa Clara Valley Mistral Vineyard 1988: Fresh and lively, with nice apple and grapefruit aromas and flavors that are refreshing and spicy on the finish. Drinkable now. $12 (7/15/91) **83**

CONGRESS SPRINGS
Chardonnay Santa Clara County Barrel Fermented 1989: Has the floral, apricot aromas and flavors of a Riesling, with the rich texture and earthy mineral overtones to tell it's Chardonnay. Soft in structure and also on the finish. 2,643 cases made. $12 (7/15/91) **85**
Chardonnay Santa Clara County Barrel Fermented 1988: This one has far too much of a vinegar aroma and flavor for the vaguely buttery flavor to overcome. Not to our tastes. Tasted twice. $14 (2/15/90) **68**
Chardonnay Santa Clara County Barrel Fermented 1983 Rel: $10 Cur: $25 (CH-4/90) **85**
Chardonnay Santa Clara County 1987 Rel: $12 Cur: $19 (CH-4/90) **84**
Chardonnay Santa Clara County 1986 Rel: $12 Cur: $18 (CH-4/90) **83**
Chardonnay Santa Clara County 1985 Rel: $12 Cur: $20 (CH-4/90) **87**
Chardonnay Santa Clara County 1984 Rel: $11 Cur: $25 (CH-4/90) **90**
Chardonnay Santa Clara County 1982 Rel: $10 Cur: $20 (CH-4/90) **79**
Chardonnay Santa Clara County San Ysidro Reserve 1989: Soft and generous, with lots of honey- and nut-tinged apple and pear flavors that are almost sweet on the finish. A likable wine that probably should be consumed soon. 2,607 cases made. $15 (7/15/91) **88**
Chardonnay Santa Clara County San Ysidro Reserve 1988: A rich, ripe and spicy wine with lots of nutmeg and clove to make the apple and lemon flavors come alive; it's silky textured, long and smooth. Drinkable now, but the long finish suggests that cellaring until 1993 wouldn't be inappropriate. 2,682 cases made. $20 (1/31/90) **89**
Chardonnay Santa Clara County San Ysidro Reserve 1987 Rel: $16 Cur: $22 (CH-4/90) **90**
Chardonnay Santa Clara County San Ysidro Reserve 1986 Rel: $15 Cur: $20 (CH-4/90) **85**
Chardonnay Santa Cruz Mountains Monmartre 1988 $30 (CH-4/90) **88**
Chardonnay Santa Cruz Mountains Monmartre 1987 Rel: $28 Cur: $32 (CH-4/90) **87**
Chardonnay Santa Cruz Mountains Private Reserve 1986 Rel: $20 Cur: $23 (CH-4/90) **85**
Chardonnay Santa Cruz Mountains Private Reserve 1985 Rel: $16 Cur: $27 (CH-4/90) **84**
Chardonnay Santa Cruz Mountains Private Reserve 1984 Rel: $16 Cur: $27 (CH-4/90) **80**
Chardonnay Santa Cruz Mountains Private Reserve 1983 Rel: $15 Cur: $28 (CH-4/90) **74**
Chardonnay Santa Cruz Mountains Private Reserve 1982 Rel: $15 Cur: $28 (CH-4/90) **87**

CONN CREEK
Chardonnay Napa Valley Barrel Select 1988: Has crisp, spicy Chardonnay flavor, with ripe pear, melon and apple notes that turn elegant. Young, intense and concentrated; should drink well through 1994. $13 (7/15/91) **86**
Chardonnay Napa Valley Barrel Select 1987: Strikes a fine balance between firm, tart acidity and lush, clean, complex fruit flavors. Tiers of pear, lemon, nutmeg and spice are all neatly woven together, finishing with a burst of fruit. May get better with a year in the cellar. Fair price. Drink now to 1995. 5,000 cases made. $12 (9/15/90) **88**
Chardonnay Napa Valley Barrel Select Lot No. 32 1985 $12 (2/15/88) **80**
Chardonnay Napa Valley Barrel Select Lot No. 139 1985 $12.50 (12/31/88) **78**
Chardonnay Napa Valley Barrel Select 1983 $14 (6/30/87) **83**
Chardonnay Napa Valley 1982 $12.50 (11/01/85) **81**
Chardonnay Napa Valley Château Maja 1984 $6.50 (4/16/86) BB **84**

COOK'S
Chardonnay California Captain's Reserve 1990: Distinctive for its ripe, peachy aromas and flavors, it offers a nice display of fruit, albeit one-dimensional. A simple wine to drink now. $5.50 (3/31/92) **77**

CORBETT CANYON
Chardonnay Central Coast 1984 $8 (3/01/86) BB **84**
Chardonnay Central Coast Coastal Classic 1990: Tastes like a dry late-harvest Riesling, if you can imagine that. Very odd, with ample honey and citrus aromas, but the flavors are thin and fall flat on the finish. $6 (7/15/92) **74**
Chardonnay Central Coast Coastal Classic 1989: Snappy, fresh and crisp, with pretty Pippin apple flavors that turn floral and spicy on the finish. Balanced, with good depth and richness and a lively aftertaste. Drink now to 1993. $7/1L (7/15/91) BB **84**
Chardonnay Central Coast Coastal Classic 1988: Has an orange and grapefruit character that offers plenty of flavor and crispness if not complexity. $6.50/1L (12/15/89) **75**
Chardonnay Central Coast Coastal Classic 1987 $7/1L (7/15/88) **79**
Chardonnay Central Coast Coastal Classic 1986 $6.50/1L (11/15/87) **68**
Chardonnay Central Coast Reserve 1988 $9.50 (7/15/91) **78**
Chardonnay Central Coast Reserve 1987 $8 (12/15/89) **80**
Chardonnay Central Coast Select 1986 $8.75 (3/15/89) **66**
Chardonnay Central Coast Select 1985 $9 (1/31/87) **83**
Chardonnay Edna Valley Winemaker's Reserve 1984 $10 (7/01/86) **67**
Chardonnay Santa Barbara County Reserve 1990 $9.50 (7/15/92) **77**

COSENTINO
Chardonnay Napa County 1990: Ripe and flavorful, with ripe pear, vanilla, honey and spice flavors that have good depth. Finish turns oaky with a hint of must. Drink now to 1995. Tasted twice. 1,200 cases made. $14 (3/31/92) **83**
Chardonnay Napa County 1989: Soft and pleasant, with a nice smack of wood to lift the otherwise simple, modest peach and apple flavors. Drinkable now. 1,900 cases made. $13 (4/15/91) **81**
Chardonnay Napa Valley 1987: Ripe and generous without losing its impeccable balance, showing depth of pear, spice and honey flavors that echo a long time on the finish. $11.50 (3/15/89) **91**
Chardonnay Napa County The Sculptor 1990 $18 (7/15/92) **83**
Chardonnay Napa Valley The Sculptor 1989: An earthy style, with lemony pear and spicy oak flavors that offer moderate depth and concentration. Lacks focus on the finish, making it taste simple and incomplete. Drink now. 850 cases made. $18 (7/15/91) **80**
Chardonnay Napa Valley The Sculptor 1988: A touch of astringency runs through the apple, pear, honey and nutmeg flavors, but this wine is well balanced, with plenty of flavor and intensity. Could use a year to settle down. Drink now to 1994. $18 (6/15/90) **86**
Chardonnay Napa Valley The Sculptor 1987: Attractive and full blown. Plenty of ripe peach and honey flavors in a rich, oaky style. Drink now. $18 (7/15/89) **84**
Chardonnay Napa Valley The Sculptor 1986 $17 (9/15/88) **80**

COTTONWOOD CANYON
Chardonnay Central Coast 1989: Broad and rich, with flavors that are much more mature than the vintage would indicate, centered around pear and honey right through the long finish. Drink soon. 2,960 cases made. $14 (7/15/91) **85**
Chardonnay Santa Barbara County Barrel Select 1989: Fat, ripe and oily, with intense tropical fruit flavors and loads of rich banana, honey, pear and butter notes that are long and full. A delicious mouthful of wine. Drink now to 1994. 489 cases made. $19/500ml (3/31/92) **90**

CRESTON
Chardonnay Central Coast 1985 $10 (11/15/87) **81**
Chardonnay Paso Robles Barrel Fermented 1989: Ripe, smooth and buttery, with generous pear and lemon flavors turning toward butterscotch on the finish. A pleasantly plump wine that's best to drink early. $10 (12/31/91) **83**
Chardonnay San Luis Obispo County 1987: Refreshing and straightforward. Crisp, grassy smelling, lean in flavor and slightly tart in balance. $12 (12/15/89) **80**

CRICHTON HALL
Chardonnay Napa Valley 1990: Rich, smooth and toasty, with ripe pear, almond and citrus flavors that are thick and bold. Could use a little more finesse on the aftertaste. Drink now to 1994. 3,000 cases made. $18 (7/15/92) **84**
Chardonnay Napa Valley 1989: Very lean and simple, with a watery texture, but it does have nice lemony pear and delicate toast flavors. Drink soon. $16.50 (7/15/91) **82**
Chardonnay Napa Valley 1988: Blunt and tannic, with authoritative ripe pineapple flavor and plenty of oak, but not much in the way of elegance or finesse. Perhaps with time it will show more charm. Drink now to 1993. 3,900 cases made. $16 (12/31/90) **82**
Chardonnay Napa Valley 1987 $16 (11/15/89) **75**

CRONIN
Chardonnay Alexander Valley 1989: A bold, rich, oaky style, with the fruit concentration to stand up to the wood. The honey, pear, spice and citrus notes hang together nicely and the finish lingers. Ready now through 1994. $14 (8/31/91) **86**
Chardonnay Alexander Valley Stuhlmuller Vineyard 1990: Tight and focused, with rich, complex honey, pear and toast flavors that are intense and lively. A solid wine from start to finish. Should soften with bottle time. Drink or hold through 1995. $16 (7/15/92) **88**

Chardonnay Alexander Valley Stuhlmuller Vineyard 1988: An oaky wine, with plenty of vanilla and toast notes, but also some pretty, elegant pear, fig and leaf flavors that are intense and spicy yet blunt. Drink now. $18 (6/30/90) **87**
Chardonnay Monterey County Ventana Vineyard 1990: Intense and buttery, with ripe, round pear, citrus and melon flavors that hang together nicely. The finish is long and complex. Drink now through 1995. $14 (7/15/92) **88**
Chardonnay Monterey County Ventana Vineyard 1988: Ripe, round and smooth, with elegant pear, apple, spice and oak flavors that blend together well. Finishes with a touch of nutmeg and plenty of fruit. Drink now. $18 (6/30/90) **84**
Chardonnay Napa Valley 1990: Ripe, round and generous, this is smooth and creamy, with bold pear, honey, butter and vanilla aromas and flavors. Fruit persists on the finish. Feels young and tight now, but has excellent potential. Drink after 1993. 275 cases made. $18 (7/15/92) **90**
Chardonnay Napa Valley 1989: Altogether a nice drink, despite an earthy edge to the pear, smoke, toast and honey flavors. Has ripe, rich flavors, but the finish tapers off, not unlike many '89s. Drink now to 1993. $18 (8/31/91) **87**
Chardonnay Napa Valley 1988: Has plenty of ripe fig and pear flavors but they taste rather simple and lack pizzazz, finishing with oak and honey flavors that taste a bit tired. Drink now. $18 (5/31/90) **78**
Chardonnay Santa Cruz Mountains 1989: Has a gamy, earthy streak that runs through the pear and apple flavors, finishing with a burnt quality that's not satisfying. Hollow in the middle, too. Of average quality. $20 (3/31/92) **74**
Chardonnay Santa Cruz Mountains 1988: A generous, spicy wine that's focused and concentrated, with hints of honey and butter rounding out the pear and citrus flavors. A bit astringent now, but cellaring until 1993 should smooth it out. $20 (4/30/91) **85**
Chardonnay Santa Cruz Mountains 1987: Rich, ripe and intense with concentrated orange, pear, spice, and pretty toasty oak flavors that combine to give it depth and complexity. Drink now to 1994. $18 (2/15/90) **90**

CRUVINET
Chardonnay California 1984 $4.50 (9/15/86) **90**

CRYSTAL VALLEY
Chardonnay North Coast 1986 $8.50 (11/15/87) **70**

CUVAISON
Chardonnay Carneros Napa Valley 1990: Tart, crisp and lemony, with hints of pear and grapefruit flavors, but it's an austere, mouth-puckering style that needs food to soften it. Tasted twice. $16 (3/31/92) **81**
Chardonnay Carneros Napa Valley 1989: Fresh, floral aromas and flavors are pleasant enough, and the peach and vanilla notes that echo on the finish are somewhat elegant. A medium-weight wine that's ultimately simple and fresh. Drinkable now. $14 (7/15/91) **82**
Chardonnay Carneros Napa Valley 1988: Remarkably elegant, crisp, clean and refreshing, with fresh, ripe apple, pear and lemon flavors that are subtle and complex, framed by just a touch of oak, leaving a long, mouth-watering finish. Drink in 1993. Rel: $15 Cur: $17 (2/28/90) SS **91**
Chardonnay Napa Valley 1987 Rel: $13.50 Cur: $17 (CH-4/90) **90**
Chardonnay Napa Valley 1986 Rel: $12.75 Cur: $18 (CH-4/90) **89**
Chardonnay Napa Valley 1985 Rel: $12 Cur: $20 (CH-4/90) **93**
Chardonnay Napa Valley 1984 Rel: $12 Cur: $20 (CH-4/90) **82**
Chardonnay Napa Valley 1983 Rel: $12 Cur: $17 (CH-4/90) **62**
Chardonnay Napa Valley 1982 Rel: $12 Cur: $17 (CH-4/90) **61**
Chardonnay Napa Valley 1981 Rel: $12 Cur: $18 (CH-4/90) **75**
Chardonnay Napa Valley 1980 Rel: $11 Cur: $26 (CH-4/90) **87**
Chardonnay Napa Valley 1979 Rel: $10 Cur: $26 (CH-4/90) **84**
Chardonnay Napa Valley 1978 Rel: $10 Cur: $28 (CH-4/90) **81**
Chardonnay Carneros Napa Valley Reserve 1988 $25 (CH-6/90) **92**
Chardonnay Carneros Napa Valley Reserve 1987 $22 (CH-7/90) **91**
Chardonnay Carneros Napa Valley Reserve 1986 Rel: $20 Cur: $28 (CH-6/90) **94**

CYPRESS LANE
Chardonnay California 1986 $6 (12/31/87) **71**
Chardonnay California 1985 $6 (1/31/87) **72**

DE LOACH
Chardonnay Russian River Valley 1990: Crisp, spicy and silky, with nutmeg-tinged peach and apricot flavors shaded by honey and almond notes that sneak in on the finish. Drinkable now. $15 (5/15/92) **85**
Chardonnay Russian River Valley 1989: Intense, crisp, lively and tart, with rich, ripe pineapple, pear, spice and citrus shadings that are deep and intriguing. The finish is crisp and tart, echoing plenty of flavor. Drink now to 1994. Rel: $15 Cur: $18 (3/31/91) **87**
Chardonnay Russian River Valley 1988: Crisp in texture, with plenty of pineapple and guava aromas and flavors to make it attractive and enough spritz to keep it delicate. Attractive to drink now. Rel: $15 Cur: $19 (11/15/89) **86**
Chardonnay Russian River Valley 1987 Rel: $15 Cur: $22 (CH-2/90) **87**
Chardonnay Russian River Valley 1986 Rel: $14 Cur: $25 (CH-2/90) **89**
Chardonnay Russian River Valley 1985 Rel: $14 Cur: $33 (CH-2/90) **90**
Chardonnay Russian River Valley 1984 Rel: $12.50 Cur: $30 (CH-2/90) **88**
Chardonnay Russian River Valley 1983 Rel: $12 Cur: $22 (CH-2/90) **83**
Chardonnay Russian River Valley 1982 Rel: $12 Cur: $20 (CH-2/90) **74**
Chardonnay Russian River Valley 1981 Rel: $10 Cur: $18 (CH-2/90) **72**
Chardonnay Russian River Valley 1980 Rel: $10 Cur: $18 (CH-2/90) **62**
Chardonnay Russian River Valley O.F.S. 1990: Ripe and intense, with a beam of crisp, clean, sharply focused grapefruit and pear-scented flavor that is fresh and lively. Tight and age-worthy. Still, there's a pretty silkiness to the texture. Drink now to 1995. 4,055 cases made. $25 (5/15/92) **90**
Chardonnay Russian River Valley O.F.S. 1989: Intense, ripe and full-bodied, with full-blown pear, fig, pineapple and oak flavors that are deep and well proportioned. The flavors taper off on the finish, but it's a big, complex mouthful of wine from start to finish. Drink now to 1994. 3,500 cases made. Rel: $22 Cur: $24 (3/31/91) **89**
Chardonnay Russian River Valley O.F.S. 1988: Very rich in fruit flavor yet light on oak, so it has considerable finesse and a long-lasting finish. Its pear, pineapple and banana flavors are almost sweet. Rel: $22 Cur: $25 (2/15/90) **88**
Chardonnay Russian River Valley O.F.S. 1987 Rel: $22 Cur: $40 (CH-5/90) **92**
Chardonnay Russian River Valley O.F.S. 1986 Rel: $22 Cur: $28 (CH-2/90) **86**
Chardonnay Russian River Valley O.F.S. 1985 Rel: $20 Cur: $47 (CH-2/90) **79**
Chardonnay Russian River Valley O.F.S. 1984 $20 (CH-2/90) **90**

DE LORIMIER
Chardonnay Alexander Valley Prism 1989: Coarse and thin, with very tart, crisp, acidic fruit flavors that display citrus and barely ripe pear notes. Ultratart. Drink now. Tasted twice. 2,500 cases made. $13.50 (3/31/92) **76**
Chardonnay Alexander Valley Prism 1988: Rich, smooth and creamy, with a silky texture and pretty pear, lemon, spice and melon flavors that are elegant and well proportioned. Finishes with delicacy and grace. Delicious now till 1993. 2,300 cases made. $13.50 (9/30/90) **90**
Chardonnay Alexander Valley Prism 1987: Firm and flavorful, with persistent peach and spice aromas and flavors plus a touch of oak, with crisp enough acidity to carry the finish a long way. $13.50 (4/15/89) **86**

DE MOOR
Chardonnay Alexander Valley Napa Cellars Black Mountain Vineyard 1981 $11 (4/16/84) **86**
Chardonnay Napa Valley 1990: Has odd flavors, showing more orange than usual, and more than a touch of oak on the finish. A lean wine that's drinkable now. 1,900 cases made. $14 (6/30/92) **76**
Chardonnay Napa Valley 1989: Complex and rich, with tiers of creamy honey, pear, butter and spice flavors. A solid value, showing more depth and intensity than many '89s. Drink now to 1994. $13 (3/15/92) **85**
Chardonnay Napa Valley Owners Select 1988: Plenty of ripe pear, pineapple, melon and toast flavors combine for a wine of richness and complexity. Has a round, smooth texture and finishes with a creamy aftertaste. Drink now to 1994. $14 (7/15/91) **87**

DEER PARK
Chardonnay Napa Valley 1989: Celery, dill and earth aromas and flavors don't remind us much of Chardonnay. Not for us. Tasted twice. 600 cases made. $14 (7/15/91) **67**

DEER VALLEY
Chardonnay California 1989: Has slight hints of melon, pear and spice flavors, but they quickly turn innocuous. $7 (7/15/91) **74**

DEHLINGER
Chardonnay Russian River Valley 1990: Moderately rich and complex, with pleasing apple, citrus, oak and spice flavors that hang together nicely and echo as they build on the finish. 3,700 cases made. $13.50 (4/15/92) **88**
Chardonnay Russian River Valley 1989: One of the better '89s we've had so far. Smooth and flavorful, with buttery notes that start in the aroma and last through the spicy, long finish. Gets better with each sip. The apple, peach and honey flavors blend harmoniously. Drink now through 1993. Rel: $13 Cur: $16 (2/28/91) **89**
Chardonnay Russian River Valley 1988: A well-balanced, well-mannered wine that has good, crisp fruit flavors reined in by acidity. Not rich or buttery, but its peach and nectarine flavors have depth. Rel: $12 Cur: $15 (2/15/90) **85**
Chardonnay Russian River Valley 1987 Rel: $11.50 Cur: $16 (CH-4/90) **90**
Chardonnay Russian River Valley 1986 Rel: $11 Cur: $16 (CH-4/90) **87**
Chardonnay Russian River Valley 1985 Rel: $10 Cur: $19 (CH-5/90) **86**
Chardonnay Russian River Valley 1984 Rel: $10 Cur: $17 (CH-4/90) **86**
Chardonnay Russian River Valley 1983 Rel: $10 Cur: $17 (CH-4/90) **85**
Chardonnay Russian River Valley 1982 $10 (9/01/85) **55**
Chardonnay Russian River Valley The Montrachet Cuvée 1990: Ripe and full, with pretty pear, nectarine, tangerine and honey notes and subtle oak shadings. Offers plenty of flavor that stays with you. Drink now to 1994. 150 cases made. $18 (4/15/92) **87**

DELICATO
Chardonnay Napa Valley Barrel Fermented Golden Anniversary 1984 $10 (4/30/87) **87**

DEVLIN
Chardonnay Santa Cruz Mountains Meyley Vineyard 1989: Tastes oxidized and flabby, with more oak than fruit showing. Barely drinkable. $10 (7/15/91) **70**

DION
Chardonnay Sonoma Valley 1986 $10 (12/31/88) **78**

DOLAN
Chardonnay Mendocino 1987 $15 (12/31/88) **88**

DOMAINE DE CLARCK
Chardonnay Monterey County 1990: Elegant and stylish, with layers of honey, pear, toast and spice flavors that are neatly woven together. The finish is long and complex. Best to drink now through 1994. 900 cases made. $14 (3/31/92) **86**
Chardonnay Monterey County Première 1989: Ripe and rich, reminiscent of a good Meursault, glowing with rich, honeyed, creamy hazelnut and pear aromas and flavors. Smooth in texture and long on the palate, it's soft and supple. Drink now. 825 cases made. $14 (4/15/91) **89**
Chardonnay Monterey County Première Réserve Unfiltered 1990: Intriguing, with strong earthy notes that add dimension to the ripe pear, melon and citrus flavors. A balanced and complex wine, with a silky texture and plenty of length. Drink now to 1994. 140 cases made. $20 (3/31/92) **86**

DOMAINE MICHEL
Chardonnay Sonoma County 1989: Intense and oaky, with firm pear, apple and wood flavors that are crisp and tight. May benefit from time in the bottle, but doesn't blossom on the finish. Lacks harmony. Drink now to 1994. $15 (6/15/92) **82**
Chardonnay Sonoma County 1988: An interesting, lively wine that has nutty aromas, lean fruit flavors accented by almond and mineral notes and a rather tight, chalky finish. Not for everyone, but we find it enjoyable. $16 (3/31/91) **83**
Chardonnay Sonoma County 1987: Earthy pear and grapefruit flavors are moderately intense and concentrated, but it lacks drama. It's a simple, middle-of-the-road wine. Drink now. $16 (6/30/90) **76**
Chardonnay Sonoma County 1986 $16 (12/31/88) **76**

DOMAINE NAPA
Chardonnay California 1989: An elegant, delicate wine, with fresh, clean nectarine, melon and spice flavors that are lively and vibrant. Lightens up on the finish. Attractive to drink now, while the fruit is pure. From Guenoc. $8 (2/28/91) BB **82**
Chardonnay Napa Valley 1990: Lean and crisp, with subdued flavors that edge toward lemon and pear, finishing with a thwack of oak. Tough to drink now, but should be better around 1993 or '94. 1,200 cases made. $14 (7/15/92) **82**
Chardonnay Napa Valley 1989: Ordinary, stale flavors lack vitality and freshness. Picks up spice notes on the aftertaste, but doesn't overcome the shortness of fruit. Drink now. Tasted twice. 1,000 cases made. $12.50 (7/15/91) **77**
Chardonnay Napa Valley 1988 $12.50 (6/30/90) **81**
Chardonnay Napa Valley 1987 $12 (7/15/89) **80**

DOMAINE DE NAPA
Chardonnay Napa Valley 1986 $9.50 (10/15/88) **82**
Chardonnay Napa Valley Barrel Fermented 1986 $14.50 (12/31/88) **73**

Key to Symbols

The scores reported here are the results of blind tastings conducted by our panel of senior editors. Wines that carry the initials below are results of individual tastings.

THE WINE SPECTATOR 100-POINT SCALE ***95-100***—Classic, a great wine; ***90-94***—Outstanding, superior character and style; ***80-89***—Good to very good, a wine with special qualities; ***70-79***—Average, drinkable wine that may have minor flaws; ***60-69***—Below average, drinkable but not recommended; ***50-59***—Poor, undrinkable, not recommended. "+"—With a score indicates a range; used primarily with barrel tastings to indicate a preliminary score.

SPECIAL DESIGNATIONS SS—Spectator Selection, CS—Cellar Selection, BB—Best Buy, ($NA)—Price not available, (NR)—Not released.

TASTER'S INITIALS (JG)—Jim Gordon, (HS)—Harvey Steiman, (JL)—James Laube, (JS)—James Suckling, (TM)—Thomas Matthews, (TR)—Terry Robards, (PM)—Per-Henrik Mansson, (BT)—Barrel Tasting (these wines were tasted blind from barrel samples), (CA-date)—*California's Great Cabernets* by James Laube, (CH-date)—*California's Great Chardonnays* by James Laube, (VP-date)—*Vintage Port* by James Suckling.

DATE TASTED Dates in parentheses represent the issue in which the rating was published.

DOMAINE POTELLE
Chardonnay California 1987: Sturdy but bitter. There is some nice peach flavor, but piny, woody flavors dominate. $7 (4/15/89) **71**
Chardonnay California 1986 $6 (4/15/88) BB **80**

DOMAINE ST. GEORGE
Chardonnay Sonoma County 1986 $4.50 (12/31/87) **77**
Chardonnay Sonoma County 1984 $5 (12/16/85) BB **91**
Chardonnay Sonoma County Select Reserve 1988: Lush and ripe, with some butter, grapefruit and pear flavors, in a straightforward and clean package. There is enough bite on the finish to make it a good meal-time wine. Drink now. $9 (6/30/90) **79**
Chardonnay Sonoma County Select Reserve Barrel Fermented Barrel Aged 1987 $8 (12/31/88) BB **86**

DOMAINE SAN MARTIN
Chardonnay Central Coast 1984 $7 (4/16/86) **66**
Chardonnay Central Coast 1983 $7 (8/01/85) **85**

DORE
Chardonnay California Limited Release Lot 101 1989: A bit on the earthy side, with cloying melon and tropical fruit flavors. Drinks better as a white table wine than as a Chardonnay. Drink now. 2,500 cases made. $8.50 (7/15/91) **74**
Chardonnay Santa Maria Valley Signature Selections 1984 $5 (4/16/86) **85**

DREYER SONOMA
Chardonnay Carneros 1990: Tightly wound, concentrated and exotic, with rich pineapple and pear flavors and spicy nuances. Drinkable now, but you might want to hold until 1993 to let the complexity develop. 1,200 cases made. $15 (6/30/92) **85**

DRY CREEK
Chardonnay Dry Creek Valley Reserve 1990: Lean and tight, with lively grapefruit and green apple aromas and flavors. A straightforward wine that could develop more grace with cellaring until 1993 or '94. Tasted twice, with consistent notes. $20 (7/15/92) **83**
Chardonnay Sonoma County Reserve 1988: An oaky wine that lacks the fruit concentration to stand up to it. The finish picks up smoky nutmeg and pear notes, but the major theme is wood. Drink now to 1993. 3,079 cases made. $20 (7/15/91) **85**
Chardonnay Dry Creek Valley Reserve 1987: Lean and intense, with deep, concentrated pineapple, pear and citrus notes that give it vitality. It's framed by toasty oak flavors and has a long, lingering aftertaste. Drink now to 1994. 3,000 cases made. $18 (4/15/90) **91**
Chardonnay Dry Creek Valley Reserve 1986 $18 (11/30/89) **86**
Chardonnay Dry Creek Valley Reserve David S. Stare 1985 $15 (10/15/88) **82**
Chardonnay Dry Creek Valley Reserve David S. Stare 1984 $15 (12/31/86) **75**
Chardonnay Dry Creek Valley David S. Stare 1982 $15 (11/01/85) **75**
Chardonnay Sonoma County Vintners Reserve 1980 $14 (7/16/84) **67**
Chardonnay Sonoma County 1990: A spicy wine, with ripe, mellow apple, pear and citrus notes that are clean and pleasant, finishing with a fruity aftertaste. Drink now to 1994. $13 (4/30/92) **82**
Chardonnay Sonoma County 1989: Charming, crisp, flavorful and fruity, with plenty of pear and apple flavors accented by spicy oak. Well-balanced, firm structured and medium-bodied. Drink now. $12.50 (12/31/90) **87**
Chardonnay Sonoma County 1988: Fresh, clean and lively, with tart apple and citric notes that are straightforward and pleasant but not especially complex. Drink now. $12.50 (5/31/90) **85**
Chardonnay Sonoma County 1987 $9.75 (2/15/89) **82**
Chardonnay Sonoma County 1986 $11 (5/31/88) **88**
Chardonnay Sonoma County 1985 $10 (3/15/87) **92**
Chardonnay Sonoma County 1984 $10 (8/31/86) **88**
Chardonnay Sonoma County 1983 $10 (2/16/85) **87**
Chardonnay Sonoma County 1982 $10 (1/01/84) **87**
Chardonnay Sonoma County 1978 $8 (7/16/84) **60**
Chardonnay Sonoma County 1976 $7 (7/16/84) **73**

DUNNEWOOD
Chardonnay Napa Valley Reserve 1987 $10.50 (12/31/88) **78**
Chardonnay North Coast 1989: A simple, understated, barely varietal wine, with subtle oak shadings and clean, ripe pear and apple-tinged flavors. Won't wow you, but doesn't have any serious flaws, either. A safe and correct style. $7 (3/31/91) **78**

DURNEY
Chardonnay Carmel Valley 1988: A complex and intriguing wine, with lean, concentrated fruit and toasty earth flavors. It gradually opens up to reveal layers of pear, melon, spice and buttery oak. Delicious now, but it should only improve. Drink now to 1994. $18 (9/30/90) **88**

EBERLE
Chardonnay Paso Robles 1990: A bizarre wine that tastes oxidized, with floral, soapy flavors turning bitter on the finish. Not our style. 4,105 cases made. $12 (7/15/92) **72**
Chardonnay Paso Robles 1989: Ripe and rich, with scads of pineapple, pear and apple flavors mixed with a nice floral touch. Echoes fruity, floral notes on the full-bodied finish. Unusual in style, but generous and easy to like. 4,264 cases made. $12 (7/15/91) **86**
Chardonnay Paso Robles 1988: Smoky aromas and tart apple flavors are pleasant, but the flavors turn hard on the finish. Drink now. $12 (6/30/90) **76**
Chardonnay Paso Robles 1987 $12 (6/30/90) **74**
Chardonnay Paso Robles 1986 $10 (12/31/88) **85**
Chardonnay Paso Robles 1982 $10 (4/16/85) **79**

EDNA VALLEY
Chardonnay Edna Valley 1990: Strives for a bold, ripe, rich style, but a sulfury note interferes with the flavors and brings the finish to an abrupt halt. Clumsy and somewhat unpleasant. Tasted three times, with consistent notes. $15 (2/15/92) **74**
Chardonnay Edna Valley 1989: Smooth and supple, this elegant wine has well-controlled peach, nectarine and tropical fruit flavors held in check by crisp acidity and fine balance. Lovely to drink now, but aging until 1993 shouldn't hurt. $15 (12/31/90) **88**
Chardonnay Edna Valley 1988: Spicy, floral aromas and flavors lend a bit of complexity to this otherwise straightforward, flavorful wine, with its focused honey and toast character. Those who want a fruity Chardonnay may want to look elsewhere. $14.75 (12/15/89) **85**
Chardonnay Edna Valley 1987 Rel: $14 Cur: $20 (CH-3/90) **91**
Chardonnay Edna Valley 1986 Rel: $13.50 Cur: $20 (CH-3/90) **88**
Chardonnay Edna Valley 1985 Rel: $13 Cur: $30 (CH-3/90) **85**
Chardonnay Edna Valley 1984 Rel: $12.50 Cur: $29 (CH-6/90) **86**
Chardonnay Edna Valley 1983 Rel: $12.50 Cur: $20 (CH-3/90) **76**
Chardonnay Edna Valley 1982 Rel: $12 Cur: $32 (CH-3/90) **70**
Chardonnay Edna Valley 1981 Rel: $12 Cur: $25 (CH-3/90) **94**
Chardonnay Edna Valley 1980 Rel: $12 Cur: $44 (CH-3/90) **87**

EL MOLINO
Chardonnay Napa Valley 1989: An elegant wine, with smoky, buttery oak notes and tart, crisp pear and melon flavors. Complex and lively. Drinks well now, but it can hold through 1994. $30 (3/31/92) **86**

ELIZABETH
Chardonnay Mendocino 1989: Ripe and oaky, with rich, creamy pear, vanilla, spice and toast flavors. The good intensity, richness and depth keeps the flavors coming. Ready now through 1994. $12.50 (7/15/91) **85**
Chardonnay Mendocino 1988: Ripe, clean, fresh and fruity; this is an elegant style, with pretty pear, apple, melon and pineapple-tinged flavors that are moderately rich and offer good length. Drink now. 200 cases made. $11.50 (7/15/91) **84**

ELLISTON
Chardonnay Central Coast Elliston Vineyard 1990: The earthy, dirty aromas and flavors in this medium-weight, otherwise well-balanced wine are not pleasant. Seems bitter on the finish. 420 cases made. $16 (4/30/92) **72**
Chardonnay Central Coast Elliston Vineyard 1989: An extremely oaky wine, where the woody nuances dominate the ripe fruit flavors. It's also a bit aldehydic, finishing heavy and bitter. The fruit is MIA. Drink now. 1,332 cases made. $12 (12/31/91) **74**
Chardonnay Central Coast Elliston Vineyard 1987: A medium-bodied, fairly ripe wine, with pear and mineral flavors, good balance and a hint of spice on the finish. Well mannered and enjoyable. $18 (7/15/91) **84**
Chardonnay Central Coast Sunol Valley Vineyard 1990 $12 (4/30/92) **84**
Chardonnay Central Coast Sunol Valley Vineyard 1989 $14 (7/15/91) **80**

ESTANCIA
Chardonnay Alexander Valley 1988: A well-balanced, straightforward wine, with rich butterscotch and ripe apple flavors and a crispness that's refreshing. $8 (4/30/90) BB **83**
Chardonnay Alexander Valley 1987: A great buy. Soft and fairly rich in flavor yet delicate. Medium weight, clean and fresh. $7 (6/30/89) **85**
Chardonnay Alexander Valley 1986 $6.50 (1/31/88) BB **84**
Chardonnay Alexander Valley 1983 $7 (4/16/86) **89**
Chardonnay Monterey 1990 $9 (2/15/92) BB **88**
Chardonnay Monterey 1989 $8 (3/31/91) BB **85**
Chardonnay Monterey 1988 $8 (4/30/90) BB **82**

ESTRELLA RIVER
Chardonnay Paso Robles 1987: Simple but good. Has earthy, buttery aromas and flavors, with some fruit underneath and medium body. $8.50 (12/15/89) **74**
Chardonnay Paso Robles 1986 $8 (4/30/88) **82**
Chardonnay Paso Robles 1985 $8 (12/31/87) **65**

EYE OF THE SWAN
Chardonnay California 1990: Extremely floral and spicy aromas are matched by canned fruit flavors. Tastes more like a mediocre Riesling than a Chardonnay. $7 (3/31/92) **74**

FALCONER
Chardonnay California 1989: Smells and tastes stale, with tart, lemony, earthy fruit flavors that turn watery and thin. A metallic, botrytis-tinged flavor is also troubling. Of marginal quality. Drink now. $12 (2/28/91) **70**

FALLENLEAF
Chardonnay Sonoma Valley 1989: Crisp and tart, with fresh grapefruit and apple flavors and a grassy finish. A lively, zingy wine that doesn't fit the mold. 2,000 cases made. $12 (3/31/91) **85**
Chardonnay Sonoma Valley Carneros Special Reserve 1989: Starts out showy, but the peach, pear and pineapple flavors are ultimately simple. Drink now. Tasted three times. 500 cases made. $15 (12/31/91) **78**

FAR NIENTE
Chardonnay Napa Valley 1990: Young and very tight, with honey, pear, spice and apple flavors held in by crisp acidity. They only begin to show through on the finish, indicating an excellent wine that needs aging to show its best stuff. Try after 1993. $30 (6/15/92) CS **90**
Chardonnay Napa Valley 1989: Spicy, elegant and unusually delicate for this winery, with a light, creamy texture and nutmeg-tinged nectarine and tangerine aromas and flavors. Flavorful and long, echoing butter and cinnamon. Drinkable now. Rel: $28 Cur: $30 (2/28/91) **89**
Chardonnay Napa Valley 1988: Beautifully elegant and well-balanced, showing fullness of fruit restrained just enough by acidity and very focused pear and apple flavors that are so well defined they seem sweet. The ripe fruit flavors linger on and on. Drink now or cellar through 1993. Rel: $26 Cur: $29 (2/15/90) **91**
Chardonnay Napa Valley 1987 Rel: $26 Cur: $30 (CH-2/90) **91**
Chardonnay Napa Valley 1986 Rel: $24 Cur: $31 (CH-2/90) **88**
Chardonnay Napa Valley 1985 Rel: $24 Cur: $33 (CH-2/90) **90**
Chardonnay Napa Valley 1984 Rel: $22 Cur: $31 (CH-2/90) **86**
Chardonnay Napa Valley 1983 Rel: $22 Cur: $35 (CH-2/90) **87**
Chardonnay Napa Valley 1983 Rel: $22 Cur: $35 (4/01/85) SS **92**
Chardonnay Napa Valley 1982 Rel: $18 Cur: $38 (CH-2/90) **86**
Chardonnay Napa Valley 1981 Rel: $16.50 Cur: $40 (CH-2/90) **88**
Chardonnay Napa Valley 1980 Rel: $16.50 Cur: $45 (CH-2/90) **93**
Chardonnay Napa Valley 1979 Rel: $15 Cur: $45 (CH-2/90) **92**
Chardonnay Napa Valley Estate 1983 Rel: $22 Cur: $38 (CH-2/90) **89**
Chardonnay Napa Valley Estate 1982 Rel: $18 Cur: $38 (CH-2/90) **91**

GARY FARRELL
Chardonnay Russian River Valley Aquarius Ranch 1987 $13.50 (12/31/88) **70**
Chardonnay Sonoma County 1989: Has more intensity and length than most '89s. Oaky and toasty style, with earthy aromas, pineapple and pear flavors and a firmly oaky finish. $16 (7/15/91) **85**
Chardonnay Sonoma County 1986 $12 (8/31/88) **82**

FELTA SPRINGS
Chardonnay Sonoma County 1986 $6 (6/15/88) BB **80**

FELTON EMPIRE
Chardonnay Monterey County 1990: Ripe, creamy and almost sweet, but it offers plenty of fruit. The intense almond, lemon, pear and spice flavors linger. Drink now to 1994. 2,300 cases made. $13 (4/30/92) **87**
Chardonnay Monterey County 1988: Plenty of fresh, ripe, rich Chardonnay flavors, with hints of apple, pear, melon and a touch of spicy oak, it's altogether well balanced and crisp on the finish. Drink now. $12 (4/15/90) **84**
Chardonnay Monterey County Reserve 1990: Fresh and spicy, with simple, light pear, honey and spice notes. Drink now. 780 cases made. $16 (4/30/92) **80**
Chardonnay Monterey County Reserve 1988: Rich and concentrated,with buttery oak adding dimension to the ripe pear, apple, spice and nutmeg. Well balanced, long and full on the finish, picking up pretty butterscotch flavors. Drink now to 1993. $15 (4/15/90) **86**

FERRARI-CARANO
Chardonnay Alexander Valley 1990: Firm, focused and generous, bursting with apple, pear, spice and vanilla aromas and flavors. Balanced and lively on the finish. A wine with backbone and a graceful way of unfolding its flavors. Drinkable now, but may be better in 1993. $20 (7/15/92) **90**
Chardonnay Alexander Valley 1989: Beautifully concentrated and fruity, with intense pear, orange and spice flavors in a rich, almost sweet package that echoes honey and toast on the finish. Firmly structured with acidity. Drink now to 1994. $19.50 (6/15/91) **91**
Chardonnay Alexander Valley 1988: Has enormous concentration of fruit, with layers of melon, apple, pear, spicy nutmeg and subtle honey and toast flavors that add a pleasant dimension to the gorgeous fruit. The texture is silky smooth and the flavors echo long and full. Drink now to 1993. Rel: $18 Cur: $29 (5/31/90) SS **93**
Chardonnay Alexander Valley 1987 Rel: $16 Cur: $27 (CH-5/90) **94**

Chardonnay Alexander Valley 1986 Rel: $16 Cur: $31 (CH-5/90) **92**
Chardonnay Alexander Valley 1985 Rel: $14 Cur: $45 (9/15/87) SS **93**
Chardonnay California Reserve 1989: Intense and lively, with ripe peach, apple, lemon and spice notes that linger. Elegant, balanced and ready to enjoy now through 1994. Tasted twice. 2,200 cases made. $32 (7/15/92) **87**
Chardonnay California Reserve 1988: Crisp and concentrated, with plenty of depth to the brilliant apple and pineapple aromas and flavors. Butterscotch notes emerge on the finish. Still youthful, but smooth enough to drink now. 1,000 cases made. $30 (6/15/91) **90**
Chardonnay California Reserve 1987: Very firm and focused, with concentrated grapefruit, toast and vanilla aromas and flavors, a smooth texture and a long, elegant finish. Has intensity and finesse for cellaring until 1994. Tasted twice. 780 cases made. Rel: $28 Cur: $35 (5/31/90) **87**
Chardonnay California Reserve 1986 Rel: $28 Cur: $42 (CH-5/90) **93**

FETZER
Chardonnay California Sundial 1990: With its fresh peach and pine needle aromas, this reminds us of a good Riesling, which makes it refreshing and easy to like. Drinkable now. $8 (9/15/91) **79**
Chardonnay California Sundial 1989: Fresh and zesty, with concentrated grapefruit and nectarine flavors and a clean finish. $8 (4/30/90) BB **82**
Chardonnay California Sundial 1988: Very fruity and lively, lean enough in texture to keep from being overwhelming and crisp and tart enough to balance the floral and apple aromas and flavors. Drink soon. $7 (5/15/89) **78**
Chardonnay California Sundial 1987 $6.50 (7/31/88) **76**
Chardonnay California Sundial 1986 $6.50 (9/15/87) BB **86**
Chardonnay Mendocino County Sundial 1985 $6.50 (9/15/86) BB **84**
Chardonnay Mendocino County 1984 $6.50 (4/16/86) **86**
Chardonnay Mendocino County Barrel Select 1990: An intense, complex wine, with ripe pear, honey and pineapple flavors that are rich and sharply focused. Finishes long and lingering, with a spicy aftertaste. Drink now to 1995. $11 (7/15/92) **89**
Chardonnay Mendocino County Barrel Select 1989: This fruity, floral wine offers ample peach and apple flavors and shows a good balance between the fruit and oak. Tasty and charming. $11 (7/15/91) **84**
Chardonnay Mendocino County Barrel Select 1988: Fresh and spicy, this Muscat-like wine has pear, apple and melon flavors that are attactive but ultimately simple. Drink now. $12 (3/15/90) **82**
Chardonnay Mendocino County Barrel Select 1987: Lean and toasty, with pear and nutmeg flavors that are crisp and structured, picking up a touch of honey on the finish. Has room to grow. $10 (3/15/89) **88**
Chardonnay Mendocino County Barrel Select 1986 $10 (8/31/88) **73**
Chardonnay California Barrel Select 1985 $8.50 (4/30/87) **79**
Chardonnay California Barrel Select 1984 $8.50 (3/01/86) **72**
Chardonnay Mendocino Barrel Select 1981 $8.50 (6/01/86) **93**
Chardonnay Mendocino County Reserve 1990: Elegant, with subtle pear, pineapple and tropical fruit notes that are smooth and polished. Drinks well now. Tasted twice. 5,000 cases made. $18.50 (7/15/92) **87**
Chardonnay Mendocino County Reserve 1989: A pleasing, supple wine, with ample pear and earth flavors accented by toasty oak notes and a lingering finish. Nicely balanced and shaped. Enjoy now. $18 (7/15/91) **87**
Chardonnay Mendocino County Reserve 1988: Elegant and understated, not a generous wine, but round and smooth with hints of pear and honey. Easy to drink. 2,400 cases made. $17.50 (5/31/90) **82**
Chardonnay Mendocino County Reserve 1987 $15 (7/15/89) **82**
Chardonnay Mendocino County Special Reserve 1986 $14 (12/31/88) **88**
Chardonnay California Special Reserve 1985 $13 (11/15/87) **86**
Chardonnay California Special Reserve 1984 $13 (6/01/86) **84**
Chardonnay California Special Reserve 1982 $10 (4/01/84) **78**
Chardonnay California Special Reserve 1981 $11 (6/01/86) **88**

FIELD STONE
Chardonnay Sonoma County 1989: Intriguing, with plenty of class. The oak is showy, toasty and buttery, while the fruit is ripe, clean and elegant, with pretty floral notes and hints of pear, grapefruit and peach. It all comes together on a long, lingering finish. Drink now to 1993. $14 (3/31/91) **87**
Chardonnay Sonoma County 1988: Austere, with tightly reined-in flavors, but they fan out on the palate and reveal more depth and complexity. The pear, nutmeg and citrus notes are fresh and clean, with good concentration. Drink now to 1993. 1,150 cases made. $14 (4/15/91) **85**

FIRESTONE
Chardonnay Santa Ynez Valley 1987: Good but not a standout. Flavors are muted, even slightly oxidized, with a candylike finish. $10 (12/15/89) **72**
Chardonnay Santa Ynez Valley 1986 $10 (12/31/88) **83**
Chardonnay Santa Ynez Valley 10th Anniversary 1985 $10 (4/15/88) **63**
Chardonnay Santa Ynez Valley 1984 $10 (5/31/87) **76**
Chardonnay Santa Ynez Valley 1983 $10 (3/01/86) **63**
Chardonnay Santa Ynez Valley Barrel Fermented 1990: Offers fig, butter and lemon flavors on top of a soft, buttery style. Easy to drink, but needs more acidity to make it really lively. $13 (1/31/92) **78**
Chardonnay Santa Ynez Valley Barrel Fermented 1989: Solid and flavorful, distinguished by toasty, oaky accents. A full-bodied, soundly made wine, with ripe pear, creamy vanilla and spice notes. $12 (4/30/91) **87**

FISHER
Chardonnay Napa-Sonoma Counties 1989: Has floral aromas and a smooth texture, with nutmeg and mint flavors. It's a decent drink, but the green flavors rob it of balance. $12 (9/30/90) **74**
Chardonnay Napa-Sonoma Counties 1988: Has complex flavors with great appeal and layers of toast, melon, pear and honey notes that are well integrated; it's smooth and supple, with great length on the finish. Complete and elegant. $11 (9/15/89) **88**
Chardonnay Napa-Sonoma Counties 1987: Spicy, with crisp pear aromas and flavors and a wee touch of toast and honey on the finish. Good now, but it should benefit from time in the cellar. Drink now. $11 (4/15/89) **85**
Chardonnay Napa-Sonoma Counties 1986 $11 (7/15/88) **86**
Chardonnay Napa-Sonoma Counties 1985 $11 (7/15/87) **82**
Chardonnay Napa-Sonoma Counties 1983 Rel: $14 Cur: $18 (CH-6/90) **82**
Chardonnay Sonoma County 1982 Rel: $14 Cur: $22 (CH-2/90) **81**
Chardonnay Sonoma County 1981 Rel: $14 Cur: $25 (CH-2/90) **88**
Chardonnay Sonoma County 1980 Rel: $14 Cur: $22 (CH-2/90) **85**
Chardonnay Sonoma County Coach Insignia 1989: Ripe and generous, with pear, oak, honey and spice flavors that stay with you. A stylish wine that's ready to drink now through 1994. Tasted twice, with consistent notes. 3,900 cases made. $15 (3/31/92) **85**
Chardonnay Sonoma County Coach Insignia 1988: This wine has a delicious core of pear, apple, pineapple and melon flavors that are smooth, elegant, well balanced, complex and enticing, with a pretty pine nut flavor on the finish. Some bottle variation. Drink now to 1993. Tasted four times. Rel: $18 Cur: $20 (6/30/90) **90**
Chardonnay Sonoma County Coach Insignia 1987: It's tightly packed, lean in structure, and shows plenty of restraint before the spicy, toasty, applelike flavors unfold on the long finish. Drink now. Rel: $18 Cur: $22 (1/31/90) **84**
Chardonnay Sonoma County Coach Insignia 1986 Rel: $17 Cur: $20 (CH-2/90) **90**
Chardonnay Sonoma County Coach Insignia 1985 Rel: $16 Cur: $20 (CH-2/90) **84**
Chardonnay Sonoma County Coach Insignia 1984 Rel: $15 Cur: $20 (CH-2/90) **82**
Chardonnay Sonoma County Whitney's Vineyard 1988 $24 (CH-2/90) **88**
Chardonnay Sonoma County Whitney's Vineyard 1987 $24 (CH-2/90) **86**
Chardonnay Sonoma County Whitney's Vineyard 1985 Rel: $24 Cur: $30 (CH-2/90) **84**
Chardonnay Sonoma County Whitney's Vineyard 1984 Rel: $20 Cur: $30 (CH-2/90) **90**
Chardonnay Sonoma County Whitney's Vineyard 1983 Rel: $20 Cur: $30 (CH-2/90) **78**
Chardonnay Sonoma County Whitney's Vineyard 1982 Rel: $20 Cur: $25 (CH-6/90) **78**
Chardonnay Sonoma County Whitney's Vineyard 1981 Rel: $20 Cur: $25 (CH-2/90) **85**
Chardonnay Sonoma County Whitney's Vineyard 1980 Rel: $20 Cur: $30 (CH-2/90) **92**

FITCH MOUNTAIN
Chardonnay Napa Valley 1986 $8 (11/15/88) **81**

FIVE PALMS
Chardonnay Napa Valley 1985 $8 (4/30/87) **87**

FLAX
Chardonnay Sonoma County 1986 $14 (12/31/88) **77**
Chardonnay Sonoma County 1985 $12 (10/15/87) **82**

FLORA SPRINGS
Chardonnay Napa Valley 1990: Smooth, supple and spicy, with tiers of nutmeg, pear, vanilla and honey flavors. Well focused and well proportioned. Best to drink now through 1994. $15 (1/31/92) **89**
Chardonnay Napa Valley 1989: This medium-weight wine has somewhat earthy but pleasantly floral pear and vanilla aromas and flavors, turning to honey and spice on the long finish. Has style and grace. $15 (7/15/91) **87**
Chardonnay Napa Valley 1988: A complex wine, with smoke, honey, pear and spicy flavors that are rich, elegant and impeccably balanced, with a clean, fruity finish. Drink now to 1993. Tasted twice. 4,700 cases made. $15 (3/15/90) **87**
Chardonnay Napa Valley 1987 $15 (6/15/89) **87**
Chardonnay Napa Valley 1986 $13 (7/15/88) **77**
Chardonnay Napa Valley 1985 $14 (2/28/87) **85**
Chardonnay Napa Valley 1984 $13.50 (10/31/86) **88**
Chardonnay Napa Valley 1983 $13 (10/01/85) **77**
Chardonnay Napa Valley 1982 $12 (5/16/84) **59**
Chardonnay Napa Valley Barrel Fermented 1990: Smooth, ripe and generous, with rich, complex, polished pear, spice, hazelnut and honey notes. The fruit zooms across the palate. A stylish wine that's delicious to drink now. 6,500 cases made. $24 (4/15/92) **92**
Chardonnay Napa Valley Barrel Fermented 1989: An extremely rich, honeyed and luxuriously textured Chardonnay, with orange blossom aromas, ripe pear flavors and a full, fruity finish that just keeps going. Tempting to drink now, but should improve through 1995. 4,000 cases made. $23 (5/15/91) **91**
Chardonnay Napa Valley Barrel Fermented 1988: Smells toasty, with oaky, buttery accents and concentrated but tight lemon, pear and honey flavors. Drink now. 5,000 cases made. Rel: $24 Cur: $27 (6/30/90) **91**
Chardonnay Napa Valley Barrel Fermented 1987 Rel: $20 Cur: $27 (CH-1/90) **95**
Chardonnay Napa Valley Barrel Fermented 1986 Rel: $20 Cur: $27 (CH-1/90) **87**
Chardonnay Napa Valley Barrel Fermented 1985 Rel: $18 Cur: $22 (CH-1/90) **85**
Chardonnay Napa Valley Barrel Fermented 1984 Rel: $18 Cur: $28 (CH-1/90) **88**
Chardonnay Napa Valley Barrel Fermented 1983 Rel: $18 Cur: $28 (CH-1/90) **94**
Chardonnay Napa Valley Barrel Fermented 1982 $15 (CH-6/88) **70**
Chardonnay Napa Valley Special Selection 1981 Rel: $12 Cur: $25 (CH-1/90) **89**
Chardonnay Napa Valley Special Selection 1980 Rel: $12 Cur: $25 (CH-1/90) **88**
Chardonnay Napa Valley 1979 Rel: $9 Cur: $25 (CH-1/90) **91**
Chardonnay Napa Valley Floréal 1990: Round and fruity, with exotic pear, peach and pineapple flavors that are broad and rich. Well balanced and ready to enjoy now. $12.50 (4/15/92) **85**

THOMAS FOGARTY
Chardonnay Carneros Napa Valley 1986 $15 (12/31/88) **83**
Chardonnay Carneros Napa Valley Winery Lake Vineyard 1985 $15 (2/15/88) **73**
Chardonnay Edna Valley 1987: A stylish wine that smells toasty and buttery, has medium-intensity fruit flavor and a smooth texture. Very good in a light style. $13.50 (12/15/89) **81**
Chardonnay Edna Valley Paragon Vineyards 1989: A tart structure gives the distinctive peach, nectarine and mineral aromas and flavors in this medium-scale wine a nice zing. Lively and drinkable now, but has the concentration and structure to develop well through 1993. 1,137 cases made. $15 (7/15/91) **88**
Chardonnay Monterey 1985 $15 (2/15/88) **88**
Chardonnay Monterey Ventana Vineyards 1986 $15 (5/31/88) **68**
Chardonnay Monterey Ventana Vineyards 1984 $13.50 (2/28/87) **84**
Chardonnay Santa Cruz Mountains 1988: Ripe, rich and buttery, with a flinty mineral flavor to complement the earthy pear and spice notes. A sturdy style that's young and concentrated. Ready now through 1994. 1,200 cases made. $18 (7/15/91) **87**
Chardonnay Santa Cruz Mountains 1985 $16.50 (2/15/88) **69**

FOLIE A DEUX
Chardonnay Napa Valley 1990: Crisp and lively, with fresh, spicy grapefruit and pear aromas and flavors and toast and nutmeg notes that emerge on the finish. A tight young wine that should blossom around 1994. 3,500 cases made. $16 (7/15/92) **87**
Chardonnay Napa Valley 1989: Ultraripe and fruity but blunt, with bold pineapple, melon, citrus and earth flavors that turn even simpler on the finish. Drink now. $16 (7/15/91) **80**
Chardonnay Napa Valley 1988: Lean, fresh and simple, with a nice core of apple and spice flavors, turning toward honey and toast on the finish. Drinkable now. Rel: $16 Cur: $18 (5/31/90) **85**
Chardonnay Napa Valley 1987 Rel: $15 Cur: $18 (CH-6/90) **90**
Chardonnay Napa Valley 1986 Rel: $15 Cur: $18 (CH-6/90) **88**
Chardonnay Napa Valley 1985 Rel: $14.50 Cur: $18 (CH-6/90) **88**
Chardonnay Napa Valley 1984 Rel: $14 Cur: $18 (CH-6/90) **87**
Chardonnay Napa Valley 1983 $12 (9/16/85) **76**
Chardonnay Napa Valley 1982 $12.50 (CH-7/90) **78**
Chardonnay Napa Valley Pas de Deux 1989: A respectable wine, with appealing pineapple and peach aromas and flavors shaded by vanilla and nutmeg notes. Medium weight, fresh and drinkable. $10 (7/15/91) **83**

Key to Symbols

The scores reported here are the results of blind tastings conducted by our panel of senior editors. Wines that carry the initials below are results of individual tastings.

THE WINE SPECTATOR 100-POINT SCALE ***95-100***—Classic, a great wine; ***90-94***—Outstanding, superior character and style; ***80-89***—Good to very good, a wine with special qualities; ***70-79***—Average, drinkable wine that may have minor flaws; ***60-69***—Below average, drinkable but not recommended; ***50-59***—Poor, undrinkable, not recommended. "+"—With a score indicates a range; used primarily with barrel tastings to indicate a preliminary score.

SPECIAL DESIGNATIONS SS—Spectator Selection, CS—Cellar Selection, BB—Best Buy, ($NA)—Price not available, (NR)—Not released.

TASTER'S INITIALS (JG)—Jim Gordon, (HS)—Harvey Steiman, (JL)—James Laube, (JS)—James Suckling, (TM)—Thomas Matthews, (TR)—Terry Robards, (PM)—Per-Henrik Mansson, (BT)—Barrel Tasting (these wines were tasted blind from barrel samples), (CA-date)—*California's Great Cabernets* by James Laube, (CH-date)—*California's Great Chardonnays* by James Laube, (VP-date)—*Vintage Port* by James Suckling.

DATE TASTED Dates in parentheses represent the issue in which the rating was published.

FOPPIANO
Chardonnay Russian River Valley 1987: Has grassy aromas, tart, simple fruit flavors and decent balance. $9 (7/15/89) **72**
Chardonnay Sonoma County 1989: A heavy, woody wine, with butter and vanilla aromas but not much fruit flavor. The oak component is nice, though, and helps the wine turn smooth and round on the finish. Tasted twice. 3,200 cases made. $10 (7/15/92) **80**
Chardonnay Sonoma County 1986 $9 (5/31/88) **75**
Chardonnay Sonoma County 1983 $10 (10/01/85) **78**

FOREST HILL
Chardonnay Napa Valley Private Reserve 1990: Soft and silky, with lovely hazelnut, honey and peach aromas and flavors, turning smooth and generous on the long finish, where the flavors linger. Has intensity while remaining graceful and elegant. Lovely now, even better in 1994. 650 cases made. $24 (3/31/92) **90**
Chardonnay Napa Valley Private Reserve 1989: The toasty oak stands out, but there isn't much fruit to stand up to it. Has decent pear and apple flavors, but they thin out and lack concentration. Drink now. $24 (7/15/91) **83**

FORMAN
Chardonnay Napa Valley 1990: Tight, firm and crisp, with intense, focused pear, pineapple, peach and citrus flavors and a pretty overlay of toasty, buttery oak notes. Drinkable now, and should only improve through 1994. Shows considerably better than two bottles we tasted earlier, which suggests some bottle variation. 2,100 cases made. $22 (6/30/92) **90**
Chardonnay Napa Valley 1989: Tight, tart and astringent now, but with plenty of fruit and acidity. The melon, pear, citrus and butterscotch flavors are ripe and attractive, finishing with good length. Drink now to 1994. Rel: $22 Cur: $25 (2/15/91) **88**
Chardonnay Napa Valley 1988: Intense, concentrated and complex, with pear, pineapple, spicy oak, peach and vanilla notes that gain prominence on the finish. Balanced, elegant and well made, but may benefit from cellaring. Drink now to 1994. Scored significantly better than an earlier bottle. Rel: $20 Cur: $40 (6/30/90) **92**
Chardonnay Napa Valley 1987 Rel: $18 Cur: $33 (CH-2/90) **89**
Chardonnay Napa Valley 1986 Rel: $18 Cur: $45 (CH-2/90) **92**
Chardonnay Napa Valley 1985 Rel: $15 Cur: $60 (CH-2/90) **93**
Chardonnay Napa Valley 1984 Rel: $15 Cur: $45 (CH-2/90) **86**

FOX MOUNTAIN
Chardonnay Sonoma County Reserve 1986: Has mature, buttery, earthy aromas and flavors that hint at almond, honey and pear on the round structure and smooth texture. Plenty of character for those who want a more mature Chardonnay. Drink soon. 2,133 cases made. $15 (4/15/91) **85**
Chardonnay Sonoma County Reserve 1985 $14 (12/31/88) **70**
Chardonnay Sonoma County Reserve 1984 $14.50 (12/31/87) **80**

FOXEN
Chardonnay Santa Maria Valley 1987: An attention-grabber. Deliciously toasty and buttery, very forward and aromatic. Emphasizes oaky character, but there's good fruit flavor underneath. $18 (12/15/89) **90**

FRANCISCAN
Chardonnay Alexander Valley 1983 $10.50 (2/01/85) **87**
Chardonnay Alexander Valley 1982 $10 (4/16/84) **83**
Chardonnay Napa Valley Oakville Estate 1990: Ripe and oaky, with intense fig, pear, vanilla and spice notes that hang together nicely. Has plenty of flavor, but could use a little more finesse and polish. Drinks well now, but may be more interesting by mid-1993. Tasted twice. $12 (7/15/92) **87**
Chardonnay Napa Valley Oakville Estate 1989: Fresh, fruity and appealing, with lots of melon and pear flavors and hints of spice to make it interesting. Soft and smooth on the finish. Drink soon. $12 (7/15/91) **83**
Chardonnay Napa Valley Oakville Estate 1988: Has plenty of generous pear and butter flavors up front, but they taper off on the finish, with hints of smoke and citrus notes. Fruit could be a bit more vibrant. Drink now. $11 (6/30/90) **82**
Chardonnay Napa Valley Oakville Estate 1987 $11 (2/15/89) **81**
Chardonnay Napa Valley Oakville Estate 1986 $9.25 (5/31/88) **87**
Chardonnay Napa Valley Oakville Estate 1984 $8.50 (3/15/87) BB **90**
Chardonnay Napa Valley Oakville Estate Bottled 1982 $9.50 (8/01/85) **84**
Chardonnay Napa Valley Oakville Estate Cuvée Sauvage 1990: Tight now, but ripe and generous, with lemon-scented pear, smoke and apricot aromas and flavors that extend into a long finish. A solid wine that needs until 1993 or '94 to unfold. 1,800 cases made. $25 (7/15/92) **88**
Chardonnay Napa Valley Oakville Estate Cuvée Sauvage 1989: Ripe, generous and graceful, with a rich texture and lots of extra nuances to the pear, pineapple and lemon flavors that hint at honey and smoke on the long, crisp finish. Could keep improving through 1993. Has plenty of style. 900 cases made. Rel: $24 Cur: $28 (7/15/91) **90**
Chardonnay Napa Valley Oakville Estate Cuvée Sauvage 1988: Smooth, subtle and rich, with opulent vanilla, toast, butter and pear aromas and flavors, turning to honey on the finish. Has a silky texture. Despite all the complexity, it has a sense of freshness and liveliness. Drinkable now, but probably best around 1993. 300 cases made. Rel: $20 Cur: $25 (6/30/90) **93**
Chardonnay Napa Valley Oakville Estate Cuvée Sauvage 1987 Rel: $20 Cur: $30 (6/15/90) **90**
Chardonnay Napa Valley Oakville Estate Reserve 1990: Fresh and appealing, with generous pear and vanilla aromas and flavors. Light and lively now, but it may be richer in 1993 or '94. $16 (7/15/92) **85**
Chardonnay Napa Valley Oakville Estate Reserve 1987: Big, rich and creamy, with buttery pear and subtle oak shadings that offer complexity and finesse and a rich toasty-smoky aftertaste that lingers. Elegant and stylish. Drink now. 600 cases made. $20 (6/15/90) **92**
Chardonnay Napa Valley Oakville Estate Reserve 1986 $14 (CH-4/90) **91**
Chardonnay Napa Valley Oakville Estate Reserve 1984 Rel: $12 Cur: $23 (CH-4/90) **86**
Chardonnay Napa Valley Oakville Estate Reserve 1983 $12 (CH-4/90) **82**
Chardonnay Carneros Reserve 1982 Rel: $9.50 Cur: $17 (CH-4/90) **84**

FREEMARK ABBEY
Chardonnay Napa Valley 1989: Soft and unimpressive, with vague pineapple and grapefruit aromas and flavors. Turns stale on the finish. Tasted twice. $15 (7/15/91) **75**
Chardonnay Napa Valley 1988: Fresh and lively, with clearly focused grapefruit aromas and flavors. Has intensity and elegance, plus the subtlety and finesse to warrant cellaring. $15 (6/30/90) **91**
Chardonnay Napa Valley 1987 Rel: $15 Cur: $17 (CH-2/90) **84**
Chardonnay Napa Valley 1986 Rel: $15 Cur: $18 (CH-2/90) **86**
Chardonnay Napa Valley 1985 Rel: $14 Cur: $25 (CH-2/90) **80**
Chardonnay Napa Valley 1984 Rel: $14 Cur: $20 (CH-2/90) **87**
Chardonnay Napa Valley 1983 Rel: $14 Cur: $20 (4/01/86) **85**
Chardonnay Napa Valley 1982 Rel: $12.75 Cur: $18 (CH-2/90) **72**
Chardonnay Napa Valley 1981 Rel: $13.50 Cur: $20 (CH-2/90) **81**
Chardonnay Napa Valley 1980 Rel: $13.50 Cur: $38 (CH-2/90) **84**
Chardonnay Napa Valley 1979 Rel: $13.25 Cur: $25 (CH-2/90) **76**
Chardonnay Napa Valley 1978 Rel: $10 Cur: $26 (CH-2/90) **70**
Chardonnay Napa Valley 1977 Rel: $10 Cur: $36 (CH-2/90) **58**
Chardonnay Napa Valley 1976 Rel: $9.75 Cur: $26 (CH-2/90) **62**
Chardonnay Napa Valley 1975 Rel: $9 Cur: $45 (CH-2/90) **82**
Chardonnay Napa Valley 1974 Rel: $7.95 Cur: $42 (CH-2/90) **74**
Chardonnay Napa Valley 1973 Rel: $6.50 Cur: $32 (CH-2/90) **77**
Chardonnay Napa Valley 1972 Rel: $6.50 Cur: $48 (CH-2/90) **77**
Chardonnay Napa Valley 1971 Rel: $7 Cur: $40 (CH-2/90) **70**
Chardonnay Napa Valley 1970 Rel: $7 Cur: $35 (CH-2/90) **55**
Chardonnay Napa Valley 1969 Rel: $6 Cur: $37 (CH-2/90) **60**
Chardonnay Napa Valley 1968 Rel: $5 Cur: $35 (CH-2/90) **73**
Chardonnay Napa Valley Carpy Ranch 1990: Tart and simple, with lively grapefruit and peach aromas and flavors and hints of vanilla and spice on the finish. Drinkable now, but may be better in 1993 or '94. Tasted twice. 1,119 cases made. $22 (7/15/92) **85**
Chardonnay Napa Valley Carpy Ranch 1989: Medium in weight, with pleasant pear, apple and spice flavors that thin out on the finish. A decent drink that's ready now. 951 cases made. $22 (7/15/91) **84**
Chardonnay Napa Valley Carpy Ranch 1988: Straightforward and ebulliently fruity, turning subtle on the finish. Shows vigorous pineapple and apple aromas and flavors plus a touch of honey at the end. Drink now to 1993. Tasted twice. 566 cases made. Rel: $22 Cur: $25 (4/30/90) **84**

FREMONT CREEK
Chardonnay Mendocino County 1988: Rich and buttery, with spicy, oaky aromas and butterscotch flavors, this wine lacks fruit concentration and seems disjointed on the finish. $9.50 (6/30/90) **75**
Chardonnay Mendocino-Napa Counties 1987: Good in a sturdy, lively style. A bit smoky in aroma, very citric and appley in flavor. $9.50 (7/15/89) **76**
Chardonnay Mendocino-Napa Counties 1986 $9.50 (4/30/88) **87**

J. FRITZ
Chardonnay Alexander Valley Gauer Ranch 1981 $10 (4/16/84) **80**
Chardonnay Dry Creek Valley 1990: A crisp lively wine, with apple and piny citrus flavors. Pleasingly fruity, simple and well made. Could stand a year of aging to balance its youthfulness. $9.50 (3/31/92) **85**
Chardonnay Russian River Valley 1990: Light and simple, with tart, vague nectarine flavors that turn watery on the finish. Drink now. $12.50 (4/30/92) **77**
Chardonnay Russian River Valley 1989: A fresh, clean, fruity wine that's elegant and balanced. Pretty peach, pear, spice and pineapple notes are well focused and linger on the palate. Ready now through 1993. 4,500 cases made. $12.50 (7/15/91) **86**
Chardonnay Russian River Valley 1986 $9 (2/29/88) **81**
Chardonnay Russian River Valley 1985 $8.50 (11/30/87) **81**
Chardonnay Sonoma County 1982 $9 (5/16/84) **72**

FROG'S LEAP
Chardonnay Carneros 1990: Bold, ripe and buttery, with rich pear, spice, pineapple and apple notes. Zingy acidity keeps the flavors bouncing across your palate. Delicious now, but should drink well through 1995. $16 (4/15/92) **90**
Chardonnay Carneros 1989: Ripe and flavorful, with more oak than fruit, but definite pear and honey flavors emerge on the finish. Full-bodied, if not rich, and can probably stand cellaring until 1993. 4,900 cases made. Rel: $16 Cur: $18 (7/15/91) **83**
Chardonnay Carneros 1988: What a find. A deliciously oak-aged wine that has great breadth and texture, plus oodles of buttery fig, peach and pear flavors and a smoky, complex finish. Rel: $16 Cur: $19 (4/30/90) **87**
Chardonnay Carneros 1987 Rel: $15 Cur: $19 (CH-3/90) **86**
Chardonnay Carneros 1986 Rel: $14 Cur: $18 (CH-6/90) **87**
Chardonnay Napa Valley 1988: Tart, light and simple, with appealing lemon and spice aromas and flavors. A fresh, zingy wine, with appreciable intensity and concentration. 2,500 cases made. Rel: $15 Cur: $18 (6/30/90) **85**
Chardonnay Napa Valley 1987 Rel: $14 Cur: $18 (CH-3/90) **88**
Chardonnay Napa Valley 1986 Rel: $12 Cur: $18 (CH-3/90) **90**
Chardonnay Napa Valley 1985 Rel: $12 Cur: $16 (CH-6/90) **84**
Chardonnay Napa Valley 1984 Rel: $12 Cur: $23 (CH-3/90) **91**

GABRIELLI
Chardonnay Mendocino 1990: Fresh and creamy, with lively pear, vanilla and spicy buttery flavors. Focused, balanced and ready to drink now. 1,417 cases made. $16 (5/31/92) **83**

GAINEY
Chardonnay Santa Barbara County 1990: Fresh, fruity and pleasantly soft and round, with simple, appealing apple and vanilla aromas and flavors. Drinkable now. 3,216 cases made. $14 (6/30/92) **83**
Chardonnay Santa Barbara County 1989: Smooth, polished and definitely marked by oak, this rich-textured wine gets around to the lively apple and pineapple flavors about midpalate. Finishes long and smooth. 3,404 cases made. $13 (5/31/91) **86**
Chardonnay Santa Barbara County 1988: A big, ripe, full-bodied wine that leans heavily on toasty oak, overshadowing the ripe pineapple, pear and spice flavors. Balanced in acidity, but still a bit awkward with oak. Drink now. 3,000 cases made. $12.50 (2/28/91) **81**
Chardonnay Santa Barbara County 1987 $12 (12/15/89) **85**
Chardonnay Santa Barbara County Limited Selection 1987: Fine, flavorful and even a bit complex. Has great toasty, nutty aromas, ripe fruit flavors and a rich, smooth texture. Good finish, too. $16 (12/15/89) **89**

E. & J. GALLO
Chardonnay California Limited Release NV $6 (4/16/86) **58**
Chardonnay California Reserve NV: A light, pleasant white wine, with a smooth texture and modest apple flavors. Simple and drinkable. Priced fairly. $5 (7/15/92) **77**
Chardonnay North Coast 1985 $5 (12/31/88) **79**
Chardonnay North Coast 1990: Simple and drinkable, but not very Chardonnay-like. Tastes like it has a high percentage of Riesling or Gewürztraminer blended in, giving this light, lively wine a spicy, piny flavor. $7 (7/15/92) **77**
Chardonnay North Coast Reserve 1989: The best Gallo Chardonnay yet, it's fresh and fruity, with lively melon, spice and grapey Chardonnay flavors that are clean and balanced. No oak intrudes on the fruit. Drink now. $6.50 (7/15/91) BB **81**
Chardonnay North Coast Reserve 1987: A good wine for this price, it's decently balanced and clean tasting, but very straightforward in its modest apple and pear flavors. A touch of almond helps it out. Tasted three times. $6 (11/30/90) **78**

GAN EDEN
Chardonnay Alexander Valley 1987: Rich and spicy, with smooth, elegant texture and lush flavors of apple, pear and honey that are absolutely lovely on the palate. Long and very fine. Just the thing for Passover—it's kosher. $9.50 (3/15/89) **89**
Chardonnay Sonoma County 1988: $12 (3/31/91) **87**

GARLAND RANCH
Chardonnay California 1991: Shows simple fruit flavors that could pass for Chenin Blanc, but at this price, it's a decent white wine. Enjoy now. $6 (7/15/92) **72**
Chardonnay Central Coast 1989: Tastes like a dessert Chardonnay, with sweet honey and peach notes similar to those found in wines affected with botrytis. Very soft and quaffable, but some will undoubtedly miss the lack of acidity. A nice aperitif wine. $5 (8/31/90) **76**

GAUER ESTATE
Chardonnay Alexander Valley 1988: Crisp and lively in structure, with modest pear and peach flavors held firmly in check by lemony acidity. Might develop more nuances with age, but for now it just seems clean and correct. Try now. $16 (12/31/90) **85**
Chardonnay Alexander Valley 1987: Elegant and creamy in texture, with light melon and pear flavors that never quite open up, held in check by green flavors and a modest structure. Hints of honey and olive sneak in on the finish and make it interesting. Drink now. 4,500 cases made. $16 (11/30/90) **84**
Chardonnay Alexander Valley Library Edition 1987: A rich, complex wine that's showing its

maturity, but offers lots of depth and flavor, with layers of honey, pear, vanilla and spice. Has plenty of intensity, so you can drink it now or cellar through 1994. 400 cases made. $18 (7/15/92) **86**

GEYSER PEAK

Chardonnay Alexander Valley Estate Reserve Barrel Fermented 1989: A young, tightly wound wine that's just beginning to show its complex spice, toast, pear, honey and almond flavors. Firmly structured, with acidity and oaky astringency, but it should develop nicely if cellared through 1996. 1,300 cases made. $13 (6/15/91) **89**
Chardonnay Alexander Valley Estate Reserve 1987: Smooth and butterscotchy, soft, oaky and almost sweet. $12 (6/30/89) **80**
Chardonnay Sonoma County 1990: An impressive wine that's fairly priced, with pure, clean, ripe flavors that take on pear, apple and citrus notes. Drink now. $8 (3/15/92) BB **83**
Chardonnay Sonoma County Carneros 1985 $7 (2/28/87) BB **84**
Chardonnay Sonoma County Carneros 1984 $8 (4/16/86) **76**
Chardonnay Sonoma County Carneros 1982 $6.75 (12/16/84) **68**

GIRARD

Chardonnay Napa Valley 1990: Firm, focused and brilliantly rich, with smoky pear, honey and spice aromas and flavors that echo on the long finish. Has the intensity, grace and style to make a delicious drink now, but should be best after 1993 or '94. $16 (7/31/92) **90**
Chardonnay Napa Valley 1989: Intense and concentrated, with spicy pear, apple and toasty oak flavors in a tightly reined-in style. Crisp and austere. Drinks well now, but can age through 1994. Tasted twice. $16 (11/30/91) **85**
Chardonnay Napa Valley 1988: This beautifully crafted wine is full-flavored, young and lively, with crisp pear, peach and spice flavors rounded out by a subtle touch of oak. Has a long-lasting finish. Should improve through 1993. 4,752 cases made. $16 (11/15/90) **90**
Chardonnay Napa Valley 1987 Rel: $14.50 Cur: $19 (CH-3/90) **81**
Chardonnay Napa Valley 1986 Rel: $13.50 Cur: $28 (8/31/88) SS **93**
Chardonnay Napa Valley 1985 Rel: $13.50 Cur: $25 (CH-3/90) **90**
Chardonnay Napa Valley 1984 Rel: $13.50 Cur: $22 (CH-3/90) **80**
Chardonnay Napa Valley 1983 Rel: $12.50 Cur: $20 (CH-3/90) **76**
Chardonnay Napa Valley 1982 Rel: $12.50 Cur: $21 (CH-3/90) **76**
Chardonnay Napa Valley 1981 Rel: $12.50 Cur: $35 (CH-3/90) **90**
Chardonnay Napa Valley 1980 Rel: $11 Cur: $25 (CH-3/90) **85**
Chardonnay Napa Valley Reserve 1988 ($NA) (CH-6/90) **91**
Chardonnay Napa Valley Reserve 1987: A large-scale wine with finesse, allowing lots of flavor to emerge without a sense of weight. Subtle pear, nutmeg, toast and earth notes make for early complexity, but it's restrained enough to suggest cellaring until 1994 for optimum results. 708 cases made. Rel: $25 Cur: $29 (11/15/90) **90**
Chardonnay Napa Valley Reserve 1986 Rel: $25 Cur: $35 (CH-3/90) **92**
Chardonnay Napa Valley Reserve 1985 Rel: $25 Cur: $30 (CH-3/90) **91**

GLASS MOUNTAIN QUARRY

Chardonnay Napa Valley 1989: Has a spicy, Riesling-like edge to the flavor, but nice honey and apple notes add dimension. Ripe and complex, the fruit sticks with you on the aftertaste. Drink now. $8 (9/15/91) BB **86**

GLEN ELLEN

Chardonnay California Proprietor's Reserve 1990: Clean and spicy, with modest varietal character and intensity. A soft, easy-drinking style that turns a bit watery on the finish. Priced right. Drink now. $7 (7/15/91) **78**
Chardonnay California Proprietor's Reserve 1989: Flavors of pear, butter and spice provide some complexity in this well-balanced, enjoyable medium-weight wine. $6 (12/31/90) **79**
Chardonnay California Proprietor's Reserve 1984 $3.50 (10/16/85) BB **85**
Chardonnay Sonoma Valley 1984 $9 (3/16/86) **60**
Chardonnay Sonoma Valley 1983 $10 (2/01/85) **80**

GOOSECROSS

Chardonnay Napa Valley 1988: Good and tasty, with the unusual range of fruit flavors including peach, apricot and orange. It picks up modest complexity on the finish. Tasted twice. 3,200 cases made. $14 (8/31/90) **81**
Chardonnay Napa Valley 1987: Broad, and earthy, this full-bodied wine has plenty of depth and concentration, but the lemon, herb and toast aromas and flavors will not appeal to everyone. A distinctive style. $15 (1/31/90) **82**
Chardonnay Napa Valley 1986 $15 (5/31/88) **71**
Chardonnay Napa Valley 1985 $14 (8/31/87) **90**
Chardonnay Napa Valley Reserve 1988: Pretty honey, pear, butterscotch and grapefruit flavor make this creamy, rich and elegant. The grapefruit adds a dash of bitterness that detracts from the quality of the wine. Drink now. Tasted twice. 1,600 cases made. $18 (8/31/90) **77**

GRAND CRU

Chardonnay Carneros Premium Selection 1989: Tightly reined in, featuring more grapefruit and lemon aromas and flavors than pear and vanilla, which sneak in on the finish. Drinkable now, but needs until 1993 or '94 to soften. $14 (3/31/92) **84**
Chardonnay Carneros Premium Selection 1988: A pleasant, fruity wine, with apple and pineapple flavors that offer richness and depth. Well balanced, with fruit flavors coming through on the finish. Drink now. Much better than a bottle tasted earlier. $13.50 (6/15/90) **84**
Chardonnay Carneros Premium Selection 1987: A wine with immediate appeal; fresh and tangy, with lively grapefruit, vanilla and delicately honeyed flavors and crisp texture, it grows tastier and more focused on the finish. Drink now. $12 (3/15/89) **88**

GREEN & RED

Chardonnay Napa Valley 1989: Elegant, clean and lively, with fresh pear, melon, spice and citrus notes that are soft and supple, gaining a pretty buttery oak and toast aftertaste. Delicious now to 1993. $14 (3/31/91) **86**
Chardonnay Napa Valley 1988: Heavy and blunt, a clumsy wine with little flavor concentration. Drinkable but not appealing. $12 (4/30/90) **72**
Chardonnay Napa Valley 1987: Subdued and shy, with some aromas of green apples and lemon, butter and oak on the palate and a decent finish. Closed in and hard to evaluate at this point. $11 (7/15/89) **78**

Key to Symbols

The scores reported here are the results of blind tastings conducted by our panel of senior editors. Wines that carry the initials below are results of individual tastings.

THE WINE SPECTATOR 100-POINT SCALE ***95-100***—Classic, a great wine; ***90-94***—Outstanding, superior character and style; ***80-89***—Good to very good, a wine with special qualities; ***70-79***—Average, drinkable wine that may have minor flaws; ***60-69***—Below average, drinkable but not recommended; ***50-59***—Poor, undrinkable, not recommended. "+"—With a score indicates a range; used primarily with barrel tastings to indicate a preliminary score.

SPECIAL DESIGNATIONS SS—Spectator Selection, CS—Cellar Selection, BB—Best Buy, ($NA)—Price not available, (NR)—Not released.

TASTER'S INITIALS (JG)—Jim Gordon, (HS)—Harvey Steiman, (JL)—James Laube, (JS)—James Suckling, (TM)—Thomas Matthews, (TR)—Terry Robards, (PM)—Per-Henrik Mansson, (BT)—Barrel Tasting (these wines were tasted blind from barrel samples), (CA-date)—*California's Great Cabernets* by James Laube, (CH-date)—*California's Great Chardonnays* by James Laube, (VP-date)—*Vintage Port* by James Suckling.

DATE TASTED Dates in parentheses represent the issue in which the rating was published.

GREENWOOD RIDGE

Chardonnay Mendocino 1990: Ripe and buttery, with layers of honey, pear, toast and spice, all neatly focused with richness and depth. Finishes with subtlety and finesse. Ready now through 1995. 662 cases made. $16 (2/15/92) **85**

GRGICH HILLS

Chardonnay Napa Valley 1989: Fresh and lively, with plenty of focused grapefruit, pineapple and nutmeg aromas and flavors that stay fresh and crisp on the finish. Has the liveliness to keep improving through 1993 to '95. Rel: $22 Cur: $28 (7/15/91) **88**
Chardonnay Napa Valley 1988: Tastes more like Riesling than Chardonnay right now with its piny, spicy, floral and peachy flavors that are rich and elegant, well balanced and lingering on the finish. Young and intense, it needs time to come around in the bottle. Try now to 1996. Rel: $22 Cur: $29 (11/15/90) **89**
Chardonnay Napa Valley 1987 Rel: $22 Cur: $31 (CH-6/90) **90**
Chardonnay Napa Valley 1986 Rel: $22 Cur: $44 (CH-3/90) **91**
Chardonnay Napa Valley 1985 Rel: $22 Cur: $41 (CH-3/90) **92**
Chardonnay Napa Valley 1984 Rel: $18 Cur: $33 (CH-3/90) **90**
Chardonnay Napa Valley 1983 Rel: $17 Cur: $33 (CH-3/90) **92**
Chardonnay Napa Valley 1983 Rel: $17 Cur: $33 (10/01/85) SS **96**
Chardonnay Napa Valley 1982 Rel: $17 Cur: $48 (CH-3/90) **87**
Chardonnay Napa Valley 1981 Rel: $17 Cur: $60 (CH-3/90) **88**
Chardonnay Napa Valley 1980 Rel: $17 Cur: $51 (CH-3/90) **88**
Chardonnay Napa Valley 1979 Rel: $16 Cur: $63 (CH-3/90) **95**
Chardonnay Napa Valley 1978 Rel: $13.75 Cur: $60 (CH-3/90) **92**
Chardonnay Napa Valley Hill's Cellars 1976 Rel: $8 Cur: $50 (CH-3/90) **85**
Chardonnay Sonoma County 1977 Rel: $11 Cur: $105 (CH-3/90) **89**

GROTH

Chardonnay Napa Valley 1990: A solid effort, showing pleasant pineapple and pear flavors and nice vanilla and nutmeg hints on the finish. Medium-bodied and drinkable now, but should improve through 1994. Tasted twice. $13.50 (6/30/92) **84**
Chardonnay Napa Valley 1989: Fresh, clean and lively, with tart, crisp apple, lemon-lime, peach and spice flavors that are very attractive and linger on the palate. Has a good concentration of fruit. Ready now through 1994. $13.50 (7/15/91) **89**
Chardonnay Napa Valley 1988: Rich, peachy and lively on the palate, this is a full-bodied and intense wine, with plenty of fruit and a firm structure. Tasted twice. $13 (6/30/90) **83**
Chardonnay Napa Valley 1987 $13 (7/15/89) **79**
Chardonnay Napa Valley 1986 $12.50 (1/31/89) **87**
Chardonnay Napa Valley 1985 $11 (2/15/88) **85**
Chardonnay Napa Valley 1984 $12 (7/31/87) **90**
Chardonnay Napa Valley 1982 $13 (4/16/84) **82**

GUENOC

Chardonnay Guenoc Valley 1989: This rambunctious, snappy wine has great fruit flavor and the benefits of oak aging. Ripe, spicy and abundantly flavorful, with peach, pear and honey flavors accented by an earthy, spicy touch and a minerallike finish. $14 (3/31/91) **88**
Chardonnay Guenoc Valley 1987: Good if you like the style. Very rich and buttery in aroma and flavor, but we'd like to taste more fruit and acidity. Tastes almost like caramel, presumably from oak aging. $10 (2/15/90) **73**
Chardonnay Guenoc Valley Estate Barrel Fermented 1990: A wine with a strong wood character, from the smoky, toasty aromas to the tight texture and woody flavors, but the tart pear and spice notes don't quite match up. Drink now to 1995. $14 (3/31/92) **80**
Chardonnay Guenoc Valley Genevieve Magoon Vineyard Reserve 1990: Rich, ripe and generous, with complex, concentrated pear, pineapple, smoke and spice flavors that are sharply focused and long. Drinks well now, but can hold through 1995. 2,244 cases made. $23 (6/30/92) **91**
Chardonnay Guenoc Valley Genevieve Magoon Vineyard Reserve 1989: Very ripe and decidedly earthy, with a rich texture and plenty of mushroom and honey flavors persisting on the finish, along with plenty of pineapple and pear notes. A soft, gentle wine that's drinkable now. $23 (12/31/91) **86**
Chardonnay Guenoc Valley Genevieve Magoon Vineyard Reserve 1988: Very crisp and tart, but loaded with butter, pineapple and grapefruit aromas and flavors. Flirts with sourness on the finish, making it seem a bit clumsy. Drink now. 2,109 cases made. $17 (12/31/90) **81**
Chardonnay Guenoc Valley Première Cuvée 1986 $17.50 (12/31/88) **70**
Chardonnay North Coast 1986 $9.75 (12/31/88) **88**
Chardonnay North Coast 1985 $9.75 (11/15/87) **80**
Chardonnay North Coast 1984 $10 (9/15/86) **83**

GUNDLACH BUNDSCHU

Chardonnay Sonoma Valley 1990: Smooth and flavorful, with lots of peach, guava and pear flavors gliding across the palate, ending with lovely citrus notes and echoing grapefruit on the long finish. Fresh and appealing now. $11 (3/31/92) **86**
Chardonnay Sonoma Valley 1989: Acceptable in quality, but not much to write home about. Appley, leafy aromas lead to earthy pineapple flavors in a firm, coarse package. $12 (7/15/91) **78**
Chardonnay Sonoma Valley 1988: Shows plenty of generous ripe apple flavors up front that turn thin and coarse on the finish. Drink now. $10 (4/30/90) **76**
Chardonnay Sonoma Valley 1987 $11 (3/15/89) **79**
Chardonnay Sonoma Valley 1986 $9 (2/15/88) **87**
Chardonnay Sonoma Valley 1985 $10 (7/31/87) **80**
Chardonnay Sonoma Valley 1984 $10 (5/31/87) **84**
Chardonnay Sonoma Valley 1983 $9.75 (4/16/86) **76**
Chardonnay Sonoma Valley Sangiacomo Ranch Special Selection 1990: A racy style, with ripe pineapple and oak shadings, but a bit hollow in the middle. Drink now. $15 (12/31/91) **84**
Chardonnay Sonoma Valley Sangiacomo Ranch Special Selection 1989: Fruity in a very simple way, with grassy aromas, fruit cocktail flavors and a tired, cidery texture. Tasted twice. 600 cases made. $15 (7/15/91) **75**
Chardonnay Sonoma Valley Sangiacomo Ranch Special Selection 1988: An oaky, earthy wine, with plenty of rich, supple, and concentrated fruit flavors that echo ripe pear and pineapple, but also earth and rubber flavors. Has limited appeal. Drink or hold through 1993. Tasted twice. 3,000 cases made. $14 (6/30/90) **79**
Chardonnay Sonoma Valley Sangiacomo Ranch Special Selection 1987 $12 (7/15/89) **77**
Chardonnay Sonoma Valley Sangiacomo Ranch Special Selection 1986 $12 (9/30/88) **89**
Chardonnay Sonoma Valley Sangiacomo Ranch Special Selection 1984 $11.50 (5/31/87) **88**
Chardonnay Sonoma Valley Sangiacomo Ranch Special Selection 1983 $12 (12/01/85) **74**

HACIENDA

Chardonnay Sonoma County Clair de Lune 1989: A buttery wine that features ripe, rich, silky pear, peach and apple flavors and a creamy texture. Balanced, fresh, lively and ready to drink now through 1993. $15 (8/31/91) **86**
Chardonnay Sonoma County Clair de Lune 1988: A lush, earthy wine that will not appeal to everyone. Full and toasty, with lots of honey, melon and spice flavors, and hints of leafiness on the aroma. Drinkable now. $15 (6/30/90) **83**
Chardonnay Sonoma County Clair de Lune 1987: A big step down from the '86. Earthy, smoky and gamy, with rich fruit and lots of concentration, but the flavors will not appeal to everyone. Lacks grace and finesse with bitterness and coarseness on the finish. Tasted four times. Rel: $12 Cur: $15 (7/15/89) **73**
Chardonnay Sonoma County Clair de Lune 1986 Rel: $12 Cur: $18 (7/15/88) SS **92**
Chardonnay Sonoma County Clair de Lune 1985 Rel: $11 Cur: $20 (CH-4/90) **87**

Chardonnay Sonoma County Clair de Lune 1984 Rel: $10 Cur: $18 (CH-4/90) **88**
Chardonnay Sonoma County Clair de Lune 1983 Rel: $10 Cur: $22 (CH-4/90) **83**
Chardonnay Sonoma County Clair de Lune 1982 Rel: $9 Cur: $20 (CH-4/90) **78**
Chardonnay Sonoma County Clair de Lune 1981 Rel: $12 Cur: $20 (CH-4/90) **74**
Chardonnay Sonoma County Clair de Lune 1980 Rel: $10.50 Cur: $22 (CH-4/90) **80**
Chardonnay Sonoma County Clair de Lune 1979 Rel: $9 Cur: $25 (CH-4/90) **86**
Chardonnay Sonoma County Clair de Lune 1978 Rel: $9 Cur: $25 (CH-4/90) **73**
Chardonnay Sonoma County Clair de Lune 1977 Rel: $8 Cur: $23 (CH-4/90) **76**
Chardonnay Sonoma County Clair de Lune 1976 Rel: $7 Cur: $40 (CH-4/90) **85**
Chardonnay Sonoma County Clair de Lune 1974 Rel: $5 Cur: $40 (CH-4/90) **80**
Chardonnay Sonoma County Clair de Lune 1973 Rel: $5 Cur: $50 (CH-4/90) **91**

HAGAFEN

Chardonnay Napa Valley 1990: Smooth and polished, with medium-intense grapefruit and bitter almond aromas and flavors. Spicy and lively on the finish. Drinkable now. $14 (7/15/92) **83**

Chardonnay Napa Valley 1989: Rich and earthy, with evident oak, this big wine is soft and round and has butterscotch and pear flavors. $12.50 (3/31/91) **85**

Chardonnay Napa Valley Reserve 1990: Tart and lemony, with crisp pineapple, pear and spice notes. Has plenty of acidity, but could use more richness and depth. Perhaps with time in the bottle that will come. Drink now to 1995. $17 (6/30/92) **86**

HALLCREST

Chardonnay California Fortuyn Cuvée 1990: An earthy, dirty flavor runs through this ripe, thick wine, turning especially unsavory on the finish. Has richness, but it's flawed. 805 cases made. $9.50 (7/15/92) **71**

Chardonnay California Fortuyn Cuvée 1989: A modestly flavorful wine, full-bodied, with a fairly rich texture. Hints of pear, vanilla and spice give it substance and the flavors linger a bit on the finish. A good value, too. $9 (4/30/91) **82**

Chardonnay California Fortuyn Cuvée 1988: Earthy, butterscotch flavors dominate this richly textured, decadently Burgundian Chardonnay. Pear flavors are evident on the finish. A good value but may be difficult to find. $9 (6/30/90) **85**

Chardonnay El Dorado County Hillside Cuvée 1988: An elegant and refined wine. Toasty aromas and mint and orange flavors make this a distinctive wine. Ripe and rich with nice vanilla notes. 220 cases made. $11 (6/30/90) **88**

Chardonnay Santa Cruz Mountains Meylay Vineyard 1989: An extremely rich, intense, buttery wine, with a honeyed texture and a long finish. Big, soft and flavorful, full of ripe pear, spice and vanilla notes in a full-blown, barrel-fermented, malolactic style. Quite a find. Drink now through 1993. 111 cases made. $16.50 (4/30/91) **91**

HANDLEY

Chardonnay Anderson Valley 1988: Bold, rich, ripe and loaded with pear, melon, toast and butter flavors. Packs plenty of punch, finishing with a touch of earth and mineral. Deep and concentrated. Drink now to 1994. 2,370 cases made. $12.50 (7/15/91) **87**

Chardonnay Dry Creek Valley 1989: Young, crisp and creamy in texture, with clearly defined lemon and pear flavors and hints of vanilla for complexity. Will benefit from aging until 1993 to '96. 2,254 cases made. $14.50 (7/15/91) **87**

Chardonnay Dry Creek Valley 1987: Big and blowsy. Assertively oaky and buttery in flavor, but there's just enough fruit flavor to balance it. Full-bodied, with firm acidity and a lingering, buttery aftertaste. $14 (7/15/89) **86**

Chardonnay Dry Creek Valley 1986 $15 (10/31/88) **81**

HANNA

Chardonnay Sonoma County 1990: Lean and earthy, with a volatile edge that takes away from the pear and spice aromas and flavors. Still, it's a solid wine that's tight and concentrated. Should be at its best in 1993 or '94. $13.50 (7/15/92) **82**

Chardonnay Sonoma County 1989: Firm, focused and harmonious, with nicely articulated pear and vanilla aromas and flavors, a rich texture and a persistent finish. Well balanced, with a sense of elegance, although the flavors are simple. Drinkable now. $13.50 (12/31/91) **85**

Chardonnay Sonoma County 1988: A rich, tannic, concentrated wine, with smoky oak flavors and plenty of ripe pear, honey, butter and spice. The flavors fan out on the finish. This clean wine shows signs of complexity and finese. Drink now to 1994. $13.50 (9/30/90) **89**

Chardonnay Sonoma County 1987 $14.50 (7/15/89) **73**
Chardonnay Sonoma County 1986 $13.50 (9/30/88) **81**
Chardonnay Sonoma County 1985 $13.50 (8/31/87) **83**

HANZELL

Chardonnay Sonoma Valley 1988 Rel: $24 Cur: $34 (CH-5/90) **90**

Chardonnay Sonoma Valley 1987: Has plenty of fresh, clean, ripe pear and citrus on the nose and up front on the palate that turns elegant and subtle on the finish. With fine fruit definition, it has more elegance than most Hanzells, and good length on the finish. Drink now to 1994. Rel: $24 Cur: $33 (2/28/90) **89**

Chardonnay Sonoma Valley 1986 Rel: $22 Cur: $38 (CH-1/90) **87**
Chardonnay Sonoma Valley 1985 Rel: $22 Cur: $46 (CH-1/90) **90**
Chardonnay Sonoma Valley 1984 Rel: $20 Cur: $45 (CH-1/90) **84**
Chardonnay Sonoma Valley 1983 Rel: $20 Cur: $47 (CH-1/90) **84**
Chardonnay Sonoma Valley 1982 Rel: $19 Cur: $45 (CH-1/90) **89**
Chardonnay Sonoma Valley 1981 Rel: $18 Cur: $50 (CH-1/90) **86**
Chardonnay Sonoma Valley 1980 Rel: $17 Cur: $60 (CH-1/90) **90**
Chardonnay Sonoma Valley 1979 Rel: $16 Cur: $70 (CH-1/90) **85**
Chardonnay Sonoma Valley 1978 Rel: $13 Cur: $68 (CH-1/90) **95**
Chardonnay Sonoma Valley 1977 Rel: $12 Cur: $85 (CH-1/90) **88**
Chardonnay Sonoma Valley 1976 Rel: $12 Cur: $90 (CH-1/90) **91**
Chardonnay Sonoma Valley 1975 Rel: $10 Cur: $70 (CH-1/90) **86**
Chardonnay Sonoma Valley 1974 Rel: $9 Cur: $70 (CH-1/90) **88**
Chardonnay Sonoma Valley 1973 Rel: $8 Cur: $100 (CH-1/90) **85**
Chardonnay Sonoma Valley 1972 Rel: $7 Cur: $75 (CH-1/90) **90**
Chardonnay Sonoma Valley 1971 Rel: $7 Cur: $120 (CH-1/90) **85**
Chardonnay Sonoma Valley 1970 Rel: $7 Cur: $110 (CH-1/90) **84**
Chardonnay Sonoma Valley 1969 Rel: $6 Cur: $140 (CH-1/90) **90**
Chardonnay Sonoma Valley 1968 Rel: $6 Cur: $140 (CH-1/90) **91**
Chardonnay Sonoma Valley 1967 Rel: $6 Cur: $125 (CH-1/90) **89**
Chardonnay Sonoma Valley 1966 Rel: $6 Cur: $170 (CH-1/90) **94**
Chardonnay Sonoma Valley 1965 Rel: $6 Cur: $180 (CH-1/90) **84**
Chardonnay California 1959 Rel: $4 Cur: $200 (CH-12/89) **88**
Chardonnay California 1957 Rel: $4 Cur: $240 (CH-12/89) **90**

HARRISON

Chardonnay Napa Valley 1990: This one really smokes. Woody, spicy, smoky notes accent the pear and peach flavors for a full-bodied, very assertive wine. Drinkable now, but should mellow out if aged until about 1993. 1,100 cases made. $24 (1/31/92) **84**

Chardonnay Napa Valley 1989: A medium-weight wine that's light on fruit concentration, but pleasing for its modest peach flavors and abundant spicy, vanillalike accents. Polished and interesting, with flavors that grow on the finish. 824 cases made. $24 (7/15/91) **87**

HAVENS

Chardonnay Carneros Napa Valley 1989: Fresh and focused, with a crisp texture and a nicely focused spectrum of pear, apple, nutmeg and honey aromas and flavors. An elegant wine, with tightly packed flavors that are long and concentrated on the finish. Built to be at its best starting 1993. $14 (7/15/91) **87**

Chardonnay Carneros Napa Valley 1988: Rich and round, with a silky-smooth texture and generous pear, vanilla and butterscotch flavors that echo honey and pear on the long finish. Delicious to drink now, but cellaring until 1993 would not be amiss. 1,150 cases made. $14 (4/30/90) **89**

HAWK CREST

Chardonnay California 1990: Nothing fancy, just straight-ahead Chardonnay, with ripe, earthy pear, apple and citrus flavors that turn a bit coarse on the finish. Ready to drink now. $9 (3/15/92) **81**

Chardonnay California 1989: Simple lemon, pear and nutmeg flavors turn vapid on the finish. $9 (7/15/91) **72**

Chardonnay California 1988: Clean and neutral, vaguely applelike and crisp in texture, with little to distinguish it. $9 (12/15/89) **74**

Chardonnay California 1987 $7.50 (10/15/88) **71**
Chardonnay California 1984 $6 (4/16/86) **67**

Chardonnay Sonoma County 1987: Clean, ripe, fat and oaky, with moderate depth and ripe pear, spice and melon flavors that are delicate and subtle on the finish. Has finesse. Good value. $9 (7/15/89) **86**

HAYWOOD

Chardonnay California Vintner's Select 1990: Tart, young and lemony, with hints of apple, nectarine and vanilla. Tight and understated, but the finish is crisp and lively. Drink now and beyond. $8 (11/15/91) BB **83**

Chardonnay Sonoma Valley Los Chamizal Vineyards 1989: An agreeable wine, but the smoky, toasty aromas promise more flavor than it delivers. The modest pear and almond flavors drop out, leaving simply woody notes on the finish. $13.50 (3/31/91) **81**

Chardonnay Sonoma Valley Los Chamizal Vineyards 1988: Spicy, toasty aromas and flavors dominate, making it oakier than most Chardonnays. Has hints of pear, but it's not for anyone seeking pure fruit. Within the style, it's drinkable, but we don't expect it to improve in the cellar. 1,288 cases made. $13.50 (11/30/90) **76**

Chardonnay Sonoma Valley Los Chamizal Vineyards 1987: This big, clumsy wine is soft, somewhat alcoholic and soapy, with simple pear, peach and toasty oak flavors that are missing fruit concentration and definition. 790 cases made. $12.50 (6/30/90) **74**

Chardonnay Sonoma Valley 1986 $9.50 (10/15/88) **82**
Chardonnay Sonoma Valley 1982 $10 (5/16/84) **80**
Chardonnay Sonoma Valley Reserve 1985 $14.50 (12/31/87) **77**

THE HESS COLLECTION

Chardonnay Napa Valley 1989: Has elegant, spicy Riesling and Muscat overtones to the pear, spice and melon flavors. Delicate in style, with finesse and grace, and a lingering finish. $14.50 (7/15/91) **86**

Chardonnay Napa Valley 1988: Very ripe and attractive, with fresh, rich peach, apple and melon flavors that are well balanced, finishing with just the right touch of wood. Tasty. Drink now. Rel: $13.75 Cur: $17 (4/15/90) **85**

Chardonnay Napa Valley 1987: Rich, full-bodied and luscious, with a ripe, fat, silky texture that's not heavy. Floats over the palate. The ripe pear, spice and vanilla flavors are very enticing, finishing with a pretty touch of orange peel. Complex and graceful. Rel: $13.25 Cur: $19 (7/15/89) **90**

Chardonnay Napa Valley 1986 Rel: $12.75 Cur: $18 (CH-4/90) **88**

HESS SELECT

Chardonnay California 1990: Strong, spicy Muscat flavors add to the tiers of vibrant apple, pineapple, citrus and spice notes that are ripe, round and gentle. Pleasant to drink now through 1993. $9.50 (12/15/91) BB **86**

Chardonnay Napa Valley 1989: Exotic melon, pineapple and pear flavors and a touch of spice make this elegant, balanced and pleasing, with good depth and richness. Drink now. $9.50 (12/31/90) **86**

Chardonnay California 1988: Lean, rich, crisp and flavorful with ripe fruit, layers of pear, spice, clove and nectarine notes that keep you coming back for another sip—and finding more complexity. Elegant and subtle, with a lingering finish. A new line for Hess. Drink now to 1994. $9 (11/30/89) SS **90**

HIDDEN CELLARS

Chardonnay Mendocino County 1990: Crisp and floral, with generous apple, honey and pear aromas and flavors, hinting at tropical fruit on the finish. Keeps its balance nicely, and should remain drinkable through 1994. 2,443 cases made. $12 (4/30/92) **85**

Chardonnay Mendocino County 1989: Clean and elegant, with simple citrus, pear and melon flavors, but like many '89s, it lacks concentration and persistence. What it does have is nice, and a touch of oak comes through on the finish. Drink now. 3,789 cases made. $12 (3/31/91) **83**

Chardonnay Mendocino County 1987: Rich but elegant. Deftly blends ripe pear, lemon, honey and tasty oak flavors in a velvety smooth package. Beautiful lingering finish. $12 (7/15/89) **89**

Chardonnay Mendocino County 1986 $10.50 (5/31/88) **78**
Chardonnay Mendocino County Grasso Vineyard 1985 $9.75 (7/31/87) **78**

Chardonnay Mendocino County Reserve 1990: Young, tight, crisp and flinty, with intense, vibrant pear and Pippin apple flavors and a hint of peach on the aftertaste. Well balanced. Drink now to 1994. 500 cases made. $16 (12/15/91) **86**

Chardonnay Mendocino County Reserve Barrel Fermented 1989: An outstanding wine. Elegant in structure, intense in its pear and spice flavors and very rich in texture. Has great concentration, yet it remains light and pleasant on the palate, with a delicious, lingering, spicy aftertaste. Only 250 cases made. $16 (7/15/91) **91**

WILLIAM HILL

Chardonnay Napa Valley Reserve 1990: A vibrant wine that's youthful and intense, with plenty of toasty, earthy apple and pear aromas and flavors. Needs until 1994 or so to settle down. Tasted twice. $18 (7/15/92) **87**

Chardonnay Napa Valley Reserve 1989: Ripe, complex and generous, with a marvelous interplay of toast, butter and smoke notes against the rich pear and pineapple flavors, turning spicy and elegant on the finish. It all weaves together nicely, which suggests cellaring until 1994 wouldn't hurt. $18 (6/30/91) **90**

Chardonnay Napa Valley Reserve 1988: A bold, concentrated wine, with vivid pear and butterscotch aromas and flavors in harmonious balance, the lively acidity on the finish adding zest to the silky-smooth texture. Drinkable now. $18 (4/30/90) **90**

Chardonnay Napa Valley Reserve 1987 Rel: $18 Cur: $20 (CH-3/90) **91**
Chardonnay Napa Valley Reserve 1986 Rel: $17 Cur: $20 (CH-3/90) **91**
Chardonnay Napa Valley Reserve 1985 Rel: $16 Cur: $24 (CH-3/90) **90**
Chardonnay Napa Valley Reserve 1984 Rel: $20 Cur: $24 (CH-3/90) **88**
Chardonnay Napa Valley Reserve 1983 Rel: $22 Cur: $28 (CH-3/90) **85**
Chardonnay Napa Valley Reserve 1982 Rel: $24 Cur: $28 (CH-3/90) **86**
Chardonnay Napa Valley Reserve 1980 Rel: $16 Cur: $30 (CH-3/90) **70**

Chardonnay Napa Valley Silver Label 1989: Tight and simple, with honey, pear and nut notes that lack polish and finesse. It's a complete wine, but it lacks drama. Drink now to 1993. $12 (1/31/91) **81**

Chardonnay Napa Valley Silver Label 1988: Has plenty of fresh, ripe, moderately rich pear, oak, citrus and spice flavors that offer good depth and complexity. Well balanced and attractive. The flavors linger. Drink now to 1993. $11.50 (6/30/90) **85**

Chardonnay Napa Valley Silver Label 1987: Clumsy, with bizarre textures and flavors reminiscent of ash, on top of more acceptable pear and honey. Not immediately likable. $13 (6/15/89) **73**

Chardonnay Napa Valley Silver Label 1986 $10 (4/30/88) **80**

HOP KILN

Chardonnay Alexander Valley 10th Anniversary Reserve 1983 $10 (10/01/85) **86**

Chardonnay Russian River Valley M. Griffin Vineyards 1990: Floral, citrusy aromas and flavors characterize this charming, lighthearted wine. Would make a nice aperitif, although it has the backbone to grow with short-term cellaring. Try in 1993. 620 cases made. $12 (2/29/92) **86**

HOUTZ

Chardonnay Santa Ynez Valley 1986: Not a show-stopper, but a well-balanced dinner wine. Ripe, fruity, slightly buttery in flavor and smoothly elegant in texture. Spice and butter notes linger on the aftertaste. $11 (12/15/89) **83**

HUSCH

Chardonnay Anderson Valley Special Reserve 1987: Intensely flavored and full-bodied, with ripe pear, vanilla, nutmeg and spice flavors that linger on the palate. It finishes with a sense of elegance. Drink now. 350 cases made. $16 (6/30/90) **82**

Chardonnay Mendocino 1990: Fresh, fruity and straightforward, a medium-bodied wine, with floral aromas, apple and pear flavors, crisp balance and a clean finish. Beautifully balanced and ready to drink now. $12 (11/15/91) **84**

Chardonnay Mendocino 1988: Plenty of fresh, ripe, rich flavor to warm up to, with juicy pear, peach, fig and citrus notes that are elegantly balanced and quite harmonious. Drink now to 1993. $11 (2/28/90) **88**

Chardonnay Mendocino 1987 $10 (11/15/88) **88**

Chardonnay Mendocino 1986 $9.75 (11/30/87) **86**

Chardonnay Mendocino 1985 $9.75 (3/31/87) **88**

Chardonnay Mendocino Estate 1989: Fresh, lively and balanced, with pear flavor and hints of peach, nutmeg and vanilla. Has a smooth texture and a long finish. Nicely balanced. Drink now. $11 (12/31/90) **88**

INGLENOOK

Chardonnay Napa Valley 1990: Crisp and firm, with ripe citrus, pear and apple flavors that are tart and clean. The finish is most impressive, as the flavors stay alive with zest and vitality. Drinks well now, but can age through 1994. $10.25 (7/15/92) **87**

Chardonnay Napa Valley 1989: Light but fruity, this zingy wine offers plenty of fresh grapefruit, peach and apple aromas and flavors, a delicate touch of oak and a crisp texture. Drinkable now, but could develop well with cellaring past 1993. Tasted twice. $7.50 (2/28/91) BB **87**

Chardonnay Napa Valley 1986 $9.50 (3/15/88) **80**

Chardonnay Napa Valley 1983 $9.50 (10/01/84) **79**

Chardonnay Napa Valley Reserve 1988 (SNA) (CH-4/90) **88**

Chardonnay Napa Valley Reserve 1987: Elegant and stylish, with pretty floral and fruity aromas, and rich, ripe pear and honey flavors to match. Picks up a rich toasty, smoky oak flavor on the aftertaste. Well balanced, complex and full. Drink now to 1993. $14 (5/31/90) **89**

Chardonnay Napa Valley Reserve 1986 $14.50 (CH-4/90) **88**

Chardonnay Napa Valley Reserve 1985 $14.50 (CH-4/90) **78**

Chardonnay Napa Valley Reserve 1984 Rel: $12.50 Cur: $18 (CH-4/90) **86**

Chardonnay Napa Valley Reserve 1983 Rel: $16 Cur: $19 (CH-4/90) **82**

INNISFREE

Chardonnay Carneros 1988: Smoky, complex aromas are pleasing, but the flavors are less pleasing, with tasty pear and stale Chardonnay flavors that flirt with bitterness. Drink now. $12 (5/31/90) **77**

Chardonnay Napa Valley 1989: Light but fruity and charming, with apple, melon and butter flavors giving it substance. Has a lively balance between acidity and fruit. $11 (4/30/91) **83**

Chardonnay Napa Valley 1988: Rich and floral, with full-bodied toast, pear, honey and vanilla flavors that are elegant and concentrated. Tight and firm, with a pretty aftertaste that echoes fruit. Drink now. $12 (6/15/90) **86**

Chardonnay Napa Valley 1987: Clean and refreshing. Has a crisp, grapefruity flavor and slightly grassy aromas. $9 (2/15/89) **80**

Chardonnay Napa Valley 1986 $9 (12/31/87) **80**

Chardonnay Napa Valley 1985 $9 (12/31/86) **92**

Chardonnay Napa Valley 1984 $9 (11/16/85) **88**

INNISKILLIN NAPA

Chardonnay Napa Valley 1988: Ripe and fruity, with layers of pear, melon, citrus and apple flavors. Some may find the non-oaky style appealing. Certainly the label will draw your attention. Drink now. $14 (7/15/91) **81**

IRON HORSE

Chardonnay Sonoma County Green Valley 1990: Crisp and focused, with a bright beam of pear and spice flavors that seem to strive for subtlety rather than sheer power. Finishes with a sense of elegance and restraint, although the flavors linger. Drinkable now, but probably better in 1993 or '94. $18 (4/30/92) **88**

Chardonnay Sonoma County Green Valley 1989: Elegant, with subtle pear, peach, vanilla and banana flavors that are creamy and smooth on the palate. Well balanced, with delicate flavors on the finish. Drink now through 1993. $18 (3/31/91) **86**

Chardonnay Sonoma County Green Valley 1988: Tart fruit flavors are tightly reined in by acidity. A lean wine that keeps peach, grapefruit and nectarine flavors in check. Drink now. $18 (2/15/90) **81**

Chardonnay Sonoma County Green Valley 1987 $17 (1/31/89) **76**

Chardonnay Sonoma County Green Valley 1986 $12 (3/31/88) **83**

Chardonnay Sonoma County Green Valley 1985 $12.50 (7/31/87) **75**

Chardonnay Sonoma County Green Valley 1984 $12 (6/16/86) **88**

Chardonnay Sonoma County Green Valley 1983 $12 (11/16/85) **76**

JEKEL

Chardonnay Arroyo Seco 1989: Crisp and tight, with lemon, pineapple and tart apple notes, but ultimately a simple wine, with a good core of flavor. Drink now to 1994. $12 (6/30/92) **80**

Chardonnay Arroyo Seco 1988: A tart, young, lean and concentrated wine, with sharply focused pear and pineapple flavors that gain elegance and finesse on the finish, with very fine balance, crisp acidity and long fruity flavors on the aftertaste. Drink now to 1993. $11 (4/15/90) **87**

Chardonnay Arroyo Seco 1986: Showy and big, gushing with butter, vanilla and butterscoth, all of which overwhelm the fruit and hurt the harmony of the wine. In the end, it comes across as unbalanced and lacking in finesse. $11 (4/30/89) **76**

Chardonnay Arroyo Seco 1985 $10.50 (12/31/88) **71**

Chardonnay Arroyo Seco 1984 $10.50 (5/31/87) **83**

Key to Symbols

The scores reported here are the results of blind tastings conducted by our panel of senior editors. Wines that carry the initials below are results of individual tastings.

THE WINE SPECTATOR 100-POINT SCALE ***95-100***—Classic, a great wine; ***90-94***—Outstanding, superior character and style; ***80-89***—Good to very good, a wine with special qualities; ***70-79***—Average, drinkable wine that may have minor flaws; ***60-69***—Below average, drinkable but not recommended; ***50-59***—Poor, undrinkable, not recommended. "+"—With a score indicates a range; used primarily with barrel tastings to indicate a preliminary score.

SPECIAL DESIGNATIONS SS—Spectator Selection, CS—Cellar Selection, BB—Best Buy, (SNA)—Price not available, (NR)—Not released.

TASTER'S INITIALS (JG)—Jim Gordon, (HS)—Harvey Steiman, (JL)—James Laube, (JS)—James Suckling, (TM)—Thomas Matthews, (TR)—Terry Robards, (PM)—Per-Henrik Mansson, (BT)—Barrel Tasting (these wines were tasted blind from barrel samples), (CA-date)—*California's Great Cabernets* by James Laube, (CH-date)—*California's Great Chardonnays* by James Laube, (VP-date)—*Vintage Port* by James Suckling.

DATE TASTED Dates in parentheses represent the issue in which the rating was published.

Chardonnay Arroyo Seco 1983 $10 (4/01/86) **66**

Chardonnay Arroyo Seco 1982 $10 (1/01/84) **88**

Chardonnay Arroyo Seco 1981 $11 (6/01/86) **86**

Chardonnay Arroyo Seco Home Vineyard Private Reserve 1985: A winner. Big, rich, oaky and loaded with pineapple, spice, custard and smoky flavors that linger on the palate. A big, strong wine with layers of flavor and fine length. $18 (4/15/89) **91**

Chardonnay Arroyo Seco Home Vineyard Private Reserve 1984 $16 (11/30/87) **79**

Chardonnay Arroyo Seco Home Vineyard Private Reserve 1982 $14 (10/01/85) **93**

Chardonnay Arroyo Seco Home Vineyard Private Reserve 1981 $15 (6/01/86) **84**

JEPSON

Chardonnay Mendocino 1989: Simple and fruity, with a somewhat watery texture, but it does have nice peach and nutmeg aromas and flavors. Drinkable now. $14 (7/15/91) **79**

Chardonnay Mendocino 1988: Firm and lively, showing good fig, pear and spice flavors in a somewhat complex but restrained style. The subtleties emerge as you sip, and the long aftertaste is pleasing, too. 3,200 cases made. $12.50 (4/30/91) **85**

Chardonnay Mendocino 1986 $12 (11/15/88) **89**

Chardonnay Mendocino 1985 $12 (1/31/88) **92**

Chardonnay Mendocino Estate Reserve 1988: Pretty floral aromas and intense, concentrated fig, honey, toast, citrus and spice flavors are all tightly wound and well focused. Has lots of pizzazz, with a finish that echoes honey and spice. Drink now to 1994. 408 cases made. $21 (11/30/91) **91**

Chardonnay Mendocino Vintage Reserve 1986: Focused and fruity, with butterscoth and straightforward pineapple, apple and piny aromas and flavors. Balanced with a pleasant finish that makes it appealing to drink now. $15 (5/31/89) **80**

JOHNSON TURNBULL

Chardonnay Knights Valley Teviot Springs Vineyard 1987: Tart and thin, it tastes stripped of its body and fruit. By the way, where's the fruit? Tasted twice. $12.50 (9/15/89) **70**

JORDAN

Chardonnay Alexander Valley 1988: Rich and buttery, with toasty butterscotch, pear, fig and spice flavors and a long, full finish. A tight, focused style that's drinking well now, but can age through 1994. Tasted twice. $20 (11/30/91) **86**

Chardonnay Alexander Valley 1987: Ripe, rich and toasty, with smooth honey, pear, apple and butterscotch flavors that are elegant and well balanced. It finishes with good length and complexity. Drink now to 1993. $20 (6/30/90) **88**

Chardonnay Alexander Valley 1986: Butterscotchy, but not quite as round and supple as some others, leaning toward slightly spicy pear aromas and flavors. Good, but lacks refinement. $20 (4/15/89) **82**

Chardonnay Alexander Valley 1985 $17 (3/15/88) **87**

Chardonnay Alexander Valley 1983 $16 (7/16/86) **67**

Chardonnay Alexander Valley 1982 $15.75 (5/16/85) **85**

Chardonnay Alexander Valley 1981 $15.75 (4/16/84) **77**

JORY

Chardonnay California 1990: A disjointed wine. Spicy, with toasty oak flavors, but the fruit intensity is modest, turning thin and light. Hints of pear come through, but it's mostly oak. Drink now to 1994. Tasted twice. 1,082 cases made. $20 (4/30/92) **78**

Chardonnay Santa Clara County San Ysidro Vineyard 1989: Soft, ripe and supple, with generous honey, pear, vanilla and butter notes. Gains complexity with a hint of almond, but it's a bit flabby and the flavors cloy on the finish. Drink now. 1,000 cases made. $17 (4/30/91) **82**

Chardonnay Santa Clara County San Ysidro Vineyard 1987 $16.50 (10/31/88) **89**

JOULLIAN

Chardonnay Carmel Valley 1989: The toasty oak turns gluey in this one, interfering with the ripe melon and spicy pear notes. Some may find the oak alluring, but most will find its presence too strong. Drink now. 1,210 cases made. $12 (7/15/91) **73**

JUSTIN

Chardonnay Paso Robles 1990: An odd, overly mature wine that's unusual from the deep color through the buttery, sherrylike aromas to the caramel flavors and sweet finish. Tastes cooked and heavy. Tasted twice, with consistent notes. 1,524 cases made. $16.50 (7/15/92) **74**

Chardonnay Paso Robles 1989: Earthy, with rich, concentrated spice, pear and toasty oak flavors that linger on the aftertaste. The oak turns somewhat bitter on the finish. Ready now through 1994. 1,153 cases made. $16.50 (7/15/91) **85**

Chardonnay Paso Robles 1988: A butterball, with lots of oak, pineapple, butter and grapefruit flavors that are rich and concentrated and vanilla and mineral notes that stay with you through the finish. A big but graceful wine. Drink now to 1994. 1,153 cases made. $14 (2/15/91) **92**

KALIN

Chardonnay Potter Valley Cuvée BL 1988: Elegant and balanced, with ripe pear, pineapple and nutmeg flavors and a touch of vinegar adding an edge. Of moderate depth and complexity. Drink now. $25 (3/31/91) **86**

Chardonnay Sonoma County Cuvée DD 1989: A strange geraniumlike character permeates the nose and palate. Not our style, but drinkable. Tasted twice, with consistent notes. $22 (7/15/92) **74**

Chardonnay Sonoma County Cuvée DD 1988: Deep and complex, with tiers of pear, honey, earth and butterscotch that are rich and concentrated. Has presence and personality, and finishes with good length. Drink now. $23 (3/31/91) **87**

Chardonnay Sonoma County Cuvée LD 1988: A rich, complex wine that's intriguing, with ripe pineapple, honey, pear and spice notes that turn smooth and creamy on the palate before picking up oak tannins on the finish. Balanced and well made. Drink now to 1994. $23 (3/15/91) **88**

Chardonnay Sonoma County Cuvée LD 1987: Dull and oxidized, with weedy, herbal, vegetal flavors that override the pear and fig notes. The finish lacks focus. Drinkable but unexciting. Drink now. $25 (3/15/91) **79**

Chardonnay Sonoma County Cuvée LR 1989: Distinctive, with characteristic rose petal aromas and flavors, this medium-weight, polished wine also shows pleasant pear and apple flavors and a hint of oak on the finish but fades fast. Drinkable now. Tasted twice. $22 (7/15/92) **80**

Chardonnay Sonoma County Cuvée LV 1989: Lean and earthy, with a metallic edge to the astringent green apple flavors. Seems bitter on the finish. $22 (7/15/92) **70**

KALINDA

Chardonnay Knights Valley 1989: Pretty melon, pear and spice flavors have a touch of menthol and mint, but the flavors turn watery, with a hint of citrus. Drink now. $7 (7/15/91) **81**

KARLY

Chardonnay California 1986 $12.50 (4/15/88) **54**

Chardonnay Santa Maria Valley 1985 $12 (8/31/87) **81**

KEENAN

Chardonnay Napa Valley 1990: Lean and crisp, with bracing acidity and tart lemon, pineapple, peach and vanilla flavors that are clean and refreshing. Relies more on subtlety than power. Drink now to 1995. $15 (4/15/92) **87**

Chardonnay Napa Valley 1989: Lean and lively, with sharply focused lemon and grapefruit flavors to balance a serious component of fresh oak that extends into the long finish. Best starting in 1993. 4,800 cases made. $15 (7/15/91) **84**

Chardonnay Napa Valley 1988: Elegant and intense, with pretty pear, spice, and oak flavors, a silky texture and excellent tension between fruit and acidity. Quite complex honey and butterscotch notes sneak in on the finish. Drink now to 1993. 4,000 cases made. $15 (6/30/90) SS **91**

Chardonnay Napa Valley 1987 $12.50 (6/15/89) **82**

Chardonnay Napa Valley 1986 $12 (7/15/88) **85**

Chardonnay Napa Valley 1985 $11 (7/31/87) **81**
Chardonnay Napa Valley 1983 $12.50 (9/16/85) **74**
Chardonnay Napa Valley Ann's Vineyard 1987: Not recommended. A weedy, earthy, vegetal wine that's sour and cloying. Tasted twice, with consistent notes. 2,000 cases made. $13.50 (6/30/90) **59**
Chardonnay Napa Valley Ann's Vineyard 1986: Tart, lean and austere, with crisp citrus, green apple and rather simple flavors. Lacks body and finesse. $14 (4/15/89) **77**
Chardonnay Napa Valley Estate 1985 $13.50 (2/15/88) **80**
Chardonnay Napa Valley Estate 1983 $12.50 (8/31/86) **70**

KENDALL-JACKSON
Chardonnay Anderson Valley Dennison Vineyard 1987 Rel: $14 Cur: $16 (CH-4/90) **82**
Chardonnay Anderson Valley Dennison Vineyard 1985 Rel: $14 Cur: $20 (CH-4/90) **85**
Chardonnay Anderson Valley DuPratt Vineyard 1988 Rel: $14 Cur: $17 (CH-4/90) **85**
Chardonnay Anderson Valley DePatie Vineyard 1987: Classy and complex. A lovely, clean and stylishly oaky wine, with loads of sweet vanilla, butter, pear and apple flavors and a touch of nutmeg. Smoky, rich and long-lasting on the finish. Rel: $14 Cur: $17 (7/15/89) **91**
Chardonnay California Proprietor's Grand Reserve 1990: Elegant and creamy, with pretty peach, pear and apple flavors and almond and floral overtones that are attractive through the finish. Balanced and ready to drink now. Tasted twice. $23 (7/15/92) **86**
Chardonnay California Proprietor's Grand Reserve 1989: Rich and generous, offering lots of buttery complexity supported by a solid core of grapefruit and pineapple crispness that extends into a long finish. Drinkable now, but has the stuff to age through 1993. $23 (5/31/91) **90**
Chardonnay California The Proprietor's 1988: Effusively fruity, moderately rich and complex with a trace of sweet Chardonnay flavor that echoes honey, melon, pear and subtle oak flavors and hints of tropical fruit. Smooth and lush texture. Drink now. $24.50 (2/28/90) **88**
Chardonnay California The Proprietor's 1987 Rel: $20 Cur: $25 (CH-4/90) **92**
Chardonnay California The Proprietor's 1986 Rel: $17 Cur: $20 (CH-4/90) **86**
Chardonnay California The Proprieter's 1985 $18 (9/15/87) **79**
Chardonnay California Proprietor's Reserve 1983 $13.50 (8/01/85) **86**
Chardonnay California Vintner's Reserve 1991: Fresh, lively, elegant and creamy, with pretty pear, vanilla and almond flavors that are nicely proportioned. The fruit lingers on the finish. Drink now to 1993. $13 (7/15/92) **84**
Chardonnay California Vintner's Reserve 1989: Soft and fragrant, with spicy, buttery aromas and flavors and a modest core of apple and grapefruit flavors. Drinkable now. $13 (7/15/91) **84**
Chardonnay California Vintner's Reserve 1988: Ripe, round and lush, with spicy overtones to the lovely peach and pineapple aromas and flavors, harmonious and beautifully balanced. Drink now. $12.50 (10/31/89) **89**
Chardonnay California Vintner's Reserve 1987 $12 (9/30/88) **85**
Chardonnay California Vintner's Reserve 1985 $9.50 (3/15/87) **84**
Chardonnay California Vintner's Reserve 1984 $7 (4/16/86) **59**
Chardonnay Santa Maria Valley Camelot Vineyard 1990: Ripe and round, with a distinctive flavor profile that features toast, butter and modest amounts of pear and nutmeg. Picks up a touch of honey on the finish. Drinkable now. $14 (7/15/92) **84**
Chardonnay Sonoma Valley Durell Vineyard 1990: Ripe, generous and sharply focused, this lean-textured wine is bursting with flavors. Pear, apple, fig and spice aromas and flavors keep darting over the palate through the long, generous finish. Best after 1993. $16 (7/15/92) **87**
Chardonnay Sonoma Valley Durell Vineyard 1989: Generous, ripe and fruity, with hints of buttery oak to spice it up. Well balanced, smooth and rich for the vintage. $16 (7/15/91) **86**
Chardonnay Sonoma Valley Durell Vineyard 1987 Rel: $14 Cur: $18 (CH-4/90) **86**
Chardonnay Sonoma Valley Durell Vineyard 1986 Rel: $14 Cur: $20 (CH-6/90) **91**
Chardonnay Sonoma Valley Durell Vineyard 1985 Rel: $14 Cur: $20 (CH-4/90) **87**
Chardonnay Redwood Valley Lolonis Vineyard 1988 $14 (CH-4/90) **85**

KENWOOD
Chardonnay Sonoma Valley 1988: Well balanced, with fresh pear and lemon flavors that are straightforward. Doesn't show much in the way of finesse, but this wines's true flavors stay with you. Drink now. $14 (5/31/90) **82**
Chardonnay Sonoma Valley 1987: Intensely and lushly fruity, with layers of pear and lemon flavor. Full-bodied, with a lingering, fruity finish. Pleasantly soft and easy to drink. $13 (7/15/89) **86**
Chardonnay Sonoma Valley 1986: Delicate and fruity, with cinnamon and nutmeg-tinged peach aromas and flavors floating gently on a fragile, lacy framework. Drink now. $12 (2/15/89) **85**
Chardonnay Sonoma Valley Beltane Ranch 1990: Crisp and ultimately a pleasant white wine, with attractive peach and melon aromas and flavors, hinting at wool on the finish. Drinkable now. $16 (1/31/92) **83**
Chardonnay Sonoma Valley Beltane Ranch 1989: Fresh, lively and a bit soft in the middle, but finishes with lots of fresh apple and melon aromas and flavors. Appealing to drink soon. Rel: $16 Cur: $19 (7/15/91) **83**
Chardonnay Sonoma Valley Beltane Ranch 1988: A rich, broad-textured wine that's distinctively toasty in aroma, full-bodied and well-balanced. Made in a nice, oaky style. Rel: $15 Cur: $17 (11/30/90) **88**
Chardonnay Sonoma Valley Beltane Ranch 1987 Rel: $15 Cur: $17 (CH-7/90) **87**
Chardonnay Sonoma Valley Beltane Ranch 1986 Rel: $14 Cur: $18 (CH-7/90) **85**
Chardonnay Sonoma Valley Beltane Ranch 1985 Rel: $14 Cur: $18 (CH-7/90) **84**
Chardonnay Sonoma Valley Yulupa Vineyard 1988: An elegant wine, offering pretty ripe peach, fig and vanilla flavors that are a bit green around the edges, but are well balanced with a crisp, clean finish. Drink now. Rel: $14 Cur: $17 (5/31/90) **87**
Chardonnay Sonoma Valley Yulupa Vineyard 1987 Rel: $14 Cur: $16 (CH-7/90) **85**
Chardonnay Sonoma Valley Yulupa Vineyard 1986 Rel: $12 Cur: $17 (CH-7/90) **82**
Chardonnay Sonoma Valley Yulupa Vineyard 1985 Rel: $12 Cur: $17 (CH-7/90) **84**
Chardonnay Sonoma Valley Yulupa Vineyard 1983 Rel: $11 Cur: $18 (CH-7/90) **85**

KISTLER
Chardonnay Russian River Valley Dutton Ranch 1990: Ripe and creamy, with fresh pear, herb, smoke and butter notes that are neatly focused and well integrated. The finish is long and concentrated. Drink now. $28 (1/31/92) **88**
Chardonnay Russian River Valley Dutton Ranch 1989: Intense and complex, with pretty floral aromas and a solid core of pear, butter, toast and spice flavors. A well-proportioned wine that reveals its concentration and depth on the finish, where the fruit sails on. Drink now to 1994. 4,355 cases made. Rel: $24 Cur: $31 (2/15/91) **89**
Chardonnay Russian River Valley Dutton Ranch 1988: A beautiful wine. Has pretty up-front pear, peach and spice aromas, with woody flavors on the palate, but it has a supple texture. Drink now to 1993. Rel: $22 Cur: $40 (2/15/90) **90**
Chardonnay Russian River Valley Dutton Ranch 1987 Rel: $18 Cur: $35 (CH-2/90) **93**
Chardonnay Russian River Valley Dutton Ranch 1986 Rel: $16.50 Cur: $28 (CH-2/90) **90**
Chardonnay Russian River Valley Dutton Ranch 1985 Rel: $15 Cur: $30 (CH-2/90) **88**
Chardonnay Russian River Valley Dutton Ranch 1984 Rel: $15 Cur: $30 (CH-2/90) **89**
Chardonnay Russian River Valley Vine Hill Road Vineyard 1990: Complex and deep, with rich, ripe Chardonnay flavors framed by toasty, buttery oak notes. The ripe pear, apple, spice and melon flavors come through and linger on the finish. Elegant and stylish. Drink now through 1994. 760 cases made. $25 (1/31/92) **90**
Chardonnay Sonoma Mountain McCrea Vineyard 1990: Exuberantly fruity and full-bodied, with tons of grapefruit, pear, cream, butter and vanilla flavors fighting to get out of a texture that's crisp with acidity. Needs time to develop. Try after 1993. 2,470 cases made. $28 (5/31/92) **90**
Chardonnay Sonoma Mountain McCrea Vineyard 1989: Broad pineapple and grapefruit flavors are generously layered with the new oak notes of vanilla and butter. Solid and ready to drink now through 1993. 1,087 cases made. Rel: $28 Cur: $33 (6/15/91) **88**
Chardonnay Sonoma Mountain McCrea Vineyard 1988: Remarkably rich, concentrated and elegant, with tiers of pear, lemon, melon and stony-mineral flavors that are sharply focused and stay with you from start to finish. Impeccably well balanced and flavorful. Drink now to 1993. Rel: $24 Cur: $32 (4/30/90) **92**
Chardonnay Sonoma Valley 1989: Ripe and full-bodied, with pear, butterscotch, toasty oak and hazelnut flavors. A very complete and well-balanced wine, with integrated flavors and good length. Drink now to 1993. 1,976 cases made. Rel: $18 Cur: $25 (2/15/91) **88**
Chardonnay Sonoma Valley Durell Vineyard Sand Hill 1990: Rich, dense and young, with toasty, buttery notes over tight fruit flavors that will need a few years to develop fully. Creamy, peachy, pearlike and intense, but still a bit raw from oak. The long finish promises further development; should be great after 1993. 2,470 cases made. $28 (5/31/92) **93**
Chardonnay Sonoma Valley Durell Vineyard 1989: Ripe, spicy and buttery in flavor, with rich pear, honey and vanilla notes that fill the mouth and really last on the finish. Multifaceted and generous. 1,520 cases made. Rel: $24 Cur: $27 (5/15/91) **90**
Chardonnay Sonoma Valley Durell Vineyard 1988: A wonderfully delicious wine, with pure, rich, elegant, subtle pear, melon, spice and citrus notes all contributing to the complexity and depth. Finish lingers. Drink now to 1993. 2,300 cases made. Rel: $17 Cur: $29 (2/28/90) **90**
Chardonnay Sonoma Valley Durell Vineyard 1988 Rel: $17 Cur: $29 (CH-2/90) **91**
Chardonnay Sonoma Valley Durell Vineyard 1987 Rel: $16 Cur: $30 (CH-2/90) **93**
Chardonnay Sonoma Valley Durell Vineyard 1986 Rel: $16 Cur: $30 (CH-2/90) **89**
Chardonnay Sonoma Valley Kistler Estate Vineyard 1990: Enormously complex and deep, with rich, concentrated pear, pineapple, citrus and hazelnut flavors that glide across the palate. Finishes with a long, smoky, toasty aftertaste that goes on and on. Drink now through 1995. 511 cases made. $32 (6/15/92) **92**
Chardonnay Sonoma Valley Kistler Estate Vineyard 1989: One of the best '89s we've had so far. Generous, ripe, buttery and packed with fruit flavors. Layers of pear, pineapple, nutmeg and vanilla unfold as you sip it. A delicious, almost sweet wine that glides across the palate. 797 cases made. Rel: $32 Cur: $36 (6/15/91) **91**
Chardonnay Sonoma Valley Kistler Estate Vineyard 1988: Oozing with rich, opulent, delicious pear, honey, vanilla, lemon and spicy nutmeg flavors that explode on the palate, displaying uncommon finesse and a smooth creamy texture that allows the flavors to glide across the palate. Has an amazingly long and intense finish. Drink now to 1993. 507 cases made. Rel: $26 Cur: $35 (4/30/90) **94**
Chardonnay Sonoma Valley Kistler Estate Vineyard 1987 Rel: $22 Cur: $45 (CH-2/90) **90**
Chardonnay Sonoma Valley Kistler Estate Vineyard 1987 Rel: $22 Cur: $45 (7/15/89) **92**
Chardonnay Sonoma Valley Kistler Estate Vineyard 1986 Rel: $18 Cur: $40 (CH-2/90) **92**

KONOCTI
Chardonnay Lake County 1990: A delightful, young, harmonious wine, brimming with fresh, ripe pear, spice and melon flavors that stay with you on the finish, where subtle oak shadings and perfumed nuances emerge. A wonderful value. Drink now. 4,998 cases made. $10 (3/15/92) **87**
Chardonnay Lake County 1989: Light and simple, with thin lemon and herb notes and a short finish. Drinkable, but very short on flavor. Tasted twice. $9.50 (4/30/91) **74**
Chardonnay Lake County 1988: A well-balanced and firmly structured wine. Luxuriously fruity flavors grow stronger on the finish. Apple, peach and pear flavors are woven into a rich, full-bodied wine. 3,208 cases made. $9 (4/15/90) **83**
Chardonnay Lake County 1987 $9 (11/15/89) **73**
Chardonnay Lake County 1986 $8 (12/31/88) **80**

KONRAD
Chardonnay Mendocino County 1990: Ripe, intense and perfumed, with pear, hazelnut, citrus and spice flavors that are well integrated and tasty. Drink now. 1,670 cases made. $14 (3/31/92) **84**
Chardonnay Mendocino County Estate 1989: A serious style from a new producer. Barrel fermented and aged on the lees, but the flinty pear, peach and nectarine flavors are very tight and austere. A balanced wine that could benefit from a year in the bottle. Drink now to 1994. 600 cases made. $12 (7/15/91) **85**

CHARLES KRUG
Chardonnay Napa Valley 1990: A crisp, earthy wine, with moderate complexity, but seems to be sagging around the edges. The chalky, mineral flavors have a hint of fig and lemon. Not to be cellared. $12 (1/31/92) **76**
Chardonnay Napa Valley 1989: Crisp and straightforward, with pleasant pear, spice and butter aromas and flavors. Drinkable now. $10 (9/15/91) **82**
Chardonnay Carneros Napa Valley 1988: Lean and firm, with lots of apple aromas and flavors, and hints of toast and spice on the finish, it is a generous wine for drinking now. $11.50 (1/31/90) **80**
Chardonnay Carneros Napa Valley Reserve 1990: Ripe, round and juicy, with generous pineapple, pear and citrus aromas and flavors framed by nutmeg and toast notes from oak on the finish. Graceful and balanced, with enough intensity to warrant cellaring until 1993 or '94, but it's drinkable now. Krug's first reserve Chardonnay. Tasted twice. 750 cases made. $16 (7/15/92) **90**

KUNDE
Chardonnay Sonoma Valley 1990: Ripe, bold and buttery, with layers of honey, pear, peach and nutmeg flavors that are rich and silky-smooth. Oak adds dimension to the flavors. A harmonious wine to drink now to 1994. $12 (12/15/91) SS **91**
Chardonnay Sonoma Valley Estate Reserve 1990: Intensely rich and fruity, with smoky, buttery oak shadings that add complexity and depth to the ripe pear, spice and apple flavors. Sharply focused, long and lingering on the finish. A real beauty. Drink now to 1995. 2,900 cases made. $19 (4/30/92) **92**

LA CREMA
Chardonnay California 1989: Floral, pear and peach aromas and flavors are appealing in this medium-weight, smooth and delicately balanced wine. Drinkable now. $12 (7/15/91) **85**
Chardonnay California 1988: A spicy, fruity wine, with simple but pleasant melon, pear, kiwi and mint flavors that are round and smooth. Picks up a touch of oak on the finish. Ready to drink now. $13.50 (6/30/90) **82**
Chardonnay California 1987 $12 (12/31/88) **88**
Chardonnay California 1986 $11.50 (7/15/88) **78**
Chardonnay California 1985 $11 (2/28/87) **93**
Chardonnay California Reserve 1989: A very pretty wine that's creamy in texture, rich and buttery in flavor and a bit light in the middle, but it echoes lovely spice, pear and caramel on the long finish. Drinkable now. $22 (7/15/91) **88**
Chardonnay California Reserve 1988: A complex wine, with elegant texture and plenty of spice and toast flavors that add dimension to the ripe pear, butter, toast and nutmeg flavors. Picks up a pretty butterscotch flavor on the finish. Drink now to 1993. $22 (5/31/90) **91**
Chardonnay California Reserve 1987: A little heavy on the wood, it's rich, toasty and flavorful with pear, nutmeg and honey on the finish. $22 (5/15/89) **84**
Chardonnay California Reserve 1986 Rel: $18 Cur: $22 (CH-6/90) **85**
Chardonnay California Reserve 1985 Rel: $18 Cur: $22 (CH-6/90) **86**
Chardonnay Monterey Ventana Vineyard 1984 Rel: $18 Cur: $24 (CH-6/90) **88**

LA REINA
Chardonnay Monterey County 1987: Very pretty and delicate, showing attractive peach and floral aromas and flavors, good concentration and depth. Drink now. $13.50 (3/31/89) **85**
Chardonnay Monterey County 1986 $13 (12/31/88) **75**
Chardonnay Monterey 1984 $12 (2/01/86) **86**

LAKESPRING
Chardonnay Alexander Valley 1981 $10 (4/16/84) **78**
Chardonnay Napa Valley 1989: A chalky style that turns bitter and stemmy. Has attractive pear

flavors, but it's clumsy and disjointed. Hard in the middle. Drink now to 1993. Tasted twice. $13.50 (1/31/92) **79**
Chardonnay Napa Valley 1988: Ripe, generous and distinctive, with honeyed peach and apricot aromas and flavors. Not typical of Chardonnay, but has a sense of crispness to keep it in balance. A well-crafted wine that should age well through 1993 or '94. Much better than two bottles tasted earlier. $13 (5/15/91) **88**
Chardonnay Napa Valley 1987: Celery flavors dominate. A good wine, but tastes more like a Sauvignon Blanc with its grassy notes. $12 (10/31/89) **72**
Chardonnay Napa Valley 1986 $11 (12/31/88) **90**
Chardonnay Napa Valley 1985 $11 (11/15/87) **71**
Chardonnay Napa Valley 1984 $12 (10/31/86) **70**

LAMBERT BRIDGE
Chardonnay Sonoma County 1985 $10 (2/15/88) **73**
Chardonnay Sonoma County 1982 $13.50 (12/16/84) **83**

LANDMARK
Chardonnay Alexander Valley Proprietor's Grown 1982 $10 (5/01/84) **76**
Chardonnay Sonoma County 1990: Piny, Riesling-like flavors dominate this lean wine. Lively, fruity and crisp, with good grapefruit notes. Simple but attractive and cleanly made. $12 (7/15/92) **84**
Chardonnay Sonoma County 1989: Strongly earthy, hard-edged and slightly sour; barely drinkable. Tasted twice, with consistent notes. $12 (11/30/91) **62**
Chardonnay Sonoma County 1988: Has plenty of delicious Chardonnay flavor laced with spice and Muscat notes. Rich, balanced and intense, yet has a seam of elegance and finishes with just a touch of oak. A very successful wine at a terrific price. Drink now to 1993. $10 (4/15/91) **87**
Chardonnay Sonoma County 1985 $10 (2/15/88) **71**
Chardonnay Sonoma County 1983 $9 (1/01/86) **80**
Chardonnay Sonoma Valley 1982 $9 (5/01/84) **78**
Chardonnay Alexander Valley Damaris Reserve 1990: Crisp and refreshing, with generous grapefruit and peach aromas and flavors and hints of toast on the finish. A lively wine, with appealing flavors. Drinkable now. Tasted twice. 1,912 cases made. $16 (7/15/92) **83**
Chardonnay Sonoma Valley Damaris Vineyard 1989: Fresh and focused, with brilliant pineapple, grapefruit and nutmeg aromas and flavors and hints of pear and butterscotch on the long, concentrated finish. Flavorful without being heavy. Drinkable now, but perhaps better in 1993. 1,455 cases made. $16 (6/30/91) **87**
Chardonnay Sonoma Valley Two Williams Vineyard 1990: This bizarre wine offers more pine and herbal aromas and flavors than anything else. Far too weedy for our tastes; gives us the willies. Tasted twice, with consistent notes. 1,936 cases made. $16 (7/15/92) **69**
Chardonnay Sonoma Valley Two Williams Vineyard 1989: A tart, appley and earthy wine that's drinkable, but awkward in its tough acidity and decadent flavors. 975 cases made. $16 (7/15/91) **78**

LAURA'S
Chardonnay Paso Robles 1987: Ripe, fruity and well balanced. Direct in its peach and pineapple flavors, astringent on the finish. $12 (12/15/89) **79**
Chardonnay San Luis Obispo 1985 $7 (12/31/87) **73**

LAURIER
Chardonnay Sonoma County 1989: Delicate, with subtle oak, pear, spice and nutmeg flavors that are soft and balanced, but not especially concentrated. The finish is pretty, picking up floral and spice notes on the aftertaste. Drink now. $16 (4/30/91) **88**
Chardonnay Sonoma County 1986 $13.50 (12/31/88) **83**
Chardonnay Sonoma County 1985 $13 (10/31/87) **71**
Chardonnay Sonoma County 1984 $13 (6/16/86) **74**
Chardonnay Sonoma County 1982 $13 (4/01/85) **89**

LAVA CAP
Chardonnay El Dorado Reserve 1989: A simple, straightforward wine, with ripe apple, pear and citrus flavors and a hint of oak. Lacks complexity, but drinks OK. 376 cases made. $14 (5/31/92) **79**

LAZY CREEK
Chardonnay Anderson Valley 1989: Distinctive for its spicy Riesling-like flavors and honeyed notes. Elegant and balanced, but the spicy floral notes may throw you off. A sound sipper to drink now. 800 cases made. $8.50 (7/15/91) **86**
Chardonnay Anderson Valley 1987 $10 (5/15/89) **90**

LEEWARD
Chardonnay Central Coast 1990: A delicious wine, with bold, ripe, rich flavors that echo spice, tangerine, honey and pear notes. The flavors glide across the palate, fanning out on the finish and echoing fruit and oak. Ready now, but can age through 1994. $11 (1/31/92) **89**
Chardonnay Central Coast 1989: Very ripe and intense, offering broad, complex pineapple, papaya, pear, lemon and spice notes and bracing acidity. The tart citrus aftertaste finishes with a hint of clove. Drink now to 1993. $11 (8/31/90) **83**
Chardonnay Central Coast 1988: Packed with ripe flavors of pear, peach, honey and butter, it shows plenty of concentration without being dominated by any one element. Tastes tight, well-balanced and focused. Delicious now. $10.50 (12/15/89) **89**
Chardonnay Central Coast 1987 $9 (10/31/88) **81**
Chardonnay Central Coast 1986 $8.50 (10/31/87) **86**
Chardonnay Central Coast 1984 $8 (6/16/86) **78**
Chardonnay Edna Valley 1989: A ripe, exotic, full-blown wine, with highly extracted pineapple, spice, lemon and citrus notes. Packs in plenty of flavor, but manages to keep in bounds. Probably best to drink now. 1,937 cases made. $15 (11/30/91) **87**
Chardonnay Edna Valley MacGregor Vineyard 1988: Mature in color, with very rich, intense, buttery pear, vanilla and apple flavors that are lively and well defined, picking up butterscotch notes on the finish. Drink now to 1993. Tasted twice. $16 (4/30/90) **86**
Chardonnay Edna Valley MacGregor Vineyard 1987: Extremely ripe and rich with tropical fruit flavors. Almost a dessert wine. Smells like honey and ripe pear, tastes unctuous and honeyed, but with plenty of orange, peach and pear flavors and a long, lingering finish. $16 (12/15/89) **90**
Chardonnay Edna Valley MacGregor Vineyard 1986 $14 (2/29/88) **85**
Chardonnay Edna Valley MacGregor Vineyard 1985 $14 (5/31/87) **70**
Chardonnay Edna Valley MacGregor Vineyard 1984 $12 (6/16/86) **93**

Key to Symbols

The scores reported here are the results of blind tastings conducted by our panel of senior editors. Wines that carry the initials below are results of individual tastings.

THE WINE SPECTATOR 100-POINT SCALE ***95-100***—Classic, a great wine; ***90-94***—Outstanding, superior character and style; ***80-89***—Good to very good, a wine with special qualities; ***70-79***—Average, drinkable wine that may have minor flaws; ***60-69***—Below average, drinkable but not recommended; ***50-59***—Poor, undrinkable, not recommended. "+"—With a score indicates a range; used primarily with barrel tastings to indicate a preliminary score.

SPECIAL DESIGNATIONS SS—Spectator Selection, CS—Cellar Selection, BB—Best Buy, ($NA)—Price not available, (NR)—Not released.

TASTER'S INITIALS (JG)—Jim Gordon, (HS)—Harvey Steiman, (JL)—James Laube, (JS)—James Suckling, (TM)—Thomas Matthews, (TR)—Terry Robards, (PM)—Per-Henrik Mansson, (BT)—Barrel Tasting (these wines were tasted blind from barrel samples), (CA-date)—*California's Great Cabernets* by James Laube, (CH-date)—*California's Great Chardonnays* by James Laube, (VP-date)—*Vintage Port* by James Suckling.

DATE TASTED Dates in parentheses represent the issue in which the rating was published.

Chardonnay Edna Valley MacGregor Vineyard 1983 $14 (11/01/84) **80**
Chardonnay Monterey County 1989: Ripe and soft with an odd salty flavor that dominates the apple and melon notes. A hint of oxidation comes through on the finish, where the flavors turn oaky and a bit sour. Drink now. 1,010 cases made. $14 (11/30/90) **74**
Chardonnay Monterey County Ventana Vineyards 1983 $8 (10/16/84) **78**
Chardonnay Santa Maria Valley Bien Nacido Vineyard 1984 $12 (12/01/85) **64**

LIBERTY SCHOOL
Chardonnay California Vintner Select Series One 1989: A good, fruity wine that tastes like apples, with a lively texture and a hint of leesy flavor. Light and clean, doesn't show much oak influence. $7.50 (2/28/91) **80**
Chardonnay California Vintner Select Series Two 1990: Has a strong spicy oak flavor that gets in the way of the ripe pear and melon flavor. Could use a little more finesse. Drink now. $7.50 (11/15/91) **78**
Chardonnay Napa Valley 1989: Spicy, woody accents give it a bit of life, but this wine is basically dull and watery. It's soft in texture and not very much fun. $7.50 (11/15/90) **72**
Chardonnay California Lot 11 1986 $6 (2/29/88) **74**
Chardonnay Napa Valley Lot 15 1987: A solid wine, featuring ripe pear and honey aromas and flavors, decent length and a touch of clove on the finish. Drinkable now. $7.50 (3/31/89) BB **83**
Chardonnay California Lot 17 NV: Slightly tangy, with very applelike flavors, this wine is cleanly made and simple in structure. $7.50 (2/28/90) **77**
Chardonnay Santa Barbara County Sierra Madre Vineyard Vintner Select Barrel Fermented Series Two 1990: A very oaky, buttery wine that's lacking generous fruit, although it's pleasant enough. Decent, but one-dimensional because of the oak flavors. 3,112 cases made. $12 (1/31/92) **79**

LIMUR
Chardonnay Napa Valley 1989: Crisp, tight, clean and refreshing, with ripe pear, melon, lemon-lime and spice notes that are sharply focused, long and lingering. A firm, concentrated wine that's best to drink now through 1994. $19 (7/15/91) **88**

LOCKWOOD
Chardonnay Monterey County 1990: A ripe, exotic, full-blown wine, with plenty of honey, citrus and pear flavors that last into the finish. Full-bodied and well balanced. Keeps you coming back for another sip. $8 (7/15/92) BB **86**
Chardonnay Monterey County 1989: Leesy apple and spice flavors turn earthy and smoky, with a trace of honey on the aftertaste. Lacks concentration and depth. 500 cases made. $14 (7/15/91) **79**
Chardonnay Monterey Partners Reserve 1990: Lots of vanilla and butter flavors from oak aging are present in this stylish, medium-weight wine. Could use more fruit to back up the oaky components, but the combination of vanilla, spice and hazelnut is compelling. $14 (7/15/92) **84**

LOGAN
Chardonnay Monterey 1990: Enticing aromas of peach, vanilla and toast overlay solid, crisp flavors of pear, apple and spice. Elegant in texture, well balanced and flavorful but not heavy. From Talbott. $12 (1/31/92) **88**
Chardonnay Monterey 1989: Smooth and generous, with a silky texture and lots of apple, pear, pineapple, honey and caramel aromas and flavors that persist on the long, harmonious finish. Crisp acidity balances it nicely. Drinkable now, but it should be better after 1993. $12 (6/30/91) **88**
Chardonnay Monterey 1988: An extremely buttery, earthy wine that goes for all the complexity the winemaker could give it. Smells like roasted almonds and buttered popcorn, and tastes like grapefruit and lemon, with a tangy finish. Good, if this is your style. 4,400 cases made. $12 (6/30/90) **84**

J. LOHR
Chardonnay California Cypress 1990: The fruit cocktail aromas and flavors have a metallic edge, turning toward butterscotch on the finish. Seems excessively tart, too. Tasted twice. $8.50 (3/31/92) **70**
Chardonnay California Cypress 1989: Has spicy Muscat and lemon notes, with a touch of oak, but it gets awfully watery. Simple. $7 (7/15/91) **76**
Chardonnay Monterey County 1987: Has plenty of fruit flavor in a basically simple package. Well made if not complex. $10 (4/15/89) **78**
Chardonnay Monterey County Cypress Vineyard Reserve 1986 $13.50 (12/31/88) **87**
Chardonnay Monterey County Greenfield Vineyards 1986 $10 (4/15/88) **89**
Chardonnay Monterey County Greenfield Vineyards 1985 $9 (6/30/87) **80**
Chardonnay Monterey County Greenfield Vineyards 1984 $9 (4/16/86) **69**
Chardonnay Monterey County Greenfield Vineyards 1983 $9 (7/01/85) **75**
Chardonnay Monterey Riverstone 1990: A bold, rich, buttery wine, loaded with butterscotch, caramel, honey and spice notes. Full-blown, concentrated, oaky and exotic but well done. Drink now to 1994. $13 (2/15/92) **87**
Chardonnay Monterey Riverstone 1989: An outstanding wine at a reasonable price. Fresh and spicy, with ripe pear and pineapple flavors and nutmeg and oak shadings. Burgundian in style, finishing with a pretty touch of butterscotch and smoky oak that lingers. Well made, balanced, moderately rich, complex and ready to drink. $12 (3/15/91) SS **90**
Chardonnay Monterey Riverstone 1988: Offers perfumed, Muscat-like aromas, with rich, intense, concentrated pear, melon, pineapple and spicy nutmeg flavors. Lively and full on the finish, with lots of sweet oak flavor. Drink now to 1994. $12 (4/30/90) **90**
Chardonnay Monterey Riverstone 1987 $12 (11/15/89) **90**

LOLONIS
Chardonnay Mendocino County 1990: A ripe, floral, very fruity wine at a fair price. Tastes a bit sweet, with orange, pineapple and grapefruit flavors to make it lively. Shows a bit of vanilla on the finish. $10 (5/31/92) **82**
Chardonnay Mendocino County Lolonis Vineyards 1989: Ripe and intense, with bold, rich fruit flavors for an '89. The pear, melon, pineapple and spice notes are rich and attractive and stay with you. Has enough intensity to cellar through 1993. 5,000 cases made. $12 (7/15/91) **86**
Chardonnay Mendocino County Lolonis Vineyards 1984 $14 (6/30/87) **74**
Chardonnay Mendocino County Private Reserve 1990: Ripe and creamy, with smoky pear, pineapple and herb notes that combine to give it complexity and depth. Drink now to 1994. 800 cases made. $15 (6/30/92) **85**
Chardonnay Mendocino County Private Reserve 1988: Bright and tangy, with brilliantly focused peach, grapefruit and pineapple aromas and flavors. Has a nice touch of vanilla. This is the kind of wine that is delicious to drink now or could develop well with cellaring until 1994. $19 (4/30/90) **91**
Chardonnay Mendocino County Private Reserve Lolonis Vineyards 1989: Soft and spicy, with orange, pear, nutmeg and cinnamon notes that carry from the aroma to the long finish. Charming, stylish and very appealing for current drinking. 700 cases made. $19 (7/15/91) **88**

LONG
Chardonnay Napa Valley 1990: Ripe, rich and creamy, with layers of honey, pear, toast and vanilla flavors that dance on the palate. Full on Burgundian treatment without getting heavy-handed. Chardonnays from Long are known to improve with age. Drink from 1993 to '96. 1,800 cases made. $29 (6/30/92) CS **90**
Chardonnay Napa Valley 1989: Rich, smooth and elegant, offering lots of nutmeg, almond, pear, peach and honey aromas and flavors. Polished and balanced for drinking soon. Has the concentration to develop through 1993. 900 cases made. Rel: $30 Cur: $33 (7/15/91) **91**
Chardonnay Napa Valley 1988: Bright, harmonious and rich without being weighty, offering lots of appealing peach, apple, nutmeg and vanilla aromas and flavors. A smooth texture makes it drinkable now, but it has the concentration to develop through 1993. Rel: $27.50 Cur: $33 (5/15/91) **89**
Chardonnay Napa Valley 1987 Rel: $27.50 Cur: $35 (CH-4/90) **90**
Chardonnay Napa Valley 1986 Rel: $27.50 Cur: $48 (CH-4/90) **92**
Chardonnay Napa Valley 1985 Rel: $27.50 Cur: $60 (CH-4/90) **91**

Chardonnay Napa Valley 1984 Rel: $27.50 Cur: $65 (CH-4/90) **88**

MACROSTIE

Chardonnay Carneros 1990: This elegant wine offers plenty of generous, ripe fruit flavor and hints of vanilla, cherry, pear and butter, all with a silky texture and firm acidity. The oak is subtle and in the background. Drink now to 1994. 4,000 cases made. $16 (12/15/91) **90**

Chardonnay Carneros 1989: A unique, complex wine, with pretty honey, pear and floral notes that balance out. Has plenty of flavor and a clean, simple finish. Drink now to 1994. 2,000 cases made. $14 (12/31/90) **87**

Chardonnay Carneros 1988: Impressive for its rich, pure, supple Chardonnay flavor and wonderful smoke, honey and butterscotch flavors. An elegant glassful of wine that keeps you yearning for a second and third taste. Drink now. $14 (2/28/90) **90**

Chardonnay Carneros 1987 $14.50 (11/30/88) **89**

MADDALENA

Chardonnay Central Coast 1990: Offers fruit complexity, with an array of ripe pineapple and pear flavors and spicy oak notes, but fails to move on to the next level of depth, richness and finesse. Still, you get plenty of flavor for the price. Drink now to 1993. $7.50 (3/31/92) **80**

Chardonnay Central Coast 1989: Ripe and straightforward, with rich pineapple, pear, citrus and spice notes that are attractive and pleasing. Doesn't go the extra distance with depth and complexity, but it's a solid deal for the price. Drink now. $8 (4/30/91) BB **83**

Chardonnay Central Coast San Simeon Collection 1990: A green, earthy edge detracts from the pear and apple flavors. It also gets coarse on the finish. Drink now. 2,000 cases made. $14 (3/31/92) **77**

Chardonnay Central Coast San Simeon Collection 1989: A graceful wine, with lip-smacking fruit, offering a nice balance of pear and fig flavors balanced with nutmeg and vanilla overtones, turning spicy and buttery on the long finish. 1,700 cases made. $14 (11/30/91) **88**

Chardonnay Napa Valley 1989: This pleasant wine has good varietal character, with hints of ripe melon, apple and pear flavors, but it's rather simple and offers little in the way of complexity or finesse. Drink now. $10 (7/15/91) **80**

Chardonnay San Luis Obispo County 1982 $6 (5/16/84) **70**

Chardonnay Santa Barbara County 1984 $5 (4/16/86) **72**

MADRONA

Chardonnay El Dorado 1989: Firm and intense, offering ripe pear and apple notes, but turns bitter, with a touch of grapefruit on the finish. Drink now. 2,210 cases made. $10 (7/15/92) **80**

Chardonnay El Dorado 1987: Ripe and creamy, with tasty pear, pineapple and oak flavors that are well proportioned, turning a bit coarse on the finish. Overall, a nice bottle of wine for the price. Drink now. 1,384 cases made. $12 (3/31/92) **82**

MANISCHEWITZ

Chardonnay Alexander Valley 1988: A lively, well-made wine, with buttery oak, floral and lemon flavors and a long vanilla finish. There's some spritz. $7 (3/31/91) **87**

MANZANITA

Chardonnay Napa Valley 1984 $12.50 (10/31/86) **71**

Chardonnay Napa Valley 1983 $12.50 (1/01/86) SS **93**

Chardonnay Napa Valley 1982 $14 (4/01/84) **84**

MANZANITA RIDGE

Chardonnay Sonoma County Barrel Fermented 1989: A serious wine, with deft balance and ripe, rich, intense Chardonnay flavor and delicate oak notes. Has beautifully proportioned peach, melon, pear and spice flavors and a smooth, elegant finish. A solid buy. Drink now to 1993. 5,000 cases made. $8 (6/30/91) BB **86**

MARION

Chardonnay California 1989: Varnish and cheesy pine and apple notes miss the mark for Chardonnay. Of marginal quality. $8 (7/15/91) **70**

Chardonnay California 1986 $5.50 (2/15/88) BB **81**

MARK WEST

Chardonnay Russian River Valley 1982 $10.50 (10/16/85) **80**

Chardonnay Russian River Valley Le Beau Vineyards 1990: Crisp and clean, with simple pear, citrus, spice and oak flavors that turn tart and bracing on the finish. Needs food to take the edge off. Drink now to 1994. 2,000 cases made. $14 (3/31/92) **80**

Chardonnay Russian River Valley Le Beau Vineyards 1987: This wine doesn't quite hit the mark. Has toasty, earthy aromas that are rich and oily on the palate, but the flavors are a bit earthy and bitter. Tasted three times and this was the best score. $12 (6/30/90) **73**

Chardonnay Russian River Valley Le Beau Vineyards 1986 $12 (9/15/88) **77**

Chardonnay Russian River Valley Le Beau Vineyards Reserve 1987: Big, full, rich and toasty, packing in plenty of flavor, with tiers of intense, concentrated pear, lemon, earth and pineapple notes that are full-bodied, yet elegant. The finish sustains the flavors. A highly successful wine. Drink now to 1994. $17 (4/15/91) **88**

Chardonnay Russian River Valley Le Beau Vineyards Reserve 1985 $16 (10/31/87) **88**

Chardonnay Russian River Valley Vintner's Library Selection 1980 $14 (10/01/85) **88**

Chardonnay Sonoma Valley 1987 $8 (12/31/88) **78**

MARKHAM

Chardonnay Napa Valley Barrel Fermented 1990: Crisp and tight, with focused grapefruit and pear flavors that are fresh and lively, and stay with you from start to finish. Drinks well now. $14 (7/15/92) **85**

Chardonnay Napa Valley 1989: This lively, intense style is light enough on its feet to let the grapefruit, nutmeg and vanilla flavors extend over a long finish. Beautifully balanced, with nice pineapple and floral overtones. Drinkable now, but could be even better by 1993 or '94. $12 (6/15/91) SS **92**

Chardonnay Napa Valley 1988: Almost like a Gewürztraminer with its spice and grapefruit flavors. Ripe and intense but it's a bit off in flavor. It's a pleasant drink, especially on the finish where the flavors echo grapefruit and pineapple. Drink now. Rel: $12 Cur: $19 (5/31/90) **82**

Chardonnay Napa Valley 1987 Rel: $12 Cur: $16 (CH-2/90) **87**

Chardonnay Napa Valley 1987 Rel: $12 Cur: $16 (4/30/89) **86**

Chardonnay Napa Valley Estate 1986 Rel: $12 Cur: $15 (CH-2/90) **84**

Chardonnay Napa Valley Estate 1985 Rel: $12 Cur: $17 (CH-2/90) **86**

Chardonnay Napa Valley 1984 Rel: $12 Cur: $17 (CH-2/90) **85**

Chardonnay Napa Valley Estate 1983 Rel: $11.50 Cur: $18 (CH-2/90) **81**

Chardonnay Napa Valley Estate 1982 Rel: $12 Cur: $17 (CH-2/90) **83**

MARTIN BROTHERS

Chardonnay Paso Robles 1988: Fruity, floral and well balanced, fine for sipping before or during dinner. Clean and straightforward in style. $10 (12/15/89) **81**

MARTINELLI

Chardonnay Russian River Valley 1989: Clean and well made, with subtle, ripe pear, apple and melon-tinged flavors that gain a touch of toasty, smoky oak on the finish. Balanced and moderate in depth and concentration. Best to drink now. 650 cases made. $9 (7/15/91) **82**

LOUIS M. MARTINI

Chardonnay California 1982 $7 (3/16/84) **71**

Chardonnay Los Carneros Las Amigas Vineyard Vineyard Selection 1989: Funky, earthy, wilted-flower aromas and flavors eventually turn smooth, fruity and spicy on the finish. The apple cider flavors may not please everyone, but it's lively and tasty. Try now to 1993. Tasted twice. 500 cases made. $20 (7/15/91) **83**

Chardonnay Napa-Sonoma Counties 1990: Crisp, ripe and fruity, with tiers of peach, pear, honey and spice flavors that are lush and creamy. A seductive wine that drinks well now. 3,200 cases made. $9 (3/15/92) BB **89**

Chardonnay Napa-Sonoma Counties 1989: Piny, resiny aromas and flavors dominate this lean, somewhat austere wine. Drinkable, but not likable. $9 (4/30/91) **75**

Chardonnay Napa Valley Reserve 1989: Intense and lively, with fresh, crisp peach, pear, melon and nutmeg flavors that are rich and full-bodied, but with a measure of elegance and grace. Echoes citrus notes on the finish. Drink now to 1994. $14 (12/31/90) **87**

Chardonnay North Coast 1986 $9.50 (5/31/88) **74**

Chardonnay North Coast 1984 $8 (4/16/86) **70**

PAUL MASSON

Chardonnay Monterey 1981 $8.50 (4/16/84) **77**

Chardonnay Monterey County 1987 $8 (11/15/88) **82**

MATANZAS CREEK

Chardonnay Sonoma Valley 1989: Soft, simple and fruity, with generous peach, apple and pear aromas and flavors, hinting at nutmeg and vanilla on the finish. Smooth, polished and drinkable now. $19 (5/15/92) **85**

Chardonnay Sonoma County 1988: Attractive with pretty tropical fruit, apple, pineapple, peach and pear flavors that are sharply defined, braced with lively acidity and finishing with fine length and traces of honey and vanilla. Drink now. $18.75 (4/30/90) **91**

Chardonnay Sonoma County 1987 Rel: $18 Cur: $22 (CH-2/90) **90**

Chardonnay Sonoma County 1986 Rel: $17.50 Cur: $24 (CH-2/90) **89**

Chardonnay Sonoma County 1985 Rel: $16.50 Cur: $28 (CH-2/90) **88**

Chardonnay Sonoma County 1984 Rel: $15 Cur: $28 (CH-2/90) **89**

Chardonnay Sonoma County 1983 Rel: $15 Cur: $25 (CH-2/90) **85**

Chardonnay Sonoma County 1982 Rel: $15 Cur: $25 (CH-2/90) **78**

Chardonnay Sonoma County 1981 Rel: $15 Cur: $28 (CH-2/90) **85**

Chardonnay Sonoma County 1980 Rel: $15 Cur: $23 (CH-2/90) **82**

Chardonnay Sonoma-Napa Counties 1979 Rel: $14.50 Cur: $40 (CH-2/90) **80**

Chardonnay Sonoma County 1978 Rel: $12.50 Cur: $50 (CH-2/90) **79**

Chardonnay Sonoma Valley Estate 1985 Rel: $18 Cur: $39 (CH-2/90) **86**

Chardonnay Sonoma Valley Estate 1984 Rel: $18 Cur: $30 (CH-2/90) **80**

Chardonnay Sonoma Valley Estate 1983 $18 (CH-2/90) **68**

Chardonnay Sonoma Valley Estate 1982 Rel: $18 Cur: $25 (7/16/84) SS **88**

Chardonnay Sonoma County Estate 1980 Rel: $18 Cur: $25 (CH-2/90) **70**

MAYACAMAS

Chardonnay Napa Valley 1989: Fresh and clean, with elegant nectarine, pear and apple notes that are correct and attractive, but don't turn into anything exciting. Fans of crisp Chardonnays may find this more appealing. Drink now. 2,200 cases made. $20 (7/15/92) **83**

Chardonnay Napa Valley 1988: Firm and flavorful, with nicely focused, toasty pineapple aromas and flavors, but could be smoother and more harmonious. Perhaps better by 1993 or '94. 1,520 cases made. $20 (7/15/91) **86**

Chardonnay Napa Valley 1987: Has loads of pear, lemon and apple flavors, but it's bound by plenty of acidity and a spicy note on the finish. Drinkable now, but this wine is a good bet to improve in the cellar through 1999. Rel: $20 Cur: $30 (9/15/90) **86**

Chardonnay Napa Valley 1986 Rel: $20 Cur: $32 (7/15/92) **86**

Chardonnay Napa Valley 1985 Rel: $20 Cur: $29 (CH-1/90) **90**

Chardonnay Napa Valley 1984 Rel: $18 Cur: $28 (CH-3/90) **88**

Chardonnay Napa Valley 1983 Rel: $16 Cur: $25 (CH-1/90) **86**

Chardonnay Napa Valley 1982 Rel: $16 Cur: $29 (CH-1/90) **85**

Chardonnay Napa Valley 1981 Rel: $16 Cur: $35 (CH-1/90) **78**

Chardonnay Napa Valley 1980 Rel: $16 Cur: $35 (CH-1/90) **74**

Chardonnay Napa Valley 1979 Rel: $15 Cur: $28 (CH-1/90) **70**

Chardonnay Napa Valley 1978 Rel: $13 Cur: $30 (CH-1/90) **75**

Chardonnay Napa Valley 1977 Rel: $12 Cur: $35 (CH-1/90) **70**

Chardonnay Napa Valley 1976 Rel: $11 Cur: $45 (CH-1/90) **81**

Chardonnay Napa Valley 1975 Rel: $9 Cur: $50 (CH-1/90) **78**

Chardonnay Napa Valley 1974 Rel: $7.50 Cur: $50 (CH-1/90) **70**

Chardonnay Napa Valley 1973 Rel: $7 Cur: $50 (CH-1/90) **60**

Chardonnay Napa Valley 1972 Rel: $7 Cur: $60 (CH-1/90) **59**

Chardonnay Napa Valley 1965 Rel: $2.50 Cur: $125 (CH-1/90) **58**

Chardonnay Napa Valley 1964 Rel: $1.75 Cur: $200 (CH-1/90) **92**

Chardonnay Napa Valley 1963 Rel: $1.75 Cur: $150 (CH-1/90) **58**

Chardonnay Napa Valley 1962 Rel: $1.75 Cur: $150 (CH-1/90) **58**

Chardonnay Napa Valley 1958 Rel: $1 Cur: $200 (CH-1/90) **60**

Chardonnay Napa Valley 1955 Rel: $1 Cur: $330 (CH-1/90) **88**

MAZZOCCO

Chardonnay Alexander Valley River Lane Vineyard 1989: Firm and fruity. Honey, pear and caramel flavors power through the palate, leaving an echo of sweet spice and honey. Drinkable now, but might settle down with cellaring until 1994. 4,600 cases made. $16.50 (4/30/92) **82**

Chardonnay Alexander Valley River Lane Vineyard 1988: This wine has plenty of attractive pear, honey, lemon and nutmeg flavors that offer good depth and intensity, but it could use a little more focus and finesse. Drink now. 4,300 cases made. $16.50 (6/30/90) **84**

Chardonnay Alexander Valley River Lane Vineyard 1987: Delicious for current drinking. An elegant, nicely complex wine that has peach and pear aromas, a delicate, smooth texture and a finish that echoes peach and vanilla. $16.50 (4/15/89) **88**

Chardonnay Alexander Valley River Lane Barrel Fermented 1986 $16.50 (2/15/88) **86**

Chardonnay Sonoma County Barrel Fermented 1989: Tart, crisp and clean, with elegant pear, spice and vanilla flavors that are balanced and well defined, but not particularly complex or rich. A light wine for drinking now. $11 (7/15/91) **85**

Chardonnay Sonoma County Barrel Fermented 1988: A bit awkward, with simple ginger and pineapple flavors that are coarse. Decent but unexciting. Drink now. $12 (11/30/89) **78**

Chardonnay Sonoma County Barrel Fermented 1987 $11 (11/15/88) **83**

Chardonnay Sonoma County Winemaster's Cuvée 1986 $10 (2/15/88) **85**

MCDOWELL VALLEY

Chardonnay California 1989: A watery, diluted wine, with faint hints of pear and lemon flavors. Tasted twice. $10 (7/15/91) **72**

Chardonnay California 1988: Crisp and light, with herbal and citrus notes to the basic apple aromas and flavors; appealing to drink now, balanced and refreshing. $8.50 (12/15/89) **78**

Chardonnay California 1987 $8 (7/15/89) **86**

Chardonnay McDowell Valley 1987: Extremely earthy, moldy aromas and flavors ruin this for us. Harsh, gamy and earthy, an unpleasant wine from the first sniff. Tasted twice. 2,428 cases made. $12 (12/15/89) **59**

Chardonnay McDowell Valley 1986 $11 (5/31/88) **76**

Chardonnay McDowell Valley 1984 $11 (2/28/87) **85**

Chardonnay McDowell Valley Estate Reserve 1988: Round in texture and generous, but earthiness and strong mineral flavors dominate, with pear and vanilla notes coming through on the finish. Some may find it too funky. Needs time to develop. Try in 1993 or '94. Tasted twice. 2,550 cases made. $13 (7/15/91) **75**

Chardonnay Mendocino 1990: Lean, crisp and focused, with citrus, pear and spice notes that hang together. Fairly priced. Attractive to drink now. $9 (7/15/92) **83**

MEADOW GLEN
Chardonnay Sonoma County Barrel Fermented 1989: Clean and correct but nothing flashy, with spicy apple, citrus and melon notes that stay true, finishing with a touch of toastiness. Drink now. $8.50 (4/30/91) **81**

MEEKER
Chardonnay Dry Creek Valley 1990: An earthy, dirty edge to the fruit and oak notes detracts from the ripe pear and apple-tinged flavors. The finish turns bitter, but perhaps with age it will show more harmony. Drink after 1993. Tasted twice, with consistent notes. $11.50 (4/30/92) **78**
Chardonnay Dry Creek Valley 1989: Ripe, rich fig, spice, mint and toasty oak flavors have good concentration and depth and blend together well, but taper off on the finish. Drink now to 1993. $12 (7/15/91) **85**
Chardonnay Dry Creek Valley 1988: A full-bodied wine that leans more toward the butterscotch and toast end of the flavor spectrum than fruit, but it's an appealing wine that should be consumed now. $13.50 (2/15/90) **75**
Chardonnay Dry Creek Valley 1987 $12 (2/15/89) **79**
Chardonnay Dry Creek Valley 1986 $11 (5/31/88) **91**

MENDOCINO ESTATE
Chardonnay Mendocino 1989: A spicy, Muscat-like flavor dominates the taste. Offers simple, pure fruit flavor and hints of melon and honey, but the finish is a bit coarse. A fair price. Drink now. 5,000 cases made. $6.50 (7/15/91) **79**
Chardonnay Mendocino 1988: Crisp and spicy, with hints of candied fruit and enough apple flavor to make it pleasant and drinkable. A lean wine with little to distinguish it. $6.25 (12/15/89) **73**
Chardonnay Mendocino 1986 $5.50 (12/31/87) **65**
Chardonnay Mendocino 1985 $5 (12/15/86) BB **89**

MERIDIAN
Chardonnay Edna Valley 1990: Bold pear, apple, honey and spice flavors are concentrated and stay with you on the aftertaste of this ripe, rich, spicy wine. Drinkable now, but perhaps smoother in 1993. $15 (7/15/92) **89**
Chardonnay Edna Valley 1989: Light and lemony, with pleasant pine and vanilla overtones that persist into the finish. Turns spicy and fresh. Drink soon. 4,000 cases made. $14 (7/15/91) **82**
Chardonnay Edna Valley 1988: Toasty and earthy with lean, elegant pear and melon flavors that turn a bit woody and dirty on the finish. An unusual style. Drink now. Tasted twice. $9.75 (9/30/90) **80**
Chardonnay Edna Valley 1987: Fresh, fruity and slightly herbal in flavor. Straightforward but concentrated. Very satisfying for current drinking. $12 (12/15/89) **78**
Chardonnay Napa Valley 1986 $12 (5/31/88) **85**
Chardonnay Napa Valley 1985 $11 (4/30/87) **88**
Chardonnay Santa Barbara County 1990: A bold, rich, ripe style, with exotic honey, pineapple, orange and nutmeg flavors. Pretty oak shadings add to its depth and richness. Drinks well now. $9.75 (1/31/92) BB **87**
Chardonnay Santa Barbara County 1989: Intense and lively, with juicy Chardonnay flavor that echoes complex lemon, pear, apple, pineapple and spice flavors and keeps repeating them. There's a pretty kiss of French oak, too, but it's subtle and in the background. Very good length. Drink now to 1993. $10 (2/28/91) **87**
Chardonnay Santa Barbara County 1988: A new wine that tastes luscious, ripe and fruity. Jam-packed with rich pear, apple and nutmeg flavors on a supple frame. Full-bodied and smooth, with a long-lasting finish. $10 (4/15/90) **89**

MERLION
Chardonnay Napa Valley 1987: A very earthy, creamy flavor turns us off. Tastes sour and dirty, with a woolly finish. Not pleasant to drink and not recommended. Tasted twice, with consistent notes. 896 cases made. $9 (12/31/90) **63**
Chardonnay Napa Valley 1985 $15 (2/15/88) **84**

MERRY VINTNERS
Chardonnay Sonoma County 1989: Exotic, with ripe, bold, buttery textures, with racy pineapple, apple and pear flavors that pick up a trace of honey on the finish. A tasty wine to drink now through 1994. 3,000 cases made. $12 (3/15/92) **86**
Chardonnay Sonoma County 1988: Refreshing and complex, with rich, intense pear, honey and pineapple flavors and a nice citrus and mineral edge that adds dimension and depth. Well balanced, long and clean on the finish. Drink in 1993. 3,000 cases made. $12 (1/31/91) **89**
Chardonnay Sonoma County 1987: Lively, refreshing and clean, with bright acidity and right-on fruit flavors that are modest but linger on the aftertaste. $12 (7/15/89) **84**
Chardonnay Sonoma County 1984 $13.75 (6/16/86) **88**
Chardonnay Sonoma County Reserve 1987: Soft yet intense with lush orange, honeysuckle, spice, vanilla and nut flavors that are long and full. 3,000 cases made. $15 (9/15/89) **86**
Chardonnay Sonoma County Reserve 1986 $14.75 (11/30/88) **85**
Chardonnay Sonoma County Reserve 1985 $15 (9/15/87) **81**
Chardonnay Sonoma County Signature Reserve 1989: Ripe and balanced, with spicy pear, apple and melon flavors that offer more depth and complexity than many 1989s. Finishes with pretty citrus notes. Drink now to 1994. 2,000 cases made. $15 (3/15/92) **86**
Chardonnay Sonoma County Signature Reserve 1988: Rich, lively, intense and spicy, with deep peach, vanilla, honey and butterscotch flavors that are elegant and supple. Impeccably balanced, with a long, full, clean finish. Delicious to drink now to 1994. 2,000 cases made. $15 (1/31/91) **90**
Chardonnay Sonoma County Sylvan Hills Vineyard 1987: Ripe and spicy in flavor, accented by citrus, ripe pear and pineapple flavors. Clean and lively, well-balanced. A touch of vanilla adds complexity. $11 (7/15/89) **85**
Chardonnay Sonoma County Vintage Preview 1986 $9.75 (7/15/88) **85**
Chardonnay Sonoma County Vintage Preview 1985 $9.75 (12/15/86) **83**

MERRYVALE
Chardonnay Napa Valley 1988: Combines subtlety and complexity with ripe pear, spice, vanilla and honey flavors, each time adding a different flavor that enhances its drinking pleasure. Well balanced and well proportioned. Drink now to 1993. 2,400 cases made. $23 (6/30/90) **91**
Chardonnay Napa Valley 1987: Very distinctive, from the toasty, earthy aromas, through the crisp acidity and intense pear and spice flavors, to the intense, lingering aftertaste, this magnificently structured wine is packed with unique flavors and is drinkable now through 1993. 2,300 cases made. $19 (2/15/90) **93**

Key to Symbols

The scores reported here are the results of blind tastings conducted by our panel of senior editors. Wines that carry the initials below are results of individual tastings.

THE WINE SPECTATOR 100-POINT SCALE ***95-100***—Classic, a great wine; ***90-94***—Outstanding, superior character and style; ***80-89***—Good to very good, a wine with special qualities; ***70-79***—Average, drinkable wine that may have minor flaws; ***60-69***—Below average, drinkable but not recommended; ***50-59***—Poor, undrinkable, not recommended. "+"—With a score indicates a range; used primarily with barrel tastings to indicate a preliminary score.

SPECIAL DESIGNATIONS SS—Spectator Selection, CS—Cellar Selection, BB—Best Buy, ($NA)—Price not available, (NR)—Not released.

TASTER'S INITIALS (JG)—Jim Gordon, (HS)—Harvey Steiman, (JL)—James Laube, (JS)—James Suckling, (TM)—Thomas Matthews, (TR)—Terry Robards, (PM)—Per-Henrik Mansson, (BT)—Barrel Tasting (these wines were tasted blind from barrel samples), (CA-date)—*California's Great Cabernets* by James Laube, (CH-date)—*California's Great Chardonnays* by James Laube, (VP-date)—*Vintage Port* by James Suckling.

DATE TASTED Dates in parentheses represent the issue in which the rating was published.

Chardonnay Napa Valley 1986 $20 (10/31/88) **72**
Chardonnay Napa Valley 1985 $16.50 (10/31/87) **90**
Chardonnay Napa Valley Reserve 1990: A complex, intriguing wine that combines rich, smoky pear and musky spice flavors that are deep and persistent. Big in style, with lots of dimensions. Drinks well now, but can age through 1995. 2,300 cases made. $23 (6/30/92) **91**
Chardonnay Napa Valley Reserve 1989: Assertively oaky, smoky and spicy, coming on strong and carrying through with lively, assertive honey and pear flavors. Has richness, body and depth rare in an '89. Drink now through 1994. 1,000 cases made. $23 (11/30/91) **90**
Chardonnay Napa Valley Starmont 1990: Strikes a pleasant balance between rich, ripe pear, melon and spice flavors and toasty, buttery oak notes. Complex and deep, with a smooth, creamy finish that echoes fruit and oak. Drink now to 1994. 2,500 cases made. $16 (11/30/91) **90**
Chardonnay Napa Valley Starmont 1989: Very fruity and lush, with layers of pear, banana, apple and honey flavors lasting through the long, generous finish. Takes a sharp turn toward honey and spice on the aftertaste. Drink now. 4,000 cases made. $16 (12/31/90) **89**
Chardonnay Stags Leap District 1990: Ripe, rich and elegant, with subtle fruit and oak shadings. Plenty of pear, spice, vanilla and hazelnut flavors turn complex and creamy on the finish, where it picks up a touch of coarseness. Altogether a very complete wine. Drink now to 1994. 500 cases made. $18 (11/30/91) **91**
Chardonnay Stags Leap District 1989: Ripe and generous, with wide-open pear, honey and spice aromas and flavors, an opulent, smooth texture and lots of cream and vanilla overtones. A hedonistic wine to drink now. Cellaring shouldn't be necessary to improve it. 360 cases made. $19 (12/31/90) **90**

PETER MICHAEL
Chardonnay Howell Mountain 1990: Ripe, round and rich, with generous, buttery apple, honey and spice aromas and flavors and a toasty, tangy finish. Has grace, style and length. Should be even better with cellaring until 1993 to '95. 1,318 cases made. $22 (6/30/92) **91**
Chardonnay Sonoma County Mon Plaisir 1989: A crowd-pleaser. Extremely rich and buttery, with lots of butterscotch, honey and brown sugar flavors that are full, oaky and assertive. Concentrated and woody on the finish. $28 (7/15/91) **88**

MICHTOM
Chardonnay Alexander Valley 1983 $8 (10/16/85) **71**

MILANO
Chardonnay California 1985 $10 (4/15/88) **79**
Chardonnay Mendocino County Sanel Valley Vineyard 1988: Ripe and concentrated, with a smooth, fleshy texture and generous pear and pineapple aromas and flavors. Hints at smoke and vanilla on the finish, which continues to echo fruit. Drinkable now. 120 cases made. $18 (7/15/91) **88**
Chardonnay Sonoma County Vine Hill Ranch 1985 $14 (12/31/88) **71**

MILL CREEK
Chardonnay Dry Creek Valley 1985 $10 (12/31/87) **75**

MIRASSOU
Chardonnay Monterey County Family Selection 1990: Rich, well balanced and ripe, with plenty of fruit flavor and attractive honey and spice accents. Smooth, harmonious and focused. $10 (6/30/92) **86**
Chardonnay Monterey County Family Selection 1989: Watery pear and apple flavors are simple and diluted. Drinkable but unexciting. Drink now. $9.75 (7/15/91) **74**
Chardonnay Monterey County Family Selection 1986 $8 (11/15/87) **77**
Chardonnay Monterey County Family Selection 1985 $8 (12/31/86) **86**
Chardonnay Monterey County Harvest Reserve 1990: Extremely ripe, with honey and spicy sage flavors that come together well in this unusual style. Pineapple flavors linger on the finish of this well-balanced and luscious wine. $12.50 (3/31/92) **86**
Chardonnay Monterey County Harvest Reserve 1989: Ultrarich and toasty, this is a lavishly oaked wine that some may find too woody and powerful. Still, plenty of roasted pear, fig and apple flavors balance it out, and the fruit is quite concentrated. Drink now to 1994. 2,228 cases made. $12.50 (5/15/91) **87**
Chardonnay Monterey County Harvest Reserve 1984 $12 (4/01/86) **68**
Chardonnay Monterey County Harvest Reserve 1983 $11 (1/01/85) **74**

MOCERI
Chardonnay Monterey County San Bernabe Vineyard 1984 $5 (7/01/86) BB **87**

CK MONDAVI
Chardonnay California 1986 $4.50 (8/31/87) **70**

ROBERT MONDAVI
Chardonnay California Woodbridge 1990: Crisp, clean and lean in flavor. Mostly appley, with good acidity but not much depth. Fine for a simple, everyday wine. $6.50 (7/15/92) **79**
Chardonnay California Woodbridge 1989: Simple and modestly varietal, with crisp apple, pear and honey flavors, but they don't stay with you very long. $7.25 (4/30/91) **74**
Chardonnay Napa Valley 1990: Crisp and pleasant, with attractive apple and spice aromas and flavors, emphasizing nutmeg on the finish. Drinkable now. $15 (12/31/91) **83**
Chardonnay Napa Valley 1989: A gentle wine, with soft pear, spice and earth flavors that are moderately rich and concentrated, picking up a pretty hint of orange blossom on the finish. Balanced and ready to drink now. $16 (4/15/91) **87**
Chardonnay Napa Valley 1988: Tart and firm, with crisp lemon, butterscotch and honey notes that offer a good measure of depth and complexity. Flavors linger on the finish. Drink now. Rel: $16 Cur: $19 (11/30/89) **86**
Chardonnay Napa Valley 1987 Rel: $17 Cur: $21 (4/30/89) **83**
Chardonnay Napa Valley 1986 $15 (7/15/88) **88**
Chardonnay Napa Valley 1985 Rel: $12 Cur: $20 (7/15/87) **79**
Chardonnay Napa Valley 1984 Rel: $10 Cur: $16 (9/15/86) **83**
Chardonnay Napa Valley 1983 Rel: $14 Cur: $17 (8/01/85) **90**
Chardonnay Napa Valley 1982 $10 (8/01/84) **82**
Chardonnay Napa Valley 1981 $15 (6/01/86) **94**
Chardonnay Napa Valley Reserve 1990: Tightly focused, spicy and lively, showing distinctive peach, pear and almond overtones that extend into a long finish. Youthful and appealing now, it should improve through 1993. $28 (12/31/91) **88**
Chardonnay Napa Valley Reserve Barrel Fermented 1989: Lacks polish and finesse, but offers nice flavors, with layers of pear, honey, toast, apple and caramel. The texture is a bit rough, but the flavors smooth out and linger on the finish. Drink now to 1994. $28 (7/15/91) **87**
Chardonnay Napa Valley Reserve 1988: A very classy wine. Extremely rich and elegant, it's marked by distinctive toasty aromas, full flavors and a very light finish. Has plenty of pear, honey, vanilla and mineral flavors. Rel: $26 Cur: $29 (8/31/90) **92**
Chardonnay Napa Valley Reserve 1987 Rel: $26 Cur: $34 (CH-6/90) **92**
Chardonnay Napa Valley Reserve 1986 Rel: $25 Cur: $30 (CH-3/90) **89**
Chardonnay Napa Valley Reserve 1985 Rel: $25 Cur: $30 (CH-3/90) **88**
Chardonnay Napa Valley Reserve 1984 Rel: $22 Cur: $41 (CH-3/90) **87**
Chardonnay Napa Valley Reserve 1983 Rel: $20 Cur: $28 (CH-3/90) **88**
Chardonnay Napa Valley Reserve 1982 Rel: $20 Cur: $25 (CH-3/90) **81**
Chardonnay Napa Valley Reserve 1981 Rel: $20 Cur: $24 (CH-3/90) **86**
Chardonnay Napa Valley Reserve 1980 Rel: $20 Cur: $30 (CH-3/90) **69**
Chardonnay Napa Valley Reserve 1979 Rel: $20 Cur: $27 (CH-3/90) **79**
Chardonnay Napa Valley Reserve 1978 Rel: $20 Cur: $24 (CH-3/90) **69**
Chardonnay Napa Valley Reserve 1977 Rel: $14 Cur: $32 (CH-3/90) **68**
Chardonnay Napa Valley Reserve 1976 Rel: $12 Cur: $32 (CH-3/90) **78**
Chardonnay Napa Valley Reserve 1975 Rel: $10 Cur: $35 (CH-3/90) **75**

Chardonnay Napa Valley Reserve 1974 Rel: $10 Cur: $45 (CH-3/90) **88**

MONT ST. JOHN
Chardonnay Carneros Napa Valley 1987: Practically melts in the mouth. Rich and buttery tasting, with a very smooth texture and soft, modest fruit flavors. One could only ask for more liveliness. $15 (7/15/89) **81**

MONTE VERDE
Chardonnay California 1988: Full-bodied but simple. Its flavors are herbal and piny. $9 (12/15/89) **71**
Chardonnay California Proprietor's Reserve 1989: Subdued but smooth, clean and light. Has modest fruit flavors and decent balance. $5.50 (3/31/91) **78**
Chardonnay California Proprietor's Reserve 1987: Ripe, round and very fruity tasting. Soft in texture, simple in structure and full of pear, orange and minty flavors. $6.50 (12/15/89) **76**

MONTEREY PENINSULA
Chardonnay Monterey Sleepy Hollow 1989: Rich and intense, with layers of ripe pear, pineapple and spice flavors, but it also has an odd earthy flavor that doesn't quite come clean on the finish. Drink now. 195 cases made. $12 (5/31/91) **83**

MONTEREY VINEYARD
Chardonnay Monterey Classic 1990: Overwhelmingly woody and very light on fruit. Butter flavors dominate but not much else. An out-of-balance wine with an off-putting finish. $6 (2/29/92) **76**
Chardonnay Central Coast Classic 1989: An inoffensive, ordinary wine with light fruit flavors and decent balance. Average, drinkable stuff. $6 (12/31/90) **77**
Chardonnay Monterey County Classic 1987: Nicely balanced and flavorful. Shows ripe apple and pear flavors with a hint of stylish oak in the aroma. A great wine for the price. $5 (2/15/89) BB **83**
Chardonnay Monterey County 1985 $7 (10/15/87) **70**
Chardonnay Monterey County Limited Release 1988: Shoots for complexity, with toasty oak up front and buttery pear and spice flavors, but altogether it's pleasant, simple and easy to drink now. $12 (2/28/91) **80**
Chardonnay Monterey County Limited Release 1986 $10 (8/31/88) **89**

MONTICELLO
Chardonnay Napa Valley Barrel Fermented 1983 Rel: $12.50 Cur: $20 (CH-2/90) **80**
Chardonnay Napa Valley Barrel Fermented 1982 Rel: $14 Cur: $20 (CH-2/90) **84**
Chardonnay Napa Valley 1982 Rel: $13.50 Cur: $20 (CH-2/90) **82**
Chardonnay Napa Valley 1981 Rel: $12 Cur: $20 (CH-2/90) **76**
Chardonnay Napa Valley 1980 Rel: $12 Cur: $20 (CH-2/90) **86**
Chardonnay Napa Valley Corley Reserve 1990: Big, bold and ripe, offering lots of pear, nectarine and spice flavors, but it's a bit rough and tannic now. We like the flavors and complexity, but it could use time in the bottle. Drink in 1993 to '95. 2,700 cases made. $17 (7/15/92) **87**
Chardonnay Napa Valley Corley Reserve 1989: Round and focused, with good concentration of pear, honey and vanilla flavors that persist into a long finish. Has balance and polish without excessive weight. Drinkable now. 3,000 cases made. $18 (7/15/91) **89**
Chardonnay Napa Valley Corley Reserve 1988: A beautiful combination of fruit and oak. Has intense, concentrated, elegant apple, pear and peach flavors neatly shaded by sweet vanilla and honey notes. Polished, long and full on the finish. A real treat. Drink now to 1994. 3,700 cases made. Rel: $17.25 Cur: $20 (1/31/91) SS **92**
Chardonnay Napa Valley Corley Reserve 1987 Rel: $17.25 Cur: $20 (CH-6/90) **86**
Chardonnay Napa Valley Corley Reserve 1986 Rel: $16.50 Cur: $20 (CH-2/90) **89**
Chardonnay Napa Valley Corley Reserve 1985 Rel: $14 Cur: $20 (CH-2/90) **85**
Chardonnay Napa Valley Corley Reserve 1984 Rel: $12.50 Cur: $25 (CH-2/90) **94**
Chardonnay Napa Valley Jefferson Ranch 1989: Tart and oaky, with piny, floral overtones to the lightish apple flavors. Drinkable now. Tasted twice. $12.50 (7/15/91) **74**
Chardonnay Napa Valley Jefferson Ranch 1988: Lean and tart, this wine has a hard edge that takes some of the gloss off the otherwise appealing peach and honey flavors, but the spicy, honeyed aftertaste is nice. $12.25 (6/30/90) **81**
Chardonnay Napa Valley Jefferson Ranch 1987: Big and round but ultimately simple, like it has a hole in the middle. Smoky aromas and flavors lean toward peach and peanuts. Rel: $12.25 Cur: $16 (4/30/89) **77**
Chardonnay Napa Valley Jefferson Ranch 1986 Rel: $11 Cur: $18 (CH-2/90) **86**
Chardonnay Napa Valley Jefferson Ranch 1985 Rel: $11 Cur: $18 (CH-2/90) **82**
Chardonnay Napa Valley Jefferson Ranch 1984 Rel: $10 Cur: $18 (CH-2/90) **86**
Chardonnay Napa Valley Jefferson Ranch 1983 Rel: $10 Cur: $20 (CH-2/90) **93**

MONTPELLIER
Chardonnay California 1990: Offers simple pear and citrus notes in an easy-to-drink, affordable wine. Drink now. $6 (7/15/92) **78**
Chardonnay California 1989: Simple and a bit on the heavy side. A solid wine, with vague fruit flavors but not much else. Drinkable now. Tasted twice. $7 (9/15/91) **76**
Chardonnay California 1988: Floral and somewhat soapy, with decent Chardonnay character and apple and pear notes. Nothing to get excited about, but a decent value. Drink now. $7 (3/31/90) **73**

MORGAN
Chardonnay Edna Valley MacGregor Vineyard 1989: Ripe and fruity, with attractive orange, peach, spice and melon flavors that are smooth and round, with pretty toasty oak notes on the lingering aftertaste. Drink now to 1993. $16.50 (7/15/91) **86**
Chardonnay Monterey 1990: Tight and lean, with more oak and vanilla flavors showing than fruit. Hints of pear and apple come through on the finish. Drink now to 1993. $16.50 (4/30/92) **82**
Chardonnay Monterey 1989: An extremely buttery wine, with butterscotch aromas and an appley, herbal flavor running underneath. The butterscotch character lingers on the finish. Has personality, but it's somewhat light in fruit substance. Rel: $16 Cur: $18 (3/31/91) **84**
Chardonnay Monterey 1988: A very oaky, toasty style, with buttery pineapple and pear flavors and a woody aftertaste. Some might fault it for woodiness, but others will love it. Rel: $15 Cur: $18 (2/28/90) **88**
Chardonnay Monterey 1987 Rel: $15 Cur: $18 (CH-5/90) **84**
Chardonnay Monterey 1986 Rel: $14 Cur: $20 (CH-5/90) **89**
Chardonnay Monterey County 1985 Rel: $14 Cur: $23 (CH-7/90) **86**
Chardonnay Monterey County 1984 Rel: $12.75 Cur: $23 (CH-5/90) **86**
Chardonnay Monterey County 1983 Rel: $12.50 Cur: $23 (CH-5/90) **80**
Chardonnay Monterey County 1982 Rel: $12 Cur: $28 (CH-5/90) **89**
Chardonnay Monterey Reserve 1989: Intense and rich, with honey, pear, vanilla and butterscotch flavors that fill the mouth. A big, impressive wine to drink now through 1993. $23 (12/31/91) **87**
Chardonnay Monterey Reserve 1988: Big, rich and full-bodied, with generous pear, pineapple, apple and spicy oak flavors, balanced with crisp acidity and picking up pretty honey and butterscotch flavors on the finish. Persistent. Drink now. 1,500 cases made. Rel: $20 Cur: $23 (5/31/90) **89**
Chardonnay Monterey Reserve 1987: Ripe with tropical fruit flavors that are rich and full-bodied, tasty and pleasant but essentially simple and one-dimensional. Rel: $19 Cur: $23 (7/15/89) **84**

J.W. MORRIS
Chardonnay California Private Reserve 1989: A perfumed aroma quickly fades to simple pineapple, lemon and citrus notes. Does have modest follow through on the finish, though. $8 (7/15/91) **79**
Chardonnay California Private Reserve 1988: Out of balance, Tasting both sweet and sour. Fruit flavors are stale. Drinkable but not recommended. $8 (5/15/90) **66**

MOUNT EDEN
Chardonnay Edna Valley MacGregor Vineyard 1989: Complex and beautifully balanced, with brilliant pineapple and pear flavors and accents of spice, toast, smoke and vanilla. A rich and multifaceted yet elegant and polished wine. Drink now through 1994. 3,600 cases made. Rel: $14.50 Cur: $23 (11/30/90) **89**
Chardonnay Edna Valley MacGregor Vineyard 1988: Tight and firm, with crisp lemon and pineapple flavors that are tart and lean but lack depth. A balanced wine, showing more oak than fruit. Drink now. Tasted twice, with consistent results. 1,551 cases made. $14 (6/30/90) **83**
Chardonnay Edna Valley M.E.V. MacGregor Vineyard 1987: Earthy, ripe and complex, without showing any heaviness. Elegant and ever-changing in the glass, mingling aromas and flavors of toast, honey, apple, pear and more. Drinkable now, but it can only improve with cellaring. Rel: $14 Cur: $20 (4/30/89) SS **93**
Chardonnay Edna Valley M.E.V. MacGregor Vineyard 1986 Rel: $13 Cur: $16 (CH-3/90) **81**
Chardonnay Edna Valley M.E.V. MacGregor Vineyard 1985 $12.50 (CH-3/90) **87**
Chardonnay Monterey County 1982 $12.50 (4/01/84) **76**
Chardonnay Santa Barbara County 1990: Earthy, ripe and concentrated, with pretty citrus, honey, pineapple and cedary oak flavors that are sharply focused and lively through the finish. Drink now to 1995. 3,979 cases made. $14.50 (6/15/92) **89**
Chardonnay Santa Cruz Mountains 1988: Firm and slightly tannic, but the smoky pear and nutmeg aromas and flavors are beautifully focused and linger enticingly on the finish. A sturdy wine. Drink now. $30 (11/30/90) **88**
Chardonnay Santa Cruz Mountains 1987: Lavishly oak aged, with butterscotch, pear and spicy flavors that are woody, but it has a smooth texture and good length on the finish. The smoky aftertaste is pretty. Rel: $28 Cur: $39 (11/15/89) **88**
Chardonnay Santa Cruz Mountains 1986 Rel: $25 Cur: $37 (CH-3/90) **88**
Chardonnay Santa Cruz Mountains 1985 Rel: $25 Cur: $57 (CH-3/90) **87**
Chardonnay Santa Cruz Mountains 1984 Rel: $23 Cur: $56 (CH-3/90) **85**
Chardonnay Santa Cruz Mountains 1983 Rel: $20 Cur: $48 (CH-3/90) **84**
Chardonnay Santa Cruz Mountains 1982 Rel: $18 Cur: $43 (CH-3/90) **76**
Chardonnay Santa Cruz Mountains 1981 Rel: $18 Cur: $50 (CH-3/90) **89**
Chardonnay Santa Cruz Mountains 1980 Rel: $30 Cur: $52 (CH-3/90) **87**
Chardonnay Santa Cruz Mountains 1979 Rel: $16 Cur: $52 (CH-3/90) **90**
Chardonnay Santa Cruz Mountains 1978 Rel: $16 Cur: $50 (CH-3/90) **66**
Chardonnay Santa Cruz Mountains 1977 Rel: $16 Cur: $70 (CH-8/90) **85**
Chardonnay Santa Cruz Mountains 1976 Rel: $16 Cur: $50 (CH-3/90) **78**
Chardonnay Santa Cruz Mountains 1975 Rel: $14 Cur: $45 (CH-3/90) **60**
Chardonnay Santa Cruz Mountains 1974 Rel: $14 Cur: $50 (CH-3/90) **59**
Chardonnay Santa Cruz Mountains 1973 Rel: $12 Cur: $55 (CH-3/90) **82**
Chardonnay Santa Cruz Mountains 1972 Rel: $20 Cur: $50 (CH-3/90) **80**

MT. MADONNA
Chardonnay San Luis Obispo County 1987: Fresh and light, but that's about the best that can be said about this short-flavored, modestly structured, vaguely appley wine. $7.50 (3/31/89) **70**

MOUNT VEEDER
Chardonnay Napa Valley 1990: Fresh, tight and sharply focused, displaying appealing pear, peach and butter aromas and flavors. Turns spicy and generous on the finish. Has elegance and charm. Best to drink around 1993 to '95. 2,850 cases made. $14 (6/30/92) **88**
Chardonnay Napa Valley 1989: Smooth and fruity, with citrus and pineapple aromas and flavors that are tangy and fresh and a nice hint of vanilla on the finish. Drink now. 2,000 cases made. $18 (4/30/91) **83**
Chardonnay Napa Valley 1988: Polished, complex, and delicious. Like a white Burgundy in aroma, with hints of toast, earth, butter and pear, and rich, concentrated and ripe on the palate, with a long, lingering finish. 1,270 cases made. $15 (6/30/90) **91**
Chardonnay Napa Valley 1987 $14 (6/15/89) **83**
Chardonnay Napa County 1986 $14 (2/29/88) **86**
Chardonnay Napa County 1985 $13.50 (5/31/87) **89**

MOUNTAIN HOUSE
Chardonnay Sonoma County 1981 $11 (2/15/84) **90**

MOUNTAIN VIEW
Chardonnay Monterey County 1990: A simple, fruity wine, with ripe apple, pear, spice and fig flavors that are balanced and tasty. Fairly priced. $6 (3/15/92) BB **80**
Chardonnay Monterey County 1989: Pure, ripe apple, melon, honey and spice notes are soft and complex, with plenty of staying power. Echoes honey and spice on the finish. Fresh and clean. You don't find many Chardonnays with this much character at this price. Drink now. $6 (4/15/91) BB **84**
Chardonnay Monterey County 1988: Excellent value in a true-to-form Chardonnay, with ripe pear, apple and melon flavors offering fruit complexity and decent depth. Drink now. $6.50 (4/30/90) BB **81**
Chardonnay Monterey County 1987 $6 (4/30/89) **79**
Chardonnay Monterey County 1985 $5 (2/15/87) BB **89**

MURPHY-GOODE
Chardonnay Alexander Valley Estate Vineyard 1990: Ripe, rich and creamy, with spicy pear, melon and toasty, buttery oak flavors, all in harmony. The texture is silky-smooth and the finish echoes fruit and oak, on and on. Drink now through 1995. $12.50 (12/31/91) **89**
Chardonnay Alexander Valley Estate Vineyard 1989: The light, simple peach, nutmeg and spice notes are pleasant and stay with you. Drink now. Tasted twice. Rel: $12 Cur: $14 (6/30/91) **82**
Chardonnay Alexander Valley Estate Vineyard 1988: Ripe and full-bodied, with layers of pineapple, pear and spice flavors, offering a lively balance between oak, fruit and acidity, with a mouth-watering finish. Decent price, too. Drink now to 1994. Rel: $11.50 Cur: $15 (11/30/89) **91**
Chardonnay Alexander Valley Premier Vineyard 1987 Rel: $11 Cur: $14 (CH-4/90) **87**
Chardonnay Alexander Valley Estate Vineyard 1986 Rel: $10 Cur: $15 (CH-4/90) **86**
Chardonnay Alexander Valley Estate Vineyard 1985 Rel: $9 Cur: $14 (CH-4/90) **85**

NAPA CELLARS
Chardonnay Napa Valley 1990: The fruit is earthy and somewhat stale, but at this price you still get a good bottle of wine, with toast, spice, pear and melon notes. Drink now. $7 (3/15/92) **80**
Chardonnay Napa Valley 1989: Has plenty of clean, ripe, pure Chardonnay flavor, with tiers of pear, apple, spice and honey notes. Well balanced, richly varietal and not too oaky. A wonderful price, too. Drink up. 3,000 cases made. $7 (4/15/91) BB **85**

NAPA CREEK
Chardonnay Napa Valley 1989: Smells ripe and almost honeyed, but tastes light, vaguely fruity and lean. Lacks fruit flavor, so it's not very satisfying, though clean and correct. 2,500 cases made. $13 (4/30/91) **77**
Chardonnay Napa Valley 1988: Lean and concentrated, with bright apple and lemon aromas and flavors, crisp yet smooth structure and a spicy finish. Polished and reaching drinkability. Drink now to 1993. $13.50 (4/15/90) **86**
Chardonnay Napa Valley 1986 $12 (5/31/88) **86**

NAPA RIDGE
Chardonnay California 1984 $5.75 (1/31/87) BB **85**
Chardonnay Central Coast 1989: An unusually light, fragrant wine that's full of peach, spice and floral flavors of moderate depth and intensity. Fruity and pleasant to drink now. $7 (11/15/90) BB **83**
Chardonnay Central Coast 1988: This soft wine is easy to like and uncomplicated, with floral and honeysuckle aromas that stand out. Peach and pear flavors and just enough lemon and acidity on the finish make it interesting. Drink now. $7 (6/30/90) **77**
Chardonnay North Coast Coastal 1989: Intense and lively, with ripe, rich, crisp citrus, pineapple,

pear, peach and spice flavors that linger on the palate. Offers more depth and concentration than most '89s and has a sense of elegance and finesse. Drink now to 1994. $7 (6/30/91) BB **88**
Chardonnay North Coast 1987 $6.50 (7/15/88) **77**

NAVARRO
Chardonnay Anderson Valley 1989: Ripe, smooth and creamy, with intense yet subtle pear, spice, apple and melon flavors that are long and lingering. An elegant style that's quite appealing. Drink now to 1993. 2,061 cases made. $11 (11/15/91) **86**
Chardonnay Mendocino 1988: Light, lean and crisp, showing pleasant, refreshing almond and peach flavors. A likable, ready-to-drink wine that develops more richness with each sip. 2,800 cases made. $9.75 (11/30/90) **87**
Chardonnay Anderson Valley 1987: A beautifully crafted wine with plenty of flavor. The peach, spice, smoke and anise flavors are rich and complex with fine structure and a long, elegant finish. Gets better with each sip. 2,771 cases made. $9.75 (9/30/89) **89**
Chardonnay Mendocino 1986 $9.75 (9/30/88) **88**
Chardonnay Mendocino 1985 $8.50 (10/31/87) **88**
Chardonnay Anderson Valley Table Wine 1989: Spicy Riesling-like flavors, with tart peach, pine and vanilla notes, turn a bit flat on the aftertaste. Drink now. 1,099 cases made. $7.50 (11/15/91) BB **81**
Chardonnay Mendocino Table Wine 1987: Delicate and spicy, with layers of buttery anise, oak and fig flavors that linger on the palate, finishing with butterscotch notes. Well balanced and nicely proportioned. 1,356 cases made. $7 (9/30/89) BB **85**
Chardonnay Mendocino Première Reserve 1989: Ripe, rich and creamy, with sharply focused pear, vanilla, butter, apple and cream flavors all combining to give this wine uncommon complexity, depth and charm. Has a wonderful sense of harmony, with good concentration of flavor. Drink now to 1994. 3,596 cases made. $14 (12/31/91) **88**
Chardonnay Anderson Valley Première Reserve 1988: Earthy, slightly herbal aromas detract from the modest fruit flavors, but the creamy texture is appealing and the overall effect is distinctive. Drinkable now. 3,400 cases made. Rel: $14 Cur: $18 (12/31/90) **89**
Chardonnay Anderson Valley Première Reserve 1987: Subtle yet distinctive, with butterscotch, caramel and smoky oak flavors along with a touch of herb and peach on the finish. Flavors grow on you. 1,813 cases made. Rel: $14 Cur: $17 (9/30/89) **84**
Chardonnay Anderson Valley Première Reserve 1986 Rel: $14 Cur: $18 (CH-3/90) **87**
Chardonnay Anderson Valley Première Reserve 1985 Rel: $12 Cur: $18 (CH-3/90) **89**
Chardonnay Anderson Valley Première Reserve 1984 Rel: $12 Cur: $22 (CH-3/90) **91**

NEWLAN
Chardonnay Napa Valley 1990: Pleasantly proportioned, with focused pear, spice, pineapple, honey and oak notes that hang together. Finishes a bit rough, but should smooth out with time. Drink now to 1994. 1,244 cases made. $14 (3/31/92) **86**
Chardonnay Napa Valley 1989: This ripe, oaky style has lots of spicy vanilla and creamy oak flavors, but also plenty of fresh, clean apple, pear and melon notes, too. Balanced, with a pretty fruit and oak aftertaste. Drink now to 1994. 731 cases made. $14 (7/15/91) **90**
Chardonnay Napa Valley 1988: Lively, supple and elegant, with generous peach flavors and a touch of vanilla and toast, focused, smooth and concentrated, echoing nutmeg and honey on the finish. Drinkable now, but better to let it grow until at least 1993 to see what develops. 2,000 cases made. $13 (6/15/90) **91**
Chardonnay Napa Valley 1987 $13 (6/30/90) **86**

NEWTON
Chardonnay Napa Valley 1989: Tight and compact, with focused pear, toast and spicy oak flavors. Blunt now, but with another year it should be smoother. Drink in 1993 to '95. $15 (5/15/92) **86**
Chardonnay Napa Valley 1988: A big, tough wine with a bite that won't quit, but the hard apple and toast flavors turn mellow and honeyed on the finish. Drink now. $14.50 (6/30/90) **90**
Chardonnay Napa Valley 1987: Lively, with plenty of apple, pear, spice and melon flavors that pick up a load of oak and a touch of oxidation on the finish. Drink now. $14 (3/15/90) **84**
Chardonnay Napa Valley 1986 $14 (CH-3/90) **85**
Chardonnay Napa Valley 1985 Rel: $12.75 Cur: $19 (CH-3/90) **85**
Chardonnay Napa Valley 1984 Rel: $11.50 Cur: $18 (CH-5/90) **86**
Chardonnay Napa Valley 1983 Rel: $12 Cur: $19 (CH-5/90) **89**
Chardonnay Napa Valley 1982 $16 (9/01/84) **82**

NEYERS
Chardonnay California 1987: A very oaky wine that will appeal to some, but it seems all wood and little fruit. Pungently earthy and woody in aroma and rough on the finish. $14 (7/15/89) **77**
Chardonnay Carneros District 1989: Tart and earthy, an angular wine, with harsh, smoky, funky aromas and flavors that pick up enough pear and pineapple notes on the finish to be drinkable. Tasted twice, with consistent notes. 1,500 cases made. $17 (7/15/92) **75**
Chardonnay Carneros 1988: Tight and concentrated, but fairly blunt and one-dimensional, with little depth to the flavors or smoothness to the texture. Pleasant pear flavors make it drinkable. 1,500 cases made. $17 (7/15/91) **81**
Chardonnay Napa Valley 1990: Elegant and balanced, with subtle pear, toast and butter notes that turn soft on the finish. Drink now. $15 (7/15/92) **82**
Chardonnay Napa Valley 1989: The watery pear, earth and melon flavors lack richness, depth and complexity. A simple wine to drink now. 5,000 cases made. $15 (7/15/91) **78**
Chardonnay Napa Valley 1988: Lean and tart, with simple apple cider and clove aromas and flavors. Decent but unexciting. 4,000 cases made. $15 (5/15/90) **79**
Chardonnay Napa Valley 1986 $12.50 (4/30/88) **81**
Chardonnay Napa Valley 1985 $12 (8/31/87) **90**

GUSTAVE NIEBAUM
Chardonnay Carneros Napa Valley Bayview Vineyard 1988: Youthful and attractive with fresh, ripe pear, orange and spice flavors, with pineapple notes, a crisp texture and a long tasty finish that echoes the fruit. 3,000 cases made. $14.50 (10/31/89) **91**
Chardonnay Carneros Napa Valley Bayview Vineyard Barrel Fermented 1989: Tart and lemony, with hints of green apple and grapefruit flavors on the finish. A lean, lively style that needs time to soften, perhaps until 1994. $15 (6/30/92) **86**
Chardonnay Carneros Napa Valley Bayview Vineyard Special Reserve 1988: A wonderful display of rich, ripe, complex fruit, with layers of concentrated pear, pineapple, honey and spice flavors that are wrapped in a silky-smooth texture and pretty smoky and toast flavors on the finish. Drink now. $18 (5/31/90) **90**
Chardonnay Carneros Napa Valley Laird Vineyards 1989: Intense pineapple and wood flavors are a bit rough early on, but the pear and citrus flavors are well defined, albeit lacking in concentration. Drink now. 2,500 cases made. $13.50 (1/31/91) **82**
Chardonnay Carneros Napa Valley Laird Vineyards 1988: Mouth-watering flavors and crisp acidity give this wine backbone, and the touch of oak and honey kick in on the finish to add another layer of complexity. Well made, with restraint and finesse. Drink now to 1993. 3,800 cases made. $13.50 (10/31/89) **90**
Chardonnay Napa Valley Reference 1990: Crisp and fruity, with focused pear, nectarine, pineapple and spice flavors that are fresh and lively. Finishes clean and fruity. Drink now to 1993. Tasted twice. $11 (7/15/92) **85**
Chardonnay Napa Valley Reference 1989: An intensely fruity, tangy wine, with a lively texture, a bit of vanilla to round it out and a lingering finish. Tight and tart in structure, but should smooth out fine by 1994. $11 (6/15/91) **86**

OAKVILLE BENCH
Chardonnay Napa Valley 1989: Smooth and buttery, with crisp citrus, pear and honey notes that show a measure of maturity. Drink now. Tasted twice. 1,000 cases made. $12 (7/15/92) **85**

OBESTER
Chardonnay Mendocino County 1988: Offers lots of toasty, buttery oak, but has a nice core of pear and lemon-tinged flavors, too. Balanced, elegant and perfectly enjoyable. A fair price. 600 cases made. $13 (7/15/91) **83**
Chardonnay Mendocino County Barrel Fermented 1989: Intense oak and vegetal Chardonnay flavors are difficult to warm up to, and the fruit is simple and turns watery. Barely decent. 600 cases made. $13 (7/15/91) **71**

OJAI
Chardonnay Santa Barbara County 1990: Ripe and full-bodied, with creamy pear, fig and melon notes that trail off on the finish. Drink now. Tasted twice. $15 (7/15/92) **81**

OLIVET LANE
Chardonnay Russian River Valley 1989: Has good intensity and flavor for an '89, with creamy, toasty oak notes and pear, melon and citrus flavors. Lacks a sense of harmony, but not by much. Best now. 4,500 cases made. $12 (7/15/91) **80**

OLSON
Chardonnay Mendocino County 1984 $9 (4/16/86) **57**

OPTIMA
Chardonnay Sonoma County 1990: Offers a strong toasty, oaky flavor, but matches it with fruit that echoes pear, spice, citrus and honey. The texture is a bit coarse, but it has all the ingredients. Cellar until 1993. 300 cases made. $25 (2/29/92) **87**
Chardonnay Sonoma County 1989: There is lots of flair in this buttery smelling, spicy and elegant-tasting wine, with layers of pear, vanilla, butterscotch and nutmeg to give it complexity. Medium-bodied and well balanced. $25 (7/15/91) **86**

ORGANIC WINE WORKS
Chardonnay Sonoma County Freiberg Vineyard 1991: Smells and tastes a bit oxidized, with candied pear and earth notes. Drinkable, but doesn't stand out as Chardonnay. Drink now. $9.50 (7/15/92) **72**

PAHLMEYER
Chardonnay Napa Valley Caldwell Vineyard 1989: Has attractive smoky, toasty oak flavors, with delicate pear, almond and spice notes that gain a nice oaky aftertaste. The Chardonnay flavors are elegant, but lack intensity and concentration. Still, it's a pretty drink that's ready now. 400 cases made. $20 (4/30/91) **86**

PARDUCCI
Chardonnay Mendocino County 1990: A lively, light, crisp, Riesling-like Chardonnay, with pleasant apple and grapefruit flavors. Clean and well made, with a nice balance, though not particularly flavorful. $10 (1/31/92) **81**
Chardonnay Mendocino County 1989: Pleasantly fruity, with crisp pear, citrus, mineral and spice notes that are elegant but simple. Turns crisp and light on the finish. Drink now. $9.50 (7/15/91) BB **83**
Chardonnay Mendocino County 1988: Attractive with crisp, spicy pear and peach notes and a touch of vanilla. An elegant, well-balanced, satisfying wine. Drink now. $9.75 (4/30/90) **83**
Chardonnay Mendocino County 1987 $7 (10/31/88) BB **85**
Chardonnay Mendocino County 1986 $8 (12/31/87) **68**
Chardonnay Mendocino County 1984 $6 (4/16/86) **55**
Chardonnay Mendocino County Cellarmaster Selection 1988: Beautifully defined Chardonnay, layers of rich, ripe apple, pear, peach, honey and pineapple flavors that glide along with a smooth, creamy texture and just the right amount of oak to give it complexity and depth. Finish goes on and on. Drink now to 1993. 1,200 cases made. $16 (6/30/90) **91**

PARKER
Chardonnay Santa Barbara County 1989: Fresh, clean and lively, with pretty peach, nectarine, pear and honey notes that are rich and elegant. The texture is smooth and creamy, finishing with zesty acidity and fine length. Ready now through 1994. $15 (8/31/91) **87**

PARSONS CREEK
Chardonnay Sonoma County Winemaker's Select 1988: A somewhat rich, oak-aged Chardonnay that's fairly priced. It's ripe and flavorful, with generous butter and pear notes and hints of toast and spice in the aromas. The flavors last on the finish. Well balanced, too. 1,300 cases made. $10 (2/28/91) **86**

PATZ & HALL
Chardonnay Napa Valley 1990: Crisp and complex, with lively, well-focused citrus, pear, honey and melon flavors. Finishes with a long, fruity aftertaste. Drink now to 1994. $23 (1/31/92) **87**
Chardonnay Napa Valley 1989: Lean, elegant and harmonious, with attractive pear, smoke and nutmeg aromas and flavors that are light and friendly, making it drinkable now. $25 (7/15/91) **86**
Chardonnay Napa Valley 1988: A modest wine with a tasty touch of spice and caramel from oak aging. Good but light. Tasted twice, with consistent scores. $24 (6/30/90) **77**

PAT PAULSEN
Chardonnay Sonoma County 1983 $11 (2/16/85) **75**

ROBERT PECOTA
Chardonnay Alexander Valley Canepa Vineyard 1988: Distintive, with honey and caramel flavors, but it comes across as rather simple and finishes slightly bitter. Lacks the fruit concentration to stand up to the oak. Drink now. Tasted twice. $16 (5/15/90) **80**
Chardonnay Alexander Valley Canepa Vineyard 1987 Rel: $16 Cur: $20 (CH-4/90) **91**
Chardonnay Alexander Valley Canepa Vineyard 1986 Rel: $16 Cur: $19 (CH-4/90) **85**
Chardonnay Alexander Valley Canepa Vineyard 1985 Rel: $16 Cur: $18 (CH-7/90) **89**
Chardonnay Alexander Valley Canepa Vineyard 1984 Rel: $14 Cur: $18 (CH-4/90) **83**
Chardonnay Alexander Valley Canepa Vineyard 1983 Rel: $14 Cur: $18 (CH-4/90) **79**
Chardonnay Alexander Valley Canepa Vineyard 1981 Rel: $12 Cur: $20 (CH-4/90) **75**
Chardonnay Alexander Valley Canepa Vineyard 1980 Rel: $12 Cur: $20 (CH-4/90) **89**

J. PEDRONCELLI
Chardonnay Dry Creek Valley 1990: A straightforward wine, with ripe apple, pear and citrus

Key to Symbols

The scores reported here are the results of blind tastings conducted by our panel of senior editors. Wines that carry the initials below are results of individual tastings.

THE WINE SPECTATOR 100-POINT SCALE ***95-100***—Classic, a great wine; ***90-94***—Outstanding, superior character and style; ***80-89***—Good to very good, a wine with special qualities; ***70-79***—Average, drinkable wine that may have minor flaws; ***60-69***—Below average, drinkable but not recommended; ***50-59***—Poor, undrinkable, not recommended. "+"—With a score indicates a range; used primarily with barrel tastings to indicate a preliminary score.

SPECIAL DESIGNATIONS SS—Spectator Selection, CS—Cellar Selection, BB—Best Buy, ($NA)—Price not available, (NR)—Not released.

TASTER'S INITIALS (JG)—Jim Gordon, (HS)—Harvey Steiman, (JL)—James Laube, (JS)—James Suckling, (TM)—Thomas Matthews, (TR)—Terry Robards, (PM)—Per-Henrik Mansson, (BT)—Barrel Tasting (these wines were tasted blind from barrel samples), (CA-date)—*California's Great Cabernets* by James Laube, (CH-date)—*California's Great Chardonnays* by James Laube, (VP-date)—*Vintage Port* by James Suckling.

DATE TASTED Dates in parentheses represent the issue in which the rating was published.

flavors, but not much in the way of oak, complexity or nuance. A fair price for a drink-now wine. $10 (3/31/92) **80**
Chardonnay Dry Creek Valley 1989: A tart, assertive wine, showing more buttery, spicy flavors from oak than fruit. A little bit of orange flavor helps, but overall it's blunt and woody. $9.50 (12/31/90) **77**
Chardonnay Dry Creek Valley 1988 $9 (12/15/89) **79**
Chardonnay Dry Creek Valley 1987 $8 (12/31/88) BB **85**
Chardonnay Dry Creek Valley 1986 $8 (6/15/88) **83**
Chardonnay Sonoma County 1985 $7.75 (7/31/87) **83**
Chardonnay Sonoma County 1984 $7.75 (3/01/86) **81**
Chardonnay Sonoma County 1983 $7.75 (6/01/85) **66**

ROBERT PEPI
Chardonnay Napa Valley 1987 $13.50 (2/15/90) **84**
Chardonnay Napa Valley 1986 $12 (10/31/88) **80**
Chardonnay Napa Valley 1985 $12 (11/15/87) **81**
Chardonnay Napa Valley 1983 $11 (3/01/86) **70**
Chardonnay Napa Valley 1982 $11 (5/01/84) **72**
Chardonnay Napa Valley Puncheon Fermented 1990: Crisp and lively, with generous peach and apple aromas and flavors that become creamy and appealing on the finish. Drinkable now. 2,552 cases made. $15 (7/15/92) **82**
Chardonnay Napa Valley Puncheon Fermented 1989: Offers spice, citrus, nutmeg and clove flavors and a touch of ripe pear and melon. Balanced with a good core of fruit, but the finish fades. Drink now to 1993. 1,000 cases made. $12 (12/31/91) **84**
Chardonnay Napa Valley Puncheon Fermented 1988: Lean and crisp, with a bright beam of pear, nectarine and spice flavor shining across the palate, broadening on the finish. Drink now. $14 (5/31/90) **88**
Chardonnay Napa Valley Puncheon Fermented Reserve 1989: Has a smooth veneer of buttery aromas and flavors wrapped around a core of pear and pineapple. Straightforward, uncomplicated and drinkable now, but perhaps better around 1993. 2,000 cases made. $20 (2/28/91) **81**

MARIO PERELLI-MINETTI
Chardonnay Napa Valley 1990: Young and sharp, with snappy apple and pear flavors that are ripe and attractive but simple. Drink now. 4,100 cases made. $12.50 (5/31/92) **81**
Chardonnay Napa Valley 1989: A decent, fruity wine that has a touch of richness in the aroma and good pineapple and pear flavors. Fairly crisp and light overall. 2,750 cases made. $12.50 (4/30/91) **83**
Chardonnay Napa Valley 1988: Crisp and straightforward, with fruit flavors that lean toward floral and piny. A good, clean, simple wine. 3,130 cases made. $11.50 (6/30/90) **80**

PERRET
Chardonnay Carneros Napa Valley Perret Vineyard 1985 $14 (12/31/88) **78**
Chardonnay Carneros Napa Valley Perret Vineyard 1984 $14.50 (10/15/87) **91**
Chardonnay Carneros Napa Valley Perret Vineyard 1982 $14.50 (11/01/84) **81**
Chardonnay Carneros Napa Valley Winery Lake Vineyard 1985 $14.50 (12/31/88) **84**

JOSEPH PHELPS
Chardonnay Carneros Sangiacomo Vineyard 1989: Soft and generous, with a lively streak of apple and lemon aromas and flavors that persist on the soft finish. An agreeable wine for early drinking. 3,000 cases made. $20 (7/15/91) **85**
Chardonnay Carneros Sangiacomo Vineyard 1988: Intense and forward, with wonderful aromas, this wine has rich, earthy pear and pineapple flavors and a distinct mineral quality, braced by crisp acidity. Has wonderful balance, a supple texture, and a long finish. Drink now. 3,500 cases made. $16 (6/30/90) **89**
Chardonnay Carneros Sangiacomo Vineyard 1987: Bitter, earthy flavors override the ripe Chardonnay flavor, leaving an awkward, clumsy wine that's disappointing. Drink now. Tasted twice. $18 (5/15/89) **68**
Chardonnay Carneros Sangiacomo Vineyard 1986 $16 (7/15/88) **93**
Chardonnay Carneros Sangiacomo Vineyard 1985 $14 (11/15/87) **84**
Chardonnay Carneros Sangiacomo Vineyard 1982 $14 (4/01/84) **79**
Chardonnay Napa Valley 1990: Ripe and spicy, with toasted almond, pear and oak shadings. Elegant and understated but well made, with pretty flavors on the finish, echoing pear and cream. Drink now to 1993. 11,000 cases made. $16 (12/15/91) **90**
Chardonnay Napa Valley 1989: Has pure ripe pineapple and spicy apple flavors, but like most '89s it lacks richness and concentration and turns watery on the finish. Drink now. $16 (7/15/91) **81**
Chardonnay Napa Valley 1988: Despite a somewhat astringent texture, this wine has enough generous peach, butter and apple aromas and flavors to make it appealing. Drink now. $16 (6/30/90) **86**
Chardonnay Napa Valley 1987 $15 (3/15/89) **81**
Chardonnay Napa Valley 1984 $13 (6/30/87) **75**
Chardonnay Napa Valley 1983 $12.75 (12/15/86) **68**
Chardonnay Napa Valley 1982 $12.50 (4/16/85) **85**

PHILIPPE-LORRAINE
Chardonnay Napa Valley 1990: Crisp and tart, with lemon and citrus notes that gain a touch of vanilla and spice. Elegant and clean. Drink now. 2,000 cases made. $10 (5/15/92) **83**

R.H. PHILLIPS
Chardonnay California 1990: Fresh, clean and lively, with pretty melon, pear, citrus and spice flavors that are moderately rich and concentrated up front, but taper off on the finish. Still a pretty good bargain. Drink now. $8 (7/15/91) BB **85**
Chardonnay California 1989: Clean, ripe and fruity, with intense pear, peach, apple and honey notes that stay from start to finish. Balanced, with moderate fruit complexity and barely a trace of wood. A fair price, too. Drink now. $7 (4/30/91) BB **83**
Chardonnay California 1987: A reasonably refreshing but basically simple wine, with citrusy flavors. $6 (2/15/89) **77**

PINE RIDGE
Chardonnay Napa Valley Knollside Cuvée 1990: A woody wine, which buries some fairly rich pear, honey and vanilla flavor trying to well up underneath it, but the oak flavors dominate and make this a gamble. Try it in 1994. Tasted twice. $14 (7/15/92) **79**
Chardonnay Napa Valley Knollside Cuvée 1989: Smells and tastes vegetal and pickle-like. Drinkable but not enjoyable. Tasted three times. $16 (7/15/91) **67**
Chardonnay Napa Valley Knollside Cuvée 1988: Extremely woody and harsh, with apple cider and honey flavors coming through on the finish. The style is not for everyone, but it could develop with cellaring through 1994. Tasted twice. Rel: $15 Cur: $17 (5/15/90) **85**
Chardonnay Napa Valley Knollside Cuvée 1987 Rel: $15 Cur: $17 (CH-4/90) **90**
Chardonnay Napa Valley Knollside Cuvée 1986 Rel: $14 Cur: $17 (CH-4/90) **88**
Chardonnay Napa Valley Knollside Cuvée 1985 Rel: $14 Cur: $16 (CH-4/90) **87**
Chardonnay Napa Valley Knollside Cuvée 1984 Rel: $14 Cur: $17 (CH-4/90) **85**
Chardonnay Napa Valley Oak Knoll Cuvée 1983 Rel: $13 Cur: $18 (CH-4/90) **88**
Chardonnay Napa Valley Oak Knoll Cuvée 1982 Rel: $13 Cur: $19 (3/16/84) SS **89**
Chardonnay Napa Valley Oak Knoll Cuvée 1981 Rel: $13 Cur: $20 (CH-4/90) **84**
Chardonnay Napa Valley Stags Leap District 1988: Rich and complex in an earthy, honeyed, hazelnut sort of way, but the lack of fruit seems to emphasize the excessive earthiness. Drinkable now. Tasted three times. 3,180 cases made. $20 (11/30/90) **78**
Chardonnay Stags Leap District Pine Ridge Stags Leap Vineyard 1988 $20 (CH-7/90) **88**
Chardonnay Stags Leap District Pine Ridge Stags Leap Vineyard 1987: Earthy, but smooth and honeyed on the palate, with tangerine-tinged peach aromas and flavors. It's medium-bodied and well balanced, but you have to like the earthiness. Rel: $20 Cur: $23 (4/30/89) **82**
Chardonnay Stags Leap District Pine Ridge Stags Leap Vineyard 1986 Rel: $19 Cur: $23 (CH-4/90) **88**
Chardonnay Stags Leap District Pine Ridge Stags Leap Vineyard 1985 Rel: $18 Cur: $23 (CH-4/90) **85**
Chardonnay Stags Leap District Pine Ridge Stags Leap Vineyard 1984 Rel: $18 Cur: $25 (CH-4/90) **84**
Chardonnay Stags Leap District Pine Ridge Stags Leap Vineyard 1983 Rel: $16 Cur: $25 (12/16/85) SS **94**
Chardonnay Stags Leap District Stags Leap Vineyard 1982 Rel: $15 Cur: $27 (CH-4/90) **82**
Chardonnay Stags Leap District Stags Leap Vineyard 1981 Rel: $15 Cur: $31 (CH-4/90) **86**
Chardonnay Stags Leap District Stags Leap Vineyard 1979 Rel: $9.50 Cur: $32 (CH-4/90) **82**

PINNACLES
Chardonnay Monterey 1990: Hard and tight, with a gamy edge. This backward wine has a good oaky edge and interesting flavors, but it's closed and not showing much at this stage. Hold until 1993. Tasted twice. 600 cases made. $16 (7/15/92) **85**

PLAM
Chardonnay Napa Valley 1989: Ripe and generous, turning soft, but the nutmeg- and toast-tinged pear and apple flavors take on hints of honey on the long finish. The texture is smooth and the flavors have style. Drinkable now. 2,800 cases made. $16 (7/15/91) **85**
Chardonnay Napa Valley 1988: Woody flavors dominate, but a core of lemon and pear flavors give it backing. Has crisp acidity and good length. 3,607 cases made. $16 (6/30/90) **85**
Chardonnay Napa Valley 1986: Rich and toasty for a medium-bodied wine, balanced and clean, with apple and a touch of honey for interest. $18 (4/15/89) **84**
Chardonnay Napa Valley 1985 $12 (7/15/88) **79**

BERNARD PRADEL
Chardonnay Napa Valley 1986 $9.50 (2/29/88) **82**

QUAIL RIDGE
Chardonnay Napa Valley 1989: Simple and fruity, with pleasant pineapple and citrus notes, but it's nothing special. Drink now. Tasted twice. $15 (4/30/92) **78**
Chardonnay Napa Valley 1988: Rich, smooth, flavorful and well balanced. Ripe, almost sweet in flavor, with intense pear, honey and apple notes, a dense, chewy texture and a long finish. $14 (2/15/90) **89**
Chardonnay Napa Valley 1987: A woody, peppery wine that's full-bodied but lacking in fruit flavor. Rough and a bit sour. $15 (7/15/89) **68**
Chardonnay Napa Valley 1986 $15 (10/31/88) **81**
Chardonnay Napa Valley 1983 $14 (9/01/85) **80**
Chardonnay Napa Valley 1982 $14 (5/16/84) **85**
Chardonnay Napa Valley Winemakers' Selection 1984 $17 (12/15/87) **80**
Chardonnay Sonoma County 1982 $9 (3/16/84) **84**

QUPE
Chardonnay Santa Barbara County Sierra Madre Reserve 1990: Crisp and lively, with a nice zing of lemon, apple and grapefruit flavors that hint at toast and honey on the finish. Drinkable now, and should improve through 1994. $22 (7/15/92) **86**
Chardonnay Santa Barbara County Sierra Madre Reserve 1989: A rich, complex and graceful wine, with many facets. The pear, apricot, citrus, butterscotch and honey aromas and flavors all come together for a long, delicious finish. Drinkable now, so why wait? 620 cases made. $25 (7/15/91) **91**
Chardonnay Santa Barbara County Sierra Madre Reserve 1988: A very easy-to-like wine. Rich, ripe and exuberantly fruity in flavor, with a smooth, soft texture and lingering aftertaste. $12.50 (12/15/89) **81**

RABBIT RIDGE
Chardonnay Sonoma County 1990: Coarse and biting, with a good dose of alcohol showing, too, but those characteristics overshadow the ripe pear and apple notes. A clumsy effort. Drink now. $12.50 (3/31/92) **76**
Chardonnay Sonoma County 1989: A very stylish wine, with lots of vanilla and spice aromas, rich buttery flavors and a lingering finish. A bit short on fruit flavor, but very appealing nonetheless. $12 (4/30/91) **85**

RANCHO SISQUOC
Chardonnay Santa Maria Valley 1987: Not a heavyweight, but it has clean, modest flavors of spices and pears and decent balance. Short on the finish. $10 (12/15/89) **76**

KENT RASMUSSEN
Chardonnay Carneros 1989: Heavy, rich and coarse, with aromas of butter, butterscotch and pear and hints of sweet botrytis and honey flavors that are wide of the mark for Chardonnay, but may be typical of some California '89s. Drink now to 1993. $20 (1/31/91) **79**
Chardonnay Carneros 1988: Elegant and concentrated, with firm, intense pear and pineapple flavors that are crisp and lively, with subtle oak shadings adding dimension and texture. Well balanced and complex on the finish. Drink now to 1994. 1,373 cases made. $19 (9/15/90) **90**
Chardonnay Carneros Napa Valley 1989: Tastes like it's made from a strong Muscat clone, with spice and floral flavors and honey and oak notes on the finish. Has a pretty aftertaste. Drink now to 1993. Much better than a bottle tasted earlier. $19 (3/15/91) **87**

RAVENSWOOD
Chardonnay Sonoma Valley Sangiacomo 1990: Strong earthy, smoky juniper aromas border on funky, but there's also a nice, rich core of ripe pear and butterscotch-tinged Chardonnay flavor. A daring style that pushes the extremes of flavor, but it's a nice drink. Ready now through 1994. $18 (5/31/92) **83**
Chardonnay Sonoma Valley Sangiacomo 1989: A flawed wine, with sulfur and sauerkraut aromas, earthy flavors and a dirty-tasting finish. Tasted twice. $18 (7/15/91) **65**
Chardonnay Sonoma Valley Sangiacomo 1988: Heavy toast and earthy flavors dominate the aroma, but on the palate the ripe lemon and pear-scented Chardonnay flavor shows through. Will appeal more to those who prefer the heavy toast flavors. Drink now to 1993. Tasted twice. $18 (2/28/90) **80**
Chardonnay Sonoma Valley Sangiacomo 1987 $15 (7/15/89) **87**
Chardonnay Sonoma Valley Sangiacomo 1986 $15 (3/15/88) **71**
Chardonnay Sonoma Valley Sangiacomo 1985 $15 (3/31/87) **91**

RAYMOND
Chardonnay California Selection 1990: Crisp, clean and simple, with citrus, pear, grapefruit and rose petal flavors. An easy-drinking wine, with an herbal edge. Drink now. $11.50 (11/15/91) **83**
Chardonnay California Selection 1989: Very fruity and straightforward, with peach, fig and spice flavors and a nicely tart structure. $11.50 (2/28/91) **83**
Chardonnay California Selection 1988: Ripe, rich and oaky, with layers of peach, vanilla, nutmeg and a touch of honey on the finish. It's full-bodied and complex. Drink now. $11 (10/31/89) **82**
Chardonnay California Selection 1987 $9 (12/31/88) **84**
Chardonnay California Selection 1986 $8.50 (11/15/87) **82**
Chardonnay California Selection 1985 $8.50 (2/28/87) **83**
Chardonnay California Selection 1984 $8.50 (3/01/86) **93**
Chardonnay California Selection 1983 $8.50 (12/01/84) **82**
Chardonnay Napa Valley 1990: Firm and straightforward, with ample pear flavors, vanilla accents and a good finish, but it lacks extra dimension. Enjoyable to drink now. $13.50 (5/31/92) **82**
Chardonnay Napa Valley 1989: Light and lean, with pleasant pear and apple aromas and flavors that hint at lemon on the finish. Drinkable now. Tasted twice. Rel: $15 Cur: $17 (7/15/91) **80**

Chardonnay Napa Valley 1988: A big, rich, smooth and supple wine, with pretty pear, apple, nutmeg and vanilla flavors that graciously unfold and stay with you from start to finish. Drink now. $15 (6/15/90) **85**
Chardonnay Napa Valley 1987 $13 (12/31/88) **85**
Chardonnay Napa Valley 1986 Rel: $13 Cur: $19 (2/15/88) **80**
Chardonnay Napa Valley 1985 $12 (9/15/87) **92**
Chardonnay Napa Valley 1983 $12 (11/01/85) **94**
Chardonnay Napa Valley 1982 Rel: $13 Cur: $15 (5/16/84) **83**
Chardonnay Napa Valley Private Reserve 1990: This well-balanced wine has ample pear and fig flavors supported by good acidity. Oak and spice notes come out on the finish. Good to drink now, but may improve through 1993. $18 (5/31/92) **87**
Chardonnay Napa Valley Private Reserve 1989: A rich, full-blown style, with layers of fig, toast, melon and citrus flavors all tightly packaged together. Concentrated and complex, with a long, rich, fruity aftertaste. Drink now to 1994. 2,500 cases made. $18 (3/31/92) **89**
Chardonnay Napa Valley Private Reserve 1988: Attractive for its spicy richness and band of pear, pineapple and apricot flavors, balanced with spicy oak notes on the aftertaste. The texture is smooth and the flavors run deep and rich. Drink now to 1993. Tasted twice. $22 (7/15/91) **85**
Chardonnay Napa Valley Private Reserve 1987 Rel: $22 Cur: $24 (5/15/90) **90**
Chardonnay Napa Valley Private Reserve 1986 Rel: $18 Cur: $21 (CH-5/90) **87**
Chardonnay Napa Valley Private Reserve 1985 Rel: $18 Cur: $21 (CH-5/90) **91**
Chardonnay Napa Valley Private Reserve 1984 $16 (7/15/87) **86**
Chardonnay Napa Valley Private Reserve 1983 $16 (9/15/86) **73**
Chardonnay Napa Valley Private Reserve 1981 Rel: $15 Cur: $25 (CH-6/90) **70**

REVERE
Chardonnay Napa Valley 1989: Lean and earthy, with a coarse texture, but fruity enough to feature nice apple and honey flavors on the finish. Tasted twice. 672 cases made. $13 (7/15/91) **79**
Chardonnay Napa Valley 1988: Fairly dry and oaky, but with enough fruit concentration to stand up to it. The pear, lemon and spicy oak flavors are austere and could use a little more drama, but they're well integrated. Drink now to 1993. 2,100 cases made. Rel: $14 Cur: $22 (2/28/91) **84**
Chardonnay Napa Valley 1987: Smells oaky and earthy and tastes rough and astringent, with the woody flavors outweighing the modest fruit component. Not for everybody. Rel: $14 Cur: $22 (9/15/90) **76**
Chardonnay Napa Valley 1986 $15 (CH-4/90) **85**
Chardonnay Napa Valley 1985 Rel: $15 Cur: $20 (CH-4/90) **85**
Chardonnay Napa Valley Berlenbach Vineyards 1989: Tight and sharply focused, with a lean texture and bright intensity of lemon, smoke, flinty mineral and pear aromas and flavors. Has elegance and length, but needs cellaring until 1994 to develop more depth. 300 cases made. $15 (7/15/91) **89**
Chardonnay Napa Valley Reserve 1989: Light and spicy, with some smoke and pear aromas, turning lemony and earthy on the palate. Has some flavor interest, but not a lot of intensity. Tasted twice. 250 cases made. $18 (7/15/91) **77**
Chardonnay Napa Valley Reserve 1988: Layers of smoke, vanilla, spice and pear flavors build up and linger on the finish of this toasty, complex, but very young wine that will need until 1995 to loosen up and show its best flavors. Tastes like it will be very elegant when it matures. 2,000 cases made. Rel: $18 Cur: $26 (5/15/91) **93**
Chardonnay Napa Valley Reserve 1987: Good and flavorful, with butter, lemon and smoke accents, but the acidity and oakiness make it a bit coarse. Drink now. $25 (9/15/90) **81**
Chardonnay Napa Valley Reserve 1986 Rel: $22 Cur: $30 (CH-4/90) **87**

RIDGE
Chardonnay Howell Mountain 1990: Ripe and rich, with generous pear and honey aromas and flavors shaded by a touch of bitterness. The oak definitely comes through on the finish. Drinkable now, but better in 1993. 2,415 cases made. $12 (3/15/92) **85**
Chardonnay Howell Mountain 1989: Has flavor but it's mostly oak, with round, broad, soft melon, pear and apple notes. Simple but drinkable. Tasted three times. $14 (7/15/91) **81**
Chardonnay Howell Mountain 1988: An earthy style, with fresh pear, melon, spice and toast notes that are well focused and linger on the finish. The fruit could be a little brighter. Drink now. $14 (7/15/91) **85**
Chardonnay Howell Mountain 1987 $14 (4/30/89) **87**
Chardonnay Santa Cruz Mountains 1989: Offers good intensity of fruit, with tiers of honey, pear, melon and apple flavors, but they thin out toward the finish and, like most '89s, get a bit watery. Still, a nice use of toasty oak. Drink now to 1994. $14 (7/15/91) **84**
Chardonnay Santa Cruz Mountains 1988: Ripe and full-bodied, with a lush, polished texture and lively pear, spice, vanilla and citrus notes that are complex and elegant. Crisp acidity sustains the flavors. Balanced and ready to drink now through 1994. $14 (7/15/91) **89**

RITCHIE CREEK
Chardonnay Napa Valley 1989: Soft and complex, with flashing hints of grapefruit, pear, toast and butter weaving in and out before settling on vanilla and toast on the long finish. Polished, elegant and drinkable now, but could continue to improve through 1994. 725 cases made. $15 (7/15/91) **88**

RIVER OAKS
Chardonnay Alexander Valley 1984 $6 (4/01/85) **79**
Chardonnay Sonoma County 1985 $6 (4/16/86) **77**

RIVERSIDE FARM
Chardonnay California 1991: Fresh, creamy, balanced and flavorful, with tasty pear, citrus and apple notes. Priced right. Drink now. $7 (7/15/92) BB **82**
Chardonnay California 1989: Light, pleasant and crisp, with slightly sweet, fruity, floral flavors. Not much like typical Chardonnay, but enjoyable in a simple way. $6.75 (12/31/90) **79**

ROCHE
Chardonnay Carneros 1990: Ripe pear, melon and spice flavors are rich and creamy, picking up a touch of smoke and vanilla on the aftertaste. Gets more complex with each sip. 3,022 cases made. $13 (3/15/92) **89**
Chardonnay Carneros 1989: This soft, velvety wine has herbal, buttery flavors, but only modest fruit character to fill it out. $13 (3/31/91) **81**
Chardonnay Carneros 1988 $11 (10/31/89) **90**

Key to Symbols

The scores reported here are the results of blind tastings conducted by our panel of senior editors. Wines that carry the initials below are results of individual tastings.

THE WINE SPECTATOR 100-POINT SCALE ***95-100***—Classic, a great wine; ***90-94***—Outstanding, superior character and style; ***80-89***—Good to very good, a wine with special qualities; ***70-79***—Average, drinkable wine that may have minor flaws; ***60-69***—Below average, drinkable but not recommended; ***50-59***—Poor, undrinkable, not recommended. "+"—With a score indicates a range; used primarily with barrel tastings to indicate a preliminary score.

SPECIAL DESIGNATIONS SS—Spectator Selection, CS—Cellar Selection, BB—Best Buy, ($NA)—Price not available, (NR)—Not released.

TASTER'S INITIALS (JG)—Jim Gordon, (HS)—Harvey Steiman, (JL)—James Laube, (JS)—James Suckling, (TM)—Thomas Matthews, (TR)—Terry Robards, (PM)—Per-Henrik Mansson, (BT)—Barrel Tasting (these wines were tasted blind from barrel samples), (CA-date)—*California's Great Cabernets* by James Laube, (CH-date)—*California's Great Chardonnays* by James Laube, (VP-date)—*Vintage Port* by James Suckling.

DATE TASTED Dates in parentheses represent the issue in which the rating was published.

ROCHIOLI
Chardonnay Russian River Valley 1990: Rich, fresh and spicy, with lots of nutmeg-scented pear and cream aromas and flavors that extend into a solid finish. Has plenty of oomph; should improve through 1993 or '94. 1,600 cases made. $15 (6/30/92) **90**
Chardonnay Russian River Valley 1989: A smooth, elegant style, with subtle pear, melon, apple and creamy oak flavors. Balanced toward the lighter side. Drink now to 1993. 2,200 cases made. $14 (12/15/91) **85**
Chardonnay Russian River Valley 1988: Hard and tart, a zesty wine with plenty of crisp grapefruit and nutmeg aromas and flavors. So assertive it seems to crave rich foods so it can cut right through. Drink now to 1993. 1,300 cases made. $15 (4/15/90) **81**
Chardonnay Russian River Valley 1987 $14 (5/31/89) **83**
Chardonnay Russian River Valley 1986 $12 (1/31/88) **72**
Chardonnay Russian River Valley J. Rochioli Reserve 1990: An impressive effort. Tight and firmly flavorful, with classic green apple, pear and nutmeg aromas and flavors that extend into a lingering finish. A medium-weight wine that's packed with flavor. Drinkable now, but probably better in 1993 or '94. 100 cases made. $24 (6/30/92) **91**

ROMBAUER
Chardonnay Napa Valley 1989: Crisp and clean, with elegant pear, spice and oak flavors that are refreshing and balanced. Ready to drink now. Better than a bottle tasted earlier. 3,819 cases made. $14 (3/15/92) **84**
Chardonnay Napa Valley 1988: Very tight and concentrated, with focused orange, honey and nutmeg notes that linger through the long aftertaste. Only needs cellar time to open it up. Try in 1993. $15 (12/31/90) **86**
Chardonnay Napa Valley 1987: This wine has a concentrated style with generous pear and spice flavors that are elegant, and a long, full finish that picks up a nice trace of oak. Drink now. Rel: $14.50 Cur: $17 (1/31/90) **88**
Chardonnay Napa Valley 1986 Rel: $14.50 Cur: $17 (CH-6/90) **85**
Chardonnay Napa Valley 1985 Rel: $14.50 Cur: $18 (CH-6/90) **84**
Chardonnay Napa Valley 1984 Rel: $14.50 Cur: $20 (CH-6/90) **78**
Chardonnay Napa Valley 1983 Rel: $14.50 Cur: $25 (CH-7/90) **87**
Chardonnay Napa Valley 1982 Rel: $14.50 Cur: $25 (CH-6/90) **84**
Chardonnay Napa Valley French Vineyard 1984 $13.50 (4/01/86) **71**
Chardonnay Napa Valley Private Reserve 1988: Exotic pineapple and tropical fruit flavors are framed by spicy, toasty oak notes. For all its showy flavors, it manages to remain elegant and refined. Drink now to 1994. 250 cases made. $20 (12/31/91) **85**
Chardonnay Napa Valley Reserve 1988 $20 (CH-6/90) **89**
Chardonnay Napa Valley Reserve 1987 $25 (CH-6/90) **87**
Chardonnay Napa Valley Reserve 1986 $24 (CH-6/90) **86**

ROUDON-SMITH
Chardonnay Mendocino Nelson Ranch 1986 $12 (9/15/88) **85**
Chardonnay Santa Cruz Mountains 1985: Lean and reticent, with some appealing mature Chardonnay flavors, but not much showing in the way of aromas. $15 (3/31/89) **70**

ROUND HILL
Chardonnay California 1990: Citrus and lemon flavors make for a tart, tight wine. Clean and well-balanced. A good white wine to have with tonight's dinner. $6 (2/29/92) BB **82**
Chardonnay California 1988: Lean, fresh and lively, with unpolished grapefruit and herbal aromas and flavors, a crisp texture and a touch of earthiness on the finish. Drinkable now. $7.50 (2/28/91) BB **81**
Chardonnay California House 1989: Ripe and fruity, with a touch of pear, citrus, grapefruit and apple notes that hang together. An easy-drinking style that's a sound value for everyday wine. Drink now. $6.50 (7/15/91) BB **83**
Chardonnay California House 1988: Fresh, clean and lively, with ripe pear, melon and apple flavors, this is one to drink now while the fruit is still crisp and fresh. Easy on the pocketbook too. $5.50 (4/15/90) BB **83**
Chardonnay California House 1987 $6.25 (11/15/88) **79**
Chardonnay California House 1986 $5.25 (11/30/87) BB **83**
Chardonnay California House 1985 $5 (9/30/86) BB **81**
Chardonnay California House 1984 $4.75 (4/16/86) **79**
Chardonnay Napa Valley 1989: Ripe, clean, crisp and fruity, with pear, citrus and melon flavors and subtle oak shadings. Has good concentration for an '89. Spicy fruit emerges on the lingering finish. Drink now to 1993. 4,843 cases made. $9 (6/30/91) **84**
Chardonnay Napa Valley Reserve 1990: Solid and youthful, with generous peach, apricot and pear flavors, edging toward nutmeg and toast on the finish. Needs until 1993 or '94 to come into focus. 1,956 cases made. $11 (7/15/92) **85**
Chardonnay Napa Valley Reserve 1989: Packed with ripe, rich pineapple, spice, apple and vanilla notes that are concentrated and elegant. The persistent flavors carry through on the finish. Drink now to 1994. 2,260 cases made. $11 (6/15/91) **89**
Chardonnay Napa Valley Reserve 1988: Bright, fruity and supple in texture, with unusual floral aromas, clean fruit flavors, good balance and a spicy finish. Light and interesting, but an atypical Chardonnay. 2,000 cases made. $11 (2/28/91) **82**
Chardonnay Napa Valley Reserve 1986 $9.50 (5/31/88) **75**
Chardonnay Napa Valley Reserve 1985 $9.50 (11/15/87) **82**
Chardonnay Napa Valley Van Asperen Reserve 1986 $11 (5/31/88) **72**
Chardonnay Napa Valley Reserve Van Asperen Selection 1990: Young, tight and stiff, especially for an '89, but a pretty beam of elegant pear, spice, nutmeg and vanilla flavors stays with you on the palate. The finish is long and complex. Drink now. 445 cases made. $12 (7/15/92) **89**
Chardonnay Napa Valley Van Asperen Vineyard 1988: Austere and toasty, with aromas and flavors more reminiscent of sulfur dioxide than fruit. Finishes earthy and very tart. Tasted twice. 700 cases made. $11 (2/28/91) **74**
Chardonnay Napa Valley Van Asperen Vineyard 1987: Long on oaky flavors with just a touch of fruit underneath. Smooth, buttery texture and clean aromas, but nothing to get excited about. $11 (7/15/89) **74**
Chardonnay North Coast 1986 $6.75 (12/15/87) **78**

RUTHERFORD ESTATE
Chardonnay Napa Valley 1990: Ripe and flavorful, with creamy pear, vanilla and apple flavors. A nice value. Drink now. $8 (7/15/92) BB **81**
Chardonnay Napa Valley 1989: Pleasant if simple pear, apple and citrus notes don't strive for complexity, but provide enough fruit interest for casual sipping. May remind you more of Chenin Blanc than Chardonnay. Drink now. $8.50 (7/15/91) **77**
Chardonnay Napa Valley 1985 $5 (11/15/87) **70**

RUTHERFORD HILL
Chardonnay Napa Valley Cellar Reserve 1987: A tempting example of a mature Chardonnay, this is ripe, rich and golden, offering a lovely balance of pineapple, honey, almond and butter flavors, all of which echo on the long, generous finish. Drinkable now. 3,000 cases made. $18 (2/15/91) **90**
Chardonnay Napa Valley Cellar Reserve 1986: A mature wine, with honey, spice and citrus notes that offer complexity and depth, good balance and plenty of flavor on the aftertaste. Ready to drink now. $18 (5/31/90) **87**
Chardonnay Napa Valley Cellar Reserve 1985 $15 (5/31/88) **87**
Chardonnay Napa Valley Jaeger Vineyards 1988: Has appealing grapefruit and pineapple aromas and flavors and a crisp texture that broadens and softens on the finish. Not very long-lasting, but the flavors are nice. Drinkable now. $13 (2/15/91) **83**
Chardonnay Napa Valley Jaeger Vineyards 1986 $12 (12/31/88) **87**

Chardonnay Napa Valley Jaeger Vineyards 1985 $11 (5/31/88) **80**
Chardonnay Napa Valley Jaeger Vineyards 1983 $10.75 (5/16/85) **77**
Chardonnay Napa Valley Jaeger Vineyards Cellar Reserve 1981 $14 (3/16/86) **89**
Chardonnay Napa Valley Partners Chardonnay 1984 $7 (4/16/86) **57**
Chardonnay Napa Valley Rutherford Knoll Special Cuvée 1987: Fresh and enticing, with various flavors such as pear, honey and green apple nicely interwoven in a pretty package. A fairly elegant and complex wine that brings you back for another sip. $11 (4/30/89) **86**
Chardonnay Napa Valley Rutherford Knoll Special Cuvée 1986 $11 (1/31/88) **83**
Chardonnay Napa Valley XVS 1988: Ripe and generous, with lots of pear, honey and vanilla aromas and flavors and a touch of mineral around the edge. Has a rich texture and a graceful structure. Drinkable now. 2,500 cases made. $18 (7/15/91) **87**

RUTHERFORD RANCH
Chardonnay Napa Valley 1987: An earthy style, with lively lemon and apple aromas and flavors to balance the herbal, wet-earth aromas and flavors. Pleasant and immediately likable. Drink soon. $11 (5/15/90) **83**
Chardonnay Napa Valley Reese Vineyard 1985 $10 (11/15/87) **72**

SADDLEBACK
Chardonnay Napa Valley 1990: Shows plenty of ripe fruit flavors, but it's disjointed, with earthy, milky notes. Finishes sour and simple; an unappealing wine. $12 (7/15/92) **72**

ST. ANDREW'S VINEYARD
Chardonnay Napa Valley 1989: Smooth and generous, with a clear, herbal, grassy edge to the subtle pear and peach flavors. A pleasant, harmonious wine that has plenty of room to grow. Best after 1993. Significantly better than a bottle tasted earlier. $14 (9/15/91) **87**
Chardonnay Napa Valley 1988: Smooth and creamy, with lots of butter, butterscotch, pear and vanilla flavors that are delicate and elegant, finishing with complexity and finesse. Well proportioned. Drink now to 1994. $13 (12/31/90) **89**
Chardonnay Napa Valley 1987: Smooth and full-bodied, with a controlled earthiness that adds depth to the pear and lemon flavors, this wine is distinctive for its flavors and silky texture. Drink now. 3,000 cases made. $14 (1/31/90) **85**
Chardonnay Napa Valley 1986 $13 (4/30/88) **90**
Chardonnay Napa Valley 1985 $13 (6/30/87) **87**
Chardonnay Napa Valley 1984 $13 (1/01/86) **92**
Chardonnay Napa Valley 1982 $12.50 (10/01/84) **89**
Chardonnay Napa Valley Limited Bottling 1989: An earthy style that doesn't show much fruit and turns papery on the finish. You get a faint hint of pear and spice flavors, but not much more. Tasted twice, with consistent notes. 200 cases made. $17 (7/15/92) **77**

ST. ANDREW'S WINERY
Chardonnay Napa Valley 1990: Ripe and appealing, with attractive pear, spice, apple and melon notes. A simple but pleasing wine to drink now. Significantly better than when reviewed earlier.. $10 (2/15/92) **83**
Chardonnay Napa Valley 1989: Tart and earthy, with a strong core of apple and lemon aromas and flavors, echoing earth and spice on the finish. Simple in the end. Drink soon. Tasted twice. $10 (7/15/91) **80**
Chardonnay Napa Valley 1988: Attractive, with plenty of ripe apple, pear and melon flavors and just the right amount of toasty oak to add dimension and depth. Well balanced and easy to drink now to 1993. $10.50 (4/15/90) **84**
Chardonnay Napa Valley 1987 $6.50 (7/15/88) **80**
Chardonnay Napa Valley 1986 $8 (8/31/87) **80**
Chardonnay Napa Valley 1985 $7.50 (11/30/86) SS **93**
Chardonnay Napa Valley 1984 $7 (2/01/86) BB **91**
Chardonnay Napa Valley House 1982 $7 (10/16/84) **79**

ST. CLEMENT
Chardonnay Carneros Abbott's Vineyard 1989: Not a typical Chardonnay, but has charming fruit and floral flavors and good balance. Almond, apple and honey nuances give it complexity, if not great depth. Drink now. Tasted twice. 971 cases made. $18 (2/28/91) **85**
Chardonnay Carneros Abbott's Vineyard 1987: Rich, ripe and full-bodied, with plenty of buttery pear, spice and honey notes that are complex. The structure is firm and well balanced, finishing with good length and a pretty aftertaste. 519 cases made. $17 (10/31/89) **89**
Chardonnay Napa Valley 1990: Tight and sharply focused, with tiers of honey, pear, spice and citrus flavors. Very compact and crisp. Should be more voluptuous starting in 1993. Rel: $16 Cur: $18 (1/31/92) **90**
Chardonnay Napa Valley 1989: Bright, firm and focused, with lots of nutmeg-scented pear and pineapple aromas and flavors. Lively and tightly wound in structure, hinting at honey and spice on the finish. It has all it needs to develop with cellaring until 1993 or '94. 4,113 cases made. $16 (5/31/91) SS **90**
Chardonnay Napa Valley 1988: Starts out with generous pear, apple and citrus aromas and flavors, turning a bit more reserved and subtle as the flavors develop on the palate. Fresh and focused through the long finish. 3,683 cases made. $15 (6/15/90) **88**
Chardonnay Napa Valley 1987 $15 (CH-3/90) **86**
Chardonnay Napa Valley 1986 Rel: $15 Cur: $18 (CH-3/90) **89**
Chardonnay Napa Valley 1985 Rel: $14.50 Cur: $18 (CH-3/90) **85**
Chardonnay Napa Valley 1984 Rel: $14.50 Cur: $18 (CH-3/90) **88**
Chardonnay Napa Valley 1983 Rel: $14.50 Cur: $18 (CH-3/90) **76**
Chardonnay Napa Valley 1982 Rel: $14.50 Cur: $20 (CH-3/90) **73**
Chardonnay Napa Valley 1981 Rel: $13.50 Cur: $25 (CH-3/90) **75**
Chardonnay Napa Valley 1980 Rel: $12 Cur: $35 (CH-3/90) **83**
Chardonnay Napa Valley 1979 Rel: $12 Cur: $27 (CH-3/90) **93**

ST. FRANCIS
Chardonnay California 1989: The simple peach flavors turn sour. Decent but uninspired. $10 (7/15/91) **70**
Chardonnay California 1988: Delicious, with rich, ripe, forward pear and peach-tinged flavors. Full-bodied and well balanced. Finish is fruity and simple. Drink now. $10 (3/31/90) **82**
Chardonnay California 1987 $9.50 (10/15/88) **79**
Chardonnay California 1986 $9 (11/15/87) **83**
Chardonnay Sonoma County 1990: Ripe, smooth and creamy, with tasty pear, buttery oak and vanilla notes that are elegant and complex. The flavors build on the finish. A tremendous value. Ready now through 1994. $10 (1/31/92) SS **89**
Chardonnay Sonoma Valley 1983 $10.75 (12/01/84) **89**
Chardonnay Sonoma Valley Barrel Select 1989: A pleasant wine, with fresh pear, spice, vanilla and subtle toast notes that are elegant and lingering. Drink now to 1993. $15 (7/15/91) **84**
Chardonnay Sonoma Valley Barrel Select 1988: Marked by floral and spicy oak flavors that tend to dominate the ripe pineapple and spice notes. More attractiave on the finish. Drink now. $15 (11/30/89) **79**
Chardonnay Sonoma Valley Barrel Select 1987 $14.50 (12/31/88) **82**
Chardonnay Sonoma Valley Barrel Select 1986 $12.50 (7/15/88) **91**
Chardonnay Sonoma Valley Barrel Select 1984 $12 (10/31/86) **69**
Chardonnay Sonoma Valley Poverello 1984 $6.75 (3/16/86) **75**

SAINT GREGORY
Chardonnay Mendocino 1990: Ripe, intense and exotic, with lush pear, pineapple and citrus flavors kept alive by a crisp beam of acidity. Drink now to 1994. 1,000 cases made. $14 (7/15/92) **84**
Chardonnay Mendocino 1989: A solid, well-made wine that improves as you sip. Has lots of grapefruit and pineapple flavors on a firm structure of alcohol and acidity. Buttery notes linger on the finish. 800 cases made. $15 (7/15/91) **87**

ST. SUPERY
Chardonnay Napa Valley Dollarhide Ranch 1990: Crisp, bordering on tart, but loaded with focused peach, apple and vanilla aromas and flavors that extend into a long finish. A solid wine that needs to pick up subtlety with cellaring until 1993 or '94. $13 (4/30/92) **86**
Chardonnay Napa Valley 1989: Very straightforward, fruity and hard-edged, with flavors of lemon, apple and papaya. A crisp, firm white wine that lacks the complexity we look for in Chardonnay. $12 (3/31/91) **81**
Chardonnay Napa Valley St.-Supery Vineyards 1988: A fruitbowl of flavors—fresh, crisp, ripe pear, pineapple and cherry—that while attractive for its fruitiness comes across as simple. $11 (11/15/89) **83**

SAINTSBURY
Chardonnay Carneros 1990: Smooth and silky, offering generous apple, pear and nutmeg aromas and flavors and echoing fruit and spice on the long finish. A beautifully balanced, attractively flavored wine that appeals to us for early drinking, but should be fine through 1994 or '95. Rel: $15 Cur: $17 (12/31/91) SS **90**
Chardonnay Carneros 1989: Has earthy, toasty, buttery aromas, with mint, honey, pear and pineapple notes emerging on the finish. A complex, concentrated wine that's drinkable now. $14 (11/15/90) **91**
Chardonnay Carneros 1988: Pretty honey, toast and butterscotch flavors are rich, full and complex. It has plenty of ripe buttery fruit flavors that are well balanced, and finishes with a spicy fruity aftertaste. Drink now to 1993. Rel: $14 Cur: $16 (3/15/90) **90**
Chardonnay Carneros 1987 Rel: $13 Cur: $18 (CH-2/90) **90**
Chardonnay Carneros 1986 Rel: $12 Cur: $19 (CH-2/90) **88**
Chardonnay Carneros 1985 Rel: $11 Cur: $19 (CH-2/90) **90**
Chardonnay Carneros 1984 Rel: $11 Cur: $25 (CH-2/90) **92**
Chardonnay Carneros 1983 Rel: $11 Cur: $20 (CH-2/90) **80**
Chardonnay Sonoma County 1982 Rel: $11 Cur: $14 (11/30/87) (JL) **86**
Chardonnay Sonoma County 1981 Rel: $10 Cur: $25 (CH-2/90) **87**
Chardonnay Carneros Reserve 1990: Feels like a wine that hasn't come together yet, offering pleasant peach and apple flavors, but seems candied and minty, as well, hinting at sweetness on the finish. May be better in 1993 or '94. 2,400 cases made. $25 (7/15/92) **80**
Chardonnay Carneros Reserve 1988: Incredibly rich, opulent and exotic, graced with tiers of rich, buttery, spicy pear and pineapple flavors that border on being overblown, but then there's a trace of elegance on the finish when the flavors come through. Drink now to 1993. 1,900 cases made. Rel: $20 Cur: $22 (5/31/90) **92**
Chardonnay Carneros Reserve 1988 Rel: $20 Cur: $22 (CH-2/90) **92**
Chardonnay Carneros Reserve 1987 Rel: $20 Cur: $22 (CH-2/90) **89**
Chardonnay Carneros Reserve 1986 Rel: $20 Cur: $25 (CH-2/90) **84**

SANFORD
Chardonnay Santa Barbara County 1990: A deep golden color and honey and spice aromas characterize this seemingly sweet, apricot-scented wine. Strange, but pleasant to drink. Better get to it soon. Tasted twice, with consistent notes. $16.50 (3/15/92) **78**
Chardonnay Santa Barbara County 1989: Intense, rich and full-bodied, with pretty flavors of spice, orange, pear, vanilla and nutmeg. Balanced, with a fruity finish that lingers. An attractive, full-blown style to drink now. Rel: $16 Cur: $18 (4/30/91) **87**
Chardonnay Santa Barbara County 1988: Smooth and complex, with layers of ripe, rich, pear, pineapple, vanillà and honey flavors that linger on the palate. The flavors are deep and concentrated yet manage to display an air of elegance. Drink now. Rel: $16 Cur: $18 (5/15/90) **91**
Chardonnay Santa Barbara County 1987 Rel: $15 Cur: $18 (CH-2/90) **92**
Chardonnay Santa Barbara County 1986 Rel: $14 Cur: $18 (CH-2/90) **88**
Chardonnay Santa Barbara County 1985 Rel: $13.50 Cur: $20 (CH-2/90) **90**
Chardonnay Central Coast 1984 Rel: $12.50 Cur: $17 (CH-2/90) **78**
Chardonnay Central Coast 1983 Rel: $12 Cur: $17 (CH-2/90) **88**
Chardonnay Santa Maria Valley 1982 Rel: $12 Cur: $20 (CH-2/90) **68**
Chardonnay Santa Maria Valley 1981 Rel: $11 Cur: $20 (CH-2/90) **74**
Chardonnay Santa Barbara County Barrel Select 1990: Broad, ripe, rich and complex, with layers of honey, pineapple, toast and citrus flavors combining to give this complexity and depth. The finish goes on and on. Drink now to 1995. 2,400 cases made. $30 (6/30/92) **91**
Chardonnay Santa Barbara County Barrel Select 1989: Rich, spicy and creamy, packed with intense layers of delicious pear, melon, cucumber and vanilla flavors. This bold style has a smooth, lush texture and a long, lingering aftertaste. Drink now to 1993. 1,200 cases made. Rel: $28 Cur: $30 (7/15/91) **90**
Chardonnay Santa Barbara County Barrel Select 1988: A real hummer. Rich, lush and fruity without being heavy, it shows tons of fruit and a long, lingering aftertaste. Has bold, complex aromas and flavors of pineapple, butter, pear, cream and honey, full-bodied with firm acidity. 1,000 cases made. Rel: $25 Cur: $28 (8/31/90) **94**
Chardonnay Santa Barbara County Barrel Select 1987 Rel: $24 Cur: $30 (12/15/89) **91**
Chardonnay Santa Barbara County Barrel Select 1985 Rel: $20 Cur: $30 (CH-2/90) **92**

SANTA BARBARA
Chardonnay Santa Barbara County 1990: Pleasantly fruity, with simple pear, apple and vanilla notes, but it's nothing special. 3,722 cases made. $12 (6/15/92) **80**
Chardonnay Santa Barbara County 1989: Simple grapefruit and lemon flavors lack richness and depth. A simple, somewhat watery wine that may have limited appeal. Drink now. 4,824 cases made. $12 (1/31/91) **80**
Chardonnay Santa Ynez Valley 1988: An awkward wine, with apple and lemon flavors. Its crisp acidity and buttery ripeness don't mesh well. The tart aftertaste is uncharacteristic. $12 (4/15/90) **74**
Chardonnay Santa Ynez Valley 1987: Beautifully balanced and enjoyable. Has fresh lemony flavors, crisp acidity and enough ripeness and smooth texture to even it out. $10 (12/15/89) **83**
Chardonnay Santa Ynez Valley 1986 $8.50 (2/29/88) **67**
Chardonnay Santa Ynez Valley Reserve 1989: Fat, ripe and buttery, with a solid core of bright pineapple and honey aromas and flavors, all of it echoing on the long finish. Drink while it's fresh and appealing. 1,067 cases made. $18 (5/15/91) **87**
Chardonnay Santa Ynez Valley Reserve 1988: A ripe, graceful, smooth-textured wine with pear, butter and nutmeg flavors and a lingering finish. Delicious now. 730 cases made. $18 (9/30/90) **86**
Chardonnay Santa Ynez Valley Reserve 1987: A nicely oaky wine that yields buttery, toasty aromas, similar flavors and a sweet-seeming, buttery finish. Has modest pear and pineapple flavors, but the oak dominates. $16 (12/15/89) **84**
Chardonnay Santa Ynez Valley Reserve 1986 $14 (10/15/88) **84**

SANTA YNEZ VALLEY
Chardonnay Santa Barbara County 1988: Has perfumed floral and melon aromas and lush, sweet-flavored melon and spice flavors that spread out on the palate. Well-defined, fruity style that's very appealing. Drink now. $13 (2/28/90) **88**

SARAH'S
Chardonnay Central Coast Estate 1988: Perfumed fruit cocktail aromas and flavors aren't for everyone. A pleasant drink, but not especially sophisticated. Tasted twice. $45 (5/31/91) **77**
Chardonnay Monterey County Ventana Vineyard 1989: Light and fruity, starting off with hard-edged apple and lemon flavors and turning pleasantly toward caramel and honey notes that linger on the finish. Well balanced and drinkable. Tasted twice. $22 (5/31/91) **82**

SAUSAL
Chardonnay Alexander Valley 1990: Crisp, bright fruit flavors dominate this lively, flavorful wine. Really packs in the peach, apricot, honey and vanilla flavors, and a firm but silky-soft texture brings it all together on the finish. Well balanced, too. Tasted twice. 2,500 cases made. $11 (7/15/92) **84**

SBARBORO
Chardonnay Alexander Valley Gauer Ranch 1985 $10 (8/31/87) **64**

SCHUG
Chardonnay Carneros Barrel Fermented 1989: Crisp, fruity and tightly wound, with tart apple flavors and a streak of astringency. Good pear and apple flavors are at the core. Drinkable now, but should age well through 1993. 2,000 cases made. $12 (3/31/92) **80**
Chardonnay Carneros Beckstoffer Vineyard 1988: An austere, somewhat dull wine, with thin, tart lemon and barely ripe pineapple flavors. Some may find this flinty style appealing, but there's barely enough weight and vibrancy to the fruit to make it interesting. Drink now. 1,512 cases made. $15 (2/28/91) **75**
Chardonnay Carneros Beckstoffer Vineyard 1987: A heavily toasted wine that is hard and oaky, rough-hewn and lacking in charm. The oaky, woody flavors dominate the ripe pear and lemon flavors. May appeal to some more than others. $15 (5/31/90) **79**
Chardonnay Carneros Napa Valley Ahollinger Vineyard 1985 $9.75 (4/30/87) **63**

SEA RIDGE
Chardonnay Sonoma Coast Mill Station Vineyard 1989: Rich and full-bodied, but the ripe pineapple and citrus flavors taste tinny. 702 cases made. $14 (4/30/92) **76**

SEBASTIANI
Chardonnay Sonoma County 1989: A spicy, medium-weight wine, with light orange and clove flavors and astringency on the finish. Not as well balanced as it could be. $10 (7/15/91) **81**
Chardonnay Sonoma County Reserve 1990: Rich and creamy, with layers of spice, pear, vanilla and honey flavors. A very pretty wine that is complex and concentrated, yet elegant and lively on the palate. Drink now. $12 (5/31/92) **88**
Chardonnay Sonoma County Reserve 1988: Elegant and spicy, with subtle melon, pear, apple and citrus flavors that show a measure of finesse and restraint. Rich and concentrated enough to drink now, or cellar through 1994. A wine that grows on you. $15 (6/30/91) **89**
Chardonnay Sonoma County Reserve 1986 $10 (10/31/88) **79**
Chardonnay Sonoma Valley Reserve 1985 $10 (2/15/88) **74**

SEBASTIANI ESTATES
Chardonnay Sonoma County Wildwood Hill 1987: Well-defined fruit flavors, with richness and depth, emerge when the ripe pear, pineapple and lemon notes combine to give it complexity and finesse. Lots of fruit and flavor, with pretty butterscotch flavors on the finish. Drink now. 2,800 cases made. $14 (6/30/90) **90**
Chardonnay Sonoma County Wilson Ranch 1987: This wine is distinctive for its ripe apple and pear flavors and moderate depth and intensity, but the finish is rather simple. Drink now. 2,000 cases made. $14 (6/30/90) **77**
Chardonnay Sonoma Valley Clark Ranch 1987: Elegant and ripe, with pretty pear, melon and butterscotch flavors, a silky texture and decent length, but it could use a shade more intensity and concentration. Drink now. 1,500 cases made. $14 (6/30/90) **83**
Chardonnay Sonoma Valley Clark Ranch 1986 $14 (3/15/88) **88**
Chardonnay Sonoma Valley Kinneybrook 1987: A ripe and creamy wine, with decent apple, butterscotch and pear flavors. This is a correct but unexciting style that is straight and simple. Drink now. $14 (6/30/90) **80**
Chardonnay Sonoma Valley Kinneybrook 1986 $14 (3/15/88) **74**
Chardonnay Sonoma Valley Niles 1986 $17 (3/15/88) **82**

SEGHESIO
Chardonnay Mendocino-Sonoma Counties 1990: For fans who like their Chardonnay pure and simple, here's one with a spicy Muscat and citrus edge, its flavors uninterrupted by oak. Drink now. $9 (3/31/92) **80**
Chardonnay Mendocino-Sonoma Counties 1989: With intense citrus, grapefruit and spice notes and fresh, ripe fig and pear flavors, this balanced, fruity wine doesn't rely on wood for flavor. The fruit is zesty through the finish. Drink now to 1993. $9 (4/30/91) **86**
Chardonnay Sonoma County 1988: A spicy, orange-scented wine that's lively and flavorful. Has fairly ripe pear and apple flavors, a smooth texture and a fruity finish. Firmly structured. Drink now. 2,400 cases made. $12 (4/30/91) **84**
Chardonnay Sonoma County 1988: A medium-weight wine, with oaky, toasty aromas, green apple flavors and a tart finish. Average quality. $8 (6/30/90) **75**
Chardonnay Sonoma County 1987 $7 (12/31/88) **79**
Chardonnay Sonoma County Reserve 1988: A heavily oaked wine with toasty, woody flavors dominating the fruit, which is thin and bland. Of average quality. 2,400 cases made. $12 (2/28/91) **71**

SEQUOIA GROVE
Chardonnay Carneros 1989: Full-bodied and firm in structure, with tart pineapple and grapefruit flavors held tight by acidity and moderate astringency. Intense fruit on the finish indicates a wine that may develop if cellared until 1994. Rel: $14 Cur: $18 (7/15/91) **86**
Chardonnay Carneros 1988: Very intense and fruity, with concentrated orange, pineapple, spice and vanilla notes on a full-bodied frame. Long on the finish. Tasty to drink now. Rel: $14 Cur: $17 (4/30/90) **89**
Chardonnay Carneros 1987: Woody and toasty, with grapefruit dominating the flavors, turns slightly bitter, but it's also ripe and woody on the finish. Pungent and direct. Drinkable now. Tasted twice. $14 (6/15/89) **79**
Chardonnay Carneros 1986 Rel: $13 Cur: $16 (CH-5/90) **78**
Chardonnay Carneros 1985 Rel: $12 Cur: $16 (CH-5/90) **88**
Chardonnay Napa Valley Estate 1989: Fruity and fresh, with pleasant lemon, apple and pear aromas and flavors that last on the finish. Needs polish. Drink now. 2,126 cases made. $16 (7/15/91) **85**
Chardonnay Napa Valley Estate 1988: Beautifully focused pineapple, pear and lemon flavors balance jauntily against a smoky, spicy touch of oak, offering impressive structure and flavor persistence. Has great finesse, supple texture and follow through on the finish. Drink now to 1993. 4,228 cases made. $16 (4/30/90) **91**
Chardonnay Napa Valley Estate 1987 $16 (CH-5/90) **88**
Chardonnay Napa Valley Estate 1986 $15 (CH-5/90) **88**
Chardonnay Napa Valley Estate 1985 $16 (CH-5/90) **89**
Chardonnay Napa Valley Estate 1984 $14 (CH-5/90) **89**
Chardonnay Napa Valley Estate 1983 $12 (CH-5/90) **87**
Chardonnay Napa Valley Estate 1982 $12 (CH-5/90) **72**
Chardonnay Napa Valley Estate 1981 $12 (CH-7/90) **88**
Chardonnay Napa Valley Estate 1980 $10 (CH-5/90) **87**
Chardonnay Sonoma County 1982 $10.50 (11/01/84) **86**

SHADOWBROOK
Chardonnay Napa Valley 1989: Has a hard streak of acidity that runs through the apple and pear flavors, and finishes with coarseness and a bite. Drink now. $9.50 (7/15/91) **76**

SHAFER
Chardonnay Napa Valley 1990: Starts off with generous pear, apple and honey flavors that are complex, rich and flavorful. Could use a little more finesse, but keeps pumping out the flavor. Drink now to 1994. $15 (3/15/92) **87**
Chardonnay Napa Valley 1989: Soft and supple, with a moderate concentration of pear, peach and lemon flavors that are balanced and well proportioned. $15 (4/30/91) **84**
Chardonnay Napa Valley 1988: The crisp texture and light pear, vanilla and lemon aromas and flavors make for a lively wine that's easy to drink already. Very smooth and appealing. Tasted twice. $13.50 (5/31/90) **83**
Chardonnay Napa Valley 1987 $13.50 (4/15/89) **79**
Chardonnay Napa Valley 1986 $12 (7/15/88) **89**
Chardonnay Napa Valley 1985 $11.50 (1/31/88) **67**
Chardonnay Napa Valley 1984 $12 (10/31/86) **66**
Chardonnay Napa Valley 1983 $12 (9/01/85) **80**
Chardonnay Napa Valley 1982 $11 (10/01/84) **79**
Chardonnay Napa Valley 1981 $11 (3/16/84) **64**

CHARLES SHAW
Chardonnay Napa Valley 1989: Clean and well balanced, with subtle pear, melon, toast and spice flavors that gain a bitter grapefruit edge on the aftertaste. Drink now to 1993. $12 (2/15/92) **84**
Chardonnay Napa Valley 1988: Smooth and well proportioned, with clean but modest flavors of pear, citrus and spice, good balance and a lingering finish. Drink now. $11 (8/31/90) **85**
Chardonnay Napa Valley 1987 $11 (CH-5/90) **85**
Chardonnay Napa Valley 1986 $11 (CH-5/90) **85**
Chardonnay Napa Valley 1985 Rel: $12 Cur: $15 (CH-5/90) **87**
Chardonnay Napa Valley 1984 Rel: $12 Cur: $15 (CH-5/90) **82**
Chardonnay Napa Valley 1983 Rel: $12 Cur: $16 (CH-5/90) **84**

SIERRA VISTA
Chardonnay El Dorado 1989: Strives for complexity with its smoky, toasty oak overtones, but tastes a little charred around the edges, marring the creamy pear, apple and butter flavors. Fans of strong oak may like it more. Drink now. $12 (3/31/92) **80**

SIGNORELLO
Chardonnay Napa Valley 1990: Smoky and elegant, with pretty fig, vanilla and spice notes that are focused and attractive. Gains complexity and nuance on the finish, so you can drink it now or hold through 1993. Tasted twice. 950 cases made. $15 (6/30/92) **88**
Chardonnay Napa Valley 1989: Good fruit, with pretty oak shadings, adds spice to the ripe pear, apple, vanilla and spice flavors. Not too rich or concentrated, but balanced and attractive. Drink now. 1,500 cases made. $15 (7/15/91) **85**
Chardonnay Napa Valley 1988: Made in a buttery, rich style, with solid lemon and pear flavors and good balance to back it up. Interesting and fairly complex in flavor. Turns spicy and toasty on the finish. Drink now through 1993. 1,500 cases made. $14.50 (2/28/91) **87**
Chardonnay Napa Valley Founder's Reserve 1990: Pungently oaky, with wood dominating the flavor profile. Has lots of butter, vanilla and toast notes and hints of pear and apple creeping through on the finish. Drink now. Tasted twice, with consistent notes. 275 cases made. $25 (5/31/92) **82**
Chardonnay Napa Valley Founder's Reserve 1989: Lacks intensity and depth and tastes stripped, with unripe apple and pineapple flavors, although it picks up a nice honey and toast note on the aftertaste. Drinkable now, but unexciting. Tasted twice. 400 cases made. $25 (7/15/91) **78**
Chardonnay Napa Valley Founder's Reserve 1986: Toasty and slightly herbal in flavor, it has earthy, oaky aromas up-front, an oily texture and modest fruit flavors underneath that start coming out on the finish. $13 (7/15/89) **77**
Chardonnay Napa Valley Founder's Reserve 1985 $12 (2/15/88) **82**

SILVERADO
Chardonnay Napa Valley 1990: Not showing as well as previous vintages, but pleasant enough. Apple and pear notes make this modestly appealing, but the intensity level is low and it seems straightforward. Tasted twice, with consistent notes. $14.50 (4/15/92) **81**
Chardonnay Napa Valley 1989: Strives for subtlety and finesse, with ripe pear and spice notes and ample oak shadings, but the fruit is only moderately concentrated, leaving a pretty aftertaste of pear, spice and wood. Drink now to 1993. $14.50 (3/31/91) **86**
Chardonnay Napa Valley 1988: Fresh, clean and ripe, more delicate and subtle than powerful. Has pretty spice, peach and honey notes that echo on the finish. Should only get better with time. Drink now to 1993. Rel: $14 Cur: $17 (11/30/89) **88**
Chardonnay Napa Valley 1987 Rel: $13.50 Cur: $17 (CH-3/90) **88**
Chardonnay Napa Valley 1986 Rel: $12 Cur: $20 (CH-3/90) **90**
Chardonnay Napa Valley 1985 Rel: $11.50 Cur: $17 (CH-3/90) **87**
Chardonnay Napa Valley 1984 Rel: $11 Cur: $20 (CH-3/90) **81**
Chardonnay Napa Valley 1983 Rel: $11 Cur: $20 (CH-3/90) **84**
Chardonnay Napa Valley 1982 Rel: $10 Cur: $20 (CH-3/90) **73**
Chardonnay Napa Valley 1981 Rel: $10 Cur: $20 (CH-3/90) **70**
Chardonnay Napa Valley Limited Reserve 1987: Rich, deep and complex, a delicious mouthful of wine, with layers of smoky fig, pear, honey and apricot that come off intense and lively. The flavors stick with you, echoing fruit and oak. Drink now to 1995. 1,392 cases made. Rel: $30 Cur: $33 (8/31/91) **92**
Chardonnay Napa Valley Limited Reserve 1986: Has mature aromas and flavors that are distinctive and complex, surrounding a core of focused apple and herb flavors. A smooth, creamy, intense style that is reaching maturity. Hints at butter on the long, complex finish. Drinkable now. 650 cases made. Rel: $25 Cur: $35 (11/15/90) **93**

SILVERADO CELLARS
Chardonnay California 1988: Wonderfully complex concentration of fresh, ripe pear, peach, honey, vanilla and nutmeg flavors that are crisp and lively with excellent depth and richness. The flavors linger on and on. Remarkably elegant and balanced. Drink now to 1993. $11 (6/30/90) **90**

SILVERADO HILL CELLARS
Chardonnay Napa Valley 1990: Crisp and focused, with tart pear, apple, peach and spice notes that offer a nice array of fruit. Young, firm and drinkable now, but can age through 1994. A solid value. $10 (6/30/92) **86**
Chardonnay Napa Valley 1989: Light and lively, with pleasant apple and leesy aromas and flavors that persist into a crisp finish. Drinkable now. $10 (7/15/91) **82**
Chardonnay Napa Valley Winemaker's Traditional Method 1988: Tastes simple and dull, with apple, floral and earthy aromas and flavors, but little intensity or focus. Drinkable, but not exciting. $10 (7/15/91) **73**

Key to Symbols

The scores reported here are the results of blind tastings conducted by our panel of senior editors. Wines that carry the initials below are results of individual tastings.

THE WINE SPECTATOR 100-POINT SCALE 95-100—Classic, a great wine; ***90-94***—Outstanding, superior character and style; ***80-89***—Good to very good, a wine with special qualities; ***70-79***—Average, drinkable wine that may have minor flaws; ***60-69***—Below average, drinkable but not recommended; ***50-59***—Poor, undrinkable, not recommended. "+"—With a score indicates a range; used primarily with barrel tastings to indicate a preliminary score.

SPECIAL DESIGNATIONS SS—Spectator Selection, CS—Cellar Selection, BB—Best Buy, ($NA)—Price not available, (NR)—Not released.

TASTER'S INITIALS (JG)—Jim Gordon, (HS)—Harvey Steiman, (JL)—James Laube, (JS)—James Suckling, (TM)—Thomas Matthews, (TR)—Terry Robards, (PM)—Per-Henrik Mansson, (BT)—Barrel Tasting (these wines were tasted blind from barrel samples), (CA-date)—*California's Great Cabernets* by James Laube, (CH-date)—*California's Great Chardonnays* by James Laube, (VP-date)—*Vintage Port* by James Suckling.

DATE TASTED Dates in parentheses represent the issue in which the rating was published.

SIMI

Chardonnay Sonoma-Mendocino-Napa Counties 1990: Hard and tight, with firm pear and apple flavors that are a touch tannic. A hint of anise comes through on the finish, but this might be better with cellaring until 1993. $12 (7/15/92) **81**

Chardonnay Sonoma-Mendocino-Napa Counties 1989: Fresh and lively, with lots of toasty, buttery apple, pear and lemon aromas and flavors that stretch into a long finish. An appealing wine to drink now. $15.50 (5/31/91) **88**

Chardonnay Sonoma County 1988: Big, rich, smooth and creamy, with intense, crisp apple, pear, melon and spice flavors that are well structured and well defined, finishing with a touch of spice and fruit. Drink now. $16 (6/15/90) **87**

Chardonnay Sonoma-Mendocino-Napa Counties 1987 $14 (11/30/89) **91**

Chardonnay Sonoma-Mendocino-Napa Counties 1986 $12 (2/15/89) **84**

Chardonnay Sonoma-Mendocino Counties 1985 $11 (3/15/88) **89**

Chardonnay Sonoma-Mendocino Counties 1984 $13 (10/31/86) **77**

Chardonnay Sonoma-Mendocino Counties 1983 $12 (10/01/85) **87**

Chardonnay Sonoma County 1982 $11 (10/16/84) **90**

Chardonnay Mendocino County 1981 $11 (6/01/86) **86**

Chardonnay Sonoma County Reserve 1988: A fully mature, buttery, honeyed wine that's soft and elegant. Nutty pear and vanilla flavors linger on the finish. Great to drink now. 2,300 cases made. $32 (5/31/92) **89**

Chardonnay Sonoma County Reserve 1987: Smooth and fruity, with a real sense of elegance to the melon, pear and honey aromas and flavors, turning spicy and honeyed on the finish. Medium weight and drinkable now. 1,800 cases made. $32 (7/15/91) **92**

Chardonnay Sonoma County Reserve 1986: Ultrarich, complex and toasty, with layers of ripe pear, apple, lemon and nutmeg flavors that unfold on the palate in this very elegant and enticing wine. Beautifully proportioned, it picks up a pretty butterscotch note on the long and pleasing finish. Drink now or in 1993. 1,600 cases made. Rel: $28 Cur: $35 (9/15/90) **92**

Chardonnay Sonoma County Reserve 1985 Rel: $28 Cur: $32 (CH-4/90) **91**

Chardonnay Sonoma County Reserve 1984 Rel: $28 Cur: $32 (CH-4/90) **89**

Chardonnay Sonoma County Reserve 1983 Rel: $22 Cur: $32 (CH-4/90) **88**

Chardonnay Sonoma County Reserve 1982 Rel: $22 Cur: $60 (CH-4/90) **94**

Chardonnay Sonoma County Reserve 1982 Rel: $22 Cur: $60 (5/01/86) SS **96**

Chardonnay Sonoma County Reserve 1981 Rel: $20 Cur: $40 (CH-4/90) **91**

Chardonnay Sonoma County Reserve 1980 Rel: $20 Cur: $40 (CH-4/90) **94**

ROBERT SINSKEY

Chardonnay Carneros 1988: Aims for elegance, with light vanilla and spice aromas, a smooth, creamy texture and peach, mineral and almond flavors. Lively and well balanced for drinking now through 1993. 3,900 cases made. $16 (2/28/91) **87**

Chardonnay Carneros Napa Valley 1987: Smells pretty and tastes rich, smooth and elegant with fresh pineapple, guava and honey flavors that are complex and enticing. Finish is crisp and lively. A touch of lemon and Muscat-like spice add dimension. $16 (10/31/89) **88**

Chardonnay Carneros Napa Valley 1986 $16.50 (7/31/88) **75**

Chardonnay Carneros Napa Valley Selected Cuvée 1989: An earthy flavor and oaky aroma dominate the modest, tart lemon and pineapple flavors underneath. Butter and spice notes develop as you sip. A decent bet for cellaring until 1994. 1,100 cases made. $16 (7/15/91) **84**

SMITH-MADRONE

Chardonnay Napa Valley 1988 $13 (CH-5/90) **88**

Chardonnay Napa Valley 1987 $13 (CH-5/90) **91**

Chardonnay Napa Valley 1986 Rel: $12.50 Cur: $16 (CH-5/90) **89**

Chardonnay Napa Valley 1985 Rel: $12.50 Cur: $16 (CH-5/90) **87**

Chardonnay Napa Valley 1984 Rel: $12 Cur: $16 (CH-5/90) **80**

Chardonnay Napa Valley 1983 Rel: $12 Cur: $15 (CH-5/90) **71**

Chardonnay Napa Valley 1982 Rel: $12 Cur: $18 (CH-5/90) **86**

Chardonnay Napa Valley 1981 Rel: $12 Cur: $18 (CH-5/90) **81**

Chardonnay Napa Valley 1980 Rel: $11 Cur: $20 (CH-5/90) **85**

Chardonnay Napa Valley 1979 Rel: $10 Cur: $28 (CH-5/90) **92**

Chardonnay Napa Valley 1978 Rel: $10 Cur: $30 (CH-5/90) **86**

SODA CANYON

Chardonnay Napa Valley 12th Leaf 1990: Tight and focused, with graceful, harmonious flavors, hints of honey, pear, spice and oak. Young and unevolved now. May be better by 1993 or '94. $10 (3/31/92) **88**

Chardonnay Napa Valley 8th Leaf 1986 $11 (10/15/88) **78**

SOLIS

Chardonnay Santa Clara County 1989: Unusual in flavor and style, with a strong juniper and citrus character that strays from the mainstream Chardonnay flavors. Drinkable now, but not too exciting. 500 cases made. $12.50 (7/15/91) **76**

SONOMA CREEK

Chardonnay Carneros Barrel Fermented 1989: Fresh, round and flavorful, with a nice tension between the citrus and pear flavors and the vanilla notes from oak, right through the long, generous finish. Tasty and drinkable now. $10 (11/30/91) **89**

SONOMA-CUTRER

Chardonnay Sonoma Coast Cutrer Vineyard 1990: Tart, tight and flinty, with crisp citrus, grapefruit and tangy pear flavors and subtle oak shadings. Long and complex. A young, unevolved wine that will benefit from cellaring. Drink after 1993. $18 (5/31/92) **87**

Chardonnay Sonoma Coast Cutrer Vineyard 1988: Tart and zingy, with tightly coiled apple and pear flavors on a firm framework of lively acidity. Earthy, toasty flavors linger on the finish, and the mouthwatering acidity keeps you coming back for another sip. Try now or in 1993. Rel: $17.50 Cur: $20 (12/31/90) **89**

Chardonnay Russian River Valley Cutrer Vineyard 1987 Rel: $17.50 Cur: $24 (CH-3/90) **91**

Chardonnay Russian River Valley Cutrer Vineyard 1986 Rel: $16 Cur: $24 (CH-3/90) **89**

Chardonnay Russian River Valley Cutrer Vineyard 1985 Rel: $14.75 Cur: $29 (CH-3/90) **87**

Chardonnay Russian River Valley Cutrer Vineyard 1984 Rel: $14.25 Cur: $25 (CH-3/90) **87**

Chardonnay Russian River Valley Cutrer Vineyard 1983 Rel: $13.75 Cur: $25 (CH-3/90) **86**

Chardonnay Russian River Valley Cutrer Vineyard 1982 Rel: $13 Cur: $25 (CH-3/90) **87**

Chardonnay Russian River Valley Cutrer Vineyard 1981 Rel: $12.50 Cur: $30 (CH-3/90) **91**

Chardonnay Sonoma Coast Les Pierres 1989: Complex and lively, with creamy pear, peach, vanilla and butterscotch flavors and a solid dose of oak. Altogether it's balanced and creamy, with good depth and a pretty follow through. Drink now or in 1993. $23 (1/31/91) **86**

Chardonnay Sonoma Valley Les Pierres 1988 Rel: $22.50 Cur: $25 (CH-7/90) **93**

Chardonnay Sonoma Valley Les Pierres 1987 Rel: $22.50 Cur: $27 (CH-3/90) **92**

Chardonnay Sonoma Valley Les Pierres 1986 Rel: $19.50 Cur: $34 (CH-3/90) **88**

Chardonnay Sonoma Valley Les Pierres 1985 Rel: $17.50 Cur: $47 (9/30/87) SS **93**

Chardonnay Sonoma Valley Les Pierres 1984 Rel: $16.50 Cur: $75 (CH-3/90) **89**

Chardonnay Sonoma Valley Les Pierres 1983 Rel: $15.50 Cur: $50 (CH-3/90) **86**

Chardonnay Sonoma Valley Les Pierres 1982 Rel: $15 Cur: $35 (CH-3/90) **88**

Chardonnay Sonoma Valley Les Pierres 1981 Rel: $14.50 Cur: $53 (CH-3/90) **94**

Chardonnay Sonoma Coast Russian River Ranches 1990: Tart, intense and lively, with subtle pear, peach and spice notes that are well focused. Tight and young. Drinks well now, but can benefit from cellaring through 1994. $13.50 (5/31/92) **86**

Chardonnay Sonoma Coast Russian River Ranches 1989: Fruity and generous, with ripe pear and spice flavors that are accented by butter and vanilla notes. A slightly rough texture holds it back, but it should smooth out if cellared until 1993. $14 (7/15/91) **82**

Chardonnay Russian River Valley Russian River Ranches 1988: Intense and elegant, with sharply defined, crisp pear and pineapple flavors that zip across the palate, held in check by zingy acidity and gaining complexity and subtlety on the finish. Drink now to 1994. Rel: $13.25 Cur: $20 (6/30/90) **88**

Chardonnay Russian River Valley Russian River Ranches 1987 Rel: $12 Cur: $16 (CH-3/90) **88**

Chardonnay Russian River Valley Russian River Ranches 1986 Rel: $12 Cur: $20 (CH-3/90) **86**

Chardonnay Russian River Valley Russian River Ranches 1985 Rel: $11.50 Cur: $25 (CH-3/90) **88**

Chardonnay Russian River Valley Russian River Ranches 1984 $11.25 (6/01/86) **88**

Chardonnay Russian River Valley Russian River Ranches 1983 Rel: $10.50 Cur: $25 (CH-3/90) **85**

Chardonnay Russian River Valley Russian River Ranches 1983 Rel: $10.50 Cur: $25 (11/16/85) SS **95**

Chardonnay Russian River Valley Russian River Ranches 1982 Rel: $10 Cur: $24 (CH-3/90) **87**

Chardonnay Russian River Valley Russian River Ranches 1982 Rel: $10 Cur: $24 (10/16/84) SS **92**

Chardonnay Russian River Valley Russian River Ranches 1981 Rel: $9.35 Cur: $40 (CH-3/90) **82**

SONOMA-LOEB

Chardonnay Alexander Valley 1990: Bold, ripe and creamy, with rich pear, smoke, vanilla and toast flavors that are tight and complex. The flavors fan out on the finish, echoing pear, honey and toast notes. Drink now to 1994. 1,000 cases made. $18 (2/29/92) **86**

Chardonnay Sonoma County Private Reserve 1990: Rich, smooth and complex, with tiers of lively pear, pineapple, spice and vanilla flavors that are tightly focused and full. Hints of nutmeg and honey emerge on the long, full finish. Drink now to 1994. Only 50 cases made. $27 (2/29/92) **90**

SOQUEL

Chardonnay Santa Cruz Mountains 1990: Tight and earthy, with crisp, hard-edged apple, mint and sage notes that stray from the mainstream Chardonnay flavors. Not for everyone. Drink now to 1994. Tasted twice, with consistent notes. 750 cases made. $16 (7/15/92) **74**

SPRING MOUNTAIN

Chardonnay Napa Valley 1987: Pleasant, clean and fruity, this wine offers spice, toast, pineapple and melon flavors that are soft and correct. $15 (11/15/89) **81**

Chardonnay Napa Valley 1985 $15 (11/15/87) **82**

Chardonnay Napa Valley 1984 $15 (12/31/86) **58**

STAGLIN FAMILY

Chardonnay Napa Valley 1989: A wine with delicate, ripe, well-focused fruit. The pineapple, peach, oak and butterscotch flavors offer harmony and finesse. Lightens up on the finish. Drink now to 1993. 370 cases made. $20 (1/31/92) **86**

STAG'S LEAP WINE CELLARS

Chardonnay Napa Valley 1990: Tart, clean and lively, with sharply focused pear, apple, citrus and spice flavors that hang together nicely. Concentrated and complex, with crisp acidity that sustains the flavors. Drink now to 1994. $19 (3/15/92) **89**

Chardonnay Napa Valley 1989: Crisp and refreshing, with intense, concentrated lemon, pear, honey and vanilla flavors that are young and lively. Has good depth and persistent fruit flavors that linger on and on. Has room to grow; drink now to 1994. Rel: $18 Cur: $22 (1/31/91) **88**

Chardonnay Napa Valley 1988: Lean, crisp and elegant, with layers of peach, citrus, spice and oak flavors that are nicely balanced with good length and aftertaste. Drink now or in 1993. $18 (2/15/90) **87**

Chardonnay Napa Valley 1987 Rel: $18 Cur: $25 (CH-3/90) **89**

Chardonnay Napa Valley 1986 Rel: $17 Cur: $20 (CH-3/90) **86**

Chardonnay Napa Valley 1985 Rel: $16 Cur: $25 (CH-3/90) **83**

Chardonnay Napa Valley 1984 Rel: $14 Cur: $17 (CH-6/90) **77**

Chardonnay Napa Valley 1983 Rel: $13.50 Cur: $17 (CH-3/90) **62**

Chardonnay Napa Valley 1982 Rel: $13.50 Cur: $17 (CH-3/90) **70**

Chardonnay Napa Valley 1981 Rel: $13.50 Cur: $60 (CH-3/90) **79**

Chardonnay Napa Valley 1980 Rel: $10.50 Cur: $17 (CH-3/90) **78**

Chardonnay Napa Valley 1977 Rel: $8 Cur: $17 (CH-3/90) **59**

Chardonnay Napa Valley 1976 Rel: $8 Cur: $17 (CH-3/90) **58**

Chardonnay Napa Valley Beckstoffer Ranch 1987: Rich, smooth and buttery, with pretty pear, spice, honey and oak flavors that are supple and elegant on the finish with traces of butterscotch. Drink now. $19 (9/15/89) **91**

Chardonnay Napa Valley Haynes 1979 Rel: $12.50 Cur: $20 (CH-3/90) **82**

Chardonnay Napa Valley Haynes 1978 Rel: $10 Cur: $20 (CH-3/90) **74**

Chardonnay Napa Valley Haynes 1977 Rel: $9 Cur: $20 (CH-3/90) **67**

Chardonnay Napa Valley Mirage 1982 Rel: $11.50 Cur: $18 (CH-3/90) **70**

Chardonnay Napa Valley Reserve 1990: Ripe and smooth, with generous, buttery spice and pineapple aromas and flavors that extend into a lovely, long finish. Has style, grace and delicious flavors. Tempting to drink now, but should last through 1994 or '95. 3,000 cases made. $28 (7/15/92) **90**

Chardonnay Napa Valley Reserve 1988: Rich and distinctive, with silky butterscotch, honey, pear and vanilla notes that are very full-bodied, complex and lingering. With fine balance and persistent flavors, this is a stylish wine that's broad and showy. Drink now to 1994. 335 cases made. $28 (1/31/91) **90**

Chardonnay Napa Valley Reserve 1987: A generous wine, with crisp acidity to balance the concentrated grapefruit and apple aromas and flavors, long but not quite as elegant or smooth as some. Turns spicy and refreshing on the finish. Drinkable now. $28 (5/31/90) **88**

Chardonnay Napa Valley Reserve 1986 $26 (CH-6/90) **88**

Chardonnay Napa Valley Reserve 1985 Rel: $22 Cur: $26 (CH-3/90) **85**

STAGS' LEAP WINERY

Chardonnay Napa Valley 1989: Has a crisp grapefruit, citrus and lemon flavor, but it's a bit bracing and tinny. The finish has a tangy quality. Decent but unexciting. Drink now. 4,771 cases made. $14.50 (12/15/91) **81**

STAR HILL

Chardonnay Napa Valley Barrel Fermented 1989: Soft and ungenerous, with modestly intense pear and earthy aromas and flavors, finishing simple and straightforward. Drink soon. Tasted twice. 900 cases made. $19 (7/15/91) **78**

Chardonnay Napa Valley Doc's Reserve Barrel Fermented 1988: A very spicy wine, with cinnamon and toast overtones mingling with dusky pear fruit flavors. Complex and well balanced, it has plenty of intensity without too much weight. $19 (6/30/90) **84**

STERLING

Chardonnay Napa Valley Estate 1990: Earthy, tart and tannic up-front, with crisp pear, apple and pineapple flavors that hang together well. Once you get used to the tart bite, it tastes better. Drink now to 1994. $15 (7/15/92) **84**

Chardonnay Napa Valley Estate 1989: A ripe, gentle wine that doesn't try to bowl you over with exotic flavors, but keeps sneaking in some extra nuances with every sip. Has nutmeg, vanilla and honey notes against a smooth background of pear and apple. Drinkable now. $15 (4/30/91) **88**

Chardonnay Napa Valley Estate 1988: A big, full, rich and oaky wine, with plenty of ripe, concentrated pear, spice, honey and vanilla flavors that are young and lively, finishing with a trace of nutmeg. Drink now to 1995. Rel: $13 Cur: $19 (3/15/90) **90**

Chardonnay Napa Valley Estate 1987 Rel: $14.50 Cur: $19 (4/15/89) **89**

Chardonnay Napa Valley Estate 1986 Rel: $14.50 Cur: $19 (3/15/88) **83**

Chardonnay Napa Valley Estate 1985 $14 (7/31/87) **69**

Chardonnay Napa Valley Estate 1984 $14 (6/16/86) **77**
Chardonnay Napa Valley Estate 1983 $14 (10/01/85) **86**
Chardonnay Napa Valley Estate 1982 Rel: $14 Cur: $17 (CH-4/90) **73**
Chardonnay Napa Valley Estate 1981 Rel: $14 Cur: $17 (CH-4/90) **71**
Chardonnay Napa Valley Estate 1980 Rel: $13 Cur: $17 (CH-4/90) **70**
Chardonnay Napa Valley Estate 1979 Rel: $13 Cur: $38 (CH-4/90) **73**
Chardonnay Napa Valley Estate 1977 Rel: $10 Cur: $31 (CH-4/90) **70**
Chardonnay Napa Valley Estate 1976 Rel: $5.25 Cur: $18 (CH-4/90) **59**
Chardonnay Napa Valley Estate 1974 Rel: $4.75 Cur: $35 (CH-4/90) **78**
Chardonnay Napa Valley Diamond Mountain Ranch 1988: Complex, intense and inviting, offering pretty toast and pear aromas and mature Chardonnay flavors, with hints of nutmeg, honey, pear and toast. It has benefited from cellaring and drinks well now. $16 (7/15/92) **88**
Chardonnay Napa Valley Diamond Mountain Ranch 1987: Broad in texture but laced with a tart core of lemony, flinty flavor. Almost Chablis-like in its profile because of the austere acidity, but complex and unformed on the finish. Drink now. Tasted twice. Rel: $16 Cur: $21 (2/28/91) **84**
Chardonnay Napa Valley Diamond Mountain Ranch 1986 Rel: $15 Cur: $20 (CH-4/90) **86**
Chardonnay Napa Valley Diamond Mountain Ranch 1985 Rel: $15 Cur: $17 (CH-7/90) **87**
Chardonnay Napa Valley Diamond Mountain Ranch 1984 Rel: $15 Cur: $17 (CH-4/90) **86**
Chardonnay Napa Valley Diamond Mountain Ranch 1983 Rel: $15 Cur: $18 (CH-4/90) **86**
Chardonnay Carneros Winery Lake 1989: Earthy, focused apple and mineral flavors carry through this light- to medium-weight wine, hinting at lemon and pear on the finish. Nice enough to drink now. $18 (7/15/91) **83**
Chardonnay Carneros Winery Lake 1988: Smooth and flavorful, with floral, spicy overtones to the basic core of pineapple and pear flavors, hinting at grapefruit on the long, crisp finish. Charming now, but could be better after 1993. $20 (7/15/91) **87**
Chardonnay Carneros Winery Lake 1988 $20 (CH-4/90) **90**
Chardonnay Carneros Winery Lake 1987 $20 (CH-4/90) **89**
Chardonnay Carneros Winery Lake 1986 Rel: $20 Cur: $23 (CH-4/90) **89**

STEVENOT

Chardonnay Calaveras County Grand Reserve 1989: Firm and concentrated, with good apple and citrus flavors but the luscious aromas of butterscotch and pear fade on the palate. A watery finish doesn't add much to this decent but unexciting wine. $9 (2/29/92) **78**
Chardonnay California 1990: Smooth, slightly sweet and appealing, with apple and pear flavors and a soft texture. Clean, simple and good. $7.50 (7/15/92) BB **80**
Chardonnay California 1987: Very smooth and appealing. Has citrus and pineapple aromas and modestly fruity flavors accented with butterscotch and spice and a touch of vanilla on the finish. $7.50 (6/30/89) **83**
Chardonnay California 1986 $6 (11/15/87) **79**

STONE CREEK

Chardonnay Alexander Valley 1989: Combines pretty toasty oak aromas with elegant, moderately rich pear, melon and spice notes. Hints of butterscotch and citrus make the finish long and interesting. A balanced wine to drink now. $10 (7/15/91) **86**
Chardonnay Napa Valley Special Selection 1989: Simple fruit flavors and subtle oak shadings render an elegant, slightly diluted, moderately interesting wine. Best to drink soon. $10 (7/15/91) **78**
Chardonnay North Coast 1988: A very simple, hard-edged and ungenerous wine that tastes like fruit cocktail, including a hint of the tin can. $7 (6/30/90) **68**

STONEGATE

Chardonnay Napa Valley 1988: Modest, simple and pleasant, but not particularly concentrated. Decent buttery oak and pear flavors on the finish keep it interesting. Drink now. Much better than a bottle tasted earlier. $15 (4/15/91) **83**
Chardonnay Napa Valley 1987: A good, straightforward and fairly crisp wine. The floral, peachy aromas are followed by light flavors of almond and pear, with a dry finish. Tasted three times. This was the best showing. $13 (6/30/90) **78**
Chardonnay Napa Valley 1986 $13 (12/31/88) **89**
Chardonnay Napa Valley 1982 $10 (3/01/85) **83**
Chardonnay Napa Valley Reserve 1988: Complex and elegant, with layers of intense honey, toast, pear and citrus flavors that are sharply focused and nicely shaded by oak. The finish is long and full, with hints of silkiness coming through. Drink now to 1994. 2,000 cases made. $20 (2/15/91) **90**
Chardonnay Napa Valley Spaulding Vineyard 1983 $14 (2/15/87) **86**
Chardonnay Napa Valley Spaulding Vineyard 1982 $14 (12/01/85) **53**

STONESTREET

Chardonnay Sonoma County 1990: Plush and ripe, with rich, intense, focused pear, hazelnut, honey and citrus flavors that are complex, smooth and creamy. Delicious to drink now through 1995. $20 (6/15/92) **91**

STONY HILL

Chardonnay Napa Valley 1988 Rel: $18 Cur: $82 (CH-6/90) **90**
Chardonnay Napa Valley 1987 Rel: $18 Cur: $65 (CH-5/90) **87**
Chardonnay Napa Valley 1986 Rel: $16 Cur: $64 (CH-7/90) **87**
Chardonnay Napa Valley 1985 Rel: $16 Cur: $76 (CH-5/90) **92**
Chardonnay Napa Valley 1984 Rel: $13 Cur: $75 (CH-5/90) **90**
Chardonnay Napa Valley 1983 Rel: $13 Cur: $70 (CH-5/90) **85**
Chardonnay Napa Valley 1982 Rel: $12 Cur: $65 (CH-5/90) **85**
Chardonnay Napa Valley 1981 Rel: $12 Cur: $68 (CH-5/90) **86**
Chardonnay Napa Valley 1980 Rel: $12 Cur: $75 (CH-5/90) **86**
Chardonnay Napa Valley 1979 Rel: $12 Cur: $92 (CH-5/90) **81**
Chardonnay Napa Valley 1978 Rel: $10 Cur: $100 (CH-5/90) **85**
Chardonnay Napa Valley 1977 Rel: $9 Cur: $95 (CH-6/90) **91**
Chardonnay Napa Valley 1976 Rel: $9 Cur: $105 (CH-6/90) **88**
Chardonnay Napa Valley 1975 Rel: $9 Cur: $150 (CH-5/90) **75**
Chardonnay Napa Valley 1974 Rel: $7 Cur: $125 (CH-5/90) **73**
Chardonnay Napa Valley 1973 Rel: $7 Cur: $120 (CH-5/90) **79**
Chardonnay Napa Valley 1972 Rel: $7 Cur: $110 (CH-5/90) **83**
Chardonnay Napa Valley 1971 Rel: $6 Cur: $110 (CH-5/90) **80**
Chardonnay Napa Valley 1970 Rel: $6 Cur: $175 (CH-5/90) **92**
Chardonnay Napa Valley 1969 Rel: $5 Cur: $175 (CH-5/90) **85**
Chardonnay Napa Valley 1968 Rel: $5 Cur: $250 (CH-5/90) **93**
Chardonnay Napa Valley 1967 Rel: $4.50 Cur: $310 (CH-5/90) **83**
Chardonnay Napa Valley 1966 Rel: $4.50 Cur: $300 (CH-5/90) **91**
Chardonnay Napa Valley 1965 Rel: $4 Cur: $420 (CH-5/90) **90**
Chardonnay Napa Valley 1964 Rel: $4 Cur: $450 (CH-5/90) **98**
Chardonnay Napa Valley 1963 Rel: $4 Cur: $450 (CH-5/90) **87**
Chardonnay Napa Valley 1962 Rel: $3.25 Cur: $470 (CH-5/90) **96**
Chardonnay Napa Valley 1960 Rel: $3 Cur: $430 (CH-5/90) **88**
Chardonnay Napa Valley SHV 1988: Ripe and intense, with distinctive but one-dimensional pineapple flavors that are fruity and generous but lacking in complexity and finesse. Drink now to 2000. Rel: $20 Cur: $90 (6/30/90) **81**
Chardonnay Napa Valley SHV 1987: A pretty wine, with a tinge of orange, toast and tropical fruit and floral notes, firm, crisp backbone, good richness and decent depth. Ready to drink now. Rel: $9 Cur: $62 (4/15/89) **84**

STORRS

Chardonnay Santa Cruz Mountains 1989: A heavily oaked style that overpowers the diluted lemon and light pear notes; mostly oak. Drink now. Tasted twice. 800 cases made. $11.50 (7/15/91) **76**
Chardonnay Santa Cruz Mountains Gaspar Vineyard 1989: Smells fresh and creamy, with pretty orange, peach, pear and melon flavors, spicy oak notes and good concentration and length. Gains complexity and length on the finish. Drink now to 1993. 180 cases made. $16 (7/15/91) **86**
Chardonnay Santa Cruz Mountains Meyley Vineyard 1989: Earthy, toasty oak notes dominate the ripe pear, nutmeg and vanilla flavors even though they turn a bit watery on the finish. Drink now. 180 cases made. $16 (7/15/91) **83**
Chardonnay Santa Cruz Mountains Vanumanutagi Vineyards 1989: Pungent and earthy, with toasty oak notes masking the fruit flavors. The finish gets a little dirty, making this a tough wine to warm up to. Drink now. 350 cases made. $14 (7/15/91) **71**

STRATFORD

Chardonnay California 1989: Smooth and flavorful, with a lovely balance of pear, peach, vanilla and nutmeg aromas and flavors that taper off a bit on the finish, but keep up enough intensity to want until 1993 to show all it has. $10 (7/15/91) BB **87**
Chardonnay California 1987: A good wine that has the smooth Chardonnay framework, but comes up somewhat short on fruit flavor. $10 (7/15/89) **75**
Chardonnay California 1986 $9.50 (2/29/88) **89**
Chardonnay California 1985 $9 (2/28/87) **80**
Chardonnay California 1984 $8.50 (2/01/86) **71**
Chardonnay California 1983 $8.50 (11/01/84) **80**
Chardonnay California Partners' Reserve 1990: Light and fruity, with lively peach and pear flavors. Simple but pleasing. Drink now. $12 (6/15/92) **81**
Chardonnay California Partners' Reserve 1988: A spicy, fresh, complex wine, with plenty of ripe pear flavor that lasts through the finish. Nutmeg and honey notes make it interesting, and crisp acidity balances it out. $14.50 (6/30/90) **88**
Chardonnay California Partners' Reserve 1987: Rich, full-bodied and buttery tasting, with a smooth texture and good dose of fruity, slightly vegetal flavors. Vanilla and peachy flavors linger on the finish. $15 (7/15/89) **82**
Chardonnay California Partners' Reserve 1986 $14.50 (12/31/88) **76**

RODNEY STRONG

Chardonnay Chalk Hill Chalk Hill Vineyard 1990: Smooth and elegant, a vanilla-scented wine, with pear, butterscotch and honey flavors coming in and out of focus on the palate. Stylish, with plenty of fresh flavors and enough lingering fruit on the finish to improve perhaps through 1994 or '95. $13 (5/31/92) **89**
Chardonnay Chalk Hill Chalk Hill Vineyard 1988: Tastes like a grapefruit and pineapple concoction, with a touch of nectarine, complete with a touch of bitterness. A bit hollow in the middle and should be consumed soon. An exotic wine that reaches the extremes of Chardonnay. $12 (3/31/91) **79**
Chardonnay Chalk Hill Chalk Hill Vineyard 1987: Rich and full-bodied, with a wealth of ripe pineapple, citrus, honey, almond and spice notes all combining to give this wine complexity and depth. Long on the finish. It's a touch coarse and intense; another year of cellaring probably will help. Drink now to 1993. Tasted twice. $12 (2/15/91) **90**
Chardonnay Chalk Hill Chalk Hill Vineyard 1985 $10 (12/31/87) **72**
Chardonnay Chalk Hill Chalk Hill Vineyard 1983 $10 (1/31/87) **73**
Chardonnay Chalk Hill Chalk Hill Vineyard 1982 $9.95 (7/01/84) **79**
Chardonnay Russian River Valley River West Vineyard 1984 $10 (3/15/87) **68**
Chardonnay Sonoma County 1990: Sweet and spicy, with strong Gewürz-like flavors that make it taste more like Gewürztraminer than Chardonnay, but it's appealing. Tasted twice. $9 (7/15/92) **82**
Chardonnay Sonoma County 1989: Fresh, clean and elegant, with supple, understated pear, melon, spice and nutmeg flavors that hang together nicely. Not too rich or concentrated, but has more persistence than most '89s. Drink now for its fresh fruit flavor. A fair price, too. $9 (7/15/91) BB **86**
Chardonnay Sonoma County 1987 $6.50 (10/15/88) **80**
Chardonnay Sonoma County 1986 $7 (12/15/87) BB **85**
Chardonnay Sonoma County 1983 $8 (11/01/84) **78**

SUNNY ST. HELENA

Chardonnay California 1989: An acceptable, light wine, with spicy, woody aromas, subtle lemon and apple flavors and a short finish. Lacks concentration. 1,150 cases made. $12 (4/30/91) **78**
Chardonnay Napa Valley 1986 $9 (10/31/87) **65**

SUTTER HOME

Chardonnay California 1990: Fresh and lively, with simple peach and vanilla aromas and flavors, very modest oak nuances and a pleasant spiciness on the finish. Drinkable now. $6 (9/15/91) BB **84**
Chardonnay California 1989: Light, fruity and floral, this has tropical fruit aromas and modestly ripe flavors, but a thin finish. Good for an inexpensive quaffing wine. $5 (11/15/90) BB **80**

JOSEPH SWAN

Chardonnay Sonoma Coast 1986 $18 (7/15/88) **73**
Chardonnay Sonoma Coast Russian River Valley 1989: This big but awkward wine won't be for everyone. The super-ripe fruit and vegetal flavors compete with an overt oakiness that turns slightly bitter on the finish. 200 cases made. $20 (5/31/91) **77**

SWANSON

Chardonnay Napa Valley 1989: Pleasant but uncomplicated pear, apple, melon and spice notes fade gracefully on the finish, picking up light honey and vanilla notes along the way. Drink now. Tasted twice. 2,500 cases made. $15 (7/15/91) **84**
Chardonnay Napa Valley 1988: A straightforward, well-made wine, with peach, pear and honey flavors. Medium-bodied, well balanced and ready to drink. 3,500 cases made. $14.50 (6/30/90) **79**
Chardonnay Napa Valley Reserve 1988: Sharply focused and shapely, with rich pear, vanilla, pineapple and honey notes that gain a touch of butter and spice. The flavors are young and tight, but very well defined. Ready now through 1994. 700 cases made. $19 (7/15/91) **90**

TAFT STREET

Chardonnay Russian River Valley 1989: Coarse and earthy, with mature pear, apple and spice notes that turn gamy and bitter on the finish. Drink now. $12 (3/31/92) **74**
Chardonnay Russian River Valley 1988: Leans toward the oaky side, but manages to stay in balance, offering ripe melon, pear, apple and citrus notes. Not too intense, and finishes with a nice soft touch. Drink now. $12 (7/15/91) **83**
Chardonnay Russian River Valley 1986 $10 (12/31/88) **86**

Key to Symbols

The scores reported here are the results of blind tastings conducted by our panel of senior editors. Wines that carry the initials below are results of individual tastings.

THE WINE SPECTATOR 100-POINT SCALE ***95-100***—Classic, a great wine; ***90-94***—Outstanding, superior character and style; ***80-89***—Good to very good, a wine with special qualities; ***70-79***—Average, drinkable wine that may have minor flaws; ***60-69***—Below average, drinkable but not recommended; ***50-59***—Poor, undrinkable, not recommended. "+"—With a score indicates a range; used primarily with barrel tastings to indicate a preliminary score.

SPECIAL DESIGNATIONS SS—Spectator Selection, CS—Cellar Selection, BB—Best Buy, ($NA)—Price not available, (NR)—Not released.

TASTER'S INITIALS (JG)—Jim Gordon, (HS)—Harvey Steiman, (JL)—James Laube, (JS)—James Suckling, (TM)—Thomas Matthews, (TR)—Terry Robards, (PM)—Per-Henrik Mansson, (BT)—Barrel Tasting (these wines were tasted blind from barrel samples), (CA-date)—*California's Great Cabernets* by James Laube, (CH-date)—*California's Great Chardonnays* by James Laube, (VP-date)—*Vintage Port* by James Suckling.

DATE TASTED Dates in parentheses represent the issue in which the rating was published.

Chardonnay Sonoma County 1990: This pleasing, fruity wine shows simple apple, spice, pear and nutmeg notes. Drink now. $8.50 (3/31/92) BB **82**
Chardonnay Sonoma County 1989: Has good fruit intensity for an '89, with fresh, ripe peach, pear, melon and spice flavors that are well focused and persistent. Drink now. $8.50 (7/15/91) BB **86**
Chardonnay Sonoma County 1988: Light and clean, with plenty of pear, fig, and pineapple flavors, it finishes with a smooth texture on the finish. A good value. $8 (1/31/90) **79**
Chardonnay Sonoma County 1987 $7.50 (10/15/88) **84**
Chardonnay Sonoma County 1986 $7 (11/15/87) **78**

TALBOTT
Chardonnay Carmel Valley Diamond T Estate 1989: Ripe, round, rich and creamy, with sharply focused pear, hazelnut, spice and earth notes that gain a touch of oak on the finish. Complex and inviting, with a long finish. Drink now to 1994. 250 cases made. $28 (4/30/92) **87**
Chardonnay Monterey 1989: Full and ripe, with generous pineapple and tropical fruit flavors and spice and butter notes that glide across the palate. Finishes with a strong burst of fruit and lively acidity. Delicious now through 1994. $24 (12/15/91) **89**

TALLEY
Chardonnay Arroyo Grande Valley 1990: Ripe peach and pear flavors are nicely matched by good buttery notes. This full-bodied wine is crisp and clean and drinkable now. Appealing and stylish. 1,572 cases made. $15 (3/31/92) **85**
Chardonnay Arroyo Grande Valley 1989: A lively wine, with a silky texture that lets the ripe, rich pear, citrus, guava and spice notes glide across the palate. Picks up a trace of oak and is well balanced and clean on the finish. Has moderate concentration and depth. Drink now to 1993. 1,166 cases made. $14.50 (7/15/91) **84**
Chardonnay San Luis Obispo County 1987: Fruity and crisp, made in a style that emphasizes strong piny, grapefruitlike aromas, tart fruit flavors and a crisp finish. Drink now. $12 (12/15/89) **78**

IVAN TAMAS
Chardonnay Livermore Valley 1988: A ripe, earthy-tasting wine that's rich in texture and almost unctuous. Good, but a bit flabby and unfocused. $7.50 (4/30/90) **75**
Chardonnay Napa Valley-Central Coast 1986 $7 (12/31/87) **77**
Chardonnay Napa Valley Reserve 1986 $15 (9/30/88) **86**

TERRA
Chardonnay Napa Valley 1987: Fresh, clean and fruity, with rich peach, melon, apple and pear flavors that are ripe and enticing. Strives for elegance and finesse, with a silky texture and a lingering finish. An impressive '87 from a new producer. Drink now to 1993. $12 (7/15/91) **87**

THOMAS-HSI
Chardonnay Napa Valley 1988: Deftly balanced, with subtle oak shadings and an elegant core of buttery pear and pineapple-tinged flavors that become more complex and enticing on the finish, picking up pretty spice and cinnamon notes. Has a sense of harmony and grace. Drink now to 1994. 240 cases made. $18 (6/30/91) **89**
Chardonnay Napa Valley 1987: A rich, woody style, this concentrated wine has a long finish, oozing with intense vanilla, toast and pear flavors. It's not harsh, but it's almost thick in texture, so it lacks the finesse of the best. Drinkable now. $18 (6/30/90) **82**

TIFFANY HILL
Chardonnay Edna Valley 1989: Bizarre flavors hint at honey, but end up reminding us of sour vegetables. Seems awkward, too. $18 (7/15/91) **73**
Chardonnay Edna Valley 1987: Ripe and soft, with well-balanced flavors of pear, caramel and honey riding on a smooth texture to a good finish. $19 (3/31/89) **85**
Chardonnay Edna Valley 1986 $19 (6/15/88) **90**

TIJSSELING
Chardonnay Mendocino 1989: Watery apple, melon and pear flavors turn bitter and musty. Tasted twice. 452 cases made. $10 (7/15/91) **69**
Chardonnay Mendocino 1988: A buttery, oaky wine that doesn't have much fruit stuffing. Drinkable. $10 (2/28/90) **70**

TIN PONY
Chardonnay Sonoma County Green Valley 1986 $8 (9/30/88) **71**

MARIMAR TORRES
Chardonnay Sonoma County Green Valley Don Miguel Vineyard 1990: Shows plenty of flavor, with layers of honey, pear, apple and vanilla. Well focused, toasty and buttery, with fine length. A complex, charming wine to drink now. 3,000 cases made. $24 (7/15/92) **87**
Chardonnay Sonoma County Green Valley Don Miguel Vineyard 1989: Concentrated and focused, with ripe fruit flavor and an almost unctuous texture. An extremely seductive style, shaped by aging in new oak that brings out lush vanilla and honey notes to complement the pear and peach flavors. Drink now through 1993. Impressive debut. 1,300 cases made. $20 (5/15/91) **90**

TREFETHEN
Chardonnay Napa Valley 1990: Tart, with a firm, citrus edge to the peach and pear flavors. A tight young wine that will need cellaring until at least 1993 for the flavors to soften and evolve. $18 (7/15/92) **83**
Chardonnay Napa Valley 1988: A correct, rather tart and appley wine that's good, well balanced and straightforward. Aging until 1993 should help. Rel: $17.50 Cur: $20 (12/31/90) **85**
Chardonnay Napa Valley 1988 Rel: $17.50 Cur: $20 (CH-3/90) **90**
Chardonnay Napa Valley 1987 Rel: $16.75 Cur: $20 (CH-3/90) **88**
Chardonnay Napa Valley 1986 Rel: $16.25 Cur: $22 (CH-3/90) **87**
Chardonnay Napa Valley 1985 Rel: $15.25 Cur: $34 (CH-3/90) **88**
Chardonnay Napa Valley 1984 Rel: $14.25 Cur: $40 (CH-3/90) **86**
Chardonnay Napa Valley 1983 Rel: $13.75 Cur: $35 (CH-3/90) **77**
Chardonnay Napa Valley 1982 Rel: $13.50 Cur: $30 (CH-3/90) **73**
Chardonnay Napa Valley 1981 Rel: $13 Cur: $30 (CH-3/90) **83**
Chardonnay Napa Valley 1980 Rel: $13 Cur: $40 (CH-3/90) **86**
Chardonnay Napa Valley 1979 Rel: $12 Cur: $30 (CH-3/90) **73**
Chardonnay Napa Valley 1978 Rel: $10 Cur: $35 (CH-3/90) **90**
Chardonnay Napa Valley 1977 Rel: $8.50 Cur: $35 (CH-3/90) **81**
Chardonnay Napa Valley 1976 Rel: $7 Cur: $40 (CH-3/90) **74**
Chardonnay Napa Valley 1975 Rel: $6.50 Cur: $45 (CH-3/90) **73**
Chardonnay Napa Valley 1974 Rel: $5.75 Cur: $50 (CH-3/90) **80**
Chardonnay Napa Valley 1973 Rel: $6.50 Cur: $50 (CH-3/90) **85**
Chardonnay Napa Valley Library Selection 1985: Fully mature, but aging extremely well. Bold, rich and concentrated, packed with deep, complex flavors and tiers of honey, pear, butter and spice notes that go on and on. Remarkably well preserved. Drink now. 1,500 cases made. $30 (3/15/92) **92**

TRUCHARD
Chardonnay Carneros Napa Valley 1990: Firm and focused, with straight-ahead apricot and pear aromas and flavors that are crisp and appealing. Drinkable now, but better in 1993. 360 cases made. $16 (3/31/92) **82**
Chardonnay Carneros 1989: A creamy, elegant style, with ripe melon, pear, spice and honey flavors that are delicate and well defined. Finish is long and lingering. Ready now through 1994. First wine from this producer. 200 cases made. $16 (11/30/91) **87**

TULOCAY
Chardonnay Napa Valley De Celles Vineyard 1989: Smooth and polished, with a charred, smoky, slightly earthy edge to the basic peach, melon and apple aromas and flavors. Has character and depth, but not everyone will like the aromas. Drinkable now, but may be better in 1993 or '94. Tasted twice. $13 (4/30/92) **84**
Chardonnay Napa Valley DeCelles Vineyard 1988: Lively, with lots of butterscotch and apple aromas and flavors. A bit leesy, but it's fresh enough to enjoy now. $14 (4/30/91) **80**

ULTRAVINO
Chardonnay Napa Valley 1984 $8.50 (2/15/87) **82**

M.G. VALLEJO
Chardonnay California 1989: Simple, flabby pear and spice notes turn diluted on the finish. Drink now. $6.50 (7/15/91) **74**
Chardonnay California 1988: Lean in flavor, but has enough butter and pear to keep you interested. Smooth texture, modest structure. $5 (4/30/90) **78**
Chardonnay California 1987: Smooth and reasonably fruity. Good quality. Has appley, piny aromas and a smooth texture. $5 (2/15/89) **74**

VAN DER HAYDEN
Chardonnay Napa Valley Private Reserve 1989: Lean and crisp, with modest peach and nectarine flavors and an austere, slightly astringent texture. Hints at honey on the finish. Tasted twice. 450 cases made. $18 (7/15/92) **78**

VEGA
Chardonnay Santa Barbara County 1986: A very concentrated, distinctive, French-style Chardonnay, with its dominant earthy aromas and flavors. Has a rich, supple, broad texture and enough fruit and honey complexity to keep it interesting through the aftertaste. $14 (12/15/89) **89**

VENDANGE
Chardonnay California 1990: A simple, clean and fruity wine, with hints of grapey pear and melon. Serve chilled; drink now. $6 (7/15/92) **79**

VENTANA
Chardonnay Monterey Barrel Fermented 1987: An oily, vegetal presence dominates the ripe pear and pineapple flavors in a style that may appeal to some more than others. $16 (10/31/89) **76**
Chardonnay Monterey Crystal Ventana Vineyards 1986: Rich with layers of honey, toast and butterscotch flavors that are full-bodied and slightly cloying on the finish. Could use a little measure of finesse. Straightforward. $16 (10/31/89) **79**
Chardonnay Monterey Gold Stripe Selection 1989: Pleasant peach, pear, earth and apple flavors are ripe, tart and clean, with good depth and intensity. Picks up interesting honey and spicy oak notes on the aftertaste. Drink now to 1993. $10 (7/15/91) **87**
Chardonnay Monterey Gold Stripe Selection 1988: Rich, opulent and juicy with pungent, somewhat oily Chardonnay flavor that offers sweetish fig, melon and spicy flavors. Gets a bit earthy on the finish, but the overall impression is positive. $10 (9/30/89) **81**
Chardonnay Monterey Gold Stripe Selection 1985 $7.50 (9/15/87) BB **87**
Chardonnay Monterey Gold Stripe Selection 1984 $8 (4/16/86) **69**
Chardonnay Monterey Ventana Vineyards Gold Stripe Selection 1987: A fine value. Very harmonious and clean in a medium-bodied style. Nicely rich but well-balanced, with appley flavors tinged by earthy notes, a smooth, viscous texture and a lingering finish. $10 (6/30/89) **88**

VIANSA
Chardonnay Napa-Sonoma Counties 1988: Ripe, clean and fruity with intense, concentrated apple, pear, citrus and melon notes blending nicely with subtle oak shadings. Well balanced, fresh and lively on the finish. Drink now to 1993. Tasted twice. $15 (9/15/90) **85**
Chardonnay Napa-Sonoma Counties 1987: Earthy and crisp, with citric aromas, grapefruit and lemon flavors, a long, delicate finish and fine structure. Drink now. $13 (4/15/89) **84**
Chardonnay Napa-Sonoma Counties 1986 $12.50 (3/31/88) **87**
Chardonnay Napa-Sonoma Counties Reserve 1988: A very spicy wine, with open aromas of fig and vanilla, creamy, pearlike flavors accented with nutmeg and a spicy finish. Modestly structured and ready to drink now. $18 (11/30/90) **84**
Chardonnay Sonoma-Napa Counties Sam J. Sebastiani 1985 $12.50 (6/30/87) **68**

VICHON
Chardonnay Napa Valley 1990: Shows correct flavors, with tiers of honey, pear, citrus and spice, but lacks pizzazz. A bit alcoholic on the finish. Drink now. Tasted twice. $15 (3/31/92) **81**
Chardonnay Napa Valley Tenth Harvest 1989: Expansive and spicy, showing a great combination of buttery oak, crisp pear and butterscotch flavors. Spicy vanilla notes linger on the finish. Rel: $16 Cur: $18 (3/31/91) **86**
Chardonnay Napa Valley 1988: Rich and complex with tiers of honey, butterscotch, citrus and oak flavors that are crisp and satisfying on the palate. Impressive length. Drink now. Rel: $17 Cur: $19 (11/15/89) **89**
Chardonnay Napa Valley 1987 Rel: $16 Cur: $18 (CH-3/90) **87**
Chardonnay Napa Valley 1986 Rel: $15 Cur: $17 (CH-3/90) **90**
Chardonnay Napa Valley 1985 Rel: $15 Cur: $17 (CH-3/90) **88**
Chardonnay Napa Valley 1984 Rel: $15 Cur: $17 (CH-3/90) **86**
Chardonnay Napa Valley 1983 Rel: $15 Cur: $18 (CH-3/90) **71**
Chardonnay Napa Valley 1982 Rel: $15 Cur: $20 (CH-3/90) **66**
Chardonnay Napa Valley 1981 Rel: $15 Cur: $25 (CH-3/90) **76**
Chardonnay Napa Valley 1980 Rel: $15 Cur: $25 (CH-3/90) **87**

VILLA MT. EDEN
Chardonnay California Cellar Select 1990: Ripe and lush, with spicy pineapple, pear and citrus notes of modest depth and concentration. Ready to drink now. $8 (6/15/92) BB **82**
Chardonnay Carneros 1989: A basic peach and apple-flavored wine that's of good quality, but somewhat diluted in fruit intensity. Drink now. Tasted twice. $12 (2/28/91) **79**
Chardonnay Carneros 1988: Vibrant and very well-balanced, this focused wine emphasizes crisp pineapple flavors, accented by spice, pear and toast. Fruit really lingers on the finish. Drink now. $13.50 (9/30/90) **87**
Chardonnay Napa Valley 1989: Stylish, but a little awkward, with vanilla and honey aromas and modest oak and peach flavors. This simple wine is charming, but it doesn't have a lot of complexity. Drinkable now. Tasted twice. $12 (2/28/91) **82**
Chardonnay Napa Valley 1986 $12 (7/31/88) **86**
Chardonnay Napa Valley 1984 $9 (4/30/87) **84**
Chardonnay Napa Valley 1983 $10 (4/16/85) **75**
Chardonnay Napa Valley Grand Reserve 1990: Firm and concentrated, with flavors that center around pear, apple and spice and continue into a long, lively finish. The flavors stay with you, suggesting this should only improve through 1994. An excellent value. 2,400 cases made. $12 (6/30/92) **89**

VILLA ZAPU
Chardonnay Napa Valley 1990: This lively, spicy wine offers pretty apple, pear and spice aromas and flavors rounded out by a pleasant tinge of oak on the finish. A pretty wine to drink now, or hold until 1994 or '95. 5,000 cases made. $11 (7/31/92) **87**
Chardonnay Napa Valley 1989: Ripe and round, with strong spice and toast overtones to the smooth-textured pear, melon and smoke flavors that persist on the rich finish. Drinkable now, but has the concentration to hang on through 1993 to '95. $17.50 (7/15/91) **86**
Chardonnay Napa Valley 1988: Intense and concentrated, with great structure from acidity. Smelling smoky and spicy, this wine tastes full-bodied and firm, with pineapple and pear flavors and a lingering finish. Should improve with cellaring till 1993. $14 (6/30/90) **88**
Chardonnay Napa Valley 1987 $14 (5/31/89) **73**
Chardonnay Napa Valley 1986 $13.75 (12/31/88) **77**

VITA NOVA
Chardonnay Santa Barbara County 1989: Ripe and intense, with earthy pineapple, apple, citrus and pear flavors that are rich and full-bodied up-front, but the finish turns a bit simple and lacks follow through. Drink now to 1994. $18 (7/15/91) **86**
Chardonnay Santa Barbara County 1988: A real butterball that's delicious and unctuous in flavor, yet still balanced with acidity. Deep gold in color, extremely rich, toasty, and buttery in aroma and rich, honeylike and very viscous on the palate. Limited availability. $13.50 (2/15/90) **91**
Chardonnay Santa Barbara County Rancho Vinedo Vineyards 1990: An earthy wine that stretches the band of Chardonnay flavors to the extreme. You get a nice taste of peach and honey flavors, but it's funky. Drink now to 1995. Tasted twice, with consistent notes. $18 (7/15/92) **83**

WEIBEL
Chardonnay Mendocino County 1989: Exotic peach, pineapple and nectarine flavors won't shortchange you on flavor, but they stray from the typical Chardonnay spectrum. The finish is clean and crisp. A complete and satisfying drink. $8 (3/31/91) BB **82**

WEINSTOCK
Chardonnay Alexander Valley 1989: A pretty wine, light but balanced, with sweet oak, pineapple and melon flavors lifted by a pleasing tartness. $11 (3/31/91) **87**
Chardonnay Alexander Valley Winemaker Selection Reserve 1989: Smells good, but fails to deliver on the palate. The ripe pear and apple notes turn watery on the finish, and it lacks concentration and depth. Tasted twice. Drink now. 500 cases made. $10 (1/31/92) **79**

WELLINGTON
Chardonnay Sonoma Valley Barrel Fermented 1990: A bit heavy-handed with the oak, which tastes like varnish, marring the pear, apple and citrus notes that are buried beneath the pile of wood. Unbalanced. Drink now. 840 cases made. $12.50 (4/30/92) **74**

WENTE BROS.
Chardonnay Arroyo Seco Reserve Arroyo Seco Vineyards 1988: Beautifully focused, long and elegant, with fine concentration of fig, honey and toast aromas and flavors that linger enticingly on the finish. Flavors are assertive, but this is a smoothly polished wine. Drink now. 6,150 cases made. $12 (4/15/90) **90**
Chardonnay Arroyo Seco Reserve Arroyo Seco Vineyards 1987: Lean and spicy, tart and turning a bit harsh and sour on the finish, echoing nutmeg and pear flavors. Drink now. $14 (10/31/89) **77**
Chardonnay Arroyo Seco Reserve Arroyo Seco Vineyards 1985 $10 (10/15/87) **84**
Chardonnay Arroyo Seco Reserve Arroyo Seco Vineyards 1984 $9 (6/01/86) **90**
Chardonnay Arroyo Seco Riva Ranch 1990: A delicious wine that's elegant and stylish, with rich, sharply focused pear, pineapple and tropical fruit flavors framed by subtle oak shadings that turn toasty on the finish. Enjoy now through 1995. 4,900 cases made. $12 (6/30/92) SS **90**
Chardonnay Arroyo Seco Vineyard Reserve 1985: Simple and fruity, with leafy, buttery pear and apple flavors that are crisp and elegant and modest varietal character that picks up honey and toast notes on the finish. 900 cases made. $30/1.5L (3/31/90) **79**
Chardonnay Central Coast Estate Grown 1991: The best Chardonnay for less than $10 on the market. Pretty, elegant and almost sweet tasting, with lots of ripe fruit flavors and a silky texture that keeps it light on its feet. Spice and vanilla notes linger on the finish. Tasted twice, with consistent notes. $8 (7/15/92) SS **91**
Chardonnay Central Coast Estate Grown 1989: Manages to offer enough concentration to avoid being watery. The melon, apricot and apple flavors are attractive. Drink now. $10.50 (7/15/91) **83**
Chardonnay Livermore Valley Herman Wente Vineyard Reserve 1990: A smooth, creamy wine, with lots of pear, peach, vanilla, grapefruit and honey notes that glide across the palate. Finishes with complexity and grace. Drink now to 1994. $18 (7/15/92) **88**
Chardonnay Livermore Valley Herman Wente Vineyard Reserve 1989: Has an intense, almost sweet fruitiness that's very appealing, rich and creamy. Earthy in aroma, then opens up with ripe pear, vanilla and honey flavors that linger on the finish. Quite distinctive. $18 (4/30/91) **88**
Chardonnay Livermore Valley Herman Wente Vineyard Reserve 1986 $11 (5/31/88) **80**

WESTWOOD
Chardonnay El Dorado 1989: A bit heavy-handed with the oak, but still manages to hang in balance. Offers plenty of pine and spice notes, with ripe pear and melon nuances. Drink now. 950 cases made. $10 (7/15/91) **75**

WILLIAM WHEELER
Chardonnay Sonoma County 1990: Light and elegant, with pear, citrus and oak flavors that are well proportioned, but thin out on the finish, where the oak dominates and earthy flavors show. Drink now to 1994. 4,900 cases made. $13 (3/31/92) **83**
Chardonnay Sonoma County 1989: Rich, concentrated and silky, with a solid core of ripe, concentrated pear, apple, honey and spice notes that are tight and well focused. Riper and bolder than most '89s; a fine value. Drink now to 1994. $13 (12/31/91) **88**
Chardonnay Sonoma County 1988: Fresh and lively, with ripe, rich melon, pineapple and apple-tinged fruit flavors that offer good depth and intensity, finishing with a touch of vanilla and pear. A balanced and flavorful wine. Better than an earlier bottle. $12 (6/30/90) **85**
Chardonnay Sonoma County 1987 $12 (7/15/89) **88**
Chardonnay Sonoma County 1986 $11.50 (1/31/88) **79**
Chardonnay Sonoma County 1984 $11 (1/31/87) **88**
Chardonnay Sonoma County 1983 $11 (6/01/85) **82**

WHITE OAK
Chardonnay Sonoma County 1990: Fruity and straightforward, with pineapple, floral and spice flavors. Not very sophisticated, but a good, fruity wine. Rel: $13 Cur: $15 (12/31/91) **81**
Chardonnay Sonoma County 1989: Focused and spicy, offering a good combination of ripe pineapple and pear flavors, with spicy oak nuances. Lively, full-bodied and flavorful. Enjoy now through 1993. $12 (3/31/91) **85**
Chardonnay Sonoma County 1988: Has generous, lively fruit, with layers of rich, ripe, pineapple, pear and apple flavors and subtle oak shadings that are long and full on the palate. A pleasant mouthful of Chardonnay that lingers. Drink now. Rel: $12 Cur: $16 (4/30/90) **88**
Chardonnay Sonoma County 1987 Rel: $11 Cur: $16 (CH-5/90) **85**
Chardonnay Sonoma County 1986 Rel: $11 Cur: $17 (CH-5/90) **86**
Chardonnay Sonoma County 1985 Rel: $10.50 Cur: $18 (CH-5/90) **89**
Chardonnay Sonoma County 1984 Rel: $10 Cur: $18 (CH-5/90) **86**

Key to Symbols

The scores reported here are the results of blind tastings conducted by our panel of senior editors. Wines that carry the initials below are results of individual tastings.

THE WINE SPECTATOR 100-POINT SCALE ***95-100***—Classic, a great wine; ***90-94***—Outstanding, superior character and style; ***80-89***—Good to very good, a wine with special qualities; ***70-79***—Average, drinkable wine that may have minor flaws; ***60-69***—Below average, drinkable but not recommended; ***50-59***—Poor, undrinkable, not recommended. "+"—With a score indicates a range; used primarily with barrel tastings to indicate a preliminary score.

SPECIAL DESIGNATIONS SS—Spectator Selection, CS—Cellar Selection, BB—Best Buy, ($NA)—Price not available, (NR)—Not released.

TASTER'S INITIALS (JG)—Jim Gordon, (HS)—Harvey Steiman, (JL)—James Laube, (JS)—James Suckling, (TM)—Thomas Matthews, (TR)—Terry Robards, (PM)—Per-Henrik Mansson, (BT)—Barrel Tasting (these wines were tasted blind from barrel samples), (CA-date)—*California's Great Cabernets* by James Laube, (CH-date)—*California's Great Chardonnays* by James Laube, (VP-date)—*Vintage Port* by James Suckling.

DATE TASTED Dates in parentheses represent the issue in which the rating was published.

Chardonnay Sonoma County Myers Limited Reserve 1990: Straightforward apple and melon flavors have hints of vanilla and spice. A young, tight, focused wine that has a sense of harmony. Drink now to 1994. $20 (2/29/92) **86**
Chardonnay Sonoma County Myers Limited Reserve 1989: A good, pleasant wine that blends modest fruit flavors, spice and butter for a complete but not concentrated package. $20 (3/31/91) **80**
Chardonnay Sonoma County Myers Limited Release 1988: Ripe and round, a fruity wine that wraps its pear and pineapple flavors with a blanket of vanilla-tinged oak. Flavorful and easy to drink. Nice tension between fruit and oak. Could use more complexity. Rel: $18 Cur: $20 (2/28/90) **82**
Chardonnay Sonoma County Myers Limited Release 1987 Rel: $18 Cur: $20 (CH-5/90) **81**
Chardonnay Sonoma County Myers Limited Release 1986 Rel: $16 Cur: $20 (CH-5/90) **87**
Chardonnay Alexander Valley Myers Limited Release 1985 Rel: $14.50 Cur: $22 (CH-5/90) **90**

WHITE ROCK
Chardonnay Napa Valley 1990: Crisp and bright, with lively peach, pineapple and floral aromas and flavors that focus sharply on the finish, resulting in a long, appealing aftertaste. Drinkable now, but tight enough to benefit from cellaring until 1994. $15 (7/15/92) **89**
Chardonnay Napa Valley Barrel Fermented 1989: Lean and crisp, with pleasant lemon and peach aromas and flavors that are firmly focused and tightly reined in. Should improve through 1993 or '94. So tightly wound it's hard to say what could develop. $16 (7/15/91) **87**

WHITEHALL LANE
Chardonnay Napa Valley Cerro Vista Vineyard 1982 $12 (9/01/84) **74**
Chardonnay Napa Valley Estate Bottled 1988: Modest in flavor, with apple and melon flavor and a bite on the finish. Tasted twice. $15 (6/30/90) **78**
Chardonnay Napa Valley Le Petit 1990: Despite an earthy edge, this wine delivers plenty of attractive pear, honey, fig and spice flavors, with moderate richness and depth. Simple but pleasing. Drink now. 4,450 cases made. $8 (3/15/92) **82**
Chardonnay Napa Valley Le Petit 1989: Acceptable, but bland tasting. Has modest apple and pear flavors and good structure, but basically not much fruit content. $9 (2/28/91) **77**
Chardonnay Napa Valley Le Petit 1988: Tastes lively and beautifully balanced. Medium-bodied, very fruity and focused, with crisp pear, melon and spice flavors and a pleasant aftertaste. Drink now. $8 (4/30/90) BB **84**
Chardonnay Napa Valley Reserve 1990: Crisp and lively, with a delicate texture and plenty of nectarine, apple and spice aromas and flavors. Hints at honey and butterscotch on the finish. Drinkable now. 982 cases made. $16 (7/15/92) **87**

WILD HORSE
Chardonnay Central Coast 1990: Rich and full-bodied, with layers of butterscotch, pear, melon and spice flavors. Round and complex, finishing with a touch of oak that turns to nutmeg. Drink now to 1994. $13 (12/31/91) **88**
Chardonnay Central Coast 1989: This open, likable wine offers lots of exotic tropical fruit aromas and flavors, a smooth texture and ready drinkability. Butter and oak notes make it more interesting on further sipping. $13 (4/30/91) **86**
Chardonnay San Luis Obispo County 1988: Ripe and toasty, with generous pineapple and pear aromas and flavors shaded with smoke, vanilla and butter flavors on the finish. Very full and fine, with lots of concentration. Drink now or in 1993. 3,222 cases made. $12 (4/15/90) **90**
Chardonnay San Luis Obispo County Wild Horse Vineyards 1987: Tart and crisp, with flavors centered around grapefruit, but some honey and floral flavors on the finish lend complexity. For those who like 'em lean. $12 (6/15/89) **81**
Chardonnay San Luis Obispo County Wild Horse Vineyards 1986 $9.75 (5/31/88) **79**

WILDHURST
Chardonnay Napa Valley 1990: Ripe, full-bodied and figgy tasting, this powerful wine has straightforward flavors and a touch of vanilla on the finish. Solid and likable. $10 (6/15/92) **85**

J. WILE & SONS
Chardonnay Napa Valley 1990: An awkward wine that combines appley, lemony flavors with a milky taste. Turns thin and earthy on the finish. Not enjoyable. Tasted twice, with consistent notes. $10 (7/15/92) **69**
Chardonnay Napa Valley 1987: Crisp, appley tasting and appealing. Pleasant but not powerful. $7 (2/15/89) **79**
Chardonnay Napa Valley 1986 $7 (9/15/87) **77**

WILLOW CREEK
Chardonnay Sonoma County 1989: This is a wine for Riesling lovers, with peach and floral aromas and a touch of the pine resin flavor that characterizes good Riesling. A balanced, harmonious wine for current drinking. $11 (9/30/90) **84**
Chardonnay Sonoma County 1988: Rich and intense yet elegant, with plenty of ripe, exotic pineapple, citrus and honey notes and a gentle oak texture. Elegant, long and juicy on the finish. An excellent value. Drink now. $10 (2/28/90) **87**

WINDEMERE
Chardonnay Edna Valley MacGregor Vineyard 1989: Ripe, fat and generous, with more fruit on the palate than on the nose, offering plenty of spice and pear notes that extend into the finish. Drinkable now. $13 (12/15/91) **83**
Chardonnay Edna Valley MacGregor Vineyard 1988: Smooth and flavorful, with lots of apple, spice and almond aromas and flavors and a long, lively finish. Drinkable now. $13 (4/30/91) **83**
Chardonnay Edna Valley MacGregor Vineyard 1987: A sophisticated, nicely balanced wine, with earthy aromas, ripe, almost sweet pear and honey flavors and a rich texture. Its long aftertaste signals extra quality. $12 (7/15/89) **88**

YORK MOUNTAIN
Chardonnay San Luis Obispo 1987: Not for everyone, although some may like this style. Has an unusual earthy, barnyardy aroma and austere, earthy flavors. The texture is rich and the finish lingers. $9 (12/15/89) **77**

ZACA MESA
Chardonnay Santa Barbara County 1990: Broad and lush, with layers of tropical fruit, pineapple, honey and citrus flavors. Finishes with plenty of fruit, but it's a bit out of focus. Drink now to 1994. $9.75 (6/15/92) **85**
Chardonnay Santa Barbara County 1989: A straightforward, satisfying wine. Young, crisp and fruity tasting, with lemony aromas, peachy flavors and good balance. $11 (11/15/90) **85**
Chardonnay Santa Barbara County 1988: Ripe and straightforward. Ripe and rich, with pineapple flavors and hints of citrus, a soft texture and a sweet, fruity finish. $10 (2/15/90) **84**
Chardonnay Santa Barbara County 1987: Lively and juicy, with sharply focused green apple and pear flavors and impressive length. Drink now. Reasonably priced, too. $10 (3/31/89) **87**
Chardonnay Santa Barbara County 1986 $9.75 (10/15/88) **74**
Chardonnay Santa Barbara County 1985 $8 (10/31/87) **77**
Chardonnay Santa Barbara County 1983 $9.75 (4/16/86) **58**
Chardonnay Santa Barbara County American Reserve 1984 $13 (2/28/87) **85**
Chardonnay Santa Barbara County Barrel Select 1985 $9.75 (10/15/88) **84**
Chardonnay Santa Barbara County Reserve 1989: A nice use of toasty oak, with spice, pear, orange and vanilla flavors underneath. Smooth, polished and elegant, with a silky texture and a smoky aftertaste where the flavors fan out. Drink now to 1993. $16.50 (7/15/91) **86**
Chardonnay Santa Barbara County Reserve 1988: Intense, rich and very complex in flavor, the layers of smoke, pear, peach, pineapple and subtle earth notes add dimension and complexity to this exotic style. Finishes tart, crisp and lemony. Drink now. $15.50 (9/15/90) **87**
Chardonnay Santa Barbara County Reserve 1987: Solidly built and somewhat stylish. Earthy and toasty smelling and tart in balance, with lemony, oaky flavors. $15 (12/15/89) **80**
Chardonnay Santa Barbara County Reserve 1986 $15 (10/15/88) **81**

ZD
Chardonnay California 1989: A flavorful, complex wine that balances crispness and good fruit flavors of peach and pear, with hints of honey, spice and vanilla lingering on the finish. Drink now through 1993. Tasted twice. $21 (2/28/91) **87**
Chardonnay California 1988 $20 (CH-3/90) **89**
Chardonnay California 1987 $18.50 (CH-3/90) **85**
Chardonnay California 1986 Rel: $18 Cur: $22 (CH-6/90) **85**
Chardonnay California 1985 Rel: $16 Cur: $28 (CH-3/90) **90**
Chardonnay California 1984 Rel: $15 Cur: $30 (CH-3/90) **90**
Chardonnay California 1983 Rel: $14 Cur: $25 (CH-3/90) **74**
Chardonnay California 1982 Rel: $14 Cur: $30 (CH-3/90) **76**
Chardonnay California 1981 Rel: $13 Cur: $28 (CH-3/90) **87**
Chardonnay California 1980 Rel: $13 Cur: $28 (CH-3/90) **81**

STEPHEN ZELLERBACH
Chardonnay Alexander Valley 1984 $6 (2/15/87) **79**
Chardonnay Alexander Valley 1983 $9.95 (1/01/85) **84**
Chardonnay Alexander Valley Warnecke Sonoma Vineyard 1982 $10 (4/16/84) **75**
Chardonnay California 1987 $7 (10/15/88) BB **82**
Chardonnay Sonoma County 1990: Fresh, smooth and creamy, with elegant pear, apple, spice and vanilla flavors that glide across the palate, finishing with hints of almond and hazelnut. Ready to drink now. $9 (3/15/92) BB **86**
Chardonnay Sonoma County 1989: Plenty of butterscotch and honey aromas and flavors flesh out the ripe pear notes in this rich, unctuous wine. A decent wine that's drinkable now. $8.50 (11/30/90) BB **85**
Chardonnay Sonoma County 1988: Very full and spicy, with generous vanilla and nutmeg-tinged apple and citrus aromas and flavors, lively and long. With its crisp acidity, this wine could be enjoyed now or cellared until 1993. $8 (4/15/90) BB **88**
Chardonnay Sonoma County Reserve 1989: Has a good dose of toasty, buttery oak and pretty ripe fruit to match. Pear, melon, caramel and toasty oak flavors and a smooth, creamy texture make this a very pleasant and attractive wine. Drink now to 1994. 1,500 cases made. $13 (7/15/91) **87**

CHENIN BLANC

ALMADEN
Chenin Blanc California NV $4/1.5L (7/31/89) **77**

BARON HERZOG
Chenin Blanc California 1988 $4.50 (7/31/89) **84**

BEAULIEU
Chenin Blanc Napa Valley Chablis 1986 $5.50 (7/31/89) **84**

BERINGER
Chenin Blanc Napa Valley 1987 $7 (7/31/89) **83**

CALLAWAY
Chenin Blanc Temecula Morning Harvest 1988 $6.50 (7/31/89) **87**
Chenin Blanc Temecula Morning Harvest 1987 $5.50 (7/31/89) **84**

CASA NUESTRA
Chenin Blanc Napa Valley Dry 1987 $6.50 (7/31/89) **82**

CHAPPELLET
Chenin Blanc Napa Valley 1986 $7.50 (7/31/89) **85**

CHRISTIAN BROTHERS
Chenin Blanc Napa Valley 1987 $5 (7/31/89) **84**

R. & J. COOK
Chenin Blanc Clarksburg 1988 $5.50 (7/31/89) **83**

DRY CREEK
Chenin Blanc Yolo & Napa Counties 1988 $6.50 (7/31/89) **86**

DURNEY
Chenin Blanc Carmel Valley 1986 $7 (7/31/89) **72**

FETZER
Chenin Blanc California 1988 $6 (7/31/89) **88**
Chenin Blanc Mendocino County 1990: Frankly sweet, fruity and flavorful, with lemon-lime flavors that turn a bit sugary on the finish. Simple and drinkable. $6.75 (11/15/91) **77**

FOLIE A DEUX
Chenin Blanc Napa Valley 1988 $7 (7/31/89) **88**

E. & J. GALLO
Chenin Blanc California 1987 $3.50/1.5L (7/31/89) **77**
Chenin Blanc California Chablis Blanc NV $2.50 (7/31/89) **83**
Chenin Blanc North Coast Dry Chablis 1987 $4 (7/31/89) **73**

GIRARD
Chenin Blanc Napa Valley Dry 1988 $7 (7/31/89) **82**

GLEN ELLEN
Chenin Blanc California Proprietor's Reserve 1988 $6 (7/31/89) **79**

GRAND CRU
Chenin Blanc Clarksburg Dry 1989: Tastes crisp, light and very fruity in a straightforward way. The label says dry, but it tastes slightly sweet, though well balanced with acidity. Enjoy now, well-chilled, as an aperitif or with light foods. $6.50 (6/30/90) **83**
Chenin Blanc Clarksburg Dry Premium Selection 1990: Dry and fruity, with lots of green apple and grapefruit flavors that extend into a lively finish. An appealing wine that has the balance to match well with food. $6.50 (11/15/91) BB **85**
Chenin Blanc Clarksburg Dry Premium Selection 1988 $7 (7/31/89) **85**

GRANITE SPRINGS
Chenin Blanc El Dorado 1988: Nectarine and toasty oak aromas and flavors run through this firm-textured, aromatic wine. It's drinkable now, but the oak tends to dominate and may need time to meld into the wine. $5.50 (7/31/89) **85**

GUENOC
Chenin Blanc Guenoc Valley 1987 $5.50 (7/31/89) **82**

HACIENDA
Chenin Blanc Clarksburg Dry 1988 $5.50 (7/31/89) **84**

HOUTZ
Chenin Blanc Santa Ynez Valley 1987: Medicinal, earthy aromas are off-putting, and the vegetable flavors don't help. $6 (7/31/89) **62**

HUSCH
Chenin Blanc Mendocino 1988 $5.75 (7/31/89) **86**

INGLENOOK-NAVELLE
Chenin Blanc California NV $3.75/1.5L (7/31/89) **76**

CHARLES KRUG
Chenin Blanc Napa Valley 1987: Off-dry, soft and smooth, with peach and floral flavors. $5.50 (7/31/89) **82**

J. LOHR
Chenin Blanc Clarksburg Pheasant's Call Vineyard 1988 $4.50 (7/31/89) **58**

LOS HERMANOS
Chenin Blanc California NV $4/1.5L (7/31/89) **74**

MARTIN BROTHERS
Chenin Blanc Paso Robles 1988 $6 (7/31/89) **85**

LOUIS M. MARTINI
Chenin Blanc Napa Valley 1987 $5 (7/31/89) **70**

PAUL MASSON
Chenin Blanc California 1988 $5/1.5L (7/31/89) **65**

MIRASSOU
Chenin Blanc Monterey 1987 $5.50 (7/31/89) **75**

ROBERT MONDAVI
Chenin Blanc Napa Valley 1989: Spicy, floral and a tad earthy, this is a dead ringer for a sweetish Vouvray. Not especially fruity, but flavorful and a little more complex than most. Drinkable now. $8 (11/15/91) **82**
Chenin Blanc Napa Valley 1988: Very basic stuff. Smells grassy and slightly musty or woody and tastes very sweet and simple, with apple flavors. Tasted twice, and this was the better score. $8 (6/30/90) **69**
Chenin Blanc Napa Valley 1987 $8 (7/31/89) **78**

MONTEREY VINEYARD
Chenin Blanc Monterey Classic 1988 $6.50 (7/31/89) **88**

PARDUCCI
Chenin Blanc Mendocino 1987 $5.75 (7/31/89) **87**

PELLIGRINI
Chenin Blanc North Coast Vintage White 1988 $4.50 (7/31/89) **79**

R.H. PHILLIPS
Chenin Blanc Yolo County Dunnigan Hills 1987 $4.50 (7/31/89) **82**

PINE RIDGE
Chenin Blanc Napa Valley Yountville Cuvée 1989: Light and effusively fruity, this is clean, crisp and a bit sweet, showing appealing peach, apple and watermelon aromas and flavors. A delight to sip now. $7 (4/30/90) **81**
Chenin Blanc Napa Valley Yountville Cuvée 1988 $7 (7/31/89) **83**

PRESTON
Chenin Blanc Dry Creek Valley 1988 $7.50 (7/31/89) **82**

SAN MARTIN
Chenin Blanc Monterey 1987 $6 (7/31/89) **58**

SANTA BARBARA
Chenin Blanc Santa Ynez Valley 1987 $7 (7/31/89) **77**

SEBASTIANI
Chenin Blanc California 1987 $5.25 (7/31/89) **65**

SIMI
Chenin Blanc Mendocino 1987 $6.50 (7/31/89) **83**

STEVENOT
Chenin Blanc Calaveras County 1987 $5.50 (7/31/89) **69**

SUTTER HOME
Chenin Blanc California 1988 $4 (7/31/89) **66**

TAYLOR
Chenin Blanc California NV $3/1.5L (7/31/89) **71**

VENTANA
Chenin Blanc Monterey 1988 $5.50 (7/31/89) **78**

VILLA MT. EDEN
Chenin Blanc Napa Valley Dry 1987 $6 (7/31/89) **81**

WEIBEL
Chenin Blanc Mendocino 1988 $5 (7/31/89) **83**

WHITE OAK
Chenin Blanc Alexander Valley 1990: Soft and fruity, with a pleasant green apple zing to it, showing a level of flavor intensity seldom seen even in Vouvray. Has style and charm. Drinkable now. 1,329 cases made. $7 (11/15/91) BB **87**
Chenin Blanc Dry Creek Valley 1988 $6.50 (7/31/89) **84**

DESSERT

ALDERBROOK
Sauvignon Blanc Late Harvest Dry Creek Valley 1989: Extremely sweet and honeyed, yet amazingly light in texture, with intense, clean flavors of honey, vanilla, spice and pear that are very appealing, if almost too sweet in balance. Liqueurlike; a dessert in itself. $24/375ml (6/15/92) **88**

ARCIERO
White Riesling Late Harvest Santa Barbara County December Harvest 1985: A rich, distinctive dessert wine. Has a deep amber color, ripe dried apricot and honey aromas and very sweet nut, butter candy and apricot flavors. A tart edge keeps it from being cloying. $10.50 (12/15/89) **84**

AUSTIN
Johannisberg Riesling Late Harvest Santa Barbara County Botrytis 1986: A very good, solid sweet wine. Ripe and fruity, with a smooth, soft texture and hints of honey and nuts to complement the apricot flavors. $8/375ml (12/15/89) **81**
Sauvignon Blanc Late Harvest Santa Barbara County Botrytis Sierra Madre Vineyard 1985: Only for the adventurous. Has pungent aromas of tobacco, salted nuts and herbs backed by modest fruit flavors and good acidity. A very unusual dessert wine. $10/375ml (12/15/89) **72**

BABCOCK
Johannisberg Riesling Late Harvest Santa Ynez Valley Cluster Selected 1987: An outstanding dessert wine that's rich and very fruity, yet retains its balance and an elegant texture. Has complex peach, apricot, honey, vanilla and nutmeg falvors that last on the finish. Delicious now through 1993 if kept in a cool place. $14/375ml (12/15/89) **89**

BARON HERZOG
Johannisberg Riesling Late Harvest California 1989 $8/375ml (3/31/91) **86**

BELVEDERE
Muscat Canelli Late Harvest Alexander Valley 1990: Rich, unctuous and smooth in texture, with pungent orange, spice and grapefruit aromas and flavors. Tasted twice. 1,130 cases made. $10/375ml (6/15/92) **80**

BONNY DOON

Grenache Late Harvest California Vin de Glacière 1987 $15/375ml (12/31/88) **90**

Muscat Canelli Late Harvest California Vin de Glacière 1990: Rich, perfumed, concentrated and sweet, with delicious, delicately spiced pear and orange blossom aromas and flavors that extend into a long, lovely finish. A wonderful after-dinner sipper. Drink soon. $15/375ml (3/31/92) **91**

Muscat Canelli Late Harvest California Vin de Glacière 1987 $15/375ml (12/31/88) **91**

Prunus Ca' del Solo California NV: Eau-de-vie fans can rejoice over this remarkable dry blend of apricot, cherry and plum brandies. Each fruit flavor asserts itself on the long, generous flavor profile. Doesn't bite too much, either. Serve chilled. $15/375ml (3/31/92) **92**

BUENA VISTA

Late Harvest Carneros Ingrid's Vineyard Late Harvest White 1989: Sweet but acidic and velvety enough to keep from being rich or voluptuous, offering plenty of peach, fig and honey aromas and flavors. Could be a bit longer and smoother, but it's very pleasant to drink. 500 cases made. $18 (4/30/91) **87**

CHALK HILL

Sémillon Late Harvest Chalk Hill 1986: Would give most Sauternes a run for their money. The salty, nutty, tobaccolike aromas and rich, ripe flavors are full and satisfying. Sweet, unctuous and long on the finish. Mature now and ready to drink. 2,262 cases made. $10/375ml (6/15/92) **91**

CHATEAU DE BAUN

Symphony Late Harvest Sonoma County Finale 1988: Floral, spicy Muscat aromas and flavors make this sweet dessert wine distinctive. The almond overtones are nice, too. Drinkable now. 900 cases made. $12/375ml (4/30/91) **87**

Symphony Late Harvest Sonoma County Finale 1987: Super sweet, thick and very concentrated in flavor, but backed with good acidity. Very assertive aromas border on soapy, but the finish is clean and long-lasting. $14/375ml (4/30/89) **85**

Symphony Late Harvest Sonoma County Finale 1986 $14/375ml (9/15/87) **81**

CHATEAU ST. JEAN

Gewürztraminer Late Harvest Alexander Valley Robert Young Vineyards 1982 $18/375ml (7/16/84) **91**

Gewürztraminer Late Harvest Alexander Valley Robert Young Vineyards Select 1983 $14/375ml (11/01/84) **92**

Johannisberg Riesling Late Harvest Alexander Valley Robert Young Vineyards 1984 $15/375ml (3/16/86) **86**

Johannisberg Riesling Late Harvest Alexander Valley Robert Young Vineyards 1983 $25/375ml (8/01/85) SS **92**

Johannisberg Riesling Late Harvest Alexander Valley Robert Young Vineyards Special Select 1982 $22/375ml (9/01/84) **92**

Johannisberg Riesling Late Harvest Alexander Valley Select 1988: An aromatic wine of moderate sweetness, but with plenty of pine, peach and floral varietal flavors, crisp acidity and good length. Drinkable now, but should show more after 1993. $20/375ml (4/30/91) **86**

Johannisberg Riesling Late Harvest Russian River Valley Select 1985 $12 (8/31/87) **84**

Sauvignon Blanc Late Harvest Sonoma County Sauvignon d'Or 1982 $15 (7/01/84) **85**

Sémillon Late Harvest Sonoma Valley Sémillon d'Or St. Jean Vineyard 1984 $15 (11/30/86) **86**

CLAIBORNE & CHURCHILL

Riesling Late Harvest Central Coast 1987: A subtle, soft earthy flavor runs through this very sweet, smooth-tasting wine. A bit of fruit lends a nice background. Balanced on the soft side. $15/375ml (12/15/89) **81**

CLOS DU BOIS

Gewürztraminer Late Harvest Alexander Valley Individual Bunch Selected 1986 $18/375ml (8/31/87) **80**

Johannisberg Riesling Late Harvest Alexander Valley Individual Bunch Selected 1986 $15/375ml (8/31/87) **89**

Muscat of Alexandria Late Harvest Alexander Valley Fleur d'Alexandra 1986 $10 (5/31/88) **90**

DE LOACH

Gewürztraminer Late Harvest Russian River Valley 1989: Ripe, rich and bursting with pineapple and apricot flavors, this is sweet without being cloying. It's balanced with plenty of acidity and an appealing nip of bitter almond on the finish. A golden wine, with plenty to offer for drinking soon. $10/375ml (4/30/91) **88**

Gewürztraminer Late Harvest Russian River Valley 1987 $10/375ml (12/31/88) **93**

Gewürztraminer Late Harvest Russian River Valley 1984 $10 (10/01/85) BB **92**

DE LORIMIER

Sauvignon Blanc Late Harvest Alexander Valley Lace 1986 $11/375ml (2/29/88) **82**

DE MOOR

Sauvignon Blanc Late Harvest Napa Valley Fie Doux 1989: On the light side for a late-harvest Sauvignon Blanc, with pleasant honey and anise aromas and flavors surrounding a pearlike core. Hints of nutmeg and walnut on the finish are pleasant. Drinkable now. $12/375ml (3/15/92) **84**

DOLCE

Late Harvest California 1989: Bold, ripe and complex, with intense, rich pear, spice, butter, nutmeg and honey flavors that fan out on the palate. Harmonious and elegant, with layers of apricot and butterscotch emerging on the long, lingering finish. Drink now to 1994. First release of Dolce from Far Niente winery. $50/375ml (6/15/92) **91**

DOMAINE CHARBAY

Dessert Chardonnay Sonoma County NV: Earthy aromas and flavors dominate what fruit is present in this sweet, otherwise nondescript dessert wine. $5/187ml (3/31/92) **71**

DRY CREEK

Sauvignon Blanc Late Harvest Dry Creek Valley Soleil Vintner's Reserve David S. Stare 1986 $15/375ml (6/15/89) **90**

FERRARI-CARANO

Sauvignon Blanc Late Harvest Alexander Valley Eldorado Gold 1989: A very focused, rich and fruity dessert wine, with clean, vivid apricot, fig and honey flavors that linger on the finish. Balanced, harmonious and delicious. $16.50/375ml (9/15/91) **88**

Key to Symbols

The scores reported here are the results of blind tastings conducted by our panel of senior editors. Wines that carry the initials below are results of individual tastings.

THE WINE SPECTATOR 100-POINT SCALE ***95-100***—Classic, a great wine; ***90-94***—Outstanding, superior character and style; ***80-89***—Good to very good, a wine with special qualities; ***70-79***—Average, drinkable wine that may have minor flaws; ***60-69***—Below average, drinkable but not recommended; ***50-59***—Poor, undrinkable, not recommended. "+"—With a score indicates a range; used primarily with barrel tastings to indicate a preliminary score.

SPECIAL DESIGNATIONS SS—Spectator Selection, CS—Cellar Selection, BB—Best Buy, ($NA)—Price not available, (NR)—Not released.

TASTER'S INITIALS (JG)—Jim Gordon, (HS)—Harvey Steiman, (JL)—James Laube, (JS)—James Suckling, (TM)—Thomas Matthews, (TR)—Terry Robards, (PM)—Per-Henrik Mansson, (BT)—Barrel Tasting (these wines were tasted blind from barrel samples), (CA-date)—*California's Great Cabernets* by James Laube, (CH-date)—*California's Great Chardonnays* by James Laube, (VP-date)—*Vintage Port* by James Suckling.

DATE TASTED Dates in parentheses represent the issue in which the rating was published.

FETZER

Johannisberg Riesling Late Harvest Sonoma County Reserve 1988: Very ripe, lush and opulent, with rich apricot, spice and honey aromas and flavors that are long, fresh and balanced on the finish despite the high level of sweetness. Drinkable now, but should be best after 1993. A good value. $10/375ml (3/31/91) **91**

FICKLIN

Port California Special Bottling No. 5 1980: Light in texture, spicy and elegant, with appealing cherry, toast and walnut aromas and flavors that are long and focused. Not as rich or dramatic as some Ports, but well crafted. $19 (4/30/91) **84**

Port California Special Bottling No. 6 1983: Rich and complex, already acquiring a definite sense of maturity, offering interesting chocolate, walnut and smoke overtones to the basic ripe plum and prune flavors. Approaching drinkability. Best from 1993 to '98. $25 (11/30/91) **87**

Port California Tinta NV: Light in texture and not as sweet as some California Ports, but a flavorful dessert wine offering cherry and walnut aromas and flavors in modest dimensions. $10 (4/30/91) **78**

FIRESTONE

Johannisberg Riesling Late Harvest Santa Barbara County Selected Harvest 1989: Silky in texture and very ripe, lush and sweet, with spicy ginger, apricot and honey aromas and flavors that turn a bit soft and unctuous on the finish. Drinkable now. 750 cases made. $12/375ml (4/30/91) **84**

Johannisberg Riesling Late Harvest Santa Ynez Valley Ambassador's Vineyard Selected Harvest 1988: An extremely sweet, soft, cleanly made dessert wine with abundant peach and pear flavors. Drink as dessert, not with dessert. Some may find it too cloying. $9.50/375ml (12/15/89) **79**

Johannisberg Riesling Late Harvest Santa Ynez Valley Ambassador's Vineyard Selected Harvest 1986: Rich, honeyed and smooth, with unctuous fruit and vanilla overtones. Spicy and almost buttery on the finish, yet clean and not too heavily sweet. $9.50/375ml (2/28/89) **89**

FRANCISCAN

Johannisberg Riesling Late Harvest Napa Valley Select 1983 $10/375ml (1/31/88) **88**

FREEMARK ABBEY

Johannisberg Riesling Late Harvest Napa Valley Edelwein Gold 1989: With its golden color and honey, apricot and subtle spice aromas and flavors, this is a knockout from the first whiff to the last echo of the long finish. A rich, sweet wine that is seductive now and should continue to develop through 1995 to 2000. 1,000 cases made. $22/375ml (7/15/90) **92**

Johannisberg Riesling Late Harvest Napa Valley Edelwein Gold 1988: Rich and delicate, with complex pine, apple, orange and tangerine flavors that are ripe and exotic, and soft and lingering on the finish. $18/375ml (6/15/89) **87**

Johannisberg Riesling Late Harvest Napa Valley Edelwein Gold 1986 $18.50/375ml (6/15/87) **87**

Johannisberg Riesling Late Harvest Napa Valley Edelwein Gold 1973 ($NA) (2/28/87) **91**

FROG'S LEAP

Sauvignon Blanc Late Harvest Napa Valley Late Leap 1989: Very nutty tasting, ripe and soft, with honey and orange nuances that linger on the finish. A rich dessert wine that's appealing to drink now. 350 cases made. $14/375ml (10/31/91) **84**

Sauvignon Blanc Late Harvest Napa Valley Late Leap 1986 $9.50/375ml (9/30/88) **85**

GEYSER PEAK

Johannisberg Riesling Late Harvest Mendocino County Selected Dried Berry 1990: Ripe, spicy and balanced, an elegant dessert wine just oozing with grapefruit, honey, apricot and spice aromas and flavors that keep echoing on the long, generous finish. Drinkable now. 300 cases made. $13/375ml (8/31/91) **93**

Opulence California NV $7.50 (1/31/87) **80**

GLEN ELLEN

Riesling Late Harvest Santa Maria Valley Imagery Series 1989: Very sweet and smooth, this syrupy wine has attractive peach and delicate spice aromas and flavors, but comes off as syrupy rather than rich. Drinkable now, but better if it gains more maturity. Try around 1994 or '95. 227 cases made. $10/375ml (3/31/92) **79**

GRAND CRU

Gewürztraminer Late Harvest Sonoma County Select 1987: The flavors are appealing, with honey and apricot dominating, but strong sulphur and leafy overtones keep it from being smooth or elegant. $10/375ml (3/31/90) **72**

GREENWOOD RIDGE

White Riesling Late Harvest Mendocino 1989: Very ripe, sweet and generous, with nutmeg- and honey-scented apricot and pear aromas and flavors. Gets very rich and unctuous on the finish. Drinkable now, but aging until 1995 to '97 should bring it into better sugar balance. 316 cases made. $18/375ml (8/31/91) **89**

HIDDEN CELLARS

Chanson d'Or Bailey J. Lovin Vineyard Mendocino County 1989: Sweet, flavorful and dramatic. Has the deep gold color of a classic late-harvest wine and modest apricot and peach flavors, but comes up a bit short on intensity for a wine of this type. 478 cases made. $15/375ml (9/15/91) **84**

Riesling Late Harvest Mendocino Bailey J. Lovin Vineyard 1984 $10 (10/16/85) **94**

INGLENOOK

Gewürztraminer Late Harvest Napa Valley 1986 $9.50/375ml (5/15/88) **78**

JEKEL

Riesling Late Harvest Arroyo Seco Gravelstone Vineyard 1987: Has short, heavy, slightly moldy aromas and light, simple, stony flavors, with hints of peach, nectarine, honey and nuts and an aftertaste of bread mold. Tasted twice. $13.50/375ml (2/28/89) **77**

KENWOOD

Johannisberg Riesling Late Harvest Sonoma Valley 1985 $10/375ml (2/28/87) BB **89**

Johannisberg Riesling Late Harvest Sonoma Valley 1984 $8.50/375ml (9/16/85) **79**

CHARLES LEFRANC

Gewürztraminer Late Harvest San Benito County Selected 1984 $11 (3/16/86) **75**

LONG

Johannisberg Riesling Late Harvest Napa Valley Botrytis 1990: Very fruity, bursting with peach and lemon aromas and flavors. Sweet and balanced, but shows little in the way of honey or other botrytis overtones. The grapefruit and lemon flavors linger. Drinkable now. $18 (9/15/91) **86**

MARK WEST

Johannisberg Riesling Late Harvest Russian River Valley 1983 $10/375ml (3/16/86) **79**

MARTIN BROTHERS

Aleatico California 1990: Spicy strawberry aromas are strong and aggressive, but this is a relatively light-weight, not-very-sweet dessert wine that's pinkish in color and aromatic. Tasted twice, with consistent notes. 2,200 cases made. $10/375ml (3/15/92) **78**

Moscato Frizzante California 1991: Light and frankly sweet, but balanced with a lean line of lacy acidity. A fragrant wine, with orange blossom, pear and litchi aromas and flavors that are utterly beguiling. Despite the name, there's not much fizz. Drink soon. 1,100 cases made. $9 (3/31/92) **88**

Vin Santo Sweet Malvasia Bianca California 1990: An odd, citrusy wine, with a mild effervescence and a nutty edge to the flavors. Best served chilled. Tasted twice. 515 cases made. $15 (3/15/92) **81**

Zinfandel Port Paso Robles Primitivo Appassito 1990: Distinctly fruity, from the first whiff to the last echo of the finish, with all the Zinfandel-like berry aromas and flavors and little of the Port complexity. Rather like a high-alcohol Zin that is not overripe. Probably best to cellar until 1994 to '96. $12 (3/15/92) **83**

MAYACAMAS
Zinfandel Late Harvest Napa Valley 1984: Jammy and Port-like, packed with raspberry aromas and flavors wrapped in tannins, but the sweetness mitigates the tannins enough to make it drinkable. Try on a cool evening with a wedge of tasty cheese. $18 (11/15/89) **84**

MERRYVALE
Muscat de Frontignan Napa Valley Antigua NV: A distinctive, amber-colored wine, with Madeira-like nuttiness, a smooth texture and a set of spicy orange aromas and flavors that linger on the finish. Well made and elegant. 600 cases made. $12 (11/30/91) **86**

MIRASSOU
Johannisberg Riesling Late Harvest Monterey Select Harvest Reserve 1987: Rich and concentrated, dark amber in color, with lots of apricot, spice and caramel aromas and flavors. Long and elegant, if a mite syrupy. Drinkable now. 1,225 cases made. $12.50/375ml (8/31/91) **87**

NAVARRO
Gewürztraminer Late Harvest Anderson Valley Sweet 1989: Delicately sweet, showing a moderate level of appealing apricot, spice and floral aromas and flavors that are balanced and harmonious. Drinkable now. 4,373 cases made. $12 (4/30/91) **86**
Gewürztraminer Late Harvest Anderson Valley Sweet Cluster Selected 1989: Dark and ripe, with an acetic edge to the otherwise sweet, honeyed flavors, turning spicy with apricot and pineapple notes that extend into a long finish. Tastes much better than it smells at this point. Try cellaring until 1994. 580 cases made. $15/375ml (3/15/92) **86**
Gewürztraminer Late Harvest Anderson Valley Vineyard Selection 1986: Very ripe and honeyed, with rich apricot, honey and slightly floral flavors that are smooth and carefully balanced. Shows restraint, but is plenty tasty. Give it some time to open up. $18.50 (2/28/89) **93**
White Riesling Late Harvest Anderson Valley Cluster Selected 1985 $10/375ml (5/15/87) **81**
White Riesling Late Harvest Anderson Valley Sweet Cluster Selected 1989: Sweet and rich, with honeyed apricot and pear aromas and flavors, plus a definite component of volatile acidity that keeps it from being as lush and seductive as it could be. Best to drink after 1994 or '95, when maturity sets in. $15 (3/31/92) **83**
White Riesling Late Harvest Anderson Valley Sweet Cluster Selected 1986: Rich, very sweet and deeply honeyed, with complex hazelnut and caramel overtones to the ripe apricot and pineapple flavors. Definitely sticky on the finish. Approachable now, but cellaring until 1993 to '95 could bring it into better balance. 782 cases made. $25 (3/31/90) **85**

PEJU
Chardonnay Late Harvest Napa Valley Select 1989: A happy surprise. Sweet but not cloying, with plenty of apricot, pineapple, honey and apple pie flavors extending into the finish. Honey on the aftertaste. Very tasty and appealing. Drinkable now. 800 cases made. $12.50/375ml (3/15/92) **88**

JOSEPH PHELPS
Johannisberg Riesling Late Harvest Napa Valley 1985 $11.75 (12/15/86) **93**
Johannisberg Riesling Late Harvest Napa Valley Special Select 1983 $25 (3/16/86) **75**
Johannisberg Riesling Late Harvest Napa Valley Special Select 1982 $22.50/375ml (4/16/84) **92**
Scheurebe Late Harvest Napa Valley 1990: Nice peach and floral flavors fill up this sweet but straightforward dessert wine. The flavors lack concentration and depth, but are appealing. Tasted twice. 200 cases made. $12.50/375ml (6/15/92) **81**
Scheurebe Late Harvest Napa Valley 1985 Rel: $15 Cur: $21 (8/31/86) SS **94**
Scheurebe Late Harvest Napa Valley 1983 $15 (9/16/84) **87**
Scheurebe Late Harvest Napa Valley 1982 Rel: $15 Cur: $21 (4/16/84) CS **90**
Scheurebe Late Harvest Napa Valley Special Select 1989: Sweet but not cloying, with focused peach, berry and tropical fruit aromas and flavors. Has elegance and plenty of flavor on the finish. Drinkable now, but cellaring until 1993 to '95 wouldn't hurt. $18/375ml (4/30/91) **88**
Scheurebe Late Harvest Napa Valley Special Select 1982 $25/375ml (5/16/85) **88**
Sémillon Late Harvest Napa Valley Délice du Sémillon 1989: The ripe peach, fig and nectarine aromas and flavors are most appealing in this sweet but balanced, richly flavored and elegant wine. Finishes drier than it starts. Drinkable now. 1,000 cases made. $12.50/375ml (4/30/91) **89**
Sémillon Late Harvest Napa Valley Délice du Sémillon 1985 $8.75/375ml (8/31/87) **91**
Sémillon Late Harvest Napa Valley Délice du Sémillon 1983 $15 (1/31/87) **61**

BERNARD PRADEL
Sauvignon Blanc Late Harvest Napa Valley Allais Vineyard Botrytis 1985 $9/375ml (5/31/88) **75**

PRESTON
Muscat Canelli Late Harvest Dry Creek Valley Muscat Brûlée 1989: Rich, ripe and sweet, turning earthy and bitter on the aftertaste. Still good, but needs food to soften the edges. Drink now. 752 cases made. $12/375ml (3/15/92) **82**
Muscat Canelli Late Harvest Dry Creek Valley Muscat Brûlée 1987: Extremely ripe and intense, this is thick, concentrated, smooth and polished, showing great depth of apricot, orange and spice aromas and flavors balanced with a nick of acidity and bitterness on the finish to complement the sweetness. A great dessert wine. $12/375ml (8/31/89) **91**

QUADY
Black Muscat California Elysium 1990: Firm in texture and ebulliently fruity, with terrific blackberry, Muscat and nutmeg aromas and flavors. The alcohol doesn't get in the way. Like a Muscat Port. Drinkable now. $12 (11/30/91) **86**
Black Muscat California Elysium 1989: Despite the light, almost magenta color, this sweet wine has plenty of peach, watermelon and berry aromas and flavors. It could be more concentrated, but it's refreshing. 4,300 cases made. $12 (10/15/90) **85**
Black Muscat California Elysium 1988: Floral and berry aromas meld into delicious complexity against a remarkably light, elegant structure. Sweet without being cloying, this is long and distinctive, with violet overtones and ripe boysenberry flavors lending considerable depth. $11 (8/31/89) **90**
Black Muscat California Elysium 1987 $6.50/375ml (9/30/88) **82**
Black Muscat California Elysium 1985 $11 (9/15/86) **85**
Black Muscat California Elysium 1984 $11 (8/01/85) **87**
Orange Muscat California Electra 1991: Fresh, crisp and spritzy, with tart, sweet orange and floral flavors that are refreshingly lively. Tastes fresher and better than a bottle reviewed earlier. $9.50 (6/15/92) **84**
Orange Muscat California Essensia 1990: Has a stronger alcohol edge than usual, but the orange and spice aromas and flavors are attractive and stay with you on the finish. Drinkable now. $12 (11/30/91) **83**
Orange Muscat California Essensia 1989: A delicious dessert in a glass, bursting with rose petal, litchi, nectarine, honey and orange aromas and flavors. This is a sensory symphony offering elegance as well as intensity. Drink soon. $12 (10/15/90) **89**
Orange Muscat California Essensia 1987: The deep color and rich, creamy texture show off the distinctive orange character in the aromas and flavors. Long, flavorful and a bit sticky. It's lacking the usual finesse associated with this wine. $11 (8/31/89) **78**
Orange Muscat California Essensia 1985 $11 (9/30/86) **79**
Orange Muscat California Essensia 1984 $11 (7/01/85) **88**
Port Amador County 1984 $9 (10/01/85) **82**
Port Amador County Frank's Vineyard 1986: Spicy and alcoholic, smelling more like grappa than Port. This spirity wine could never be described as smooth, but it has complex chocolate, cherry and spice flavors that linger on the finish. May be worth drinking after 1995. 1,500 cases made. $12 (10/15/90) **75**
Port Amador County Frank's Vineyard 1985: Smells like it was fortified with grappa, not brandy. Harsh and hot, a wine that singes—not sings. $16 (8/31/89) **65**
Port California 1985: A harsh, bitter edge takes away from the sweet, plummy flavors and overcomes whatever smoothness and elegance it has. Drinkable with of strong cheese. $9.50 (8/31/89) **73**
Starboard Amador County 1987: Ripe and sweet, but spirity, showing more alcoholic harshness than is desirable. Still, the cherry and berry flavors are appealing. $25 (3/31/91) **81**
Starboard Amador County Batch 88 Rich Ruby 1988: Very rich and spicy, a well-crafted, Port-like wine with concentration and character. A brilliant berry flavor extends through the finish, shaded by smoky, spicy overtones. Best to drink after 1998 to 2000. 600 cases made. $15 (11/30/91) **87**

RANCHO SISQUOC
Johannisberg Riesling Late Harvest Santa Maria Valley Special Select 1986: An acceptable dessert wine that misses the mark because of its herbal, volatile aromas and salty, tobaccolike flavors. $18/375ml (12/15/89) **68**

RAYMOND
Johannisberg Riesling Late Harvest Napa Valley 1985 $8.50 (9/15/86) **91**

RUTHERFORD HILL
Port Napa Valley Vintage 1983 $18 (11/15/87) **66**

ST. FRANCIS
Muscat Canelli Sonoma County 1990: Fruity, creamy and refreshing, with a nice bite of acidity to balance the sweet pear and peach aromas and flavors. Drinkable now. $10 (11/30/91) **80**

SANTA BARBARA
Johannisberg Riesling Late Harvest Santa Ynez Valley Botrytised Grapes 1986 $15/375ml (10/15/87) **88**
Zinfandel Late Harvest Santa Ynez Valley Essence 1987: Think of it as a late-harvest iced tea. Orange-brown in color, tealike in aroma and very sweet, but not very flavorful. The texture is smooth and rich. $15/375ml (12/15/89) **74**

SANTINO
Johannisberg Riesling Late Harvest Sonoma County Dry Berry Select 1989: Dark, sweet and spicy, with natural caramel color and caramel flavors, hinting at apricot, honey and walnut on the unctuous finish. Incredibly concentrated and rich but not heavy. Drinkable now. 975 cases made. $18/375ml (11/30/91) **92**

SHENANDOAH
Orange Muscat Amador County 1990: This charming, off-beat wine is spicy, with distinct Muscat and orange flavors that are rich and sweet. 616 cases made. $10 (6/15/92) **84**

STAG'S LEAP WINE CELLARS
White Riesling Late Harvest Napa Valley Birkmyer Vineyards Selected Bunches 1983 $13.50/375ml (10/01/84) **85**

ROBERT STEMMLER
Sauvignon Blanc Late Harvest Sonoma County 1985 $10/375ml (9/30/88) **68**

STONEGATE
Late Harvest Napa Valley 1990: Mildly sweet, with subtle herbal, earthy notes and a lean core of pear and fig flavors. Finishes nicely. Drinkable now. 80 percent Sauvignon Blanc and 20 percent Sémillon. 767 cases made. $9.50/375ml (3/31/92) **83**
Late Harvest Napa Valley 1989: Very sweet and rich, with lots of fig and pineapple aromas and flavors and a smooth texture. Long and just the tiniest bit cloying on the finish, but cellaring until 1993 or '94 should take care of that. 60 percent Sauvignon Blanc and 40 percent Sémillon. $13/375ml (4/30/91) **87**

TOPAZ
Sauvignon Blanc -Sémillon Late Harvest Napa Valley Special Select 1989: Ripe, rich and sweet, with lots of fig, herb and honey aromas and flavors that extend into a long, concentrated finish. Beautifully balanced, elegant and drinkable now, but should improve at least through 1994 or '95. 710 cases made. $19/375ml (8/31/91) **90**

VEGA
Johannisberg Riesling Late Harvest Santa Barbara County Special Selection 1987: Enjoyable, with tasty orange and sweet apricot flavors and a smooth, soft structure. $10.50/375ml (12/15/89) **78**

VENTANA
White Riesling Late Harvest Monterey Ventana Vineyards Hand-Selected Clusters 1987: Soft and sweet, but a bit watery and earthy on the finish. It starts out smelling rich, buttery and honeylike, but the lack of balancing acidity keeps it from being as good as it could be. $14/375ml (8/31/89) **70**

VICHON
Sémillon Late Harvest Napa Valley Botrytis 1986 $15/375ml (12/31/88) **86**
Sémillon Late Harvest Napa Valley Botrytis 1985 $15/375ml (7/15/88) **88**

VILLA MT. EDEN
Sauvignon Blanc Late Harvest Napa Valley 1989: A rich wine, with very ripe, lush, honeyed aromas and flavors of botrytised pineapple and fig. Smooth and sweet on the finish. An acetic edge knocks it down a peg, but it's still a fine drink. $13/375ml (4/30/91) **83**
Sauvignon Blanc Late Harvest Napa Valley 1986 $10/375ml (5/15/88) **89**

WENTE BROS.
Riesling Late Harvest Arroyo Seco Auslese 1973 ($NA) (2/28/87) **95**
Riesling Late Harvest Arroyo Seco November Harvest Reserve Arroyo Seco Vineyard 1987: Not as smooth, sweet and opulent as the deep golden color suggests, and lacking the richness and honeyed fruit flavor one expects in this type of wine. Only hints of honey come through on the finish. 905 cases made. $12 (7/15/90) **76**

WOODBURY
Port Alexander Valley Old Vines 1981 $10 (1/01/86) **91**

GAMAY

BEAULIEU
Gamay Beaujolais Napa Valley 1988: Very light in color and light on the palate as well, with pleasant red cherry flavors. Best served slightly chilled. $6.50 (8/31/89) **73**

BUENA VISTA
Gamay Beaujolais Carneros 1988: Lively, charmingly fruity and full of strawberry, cherry and grass flavors. A nip of astringency in the aftertaste is welcome, but not everyone will like the grassiness. $7.50 (7/15/89) **84**

DUXOUP
Napa Gamay Dry Creek Valley 1988: Effusively fruity and fresh in aroma, but heavier on the palate, with tart, grapey flavors and a short, dry finish. $7.50 (2/28/90) **76**
Napa Gamay Dry Creek Valley 1987: One to sink your teeth into. A lively, flavorful red with a bright purple color, berry and pepper flavors and a firm structure. Drink now. $7 (2/28/89) BB **86**

FETZER
Gamay Beaujolais Mendocino County 1988: Light, fresh and sweet, like a simple French Beaujolais. Fine for quaffing. $5 (7/15/89) **74**

PRESTON
Gamay Beaujolais Dry Creek Valley 1988: Offers gobs of fresh, ripe, grapey, plum-tinged flavors that are soft and supple and a pretty floral aftertaste. Delicious to drink chilled or otherwise. $7 (2/15/89) **85**

CHARLES SHAW
Gamay Beaujolais Napa Valley 1988: Effusively fruity, clean and light, making this an easy-to-like quaffing wine for the lunch table. $6.50 (7/15/89) **78**

WEINSTOCK
Gamay Sonoma County 1989 $8 (3/31/91) **75**

GEWÜRZTRAMINER

ALEXANDER VALLEY VINEYARDS
Gewürztraminer Alexander Valley 1988: Acceptable in a pinch. Sweet, soft and fruity but doesn't have much freshness or complexity. 500 cases made. $6.50 (6/30/90) **69**

BABCOCK
Gewürztraminer Santa Ynez Valley 1987: An awkward wine that's refreshing but out of balance. Tastes sweet at first, then turns aggressively tart on the finish. Has 1.5 percent residual sugar. $6.50 (2/28/89) **73**

LAWRENCE J. BARGETTO
Gewürztraminer Monterey County 1990: Fresh and grapefruity, with lovely rose petal and nutmeg overtones. Echoes peach and grapefruit on the finish, where a nice zing of acidity makes it balanced and refreshing. Drink soon. 1,312 cases made. $8 (9/30/91) BB **84**
Gewürztraminer Monterey County Dry Pinnacles Vineyard 1990: Lean and racy, with a crisp texture and pleasant grapefruit, melon and spice aromas and flavors. On the dry side, balanced and refreshing. Drink soon. 1,407 cases made. $8 (9/30/91) BB **83**

BOUCHAINE
Gewürztraminer Carneros 1989: Fruity and fresh, with a gentle softness that lets the apricot, pear and grapefruit flavors unfold across the palate. Lightly spicy on the finish. 500 cases made. $8.50 (6/15/91) **84**
Gewürztraminer Russian River Valley Dry 1990: Floral and spicy, with traditional grapefruit and pineapple flavors. Refreshingly crisp and dry, though not particularly complex. 1,000 cases made. $8.50 (3/31/92) **82**

CHATEAU ST. JEAN
Gewürztraminer Sonoma County 1988: An aggressive wine, with piney flavors and an almost picklelike aroma. Flavorful, but simple and rough-edged. $8 (1/31/90) **72**

CLOS DU BOIS
Gewürztraminer Alexander Valley Early Harvest 1990: Somewhat sweet, but with enough tart apple flavors to keep it lively and appealing. A light, charming wine that would be a good candidate for picnic fare. $8 (3/31/92) **81**
Gewürztraminer Alexander Valley Early Harvest 1989: Pleasantly fruity, with nice orange and grapefruit aromas and flavors, turning soft and a bit metallic on the finish. $8 (2/15/91) **76**
Gewürztraminer Alexander Valley Early Harvest 1988: Balanced on the dry side, with lemony, peachy flavors. Almost like a Riesling, but with hints of spice. Needs to lose some of that lemony quality, but then it should be fine. $8 (11/15/89) **77**

DE LOACH
Gewürztraminer Russian River Valley Early Harvest 1990: Sturdy and broad in texture, with pear, grapefruit and rose petal aromas and flavors. On the dry side, but drinkable now. 3,760 cases made. $8 (4/30/91) **81**
Gewürztraminer Russian River Valley Early Harvest 1989: A good wine that's fairly crisp and fruity, with slightly sweet grapefruit and apple flavors complemented by a touch of spice and butter on the finish. 2,330 cases made. $7.50 (6/30/90) **83**

FETZER
Gewürztraminer California 1990: On the sweet side, but has very pleasant floral and apple aromas and flavors and hints of ginger. Drink cold. $6.75 (4/30/91) **75**
Gewürztraminer California 1989: Fruity, soft and sweet, with plenty of peach and apricot flavors and a touch of spritz that picks it up a bit. Drink it while it's fresh. $6 (6/30/90) **79**
Gewürztraminer California 1988: Clean and spicy, with delicious peach and melon flavors and hints of spice that seem to dance on the aromas and flavors, making this an elegant wine. Slightly off-dry, delicate and long, with a pretty finish. $6.50 (2/28/89) BB **88**

FIELD STONE
Gewürztraminer Alexander Valley 1987: A good white wine that nevertheless lacks the freshness and vivid flavors we look for in Gewürz. Tastes slightly tired and earthy. $7 (2/28/89) **69**

FIRESTONE
Gewürztraminer Santa Ynez Valley 1990: Simple and slightly bitter, this floral wine has a firm texture and a hint of soapiness on the finish. Drinkable now. $8 (11/15/91) **73**

THOMAS FOGARTY
Gewürztraminer Monterey Ventana Vineyards 1990: Simple and uninspired. The grapefruit flavors become almost sour on the finish. 2,225 cases made. $9 (3/31/92) **73**

GRAND CRU
Gewürztraminer Alexander Valley 1990: Soft, fruity and a bit sweet, with pleasant melon, mineral and floral aromas and flavors. Drink soon. $9.50 (9/30/91) **75**

HALLCREST
Gewürztraminer Mendocino County Dry Talmage Town 1989: On the dry side, with lemony, somewhat soapy flavors hinting at pineapple on the finish. Has some of the spice associated with Gewürztraminer, but not in abundance. Drinkable now. 735 cases made. $8.50 (9/30/91) **78**

HANDLEY
Gewürztraminer Anderson Valley 1988: California Gewurtztraminer at its best. Dry but full of ripe peach and pineapple flavors that linger on the finish. Crisp and full-bodied, with complex aromas and flavors. $7 (1/31/90) BB **89**
Gewürztraminer Anderson Valley 1987: A dry, lean wine with good flavors. Well balanced and delicately grapefruity, with rose petal aromas and a touch of honey on the finish. $7 (2/28/89) **86**

Key to Symbols

The scores reported here are the results of blind tastings conducted by our panel of senior editors. Wines that carry the initials below are results of individual tastings.

THE WINE SPECTATOR 100-POINT SCALE ***95-100***—Classic, a great wine; ***90-94***—Outstanding, superior character and style; ***80-89***—Good to very good, a wine with special qualities; ***70-79***—Average, drinkable wine that may have minor flaws; ***60-69***—Below average, drinkable but not recommended; ***50-59***—Poor, undrinkable, not recommended. "+"—With a score indicates a range; used primarily with barrel tastings to indicate a preliminary score.

SPECIAL DESIGNATIONS SS—Spectator Selection, CS—Cellar Selection, BB—Best Buy, ($NA)—Price not available, (NR)—Not released.

TASTER'S INITIALS (JG)—Jim Gordon, (HS)—Harvey Steiman, (JL)—James Laube, (JS)—James Suckling, (TM)—Thomas Matthews, (TR)—Terry Robards, (PM)—Per-Henrik Mansson, (BT)—Barrel Tasting (these wines were tasted blind from barrel samples), (CA-date)—*California's Great Cabernets* by James Laube, (CH-date)—*California's Great Chardonnays* by James Laube, (VP-date)—*Vintage Port* by James Suckling.

DATE TASTED Dates in parentheses represent the issue in which the rating was published.

HIDDEN CELLARS
Gewürztraminer Mendocino County 1987: Dry but not bitter, this is delicately scented with rose petal and grapefruit aromas and clean and austere on the palate. $7 (2/28/89) **83**

HOP KILN
Gewürztraminer Russian River Valley 1988: Floral and grassy smelling, an acceptable, fruity wine that's hard to get excited about. 535 cases made. $7.50 (1/31/90) **72**

HUSCH
Gewürztraminer Anderson Valley 1990: Crisp, fruity and somewhat dry, but generous with its grapefruit, peach and spice aromas and flavors. Drinkable and refreshing. $8.50 (10/31/91) **84**
Gewürztraminer Anderson Valley 1989: Very fruity, soft and easy to like, offering plenty of ripe peach, grapefruit and rose petal characteristics. $8 (6/30/90) **81**
Gewürztraminer Anderson Valley 1987 $7 (9/15/88) **90**

CHARLES KRUG
Gewürztraminer Napa Valley 1988: Fresh and fruity, with distinct apple aromas and flavors and hints of pine and spice. Off-dry but balanced and smooth. $7.25 (1/31/90) **78**

MADDALENA
Gewürztraminer Central Coast 1990: Soft in texture and bordering on sweet, with simple peach and floral aromas and flavors. Finishes sweeter than it starts. 2,000 cases made. $6 (9/30/91) **78**

LOUIS M. MARTINI
Gewürztraminer Russian River Valley Los Vinedos del Rio 1987: A sweet-style Gewürztraminer that's simple and pleasant, with earthy aromas and grassy, fruity flavors. $7 (1/31/90) **71**

MONTICELLO
Gewürztraminer Napa Valley 1986: Has a personality of its own, but comes off light and a bit too simple. Lively on the palate, strongly grapefruity in flavor and dry. $7.50 (2/28/89) **76**

Z. MOORE
Gewürztraminer Russian River Valley 1987: A welcome departure from the usual soft, simple California Gewürztraminer. Nearly dry and well made in the style of Alsace. Has rich, assertive, pleasantly bitter varietal flavors of spice and grapefruit and a lingering finish. $8.50 (2/28/89) **86**

NAVARRO
Gewürztraminer Anderson Valley 1989: Smells great, with floral and grapefruit aromas that echo on the palate. Tastes drier than most California Gewürztraminers, echoing floral and fruit flavors on the finish. Drinkable now. 4,373 cases made. $8.50 (4/30/91) BB **89**
Gewürztraminer Anderson Valley 1988: Very floral and fruity smelling, this is dry and full-bodied, with fruit aromas that aren't matched by the subdued flavors. A serious wine. $8.50 (1/31/90) **79**
Gewürztraminer Anderson Valley 1987: One of California's best. Fresh, vibrant and complex in flavor. Fragrant almond and floral aromas are followed by lively, off-dry grapefruit flavors with floral accents. Full-bodied. $7.50 (2/28/89) **89**

PARDUCCI
Gewürztraminer Mendocino County 1990: Lightly spritzy, with ripe aromas, but has off-dry grapefruit flavors. Floral and spice notes also add to this unique, appealing wine. 5,000 cases made. $8 (3/31/92) BB **84**

J. PEDRONCELLI
Gewürztraminer Sonoma County 1987: Simple, sweet and syrupy. Tastes like peaches and nectarines but doesn't have much backbone. $5.50 (2/28/89) **71**

JOSEPH PHELPS
Gewürztraminer Napa Valley 1988: Full-bodied and mostly dry, with grapefruit and spice flavors in an Alsace style, rose petal aromas and a rich texture. $8.50 (6/30/90) **81**

QUAFF
Gewürztraminer Sonoma County 1990: The name says it—drink at a picnic. Light and simple, with appealing apple, pear and floral aromas and flavors. Balanced and easy to drink. $6.25 (4/30/91) **78**
Gewürztraminer Sonoma County 1987: A fruity wine with varietal personality, offering rose petal and earth aromas. Slightly sweet and fairly complex in flavor. $6.50 (2/28/89) **78**

ROUND HILL
Gewürztraminer Napa Valley 1989: Light in texture and fragrant, with litchi, grapefruit and spice aromas, but seems soft and surprisingly bland on the palate. A pleasant drink, though. Drink now. 3,000 cases made. $6 (2/15/91) **79**
Gewürztraminer Napa Valley 1988: An easy-to-like, well-balanced wine, with earthy aromas and nice peach flavors that linger on the finish. Slightly sweet. $6.25 (1/31/90) BB **84**

ST. FRANCIS
Gewürztraminer Sonoma County 1990: Sweet and simple, with straightforward peach and spice flavors. Heavy-handed and unexciting. $10 (3/31/92) **75**
Gewürztraminer Sonoma Valley 1988: Fruity and easy to like, with peachy flavors and exuberant aromas. This slightly sweet wine is great for a picnic. $7.50 (1/31/90) **80**

RODNEY STRONG
Gewürztraminer Sonoma County 1990: Ripe and flavorful, with a firm texture and a sweet edge, but balanced enough to keep a tight rein on the grapefruit and apple aromas and flavors. Refreshing and distinctive. $7 (9/30/91) BB **83**
Gewürztraminer Sonoma County 1987: Crisp, clean, slightly off-dry and vaguely floral, a pale reflection of the robust flavors one expects from Gewürz. $5.50 (2/28/89) **75**

WENTE BROS.
Gewürztraminer Arroyo Seco Vintner Grown Arroyo Seco Vineyards 1987: The sweet-and-sour flavors have little varietal character, just sugar and earthiness. $9 (12/15/89) **64**

MERLOT

ACACIA
Merlot Napa Valley 1984 $15 (2/28/87) **83**

ALEXANDER VALLEY VINEYARDS
Merlot Alexander Valley 1991: Young and lively, with a solid core of tight berry flavors. Not too tannic, balanced and tasty. (NR) (5/15/92) (BT) **83+**
Merlot Alexander Valley 1990 (NR) (5/15/91) (BT) **85+**
Merlot Alexander Valley 1989: Pleasantly ripe and fruity, with hints of herb, cherry and currant flavors. Also has a distinct oaky edge but isn't too tannic. Drink now through 1994. 4,821 cases made. $13 (11/15/91) **84**
Merlot Alexander Valley 1985 $11 (10/31/87) **88**

ANGELS CREEK
Merlot California 1989: Pungent herb and raw oak aromas continue through the flavors and the finish. Heavy-handed and awkward, but drinkable if you really like wood. 1,500 cases made. $9 (5/31/92) **71**

ARMIDA
Merlot Russian River Valley 1990: Tough, tannic and young, this will need until at least 1995 to come around. A decent core of fruit backs it up now, but will it last until the tannins back off? 1,800 cases made. $14 (5/31/92) **78**

ARROWOOD
Merlot Sonoma County 1988: Bright, rich and concentrated, offering plenty of fresh berry and

currant flavors shaded by anise and toast on the smooth finish. Drinkable now but should improve through 1994. Tasted twice. 600 cases made. $25 (5/31/92) **88**

ESTATE WILLIAM BACCALA

Merlot Alexander Valley 1984 $10 (2/28/87) **72**

BEAUCANON

Merlot Napa Valley 1989: Offers a strange concoction of pickley herb and stale, spicy Merlot flavors that are dull. Drink now. Tasted twice. $10 (5/31/92) **73**

Merlot Napa Valley 1988: Very firm and focused, with a moderate level of intensity to the smoky berry and currant flavors. The nicely integrated tannins will need until about 1994 to soften, but it's drinkable now with food. 1,500 cases made. $13 (3/31/91) **84**

Merlot Napa Valley 1986 $13 (12/31/88) **78**

BELLEROSE

Merlot Dry Creek Valley Reserve 1988: Intense raspberry, cherry and strawberry flavors enliven this crisp, medium-bodied wine that's straightforward, charming and easy to drink now. 600 cases made. $16 (5/31/92) **84**

Merlot Sonoma County 1986: Dry, leathery and tannic, not showing much in the way of fruit and finishing on the dry, oaky side. Avoid. Tasted twice. 1,036 cases made. $16 (4/15/90) **69**

Merlot Sonoma County 1985: Very woody and tough, with hard-nosed cherry and berry flavors buried beneath the prickly exterior. Has a tart balance and a woody finish. $16 (2/28/89) **73**

Merlot Sonoma County 1984 $12 (12/31/87) **77**

BELVEDERE

Merlot Alexander Valley Robert Young Vineyards 1986: Attractive and elegant, with rich berry, plum, herb and cedary oak flavors that are sharply defined and well balanced. The finish is long and fruity, with the kind of structure that bodes well for aging. Try in 1993. $13 (6/30/89) **87**

Merlot Alexander Valley Robert Young Vineyards 1984 $13 (8/31/88) **90**

Merlot Alexander Valley Robert Young Vineyards 1983 $12 (12/31/87) **70**

Merlot Alexander Valley Robert Young Vineyards 1982 $12 (3/16/86) **94**

BENZIGER

Merlot Sonoma County 1989: Light and elegant, with pleasant cherry and spice notes. Firmly tannic on the finish, but generous enough to drink now. 900 cases made. $14 (5/31/92) **81**

Merlot Sonoma County 1988: Pleasant and enticing, with a pretty core of cherry and plum flavor balanced by moderate tannins. Ready now through 1993. $12 (11/15/91) **87**

Merlot Sonoma Valley 1987: Distinctively herbal and spicy, but warm and supple on the palate, with ripe black cherry, blackberry, currant and plum flavors that are elegant and fan out. Not too tannic and ready to drink now to 1994. $12 (3/31/91) **86**

Merlot Sonoma Valley 1986: Smooth and lush, with herbal edges to the cassis aromas and flavors, plus hints of Bordeaux-like cedar aromas to lend further interest. Supple, lively and drinkable now. $16 (7/31/89) **84**

BERGFELD

Merlot Napa Valley 1989: A clean single into center field. Fresh, lively and fruity, with moderate tannins and a finish that lingers. Tastes great right now, but could be aged through about 1995. 2,200 cases made. $15 (5/31/92) **87**

BERINGER

Merlot Howell Mountain Bancroft Ranch 1989: Enormously concentrated, smelling of smoke and coffee and tasting of chocolate and black cherry. An extreme wine that swings for the fences. A long, toasty finish brings the oak flavors back for an encore. Tannic and young enough to require cellaring until about 1995 to start drinking. (NR) (5/31/92) **91**

Merlot Howell Mountain Bancroft Ranch 1988: Rich and complex, lavishly spread with buttery oak and bursting with berry and currant flavors underneath. The tannins are well integrated in this mouth-filling but elegantly balanced wine. Distinctive. Can use until 1995 to develop all its complexity. 385 cases made. $28 (5/31/92) **90**

Merlot Howell Mountain Bancroft Ranch 1987: Warm, ripe and generous, with plush herb, plum, chocolate and toasty oak flavors and the concentration, suppleness and finesse you expect from Merlot. The pretty finish echoes the plum and herb notes. A fine expression. Drink now to 1996 and beyond. 400 cases made. $29 (12/31/90) **91**

BOEGER

Merlot El Dorado 1989: Fruity, fairly tight and well balanced, with tart raspberry and plum flavors, moderate tannins and a crisp, fruity finish. Drink now to 1995. 1,200 cases made. $12.50 (2/29/92) **86**

Merlot El Dorado 1988: Earthy, gamy aromas and flavors prevail over the modest level of ripe cherry and currant characteristics. A bit tight and tannic now, this needs until 1993 to begin to soften. 625 cases made. $12.50 (3/31/91) **78**

Merlot El Dorado 1987: Don't let the earthy aromas put you off. Straightforward and well balanced, with smooth, polished plum and black cherry flavors, moderate tannins and typical Merlot tobacco characteristics. Drink now. $12.50 (7/15/90) **81**

Merlot El Dorado 1986 $12.50 (1/31/89) **73**

Merlot El Dorado 1985 $12.50 (2/15/88) **82**

Merlot El Dorado 1982 $10 (10/01/84) **74**

BOGLE

Merlot California 1990: Refreshingly fruity and lively, with pretty ripe cherry, plum and berry notes. Drinks well now and is priced right. 4,000 cases made. $8 (5/31/92) **82**

BRANDER

Merlot Santa Ynez Valley Three Flags 1989: A stylish, plummy, herbal wine wrapped in a robe of toasty oak. Vanilla, spice and maple aromas lead to decent fruit flavors and good balance. $12 (5/31/92) **82**

Merlot Santa Ynez Valley Three Flags 1988: Fresh, fruity and light, with pleasant cherry and strawberry flavors and light tannins. Easy to drink now. $12 (5/31/92) **81**

BRAREN PAULI

Merlot Alexander Valley Mauritson Vineyard 1989: Simple and straightforward, with decent but uninspired herb and plum flavors. Drink now. Tasted twice. 1,800 cases made. $12 (5/31/92) **77**

Merlot Alexander Valley Mauritson Vineyard 1987: Big, ripe and exotic, with rich cherry, raspberry and currant flavors that gain herb and dill-tinged oak notes. Well balanced, neatly proportioned and drinkable now, but better around 1995. $11 (3/31/91) **84**

BRUTOCAO

Merlot Mendocino 1988: A light but flavorful red, with plenty of plum and strawberry flavors and mild tannins. The fruit lasts nicely on the finish. Fine for drinking right away. 300 cases made. $12.50 (5/31/92) **84**

BUENA VISTA

Merlot Carneros 1989: An odd chemical taste gets in the way of the tart fruit flavors. Something went wrong along the line. Tasted twice. $11 (5/31/92) **71**

Merlot Carneros 1985 $11 (6/30/88) **80**

Merlot Carneros Private Reserve 1988: Light and elegant, with tart cherry and plum notes and modest tannins. Drinkable now through 1995. 2,800 cases made. $16.50 (5/31/92) **82**

Merlot Carneros Private Reserve 1987: Sharp and fruity, with raspberry and tart cherry flavors that are inviting but don't really linger on the finish. Might mellow out a bit if aged. Drink now to 1993. $18 (3/31/91) **84**

Merlot Carneros Private Reserve 1986: Soft and supple, with ample herb, currant and cedar aromas and flavors that turn vibrant and rich on the finish. The richness is reined in by zingy acidity and sufficient tannins to warrant holding it until at least 1994. $16.50 (10/31/89) **86**

Merlot Carneros Private Reserve 1984 $14.50 (2/15/88) **87**

Merlot Sonoma County 1987: Smooth and supple, with elegant currant, blackberry and herb aromas and flavors. A balanced, welcoming wine that's drinkable now. $11 (7/31/90) **86**

BUTTERFLY CREEK

Merlot California 1989: Rough and tannic, with plenty of spice and vanilla notes from oak aging, but only modest fruit flavors to back them up. Will need until about 1995 for the tannins to mellow, but is probably best to drink now, while there's still fruit. 223 cases made. $15 (5/31/92) **77**

CAFARO

Merlot Napa Valley 1988: Rich, lively and concentrated, packed with herb, cherry, plum and currant flavors that are a bit tight and tannic now, but shows a sense of harmony and finesse. Probably best to cellar until 1994. 229 cases made. $20 (11/15/91) **89**

Merlot Napa Valley 1987: Big and concentrated, but elegant enough to let the cedary, spicy overtones shine through the focused currant and blackberry aromas and flavors. Seems woody on the finish. Complex already, but should improve with cellaring until 1994. $18 (12/31/90) **86**

Merlot Napa Valley 1986: Lean and tannic now, with an elegant core of tobacco, cherry and currant flavors that dry out on the palate. Doesn't appear to have the depth and concentration for long-term cellaring. Best now to 1994. $18 (12/31/89) **84**

CAIN

Merlot Napa Valley 1990 (NR) (5/15/91) (BT) **90+**

Merlot Napa Valley 1986: A woody wine, with rich, ripe plum, spice and chalk flavors that are lean and tannic on the finish. Well balanced. Drink now. $14 (2/28/89) **83**

Merlot Napa Valley 1984 $12 (9/30/88) **89**

Merlot Napa Valley 1982 $11 (2/01/85) **78**

CANTERBURY

Merlot California 1990: Ripe and fruity but ultimately simple, with cherry and plum flavors that thin out on the aftertaste, where a touch of oak emerges. Drink now. 1,500 cases made. $7 (5/31/92) **79**

CAPARONE

Merlot Santa Maria Valley Tepusquet Vineyard 1981 $10 (3/16/84) **88**

CAREY

Merlot Santa Ynez Valley La Cuesta Vineyard 1988: Not our style. The pungent pickle and green bean flavors throw it all out of whack. Drinkable, but difficult to appreciate as Merlot. Tasted twice, with consistent notes. $16 (5/31/92) **68**

Merlot Santa Ynez Valley La Cuesta Vineyard 1986: Fresh, fruity and medium-bodied. Should be a versatile dinner wine with its berry and herbal flavors, good acidity and moderate tannins. Drink now. $12 (12/15/89) **82**

CARNEROS CREEK

Merlot Napa Valley 1985 $12.50 (2/15/88) **84**

Merlot Napa Valley 1984 $10.50 (8/31/87) **87**

Merlot Napa Valley 1982 $9.50 (2/16/86) **80**

Merlot Napa Valley Truchard Vineyard 1983 $10 (10/01/85) **84**

CECCHETTI SEBASTIANI

Merlot Sonoma County 1989: Leans toward the herbal spectrum of Merlot, but the cherry and currant flavors are attractive and balanced. Has plenty of tannins for the cellar. Hold until 1995. Better than bottles tasted earlier. 350 cases made. $10 (5/31/92) **83**

CHAPPELLET

Merlot Napa Valley 1989: Earthy and strongly mossy, showing little fruit and mostly leafy aromas and flavors. We thought it was corky, but three bottles tasted blind all tasted this way. 1,200 cases made. $16 (5/31/92) **68**

Merlot Napa Valley 1988: Ripe, lively and intense for this vintage, with raspberry and cherry flavors, moderate tannins and a good shot of spice from oak aging. The fruit lingers on the finish. Tasted three times. 5 percent Cabernet Sauvignon. 486 cases made. $15 (4/15/92) **85**

Merlot Napa Valley 1987: Tight and herbal, with firmly reined-in currant and red pepper flavors and hints of tobacco and leather on the finish. Similar to Bordeaux and a bit tannic. Cellar until 1993. 800 cases made. $15 (12/31/90) **89**

Merlot Napa Valley 1986 $15 (1/31/90) **80**

Merlot Napa Valley 1985 $12 (12/31/88) **78**

CHATEAU CHEVRE

Merlot Napa Valley 1985 $16 (8/31/88) **87**

Merlot Napa Valley 1984 $12.50 (10/31/87) **91**

Merlot Napa Valley 1983 $12.50 (10/15/87) **85**

Merlot Napa Valley 1982 $12 (10/01/85) **84**

Merlot Napa Valley Reserve 1986: Has plenty of rich plum and currant aromas and velvety flavors, with a meaty nuance and a touch of tobacco and wood on the finish. $25 (7/31/89) **80**

Merlot Napa Valley Reserve 1984 $15 (12/15/87) **78**

CHATEAU JULIEN

Merlot Monterey County 1989: Deeply colored, rich, ripe and chocolaty in flavor and backed by firm tannins. Has fine flavor concentration, good structure and a lingering finish. Needs until about 1994 to smooth out. 680 cases made. $9 (5/31/92) **86**

Merlot Monterey County 1988: An average-quality Merlot, with vegetal aromas and flavors tinged by an unappealing dirty note. 2,410 cases made. $9 (5/31/92) **72**

Merlot Monterey County 1986: Lean, mean and very herbal, this is overwhelmingly minty and oaky. Not much fun to drink now and doesn't seem as if it will develop. $10 (4/15/89) **60**

Merlot Santa Barbara County Bien Nacido Vineyard 1984 $12 (2/29/88) **76**

CHATEAU SOUVERAIN

Merlot Alexander Valley 1991: Firm and austere, with herbal-tinged currant and berry flavors. Shows plenty of tough tannins, too, but they're in line for a barrel sample. 20 percent Cabernet Franc. 500 cases made. (NR) (5/15/92) (BT) **83+**

Merlot Alexander Valley 1989: Ripe, full and generous, with focused plum, cherry and currant flavors that are supple and tasty. Not too tannic and holds together nicely, with an elegant aftertaste. Best around 1995. Much better than bottles tasted earlier. $10 (5/31/92) **89**

Merlot North Coast 1981 $6.75 (10/01/85) **89**

Merlot Sonoma County 1990: Ripe and round, with plump cherry and currant flavors. Finishes with firm tannins, a hint of cola and smoky, buttery oak notes. Needs until 1995. $10 (5/31/92) **86**

Merlot Sonoma County 1986: An herbal, vegetal wine that's soft in structure, with tarry elements to give it interest. Short on the finish. $10 (3/31/89) **74**

Merlot Sonoma County 1984 $8.50 (7/31/87) **86**

CHESTNUT HILL

Merlot Napa Valley 1989: Has distinct herb and spice notes, but the plum and currant flavors taste light and thin. The tannins suggest it needs time, but without the fruit concentration it's probably best to drink soon. Try now to 1993. $10 (11/15/91) **81**

Merlot North Coast 1985 $8.50 (12/15/87) **84**

CHRISTIAN BROTHERS

Merlot Napa Valley 1985 $8 (8/31/88) **80**

CILURZO

Merlot Temecula Unfiltered Proprietor's Reserve 1990: A strong menthol flavor marks this full-bodied, unusual Merlot. Offers plenty to sink your teeth into, but be sure to try a bottle to see if this is your style before buying a case. Drinkable now through 1994. 1,000 cases made. $12 (5/31/92) **79**

CLAIRVAUX
Merlot Napa Valley 1989: A bit lean, but nicely flavorful and well balanced with cherry and herb flavors accented by spicy oak notes. Very satisfying and full on the finish. 1,600 cases made. $12 (5/31/92) **85**

CLINE
Merlot California 1989: An average-quality red that's medium-bodied and mostly vegetal in flavor. Decent but very simple. Tasted twice. 361 cases made. $16.50 (5/31/92) **75**

CLOS DU BOIS
Merlot Sonoma County 1989: Light in color and flavor, but the light cherry and cola notes compete with oak. The tannic finish suggests you can drink it now or hold until 1995. $15 (5/31/92) **82**
Merlot Sonoma County 1988: Leans toward the herbal, vegetal spectrum, with more vegetable than fruit flavors. The herb, mint, olive and spice characteristics overshadow the currant notes. Drink in 1993 to '95. $15 (5/31/91) **81**
Merlot Sonoma County 1987: Offers wonderful aromas and plenty of ripe plum, currant, smoke and spice flavors that are rich yet elegant and intense without being weighty. The crisp acidity carries the flavors on the finish. Has just the right amount of tannin. Start drinking now. $12 (4/15/90) **89**
Merlot Sonoma County 1986 $10.75 (10/15/88) **86**
Merlot Sonoma County 1985 Rel: $10 Cur: $16 (10/31/87) SS **92**
Merlot Sonoma County 1984 $9 (5/16/86) **87**
Merlot Sonoma County 1983 $9 (10/01/85) **86**

CLOS DU VAL
Merlot Stags Leap District 1990 (NR) (5/15/91) (BT) **90+**
Merlot Stags Leap District 1989: Tight, firm and oaky now and not showing much fruit. The cherry, currant and anise flavors that do peek through are hard and focused. Simply needs time to evolve. Try after 1994. $21 (5/31/92) **86**
Merlot Stags Leap District 1988: Very ripe, rich and concentrated, with firm but soft tannins, plenty of cherry and plum flavors and a nice overlay of spicy oak seasoning. Well balanced and tempting to drink now but should age through 1996. $20 (3/31/91) **89**
Merlot Stags Leap District 1987: Intense and concentrated, with heavy smoke, currant, plum and spice flavors tightly packaged with firm tannins and plenty of oak. Altogether well balanced, with a long aftertaste. Drink in 1993 and beyond. $17 (3/31/90) **85**
Merlot Stags Leap District 1986 $16 (8/31/89) **86**
Merlot Stags Leap District 1985 $15.50 (4/30/88) **87**
Merlot Stags Leap District 1984 $15 (7/31/87) **88**
Merlot Stags Leap District 1983 $14 (6/16/86) **92**
Merlot Stags Leap District 1982 $12.50 (10/01/85) **80**
Merlot Stags Leap District 1981 $13.50 (2/15/84) **88**

CLOS PEGASE
Merlot Napa Valley 1988: Ripe and cedary, with a firm texture and modest cherry flavor shaded by dill and bay leaf notes on the finish. Could improve with cellaring until 1993. 1,300 cases made. $15 (11/15/91) **82**
Merlot Napa Valley 1986: Lean and focused, with cherry and currant flavors buried beneath a layer of firm tannins. Minty on the nose and long on the finish, this wine could develop well in the cellar through at least 1993. $15.50 (7/15/90) **84**

B.R. COHN
Merlot Napa Valley Silver Label 1989: Definitely herbal, with heavy dill and pine overtones to the basic currant flavor, turning tannic and tough on the finish. Needs until 1995 to '97 to soften and gain polish. 1,400 cases made. $14 (11/15/91) **82**

CONGRESS SPRINGS
Merlot Santa Clara County 1988: Herbal, slightly gamy overtones shade the modest currant flavor in this lightweight, supple-textured wine. Not for everyone. 712 cases made. $14 (3/31/91) **74**

CONN CREEK
Merlot Napa Valley Barrel Select 1988: Offers bright, lively fruit flavors with tiers of black cherry, currant, plum and spice notes that are very likable and linger on the finish. The tannins are soft and friendly. A pretty expression of Merlot to drink now to 1995. 860 cases made. $22 (11/15/91) **86**
Merlot Napa Valley Collins Vineyard 1985 $14 (3/31/88) **84**
Merlot Napa Valley Collins Vineyard Barrel Select Limited Bottling 1987: A strong minty quality dominates the rich, concentrated currant and cherry flavors. Balanced and fruity, with firm, somewhat sharp tannins, but altogether has good length and focus. Cellar until 1993 to '96. 800 cases made. $22 (12/31/90) **87**

R. & J. COOK
Merlot Clarksburg 1989: Supple, firm and fruity, with pretty oak shadings adding dimension to the ripe plum and currant notes. Drink now through 1995. 600 cases made. $9.50 (5/31/92) **82**

COOK'S
Merlot California Captain's Reserve 1989: Simple and fruity, with plum and cherry notes. Priced accordingly. Drink now. $5.50 (5/31/92) **77**

CORBETT CANYON
Merlot California Coastal Classic 1989: Pleasantly fruity with a biting edge, offering concentrated raspberry and strawberry flavors shaded by slightly bitter citrus characteristics. Drinkable now but probably better after 1993. $7 (11/15/91) BB **81**

COSENTINO
Merlot Napa County 1988: Has plenty of oak, herb, tea and cedar notes and a core of supple cherry and currant flavors. The tannins are firm and drying on the finish. Drink now to 1996. Tasted twice. 1,000 cases made. $18 (4/15/91) **82**
Merlot Napa County 1986 $14 (9/30/88) **85**
Merlot Napa County Reserve 1987: A bit green and austere, with tea, currant, bell pepper and cherry notes and firm tannins. Could use a little more generosity, but it's balanced and just needs another two to three years' aging. Drink now to 1995. Tasted twice. $18 (7/31/90) **80**
Merlot Napa Valley 1989: Lean and earthy, with currant and cherry flavors steaming through on the finish, lending charm to this modestly built wine. Has enough tannin to want until 1993 or '94 to show its best. 800 cases made. $18 (5/31/92) **85**

Key to Symbols

The scores reported here are the results of blind tastings conducted by our panel of senior editors. Wines that carry the initials below are results of individual tastings.

THE WINE SPECTATOR 100-POINT SCALE 95-100—Classic, a great wine; ***90-94***—Outstanding, superior character and style; ***80-89***—Good to very good, a wine with special qualities; ***70-79***—Average, drinkable wine that may have minor flaws; ***60-69***—Below average, drinkable but not recommended; ***50-59***—Poor, undrinkable, not recommended. "+"—With a score indicates a range; used primarily with barrel tastings to indicate a preliminary score.

SPECIAL DESIGNATIONS SS—Spectator Selection, CS—Cellar Selection, BB—Best Buy, ($NA)—Price not available, (NR)—Not released.

TASTER'S INITIALS (JG)—Jim Gordon, (HS)—Harvey Steiman, (JL)—James Laube, (JS)—James Suckling, (TM)—Thomas Matthews, (TR)—Terry Robards, (PM)—Per-Henrik Mansson, (BT)—Barrel Tasting (these wines were tasted blind from barrel samples), (CA-date)—*California's Great Cabernets* by James Laube, (CH-date)—*California's Great Chardonnays* by James Laube, (VP-date)—*Vintage Port* by James Suckling.

DATE TASTED Dates in parentheses represent the issue in which the rating was published.

CUVAISON
Merlot Napa Valley 1989: Ripe, rich and complex, with concentrated currant, cherry, anise and spice notes that are well proportioned and lively. The long, persistent finish echoes fruit and oak. Tempting now, but can be cellared. Drink now to 1994. $23 (5/31/92) **89**
Merlot Napa Valley 1988: A bit woody now but pleasant, with spice, tobacco, plum and mint notes that are supple and balanced by moderate richness and complexity. Finishes with delicate tannins. Ready now through 1994. Tasted twice. 3,200 cases made. $24 (4/15/91) **86**
Merlot Napa Valley 1985 $19 (6/30/88) **89**
Merlot Napa Valley Anniversary Release 1984 $13.50 (8/31/87) **90**

DE LOACH
Merlot Russian River Valley 1991: Distinct herb, olive and vegetal flavors are quite pungent, dominating the flavor spectrum. Hard to judge. 450 cases made. (NR) (5/15/92) (BT) **78+**

DEER VALLEY
Merlot California 1990: Lean, hard and tightly tannic, with plum and berry flavors struggling to emerge. Needs time to mellow. Best after 1994. $6 (5/31/92) **77**

DEHLINGER
Merlot Sonoma County 1986: Very pleasant, ripe and generous with plum, spice and anise notes, simple tannins and decent length. Ready to enjoy now. $13 (7/31/89) **83**
Merlot Sonoma County 1985 $10.50 (4/30/88) **89**
Merlot Sonoma County 1984 Rel: $12 Cur: $18 (6/15/87) SS **94**

DEVLIN
Merlot Central Coast 1982 $8 (7/16/85) **80**

DIABLO VISTA
Merlot Dry Creek Valley 1981 $7.50 (5/01/84) **79**

R.W. DOLAN
Merlot California 1986: A fine value that reminds us of a youthful Pomerol. Intense, rich, young and fruity, with plenty of vanillalike, new-oak flavors. Seductive now. $8 (1/31/89) **88**

DOMAINE NAPA
Merlot Napa Valley 1990: Simple, fruity and light, an amiable wine with modest berry and currant flavors. Drinkable now, but may be better after 1993. 1,200 cases made. $14.50 (5/31/92) **84**

DRY CREEK
Merlot Dry Creek Valley 1989: Soft and supple, with elegant currant and raspberry flavors framed by spicy, buttery oak. Firms up on the finish, where the tannins are more evident. Drinkable now through 1996. 5,000 cases made. $14 (4/15/92) **86**
Merlot Dry Creek Valley 1988: Simple, pleasant, fruity and fresh, with toasty cherry and plum aromas and flavors of modest intensity. Already drinkable. 1,050 cases made. $15 (3/31/91) **83**
Merlot Dry Creek Valley 1985 $7.50 (2/15/88) **80**
Merlot Sonoma County 1986: An herbal, plummy wine with a firm texture and generous tannins. With a little age it might soften and become more supple. $15 (3/31/89) **78**

DUCKHORN
Merlot Napa Valley 1990 (NR) (5/15/91) (BT) **85+**
Merlot Napa Valley 1989: A strong earthy, leathery quality takes away from the core of plum and cherry flavors. The tannins are firm but supple, with good depth. Best to start drinking between 1994 and '96. Tasted three times. Rel: $20 Cur: $25 (4/15/92) **82**
Merlot Napa Valley 1988: Rough, austere and gawky, with currant, bell pepper, spice and oak flavors that are tight, firm and in need of cellaring for two to three years. Should come around by 1993. Rel: $19 Cur: $28 (12/31/90) **86**
Merlot Napa Valley 1987: Deep in color and flavor, this is rich, dense but flavorful, with tiers of currant, plum and cherry flavors flanked by toasty oak. Has generous fruit, a pretty aftertaste and the tannins to stand up to a decade of cellaring. Best between 1993 and '97. 3,987 cases made. Rel: $18 Cur: $25 (12/31/89) **91**
Merlot Napa Valley 1986 Rel: $17 Cur: $30 (1/31/89) **86**
Merlot Napa Valley 1985 Rel: $16 Cur: $35 (12/31/87) CS **93**
Merlot Napa Valley 1984 Rel: $15 Cur: $40 (12/31/86) SS **94**
Merlot Napa Valley 1983 Rel: $15 Cur: $28 (11/01/85) CS **94**
Merlot Napa Valley 1982 Rel: $13 Cur: $56 (12/16/84) SS **92**
Merlot Napa Valley Three Palms Vineyard 1989: Dense and fruity, with layers of chunky plum, currant and blackberry flavors piling on the palate and expanding on the finish to include hints of anise and toast. An appealing wine that could use until 1993 to '95 to settle down. 3,000 cases made. Rel: $25 Cur: $29 (5/31/92) **89**
Merlot Napa Valley Three Palms Vineyard 1988: A disappointing wine that's lighter and less immediately appealing than previous vintages. Crisp and tart, with a definite layer of oak to accentuate the plum and slight raisin aromas and flavors. Balanced enough to keep until 1994 or '95 to see how it develops. Rel: $25 Cur: $46 (11/15/91) **84**
Merlot Napa Valley Three Palms Vineyard 1987: Very firm and tannic, with a lean intensity of complex cherry and blackberry flavors. Spicy and slightly herbal. The oak dominates at this point and it needs at least until 1993 to '95 to shed enough tannin, but it is a well proportioned wine for the long term. Tasted twice. 770 cases made. Rel: $25 Cur: $55 (7/31/90) **92**
Merlot Napa Valley Three Palms Vineyard 1986 Rel: $20 Cur: $58 (7/31/89) **88**
Merlot Napa Valley Three Palms Vineyard 1985 Rel: $20 Cur: $63 (6/30/88) **91**
Merlot Napa Valley Three Palms Vineyard 1984 Rel: $18 Cur: $50 (7/31/87) **89**
Merlot Napa Valley Vine Hill Ranch 1987: Smooth and elegant, with a solid core of black currant and cherry flavors that threads its way through the supple tannins and firm oak. A wine with immense charm that needs until about 1994 to show all it has. Tasted twice. 548 cases made. $18 (7/31/90) **87**
Merlot Napa Valley Vine Hill Ranch 1986: Lean, hard and very woody, with a dense color and concentrated oak and ripe Merlot aromas and flavors that thin out a bit on the palate. Needs a little time to smooth out, but will never be opulent. $18 (7/31/89) **80**
Merlot Napa Valley Vine Hill Ranch 1985 $16 (6/30/88) **91**

FARVIEW FARM
Merlot California Templeton 1980 $6.50 (3/16/84) **78**

FENESTRA
Merlot Livermore Valley 1989: Plush, smooth and intensely fruity, with plenty of black cherry and blackberry flavors, firm tannins and a rich, lingering finish. The youthful tannins make it a bit rough to drink now, but should be fine from 1993 to '96. 392 cases made. $13 (5/31/92) **87**
Merlot Livermore Valley Special Reserve 1989: Lush, plush and flavorful. A stiff dose of spicy French oak blends well with the ample cassis and black cherry flavors in this rich, full-bodied wine. Fruit and spice linger on the finish. Fine to drink now if you like spicy oak, or cellar through about 1996. 50 cases made. $40/1.5L (5/31/92) **89**
Merlot Sonoma County 1986: Ripe cherry and currant flavors run through this pleasant, medium-bodied, simple wine. $11 (10/15/89) **83**

FERRARI-CARANO
Merlot Alexander Valley 1987: Distinctively herbal, with a solid core of black currant flavor. Soft, supple and elegant, this is a wine to drink soon rather than cellar for ages, but it should hold up through 1993 or '94. $16.50 (7/31/90) **84**
Merlot Alexander Valley 1986: Sharply focused, with a fleshy texture, firm, tight tannins and bright cherry, currant and cedar flavors that are long and full. Just a baby, this needs cellaring until about 1993. $15 (6/30/89) **87**
Merlot Sonoma County 1989: Straightforward and almost sweet, with sturdy cherry and berry flavors, firm tannins and a bit of a finish. Very good. Drink now through 1994. $15 (5/31/92) **86**

Merlot Sonoma County 1988: A fresh, fruity, exuberant wine, with modest tannins and crisp acidity supporting the strawberry and cherry flavors. Probably best to drink now through 1994. $17.50 (8/31/91) **85**

FIRESTONE

Merlot Santa Ynez Valley 1989: Crisp and fruity, with marvelous plum, raspberry and chocolate aromas and flavors that get a little spicy on the finish. Drinkable now, so why wait? $12 (8/31/91) **86**
Merlot Santa Ynez Valley 1988: Tightly wound, with a tough veneer of tannin around the core of currant and mint aromas and flavors. The fruit flavors just about balance the tannins on the finish. Try after 1994 or '95. $11 (3/31/91) **82**
Merlot Santa Ynez Valley 1987: Nicely styled, with ripe fruit flavors enhanced by oak and herb accents. Has firm tannins, good balance and a lingering finish. Drink now. $9 (12/15/89) **83**
Merlot Santa Ynez Valley 1986 $9 (9/30/88) **83**
Merlot Santa Ynez Valley 1985 $9 (4/30/88) **78**
Merlot Santa Ynez Valley 1981 $6.50 (5/16/86) **50**

FITCH MOUNTAIN

Merlot Napa Valley 1986 $9 (9/30/88) **84**
Merlot Napa Valley 1985 $9 (12/15/87) **89**

FLORA SPRINGS

Merlot Napa Valley 1990 (NR) (5/15/91) (BT) **85+**
Merlot Napa Valley 1988: A tough, oaky edge gives way to tart, firm currant, berry and spice notes in this supple wine. Balanced and ready to drink now to 1994. Tasted twice. $15 (8/31/91) **83**
Merlot Napa Valley 1987: Dense and concentrated, with plenty of oak and herb overtones to the focused cherry and black currant flavors. Long and rich on the finish. Drink now to 1994. Tasted twice. $16.50 (7/31/90) **87**
Merlot Napa Valley 1985 $15 (6/30/88) **82**
Merlot Napa Valley Floréal 1989: Tightly wound, but full of fresh, tasty berry, cherry and spice flavors that are very focused and direct. The tannins are firm and the finish lingers. Will need until about 1994 or '95 to show its best stuff. Tasted twice. 700 cases made. $12.50 (5/31/92) **84**

FOLIE A DEUX

Merlot Napa Valley 1988: A bit heavy-handed, with mint, menthol, wood and spice notes, but pretty herb and raspberry flavors show through along with hints of wildflowers. Not too tannic, elegant, balanced and exotic. Drink now to 1994. 300 cases made. $18 (3/31/91) **82**

FRANCISCAN

Merlot Napa Valley 1981 $8.50 (10/01/85) **91**
Merlot Napa Valley Oakville Estate 1989: A straightforward, herbaceous wine that's medium-bodied and dressed up with a flash of sweet oak. Not deep or complex, but decent. Tasted twice, with consistent notes. $12 (5/31/92) **79**
Merlot Napa Valley Oakville Estate 1988 ($NA) (4/30/90) (BT) **80+**
Merlot Napa Valley Oakville Estate 1987: Tightly structured, with lots of raspberry and red cherry flavors packed into a tannic package. Focused, balanced and long, this is firm without being harsh. Needs cellaring until 1994 or '95, but gorgeous flavors should emerge after that. 5,000 cases made. $12.50 (6/15/90) **88**
Merlot Napa Valley Oakville Estate 1986: Lean and ripe, with leathery, spicy plum aromas and flavors clinging to the spare frame. Drink now. $12 (7/31/89) **80**
Merlot Napa Valley Oakville Estate 1985 Rel: $9.25 Cur: $15 (5/31/88) **89**
Merlot Napa Valley Oakville Estate 1984 Rel: $8.50 Cur: $15 (6/30/87) SS **90**
Merlot Napa Valley Oakville Estate 1983 $8.50 (2/28/87) **88**

FREEMARK ABBEY

Merlot Napa Valley 1985 $10 (12/31/88) **90**

GAINEY

Merlot Santa Barbara County 1989: Pungently earthy and vegetal, with tarry plum and cherry notes. Most will find it too vegetal. Tasted twice. 1,212 cases made. $14 (5/31/92) **70**
Merlot Santa Barbara County 1988: Firm, tannic and a bit soft on the finish, but the oak-framed currant and plum flavors have enough concentration to suggest it might be better after cellaring until 1993 or '94. 549 cases made. $13 (4/15/91) **82**
Merlot Santa Ynez Valley Limited Selection 1988: Very supple, elegant and silky, with plenty of vanilla, butter and spice notes from oak aging on top of ample plum and currant flavors, backed with good acidity and moderate tannins. Drinkable now through 1995. 70 cases made. $20 (2/29/92) **89**

GARLAND RANCH

Merlot California 1986: Strives for concentration and character, but is so extreme in style that it will turn some people off. The pungent, earthy aromas and powerful herb flavors need more fruit to back them up. Pretty tannic but ready to drink now through about 1995. 1,122 cases made. $6 (5/31/92) **76**

GEORIS

Merlot Carmel Valley 1987: Tastes full, warm and inviting, with lots of spicy, rich accents from oak aging piled on top of ripe plum, cherry and herb flavors. Has fine tannins, a plush texture and a lingering, spicy finish. Tempting now, but could be cellared until at least 1995. $27 (3/31/91) **89**
Merlot Carmel Valley 1986: A distinctively weedy, tannic wine that clamps down on the palate. The subtle currant and plum flavors are buried beneath the drying tannins. Perhaps with time this wine will show more fruit and finesse, but for now it's very dense and awkward. Drink in 1993 or '94, but try a bottle before you cellar much. $25 (12/31/90) **77**
Merlot Carmel Valley 1985: Lean but concentrated, with beautiful berry and black cherry aromas and flavors nestled into a background of sweet oak. A bit harsh at this point and in need of time to smooth out. Drink now to 1993. $20 (4/15/89) **83**

GEYSER PEAK

Merlot Alexander Valley 1989: Big, tart and tannic, obscuring most of the black cherry flavors. Will need until about 1995 to soften, but it's difficult to tell how much fruit will be left. 4,900 cases made. $9 (5/31/92) **79**
Merlot Alexander Valley 1987: This medium-weight, juicy, herbal wine has moderate tannins and solid fruit flavor to back it up. Drinkable now. Tasted twice. $8 (7/15/90) **82**
Merlot Alexander Valley 1985 $7.75 (10/15/88) **77**
Merlot Alexander Valley 1984 $7 (2/29/88) **69**
Merlot Alexander Valley 1983 $7 (12/31/86) **80**

GLEN ELLEN

Merlot California Proprietor's Reserve 1990: Supple, simple and fruity, with an earthy edge to the sweet cherry and berry notes. Balanced and ready to drink. A fair price. $6 (5/31/92) **79**
Merlot California Proprietor's Reserve 1986: Easy to drink and delicate, with nicely focused berry and herbal flavors accented by a touch of vanilla. Has a sweet, fruity aftertaste. Drink now. $6 (1/31/89) BB **84**

GOLDEN CREEK

Merlot Sonoma County 1989: Herbaceous, with decent plum and cherry notes to round it out. Moderately tannic but drinkable now for its freshness. 320 cases made. $12.50 (5/31/92) **81**
Merlot Sonoma County Reserve 1989: Lean, crisp and lively, with focused cherry, spice and currant flavors that finish with a solid dose of tannin and firm oak shadings. Best to cellar until 1995. 200 cases made. $16 (5/31/92) **87**

GREENWOOD RIDGE

Merlot Anderson Valley 1989: Fresh and fruity, with lively black cherry, spice, currant and herb notes that are crisp and smooth. Has enough tannin for aging but is awfully good right now. Drink now to 1995. 205 cases made. $16 (11/15/91) **85**

GUENOC

Merlot Guenoc Valley 1985: This fragrant wine has floral, minty, herbal elements and is rich and smooth on the palate, showing ripe cherry flavor that carries through on the finish. Drinkable now. $15 (3/31/89) **85**
Merlot Lake-Napa Counties 1987: Firm and focused, with well-articulated berry and currant aromas and flavors and hints of plum on the finish. Smooth enough to drink now but could benefit from cellaring until 1993. $14 (11/15/91) **86**
Merlot Lake-Napa Counties 1986: A mature, medium-bodied wine to drink now, with tea and herb aromas and cherry and tomato flavors. Good but simple and maturing fast. $12 (6/15/90) **80**

GUNDLACH BUNDSCHU

Merlot Sonoma Valley Rhinefarm Vineyards 1989: A sturdy, tannic, young wine that will need until about 1995 to smooth out. Has enough focused fruit and spice flavors to make it promising. Tasted twice. $16 (5/31/92) **80**
Merlot Sonoma Valley Rhinefarm Vineyards 1988: Firm and tight, with modest, ripe plum, currant, herb and spice notes that are compact and firmly tannic now. Moderately rich and deep. Drinkable now through 1995. Rel: $16 Cur: $20 (5/31/91) **81**
Merlot Sonoma Valley Rhinefarm Vineyards 1987: Defines Merlot character. Concentrated, intense and supple, with integrated plum, cherry, tobacco and cedar aromas and flavors and a lush, chocolaty finish. Delicious now but should develop until 1994. Rel: $13 Cur: $16 (10/31/89) SS **93**
Merlot Sonoma Valley Rhinefarm Vineyards 1986 Rel: $12 Cur: $18 (12/31/88) **91**
Merlot Sonoma Valley Rhinefarm Vineyards 1985 Rel: $12 Cur: $20 (2/29/88) SS **92**
Merlot Sonoma Valley Rhinefarm Vineyards 1984 Rel: $12 Cur: $20 (2/28/87) **88**
Merlot Sonoma Valley Rhinefarm Vineyards 1983 Rel: $12 Cur: $20 (5/01/86) **92**
Merlot Sonoma Valley Rhinefarm Vineyards 1982 $8.50 (10/01/85) **88**

HAHN

Merlot Monterey 1990: Concentrated and full-bodied, with dense black cherry and herb flavors framed by rough oak. Turns tough and astringent on the finish but is a pretty nice ride. 4,200 cases made. $10 (5/31/92) **83**
Merlot Monterey 1989: Tight and firm, with a rich, smooth core of currant and cherry-tinged flavor and tannins and oak clamping down on the finish. Has fine potential but needs cellaring until 1995. 2,000 cases made. $10 (5/31/92) **86**

HALLCREST

Merlot El Dorado County De Cascabel Vineyard 1989: Thin flavors are wrapped in a stiff coat of acidity and tannins, making this very tough and lean. It's difficult to say if time will help much. Try in 1993 if you like them tannic. 70 cases made. $14.50 (5/31/92) **74**
Merlot El Dorado County De Cascabel Vineyard 1988: A full-bodied, tannic, hot-tasting wine that's rough in texture but has decent black cherry flavors. Drink now through 1993. 55 cases made. $14.50 (5/31/92) **78**

HART

Merlot Temecula 1989: Full-bodied and flavorful, with plenty of raspberry and apple skin flavors, tart acidity and moderate tannins. Overall a simple, straightforward wine. 249 cases made. $15 (5/31/92) **80**

HAVENS

Merlot Carneros Napa Valley Truchard Vineyard 1988: The ripe, jammy, floral aroma doesn't follow through on the palate, where it's tight and biting with hard-edged tannins. Modest fruit sneaks through on the finish, but overall it's a tough wine. Drink now to 1995. $20 (8/31/91) **76**
Merlot Carneros Napa Valley Truchard Vineyard Reserve 1989: Lean and tough, with a strong tannic backbone and cedary, earthy aromas and flavors. A hint of berry and currant emerges on the finish, which broadens out a little, suggesting it might come around by 1993 to '95. 475 cases made. $20 (5/31/92) **82**
Merlot Napa Valley 1989: Ripe and balanced, with a tight core of plum, oak, currant and spice flavor that stays with you. Drinkable now but has enough tannin to carry it through 1995. $14 (5/31/92) **84**
Merlot Napa Valley 1988: Weedy, herbal aromas and flavors crowd out the modest streak of currant flavor in this lean, somewhat tannic wine until it all comes together on the finish. Worth cellaring until 1994 or '95. $14 (3/31/91) **82**
Merlot Napa Valley 1987: Generous, supple and distinctive, with caramel- and smoke-tinged cherry and strawberry aromas and flavors. Firm enough without being harsh, this elegant wine is drinkable now but could use cellaring until 1994 to soften the tannins. 1,350 cases made. $14 (7/15/90) **89**
Merlot Napa Valley 1986 $13.50 (3/31/90) **72**
Merlot Napa Valley 1985 $12.50 (5/31/88) **84**

THE HESS COLLECTION

Merlot Napa Valley 1989: Very attractive and ripe, with a supple texture and plenty of plum and cherry flavors. Tastes round and smooth, emphasizing fruit, but is accented by spicy oak. Best to drink in 1993 through '95. 400 cases made. $25 (5/31/92) **86**

HUNTER ASHBY

Merlot Napa Valley 1985: Solid, flavorful and even a bit complex, this rich wine has plum and tobaccolike flavors, earthy aromas and firm tannins and acidity. Drink now. $9.75 (7/31/89) **84**
Merlot Napa Valley 1982 $6.50 (12/15/87) **65**

INGLENOOK

Merlot Napa Valley 1981 $12 (10/01/85) **77**
Merlot Napa Valley Limited Bottling 1982 $8.50 (5/16/86) **67**
Merlot Napa Valley Limited Cask Reserve Selection 1981 $12 (2/16/85) **80**
Merlot Napa Valley Reserve 1988: Tight and tough, with lean currant and cherry notes that turn tannic on the finish. Balanced and ready to drink now through 1996. $11.50 (5/31/92) **83**
Merlot Napa Valley Reserve 1986: Harsh, woody, acidic and tough to like now, but the plum and cherry flavors could come through when the tannins soften. Drink in 1993 to '96. Tasted twice. $12 (10/31/89) **81**
Merlot Napa Valley Reserve 1985 Rel: $10.50 Cur: $14 (10/15/88) SS **91**
Merlot Napa Valley Reserve 1983 $9.50 (10/15/87) **85**

JAEGER

Merlot Napa Valley Inglewood Vineyard 1987: A rustic wine that's tough and unfocused, with ripe plum and berry flavors lurking behind a wall of tannin. Tastes woody and metallic rather than fruity. Try in 1995 or '96. $15 (5/31/92) **81**
Merlot Napa Valley Inglewood Vineyard 1986: Firm, focused and flavorful, leaning toward earthy flavors, but offers a nice array of ripe berry and currant notes and hints of chocolate and tea sneaking in on the finish. A harmonious wine that's still intense and lively. Good now and may be better around 1993 to '95. Better than bottles tasted earlier. $15 (5/31/92) **88**
Merlot Napa Valley Inglewood Vineyard 1985: Very concentrated and delicious, with loads of ripe black cherry flavors, full, firm tannins and good acidity to back them up. Drink now through 1995. $16 (2/15/90) **89**
Merlot Napa Valley Inglewood Vineyard 1983 $14 (2/29/88) **87**

KEENAN

Merlot Napa Valley 1989: A rough-hewn wine, with hard oak and tannins overshadowing the currant and berry notes. Time may soften the edges, but for now it's a gamble to age. Drink after 1994. Tasted twice. 3,150 cases made. $18 (5/31/92) **82**
Merlot Napa Valley 1988: Firm and tight, with gritty tannins, but also has enough ripe plum, blueberry and cherry flavors that turn supple and smooth. Still, the tannins on the finish suggest cellaring until 1994 or '95. Tasted twice. Rel: $18 Cur: $21 (5/31/92) **84**
Merlot Napa Valley 1987: Lean, rich and concentrated, with pretty herb, raspberry, currant and spicy

Merlot flavors that are impeccably balanced and framed by toasty oak and firm tannins. Drink now to 1995. Rel: $18 Cur: $20 (3/31/90) **88**
Merlot Napa Valley 1986 Rel: $18 Cur: $20 (6/30/89) **90**
Merlot Napa Valley 1985 $18 (5/31/88) **83**
Merlot Napa Valley 1984 Rel: $16.50 Cur: $20 (7/31/87) CS **94**

KENDALL-JACKSON
Merlot Alexander Valley 1986 $16 (12/31/88) **93**
Merlot California Vintner's Reserve 1989: Lean, earthy and vegetal, with tart plum and tobacco notes. Not quite ripe, but drinkable now. Tasted three times, with consistent notes. $14 (5/31/92) **75**
Merlot California Vintner's Reserve 1988: A lively wine, with generous spice, red plum and berry aromas and flavors that come together on the finish. Drinkable now. $13.50 (11/15/91) **84**
Merlot Sonoma County The Proprietor's 1987: Well proportioned with ripe currant and cherry flavors and toasty oak notes that add amplitude to the flavors. The tannins finish strong with a hint of herbs and spice. Best to start drinking now to 1996. $20 (12/31/90) **87**

KONOCTI
Merlot Lake County 1989: Offers attractive dark cherry and blackberry flavors and a hint of plum. A lean, crisp wine that's not too tannic. Ready now through 1995. $10 (2/29/92) **85**
Merlot Lake County 1988: More tannic than the gentle currant and berry aromas would suggest, but the flavors manage to peek through the tough texture on the finish. It's a gamble, but worth waiting until 1994 to '96. 2,086 cases made. $9.50 (3/31/91) BB **83**
Merlot Lake County 1987: Lean and citrusy, with vaguely defined olive and toast aromas and flavors and not much intensity to stand up to the tough tannins. 2,558 cases made. $9.50 (12/31/90) **73**
Merlot Lake County 1985 $8 (12/31/88) **83**

CHARLES KRUG
Merlot Napa Valley 1989: Crisp and lean, with tart cherry and sage notes adding complexity. Not too oaky, and firm and tannic enough to cellar until 1994. 1,500 cases made. $13 (5/31/92) **84**

LAKE SONOMA
Merlot Dry Creek Valley Yoakim Bridge Ranch 1990: Lively and complex, with earthy aromas to the concentrated, fresh cherry flavors. The firm tannins and good depth bode well for aging through about 1996. 346 cases made. $13.50 (5/31/92) **86**

LAKESPRING
Merlot Napa Valley 1987: Spicy, toasty and tough, made for longer cellaring than most Merlots. Offers gamy currant and black pepper aromas and flavors and echoes cherry and spice on the long finish. Will need cellaring until at least 1993 or '94 to soften the tannins. 3,000 cases made. $14 (6/15/90) **85**
Merlot Napa Valley 1986: Shows the minty herb and vegetal side of Merlot, with plummy flavor underneath. Tart, tannic and hard, with a dry, rough finish. Needs time. Begin drinking in 1993. $14 (3/31/89) **79**
Merlot Napa Valley 1985 Rel: $12 Cur: $15 (3/31/88) SS **91**
Merlot Napa Valley 1984 $12 (5/15/87) **88**
Merlot Napa Valley 1983 $11 (5/16/86) **87**
Merlot Napa Valley 1982 $10 (10/01/85) **78**
Merlot Napa Valley Yountmill Vineyard 1988: Tight and austere, with strong oak and menthol notes, and packs in plenty of flavor, with tiers of currant, plum and cherry-scented characteristics. Balanced but needs cellaring until 1994 to soften. $15 (2/29/92) **85**

LAMBERT BRIDGE
Merlot Sonoma County 1985 $10 (12/15/87) **69**
Merlot Sonoma County 1982 $11.50 (12/16/84) **79**

LEEWARD
Merlot Napa Valley 1989: Crisp and fruity, with well-defined berry and currant aromas and flavors and hints of toast and vanilla on the finish. Drinkable now but could improve through 1994. $14 (11/15/91) **83**
Merlot Napa Valley 1985 $10 (5/15/87) **88**

CHARLES LEFRANC
Merlot Monterey County San Lucas Ranch 1984 $8.50 (12/15/87) **70**

J. LOHR
Merlot California Cypress 1989: A pure fruit style of Merlot, with raspberry and cherry flavors that are ripe and up-front. Medium-bodied, moderate in tannins and value priced. Drinkable now or cellar until about 1994. $8.50 (2/29/92) BB **85**

MADDALENA
Merlot Central Coast San Simeon Collection 1989: Hard, green and vegetal, with flavors that don't taste ripe. Marginal quality. Tasted twice, with consistent notes. 2,500 cases made. $12 (5/31/92) **73**

MARILYN MERLOT
Merlot Napa Valley 1989: Lean and lively, with a nice core of raspberry and currant flavors splashed with enough tannin to give it dimension. Finishes smooth and inviting and makes you want another sip. Drinkable now, but the tannins can use until 1993 or '94 to soften. 4,000 cases made. $13.50 (5/31/92) **87**
Merlot Napa Valley 1988: Soft, ripe and generous, with lots of blackberry and currant aromas and flavors that lean toward chocolate on the finish. Smooth in texture and tempting to drink soon but the tannins can use until about 1993 to soften a bit. 3,600 cases made. $12.50 (5/31/91) **85**
Merlot Napa Valley 1986 $13 (12/31/88) **85**

MARKHAM
Merlot Napa Valley 1990 (NR) (5/15/91) (BT) **85+**
Merlot Napa Valley 1989: A pleasant core of ripe fruit echoes plum and cherry flavors and a touch of oak adds dimension. Has a smooth, supple texture. Drink now. Tasted twice. $15 (5/31/92) **85**
Merlot Napa Valley 1988: Rich and flavorful, with intense yet supple currant, cherry, raspberry and anise flavors that are silky-smooth in texture, with a persistence that echoes fruit. Delicious to drink now or hold through 1996. $13.50 (4/15/91) **90**
Merlot Napa Valley 1987: Offers sweet currant, cherry and plum aromas and flavors and a pretty kiss of oak. The flavors are rich, deep, intense, lively and long on the finish, with ample tannins for development over the next decade. Drink now. $13.50 (10/15/89) **91**

Key to Symbols

The scores reported here are the results of blind tastings conducted by our panel of senior editors. Wines that carry the initials below are results of individual tastings.

THE WINE SPECTATOR 100-POINT SCALE ***95-100***—Classic, a great wine; ***90-94***—Outstanding, superior character and style; ***80-89***—Good to very good, a wine with special qualities; ***70-79***—Average, drinkable wine that may have minor flaws; ***60-69***—Below average, drinkable but not recommended; ***50-59***—Poor, undrinkable, not recommended. "+"—With a score indicates a range; used primarily with barrel tastings to indicate a preliminary score.

SPECIAL DESIGNATIONS SS—Spectator Selection, CS—Cellar Selection, BB—Best Buy, ($NA)—Price not available, (NR)—Not released.

TASTER'S INITIALS (JG)—Jim Gordon, (HS)—Harvey Steiman, (JL)—James Laube, (JS)—James Suckling, (TM)—Thomas Matthews, (TR)—Terry Robards, (PM)—Per-Henrik Mansson, (BT)—Barrel Tasting (these wines were tasted blind from barrel samples), (CA-date)—*California's Great Cabernets* by James Laube, (CH-date)—*California's Great Chardonnays* by James Laube, (VP-date)—*Vintage Port* by James Suckling.

DATE TASTED Dates in parentheses represent the issue in which the rating was published.

Merlot Napa Valley 1985 $11 (4/30/88) **88**
Merlot Napa Valley 1981 $8.75 (8/01/84) **86**

LOUIS M. MARTINI
Merlot North Coast 1989: An unusually spicy aroma and sparse fruit flavors make this atypical and lean. Mature for its age. Drink now. $9 (5/31/92) **74**
Merlot North Coast 1988: Crisp and tightly structured, with reined-in plum and herb flavors that loosen up on the finish. Firm acidity is its hallmark. Graceful and rather restrained, with no woody taste and no excess tannins. Drinkable now but should improve through 1994. 13,000 cases made. $10 (8/31/91) **85**
Merlot North Coast 1986: Light and a bit tart, with ample cedar and spice notes to the crisp, berrylike flavors. Drink now. $12 (10/31/89) **79**
Merlot North Coast 1984 $6.75 (2/15/88) **79**
Merlot North Coast 1982 $5.85 (2/16/86) **71**
Merlot Russian River Valley Los Vinedos del Rio 1988: Tart and gamy, with earthy, oaky plum and currant notes that turn hard and tannic on the finish. An oddball wine that lacks focus and finesse. Drink after 1993. Tasted twice. 1,000 cases made. $22 (5/31/92) **74**
Merlot Russian River Valley Los Vinedos del Rio 1986: Dry, thin and oaky, without the fruit concentration or generosity to stand up to the wood, but the cherry and berry flavors are pretty. May be more attractive once the woodiness softens. Drink now. $20 (3/31/90) **79**
Merlot Russian River Valley Los Vinedos del Rio 1984 $12 (2/15/88) **82**
Merlot Russian River Valley Los Vinedos del Rio 1981 $10 (10/01/85) **81**

PAUL MASSON
Merlot California Vintners Selection 1989: A hearty, tannic red at a fabulous price, with simple, honest fruit flavors. Fine for everyday drinking. Doesn't need cellaring. $4.50/1.5L (4/15/92) BB **80**
Merlot Monterey County Masson 1988: Light, fruity and not too tannic, with hints of plum and currant flavors. Easy to drink and fairly priced. 4,000 cases made. $8 (5/31/92) **79**
Merlot Monterey County Vintage Selection Masson 1987: A good, full-bodied wine, with powerful oak and menthol aromas, spicy, plummy flavors and a texture that's rough at this stage. Deep and tannic. A good value. Drinkable now. $8.50 (7/15/90) **83**

MATANZAS CREEK
Merlot Sonoma County 1987: Deep, elegant and rich, with plenty of complex, toasty, spicy currant, plum and berry aromas and flavors. Long and smooth, with a supple structure and lots of finesse. Drinkable already but cellaring until about 1994 wouldn't hurt a bit. A California Merlot for Pomerol lovers. Rel: $25 Cur: $29 (6/15/90) SS **92**
Merlot Sonoma County 1986: Enormously rich, tannic and complex, with layers of concentrated cedar, plum, cherry and herb flavors framed by firm tannins and oak. Gets better with every sip. Drink now. $20 (6/30/89) **92**
Merlot Sonoma Valley 1989: Rich, smooth and complex, with concentrated layers of cherry, currant and smoky, buttery oak flavors. Deep, lively and stays with you. Delicious now but still firm and tannic enough to cellar through 1995. $28 (4/15/92) **90**
Merlot Sonoma Valley 1988: Stylish and plush in texture, with enticing herb and cherry flavors definitely influenced by toasty oak. Firm tannins emerge on the lingering finish. Try in 1993 and later. $28 (8/31/91) **88**
Merlot Sonoma Valley 1985 Rel: $18 Cur: $40 (5/31/88) **88**
Merlot Sonoma Valley 1984 Rel: $14.50 Cur: $25 (6/30/87) **91**
Merlot Sonoma Valley 1982 Rel: $13.50 Cur: $28 (10/01/85) **88**
Merlot Sonoma Valley 1981 Rel: $12.50 Cur: $30 (4/16/84) **80**

MAZZOCCO
Merlot Dry Creek Valley Estate Unfiltered 1989: Not flashy, but solid and satisfying. Very supple, flavorful and complex, with nicely modulated cherry, cedar, chocolate and earth flavors on a frame of moderate tannins and good acidity. Drink in 1993 to '96. 200 cases made. $14 (5/31/92) **89**

MEADOW GLEN
Merlot Napa Valley 1989: Starts out ripe and generous, but turns tough, oaky and tannic, with a firm grip. The currant and cherry flavors are lean and tart. Needs until 1995 to soften. 3,000 cases made. $8 (5/31/92) **81**

MERRYVALE
Merlot Napa Valley 1989: Tough and hard-edged, with firm, drying tannins and a tight core of currant and plum flavors. Not showing much depth or suppleness and needs time to soften, but may always be tannic and lean. Drink in 1995. 1,200 cases made. $16 (5/31/92) **84**

MIETZ
Merlot Sonoma County 1989: A beautifully harmonious wine, with intense fruit flavors that blend seamlessly with accents of spicy oak. Velvety in texture, moderately tannic and long on the finish. The cherry and plum flavors have finesse. Drinkable now but should continue to develop through 1997. 400 cases made. $13.50 (4/15/92) **91**

MILL CREEK
Merlot Dry Creek Valley 1988: Weedy, herbaceous and grassy, with a touch of floral and plum-scented flavors. An odd wine that lacks harmony and finesse. Drink after 1994. Tasted twice, with consistent notes. 1,273 cases made. $12 (5/31/92) **77**
Merlot Dry Creek Valley 1987: Spicy, herbal overtones add interest to this medium-weight wine, with focused cherry and plum flavors echoing cedar and tobacco notes on the finish. Smooth, amiable and drinkable now. 2,338 cases made. $12 (11/15/91) **84**
Merlot Dry Creek Valley 1984 $8.50 (2/15/88) **68**
Merlot Dry Creek Valley 1983 $9 (10/01/85) **80**
Merlot Dry Creek Valley 1982 $8.50 (4/01/85) **85**

ROBERT MONDAVI
Merlot Napa Valley 1989: Mondavi's first Merlot is ripe and tannic, with plenty of plum and currant aromas and flavors, but for now it's all buried under a layer of gritty tannins that need until 1996 to '98 to soften. 2,500 cases made. $21 (5/31/92) **87**

MONTEREY PENINSULA
Merlot Monterey Doctors' Reserve 1986: Serious, full-bodied and tannic, with a nice kiss of oak to the deep cherry and earth flavors. It needs until about 1994 for the tannins to soften more. Not complex but powerful and solid. 1,419 cases made. $16 (5/31/92) **83**
Merlot Monterey Doctors' Reserve 1985: Elegant, beautifully focused and rich in flavor, with honey-shaded pear, apple and nutmeg aromas and flavors that linger for minutes on the finish and get prettier with every sip. A beautiful wine with no exaggeration of flavors. Tempting to drink now, but best after 1993 or '94. 250 cases made. $14 (1/31/89) **83**
Merlot Monterey Doctors' Reserve 1984 $12 (12/15/87) **74**

MONTEREY VINEYARD
Merlot Monterey Classic 1989: An element of spice, presumably from French oak, adds an extra dimension to this well-rounded wine, with good herbal, plummy, earthy flavors backed by firm tannins. Drink now through 1994. $6 (2/29/92) BB **84**
Merlot Monterey County Classic 1988: Extremely earthy and herbal, with more olive flavor than fruit. A hint of black cherry tries to make its presence felt but loses in the end. $6 (12/31/90) **76**

MONTICELLO
Merlot Napa Valley 1991: Young, crisp and lively, full of ripe berry and plum flavors. The finish is long and crisp. 2,000 cases made. (NR) (5/15/92) (BT) **85+**

MT. MADONNA
Merlot San Luis Obispo County 1987: Extremely herbaceous and thin. Misses the mark for Merlot. Tasted twice, with consistent notes. 1,900 cases made. $8 (5/31/92) **69**

MOUNTAIN VIEW
Merlot Napa County 1989: A light, fruity, simple Merlot that's closer to a red table wine than a varietal expression. The plum and cedar flavors are decent but unexciting. At $6 it's price driven. Drink now. $6 (5/31/91) **72**

MURPHY-GOODE
Merlot Alexander Valley Murphy Ranch 1989: Well balanced and freshly fruity, with cola and sassafras accents to the cherry flavors. Moderate tannins make it drinkable now through 1993. Tasted three times. 1,300 cases made. $15 (5/31/92) **82**
Merlot Alexander Valley Premier Vineyard 1986: Spicy, floral berry flavors characterize this smooth, lithe, elegant young wine, framed with a touch of tasty vanilla from oak and a firm blanket of soft tannin. With the polish of a few years' aging, it should be lovely. $14 (1/31/89) **90**

NAPA CELLARS
Merlot California 1990: Lean, hard and oaky, with peppery berry notes. It's priced to drink now, but the tannins and oak make it tough and tight. Drink after 1994. 700 cases made. $7 (5/31/92) **79**
Merlot California 1989: Strongly herbal and spicy, with more tar flavor than fruit. Flavorful, but not appealing to us. Tasted twice. $7 (5/31/91) **70**

NAPA CREEK
Merlot Napa Valley 1988: Simple in flavor but delicate and creamy in texture, showing hints of spice and toast in the nose and cherry and orange on the palate. $13 (3/31/91) **75**
Merlot Napa Valley 1987: Closed and tight, with more oak than fruit showing. The herb and berry flavors are firmly tannic and currant and cherry notes come through on the finish. Drink now to 1993. 540 cases made. $13.50 (6/15/90) **83**

NEVADA CITY
Merlot Nevada County 1989: Ripe and straightforward, with decent cherry flavors and firm tannins. May develop complexity and smoothness if aged until about 1994. 163 cases made. $14 (5/31/92) **80**

NEWTON
Merlot Napa Valley 1989: Plush and concentrated, with rich currant, earth and toasty, buttery oak flavors, all of which add up to a complex, tasty wine. Has plenty of spice and length. Drink now or hold until 1994. $20 (5/31/92) **88**
Merlot Napa Valley 1987: Offers plenty of herb, cherry, currant and bell pepper flavors in an austere, narrowly focused wine that finishes on the tannic side. Needs a little more body and richness. Drink now to 1994. Tasted twice. $17 (7/31/90) **81**
Merlot Napa Valley 1986 $15 (12/31/88) **83**
Merlot Napa Valley 1985 $14 (3/31/88) **93**
Merlot Napa Valley 1983 $11.50 (2/28/87) **90**
Merlot Napa Valley 1982 $12.50 (2/16/86) **83**
Merlot Napa Valley 1981 $12.50 (12/16/84) **91**
Merlot Napa Valley Reserve 1987 Rel: $17 Cur: $20 (4/15/89) (BT) **85+**

OLSON
Merlot California 1989: Full-bodied and tannic, with fruit and herb flavors that get a bit muddy and turn bitter on the finish. A gamble to cellar but should soften up a bit by 1994. Organically grown. Tasted twice. $11 (5/31/92) **76**

ORGANIC WINE WORKS
Merlot Napa Valley Thompson Ranch 1991: Ripe and compact, with rich, generous berry, cherry and plum flavors. Tastes young—like a Dolcetto barrel sample—and the finish sizzles with alcohol and tannin. Cellar until 1995. 158 cases made. $12.50 (5/31/92) **84**

PAGOR
Merlot Santa Maria Valley 1984 $10.25 (4/30/88) **70**

PARDUCCI
Merlot Mendocino County 1983 $8 (12/15/87) **75**
Merlot North Coast 1989: Light, smooth and fruity, with a pleasantly tannic edge to the lively currant and black cherry flavors. A simple, stylish wine that's drinkable now. $10 (11/15/91) **85**
Merlot North Coast 1988: Light in texture, with modest, vaguely berrylike flavors shaded by herb and green bean overtones. Drinkable now. $9.50 (4/30/91) **78**

PEBBLEWOOD
Merlot Alexander Valley Limited Release 1987: Earthy, barnyardy notes dominate the plum and cherry-scented flavors and the firm, tannic finish turns murky. Drink now to 1995. Tasted twice, with consistent notes. $9 (5/31/92) **76**

ROBERT PECOTA
Merlot Napa Valley Steven André 1991: Already quite smoky and toasty but has a nice beam of floral and berry-tinged flavors. (NR) (5/15/92) (BT) **86+**
Merlot Napa Valley Steven André 1990: Fruity and focused, with generous currant, cherry and berry aromas and flavors that persist on the palate. Lean in texture, with plenty of flavor and enough tannin to keep it growing through 1993 to '95. 800 cases made. $16.50 (5/31/92) **86**
Merlot Napa Valley Steven André 1989: Has nice blackberry and currant aromas and flavors but seems hard and a bit woody now. Perhaps cellaring until 1994 or '95 will soften it enough to be smooth. 800 cases made. $16.50 (11/15/91) **86**

J. PEDRONCELLI
Merlot Sonoma County 1989: Bitter and murky, with green, stemmy menthol nuances that interfere with the barely ripe flavors. Tobacco notes and hints of black cherry come through on the finish. Drink now to 1994. $12.50 (2/29/92) **76**

JOSEPH PHELPS
Merlot Napa Valley 1989: Firm and tight, with concentrated raspberry and cherry-scented flavors and oak notes lingering in the background. Has all the ingredients and should be a little more generous by 1995. 2,200 cases made. $15 (5/31/92) **88**
Merlot Napa Valley 1987: So herbal and spicy you could use it as a ready-made marinade. Overloaded with herb, bay leaf, soy sauce and vegetal aromas and flavors that totally overwhelm the currant notes. A surreal wine that's not designed to appeal to a wide spectrum. $18 (7/31/90) **80**
Merlot Napa Valley 1986 $15 (6/30/88) **84**

PHILIPPE-LORRAINE
Merlot Napa Valley 1989: Generous and smooth, with beautifully articulated berry flavors dressed in luxurious, spicy oak. A supple wine, with polished tannins that make it drinkable already. May be better after 1994. A new wine from Philip Baxter. 650 cases made. $15 (5/31/92) **89**

PINE RIDGE
Merlot Napa Valley Selected Cuvée 1990 (NR) (5/15/91) (BT) **85+**
Merlot Napa Valley Selected Cuvée 1989: Overwhelmingly woody tasting, with intense oak aromas and flavors suffocating the nice fruit underneath. A very overwrought wine. Tasted twice, with consistent notes. 4,750 cases made. $16.50 (5/31/92) **73**
Merlot Napa Valley Selected Cuvée 1988: The oak is strong, with a menthol-dill note that turns dry and masks the ripe plum and cherry-tinged flavors. Clean and fresh but not especially rich or distinctive. Drink now to 1993. Tasted twice. $17 (8/31/91) **80**
Merlot Napa Valley Selected Cuvée 1987: Has plenty of oak and herb notes and lean, elegant currant and plum-scented flavors to complement them. Well balanced with firm tannins and decent length. Drink now. $15 (4/15/90) **88**
Merlot Napa Valley Selected Cuvée 1986 $15 (6/30/89) **80**
Merlot Napa Valley Selected Cuvée 1985 Rel: $13 Cur: $18 (2/15/88) SS **91**
Merlot Napa Valley Selected Cuvée 1984 $13 (5/15/87) **80**
Merlot Napa Valley Selected Cuvée 1983 $13 (12/16/85) **83**
Merlot Napa Valley Selected Cuvée 1982 $13 (10/01/85) **90**
Merlot Napa Valley Selected Cuvée 1981 $12.50 (3/16/84) **82**

QUAIL RIDGE
Merlot Napa Valley 1988: Light, smooth and pleasantly full on the palate, with herb-scented plum and cherry flavors rounding nicely toward spice and vanilla on the finish. Not a powerful wine but smooth and appealing. Drinkable now. Tasted twice, with consistent notes. 4,000 cases made. $15 (5/31/92) **84**
Merlot Napa Valley 1987: Wild and exotic, bursting with jammy berry and plum aromas and flavors, turning tight and tart without diminishing the fruitiness. Drink now. $15 (6/15/90) **86**
Merlot Napa Valley 1985: Thick, rich, soft and luscious, with black cherry, herb and chocolate flavors, fine tannins and a plummy aftertaste. Drink now. $13.50 (3/31/89) **90**

RAMSAY
Merlot Napa Valley 1989: A decadent wine that nonetheless has plenty of lively fruit flavors to back up the earthy, barnyardy aromas and finish. Firmly tannic but supple enough to drink in 1993 to '96. Tasted twice. From Kent Rasmussen. 484 cases made. $12 (4/15/92) **86**

RANCHO SISQUOC
Merlot Santa Maria Valley 1989: Intense and firmly tannic, with ripe currant and berry flavors wrapped up tightly. Balanced and well made but needs a year or two for the tannins to soften. Drink after 1993. 900 cases made. $12 (5/31/92) **81**
Merlot Santa Maria Valley 1986: Shows a nice blending of fruit and wood-aged flavors and interesting spice, cedar and leather aromas. Medium-bodied and slightly tannic but ready to drink now. $9 (12/15/89) **77**

RAVENSWOOD
Merlot Carneros Sangiacomo 1989: A chunky, lively wine, with lots of flavor packed into a still-rough frame, but the balance is good. Offers dynamic currant, cherry and blackberry flavors shaded by anise and cedar notes. Best to drink after 1994 or '95. 475 cases made. $20 (11/15/91) **90**
Merlot North Coast Vintners Blend 1990: Fruity and refreshing, with plenty of ripe strawberry, plum and herb flavors and a touch of chocolate on the finish. The smooth texture and forward fruit make it pleasant to drink now. $9.50 (5/31/92) BB **84**
Merlot Sonoma County 1989: Dense and tannic, with austere plum and currant flavors framed by hard-edged oak notes. A tough wine to warm up to now—will need time to soften—but may always display a tough personality. Drink in 1994. Tasted twice. $15 (5/31/92) **86**
Merlot Sonoma County 1987: Soft and generous at first, this is tightly structured with the sort of sharply focused cherry and plum aromas and flavors that linger appealing on the finish. Start drinking now. 1,600 cases made. $18 (1/31/90) **87**
Merlot Sonoma County 1986 $18 (12/31/88) **80**
Merlot Sonoma County 1984 $11 (2/28/87) **85**
Merlot Sonoma County 1983 $11 (5/16/86) **61**
Merlot Sonoma County Vintners Blend 1989: Crisp and fruity, with lots of cherry and red pepper aromas and flavors, a light texture and soft tannins. Already drinkable. 4,000 cases made. $9 (3/31/91) BB **84**

RICHARDSON
Merlot Carneros Sonoma Valley Gregory 1989: Youthful, lively, tannic and focused, with a strong streak of currant flavor shaded by chocolate and cedar notes and an herbal overlay. Needs until 1993 to '95 to settle the tannin question. 400 cases made. $14 (3/31/91) **83**
Merlot Sangiacomo 1990: Very thick and flavorful, with tons of herb, plum and currant flavors backed by full but soft tannins and a lingering finish. A distinctive, powerful wine to drink now through 1997. 700 cases made. $14.50 (5/31/92) **87**
Merlot Sonoma Valley Los Carneros Gregory 1990: A major wine that has plenty of flavor and a character of its own. Its deep color and full cassis, earth and smoke aromas are backed up by deep, complex fruit flavors and a lingering finish. 400 cases made. $14.50 (5/31/92) **89**

RIDGE
Merlot Sonoma County Bradford Mountain 1987: Despite pretty ripe plum aromas, this is tight and tannic on the palate, with a green edge and a little stemminess. It needs a little fruit on its bones. Drinkable now. $17 (7/15/90) **75**
Merlot Sonoma County Bradford Mountain 1986: Extremely woody and vegetal, with thin, boring, uninspired red-wine flavors. Tasted twice. $16 (7/31/89) **64**

ROMBAUER
Merlot Napa Valley 1989: Heavy-handed with spicy oak, making it difficult to detect whether there are sufficient currant and cherry flavors to stand up to it in the long run. Curious now and best to try after 1993. 1,261 cases made. $16 (11/15/91) **84**
Merlot Napa Valley 1987: Attractive for its suppleness, elegance and ripe plum, tobacco and herb notes. Not too tannic and the flavors linger on the finish. Drink now to 1994. $14 (2/15/90) **87**
Merlot Napa Valley 1986: Excessively woody, with firm tannins and ripe cherry and currant flavors. Drink now to 1994. $14 (7/31/89) **78**

ROSENBLUM
Merlot Napa Valley Holbrook Mitchell Vineyard 1989: Shows attractive plum and cherry flavors up front, but then the tannins dominate with a vicelike grip that won't let go. Concentrated but tough. $20 (5/31/92) **80**
Merlot Russian River Valley 1989: Dark, tight and concentrated, with ripe cherry, currant and mint flavors that are fresh and lively with crisp acidity and firm tannins. A good candidate for the cellar. Try after 1995. 300 cases made. $14 (5/31/92) **85**

ROUND HILL
Merlot Napa Valley 1984 $9 (5/15/87) **87**
Merlot Napa Valley 1983 $7.50 (1/31/87) SS **92**
Merlot Napa Valley 1982 $7.50 (2/16/86) **65**
Merlot Napa Valley Reserve 1989: Light, crisp and lean, with simple herb and plum flavors. Ready to drink now. Tasted twice. 4,074 cases made. $11 (5/31/92) **78**
Merlot Napa Valley Reserve 1988: Simple and fresh, with a crisp edge to the strawberry and cherry flavors and hints of cinnamon on the finish. A bit watery in the middle but pleasant to sip. Tasted twice. $11 (11/15/91) **80**
Merlot Napa Valley Reserve 1986 $10.75 (12/31/88) **82**
Merlot Napa Valley Reserve 1985 $10 (5/31/88) **84**

RUBISSOW-SARGENT
Merlot Mt. Veeder 1988: Crisp and flavorful, with lively, appealing currant and berry aromas and flavors. Not an intense wine, but glides nicely across the palate. Best to drink in 1993 to '95. Tasted twice. 440 cases made. $15 (5/31/92) **84**

RUTHERFORD HILL
Merlot Napa Valley 1989: Thin, harsh and ultimately bland, with little more than tannin and greenish fruit flavor to distinguish it. Tasted three times. $14 (5/31/92) **70**
Merlot Napa Valley 1988: Herbal, earthy and a bit light in flavor concentration, but smooth and almost ready to drink. Has modest cherry and plum flavors and moderate tannins. Try now to 1994. $14.50 (5/31/92) **82**
Merlot Napa Valley 1987: Despite awkward green bean overtones, this medium-weight wine shows modest currant and berry flavors. It might be worth saving until 1993, when the tannins should settle down, but it seems thin. Tasted twice. $14 (3/31/91) **74**
Merlot Napa Valley 1986 $13 (6/15/90) **68**
Merlot Napa Valley 1985 $12 (1/31/89) **92**
Merlot Napa Valley 1984 $11 (4/30/88) **84**

Merlot Napa Valley 1983 $10 (8/31/87) **87**
Merlot Napa Valley 1982 $10.50 (5/16/86) **79**
Merlot Napa Valley 1981 $10 (10/01/85) **78**

RUTHERFORD RANCH
Merlot Napa Valley 1988: Light and elegant, with complex spice, clove and oak aromas, but has simple fruit flavors underneath that border on watery. Drink now. $12 (8/31/91) **80**
Merlot Napa Valley 1986 $11.75 (12/31/88) **87**
Merlot Napa Valley 1985 $10.50 (4/30/88) **92**
Merlot Napa Valley 1984 $9.75 (10/15/87) **83**

ST. CLEMENT
Merlot Napa Valley 1989: Ripe and round, with generous butter- and cedar-scented currant aromas and flavors. Firm on the palate and needs until 1994 or '95 to smooth the rough edges. 650 cases made. $18 (5/31/92) **87**
Merlot Napa Valley 1987: Elegant and well proportioned, with attractive cherry, currant and spicy herb notes that all add up to an appealing wine with good richness and depth. Needs to shed some tannin. Should be ready between 1993 to '97. 570 cases made. $16 (12/31/90) **85**
Merlot Napa Valley 1986: Hard and tannic, with tightly wound currant and citrus flavors barely peeking through the tannins and harsh acidity. Hard to like now but could be better when it softens up, say in 1993 to '95. 651 cases made. $15 (10/31/89) **74**
Merlot Napa Valley 1985 $15 (3/31/89) **91**
Merlot Napa Valley 1983 $14.50 (5/31/88) **81**

ST. FRANCIS
Merlot Sonoma Valley 1989: Drinkable but odd, with smoke and bacon aromas, rhubarb and plum flavors and a smoky finish. Soft and ready to drink. Tasted three times. $14 (5/31/92) **79**
Merlot Sonoma Valley 1988: Lavishly oaked, with layers of herb, tea, currant and spice notes and ripe fruit flavors that lean toward the oak and herb spectrum of Merlot. If you like a good slap of oak in your wine, this may be for you. Drink now to 1995. $16 (11/15/91) **82**
Merlot Sonoma Valley 1987: Extremely herbal, tobaccolike and smoky. A good wine, with odd flavors that are more vegetal and floral than fruity. Soft, generous and distinctive but not for everyone. Not typical of this winery's style. $14 (6/15/90) **80**
Merlot Sonoma Valley 1986 $14 (6/30/89) **85**
Merlot Sonoma Valley 1985 $12 (10/15/88) **66**
Merlot Sonoma Valley 1984 $12 (10/31/87) **88**
Merlot Sonoma Valley 1983 $11 (7/31/87) **80**
Merlot Sonoma Valley 1982 $10.75 (10/01/85) **78**
Merlot Sonoma Valley Reserve 1989: Stylish and appealing. Exotic and almost floral-smelling, with plenty of expensive oak accents over an exuberant base of blueberry and herb flavors. The tannins are smooth and the finish lingers. Drink now to 1995. 1,900 cases made. $24 (5/31/92) **90**
Merlot Sonoma Valley Reserve 1988: Weedy herb and black cherry flavors turn medicinal on the aftertaste. The tannins are soft and it's balanced but the flavors may not appeal to everyone. Drink now to 1995. $24 (11/15/91) **82**
Merlot Sonoma Valley Reserve 1986: Haul out the thesaurus. This one deserves all the adjectives you can find. Rich, opulent, supple and complex, with generous plum and vanilla aromas and flavors, magnificent depth and concentration. Drinkable now but should age at least through 1994. 1,042 cases made. $20 (1/31/90) **94**
Merlot Sonoma Valley Reserve 1985 $14.50 (12/31/88) **81**
Merlot Sonoma Valley Reserve 1984 $16 (2/15/88) **74**

ST. SUPERY
Merlot Napa Valley Dollarhide Ranch 1989: Firm and fresh, with generous currant and berry aromas and flavors that bounce appealingly across the palate. The fruit stays with you on the long finish, echoing raspberry and plum. Needs until 1993 to '95 to settle the tannins. 1,755 cases made. $13.50 (5/31/92) **89**

SANFORD
Merlot Santa Barbara County 1984 $18 (12/31/87) **66**

SANTA CRUZ MOUNTAIN
Merlot California 1983 $10 (10/01/85) **82**
Merlot Central Coast 1988 ($NA) (4/30/90) (BT) **90+**
Merlot Central Coast 1987 ($NA) (4/15/89) (BT) **80+**

SARAH'S
Merlot San Luis Obispo County John Radike Vineyard 1987: Bizarre beet, cola and vegetal flavors miss the mark for Merlot. Not our style. Tasted twice, with consistent notes. $30 (5/31/92) **65**

SEA RIDGE
Merlot Sonoma Coast Occidental Vineyards 1989: Stiff for a Merlot, but deeply flavored with intense, almost chocolaty flavors of black cherry and black pepper. The tannins are plenty firm, not rough, but the wine is tightly wound so it should improve if aged until at least 1995. Only 106 cases made. $15 (5/31/92) **86**

SEBASTIANI
Merlot Sonoma County 1989: Spicy and elegant, with a pretty beam of cherry and raspberry flavors sustained by crisp, lively acidity. The tannins on the finish are firm but polished. Approachable now, but may be better after 1994. Tasted twice. $9 (5/31/92) **85**
Merlot Sonoma County Family Selection 1985 $7 (9/30/88) **85**

AUGUST SEBASTIANI
Merlot California Country NV: Undistinguished, with herb and plum aromas and a tart, vinegary taste. Drinkable now. $4.50 (5/31/92) **72**

SHAFER
Merlot Napa Valley 1991: Rich, ripe and complex, already showing nice toasty oak notes and a pretty core of fruit flavor behind it. Floral and chocolate nuances add dimension. (NR) (5/15/92) (BT) **90+**
Merlot Napa Valley 1990: Full, rich and generous, with complex currant, chocolate and herb aromas and flavors shaded by sweet oak. A lively wine, with deep flavors and pretty spice notes on the finish. The tannins are present but not intrusive. Give it until 1994 or '95. $18 (5/31/92) **91**
Merlot Napa Valley 1989: A wine with a pretty core of ripe black cherry, currant, spice and cedar flavors that are elegant and polished. Drink now or cellar through 1995. $18 (8/31/91) **87**
Merlot Napa Valley 1988 $16.50 (12/31/90) **83**
Merlot Napa Valley 1987 $15 (10/15/89) **92**
Merlot Napa Valley 1986 $13 (12/31/88) **91**
Merlot Napa Valley 1985 $12.50 (12/15/87) **90**
Merlot Napa Valley 1984 $12.50 (2/28/87) **87**
Merlot Napa Valley 1983 $10 (2/16/86) **93**

SILVERADO
Merlot Stags Leap District 1989: Intense, focused blueberry and cherry flavors mark this supple, medium-bodied wine that's tempting to drink now for its freshness and fruit, but should develop well through about 1995. $16 (4/15/92) **87**
Merlot Stags Leap District 1988: Ripe, crisp and juicy, with elegant black cherry, plum and currant-tinged flavors. Not too tannic or rich and ready to drink now through 1994. 1,025 cases made. $15.50 (5/31/91) **86**
Merlot Stags Leap District 1987: Big and firm, with plenty of generous raspberry and plum aromas and flavors, opening up beautifully on the palate to a long finish. The tannins are tough enough to indicate cellaring until 1993 or '94. A harmonious wine that just needs time. 1,941 cases made. $14 (4/15/90) **92**
Merlot Stags Leap District 1986 $12 (8/31/89) **91**
Merlot Stags Leap District 1984 $12.50 (12/15/87) **78**

ROBERT SINSKEY
Merlot Napa Valley 1987: Elegant and harmonious, with wonderful balance and finesse. The rich, ripe currant, plum, black cherry and oak flavors are well integrated and there's a suppleness to the texture, but it's also structured, finishing with firm, fine tannins. Cellar until 1994 to '97. 600 cases made. $18 (3/31/91) **88**
Merlot Napa Valley 1986: Deeply colored, rich and supple, with herb, spice and currant flavors framed by leathery oak notes. Try now. $17 (10/15/89) **83**
Merlot Napa Valley Los Carneros 1989: Lean and crisp, with earthy, slightly minerallike aromas and flavors, modest fruit and enough tannin to need until 1995 or '96 to settle down. 2,200 cases made. $18 (5/31/92) **83**
Merlot Napa Valley Los Carneros Aries 1989: Crisp and lively, with generous raspberry and leather aromas and flavors that focus nicely on the finish with a hint of citrus. A well-crafted wine that's drinkable now but should improve through 1993 or '94. 1,700 cases made. $18 (5/31/92) **86**

SMITH & HOOK
Merlot Monterey Santa Lucia Highlands 1989: An extreme wine that smells vegetal and rubbery, tastes smoky and tannic and finishes a bit harsh. Raw and unappealing. Time in the cellar may help, but it's a gamble. 1,400 cases made. $15 (5/31/92) **70**
Merlot Monterey Santa Lucia Highlands 1988: Pleasant and medium-bodied, with straightforward plum and herb flavors and good balance. Simple but easy to like. Much better than bottles tasted earlier. 2,100 cases made. $15 (5/31/92) **80**
Merlot Napa County 1987: Bell pepper and herbal aromas and flavors distinguish this, but the ripe currant flavor manages to make itself heard over the peppery din. Overall a fairly elegant wine that's drinkable now. Better than a bottle tasted earlier. $15 (12/31/90) **83**
Merlot Napa County 1986: Rich, soft, lush and appealing, with hints of herb, bell pepper, chocolate and plum flavors that are pleasant and well defined. Has just enough tannin to lay it away for a while. Drink now to 1995. $20 (8/31/89) **86**

SOLIS
Merlot Monterey County 1988: Oaky and vegetal, with a touch of cherry and berry flavors on the aftertaste. Drink now. Tasted twice. 500 cases made. $10.50 (5/31/92) **73**

STAG'S LEAP WINE CELLARS
Merlot Napa Valley 1985 $16 (5/31/88) **86**
Merlot Napa Valley 1984 $15 (5/15/87) **78**
Merlot Napa Valley 1982 $13.50 (10/01/85) **78**
Merlot Napa Valley 1981 $13.50 (4/16/84) **82**

STAGS' LEAP WINERY
Merlot Napa Valley 1989: Plush, spicy, plummy and generous, with opulent currant, plum and chocolate aromas and flavors, finely integrated tannins and a sense of elegance than persists through the tasty finish. Best to drink after 1995. $17 (5/31/92) **88**
Merlot Napa Valley 1987: Firm and fruity, with a nice oaky edge to the ripe plum and currant flavors. Balanced and ready to drink now through 1995. 2,982 cases made. $17 (11/15/91) **85**
Merlot Napa Valley 1986: Distinctively Merlot, with ripe cherry and spice notes, an herbal edge, a supple oak texture and firm but soft tannins. It's nearing its peak. Probably best to drink now through 1996. $17 (12/31/90) **84**
Merlot Napa Valley 1981 $12 (2/16/85) **83**

STELTZNER
Merlot Stags Leap District 1990 (NR) (5/15/91) (BT) **85+**
Merlot Stags Leap District 1989: Firm, spicy and marked by oak, but has a solid foundation of ripe cherry flavor lurking in the background, shaded by toffee and walnut notes. Needs until 1994 for the tannins to settle down. $15 (11/15/91) **85**

STERLING
Merlot Carneros Winery Lake 1987: Firm and well structured, with plenty of cedar, cherry, chocolate and currant flavors that have amplitude, depth and complexity. Has plenty of tannins and fruit concentration to cellar until 1994 or '95. 400 cases made. $25 (12/31/90) **90**
Merlot Napa Valley 1991: Firm, tight and concentrated, with loads of ripe black cherry and berry flavors and a touch of smoky oak adding complexity to the long aftertaste. 5 percent Cabernet Franc. (NR) (5/15/92) (BT) **88+**
Merlot Napa Valley 1990 (NR) (5/15/91) (BT) **85+**
Merlot Napa Valley 1989: Nice, forward plum and raspberry aromas and flavors shaded by a smooth touch of oak make for a softish, medium-weight wine that's drinkable now. Tasted three times. $15 (5/31/92) **82**
Merlot Napa Valley 1988: Tight and compact, with layers of herb, raspberry, spice and plum flavors that turn firm and tannic on the finish. Moderately deep and concentrated. Drink in 1993 to '97. $15 (4/15/91) **83**
Merlot Napa Valley 1987 $13 (6/15/90) **83**
Merlot Napa Valley 1986 $14 (3/31/89) **85**
Merlot Napa Valley 1985 $14 (3/31/88) **87**
Merlot Napa Valley 1984 $11.50 (4/30/87) **93**
Merlot Napa Valley 1983 $11 (6/01/86) **91**
Merlot Napa Valley 1982 $12 (10/01/85) **83**
Merlot Napa Valley 1981 $11 (3/01/84) **83**

STEVENOT
Merlot North Coast Reserve 1989: Very solid and sturdy in texture, showing currant and herb flavors and chunky tannins. Probably best to cellar until about 1994 or beyond. 4,200 cases made. $10 (5/31/92) **83**

STONE CREEK
Merlot California Special Selection 1989: A decent wine at $6, with firm plum and cherry flavors and tight tannins. Best to drink now while the fruit is fresh. $6 (5/31/92) **79**

Key to Symbols

The scores reported here are the results of blind tastings conducted by our panel of senior editors. Wines that carry the initials below are results of individual tastings.

THE WINE SPECTATOR 100-POINT SCALE ***95-100***—Classic, a great wine; ***90-94***—Outstanding, superior character and style; ***80-89***—Good to very good, a wine with special qualities; ***70-79***—Average, drinkable wine that may have minor flaws; ***60-69***—Below average, drinkable but not recommended; ***50-59***—Poor, undrinkable, not recommended. "+"—With a score indicates a range; used primarily with barrel tastings to indicate a preliminary score.

SPECIAL DESIGNATIONS SS—Spectator Selection, CS—Cellar Selection, BB—Best Buy, ($NA)—Price not available, (NR)—Not released.

TASTER'S INITIALS (JG)—Jim Gordon, (HS)—Harvey Steiman, (JL)—James Laube, (JS)—James Suckling, (TM)—Thomas Matthews, (TR)—Terry Robards, (PM)—Per-Henrik Mansson, (BT)—Barrel Tasting (these wines were tasted blind from barrel samples), (CA-date)—*California's Great Cabernets* by James Laube, (CH-date)—*California's Great Chardonnays* by James Laube, (VP-date)—*Vintage Port* by James Suckling.

DATE TASTED Dates in parentheses represent the issue in which the rating was published.

STONEGATE
Merlot Napa Valley 1991: Firmly tannic and fruity, but missing richness and concentration. One-dimensional at this stage. 2,500 cases made. (NR) (5/15/92) (BT) **80+**
Merlot Napa Valley 1988: Hard and oaky, with a strong woody component that shoulders past the modest fruit characteristics. Berry flavors sneak in on the finish, suggesting this might be at its best around 1993. 662 cases made. $16.50 (5/31/92) **81**
Merlot Napa Valley 1986: Oaky and woody, but the currant and plum flavors stand up to it. Still, it's somewhat bitter on the finish and needs time. Drink in 1993. 1,000 cases made. $15 (4/15/90) **84**
Merlot Napa Valley Pershing Vineyard 1990 (NR) (5/15/91) (BT) **85+**
Merlot Napa Valley Pershing Vineyard 1987: Offers toast, herb and spice aromas, but woody, oaky notes override the ripe plum and currant flavors and leave a heavy, oaky, woody aftertaste that seems unbalanced. Bitterness comes through on the finish. Perhaps with time it will mellow. Drink in 1995 to 2000. 700 cases made. $16.50 (3/31/91) **83**
Merlot Napa Valley Spaulding Vineyard 1987: Elegant, ripe and supple, with plenty of herb, menthol, currant and plum flavors that ride softly on the palate. The tannins are moderate and the finish is full and pleasant. Drink now to 1994. 600 cases made. $16.50 (3/31/91) **86**
Merlot Napa Valley Spaulding Vineyard 1982 $14 (2/28/87) **84**
Merlot Napa Valley Spaulding Vineyard Proprietor's Reserve 1984 $15 (12/31/88) **85**

STONESTREET
Merlot Alexander Valley 1989: Ripe, intense and concentrated, with pretty spice, currant and anise flavors framed by toasty, smoky oak notes. Firm tannins on the finish suggest cellaring until 1996. $24 (5/31/92) **88**

STRATFORD
Merlot California 1990: Solidly fruity and flavorful, with nice black cherry flavors accented by spice and earth notes. Moderately tannic, full-bodied and ready to drink now. 3,000 cases made. $9.75 (5/31/92) BB **85**
Merlot California 1987: Lean and crisp, with pretty vanilla overtones to the tightly focused red cherry and berry aromas and flavors. Drinkable now, but can use cellaring until 1993 to soften the grip a bit. $13 (10/31/89) **83**
Merlot California 1986: Raw, cedary and ripe in aroma and youthful and tannic on the palate, with plenty of currant and cedar flavors and a good finish. $10 (1/31/89) **78**
Merlot California 1983 $8.50 (9/30/86) **79**

STRAUSS
Merlot Napa Valley 1989: Hard-edged and woody, with a strong fruit component but not much grace or finesse. A chunky wine that might grow into itself with cellaring through 1993 to '95. 2,800 cases made. $15 (11/15/91) **81**
Merlot Napa Valley 1988: A weedy, herbal wine, with more herbs and spice than fruit, but not out of the proper range for Merlot. The tannins are firm and the flavors turn vegetal on the finish. Drink now to 1993. 1,900 cases made. $14 (12/31/90) **82**
Merlot Napa Valley 1987: Deliciously focused and concentrated, with marvelous plum and cherry aromas and flavors, a firm texture and a light film of tannin. 1,800 cases made. $12 (2/15/90) **90**
Merlot Napa Valley 1986 $11 (2/28/89) **93**
Merlot Napa Valley 1985 $10 (2/15/88) **81**

STREBLOW
Merlot Napa Valley 1989: Sharply focused, with tart black cherry and currant flavors and toasty, smoky oak notes adding a nice dimension. The flavors fan out on the finish, echoing fruit and oak, and the texture is smooth and supple. Drink now through 1996. 350 cases made. $20 (5/31/92) **89**

RODNEY STRONG
Merlot Russian River Valley River West Vineyard 1985: Hard, thin, herbal and minty, not offering much flesh or body. Has modest, tangy fruit flavor, tannins and a woody finish. Drink now. $12 (2/28/89) **79**

SULLIVAN
Merlot Napa Valley 1989: Bold, rich and fruity, with ripe, concentrated plum, currant and raspberry flavors that run deep. Has subtle oak shadings on the finish and well-integrated tannins that are present but not overbearing. Beautifully crafted but needs until 1995. 800 cases made. $20 (4/15/92) **92**

SWANSON
Merlot Napa Valley 1990: Hard and tannic, a medium-weight wine, with modest fruit flavors and a strong leafy, woody component. The tannins need until 1995 to sort themselves out. 1,800 cases made. $16 (5/31/92) **82**

TAFT STREET
Merlot Sonoma County 1990: Very fresh and lively, with well-defined currant and berry aromas and flavors and hints of cedar and spice on the finish. A bit rough around the edges but cellaring until 1994 or '95 should do the trick. 2,851 cases made. $11.50 (5/31/92) **89**
Merlot Sonoma County 1989: Ripe, sweet and jammy, with generous berry and cherry flavors. Firm tannins on the finish indicate it needs until 1995 to soften. 1,067 cases made. $12 (5/31/92) **85**
Merlot Sonoma County 1985 $10 (5/31/88) **83**

TERRA
Merlot Napa Valley 1988: Strikes a nice balance between oak and herb-tinged currant and berry flavors. Spicy, not too tannic and drinkable now through 1995. Better than bottles tasted earlier. 500 cases made. $14 (5/31/92) **84**

TRUCHARD
Merlot Carneros Napa Valley 1989: A sturdy wine, with simple raspberry and plum flavors. Has a lean texture and turns citrusy on the crisp finish. Drinkable now but can use until 1993 or '94 to soften the hard edges. 200 cases made. $18 (5/31/92) **81**

M.G. VALLEJO
Merlot California 1990: Tannic and smoky, with firm berry and plum flavors. Offers more character than many wines at this price. 3,740 cases made. $6 (5/31/92) BB **80**
Merlot California 1987: Light and herbal, with fresh berry notes. An easy-to-drink wine with enough Merlot character to convince you it is varietal. A fair price. Drink now. $5 (6/15/90) **77**

VENDANGE
Merlot California 1990: A light, fresh-tasting wine, with strawberry and cherry flavors. Pleasant to drink now while it's fresh. $6 (5/31/92) BB **80**

VICHON
Merlot Napa Valley 1988: Has decent Merlot flavor but lacks concentration and depth. The light currant, cherry and plum flavors are ripe and attractive and there's enough tannin to warrant cellaring until 1993. 1,944 cases made. $16 (12/31/90) **81**
Merlot Napa Valley 1987: An intense wine, with layers of rich, ripe, round, supple plum and currant flavors that are well oaked and elegantly balanced. Tempting to drink now, but can age through 1995. 2,460 cases made. $16 (2/15/90) **91**
Merlot Napa Valley 1986: Offers pretty aromas and an elegant framework. Medium-bodied, with spice, herb and currant flavors that are persistent from start to finish. Has the structure and tannins for cellaring. Drink now through 1995. $16 (8/31/89) **86**
Merlot Napa Valley 1985 $14 (12/15/87) **88**
Merlot Napa Valley Tenth Harvest 1989: Ripe, spicy and rounded with classy-tasting oak, this supple, fleshy wine has plenty to offer for current drinking but could continue to develop with aging through 1994. Currant, tobacco and vanilla flavors predominate. 3,400 cases made. $17 (4/15/92) **88**

VINA VISTA
Merlot Alexander Valley 1988: Tart, crisp and fruity, with ripe cherry, currant and spice notes. Lively acidity sustains the flavors on the finish. Not too tannic and can still be aged until 1994 for it to soften. 720 cases made. $12 (5/31/92) **86**
Merlot Alexander Valley 1985 $8 (10/31/87) **90**

WHITEHALL LANE
Merlot Knights Valley 1987: Pungent and fruity, offering pickle and raspberry aromas and flavors and hinting at tarragon on the finish. A unique wine but more like Zinfandel than Merlot. Tasted twice. 788 cases made. $16 (7/15/90) **77**
Merlot Knights Valley 1986 ($NA) (4/15/88) (BT) **90+**
Merlot Knights Valley 1984 $14 (12/31/87) **87**
Merlot Knights Valley 1983 $12 (10/01/85) **85**
Merlot Knights Valley 1982 Rel: $10 Cur: $19 (6/01/85) CS **92**
Merlot Knights Valley Reserve 1986: A racy wine that's very ripe and alcoholic. Hot on the palate and finish, with hard fruit and tannins overshadowing the ripe raisiny flavors. Coarse on the finish. Needs a few years' cellaring. Tasted twice. $15 (7/31/89) **72**
Merlot Knights Valley Summers Ranch 1989: A wrapping of stylish, sweet oak surrounds the lush cherry and raspberry flavors for a spicy but fruity, well-balanced wine, with moderate tannins. Enjoyable now through about 1995. Tasted twice. 3,800 cases made. $18 (4/15/92) **84**
Merlot Knights Valley Summers Ranch 1988: Supple, fruity, well balanced and medium-bodied, with nice cherry, herb and plum flavors of medium intensity. Drink now through 1993. 1,450 cases made. $18 (3/31/91) **82**

WILD HORSE
Merlot Central Coast 1989: Very earthy, rustic and wild, with leather aromas and extra-ripe fruit flavors that are almost overwhelming. Heavy on the oak and tannins. Not a wine for everyone but sure is flavorful. Try drinking in 1994. $15 (5/31/92) **76**
Merlot Central Coast 1986: Very soft but also tannic, showing gorgeous plum, cherry and smoke aromas but turning mushy on the palate. A pleasant wine that lacks the depth to develop much. $11 (7/31/89) **77**

WILDCAT
Merlot Sonoma Valley 1989: Tastes harsh, green and tannic, with very little fruit underneath. Oaky tannins and flavors dominate. Tasted twice, with consistent notes. 250 cases made. $20 (5/31/92) **74**
Merlot Sonoma Valley 1988: Distinctive, with ripe raisin and rhubarb flavors and plenty of oak. A bit clumsy on the finish, where the oak and fruit collide rather than embrace. Drink after 1994. Tasted twice. 250 cases made. $18 (5/31/92) **78**

J. WILE & SONS
Merlot Napa Valley 1989: Light and simple, with ripe cherry and berry notes and a splash of oak but nothing more. Drink now. Tasted twice. $10 (5/31/92) **77**

WINDSOR
Merlot Russian River Valley Signature Series 1987: Smells attractive, with smoky vanilla and oak aromas, but is lean and tight on the palate, with cherry and plum notes that turn supple on the finish. Balanced and ready to drink now through 1995. 1,800 cases made. $25 (5/31/92) **84**

WOLTNER
Merlot Alexander Valley Cask 465 1982 $4.75 (4/16/85) **60**

YORK MOUNTAIN
Merlot San Luis Obispo County 1989: Broad, ripe and flavorful, with herb, cherry and plum notes and soft tannins. Supple enough to drink now or through 1994. 775 cases made. $13 (5/31/92) **84**
Merlot San Luis Obispo County 1986: Very ripe and soft. Smells and tastes like blackberries and has a deep but soft texture, medium body and mild tannins. Doesn't need cellaring. $10 (12/15/89) **80**

STEPHEN ZELLERBACH
Merlot Alexander Valley 1982 $8.50 (10/01/85) **84**
Merlot Alexander Valley 1980 $8.50 (5/01/84) **68**

MUSCAT

ALDERBROOK
Muscat Canelli Sonoma County 1989: Light, dry and slightly sparkling, with muted fruit flavors and a sappy finish. 800 cases made. $7.50 (7/15/90) **75**

ARCIERO
Muscat Canelli Paso Robles 1988: Smells nutty, tastes simple, sweet and bland with little of the distinctive Muscat tang. $6 (12/15/89) **67**

AUSTIN
Muscat Canelli Santa Barbara County 1988: Decent quality. Has an earthy, slightly musty aroma backed up by simple fruit flavors and good acidity. $8.50 (12/15/89) **72**

BENZIGER
Muscat Canelli Sonoma County 1987: Delicate and refreshing, lightly sweet, with very pleasant peach and floral aromas and flavors, smooth and silky through the finish. Neither too dry nor too sweet. $10 (8/31/89) **80**

BONNY DOON
Muscat Monterey Moscato del Solo Ca' del Solo 1990: A flavorful, sweet wine that comes off as heavy-handed; could be an apricot wine. Very fruity, spicy and floral, with a good dose of effervescence and sugar. 950 cases made. $9 (8/31/91) **77**

CLAIBORNE & CHURCHILL
Muscat Canelli California Dry Alsatian Style 1987: Exuberant and flavorful, with abundant flavors of apricot and spice. Rich and full in texture and slightly sweet, balanced toward the soft side. $8 (12/15/89) **78**

EBERLE
Muscat Canelli Paso Robles 1990: Fresh, spicy and soft in texture, with classic Muscat litchi and nutmeg aromas and flavors, delicately sweet and fruity on the finish. Drink as soon as possible. 1,158 cases made. $8.50 (8/31/91) **83**
Muscat Canelli Paso Robles 1988: An interesting sweet wine. Has a smoky, herbal aroma, clean but soft fruit flavors and reasonable balance. $7.50 (12/15/89) **76**

FOLIE A DEUX
Muscat Canelli Napa Valley Muscat à Deux 1990: Fragrant, with all the characteristic litchi and spice aromas of Muscat, but drier on the palate than most, offering tightly controlled fruit and spice flavors. Simple but refreshing. 1,143 cases made. $8.50 (8/31/91) **80**
Muscat Canelli Napa Valley Muscat à Deux 1988: Dry and crisp, with delicate spicy, almond and sweet anise aromas and flavors. $7.50 (8/31/89) **83**

MARKHAM
Muscat Napa Valley Blanc 1989: A floral wine that's lightly sweet and fruity. A fresh, simple wine that seems almost subdued, rather than aggressively spicy. $9 (7/15/90) **79**
Muscat Napa Valley Blanc Markham Vineyard 1988: Lively and very fruity, with a cornucopia of grassy, sweet apricot, grapefruit and peach flavors and a long, fruity finish. $9 (4/30/89) **84**

MISSION VIEW
Muscat Canelli Paso Robles 1988: An earthy, decayed aroma is unappealing and the sweet, simple fruit flavors don't make up for it. $7 (12/15/89) **68**

ROBERT MONDAVI
Muscat Napa Valley Moscato d'Oro 1990: The perfumed aromas and soapy flavors do not

distinguish this sweet wine, which hints not very successfully at fruitiness on the finish. Tasted twice. $12 (11/30/91) **72**

Muscat Napa Valley Moscato d'Oro 1988: Packed with apricot and menthol flavors, sweet and soft in texture. Try it well chilled as an aperitif. Tasted twice. $10 (4/30/90) **78**

Muscat Napa Valley Moscato d'Oro 1987: Smells great but disappoints, with its lack of intensity and richness on the palate. In an effort to keep it from being too sweet, it comes off as insipid. Peach, litchi and almond aromas are attractive. $11 (11/15/89) **79**

ROBERT PECOTA

Muscato di Andrea Napa Valley 1990: Has the appealing litchi aromas and flavors of a ripe Muscat bundled into a delicate package. Sweet but not unctuous. The flavors persist on the balanced finish. Drinkable now. A good value. $9.75 (9/15/91) **87**

Muscato di Andrea Napa Valley 1989: Light, sweet and fruity, with nice hints of sweet spices on the finish to remind you that it's Muscat. Just the thing for summer fruit desserts. 2,000 cases made. $9.25 (7/15/90) **86**

PRESTON

Muscat Canelli Dry Creek Valley 1987: Clean and fruity, but the watery texture does not allow much fruit flavor or aroma to emerge. Seems delicate and pleasant. $7 (8/31/89) **78**

SUTTER HOME

Muscat Alexandria California 1990: Spicy, floral, heavily perfumed and definitely sweet, although not sticky. The aromas are strong and not as pleasant as they could be. Drinkable now, while it's fresh. $5 (11/30/91) **77**

PETITE SIRAH

BLACK MOUNTAIN

Petite Sirah Alexander Valley Bosun Crest 1987: Full-bodied, soft and generous, oozing with plum and currant flavors that persist on the finish. Well-integrated tannins wouldn't get in the way of a hearty dish now, but the tannins should resolve by 1993 to '95. 785 cases made. $8.50 (10/31/91) BB **87**

Petite Sirah Alexander Valley Bosun Crest 1986: Firm, tannic and somewhat sour, with an unfortunate moldy edge that takes away what little plum flavor is present. Tasted twice. 900 cases made. $8.50 (10/31/91) **67**

Petite Sirah Alexander Valley Bosun Crest 1985: Warm and generous on the nose, tannic and tough on the palate. The ripe cherry, cinnamon and black pepper aromas are beguiling, but it's going to take a while for the personality to show through all that tannin. Needs until 1994. It's $9 (2/15/89) **81**

BOGLE

Petite Sirah Clarksburg 1988: Ebulliently fruity, with the tropical fruit overtones of carbonic maceration, turning a bit bitter on the finish. Eccentric style that no one would ever guess is a Petite Sirah. $7 (10/31/89) **70**

CLOS PEGASE

Petite Sirah Napa Valley Petite Syrah 1988: Firm and flavorful, with generous blackberry and raspberry flavors, integrated tannins and a solid level of intensity on the finish. Drinkable now. 298 cases made. $14.50 (10/31/91) **83**

CONCANNON

Petite Sirah Livermore Valley 1987: Oaky dill and vinegar overtones make the blackberry aromas and flavors less appealing, but it's a legitimate wine. Drink after 1993 or '94. $11 (8/31/91) **77**

Petite Sirah Livermore Valley Reserve 1985: Broad and flavorful, with earthy cherry and chocolate flavors. Tannic, but not heavy or tough. Best after 1993 or '94. $15 (8/31/91) **83**

DEER PARK

Petite Sirah Howell Mountain Parks-Muscatine Vineyards 1987: Crisp in texture, with firm tannins and lively acidity supporting a range of flavors that include berry, plum, chocolate and spice. Tannic enough to need until 1995 to '98 to soften. 300 cases made. $14 (10/31/91) **82**

FETZER

Petite Sirah California Petite Syrah Reserve 1986: Promises more than it delivers. Woody, buttery flavors and full tannins overwhelm the fruit flavors. Too tannic to drink now, and it's difficult to tell whether it will get better with age. $14 (8/31/90) **74**

FIELD STONE

Petite Sirah Alexander Valley 1988: Ripe, generous and not lacking in the tannin department, but mellow enough to let the black pepper and cherry flavors come through. Cellaring until 1993 to '95 should smooth it out somewhat, but this will never be a polished wine. Drink when you want something hearty. 1,900 cases made. $15 (12/31/90) **85**

Petite Sirah Alexander Valley 1987: Firm in texture, but generous, offering blueberry and cherry aromas and flavors. This broad, soft wine is almost drinkable now, but could use cellaring until 1993 or '94 to soften the tannins. $15 (12/31/90) **84**

Petite Sirah Alexander Valley 1986: Ripe and loaded with the characteristic black pepper aromas, very firm and tannic, thick and a bit coarse on the finish. Tannin needs until at least 1993 to soften a bit. $15 (9/30/89) **79**

Petite Sirah Alexander Valley 1985 $11 (2/15/89) **83**

FOPPIANO

Petite Sirah Russian River Valley 1988: Jammy, berrylike notes and ripe, fresh fruit flavors dominate this broad, tannic wine, but it's still lively. Offers nice touches of oak. Cleanly made and delicious now. A good value. $8.25 (8/31/90) **86**

Petite Sirah Russian River Valley 1986: Big and full-bodied. Its flavor owes a lot to oak at this stage, but it has the concentrated blueberry, pepper and cherry flavors to expect it to develop nicely by 1993 or later. $8 (6/15/89) **83**

Petite Sirah Russian River Valley Reserve Le Grande Petite 1987: Somewhat harsh and tannic despite the black cherry flavor, this is a big wine that lacks focus, but it's still likable. Drink now. $20 (8/31/90) **79**

Petite Sirah Sonoma County 1990: Dark in color, full-bodied, very concentrated and tannic, with ripe blackberry flavors accented by vanilla and spice notes from oak aging. Despite its heavy profile, this is well balanced and should be fine to drink now through at least 1996. $10 (6/30/92) **87**

FRICK

Petite Sirah Monterey County 1985: Dense, dark and peppery, with more spice and toast than the well-focused plum and cherry flavor can take right now. A chewy wine with a lot of personality and style. Drink now. $8 (2/15/89) **87**

GEYSER PEAK

Petite Sirah Alexander Valley 1989: A wall of tannin blocks entry to this deep, dark wine, overshadowing the tart black cherry and berry flavors. Smells inviting, but tastes very harsh and closed. Would need many years for the tannins to subside, but it's a gamble to cellar because of the heavy-handed style. 165 cases made. $15 (6/30/92) **79**

GLASS MOUNTAIN QUARRY

Petite Sirah Napa Valley 1988: A firm, spicy wine, with definite black pepper overtones to the modest cherry flavor. Tannic enough to need until 1993 to '96 to soften. From Markham. 244 cases made. $8 (10/31/91) BB **81**

GUENOC

Petite Sirah Guenoc Valley 1988: Sturdy and fruity, with plenty of plum and oak aromas and flavors. Generous, stylish and well balanced. The tannins need until 1993 or '94, but it has plenty of appeal already. $10 (8/31/91) **86**

Petite Sirah Guenoc Valley 1985: Sweet plum flavor tinged with vanilla and anise runs through this balanced, harmonious and velvety wine from start to finish. A good value. $7 (2/15/89) **83**

Petite Sirah North Coast 1989: Big and hearty, with tons of tannin and a flavor that owes a lot to oak. Deep in color, spicy and rich in aroma and tannic and firm on the palate. Too tannic to enjoy now; cellar until about 1996 if this is your style of wine. $14 (6/30/92) **82**

HOP KILN

Petite Sirah Russian River Valley M. Griffin Vineyards 1987: Generous fruit and firm tannins manage to strike a balance that makes this wine drinkable with hearty food, but the soft texture does not bode well for cellaring. Drink it soon. 413 cases made. $11 (2/28/90) **82**

KARLY

Petite Sirah Amador County 1989: Earthy animal aromas and flavors add up to a classic barnyardy, gamy wine. Not our style at all. Tasted twice. $11.50 (3/15/92) **65**

Petite Sirah Amador County Not So Petite Sirah 1988: Sturdy, funky and generous, with ripe flavors reminiscent of Concord grapes, layered with earthy, gamy and spicy overtones. Should develop well with cellaring through 1993 to '95. Love the label. $14 (12/31/90) **81**

MARIETTA

Petite Sirah Sonoma County 1988: Dark, dense and tannic, with generous plum and blueberry flavors peeking through the veneer of astringency. Best to drink after 1994. 850 cases made. $10 (3/15/92) **84**

LOUIS M. MARTINI

Petite Sirah Napa Valley 1985: Generous and flavorful, offering plenty of blackberry and black pepper aromas and flavors, soft and velvety, not at all harsh. Blueberry flavors on the finish are appealing enough to make this drinkable now, but can age until 1994. $7 (10/31/89) BB **85**

Petite Sirah Napa Valley Reserve 1987: Firm, tannic and fruity, with generous blueberry and red plum flavors, but the tannins are tough enough to wrestle the fruit down on the finish. Try in 1995. $11 (11/30/91) **85**

Petite Sirah Napa Valley Reserve 1986: Firm and fruity, with plenty of tannin, but the generous cherry and berry flavors manage to inch past the oak and tannin. Probably best around 1995 to '97. $12 (10/31/90) **81**

MIRASSOU

Petite Sirah Monterey County Fifth Generation Family Selection 1989: A sturdy red, with significant tannins and simple berry aromas and flavors. Drink now. $7.50 (3/15/92) **79**

RIDGE

Petite Sirah Napa County York Creek 1987: The inky black color foreshadows the licorice and black leather flavors that dominate this rich, intense wine. Will appeal to lovers of concentrated wines. May live forever. Distinctive, but not for everyone. Tasted twice, with consistent notes. $11.50 (8/31/91) **76**

Petite Sirah Napa County York Creek 1985: Ripe and pretty, with crushed pepper and floral notes to complement the fresh berry flavors. Rich and full-bodied, robust and satisfying. Drink now to 1999. $9 (10/31/89) **87**

Petite Sirah Napa Valley 1988: Earthy, gamy aromas and flavors persist through the finish, making the peppery plum flavors recede. The tannins clench the finish. Needs until 1995 or '96. 1,040 cases made. $16 (3/15/92) **80**

STAG'S LEAP WINE CELLARS

Petite Sirah Napa Valley 1987: This fine example of the varietal has intense color, nice cassis and blackberry aromas and dominating black cherry flavors. Tannic, full-bodied and well balanced, the fruit lingers on the finish. Try now to 1995. $12 (8/31/90) **87**

STAGS' LEAP WINERY

Petite Sirah Napa Valley Petite Syrah 1987: Firm, tannic and flavorful, with a generous level of blackberry, black cherry and smoke aromas and flavors, plus a definite earthy edge to the finish. Needs until 1994 to '96 to soften. 4,267 cases made. $13.50 (10/31/91) **82**

SEAN H. THACKREY

Petite Sirah Napa Valley Sirius Marston Vineyard Old Vines 1989: Chewy blackberry and plum flavors emerge from the rich tannic stew, and mint, licorice and alcohol come out on the finish. A dense, highly concentrated wine that needs cellaring until 1995. $24 (8/31/91) **87**

PINOT BLANC

AU BON CLIMAT

Pinot Blanc Santa Barbara County 1990: A gentle wine, with appealing caramel and honey overtones to the ripe pear and melon aromas and flavors. Smooth and nicely balanced. Drink soon. $12.50 (7/15/91) **83**

BENZIGER

Pinot Blanc Sonoma County 1989: Fresh, clean and fruity, with ripe nectarine, pear, fig, spice and vanilla notes that are neatly woven together. The texture is soft and silky, with a pretty aftertaste. Ready now through 1993. $9 (11/15/91) **85**

BUEHLER

Pinot Blanc Napa Valley 1987: Artfully balancing ripe fig and peach fruit with spicy oak, this is a lively, crisp and harmonious wine with impressive fruit complexity. Drink it now. $9 (3/31/89) **87**

Pinot Blanc Napa Valley Buehler Vineyards 1988: Very rich and round, with honey and butter aromas and flavors that soften on the finish, echoing pear and fig. Drink now. $9 (2/15/90) **84**

CHALONE

Pinot Blanc Chalone 1990: Intense and lively, with rich pear and citrus notes, but they turn earthy and papery on the finish, leaving a trace of bitterness. This wine typically needs three to five years' cellaring to develop; cellar until 1994. Tasted twice, with consistent notes. 2,143 cases made. Rel: $17.50 Cur: $22 (2/29/92) **80**

Pinot Blanc Chalone 1989: Ripe and buttery, with enough elegance and suppleness to keep it from being ponderous. Has lots of pear, butterscotch, vanilla and nutmeg flavors reminiscent of Chardonnay, but it's rounder and broader. Drinkable now. 1,824 cases made. Rel: $17 Cur: $25 (11/30/90) **88**

Pinot Blanc Chalone 1988: Floral overtones to the generous peach, pear and fig flavors make this immediately appealing, but it also has the structure and earthy, hazelnut notes on the finish to make it graceful. Rel: $17 Cur: $29 (2/15/90) **88**

Pinot Blanc Chalone 1987 Rel: $17 Cur: $30 (12/15/88) **87**

Key to Symbols

The scores reported here are the results of blind tastings conducted by our panel of senior editors. Wines that carry the initials below are results of individual tastings.

THE WINE SPECTATOR 100-POINT SCALE *95-100*—Classic, a great wine; *90-94*—Outstanding, superior character and style; *80-89*—Good to very good, a wine with special qualities; *70-79*—Average, drinkable wine that may have minor flaws; *60-69*—Below average, drinkable but not recommended; *50-59*—Poor, undrinkable, not recommended. "+"—With a score indicates a range; used primarily with barrel tastings to indicate a preliminary score.

SPECIAL DESIGNATIONS SS—Spectator Selection, CS—Cellar Selection, BB—Best Buy, ($NA)—Price not available, (NR)—Not released.

TASTER'S INITIALS (JG)—Jim Gordon, (HS)—Harvey Steiman, (JL)—James Laube, (JS)—James Suckling, (TM)—Thomas Matthews, (TR)—Terry Robards, (PM)—Per-Henrik Mansson, (BT)—Barrel Tasting (these wines were tasted blind from barrel samples), (CA-date)—*California's Great Cabernets* by James Laube, (CH-date)—*California's Great Chardonnays* by James Laube, (VP-date)—*Vintage Port* by James Suckling.

DATE TASTED Dates in parentheses represent the issue in which the rating was published.

CHATEAU ST. JEAN
Pinot Blanc Alexander Valley Robert Young Vineyards 1988: Flavorful and concentrated, offering lots of pear, pineapple and spice aromas and flavors and hints of butter on the long finish. Refreshing thread of acidity. Drinkable now, but can probably improve through 1993. 2,640 cases made. $9 (5/31/91) BB **89**
Pinot Blanc Alexander Valley Robert Young Vineyards 1987: Earthy, toasty, round and buttery, a rich, supple wine with smooth texture. A bit soft and fat but stylish and easily approachable, echoing honey and toast on the finish. Drink now. A good value. $9 (5/31/90) **88**
Pinot Blanc Alexander Valley Robert Young Vineyards 1985: Almond and pineapple aromas and flavors distinguish this ripe, round wine that turns honeylike on the finish. A generous wine that calls for another sip. Drink now. $9 (12/15/89) **85**
Pinot Blanc Alexander Valley Robert Young Vineyards 1984 $9 (8/31/87) **91**

CONGRESS SPRINGS
Pinot Blanc Santa Clara County 1989: Flavorful but a bit clumsy, with a chunky texture offering modest apple, nectarine and nutmeg aromas and flavors that turn a bit chalky on the finish. 2,138 cases made. $9 (4/30/91) **78**
Pinot Blanc Santa Clara County San Ysidro Vineyard 1988: Attractive with pretty floral flavors, but somewhat one-dimensional on the palate, with tight, firm, crisp lemon and spicy pear flavor. Give it a year or two to develop. $9.50 (8/31/89) **84**

ELLISTON
Pinot Blanc Central Coast Sunol Valley Vineyard 1989: An earthy, funky wine that misses the mark in flavor. Turns thin and watery. Of average quality. 637 cases made. $10 (11/15/91) **75**
Pinot Blanc Central Coast Sunol Valley Vineyard 1987: Lean and earthy, with smoke and mineral aromas and flavors turning toward fig and butter on the finish. A stylish wine, holding a lot in reserve, but not especially generous. Drinkable now. $10 (5/31/91) **82**

JEKEL
Pinot Blanc Arroyo Seco Arroyo Blanc 1985: Rich and woody. Has Chardonnay body and texture but pleasant earthy and figgy flavors dominate. Nice vanilla overtones, full-bodied and ripe. Starts with decadent aromas and finishes with a lingering aftertaste. $6 (6/15/89) BB **83**
Pinot Blanc Arroyo Seco Home Vineyard 1984: Ripe and full-blown, with intense bottle bouguet, pineapple and peach flavor, a good shot of oak and the impression of sweetness on the finish, stylishly knit into a well-made wine. $8 (3/31/89) **81**

MERLION
Pinot Blanc Napa Valley Coeur de Melon 1987: A gentle, generous wine, with a steely backbone of crisp, lemony acidity rounded off by melon, butter and fig aromas and flavors. Good to drink soon. 1,307 cases made. $9 (11/30/90) **82**

MIRASSOU
Pinot Blanc Monterey County Limited Bottling Fifth Generation Harvest Reserve 1989: Ripe, broad and stylish, with generous melon and pear flavors and hints of nutmeg and fig around the edges. Buttery and smooth on the long finish. Drinkable now. 1,200 cases made. $12.50 (5/31/91) **86**
Pinot Blanc Monterey County White Burgundy 1989: Round and citrusy, with lots of grapefruit and pineapple aromas and flavors wrapped in a cloak of vanilla and spice notes. Likable, with more heft that most Chardonnays. Drinkable now. $7 (12/31/91) BB **83**

MONTEREY PENINSULA
Pinot Blanc Monterey Doctor's Reserve 1988: Generous, aromatic and flavorful, with earth, vanilla, honey and almond overtones to the ripe pear character. Long, flavorful, balanced and full of personality. Drinkable now, but perhaps better in 1993. $12 (4/30/91) **87**

PARAISO SPRINGS
Pinot Blanc Monterey County 1990: Simple but pleasant, with nutty peach, pear and spice notes that display moderate richness and complexity. Drink now to 1994. 1,600 cases made. $8 (2/29/92) **82**

Pinot Noir

ACACIA
Pinot Noir Carneros Napa Valley 1989: Disappointing for Acacia. Has a definite barnyardy edge to the cherry and strawberry flavors. Gets muddled and murky on the aftertaste. Drink now. Tasted twice, with consistent notes. $14 (11/15/91) **71**
Pinot Noir Carneros Napa Valley 1988: Light in texture, but sharply focused, with a good concentration of strawberry and currant aromas and flavors that linger on the finely crafted finish. A wine to drink now or hold until 1993 or '94. Tasted twice. 4,904 cases made. $14 (2/28/91) **89**
Pinot Noir Carneros Napa Valley 1987: Light, fresh and elegant, with delicate spicy cherry and toasty oak nuances that make it very appealing to drink now. This is not a wine to lay away in the cellar. Best to enjoy its complexities now. Rel: $13 Cur: $15 (2/15/90) **87**
Pinot Noir Carneros Napa Valley 1986 $15 (6/15/88) **88**
Pinot Noir Carneros Napa Valley 1985 Rel: $12 Cur: $14 (12/15/87) **84**
Pinot Noir Carneros Napa Valley 1984 $11 (12/15/86) SS **95**
Pinot Noir Carneros Napa Valley Iund Vineyard 1984 $15 (3/15/87) **81**
Pinot Noir Carneros Napa Valley Iund Vineyard 1983 $15.50 (8/31/86) **77**
Pinot Noir Carneros Napa Valley Iund Vineyard 1982 Rel: $15 Cur: $31 (7/16/84) CS **91**
Pinot Noir Carneros Napa Valley Lee Vineyard 1983 Rel: $15.50 Cur: $20 (8/31/86) **89**
Pinot Noir Carneros Napa Valley Lee Vineyard 1982 $15 (7/16/84) **90**
Pinot Noir Carneros Napa Valley Madonna Vineyard 1986 $18 (6/15/88) **88**
Pinot Noir Carneros Napa Valley Madonna Vineyard 1985 $16 (12/15/87) **88**
Pinot Noir Carneros Napa Valley Madonna Vineyard 1984 $16 (3/15/87) **88**
Pinot Noir Carneros Napa Valley Madonna Vineyard 1983 $15.50 (8/31/86) **93**
Pinot Noir Carneros Napa Valley St. Clair Vineyard 1988: Very firm and concentrated, with nicely modulated plum, cherry and currant aromas and flavors and sufficient tannins to hold the wine without getting in the way. Concentrated enough to develop well through 1995. Tasted twice. 2,588 cases made. $20 (2/28/91) **91**
Pinot Noir Carneros Napa Valley St. Clair Vineyard 1987: Plenty of elegant and well-defined Pinot Noir character. The pretty spice, cherry and smoke flavors are rich and concentrated and marry well on the palate. Good length on the aftertaste; altogether delicate and pleasing. Best now through 1993. Rel: $18 Cur: $22 (2/15/90) **89**
Pinot Noir Carneros Napa Valley St. Clair Vineyard 1986 Rel: $18 Cur: $30 (6/15/88) **91**
Pinot Noir Carneros Napa Valley St. Clair Vineyard 1985 $16 (12/15/87) **91**
Pinot Noir Carneros Napa Valley St. Clair Vineyard 1984 Rel: $16 Cur: $30 (11/30/86) **93**
Pinot Noir Carneros Napa Valley St. Clair Vineyard 1983 Rel: $15 Cur: $30 (10/01/85) CS **95**
Pinot Noir Carneros Napa Valley St. Clair Vineyard 1982 Rel: $15 Cur: $25 (7/16/84) **89**
Pinot Noir Carneros Napa Valley Winery Lake Vineyard 1983 $15 (11/16/85) **78**
Pinot Noir Carneros Napa Valley Winery Lake Vineyard 1982 $15 (7/16/84) **90**

ALEXANDER VALLEY VINEYARDS
Pinot Noir Alexander Valley 1989: Very firm and almost harsh, with earthy flavors and little fruit to rescue it. Not our style. Tasted twice, with consistent notes. 2,247 cases made. $10 (10/31/91) **65**
Pinot Noir Alexander Valley 1987: Grapey in flavor, this wine is tannic and blunt. Woody and tannic on the finish. Drink now. $9 (5/31/90) **74**
Pinot Noir Alexander Valley 1985 $8 (4/15/88) **81**
Pinot Noir Alexander Valley 1984 $7 (2/15/88) **87**
Pinot Noir Alexander Valley 1982 $6.50 (11/01/84) **75**

ALMADEN
Pinot Noir San Benito County 1982 $5 (6/30/87) **69**

ARIES
Pinot Noir Los Carneros Cuvée Vivace 1989: A strong horsey, leathery flavor detracts from the wine. Some may find it barnyardy. Hard to swallow. $8 (4/30/91) **70**

AU BON CLIMAT
Pinot Noir Santa Barbara County 1988: Rich, earthy and generous, with lavish black cherry, cola and smoke aromas and flavors, a firm texture and a solid finish. Needs until 1993 or '94 to settle down. $16 (4/30/91) **80**
Pinot Noir Santa Barbara County 1987: Firm and concentrated, with lovely rose-scented cherry flavors, crisp acidity and smoky, plummy overtones on the aroma and finish. Very well made. Watch the fine print; make sure you get the right bottling. $16 (12/15/89) **84**
Pinot Noir Santa Barbara County 1985 $12 (6/15/88) **73**
Pinot Noir Santa Ynez Valley Benedict Vineyard 1987: An intense, nicely balanced Pinot Noir with full fruit flavors accented by slightly smoky, peppery aromas. It tastes concentrated and lively. Drinkable now. $30 (12/15/89) **88**
Pinot Noir Santa Ynez Valley Rancho Vinedo Vineyard 1988: A really vibrant, fruity wine that bowls you over with strawberry and cherry flavors. Not subtle or complex, but very tasty and well balanced. $12.50 (12/15/89) **83**

AUSTIN
Pinot Noir Santa Barbara County 1987: A good, solid wine, with very ripe, almost pruny flavors that are balanced toward the soft side. Enjoyable, but without many of the complexities and distinct Pinot Noir flavors you might expect. $15 (12/15/89) **77**
Pinot Noir Santa Barbara County 1983: A light, mature tasting wine with lots of meaty, herbal aromas and similar flavors. Smooth and pleasant for current drinking. $25 (12/15/89) **78**
Pinot Noir Santa Barbara County Artist Series 1988: Tastes young, fresh and ripe, like a Beaujolais, with simple berry and prune flavors and a soft structure. $10 (12/15/89) **75**
Pinot Noir Santa Barbara County Bien Nacido Vineyard 1982 $10 (3/16/85) **88**
Pinot Noir Santa Barbara County Sierra Madre Vineyards 1982 $12 (5/01/84) **87**

LAWRENCE J. BARGETTO
Pinot Noir Carneros Madonna Vineyard 1985 $12.50 (9/15/88) **83**
Pinot Noir Santa Maria Valley 1987: A fairly light wine that's heavily influenced by tea and herb notes, backed by a modest amount of fruit flavor. Medium-bodied and not very tannic, but lean in structure. A blend from Sierra Madre and Bien Nacido vineyards. $16 (2/28/91) **81**

BARROW GREEN
Pinot Noir California 1987: Light in color, with aromas and flavors that owe more to wood than fruit, offering minty herbal and smoke notes. Lean and caramellike on the finish. Drinkable, if somewhat unusual. $14.50 (10/31/91) **79**
Pinot Noir California 1986: Decent, correct Pinot Noir, but it lacks excitement and charm. The plum and leathery flavors are straightforward. Drink now. $16 (10/15/89) **76**

BAY CELLARS
Pinot Noir Los Carneros 1985 $15 (6/15/88) **77**

BEAULIEU
Pinot Noir Carneros Napa Valley Reserve 1989: Tart and lively, with nicely focused raspberry and blueberry aromas and flavors shaded by herbal and oak overtones. Snappy and crisp, a good wine to wash down a plate of roast chicken. Drink soon. $13 (4/30/91) **85**
Pinot Noir Carneros Napa Valley Reserve 1988: Light, smooth and fruity, with generous cherry, rhubarb and vanilla aromas and flavors on a delicate structure. Firm enough around the edges to survive cellaring through 1993, but drinkable and enjoyable now. An excellent value. $9.50 (4/15/90) **87**
Pinot Noir Carneros Napa Valley Reserve 1987 $9.50 (12/31/88) **90**
Pinot Noir Napa Valley Beaumont 1986 $7 (6/15/88) **74**
Pinot Noir Napa Valley Beaumont 1985 $6.25 (6/15/88) **78**
Pinot Noir Napa Valley Los Carneros 1980 $10 (8/31/86) **88**
Pinot Noir Napa Valley Los Carneros Reserve 1986 $9.50 (9/15/88) **88**
Pinot Noir Napa Valley Los Carneros Reserve 1985 $9.50 (1/31/88) **74**

BELVEDERE
Pinot Noir Los Carneros Winery Lake 1983 $12 (12/15/87) **73**
Pinot Noir Los Carneros Winery Lake 1982 $12 (8/31/86) **58**
Pinot Noir Sonoma County Bacigalupi 1985 $12 (6/15/88) **73**
Pinot Noir Sonoma County Bacigalupi 1982 $12 (11/16/85) **65**

BON MARCHE
Pinot Noir Napa Valley 1990: A decent value. Firm and crisp, with modest cherry and toast aromas and flavors that are simple and direct. Drinkable now. 1,635 cases made. $7 (11/15/91) **79**

BONNY DOON
Pinot Noir Sonoma County 1981 $9 (3/01/84) **65**

BOUCHAINE
Pinot Noir Carneros 1987: Attractive, with light strawberry and spicy cherry flavors and subtle oak and spice shadings. A well-balanced, elegant wine that's ready to drink now. There's a nip of tannin on the finish. 2,300 cases made. $13 (10/31/90) **82**
Pinot Noir Carneros Napa Valley 1988: Simple, light and fruity, with ripe cherry and spice flavors and a slight sulfury quality that comes across in the aroma and on the finish. Drink now. 3,000 cases made. $15 (7/31/91) **78**
Pinot Noir Carneros Napa Valley 1986: A lean, supple, elegant style with earth, cherry, plum and spicy flavors that are well focused on the palate. Has the tannins for aging, but it's drinkable now. $12 (5/31/89) **86**
Pinot Noir Carneros Napa Valley 1985 $11.50 (12/31/88) **82**
Pinot Noir Carneros Napa Valley Reserve 1988: Smooth and appealing, with a solid core of currant and berry aromas and flavors, plus a significant component of oak that manages to stay in bounds. Try in 1993. 500 cases made. $25 (3/31/92) **83**
Pinot Noir Carneros Reserve 1987: Well made, sturdy and balanced, this has pretty cherry, wild berry and cassis flavors that are young and vibrant, but the tannins need time to soften and mellow. Try now to 1994. 492 cases made. $20 (10/31/90) **85**
Pinot Noir Napa Valley 1982 $20 (6/30/87) **81**
Pinot Noir Napa Valley Los Carneros 1985 $7.50 (6/30/87) **76**
Pinot Noir Napa Valley Los Carneros 1982 $12.50 (7/16/85) **87**
Pinot Noir Napa Valley Los Carneros Winery Lake Vineyard 1982 Rel: $15 Cur: $18 (3/01/86) CS **91**

BRANDBORG
Pinot Noir Anderson Valley 1989: Tart and concentrated, with a decidedly woody edge to the ripe plum and berry aromas and flavors. Needs time to become more polished, but has all the pieces to come together around 1993 to '95. 125 cases made. $11 (11/15/91) **86**
Pinot Noir Santa Barbara County 1989: A pretty, fruit-packed wine, showing plenty of cherry, currant and spice flavors. Moderate tannins, a plush texture and a polished finish make it tempting to drink now, but it could be cellared through 1994. 200 cases made. $13 (11/15/91) **87**

DAVID BRUCE
Pinot Noir Santa Cruz Mountains 1986: Extremely earthy, dirty and gamy, a bizarre wine that is flawed. Avoid. Tasted twice. $18 (3/31/90) **59**
Pinot Noir Santa Cruz Mountains 1984 $15 (6/30/87) **81**
Pinot Noir Santa Cruz Mountains 1983 $15 (8/31/86) **78**

BUENA VISTA
Pinot Noir Carneros 1989: Lean and silky, with nice, toasty orange peel shades to the plum and tomato aromas and flavors, echoing spice notes on the finish. A stylish wine that might be better in 1993, when it might pick up more depth. 5,000 cases made. $7/500ml (7/31/91) **81**
Pinot Noir Carneros 1988: Toasty, spicy aromas make this distinctive, but the raspberry and red cherry flavors come through on the palate and it comes off as smooth and elegant on the finish. Drink now. $11 (12/15/90) **82**
Pinot Noir Carneros Private Reserve 1987: Ripe and fruity but simple, with pleasant plum and cherry notes. Drink now. Tasted twice. $14 (6/30/91) **80**
Pinot Noir Carneros Private Reserve 1986: Ripe, with spicy cherry flavor and plenty of toasty oak. All the elements are there, but it needs time to develop. Drink now to 1994. $14 (3/31/90) **85**
Pinot Noir Carneros Private Reserve 1984 $14.50 (2/15/88) **81**
Pinot Noir Sonoma Valley Carneros 1983 $14 (8/31/86) **75**
Pinot Noir Sonoma Valley Carneros 1980 $7 (4/16/84) **71**
Pinot Noir Sonoma Valley Carneros Private Reserve 1981 $14 (8/31/86) **88**

BYINGTON
Pinot Noir California 1988: Simple, sturdy, ripe and generous. This fruity wine has a smooth texture and is perhaps a bit soft on the finish, but it's tasty and ready to drink. $15 (4/30/91) **83**
Pinot Noir Napa Valley 1987: Thin and uninspired, with cooked cherry and spice notes. Drinkable but uninspired. Better than a bottle tasted earlier. $15 (4/30/91) **74**

DAVIS BYNUM
Pinot Noir Russian River Valley Artist Series 1985 $15 (6/15/88) **82**
Pinot Noir Russian River Valley Limited Release 1988: Rich and intense yet elegant, with bright, fresh black cherry, strawberry, tea and spice notes that fan out on the palate, rendering a complex, enticing wine with flavors that linger. Balanced and firmly tannic, but drinkable. Best in 1993 to '95. $16 (4/30/91) **86**
Pinot Noir Russian River Valley Limited Release 1986: Attractive and ready to drink. Tastes lean and mature, medium-bodied, with tight but long-lasting cherry and spice flavors and good balance. $14 (3/31/90) **83**
Pinot Noir Russian River Valley Limited Release 1984 $14 (5/31/88) **89**
Pinot Noir Russian River Valley Westside Road 1983 $10 (7/16/86) **71**
Pinot Noir Sonoma County Reserve Bottling 1986 $9 (9/15/88) **82**
Pinot Noir Sonoma County Reserve Bottling 1985 $7 (1/31/88) **67**

BYRON
Pinot Noir Santa Barbara County 1986 $12 (6/15/88) **88**
Pinot Noir Santa Barbara County 1985 $12 (6/15/88) **81**
Pinot Noir Santa Barbara County Reserve 1987: Nicely balanced, medium-weight wine that starts with distinctive leathery, earthy aromas, then shows ripe plum and cherry flavors that linger on the refreshingly tart finish. Drink now. $16 (12/15/89) **85**
Pinot Noir Santa Barbara County Reserve 1986 $12 (6/15/88) **84**
Pinot Noir Santa Barbara County Sierra Madre Vineyards 1984 $12.50 (8/31/86) **85**

CALERA
Pinot Noir Central Coast 1990: Ripe and perfumed, with pretty cherry, plum, herb and spice notes that are elegant and balanced. Lively, fresh and delicious to drink now or cellar through 1995. $14 (3/31/92) **87**
Pinot Noir Central Coast 1989: An assertive, cherry-flavored wine, with minty menthol aromas, solid fruit flavors and a very tart edge that won't appeal to everyone. $14 (11/15/91) **85**
Pinot Noir Central Coast 1987: Has a pleasant balance of toast, cherry and gamy nuances that come together for an attractive wine for those who like a touch of leafy, green flavor in their Pinot Noir. Best to drink it soon while the fruit's showing well. 573 cases made. $14 (2/15/90) **82**
Pinot Noir Mt. Harlan Jensen 1988: Packs in a load of fresh, ultraripe, rich black cherry, currant, herb and spicy earth overtones. Deeply flavored and very concentrated, with smooth, supple tannins and a long, full, fruity finish. A distinctive wine. Drink now through 1997. 437 cases made. $35 (11/15/91) **92**
Pinot Noir San Benito County Jensen 1987: Deep, rich, enormously complex and concentrated, with intense, sharply focused plum, currant, black cherry, raspberry, mineral and spice flavors that have uncommon depth and grace. Has enough tannin to warrant cellaring through 1994. 2,178 cases made. $30 (4/30/91) **93**
Pinot Noir San Benito County Jensen 1986: A sensational wine, with a magnificent interplay of plum, currant, nutmeg and vanilla flavors, a supple texture and vibrant acidity. It's beautifully balanced and long and almost sweet on the finish, echoing all the flavors for minutes. Can only become richer and more complex with cellaring past 1995 to 2000. 125 cases made. $25 (5/31/89) **88**
Pinot Noir San Benito County Jensen 1985 $25 (6/15/88) **88**
Pinot Noir San Benito County Jensen 1983 $22 (8/31/86) **80**
Pinot Noir California Jensen 1982 $23 (1/01/85) **88**
Pinot Noir Mt. Harlan Mills 1988: Dense and austere, but has plenty of stuffing. The black cherry and currant flavors are tightly wrapped in tannins now, but it should evolve into a very attractive wine. Best between 1994 and '98. $30 (11/15/91) **89**
Pinot Noir Mt. Harlan Reed 1988: Ripe and intense, with pepper, stewed plum, herb and black cherry flavors that come with some alcoholic heat. Firm tannins and crisp acidity sustain the flavors. Ready now, but can age through 1994. $30 (11/15/91) **85**
Pinot Noir San Benito County Reed 1987: Spicy and slightly cooked, with cherry and beet flavors that are concentrated and rich, but also a bit earthy. An eccentric wine, with limited appeal. Drink now to 1994. Tasted twice. 318 cases made. $35 (4/30/91) **80**
Pinot Noir San Benito County Reed 1982 $23 (8/31/86) **75**
Pinot Noir Mt. Harlan Selleck 1987: Hard and tight now, but with a solid core of rich, concentrated, deeply perfumed black cherry, currant, plum and spice flavors. The finish picks up plenty of firm, chewy tannins and a good blast of oak. 514 cases made. $30 (11/15/91) **92**
Pinot Noir San Benito County Selleck 1986: Plenty of fresh, ripe berry and cherry-scented Pinot Noir flavors in a full-bodied, tannic style that could use a year or two to mellow. Plenty of oak and tannin on the finish, but the fruit comes through. Drink now to 1996. $30 (3/31/90) **85**
Pinot Noir Santa Barbara County Bien Nacido Vineyard 1985 $12.50 (6/15/88) **82**
Pinot Noir Santa Barbara County Los Alamos Vineyard 1982 $10 (11/16/85) **62**

Key to Symbols

The scores reported here are the results of blind tastings conducted by our panel of senior editors. Wines that carry the initials below are results of individual tastings.

THE WINE SPECTATOR 100-POINT SCALE ***95-100***—Classic, a great wine; ***90-94***—Outstanding, superior character and style; ***80-89***—Good to very good, a wine with special qualities; ***70-79***—Average, drinkable wine that may have minor flaws; ***60-69***—Below average, drinkable but not recommended; ***50-59***—Poor, undrinkable, not recommended. "+"—With a score indicates a range; used primarily with barrel tastings to indicate a preliminary score.

SPECIAL DESIGNATIONS SS—Spectator Selection, CS—Cellar Selection, BB—Best Buy, (SNA)—Price not available, (NR)—Not released.

TASTER'S INITIALS (JG)—Jim Gordon, (HS)—Harvey Steiman, (JL)—James Laube, (JS)—James Suckling, (TM)—Thomas Matthews, (TR)—Terry Robards, (PM)—Per-Henrik Mansson, (BT)—Barrel Tasting (these wines were tasted blind from barrel samples), (CA-date)—*California's Great Cabernets* by James Laube, (CH-date)—*California's Great Chardonnays* by James Laube, (VP-date)—*Vintage Port* by James Suckling.

DATE TASTED Dates in parentheses represent the issue in which the rating was published.

CAMBRIA
Pinot Noir Santa Maria Valley Julia's Vineyard 1988: Ripe, generous and complex, with raspberry and plum flavors and hints of coffee, toast and chocolate on the long, complex finish. The silky texture has just enough tannin to warrant cellaring until 1994, but it's also drinkable now. 2,300 cases made. $16 (12/15/90) **88**

CARNEROS CREEK
Pinot Noir Carneros Fleur de Carneros 1989: Light but flavorful, with a silky texture and cola-tinged berry and currant flavors. Smooth and appealing. Drink now. $9 (4/30/91) **82**
Pinot Noir Carneros Fleur de Carneros 1988: Attractive with its fresh, crisp, ripe strawberry, cherry and spice notes, delicate balance and fine tannins. Ready to drink now. $10 (2/15/90) **85**
Pinot Noir Carneros Fleur de Carneros 1987: An elegant, precisely balanced wine for current drinking. Beautifully aromatic with spicy plum, cranberry and toast flavors and uncommon intensity. Has finesse and subtlety, finishing with spicy cinnamon and flavor complexities that linger on the finish. $9 (2/28/89) SS **92**
Pinot Noir Carneros Signature Reserve 1988: Has plenty of depth, intensity, sophistication and elegance, with chocolate and toasty oak aromas and firm, rich, concentrated and complex black cherry and plummy oak flavors. Sharply focused, long and full on the finish. Drink now to 1995. 500 cases made. $28 (10/31/90) **89**
Pinot Noir Carneros Signature Reserve First Release 1987: A rich, supple style, with intense, concentrated spice, cola and cherry flavors rounded out by a touch of toasty oak. The smooth, firm tannins bode well for cellaring. Drink now to 1995. $28 (10/31/90) **87**
Pinot Noir Los Carneros 1989: A solid wine, with a nice tension between the fruit and oak. Features plum, toast, smoke and sassafras aromas and flavors and hints at tea leaf on the finish. Drinkable now through 1995. $15 (3/31/92) **85**
Pinot Noir Los Carneros 1988: Ripe and rich, with supple black cherry, spice and oak flavors that are youthful, intense and concentrated. Firmly tannic with very good balance and length. Drink now to 1994. $15.50 (10/31/90) **83**
Pinot Noir Los Carneros 1987: Plenty of ripe, spicy cherry and raspberry flavors up-front, with fine balance and good length. Pleasant, intense and crisp. Drink now to 1995. $15 (2/15/90) **85**
Pinot Noir Los Carneros 1986 $14.50 (12/31/88) **92**
Pinot Noir Los Carneros 1985 $13 (4/15/88) **88**
Pinot Noir Los Carneros 1984 $15 (3/15/87) **92**
Pinot Noir Los Carneros 1983 $12.50 (8/31/86) **92**

CARNEROS QUALITY ALLIANCE
Pinot Noir Carneros 1986: A pleasant wine, with modest varietal raspberry aromas and flavors. Taut and a bit tannic, but there is enough cherry-cinnamon flavor wrapped up in the tight structure to make it worth cellaring until 1993. $23 (7/31/89) **81**
Pinot Noir Carneros 1985 $25 (12/31/87) **90**

CASTORO
Pinot Noir Central Coast 1987: Very good but light. For drinking now. Fruity, clean-tasting and supple in texture, with cherry and mint aromas and cherry and plum flavors. $4.50 (12/15/89) BB **82**

CAYMUS
Pinot Noir Napa Valley 1981 $7.50 (5/01/84) BB **85**
Pinot Noir Napa Valley 1980 $6.50 (3/16/84) **81**
Pinot Noir Napa Valley Special Selection 1988: An earthy wine with bark and cedar notes, but also a pretty core of supple black cherry flavor. Intense and barnyardy on the finish. Ready now through 1994. 1,624 cases made. $18 (11/15/91) **82**
Pinot Noir Napa Valley Special Selection 1987: Very firm and tannic, with flavors that lean toward smoke and toast but are nonetheless elegant, hinting at meat and cherry flavors on the finish. Needs time to smooth the tannins and bring out the fruit. Try now to 1993. $14 (12/15/90) **86**
Pinot Noir Napa Valley Special Selection 1986: A charming wine with good concentration of cherry and plum flavors. It's blunt but generous, and needs cellaring to soften the tannins and bring out its best. Try it around 1994. $15 (12/31/89) **82**
Pinot Noir Napa Valley Special Selection 1985 $15 (12/31/88) **90**
Pinot Noir Napa Valley Special Selection 1984 $12.50 (2/15/88) **79**
Pinot Noir Napa Valley Special Selection 1982 $12.50 (8/31/86) **85**

CHALONE
Pinot Noir Chalone 1986: Aromatic, tight and flavorful, with dark cherry, toast and tobacco aromas and flavors that manage to hang on even after the somewhat tough tannins cross the palate. Long and remarkably Burgundian in style. Cellaring until 1993 or '94 should soften the tannins. 2,456 cases made. $25 (12/15/90) **89**
Pinot Noir Chalone 1985: Smooth, rich and varietal in character, with earthy, toasty plum and cherry-scented flavors that are fully mature and ready to drink. Well balanced, not too tannic. Drink now to 1994. Rel: $17.50 Cur: $30 (2/15/90) **85**
Pinot Noir Chalone 1984 Rel: $18.50 Cur: $24 (12/15/87) **88**
Pinot Noir Chalone 1983 Rel: $18.50 Cur: $34 (8/31/86) **89**
Pinot Noir Chalone 1982 Rel: $20 Cur: $50 (8/31/86) **66**
Pinot Noir Chalone 1981 Rel: $18.50 Cur: $45 (12/16/84) **83**
Pinot Noir Chalone Red Table Wine 1983 $9 (8/31/86) **71**
Pinot Noir Chalone Reserve 1981 $28 (8/31/86) **92**

CHATEAU DE LEU
Pinot Noir Solano County Green Valley 1985: A distinctly peppery wine with good fruit flavors and a substantial coating of tannins. A bit soft in structure and drying on the finish. $7 (2/28/89) **77**

CHATEAU ST. JEAN
Pinot Noir Sonoma Valley McCrea Vineyards 1983 $12 (9/30/87) **75**

CHRISTOPHE
Pinot Noir Carneros Napa Valley Reserve 1989: Very light in color, this is a polished wine, with focused strawberry and raspberry flavors, a smooth texture and a crisp finish. Very well made and appealing in flavor. Drinkable now, but could evolve through 1993 to '95. $12 (11/15/91) **85**

CLOS DU BOIS
Pinot Noir Dry Creek Valley Proprietor's Reserve 1980 $10.75 (7/16/84) **86**
Pinot Noir Sonoma County 1989: Lean and leathery, with nice strawberry and watermelon flavors sneaking in on the finish. Would be better to sip slightly chilled. $13 (10/31/91) **78**
Pinot Noir Sonoma County 1988: A simple but complete Pinot Noir, with fresh strawberry and cherry flavors and firm oak and tannins. Modest length on the finish. Drink now. $12 (4/30/91) **80**
Pinot Noir Sonoma County 1987: An austere wine, earthy and somewhat flat, lacking flavor, depth and richness. Decent, showing more wood than fruit. Drink now. $12 (5/31/90) **73**
Pinot Noir Sonoma County 1986 $11 (10/15/89) **87**
Pinot Noir Sonoma County 1985 $10.50 (6/15/88) **70**
Pinot Noir Sonoma County 1984 $8 (8/31/86) **86**
Pinot Noir Sonoma County 1983 $8 (8/31/86) **70**
Pinot Noir Sonoma County 1982 $8 (7/16/85) **60**

CLOS DU VAL
Pinot Noir Napa Valley 1987: Strong mint and menthol aromas detract from the bright beam of ripe cherry and berry flavors, making it seem woody and tough. Worth cellaring until 1993 to '95 to see what develops. $13.50 (4/30/91) **84**
Pinot Noir Napa Valley 1986: Intense, full-bodied and tannic with a stemmy quality, but it has adequate cherry flavors, with a woody, dry finish. Drink now to 1994. Tasted twice. $16 (2/15/90) **80**
Pinot Noir Napa Valley 1985 $12.50 (6/15/88) **80**
Pinot Noir Napa Valley 1984 $11.50 (9/30/87) **78**

Pinot Noir Napa Valley 1983 $11.50 (8/31/86) **66**
Pinot Noir Napa Valley 1982 $10.75 (9/01/84) **75**

CONGRESS SPRINGS
Pinot Noir Santa Clara County 1989: Tart and crisp, with fresh cherry, strawberry, nutmeg and spice notes that are light and elegant. Not too tannic and drinks well now, but can age through 1993 or so. 3,513 cases made. $10 (4/30/91) **84**
Pinot Noir Santa Clara County San Ysidro Vineyard 1988: Has wonderful chocolate, coffee and wild berry aromas and flavors to match, all in a rich, smooth, elegant style that is very attractive. A harmonious wine that's ready now or can age a few years. Drink now to 1994. $9 (3/31/90) **87**

CORBETT CANYON
Pinot Noir Central Coast Reserve 1989: Smooth and exotic, with a meaty aroma and flavor shaded by berry and dried citrus peel overtones. Turns spicy on the finish. Different but appealing. $9.50 (11/15/91) **81**
Pinot Noir Central Coast Reserve 1986: Has fresh aromas of cherries and cedar, full fruit flavors that are stemmy but deep, lively acidity and a lingering vanillalike aftertaste. Drinkable now. $8 (12/15/89) **83**
Pinot Noir Santa Maria Valley Sierra Madre Vineyard Reserve 1985 $12 (2/15/88) **81**

COSENTINO
Pinot Noir Sonoma County 1989: Light and elegant, with complex aromas of cherry, spice, brown sugar and oak and a trace of tea and spice coming through on the finish. Drink now to 1993. 200 cases made. $13 (6/30/91) **82**

CRESTON
Pinot Noir Paso Robles 1990: Smells like Beaujolais, tastes like butter and cream and finishes bitter. A very weird wine that misses the mark. $8 (11/15/91) **70**
Pinot Noir San Luis Obispo County Petit d'Noir 1987 $8 (8/31/88) **80**
Pinot Noir San Luis Obispo County Petit d'Noir Maceration Carbonique 1988: Good but a bit off-balance. Shows its oak aging in very toasty aromas and drying tannins. There are intriguing ripe fruit flavors and a touch of Burgundian earthiness underneath. $8 (12/15/89) **74**

CRONIN
Pinot Noir Santa Cruz Mountains Peter Martin Ray Vineyard 1988: Ripe and bold, with tiers of plum, currant, herb and rhubarb flavors shaded by toasty, buttery oak notes and firm tannins. An exotic wine that turns earthy on the finish. Drink now to 1995. Tasted twice. $27 (3/31/92) **81**

CRYSTAL VALLEY
Pinot Noir North Coast Reserve Edition 1986 $10.50 (6/15/88) **74**

DE LOACH
Pinot Noir Russian River Valley 1986: A rich, full-bodied yet graceful wine that won't shortchange you on flavor, with pretty cherry, herb, earth and spice notes that offer complexity and depth. Has tannins for another two to three years' cellaring, but it's ready to drink now. 1,060 cases made. $12 (5/31/90) **87**
Pinot Noir Russian River Valley 1985 $12 (6/15/88) **72**
Pinot Noir Russian River Valley 1983 $10 (3/01/86) **75**
Pinot Noir Russian River Valley 1982 $10 (8/31/86) **76**
Pinot Noir Russian River Valley O.F.S. 1987: An austere wine, with tightly knit cassis and cherry flavors and a nice, spicy character framed by solid oak. Needs two to three years to soften and mellow. Drink now to 1994. 600 cases made. $25 (10/31/90) **82**

DEHLINGER
Pinot Noir Russian River Valley 1989: This smoky, woody-tasting wine has modest plum flavors underneath. The spice and oak component is tasty, but needs more fleshing out. A good wine, but disappointing for Dehlinger. Tasted twice, with consistent notes. 800 cases made. $16.50 (3/31/92) **80**
Pinot Noir Russian River Valley 1987: Tasty, with complex toasty oak, fresh, ripe cherries and deep smoke flavors that gain intensity on the palate, well balanced with a velvety texture, yet also has enough tannin for cellaring. Pretty fruit flavors echo on the finish. Drink now to 1994. 1,900 cases made. $14 (2/15/90) **91**
Pinot Noir Russian River Valley 1986: Very ripe and supple with spicy currant, plum and cherry flavors, finishing with smoky toast and floral notes, finishing with complexity and finesse. Charming now but should improve in the next two to three years. $13 (5/31/89) **88**
Pinot Noir Russian River Valley 1985 $12 (2/15/88) **85**
Pinot Noir Russian River Valley 1984 $11 (6/30/87) **89**
Pinot Noir Russian River Valley 1983 $10 (8/31/86) **89**
Pinot Noir Russian River Valley 1982 $10 (10/01/85) **86**

DOMAINE DE CLARCK
Pinot Noir Monterey County Villages 1990: Tart and earthy, with ripe plum and cherry flavors that turn to rhubarb on the finish. Not too tannic; enjoyable now. 500 cases made. $10 (3/31/92) **82**
Pinot Noir Monterey Première 1989: Light and uninspired, this is silky in texture and muddy in flavor, hinting at strawberry on the finish. Drink now. 108 cases made. $15 (4/30/91) **77**
Pinot Noir Sonoma County Villages 1989: Extreme leather and oak flavors mar the Pinot Noir flavor underneath. The wood flavors turn bitter on the finish. Not our style. Drink now. 500 cases made. $10 (3/31/92) **72**

DOMAINE LAURIER
Pinot Noir Sonoma County Green Valley 1986 $10 (6/15/88) **90**
Pinot Noir Sonoma County Green Valley 1982 $10 (11/15/87) **63**
Pinot Noir Sonoma County Green Valley 1981 $10 (2/16/85) **78**

DONNA MARIA
Pinot Noir Chalk Hill 1981 $6 (9/16/84) **79**

DURNEY
Pinot Noir Carmel Valley 1988: Firm and concentrated, with a tannic edge and mildly earthy cherry and beet aromas and flavors. Has all the pieces to develop with cellaring through 1994. 200 cases made. $16 (4/30/91) **80**

EDMEADES
Pinot Noir Anderson Valley 1982 $10 (2/16/85) **89**

EDNA VALLEY
Pinot Noir Edna Valley 1986: Crisp and lean, with berrylike flavors that make up for the leafy, vegetal aromas, echoing cherry on the finish. Drink now. Tasted twice. $15 (12/15/89) **76**
Pinot Noir Edna Valley 1985 $15 (6/15/88) **78**
Pinot Noir Edna Valley 1984 $10 (12/15/87) **85**
Pinot Noir Edna Valley 1983 $10 (4/15/87) **57**
Pinot Noir Edna Valley 1982 $11.50 (8/31/86) **80**

EL MOLINO
Pinot Noir Napa County 1988: Decidedly herbal, but it has attractive plum and cherry-scented fruit flavors and a toasty oak overlay, with hints of tea and mint. The texture is smooth and lush, with crisp acidity and good length. Drink now through 1994. $30 (11/15/91) **82**
Pinot Noir Napa County 1987: Very mature, chocolaty and spicy, with little fruit, but plenty of nutmeg and earth notes and a hint of cherry emerge on the finish. Tastes older than it is, but fans of earthier wines will like it. Drink soon. Very limited availability. $29 (10/31/91) **85**

ETUDE
Pinot Noir Carneros 1989: Soft, round and easy to like, with ample plum and soft cherry flavors in a medium-bodied, spicy wine. Very accessible and ready to drink now. $20 (11/15/91) **85**
Pinot Noir Napa Valley 1988: Ripe, generous and fruity, with soft wild plum and cherry notes and pretty spice and oak nuances. Well balanced, charming and best to drink now. $20 (12/15/90) **86**
Pinot Noir Napa Valley 1985 $16 (6/15/88) **83**

EYE OF THE SWAN
Pinot Noir California 1989: Spicy and fruity with hints of mint, cherry and anise. A tasty wine that's priced right. Drink now. $6 (4/30/92) **77**

GARY FARRELL
Pinot Noir Russian River Valley 1989: Aromatic and rich in fruit, with lovely berry and currant aromas and flavors that persist through the crisp, lively finish. This zesty wine has lots of appealing flavors and enough tannins to want until 1993 to '95 to be at its best. $16 (7/31/91) **88**
Pinot Noir Russian River Valley 1988: An elegant and intense wine, with distinctive black cherry, plum and raspberry flavors nicely shaded by toasty oak. Smooth and complex, with fine intensity, it turns almost jammy on the finish. Drinkable now through 1993. $16 (10/31/90) **88**
Pinot Noir Russian River Valley 1986 $15 (6/15/88) **90**
Pinot Noir Russian River Valley 1985 $13.50 (6/15/88) **62**
Pinot Noir Russian River Valley 1984 $12 (4/15/87) **79**
Pinot Noir Russian River Valley 1983 $12 (8/31/86) **88**
Pinot Noir Russian River Valley Allen Vineyard 1988: Rich, deep and complex, with lavish vanilla-tinged oak and bright cherry, strawberry, nutmeg and spice flavors that are sharply focused, picking up a touch of tannin and a hint of vinegar on the finish. Drink now to 1994. $25 (10/31/90) **87**
Pinot Noir Sonoma County Howard Allen Vineyard 1987: A complex little wine, with plenty of plum and cherry flavors and a touch of earth and hay, but also a pretty delicacy on the finish that makes it quite appealing. Drink now to 1995. 700 cases made. $20 (2/15/90) **84**

FELTON EMPIRE
Pinot Noir California Tonneaux Français 1984 $12 (5/15/87) **77**

FETZER
Pinot Noir California Special Reserve 1980 $13 (8/31/86) **65**
Pinot Noir Mendocino 1981 $5.50 (4/01/84) **80**
Pinot Noir Mendocino County Reserve 1986: Very ripe, plummy and supple, with a smooth texture and pretty spice, oak, cherry and anise notes, finishing with firm tannins and good length. Balanced, with rich, complex flavors. Drink now to 1994. $17.50 (10/31/90) **87**
Pinot Noir Mendocino County Special Reserve 1985 $13 (6/15/88) **78**

FIRESTONE
Pinot Noir Santa Ynez Valley 1986: An old style that's dark in color and deep in flavor. Tastes full-bodied, tannic, pruny and stemmy. Drink now if you like the robust style. $10 (12/15/89) **77**
Pinot Noir Santa Ynez Valley 1983 $9 (11/15/87) **71**
Pinot Noir Santa Ynez Valley 1981 $8.25 (5/16/86) **73**

THOMAS FOGARTY
Pinot Noir Carneros Napa Valley 1985 $15 (6/15/88) **73**
Pinot Noir Napa Valley 1988: Wonderfully fruity and generous, but the woody tannins gang up on the aftertaste and make it a bit rough. Cherry and ripe strawberry flavors are focused and deep and carry over on the finish. Drink now. $15 (2/28/91) **86**
Pinot Noir Santa Cruz Mountains Estate 1988: Full of attractive spice, plum and berrylike flavors on a medium-bodied frame of moderate tannins and acidity. Very drinkable and somewhat complex. $15 (2/28/91) **83**
Pinot Noir Santa Cruz Mountains Estate 1986 $20 (6/15/88) **64**
Pinot Noir Santa Cruz Mountains Estate 1985 $20 (6/15/88) **58**

FOXEN
Pinot Noir Santa Maria Valley 1987: Packed with fruit flavor, but a bit woody and tart. Has meaty, herbal, cherrylike aromas, full acidity and stiff tannins. Drink now. $16 (12/15/89) **78**

FRICK
Pinot Noir California 1981 $12 (8/31/86) **89**
Pinot Noir Santa Maria Valley 1984: Lean and woody, with more leathery, spicy and earthy aromas and flavors than fruit, which appears to be submerged behind the wood and mature-wine characteristics. $12 (2/28/89) **75**

GAINEY
Pinot Noir Santa Barbara County 1986: Full-bodied, complex and oaky tasting with aromas and flavors of leather, spices, and cherries, firm tannins and lively acidity. The fruit flavors linger. Drink now. $15 (12/15/89) **88**
Pinot Noir Santa Ynez Valley Limited Selection 1988: Ripe and decadent, with a distinctive earthy, leathery streak that adds character to the basic black cherry and currant flavors. Turns a bit smoky and peppery on the finish. Drinkable now, but should improve through 1994. 288 cases made. $25 (11/15/91) **86**

GEYSER PEAK
Pinot Noir Sonoma County Carneros 1985 $6 (6/15/88) **82**
Pinot Noir Sonoma County Carneros 1981 $5.75 (8/31/86) **82**

GREENWOOD RIDGE
Pinot Noir Anderson Valley 1989: Bright and fruity, with lots of tasty cherry and currant aromas and flavors and hints of toast on the finish. A solid, drinkable wine. 376 cases made. $13.50 (6/30/91) **87**

GUNDLACH BUNDSCHU
Pinot Noir Sonoma Valley Rhinefarm Vineyards 1989: Light in color, but offers pretty strawberry, cherry and plum jam flavors. Not too tannic, and finishes with a hint of orange peel. Tasty, but lacks refinement. $14 (10/31/91) **83**
Pinot Noir Sonoma Valley Rhinefarm Vineyards 1988: Smooth and supple, with gently unfolding cherry, strawberry and spice aromas and flavors. Focused and flavorful without weight, this is a very pretty wine for current drinking, though it may evolve in the cellar through 1993. $16 (2/28/91) **88**
Pinot Noir Sonoma Valley Rhinefarm Vineyards 1986 $12 (6/15/88) **89**
Pinot Noir Sonoma Valley Rhinefarm Vineyards 1985 $7 (2/29/88) **81**
Pinot Noir Sonoma Valley Rhinefarm Vineyards 1984 $12 (6/30/87) **53**
Pinot Noir Sonoma Valley Rhinefarm Vineyards 1982 $8.50 (5/01/84) **75**

HACIENDA
Pinot Noir Sonoma Valley 1982 $12 (12/16/84) **85**
Pinot Noir Sonoma Valley Estate Reserve 1987: Distinctive mint and menthol aromas and flavors lend a hard edge to this medium-weight, slightly plummy wine. Drinkable, but very distinctive. Try now. 500 cases made. $15 (10/31/90) **78**
Pinot Noir Sonoma Valley Estate Reserve 1986 $15 (6/15/88) **80**
Pinot Noir Sonoma Valley Estate Reserve 1985 $15 (6/15/88) **86**

HANZELL
Pinot Noir Sonoma Valley 1987: Ripe, rich and concentrated, with earthy plum, cherry and currant flavors framed by tight tannins and a good dose of fresh oak. Best to cellar until about 1994 to allow the tannins to soften. Tasted twice. $19 (2/15/92) **84**
Pinot Noir Sonoma Valley 1986: With ripe cherry, plum and spice notes, this intense, earthy wine has plenty of flavor and depth, but it's not for everyone. The firm tannins suggest cellaring for another three to four years. Drink in 1993 to '96. $19 (10/31/90) **84**
Pinot Noir Sonoma Valley 1985: Extremely earthy, tannic and dry, but with concentrated leather, chocolate and berry flavors. More austere and rugged than you'd expect for a Pinot Noir, but in sync with Hanzell's style. It's distinctive and stylistic. Drink in 1993 to '98. Tasted twice. Rel: $19 Cur: $29 (3/31/90) **82**

Pinot Noir Sonoma Valley 1984 Rel: $17 Cur: $32 (5/31/89) **78**
Pinot Noir Sonoma Valley 1983 Rel: $17 Cur: $38 (4/15/88) **70**
Pinot Noir Sonoma Valley 1981 Rel: $17 Cur: $21 (8/31/86) **93**

HMR
Pinot Noir Paso Robles 1979 $6.50 (2/01/85) **72**

HULTGREN & SAMPERTON
Pinot Noir Sonoma County 1980 $5.75 (9/01/84) **55**

HUSCH
Pinot Noir Anderson Valley 1989: Packs lots of flavor into a light, easy-to-drink structure. A medium-bodied, delicate, nicely flavored wine, with fresh, spicy plum and cherry flavors and great balance. Drink now through 1993. $14 (11/15/91) **87**
Pinot Noir Anderson Valley 1988: Tough and tannic, but not heavy-handed, with tea-scented, somewhat herbal plum aromas and flavors. An exotic wine that will not appeal to everyone, but has the delicate structure and firm tannins to cellar until 1994. $13 (12/15/90) **84**
Pinot Noir Anderson Valley 1987: Decent, with ripe berry, brown sugar and cherry flavors, but it's also rather simple and lacking complexity. Won't disappoint, though. Drink now to 1993. $13 (2/15/90) **80**
Pinot Noir Anderson Valley 1986 $13 (10/15/89) **81**
Pinot Noir Anderson Valley 1985 $10 (6/15/88) **84**
Pinot Noir Anderson Valley 1983 $9 (5/31/88) **74**
Pinot Noir Anderson Valley 1982 $9 (8/31/86) **88**

INGLENOOK
Pinot Noir Napa Valley 1985 $9.50 (6/15/88) **82**
Pinot Noir Napa Valley 1982 $7.50 (12/31/86) **64**
Pinot Noir Napa Valley 1981 $7.50 (2/01/85) **62**
Pinot Noir Napa Valley 1980 $6 (3/01/84) **71**

INNISFREE
Pinot Noir California 1989: Fruity, elegant and pleasing, with hints of black cherry, nutmeg and spice flavors. The finish lingers and it's not too tannic. Ready to drink now through 1993. $11 (4/30/91) **84**

IRON HORSE
Pinot Noir Sonoma County Green Valley 1987: A tight, hard-edged wine, with firm, tannic plum, cherry and strawberry flavors that are overshadowed by oak. The wood really intrudes on the finish. Drink now. 700 cases made. $19 (10/31/90) **72**
Pinot Noir Sonoma County Green Valley 1986 $18 (6/15/88) **92**
Pinot Noir Sonoma County Green Valley 1985 $18 (6/15/88) **77**
Pinot Noir Sonoma County Green Valley 1982 $10 (10/01/85) **76**

JEKEL
Pinot Noir Arroyo Seco Home Vineyard 1982 Rel: $9 Cur: $20 (6/30/87) **57**

JORY
Pinot Noir Santa Clara County 1986 $19 (6/15/88) **76**

KALIN
Pinot Noir Sonoma County Cuvée DD 1986: The menthol edge may not be for everyone, but this sturdy, lively wine shows enough cherry flavor to be likable. Already drinkable. $20 (4/30/91) **80**

KENDALL-JACKSON
Pinot Noir Santa Maria Valley Julia's Vineyard 1988: An elegant wine, with spicy cherry, leather and smoke flavors and moderate depth and concentration. Ready to drink now. $14 (11/15/91) **82**

KENWOOD
Pinot Noir Sonoma Valley Jack London Vineyard 1989: Tart and light, with modest cherry and plum aromas and flavors that linger on the finish, but it seems light and ungenerous overall. May be best after 1993. $15 (10/31/91) **80**
Pinot Noir Sonoma Valley Jack London Vineyard 1984: Bitter, woody tannins override the spicy, ripe plum and cherry flavor. Drink now. $15 (5/31/89) **77**

KISTLER
Pinot Noir Russian River Valley Dutton Ranch 1987: Smoky, earthy and tannic, the cherry and berry flavor is trapped beneath the wood and tannins. It will always be on the oaky side. Drink now to 1994. $15 (3/31/90) **85**
Pinot Noir Russian River Valley Dutton Ranch 1986 $13.50 (6/15/88) **89**

CHARLES KRUG
Pinot Noir Carneros 1987: Well balanced and sharply focused, with a tight core of cherry and plum flavors. Firm tannins and toasty oak notes add dimension and echo on the finish. Drink now to 1994. $8.50 (2/28/91) BB **87**
Pinot Noir Carneros Napa Valley 1989: Light and silky with hints of currant, cherry and spice. Picks up a touch of vanilla on the aftertaste. Pleasant to drink now. A good value. $10 (2/15/92) **82**
Pinot Noir Carneros Napa Valley 1985: Light, spicy and tealike, an austere wine with some richness of strawberry and toast flavor on the finish where it turns silky and more generous. Drinkable now. $8.50 (2/15/90) **81**

LA CREMA
Pinot Noir California 1986 $11.75 (12/31/88) **89**
Pinot Noir California 1985 $11 (9/30/87) **90**
Pinot Noir California 1984 $11 (3/15/87) **89**
Pinot Noir California Reserve 1986: Extremely ripe with plum and cherry jam flavors that are rich and powerful with hints of black cherry. Soft tannins make it approachable soon. $22 (5/31/89) **85**
Pinot Noir California Reserve 1985 $17.50 (12/31/87) **82**

LANE TANNER
Pinot Noir Santa Barbara County Benedict Vineyard 1989: Ripe, rich and round, with generous cherry, raspberry and tobaccolike aromas and flavors that persist into a solid finish. Drinkable now, but the tannins can use until 1993 or '94 to soften. 285 cases made. $25 (11/15/91) **85**

LEEWARD
Pinot Noir Santa Barbara County 1989: Woody, bitter, barnyardy aromas and flavors overwhelm this unpleasant wine. Tasted three times, with consistent notes. $16 (2/15/92) **59**

MANISCHEWITZ
Pinot Noir Russian River Valley 1989 $9 (3/31/91) **74**

MARK WEST
Pinot Noir Russian River Valley 1983 $10 (5/16/86) **67**
Pinot Noir Russian River Valley Ellis Vineyard 1986: Light in color and broad in flavor, but lacking the crispness that could carry it further in the cellar. The smoky wild berry aromas and flavors are attractive for current drinking. $14 (3/31/90) **81**
Pinot Noir Russian River Valley Ellis Vineyard 1984 $10 (3/15/87) **84**
Pinot Noir Sonoma County 1986: Very light in color, almost like a rosé, but there's nice intensity of leather-tinged berry flavor that threads through the silky texture of this wine. Drink now. $8 (2/28/89) **80**

LOUIS M. MARTINI
Pinot Noir Carneros 1987: This straightforward wine is nothing fancy, with direct Pinot Noir, plum, mint and berry-tinged flavors, subtle oak shadings and good balance. Attractively priced. Drink now to 1994. $7 (2/28/91) BB **82**
Pinot Noir Carneros Napa Valley La Loma Vineyard 1988: Unusual and crisp, offering apple and spice flavors. A decent but tart wine that doesn't remind us much of Pinot Noir. Tasted twice. 800 cases made. $18 (3/31/92) **75**
Pinot Noir Carneros Napa Valley Las Amigas 1982: A fully mature, harmonious wine, with well-preserved cherry and spice aromas and flavors that are full-bodied without being overly rich. Although drinkable now, it has the balance to age. $12 (3/31/90) **85**
Pinot Noir Los Carneros 1988: Smooth and generous, with nicely focused currant aromas and flavors that are crisply balanced and linger on the finish, hinting at toast and vanilla. Almost ready for drinking; best in 1993 or '94. $8 (7/15/91) BB **85**
Pinot Noir Napa Valley 1986: Spicy, black pepper aromas and flavors make this lean, lithe wine distinctive. Drinkable now, but there is enough ripe berry flavor in the flavors to develop with cellaring until 1994. $8 (12/31/89) BB **85**
Pinot Noir Napa Valley Las Amigas Vineyard Selection 1980 $10 (3/15/87) **68**

MAYACAMAS
Pinot Noir Napa Valley 1987: Firm and tannic, with very ripe, almost rustic aromas and flavors of plum, prune and pepper. Hard enough to need until 1994 or '95 to settle down, but the intensity is low enough to be a risk. 550 cases made. $14 (4/30/91) **80**
Pinot Noir Napa Valley 1986: Light in color, meaty tasting and meager, with barnyardy aromas and cherry and spice notes. An extreme wine. The flavors come up shallow. Tasted three times. $14 (3/31/90) **67**
Pinot Noir Napa Valley 1985 $12 (6/15/88) **72**
Pinot Noir Napa Valley 1984 $12 (12/31/88) **71**

MCHENRY
Pinot Noir Santa Cruz Mountains 1985 $13 (6/15/88) **75**

MERIDIAN
Pinot Noir Santa Barbara County Riverbench Vineyard 1988: Besides herbaceous aromas, this offers a smooth texture and tasty, spicy strawberry and cedar flavors that linger crisply on the finish. A stylish wine that's drinkable now. $14 (2/28/91) **86**

MERLION
Pinot Noir Los Carneros Hyde Vineyards 1986: Peppery, earthy, somewhat harsh and woody, lacking the warmth and silky texture that such a light-bodied Pinot should have. $13.50 (2/28/89) **66**

MIRASSOU
Pinot Noir Monterey County Fifth Generation Family Selection 1988: Offers pretty good character, especially at this price. The spice and cherry aromas carry over on the palate, and the flavors stay with you. Has mild tannins. Drink now to 1993. 2,248 cases made. $7.50 (4/30/91) BB **81**
Pinot Noir Monterey County Harvest Reserve 1988: This wine combines delicate cherry and floral-scented Pinot Noir flavor with pretty toasty oak. Balanced and intense yet measured in its restraint, it's quite attractive to drink now through 1995. $13 (4/30/92) **84**
Pinot Noir Monterey County Harvest Reserve 1986: Distinctive for its spicy, peppery sassafras notes, as well as its tough oaky veneer, this is a varietally correct wine, but it lacks flair and intrigue. Drink now to 1993. $12 (4/30/91) **78**

ROBERT MONDAVI
Pinot Noir Napa Valley 1990: Light, fresh and fruity, with lively cherry and strawberry flavors accented by sweet oak notes. Bracing acidity keeps the fruit bright. An elegant wine for drinking now through 1994. Rel: $15 Cur: $18 (3/31/92) **86**
Pinot Noir Napa Valley 1989: Smells pretty, with currant, cherry and oak aromas, and it's warm and supple on the palate, with hints of nutmeg and spice. Has moderate richness, good depth and rounded tannins. Drink now to 1995. Tasted twice. $15 (4/30/91) **86**
Pinot Noir Napa Valley 1988: Deep in color and ripe in flavor, with a distinct mintiness that adds dimension to the fresh, full, rich, broad black cherry and spice notes. Big and tannic, it can be enjoyed today, but may benefit from short-term cellaring. Drink now to 1994. $13 (2/15/90) **89**
Pinot Noir Napa Valley 1987 $12 (7/31/89) **88**
Pinot Noir Napa Valley 1985 $10.50 (6/15/88) **79**
Pinot Noir Napa Valley 1984 $8.25 (11/15/87) **75**
Pinot Noir Napa Valley 1982 $9.50 (8/31/86) **79**
Pinot Noir Napa Valley 1981 $7.50 (11/01/84) **80**
Pinot Noir Napa Valley Reserve 1990: Powerful and complete, with depth, complexity and great balance. The black cherry and currant flavors are focused, and a kiss of sweet oak lasts through the long finish. For all its flavor, it remains light on its feet. Drinkable now, but should improve in the cellar through about 1995. 2,000 cases made. $28 (3/31/92) **92**
Pinot Noir Napa Valley Reserve 1988: A bit disappointing from a winery making big strides with Pinot Noir, this is an intense, gutsy wine, with ripe, concentrated black cherry and plum flavors. Very smoky right through the finish. Needs to develop some smoothness and grace; perhaps cellaring until 1993 to '94 will do it. Rel: $23 Cur: $26 (10/31/90) **82**
Pinot Noir Napa Valley Reserve 1986: Possesses classic Burgundian aromas and it's lavishly oaked. It's tart on the palate, with true Pinot Noir flavors that are elegant and complex, echoing plum and cherry notes on a long, full aftertaste. Drink now to 1995. $22 (10/15/89) **91**
Pinot Noir Napa Valley Reserve 1985 Rel: $19 Cur: $31 (4/15/89) SS **92**
Pinot Noir Napa Valley Reserve 1983 Rel: $16 Cur: $25 (11/15/87) **80**
Pinot Noir Napa Valley Reserve 1982 Rel: $15 Cur: $25 (8/31/86) **78**
Pinot Noir Napa Valley Reserve 1981 Rel: $14 Cur: $17 (8/31/86) **86**
Pinot Noir Napa Valley Reserve 1980 $13.25 (8/01/84) **81**

MONT ST. JOHN
Pinot Noir Carneros Napa Valley 1988: Has simple but pleasant Pinot Noir character, with nutmeg, cherry and vanilla notes that are ripe and full-bodied. The firm tannins suggest drinking in 1993 to '95. Tasted twice. $14 (4/30/91) **81**
Pinot Noir Carneros Napa Valley 1987: A good but modest wine. Tart, lean and light in structure, with attractive spicy aromas, and modest cherry and strawberry flavors. $15 (3/31/90) **76**
Pinot Noir Carneros Napa Valley 1985: Lean and tight, with reined-in cherry and toast aromas and flavors, crisp acidity and good length. Drink now. $15 (10/15/89) **82**
Pinot Noir Carneros Napa Valley 1981 $9.75 (5/16/84) **73**
Pinot Noir Carneros Napa Valley Madonna Vineyard 1985 $11 (6/15/88) **78**

Key to Symbols

The scores reported here are the results of blind tastings conducted by our panel of senior editors. Wines that carry the initials below are results of individual tastings.

THE WINE SPECTATOR 100-POINT SCALE 95-100—Classic, a great wine; ***90-94***—Outstanding, superior character and style; ***80-89***—Good to very good, a wine with special qualities; ***70-79***—Average, drinkable wine that may have minor flaws; ***60-69***—Below average, drinkable but not recommended; ***50-59***—Poor, undrinkable, not recommended. "+"—With a score indicates a range; used primarily with barrel tastings to indicate a preliminary score.

SPECIAL DESIGNATIONS SS—Spectator Selection, CS—Cellar Selection, BB—Best Buy, ($NA)—Price not available, (NR)—Not released.

TASTER'S INITIALS (JG)—Jim Gordon, (HS)—Harvey Steiman, (JL)—James Laube, (JS)—James Suckling, (TM)—Thomas Matthews, (TR)—Terry Robards, (PM)—Per-Henrik Mansson, (BT)—Barrel Tasting (these wines were tasted blind from barrel samples), (CA-date)—*California's Great Cabernets* by James Laube, (CH-date)—*California's Great Chardonnays* by James Laube, (VP-date)—*Vintage Port* by James Suckling.

DATE TASTED Dates in parentheses represent the issue in which the rating was published.

MONTEREY PENINSULA
Pinot Noir Monterey Sleepy Hollow 1987: A dark, ripe, intense wine. Tannic and concentrated, with a sharply focused, deep plum, herb, earth and cherry flavors. Drink now to 1996. $18 (2/28/91) **86**

MONTEREY VINEYARD
Pinot Noir Monterey County 1987: Made in a very distinctive, earthy style, with ripe fruit flavors and an almost chocolaty richness on mid-palate. Drink now. $8.50 (3/31/90) **84**
Pinot Noir Monterey County 1986 $7 (6/15/88) **83**
Pinot Noir Monterey County Limited Release 1988: Intense, leathery and tannic, an attempt at a serious wine, but for now it's tight and closed, showing plenty of oak and cherry notes. Best to cellar until 1993. $9 (2/28/91) **80**

MONTICELLO
Pinot Noir Napa Valley 1987: A refreshing, lively wine, with brambly herb and cherry-scented flavors that broaden into tea, rose petal, and toasty flavors. An intriguing wine that keeps changing in the glass. Has the tannins to develop through 1994. $14.50 (10/15/89) **85**
Pinot Noir Napa Valley 1986 $12 (6/15/88) **89**
Pinot Noir Napa Valley 1985 $12 (12/15/87) **89**

MORGAN
Pinot Noir California 1989: Very light in color, but it has a rich texture and pretty berry, cherry and vanilla aromas and flavors. Smooth and very appealing on the finish, where it shows a nice twinge of herb. $14 (3/31/92) **85**
Pinot Noir California 1988: Mint, menthol and camphor aromas dominate the bright cherry flavor, but it thins out on the palate. Some may find the mintiness to their tastes, but it lacks sufficient flavor and concentration. Has a biting finish. Drink now to 1994. Tasted twice. 3,000 cases made. $14 (4/30/91) **75**
Pinot Noir California 1987: Smooth and spicy, with rhubarblike flavors and pleasant cinnamon-clove overtones, finishing nicely with black cherry and plum on the finish. More like a good Beaujolais than Burgundy. $15 (7/31/89) **81**
Pinot Noir California 1986 $14 (6/15/88) **84**

MOUNT EDEN
Pinot Noir Santa Cruz Mountains 1987: A sturdy wine, with smoke, raspberry and green fruit aromas and flavors that are tart and somewhat tannic. Could be smoother. Try cellaring until 1994. Rel: $20 Cur: $25 (4/15/90) **79**
Pinot Noir Santa Cruz Mountains 1985 Rel: $25 Cur: $30 (6/15/88) **90**
Pinot Noir Santa Cruz Mountains 1984 Rel: $20 Cur: $30 (4/15/88) **86**
Pinot Noir Santa Cruz Mountains 1983 Rel: $18 Cur: $28 (8/31/86) **77**

MOUNTAIN VIEW
Pinot Noir Carneros 1986: Nicely balanced. A light, lean, spice- and cherry-flavored wine for current drinking. $6 (2/28/89) BB **80**
Pinot Noir Monterey-Napa Counties 1990: Tastes a bit like Gamay, but you get a very pleasantly fruity wine for the money, with hints of plum, rose petal and black cherry. Offers just a touch of tannin on the finish. Best to drink now while the fruit is fresh and lively. $6 (4/30/92) BB **82**
Pinot Noir Monterey-Napa Counties 1989: Young and fruity, with a mild tannic bite, made in a style for early drinking. Offers simple but attractive cherry, spice, plum and anise notes. Drink now to 1993. $6 (2/28/91) BB **82**
Pinot Noir Monterey-Napa Counties 1988: Light, fruity and ultimately simple, with faint berry and cherry notes that are clean. Drink now. $6.50 (3/31/90) **72**

NAPA RIDGE
Pinot Noir North Coast Coastal 1989: Has an earthy, gamy edge, but stays within bounds, offering nice spice and toast shades to the black cherry flavor. Seems a bit mature for an '89, but it's enjoyable. $7.50 (7/31/91) BB **82**

NAVARRO
Pinot Noir Anderson Valley 1984 $12 (1/31/88) **91**
Pinot Noir Anderson Valley 1982 $9.75 (4/15/87) **82**
Pinot Noir Anderson Valley Méthode à l'Ancienne 1988: Ripe and yummy, with delicate cherry, raspberry, vanilla and spice flavors that are focused and elegant. The fruit and oak flavors stay with you on the finish. Drinks well now, but can age through 1995. $14 (3/31/92) **89**
Pinot Noir Anderson Valley Méthode à l'Ancienne 1987: Earthy, gamy aromas and flavors tend to shoulder past what fruit is present, but a hint of cherry manages to come through on the finish. Firm and rich in texture, and the flavors are promising enough to warrant waiting until 1993. 1,428 cases made. $14 (4/30/91) **85**
Pinot Noir Anderson Valley Méthode à l'Ancienne 1986: A value-priced wine that's crisp but concentrated, with generous cherry and strawberry flavors that have depth and linger on the aftertaste. The supple texture and complex fruit notes lend extra interest. Drink now. 1,411 cases made. $14 (3/31/90) **87**
Pinot Noir Anderson Valley Méthode à l'Ancienne 1985: Light and spicy, with tasty cherry and plum flavor delicately framed by a touch of vanilla-laced oak flavors. Delicious flavors are easy to like already, but should gain in the bottle. Start drinking now. $14 (2/28/89) **85**
Pinot Noir Anderson Valley Whole Berry Fermentation 1987: Fresh, light and plummy, more like Beaujolais, but there's some meaty texture and smoky flavor to give it some interest. Fruit flavors extend well into the finish, but there's also more than a touch of wood. $9.75 (2/28/89) **81**

NEWLAN
Pinot Noir Napa Valley 1988: Firm, tart and focused, with lots of spice and vanilla notes that are hard-edged from too much oak. May be better around 1995, when the blackberry flavors can emerge. 638 cases made. $18 (11/15/91) **81**
Pinot Noir Napa Valley 1987: Ripe and broad in flavor, with minty aromas and full flavors of cherry and strawberry in a velvety texture. Soft balance and moderate tannins. $16 (3/31/90) **81**
Pinot Noir Napa Valley 1985 $12 (6/15/88) **88**
Pinot Noir Napa Valley Vieilles Vignes 1986: Earthy and tannic, with juniper berry flavors but not much in the way of fresh, ripe Pinot Noir flavor. With time it may be more appealing, but for now it's very tight and closed. Drink now to 1995. $19 (3/31/90) **76**
Pinot Noir Napa Valley Vieilles Vignes 1985 $16 (6/15/88) **80**

OCTOPUS MOUNTAIN
Pinot Noir Anderson Valley 1989: Light and smooth, with appealing plum, cherry and spice aromas and flavors, crisp balance and polished, soft tannins to round it out. A pretty wine that's ready to drink now. $12.50 (10/31/91) **86**

OLIVET LANE
Pinot Noir Russian River Valley 1988: Light in color but smooth and flavorful, with abundant black cherry, pepper and spice aromas and flavors on a modest structure. Drinkable now. 1,000 cases made. $9 (6/30/91) BB **85**

PAGE MILL
Pinot Noir Santa Barbara County Bien Nacido Vineyard 1985 $12.50 (6/15/88) **87**

PAGOR
Pinot Noir Santa Barbara County 1987: Interesting and very flavorful. Has distinctive earthy, herbal aromas and full, spicy flavors on a medium frame of acid and tannins. $10.50 (12/15/89) **85**

PARDUCCI
Pinot Noir Mendocino County 1988: Light and delicate, with fresh, lively cherry and berry aromas and flavors and overtones of vanilla and spice, all wrapped in a lacy structure that has just the right acidity. Drink soon. $7.50 (4/15/90) BB **85**
Pinot Noir Mendocino County 1986 $7 (6/15/88) **70**
Pinot Noir Mendocino County 1985 $5.50 (11/15/87) **76**
Pinot Noir Mendocino County 1983 $6 (8/31/86) **65**
Pinot Noir Mendocino County 1980 $5.65 (8/01/84) **56**
Pinot Noir Mendocino County Cellarmaster Selection 1987: Gentle and fragrant, offering lovely spice, berry and currant aromas and flavors shaded by a touch of tea leaf on the finish. Not a grand wine, but harmonious and nicely balanced. Drinkable now. $15 (4/30/91) **84**

J. PEDRONCELLI
Pinot Noir Dry Creek Valley 1989: An earthy, leathery style, with attractive black cherry notes, but the flavor of American oak is strong and interrupts the flow. Tannic, too. Try after 1993. 4,050 cases made. $8.50 (3/31/92) **75**
Pinot Noir Dry Creek Valley 1988: Tight and firm, with a hard-edged core of cherry and currant flavors that fan out with spice, oak and herb notes. It's backed by sufficient tannins to warrant cellaring until 1993. 3,230 cases made. $8 (2/28/91) BB **84**
Pinot Noir Dry Creek Valley 1986: Light in aroma and flavor and tough and tannic on the palate. Grapey, but otherwise undistinguished. Tasted twice. 3,600 cases made. $7 (5/31/90) **70**
Pinot Noir Dry Creek Valley 1985 $7.50 (6/15/88) **76**
Pinot Noir Sonoma County 1983 $6 (4/15/88) **67**
Pinot Noir Sonoma County 1982 $5.50 (6/30/87) **68**

PINNACLES
Pinot Noir Monterey Pinnacles Vineyard 1988: Earthy, oxidized aromas and flavors turn tealike and funky on the finish. Interesting, but lacks fruit. Tasted twice. 900 cases made. $16 (10/31/91) **74**

KENT RASMUSSEN
Pinot Noir Carneros 1988: An earthy, juniper flavor overrides the spicy cherry and plum notes now, which we find rather clumsy. The finish shows off more wood and more of the juniper flavor, but with time it may come together. Drink in 1993 and beyond. 1,027 cases made. $22 (10/31/90) **84**

RICHARDSON
Pinot Noir Sonoma Valley Los Carneros Sangiacomo 1989: Deep in color, with plenty of fruit and charm. Has ripe, rich raspberry, spice, loganberry and currant flavors, and the acidity carries them to a pretty aftertaste. The tannins are supple and in proportion. Drink now to 1994. 600 cases made. $14 (4/30/91) **86**
Pinot Noir Sonoma Valley Carneros Sangiacomo 1987: Distinctive, rich and enticing, with layers of smoky bacon, plum and black cherry flavors that flow easily on the palate. Delicious now, but can age till 1994 with ease. $12 (10/15/89) **88**
Pinot Noir Sonoma Valley Carneros Sangiacomo 1986 $12 (6/15/88) **87**

ROCHE
Pinot Noir Carneros 1989: Light, tart and flavorful, with a lively sour cherry, candied, raspberry flavor profile. Pleasant and crisp, but not especially deep. Drink soon. $15 (4/30/91) **81**
Pinot Noir Carneros 1988: Marvelously concentrated and spicy, all its complex flavors artfully contained in a rounded, supple frame. Cinnamon- and nutmeg-scented cherry and plum flavors show a lot of finesse and complexity already. Drink soon, but it should last through 1993 to '94. $14 (12/31/89) **89**
Pinot Noir Carneros Unfiltered 1989: Woody, varnishlike aromas and flavors are not to our liking in this light, hard-edged wine. Needs to soften, but not necessarily built to last. Try in 1993. $19 (4/30/91) **78**

ROCHIOLI
Pinot Noir Russian River Valley 1989: Crisp and flavorful, with bright strawberry and cherry aromas and flavors that turn lemony and tart on the finish. Needs to soften, perhaps by 1993 or '94. 1,200 cases made. $16 (11/15/91) **84**
Pinot Noir Russian River Valley 1988: Deliciously rich and fruity with a wide array of ripe, vivid berry, cherry and raspberry flavors and a touch of spicy seasoning. A big, full-bodied concentrated wine that keeps oozing with fresh fruit. Drink now to 1995. $15 (10/31/90) **85**
Pinot Noir Russian River Valley 1987: Offers plenty of generous cherry, berry and spicy flavors up-front, with complex nutmeg and spice notes that add subtlety and nuance. The texture is rich and supple. Well balanced, with a pretty fruit aftertaste. Drink now. 475 cases made. $15 (5/31/90) **89**
Pinot Noir Russian River Valley 1986 $14.25 (10/15/89) **87**
Pinot Noir Russian River Valley 1985 $12.50 (6/15/88) **92**
Pinot Noir Russian River Valley 1984 $12 (11/15/87) **84**
Pinot Noir Russian River Valley 1982 $12.50 (8/31/86) **89**

ROLLING HILLS
Pinot Noir Santa Maria Valley 1985 $6 (6/15/88) **77**

ROUDON-SMITH
Pinot Noir Santa Cruz Mountains 1985 $15 (6/15/88) **86**
Pinot Noir Santa Cruz Mountains Cox Vineyard 1987: Elegant and well defined, with pretty fruit flavors that echo cherry, plum, spice and toast notes, framed by firm but fine tannins and finishing with good length. Best to cellar until 1993. $15 (2/28/91) **84**

ST. FRANCIS
Pinot Noir Sonoma Valley 1986 $14 (6/15/88) **74**

SAINTSBURY
Pinot Noir Carneros 1989: A step back from the usual high quality, but still crisp and focused, with lots of ripe black cherry, plum and toast flavors that persist into a long finish. Has the stuff to age through 1993 or '94. $16.50 (2/15/92) **85**
Pinot Noir Carneros 1988: Difficult to find a better Pinot Noir at this reasonable price. Aromatic, flavorful and elegant, offering plenty of spicy raspberry and cherry flavors up-front and turning supple and warm on the palate. Nuances of oak are carefully folded in. Drinkable now, but should improve through 1994. Rel: $15 Cur: $17 (12/15/90) SS **91**
Pinot Noir Carneros 1987: A step down from the great '85 and '86, ripe and opulent on the nose, concentrated and bit tannic on the palate, but the cherry, cinnamon and strawberry flavors come bubbling up on the finish. Drink now. $15 (7/31/89) **86**
Pinot Noir Carneros 1986 $14 (6/15/88) **92**
Pinot Noir Carneros 1985 $13 (9/15/87) **92**
Pinot Noir Carneros 1984 $12 (12/15/86) **93**
Pinot Noir Carneros 1983 $12 (12/01/85) **93**
Pinot Noir Carneros 1982 $8 (11/30/87) (JL) **86**
Pinot Noir Carneros Garnet 1990: Tart and lean, with raw plum and black cherry flavors that turn flinty on the finish. A young, assertive style that may benefit from cellaring. Drink after 1993. $10 (2/15/92) **86**
Pinot Noir Carneros Garnet 1989: Generous, smooth and delicately fruity, offering lots of strawberry, plum and cinnamon aromas and flavors. This pretty wine is a knockout to drink now and probably will not get any better with cellaring. Drink it while it's fresh. $9 (12/15/90) **88**
Pinot Noir Carneros Garnet 1988: Light, fruity, simple and pleasant, with fresh strawberry, spice, oak and berry notes. Not quite up to previous Garnet bottlings, but still attractive. Drink now. $9 (3/31/90) **84**
Pinot Noir Carneros Garnet 1987 $9 (12/31/88) **91**
Pinot Noir Carneros Garnet 1986 $8 (12/15/87) **87**
Pinot Noir Carneros Garnet 1985 $9 (3/15/87) **86**
Pinot Noir Carneros Garnet 1984 $8 (8/31/86) **76**
Pinot Noir Carneros Garnet 1983 $8 (11/30/87) (JL) **73**
Pinot Noir Carneros Rancho 1981 ($NA) (11/30/87) (JL) **80**

SANFORD
Pinot Noir Central Coast 1984 $12 (5/15/87) **85**
Pinot Noir Santa Barbara County 1989: Leans toward the earthy, leathery spectrum of Pinot Noir, with herb, tea and rhubarb notes adding to the ripe cherry and plum flavors. Balanced and a touch tannic, with meaty, peppery notes on the finish. Drinkable now, but capable of being cellared through 1995. 3,900 cases made. $15 (3/31/92) **85**
Pinot Noir Santa Barbara County 1988: Extremely earthy, gamy tea leaf aromas and flavors turn a bit sour on the finish. Despite modest beet and dried cherry flavors, it's not much above average. Tasted twice. 4,000 cases made. $15 (6/30/91) **78**
Pinot Noir Santa Barbara County 1987: Extremely earthy and vegetal flavors dominate the cherry and anise notes. An extreme wine that brings out the herbal, weedy component of Pinot Noir that some people love. Tasted twice, with consistent notes. Drink now. 3,000 cases made. $14 (2/28/91) **76**
Pinot Noir Santa Barbara County 1986 $14 (12/15/89) **75**
Pinot Noir Santa Barbara County 1985 $14 (6/15/88) **74**
Pinot Noir Santa Barbara County Barrel Select 1986: A rough, unbalanced wine at this age, it smells like herbs and vanilla, tastes woody, earthy, herbal and tannic and finishes dry. Drink now if this is your style. $20 (12/15/89) **78**
Pinot Noir Santa Barbara County Barrel Select 1985 $20 (6/15/88) **75**
Pinot Noir Santa Maria Valley 1982 $11 (12/01/84) **63**

SANTA BARBARA
Pinot Noir Santa Barbara County 1989: Light and velvety, with spicy, tea-scented cherry and plum aromas and flavors. Turns slightly tannic on the finish, but cellaring until 1993 or '94 should take care of it. 1,400 cases made. $11 (7/31/91) **84**
Pinot Noir Santa Barbara County 1986 $11 (6/15/88) **80**
Pinot Noir Santa Barbara County Reserve 1989: Ripe, smoky, silky and polished, with lots of exotic flavors on a lean frame. Has a nice edge of bacon and earthiness to the plum and blackberry aromas and flavors. A distinctive wine with character. 385 cases made. $20 (11/15/91) **87**
Pinot Noir Santa Ynez Valley Reserve 1987: An elegant, beautifully balanced wine. Has toasty, complex aromas and lively acidity, and it's very flavorful with cherries and strawberries and a hint of vanilla. Finish lingers. $20 (12/15/89) **89**

SANTA CRUZ MOUNTAIN
Pinot Noir Santa Cruz Mountains 1985 $15 (6/15/88) **89**
Pinot Noir Santa Cruz Mountains Jarvis Vineyard 1981 $15 (8/31/86) **89**

SANTA YNEZ VALLEY
Pinot Noir Santa Maria Valley 1987: Tart and sour, with earthy, gamy Pinot Noir flavors. Avoid. Tasted twice. $13 (3/31/90) **62**

SCHUG
Pinot Noir Carneros Beckstoffer Vineyard 1987: Has a tough, leather and mushroom quality that some may find appealing, but the hard edges need a year or two to mellow. Hints of black cherry come through on the finish. Drink now to 1994. 1,789 cases made. $13 (2/28/91) **81**
Pinot Noir Carneros Beckstoffer Vineyard 1986: Aromatically pleasing, with complex spice, tea and cherry aromas and flavors to match. An elegant, crisp, supple wine that's still a bit chewy and firm on the finish. Drink now to 1994. 1,100 cases made. $13 (10/31/90) **87**
Pinot Noir Napa Valley Heinemann Vineyard Reserve 1985: A very crisp, tight-textured wine, with complex, mature tea, spice and plum aromas. Turns lean and dry on the palate. Not lush, but tasty and tart. 950 cases made. $15 (11/15/91) **83**

SEA RIDGE
Pinot Noir Sonoma Coast Hirsch Vinyard 1990: Tastes and smells like a peppery Beaujolais rather than Pinot Noir, but it's a pleasant drink, with fresh, ripe flavors. Drink now. 200 cases made. $20 (3/31/92) **82**
Pinot Noir Sonoma Coast Hirsch Vinyard 1989: A rich wine, with nice plum and cherry flavors, but a stemmy, greenish edge turns peppery and slightly bitter on the finish. May be better after 1993. 127 cases made. $18 (3/31/92) **81**
Pinot Noir Sonoma County 1982 $10.50 (8/31/86) **72**

SEGHESIO
Pinot Noir Northern Sonoma 1983 $5 (4/15/87) **72**
Pinot Noir Russian River Valley 1988: Crisp, tart and juicy, with bracing acidity to support the slightly jammy plum and wild berry flavors. Hints of menthol make it unusual. Drinkable now, but better around 1993. 4,480 cases made. $9 (10/31/91) **83**
Pinot Noir Russian River Valley 1987: Light and smooth, with pretty strawberry and peach aromas and flavors that are very pleasant and appealing. Flavors persist on the finish, making this a welcome wine for current drinking. $8 (4/15/90) **84**
Pinot Noir Russian River Valley Reserve 1987: Firm and concentrated, with a sense of restraint on the structure, offering strawberry and cherry aromas and flavors, plus a bit of tannin that needs until 1994 to resolve. $13 (4/15/90) **83**
Pinot Noir Sonoma County 1989: Delicate in style, offering subtle ripe cherry and spice notes with pretty oak shadings. Attractively balanced, it drinks well now. 2,300 cases made. $9 (4/30/92) **79**
Pinot Noir Sonoma-Mendocino Counties 1984 $6.75 (5/31/88) **84**

SIGNORELLO
Pinot Noir Napa Valley 1988: A ripe, stylish wine that emphasizes the spicy vanilla flavors from aging in new oak barrels. Its fruit component is modest, but the whole package is seductive and impressive. 440 cases made. $25 (2/28/91) **85**
Pinot Noir Napa Valley Founder's Reserve 1989: Mint, dill and pickle flavors overshadow the plum and cherry notes. Has lots of oak and tannin, too, making for a heavy-handed, rustic wine that lacks finesse. Drink now. 500 cases made. $25 (11/15/91) **78**

SIMI
Pinot Noir North Coast 1981 $7 (9/16/85) **64**

ROBERT SINSKEY
Pinot Noir Carneros 1988: Ripe and generous, with leather- and earth-tinged plum flavors. A bit tannic and tough on the finish, but probably best to drink soon. Tasted twice. 1,500 cases made. $18 (2/28/91) **81**
Pinot Noir Carneros Napa Valley 1987: Has fine fruit intensity, with layers of rich, elegant plum, spice and cherry flavors that dance on the palate. It has more depth and tannins on each taste. Drink now to 1995. $14 (3/31/90) **86**
Pinot Noir Carneros Napa Valley 1986 $12 (6/15/88) **79**

SMITH-MADRONE
Pinot Noir Napa Valley 1984 $10 (12/15/87) **65**

SOLETERRA
Pinot Noir Napa Valley Three Palms Vineyard 1982 $12 (10/16/84) **80**

SOLIS
Pinot Noir Santa Clara County 1988: A pleasant wine, with simple plum and cherry flavors, a trace of Pinot Noir character and mild tannins. Ready to drink now. 300 cases made. $9 (4/30/91) **78**

STAR HILL
Pinot Noir Napa Valley Doc's Reserve 1988: Ripe and oaky, with generous black cherry and currant flavors lavishly spread with a toasty, minty oak character. A stylish wine, with slightly skewed flavors. Best to drink after 1994. Significantly better than when reviewed earlier. $19 (2/15/92) **82**
Pinot Noir Napa Valley Doc's Reserve 1987: The intriguing flavors of vanilla, chocolate, cherry and spice are generous and distinctive, finishing with crisp acidity and good length. Complex and well balanced with good concentration of fruit. Drink now to 1993. $19 (5/31/90) **87**

ROBERT STEMMLER
Pinot Noir Sonoma County 1987: Austere style, firm and tannic but with attractive coffee, cedar, cherry and toasty notes that add complexity of flavor, but it could use a little more subtlety and finesse. Drink now to 1994. $19 (10/31/90) **82**
Pinot Noir Sonoma County 1986 $18 (6/15/88) **84**
Pinot Noir Sonoma County 1985 $18 (9/30/87) **79**
Pinot Noir Sonoma County 1984 $16 (8/31/86) **90**
Pinot Noir Sonoma County 1983 $15 (3/16/85) SS **93**

STERLING
Pinot Noir Carneros Napa Valley Winery Lake 1989: Complex and elegant with tiers of cherry, spice, smoke and strawberry. Picks up a pleasant earthy edge on the aftertaste, but maintains its satiny texture. Drink now to 1995. $14 (3/31/92) **87**
Pinot Noir Carneros Napa Valley Winery Lake 1988: Light in texture but fragrant, spicy and oaky, with very nice raspberry, caramel and nutmeg flavors that linger on the finish. A lively, flavorful wine that's just about drinkable now. $14 (4/30/91) **87**
Pinot Noir Carneros Napa Valley Winery Lake 1987: Ebulliently fruity and spicy, with cinnamon-tinged strawberry and red cherry aromas and flavors, appealing from the first sip to the last echo of fruit and oak. Drinkable now, but it has enough structure to hold in the cellar through at least 1993. $18 (12/31/89) **86**
Pinot Noir Carneros Napa Valley Winery Lake 1986 $18 (2/28/89) **89**

RODNEY STRONG
Pinot Noir Russian River Valley River East Vineyard 1985: Elegant and balanced, with mature but pretty cherry, toast, herb and plum flavors that are nicely integrated and well proportioned. Not too tannic; fairly priced. Drink now through 1993. 4,000 cases made. $10 (2/28/91) **83**
Pinot Noir Russian River Valley River East Vineyard 1984 $8 (11/15/87) **78**
Pinot Noir Russian River Valley River East Vineyard 1981 $8.50 (8/31/86) **63**
Pinot Noir Russian River Valley River East Vineyard 1980 $10 (7/01/84) **78**

SUNRISE
Pinot Noir Santa Clara County San Ysidro Vineyard 1985 $12 (6/15/88) **71**
Pinot Noir Sonoma County Green Valley Dutton Ranch Vineyard 1986 $10 (6/15/88) **60**

JOSEPH SWAN
Pinot Noir 1982 $17 (8/31/86) **82**
Pinot Noir Sonoma Coast 1985 $18 (6/15/88) **89**
Pinot Noir Sonoma Coast Russian River Valley 1988: Smells attractive, but on the palate it's extremely woody, tannic and dry and doesn't give the peppery cherry flavor much of a chance. Perhaps with time the wood will soften a bit, but our guess is it will always show its wood. Drink in 1993 or '94. 240 cases made. $20 (6/30/91) **79**

TAFT STREET
Pinot Noir Monterey County 1982 $7.50 (5/01/84) **76**
Pinot Noir Santa Maria Valley 1983 $9 (4/15/87) **76**

TALLEY
Pinot Noir Arroyo Grande Valley 1989: Very firm and tannic, with pleasant cherry and blackberry aromas and modest spice flavors, but it needs until 1994 or '95 to soften. And then what? 822 cases made. $17 (10/31/91) **75**

TREFETHEN
Pinot Noir Napa Valley 1986: Has stemmy, peppery aromas, and it's thin and bitter on the palate. Tasted twice. $13 (7/31/89) **68**
Pinot Noir Napa Valley 1985 $12 (6/15/88) **74**
Pinot Noir Napa Valley 1984 $9.25 (5/31/88) **80**

TRUCHARD
Pinot Noir Carneros 1989: This wine offers a rich array of ripe cherry, plum and currant flavor with hints of anise and spicy oak. Beautifully integrated, with a supple texture and just the right amount of tannin. Ready now but capable of improving through 1994. Finish lingers on and on. 300 cases made. $18 (10/31/91) **90**

TULOCAY
Pinot Noir Napa Valley Haynes Vineyard 1989: Sweet oak flavors of vanilla and spice dominate the modest cherry and cola notes in this medium-bodied wine. Easy to drink, but lacks strong fruit character and definition. Tasted twice, with consistent notes. $16 (3/31/92) **76**
Pinot Noir Napa Valley Haynes Vineyard 1988: Very little Pinot Noir character is evident in this leathery, swampy-smelling wine. The flavors are muddy and only slightly fruity. Might be someone's idea of a Burgundian wine, but not ours. Tasted twice, with consistent notes. $15 (3/31/92) **75**
Pinot Noir Napa Valley Haynes Vineyard 1985: Tea, mint and raspberry aromas and flavors are tightly packed into this firmly structured, somewhat leathery wine. An old-style California Pinot, hinting more at mushrooms than fruit. Drinkable now. $18 (2/28/91) **83**

VILLA MT. EDEN
Pinot Noir Napa Valley 1988: A lean, woody style, with ripe, well-proportioned strawberry, herb and plum flavors and a good dose of tannin on the finish. Ultimately simple but pleasant. Drink now to 1994. 1,200 cases made. $12 (2/28/91) **82**
Pinot Noir Napa Valley Tres Niños Vineyard 1981 $5 (4/16/85) BB **86**

WATSON
Pinot Noir Santa Maria Valley Bien Nacido Vineyard 1986: Think of it as a sturdy red wine and it will be satisfying. Shows herb and tomato flavors and a rough texture. $9 (12/15/89) **77**

WEIBEL
Pinot Noir Mendocino County 1988: Simple and fruity, but priced right. The cherry and plum flavors won't wow you, but it's more than passable, with enough varietal character to call it Pinot Noir. Drink now. $6 (2/28/91) **74**

WEINSTOCK
Pinot Noir Sonoma County Winemaker Selection Reserve 1989: Lean and extremely minty,

Key to Symbols

The scores reported here are the results of blind tastings conducted by our panel of senior editors. Wines that carry the initials below are results of individual tastings.

THE WINE SPECTATOR 100-POINT SCALE ***95-100***—Classic, a great wine; ***90-94***—Outstanding, superior character and style; ***80-89***—Good to very good, a wine with special qualities; ***70-79***—Average, drinkable wine that may have minor flaws; ***60-69***—Below average, drinkable but not recommended; ***50-59***—Poor, undrinkable, not recommended. "+"—With a score indicates a range; used primarily with barrel tastings to indicate a preliminary score.

SPECIAL DESIGNATIONS SS—Spectator Selection, CS—Cellar Selection, BB—Best Buy, (\$NA)—Price not available, (NR)—Not released.

TASTER'S INITIALS (JG)—Jim Gordon, (HS)—Harvey Steiman, (JL)—James Laube, (JS)—James Suckling, (TM)—Thomas Matthews, (TR)—Terry Robards, (PM)—Per-Henrik Mansson, (BT)—Barrel Tasting (these wines were tasted blind from barrel samples), (CA-date)—*California's Great Cabernets* by James Laube, (CH-date)—*California's Great Chardonnays* by James Laube, (VP-date)—*Vintage Port* by James Suckling.

DATE TASTED Dates in parentheses represent the issue in which the rating was published.

hinting at camphor, with a modest streak of black cherry flavor to keep it more or less in balance. Simple and direct. Drinkable now. Tasted twice. 1,075 cases made. $12.50 (11/15/91) **79**

WHALER
Pinot Noir California 1989: Only a faint hint of Pinot Noir character is evident in the plummy flavor. An otherwise simple, decent table wine. Drink now. 450 cases made. $9.75 (4/30/91) **75**

WHITEHALL LANE
Pinot Noir Alexander Valley 1988: Lavishly oaked to the point where you get more wood than fruit flavors. Underneath there are elegant cherry and spice flavors, but this style is for fans of toasty oak. Drink now to 1994. 750 cases made. $13.50 (10/31/90) **82**
Pinot Noir Napa Valley 1987: Pretty fruity aromas of red cherry, blueberry, oak and spice with flavors to match, packaged in a crisp, firm, smooth texture, with fruit flavors that echo on the finish. Drink now to 1993. $12 (10/15/89) **88**
Pinot Noir Napa Valley 1985 $7.50 (6/15/88) **82**
Pinot Noir Napa Valley 1984 $7.50 (3/01/86) **86**

WILD HORSE
Pinot Noir Paso Robles 1987 $14 (10/15/89) **90**
Pinot Noir Santa Barbara County 1988: Provides a wide range of spicy cherry and berry flavors, with what appears to be a good dose of volatile acidity and oak. Tea, spice and vinegar notes come through on the finish. Drink now to 1993. Tasted twice. $14 (4/30/91) **79**
Pinot Noir Santa Barbara County 1987: An elegant wine, with fresh strawberry, earth and cherry fruit of moderate depth and intensity. Well balanced, somewhat tannic and ready to drink now to 1993. $13.50 (3/31/90) **82**
Pinot Noir Santa Barbara County 1986 $13.50 (6/15/88) **85**
Pinot Noir Santa Barbara County 1985 $12.50 (6/15/88) **86**

WILLIAMS SELYEM
Pinot Noir Russian River Valley Allen Vineyard 1988: Elegant and subtle, with pretty oak and spice notes, and well-defined cherry, chocolate and cola flavors that are young and intense. Start drinking now. 317 cases made. $40 (5/31/90) **88**
Pinot Noir Russian River Valley Allen Vineyard 1987: A remarkably rich and complex wine, with layers of black cherry, raspberry, chocolate and vanilla flavors that are very harmonious and elegant, finishing with subtley and delicacy. Has the tannin to age three to five years, but it's hard to wait. $20 (5/31/89) **92**
Pinot Noir Russian River Valley Olivet Lane Vineyard 1989: Ripe, round and fruity, with plenty of plum and black cherry flavors accented by toast and spice notes. A medium-bodied, well-balanced, plush-textured wine for drinking now through 1994. $25 (11/15/91) **90**
Pinot Noir Russian River Valley Rochioli Vineyard 1988: A beautifully proportioned Pinot Noir that's aromatic, elegant and long, with lots of raspberry, plum and cherry flavors to balance the vanilla and spice of oak, all of which keeps growing on the finish. Wonderful now, but cellaring until 1993 or '94 should only make it better. 182 cases made. $40 (2/28/91) **92**
Pinot Noir Sonoma Coast 1988: Remarkable for its rich, deep, complex chocolate, cherry, toast and vanilla flavors that are smooth and concentrated, backed with toasty oak and firm, supple tannins. It glides across the palate. Elegant and stylish, delicious to drink now, but should improve through 1993. 597 cases made. $40 (5/31/90) **92**
Pinot Noir Sonoma Coast Summa Vineyard 1988: An earthy wine supported by plenty of rich, ripe berry and cherry flavors that come across as complex, with hints of herb, spice, and plum notes on the finish. Has attractive toasty oak notes and an elegant aftertaste. Drink now to 1993. 108 cases made. $40 (5/31/90) **88**
Pinot Noir Sonoma County 1987 $16 (5/31/89) **88**
Pinot Noir Sonoma County 1986 $16 (6/15/88) **91**

WINDSOR
Pinot Noir Russian River Valley Winemaster's Private Reserve 1985 $8 (6/15/88) **83**

YORK MOUNTAIN
Pinot Noir Central Coast 1986 $6 (6/15/88) **81**
Pinot Noir San Luis Obispo County 1985 $9 (6/15/88) **80**

ZACA MESA
Pinot Noir Santa Barbara County Reserve 1988: A tart, earthy, compact style, with subtle cassis, cherry and strawberry flavors that are tightly reined in now, but show their best on the finish where they reveal complexity and length. A nip of oak on the finish will soften by 1993. $15.50 (10/31/90) **86**
Pinot Noir Santa Barbara County Reserve 1987: Smooth, supple and flavorful. A fruity, medium-bodied, elegant wine, with hints of oak and herbs in the flavors. $15 (12/15/89) **82**
Pinot Noir Santa Barbara County Reserve 1986 $15 (6/15/88) **91**
Pinot Noir Santa Barbara County American Reserve 1984 $12.75 (2/15/87) **93**
Pinot Noir Santa Barbara County American Reserve 1983 $13 (8/31/86) **60**
Pinot Noir Santa Ynez Valley 1981 $12 (4/01/84) **59**

ZD
Pinot Noir Carneros Napa Valley 1989: A tart, tight wine that's tannic and tough in texture, with raspberry and red cherry flavors and a drying finish. May soften up with time in the cellar; try in 1993. 1,646 cases made. $16 (11/15/91) **82**
Pinot Noir Carneros Napa Valley 1988: An earthy wine, with tiers of spice, pepper, plum and leather notes that keep it interesting. Balanced, full-bodied and quite approachable now. 1,058 cases made. $17 (6/30/91) **82**
Pinot Noir Carneros Napa Valley 1985: Hard-edged and woody, with an undercurrent of concentrated black cherry flavors plus hints of cassis and cinnamon. Drink now. $14 (7/31/89) **79**
Pinot Noir Napa Valley 1982 $12.50 (8/31/86) **75**

RHÔNE-TYPE RED

BONNY DOON
Ca' del Solo Big House Red California 1990: Wow. Talk about a peppery red wine—from the aroma to the finish this medium-bodied, lively wine is dominated by black pepper, but it's backed by enough ripe cherry flavor to keep it fruity and satisfying. Moderate tannins make it drinkable now. As fun to drink as the new label is to look at. $7.50 (6/30/92) BB **85**
Grahm Crew Vin Rouge California 1989: Strong berry aromas and flavors are vivid from the first whiff to the last echo of the finish in this effusively fruity wine that's lively and spicy. An herbal note draws attention away from the fruit, but it's a good quaffer. $7.50 (10/31/90) BB **82**
Grahm Crew Vin Rouge California 1988: A clean and lively wine, with fresh strawberry and cherry aromas. Light-bodied and well balanced with a nice hint of vanilla and very fruity flavors. $7.50 (2/15/90) **83**
Grahm Crew Vin Rouge California 1987 $8 (11/30/88) **85**
Grahm Crew Vin Rouge California 1985 $6.25 (9/30/87) BB **80**
Grenache California Clos de Gilroy 1990: Vibrantly fruity, crisp in texture and broad enough in flavor to let the plum, cherry, strawberry and black pepper flavors roll on. A wine to enjoy with hearty food or to sip by itself. Drinkable now. 4,500 cases made. $8 (2/15/91) BB **87**
Grenache California Clos de Gilroy 1988: Crisp and refreshing, with hints of perfume, tar, cherry and spice. Soft and lush, with herb and mineral flavors on the finish. $6.75 (2/15/89) BB **85**
Grenache California Clos de Gilroy 1987 $6.50 (2/29/88) BB **87**
Grenache California Clos de Gilroy 1986 $6.50 (4/30/87) **84**
Grenache California Clos de Gilroy Cuvée Tremblement de Terre 1989: A vibrant, jammy, effusively flavored wine, with great blackberry flavors that linger incredibly long on the finish. Has moderate tannins, and it's well balanced for drinking now. Check the label for an earthquake dedication. $7.50 (2/15/90) BB **88**
Le Cigare Volant California 1989: A firm, tightly tannic wine, with a lean beam of earthy cherry and plum aromas and flavors and hints of pepper on the nose. A little tannic, but drinkable now. Tasted twice, with consistent notes. $20 (3/15/92) **80**
Le Cigare Volant California 1988: Blackberry and currant aromas jump out of the glass at first whiff, joined by hints of leather and smoke on the palate. A polished wine, with a lighter texture than previous Cigares, but with plenty of intensity. Drink now. Rel: $19 Cur: $23 (12/31/90) **86**
Le Cigare Volant California 1987: Warm and generous, with nicely focused plum and black pepper aromas and flavors plus a welcome touch of spice on the finish. Soft and supple, drinkable now. Tastes a bit more subdued, less intense than recent vintages. Rel: $15 Cur: $24 (12/15/89) **85**
Le Cigare Volant California 1986 Rel: $13.50 Cur: $25 (11/15/88) **92**
Le Cigare Volant California 1985 Rel: $12.50 Cur: $25 (1/31/88) **90**
Le Cigare Volant California 1984 Rel: $10.50 Cur: $30 (8/31/86) **87**
Mourvèdre California Old Telegram 1988: Vibrant cherry, blackberry and rose petal aromas and flavors leap out of the glass from the very first whiff, and the firm, slightly tannic texture holds the medium-weight concentration together neatly. Drink now. Rel: $20 Cur: $26 (12/31/90) **85**
Mourvèdre California Old Telegram 1986 $13.50 (11/15/88) **90**
Syrah Santa Cruz Mountains 1988: A lively, stylish wine that doesn't seem like a Rhône, but it's very firm, with well-integrated tannins and plenty of ripe blackberry, cranberry and plum aromas and flavors shaded by lovely violet and other floral overtones. A unique wine that is tempting to drink now, but it should evolve nicely with cellaring until 1993 or '94. $25 (2/15/91) **88**

DAVID BRUCE
Côte de Shandon Vin Rouge San Luis Obispo County 1987 $7.50 (12/31/88) **81**

CHATEAU LA GRANDE ROCHE
Napa Valley 1988 $13 (10/15/90) **86**

CLAIRVAUX
Grenache California 1989: Very light in color, but smooth and oaky on the palate, with distinctive caramel, butter and toast flavors that extend into the finish. Drinkable now. $7 (3/31/92) BB **83**

CLINE
Côtes d'Oakley Contra Costa County 1989: Light in color and concentration, but the bright, spicy cherry and strawberry aromas and flavors are pleasant. Drink slightly chilled. $7.50 (5/31/91) **80**
Côtes d'Oakley Contra Costa County 1988: Tastes fresh, frank and fruity, a wine made to drink while it's young. Medium-bodied, with mild tannins, plenty of cherry and plum flavors and a touch of vanilla on the finish. 1,200 cases made. $9 (4/30/90) **83**
Mourvèdre Contra Costa County 1989: Tough in texture, which tends to obscure the pleasant blueberry and plum flavors that extend long enough into the finish to suggest that cellaring will bring it around by 1993 or '94. For all the tannin, it seems fleshy. 2,577 cases made. $18 (11/30/91) **86**
Mourvèdre Contra Costa County 1988: What a discovery. Full of sophisticated, rich currant, plum and sweet cherry flavors, with the roundness and vanilla scent of oak aging. Intense, well balanced and long on the finish. Delicious to drink now. 1,400 cases made. $18 (4/30/90) **91**
Mourvèdre Contra Costa County 1987: Very rich and spicy, with minty overtones to the effusive plum and wild strawberry flavors, quite tannic and chewy. Needs to age at least until 1993. A tough wine to judge. $18 (4/15/89) **82**
Mourvèdre Contra Costa County Reserve 1989: A clumsy wine, featuring ripe plum and mint flavors that come across as disjointed and out of focus. Drink in 1994. Tasted twice. 613 cases made. $26 (3/15/92) **78**
Oakley Cuvée Contra Costa County 1989: Brilliantly fresh, fruity and concentrated, offering all sorts of berry and cherry aromas and flavors on a medium frame. Immediately likable and drinkable. 3,427 cases made. $12 (5/31/91) **88**
Oakley Cuvée Contra Costa County 1988: Well knit, supple and beautifully flavored with vivid black cherry, spice and blackberry. Elegant in texture and nicely balanced with good acidity and moderate tannins. Drink soon. 3,100 cases made. $12 (2/28/90) **90**
Oakley Cuvée Contra Costa County NV: Minty, herbal aromas and flavors mark this very ripe, late-harvest Zin-like wine, round and easy to drink, simple. $12 (4/15/89) **78**

CLOS PEGASE
Grenache California 1989: Light in color but rich in flavor, with generous berry, cherry and chocolate aromas and flavors that persist into the finish. Drinkable now, but cellaring until 1993 or '94 wouldn't hurt. 295 cases made. $9.50 (8/31/91) **84**

DOMAINE DE LA TERRE ROUGE
Sierra Foothills 1986: Very smooth and harmonious, with well-defined plum and berry aromas and flavors, firm and supple. The fruit carries on and on. Drinkable now, but it could age for three or four years. $12 (4/15/89) **89**

DUXOUP
Syrah Dry Creek Valley 1987: Very youthful color, vibrantly fruity and nicely focused, showing raspberry and floral aromas and flavors and an underlying gentle tannin structure to keep it healthy through at leat 1993. $12 (4/15/89) **87**
Syrah Dry Creek Valley 1986: Very fragrant and flavorful, exuding good concentration of berry and slightly floral aromas and flavors, supported by soft tannin. Drink now. $9 (4/15/89) **85**
Syrah Sonoma County 1982 $9 (3/16/84) **78**

EDMUNDS ST. JOHN
Les Côtes Sauvages California 1989: Herbal, earthy cedar, bay leaf and mineral aromas tend to push past the modest fruit in this tough, tannic wine. Needs until 1994 or '95 to show what it has, but it's hard to tell at this stage what that might be. $19 (7/15/91) **79**
Les Côtes Sauvages California 1986: Full and rich on the nose, with black pepper-tinged cherry and berry aromas and flavors, plus a touch of leather on the finish. Long and firm. Similar to northern Rhônes, despite the predominance of Grenache. Drink now. $13.50 (4/15/89) **88**
Mourvèdre Napa Valley 1986: Very peppery and ripe, with delicious black cherry flavor on the lean, complex finish. Not for everyone, but if you like Châteauneuf, this one has the character for you. $15 (4/15/89) **87**
Port o'Call New World Red California 1989: Ripe and exotic, with a leathery edge to the plum, spice and tobacco aromas and flavors. Hints at tropical spices. Tannic enough to need until 1994 to soften sufficiently. 350 cases made. $9.50 (8/31/91) **84**
Syrah California 1987: Vegetal aromas and flavors tend to shoulder past the generous plum and berry flavors, but the richness emerges on the finish, turning ripe and open. A distinctive wine that probably needs until 1994 to reach a sense of balance. $18 (12/15/89) **81**
Syrah Sonoma County 1986: Beautifully concentrated and long, with enough fine tannin to hold it for years in the cellar. After a touch of earthiness on the nose, blueberry, plum and anise aromas and flavors burst over the palate. Should be an elegant wine by 1993. $12 (4/15/89) **91**
Syrah Sonoma Valley 1988: Very firm and tannic, with a wonderful concentration of cherry, blackberry and chocolate flavors beating out the tannins on the long, solid finish. Has all the pieces, but needs until 1994 to '96 to soften sufficiently. 200 cases made. $19 (8/31/91) **85**

ESTRELLA RIVER
Syrah Paso Robles 1986: Lean in texture but smooth and round, with tart cranberry flavors balanced against the spice and vanilla of new oak, harmonious and well balanced. $8 (9/30/89) **82**
Syrah Paso Robles 1985 $6.50 (3/31/88) **79**
Syrah Paso Robles 1983 $6.50 (1/31/88) BB **80**

FREY
Syrah Mendocino Bulow Vineyard 1986: Tight and tannic, with a generous streak of rose-tinged

blackberry flavor, drying on the finish from a high level of tannin. But the fruit has enough oomph to suggest cellaring will bring it around, but not before 1994. $10 (4/15/89) **82**

FRICK
Grenache Napa County 1985: Tart and lively, with very smooth, round, vanilla- and chocolate-tinged berry and cherry flavors with a touch of pepper. $7.50 (4/15/89) **86**

HALLCREST
Syrah California Doe Mill Cuvée 1989: Manages to balance the firm dry tannins with ripe raspberry and spicy plum flavors that persist on the finish. Tempting now, but it's also cellar-worthy through 1994 or '95. $7 (4/30/91) **86**

JADE MOUNTAIN
La Provençale California 1990: Sturdy and simple, with appealing blackberry and pepper aromas and flavors that persist nicely on the finish. Drinkable now, but could improve through 1994. 530 cases made. $12 (3/15/92) **80**
Mourvèdre California 1990: Crisp and fruity, with a gamy, peppery edge that hints at olive on the finish. Drinkable now, but might be better in 1993 or '94, when the tannins settle down. 1,300 cases made. $15 (3/15/92) **81**
Mourvèdre California Unfiltered 1990: A firm, sturdy wine, with pleasant blackberry, toast and vanilla aromas and flavors. Has some tannin to lose, but it's drinkable now. Might be better in 1993 or '94. 380 cases made. $15 (3/15/92) **83**

KENDALL-JACKSON
Syrah Sonoma Valley Durell Vineyard 1988: Ripe and smooth, with generous berry and plum aromas and flavors nicely tuned by a light touch of new oak. The tannins are well integrated, and it's intense and elegant on the long finish. Best now to 1994. $24 (8/31/91) **89**
Syrah Sonoma Valley Durell Vineyard 1987: Ripe, round and generous, with a burst of plum and berry flavors surrounded by nuances of vanilla, toast and black pepper. Drink now. $17 (12/15/89) **90**
Syrah Sonoma Valley Durell Vineyard 1986 $14 (11/30/88) **92**

MCDOWELL VALLEY
Grenache McDowell Valley Rosé Les Vieux Cépages 1988: Shows plenty of fruit flavors, including strawberry, berry and apple, in a light-bodied, off-dry wine with soft texture. Drink it while it's fresh. 1,437 cases made. $6.50 (11/15/89) BB **80**
Les Trésor McDowell Valley Les Vieux Cépages 1988: A lean, mature wine, with earthy, leathery aromas and tart, tight cherry flavors. Pretty miserly with the fruit, and turns very dry on the finish. $12 (6/30/92) **75**
Les Trésor McDowell Valley Les Vieux Cépages 1987: Light and pleasant, with strawberry and raspberry flavors and modest tannins balanced by good acidity. The buttery finish and soft structure give it style. Drink now. 1,288 cases made. $14 (8/31/90) **82**
Les Trésor McDowell Valley Les Vieux Cépages 1986: Generous in flavor and supple in texture, showing plum and cherry aromas and flavors plus a touch of characteristic spiciness on the finish. With a bit more concentration, this would age into a beauty, but it's delightful to drink now. 393 cases made. $13 (9/30/89) **86**
Syrah McDowell Valley 1985: Very firm and tasty, with plum, smoke and berry flavors packed into a full-bodied, harmonious, powerful wine. The aromas and finish are especially appealing. Best McDowell Syrah yet. Needs cellaring to tame the tannins, perhaps until 1993. 2,300 cases made. $12 (9/30/89) **90**
Syrah McDowell Valley 1984: Attractive, elegant aromas of blackberry, cherry and orange peel are the best thing about this otherwise lean, tannic, rather hard wine. The fruit should outlast the tannin, and then it should be wonderful. Try it in 1993. $9.50 (2/15/89) **86**
Syrah McDowell Valley 1983 $10 (5/31/88) **69**
Syrah McDowell Valley 1982 $10 (1/31/87) **75**
Syrah McDowell Valley 1981 $10 (12/16/84) **90**
Syrah McDowell Valley Bistro Syrah Les Vieux Cépages 1990: A flavorful but awkward wine, with effusively fruity, floral, Muscat-like aromas that don't jibe with the tannic, lean flavors. Drinkable, but not well balanced. 900 cases made. $9 (6/30/92) **76**
Syrah McDowell Valley Les Vieux Cépages 1987: Tough and tannic. The tobacco and cedar overtones are interesting, but the fruit flavor seems dull. Drinkable, but clumsy. 1,300 cases made. $16 (3/31/91) **74**
Syrah McDowell Valley Les Vieux Cépages 1986: Fully tannic, with hearty, full-bodied plum and chocolate flavors, this isn't very complex or deep, but it's straightforward. Has toasty aromas and it's fairly well balanced. 1,470 cases made. $14 (8/31/90) **80**

MERIDIAN
Syrah Paso Robles 1988: Dense, dark and rich, with spicy, cedary and focused blackberry and wild raspberry aromas and flavors. A tough wine with a soft heart. Long and elegant, turning complex and especially delicious on the finish. Drinkable now, but cellaring until 1993 or '94 couldn't hurt. 4,000 cases made. $14 (3/31/91) **91**

OJAI
Syrah California 1986: Light color, light texture, very mature, leathery and slightly smoky, A very different wine; drinkable now. $7.50 (4/15/89) **77**

JOSEPH PHELPS
Vin du Mistral Rouge California 1989: Fruity and lively, with a strain of tannin running through that keeps it from being too light. Flavors tend toward plum and berry, with a distinctive salt-and-pepper edge. Drinkable now, but the tannins could benefit from aging until 1993. 900 cases made. $14 (7/15/91) **85**
Syrah Napa Valley 1984 $8.50 (11/15/88) **89**
Syrah Napa Valley 1983 $8.50 (11/15/87) **71**
Syrah Napa Valley 1979 $7.50 (9/16/84) **78**
Syrah Napa Valley Vin du Mistral 1988: This complex, flavorful wine keeps the gamy, earthy aromas and ample grapey, berry flavors in good balance with the moderate tannins and supple texture. Fine to drink now through 1995. Tasted twice. $16 (6/30/92) **87**
Syrah Napa Valley Vin du Mistral 1987: Earthy pepper, herb and dill aromas and flavors tend to dominate this sturdy, rustic wine. Not a typical California red, but distinctive. 400 cases made. $14 (8/31/91) **81**
Syrah Napa Valley Vin du Mistral 1986: Smooth, focused and harmonious, with gentle black cherry, leather and nutmeg aromas and flavors and velvety tannins. One of the gentler California Syrahs around. Best now to 1995. 1,400 cases made. $14 (10/31/90) **88**

R.H. PHILLIPS
Alliance California 1989: Firm and flavorful, with a nice range of cherry, raspberry and plum flavors shaded by black pepper and spice notes. The tannins are soft enough to be ready around 1993 to '95, and the flavors persist into a long finish. 2,604 cases made. $10 (11/30/91) **88**
Mourvèdre California EXP 1988: Smells fine, but hits a snag of dill and vinegar notes that overwhelm the modest berry flavor. Not very appealing. Tasted twice. 500 cases made. $13/375ml (4/30/91) **74**
Syrah California EXP 1988: Ripe, rich and opulent, with a luscious concentration of black cherry, plum and strawberry aromas and flavors and hints of pepper and smoke on the long finish. A dense, profound wine that's round in texture. Tempting to drink now for its richness, but cellaring until 1995 seems appropriate. 1,670 cases made. $15 (11/15/91) **91**
Syrah California Reserve 1987: Modest in flavor and firm in structure, but not much to excite the senses. A nicely proportioned wine that may just need time in the cellar to open up. Try in 1993 or '94. 1,300 cases made. $13 (12/31/90) **80**

PRESTON
Sirah-Syrah Dry Creek Valley 1989: The crisp, lean texture lacks generosity, but the wine shows nice plum and cherry flavors. Could be a lot more intense. Not as good as in most years. Tasted twice, with consistent notes. 750 cases made. $18 (3/15/92) **78**
Sirah-Syrah Dry Creek Valley 1986: With its vibrant purple color and intensely floral aromas, this announces itself as something different, and the oak-tinged blackberry and blueberry flavors sail on and on. A real achievement, and delicious to drink now. $11 (2/15/89) **90**
Sirah-Syrah Dry Creek Valley 1985 $9.50 (1/31/88) **91**

QUPE
Los Olivos Cuvée Santa Barbara County 1989: Hearty and full-bodied, with a smooth texture and an earthy edge to the generous plum, cherry and spice aromas and flavors. Has a murky feel and vegetal overtones that are not so appealing, but has the style and substance to age well through 1993 to '95. $15 (8/31/91) **85**
Syrah Central Coast 1989: Very smooth and focused, with generous berry and spice aromas and flavors that edge toward pleasant cedary, earthy complexity on the finish. Has enough tannin to suggest it might be best after 1993. $12.50 (8/31/91) **87**
Syrah Central Coast 1988 $10.25 (12/15/89) **90**
Syrah Central Coast 1987: Firm and flavorful but reined in, with nicely focused raspberry, floral, toast and vanilla aromas and flavors, supple but balanced, with crisp acidity. Tannins are well incorporated. Drinkable now. $9 (4/15/89) **88**
Syrah Central Coast 1986: Not as rich and powerful as many other Syrahs, but well-crafted and lively on the palate, a nice wine but not particularly distinctive. $9.50 (4/15/89) **79**
Syrah Central Coast 1985 $5.75 (4/15/88) **78**
Syrah Santa Barbara County Bien Nacido Vineyard 1989: Powerful and spicy, with lots of cedar, toast and pepper edges to the central core of plum and cherry flavors. Full-bodied and flavorful; goes for lots of gusto, but stays in balance. Best after 1993 or '94. $20 (8/31/91) **89**
Syrah Santa Barbara County Bien Nacido Vineyard 1987: Distinctive, robust and ripe. Extremely dark in color, peppery and gamy in flavor, with smoke, anise and black cherry notes to add complexity. Moderately tannic, but soft in structure. Drink now through 1993. $20 (2/28/90) **81**

RIDGE
Mourvèdre California Evangelo Vineyards Mataro 1990: Gamy, smoky, toasty aromas and flavors shoulder past the modest fruit in this medium-weight, closed-in wine. May be better after 1994. 753 cases made. $14 (3/15/92) **73**

SARAH'S
Grenache California Cadenza 1988: Tart and fruity, with lively blueberry and raspberry flavors and a touch of tannin, crisp and lively on the finish. Tasty, if a bit short. Drink now. ($NA) (4/15/89) **80**

SHENANDOAH
Serene Varietal Adventure Series Amador County 1989: A straightforward, slightly spicy, lightly fruity wine that's smooth and drinkable, but very light on flavor. 716 cases made. $8 (3/31/91) **74**

SIERRA VISTA
Syrah El Dorado Sierra Syrah 1985: Has mature, spicy aromas and flavors, scented with vanilla and chocolate, smooth but a bit woody for the gentle cherry flavors. Drink now. $9.75 (4/15/89) **82**
Syrah El Dorado Sierra Syrah 1983: Has sharply focused plum and leathery aromas and flavors, with floral and nutmeg overtones on the finish, it's round and velvety, harmonious and coming together beautifully. Drinkable now, but can be cellared through 1993. $9 (4/15/89) **89**

SOTOYOME
Syrah Russian River Valley 1986: Firm and tannic, with earthy overtones to the concentrated plum and cherry flavors. Some may find it too earthy. Drinkable now. $7 (4/15/89) **85**
Syrah Russian River Valley 1985: Earthy, leathery, relatively light-bodied, showing strawberry flavor against the smoky and earthy character. $7 (4/15/89) **77**

SEAN H. THACKREY
Mourvèdre California Taurus 1989: The velvety texture carries pretty plum, herb and coffee flavors over rich, ripe tannins. Integrated and not too heavy, but could use until 1994 or '95 to soften. $24 (8/31/91) **86**
Mourvèdre California Taurus 1988: Soft, supple and generous, offering ripe blackberry and vanilla aromas and flavors and significant but not overwhelming tannins. Drink now. 120 cases made. $24 (9/30/90) **86**
Syrah Napa Valley Orion 1989: Intense, ripe, deep, rich and plummy, with tiers of cherry and chocolate flavors. Offers firm but not overpowering tannins and a pretty overlay of oak. Needs cellaring until 1994 to soften. $45 (12/31/91) **90**
Syrah Napa Valley Orion 1988: Ripe, rich, generous and glowing with meaty berry and pepper aromas and flavors that are smooth, polished and tannic without being rough. It's long lasting and hints at elegance on the finish. Tempting now, but give it until 1993 to '95 to settle down. 600 cases made. $30 (9/30/90) **89**
Syrah Napa Valley Orion 1987: Dark, dense and remarkably supple, with gorgeous plum, peach and cherry flavor graced with hints of mint and spice, rounded out with delicious oak. Comes off like a Bordeaux with Rhône flavors, very seductive. Drinkable now if you don't mind some velvety tannin. Not cheap. $30 (9/30/89) **92**
Syrah Napa Valley Orion 1986 $26 (4/15/89) **83**

TRUMPETVINE
Syrah California Berkeley Red NV: More tannin than you might expect from a non-vintage wine, but it's very firm and balanced, showing ripe, plum flavor and supple texture. $5 (4/15/89) **79**

WILLIAM WHEELER
RS Reserve California 1989: Lean and tart, with a firm backbone of acidity and tannin that makes it seem austere rather than generous. Drink with hearty food. Start drinking in 1993. 3,400 cases made. $10.50 (10/31/91) **77**
RS Reserve California 1988: Full-bodied and moderately tannic. Pepper and spice notes accent the rich core of fruit flavors in this firm, rugged wine. Plum and cherry aromas linger on the finish. Drink now. 2,775 cases made. $10 (8/31/90) **83**

ZACA MESA
Syrah Santa Barbara County 1989: Rich and focused, with lots of berry and cherry flavors and shades of black pepper, tea and leather overtones. Tannic enough to want until 1994 to settle down. 541 cases made. $12 (8/31/91) **83**

Key to Symbols

The scores reported here are the results of blind tastings conducted by our panel of senior editors. Wines that carry the initials below are results of individual tastings.

THE WINE SPECTATOR 100-POINT SCALE ***95-100***—Classic, a great wine; ***90-94***—Outstanding, superior character and style; ***80-89***—Good to very good, a wine with special qualities; ***70-79***—Average, drinkable wine that may have minor flaws; ***60-69***—Below average, drinkable but not recommended; ***50-59***—Poor, undrinkable, not recommended. "+"—With a score indicates a range; used primarily with barrel tastings to indicate a preliminary score.

SPECIAL DESIGNATIONS SS—Spectator Selection, CS—Cellar Selection, BB—Best Buy, ($NA)—Price not available, (NR)—Not released.

TASTER'S INITIALS (JG)—Jim Gordon, (HS)—Harvey Steiman, (JL)—James Laube, (JS)—James Suckling, (TM)—Thomas Matthews, (TR)—Terry Robards, (PM)—Per-Henrik Mansson, (BT)—Barrel Tasting (these wines were tasted blind from barrel samples), (CA-date)—*California's Great Cabernets* by James Laube, (CH-date)—*California's Great Chardonnays* by James Laube, (VP-date)—*Vintage Port* by James Suckling.

DATE TASTED Dates in parentheses represent the issue in which the rating was published.

RHÔNE-TYPE WHITE

BONNY DOON
Le Sophiste Santa Cruz Mountains 1989: Complex and flavorful, with oodles of rich pear, honey, vanilla and citrus flavors that are framed by oak. Echoes pineapple and orange notes on the finish. A tasty concoction. Drink now. $25 (3/15/92) **86**
Le Sophiste Santa Cruz Mountains 1989 $25 (1/31/91) **90**
Le Sophiste Santa Cruz Mountains 1987: Very spicy and slightly sappy, but it's fragrant, buttery, smooth and round, with flavors of peach and almond echoing on the finish. Complex and interesting now, with lots of room to develop in the next year or so. ($NA) (4/15/89) **87**

CALERA
Viognier San Benito County 1987: Has more reserve than the others, but the first impression is like biting into a fresh apple, then comes an overlay of spice and walnut, turning toward delicacy on the finish. A sturdy, well-balanced wine. Only 50 bottles made. ($NA) (4/15/89) **86**

LA JOTA
Viognier Howell Mountain 1989: Has plenty of ripe flavors, with honey, spice, floral and butter notes that are complex and engaging. Finishes with a touch of coarseness and tannin, but altogether very pleasant. Limited supply. Drink now to 1993. $25 (1/31/91) **88**
Viognier Howell Mountain 1987: Fragrant, exotic, full-bodied and spicy, with caramel and honey overtones to the pear and floral aromas and flavors. A big wine with plenty of flavor to back up the muscle. Very long and rich, but some would find it awkward. 100 cases made. $18 (4/15/89) **84**

JOSEPH PHELPS
Viognier Napa Valley Vin du Mistral 1990: Ripe, generous and full-bodied, with exotic mango, papaya and pineapple aromas and flavors that are refreshing despite the richness and body. Distinctive and full of personality; could develop nicely with cellaring through 1993 or '94. 800 cases made. $20 (6/15/91) **89**

QUPE
Marsanne Santa Barbara County 1988: A fine discovery. This varietal, rare in California, tastes intriguingly rich and honeylike in flavor, with a buttery texture, vanilla, honey and underlying, focused peach and apricot flavors. $12.50 (12/15/89) **87**

RITCHIE CREEK
Viognier Napa Valley 1987: Firm and focused, with bright flavors of pineapple, melon and pear with hints of spice. Tart and streamlined on the finish. The floral overtones give it plenty of interest, making it more subtle than the others. $13 (4/15/89) **89**

RIESLING

ALEXANDER VALLEY VINEYARDS
Johannisberg Riesling Alexander Valley 1991: Generous apple, peach and floral aromas and flavors are fresh and lively in this soft, modestly sweet Riesling. The fruit is charming and the wine has enough of an acidic backbone to keep it in balance. 1,201 cases made. $8 (5/31/92) **86**

AUSTIN
White Riesling Santa Barbara County Los Alamos Vineyards 1987: Spicy and complex in flavor like an Alsatian Riesling. Has pretty aromas of flowers, spices and peaches. Tastes smooth and quite fruity. $6.50 (12/15/89) **83**

BABCOCK
Johannisberg Riesling Santa Ynez Valley 1986: Quite a find. Has developed into a complex, interesting wine with an array of honey, peach and almond flavors while retaining great acidity and balance. Mildly sweet. $6 (12/15/89) **88**

BALLARD CANYON
Johannisberg Riesling Santa Ynez Valley 1988: Grassy, grapefruitlike aromas and sweet pineapple flavors combine to make a simple, soft, fruity wine. $7 (12/15/89) **74**
Johannisberg Riesling Santa Ynez Valley Reserve 1988: Has exuberantly fruity Riesling aromas, with sweet, simple, soft fruit flavors. Almost a dessert wine. $9 (12/15/89) **75**

BERINGER
Johannisberg Riesling North Coast 1989: A soft, fat texture and sweet, floral, nutty flavors add up to an easy drinking, simple and rather dull wine. $8 (12/31/90) **75**

BOEGER
Johannisberg Riesling El Dorado 1990: Everything an off-dry Riesling should be: Delicate, refreshing and slightly sweet but balanced, with crisp grapefruit undertones to the peach and floral aromas and flavors. Drinkable now. 700 cases made. $7 (9/15/91) **89**

BUENA VISTA
Johannisberg Riesling Carneros 1987: Deep gold in color and somewhat earthy aromas and flavors mark this as more mature, but it has not developed the generosity or complexity to replace the bloom of youth. $7 (7/31/89) **78**

CALLAWAY
White Riesling Temecula 1990: A light wine that's fresh, fruity and soft around the edges, but shows modest concentration of peach and vanilla aromas and flavors. Drink up. $6.75 (5/15/91) **82**
White Riesling Temecula 1989: A very sweet wine that smells herbal and melony and tastes mildy fruity and almost unctuous. Not bad, but simple. $6.75 (5/31/90) **73**
White Riesling Temecula 1988: Fresh, lively and tasty, soft in texture but balanced with enough zingy acidity to carry the orange-tinged peach and apple flavors. Enjoy it now while the fruit is so exuberant. $6.25 (7/31/89) **84**

CLAIBORNE & CHURCHILL
Riesling Central Coast Dry Alsatian Style 1991: Softer and less racy than most dry Rieslings, with generous peach, apricot and almond aromas and flavors shaded by vanilla and spice notes on the finish. Unusual, but appealing. 841 cases made. $9.50 (5/31/92) **85**
Riesling Edna Valley Dry Alsatian Style 1987: A very unusual wine. Has a deep gold color, ripe, honeylike aromas and butterscotchy flavors. The result is a round and rich wine, rather than the usual crisp and fruity. $8 (12/15/89) **76**

DRY CREEK
Johannisberg Riesling Sonoma County 1988: Lightly sweet and delicately fruity, like biting into a ripe peach, complete with the refreshing astringency of the skin. Appealing and balanced well enough to let the flavors linger. $7 (7/31/89) **86**

ESTRELLA RIVER
Johannisberg Riesling Paso Robles 1988: A simple, sweet wine for drinking well-chilled. Has fruit cocktail flavors and a slightly grassy aroma. $6 (12/15/89) **71**

FETZER
Johannisberg Riesling California 1990: Fresh and spicy, with nice cinnamon and nutmeg overtones to the basic grapefruit and peach flavors. Has good intensity and agile balance on the finish. Drinkable now. $6.75 (5/15/91) BB **85**
Johannisberg Riesling California 1988: Very floral, spicy and fruity, tending toward orange-scented peaches, but also a bit coarse and lacking in elegance. Off-dry. $6 (7/31/89) BB **81**

FIRESTONE
Johannisberg Riesling Santa Barbara County Dry 1990: Off-dry, with a rich, unctuous texture and tart green apple and apricot flavors. An unusual, full-bodied wine for a Riesling. 3,000 cases made. $9 (7/15/91) **82**
Johannisberg Riesling Santa Ynez Valley 1990: This fruity, sweet wine has a soft texture, peach and apricot flavors and good balance. $7.50 (7/15/91) **84**
Johannisberg Riesling Santa Ynez Valley 1989: A silky-textured, soft and delicately sweet wine, with plenty of fruit flavor. Shows good balance and harmony. Nicely made. $7.50 (12/31/90) **84**
Johannisberg Riesling Santa Ynez Valley 1988: Sweet but nicely balanced by vivid fruit flavors and crisp acidity. Fruit lingers nicely on the aftertaste. $7 (12/15/89) **82**
Johannisberg Riesling Santa Ynez Valley 1987 $6.50 (2/28/89) **74**

FORTINO
Johannisberg Riesling Santa Clara County 1988: Ripe and smooth, almost buttery-rich, turning delicate and silky on the palate, off-dry, soft and flavorful. Aftertaste of sulfur needs time to dissipate. Drink now. $5.50 (7/31/89) **77**

FREEMARK ABBEY
Johannisberg Riesling Napa Valley 1990: On the dry side, showing focused grapefruit, peach and pine aromas and flavors that are harmonious and balanced toward smoothness. Refreshing, with beautifully realized fruit. $8 (4/30/91) BB **85**
Johannisberg Riesling Napa Valley 1988: Fresh and aromatic, with lovely melon, rose petal, pear, spice and peachy-nectarine flavors that are crisp and delicate, finishing with a full bowl of fruit. California Riesling doesn't get much better. Best Freemark Abbey in years. $8 (8/31/89) **90**

GAINEY
Johannisberg Riesling Santa Barbara County 1989: This very delicate wine is so light it becomes almost watery on the finish. It offers hints of peach and pine flavors, but it's ultimately simple and uninspired. 2,300 cases made. $7.75 (9/15/90) **76**
Johannisberg Riesling Santa Barbara County 1988: Very good. Smells slightly earthy and tastes sweet, but it's lively, with fine pineapple and peach flavors and a lingering, fruity aftertaste. $7.50 (12/15/89) **84**
Johannisberg Riesling Santa Ynez Valley 1990: Soft and frankly sweet, with pleasant peach and apricot aromas and flavors and more than a hint of spritz to keep it refreshing and balanced. Drink soon at a picnic. 2,580 cases made. $8 (6/15/91) **82**

GEYSER PEAK
Johannisberg Riesling California Soft 1989: Decent but lackluster. Sweet, slightly spritzy, with peachy, piny flavors. Herbal aftertaste. $6 (7/31/90) **71**

GREENWOOD RIDGE
White Riesling Anderson Valley 1991: Moderately sweet, soft and flavorful, with floral and almond aromas and flavors and hints of apple and pear on the finish. Drinkable now. 700 cases made. $8.50 (5/31/92) **82**
White Riesling Mendocino 1987: A sweet-and-sour balance pits hints of vinegar against the spicy peach aromas and flavors, suggesting chutney more than anything else. Oddly appealing, despite its flaws. $8 (7/31/89) **77**

GRGICH HILLS
Johannisberg Riesling Napa Valley 1987: Distinctive for its earthy, slatelike aromas and juicy, crisp, nectarine, peach, spice, pine and pear flavors that are complex and very attractive. Exceptionally well-made Riesling. $7.75 (8/31/89) **90**

HAGAFEN
Johannisberg Riesling Napa Valley 1991: Soft and fruity, with fresh, appealing apple and floral aromas and flavors that turn slightly spicy on the finish. Drinkable now. Mevushal kosher. 1,000 cases made. $9 (5/31/92) **84**
Johannisberg Riesling Napa Valley 1989: The floral and petrol notes on the nose are all Riesling. The sweet fruit isn't quite lifted by the acidity, making the wine a little dull. $8.75 (3/31/91) **81**
Johannisberg Riesling Napa Valley 1988: Soft and sappy, seeming resiny at first, but then the delicate peach flavor emerges to bring the wine to a very pretty finish. $8.75 (7/31/89) **74**

HIDDEN CELLARS
Johannisberg Riesling Potter Valley 1990: Offers a lively balance of ripe nectarine, pear and nutmeg aromas and flavors against a hint of sweetness. An off-dry wine with immediate appeal that's light enough to sip when it's warm. 1,788 cases made. $7.50 (6/30/91) BB **85**
Johannisberg Riesling Potter Valley 1989 $8 (9/15/90) **83**

HOP KILN
Johannisberg Riesling Russian River Valley M. Griffin Vineyards 1990: Pleasantly sweet and fruity, with lovely peach and pear flavors plus just enough acidity to keep it from seeming too sweet. Has delicacy and charm. Drinkable now. 605 cases made. $7.50 (12/31/91) BB **87**

JEKEL
White Riesling Arroyo Seco 1987: Fruit aromas and flavors are masked by a high level of sulfur, making this a difficult wine to like. Crisp structure. Drink now. $6.75 (2/28/89) **75**
White Riesling Arroyo Seco Gravelstone Vineyard Dry Styled 1987: Fresh and spicy, with delicate peach and floral aromas and flavors, simple and attractive, with crisp, barely off-dry balance, flavorful and long. $11.50 (2/28/89) **85**
White Riesling Arroyo Seco Gravelstone Vineyard Sweet Styled 1987: Delicately fruity, floral and sweet, a charming wine with beguiling peach, apricot and honey flavors, long and beautifully focused. An artfully balanced wine. $11.50 (2/28/89) **90**

KENDALL-JACKSON
Johannisberg Riesling Clear Lake Vintners Reserve 1989: Light, crisp and slightly spritzy in texture, with herb and apple flavors and good balance. Lingering notes of honey and peach on the finish add some interest. $9 (12/31/90) **80**

J. LOHR
Johannisberg Riesling California Bay Mist 1990: A sweet, ripe wine, with a component of delicate carbonation to keep it from going over the edge. Still, its apricot flavors need more acidity for better balance. Drink it cold. $7.75 (12/31/91) **77**
Johannisberg Riesling Monterey County Greenfield Vineyards 1989: An off-dry wine, with beautifully fruity aromas, apricot flavors and fruit and honey notes. Simple in structure and short on the finish, but easy to like. $6.50 (12/31/90) **82**

MADRONA
Johannisberg Riesling El Dorado 1987: Light, slightly sweet and soft in texture, surprisingly short in fruit aromas and flavors, comes off as a floral- and herbal-accented wine. $6 (7/31/89) **79**

MARION
Johannisberg Riesling California 1987: Very floral aromas and flavors, soft structure and not much length mark this one as drinkable but ordinary. $4.50 (2/28/89) **74**

MIRASSOU
Riesling Monterey County Monterey Riesling 1988: Sappy, petrol-tinged scents compete with lovely apricot and vanilla flavors. It has good structure and fine balance of sweetness and acidity, but the flavors are troublesome. $6.75 (7/31/89) **79**

ROBERT MONDAVI
Johannisberg Riesling Napa Valley 1989: A watery texture and green, resiny flavors do not add up to a pleasant wine. $8.25 (5/15/91) **69**
Johannisberg Riesling Napa Valley 1988: Musty and sour, this tastes tired, oxidized and dirty. It's candylike on the finish and obviously flawed. Tasted twice. $8 (9/15/90) **55**

NAVARRO
White Riesling Anderson Valley 1989: Pine, apple and apricot aromas and flavors run through this

sweetish, somewhat earthy wine. Not a dessert wine, but balanced enough to make it a before-dinner sipper. 1,071 cases made. $8.50 (4/30/91) **83**
White Riesling Anderson Valley 1986 $7.50 (4/30/88) **90**

PARDUCCI
Johannisberg Riesling North Coast 1990: Earthy flavors dominate, although it has a modicum of grapefruit and pineapple to go with the dry, simple structure. Drinkable now. $7 (5/31/92) **80**

PARKER
Johannisberg Riesling Santa Barbara County 1989: The fruit seems stale and gluey, and the flavors lean toward watermelon and resin. An unusual wine, with little charm. The gilt coonskin cap on the label doesn't help. $7.50 (9/15/91) **74**

J. PEDRONCELLI
White Riesling Dry Creek Valley 1989: Fresh, smooth and slightly off-dry, offering ebullient orange and floral aromas and flavors that are somewhat sappy, but still appealing and refreshing. Drinkable now. 2,000 cases made. $5.50 (9/30/90) BB **81**
White Riesling Dry Creek Valley 1988 $5.50 (8/31/89) BB **87**

JOSEPH PHELPS
Johannisberg Riesling Napa Valley 1987: An elegantly fruity, off-dry Riesling. Has attractive nectarine aromas, with melon and honey on the palate and lively balance. $8.50 (2/28/89) **86**
Johannisberg Riesling Napa Valley Early Harvest 1987: Delicate and fresh, with crisp pine, apple, pear and spice flavors that are well focused and long on the finish. $8 (8/31/89) **85**

RANCHO SISQUOC
Johannisberg Riesling Santa Maria Valley 1988: A good, solid, fruity wine, with pleasantly ripe peach and pear flavors and a bit of sweetness to balance the firm acidity. $6.50 (12/15/89) **78**
Riesling Santa Maria Valley Franken Riesling Sylvaner 1988: Tastes crisp and refreshing, with lively grapefruit and peach flavors and good acidity. Very clean and well made. $7 (12/15/89) **81**

RENAISSANCE
Riesling North Yuba Dry 1989: Light, tart and tangy, with pleasant grapefruit and peach aromas and flavors, a crisp texture and a clean, dry finish. Drinkable now. 2,000 cases made. $8 (5/15/91) **83**

ST. FRANCIS
Johannisberg Riesling Sonoma Valley 1988: Clean and vivid in flavor, with slightly sweet piny, lemony flavors and a sense of delicacy and balance. Well made and easy to like. $7.50 (7/31/90) **80**

SANTA BARBARA
Johannisberg Riesling Santa Ynez Valley 1988: Good and simple. A pleasant, slightly sweet, fruity tasting wine that's soft in structure. $7.50 (12/15/89) **76**
Johannisberg Riesling Santa Ynez Valley 1987: Very flavorful and focused, with full peach and pineapple flavors, a sense of depth and a lingering, fruity finish. Off-dry and well balanced. $7 (12/15/89) **84**

SMITH-MADRONE
Riesling Napa Valley 1988: Piny aromas and flavors and a touch of peach make this somewhat appealing, but the brittle structure makes it seem coarse and simple. Drinkable. 850 cases made. $8.50 (9/15/90) **76**

TREFETHEN
White Riesling Napa Valley 1988: Generous fruit on a crisp, lean, almost-dry structure makes this a classic Riesling in the Spätlese style. Its peach and apple flavor permeates the wine right through the long finish without sacrificing a bit of delicacy. $8.25 (7/31/89) **87**

ZACA MESA
Johannisberg Riesling Santa Barbara County 1987: A change from the average bland California Riesling. Has the earthy, austere aromas of a Mosel Riesling complemented by good peachy flavors and firm acidity. $6 (12/15/89) BB **85**

Sauvignon Blanc

ADLER FELS
Fumé Blanc Sonoma County 1990: Tightly structured and sharply focused, with flavors that lean strongly toward green pepper and quince, making it a wine not everyone will love. Has character, though. 4,200 cases made. $9.50 (4/15/92) **82**
Fumé Blanc Sonoma County 1989: Smells and tastes remarkably like an Alsace Gewürztraminer, full-bodied, and rose petal and spice aromas and flavors. A bit soft, but pleasant to drink soon. $10 (4/30/91) **80**

ALDERBROOK
Sauvignon Blanc Dry Creek Valley 1990: A crisp, straightforward wine, with apple and herb flavors and good balance. $7.50 (6/15/92) **80**
Sauvignon Blanc Dry Creek Valley 1989: Very crisp and dry, with a leesy, apple skin flavor, but not a lot of fruit to fill it out. Tasted twice. 4,063 cases made. $8 (11/15/91) **79**
Sauvignon Blanc Dry Creek Valley 1988: A crisp, lean wine that's appealing for its restraint. Has modest peachy, piny aromas and snappy grapefruit flavors. Very dry but well balanced. 3,700 cases made. $9 (3/31/90) **85**
Sauvignon Blanc Dry Creek Valley 1987 $7.50 (4/15/89) **86**

BABCOCK
Sauvignon Blanc Santa Ynez Valley 1987: Toasted onion and vegetable aromas are not appealing, and the lingering taste of smoke and lemon helps only a little. $8 (12/15/89) **65**

BARON HERZOG
Sauvignon Blanc California 1989: Reminiscent of a Sancerre, with delicate, grassy aromas, good acidity and bright, crisp fruit flavor. $8 (3/31/91) **83**
Sauvignon Blanc Sonoma County Special Reserve 1988: $10 (3/31/91) **67**

BEAULIEU
Fumé Blanc Napa Valley Beau Tour 1989: Crisp and light, with modest floral and sweet pea overtones to the lively lemon flavor. A pleasant wine that won't overwhelm. $7.75 (10/15/91) **83**
Sauvignon Blanc Napa Valley Dry 1990: Light and simple, with fresh lemon and grass notes. A decent drink, but nothing to get excited about. $9.50 (2/15/92) **78**
Sauvignon Blanc Napa Valley Dry 1989: Light and refreshing, with attractive melon and herb aromas and flavors and a soft texture. Smooth and subtle on the finish, well made and harmonious. Drink soon. $8.50 (4/30/91) **81**
Sauvignon Blanc Napa Valley Dry 1988: Crisp, fresh and oaky with herb, lemon, citrus and fig flavors that sit nicely on the palate. $8.50 (9/15/89) **83**

BELLEROSE
Sauvignon Blanc Dry Creek Valley Barrel Fermented Reserve 1990: Soft and floral, with lemony flavors that hint at rose petal on the finish. A pretty wine that finishes a little bitter. Drinkable now. $10.50 (4/15/92) **77**
Sauvignon Blanc Sonoma County Barrel Fermented 1987: Smells terrible—totally undrinkable. Tasted twice. 950 cases made. $10.50 (5/15/90) **56**

BENZIGER
Fumé Blanc Sonoma County 1990: A lively, crisp wine with grapefruit and grassy flavors. Clean, refreshing and ready to drink. Significantly better than when reviewed earlier. $9 (2/15/92) **84**
Fumé Blanc Sonoma County 1988: Fairly oaky, with pleasant sweet pea, fig and melon flavors that are attractively balanced. The texture is smooth and fine, offering a measure of complexity. $8.50 (10/31/89) **84**
Sauvignon Blanc Sonoma Mountain 1989: An exotic wine, with strong herb and wood notes, but also an intriguing range of pineapple and tropical fruit flavors that hang with you. Complex and balanced even if it strays from the mainstream. Drink now to 1993. $13 (11/30/91) **87**

BERINGER
Fumé Blanc Napa Valley 1988: This unusual wine has pungent sweet pea, hay, grass and honey aromas and flavors and is soft and flabby on the palate, with sweet butter tones. Definitely not for everyone. $7.50 (8/31/90) **74**
Sauvignon Blanc Knights Valley 1990: Ripe, rich and concentrated, this is smooth and polished, with pear flavor touched by a hint of celery and a definite oak component that melds nicely with the other flavors on the long finish. Seems tight and sharply focused. Drinkable now, but might be better in 1993 or '94. $9 (6/15/92) **86**
Sauvignon Blanc Knights Valley 1989: Firm and fruity, with ripe pineapple and grapefruit aromas and flavors. Full-bodied and generous on the finish. Not typical, but it has appeal. $8.50 (7/31/91) **85**
Sauvignon Blanc Knights Valley 1988: Stylishly oaky in aroma and flavor, with minty, floral aromas and buttery, toasty flavors that surround a modest core of lemon and apple flavor. Buttery notes linger on the finish. $8.50 (6/30/90) **85**
Sauvignon Blanc Knights Valley 1987 $8.50 (3/15/89) **77**

BOEGER
Sauvignon Blanc El Dorado 1990: Has a definite Riesling-like caste, with pretty floral and pine-scented lemon and pear aromas and flavors. A light, crisp wine with style. Drinkable now. 1,950 cases made. $7.50 (11/15/91) **82**

BOGLE
Fumé Blanc California 1988: Clean and refreshing, with modest fruit flavors and typically grassy aromas. On the soft side, without much acidity or depth. Almost colorless. $6/1L (7/31/89) **73**

BRANDER
Sauvignon Blanc Santa Ynez Valley 1987: Intense, lively and flavorful. Has aromas of grapefruit and herbs and tastes dry and full of fruit. $8 (3/15/89) **85**
Sauvignon Blanc Santa Ynez Valley Reserve 1987: Attractive for its rich fig, spice, onion and herb-tinged flavors. Won't disappoint you with its varietal character. $11 (12/15/89) **82**
Sauvignon Blanc Santa Ynez Valley Tête de Cuvée 1990: Herbal, slightly bitter flavors tend to obscure the modest peach and pear aromas and flavors. Finishes tart, needing until 1993 to soften. 2,800 cases made. $9.75 (4/15/92) **81**
Sauvignon Blanc Santa Ynez Valley Tête de Cuvée 1989: Light, crisp and toasty, with a strongly herbal edge to the lemony flavors. Drinkable now. $9.50 (4/30/91) **79**

BUENA VISTA
Fumé Blanc Alexander Valley 1987: Distinctively grassy, with pungent herbal aromas and flavors, yet it's crisp and well balanced. Very well made. Drink now. $8.50 (3/15/89) **86**
Sauvignon Blanc Lake County 1990: Fresh and citrusy, this light-textured wine has pleasant fruit flavors and a nice sense of crispness on the finish. Drinkable now. $6.50 (10/31/91) BB **84**
Sauvignon Blanc Lake County 1989: Has a very smooth and supple texture, with a nice tension between the fruit, spice and herb components. It's long and delicate on the finish, echoing grapefruit and vanilla. Tasted twice. $7.50 (8/31/90) **85**
Sauvignon Blanc Lake County 1988: Crisp and clean, with tart, lively, herb, grass, spice, melon and honey on the finish. Drinks very well. $7.50 (9/15/89) **88**
Sauvignon Blanc Lake County 1986 $7.25 (7/15/87) SS **91**

BYRON
Sauvignon Blanc Santa Barbara County 1989: Smooth and flavorful, with a crisp texture and lots of grapefruit and spice aromas and flavors and a hint of grassiness on the finish. A tangy wine to drink soon. 2,828 cases made. $9 (4/30/91) **84**
Sauvignon Blanc Santa Barbara County 1988: Very good quality. Tastes crisp and lively, not heavy, with plenty of fruit flavor, a grassy aroma and a pleasant, lingering aftertaste. 1,902 cases made. $8.50 (12/15/89) **85**

CAIN
Sauvignon Blanc Napa Valley Musqué 1990: This rich, lavishly oak-accented wine is full-bodied and ripe, with pear and butter flavors. Good, but could use a bit more polish and liveliness. 600 cases made. $12 (6/15/92) **82**
Sauvignon Blanc Napa Valley Musqué 1989: A round texture and spicy vanilla aromas and flavors from oak make this an interesting wine that shows enough ripe pear and butter on the finish to warrant some attention. Drink soon. 450 cases made. $12 (3/15/91) **83**

CALLAWAY
Fumé Blanc Temecula 1989: A well-modulated wine, with ample grassy and fruity flavors rounded out by smooth vanilla tones, presumably from oak aging. Pleasant and well balanced. $6.50 (2/15/92) BB **83**
Fumé Blanc Temecula 1988: The grassy, herbal, almost garlicky aromas and flavors aren't for everyone. Crisp, with odd, almost sour flavors. Tasted twice, with identical scores. $8 (7/31/91) **68**
Fumé Blanc Temecula 1987: Extremely varietal, with pungent grassy aromas, a smooth texture, melon, mint and grapefruit flavors and a crisp, lingering finish. Fine, if this is your style. Tasted twice. $8.25 (6/30/90) **78**
Sauvignon Blanc Temecula 1990: A soft, floral-tasting wine with simple flavors and some sweetness. $6.50 (2/15/92) **77**
Sauvignon Blanc Temecula 1989: Earthy and herbal, this has plenty of crisp grapefruit flavor at the core and is slightly sweet on the finish. A lively wine that's drinkable now. $8 (10/31/90) **79**
Sauvignon Blanc Temecula 1988: Tart, clean and simple, with lemon and herb flavors and delicate balance. Fresh and clean on the finish. $8 (10/31/89) **82**
Sauvignon Blanc Temecula 1987 $7.75 (3/15/89) **71**

CANTERBURY
Sauvignon Blanc California 1988: Herbal and earthy, with a touch of greenish apricot flavor to liven it up. $5 (10/31/89) **75**

CAREY
Sauvignon Blanc Santa Ynez Valley 1990: Light and fruity, with tart citrus and grapefruit flavors. Moderate in depth and intensity. Drink now. 880 cases made. $9 (6/15/92) **79**
Sauvignon Blanc Santa Ynez Valley 1988: Fresh and zingy, with lively grapefruit flavors and

Key to Symbols

The scores reported here are the results of blind tastings conducted by our panel of senior editors. Wines that carry the initials below are results of individual tastings.

THE WINE SPECTATOR 100-POINT SCALE ***95-100***—Classic, a great wine; ***90-94***—Outstanding, superior character and style; ***80-89***—Good to very good, a wine with special qualities; ***70-79***—Average, drinkable wine that may have minor flaws; ***60-69***—Below average, drinkable but not recommended; ***50-59***—Poor, undrinkable, not recommended. "+"—With a score indicates a range; used primarily with barrel tastings to indicate a preliminary score.

SPECIAL DESIGNATIONS SS—Spectator Selection, CS—Cellar Selection, BB—Best Buy, ($NA)—Price not available, (NR)—Not released.

TASTER'S INITIALS (JG)—Jim Gordon, (HS)—Harvey Steiman, (JL)—James Laube, (JS)—James Suckling, (TM)—Thomas Matthews, (TR)—Terry Robards, (PM)—Per-Henrik Mansson, (BT)—Barrel Tasting (these wines were tasted blind from barrel samples), (CA-date)—*California's Great Cabernets* by James Laube, (CH-date)—*California's Great Chardonnays* by James Laube, (VP-date)—*Vintage Port* by James Suckling.

DATE TASTED Dates in parentheses represent the issue in which the rating was published.

refreshing hints of sweet peas to let you know its varietal heritage. Crisp and artfully balanced for drinking now. $8 (12/15/89) **87**

CASTORO

Fumé Blanc San Luis Obispo County 1988: Lean, earthy and toasty, an austere wine with crisp acidity that could use more flavor on its bones. Drink now. $5.25 (12/15/89) **78**

CAYMUS

Sauvignon Blanc Napa Valley 1989: A lively, almost elegant wine, showing the stylish notes of new-oak aging in its spicy vanilla aromas. Herbal, lemony flavors give it life. Has a round texture and a buttery finish. 5,000 cases made. $9 (10/31/90) **88**

Sauvignon Blanc Napa Valley 1988: Tart, lemony, slightly herbaceous with a touch of sweet pea flavor. Well balanced, likable and drinkable. $9 (9/15/89) **83**

Sauvignon Blanc Napa Valley Barrel Fermented 1990: Lavishly oaked, with pretty layers of butter and vanilla notes adding a nice edge to the pear, melon, spice and nutmeg flavors. Has plenty of oak, but it's carried well. Drink now to 1993. 4,487 cases made. $10 (11/15/91) **89**

CHALK HILL

Sauvignon Blanc Chalk Hill 1990: Has nearly everything you could ask for in a Sauvignon Blanc: lots of fruit, crisp balance, spicy oak accents and a lingering finish. $8.50 (4/15/92) **88**

Sauvignon Blanc Chalk Hill 1989: Crisp and lively, with nicely focused peach and grapefruit aromas and flavors shaded by sweet peas and herbs. Balanced, fresh and drinkable. $8 (7/31/91) **85**

Sauvignon Blanc Chalk Hill 1987: Vegetal aromas and flavors make this so distinctive not everyone will like it—tastes like celery and radicchio at first, turning to dill and honey on the finish. Drinkable now, if you like the style. $7 (10/31/89) **82**

CHATEAU POTELLE

Sauvignon Blanc Napa Valley 1990: Fresh and lively, with pleasant grapefruit and vanilla aromas and flavors on the palate. Vanilla notes echo on the finish. Drinkable now. $9 (11/15/91) **85**

CHATEAU SOUVERAIN

Sauvignon Blanc Alexander Valley Barrel Fermented 1990: A mature wine that's figgy, earthy and peachy in flavor, round in texture and ready to drink. $7.50 (6/15/92) BB **82**

CHATEAU ST. JEAN

Fumé Blanc Russian River Valley La Petite Etoile 1988: Fresh and juicy, with layers of tart citrus, fig and toasty oak flavors and a polished texture that lets the flavors dance across the palate. Good length. $10.50 (11/30/89) **89**

Fumé Blanc Sonoma County 1989: Lively, lemony and fresh, with herbal overtones and a tight structure. Overall very tangy, clean and refreshing. $8 (4/30/91) **85**

Fumé Blanc Sonoma County 1988: Earthy, herbal and musty but lively on the palate, lean and austere rather than generous, lemony on the finish. Not for everyone. Tasted twice. $8 (5/15/90) **73**

Fumé Blanc Sonoma County La Petite Etoile 1989: Almost sweet, full of rich, ripe honey and grapefruit flavors, herb notes and buttery overtones. Has lively acidity, aggressive fruit flavors and a crisp finish. It's difficult to think of a Sauvignon Blanc with more flavor, but it could use more elegance. $10.50 (4/30/91) **84**

CHESTNUT HILL

Sauvignon Blanc North Coast 1990: Earthy pear and lemon aromas and flavors dominate this wine, turning sweet-and-sour on the finish. Not a thrill. $6 (11/15/91) **73**

CHIMNEY ROCK

Fumé Blanc Stags Leap District 1989: Crisp and simple, this lively wine has modest grapefruit and grass aromas and flavors, hinting at resin and herbs on the finish. Drinkable now. Tasted twice, with consistent notes. 1,700 cases made. $11 (7/31/91) **81**

Fumé Blanc Stags Leap District 1988: Overwhelmingly grassy and vegetal smelling, tastes like cabbage and broccoli. Difficult to like. Tasted twice. $15 (5/15/90) **65**

Fumé Blanc Stags Leap District 1987: Pronounced sweet pea flavors are rich and concentrated but come up short and bitter. $10 (1/31/89) **77**

CHRISTOPHE

Sauvignon Blanc California 1987: An earthy, herbal wine for drinking now. Grapefruity and light in flavor, but it's pleasant and finishes dry. $7 (4/30/89) BB **82**

CLOS DU BOIS

Sauvignon Blanc Alexander Valley 1989: The refreshing lemon and pine flavors in this wine lack intensity but are still attractive. It turns tart and slightly bitter on the finish. $8 (8/31/90) **76**

Sauvignon Blanc Alexander Valley 1988: Leans toward the oaky end of the spectrum, with crisp, tart grassy and citrus flavors that turn watery on the finish. $11 (7/31/89) **78**

Sauvignon Blanc Alexander Valley Barrel Fermented 1990: A sturdy, medium-bodied wine, with grassy aromas and good fruit flavors. Ready to drink now. $8 (4/15/92) **79**

CLOS PEGASE

Sauvignon Blanc Lake County 1987: Ripe and herbal, with sweet pea, melon and spice flavors, fine structure and balanced, elegant flavors that linger on the palate. Drink now. $9.50 (5/15/90) **84**

Sauvignon Blanc Napa Valley 1989: Herbal, borderline vegetal flavors emphasize lime and oak, making this an unusual style that's ultimately simple and unappealing. $9.50 (6/15/92) **72**

CONCANNON

Fumé Blanc California Selected Vineyards 1987: A basic, drinkable wine with strong grassy aromas and flavors, but little to make it stand out. Very dry. $9.50 (4/30/91) **73**

Sauvignon Blanc Livermore Valley 1990: Fruity and lively, with pleasant melon, grape and slightly sweet pea aromas and flavors. Drinkable now. $8 (2/15/92) BB **85**

Sauvignon Blanc Livermore Valley Reserve 1988: Tart and crisp, with a modest level of citrus and vaguely oniony aromas and flavors. Seems a little watery. Drinkable now. $10 (4/15/92) **79**

Sauvignon Blanc Santa Clara County Mistral Vineyard 1989: Lemony, vegetal aromas and flavors turn a bit stale and simple, finishing a tad sweet. An unusual wine that not everyone will like. $7.50 (11/15/91) **79**

CONN CREEK

Sauvignon Blanc Napa Valley Barrel Select 1987: Rich and smooth, emphasizing figgy fruit flavors. Round in structure, harmonious and well knit, with good length. Drink now. $10 (4/30/89) **83**

CORBETT CANYON

Sauvignon Blanc Central Coast Coastal Classic 1988: Rather delicate and medium-bodied, attractive in a subtle way. Its clean fruit flavors have just a hint of grassiness. $5.50/1L (12/15/89) **78**

Sauvignon Blanc Central Coast Reserve 1988: Pleasant and simple, a lightly fruity, cleanly made wine with modest flavors of melon and peach and a delicate texture. $6 (12/15/89) **77**

CRESTON

Sauvignon Blanc San Luis Obispo County 1987: A good-quality wine, with grassy, slightly woody and musty aromas and lively, fairly intense fruit flavors. $8.25 (12/15/89) **72**

DE LOACH

Fumé Blanc Russian River Valley 1990: Smooth and supple, with engaging peach, almond and vanilla aromas and flavors and just enough of an herbal edge to distinguish it as Sauvignon Blanc. Drinkable now. $9 (11/15/91) **84**

Fumé Blanc Russian River Valley 1988: Rich and concentrated, with tiers of pear, fig, lemon and grassy flavors that are supple and enticing with crisp acidity and good length. $9 (7/31/89) **86**

Sauvignon Blanc Russian River Valley 1989: Very aromatic, and even better on the palate, where the pungent herbal notes pick up lemon, lime and grapefruit flavors. Has a lean texture and a clean finish. 2,500 cases made. $9 (5/15/90) **84**

Sauvignon Blanc Russian River Valley 1988: A crisp, lean, lemony wine with a kiss of wood and herbs. Ultimately simple but very good. $9 (7/31/89) **81**

DRY CREEK

Fumé Blanc Sonoma County 1990: Has an oaky, earthy, grassy edge to the citrus and grapefruit flavors. Balanced, but with a few rough spots on the palate. Drink now. $9 (11/15/91) **82**

Sauvignon Blanc Sonoma County 1989: Crisp, delicate and elegant, with well-defined grapefruit, vanilla and sweet pea aromas and flavors in harmonious proportions. A likable wine to drink with seafood. Drinkable now. $9 (12/31/90) **87**

DUCKHORN

Sauvignon Blanc Napa Valley 1990: Rich and complex, with intriguing pear, fig, melon and toast flavors that are well integrated and balanced. Picks up a pretty caramel flavor on the finish. Drink now through 1994. A good value. $10 (2/15/92) **89**

Sauvignon Blanc Napa Valley 1989: Has tight, firm melon and grapefruit flavors that are crisp and lively, with a pretty touch of vanilla on the finish. Well balanced, nicely proportioned and ready to drink now. $10 (12/31/90) **87**

Sauvignon Blanc Napa Valley 1988: Lean and crisp with sharply defined grapefruit, vanilla and spicy pear flavor, all combining to give this wine plenty of flavor. Crisp aftertaste. Drink now or in 1993. $10 (2/15/90) **86**

ESTANCIA

Sauvignon Blanc Alexander Valley 1989: Pleasantly fruity, with a nice hint of pine to complement the pineapple and peach aromas and flavors. Light and lively right through the finish. $7 (3/15/91) **79**

Sauvignon Blanc Alexander Valley 1988: Round, rich and buttery, but it turns supple on the palate, echoing hints of almond and vanilla and a touch of grassiness. A smooth, stylish wine for current drinking. $6 (5/15/90) BB **82**

Sauvignon Blanc Monterey 1990: Crisp and citrusy, with strong oaky overtones and modest herbal, spicy flavors sneaking in on the finish. A sturdy style of Sauvignon Blanc. 4,000 cases made. $7.50 (6/15/92) BB **81**

ESTRELLA RIVER

Sauvignon Blanc Paso Robles 1987: A very aromatic, grassy wine that's well-balanced and fairly intense, with crisp citrus flavors backing up the strong herbal notes. $6 (12/15/89) **81**

FALLENLEAF

Sauvignon Blanc Sonoma Valley 1990: Full-bodied and heavy, without much charm or crisp fruit flavor. Earthy, chalky notes dominate, and it turns a bit sour on the finish. Tasted twice. 2,500 cases made. $9 (6/15/92) **73**

FERRARI-CARANO

Fumé Blanc Sonoma County 1990: A big, rich wine, with ripe peach and pineapple flavors, herbal overtones and an almost sweet, fruity finish. Full-bodied, full flavored and immediately appealing. $10 (7/15/91) **87**

Fumé Blanc Sonoma County 1989: Elegant and perfumed, light and tasty, with moderate depth and concentration. The pear, grapefruit and melon notes are attractive, but they thin out on the finish. $10 (10/15/90) **80**

Fumé Blanc Sonoma County 1988: Rich, intense and concentrated with round, smooth fruit that offers grapefruit, citrus, fig and stone flavors that finish with a soft touch. $9 (9/15/89) **88**

Fumé Blanc Sonoma County 1987 $9 (3/15/89) **89**

FETZER

Fumé Blanc California Valley Oaks Fumé 1989: Unusual melon and toast aromas and flavors are appealing in this off-dry, fruity wine. Sweet and simple; drink cold. $6.50 (12/31/90) **76**

Fumé Blanc California Valley Oaks Fumé 1988: Medium-bodied with nice fresh fruit flavors. Noticeable spritz adds to the crispness. Grassy and citrus flavors are intense enough to provide interest to typical varietal characteristics. Decent lemony aftertaste. $6.50 (7/31/89) **79**

Sauvignon Blanc California Barrel Select 1990: Fruity in flavor and soft in texture, medium-bodied, with character from its herb and apple notes. $9 (2/15/92) **80**

FIRESTONE

Sauvignon Blanc Santa Ynez Valley 1987: Herbal, vegetal aromas and flavors are an acquired taste, but the finish is clean and some fig fruit shows at the end. $7.50 (12/15/89) **77**

FLORA SPRINGS

Sauvignon Blanc Napa Valley 1990: One of the best Sauvignon Blancs available, and at a good price, too. Intense and flavorful, with creamy pear, vanilla, spice and honeyed nutmeg notes and a soft finish. A complex, ripe wine. Drink now to 1993. 4,500 cases made. $9.25 (11/30/91) SS **90**

Sauvignon Blanc Napa Valley 1988: Odd mossy, musty aromas override the crisp lemon and fig flavors. Tastes flat and dull overall. Tasted three times. $8.50 (3/31/90) **67**

Sauvignon Blanc Napa Valley Soliloquy Special Select 1989: A lively, light wine, showing finesse and subtlety to the lemon and vanilla-tinged grapefruit flavors. Has better length than most '89s. 350 cases made. $20 (3/15/91) **88**

FREMONT CREEK

Sauvignon Blanc Mendocino-Napa Counties 1989: Crisp and herbal, with nice vanilla notes to round out the lemon and bay leaf varietal character. Drinkable now. 3,000 cases made. $5.50 (10/15/91) BB **82**

J. FRITZ

Sauvignon Blanc Dry Creek Valley 1989: Straightforward, fruity and somewhat resiny and stale on the finish. Not for everyone. 3,000 cases made. $8 (10/15/91) **72**

FROG'S LEAP

Sauvignon Blanc Napa Valley 1990: Definitely oaky, but light enough to show off pleasant grapefruit flavor, as well. Keeps a delicate enough touch to have finesse. Drinkable now. $10 (10/15/91) **85**

Sauvignon Blanc Napa Valley 1989: Has good intensity and focus of flavors, with perfumed lemon, citrus, pear and melon notes that are lively and elegant. Finishes with a hint of almond. Drink now. $9.50 (10/31/90) **87**

Sauvignon Blanc Napa Valley 1988: A bit thin and watery with oak and grapefruit flavors that are decent but unexciting. $9.50 (11/30/89) **76**

GAINEY

Sauvignon Blanc Santa Barbara County 1987: Shows welcome restraint, with careful balance between acidity and fruit, offering delicate peach and lemon aromas and flavors plus a hint of varietal grassiness. Drink now. $8.50 (12/15/89) **82**

E. & J. GALLO

Sauvignon Blanc California Reserve 1989: Mostly crisp and grassy in flavor, with hints of peach and vanilla in the background. Clean and refreshing. $4 (7/31/91) BB **82**

GAN EDEN

Sauvignon Blanc Sonoma County 1988: Brutally aggressive, with a strong vegetal aroma and dull asparagus flavors. A disappointment from this winery. $9 (3/31/91) **72**

GEYSER PEAK

Sauvignon Blanc Sonoma County 1990: A racy wine, with hints of herb, spice and pepper seasoning the pear, grapefruit and melon notes; a complex wine. Drink now. $6.50 (4/15/92) BB **85**

GLEN ELLEN

Sauvignon Blanc California Proprietor's Reserve 1990: Has floral, piny aromas and flavors that are reminiscent of Riesling, with hints of melon and grapefruit. A pleasant, off-dry sipping wine. Drink soon. $6 (7/31/91) BB **80**

Sauvignon Blanc California Proprietor's Reserve 1989: Light, smooth, silky and a bit sweet, this wine has herb, orange and pear aromas and flavors that are not too aggressive. $5 (8/31/90) **77**

GREENWOOD RIDGE

Sauvignon Blanc Anderson Valley 1989: Soft and broad in texture, with lemon and toast aromas and flavors on the palate. Drinkable now. 725 cases made. $8 (10/15/91) **78**

GRGICH HILLS

Fumé Blanc Napa Valley 1990: A very concentrated, classic Sauvignon Blanc, with intense, crisp fruit and herb flavors that linger a long time on the finish. Has great balance and depth. Tastes fine now, but should develop more complexity if cellared till about 1993. $12 (2/15/92) **90**

Fumé Blanc Napa Valley 1989: An extreme wine, but it has lots of rich fig and pear flavors with onion and herb aromas. Smooth and floral on the palate. $11 (3/15/91) **85**

Fumé Blanc Napa Valley 1988: Rich and opulent, with sharply focused sweet pea, fig, melon and herbal notes that are intense and lively. Has fine depth, elegant balance and flavors that linger long and full on the finish. Drink now to 1993. $10 (3/31/90) **90**

Fumé Blanc Napa Valley 1987 $10 (7/31/89) **89**

GROTH

Sauvignon Blanc Napa Valley 1990: Fresh and lively, with pretty gooseberry, citrus, pear and nutmeg flavors that give it complexity. Has a smooth texture and picks up a grassy note on the finish. Drink now. $8.50 (11/30/91) **87**

Sauvignon Blanc Napa Valley 1989: Spicy, woody aromas and flavors don't quite cover the steely grapefruit and herbal qualities that come through on the finish. Lively and drinkable now. $8.50 (10/31/90) **81**

Sauvignon Blanc Napa Valley 1988: There's an attractive richness and fig-flavored quality to this wine, but it's also very woody, offering a roundness on the palate that's appealing, finishing with a touch of honey. Drink now. $8 (2/15/90) **85**

GUENOC

Sauvignon Blanc Guenoc Valley 1989: Smells extremely earthy and grassy, but comes together reasonably well on the palate in a crisp, earthy, almond-scented way. Not for everyone, but good within its style. $10 (4/30/91) **77**

Sauvignon Blanc Guenoc Valley Estate 1990: Intensely herbaceous and vegetal, an extreme wine that some may find too demanding, but for fans of open-throttle Sauvignon Blanc shaded by toasty oak, this may be your cup of wine. Drink now. $10 (4/15/92) **82**

HANDLEY

Sauvignon Blanc Dry Creek Valley 1988: A full, well-rounded wine with lemon and citrus aromas. The crisp citrus, grapefruit and pear flavors are backed by oaky richness, and the finish is smooth and buttery. $8 (8/31/90) **84**

HANNA

Sauvignon Blanc Sonoma County 1989: Crisp and light, with lots of agreeable floral, grapefruit and sweet pea aromas and flavors on a flexible frame. Pleasant to drink now. 4,600 cases made. $8.50 (7/15/91) **87**

Sauvignon Blanc Sonoma County 1988: Simple, watery and soft, with unusual anise aromas and flavors. Very dry and verging on bitter, with hints of lemon and herb. Tasted twice, with consistent results. 4,148 cases made. $8.75 (8/31/90) **71**

HAWK CREST

Sauvignon Blanc California 1989: Light, slightly grassy, very fruity and generous, with tutti frutti flavors echoing on the finish. A pleasant, clearly varietal wine. $6 (8/31/90) BB **80**

Sauvignon Blanc California 1988: Light and lemony, with hints of herbs and onion skin aromas and flavors, fresh and easy to drink. $6 (5/15/90) **76**

Sauvignon Blanc California 1987: Rich, round and ripe, with a sense of restraint that reins in the finish and keeps it from being overblown. Fig and toast flavors prevail. A good value. $6 (10/31/89) BB **83**

HAYWOOD

Fumé Blanc Sonoma Valley 1988: Crisp, tart and lively with fresh, clean fig, lemon and citrus notes that keep you coming back for another glass. Gains complexity. 729 cases made. $9.50 (11/30/89) **88**

Fumé Blanc Sonoma Valley Los Chamizal Vineyards 1990: An earthy, herbal-tasting wine that shows oak influence in the stylish spice and vanilla aromas. The fruit component is modest, with herbal-oak complexity taking the lead. 820 cases made. $9.50 (6/15/92) **81**

HIDDEN CELLARS

Sauvignon Blanc Mendocino County 1990: Fresh, clean and lively, with rich fig, herb, citrus and melon flavors that are elegant and sharply focused. Finishes with subtle oak shadings. Delicious to drink now. 1,676 cases made. $9 (4/15/92) **88**

Sauvignon Blanc Mendocino County 1989: Crisp and lemony, with a fragrant edge of oak that perfumes the basic citrus and herb flavors, which persist into the finish. Drinkable now. 2,130 cases made. $9 (11/15/91) **87**

Sauvignon Blanc Mendocino County White Table Wine Alchemy 1989: Ripe and spicy, with a wonderful round texture. Offers honey, lemon and pear aromas and flavors and hints of butterscotch and nutmeg on the long finish. A grand wine, with a distinctive style; comes in a tall bottle with a long cork. 295 cases made. $18 (7/31/91) **90**

HONIG

Sauvignon Blanc Napa Valley 1990: Very fresh, fruity and crisp, with lively apple and citrus flavors and hints of herbs and vanilla on the finish. A zingy, nicely balanced wine. $9.25 (6/15/92) **85**

Sauvignon Blanc Napa Valley 1989: Fresh and fruity, with generous peach, grapefruit and slightly herbal overtones and a perfumed finish. Drinkable now for its refreshing balance. $9 (11/15/91) **84**

Sauvignon Blanc Napa Valley 1988: Lean and crisp, with nicely focused grapefruit and herb aromas and flavors. Simple and straightforward. Drinkable now. $8.75 (5/15/90) **78**

Sauvignon Blanc Napa Valley 1987 $8.75 (7/31/89) **84**

HUSCH

Sauvignon Blanc Mendocino 1990: Smooth and flavorful, with beautifully modulated pear, grapefruit and spice aromas and flavors persisting into a long finish. Emphasizes fruit and delicacy without sacrificing intensity. Drinkable now. $8.50 (11/15/91) **87**

Key to Symbols

The scores reported here are the results of blind tastings conducted by our panel of senior editors. Wines that carry the initials below are results of individual tastings.

THE WINE SPECTATOR 100-POINT SCALE ***95-100***—Classic, a great wine; ***90-94***—Outstanding, superior character and style; ***80-89***—Good to very good, a wine with special qualities; ***70-79***—Average, drinkable wine that may have minor flaws; ***60-69***—Below average, drinkable but not recommended; ***50-59***—Poor, undrinkable, not recommended. "+"—With a score indicates a range; used primarily with barrel tastings to indicate a preliminary score.

SPECIAL DESIGNATIONS SS—Spectator Selection, CS—Cellar Selection, BB—Best Buy, ($NA)—Price not available, (NR)—Not released.

TASTER'S INITIALS (JG)—Jim Gordon, (HS)—Harvey Steiman, (JL)—James Laube, (JS)—James Suckling, (TM)—Thomas Matthews, (TR)—Terry Robards, (PM)—Per-Henrik Mansson, (BT)—Barrel Tasting (these wines were tasted blind from barrel samples), (CA-date)—*California's Great Cabernets* by James Laube, (CH-date)—*California's Great Chardonnays* by James Laube, (VP-date)—*Vintage Port* by James Suckling.

DATE TASTED Dates in parentheses represent the issue in which the rating was published.

INNISFREE

Sauvignon Blanc Napa Valley 1989: Very pretty floral aromas and flavors enhance the soft grapefruit and peach notes at the core. A supple wine, with understated varietal character. Balanced to drink soon. $7.50 (4/30/91) **82**

IRON HORSE

Fumé Blanc Alexander Valley Barrel Fermented 1989: Straightforward and fruity, with grass and mineral notes, this wine is balanced and clean on the finish. Drink now. Tasted twice. 4,500 cases made. $11 (8/31/90) **77**

Fumé Blanc Alexander Valley Barrel Fermented 1988: Has an oaky style, with vanilla, spice and woodsy aromas. The crisp Sauvignon Blanc flavor marries well with the oak on the palate. $11 (11/30/89) **84**

Fumé Blanc Alexander Valley T-T Vineyards Barrel Fermented 1990: Full-bodied, rich and spicy, with roundness from oak and lots of herb, grapefruit and pear aromas and flavors, all packaged smoothly and gracefully. Drinkable now, but could improve with cellaring until 1993. 3,500 cases made. $15 (10/15/91) **89**

JEPSON

Sauvignon Blanc Mendocino 1987: Dull, earthy, very soft and herbal. Drinkable now, but don't wait. $7 (7/31/89) **66**

KENDALL-JACKSON

Sauvignon Blanc Lake County Vintner's Reserve 1989: With powerful grassy, fruity aromas, full, crisp flavors and a lingering, light finish, this is unmistakably Sauvignon Blanc. Herb, vanilla and tasty peach flavors fill out the profile. $9 (10/31/90) **90**

Sauvignon Blanc Lake County Vintner's Reserve 1988: One sip calls for more. Deliciously fruity, juicy and refreshing. A harmonious combination of long-lasting peach, green apple and herb flavors in a very clean package. $9 (3/31/90) **89**

KENWOOD

Sauvignon Blanc Sonoma County 1990: A different beast from this consistent producer. Strongly herbal, almost oniony, with just enough citrus flavors to make it approachable. Drinkable now. Tasted twice. $9.50 (11/15/91) **78**

Sauvignon Blanc Sonoma County 1988: Smells like orange blossoms, tastes crisp and tart, with good varietal character, and a touch of the orange and citrus flavors coming through. Intriguing flavors. $9 (11/30/89) **85**

KONOCTI

Fumé Blanc Lake County 1990: Crisp and floral, with generous grapefruit, melon and sweet pea aromas and flavors broadening on the finish. A lovely wine to drink now. $7.50 (2/15/92) BB **87**

KUNDE

Sauvignon Blanc Sonoma Valley 1990: A light, simple wine, with modest citrus and spice aromas and flavors. Rests gently on the palate and finishes with slightly sweet vanilla flavors. Tasted twice. $9 (6/15/92) **81**

LAKESPRING

Sauvignon Blanc Napa Valley 1988: Has barnyardy aromas and similar flavors. Intense and tart, but it lacks the fruit flavor to offset the hard, vegetal tartness. Some may like its earthiness. 5,000 cases made. $8.50 (11/30/89) **76**

Sauvignon Blanc Napa Valley Yountmill Vineyard 1990: Crisp and lively, with a solid streak of grapefruit flavor that persists into the finish, balancing an odd onion character on the nose. Has a nice tweak of oak to round it off. Drinkable now. $8.50 (10/15/91) **83**

LONG

Sauvignon Blanc Napa Valley 1989: Lean and austere, with modest earth and lemon aromas and flavors. Drinkable. Tasted three times. $12 (7/15/91) **78**

Sauvignon Blanc Sonoma County 1987: Crisp, tart and structured, with buttery, citrus and vanilla flavors along with a measure of finesse and charm. $11 (1/31/89) **87**

MARKHAM

Sauvignon Blanc Napa Valley 1990: Crisp and fresh, with well-defined, concentrated nectarine, lemon and herb aromas and flavors that are lively and refreshing on the finish. Easy to like. Drink soon. $8 (10/15/91) **87**

Sauvignon Blanc Napa Valley 1989: A touch of oak adds spice to this focused, tasty wine that's very interesting, refreshing and fruity. Grapefruit flavors last through the aftertaste. 3,000 cases made. $7 (10/31/90) BB **87**

Sauvignon Blanc Napa Valley 1988: A mild-mannered, clean and supple wine, with herb, spice and citrus flavors that are delicate and understated. $7 (9/15/89) **82**

Sauvignon Blanc Napa Valley 1987 $7 (4/15/89) **86**

LOUIS M. MARTINI

Sauvignon Blanc Napa Valley 1989: Soft and fruity, offering light grapefruit and mineral aromas and flavors. Drinkable now. $8 (4/30/91) **80**

MATANZAS CREEK

Sauvignon Blanc Sonoma County 1990: Tangy and delicious, a very flavorful wine, with loads of grapefruit, pineapple and apricot flavors that are focused and crisp. $12 (4/15/92) **87**

Sauvignon Blanc Sonoma County 1989: Fairly full-bodied and flavorful, with generous pear, vanilla and grapefruit aromas and flavors. This is a polished, stylish wine. Drink soon. $12 (7/15/91) **85**

Sauvignon Blanc Sonoma County 1988: Big, rich and full-bodied, with well-defined fig, pear and spice notes and hints of herb, vanilla and oak on the finish. Drink now or in 1993. $12 (2/15/90) **86**

Sauvignon Blanc Sonoma County 1987 $12 (3/15/89) **85**

MAYACAMAS

Sauvignon Blanc Napa Valley 1989: An earthy wine, with strong oak and mineral aromas and flavors and hints of honey and toast on the finish. Has very little fruit flavor. Tasted twice, with consistent notes. 780 cases made. $11 (10/15/91) **75**

Sauvignon Blanc Napa Valley 1988: Tastes and smells swampy and weedy. There's intensity, but not enough to overpower the off-putting flavors. $11 (8/31/90) **66**

Sauvignon Blanc Napa Valley 1987: Elegant, smooth and creamy, with vanilla, delicate pear and citrus flavors that are clean and refreshing. An appealing wine that doesn't attempt to overwhelm you with varietal intensity. $11 (9/15/89) **87**

MCDOWELL VALLEY

Fumé Blanc Mendocino 1989: Extremely earthy, but grapefruit and pineapple flavors sneak through on the finish to rescue it. Drinkable now. $8.50 (11/15/91) **73**

Fumé Blanc Mendocino 1988: A good-quality wine, with grassy, oniony aromas and lemon and melon flavors. Balanced toward the soft side. Easy to drink now. $7.50 (3/31/90) **79**

MERRYVALE

Sauvignon Blanc Napa Valley Meritage 1989: Crisp and fruity, focusing on grapefruit, with strong overtones of herbs and onion skins. A distinctive wine for those who like the herbal style. Drink soon. 1,000 cases made. $12 (4/30/91) **80**

ROBERT MONDAVI

Fumé Blanc Napa Valley 1989: Complex and lively, with pretty pear, sweet pea, spice and citrus flavors that are crisp and well proportioned. Shows good concentration of flavors for an '89. Drink now. $9.50 (11/15/91) **87**

Fumé Blanc Napa Valley 1988: Soft, broad and herbal, with candied, leafy, green aromas and flavors. An odd duck, not for everyone, but it has decent lemon-grapefruit aromas and flavors. Tasted twice. $9.50 (5/15/90) **74**

Fumé Blanc Napa Valley 1987: Snappy, lean and lively, sporting vivid pear and melon aromas and

flavors balanced artfully with the varietal grassiness and herbal component. Long and impressively complex. Drink now. $9.50 (7/31/89) **87**
Fumé Blanc Napa Valley To-Kalon Vineyard Reserve 1990: Spicy oak dominates the fruit in this full-bodied wine. Ginger, nutmeg and vanilla flavors make it very interesting, though one-dimensional. We'd like more depth of fruit, but it's still pretty dazzling. $17.50 (2/15/92) **82**
Fumé Blanc Napa Valley To-Kalon Vineyard Reserve 1989: Herbal, grassy and decidedly oaky, this has a polished texture and a spicy flavor from the sweet oak. A Graves style that obscures the fruit in favor of oak. $15 (7/15/91) **83**
Fumé Blanc Napa Valley To-Kalon Vineyard Reserve 1988: Distinctive and unusually oaky in style, this has pleasant butter and cedar flavors, but not much fruit except for a little orange and apricot. Finishes nice and smooth. $15 (8/31/90) **84**
Fumé Blanc Napa Valley To-Kalon Vineyard Reserve 1987 $15 (3/31/90) **80**
Fumé Blanc Napa Valley To-Kalon Vineyard Reserve 1986 $15 (7/31/89) **77**
Sauvignon Blanc California White 1987: A fine wine for the money. Lean and simple, with a slightly sweet lemon flavor, good length and herbal, sweet pea flavor on the finish. $5 (3/15/89) BB **81**
Sauvignon Blanc California Woodbridge 1990: Crisp and refreshing, with a nice core of citrus, pear, spice and melon flavors. An elegant, refined wine to drink now. $5.50 (6/15/92) BB **83**
Sauvignon Blanc California Woodbridge 1989: Solid, fruity and flavorful, with more than a hint of herb and onion to go along with the appealing peach and melon flavors. The taste lingers. Drink soon. $5 (4/30/91) BB **80**
Sauvignon Blanc California Woodbridge 1988: Smooth and simple, but the crisp zest of lemony acidity lingers long after the attractive peach and herbal aromas and flavors fade. $5 (10/31/89) **78**

MONTEREY VINEYARD
Sauvignon Blanc Monterey County Classic 1989: An assertively fruity tasting wine that shows off Sauvignon Blanc's grassy, sweet pea notes, plus a touch of grapefruit. It's well balanced and very flavorful, but will be too herbaceous for some. $5.50 (3/31/91) **79**

MORGAN
Sauvignon Blanc Alexander Valley 1988: Lean and crisp, with tightly focused lemon, melon and green pepper aromas and flavors intermingling attractively. A neatly proportioned, somewhat austere wine offering more harmony than most. $8.50 (11/30/89) **83**

MURPHY-GOODE
Fumé Blanc Alexander Valley 1987: Distinctive and flavorful, leaning toward woody and celerylike vegetal characteristics, balanced, lean and concentrated. Drink soon if you like the style. $7.50 (3/15/89) **76**
Fumé Blanc Alexander Valley Barrel Fermented Reserve 1990: Stands out from the pack. A rich-tasting, rich-textured wine, with butter and vanilla overtones to the citrus and pear flavors. Has depth, elegance and a long finish. $12.50 (2/15/92) **90**
Fumé Blanc Alexander Valley Estate Vineyard 1990: Unusually satisfying, with plenty of flavor and a rich texture. Very fruity, lush and broad, with ripe pineapple and papaya flavors and a lingering finish. $9 (7/15/91) **87**
Fumé Blanc Alexander Valley Estate Vineyard 1988: An intense, concentrated wine, with layers of nectarine, peach and herb overtones framed by toasty oak. Complex and enticing. Drink now. $8 (11/30/89) **89**

NAVARRO
Sauvignon Blanc Anderson Valley Cuvée 128 1990: Crisp, intense and sharply focused, with concentrated pear, citrus, melon and spice flavors framed by toasty oak notes. A rich, complex wine that can be enjoyed now or cellared through 1994. A very good value. $9.75 (6/15/92) **88**

OCTOPUS MOUNTAIN
Sauvignon Blanc Anderson Valley 1989: Steely, austere and extremely grassy and herbal. Tart, with plenty of flavor and enough sweet oak notes on the finish to keep it in balance. Drinkable now, but cellaring until 1993 wouldn't hurt. $9 (10/15/91) **87**

PARDUCCI
Fumé Blanc Mendocino County Cellarmaster Selection 1988: Lean and austere, with flavors that lean more toward onion and herbs than fruit. Fresh and clean, however, and best to drink soon. $12 (4/30/91) **82**
Sauvignon Blanc Mendocino County 1988: Tastes sweet and grassy, in a light, non-oaky style. Has citrus and herbal flavors and a fairly crisp finish. $7.50 (5/15/90) **78**

ROBERT PECOTA
Sauvignon Blanc Napa Valley 1989: Butterscotch, honey and grass notes make this an interesting wine, but more fruit flavors would round out the package. 5,000 cases made. $9.25 (8/31/90) **78**
Sauvignon Blanc Napa Valley 1985 $9.25 (10/15/86) SS **94**

J. PEDRONCELLI
Fumé Blanc Sonoma County 1990: Ripe and flavorful, with lots of pear and pineapple flavors to liven it up. The crisp texture is rounded on the finish, with a nice touch of vanilla. Drinkable now. 4,000 cases made. $8 (10/15/91) **85**
Fumé Blanc Dry Creek Valley 1989: Aromatic, with grassy, almost onionlike scents and a nice core of grapefruit and guava flavor. Crisp, lively, flavorful and distinctive. Drink now. $7 (4/30/91) BB **84**
Fumé Blanc Dry Creek Valley 1988: Concentrated and exuberantly fruity. Smells and tastes lively, with full orange and grapefruit flavors and a lingering finish. 2,000 cases made. $6 (9/15/89) BB **83**
Fumé Blanc Dry Creek Valley 1987: Intense, lively and true to type. Aggressively grassy in aroma, with lemon, melon and herbal flavors. $6 (4/30/89) **79**

ROBERT PEPI
Sauvignon Blanc Napa Valley 1987: Simple but likable, with smoke, lemon and grass hues that taste stale. The finish tapers off. $8.50 (11/30/89) **76**
Sauvignon Blanc Napa Valley Two-Heart Canopy 1990: Intense lemon, grapefruit and floral notes soften on the palate. Has plenty of flavor. Ready to drink now. $9.50 (11/15/91) **81**
Sauvignon Blanc Napa Valley Two-Heart Canopy 1989: Firm and sharply focused, with concentrated peach, orange and herbal aromas and flavors lightly framed by oak. Balanced and nicely focused. A lovely wine to drink now or hold until late 1993. $9.50 (3/31/91) **88**
Sauvignon Blanc Napa Valley Two-Heart Canopy 1988: Has plenty of fresh, ripe fruit and spicy oak, with layers of herb, vanilla, pear and spice in a crisp, well-focused wine that finishes with vanilla and grapefruit. Drink now. $9.50 (2/15/90) **87**

JOSEPH PHELPS
Sauvignon Blanc Napa Valley 1990: An earthier, oakier wine, but it succeeds with enough rich pear and melon flavors underneath. Drink now. $10 (4/15/92) **82**
Sauvignon Blanc Napa Valley 1988: We can't get past the awful aromas of decaying vegetables and rubber. A bit better on the palate, but still undrinkable. Tasted twice, with consistent results. $9.50 (6/30/90) **55**

R.H. PHILLIPS
Sauvignon Blanc California Night Harvest 1991: A classic, with all the crisp fruitiness you could want. Apple, quince and lightly herbal flavors combine for a concentrated, focused wine, with fine balance and a good finish. 4,050 cases made. $3.50/500ml (6/15/92) BB **86**
Sauvignon Blanc Yolo County Dunnigan Hills Night Harvest 1987: Tart but not fresh or fruity. Has a bit of varietal grassiness, but it's difficult to like. $4 (3/15/89) **67**

PLAM
Fumé Blanc Napa Valley 1989: Oak aging has given this wine a buttery, vanilla aftertaste, and its fruit flavors are lean and simple. Of good quality. 1,710 cases made. $9 (11/15/91) **80**

PRESTON
Sauvignon Blanc Dry Creek Valley Cuvée de Fumé 1990: A classic that blends grassy, sweet pea flavors with ripe pineapple and melon notes for a rich style that's true to the variety. Very crisp and well balanced, with lingering fruit flavors on the finish. $9.50 (7/15/91) **87**
Sauvignon Blanc Dry Creek Valley Cuvée de Fumé 1989: Very good. Lean, crisp and fairly tart, with good concentration of pineapple and grapefruit flavors and a lingering finish. $8 (5/15/90) **86**
Sauvignon Blanc Dry Creek Valley Cuvée de Fumé 1988: Fresh and fruity with herb, grass, melon and spice flavors that are rich, intense and lively. $8 (9/15/89) **86**
Sauvignon Blanc Dry Creek Valley Estate Reserve 1989: Strives for complexity, with toasty oak flavors, but underneath the fruit is clean, simple and crisp. Has citrus, melon and herb flavors, but they fan out and get watery on the finish. Drink now. 2,700 cases made. $12 (12/31/90) **82**
Sauvignon Blanc Dry Creek Valley Estate Reserve 1988: Tart and refreshing, with crisp, delicate grapefruit, spice and herb flavors that are clean and lively all the way to the finish. 2,100 cases made. $10 (11/30/89) **87**

QUAIL RIDGE
Sauvignon Blanc Napa Valley 1990: The lightly perfumed aromas are attractive, but the palate lacks richness and depth. Has full-bodied herb, fig and melon notes that gain on the finish. Drink now. 4,900 cases made. $8 (4/15/92) **84**
Sauvignon Blanc Napa Valley 1989: Tightly wound, with modest peach, floral and pear flavors kept in check by firm tannins and acidity. Austere on the finish. Drink now. $8 (12/31/90) **80**
Sauvignon Blanc Napa Valley 1988: Earthy with herb, grapefruit, apple and tobacco notes, it's mellow and smooth on the palate. Crisp and refreshing. $8 (11/30/89) **85**
Sauvignon Blanc Napa Valley 1987 $7.50 (3/15/89) **89**

QUIVIRA
Sauvignon Blanc Dry Creek Valley 1990: Has a pretty core of rich citrus, pear and lemon flavors. Tight and focused, with balance and length. Drink now or in 1993. $10 (11/15/91) **84**
Sauvignon Blanc Dry Creek Valley 1989: Has true varietal herb and citus notes, but the flavors turn simple and diluted on the finish. Pleasant but unexciting. $9.25 (10/31/90) **83**
Sauvignon Blanc Dry Creek Valley 1988: Intense and lively with rich, concentrated but not overblown Sauvignon Blanc flavor that offers layers of herb, fig and oak flavors that finish with a kiss of apple. $9.50 (11/30/89) **88**

RAYMOND
Sauvignon Blanc Napa Valley 1989: Tart, lemony and decidedly herbal, this lean, crisp wine would be refreshing with a light seafood dish. $10 (4/30/91) **80**
Sauvignon Blanc Napa Valley 1988: Crisp, light and delicately balanced, with sharply focused grapefruit and subtle herb flavors that echo nicely on the finish. Drinkable now. $8.50 (11/30/89) **88**
Sauvignon Blanc Napa Valley 1987: Won't shortchange you on rich, concentrated fruit. The ripe fig, citrus and grapefruit flavors are well knit and well focused, and the finish follows through with nice flavors. $8 (1/31/89) **85**

RENAISSANCE
Sauvignon Blanc North Yuba 1988: Dull, woody aromas and flavors obscure the fruit, making this soft wine uninteresting. Drinkable now. 5,000 cases made. $10 (11/15/91) **75**

ROCHIOLI
Sauvignon Blanc Russian River Valley 1990: A racy, herbaceous wine, with lively, concentrated citrus, grapefruit, melon and pear flavors and a nice touch of sage and spice. Balanced and complex. Drink now or in 1993. $9 (11/15/91) **87**

ROUND HILL
Fumé Blanc Napa Valley House 1989: Smoky, toasty, spicy aromas and flavors rest on a lean, almost delicate frame in this stylish wine that could use a touch more fruit to round it out. Should be fine with a fish dish. $5.75 (11/30/90) BB **83**

RUTHERFORD HILL
Sauvignon Blanc Napa Valley 1987: Toasty and herbal, with celery and toasted onion overtones to the melon flavor. Well structured, but the odd flavors will make its appeal a matter of personal taste. $8 (7/31/89) **75**

ST. CLEMENT
Sauvignon Blanc Napa Valley 1990: A distinctive, concentrated wine, with spicy caramel tinges that add to the basic floral, herbal, grapefruit aromas and flavors. Crisp, tasty and drinkable now. 2,800 cases made. $9.75 (10/15/91) **88**
Sauvignon Blanc Napa Valley 1989: Has the usual grass, lemon and sweet pea aromas and flavors, and it's medium-bodied, with pretty good length. Drink now. 3,140 cases made. $9.50 (8/31/90) **81**
Sauvignon Blanc Napa Valley 1988: A grassy, herbal style that's clean, elegant and balanced, with quince, sweet pea and tart fig notes of moderate depth and intensity. Drink now. $9.50 (3/31/90) **78**
Sauvignon Blanc Napa Valley 1987 $9.50 (7/31/89) **68**

ST. SUPERY
Sauvignon Blanc Napa Valley Dollarhide Ranch 1989: Lean and lemony, with spicy cucumber flavors that won't appeal to everyone but are definitely refreshing. Drink soon. $8 (3/15/91) **82**
Sauvignon Blanc Napa Valley Dollarhide Ranch 1988: Pineapple and grapefruit aromas and flavors enliven this wine, making this one of the most exotic Sauvignon Blancs we've tasted. It's also appealing for its liveliness and toasty oak character. Drink now. $7.50 (10/31/89) **87**

SANFORD
Sauvignon Blanc Santa Barbara County 1989: An awkward wine that has little to recommend it. Vegetal, very soft and almost sweet. Tasted twice. 4,000 cases made. $9 (7/31/91) **65**
Sauvignon Blanc Santa Barbara County 1987: The distinctly varietal fresh, grassy aromas are balanced against the ripe melon and crisp lemon flavors that carry through to the long finish. A distinctive wine. Drink soon. $8.50 (12/15/89) **85**

SANTA BARBARA
Sauvignon Blanc Santa Ynez Valley Reserve 1987: Oaky, earthy aromas and flavors dominate this heavy-handed wine. $11 (12/15/89) **68**
Sauvignon Blanc Santa Ynez Valley Valley View Vineyards 1987: Very oaky. A buttery character dominates the aromas and flavors, but there' s just enough fruit underneath to keep it in line. $8.50 (12/15/89) **72**

SHENANDOAH
Sauvignon Blanc Amador County 1990: An ebulliently fruity, ripe wine, with exotic tropical fruit flavors, a spicy accent from oak aging and a big, round texture. Assertive and flavorful. $7.50 (10/15/91) **84**

SIGNORELLO
Sauvignon Blanc Napa Valley 1987: Lively on the palate with typical sweet pea flavors. Nicely balanced. $8.25 (4/30/89) **78**

SILVERADO
Sauvignon Blanc Napa Valley 1990: Clean and simple, with modest citrus and pear-scented flavors. Picks up a touch of oak and spice on the finish. Drink now. $9 (11/30/91) **84**
Sauvignon Blanc Napa Valley 1989: Herbal, grassy aromas and flavors are moderately rich and well balanced, with hints of onion, pear and melon, finishing with crisp lemony notes. Has moderate concentration. Drink up. $9 (10/31/90) **83**
Sauvignon Blanc Napa Valley 1988: Hard to imagine a better California Sauvignon Blanc. Rich, intense and loaded with ripe fig, lemon, herb and spice flavors. Has a very enticing, fine structure, with lively flavors that build to the finish and linger. Drink now. $8.50 (2/15/90) SS **90**

UNITED STATES
CALIFORNIA/SAUVIGNON BLANC

SIMI
Sauvignon Blanc Mendocino-Sonoma-Napa Counties 1990: Grassy and herbal, with a strong weedy character that turns to citrus and grapefruit on the finish, with a trace of bitterness. Ready now. $9 (2/15/92) **83**
Sauvignon Blanc Sonoma County 1989: An extremely bold, flavorful wine, with pine, pineapple and herbaceous aromas that lead to vibrant grapefruit flavors. Makes up in power what it lacks in finesse. $9.50 (4/30/91) **84**
Sauvignon Blanc Sonoma County 1988: A polished, distinctive wine that's crisp and flavorful, with ripe, spicy, concentrated flavors of rich, honeyed quince and fig. Has hints of grassiness and impressive length. Drinkable now. $8 (10/31/90) **90**
Sauvignon Blanc Sonoma County 1987: Extremely tart, leaves your mouth watering, but it could use a little more richness and fruit. For fans of steely wines. $9.50 (7/31/89) **72**

SPOTTSWOODE
Sauvignon Blanc Napa Valley 1989: Fresh, lively, dry and crisp, with lovely lemon, melon and grassy aromas and flavors. It's not complex. Drink now. 2,400 cases made. $11 (8/31/90) **81**

STAG'S LEAP WINE CELLARS
Sauvignon Blanc Napa Valley Rancho Chimiles 1990: Tart, thin and lemony, with a narrow flavor band and a heavy splash of oak. Could use a little more concentration. Drink now. Tasted twice. $10 (11/15/91) **78**
Sauvignon Blanc Napa Valley Rancho Chimiles 1988: An earthy, bitter wine with sour edges and just enough fruit to make it drinkable. Tasted twice. $9 (11/30/89) **76**
Sauvignon Blanc Napa Valley Rancho Chimiles 1987: Rich, concentrated and a bit exaggerated with spice, herb and smoke flavors that are well focused but a shade coarse around the edges. $9 (1/31/89) **80**

STERLING
Sauvignon Blanc Napa Valley 1990: Tart and earthy, with citrus, grapefruit and tobacco flavors. Spritzy and light, but it has pleasant tart apple notes. Drink now. $8.50 (11/30/91) **80**
Sauvignon Blanc Napa Valley 1989: A disappointing vintage. Has lots of lemon and grapefruit aromas and flavors, plus a touch of herbs, but lacks in structure and hints at bitterness on the finish. Tasted twice. $9 (3/15/91) **79**
Sauvignon Blanc Napa Valley 1988: Plenty of herb, sage and lemony flavors in a clean, crisp, firm wine that finishes with tart acidity. Well balanced and likable. $9 (11/30/89) **84**

STONEGATE
Sauvignon Blanc Napa Valley 1990: Tight and austere, with flinty citrus, pear and spice flavors. Crisp and focused; an elegant wine that's ready to drink now through 1993. 1,700 cases made. $9.50 (11/15/91) **87**
Sauvignon Blanc Napa Valley 1988: Well balanced and packed with fruit complexity, a very good wine. Has fresh citrus aromas, ripe but crisp apple, pear and grapefruit flavors and a long finish. 2,000 cases made. $8.50 (6/30/90) **87**

STRATFORD
Sauvignon Blanc California 1988: A big, rich, fruity wine, with fig, herb, and ripe fruit flavors. Full-bodied, oaky and assertive. $8 (5/15/90) **83**
Sauvignon Blanc California Partners' Reserve 1989: Fresh and lively, with pleasant grapefruit, spice and vanilla aromas and flavors that spread nicely on the palate. Drink now, while it's crisp. $9.50 (11/15/91) **85**

RODNEY STRONG
Sauvignon Blanc Alexander Valley Charlotte's Home Vineyard 1989: Odd fruit cocktail aromas and flavors make this seem inelegant and unimpressive. It's drinkable, though. $9 (11/15/91) **75**

SUNNY ST. HELENA
Sauvignon Blanc Napa Valley 1989: Light, fresh and floral, with modest melon and herb flavors. Drinkable now. 820 cases made. $9 (4/30/91) **79**

SUTTER HOME
Sauvignon Blanc California 1989: Tastes very clean and fruity, in a style that many people will like. It has generous grapefruit, melon and grassy flavors of moderate depth. Seems a bit sweet on the finish. $4.50 (4/30/91) **79**

TAFT STREET
Sauvignon Blanc Sonoma County 1990: Crisp and lively, with generous herb, apple and grapefruit aromas and flavors. Drink it soon. $6.50 (6/15/92) BB **83**
Sauvignon Blanc Sonoma County 1989: Very light, thin, almost stale and decidedly earthy on the finish. Not a fun wine. $8 (10/15/91) **68**

PHILIP TOGNI
Sauvignon Blanc Napa Valley 1989: Undeniably flavorful, but it won't be everyone's style. A distinctive example of a grassy, vegetal-tasting Sauvignon Blanc. It has the whole produce section: bell peppers, onion, celery and more. Drink soon. 620 cases made. $12.50 (7/15/91) **82**

M.G. VALLEJO
Fumé Blanc California 1988: Spicy floral and vanilla aromas and delicate pineapple flavors make this an immediately appealing wine, and the herbal hints on the finish put a nice touch on it. Drink now. $4 (5/15/90) BB **81**

VENTANA
Sauvignon Blanc Monterey 1988: Made in a ripe, almost butterscotchy style, rich but not heavy. Has grassy, herbal notes that could blend better with the ripe flavors. $8 (3/31/90) **81**
Sauvignon Blanc Monterey 1987: A tight, nicely balanced wine, with crisp texture, toasted onion aromas and lemon, slightly herbal flavors. None of it is excessive, making a wine that ought to be good companion to a chunk of grilled fish. $8 (10/31/89) **85**

VIANSA
Sauvignon Blanc Napa-Sonoma Counties 1988: Pungent and vegetal, with onion, red bell pepper and spice flavors galore, but not much in the way of fruit. Simple and somewhat diluted, lacking depth and concentration. 3,775 cases made. $10 (10/31/90) **73**
Sauvignon Blanc Sonoma-Napa Counties 1987: Balanced and pleasant, displaying a nice touch of melon and peach flavors that are balanced against an herbal backdrop. A well-made wine with a rather intense finish. Drink now. $9.50 (4/30/89) **81**

Key to Symbols

The scores reported here are the results of blind tastings conducted by our panel of senior editors. Wines that carry the initials below are results of individual tastings.

THE WINE SPECTATOR 100-POINT SCALE ***95-100***—Classic, a great wine; ***90-94***—Outstanding, superior character and style; ***80-89***—Good to very good, a wine with special qualities; ***70-79***—Average, drinkable wine that may have minor flaws; ***60-69***—Below average, drinkable but not recommended; ***50-59***—Poor, undrinkable, not recommended. "+"—With a score indicates a range; used primarily with barrel tastings to indicate a preliminary score.

SPECIAL DESIGNATIONS SS—Spectator Selection, CS—Cellar Selection, BB—Best Buy, ($NA)—Price not available, (NR)—Not released.

TASTER'S INITIALS (JG)—Jim Gordon, (HS)—Harvey Steiman, (JL)—James Laube, (JS)—James Suckling, (TM)—Thomas Matthews, (TR)—Terry Robards, (PM)—Per-Henrik Mansson, (BT)—Barrel Tasting (these wines were tasted blind from barrel samples), (CA-date)—*California's Great Cabernets* by James Laube, (CH-date)—*California's Great Chardonnays* by James Laube, (VP-date)—*Vintage Port* by James Suckling.

DATE TASTED Dates in parentheses represent the issue in which the rating was published.

WHITE OAK
Sauvignon Blanc Sonoma County 1990: Light and refreshing, with appealing spice, pineapple and pear aromas and flavors. Fades a bit on the finish. Drinkable now. $9 (11/15/91) **81**

ZACA MESA
Sauvignon Blanc Santa Barbara County 1988: Lean and austere, with toasted onion aromas and flavors obscuring the fruit. A well made wine with odd flavors. $8 (12/15/89) **71**

STEPHEN ZELLERBACH
Sauvignon Blanc Sonoma County 1989: Light and refreshing, offering grapefruit aromas and flavors along with the varietal grassiness. Drink now, chilled. $5.50 (12/31/90) BB **82**

SAUVIGNON BLANC BLENDS

BENZIGER
A Tribute Sonoma Mountain 1989: Ripe and concentrated, with nicely focused tropical fruit and grapefruit aromas and flavors shaded by a distinct touch of oak. A tasty wine that has restraint in its favor. Drinkable now, but probably better around 1993. $16 (12/31/91) **87**
A Tribute Sonoma Mountain 1988: Rich, deep and complex, with intense fig, melon, citrus, vanilla and nutmeg flavors that are woven together in an elegant wine. The texture is crisp up-front and smooths out on the finish. Drink now. $11.50 (12/31/90) **89**

BRANDER
Novissimo Santa Ynez Valley 1991: A fruity, lively wine, with generous pear, fig and floral aromas and flavors, finishing with an herbal edge. Drinkable now. $9.50 (3/15/92) **82**

CARMENET
Reserve Edna Valley 1988: Ripe and buttery like a Chardonnay, but the crisp lemony backbone supports pleasant fig flavors. Easy to drink and stylish. Drink soon. $12 (1/31/91) **84**
Sonoma County 1987: An intense, vegetal wine, with plenty of rich onion, fig, herb and celery flavors that finish with intensity. $9.50 (3/31/90) **77**
Sonoma County 1986: Distinct juniper berry flavor dominates this unusual wine, but it's well made and a hint of anise comes through on the finish. Rich, concentrated and balanced. $9.50 (1/31/89) **85**

CAYMUS
Conundrum California 1989: A unique, complex white wine, with toasty, herbal, buttery aromas, rich fig, lemon and spice flavors and a lingering aftertaste. The fruit flavors are crisp and long lasting. 1,000 cases made. $18 (4/30/91) **89**

CONCANNON
Assemblage Livermore Valley 1986: A very mature-smelling wine that's showing its age. The aromas have turned somewhat interesting with smoky notes, but there's nuttier, tastier flavor than fruit, and it finishes very dry and astringent. For the adventurous. $20 (3/15/92) **80**

CRONIN
Sauvignon Blanc Sémillon Robison Vineyard Stags Leap District 1989: A curious wine that's lavishly oaked, but supported by a cast of ripe, rich fig and honey flavors that turn earthy on the finish. Tastes oxidized and tired for an '89. $8 (4/30/92) **79**

DE LORIMIER
Spectrum Alexander Valley 1989: Crisp, tart and lemony, with a buttery vanilla edge that persists into the long finish. A solid wine that's balanced and flavorful. Drinkable now. $10 (10/31/91) **86**
Spectrum Alexander Valley 1988: Creamy and buttery up-front, with appealing melon, spice and toast notes. Only moderately rich and concentrated, the flavors taper off on the finish. Drink now. $8.50 (9/30/90) **83**
Spectrum Alexander Valley 1987: Lean in structure and generous in flavor, with celery-tinged grapefruit and melon aromas and flavors. Broad and well balanced with a lemony finish. $8.50 (3/31/89) **81**

FLORA SPRINGS
Sauvignon Blanc Napa Valley Soliloquy Special Select 1990: Fresh, polished and complex, its sharply focused orange, pear and vanilla aromas and flavors turn opulent and generous on the creamy finish. Has style and richness, but never gets too heavy. Drinkable now. $20 (6/15/92) **88**

GEYSER PEAK
Château Alexandre Meritage Alexander Valley 1990: A woody, toasty, spicy wine that owes a lot to oak, but it's intriguing and well made. It's crisp and tangy, even minerally in flavor, all of which makes it distinctive. 800 cases made. $13 (4/30/92) **86**

INGLENOOK
Gravion Napa Valley 1987: Rich, flavorful and elegant, with supple texture and pretty fig, sweet pea, citrus and spice flavors backed with generous oak. The flavors are lively and lingering on the finish. $9.50 (2/28/89) **89**
Gravion Napa Valley 1986 $9.50 (4/30/88) SS **91**

KONOCTI
Meritage Clear Lake 1989: A frankly grassy, herbal wine that turns soft and simple on the finish. Decent quality. Tasted twice. 1,050 cases made. $14 (2/15/92) **75**
Meritage Clear Lake 1988: Smooth, generous and round in texture, with lively acidity, ripe fruit aromas and flavors and a delicate touch of grass and herbs to identify it as Sauvignon Blanc. Hints of butter, almond and spice enhance the finish. Drinkable now. 740 cases made. $14 (4/30/91) **89**

LYETH
White Alexander Valley 1988: Becoming quite complex and mature, this has toasty, buttery, earthy aromas, smooth almond and honey flavors and a lingering, slightly nutty finish. A very distinctive and appealing style that's reminiscent of a good Graves. $12 (10/31/90) **89**
White Alexander Valley 1986: Perfumed and spicy with floral notes, more like a Gewürztraminer than a Sauvignon Blanc, finishing dry, flat and slightly bitter. Tasted twice. $12 (9/15/89) **78**

MERLION
Chevrier Hyde Vineyards Los Carneros 1987: Distinctive and earthy, with fig and melon notes and a tart finish, this is interesting to smell but lacks elegance. Tasted twice, with consistent notes. 849 cases made. $10 (8/31/90) **70**

MERRYVALE
Meritage Napa Valley 1990: A serious, complex, full-bodied wine, with toasty, spicy aromas, crisp pear and lemon flavors and a buttery, nutty finish. Evolves nicely as you sip. Drinkable now, but could be cellared through 1993. 1,150 cases made. $12 (7/15/91) **89**

GUSTAVE NIEBAUM
Chevrier Herrick Vineyard Napa Valley 1988: Crisp and refreshing, with complex lemon-grapefruit aromas and flavors plus a tinge of herbs and onion. Drinkable now, especially with fish or grilled chicken breast. 1,700 cases made. $11.50 (12/15/89) **88**

OJAI
Cuvée Spéciale Sainte Hélène California 1989: Crisp and flavorful, with distinctive herbal and celery aromas and flavors and melon notes to give it a fruity core, but perhaps a bit soft and sweet on the finish. Drink soon. $12.50 (9/15/91) **76**

VICHON
Chevrignon Napa Valley 1990: Lively, fruity and fresh, with plenty of zingy citrus and peach flavors. Crisp in balance, with good depth and a lingering fruity finish. Tasted twice. $9.75 (3/15/92) **85**
Chevrignon Napa Valley 1989: Firm in texture and tight in structure, with a Graves-like austerity that keeps a tight rein on the mineral-tinged peach and lemon flavors. Drink now. $9.75 (5/31/91) **81**

Chevrignon Napa Valley 1988: Elegant and well balanced, with delicate spice, herb, melon and grapefruit notes that are complex and pleasant. Ready to drink now. $9.75 (1/31/91) **86**
Chevrignon Napa Valley 1986 $9.75 (1/31/89) **74**

SÉMILLON

ALDERBROOK
Sémillon Dry Creek Valley 1990: Fruity, round and aromatic, with buttery vanilla overtones to the basic peach and pear flavors. Nicely balanced and flavorful. Drinkable now. 2,228 cases made. $8.50 (11/15/91) **85**
Sémillon Dry Creek Valley 1988: Crisp and delicate, offering just a hint of the Sémillon's usual fig and tobacco flavors. Its firm texture and subtle flavors set it apart and make it particularly appealing. Drink now. 1,800 cases made. $9 (2/15/90) **83**
Sémillon Dry Creek Valley Rued Vineyard 1987: Round and earthy, with an intriguing overlay of cigar box aromas and flavors to the rich fig and apricot flavor, plus a touch of honey on the finish. Well balanced, long and focused. Drink up now. $7.50 (5/15/89) BB **87**

BENZIGER
Sémillon Sonoma Mountain 1989: A ripe, fruity wine, with strong grapefruit, peach and pineapple aromas and flavors. Finishes on the crisp side. Drinkable now. $13 (11/15/91) **81**

CAREY
Sémillon Santa Ynez Valley Buttonwood Farm 1987: Tight and austere in flavor and not showing much fruit, but it has good acid balance and is crisp and dry on the finish. Drink up. $8 (12/15/89) **77**

CLINE
Sémillon California Barrel Fermented 1990: Ripe, soft and generous, with tropical fruit aromas and flavors that pump up the volume through a generous finish. Has the tang of citrus on the finish to balance it. Drinkable now. 1,395 cases made. $9 (12/31/91) BB **86**

CLOS PEGASE
Sémillon Napa Valley 1989: Broad and smooth, with ripe fig and vanilla flavors. A craftsmanlike wine without the intensity it could have. Drinkable now. 327 cases made. $9.50 (9/15/91) **81**

CLOS DU VAL
Sémillon California 1987: A figgy-tasting wine, with crisp pineapple and lemon flavors that broaden into a strong finish. Straightforward and true to type. Tasted twice. $10 (7/15/91) **82**

DUCKHORN
Sémillon Napa Valley Decoy 1990: The flavors are bright and fruity and the structure is light and graceful in this medium-bodied, slightly herbal wine. Drinkable now. $7.25 (12/31/91) BB **80**

GIRARD
Sémillon Napa Valley Estate Grown 1989: Very crisp and tart, with almond overtones to the modest lemon flavor. Drinkable now. $11 (11/15/91) **80**

MONTICELLO
Sémillon Napa Valley Chevrier Blanc 1986: Crisp, emphasizing bright fruity flavors and a bit of celery on a solid framework. No single personality stands out. $7.50 (1/31/89) **77**

SPARKLING/BLANC DE BLANCS

BEAULIEU
Brut Napa Valley Champagne de Chardonnay 1982: Holding up well. A first decadent whiff is followed by mature and complex creamy, honey, nutty flavors with hints of anise, nutmeg and smoke. Lovely finish. $16 (5/31/89) **87**

CHATEAU ST. JEAN
Brut Blanc de Blancs Sonoma County 1987: Spicy and floral, with lemony flavors, crisp acidity and green apple flavors on the off-dry finish. $12 (12/31/89) **81**
Brut Blanc de Blancs Sonoma County 1984: Rich, full-bodied and ripe with lavish oak, berries, currant and spice in a reserved, understated, austere style. Fruit echoes on the finish. Drink in 1994 to 2000. $11 (5/31/89) **88**
Brut Blanc de Blancs Sonoma County 1983 $11 (7/31/87) **76**
Brut Blanc de Blancs Sonoma County 1982 $13 (5/16/86) **79**
Brut Blanc de Blancs Sonoma County 1981 $14 (11/01/84) **82**
Brut Blanc de Blancs Sonoma County NV $12 (5/15/91) **86**

RICHARD CUNEO
Blanc de Blancs Sonoma County Cuvée de Chardonnay 1987: Crisp and fruity, with a firm texture and lots of nectarine and lemon and modest butter aromas and flavors. A flavorful wine that finishes refreshing. $14 (11/15/91) **84**

ESTRELLA RIVER
Blanc de Blancs Paso Robles Star Cuvée 1983 $13 (2/29/88) **81**

FALCONER
Brut Blanc de Blancs Russian River Valley 1984: A perfumed, full-bodied wine, showing all the positive aspects of age with none of the defects. Lots of bread dough, tart apple and honey flavors, graced by wildflower overtones, make this mouthfilling wine a serious drink. $15 (3/15/91) **89**

IRON HORSE
Blanc de Blancs Sonoma County Green Valley 1987: Lean and elegant, with a modest flavor profile carried by spicy, toasty accents and a brisk sense of balance. Focused but delicate, it keeps bringing you back for another sip. Gains richness on the finish. $25 (12/31/91) **89**
Blanc de Blancs Sonoma County Green Valley 1986: An intense, spicy, grassy, herbal wine, with tart, crisp grapefruit flavors that have hints of toast and butter. Not a style for everyone, but it packs in plenty of flavor. Drink in now to 1993. 1,200 cases made. $22 (12/31/90) **87**
Blanc de Blancs Sonoma County Green Valley 1985: Delicate and fragrant, with basic green apple flavor and hints of lemon, spice and toast. Lean and crisp. $21 (12/31/89) **85**
Blanc de Blancs Sonoma County Green Valley 1982 $16.50 (5/16/86) **78**
Blanc de Blancs Sonoma County Green Valley 1981 $18 (11/01/84) **86**
Blanc de Blancs Sonoma County Green Valley Late Disgorged 1982 $24 (12/31/87) **85**

JEPSON
Blanc de Blancs Mendocino 1986: Crisp in texture, with rich grapefruit, layers of roasted almond and a touch of pear and vanilla flavor on the finish. Moderate in depth and complexity and elegant in style. Drink now. 3,000 cases made. $16 (4/30/91) **86**

KORBEL
Blanc de Blancs California NV: Tart lemon and fruit cocktail flavors turn coarse and bitter. A simple, drink-now style. $14 (5/15/92) **72**
Blanc de Blancs California NV: Tinny and brassy, with a canned grapefruit flavor. Aggressively fruity, but strays from the mainstream. Drink now. 5,000 cases made. $13 (6/15/91) **79**
Blanc de Blancs California NV: Good in a straightforward, off-dry style. Has simple flavors of apple and fruit cocktail and decent acidity. $13 (8/31/89) **73**
Blanc de Blancs California Private Reserve 1981 $34/1.5L (2/29/88) **69**

HANNS KORNELL
Blanc de Blancs California 1982 $14.75 (11/30/86) **77**

SCHARFFENBERGER
Blanc de Blancs Mendocino County 1987: Soft, pleasant and almost sweet, with floral, apple and honeylike flavors that remind us of sparkling Vouvray. Gentle, easygoing and easy to like. 3,000 cases made. $20 (12/31/91) **83**
Blanc de Blancs Mendocino County 1986: Delicate, dry and creamy, with plenty of flavor to go along with the finesse. Lemon, vanilla and fig aromas and flavors are harmoniously balanced and shaded by just enough hazelnut to keep it interesting. 3,000 cases made. $20 (3/15/91) **91**
Blanc de Blancs Mendocino County 1985 $18 (12/31/88) **85**
Blanc de Blancs Mendocino County 1984 $17.50 (12/31/87) **78**

SCHRAMSBERG
Blanc de Blancs Napa Valley 1987: A smooth, off-dry wine that's pleasant and mildly fruity. Lemon and green apple flavors are shaded by spice notes on the finish. Soft and elegant. $21 (12/15/91) **87**
Blanc de Blancs Napa Valley 1986: Rich, elegant and complex, with attractive, creamy pear, butterscotch, vanilla and spice notes that dance on the palate. A very appealing, classy wine that comes up short on the finish. Drink now to 1993. $20 (12/31/90) **89**
Blanc de Blancs Napa Valley 1985: Zesty and youthful tasting, with green apple, grass and lemon flavors. Has pretty good balance but a tart finish. $20 (5/31/89) **84**
Blanc de Blancs Napa Valley 1983 $17.50 (5/16/86) **82**
Blanc de Blancs Napa Valley Late Disgorged 1985: Lively, fruity, crisp and solid, with tart grapefruit, lemon and apple flavors wrapped in a firm structure of acidity. Hints of almond add complexity on the finish. 400 cases made. $27 (6/15/91) **87**

SHADOW CREEK
Blanc de Blancs California 1984 $14.50 (1/31/88) **77**
Blanc de Blancs Sonoma County 1983 $15 (5/16/86) **88**
Blanc de Blancs Sonoma County 1982 $15 (10/16/85) **89**

TIJSSELING
Blanc de Blancs Mendocino 1986: Very toasty, earthy and woody, with some fruit flavor. Drinkable, but not for everyone. Tasted twice, with consistent notes. 804 cases made. $13 (12/31/91) **72**
Blanc de Blancs Mendocino Cuvée de Chardonnay 1985: Smooth, creamy textured and nicely mature in flavor, with fruity, herbal and honey notes. Almost delicate in style. $13 (12/31/89) **80**

BLANC DE NOIRS

S. ANDERSON
Blanc de Noirs Napa Valley 1987: Full-bodied and generous, offering orange peel, pear and spice aromas and flavors and a round structure. Echoes freshness and toast notes on the finish. 2,100 cases made. $19 (6/15/91) **86**
Blanc de Noirs Napa Valley 1986: A doughy-yeasty flavored wine, with ample cherry and pear flavors backing it. Unusual in that it has wild fruit flavors in a straight-laced structure of firm acidity. Off-dry in balance. $20 (12/31/90) **83**
Blanc de Noirs Napa Valley 1985: Has ripe, intense fruit and straightfoward pear and lemon flavors. A fine example of a solidly structured sparkling wine. $16 (5/31/89) **87**
Blanc de Noirs Napa Valley 1984 $16 (10/15/88) **79**
Blanc de Noirs Napa Valley 1983 $28 (5/31/89) **85**

CHATEAU DIANA
Blanc de Noirs Monterey Special Reserve 1986: Has soapy, oily aromas and ripe Pinot Noir flavors that are off-dry and a bit cloying; not our cup of tea. Drink now. $7 (6/15/91) **71**

CULBERTSON
Blanc de Noir California 1983 $14 (5/16/86) **68**
Blanc de Noir California NV: Vivid pink in color, off-dry, straightforward, very fruity and herbal in flavor. Nothing subtle about this colorful, strawberry-scented sparkler. $14 (12/31/90) **77**

DOMAINE CHANDON
Blanc de Noirs Napa Valley NV: A lively, very fruity, fresh wine, with clean citrus and vivid cherry flavors and a crisp, fruity finish. Pale pink in color. Straightforward, satisfying stuff. $14 (5/31/89) **84**
Blanc de Noirs Napa-Sonoma Counties NV: Fruity, showing plenty of cherry aromas and flavors plus a hint of lemon to keep it in balance. Clean and simple, but very well made. $15 (12/31/89) **80**

FIRESTONE
Blanc de Noirs Santa Ynez Valley 1985 $15 (12/31/88) **79**

ROBERT HUNTER
Blanc de Noirs Sonoma Valley Brut de Noirs 1984 $15 (10/15/88) **84**
Blanc de Noirs Sonoma Valley Brut de Noirs 1983 $15 (1/31/88) **84**
Blanc de Noirs Sonoma Valley Brut de Noirs 1982 $14 (12/31/86) **90**
Blanc de Noirs Sonoma Valley Brut de Noirs 1981 $14 (12/16/84) **87**
Blanc de Noirs Sonoma Valley Brut de Noirs Late Disgorged 1981 $14 (2/01/86) **69**

IRON HORSE
Blanc de Noirs Sonoma County Green Valley Wedding Cuvée 1988: Lots of fruit balanced against a strong strain of earthiness makes for an unusual wine, but the raspberry, cherry and pear flavors manage to win in the end. Solid, with good flavor and a dry finish. Drinkable now. 1,000 cases made. $24 (10/31/91) **84**
Blanc de Noirs Sonoma County Green Valley Wedding Cuvée 1986: Intense and fruity, lively and refreshing. Lots of black cherry, with pear and lemon flavors. Almost rosé in color, it's rich on the palate, with fully ripe, somewhat sweet flavors on a solid, firm framework. $19 (5/31/89) **90**
Blanc de Noirs Sonoma County Green Valley Wedding Cuvée 1985 $17 (12/31/88) **86**
Blanc de Noirs Sonoma County Green Valley Wedding Cuvée 1984 $16.50 (12/31/87) **85**
Blanc de Noirs Sonoma County Green Valley Wedding Cuvée 1983 $16.50 (12/31/86) **82**

JUSTIN
Blanc de Noir Paso Robles 1985: A lightly pink wine with cherry and strawberry flavors. Fresh, lively and charming, with plenty of Pinot Noir character. Off-dry, but balanced. $23 (12/31/91) **84**

KORBEL
Blanc de Noirs California NV: Attractive for its fresh cherry and strawberry flavors, this is soft and fleshy, turning creamy on the finish. Drink now. $14 (5/15/92) **80**
Blanc de Noirs California NV: A good bottle of wine with simple, slightly coarse fruit flavors, a suitably smooth texture and clean finish. $14 (12/31/89) **71**

HANNS KORNELL
Blanc de Noirs California 1987: Kornell's best in a long time. Tart and tightly structured, with lemon and crisp cherry flavors that are beautifully articulated. Zesty, fresh and vibrant. $15 (6/15/91) **87**
Blanc de Noirs California 1986: Difficult to get excited about, but there's a lingering flavor of strawberry that saves it. Smells very weedy and vegetal, and tastes the same until the finish. $15 (5/31/89) **69**

MARK WEST
Blanc de Noirs Russian River Valley 1984 $16.50 (12/31/88) **71**

PAUL MASSON
Blanc de Noirs Monterey Centennial Cuvée 1984 $9 (12/31/87) **83**

MIRASSOU
Blanc de Noirs Monterey 1983 $11 (12/31/88) **69**
Blanc de Noirs Monterey 1982 $10 (8/31/87) **66**
Blanc de Noirs Monterey Fifth Generation Cuvée 1989: Tastes as if there's plenty of Pinot Noir in this pinkish, generous, cherry-flavored sparkler. Off-dry, very fruity and soft. $13 (5/15/92) **82**
Blanc de Noirs Monterey Fifth Generation Cuvée 1987: Simple and slightly sweet with vague berry flavors on the finish. Drinkable, with minimal personality. 2,400 cases made. $12 (11/15/91) **77**

ROBERT MONDAVI
Brut Napa Valley Chardonnay Reserve 1985: This stylish wine has buttery, doughy aromas, lean citrus flavors and spice notes that show maturity. Easy to drink and enjoy. 750 cases made. $35 (12/31/91) **85**

MUMM NAPA VALLEY
Blanc de Noirs Napa Valley Cuvée Napa NV: A smoky, toasty style with tart cherry and strawberry flavors that turn elegant and spicy, picking up a citrus flavor on the finish. Plenty of fresh fruit flavors. $15 (11/15/90) **83**

PIPER SONOMA
Blanc de Noirs Sonoma County 1988: The creamy texture is appealing, and the cherry and strawberry flavors nose into the fray without turning sweet. A graceful wine, with modest flavors. Drinkable now. $13.50 (1/31/92) **86**
Blanc de Noirs Sonoma County 1987: Lacks refinement, but it's a distinctive style, with toasty, yeasty aromas and a touch of earth, anise and cider on the aftertaste. Drink now. $16 (6/15/91) **83**
Blanc de Noirs Sonoma County 1986: Lively and refreshing. Young, intense and crisp, with green apple and slightly tart, grassy aromas and flavors. $15 (5/31/89) **87**
Blanc de Noirs Sonoma County 1983 $15 (12/31/86) **88**
Blanc de Noirs Sonoma County 1982 $15 (4/01/86) **86**

SCHRAMSBERG
Blanc de Noirs Napa Valley 1985: Has a spicy, floral flavor that's mature and pleasant on a smooth, round texture. Hints of butter and almond lend complexity. $22 (12/31/91) **83**
Blanc de Noirs Napa Valley 1984: Fresh, firm, lean and toasty, with vague hints of black cherry, spice and vanilla. A decent wine that could use a little more flavor. Drink now. $22 (12/31/90) **82**
Blanc de Noirs Napa Valley 1983: Woody, vegetal aromas and flavors overpower whatever fruit might be there, and it's rough and tannic for such a light wine. $21 (5/31/89) **90**
Blanc de Noirs Napa Valley 1981 $20 (5/16/86) **91**
Blanc de Noirs Napa Valley Late Disgorged 1983: A mature wine, with toasty, nutty, earthy flavors that have a touch of pear, vanilla, ginger and spice. Not for everyone, but we find it complex and distinctive. Drink now. 400 cases made. $28 (6/15/91) **87**

SEBASTIANI
Blanc de Noirs Sonoma County Five Star NV: Assertive, robust and dry, with ample cherry and herbal flavors and a firm structure. $11 (4/30/90) **77**

SHADOW CREEK
Blanc de Noirs California 1984 $12.50 (5/31/87) **86**
Blanc de Noirs California NV: Creamy in texture and spicy. Accented by cherry and grapefruit flavors. Tasted twice. $11 (6/15/91) **80**
Blanc de Noirs California NV: Firm and a bit blunt, with delicate watermelon and cherry flavor that tastes a bit candied, fresh and perhaps a bit sweet. $13 (12/31/89) **77**
Blanc de Noirs California NV: Pale rosé in color. Soft, fruity and slightly herbal in flavor. Has an attractive, round, fruity quality and a hint of toasty complexity. $12 (5/31/89) **83**
Blanc de Noirs Sonoma County 1982 $13 (5/16/86) **79**

M. TRIBAUT
Blanc de Noirs Monterey County NV: Fruity but dry, almost austere on the palate, with a touch of astringency to balance the assertive cherry and raspberry flavors. Tart enough to be refreshing. Drinkable now. $10 (1/31/92) **82**

WENTE BROS.
Blanc de Noir Arroyo Seco 1983: A good, sturdy, full-bodied wine. Shows clean, ripe fruit flavors with a touch of cherry and good balance. $15 (3/31/89) **78**

BRUT

S. ANDERSON
Brut Napa Valley 1986: Has the yeasty aromas and crisp, fruity flavors we look for in a fine sparkling wine, plus a long finish that echoes the spicy fruit. Clean and well balanced. $18 (12/15/91) **86**
Brut Napa Valley 1985: Light and creamy, with a delicate texture and attractive spicy, toasty aromas and flavors. Refreshing pear and melon flavors sneak through on the finish. A well-made wine. 3,000 cases made. $18 (6/15/91) **87**
Brut Napa Valley 1984 $18 (10/15/88) **82**
Brut Napa Valley 1983 $16 (5/31/87) **72**

BEAULIEU
Brut Napa Valley 1982: Nicely mature and developed in flavor. Shows dry, austere fruit flavors, good balance and a lingering finish. Just drink and enjoy. $12 (5/31/89) **81**

CHASE-LIMOGERE
Brut California NV: Crisp and light, with toasty pear and vanilla aromas and flavors. A refreshing, lively wine with simple, appealing flavors. $5 (5/15/92) **79**
Brut California NV: Simple, fruity and crisp in flavor, reminiscent of Chenin Blanc. Tastes soft and off-dry. $7 (12/31/89) **72**

CHATEAU DE BAUN
Brut Sonoma County Symphony Romance 1988: Very fruity and floral, with the sort of rose petal aromas and flavors associated with Gewürztraminer. Off-dry rather than sweet, and much more aggressively fruity than most bruts. Best to enjoy while it's fresh. 3,400 cases made. $11 (7/15/91) **84**
Brut Sonoma County Symphony Romance 1987: An effusively spicy, floral-tasting wine that's slightly sweet, with plenty of fruit flavor and a lingering finish. Good as an apertif or dessert wine. 1,800 cases made. $12 (4/30/90) **80**
Brut Sonoma County Symphony Romance 1986 $12 (7/31/88) **74**

CHATEAU ST. JEAN
Brut Sonoma County 1987: Tart with distinctive nectarine and peach flavors that pick up a touch of toast and vanilla. It gets astringent on the finish. Drink now or in 1993. $12 (4/30/90) **82**
Brut Sonoma County 1986: Crisp and light, with delicate hints of guava and lime. Fragrant and fruity, yet it has a sense of restraint that makes it an ideal aperitif. A stylish wine. $12 (12/31/89) **87**
Brut Sonoma County 1985 $11 (12/31/88) **86**
Brut Sonoma County 1984 $11 (7/15/88) **84**
Brut Sonoma County 1983 $11 (5/31/87) **67**
Brut Sonoma County 1982 $13 (5/16/86) **67**
Brut Sonoma County 1981 $14 (11/01/84) **81**
Brut Sonoma County NV $12 (5/15/91) **86**
Brut Sonoma County Grande Cuvée 1982: A mature wine that's approaching retirement age, but shows the benefits of time in its nutty, doughy, earthy aromas. Has spicy almond and pear flavors, but it's getting a bit tired. Drink now. Tasted twice. 2,000 cases made. $19 (6/15/91) **80**

CODORNIU NAPA
Brut Napa Valley NV: Pleasant but simple, with soft, ripe, fresh apple and citrus notes that stay with you. Lacks drama and excitement, but it's well made. Serve well chilled. $15 (11/15/91) **82**

CONGRESS SPRINGS
Brut Santa Clara County Brut de Pinot 1986 $8 (3/31/88) **77**

CULBERTSON
Brut California 1985: A remarkably flavorful wine, round and smooth, with spicy, vanilla and pear aromas and flavors like a Chardonnay. Dry and crisp on the finish. Drink now. $14 (5/31/89) **83**
Brut California 1983 $14 (5/16/86) **66**
Brut California NV: Zesty and spicy, almost like a Gewürztraminer, with enough richness to keep your attention. Not a Champagne-style bubbly, but it's well balanced and enjoyable. $12 (5/15/92) **80**

DOMAINE CARNEROS
Brut Carneros NV: An intense wine, with a concentrated beam of finely focused peach, pear and pineapple flavors and hints of spice and toast that give it complexity. This is a generous, almost supple wine in a distinctive style. $14 (11/15/90) **88**

DOMAINE CHANDON
Brut Napa County Etoile NV: Distinctive for its ripe, crisp cherry and sweet-and-sour flavors. The texture is smooth and creamy, but the flavors come across as simple. Drink now. 2,600 cases made. $23 (12/31/91) **85**
Brut Napa Valley Club Cuvée NV: Earthy, musty notes detract from the core of ripe pear and butter. Some may find the wine appealing, but others may find it stale and overly mature for a new release. Drink now. $17 (6/15/91) **77**
Brut Napa Valley Reserve NV: Rich and concentrated, with earthy aromas and toasty lemon and honey flavors unfolding nicely on the palate. Appears mature in color, with gold and brown tinges. Complex and extremely appealing. $38/1.5L (5/31/89) **89**
Brut Napa Valley Reserve NV $38/1.5L (5/16/86) **80**
Brut Napa-Sonoma Counties NV: Round, flavorful and fruity, but dry enough to drink happily as an aperitif, clean and crisp on the finish. $15 (12/31/89) **80**

EDEN ROC
Brut California NV: Sweet and simple, with a one-note grassy, grapey flavor and a soft, sweet finish. Tasted twice. $4 (5/15/92) **76**

GLORIA FERRER
Brut Carneros Cuvée 1985: Extremely tart, lemony, earthy aromas and flavors make this wine so acidic it will pucker most palates. For fans of the lean, racy style. Tasted twice. $20 (5/15/92) **81**
Brut Carneros Royal Cuvée 1987: Combines tart apple and lemon flavors with hints of butter and toast. Has an incredibly thick foam that really lasts. Tart and tangy on the finish. Refreshing and a bit complex. $17 (5/15/92) **84**
Brut Carneros Royal Cuvée 1986: Lively and peachy in flavor, with cherry and spice accents and plenty of crisp acidity. Fruity, flavorful and satisfying. $17 (12/31/91) **84**
Brut Sonoma County NV: A lean, lively wine that's tart, light and appley in flavor and long on the finish. Well made in a very dry, crisp style. $14 (5/15/92) **84**
Brut Sonoma County Royal Cuvée 1986: Crisp and delicate, with lively citrus, grapefruit, pear and vanilla flavors that are concentrated and rich, finishing with good depth and intensity. A touch of earthiness creeps through on the finish. Drink now. $16 (4/30/91) **84**
Brut Sonoma County Royal Cuvée 1985: A tart, fruity wine that's clean and lively on the palate, with very pleasant, simple, modest flavors of green apple and almond. Tasted twice. $16 (3/15/91) **83**
Brut Sonoma County Royal Cuvée 1984 $15 (4/15/88) **89**

FOLIE A DEUX
Brut Napa Valley Fantasie 1989: A dry wine that's fruity and spicy like a Muscat, but without the sugar, with well-defined peach aromas and flavors. Charming and fresh. 1,040 cases made. $18 (6/15/91) **81**

HANDLEY
Brut Anderson Valley 1984 $15 (10/15/88) **81**

IRON HORSE
Brut Sonoma County Green Valley 1987: A delicate, creamy wine, with lovely spice and grapefruit aromas and flavors held in check by a fragile framework of crisp acidity. Hints of orange, peach and nutmeg make for a complex finish. An elegant wine, near the head of the pack. $21 (11/15/90) **89**
Brut Sonoma County Green Valley 1986: Full-bodied, frothy, round and creamy, with ripe cherry flavor showing in the nose and palate. $20 (12/31/89) **82**
Brut Sonoma County Green Valley 1985 $17.50 (12/31/88) **83**
Brut Sonoma County Green Valley 1984 $16.50 (12/31/87) **79**
Brut Sonoma County Green Valley 1983 $16.50 (12/31/86) **87**
Brut Sonoma County Green Valley 1982 $16.50 (5/16/86) **80**
Brut Sonoma County Green Valley Late Disgorged 1986: Tart, crisp and intense, with deeply concentrated apple, citrus and earth flavors that are complex and lively. The acidity is crisp and tart, creating an appealing style. Shows a touch of butter and vanilla on the finish. Drink now. 1,200 cases made. $24 (11/30/91) **91**
Brut Sonoma County Green Valley Late Disgorged 1984: Crisp and lively, with spicy, peppery flavors, but lean and austere on the finish. Doesn't quite have the finesse of previous vintages. $23 (12/31/89) **80**
Brut Sonoma County Green Valley Late Disgorged Vrais Amis 1986: A classy, complex wine. Bracing and crisp, but backed by lovely green apple and spice flavors that are shaded by doughy, toasty notes. Has good length on the finish, too. 700 cases made. $25 (12/15/91) **90**

JEPSON
Brut Mendocino 1985 $16 (12/31/88) **82**

KORBEL
Brut California NV: Tastes soft and creamy, spicy and floral in flavor and off-dry in balance. Tasty but not complex. Fine for most occasions. $10 (5/15/92) **80**

HANNS KORNELL
Brut California NV: Dry and nutty, with floral aromas, mature flavors and a broad texture. Sturdy and simple. $11.50 (6/15/91) **79**

LE DOMAINE
Brut California NV: Sweet with perfumed aromas. Drinkable, but cloying and unbalanced. $5 (2/28/89) **67**

MAISON DEUTZ
Brut San Luis Obispo County Reserve 1987: An attractive wine, with creamy black cherry, vanilla, spice and toast notes that are rich and elegant, with good depth and concentration. A balanced wine that's ready to drink now to 1994. 1,000 cases made. $22 (10/31/91) **88**
Brut San Luis Obispo County Reserve 1986: Not nearly as appealing as this label's regular bottling. Balanced and flavorful, with earthy, slightly gamy aromas and flavors that manage to stay in bounds. This dry, medium-bodied wine is not for everyone. Tasted twice. 500 cases made. $22 (4/30/91) **77**

Key to Symbols

The scores reported here are the results of blind tastings conducted by our panel of senior editors. Wines that carry the initials below are results of individual tastings.

THE WINE SPECTATOR 100-POINT SCALE ***95-100***—Classic, a great wine; ***90-94***—Outstanding, superior character and style; ***80-89***—Good to very good, a wine with special qualities; ***70-79***—Average, drinkable wine that may have minor flaws; ***60-69***—Below average, drinkable but not recommended; ***50-59***—Poor, undrinkable, not recommended. "+"—With a score indicates a range; used primarily with barrel tastings to indicate a preliminary score.

SPECIAL DESIGNATIONS SS—Spectator Selection, CS—Cellar Selection, BB—Best Buy, ($NA)—Price not available, (NR)—Not released.

TASTER'S INITIALS (JG)—Jim Gordon, (HS)—Harvey Steiman, (JL)—James Laube, (JS)—James Suckling, (TM)—Thomas Matthews, (TR)—Terry Robards, (PM)—Per-Henrik Mansson, (BT)—Barrel Tasting (these wines were tasted blind from barrel samples), (CA-date)—*California's Great Cabernets* by James Laube, (CH-date)—*California's Great Chardonnays* by James Laube, (VP-date)—*Vintage Port* by James Suckling.

DATE TASTED Dates in parentheses represent the issue in which the rating was published.

Brut Santa Barbara County Cuvée NV $15 (1/31/88) **85**
Brut Santa Barbara County Cuvée 3 NV: Complex and elegant, with interesting, delicate flavors. Doughy aromas are followed by layers of creamy, smoky, toasty lemon flavors. Smooth and enticing flavors make you want to go back for more. $17 (5/31/89) **89**

MIRABELLE
Brut North Coast NV: A creamy, buttery wine that strives for complexity in an oaky, toasty style and achieves it. Full, round and a bit sweet. A new label from Schramsberg. $12 (5/15/92) **84**

MIRASSOU
Brut Monterey 1983 $10 (7/31/88) **66**
Brut Monterey 1982 $12 (9/16/85) **78**
Brut Monterey County 1987: The earthy, spicy flavors are palatable, but rather coarse and simple. Of decent quality. $13 (12/31/91) **76**
Brut Monterey Cuvée 1984: This mature, spicy, nutty tasting wine is interesting, but fades on the finish. Grapefruit and cherry flavors keep it lively. $12 (6/15/91) **84**
Brut Monterey Fifth Generation Cuvée 1988: Very fruity, straightforward and easy to drink. Slightly sweet, with simple fruit cocktail flavors and a short finish. $13 (5/15/92) **78**
Brut Monterey Fifth Generation Cuvée Reserve 1984: Generously fruity, very crisp and youthful. Pear, vanilla, toast and apple flavors give it life, and the finish lingers. $15 (12/31/91) **85**
Brut Monterey Reserve 1983: Earthy, with enough creaminess and richness to offset a hint of staleness that detracts from the aroma and flavor. $15 (12/31/89) **76**

ROBERT MONDAVI
Brut Napa Valley Reserve 1985: Mature, with a distinctive, stylish character. Has the smoky caramel aromas that come with age, plus nutty, yeasty flavors and a smooth texture. 750 cases made. $35 (12/31/91) **90**

MONTREAUX
Brut Napa Valley 1986: A toasty, lemony, mature wine, with broad, spicy flavors and a good finish. Hints of nutmeg and almond give complexity to the lemon and apple notes. $26 (12/15/91) **88**
Brut Napa Valley 1985: A very assertive sparkling wine that's flavorful but rough. Has doughy, toasty aromas and a slightly pink hue that may explain the Pinot Noir cherry flavors accompanying the lemon and tart apple notes. 750 cases made. $32 (12/31/90) **79**

MUMM NAPA VALLEY
Brut Carneros Napa Valley Winery Lake Cuvée Napa 1988: Crisp and refreshing, with tart, fresh, clean apple, vanilla, spice and peach notes that are long and lively. Finishes with bracing acidity and lots of delicious fruit flavors. Ready to drink now. 3,300 cases made. $22 (11/15/91) **89**
Brut Carneros Napa Valley Winery Lake Cuvée Napa 1987: Elegant, complex and toasty, with tart lemon, honey and spice flavors extending into a long finish. It's a mouthful of flavor but not full-bodied. It's balanced, creamy and strikes a middle chord between lightness and richness. 2,000 cases made. $22 (11/15/90) **91**
Brut Carneros Napa Valley Winery Lake Cuvée Napa 1986: Fruity, assertive and straightfoward, tart and appealing with a lingering lemony finish. It's pleasant to drink and develops complexity in the glass. $23 (5/31/89) **87**
Brut Napa Valley Cuvée Napa NV $14 (12/31/87) **89**
Brut Napa Valley Prestige Cuvée Napa NV: Spicy and lively, with black cherry, spice, grapefruit and citrus notes that are ripe, tasty and simple but pleasant. Drink now. $15 (12/31/90) **82**
Brut Napa Valley Prestige Cuvée Napa NV: Generous and supple up-front before the tannins kick in. The plum, cherry, spice and cedar flavors are concentrated and very rich, finishing with good length. Drink in 1995 and beyond. $14 (5/31/89) **87**
Brut Napa Valley Prestige Cuvée Napa NV $14 (12/31/88) **88**
Brut Napa Valley Reserve Cuvée Napa 1987: Elegant and lively, with fresh, ripe pear, spice, vanilla and toast notes offering complexity and finesse. Well balanced, with a long, clean finish. Drink now. $22 (12/31/90) **87**
Brut Napa Valley Reserve Cuvée Napa 1985: Straightforward and well-balanced, with intense and concentrated lemon and toast flavors and an appealing finish. $21 (5/31/89) **86**

NAVARRO
Brut Anderson Valley Gewürztraminer 1989: Pleasant floral and spice flavors from the Gewürztraminer and a touch of sweetness add up to a fruity, likable bubbly at a good price. $8.50 (5/15/92) **82**

PARSONS CREEK
Brut Mendocino County Reserve NV: Simple in flavor but delicate and creamy in texture. Shows hints of spice and toast in the nose and cherry and orange on the palate. $15 (5/31/89) **79**

PIPER SONOMA
Brut Sonoma County 1988: Lively fruit flavors center around strawberry and grapefruit, and a crisp structure and steely finish give it a bracing, refreshing quality. Not sweet, but not bone dry, either. Has a wisp of a pink tinge to the color. $13.50 (1/31/92) **88**
Brut Sonoma County 1987: Lively and fruity, with spice, cherry, citrus and toast notes that turn elegant and dry on the finish. An austere wine that succeeds. Drink now to 1993. $16 (6/15/91) **87**
Brut Sonoma County 1986: Lemony and almost minerallike in flavor, balanced toward leanness and lightness. Attractive in a restrained, fragile style. $14 (5/31/89) **82**
Brut Sonoma County 1985 $14 (7/15/88) **79**
Brut Sonoma County 1983 $13 (12/31/86) **79**
Brut Sonoma County 1982 $13 (5/01/86) **62**
Brut Sonoma County Reserve 1982: Crisp and appley, with delicate hints of ginger and other spices, light as a feather on the palate, but flavorful and extremely long-lasting as well. Mouth-watering now, but it feels as though it can age, too. $20 (12/31/89) **93**
Brut Sonoma County Tête de Cuvée 1981: Restrained for its age, but the toast and complexity of aging peeks through. Tastes fresh and creamy, with ginger flavor on the aftertaste. Time in the cellar has definitely improved its quality. $29 (5/31/89) **88**

ROEDERER ESTATE
Brut Anderson Valley NV: Big and full flavored. Creamy and doughy on the nose, with tart grapefruit and pineapple flavors. A solid wine that doesn't attempt to be delicate. May develop more complexity with a couple of years' cellaring. $16 (5/31/89) **88**

ST. FRANCIS
Brut Sonoma Valley 1984 $9.50 (12/16/85) **82**

SCHARFFENBERGER
Brut Mendocino County 1983 $13 (9/30/87) **84**
Brut Mendocino County 1982 $12.50 (2/01/86) **85**
Brut Mendocino County NV: Zesty and inviting. Very crisp, flavorful and fruity, with tart cherry, lemon and spice flavors. Beautifully balanced and lively, with a crisp but lingering finish. $16.50 (12/31/91) **90**

SCHRAMSBERG
Brut Napa Valley Reserve 1983: Mature, with earthy, nutty aromas and similar flavors that some may find quite attractive, but others may find overly mature. For fans of older California bubbly. Drink now. $29 (12/31/90) **82**
Brut Napa Valley Reserve 1982: Attractive and mature, with flavors of walnuts, toast, pear and honey. It has some appealing complexity, but it lacks pizzazz and freshness. $28 (5/31/89) **85**
Brut Napa Valley Reserve 1981 $27 (7/31/87) **78**
Brut Napa Valley Reserve 1980 $30 (5/16/86) **61**

SEBASTIANI
Brut Sonoma County Five Star NV: A sturdy wine whose vegetal and herbal flavors are coarse but acceptable. A touch of doughy complexity on the finish helps. $11 (4/30/90) **72**

SHADOW CREEK
Brut California NV: The nutty, cidery notes provide a bit of flavor in this austere, earthy wine. Has a very dry finish. $11 (6/15/91) **76**
Brut California Reserve Cuvée 1983: A distinctive, complex wine that's rich, round and creamy in flavor with hints of earthy berry aromas. Tangy and refreshing on the finish. $20 (5/31/89) **87**

STANFORD
Brut California Governor's Cuvée NV: Slightly sweet, simple and fruity, with fruit cocktail and almond flavors. Not bad, but it doesn't stand out. $5 (12/31/90) **76**

TIJSSELING
Brut Mendocino 1987: Extremely tart and crisp, with lemon and grapefruit flavors and floral aromas, but the severe mouth-feel partly obscures the fruit flavors. 2,741 cases made. $11.50 (12/31/91) **81**
Brut Mendocino 1986: A rich but delicately textured wine that packs a great concentration of ripe fruit. Nicely balanced and complex in flavor, with plenty of ripe pear and honey flavors. $11.50 (12/31/89) **89**

TOTT'S
Brut California NV: Light and off-dry, with ginger, spice and pear flavors that turn creamy, earthy and simple on the finish. Drink now. $8 (5/15/92) **77**
Brut California Reserve Cuvée NV: Fruity and simple, pleasant, clean and slightly gingery, attractive and easy to drink. Balanced on the finish. Much better then two bottles tasted earlier, so beware of bottle variation. $8 (5/31/89) **80**

M. TRIBAUT
Brut Monterey County 1985: Rich and ripe, showing lovely Pinot Noir cherry flavors in the nose, with an herbal hint in the aromas. Nutty on the palate and complex, with a long, terrific finish that really makes this one stand out from the crowd. Full flavored and impressive. $13 (5/31/89) **91**
Brut Monterey County 1984 $14 (12/31/87) **85**
Brut Monterey County 1983 $14 (2/15/87) **81**

VAN DER KAMP
Brut Sonoma Valley 1985: A crisp, well-balanced wine, with lemon and apple flavors and a clean finish. It has enough dryness and character to drink with dinner. $15 (12/15/91) **84**
Brut Sonoma Valley 1984: Exotic and attractive. Full of crisp, spicy, lime, cherry and ginger flavors. Lively, spicy and delicious. $15 (5/31/89) **86**
Brut Sonoma Valley 1983 $17.50 (12/31/87) **86**

WEIBEL
Brut Mendocino County 1982 $13 (9/15/86) **77**

WENTE BROS.
Brut Arroyo Seco 1983 $10 (8/31/88) **79**
Brut Arroyo Seco 1982 $8 (12/31/86) **84**
Brut Arroyo Seco 1981 $8 (4/01/86) **78**

Rosé

CHASE-LIMOGERE
Brut Rosé California NV: Has a beautiful pink color but is frankly sweet and loaded with watermelon, cherry and strawberry flavors that taste almost artificial. Not a success. $7 (12/31/89) **68**

CHATEAU DE BAUN
Brut Rosé Sonoma County Symphony Rhapsody 1988: Fruity and creamy, with aromas and flavors that remind us of a fruit bowl, with cherry and pear predominating. Very fresh and lively—neither sweet nor dry—but definitely soft and creamy in texture. Enjoy while it's fresh. 4,000 cases made. $11 (7/15/91) **83**
Rosé Sonoma County Symphony Rhapsody Sec 1987: Sweet, pink, heavily floral and spicy in flavor, like a strong perfume. Lacks delicacy but is great for fans of all-out flavor. 810 cases made. $12 (5/31/90) **78**
Rosé Sonoma County Symphony Rhapsody Sec 1986 $12 (9/15/88) **88**

CULBERTSON
Brut Rosé California 1986: Light salmon in color, with earthy Pinot Noir aromas and similar flavors. Creamy and smooth in texture and clean, with a subtle cherry aftertaste. $17.50 (5/31/89) **80**
Cuvée Rouge California NV: A horse of a different color. Deep red, with grapey raspberry flavors and a long, fruity finish. Sweet and jammy but not sugary. $14 (12/31/90) **79**
Cuvée Rouge California NV: Slightly sweet and fire-engine red, with soft plum and cherry flavors and a hint of herbs. Delicate and unusual. $12 (3/31/89) **80**

HANDLEY
Rosé Anderson Valley 1984 $16.75 (12/31/88) **75**

IRON HORSE
Brut Rosé Sonoma County Green Valley 1988: The coppery pink color is deeper than most rosés, but it's crisp and dry, with definite cherry and spice characteristics. Finishes creamy and smooth. Classy and dry. $28 (12/15/91) **87**
Brut Rosé Sonoma County Green Valley 1987: A deep rose color and ripe black cherry, plum and spice flavors are quite appealing in this fruity wine that has a soft, creamy aftertaste. Serve as a holiday quaffer. Drink now. 500 cases made. $28 (12/31/90) **84**
Brut Rosé Sonoma County Green Valley 1986: Fruity but balanced, showing hints of herbs and toast to offset the delicate sweetness. This isn't one of those sugary rosés. The crisp structure and clean strawberry flavor make it appealing. $23 (12/31/89) **80**
Brut Rosé Sonoma County Green Valley 1985 $20 (12/31/88) **88**

KORBEL
Brut Rosé California NV: Spicy, with anise, cherry and vanilla flavors that are soft and creamy. Pleasant and ready to drink. $11 (5/15/92) **82**

MAISON DEUTZ
Brut Rosé Santa Barbara County NV: Crisp and tasty, with appealing strawberry, raspberry and vanilla aromas and flavors. Dry and slightly chalky but refreshing and flavorful. Drinkable now. $24 (5/15/92) **85**

J. PEDRONCELLI
Brut Rosé Sonoma County 1986: Unusual, attractive and assertive, this is more red than rosé, with cherry, berry and vanilla flavors, moderate tannins and a spicy finish. $10 (7/31/89) **84**

SCHARFFENBERGER
Brut Rosé Mendocino County NV: Lively and dry, but full of cherry and apple flavors and hints of toast and spice. Firm, direct and straightforward. 3,000 cases made. $18 (12/31/91) **82**

SCHRAMSBERG
Brut Rosé Napa Valley Cuvée de Pinot 1987: Copper in color, with simple but pleasant earth, cherry and citrus notes that are elegant and easy to like, but missing that extra dimension. Drink now. $20 (12/31/90) **81**
Brut Rosé Napa Valley Cuvée de Pinot 1986: Medium- to light-bodied, with simple fruit flavors, a short finish and a touch of toast. $19 (5/31/89) **76**
Brut Rosé Napa Valley Cuvée de Pinot 1985 $17 (4/30/88) **80**
Brut Rosé Napa Valley Cuvée de Pinot 1984 $17 (5/31/87) **83**

M. TRIBAUT
Rosé Monterey County 1984 $14 (12/31/87) **80**
Rosé Monterey County NV: Definitely salmon or sunset in color, with dull flavors reminiscent of tangerines and strawberries. Simple and unexciting. Tasted twice. $13 (1/31/92) **77**

VAN DER KAMP
Brut Rosé Sonoma Valley Midnight Cuvée 1988: Smells earthy and funky, with similar flavors. Hints of cherry, tobacco and earth emerge on the finish. Drink now. $12 (5/15/92) **75**
Brut Rosé Sonoma Valley Midnight Cuvée 1987: Fresh, crisp and lively, with minty cherry flavors that are tart and balanced. A summer quaffer that goes down easy. Drink now. $15 (11/15/90) **81**
Brut Rosé Sonoma Valley Midnight Cuvée 1986: Very user-friendly. Pleasant and fruity in an off-dry style, like a good sparkling white Zinfandel. Has strawberry and slightly herbal flavors. $15 (5/31/89) **83**
Brut Rosé Sonoma Valley Midnight Cuvée 1985 $17.50 (12/31/87) **84**

Other Sparkling

ADLER FELS
Melange à Deux Sonoma County 1985 $15 (10/15/87) **74**

S. ANDERSON
Blanc de Noirs Tivoli Brut Noir NV: Distinctive for its earthy mushroom flavors that taste more like stale ginger ale. An unusual combination of flavors. Drink now. 1,400 cases made. $12 (6/15/91) **73**

BALLATORE
California NV $4 (5/01/86) BB **87**

CULBERTSON
Demi-Sec California Cuvée de Frontignan NV: Frankly sweet, with just enough crisp fruit flavor to balance out the sugar. Good quality, but think of it as an after-dinner wine. Too sweet for most foods. 2,000 cases made. $12 (5/15/92) **81**
Natural California 1986: Coarse and rough around the edges, but fruity and perfumed, as well. Doesn't have much subtlety but is drinkable. 2,900 cases made. $18.50 (12/31/90) **74**
Natural California 1985: Austere, with razor-sharp acidity. Very dry and verging on coarse, with earthy, doughy aromas and lemon and nut flavors. $17.50 (5/31/89) **81**
Natural California 1983 $16.50 (5/16/86) **72**

EDEN ROC
Extra Dry California NV: Sweet, floral, simple and fruity, echoing peach on the finish. A clean bubbly to sip with or after dessert. $4 (5/15/92) **78**

GLORIA FERRER
Natural Sonoma County Cuvée Emerald NV $11 (5/16/86) **89**

JORDAN
J Sonoma County 1987: Good, solid, crisp and clean, with tart apple and floral flavors rounded out by creamy, slightly nutty accents. The first sparkling wine from Jordan. $22 (5/15/91) **88**

KORBEL
Extra Dry California NV: Simple pear and spice flavors make this sweet wine appealing. The fruit lingers on the finish and the texture has creaminess. $11 (5/15/92) **78**
Natural California NV: Crisp and dry, with light strawberry and grass flavors and a clean, bracing finish. Well balanced, straightforward and appealing. $14 (5/15/92) **83**
Sec California NV: Simple and very fruity. Has effusive herbal and fruit cocktail aromas, sweet, fruity flavors and a short finish. $10 (8/31/89) **73**

HANNS KORNELL
Extra Dry California NV: Has a tutti-frutti, grassy aroma not associated with sophisticated sparkling wines, but it's basically clean, fruity and enjoyable served very cold. $11 (5/31/89) **73**
Sehr Trocken California 1984: Mildly spicy, but not lively or elegant. Seems stale and oxidized. Tasted twice. $14.50 (6/15/91) **74**

MIRASSOU
Natural Monterey Au Naturel 1988: Enjoyable, clean, dry and crisp, with good underpinnings of subtle fruit flavor. Appley, spicy notes give it vibrancy and linger on the finish. $15 (5/15/92) **85**
Natural Monterey Cuvée Au Naturel 1984: Has doughy aromas, mature, ripe Chardonnay and soft-textured green apple flavors and a hint of fig. A distinctive wine that's easy to drink. 1,200 cases made. $15 (6/15/91) **83**
Natural Monterey Fifth Generation Cuvée Au Naturel 1987: Pleasantly creamy and tart, a smooth-textured wine, with nice vanilla, peach and toast notes. Straightforward and crisply balanced. 1,550 cases made. $15 (11/15/91) **85**

SCHARFFENBERGER
Crémant Mendocino County NV: Smooth and well rounded, with a hint of sweet peach adding to the lemon and apple flavors. 2,000 cases made. $18 (12/31/91) **83**

SCHRAMSBERG
Demi-Sec Crémant Napa Valley 1987: A soft, sweet wine, with strawberry, apple and spice flavors. Floral aromas mark it as something different to drink with or after dessert. $20 (12/31/91) **80**
Demi-Sec Crémant Napa Valley 1986: Sweet, simple and drinkable but uninteresting. Offers decent pear and lemon flavors, but the balance is soft and it's not complex or deep. $20 (12/31/90) **77**
Demi-Sec Crémant Napa Valley 1985: A fine, well-balanced dessert wine. The tasty honey, nut and mint flavors are sweet without being cloying and are soft and lingering on the finish. $19 (5/31/89) **85**

SCHUG
Rouge de Noir Pinot Noir Carneros 1987: Almost like a sparkling Beaujolais, offering plenty of Gamay-like Pinot Noir characteristics and an unusually distinctive orange peel and spice component. An interesting wine for the more adventurous. 215 cases made. $18 (12/15/91) **85**

STANFORD
Extra Dry California Governor's Cuvée NV: Drinkable and semisweet, with simple, grapey flavors. $5 (12/31/90) **73**

Key to Symbols

The scores reported here are the results of blind tastings conducted by our panel of senior editors. Wines that carry the initials below are results of individual tastings.

THE WINE SPECTATOR 100-POINT SCALE ***95-100***—Classic, a great wine; ***90-94***—Outstanding, superior character and style; ***80-89***—Good to very good, a wine with special qualities; ***70-79***—Average, drinkable wine that may have minor flaws; ***60-69***—Below average, drinkable but not recommended; ***50-59***—Poor, undrinkable, not recommended. "+"—With a score indicates a range; used primarily with barrel tastings to indicate a preliminary score.

SPECIAL DESIGNATIONS SS—Spectator Selection, CS—Cellar Selection, BB—Best Buy, ($NA)—Price not available, (NR)—Not released.

TASTER'S INITIALS (JG)—Jim Gordon, (HS)—Harvey Steiman, (JL)—James Laube, (JS)—James Suckling, (TM)—Thomas Matthews, (TR)—Terry Robards, (PM)—Per-Henrik Mansson, (BT)—Barrel Tasting (these wines were tasted blind from barrel samples), (CA-date)—*California's Great Cabernets* by James Laube, (CH-date)—*California's Great Chardonnays* by James Laube, (VP-date)—*Vintage Port* by James Suckling.

DATE TASTED Dates in parentheses represent the issue in which the rating was published.

TOTT'S
Extra Dry California NV: Simple, pungently perfumed aromas and flavors characterize this basically grapey wine. A touch of bitterness keeps it from being terribly sweet. $8 (5/15/92) **75**
Extra Dry California Reserve Cuvée NV: A simple, pleasant wine from Gallo. Ripe and smooth, with lots of fresh fig and pineapple flavors that are lively, sweet and well balanced. $8 (2/28/89) **75**

Zinfandel

ADELAIDA
Zinfandel Paso Robles 1988: Very ripe and rich, with big, concentrated cherry, plum and spice flavors, high alcohol and deep color reminiscent of a late-harvest wine, but it manages to stay in balance. A heady wine to drink now or wait until 1993 or '94 to see what develops. 616 cases made. $12 (4/30/91) **88**

AHERN
Zinfandel Amador County 1980 $6.50 (2/15/84) **78**

ALEXANDER VALLEY VINEYARDS
Zinfandel Alexander Valley 1987: Ripe and moderately intense, with raspberry and jammy notes of moderate depth and complexity and firm tannins of the finish. Drink now. $9 (3/31/90) **82**

AMADOR FOOTHILL
Zinfandel Fiddletown Eschen Vineyard 1986: Tasty and distinctive. A spicy, attractively oaky nuance predominates, but there is sufficient raspberry flavor to back it up. $9 (6/15/89) **82**
Zinfandel Fiddletown Eschen Vineyard 1984 $9 (10/15/88) **86**
Zinfandel Fiddletown Eschen Vineyard Special Selection 1982 $9 (4/15/87) **74**
Zinfandel Shenandoah Valley Ferrero Vineyard Special Selection 1989: A good core of berrylike flavor is wrapped in a heavy coat of tannins, oak and alcohol. Too tough to drink now. Cellar until 1994. Good quality, but difficult to say how it will develop. 1,044 cases made. $10 (3/31/92) **81**
Zinfandel Shenandoah Valley Grand-Père Vineyard Special Selection 1988: Light in color and fruity smelling, but seems tannic and watery on the palate. $10 (8/31/91) **75**

ARCIERO
Zinfandel Paso Robles 1985: Square jawed and full-bodied, showing plenty of chewy tannins, good but simple berry flavors and an astringent finish. $7.50 (12/15/89) **78**

AUDUBON
Zinfandel San Luis Obispo County 1983 $7 (7/15/88) **84**

BALDINELLI
Zinfandel Shenandoah Valley 1988: Light, crisp and pleasantly tart, offering modest strawberry and leafy, spicy aromas and flavors. Simple and easy to drink soon. $7.75 (12/31/90) **82**
Zinfandel Shenandoah Valley 1987: Aggressively fruity and tannic, with concentrated plum, cherry and berry flavors, American oak notes and hints of chocolate on the finish. A rich wine but loaded with enough tannin that it will need time in the cellar to soften. Try in 1993 or '94. $8 (5/15/90) **85**
Zinfandel Shenandoah Valley Reserve 1986 $6.75 (12/15/88) BB **83**

BELVEDERE
Zinfandel Dry Creek Valley 1989: Intense and oaky, but with a solid core of cherry and raspberry-tinged flavors. Fine tannins on the finish make it drinkable now through 1995. 2,400 cases made. $9 (5/15/92) BB **85**

BERINGER
Zinfandel North Coast 1988: Soft and flavorful, with lots of blackberry and plum flavors and not many tannins. Broad, appealing and medium-bodied. $8.50 (2/29/92) BB **85**
Zinfandel North Coast 1987: Don't let the light color fool you. This wine has real depth of character, with toast and earth nuances to the cherry and cassis aromas and flavors, pretty good length and enough tannin to stand cellaring until 1993. A decent value. $8 (9/15/90) **86**
Zinfandel North Coast 1985 $6 (4/30/88) BB **87**

BLACK MOUNTAIN
Zinfandel Alexander Valley Cramer Ridge 1987: Smells musty but tastes fruity, with plenty of blackberry flavor, but the drying texture is troubling. Seems too tannic for the fruit or it might be corky. Tasted twice. 2,477 cases made. $10 (9/30/91) **77**
Zinfandel Alexander Valley Cramer Ridge 1986: An intense, tannic wine that's hard and unyielding now, with a dry finish, but has a decent core of peppery, ripe flavor. It just needs a year or two to soften. Drinkable now. $9 (3/31/90) **82**

BOEGER
Zinfandel El Dorado Walker Vineyard 1989: A lighter wine that's fresh and fruity, with lots of spice-tinged raspberry aromas and flavors, a lean texture and a solid finish. Drinkable now through 1993. 725 cases made. $9.50 (9/30/91) **84**
Zinfandel El Dorado Walker Vineyard 1988: Big and firm, with loads of delicious fruit flavors, full body and moderate tannins. Drink now through 1993 for its exuberant plum and berry flavors. 700 cases made. $8.50 (2/15/91) **85**
Zinfandel El Dorado Walker Vineyard 1987: A ripe, jammy wine that's well balanced, with full, supple plum and raspberry jam flavors, firm tannins and a full, fruity aftertaste. Drink now to 1994. $8.50 (3/31/90) **86**
Zinfandel El Dorado Walker Vineyard 1986 $7 (7/31/88) **73**
Zinfandel El Dorado Walker Vineyard 1981 $6 (7/16/85) **76**
Zinfandel Napa Valley Joseph A. Nichelini Vineyards 1988: Ripe, smooth and fruity, with generous blackberry and vanilla aromas and flavors. A stylish wine, with focused fruit and plenty of extract. Drinkable now. 450 cases made. $12 (8/31/91) **85**

DAVID BRUCE
Zinfandel San Luis Obispo County 1990: Big and rangy, with attractive berry and spice aromas and flavors that persist through the finish. The concentrated, seductive flavors make this drinkable now despite a firm tannin foundation. 706 cases made. $12 (5/15/92) **90**

BUEHLER
Zinfandel Napa Valley 1989: A rough-cut red, with earthy, peppery flavors and a little raspberry and anise. Straightforward and easy to drink. Tasted twice. 2,453 cases made. $9.75 (3/31/92) **83**
Zinfandel Napa Valley 1987: Ripe and concentrated, with distinct, intense blueberry and raspberry flavors, a polished texture and a welcome hint of smoke and pepper on the finish. A stylish wine with flavor to burn. $9.50 (5/15/90) **89**
Zinfandel Napa Valley 1986 $8.50 (12/15/88) **83**
Zinfandel Napa Valley 1985 $8 (12/31/87) **89**
Zinfandel Napa Valley 1983 $6.50 (3/15/87) **71**
Zinfandel Napa Valley 1982 $6 (3/01/85) **91**
Zinfandel Napa Valley 1981 $6 (9/16/84) **80**

BUENA VISTA
Zinfandel North Coast 1984 $7.25 (4/30/88) **77**
Zinfandel Sonoma County 1982 $6 (4/01/85) **80**

BURGESS
Zinfandel Napa Valley 1988: Rich and highly extracted, with plum and chocolate flavors, but lacks acidity and lift and cruises to a listless finish of alcohol and wood. The full tannins will smooth with time. Drink in 1994 or '95. 4,500 cases made. $12 (7/31/91) **80**
Zinfandel Napa Valley 1987: Tastes big, assertive and robust, offering plenty of fruit flavor on a rough-hewn frame of woody tannins and firm acidity. Drink now with hearty foods. $10 (5/31/90) **82**
Zinfandel Napa Valley 1986: Despite the pretty peppery aromas, this is very woody and tannic on

the palate, overshadowing the fruit flavors. Will need time to strut its stuff. Drink in 1994 and beyond. $9.50 (7/31/89) **82**
Zinfandel Napa Valley 1985 $9 (6/30/88) **87**
Zinfandel Napa Valley 1984 $8 (11/15/87) **89**
Zinfandel Napa Valley 1983 $7.50 (10/31/86) **81**
Zinfandel Napa Valley 1982 $6.50 (7/16/85) **85**
Zinfandel Napa Valley 1981 $6 (4/16/84) **81**

CALERA
Zinfandel California NV $5 (7/31/88) **71**
Zinfandel Cienega Valley 1981 $7 (4/16/84) **81**
Zinfandel Cienega Valley Reserve 1981 $8.50 (1/01/85) **82**

CASTORO
Zinfandel Paso Robles 1987: Don't let the amateurish label fool you. This is classic, elegant and stylish, with deep, fragrant fruit and spice aromas and rich, spicy, cedary flavors. Shows oak influence in the proper balance with the raspberry and cassis flavors and soft but firm tannins. Fruit lingers on the finish. $7.50 (12/15/89) **90**

CAYMUS
Zinfandel California 1976 $35 (6/16/85) **79**
Zinfandel California 1974 $45 (6/16/85) **83**
Zinfandel California Lot 31-J 1975 $40 (6/16/85) **77**
Zinfandel Napa Valley 1989: Tight and austere, with pretty raspberry and currant aromas and flavors and barnyardy hints on the palate. A bit rough around the edges but may develop well through 1994 or '95. 2,000 cases made. $10 (11/15/91) **83**
Zinfandel Napa Valley 1988: Distinctive dill and anise overtones color the dark cherry and berry aromas and flavors in this firm, concentrated wine. An attempt at a claret style that could use more Zin character and less oak. $9 (10/15/90) **80**
Zinfandel Napa Valley 1987: A delicious claret-type Zinfandel, with fresh, toasty oak notes to complement the raspberry and spicy cherry flavors. Easy to warm up to. Drink now to 1995. $9.75 (10/31/89) **85**
Zinfandel Napa Valley 1986 $9 (12/15/88) **89**
Zinfandel Napa Valley 1985 $8 (12/31/87) **85**
Zinfandel Napa Valley 1984 $8 (5/15/87) **90**
Zinfandel Napa Valley 1983 $7.50 (12/31/86) **79**
Zinfandel Napa Valley 1982 $7.50 (5/16/86) **92**
Zinfandel Napa Valley 1981 $6.50 (12/01/84) **84**

CHATEAU MONTELENA
Zinfandel Napa Valley 1987: An anomoly for this usually consistent winery. Tough and earthy, with hard-edged oak and leaf aromas and flavors that are minty and stony on the finish. Not a likable wine. Try in 1993. Tasted twice. $10 (7/31/90) **69**
Zinfandel Napa Valley 1986: Firm, tight and slightly hard, with decent ripe plum and cherry flavors and a touch of spice. Lacks the hand-over-fist fruit of most Montelena Zins. Drink now to 1993. Tasted three times. Rel: $10 Cur: $12 (9/15/89) **80**
Zinfandel Napa Valley 1985 $10 (4/30/88) **90**
Zinfandel Napa Valley John Rolleri Vineyard 1984 Rel: $10 Cur: $15 (5/15/87) **91**
Zinfandel Napa Valley 1983 $10 (5/01/86) **84**
Zinfandel Napa Valley 1982 Rel: $10 Cur: $18 (5/01/84) **91**
Zinfandel Napa Valley 1981 Rel: $8 Cur: $20 (4/16/84) **80**
Zinfandel North Coast 1976 $25 (6/16/85) **78**
Zinfandel Napa-Alexander Valleys 1974 $40 (6/16/85) **92**
Zinfandel Napa Valley 1973 $50 (6/16/85) **90**

CHATEAU SOUVERAIN
Zinfandel Dry Creek Valley 1989: Firm and flavorful, with pleasant, bright berry and cherry flavors that bounce through the finish. The tannins are present but the fruit wins in the end. Drinkable now with hearty food. 3,400 cases made. $7.50 (5/15/92) BB **82**
Zinfandel Dry Creek Valley 1987: Light and lively, with generous raspberry and spice aromas and flavors that linger delicately, yet shows enough firm tannin to keep for a while. A stylish wine that is delicious to drink now. Tasted twice. $9.50 (5/15/90) **82**
Zinfandel Dry Creek Valley 1986: A bit more austere and woody than most Dry Creek-area Zins, but has plenty of strawberry and raspberry flavors. A good drink, althought it could be a bit more concentrated. $5 (3/31/89) BB **81**
Zinfandel Dry Creek Valley Bradford Mountain Vineyard 1987: Fresh and unpolished, with lush raspberry, cherry and vanilla aromas and flavors and a plush texture. Generous right through to the finish. Drinkable now, but probably best after the tannins soften. $15 (5/15/90) **85**

CHESTNUT HILL
Zinfandel San Luis Obispo 1988: Fruity and lively, with lots of familiar flavors—berries, pepper and flowers—and a firm texture, but balanced toward smoothness with plenty of flavor. Drinkable now. 3,000 cases made. $6 (8/31/91) BB **86**

CHRISTIAN BROTHERS
Zinfandel Napa Valley 1986 $5.50 (6/30/88) **79**

CLINE
Zinfandel Contra Costa County 1989: Big and generous, with a nice tension between the ripe blackberry and plum flavors and oak notes. Has a firm texture and even a touch of elegance on the finish. Drinkable now. 2,200 cases made. $9 (5/15/91) **86**
Zinfandel Contra Costa County 1987: Ripe, fruity and generous, with a deep color and nicely focused raspberry and cherry aromas and flavors. The tannins are firm but not harsh or heavy. An exuberant wine with plenty to offer. Drink now. $9 (5/15/90) **89**
Zinfandel Contra Costa County Reserve 1989: A bit tannic and oaky, but the ripe berry and currant flavors emerge on the finish and spread across the palate nicely. Appealing flavors and a smooth texture make this drinkable now, although the tannins could use until 1994 to settle down. 290 cases made. $12 (12/31/91) **84**
Zinfandel Contra Costa County Reserve 1987: Classic old-fashioned Zinfandel, from the briary aromas to the ripe raspberry and cherry flavors that are rich, dense and chocolaty on the finish. Has the restraint to be agreeable now. Very well made. $12 (5/15/90) **87**

CLOS DU VAL
Zinfandel Stags Leap District 1987: Has Zinfandel character in spades, from the effusively fruity, herbal aromas to the slightly pickley flavor associated with American oak. Lively, flavorful and ready to drink now. $12.50 (5/31/90) **83**
Zinfandel Napa Valley 1986: A bit tannic, but the spicy raspberry aromas and flavors ride over the storm to finish clearly and sharply defined. Drinkable now. $12 (5/31/89) **87**
Zinfandel Napa Valley 1985 $12 (4/30/88) **90**
Zinfandel Napa Valley 1984 $12 (5/31/87) **81**
Zinfandel Napa Valley 1981 Rel: $9 Cur: $18 (5/16/84) CS **90**
Zinfandel Napa Valley 1974 $45 (6/16/85) **77**
Zinfandel Napa Valley 1973 $50 (6/16/85) **86**
Zinfandel Napa Valley 1972 ($NA) (6/16/85) **90**

CONGRESS SPRINGS
Zinfandel Santa Cruz Mountains 1987: Resembles Port. Extremely concentrated, intense and almost sweet, with alcohol and ripe fruit flavors. Full-bodied, tannic and loaded with ripe berry and pepper flavors. 510 cases made. $12 (3/15/90) **83**

CONN CREEK
Zinfandel Napa Valley 1979 $7.50 (3/16/84) **60**
Zinfandel Napa Valley Barrel Select 1987: The flavors are ripe but the structure is a little tough and the intensity level is not high. Tries to be elegant but succeeds only at being modest. Drinkable. 586 cases made. $10 (11/15/91) **80**
Zinfandel Napa Valley Barrel Select 1986: Lively and peppery, with plenty of spice and concentration, echoing black pepper on the crisp finish. Doesn't show much subtlety but is an exuberant wine with plenty of character. Drinkable now. A good value. 1,500 cases made. $9 (10/15/90) **86**
Zinfandel Napa Valley Collins Vineyard 1983 $10 (12/15/88) **84**

CORBETT CANYON
Zinfandel San Luis Obispo County Select 1984 $7.50 (5/15/88) **87**

CUVAISON
Zinfandel Napa Valley 1986 $10 (3/15/89) **85**
Zinfandel Napa Valley 1983 $8.50 (9/15/87) **75**

DALLA VALLE
Zinfandel Napa Valley 1986: Ripe and complex but tightly tannic, with a hard edge of woody astringency keeping the plum, raspberry and spice flavors in check for now. Better to keep until 1994 or '95 to polish the tannins, but it's a gamble. $25 (2/15/91) **84**

DE LOACH
Zinfandel Russian River Valley 1990: Ripe, rich, polished and robust, with plenty of berry, plum and vanilla flavors and hints of toast and anise on the long finish. It's all wrapped up tight now, but should be fine by 1993 or '94. $11.50 (5/15/92) **89**
Zinfandel Russian River Valley 1989: A lighter wine, like many '89s, but the peppery raspberry and strawberry flavors come through. Can be served chilled. Drink now to 1993. 4,140 cases made. $11 (9/30/91) **82**
Zinfandel Russian River Valley 1988: Along with the simple pepper and raspberry notes, the drying oak is overpowering right now. Fans of oaky wines should try this now to 1994. $11 (9/15/90) **78**
Zinfandel Russian River Valley 1987 $10 (9/15/89) **90**
Zinfandel Russian River Valley 1986 $9 (10/15/88) **88**
Zinfandel Russian River Valley 1984 $8.50 (7/31/87) **84**
Zinfandel Russian River Valley 1983 $8 (10/15/86) **69**
Zinfandel Russian River Valley 1982 $8 (11/01/85) **77**
Zinfandel Russian River Valley 1981 $7.50 (6/01/85) **89**
Zinfandel Russian River Valley Barbieri Ranch 1990: Youthful, exuberant flavors lean toward wild berry, wild cherry and smoky oak with a touch of gaminess. A medium-weight wine that needs until 1993 or so to settle down, but not more. 507 cases made. $14 (5/15/92) **82**
Zinfandel Russian River Valley Papera Ranch 1990: Earthy flavors flit in and out as the ripe plum and cherry notes try to get focused on the palate. Winds up seeming unfocused and a bit murky. The flavors are fine, though. Drinkable now. 504 cases made. $14 (5/15/92) **81**
Zinfandel Russian River Valley Pelletti Ranch 1990: Tight and tannic, with a solid core of blackberry and black cherry aromas and flavors that persist through a lively finish. Has distinctive character, moderate tannins and a sense of style. Drinkable now for its youthful zeal. 505 cases made. $14 (5/15/92) **87**

DE MOOR
Zinfandel Napa Valley 1988: A hard, tough wine with a tart peppery flavor that borders on sour. The flavors lack richness and depth and are simple and uninspiring. Drink now. $10 (4/30/91) **72**

DEER PARK
Zinfandel Howell Mountain Beatty Ranch 1987: Shows maturity in the aromas and flavors, but is still tannic and scratchy on the palate. The plum and spice flavors are appealing if modest in intensity. Probably best after about 1993. 1,000 cases made. $14 (8/31/91) **79**
Zinfandel Howell Mountain Beatty Ranch Reserve 1987: Still firm and tannic but generous, with ripe blackberry, cherry and tar aromas and flavors and nice spice and toast overtones that persist on the finish. A bit hot but should be at its best in 1993 to '95. 150 cases made. $18 (8/31/91) **85**

DEHLINGER
Zinfandel Sonoma County 1983 $8 (7/31/87) **73**

DOMAINE BRETON
Zinfandel Lake County 1989: Light in color and flavor, emphasizing modest berry and tropical fruit characteristics. Might be best served slightly chilled to freshen the fruit. $8 (2/29/92) **79**
Zinfandel Lake County 1988: Fruity and fresh, with loads of raspberry and blackberry flavors and a texture that's slightly spritzy. A light wine with plenty of flavor to drink now. $8 (2/15/91) **82**

DOMAINE ST. GEORGE
Zinfandel California 1989: Soft in texture, very youthful, intense and almost wild tasting, with ebullient wild plum and berry flavors. Hints at sourness in the aromas and on the finish but is pleasant nonetheless. $5 (2/15/91) **77**

DRY CREEK
Zinfandel Dry Creek Valley 1986: Very deep, concentrated and complex, loaded with ripe berry and cherry aromas and flavors balanced by a healthy dose of oak that needs time to meld itself into the wine. Try now. $9 (4/15/89) **85**
Zinfandel Dry Creek Valley Old Vines 1989: Ripe and a little raisiny, with a strong chorus of raspberry and black currant flavor that keeps singing through the finish. The tannins are well integrated in this claret-style red. Drinkable now. 2,800 cases made. $11 (5/15/92) **85**
Zinfandel Dry Creek Valley Old Vines 1988: Delicious fruit flavor makes this immediately appealing, offering beautiful raspberry and strawberry aromas and flavors on a medium frame. Perhaps it could be longer lasting, but it sure is fun to drink. 2,500 cases made. $11 (2/15/91) **86**

EDMEADES
Zinfandel Mendocino Ciapusci Vineyard 1981 $9 (3/01/85) **87**

ELYSE
Zinfandel Napa Valley Rutherford Bench Morisoli Ranch 1989: Lean and sharply focused, with bright raspberry and spice aromas and flavors that are tart and lively on the finish. Needs food to bring out its best. 586 cases made. $12.50 (8/31/91) **85**

ESTRELLA RIVER
Zinfandel Paso Robles 1987: Well structured and balanced, but the slightly cooked vegetal aromas need more fruit flavors to back them up. Good but not for everyone. $8 (12/15/89) **72**
Zinfandel San Luis Obispo County 1980 $6 (12/01/84) **77**

GARY FARRELL
Zinfandel Sonoma County 1985 $10 (4/30/88) **91**

FARVIEW FARM
Zinfandel San Luis Obispo Reserve 1980 $7 (3/16/84) **62**

FETZER
Zinfandel California 1989: Soft and almost delicate in flavor, this lighter wine shows generous raspberry and strawberry aromas but lacks the generosity and finish that would lift it up a few notches. $6.50 (11/30/90) **76**
Zinfandel California 1986 $6 (9/15/88) **78**
Zinfandel Lake County 1986 $6 (2/15/88) BB **83**
Zinfandel Lake County 1984 $5 (4/15/87) **81**
Zinfandel Lake County 1983 $4.50 (7/16/86) BB **83**
Zinfandel Mendocino 1982 $5.50 (4/01/85) **81**

Zinfandel Mendocino 1980 $5.50 (4/01/84) **78**
Zinfandel Mendocino County Reserve 1986: A broad wine, with rich, ripe plum flavors, hints of pepper and spice and a toasty finish. Full-flavored and tannic, it tries to be a Cabernet. Drink now to 1993. $14 (7/31/90) **83**
Zinfandel Mendocino Home Vineyard 1982 $8 (11/01/84) **77**
Zinfandel Mendocino Lolonis Vineyards 1982 $8 (11/01/84) **79**
Zinfandel Mendocino Ricetti Vineyard 1985 $14 (10/15/88) **79**
Zinfandel Mendocino Ricetti Vineyard 1983 $8.50 (2/16/86) **82**
Zinfandel Mendocino Ricetti Vineyard 1982 $8 (10/16/84) **79**
Zinfandel Mendocino Ricetti Vineyard Reserve 1986: A wine with a lot of wood, offering mature, tealike flavors and modest cherry nuances, but overpowering tannins. The swampy, pickley aromas don't help much. Not worth the extra price. $14 (7/31/90) **74**
Zinfandel Mendocino Scharffenberger Vineyard 1982 $8 (10/16/84) **85**
Zinfandel Mendocino Special Reserve 1985 $14 (12/15/88) **81**
Zinfandel Mendocino Special Reserve 1983 $8.50 (5/01/86) **63**

FITCH MOUNTAIN
Zinfandel Dry Creek Valley 1989: Crisp and fruity, with generous raspberry and cranberry aromas and flavors and hints of spice and toast on the finish. Drinkable now. Limited availability. 383 cases made. $10 (3/31/92) **86**

FOPPIANO
Zinfandel Dry Creek Valley Proprietor's Reserve 1987: Herbal, briary aromas and flavors tend to overshadow the softly focused strawberry and raspberry flavors at first, but they reappear on the finish. A fleshy wine that tastes better than it smells. Drinkable now. $12 (12/31/90) **86**

FRANCISCAN
Zinfandel Napa Valley Oakville Estate 1989: Tough and concentrated, with powerful plum and cherry aromas and flavors that hint at herbs and cedar at the edge. Tart in balance but powerful and perhaps a bit alcoholic. A big-scale wine that should be best after 1993 or '94. $10 (7/31/91) **88**
Zinfandel Napa Valley Oakville Estate 1988: Raspberry, cherry and chocolate aromas and flavors pervade this lively, focused, effusive but sharply defined wine. Excellent. Should soften in the cellar through 1993. $9 (5/31/90) **87**

J. FRITZ
Zinfandel Dry Creek Valley 1986: A deliciously fruity wine to drink now. Crisp and fresh, full of raspberry flavor and a hint of herbs. Fruit lingers on the finish. $9 (3/15/89) **86**
Zinfandel Dry Creek Valley 1984 $7 (2/15/88) **84**
Zinfandel Dry Creek Valley Eighty-Year-Old Vines 1988: This sturdy wine has pleasant plum and berry aromas but lacks intensity and polish on the palate. Drinkable now, but perhaps cellaring until 1993 will soften it up. 600 cases made. $10 (7/31/91) **79**
Zinfandel Dry Creek Valley Eighty-Year-Old Vines 1989: Light and fruity, with pleasant strawberry, raspberry and spice aromas and flavors. A lean, crisp-textured wine with appealing flavor. Drinkable now. $10 (3/31/92) **84**

FROG'S LEAP
Zinfandel Napa Valley 1989: Starts off fruity and plummy, but the texture sort of veers off and turns flat and slightly watery on the finish instead of muscling through with the flavors. Drinkable now. Tasted twice, with consistent notes. 3,800 cases made. $12 (11/15/91) **83**
Zinfandel Napa Valley 1988: Supple, smooth and generous, with plenty of cherry, plum and raspberry flavors that fill the mouth and are velvety and long on the finish. The nose is deceptively shy but the flavors are marvelous. Drinkable now. 4,206 cases made. $11.50 (12/15/90) **88**
Zinfandel Napa Valley 1987: Very appealing, with moderate tannins and great fruit flavor. Ripe but well balanced and smooth, with plum flavor. Drink now to 1993. Tasted twice. $10.50 (3/15/90) **86**
Zinfandel Napa Valley 1986 $10 (12/15/88) **85**
Zinfandel Napa Valley 1985 $9 (11/15/87) **79**

GEYSER PEAK
Zinfandel Alexander Valley 1984 $7.75 (7/31/88) **79**

GREEN & RED
Zinfandel Napa Valley 1987: Fresh and fruity but tannic and crisp in texture. The rough mouth-feel tends to negate the promising strawberry and spice aromas. $9.50 (2/15/91) **77**
Zinfandel Napa Valley 1986: Tough, tart and green, with very intense plum and cherry flavors. The oak assaults the palate and the wine is hard as nails on the finish. Drink in 1993 at the earliest. $9 (3/15/90) **76**
Zinfandel Napa Valley 1985: A solid red wine that's lean in flavor and has leathery, herbal aromas and a minimum amount of fruit. Good but austere. $8.50 (6/15/89) **73**
Zinfandel Napa Valley 1984 $7.75 (11/15/87) **82**
Zinfandel Napa Valley 1983 $7.25 (7/31/87) **64**
Zinfandel Napa Valley 1982 $7.50 (12/16/85) **82**

GREENWOOD RIDGE
Zinfandel Sonoma County 1988: Firm and fruity, with lots of appealing plum, raspberry and vanilla aromas and flavors on a medium frame. Hints of pepper emerge on the finish. Drinkable now, but should be fine in the cellar until 1993. 255 cases made. $11 (5/15/91) **86**

GRGICH HILLS
Zinfandel Alexander Valley 1986: Plump, concentrated and smooth, with lots of blueberry and raspberry flavors. Rich and chocolaty on the finish and a bit on the oaky, buttery side, but balanced enough to qualify as a wine with moderate finesse. Drinkable now, but the depth of flavor could carry it for aging until 1994. Rel: $12 Cur: $16 (5/15/90) **85**
Zinfandel Alexander Valley 1985: Austere, extremely dry and tannic, with raspberry flavors buried underneath. A very good wine in an extreme style. Will need until 1994 to '96. Rel: $12 Cur: $16 (7/31/89) **84**
Zinfandel Alexander Valley 1984 Rel: $10 Cur: $18 (3/15/87) **90**
Zinfandel Alexander Valley 1983 Rel: $10 Cur: $18 (5/01/86) **85**
Zinfandel Alexander Valley 1982 Rel: $10 Cur: $18 (5/16/85) SS **91**
Zinfandel Sonoma County 1988: Ripe and rich on the nose, with a stiff push of tannin on the palate, but the berry, red cherry and tart plum flavors sneak through. Has a sense of roundness on the aftertaste. Best to drink after 1994. $12 (3/31/92) **85**

Key to Symbols

The scores reported here are the results of blind tastings conducted by our panel of senior editors. Wines that carry the initials below are results of individual tastings.

THE WINE SPECTATOR 100-POINT SCALE ***95-100***—Classic, a great wine; ***90-94***—Outstanding, superior character and style; ***80-89***—Good to very good, a wine with special qualities; ***70-79***—Average, drinkable wine that may have minor flaws; ***60-69***—Below average, drinkable but not recommended; ***50-59***—Poor, undrinkable, not recommended. "+"—With a score indicates a range; used primarily with barrel tastings to indicate a preliminary score.

SPECIAL DESIGNATIONS SS—Spectator Selection, CS—Cellar Selection, BB—Best Buy, ($NA)—Price not available, (NR)—Not released.

TASTER'S INITIALS (JG)—Jim Gordon, (HS)—Harvey Steiman, (JL)—James Laube, (JS)—James Suckling, (TM)—Thomas Matthews, (TR)—Terry Robards, (PM)—Per-Henrik Mansson, (BT)—Barrel Tasting (these wines were tasted blind from barrel samples), (CA-date)—*California's Great Cabernets* by James Laube, (CH-date)—*California's Great Chardonnays* by James Laube, (VP-date)—*Vintage Port* by James Suckling.

DATE TASTED Dates in parentheses represent the issue in which the rating was published.

Zinfandel Sonoma County 1987: Straightforward and not as elegant as in most years, but sharply focused blackberry aromas and flavors carry through the long, somewhat tannic finish. Drinkable now, but better in about 1994. Rel: $12 Cur: $17 (10/15/90) **84**
Zinfandel Sonoma County 1984 $11 (10/31/88) **86**
Zinfandel Sonoma County 1981 $10 (4/01/84) **80**

GUENOC
Zinfandel California 1989: Firm and tight, packing in plenty of spicy, minty, berry-scented flavors. Intense and lively. Drink now through 1995. $9.50 (5/15/92) **85**
Zinfandel California 1988: Wood-tinged cherry and spice aromas and flavors are modest and unassuming in this soft wine that's a bit flabby and awkward. Drinkable now. $7.50 (9/15/90) **76**
Zinfandel Guenoc Valley 1987: Very ripe and fruity, with juicy plum and earthy raspberry notes that are very appealing. Not too tannic. Drink now. $8 (5/15/90) **84**
Zinfandel Guenoc Valley 1984 $5.50 (9/15/87) **67**
Zinfandel Lake County 1985: Tart, lean and compact, with spicy, peppery flavors, moderate tainnins and decent length. A solid everyday wine to drink now. $5.50 (3/31/89) **79**
Zinfandel Lake County 1981 $5 (5/16/84) **78**

GUNDLACH BUNDSCHU
Zinfandel Sonoma Valley 1989: Fresh and flavorful, running more toward rhubarb than the typical raspberry flavors. Finishes sweet and smooth. Drinkable now. A good value. 600 cases made. $7.50 (7/31/91) **84**
Zinfandel Sonoma Valley 1988: A claret-style Zin, offering delicious berry, plum, violet and toast aromas and flavors plus a sense of restraint that frames the juicy fruit with a frank dose of tannin. $16 (5/31/90) BB **88**
Zinfandel Sonoma Valley 1987: A Beaujolais-style wine, and a charming example of it. Youthful from the color through the delicate finish, bursting with fresh, appealing strawberry and cherry aromas and flavors. Drink now. $7.75 (3/31/89) **87**
Zinfandel Sonoma Valley Rhinefarm Vineyards 1989: Rough and ready, with generous, ripe plum and pepper aromas and flavors, full body and concentration that persists on the finish. Good now and maybe better in 1993. 500 cases made. $12 (7/31/91) **87**
Zinfandel Sonoma Valley Rhinefarm Vineyards 1988: Lovely black cherry and black pepper aromas and flavors seem to jump out of the glass in this smooth-textured, firmly structured wine. Has plenty to offer for current drinking or short-term aging. Drink by 1993. 1,720 cases made. $16 (12/15/90) **88**
Zinfandel Sonoma Valley Rhinefarm Vineyards 1987: Oak overtones detract from the quality. The flavors are simple and decent but unexciting. Drink now. $8.50 (9/15/89) **71**
Zinfandel Sonoma Valley Rhinefarm Vineyards 1986 $12 (9/15/88) **90**
Zinfandel Sonoma Valley Rhinefarm Vineyards 1985 $7 (2/29/88) **84**
Zinfandel Sonoma Valley Rhinefarm Vineyards 1984 $12 (4/30/87) BB **87**
Zinfandel Sonoma Valley Rhinefarm Vineyards 1982 $8.50 (2/16/86) **87**

HAYWOOD
Zinfandel Sonoma Valley 1986 $11 (9/15/88) **89**
Zinfandel Sonoma Valley 1985 $9.50 (11/15/87) **85**
Zinfandel Sonoma Valley 1984 $9 (5/31/87) **92**
Zinfandel Sonoma Valley 1983 $8 (1/01/86) **85**
Zinfandel Sonoma Valley 1982 $8 (11/01/84) **89**
Zinfandel Sonoma Valley Los Chamizal Vineyards 1989: Spicy, earthy flavors add grace to the crisply focused, intense plum and berry aromas and flavors. Finishes crisp and tart, with tannins that could use until 1993 to '95 to settle down. 2,200 cases made. $14 (11/15/91) **85**
Zinfandel Sonoma Valley Los Chamizal Vineyards 1988: Lean in texture but concentrated in flavor, with lip-smacking raspberry and cherry flavors lasting well into the long finish. A fairly elegant wine with overtones of vanilla and nutmeg. Drinkable now, but should last through 1993 or '94. 1,316 cases made. $12.50 (11/30/90) **89**

HIDDEN CELLARS
Zinfandel Mendocino County Pacini Vineyard 1989: Offers plenty of fresh berry flavor accented by spice notes, but has a vinegary edge that not everyone will like. Fine to drink now. 1,328 cases made. $10 (2/29/92) **81**
Zinfandel Mendocino County Pacini Vineyard 1988: Bursting at the seams with appealing cherry and mixed berry aromas and flavors, but held in check by a firm structure that just focuses the spicy fruit on the long finish. Less polished than some at this point. Perhaps cellaring until 1993 or '94 will shine it up. 1,250 cases made. $10 (12/31/90) **85**
Zinfandel Mendocino County Pacini Vineyard 1986 $7.50 (10/31/88) **86**
Zinfandel Mendocino County Pacini Vineyard 1984 $7.50 (4/15/87) **88**

HOP KILN
Zinfandel Russian River Valley 1988: Ripe and rich, with generous plum, cherry and vanilla aromas and flavors held in check by a structure of firm tannin and alcohol. Balanced but not at all shy. Has enough tannin to carry it through 1993 to '95 in the cellar, but is probably best to drink before then. $12 (12/15/90) **88**
Zinfandel Russian River Valley 1986: What good Zinfandel is all about. Smooth, velvety and ripe on a firm framework of acidity and moderate tannins. The wild berry flavors are fresh and full. Drink now. $10 (6/15/89) **85**
Zinfandel Russian River Valley 1982 $8.50 (11/01/85) **85**
Zinfandel Russian River Valley Primitivo 1985 $12 (3/15/88) **80**
Zinfandel Russian River Valley Primitivo Reserve 1985: Packs a wallop. Deeply colored with equally deep blackberry and black cherry flavors and plenty of soft tannins. Full-bodied. Smells dusty and oaky at first, but has a well of fruit in the flavor. Drink now to 1993. $12 (6/15/89) **90**
Zinfandel Sonoma County Primitivo 1988: Deep, dark, ripe, intense and powerful, with plenty of tannin to complement the muscular plum, raspberry and cherry flavors. There's nothing subtle about it, but the intensity of fruit is so enjoyable that it almost makes you forget the tannin. Drink now to 1994. Limited availability. $14 (12/31/90) **89**

INGLENOOK
Zinfandel Napa Valley 1986: Hard-edged and peppery, with drying oak dominating. The fruit tastes simple, barely ripe and shallow. Of marginal quality. Drink now. 5,000 cases made. $8 (4/30/91) **73**
Zinfandel Napa Valley 1983 $7.50 (3/15/88) **81**
Zinfandel Napa Valley 1981 $7 (2/01/85) **79**

IRON HORSE
Zinfandel Alexander Valley 1982 $7 (10/16/84) **81**

KARLY
Zinfandel Amador County 1988: Earthy and smoky, with very ripe fruit flavor that could use a firmer, more muscular structure. For such a big wine it comes off as simple and gentle on the finish. Drinkable now. $9.50 (12/31/90) **83**
Zinfandel Amador County 1987: Lavishly oaked and elegant in style, with clean, simple, ripe flavors in an easy-to-drink wine. Fruit comes through on the finish. Drink now. $9.50 (3/31/90) **83**
Zinfandel Amador County 1986: Not for the faint of palate. Powerfully oaky and herbal in flavor and quite tannic. The plum and berry flavors seem strong enough to balance the tannins. Drink now to 1994. $9 (3/31/89) **79**
Zinfandel Amador County 1985 $8.50 (12/31/87) **72**
Zinfandel Amador County Sadie Upton 1989: A very earthy aroma throws you off, but the raspberry and herb flavors make a recovery. Good quality overall. $15 (3/31/92) **81**

KENDALL-JACKSON
Zinfandel Anderson Valley DuPratt Vineyard 1987: Ripe and focused, with richness, elegance and

plenty of plum, raspberry, vanilla and toast aromas and flavors. Echoes coffee and cocoa notes on the long finish. Shows maturity but has plenty of life. Drink now. 1,000 cases made. $20 (7/31/91) **90**
Zinfandel Anderson Valley DuPratt-DePatie Vineyard 1986: Thick and intense, a wine for those who like the bold, assertive style. Has rich pepper and berry notes and lots of oak. Very intense and may be less appealing to most Zin fans. Drink now. $16 (12/15/89) **85**
Zinfandel Anderson Valley DuPratt-DePatie Vineyard 1983 $10 (11/01/85) **76**
Zinfandel California Vintner's Reserve 1989: Light and fruity, with nicely focused raspberry and currant aromas and flavors, a smooth texture and drinkable balance. Best to drink soon. $11 (9/30/91) **84**
Zinfandel Clear Lake Viña Las Lomas Vineyard 1983 $7 (6/01/85) **80**
Zinfandel Mendocino 1987: Earthy and complex, with fresh, ripe cherry, plum and raspberry flavors that are rich and intense and finish with fine length. The tannins are well proportioned. Drink now to 1994. $9 (3/15/90) **88**
Zinfandel Mendocino 1986 $9 (9/15/88) **86**
Zinfandel Mendocino Ciapusci Vineyard 1984: A claret-style Zinfandel, with all the character you would want. The spice, pepper and ripe raspberry notes are in harmony, but the tannins sneak up on the finish. Ready now. $16 (12/15/89) **86**

KENWOOD
Zinfandel Sonoma Valley 1988: Drinkable and pleasant, with appealing wild berry and toast flavors, but the structure seems relatively flat and unexceptional. Tasted twice. $11 (12/31/90) **82**
Zinfandel Sonoma Valley 1987: Rich, elegant and well balanced, with pretty, supple, ripe raspberry, cherry and spicy plum flavors that are fresh, lively and long on the finish. Has a gorgeous aftertaste. Drink now to 1995. $11 (10/31/89) **90**
Zinfandel Sonoma Valley 1985 $9.50 (5/15/88) **89**
Zinfandel Sonoma Valley 1984 $8.50 (9/15/87) **90**
Zinfandel Sonoma Valley 1983 $7.50 (11/15/86) **88**
Zinfandel Sonoma Valley 1982 $7.50 (7/16/86) **90**
Zinfandel Sonoma Valley Jack London Vineyard 1989: Crisply focused and tart, with lively plum and berry aromas and flavors that finish strong. Drinkable now, but probably better after it softens in 1993 or '94. $14 (9/30/91) **83**
Zinfandel Sonoma Valley Jack London Vineyard 1987: Attractive for its ripe raspberry, cherry and vanilla notes and elegant balance, but its firmness and tannic structure bode well for aging. Try now. $12 (12/15/89) **88**

KONRAD
Zinfandel Mendocino County 1989: Packed with ripe berry flavors and accented by cinnamon notes, this is well balanced to begin drinking in about 1994. The tight tannins on the finish need time to settle down. 1,008 cases made. $10 (3/31/92) **84**

CHARLES KRUG
Zinfandel Napa Valley 1989: Lean, crisp and fruity, with energetic raspberry and strawberry aromas that are less intense on the palate, leaving it rather light and crisp. Drink now with chicken or pork. $6 (12/15/90) BB **83**

LA JOTA
Zinfandel Howell Mountain 1987: Very tough and tannic, but has enough rich, intense cherry flavor trying to pry its way loose. Drink now. 850 cases made. $12 (10/31/89) **83**
Zinfandel Howell Mountain 1986 $10 (10/31/88) **89**
Zinfandel Howell Mountain 1985 $10 (4/30/88) **85**
Zinfandel Howell Mountain 1984 $10 (11/15/87) **88**

LAMBORN FAMILY
Zinfandel Howell Mountain 1988: Big, tough and flavorful, with lots of ripe blackberry, cedar and toast aromas and flavors that are mouth-filling and long. Hold until at least 1993 or '94 to let the tannins subside. $11 (2/15/91) **89**
Zinfandel Howell Mountain 1987: Intense and tannic, with dry raspberry and cherry flavors that are very tight and concentrated. You'll need to give this one time to soften and mellow, but then it should be a beauty. One to watch. Drink in 1993 at the earliest. $10 (3/15/90) **84**

LOLONIS
Zinfandel Mendocino County Lolonis Vineyards Private Reserve 1989: Rich and flavorful, with plenty of oak-rounded ripe blackberry and cherry flavors that are focused and spicy on the finish. Shows a hint of pickle on the aroma, but is a solid wine that delivers plenty of flavor. Drinkable now. 1,000 cases made. $12 (8/31/91) **83**

LYTTON SPRINGS
Palette Sonoma-Mendocino Counties NV: A curious blend of Merlot and Zinfandel, this ultraripe wine offers lush black cherry, plum, anise and herb notes. Pleasant to enjoy now through 1994. Tasted twice. 1,500 cases made. $10 (11/15/91) **83**
Zinfandel Sonoma County 1989: Ripe, generous and full-bodied, with lots of plum and spice aromas, earthy, barnyardy toast and ripe fruit flavors and echoes of plum and vanilla. $15 (8/31/91) **84**
Zinfandel Sonoma County 1988: Ripe and jammy, with beautifully defined raspberry aromas and flavors and hints of plum, nutmeg, vanilla and toast to make it more interesting. Claret-style in structure and well balanced. Lovely now but should continue to develop through 1994. $12 (7/31/90) **90**
Zinfandel Sonoma County 1987: Very ripe, powerful and toasty, with concentrated pepper, raspberry and plum flavors held in careful check by a firm structure and fine tannins. Drink now. $12 (5/31/89) **88**
Zinfandel Sonoma County 1986 $10 (10/15/88) **87**
Zinfandel Sonoma County 1985 $8 (8/31/87) **90**
Zinfandel Sonoma County 1984 $8 (10/31/86) **70**
Zinfandel Sonoma County Valley Vista Vineyard Private Reserve 1981 $12 (1/01/85) **85**

MARIETTA
Zinfandel Sonoma County 1988: Dense and flavorful, with generous berry, plum and spice aromas and flavors. Thick and chewy, but the fruit and chocolate flavors manage to outrun the tannins. Best to drink in 1993 to '97. 2,200 cases made. $8 (12/31/91) BB **87**
Zinfandel Sonoma County 1987: An austere wine, with more tannin than the modest intensity of black cherry flavor can support. Lacks the generosity and power to be the big wine it wants to be, but may soften with time. Drinkable now. 2,800 cases made. $8 (11/30/90) **79**
Zinfandel Sonoma County 1985 $7.50 (12/31/87) **87**
Zinfandel Sonoma County 1984 $7.50 (1/31/87) **90**
Zinfandel Sonoma County 1982 $6.50 (6/16/84) **73**
Zinfandel Sonoma County Reserve 1985 $10 (12/31/87) **88**

MARK WEST
Zinfandel Sonoma County Robert Rue Vineyard 1987: Ripe, tight and peppery, with tannic raspberry, cherry and plum flavors. Shows more depth than most, but is tightly wound and should benefit from cellaring through 1994. 600 cases made. $16.50 (5/15/92) **86**
Zinfandel Sonoma County Robert Rue Vineyard 1986: Big and brawny, with Port-like aromas and flavors suggesting wild berries and plums. The tannins are present without being overwhelming and the aromatic pepper notes are appealing. Drink with cheese. $14 (3/15/90) **83**
Zinfandel Sonoma County Robert Rue Vineyard 1985 $14 (7/31/88) **85**

MARTIN BROTHERS
Zinfandel Paso Robles 1986: Light in color and body, this is ready to enjoy now for its freshness and crisp balance. Has clean plum and strawberry flavors. $8 (12/15/89) **78**
Zinfandel Paso Robles 1985 $6.50 (2/15/88) **83**

MARTINELLI
Zinfandel Russian River Valley 1988: A peppery, fruity wine that's light and charming to drink now. Well balanced, with cherry, strawberry and spice accents. $11 (4/30/91) **85**

LOUIS M. MARTINI
Zinfandel California 1974 $22 (6/16/85) **78**
Zinfandel California 1973 $25 (6/16/85) **87**
Zinfandel North Coast 1985: Clean, crisp and nicely proportioned, with spicy cedar and pepper notes that should play well off a zesty pasta dish. Drink now. $6.25 (3/31/89) **80**
Zinfandel North Coast 1984 $6 (2/15/88) BB **84**
Zinfandel North Coast 1983 $7.75 (10/15/86) **87**
Zinfandel Paso Robles 1989: Light and bursting with raspberry aromas and flavors, this Beaujolais-style quaffing wine is immediately likable. Drink soon. $8 (8/31/91) **83**
Zinfandel Sonoma County 1986: Lean and austere, with herbal tobacco aromas and flavors. Crisp and tannic enough to need until about 1994 to show what it has. $7 (10/31/89) **79**

MASTANTUONO
Zinfandel San Luis Obispo County Dante Dusi Vineyards 1986: Richly aromatic and rustic, with brilliant cherry, blueberry and vanilla aromas and flavors. Perhaps a bit volatile on the finish but generous and drinkable. Ripe and ready to drink soon. $9 (8/31/91) **84**
Zinfandel San Luis Obispo County Dante Dusi Vineyards Unfined & Unfiltered 1984: A mature wine, with so many tar, leather and smoke flavors that it's almost medicinal. Has ripe cherry notes but seems earthy and stale. $18 (7/31/91) **73**

MAZZOCCO
Zinfandel Sonoma County Traditional Style 1988: Ripe and rich, with deep, concentrated cherry and berry aromas and flavors rounded by spicy oak notes. Is a bit blunt on the finish, but balanced and flavorful. Drink now. 1,700 cases made. $13 (10/15/90) **89**
Zinfandel Sonoma County Traditional Style 1986 $10 (12/15/88) **90**

MCDOWELL VALLEY
Zinfandel McDowell Valley 1988: Firm and fairly full-bodied, with solid plum and vaguely herbal aromas and flavors that veer away from the usual pure fruit. Signficant tannins need hearty food or cellaring until 1993 or '94 to soften. $9.50 (12/31/90) **80**
Zinfandel McDowell Valley 1987: With its cherry and blackberry flavors focused sharply on a lean frame, this has immediate appeal for the dinner table. A firm texture and hints of vanilla and spice on the finish make it distinctive. Start drinking now. $8 (12/15/89) BB **87**

MEEKER
Zinfandel Dry Creek Valley 1988: Ripe and tart at the same time, with a sharply focused range of blackberry, plum and toast aromas and flavors that are a bit awkward now, but should settle down with cellaring until 1993 or '94. $10 (8/31/91) **82**
Zinfandel Dry Creek Valley 1987: Elegantly balanced with fresh, crisp, lively raspberry and cherry notes and just the right touch of oak. Has firm tannins and a clean, fruity aftertaste. Drink now to 1994. $10 (3/31/90) **85**
Zinfandel Dry Creek Valley 1986: Bright, fresh raspberry and cherry aromas mark it as a light but firmly tannic wine to drink now. Tasty and well balanced. $9 (3/15/89) **83**
Zinfandel Dry Creek Valley 1985 $8 (5/15/88) **90**

MENDOCINO ESTATE
Zinfandel Mendocino 1985 $4.75 (2/15/88) **79**
Zinfandel Mendocino 1984 $4.25 (5/31/87) **68**

MILANO
Zinfandel Mendocino County 1981 $6 (10/01/84) **80**
Zinfandel Mendocino County Sanel Valley Vineyard 1988: A pretty core of ripe, elegant raspberry and black cherry flavors pours through this youngster before the tannins clamp down. Enjoy now for its fruitiness or let it mellow. Drink now to 1994. 461 cases made. $8 (4/30/91) **85**

MIRASSOU
Zinfandel California Dry Red Lot No. 3 NV: A reasonably smooth but awkward wine that tastes like a blend of old and new lots. Acceptable but just average quality. $5 (7/31/91) **73**
Zinfandel California Lot No. 4 NV: Fruity and true to type, this medium-weight wine has appealing blackberry and cherry aromas and flavors and hints of spices on the finish. Drinkable now. $5.50 (7/31/91) BB **81**

MONTEREY PENINSULA
Zinfandel Amador County Ferrero Ranch Doctors' Reserve 1987: Ripe and full-bodied, this old-style, rock 'em, sock 'em wine has generous berry and plum aromas and flavors and is a bit leathery on the finish. Enjoyable with hearty food. 250 cases made. $15 (5/15/91) **83**
Zinfandel Amador County Ferrero Ranch Doctors' Reserve 1982 $10 (2/29/88) **83**

MONTEVINA
Zinfandel Amador County 1987: Light and simple, with more earthy, oaky flavors showing than fruit. Decent and well balanced but unexciting. For fans of understated wines. Drink now. $7.50 (3/31/90) **75**
Zinfandel Shenandoah Valley Montino 1985 $5.50 (10/15/88) **75**
Zinfandel Shenandoah Valley Winemaker's Choice 1984 $9 (8/31/87) **75**
Zinfandel Shenandoah Valley Winemaker's Choice 1980 $9 (4/16/84) **78**

MOUNT VEEDER
Zinfandel Napa County 1982 $8.50 (3/16/85) **86**

NALLE
Zinfandel Dry Creek Valley 1989: Fresh and fruity, with solid blackberry and black cherry aromas and flavors that spread nicely on the palate and hint at vanilla on the finish. Drinkable now. $13.50 (7/31/91) **85**
Zinfandel Dry Creek Valley 1988: Every berry aroma and flavor you can imagine wafts across the palate in this supple, almost elegant wine, hinting at toast and black pepper on the finish. Long and beautifully balanced, this is a Zinfandel for Cabernet lovers. Drinkable now. 2,100 cases made. Rel: $12.50 Cur: $15 (7/31/90) **89**
Zinfandel Dry Creek Valley 1987: A mouthful of pure Zin-ful pleasure. Extremely youthful, exuberant, firm textured and bustin' out all over with raspberry, vanilla and floral complexity. Long and almost elegant on the finish. Best yet from Doug Nalle. Drinkable now. $10 (5/31/89) SS **92**
Zinfandel Dry Creek Valley 1986 $9 (6/30/88) **90**
Zinfandel Dry Creek Valley 1985 $8 (9/15/87) **91**
Zinfandel Dry Creek Valley 1984 $7.50 (10/15/86) **91**

PARDUCCI
Zinfandel Mendocino County 1986 $5.75 (7/15/88) **80**

PEACHY CANYON
Zinfandel Paso Robles 1989: Wild berry and beet aromas and flavors are a little strange in this tart, otherwise racy wine. Finishes with a touch of greenish fruit. Best in 1993 to '95. 650 cases made. $10 (12/31/91) **82**
Zinfandel Paso Robles Especial Reserve 1989: Ripe, supple and generous, with lots of plum, black cherry and spice aromas and flavors that expand over the palate and join hints of chocolate and cedar on the finish. Drinkable now if you want something hearty, but probably at its best around 1994. 240 cases made. $12 (12/31/91) **89**

J. PEDRONCELLI
Zinfandel Dry Creek Valley 1988: Smooth, supple and flavorful, with bright raspberry, strawberry

and cherry flavors. Not particularly intense but pleasant, lively and ready to drink tonight. $7 (11/30/90) BB **84**
Zinfandel Dry Creek Valley 1987: Extremely dry and almost sour on the finish. The modest cherry flavor gets buried under the tannins and off-putting aromas make this hard to like. Tasted twice, with identical scores. $7 (7/31/90) **65**
Zinfandel Dry Creek Valley 1986: Very spicy and floral, with zippy ripe berry and plum flavors that are focused and concentrated, framed with enough austere tannin to want time in the cellar to smooth out. Drinkable now. $6 (3/31/89) BB **86**
Zinfandel Dry Creek Valley 1984 $5.50 (7/15/88) BB **88**
Zinfandel Sonoma County 1983 $4.50 (9/15/87) **77**
Zinfandel Sonoma County 1982 $4.50 (10/31/86) BB **79**
Zinfandel Sonoma County 1981 $4.50 (1/01/85) **78**
Zinfandel Sonoma County Reserve 1981 $8 (11/15/87) **82**

PESENTI
Zinfandel San Luis Obispo County Family Reserve 1984: Agreeably mature, showing leathery, tealike aromas, muted fruit flavors and a lush texture, with moderate tannins and soft balance. Drink now. $6 (12/15/89) **79**

JOSEPH PHELPS
Zinfandel Alexander Valley 1985 $10 (7/31/87) **74**
Zinfandel Alexander Valley 1981 $6.75 (4/16/85) **80**
Zinfandel Alexander Valley 1980 $6.75 (7/16/84) **85**
Zinfandel Napa Valley 1985 $6 (12/31/86) **82**
Zinfandel Napa Valley 1980 $6.75 (1/01/86) **60**
Zinfandel Napa Valley 1979 $6.75 (4/16/84) **60**

PRESTON
Zinfandel Dry Creek Valley 1988: Lighter in style, with charming strawberry and blackberry aromas and flavors that are stylish, pleasant and immediately likable. Drinkable now but should hold through the mid-1990s. 4,100 cases made. $10 (10/15/90) **86**
Zinfandel Dry Creek Valley 1987: Intense and concentrated, with plenty of ripe raspberry and cherry flavors framed by toasty oak notes. A bit alcoholic but still balanced. Slightly below Preston's usual standard. Drink now to 1995. 3,840 cases made. $10 (3/15/90) **83**
Zinfandel Dry Creek Valley 1986 $8.50 (12/15/88) **84**
Zinfandel Dry Creek Valley 1985 $8.50 (11/15/87) **91**
Zinfandel Dry Creek Valley 1984 $8 (12/31/86) **80**

QUIVIRA
Zinfandel Dry Creek Valley 1989: Lively and focused, with wild berry and plum aromas and flavors and a hint of earthiness on the finish. Balanced and drinkable. Has enough to wait until 1993 or '94 to be smoother. $13 (7/31/91) **84**
Zinfandel Dry Creek Valley 1988: The beautiful plum, black pepper and wild berry aromas are as seductive as they could be, braced by a firm backbone of supple tannins and toasty oak. A classy wine that's drinkable now. $12 (5/31/90) **88**
Zinfandel Dry Creek Valley 1987: Refreshing and effusively fruity, teeming with pepper, raspberry, spice and jam notes framed by balanced tannins and a touch of wood, but not overdone. Fruit echos on the finish. Delicious now but should age until 1994 and beyond. $11 (7/31/89) **88**
Zinfandel Dry Creek Valley 1986 $9.75 (12/15/88) **88**
Zinfandel Dry Creek Valley 1984 $7 (4/15/87) **88**
Zinfandel Dry Creek Valley 1983 $7 (1/01/86) **75**

RABBIT RIDGE
Zinfandel Russian River Valley Rabbit Ridge Ranch 1988: A firm, focused, claret-style wine that offers attractive blackberry and cherry aromas and flavors and the sort of well-integrated tannins that should have this at its best around 1995. $8 (4/30/91) **86**
Zinfandel Sonoma County 1989: Firm and concentrated, with a strong dose of blackberry and plum aromas and flavors shaded by cedar and slightly leafy overtones. Tannic enough to need until 1993 to '95 to settle down. $9.50 (8/31/91) **86**

A. RAFANELLI
Zinfandel Dry Creek Valley 1989: Aromatic, with a firm, crisp texture and plenty of plum and blackberry flavors to ride a solid stream of fine tannins. Drinkable now with hearty food, but probably better around 1993 to '95. $11 (9/30/91) **85**
Zinfandel Dry Creek Valley 1988: Massively proportioned, with elegance and finesse. Tiers of ripe raspberry, plum and cherry flavors are complex and concentrated, seasoned by the spicy dill flavors of American oak. Drink now to 1995. 5,000 cases made. $9.75 (9/15/90) **90**
Zinfandel Dry Creek Valley 1987: Offers juicy flavors with a touch of gaminess on the finish. Bright raspberry and berry notes come through despite the earthiness. Has a tannic finish. Drink now. $9 (12/15/89) **84**
Zinfandel Dry Creek Valley 1986 $7 (9/15/88) **91**
Zinfandel Dry Creek Valley 1985 $6.25 (12/31/87) **77**
Zinfandel Dry Creek Valley 1983 $6.50 (3/01/86) BB **91**

RAVENSWOOD
Zinfandel Napa Valley Canard 1988: A tough, tannic wine that lacks the fruit to fill it out. Has pleasant spice and toasty oak aromas, but shuts down on the finish and lacks overall harmony and grace. Cellar until 1996. 400 cases made. $11.50 (8/31/91) **75**
Zinfandel Napa Valley Canard 1986: Firm and tannic, balanced by spicy, oaky, peppery notes that are correct but unexciting. Drink now. $11 (3/15/90) **81**
Zinfandel Napa Valley Canard 1985 $10 (3/15/89) **85**
Zinfandel Napa Valley Dickerson Vineyard 1989: Spicy, oaky flavors hit you first, but a core of raspberry emerges on the palate and sneaks in on the finish. Has a bold personality that should keep developing through 1994. 1,000 cases made. $13 (11/15/91) **87**
Zinfandel Napa Valley Dickerson Vineyard 1988: Light in texture but focused in flavor, with an odd eucalyptus and menthol edge to the vivid red cherry and raspberry aromas and flavors that persist on the long finish. A little rambunctious now, but cellaring until 1993 or '94 should make it fine. Tasted twice. 1,000 cases made. $13 (8/31/91) **84**
Zinfandel Napa Valley Dickerson Vineyard 1987: Intense and tannic, with very ripe, powerful plum, blueberry and cherry flavors that are sharply focused. For fans of tart, intense wines. Best to drink in 1993 and beyond. $13 (3/15/90) **86**
Zinfandel Napa Valley Dickerson Vineyard 1986 $12 (12/15/88) **88**
Zinfandel Napa Valley Dickerson Vineyard 1985 $10.50 (12/31/87) **80**
Zinfandel Napa Valley Vintners Blend 1985 $6.25 (5/31/87) **80**
Zinfandel North Coast Vintners Blend 1989: A solid wine, with a firm texture and lots of plum and raspberry aromas and flavors. Hints at vanilla and turns a mite tannic on the finish, so probably best to drink after 1993. $7.50 (7/31/91) BB **83**
Zinfandel North Coast Vintners Blend 1988: Simple, straightforward, balanced and generous in flavor, echoing cherry and toast on a moderately long finish. Easy to approach but firm enough in texture to complement serious food. $7.25 (10/15/90) BB **81**
Zinfandel Sonoma County 1987: Despite the tannins, this has attractive flavors that are spicy, peppery and well balanced. Raspberry notes peek through on the finish. Drink now to 1993. $11 (3/15/90) **88**
Zinfandel Sonoma County 1986 $9 (12/15/88) **90**
Zinfandel Sonoma County 1985 $8.25 (12/31/87) **80**
Zinfandel Sonoma County 1983 $8 (5/01/86) **57**
Zinfandel Sonoma County Dry Creek Benchland 1981 $6.50 (4/01/84) **81**
Zinfandel Sonoma County Old Vines 1989: Solid and chewy, with a firm texture and enough plum and berry flavors coming through on the finish. Needs until 1994 to sort out the tannins. $11 (12/31/91) **82**
Zinfandel Sonoma County Old Vines 1988: Firm, tannic and tart, with well-defined plum and berry aromas and flavors that linger on the finish. Doesn't have the intensity of some wines but should cut rich food nicely. Drinkable now. 4,133 cases made. $11 (11/30/90) **87**
Zinfandel Sonoma County Vintners Blend 1987: Simply luscious, and a great bargain. Tastes deep, lively and supple, with smooth, ripe cherry and berry flavors and a little cherry and spice seasoning. Drink now. $6 (6/15/89) BB **88**
Zinfandel Sonoma County Vogensen Vineyard 1981 $8 (4/16/84) **68**
Zinfandel Sonoma-Napa Counties Vintners Blend 1986 $5.75 (6/30/88) BB **85**
Zinfandel Sonoma Valley Cooke 1987: An intense, lively wine that's dense, deep, rich and concentrated, with pretty raspberry and pepper notes coming through on the finish. Drink now. $13 (3/15/90) **84**
Zinfandel Sonoma Valley Old Hill Vineyard 1987: Intensely tannic and packed with ripe raspberry, cherry, plum and spice flavors that are powerful and enduring. Drink in 1994 at the earliest. $15 (3/15/90) **87**
Zinfandel Sonoma Valley Old Hill Vineyard 1986 $13 (12/15/88) **92**
Zinfandel Sonoma Valley Old Hill Vineyard 1985 $12 (12/31/87) **87**

RICHARDSON
Geyserville Sonoma County 1989: Full-bodied, flavorful and velvety in texture, with straightforward blueberry and blackberry aromas and flavors. A solid wine. 2,266 cases made. $14 (11/15/91) **84**
Zinfandel Sonoma Valley NV: Very flavorful and deeply colored, with spicy, oaky aromas of nutmeg and ginger and broad, sweet-tasting raspberry and blackberry flavors. Needs only firmer acidity. $9 (7/31/89) **76**

RIDGE
Zinfandel Howell Mountain 1989: A densely flavored, deeply colored wine that piles pepper and well-extracted blackberry flavors on top of firm, chewy tannins and full body. Perhaps best in 1993. $12 (3/31/92) **87**
Zinfandel Howell Mountain 1988: Ripe and earthy, with strong burnt coffee overtones to the dark plum and cherry flavors. A rough, tough wine that needs something such as barbecued steak to do it justice. Drink in 1993 to '95. Tasted twice. 2,775 cases made. $12 (7/31/91) **82**
Zinfandel Howell Mountain 1987: A ripe, earthy-smelling wine that's full of fruit, supple in texture and moderately tannic on the finish. Medium-bodied and ready to drink now to 1993. $10 (5/31/90) **83**
Zinfandel Howell Mountain 1985 $9 (5/15/88) **73**
Zinfandel Howell Mountain 1984 $9 (6/30/87) **81**
Zinfandel Howell Mountain 1983 $9 (5/01/86) **89**
Zinfandel Howell Mountain 1982 $9 (6/01/85) **85**
Zinfandel Napa County York Creek 1985 $10.50 (12/31/87) **82**
Zinfandel Napa County York Creek 1984 $10.50 (3/15/87) **86**
Zinfandel Napa County York Creek 1982 $10.50 (7/16/85) SS **91**
Zinfandel Napa County York Creek 1981 $9.50 (1/01/84) **89**
Zinfandel Paso Robles 1989: Ripe and rich, with definite oak and modest barnyardy overtones to the ripe raspberry and plum aromas and flavors. Has enough to want until 1994 but you could enjoy it sooner with hearty food. Tasted twice. $10 (11/15/91) **84**
Zinfandel Paso Robles 1987: Earthy and gamy, with attractive wild berry and spice notes to make it complete. Well balanced with enough tannin for cellaring. Drink now to 1994. $10 (3/15/90) **85**
Zinfandel Paso Robles 1986 $7.25 (10/31/88) **81**
Zinfandel Paso Robles 1982 $8.50 (1/01/85) **90**
Zinfandel Sonoma County 1989: Distinctive on the earthy side of the flavor spectrum, with dill and mineral notes backed by straightforward berry flavor. Drink now to 1994. $8.50 (3/31/92) **80**
Zinfandel Sonoma County 1988: Makes a real style statement. Earthy, leather scented and firmly tannic, with the earthiness almost overpowering the berry and cherry flavors at first sip. Still, it's smooth, generous and ripe and gains fruit complexity on the long finish. $8.50 (2/15/91) BB **88**
Zinfandel Sonoma County Geyserville 1988: Spicy vanilla nuances add grace and complexity to this lively, distinctive wine that's oozing with blackberry and boysenberry flavors on a supple, generous framework. Powerful but not terribly tannic or overbearing. Drinkable now. 3,969 cases made. $14 (11/30/90) SS **90**
Zinfandel Sonoma County Geyserville 1987 $14 (10/31/89) **90**
Zinfandel Sonoma County Geyserville 1986 Rel: $12 Cur: $30 (10/31/88) **79**
Zinfandel Sonoma County Geyserville 1985 Rel: $10.50 Cur: $15 (9/15/87) **83**
Zinfandel Sonoma County Geyserville 1984 $10.50 (12/31/86) **79**
Zinfandel Sonoma County Geyserville 1982 Rel: $9.50 Cur: $32 (9/16/84) **90**
Zinfandel Sonoma County Geyserville 1975 $28 (6/16/85) **67**
Zinfandel Sonoma County Geyserville 1974 $44 (6/16/85) **79**
Zinfandel Sonoma County Geyserville 1973 $55 (6/16/85) **80**
Zinfandel Sonoma County Lytton Springs 1989: Firm and tannic, with a delicate balance between the distinctive oaky, barnyardy flavor profile and the fruit flavor profile. It's a tie on the finish. Should need until 1994 to '96 to soften the tannins. Tasted twice. 3,707 cases made. $13 (11/15/91) **82**
Zinfandel Sonoma County Lytton Springs 1988: Tart and fruity, with berry and plum flavors that turn a bit sour, but the finish is spicy and toasty. Overall a pleasant drink, but where's the beef? 3,258 cases made. $12 (11/30/90) **82**
Zinfandel Sonoma County Lytton Springs 1987: Enormously ripe, fruity and complex, teeming with jammy flavors and finishing with richness and finesse. Drink now to 1994. 3,448 cases made. $11 (10/31/89) **91**
Zinfandel Sonoma County Lytton Springs 1986 Rel: $10 Cur: $14 (10/15/88) **88**
Zinfandel Sonoma County Lytton Springs 1985 $9 (9/15/87) **81**
Zinfandel Sonoma County Lytton Springs 1984 Rel: $9 Cur: $17 (11/15/86) **79**

ROSENBLUM
Zinfandel Napa Valley 1987: Earthy, herbal aromas and flavors tend to overshadow what raspberry characteristics peek through. $9 (10/31/89) **77**
Zinfandel Napa Valley Hendry Vineyard Reserve 1988: Firm and tannic, with spicy, earthy

Key to Symbols

The scores reported here are the results of blind tastings conducted by our panel of senior editors. Wines that carry the initials below are results of individual tastings.

THE WINE SPECTATOR 100-POINT SCALE ***95-100***—Classic, a great wine; ***90-94***—Outstanding, superior character and style; ***80-89***—Good to very good, a wine with special qualities; ***70-79***—Average, drinkable wine that may have minor flaws; ***60-69***—Below average, drinkable but not recommended; ***50-59***—Poor, undrinkable, not recommended. "+"—With a score indicates a range; used primarily with barrel tastings to indicate a preliminary score.

SPECIAL DESIGNATIONS SS—Spectator Selection, CS—Cellar Selection, BB—Best Buy, ($NA)—Price not available, (NR)—Not released.

TASTER'S INITIALS (JG)—Jim Gordon, (HS)—Harvey Steiman, (JL)—James Laube, (JS)—James Suckling, (TM)—Thomas Matthews, (TR)—Terry Robards, (PM)—Per-Henrik Mansson, (BT)—Barrel Tasting (these wines were tasted blind from barrel samples), (CA-date)—*California's Great Cabernets* by James Laube, (CH-date)—*California's Great Chardonnays* by James Laube, (VP-date)—*Vintage Port* by James Suckling.

DATE TASTED Dates in parentheses represent the issue in which the rating was published.

blackberry and cherry aromas and flavors. Tough enough to need until 1993 to soften around the edges. $14 (4/30/91) **84**

ROSS VALLEY
Zinfandel Sonoma County Tom and Kelley Parsons' Vineyard 1988: Ripe and rich, with focused plum, prune, nutmeg and vanilla aromas and flavors. Tastes more like cooked than fresh fruit, but is a big, generous wine to drink with hearty food. $11 (8/31/91) **83**

ROUDON-SMITH
Zinfandel Sonoma County 1988: A good example of the claret style, offering focused, polished ripe raspberry, toast and spice aromas and flavors, a firm texture and good length. Has the grace and style to give a lot of Cabernets a run for their money. Should develop with cellaring until 1993 or '94. $12 (2/15/91) **87**
Zinfandel Sonoma Valley Chauvet Vineyard 1985: Smells mature but tastes overripe, leathery, tannic, heavy and distinctive. When the tannin subsides it should appeal to those who like funky wines. Try in 1993. $8.50 (3/31/89) **80**

ROUND HILL
Zinfandel Napa Valley 1989: Lean and crisp, with laser-sharp raspberry flavors and a strong overtone of anise and toast. Drinkable now but could be cellared until 1993. $6 (3/31/92) BB **81**
Zinfandel Napa Valley 1988: Very well made in the claret style, with oak-tinged blackberry, cherry and nutmeg aromas and flavors expanding enticingly on the long finish. A seductive wine with a firm backbone. Drinkable now. 2,500 cases made. $6.50 (2/15/91) BB **89**
Zinfandel Napa Valley 1985 $5.50 (5/15/88) BB **82**
Zinfandel Napa Valley 1981 $5 (4/16/84) **84**
Zinfandel Napa Valley Select 1987: Offers plenty of fresh, clean flavors with hints of oak, pepper and berry. Well balanced, showing just a touch of tannin. A ready-to-drink wine with character. Drink now to 1993. $6 (3/31/90) BB **84**

RUTHERFORD RANCH
Zinfandel Napa Valley 1986 $7.75 (10/31/88) **62**
Zinfandel Napa Valley 1985 $7.75 (3/15/88) **89**
Zinfandel Napa Valley 1982 $6 (9/16/85) **80**

ST. FRANCIS
Zinfandel Sonoma Valley Old Vines 1989: Earthy, toasty anise flavors dominate the modest berrylike notes, making this slightly hot-finishing wine one not everyone will love. Has distinctive character, however. Try in 1993 or '94. 850 cases made. $12 (3/31/92) **76**

SANDERLING
Zinfandel Amador County 1984 $6 (5/01/86) **70**

SANTA BARBARA
Zinfandel Santa Ynez Valley 1987: Very tasty, fresh, jammy strawberry and raspberry flavors and an almost sweet finish mark this as a wine to be enjoyed in its youth. Drink now. $8.50 (12/15/89) **82**
Zinfandel Santa Ynez Valley Beaujour 1988: Enjoy this now for its freshness and youth. Has ripe, jammy aromas and fresh Nouveau flavors backed by moderate, chewy tannins. $7 (12/15/89) **80**

SANTA YNEZ VALLEY
Zinfandel Paso Robles 1987: Effusively fruity and jammy, showing plum, berry, oak and spice flavors in a ready-to-drink wine that's not too tannic. Drink now to 1993. $8 (3/31/90) **84**

SANTINO
Zinfandel Amador County Aged Release 1988: The flavors are murky and tired, with tomato, anise and earth notes. Drinkable, but not much to get excited about. 1,903 cases made. $7 (2/29/92) **75**
Zinfandel Amador County Aged Release 1984: A mature, claret-style wine without much fruit or depth. More chalky and austere than one expects from this variety. $7 (3/31/89) **67**
Zinfandel Fiddletown Eschen Vineyards 1983 $7.50 (4/15/87) **84**
Zinfandel Shenandoah Valley Grandpère Vineyards 1988: Lean in texture, with herbal bay leaf aromas and flavors that tend to push past the ripe black cherry notes hiding in the background. A simple wine that's best with hearty food. 693 cases made. $12 (8/31/91) **79**

SARAFORNIA
Zinfandel Napa Valley 1988: Sturdy and drinkable, offering cedar- and smoke-tinged berry aromas and flavors and firm tannins. Finishes coarse and simple. 1,200 cases made. $8 (2/15/91) **81**
Zinfandel Napa Valley 1987: Almost overripe, with aromas and flavors of plums and peppers. Medium-bodied and drinkable now. The second label of Storybook Mountain. $7 (3/15/90) **78**

SAUCELITO CANYON
Zinfandel San Luis Obispo County 1986: Rich and seductive, like a full-bodied Burgundy, with slightly earthy, exotic aromas and polished fruit and black pepper flavors. A tasty accent of oak runs from the aroma to the finish. $9.50 (12/15/89) **87**

SAUSAL
Zinfandel Alexander Valley 1989: The salt and pepper aromas and earthy berry flavors are pleasant but unfocused. A good drink, but may be a bit tired already. Tasted twice. 5,000 cases made. $8.50 (3/31/92) **79**
Zinfandel Alexander Valley 1988: Ripe and full-bodied, with rich fruit flavor and firm tannins, but the plum, cherry and spice flavors are closed in now. Drink now or cellar for up to five years, but best to hold until about 1993. $8.50 (4/30/91) **82**
Zinfandel Alexander Valley 1987: Lean and tight, with leafy, green overtones to the raspberry flavors. Drink now. $7.75 (9/15/89) **83**
Zinfandel Alexander Valley 1986 $6.75 (3/31/89) SS **90**
Zinfandel Alexander Valley 1985 $6.25 (10/15/88) **72**
Zinfandel Alexander Valley 1984 $6.75 (5/31/88) **78**
Zinfandel Alexander Valley 1983 $5.75 (9/15/87) BB **82**
Zinfandel Alexander Valley Private Reserve 1988: Ripe and focused but not weighty, showing a nice balance of berry, currant and vanilla aromas and flavors and hints of smoke on the smooth finish. The tannins are well integrated, so it's drinkable now. 1,300 cases made. $14 (4/30/91) **88**
Zinfandel Alexander Valley Private Reserve 1984 $10 (2/15/88) **86**

SEBASTIANI
Zinfandel Sonoma County Family Selection 1985 $5 (9/15/88) BB **88**
Zinfandel Sonoma Valley Proprietor's Reserve Black Beauty 1980 $9 (12/16/85) **76**

SEGHESIO
Zinfandel Alexander Valley Reserve 1988: Rich, fruity and almost opulent, with generous berry, cherry and plum flavors on a smooth-textured background, balanced by lively acidity on the finish. Drinkable now. 1,429 cases made. $12 (8/31/91) **88**
Zinfandel Alexander Valley Reserve 1986: A woody wine, with toast and cedar aromas and flavors that dominate from the first whiff to the last echo of the finish, where the ripe cherry flavor finally kicks in. Fairly smooth now, so drink soon. $9 (10/31/89) **80**
Zinfandel Northern Sonoma 1987: Full-bodied, clean and well structured, with firm tannins and nice blueberry and cherry flavors. Drinkable now, but has enough acidity to last through 1993. $6.50 (7/31/90) BB **85**
Zinfandel Northern Sonoma 1986: Crisp, lively and elegant, with attractive berry and oak flavors of moderate depth and intensity. Ready to drink now. $6.50 (5/15/90) BB **80**
Zinfandel Northern Sonoma 1985: Offers focused berry flavors, good structure and balance and straightforward varietal character. $5.50 (3/15/89) BB **80**
Zinfandel Northern Sonoma 1984 $5.50 (6/30/88) **76**
Zinfandel Sonoma County 1988: Crisp, fruity and smooth in texture, with generous raspberry, blackberry and cinnamon aromas and flavors that echo nicely on the finish. Drink now through 1993. $6.50 (9/30/91) BB **86**

SHAFER
Zinfandel Napa Valley Last Chance 1983 $7 (2/16/86) **73**

SHENANDOAH
Zinfandel Amador County Classico Varietal Adventure Series 1989: Very light and fruity, rather like a Beaujolais, with lots of strawberry and floral flavors. Drink slightly chilled. 841 cases made. $6 (4/30/91) BB **82**
Zinfandel Amador County Special Reserve 1989: Spicy and well balanced, with a lean texture and moderate raspberry and cedar flavors. 4,800 cases made. $8.50 (2/29/92) **84**
Zinfandel Amador County Special Reserve 1987: Ripe and full of fruit, but with firm tannins and a dash of the herbal, briary flavor typical of some Zins. A medium-bodied wine to drink now. $8.50 (7/31/89) **81**
Zinfandel Amador County Special Reserve 1986 $7.50 (7/15/88) **86**
Zinfandel Amador County Special Reserve 1985 $7.50 (2/15/88) **85**
Zinfandel Fiddletown Special Reserve 1983 $7 (10/15/86) **74**

SHOWN AND SONS
Zinfandel Napa Valley 1981 $7.50 (4/16/84) **85**

SIERRA VISTA
Zinfandel El Dorado 1989: Crisp in texture and earthy in flavor, with American oak aromas and flavors that color the modest raspberry notes. Drinkable now, but might be better around 1993 or '94. 1,580 cases made. $9 (3/31/92) **78**
Zinfandel El Dorado Herbert Vineyards 1986: Spicy and charming, with a lean, crisp structure and generous berry aromas and flavors. Drinkable now. $8 (3/31/89) **84**
Zinfandel El Dorado Reeves Vineyard Special Reserve 1985 $12 (4/30/88) **73**

SIMI
Zinfandel Sonoma County 1982 $6.25 (5/01/86) **60**

SKY
Zinfandel Napa Valley 1988: The herb and raspberry aromas promise more than this lean, tart wine delivers on the palate now. The finish is all tannin and herbs. Give it until 1994 to soften. $12 (8/31/91) **78**
Zinfandel Napa Valley 1987: Bold, rich and thick, oozing with fresh, ripe blackberry, cherry and jam flavors that are smooth and supple. Not too tannic, but balanced to drink now or hold. Best now to 1994. Rel: $12 Cur: $17 (10/15/90) **90**
Zinfandel Napa Valley 1985 $9 (10/31/88) **88**

SOBON ESTATE
Zinfandel Shenandoah Valley 1988: Full-bodied, ripe and powerful, with generous plum, toast, chocolate and vanilla aromas and flavors supported by lively acidity and firm tannins. A good example of Foothills Zin, offering more depth and structure than most. Probably best now to around 1994. 800 cases made. $10 (11/30/90) **88**

STEVENOT
Zinfandel Amador County Grand Reserve 1985 $7.50 (12/31/87) **72**
Zinfandel Calaveras County 1986: You could drink this every day. Very lively and well balanced, with ripe berry and black cherry flavors on a firm framework of acidity and tannins. $7.50 (7/31/89) BB **84**
Zinfandel Calaveras County 1984 $6 (6/30/87) **73**

STONY RIDGE
Zinfandel Livermore Valley 1980 $7 (6/16/84) **75**

STORY
Zinfandel Amador County 1987: Ripe and jammy up front, with ripe raspberry and pepper notes, but also fairly woody and dry. A big, ripe style that manages to have a seam of elegance. Balanced and firmly tannic, but drinkable now to 1994. $8.50 (4/30/91) **84**
Zinfandel Amador County 1986: Firm in texture but fruity enough, with a vanilla and caramel edge that adds depth. The tannins could use rich food to soften, or cellar until 1993 or '94. $8.50 (8/31/91) **80**
Zinfandel Amador County 1980 $6 (4/01/84) **73**
Zinfandel Amador County Shenandoah Valley Private Reserve 1984: A bit heavy-handed with oak, leaving a dry, woody impression and a touch of bitterness. The lighter and more delicate fruit is overshadowed by the oaky presence. Drink now to 1993. $14 (4/30/91) **79**

STORYBOOK MOUNTAIN
Zinfandel Napa Valley 1989: Very peppery, tannic and woodsy smelling, with lean fruit flavors and an earthy, tannic finish. Tasted twice, with consistent notes. Rel: $13 Cur: $18 (3/31/92) **80**
Zinfandel Napa Valley 1988: Ripe and peppery, with a solid, tannic core of crushed pepper and berries. Lacks harmony and grace, but perhaps will soften and mellow with cellaring. Drink now. 4,000 cases made. $12.50 (12/31/90) **75**
Zinfandel Napa Valley 1987: A mouthful of fruit and tannin, this rich wine has bright raspberry, berry and spice flavors that are generous and full-bodied and finishes with a cloak of tannin. Drink now to 1996. $11.50 (12/15/89) **88**
Zinfandel Napa Valley 1986 $10.50 (12/15/88) **88**
Zinfandel Napa Valley 1985 $10 (12/31/87) **90**
Zinfandel Napa Valley 1984 $9.50 (3/15/87) **80**
Zinfandel Napa Valley 1983 $8.75 (4/16/86) **90**
Zinfandel Napa Valley 1982 $8.50 (12/01/84) **86**
Zinfandel Napa Valley Reserve 1988: Powerful, full-bodied, tannic and peppery smelling, packing in ample blackberry, tart cherry and spice flavors. Not supple or elegant, but provides a mouthful of flavor. Rel: $20 Cur: $22 (3/31/92) **84**
Zinfandel Napa Valley Reserve 1987: Amazingly ripe and powerful, with deep, rich, complex berry, cherry and peppery, spicy flavors. Is also quite tannic, but not out of bounds for all the fruit. Tasty enough to enjoy now, but should hold up well through 1993 to '95. 950 cases made. Rel: $17.50 Cur: $27 (12/31/90) **89**
Zinfandel Napa Valley Reserve 1986: Spicy, firm in texture and fragrant, with black pepper and raspberry aromas. Approach this big, powerful wine with caution. It has so much tannin that it needs cellaring to soften the edges. Try in 1993 to '95. Rel: $17.50 Cur: $24 (5/15/90) **82**
Zinfandel Napa Valley Reserve 1985 Rel: $16.50 Cur: $22 (5/31/89) **88**
Zinfandel Napa Valley Reserve 1984 Rel: $14.50 Cur: $24 (4/30/88) **92**
Zinfandel Napa Valley Reserve 1983 Rel: $12.50 Cur: $22 (7/31/87) **81**
Zinfandel Napa Valley Reserve 1981 $9.50 (4/16/84) **86**
Zinfandel Sonoma County 1986 $8.50 (10/15/88) **87**
Zinfandel Sonoma County 1982 $7.50 (9/16/85) **81**

RODNEY STRONG
Zinfandel Russian River Valley Old Vines River West Vineyard 1987: Light in color, with more vanilla and spice characteristics of oak than cherry and strawberry flavors. A round, polished wine that's drinkable now. 1,100 cases made. $14 (8/31/91) **82**
Zinfandel Russian River Valley Old Vines River West Vineyard 1980 $12 (11/15/87) **68**
Zinfandel Russian River Valley Old Vines River West Vineyard 1979 $10 (3/15/87) **71**
Zinfandel Sonoma County 1986: Medium-bodied and well made, this tastes smooth, plummy, spicy and soft at first, but has a nip of woody tannins on the finish. $5.50 (3/31/89) **79**
Zinfandel Sonoma County 1982 $5.50 (12/31/87) **70**

SUMMIT LAKE
Zinfandel Howell Mountain 1987: Intense, ripe and jammy, with lively black pepper and berry flavors that are full-bodied, deep and echo on the finish. Straightforward Napa Valley Zinfandel. Drink now to 1994. 1,200 cases made. $11 (2/15/91) **87**
Zinfandel Howell Mountain 1986: Tart, with fresh berry, raspberry and spice notes and lots of acidity. Some may find it too tough and tannic. Drink in 1993 to '97. 900 cases made. $11 (3/15/90) **84**
Zinfandel Howell Mountain 1985 $9.50 (12/15/88) **88**
Zinfandel Howell Mountain 1984 $8.50 (4/30/88) **90**

SUTTER HOME
Zinfandel Amador County 1981 $6.25 (5/16/84) **80**
Zinfandel Amador County 1973 $30 (6/16/85) **86**
Zinfandel Amador County 1972 $8 (6/16/85) **85**
Zinfandel Amador County 1970 $25 (6/16/85) **80**
Zinfandel Amador County Reserve 1988: Big and full-bodied, with extra-ripe prune and blackberry flavors that cruise on through the finish. The tannins are moderate, but high alcohol gives it plenty of punch. $10 (3/31/92) **84**
Zinfandel Amador County Reserve 1987: A sturdy wine, with modest cherry aromas and flavors and perhaps a bit more tannin than you might want, but should be fine with hearty food. 3,400 cases made. $9.50 (5/15/91) **79**
Zinfandel Amador County Reserve 1985: Unusually mature and spicy, offering more toast and tea aromas and flavors than fruit. This lean, somewhat austere wine won't appeal to everyone, but it offers modest complexity. Drink with rich food. Tasted twice. $8.75 (11/30/90) **81**
Zinfandel Amador County Reserve 1984 $9.50 (7/31/89) **82**
Zinfandel California 1989: Light, fruity and accessible, with fresh, ripe raspberry, currant, plum and spice notes that have just the right tannic edge for drinking now through 1993. The finish picks up a touch of raisin that adds a nice dimension. $5 (5/15/91) BB **85**
Zinfandel California 1988: Very light in color and texture, this is a wine of modest dimensions. Simple, drinkable and more vinous than distinctive. Could be fresher. $5 (3/31/91) **72**
Zinfandel California 1987: Won't disappoint. Well balanced and ripe, with blackberry and herbal flavors and a clean, almost sweet finish. A good value. $5.50 (7/31/89) **78**
Zinfandel California 1986 $7 (10/15/88) **76**
Zinfandel California 1984 $6 (12/31/86) **77**

JOSEPH SWAN
Zinfandel California 1973 $55 (6/16/85) **84**
Zinfandel California 1969 $80 (6/16/85) **83**
Zinfandel Sonoma Coast 1986: Attractive for its pure, rich, ripe, spicy flavors and peppery notes that play off the delicious cherry and jam nuances. Tannic but balanced. Reminds you of the old style, but with a sense of elegance. Drink now to 1994. Rel: $12.50 Cur: $17 (3/15/90) **89**
Zinfandel Sonoma Coast 1985 Rel: $12 Cur: $17 (3/15/89) **82**
Zinfandel Sonoma Coast Ziegler Vineyard 1987: Very ripe, with cherry and raspberry notes and pepper seasoning. Not too tannic, and the well-balanced flavors linger on the aftertaste. Best now to 1993. $12.50 (9/15/90) **86**
Zinfandel Sonoma County 1988: Exotic pepper and spice aromas and flavors are built on a firm foundation of well-integrated tannins, but the blackberry notes recede somewhat into the background. Drink soon with hearty food. 850 cases made. $12.50 (8/31/91) **82**
Zinfandel Sonoma County 1987: Relatively light and bright, with jammy berry and toast aromas and flavors and firm tannins, but is ultimately gentle and balanced. Drink now. $12.50 (7/31/90) **86**
Zinfandel Sonoma Valley Stellwagen Vineyard 1987: Firm and tannic, with pepper, cherry, raspberry and jam flavors seasoned by nutmeg and spice notes. Drinkable now, but can be cellared through 1993. $12.50 (9/15/90) **86**

SYCAMORE CREEK
Zinfandel California 1982 $9 (6/16/84) **87**

TERRACES
Zinfandel Napa Valley 1988: Nicely blends smoky, spicy aromas with blueberry and ripe cherry flavors for a stylish, complex wine. Supple enough to drink now, but could be cellared until about 1994. 310 cases made. $12.50 (2/29/92) **86**
Zinfandel Napa Valley 1987: Concentrated, intense raspberry and plum aromas and flavors are framed by lavish spice and mint nuances from oak. A stylish wine that can please today or gain in the cellar through 1993 or '94. 400 cases made. $12.50 (2/15/91) **89**
Zinfandel Napa Valley Hogue Vineyard 1985 $12.50 (10/31/88) **87**

TOPOLOS
Zinfandel Sonoma County Ultimo 1988: Earthy, tannic and rustic, with hard-edged berry and cherry flavors buried under the tannins. Time in the bottle may make this more generous, but it may always be on the earthy side. Drink after 1994. $12 (5/15/92) **77**

VALLEY OF THE MOON
Zinfandel Sonoma Valley 1984: A mature, woody wine that offers berry and pepper notes, but the finish gets dry and tannic. Will need time to soften, but will it get better? We doubt it. Drink now to 1993. $9 (3/15/90) **76**

VALLEY RIDGE
Zinfandel Sonoma County 1988: Smooth, lively and delicate in texture, with appealing raspberry, nutmeg and cinnamon flavors that persist into a balanced finish. Drinkable now through 1994. $9 (11/15/91) **86**

VENDANGE
Zinfandel California 1987: A drinkable wine, with modest cherry and spice aromas and flavors. Smooth and simple, but a bit short on the finish. From Sebastiani. $5.50 (9/15/90) **78**

VILLA MT. EDEN
Zinfandel Napa Valley 1986 $8.50 (12/15/88) **90**

WENTE BROS.
Zinfandel Livermore Valley Special Selection Raboli Vineyards 1985: Rough, stemmy and a bit austere, but enough ripe cherry and raspberry aromas and flavors come through on the finish to make it appealing. Drink now. $10 (12/15/89) **77**

WHITE OAK
Zinfandel Sonoma County 1989: Very solid, full-bodied and deeply flavored, packed with ripe blackberry and raspberry flavors that linger on the finish. Firmly tannic but not overpowering. Best to cellar until about 1993. $10 (2/29/92) **87**

WILLIAMS SELYEM
Zinfandel Russian River Valley Leno Martinelli Vineyard 1985 $10 (7/31/88) **79**

YORK MOUNTAIN
Zinfandel San Luis Obispo County 1986: Ripe, complex and tannic, with clean cherry, berry, cinnamon and nutmeg flavors, stiff tannins and good acidity. Needs until about 1994 to show its potential. $8 (12/15/89) **85**

OTHER CALIFORNIA RED

ATLAS PEAK
Sangiovese Napa Valley 1989: Solid, with a firm texture and a meaty core of cherry, rhubarb and nutmeg aromas and flavors. Not a big wine, but generous and approaching drinkability. May be best after 1993. First release from this new winery. $24 (11/15/91) **86**

BEAULIEU
Burgundy Napa Valley 1987: A hearty, fruity, full-bodied red that's simple but satisfying. Tastes almost like a Zinfandel. $5 (1/31/91) BB **80**
Burgundy Napa Valley 1984: Light, fruity and smooth, a clean, polished wine, with a bit of plummy flavor to balance the maturity and lift it out of the ordinary. $5 (8/31/89) **78**

BOEGER
Barbera El Dorado 1989: Crisp, flavorful and distinctive, offering lots of wild berry and plum aromas and flavors that hint at sage and spices on the finish. Should be great with meat-sauced pasta. Drinkable now. 550 cases made. $10 (10/31/91) **85**
Hangtown Red California 1988: Clean and straightforward, with strawberry and cherry aromas and flavors, medium body and modest tannins. Very intense but still likable. 1,200 cases made. $5.25 (8/31/90) **78**
Hangtown Red California 1987: A sturdy, austere but likable red wine for hearty foods, with peppery, floral, berrylike flavors and firm tannins and acidity. Drink now. $5.25 (2/28/90) BB **82**
Hangtown Red Lot No. 16 California NV: Firm and fruity, like a good Zinfandel, echoing lively raspberry and spice flavors on the slightly tannic finish. Drinkable now with hearty food. 800 cases made. $5.75 (10/31/91) BB **80**

BRANDBORG
Charbono Napa Valley 1989: Velvety in texture and keenly balanced, offering effusive plum and blackberry aromas and flavors that spread and soften on the finish. Drinkable now, but should keep improving through 1993 to '95. 135 cases made. $12 (10/31/91) **85**

DAVID BRUCE
Mrs. Baggins California 1990: A rich, full-bodied, Rhône-style red, with focused fruit flavors rounded out by the vanilla notes of oak barrels. Firmly tannic, but well balanced for drinking now through about 1994. 241 cases made. $10 (6/30/92) **84**

CHRISTOPHE
Joliesse California 1987: Good, solid, firmly structured and tight in flavor, with hints of bell pepper and cherry supplemented by oaky tannins. $5 (2/28/90) **79**

CLOS DU BOIS
Malbec Alexander Valley L'Etranger Winemaker's Reserve 1987: Wildly aromatic, with floral notes and warm, ripe, soft plum, currant, berry and cherry flavors that are bright and vivid. The tannins are smooth and polished and the finish is long and full. Tempting now for its voluptuous flavors, but should age well. Drink now to 1995. $20 (1/31/91) **87**

CLOS DU VAL
Le Clos Napa Valley NV: This hearty, full-bodied, firmly tannic red has good, deep plum and cherry flavors. Delicious and easy to drink now. A blend of Cabernet Sauvignon, Pinot Noir and Zinfandel. 1,800 cases made. $5.50 (8/31/90) BB **85**

COTES DE SONOMA
Deux Cépages Sonoma County 1990: Light in color and resembling Kool-Aid on the palate, with a stalky edge that intrudes. Better to drink chilled. 1,200 cases made. $6 (11/15/91) **73**

DEHLINGER
Young Vines Russian River Valley 1985: Tart and meager, with tannin and acidity-drowned fruit flavors that can't quite peek out from behind the screen of harshness now. Try again in 1993. Not at all what you expect from a quality label such as Dehlinger. $9 (4/15/89) **68**

DICKERSON
Ruby Cabernet Napa Valley 1988: A very deeply colored, full-bodied, tannic, awkward wine that's rough on the palate at this young age. It's questionable whether the currant and cherry flavors will shoulder past the oaky harshness after a few years in the cellar. Save until at least 1995 if this is your style of wine. $9 (2/28/91) **79**

DUNNEWOOD
Reserve Red California NV: Plummy, berrylike flavors stand out in this hearty if unremarkable wine. Fairly well balanced and good for everyday drinking. $3.75 (2/28/89) **76**

DUXOUP
Charbono Napa Valley 1987: An unusual wine for the cellar. Extremely deep in color, with extremely concentrated blackberry and spice aromas, intense berry flavors and a tangy, lingering finish. Hold until at least 1993. $9.50 (6/15/89) **88**

ELYSE
Nero Misto Napa Valley 1990: Rich and almost jammy, with lots of grapey, plummy flavors, moderate tannins and a good accent of vanilla from oak aging. Flavorful, smooth and easy to drink. 120 cases made. $15 (6/30/92) **86**

FIRESTONE
Red Table Wine Santa Ynez Valley 1990: Light and simple, with fresh berry and cherry notes but not much more. A drink-now wine that's devoid of richness or depth. $6 (4/30/92) **74**

GEYSER PEAK
Trione Vineyards California 1987: A good value. Simple but hearty, resembling Cabernet in aroma, this is a bit sweet, with berrylike flavors, a soft structure and light tannins. $3.25 (2/28/90) **77**

GLASS MOUNTAIN QUARRY
Rubis du Val Napa Valley 1988: Simple, fruity and generous, with enough firmness of texture to make it a good companion to hearty chicken or beef. Drinkable now. 587 cases made. $8 (10/31/91) BB **82**

GLEN ELLEN
Petite Verdot Alexander Valley Imagery Series 1988: Light and lively, with bright, fresh, snappy, violet-tinged currant flavors and hints of bay leaf and oregano on the finish. Not a rich wine, but has verve and flavor. The tannins are well submerged. Best after 1993. 312 cases made. $16 (3/31/92) **88**

GUNDLACH BUNDSCHU
No. 2 Sonoma Red Sonoma Valley NV: Salty, nutty aromas and flavors are pleasant enough, but an overtone of pickles detracts from the hints of currant and cherry that poke through on the finish. Drinkable, if a bit odd. $5 (11/15/89) **77**

Key to Symbols

The scores reported here are the results of blind tastings conducted by our panel of senior editors. Wines that carry the initials below are results of individual tastings.

THE WINE SPECTATOR 100-POINT SCALE 95-100—Classic, a great wine; ***90-94***—Outstanding, superior character and style; ***80-89***—Good to very good, a wine with special qualities; ***70-79***—Average, drinkable wine that may have minor flaws; ***60-69***—Below average, drinkable but not recommended; ***50-59***—Poor, undrinkable, not recommended. "+"—With a score indicates a range; used primarily with barrel tastings to indicate a preliminary score.

SPECIAL DESIGNATIONS SS—Spectator Selection, CS—Cellar Selection, BB—Best Buy, ($NA)—Price not available, (NR)—Not released.

TASTER'S INITIALS (JG)—Jim Gordon, (HS)—Harvey Steiman, (JL)—James Laube, (JS)—James Suckling, (TM)—Thomas Matthews, (TR)—Terry Robards, (PM)—Per-Henrik Mansson, (BT)—Barrel Tasting (these wines were tasted blind from barrel samples), (CA-date)—*California's Great Cabernets* by James Laube, (CH-date)—*California's Great Chardonnays* by James Laube, (VP-date)—*Vintage Port* by James Suckling.

DATE TASTED Dates in parentheses represent the issue in which the rating was published.

HAGAFEN
Red Table Wine Napa Valley NV: A very basic red wine that's light on flavor and lean in texture, with a bit of cherry added to a generic, herbal character. $7.50 (6/30/92) **75**

HALLCREST
Clos de Jeannine California 1989: Firm, flavorful and solidly built, but supple enough to show off nice currant and berry aromas and flavors. Hints at vanilla on the finish. Drinkable now. 900 cases made. $8.50 (10/31/91) **82**

HAYWOOD
Spaghetti Red California NV: OK for some occasions, but overdone. Very ripe tasting, with extremely spicy, sweet, raisiny flavors, a soft texture and moderate tannins. $6 (2/15/90) **74**

HEITZ
Ryan's Red Napa Valley NV: An unusual, medium-weight wine that tastes spicy, almost floral, and wears a heavy jacket of tannins for its modest fruit. $6 (2/28/89) **74**

HOP KILN
Marty Griffin's Big Red Russian River Valley 1988: Deep in color and intense in aroma and flavor, yet relatively gentle on the palate, offering appealing berry and plum flavors, a supple texture and charming balance. Enjoy while it's still lively. Drinkable now. $7.50 (11/30/90) BB **85**
Marty Griffin's Big Red Russian River Valley 1987: A powerful wine that lets its blueberry, raspberry and plum flavors shine through. The tannins are subdued. Enjoy it now, but it should hold through 1994 or '95. A blend of mostly Zinfandel and Petite Syrah. 661 cases made. $7.50 (12/15/89) BB **89**
Marty Griffin's Big Red Russian River Valley 1986: Firm, tannic, clean and concentrated, with fresh cherry and blackberry flavors, crisp acidity and nice oaky accents. Very good now, but better in about 1993. $6.50 (6/15/89) BB **85**
Valdiguié M. Griffin Vineyards Russian River Valley 1990: Tannic and ripe, with stewed plum and cherry aromas and flavors and hints of nutmeg and toast on the finish. A bigger wine than you might expect from this grape variety, which usually travels as Gamay in California. Drink in 1993 or '94. 235 cases made. $15 (6/30/92) **77**

KENWOOD
Vintage Red California 1988: Decent and simple. The fresh fruitiness is marred by a drying, tannic finish, leaving an overall impression of awkwardness. $5 (12/31/90) **77**

MARIETTA
Old Vine Red Lot No. Eight Sonoma County NV: A bargain-priced, straightforward, fruity wine that's vibrant and almost sweet, with ripe cherry and berry flavors. Smooth and easy to drink. $5.50 (5/31/90) BB **81**
Old Vine Red Lot No. Seven Sonoma County NV: A claret-style wine that's ripe and toasty, with a firm texture and broad cherry and currant flavors. A likable, lively wine to drink now. $6 (11/15/89) BB **82**
Old Vine Red Lot No. Ten Sonoma County NV: Simple everyday wine, with plenty of punch and tannin. Has enough cherry and berry-scented flavors to stand up to a hearty plate of pasta or grilled meat. Drink now. $6 (4/30/92) **79**

MARTIN BROTHERS
Nebbiolo California 1989: A light, raspberry-tinged wine, with a strong herb and vegetal edge and a floral touch in the aroma. A decent red to drink now. 2,881 cases made. $9 (11/15/91) **76**
Nebbiolo California 1987: Light in color but firmly structured, with modest pepper and herbal flavors and a crisp finish. Ready to drink now. $12 (12/15/89) **75**
Nebbiolo California 1986: Rich, almost sweet berry and cherry flavors are carried on a soft frame of mild tannins and acidity. Drink while it's young and fresh. $12 (12/15/89) **75**
Nebbiolo Paso Robles 1987: Exuberant and lively, with plenty of fresh strawberry and raspberry flavors, firm tannins and crisp acidity. Drink now. $12 (12/15/89) **85**

LOUIS M. MARTINI
Barbera California 1987: Crisp and zesty, with appealing berry aromas and flavors, smoke and dill overtones, lively acidity, moderate tannins and all-around drinkability. Best to drink soon. $6 (12/31/90) BB **83**
Barbera California 1984: Mature and spicy, with very ripe, almost raisiny flavors, but crisply balanced to keep it from getting unctuous. Drinkable now, perhaps with a roast chicken. $7 (11/15/89) **80**

MASTANTUONO
Carminello California 1988: Firm in texture and a bit on the austere side, with simple, grapey, spicy aromas and flavors. A bit tannic on the finish. $7 (7/15/91) **79**

MCDOWELL VALLEY
Bistro Red LVC Mendocino NV: Solid and hearty, with generic fruit flavors and a hint of pepper. Fairly tannic but ready to drink now. $7 (6/30/92) **79**

MONTEREY PENINSULA
California NV: Full-bodied and somewhat tannic, offering plum, raisin and spice flavors. A ripe, hearty, flavorful wine, with more guts than finesse. Drink with hearty food. 2,000 cases made. $6.50 (7/15/91) BB **82**

MONTEVINA
Barbera Amador County Reserve Selection 1987: Ripe and fruity, with a lean texture, but bursting with raspberry and plum aromas and flavors that hint at anise around the edges. Very well balanced and drinkable now, but should continue to improve through 1993 or '94. 600 cases made. $14 (5/31/91) **89**

J.W. MORRIS
Private Reserve California 1987: Simple but hearty, deep in color and very ripe, almost pruny tasting. A slightly sweet wine. $3.50 (6/30/90) **70**

OJAI
Cabernet Sauvignon Syrah Red California 1986: Very mature, mossy and sappy in aroma and flavor and light in color. An attempt at subtlety that's perfectly drinkable, but loses the vigor of either Syrah or Cabernet. An odd style. $7.50 (4/15/89) **74**

ROBERT PEPI
Sangiovese Napa Valley Colline di Sassi Sangiovese Grosso 1989: The second release of this unusual wine from a Tuscan grape. Firm and smooth, with lots of oak notes, but also has attractive cherry, plum and raspberry flavors. A light style of wine that's ready to drink now. 630 cases made. $25 (10/31/91) **83**

R.H. PHILLIPS
Cuvée Night Harvest California NV: Fresh and rich, with lively plum, cedar and strawberry aromas and spicy, refreshing, complex flavors that are beguiling. Drink now. $5 (5/15/89) BB **86**
Cuvée Rouge Night Harvest California NV: A stylish, distinctive wine that's fruity, spicy and generous, with lots of nutmeg, cherry and anise flavors. Smooth, balanced and ready to drink. A blend of Syrah, Mourvèdre and Duriff. $6 (5/31/91) BB **84**

PRESTON
Barbera Dry Creek Valley 1989: Tart, crisp and fruity, with intense, moderately rich berry, plum and raspberry flavors that aren't too tannic. Enjoy now or cellar through 1995. 625 cases made. $12.50 (3/15/92) **86**
Estate Red Dry Creek Valley 1989: Good for everyday consumption. Fresh, light and simple, with cherry and herb flavors, mild tannins and a clean finish. Tasted twice. 2,200 cases made. $5.50 (6/30/90) **77**
Estate Red Dry Creek Valley 1988: Wild berry aromas and flavors make this attractive at first sip and the flavors stay with you right through to the well-balanced finish. $5 (8/31/89) BB **82**
Faux-Castel Rouge Dry Creek Valley 1990: Tough and tannic, with a core of raspberry and blackberry flavors pressing against the veil of astringency. Has plenty of character, but it's a gamble to hope the tannins will subside. Best after 1994. 1,298 cases made. $9 (6/30/92) **82**

KENT RASMUSSEN
Dolcetto Napa Valley 1990: A blue bottle? Seems appropriate for a fresh, snappy wine, with nice blueberry and plum aromas and flavors. Gets a little tannic on the finish, but food should take care of that. Drinkable now. 75 cases made. $20 (3/15/92) **85**

ROUDON-SMITH
Claret Cuvée Five California NV: Full-flavored, with ripe, simple berry and cherry flavors and an agreeably sturdy structure of acidity and tannins. $4.50 (3/31/89) **78**

SANTINO
Alfresco Amador County NV: Light and smooth in texture, but ebulliently fruity, with lots of jammy strawberry and raspberry aromas and flavors that persist on the finish. 5,000 cases made. $6 (8/31/91) BB **83**
Barbera Amador County Aged Release 1988: Ripe and generous, with lots of cherry, cola and chocolate flavors, but has less to offer in the way of aroma. Firm and tannic enough to need until 1993 to polish the texture and let the rich flavors come through. 412 cases made. $12 (10/31/91) **85**
Satyricon California 1988: Warm, rich, flavorful and generous, offering plum, berry and spice aromas and flavors that linger on the finish. Drinkable now, but should be fine through 1994 or '95. Limited quantity. 220 cases made. $14 (10/31/91) **83**

SEBASTIANI
Barbera Sonoma Valley 1987: Ripe and fruity, with generous blackberry and raspberry aromas and flavors and firm acidity, but round in texture. Balanced, flavorful and drinkable now. $11 (4/30/91) **86**

SEGHESIO
Sonoma Red Lot 4 Sonoma County NV: Fine as a carafe wine. Very ripe, straightforward and fruity, with cherry aromas turning to prune, raisin and a hint of pepper on the finish. $5 (6/30/90) **75**

SEAN H. THACKREY
Pleiades California NV: Has a lot of personality, offering gamy cherry and pepper aromas and flavors on a medium-weight frame. Modestly tannic and drinkable now, but better around 1993 or '94. 750 cases made. $15 (6/30/92) **83**

TREFETHEN
Eschol Red Napa Valley NV: A medium-bodied, claret-style wine, with berry flavors, a solid dose of oak seasoning and a fruity finish. Moderate tannins and good acidity give it structure. $6 (2/15/91) **79**
Eshcol Red No. 3 Napa Valley NV: A fine generic red from Trefethen. Sturdy and flavorful, echoing cherry and spice flavors through the finish, with enough velvety tannin to give it bite. Drink now with a roast or a steak. A blend of mostly Cabernet Sauvignon and Zinfandel. $6.25 (11/15/89) BB **80**

M.G. VALLEJO
M.G.V. Red California NV: Ripe, pruny and herbal tasting, a simple wine with lots of fruit flavor. $3 (5/31/90) **74**

WELLINGTON
Criolla Old Vines Sonoma Valley 1990: Smooth and generous, with well-defined raspberry and blackberry aromas and flavors, a supple texture and a velvety finish. Drinkable now, but the tannins can use until 1994 to settle. Made from 80 percent Mission, the rest Carignane and Béclan. 292 cases made. $7 (3/31/92) **85**

OTHER CALIFORNIA WHITE

BEAULIEU
Chablis Napa Valley 1988: Dry and fruity, but with an earthy, musty component that detracts. $5 (12/31/90) **72**

BONNY DOON
Grahm Crew Vin Blanc California 1990: Fresh, light and sweet, with hints of cherry and strawberry flavors. A decent quaffer. Serve chilled. Drink now. 2,500 cases made. $7 (10/31/91) **76**
Malvasia Bianca Ca' del Solo Monterey 1990: Fragrant, with seductive spice, litchi and pear aromas that carry through on the light-bodied, soft-textured finish. Shows plenty of personality without weight. $8 (6/15/91) BB **84**

BUENA VISTA
Chardonnay-Sémillon Bistro Style Napa Valley 1990: Very fruity, crisp and lively on balance, with plenty of floral, pine-edged melon and grapefruit aromas and flavors that persist on the finish. Drinkable now for its freshness and should be fine through 1993. 5,000 cases made. $11 (9/15/91) **83**

CAYMUS
Conundrum California 1990: A unique, complex wine, with toasted herbal, buttery aromas, rich fig, lemon and spice flavors and a lingering aftertaste. The fruit flavors are crisp and long-lasting. 1,000 cases made. $18 (11/30/91) **91**

CHATEAU DE BAUN
Château Blanc Reserve Sonoma County 1989: Fresh and floral. Despite the barrel fermentation, this is a lighter style of dry white wine, with lively pear and apple aromas and flavors that turn lightly spicy on the finish. A blend of 60 percent Symphony and 40 percent Chardonnay. 2,200 cases made. $5 (6/15/91) BB **82**
Symphony Sonoma County Dry Overture 1987: Has extremely spicy, floral aromas and dry apricot and peach flavors. Fine for a picnic, but comes up a little short on flavor. 3,000 cases made. $8.50 (4/30/90) **75**
Symphony Sonoma Valley Prelude Off-Dry 1987: Soft and lightly sweet, with appealing nectarine and almond aromas and flavors that are generally pleasant but a touch bitter on the finish. 3,000 cases made. $8.50 (3/31/90) **80**

CHATEAU ST. JEAN
Vin Blanc Sonoma County 1989: Very assertive and up front, with floral, fruity, piny flavors, but it's drier than you'd expect. It's fun to pick out the aromas from the wines blended into this one; Riesling and Sauvignon Blanc are good guesses. Flavorful but not sophisticated. A fine value. $5 (2/15/91) BB **80**

CHRISTOPHE
Joliesse California NV: Modestly fruity and reminiscent of Chardonnay, with citrus aromas and a touch of maturity. Clean, light-bodied and short on the finish. $4 (6/15/89) **78**

CLOS DU VAL
Le Clos Napa Valley 1989: Attractive for the price, with ripe, moderately rich pear, fig, apple, citrus and spice notes. Nothing fancy but drinks easy. Drink now. 100 percent Chardonnay. 2,700 cases made. $6 (3/15/92) BB **82**
Le Clos Napa Valley 1988: Very basic. About the only thing going for it is body. Has dull fruit flavors and a soft structure, but a little bit of spicy, woody flavor on the finish helps. $5.50 (12/31/90) **73**

GEYSER PEAK
Semchard California 1990: Crisp in texture, citrusy in flavor and lively, with generous pear, orange and peach aromas and flavors that persist into a long finish. Not elegant, but definitely flavorful and worth another sip. $8 (9/15/91) BB **88**

UNITED STATES

CALIFORNIA/OTHER CALIFORNIA WHITE

Semchard California 1989: A really good wine with a graceless name. Ripe, round and spicy, with a smooth texture and generous fig, apple, honey and butter aromas and flavors. Stylish, with a distinctive flavor profile. Drinkable now. 2,186 cases made. $8 (2/15/91) BB **87**

HEITZ
Joe's White Napa Valley NV: Floral and rich, with toffee, caramel and butter aromas and flavors and crisp acidity to balance the richness. Long and soft on the finish. Drink now. $5 (4/30/89) BB **83**

LA CREMA
Crème de Tête Select White California 1988: An earthy, toasty, French-style wine that flirts with funkiness. Tastes full and rich, with toasty flavors backed by green apple acidity and a lingering finish. $5.50 (12/15/89) BB **83**

LIBERTY SCHOOL
Three Valley Select Series One California 1989: The Muscat in the blend keeps this light, fruity wine fragrant. An appealing summer wine for drinking by itself or perhaps with a seafood salad. A blend of Sauvignon Blanc, Muscat and Chardonnay. 4,600 cases made. $4.50 (6/15/91) BB **83**

PRESTON
Estate White Dry Creek Valley 1988: Crisp and well balanced, a lot like Sauvignon Blanc. Light, pleasant and grassy scented, with good clean fruit flavors and a lingering finish. $5 (9/15/89) BB **83**

RABBIT RIDGE
Mystique Sonoma County 1989: Don't let the barrel-fermented designation mislead you. This fresh, fruity wine emphasizes its pear, sweet pea and apple flavors, keeping any grassiness from the Sauvignon to a bare minimum. Perfect for a warm day. A blend of Sauvignon Blanc, Sémillon and Chardonnay. $7 (6/30/91) BB **82**

RAYMOND
Vintage Select White California 1987: A pleasant everyday wine. Clean, crisp and fairly concentrated, with fruity, grassy flavors. $4.25 (2/28/89) **76**

SEBASTIANI
La Sorella California 1988: Agreeably grassy and peachy in flavor, this is soft, simple and easy to drink. A great buy. $4 (3/31/90) **79**

IVAN TAMAS
Trebbiano Livermore Valley 1990: Fresh, fruity and simple, with pleasant, spicy melon aromas and flavors. Appealing to drink soon, while it's lively and fruity. $8 (9/15/91) **81**

TREFETHEN
Eschol White Napa Valley NV: Made mostly from Chardonnay, this is dry, with tart apple and lemon flavors, good balance and a crisp finish. Lean and straightforward. Should be versatile at the table. A good bargain, too. $6.50 (1/31/91) BB **81**
Eshcol White Napa Valley NV: A solid white with a touch of oak flavor, though basically simple. Has decent structure and crispness. Made of 75 percent Chardonnay and two other grapes. $6.25 (9/15/89) **78**

NEW YORK/CABERNET SAUVIGNON & BLENDS

BEDELL
Cabernet Sauvignon North Fork of Long Island 1988 $15 (6/30/91) (TM) **86**

BIDWELL
Cabernet Sauvignon North Fork of Long Island 1988 $12 (6/30/91) (TM) **82**
Cabernet Sauvignon North Fork of Long Island 1987: A smoky, somewhat vegetal wine. Lean and hard-edged, with lots of woody, weedy flavors and not much fruit. Fans of the austere style should cellar this until 1994 to '95 to see what develops. $12 (6/15/90) **76**

BRIDGEHAMPTON
Cabernet Sauvignon Long Island 1988 $14 (6/30/91) (TM) **84**
Cabernet Sauvignon Long Island 1987 $14 (6/30/91) (TM) **87**
Reserve Red Grand Vineyard North Fork of Long Island 1987 $17 (6/30/91) (TM) **80**

GRISTINA
Cabernet Sauvignon North Fork of Long Island 1988 $14 (6/30/91) (TM) **90**

HARGRAVE
Cabernet Franc North Fork of Long Island 1988 $14 (6/30/91) (TM) **81**

JAMESPORT
Cabernet Sauvignon North Fork of Long Island North House 1987 $10 (6/30/91) (TM) **78**

MATTITUCK HILLS
Cabernet Sauvignon North Fork of Long Island 1987 $9 (6/30/91) (TM) **82**

PALMER
Cabernet Franc North Fork of Long Island Proprietor's Reserve 1989: A strong herbal, green bean aroma dissipates, but the strong, harsh, woody flavors make it ultratight and austere. Gains more smoke than fruit on the finish. Drink in 1993. $13 (11/15/91) **76**
Cabernet Sauvignon North Fork of Long Island 1988 $13.50 (6/30/91) (TM) **83**

PECONIC BAY
Cabernet Sauvignon North Fork of Long Island 1988 $13 (6/30/91) (TM) **81**
Cabernet Sauvignon North Fork of Long Island 1987 $13 (6/30/91) (TM) **78**

PETITE CHATEAU
Cabernet Sauvignon North Fork of Long Island NV $10 (6/30/91) (TM) **79**

PINDAR
Cabernet Sauvignon North Fork of Long Island Reserve 1988 $14 (6/30/91) (TM) **85**
Mythology North Fork of Long Island 1988 $20 (6/30/91) (TM) **83**
Mythology North Fork of Long Island 1987: Lean and juicy, with complex aromas and flavors of currant, nutmeg and cedar. Sharply focused, long and lively but also young and raw. This wine needs cellaring until 1993 or '95 before it softens enough to make a comfortable dinner companion. $20 (3/31/90) **86**

Key to Symbols

The scores reported here are the results of blind tastings conducted by our panel of senior editors. Wines that carry the initials below are results of individual tastings.

THE WINE SPECTATOR 100-POINT SCALE ***95-100***—Classic, a great wine; ***90-94***—Outstanding, superior character and style; ***80-89***—Good to very good, a wine with special qualities; ***70-79***—Average, drinkable wine that may have minor flaws; ***60-69***—Below average, drinkable but not recommended; ***50-59***—Poor, undrinkable, not recommended. "+"—With a score indicates a range; used primarily with barrel tastings to indicate a preliminary score.

SPECIAL DESIGNATIONS SS—Spectator Selection, CS—Cellar Selection, BB—Best Buy, (SNA)—Price not available, (NR)—Not released.

TASTER'S INITIALS (JG)—Jim Gordon, (HS)—Harvey Steiman, (JL)—James Laube, (JS)—James Suckling, (TM)—Thomas Matthews, (TR)—Terry Robards, (PM)—Per-Henrik Mansson, (BT)—Barrel Tasting (these wines were tasted blind from barrel samples), (CA-date)—*California's Great Cabernets* by James Laube, (CH-date)—*California's Great Chardonnays* by James Laube, (VP-date)—*Vintage Port* by James Suckling.

DATE TASTED Dates in parentheses represent the issue in which the rating was published.

CHARDONNAY

BANFI
Chardonnay Nassau County Old Brookville 1988 $11 (6/30/91) (TM) **70**
Chardonnay Nassau County Old Brookville 1987: Relatively dark and brassy in color, with ripe fig, honey and butter aromas and flavors that round out nicely on the finish. Not dramatic or complex, but it's balanced and likable. Drinkable now. $11.50 (12/15/90) **85**

BEDELL
Chardonnay North Fork of Long Island 1989 $12 (6/30/91) (TM) **83**
Chardonnay North Fork of Long Island Reserve 1988: Earthy, somewhat musty aromas and flavors detract from this simple, slightly buttery wine. It becomes ripe and unctuous on the lingering finish. Not typical, but it's interesting to drink. Ready now. 700 cases made. $14 (12/15/90) **81**

BIDWELL
Chardonnay North Fork of Long Island 1988 $9 (6/30/91) (TM) **81**
Chardonnay North Fork of Long Island 1986: Has zingy acidity but a sense of richness develops on the palate, and the sharply focused grapefruit and toast aromas and flavors make an appealing package. A big, distinctive wine. $9 (3/31/90) **87**

BRIDGEHAMPTON
Chardonnay Long Island Grand Vineyard Selection 1989 $17 (6/30/91) (TM) **81**
Chardonnay Long Island Grand Vineyard Selection 1988: Very smooth, harmonious and balanced, offering well-defined pear, orange and vanilla aromas and flavors, hinting at butterscotch and honey on the long finish. A delicious wine for drinking now or in 1993. 400 cases made. $18 (3/31/90) **91**
Chardonnay Long Island The Hamptons Estate Reserve 1989 $14.50 (6/30/91) (TM) **78**

CROSSWOODS
Chardonnay North Fork of Long Island Ressler Vineyards 1988: Smells earthy, but comes off as light and spicy on the palate, with hints of pear and earthiness on the finish. Drinkable. $10 (2/29/92) **75**

GRISTINA
Chardonnay North Fork of Long Island 1989 $13 (6/30/91) (TM) **90**

HARGRAVE
Chardonnay North Fork of Long Island 1988 $15 (6/30/91) (TM) **82**

LENZ
Chardonnay North Fork of Long Island 1989 $10 (6/30/91) (TM) **81**
Chardonnay North Fork of Long Island Barrel Fermented 1989 $15 (6/30/91) (TM) **84**

MATTITUCK HILLS
Chardonnay North Fork of Long Island 1988 $11 (6/30/91) (TM) **77**

PALMER
Chardonnay North Fork of Long Island 1989 $11.50 (6/30/91) (TM) **84**
Chardonnay North Fork of Long Island Barrel Fermented 1989 $15 (6/30/91) (TM) **82**

PAUMANOK
Chardonnay North Fork of Long Island 1989 $10 (6/30/91) (TM) **80**

PECONIC BAY
Chardonnay North Fork of Long Island 1989 $11 (6/30/91) (TM) **80**
Chardonnay North Fork of Long Island Reserve 1989 $15 (6/30/91) (TM) **79**

PINDAR
Chardonnay North Fork of Long Island 1988 $9 (6/30/91) (TM) **86**
Chardonnay North Fork of Long Island Reserve 1988 $12 (6/30/91) (TM) **82**

PUGLIESE
Chardonnay North Fork of Long Island 1988 $10 (6/30/91) (TM) **78**

RIVENDELL
Chardonnay New York 1989: Clean and fruity, with ripe apple, melon and spice notes and just a touch of oak in the background. The finish lingers. Drink now. 725 cases made. $12 (6/30/91) **80**
Chardonnay New York Barrel Selection 1989 $14 (6/30/91) (TM) **85**
Chardonnay New York Reserve 1989: Rich, oaky and full-bodied, with full-blown apple, custard, melon and pear flavors that are deep and complex. The soft, persistent finish echoes fruit and oak. Has wonderful balance and intensity. Drink now or in 1993. 350 cases made. $17 (6/30/91) **86**
Chardonnay North Fork of Long Island Cuvée 1988 $12 (6/30/91) (TM) **87**

WAGNER
Chardonnay Finger Lakes Barrel Fermented 1988: Strong oak flavors turn gluey and interfere with the ripe pear and melon notes. Decent. 2,800 cases made. $13 (8/31/91) **76**
Chardonnay Finger Lakes Reserve 1988: A strong herbaceous flavor dominates the ripe pear and melon flavor. Intense and flavorful, if lacking finesse and grace. Drink now. $17 (8/31/91) **77**

MERLOT

BEDELL
Merlot North Fork of Long Island 1987: Fragrant and supple, bursting with ripe cherry and berry aromas and flavors seasoned with tobacco and toast nuances. Concentrated, balanced, stylish and likable. Drinkable now, but cellaring until 1994 shouldn't hurt. $18 (3/31/90) **90**
Merlot North Fork of Long Island Reserve 1988 $14 (6/30/91) (TM) **90**

BIDWELL
Merlot North Fork of Long Island 1988 $11 (6/30/91) (TM) **85**
Merlot North Fork of Long Island Reserve 1987: An herbal, tobacco-tinged wine, with firm tannins and enough cassis and berry flavor coming through on the finish to indicate cellaring until at 1993. $16 (3/31/90) **83**

BRIDGEHAMPTON
Merlot Long Island 1988 $16 (6/30/91) (TM) **89**

CROSSWOODS
Merlot North Fork of Long Island Ressler Vineyards 1987: Firm in texture, with solid cherry and currant aromas and flavors and plenty of smoky, toasty overtones. A flavorful wine that needs until 1994 to soften the tannins. $10 (2/29/92) **84**

GRISTINA
Merlot North Fork of Long Island 1988 $13 (6/30/91) (TM) **81**

HARGRAVE
Merlot North Fork of Long Island 1988 $17.50 (6/30/91) (TM) **81**

JAMESPORT
Merlot North Fork of Long Island 1986 $9 (6/30/91) (TM) **72**

LENZ
Merlot North Fork of Long Island 1987 $12 (6/30/91) (TM) **80**

PALMER
Merlot North Fork of Long Island 1988 $13 (6/30/91) (TM) **86**

PECONIC BAY
Merlot North Fork of Long Island 1989 $13 (6/30/91) (TM) **78**

PINDAR
Merlot North Fork of Long Island 1987: True to the varietal. Lean, with smoke and tobacco aromas and hints of riper currant flavor, but it lacks depth and complexity. Not too tannic. Balanced and pleasant. Drink now to 1994. 1,200 cases made. $13 (12/15/90) **80**
Merlot North Fork of Long Island Reserve 1988 $14 (6/30/91) (TM) **83**

SPARKLING

BULLY HILL
Brut Seyval Blanc Finger Lakes 1988: Clean and crisp, but very austere. It's lean in texture, with green melon and cucumber flavors and a dry finish. $15 (12/31/90) **74**

CASA LARGA
Blanc de Blancs Finger Lakes NV: A not-quite-dry wine that tastes smooth and mature. It has nice doughy aromas, a soft, creamy texture, figgy, buttery, lemony flavors and a lingering finish. $13 (12/31/90) **78**
Brut Blanc de Blancs Finger Lakes NV: A crisp, dry wine that's clean and simple, but won't disappoint anyone. Has citrus and herbal flavors. $11 (12/31/90) **77**

CHATEAU FRANK
Brut Finger Lakes 1985: A good, clean, crisp wine, with lemon and pear flavors, good balance and a hint of doughy complexity. $18 (12/31/90) **80**

GLENORA
Blanc de Blancs Finger Lakes 1987: A bright gold bubbly that tastes clean, rich and buttery. It's smooth textured, spicy, flavorful and a bit complex. Best sparkling wine that we've tasted from New York. 1,037 cases made. $12 (12/31/90) **85**
Brut New York 1987: Smooth and mature tasting, with well-integrated fruit, spice and butter flavors. Firm on the palate and easy to enjoy. 2,661 cases made. $12 (12/31/90) **81**

GOLD SEAL
Brut Bottle Fermented New York NV: Tastes sweet, simple and reminds us of Labrusca. Drinkable, but very basic. Best for mixing with orange juice. $7 (12/31/90) **69**

GREAT WESTERN
Blanc de Blancs New York NV: Decent quality, but not much complexity or fruit flavor to warm up to. Very dry, offering austere but earthy grapefruit and walnut flavors. $14 (6/30/90) **76**
Brut Very Dry New York NV: Has the grapey, grassy flavors of Labrusca grapes. Simple and coarse tasting but drinkable. $9.75 (12/31/90) **69**
Extra Dry New York NV: Very sweet and simple tasting. Flavors are a bit like celery. Drinkable in a pinch. $9.75 (12/31/90) **68**
Natural New York NV: Very dry and somewhat rough in texture. It's lean tasting, with nutty, slightly herbal, earthy flavors and a short, dry finish. $14 (6/30/90) **74**
Rosé New York NV: Sweet and simple but fresh tasting, with a bright pink color, floral aromas and sweet, plummy flavors. $9.75 (12/31/90) **71**

KEDEM
Charmat Kosher New York NV: A sweet, simple wine with floral, bubble gum aromas, and sugary, banana flavors. Probably best mixed with orange juice. $6 (12/31/90) **72**

LENZ
North Fork of Long Island 1986: Extremely earthy and barnyardy in aroma and flavor. Sour on the finish. Tasted twice. $17.50 (12/31/90) **68**

MCGREGOR
Blanc de Blancs Finger Lakes 1985: An unpleasantly bitter flavor and aftertaste override any decent sparkling wine characteristics. It's dry and then some. Tasted twice. $15 (12/31/90) **64**

PINDAR
Brut North Fork Première Cuvée North Fork of Long Island 1986: Tastes lemony and refreshing, in a simple, crisp, light style. Clean cherry and citrus flavors are strong enough to give it substance. $13 (12/31/90) **80**

TAYLOR
Brut Bottle Fermented New York NV: Tastes sweet, grapey, earthy and oxidized. Very simple and unenjoyable. $6.50 (12/31/90) **61**

WOODBURY
Blanc de Noirs New York 1987: Tastes simple and rough, but it's drinkable, with grapey, floral flavors and a slightly sweet finish. Tasted twice. $12 (12/31/90) **70**
Brut Blanc de Blancs New York 1987: An interesting, flavorful wine with ripe pear and fig flavors, and a touch of earthiness that makes it stand out. Rich, ripe and assertive. Limited production. $12 (12/31/90) **82**

OTHER NEW YORK

WAGNER
Gewürztraminer Finger Lakes 1987: Light and dry, with delicate floral and grapefruit aromas and flavors. A low-profile wine that has refreshing character. Drinkable now. 700 cases made. $8 (1/31/92) **80**
Johannisberg Riesling Late Harvest Finger Lakes Ice Wine 1989: Very crisp and tart beneath the veneer of sweet honey and apricot flavors, like a sour lemon candy. Refreshing and appealing. Drinkable now, but should improve through 1993. 270 cases made. $14/375ml (1/31/92) **85**
Seyval Blanc Finger Lakes Barrel Fermented 1988: Broad, almost coarse, but the lime, melon and earthy flavors are pleasant and there's enough acidity to keep it interesting. 5,000 cases made. $6 (3/31/92) **75**

OREGON/*CHARDONNAY*

ARGYLE
Chardonnay Oregon Barrel Fermented 1987: Best Oregon Chardonnay we've ever tasted. Full-bodied and rich but graceful, with plenty of fruit flavor and complex accents of honey, spice and vanilla. Its elegant, supple style supports classic pear, apple and melon notes. Drink now through 1994. 1,000 cases made. $18.50 (12/15/90) **93**

ARTERBERRY
Chardonnay Willamette Valley 1988: A creamy, buttery wine, with complex butterscotch, pear, vanilla and spice notes that are engagingly complex. The richness and smooth texture add dimension and depth, and it finishes with a long, full aftertaste. Drink now to 1994. 448 cases made. $10 (1/31/91) **90**

ASHLAND
Chardonnay Rogue Valley Layne Vineyards Reserve 1989: A cheesy aroma and canned fruit flavors mark this simple, leesy-tasting wine. A pretty ordinary wine. $15 (6/15/92) **70**

BRIDGEVIEW
Chardonnay Oregon 1990: Crisp and juicy, with lots of fresh nectarine and grapefruit aromas and flavors that extend into a lively finish. A light wine, with plenty of charm. Drinkable now. $6.50 (11/15/91) BB **83**
Chardonnay Oregon Barrel Select 1989: Soft, gentle and flavorful, offering apple and pear flavors at the core that are enhanced by a touch of butter and toast. The flavors linger nicely on the finish. Drinkable now. 1,200 cases made. $12 (3/31/91) **84**
Chardonnay Oregon Barrel Select 1988: Full and flavorful, with lots of pear and spice aromas and flavors that are sturdy rather than elegant. Drinkable now. 600 cases made. $12 (3/31/91) **81**

CAMERON
Chardonnay Willamette Valley 1990: A buttery wine that's soft and spicy, with a modest core of orange and pear flavors. Soft and simple on the finish. Drinkable now. 560 cases made. $14 (6/15/92) **79**

ELK COVE
Chardonnay Willamette Valley 1989: Ripe and perfumed, dominated by strong Muscat and apple flavors. Turns a bit flat and simple on the finish. Drinkable but unexciting. Ready now. Tasted twice. 1,535 cases made. $12 (3/31/92) **74**
Chardonnay Willamette Valley 1988: A blunt, woody wine that's a bit rough around the edges, but has lots of buttery, toasty flavors and a lean core of apple and pear notes. Needs to settle down with cellaring until 1993 or '94. 832 cases made. $12 (3/31/91) **75**

KNUDSEN ERATH
Chardonnay Willamette Valley 1988: Earthy, extremely buttery and more than a little musty. Tasted twice. 2,750 cases made. $11 (8/31/91) **67**

MONTINORE
Chardonnay Washington County 1988: Sturdy and flavorful, with straightforward apple and spice aromas and flavors. Drinkable now. 790 cases made. $11 (3/31/91) **77**

OAK KNOLL
Chardonnay Willamette Valley 1988: Very fruity, full and forward, with apple cider aromas and flavors shaded by oak. Generous and toasty on the finish. Drinkable, but probably better after 1993. $11 (3/31/91) **83**

ST. JOSEF'S
Chardonnay Oregon 1987: Has orange and spice aromas and flavors, but seems tired and oxidized, with metallic flavors. Tasted twice. $11.50 (8/31/91) **68**

SOKOL BLOSSER
Chardonnay Yamhill County Redland 1988: A smooth, spicy, buttery wine, crisply accented by lemon, nutmeg and butter notes harmoniously balanced with a core of peach and pear flavor. No shortage of oak here, but it's well integrated. The flavors linger. Drinkable now. 1,400 cases made. $12 (3/31/91) **87**

TUALATIN
Chardonnay Willamette Valley 1989: Crisp and refreshing, with an elegant structure and well-defined apple, pear and spice aromas and flavors. Focused, flavorful and drinkable now. 2,000 cases made. $14 (6/15/92) **88**
Chardonnay Willamette Valley Barrel Fermented 1988: Despite the barrel-fermented indication, this is crisp and lemony, with enough softness around the edges to make it immediately likable. Hints of butter and spice enhance the finish. Well made in a light style. $14 (3/31/91) **86**
Chardonnay Willamette Valley Barrel Fermented Private Reserve 1988: Rich, flavorful, smooth textured and generous, offering plenty of spice- and butter-enhanced peach and pineapple flavors. Has a sense of delicacy despite the rich flavors. Drinkable now, but it should hold through 1993. $20 (3/31/91) **91**
Chardonnay Willamette Valley Selected Private Reserve 1989: Crisp at the center, but nicely rounded and polished around the edges, featuring toasty hazelnut, pear and honey aromas and flavors that extend into a long finish. Reminiscent of a good Puligny-Montrachet. Has style and grace. Drinkable now. 700 cases made. $20 (6/15/92) **91**

VALLEY VIEW
Chardonnay Oregon Barrel Select 1988: Very firm and concentrated, with a nice array of butter, toast and spice nuances to the core of apple and lemon flavors. Tight in structure, but might be worth cellaring until 1993 to see what develops. 800 cases made. $12 (3/31/91) **81**
Chardonnay Rogue Valley 1990: Decent and simple, with crisp apple and peach flavors and a clean finish. Nothing remarkable, but OK for everyday drinking. 3,000 cases made. $7.50 (6/15/92) **78**
Chardonnay Rogue Valley Barrel Select 1989: This fresh, medium-weight wine leans toward buttery vanilla and oak flavors around a light core of pear. Drinkable now. $12.50 (6/15/92) **83**

VAN DUZER
Chardonnay Oregon Reserve 1990: Smooth and polished but ultimately simple, featuring nice pear and oak aromas and flavors. Finishes with attractive fruit notes. Drinkable now. 3,500 cases made. $16 (6/15/92) **82**
Chardonnay Oregon Reserve 1989: A smooth, generous wine, with tart pear and apple flavors that come across as ripe and decidedly woody, echoing butter and spice on the finish. Balanced and pleasing to drink. Try now to 1993. $16 (11/15/91) **86**

VERITAS
Chardonnay Willamette Valley 1988: Crisp, light and fresh, with lively lemon, apple and gingersnap aromas and flavors that linger nicely on the tart finish. A refreshing wine to drink soon with a plate of oysters. 769 cases made. $12 (3/31/91) **83**

YAMHILL VALLEY
Chardonnay Willamette Valley 1988: Very taut and crisp, with minerallike overtones to the crisp grapefruit and lemon flavors. Reminiscent of a French Chablis. It will probably be better after 1993. Try with oysters. 2,000 cases made. $12 (3/31/91) **84**

PINOT NOIR

ADAMS
Pinot Noir Yamhill County 1985: Fresh, pure and lively, with distinct, complex black cherry flavor that is well defined and well focused. Good length on the finish. Drink now. $25 (2/15/90) **89**

PETER F. ADAMS
Pinot Noir Yamhill County 1983: Complex, mature, fragrant and generous, with the texture of silk. Has a delicious balance of spice against ripe cherry and raisin flavor and toasty oak against mature brown sugar flavors. It broadens appealingly on the finish. Drinkable now. ($NA) (2/15/90) **91**

ADELSHEIM
Pinot Noir Oregon 1987: Offers decent cherry and spice notes, but it's also earthy, dry and tannic, lacking in depth and concentration. Drink now. $13 (2/15/90) **72**
Pinot Noir Oregon 1985: Oaky, but it offers pretty cherry notes that rise to the surface. Drink now. Tasted twice. $25 (2/15/90) **75**
Pinot Noir Polk County 1986 $15 (6/15/88) **87**
Pinot Noir Polk County The Eola Hills 1987: Light and simple with faint cherry notes, but not much depth or concentration. Decent but uninspired. Drink now. $16 (2/15/90) **70**
Pinot Noir Willamette Valley 1988: Warm, rich and supple, with lovely currant, berry, cherry and spice flavors. An elegant, balanced, appealing style, with fine length and finesse. Drink now to 1994. Tasted twice. 1,457 cases made. $13 (4/15/91) **89**
Pinot Noir Yamhill County 1985 $16 (6/15/87) **88**
Pinot Noir Yamhill County 1983: Offers mature Pinot Noir aromas, but it's earthy and watery on the palate, lacking in fruit definition and concentration. Fading and past its prime. Drink now, before it's too late. $40 (2/15/90) **70**
Pinot Noir Yamhill County Elizabeth's Reserve 1987: There are pretty cherry notes, but this wine quickly turns watery and tannic. Best to drink it soon while fruit is showing. Drink now. Tasted three times. $19 (2/15/90) **73**

AIRLIE
Pinot Noir Willamette Valley 1987: Simple and pleasant with decent cherry-scented flavor. But a hard edge takes away from its charm, and it lacks depth. Drink now. $9 (2/15/90) **75**

ALPINE
Pinot Noir Willamette Valley Vintage Select 1985 $17 (6/15/87) **80**

AMITY
Pinot Noir Oregon 1988: A tight, tannic, slightly stemmy wine, with ripe cherry and currant flavors, but also a tough edge on the finish. The flavors are attractive, but it needs a year or so to round out. Drink now to 1994. 1,500 cases made. $10 (5/31/91) **82**
Pinot Noir Oregon 1983: A lean, hard wine that offers meager aromas that lean toward earthiness and smoke. Not a generous wine. Drinkable now. $30 (2/15/90) **73**
Pinot Noir Oregon Gamay Noir 1988: Dead ringer for a nouveau Beaujolais, but it's quite pleasant, with crisp berry and pepper notes. Drink now, chilled. $9 (2/15/90) **84**
Pinot Noir Oregon Winemaker's Reserve 1985: Crisp and tart, with maturing aromas and flavors of toast, chocolate and coffee, and a thin thread of berry and plum flavor that emerges on the finish. Drinkable now, or cellar through 1994. 509 cases made. ($NA) (2/15/90) **80**
Pinot Noir Oregon Winemaker's Reserve 1983: Earthy, woody and slightly bitter, not appealing in texture or flavor. OK if you like the style. Drinkable now. $30 (2/15/90) **75**
Pinot Noir Willamette Valley 1987: Tough and tannic, very tight and closed with hard oak flavors. There are some pretty cherry and plum flavors, but it's going to take a while for the tannins to simmer down. Drink in 1993 to '96. Tasted twice. $15 (2/15/90) **81**
Pinot Noir Willamette Valley 1986: Rich, full, intense and tannic but ultimately rather simple. The berry and cherry flavors are pleasant but nothing to get excited about. It finishes with a hard edge. Drink now or in 1993. $12.50 (2/15/90) **74**
Pinot Noir Willamette Valley 1985: Broad and tannic, but there is enough black cherry flavor behind it to fit snugly into a frame of toasty oak and suggest that cellaring through 1995 will soften the tannins. $25 (2/15/90) **85**
Pinot Noir Willamette Valley 1982 $9.50 (3/01/86) **77**
Pinot Noir Willamette Valley Estate 1987: There are some pretty berry and cherry flavors in this, wine but it's overly dry and tannic, which tends to override the fruitiness. May never shed its woodiness. Drink now to 1996. Tasted twice. $25 (2/15/90) **79**
Pinot Noir Willamette Valley Estate 1985: Simple, with a velvety texture, mature brown sugar and black cherry flavors and a long finish. A bit lean; it needs cellaring until 1993 to smooth things out. $25 (2/15/90) **79**
Pinot Noir Willamette Valley Estate 1983: Ripe and mature with cherry and plum notes, but vegetal, herbal notes detract from the main focus of fruit. Finish is simple and unfocused. $30 (2/15/90) **76**
Pinot Noir Willamette Valley Winemaker's Reserve 1987: Generously fragrant and flavorful but tannic. This wine has the sort of concentrated wild berry flavor to stand up to the astringency and the structure to age. Try in 1993 and see what develops. Tasted twice. $30 (2/15/90) **83**

ANKENY
Pinot Noir Willamette Valley Estate Bottled 1986 $9 (6/15/88) **68**

ARTERBERRY
Pinot Noir Willamette Valley Weber Vineyards 1989: Smells and looks a little light, but the flavors are attractive, offering pretty strawberry, earth, tar and orange peel notes with a touch of tea on the finish. A wine with elegance and grace and flavors that linger. Drink now to 1994. $12 (11/15/91) **85**
Pinot Noir Willamette Valley Winemaker's Reserve 1989: Austere and astringent, with stemmy tannins and a hard edge, but it also shows attractive plum and cherry-tinged flavors. Best to cellar until 1993. $12 (11/15/91) **75**
Pinot Noir Willamette Valley Winemaker's Reserve 1988: Ripe and aromatic but surprisingly muted on the palate. The plum, cinnamon and vanilla aromas are lovely, but they don't come through on the palate, where the flavors are flat and uninspiring. Cellaring until 1994 might help. $14 (1/31/91) **79**
Pinot Noir Yamhill County Red Hills Vineyard Winemaker's Reserve 1986 $14.75 (6/15/88) **74**
Pinot Noir Yamhill County Red Hills Vineyard Winemaker's Reserve 1985 $16 (6/15/87) **95**
Pinot Noir Yamhill County Red Hills Vineyard Winemaker's Reserve 1983: Ripe, rich and fragrant, with vegetal hints that come off as minty and herbal on the palate; smooth and generous, opening up on the finish. Drink now. $16 (2/15/90) **86**
Pinot Noir Yamhill County Weber Vineyards Winemaker's Reserve 1987: A seductive wine, with supple texture, appealing raspberry and floral aromas and generous berry and spice flavors that linger dramatically. There is also plenty of juicy acidity to carry it well past 1995, though you can start drinking it now. Tasted twice. $14 (2/15/90) **90**

AUTUMN WIND
Pinot Noir Willamette Valley 1988: Light and austere, with woody aromas and flavors dominating the modest cherry notes. Needs time to soften the oak; try after 1994. 500 cases made. $12 (4/15/91) **80**
Pinot Noir Willamette Valley 1987: Ripe and plummy, with attractive, generous fruit that turns astringent on the finish. Austerity and tannins on the finish detract from its potential now. Drink now or in 1993. Tasted twice. 390 cases made. $15 (2/15/90) **83**

BAY CELLARS
Pinot Noir Willamette Valley 1985 $18 (6/15/88) **85**

BETHEL HEIGHTS
Pinot Noir Willamette Valley 1988: Flavorful and lively, showing lots of plum and berry aromas and flavors that are focused and elegant. The tannins are well integrated and the flavors make it tempting to drink now. A bit tart on the finish, but it could hold until 1994. 1,095 cases made. $15 (4/15/91) **87**
Pinot Noir Willamette Valley 1987: A delicate, elegant wine, with pretty cherry and raspberry flavors. Better balanced than most '87s; deceptively concentrated. The fruit really comes through on the finish. Drink now to 1994. Tasted twice. $12 (2/15/90) **86**
Pinot Noir Willamette Valley 1986 $15 (6/15/88) **86**
Pinot Noir Willamette Valley 1985 $12 (2/15/90) **79**
Pinot Noir Willamette Valley Reserve 1988: Generous, flavorful and tart, but loaded with black cherry, wild plum and smoke aromas and flavors. Should be at its best after 1993. 400 cases made. $18 (4/15/91) **86**
Pinot Noir Willamette Valley Unfiltered 1985: Ripe, fruity and concentrated, bursting with raspberry and blackberry aromas and flavors; smooth and vibrant. Has plenty of flavor—cellaring until 1993 could bring out more. $12 (2/15/90) **86**

BONNY DOON
Pinot Noir Oregon Bethel Heights Vineyard 1985 $18 (6/15/88) **90**
Pinot Noir Oregon Temperance Hill Vineyard 1985 $18 (6/15/88) **88**

BRIDGEVIEW
Pinot Noir Oregon 1986: Light and earthy with distinct mushroom flavors, but it also has a pleasant touch of cherry flavor. Drink 1990 to '93. $8 (2/15/90) **79**
Pinot Noir Oregon Estate Bottled 1988: Attractive for its fresh, ripe, supple strawberry and cherry-scented flavors that are smooth and even. Well balanced with pretty fruit concentration coming through on the finish. Drink now to 1994. Tasted twice. $8 (2/15/90) **88**
Pinot Noir Oregon Estate Bottled 1986 $8 (6/15/88) **87**
Pinot Noir Oregon Special Reserve 1987: Don't let the light color fool you. This wine has plenty of concentrated cherry, vanilla and cinnamon flavors in an elegant package. It has firm structure and modulated tannins that won't need a long time to soften, but should carry the wine well past 1995. Start drinking now. Tasted twice. $12 (2/15/90) **80**
Pinot Noir Oregon Winemaker's Reserve 1988: An elegant, subtle wine, with attractive cherry, oak, currant and strawberry flavors that are smooth and polished. Picks up a trace of tannin on the finish, but it's drinkable now through 1994. 1,200 cases made. $12 (11/15/91) **87**
Pinot Noir Oregon Winemaker's Reserve 1987: Earthy, with plenty of oak, but the cherry and berry flavors shine through. It's balanced with good depth and length. Drink now to 1994. Tasted twice. $15 (2/15/90) **89**

BROADLEY
Pinot Noir Oregon 1987: This dark-colored wine offers ripe, supple, fresh raspberry and cherry flavors, with a touch of volatile acidity and oak that may appeal to some more than others. Best to drink now. $8 (2/15/90) **76**
Pinot Noir Oregon Reserve 1987: Pleasing for its rich, ripe sweet cherry and raspberry flavors and toasty oak. Well balanced, with depth and concentration and a long aftertaste that echoes cherry flavor. Impressive. Drink now to 1995. $12 (2/15/90) **88**
Pinot Noir Oregon Reserve 1986 $11.50 (6/15/88) **73**

CALLAHAN RIDGE
Pinot Noir Oregon Elkton Vineyards 1987: Has yummy fruit. It's smooth and supple, with fresh berry and cherry flavors that are quite attractive and a long, satisfying finish. Youthful and vibrant, enticing now but capable of cellaring a few years. More than a fair price. Drink now to 1994. Tasted twice. $8 (2/15/90) **88**

CAMERON
Pinot Noir Willamette Valley 1987: Ripe with cherry and plum notes, but fairly dry and tannic. Best to drink it soon before it dries up further. The nose is very aromatic. Drink now. $14 (2/15/90) **81**
Pinot Noir Willamette Valley 1986 $15 (6/15/88) **86**
Pinot Noir Willamette Valley 1985: Very firm, tannic and hard-edged. It tastes herbal and toasty at first but ends up tasting barklike and dry. Has an underlying strand of ripe fruit. Try now. $14 (2/15/90) **82**
Pinot Noir Willamette Valley Abbey Ridge Vineyard Unfiltered Reserve 1989: Burgundian in style, with lavish oak and rich currant flavors that take on an herbal edge. The tannins are firm, but the texture is smooth and polished. Drink now to 1996. 300 cases made. $19 (3/31/92) **86**
Pinot Noir Willamette Valley Vintage Reserve 1987: Attractive for its richness and purity of flavor, the ripe cherry and plum notes are pretty, but the oak and tannins are harsh on the finish. Drink now to 1994. $18 (2/15/90) **86**
Pinot Noir Willamette Valley Reserve 1986: Rich and meaty with pepper and black cherry flavors that are tight and austere but could come through on the finish. Could use a shade more richness and depth. Drink now through 1993. $18 (2/15/90) **80**
Pinot Noir Willamette Valley Reserve 1985: Earthy and gamy, lacking in fruit and charm. Dry and bitter on the finish. $25 (2/15/90) **63**

CHATEAU BENOIT
Pinot Noir Oregon 1986 $15 (6/15/88) **55**
Pinot Noir Oregon 1985 $14 (6/15/88) **55**

COOPER MOUNTAIN
Pinot Noir Willamette Valley 1988: Very firm and fruity, with lively raspberry and plum aromas and flavors and coarse tannins. Cellaring until 1993 or '94 should take the edge off. 600 cases made. $13 (4/15/91) **83**
Pinot Noir Willamette Valley 1987: Has plenty of fresh, ripe, rich berry and cherry flavors that are lively and intense with good depth. The flavors stay with you on the finish. Balanced with just the right amount of tannin for developing in the next three to five years. Drink now to 1994. Tasted twice. $13 (2/15/90) **87**
Pinot Noir Willamette Valley Reserve 1988: On the tannic side, but showing lots of generous, ripe plum and cherry aromas and flavors shaded by sweet oak and vanilla notes. Tight enough to need until 1994 to loosen up. 200 cases made. $20 (4/15/91) **83**

DOMAINE DROUHIN
Pinot Noir Oregon 1989: Ripe and spicy, with pretty cherry, plum and nutmeg flavors that are sustained by crisp acidity and firm tannins. Drinkable now, but a good bet to improve with a year or two in the cellar. Drink in 1993 and beyond. $32 (1/31/92) **87**
Pinot Noir Oregon 1988: Pretty toast and smoky oak notes and a tight core of cherry, vanilla, plum and currant flavors come together nicely and stay with you. Echoes fruit and oak on the finish. Delicious now through 1994. An impressive debut. 1,800 cases made. $32 (5/31/91) **89**

ELK COVE
Pinot Noir Willamette Valley 1989: Attractive fruit and spice flavors have hints of berry and cherry, turning silky on the palate and picking up a trace of oak on the finish. Drink now to 1994. A fine value. 1,800 cases made. $10 (3/31/92) **88**
Pinot Noir Willamette Valley 1988: Aromatic but tannic, suffering from a chalky texture and flavor in addition to the slightly decadent cherry and toast aromas and flavors. An earthy style that not everyone will appreciate. Try in 1993. 1,073 cases made. $15 (1/31/91) **78**
Pinot Noir Willamette Valley Dundee Hills Vineyard 1989: A meaty, gamy wine, with lean berry and spice notes of moderate depth. Tannic and oaky on the finish, but not overbearing. May be more appealing in a year or so. Drink after 1993. 145 cases made. $18 (3/31/92) **84**
Pinot Noir Willamette Valley Dundee Hills Vineyard 1987: More generous than most '87s, with supple ripe cherry and oaky flavors that fade on the finish. The harshness detracts from the overall appeal. Drink now. 420 cases made. $15 (2/15/90) **81**
Pinot Noir Willamette Valley Dundee Hills Vineyard 1986 $15 (6/15/88) 78
Pinot Noir Willamette Valley Dundee Hills Vineyard 1985 $15 (6/15/87) **85**
Pinot Noir Willamette Valley Estate Bottled 1987: Attractive for its cherry and menthol notes, but it could use a little more richness and depth. Tasted twice. $15 (2/15/90) **78**
Pinot Noir Willamette Valley Estate Bottled 1986: Extremely gamy with juniper berry flavors that don't remind us of Pinot Noir whatsoever. Avoid. $15 (2/15/90) **65**
Pinot Noir Willamette Valley Reserve 1987: Lean and focused, with plum and cherry flavors carrying through the long finish. Not rich or complex, but well made in a lighter style. Needs to develop softness and depth, which cellaring until 1993 should accomplish. 539 cases made. $15 (12/15/90) **85**
Pinot Noir Willamette Valley Reserve 1985: Light in color and texture, with subtle wild strawberry and mushroom aromas and flavors blending harmoniously with a touch of brown sugar and toast. A delicate wine with crisp acidity. Drink now or in 1993. $15 (2/15/90) **79**
Pinot Noir Willamette Valley Reserve 1983: Earthy and peppery with herb, wood and plum-scented

Key to Symbols

The scores reported here are the results of blind tastings conducted by our panel of senior editors. Wines that carry the initials below are results of individual tastings.

THE WINE SPECTATOR 100-POINT SCALE ***95-100***—Classic, a great wine; ***90-94***—Outstanding, superior character and style; ***80-89***—Good to very good, a wine with special qualities; ***70-79***—Average, drinkable wine that may have minor flaws; ***60-69***—Below average, drinkable but not recommended; ***50-59***—Poor, undrinkable, not recommended. "+"—With a score indicates a range; used primarily with barrel tastings to indicate a preliminary score.

SPECIAL DESIGNATIONS SS—Spectator Selection, CS—Cellar Selection, BB—Best Buy, ($NA)—Price not available, (NR)—Not released.

TASTER'S INITIALS (JG)—Jim Gordon, (HS)—Harvey Steiman, (JL)—James Laube, (JS)—James Suckling, (TM)—Thomas Matthews, (TR)—Terry Robards, (PM)—Per-Henrik Mansson, (BT)—Barrel Tasting (these wines were tasted blind from barrel samples), (CA-date)—*California's Great Cabernets* by James Laube, (CH-date)—*California's Great Chardonnays* by James Laube, (VP-date)—*Vintage Port* by James Suckling.

DATE TASTED Dates in parentheses represent the issue in which the rating was published.

flavors. Decent as a red wine but not distinctive as Pinot Noir. Mature and ready to drink now. $20 (2/15/90) **79**
Pinot Noir Willamette Valley Wind Hills Vineyard 1989: A gangly wine, with smooth, appealing berry and cherry notes that turn earthy and leathery on the finish. Drinks well now. 420 cases made. $25 (3/31/92) **82**
Pinot Noir Willamette Valley Wind Hills Vineyard 1988: Aromatic, floral and more stemmy and earthy than fruity, but a touch of strawberry flavor keeps it in bounds. Needs cellaring until 1993 or '94. 447 cases made. $18 (1/31/91) **80**
Pinot Noir Willamette Valley Wind Hills Vineyard 1987: Thin and shallow, with a faint hint of cherry and spice that fails to sustain much interest. Drink now. 800 cases made. $15 (2/15/90) **75**
Pinot Noir Willamette Valley Wind Hills Vineyard 1986 $15 (6/15/88) **85**
Pinot Noir Willamette Valley Wind Hills Vineyard 1985 $15 (6/15/87) **91**

ELLENDALE
Pinot Noir Willamette Valley Estate Bottled 1986 $12 (6/15/88) **71**
Pinot Noir Willamette Valley Estate Bottled 1985 $15 (6/15/88) **78**

EOLA HILLS
Pinot Noir Oregon 1987: It's heavy-handed with oak, but there are attractive strawberry and watermelon flavors that are decent. Drink now. Tasted twice. $12 (2/15/90) **76**
Pinot Noir Oregon 1986: Tannic, thin and smoky with tart berry flavor. It could use a year or two more in the cellar, though it's drinkable now. $12 (2/15/90) **77**

EVESHAM WOOD
Pinot Noir Willamette Valley 1986: Excessively dry and leathery; an extremely difficult wine to make friends with. The dryness wipes out the fruit. Drink now to 1994. $12 (2/15/90) **68**

EYRIE
Pinot Noir Willamette Valley 1987: Attractive for its rich, smooth, supple cherry and raspberry flavors that pick up a touch of spice and herb notes. Well balanced with decent length. Drink now. Tasted three times. $20 (2/15/90) **80**
Pinot Noir Willamette Valley 1986 $19.50 (6/15/88) **83**
Pinot Noir Willamette Valley 1985: Ripe and round, though not concentrated, with a sense of elegance to the silky texture and supple structure. Spicy chocolate and coffee nuances make the finish smooth and delicious. Drinkable now, but it should hold until 1995. $19 (2/15/90) **91**
Pinot Noir Willamette Valley 1984 $15 (8/31/86) **84**
Pinot Noir Willamette Valley 1983 $30 (2/15/90) **87**
Pinot Noir Willamette Valley Reserve 1987: Rich, supple and complex, showing grace and harmony. The smoky cherry, spice and earthy notes finish with a soft landing. More attractive than most Oregon '87s. Drink now or in 1993. $25 (2/15/90) **86**

FORGERON
Pinot Noir Oregon 1985: Very ripe and fruity, oozing with intense, concentrated black cherry flavor. But it's also fairly oaky and still needs time for the wood to soften a bit. Drink now to 1994. $19 (2/15/90) **89**
Pinot Noir Oregon Vinters Reserve 1987: Tannic and austere, but there are also enough cherry and berry flavors to suggest that it might survive cellaring until 1994 to '96. $12 (2/15/90) **76**

GIRARD
Pinot Noir Oregon 1987: As appealing as this wine smells, the austere tannins are just too drying and gripping for us to recommend it. Tasted twice. $12 (2/15/90) **67**

GIRARDET
Pinot Noir Umpqua Valley 1987: Hard and moldy tasting and overly tannic. Lacks charm, but it has a decent smoky aftertaste to go with the earthy, gamy flavors. Limited appeal. Drink now to 1994. $12 (2/15/90) **75**

GRATEFUL RED
Pinot Noir Willamette Valley 1990: Soft and generous, with spicy cherry and plum aromas and flavors, yet remains light on its feet and crisp through the finish. Has a touch of tannin, but it's drinkable now through 1994. $10 (6/15/92) **84**

HENRY
Pinot Noir Umpqua Valley 1986: Spicy, cedary aromas and flavors pervade this medium-weight, fairly supple wine, showing plenty of tea and herb flavors and enough maturity to drink soon despite a light smack of tannin. $10 (4/15/91) **81**
Pinot Noir Umpqua Valley 1985: Very light in color, with very little aroma and a modest intensity of mature brown sugar and black cherry flavors that persist on the finish. A subtle wine that's worth noticing. Drinkable now. $15 (2/15/90) **85**

HIDDEN SPRINGS
Pinot Noir Oregon 1985 $12 (6/15/88) **78**

HONEYWOOD
Pinot Noir Willamette Valley 1986 $9 (6/15/88) **86**

KNUDSEN ERATH
Pinot Noir Willamette Valley 1988: Tough and tannic, with tart cherry and blackberry flavors and hints of chocolate, finishing with firm, drying tannins. Best to cellar until 1994. Tasted twice. $11 (5/31/91) **82**
Pinot Noir Willamette Valley 1987: Extremely earthy and mossy with a corky flavor that dominates. The mossiness and tannin override the fruit. Drink now to '94. Tasted twice. $11 (2/15/90) **65**
Pinot Noir Willamette Valley 1986: Tart, thin, woody and bitter. Not what we've come to expect from this producer. $9 (2/15/90) **64**
Pinot Noir Willamette Valley NV $6 (6/16/86) BB **81**
Pinot Noir Willamette Valley Leland Vineyards Reserve 1987: Has mouthfilling, supple, generous flavors, with marvelous concentration of strawberry and red cherry flavors framed by sweet oak. The fruit character is brilliantly realized and the velvety texture makes it drinkable now, though it can age through at least 1994. $24 (2/15/90) **89**
Pinot Noir Willamette Valley Vintage Select 1986 $15 (6/15/88) **87**
Pinot Noir Willamette Valley Vintage Select 1985 ($NA) (9/30/87) **90**
Pinot Noir Yamhill County Vintage Select 1985: A mature but uninspired wine with fruity flavors, but it's nothing to get excited about. Dry and gamy on the finish. Drink now. $20 (2/15/90) **75**
Pinot Noir Yamhill County Vintage Select 1983: Developing mature aromas and flavors, with pleasant hints of brown sugar and prunes to make the basic spice and cherry character more interesting. A bit blunt, barklike and vegetal on the finish. Drink now. $35 (2/15/90) **81**
Pinot Noir Yamhill County Vintage Select 1983 Rel: $12 Cur: $19 (7/01/86) SS **94**

MCKINLAY
Pinot Noir Willamette Valley 1988: Sleek and moderately tannic, with some concentration of cassis fruit and cedary overtones, finishing firm and flavorful. A good bet to improve with cellaring. Drink now to 1995. $13 (4/15/91) **90**

MONTINORE
Pinot Noir Washington County 1988: Rich and plummy, both in color and in flavor, with concentrated fruit and spice aromas and flavors. Firmly tannic, but balanced, suggesting elegance on the finish. Give it until 1993 or '94 to soften the tannins. 782 cases made. Rel: $13.50 Cur: $35 (4/15/91) **88**
Pinot Noir Washington County 1987: Ripe, fresh, supple and fruity, not exactly classic Pinot Noir but fruity nonetheless. There's a touch of dryness on the finish, but otherwise this is a pleasant, well-balanced, perfectly enjoyable wine. Drink now to 1993. Tasted twice. $12.50 (2/15/90) **81**

OAK KNOLL
Pinot Noir Oregon Vintage Select 1983: Shows lots of sediment and mature, gentle aromas of spice and ripe cherry. A bit blunt but flavorful. A year or two longer in the cellar could soften it more, but it's drinkable now. $20 (2/15/90) **78**
Pinot Noir Oregon Vintage Select 1982: Mature, with smoky ripe plum and cherry flavor that is attractive but ultimately simple. The finish is drying out. Drink now or in 1993. $25 (2/15/90) **77**
Pinot Noir Willamette Valley 1988: Firm and focused, with plum, spice and cedar aromas and flavors wrapped in a solid layer of tannin, making it seem a little bitter on the finish. Should be softened by 1993 or '94. 1,566 cases made. $11 (4/15/91) **81**
Pinot Noir Willamette Valley 1985 $10 (6/15/87) **65**
Pinot Noir Willamette Valley Vintage Select 1988: Offers tart, greenish Pinot Noir flavor in a fairly tannic, dry package. The herbal cola and cherry flavors bite on the finish. Cellar until 1993. 1,258 cases made. $18 (5/31/91) **81**
Pinot Noir Willamette Valley Vintage Select 1987: Tart and a bit tannic, a sharp-edged wine with appealing peppermint and raspberry flavors. Needs cellaring to soften, at least until 1993 to '94. Tasted twice. $17.50 (2/15/90) **77**
Pinot Noir Willamette Valley Vintage Select 1985: Despite a healthy color, this is a dry, bitter, earthy wine that is simply unpalatable. Tasted twice. $17.50 (2/15/90) **59**

PANTHER CREEK
Pinot Noir Willamette Valley 1988: Woody aromas and flavors tend to permeate this firmly structured wine. Has minty, cedary, almost cheesy aromas and flavors and tannins that need until 1993 to '95 to mellow. 1,050 cases made. $15 (4/15/91) **75**
Pinot Noir Willamette Valley 1987: Aromatic, floral and bursting with fruit aromas, turning hard, metallic and tannic on the palate. Awkward now and not likely to improve. Better than two bottles tasted earlier that were undergoing malolactic fermentation. $17 (4/15/90) **74**
Pinot Noir Willamette Valley Oak Grove Vineyard Abbey Ridge Vineyard 1986 $15 (6/15/88) **69**
Pinot Noir Willamette Valley Oak Knoll and Freedom Hill Vineyards 1987: Spritzy with malolacticlike flavors. Undrinkable. Tasted twice. 800 cases made. $17 (2/15/90) **58**

PELLIER
Pinot Noir Willamette Valley 1985 $8 (6/15/88) **73**

PONZI
Pinot Noir Willamette Valley 1988: The strong earthy note that runs through this wine overpowers the cherry- and currant-tinged flavors, and the finish gets a bit dry and tannic. Drink now to 1995. Tasted twice. $16 (5/31/91) **76**
Pinot Noir Willamette Valley 1987: Gentle, ripe and rewarding, with ripe cherry, raspberry, spice and cinnamon flavors that are quite appealing. The aftertaste lingers, inviting you back for another glass. Drink now or in 1993. $15 (2/15/90) **88**
Pinot Noir Willamette Valley 1985: The crisp texture and berrylike aromas and flavors make this immediately appealing, especially on the nose and again on the finish. The flavors are persistent, ending with an engaging plumminess. Drink now. $20 (2/15/90) **84**
Pinot Noir Willamette Valley Reserve 1988: Firm and tannic, but opulently ripe and complex, with smoky, toasty cola and plum aromas and flavors. A bit shy on the finish and somewhat woody and rough now, but try after 1994 and see what develops. $25 (4/15/91) **86**
Pinot Noir Willamette Valley Reserve 1987: Deliciously rich and complex, with ripe, concentrated plum, cherry and spice notes that offer depth and grace. The finish follows through, showcasing the plummy richness. The toasty oak echoes on the finish. Drink now to 1995. $20 (2/15/90) **91**
Pinot Noir Willamette Valley Reserve 1986 $15 (6/15/88) **81**

REX HILL
Pinot Noir Oregon 1985: Intense, tannic and woody, yet it has a core of concentrated cherry, chocolate and vanilla notes from the oak. A big, full-bodied, oaky wine. Drink now to 1994. $15 (2/15/90) **81**
Pinot Noir Oregon Archibald Vineyards 1985: Mature with sassafras, cherry and cola notes along with a solid dose of tannin. A distinct style that's fairly tannic, but also has plenty of fruit to stand up to it. Drink now to 1994. $30 (2/15/90) **84**
Pinot Noir Oregon Dundee Hills Vineyards 1985: Dry, earthy and tannic with a juniper berry flavor. There are also some cherry and berry flavors, but they're awfully dry and tannic on the finish. Drink now. $25 (2/15/90) **74**
Pinot Noir Oregon Dundee Hills Vineyards 1983: Woody, vegetal aromas and flavors are wrapped in a thin veil of tannin. Drinkable now, if you like this style. $35 (2/15/90) **77**
Pinot Noir Oregon Maresh Vineyards 1985: Extremely tannic and dry for a Pinot Noir. It's also high in volatile acidity. For fans of that style only. Drink now. $40 (2/15/90) **66**
Pinot Noir Oregon Maresh Vineyards 1983: Distinctive for its mintiness, but that's about the only flavor. Hardly reminiscent of Pinot Noir. Dry and earthy on the finish. $40 (2/15/90) **64**
Pinot Noir Oregon Medici Vineyard 1985: Dry and tannic, with peppery berry and cherry flavors that aren't strong enough to stand up to the dryness. Drink now or in 1993. $28 (2/15/90) **77**
Pinot Noir Oregon Wirtz Vineyards 1985 $18 (6/15/88) **82**
Pinot Noir Willamette Valley 1988: Ripe, polished, supple and brightly focused, showing lovely strawberry, raspberry and cinnamon aromas and flavors shaded by rose petal notes on the finish. A light style, with generous flavors. Drinkable now, but possibly better around 1993 or '94. 1,500 cases made. $18 (4/15/91) **88**
Pinot Noir Willamette Valley 1985 $15 (6/15/88) **79**

ST. JOSEF'S
Pinot Noir Oregon 1987: Lean and tannic, with coffee and cola overtones to the modest cherry flavor. Turns dry and hard on the finish; a risk to cellar. $8 (4/15/91) **76**
Pinot Noir Oregon 1985: Ripe and generous, with well-defined black cherry flavor that's fresh and lively; supple and smooth. It's in fine balance and simply delicious to drink. Just the right kiss of oak for complexity. Drink now or in 1993. $16 (2/15/90) **89**

SCHWARZENBERG
Pinot Noir Oregon 1987: Oaky flavors mute the fruit. An unapproachable, grapey, somewhat flat wine that lacks charm and varietal definition. Drink now. $13.50 (2/15/90) **70**

SILVER FALLS
Pinot Noir Willamette Valley 1987: Thin and shallow with ivy, smoke and leafy tobacco notes that overshadow the cherry notes. Drink now. $10 (2/15/90) **75**

SISKIYOU
Pinot Noir Oregon Estate 1987: Firm and structured with ripe raspberry and spice notes; simple, correct and well balanced. A light style that's appealing. Drink now. Tasted twice. $13 (2/15/90) **80**

SOKOL BLOSSER
Pinot Noir Willamette Valley Red Hills Vineyard 1985 ($NA) (9/30/87) **92**
Pinot Noir Yamhill County 1986 $10 (6/15/88) **59**
Pinot Noir Yamhill County 1982 $8.95 (2/16/85) **63**
Pinot Noir Yamhill County Hyland Vineyards 1986 $15 (6/15/88) **79**
Pinot Noir Yamhill County Hyland Vineyards 1985 $15 (6/15/87) **86**
Pinot Noir Yamhill County Hyland Vineyards 1983 $14 (8/31/86) **82**
Pinot Noir Yamhill County Hyland Vineyards Reserve 1985 $18 (6/15/88) **86**
Pinot Noir Yamhill County Hyland Vineyards Reserve 1983: Earthy, dry and tannic, not showing much in the way of fruit. Disappointing. Tasted twice. $30 (2/15/90) **67**
Pinot Noir Yamhill County Red Hills Vineyard 1986 $15 (6/15/88) **77**
Pinot Noir Yamhill County Red Hills Vineyard 1985 $15 (6/15/87) **80**
Pinot Noir Yamhill County Red Hills Vineyard Reserve 1985: Fruity, more like a Gamay than a

Pinot Noir. Simple and pleasant, but it has gamy flavors that bring up the rear. It's tannic too. Drink now. $30 (2/15/90) **74**
Pinot Noir Yamhill County Redland 1988: Earthy, gamy, barnyardy aromas and flavors will not please everyone, but it has the character many Burgundy fanciers like. A bit tannic; best to drink starting 1993. 2,300 cases made. $13 (4/15/91) **82**
Pinot Noir Yamhill County Redland 1987: Thin and mediocre, lacking fruit and character. Boring. Avoid. Tasted twice. $13 (2/15/90) **66**

STATON HILLS
Pinot Noir Oregon 1987: Wild, jammy and gamy, this rambunctious wine offers plenty of wild cherry, berry, menthol and tea leaf flavors, but finishes better than it starts. Seems hard enough on the finish to need cellaring until 1993 or '94. 1,300 cases made. $13 (4/15/91) **84**
Pinot Noir Oregon 1986: Bizarre; earthy and funky, with an overabundance of unappetizing oak and picklelike green flavors. $13 (2/15/90) **64**

TUALATIN
Pinot Noir Willamette Valley 1983 $10 (8/31/86) **64**
Pinot Noir Willamette Valley Estate Bottled 1987: Has pretty aromas of cherries and wild berries, but the palate is rather dry and tannic. Simple and correct but unexciting for now. Very tannic and austere. May get better with time. Drink now to 1995. Tasted twice. $14 (2/15/90) **79**
Pinot Noir Willamette Valley Estate Bottled 1986 $13.50 (6/15/88) **85**
Pinot Noir Willamette Valley Private Reserve 1985: Light and crisp, with some interplay of plum flavor and toasty oak, but it's short on harmony and complexity. Drink now. $14 (2/15/90) **84**

VALLEY VIEW
Pinot Noir Oregon 1982 $8.50 (3/01/86) **73**
Pinot Noir Oregon 1980 $7.50 (9/16/84) **76**

VAN DUZER
Pinot Noir Willamette Valley Reserve 1989: Tight, lean and concentrated, with rich, sharply focused cherry, cola, spice and toasty oak notes. The finish is complex and lingering. Drinks well now, but it can age through 1995. 4,200 cases made. $16 (6/15/92) **87**

VERITAS
Pinot Noir Oregon 1985 $15 (6/15/87) **88**
Pinot Noir Willamette Valley 1988: Rich and elegant, with ripe, concentrated raspberry, black cherry, toast and vanilla flavors that stay with you from start to finish, where the flavors turn simple. Drink now to 1994. 2,312 cases made. $15 (5/31/91) **87**
Pinot Noir Willamette Valley 1987: Attractive and supple up front, with cherry and spice notes, but the finish ends up astringent and lacks charm. Drink now. $15 (2/15/90) **77**

WASSON BROS
Pinot Noir Oregon 1985 ($NA) (9/30/87) **93**

YAMHILL VALLEY
Pinot Noir Oregon 1985 $16 (6/15/87) **86**
Pinot Noir Oregon 1983 $17 (8/31/86) **92**
Pinot Noir Willamette Valley 1988: Tart and bordering on sour, with earthy, mulchy flavors detracting from the cherry and plum notes. Not for everyone; best to drink now or in 1993. 2,000 cases made. $12 (1/31/91) **76**
Pinot Noir Willamette Valley 1983: Intensely ripe and concentrated, with vibrant fruit, moderately complex raisin, cherry and herb notes and ample oak flavor. Fully mature with a healthy red color. Ready to drink, but it can last until 1994. $35 (2/15/90) **87**
Pinot Noir Willamette Valley Estate Reserve 1988: Despite attractive cherry and plum flavors, it turns dry and leathery, with a mild barnyardy character. Not for everyone. Drink now. Tasted twice, with consistent notes. $18 (11/15/91) **78**

OTHER OREGON

ARGYLE
Blanc de Blancs Willamette Valley Cuvée Limited 1987: Ripe and intense, with bold pineapple, citrus and spice notes that are simple but pleasant. Make sure it's well chilled. Drink now. 2,500 cases made. $23 (11/15/91) **83**
Brut Oregon Cuvée Limited 1987: Fruity and appealing, with fruit cocktail aromas and flavors and a clean texture; fresh and simple. A charming wine. $18.50 (12/31/90) **82**
Brut Willamette Valley Cuvée Limited 1988: A very good wine, with the toasty, buttery aroma of oak-aged Chardonnay and a distinctive figgy, spicy flavor that's full and satisfying. Remains light and elegant overall. $18 (5/15/92) **87**
Rosé Willamette Valley Cuvée Limited 1987: Soft and fruity but not sweet, with well-defined cherry and strawberry aromas and flavors that turn delicate and crisp on the finish. Drinkable now. An unusual style, with a dark color. $23 (11/15/91) **82**

BONNY DOON
Gewürztraminer Vin de Glacière Oregon 1990: Rich, sweet and a little syrupy, but loaded with apricot and pear flavors and a delicious Gewürztraminer-like spicy tang on the palate. Drinkable now through 1995. $15/375ml (3/31/92) **90**

BRIDGEVIEW
Pinot Gris Oregon 1990: Spicy, fragrant and likable, showing plenty of peach and floral aromas and flavors and hints of cherry on the finish. A solid wine, with polish to its texture. Drinkable now. 500 cases made. $11 (11/15/91) **86**
Riesling Oregon Dry Vintage Select 1990: Crisp and appley, with pleasant fruit flavors and hints of mineral and spice sneaking in. Drinkable now. 450 cases made. $6 (6/15/92) BB **83**

ELK COVE
Cabernet Sauvignon Willamette Valley Dundee Hills Vineyard Commander's Cabernet 1987: Smells better than it tastes. Tart and lively, with a modest concentration of berry flavor and a shade more tannin than the wine seems willing to support. Perhaps cellaring until 1993 to '95 will resolve the tannins, but it seems a bit out of balance. $15 (3/31/91) **80**

FLYNN
Brut Willamette Valley Première Cuvée 1987: A dry, easy-to-drink blancs de noir, with light, pleasant cherry flavors and a soft, fruity finish. $14 (5/15/92) **81**

Key to Symbols

The scores reported here are the results of blind tastings conducted by our panel of senior editors. Wines that carry the initials below are results of individual tastings.

THE WINE SPECTATOR 100-POINT SCALE *95-100*—Classic, a great wine; *90-94*—Outstanding, superior character and style; *80-89*—Good to very good, a wine with special qualities; *70-79*—Average, drinkable wine that may have minor flaws; *60-69*—Below average, drinkable but not recommended; *50-59*—Poor, undrinkable, not recommended. "+"—With a score indicates a range; used primarily with barrel tastings to indicate a preliminary score.

SPECIAL DESIGNATIONS SS—Spectator Selection, CS—Cellar Selection, BB—Best Buy, ($NA)—Price not available, (NR)—Not released.

TASTER'S INITIALS (JG)—Jim Gordon, (HS)—Harvey Steiman, (JL)—James Laube, (JS)—James Suckling, (TM)—Thomas Matthews, (TR)—Terry Robards, (PM)—Per-Henrik Mansson, (BT)—Barrel Tasting (these wines were tasted blind from barrel samples), (CA-date)—*California's Great Cabernets* by James Laube, (CH-date)—*California's Great Chardonnays* by James Laube, (VP-date)—*Vintage Port* by James Suckling.

DATE TASTED Dates in parentheses represent the issue in which the rating was published.

FORGERON
Chenin Blanc Oregon 1987 $7.50 (7/31/89) **69**

KNUDSEN ERATH
Gewürztraminer Willamette Valley Dry 1989: A light sipping wine that's gently fruity and soft, not sweet. Not particularly spicy, either. $7 (6/30/91) **81**
Riesling Willamette Valley Dry 1989: A dry, steely, austere wine that's earthy around the edges, offering modest peach and pine aromas and flavors. Should be perfect for drinking with oysters. $7 (8/31/91) **79**

MONTINORE
White Riesling Late Harvest Yamhill County 1989: Very light and spicy, and not nearly as sweet as the 5.2 percent residual sugar statement might suggest. Delicate and floral enough to be a nice aperitif. Drink soon. 2,065 cases made. $7 (3/31/91) **84**
White Riesling Ultra Late Harvest Oregon 1987: Very spicy and floral, this lean-textured, crisp, delicate and sweet wine has distinctive ginger, cinnamon and rose petal aromas and flavors; not the typical Riesling character. A charming wine for dessert. $22/375ml (3/31/91) **83**

ST. JOSEF'S
Cabernet Sauvignon Oregon 1986: Tannic, but ripe and earthy, showing modest currant and plum flavors overshadowed by tannin and leather notes. Seems unbalanced. Tasted twice. $12 (8/31/91) **68**
Cabernet Sauvignon Oregon 1985: Smooth and supple, with plenty of focused plum and currant aromas and flavors shaded by sweet oak and well-integrated tannins. Has a sense of balance and elegance that should be enhanced by cellaring through 1993 to '97. $15 (3/31/91) **87**
Gewürztraminer Oregon l'Esprit NV: Earthy, soft and unbalanced. It's too sweet for the modest fruit flavor, and it hints at bubble gum. Not for us. $7 (8/31/91) **65**
White Riesling Oregon 1989: Piny, peachy aromas are definitely Riesling, and the crisp structure and flinty texture makes this a racy wine. Drink now. $6.25 (8/31/91) **80**

STATON HILLS
Oregon 1988: Tight and firm, with ripe currant, plum and vanilla flavors of modest depth and intensity and green tannins on the finish. Needs time to soften; try around 1994. 1,000 cases made. $15 (3/31/92) **85**

TUALATIN
White Riesling Willamette Valley 1989: Dry and resiny, emphasizing the earthy, piny side of Riesling rather than the fruit side. Lean and lithe but not especially charming. $6.50 (6/30/91) **80**
White Riesling Willamette Valley 1988: Exotic mango aromas and flavors permeate this lean, crisp wine, making it distinctive. Balanced beautifully, so the flavors linger appealingly. $6 (7/31/89) BB **89**

VALLEY VIEW
Cabernet Sauvignon Rogue Valley Barrel Select 1989: Strikes a nice balance between ripe, intense currant-tinged Cabernet flavor and toasty oak notes. Firmly tannic. Enjoyable now through 1996. $12.50 (6/15/92) **83**

VAN DUZER
Riesling Oregon Dry 1990: Lean and racy, with a focused beam of peach and floral aromas and flavors. A mouthfilling wine with a lively acidity that carries everything through the finish. Drinkable now. 4,500 cases made. $8(6/15/92) **87**

WHITTLESEY MARK
Brut de Noir Willamette Valley Sans Année NV: A nice doughy nose and light fruit flavors are marred by a bitter finish. Not well balanced overall, but drinkable. 460 cases made. $16.50 (5/15/92) **74**
Brut Oregon 1987: Tastes quite dry and austere, with tart lemon and grapefruit flavors that almost seem green. A decent drink, but it's rough around the edges. 460 cases made. $16.50 (5/15/92) **78**

YAMHILL VALLEY
Pinot Gris Willamette Valley 1990: Fruity and floral, this attractive wine has melon and rose petal flavors that stand out in an overall pleasant wine. Finishes dry and crisp, making it an ideal food companion. A good value. $10 (6/30/91) **85**

WASHINGTON / *CABERNET SAUVIGNON & BLENDS*

ARBOR CREST
Cabernet Sauvignon Columbia Valley 1988: Aromatic and elegant, with opulent aromas of sweet oak, currant, plum and spice. A bit less expansive on the palate, but balanced and built to keep growing through at least 1994 or '95. Needs that time to shed some tannin. $11 (9/30/91) **87**
Cabernet Sauvignon Columbia Valley Bacchus Vineyard 1985: The spicy currant aromas smell great, but the wine lacks the concentration on the palate that the aromas promise. It's flavorful and tart nonetheless. $11 (10/15/89) **80**
Cabernet Sauvignon Columbia Valley Bacchus Vineyard 1983 $12.50 (12/15/87) **77**

CHATEAU STE. MICHELLE
Cabernet Sauvignon Benton County Cold Creek Vineyards Château Reserve 1980: Smells mature and smoky, but still crisp and tart on the palate, showing enough berry flavor on the finish to suggest this could develop further with time. $21 (10/15/89) **85**
Cabernet Sauvignon Columbia Valley 1988: More mature than one might expect from an '88. It has lovely plum and smoke flavors that continue into a long finish, suggesting that it might continue to improve through 1993 to '96, though it's drinkable now. $12.50 (8/31/91) **84**
Cabernet Sauvignon Columbia Valley 1986: Difficult to resist. A lush, smooth, flavorful wine, with ripe cherry and plum flavors, moderate tannins, good balance and a lasting, fruity aftertaste. Drink now through 1993. $12 (9/30/90) **88**
Cabernet Sauvignon Columbia Valley Cold Creek Vineyard Limited Bottling 1987: Has a good dose of tannin and oak, but a core of mineral, plum, currant and cherry flavor is firm and tightly packed. The level of tannin suggests it's best to cellar until 1995. Tasted twice, with consistent notes. $20 (8/31/91) **83**
Cabernet Sauvignon Columbia Valley River Ridge Vineyard Limited Bottling 1987: Very firm and focused, this lean-structured wine is packed with raspberry, currant, toast and cola flavors that persist on the long, concentrated finish. Has excellent potential to soften into a real beauty, but for now, it's tight and concentrated; try after 1995 to '97. $18 (8/31/91) **87**
Cabernet Sauvignon Columbia Valley Twentieth Vintage 1987: This tight, youthful wine has plenty of plum and black currant flavors underneath the tart acidity and firm tannins. It's clean, and well balanced, except for the stiff tannins. Should be much smoother by 1994. $12 (9/30/90) **85**
Cabernet Sauvignon Washington 1985: Starts off tart and tannic, but the jammy raspberry and currant flavors develop nicely on the palate, turning rich and vibrant on the finish. Almost drinkable now. $11.50 (10/15/89) **85**
Cabernet Sauvignon Washington 1984 $11 (12/31/88) **89**
Cabernet Sauvignon Washington 1983 $10 (11/15/87) **81**
Cabernet Sauvignon Washington 1980 $9 (3/01/85) **65**
Cabernet Sauvignon Washington Cold Creek Vineyard Limited Bottling 1985: A complex wine that's dominated by tannins. It's deeply flavored and massively structured, developing a bottle bouquet of spice, smoke and earth, with deep cherry and currant flavors. Drink now. $19 (12/15/90) **83**
Cabernet Sauvignon Washington River Ridge Vineyard Limited Bottling 1985: A mature, spicy, smoky character adds to the black cherry and nutmeg aromas and flavors, which broaden into an enticing array of complex spices on the finish. Has the structure to keep developing through the mid-1990s. 2,400 cases made. $17 (11/30/90) **90**

COLUMBIA
Cabernet Sauvignon Columbia Valley 1988: Very firm and concentrated, with a solid center of

berry and currant flavors shaded by hints of oak, smoke and chocolate. The tannins are well integrated and only need until 1993 to '96 to resolve themselves. $10 (3/31/91) **86**

Cabernet Sauvignon Columbia Valley 1987: A herbaceous style that's elegant and supple, with currant and cherry flavors peeking through on the finish. You taste more fruit with every sip. Delicious to drink already. A good value. $9.50 (6/15/90) **87**

Cabernet Sauvignon Columbia Valley 1986: Ripe Cabernet flavor is set against a crisp structure and tempered with a supple streak of sweet oak. Drink now or in 1993. $10 (10/15/89) **85**

Cabernet Sauvignon Columbia Valley 1985 $9.50 (7/15/88) **79**

Cabernet Sauvignon Columbia Valley David Lake Sagemoor Vineyards 1986: Bright and lively, with intense herb, plum and currant flavors that turn supple on the palate. The finish picks up plenty of tannin. Best to drink in 1993 to '98. 600 cases made. $16 (5/15/91) **85**

Cabernet Sauvignon Columbia Valley Sagemoor Vineyards 1985: Ripe aromas and flavors of currant and plum are tempered with a welcome sense of restraint. The wine seems tightly wrapped, waiting for cellaring to bring out its best, perhaps by 1993 to '95. $15 (10/15/89) **85**

Cabernet Sauvignon Columbia Valley Signature Series Otis Vineyard 1988: Dark and dense, with ripe cherry and plum aromas and flavors that are focused and not complicated by too much oak. Has enough tannin to carry it through at least 1995 or '96. 923 cases made. $20 (4/15/92) **89**

Cabernet Sauvignon Columbia Valley Signature Series Red Willow Vineyard 1988: Crisp and lively, with plenty of cedar- and cola-tinged currant and black cherry flavors supported by fine tannins and firm acidity. Has a nice balance between fruit and oak. Should be best after 1996 or '97. 637 cases made. $20 (4/15/92) **86**

Cabernet Sauvignon Columbia Valley Signature Series Sagemoor Vineyards 1988: Lean and astringent, with tannic tea, oak and currant flavors. Needs time to soften, but it may always be tannic. Drink after 1995. Tasted twice. 640 cases made. $20 (4/30/92) **81**

Cabernet Sauvignon Washington Bacchus Vineyard 1981 $12 (8/01/84) **86**

Cabernet Sauvignon Yakima Valley 1981 $8 (8/01/84) **76**

Cabernet Sauvignon Yakima Valley Otis Vineyard 1985: So impeccably balanced you almost don't notice the tannins, which give just the right nudge of toughness to this supple, elegant, harmonious wine. The ripe Cabernet flavor plays beautifully against the sweet oak now, but with cellaring until 1993 to '95, this should be a beauty. $15 (10/15/89) **91**

Cabernet Sauvignon Yakima Valley Otis Vineyard 1981 $13 (8/01/84) **83**

Cabernet Sauvignon Yakima Valley Red Willow Vineyard 1985: Has ideal aromas and flavors of currantlike Cabernet flavor that aren't particularly intense, but are balanced with a nice touch of oak. Drink now. $15 (10/15/89) **82**

Cabernet Sauvignon Yakima Valley Red Willow Vineyard 1981: Balanced toward lightness and elegance rather than richness, with mature, smoky, cedary aromas and a supple smoothness on the palate. Drink now. $35 (10/15/89) **84**

COLUMBIA CREST

Cabernet Sauvignon Columbia Valley 1987: Firm in texture and flavorful without being terribly concentrated or expansive, offering nicely articulated ripe currant and plum aromas and flavors, hinting at chocolate on the finish. Should be best after 1993 or '94. $10 (8/31/91) **85**

Cabernet Sauvignon Columbia Valley 1986: Firm, focused and balanced, with plenty of attractive plum, currant and berry flavors tightly wrapped in fine tannins and supported by crisp acidity. Cellar until about 1994. $8 (1/31/91) BB **88**

Cabernet Sauvignon Columbia Valley 1985: Ripe and rich, with earthy undertones to the cherry and berry flavor. Almost drinkable now; better than a bottle tasted earlier. $8 (10/15/89) **81**

Cabernet Sauvignon Columbia Valley 1984 $7.50 (7/15/88) **79**

COVEY RUN

Cabernet Sauvignon Yakima Valley 1988: Tart, lean and crisp, with pretty plum, currant, anise and smoke flavors and tight but supple tannins. Drinkable now, but should age through 1995 with ease. $11 (4/30/92) **85**

Cabernet Sauvignon Yakima Valley 1986: Crisp and tart, but the jammy raspberry flavor carries through to the finish, balancing the tartness. Drink now. $10 (10/15/89) **80**

FRENCH CREEK

Cabernet Sauvignon Washington 1988: An oddball wine, with leathery, barnyardy aromas that give way to tart raspberry and pine flavors. Of average quality. Tasted twice, with consistent notes. $9.50 (4/15/92) **73**

Cabernet Sauvignon Washington 1985 $8 (10/15/88) **82**

GORDON BROTHERS

Cabernet Sauvignon Washington 1988: Crisp in texture, but it rolls out smoothly with lovely raspberry and currant flavors that echo nicely on the long finish. Fruit and spice flavors keep piling up with each sip. A delicious wine to drink now, but it should keep improving through 1995. $19 (11/15/91) **89**

HEDGES

Cabernet-Merlot Columbia Valley 1990: Firm and focused, with currant and plum aromas and flavors shaded by oak and cedar on the finish. A nicely balanced wine, but its tannins need until 1995 or '96 to soften. $9 (6/15/92) BB **88**

Cabernet-Merlot Columbia Valley 1989: A charming wine with pretty oak shadings and plenty of fruit. Layers of ripe, supple currant, herb, berry and cherry flavors are long and lingering. The smooth tannins make this easy to enjoy now. Drink at its peak in 1993 to '95. $7 (9/30/91) BB **89**

HOGUE

Cabernet Sauvignon Washington 1989: Tart, tightly structured and amply flavored, with mint and cassis notes. Firm tannins make it rough to drink now. Cellar until at least 1993. $12 (11/15/91) **84**

Cabernet Sauvignon Washington 1988: Firm and concentrated, with clear, sharply focused cherry, currant, anise and plum flavors that are rich and complex. A pretty touch of chocolate and vanilla oak shadings add to a pleasing aftertaste. Drink in 1995. $12 (3/31/92) **88**

Cabernet Sauvignon Washington Reserve 1988: Supple in texture and almost chocolaty in richness, but firm, integrated tannins balance out the ripe, crisp blackberry and black cherry flavors. Too tight to drink now; probably best in 1994 to '96. 740 cases made. $18 (11/15/91) **89**

Cabernet Sauvignon Washington Reserve 1987: Very spicy, toasted and rich, with concentrated currant and raspberry aromas and flavors shaded by nutmeg and chocolate. The smoothly integrated tannins will need until 1993 to '95 to resolve, but it's approaching drinkability already. $19 (3/31/91) **88**

Cabernet Sauvignon Washington Reserve 1985: Lean and relatively light, but the aromas and flavors are ripe and focused with a nice balance of ripe currant and toasted oak. $18 (10/15/89) **81**

KIONA

Cabernet Sauvignon Yakima Valley Estate Bottled 1986: Ripe, concentrated, smooth and elegant, with well-defined Cabernet flavor emerging on the finish against a firm underpinning of tannin. Drinkable now. $14 (10/15/89) **89**

Cabernet Sauvignon Yakima Valley Tapteil Vineyard 1988: Lean and firm, with enough currant and berry flavors poking around on the palate to overcome the tannic structure. Not a big wine, but it could develop with cellaring through 1993 to '95. $12 (3/31/92) **85**

LATAH CREEK

Cabernet Sauvignon Washington 1986 $13 (10/15/88) **80**

Cabernet Sauvignon Washington Limited Bottling 1988: Focused and flavorful, a solid mouthful of currant, berry and spice flavors echoing anise and vanilla on the crisp finish. The tannins are balanced for aging through 1993 to '95. 512 cases made. $12.50 (10/15/91) **91**

Cabernet Sauvignon Washington Limited Bottling 1987: Ripe, fresh and generous but very tannic and rough at this age. The flavors of currants, plums and cherries are intense and bode well for aging. Drink now. $13 (7/31/89) **83**

LEONETTI

Cabernet Sauvignon Columbia Valley 1986: Warm, ripe and mellow. The ripe cherry and currant flavors are overshadowed by earthier aromas and flavors. Try now or in 1993. $20 (10/15/89) **81**

Cabernet Sauvignon Walla Walla Valley Seven Hills Vineyard 1988: Has a good slap of toasty oak, but also ripe, rich currant and plum flavors that are concentrated enough to stand up to the wood. A distinctive wine, with a long, lingering finish that echoes black cherry and spice notes. Drink in 1994 to '98. 240 cases made. $25 (8/31/91) **91**

Cabernet Sauvignon Walla Walla Valley Seven Hills Vineyard 1985: Ripe cherry and spice aromas and flavors burst forth from this generous, full-bodied but artfully balanced wine. A hint of earthiness intrudes on the palate and tannin envelops the flavors. Try now or in 1993. $22 (10/15/89) **85**

Cabernet Sauvignon Washington 1988: Crisp and focused, with a firm core of currant and plum aromas and flavors tightly wrapped in tannin and supported by sufficient acidity to require until 1994 to '96 to soften. 1,000 cases made. $22 (8/31/91) **87**

Cabernet Sauvignon Washington 1987: Loaded with layers of fresh currant, plum and cherry flavors framed by toasty, cedary oak that echoes vanilla and chocolate notes. Rich and concentrated, with flavors that linger on the finish. Elegantly balanced and tannic enough to cellar until 1994. 605 cases made. $22 (6/15/90) **91**

Cabernet Sauvignon Washington Reserve 1985: A gutsy wine that's tough, tannic and tightly wound, with lots of cedar and herb overtones to the very ripe plum and cherry flavors and a definite streak of leather that runs through the finish. Tannic enough to need until 1996 to 2000 to soften. Tasted twice. 240 cases made. $40 (6/15/91) **84**

MERCER RANCH

Cabernet Sauvignon Columbia Valley Mercer Ranch Vineyard Block 1 1985: Tart and tannic, with berry and currant flavors tightly wrapped in a cloak of acidity. Maybe it will soften with time; perhaps by 1993. $13 (10/15/89) **81**

MOUNT BAKER

Cabernet Sauvignon Washington 1988: Ripe and generous, with lots of concentrated currant and plum aromas and flavors and a strong component of chocolaty, buttery oak. Hints at cranberry on the finish. A complex wine with plenty of flavor, but seems a little soft on the finish. 600 cases made. $16 (3/31/92) **84**

PORTTEUS

Cabernet Sauvignon Yakima Valley 1987: Tight, firm and tannic, but pretty cherry and currant flavors are beginning to show through. The finish gets dry and chewy, so it's best to let this one rest in your cellar until around 1995. 500 cases made. $18 (3/31/92) **86**

PRESTON WINE CELLARS

Cabernet Sauvignon Washington 1982 $8 (5/31/88) **84**

Cabernet Sauvignon Washington Oak Aged 1989: A nicely balanced, fruity, fresh wine, with herb, currant and plum flavors, medium-strength tannins and good acidity to back it all up. Altogether a pleasing package for drinking now. $10 (5/15/91) **85**

Cabernet Sauvignon Washington Preston Vineyard Oak Aged 1990: Decidedly herbal, vegetal and oaky, with hints of barely ripe plum and currant. Stylistic, but some may like the greenish, herbal character. Drinkable now. $12 (4/30/92) **76**

Cabernet Sauvignon Washington Preston Vineyard Reserve 1990: Complex and harmonious, with lovely currant, anise, cherry and spice flavors framed by toasty, buttery oak nuances. Balanced and long on the finish. A delicious wine that should age well throughout the decade. 125 cases made. $21 (3/31/92) **91**

Cabernet Sauvignon Washington Preston Vineyard Selected Reserve 1987: A big disappointment. Extremely earthy, leathery, harsh and tannic. Tart, too. Tasted twice. $13.50 (10/15/89) **62**

Cabernet Sauvignon Washington Reserve 1989: Ripe, rich, dark and dense, with expansive black cherry, boysenberry and currant aromas and flavors that are almost jammy on the palate and firm tannins that should carry this well through the late 1990s. The spice of oak sneaks in on the finish. 65 cases made. $24 (8/31/91) **90**

QUARRY LAKE

Cabernet Sauvignon Washington 1986: Distinctly herbal, lean and tannic. It's ripe, but not as concentrated as it could be. $10 (10/15/89) **78**

QUILCEDA CREEK

Cabernet Sauvignon Washington 1985: Ripe, grapey and tannic, with a bitter edge to the finish and a clumsy feel to the structure. $16.50 (10/15/89) **74**

STE. CHAPELLE

Cabernet Sauvignon Washington 1988: An exotic style that stretches the cherry and currant flavors to include touches of herb and oak, giving it a sense of complexity. Fairly tannic on the finish. Best to cellar until 1996. $10 (2/29/92) **84**

Cabernet Sauvignon Washington 1986: Crisp and flavorful, with nicely focused currant and black cherry aromas and flavors. Moderately intense and firm, but not too tannic. Drinkable now, but better around 1993 to '95. 1,800 cases made. $10 (8/31/91) **83**

SEVEN HILLS

Cabernet Sauvignon Walla Walla Valley 1989: A deep, rich, powerful wine that packs a wallop with the tannins, but it's also loaded with complex cherry, currant, wild berry and spicy, toasty oak flavors. The tannin level warrants cellaring until 1997. 240 cases made. $20 (3/31/92) **85**

SNOQUALMIE

Cabernet Sauvignon Columbia Valley 1987: Rich, jammy, ripe and seductive, overflowing with great fruit flavor and backed by a good structure of tannins and acidity; this wine is pure pleasure. Drinkable now, but should improve through 1993. 3,000 cases made. $10 (9/30/90) **90**

STATON HILLS

Cabernet Sauvignon Washington 1988: An unusual wine that features cranberry, beet and herb flavors, but it also has ripe currant and cherry notes. Tastes best on the finish, where the flavors combine. Not too tannic. Drink after 1994. 2,000 cases made. $15 (3/31/92) **81**

Cabernet Sauvignon Washington 1987: Ripe and generous, this broad-textured wine has slightly gamy cherry and currant aromas and flavors and hints of vanilla and smoke on the finish where the flavors fade a bit. It's well balanced and worth cellaring until 1995 or '96 to see what develops. $13 (3/31/91) **86**

Cabernet Sauvignon Washington 1986: Has nice fruit, albeit somewhat simple, a supple texture, and enough tannin to give it structure. Drink now. $12 (10/15/89) **80**

Cabernet Sauvignon Washington 1983 $9 (4/30/88) **77**

Cabernet Sauvignon Washington 1981 $9 (5/15/87) **80**

Cabernet Sauvignon Washington Collectors' Series 1981: Mature, but basically simple and spicy. At its best right now. $18 (10/15/89) **81**

Cabernet Sauvignon Washington Estate 1987: Thick in texture, tasting cooked rather than fresh, with cherry and beet aromas and flavors. Not tannic but soft on the finish. Drinkable now. 400 cases made. $20 (2/29/92) **79**

Cabernet Sauvignon Washington Estate Bottled 1986: Extremely ripe and tannic. Though it's not heavy-handed, the cherry, raisin and prune aromas and flavors are wrapped in enough tannin to need until 1995 to settle down. 268 cases made. $20 (3/31/91) **83**

Cabernet Sauvignon Washington Reserve 1987: Ripe and generous, in tannin as well as in flavor, with distinctive stewed plum and black cherry aromas and flavors and a smooth texture underneath the fierce tannins. Should be fine after 1995. 450 cases made. $22 (3/31/92) **85**

Cabernet Sauvignon Washington Reserve 1986: Ripe and herbal, with generous plum and currant flavors shaded strongly by bay leaf, dill and toast notes. The tannins are present without being too strong. Should be best after 1994 or '95. 250 cases made. $22 (8/31/91) **83**

STEWART
Cabernet Sauvignon Columbia Valley 1988: Strong bay leaf aromas and flavors permeate this wine, rendering it highly distinctive and not for everyone. Seems raw and lacks fruit. Drink after 1994. 900 cases made. $11 (8/31/91) **79**

PAUL THOMAS
Cabernet Sauvignon Washington 1989: Tart and fresh, with simple plum and cherry flavors. A pleasant but uncomplicated wine. 2,200 cases made. $12 (3/31/92) **80**
Cabernet Sauvignon Washington 1986: Clean, straightforward and dry, very firm and crisp, with sufficient cherry and plum flavors, firm tannins and good balance. $14 (9/30/90) **84**
Cabernet Sauvignon Washington 1985: Impressively ripe but balanced with juicy acidity, making the currant and cherry aromas and flavors turn snappy and more concentrated as the finish unfolds. $20 (10/15/89) **88**
Cabernet Sauvignon Washington Reserve 1987: Tight and astringent, but the flavors are fresh and vibrant, offering black cherry, blackberry and currant and hints of coffee and spice on the finish. Finishes smoother than it starts. Drink after 1994. 520 cases made. $16 (3/31/92) **86**

WATERBROOK
Cabernet Sauvignon Columbia Valley 1988: Firm and flavorful, with more than a hint of green bean against a nice background of currant and plum flavors. The tannins are nicely integrated. Should need until 1995 or '96 to soften. 510 cases made. $14 (4/15/92) **85**

WHITE HERON
Chantepierre Washington 1988: Light and lean in flavor, with touches of jam and spice and a sweet finish. Drinkable but simple. Drink now. $11 (4/15/92) **80**

WOODWARD CANYON
Cabernet Sauvignon Columbia Valley 1989: Bold, ripe and intense, with layers of plum, cedar, spice, anise and currant flavors that are rich, deep and concentrated. Has firm but polished tannins and a long, lingering aftertaste that keeps repeating the fruit themes. 1,600 cases made. $27 (5/15/92) **92**
Cabernet Sauvignon Columbia Valley 1988: Firm, beautifully structured and rich, with ripe plum, black cherry and anise flavors. A fairly tight frame of crisp acidity and firm tannins gives it a taut balance that indicates cellaring until at least 1995 to '98 will ensure optimum enjoyment. Classy spice and oak nuances linger on the finish. 1,504 cases made. $24 (10/15/91) **93**
Cabernet Sauvignon Columbia Valley 1987: Incredibly fruity, very rich, supple, smooth and elegant. Has ripe currant, black cherry, plum and anise flavors layered with spicy tannins and a firm overlay of earth and oak on the finish. One of the greatest Washington Cabs we've tasted. Should peak in 1994 or '95. 804 cases made. Rel: $18.50 Cur: $24 (12/31/90) **95**
Cabernet Sauvignon Columbia Valley 1986 Rel: $18.50 Cur: $24 (10/15/89) **93**
Cabernet Sauvignon Columbia Valley 1985 ($NA) (4/15/92) (JL) **86**
Cabernet Sauvignon Columbia Valley 1984 ($NA) (4/15/92) (JL) **81**
Cabernet Sauvignon Columbia Valley 1983 ($NA) (4/15/92) (JL) **88**
Cabernet Sauvignon Columbia Valley 1982 ($NA) (4/15/92) (JL) **83**
Cabernet Sauvignon Columbia Valley 1981 ($NA) (4/15/92) (JL) **85**
Charbonneau Walla Walla County 1989: Very tight, compact and austere, with hints of plum, cherry, anise and cedar. Deeply concentrated, but youthful and unevolved. A nice core of prune and currant flavor emerges on the finish. Hands off until 1995. 418 cases made. $30 (5/15/92) **88**
Charbonneau Walla Walla County 1988: A very seductive, supple, flavor-packed wine that wraps spicy French oak around a solid, concentrated core of ripe cherry, currant and herb flavors. The overall effect is gentle power because the tannins are abundant but soft. Tempting now, but it could be cellared until 1997 or beyond. 404 cases made. $26 (10/15/91) **95**
Charbonneau Walla Walla County 1987: Lavishly oaked, with exotic herb and spice notes complementing the ripe cranberry and cherry flavors. The texture is smooth, and the finish echoes chocolate and herbs. Fans of this style will love it. Drink now to 1995. $20 (12/31/90) **89**
Charbonneau Walla Walla County 1985 $30 (4/15/92) (JL) **86**

WORDEN
Cabernet Merlot Washington 1989: Ripe and concentrated, but wrapped in a cloak of thick tannins. Has plenty of dark cherry and currant flavors at the core, with hints of cranberry on the finish. Best after 1995. $10 (2/29/92) **86**

YAKIMA RIVER
Cabernet Sauvignon Columbia Valley 1988: An earthy, funky wine, with strong gamy aromas and flavors that compete with oak and ripe currant notes on the finish. Seems unbalanced; not likely to improve even if you cellar it through 1995. 3,420 cases made. $15 (3/31/92) **74**

CHARDONNAY

ARBOR CREST
Chardonnay Columbia Valley 1988: Crisp and lively, with attractive grapefruit aromas and flavors, a juicy texture and long finish. Not especially complex, but highly appealing. Drink now. $9.50 (3/31/90) **85**
Chardonnay Columbia Valley 1987: Lean and crisp, but the predominant aromas and flavors are those of oak aging. The balance is fine for a lighter style. $9.25 (10/15/89) **84**
Chardonnay Columbia Valley 1984 $9.25 (7/31/87) **78**
Chardonnay Washington Sagemoore Vineyards 1983 $10 (11/01/85) **69**
Chardonnay Washington Sagemoore Vineyards 1982 $14 (1/01/85) **85**

CHATEAU STE. MICHELLE
Chardonnay Columbia Valley 1988: Light, delicate and well crafted, this seems straightforward at first but develops exotic complexity and intensity on the finish. Likable and drinkable now. $10 (9/30/90) **84**
Chardonnay Columbia Valley Cold Creek Vineyard 1990: Fresh and lively, with tiers of tart apple, melon, lemon and pear flavors that are sharply focused, well defined and linger on the aftertaste. This tight, young wine can stand cellaring through 1993. $17 (3/31/92) **89**
Chardonnay Columbia Valley River Ridge Vineyard 1990: Crisp and lean, with a beam of tart apple, lemon and spice flavors. Well focused, but lacking depth and richness. Perhaps with time it will show more complexity. Drink now to 1994. $15 (3/31/92) **83**
Chardonnay Washington 1987: Fresh and lively, with simple Chardonnay flavor and a nice touch of oak to provide some tension. $10 (10/15/89) **81**
Chardonnay Washington 1984 $10 (7/31/87) **67**
Chardonnay Washington 1982 $9 (4/16/86) **73**
Chardonnay Washington Cold Creek Vineyard Limited Bottling 1987: Complexity on a racy structure equals elegance in this medium-weight but sharply focused wine. Apple, lemon, pear and spice aromas and flavors compete for attention without becoming unruly. $13 (10/15/89) **87**
Chardonnay Washington Cold Creek Vineyard Limited Bottling 1986 $13 (12/31/88) **82**
Chardonnay Washington River Ridge Vineyard Château Reserve 1983 $18 (7/31/87) **81**
Chardonnay Washington River Ridge Vineyard Limited Bottling 1987: Concentrated but light and crisp in texture; the apple-lemon flavor is touched by enough oak to make this a snappy wine for current drinking. $13 (10/15/89) **85**

CHINOOK
Chardonnay Washington 1987: Ripe and toasty, a concentrated wine with good balance and fruit complexity, but it's broad and unfocused. $11 (10/15/89) **82**

COLUMBIA
Chardonnay Columbia Valley 1989: Light, lean and earthy, a sort of Mâcon style that makes for simple, short-term drinking. Tasted twice. $7 (5/31/91) **78**
Chardonnay Columbia Valley 1988: Oozing with butterscotch aromas and flavors, it's lean and slightly tart on the palate. Oak flavors remain on the finish. Drinkable now. $8.50 (9/30/90) **79**
Chardonnay Columbia Valley Sagemoor Vineyards Barrel Fermented The Woodburne Collection 1989: Ripe, round and rich, but not weighty, making this an elegant, flavorful Chardonnay. The flavors lean toward pear, butter and honey, with a nice hint of nutmeg on the long finish. Highly enjoyable now, but cellaring until 1993 could bring out more. $10 (3/31/91) **89**
Chardonnay Columbia Valley Woodburne Cuvée 1990: A lean wine, offering sharply defined grapefruit and almond aromas and flavors and earthy nuances around the edges, but it's sound, and should continue to improve through 1993. $12 (11/30/91) **84**
Chardonnay Washington 1985 $8 (7/31/87) **79**
Chardonnay Washington Barrel Fermented The Woodburne Collection 1987: Sturdy, ripe and generous, with lots of honey, fig and pineapple aromas and flavors, firm acidity and lively flavors on the long finish. Not elegant, but well-proportioned and drinkable. 900 cases made. $10 (3/31/91) **83**
Chardonnay Washington Jolona Vineyard 1982 $12 (9/01/84) **80**
Chardonnay Yakima Valley Brookside Vineyards 1987: Light and snappy; a lean, crisp wine with delicate lemon and pear aromas and flavors. Takes subtlety a bit too far; with a little more concentration, this would be a winner. $15 (10/15/89) **80**
Chardonnay Yakima Valley Wyckoff Vineyard 1983 $8.50 (4/16/86) **46**

COLUMBIA CREST
Chardonnay Columbia Valley 1989: Lean and delicate, this wine packs ripe fig and pear flavors in a compact frame, with hints of toast, lemon and nutmeg. A fresh, lively wine. Drink now. $7 (9/30/90) BB **86**
Chardonnay Columbia Valley 1987 $7 (12/31/88) **80**
Chardonnay Columbia Valley 1986 $8 (12/31/87) **79**
Chardonnay Columbia Valley Barrel Select 1989: Firm and focused, with toasty, earthy Burgundian overtones to the narrow range of pear and apple flavors. Balanced and very pretty on the finish. Drinkable now. 2,500 cases made. $15 (5/31/91) **86**
Chardonnay Columbia Valley Vintage Select 1987: An earthy edge gives the apple flavor a ciderlike flavor in this medium-weight, already mature-tasting wine. $7 (10/15/89) **77**

COVEY RUN
Chardonnay Yakima Valley 1990: Fresh, inviting, intensely fruity, round in texture and easy to drink. Packs in a lot of pear, peach and floral flavors without much interference from oak. $10 (4/30/92) **84**
Chardonnay Yakima Valley 1989: Very crisp and lively in texture, with well-proportioned green apple, spice and toast flavors that linger on the finish. Very fruity and fresh. Pleasant for drinking now. $10 (3/31/91) **86**
Chardonnay Yakima Valley 1987: Firm and concentrated, almost hard-edged. The toasted vanilla character of oak edges out the Chardonnay flavor. Drink now. $9 (10/15/89) **82**
Chardonnay Yakima Valley Reserve 1989: Bright, flavorful and lively, with plenty of peach and pear flavors accented by lavish butter, vanilla and spice notes from new oak. The fruit and spice really linger on the seemingly sweet finish. $15 (7/15/91) **89**

FRENCH CREEK
Chardonnay Washington 1989: A butterscotch aroma from oak is about the only lively thing in this tired, brown, medicinal-tasting Chardonnay. There's not much fruit, and what there is, is overly mature. Not recommended. Tasted twice, with consistent notes. $9.50 (4/30/92) **66**

HOGUE
Chardonnay Washington 1990: Deep, rich, ripe and complex, with all the barrel-fermented spice and honey notes to round out a core of pear and apple flavors. Lavishly oaked and full-bodied, with the grace and balance to keep developing through 1993 to '95, although the finish could expand a bit more than it does. $9 (4/30/92) **89**
Chardonnay Washington 1988: Lively and zesty, with ripe apple and honey notes that offer richness but turn a bit tart on the finish. Drink now. $8 (6/15/90) **80**
Chardonnay Washington 1987: Toasted, resiny aromas and flavors dominate this medium-weight, richly textured wine. A bit of peach flavor peeks through on the finish. Drink now. $8 (10/15/89) **83**
Chardonnay Washington 1986 $8 (12/31/87) **81**
Chardonnay Washington Reserve 1989: Fruity, spicy, lively and delicate, with nicely focused apple, peach, pear and nutmeg aromas and flavors. Crisply balanced, showing a good deal of finesse and flavor. Drinkable now. $13 (5/31/91) **86**
Chardonnay Yakima Valley Reserve 1987: Ripe and toasty, with a smooth texture and a hint of vanilla and honey on the long finish. There is a lot of subtlety here, and a nice tension between fruit and oak. $10 (10/15/89) **88**

KIONA
Chardonnay Yakima Valley Barrel Fermented 1987: With its lovely peach and vanilla aromas and flavors, this strikes an extraordinary balance between fruit and oak, all of which is supported firmly and harmoniously. Beautiful to drink now. $10 (10/15/89) **91**

LATAH CREEK
Chardonnay Washington 1990: Ripe, rich and generous, with a bold streak of grapefruit giving a lift to the spice, honey and pear aromas and flavors. Round and polished, this has enough underlying acidity to give it a sense of urgency. Drinkable now. $8.50 (1/31/92) **86**
Chardonnay Washington 1987: A spicy wine, with lots of ginger and nutmeg "seasoning" on the complex fruit; heavy and thick in texture, broad and fairly long. $9 (10/15/89) **82**
Chardonnay Washington 1986 $8.50 (12/31/87) **70**
Chardonnay Washington Feather 1988: Fruity and spicy, with more Riesling-like character than Chardonnay, but it's fresh and appealing. $6 (10/15/89) **80**

STEVEN THOMAS LIVINGSTONE
Chardonnay Columbia Valley 1990: Light and crisp. A simple wine, with modest apple and lemon aromas and flavors. Drinkable now. $10 (11/30/91) **80**

PRESTON WINE CELLARS
Chardonnay Washington Barrel Fermented 1990: An odd wine, with musty, earthy overtones and peachy, floral flavors that remind us more of a late-harvest Riesling than Chardonnay. Not bad, just different. $12 (11/30/91) **81**
Chardonnay Washington Barrel Fermented 1989: Full-bodied, complex, earthy and oaky, but the grapefruit and pear flavors come through on the rich finish. A stylish wine that gets better with each sip. Drinkable now, but should be better around 1993. 700 cases made. $12 (5/31/91) **91**
Chardonnay Washington Preston Vineyard Hand Harvested 1987: Gewurztraminer-like spicy

Key to Symbols

The scores reported here are the results of blind tastings conducted by our panel of senior editors. Wines that carry the initials below are results of individual tastings.

THE WINE SPECTATOR 100-POINT SCALE 95-100—Classic, a great wine; ***90-94***—Outstanding, superior character and style; ***80-89***—Good to very good, a wine with special qualities; ***70-79***—Average, drinkable wine that may have minor flaws; ***60-69***—Below average, drinkable but not recommended; ***50-59***—Poor, undrinkable, not recommended. "+"—With a score indicates a range; used primarily with barrel tastings to indicate a preliminary score.

SPECIAL DESIGNATIONS SS—Spectator Selection, CS—Cellar Selection, BB—Best Buy, ($NA)—Price not available, (NR)—Not released.

TASTER'S INITIALS (JG)—Jim Gordon, (HS)—Harvey Steiman, (JL)—James Laube, (JS)—James Suckling, (TM)—Thomas Matthews, (TR)—Terry Robards, (PM)—Per-Henrik Mansson, (BT)—Barrel Tasting (these wines were tasted blind from barrel samples), (CA-date)—*California's Great Cabernets* by James Laube, (CH-date)—*California's Great Chardonnays* by James Laube, (VP-date)—*Vintage Port* by James Suckling.

DATE TASTED Dates in parentheses represent the issue in which the rating was published.

aromas and flavors make this medium-weight wine distinctive and attractive, if unusual for a Chardonnay. $10 (10/15/89) **82**

QUARRY LAKE
Chardonnay Washington 1987: More resin and pine aromas and flavors than fruit make this a wine not everyone will like. $10 (10/15/89) **74**

SILVER LAKE
Chardonnay Columbia Valley Reserve 1989: Crisp, lively, spicy and fresh, with nicely focused apple, lemon and vanilla aromas and flavors that persist on the finish. A wine with subtlety and style. Drinkable now for its freshness. 1,000 cases made. $16 (5/31/91) **88**

SNOQUALMIE
Chardonnay Columbia Valley 1987: A lean, spicy, concentrated wine that appears to be light on its feet due to its bracing, lemony acidity. $8 (10/15/89) **83**
Chardonnay Yakima Valley 1984 $9 (4/16/86) **53**
Chardonnay Yakima Valley Early Release 1984 $7 (4/16/86) **70**
Chardonnay Columbia Valley Reserve 1987: Ripe and generous in flavor, contained in a framework of crisp acidity and smooth, barrel-fermented texture that shows off the peach and apple flavor with a harmonious overlay of toast and nutmeg. $13 (10/15/89) **85**

STATON HILLS
Chardonnay Washington 1989: Stylish but light for a Chardonnay, with crisp fruit flavor complemented by spicy, buttery notes from aging in new oak. Charming and ready to drink now. 2,000 cases made. $10 (7/15/91) **82**
Chardonnay Washington 1988: A gentle wine, with spicy apple cider aromas and flavors. Tasty enough, but lacking the crisp backbone to be all that it can be. Tasted twice. $10 (5/31/91) **79**
Chardonnay Washington 1987: Ripe in pear and spice flavors and broad in texture, but basically a simple, tasty wine to drink now. $10 (10/15/89) **81**

STEWART
Chardonnay Columbia Valley 1988: A crisp texture and appley aromas and flavors make this a lively wine, with a streak of spice and honey adding nice nuances. Drinkable, but the hard-edged acidity can use until 1993 or '94 to soften. 4,500 cases made. $10 (3/31/91) **85**
Chardonnay Columbia Valley Reserve 1988: Maturing fast, showing lots of spice and toast aromas and flavors against a core of orange and apple, looking dark and not quite as lively as it could. Drink soon. 450 cases made. $17 (5/31/91) **78**
Chardonnay Columbia Valley Reserve 1987: Ripe and rich, but refreshingly balanced with snappy acidity. Very smoky aromas, but bursting with pear, grapefruit, vanilla and honey flavors right through the long finish. Drinkable now, but it should develop nicely through 1994. 250 cases made. $15 (3/31/90) **90**

PAUL THOMAS
Chardonnay Washington 1990: Fresh, crisp and lively, with layers of pear, spice, citrus and oak flavors. It zings across the palate, echoing grapefruit and floral notes on the aftertaste. The flavors linger on and on. Drink now to 1995. 4,600 cases made. $12 (3/31/92) **89**
Chardonnay Washington 1988: Smooth and remarkably well balanced, with concentrated Chardonnay flavor graced with overtones of ginger and vanilla, showing Burgundian complexity and richness. Drink now. $11 (10/15/89) **89**
Chardonnay Washington 1987: A subtle wine, with shy, delicate flavors of apple and spice; light in flavor and texture but clean and appealing. $10 (10/15/89) **81**
Chardonnay Washington Private Reserve 1987: Ripe and concentrated, but lean and snappy at the same time, with a lively balance of lemony acidity and pear and vanilla richness making this a promising dinner companion. $18 (10/15/89) **85**
Chardonnay Washington Reserve 1989: A bit heavy-handed with the oak, making the tart pear and lemon flavors taste gluey and metallic. Drink now. 890 cases made. $18 (3/31/92) **76**

WATERBROOK
Chardonnay Columbia Valley 1990: Firm and focused, with lively grapefruit, pineapple and toast aromas and flavors, hinting at nutmeg and vanilla on the finish. Drinkable now, but could get smoother with cellaring until 1993 or '94. $8 (4/30/92) BB **87**
Chardonnay Columbia Valley 1989: Smells woody, but comes up with nice fruit on the palate, offering apple, butter and spice flavors that linger into the finish. A medium-weight wine, with attractive flavors. Drinkable now. $6.50 (11/30/91) **84**
Chardonnay Columbia Valley Barrel Fermented Reserve 1990: Fruity and floral, with generous apple, pear, butter and rose petal aromas and flavors. Full-bodied, with attractive flavors. Drinkable now. 600 cases made. $13 (4/30/92) **87**

WOODWARD CANYON
Chardonnay Columbia Valley 1990: Silky, complex and very Burgundian in style. Smells very toasty and buttery, with rich, almost unctuous pear, butterscotch and spice flavors accented by hazelnut, honey and cream notes. The flavors linger a long time on the finish. 1,553 cases made. $18.50 (11/15/91) **93**
Chardonnay Columbia Valley 1987: Oaky, ripe and spicy; a big, powerful wine that could use more finesse. $18 (10/15/89) **81**
Chardonnay Walla Walla Valley Reserve 1990: Like an Aussie Chardonnay: it's deep in color, with plenty of smoky, toasty aromas from wood aging backed by rich, ripe pear and honey flavors. Spicy, toasted notes linger nicely on the finish. 443 cases made. $25 (11/15/91) **90**
Chardonnay Washington 1986 $16 (4/30/88) **85**
Chardonnay Washington 1984 $21 (5/15/87) **81**
Chardonnay Washington Roza Berge' Vineyard 1990: Solid, very concentrated and fruity, with spice and butter accents. The nectarine and pear flavors are backed with plenty of acidity. Very good quality. 495 cases made. $23 (11/15/91) **87**

DESSERT

BAINBRIDGE ISLAND
Siegerrebe Botrytis Affected Washington 1987: Perfumed, somewhat soapy aromas and flavors detract from the fruit in this sweet, sticky wine. $15/375ml (10/15/89) **71**

BONNY DOON
Eau-de-vie Poire Washington NV: Offers essence of pears in a brandy that is smooth and flavorful, as well as dramatically aromatic. They don't do it much better in France or Switzerland. $18/375ml (3/31/92) **90**

BOOKWALTER
White Riesling Late Harvest Washington 1987: Sweet and generous in flavor, fairly round and rich. Pleasant but simple. $5.50/375ml (10/15/89) **78**

CHATEAU STE. MICHELLE
White Riesling Late Harvest Columbia Valley River Ridge Vineyards Hand-Selected Clusters 1989: Strong resiny aromas and flavors keep the fruit from coming through in this wine, but it's clean, sweet and pleasant. $18 (9/30/91) **82**
White Riesling Late Harvest Yakima Valley Château Reserve Hand-Selected Clusters 1985 $22 (7/31/89) **91**

COLUMBIA
Johannisberg Riesling Late Harvest Columbia Valley Cellarmaster's Reserve 1988: Has beautifully defined Riesling flavor with overtones of pine and honey, especially on the finish; sweet but balanced with snappy acidity. $7 (10/15/89) BB **85**

COVEY RUN
White Riesling Late Harvest Yakima Valley Ice Wine 1987: Concentrated, ripe, rich and very sweet, oozing honey, apricot and vanilla flavors on the long finish. A touch of volatility keeps it from being outstanding. $24/375ml (10/15/89) **87**
White Riesling Late Harvest Yakima Valley Mahre Vineyards Botrytis 1986: Has the ripe, honeyed richness you expect in a botrytis-affected Riesling. Very tasty and solidly structured. $7 (10/15/89) **83**

HINZERLING
Gewüztraminer Late Harvest Yakima Valley Selected Cluster Die Sonne 1985: Dark color and caramelized, sherrylike flavors overcome whatever Gewürztraminer character is there. A very pleasant, even distinctive dessert wine, but not what you might expect from reading the label. $12/375ml (10/15/89) **82**

HOGUE
White Riesling Late Harvest Yakima Valley Markin Vineyard 1987: Has little of the honey or buttery character you might expect from a late-harvest wine, but the peachy Riesling flavor is well defined and the balance is good. $7.50 (10/15/89) **79**

HYATT
Riesling Late Harvest Yakima Valley 1987: Very pretty floral, apricot and honey aromas and flavors ride smoothly on a rich texture, finishing sweet but balanced, fresh and long. $8 (10/15/89) **87**

KIONA
Ice Wine Yakima Valley 1989: Smells and tastes like the syrup from canned pears, not wine. $15/375ml (6/15/91) **75**

PRESTON WINE CELLARS
White Riesling Late Harvest Washington Ice Wine 1986: Very sweet, but rather light on its feet, almost delicate in texture despite 20 percent residual sugar. $38 (10/15/89) **80**

SILVER LAKE
Ice Wine Columbia Valley 1989: Very sweet and rich, with smooth texture and lively apricot, melon and lemon aromas and flavors that extend into a sweet, slightly sugary finish. Drinkable now. 250 cases made. $25/375ml (6/15/91) **85**

SNOQUALMIE
White Riesling Late Harvest Columbia Valley 1988: Ripe and sweet, yet it retains a sense of delicacy that suits the light peach and apricot flavors well. $7 (10/15/89) **84**

STATON HILLS
Riesling Late Harvest Washington 1987: The dark caramel color and developed aromas mark this as a mature example of Riesling, although it's not very sweet. Apricot and honey flavors come through on a medium-sweet, soft structure. Drinkable now. 200 cases made. $10/375ml (3/31/92) **82**

STEWART
White Riesling Late Harvest Columbia Valley 1987: The opulent, honeyed richness of the aromas becomes too restrained on the palate, as if it can't make up its mind. Smells great, but it could taste better. $8/375ml (7/31/89) **83**
White Riesling Late Harvest Columbia Valley Select 1986: Very dark in color, honeyed and full of caramel aromas and flavors, but curiously lacking in intensity and depth. $6.50/375ml (10/15/89) **80**

TENREBAC
Port Washington 1989: Not as sweet as most Ports, and it has a distinct vegetal edge. It's not easy to like. Not for most Port enthusiasts. $24 (11/30/91) **74**

THURSTON WOLFE
Black Muscat Washington 1987: Sweet, but not like treacle, and its exuberant aromas of berries, plums, vanilla and honey continue through the flavors and the finish. A delicious dessert wine that has style and character. $9 (10/15/89) **85**
Sauvignon Blanc Late Harvest Washington Sweet Rebecca 1987: Sweet and simple, with hints of herbs and spices on the finish, which is a clear indication of the grape variety. A very tasty wine. $9 (10/15/89) **83**

GEWÜRZTRAMINER

CHATEAU STE. MICHELLE
Gewürztraminer Columbia Valley 1990: Bright, fruity and slightly sweet, with a nice tension between the grapefruit and peach flavors and a pleasant floral note. A broad-textured wine, with plenty of flavor to enjoy. $6.50 (8/31/91) BB **84**
Gewürztraminer Columbia Valley 1988: Fresh and fruity but not reminiscent of Gewürztraminer. Flavors run toward pear and nuts in this off-dry wine. $6.50 (10/15/89) **79**

COLUMBIA CREST
Gewürztraminer Columbia Valley 1990: Soft and floral, with modest peach and apricot flavors, but mostly sweet and simple. Drink soon; serve cold. $6 (8/31/91) **76**
Gewürztraminer Columbia Valley 1987: A pleasant, off-dry wine with distinctive varietal spice, including rose petal aromas and grapefruit flavors; balanced toward softness on the finish. $6 (10/15/89) **81**

COVEY RUN
Gewürztraminer Yakima Valley 1989: The earthy, floral aromas and flavors could use some fruit to back them up. An average wine. $7 (6/15/91) **76**
Gewürztraminer Yakima Valley 1988: Off-dry, flavorful, emphasizing fruit without the varietal spice, except for a touch of bitterness on the finish. $5.50 (10/15/89) **77**

HOODSPORT
Gewürztraminer Washington 1988: Clean, fresh and fruity, with grapefruit and vanilla aromas and flavors, off-dry but impeccably balanced. $6 (10/15/89) BB **85**

SNOQUALMIE
Gewürztraminer Columbia Valley 1988: Soft, fresh and fruity but not particuarly varietal. A pleasant sipper. $6 (10/15/89) **79**

STATON HILLS
Gewürztraminer Washington 1990: Sweet and candylike, with earthy flavors and a flat structure. Not an enjoyable wine. 1,500 cases made. $7 (10/15/91) **66**

STEWART
Gewürztraminer Yakima Valley 1988: Soft and pleasant but not very flavorful. The fruit seems tired. $5.50 (10/15/89) **69**

WORDEN
Gewürztraminer Washington 1990: Soft and spicy, with pleasantly floral, peppery aromas and flavors that rest gently on a smooth-textured background. A flavorful wine that's refreshing to drink now. 700 cases made. $6.50 (10/15/91) BB **83**

MERLOT

ARBOR CREST
Merlot Columbia Valley 1990: Bursting with plummy berry and rose petal-tinged fruit flavors, but they fight to be heard above the din of tough tannins. Should be fine with cellaring until 1996 to '98, but until then, approach with caution, or at least rich food. $11.50 (4/15/92) **88**
Merlot Columbia Valley 1988: Much more tannic than the lean texture and modest currant and berry

flavors want to carry, which means this will need until 1994 to '97 to be approachable. A longshot, but could be fine. $9 (8/31/91) **81**
Merlot Columbia Valley 1987: Tight and tannic, packed with ripe cherry and berry flavor, velvety and rich, though a bit short. $8 (10/15/89) **83**
Merlot Columbia Valley Bacchus Vineyard 1985 $8 (7/31/87) **75**
Merlot Columbia Valley Bacchus Vineyard 1982 $8.25 (11/01/84) **82**
Merlot Columbia Valley Cameo Reserve 1989: Hard and tart, with greenish aromas that seem to avoid fruit until it gets to the finish, when plum and currant notes sneak in. A tough wine to like now, but might improve with cellaring through 1995. Tasted twice. $12 (3/31/92) **77**
Merlot Columbia Valley Cameo Reserve 1988: Hard-edged and austere, with firm tannins and plenty of oak, but there's also a solid core of plum and currant flavor, too. Tannins are drying on the aftertaste. Best to cellar until 1994. $12 (8/31/91) **83**
Merlot Columbia Valley Cameo Reserve 1987: An attractive, fruity style, with ripe cherry and berry notes and a touch of oak. Good balance of fruit and tannins and a supple texture make it easy and enjoyable to drink now. $11 (6/15/90) **85**
Merlot Columbia Valley Bacchus Vineyard Cameo Reserve 1985 $10 (12/15/87) **83**

CHATEAU STE. MICHELLE
Merlot Columbia Valley 1988: Complex and elegant, with pretty cherry, plum, anise and raspberry flavors that are crisp and lively. Finishes with firm tannins. Drinkable now, but probably better around 1994. $14.50 (3/31/92) **84**
Merlot Columbia Valley 1987: The spice and cedar character of new French oak barrels highlights the clean plum and cherry flavors in this tannic, full-bodied wine. Try now. $12 (9/30/90) **84**
Merlot Columbia Valley 1986: Herbal and plummy, with firm tannins and a somewhat woody character overlaying the soft fruit flavors. This is a very good, straightforward Merlot. Ready to drink now. $12 (9/30/90) **84**
Merlot Columbia Valley Cold Creek Vineyard Limited Bottling 1987: A muted style, with firm tannins and a halo of oak aromas and flavors obscuring the fruit, which seems to center around currant and rhubarb. Could turn out to be a pleasant wine after 1993 or '94. $19 (8/31/91) **81**
Merlot Columbia Valley River Ridge Vineyard 1985: Deep, rich and full-flavored, with good structure and plenty of fine tannins. Ripe, full-bodied and delicious, it's almost drinkable now but should improve through at least 1993. $17.50 (9/30/90) **89**
Merlot Washington 1983 $10 (12/31/88) **80**
Merlot Washington River Ridge Vineyard 1985: Has the concentration and toasted, chocolaty oak to show off the focused flavors of delicious cherry and berry flavor. With crisp acidity and velvety tannins, it's drinkable now, but it ought to get better with cellaring, perhaps until 1994. $14 (10/15/89) **87**
Merlot Washington River Ridge Vineyard Château Reserve 1983 $15 (12/31/88) **87**

CHINOOK
Merlot Washington 1986: Ripe and velvety, with distinctly earthy overtones to the ripe cherry flavor. $12.50 (10/15/89) **83**

COLUMBIA
Merlot Columbia Valley 1989: An oaky, herbal style, with crisp cherry and stewed plum flavors underneath. Has plenty of wood and tannin for cellaring until 1994, but it's drinkable now. 5,000 cases made. $12 (3/31/92) **80**
Merlot Columbia Valley 1988: Very tart and crisp. A heavy green bean edge to the blackberry and currant flavors makes this seem simple and one-dimensional. Drink now or in 1993. Tasted twice. $10 (3/31/91) **81**
Merlot Columbia Valley 1986: A little rough around the edges, but the ebullient cherry and berry flavors show beautifully against a steely backdrop of acidity. Drink now. $10 (10/15/89) **84**
Merlot Columbia Valley 1985 $9.50 (5/31/88) **86**
Merlot Washington 1984 $9 (5/15/87) **75**
Merlot Washington 1981: Has matured beautifully into a spicy, elegant wine, especially in its expansive aromas of ripe cherry, plum, toast and cinnamon; crisp and elegant on the palate. Limited availability. $25 (10/15/89) **87**
Merlot Yakima Valley Red Willow Vineyard 1989: Packed with ripe, rich layers of currant, black cherry, berry and spice flavors and tannins that are round, smooth and supple. The flavors stick with you, making this a wine to enjoy now or cellar through 1994. $20 (11/15/91) **89**
Merlot Yakima Valley Red Willow Vineyard Milestone David Lake 1989: Brilliantly flavorful, with generous black cherry and currant flavor that sails on and on through the long finish. Has smooth, polished texture and suppleness to give the flavors a good ride. Drinkable now. $18 (6/15/92) **88**
Merlot Yakima Valley Red Willow Vineyard Milestone David Lake 1988: Firm, tannic and focused, with berry aromas and flavors shaded by hints of smoke and herbs. A straightforward wine worth cellaring until 1994. This vineyard's wines tend to improve with bottle age. 2,000 cases made. $16 (3/31/91) **82**
Merlot Yakima Valley Red Willow Vineyard Milestone 1987: Lean and tight, with focused berry and cherry flavors wrapped in a cocoon of tannins. Try now. $15 (10/15/89) **80**

COLUMBIA CREST
Merlot Columbia Valley 1989: Very good quality and a great value. Ripe and generous, with a round texture and deep cherry, currant and plum aromas and flavors, hinting around the edges at chocolate and toast. Drinkable now, but should improve through 1994 or '95. $10 (2/29/92) SS **88**
Merlot Columbia Valley 1987: The toasted oak aromas, crisp cherry and berry flavors and fine balance add up to a stylish, clean, flavorful wine for drinking now or through 1993. $8 (9/30/90) BB **86**
Merlot Columbia Valley 1985: Lean and racy, but there are enough concentrated, berry and chocolate aromas and flavors on a firm, medium-weight frame to warrant cellaring for a year or two to see what develops. $8 (10/15/89) **85**
Merlot Columbia Valley 1984 $7.50 (5/31/88) **78**
Merlot Columbia Valley Barrel Select 1987: A solid wine, with plenty of currant and chocolate flavors that persist through a long finish, along with enough oak notes and tannins to want until 1993 to '95 to come into balance. 2,500 cases made. $15 (5/31/91) **84**

COVEY RUN
Merlot Yakima Valley 1989: Intense cedar and juniper aromas carry over to the flavors in this crisp, juicy wine. Fresh tasting and light in tannins. Good to drink now if you don't mind the strong evergreen character. $11 (6/15/92) **79**

Key to Symbols

The scores reported here are the results of blind tastings conducted by our panel of senior editors. Wines that carry the initials below are results of individual tastings.

THE WINE SPECTATOR 100-POINT SCALE 95-100—Classic, a great wine; ***90-94***—Outstanding, superior character and style; ***80-89***—Good to very good, a wine with special qualities; ***70-79***—Average, drinkable wine that may have minor flaws; ***60-69***—Below average, drinkable but not recommended; ***50-59***—Poor, undrinkable, not recommended. "+"—With a score indicates a range; used primarily with barrel tastings to indicate a preliminary score.

SPECIAL DESIGNATIONS SS—Spectator Selection, CS—Cellar Selection, BB—Best Buy, ($NA)—Price not available, (NR)—Not released.

TASTER'S INITIALS (JG)—Jim Gordon, (HS)—Harvey Steiman, (JL)—James Laube, (JS)—James Suckling, (TM)—Thomas Matthews, (TR)—Terry Robards, (PM)—Per-Henrik Mansson, (BT)—Barrel Tasting (these wines were tasted blind from barrel samples), (CA-date)—*California's Great Cabernets* by James Laube, (CH-date)—*California's Great Chardonnays* by James Laube, (VP-date)—*Vintage Port* by James Suckling.

DATE TASTED Dates in parentheses represent the issue in which the rating was published.

Merlot Yakima Valley 1988: Tough and youthful, but has a lovely concentration of currant, plum and cedar flavors that outmuscle the tannins on the long finish. Needs until 1995 to '98 to soften the tannins, but seems to have the concentration to win in the end. $10 (3/31/91) **87**
Merlot Yakima Valley 1986: Light, fruity and crisp; the boysenberry and raspberry flavors ride a racy streak of lemony acidity. Drinkable now. $9 (10/15/89) **82**
Merlot Yakima Valley 1985 $9 (4/15/89) **85**
Merlot Yakima Valley 1984 $8.50 (11/15/87) **82**
Merlot Yakima Valley Reserve 1989: Fresh and firm in texture, with smooth-sailing currant, plum and pepper flavors that glide over the palate just before the tannins close in on the finish. Needs until 1994 or '95 to soften. $17 (3/31/92) **83**

FRENCH CREEK
Merlot Washington 1985 $11.50 (12/31/88) **83**

HAVILAND
Merlot Washington 1982 $8 (10/01/84) **76**

HOGUE
Merlot Washington 1989: An exciting wine at a good price. Crisp, bright and concentrated, with sharply focused blueberry, currant and raspberry aromas and flavors that gush across the palate. Delicious to drink now, but has the structure and power to age gracefully well into the late 1990s. $12 (10/15/91) SS **92**
Merlot Washington 1986: Lean and crisp, with a sense of austerity to hold back the black cherry flavor wrapped with more than a hint of toasted wood. Very similar to some Bordeaux. $12 (4/15/89) **85**
Merlot Washington 1985 $12 (11/15/87) **80**
Merlot Washington Reserve 1988: Spicy and cedary, marked strongly by new French oak, with generous cherry and plum flavors echoing on the finish. A smooth wine with a silky texture. Drinkable now, but should keep deepening with cellaring through 1993 or '94. 700 cases made. $18 (11/15/91) **90**
Merlot Washington Reserve 1987: A supple, elegant wine, with ripe currant and prune aromas and flavors shaded by spice, cedar and chocolate. The fruit persists through the long finish. Tannic enough to need until 1995 to show its true colors. $19 (3/31/91) **89**

KIONA
Merlot Columbia Valley 1989: Crisply focused, with a bright beam of cherry, plum and currant flavors that broadens and deepens on the finish, hinting at tobacco. A pleasant drink with a Bordeaux profile. Drinkable now. $12 (3/31/92) **86**
Merlot Columbia Valley 1988: Fragrant, with currant, cherry, spice and vanilla aromas. This medium-weight wine has plenty of style and grace, but needs until 1994 to soften the still-scratchy tannins. $12 (5/31/91) **84**

LATAH CREEK
Merlot Washington 1986 $10 (5/31/88) **89**
Merlot Washington Limited Bottling 1989: Effusively fruity, with layers of ripe, rich, concentrated blackberry, raspberry, cherry and currant flavors that border on being jammy. The tannins are supple, but sufficient to sustain it another five to 10 years. Tempting now, but probably best around 1993. 1,250 cases made. $11 (9/30/91) **91**
Merlot Washington Limited Bottling 1987: A deep color and dense, concentrated raspberry and spice aromas mark this as something special even before the elegant plummy richness hits the palate. A velvety texture and sense of harmony make it deceptively drinkable today, but it can age, at least through 1993 to '95. Showed much better than a bottle tasted earlier. $10 (10/15/89) **90**

L'ECOLE NO. 41
Merlot Washington 1987: Ripe and complex, full of fruit flavor, with a soft, lush texture, but has good acidity on the finish. Rich, lingering cherry, cassis and mint flavors mark it as special. Modest tannins make it drinkable now through 1994. 600 cases made. $13 (11/30/91) **90**

LEONETTI
Merlot Columbia Valley 1987: Extremely youthful and vibrant, reverberating with concentrated raspberry, cherry and plum aromas and flavors. Cedary aromas add to the tension of a wine that needs at least until 1994 to simmer down and develop some harmony. $16 (10/15/89) **88**
Merlot Washington 1990: A real mouthful of richness and flavor, brimming with spicy, chocolaty currant, plum and black cherry character; smooth and polished to a warm glow. Tannins are present but well-integrated, and the flavors extend into a long and complex finish. Tempting to drink now, but probably better around 1994 or '95. 916 cases made. $22 (6/15/92) **92**
Merlot Washington 1989: A rich, supple, generous wine, with lavish oak, herb, chocolate, plum and currant flavors that gently unfold on the palate. The tannins are firm but round, making this a delicious wine to enjoy now or cellar through 1995. Has plenty of flavor and finesse. 900 cases made. $18 (5/31/91) **93**
Merlot Washington 1988: Perfumed and elegant, with spicy, cedary overtones to the rich core of currant and vanilla aromas and flavors, turning floral and elegant on the finish. Drink now or in 1993. 969 cases made. $17 (4/15/90) **90**

STEVEN THOMAS LIVINGSTONE
Merlot Columbia Valley 1989: Firm and flavorful, with generous aromas of black cherry and currant that turn toward mineral and spice on the palate. The tannins tend to intrude, suggesting this should be better around 1993 to '95. $11 (8/31/91) **84**

PRESTON WINE CELLARS
Merlot Washington Oak Aged 1988: Strong herb and green bean flavors dominate this light wine. Lacks focus and concentration, plus the flavors stray from the mainstream of Merlot. Drink now or in 1993. $7 (8/31/91) **77**

QUARRY LAKE
Merlot Washington 1986: Velvety and ripe, a supple wine with simple black cherry fruit and cedary overtones. Drink now. $10 (10/15/89) **81**

STE. CHAPELLE
Merlot Washington 1987: An acceptable wine for current drinking that is simple and vegetal tasting. It seems tired and mature already. $10 (9/30/90) **73**
Merlot Washington Dionysus Vineyard 1986 $12 (5/31/88) **81**

SNOQUALMIE
Merlot Columbia Valley Reserve 1987: This unusually concentrated youthful wine is not yet elegant or complex, but it has vivid, focused black cherry and grape flavors in a lush texture, with stiff, young tannins that will need till 1993 or beyond to loosen up. 1,140 cases made. $12 (9/30/90) **91**

STATON HILLS
Merlot Washington 1988: Distinctive for its bright, ripe cherry flavor and picks up a touch of raspberry, but turns tart and oaky on the finish. Drink now to 1995. 3,500 cases made. $15 (3/31/92) **82**
Merlot Washington 1987: Strong herbal, oaky overtones mark this medium-bodied, moderately tannic wine. Good for drinking now through 1994. Tasted twice. 2,500 cases made. $14 (8/31/91) **79**

STONE CREEK
Merlot Columbia Valley 1989: Brightly fruity, with ripe blackberry and currant aromas and flavors shaded by vanilla and toast overtones. A fresh, focused wine that incorporates its tannins smoothly. Good now, but best in 1993. $7 (5/31/91) BB **86**
Merlot Columbia Valley 1988: Despite fresh, tempting flavors, this tastes rough, and the youthful fruit and herbal flavors don't seem to have the depth to match the firm tannins. Drink now if you don't mind the roughness. $6 (9/30/90) **78**

PAUL THOMAS
Merlot Washington 1987: Offering vivid raspberry flavors, pleasant herbal aromas and firm tannins, this lively, fruity wine is very distinctive and flavorful. Drink now. $16 (9/30/90) **89**
Merlot Washington Reserve 1989: Crisp and flavorful, with definite menthol aromas and flavors and a modest berry component. A bit tannic. Better after 1994. 960 cases made. $15 (3/31/92) **79**

WATERBROOK
Merlot Columbia Valley 1989: Bold, rich, complex and concentrated, with layers of smoky oak, ripe plum, currant and cherry flavors that glide across the palate. Intense, with fine tannins, a remarkably complex and well-integrated wine. Drinks well now, but should improve with cellaring through 1996. 600 cases made. $14 (4/30/92) **94**

YAKIMA RIVER
Merlot Columbia Valley 1988: An attractive Merlot, with well-focused cherry, currant, herb and spicy cedar flavors that are elegant and not too tannic. Drinks well now, but can be cellared through 1994. 2,850 cases made. $15 (4/15/92) **83**

RIESLING

ARBOR CREST
Riesling Columbia Valley Dry 1990: Dry and almost austere, with pleasant floral and greenish peach aromas and flavors. Drinkable now. 1,200 cases made. $5.75 (11/15/91) **78**

BARNARD GRIFFIN
Johannisberg Riesling Columbia Valley 1987: Delicious nectarine and peach flavors get richer and truer with every sip in this medium-weight, slightly off-dry wine. $6.50 (10/15/89) BB **88**

BLACKWOOD CANYON
White Riesling Columbia Valley Claar Vineyard Dry 1987: Woody, broad and slightly sour, not a pure expression of Riesling. $9 (10/15/89) **66**

BONAIR
Johannisberg Riesling Yakima Valley 1987: Medium-weight and slightly sweet. The sappy flavors cover the fruit. $5.50 (10/15/89) **74**

CASCADE CREST
Johannisberg Riesling Yakima Valley 1987: There is some appealing fruit flavor in this wine, but it starts off so coarse and unappealing that it never quite recovers. $6 (10/15/89) **75**

CHATEAU STE. MICHELLE
Johannisberg Riesling Columbia Valley 1990: A slightly sweet wine that's well made and straightforward, with simple fruit flavors. $7 (8/31/91) **79**
Johannisberg Riesling Columbia Valley 1988: Light and delicately sweet, with nectarine aromas and flavors that carry through to a smooth, balanced finish that echoes grapefruit and peach. $6.50 (10/15/89) **85**
Johannisberg Riesling Washington 1987: Nicely balanced. Crisp and peachy in flavor, clean and light on the palate. Fine before or during the meal. $6 (4/15/89) **82**
Riesling Columbia Valley Dry River Ridge Vineyard 1990: The label says dry and it is off-dry, but the pear and peach aromas and flavors remain fresh, lively and clean, balanced toward softness. A real charmer. $7 (6/15/91) BB **85**
White Riesling Columbia Valley Sweet Select 1990: Sweet and straightforward, with floral aromas and apple and pear flavors. Light, fruity and sweet but not unctuous. $7 (6/15/92) **80**
White Riesling Columbia Valley Sweet Select 1988: Sweet but balanced with sufficient acidity to bring out the fruit; it tastes sugary. $7 (10/15/89) **78**

COLUMBIA
Johannisberg Riesling Columbia Valley Cellarmaster's Reserve 1990: Sweet, simple and fresh, but it lacks fruit concentration and complexity. $7 (6/15/92) **77**

COLUMBIA CREST
Johannisberg Riesling Columbia Valley 1990: A very straightforward Riesling, with sweet apple and peach flavors, a soft structure and medium body. $6 (8/31/91) BB **81**
Johannisberg Riesling Columbia Valley 1986: Fruit seems subdued in this sweet wine, which is covered by an unfortunate cardboard overtone. $6 (10/15/89) **70**
Riesling Columbia Valley Dry 1990: Light and fresh, with modest apple and apricot flavors and a crisp mouth-feel. Drinkable and simple. $6 (8/31/91) **77**

COVEY RUN
Johannisberg Riesling Washington 1988: Smooth, off-dry, pleasantly peachy and clean. $5.50 (10/15/89) **79**
Johannisberg Riesling Yakima Valley 1989: Hints of grapefruit and peach carry through on the long, elegant finish in this fresh, lively and delicate wine. The lightness and complexity make this an especially appealing package. Slightly off-dry, but drinkable now. $7 (8/31/90) BB **88**
Riesling Yakima Valley Dry 1990: Light and simple, with earthy, grapey flavors that never quite come into focus. Drinkable now. $8 (6/15/92) **74**

FACELLI
Johannisberg Riesling Washington Dry 1988: Aside from a hint of floral character, this medium-bodied dry white wine has little to remind one of Riesling, but it finishes smooth and fresh. $7.50 (10/15/89) **78**

FRENCH CREEK
Riesling Washington Dry 1990: A dry wine that's round in texture. Has pine and peach aromas and flavors and finishes crisp and simple. Drinkable now, but should be better in 1993. 600 cases made. $4 (11/15/91) **80**

HOGUE
Johannisberg Riesling Yakima Valley 1988: Firm and flavorful, with beautifully defined peach aromas and flavors and hints of the typical piny character as well; slightly off-dry, balanced and very appealing. $6 (10/15/89) BB **90**
Johannisberg Riesling Yakima Valley Dry Schwartzman Vineyard 1988: Dry, medium-bodied, fruity and varietally peachlike, with flavors that carry well into a long finish. Better than a bottle tasted earlier. $6.50 (10/15/89) **84**
Riesling Washington Dry Schwartzman Vineyard Reserve 1989: Light and delicate, but loaded with fruit flavor, primarily nectarine and a whisper of grapefruit. A touch of astringency makes the texture seem a bit rough. Drink now or in 1993. $8.50 (6/15/91) **80**

HOODSPORT
Johannisberg Riesling Washington 1988: Clearly defined nectarine flavor carries through this medium-bodied, slightly sweet wine, getting richer with every sip. $6 (10/15/89) BB **87**

KIONA
White Riesling Columbia Valley 1988: Fruit cockail aromas and flavors lack finesse or elegance and come off as a bit metallic or bitter in this off-dry wine. $6 (10/15/89) **74**

LATAH CREEK
Johannisberg Riesling Washington 1990: A crisp, barely off-dry wine, with modest resin and peach aromas and flavors that are clean and refreshing. Could be prettier. Drinkable now. Tasted twice. $7 (1/31/92) **79**
Johannisberg Riesling Washington 1987: Herbal and floral aromas turn crisp and peachy on the palate, finishing with a dry sensation. A refreshing wine that should be great with food. $5.50 (4/15/89) BB **82**

STEVEN THOMAS LIVINGSTONE
Johannisberg Riesling Columbia Valley 1990: An off-dry Riesling, with up-front peach and papaya flavors, good acidity and a bit of effervescence. Fresh, clean and charming. 700 cases made. $6 (8/31/91) **85**
Riesling Columbia Valley Dry 1990: Charming and fruity, made in a light style, but has the floral aromas and fresh peach and grapefruit flavors that we love in Riesling. Off-dry and ready to drink now. 120 cases made. $7 (8/31/91) **87**

NEUHARTH
Johannisberg Riesling Washington 1987: Earthy, herbal, slightly vegetal aromas and flavors are not typical of Riesling. $8.75 (10/15/89) **65**

PRESTON WINE CELLARS
Johannisberg Riesling Washington Preston Vineyard 1989: Lean and aromatic, with a strong thread of kerosene running through the modest apple and spice aromas and flavors. $6 (6/15/92) **78**
Johannisberg Riesling Washington Preston Vineyard Hand Harvested 1987: Frankly sweet and soft, bordering on flat, with little flavor distinction as a result. $5.75 (10/15/89) **71**

SALISHAN
White Riesling Washington Dry 1988: Has fresh peach aromas and flavors, but could use more delicacy and finesse. A big, firm dry Riesling. Good value. $5 (10/15/89) **79**

SEVEN HILLS
White Riesling Columbia Valley 1990: Soft and generous, with spicy apple and peach aromas and flavors that linger on the finish. Reminds us of Alsace flavors on a slightly sweet structure. Drinkable now. 800 cases made. $6 (6/15/92) BB **84**

SILVER LAKE
Riesling Columbia Valley Dry 1989: Says dry, but tastes off-dry, with nicely concentrated nectarine and grapefruit flavors and a pleasant hint of slate and mineral notes. A terrific summer sipper. 1,100 cases made. $6 (6/15/91) BB **87**

SNOQUALMIE
Johannisberg Riesling Columbia Valley 1988: Fresh and fruity, with delicate peach aromas and flavors and a tinge of bitterness to remind you that it is dry. $6 (10/15/89) **80**
Johannisberg Riesling Columbia Valley (Residual Sugar 1.8 Percent) 1988: A lean style with resiny grace notes to the crisp peach fruit; off-dry but balanced with zingy acidity. $6 (10/15/89) **81**

STATON HILLS
Johannisberg Riesling Washington 1990: Light and dry, with pleasant apricot and berry aromas and flavors that persist on the finish. Tastes ripe and elegant. Drinkable now. 2,100 cases made. $6 (11/15/91) BB **86**

STEWART
Johannisberg Riesling Columbia Valley 1988: Has the honey overtones of botrytis, but also a tinny, sour edge to the flavor that keeps it from being more appealing. $6.50 (10/15/89) **72**
Johannisberg Riesling Columbia Valley 1987: Very aromatic, floral and fresh, with slightly honeyed, soft and earthy flavors. The flavors stay with you; it's a satisfying wine for Sunday sipping. $6 (4/15/89) **80**
White Riesling Columbia Valley 1988: Oddly herbal aromas and flavors detract from the honeyed richess of this wine, leaving it unbalanced. $15/375ml (10/15/89) **68**

PAUL THOMAS
Johannisberg Riesling Washington 1988: Fresh and lively, fairly broad for a Riesling, with crisp balance and dead-on peach flavor. The flavors linger without a sense of weight. $7 (10/15/89) **85**
Riesling Washington Dry 1988: Light and slightly sweet, with a subtle fruit complexity that centers around nectarine but hints at more exotic fruits as well. Smooth and well made. $7 (10/15/89) **85**
Riesling Washington Dry 1987: Kerosene aromas and flavors are distinctly varietal, but they would be more appealing against more generous fruit flavors. It comes off as earthy. $7 (7/31/89) **77**

WHITE HERON
Johannisberg Riesling Washington 1987: Exotic almond and spice aromas and flavors are missing the fruit to round them out, and the modest acidity leaves the finish tasting flat. $5 (7/31/89) **68**

WORDEN
Johannisberg Riesling Washington Charbonneau Vineyards 1988: Frankly sweet, but beautifully balanced with a firm underpinning of acidity and a fruit expression that starts with crisp, fresh peach and then adds grace notes of nutmeg, vanilla and orange flowers. $6 (10/15/89) **85**

SAUVIGNON BLANC

ARBOR CREST
Sauvignon Blanc Columbia Valley 1989: Onion skin aromas and flavors add depth and interest to this rich-textured, vanilla-scented wine, all surrounding a core of fig flavor. Drinkable now. $7.50 (8/31/91) **85**
Sauvignon Blanc Columbia Valley Wahluke Slope 1987: Has a firm structure and silky texture; varietally true, showing pear, vanilla and herbal flavors. The finish is so rich it almost seems a bit sticky. $7.50 (10/15/89) **85**

BARNARD GRIFFIN
Fumé Blanc Washington Barrel Fermented 1987: Herbal, toasty, slightly coarse and hot, but it is flavorful and true to type. $9 (10/15/89) **75**

CHATEAU STE. MICHELLE
Fumé Blanc Columbia Valley 1989: Crisp and flavorful, a lean-textured wine with sour lemon candy and herbal aromas and flavors. Interesting, but not a mainstream kind of Fumé. $9 (8/31/91) **80**
Sauvignon Blanc Columbia Valley 1990: A real zinger, combining great value and outstanding quality. Crisp and lively, with a creamy richness that lifts it out of the ordinary. Citrus, floral and pear aromas and flavors slip in and out of the spotlight, and it remains refreshing through the long finish. Drinkable now. $8.50 (4/30/92) SS **91**
Sauvignon Blanc Columbia Valley 1988: Very unusual for its smoky bacon flavors, probably stemming from aging in new oak barrels. Has only modest fruit to back it up. For fans of assertive styles. $7 (12/31/90) **78**

CHINOOK
Sauvignon Blanc Washington 1987: The distinctive aromas and texture of sweet oak permeate this wine, making it round and rich in the style of a top white Bordeaux. The structure and concentration of pear flavor are impeccable if light, and a touch of honey on the finish is especially ingratiating. $8.25 (10/15/89) **89**

COLUMBIA CREST
Sauvignon Blanc Columbia Valley 1986: Has very herbal aromas, but the flavors emphasize melon. Has a firm texture and good length, echoing toasty vanilla flavors on the finish. $7 (10/15/89) **82**

COVEY RUN
Fumé Blanc Washington 1988: Earthy, with crisp, grapefruit flavors carrying through to the finish. Not for every palate, but it's a legitimate style. $8 (10/15/89) **80**

HOGUE
Fumé Blanc Washington 1988: Soft, subtle and flavorful, with lively peach and melon fruit, herbal overtones and a hint of orange on the finish; it's long and delicate. $8 (10/15/89) **88**

PRESTON
Fumé Blanc Washington Oak Aged 1989: Has unusual flavors for Sauvignon Blanc, offering honey,

almond and walnut. Interesting and full-bodied, but difficult to like as a Sauvignon Blanc. Where's the fruit? $7 (7/15/91) **78**

QUARRY LAKE
Sauvignon Blanc Washington 1987: Earthy, soft and unfocused, not for everyone. $7.50 (10/15/89) **68**

SADDLE MOUNTAIN
Fumé Blanc Columbia Valley 1988: Crisp and delicately herbal, with a bright beam of peach flavor carrying through from the nose to the finish; an appealing style to drink now. $5 (10/15/89) BB **86**

SNOQUALMIE
Fumé Blanc Columbia Valley 1987: A clean, herbal wine that's light on the palate, but the focused pear and vanilla flavors carry through to a long finish. Very well made. $7 (10/15/89) BB **88**

STATON HILLS
Sauvignon Blanc Washington 1987: Flavors lean toward wood and the structure seems flat and hot on the finish. Not much distinction. $8 (10/15/89) **71**

STEWART
Sauvignon Blanc Yakima Valley 1988: Clean herbal and citrus aromas and flavors get a bumpy ride from a softer structure than they need. The finish is metallic. $8 (10/15/89) **78**

TAGARIS
Fumé Blanc Washington 1988: Extremely herbal, bordering on vegetal, with aromas and flavors of celery and bay leaf overpowering whatever fruit might be there. $8 (10/15/89) **76**

PAUL THOMAS
Sauvignon Blanc Washington 1987: Clean and fresh, with pleasant orange overtones to the aroma and herbal flavors developing nicely on the finish. Well balanced. $9 (10/15/89) **85**

WATERBROOK
Sauvignon Blanc Washington 1987: Aromas and flavors lean strongly toward wood, but there is enough pear flavor peeking through to keep it in balance. $9 (10/15/89) **85**

WORDEN
Fumé Blanc Washington 1987: Soft and smooth, but it's dominated by an orange flower scent and finishing with a touch of bitterness. $7 (10/15/89) **73**

SÉMILLON

BLACKWOOD CANYON
Sémillon Yakima Valley Barrel Fermented 1987: Buttery, honeylike aromas and flavors make this rich, full-bodied wine feel broad and muscular. A touch of tobacco reminds us it is Sémillon. $9 (10/15/89) **83**

CASCADE CREST
Sémillon Yakima Valley Blanc 1987: Clean citrus aromas reminiscent of grapefruit mesh with the fig and pear flavor on the palate to make this an appealing, harmoniously balanced wine. Drink it now. $5.50 (10/15/89) BB **87**

CHATEAU STE. MICHELLE
Sémillon Columbia Valley 1990: Elegant and fruity, with pretty fig, melon, spice and tobacco notes. A balanced, flavorful Washington wine to drink now. $7 (4/15/92) BB **84**

COLUMBIA
Sémillon Columbia Valley 1988: Light, lean and flavorful, with lemon and grapefruit aromas and flavors plus an edge of herbal flavor emerging on the finish. $6 (10/15/89) BB **84**
Sémillon Columbia Valley Sur Lie Chevrier 1990: Like a cross between Bordeaux and Muscadet, this has the fig and tobacco flavors of Sémillon and the crisp texture and leesy overtones of a Muscadet. Attractive, if offbeat. Drinkable now. $12 (1/31/92) **84**

COLUMBIA CREST
Sémillon Columbia Valley 1990: Very light on its feet. Crisp, fruity and fresh, with lots of bright pear and apple flavors, zingy acidity and a clean finish. Light- to medium-bodied and ready to drink now. $6 (7/15/91) BB **86**
Sémillon Columbia Valley 1986: Earthy, cedary aromas and tobacco-tinged fig flavors make this a bold, assertive wine that is soft enough in texture to hint at a bit of honeyed sweetness on the finish. $5.75 (10/15/89) **78**

FACELLI
Sémillon Washington 1988: Has fresh, floral aromas and flavors, and it's lean, clean and zesty. Firm textured, but not particularly complex. $8 (10/15/89) **82**

HOGUE
Sémillon Washington 1990: Crisp and straightforward, showing ripe apricot and apple flavors, good acidity and a short, clean finish. Tastes fresh and lively. $7 (6/15/92) **83**
Sémillon Washington 1989: Smooth and ripe, with definite fig and lemon aromas and flavors, finishing with a lively zing of acidity to keep it in balance and hints of butterscotch. A tasty wine that's drinkable now. $6.50 (11/30/91) BB **84**
Sémillon Washington Reserve 1986: A sour, vegetal edge to the flavor takes this one down a peg. Not much fruit to balance it, but the finish hints at honey and butter. $8 (10/15/89) **72**

LATAH CREEK
Sémillon Washington 1986: Strongly herbal aromas and flavors get even stronger on the finish of this lean but flavorful wine. $6 (10/15/89) **79**

L'ECOLE NO. 41
Sémillon Washington 1989: Earthy, candied aromas and flavors lack depth and substance. A simple wine with oddball flavors. Drinkable now. 600 cases made. $10 (1/31/92) **72**

PORTTEUS
Sémillon Yakima Valley 1987: With its brassy color and nutlike aromas and flavors, this seems old and tired before its time. $7 (10/15/89) **67**

SNOQUALMIE
Sémillon Columbia Valley 1988: Has sweet, floral aromas and flavors with a slightly soapy edge that gets in the way. $6 (10/15/89) **74**

SPARKLING

DOMAINE STE. MICHELLE
Blanc de Blancs Columbia Valley 1986: A dry sparkling wine, with plenty of flavor complexity and a lingering finish that echoes the almond, butter and spice flavors. Balanced on the lean, crisp side. $14 (1/31/92) **86**
Blanc de Noirs Columbia Valley 1986: A smooth, fruity, easy-to-drink sparkling wine, with pear and apple flavors and a soft finish. Straightforward and enjoyable. $17 (1/31/92) **80**
Blanc de Noirs Columbia Valley 1985: Fresh cherry in the aroma and flavor is presumably from Pinot Noir grapes; it's smooth, complete and well-balanced. Lively and youthful. $20 (12/31/90) **86**
Brut Columbia Valley NV: Dry, smooth and fruity if not elegant, the simple fruit flavors are smoothed by a creamy, soft texture and very fine bubbles. $10 (12/31/90) **78**
Brut Columbia Valley NV: A lively, dry, crisp wine, with delicate apple and spice flavors and a dry finish. Refreshing acidity should make it versatile as an aperitif or a dinner companion. $9 (1/31/92) BB **84**

HOGUE
Brut Yakima Valley NV: Spicy, gingerlike aromas and flavors enliven this generally soft, broad-textured sparkler that's on the dry side but not steely. Lots of toasty character makes it a good drink. $12 (10/15/89) **82**

STATON HILLS
Blanc de Noir Washington NV: Toasted berry aromas and flavors run through this soft, almost velvety wine that's pink in color, simple, pleasant and a bit sweet. $16 (10/15/89) **77**
Brut Rosé Washington NV: An eminently drinkable, off-dry rosé, with mild cherry and berry flavors, good balance and hints of earthiness and maturity that give it character. 2,000 cases made. $16 (4/30/92) **84**

OTHER WASHINGTON RED

CAVATAPPI
Nebbiolo Maddalena Red Willow Vineyards Washington 1988: Spicy aromas and flavors make this medium-weight, barrel-aged wine immediately appealing. Has a style of its own, offering modest berry flavors and cinnamon, nutmeg and vanilla notes. Drinkable now. $19 (6/15/91) **83**

CHATEAU STE. MICHELLE
Pinot Noir Columbia Valley Limited Bottling 1987: Doesn't have a lot of flesh on its bones, but it's nicely balanced. A light Pinot, with cherry and spice flavors in a lean, tight package. $11 (8/31/91) **79**

COLUMBIA
Pinot Noir Washington The Woodburne Collection 1987: Complex and stylish, with an elegant, supple texture and pretty black cherry, cola, spice, toasty oak and currant flavors that are woven together in fine fashion. Ready now, but should improve as the fine tannins mellow. Best to start drinking now to 1995. 900 cases made. $10 (3/31/91) **88**
Pinot Noir Washington Woodburne Cuvée 1990: A light, lean Pinot, with mostly spicy, woody flavors and not much fruit. Decent but uninspired. Drink now. 900 cases made. $12 (3/31/92) **77**
Pinot Noir Washington Woodburne Cuvée 1989: Crisp and lively, with generous red cherry and strawberry aromas and flavors, hinting at plum and spice on the supple finish. Drinkable now, but might improve through 1994. Better than a bottle tasted earlier. $12 (6/15/92) **84**
Syrah Yakima Valley Red Willow Vineyard 1988: Rich, concentrated and elegant, offering lots of vanilla-tinged plum and blackberry aromas and flavors. Has firm, but not excessive tannins that are long and very fine, and echoes fruit and spice notes on the finish. Approaching drinkability, but probably better after 1993. 320 cases made. $25 (5/15/91) **90**

KIONA
Lemberger Columbia Valley 1989: A simple, berry-flavored wine that would likely benefit when paired with food. $9 (5/15/92) **76**

LATAH CREEK
Red Table Wine Lemberger Washington 1990: Brilliantly fruity and fresh-tasting, with flavors reminiscent of a young Grenache, leaning toward blackberries and boysenberries. There's just enough tannin to give it a slight burr, but it's drinkable now with food. 100 percent Lemberger. $8.50 (1/31/92) **85**

PATRICK M. PAUL
Cabernet Franc Walla Walla Valley 1988: Plum, cherry and berry flavors have matured into a rounded, complex wine. Ripe with well-integrated tannins. Drink now or hold until 1993. $12 (2/29/92) **84**

YAKIMA RIVER
Lemberger Rendezvous Yakima Valley 1989: Straightforward and flavorful, with simple plum and cherry flavors accented by a hint of herbs. Fine for drinking now. 100 percent Lemberger. 2,560 cases made. $7.50 (3/31/92) **81**

OTHER WASHINGTON WHITE

BAINBRIDGE ISLAND
Müller-Thurgau Washington 1987: Here is an everyday sipping wine with distinction—piny aromas and flavors surround a slender core of nectarine flavor, and it's clean with a flavorful finish. $6 (10/15/89) **84**
Müller-Thurgau Washington Dry 1987: Has distinctive snappy, piny aromas on a light frame; it's soft, and smells better than it tastes. $6 (10/15/89) **77**

BOOKWALTER
Chenin Blanc Washington Joseph Roberts Vineyards 1988: Sweet, but balanced with refreshing acidity, showing pleasant grapey aromas and flavors. $6 (10/15/89) **78**

CASCADE MOUNTAIN
Chenin Blanc Washington Vouvray 1987: Fruity and sweet, with a slightly stemmy edge to the apple flavor. $5.25 (10/15/89) **75**

CHATEAU STE. MICHELLE
Chenin Blanc Columbia Valley 1990: Crisp and fruity, with pleasant nectarine and apple aromas and flavors. Just a little sweet on the finish, but stays in balance. Drinkable now. $6 (11/15/91) **83**
Chenin Blanc Columbia Valley 1988 $6 (7/31/89) **88**
Chenin Blanc Washington 1987: Lean and snappy, with a resiny edge to the melon flavors that persist through the finish. $6 (10/15/89) **80**
Chenin Blanc Washington 1986 $4 (7/31/89) **84**
Muscat Canelli Columbia Valley 1990: Crisp in texture, lightly sweet and pointedly fruity, with appealing peach, grapefruit and slight pine aromas and flavors. Drinkable now. 2,000 cases made. $6.50 (11/30/91) BB **83**

COLUMBIA CREST
Chenin Blanc Columbia Valley 1986: Crisp, lean and not very fruity. $5.25 (10/15/89) **77**
Sémillon-Chardonnay Columbia Valley 1989: An oaky, earthy flavor outweighs the lean fruit component in this dry, austere, medium-bodied wine. Tasted twice. $7 (7/15/91) **73**

Key to Symbols

The scores reported here are the results of blind tastings conducted by our panel of senior editors. Wines that carry the initials below are results of individual tastings.

THE WINE SPECTATOR 100-POINT SCALE ***95-100***—Classic, a great wine; ***90-94***—Outstanding, superior character and style; ***80-89***—Good to very good, a wine with special qualities; ***70-79***—Average, drinkable wine that may have minor flaws; ***60-69***—Below average, drinkable but not recommended; ***50-59***—Poor, undrinkable, not recommended. "+"—With a score indicates a range; used primarily with barrel tastings to indicate a preliminary score.

SPECIAL DESIGNATIONS SS—Spectator Selection, CS—Cellar Selection, BB—Best Buy, ($NA)—Price not available, (NR)—Not released.

TASTER'S INITIALS (JG)—Jim Gordon, (HS)—Harvey Steiman, (JL)—James Laube, (JS)—James Suckling, (TM)—Thomas Matthews, (TR)—Terry Robards, (PM)—Per-Henrik Mansson, (BT)—Barrel Tasting (these wines were tasted blind from barrel samples), (CA-date)—*California's Great Cabernets* by James Laube, (CH-date)—*California's Great Chardonnays* by James Laube, (VP-date)—*Vintage Port* by James Suckling.

DATE TASTED Dates in parentheses represent the issue in which the rating was published.

HOGUE
Chenin Blanc Washington 1988: Sweet, with toasted flavors obscuring the freshness of the fruit. $6 (10/15/89) **74**

KIONA
Chenin Blanc Yakima Valley Estate Bottled 1988: Fruity, simple and pleasant. $5.75 (10/15/89) **76**

LAKESIDE
Chenin Blanc Washington NV $6 (7/31/89) **68**

LATAH CREEK
Muscat Canelli Washington 1987: Unusually delicate, fragrant and fruity, emphasizing the sweet peach and litchi flavors over the spice. Well balanced and snappy on the finish. $6 (10/15/89) **81**

MOUNT BAKER
Müller-Thurgau Washington 1988: Bitter, almost coffeelike flavors detract from this otherwise simple, fruity wine. $6 (10/15/89) **63**

PONTIN DEL ROZA
Roza Sunset Yakima Valley 1988: Exotic guava and berry aromas and flavors give this lightly sweet, delicate wine some distinction. $6 (10/15/89) **80**

QUARRY LAKE
Chenin Blanc Washington 1987: Sweet, pleasant and fruity, with touch of honey on the aftertaste that persists nicely. $5.50 (10/15/89) **83**

SADDLE MOUNTAIN
Chenin Blanc Columbia Valley 1988: Fruity and fairly concentrated, a bit sweet and sticky on the finish. $5 (10/15/89) **76**

SALISHAN
Chenin Blanc Washington Dry 1988: Oxidized, slightly bitter flavors keep this from being as clean and pleasant as it could be. $6.25 (10/15/89) **71**

SNOQUALMIE
Chenin Blanc Columbia Valley 1988: Off-dry, snappy and crisp, with appealing tension between the acidity and fruit. The flavors could be more concentrated, but this is a nicely balanced sipping wine. $6 (10/15/89) **80**

STATON HILLS
Muscat Canelli Washington 1990: Fruity and frankly sweet, featuring spicy pear flavors, balanced by a touch of bitterness on the finish. Soft and simple. Drinkable now. 500 cases made. $8 (11/15/91) **78**

PAUL THOMAS
Chenin Blanc Washington 1988: A significant amount of spritz keeps this tasting fresh and lively, yet the wine remains delicately sweet and appealing, with disarming fruit flavors. $7 (10/15/89) **84**

WORDEN
Chenin Blanc Washington 1988: Bracing acidity balances the sweetness, and a touch of spritz lends extra texture to the rather delicate apple flavor. $6 (10/15/89) **81**

OTHER UNITED STATES/*AMERICAN*

BEL ARBORS
Cabernet Sauvignon American Cask 88 NV: A simple, sturdy red, with pleasant cherry and toast aromas and flavors. Drinkable now. $6 (11/15/91) **78**
Cabernet Sauvignon American Founder's Selection NV: Light and crisply balanced, offering appealing berry and currant aromas and flavors and a touch of toast for complexity. A harmonious wine. Drink now. $5 (10/15/89) BB **82**
Chardonnay American Cask 90 NV: Fresh, clean and fruity, with ripe melon, pear and apple flavors that are crisp and refreshing. Balanced, ready to drink and easy on the pocketbook. $6 (8/31/91) **79**
Chardonnay American Founder's Selection NV: Soft and generous, with peach and pear aromas and flavors that remain lush and appealing through the finish. Drink now. $5 (10/31/89) BB **81**
Merlot American Cask 89 NV: Alive and fruity, with supple plum and black cherry flavors. Tasty, fresh and fruity. A terrific value. Drink now. $6 (11/15/91) BB **81**
Merlot American Founder's Selection American Grown NV: A tannic wine without the fruit flavor to balance it out. Tastes broad and lush but very oaky. Has minty, woody aromas, soft plum and berry flavors and heavy tannins that gang up on the finish. $5 (6/15/90) **72**
Sauvignon Blanc American Founder's Selection NV: Fruity, soft and pleasantly varietal, a simple, refreshing wine with enough character to keep you coming back for another sip. Drink now. $5 (10/15/89) BB **81**

COOK'S
Brut American Champagne NV: Sweet and floral, with candy-watermelon aromas and flavors. Simple and coarse but pleasant. $4 (3/31/92) **74**
Extra Dry American NV: Earthy, sweet and simple. Pear flavors sneak through on the finish and the texture turns creamy. $4 (3/31/92) **76**
Extremely Dry Grand Reserve American NV: Earthy-spicy flavors obscure any fruit or liveliness in this dull, drab bubbly. $4 (3/31/92) **70**

GOLD SEAL
American Charles Fournier Special Selection NV: Refreshing, clean and dry, but the flavors are very simple, almost watery. Has a slightly floral aroma, good effervescence and a lemony finish. $10 (6/30/90) **77**
Blanc de Blancs American Charles Fournier Special Selection NV: Refreshing, clean and dry, but the flavors are very simple, almost watery. Has a slightly floral aroma, good effervescence and a lemony finish. $10 (6/30/90) **77**

GRAYSON
White Zinfandel American NV $4 (6/15/89) **82**

GREAT WESTERN
Blanc de Noirs American NV: Good but simple, with a soft texture and decent fruit flavors. Off-dry in style. $14 (3/31/90) **70**

JADE MOUNTAIN
Grenache American Grenache NV: A nice, medium-weight wine, with generous fruit flavors and a sense of liveliness. Hints at plum, rhubarb and cherry, finishing crisp and fruity. Drink soon. 600 cases made. $8.50 (3/31/92) **82**

ARIZONA

SONOITA
Cabernet Sauvignon Soñoita Private Reserve 1987: An earthy wine, with definite smoky cherry aromas and flavors that turn spicy and earthy on the finish. The crisp texture means it could develop nicely through 1993 or '94. Tasted three times. $15 (2/29/92) **79**
Cabernet Sauvignon Soñoita Private Reserve 1985: Soft and somewhat tannic, with vague flavors reminiscent of tobacco, prune and beet. Has a cooked flavor. $22 (2/29/92) **71**
Pinot Noir Soñoita 1989: A medium-weight wine, with bitter, earthy flavors perked up a little by a streak of spiciness. Try after 1993. Tasted twice. $30 (2/29/92) **75**

ARKANSAS

WIEDERKEHR
Altus Spumante Arkansas NV: Sweet bubble gum aromas and flavors turn surprisingly delicate and charming, seeming more like pear and tropical fruit. Similar to an Italian Asti Spumante. Finishes clean, fruity and sweet. $6.50 (2/29/92) **80**
Cabernet Sauvignon Arkansas Mountain 1978: Ripe but cooked aromas and flavors characterize this soft-textured wine, hinting at green bean on the finish. Still, impressively fruity for its age. $35 (2/29/92) **70**
Muscat di Tanta Maria Altus Arkansas 1990: Sweet, with flavors that remind us of bubble gum and orange or nectarine. The texture is odd, gritty rather than smooth. $9 (2/29/92) **71**

COLORADO

COLORADO CELLARS
Alpenglo Riesling Turley Vineyards Colorado 1990: A rosé-colored wine that's frankly sweet, with orange-peel and strawberry aromas and flavors. Finishes sweet, but it's clean and fresh. $8.50 (2/29/92) **77**
Cherry Wine Colorado 1990: Very tart, with flavors exactly like tart pie cherries. Tastes like it needs a scoop of ice cream to soften it. Best served chilled. $5 (2/29/92) **73**
Grand Gamé Rocky Mountain 1988: Attractive cassis and floral aromas lead to soft, full fruit flavors. There's not much tannin, but it gets austere and spicy on the finish. Drinkable now. $8.50 (2/29/92) **79**

CONNECTICUT

CROSSWOODS
Chardonnay Southeastern New England 1986: Pungently mature, with all the butter and oak aromas and flavors you could want, broad and rangy, generous but not finely balanced. $15 (10/31/89) **77**
Scrimshaw White Connecticut NV: Peach and pine aromas turn crisp and tart on the palate, where the main flavor is grapefruit. Steely and slightly one-dimensional, but refreshing. $5 (2/29/92) **75**

FLORIDA

LAFAYETTE
Blanc de Fleur Florida NV: Floral, perfumed aromas and flavors pervade this sweet, peach-flavored wine. Has a coarse texture and simple flavors. $11 (2/29/92) **73**
Stover Special Reserve Florida 1988: Big and solid, with vegetal flavors tinged with honey. Neither sweet nor tart, with an anise finish. Distinctive and still fresh, but not complex. We've never tasted the Stover grape before. $9 (2/29/92) **74**
Sunblush Florida NV: Distinctive foxy, gamy overtones give this rosé its personality. Could be sweeter or fruitier. $7 (2/29/92) **75**

LAKERIDGE
Crescendo Florida NV: Definitely sweet, more of a dessert style than an aperitif, with simple floral and pear aromas and flavors. A generous wine that starts clean and finishes on the sweet side. Made from Magnolia, a variety of Muscadine. $12 (2/29/92) **79**
Cuvée Blanc Florida NV: Soft, round and slightly sweet, with honey and earth flavors. Made from Suwanee and Stover. $9 (2/29/92) **73**
Southern White Wine Florida NV: Round, full-bodied and sweet, with the unmistakable spiciness of Muscadine. Balanced, off-dry and lacks subtlety, but has a frank appeal. Made from Carlos, a variety of Muscadine. $7 (2/29/92) **77**

GEORGIA

CHATEAU ELAN
Chardonnay Georgia Founder's Reserve 1987: Light in body, with a smooth texture and modest flavors that lean toward apple and honey, with definite earthy overtones. Drink soon. $9 (2/29/92) **74**
Essence de Cabernet Founder's Reserve Georgia 1988: An earthy wine that cleans up and becomes crisp and spicy on the finish. Buttery and smooth on the palate, with modest tannins that make it drinkable now. $11 (2/29/92) **76**
Summer Wine Georgia 1990: Aromas and flavors of peaches and bubble gum, a silky texture, considerable sweetness and a candied, slightly gamy finish make this a well-made wine that is true to what it is: Muscadine blended with peach juice. Only 7 percent alcohol. $6 (2/29/92) **78**

CHESTNUT MOUNTAIN
Cabernet Sauvignon Georgia Mossy Creek Vineyard 1989: Bursting with cherry and eucalyptus aromas, the palate is lush with plum, chocolate and mint flavors. Intense, but not too tannic. Attractive for early drinking. $16 (2/29/92) **83**
Chardonnay Georgia Mossy Creek Vineyard 1989: A hard, acidic texture and apple cider aromas and flavors are not charming, but the spiciness on the nose has some appeal. Seems a bit oxidized, too. $16 (2/29/92) **70**
Merlot Georgia 1990: Lean and lively, with well-articulated berry and cherry flavors shaded by minty herbal notes. Crisp acidity and fine tannins make this appealing now. Should be fine through 1994. $14 (2/29/92) **83**

HAWAII

TEDESCHI VINEYARDS
Blanc Pineapple Wine Maui NV: Made from pineapples—the pineapple aromas and flavors are clean and well defined. Refreshing, if a little odd, with a touch of sweetness. Distinctive and pleasing. $6.75 (2/29/92) **80**
Brut Blanc de Noirs Maui 1984: Spicy, creamy aromas and flavors are pleasant in this off-dry sparkler. Has enough acidity to keep it clean and balanced on the finish. $19 (2/29/92) **79**
Nouveau Maui 1991: A Nouveau style, with candied overtones to the lively berry and plum flavors, but it has a level of tannin that will need until 1993 or '94 to settle down. Could drink now with rich food. $15 (2/29/92) **78**
Rosé Hawaii Ranch Cuvée 1984: Simple and fruity, with definite strawberry and watermelon aromas and flavors. Crisp acidity balances the sugar to make it not too sweet. The color is a brazen pink, and the wine has charm. $20 (2/29/92) **79**

IDAHO

PINTLER
Cabernet Sauvignon Idaho 1988: Sweet cassis and strawberry flavors are kept lively and fresh by crisp acidity, giving the wine a pleasant, delicate sweet-and-sour character. Drinkable now. $16 (2/29/92) **81**
Chardonnay Idaho Vickers Vineyard Barrel Fermented 1990: Crisp and flavorful, with definite butterscotch and caramel overtones to the basic green apple and lime flavors. Finishes with plenty of fruit and lively acidity, suggesting it will improve through 1993. $11 (2/29/92) **84**
White Riesling Idaho Dry 1989: A spicy, silky wine, with well-defined peach, apple, cookie dough and mineral aromas and flavors and hints of honey on the finish. Finishes dry and refreshing. Drink soon. $6.25 (2/29/92) **82**

ROSE CREEK
Chardonnay Idaho 1990: A simple, straightforward white wine, with a slightly medicinal edge. $13 (2/29/92) **72**

Johannisberg Riesling Idaho 1990: Light and fruity, with generous peach and melon aromas and flavors. Slightly floral on the finish. Off-dry, bordering on sweet, with good underlying acidity. $6 (2/29/92) BB **83**

STE. CHAPELLE

Cabernet Sauvignon Idaho Reserve 1988: Crisp and simple, with definite green bean, beet and mint aromas and flavors overshadowing the modest Cabernet flavor. Approaching drinkability. Tasted three times. $20 (2/29/92) **74**

Chardonnay Idaho 1988: Has ripe, rich flavors but such a stiff backbone of acidity that it seems to stand out rather than fold itself into a harmonious package. Maybe by now the honeyed pear and butter flavors smooth out. Try now. $10 (12/15/90) **83**

Chardonnay Idaho Reserve 1988: Crisp and spicy, this lean-textured wine has lemon and nutmeg flavors and finishes creamy and buttery, but still zingy from lively acidity. Drinkable now. $15 (2/29/92) **84**

Fumé Blanc Idaho Dry 1989: Light and floral, like a Riesling, this is slightly citrusy in flavor, smooth and easy to drink. 2,300 cases made. $8 (8/31/91) **81**

Pinot Noir Idaho 1988: An intriguing Pinot Noir that offers attractive berry and beet flavors, but also turns leathery and a touch metallic on the finish. $8 (2/29/92) **74**

Johannisberg Riesling Idaho 1990: Light and refreshing, with appealing grapefruit, peach and lemon aromas and flavors, balanced with a hint of tartness on the finish. Drinkable now. $6 (11/15/91) BB **84**

Johannisberg Riesling Idaho 1989: Very light in color, this slightly spritzy, delicate and fruity wine has litchi, apricot and lemon aromas and flavors that persist on the long finish. A bit sweet and simple at the very end, but a good wine to drink cold. $6 (12/15/90) BB **81**

Johannisberg Riesling Idaho 1988: Fresh peach and loquat aromas and flavors permeate this smooth, silky, artfully balanced wine. Each sip reveals another nuance, and the finish is generous and lightly sweet. What a value! $6 (7/31/89) BB **88**

Johannisberg Riesling Idaho Dry Vineyard Select 1990: Fruity, aromatic and clean, with plenty of apricot and citrus aromas and flavors. Off-dry, balanced and refreshing. There's a lot to like here. $6 (2/29/92) BB **85**

Johannisberg Riesling Idaho Dry Vineyard Select 1989: A well made, refreshing, off-dry (despite the label calling it "dry") Riesling for current drinking. Light and fruity, with attractive peach and grapefruit aromas and flavors that are long and spicy. $6 (8/31/91) BB **84**

INDIANA

OLIVER

Gewürztraminer Indiana 1989: Earthy aromas and flavors obscure any fruit that might be present. Has little varietal character to speak of. $8.75 (2/29/92) **73**

Merlot Indiana 1988: Light and pleasant, with plummy, herbal aromas and flavors, a smooth texture and modest tannins. Hints of anise and earth emerge on the finish. A well-made wine that's drinkable now. $15 (2/29/92) **82**

Sauvignon Blanc Indiana 1990: A vivid streak of lemon lifts this wine, and herb and ginger notes give it complexity. Balanced and fresh. $10 (2/29/92) **84**

KANSAS

FIELDS OF FAIR

Concord Kansas 1991: Offers very sweet strawberry and grape-juice flavors on a light, simple frame. Drink well chilled. Made from Concord grapes. $5 (2/29/92) **70**

Flint Hills Red Proprietor's Reserve Kansas 1990: The gamy, jammy fruit flavors lack depth and structure. Quite sweet; not in the mainstream. Made from Maréchal Foch grapes. $6.50 (2/29/92) **70**

Vintage One Proprietor's Reserve Kansas 1991: Honey, pear and vanilla flavors stand out in this rather coarse, sweet wine. The finish is not quite clean. Made from Vignole grapes. $7 (2/29/92) **70**

MARYLAND

BOORDY

Cabernet Sauvignon Maryland 1989: Very soft, almost sweet, with candied cherry and brown sugar flavors. Doesn't have much structure, so drink soon. $11 (2/29/92) **73**

Seyval Blanc Maryland Sur Lie Reserve 1989: Big-boned and rather flabby, with honey and spice flavors, but not much fruit. Quaffable, but short on definition and character. $6.75 (2/29/92) **73**

Vidal Blanc Maryland Semi-Dry 1990: Perfumed peach aromas give way to a slightly sweet, slightly spritzy wine that's charming and easy to drink. Not complex, but refreshing. $6 (2/29/92) BB **81**

CATOCTIN

Cabernet Sauvignon Maryland 1985: Tart and herbal, with modest blackberry flavor threading through the hard-edged tannins. A solid wine that needs until 1994 or '95 to soften as it unwinds. $8 (2/29/92) BB **82**

Chardonnay Maryland 1989: Fruity, lively aromas and flavors are balanced and rich enough to show modest depth. The flavors run toward pear, pineapple and nutmeg, with a definite vanilla sweetness on the finish. An attractive wine to drink soon. $8 (2/29/92) BB **82**

Chardonnay Maryland Oak Fermented 1988: Ripe and almost sweet, with honeyed pineapple flavors and a structure that seems a little soft, making the wine seem simple. Honey flavors are pleasant on the finish. $9 (2/29/92) **78**

MICHIGAN

CHATEAU GRAND TRAVERSE

Chardonnay Old Mission Penisula Reserve 1989: Medicinal menthol notes tend to obscure the modest peach and apple flavors, and the acidity jabs at the palate, too. $13 (2/29/92) **73**

Johannisberg Riesling Late Harvest Michigan 1990: A medium-bodied, clean, taut style of dessert wine, offering a crisp texture and an intriguing balance of ripe apricot and green peach flavors. Finishes crisp and a bit tart. $10 (2/29/92) **78**

Johannisberg Riesling Old Mission Penisula Dry 1990: Crisp and floral, with citrus, nectarine and flinty mineral aromas and flavors that remind us of wines from the Rheingau. A clean, brisk style of Riesling that should be great with trout. $8.50 (2/29/92) **84**

Key to Symbols

The scores reported here are the results of blind tastings conducted by our panel of senior editors. Wines that carry the initials below are results of individual tastings.

THE WINE SPECTATOR 100-POINT SCALE ***95-100***—Classic, a great wine; ***90-94***—Outstanding, superior character and style; ***80-89***—Good to very good, a wine with special qualities; ***70-79***—Average, drinkable wine that may have minor flaws; ***60-69***—Below average, drinkable but not recommended; ***50-59***—Poor, undrinkable, not recommended. "+"—With a score indicates a range; used primarily with barrel tastings to indicate a preliminary score.

SPECIAL DESIGNATIONS SS—Spectator Selection, CS—Cellar Selection, BB—Best Buy, ($NA)—Price not available, (NR)—Not released.

TASTER'S INITIALS (JG)—Jim Gordon, (HS)—Harvey Steiman, (JL)—James Laube, (JS)—James Suckling, (TM)—Thomas Matthews, (TR)—Terry Robards, (PM)—Per-Henrik Mansson, (BT)—Barrel Tasting (these wines were tasted blind from barrel samples), (CA-date)—*California's Great Cabernets* by James Laube, (CH-date)—*California's Great Chardonnays* by James Laube, (VP-date)—*Vintage Port* by James Suckling.

DATE TASTED Dates in parentheses represent the issue in which the rating was published.

FENN VALLEY

Chancellor Lake Michigan Shore 1989: A gutsy wine with a few rough edges, full of plum, cherry and earth flavors. Moderate tannins and high acidity suggest cellaring until 1993. $9.50 (2/29/92) **81**

Johannisberg Riesling Lake Michigan Shore 1989: Light and crisp, with pleasant green apple and spice aromas and flavors that stay with you on the finish, turning toward honey on the aftertaste. $8 (2/29/92) **85**

MADRON LAKE HILLS

Chardonnay Michigan Lake Erie Heartland Vineyards 1990: A solid wine, with simple, earthy, buttery flavors and a hint of sweet pear coming through on the finish. Drinkable now. $13.50 (2/29/92) **79**

White Riesling Late Harvest Michigan Lake Erie Semi-Dry Heartland Vineyards 1990: Only slightly sweet, with modest apricot flavor coming through, but basically a simple, lean wine. Drink soon. $10 (2/29/92) **74**

ST. JULIAN

Chambourcin Lake Michigan Shore 1989: Has ripe cherry, grape and somewhat foxy aromas and is straightforward, fruity and simple in flavor. Ripe but not sweet. Drinkable now. $8.50 (2/29/92) **76**

Chardonnay Lake Michigan Shore Barrel Fermented 1990: Fresh and peachlike in aroma and flavor, with definite sweet oak overtones. Almost syrupy soft on the finish. A pleasant wine to sip cold. $12 (2/29/92) **78**

Solera Light Cream Sherry Michigan NV: Spicy and complex, with all the coffee, toffee, walnut and spice aromas and flavors you could want. Definitely sweet, but not cloying or syrupy. A very well-made dessert sherry. $12 (2/29/92) **88**

MINNESOTA

ALEXIS BAILLY

Country Red Minnesota NV: Tarry, vegetal aromas give way to ripe cherry, menthol and eucalyptus flavors that suggest American oak. Chunky but soft. Drinkable now. A blend of several unnamed hybrid grapes. $7 (2/29/92) **78**

Léon Millot Minnesota 1990: Smoky, meaty berry flavors remind us of Syrah, although it doesn't have the depth. Drinkable but odd. $9 (2/29/92) **74**

Maréchal Foch Minnesota 1990: Gamy, smoky aromas promise more than the soft, almost diluted flavors deliver, but it has definite character. Reminiscent of Syrah. $9 (2/29/92) **77**

MISSISSIPPI

CLAIBORNE

Sauvignon Blanc Mississippi Delta 1987: The dark color suggests this might be oxidized, but the delicate flavors run toward honey and slightly herbal pear notes. Drinkable, but soft around the edges. $10.50 (2/29/92) **76**

MISSOURI

MOUNT PLEASANT

Chardonnay Augusta Estate Limited Bottling 1989: Spicy, grassy aromas and flavors have their appeal, but it seems an odd duck, finishing sweet and buttery. Seems tired and old before its time. 42 cases made. $18 (2/29/92) **75**

Port Augusta 1988: A soft, ripe style, with flavors that border on stewed plum and prune, hinting at toast and coffee on the finish. The alcohol is not obtrusive—it lacks grip. A pleasant dessert wine. $19 (2/29/92) **80**

Vidal Blanc Missouri Parkers' Point 1989: The toasted, spicy oak flavors are appealing, but they overwhelm the light pear notes and leave the wine out of balance. Still, it's smooth and polished and will appeal to *barrique* fans. $12 (2/29/92) **77**

Vidal Late Harvest Augusta Ice Wine 1989: Full-bodied, rich and sweet, with a bitter edge that cuts the sweetness, offering fig, honey and bitter almond flavors. Tastes almost like a minor Sauternes. $20 (2/29/92) **78**

NEW JERSEY

TEWKSBURY

Cherry Wine New Jersey NV: Looks like cherries, smells like cherries, tastes like cherries. Off-dry, distinctive and refreshing. Drink chilled. A blend of Montmorency and Morello cherries. $6.25 (2/29/92) **78**

Sunset New Jersey 1990: An off-dry rosé, with distinctive watermelon and mineral aromas and flavors. A bit on the shy side, but balanced and friendly on the finish. $7 (2/29/92) **78**

Vidal Blanc New Jersey 1990: Austere and rather coarse, without much fruit flavor to flesh out the tart acidity. $8 (2/29/92) **73**

NEW MEXICO

ANDERSON VALLEY

Cabernet Sauvignon New Mexico 1986: A hearty, full-bodied and likable wine without a lot of complexity. Has currant, cherry and herb flavors, a deep color, firm tannins and good balance. $11 (7/31/89) **80**

Cabernet Sauvignon New Mexico Reserve 1987: Lively, fruity aromas and flavors center around cassis and raspberry, with hints of toast and herb, finishing with vibrant fruit. A very appealing wine. $14 (2/29/92) **84**

Chardonnay New Mexico Barrel Fermented 1987: An appealing wine from an unusual appellation. Spicy and buttery in flavor, smooth in texture and modestly fruity. $8.50 (4/15/89) **79**

Muscat Canelli New Mexico 1990: Strong in aroma but lean in texture, turning austere and short on the palate. The flavors are more vegetal than fruity. $6 (2/29/92) **70**

Sauvignon Blanc New Mexico 1990: Offers pretty toast and lime aromas, but gets bland and short on the palate. Has acidity, but not much varietal character. $6 (2/29/92) **76**

Sauvignon Blanc New Mexico 1987: A straightforward wine that doesn't disappoint. Ripe and figgy in flavor, thick and rich in texture. $7 (4/15/89) **79**

DOMAINE CHEURLIN

Brut New Mexico NV: A simple, tasty sparkler, with modest toast and pear aromas and flavors and hints of honey on the finish. An attractive wine that's cleanly made. $12 (2/29/92) **82**

Extra Dry New Mexico NV: Coarse in texture, with a sweet-tart balance that accentuates the smoky pear and spice aromas and flavors. Could use more polish or subtlety, but it's a mouthful of flavor. $12 (2/29/92) **77**

GRUET

Brut Blanc de Noirs New Mexico NV: Refreshing and flavorful in an off-dry style. A very crisp, fruity sparkling wine with strawberry and grapefruit flavors that are creamy, with a lively texture and clean finish. $13 (3/31/90) **80**

Brut New Mexico NV: A good sparkling wine with Chardonnay flavors. Very clean in aroma, almost austere and heavy in flavor, but hints of pear and vanilla give it personality. $13 (3/31/90) **79**

NORTH CAROLINA

BILTMORE ESTATE

Cabernet Sauvignon American 1987: A balanced wine, with concentrated black cherry and berry flavors and a touch of new oak toastiness. Well made, pleasingly complex and drinkable now. $16 (2/29/92) **84**

Chardonnay American Sur Lie 1990: A lean, austere wine, with hints of melon and green apple flavor. Basically a crisp white wine reminiscent of French Petit Chablis. $13 (2/29/92) **78**

CHATEAU BILTMORE

Blanc de Blancs North Carolina NV: Shows simple, sappy flavors in a medium-weight bubbly. Gets a little sticky on the finish; serve well chilled. $21 (2/29/92) **74**

Cabernet Sauvignon North Carolina 1987: Earthy, gamy flavors ride a rugged frame of firm tannins. The fruit is there but submerged. Could be going through malolactic fermentation in the bottle. $16 (2/29/92) **76**

Chardonnay North Carolina 1990: Crisp and fruity, with lime-scented grapefruit and pineapple flavors and a lean texture, opening out to a long, graceful finish. Appealing to drink now. $13 (2/29/92) **86**

OHIO

DEBONNE

Chambourcin Ohio Lake Erie 1989: Simple, fruity and just a touch sweet, with cherry and berry flavors on a light frame. Drinkable now. $6 (2/29/92) **79**

Chardonnay Ohio Lake Erie Proprietor's Reserve 1989: Thin, tart and extremely modest in flavor. All texture and no character. $12 (2/29/92) **70**

Johannisberg Riesling Grand River Valley 1990: A soft, floral wine, with modest fruit flavors and a sweet finish. Light in style. Best served chilled. $7.50 (2/29/92) **76**

FIRELANDS

Brut American Champagne NV: Simple, floral and undistinguished, with flavors that run toward pear and celery. Off-dry, simple and drinkable. $12 (2/29/92) **73**

Cabernet Sauvignon Ohio Lake Erie 1988: The cherry and smoke flavors are simple but attractive, braced by light, firm tannins. A peppery note gives it some of the character of a Côtes du Rhône. Drinkable now. $10 (2/29/92) **82**

Chardonnay Ohio Lake Erie Barrel Select 1990: Fruity and lively, with a creamy texture and gently oak-accented grapefruit and pineapple aromas and flavors. Finishes flavorful and delicate. An attractive wine to drink now. $10 (2/29/92) **86**

MARKKO

Cabernet Sauvignon Conneaut 1988: Light and lively, with plenty of tart raspberry and cranberry aromas and flavors and tight tannins that make it finish with cheek-numbing astringency. Better hold until 1995. $10 (2/29/92) **76**

Pinot Noir Conneaut 1989: Light in color and flavor, with anise and berry flavors, turning toward orange peel on the finish. An honest wine, with modest character. $15 (2/29/92) **76**

PENNSYLVANIA

CHADDSFORD

Chambourcin Pennsylvania Proprietor's Reserve 1989: Has Beaujolais-like fruitiness, with crisp acidity to support the appealing currant and plum flavors. A graceful wine. Drinkable now. $10 (2/29/92) **80**

Chambourcin Pennsylvania Seven Valleys Vineyard 1989: Fruity and concentrated, with an underlying set of barnyardy aromas and flavors that not everyone will like. The fruit leans toward blackberry and currant, and has plenty of zip. $13 (2/29/92) **81**

Chardonnay Pennsylvania Philip Roth Vineyard 1989: Rich and generous, with complex apple, pear and spice aromas and flavors, turning buttery and honeylike on the finish. Has all the ripe fruit and leesy overtones you could want, and remains graceful and appealing. Drinkable now. $24 (2/29/92) **90**

Chardonnay Pennsylvania Stargazers Vineyard 1988: An earthy wine, with distinctive spice and butterscotch flavors and pear notes, turning silky and generous on the finish. Balanced toward tartness. Should be fine to drink through 1993. $24 (2/29/92) **84**

Pinot Noir Pennsylvania Lake Erie Region 1988: Fruity and lively, with a smooth texture and attractive berry and toast aromas and flavors. Crisp acidity keeps it together and suggests this should keep through 1993 or '94 at least. $28 (2/29/92) **82**

Proprietor's Reserve Pennsylvania 1990: Light, fruity and refreshing, this simple, grapey wine has a hint of pear on the finish. Drinkable now. $9 (2/29/92) **78**

NAYLOR

Chambourcin York County 1986: Ripe plum flavors are undermined by a leathery, gamy note in this big, soft wine. $10 (2/29/92) **70**

Chardonnay York County 1990: A light style, with modest pear and mineral flavors that dwindle on the finish, but the spice and pear aromas are strong. Drinkable now. $10 (2/29/92) **80**

Ekem York County 1990: The name is a play on "Yquem," but this is dry enough to drink as an aperitif. Made from Vignoles, this crisply balanced, sweet wine has flavors that remind us of peach and almond and finishes crisp and citrusy. $9 (2/29/92) **77**

RHODE ISLAND

SAKONNET

Chardonnay Southeastern New England Barrel Select 1989: Crisp and spicy, with attractive buttery overtones to the green apple and pear flavors. A graceful wine, with a lively balance and plenty of flavor. Drinkable now. $14 (2/29/92) **87**

Gewürztraminer Southeastern New England Apponagansett Bay Vineyards 1990: Lean and fruity, with earthy mineral overtones that detract from the modest pear and apple flavors. Off-dry and drinkable, but unexceptional. $11 (2/29/92) **75**

Vidal Blanc Southeastern New England 1990: Fruity, with melon and peach flavors, but a little coarse and anonymous. Has good balance of acidity and sweetness. $8 (2/29/92) **78**

TENNESSEE

MOUNTAIN VALLEY

Blackberry Table Wine Tennessee 1991: Bright red in color, with sweet berry flavors that are pleasant. Not a sophisticated wine, but a nice afternoon or after-dinner sipper. $8 (2/29/92) **75**

Mountain Valley White Tennessee 1990: The sweet pineapple flavors spiced with honey and cinnamon notes are tasty, but the wine is dull and very sweet. Lacks clarity and nerve. 80 percent Seyval and 10 percent each Catawba and Vidal. $8 (2/29/92) **74**

TENNESSEE VALLEY

Cabernet Sauvignon Tennessee 1988: A soft, watery texture makes this seem thin, with very modest, tart berry aromas and flavors. $14 (2/29/92) **72**

TEXAS

BELL MOUNTAIN

Cabernet Sauvignon Bell Mountain 1989: Offers cassis, plum and earth aromas and flavors, with good concentration, lush tannins and a long, fruity finish. Drinkable now, but should refine through 1994. $13 (2/29/92) **85**

Pinot Noir Bell Mountain 1989: Spicy cherry aromas show varietal character and the flavors follow through, though the tannins are a little mean. Not a big wine. Drinkable now. $12 (2/29/92) **76**

Sémillon Bell Mountain 1990: Soft and simple, with noticeable sweetness and modest pear, fig and herbal flavors. $9 (2/29/92) **77**

FALL CREEK

Cabernet Sauvignon Texas 1989: A simple wine without much in the way of varietal character or even flavor. Earthy berry notes surface from under the tannins, and the finish is vegetal. Tasted in Texas, it was fruitier, but still odd. $13 (2/29/92) (HS) **75**

Cabernet Sauvignon Texas 1988: The ripe raspberry flavor turns a bit earthy and gamy, with dill and oak nuances. Could use a little more fruit and finesse, but perhaps with time it will gain those attributes. Drink in 1993 to '95. 835 cases made. $13 (7/15/91) **78**

Carnelian Llano County 1988: The simple plum and cherry flavors have a touch of leather and spice that dries out on the finish. A decent red table wine, but nothing special. 154 cases made. $13 (7/15/91) **73**

Chardonnay Texas Grand Reserve 1990: Balanced, elegant and silky in texture, with rich pear, honey and spice aromas and flavors. A gentle wine, with appealing fruit and texture. Drinkable now, but seems to be getting better. $16 (2/29/92) (HS) **88**

Sauvignon Blanc Llano County 1991: An appealingly citrusy, crisp and sappy wine. $9 (2/29/92) (HS) **81**

Sauvignon Blanc Llano County 1990: Showing appealing grapefruit aromas bending toward floral and herbal notes on the palate. $9 (2/29/92) (HS) **79**

Sauvignon Blanc Texas 1989: Pleasantly crisp, with mineral tones shading the generous peach and melon flavors. Fairly long and full on the finish. Drink now. $8.50 (7/15/91) **83**

LLANO ESTACADO

Cabernet Sauvignon Texas 1988: The plummy, spicy aromas are more exciting than the fruity, simple flavors. A lean wine, with firm tannins. Would go well with burgers on the grill. Drinkable now. $12 (2/29/92) **81**

Chardonnay Texas 1990: Crisp and light, with modest peach and pear aromas and flavors layered with attractive oak flavors. Turns appley and pleasant on the finish. $12 (2/29/92) **83**

Chenin Blanc Texas 1988 $6.50 (7/31/89) **82**

Johannisberg Riesling Texas 1990: A very pretty wine that's light and delicately sweet, with lovely pine, honey and peach aromas and flavors. $9 (2/29/92) (HS) **84**

Sauvignon Blanc Lubbock County 1990: Lean and crisp, with classic grass and citrus flavors. Fresh and lively on the palate. A good aperitif or shellfish wine. $8 (2/29/92) BB **85**

MESSINA HOF

Chardonnay Texas Bell Brothers Vineyard Private Reserve 1989: A spicy wine, with a definite clove character on the aroma and flavor, with modest apple intensity and a touch of butter on the finish. Seems a little candied and coarse. $15 (2/29/92) **76**

Chenin Blanc Brazos Valley 1988 $7 (7/31/89) **86**

Johannisberg Riesling Late Harvest Texas Angel 1990: Sweet and silky, with lovely apricot, pear and floral aromas and flavors, turning rich and honeyed on the long finish. Has a solid frame for the delicate flavors to hang on. Well made, showing all the signs of developing with cellaring. Try in 1994 or '95. $15 (2/29/92) **90**

Reflections Texas 1988: Lean and firm, with modest berry and herbal aromas and flavors. Should be ready around 1993. A blend of Cabernet Sauvignon, Cabernet Franc and Merlot. $15 (2/29/92) **77**

MOYER

Brut Texas NV: On the dry side, with toasty, buttery aromas and flavors that stay with you on the finish, echoing toast and pear notes. A well-made sparkler of modest dimensions. $13 (2/29/92) **80**

Brut Texas Especial NV: An earthy style, with attractive toast and spice aromas, turning simple and slightly sweet on the palate. A pleasant wine to drink cold. $9 (2/29/92) **78**

Extra Dry Texas NV: Fruity and refreshing, with definite pear and apple aromas and flavors, hinting at vanilla and spice on the finish. A clean, tasty bubbly. $9 (2/29/92) **81**

Texas Natural NV: Mature, robust and fairly complex in flavor. Tastes toasty and nutty, with earthy aromas, a creamy texture and lingering finish. $11 (7/31/89) **79**

PHEASANT RIDGE

Cabernet Franc Lubbock County Cox Family Vineyards 1988: Crisp in texture, with severe tannins that almost obscure the minty cherry and currant flavors that emerge on the finish. A tight wine that needs until 1995 to '97 to shed some tannin. $12 (2/29/92) **79**

Cabernet Sauvignon Lubbock County 1988: Firm textured and richly tannic, showing a solid thread of plum and currant flavor, smoky overtones and enough restraint to promise an elegant wine when the tannins become polished. Try in 1995 to '97. $13 (2/29/92) **83**

Chardonnay Lubbock County 1989: This distinctive wine is dark in color, soft in texture and marked by smoky oak aromas and flavors. An offbeat Chardonnay, with plenty of pear and apricot flavors and a generous soul. The slight bitterness of the smoky flavors may put off some. $13 (2/29/92) **83**

Chenin Blanc Lubbock County 1989: A dry, medium-weight wine, with simple green apple and vanilla flavors and modest complexity from toasty, slightly herbal overtones. Drinkable now. $6 (2/29/92) **79**

STE. GENEVIEVE

Chardonnay Texas Grand Reserve 1989: Simple and slightly grassy, with modest green apple flavors and a light texture. Hints at honey on the finish, making it modestly appealing and drinkable now. $8 (2/29/92) **79**

Fumé Blanc Texas NV: Effusively fruity, with distinctive quince and pear aromas and flavors. Simple, attractive and slightly sweet. $6/1.5L (2/29/92) (HS) **82**

Fumé Blanc Texas Grand Reserve 1989: Pretty grapefruit and spice aromas don't quite carry through to the soft, simple palate, but a touch of honey on the finish makes this an easy-drinking wine. $6 (2/29/92) **78**

Sauvignon Blanc Texas 1990: Shows pretty spice, pear and citrus aromas and flavors along with a strong hint of sweetness, which is more pleasing than distracting. $6 (2/29/92) **81**

SCHOPPAUL HILL

Chenin Blanc Texas 1990: Offers strong peach flavors and is quite sweet, but has good acidity. A vibrant wine that shows good varietal character. Flavorful, refreshing and charming. $7 (2/29/92) BB **82**

Muscat Canelli Texas 1990: Fresh and fruity, with pleasant peach, grapefruit and cream aromas and flavors. A little sweet, but refreshingly balanced. Drinkable now. $8 (2/29/92) **81**

Sauvignon Blanc Texas 1989: Round and almost honeyed on the palate, with butter, vanilla, fig and pineapple flavors. Tastes like a dry Sauternes. Rich, but its slight sweetness is a little unusual for this varietal. $7 (2/29/92) **81**

Sauvignon Blanc Texas 1989 $7 (2/29/92) **81**

SLAUGHTER LEFTWICH

Cabernet Sauvignon Texas 1989: Fruity and spicy, with a harsh edge of oak that will need time to soften, perhaps until 1994, but the wine is soft and needs to be drunk soon. Try it with hearty food. $9 (2/29/92) **76**

Sauvignon Blanc Texas 1990: A friendly quaffing wine, with lime, pineapple and vanilla flavors in a soft frame and just enough acidity to keep it interesting. $7 (2/29/92) **80**

TEYSHA

Cabernet Sauvignon Texas Late Harvest 1990: An earthy style of red dessert wine, offering plum and prune aromas and flavors. Simple and not terribly tannic. Like a ruby Port without the high alcohol. (Residual sugar 5.8 percent.) Drink soon. $10 (2/29/92) **78**

Gewürztraminer Texas Casa Nueva Vineyards 1989: Has the familiar Gewürz spice and rose petal aromas and flavors, with a nice balance of pear and almond notes at the core. On the dry side; clean, flavorful and easy to drink. $10 (2/29/92) **84**

Rosé of Cabernet Sauvignon Texas Cabernet Royale 1990: Very fruity and full-bodied, with distinctive rhubarb and berry aromas and flavors, hinting at meatiness on the palate. Off-dry but balanced. $9 (2/29/92) **77**

Virginia

BARBOURSVILLE

Cabernet Sauvignon Monticello Reserve 1983: Light in texture and still has a hard edge of tannin and acidity supporting the modest stewed cherry flavors. Has a menthol edge. $15 (2/29/92) **73**

Chardonnay Monticello Reserve 1989: Crisp and lively, with nicely focused lemon and pear aromas and flavors definitely shaded by the sweet vanilla of oak. Has richness despite a lean texture. Drinkable now, but feels as though it could gain with cellaring until 1993. $14 (2/29/92) **87**

Sauvignon Blanc Monticello 1989: Lush, almost sweet, with pear and honey flavors accented by herbal notes. Has enough acidity to keep it refreshing, and recognizable varietal character. $10 (2/29/92) **80**

LINDEN

Cabernet Virginia 1988: A solid wine, with firm tannins and a focused thread of blackberry flavor extending into a finish that features hints of toast and anise. Needs until 1995 or '96 to settle the tannins. A blend of Cabernet Sauvignon and Cabernet Franc. $15 (2/29/92) **84**

Chardonnay Virginia 1990: An earthy, generous wine, with a firm texture and sweet pineapple, pear and butter aromas and flavors. Ever-so-slightly bitter on the finish. Could be smoother, but it's a solid effort. $12 (2/29/92) **79**

Chardonnay Virginia 1989: Crisp and focused, with nicely balanced gingerbread-scented apple and pear flavors, turning a tiny bit herbal or bitter on the finish. An attractive wine; drink now. $12 (2/29/92) **80**

Seyval Blanc Virginia 1990: A lively wine, with grapefruit and pineapple flavors that are crisp and clean, but fade quickly. A nice aperitif. $9 (2/29/92) **78**

MEREDYTH

Cabernet Sauvignon Virginia 1989: Modest black cherry and blackberry flavors are ripe and lush, but not very well defined. The firm tannins need hearty food, but hearty and simple is what this wine is all about. $11 (2/29/92) **79**

Merlot Virginia 1989: Firm and flavorful, with well-defined currant and rhubarb characteristics plus a nice hint of toastiness. Lacks polish, but the flavors are attractive. Drinkable now. $25 (2/29/92) **81**

Seyval Blanc Virginia 1989: Round and fruity, with creamy honey and melon flavors. Not sophisticated, but lively and easy to drink. $7.50 (2/29/92) **80**

MISTY MOUNTAIN

Cabernet Sauvignon Virginia 1988: Expressive plum and black olive flavors say Cabernet, following through with currant and plum flavors. Rich, warm and sturdy, but not too tannic. Drink now. $18 (2/29/92) **82**

Chardonnay Virginia Barrel Fermented Vintners Reserve 1989: Firm and flavorful, with simple pear, melon and honey flavors that extend into a solid finish. Drinkable now. $16 (2/29/92) **80**

Merlot Virginia 1988: Light in texture, with tart, lemony, berry aromas and flavors. Reminds us of cranberry juice. Pleasant enough, but nothing exceptional. $18 (2/29/92) **77**

MONTDOMAINE

Heritage Monticello 1988: Spicy oak and cherry aromas and flavors supported by firm tannins give this wine structure and depth. A strong minty note makes it distinctive. Drinkable now, but should soften by 1993. A Bordeaux blend. $14 (2/29/92) **82**

Merlot Monticello Reserve 1987: Rich and generous, with well-modulated currant and berry aromas and flavors, a velvety texture from well-integrated tannins and a lively balance that lets the flavors glide across the palate. A well-made, stylish wine. Drinkable now, but better around 1993 or '94. $15 (2/29/92) **86**

PIEDMONT

Chardonnay Virginia Barrel Fermented Special Reserve 1990: Crisp and lively, with appealing pineapple and pear aromas and flavors that extend into a clean, long finish. A light style with plenty of flavor. $12 (2/29/92) **83**

Sémillon Virginia 1989: Lean, crisp, austere and earthy, with peach and apple aromas that fade quickly. $15 (2/29/92) **74**

PRINCE MICHEL

Chardonnay Virginia 1990: Simple and chunky, with definite oaky aromas and flavors that tend to overshadow whatever fruit is present. Hints at candy or apple on the finish. $13 (2/29/92) **75**

Chardonnay Virginia 1989: Tastes sweet with ultraripe apple, pear and melon flavors that are clean and well defined. May be too sweet for some, but it won't shortchange you on ripe fruit. Drink now. $9 (8/31/91) **79**

Chardonnay Virginia Barrel Select 1990: Lean and assertive, with a heavy thread of toasty, slightly bitter lemon and apple flavors that turn thick on the finish. $15 (2/29/92) **76**

Chardonnay Virginia Barrel Select 1988: Rich but delicate; full of ripe pear and tropical fruit flavors with a bit of spice and vanilla for complexity. Texture is soft and velvety, and the flavors linger on the finish. Delicious now if you can afford the tariff. $15 (6/30/90) **87**

Le Ducq Lot 87 NV: Big and tannic, with ripe cherry, stewed plum and almost Port-like flavors. It's a little tough, but there's a lot going on. Hold until 1993 for the tannins to soften. A Bordeaux blend of Virginia and California grapes; an ambitious effort that isn't paying off yet. $50 (2/29/92) **79**

RAPIDAN RIVER

Gewürztraminer Virginia 1990: Has all the Gewürz aromas and flavors on a gentle, off-dry frame, offering pleasant rose petal, grapefruit and almond aromas and flavors and a smooth finish. Drink soon. $13 (2/29/92) **83**

TARARA

Cabernet Frederick County 1989: Smells sunbaked, with leather and dried tomato aromas; the palate is more herbal, with rhubarb and dried cherry notes. Has distinctive flavors, but the structure is fine. A blend of Cabernet Franc and Cabernet Sauvignon. $12 (2/29/92) **82**

Chardonnay Virginia 1990: Crisp in texture, with buttery overtones to the basic pear and almond flavors, turning round and nicely balanced on the finish. A charming wine to drink now. $11 (2/29/92) **85**

Charval Virginia 1990: Crisp and quite lively, this balanced, fresh wine has clean apple flavors and a touch of toast and honey. A blend of Chardonnay and Seyval. $8 (2/29/92) **79**

WILLIAMSBURG

Chardonnay Virginia Acte 12 of 1619 1990: Lean and lively, with a definite splash of oak aroma that slowly evolves toward grapefruit and apple on the finish. Nicely balanced for current drinking. $12 (2/29/92) **88**

Chardonnay Virginia Barrel Fermented Vintage Reserve 1990: Smooth and generous, with appealing vanilla-scented pear and peach flavors, turning soft and delicate on the finish, although the flavors linger nicely. Drinkable now. $16 (2/29/92) **87**

Wisconsin

CEDAR CREEK

American 1990: Has spicy strawberry, cherry and smoke aromas and flavors that are round and soft, but the wine turns lean and crisp on the finish. Made from 100 percent Michigan-grown Chancellor. $6 (2/29/92) **78**

American Cranberry Blush 1990: Sweet and spicy, a light rosé, with pleasant watermelon and rhubarb aromas and flavors that fill the mouth. Drink chilled. A blend of Seyval, Vidal Blanc and cranberry juice. $7 (2/29/92) **78**

Vidal Blanc American Red 1990: Orange and spice flavors enliven this rather coarse, off-dry wine that's lively and fresh. $7 (2/29/92) **76**

WOLLERSHEIM

Domaine Reserve Wisconsin 1989: A modest wine, with light cherry and cinnamon flavors. Quite acidic and finishes short. Made from 100 percent Maréchal Foch. $12 (2/29/92) **73**

Domaine du Sac Dry Red Wine Wisconsin 1990: Round and polished, with ripe black cherry and blackberry flavors. Sturdy, flavorful, not too tannic and easy to drink. Made from 100 percent Maréchal Foch. $8 (2/29/92) **81**

Pinot Noir Wisconsin Sugarloaf Hill 1989: Light and smooth, with vague flavors reminiscent of sour-cherry candy. Simple and drinkable. (NR) (2/29/92) **75**

Seyval Blanc American Prairie Fumé 1990: Round and off-dry, with pleasant melon and spice flavors. Not complex, but has enough acidity to balance the sweetness. $6 (2/29/92) **78**

Key to Symbols

The scores reported here are the results of blind tastings conducted by our panel of senior editors. Wines that carry the initials below are results of individual tastings.

THE WINE SPECTATOR 100-POINT SCALE ***95-100***—Classic, a great wine; ***90-94***—Outstanding, superior character and style; ***80-89***—Good to very good, a wine with special qualities; ***70-79***—Average, drinkable wine that may have minor flaws; ***60-69***—Below average, drinkable but not recommended; ***50-59***—Poor, undrinkable, not recommended. "+"—With a score indicates a range; used primarily with barrel tastings to indicate a preliminary score.

SPECIAL DESIGNATIONS SS—Spectator Selection, CS—Cellar Selection, BB—Best Buy, ($NA)—Price not available, (NR)—Not released.

TASTER'S INITIALS (JG)—Jim Gordon, (HS)—Harvey Steiman, (JL)—James Laube, (JS)—James Suckling, (TM)—Thomas Matthews, (TR)—Terry Robards, (PM)—Per-Henrik Mansson, (BT)—Barrel Tasting (these wines were tasted blind from barrel samples), (CA-date)—*California's Great Cabernets* by James Laube, (CH-date)—*California's Great Chardonnays* by James Laube, (VP-date)—*Vintage Port* by James Suckling.

DATE TASTED Dates in parentheses represent the issue in which the rating was published.

SECTION C: WINES LISTED ALPHABETICALLY BY PRODUCER

ABBAYE DE VALMAGNE (France/Other)
Côteaux du Languedoc 1988 $12 (8/31/91) **80**

ABBAZIA DI ROSAZZO (Italy/Other)
Chardonnay 1990 $22 (1/31/92) **75**
Colli Orientali del Friuli Ribolla Gialla 1990 $21 (1/31/92) **76**
Pignolo 1987 $36 (6/30/91) **85**
Ronco delle Acacie 1989 $36 (7/15/91) **89**
Ronco della Abbazia 1988 $11/375ml (7/15/91) **73**
Ronco di Corte 1989 $27 (7/15/91) **84**
Ronco dei Roseti 1987 $35 (7/15/91) **87**
Ronco dei Roseti 1986 $22 (3/15/89) **85**
Ronco dei Roseti 1983 $20 (9/15/88) (TM) **87**
Sauvignon Colli Orientali del Friuli 1989 $19 (7/15/91) **83**

ABBAZIA DI VALLE CHIARA (Italy/Piedmont)
Dolcetto d'Ovada 1989 $13 (7/15/91) **79**
Torre Albarola 1988 $24 (1/31/92) **87**

MARZIANO & ENRICO ABBONA (Italy/Piedmont)
Roero Arneis 1990 $13/375ml (5/15/92) **85**

HENRI ABELE (France/Champagne)
Brut Champagne NV $24 (12/31/91) **89**
Brut Champagne Grande Marque Impériale 1982 $29 (7/31/87) **90**
Brut Champagne Le Sourire de Reims NV $24 (7/31/87) **79**
Brut Rosé Champagne NV $29 (7/31/87) **77**
Brut Rosé Champagne Cuvée Reserve 1983 $50 (3/31/92) **88**
Brut Rosé Champagne Grande Marque Impériale 1982 $25 (3/31/92) **88**

ABREU (United States/California)
Cabernet Sauvignon Napa Valley Madrona Ranch 1987 $25 (7/31/91) **89**

ACACIA (United States/California)
Cabernet Sauvignon Napa Valley 1984 $15 (12/15/86) **75**
Chardonnay Carneros Napa Valley 1990 $16.50 (6/30/92) **85**
Chardonnay Carneros Napa Valley 1989 $16 (12/31/90) **84**
Chardonnay Carneros Napa Valley 1988 $16 (1/31/90) **89**
Chardonnay Carneros Napa Valley 1987 $17 (CH-1/90) **84**
Chardonnay Carneros Napa Valley 1986 Rel: $15 Cur: $18 (CH-1/90) **87**
Chardonnay Carneros Napa Valley 1985 Rel: $15 Cur: $20 (CH-1/90) **80**
Chardonnay Carneros Napa Valley 1984 Rel: $14 Cur: $20 (CH-1/90) **84**
Chardonnay Carneros Napa Valley 1983 Rel: $12 Cur: $19 (12/01/84) **84**
Chardonnay Carneros Napa Valley Marina Vineyard 1990 $18.50 (6/30/92) **82**
Chardonnay Carneros Napa Valley Marina Vineyard 1989 $21 (5/15/92) **85**
Chardonnay Carneros Napa Valley Marina Vineyard 1988 Rel: $20 Cur: $23 (1/31/90) **90**
Chardonnay Carneros Napa Valley Marina Vineyard 1987 Rel: $18 Cur: $21 (CH-1/90) **85**
Chardonnay Carneros Napa Valley Marina Vineyard 1986 Rel: $18 Cur: $22 (CH-1/90) **86**
Chardonnay Carneros Napa Valley Marina Vineyard 1985 Rel: $18 Cur: $22 (CH-1/90) **80**
Chardonnay Carneros Napa Valley Marina Vineyard 1984 Rel: $16 Cur: $22 (CH-1/90) **86**
Chardonnay Carneros Napa Valley Marina Vineyard 1983 Rel: $16 Cur: $22 (CH-1/90) **79**
Chardonnay Carneros Napa Valley Winery Lake Vineyard 1985 Rel: $18 Cur: $25 (CH-1/90) **82**
Chardonnay Carneros Napa Valley Winery Lake Vineyard 1984 Rel: $18 Cur: $30 (CH-1/90) **88**
Chardonnay Carneros Napa Valley Winery Lake Vineyard 1983 Rel: $18 Cur: $25 (CH-1/90) **87**
Chardonnay Carneros Napa Valley Winery Lake Vineyard 1979 Rel: $16 Cur: $26 (CH-1/90) **76**
Chardonnay Napa Valley 1986 Rel: $15 Cur: $17 (CH-1/90) **81**
Chardonnay Napa Valley 1985 Rel: $12.50 Cur: $16 (CH-1/90) **79**
Chardonnay Napa Valley 1984 Rel: $12.50 Cur: $16 (CH-7/90) **89**
Chardonnay Napa Valley 1983 Rel: $12 Cur: $18 (CH-1/90) **80**
Chardonnay Napa Valley 1982 Rel: $12 Cur: $18 (CH-1/90) **80**
Merlot Napa Valley 1984 $15 (2/28/87) **83**
Pinot Noir Carneros Napa Valley 1989 $14 (11/15/91) **71**
Pinot Noir Carneros Napa Valley 1988 $14 (2/28/91) **89**
Pinot Noir Carneros Napa Valley 1987 Rel: $13 Cur: $15 (2/15/90) **87**
Pinot Noir Carneros Napa Valley 1986 $15 (6/15/88) **88**
Pinot Noir Carneros Napa Valley 1985 Rel: $12 Cur: $14 (12/15/87) **84**
Pinot Noir Carneros Napa Valley 1984 $11 (12/15/86) SS **95**
Pinot Noir Carneros Napa Valley Iund Vineyard 1984 $15 (3/15/87) **81**
Pinot Noir Carneros Napa Valley Iund Vineyard 1983 $15.50 (8/31/86) **77**
Pinot Noir Carneros Napa Valley Iund Vineyard 1982 Rel: $15 Cur: $31 (7/16/84) CS **91**
Pinot Noir Carneros Napa Valley Lee Vineyard 1983 Rel: $15.50 Cur: $20 (8/31/86) **89**
Pinot Noir Carneros Napa Valley Lee Vineyard 1982 $15 (7/16/84) **90**
Pinot Noir Carneros Napa Valley Madonna Vineyard 1986 $18 (6/15/88) **88**
Pinot Noir Carneros Napa Valley Madonna Vineyard 1985 $16 (12/15/87) **88**
Pinot Noir Carneros Napa Valley Madonna Vineyard 1984 $16 (3/15/87) **88**
Pinot Noir Carneros Napa Valley Madonna Vineyard 1983 $15.50 (8/31/86) **93**
Pinot Noir Carneros Napa Valley St. Clair Vineyard 1989 Rel: $21 Cur: $23 (10/31/91) **86**
Pinot Noir Carneros Napa Valley St. Clair Vineyard 1988 $20 (2/28/91) **91**
Pinot Noir Carneros Napa Valley St. Clair Vineyard 1987 Rel: $18 Cur: $22 (2/15/90) **89**
Pinot Noir Carneros Napa Valley St. Clair Vineyard 1986 Rel: $18 Cur: $30 (6/15/88) **91**
Pinot Noir Carneros Napa Valley St. Clair Vineyard 1985 $16 (12/15/87) **91**
Pinot Noir Carneros Napa Valley St. Clair Vineyard 1984 Rel: $16 Cur: $30 (11/30/86) **93**
Pinot Noir Carneros Napa Valley St. Clair Vineyard 1983 Rel: $15 Cur: $30 (10/01/85) CS **95**
Pinot Noir Carneros Napa Valley St. Clair Vineyard 1982 Rel: $15 Cur: $25 (7/16/84) **89**
Pinot Noir Carneros Napa Valley Winery Lake Vineyard 1983 $15 (11/16/85) **78**
Pinot Noir Carneros Napa Valley Winery Lake Vineyard 1982 $15 (7/16/84) **90**

Key to Symbols

The scores reported here are the results of blind tastings conducted by our panel of senior editors. Wines that carry the initials below are results of individual tastings.

THE WINE SPECTATOR 100-POINT SCALE 95-100—Classic, a great wine; ***90-94***—Outstanding, superior character and style; ***80-89***—Good to very good, a wine with special qualities; ***70-79***—Average, drinkable wine that may have minor flaws; ***60-69***—Below average, drinkable but not recommended; ***50-59***—Poor, undrinkable, not recommended. "+"—With a score indicates a range; used primarily with barrel tastings to indicate a preliminary score.

SPECIAL DESIGNATIONS SS—Spectator Selection, CS—Cellar Selection, BB—Best Buy, ($NA)—Price not available, (NR)—Not released.

TASTER'S INITIALS (JG)—Jim Gordon, (HS)—Harvey Steiman, (JL)—James Laube, (JS)—James Suckling, (TM)—Thomas Matthews, (TR)—Terry Robards, (PM)—Per-Henrik Mansson, (BT)—Barrel Tasting (these wines were tasted blind from barrel samples), (CA- date)—*California's Great Cabernets* by James Laube, (CH-date)—*California's Great Chardonnays* by James Laube, (VP -date)—*Vintage Port* by James Suckling.

DATE TASTED Dates in parentheses represent the issue in which the rating was published.

LES ACACIAS (France/Burgundy)
Brut Crémant de Bourgogne Cépage Chardonnay NV $11 (6/15/90) **78**
Mâcon-Villages Cave de Viré 1989 $11 (2/28/91) **71**
Mâcon-Viré Vieilles Vignes 1988 $9 (8/31/90) **76**

GIOVANNI ACCOMASSO & FIGLIO (Italy/Piedmont)
Barolo Vigneto Rocchette 1985 $24 (1/31/92) **75**
Nebbiolo delle Langhe 1982 $14 (7/31/89) **65**

J.B. ADAM (France/Alsace)
Gewürztraminer Alsace Vendange Tardive 1990 $40 (2/15/92) (BT) **80+**
Muscat Alsace 1990 (NR) (2/15/92) **87**
Pinot Blanc Alsace 1990 (NR) (2/15/92) **87**
Riesling Alsace Cuvée Jean-Baptiste Kaefferkopf 1990 $19 (2/15/92) **87**
Riesling Alsace Réserve 1990 $11.50 (2/15/92) **85**
Riesling Alsace Vendange Tardive 1990 $40 (2/15/92) (BT) **90+**
Tokay Pinot Gris Alsace Cuvée Jean-Baptiste 1990 $16 (2/15/92) **87**
Tokay Pinot Gris Alsace Réserve 1990 $13 (2/15/92) **83**
Tokay Pinot Gris Alsace Sélection de Grains Nobles 1990 (NR) (2/15/92) (BT) **85+**
Tokay Pinot Gris Alsace Vendange Tardive 1990 $40 (2/15/92) (BT) **85+**

ADAMS (United States/Oregon)
Pinot Noir Yamhill County 1985 $25 (2/15/90) **89**
Pinot Noir Yamhill County Peter F. Adams 1983 (NR) (2/15/90) **91**

ADELAIDA (United States/California)
Cabernet Sauvignon Paso Robles 1987 $14 (2/28/91) **89**
Cabernet Sauvignon Paso Robles 1983 $12 (12/15/89) **75**
Cabernet Sauvignon Paso Robles 1981 $7.25 (3/01/84) **88**
Chardonnay Paso Robles 1988 $14 (2/15/91) **89**
Chardonnay Paso Robles 1987 $12.50 (12/15/89) **84**
Zinfandel Paso Robles 1988 $12 (4/30/91) **88**

ADELSHEIM (United States/Oregon)
Pinot Noir Oregon 1987 $13 (2/15/90) **72**
Pinot Noir Oregon 1985 $25 (2/15/90) **75**
Pinot Noir Polk County 1986 $15 (6/15/88) **87**
Pinot Noir Polk County The Eola Hills 1987 $16 (2/15/90) **70**
Pinot Noir Willamette Valley 1988 $13 (4/15/91) **89**
Pinot Noir Yamhill County 1985 $16 (6/15/87) **88**
Pinot Noir Yamhill County 1983 $40 (2/15/90) **70**
Pinot Noir Yamhill County Elizabeth's Reserve 1987 $19 (2/15/90) **73**

ADLER FELS (United States/California)
Cabernet Sauvignon Napa Valley 1980 $10 (10/01/84) **74**
Chardonnay Carneros Sangiacomo Vineyards 1989 $12.50 (4/30/91) **80**
Chardonnay Sonoma Valley Sobra Vista Vineyards 1989 $12 (4/15/91) **82**
Fumé Blanc Sonoma County 1990 $9.50 (4/15/92) **82**
Fumé Blanc Sonoma County 1989 $10 (4/30/91) **80**
Melange à Deux Sonoma County 1985 $15 (10/15/87) **74**

CHATEAU D'AGASSAC (France/Bordeaux)
Haut-Médoc 1989 (NR) (3/15/92) **88**

AGE (Spain)
Rioja White Siglo 1988 (NR) (5/31/92) **78**

AHERN (United States/California)
Chardonnay Edna Valley Paragon Vineyard 1982 $10 (2/15/84) **84**
Zinfandel Amador County 1980 $6.50 (2/15/84) **78**

CHATEAU D'AIGUEVILLE (France/Rhône)
Côtes du Rhône 1987 $5 (1/31/89) **73**
Côtes du Rhône 1984 $4.50 (10/15/87) **68**

AIRLIE (United States/Oregon)
Pinot Noir Willamette Valley 1987 $9 (2/15/90) **75**

ALAMEDA (Chile)
Cabernet Sauvignon Maipo Valley 1988 $5.50 (6/15/92) BB **84**
Merlot Maipo Valley Santa Maria Vineyard 1987 $5.50 (6/15/92) BB **82**
Sauvignon Blanc Maipo Valley 1989 $7 (10/15/91) **75**

CASTELLO D'ALBOLA (Italy/Tuscany)
Acciaiolo 1988 $40 (9/15/91) **88**
Chardonnay 1989 $50 (2/15/91) **90**
Chianti Classico 1988 $10 (9/15/91) **89**
Chianti Classico 1986 $7.50 (11/30/89) **85**
Chianti Classico Riserva 1985 $12 (11/30/89) **76**

DOMAINE LUCIEN ALBRECHT (France/Alsace)
Gewürztraminer Alsace Cuvée Martine Albrecht 1990 (NR) (2/15/92) **85**
Gewürztraminer Alsace Sélection de Grains Nobles 1989 (NR) (11/15/90) **93**
Gewürztraminer Alsace Vendange Tardive 1989 (NR) (11/15/90) **85**
Pinot Blanc Alsace 1989 $7 (11/15/90) **75**
Pinot Blanc Alsace Vieilles Vignes Barrel Fermented 1990 (NR) (2/15/92) **72**
Riesling Alsace Pfingstberg Sélection de Grains Nobles 1989 (NR) (11/15/90) **87**
Tokay Pinot Gris Alsace Pfingstberg 1990 (NR) (2/15/92) **84**
Tokay Pinot Gris Alsace Pfingstberg 1989 (NR) (11/15/90) **80**
Tokay Pinot Gris Alsace Réserve du Domaine 1989 (NR) (11/15/90) **80**
Tokay Pinot Gris Alsace Sélection de Grains Nobles 1990 (NR) (2/15/92) (BT) **80+**
Tokay Pinot Gris Alsace Vendange Tardive 1990 (NR) (2/15/92) (BT) **90+**
Tokay Pinot Gris Alsace Vendange Tardive 1989 (NR) (11/15/90) **88**

ALDERBROOK (United States/California)
Chardonnay Dry Creek Valley 1990 $10 (6/30/92) **82**
Chardonnay Dry Creek Valley 1989 $10 (3/31/91) **82**
Chardonnay Dry Creek Valley 1988 $10 (2/15/90) **82**
Chardonnay Dry Creek Valley 1987 $9.75 (2/15/89) **90**
Chardonnay Dry Creek Valley 1986 $9.25 (4/15/88) **84**
Chardonnay Dry Creek Valley 1985 $8.75 (2/15/87) **79**
Chardonnay Dry Creek Valley Reserve 1988 $16 (4/15/90) **82**
Muscat Canelli Sonoma County 1989 $7.50 (7/15/90) **75**
Sauvignon Blanc Dry Creek Valley 1990 $7.50 (6/15/92) **80**
Sauvignon Blanc Dry Creek Valley 1989 $8 (11/15/91) **79**
Sauvignon Blanc Dry Creek Valley 1988 $9 (3/31/90) **85**
Sauvignon Blanc Dry Creek Valley 1987 $7.50 (4/15/89) **86**
Sauvignon Blanc Late Harvest Dry Creek Valley 1989 $24/375ml (6/15/92) **88**
Sémillon Dry Creek Valley 1990 $8.50 (11/15/91) **85**
Sémillon Dry Creek Valley 1988 $9 (2/15/90) **83**

Sémillon Dry Creek Valley Rued Vineyard 1987 $7.50 (5/15/89) BB **87**

ALEXANDER VALLEY VINEYARDS (United States/California)
Cabernet Sauvignon Alexander Valley 1991 (NR) (5/15/92) (BT) **86+**
Cabernet Sauvignon Alexander Valley 1990 (NR) (5/15/91) (BT) **90+**
Cabernet Sauvignon Alexander Valley 1989 $14 (5/15/91) (BT) **85+**
Cabernet Sauvignon Alexander Valley 1988 $12 (9/30/91) **88**
Cabernet Sauvignon Alexander Valley 1987 Rel: $12 Cur: $15 (5/31/90) **87**
Cabernet Sauvignon Alexander Valley 1986 Rel: $11.50 Cur: $16 (CA-3/89) **88**
Cabernet Sauvignon Alexander Valley 1985 Rel: $11 Cur: $18 (CA-3/89) **88**
Cabernet Sauvignon Alexander Valley 1984 Rel: $10.50 Cur: $18 (CA-3/89) **92**
Cabernet Sauvignon Alexander Valley 1984 Rel: $10.50 Cur: $18 (5/15/87) SS **93**
Cabernet Sauvignon Alexander Valley 1983 Rel: $10.50 Cur: $18 (CA-3/89) **90**
Cabernet Sauvignon Alexander Valley 1982 Rel: $10 Cur: $16 (CA-3/89) **90**
Cabernet Sauvignon Alexander Valley 1982 Rel: $10 Cur: $16 (11/01/84) SS **92**
Cabernet Sauvignon Alexander Valley 1981 Rel: $9 Cur: $18 (CA-3/89) **87**
Cabernet Sauvignon Alexander Valley 1980 Rel: $9 Cur: $16 (CA-3/89) **83**
Cabernet Sauvignon Alexander Valley 1979 Rel: $7 Cur: $18 (CA-3/89) **86**
Cabernet Sauvignon Alexander Valley 1978 Rel: $6.50 Cur: $20 (CA-3/89) **80**
Cabernet Sauvignon Alexander Valley 1976 Rel: $5.50 Cur: $18 (CA-3/89) **60**
Cabernet Sauvignon Alexander Valley 1975 Rel: $5.50 Cur: $20 (CA-3/89) **75**
Chardonnay Alexander Valley 1990 $11 (7/15/92) **83**
Chardonnay Alexander Valley 1988 $12 (6/30/90) **88**
Chardonnay Alexander Valley 1987 $11 (1/31/89) **77**
Chardonnay Alexander Valley 1986 $11 (4/30/88) **83**
Chardonnay Alexander Valley 1985 $10.50 (5/31/87) **79**
Chardonnay Alexander Valley 1983 $10 (4/01/85) **87**
Chardonnay Alexander Valley 1982 $10 (3/01/84) **85**
Gewürztraminer Alexander Valley 1988 $6.50 (6/30/90) **69**
Johannisberg Riesling Alexander Valley 1991 $8 (5/31/92) **86**
Merlot Alexander Valley 1991 (NR) (5/15/92) (BT) **83+**
Merlot Alexander Valley 1990 (NR) (5/15/91) (BT) **85+**
Merlot Alexander Valley 1989 $13 (11/15/91) **84**
Merlot Alexander Valley 1985 $11 (10/31/87) **88**
Pinot Noir Alexander Valley 1989 $10 (10/31/91) **65**
Pinot Noir Alexander Valley 1987 $9 (5/31/90) **74**
Pinot Noir Alexander Valley 1985 $8 (4/15/88) **81**
Pinot Noir Alexander Valley 1984 $7 (2/15/88) **87**
Pinot Noir Alexander Valley 1982 $6.50 (11/01/84) **75**
Zinfandel Alexander Valley 1987 $9 (3/31/90) **82**

CAVES ALIANCA (Portugal)
Bairrada Colheita 1990 $5 (11/15/91) **74**
Bairrada Garrafeira 1984 $8 (7/15/91) **78**
Bairrada Reserva 1987 $5 (7/15/91) **77**
Beiras Garrafeira 1982 $9 (7/15/91) **84**
Dão Vinho Tinto 1984 $8 (7/15/91) **74**

ALIGNE (France/Rhône)
Côtes du Rhône 1985 $6 (2/28/87) **74**

MARQUES DE ALLELLA (Spain)
Alella 1989 $17 (12/15/90) **80**

ROBERT ALLISON (Chile)
Merlot Maipo Valley 1987 $5 (6/30/90) **77**

ALMADEN (United States/California)
Cabernet Sauvignon Monterey County 1981 $6 (7/01/84) **80**
Cabernet Sauvignon Monterey County Vintage Classic Selection 1983 $5 (10/15/87) **74**
Chenin Blanc California NV $4/1.5L (7/31/89) **77**
Pinot Noir San Benito County 1982 $5 (6/30/87) **69**

DOMAINE DE L'ALOUETTE (France/Loire)
Muscadet de Sèvre et Maine Sur Lie 1989 $7 (11/30/90) **74**

CHATEAU LES ALOUETTES (France/Bordeaux)
Bordeaux Kosher 1986 $10 (3/31/90) **70**

ALPHA (France/Bordeaux)
Bordeaux Blanc 1990 (NR) (9/30/91) (BT) **75+**
Bordeaux Blanc 1989 $16 (2/28/91) **84**

ALPINE (United States/Oregon)
Pinot Noir Willamette Valley Vintage Select 1985 $17 (6/15/87) **80**

ALTAMURA (United States/California)
Chardonnay Napa Valley 1988 $18 (5/31/92) **86**
Chardonnay Napa Valley 1987 Rel: $16.50 Cur: $21 (6/30/90) **87**
Chardonnay Napa Valley 1986 Rel: $15 Cur: $21 (CH-1/90) **88**
Chardonnay Napa Valley 1985 Rel: $14 Cur: $21 (CH-1/90) **91**

ELIO ALTARE (Italy/Piedmont)
1989 $11.50 (7/15/91) **85**
Barbera d'Alba 1989 $13 (3/15/91) **91**
Barbera d'Alba 1988 $10 (3/31/90) **84**
Barbera d'Alba 1987 $12 (8/31/89) **92**
Barolo 1985 $24 (1/31/90) **92**
Barolo 1982 $13 (6/30/87) **88**
Barolo Vigneto Arborina 1982 $15 (9/15/87) **87**
Dolcetto d'Alba 1989 $12 (7/15/91) **81**
Dolcetto d'Alba 1988 $10 (3/31/90) **82**
Dolcetto d'Alba 1987 $9 (2/28/89) **90**
Nebbiolo delle Langhe 1988 $10 (3/31/90) **81**
Nebbiolo delle Langhe 1987 $9 (7/31/89) **85**

Key to Symbols

The scores reported here are the results of blind tastings conducted by our panel of senior editors. Wines that carry the initials below are results of individual tastings.

THE WINE SPECTATOR 100-POINT SCALE ***95-100***—Classic, a great wine; ***90-94***—Outstanding, superior character and style; ***80-89***—Good to very good, a wine with special qualities; ***70-79***—Average, drinkable wine that may have minor flaws; ***60-69*** —Below average, drinkable but not recommended; ***50-59*** —Poor, undrinkable, not recommended. "+"—With a score indicates a range; used primarily with barrel tastings to indicate a preliminary score.

SPECIAL DESIGNATIONS SS—Spectator Selection, CS—Cellar Selection, BB—Best Buy, ($NA)—Price not available, (NR)—Not released.

TASTER'S INITIALS (JG)—Jim Gordon, (HS)—Harvey Steiman, (JL)—James Laube, (JS)—James Suckling, (TM)—Thomas Matthews, (TR)—Terry Robards, (PM)—Per-Henrik Mansson, (BT)—Barrel Tasting (these wines were tasted blind from barrel samples), (CA-date)—*California's Great Cabernets* by James Laube, (CH-date)—*California's Great Chardonnays* by James Laube, (VP-date)—*Vintage Port* by James Suckling.

DATE TASTED Dates in parentheses represent the issue in which the rating was published.

Nebbiolo Vigna Arborina 1987 $32 (9/15/90) **84**
Nebbiolo Vigna Arborina 1986 $20 (2/28/89) **90**
Nebbiolo Vigna Larigi 1987 $28 (5/31/90) **89**

ALTESINO (Italy/Tuscany)
Alte d'Altesi 1988 $35 (9/15/91) **92**
Alte d'Altesi 1987 $35 (1/31/92) **69**
Alte d'Altesi 1986 $32 (7/15/89) **85**
Brunello di Montalcino 1982 $22 (9/15/86) **85**
Brunello di Montalcino 1981 $22 (9/15/86) **80**
Brunello di Montalcino 1980 $18 (9/15/86) **91**
Brunello di Montalcino 1979 $20 (9/15/86) **82**
Brunello di Montalcino Riserva 1983 $29 (11/30/89) **86**
Brunello di Montalcino Vigna Altesino 1985 $32 (9/30/90) **91**
Brunello di Montalcino Vigna Altesino 1983 $26 (1/31/90) **84**
Palazzo Altesi 1988 $26 (9/15/91) **90**
Palazzo Altesi 1987 $25 (1/31/92) **78**
Palazzo Altesi 1985 $23 (10/31/90) **82**
Palazzo Altesi 1983 $17 (2/15/88) **88**
Rosso di Altesino 1989 $8 (1/31/92) BB **86**
Rosso di Montalcino 1988 $14.50 (7/15/91) **73**
Rosso di Montalcino 1986 $10 (7/15/89) **80**

FATTORIA DI AMA (Italy/Tuscany)
Castello di Ama Vigna il Chiuso 1988 (NR) (9/15/91) **90**
Chardonnay Colline di Ama 1988 $17 (9/15/89) **82**
Chardonnay Colline di Ama 1987 $17 (9/15/89) **82**
Chardonnay Colline di Ama 1986 $17 (9/15/89) **79**
Chianti Classico Castello di Ama 1988 $18 (4/15/91) **87**
Chianti Classico Castello di Ama 1987 $9 (11/30/89) (HS) **87**
Chianti Classico Castello di Ama 1986 $8 (1/31/89) **87**
Chianti Classico Castello di Ama Vigneto Bellavista 1986 $36 (11/30/89) (HS) **90**
Chianti Classico Castello di Ama Vigneto Bellavista 1985 $30 (7/31/89) **94**
Chianti Classico Castello di Ama Vigneto Bellavista 1983 $25 (12/15/87) **90**
Chianti Classico Castello di Ama Vigneto La Casuccia Riserva 1986 $40 (11/30/89) (HS) **87**
Chianti Classico Castello di Ama Vigneto La Casuccia Riserva 1985 $40 (9/15/91) **89**
Chianti Classico Castello di Ama Vigneto San Lorenzo 1986 $36 (11/30/89) (HS) **84**
Chianti Classico Castello di Ama Vigneto San Lorenzo 1985 $32 (11/30/89) (HS) **86**
Colline di Ama 1986 $9 (11/15/87) **82**
Vigna l'Apparita Merlot 1988 (NR) (9/15/91) **93**
Vigna l'Apparita Merlot 1986 (NR) (11/30/89) (HS) **87**
Vigna l'Apparita Merlot 1985 (NR) (11/30/89) (HS) **92**

AMADOR FOOTHILL (United States/California)
Zinfandel Fiddletown Eschen Vineyard 1986 $9 (6/15/89) **82**
Zinfandel Fiddletown Eschen Vineyard 1984 $9 (10/15/88) **86**
Zinfandel Fiddletown Eschen Vineyard Special Selection 1982 $9 (4/15/87) **74**
Zinfandel Shenandoah Valley Ferrero Vineyard Special Selection 1989 $10 (3/31/92) **81**
Zinfandel Shenandoah Valley Grand-Père Vineyard Special Selection 1988 $10 (8/31/91) **75**

AMBRA (Italy/Tuscany)
Barco Reale 1985 $7 (4/15/88) **76**
Carmignano 1986 $12.50 (5/15/89) **80**

BERTRAND AMBROISE (France/Burgundy)
Bourgogne Blanc Chardonnay Blanc 1989 $15 (8/31/91) **86**
Corton Le Rognet 1989 $45 (1/31/92) **93**
Côte de Nuits-Villages 1989 $20 (1/31/92) **86**
Nuits-St.-Georges 1989 $30 (1/31/92) **90**
Nuits-St.-Georges en Rue de Chaux 1989 $38 (1/31/92) **91**
Nuits-St.-Georges en Rue de Chaux 1988 $40 (5/15/91) **93**
Nuits-St.-Georges Les Vaucrains 1989 $38 (1/31/92) **94**

MAISON AMBROISE (France/Burgundy)
Corton Le Rognet 1988 $43 (11/30/90) **92**
Corton Le Rognet 1987 $38 (3/31/90) **90**
Côte de Nuits-Villages 1987 $15 (2/28/90) **82**

DOMAINE DE L'AMEILLAUD (France/Rhône)
Côtes du Rhône 1984 $4.50 (6/01/86) **72**

AMIOT-BONFILS (France/Burgundy)
Chassagne-Montrachet Les Caillerets 1988 $27 (5/15/90) **70**
Chassagne-Montrachet Les Champs--Gains 1988 $27 (3/31/90) **86**
Montrachet 1988 $135 (2/28/90) **90**
Puligny-Montrachet Les Demoiselles 1988 $33 (3/15/90) **87**

AMIOT-PONSOT (France/Burgundy)
Chassagne-Montrachet Les Champs-Gains 1987 $42 (5/31/89) **86**

DOMAINE PIERRE AMIOT (France/Burgundy)
Clos de la Roche 1988 $75 (3/15/91) **86**
Clos de la Roche 1987 $49 (12/15/89) **86**
Clos de la Roche 1982 $28 (6/16/85) SS **93**
Gevrey-Chambertin Les Combottes 1988 $64 (3/15/91) **89**
Gevrey-Chambertin Les Combottes 1987 $42 (12/15/89) **88**
Morey-St.-Denis Aux Charmes 1982 $18 (7/01/85) **88**
Morey-St.-Denis Les Ruchots 1988 $57 (2/28/91) **80**

AMITY (United States/Oregon)
Pinot Noir Oregon 1988 $10 (5/31/91) **82**
Pinot Noir Oregon 1983 $30 (2/15/90) **73**
Pinot Noir Oregon Gamay Noir 1988 $9 (2/15/90) **84**
Pinot Noir Oregon Winemaker's Reserve 1985 (NR) (2/15/90) **80**
Pinot Noir Oregon Winemaker's Reserve 1983 $30 (2/15/90) **75**
Pinot Noir Willamette Valley 1987 $15 (2/15/90) **81**
Pinot Noir Willamette Valley 1986 $12.50 (2/15/90) **74**
Pinot Noir Willamette Valley 1985 $25 (2/15/90) **85**
Pinot Noir Willamette Valley 1982 $9.50 (3/01/86) **77**
Pinot Noir Willamette Valley Estate 1987 $25 (2/15/90) **79**
Pinot Noir Willamette Valley Estate 1985 $25 (2/15/90) **79**
Pinot Noir Willamette Valley Estate 1983 $30 (2/15/90) **76**
Pinot Noir Willamette Valley Winemaker's Reserve 1987 $30 (2/15/90) **83**

AMIZETTA (United States/California)
Cabernet Sauvignon Napa Valley 1985 $16 (5/31/88) **70**

ANCIEN DOMAINE DU CHAPITRE DE MACON (France/Burgundy)
St.-Véran Les Colombières 1988 $12 (8/31/90) **75**

ANDERSON VALLEY (United States/New Mexico)
Cabernet Sauvignon New Mexico 1986 $11 (7/31/89) **80**
Cabernet Sauvignon New Mexico Reserve 1987 $14 (2/29/92) **84**
Chardonnay New Mexico Barrel Fermented 1987 $8.50 (4/15/89) **79**

Muscat Canelli New Mexico 1990 $6 (2/29/92) **70**
Sauvignon Blanc New Mexico 1990 $6 (2/29/92) **76**
Sauvignon Blanc New Mexico 1987 $7 (4/15/89) **79**

S. ANDERSON (United States/California)
Blanc de Noirs Napa Valley 1987 $19 (6/15/91) **86**
Blanc de Noirs Napa Valley 1986 $20 (12/31/90) **83**
Blanc de Noirs Napa Valley 1985 $16 (5/31/89) **87**
Blanc de Noirs Napa Valley 1984 $16 (10/15/88) **79**
Blanc de Noirs Napa Valley 1983 $28 (5/31/89) **85**
Blanc de Noirs Tivoli Brut Noir NV $12 (6/15/91) **73**
Brut Napa Valley 1986 $18 (12/15/91) **86**
Brut Napa Valley 1985 $18 (6/15/91) **87**
Brut Napa Valley 1984 $18 (10/15/88) **82**
Brut Napa Valley 1983 $16 (5/31/87) **72**
Cabernet Sauvignon Stags Leap District Richard Chambers Vineyard 1991 (NR) (5/15/92) (BT) **92+**
Cabernet Sauvignon Stags Leap District Richard Chambers Vineyard 1990 (NR) (5/15/91) (BT) **90+**
Cabernet Sauvignon Stags Leap District Richard Chambers Vineyard 1989 (NR) (5/15/91) (BT) **90+**
Chardonnay Stags Leap District 1990 $19 (7/15/92) **82**
Chardonnay Stags Leap District 1989 $18 (12/31/91) **84**
Chardonnay Stags Leap District 1988 $18 (12/31/90) **79**
Chardonnay Stags Leap District 1987 Rel: $16 Cur: $18 (CH-6/90) **85**
Chardonnay Stags Leap District 1986 Rel: $16 Cur: $18 (CH-3/90) **81**
Chardonnay Stags Leap District 1985 Rel: $14 Cur: $25 (CH-3/90) **92**
Chardonnay Stags Leap District 1984 Rel: $12.50 Cur: $25 (CH-3/90) **89**
Chardonnay Stags Leap District 1983 Rel: $12.50 Cur: $25 (CH-3/90) **86**
Chardonnay Stags Leap District 1982 Rel: $12.50 Cur: $21 (CH-3/90) **72**
Chardonnay Stags Leap District 1981 Rel: $12.50 Cur: $25 (CH-3/90) **80**
Chardonnay Stags Leap District 1980 Rel: $12.50 Cur: $30 (CH-3/90) **83**
Chardonnay Stags Leap District Proprietor's Reserve 1987 $20 (CH-3/90) **89**
Chardonnay Stags Leap District Proprietor's Selection 1983 Rel: $16 Cur: $40 (CH-3/90) **87**

ANDERSON'S CONN VALLEY (United States/California)
Cabernet Sauvignon Napa Valley Estate Reserve 1988 $24 (11/15/91) **92**

PIERRE ANDRE (France/Burgundy)
Châteauneuf-du-Pape 1988 $23 (3/31/91) **84**
Châteauneuf-du-Pape Blanc 1990 $19 (11/15/91) **83**
Châteauneuf-du-Pape Blanc 1984 $17 (10/01/85) **84**
Corton Clos du Roi 1985 $45 (7/15/88) **88**
Corton Pougets 1985 $45 (7/15/88) **90**
Meursault 1989 $23 (8/31/91) **84**
Puligny-Montrachet 1989 $32 (8/31/91) **87**
Savigny-lès-Beaune Clos des Guettes 1985 $20 (7/31/88) **85**

CHATEAU ANDRON BLANQUET (France/Bordeaux)
St.-Estèphe 1990 (NR) (5/15/92) (BT) **80+**

ANGAS (Australia)
Brut Australia NV $8 (12/31/87) **76**
Brut Rosé Australia NV $8 (12/31/87) **78**

D'ANGELO (Italy/Other)
Aglianico del Vulture 1985 $18 (9/15/89) **70**

ANGELS CREEK (United States/California)
Merlot California 1989 $9 (5/31/92) **71**

CHATEAU L'ANGELUS (France/Bordeaux)
St.-Emilion 1990 (NR) (5/15/92) (BT) **90+**
St.-Emilion 1989 $53 (3/15/92) **94**
St.-Emilion 1988 $41 (3/31/91) **93**
St.-Emilion 1987 $30 (5/15/90) **85**
St.-Emilion 1986 Rel: $26 Cur: $30 (6/30/89) **94**
St.-Emilion 1985 Rel: $26 Cur: $32 (3/31/88) CS **94**
St.-Emilion 1983 Rel: $22 Cur: $30 (3/16/86) **92**
St.-Emilion 1982 Rel: $20 Cur: $32 (5/15/89) (TR) **88**
St.-Emilion 1979 $27 (10/15/89) (JS) **82**
St.-Emilion 1962 $45 (11/30/87) (JS) **68**

CHATEAU D'ANGLUDET (France/Bordeaux)
Margaux 1991 (NR) (5/15/92) (BT) **85+**
Margaux 1990 (NR) (5/15/92) (BT) **90+**
Margaux 1989 $33 (3/15/92) **87**
Margaux 1988 $22 (2/28/91) **85**
Margaux 1987 Rel: $13 Cur: $16 (5/15/90) **78**
Margaux 1986 Rel: $17 Cur: $25 (11/30/89) (JS) **90**
Margaux 1986 Rel: $17 Cur: $25 (6/15/89) **91**
Margaux 1985 Rel: $17 Cur: $23 (4/15/88) **90**
Margaux 1983 Rel: $17 Cur: $38 (10/15/86) **93**
Margaux 1982 Rel: $15 Cur: $25 (11/30/89) (JS) **90**
Margaux 1982 Rel: $15 Cur: $25 (12/01/85) CS **95**

ANKENY (United States/Oregon)
Pinot Noir Willamette Valley Estate Bottled 1986 $9 (6/15/88) **68**

PERE ANSELME (France/Rhône)
Châteauneuf-du-Pape 1986 $14 (10/15/91) **84**
Châteauneuf-du-Pape 1985 $14 (10/15/91) **86**
Châteauneuf-du-Pape 1983 Rel: $12 Cur: $23 (10/15/91) **89**
Châteauneuf-du-Pape 1981 $25 (10/15/91) **88**
Châteauneuf-du-Pape Blanc 1990 $20 (10/15/91) **82**
Châteauneuf-du-Pape Clos-Bimard 1989 (NR) (10/15/91) **84**
Châteauneuf-du-Pape Clos Bimard Cuvée Prestige 1988 $20 (10/15/91) **88**
Châteauneuf-du-Pape La Fiole 1984 $12 (10/31/87) **88**
Châteauneuf-du-Pape La Fiole Grand Cuvée 1984 $13 (10/31/87) **74**
Châteauneuf-du-Pape La Fiole du Pape NV $14 (9/30/89) **86**
Châteauneuf-du-Pape La Fiole du Pape Uno Bono Fiolo NV $13 (1/31/88) **82**
Côte-Rôtie Tête de Cuvée 1982 $13 (10/15/87) **68**
Côtes du Rhône-Villages Marescal 1985 $5.25 (12/31/87) **75**
Côtes du Rhône-Villages Seguret 1986 $5.25 (5/15/89) **72**
Crozes-Hermitage 1986 $7.75 (7/31/89) **80**
Crozes-Hermitage 1983 $7.50 (10/15/87) BB **84**
Merlot Vin de Pays des Côteaux d'Enserune NV $5.50 (7/15/89) **78**

ANSELMI (Italy/Other)
Recioto della Valpolicella 1985 $19 (6/30/91) **86**
Soave Classico Capitel Foscarino 1989 $20 (7/15/91) **76**
Soave Classico Superiore 1989 $8 (7/15/91) **81**

ANTINORI (Italy/Tuscany)
Bianco Toscano 1988 $6.50 (10/15/89) BB **85**
Castello della Sala Borro della Sala 1990 $13 (1/31/92) **79**
Castello della Sala Borro della Sala 1989 $11.50 (1/31/91) **86**
Castello della Sala Borro della Sala 1987 $10 (10/15/89) **77**
Castello della Sala Cervaro della Sala 1989 $23 (1/31/92) **85**
Castello della Sala Cervaro della Sala 1988 $21 (1/31/91) **89**
Castello della Sala Cervaro della Sala 1987 $20 (4/30/90) **83**
Chianti Classico 1988 $11 (9/15/91) **86**
Chianti Classico Pèppoli 1988 $19 (9/15/91) **88**
Chianti Classico Pèppoli 1987 Rel: $17 Cur: $22 (5/15/90) **83**
Chianti Classico Pèppoli 1986 Rel: $17 Cur: $22 (7/15/89) **90**
Chianti Classico Pèppoli 1985 Rel: $16 Cur: $22 (5/31/88) **92**
Chianti Classico Riserva 1985 $9 (10/15/89) **89**
Chianti Classico Riserva 1982 $10 (11/30/89) (HS) **87**
Chianti Classico Santa Cristina 1985 $6 (10/31/88) BB **90**
Chianti Classico Tenute Marchese Riserva 1987 (NR) (11/30/89) (HS) **88**
Chianti Classico Tenute Marchese Riserva 1985 $21 (9/15/91) **91**
Chianti Classico Tenute Marchese Riserva 1983 $16 (11/30/89) (HS) **90**
Chianti Classico Tenute Marchese Riserva 1982 Rel: $16 Cur: $19 (5/31/89) **90**
Chianti Classico Tenute Marchese Riserva 1980 $16 (9/15/87) **90**
Chianti Classico Tenute Marchesi Riserva 1985 $21 (10/31/91) **88**
Chianti Classico Villa Antinori Riserva 1987 $11 (11/30/91) **82**
Chianti Classico Villa Antinori Riserva 1983 $9.25 (3/31/89) **79**
Galestro 1990 $7 (8/31/91) **75**
Galestro 1989 $7 (12/31/90) **79**
Orvieto Classico 1987 $5 (5/15/89) **78**
Orvieto Classico Campogrande Secco 1990 $7.25 (3/31/92) **78**
Orvieto Classico Campogrande Secco 1989 $7.25 (7/15/91) **80**
Orvieto Classico Castello della Sala 1990 $13 (3/31/92) **83**
Santa Cristina 1989 $7 (7/15/91) **80**
Santa Cristina 1988 $6.50 (1/31/91) BB **85**
Santa Cristina 1987 $6 (4/30/89) BB **81**
Solàia 1988 $65 (9/15/91) **92**
Solàia 1985 Rel: $62 Cur: $110 (12/15/89) **92**
Solàia 1982 $62 (7/31/87) **81**
Tignanello 1988 Rel: $33 Cur: $41 (9/15/91) **91**
Tignanello 1985 Rel: $30 Cur: $40 (4/15/90) **87**
Tignanello 1983 Rel: $25 Cur: $41 (12/15/89) **88**
Tignanello 1982 Rel: $37 Cur: $43 (7/15/87) CS **91**

PHILIPPE ANTOINE (France/Beaujolais)
Beaujolais-Villages 1988 $5.50 (5/31/89) (TM) **77**
Brouilly 1988 $11.50 (5/31/89) (TM) **82**
Fleurie 1988 $11.50 (5/31/89) (TM) **84**
Juliénas 1988 $11.50 (5/31/89) (TM) **85**
Moulin-à-Vent 1988 $11.50 (5/31/89) (TM) **88**
Régnié 1988 $11.50 (5/31/89) (TM) **81**
Pouilly-Fuissé 1986 $15 (4/30/88) **79**
St.-Véran 1986 $10 (4/30/88) **83**

ANTONUTTI (Italy/Other)
Poggio Alto 1986 $15 (4/15/90) **86**

ARBOR CREST (United States/Washington)
Cabernet Sauvignon Columbia Valley 1988 $11 (9/30/91) **87**
Cabernet Sauvignon Columbia Valley Bacchus Vineyard 1985 $11 (10/15/89) **80**
Cabernet Sauvignon Columbia Valley Bacchus Vineyard 1983 $12.50 (12/15/87) **77**
Chardonnay Columbia Valley 1988 $9.50 (3/31/90) **85**
Chardonnay Columbia Valley 1987 $9.25 (10/15/89) **84**
Chardonnay Columbia Valley 1984 $9.25 (7/31/87) **78**
Chardonnay Washington Sagemoore Vineyards 1983 $10 (11/01/85) **69**
Chardonnay Washington Sagemoore Vineyards 1982 $14 (1/01/85) **85**
Merlot Columbia Valley 1990 $11.50 (4/15/92) **88**
Merlot Columbia Valley 1988 $9 (8/31/91) **81**
Merlot Columbia Valley 1987 $8 (10/15/89) **83**
Merlot Columbia Valley Bacchus Vineyard 1985 $8 (7/31/87) **75**
Merlot Columbia Valley Bacchus Vineyard 1982 $8.25 (11/01/84) **82**
Merlot Columbia Valley Bacchus Vineyard Cameo Reserve 1985 $10 (12/15/87) **83**
Merlot Columbia Valley Cameo Reserve 1989 $12 (3/31/92) **77**
Merlot Columbia Valley Cameo Reserve 1988 $12 (8/31/91) **83**
Merlot Columbia Valley Cameo Reserve 1987 $11 (6/15/90) **85**
Riesling Columbia Valley Dry 1990 $5.75 (11/15/91) **78**
Sauvignon Blanc Columbia Valley 1989 $7.50 (8/31/91) **85**
Sauvignon Blanc Columbia Valley Wahluke Slope 1987 $7.50 (10/15/89) **85**

CHATEAU D'ARCHE (France/Sauternes)
Sauternes 1988 $20/375ml (4/30/91) **87**
Sauternes 1987 (NR) (6/15/90) **85**
Sauternes 1986 $32 (12/31/89) **85**
Sauternes 1983 Rel: $23 Cur: $39 (1/31/88) **93**

CHATEAU D'ARCHE-PUGNEAU (France/Sauternes)
Sauternes 1989 (NR) (6/15/90) (BT) **75+**
Sauternes 1988 (NR) (6/15/90) (BT) **75+**
Sauternes 1987 (NR) (6/15/90) **71**

ARCIERO (United States/California)
Cabernet Sauvignon Paso Robles 1986 $8.50 (11/15/90) **80**
Cabernet Sauvignon Paso Robles 1985 $6 (12/31/87) **77**
Chardonnay Paso Robles 1987 $9 (12/15/89) **72**
Muscat Canelli Paso Robles 1988 $6 (12/15/89) **67**
White Riesling Late Harvest Santa Barbara County December Harvest 1985 $10.50 (12/15/89) **84**
Zinfandel Paso Robles 1985 $7.50 (12/15/89) **78**

VIGNERONS ARDECHOIS (France/Other)
Vin de Pays des Côteaux de l'Ardeche 1988 $4.50 (4/30/90) BB **79**

ARGIANO (Italy/Tuscany)
Brunello di Montalcino 1979 $11 (9/15/86) **77**
Brunello di Montalcino Riserva 1978 $12 (9/15/86) **68**
Brunello di Montalcino Riserva 1977 $13 (9/15/86) **67**

ARGYLE (United States/Oregon)
Blanc de Blancs Willamette Valley Cuvée Limited 1987 $23 (11/15/91) **83**
Brut Oregon Cuvée Limited 1987 $18.50 (12/31/90) **82**
Brut Willamette Valley Cuvée Limited 1988 $18 (5/15/92) **87**
Chardonnay Oregon Barrel Fermented 1987 $18.50 (12/15/90) **93**
Rosé Willamette Valley Cuvée Limited 1987 $23 (11/15/91) **82**

MARQUES DE ARIENZO (Spain)
Rioja 1987 $7.50 (3/31/92) **84**
Rioja 1986 $7.50 (3/31/92) **81**
Rioja 1985 $8 (7/31/89) BB **84**
Rioja 1983 $5 (6/30/88) BB **81**

Rioja Gran Reserva 1982 $23 (3/31/92) **83**
Rioja Gran Reserva 1981 $18 (3/31/92) **84**
Rioja Gran Reserva 1978 $18 (3/31/90) (TM) **78**
Rioja Gran Reserva 1976 $18 (3/31/92) **87**
Rioja Reserva 1985 $12 (3/31/92) **84**
Rioja Reserva 1983 $12 (3/31/92) **85**
Rioja Reserva 1981 $12 (7/31/89) **83**
Rioja Reserva 1980 $8 (6/30/88) **76**

ARIES (United States/California)
Pinot Noir Los Carneros Cuvée Vivace 1989 $8 (4/30/91) **70**

ARLAUD (France/Burgundy)
Bonnes Mares 1983 $30 (12/01/85) **91**

DOMAINE DE L'ARLOT (France/Burgundy)
Côte de Nuits-Villages Clos du Châpeau 1989 (NR) (1/31/92) **83**
Côte de Nuits-Villages Clos du Châpeau 1988 $21 (3/31/91) **80**
Nuits-St.-Georges Blanc Clos de l'Arlot 1988 $27/375ml (4/30/91) **84**
Nuits-St.-Georges Clos de l'Arlot 1989 (NR) (1/31/92) **78**
Nuits-St.-Georges Clos de l'Arlot 1988 $43 (3/31/91) **87**
Nuits-St.-Georges Clos des Forêts St.-Georges 1989 (NR) (1/31/92) **90**
Nuits-St.-Georges Clos des Forêts St.-Georges 1988 $53 (3/31/91) **85**
Nuits-St.-Georges Clos des Forêts St.-Georges 1987 $43 (3/31/90) **83**

CHATEAU ARMAILHAC (France/Bordeaux)
Pauillac 1991 (NR) (5/15/92) (BT) **85+**
Pauillac 1990 (NR) (5/15/92) (BT) **85+**
Pauillac 1989 $26 (3/15/92) **94**

CHATEAU D'ARMAJAN-DES-ORMES (France/Sauternes)
Sauternes 1989 (NR) (6/15/90) (BT) **90+**
Sauternes 1987 (NR) (6/15/90) **72**

COMTE ARMAND (France/Burgundy)
Pommard Clos des Epeneaux 1988 $46 (2/28/91) **90**
Pommard Clos des Epeneaux 1987 $41 (8/31/90) **81**
Pommard Clos des Epeneaux 1985 $44 (3/15/88) **91**

ARMIDA (United States/California)
Chardonnay Russian River Valley 1990 $14 (2/15/92) **81**
Merlot Russian River Valley 1990 $14 (5/31/92) **78**

CHATEAU ARNAULD (France/Bordeaux)
Haut-Médoc 1991 (NR) (5/15/92) (BT) **75+**
Haut-Médoc 1990 (NR) (5/15/92) (BT) **80+**
Haut-Médoc 1989 $14 (3/15/92) **88**
Haut-Médoc 1988 $15 (4/30/91) **84**
Haut-Médoc 1987 $13 (11/30/89) (JS) **79**
Haut-Médoc 1986 $18 (11/30/89) (JS) **82**
Haut-Médoc 1985 $15 (2/15/88) **82**
Haut-Médoc 1983 $8 (1/01/86) **75**
Haut-Médoc 1982 $17 (11/30/89) (JS) **71**

ROBERT ARNOUX (France/Burgundy)
Clos Vougeot 1988 $70 (3/15/91) **78**
Romanée-St.-Vivant 1988 $250 (11/15/90) **91**
Vosne-Romanée Les Chaumes 1988 $45 (2/28/91) **80**
Vosne-Romanée Les Suchots 1988 $60 (2/28/91) **86**
Vosne-Romanée Les Suchots 1985 $52 (7/31/88) **90**

B. ARRIGONI (Italy/Tuscany)
Chianti Putto 1987 $4.50 (11/30/89) **78**

CHATEAU L'ARROSEE (France/Bordeaux)
St.-Emilion 1989 $40 (4/30/92) **93**
St.-Emilion 1988 $34 (3/15/91) **94**
St.-Emilion 1987 $25 (5/15/90) **82**
St.-Emilion 1986 Rel: $31 Cur: $36 (2/15/89) **87**
St.-Emilion 1985 Rel: $24 Cur: $47 (2/29/88) **85**
St.-Emilion 1983 Rel: $20 Cur: $34 (5/16/86) **87**
St.-Emilion 1982 $45 (5/15/89) (TR) **91**

ARROWFIELD (Australia)
Chardonnay South Eastern Australia 1990 $4 (5/31/92) **77**

ARROWOOD (United States/California)
Cabernet Sauvignon Sonoma County 1988 Rel: $23 Cur: $26 (11/15/91) **88**
Cabernet Sauvignon Sonoma County 1987 Rel: $22 Cur: $25 (11/15/90) **87**
Cabernet Sauvignon Sonoma County 1986 Rel: $20 Cur: $25 (10/15/89) **92**
Cabernet Sauvignon Sonoma County 1985 Rel: $19 Cur: $35 (12/15/88) **94**
Chardonnay Sonoma County 1989 Rel: $19 Cur: $21 (7/15/91) **85**
Chardonnay Sonoma County 1988 Rel: $18 Cur: $21 (4/30/90) **92**
Chardonnay Sonoma County 1987 Rel: $18 Cur: $21 (CH-4/90) **89**
Chardonnay Sonoma County 1986 Rel: $18 Cur: $25 (CH-4/90) **89**
Chardonnay Sonoma County Réserve Spéciale 1989 $45/1.5L (1/31/92) **92**
Chardonnay Sonoma County Réserve Spéciale 1988 Rel: $50/1.5L Cur: $60/1.5L (CH-4/90) **92**
Merlot Sonoma County 1988 $25 (5/31/92) **88**

BODEGAS ISMAEL ARROYO (Spain)
Ribera del Duero Mesoñeros de Castilla 1986 $6 (4/30/88) **60**

VINCENT ARROYO (United States/California)
Cabernet Sauvignon Napa Valley 1987 $12 (11/15/90) **91**

CHATEAU D'ARSAC (France/Bordeaux)
Haut-Médoc 1989 $9 (3/15/92) **82**

Key to Symbols

The scores reported here are the results of blind tastings conducted by our panel of senior editors. Wines that carry the initials below are results of individual tastings.

THE WINE SPECTATOR 100-POINT SCALE 95-100—Classic, a great wine; ***90-94***—Outstanding, superior character and style; ***80-89***—Good to very good, a wine with special qualities; ***70-79***—Average, drinkable wine that may have minor flaws; ***60-69***—Below average, drinkable but not recommended; ***50-59***—Poor, undrinkable, not recommended. "+"—With a score indicates a range; used primarily with barrel tastings to indicate a preliminary score.

SPECIAL DESIGNATIONS SS—Spectator Selection, CS—Cellar Selection, BB—Best Buy, ($NA)—Price not available, (NR)—Not released.

TASTER'S INITIALS (JG)—Jim Gordon, (HS)—Harvey Steiman, (JL)—James Laube, (JS)—James Suckling, (TM)—Thomas Matthews, (TR)—Terry Robards, (PM)—Per-Henrik Mansson, (BT)—Barrel Tasting (these wines were tasted blind from barrel samples), (CA-date)—*California's Great Cabernets* by James Laube, (CH-date)—*California's Great Chardonnays* by James Laube, (VP-date)—*Vintage Port* by James Suckling.

DATE TASTED Dates in parentheses represent the issue in which the rating was published.

Haut-Médoc 1988 $7 (6/30/89) (BT) **70+**
Haut-Médoc 1987 $6 (6/30/89) (BT) **70+**
Haut-Médoc 1985 $5.75 (2/15/89) **75**

ARTADI (Spain)
Rioja Alavesa 1987 $6 (4/30/88) **80**

ARTERBERRY (United States/Oregon)
Chardonnay Willamette Valley 1988 $10 (1/31/91) **90**
Pinot Noir Willamette Valley Weber Vineyards 1989 $12 (11/15/91) **85**
Pinot Noir Willamette Valley Winemaker Reserve 1989 $12 (11/15/91) **75**
Pinot Noir Willamette Valley Winemaker's Reserve 1988 $14 (1/31/91) **79**
Pinot Noir Yamhill County Red Hills Vineyard Winemaker's Reserve 1986 $14.75 (6/15/88) **74**
Pinot Noir Yamhill County Red Hills Vineyard Winemaker's Reserve 1985 $16 (6/15/87) **95**
Pinot Noir Yamhill County Red Hills Vineyard Winemaker's Reserve 1983 $16 (2/15/90) **86**
Pinot Noir Yamhill County Weber Vineyards Winemaker's Reserve 1987 $14 (2/15/90) **90**

DAVID ARTHUR (United States/California)
Chardonnay Napa Valley 1989 $15 (4/15/92) **80**
Chardonnay Napa Valley 1985 $13 (4/15/88) **70**

GEHEIMRAT ASCHROTT (Germany)
Riesling Kabinett Rheingau Hochheimer Kirchenstück 1988 (NR) (9/30/89) **79**
Riesling Kabinett Rheingau Hochheimer Stielweg 1988 (NR) (9/30/89) **87**
Riesling Spätlese Halbtrocken Rheingau Hochheimer Hölle 1988 (NR) (9/30/89) **92**
Riesling Spätlese Rheingau Hochheimer Hölle 1988 (NR) (9/30/89) **85**

HUNTER ASHBY (United States/California)
Merlot Napa Valley 1982 $6.50 (12/15/87) **65**

ASHLAND (United States/Oregon)
Chardonnay Rogue Valley Layne Vineyards Reserve 1989 $15 (6/15/92) **70**

ASHLY (United States/California)
Chardonnay Monterey 1986 $16.50 (10/31/88) **65**

ATLAS PEAK (United States/California)
Sangiovese Napa Valley 1989 $24 (11/15/91) **86**

AU BON CLIMAT (United States/California)
Chardonnay Arroyo Grande Valley 1990 $30 (7/15/92) **87**
Chardonnay Santa Barbara County 1990 $16 (7/15/92) **84**
Chardonnay Santa Barbara County 1988 $12.50 (12/15/89) **82**
Chardonnay Santa Barbara County 1987 $14 (3/15/89) **58**
Chardonnay Santa Barbara County Reserve 1989 $25 (7/15/91) **86**
Chardonnay Santa Barbara County Reserve 1988 $35 (3/15/91) **91**
Chardonnay Santa Barbara County Reserve 1987 $20 (12/15/89) **87**
Chardonnay Santa Barbara County Reserve 1986 $20 (6/15/88) **84**
Chardonnay Santa Barbara County Reserve Bien Nacido 1990 $25 (7/15/92) **90**
Chardonnay Santa Barbara County Reserve Los Alamos Vineyard 1987 $20 (12/15/89) **82**
Chardonnay Santa Ynez Valley Benedict Vineyard 1987 $30 (12/15/89) **80**
Pinot Blanc Santa Barbara County 1990 $12.50 (7/15/91) **83**
Pinot Noir Santa Barbara County 1988 $16 (4/30/91) **80**
Pinot Noir Santa Barbara County 1987 $16 (12/15/89) **84**
Pinot Noir Santa Barbara County 1985 $12 (6/15/88) **73**
Pinot Noir Santa Ynez Valley Benedict Vineyard 1987 $30 (12/15/89) **88**
Pinot Noir Santa Ynez Valley Rancho Vinedo Vineyard 1988 $12.50 (12/15/89) **83**

AUDUBON (United States/California)
Cabernet Sauvignon Napa Valley 1985 $11 (6/15/88) **77**
Zinfandel San Luis Obispo County 1983 $7 (7/15/88) **84**

DOMAINE AUFFRAY (France/Chablis)
Chablis 1986 $13 (11/15/87) **66**
Chablis Champs Royaux 1989 $19 (1/31/91) **86**
Chablis Champs Royaux 1988 $12 (3/31/90) **79**
Chablis Champs Royaux 1986 $17 (9/15/88) **88**
Chablis Les Clos 1989 $50 (1/31/91) **92**
Chablis Les Clos 1988 $38 (3/31/90) **92**
Chablis Les Clos 1986 $36 (10/15/88) **70**
Chablis Fourchaume 1986 $24 (9/15/88) **85**
Chablis Montée de Tonnerre 1989 $25 (2/28/91) **74**
Chablis Montée de Tonnerre 1988 $21 (3/31/90) **87**
Chablis Montée de Tonnerre 1986 $24 (10/15/88) **75**
Chablis Les Preuses 1986 $36 (9/15/88) **88**
Chablis Les Preuses 1984 $30 (4/15/87) **92**
Chablis Vaillon 1989 $27 (1/31/91) **88**
Chablis Vaillon 1988 $20 (12/15/89) **93**
Chablis Valmur 1988 $32 (12/15/89) **80**
Chardonnay Vin de Pays de l'Yonne 1988 $8 (4/15/90) **75**

AUGEY (France/Bordeaux)
Bordeaux Blanc 1984 $4.50 (10/15/86) **75**

CHATEAU AUSONE (France/Bordeaux)
St.-Emilion 1990 (NR) (5/15/92) (BT) **95+**
St.-Emilion 1989 $180 (3/15/92) **93**
St.-Emilion 1988 Rel: $76 Cur: $98 (8/31/90) (BT) **95+**
St.-Emilion 1987 Rel: $55 Cur: $68 (6/30/89) (BT) **85+**
St.-Emilion 1986 Rel: $90 Cur: $115 (6/30/89) **85**
St.-Emilion 1985 $100 (5/31/88) **87**
St.-Emilion 1983 $130 (11/30/87) (TR) **96**
St.-Emilion 1982 $170 (5/15/89) (TR) **93**
St.-Emilion 1981 $86 (11/30/87) (TR) **90**
St.-Emilion 1980 $40 (11/30/87) (TR) **86**
St.-Emilion 1979 $100 (10/15/89) (JS) **92**
St.-Emilion 1978 $90 (11/30/87) (TR) **93**
St.-Emilion 1977 $29 (11/30/87) (TR) **83**
St.-Emilion 1976 $130 (11/30/87) (TR) **89**
St.-Emilion 1974 $28 (11/30/87) (TR) **76**
St.-Emilion 1973 $45 (11/30/87) (TR) **77**
St.-Emilion 1972 $30 (11/30/87) (TR) **75**
St.-Emilion 1971 $105 (11/30/87) (TR) **83**
St.-Emilion 1970 $130 (11/30/87) (TR) **82**
St.-Emilion 1969 $27 (11/30/87) (TR) **76**
St.-Emilion 1967 $64 (11/30/87) (TR) **79**
St.-Emilion 1966 $125 (11/30/87) (TR) **85**
St.-Emilion 1964 $87 (11/30/87) (TR) **78**
St.-Emilion 1962 $170 (11/30/87) (JS) **85**
St.-Emilion 1961 $300 (11/30/87) (TR) **82**
St.-Emilion 1959 $230 (10/15/90) (JS) **79**
St.-Emilion 1958 $95 (11/30/87) (TR) **79**
St.-Emilion 1957 $250 (11/30/87) (TR) **74**

St.-Emilion 1956 $175 (11/30/87) (TR) **86**
St.-Emilion 1955 $230 (11/30/87) (TR) **91**
St.-Emilion 1954 $180 (11/30/87) (TR) **87**
St.-Emilion 1953 $280 (11/30/87) (TR) **78**
St.-Emilion 1952 $150 (11/30/87) (TR) **85**
St.-Emilion 1950 $230 (11/30/87) (TR) **78**
St.-Emilion 1949 $500 (11/30/87) (TR) **91**
St.-Emilion 1947 $220 (11/30/87) (TR) **83**
St.-Emilion 1945 $320 (3/16/86) (JL) **75**
St.-Emilion 1943 $350 (11/30/87) (TR) **84**
St.-Emilion 1942 $250 (11/30/87) (TR) **81**
St.-Emilion 1937 $175 (11/30/87) (TR) **83**
St.-Emilion 1936 $300 (11/30/87) (TR) **82**
St.-Emilion 1929 $330 (11/30/87) (TR) **83**
St.-Emilion 1928 $600 (11/30/87) (TR) **83**
St.-Emilion 1926 $620 (11/30/87) (TR) **82**
St.-Emilion 1925 $175 (11/30/87) (TR) **75**
St.-Emilion 1924 $250 (11/30/87) (TR) **95**
St.-Emilion 1923 $200 (11/30/87) (TR) **76**
St.-Emilion 1921 $250 (11/30/87) (TR) **94**
St.-Emilion 1918 $480 (11/30/87) (TR) **87**
St.-Emilion 1916 $430 (11/30/87) (TR) **86**
St.-Emilion 1914 $380 (11/30/87) (TR) **79**
St.-Emilion 1913 $380 (11/30/87) (TR) **81**
St.-Emilion 1912 $380 (11/30/87) (TR) **79**
St.-Emilion 1905 $600 (11/30/87) (TR) **82**
St.-Emilion 1902 $300 (11/30/87) (TR) **83**
St.-Emilion 1900 $1,000 (11/30/87) (TR) **78**
St.-Emilion 1899 $1,200 (11/30/87) (TR) **77**
St.-Emilion 1894 $800 (11/30/87) (TR) **85**
St.-Emilion 1879 $700 (11/30/87) (TR) **93**
St.-Emilion 1877 $2,200 (11/30/87) (TR) **92**

DOMAINE LES AUSSELONS (France/Rhône)
Côtes du Rhône Vinsobres 1987 $8 (6/30/90) **75**

AUSTIN (United States/California)
Cabernet Franc Santa Barbara County 1988 $12 (11/15/90) **76**
Genoux Santa Barbara County 1986 $15 (12/15/89) **74**
Johannisberg Riesling Late Harvest Santa Barbara County Botrytis 1986 $8/375ml (12/15/89) **81**
Muscat Canelli Santa Barbara County 1988 $8.50 (12/15/89) **72**
Pinot Noir Santa Barbara County 1987 $15 (12/15/89) **77**
Pinot Noir Santa Barbara County 1983 $25 (12/15/89) **78**
Pinot Noir Santa Barbara County Artist Series 1988 $10 (12/15/89) **75**
Pinot Noir Santa Barbara County Bien Nacido Vineyard 1982 $10 (3/16/85) **88**
Pinot Noir Santa Barbara County Sierra Madre Vineyards 1982 $12 (5/01/84) **87**
Sauvignon Blanc Late Harvest Santa Barbara County Sierra Madre Vineyard Botrytis 1985 $10/375ml (12/15/89) **72**
White Riesling Santa Barbara County Los Alamos Vineyards 1987 $6.50 (12/15/89) **83**

AUTUMN WIND (United States/Oregon)
Pinot Noir Willamette Valley 1988 $12 (4/15/91) **80**
Pinot Noir Willamette Valley 1987 $15 (2/15/90) **83**

DOMAINE D'AUVENAY (France/Burgundy)
Auxey-Duresses Rouge 1989 $42 (1/31/92) **88**
Meursault Les Narvaux 1989 $60 (8/31/91) **96**
Puligny-Montrachet Les Folatières 1989 $95 (8/31/91) **97**

AVIA (Yugoslavia)
Cabernet Sauvignon Yugoslavia Primorska 1985 $3 (3/31/89) **77**
Merlot Yugoslavia Primorska Hrvatska-Istra 1985 $3 (3/31/89) **75**

AVIGNONESI (Italy/Tuscany)
1988 $45 (9/15/91) **93**
Chardonnay Il Marzocco 1987 Rel: $18 Cur: $23 (9/15/89) **90**
Chardonnay Il Marzocco 1986 $16 (2/15/88) **92**
Grifi 1988 $25 (9/15/91) **91**
Grifi 1987 $21 (4/15/91) **86**
Grifi 1986 $18 (1/31/89) **86**
Grifi 1985 Rel: $16 Cur: $36 (2/15/88) **85**
Grifi 1983 Rel: $12 Cur: $30 (6/01/86) **91**
Grifi 1982 Rel: $10 Cur: $30 (6/16/85) **87**
Rosso di Montepulciano 1989 $12 (4/30/91) **83**
Sauvignon Blanc Il Vignola 1988 $20 (10/15/89) **87**
Terre di Cortona 1987 Rel: $12 Cur: $23 (3/31/89) **83**
Terre di Cortona 1986 $9.50 (2/15/88) **87**
Vin Santo 1977 $18 (10/01/85) **92**
Vino Nobile di Montepulciano 1985 $12 (2/15/88) **86**
Vino Nobile di Montepulciano 1981 $7.25 (10/01/85) **86**
Vino Nobile di Montepulciano 1980 $6.75 (7/01/85) **85**

AYALA (France/Champagne)
Brut Blanc de Blancs Champagne 1985 $33 (12/31/90) **90**
Brut Blanc de Blancs Champagne 1982 $29 (4/15/88) **85**
Brut Champagne 1985 $59 (12/31/90) **89**
Brut Champagne 1983 $30 (12/31/89) **80**
Brut Champagne 1982 $27 (4/15/88) **86**
Brut Champagne NV $30 (12/31/91) **86**
Brut Champagne NV $23 (4/15/88) **83**
Brut Champagne Extra Quality NV $28 (12/31/87) **78**
Brut Champagne Grand Cuvée 1985 $57 (12/31/89) **84**
Brut Champagne Grand Cuvée 1982 $52 (4/15/88) **87**
Brut Rosé Champagne NV $26 (4/15/88) **85**
Brut Rosé Champagne Extra Quality NV $20 (5/31/87) **80**

BABCOCK (United States/California)
Chardonnay Santa Barbara County 1990 $13 (7/15/92) **82**
Chardonnay Santa Barbara County 1989 $16 (5/15/92) **77**
Chardonnay Santa Ynez Valley 1987 $12 (12/15/89) **82**
Chardonnay Santa Ynez Valley 1986 $11 (2/15/88) **66**
Chardonnay Santa Ynez Valley Reserve 1986 $14 (2/15/88) **80**
Chardonnay Santa Ynez Valley Reserve Selected Barrels 1987 $20 (12/15/89) **90**
Gewürztraminer Santa Ynez Valley 1987 $6.50 (2/28/89) **73**
Johannisberg Riesling Late Harvest Santa Ynez Valley Cluster Selected 1987 $14/375ml (12/15/89) **89**
Johannisberg Riesling Santa Ynez Valley 1986 $6 (12/15/89) **88**
Sauvignon Blanc Santa Ynez Valley 1987 $8 (12/15/89) **65**

BABICH (New Zealand)
Cabernet Sauvignon Hawke's Bay 1989 $10 (7/15/91) **74**
Chardonnay Hawke's Bay 1989 $12 (9/15/91) **71**
Chardonnay Hawke's Bay Irongate 1989 $17 (3/31/91) **88**
Chardonnay Henderson Valley 1986 $10 (5/15/88) **86**

ESTATE WILLIAM BACCALA (United States/California)
Chardonnay Mendocino 1984 $11 (1/31/87) **70**
Merlot Alexander Valley 1984 $10 (2/28/87) **72**

DOMAINE BACHELET (France/Burgundy)
Charmes-Chambertin Vieilles Vignes 1986 $43 (7/15/89) **87**
Gevrey-Chambertin Les Corbeaux Vieilles Vignes 1986 $30 (7/15/89) **83**
Gevrey-Chambertin Vieilles Vignes 1986 $24 (7/15/89) **88**

BACHELET-RAMONET (France/Burgundy)
Bienvenues-Bâtard-Montrachet 1979 (NR) (2/29/88) **93**
Chassagne-Montrachet 1988 $37 (4/30/91) **80**
Chassagne-Montrachet 1987 $36 (11/15/89) **87**
Chassagne-Montrachet Caillerets 1987 $35 (5/15/90) **87**
Chassagne-Montrachet Caillerets 1985 $41 (2/29/88) **91**

BADIA A COLTIBUONO (Italy/Tuscany)
Chianti Cetamura 1988 $7 (12/15/90) BB **82**
Chianti Classico 1987 $8 (11/30/89) (HS) **85**
Chianti Classico Riserva 1985 $16 (9/15/91) **90**
Chianti Classico Riserva 1983 $15 (11/30/89) (HS) **78**
Chianti Classico Riserva 1982 $13 (7/31/88) **88**
Coltibuono Rosso 1986 $6.75 (7/31/88) **81**
Sangioveto 1985 ($NA) (11/30/89) (HS) **85**
Sangioveto 1983 $20 (11/30/89) (HS) **84**
Sangioveto 1983 $20 (9/15/87) (HS) **93**
Sangioveto 1982 $20 (11/30/89) (HS) **87**
Sangioveto 1981 $21 (9/15/87) (HS) **87**

FATTORIA BAGGIOLINO (Italy/Tuscany)
Poggio Brandi 1986 $19 (8/31/91) **86**
Poggio Brandi 1985 $19 (9/15/89) **84**

CHATEAU BAHANS-HAUT-BRION (France/Bordeaux)
Pessac-Léognan 1991 (NR) (5/15/92) (BT) **85+**
Pessac-Léognan 1990 (NR) (5/15/92) (BT) **90+**
Pessac-Léognan 1989 $32 (3/15/92) **90**
Pessac-Léognan 1988 $20 (8/31/90) (BT) **80+**
Pessac-Léognan 1987 $19 (6/30/89) (BT) **75+**
Pessac-Léognan 1986 Rel: $22 Cur: $26 (9/15/89) **86**
Graves 1985 $20 (5/15/87) (BT) **80+**

ALEXIS BAILLY (United States/Minnesota)
Country Red Minnesota NV $7 (2/29/92) **78**
Maréchal Foch Minnesota 1990 $9 (2/29/92) **77**
Léon Millot Minnesota 1990 $9 (2/29/92) **74**

BAINBRIDGE ISLAND (United States/Washington)
Müller-Thurgau Washington 1987 $6 (10/15/89) **84**
Müller-Thurgau Washington Dry 1987 $6 (10/15/89) **77**
Siegerrebe Botrytis Affected Washington 1987 $15/375ml (10/15/89) **71**

CANTINE BAIOCCHI (Italy/Tuscany)
Vino Nobile di Montepulciano 1986 $15 (3/15/91) **87**
Vino Nobile di Montepulciano Riserva 1985 $10 (11/30/89) **85**

BALADA (Spain)
Penedès Macabeo Gran Blanc 1988 $8 (3/31/90) **75**

BALBACH (Germany)
Riesling Auslese Rheinhessen Niersteiner Hipping 1989 (NR) (12/15/90) **80**
Riesling Auslese Rheinhessen Niersteiner Oelberg 1990 (NR) (12/15/91) **90**
Riesling Auslese Rheinhessen Niersteiner Pettenthal 1989 (NR) (12/15/90) **84**
Riesling Auslese Rheinhessen Niersteiner Pettenthal 1985 $16 (1/31/87) **79**
Riesling Beerenauslese Rheinhessen Niersteiner Pettenthal 1989 (NR) (12/15/90) **84**
Riesling Kabinett Halbtrocken Rheinhessen Niersteiner Bildstock 1990 (NR) (12/15/91) **84**
Riesling Kabinett Rheinhessen 1989 (NR) (12/15/90) **69**
Riesling Kabinett Rheinhessen Niersteiner Bildstock 1983 $7 (3/01/85) **80**
Riesling Kabinett Rheinhessen Niersteiner Klostergarten 1990 $17 (12/15/91) **85**
Riesling Kabinett Rheinhessen Niersteiner Klostergarten 1985 $8 (1/31/87) **60**
Riesling Kabinett Rheinhessen Niersteiner Rehbach 1988 $9 (9/30/89) **82**
Riesling Spätlese Rheinhessen Niersteiner Hipping 1990 $21 (12/15/91) **86**
Riesling Spätlese Rheinhessen Niersteiner Hipping 1989 (NR) (12/15/90) **84**
Riesling Spätlese Rheinhessen Niersteiner Hipping 1988 $12 (9/30/89) **85**
Riesling Spätlese Rheinhessen Niersteiner Pettenthal 1990 (NR) (12/15/91) **85**
Riesling Spätlese Rheinhessen Niersteiner Pettenthal 1989 (NR) (12/15/90) **85**
Riesling Spätlese Rheinhessen Niersteiner Pettenthal 1988 $12 (9/30/89) **86**
Riesling Spätlese Rheinhessen Niersteiner Pettenthal 1985 $10 (1/31/87) **61**
Riesling Spätlese Rheinhessen Niersteiner Pettenthal 1983 $9 (4/16/85) **83**
Riesling Spätlese Rheinhessen Niersteiner Rehbach 1989 (NR) (12/15/90) **88**
Riesling Spätlese Rheinhessen Niersteiner Rehbach 1988 $12 (9/30/89) **88**
Riesling Spätlese Rheinhessen Niersteiner Spiegelberg 1989 (NR) (12/15/90) **81**
Riesling Spätlese Trocken Rheinhessen Niersteiner Oelberg 1990 (NR) (12/15/91) **79**

BODEGAS BALBAS (Spain)
Ribera del Duero 1988 $15 (9/30/91) **88**
Ribera del Duero 1987 $14 (9/30/90) **81**
Ribera del Duero 1986 $15 (7/31/89) **87**
Ribera del Duero 1985 $13 (9/15/88) **83**
Ribera del Duero Reserva 1985 (NR) (3/31/90) (TM) **75**

BALDINELLI (United States/California)
Cabernet Sauvignon Shenandoah Valley 1983 $7.75 (11/30/88) **86**
Zinfandel Shenandoah Valley 1988 $7.75 (12/31/90) **82**
Zinfandel Shenandoah Valley 1987 $8 (5/15/90) **85**
Zinfandel Shenandoah Valley Reserve 1986 $6.75 (12/15/88) BB **83**

CHATEAU BALESTARD LA TONNELLE (France/Bordeaux)
St.-Emilion 1990 (NR) (4/30/91) (BT) **80+**
St.-Emilion 1989 $28 (3/15/92) **85**
St.-Emilion 1988 $25 (4/30/91) **91**
St.-Emilion 1987 $20 (6/30/89) (BT) **75+**
St.-Emilion 1986 $22 (6/30/88) (BT) **80+**
St.-Emilion 1982 $25 (5/15/89) (TR) **83**

BALGOWNIE (Australia)
Chardonnay Coonawarra Series One Première Cuvée 1987 $6.50 (9/30/88) **74**

BALKAN CREST (Other/Bulgaria)
Cabernet Sauvignon Stara Zagora Oriahovitza Vineyards Reserve 1985 $6 (7/15/91) **58**
Chardonnay Shoumen Khan Krum Vineyards Reserve 1987 $6 (7/15/91) **79**

BALLARD CANYON (United States/California)
Chardonnay Santa Ynez Valley 1988 $14 (12/15/89) **86**
Chardonnay Santa Ynez Valley Dr.'s Fun Baby 1988 $10 (12/15/89) **79**
Johannisberg Riesling Santa Ynez Valley 1988 $7 (12/15/89) **74**
Johannisberg Riesling Santa Ynez Valley Reserve 1988 $9 (12/15/89) **75**

BALLATORE (United States/California)
California NV $4 (5/01/86) BB **87**

R. BALLOT-MILLOT & FILS (France/Burgundy)
Meursault Les Charmes 1987 $34 (8/31/90) **77**
Meursault Les Criots 1985 $34 (4/30/88) **88**

CHATEAU BALLUE-MONDON (France/Bordeaux)
Bordeaux Blanc Sauvignon Blanc Sec 1988 $8 (3/31/90) **71**

BALVERNE (United States/California)
Cabernet Sauvignon Chalk Hill Laurel Vineyard 1983 $13 (2/15/89) **86**
Cabernet Sauvignon Sonoma County 1982 $12 (8/31/88) **88**
Chardonnay Chalk Hill Deerfield Vineyard 1984 $11 (11/15/87) **79**

BANCROFT (United States/California)
Chardonnay Howell Mountain 1990 $13.50 (5/31/92) **84**
Chardonnay Howell Mountain 1988 $14 (12/31/90) **88**

BANDIERA (United States/California)
Cabernet Sauvignon Napa Valley 1988 $6.50 (4/15/92) BB **80**
Cabernet Sauvignon Napa Valley 1987 $7 (11/15/91) BB **89**
Cabernet Sauvignon Napa Valley 1986 $6.50 (10/31/89) BB **85**
Chardonnay Napa County 1990 $6.50 (3/15/92) BB **80**
White Zinfandel California 1988 $5.25 (6/15/89) **74**

BANEAR (Italy/North)
Pinot Grigio Grave del Friuli 1990 $8 (1/31/92) **80**

BANFI (United States/New York)
Chardonnay Nassau County Old Brookville 1988 $11 (6/30/91) (TM) **70**
Chardonnay Nassau County Old Brookville 1987 $11.50 (12/15/90) **85**

CASTELLO BANFI (Italy/Piedmont)
Brunello di Montalcino 1985 $30 (10/15/90) **92**
Brunello di Montalcino 1982 Rel: $28 Cur: $35 (12/15/87) **89**
Brunello di Montalcino 1981 Rel: $23 Cur: $32 (3/31/87) CS **92**
Brunello di Montalcino 1980 Rel: $20 Cur: $33 (9/15/86) **90**
Brunello di Montalcino 1979 $18 (4/16/85) SS **90**
Brunello di Montalcino Poggio all'Oro 1985 $30 (12/15/91) CS **92**
Brut 1986 $20 (3/31/92) **83**
Brut 1985 $15.50 (6/30/90) **81**
Cabernet Sauvignon Tavernelle 1988 (NR) (9/15/91) **87**
Cabernet Sauvignon Tavernelle 1984 $18 (1/31/88) **89**
Cabernet Sauvignon Tavernelle 1982 $15 (8/01/85) **88**
Chardonnay Centine 1988 $8 (4/30/90) **78**
Chardonnay Centine 1987 $8 (3/31/89) **84**
Chardonnay Fontanelle 1988 $11 (12/31/90) **86**
Chardonnay Fontanelle 1987 $16 (9/15/89) **80**
Chardonnay Fontanelle 1986 $16 (9/15/89) **86**
Chianti 1987 $7.50/1L (11/30/89) BB **85**
Chianti Classico Riserva 1985 $9 (5/15/90) **86**
Chianti Classico Riserva 1982 $7 (12/15/87) **83**
Chianti Classico Riserva 1981 $7 (8/31/86) **80**
Gavi Principessa 1989 $12 (12/31/90) **83**
PNE 1988 (NR) (9/15/91) **86**
Rosso di Montalcino Centine 1988 $8 (12/15/91) BB **81**
Rosso di Montalcino Centine 1987 $8 (6/15/90) BB **85**
Rosso di Montalcino Centine 1986 $7 (11/30/89) BB **87**
Rosso di Montalcino Centine 1985 $7 (11/30/87) BB **88**
Rosso di Montalcino Centine 1983 $7 (4/30/87) BB **89**
Summus 1988 (NR) (9/15/91) **87**

BANNISTER (United States/California)
Chardonnay Russian River Valley 1990 $16 (3/31/92) **88**
Chardonnay Sonoma County 1989 $15 (7/15/91) **85**

BANNOCKBURN (Australia)
Pinot Noir Geelong 1986 $26 (1/31/90) **73**
Pinot Noir Geelong 1985 $16.50 (3/15/88) **74**
Shiraz Geelong 1984 $13 (10/31/89) **81**

PAUL BARA (France/Champagne)
Brut Champagne 1982 $34 (12/31/88) **89**

BARANCOURT (France/Champagne)
Brut Blanc de Blancs Champagne Cramant NV $20 (5/31/87) **71**
Brut Blanc de Blancs Champagne Cramant Grand Cru NV $30 (12/31/90) **85**
Cuvée de Fondateurs Champagne 1985 (NR) (12/31/90) **90**

FATTORIA DEI BARBI (Italy/Tuscany)
Brunello di Montalcino 1982 Rel: $20 Cur: $25 (3/15/89) **78**
Brunello di Montalcino 1981 Rel: $20 Cur: $24 (9/15/86) **85**
Brunello di Montalcino Blue Label 1986 Rel: $28 Cur: $34 (8/31/91) **84**
Brunello di Montalcino Blue Label 1981 Rel: $20 Cur: $24 (1/31/91) **81**
Brunello di Montalcino Riserva 1985 $46 (11/30/91) **87**
Brunello di Montalcino Riserva 1977 $20 (9/15/86) **86**
Brunello di Montalcino Vigna del Fiore 1982 $22 (3/15/89) **64**
Brusco dei Barbi 1988 $12 (9/15/91) **86**
Brusco dei Barbi 1986 $9 (4/30/89) **79**
Brusco dei Barbi 1985 $9 (10/15/88) **85**
Bruscone dei Barbi 1988 (NR) (9/15/91) **84**

RENE BARBIER (Spain)
Cabernet Sauvignon Penedès 1981 $5 (3/31/90) **74**
Penedès 1982 $3 (1/31/87) **77**
Penedès Reserva 1978 $4.50 (3/31/90) **77**
Red Table Wine 1983 $3 (3/31/90) BB **80**

BARBOURSVILLE (United States/Virginia)
Cabernet Sauvignon Monticello Reserve 1983 $15 (2/29/92) **73**
Chardonnay Monticello Reserve 1989 $14 (2/29/92) **87**
Sauvignon Blanc Monticello 1989 $10 (2/29/92) **80**

HIJOS DE ANTONIO BARCELO (Spain)
Rueda Vino Blanco Santorcal 1989 $6 (7/15/91) **77**

CHATEAU BARET (France/Bordeaux)
Pessac-Léognan 1989 $18 (3/15/92) **93**
Pessac-Léognan 1988 $15 (6/30/89) (BT) **70+**
Pessac-Léognan 1987 $14 (6/30/89) (BT) **75+**
Pessac-Léognan 1986 $16 (5/15/87) (BT) **70+**
Pessac-Léognan Blanc 1990 (NR) (9/30/91) (BT) **80+**
Pessac-Léognan Blanc 1988 $19 (6/30/89) (BT) **80+**
Pessac-Léognan Blanc 1987 $15 (6/30/89) (BT) **75+**

PIERRE BARGE (France/Rhône)
Côte-Rôtie 1988 $42 (7/31/91) **84**

LAWRENCE J. BARGETTO (United States/California)
Cabernet Sauvignon Sonoma County Cypress 1985 $8.50 (11/15/89) **79**
Chardonnay Central Coast Cypress 1990 $9.50 (7/15/92) **82**
Chardonnay Central Coast Cypress 1989 $9 (7/15/91) **79**
Chardonnay Santa Cruz Mountains 1990 $18 (6/15/92) **85**
Chardonnay Santa Cruz Mountains 1989 $18 (2/28/91) **82**
Chardonnay Santa Cruz Mountains 1988 $18 (6/30/90) **78**
Chardonnay Santa Cruz Mountains Miller Ranch 1987 $15 (4/15/89) **82**
Chardonnay Santa Maria Valley 1985 $10 (11/15/87) **81**
Gewürztraminer Monterey County 1990 $8 (9/30/91) BB **84**
Gewürztraminer Monterey County Dry Pinnacles Vineyard 1990 $8 (9/30/91) BB **83**
Pinot Noir Carneros Madonna Vineyard 1985 $12.50 (9/15/88) **83**
Pinot Noir Santa Maria Valley 1987 $16 (2/28/91) **81**

GUY DE BARJAC (France/Rhône)
Cornas 1985 $17 (10/15/88) **81**

DOMAINE DE BARJUNEAU-CHAUVIN (France/Sauternes)
Sauternes 1989 (NR) (6/15/90) (BT) **85+**
Sauternes 1987 (NR) (6/15/90) **74**

BARNARD GRIFFIN (United States/Washington)
Fumé Blanc Washington Barrel Fermented 1987 $9 (10/15/89) **75**
Johannisberg Riesling Columbia Valley 1987 $6.50 (10/15/89) BB **88**

DR. BAROLET (France/Burgundy)
Aloxe-Corton Villamont 1952 $75 (8/31/90) (TR) **92**

CHATEAU BARON DE BRANE (France/Bordeaux)
Margaux 1989 (NR) (3/15/92) **89**

BARON HERZOG (United States/California)
Cabernet Sauvignon Sonoma County 1989 $11 (3/31/91) **73**
Cabernet Sauvignon Sonoma County Special Reserve 1986 $16 (3/31/91) **74**
Chardonnay California Selection 1990 $10 (9/15/91) **83**
Chardonnay Sonoma County 1989 $11 (3/31/91) **75**
Chenin Blanc California 1988 $4.50 (7/31/89) **84**
Johannisberg Riesling Late Harvest California 1989 $8/375ml (3/31/91) **86**
Sauvignon Blanc California 1989 $8 (3/31/91) **83**
White Zinfandel California 1989 $7 (3/31/91) **79**
White Zinfandel California 1988 $6 (6/15/89) **80**

DOMAINES BARONS DE ROTHSCHILD (France/Bordeaux)
Pauillac Réserve Spéciale 1987 $12 (12/31/90) **81**
Pauillac Réserve Spéciale NV $12 (2/15/90) **85**

BAROSSA VALLEY (Australia)
Cabernet Sauvignon South Australia 1987 $11 (1/31/90) **83**
Chardonnay South Australia 1988 $11 (3/15/90) **81**
Shiraz Cabernet Sauvignon Barossa Valley 1985 $8 (9/30/89) BB **86**

G. BAROUX (France/Rhône)
Côtes du Rhône Château de Bourdines 1988 $8 (12/15/90) **79**

CHATEAU BARRABAQUE (France/Bordeaux)
Canon-Fronsac Cuvée Prestige 1991 (NR) (5/15/92) (BT) **80+**

CHATEAU LE BARRADIS (France/Other)
Monbazillac 1988 $20 (7/15/91) **76**

DOMAINE BARRE (France/Loire)
Muscadet de Sèvre et Maine 1990 $9.50 (9/30/91) **83**

CHATEAU BARREYRES (France/Bordeaux)
Haut-Médoc 1986 $8.25 (6/30/89) **78**

BARROS (Portugal)
Tawny Port 20 Year Old NV $35 (2/28/90) (JS) **96**
Vintage Port 1987 $28 (VP-1/90) **81**
Vintage Port 1985 Rel: $24 Cur: $29 (VP-1/90) **80**
Vintage Port 1983 Rel: $8 Cur: $30 (VP-1/90) **76**
Vintage Port 1978 Rel: $7 Cur: $30 (VP-1/90) **75**
Vintage Port 1974 $40 (VP-1/90) **74**
Vintage Port 1970 $60 (VP-1/90) **82**

DOMAINE LUCIEN BARROT (France/Rhône)
Châteauneuf-du-Pape 1989 $20 (10/15/91) **88**
Châteauneuf-du-Pape 1988 $18 (10/15/91) **87**
Châteauneuf-du-Pape 1986 $18 (10/15/91) **89**
Châteauneuf-du-Pape 1981 $16 (9/30/87) **87**

BARROW GREEN (United States/California)
Chardonnay California 1988 $14.50 (7/15/91) **75**
Chardonnay California 1987 $16 (11/15/89) **90**
Pinot Noir California 1987 $14.50 (10/31/91) **79**
Pinot Noir California 1986 $16 (10/15/89) **76**

GHISLAINE BARTHOD (France/Burgundy)
Bourgogne 1988 $20 (3/31/91) **82**
Chambolle-Musigny 1988 $50 (3/15/91) **88**

Key to Symbols

The scores reported here are the results of blind tastings conducted by our panel of senior editors. Wines that carry the initials below are results of individual tastings.

THE WINE SPECTATOR 100-POINT SCALE 95-100—Classic, a great wine; ***90-94***—Outstanding, superior character and style; ***80-89***—Good to very good, a wine with special qualities; ***70-79***—Average, drinkable wine that may have minor flaws; ***60-69***—Below average, drinkable but not recommended; ***50-59***—Poor, undrinkable, not recommended. "+"—With a score indicates a range; used primarily with barrel tastings to indicate a preliminary score.

SPECIAL DESIGNATIONS SS—Spectator Selection, CS—Cellar Selection, BB—Best Buy, ($NA)—Price not available, (NR)—Not released.

TASTER'S INITIALS (JG)—Jim Gordon, (HS)—Harvey Steiman, (JL)—James Laube, (JS)—James Suckling, (TM)—Thomas Matthews, (TR)—Terry Robards, (PM)—Per-Henrik Mansson, (BT)—Barrel Tasting (these wines were tasted blind from barrel samples), (CA-date)—*California's Great Cabernets* by James Laube, (CH-date)—*California's Great Chardonnays* by James Laube, (VP-date)—*Vintage Port* by James Suckling.

DATE TASTED Dates in parentheses represent the issue in which the rating was published.

Chambolle-Musigny Les Beaux-Bruns 1988 $45 (2/28/91) **83**
Chambolle-Musigny Les Crâs 1988 $45 (2/28/91) **87**
Chambolle-Musigny Les Véroilles 1988 $45 (2/28/91) **81**

G. BARTHOD-NOELLAT (France/Burgundy)
Chambolle-Musigny Les Charmes 1984 $27 (10/31/87) **82**
Chambolle-Musigny Les Crâs 1985 $37 (7/31/88) **88**

MARCO DE BARTOLI (Italy/Dessert)
Marsala Superiore Vigna la Miccia 1985 $16 (3/31/90) **87**
Moscato di Pantelleria 1987 $16 (3/31/90) **87**

BARTON & GUESTIER (France/Bordeaux)
Beaujolais-Villages 1988 $9 (5/31/89) (TM) **77**
Beaujolais-Villages St.-Louis 1988 $7.50 (5/31/89) (TM) **75**
Bordeaux Blanc Fondation 1725 1990 $9 (9/15/91) **81**
Bordeaux Blanc Sauvignon Blanc 1988 $6 (3/31/90) **78**
Bordeaux Cabernet Sauvignon 1988 $6 (2/15/90) **73**
Bordeaux Fondation Rouge 1989 $9 (7/31/91) **75**
Bordeaux Merlot 1988 $6 (2/15/90) BB **84**
Brouilly 1988 $11 (5/31/89) (TM) **82**
Châteauneuf-du-Pape 1983 $11 (9/30/87) **74**
Gevrey-Chambertin 1985 $21 (4/30/88) **89**
Mâcon St.-Louis Chardonnay 1990 $8 (3/31/92) **72**
Mâcon-Villages 1988 $9 (9/30/89) **81**
Margaux 1985 $12 (4/30/88) **75**
Moulin-à-Vent 1988 $13 (5/31/89) (TM) **84**
Pommard 1985 $21 (11/30/87) **81**
Sauternes 1985 $12 (5/31/88) **75**
St.-Julien 1985 $13 (2/15/88) **83**

CASE BASSE (Italy/Tuscany)
Soldera Intistiei 1987 $68 (1/31/92) **87**

BASSERMANN-JORDAN (Germany)
Riesling Auslese Rheinpfalz Deidesheimer Hohenmorgen 1989 (NR) (12/15/90) **87**
Riesling Auslese Rheinpfalz Deidesheimer Hohenmorgen 1990 $38 (12/15/91) **90**
Riesling Beerenauslese Rheinhessen Deidesheimer Kieselberg 1990 $150 (12/15/91) **93**
Riesling Kabinett Rheinpfalz Deidesheimer 1989 $9 (12/15/90) **89**
Riesling Kabinett Rheinpfalz Deidesheimer Herrgottsaker 1983 $7 (3/16/85) **74**
Riesling Kabinett Rheinpfalz Deidesheimer Hohenmorgen 1989 $10 (12/15/90) **86**
Riesling Kabinett Rheinpfalz Deidesheimer Leinhöhle 1990 $14 (12/15/91) **88**
Riesling Kabinett Rheinpfalz Deidesheimer Paradiesgarten 1990 $15 (12/15/91) **89**
Riesling Spätlese Rheinpfalz Forster Jesuitengarten 1990 $26 (12/15/91) **91**
Riesling Spätlese Rheinpfalz Forster Kirchenstück 1990 $19 (12/15/91) **92**

THOMAS BASSOT (France/Burgundy)
Clos de Vougeot 1942 (NR) (8/31/90) (TR) **84**

CHATEAU BASTOR-LAMONTAGNE (France/Sauternes)
Sauternes 1989 (NR) (6/15/90) (BT) **95+**
Sauternes 1988 $18 (2/15/91) **82**
Sauternes 1987 $17 (6/15/90) **67**
Sauternes 1985 $20 (5/31/88) **82**
Sauternes 1983 $20 (1/31/88) **82**

CHATEAU BATAILLEY (France/Bordeaux)
Pauillac 1990 (NR) (4/30/91) (BT) **85+**
Pauillac 1989 $28 (3/15/92) **81**
Pauillac 1988 Rel: $23 Cur: $27 (4/30/91) **90**
Pauillac 1987 $18 (6/30/89) (BT) **75+**
Pauillac 1986 $34 (6/30/88) (BT) **80+**
Pauillac 1961 $100 (3/16/86) (TR) **84**
Pauillac 1945 $300 (3/16/86) (JL) **87**

BENI DI BATASIOLO (Italy/Piedmont)
Barbera d'Alba 1989 $11.50 (2/15/92) **84**
Barbera d'Alba 1988 $10.50 (4/15/91) **88**
Barolo 1985 $15 (3/31/90) **84**
Barolo la Corda della Briccolina 1987 $35 (1/31/92) **84**
Barolo Riserva 1982 $17 (3/31/90) **79**
Chardonnay delle Langhe 1990 $12 (1/31/92) **79**
Chardonnay delle Langhe 1989 $14 (7/15/91) **79**
Chardonnay delle Langhe Vigneto Morino 1989 $27 (7/15/91) **82**
Chardonnay delle Langhe Vigneto Morino 1988 $25 (12/31/90) **87**
Dolcetto d'Alba 1989 $12 (7/15/91) **82**
Dolcetto d'Alba 1988 $10.50 (12/31/90) **85**
Gavi 1989 $10.50 (8/31/91) **82**
Moscato d'Asti 1989 $14 (7/15/91) **85**

WILLIAM BATES (United States/California)
White Zinfandel California 1988 $4 (6/15/89) **72**

CHATEAU LA BATISSE (France/Bordeaux)
Haut-Médoc 1985 $10 (6/30/88) **82**

LA BATTISTINA (Italy/Piedmont)
Gavi 1987 $18 (4/30/90) **83**

CHATEAU BAULOS (France/Bordeaux)
Bordeaux Prince Albert Poniatowski 1988 $8.75 (8/31/91) **69**

BAUM (Germany)
Riesling Eiswein Mosel-Saar-Ruwer Ockenheimer St. Rochuskapelle 1983 $25 (10/01/84) **86**
Riesling Kabinett Rheinhessen Mainzer Domherr 1985 $5 (10/15/86) BB **82**
Riesling Qualitätswein Mosel-Saar-Ruwer Piesporter Michelsberg 1983 $4 (4/01/84) **79**
Riesling Qualitätswein Rheinhessen Niersteiner Gutes Domtal 1984 $4.50 (5/16/85) **76**
Riesling Spätlese Mosel-Saar-Ruwer Piesporter Goldtröpfchen 1983 $11 (10/01/84) **85**
Riesling Spätlese Mosel-Saar-Ruwer Weingartener Trappenberg 1983 $5 (10/01/84) **77**

DOMAINE DES BAUMARD (France/Loire)
Côteaux du Layon 1990 $20 (3/31/92) **87**
Côteaux du Layon Clos de Ste.-Catherine 1988 $10.50 (4/15/90) **81**
Quarts de Chaume 1990 $45 (3/31/92) **89**
Quarts de Chaume 1988 $20 (4/15/90) **82**
Sancerre 1990 $17 (3/31/92) **88**
Savennières 1988 $8.75 (4/15/90) **78**
Savennières Clos du Papillon 1988 $9.50 (4/15/90) **85**
Savennières Clos de St.-Yves 1981 $18 (3/31/92) **87**
Savennières Trie Spéciale 1990 $23 (3/31/92) **82**

BAVA (Italy/Piedmont)
Barbaresco 1982 $23 (4/30/91) **83**
Barbera d'Asti 1985 $13 (3/15/91) **87**
Barolo 1985 $19 (4/30/91) **83**
Gavi 1989 $13 (7/15/91) **78**

BAY CELLARS (United States/California)
Pinot Noir Los Carneros 1985 $15 (6/15/88) **77**
Pinot Noir Willamette Valley 1985 $18 (6/15/88) **85**

BEAU MAYNE (France/Bordeaux)
Bordeaux 1983 $5 (3/31/87) BB **81**
Bordeaux Blanc 1985 $5 (4/30/87) **80**

CHATEAU BEAU-SEJOUR BECOT (France/Bordeaux)
St.-Emilion 1988 $21 (6/30/91) **87**
St.-Emilion 1986 $22 (7/31/89) **79**
St.-Emilion 1982 $25 (5/15/89) (TR) **85**

CHATEAU BEAU-SITE (France/Bordeaux)
St.-Estèphe 1991 (NR) (5/15/92) (BT) **80+**
St.-Estèphe 1990 (NR) (5/15/92) (BT) **90+**
St.-Estèphe 1989 Rel: $17 Cur: $20 (3/15/92) **90**
St.-Estèphe 1988 $14 (6/30/89) (BT) **80+**
St.-Estèphe 1987 $12 (11/30/89) (JS) **81**
St.-Estèphe 1986 Rel: $15 Cur: $18 (11/30/89) (JS) **86**
St.-Estèphe 1982 $18 (11/30/89) (JS) **86**

CHATEAU DU BEAU-VALLON (France/Bordeaux)
St.-Emilion 1987 $10 (5/15/90) **81**
St.-Emilion 1986 $10 (9/30/89) **84**
St.-Emilion 1985 $8.50 (9/30/88) **82**

BEAUCANON (United States/California)
Cabernet Sauvignon Napa Valley 1986 $15 (12/31/88) **85**
Chardonnay Napa Valley 1990 $9 (7/15/92) BB **83**
Chardonnay Napa Valley 1988 $10 (7/15/91) **87**
Chardonnay Napa Valley 1987 $12 (1/31/89) **85**
Merlot Napa Valley 1989 $10 (5/31/92) **73**
Merlot Napa Valley 1988 $13 (3/31/91) **84**
Merlot Napa Valley 1986 $13 (12/31/88) **78**

CHATEAU DE BEAUCASTEL (France/Rhône)
Châteauneuf-du-Pape 1989 $35 (10/15/91) CS **97**
Châteauneuf-du-Pape 1988 $28 (10/15/91) **90**
Châteauneuf-du-Pape 1987 Rel: $17 Cur: $20 (9/30/89) **86**
Châteauneuf-du-Pape 1986 Rel: $25 Cur: $30 (10/15/91) **91**
Châteauneuf-du-Pape 1985 Rel: $16 Cur: $37 (10/15/91) **91**
Châteauneuf-du-Pape 1984 Rel: $12 Cur: $23 (11/30/89) (HS) **89**
Châteauneuf-du-Pape 1984 Rel: $12 Cur: $23 (9/30/87) **82**
Châteauneuf-du-Pape 1983 Rel: $17 Cur: $35 (10/15/91) **90**
Châteauneuf-du-Pape 1982 $30 (11/30/89) (HS) **92**
Châteauneuf-du-Pape 1981 $47 (10/15/91) **96**
Châteauneuf-du-Pape 1980 $30 (11/30/89) (HS) **83**
Châteauneuf-du-Pape Blanc 1989 $34 (10/15/91) **91**
Châteauneuf-du-Pape Blanc 1986 $29 (2/29/88) **84**
Châteauneuf-du-Pape Blanc 1985 $27 (11/15/87) **82**
Châteauneuf-du-Pape Blanc Roussanne Vieilles Vignes 1988 $46 (12/31/90) **87**

BEAUCLAIRE (France/Bordeaux)
Bordeaux Supérieur 1988 $6 (12/31/90) **79**
Vin de Pays des Côtes de Gascogne 1990 $5 (6/30/92) BB **83**

BEAULIEU (United States/California)
Brut Napa Valley 1982 $12 (5/31/89) **81**
Brut Napa Valley Champagne de Chardonnay 1982 $16 (5/31/89) **87**
Burgundy Napa Valley 1987 $5 (1/31/91) BB **80**
Burgundy Napa Valley 1984 $5 (8/31/89) **78**
Cabernet Sauvignon Napa Valley Beau Tour 1988 $7 (9/30/90) **79**
Cabernet Sauvignon Napa Valley Beau Tour 1987 $8 (5/31/89) BB **81**
Cabernet Sauvignon Napa Valley Beau Tour 1986 $7 (10/31/88) **83**
Cabernet Sauvignon Napa Valley Beau Tour 1985 $7 (6/15/88) **83**
Cabernet Sauvignon Napa Valley Beau Tour 1982 $7.50 (10/15/86) **64**
Cabernet Sauvignon Napa Valley Georges de Latour Private Reserve 1990 (NR) (5/15/91) (BT) **85+**
Cabernet Sauvignon Napa Valley Georges de Latour Private Reserve 1989 (NR) (5/15/91) (BT) **85+**
Cabernet Sauvignon Napa Valley Georges de Latour Private Reserve 1987 Rel: $35 Cur: $39 (11/15/91) **92**
Cabernet Sauvignon Napa Valley Georges de Latour Private Reserve 1986 Rel: $31 Cur: $40 (3/31/91) (JL) **93**
Cabernet Sauvignon Napa Valley Georges de Latour Private Reserve 1985 Rel: $25 Cur: $46 (3/31/91) (JL) **95**
Cabernet Sauvignon Napa Valley Georges de Latour Private Reserve 1984 Rel: $25 Cur: $36 (3/31/91) (JL) **92**
Cabernet Sauvignon Napa Valley Georges de Latour Private Reserve 1983 Rel: $24 Cur: $31 (3/31/91) (JL) **82**
Cabernet Sauvignon Napa Valley Georges de Latour Private Reserve 1982 Rel: $24 Cur: $40 (3/31/91) (JL) **90**
Cabernet Sauvignon Napa Valley Georges de Latour Private Reserve 1982 Rel: $24 Cur: $40 (3/15/87) CS **93**
Cabernet Sauvignon Napa Valley Georges de Latour Private Reserve 1981 Rel: $24 Cur: $35 (3/31/91) (JL) **86**
Cabernet Sauvignon Napa Valley Georges de Latour Private Reserve 1980 Rel: $24 Cur: $49 (3/31/91) (JL) **93**
Cabernet Sauvignon Napa Valley Georges de Latour Private Reserve 1980 Rel: $24 Cur: $49 (9/16/85) SS **93**
Cabernet Sauvignon Napa Valley Georges de Latour Private Reserve 1979 Rel: $21 Cur: $55 (3/31/91) (JL) **87**
Cabernet Sauvignon Napa Valley Georges de Latour Private Reserve 1979 Rel: $21 Cur: $55 (3/01/84) SS **93**
Cabernet Sauvignon Napa Valley Georges de Latour Private Reserve 1978 Rel: $19 Cur: $61 (3/31/91) (JL) **90**
Cabernet Sauvignon Napa Valley Georges de Latour Private Reserve 1977 Rel: $16 Cur: $45 (3/31/91) (JL) **79**
Cabernet Sauvignon Napa Valley Georges de Latour Private Reserve 1976 Rel: $19 Cur: $58 (3/31/91) (JL) **88**
Cabernet Sauvignon Napa Valley Georges de Latour Private Reserve 1975 Rel: $16 Cur: $53 (3/31/91) (JL) **83**
Cabernet Sauvignon Napa Valley Georges de Latour Private Reserve 1974 Rel: $12 Cur: $77 (3/31/91) (JL) **79**
Cabernet Sauvignon Napa Valley Georges de Latour Private Reserve 1973 Rel: $9 Cur: $56 (3/31/91) (JL) **75**
Cabernet Sauvignon Napa Valley Georges de Latour Private Reserve 1972 Rel: $6 Cur: $46 (3/31/91) (JL) **71**
Cabernet Sauvignon Napa Valley Georges de Latour Private Reserve 1971 Rel: $8 Cur: $60 (3/31/91) (JL) **79**

Cabernet Sauvignon Napa Valley Georges de Latour Private Reserve 1970 Rel: $8 Cur: $135 (3/31/91) (JL) **93**
Cabernet Sauvignon Napa Valley Georges de Latour Private Reserve 1969 Rel: $6.50 Cur: $110 (3/31/91) (JL) **92**
Cabernet Sauvignon Napa Valley Georges de Latour Private Reserve 1968 Rel: $6 Cur: $170 (3/31/91) (JL) **92**
Cabernet Sauvignon Napa Valley Georges de Latour Private Reserve 1967 Rel: $5.25 Cur: $105 (3/31/91) (JL) **82**
Cabernet Sauvignon Napa Valley Georges de Latour Private Reserve 1966 Rel: $5.25 Cur: $145 (3/31/91) (JL) **87**
Cabernet Sauvignon Napa Valley Georges de Latour Private Reserve 1965 Rel: $5.25 Cur: $115 (3/31/91) (JL) **77**
Cabernet Sauvignon Napa Valley Georges de Latour Private Reserve 1964 Rel: $4.25 Cur: $130 (3/31/91) (JL) **72**
Cabernet Sauvignon Napa Valley Georges de Latour Private Reserve 1963 Rel: $3.50 Cur: $115 (3/31/91) (JL) **74**
Cabernet Sauvignon Napa Valley Georges de Latour Private Reserve 1962 Rel: $3.50 Cur: $120 (3/31/91) (JL) **75**
Cabernet Sauvignon Napa Valley Georges de Latour Private Reserve 1961 Rel: $3.50 Cur: $200 (3/31/91) (JL) **77**
Cabernet Sauvignon Napa Valley Georges de Latour Private Reserve 1960 Rel: $3.50 Cur: $135 (3/31/91) (JL) **85**
Cabernet Sauvignon Napa Valley Georges de Latour Private Reserve 1959 Rel: $3.50 Cur: $330 (3/31/91) (JL) **89**
Cabernet Sauvignon Napa Valley Georges de Latour Private Reserve 1958 Rel: $3 Cur: $510 (3/31/91) (JL) **97**
Cabernet Sauvignon Napa Valley Georges de Latour Private Reserve 1957 Rel: $2.50 Cur: $240 (3/31/91) (JL) **69**
Cabernet Sauvignon Napa Valley Georges de Latour Private Reserve 1956 Rel: $2.50 Cur: $600 (3/31/91) (JL) **88**
Cabernet Sauvignon Napa Valley Georges de Latour Private Reserve 1955 Rel: $2.50 Cur: $550 (3/31/91) (JL) **85**
Cabernet Sauvignon Napa Valley Georges de Latour Private Reserve 1954 Rel: $2.50 Cur: $330 (3/31/91) (JL) **86**
Cabernet Sauvignon Napa Valley Georges de Latour Private Reserve 1953 Rel: $2.50 Cur: $600 (3/31/91) (JL) **91**
Cabernet Sauvignon Napa Valley Georges de Latour Private Reserve 1952 Rel: $2.50 Cur: $600 (3/31/91) (JL) **91**
Cabernet Sauvignon Napa Valley Georges de Latour Private Reserve 1951 Rel: $1.82 Cur: $1,000 (3/31/91) (JL) **92**
Cabernet Sauvignon Napa Valley Georges de Latour Private Reserve 1950 Rel: $1.82 Cur: $760 (3/31/91) (JL) **88**
Cabernet Sauvignon Napa Valley Georges de Latour Private Reserve 1949 Rel: $1.82 Cur: $950 (3/31/91) (JL) **88**
Cabernet Sauvignon Napa Valley Georges de Latour Private Reserve 1948 Rel: $1.82 Cur: $1,040 (3/31/91) (JL) **79**
Cabernet Sauvignon Napa Valley Georges de Latour Private Reserve 1947 Rel: $1.82 Cur: $1,350 (3/31/91) (JL) **89**
Cabernet Sauvignon Napa Valley Georges de Latour Private Reserve 1946 Rel: $1.47 Cur: $1,000 (3/31/91) (JL) **87**
Cabernet Sauvignon Napa Valley Georges de Latour Private Reserve 1945 Rel: $1.47 Cur: $700 (3/31/91) (JL) **70**
Cabernet Sauvignon Napa Valley Georges de Latour Private Reserve 1944 Rel: $1.47 Cur: $680 (3/31/91) (JL) **75**
Cabernet Sauvignon Napa Valley Georges de Latour Private Reserve 1943 Rel: $1.45 Cur: $500 (3/31/91) (JL) **87**
Cabernet Sauvignon Napa Valley Georges de Latour Private Reserve 1942 Rel: $1.45 Cur: $1,300 (3/31/91) (JL) **85**
Cabernet Sauvignon Napa Valley Georges de Latour Private Reserve 1941 Rel: $1.45 Cur: $1,200 (3/31/91) (JL) **89**
Cabernet Sauvignon Napa Valley Georges de Latour Private Reserve 1940 Rel: $1.45 Cur: $1,200 (3/31/91) (JL) **89**
Cabernet Sauvignon Napa Valley Georges de Latour Private Reserve 1939 Rel: $1.45 Cur: $1,500 (3/31/91) (JL) **91**
Cabernet Sauvignon Napa Valley Georges de Latour Private Reserve 1936 Rel: $1.45 Cur: $1,500 (3/31/91) (JL) **86**
Cabernet Sauvignon Napa Valley Rutherford 1990 (NR) (5/15/91) (BT) **85+**
Cabernet Sauvignon Napa Valley Rutherford 1989 $11 (3/31/92) **81**
Cabernet Sauvignon Napa Valley Rutherford 1988 Rel: $11 Cur: $13 (7/15/91) **86**
Cabernet Sauvignon Napa Valley Rutherford 1987 Rel: $10 Cur: $13 (12/15/90) **85**
Cabernet Sauvignon Napa Valley Rutherford 1986 $11.25 (9/15/89) **85**
Cabernet Sauvignon Napa Valley Rutherford 1985 Rel: $9.50 Cur: $13 (6/15/88) **85**
Cabernet Sauvignon Napa Valley Rutherford 1984 Rel: $9.50 Cur: $15 (8/31/87) **78**
Cabernet Sauvignon Napa Valley Rutherford 1983 Rel: $6.50 Cur: $12 (6/15/87) **80**
Cabernet Sauvignon Napa Valley Rutherford 1982 Rel: $8.50 Cur: $14 (4/16/86) **81**
Cabernet Sauvignon Napa Valley Rutherford 1981 Rel: $9 Cur: $19 (5/16/85) **81**
Cabernet Sauvignon Napa Valley Rutherford 1980 Rel: $9 Cur: $30 (6/01/85) (JL) **88**
Cabernet Sauvignon Napa Valley Rutherford 1979 Rel: $9 Cur: $25 (6/01/85) (JL) **89**
Cabernet Sauvignon Napa Valley Rutherford 1970 $70 (6/01/85) (JL) **90**
Chablis Napa Valley 1988 $5 (12/31/90) **72**
Chardonnay Carneros Napa Valley Carneros Reserve 1990 $17 (6/30/92) **83**
Chardonnay Carneros Napa Valley Carneros Reserve 1989 $17 (5/31/91) **81**
Chardonnay Carneros Napa Valley Carneros Reserve 1988 $14 (CH-6/90) **89**
Chardonnay Carneros Napa Valley Los Carneros Reserve 1987 Rel: $14 Cur: $16 (CH-5/90) **87**
Chardonnay Carneros Napa Valley Los Carneros Reserve 1986 Rel: $12 Cur: $15 (CH-6/90) **86**
Chardonnay Carneros Napa Valley Los Carneros Reserve 1985 Rel: $12 Cur: $16 (CH-6/90) **84**
Chardonnay Carneros Napa Valley Los Carneros Reserve 1984 Rel: $10 Cur: $16 (CH-4/90) **79**
Chardonnay Carneros Napa Valley Los Carneros Reserve 1983 Rel: $10 Cur: $15 (CH-4/90) **74**

Key to Symbols

The scores reported here are the results of blind tastings conducted by our panel of senior editors. Wines that carry the initials below are results of individual tastings.

THE WINE SPECTATOR 100-POINT SCALE ***95-100***—Classic, a great wine; ***90-94***—Outstanding, superior character and style; ***80-89***—Good to very good, a wine with special qualities; ***70-79***—Average, drinkable wine that may have minor flaws; ***60-69***—Below average, drinkable but not recommended; ***50-59***—Poor, undrinkable, not recommended. "+"—With a score indicates a range; used primarily with barrel tastings to indicate a preliminary score.

SPECIAL DESIGNATIONS SS—Spectator Selection, CS—Cellar Selection, BB—Best Buy, ($NA)—Price not available, (NR)—Not released.

TASTER'S INITIALS (JG)—Jim Gordon, (HS)—Harvey Steiman, (JL)—James Laube, (JS)—James Suckling, (TM)—Thomas Matthews, (TR)—Terry Robards, (PM)—Per-Henrik Mansson, (BT)—Barrel Tasting (these wines were tasted blind from barrel samples), (CA-date)—*California's Great Cabernets* by James Laube, (CH-date)—*California's Great Chardonnays* by James Laube, (VP-date)—*Vintage Port* by James Suckling.

DATE TASTED Dates in parentheses represent the issue in which the rating was published.

Chardonnay Carneros Napa Valley Los Carneros Reserve 1982 Rel: $10 Cur: $16 (CH-4/90) **72**
Chardonnay Carneros Napa Valley Los Carneros Reserve 1981 Rel: $10 Cur: $18 (CH-4/90) **70**
Chardonnay Napa Valley Beaufort 1990 $9 (3/31/92) **82**
Chardonnay Napa Valley Beaufort 1989 $11 (7/15/91) **81**
Chardonnay Napa Valley Beaufort 1988 $9.50 (4/30/90) **79**
Chardonnay Napa Valley Beaufort 1987 $12.50 (6/15/89) **79**
Chardonnay Napa Valley Beaufort 1986 $9 (7/15/88) **85**
Chardonnay Napa Valley Beaufort 1983 $10.50 (10/01/85) **77**
Chardonnay Napa Valley Beaufort 1979 Rel: $6 Cur: $20 (CH-4/90) **70**
Chardonnay Napa Valley Beaufort 1978 Rel: $6 Cur: $22 (CH-4/90) **70**
Chardonnay Napa Valley Beaufort 1977 Rel: $6 Cur: $22 (CH-4/90) **64**
Chardonnay Napa Valley Beaufort 1976 Rel: $6 Cur: $22 (CH-4/90) **62**
Chardonnay Napa Valley Beaufort 1975 Rel: $5 Cur: $28 (CH-4/90) **61**
Chardonnay Napa Valley Beaufort 1974 Rel: $5 Cur: $25 (CH-4/90) **62**
Chardonnay Napa Valley Beaufort 1973 Rel: $5 Cur: $30 (CH-4/90) **60**
Chardonnay Napa Valley Beaufort 1972 Rel: $5 Cur: $30 (CH-4/90) **60**
Chardonnay Napa Valley Beaufort 1971 Rel: $4 Cur: $30 (CH-4/90) **58**
Chardonnay Napa Valley Beaufort 1970 Rel: $4 Cur: $32 (CH-4/90) **59**
Chardonnay Napa Valley Beaufort 1969 Rel: $2 Cur: $35 (CH-4/90) **57**
Chardonnay Napa Valley Beaufort 1968 Rel: $2 Cur: $35 (CH-4/90) **59**
Chardonnay Napa Valley Beautour 1990 $7.75 (11/15/91) **80**
Chenin Blanc Napa Valley Chablis 1986 $5.50 (7/31/89) **84**
Fumé Blanc Napa Valley Beau Tour 1989 $7.75 (10/15/91) **83**
Gamay Beaujolais Napa Valley 1988 $6.50 (8/31/89) **73**
Pinot Noir Carneros Napa Valley Reserve 1989 $13 (4/30/91) **85**
Pinot Noir Carneros Napa Valley Reserve 1987 $9.50 (12/31/88) **90**
Pinot Noir Napa Valley Beaumont 1986 $7 (6/15/88) **74**
Pinot Noir Napa Valley Beaumont 1985 $6.25 (6/15/88) **78**
Pinot Noir Napa Valley Los Carneros 1980 $10 (8/31/86) **88**
Pinot Noir Napa Valley Los Carneros Reserve 1988 $9.50 (4/15/90) **87**
Pinot Noir Napa Valley Los Carneros Reserve 1986 $9.50 (9/15/88) **88**
Pinot Noir Napa Valley Los Carneros Reserve 1985 $9.50 (1/31/88) **74**
Sauvignon Blanc Napa Valley Dry 1990 $9.50 (2/15/92) **78**
Sauvignon Blanc Napa Valley Dry 1989 $8.50 (4/30/91) **81**
Sauvignon Blanc Napa Valley Dry 1988 $8.50 (9/15/89) **83**

BEAULT-FORGEOT (France/Burgundy)
Mazis-Chambertin Hospice de Beaune Cuvée Madeleine-Collignon 1980 $56 (7/01/84) **91**
Nuits-St.-Georges Les Plateaux 1981 $17 (7/01/84) **83**

BEAUMET (France/Champagne)
Brut Blanc de Blancs Champagne NV $30 (12/31/90) **85**
Brut Blanc de Blancs Champagne Cuvée Malakoff 1982 $41 (12/31/90) **91**
Brut Blanc de Blancs Champagne Cuvée Malakoff 1979 $30 (5/31/87) **89**
Brut Blanc de Noirs Champagne 1985 $30 (12/31/90) **90**
Brut Blanc de Noirs Champagne 1983 $30 (12/31/89) **89**
Brut Champagne NV $26 (12/31/91) **86**
Brut Rosé Champagne 1983 $30 (12/31/89) **90**
Brut Rosé Champagne 1979 $16 (12/16/85) **79**

CHATEAU BEAUMONT (France/Bordeaux)
Haut-Médoc 1991 (NR) (5/15/92) (BT) **80+**
Haut-Médoc 1990 (NR) (5/15/92) (BT) **85+**
Haut-Médoc 1989 $14 (3/15/92) **82**
Haut-Médoc 1988 $15 (7/15/91) **82**
Haut-Médoc 1987 $13 (6/30/89) (BT) **75+**
Haut-Médoc 1986 $9 (6/30/89) **84**
Haut-Médoc 1985 $8.50 (4/30/88) **74**

BEAUMONT DES CRAYERES (France/Champagne)
Brut Champagne Cuvée Prestige NV (NR) (12/31/91) **82**
Brut Champagne Cuvée Réserve NV (NR) (12/31/91) **91**

BEAUREGARD (United States/California)
Chardonnay Napa Valley 1987 $10 (7/15/91) **75**

CHATEAU BEAUREGARD (France/Bordeaux)
Pomerol 1991 (NR) (5/15/92) (BT) **75+**
Pomerol 1990 (NR) (5/15/92) (BT) **90+**
Pomerol 1988 $36 (7/31/91) **90**
Pomerol 1986 Rel: $22 Cur: $24 (6/15/89) **87**
Pomerol 1982 Rel: $16 Cur: $20 (5/15/89) (TR) **89**

CHATEAU DE BEAUREGARD (France/Other)
Côteaux du Languedoc 1989 $5 (12/15/91) BB **81**

CHATEAU DE BEAUREGARD (France/Burgundy)
Pouilly-Fuissé 1983 $15 (3/16/85) **78**

DOMAINE DE BEAURENARD (France/Rhône)
Châteauneuf-du-Pape 1989 $21 (10/15/91) **86**
Châteauneuf-du-Pape 1988 $20 (10/15/91) **89**
Châteauneuf-du-Pape 1986 $24 (10/15/91) **88**
Châteauneuf-du-Pape 1985 Rel: $16 Cur: $20 (10/15/91) **87**
Châteauneuf-du-Pape 1983 $20 (10/15/91) **87**
Châteauneuf-du-Pape 1982 $9 (4/01/85) BB **85**
Châteauneuf-du-Pape 1981 $20 (10/15/91) **88**
Châteauneuf-du-Pape Blanc 1990 $25 (10/15/91) **86**
Châteauneuf-du-Pape Blanc 1989 $25 (10/15/91) **75**

CHATEAU BEAUSEJOUR (France/Bordeaux)
Côtes de Castillon 1986 $5 (6/15/89) BB **80**

CHATEAU BEAUSEJOUR-DUFFAU-LAGARROSSE (France/Bordeaux)
St.-Emilion 1990 (NR) (5/15/92) (BT) **95+**
St.-Emilion 1989 $44 (3/15/92) **91**
St.-Emilion 1988 $32 (4/30/91) **87**
St.-Emilion 1987 $20 (6/30/89) (BT) **85+**
St.-Emilion 1986 Rel: $27 Cur: $34 (6/30/89) **91**
St.-Emilion 1982 $30 (5/15/89) (TR) **90**

BEAUVOLAGE (France/Other)
Brut Blanc de Blancs Touraine Reserve 1989 $24 (1/31/92) **83**
Brut Rosé Touraine Reserve NV $29 (1/31/92) **84**
Brut Touraine Reserve 1989 $24 (1/31/92) **84**
Brut Vouvray Suprême Cuvée Comtesse Anne 1985 $39 (1/31/92) **80**
Cuvée Rouge et Noir Haut Poitou 1985 $35 (1/31/92) **81**

CHATEAU BECHEREAU (France/Sauternes)
Sauternes 1989 (NR) (6/15/90) (BT) **80+**

BEDELL (United States/New York)
Cabernet Sauvignon North Fork of Long Island 1988 $15 (6/30/91) (TM) **86**
Chardonnay North Fork of Long Island 1989 $12 (6/30/91) (TM) **83**

Chardonnay North Fork of Long Island Reserve 1988 $14 (12/15/90) **81**
Merlot North Fork of Long Island 1987 $18 (3/31/90) **90**
Merlot North Fork of Long Island Reserve 1988 $14 (6/30/91) (TM) **90**

CHATEAU BEL AIR (France/Bordeaux)
Haut-Médoc 1988 $15 (4/30/91) **85**

BEL ARBORS (United States/Other US)
Cabernet Sauvignon American Cask 88 NV $6 (11/15/91) **78**
Cabernet Sauvignon American Founder's Selection NV $5 (10/15/89) BB **82**
Chardonnay American Cask 90 NV $6 (8/31/91) **79**
Chardonnay American Founder's Selection NV $5 (10/31/89) BB **81**
Merlot American Cask 89 NV $6 (11/15/91) BB **81**
Merlot American Founder's Selection American Grown NV $5 (6/15/90) **72**
Sauvignon Blanc American Founder's Selection NV $5 (10/15/89) BB **81**

BEL ARBRES (United States/California)
White Zinfandel California 1988 $5.25 (6/15/89) **83**

BEL COLLE (Italy/Piedmont)
Barolo Riserva 1982 $15 (3/31/90) **85**
Barolo Vigna Monvigliero 1985 $20 (10/15/90) **87**

CHATEAU BEL-AIR (France/Bordeaux)
Haut-Médoc 1986 $9 (11/15/89) BB **88**
Haut-Médoc 1985 $5 (3/15/88) BB **80**
Haut-Médoc 1983 $6 (12/31/86) **83**
Haut-Médoc 1981 $6 (5/01/84) **72**

CHATEAU DE BEL-AIR (France/Bordeaux)
Lalande-de-Pomerol 1985 $18 (9/30/88) **85**

CHATEAU BELAIR (France/Bordeaux)
St.-Emilion 1990 (NR) (5/15/92) (BT) **90+**
St.-Emilion 1989 $34 (3/15/92) **89**
St.-Emilion 1988 $28 (8/31/90) (BT) **80+**
St.-Emilion 1987 $25 (6/30/89) (BT) **85+**
St.-Emilion 1986 Rel: $26 Cur: $35 (3/31/90) **82**
St.-Emilion 1985 $29 (4/16/86) (BT) **80+**
St.-Emilion 1982 $36 (5/15/89) (TR) **90**
St.-Emilion 1961 $125 (3/16/86) (TR) **75**

CHATEAU DE BELCIER (France/Bordeaux)
Côtes de Castillon 1985 $5 (6/30/88) **76**

CHATEAU BELGRAVE (France/Bordeaux)
Haut-Médoc 1988 $28 (7/31/91) **79**
Haut-Médoc 1986 $16 (3/31/90) **81**

JULES BELIN (France/Burgundy)
Nuits-St.-Georges Les St.-Georges 1943 (NR) (8/31/90) (TR) **91**

BELL MOUNTAIN (United States/Texas)
Cabernet Sauvignon Bell Mountain 1989 $13 (2/29/92) **85**
Pinot Noir Bell Mountain 1989 $12 (2/29/92) **76**
Sémillon Bell Mountain 1990 $9 (2/29/92) **77**

ADRIEN BELLAND (France/Burgundy)
Corton Grèves 1982 $16.50 (9/01/85) **87**
Puligny-Montrachet 1985 $35 (9/15/87) **89**
Puligny-Montrachet 1984 $27 (1/31/87) **75**
Puligny-Montrachet 1983 $20 (9/16/85) **88**
Santenay Comme 1987 $22 (11/15/90) **78**
Santenay Comme 1982 Rel: $12 Cur: $25 (8/01/85) CS **91**

JEAN-CLAUDE BELLAND (France/Burgundy)
Corton-Charlemagne 1986 $58 (3/31/89) **89**

BELLAVISTA (Italy/North)
Chardonnay Uccellanda 1987 $30 (9/15/89) **83**
Chardonnay Uccellanda 1986 $30 (9/15/89) **92**
Solesine 1986 $30 (5/15/89) **92**

CHATEAU BELLEGRAVE-VAN DER VOORT (France/Bordeaux)
Pauillac 1988 $20 (8/31/91) **83**
Pauillac 1986 $19 (10/31/91) **80**

CHATEAU BELLERIVE (France/Bordeaux)
Bordeaux Supérieur 1985 $7 (11/15/87) **70**
Bordeaux Supérieur 1982 $8 (12/16/85) **72**
Médoc 1986 $4.50 (2/15/89) **79**

BELLEROSE (United States/California)
Cabernet Sauvignon Dry Creek Valley Cuvée Reserve 1987 $18 (11/15/91) **83**
Cuvée Bellerose Sonoma County 1986 $18 (1/31/90) **83**
Cuvée Bellerose Sonoma County 1985 $16 (12/15/88) **82**
Cuvée Bellerose Sonoma County 1984 $14 (11/15/87) **77**
Cuvée Bellerose Sonoma County 1983 $12 (1/31/87) **74**
Cuvée Bellerose Sonoma County 1980 $10.50 (11/01/84) **79**
Merlot Dry Creek Valley Reserve 1988 $16 (5/31/92) **84**
Merlot Sonoma County 1986 $16 (4/15/90) **69**
Merlot Sonoma County 1985 $16 (2/28/89) **73**
Merlot Sonoma County 1984 $12 (12/31/87) **77**
Sauvignon Blanc Dry Creek Valley Barrel Fermented Reserve 1990 $10.50 (4/15/92) **77**
Sauvignon Blanc Sonoma County Barrel Fermented 1987 $10.50 (5/15/90) **56**

BELVEDERE (United States/California)
Cabernet Sauvignon Alexander Valley Robert Young Vineyards Gifts of the Land 1985 $16 (1/31/91) **81**
Cabernet Sauvignon Alexander Valley Robert Young Vineyards 1984 $13 (7/15/88) **88**
Cabernet Sauvignon Alexander Valley Robert Young Vineyards 1983 $12 (5/15/87) **88**
Cabernet Sauvignon Alexander Valley Robert Young Vineyards 1982 Rel: $12 Cur: $17 (12/01/85) SS **95**
Cabernet Sauvignon Lake County Discovery Series 1982 $4 (4/01/85) BB **80**
Cabernet Sauvignon Napa Valley Discovery Series 1982 $4 (2/16/86) **71**
Cabernet Sauvignon Sonoma County Discovery Series 1987 $6 (6/15/90) **75**
Cabernet Sauvignon Napa Valley York Creek Vineyard 1983 $12 (12/31/87) **79**
Cabernet Sauvignon Napa Valley York Creek Vineyard 1982 $12 (9/15/86) **72**
Chardonnay Alexander Valley 1990 $8 (3/31/92) **80**
Chardonnay Carneros 1987 $13 (4/30/89) **84**
Chardonnay Carneros 1986 $13 (7/15/88) **88**
Chardonnay Los Carneros Winery Lake 1983 $12 (6/01/85) **91**
Chardonnay Los Carneros Winery Lake 1982 $12 (8/01/84) **60**
Chardonnay Sonoma County Bacigalupi 1986 $13 (7/15/88) **80**
Chardonnay Sonoma County Bacigalupi 1985 $12 (12/15/87) **91**
Chardonnay Sonoma County Bacigalupi 1983 $12 (11/16/85) **73**
Chardonnay Russian River Valley 1990 $11 (7/15/92) **85**
Chardonnay Russian River Valley Reserve 1989 $9 (3/31/91) **85**
Chardonnay Russian River Valley Reserve 1988 $9 (2/15/90) **85**
Chardonnay Russian River Valley 1987 $11 (7/15/89) **88**
Chardonnay Sonoma County 1989 $6 (7/15/91) **71**
Chardonnay Sonoma County Discovery Series 1989 $6 (12/31/90) BB **80**
Chardonnay Sonoma County Discovery Series 1987 $5.25 (7/31/88) **78**
Chardonnay Central Coast Discovery Series 1984 $4.75 (10/16/85) BB **83**
Chardonnay North Coast Discovery Series 1984 $5 (1/01/86) BB **83**
Chardonnay Monterey County Discovery Series 1983 $4.75 (2/01/85) **58**
Merlot Alexander Valley Robert Young Vineyards 1986 $13 (6/30/89) **87**
Merlot Alexander Valley Robert Young Vineyards 1984 $13 (8/31/88) **90**
Merlot Alexander Valley Robert Young Vineyards 1983 $12 (12/31/87) **70**
Merlot Alexander Valley Robert Young Vineyards 1982 $12 (3/16/86) **94**
Muscat Canelli Late Harvest Alexander Valley 1990 $10/375ml (6/15/92) **80**
Pinot Noir Los Carneros Winery Lake 1983 $12 (12/15/87) **73**
Pinot Noir Los Carneros Winery Lake 1982 $12 (8/31/86) **58**
Pinot Noir Sonoma County Bacigalupi 1985 $12 (6/15/88) **73**
Pinot Noir Sonoma County Bacigalupi 1982 $12 (11/16/85) **65**
White Zinfandel California Discovery Series 1988 $4 (6/15/89) **78**
Zinfandel Dry Creek Valley 1989 $9 (5/15/92) BB **85**

BENZIGER (United States/California)
A Tribute Sonoma Mountain 1988 $26 (1/31/92) **88**
A Tribute Sonoma Mountain 1987 $20 (12/31/90) **85**
A Tribute White Sonoma Mountain 1989 $16 (12/31/91) **87**
A Tribute White Sonoma Mountain 1988 $11.50 (12/31/90) **89**
Cabernet Sauvignon Sonoma County 1988 $12 (11/15/91) **84**
Cabernet Sauvignon Sonoma County 1987 Rel: $10 Cur: $20 (9/30/90) SS **93**
Cabernet Sauvignon Sonoma County 1986 $10 (7/31/89) **82**
Cabernet Sauvignon Sonoma Mountain 1988 $25 (11/15/91) **85**
Cabernet Sauvignon Sonoma Valley Estate Bottled 1987 $12 (11/15/90) **85**
Cabernet Sauvignon Sonoma Valley 1986 $17 (4/30/90) **78**
Cabernet Sauvignon Sonoma Valley 1985 $16 (12/15/88) **83**
Chardonnay Carneros Première Vineyard 1989 $14 (2/15/92) **91**
Chardonnay Sonoma County 1990 $12 (5/31/92) **82**
Chardonnay Sonoma County 1989 $12 (11/15/91) **85**
Chardonnay Sonoma County 1988 $10 (6/30/90) **85**
Chardonnay Sonoma County 1987 $9.50 (7/15/89) **87**
Fumé Blanc Sonoma County 1990 $9 (2/15/92) **84**
Fumé Blanc Sonoma County 1988 $8.50 (10/31/89) **84**
Merlot Sonoma County 1989 $14 (5/31/92) **81**
Merlot Sonoma County 1988 $12 (11/15/91) **87**
Merlot Sonoma Valley 1987 $12 (3/31/91) **86**
Merlot Sonoma Valley 1986 $16 (7/31/89) **84**
Muscat Canelli Sonoma County 1987 $10 (8/31/89) **80**
Pinot Blanc Sonoma County 1989 $9 (11/15/91) **85**
Sauvignon Blanc Sonoma Mountain 1989 $13 (11/30/91) **87**
Sémillon Sonoma Mountain 1989 $13 (11/15/91) **81**

BERA (Italy/Sparkling)
Asti Spumante NV $15 (7/15/91) **83**
Moscato d'Asti NV $14 (7/15/91) **84**

BODEGAS BERBERANA (Spain)
Rioja Carta de Oro 1988 (NR) (3/31/92) **78**
Rioja Carta de Oro 1987 (NR) (3/31/92) **87**
Rioja Carta de Oro 1986 $8 (3/31/90) **81**
Rioja Carta de Oro 1985 $6 (7/31/89) **78**
Rioja Carta de Plata 1989 $8.50 (3/31/92) **77**
Rioja Carta de Plata 1988 $7.50 (9/30/91) BB **83**
Rioja Carta de Plata 1987 $7.50 (12/15/90) BB **84**
Rioja Carta de Plata 1986 $6 (5/15/89) BB **88**
Rioja Carta de Plata 1985 $6 (10/31/88) BB **89**
Rioja Gran Reserva 1982 $20 (3/31/92) **83**
Rioja Gran Reserva 1980 $9 (10/31/88) **82**
Rioja Gran Reserva 1975 (NR) (3/31/92) **88**
Rioja Gran Reserva 1973 (NR) (3/31/92) **89**
Rioja Reserva 1986 (NR) (3/31/92) **81**
Rioja Reserva 1985 Rel: $10 Cur: $13 (3/31/92) **82**
Rioja Reserva 1985 Rel: $10 Cur: $13 (2/28/90) **90**
Rioja Reserva 1983 $12 (3/31/92) **82**
Rioja Reserva 1982 $20 (3/31/92) **85**
Rioja White Carta de Oro Crianza 1988 $7 (5/31/92) **88**

VINA BERCEO (Spain)
Rioja Crianza 1988 $5 (9/30/90) **70**
Rioja Crianza 1987 $5 (4/15/89) BB **86**
Rioja Crianza 1986 $7 (9/30/90) BB **87**
Rioja Crianza 1984 $5.75 (10/15/88) **76**
Rioja Gran Reserva 1982 $25 (11/30/91) (TM) **87**
Rioja Reserva 1985 $10 (3/31/90) **76**
Rioja Reserva 1983 $10 (11/15/89) **69**
Rioja Reserva 1982 $8.50 (10/15/88) **76**
Rioja Reserva 1980 $8.50 (10/15/88) **77**

CHATEAU BERGAT (France/Bordeaux)
St.-Emilion 1989 (NR) (4/30/90) (BT) **80+**

C. BERGERET (France/Burgundy)
Chassagne-Montrachet 1985 $31 (8/31/87) **69**
Chassagne-Montrachet Morgeot 1985 $35 (8/31/87) **71**

CHATEAU BERGEY (France/Bordeaux)
Entre-Deux-Mers 1990 $6 (11/15/91) BB **82**

BERGFELD (United States/California)
Cabernet Sauvignon Napa Valley 1988 $14 (11/15/91) **83**
Merlot Napa Valley 1989 $15 (5/31/92) **87**

BERINGER (United States/California)
Cabernet Sauvignon Knights Valley 1989 (NR) (5/15/91) (BT) **85+**
Cabernet Sauvignon Knights Valley 1988 $16 (11/15/91) **86**
Cabernet Sauvignon Knights Valley 1987 $15.50 (11/15/90) **90**
Cabernet Sauvignon Knights Valley 1985 $12 (5/31/88) **87**
Cabernet Sauvignon Knights Valley 1983 $9 (4/15/87) **83**
Cabernet Sauvignon Knights Valley 1982 $9 (4/15/87) **90**
Cabernet Sauvignon Knights Valley 1981 $9 (10/01/85) **86**
Cabernet Sauvignon Knights Valley 1980 $8 (2/15/84) **88**
Cabernet Sauvignon Napa Valley Chabot Vineyard 1989 (NR) (5/15/91) (BT) **85+**
Cabernet Sauvignon Napa Valley Chabot Vineyard 1988 (NR) (5/15/90) (BT) **90+**

Cabernet Sauvignon Napa Valley Chabot Vineyard 1987 (NR) (4/15/89) (BT) **90+**
Cabernet Sauvignon Napa Valley Chabot Vineyard 1986 $30 (CA-3/89) **93**
Cabernet Sauvignon Napa Valley Chabot Vineyard 1985 $30 (11/15/91) **90**
Cabernet Sauvignon Napa Valley Chabot Vineyard 1984 Rel: $30 Cur: $34 (9/15/90) **85**
Cabernet Sauvignon Napa Valley Chabot Vineyard 1983 Rel: $27 Cur: $34 (CA-3/89) **85**
Cabernet Sauvignon Napa Valley Chabot Vineyard 1982 Rel: $25 Cur: $40 (CA-3/89) **89**
Cabernet Sauvignon Napa Valley Chabot Vineyard 1981 Rel: $23 Cur: $40 (CA-3/89) **87**
Cabernet Sauvignon Napa Valley Private Reserve 1989 (NR) (5/15/91) (BT) **85+**
Cabernet Sauvignon Napa Valley Private Reserve 1988 (NR) (5/15/90) (BT) **95+**
Cabernet Sauvignon Napa Valley Private Reserve 1987 Rel: $40 Cur: $47 (10/31/91) **94**
Cabernet Sauvignon Napa Valley Private Reserve 1986 Rel: $35 Cur: $49 (9/15/90) CS **95**
Cabernet Sauvignon Napa Valley Private Reserve 1985 Rel: $30 Cur: $75 (12/15/89) SS **95**
Cabernet Sauvignon Napa Valley Private Reserve 1984 Rel: $25 Cur: $45 (2/15/89) CS **94**
Cabernet Sauvignon Napa Valley Private Reserve 1983 Rel: $19 Cur: $44 (CA-3/89) **89**
Cabernet Sauvignon Napa Valley Private Reserve 1982 Rel: $19 Cur: $51 (CA-3/89) **92**
Cabernet Sauvignon Napa Valley Private Reserve 1981 Rel: $18 Cur: $31 (6/01/86) CS **92**
Cabernet Sauvignon Napa Valley Private Reserve Lemmon-Chabot Vineyard 1981 Rel: $23 Cur: $40 (4/15/87) **93**
Cabernet Sauvignon Napa Valley Private Reserve Lemmon-Chabot Vineyard 1980 Rel: $20 Cur: $42 (8/01/84) CS **93**
Cabernet Sauvignon Napa Valley Private Reserve State Lane Vineyard 1980 Rel: $15 Cur: $40 (CA-3/89) **85**
Cabernet Sauvignon Napa Valley Private Reserve State Lane Vineyard 1979 Rel: $15 Cur: $42 (CA-3/89) **89**
Cabernet Sauvignon Napa Valley Private Reserve Lemmon Ranch Vineyard 1978 Rel: $15 Cur: $36 (4/30/87) **92**
Cabernet Sauvignon Napa Valley Private Reserve Lemmon Ranch Vineyard 1977 Rel: $12 Cur: $75 (CA-3/89) **88**
Chardonnay Napa Valley 1990 $12 (2/15/92) **88**
Chardonnay Napa Valley 1989 $14 (3/15/91) **81**
Chardonnay Napa Valley 1988 $13 (4/15/90) **87**
Chardonnay Napa Valley 1987 $10 (7/15/89) **80**
Chardonnay Napa Valley 1986 $10.50 (1/31/88) **83**
Chardonnay Napa Valley 1985 $10 (4/30/87) **84**
Chardonnay Napa Valley 1984 $9 (4/15/87) **90**
Chardonnay Napa Valley 1983 $10 (9/01/85) **82**
Chardonnay Napa Valley 1982 $9.75 (4/16/84) **80**
Chardonnay Napa Valley 1981 $10 (6/01/86) **85**
Chardonnay Napa Valley Centennial Cask Selection 1974 Rel: $5 Cur: $40 (CH-4/90) **70**
Chardonnay Napa Valley Private Reserve 1990 Rel: $19 Cur: $23 (5/31/92) **90**
Chardonnay Napa Valley Private Reserve 1989 Rel: $19 Cur: $23 (7/15/91) **85**
Chardonnay Napa Valley Private Reserve 1988 Rel: $19 Cur: $21 (6/30/90) **76**
Chardonnay Napa Valley Private Reserve 1987 Rel: $17 Cur: $19 (CH-4/90) **79**
Chardonnay Napa Valley Private Reserve 1986 Rel: $16 Cur: $22 (CH-4/90) **90**
Chardonnay Napa Valley Private Reserve 1985 Rel: $15 Cur: $24 (CH-4/90) **86**
Chardonnay Napa Valley Private Reserve 1984 Rel: $15 Cur: $24 (CH-4/90) **88**
Chardonnay Napa Valley Private Reserve 1983 Rel: $15 Cur: $24 (CH-4/90) **76**
Chardonnay Napa Valley Private Reserve 1982 Rel: $15 Cur: $22 (CH-4/90) **74**
Chardonnay Napa Valley Private Reserve 1981 Rel: $15 Cur: $26 (CH-4/90) **86**
Chardonnay Napa Valley Private Reserve 1980 Rel: $15 Cur: $25 (CH-4/90) **75**
Chardonnay Napa Valley Private Reserve 1979 Rel: $14 Cur: $25 (CH-4/90) **78**
Chardonnay Napa Valley Private Reserve 1978 Rel: $12 Cur: $15 (CH-4/90) **70**
Chardonnay Santa Barbara County 1974 $5 (CH-4/90) **88**
Chenin Blanc Napa Valley 1987 $7 (7/31/89) **83**
Fumé Blanc Napa Valley 1988 $7.50 (8/31/90) **74**
Johannisberg Riesling North Coast 1989 $8 (12/31/90) **75**
Merlot Howell Mountain Bancroft Ranch 1989 (NR) (5/31/92) **91**
Merlot Howell Mountain Bancroft Ranch 1988 $28 (5/31/92) **90**
Merlot Howell Mountain Bancroft Ranch 1987 $29 (12/31/90) **91**
Sauvignon Blanc Knights Valley 1990 $9 (6/15/92) **86**
Sauvignon Blanc Knights Valley 1989 $8.50 (7/31/91) **85**
Sauvignon Blanc Knights Valley 1988 $8.50 (6/30/90) **85**
Sauvignon Blanc Knights Valley 1987 $8.50 (3/15/89) **77**
White Zinfandel North Coast 1988 $7.50 (6/15/89) **72**
Zinfandel North Coast 1988 $8.50 (2/29/92) BB **85**
Zinfandel North Coast 1987 $8 (9/15/90) **86**
Zinfandel North Coast 1985 $6 (4/30/88) BB **87**

CHATEAU BERLIQUET (France/Bordeaux)
St.-Emilion 1983 $12 (12/31/86) **90**

GUIDO BERLUCCHI (Italy/Sparkling)
Cuvée Impériale NV $12.50 (9/15/89) **81**

CHATEAU BERNADOTTE (France/Bordeaux)
Pauillac 1988 $20 (6/30/89) (BT) **80+**
Pauillac 1987 $20 (11/30/89) (JS) **79**
Pauillac 1986 Rel: $20 Cur: $22 (11/30/89) (JS) **92**
Pauillac 1985 $19 (3/31/88) **89**
Pauillac 1983 $14 (2/15/87) **90**

GUY BERNARD (France/Rhône)
Côte-Rôtie 1988 $30 (10/15/90) **78**

DOMAINE MICHEL BERNARD (France/Rhône)
Côtes du Rhône Domaine de la Serrière 1987 $7 (3/15/91) **77**

DOMAINE PAUL BERNARD (France/Beaujolais)
Fleurie 1990 $13 (10/31/91) **87**

BODEGAS BERONIA (Spain)
Rioja Reserva 1982 $12 (3/31/90) (TM) **82**

Key to Symbols

The scores reported here are the results of blind tastings conducted by our panel of senior editors. Wines that carry the initials below are results of individual tastings.

THE WINE SPECTATOR 100-POINT SCALE ***95-100***—Classic, a great wine; ***90-94***—Outstanding, superior character and style; ***80-89***—Good to very good, a wine with special qualities; ***70-79***—Average, drinkable wine that may have minor flaws; ***60-69***—Below average, drinkable but not recommended; ***50-59***—Poor, undrinkable, not recommended. "+"—With a score indicates a range; used primarily with barrel tastings to indicate a preliminary score.

SPECIAL DESIGNATIONS SS—Spectator Selection, CS—Cellar Selection, BB—Best Buy, ($NA)—Price not available, (NR)—Not released.

TASTER'S INITIALS (JG)—Jim Gordon, (HS)—Harvey Steiman, (JL)—James Laube, (JS)—James Suckling, (TM)—Thomas Matthews, (TR)—Terry Robards, (PM)—Per-Henrik Mansson, (BT)—Barrel Tasting (these wines were tasted blind from barrel samples), (CA-date)—*California's Great Cabernets* by James Laube, (CH-date)—*California's Great Chardonnays* by James Laube, (VP-date)—*Vintage Port* by James Suckling.

DATE TASTED Dates in parentheses represent the issue in which the rating was published.

Rioja White Crianza 1988 $7.50 (5/31/92) **83**

BERRI (Australia)
Cabernet Sauvignon Barossa Valley 1985 $7 (4/30/88) **76**
Cabernet Shiraz Australia 1985 $10 (7/01/87) **89**
Chardonnay Barossa Valley 1986 $12 (5/31/87) **89**
Chardonnay South Australia Vintage Selection 1986 $7.75 (2/15/88) **89**
Shiraz Barossa Valley 1985 $9.25 (2/15/88) **85**
Shiraz Cabernet South Australia Vintage Selection 1986 $9.50 (3/15/88) **80**

BERSANO (Italy/Piedmont)
Barbaresco 1983 $7.75 (1/31/89) **79**
Barbaresco 1975 (NR) (9/15/88) (HS) **76**
Barbaresco 1971 (NR) (9/15/88) (HS) **78**
Barbaresco 1964 (NR) (9/15/88) (HS) **85**
Barbera d'Asti 1987 $9 (3/15/91) **80**
Barolo 1985 $10 (10/15/90) **79**
Barolo 1983 $9 (11/15/88) **81**
Barolo 1974 (NR) (9/15/88) (HS) **79**
Barolo 1971 (NR) (9/15/88) (HS) **77**
Barolo 1964 (NR) (9/15/88) (HS) **80**
Castellengo 1986 $16 (4/15/91) **88**

DOMAINE BERTAGNA (France/Burgundy)
Nuits-St.-Georges Aux Murgers 1985 $41 (2/28/89) **85**
Vosne-Romanée Les Beaux Monts Bas 1985 $35 (10/15/88) **82**
Vougeot Clos de la Perrière 1985 $40 (4/15/89) **87**
Vougeot Les Crâs 1985 $30 (3/31/88) **85**

BERTANI (Italy/North)
Catullo 1987 $8 (3/31/89) **86**
Catullo 1984 $9 (2/15/89) **86**

A. BERTELLI (Italy/Other)
I Fossaretti 1985 $34 (12/31/90) **92**

DOMAINE BERTHEAU (France/Burgundy)
Bonnes Mares 1987 $55 (6/15/90) **89**
Chambolle-Musigny 1987 $25 (6/15/90) **80**
Chambolle-Musigny Les Amoureuses 1987 $50 (6/15/90) **84**
Chambolle-Musigny Les Charmes 1987 $35 (6/15/90) **81**

CHATEAU BERTINERIE (France/Bordeaux)
Premières Côtes de Blaye 1988 $10 (7/15/90) **85**

DANIEL BESSIERE (France/Other)
Côteaux du Languedoc 1987 $5 (9/30/89) BB **83**
Faugères 1987 $6 (9/15/89) **73**
Minervois 1986 $6 (9/15/89) BB **81**
St.-Chinian 1987 $6 (8/31/89) **79**

ANDRE BESSON (France/Burgundy)
Pouilly-Fuissé Domaine de Pouilly 1988 $15 (7/31/90) **86**

BETHEL HEIGHTS (United States/Oregon)
Pinot Noir Willamette Valley 1988 $15 (4/15/91) **87**
Pinot Noir Willamette Valley 1987 $12 (2/15/90) **86**
Pinot Noir Willamette Valley 1986 $15 (6/15/88) **86**
Pinot Noir Willamette Valley 1985 $12 (2/15/90) **79**
Pinot Noir Willamette Valley Reserve 1988 $18 (4/15/91) **86**
Pinot Noir Willamette Valley Unfiltered 1985 $12 (2/15/90) **86**

CHATEAU BEYCHEVELLE (France/Bordeaux)
St.-Julien 1991 (NR) (5/15/92) (BT) **80+**
St.-Julien 1990 (NR) (5/15/92) (BT) **90+**
St.-Julien 1989 $48 (3/15/92) **95**
St.-Julien 1988 $40 (4/30/91) **93**
St.-Julien 1987 $28 (5/15/90) **79**
St.-Julien 1986 $37 (5/31/89) **93**
St.-Julien 1985 Rel: $35 Cur: $39 (8/31/88) CS **95**
St.-Julien 1984 $32 (5/15/87) **78**
St.-Julien 1983 Rel: $25 Cur: $30 (3/01/86) **88**
St.-Julien 1982 Rel: $35 Cur: $47 (12/31/89) (TM) **89**
St.-Julien 1981 Rel: $17 Cur: $26 (5/01/84) **81**
St.-Julien 1979 $47 (10/15/89) (JS) **92**
St.-Julien 1978 $44 (12/31/89) (TM) **86**
St.-Julien 1971 $44 (12/31/89) (TM) **85**
St.-Julien 1967 $37 (12/31/89) (TM) **83**
St.-Julien 1962 $89 (11/30/87) (JS) **95**
St.-Julien 1961 $155 (3/16/86) (TR) **68**
St.-Julien 1959 $130 (10/15/90) (JS) **80**
St.-Julien 1948 $175 (12/31/89) (TM) **92**
St.-Julien 1945 $410 (3/16/86) (JL) **88**
St.-Julien 1929 $500 (12/31/89) (TM) **95**

LEON BEYER (France/Alsace)
Gewürztraminer Alsace 1990 $17 (2/15/92) **84**
Gewürztraminer Alsace 1989 $16 (11/15/90) **90**
Gewürztraminer Alsace 1988 $11.50 (10/15/89) **85**
Gewürztraminer Alsace Cuvée des Comtes d'Eguisheim 1990 $38 (2/15/92) **91**
Gewürztraminer Alsace Cuvée des Comtes d'Eguisheim 1989 $33 (11/15/90) **91**
Gewürztraminer Alsace Cuvée des Comtes d'Eguisheim 1988 $25 (10/15/89) **89**
Gewürztraminer Alsace Sélection de Grains Nobles 1990 (NR) (2/15/92) (BT) **70+**
Gewürztraminer Alsace Sélection de Grains Nobles 1989 (NR) (11/15/90) **96**
Gewürztraminer Alsace Vendange Tardive 1990 (NR) (2/15/92) (BT) **80+**
Gewürztraminer Alsace Vendange Tardive 1989 (NR) (11/15/90) **75**
Muscat Alsace Cuvée Particulière 1990 (NR) (2/15/92) **79**
Pinot Blanc Alsace 1989 $12 (11/15/90) **78**
Pinot Blanc Alsace Blanc de Blancs 1990 $12.50 (2/15/92) **88**
Pinot Blanc Alsace Blanc de Blancs 1988 $8.75 (10/15/89) **79**
Pinot Blanc Alsace Blanc de Blancs 1987 $9 (7/31/89) **84**
Pinot Gris Alsace 1989 $16.50 (10/31/91) **82**
Pinot Gris Alsace Sélection de Grains Nobles 1983 $48/375ml (7/31/89) **87**
Riesling Alsace 1989 (NR) (11/15/90) **84**
Riesling Alsace 1988 $10.50 (10/15/89) **80**
Riesling Alsace Cuvée Particulière 1990 (NR) (2/15/92) **88**
Riesling Alsace Cuvée Particulière 1989 $29 (11/15/90) **92**
Riesling Alsace Réserve 1987 $13 (7/31/89) **76**
Riesling Alsace Sélection de Grains Nobles 1989 (NR) (11/15/90) **80**
Riesling Alsace Sélection de Grains Nobles 1988 $25 (10/15/89) **87**
Riesling Alsace Vendange Tardive 1989 (NR) (11/15/90) **79**
Tokay Pinot Gris Alsace Cuvée Particulière 1988 $12 (10/15/89) **78**
Tokay Pinot Gris Alsace Réserve 1990 (NR) (2/15/92) **88**

Tokay Pinot Gris Alsace Réserve 1989 (NR) (11/15/90) **84**
Tokay Pinot Gris Alsace Sélection de Grains Nobles 1989 (NR) (11/15/90) **93**
Tokay Pinot Gris Alsace Vendange Tardive 1990 (NR) (2/15/92) (BT) **85+**
Tokay Pinot Gris Alsace Vendange Tardive 1989 (NR) (11/15/90) **77**

VALENTIN BIANCHI (Other/Argentina)
Cabernet Sauvignon Mendoza Elsa's Vineyard 1987 $7 (7/15/91) **77**
Malbec Mendoza Elsa's Vineyard 1985 $6 (7/15/91) **76**

VILLA BIANCHI (Italy/Other)
Verdicchio dei Castelli di Jesi Classico 1989 $7 (6/30/91) BB **83**

DOMAINE DU BICHERON (France/Other)
Blanc de Blancs Crémant de Bourgogne NV $12 (3/31/90) **84**

BICHOT (France/Burgundy)
Aloxe-Corton 1983 $18 (11/30/86) **68**
Bâtard-Montrachet 1983 $60 (2/29/88) **90**
Beaune 1988 $15 (8/31/90) **82**
Beaune Bressandes 1986 $24 (7/31/88) **80**
Beaune Hospices de Beaune Cuvée Guigone-de-Salins 1989 $68 (1/31/92) **83**
Bienvenues-Bâtard-Montrachet 1989 $84 (8/31/91) **84**
Bourgogne Blanc Le Bourgogne Bichot 1988 $8 (4/30/90) **76**
Bourgogne Blanc Le Bourgogne Bichot 1987 $8 (5/15/89) **79**
Bourgogne Le Bourgogne Bichot Pinot Noir 1985 $8 (11/15/87) **81**
Bourgogne Château de Dracy Pinot Noir 1989 $9 (6/15/92) **82**
Bourgogne Château de Dracy Pinot Noir 1986 $6.50 (12/31/88) **76**
Bourgogne Château de Montpatey Pinot Noir 1989 $10 (6/15/92) BB **85**
Bourgogne Croix St.-Louis Pinot Noir 1989 $9 (6/15/92) BB **83**
Bourgogne Croix St.-Louis Pinot Noir 1986 $6 (10/31/88) **77**
Chablis 1988 $17 (3/31/90) **84**
Chablis 1987 $11 (3/31/89) **85**
Chablis 1984 $9 (2/16/86) **65**
Chablis Les Vaillons 1988 $17 (12/15/89) **82**
Chassagne-Montrachet Morgeot-Vignes-Blanches 1988 $40 (2/15/91) **82**
Chassagne-Montrachet La Romanée 1986 $32 (4/30/88) **90**
Châteauneuf-du-Pape 1988 $13 (9/30/90) **84**
Châteauneuf-du-Pape 1987 $10 (3/15/90) **82**
Châteauneuf-du-Pape 1986 $9 (11/30/88) **86**
Châteauneuf-du-Pape 1985 $12 (11/15/87) **86**
Corton-Charlemagne 1985 $63 (3/15/88) **87**
Corton Hospices de Beaune Cuvée Docteur-Peste 1989 $100 (1/31/92) **88**
Côtes de Duras 1989 $6 (3/31/92) BB **81**
Côtes de Duras Blanc 1987 $4 (5/15/89) **77**
Côtes du Rhône 1987 $3.50 (11/15/88) **72**
Côtes du Rhône 1985 $5.75 (12/15/87) **75**
Côtes du Rhône Château d'Orsan 1989 $7 (6/15/92) **74**
Gevrey-Chambertin 1983 $13 (2/01/86) **58**
Mâcon-Villages 1989 $9 (7/15/90) **83**
Mâcon-Villages 1987 $6 (1/31/89) BB **82**
Meursault 1989 $26 (8/31/91) **84**
Meursault 1987 $24 (9/30/89) **75**
Meursault Les Charmes 1988 $40 (7/15/90) **92**
Meursault Les Charmes 1986 $37 (3/15/88) **82**
Meursault Les Charmes 1985 $30 (2/15/88) **93**
Meursault Les Genevrières 1989 $33 (8/31/91) **90**
Meursault Goutte-d'Or 1988 $35 (1/31/92) **82**
Meursault Hospices de Beaune Cuvée Goureau 1986 $55 (2/15/88) **92**
Meursault Poruzots 1989 $31 (8/31/91) **90**
Meursault Poruzots 1988 $36 (7/15/90) **85**
Monthélie Hospices de Beaune Cuvée Lebelin 1985 $52 (10/15/87) **86**
Montrachet 1989 $170 (8/31/91) **85**
Nuits-St.-Georges Les Boudots Hospices de Nuits Cuvée Mesny de Boissea 1986 $36 (3/31/90) **77**
Nuits-St.-Georges Les Maladières Hospices de Nuits 1986 $33 (2/28/89) **75**
Nuits-St.-Georges Les Maladières Hospices de Nuits Cuvée Grangier 1986 $30 (3/31/90) **80**
Nuits-St.-Georges Les Vignerondes Hospices de Nuits Cuvée Richard de Blagny 1986 $40 (2/28/89) **85**
Pommard 1988 $25 (8/31/90) **87**
Pommard 1986 $20 (9/15/89) **79**
Pommard 1983 $19 (9/15/86) **83**
Pommard Hospices de Beaune Cuvée Cyrot-Chaudron 1989 $70 (1/31/92) **86**
Pommard Hospices de Beaune Cuvée Cyrot-Chaudron 1985 $60 (10/31/88) **91**
Pommard Rugiens 1988 $40 (7/15/90) (BT) **80+**
Pouilly-Fuissé 1988 $13 (12/31/90) **73**
Pouilly-Fuissé 1987 $10 (4/30/89) **84**
Pouilly-Fuissé 1986 $11 (3/15/88) **79**
Pouilly-Fuissé 1985 $16 (3/31/87) **85**
Puligny-Montrachet 1989 $30 (8/31/91) **88**
Puligny-Montrachet 1987 $28 (9/30/89) **77**
Puligny-Montrachet Les Chalumeaux 1989 $35 (8/31/91) **88**
Puligny-Montrachet Les Chalumeaux 1988 $39 (6/30/90) **76**
Puligny-Montrachet Hameau de Blagny 1989 $38 (1/31/92) **87**
Rully Blanc 1984 $8 (6/01/86) **50**
Santenay 1986 $12 (10/15/89) **78**
Santenay Clos Rousseau 1988 $20 (7/15/90) (BT) **70+**
Santenay Les Gravières 1985 $15 (3/15/88) **66**
Savigny-lès-Beaune 1988 $17 (7/15/90) (BT) **80+**
Savigny-lès-Beaune 1986 $10 (10/15/89) **81**
Savigny-lès-Beaune Blanc Savigny Blanc 1989 $19 (8/31/91) **83**
Savigny-lès-Beaune Hospices de Beaune Cuvée Fouquerand 1988 $39 (1/31/92) **78**
Vin Rouge NV $3 (8/31/89) **75**
Volnay 1988 $25 (8/31/90) **84**
Volnay 1983 $18 (9/15/86) **68**
Volnay Hospices de Beaune Cuvée Blondeau 1988 $60 (6/15/92) **87**
Volnay Hospices de Beaune Cuvée Blondeau 1985 $53 (4/30/89) **88**
Volnay Hospices de Beaune Cuvée Blondeau 1982 Rel: $26 Cur: $38 (8/01/84) SS **92**
Volnay Premier Cru 1986 $25 (7/31/88) **84**
Volnay-Santenots 1986 $22 (10/31/89) **77**
Vosne-Romanée Les Beaux Monts 1988 $34 (7/15/90) **87**

BIDWELL (United States/New York)
Cabernet Sauvignon North Fork of Long Island 1988 $12 (6/30/91) (TM) **82**
Cabernet Sauvignon North Fork of Long Island 1987 $12 (6/15/90) **76**
Chardonnay North Fork of Long Island 1988 $9 (6/30/91) (TM) **81**
Chardonnay North Fork of Long Island 1986 $9 (3/31/90) **87**
Merlot North Fork of Long Island 1988 $11 (6/30/91) (TM) **85**
Merlot North Fork of Long Island Reserve 1987 $16 (3/31/90) **83**

BIGI (Italy/Tuscany)
Vino Nobile di Montepulciano 1985 $11.50 (11/30/90) **81**
Vino Nobile di Montepulciano Riserva 1982 $9 (1/31/88) **77**
Vino Nobile di Montepulciano Riserva 1980 $8 (9/01/85) **84**

BODEGAS BILBAINAS (Spain)
Rioja Viña Pomal 1983 $8 (6/30/90) **79**
Rioja Viña Pomal Gran Reserva 1978 $20 (3/31/90) **88**

J. BILLAUD-SIMON (France/Chablis)
Chablis Montée de Tonnerre 1985 $19 (9/30/87) **72**

BILLECART-SALMON (France/Champagne)
Brut Blanc de Blancs Champagne 1983 $50 (12/31/89) **88**
Brut Blanc de Blancs Champagne 1982 $43 (5/31/87) **86**
Brut Champagne 1983 $47 (12/31/89) **89**
Brut Champagne NV $28 (12/31/91) **86**
Brut Rosé Champagne NV $28 (12/16/85) **80**

BILTMORE ESTATE (United States/North Carolina)
Cabernet Sauvignon American 1987 $16 (2/29/92) **84**
Chardonnay American Sur Lie 1990 $13 (2/29/92) **78**

BINDELLA (Italy/Tuscany)
Vino Nobile di Montepulciano Riserva 1985 $27 (10/31/90) **68**

BIONDI-SANTI (Italy/Tuscany)
Brunello di Montalcino Il Greppo 1983 Rel: $66 Cur: $75 (11/30/89) **91**
Brunello di Montalcino Il Greppo 1982 Rel: $45 Cur: $62 (10/15/88) **92**
Brunello di Montalcino Il Greppo 1981 Rel: $40 Cur: $53 (9/15/86) **93**
Brunello di Montalcino Il Greppo 1980 $40 (9/15/86) **88**
Brunello di Montalcino Il Greppo 1978 Rel: $45 Cur: $55 (9/15/86) **70**
Brunello di Montalcino Riserva 1985 $180 (3/31/92) **82**
Brunello di Montalcino Riserva 1982 Rel: $80 Cur: $97 (10/15/88) CS **94**
Rosso di Montalcino Il Greppo 1984 $22 (1/31/90) **82**

BISCHOFLICHE WEINGUTER (Germany)
Riesling Auslese Mosel-Saar-Ruwer Dhroner Hofberger 1988 (NR) (9/30/89) **78**
Riesling Auslese Mosel-Saar-Ruwer Kaseler Neis'chen 1988 (NR) (9/30/89) **90**
Riesling Auslese Mosel-Saar-Ruwer Kaseler Neis'chen 1983 $10.50 (4/01/85) **86**
Riesling Kabinett Mosel-Saar-Ruwer Trittenheimer Apotheke 1983 $8 (5/01/85) **79**
Riesling Spätlese Mosel-Saar-Ruwer Ayler Kupp 1988 (NR) (9/30/89) **84**
Riesling Spätlese Mosel-Saar-Ruwer Kaseler Nies'chen 1983 $8.50 (5/01/85) **76**
Riesling Spätlese Mosel-Saar-Ruwer Trittenheimer Apotheke 1988 (NR) (9/30/89) **85**

BISCHOFLICHES PRIESTERSEMINAR (Germany)
Riesling Auslese Mosel-Saar-Ruwer Erdener Treppchen 1985 $14 (11/30/87) **86**

PIERRE BITOUZET (France/Burgundy)
Aloxe-Corton Valozières 1986 $19 (8/31/90) **78**
Corton-Charlemagne 1988 $75 (12/31/90) **91**
Corton-Charlemagne 1987 $68 (11/15/89) **92**
Corton-Charlemagne 1986 $72 (9/30/88) **95**
Savigny-lès-Beaune Lavières 1986 $15 (3/31/90) **87**
Savigny-lès-Beaune Lavières 1985 $19 (3/15/88) **67**

BITOUZET-PRIEUR (France/Burgundy)
Meursault 1987 $28 (7/15/90) **86**
Meursault Les Charmes 1987 $41 (2/28/91) **87**
Meursault Clos du Cromin 1987 $34 (8/31/90) **87**
Volnay Clos des Chênes 1987 $36 (12/31/90) **80**
Volnay Pitures 1985 $36 (7/31/88) **91**

SIMON BIZE & FILS (France/Burgundy)
Bourgogne Blanc Chardonnay Les Champlains 1989 (NR) (8/31/91) **84**
Savigny-lès-Beaune Blanc 1989 $22 (8/31/91) **88**
Savigny-lès-Beaune Les Bourgeots 1989 $19 (1/31/92) **85**
Savigny-lès-Beaune Aux Vergelesses 1989 $27 (1/31/92) **87**

BLACK MOUNTAIN (United States/California)
Cabernet Sauvignon Alexander Valley Fat Cat 1986 $20 (11/15/91) **86**
Cabernet Sauvignon Alexander Valley Fat Cat 1985 $18 (4/30/90) **87**
Chardonnay Alexander Valley Douglass Hill 1989 $11 (9/15/91) **88**
Chardonnay Alexander Valley Douglass Hill 1988 $10 (4/15/90) **88**
Chardonnay Alexander Valley Douglass Hill 1987 $10 (12/31/88) **86**
Chardonnay Alexander Valley Douglass Hill 1985 $10 (8/31/87) **72**
Chardonnay Alexander Valley Gravel Bar 1989 $18 (7/15/92) **74**
Chardonnay Alexander Valley Gravel Bar 1988 $20 (8/31/91) **81**
Chardonnay Alexander Valley Gravel Bar 1987 $18 (4/15/90) **88**
Petite Sirah Alexander Valley Bosun Crest 1987 $8.50 (10/31/91) BB **87**
Petite Sirah Alexander Valley Bosun Crest 1986 $8.50 (10/31/91) **67**
Petite Sirah Alexander Valley Bosun Crest 1985 $9 (2/15/89) **81**
Zinfandel Alexander Valley Cramer Ridge 1987 $10 (9/30/91) **77**
Zinfandel Alexander Valley Cramer Ridge 1986 $9 (3/31/90) **82**

BLACK OPAL (Australia)
Cabernet Sauvignon Hunter Valley 1985 $8 (7/15/88) BB **81**
Cabernet Sauvignon South Eastern Australia 1987 $8 (2/28/90) BB **85**
Chardonnay Hunter Valley 1987 $9 (7/31/89) **85**
Chardonnay Hunter Valley 1986 $8 (12/31/87) **79**
Chardonnay Hunter Valley 1985 $8 (5/15/87) BB **87**

BLACKWOOD CANYON (United States/Washington)
Sémillon Yakima Valley Barrel Fermented 1987 $9 (10/15/89) **83**
White Riesling Columbia Valley Claar Vineyard Dry 1987 $9 (10/15/89) **66**

BLAIN-GAGNARD (France/Burgundy)
Chassagne-Montrachet Caillerets 1985 $45 (5/31/88) **88**

FRANCIS BLANCHET (France/Loire)
Pouilly-Fumé Vieilles Vignes 1990 $13 (9/30/91) **85**

DOMAINE PAUL BLANCK (France/Alsace)
Gewürztraminer Alsace 1990 (NR) (2/15/92) **84**
Gewürztraminer Alsace Altenbourg 1990 (NR) (2/15/92) **83**
Gewürztraminer Alsace Altenbourg Vieilles Vignes 1990 (NR) (2/15/92) **84**
Gewürztraminer Alsace Furstentum Vieilles Vignes 1990 (NR) (2/15/92) **79**
Muscat d'Alsace Alsace 1990 (NR) (2/15/92) **86**
Pinot d'Alsace Alsace 1990 (NR) (2/15/92) **89**
Pinot Blanc Alsace Kientzheim Klevner 1990 (NR) (2/15/92) **88**
Pinot Blanc Alsace Klevner 1990 (NR) (2/15/92) **87**
Pinot Blanc Alsace Riquewihr Klevner 1990 (NR) (2/15/92) **90**
Riesling Alsace Furstentum Jeunes Vignes 1990 (NR) (2/15/92) **83**
Riesling Alsace Furstentum Vieilles Vignes 1990 (NR) (2/15/92) **89**
Riesling Alsace Kientzheim 1990 (NR) (2/15/92) **82**
Riesling Alsace Patergarten 1990 (NR) (2/15/92) **87**
Riesling Alsace Riquewihr 1990 (NR) (2/15/92) **88**
Riesling Alsace Sand 1990 (NR) (2/15/92) **86**

Riesling Alsace Schlossberg Jeunes Vignes 1990 (NR) (2/15/92) **86**
Riesling Alsace Schlossberg Vieilles Vignes 1990 (NR) (2/15/92) **88**
Tokay Pinot Gris Alsace 1990 (NR) (2/15/92) **87**
Tokay Pinot Gris Alsace Altenberg 1990 (NR) (2/15/92) **79**
Tokay Pinot Gris Alsace Furstentum 1990 (NR) (2/15/92) **85**
Tokay Pinot Gris Alsace Graffreben 1990 (NR) (2/15/92) **83**
Tokay Pinot Gris Alsace Patergarten 1990 (NR) (2/15/92) **87**

MAISTRE BLANQUETIER (France/Other)
Brut Blanquette de Limoux Le Berceau NV $9 (4/15/90) **81**

WOLF BLASS (Australia)
Cabernet Merlot South Australia Black Label 1983 $25 (4/30/89) **77**
Cabernet Sauvignon South Australia President's Selection 1986 $18 (3/15/92) **78**
Cabernet Sauvignon South Australia President's Selection 1983 $13.50 (4/30/88) **76**
Cabernet Sauvignon South Australia Yellow Label 1988 $10 (3/15/92) **88**
Cabernet Sauvignon South Australia Yellow Label 1984 $10 (4/30/89) **78**
Cabernet Sauvignon South Australia Yellow Label 1983 $9 (12/15/87) **86**
Cabernet Shiraz Australia Black Label 1980 $18 (7/01/87) **89**
Cabernet Shiraz Australia Yellow Label 1983 $8 (7/01/87) **87**
Cabernet Shiraz Clare-Barossa Valleys Black Label 1982 $25 (4/15/88) **88**
Cabernet Shiraz Langhorne Creek 1981 $18 (7/01/87) **90**
Chardonnay South Australia Première Release 1987 $9 (4/15/89) **82**
Chardonnay South Australia Première Release 1986 $10 (5/15/88) **81**

H. BLIN (France/Champagne)
Brut Champagne NV $18 (12/31/91) **85**

CHATEAU DE BLOMAC (France/Other)
Minervois Cuvée Tradition 1988 $6 (12/31/91) BB **82**

BLOSSOM HILL (United States/California)
White Zinfandel California 1988 $7/1.5L (6/15/89) **79**

BLUE HERON LAKE (United States/California)
Chardonnay Napa County 1985 $13 (8/31/87) **86**
Chardonnay Wild Horse Valley 1988 $13 (3/31/91) **76**

BLUE PYRENEES (Australia)
Cabernet Sauvignon Australia 1982 $20 (5/31/87) **89**

LA BOATINA (Italy/North)
Pinot Grigio Collio 1990 $14 (1/31/92) **71**
Verduzzo 1989 $17 (1/31/92) **84**

GUY BOCARD (France/Burgundy)
Meursault Les Charmes 1985 $32 (4/30/87) **91**
Meursault Les Grands Charrons 1986 $27 (10/15/88) **69**
Meursault Limozin 1986 $28 (10/15/88) **84**
Meursault Limozin 1985 $28 (4/30/87) **85**

E. BOECKEL (France/Alsace)
Gewürztraminer Alsace 1990 $14.50 (2/15/92) **84**
Gewürztraminer Alsace Vendange Tardive 1990 $36 (2/15/92) (BT) **90+**
Pinot Blanc Alsace Réserve 1990 $9 (2/15/92) **82**
Riesling Alsace Vendange Tardive 1990 (NR) (2/15/92) (BT) **80+**
Riesling Alsace Wiebelsberg 1990 $17 (2/15/92) **92**

BOEGER (United States/California)
Barbera El Dorado 1989 $10 (10/31/91) **85**
Cabernet Sauvignon El Dorado 1987 $11 (3/15/91) **85**
Cabernet Sauvignon El Dorado 1985 $11 (2/15/89) **77**
Cabernet Sauvignon El Dorado 1984 $11 (5/31/88) **81**
Cabernet Sauvignon El Dorado 1983 $10 (8/31/87) **82**
Cabernet Sauvignon El Dorado 1980 $8.50 (4/16/84) **76**
Chardonnay El Dorado 1989 $11.50 (5/31/91) **82**
Chardonnay El Dorado 1986 $10.50 (9/30/88) **89**
Hangtown Red California 1988 $5.25 (8/31/90) **78**
Hangtown Red California 1987 $5.25 (2/28/90) BB **82**
Hangtown Red California Lot No. 16 NV $5.75 (10/31/91) BB **80**
Johannisberg Riesling El Dorado 1990 $7 (9/15/91) **89**
Merlot El Dorado 1989 $12.50 (2/29/92) **86**
Merlot El Dorado 1988 $12.50 (3/31/91) **78**
Merlot El Dorado 1987 $12.50 (7/15/90) **81**
Merlot El Dorado 1986 $12.50 (1/31/89) **73**
Merlot El Dorado 1985 $12.50 (2/15/88) **82**
Merlot El Dorado 1982 $10 (10/01/84) **74**
Sauvignon Blanc El Dorado 1990 $7.50 (11/15/91) **82**
White Zinfandel El Dorado 1988 $7.50 (6/15/89) **65**
Zinfandel El Dorado Walker Vineyard 1989 $9.50 (9/30/91) **84**
Zinfandel El Dorado Walker Vineyard 1988 $8.50 (2/15/91) **85**
Zinfandel El Dorado Walker Vineyard 1987 $8.50 (3/31/90) **86**
Zinfandel El Dorado Walker Vineyard 1986 $7 (7/31/88) **73**
Zinfandel El Dorado Walker Vineyard 1981 $6 (7/16/85) **76**
Zinfandel Napa Valley Joseph A. Nichelini Vineyards 1988 $12 (8/31/91) **85**

BOGLE (United States/California)
Fumé Blanc California 1988 $6/1L (7/31/89) **73**
Merlot California 1990 $8 (5/31/92) **82**
Petite Sirah Clarksburg 1988 $7 (10/31/89) **70**

HENRI BOILLOT (France/Burgundy)
Bourgogne 1985 $13 (12/31/88) **76**
Puligny-Montrachet Clos de la Moushere 1986 $36 (9/30/88) **75**

JEAN-MARC BOILLOT (France/Burgundy)
Bâtard-Montrachet 1989 (NR) (8/31/91) **93**
Beaune Montrevenots 1988 $37 (5/15/91) **88**
Meursault 1989 (NR) (8/31/91) **91**
Montagny Premier Cru 1988 $22 (8/31/90) **79**
Pommard Saucilles 1988 $47 (5/15/91) **77**
Puligny-Montrachet 1989 (NR) (8/31/91) **91**
Puligny-Montrachet Les Pucelles 1986 $43 (9/30/88) **92**

DOMAINE LUCIEN BOILLOT (France/Burgundy)
Gevrey-Chambertin Les Cherbaudes 1987 $25 (5/31/90) **85**
Nuits-St.-Georges Les Pruliers 1987 $25 (7/15/90) **88**
Volnay Les Angles 1985 $33 (7/15/88) **86**

PIERRE BOILLOT (France/Burgundy)
Bourgogne Aligoté 1987 $13 (7/31/90) **75**
Meursault 1988 $37 (8/31/90) **87**
Meursault Les Charmes 1988 $47 (8/31/90) **90**
Meursault Les Charmes 1987 $44 (8/31/90) **79**
Volnay-Santenots 1988 $37 (8/31/90) **85**
Volnay-Santenots 1987 $37 (6/15/90) **86**

HENRI BOIRON (France/Rhône)
Châteauneuf-du-Pape 1983 $11 (8/31/86) **79**
Châteauneuf-du-Pape Les Relagnes 1984 $13 (11/15/87) **76**

DOMAINE DU BOIS DAUPHIN (France/Rhône)
Châteauneuf-du-Pape 1983 $12 (11/15/87) **62**

CHATEAU DU BOIS DE LA GARDE (France/Rhône)
Côtes du Rhône 1989 $8 (5/31/91) **83**
Côtes du Rhône 1988 $7 (10/31/90) BB **82**

CHATEAU BOIS-VERT (France/Bordeaux)
Bordeaux 1983 $3.75 (11/16/85) **53**

JEAN CLAUDE BOISSET (France/Burgundy)
Beaujolais 1988 $6.75 (11/15/90) **77**
Beaujolais-Villages 1988 $7.50 (11/15/90) **76**
Bourgogne Confèrie des Chevaliers du Tastevin 1989 $7 (6/15/92) **76**
Bourgogne Rouge Tastevinage 1988 $11 (8/31/91) **72**
Cabernet Sauvignon Napa Valley 1984 $7 (12/31/87) **72**
Cabernet Sauvignon Napa Valley 1981 $9 (5/01/85) **80**
Chablis 1985 $14 (1/31/87) **75**
Chablis Les Grenouilles 1982 $15 (6/16/85) **85**
Chardonnay Napa Valley 1983 $9.50 (4/16/86) **86**
Chassagne-Montrachet 1988 $28 (2/15/91) **86**
Chassagne-Montrachet Les Vergers 1989 $38 (8/31/91) **86**
Châteauneuf-du-Pape 1986 $12 (11/30/88) **80**
Côte de Beaune-Villages 1982 $5 (7/01/85) BB **86**
Côte de Nuits-Villages 1983 $13 (2/01/86) **78**
Côtes du Rhône 1987 $4.50 (7/31/89) **78**
Côtes du Rhône 1986 $4 (10/31/87) **73**
Côtes du Rhône 1985 $3.75 (11/30/86) BB **77**
Côtes du Rhône Blanc 1988 $4.50 (10/31/90) **76**
Côtes du Rhône Blanc 1986 $4.50 (11/15/87) **70**
Côtes du Ventoux 1988 $4 (10/15/90) **75**
Gevrey-Chambertin 1982 $9 (6/01/85) **74**
Mâcon-Blanc-Villages 1988 $9 (12/31/90) **76**
Mâcon-Blanc-Villages 1987 $8.50 (9/15/89) **76**
Meursault 1988 $28 (5/31/91) **83**
Nuits-St.-Georges 1985 $25 (4/30/88) **79**
Pommard 1985 $28 (4/30/88) **78**
Pommard Rugiens 1985 $33 (3/15/88) **76**
Pouilly-Fuissé 1986 $10 (9/30/87) **90**
Pouilly-Fuissé 1985 $16 (3/31/87) **77**
Puligny-Montrachet 1988 $29 (6/30/90) **81**
Puligny-Montrachet 1987 $33 (7/31/89) **70**
Puligny-Montrachet Les Folatières 1989 $38 (8/31/91) **88**
St.-Aubin Les Charmois 1989 $19 (8/31/91) **78**
St.-Véran 1989 $12 (7/31/91) **68**
St.-Véran 1988 $9.50 (7/31/90) **81**
St.-Véran 1984 $10 (3/31/87) **68**
Volnay Clos des Chênes 1985 $28 (4/15/88) **86**

BOIZEL (France/Champagne)
Brut Champagne Réserve NV $30 (12/31/91) **86**

BOKOBSA (France/Rhône)
Côtes du Rhône Cuvée du Centenaire 1986 $6.50 (2/28/90) **68**

BOLLA (Italy/North)
Bardolino 1990 $8 (1/31/92) **79**
Chardonnay 1989 $6 (4/30/90) **76**
Chardonnay 1988 $6 (9/15/89) (JS) **82**
Creso Rosso 1986 $25 (4/15/90) **88**
Gavi di Gavi 1987 $8 (10/15/89) **81**
Soave Classico Vigneti di Castellaro 1989 $12 (12/31/90) **81**
Valpolicella 1986 $6 (12/15/89) **71**
Valpolicella Vigneti di Jago Classico 1986 $12 (12/31/90) **78**

BOLLINGER (France/Champagne)
Brut Champagne Extra RD 1982 $100 (11/15/91) **87**
Brut Champagne Extra RD 1979 Rel: $79 Cur: $87 (12/31/89) **94**
Brut Champagne Extra RD 1976 Rel: $59 Cur: $73 (4/15/88) **88**
Brut Champagne Extra RD 1975 Rel: $64 Cur: $90 (5/16/86) **89**
Brut Champagne Grand Année 1985 Rel: $45 Cur: $50 (12/31/90) **96**
Brut Champagne Grand Année 1983 $43 (12/31/89) **86**
Brut Champagne Grand Année 1982 $30 (7/15/88) **93**
Brut Champagne Spécial Cuvée NV $38 (12/31/91) **92**
Brut Champagne Spécial Cuvée NV $25 (12/31/87) SS **92**
Brut Rosé Champagne Grand Année 1985 $60 (11/15/91) **85**
Brut Rosé Champagne Grand Année 1983 $50 (12/31/89) **89**
Brut Rosé Champagne Grand Année 1982 $35 (7/15/88) **80**
Brut Rosé Champagne Grand Année 1979 $40 (12/16/85) **94**

BOLLINI (Italy/North)
Chardonnay Trentino 1990 $9 (1/31/92) **82**
Chardonnay Trentino 1988 $7 (9/15/89) **85**
Chardonnay Trentino 1987 $7.25 (9/15/89) **84**

GIACOMO BOLOGNA (Italy/Piedmont)
Barbera Bricco della Bigotta 1988 $40 (3/15/91) **92**

Key to Symbols

The scores reported here are the results of blind tastings conducted by our panel of senior editors. Wines that carry the initials below are results of individual tastings.

THE WINE SPECTATOR 100-POINT SCALE *95-100*—Classic, a great wine; *90-94*—Outstanding, superior character and style; *80-89*—Good to very good, a wine with special qualities; *70-79*—Average, drinkable wine that may have minor flaws; *60-69*—Below average, drinkable but not recommended; *50-59*—Poor, undrinkable, not recommended. "+"—With a score indicates a range; used primarily with barrel tastings to indicate a preliminary score.

SPECIAL DESIGNATIONS SS—Spectator Selection, CS—Cellar Selection, BB—Best Buy, ($NA)—Price not available, (NR)—Not released.

TASTER'S INITIALS (JG)—Jim Gordon, (HS)—Harvey Steiman, (JL)—James Laube, (JS)—James Suckling, (TM)—Thomas Matthews, (TR)—Terry Robards, (PM)—Per-Henrik Mansson, (BT)—Barrel Tasting (these wines were tasted blind from barrel samples), (CA-date)—*California's Great Cabernets* by James Laube, (CH-date)—*California's Great Chardonnays* by James Laube, (VP-date)—*Vintage Port* by James Suckling.

DATE TASTED Dates in parentheses represent the issue in which the rating was published.

Barbera Bricco della Bigotta 1987 $34 (3/15/91) **88**
Barbera Bricco della Bigotta 1986 $34 (3/15/91) **88**
Barbera Bricco dell' Uccellone 1988 $45 (3/15/91) **91**
Barbera Bricco dell' Uccellone 1987 $45 (3/15/91) **88**
Barbera Bricco dell' Uccellone 1986 $38 (3/15/91) **89**
Barbera Bricco dell' Uccellone 1985 $33 (8/31/89) **88**
Brachetto d'Acqui 1987 $16 (3/31/90) **84**

BON MARCHE (United States/California)
Cabernet Sauvignon Alexander Valley 1989 $8 (2/28/91) BB **87**
Chardonnay Alexander Valley 1989 $8 (3/31/91) BB **88**
Chardonnay Sonoma County 1990 $8 (1/31/92) **76**
Pinot Noir Napa Valley 1990 $7 (11/15/91) **79**

CHATEAU LE BON-PASTEUR (France/Bordeaux)
Pomerol 1990 (NR) (5/15/92) (BT) **90+**
Pomerol 1989 $35 (4/30/92) **88**
Pomerol 1988 $23 (2/28/91) **85**
Pomerol 1987 $22 (5/15/90) **81**
Pomerol 1986 Rel: $22 Cur: $25 (6/15/89) **92**
Pomerol 1985 Rel: $20 Cur: $29 (5/15/88) **92**
Pomerol 1984 Rel: $12 Cur: $23 (6/15/87) **86**
Pomerol 1983 Rel: $22 Cur: $28 (6/16/86) **86**
Pomerol 1982 $54 (5/15/89) (TR) **91**
Pomerol 1979 $28 (10/15/89) (JS) **91**

BONAIR (United States/Washington)
Johannisberg Riesling Yakima Valley 1987 $5.50 (10/15/89) **74**

CHATEAU BONALGUE (France/Bordeaux)
Pomerol 1989 (NR) (4/30/91) (BT) **85+**
Pomerol 1988 (NR) (6/30/89) (BT) **85+**
Pomerol 1987 $18 (6/30/89) (BT) **80+**
Pomerol 1986 $27 (6/30/88) (BT) **85+**

BONARDI (Italy/Sparkling)
Moscato d'Asti NV $12 (3/31/90) **81**

FEDERICO BONFIO (Italy/Tuscany)
Chianti Le Poggiolo Riserva 1985 $10.50 (3/31/90) **76**
Chianti Le Poggiolo Riserva 1982 $7 (11/15/87) **73**
Chianti Le Portine Riserva 1985 $9.50 (3/31/90) **85**
Chianti Le Portine Riserva 1982 $9 (11/15/87) **79**
Chianti Proprietor's Reserve 1985 $15 (3/31/90) **85**

BONNAIRE (France/Champagne)
Brut Blanc de Blancs Champagne Cramant 1985 $42 (12/31/89) **83**
Brut Blanc de Blancs Champagne Cramant 1983 $38 (2/29/88) **87**
Brut Blanc de Blancs Champagne Cramant 1979 $40 (5/31/87) **86**
Brut Blanc de Blancs Champagne Cramant NV $30 (12/31/89) **90**

CHATEAU LE BONNAT (France/Bordeaux)
Graves 1989 $18 (4/30/92) **81**
Graves 1988 $18 (12/31/90) **87**
Graves 1987 $12 (4/15/90) **83**
Graves Blanc 1988 $17 (3/31/90) **84**

BONNEAU DU MARTRAY (France/Burgundy)
Corton 1985 $62 (10/15/88) **91**
Corton-Charlemagne 1989 $80 (8/31/91) **95**
Corton-Charlemagne 1988 $78 (9/15/91) **92**
Corton-Charlemagne 1986 Rel: $60 Cur: $73 (2/28/90) **88**
Corton-Charlemagne 1985 Rel: $65 Cur: $77 (5/31/88) **84**

HENRI BONNEAU (France/Rhône)
Châteauneuf-du-Pape Réserve des Celestins 1986 $19 (5/31/89) **82**

CHATEAU BONNET (France/Bordeaux)
Bordeaux 1989 (NR) (4/30/91) (BT) **80+**
Bordeaux 1988 $7.50 (4/30/91) **77**
Bordeaux 1987 $7 (4/15/90) **79**
Bordeaux 1986 $6 (5/15/89) **73**
Bordeaux 1983 $4.75 (5/01/86) **72**
Bordeaux 1982 $4.50 (4/16/85) **73**
Bordeaux Réserve 1988 $11 (7/15/91) **78**
Entre-Deux-Mers 1990 $9 (7/31/91) BB **85**
Entre-Deux-Mers 1988 $7 (5/31/90) BB **80**
Entre-Deux-Mers 1987 $6 (8/31/88) **79**
Entre-Deux-Mers 1986 $4.50 (4/30/88) **79**
Entre-Deux-Mers Oak Aged 1989 $13 (9/30/91) **85**
Graves 1985 $5.50 (4/15/88) BB **84**

BONNY DOON (United States/California)
Ca' del Solo Big House Red California 1990 $7.50 (6/30/92) BB **85**
California Vin Gris de Cigare 1990 $7 (7/15/91) BB **84**
California Vin Gris de Cigare 1989 $7.50 (10/31/90) **78**
California Vin Gris de Cigare 1988 $6.75 (7/31/89) BB **89**
California Vin Gris de Cigare 1987 $6.50 (4/15/89) **84**
Chardonnay California Grahm Crew 1989 $9 (9/30/90) BB **84**
Chardonnay Sonoma County Grahm Crew 1986 $8.50 (10/15/87) **85**
Chardonnay Monterey County La Reina Vineyard Cuvée Fin de Linea 1990 $12 (3/31/92) **78**
Chardonnay Monterey County La Reina Vineyard 1989 $14 (3/15/91) **90**
Chardonnay Monterey County La Reina Vineyard 1987 $15 (12/31/88) **88**
Chardonnay Monterey County La Reina Vineyard 1986 $13.25 (3/31/88) **91**
Chardonnay Monterey County La Reina Vineyard 1985 $13 (4/30/87) **73**
Chardonnay Santa Cruz Mountains Estate Bottled 1990 $25 (6/30/92) **83**
Chardonnay Santa Cruz Mountains Estate Bottled 1989 $25 (3/31/92) **83**
Gewürztraminer Oregon Vin de Glacière 1990 $15/375ml (3/31/92) **90**
Grahm Crew Vin Blanc California 1990 $7 (10/31/91) **76**
Grahm Crew Vin Rouge California 1989 $7.50 (10/31/90) BB **82**
Grahm Crew Vin Rouge California 1988 $7.50 (2/15/90) **83**
Grahm Crew Vin Rouge California 1987 $8 (11/30/88) **85**
Grahm Crew Vin Rouge California 1985 $6.25 (9/30/87) BB **80**
Grenache California Clos de Gilroy 1990 $8 (2/15/91) BB **87**
Grenache California Clos de Gilroy 1988 $6.75 (2/15/89) BB **85**
Grenache California Clos de Gilroy 1987 $6.50 (2/29/88) BB **87**
Grenache California Clos de Gilroy 1986 $6.50 (4/30/87) **84**
Grenache California Clos de Gilroy Cuvée Tremblement de Terre 1989 $7.50 (2/15/90) BB **88**
Grenache Late Harvest California Vin de Glacière 1987 $15/375ml (12/31/88) **90**
Le Cigare Volant California 1989 $20 (3/15/92) **80**
Le Cigare Volant California 1988 Rel: $19 Cur: $23 (12/31/90) **86**
Le Cigare Volant California 1987 Rel: $15 Cur: $24 (12/15/89) **85**
Le Cigare Volant California 1986 Rel: $13.50 Cur: $25 (11/15/88) **92**
Le Cigare Volant California 1985 Rel: $12.50 Cur: $25 (1/31/88) **90**
Le Cigare Volant California 1984 Rel: $10.50 Cur: $30 (8/31/86) **87**
Le Sophiste Santa Cruz Mountains 1989 $25 (3/15/92) **86**
Le Sophiste Santa Cruz Mountains 1989 $25 (1/31/91) **90**
Le Sophiste Santa Cruz Mountains 1987 (NR) (4/15/89) **87**
Malvasia Bianca Ca' del Solo Monterey 1990 $8 (6/15/91) BB **84**
Mourvèdre California Old Telegram 1988 Rel: $20 Cur: $26 (12/31/90) **85**
Mourvèdre California Old Telegram 1986 $13.50 (11/15/88) **90**
Muscat Canelli Late Harvest California Vin de Glacière 1990 $15/375ml (3/31/92) **91**
Muscat Canelli Late Harvest California Vin de Glacière 1987 $15/375ml (12/31/88) **91**
Muscat Monterey Moscato del Solo Ca' del Solo 1990 $9 (8/31/91) **77**
Eau-de-vie Poire Washington NV $18/375ml (3/31/92) **90**
Pinot Noir Oregon Bethel Heights Vineyard 1985 $18 (6/15/88) **90**
Pinot Noir Oregon Temperance Hill Vineyard 1985 $18 (6/15/88) **88**
Pinot Noir Sonoma County 1981 $9 (3/01/84) **65**
Prunus Ca' del Solo California NV $15/375ml (3/31/92) **92**
Syrah Santa Cruz Mountains 1988 $25 (2/15/91) **88**

BOOKWALTER (United States/Washington)
Chenin Blanc Washington Joseph Roberts Vineyards 1988 $6 (10/15/89) **78**
White Riesling Late Harvest Washington 1987 $5.50/375ml (10/15/89) **78**

BOORDY (United States/Maryland)
Cabernet Sauvignon Maryland 1989 $11 (2/29/92) **73**
Seyval Blanc Maryland Sur Lie Reserve 1989 $6.75 (2/29/92) **73**
Vidal Blanc Maryland Semi-Dry 1990 $6 (2/29/92) **81**

LE BORDEAUX PRESTIGE (France/Bordeaux)
Bordeaux 1985 $9.50 (9/30/88) **80**

CASCINA BORDINO (Italy/Piedmont)
Dolcetto d'Alba 1988 $9.50 (3/31/90) **84**

BORGES (Portugal)
Vintage Port 1985 $15 (VP-5/90) **70**
Vintage Port 1983 Rel: $12 Cur: $26 (VP-5/90) **70**
Vintage Port 1982 Rel: $12 Cur: $30 (VP-5/90) **79**
Vintage Port 1980 Rel: $11 Cur: $23 (VP-5/90) **70**
Vintage Port 1979 Rel: $11 Cur: $22 (VP-5/90) **65**
Vintage Port 1970 $86 (VP-5/90) **59**

VILLA BORGHETTI (Italy/North)
Valpolicella Classico 1989 $7 (4/30/92) **78**

BORGIANNI (Italy/Tuscany)
Chianti Classico 1982 $3.50 (4/01/85) **71**

CHATEAU LA BORIE (France/Rhône)
Côtes du Rhône Cuvée de Prestige 1985 $6 (7/15/87) **74**
Côtes du Rhône Cuvée de Prestige 1983 $4 (3/16/85) BB **87**

BORTOLUZZI (Italy/North)
Chardonnay 1988 $11 (9/15/89) **87**
Chardonnay 1987 $11 (5/15/89) **72**

BOSCAINI (Italy/North)
Soave Classico Monteleone 1989 $8 (6/30/91) BB **82**

BOSCARELLI (Italy/Tuscany)
1985 $30 (2/15/89) **92**
1983 $29 (6/30/88) **85**
Chianti Colli Senesi 1986 $8 (1/31/89) **78**
Chianti Colli Senesi 1984 $6 (9/15/87) **72**
Vino Nobile di Montepulciano 1981 $10 (7/01/86) **71**
Vino Nobile di Montepulciano Riserva 1985 $15 (6/15/90) **76**
Vino Nobile di Montepulciano Riserva 1981 $11 (10/31/86) **70**

CA' DEL BOSCO (Italy/North)
Chardonnay Franciacorta 1989 $31 (1/31/92) **85**
Chardonnay Franciacorta 1986 $38 (9/15/89) **85**
Franciacorta 1989 $11 (9/15/91) **82**
Franciacorta 1988 $11 (1/31/92) **81**
Franciacorta 1988 $17 (4/30/90) **78**
Franciacorta 1987 $16 (12/31/90) **77**
Franciacorta Brut NV $41 (12/31/91) **86**
Franciacorta Crémant NV $46 (12/31/91) **90**
Franciacorta Dosage Zero NV $35 (12/31/91) **89**
Franciacorta Rosé NV $42 (12/31/91) **83**
Maurizio Zanella 1988 Rel: $32 Cur: $57 (9/30/91) **93**
Maurizio Zanella 1987 Rel: $40 Cur: $45 (4/15/90) **92**
Maurizio Zanella 1985 $38 (9/15/88) **92**
Pinot Nero Pinero 1988 $50 (1/31/92) **83**
Pinot Nero Pinero 1987 $69 (6/15/90) **82**

CASTIGLIONE DEL BOSCO (Italy/Tuscany)
Brunello di Montalcino 1979 $14 (4/30/87) **93**
Rosso di Montalcino 1988 $11 (7/15/91) **82**

TENUTA IL BOSCO (Italy/North)
Pinot Nero Oltrepò Pavese 1988 $9.50 (6/30/91) **81**

CHATEAU LE BOSCQ (France/Bordeaux)
Médoc 1988 $20 (4/30/91) **84**
Médoc 1986 $10 (6/30/89) **75**
Médoc 1983 $8 (1/01/86) **70**
Médoc 1982 $6 (10/01/85) BB **76**

BOSQUET DES PAPES (France/Rhône)
Châteauneuf-du-Pape 1989 $18 (10/15/91) **85**
Châteauneuf-du-Pape 1988 $18 (10/15/91) **83**
Châteauneuf-du-Pape 1986 $18 (10/15/91) **90**
Châteauneuf-du-Pape 1985 $18 (10/15/91) **86**
Châteauneuf-du-Pape 1984 $17 (11/15/87) **91**
Châteauneuf-du-Pape 1983 $20 (10/15/91) **86**
Châteauneuf-du-Pape 1981 $30 (10/15/91) **93**
Châteauneuf-du-Pape Blanc 1990 $22 (10/15/91) **82**
Châteauneuf-du-Pape Blanc 1989 $18 (10/15/91) **87**

BOTT FRERES (France/Alsace)
Gewürztraminer Alsace Cuvée Exceptionnelle 1990 $15 (2/15/92) **87**
Gewürztraminer Alsace Cuvée Exceptionnelle 1989 $13.50 (6/30/91) **87**
Gewürztraminer Alsace Réserve Personnelle 1990 $18 (2/15/92) **84**
Gewürztraminer Alsace Réserve Personnelle 1989 $17 (6/30/91) **88**
Gewürztraminer Alsace Vendange Tardive 1990 $38 (2/15/92) (BT) **80+**
Gewürztraminer Alsace Vendange Tardive 1988 $40 (7/31/91) **63**
Pinot d'Alsace Alsace Sélection 1990 $13 (2/15/92) **78**

Riesling Alsace Cuvée Exceptionnelle 1989 $13 (7/31/91) **81**
Riesling Alsace Réserve 1990 $14 (2/15/92) **88**
Riesling Alsace Vendange Tardive 1990 $35 (2/15/92) (BT) **90+**
Riesling Alsace Vin de Prestige des Vignobles Réserve Personnelle 1990 $16 (2/15/92) **91**
Tokay d'Alsace Alsace Cuvée Exceptionnelle 1989 $13.50 (7/31/91) **80**
Tokay Pinot Gris Alsace Réserve Personnelle 1990 $18 (2/15/92) **89**
Tokay Pinot Gris Alsace Vendange Tardive 1990 $38 (2/15/92) (BT) **85+**

BOUCHAINE (United States/California)
Chardonnay Alexander Valley 1982 Rel: $14 Cur: $18 (CH-2/90) **79**
Chardonnay Alexander Valley 1982 Rel: $12.50 Cur: $18 (11/01/84) **82**
Chardonnay Carneros 1988 $15 (11/30/90) **82**
Chardonnay Carneros 1987 Rel: $14 Cur: $16 (8/31/90) **89**
Chardonnay Carneros 1985 Rel: $15 Cur: $20 (CH-2/90) **87**
Chardonnay Carneros 1984 Rel: $14 Cur: $20 (CH-2/90) **85**
Chardonnay Carneros 1983 Rel: $14 Cur: $23 (CH-2/90) **77**
Chardonnay Carneros Estate Reserve 1988 $20 (2/29/92) **88**
Chardonnay Carneros Estate Reserve 1987 $19 (5/31/90) **89**
Chardonnay Carneros Estate Reserve 1986 Rel: $19 Cur: $22 (CH-2/90) **88**
Chardonnay Carneros Winery Lake Vineyard 1984 $22 (CH-2/90) **71**
Chardonnay Napa Valley 1990 $15 (7/15/92) **85**
Chardonnay Napa Valley 1989 $15 (2/15/92) **84**
Chardonnay Napa Valley 1986 Rel: $13 Cur: $17 (CH-2/90) **88**
Chardonnay Napa Valley 1985 Rel: $13 Cur: $17 (CH-2/90) **87**
Chardonnay Napa Valley 1984 Rel: $12.50 Cur: $16 (CH-2/90) **66**
Chardonnay Napa Valley 1983 Rel: $12.50 Cur: $18 (CH-2/90) **75**
Chardonnay Napa Valley 1982 Rel: $14.50 Cur: $18 (6/16/84) SS **90**
Chardonnay Napa Valley Cask 85-86 NV $7.50 (7/31/87) BB **81**
Gewürztraminer Carneros 1989 $8.50 (6/15/91) **84**
Gewürztraminer Russian River Valley Dry 1990 $8.50 (3/31/92) **82**
Pinot Noir Los Carneros 1985 $7.50 (6/30/87) **76**
Pinot Noir Napa Valley 1982 $20 (6/30/87) **81**
Pinot Noir Napa Valley Los Carneros 1988 $15 (7/31/91) **78**
Pinot Noir Napa Valley Los Carneros 1987 $13 (10/31/90) **82**
Pinot Noir Napa Valley Los Carneros 1986 $12 (5/31/89) **86**
Pinot Noir Napa Valley Los Carneros 1985 $11.50 (12/31/88) **82**
Pinot Noir Napa Valley Los Carneros 1982 $12.50 (7/16/85) **87**
Pinot Noir Napa Valley Los Carneros Reserve 1988 $25 (3/31/92) **83**
Pinot Noir Napa Valley Los Carneros Reserve 1987 $20 (10/31/90) **85**
Pinot Noir Napa Valley Los Carneros Winery Lake Vineyard 1982 Rel: $15 Cur: $18 (3/01/86) CS **91**

BOUCHARD AINE (France/Burgundy)
Chambertin Clos de Bèze 1959 $90 (8/31/90) (TR) **84**
Chambertin Clos de Bèze Domaine Marion 1989 (NR) (1/31/92) **88**
Merlot Vin de Pays de l'Aude NV $5 (6/30/90) **72**
Pouilly-Fuissé Réserve 1985 $18 (3/31/87) **87**

BOUCHARD PERE & FILS (France/Burgundy)
Aloxe-Corton 1989 $36 (1/31/92) **87**
Beaune Blanc Clos St.-Landry Domaines du Château de Beaune 1989 $50 (8/31/91) **79**
Beaune Blanc Clos St.-Landry Domaines du Château de Beaune 1986 $33 (2/28/89) **81**
Beaune Clos de la Mousse Domaines du Château de Beaune 1989 $36 (7/15/90) (BT) **85+**
Beaune Clos de la Mousse Domaines du Château de Beaune 1986 $33 (7/31/88) **78**
Beaune Grèves Vigne de l'Enfant Jésus 1989 $59 (7/15/90) (BT) **95+**
Beaune Grèves Vigne de l'Enfant Jésus 1988 $59 (4/30/91) **91**
Beaune Grèves Vigne de l'Enfant Jésus 1986 $47 (7/31/88) **82**
Beaune Grèves Vigne de l'Enfant Jésus 1985 $61 (1/31/89) **91**
Beaune Grèves Vigne de l'Enfant Jésus 1983 Rel: $30 Cur: $34 (9/15/86) **85**
Beaune Marconnets Domaines du Château de Beaune 1989 $39 (1/31/92) **90**
Beaune Marconnets Domaines du Château de Beaune 1986 $24 (7/31/88) **83**
Beaune Marconnets Domaines du Château de Beaune 1985 $35 (1/31/89) **89**
Beaune Teurons Domaines du Château de Beaune 1988 $36 (7/15/90) (BT) **70+**
Beaune Teurons Domaines du Château de Beaune 1986 $32 (7/31/88) **81**
Beaune Teurons Domaines du Château de Beaune 1985 $35 (1/31/89) **85**
Beaune Teurons Domaines du Château de Beaune 1983 $21 (9/15/86) **71**
Chablis 1985 $15 (10/15/87) **83**
Chambertin 1989 (NR) (7/15/90) (BT) **90+**
Chambertin 1986 $78 (7/31/88) **81**
Chambertin Clos de Bèze 1989 $92 (1/31/92) **92**
Chambertin Clos de Bèze 1988 $82 (4/30/91) **89**
Chambolle-Musigny 1989 (NR) (7/15/90) (BT) **85+**
Chambolle-Musigny 1986 $29 (7/31/88) **73**
Chardonnay Vin de Pays d'Oc Première 1989 $9 (4/30/91) **75**
Chassagne-Montrachet 1989 $17 (4/30/91) **88**
Chassagne-Montrachet 1982 $17 (7/01/84) **80**
Chassagne-Montrachet Rouge 1988 $22 (4/30/91) **85**
Châteauneuf-du-Pape 1985 $11 (9/30/87) **82**
Chevalier-Montrachet Domaines du Château de Beaune 1989 $148 (8/31/91) **92**
Chevalier-Montrachet Domaines du Château de Beaune 1986 $92 (2/28/89) **68**
Clos de la Roche 1989 (NR) (1/31/92) **89**
Clos de Vougeot 1959 $120 (8/31/90) (TR) **85**
Corton Le Corton Domaines du Château de Beaune 1989 $79 (1/31/92) **92**
Corton Le Corton Domaines du Château de Beaune 1988 $77 (3/31/91) **91**
Corton Le Corton Domaines du Château de Beaune 1986 $47 (7/31/88) **85**
Corton Le Corton Domaines du Château de Beaune 1983 $37 (9/15/86) **83**
Corton-Charlemagne 1989 $77 (8/31/91) **87**
Côte de Beaune-Villages 1982 $19 (5/16/84) SS **88**
Côte de Beaune-Villages Clos des Topes Bizot 1983 $22 (9/15/86) **82**
Côtes du Rhône 1989 $8.50 (7/15/91) BB **82**

Key to Symbols

The scores reported here are the results of blind tastings conducted by our panel of senior editors. Wines that carry the initials below are results of individual tastings.

THE WINE SPECTATOR 100-POINT SCALE ***95-100***—Classic, a great wine; ***90-94***—Outstanding, superior character and style; ***80-89***—Good to very good, a wine with special qualities; ***70-79***—Average, drinkable wine that may have minor flaws; ***60-69***—Below average, drinkable but not recommended; ***50-59***—Poor, undrinkable, not recommended. "+"—With a score indicates a range; used primarily with barrel tastings to indicate a preliminary score.

SPECIAL DESIGNATIONS SS—Spectator Selection, CS—Cellar Selection, BB—Best Buy, ($NA)—Price not available, (NR)—Not released.

TASTER'S INITIALS (JG)—Jim Gordon, (HS)—Harvey Steiman, (JL)—James Laube, (JS)—James Suckling, (TM)—Thomas Matthews, (TR)—Terry Robards, (PM)—Per-Henrik Mansson, (BT)—Barrel Tasting (these wines were tasted blind from barrel samples), (CA-date)—*California's Great Cabernets* by James Laube, (CH-date)—*California's Great Chardonnays* by James Laube, (VP-date)—*Vintage Port* by James Suckling.

DATE TASTED Dates in parentheses represent the issue in which the rating was published.

Echézeaux 1989 $62 (1/31/92) **88**
Gevrey-Chambertin 1982 $18 (6/16/84) **80**
Meursault 1989 $37 (4/30/91) **83**
Meursault 1983 $20 (4/30/87) **75**
Meursault Clos des Corvées de Citeaux 1986 $26 (3/15/89) **83**
Meursault Les Genevrières Domaines du Château de Beaune 1989 $63 (8/31/91) **85**
Meursault Les Genevrières Domaines du Château de Beaune 1986 $44 (3/15/89) **77**
Montrachet Domaines du Château de Beaune 1989 $230 (8/31/91) **94**
Nuits-St.-Georges 1983 $21 (9/15/86) **68**
Nuits-St.-Georges Les Cailles 1959 $90 (8/31/90) (TR) **87**
Nuits-St.-Georges Clos-St.-Marc 1989 $59 (1/31/92) **89**
Nuits-St.-Georges Clos-St.-Marc 1988 $52 (7/15/90) (BT) **75+**
Nuits-St.-Georges Clos-St.-Marc 1985 $53 (2/28/89) **87**
Nuits-St.-Georges Clos-St.-Marc 1983 $33 (9/15/86) **74**
Nuits-St.-Georges La Richemone 1989 (NR) (1/31/92) **89**
Pommard 1989 $38 (7/15/90) (BT) **80+**
Pommard 1988 $37 (4/30/91) **90**
Pommard 1983 $23 (9/15/86) **74**
Pommard Clos du Pavillon 1989 (NR) (1/31/92) **92**
Pommard Premier Cru Domaines du Château de Beaune 1988 $53 (3/31/91) **89**
Pommard Premier Cru Domaines du Château de Beaune 1986 $41 (7/31/88) **87**
Pouilly-Fuissé 1989 $25 (4/30/91) **85**
Pouilly-Fuissé 1984 $20 (3/31/87) **87**
Pouilly-Vinzelles 1984 $13 (3/31/87) **79**
Puligny-Montrachet 1986 $31 (2/28/89) **87**
Puligny-Montrachet 1982 $18 (6/16/84) **87**
Puligny-Montrachet Les Champs-Gains 1989 (NR) (8/31/91) **85**
Puligny-Montrachet Les Folatières 1986 $33 (2/28/89) **90**
Puligny-Montrachet Les Folatières 1985 $33 (2/29/88) **85**
Puligny-Montrachet Les Pucelles 1989 $50 (8/31/91) **90**
La Romanée Château de Vosne-Romanée 1989 $298 (7/15/90) (BT) **90+**
La Romanée Château de Vosne-Romanée 1988 $238 (7/15/90) (BT) **90+**
La Romanée Château de Vosne-Romanée 1986 $200 (7/31/88) **91**
Savigny-lès-Beaune 1989 $29 (1/31/92) **82**
Savigny-lès-Beaune Les Lavières Domaines du Château de Beaune 1989 $29 (7/15/90) (BT) **80+**
Savigny-lès-Beaune Les Lavières Domaines du Château de Beaune 1988 $29 (4/30/91) **83**
Savigny-lès-Beaune Les Lavières Domaines du Château de Beaune 1986 $25 (7/31/88) **78**
Volnay Caillerets Ancienne Cuvée Carnot Château de Beaune 1989 $52 (2/29/92) CS **94**
Volnay Caillerets Ancienne Cuvée Carnot Château de Beaune 1988 $47 (3/31/91) **87**
Volnay Caillerets Ancienne Cuvée Carnot Château de Beaune 1986 $34 (7/31/88) **83**
Volnay Caillerets Ancienne Cuvée Carnot Château de Beaune 1985 $44 (1/31/89) **87**
Volnay Frémiets Clos de la Rougeotte Domaines du Château 1985 $35 (1/31/89) **88**
Volnay Taillepieds Domaines du Château de Beaune 1989 $48 (1/31/92) **88**
Volnay Taillepieds Domaines du Château de Beaune 1988 $50 (3/31/91) **88**
Vosne-Romanée Aux Reignots Château de Vosne-Romanée 1989 (NR) (1/31/92) **93**
Vosne-Romanée Aux Reignots Château de Vosne-Romanée 1988 $50 (7/15/90) (BT) **70+**
Vosne-Romanée Aux Reignots Château de Vosne-Romanée 1986 $50 (7/31/88) **89**
Vosne-Romanée Aux Reignots Château de Vosne-Romanée 1985 $51 (2/28/89) **90**

DOMAINE PASCAL BOUCHARD (France/Chablis)
Chablis 1989 $15 (11/30/91) **84**
Chablis Les Clos 1989 $36 (11/30/91) **89**

BOUCHE PERE & FILS (France/Champagne)
Brut Champagne Cuvée Réserve NV $20 (1/31/92) **87**

VALENTIN BOUCHOTTE (France/Burgundy)
Savigny-lès-Beaune Hauts-Jarrons 1988 $31 (2/28/91) **83**

DOMAINE JEAN-MARC BOULEY (France/Burgundy)
Pommard Les Rugiens 1987 $34 (11/15/90) **63**
Pommard Les Rugiens 1985 $30 (10/31/88) **92**
Volnay Les Caillerets 1985 $27 (10/15/88) **90**
Volnay Clos des Chênes 1985 $27 (10/15/88) **87**

PIERRE BOUREE FILS (France/Burgundy)
Beaune Epenottes 1989 $30 (1/31/92) **91**
Beaune Epenottes 1987 $35 (6/15/90) **88**
Bonnes Mares 1985 $85 (5/31/88) **91**
Bourgogne 1988 $15 (3/31/92) **73**
Chambertin 1987 $100 (5/31/90) **90**
Chambertin 1985 $113 (5/31/88) **92**
Chambolle-Musigny 1987 $44 (6/15/90) **82**
Chambolle-Musigny Charmes 1987 $56 (6/15/90) **82**
Charmes-Chambertin 1988 $75 (3/31/91) **89**
Charmes-Chambertin 1987 $66 (5/31/90) **87**
Charmes-Chambertin 1985 Rel: $68 Cur: $85 (5/31/88) **88**
Clos de la Roche 1989 $65 (1/31/92) **94**
Clos de la Roche 1988 $85 (3/31/91) **91**
Clos de la Roche 1987 $86 (6/15/90) **85**
Gevrey-Chambertin 1989 $35 (1/31/92) **85**
Gevrey-Chambertin Les Cazetiers 1987 $66 (5/31/90) **80**
Gevrey-Chambertin Les Cazetiers 1985 $67 (5/31/88) **91**
Gevrey-Chambertin Clos de la Justice 1988 $54 (3/31/92) **78**
Gevrey-Chambertin Clos de la Justice 1985 $51 (5/31/88) **85**
Gevrey-Chambertin Clos St.-Jacques 1987 $56 (5/31/90) **86**
Latricières-Chambertin 1959 $150 (8/31/90) (TR) **98**
Morey-St.-Denis 1987 $35 (5/15/90) **74**
Nuits-St.-Georges Les Vaucrains 1985 $68 (5/31/88) **93**
Santenay Gravières 1985 $30 (5/31/88) **88**
Vosne-Romanée 1987 $44 (7/15/90) **68**

HENRI BOURGEOIS (France/Loire)
Pouilly-Fumé Le Demoiselle de Bourgeois 1990 $20 (9/30/91) **84**
Sancerre Les Baronnes 1990 $18 (9/30/91) **87**
Sancerre Etienne Henri 1989 $30 (9/30/91) **83**
Sancerre Le MD de Bourgeois 1990 $22.50 (9/30/91) **90**

CHATEAU BOURGNEUF-VAYRON (France/Bordeaux)
Pomerol 1990 (NR) (5/15/92) (BT) **90+**
Pomerol 1989 $32 (3/15/92) **90**
Pomerol 1988 $19 (6/30/91) **90**
Pomerol 1987 $13 (6/30/89) (BT) **75+**
Pomerol 1986 Rel: $22 Cur: $26 (6/30/88) (BT) **80+**
Pomerol 1985 $28 (11/30/88) **86**
Pomerol 1982 $23 (5/15/89) (TR) **83**

BOURGOGNE ST.-VINCENT (France/Rhône)
Châteauneuf-du-Pape 1983 $8.50 (7/16/85) **81**

CHATEAU BOUSCAUT (France/Bordeaux)
Pessac-Léognan 1991 (NR) (5/15/92) (BT) **75+**
Pessac-Léognan 1990 (NR) (4/30/91) (BT) **90+**
Pessac-Léognan 1989 $22 (3/15/92) **93**
Pessac-Léognan 1988 $20 (4/30/91) **87**
Pessac-Léognan 1987 $10 (6/30/89) (BT) **80+**
Pessac-Léognan 1986 Rel: $9 Cur: $14 (2/15/89) **78**
Graves 1985 $15 (12/31/88) **90**
Graves 1981 $12 (5/01/84) **86**
Pessac-Léognan Blanc 1990 (NR) (9/30/91) (BT) **80+**
Pessac-Léognan Blanc 1989 $17 (9/30/91) **79**
Pessac-Léognan Blanc 1988 $15 (6/30/89) (BT) **80+**
Pessac-Léognan Blanc 1987 $13 (6/30/89) (BT) **85+**

DOMAINE DE LA BOUSQUETTE (France/Other)
St.-Chinian 1986 $8 (3/31/90) **82**

LA BOUVERIE (France/Rhône)
Costières de Nimes 1989 $6 (7/15/91) **79**
Costières de Nimes Blanc 1989 $6 (7/15/91) **79**

BOUVET (France/Other)
Brut Rosé NV $10 (6/15/90) **80**
Brut Rosé Excellence NV $12 (6/15/90) **80**
Brut Saumur Saphir 1988 $14 (1/31/92) **82**
Brut Saumur Saphir 1985 $12 (6/15/90) **84**
Brut Saumur Signature NV $11.50 (6/15/90) **75**
Rubis NV $10 (6/15/90) **72**

CHATEAU BOUYOT (France/Sauternes)
Barsac 1988 (NR) (6/15/90) (BT) **70+**
Barsac 1987 (NR) (6/15/90) **74**

HUBERT BOUZEREAU (France/Burgundy)
Chassagne-Montrachet 1985 $35 (8/31/87) **93**
Meursault Limozin 1985 $27 (8/31/87) **88**
Meursault Les Narvaux 1985 $25 (4/30/87) **73**

MICHEL BOUZEREAU (France/Burgundy)
Meursault Les Genevrières 1989 $46 (5/31/91) **93**
Meursault Les Genevrières 1988 $37 (7/15/90) **93**
Meursault Les Grands Charrons 1989 $33 (5/31/91) **90**
Meursault Les Grands Charrons 1988 $25 (8/31/90) **91**
Meursault Les Tessons 1989 $35 (5/31/91) **87**
Meursault Les Tessons 1988 $28 (8/31/90) **90**
Meursault Les Tessons 1985 $25 (5/31/88) **70**
Puligny-Montrachet 1985 $30 (5/31/88) **88**
Puligny-Montrachet Les Champs-Gains 1989 $42 (5/31/91) **91**
Puligny-Montrachet Les Champs-Gains 1988 $32 (7/31/90) **90**

PHILIPPE BOUZEREAU (France/Burgundy)
Chassagne-Montrachet Les Meix Goudard 1986 $29 (11/15/88) **77**
Meursault Les Charmes 1987 $37 (11/15/89) **75**
Meursault Les Genevrières 1987 $37 (7/15/90) **80**
Meursault Les Narvaux 1989 $37 (11/30/91) **74**
Meursault Les Narvaux 1986 $31 (3/15/89) **81**
Meursault Poruzots 1987 $36 (11/15/89) **83**
Puligny-Montrachet Les Champs-Gains 1986 $38 (11/15/88) **86**
Puligny-Montrachet Les Champs-Gains 1985 $34 (4/15/87) **94**

CHATEAU BOYD-CANTENAC (France/Bordeaux)
Margaux 1988 $20 (6/30/89) (BT) **85+**
Margaux 1987 $15 (6/30/89) (BT) **75+**
Margaux 1986 $15 (5/15/87) (BT) **80+**
Margaux 1985 Rel: $22 Cur: $24 (4/15/88) **90**
Margaux 1983 $19 (4/16/86) **86**
Margaux 1982 Rel: $15 Cur: $25 (5/01/85) **91**
Margaux 1961 $120 (3/16/86) (TR) **65**

BOYER (United States/California)
Chardonnay Monterey County Ventana Vineyard 1990 $12 (7/15/92) **80**
Chardonnay Monterey County Ventana Vineyard 1989 $15 (7/15/91) **87**

BOYER-MARTENOT (France/Burgundy)
Meursault Les Narvaux 1983 $15 (2/16/86) **60**

CHATEAU BRANAIRE-DUCRU (France/Bordeaux)
St.-Julien 1991 (NR) (5/15/92) (BT) **80+**
St.-Julien 1990 (NR) (5/15/92) (BT) **90+**
St.-Julien 1989 $35 (3/15/92) **90**
St.-Julien 1988 Rel: $16 Cur: $22 (8/31/90) (BT) **85+**
St.-Julien 1987 $15 (6/30/89) (BT) **80+**
St.-Julien 1986 Rel: $16 Cur: $27 (6/30/88) (BT) **85+**
St.-Julien 1985 Rel: $25 Cur: $29 (6/30/88) **89**
St.-Julien 1983 $24 (3/01/86) **88**
St.-Julien 1961 $125 (3/16/86) (TR) **79**
St.-Julien 1959 $140 (10/15/90) (JS) **86**
St.-Julien 1945 $175 (3/16/86) (JL) **67**

BODEGAS BRANAVIEJA (Spain)
Navarra Pleno 1988 $6 (12/15/90) BB **85**

BRANDBORG (United States/California)
Charbono Napa Valley 1989 $12 (10/31/91) **85**
Pinot Noir Anderson Valley 1989 $11 (11/15/91) **86**
Pinot Noir Santa Barbara County 1989 $13 (11/15/91) **87**

BRANDER (United States/California)
Bouchet Santa Ynez Valley Tête de Cuvée 1989 $20 (3/31/92) **84**
Chardonnay Santa Ynez Valley 1990 $14 (7/15/92) **64**
Chardonnay Santa Ynez Valley 1987 $13 (12/15/89) **84**
Chardonnay Santa Ynez Valley Tête de Cuvée 1989 $22 (7/15/91) **84**
Merlot Santa Ynez Valley Three Flags 1989 $12 (5/31/92) **82**
Merlot Santa Ynez Valley Three Flags 1988 $12 (5/31/92) **81**
Novissimo Santa Ynez Valley 1991 $9.50 (3/15/92) **82**
Sauvignon Blanc Santa Ynez Valley 1987 $8 (3/15/89) **85**
Sauvignon Blanc Santa Ynez Valley Reserve 1987 $11 (12/15/89) **82**
Sauvignon Blanc Santa Ynez Valley Tête de Cuvée 1990 $9.75 (4/15/92) **81**
Sauvignon Blanc Santa Ynez Valley Tête de Cuvée 1989 $9.50 (4/30/91) **79**

CHATEAU BRANE-CANTENAC (France/Bordeaux)
Margaux 1989 $42 (3/15/92) **94**
Margaux 1988 $42 (8/31/91) **76**
Margaux 1987 $25 (6/30/89) (BT) **80+**
Margaux 1986 Rel: $26 Cur: $30 (6/15/89) **87**
Margaux 1985 Rel: $24 Cur: $30 (6/30/88) **89**
Margaux 1983 Rel: $19 Cur: $28 (4/16/86) **94**
Margaux 1982 Rel: $22 Cur: $33 (5/01/85) **88**
Margaux 1979 $23 (10/15/89) (JS) **80**
Margaux 1962 $65 (11/30/87) (JS) **60**
Margaux 1961 $115 (3/16/86) (TR) **64**
Margaux 1945 $200 (3/16/86) (JL) **87**

BRAREN PAULI (United States/California)
Cabernet Sauvignon Mendocino 1987 $8.50 (3/31/91) BB **84**
Merlot Alexander Valley Mauritson Vineyard 1989 $12 (5/31/92) **77**
Merlot Alexander Valley Mauritson Vineyard 1987 $11 (3/31/91) **84**

CHATEAU BRASSAC (France/Bordeaux)
Bordeaux Supérieur 1986 $5.50 (8/31/88) BB **80**

MARC BREDIF (France/Loire)
Vouvray 1988 $11 (4/30/91) **87**
Vouvray Vin Moelleux Nectar 1985 $9/375ml (6/15/91) **75**

ANDRE-MICHEL BREGEON (France/Loire)
Muscadet de Sèvre et Maine Sur Lie 1988 $6.75 (11/15/90) **77**

BODEGAS BRETON (Spain)
Rioja Lorinon Crianza 1985 $9 (3/31/90) **85**

BRETON LORINON (Spain)
Rioja White 1990 (NR) (5/31/92) **85**
Rioja White Crianza 1989 (NR) (5/31/92) (BT) **85+**

GEORG BREUER (Germany)
Riesling Auslese Rheingau Charta 1990 $10 (12/15/91) **83**
Riesling Auslese Rheingau Rüdesheimer Bischofsberg 1990 $25 (12/15/91) **86**
Riesling Beerenauslese Rheingau Rüdesheimer Bischofsberg 1990 $100 (12/15/91) **97**
Riesling Kabinett Halbtrocken Rheingau Rüdesheimer Berg Schlossberg Charta 1988 $22 (9/30/89) **83**
Riesling Kabinett Halbtrocken Rheingau Rüdesheimer Bischofsberg Charta 1988 $16 (9/30/89) **82**
Riesling Kabinett Rheingau Rüdesheimer Berg Schlossberg Charta 1990 $12 (12/15/91) **82**
Riesling Qualitätswein Rheingau Charta 1988 $14 (9/30/89) **81**
Riesling Qualitätswein Rheingau Rüdesheimer Berg Roseneck Charta 1988 $14 (9/30/89) **85**
Riesling Qualitätswein Rheingau Rüdesheimer Berg Rottland Charta 1988 $14 (9/30/89) **85**
Riesling Spätlese Rheingau Rauenthaler Nonnenberg Charta 1990 $15 (12/15/91) **88**

CHATEAU BREUIL (France/Bordeaux)
Haut-Médoc 1991 (NR) (5/15/92) (BT) **70+**

BRICOUT (France/Champagne)
Brut Blanc de Blancs Champagne NV $21 (12/31/87) **85**
Brut Champagne 1985 (NR) (12/31/90) **81**
Brut Champagne Carte Noire Réserve NV $30 (12/31/91) **90**
Brut Champagne Carte d'Or Prestige 1986 $40 (12/31/91) **86**
Brut Champagne Carte d'Or Prestige 1983 $25 (12/31/89) **75**
Brut Champagne Carte d'Or Prestige NV $30 (12/31/91) **83**
Brut Champagne Elegance de Bricout 1985 (NR) (12/31/90) **85**
Brut Champagne Elegance de Bricout 1982 $50 (12/31/88) **90**
Brut Rosé Champagne NV $28 (12/31/88) **90**

MICHEL BRIDAY (France/Burgundy)
Rully Champ Clou 1987 $16 (12/31/90) **68**

BRIDGEHAMPTON (United States/New York)
Cabernet Sauvignon Long Island 1988 $14 (6/30/91) (TM) **84**
Cabernet Sauvignon Long Island 1987 $14 (6/30/91) (TM) **87**
Chardonnay Long Island Grand Vineyard Selection 1989 $17 (6/30/91) (TM) **81**
Chardonnay Long Island Grand Vineyard Selection 1988 $18 (3/31/90) **91**
Chardonnay Long Island The Hamptons Estate Reserve 1989 $14.50 (6/30/91) (TM) **78**
Merlot Long Island 1988 $16 (6/30/91) (TM) **89**
Reserve Red Grand Vineyard North Fork of Long Island 1987 $17 (6/30/91) (TM) **80**

BRIDGEVIEW (United States/Oregon)
Chardonnay Oregon 1990 $6.50 (11/15/91) BB **83**
Chardonnay Oregon Barrel Select 1989 $12 (3/31/91) **84**
Chardonnay Oregon Barrel Select 1988 $12 (3/31/91) **81**
Pinot Gris Oregon 1990 $11 (11/15/91) **86**
Pinot Noir Oregon 1986 $8 (2/15/90) **79**
Pinot Noir Oregon Estate Bottled 1988 $8 (2/15/90) **88**
Pinot Noir Oregon Estate Bottled 1986 $8 (6/15/88) **87**
Pinot Noir Oregon Special Reserve 1987 $12 (2/15/90) **80**
Pinot Noir Oregon Winemaker's Reserve 1988 $12 (11/15/91) **87**
Pinot Noir Oregon Winemaker's Reserve 1987 $15 (2/15/90) **89**
Riesling Oregon Dry Vintage Select 1990 $6 (6/15/92) BB **83**

JOSEF BRIGL (Italy/North)
Chardonnay Alto Adige 1989 $10 (7/15/91) **77**

CHATEAU BRILLETTE (France/Bordeaux)
Moulis 1991 (NR) (5/15/92) (BT) **70+**
Moulis 1989 $17 (3/15/92) **86**
Moulis 1988 $15 (8/31/91) **81**
Moulis 1987 $15 (11/30/89) (JS) **72**
Moulis 1986 $14 (11/30/89) (JS) **78**
Moulis 1982 $23 (11/30/89) (JS) **85**

CHATEAU BRIOT (France/Bordeaux)
Bordeaux 1985 $4 (5/15/87) **75**

BROADLEY (United States/Oregon)
Pinot Noir Oregon 1987 $8 (2/15/90) **76**
Pinot Noir Oregon Reserve 1987 $12 (2/15/90) **88**
Pinot Noir Oregon Reserve 1986 $11.50 (6/15/88) **73**

JEAN-MARC BROCARD (France/Chablis)
Chablis Domaine Ste.-Claire 1989 $13 (1/31/91) **86**

VILLA BROTINI (Italy/Tuscany)
Chianti Classico Villa Brotini 1984 $5.75 (12/31/87) **77**

LAURENT CHARLES BROTTE (France/Rhône)
Châteauneuf-du-Pape Blanc 1987 $14 (10/31/89) **74**
Côtes du Rhône-Villages Seguret 1986 $6 (9/30/89) BB **80**
Vin de Pays d'Oc Viognier 1991 $8 (6/30/92) BB **81**

CHATEAU BROUSTET (France/Sauternes)
Barsac 1989 (NR) (6/15/90) (BT) **90+**
Barsac 1988 $19/375ml (3/31/91) **83**
Barsac 1986 $20 (6/30/88) (BT) **75+**

CHATEAU BROWN (France/Bordeaux)
Pessac-Léognan 1988 $17 (6/30/89) (BT) **80+**
Pessac-Léognan 1987 $15 (6/30/89) (BT) **75+**
Pessac-Léognan 1986 $19 (5/15/87) (BT) **80+**

BROWN BROTHERS (Australia)
Cabernet Sauvignon Victoria Family Reserve 1987 $11.50 (9/15/90) **83**
Cabernet Sauvignon Victoria Family Selection 1987 $9.50 (7/15/90) **82**
Cabernet Sauvignon Victoria Family Selection 1985 $7.50 (5/15/89) **76**
Cabernet Sauvignon Victoria St.-George Vineyard 1984 $8 (5/31/87) **86**
Chardonnay Australia Family Reserve NV $9 (5/31/87) **86**
Chardonnay King Valley 1987 $11 (7/31/89) **84**
Chardonnay King Valley Family Reserve 1988 $17 (9/15/91) **90**
Chardonnay King Valley Family Reserve 1987 $15.50 (7/15/90) SS **91**
Chardonnay King Valley Family Selection 1988 $11.50 (7/15/90) **80**
Chardonnay Victoria Estate Selection 1985 $8 (8/31/87) **85**
Muscat of Alexandria Victoria Lexia 1986 $8 (5/15/89) **77**
Muscat of Alexandria Victoria Lexia Family Selection 1987 $8.50 (7/31/90) **73**
Pinot Noir Victoria 1983 $9 (7/01/87) **83**
Port Victoria Family Selection 1987 $12.50 (7/31/90) **84**
Sauvignon Blanc Victoria Family Selection Limited Production 1988 $15 (6/30/92) **83**
Shiraz Australia 1983 $9 (7/15/87) **92**
Shiraz Mondeuse Cabernet Sauvignon Australia 1983 $10 (7/01/87) **87**
Shiraz Victoria 1985 $7 (5/15/89) BB **83**
Shiraz Victoria Family Selection 1986 $8 (7/15/90) **85**

DAVID BRUCE (United States/California)
Cabernet Sauvignon California Vintner's Select 1983 $12.50 (9/30/86) **79**
Chardonnay California 1984 $10 (7/16/86) **79**
Chardonnay Santa Cruz Mountains 1990 $18 (4/30/92) **85**
Chardonnay Santa Cruz Mountains 1987 $18 (2/15/90) **77**
Chardonnay Santa Cruz Mountains 1983 $18 (9/30/86) **69**
Chardonnay Santa Cruz Mountains Estate Reserve 1990 $25 (5/31/92) **84**
Chardonnay Santa Cruz Mountains Meyley Vineyard 1990 $18 (7/15/92) **69**
Chardonnay Santa Cruz Mountains Vineyard Selection 1990 $15 (5/31/92) **74**
Côte de Shandon Vin Rouge San Luis Obispo County 1987 $7.50 (12/31/88) **81**
Mrs. Baggins California 1990 $10 (6/30/92) **84**
Pinot Noir Santa Cruz Mountains 1986 $18 (3/31/90) **59**
Pinot Noir Santa Cruz Mountains 1984 $15 (6/30/87) **81**
Pinot Noir Santa Cruz Mountains 1983 $15 (8/31/86) **78**
Zinfandel San Luis Obispo County 1990 $12 (5/15/92) **90**

LIONEL J. BRUCK (France/Burgundy)
Bourgogne Blanc St.-Vincent Pinot Chardonnay 1984 $10 (3/31/87) **79**
Bourgogne St.-Vincent Pinot Noir 1983 $10 (2/15/87) **78**

BRUGNANO (Italy/Tuscany)
Chianti Colli Fiorentini 1986 $5 (1/31/89) BB **85**

BRUMMELL (France/Other)
Blanc de Blancs Carte Noir NV $7.25 (6/15/90) **79**

DANIEL BRUSSET (France/Rhône)
Gigondas Les Hauts de Montmirail 1989 $22 (11/15/91) **91**
Gigondas Les Hauts de Montmirail 1988 $17 (9/30/90) **90**

DOMAINE BRUSSET (France/Rhône)
Côtes du Rhône-Villages Cairanne Côteaux des Trabers 1986 $7 (6/15/89) **61**
Côtes du Rhône-Villages Côteaux des Trabers 1988 $7.75 (12/15/90) BB **86**

BRUTOCAO (United States/California)
Cabernet Sauvignon Mendocino 1988 $12.50 (3/31/92) **83**
Cabernet Sauvignon Mendocino 1986 $12.50 (3/31/92) **82**
Cabernet Sauvignon Mendocino 1982 $9 (11/30/88) **83**
Chardonnay Mendocino 1988 $10 (5/15/92) **81**
Merlot Mendocino 1988 $12.50 (5/31/92) **84**
White Zinfandel Mendocino 1987 $7 (6/15/89) **69**

BUCCI (Italy/Other)
Verdicchio dei Castelli di Jesi Classico 1988 $14 (12/31/90) **73**

BUEHLER (United States/California)
Cabernet Sauvignon Napa Valley 1988 (NR) (5/15/90) (BT) **80+**
Cabernet Sauvignon Napa Valley 1987 Rel: $16 Cur: $19 (7/31/90) **85**
Cabernet Sauvignon Napa Valley 1986 Rel: $15 Cur: $18 (4/30/89) **85**
Cabernet Sauvignon Napa Valley 1985 Rel: $14 Cur: $18 (CA-3/89) **93**
Cabernet Sauvignon Napa Valley 1984 Rel: $13 Cur: $23 (CA-3/89) **87**
Cabernet Sauvignon Napa Valley 1983 Rel: $12 Cur: $23 (7/16/86) SS **93**
Cabernet Sauvignon Napa Valley 1982 Rel: $12 Cur: $28 (CA-3/89) **88**
Cabernet Sauvignon Napa Valley 1981 Rel: $11 Cur: $20 (CA-3/89) **85**
Cabernet Sauvignon Napa Valley 1980 Rel: $10 Cur: $25 (CA-3/89) **82**
Cabernet Sauvignon Napa Valley 1978 Rel: $10 Cur: $35 (CA-3/89) **87**
Pinot Blanc Napa Valley 1987 $9 (3/31/89) **87**
Pinot Blanc Napa Valley Buehler Vineyards 1988 $9 (2/15/90) **84**
White Zinfandel Napa Valley 1988 $6 (6/15/89) **88**
Zinfandel Napa Valley 1989 $9.75 (3/31/92) **83**
Zinfandel Napa Valley 1987 $9.50 (5/15/90) **89**
Zinfandel Napa Valley 1986 $8.50 (12/15/88) **83**
Zinfandel Napa Valley 1985 $8 (12/31/87) **89**
Zinfandel Napa Valley 1983 $6.50 (3/15/87) **71**
Zinfandel Napa Valley 1982 $6 (3/01/85) **91**
Zinfandel Napa Valley 1981 $6 (9/16/84) **80**

Key to Symbols

The scores reported here are the results of blind tastings conducted by our panel of senior editors. Wines that carry the initials below are results of individual tastings.

THE WINE SPECTATOR 100-POINT SCALE 95-100—Classic, a great wine; ***90-94***—Outstanding, superior character and style; ***80-89***—Good to very good, a wine with special qualities; ***70-79***—Average, drinkable wine that may have minor flaws; ***60-69***—Below average, drinkable but not recommended; ***50-59***—Poor, undrinkable, not recommended. "+"—With a score indicates a range; used primarily with barrel tastings to indicate a preliminary score.

SPECIAL DESIGNATIONS SS—Spectator Selection, CS—Cellar Selection, BB—Best Buy, ($NA)—Price not available, (NR)—Not released.

TASTER'S INITIALS (JG)—Jim Gordon, (HS)—Harvey Steiman, (JL)—James Laube, (JS)—James Suckling, (TM)—Thomas Matthews, (TR)—Terry Robards, (PM)—Per-Henrik Mansson, (BT)—Barrel Tasting (these wines were tasted blind from barrel samples), (CA-date)—*California's Great Cabernets* by James Laube, (CH-date)—*California's Great Chardonnays* by James Laube, (VP-date)—*Vintage Port* by James Suckling.

DATE TASTED Dates in parentheses represent the issue in which the rating was published.

BUENA VISTA (United States/California)
Bistro Style Napa Valley 1990 $11 (7/15/91) **83**
Cabernet Sauvignon Carneros 1988 $8 (11/15/91) **79**
Cabernet Sauvignon Carneros 1987 $11 (10/15/90) **83**
Cabernet Sauvignon Carneros 1986 $11 (10/15/89) **91**
Cabernet Sauvignon Carneros 1985 $10 (11/15/88) **84**
Cabernet Sauvignon Carneros 1984 $10 (8/31/87) **94**
Cabernet Sauvignon Carneros 1983 $9.75 (6/15/87) **77**
Cabernet Sauvignon Carneros 1982 $11 (9/16/85) **85**
Cabernet Sauvignon Sonoma Valley 1978 Rel: $12 Cur: $30 (6/01/86) **94**
Cabernet Sauvignon Sonoma Valley 1976 Rel: $12 Cur: $40 (CA-3/89) **66**
Cabernet Sauvignon Sonoma Valley 1975 Rel: $12 Cur: $30 (CA-3/89) **64**
Cabernet Sauvignon Carneros Private Reserve 1986 Rel: $25 Cur: $28 (10/15/90) **93**
Cabernet Sauvignon Carneros Private Reserve 1985 Rel: $18 Cur: $26 (10/15/89) SS **94**
Cabernet Sauvignon Carneros Private Reserve 1984 Rel: $18 Cur: $25 (CA-3/89) **90**
Cabernet Sauvignon Carneros Private Reserve 1983 Rel: $18 Cur: $25 (CA-3/89) **87**
Cabernet Sauvignon Carneros Private Reserve 1982 Rel: $18 Cur: $30 (CA-3/89) **85**
Cabernet Sauvignon Carneros Private Reserve Special Selection 1981 Rel: $18 Cur: $30 (CA-3/89) **86**
Cabernet Sauvignon Carneros Special Selection 1980 Rel: $18 Cur: $28 (CA-3/89) **84**
Cabernet Sauvignon Carneros Special Selection 1979 Rel: $18 Cur: $35 (CA-3/89) **92**
Cabernet Sauvignon Carneros Special Selection 1978 Rel: $18 Cur: $50 (CA-3/89) **90**
Cabernet Sauvignon Sonoma Valley Cask 34 1977 Rel: $12 Cur: $40 (CA-3/89) **72**
Cabernet Sauvignon Sonoma Valley Cask 25 1974 Rel: $12 Cur: $37 (CA-3/89) **68**
Cabernet Sauvignon Sonoma County 1986 $11 (11/15/89) **90**
Chardonnay Carneros 1990 $12 (11/15/91) **85**
Chardonnay Carneros 1989 $11 (7/15/91) **85**
Chardonnay Carneros 1987 $10 (10/15/88) **88**
Chardonnay Carneros 1986 $11.50 (6/30/87) **83**
Chardonnay Carneros 1984 $11 (3/01/86) **78**
Chardonnay Carneros Jeanette's Vineyard 1988 $26 (3/31/91) **83**
Chardonnay Carneros Jeanette's Vineyard 1986 $8.50 (2/15/88) **81**
Chardonnay Carneros Jeanette's Vineyard 1985 $13.25 (2/28/87) **83**
Chardonnay Carneros Private Reserve 1988 $16.50 (3/31/91) **82**
Chardonnay Carneros Private Reserve 1987 Rel: $16.50 Cur: $20 (CH-3/90) **82**
Chardonnay Carneros Private Reserve 1986 $16.50 (CH-3/90) **91**
Chardonnay Carneros Private Reserve 1985 $16.50 (CH-3/90) **86**
Chardonnay Carneros Private Reserve 1984 $14.50 (CH-6/90) **75**
Chardonnay Carneros Private Reserve 1983 Rel: $14.50 Cur: $18 (CH-3/90) **84**
Chardonnay Carneros Private Reserve 1982 $16.50 (3/16/86) **70**
Chardonnay Sémillon Bistro Style Napa Valley 1990 $11 (9/15/91) **83**
Fumé Blanc Alexander Valley 1987 $8.50 (3/15/89) **86**
Gamay Beaujolais Carneros 1988 $7.50 (7/15/89) **84**
Johannisberg Riesling Carneros 1987 $7 (7/31/89) **78**
L'Année Carneros 1986 $35 (2/28/91) **87**
L'Année Carneros 1984 $32/1.5L (2/15/88) **88**
Late Harvest Carneros Ingrid's Vineyard White 1989 $18 (4/30/91) **87**
Merlot Carneros 1989 $11 (5/31/92) **71**
Merlot Carneros 1985 $11 (6/30/88) **80**
Merlot Carneros Private Reserve 1988 $16.50 (5/31/92) **82**
Merlot Carneros Private Reserve 1987 $18 (3/31/91) **84**
Merlot Carneros Private Reserve 1986 $16.50 (10/31/89) **86**
Merlot Carneros Private Reserve 1984 $14.50 (2/15/88) **87**
Merlot Sonoma County 1987 $11 (7/31/90) **86**
Pinot Noir Carneros 1989 $7/500ml (7/31/91) **81**
Pinot Noir Carneros 1988 $11 (12/15/90) **82**
Pinot Noir Carneros Private Reserve 1987 $14 (6/30/91) **80**
Pinot Noir Carneros Private Reserve 1986 $14 (3/31/90) **85**
Pinot Noir Carneros Private Reserve 1984 $14.50 (2/15/88) **81**
Pinot Noir Sonoma Valley Carneros 1983 $14 (8/31/86) **75**
Pinot Noir Sonoma Valley Carneros 1980 $7 (4/16/84) **71**
Pinot Noir Sonoma Valley Carneros Private Reserve 1981 $14 (8/31/86) **88**
Sauvignon Blanc Lake County 1990 $6.50 (10/31/91) BB **84**
Sauvignon Blanc Lake County 1989 $7.50 (8/31/90) **85**
Sauvignon Blanc Lake County 1988 $7.50 (9/15/89) **88**
Sauvignon Blanc Lake County 1986 $7.25 (7/15/87) SS **91**
Zinfandel North Coast 1984 $7.25 (4/30/88) **77**
Zinfandel Sonoma County 1982 $6 (4/01/85) **80**

DOMAINE F. BUFFET (France/Burgundy)
Pommard Rugiens 1985 $40 (10/15/88) **88**
Volnay Champans 1985 $35 (10/15/88) **91**
Volnay Clos de la Rougeotte 1985 $35 (10/15/88) **91**

BODEGAS MARTINEZ BUJANDA (Spain)
Rioja Conde de Valdemar 1987 $8.50 (3/31/92) BB **90**
Rioja Conde de Valdemar 1986 $7 (3/31/92) **83**
Rioja Conde de Valdemar 1985 $7 (12/15/88) BB **89**
Rioja Conde de Valdemar Gran Reserva 1982 $20 (11/30/91) (TM) **89**
Rioja Conde de Valdemar Gran Reserva 1981 $20 (3/31/92) **89**
Rioja Conde de Valdemar Gran Reserva 1975 $25 (3/31/92) **87**
Rioja Conde de Valdemar Gran Reserva 1973 $25 (3/31/92) **86**
Rioja Conde de Valdemar Gran Reserva 1970 $30 (3/31/92) **89**
Rioja Conde de Valdemar Reserva 1986 $10 (3/31/92) **83**
Rioja Conde de Valdemar Reserva 1985 $9 (3/31/92) **91**
Rioja Conde de Valdemar Reserva 1983 (NR) (3/31/92) **88**
Rioja Conde de Valdemar Reserva 1982 $19 (3/31/92) **89**
Rioja Valdemar Vino Tinto 1989 $7 (6/30/90) BB **83**
Rioja White Conde de Valdemar 1990 $6.50 (5/31/92) **85**
Rioja White Valdemar 1990 $7 (11/15/91) **72**

BULLY HILL (United States/New York)
Brut Seyval Blanc Finger Lakes 1988 $15 (12/31/90) **74**

BURATI (Italy/Sparkling)
Asti Spumante NV $6.50 (3/15/89) **75**

BERNARD BURGAUD (France/Rhône)
Côte-Rôtie 1989 $32 (1/31/92) **84**
Côte-Rôtie 1988 $40 (3/31/91) **87**
Côte-Rôtie 1987 $29 (2/28/90) **85**
Côte-Rôtie 1986 $31 (1/31/89) **93**
Côte-Rôtie 1984 $22 (10/15/87) **90**
Côte-Rôtie 1983 $18 (5/01/86) **92**

BURGESS (United States/California)
Cabernet Sauvignon Napa Valley Vintage Selection 1987 Rel: $20 Cur: $23 (10/15/91) **85**
Cabernet Sauvignon Napa Valley Vintage Selection 1986 Rel: $20 Cur: $23 (7/15/90) **88**
Cabernet Sauvignon Napa Valley Vintage Selection 1985 Rel: $18 Cur: $22 (7/15/89) **92**
Cabernet Sauvignon Napa Valley Vintage Selection 1984 Rel: $17 Cur: $25 (CA-3/89) **93**

Cabernet Sauvignon Napa Valley Vintage Selection 1983 Rel: $17 Cur: $21 (CA-3/89) **87**
Cabernet Sauvignon Napa Valley Vintage Selection 1982 Rel: $16 Cur: $29 (CA-3/89) **88**
Cabernet Sauvignon Napa Valley Vintage Selection 1981 Rel: $16 Cur: $35 (9/16/85) **87**
Cabernet Sauvignon Napa Valley Vintage Selection 1980 Rel: $16 Cur: $46 (CA-3/89) **88**
Cabernet Sauvignon Napa Valley Vintage Selection 1980 Rel: $16 Cur: $46 (5/01/84) SS **90**
Cabernet Sauvignon Napa Valley Vintage Selection 1979 Rel: $16 Cur: $43 (CA-3/89) **87**
Cabernet Sauvignon Napa Valley Vintage Selection 1978 Rel: $14 Cur: $47 (CA-3/89) **93**
Cabernet Sauvignon Napa Valley Vintage Selection 1977 Rel: $12 Cur: $38 (CA-3/89) **92**
Cabernet Sauvignon Napa Valley Vintage Selection 1976 Rel: $12 Cur: $40 (CA-3/89) **87**
Cabernet Sauvignon Napa Valley Vintage Selection 1975 Rel: $9 Cur: $37 (CA-3/89) **88**
Cabernet Sauvignon Napa Valley Vintage Selection 1974 Rel: $9 Cur: $65 (CA-3/89) **86**
Chardonnay Napa Valley Triere Vineyard 1990 Rel: $15 Cur: $17 (5/31/92) SS **91**
Chardonnay Napa Valley Triere Vineyard 1989 Rel: $16 Cur: $18 (7/15/91) **82**
Chardonnay Napa Valley Triere Vineyard 1988 $16 (4/30/90) **90**
Chardonnay Napa Valley Triere Vineyard 1987 Rel: $14.50 Cur: $17 (CH-12/89) **85**
Chardonnay Napa Valley Triere Vineyard 1986 Rel: $14 Cur: $19 (CH-12/89) **87**
Chardonnay Napa Valley Vintage Reserve 1985 Rel: $13 Cur: $19 (CH-12/89) **88**
Chardonnay Napa Valley Vintage Reserve 1984 Rel: $13 Cur: $19 (CH-12/89) **79**
Chardonnay Napa Valley Vintage Reserve 1983 Rel: $12 Cur: $20 (CH-12/89) **69**
Chardonnay Napa Valley Vintage Reserve 1982 $12 (CH-12/89) **68**
Chardonnay Napa Valley 1981 Rel: $11 Cur: $16 (CH-12/89) **74**
Chardonnay Napa Valley 1980 Rel: $11 Cur: $18 (CH-12/89) **75**
Chardonnay Napa Valley 1979 Rel: $11 Cur: $18 (CH-12/89) **78**
Chardonnay Napa Valley 1978 Rel: $11 Cur: $18 (CH-12/89) **77**
Chardonnay Napa Valley 1977 Rel: $11 Cur: $23 (CH-12/89) **80**
Chardonnay Carneros Winery Lake Vineyard 1976 Rel: $10 Cur: $20 (CH-12/89) **70**
Chardonnay Carneros Winery Lake Vineyard 1975 Rel: $9 Cur: $40 (CH-12/89) **84**
Chardonnay Carneros Winery Lake Vineyard 1974 Rel: $6 Cur: $25 (CH-12/89) **79**
Chardonnay Napa Valley 1973 Rel: $6 Cur: $30 (CH-12/89) **85**
Zinfandel Napa Valley 1988 $12 (7/31/91) **80**
Zinfandel Napa Valley 1987 $10 (5/31/90) **82**
Zinfandel Napa Valley 1986 $9.50 (7/31/89) **82**
Zinfandel Napa Valley 1985 $9 (6/30/88) **87**
Zinfandel Napa Valley 1984 $8 (11/15/87) **89**
Zinfandel Napa Valley 1983 $7.50 (10/31/86) **81**
Zinfandel Napa Valley 1982 $6.50 (7/16/85) **85**
Zinfandel Napa Valley 1981 $6 (4/16/84) **81**

ALAIN BURGUET (France/Burgundy)
Gevrey-Chambertin Vieilles Vignes 1988 $45 (12/31/90) **88**
Gevrey-Chambertin Vieilles Vignes 1986 $33 (7/15/89) **84**

DR. BURKLIN-WOLF (Germany)
Riesling Auslese Rheinpfalz Forster Pechstein 1990 (NR) (12/15/91) **90**
Riesling Auslese Rheinpfalz Forster Pechstein 1989 $25 (12/15/90) **94**
Riesling Auslese Rheinpfalz Wachenheimer Gerümpel 1989 $34 (12/15/90) **95**
Riesling Beerenauslese Rheinpfalz Wachenheimer Gerümpel 1990 $130/375ml (12/15/91) **96**
Riesling Beerenauslese Rheinpfalz Wachenheimer Gerümpel 1989 (NR) (12/15/90) **95**
Riesling Beerenauslese Rheinpfalz Wachenheimer Goldbächel 1988 $30 (9/30/89) **87**
Riesling Beerenauslese Rheinpfalz Wachenheimer Rechbächel 1989 $95/375ml (12/15/90) **93**
Riesling Kabinett Halbtrocken Rheinpfalz 1988 $8 (9/30/89) **85**
Riesling Kabinett Rheinpfalz Deidesheimer Hohenmorgen 1985 $6.25 (6/30/87) **61**
Riesling Kabinett Rheinpfalz Forster Mariengarten 1990 $12 (12/15/91) **89**
Riesling Kabinett Rheinpfalz Ruppertsberger 1990 $12 (12/15/91) **80**
Riesling Kabinett Rheinpfalz Ruppertsberger Hoheburg 1989 (NR) (12/15/90) **87**
Riesling Kabinett Rheinpfalz Wachenheimer Gerümpel 1989 $9 (12/15/90) **83**
Riesling Kabinett Rheinpfalz Wachenheimer Rechbächel 1989 (NR) (12/15/90) **78**
Riesling Spätlese Rheinpfalz Deidesheimer Hohenmorgen 1989 $14 (12/15/90) **84**
Riesling Spätlese Rheinpfalz Forster Jesuitengarten 1990 $23 (12/15/91) **90**
Riesling Spätlese Rheinpfalz Forster Jesuitgartener 1989 $18 (12/15/90) **90**
Riesling Spätlese Rheinpfalz Wachenheimer Gerümpel 1989 $15 (12/15/90) **85**
Riesling Spätlese Rheinpfalz Wachenheimer Rechbächel 1990 $15 (12/15/91) **89**
Riesling Spätlese Trocken Rheinpfalz Geheimrat Dr. Albert Bürklin-Wolf 1990 (NR) (12/15/91) **85**
Riesling Spätlese Trocken Rheinpfalz Geheimrat Dr. Albert Bürklin-Wolf 1989 (NR) (12/15/90) **80**
Riesling Spätlese Trocken Rheinpfalz Wachenheimer Gerümpel 1988 $10 (9/30/89) **88**
Riesling Trockenbeerenauslese Rheinpfalz Ehrenfelser Wachenheimer Mandelgarten 1990 (NR) (12/15/91) **93**
Riesling Trockenbeerenauslese Rheinpfalz Ruppertsberger Linsenbusch 1988 $9 (9/30/89) **79**
Riesling Trockenbeerenauslese Rheinpfalz Wachenheimer Luginsland 1989 $165 (12/15/90) **95**

BURMESTER (Portugal)
Tawny Port 20-Year-Old NV $40 (2/28/90) (JS) **95**
Vintage Port 1985 $25 (VP-1/90) **93**
Vintage Port 1984 (NR) (VP-1/90) **84**
Vintage Port 1980 Rel: $18 Cur: $35 (VP-1/90) **88**
Vintage Port 1977 Rel: $11 Cur: $35 (VP-1/90) **82**
Vintage Port 1970 $50 (VP-1/90) **86**
Vintage Port 1963 $120 (VP-1/90) **83**

LEO BURNING (Australia)
Chardonnay South Australia 1987 $7 (5/31/88) **72**

MESSMER BURRWEILER (Germany)
Riesling Kabinett Halbtrocken Rheinpfalz Schlossgarten 1988 $8 (9/30/89) **87**
Riesling Kabinett Rheinpfalz Schlossgarten 1988 (NR) (9/30/89) **90**
Riesling Spätlese Rheinpfalz Schäwer 1988 $9 (9/30/89) **87**
Riesling Spätlese Trocken Rheinpfalz Schlossgarten 1988 $10 (9/30/89) **94**

BUTTERFLY CREEK (United States/California)
Merlot California 1989 $15 (5/31/92) **77**

CAVE DES VIGNERONS DE BUXY (France/Burgundy)
Bourgogne Pinot Noir Grande Réserve 1985 $7 (6/30/88) **75**
Bourgogne Pinot Noir Grande Réserve 1983 $5 (2/01/86) **73**

BYINGTON (United States/California)
Cabernet Sauvignon Napa Valley 1987 $16 (11/15/91) **86**
Chardonnay Napa Valley 1990 $15 (6/30/92) **78**
Chardonnay Napa Valley 1989 $15 (12/31/91) **77**
Pinot Noir California 1988 $15 (4/30/91) **83**
Pinot Noir Napa Valley 1987 $15 (4/30/91) **74**

DAVIS BYNUM (United States/California)
Cabernet Sauvignon Napa Valley Reserve Bottling 1984 $7 (12/15/87) **71**
Cabernet Sauvignon Sonoma County 1987 $10.50 (11/15/90) **79**
Cabernet Sauvignon Sonoma County 1986 $10 (11/15/89) **84**
Chardonnay Russian River Valley 1988 $10 (4/30/90) **79**
Chardonnay Russian River Valley Limited Release 1989 $13 (4/30/91) **79**
Chardonnay Russian River Valley Limited Release 1987 $14 (9/30/89) **80**
Chardonnay Sonoma County Reserve Bottling 1987 $9 (7/15/89) **82**
Pinot Noir Russian River Valley Artist Series 1985 $15 (6/15/88) **82**
Pinot Noir Russian River Valley Limited Release 1988 $16 (4/30/91) **86**
Pinot Noir Russian River Valley Limited Release 1986 $14 (3/31/90) **83**
Pinot Noir Russian River Valley Limited Release 1984 $14 (5/31/88) **89**
Pinot Noir Russian River Valley Westside Road 1983 $10 (7/16/86) **71**
Pinot Noir Sonoma County Reserve Bottling 1986 $9 (9/15/88) **82**
Pinot Noir Sonoma County Reserve Bottling 1985 $7 (1/31/88) **67**

BYRON (United States/California)
Cabernet Sauvignon Central Coast 1985 $14 (12/15/89) **76**
Chardonnay Santa Barbara County 1990 $14 (6/30/92) **85**
Chardonnay Santa Barbara County 1989 $13 (7/15/91) **80**
Chardonnay Santa Barbara County 1988 $12 (4/30/90) SS **92**
Chardonnay Santa Barbara County 1987 $11 (12/15/89) **91**
Chardonnay Santa Barbara County Reserve 1989 $18 (5/31/92) **82**
Chardonnay Santa Barbara County Reserve 1988 $17 (11/15/90) **86**
Chardonnay Santa Barbara County Reserve Barrel Fermented 1987 $16 (12/15/89) **78**
Chardonnay Santa Barbara County Reserve 1985 $13 (10/31/87) **73**
Pinot Noir Santa Barbara County 1986 $12 (6/15/88) **88**
Pinot Noir Santa Barbara County 1985 $12 (6/15/88) **81**
Pinot Noir Santa Barbara County Reserve 1987 $16 (12/15/89) **85**
Pinot Noir Santa Barbara County Reserve 1986 $12 (6/15/88) **84**
Pinot Noir Santa Barbara County Sierra Madre Vineyards 1984 $12.50 (8/31/86) **85**
Sauvignon Blanc Santa Barbara County 1989 $9 (4/30/91) **84**
Sauvignon Blanc Santa Barbara County 1988 $8.50 (12/15/89) **85**

LA CA' NOVA (Italy/Piedmont)
Barbaresco 1986 $14.50 (10/31/90) **87**

CA' ROME (Italy/Piedmont)
Barbaresco 1985 $28 (1/31/90) **88**
Barbaresco Maria di Brun 1985 $37 (1/31/90) **92**
Barolo 1985 $35 (10/15/90) **89**

TENUTA CA DU RUSS (Italy/Piedmont)
Arneis del Pidemonte 1989 $16 (1/31/92) **84**

CHATEAU LA CABANNE (France/Bordeaux)
Pomerol 1991 (NR) (5/15/92) (BT) **80+**
Pomerol 1990 (NR) (5/15/92) (BT) **90+**
Pomerol 1989 $30 (3/15/92) **92**
Pomerol 1987 $20 (6/30/89) (BT) **80+**
Pomerol 1986 $30 (6/30/88) (BT) **85+**
Pomerol 1985 $30 (5/15/87) (BT) **80+**

DOMAINE DU PERE CABOCHE (France/Rhône)
Châteauneuf-du-Pape 1989 $20 (10/15/91) **84**
Châteauneuf-du-Pape 1988 $20 (10/15/91) **87**
Châteauneuf-du-Pape 1986 $20 (10/15/91) **81**
Châteauneuf-du-Pape 1985 $20 (10/15/91) **85**
Châteauneuf-du-Pape 1983 $18 (10/15/91) **77**
Châteauneuf-du-Pape 1981 $30 (10/15/91) **87**
Châteauneuf-du-Pape Blanc 1990 $20 (10/15/91) **85**

CHATEAU CABRIERES (France/Rhône)
Châteauneuf-du-Pape 1988 $17 (11/30/90) **82**

CASTELLO DI CACCHIANO (Italy/Tuscany)
Chianti Classico 1988 ($NA) (9/15/91) **90**
Chianti Classico 1986 $8 (5/15/90) **86**
Chianti Classico 1985 $10 (10/31/88) **87**
Chianti Classico 1983 $6 (9/15/87) **73**
Chianti Classico Millennio Riserva 1985 $18 (9/15/90) **80**
RF 1988 $20 (9/15/91) **90**
RF 1986 $16 (6/15/90) **85**
RF 1985 $15 (8/31/88) **91**

MARQUES DE CACERES (Spain)
Rioja 1987 ($NA) (3/31/92) **88**
Rioja 1986 $9 (3/31/92) **82**
Rioja 1985 $9.50 (3/31/90) **80**
Rioja 1982 $7.50 (11/15/87) (JL) **87**
Rioja 1981 $5.50 (11/01/85) BB **88**
Rioja Gran Reserva 1982 $25 (3/31/92) **89**
Rioja Gran Reserva 1975 $26 (3/31/92) **89**
Rioja Gran Reserva 1973 ($NA) (3/31/92) **83**
Rioja Reserva 1985 $18.50 (3/31/92) **87**
Rioja Reserva 1982 $25 (3/31/92) **83**
Rioja Reserva 1981 $20 (3/31/90) **69**
Rioja Reserva 1975 $9.50 (12/01/85) **67**
Rioja White 1989 $10 (5/31/92) **87**
Rioja White 1988 $7.50 (3/31/90) **78**
Rioja White Reserva 1987 ($NA) (5/31/92) **85**

LA CADALORA (Italy/North)
Chardonnay della Vallagarina 1988 $11.25 (9/15/89) **79**
Chardonnay della Vallagarina 1987 $8.25 (3/31/89) **84**

CHATEAU CADET-PIOLA (France/Bordeaux)
St.-Emilion 1989 $24 (4/30/91) (BT) **80+**
St.-Emilion 1988 $20 (7/15/91) **89**
St.-Emilion 1987 $16 (6/30/89) (BT) **70+**
St.-Emilion 1982 $23 (5/15/89) (TR) **88**

VILLA CAFAGGIO (Italy/Tuscany)
Chianti Classico 1988 $10 (11/30/90) **83**
Chianti Classico 1987 $9 (9/15/89) **86**
Chianti Classico 1986 $9 (3/31/90) **89**
Chianti Classico 1985 $8 (5/31/88) **84**
Chianti Classico 1983 $10.50 (9/15/87) **91**
Chianti Classico 1982 $4 (10/16/85) **66**
Chianti Classico Riserva 1986 $18 (12/15/90) **86**
Chianti Classico Riserva 1985 $13 (9/15/91) **91**
Chianti Classico Riserva 1983 $10 (5/31/88) **80**
San Martino 1985 $20 (9/30/89) **79**
Solatio Basilica 1985 $20 (8/31/91) **83**

CAFARO (United States/California)
Cabernet Sauvignon Napa Valley 1988 Rel: $25 Cur: $27 (11/15/91) **81**
Cabernet Sauvignon Napa Valley 1987 $20 (11/15/90) **84**
Cabernet Sauvignon Napa Valley 1986 $18 (11/15/89) **93**
Merlot Napa Valley 1988 $20 (11/15/91) **89**
Merlot Napa Valley 1987 $18 (12/31/90) **86**
Merlot Napa Valley 1986 $18 (12/31/89) **84**

ROGER CAILLOT (France/Burgundy)
Bâtard-Montrachet 1985 $90 (5/31/88) **93**
Pommard 1987 $35 (9/15/89) **79**
Puligny-Montrachet Les Folatières 1988 $40 (6/30/90) **73**

CHATEAU CAILLOU (France/Sauternes)
Barsac 1989 $24 (6/15/90) (BT) **95+**
Barsac 1988 Rel: $37 Cur: $41 (6/15/90) (BT) **85+**
Barsac 1987 ($NA) (6/15/90) **85**
Barsac 1986 $30 (6/30/88) (BT) **75+**
Barsac 1983 Rel: $22 Cur: $28 (1/31/88) **76**

DOMAINE DU CAILLOU (France/Rhône)
Châteauneuf-du-Pape 1988 $22 (3/31/91) **86**

LES CAILLOUX (France/Rhône)
Châteauneuf-du-Pape 1989 $19 (10/15/91) **93**
Châteauneuf-du-Pape 1988 $18 (10/15/91) **88**
Châteauneuf-du-Pape 1986 $18 (10/15/91) **79**
Châteauneuf-du-Pape 1985 $20 (10/15/91) **82**
Châteauneuf-du-Pape 1983 $25 (10/15/91) **88**
Châteauneuf-du-Pape 1981 $30 (10/15/91) **76**
Châteauneuf-du-Pape Blanc 1990 $18 (10/15/91) **88**
Châteauneuf-du-Pape Blanc 1989 $17 (10/15/91) **89**
Châteauneuf-du-Pape Sélection Reflets 1986 $14 (5/31/89) **89**

CAIN (United States/California)
Cabernet Sauvignon Napa Valley Estate 1987 $25 (10/15/90) **92**
Cabernet Sauvignon Napa Valley 1986 $16 (8/31/90) **85**
Cabernet Sauvignon Napa Valley 1985 $16 (4/15/89) **81**
Cabernet Sauvignon Napa Valley 1984 $14 (5/31/88) **79**
Cabernet Sauvignon Napa Valley 1983 $14 (8/31/87) **75**
Cabernet Sauvignon Napa Valley 1982 $11 (9/30/86) **78**
Chardonnay Carneros 1990 $12 (7/15/92) **83**
Chardonnay Carneros 1989 $16 (7/15/91) **83**
Chardonnay Carneros 1988 $16 (11/30/90) **84**
Chardonnay Carneros 1987 $16 (12/31/89) **86**
Chardonnay Carneros 1986 $16 (9/15/88) **88**
Chardonnay Carneros 1985 $16 (10/31/87) **82**
Chardonnay Napa Valley 1987 $10 (4/30/89) **83**
Chardonnay Napa Valley 1986 $10 (9/30/88) **87**
Chardonnay Napa Valley 1984 $10 (10/31/86) **62**
Chardonnay Napa Valley 1983 $10 (1/01/85) **60**
Chardonnay Napa-Sonoma Counties 1985 $10 (7/31/87) **74**
Five Napa Valley 1991 (NR) (5/15/92) (BT) **92+**
Five Napa Valley 1990 (NR) (5/15/91) (BT) **90+**
Five Napa Valley 1989 (NR) (5/15/91) (BT) **90+**
Five Napa Valley 1987 $30 (4/30/91) **91**
Five Napa Valley 1986 $30 (2/15/90) **91**
Five Napa Valley 1985 $26 (6/15/89) **87**
Merlot Napa Valley 1990 (NR) (5/15/91) (BT) **90+**
Merlot Napa Valley 1986 $14 (2/28/89) **83**
Merlot Napa Valley 1984 $12 (9/30/88) **89**
Merlot Napa Valley 1982 $11 (2/01/85) **78**
Sauvignon Blanc Napa Valley Musqué 1990 $12 (6/15/92) **82**
Sauvignon Blanc Napa Valley Musqué 1989 $12 (3/15/91) **83**

CAVE DES COTEAUX CAIRANNE (France/Rhône)
Côtes du Rhône 1986 $7.25 (7/31/88) **86**
Côtes du Rhône Domaine le Château 1985 $6.25 (8/31/87) BB **85**
Côtes du Rhône Le Château a Cairanne 1987 $7 (12/15/89) **77**
Côtes du Rhône Le Château a Cairanne 1986 $6 (7/31/88) BB **82**
Côtes du Rhône-Villages 1988 $6.50 (2/28/90) BB **81**
Côtes du Rhône-Villages Cairanne 1988 $6.25 (6/30/90) **76**

CAKEBREAD (United States/California)
Cabernet Sauvignon Napa Valley 1988 $24 (11/15/91) **86**
Cabernet Sauvignon Napa Valley 1987 Rel: $18 Cur: $23 (10/15/90) **90**
Cabernet Sauvignon Napa Valley 1986 Rel: $18 Cur: $21 (8/31/89) **90**
Cabernet Sauvignon Napa Valley 1985 Rel: $17 Cur: $20 (CA-3/89) **84**
Cabernet Sauvignon Napa Valley 1984 Rel: $16 Cur: $25 (CA-3/89) **89**
Cabernet Sauvignon Napa Valley 1983 Rel: $16 Cur: $25 (CA-3/89) **77**
Cabernet Sauvignon Napa Valley 1982 Rel: $16 Cur: $28 (CA-3/89) **86**
Cabernet Sauvignon Napa Valley 1981 Rel: $16 Cur: $30 (CA-3/89) **88**
Cabernet Sauvignon Napa Valley 1980 Rel: $14 Cur: $30 (CA-3/89) **84**
Cabernet Sauvignon Napa Valley 1979 Rel: $13 Cur: $30 (CA-3/89) **82**
Cabernet Sauvignon Napa Valley 1978 Rel: $12 Cur: $35 (CA-3/89) **85**
Cabernet Sauvignon Napa Valley Lot 2 1978 Rel: $12 Cur: $50 (CA-3/89) **86**
Cabernet Sauvignon Napa Valley Rutherford Reserve 1986 $43 (11/15/91) **89**
Cabernet Sauvignon Napa Valley Rutherford Reserve 1985 $40 (CA-3/89) **85**
Cabernet Sauvignon Napa Valley Rutherford Reserve 1984 $35 (2/15/90) **85**
Cabernet Sauvignon Napa Valley Rutherford Reserve 1983 $35 (CA-3/89) **88**
Chardonnay Napa Valley 1990 $21 (1/31/92) **86**
Chardonnay Napa Valley 1989 $19.50 (7/15/91) **79**
Chardonnay Napa Valley 1988 $17.50 (3/15/90) **89**
Chardonnay Napa Valley 1987 $21 (6/30/89) **86**
Chardonnay Napa Valley 1986 $20 (2/15/88) **70**
Chardonnay Napa Valley Reserve 1988 $30 (11/30/91) **86**
Chardonnay Napa Valley Reserve 1986 $26 (2/15/90) **88**

VILLA CALCINAIA (Italy/Tuscany)
Cerviolo 1987 $18 (3/31/90) **79**
Cerviolo 1986 $18.50 (3/31/90) **82**
Chianti Classico 1988 $11.50 (9/15/91) **89**
Chianti Classico Riserva 1985 ($NA) (9/15/91) **84**

LUIGI CALDI (Italy/Piedmont)
Barbera d'Asti 1985 $7 (7/31/89) **78**
Gattinara 1982 $12 (1/31/90) **69**

CALE (United States/California)
Chardonnay Carneros Sangiacomo Vineyard 1990 $18 (3/31/92) **90**

CALEM (Portugal)
Tawny Port 20 Años NV $35 (4/15/90) (JS) **83**
Vintage Port 1985 Rel: $25 Cur: $40 (VP-6/90) **88**
Vintage Port 1983 Rel: $18 Cur: $44 (VP-6/90) **84**
Vintage Port 1980 Rel: $14 Cur: $42 (VP-6/90) **78**
Vintage Port 1977 Rel: $11 Cur: $58 (VP-11/89) **69**
Vintage Port 1975 $45 (VP-2/90) **86**
Vintage Port 1970 $50 (VP-11/89) **80**
Vintage Port 1966 $65 (VP-11/89) **82**
Vintage Port 1963 $85 (VP-12/89) **82**
Vintage Port Quinta do Foz 1987 $28 (VP-6/90) **84**
Vintage Port Quinta do Foz 1982 Rel: $16 Cur: $37 (VP-6/90) **82**

CALERA (United States/California)
Chardonnay Central Coast 1990 $14 (3/31/92) **88**
Chardonnay Central Coast 1989 $14 (1/31/92) **84**
Chardonnay Central Coast 1988 $14 (11/30/90) **86**
Chardonnay Central Coast 1987 $12 (3/15/90) **82**
Chardonnay Central Coast 1986 $12 (7/31/89) **83**
Chardonnay San Benito County Mount Harlan Vineyard Young Vines 1987 $22 (4/15/89) **86**
Chardonnay Santa Barbara County 1985 $11.75 (7/31/87) **80**
Chardonnay Santa Barbara County 1984 $11.25 (3/16/86) **64**
Chardonnay Santa Barbara County Los Alamos Vineyard 1983 $10.75 (2/01/85) **83**
Pinot Noir Blanc California 1990 $7 (10/31/91) BB **84**
Pinot Noir Central Coast 1990 $14 (3/31/92) **87**
Pinot Noir Central Coast 1989 $14 (11/15/91) **85**
Pinot Noir Central Coast 1987 $14 (2/15/90) **82**
Pinot Noir Mt. Harlan Mills 1988 $30 (11/15/91) **89**
Pinot Noir Mt. Harlan Jensen 1988 $35 (11/15/91) **92**
Pinot Noir San Benito County Jensen 1987 $30 (4/30/91) **93**
Pinot Noir San Benito County Jensen 1986 $25 (5/31/89) **88**
Pinot Noir San Benito County Jensen 1985 $25 (6/15/88) **88**
Pinot Noir San Benito County Jensen 1983 $22 (8/31/86) **80**
Pinot Noir California Jensen 1982 $23 (1/01/85) **88**
Pinot Noir Mt. Harlan Reed 1988 $30 (11/15/91) **85**
Pinot Noir San Benito County Reed 1987 $35 (4/30/91) **80**
Pinot Noir San Benito County Reed 1982 $23 (8/31/86) **75**
Pinot Noir Mt. Harlan Selleck 1987 $30 (11/15/91) **92**
Pinot Noir San Benito County Selleck 1986 $30 (3/31/90) **85**
Pinot Noir Santa Barbara County Bien Nacido Vineyard 1985 $12.50 (6/15/88) **82**
Pinot Noir Santa Barbara County Los Alamos Vineyard 1982 $10 (11/16/85) **62**
Viognier San Benito County 1987 ($NA) (4/15/89) **86**
Zinfandel California NV $5 (7/31/88) **71**
Zinfandel Cienega Valley 1981 $7 (4/16/84) **81**
Zinfandel Cienega Valley Reserve 1981 $8.50 (1/01/85) **82**

CHATEAU DE CALISSANNE (France/Other)
Côteaux d'Aix en Provence Cuvée Prestige 1988 $12 (8/31/91) **78**

CALITERRA (Chile)
Cabernet Sauvignon Maipo 1989 $6 (6/15/92) BB **87**
Cabernet Sauvignon Maipo 1988 $6 (10/15/91) **79**
Cabernet Sauvignon Maipo 1987 $6 (9/15/90) BB **86**
Cabernet Sauvignon Maipo 1986 $6 (7/31/89) BB **85**
Chardonnay Curicó 1991 $6 (6/15/92) BB **86**
Chardonnay Curicó 1990 $6 (6/15/91) **78**
Chardonnay Curicó 1989 $7 (9/15/90) **79**
Sauvignon Blanc Curicó 1991 $5 (6/15/92) **79**
Sauvignon Blanc Curicó 1990 $5 (10/15/91) **78**

CALLAHAN RIDGE (United States/Oregon)
Pinot Noir Oregon Elkton Vineyards 1987 $8 (2/15/90) **88**

CALLAWAY (United States/California)
Cabernet Sauvignon California America's Cup 1989 $10 (11/15/91) **82**
Chardonnay Temecula Calla-Lees 1990 $8 (11/30/91) **88**
Chardonnay Temecula Calla-Lees 1989 $10 (2/28/91) **72**
Chardonnay Temecula Calla-Lees 1988 $10 (2/28/90) **86**
Chardonnay Temecula Calla-Lees 1987 $9.75 (12/31/88) **84**
Chardonnay Temecula Calla-Lees 1986 $9.50 (11/15/87) **82**
Chardonnay Temecula Calla-Lees 1985 $9.25 (3/15/87) **86**
Chenin Blanc Temecula Morning Harvest 1988 $6.50 (7/31/89) **87**
Chenin Blanc Temecula Morning Harvest 1987 $5.50 (7/31/89) **84**
Fumé Blanc Temecula 1989 $6.50 (2/15/92) BB **83**
Fumé Blanc Temecula 1988 $8 (7/31/91) **68**
Fumé Blanc Temecula 1987 $8.25 (6/30/90) **78**
Sauvignon Blanc Temecula 1990 $6.50 (2/15/92) **77**
Sauvignon Blanc Temecula 1989 $8 (10/31/90) **79**
Sauvignon Blanc Temecula 1988 $8 (10/31/89) **82**
Sauvignon Blanc Temecula 1987 $7.75 (3/15/89) **71**
White Riesling Temecula 1990 $6.75 (5/15/91) **82**
White Riesling Temecula 1989 $6.75 (5/31/90) **73**
White Riesling Temecula 1988 $6.25 (7/31/89) **84**

CHATEAU CALON-SEGUR (France/Bordeaux)
St.-Estèphe 1991 (NR) (5/15/92) (BT) **80+**
St.-Estèphe 1990 (NR) (4/30/91) (BT) **85+**
St.-Estèphe 1989 $41 (3/15/92) **95**
St.-Estèphe 1988 $30 (7/15/91) **85**
St.-Estèphe 1987 $25 (6/30/89) (BT) **75+**
St.-Estèphe 1986 $32 (5/31/89) **86**
St.-Estèphe 1985 $30 (5/31/88) **88**
St.-Estèphe 1983 Rel: $16 Cur: $28 (10/31/86) **83**
St.-Estèphe 1962 $69 (11/30/87) (JS) **70**
St.-Estèphe 1961 $110 (3/16/86) (TR) **84**
St.-Estèphe 1959 $110 (10/15/90) (JS) **82**
St.-Estèphe 1945 $420 (3/16/86) (JL) **94**

CALVET (France/Burgundy)
Bourgogne Blanc Chardonnay Première 1987 $10 (4/30/89) **83**

Key to Symbols

The scores reported here are the results of blind tastings conducted by our panel of senior editors. Wines that carry the initials below are results of individual tastings.

THE WINE SPECTATOR 100-POINT SCALE ***95-100***—Classic, a great wine; ***90-94***—Outstanding, superior character and style; ***80-89***—Good to very good, a wine with special qualities; ***70-79***—Average, drinkable wine that may have minor flaws; ***60-69***—Below average, drinkable but not recommended; ***50-59***—Poor, undrinkable, not recommended. "+"—With a score indicates a range; used primarily with barrel tastings to indicate a preliminary score.

SPECIAL DESIGNATIONS SS—Spectator Selection, CS—Cellar Selection, BB—Best Buy, ($NA)—Price not available, (NR)—Not released.

TASTER'S INITIALS (JG)—Jim Gordon, (HS)—Harvey Steiman, (JL)—James Laube, (JS)—James Suckling, (TM)—Thomas Matthews, (TR)—Terry Robards, (PM)—Per-Henrik Mansson, (BT)—Barrel Tasting (these wines were tasted blind from barrel samples), (CA-date)—*California's Great Cabernets* by James Laube, (CH-date)—*California's Great Chardonnays* by James Laube, (VP-date)—*Vintage Port* by James Suckling.

DATE TASTED Dates in parentheses represent the issue in which the rating was published.

CAMBIASO (United States/California)
Cabernet Sauvignon Dry Creek Valley 1981 $4.75 (6/16/84) **60**

CAMBRIA (United States/California)
Chardonnay Santa Barbara County Cambria Vineyard Sur Lie 1988 $16 (12/15/89) **84**
Chardonnay Santa Barbara County Reserve 1986 $25 (12/15/89) **86**
Chardonnay Santa Maria Valley Katherine's Vineyard 1990 $16 (4/30/92) **90**
Chardonnay Santa Maria Valley Katherine's Vineyard 1989 $16 (12/31/90) **84**
Chardonnay Santa Maria Valley Reserve 1989 $25 (7/15/92) **89**
Chardonnay Santa Maria Valley Reserve 1988 $25 (12/31/90) **85**
Pinot Noir Santa Maria Valley Julia's Vineyard 1988 $16 (12/15/90) **88**

CHATEAU DE CAMENSAC (France/Bordeaux)
Haut-Médoc 1989 $22 (3/15/92) **86**
Haut-Médoc 1988 $16 (7/15/91) **55**
Haut-Médoc 1987 $12 (6/30/89) (BT) **75+**
Haut-Médoc 1986 $14 (6/30/89) **83**
Haut-Médoc 1985 $16 (5/15/87) (BT) **90+**
Haut-Médoc 1979 $22 (10/15/89) (JS) **82**

CAMERON (United States/Oregon)
Chardonnay Willamette Valley 1990 $14 (6/15/92) **79**
Pinot Noir Willamette Valley 1987 $14 (2/15/90) **81**
Pinot Noir Willamette Valley 1986 $15 (6/15/88) **86**
Pinot Noir Willamette Valley 1985 $14 (2/15/90) **82**
Pinot Noir Willamette Valley Abbey Ridge Vineyard Unfiltered Reserve 1989 $19 (3/31/92) **86**
Pinot Noir Willamette Valley Reserve 1986 $18 (2/15/90) **80**
Pinot Noir Willamette Valley Reserve 1985 $25 (2/15/90) **63**
Pinot Noir Willamette Valley Vintage Reserve 1987 $18 (2/15/90) **86**

CHATEAU CAMERON (France/Sauternes)
Sauternes 1989 ($NA) (6/15/90) (BT) **85+**
Sauternes 1988 ($NA) (6/15/90) (BT) **85+**
Sauternes 1987 ($NA) (6/15/90) **82**

CAMIGLIANO (Italy/Tuscany)
Brunello di Montalcino 1980 $8.50 (9/15/86) **72**
Brunello di Montalcino Riserva 1977 $11 (8/01/85) **85**
Chianti Colli Senesi 1985 $3.50 (12/15/87) **77**
Chianti Colli Senesi 1983 $2.75 (5/16/85) BB **82**

LAS CAMPANAS (Spain)
Navarra 1984 $6 (3/31/90) BB **86**

CAMPBELLS (Australia)
Muscat Rutherglen Old NV $15 (7/01/87) **92**
Tokay Rutherglen Old NV $15 (7/01/87) **91**

BODEGAS CAMPO VIEJO (Spain)
Rioja 1988 ($NA) (3/31/92) **83**
Rioja 1987 $6.50 (3/31/92) BB **83**
Rioja 1986 $6.50 (3/31/92) **81**
Rioja 1985 $6.50 (3/15/90) BB **83**
Rioja 1984 $5.25 (1/31/88) BB **82**
Rioja Gran Reserva 1981 ($NA) (3/31/92) **83**
Rioja Gran Reserva 1980 $15 (9/30/91) **88**
Rioja Gran Reserva 1978 $13.50 (9/30/90) **83**
Rioja Marqués de Villamagna Gran Reserva 1982 $20 (3/31/92) **81**
Rioja Marqués de Villamagna Gran Reserva 1978 $19 (11/15/91) **84**
Rioja Marqués de Villamagna Gran Reserva 1975 $20 (3/31/92) **88**
Rioja Marqués de Villamagna Gran Reserva 1973 ($NA) (3/31/92) **74**
Rioja Marqués de Villamagna Gran Reserva 1970 ($NA) (3/31/92) **87**
Rioja Reserva 1985 $9 (3/31/92) **83**
Rioja Reserva 1983 $9 (3/31/92) **81**
Rioja Reserva 1982 $9 (3/31/92) **84**
Rioja Reserva 1981 $7.25 (11/15/88) **78**
Rioja Viña Alcorta 1985 $10 (9/30/90) **85**
Rioja Viña Alcorta 1981 $7.25 (10/31/88) **76**
Rioja Viña Alcorta Reserva 1982 ($NA) (11/15/87) (JL) **87**
Rioja Viña Alcorta Tempranillo 1981 $7 (3/31/90) **64**
Rioja White Selección José Bezares Crianza 1987 ($NA) (5/31/92) **85**

CANARD-DUCHENE (France/Champagne)
Brut Champagne Cuvée Bicentenaire NV $29 (11/15/91) **87**
Brut Champagne Cuvée Spéciale de Charles VII NV $75 (12/31/89) **85**
Brut Champagne Patrimoine 1983 $42 (12/31/89) **80**
Brut Champagne Patrimoine NV $34 (12/31/91) **85**

CHATEAU CANDELAY (France/Bordeaux)
Bordeaux Supérieur 1986 $5 (6/15/89) **78**

CANEPA (Chile)
Cabernet Sauvignon Maipo Valley 1990 $6 (6/15/92) BB **81**
Cabernet Sauvignon Maipo Valley 1986 $6 (6/15/90) **75**
Cabernet Sauvignon Maipo Valley 1985 $4 (11/15/87) **75**
Cabernet Sauvignon Maipo Valley Finisismo 1983 $9 (6/30/90) **76**
Cabernet Sauvignon Maipo Valley Reserva 1988 $6.50 (6/15/90) BB **84**
Chardonnay Maipo Valley 1989 $6.50 (6/30/90) **72**
Merlot Maipo Valley 1990 $6 (6/15/92) BB **84**
Merlot Maipo Valley 1988 $6 (6/30/90) BB **79**
Sauvignon Blanc Maipo Valley 1991 $5 (5/15/92) BB **88**

CHATEAU CANET (France/Other)
Minervois Cuvée Elevée en Futs Grande Réserve 1988 $6 (5/31/90) **69**

CHATEAU CANON (France/Bordeaux)
St.-Emilion 1990 (NR) (5/15/92) (BT) **90+**
St.-Emilion 1989 $53 (3/15/92) **90**
St.-Emilion 1988 $40 (6/30/91) **90**
St.-Emilion 1987 $32 (5/15/90) **79**
St.-Emilion 1986 $45 (6/30/89) **93**
St.-Emilion 1985 Rel: $34 Cur: $47 (5/15/89) (TM) **91**
St.-Emilion 1983 Rel: $31 Cur: $42 (5/15/89) (TM) **88**
St.-Emilion 1982 $64 (5/15/89) (TM) **91**
St.-Emilion 1981 $28 (5/15/89) (TM) **82**
St.-Emilion 1980 $19 (5/15/89) (TM) **80**
St.-Emilion 1979 $40 (5/15/89) (TM) **89**
St.-Emilion 1978 $50 (5/15/89) (TM) **84**
St.-Emilion 1975 $38 (5/15/89) (TM) **84**
St.-Emilion 1971 $45 (5/15/89) (TM) **85**
St.-Emilion 1970 $60 (5/15/89) (TM) **93**
St.-Emilion 1966 $75 (5/15/89) (TM) **91**
St.-Emilion 1964 $75 (5/15/89) (TM) **89**
St.-Emilion 1962 $100 (5/15/89) (TM) **93**
St.-Emilion 1961 $100 (5/15/89) (TM) **88**
St.-Emilion 1959 $125 (5/15/89) (TM) **95**
St.-Emilion 1955 $110 (5/15/89) (TM) **88**
St.-Emilion 1953 $125 (5/15/89) (TM) **88**
St.-Emilion 1947 $250 (5/15/89) (TM) **91**

CHATEAU CANON DE BREM (France/Bordeaux)
Canon-Fronsac 1990 (NR) (5/15/92) (BT) **80+**
Canon-Fronsac 1989 $23 (3/15/92) **84**
Canon-Fronsac 1988 $13 (6/30/89) (BT) **80+**
Canon-Fronsac 1987 $14 (6/30/89) (BT) **80+**
Canon-Fronsac 1986 $15 (3/31/90) **86**
Canon-Fronsac 1985 $19 (5/15/87) (BT) **80+**

CHATEAU CANON-FRONSAC (France/Bordeaux)
Canon-Fronsac 1990 (NR) (5/15/92) (BT) **85+**
Canon-Fronsac 1989 (NR) (3/15/92) **82**

CHATEAU CANON-LA-GAFFELIERE (France/Bordeaux)
St.-Emilion 1990 (NR) (4/30/91) (BT) **90+**
St.-Emilion 1989 $29 (3/15/92) **88**
St.-Emilion 1988 $30 (6/30/91) **86**
St.-Emilion 1987 $15 (6/30/89) (BT) **70+**
St.-Emilion 1986 Rel: $21 Cur: $28 (6/30/89) **91**
St.-Emilion 1985 Rel: $20 Cur: $37 (5/15/87) (BT) **90+**

CHATEAU CANON MOUEIX (France/Bordeaux)
Canon-Fronsac 1990 (NR) (5/15/92) (BT) **80+**
Canon-Fronsac 1989 $22 (3/15/92) **86**
Canon-Fronsac 1988 $16 (8/31/90) (BT) **85+**
Canon-Fronsac 1987 $14 (6/30/89) (BT) **75+**
Canon-Fronsac 1986 Rel: $15 Cur: $18 (6/30/88) (BT) **80+**
Canon-Fronsac 1985 Rel: $15 Cur: $19 (5/15/87) (BT) **80+**

ANTICHI VIGNETI DI CANTALUPO (Italy/Piedmont)
Ghemme Collis Breclemae 1985 $25 (1/31/92) **81**

CHATEAU CANTEGRIL (France/Sauternes)
Barsac 1989 ($NA) (6/15/90) (BT) **85+**

CHATEAU CANTELAUDE (France/Bordeaux)
Haut-Médoc 1986 $17 (6/30/89) **78**

CHATEAU CANTEMERLE (France/Bordeaux)
Haut-Médoc 1991 (NR) (5/15/92) (BT) **75+**
Haut-Médoc 1990 (NR) (5/15/92) (BT) **85+**
Haut-Médoc 1989 $35 (3/15/92) **91**
Haut-Médoc 1988 $25 (3/15/91) **85**
Haut-Médoc 1987 $21 (5/15/90) **87**
Haut-Médoc 1986 $30 (6/30/89) **89**
Haut-Médoc 1985 $30 (8/31/88) **88**
Haut-Médoc 1984 $17 (6/15/87) **85**
Haut-Médoc 1982 $30 (5/01/89) **92**
Haut-Médoc 1981 Rel: $13 Cur: $17 (5/01/84) **70**
Haut-Médoc 1979 $20 (10/15/89) (JS) **78**
Haut-Médoc 1962 $113 (11/30/87) (JS) **90**
Haut-Médoc 1961 $150 (3/16/86) (TR) **78**
Haut-Médoc 1945 $300 (3/16/86) (JL) **92**

CHATEAU CANTENAC-BROWN (France/Bordeaux)
Margaux 1991 (NR) (5/15/92) (BT) **80+**
Margaux 1990 (NR) (5/15/92) (BT) **90+**
Margaux 1989 $32 (3/15/92) **89**
Margaux 1988 $25 (4/30/91) **89**
Margaux 1987 Rel: $18 Cur: $22 (2/15/90) **78**
Margaux 1986 Rel: $24 Cur: $26 (6/30/88) (BT) **85+**
Margaux 1984 $19 (5/15/87) **85**
Margaux 1982 Rel: $12 Cur: $21 (5/01/85) **91**
Margaux 1981 Rel: $12 Cur: $18 (3/01/85) **91**
Margaux 1959 $100 (10/15/90) (JS) **89**
Margaux 1945 $150 (3/16/86) (JL) **75**

CANTERBURY (United States/California)
Cabernet Sauvignon California 1989 $6 (11/15/91) BB **80**
Cabernet Sauvignon Yugoslavia Istria 1985 $5.50 (9/30/89) BB **81**
Chardonnay California 1990 $8 (7/15/92) BB **83**
Chardonnay California 1989 $7.50 (7/15/91) BB **82**
Chardonnay California 1985 $6.50 (11/15/86) BB **83**
Merlot California 1990 $7 (5/31/92) **79**
Sauvignon Blanc California 1988 $5 (10/31/89) **75**

CANTINA DELLA PORTA ROSSA (Italy/Piedmont)
Diano d'Alba Vigna Bruni 1988 $25 (2/15/91) **85**

CHATEAU CANUET (France/Bordeaux)
Margaux 1991 (NR) (5/15/92) (BT) **80+**
Margaux 1990 (NR) (5/15/92) (BT) **90+**
Margaux 1989 $18 (3/15/92) **82**
Margaux 1988 $15 (8/31/90) (BT) **85+**
Margaux 1987 $12.50 (5/15/90) **74**
Margaux 1986 $15 (11/30/89) (JS) **88**

CHATEAU CAP DE MOURLIN (France/Bordeaux)
St.-Emilion 1989 $23 (3/15/92) **87**
St.-Emilion 1988 $20 (4/30/91) **84**
St.-Emilion 1987 $15 (6/30/89) (BT) **70+**
St.-Emilion 1986 $18 (6/30/89) **87**
St.-Emilion 1985 $15 (5/15/87) (BT) **80+**

CHATEAU CAP DE MOURLIN (JACQUES) (France/Bordeaux)
St.-Emilion 1982 ($NA) (5/15/89) (TR) **86**

CHATEAU CAP DE MOURLIN (JEAN) (France/Bordeaux)
St.-Emilion 1982 ($NA) (5/15/89) (TR) **81**

PODERE CAPACCIA (Italy/Tuscany)
Chianti Classico 1988 ($NA) (9/15/91) **89**
Chianti Classico Riserva 1985 ($NA) (9/15/91) **88**

CAPARONE (United States/California)
Cabernet Sauvignon Santa Maria Valley Tepusquet Vineyard 1981 $10 (3/16/84) **80**
Merlot Santa Maria Valley Tepusquet Vineyard 1981 $10 (3/16/84) **88**

CAPARZO (Italy/Tuscany)
Brunello di Montalcino 1985 $34 (7/15/91) **83**

Brunello di Montalcino 1982 $31 (9/15/86) **95**
Brunello di Montalcino 1981 $18 (9/15/86) **90**
Brunello di Montalcino 1980 $23 (9/15/86) **88**
Brunello di Montalcino La Casa 1985 $53 (7/15/91) **88**
Brunello di Montalcino La Casa 1982 $50 (11/30/89) **67**
Brunello di Montalcino La Casa 1981 $50 (6/15/90) **83**
Brunello di Montalcino La Casa 1979 $27 (9/15/86) **89**
Brunello di Montalcino Riserva 1981 $23 (6/15/90) **70**
Ca' del Pazzo 1987 $24 (8/31/91) **85**
Ca' del Pazzo 1985 $28 (5/15/90) **77**
Rosso di Montalcino 1988 $14 (4/30/91) **81**
Rosso di Montalcino 1986 $10 (9/30/89) **86**

CHATEAU CAPBERN-GASQUETON (France/Bordeaux)
St.-Estèphe 1991 (NR) (5/15/92) (BT) **75+**
St.-Estèphe 1989 $27 (3/15/92) **84**
St.-Estèphe 1988 ($NA) (6/30/89) (BT) **75+**
St.-Estèphe 1986 $20 (11/30/89) (JS) **76**
St.-Estèphe 1985 Rel: $18 Cur: $23 (8/31/88) **85**
St.-Estèphe 1983 $19 (2/15/88) **66**
St.-Estèphe 1982 Rel: $11 Cur: $24 (11/30/89) (JS) **83**

CAPE MENTELLE (Australia)
Cabernet Sauvignon Margaret River 1988 $19 (6/30/92) **79**
Cabernet Sauvignon Western Australia 1987 $18.50 (3/31/91) **84**
Chardonnay Margaret River 1990 $20 (5/31/92) **91**
Chardonnay Margaret River 1989 $19 (2/29/92) **80**
Shiraz Margaret River 1989 $15 (5/31/92) **84**
Shiraz Margaret River 1988 $15 (2/28/91) **88**

CHATEAU CAPENDU (France/Other)
Corbières Cuvée Elevée en Futs Grande Réserve 1988 $6 (5/31/90) **77**

CAPEZZANA (Italy/Tuscany)
Barco Reale 1987 $11.50 (7/15/91) **78**
Carmignano 1986 $15 (7/15/91) **81**
Carmignano Riserva 1985 $25 (7/15/91) **83**
Chardonnay 1988 $14 (9/15/89) **84**
Chardonnay 1987 $14 (9/15/89) **82**
Chianti Montalbano 1983 $6 (9/15/86) BB **83**
Chianti Montalbano Conte Contini Bonacossi 1988 $8 (10/31/91) **79**
Ghiaie della Furba 1987 $30 (12/15/91) **79**
Ghiaie della Furba 1985 $20 (1/31/90) **91**

DOMAINE CAPION (France/Other)
Cabernet Sauvignon Vin de Pays d'Oc Merlot 1989 $9 (1/31/92) **77**
Syrah Vin de Pays d'Oc 1989 $9 (12/15/91) **82**

DOMAINE DE CAPLANE (France/Sauternes)
Sauternes 1985 $11 (9/30/88) **81**

CAPRILI (Italy/Tuscany)
Rosso di Montalcino 1986 $10 (1/31/89) **78**

CAPTAIN-GAGNEROT (France/Burgundy)
Clos Vougeot 1985 $67 (12/31/88) **86**
Corton Les Renardes 1985 $70 (12/31/88) **92**

CARATELLO (Italy/Tuscany)
Chianti Classico 1988 $9 (12/15/90) **77**
Chianti Classico 1986 $6.75 (1/31/89) **68**
Chianti Classico 1983 $4 (8/31/86) **70**
Chianti Classico 1982 $3.50 (3/01/86) BB **85**

CARBALLO DO REI CONDADO (Spain)
Rias Baixas 1990 $14 (7/15/91) **84**

CHATEAU CARBONNIEUX (France/Bordeaux)
Pessac-Léognan 1991 (NR) (5/15/92) (BT) **75+**
Pessac-Léognan 1990 (NR) (5/15/92) (BT) **85+**
Pessac-Léognan 1989 $22 (3/15/92) **85**
Pessac-Léognan 1988 $20 (2/28/91) **86**
Pessac-Léognan 1987 $15 (5/15/90) **80**
Pessac-Léognan 1986 $18 (9/15/89) **87**
Graves 1985 Rel: $16 Cur: $18 (11/30/88) **87**
Pessac-Léognan Blanc 1990 $18 (9/30/91) (BT) **85+**
Pessac-Léognan Blanc 1989 $22 (2/28/91) **81**
Pessac-Léognan Blanc 1988 $20 (6/30/89) (BT) **80+**
Pessac-Léognan Blanc 1987 $15 (6/30/89) (BT) **80+**
Graves Blanc 1985 Rel: $13 Cur: $19 (3/31/87) **81**
Graves Blanc 1982 Rel: $11 Cur: $26 (2/15/84) **81**

LE CARDINALE (France/Other)
Brut NV $5.25 (6/15/90) BB **80**

CHATEAU LA CARDONNE (France/Bordeaux)
Médoc 1991 (NR) (5/15/92) (BT) **75+**
Médoc 1990 (NR) (5/15/92) (BT) **80+**
Médoc 1989 $11 (4/30/91) (BT) **80+**
Médoc 1987 $10 (6/30/88) (BT) **70+**
Médoc 1986 $10 (2/15/90) **84**
Médoc 1985 Rel: $9 Cur: $11 (12/31/88) **83**
Médoc 1983 $7 (10/15/86) **79**

CAREY (United States/California)
Cabernet Sauvignon Santa Ynez Valley 1985 $10 (11/15/89) **83**

Key to Symbols

The scores reported here are the results of blind tastings conducted by our panel of senior editors. Wines that carry the initials below are results of individual tastings.

THE WINE SPECTATOR 100-POINT SCALE 95-100—Classic, a great wine; ***90-94***—Outstanding, superior character and style; ***80-89***—Good to very good, a wine with special qualities; ***70-79***—Average, drinkable wine that may have minor flaws; ***60-69***—Below average, drinkable but not recommended; ***50-59***—Poor, undrinkable, not recommended. "+"—With a score indicates a range; used primarily with barrel tastings to indicate a preliminary score.

SPECIAL DESIGNATIONS SS—Spectator Selection, CS—Cellar Selection, BB—Best Buy, ($NA)—Price not available, (NR)—Not released.

TASTER'S INITIALS (JG)—Jim Gordon, (HS)—Harvey Steiman, (JL)—James Laube, (JS)—James Suckling, (TM)—Thomas Matthews, (TR)—Terry Robards, (PM)—Per-Henrik Mansson, (BT)—Barrel Tasting (these wines were tasted blind from barrel samples), (CA-date)—*California's Great Cabernets* by James Laube, (CH-date)—*California's Great Chardonnays* by James Laube, (VP-date)—*Vintage Port* by James Suckling.

DATE TASTED Dates in parentheses represent the issue in which the rating was published.

Cabernet Sauvignon Santa Ynez Valley 1984 $9 (3/31/88) **72**
Cabernet Sauvignon Santa Ynez Valley Alamo Pintado Vineyard 1981 $9.50 (6/16/84) **76**
Cabernet Sauvignon Santa Ynez Valley La Cuesta Vineyard 1983 $9.50 (12/15/89) **83**
Cabernet Sauvignon Santa Ynez Valley La Cuesta Vineyard Reserve 1987 $16 (5/31/91) **81**
Chardonnay Santa Barbara County 1989 $13 (4/30/91) **82**
Chardonnay Santa Ynez Valley 1988 $12 (6/30/90) **83**
Chardonnay Santa Ynez Valley 1987 $10 (12/15/89) **85**
Merlot Santa Ynez Valley La Cuesta Vineyard 1988 $16 (5/31/92) **68**
Merlot Santa Ynez Valley La Cuesta Vineyard 1986 $12 (12/15/89) **82**
Sauvignon Blanc Santa Ynez Valley 1990 $9 (6/15/92) **79**
Sauvignon Blanc Santa Ynez Valley 1988 $8 (12/15/89) **87**
Sémillon Santa Ynez Valley Buttonwood Farm 1987 $8 (12/15/89) **77**

LOUIS CARILLON (France/Burgundy)
Puligny-Montrachet 1989 $50 (8/31/91) **88**
Puligny-Montrachet 1988 $36 (2/28/91) **85**
Puligny-Montrachet 1987 $36 (9/30/89) **82**
Puligny-Montrachet Les Champs-Gains 1989 $50 (8/31/91) **87**
Puligny-Montrachet Les Perrières 1989 $50 (8/31/91) **89**
Puligny-Montrachet Les Perrières 1988 $39 (2/28/91) **88**

CHATEAU DE CARLES (France/Bordeaux)
Fronsac 1990 (NR) (5/15/92) (BT) **85+**
Fronsac 1989 (NR) (4/30/91) (BT) **80+**

S. CARLO (Italy/Tuscany)
Brunello di Montalcino 1983 $23 (6/15/90) **86**
Rosso di Montalcino 1986 $10 (7/15/89) **82**

CARMEL (Other/Israel)
Cabernet Sauvignon Samson 1986 $7.50 (3/31/91) **78**
Chenin Blanc Galil 1989 $6 (3/31/91) **72**

CARMENET (United States/California)
Red Sonoma Valley 1989 (NR) (5/15/91) (BT) **85+**
Red Sonoma Valley 1988 Rel: $21 Cur: $25 (11/15/91) **87**
Red Sonoma Valley 1987 Rel: $20 Cur: $24 (11/15/90) **89**
Red Sonoma Valley 1986 Rel: $20 Cur: $27 (7/31/89) **91**
Red Sonoma Valley 1985 Rel: $18.50 Cur: $28 (CA-3/89) **91**
Red Sonoma Valley 1984 Rel: $16 Cur: $30 (CA-3/89) **92**
Red Sonoma Valley 1983 Rel: $18 Cur: $27 (CA-3/89) **85**
Red Sonoma Valley 1982 Rel: $16 Cur: $33 (CA-3/89) **87**
White Reserve Edna Valley 1988 $12 (1/31/91) **84**
White Sonoma County 1987 $9.50 (3/31/90) **77**
White Sonoma County 1986 $9.50 (1/31/89) **85**

CHATEAU CARMES-HAUT-BRION (France/Bordeaux)
Pessac-Léognan 1988 $22 (6/30/89) (BT) **75+**
Pessac-Léognan 1987 $20 (6/30/89) (BT) **75+**
Pessac-Léognan 1986 $26 (6/30/88) (BT) **80+**

CARNEROS CREEK (United States/California)
Cabernet Sauvignon Los Carneros 1985 $15 (10/31/89) **90**
Cabernet Sauvignon Napa Valley 1983 $10.50 (8/31/87) **62**
Cabernet Sauvignon Napa Valley 1982 $11 (2/16/86) **71**
Cabernet Sauvignon Napa Valley 1981 $12 (12/16/84) **77**
Cabernet Sauvignon Napa Valley Fay Vineyard 1982 $13.50 (5/15/87) **70**
Cabernet Sauvignon Napa Valley Reserve 1983 $13.50 (10/15/88) **83**
Chardonnay Los Carneros 1990 $12.50 (3/31/92) SS **90**
Chardonnay Los Carneros 1989 $13 (5/15/91) **78**
Chardonnay Los Carneros 1988 $13 (2/15/90) **85**
Chardonnay Los Carneros 1987 $13 (7/15/89) **81**
Chardonnay Los Carneros 1986 $11.50 (7/15/88) **87**
Chardonnay Los Carneros 1985 $10.50 (11/15/87) **79**
Chardonnay Los Carneros 1984 $10.50 (4/30/87) **86**
Chardonnay Napa Valley 1983 $11 (9/01/85) **80**
Chardonnay Napa Valley 1982 $12 (12/16/84) **71**
Chardonnay Napa Valley 1981 $10 (1/01/84) **81**
Chardonnay Los Carneros Fleur de Carneros 1989 $9 (6/30/91) BB **86**
Chardonnay Sonoma County 1981 $10 (1/01/84) **79**
Merlot Napa Valley 1985 $12.50 (2/15/88) **84**
Merlot Napa Valley 1984 $10.50 (8/31/87) **87**
Merlot Napa Valley 1982 $9.50 (2/16/86) **80**
Merlot Napa Valley Truchard Vineyard 1983 $10 (10/01/85) **84**
Pinot Noir Los Carneros 1989 $15 (3/31/92) **85**
Pinot Noir Los Carneros 1988 $15.50 (10/31/90) **83**
Pinot Noir Los Carneros 1987 $15 (2/15/90) **85**
Pinot Noir Los Carneros 1986 $14.50 (12/31/88) **92**
Pinot Noir Los Carneros 1985 $13 (4/15/88) **88**
Pinot Noir Los Carneros 1984 $15 (3/15/87) **92**
Pinot Noir Los Carneros 1983 $12.50 (8/31/86) **92**
Pinot Noir Los Carneros Fleur de Carneros 1989 $9 (4/30/91) **82**
Pinot Noir Los Carneros Fleur de Carneros 1988 $10 (2/15/90) **85**
Pinot Noir Los Carneros Fleur de Carneros 1987 $9 (2/28/89) SS **92**
Pinot Noir Los Carneros Signature Reserve 1988 $28 (10/31/90) **89**
Pinot Noir Los Carneros Signature Reserve First Release 1987 $28 (10/31/90) **87**

CARNEROS QUALITY ALLIANCE (United States/California)
Pinot Noir Carneros 1986 $23 (7/31/89) **81**
Pinot Noir Carneros 1985 $25 (12/31/87) **90**

CHATEAU CARONNE STE.-GEMME (France/Bordeaux)
Haut-Médoc 1989 (NR) (4/30/91) (BT) **80+**
Haut-Médoc 1988 ($NA) (6/30/89) (BT) **75+**
Haut-Médoc 1987 ($NA) (6/30/89) (BT) **75+**

CARPINETO (Italy/Tuscany)
Chianti Classico 1988 $12 (9/15/91) **87**
Chianti Classico Riserva 1985 $19 (9/15/91) **89**

BODEGAS JAIME CARRERAS (Spain)
Valencia 1985 $4 (3/31/90) BB **80**

CARRETTA (Italy/Piedmont)
Barolo Poderi Cannubi 1985 $26 (1/31/92) **82**
Barolo Poderi Cannubi 1982 $22 (10/15/90) **86**
Barolo Poderi Cannubi 1980 $14 (9/15/87) **62**
Bianco del Poggio 1990 $14 (1/31/92) **78**
Quercia Bric 1989 $20 (1/31/92) **84**

MAURICE CARRIE (United States/California)
Chardonnay Temecula 1989 $7.50 (7/15/92) BB **83**

CARRUADES DE LAFITE (France/Bordeaux)
Pauillac 1991 (NR) (5/15/92) (BT) **80+**
Pauillac 1990 (NR) (5/15/92) (BT) **85+**
Pauillac 1989 Rel: $24 Cur: $27 (3/15/92) **89**
Pauillac 1988 Rel: $19 Cur: $25 (8/31/90) (BT) **80+**
Pauillac 1987 $19 (6/30/89) (BT) **75+**
Pauillac 1986 $30 (5/15/87) (BT) **70+**
Pauillac 1967 $29 (11/30/87) **82**
Pauillac 1964 $49 (11/30/87) **81**
Pauillac 1962 $68 (11/30/87) (JS) **75**
Pauillac 1961 $80 (11/30/91) (JG) **90**
Pauillac 1959 $100 (11/30/91) (JG) **90**
Pauillac 1937 $125 (11/30/87) **77**
Pauillac 1934 $145 (11/30/87) **84**
Pauillac 1902 $280 (11/30/87) **80**

CARTA VIEJA (Chile)
Cabernet Sauvignon Maule Valley 1987 $6 (6/15/91) **78**
Cabernet Sauvignon Maule Valley 1986 $4 (6/15/90) **75**
Cabernet Sauvignon Maule Valley 1985 $3 (7/31/89) **68**
Cabernet Sauvignon Maule Valley Antiqua Selection 1986 $8 (6/15/91) **75**
Sauvignon Blanc Maule Valley 1989 $6 (10/15/91) **75**

CHATEAU CARTEYRON (France/Bordeaux)
St.-Emilion 1982 $7.25 (9/01/85) **79**

CARTLIDGE & BROWNE (United States/California)
Chardonnay Napa Valley 1989 $9.75 (5/31/91) **84**
Chardonnay Napa Valley 1987 $11 (4/15/90) **81**
Chardonnay Napa Valley 1986 $10 (5/31/88) **83**
Chardonnay Napa Valley 1985 $9.75 (3/31/87) **91**
Chardonnay Napa Valley 1984 $11.50 (1/01/86) **66**
Chardonnay Napa Valley 1983 $11.50 (2/16/85) **78**

CASA DE LA VINA (Spain)
Valdepeñas Cencibel 1985 $6.50 (3/31/90) **82**

CASA FRANCESCO (Italy/Tuscany)
Chianti Classico 1982 $6 (11/30/89) **81**

CASA LARGA (United States/New York)
Blanc de Blancs Finger Lakes NV $13 (12/31/90) **78**
Brut Blanc de Blancs Finger Lakes NV $11 (12/31/90) **77**

CASA NUESTRA (United States/California)
Chenin Blanc Napa Valley Dry 1987 $6.50 (7/31/89) **82**

CASAL THAULERO (Italy/Piedmont)
Abbazia di Propezzano 1986 $19 (7/15/91) **89**
Montepulciano d'Abruzzo 1989 $6 (6/30/91) BB **81**
Montepulciano d'Abruzzo 1988 $5 (5/31/90) BB **80**

E. CASASLTE (Italy/Tuscany)
Vino Nobile di Montepulciano 1983 $9 (11/30/87) **86**

CASCADE CREST (United States/Washington)
Johannisberg Riesling Yakima Valley 1987 $6 (10/15/89) **75**
Sémillon Yakima Valley Blanc 1987 $5.50 (10/15/89) BB **87**

CASCADE MOUNTAIN (United States/Washington)
Chenin Blanc Washington Vouvray 1987 $5.25 (10/15/89) **75**

CASCINACASTLE'T (Italy/Piedmont)
Passum 1984 $25 (12/31/88) **61**

CASCINETTA (Italy/Sparkling)
Moscato d'Asti 1987 $9 (12/31/90) **80**

IL CASELLO (Italy/Tuscany)
Brunello di Montalcino 1982 $18 (7/31/88) **84**
Brunello di Montalcino 1981 $15 (10/31/87) **84**

CASETTA (Italy/Piedmont)
Barbera d'Alba Vigna Lazaretto 1987 $9 (3/15/91) BB **89**

CASSEGRAIN (Australia)
Cabernet Sauvignon Pokolbin 1986 $18 (3/31/91) **83**
Cabernet Shiraz Merlot South Eastern Australia 1988 $8 (9/30/91) **69**
Chambourcin South Eastern Australia 1990 $12 (2/15/92) **77**
Chardonnay Hastings Valley Fromenteau Vineyard 1989 $25 (3/31/91) **89**
Chardonnay Hunter Valley Vintage Selection 1989 $20 (2/15/92) **86**
Chardonnay South Eastern Australia 1989 $14.50 (3/31/91) **87**
Pinot Noir New South Wales Morrillon Vinyard 1988 $20 (2/29/92) **80**
Sémillon Hunter Valley Vintage Selection 1989 $20 (9/30/91) **81**
Shiraz Pokolbin Leonard Select Vineyard 1987 $20 (3/15/91) **87**
Shiraz South Eastern Australia 1988 $12.50 (2/15/92) **77**

GUY CASTAGNIER (France/Burgundy)
Bonnes Mares 1989 $67 (1/31/92) **91**
Bonnes Mares 1988 $67 (7/15/91) **87**
Bonnes Mares 1986 $50 (4/15/89) **91**
Chambolle-Musigny 1989 $39 (1/31/92) **88**
Chambolle-Musigny 1986 $31 (7/15/89) **84**
Charmes-Chambertin 1989 $62 (1/31/92) **90**
Clos de la Roche 1989 $62 (1/31/92) **90**
Clos de la Roche 1988 $63 (7/15/91) **91**
Clos de la Roche 1986 $43 (7/15/89) **75**
Clos St.-Denis 1989 $62 (1/31/92) **91**
Clos St.-Denis 1988 $63 (7/15/91) **89**
Clos St.-Denis 1986 $43 (7/15/89) **84**
Clos de Vougeot 1989 $64 (1/31/92) **85**
Clos de Vougeot 1988 $65 (8/31/91) **86**
Latricières-Chambertin 1989 $62 (1/31/92) **93**
Latricières-Chambertin 1988 $63 (7/15/91) **93**
Mazis-Chambertin Mazy-Chambertin 1989 $62 (1/31/92) **93**
Mazis-Chambertin Mazy-Chambertin 1988 $63 (7/15/91) **91**
Morey-St.-Denis 1989 (NR) (1/31/92) **86**
Morey-St.-Denis 1986 $28 (7/15/89) **66**

CASTELCOSA (Italy/North)
Chardonnay 1987 $12.50 (9/15/89) **82**
Chardonnay 1986 $9.50 (9/15/89) **85**
Chardonnay Pra di Pradis 1986 $13 (9/15/89) **83**

CASTELL'IN VILLA (Italy/Tuscany)
Chianti Classico 1988 $13 (9/15/91) **88**
Chianti Classico 1986 $13 (9/15/90) **79**
Chianti Classico 1985 $11.50 (6/30/89) **86**
Chianti Classico 1983 $7 (9/15/87) **87**
Chianti Classico Riserva 1985 ($NA) (9/15/91) **83**
Chianti Classico Riserva 1982 $18 (11/30/90) **86**

LA CASTELLADA (Italy/North)
Chardonnay 1988 $14 (3/31/90) **86**

DE CASTELLANE (France/Champagne)
Brut Blanc de Blancs Champagne 1981 $33 (4/15/88) **84**
Brut Blanc de Blancs Champagne 1980 $22 (5/31/87) **91**
Brut Blanc de Blancs Champagne Chardonnay 1983 ($NA) (12/31/90) **90**
Brut Blanc de Blancs Champagne Chardonnay NV $30 (12/31/91) **84**
Brut Champagne 1985 $27 (12/31/90) **84**
Brut Champagne NV $38 (12/31/91) **83**
Brut Champagne Cuvée Florens de Castellane 1982 $59 (12/31/90) **88**
Brut Rosé Champagne NV $29 (12/31/90) **88**
Cuvée Commodore Champagne 1981 $50 (4/15/88) **87**

CASTELLARE DI CASTELLINA (Italy/Tuscany)
Canonico di Castellare 1988 $18 (12/31/90) **79**
Chianti Classico 1988 $12.50 (11/30/90) **82**
Chianti Classico 1987 $11 (11/30/89) **81**
Chianti Classico 1986 $11 (10/15/89) **82**
Chianti Classico 1985 $11 (3/31/88) **85**
Chianti Classico Riserva 1985 $17 (9/15/91) **77**
Coniale di Castellare 1988 $35 (9/15/91) **92**
Coniale di Castellare 1987 $31 (10/31/90) **87**
I Sodi di San Niccolò 1988 $35 (9/15/91) **88**
I Sodi di San Niccolò 1987 $32 (4/15/91) **86**
I Sodi di San Niccolò 1986 $25 (11/30/89) **94**
I Sodi di San Niccolò 1985 $25 (5/31/88) **96**
I Sodi di San Niccolò 1983 $18 (5/31/88) **87**
I Sodi di San Niccolò 1982 ($NA) (9/15/87) (HS) **89**
I Sodi di San Niccolò 1981 ($NA) (9/15/87) (HS) **87**
Vin Santo 1984 $28/375ml (9/30/90) **88**

CASTELLBLANCH (Spain)
Brut Cava Extra NV $6 (2/29/92) BB **82**

CASTELVECCHI (Italy/Tuscany)
Chianti Classico Riserva 1982 $13 (5/15/90) **85**

CASTORO (United States/California)
Cabernet Sauvignon Paso Robles Hope Farms 1986 $8.50 (12/15/89) **80**
Chardonnay San Luis Obispo County 1990 $9.50 (6/30/92) **80**
Chardonnay San Luis Obispo County 1988 $8.50 (12/15/89) **75**
Fumé Blanc San Luis Obispo County 1988 $5.25 (12/15/89) **78**
Pinot Noir Central Coast 1987 $4.50 (12/15/89) BB **82**
White Zinfandel San Luis Obispo 1988 $6 (6/15/89) **67**
Zinfandel Paso Robles 1987 $7.50 (12/15/89) **90**

LOS CATADORES (Chile)
Cabernet Sauvignon Lontue Selección Especial 1986 $5 (6/15/92) BB **84**
Sauvignon Blanc Lontue Selección Especial 1990 $5 (6/15/92) **79**

CATHIARD-MOLINIER (France/Burgundy)
Nuits-St.-Georges Les Meurgers 1986 $22 (2/28/89) **77**

CATOCTIN (United States/Maryland)
Cabernet Sauvignon Maryland 1985 $8 (2/29/92) **82**
Chardonnay Maryland 1989 $8 (2/29/92) **82**
Chardonnay Maryland Oak Fermented 1988 $9 (2/29/92) **78**

CATTIER (France/Champagne)
Brut Champagne NV $17 (12/31/89) **82**
Brut Champagne Chigny-les-Roses Premier Cru NV $30 (12/31/91) **92**
Brut Champagne Clos du Moulin NV $65 (12/31/91) **89**

CHATEAU DU CAUZE (France/Bordeaux)
St.-Emilion 1986 $15 (6/30/89) **84**

DOMAINE DE LA CAVALE (France/Rhône)
Côtes du Lubéron Blanc 1987 $7 (2/15/89) **77**

CAVALOTTO (Italy/Piedmont)
Barbaresco Vigna San Giuseppe Riserva 1985 $22 (2/28/91) **90**
Dolcetto d'Alba Mallera 1987 $10 (3/15/89) **83**

CAVATAPPI (United States/Washington)
Nebbiolo Maddalena Red Willow Vineyards Washington 1988 $19 (6/15/91) **83**

LA CAVE TROISGROS (France/Bordeaux)
Bordeaux Blanc Blanc 1990 $9 (6/15/91) **75**
Bordeaux Rouge 1989 $9.50 (5/15/91) **82**

LES CAVES ST.-PIERRE (France/Rhône)
Châteauneuf-du-Pape Clefs des Prelats 1988 $13 (1/31/91) **87**
Côte-Rôtie Marquis de Tournelles 1987 $23 (1/31/91) **84**
Côtes du Rhône-Villages Les Lissandres 1988 $7.25 (12/15/90) BB **84**
Hermitage Tertre des Carmes 1988 $23 (12/31/90) **88**

CAVIT (Italy/North)
Chardonnay Trentino 1988 $6 (9/15/89) **84**

CHATEAU CAYLA (France/Bordeaux)
Premières Côtes de Bordeaux 1986 $7 (6/30/89) **76**
Premières Côtes de Bordeaux 1985 $4 (5/31/88) **73**

CAYMUS (United States/California)
Cabernet Sauvignon Napa Valley 1988 $20 (1/31/92) **87**
Cabernet Sauvignon Napa Valley 1987 Rel: $16 Cur: $23 (9/15/90) **93**
Cabernet Sauvignon Napa Valley 1986 Rel: $22 Cur: $33 (3/15/90) SS **94**
Cabernet Sauvignon Napa Valley 1985 Rel: $18 Cur: $55 (CA-3/89) **92**
Cabernet Sauvignon Napa Valley 1984 Rel: $16 Cur: $50 (CA-3/89) **91**
Cabernet Sauvignon Napa Valley 1983 Rel: $15 Cur: $54 (CA-3/89) **87**
Cabernet Sauvignon Napa Valley 1983 Rel: $15 Cur: $54 (11/30/86) CS **94**
Cabernet Sauvignon Napa Valley 1982 Rel: $14 Cur: $50 (CA-3/89) **90**
Cabernet Sauvignon Napa Valley 1981 Rel: $14 Cur: $52 (CA-3/89) **88**
Cabernet Sauvignon Napa Valley 1980 Rel: $12.50 Cur: $53 (CA-3/89) **90**
Cabernet Sauvignon Napa Valley 1979 Rel: $12 Cur: $63 (CA-3/89) **92**
Cabernet Sauvignon Napa Valley 1978 Rel: $12 Cur: $68 (CA-3/89) **87**
Cabernet Sauvignon Napa Valley 1977 Rel: $10 Cur: $36 (CA-3/89) **77**
Cabernet Sauvignon Napa Valley 1976 Rel: $10 Cur: $60 (CA-3/89) **85**
Cabernet Sauvignon Napa Valley 1975 Rel: $8.50 Cur: $85 (CA-3/89) **89**
Cabernet Sauvignon Napa Valley 1974 Rel: $7 Cur: $105 (2/15/90) (JG) **91**
Cabernet Sauvignon Napa Valley 1973 Rel: $6 Cur: $145 (CA-3/89) **93**

Cabernet Sauvignon Napa Valley 1972 Rel: $4.50 Cur: $110 (CA-3/89) **86**
Cabernet Sauvignon Napa Valley Cuvée 1986 $15 (8/31/89) **90**
Cabernet Sauvignon Napa Valley Cuvée 1985 $12 (7/15/88) **92**
Cabernet Sauvignon Napa Valley Cuvée 1984 $12 (8/31/87) **88**
Cabernet Sauvignon Napa Valley Special Selection 1987 Rel: $60 Cur: $82 (10/31/91) CS **98**
Cabernet Sauvignon Napa Valley Special Selection 1986 Rel: $50 Cur: $122 (CA-3/89) **98**
Cabernet Sauvignon Napa Valley Special Selection 1985 Rel: $50 Cur: $190 (4/30/90) **99**
Cabernet Sauvignon Napa Valley Special Selection 1984 Rel: $35 Cur: $185 (7/15/89) CS **98**
Cabernet Sauvignon Napa Valley Special Selection 1983 Rel: $35 Cur: $110 (CA-3/89) **91**
Cabernet Sauvignon Napa Valley Special Selection 1982 Rel: $35 Cur: $140 (CA-3/89) **92**
Cabernet Sauvignon Napa Valley Special Selection 1981 Rel: $35 Cur: $120 (CA-3/89) **93**
Cabernet Sauvignon Napa Valley Special Selection 1980 Rel: $30 Cur: $145 (CA-3/89) **92**
Cabernet Sauvignon Napa Valley Special Selection 1980 Rel: $30 Cur: $145 (3/16/86) SS **96**
Cabernet Sauvignon Napa Valley Special Selection 1979 Rel: $30 Cur: $220 (CA-3/89) **97**
Cabernet Sauvignon Napa Valley Special Selection 1979 Rel: $30 Cur: $220 (6/01/85) SS **93**
Cabernet Sauvignon Napa Valley Special Selection 1978 Rel: $30 Cur: $230 (CA-3/89) **97**
Cabernet Sauvignon Napa Valley Special Selection 1978 Rel: $30 Cur: $230 (6/16/84) CS **95**
Cabernet Sauvignon Napa Valley Special Selection 1976 Rel: $35 Cur: $430 (CA-3/89) **90**
Cabernet Sauvignon Napa Valley Special Selection 1975 Rel: $22 Cur: $250 (CA-3/89) **92**
Chardonnay Napa Valley 1986 $12 (8/31/88) **83**
Conundrum California 1990 $18 (11/30/91) **91**
Conundrum California 1989 $18 (4/30/91) **89**
Pinot Noir Napa Valley 1981 $7.50 (5/01/84) BB **85**
Pinot Noir Napa Valley 1980 $6.50 (3/16/84) **81**
Pinot Noir Napa Valley Special Selection 1988 $18 (11/15/91) **82**
Pinot Noir Napa Valley Special Selection 1987 $14 (12/15/90) **86**
Pinot Noir Napa Valley Special Selection 1986 $15 (12/31/89) **82**
Pinot Noir Napa Valley Special Selection 1985 $15 (12/31/88) **90**
Pinot Noir Napa Valley Special Selection 1984 $12.50 (2/15/88) **79**
Pinot Noir Napa Valley Special Selection 1982 $12.50 (8/31/86) **85**
Sauvignon Blanc Napa Valley 1989 $9 (10/31/90) **88**
Sauvignon Blanc Napa Valley 1988 $9 (9/15/89) **83**
Sauvignon Blanc Napa Valley Barrel Fermented 1990 $10 (11/15/91) **89**
Zinfandel California 1976 $35 (6/16/85) **79**
Zinfandel California 1974 $45 (6/16/85) **83**
Zinfandel California Lot 31-J 1975 $40 (6/16/85) **77**
Zinfandel Napa Valley 1989 $10 (11/15/91) **83**
Zinfandel Napa Valley 1988 $9 (10/15/90) **80**
Zinfandel Napa Valley 1987 $9.75 (10/31/89) **85**
Zinfandel Napa Valley 1986 $9 (12/15/88) **89**
Zinfandel Napa Valley 1985 $8 (12/31/87) **85**
Zinfandel Napa Valley 1984 $8 (5/15/87) **90**
Zinfandel Napa Valley 1983 $7.50 (12/31/86) **79**
Zinfandel Napa Valley 1982 $7.50 (5/16/86) **92**
Zinfandel Napa Valley 1981 $6.50 (12/01/84) **84**

CHARLES DE CAZANOVE (France/Champagne)
Brut Champagne NV $28 (12/31/91) **84**
Brut Champagne Ruban Azur NV $32 (12/31/91) **87**
Champagne Stradivarius 1985 $48 (12/31/91) **85**

CECCHETTI SEBASTIANI (United States/California)
Cabernet Sauvignon Alexander Valley 1986 $8.50 (4/15/89) **83**
Cabernet Sauvignon Sonoma County 1983 $12.50 (9/30/86) **76**
Chardonnay Napa Valley 1989 $6.50 (4/30/91) **80**
Chardonnay Napa Valley Cask Lot 1 1987 $9.50 (4/15/89) **64**
Chardonnay Napa Valley Cask Lot 2 1986 $9.50 (12/15/87) **85**
Merlot Sonoma County 1989 $10 (5/31/92) **83**

CECCHI (Italy/Tuscany)
Chianti 1986 $5 (1/31/89) **80**
Chianti Classico 1986 $7 (7/15/89) **86**
Spargolo Predicato di Cardisco 1988 $16 (9/15/91) **84**
Spargolo Predicato di Cardisco 1985 $36 (1/31/92) **78**
Spargolo Predicato di Cardisco 1983 $25 (3/15/91) **75**
Spargolo Predicato di Cardisco 1982 $12 (9/30/89) **68**
Vernaccia di San Gimignano 1987 $6 (5/15/89) BB **82**
Vino Nobile di Montepulciano 1987 $13 (3/31/92) **77**
Vino Nobile di Montepulciano 1983 $9 (5/15/89) **77**

DOMAINE CECI (France/Burgundy)
Chambolle-Musigny Aux Echanges 1988 $33 (7/15/91) **91**
Chambolle-Musigny Aux Echanges 1987 $20 (3/31/90) **72**
Clos de Vougeot 1988 $48 (7/15/91) **93**
Clos de Vougeot 1987 $40 (3/31/90) **82**

CEDAR CREEK (AUSTRALIA) (Australia)
Chardonnay South Eastern Australia Bin 33 1990 $6 (5/31/92) BB **85**

CEDAR CREEK (United States/Other US)
American 1990 $6 (2/29/92) **78**
American Cranberry Blush 1990 $7 (2/29/92) **78**
Vidal Blanc American Red 1990 $7 (2/29/92) **76**

CEDAR MOUNTAIN (United States/California)
Chardonnay Livermore Valley Blanches Vineyard 1990 $13.50 (5/15/92) **79**

DOMAINE DU CEDRE (France/Other)
Cahors 1988 $10 (8/31/91) **83**
Cahors 1987 $11 (8/31/91) **81**
Cahors Le Prestige 1988 $14 (8/31/91) **84**
Cahors Le Prestige 1987 $14 (3/15/90) **75**

Key to Symbols

The scores reported here are the results of blind tastings conducted by our panel of senior editors. Wines that carry the initials below are results of individual tastings.

THE WINE SPECTATOR 100-POINT SCALE 95-100—Classic, a great wine; ***90-94***—Outstanding, superior character and style; ***80-89***—Good to very good, a wine with special qualities; ***70-79***—Average, drinkable wine that may have minor flaws; ***60-69***—Below average, drinkable but not recommended; ***50-59***—Poor, undrinkable, not recommended. "+"—With a score indicates a range; used primarily with barrel tastings to indicate a preliminary score.

SPECIAL DESIGNATIONS SS—Spectator Selection, CS—Cellar Selection, BB—Best Buy, ($NA)—Price not available, (NR)—Not released.

TASTER'S INITIALS (JG)—Jim Gordon, (HS)—Harvey Steiman, (JL)—James Laube, (JS)—James Suckling, (TM)—Thomas Matthews, (TR)—Terry Robards, (PM)—Per-Henrik Mansson, (BT)—Barrel Tasting (these wines were tasted blind from barrel samples), (CA-date)—*California's Great Cabernets* by James Laube, (CH-date)—*California's Great Chardonnays* by James Laube, (VP-date)—*Vintage Port* by James Suckling.

DATE TASTED Dates in parentheses represent the issue in which the rating was published.

DOMAINE DES CEDRES (France/Rhône)
Côtes du Rhône Pons Dominique 1986 $10 (3/31/90) **82**

CELLIER DE LA DONA (France/Other)
Côtes du Roussillon-Villages 1988 $8.50 (10/15/90) BB **85**

CERBAIONA (Italy/Tuscany)
Brunello di Montalcino 1985 $60 (11/30/91) **71**
Rosso di Montalcino 1988 $21 (1/31/92) **82**

CEREQUIO (Italy/Piedmont)
Barolo 1982 $19 (11/15/88) **91**
Barolo 1979 $13 (7/31/89) **69**
Barolo Riserva 1980 $13 (7/31/89) **80**

CERETTO (Italy/Piedmont)
Arneis Blangé 1990 $19 (8/31/91) **83**
Arneis Blangé 1989 $19 (7/15/91) **82**
Barbaresco Asij 1987 $22 (7/15/91) **86**
Barbaresco Asij 1985 $15 (1/31/90) **64**
Barbaresco Bricco Asili Bricco Asili 1987 Rel: $40 Cur: $50 (4/30/91) **89**
Barbaresco Bricco Asili Bricco Asili 1986 $35 (4/15/90) **85**
Barbaresco Bricco Asili Bricco Asili 1985 Rel: $35 Cur: $41 (8/31/89) **89**
Barbaresco Bricco Asili Bricco Asili 1984 Rel: $15 Cur: $20 (9/15/88) (HS) **80**
Barbaresco Bricco Asili Bricco Asili 1982 Rel: $19 Cur: $63 (9/15/88) (HS) **87**
Barbaresco Bricco Asili Bricco Asili 1978 $55 (3/01/86) (JS) **90**
Barbaresco Bricco Asili Bricco Asili 1976 ($NA) (9/15/88) (HS) **89**
Barbaresco Bricco Asili Bricco Asili 1974 ($NA) (3/01/86) (JS) **90**
Barbaresco Bricco Asili Faset 1987 $31 (7/15/91) **89**
Barbaresco Bricco Asili Faset 1985 $31 (1/31/90) **87**
Barolo Bricco Rocche Bricco Rocche 1986 $119 (4/30/91) **89**
Barolo Bricco Rocche Bricco Rocche 1985 Rel: $56 Cur: $98 (3/31/90) **86**
Barolo Bricco Rocche Bricco Rocche 1982 $95 (9/15/88) (HS) **91**
Barolo Bricco Rocche Bricco Rocche 1980 $60 (3/01/86) (JS) **90**
Barolo Bricco Rocche Brunate 1986 $40 (4/30/91) **80**
Barolo Bricco Rocche Brunate 1985 $41 (1/31/90) **92**
Barolo Bricco Rocche Brunate 1983 Rel: $27 Cur: $37 (7/31/89) **85**
Barolo Bricco Rocche Brunate 1979 $42 (3/01/86) (JS) **86**
Barolo Bricco Rocche Brunate 1978 $92 (9/15/88) (HS) **86**
Barolo Bricco Rocche Brunate 1967 ($NA) (10/20/87) **90**
Barolo Bricco Rocche Prapò 1986 $50 (2/28/91) **91**
Barolo Bricco Rocche Prapò 1985 $50 (3/31/90) **78**
Barolo Bricco Rocche Prapò 1983 $31 (7/31/89) **86**
Barolo Bricco Rocche Prapò 1978 $95 (3/01/86) (JS) **95**
Barolo Bricco Rocche Prapò 1976 ($NA) (9/15/88) (HS) **82**
Barolo Bricco Rocche Prapò 1971 ($NA) (10/30/87) **88**
Barolo Cannubi 1971 ($NA) (3/01/86) (JS) **85**
Barolo Zonchera 1987 $23 (8/31/91) **86**
Barolo Zonchera 1985 $16 (6/15/90) **82**
Barolo Zonchera 1984 $16 (9/15/88) (HS) **83**
Barolo Zonchera 1982 $16 (6/30/87) **90**
Barolo Zonchera 1980 Rel: $9.50 Cur: $16 (2/16/86) SS **96**
Dolcetto d'Alba Rossana 1989 $16 (4/30/91) **79**
Dolcetto d'Alba Rossana 1987 $12 (3/15/89) **86**
Dolcetto d'Alba Vigna 1985 $11 (3/15/89) **77**
Nebbiolo d'Alba Lantasco 1988 $18 (4/30/91) **81**

VILLA CERNA (Italy/Tuscany)
Chianti Classico 1988 $9.50 (9/15/91) **89**
Chianti Classico Riserva 1985 $16 (9/15/91) **87**
Chianti Classico Riserva 1983 $8.25 (3/31/89) BB **84**
Vigneto La Gavina 1988 ($NA) (9/15/91) **91**

FATTORIA DEL CERRO (Italy/Tuscany)
Chianti Colli Senesi 1987 $5 (7/31/89) **74**

CHATEAU CERTAN DE MAY (France/Bordeaux)
Pomerol 1990 (NR) (5/15/92) (BT) **95+**
Pomerol 1989 $75 (4/30/91) (BT) **90+**
Pomerol 1988 $66 (6/30/91) **90**
Pomerol 1987 $50 (6/30/89) (BT) **85+**
Pomerol 1986 Rel: $53 Cur: $71 (9/15/89) **93**
Pomerol 1985 Rel: $70 Cur: $84 (4/30/88) **86**
Pomerol 1982 $150 (5/15/89) (TR) **92**
Pomerol 1979 $76 (10/15/89) (JS) **90**

CHATEAU CERTAN-GIRAUD (France/Bordeaux)
Pomerol 1988 $23 (2/28/91) **89**
Pomerol 1987 $18 (6/30/89) (BT) **75+**
Pomerol 1986 $22 (6/30/89) **86**
Pomerol 1985 $25 (4/30/88) **85**
Pomerol 1982 $39 (5/15/89) (TR) **90**

PIO CESARE (Italy/Piedmont)
Barbera d'Alba 1987 $12 (4/15/91) **81**
Barbera d'Alba 1985 $11.50 (11/15/88) **78**
Barolo 1985 $38 (5/15/91) **89**
Barolo 1983 $34 (9/15/88) (HS) **88**
Barolo 1982 $36 (9/15/88) (HS) **91**
Barolo 1981 $25 (9/15/88) (HS) **87**
Barolo 1978 Rel: $19 Cur: $28 (9/15/88) (HS) **85**
Barolo 1974 $40 (9/15/88) (HS) **77**
Barolo 1971 $38 (9/15/88) (HS) **80**
Barolo Ornato Riserva 1985 $48 (5/15/91) **91**
Barolo Riserva 1982 $31 (11/15/88) **86**
Barolo Riserva 1980 $19 (2/15/87) **72**
Barolo Riserva 1978 Rel: $19 Cur: $28 (10/01/84) SS **89**
Bianco del Piemonte 1990 $12 (9/15/91) **81**
Chardonnay 1988 $37 (9/15/91) **86**
Chardonnay 1987 $29 (9/15/89) **92**
Chardonnay 1986 $29 (9/15/89) **88**
Nebbiolo 1983 $8 (2/16/86) **88**
Ornato 1983 $16 (3/31/88) **82**
Rosso del Piemonte 1989 $12 (1/31/92) **83**

LA CHABLISIENNE (France/Chablis)
Chablis 1987 $13 (3/31/89) **82**
Chablis Beauroy 1986 ($NA) (3/31/89) **84**
Chablis Les Clos 1986 ($NA) (3/31/89) **88**
Chablis Fourchaume 1987 $18 (3/31/89) **85**
Chablis Grande Cuvée 1987 ($NA) (3/31/89) **87**
Chablis Grande Cuvée 1986 ($NA) (3/31/89) **90**

Chablis Les Grenouilles 1986 ($NA) (3/31/89) **88**
Chablis Montée de Tonnerre 1986 ($NA) (3/31/89) **86**
Chablis Vaudésir 1986 ($NA) (3/31/89) **90**
Petit Chablis 1987 ($NA) (3/31/89) **77**

CHADDSFORD (United States/Pennsylvania)
Chambourcin Pennsylvania Proprietor's Reserve 1989 $10 (2/29/92) **80**
Chambourcin Pennsylvania Seven Valleys Vineyard 1989 $13 (2/29/92) **81**
Chardonnay Pennsylvania Philip Roth Vineyard 1989 $24 (2/29/92) **90**
Chardonnay Pennsylvania Stargazers Vineyard 1988 $24 (2/29/92) **84**
Pinot Noir Pennsylvania Lake Erie Region 1988 $28 (2/29/92) **82**
Proprietor's Reserve Pennsylvania 1990 $9 (2/29/92) **78**

BARON CHAGALE (France/Other)
Brut Blanc de Blancs NV $6 (6/15/90) **70**

CHATEAU DU CHALET (France/Bordeaux)
Bordeaux 1987 $6 (4/15/90) **78**

CHALK HILL (United States/California)
Cabernet Sauvignon Chalk Hill 1988 $12 (6/15/91) **87**
Cabernet Sauvignon Chalk Hill 1983 $10 (11/15/86) **78**
Cabernet Sauvignon Chalk Hill 1982 $9 (11/01/85) **66**
Cabernet Sauvignon Chalk Hill 1981 $8 (4/01/84) **83**
Chardonnay Chalk Hill 1990 $15 (6/15/92) SS **91**
Chardonnay Chalk Hill 1989 $14 (5/15/91) SS **90**
Chardonnay Chalk Hill 1986 $10 (1/31/88) **68**
Chardonnay Chalk Hill 1984 $8 (12/01/85) **82**
Sauvignon Blanc Chalk Hill 1990 $8.50 (4/15/92) **88**
Sauvignon Blanc Chalk Hill 1989 $8 (7/31/91) **85**
Sauvignon Blanc Chalk Hill 1987 $7 (10/31/89) **82**
Sémillon Late Harvest Chalk Hill 1986 $10/375ml (6/15/92) **91**

CHALONE (United States/California)
Chardonnay Chalone 1990 Rel: $22 Cur: $27 (2/15/92) **89**
Chardonnay Chalone 1989 Rel: $25 Cur: $27 (11/30/90) **90**
Chardonnay Chalone 1988 Rel: $22 Cur: $29 (2/28/90) **89**
Chardonnay Chalone 1987 Rel: $22 Cur: $37 (12/31/88) **90**
Chardonnay Chalone 1986 Rel: $22 Cur: $48 (CH-1/90) **94**
Chardonnay Chalone 1985 Rel: $22 Cur: $68 (CH-4/90) **80**
Chardonnay Chalone 1984 Rel: $18 Cur: $53 (CH-1/90) **88**
Chardonnay Chalone 1983 Rel: $18 Cur: $50 (CH-1/90) **90**
Chardonnay Chalone 1982 Rel: $18 Cur: $65 (CH-1/90) **95**
Chardonnay Chalone 1981 Rel: $17 Cur: $68 (CH-4/90) **93**
Chardonnay Chalone 1980 Rel: $17 Cur: $48 (CH-1/90) **92**
Chardonnay Chalone 1979 Rel: $14 Cur: $55 (CH-1/90) **89**
Chardonnay Chalone Gavilan 1990 $12.50 (6/30/92) **86**
Chardonnay California Gavilan 1989 $12 (12/31/90) **85**
Chardonnay Chalone Gavilan 1988 $12 (4/15/90) **87**
Chardonnay Chalone Reserve 1988 Rel: $40 Cur: $45 (CH-6/90) **89**
Chardonnay Chalone Reserve 1987 Rel: $35 Cur: $85 (CH-5/90) **87**
Chardonnay Chalone Reserve 1986 Rel: $28 Cur: $80 (CH-5/90) **85**
Chardonnay Chalone Reserve 1985 Rel: $28 Cur: $80 (CH-6/90) **94**
Chardonnay Chalone Reserve 1983 Rel: $25 Cur: $53 (CH-5/90) **87**
Chardonnay Chalone Reserve 1982 Rel: $25 Cur: $48 (CH-5/90) **93**
Chardonnay Chalone Reserve 1981 Rel: $20 Cur: $100 (CH-5/90) **86**
Chardonnay Chalone Reserve 1980 Rel: $18 Cur: $125 (CH-5/90) **94**
Pinot Blanc Chalone 1990 Rel: $17.50 Cur: $22 (2/29/92) **80**
Pinot Blanc Chalone 1989 Rel: $17 Cur: $25 (11/30/90) **88**
Pinot Blanc Chalone 1988 Rel: $17 Cur: $29 (2/15/90) **88**
Pinot Blanc Chalone 1987 Rel: $17 Cur: $30 (12/15/88) **87**
Pinot Noir Chalone 1986 $25 (12/15/90) **89**
Pinot Noir Chalone 1985 Rel: $17.50 Cur: $30 (2/15/90) **85**
Pinot Noir Chalone 1984 Rel: $18.50 Cur: $24 (12/15/87) **88**
Pinot Noir Chalone 1983 Rel: $18.50 Cur: $34 (8/31/86) **89**
Pinot Noir Chalone 1982 Rel: $20 Cur: $50 (8/31/86) **66**
Pinot Noir Chalone 1981 Rel: $18.50 Cur: $45 (12/16/84) **83**
Pinot Noir Chalone Red Table Wine 1983 $9 (8/31/86) **71**
Pinot Noir Chalone Reserve 1981 $28 (8/31/86) **92**

CHATEAU DE CHAMBERT (France/Other)
Cahors 1986 $12 (8/31/89) **87**

CHATEAU CHAMBERT-MARBUZET (France/Bordeaux)
St.-Estèphe 1991 (NR) (5/15/92) (BT) **80+**
St.-Estèphe 1990 (NR) (5/15/92) (BT) **90+**
St.-Estèphe 1989 $21 (4/30/91) (BT) **85+**
St.-Estèphe 1988 $26 (8/31/90) (BT) **75+**
St.-Estèphe 1987 $18 (11/30/89) (JS) **79**
St.-Estèphe 1986 Rel: $25 Cur: $28 (11/30/89) (JS) **89**
St.-Estèphe 1985 Rel: $28 Cur: $32 (6/30/88) **87**
St.-Estèphe 1983 $15 (9/30/86) **77**
St.-Estèphe 1982 $30 (11/30/89) (JS) **88**

PAUL CHAMBLAIN (France/Other)
Brut Blanc de Blancs NV $6.75 (6/15/90) **74**

CHATEAU DE CHAMIREY (France/Burgundy)
Mercurey Blanc 1985 $14 (1/31/87) **85**

CHAMISAL (United States/California)
Chardonnay Edna Valley 1989 $14 (7/15/91) **82**
Chardonnay Edna Valley 1988 $14 (6/30/90) **78**
Chardonnay Edna Valley 1987 $14 (7/15/89) **85**
Chardonnay Edna Valley 1986 $13 (5/31/88) **90**
Chardonnay Edna Valley 1985 $10 (11/15/87) **78**
Chardonnay Edna Valley 1984 $10 (6/01/86) **70**
Chardonnay Edna Valley Special Reserve 1989 $18 (11/30/91) **91**
Chardonnay Edna Valley Special Reserve 1988 $18.50 (11/30/90) **90**

CHAMPALIMAUD (Portugal)
Vintage Port 1982 $20 (VP-2/90) **86**

CHAMPALOU (France/Loire)
Vouvray 1990 $13 (9/30/91) **84**

JEANNE-MARIE DE CHAMPS (France/Burgundy)
Corton Hospices de Beaune Cuvée Charlotte-Dumay 1985 $76 (10/15/88) **87**
Meursault Charmes Cuvée de Bahèzre-de-Lanlay Hopices de Beaune 1989 $75 (8/31/91) **82**
Nuits-St.-Georges Les Didiers Hospices de Nuits Cuvée Cabet 1988 $49 (9/30/90) **83**
Nuits-St.-Georges Les Didiers Hospices de Nuits Cuvée Cabet 1985 $53 (3/15/88) **96**
Nuits-St.-Georges Les Didiers Hospices de Nuits Cuvée Jacques Duret 1988 $49 (9/30/90) **89**
Nuits-St.-Georges Les Terres Blanches 1988 $39 (7/15/91) **90**

DOMAINE CHANDON DE BRIAILLES (France/Burgundy)
Aloxe-Corton 1983 $25 (9/15/86) **84**
Corton Blanc 1988 $88 (2/28/91) **84**
Corton Bressandes 1988 $75 (2/28/91) **89**
Corton Bressandes 1986 $43 (2/28/90) **88**
Corton Clos du Roi 1986 $47 (2/28/90) **85**
Pernand-Vergelesses Ile des Vergelesses 1988 $35 (2/28/91) **83**
Savigny-lès-Beaune Les Lavières 1988 $31 (2/28/91) **86**

CHATEAU CHANGROLLE (France/Bordeaux)
Lalande-de-Pomerol 1982 $6 (12/16/84) **78**

CHANSA (United States/California)
Chardonnay Santa Barbara County 1989 $10 (4/30/91) **77**

CHANSON PERE & FILS (France/Burgundy)
Beaune Blanc Clos des Mouches 1989 $15 (8/31/91) **79**
Beaune Clos des Fèves 1988 $35 (8/31/90) **84**
Beaune Clos des Fèves 1987 Rel: $23 Cur: $27 (7/31/89) **85**
Beaune Clos des Fèves 1985 Rel: $25 Cur: $33 (1/31/89) **92**
Beaune Clos des Marconnets 1986 $20 (5/31/89) **81**
Bourgogne Blanc Chardonnay 1989 $10 (8/31/91) **81**
Bourgogne Hautes Côtes de Beaune 1989 $12 (8/31/91) **75**
Chassagne-Montrachet Les Embazées 1989 $37 (8/31/91) **85**
Corton 1986 $30 (4/30/89) **90**
Givry 1988 $13 (12/31/90) **78**
Meursault 1989 $30 (8/31/91) **78**
Pernand-Vergelesses Blanc 1989 $18 (8/31/91) **80**
Pernand-Vergelesses Blanc 1986 $16 (7/31/89) **79**
Pernand-Vergelesses Blanc Les Caradeux 1988 $25 (8/31/90) **72**
Pernand-Vergelesses Les Vergelesses 1988 $24 (8/31/90) **85**
Puligny-Montrachet 1989 $37 (8/31/91) **84**
Puligny-Montrachet 1988 $44 (10/15/90) **71**
Vosne-Romanée Suchots 1988 $55 (9/30/90) **87**

CHANTE CIGALE (France/Rhône)
Châteauneuf-du-Pape 1989 $14 (10/15/91) **84**
Châteauneuf-du-Pape 1988 $18 (10/15/91) **89**
Châteauneuf-du-Pape 1986 $18 (10/15/91) **89**
Châteauneuf-du-Pape Blanc 1990 $25 (10/15/91) **90**
Châteauneuf-du-Pape Blanc 1989 $15 (10/15/91) **85**

DOMAINE CHANTE PERDRIX (France/Rhône)
Châteauneuf-du-Pape 1988 $17 (5/31/91) **82**

CHANTEFLEUR (France/Other)
Cabernet Sauvignon Vin de Pays de l'Ardèche 1988 $6 (5/31/90) BB **80**
Chardonnay Vin de Pays d'Oc 1988 $6 (4/30/90) **79**
Merlot Vin de Pays d'Oc 1988 $6 (5/31/90) **75**

CHATEAU DE CHANTEGRIVE (France/Bordeaux)
Pessac-Léognan 1989 (NR) (3/15/92) **88**
Pessac-Léognan Cuvée Edouard 1989 (NR) (3/15/92) **85**
Graves Blanc Cuvée Caroline 1990 (NR) (9/30/91) (BT) **85+**
Graves Blanc Cuvée Caroline 1989 $12 (9/30/91) **83**

DOMAINE CHANTEL-LESCURE (France/Burgundy)
Côte de Beaune Blanc Les Grande Chatelaine 1989 $38 (8/31/91) **84**

CHANTOVENT (France/Other)
Cabernet Sauvignon Vin de Pays d'Oc Prestige 1988 $6 (3/15/90) BB **81**
Cabernet Sauvignon Vin de Pays d'Oc Prestige 1987 $5 (10/31/89) **78**
Cabernet Sauvignon Vin de Pays d'Oc Prestige 1986 $6.50 (5/15/89) **79**
Merlot Vin de Pays d'Oc Prestige 1988 $6 (3/15/90) **73**
Merlot Vin de Pays d'Oc Prestige 1986 $6.50 (5/15/89) **69**

M. CHAPOUTIER (France/Rhône)
Châteauneuf-du-Pape La Bernardine 1989 $20 (8/31/91) **84**
Châteauneuf-du-Pape La Bernardine 1988 $17 (12/31/91) **81**
Châteauneuf-du-Pape La Bernardine 1985 $25 (3/15/90) **89**
Châteauneuf-du-Pape La Bernardine 1983 Rel: $15 Cur: $26 (9/30/87) **89**
Côte-Rôtie 1989 $30 (7/31/91) **86**
Côte-Rôtie 1988 $27 (11/15/91) **84**
Côtes du Rhône 1987 $9 (12/31/91) **79**
Côtes du Rhône Blanc 1988 $13 (12/31/91) **83**
Côtes du Rhône Cuvée de Belleruche 1989 $13 (6/15/92) **82**
Côtes du Rhône Cuvée de Belleruche 1986 $12 (12/15/89) **87**
Hermitage Blanc Chante-Alouette 1989 $26 (12/31/91) **79**
Hermitage Blanc Chante-Alouette 1988 $20 (12/31/91) **84**
Hermitage Blanc Chante-Alouette 1985 $23 (3/15/90) **80**
Hermitage Blanc Chante-Alouette 1983 $16 (5/01/86) **70**
Hermitage Blanc Spécial Cuvée 180th Anniversary 1986 $24 (12/31/90) **83**
Hermitage Monier de la Sizeranne Grande Cuvée NV $14 (5/01/86) **83**
Hermitage Monier de la Sizeranne 1989 $30 (8/31/91) **89**
Hermitage Monier de la Sizeranne 1988 $25 (12/31/91) **85**
Hermitage Monier de la Sizeranne 1983 Rel: $19 Cur: $28 (5/01/86) **83**
Hermitage Monier de la Sizeranne 1981 Rel: $10 Cur: $25 (11/01/84) **88**
Hermitage Le Pavillon NV $60 (1/31/89) **88**

CHAPPELLET (United States/California)
Cabernet Sauvignon Napa Valley Reserve 1987 Rel: $18 Cur: $21 (10/15/91) **94**
Cabernet Sauvignon Napa Valley Reserve 1986 Rel: $18 Cur: $21 (CA-3/89) **92**
Cabernet Sauvignon Napa Valley Reserve 1985 Rel: $20 Cur: $25 (2/15/90) **84**
Cabernet Sauvignon Napa Valley Reserve 1984 Rel: $18 Cur: $21 (CA-3/89) **87**
Cabernet Sauvignon Napa Valley 1983 Rel: $12 Cur: $17 (CA-3/89) **77**
Cabernet Sauvignon Napa Valley 1982 Rel: $9.25 Cur: $25 (CA-3/89) **80**
Cabernet Sauvignon Napa Valley 1981 Rel: $11 Cur: $25 (CA-3/89) **79**
Cabernet Sauvignon Napa Valley 1980 Rel: $18 Cur: $31 (CA-3/89) **91**
Cabernet Sauvignon Napa Valley 1979 Rel: $13 Cur: $25 (CA-3/89) **79**
Cabernet Sauvignon Napa Valley 1978 Rel: $13 Cur: $30 (CA-3/89) **88**
Cabernet Sauvignon Napa Valley 1977 Rel: $12 Cur: $24 (CA-3/89) **82**
Cabernet Sauvignon Napa Valley 1976 Rel: $12 Cur: $49 (CA-3/89) **76**
Cabernet Sauvignon Napa Valley 1975 Rel: $10 Cur: $37 (CA-3/89) **78**
Cabernet Sauvignon Napa Valley 1974 Rel: $7.50 Cur: $63 (CA-3/89) **70**
Cabernet Sauvignon Napa Valley 1973 Rel: $7.50 Cur: $65 (CA-3/89) **69**
Cabernet Sauvignon Napa Valley 1972 Rel: $6.50 Cur: $41 (CA-3/89) **67**
Cabernet Sauvignon Napa Valley 1971 Rel: $7.50 Cur: $60 (CA-3/89) **65**
Cabernet Sauvignon Napa Valley 1970 Rel: $7.50 Cur: $95 (CA-3/89) **93**
Cabernet Sauvignon Napa Valley 1969 Rel: $10 Cur: $110 (CA-3/89) **87**
Cabernet Sauvignon Napa Valley 1968 Rel: $5.50 Cur: $90 (CA-3/89) **88**
Chardonnay Napa Valley 1989 $14 (3/31/92) **83**
Chardonnay Napa Valley 1988 Rel: $14 Cur: $16 (5/31/91) **88**

Chardonnay Napa Valley 1987 Rel: $14 Cur: $17 (6/30/90) **82**
Chardonnay Napa Valley 1986 $14 (CH-3/90) **90**
Chardonnay Napa Valley 1985 Rel: $12.50 Cur: $15 (CH-3/90) **87**
Chardonnay Napa Valley 1984 Rel: $12 Cur: $20 (CH-3/90) **87**
Chardonnay Napa Valley 1983 Rel: $12 Cur: $18 (CH-3/90) **79**
Chardonnay Napa Valley 1982 Rel: $12.50 Cur: $20 (CH-3/90) **85**
Chardonnay Napa Valley 1981 Rel: $14 Cur: $22 (CH-3/90) **80**
Chardonnay Napa Valley 1980 Rel: $14 Cur: $25 (CH-3/90) **84**
Chardonnay Napa Valley 1979 Rel: $12 Cur: $30 (CH-3/90) **79**
Chardonnay Napa Valley 1978 Rel: $11.75 Cur: $40 (CH-3/90) **76**
Chardonnay Napa Valley 1977 Rel: $11.75 Cur: $40 (CH-6/90) **90**
Chardonnay Napa Valley 1976 Rel: $9.75 Cur: $30 (CH-3/90) **71**
Chardonnay Napa Valley 1975 Rel: $6.75 Cur: $40 (CH-3/90) **82**
Chardonnay Napa Valley 1974 Rel: $6.75 Cur: $40 (CH-3/90) **72**
Chardonnay Napa Valley 1973 Rel: $6.75 Cur: $50 (CH-3/90) **91**
Chardonnay Napa Valley 1972 Rel: $6 Cur: $50 (4/16/85) (JG) **90**
Chardonnay Napa Valley 1971 Rel: $6 Cur: $50 (4/16/85) (JG) **78**
Chardonnay Napa Valley 1970 Rel: $6 Cur: $50 (4/16/85) (JG) **86**
Chenin Blanc Napa Valley 1986 $7.50 (7/31/89) **85**
Merlot Napa Valley 1989 $16 (5/31/92) **68**
Merlot Napa Valley 1988 $15 (4/15/92) **85**
Merlot Napa Valley 1987 $15 (12/31/90) **89**
Merlot Napa Valley 1986 $15 (1/31/90) **80**
Merlot Napa Valley 1985 $12 (12/31/88) **78**

DOMAINE ANTOINE CHAPUIS (France/Chablis)
Chablis Montée de Tonnerre 1985 $21 (8/31/87) **90**

MAURICE CHAPUIS (France/Burgundy)
Bourgogne Blanc Chardonnay 1989 ($NA) (8/31/91) **82**

A. CHARBAUT (France/Champagne)
Brut Blanc de Blancs Champagne 1982 $43 (4/15/90) **90**
Brut Blanc de Blancs Champagne 1979 $34 (5/31/87) **96**
Brut Blanc de Blancs Champagne NV $40 (12/31/90) **83**
Brut Blanc de Blancs Champagne Certificate 1982 $82 (12/31/89) **87**
Brut Blanc de Blancs Champagne Certificate 1979 $80 (7/15/88) **92**
Brut Blanc de Blancs Champagne Certificate 1976 Rel: $63 Cur: $82 (2/01/86) SS **97**
Brut Champagne 1985 $49 (12/31/90) **94**
Brut Champagne 1979 $23 (2/01/86) **74**
Brut Champagne NV $30 (12/31/91) **84**
Brut Champagne Cuvée de Réserve NV $35 (12/31/91) **90**
Brut Champagne Extra Quality NV $30 (12/31/91) **86**
Brut Rosé Champagne NV $32 (12/31/88) **86**
Brut Rosé Champagne Certificate 1982 $82 (12/31/89) **88**
Brut Rosé Champagne Certificate 1979 $80 (7/15/88) **89**
Extra Dry Champagne NV $22 (12/31/88) **87**

CHARBAUT FRERES (France/Other)
Brut Blanc de Blancs Crémant de Bourgogne 1986 $15 (1/31/92) **80**
Brut Rosé Crémant de Bourgogne 1986 $11.50 (12/31/90) **79**

CAVE DE CHARDONNAY (France/Burgundy)
Mâcon-Chardonnay Chardonnay de Chardonnay 1988 $9 (7/15/90) BB **81**

PHILLIPE CHARLOPIN (France/Burgundy)
Chambertin 1989 $35 (11/15/91) **91**

CHARLOPIN-PARIZOT (France/Burgundy)
Gevrey-Chambertin 1985 $22 (11/30/87) **64**
Gevrey-Chambertin Cuvée Vieilles Vignes 1990 $40 (4/30/92) **90**
Gevrey-Chambertin Cuvée Vieilles Vignes 1989 $75 (11/15/91) **88**
Gevrey-Chambertin Cuvée Vieilles Vignes 1988 $31 (12/31/90) **79**
Marsannay en Montchenovoy 1990 $19 (4/30/92) **84**

CHATEAU LES CHARMES-GODARD (France/Bordeaux)
Côtes de Francs 1989 (NR) (3/15/92) **86**

CHATEAU LES CHARMILLES (France/Bordeaux)
Bordeaux Supérieur 1985 $8 (2/15/88) **71**

CHATEAU DE LA CHARTREUSE (France/Sauternes)
Sauternes 1988 ($NA) (6/15/90) (BT) **80+**
Sauternes 1987 ($NA) (6/15/90) **77**
Sauternes 1983 Rel: $10 Cur: $26 (1/31/88) **90**

DOMAINE JEAN CHARTRON (France/Burgundy)
Beaune Hospices de Beaune Cuvée Cyrot-Chaudron 1988 $40 (2/15/91) **88**
Bourgogne Clos de la Combe 1990 $11 (3/31/92) **85**
Bourgogne Pinot Noir l'Orme 1988 ($NA) (7/15/90) (BT) **75+**
Chevalier-Montrachet 1990 $120 (3/31/92) **86**
Chevalier-Montrachet 1989 $125 (2/28/91) **94**
Chevalier-Montrachet 1988 Rel: $95 Cur: $117 (2/28/90) **97**
Chevalier-Montrachet 1987 $100 (2/28/89) **92**
Chevalier-Montrachet 1986 $125 (5/31/88) **95**
Chevalier-Montrachet 1985 $75 (10/31/87) **91**
Puligny-Montrachet Clos du Cailleret 1990 $57 (3/31/92) **88**
Puligny-Montrachet Clos du Cailleret 1989 $79 (2/28/91) **89**
Puligny-Montrachet Clos de la Pucelle 1990 $53 (3/31/92) **91**
Puligny-Montrachet Clos de la Pucelle 1989 $69 (2/28/91) **88**
Puligny-Montrachet Clos de la Pucelle 1988 Rel: $40 Cur: $48 (3/15/90) **85**
Puligny-Montrachet Clos de la Pucelle 1987 $45 (2/28/89) **81**
Puligny-Montrachet Clos de la Pucelle 1986 $50 (5/31/88) **94**
Puligny-Montrachet Clos de la Pucelle 1985 $39 (11/15/87) **74**

Key to Symbols

The scores reported here are the results of blind tastings conducted by our panel of senior editors. Wines that carry the initials below are results of individual tastings.

THE WINE SPECTATOR 100-POINT SCALE 95-100—Classic, a great wine; ***90-94***—Outstanding, superior character and style; ***80-89***—Good to very good, a wine with special qualities; ***70-79***—Average, drinkable wine that may have minor flaws; ***60-69***—Below average, drinkable but not recommended; ***50-59***—Poor, undrinkable, not recommended. "+"—With a score indicates a range; used primarily with barrel tastings to indicate a preliminary score.

SPECIAL DESIGNATIONS SS—Spectator Selection, CS—Cellar Selection, BB—Best Buy, ($NA)—Price not available, (NR)—Not released.

TASTER'S INITIALS (JG)—Jim Gordon, (HS)—Harvey Steiman, (JL)—James Laube, (JS)—James Suckling, (TM)—Thomas Matthews, (TR)—Terry Robards, (PM)—Per-Henrik Mansson, (BT)—Barrel Tasting (these wines were tasted blind from barrel samples), (CA-date)—*California's Great Cabernets* by James Laube, (CH-date)—*California's Great Chardonnays* by James Laube, (VP-date)—*Vintage Port* by James Suckling.

DATE TASTED Dates in parentheses represent the issue in which the rating was published.

Puligny-Montrachet Les Folatières 1990 $48 (3/31/92) **89**
Puligny-Montrachet Les Folatières 1989 $62 (2/28/91) **88**
Puligny-Montrachet Les Folatières 1988 $38 (3/15/90) **94**
Puligny-Montrachet Les Folatières 1987 $45 (2/28/89) **88**
Puligny-Montrachet Les Folatières 1986 $50 (5/31/88) **88**
Puligny-Montrachet Rouge Clos du Caillerets 1989 (NR) (7/15/90) (BT) **85+**
Puligny-Montrachet Rouge Clos du Caillerets 1988 ($NA) (7/15/90) (BT) **85+**

CHARTRON LA FLEUR (France/Bordeaux)
Bordeaux 1986 $4.50 (5/15/89) **74**

CHARTRON & TREBUCHET (France/Burgundy)
Bâtard-Montrachet 1990 $108 (3/31/92) **91**
Bâtard-Montrachet 1989 $120 (2/28/91) **92**
Bâtard-Montrachet 1988 Rel: $90 Cur: $100 (2/28/90) **95**
Bâtard-Montrachet 1987 $100 (3/31/89) **92**
Beaune Blanc 1987 $30 (2/28/89) **83**
Bourgogne 1989 (NR) (7/15/90) (BT) **75+**
Bourgogne Blanc Aligoté les Equinces 1985 $9 (4/30/87) **70**
Bourgogne Blanc Blanc Hommage à Victor Hugo 1988 $10 (3/31/90) **83**
Bourgogne Blanc Blanc Hommage à Victor Hugo 1987 $13 (3/15/89) **78**
Bourgogne Blanc Blanc Hommage à Victor Hugo 1986 $13 (5/31/88) **70**
Bourgogne Blanc Chardonnay 1990 $11 (3/31/92) **74**
Bourgogne Blanc Chardonnay 1989 $10 (2/28/91) **78**
Chassagne-Montrachet 1989 $46 (2/15/91) **88**
Chassagne-Montrachet 1988 $26 (2/28/90) **91**
Chassagne-Montrachet Les Morgeots 1990 $40 (3/31/92) **86**
Chassagne-Montrachet Les Morgeots 1989 $54 (2/15/91) **94**
Chassagne-Montrachet Les Morgeots 1988 $34 (2/28/90) **96**
Chassagne-Montrachet Les Morgeots 1987 $40 (3/15/89) **90**
Corton-Charlemagne 1989 $105 (2/28/91) **85**
Corton-Charlemagne 1988 $70 (2/28/90) **95**
Corton-Charlemagne 1987 $79 (3/31/89) **91**
Corton-Charlemagne 1986 $92 (5/31/88) **95**
Côte de Beaune-Villages 1988 $16 (2/28/91) **79**
Mercurey Blanc 1986 $20 (5/31/88) **69**
Meursault 1989 $41 (2/28/91) **88**
Meursault Les Charmes 1990 $44 (3/31/92) **87**
Meursault Les Charmes 1989 $57 (2/28/91) **91**
Meursault Les Charmes 1986 $45 (5/31/88) **87**
Meursault Les Genevrières Hospices de Beaune Cuvée Baudot 1987 $87 (3/15/89) **91**
Montrachet Le Montrachet 1987 $240 (2/28/89) **93**
Pernand-Vergelesses Blanc 1988 $18 (3/15/90) **83**
Pommard Les Epenottes 1988 $45 (2/28/91) **87**
Puligny-Montrachet 1988 $30 (3/15/90) **90**
Puligny-Montrachet Les Garennes 1988 $38 (3/15/90) **91**
Puligny-Montrachet Les Garennes 1987 $40 (2/28/89) **90**
Puligny-Montrachet Les Garennes 1986 $49 (5/31/88) **93**
Puligny-Montrachet Les Referts 1988 $35 (3/15/90) **89**
Puligny-Montrachet Les Referts 1987 $40 (2/28/89) **79**
Puligny-Montrachet Les Referts 1986 $46 (5/31/88) **91**
Rully Blanc La Chaume 1990 $20 (3/31/92) **82**
Rully Blanc La Chaume 1989 $18 (4/30/91) **78**
Rully Blanc La Chaume 1988 $14 (3/15/90) **88**
Rully Blanc La Chaume 1987 $15 (4/30/89) **74**
Santenay Blanc Sous la Fée 1988 $18 (3/15/90) **87**
Santenay Blanc Sous la Fée 1987 $23 (4/30/89) **79**
St.-Aubin La Chatenière 1989 $24 (2/28/91) **86**
St.-Aubin La Chatenière 1988 $18 (3/15/90) **85**
St.-Aubin La Chatenière 1987 $20 (4/15/89) **83**
St.-Aubin Les Combes 1990 $23 (3/31/92) **84**
St.-Romain 1990 $20 (3/31/92) **86**
St.-Romain 1989 $20 (2/28/91) **85**

CHARTRONS (United States/California)
Claret California 1986 $14.50 (11/15/91) **78**

CHASE-LIMOGERE (United States/California)
Brut California NV $5 (5/15/92) **79**
Brut Rosé California NV $7 (12/31/89) **68**

CHATEAU CHASSE-SPLEEN (France/Bordeaux)
Moulis 1991 (NR) (5/15/92) (BT) **85+**
Moulis 1990 (NR) (4/30/91) (BT) **85+**
Moulis 1989 $35 (3/15/92) **95**
Moulis 1988 $26 (3/31/91) **89**
Moulis 1987 Rel: $15 Cur: $17 (2/15/90) **78**
Moulis 1986 $26 (11/30/89) (JS) **90**
Moulis 1985 Rel: $22 Cur: $30 (5/15/88) **86**
Moulis 1984 Rel: $13 Cur: $15 (6/15/87) **74**
Moulis 1983 Rel: $16.50 Cur: $24 (4/16/86) **87**
Moulis 1982 Rel: $15 Cur: $36 (11/30/89) (JS) **90**

CHATEAU BENOIT (United States/Oregon)
Pinot Noir Oregon 1986 $15 (6/15/88) **55**
Pinot Noir Oregon 1985 $14 (6/15/88) **55**

CHATEAU BILTMORE (United States/North Carolina)
Blanc de Blanc North Carolina NV $21 (2/29/92) **74**
Cabernet Sauvignon North Carolina 1987 $16 (2/29/92) **76**
Chardonnay North Carolina 1990 $13 (2/29/92) **86**

CHATEAU CHEVALIER (United States/California)
Cabernet Sauvignon Napa Valley 1980 $11.25 (1/01/84) **82**

CHATEAU CHEVRE (United States/California)
Cabernet Franc Napa Valley 1985 $16 (7/31/88) **85**
Chev Reserve Napa Valley 1986 $25 (7/31/89) **88**
Merlot Napa Valley 1985 $16 (8/31/88) **87**
Merlot Napa Valley 1984 $12.50 (10/31/87) **91**
Merlot Napa Valley 1983 $12.50 (10/15/87) **85**
Merlot Napa Valley 1982 $12 (10/01/85) **84**
Merlot Napa Valley Reserve 1986 $25 (7/31/89) **80**
Merlot Napa Valley Reserve 1984 $15 (12/15/87) **78**

CHATEAU DE BAUN (United States/California)
Brut Rosé Sonoma County Symphony Rhapsody 1988 $11 (7/15/91) **83**
Brut Rosé Sonoma County Symphony Rhapsody Sec 1987 $12 (5/31/90) **78**
Brut Rosé Sonoma County Symphony Rhapsody Sec 1986 $12 (9/15/88) **88**
Brut Sonoma County Symphony Romance 1988 $11 (7/15/91) **84**
Brut Sonoma County Symphony Romance 1987 $12 (4/30/90) **80**
Brut Sonoma County Symphony Romance 1986 $12 (7/31/88) **74**

Chardonnay Russian River Valley Barrel Fermented 1990 $10 (3/15/92) **82**
Chardonnay Russian River Valley Barrel Fermented 1989 $10 (6/15/91) **81**
Château Blanc Reserve Sonoma County 1989 $5 (6/15/91) BB **82**
Symphony Late Harvest Sonoma County Finale 1988 $12/375ml (4/30/91) **87**
Symphony Late Harvest Sonoma County Finale 1987 $14/375ml (4/30/89) **85**
Symphony Late Harvest Sonoma County Finale 1986 $14/375ml (9/15/87) **81**
Symphony Sonoma County Dry Overture 1987 $8.50 (4/30/90) **75**
Symphony Sonoma Valley Prelude Off-Dry 1987 $8.50 (3/31/90) **80**

CHATEAU DE LEU (United States/California)
Chardonnay Solano County Green Valley 1989 $8 (7/15/91) **83**
Pinot Noir Solano County Green Valley 1985 $7 (2/28/89) **77**

CHATEAU DIANA (United States/California)
Blanc de Noirs Monterey Special Reserve 1986 $7 (6/15/91) **71**
Cabernet Sauvignon California Limited Edition 1989 $5 (11/15/91) **69**
Cabernet Sauvignon California Limited Edition 1988 $5 (10/15/91) **72**
Cabernet Sauvignon California Limited Edition 1986 $5 (10/15/91) BB **82**
Cabernet Sauvignon Central Coast Limited Edition 1984 $6 (11/30/88) BB **82**

CHATEAU ELAN (United States/Georgia)
Chardonnay Georgia Founder's Reserve 1987 $9 (2/29/92) **74**
Essence de Cabernet Founder's Reserve Georgia 1988 $11 (2/29/92) **76**
Summer Wine Georgia 1990 $6 (2/29/92) **78**

CHATEAU FRANK (United States/New York)
Brut Finger Lakes 1985 $18 (12/31/90) **80**

CHATEAU GRAND TRAVERSE (United States/Michigan)
Chardonnay Old Mission Penisula Reserve 1989 $13 (2/29/92) **73**
Johannisberg Riesling Late Harvest Michigan 1990 $10 (2/29/92) **78**
Johannisberg Riesling Old Mission Penisula Dry 1990 $8.50 (2/29/92) **84**

CHATEAU JULIEN (United States/California)
Chardonnay Monterey County Barrel Fermented 1990 $8 (6/30/92) **81**
Chardonnay Monterey County Paraiso Springs Vineyard 1984 $12 (2/15/87) **76**
Chardonnay Monterey County Sur Lie Private Reserve 1990 $15 (6/15/92) **85**
Merlot Monterey County 1989 $9 (5/31/92) **86**
Merlot Monterey County 1988 $9 (5/31/92) **72**
Merlot Monterey County 1986 $10 (4/15/89) **60**
Merlot Santa Barbara County Bien Nacido Vineyard 1984 $12 (2/29/88) **76**

CHATEAU LA GRANDE ROCHE (United States/California)
Chardonnay Napa Valley 1989 $13 (11/15/90) **85**
Napa Valley 1988 $13 (10/15/90) **86**

CHATEAU MONTELENA (United States/California)
Cabernet Sauvignon Napa Valley 1991 (NR) (5/15/92) (BT) **83+**
Cabernet Sauvignon Napa Valley 1987 Rel: $30 Cur: $37 (10/31/91) SS **95**
Cabernet Sauvignon Napa Valley 1986 Rel: $25 Cur: $35 (10/15/90) **93**
Cabernet Sauvignon Napa Valley 1985 Rel: $25 Cur: $57 (11/15/89) CS **92**
Cabernet Sauvignon Napa Valley 1984 Rel: $20 Cur: $55 (CA-3/89) **94**
Cabernet Sauvignon Napa Valley 1983 Rel: $18 Cur: $34 (CA-3/89) **92**
Cabernet Sauvignon Napa Valley 1983 Rel: $18 Cur: $34 (11/15/87) CS **93**
Cabernet Sauvignon Napa Valley 1982 Rel: $16 Cur: $50 (CA-3/89) **92**
Cabernet Sauvignon Napa Valley 1981 Rel: $16 Cur: $41 (CA-3/89) **80**
Cabernet Sauvignon Napa Valley 1980 Rel: $16 Cur: $56 (CA-3/89) **86**
Cabernet Sauvignon Napa Valley 1979 Rel: $16 Cur: $57 (CA-3/89) **87**
Cabernet Sauvignon Napa Valley 1978 Rel: $16 Cur: $84 (CA-3/89) **93**
Cabernet Sauvignon Napa Valley 1977 Rel: $12 Cur: $75 (CA-3/89) **94**
Cabernet Sauvignon North Coast 1976 Rel: $10 Cur: $75 (CA-3/89) **90**
Cabernet Sauvignon North Coast 1975 Rel: $9 Cur: $38 (CA-3/89) **86**
Cabernet Sauvignon Napa Valley 1974 Rel: $9 Cur: $95 (CA-3/89) **90**
Cabernet Sauvignon Alexander Valley Sonoma 1979 Rel: $14 Cur: $45 (CA-3/89) **88**
Cabernet Sauvignon Alexander Valley Sonoma 1978 Rel: $12 Cur: $68 (CA-3/89) **87**
Cabernet Sauvignon Alexander Valley Sonoma 1977 Rel: $12 Cur: $55 (CA-3/89) **91**
Cabernet Sauvignon Alexander Valley Sonoma 1974 Rel: $9 Cur: $88 (CA-3/89) **87**
Cabernet Sauvignon Alexander Valley Sonoma 1973 Rel: $8 Cur: $100 (CA-3/89) **87**
Chardonnay Alexander Valley 1988 Rel: $20 Cur: $28 (6/30/90) **85**
Chardonnay Alexander Valley 1987 Rel: $20 Cur: $25 (6/30/89) **90**
Chardonnay Alexander Valley 1986 Rel: $18 Cur: $35 (CH-2/90) **91**
Chardonnay Alexander Valley 1985 Rel: $16 Cur: $38 (CH-2/90) **91**
Chardonnay Alexander Valley 1984 Rel: $16 Cur: $35 (CH-2/90) **90**
Chardonnay Alexander Valley 1983 Rel: $14 Cur: $50 (CH-2/90) **84**
Chardonnay Alexander Valley 1982 Rel: $14 Cur: $40 (CH-2/90) **92**
Chardonnay Alexander Valley 1981 Rel: $14 Cur: $42 (CH-2/90) **91**
Chardonnay Napa Valley 1989 $23 (7/15/91) **83**
Chardonnay Napa Valley 1988 Rel: $20 Cur: $23 (11/30/90) **86**
Chardonnay Napa Valley 1987 Rel: $20 Cur: $23 (2/15/90) **72**
Chardonnay Napa Valley 1986 Rel: $18 Cur: $28 (CH-2/90) **91**
Chardonnay Napa Valley 1985 Rel: $18 Cur: $38 (CH-2/90) **90**
Chardonnay Napa Valley 1984 Rel: $18 Cur: $40 (CH-2/90) **88**
Chardonnay Napa Valley 1983 Rel: $16 Cur: $50 (CH-2/90) **85**
Chardonnay Napa Valley 1982 Rel: $16 Cur: $40 (CH-2/90) **85**
Chardonnay Napa Valley 1981 Rel: $16 Cur: $42 (CH-2/90) **88**
Chardonnay Napa Valley 1980 Rel: $16 Cur: $39 (CH-2/90) **79**
Chardonnay Napa Valley 1979 Rel: $16 Cur: $40 (CH-2/90) **78**
Chardonnay Napa Valley 1978 Rel: $15 Cur: $45 (CH-2/90) **77**
Chardonnay Napa Valley 1977 Rel: $15 Cur: $60 (CH-2/90) **85**
Chardonnay Napa-Alexander Valleys 1976 Rel: $11 Cur: $50 (CH-2/90) **77**
Chardonnay Napa Valley 1975 Rel: $9 Cur: $75 (CH-2/90) **87**
Chardonnay Napa Valley 1974 Rel: $8 Cur: $75 (CH-2/90) **88**
Chardonnay Napa-Alexander Valleys 1973 Rel: $6.50 Cur: $100 (CH-2/90) **93**
Chardonnay Napa-Alexander Valleys 1972 Rel: $6 Cur: $110 (CH-2/90) **95**
Zinfandel Napa Valley 1987 $10 (7/31/90) **69**
Zinfandel Napa Valley 1986 Rel: $10 Cur: $12 (9/15/89) **80**
Zinfandel Napa Valley 1985 $10 (4/30/88) **90**
Zinfandel Napa Valley 1983 $10 (5/01/86) **84**
Zinfandel Napa Valley 1982 Rel: $10 Cur: $18 (5/01/84) **91**
Zinfandel Napa Valley 1981 Rel: $8 Cur: $20 (4/16/84) **80**
Zinfandel Napa-Alexander Valleys 1974 $40 (6/16/85) **92**
Zinfandel Napa Valley 1973 $50 (6/16/85) **90**
Zinfandel Napa Valley John Rolleri Vineyard 1984 Rel: $10 Cur: $15 (5/15/87) **91**
Zinfandel North Coast 1976 $25 (6/16/85) **78**

CHATEAU POTELLE (United States/California)
Cabernet Sauvignon Alexander Valley 1987 $16 (8/31/91) **83**
Cabernet Sauvignon Alexander Valley 1986 $14.50 (10/31/90) **84**
Cabernet Sauvignon Alexander Valley 1984 $13 (12/31/88) **83**
Chardonnay Carneros 1988 $14 (7/15/91) **79**
Chardonnay Napa Valley 1989 $15 (3/31/92) **84**
Chardonnay Napa Valley 1987 $13 (3/31/90) **85**
Chardonnay Napa Valley 1986 $13 (11/15/88) **77**
Sauvignon Blanc Napa Valley 1990 $9 (11/15/91) **85**

CHATEAU REYNELLA (Australia)
Brut South Australia NV $9 (11/15/91) **79**
Cabernet Sauvignon Coonawarra 1988 $8.50 (4/30/91) **86**
Cabernet Sauvignon Coonawarra 1984 $7.50 (4/30/88) **80**
Cabernet Sauvignon Coonawarra 1980 $15 (5/31/87) **84**
Chardonnay McLaren Vale 1990 $10.50 (11/30/91) **84**
Chardonnay McLaren Vale 1988 $9 (7/31/90) **85**
Chardonnay McLaren Vale 1987 $11.50 (12/31/88) **82**
Chardonnay McLaren Vale 1985 $7 (5/15/88) BB **89**
Port South Australia 1981 $11.50 (11/15/91) **85**
Tawny Port South Australia Old Cave Fine Old NV $12 (11/15/91) **77**

CHATEAU SOUVERAIN (United States/California)
Cabernet Sauvignon Alexander Valley 1990 (NR) (5/15/91) (BT) **85+**
Cabernet Sauvignon Alexander Valley 1989 (NR) (5/15/91) (BT) **90+**
Cabernet Sauvignon Alexander Valley 1988 $10 (11/15/91) **85**
Cabernet Sauvignon Alexander Valley 1987 $9.50 (11/15/90) **87**
Cabernet Sauvignon Alexander Valley 1986 $8.50 (11/15/89) BB **85**
Cabernet Sauvignon Alexander Valley Private Reserve 1991 (NR) (5/15/92) (BT) **87+**
Cabernet Sauvignon Alexander Valley Private Reserve 1987 $15 (5/15/91) **83**
Cabernet Sauvignon North Coast Vintage Selection 1980 $13 (9/16/85) **83**
Cabernet Sauvignon Sonoma County 1985 $8 (11/30/88) **87**
Cabernet Sauvignon Sonoma County 1984 $8.50 (8/31/87) **83**
Cabernet Sauvignon Sonoma County Vintage Selection 1974 $50 (2/15/90) (JG) **84**
Chardonnay Russian River Valley Allen Vineyard 1990 $13.50 (7/15/92) **88**
Chardonnay Sonoma County 1986 $9 (12/31/87) **83**
Chardonnay Sonoma County Barrel Fermented 1990 $10 (12/31/91) BB **88**
Chardonnay Sonoma Valley Durell Vineyard 1990 $13.50 (7/15/92) **85**
Chardonnay Sonoma Valley Carneros Private Reserve 1987 $12 (4/15/89) **74**
Chardonnay Sonoma Valley Carneros Reserve 1986 $12 (4/30/88) **78**
Chardonnay Sonoma Valley Carneros Sangiacomo Vineyard 1990 $13.50 (7/15/92) **90**
Merlot Alexander Valley 1991 (NR) (5/15/92) (BT) **83+**
Merlot Alexander Valley 1989 $10 (5/31/92) **89**
Merlot North Coast 1981 $6.75 (10/01/85) **89**
Merlot Sonoma County 1990 $10 (5/31/92) **86**
Merlot Sonoma County 1986 $10 (3/31/89) **74**
Merlot Sonoma County 1984 $8.50 (7/31/87) **86**
Sauvignon Blanc Alexander Valley Barrel Fermented 1990 $7.50 (6/15/92) BB **82**
White Zinfandel California 1988 $5.75 (6/15/89) **77**
Zinfandel Dry Creek Valley 1989 $7.50 (5/15/92) BB **82**
Zinfandel Dry Creek Valley 1987 $9.50 (5/15/90) **82**
Zinfandel Dry Creek Valley 1986 $5 (3/31/89) BB **81**
Zinfandel Dry Creek Valley Bradford Mountain Vineyard 1987 $15 (5/15/90) **85**

CHATEAU ST. JEAN (United States/California)
Brut Blanc de Blancs Sonoma County 1987 $12 (12/31/89) **81**
Brut Blanc de Blancs Sonoma County 1984 $11 (5/31/89) **88**
Brut Blanc de Blancs Sonoma County 1983 $11 (7/31/87) **76**
Brut Blanc de Blancs Sonoma County 1982 $13 (5/16/86) **79**
Brut Blanc de Blancs Sonoma County 1981 $14 (11/01/84) **82**
Brut Blanc de Blancs Sonoma County NV $12 (5/15/91) **86**
Brut Sonoma County 1987 $12 (4/30/90) **82**
Brut Sonoma County 1986 $12 (12/31/89) **87**
Brut Sonoma County 1985 $11 (12/31/88) **86**
Brut Sonoma County 1984 $11 (7/15/88) **84**
Brut Sonoma County 1983 $11 (5/31/87) **67**
Brut Sonoma County 1982 $13 (5/16/86) **67**
Brut Sonoma County 1981 $14 (11/01/84) **81**
Brut Sonoma County NV $12 (5/15/91) **86**
Brut Sonoma County Grande Cuvée 1982 $19 (6/15/91) **80**
Cabernet Sauvignon Alexander Valley 1987 $16 (6/30/91) SS **92**
Cabernet Sauvignon Alexander Valley 1986 $19 (10/15/89) **90**
Cabernet Sauvignon Alexander Valley 1985 Rel: $19 Cur: $22.5 (11/15/88) **86**
Cabernet Sauvignon Sonoma County 1981 Rel: $15 Cur: $20 (11/30/86) **72**
Cabernet Sauvignon Sonoma Valley Wildwood Vineyards 1980 $17 (9/01/85) **82**
Cabernet Sauvignon Sonoma Valley Wildwood Vineyards 1979 $17 (7/01/84) **76**
Chardonnay Alexander Valley Belle Terre Vineyards 1989 Rel: $18 Cur: $23 (6/30/92) **87**
Chardonnay Alexander Valley Belle Terre Vineyards 1988 Rel: $16 Cur: $20 (5/31/90) **90**
Chardonnay Alexander Valley Belle Terre Vineyards 1987 Rel: $16 Cur: $21 (5/15/89) **85**
Chardonnay Alexander Valley Belle Terre Vineyards 1986 Rel: $16 Cur: $20 (CH-3/90) **90**
Chardonnay Alexander Valley Belle Terre Vineyards 1985 Rel: $16 Cur: $25 (CH-3/90) **92**
Chardonnay Alexander Valley Belle Terre Vineyards 1984 Rel: $16 Cur: $27 (CH-3/90) **85**
Chardonnay Alexander Valley Belle Terre Vineyards 1983 Rel: $16.75 Cur: $30 (CH-3/90) **89**
Chardonnay Alexander Valley Belle Terre Vineyards 1982 Rel: $15.50 Cur: $20 (CH-3/90) **86**
Chardonnay Alexander Valley Belle Terre Vineyards 1981 Rel: $15 Cur: $18 (CH-3/90) **83**
Chardonnay Alexander Valley Belle Terre Vineyards 1980 Rel: $15 Cur: $24 (CH-3/90) **88**
Chardonnay Alexander Valley Belle Terre Vineyards 1979 Rel: $12 Cur: $22 (CH-3/90) **84**
Chardonnay Alexander Valley Belle Terre Vineyards 1978 Rel: $14 Cur: $20 (CH-3/90) **73**
Chardonnay Alexander Valley Belle Terre Vineyards 1977 Rel: $12 Cur: $22 (CH-3/90) **80**
Chardonnay Alexander Valley Belle Terre Vineyards 1976 Rel: $7.50 Cur: $22 (CH-7/90) **77**
Chardonnay Alexander Valley Belle Terre Vineyards 1975 Rel: $7.50 Cur: $22 (CH-7/90) **88**
Chardonnay Alexander Valley Gauer Ranch 1980 Rel: $14 Cur: $18 (CH-3/90) **74**
Chardonnay Alexander Valley Gauer Ranch 1979 Rel: $14 Cur: $18 (CH-3/90) **70**
Chardonnay Alexander Valley Jimtown Ranch 1989 $24 (3/31/92) **84**
Chardonnay Alexander Valley Jimtown Ranch 1988 ($NA) (CH-7/90) **88**
Chardonnay Alexander Valley Jimtown Ranch 1987 $15 (CH-3/90) **87**
Chardonnay Alexander Valley Jimtown Ranch 1983 Rel: $16 Cur: $20 (CH-7/90) **87**
Chardonnay Alexander Valley Jimtown Ranch 1981 Rel: $14.75 Cur: $22 (CH-3/90) **87**
Chardonnay Alexander Valley Jimtown Ranch 1980 Rel: $14 Cur: $16 (CH-3/90) **77**
Chardonnay Alexander Valley Riverview Vineyards 1976 Rel: $9.50 Cur: $22 (CH-7/90) **88**
Chardonnay Alexander Valley Robert Young Vineyards 1990 $22 (6/30/92) **89**
Chardonnay Alexander Valley Robert Young Vineyards 1988 Rel: $18 Cur: $25 (6/30/91) **90**
Chardonnay Alexander Valley Robert Young Vineyards 1987 Rel: $18 Cur: $24 (CH-3/90) **91**
Chardonnay Alexander Valley Robert Young Vineyards 1986 Rel: $18 Cur: $30 (CH-3/90) **92**
Chardonnay Alexander Valley Robert Young Vineyards 1985 Rel: $18 Cur: $33 (CH-3/90) **91**
Chardonnay Alexander Valley Robert Young Vineyards 1984 Rel: $20 Cur: $30 (CH-3/90) **88**
Chardonnay Alexander Valley Robert Young Vineyards 1983 Rel: $18 Cur: $33 (CH-3/90) **88**
Chardonnay Alexander Valley Robert Young Vineyards 1982 Rel: $18 Cur: $20 (CH-3/90) **75**
Chardonnay Alexander Valley Robert Young Vineyards 1981 Rel: $18 Cur: $60 (CH-3/90) **86**
Chardonnay Alexander Valley Robert Young Vineyards 1980 Rel: $18 Cur: $30 (CH-3/90) **85**
Chardonnay Alexander Valley Robert Young Vineyards 1979 Rel: $17 Cur: $30 (CH-3/90) **85**
Chardonnay Alexander Valley Robert Young Vineyards 1978 Rel: $17 Cur: $25 (CH-3/90) **84**
Chardonnay Alexander Valley Robert Young Vineyards 1977 Rel: $17 Cur: $22 (CH-3/90) **68**
Chardonnay Alexander Valley Robert Young Vineyards 1976 Rel: $8.75 Cur: $25 (CH-7/90) **92**

Chardonnay Alexander Valley Robert Young Vineyards 1975 Rel: $7.75 Cur: $22 (CH-7/90) **63**
Chardonnay Alexander Valley Robert Young Vineyards Reserve 1987 ($NA/1.5L) (CH-7/90) **96**
Chardonnay Alexander Valley Robert Young Vineyards Reserve 1986 ($NA/1.5L) (CH-7/90) **91**
Chardonnay Alexander Valley Robert Young Vineyards Reserve 1985 Rel: $40/1.5L Cur: $88/1.5L (9/30/90) **93**
Chardonnay Alexander Valley Robert Young Vineyards Reserve 1984 Rel: $40/1.5L Cur: $50/1.5L (CH-3/90) **87**
Chardonnay Alexander Valley Robert Young Vineyards Reserve 1982 Rel: $45/1.5L Cur: $99/1.5L (7/01/86) **76**
Chardonnay Dry Creek Valley Frank Johnson Vineyards 1986 Rel: $14 Cur: $19 (CH-7/90) **89**
Chardonnay Dry Creek Valley Frank Johnson Vineyards 1985 $14 (CH-3/90) **87**
Chardonnay Dry Creek Valley Frank Johnson Vineyards 1984 Rel: $14 Cur: $20 (CH-7/90) **88**
Chardonnay Dry Creek Valley Frank Johnson Vineyards 1981 $14.75 (1/01/84) **88**
Chardonnay Dry Creek Valley Frank Johnson Vineyards 1980 Rel: $14 Cur: $16 (CH-3/90) **79**
Chardonnay Dry Creek Valley Frank Johnson Vineyards 1979 $13.50 (CH-3/90) **78**
Chardonnay Sonoma County 1990 $12 (6/30/92) **84**
Chardonnay Sonoma County 1988 $12 (5/31/90) **86**
Chardonnay Sonoma County 1987 $12 (5/15/89) **83**
Chardonnay Sonoma County 1986 $11 (5/31/88) **83**
Chardonnay Sonoma County 1985 $11 (4/30/87) **88**
Chardonnay Sonoma County 1984 $12 (11/16/85) **71**
Chardonnay Sonoma County Bacigalupi 1975 Rel: $10 Cur: $21 (CH-7/90) **86**
Chardonnay Sonoma County Beltane Ranch 1976 Rel: $7.75 Cur: $18 (CH-7/90) **69**
Chardonnay Sonoma County Beltane Ranch 1975 Rel: $12.50 Cur: $21 (CH-7/90) **88**
Chardonnay Sonoma Valley Estate Selection 1990 $15 (6/30/92) **85**
Chardonnay Sonoma Valley Estate Selection 1989 $14 (7/15/91) **85**
Chardonnay Sonoma Valley Hunter Farms 1981 Rel: $14.75 Cur: $19 (CH-3/90) **81**
Chardonnay Sonoma Valley Hunter Farms 1980 Rel: $14 Cur: $17 (CH-3/90) **67**
Chardonnay Sonoma Valley Hunter Farms 1979 Rel: $14 Cur: $20 (CH-3/90) **80**
Chardonnay Sonoma Valley Hunter Farms 1978 Rel: $11.25 Cur: $18 (CH-3/90) **65**
Chardonnay Sonoma Valley Hunter Farms 1977 Rel: $10.25 Cur: $25 (CH-3/90) **81**
Chardonnay Sonoma Valley Les Pierres Vineyards 1978 Rel: $13.75 Cur: $22 (CH-3/90) **81**
Chardonnay Sonoma Valley Les Pierres Vineyards 1977 Rel: $13.75 Cur: $21 (CH-3/90) **79**
Chardonnay Sonoma Valley McCrea Vineyards 1987 $15 (CH-3/90) **88**
Chardonnay Sonoma Valley McCrea Vineyards 1986 Rel: $15 Cur: $17 (CH-3/90) **87**
Chardonnay Sonoma Valley McCrea Vineyards 1985 Rel: $14.25 Cur: $18 (CH-7/90) **86**
Chardonnay Sonoma Valley McCrea Vineyards 1984 Rel: $14.25 Cur: $17 (CH-3/90) **87**
Chardonnay Sonoma Valley McCrea Vineyards 1983 Rel: $15.25 Cur: $18 (CH-7/90) **85**
Chardonnay Sonoma Valley McCrea Vineyards 1982 Rel: $13 Cur: $18 (CH-7/90) **88**
Chardonnay Sonoma Valley McCrea Vineyards 1981 Rel: $15 Cur: $18 (CH-3/90) **75**
Chardonnay Sonoma Valley McCrea Vineyards 1980 Rel: $15 Cur: $18 (CH-3/90) **70**
Chardonnay Sonoma Valley McCrea Vineyards 1979 Rel: $14 Cur: $18 (CH-3/90) **70**
Chardonnay Sonoma Valley McCrea Vineyards 1978 Rel: $12 Cur: $20 (CH-3/90) **70**
Chardonnay Sonoma Valley McCrea Vineyards 1977 Rel: $10.25 Cur: $25 (CH-3/90) **85**
Chardonnay Sonoma Valley McCrea Vineyards 1976 Rel: $9.25 Cur: $20 (CH-7/90) **75**
Chardonnay Sonoma Valley McCrea Vineyards 1975 Rel: $8.75 Cur: $20 (CH-7/90) **78**
Chardonnay Sonoma Valley St. Jean Vineyards 1984 $14 (7/31/87) **74**
Chardonnay Sonoma Valley St. Jean Vineyards 1983 $14.75 (3/16/86) **70**
Chardonnay Sonoma Valley St. Jean Vineyards 1982 $14 (2/01/85) **91**
Chardonnay Sonoma Valley Wildwood Vineyards 1980 Rel: $13 Cur: $19 (CH-7/90) **71**
Chardonnay Sonoma Valley Wildwood Vineyards 1978 Rel: $12 Cur: $19 (CH-3/90) **65**
Chardonnay Sonoma Valley Wildwood Vineyards 1977 Rel: $15 Cur: $22 (CH-3/90) **73**
Chardonnay Sonoma Valley Wildwood Vineyards 1976 Rel: $10 Cur: $20 (CH-7/90) **82**
Chardonnay Sonoma Valley Wildwood Vineyards 1975 Rel: $9.50 Cur: $20 (CH-7/90) **70**
Fumé Blanc Russian River Valley La Petite Etoile 1988 $10.50 (11/30/89) **89**
Fumé Blanc Sonoma County La Petite Etoile 1989 $10.50 (4/30/91) **84**
Fumé Blanc Sonoma County 1989 $8 (4/30/91) **85**
Fumé Blanc Sonoma County 1988 $8 (5/15/90) **73**
Gewürztraminer Late Harvest Alexander Valley Robert Young Vineyards Select 1983 $14/375ml (11/01/84) **92**
Gewürztraminer Late Harvest Alexander Valley Robert Young Vineyards 1982 $18/375ml (7/16/84) **91**
Gewürztraminer Sonoma County 1988 $8 (1/31/90) **72**
Johannisberg Riesling Late Harvest Alexander Valley Robert Young Vineyards 1984 $15/375ml (3/16/86) **86**
Johannisberg Riesling Late Harvest Alexander Valley Robert Young Vineyards 1983 $25/375ml (8/01/85) SS **92**
Johannisberg Riesling Late Harvest Alexander Valley Robert Young Vineyards Special Selection 1982 $22/375ml (9/01/84) **92**
Johannisberg Riesling Late Harvest Alexander Valley Select 1988 $20/375ml (4/30/91) **86**
Johannisberg Riesling Late Harvest Russian River Valley Select 1985 $12 (8/31/87) **84**
Pinot Blanc Alexander Valley Robert Young Vineyards 1988 $9 (5/31/91) BB **89**
Pinot Blanc Alexander Valley Robert Young Vineyards 1987 $9 (5/31/90) **88**
Pinot Blanc Alexander Valley Robert Young Vineyards 1985 $9 (12/15/89) **85**
Pinot Blanc Alexander Valley Robert Young Vineyards 1984 $9 (8/31/87) **91**
Pinot Noir Sonoma Valley McCrea Vineyards 1983 $12 (9/30/87) **75**
Sauvignon Blanc Late Harvest Sonoma County Sauvignon d'Or 1982 $15 (7/01/84) **85**
Sémillon d'Or Late Harvest Sonoma Valley St. Jean Vineyard 1984 $15 (11/30/86) **86**
Vin Blanc Sonoma County 1989 $5 (2/15/91) BB **80**

CHATEAU STE. MICHELLE (United States/Washington)
Blush Riesling Columbia Valley 1988 $5 (10/15/89) **75**
Cabernet Sauvignon Benton County Cold Creek Vineyards Château Reserve 1980 $21 (10/15/89) **85**
Cabernet Sauvignon Columbia Valley 1988 $12.50 (8/31/91) **84**
Cabernet Sauvignon Columbia Valley 1986 $12 (9/30/90) **88**
Cabernet Sauvignon Columbia Valley Cold Creek Vineyard Limited Bottling 1987 $20 (8/31/91) **83**
Cabernet Sauvignon Columbia Valley River Ridge Vineyard Limited Bottling 1987 $18 (8/31/91) **87**
Cabernet Sauvignon Columbia Valley Twentieth Vintage 1987 $12 (9/30/90) **85**
Cabernet Sauvignon Washington 1985 $11.50 (10/15/89) **85**
Cabernet Sauvignon Washington 1984 $11 (12/31/88) **89**
Cabernet Sauvignon Washington 1983 $10 (11/15/87) **81**
Cabernet Sauvignon Washington 1980 $9 (3/01/85) **65**
Cabernet Sauvignon Washington Cold Creek Vineyard Limited Bottling 1985 $19 (12/15/90) **83**
Cabernet Sauvignon Washington River Ridge Vineyard Limited Bottling 1985 $17 (11/30/90) **90**
Chardonnay Columbia Valley 1988 $10 (9/30/90) **84**
Chardonnay Columbia Valley Cold Creek Vineyard 1990 $17 (3/31/92) **89**
Chardonnay Columbia Valley River Ridge Vineyard 1990 $15 (3/31/92) **83**
Chardonnay Washington 1987 $10 (10/15/89) **81**
Chardonnay Washington 1984 $10 (7/31/87) **67**
Chardonnay Washington 1982 $9 (4/16/86) **73**
Chardonnay Washington Cold Creek Vineyard Limited Bottling 1987 $13 (10/15/89) **87**
Chardonnay Washington Cold Creek Vineyard Limited Bottling 1986 $13 (12/31/88) **82**
Chardonnay Washington River Ridge Vineyard Château Reserve 1983 $18 (7/31/87) **81**
Chardonnay Washington River Ridge Vineyard Limited Bottling 1987 $13 (10/15/89) **85**
Chenin Blanc Columbia Valley 1990 $6 (11/15/91) **83**
Chenin Blanc Columbia Valley 1988 $6 (7/31/89) **88**
Chenin Blanc Washington 1987 $6 (10/15/89) **80**
Chenin Blanc Washington 1986 $4 (7/31/89) **84**
Fumé Blanc Columbia Valley 1989 $9 (8/31/91) **80**
Gewürztraminer Columbia Valley 1990 $6.50 (8/31/91) BB **84**
Gewürztraminer Columbia Valley 1988 $6.50 (10/15/89) **79**
Johannisberg Riesling Columbia Valley 1990 $7 (8/31/91) **79**
Johannisberg Riesling Columbia Valley 1988 $6.50 (10/15/89) **85**
Johannisberg Riesling Washington 1987 $6 (4/15/89) **82**
Merlot Columbia Valley 1988 $14.50 (3/31/92) **84**
Merlot Columbia Valley 1987 $12 (9/30/90) **84**
Merlot Columbia Valley 1986 $12 (9/30/90) **84**
Merlot Columbia Valley Cold Creek Vineyard Limited Bottling 1987 $19 (8/31/91) **81**
Merlot Columbia Valley River Ridge Vineyard 1985 $17.50 (9/30/90) **89**
Merlot Washington 1983 $10 (12/31/88) **80**
Merlot Washington River Ridge Vineyard 1985 $14 (10/15/89) **87**
Merlot Washington River Ridge Vineyard Château Reserve 1983 $15 (12/31/88) **87**
Muscat Canelli Columbia Valley 1990 $6.50 (11/30/91) BB **83**
Pinot Noir Columbia Valley Limited Bottling 1987 $11 (8/31/91) **79**
Riesling Columbia Valley Dry River Ridge Vineyard 1990 $7 (6/15/91) BB **85**
Sauvignon Blanc Columbia Valley 1990 $8.50 (4/30/92) SS **91**
Sauvignon Blanc Columbia Valley 1988 $7 (12/31/90) **78**
Sémillon Columbia Valley 1990 $7 (4/15/92) BB **84**
White Riesling Columbia Valley Sweet Select 1990 $7 (6/15/92) **80**
White Riesling Columbia Valley Sweet Select 1988 $7 (10/15/89) **78**
White Riesling Late Harvest Columbia Valley River Ridge Vineyard Hand-Selected Cluster 1989 $18 (9/30/91) **82**
White Riesling Late Harvest Yakima Valley Château Reserve Hand-Selected Cluster 1985 $22 (7/31/89) **91**

CHATEAU TAHBILK (Australia)
Cabernet Sauvignon Goulburn Valley 1988 $12 (3/31/91) **87**
Cabernet Sauvignon Goulburn Valley 1987 $11 (7/31/90) **89**
Cabernet Sauvignon Goulburn Valley 1986 $10 (3/31/89) **88**
Cabernet Sauvignon Goulburn Valley 1984 $7.50 (11/15/87) **81**
Marsanne Goulburn Valley 1989 $10 (7/15/91) **80**
Shiraz Goulburn Valley 1988 $10 (2/15/92) **82**
Shiraz Goulburn Valley 1987 $11 (3/15/91) **87**
Shiraz Goulburn Valley 1984 $6 (11/15/87) **77**
Shiraz Victoria 1986 $10 (3/31/89) **88**

CHATEAU WOLTNER (United States/California)
Chardonnay Howell Mountain 1991 $12 (7/15/92) **84**
Chardonnay Howell Mountain 1989 $12 (11/30/90) **83**
Chardonnay Howell Mountain Estate Reserve 1990 $26 (7/15/92) **88**
Chardonnay Howell Mountain Estate Reserve 1988 $24 (CH-4/90) **86**
Chardonnay Howell Mountain Estate Reserve 1987 $24 (CH-4/90) **88**
Chardonnay Howell Mountain Estate Reserve 1986 $24 (CH-4/90) **91**
Chardonnay Howell Mountain Woltner Estates 1985 Rel: $18 Cur: $28 (11/15/87) **79**
Chardonnay Howell Mountain Estate Vineyards 1989 $16 (7/15/91) **82**
Chardonnay Howell Mountain Frederique Vineyard 1990 $58 (7/15/92) **89**
Chardonnay Howell Mountain St. Thomas Vineyard 1990 $39 (7/15/92) **90**
Chardonnay Howell Mountain St. Thomas Vineyard 1988 $36 (CH-4/90) **86**
Chardonnay Howell Mountain St. Thomas Vineyard 1987 $36 (CH-4/90) **87**
Chardonnay Howell Mountain St. Thomas Vineyard 1986 $36 (CH-4/90) **89**
Chardonnay Howell Mountain St. Thomas Vineyard 1985 $30 (11/15/87) **68**
Chardonnay Howell Mountain Titus Vineyard 1990 $58 (7/15/92) **88**
Chardonnay Howell Mountain Titus Vineyard 1988 $54 (CH-4/90) **86**
Chardonnay Howell Mountain Titus Vineyard 1987 $54 (CH-4/90) **85**
Chardonnay Howell Mountain Titus Vineyard 1986 $54 (CH-4/90) **88**
Chardonnay Howell Mountain Titus Vineyard 1985 $40 (11/15/87) **75**

JEAN-CLAUDE CHATELAIN (France/Loire)
Pouilly-Fumé Domaine des Chailloux 1989 $18 (3/31/91) **87**
Pouilly-Fumé Domaine des Chailloux 1988 $17.50 (9/15/90) **87**

CHAUFFE-EAU (United States/California)
Chardonnay Carneros Sangiacomo 1990 $16 (6/15/92) **86**

F. CHAUVENET (France/Burgundy)
Auxey-Duresses Rouge Le Val 1989 (NR) (1/31/92) **79**
Beaune Clos des Mouches 1986 $27 (12/31/88) **82**
Beaune Grèves 1989 $30 (1/31/92) **91**
Beaune Grèves 1988 $25 (7/15/90) (BT) **85+**
Beaune Grèves 1986 $25 (12/31/88) **79**
Beaune Hospices de Beaune Rosseau-Deslandes 1980 $36 (6/16/86) **91**
Beaune Theurons 1988 $25 (7/15/90) (BT) **70+**
Beaune Theurons 1985 $23 (7/31/87) **88**
Bourgogne Pinot Noir Château Marguerite de Bourgogne 1985 $10 (6/30/88) **80**
Chablis Les Montmains 1982 $10 (7/01/85) **82**
Chambolle-Musigny Les Charmes 1982 $33 (4/30/87) **83**
Charmes-Chambertin 1988 $78 (7/15/90) (BT) **90+**
Charmes-Chambertin 1986 $65 (7/31/88) **90**
Charmes-Chambertin 1985 $72 (7/31/87) **97**
Charmes-Chambertin 1983 $24 (9/15/86) **88**
Chassagne-Montrachet 1985 Rel: $35 Cur: $43 (3/15/87) SS **96**
Chassagne-Montrachet 1982 $13 (3/16/85) **86**
Chassagne-Montrachet Les Caillerets 1989 ($NA) (8/31/91) **87**
Chassagne-Montrachet Clos St.-Marc 1986 $38 (6/30/88) **87**
Chassagne-Montrachet Clos St.-Marc 1985 $43 (6/15/87) **91**
Chassagne-Montrachet Morgeot 1986 $45 (5/31/88) **93**
Chassagne-Montrachet Morgeot 1985 Rel: $37 Cur: $52 (5/15/87) CS **96**
Clos St.-Denis 1989 $60 (1/31/92) **87**

Key to Symbols

The scores reported here are the results of blind tastings conducted by our panel of senior editors. Wines that carry the initials below are results of individual tastings.

THE WINE SPECTATOR 100-POINT SCALE 95-100—Classic, a great wine; ***90-94***—Outstanding, superior character and style; ***80-89***—Good to very good, a wine with special qualities; ***70-79***—Average, drinkable wine that may have minor flaws; ***60-69***—Below average, drinkable but not recommended; ***50-59***—Poor, undrinkable, not recommended. "+"—With a score indicates a range; used primarily with barrel tastings to indicate a preliminary score.

SPECIAL DESIGNATIONS SS—Spectator Selection, CS—Cellar Selection, BB—Best Buy, ($NA)—Price not available, (NR)—Not released.

TASTER'S INITIALS (JG)—Jim Gordon, (HS)—Harvey Steiman, (JL)—James Laube, (JS)—James Suckling, (TM)—Thomas Matthews, (TR)—Terry Robards, (PM)—Per-Henrik Mansson, (BT)—Barrel Tasting (these wines were tasted blind from barrel samples), (CA-date)—*California's Great Cabernets* by James Laube, (CH-date)—*California's Great Chardonnays* by James Laube, (VP-date)—*Vintage Port* by James Suckling.

DATE TASTED Dates in parentheses represent the issue in which the rating was published.

Clos St.-Denis 1988 $48 (7/15/90) (BT) **85+**
Clos St.-Denis 1986 $50 (2/28/89) **90**
Clos St.-Denis 1985 $67 (7/31/87) **94**
Clos de Vougeot 1989 $60 (1/31/92) **90**
Clos de Vougeot 1986 $57 (12/31/88) **79**
Corton 1989 $50 (1/31/92) **93**
Corton 1986 $50 (7/31/88) **87**
Corton 1985 $53 (7/31/87) **96**
Corton Blanc Vergennes Hospices de Beaune Cuvée Paul Chanson 1982 $83 (8/01/85) **95**
Corton-Bressandes 1988 $58 (7/15/90) (BT) **90+**
Corton Hospices de Beaune Docteur-Peste 1985 $133 (7/15/88) **97**
Corton-Charlemagne 1985 $70 (4/30/87) **96**
Corton-Charlemagne Hospices de Beaune Cuvée François de Salins 1985 $140 (7/31/87) **96**
Côte de Beaune-Villages 1985 $16 (7/31/87) **84**
Criots-Bâtard-Montrachet 1989 ($NA) (8/31/91) **94**
Echézeaux 1989 $56 (1/31/92) **92**
Echézeaux 1988 $50 (7/15/90) (BT) **90+**
Echézeaux 1985 $47 (7/31/87) **89**
Gevrey-Chambertin Charreux 1985 $33 (10/15/87) **88**
Gevrey-Chambertin Clos St.-Jacques 1989 $45 (1/31/92) **89**
Gevrey-Chambertin Clos St.-Jacques 1986 $35 (7/31/88) **85**
Gevrey-Chambertin Estournelles St.-Jacques 1989 $40 (1/31/92) **91**
Gevrey-Chambertin Estournelles St.-Jacques 1986 $35 (7/31/88) **89**
Gevrey-Chambertin Lavaux St.-Jacques 1989 $45 (1/31/92) **88**
Gevrey-Chambertin Lavaux St.-Jacques 1988 $48 (7/15/90) (BT) **70+**
Gevrey-Chambertin Lavaux St.-Jacques 1986 $35 (7/31/88) **86**
Gevrey-Chambertin Petite Chapelle 1988 $40 (7/15/90) (BT) **70+**
Mazis-Chambertin 1983 $27 (6/30/87) **72**
Meursault Les Boucheres 1986 $40 (6/30/88) **77**
Meursault Les Casse Têtes 1989 $26 (8/31/91) **85**
Meursault Les Casse Têtes 1985 $32 (8/31/87) **84**
Meursault Les Casse Têtes 1984 $19 (7/16/86) **71**
Meursault Les Casse Têtes 1982 $11 (3/01/85) **82**
Meursault Charmes Hospices de Beaune Cuvée de Bahèzre-de-Lanlay 1985 $141 (3/15/89) **86**
Meursault Les Genevrières 1989 $42 (8/31/91) **94**
Meursault Les Genevrières 1986 $40 (4/30/88) **85**
Meursault Les Genevrières Hospices de Beaune Cuvée Baudot 1983 $55 (11/01/85) **88**
Meursault Les Gouttes d'Or 1989 ($NA) (8/31/91) **86**
Meursault Hospices de Beaune Cuvée Jehan-Humblot 1985 $90 (7/31/87) **91**
Meursault Hospices de Beaune Cuvée Loppin 1982 Rel: $33 Cur: $65 (1/01/85) CS **92**
Meursault Les Perrières 1989 $41 (8/31/91) **91**
Meursault Les Perrières 1986 $40 (4/30/88) **86**
Meursault Les Poruzots 1989 $53 (8/31/91) **94**
Meursault Les Poruzots 1986 $40 (4/30/88) **92**
Monthélie Champs-Fulliot 1989 $20 (1/31/92) **81**
Nuits-St.-Georges Les Chaignots 1989 $45 (1/31/92) **91**
Nuits-St.-Georges Les Chaignots 1988 $38 (7/15/90) (BT) **80+**
Nuits-St.-Georges Les Chaignots 1986 $40 (7/31/88) **87**
Nuits-St.-Georges Les Perrières 1985 $48 (7/31/87) **80**
Nuits-St.-Georges Les Plateaux 1985 $34 (7/31/87) **84**
Nuits-St.-Georges Les Plateaux 1982 $16 (1/01/85) **78**
Nuits-St.-Georges Les Pruliers 1989 $45 (1/31/92) **88**
Pommard Les Chanlins 1989 $45 (1/31/92) **86**
Pommard Les Chanlins 1988 $55 (7/15/90) (BT) **85+**
Pommard Les Chanlins 1986 $40 (7/31/88) **90**
Pommard Epenottes 1989 $45 (1/31/92) **94**
Pommard Epenottes 1985 $48 (7/31/87) **95**
Pommard Hospices de Beaune Cuvée Dames-de-la-Charite 1982 Rel: $36 Cur: $55 (2/01/85) CS **91**
Pouilly-Fuissé 1982 $8.50 (3/01/84) **76**
Pouilly-Fuissé Clos de France 1987 $13 (4/30/89) **78**
Pouilly-Fuissé Clos de France 1986 $14 (10/15/87) **79**
Puligny-Montrachet Les Champs-Gains 1989 $30 (8/31/91) **87**
Puligny-Montrachet Les Champs-Gains 1984 $40 (4/30/87) **88**
Puligny-Montrachet Les Champs-Gains 1982 $17 (3/16/85) **88**
Puligny-Montrachet La Garenne 1989 ($NA) (8/31/91) **86**
Puligny-Montrachet Reuchaux 1985 $35 (2/28/87) **66**
Puligny-Montrachet Reuchaux 1982 $20 (9/16/85) **85**
Puligny-Montrachet Rouge 1985 $16 (6/15/87) **81**
St.-Romain 1989 ($NA) (8/31/91) **77**
St.-Véran 1985 $12 (3/31/87) **81**
St.-Véran 1983 $6 (12/16/85) **62**
Santenay 1985 $18 (7/31/87) **84**
Volnay Clos des Chênes 1989 $40 (1/31/92) **90**
Volnay Premier Cru 1989 $36 (1/31/92) **88**
Vosne-Romanée Les Suchots 1985 $46 (7/31/87) **92**

JEAN CHAUVENET (France/Burgundy)
Nuits-St.-Georges Les Bousselots 1985 $49 (5/31/88) **88**

CHATEAU CHAUVIN (France/Bordeaux)
St.-Emilion 1988 $20 (6/30/91) **84**
St.-Emilion 1986 $15 (6/30/89) **75**

BERNARD CHAVE (France/Rhône)
Crozes-Hermitage 1988 $14 (2/15/91) **78**
Crozes-Hermitage 1985 $12 (11/30/88) **86**
Hermitage 1989 $40 (12/31/91) **91**
Hermitage 1986 $32 (11/30/88) **86**

J.L. CHAVE (France/Rhône)
Hermitage 1987 $48 (6/30/90) **89**
Hermitage 1984 Rel: $25 Cur: $30 (8/31/87) **89**
Hermitage 1980 Rel: $25 Cur: $37 (5/01/86) **83**
Hermitage Blanc 1983 Rel: $20 Cur: $48 (5/01/86) **81**

DOMAINE CHAVET (France/Loire)
Menetou-Salon 1987 $9.50 (7/15/89) **84**

GERARD CHAVY (France/Burgundy)
Puligny-Montrachet 1985 $28 (12/31/87) **82**
Puligny-Montrachet 1984 $22 (11/15/87) **69**
Puligny-Montrachet Les Pucelles 1986 $30 (12/15/88) **91**

CHATEAU CHENE VERT (France/Bordeaux)
Pessac-Léognan 1987 ($NA) (6/30/89) (BT) **65+**

MAURICE CHENU (France/Burgundy)
Côte de Beaune-Villages 1989 (NR) (7/15/90) (BT) **85+**
Côte de Beaune-Villages 1988 ($NA) (7/15/90) (BT) **80+**
Pommard 1989 (NR) (7/15/90) (BT) **70+**
Pommard 1988 ($NA) (7/15/90) (BT) **75+**
Savigny-lès-Beaune 1989 (NR) (7/15/90) (BT) **75+**
Savigny-lès-Beaune 1988 ($NA) (7/15/90) (BT) **75+**

CHATEAU CHERCHY (France/Bordeaux)
Graves Blanc 1986 $6.50 (5/31/88) **77**
Graves Blanc 1985 $5 (6/30/87) BB **80**

CHERRIER PERE (France/Loire)
Sancerre Domaine des Chasseignes 1989 $16 (3/31/91) **86**

CHESTNUT HILL (United States/California)
Cabernet Sauvignon California 1988 $7.50 (10/15/91) BB **81**
Cabernet Sauvignon Napa Valley 1983 $7 (10/31/86) BB **91**
Cabernet Sauvignon Sonoma County 1987 $9 (3/31/90) **80**
Cabernet Sauvignon Sonoma County 1985 $7.75 (10/15/88) **77**
Chardonnay California 1988 $8 (4/15/90) **74**
Chardonnay Napa Valley 1984 $7.50 (4/16/86) **72**
Chardonnay Napa Valley Draper Vineyards Reserve 1990 $12.50 (11/30/91) **87**
Chardonnay Sonoma County 1989 $7 (7/15/91) **69**
Chardonnay Sonoma County 1986 $8 (12/31/87) **75**
Merlot Napa Valley 1989 $10 (11/15/91) **81**
Merlot North Coast 1985 $8.50 (12/15/87) **84**
Sauvignon Blanc North Coast 1990 $6 (11/15/91) **73**
Zinfandel San Luis Obispo 1988 $6 (8/31/91) BB **86**

CHESTNUT MOUNTAIN (United States/Georgia)
Cabernet Sauvignon Georgia Mossy Creek Vineyard 1989 $16 (2/29/92) **83**
Chardonnay Georgia Mossy Creek Vineyard 1989 $16 (2/29/92) **70**
Merlot Georgia 1990 $14 (2/29/92) **83**

CHATEAU CHEVAL BLANC (France/Bordeaux)
Bordeaux Blanc 1989 $5 (7/31/91) **76**
St.-Emilion 1990 (NR) (5/15/92) (BT) **95+**
St.-Emilion 1989 $150 (3/15/92) **90**
St.-Emilion 1988 $105 (12/31/90) CS **93**
St.-Emilion 1987 $57 (2/15/91) (JS) **82**
St.-Emilion 1986 Rel: $80 Cur: $85 (2/15/91) (JS) **93**
St.-Emilion 1986 Rel: $80 Cur: $85 (6/30/89) CS **98**
St.-Emilion 1985 Rel: $80 Cur: $91 (2/15/91) (JS) **98**
St.-Emilion 1984 $69 (2/15/91) (HS) **85**
St.-Emilion 1983 Rel: $63 Cur: $80 (2/15/91) (JS) **96**
St.-Emilion 1982 Rel: $69 Cur: $150 (2/15/91) (JS) **97**
St.-Emilion 1982 Rel: $69 Cur: $150 (2/16/85) CS **96**
St.-Emilion 1981 Rel: $46 Cur: $80 (2/15/91) (JS) **90**
St.-Emilion 1980 $46 (2/15/91) (JS) **84**
St.-Emilion 1979 $78 (2/15/91) (JS) **88**
St.-Emilion 1978 $115 (2/15/91) (JS) **94**
St.-Emilion 1977 $32 (2/15/91) (JS) **74**
St.-Emilion 1976 $80 (2/15/91) (JS) **88**
St.-Emilion 1975 $140 (2/15/91) (JS) **91**
St.-Emilion 1974 $46 (2/15/91) (JS) **83**
St.-Emilion 1973 $60 (2/15/91) (JS) **83**
St.-Emilion 1972 $40 (2/15/91) (JS) **82**
St.-Emilion 1971 $120 (2/15/91) (JS) **89**
St.-Emilion 1970 $165 (2/15/91) (JS) **88**
St.-Emilion 1969 $41 (2/15/91) (JS) **75**
St.-Emilion 1967 $90 (2/15/91) (JS) **85**
St.-Emilion 1966 $160 (2/15/91) (JS) **87**
St.-Emilion 1964 $220 (2/15/91) (HS) **94**
St.-Emilion 1962 $125 (2/15/91) (JS) **85**
St.-Emilion 1961 $480 (2/15/91) (JS) **96**
St.-Emilion 1960 $125 (2/15/91) (JS) **81**
St.-Emilion 1959 $270 (2/15/91) (JS) **90**
St.-Emilion 1958 $180 (2/15/91) (JS) **86**
St.-Emilion 1955 $280 (2/15/91) (JS) **94**
St.-Emilion 1953 $430 (2/15/91) (JS) **87**
St.-Emilion 1952 $270 (2/15/91) (JS) **91**
St.-Emilion 1951 $150 (2/15/91) (JS) **76**
St.-Emilion 1950 $300 (2/15/91) (JS) **89**
St.-Emilion 1949 $570 (2/15/91) (JS) **84**
St.-Emilion 1948 $300 (2/15/91) (JS) **97**
St.-Emilion 1947 $1,150 (2/15/91) (JS) **100**
St.-Emilion 1946 $340 (2/15/91) (JS) **87**
St.-Emilion 1945 $580 (3/16/86) (JL) **95**
St.-Emilion 1943 $185 (2/15/91) (JS) **85**
St.-Emilion 1941 $175 (2/15/91) (JS) **71**
St.-Emilion 1940 $520 (2/15/91) (JS) **83**
St.-Emilion 1938 $125 (2/15/91) (JS) **75**
St.-Emilion 1937 $400 (2/15/91) (JS) **93**
St.-Emilion 1936 $280 (2/15/91) (JS) **81**
St.-Emilion 1934 $330 (2/15/91) (JS) **93**
St.-Emilion 1933 $280 (2/15/91) (JS) **88**
St.-Emilion 1931 $230 (2/15/91) (JS) **72**
St.-Emilion 1930 $280 (2/15/91) (JS) **82**
St.-Emilion 1929 $450 (2/15/91) (JS) **90**
St.-Emilion 1928 $480 (2/15/91) (JS) **92**
St.-Emilion 1926 $400 (2/15/91) (JS) **85**
St.-Emilion 1924 $380 (2/15/91) (JS) **69**
St.-Emilion 1923 $200 (2/15/91) (JS) **65**
St.-Emilion 1921 $2,000 (2/15/91) (JS) **100**
St.-Emilion 1919 $500 (2/15/91) (JS) **70**
St.-Emilion 1917 $500 (2/15/91) (JS) **70**
St.-Emilion 1916 $400 (2/15/91) (JS) **71**
St.-Emilion 1915 $500 (2/15/91) (JS) **72**
St.-Emilion 1908 $500 (2/15/91) (JS) **71**
St.-Emilion 1905 $600 (2/15/91) (JS) **70**
St.-Emilion 1899 $1,200 (2/15/91) (JS) **90**

DOMAINE DE CHEVAL BLANC (France/Bordeaux)
Bordeaux 1985 $5 (5/15/88) **78**

CHATEAU DU CHEVALIER (France/Bordeaux)
Montagne-St.-Emilion 1986 $19 (3/31/91) **71**

DOMAINE DE CHEVALIER (France/Bordeaux)
Pessac-Léognan 1991 (NR) (5/15/92) (BT) **85+**
Pessac-Léognan 1990 (NR) (5/15/92) (BT) **95+**
Pessac-Léognan 1989 $59 (3/15/92) **96**
Pessac-Léognan 1988 $37 (7/15/91) **91**
Pessac-Léognan 1987 $29 (6/30/89) (BT) **80+**
Pessac-Léognan 1986 Rel: $33 Cur: $38 (6/15/89) **89**

Graves 1985 Rel: $43 Cur: $62 (9/30/88) CS **92**
Graves 1984 Rel: $20 Cur: $35 (8/31/87) **90**
Graves 1979 $47 (10/15/89) (JS) **87**
Graves 1961 $180 (3/16/86) (TR) **76**
Graves 1959 $100 (10/15/90) (JS) **97**
Graves 1945 $180 (3/16/86) (JL) **59**
Pessac-Léognan Blanc 1990 (NR) (9/30/91) (BT) **90+**
Pessac-Léognan Blanc 1989 Rel: $60 Cur: $93 (9/30/91) **90**
Pessac-Léognan Blanc 1988 $62 (6/30/89) (BT) **90+**
Pessac-Léognan Blanc 1987 $49 (6/30/89) (BT) **95+**
Graves Blanc 1985 $99 (5/15/87) (BT) **90+**
Graves Blanc 1983 Rel: $65 Cur: $96 (11/15/87) **86**

GUY CHEVALIER (France/Other)
Cabernet Syrah Vin de Pays de l'Aude 1990 $8.50 (12/31/91) **79**
Corbières La Coste 1989 $9 (8/31/91) **72**
Vin de Pays de l'Aude le Texas 1989 $9 (7/15/91) **74**

CHEVALIER DE BEAUBASSIN (France/Burgundy)
Meursault 1985 $24 (4/30/88) **81**
Nuits-St.-Georges 1985 $31 (4/30/88) **84**

CHEVALIER DUCLA (France/Bordeaux)
Bordeaux 1986 $5.50 (5/15/89) BB **80**

CHEVALIER PERE & FILS (France/Burgundy)
Aloxe-Corton 1983 $19 (9/15/86) **85**

CHEVALIER VEDRINES (France/Bordeaux)
Bordeaux 1985 $6 (6/30/88) **77**
Bordeaux Blanc Sauvignon Blanc 1986 $6 (5/31/88) **77**

DENIS CHEVILLON (France/Burgundy)
Meursault Les Charmes 1959 ($NA) (8/31/90) (TR) **86**
Nuits-St.-Georges Les Chaignots 1987 $33 (7/15/90) **87**
Nuits-St.-Georges Les Pruliers 1987 $38 (7/15/90) **84**

ROBERT CHEVILLON (France/Burgundy)
Bourgogne 1989 $16 (1/31/92) **77**
Nuits-St.-Georges 1989 $36 (1/31/92) **89**
Nuits-St.-Georges 1986 $37 (12/15/89) **74**
Nuits-St.-Georges 1985 $40 (4/30/88) **85**
Nuits-St.-Georges Les Vaucrains 1989 $65 (1/31/92) **89**

DOMAINE DES CHEZEAUX (France/Burgundy)
Chambolle-Musigny Les Charmes 1985 $75 (6/15/88) **91**
Griotte-Chambertin 1988 $110 (5/15/91) **90**
Griotte-Chambertin 1985 $100 (6/15/88) **91**

MICHELE CHIARLO (Italy/Piedmont)
Barbaresco Rabajà 1988 $47 (1/31/92) **90**
Barbera d'Asti Granduca Superiore 1989 $10 (2/15/92) **84**
Barbera d'Asti Superiore 1986 $18 (3/15/91) **86**
Barbera d'Asti Superiore Valle del Sole 1987 $19 (2/15/92) **84**
Barilot 1986 $27 (2/28/91) **80**
Barolo Granduca 1985 $20 (2/28/91) **89**
Barolo Rocche di Castiglione Riserva 1985 $43 (1/31/92) **88**
Barolo Rocche di Castiglione Riserva 1983 $30 (2/28/91) **78**
Barolo Vigna Rionda di Serralunga Riserva 1985 $39 (2/28/91) **81**
Barolo Vigna Rionda di Serralunga Riserva 1983 $36 (2/28/91) **87**
Barolo Vigna Rionda di Serralunga Riserva 1982 $32 (1/31/90) **89**
Gavi Granduca 1989 $12 (1/31/91) **84**

LA CHIESA DI S. RESTITUTA (Italy/Tuscany)
Brunello di Montalcino 1982 $23 (3/15/89) **56**

CHIMERE (United States/California)
Chardonnay Edna Valley 1989 $15 (7/15/91) **83**

CHIMNEY ROCK (United States/California)
Cabernet Sauvignon Stags Leap District 1991 (NR) (5/15/92) (BT) **86+**
Cabernet Sauvignon Stags Leap District 1988 $18 (5/15/90) (BT) **80+**
Cabernet Sauvignon Stags Leap District 1987 $18 (7/31/91) SS **90**
Cabernet Sauvignon Stags Leap District 1986 Rel: $15 Cur: $19 (9/30/89) **87**
Cabernet Sauvignon Stags Leap District 1985 Rel: $15 Cur: $19 (CA-3/89) **87**
Cabernet Sauvignon Stags Leap District 1984 Rel: $15 Cur: $19 (CA-3/89) **82**
Chardonnay Stags Leap District 1989 $16 (7/15/91) **72**
Chardonnay Stags Leap District 1988 $15 (12/31/90) **77**
Chardonnay Stags Leap District 1987 $15 (2/15/90) **81**
Chardonnay Stags Leap District 1986 $14 (10/15/88) **80**
Elevage Napa Valley 1991 (NR) (5/15/92) (BT) **89+**
Fumé Blanc Stags Leap District 1989 $11 (7/31/91) **81**
Fumé Blanc Stags Leap District 1988 $15 (5/15/90) **65**
Fumé Blanc Stags Leap District 1987 $10 (1/31/89) **77**

CHINOOK (United States/Washington)
Chardonnay Washington 1987 $11 (10/15/89) **82**
Merlot Washington 1986 $12.50 (10/15/89) **83**
Sauvignon Blanc Washington 1987 $8.25 (10/15/89) **89**

CHIONETTI (Italy/Piedmont)
Dolcetto di Dogliani Briccolero 1989 $16 (4/30/91) **87**

CHITTERING (Australia)
Cabernet Sauvignon Merlot Western Australia 1988 $18 (9/30/91) **79**
Chardonnay Western Australia 1988 $18 (9/15/91) **88**
Western Australia 1988 $10 (9/30/91) **75**

Key to Symbols

The scores reported here are the results of blind tastings conducted by our panel of senior editors. Wines that carry the initials below are results of individual tastings.

THE WINE SPECTATOR 100-POINT SCALE 95-100—Classic, a great wine; ***90-94***—Outstanding, superior character and style; ***80-89***—Good to very good, a wine with special qualities; ***70-79***—Average, drinkable wine that may have minor flaws; ***60-69*** —Below average, drinkable but not recommended; ***50-59*** —Poor, undrinkable, not recommended. "+"—With a score indicates a range; used primarily with barrel tastings to indicate a preliminary score.

SPECIAL DESIGNATIONS SS—Spectator Selection, CS—Cellar Selection, BB—Best Buy, ($NA)—Price not available, (NR)—Not released.

TASTER'S INITIALS (JG)—Jim Gordon, (HS)—Harvey Steiman, (JL)—James Laube, (JS)—James Suckling, (TM)—Thomas Matthews, (TR)—Terry Robards, (PM)—Per-Henrik Mansson, (BT)—Barrel Tasting (these wines were tasted blind from barrel samples), (CA-date)—*California's Great Cabernets* by James Laube, (CH-date)—*California's Great Chardonnays* by James Laube, (VP-date)—*Vintage Port* by James Suckling.

DATE TASTED Dates in parentheses represent the issue in which the rating was published.

JEAN CHOFFLET (France/Burgundy)
Givry 1985 $12 (11/15/87) **70**

A. CHOPIN (France/Burgundy)
Côte de Nuits-Villages 1985 $9 (10/31/87) BB **83**
Nuits-St.-Georges Aux Murgers 1988 $28 (7/15/90) **91**
Nuits-St.-Georges Aux Murgers 1987 $26 (12/15/89) **85**
Nuits-St.-Georges Aux Murgers 1986 $29 (10/15/88) **78**

CHOPIN-GROFFIER (France/Burgundy)
Chambolle-Musigny 1989 $32 (1/31/92) **90**
Clos Vougeot 1989 $72 (1/31/92) **94**
Clos Vougeot 1988 $70 (5/15/91) **87**
Nuits-St.-Georges 1989 $32 (1/31/92) **91**
Nuits-St.-Georges Les Chaignots 1989 $40 (1/31/92) **93**
Vougeot 1989 $32 (1/31/92) **93**
Vougeot 1988 $32 (5/15/91) **92**

A.R. CHOPPIN (France/Burgundy)
Beaune Bressandes 1985 $32 (9/30/87) **90**
Beaune Cent Vignes 1985 $32 (10/31/87) **81**
Beaune Grèves 1985 $32 (9/30/87) **79**
Beaune Teurons 1987 $30 (2/28/90) **87**
Beaune Teurons 1985 $32 (10/31/87) **87**
Beaune Toussaints 1987 $30 (2/28/90) **83**
Savigny-lès-Beaune Vergelesses 1987 $32 (2/28/90) **79**
Savigny-lès-Beaune Vergelesses 1985 $25 (10/31/87) **87**

CHRISTIAN BROTHERS (United States/California)
Cabernet Napa Valley-Bordeaux Montage Premier Cuvée NV $15 (10/15/88) **84**
Cabernet Sauvignon Napa Valley 1988 $6.75 (11/15/91) **76**
Cabernet Sauvignon Napa Valley 1987 $7.50 (10/15/91) **79**
Cabernet Sauvignon Napa Valley 1986 Rel: $9.50 Cur: $12 (11/15/90) **88**
Cabernet Sauvignon Napa Valley 1985 $8 (6/15/88) **90**
Cabernet Sauvignon Napa Valley 1984 $7 (10/15/87) BB **87**
Cabernet Sauvignon Napa Valley 1980 $6.75 (10/01/85) **58**
Chardonnay Napa Valley 1989 $7 (1/31/92) **79**
Chardonnay Napa Valley 1988 $7.50 (6/30/91) **78**
Chardonnay Napa Valley 1987 $10 (11/30/89) **69**
Chardonnay Napa Valley 1984 $8.50 (6/16/86) **76**
Chardonnay Napa Valley Barrel Fermented 1985 $11 (7/31/87) **88**
Chardonnay Napa Valley Private Reserve Barrel Fermented 1987 $11.50 (9/15/89) **83**
Chardonnay Napa Valley Private Reserve Barrel Fermented 1986 $12 (12/31/88) **87**
Chardonnay Napa Valley-Burgundy Montage Premier Cuvée NV $15 (10/15/88) **86**
Chenin Blanc Napa Valley 1987 $5 (7/31/89) **84**
Merlot Napa Valley 1985 $8 (8/31/88) **80**
White Zinfandel Napa Valley 1988 $5.50 (6/15/89) **77**
Zinfandel Napa Valley 1986 $5.50 (6/30/88) **79**

JOH. JOS. CHRISTOFFEL (Germany)
Riesling Auslese Mosel-Saar-Ruwer Erdener Treppchen 1990 (NR) (12/15/91) **87**
Riesling Auslese Mosel-Saar-Ruwer Erdener Treppchen 1988 ($NA) (9/30/89) **92**
Riesling Auslese Mosel-Saar-Ruwer Urziger Würzgarten 1990 $25 (12/15/91) **86**
Riesling Auslese Mosel-Saar-Ruwer Urziger Würzgarten Gold Cap (AP991) 1990 (NR) (12/15/91) **90**
Riesling Spätlese Mosel-Saar-Ruwer Erdener Treppchen 1990 (NR) (12/15/91) **86**
Riesling Spätlese Mosel-Saar-Ruwer Erdener Treppchen 1988 $10 (9/30/89) **84**
Riesling Spätlese Mosel-Saar-Ruwer Urziger Würzgarten 1990 $15 (12/15/91) **80**
Riesling Spätlese Mosel-Saar-Ruwer Urziger Würzgarten 1988 ($NA) (9/30/89) **85**

CHRISTOPHE (United States/California)
Cabernet Sauvignon California 1988 $9 (3/31/91) **83**
Cabernet Sauvignon California 1982 $4.50 (12/16/85) BB **85**
Cabernet Sauvignon Napa Valley Reserve 1987 $12 (11/15/91) **83**
Cabernet Sauvignon Napa Valley Reserve 1986 $12 (11/15/90) **78**
Cabernet Sauvignon Napa Valley Reserve 1985 $12.50 (11/15/89) **74**
Cabernet Sauvignon Napa Valley Reserve 1983 $9.50 (3/31/88) **82**
Chardonnay California 1990 $7 (7/15/92) BB **81**
Chardonnay California 1989 $9 (7/15/91) **78**
Chardonnay California 1988 $7.50 (4/30/90) BB **83**
Chardonnay California 1987 $8.50 (3/31/89) **74**
Chardonnay California 1985 $6.50 (11/15/86) **73**
Chardonnay California 1984 $5.50 (12/01/85) BB **84**
Chardonnay California Reserve 1989 $12 (7/15/91) **80**
Chardonnay California Reserve 1986 $9.50 (4/15/88) **77**
Joliesse California 1987 $5 (2/28/90) **79**
Joliesse California NV $4 (6/15/89) **78**
Pinot Noir Napa Valley Carneros Reserve 1989 $12 (11/15/91) **85**
Sauvignon Blanc California 1987 $7 (4/30/89) BB **82**

CHURCHILL (Portugal)
Vintage Character Port Finest NV $19 (4/15/91) **83**
Vintage Port 1985 Rel: $22 Cur: $51 (VP-2/90) **81**
Vintage Port 1982 $24 (VP-6/90) **78**
Vintage Port Agua Alta 1987 Rel: $37 Cur: $41 (4/15/91) **83**
Vintage Port Agua Alta 1983 Rel: $22 Cur: $40 (VP-7/90) **69**
Vintage Port Fojo 1986 ($NA) (VP-2/90) **78**
Vintage Port Fojo 1984 ($NA) (VP-2/90) **79**

CAVE DES VIGNERONS A CHUSCLAN (France/Rhône)
Côtes du Rhône Prieure St.-Julien 1985 $4.25 (12/31/87) BB **79**

CIACCI PICCOLOMINI D'ARAGONA (Italy/Tuscany)
Brunello di Montalcino 1984 $25 (6/15/90) **91**
Rosso di Montalcino 1988 $16 (4/30/91) **82**

FRATELLI CIGLIUTI (Italy/Piedmont)
Barbaresco Serraboella 1986 $20 (8/31/89) **86**
Barbera d'Alba Serraboella 1989 $15 (11/30/91) **87**

VILLA CILNIA (Italy/Tuscany)
Campo del Sasso 1988 $14 (8/31/91) **76**
Chianti Colli Aretini 1990 $10 (1/31/92) **86**
Chianti Colli Aretini 1989 $10 (4/30/91) **85**
Chianti Colli Aretini 1988 $10 (4/15/91) **89**
Chianti Colli Aretini 1987 $8.25 (10/15/89) **76**
Chianti Colli Aretini 1986 $9 (5/31/89) BB **87**
Chianti Colli Aretini Riserva 1986 $18 (10/31/87) **76**
Le Vignacce 1988 $24 (9/15/91) **89**
Le Vignacce 1986 $19 (11/30/89) **90**
Le Vignacce 1985 $20 (7/15/89) **88**
Poggio Garbato 1989 $9.25 (7/15/91) **80**

Vocato 1986 $10.50 (5/15/89) **86**

CILURZO (United States/California)
Merlot Temecula Unfiltered Proprietor's Reserve 1990 $12 (5/31/92) **79**

CINNABAR (United States/California)
Cabernet Sauvignon Santa Cruz Mountains Saratoga Vineyard 1988 $20 (3/15/92) **82**
Cabernet Sauvignon Santa Cruz Mountains 1987 $18 (3/31/91) **84**
Cabernet Sauvignon Santa Cruz Mountains 1986 $15 (11/15/89) **93**
Chardonnay Santa Cruz Mountains 1990 $20 (3/31/92) **88**
Chardonnay Santa Cruz Mountains 1989 $18 (3/31/91) **79**

CHATEAU CISSAC (France/Bordeaux)
Haut-Médoc 1991 (NR) (5/15/92) (BT) **80+**
Haut-Médoc 1989 $19 (3/15/92) **85**
Haut-Médoc 1987 $14 (11/30/89) (JS) **81**
Haut-Médoc 1986 $20 (11/30/89) (JS) **79**
Haut-Médoc 1985 $16 (7/31/88) **79**
Haut-Médoc 1982 $20 (11/30/89) (JS) **81**

CHATEAU CITRAN (France/Bordeaux)
Haut-Médoc 1991 (NR) (5/15/92) (BT) **85+**
Haut-Médoc 1990 (NR) (5/15/92) (BT) **90+**
Haut-Médoc 1989 $20 (3/15/92) **93**
Haut-Médoc 1988 Rel: $15 Cur: $20 (4/30/91) **91**
Haut-Médoc 1987 $14 (6/30/89) (BT) **75+**
Haut-Médoc 1983 Rel: $10 Cur: $12 (4/01/86) **82**
Haut-Médoc 1982 Rel: $6 Cur: $12 (4/01/85) **78**

CLAIBORNE (United States/Mississippi)
Sauvignon Blanc Mississippi Delta 1987 $10.50 (2/29/92) **76**

CLAIBORNE & CHURCHILL (United States/California)
Muscat Canelli California Dry Alsatian Style 1987 $8 (12/15/89) **78**
Riesling Central Coast Dry Alsatian Style 1991 $9.50 (5/31/92) **85**
Riesling Edna Valley Dry Alsatian Style 1987 $8 (12/15/89) **76**
Riesling Late Harvest Central Coast 1987 $15/375ml (12/15/89) **81**

DOMAINE BRUNO CLAIR (France/Burgundy)
Bourgogne Blanc 1989 $13 (8/31/91) **82**
Gevrey-Chambertin Les Cazetiers 1989 $61 (1/31/92) **89**
Marsannay 1988 $16 (11/15/91) **80**
Marsannay Blanc Rosé 1989 $13 (11/15/91) **86**
Marsannay Les Longeroies 1989 $18 (1/31/92) **87**
Marsannay Les Vaudenelles 1989 $18 (1/31/92) **81**
Morey-St.-Denis 1985 $20 (5/15/88) **73**
Morey-St.-Denis Blanc en la rue de Vergy 1989 $30 (8/31/91) **86**
Morey-St.-Denis en la rue de Vergy 1989 $36 (1/31/92) **90**
Savigny-lès-Beaune La Dominode 1989 (NR) (1/31/92) **89**
Savigny-lès-Beaune La Dominode 1985 $24 (3/15/88) **80**
Vosne-Romanée Les Champs Pedrix 1989 (NR) (1/31/92) **91**

FRANCOISE & DENIS CLAIR (France/Burgundy)
Santenay Clos de la Comme 1988 $25 (6/15/92) **85**

LOUIS CLAIR (France/Burgundy)
Santenay Gravières Domaine de l'Abbaye 1985 $17 (10/15/87) **88**

CHATEAU CLAIRAC (France/Bordeaux)
Premières Côtes de Blaye 1985 $4.50 (4/15/88) **76**

CHATEAU DE CLAIREFONT (France/Bordeaux)
Margaux 1985 $9.25 (4/30/88) **79**

CLAIRVAUX (United States/California)
Grenache California 1989 $7 (3/31/92) BB **83**
Merlot Napa Valley 1989 $12 (5/31/92) **85**

A. CLAPE (France/Rhône)
Cornas 1986 $22 (1/31/89) **88**
Cornas 1984 $12.50 (8/31/87) **78**

CHATEAU CLARKE (France/Bordeaux)
Listrac 1991 (NR) (5/15/92) (BT) **70+**
Listrac 1989 $16 (3/15/92) **85**
Listrac 1988 $18 (4/30/91) **81**
Listrac 1987 Rel: $15 Cur: $24 (6/30/89) (BT) **75+**
Listrac 1986 $17 (11/15/89) **90**
Listrac 1982 $13 (10/15/86) **68**

CHATEAU LA CLAVERIE (France/Bordeaux)
Côtes de Francs 1989 $21 (3/15/92) **88**
Côtes de Francs 1988 $18 (8/31/90) (BT) **80+**

CLEMANCEY FRERES (France/Burgundy)
Fixin Les-Hervelets 1985 $21 (4/30/88) **71**

ABEL CLEMENT (France/Rhône)
Côtes du Rhône 1988 $6 (2/28/90) BB **80**
Côtes du Rhône 1985 $5 (1/31/87) BB **78**

CHATEAU CLEMENT-PICHON (France/Bordeaux)
Haut-Médoc 1988 $15 (8/31/91) **78**
Haut-Médoc 1987 $14 (11/30/89) (JS) **73**

GUASTI CLEMENTE & FIGLI (Italy/Piedmont)
Barbaresco 1978 $20 (1/31/92) **84**
Barolo 1985 $27 (1/31/92) **81**

DOMAINE HENRI CLERC & FILS (France/Burgundy)
Bâtard-Montrachet 1986 $104 (3/31/89) **90**
Beaune Blanc Chaume Gaufriot 1989 $30 (8/31/91) **81**
Beaune Chaume Gaufriot 1985 $29 (11/15/88) **81**
Bienvenues-Bâtard-Montrachet 1989 $113 (8/31/91) **89**
Bienvenues-Bâtard-Montrachet 1986 $69 (2/29/88) **90**
Bourgogne Blanc 1984 $10 (3/31/87) **68**
Bourgogne Blanc Chardonnay Les Champs Perriers 1989 $20 (8/31/91) **86**
Puligny-Montrachet Les Combettes 1987 $41 (7/31/89) **75**
Puligny-Montrachet Les Folatières 1989 $64 (8/31/91) **76**
Puligny-Montrachet Les Folatières 1987 $41 (7/31/89) **79**
Puligny-Montrachet Les Folatières 1986 $44 (11/15/88) **93**

CHATEAU CLERC-MILON (France/Bordeaux)
Pauillac 1991 (NR) (5/15/92) (BT) **80+**
Pauillac 1990 (NR) (5/15/92) (BT) **95+**
Pauillac 1989 $32 (3/15/92) **96**
Pauillac 1988 $26 (4/30/91) SS **94**
Pauillac 1987 $19 (6/30/89) (BT) **80+**
Pauillac 1986 Rel: $23 Cur: $37 (5/31/89) **97**
Pauillac 1985 Rel: $18 Cur: $28 (5/15/88) **91**
Pauillac 1984 $18 (6/15/87) **78**
Pauillac 1983 Rel: $16 Cur: $18 (4/01/86) **91**
Pauillac 1982 Rel: $15 Cur: $29 (4/01/85) **86**

GEORGES CLERGET (France/Burgundy)
Vosne-Romanée Les Violettes 1986 $23 (8/31/89) **71**

MICHEL CLERGET (France/Burgundy)
Chambolle-Musigny 1986 $23 (8/31/89) **78**
Chambolle-Musigny 1985 $38 (5/15/88) **73**
Chambolle-Musigny Les Charmes 1986 $33 (8/31/89) **76**
Chambolle-Musigny Les Charmes 1985 $56 (5/15/88) **83**
Echézeaux 1986 $31 (8/31/89) **85**
Echézeaux 1985 $51 (7/31/88) **82**

RAOUL CLERGET (France/Burgundy)
Pouilly-Fuissé 1986 $10 (10/15/88) **67**

CLERICO (Italy/Piedmont)
Arte 1988 $26 (2/28/91) **90**
Arte 1987 $22 (1/31/90) **78**
Arte 1986 $22 (2/15/89) **88**
Arte 1985 $22 (1/31/88) **91**
Barbera d'Alba 1988 $12 (3/15/91) **84**
Barbera d'Alba 1987 $8 (8/31/89) **85**
Barbera d'Alba 1985 $8.25 (11/30/87) **84**
Barolo 1984 $13 (8/31/88) **85**
Barolo Ciabot Mentin Ginestra 1985 Rel: $27 Cur: $40 (4/15/90) CS **92**
Barolo Ciabot Mentin Ginestra 1983 $19 (12/15/87) **88**
Barolo Vigna Bricotto della Bussia 1980 $8.25 (9/01/85) BB **86**

CANTINA DEL GLICINE (Italy/Piedmont)
Barbaresco 1985 $27 (8/31/91) **75**
Dolcetto d'Alba 1989 $12.50 (11/30/91) **79**

CHATEAU CLIMENS (France/Sauternes)
Barsac 1989 $60 (6/15/90) (BT) **90+**
Barsac 1988 $48 (6/15/90) (BT) **90+**
Barsac 1986 $48 (12/31/89) **84**
Barsac 1983 Rel: $50 Cur: $55 (1/31/88) CS **95**

CLINE (United States/California)
Côtes d'Oakley Contra Costa County 1989 $7.50 (5/31/91) **80**
Côtes d'Oakley Contra Costa County 1988 $9 (4/30/90) **83**
Merlot California 1989 $16.50 (5/31/92) **75**
Mourvèdre Contra Costa County 1989 $18 (11/30/91) **86**
Mourvèdre Contra Costa County 1988 $18 (4/30/90) **91**
Mourvèdre Contra Costa County 1987 $18 (4/15/89) **82**
Mourvèdre Contra Costa County Reserve 1989 $26 (3/15/92) **78**
Oakley Cuvée Contra Costa County 1989 $12 (5/31/91) **88**
Oakley Cuvée Contra Costa County 1988 $12 (2/28/90) **90**
Oakley Cuvée Contra Costa County NV $12 (4/15/89) **78**
Sémillon California Barrel Fermented 1990 $9 (12/31/91) BB **86**
Zinfandel Contra Costa County 1989 $9 (5/15/91) **86**
Zinfandel Contra Costa County 1987 $9 (5/15/90) **89**
Zinfandel Contra Costa County Reserve 1989 $12 (12/31/91) **84**
Zinfandel Contra Costa County Reserve 1987 $12 (5/15/90) **87**

CHATEAU CLINET (France/Bordeaux)
Pomerol 1991 (NR) (5/15/92) (BT) **85+**
Pomerol 1990 (NR) (5/15/92) (BT) **95+**
Pomerol 1989 $56 (4/30/91) (BT) **90+**
Pomerol 1988 $31 (2/28/91) **92**
Pomerol 1987 $25 (6/30/89) (BT) **90+**
Pomerol 1986 Rel: $25 Cur: $29 (9/15/89) **78**
Pomerol 1985 $34 (4/30/88) **91**
Pomerol 1982 $38 (5/15/89) (TR) **78**

LES CLOCHERS DU HAUT-MEDOC (France/Bordeaux)
Haut-Médoc 1983 $7 (6/15/87) **60**

CLONINGER (United States/California)
Chardonnay Monterey 1989 $15 (7/15/91) **85**

CLOS DE L'ABBAYE (France/Loire)
Bourgueil 1986 $16 (8/31/89) **86**

CLOS DE BEAUREGARD (France/Loire)
Muscadet de Sèvre et Maine Sur Lie 1988 $6.75 (4/15/90) BB **84**

CLOS DU BOIS (United States/California)
Cabernet Sauvignon Alexander Valley 1988 $14 (7/15/91) **77**
Cabernet Sauvignon Alexander Valley 1987 $11 (2/15/90) **86**
Cabernet Sauvignon Alexander Valley 1986 $12 (5/31/89) **86**
Cabernet Sauvignon Alexander Valley 1985 $10.50 (4/15/88) **87**
Cabernet Sauvignon Alexander Valley 1984 $10 (6/15/87) **87**
Cabernet Sauvignon Alexander Valley 1981 $9 (3/01/86) **91**
Cabernet Sauvignon Alexander Valley Briarcrest Vineyard 1987 Rel: $18 Cur: $20 (11/15/91) **88**
Cabernet Sauvignon Alexander Valley Briarcrest Vineyard 1986 Rel: $17 Cur: $20 (8/31/90) **87**
Cabernet Sauvignon Alexander Valley Briarcrest Vineyard 1985 Rel: $16 Cur: $24 (6/15/89) **86**
Cabernet Sauvignon Alexander Valley Briarcrest Vineyard 1984 Rel: $16 Cur: $24 (CA-3/89) **87**
Cabernet Sauvignon Alexander Valley Briarcrest Vineyard 1983 Rel: $12 Cur: $28 (CA-3/89) **74**
Cabernet Sauvignon Alexander Valley Briarcrest Vineyard 1982 Rel: $12 Cur: $32 (CA-3/89) **66**
Cabernet Sauvignon Alexander Valley Briarcrest Vineyard 1981 Rel: $12 Cur: $30 (CA-3/89) **88**
Cabernet Sauvignon Alexander Valley Briarcrest Vineyard 1980 Rel: $12 Cur: $32 (CA-3/89) **80**
Cabernet Sauvignon Dry Creek Valley Proprietor's Reserve 1982 $19 (9/15/87) **88**
Cabernet Sauvignon Sonoma County Dry Creek 1974 $40 (2/15/90) (JG) **74**
Chardonnay Alexander Valley Barrel Fermented 1990 $13 (3/31/92) **81**
Chardonnay Alexander Valley Barrel Fermented 1989 $11 (12/31/90) **80**
Chardonnay Alexander Valley Barrel Fermented 1988 $11 (2/15/90) **84**
Chardonnay Alexander Valley Barrel Fermented 1987 $11 (CH-2/90) **87**
Chardonnay Alexander Valley Barrel Fermented 1986 Rel: $10 Cur: $13 (CH-12/89) **80**
Chardonnay Alexander Valley Barrel Fermented 1985 Rel: $9 Cur: $12 (CH-2/90) **84**
Chardonnay Alexander Valley Barrel Fermented 1984 Rel: $8 Cur: $12 (CH-2/90) **84**
Chardonnay Alexander Valley Barrel Fermented 1982 $9 (4/16/84) **85**
Chardonnay Alexander Valley Barrel Fermented 1980 $15 (4/16/84) **92**
Chardonnay Alexander Valley Calcaire Vineyard 1990 $18 (7/15/92) **83**
Chardonnay Alexander Valley Calcaire Vineyard 1989 $17 (7/15/91) **82**
Chardonnay Alexander Valley Calcaire Vineyard 1988 Rel: $17 Cur: $22 (5/15/90) **91**
Chardonnay Alexander Valley Calcaire Vineyard 1987 $20 (CH-2/90) **88**
Chardonnay Alexander Valley Calcaire Vineyard 1986 Rel: $16 Cur: $22 (CH-2/90) **85**

Chardonnay Alexander Valley Calcaire Vineyard 1985 Rel: $18 Cur: $25 (CH-2/90) **83**
Chardonnay Alexander Valley Calcaire Vineyard 1984 Rel: $12 Cur: $30 (CH-2/90) **90**
Chardonnay Alexander Valley Calcaire Vineyard 1983 Rel: $12 Cur: $30 (CH-2/90) **91**
Chardonnay Alexander Valley Calcaire Vineyard 1982 $11.25 (7/01/84) **92**
Chardonnay Russian River Valley Winemaker's Reserve 1988 Rel: $24 Cur: $28 (12/31/91) **86**
Chardonnay Alexander Valley Winemaker's Reserve 1987 $24 (2/28/90) **93**
Chardonnay Alexander Valley Proprietor's Reserve 1986 Rel: $22.50 Cur: $25 (CH-5/90) **78**
Chardonnay Alexander Valley Proprietor's Reserve 1985 Rel: $22 Cur: $25 (CH-5/90) **85**
Chardonnay Alexander Valley Proprietor's Reserve 1984 Rel: $18 Cur: $21 (10/31/86) **87**
Chardonnay Alexander Valley Proprietor's Reserve 1981 Rel: $15 Cur: $22 (CH-5/90) **70**
Chardonnay Dry Creek Valley Flintwood Vineyard 1989 Rel: $17 Cur: $22 (7/15/91) **89**
Chardonnay Dry Creek Valley Flintwood Vineyard 1988 $18 (6/30/90) **89**
Chardonnay Dry Creek Valley Flintwood Vineyard 1987 $20 (CH-2/90) **87**
Chardonnay Dry Creek Valley Flintwood Vineyard 1986 Rel: $19.50 Cur: $23 (CH-2/90) **88**
Chardonnay Dry Creek Valley Flintwood Vineyard 1985 Rel: $18 Cur: $28 (CH-5/90) **70**
Chardonnay Dry Creek Valley Flintwood Vineyard 1984 Rel: $11.25 Cur: $38 (CH-5/90) **74**
Chardonnay Dry Creek Valley Flintwood Vineyard 1983 Rel: $10.50 Cur: $37 (CH-5/90) **69**
Chardonnay Dry Creek Valley Flintwood Vineyard 1982 $11.25 (7/01/84) **79**
Chardonnay Dry Creek Valley Flintwood Vineyard 1980 Rel: $17 Cur: $32 (CH-2/90) **87**
Gewürztraminer Alexander Valley Early Harvest 1990 $8 (3/31/92) **81**
Gewürztraminer Alexander Valley Early Harvest 1989 $8 (2/15/91) **76**
Gewürztraminer Alexander Valley Early Harvest 1988 $8 (11/15/89) **77**
Gewürztraminer Late Harvest Alexander Valley Individual Bunch Selected 1986 $18/375ml (8/31/87) **80**
Johannisberg Riesling Late Harvest Alexander Valley Individual Bunch Selected 1986 $15/375ml (8/31/87) **89**
Malbec Alexander Valley l'Etranger Winemaker's Reserve 1987 $20 (1/31/91) **87**
Marlstone Vineyard Alexander Valley 1987 $20 (7/31/91) **90**
Marlstone Vineyard Alexander Valley 1986 Rel: $20 Cur: $23 (8/31/90) **85**
Marlstone Vineyard Alexander Valley 1985 Rel: $19.50 Cur: $23 (6/15/89) **81**
Marlstone Vineyard Alexander Valley 1984 Rel: $19.50 Cur: $30 (CA-3/89) **89**
Marlstone Vineyard Alexander Valley 1983 Rel: $20 Cur: $25 (CA-3/89) **70**
Marlstone Vineyard Alexander Valley 1982 Rel: $16 Cur: $30 (CA-3/89) **79**
Marlstone Vineyard Alexander Valley 1981 Rel: $15 Cur: $30 (CA-3/89) **85**
Marlstone Vineyard Alexander Valley 1980 Rel: $15 Cur: $29 (CA-3/89) **77**
Marlstone Vineyard Alexander Valley 1979 Rel: $16 Cur: $38 (CA-3/89) **75**
Marlstone Vineyard Alexander Valley 1978 Rel: $16 Cur: $30 (CA-3/89) **72**
Merlot Sonoma County 1989 $15 (5/31/92) **82**
Merlot Sonoma County 1988 $15 (5/31/91) **81**
Merlot Sonoma County 1987 $12 (4/15/90) **89**
Merlot Sonoma County 1986 $10.75 (10/15/88) **86**
Merlot Sonoma County 1985 Rel: $10 Cur: $16 (10/31/87) SS **92**
Merlot Sonoma County 1984 $9 (5/16/86) **87**
Merlot Sonoma County 1983 $9 (10/01/85) **86**
Muscat of Alexandria Late Harvest Alexander Valley Fleur d'Alexandra 1986 $10 (5/31/88) **90**
Pinot Noir Dry Creek Valley Proprietor's Reserve 1980 $10.75 (7/16/84) **86**
Pinot Noir Sonoma County 1989 $13 (10/31/91) **78**
Pinot Noir Sonoma County 1988 $12 (4/30/91) **80**
Pinot Noir Sonoma County 1987 $12 (5/31/90) **73**
Pinot Noir Sonoma County 1986 $11 (10/15/89) **87**
Pinot Noir Sonoma County 1985 $10.50 (6/15/88) **70**
Pinot Noir Sonoma County 1984 $8 (8/31/86) **86**
Pinot Noir Sonoma County 1983 $8 (8/31/86) **70**
Pinot Noir Sonoma County 1982 $8 (7/16/85) **60**
Sauvignon Blanc Alexander Valley 1989 $8 (8/31/90) **76**
Sauvignon Blanc Alexander Valley 1988 $11 (7/31/89) **78**
Sauvignon Blanc Alexander Valley Barrel Fermented 1990 $8 (4/15/92) **79**

DOMAINE LE CLOS DES CAZAUX (France/Rhône)
Vacqueyras Cuvée des Templiers 1983 $11 (1/31/87) **83**

CLOS DU CLOCHER (France/Bordeaux)
Pomerol 1989 (NR) (4/30/91) (BT) **85+**
Pomerol 1988 $22 (6/30/89) (BT) **80+**
Pomerol 1987 $18 (6/30/89) (BT) **80+**
Pomerol 1986 $20 (6/30/88) (BT) **80+**
Pomerol 1985 Rel: $17 Cur: $20 (2/29/88) **88**
Pomerol 1982 $33 (5/15/89) (TR) **83**

CLOS L'EGLISE (France/Bordeaux)
Pomerol 1990 (NR) (5/15/92) (BT) **90+**
Pomerol 1989 $24 (4/30/91) (BT) **95+**
Pomerol 1988 Rel: $24 Cur: $26 (6/30/91) **83**
Pomerol 1987 $20 (6/30/89) (BT) **75+**
Pomerol 1986 $28 (2/15/90) **86**
Pomerol 1985 Rel: $21 Cur: $25 (5/15/87) (BT) **80+**
Pomerol 1982 $27 (5/15/89) (TR) **88**
Pomerol 1961 $75 (3/16/86) (TR) **63**
Pomerol 1945 $230 (3/16/86) (JL) **87**

CLOS DE L'EGLISE (France/Other)
Madiran 1988 $12.50 (8/31/91) **79**

CLOS DOFI (Spain)
Eger Costers del Siurana 1989 $40 (1/31/92) **89**

CLOS FOURTET (France/Bordeaux)
St.-Emilion 1990 (NR) (4/30/91) (BT) **85+**
St.-Emilion 1989 Rel: $26 Cur: $31 (3/15/92) **89**
St.-Emilion 1988 $23 (10/31/91) **86**
St.-Emilion 1987 $20 (6/30/89) (BT) **80+**
St.-Emilion 1986 Rel: $29 Cur: $41 (6/30/89) **80**
St.-Emilion 1982 Rel: $20 Cur: $31 (5/15/89) (TR) **87**
St.-Emilion 1961 $120 (3/16/86) (TR) **66**
St.-Emilion 1945 $280 (3/16/86) (JL) **68**

DOMAINE DU CLOS FRANTIN (France/Burgundy)
Chambertin 1989 $73 (1/31/92) **88**
Chambertin 1986 $63 (2/28/89) **90**
Clos de Vougeot 1989 $56 (1/31/92) **91**
Clos de Vougeot 1987 $56 (7/15/90) **85**
Clos de Vougeot 1986 $37 (11/30/88) **87**
Corton 1989 (NR) (1/31/92) **86**
Corton 1988 $52 (7/15/90) (BT) **75+**
Corton-Charlemagne 1989 ($NA) (8/31/91) **85**
Corton-Charlemagne 1988 $66 (4/30/91) **71**
Corton-Charlemagne 1986 $55 (3/31/89) **87**
Echézeaux 1989 $45 (1/31/92) **93**
Echézeaux 1988 $56 (7/15/90) (BT) **95+**
Echézeaux 1986 $30 (11/30/88) **90**
Echézeaux 1985 $37 (9/15/87) **96**
Gevrey-Chambertin 1989 $29 (1/31/92) **84**
Gevrey-Chambertin 1988 $37 (7/15/90) **87**
Gevrey-Chambertin 1987 $20 (3/31/90) **82**
Grands Echézeaux 1989 $56 (1/31/92) **90**
Grands Echézeaux 1987 $56 (7/15/90) **86**
Grands Echézeaux 1986 $60 (2/28/89) **87**
Nuits-St.-Georges 1989 $29 (2/29/92) **91**
Nuits-St.-Georges 1988 $37 (7/15/90) (BT) **80+**
Nuits-St.-Georges 1986 $20 (11/15/88) **82**
Nuits-St.-Georges 1983 $18 (2/01/86) **83**
Richebourg 1989 $117 (1/31/92) **95**
Richebourg 1986 $100 (8/31/89) **88**
Vosne-Romanée 1989 $30 (1/31/92) **89**
Vosne-Romanée 1986 $19 (12/31/88) **80**
Vosne-Romanée 1985 $29 (10/15/87) **91**
Vosne-Romanée Les Malconsorts 1989 $32 (7/15/90) (BT) **85+**
Vosne-Romanée Les Malconsorts 1988 $58 (7/15/90) (BT) **85+**
Vosne-Romanée Les Malconsorts 1987 $30 (7/15/90) **88**
Vosne-Romanée Les Malconsorts 1986 $30 (10/31/88) **79**
Vosne-Romanée Les Malconsorts 1985 $40 (9/30/87) **95**

CHATEAU CLOS HAUT-PEYRAGUEY (France/Sauternes)
Sauternes 1989 ($NA) (6/15/90) (BT) **80+**
Sauternes 1988 $26 (6/15/90) (BT) **85+**
Sauternes 1987 ($NA) (6/15/90) **83**
Sauternes 1986 $23 (6/30/88) (BT) **80+**

CHATEAU CLOS DES JACOBINS (France/Bordeaux)
St.-Emilion 1991 (NR) (5/15/92) (BT) **80+**
St.-Emilion 1990 (NR) (5/15/92) (BT) **85+**
St.-Emilion 1989 $45 (3/15/92) **85**
St.-Emilion 1988 $26 (4/15/91) **90**
St.-Emilion 1987 $23 (5/15/90) **73**
St.-Emilion 1986 $34 (6/30/89) **94**
St.-Emilion 1985 $31 (9/30/88) **89**
St.-Emilion 1984 $20 (5/15/87) **83**
St.-Emilion 1982 $39 (5/15/89) (TR) **83**
St.-Emilion 1981 Rel: $16 Cur: $31 (6/01/84) **81**

CLOS J. KANON (France/Bordeaux)
St.-Emilion 1987 $10 (5/15/90) **77**
St.-Emilion 1986 $17 (11/15/89) **91**

CLOS LABARDE (France/Bordeaux)
St.-Emilion 1986 $15 (6/30/89) **82**

CLOS LARCIS (France/Bordeaux)
St.-Emilion 1991 (NR) (5/15/92) (BT) **70+**
St.-Emilion 1989 $28 (3/15/92) **92**

CLOS DES LITANIES (France/Bordeaux)
Pomerol 1982 ($NA) (5/15/89) (TR) **83**

CHATEAU CLOS LA MADELAINE (France/Bordeaux)
St.-Emilion 1982 ($NA) (5/15/89) (TR) **83**

CLOS DU MARQUIS (France/Bordeaux)
St.-Julien 1988 $19 (10/31/91) **80**
St.-Julien 1987 Rel: $12 Cur: $14 (5/15/90) **79**
St.-Julien 1986 Rel: $17 Cur: $20 (9/15/89) **84**
St.-Julien 1985 Rel: $14 Cur: $20 (9/30/88) **84**

CLOS DU MONT-OLIVET (France/Rhône)
Châteauneuf-du-Pape 1989 $29 (10/15/91) **85**
Châteauneuf-du-Pape 1988 $19 (10/15/91) **88**
Châteauneuf-du-Pape 1986 $17 (10/15/91) **87**
Châteauneuf-du-Pape 1985 Rel: $15 Cur: $20 (10/15/91) **92**
Châteauneuf-du-Pape 1983 Rel: $14 Cur: $28 (10/15/91) **86**
Châteauneuf-du-Pape 1982 $12 (3/16/86) **91**
Châteauneuf-du-Pape 1981 $30 (10/15/91) **87**
Châteauneuf-du-Pape Blanc 1990 $20 (10/15/91) **86**
Châteauneuf-du-Pape Blanc 1989 $20 (10/15/91) **78**

DOMAINE DU CLOS NAUDIN (France/Loire)
Vouvray Demi-Sec 1989 $19.50 (3/31/91) **88**
Vouvray Moelleux 1989 $34 (4/30/91) **83**
Vouvray Moelleux Réserve 1989 $54 (3/31/91) **89**
Vouvray Sec 1989 $17 (3/31/91) **83**

CLOS DE L'ORATOIRE (France/Bordeaux)
St.-Emilion 1989 (NR) (4/30/91) (BT) **80+**
St.-Emilion 1988 ($NA) (6/30/89) (BT) **75+**
St.-Emilion 1987 ($NA) (6/30/89) (BT) **75+**
St.-Emilion 1982 ($NA) (5/15/89) (TR) **78**

CLOS DE L'ORATOIRE DES PAPES (France/Rhône)
Châteauneuf-du-Pape 1985 $10 (7/31/88) **87**

CLOS DES PAPES (France/Rhône)
Châteauneuf-du-Pape 1989 $20 (10/15/91) **86**
Châteauneuf-du-Pape 1988 $19 (10/15/91) **86**
Châteauneuf-du-Pape 1986 $18 (10/15/91) **74**
Châteauneuf-du-Pape 1985 $17 (10/15/91) **89**
Châteauneuf-du-Pape 1983 $25 (10/15/91) **88**
Châteauneuf-du-Pape 1981 $30 (10/15/91) **87**

Key to Symbols

The scores reported here are the results of blind tastings conducted by our panel of senior editors. Wines that carry the initials below are results of individual tastings.

THE WINE SPECTATOR 100-POINT SCALE *95-100*—Classic, a great wine; *90-94*—Outstanding, superior character and style; *80-89*—Good to very good, a wine with special qualities; *70-79*—Average, drinkable wine that may have minor flaws; *60-69*—Below average, drinkable but not recommended; *50-59*—Poor, undrinkable, not recommended. "+"—With a score indicates a range; used primarily with barrel tastings to indicate a preliminary score.

SPECIAL DESIGNATIONS SS—Spectator Selection, CS—Cellar Selection, BB—Best Buy, ($NA)—Price not available, (NR)—Not released.

TASTER'S INITIALS (JG)—Jim Gordon, (HS)—Harvey Steiman, (JL)—James Laube, (JS)—James Suckling, (TM)—Thomas Matthews, (TR)—Terry Robards, (PM)—Per-Henrik Mansson, (BT)—Barrel Tasting (these wines were tasted blind from barrel samples), (CA-date)—*California's Great Cabernets* by James Laube, (CH-date)—*California's Great Chardonnays* by James Laube, (VP-date)—*Vintage Port* by James Suckling.

DATE TASTED Dates in parentheses represent the issue in which the rating was published.

Châteauneuf-du-Pape Blanc 1990 $25 (10/15/91) **85**
Châteauneuf-du-Pape Blanc 1989 $25 (10/15/91) **85**

CLOS PEGASE (United States/California)
Cabernet Franc California 1988 $14.50 (10/15/91) **69**
Cabernet Sauvignon Napa Valley 1986 $16.50 (9/30/90) **88**
Cabernet Sauvignon Napa Valley 1985 $17 (5/31/88) **86**
Chardonnay Alexander Valley 1985 Rel: $13 Cur: $15 (CH-3/90) **87**
Chardonnay Carneros 1988 $16.50 (5/15/90) **90**
Chardonnay Carneros 1987 $15.50 (2/15/90) **89**
Chardonnay Carneros 1986 $15.50 (CH-3/90) **89**
Chardonnay Napa Valley 1990 $13 (7/15/92) **85**
Chardonnay Napa Valley 1989 $13 (9/15/91) **88**
Chardonnay Napa Valley 1988 $12 (6/30/90) **86**
Chardonnay Napa Valley 1987 $12 (CH-3/90) **86**
Chardonnay Napa Valley 1986 Rel: $12 Cur: $14 (CH-3/90) **85**
Chardonnay Sonoma County Hommage 1989 $18.50 (8/31/91) **87**
Grenache California 1989 $9.50 (8/31/91) **84**
Hommage California 1987 $20 (8/31/91) **90**
Merlot Napa Valley 1988 $15 (11/15/91) **82**
Merlot Napa Valley 1986 $15.50 (7/15/90) **84**
Petite Sirah Napa Valley 1988 $14.50 (10/31/91) **83**
Sauvignon Blanc Lake County 1987 $9.50 (5/15/90) **84**
Sauvignon Blanc Napa Valley 1989 $9.50 (6/15/92) **72**
Sémillon Napa Valley 1989 $9.50 (9/15/91) **81**

CLOS RENE (France/Bordeaux)
Pomerol 1988 $24 (4/30/91) **88**
Pomerol 1987 $20 (6/30/89) (BT) **75+**
Pomerol 1986 Rel: $19 Cur: $24 (6/15/89) SS **94**
Pomerol 1985 Rel: $17 Cur: $20 (3/15/88) **92**
Pomerol 1983 Rel: $17 Cur: $23 (3/16/86) **91**
Pomerol 1982 $27 (5/15/89) (TR) **87**
Pomerol 1962 $35 (11/30/87) (JS) **60**
Pomerol 1959 $50 (10/15/90) (JS) **88**
Pomerol 1945 $100 (3/16/86) (JL) **79**

CLOS ROBERT (United States/California)
Cabernet Sauvignon Napa Valley Proprietor's Reserve 1984 $7 (12/31/87) **71**
Chardonnay Napa Valley 1985 $6 (7/31/87) **68**
Chardonnay Napa Valley Lot 3 1989 $9 (7/15/91) **78**

CHATEAU CLOS ST.-MARTIN (France/Bordeaux)
St.-Emilion 1991 (NR) (5/15/92) (BT) **65+**
St.-Emilion 1989 (NR) (3/15/92) **86**
St.-Emilion 1988 ($NA) (6/30/89) (BT) **90+**
St.-Emilion 1987 ($NA) (6/30/89) (BT) **80+**

CLOS STE. NICOLE (France/Other)
Cabernet Sauvignon FrenCH-California Cuvée NV $5 (10/31/89) **77**
Merlot FrenCH-California Cuvée NV $5 (10/31/89) **79**

CLOS TRIGUEDINA (France/Other)
Cahors 1983 $11 (2/28/91) **80**
Cahors Prince Probus 1985 $17 (2/28/91) **82**

CLOS DU VAL (United States/California)
Cabernet Sauvignon Stags Leap District 1989 (NR) (5/15/91) (BT) **85+**
Cabernet Sauvignon Stags Leap District 1988 Rel: $18 Cur: $20 (3/31/92) **86**
Cabernet Sauvignon Stags Leap District 1987 Rel: $18.50 Cur: $22 (6/30/91) **92**
Cabernet Sauvignon Stags Leap District 1986 Rel: $17.50 Cur: $21 (5/31/90) **91**
Cabernet Sauvignon Stags Leap District 1985 Rel: $16 Cur: $28 (6/15/89) **90**
Cabernet Sauvignon Stags Leap District 1983 Rel: $15 Cur: $21 (CA-3/89) **86**
Cabernet Sauvignon Stags Leap District 1982 Rel: $13.25 Cur: $28 (CA-3/89) **88**
Cabernet Sauvignon Stags Leap District 1981 Rel: $12.50 Cur: $25 (CA-3/89) **82**
Cabernet Sauvignon Stags Leap District 1980 Rel: $12.50 Cur: $31 (CA-3/89) **88**
Cabernet Sauvignon Stags Leap District 1980 Rel: $12.50 Cur: $31 (2/01/84) CS **88**
Cabernet Sauvignon Stags Leap District 1979 Rel: $12.50 Cur: $35 (CA-3/89) **90**
Cabernet Sauvignon Stags Leap District 1978 Rel: $12 Cur: $37 (CA-3/89) **92**
Cabernet Sauvignon Stags Leap District 1977 Rel: $10 Cur: $28 (CA-3/89) **89**
Cabernet Sauvignon Stags Leap District 1975 Rel: $9 Cur: $40 (CA-3/89) **89**
Cabernet Sauvignon Stags Leap District 1974 Rel: $7.50 Cur: $71 (CA-3/89) **91**
Cabernet Sauvignon Stags Leap District 1973 Rel: $6 Cur: $70 (CA-3/89) **86**
Cabernet Sauvignon Stags Leap District 1972 Rel: $6 Cur: $75 (CA-3/89) **90**
Cabernet Sauvignon Napa Valley 1976 Rel: $9 Cur: $55 (CA-3/89) **82**
Cabernet Sauvignon Napa Valley Gran Val 1985 $8.50 (5/31/88) **88**
Cabernet Sauvignon Napa Valley Gran Val 1984 $8.50 (2/15/87) BB **85**
Cabernet Sauvignon Napa Valley Gran Val 1982 $7.50 (4/16/84) **88**
Cabernet Sauvignon Napa Valley Joli Val 1988 $13 (7/31/91) **82**
Cabernet Sauvignon Napa Valley Joli Val 1986 $12.50 (12/15/89) **87**
Cabernet Sauvignon Stags Leap District Reserve 1979 Rel: $25 Cur: $55 (CA-3/89) **92**
Cabernet Sauvignon Stags Leap District Reserve 1979 Rel: $25 Cur: $55 (9/01/84) SS **91**
Cabernet Sauvignon Stags Leap District Reserve 1978 Rel: $30 Cur: $64 (CA-3/89) **94**
Cabernet Sauvignon Stags Leap District Reserve 1977 Rel: $20 Cur: $53 (CA-3/89) **87**
Cabernet Sauvignon Stags Leap District Reserve 1973 Rel: $10 Cur: $100 (CA-3/89) **90**
Chardonnay California Gran Val 1986 $8.50 (4/15/88) **77**
Chardonnay California Gran Val 1984 $6.50 (4/16/86) **75**
Chardonnay Carneros Napa Valley Carneros Estate 1990 $16 (3/31/92) **75**
Chardonnay Carneros Napa Valley Carneros Estate 1989 Rel: $15 Cur: $17 (3/31/91) **89**
Chardonnay Carneros Napa Valley Carneros Estate 1988 Rel: $16 Cur: $18 (6/30/90) **83**
Chardonnay Carneros Napa Valley Carneros Estate 1987 Rel: $13 Cur: $17 (CH-6/90) **89**
Chardonnay Carneros Napa Valley Carneros Estate 1986 Rel: $12 Cur: $14 (CH-6/90) **84**
Chardonnay Napa Valley 1987 $12 (CH-6/90) **87**
Chardonnay Napa Valley 1985 Rel: $11.50 Cur: $17 (CH-6/90) **87**
Chardonnay Napa Valley 1984 Rel: $11.50 Cur: $15 (CH-6/90) **85**
Chardonnay Napa Valley 1983 Rel: $11.50 Cur: $15 (CH-6/90) **82**
Chardonnay California 1982 Rel: $11.50 Cur: $16 (6/01/90) **78**
Chardonnay Napa Valley 1981 Rel: $12.50 Cur: $18 (CH-6/90) **78**
Chardonnay Napa Valley 1980 Rel: $12.50 Cur: $18 (CH-6/90) **80**
Chardonnay Napa Valley Joli Val 1989 $13 (7/15/91) **79**
Chardonnay Napa Valley Joli Val 1988 $12.50 (1/31/90) **86**
Le Clos Napa Valley 1989 $6 (3/15/92) BB **82**
Le Clos Napa Valley 1988 $5.50 (12/31/90) **73**
Le Clos Napa Valley NV $5.50 (8/31/90) BB **85**
Merlot Stags Leap District 1990 (NR) (5/15/91) (BT) **90+**
Merlot Stags Leap District 1989 $21 (5/31/92) **86**
Merlot Stags Leap District 1988 $20 (3/31/91) **89**
Merlot Stags Leap District 1987 $17 (3/31/90) **85**
Merlot Stags Leap District 1986 $16 (8/31/89) **86**
Merlot Stags Leap District 1985 $15.50 (4/30/88) **87**
Merlot Stags Leap District 1984 $15 (7/31/87) **88**
Merlot Stags Leap District 1983 $14 (6/16/86) **92**
Merlot Stags Leap District 1982 $12.50 (10/01/85) **80**
Merlot Stags Leap District 1981 $13.50 (2/15/84) **88**
Pinot Noir Napa Valley 1987 $13.50 (4/30/91) **84**
Pinot Noir Napa Valley 1986 $16 (2/15/90) **80**
Pinot Noir Napa Valley 1985 $12.50 (6/15/88) **80**
Pinot Noir Napa Valley 1984 $11.50 (9/30/87) **78**
Pinot Noir Napa Valley 1983 $11.50 (8/31/86) **66**
Pinot Noir Napa Valley 1982 $10.75 (9/01/84) **75**
Reserve Stags Leap District 1985 Rel: $45 Cur: $53 (11/15/90) **94**
Reserve Stags Leap District 1982 Rel: $28 Cur: $40 (CA-3/89) **90**
Sémillon California 1987 $10 (7/15/91) **82**
Zinfandel Napa Valley 1986 $12 (5/31/89) **87**
Zinfandel Napa Valley 1985 $12 (4/30/88) **90**
Zinfandel Napa Valley 1984 $12 (5/31/87) **81**
Zinfandel Napa Valley 1981 Rel: $9 Cur: $18 (5/16/84) CS **90**
Zinfandel Napa Valley 1974 $45 (6/16/85) **77**
Zinfandel Napa Valley 1973 $50 (6/16/85) **86**
Zinfandel Napa Valley 1972 $60 (6/16/85) **90**
Zinfandel Stags Leap District 1987 $12.50 (5/31/90) **83**

CHATEAU LA CLOTTE (France/Bordeaux)
St.-Emilion 1985 Rel: $27 Cur: $32 (5/15/88) **87**
St.-Emilion 1983 $12 (5/16/86) **68**

CLOUDY BAY (New Zealand)
Sauvignon Blanc Marlborough 1990 $14 (4/15/92) **84**

CLOVERDALE RANCH (United States/California)
Cabernet Sauvignon Alexander Valley Estate Cuvée 1989 $11 (3/31/92) **84**

DOMAINE CLUSEL (France/Rhône)
Côte-Rôtie 1988 $36 (11/15/91) **87**

GILBERT CLUSEL (France/Rhône)
Côte-Rôtie La Viallière 1986 $23 (4/15/89) **85**

CHATEAU LA CLUSIERE (France/Bordeaux)
St.-Emilion 1989 (NR) (4/30/91) (BT) **80+**
St.-Emilion 1988 $20 (6/30/89) (BT) **65+**
St.-Emilion 1982 $20 (5/15/89) (TR) **88**

CLYDE PARK (Australia)
Cabernet Sauvignon Geelong 1984 $15 (3/15/88) **79**
Chardonnay Geelong 1986 $15 (2/15/88) **90**

J.-F. COCHE-DURY (France/Burgundy)
Auxey-Duresses Rouge 1987 $30 (2/28/90) **87**
Bourgogne Pinot Noir 1987 $25 (2/28/90) **79**
Corton-Charlemagne 1987 $122 (2/28/90) **88**
Meursault 1987 $33 (2/28/90) **86**
Meursault Les Chevalières 1987 $36 (2/28/90) **91**
Meursault Les Perrières 1987 $50 (2/28/90) **90**
Meursault Rouge 1987 $30 (2/28/90) **80**
Meursault Les Rougeots 1987 $33 (2/28/90) **90**

COCKATOO RIDGE (Australia)
Cabernet Merlot South Eastern Australia 1990 $7 (6/30/92) BB **82**

COCKBURN (Portugal)
Tawny Port 20 Year Old NV $35 (2/28/90) (JS) **86**
Vintage Port 1985 Rel: $33 Cur: $45 (VP-6/90) **90**
Vintage Port 1983 Rel: $22 Cur: $45 (8/31/87) CS **92**
Vintage Port 1975 $40 (VP-1/90) **77**
Vintage Port 1970 $63 (VP-12/89) **86**
Vintage Port 1967 $61 (VP-12/89) **85**
Vintage Port 1963 $99 (VP-12/89) **88**
Vintage Port 1960 $74 (VP-8/88) **80**
Vintage Port 1958 ($NA) (VP-11/89) **84**
Vintage Port 1955 $132 (VP-11/89) **90**
Vintage Port 1950 $112 (VP-11/89) **76**
Vintage Port 1947 $162 (VP-11/89) **90**
Vintage Port 1935 $350 (VP-2/90) **92**
Vintage Port 1931 $500 (VP-1/90) **89**
Vintage Port 1927 $360 (VP-12/89) **91**
Vintage Port 1912 $350 (VP-10/87) **91**
Vintage Port 1908 $380 (VP-10/87) **89**
Vintage Port 1904 $500 (VP-10/87) **75**
Vintage Port 1896 $400 (VP-2/90) **82**

MARTIN CODAX (Spain)
Rias Baixas Albariño 1990 $12 (5/31/92) **78**

CODICE (Spain)
Rioja 1988 $6 (6/15/91) **78**

CODORNIU (Spain)
Brut Blanc de Blancs Cava 1988 $9 (12/31/90) BB **84**
Brut Blanc de Blancs Cava 1986 $8 (7/31/89) **77**
Brut Cava Anna de Codorniu 1989 $8 (5/15/92) **79**
Brut Cava Anna de Codorniu 1988 $8 (12/31/90) **78**
Brut Cava Anna de Codorniu 1987 $7 (8/31/90) **75**
Brut Cava Anna de Codorniu 1985 $6.50 (7/31/89) **76**
Brut Cava Chardonnay 1988 $15 (5/15/92) **85**
Brut Cava Chardonnay 1986 $12 (7/31/89) **84**
Brut Cava Clásico 1989 $9 (5/15/92) **75**
Brut Cava Clásico 1986 $6 (5/15/89) BB **82**

CODORNIU NAPA (United States/California)
Brut Napa Valley NV $15 (11/15/91) **82**

FERNAND COFFINET (France/Burgundy)
Bâtard-Montrachet 1988 $95 (3/31/92) **85**
Chassagne-Montrachet 1989 $34 (3/31/92) **80**
Chassagne-Montrachet 1985 $25 (5/15/87) **94**
Chassagne-Montrachet Blanchot-Dessus 1989 $36 (3/31/92) **85**

B.R. COHN (United States/California)
Cabernet Sauvignon Napa Valley Silver Label 1988 $12 (9/30/91) **87**
Cabernet Sauvignon Sonoma Valley Olive Hill Vineyard 1990 (NR) (5/15/91) (BT) **85+**
Cabernet Sauvignon Sonoma Valley Olive Hill Vineyard 1989 (NR) (5/15/91) (BT) **85+**
Cabernet Sauvignon Sonoma Valley Olive Hill Vineyard 1988 $25 (5/15/91) **89**
Cabernet Sauvignon Sonoma Valley Olive Hill Vineyard 1987 Rel: $25 Cur: $28 (6/30/90) **92**
Cabernet Sauvignon Sonoma Valley Olive Hill Vineyard 1986 Rel: $18 Cur: $26 (5/31/89) **94**

Cabernet Sauvignon Sonoma Valley Olive Hill Vineyard 1985 Rel: $16 Cur: $50 (CA-3/89) **94**
Cabernet Sauvignon Sonoma Valley Olive Hill Vineyard 1984 Rel: $15 Cur: $35 (CA-3/89) **93**
Chardonnay Sonoma Valley Olive Hill Vineyard 1989 $14 (5/31/91) **78**
Chardonnay Sonoma Valley Olive Hill Vineyard 1988 $15 (10/31/89) **82**
Chardonnay Sonoma Valley Olive Hill Vineyard 1986 $12 (10/31/88) **87**
Chardonnay Sonoma Valley Olive Hill Vineyard Barrel Reserve 1985 $21 (6/30/87) **88**
Chardonnay Sonoma Valley Olive Hill Vineyard Silver Label 1990 $14 (7/31/92) **85**
Merlot Napa Valley Silver Label 1989 $14 (11/15/91) **82**

COL D'ORCIA (Italy/Tuscany)
Brunello di Montalcino 1985 $23 (11/30/90) **88**
Brunello di Montalcino 1981 $22 (9/15/86) **70**
Brunello di Montalcino 1979 Rel: $15 Cur: $24 (9/15/86) CS **94**
Brunello di Montalcino Poggio al Vento Riserva 1982 $40 (4/15/91) **89**
Brunello di Montalcino Riserva 1981 $22 (7/31/88) **89**
Brunello di Montalcino Riserva 1978 $18 (9/15/86) **65**
Ghiaie Bianche 1989 $12 (12/31/90) **87**
Rosso di Montalcino 1988 $9 (4/30/91) **84**

COLBY (United States/California)
Chardonnay Napa Valley 1988 $15 (9/15/91) **82**
Chardonnay Napa Valley 1986 $11 (5/31/89) **81**
Chardonnay Napa Valley 1985 $10.75 (11/15/87) **87**

COLDRIDGE (Australia)
Sémillon Chardonnay Victoria 1990 $6 (4/15/91) BB **82**

COLDSTREAM HILLS (Australia)
Cabernet Sauvignon Lilydale 1987 $20 (1/31/90) **84**
Chardonnay Lilydale Three Vineyards Blend 1987 $20 (1/31/90) **87**
Chardonnay Lilydale Three Vineyards Blend 1986 $18 (5/31/88) **72**
Chardonnay Lilydale Yarra Ridge Vineyard 1987 $19 (10/15/90) **87**
Chardonnay Lilydale Yarra Ridge Vineyard 1986 $18 (5/31/88) **68**

COLEGIATA (Spain)
Toro Gran Colegiata Tinto de Crianza 1986 $7 (11/30/89) **77**
Toro Tinto 1986 $5 (11/30/89) BB **82**
Toro Tinto 1985 $5 (11/30/89) BB **88**

COLI (Italy/Tuscany)
Chianti 1987 $6 (11/30/89) **76**

MARC COLIN (France/Burgundy)
Chassagne-Montrachet 1989 ($NA) (8/31/91) **90**
Chassagne-Montrachet Les Caillerets 1989 ($NA) (8/31/91) **86**
Chassagne-Montrachet Les Champ-Gains 1989 ($NA) (8/31/91) **86**
Montrachet 1989 ($NA) (8/31/91) **90**
St.-Aubin La Chatenière 1989 ($NA) (8/31/91) **85**
St.-Aubin Les Combes 1989 ($NA) (8/31/91) **83**

MADAME FRANCOIS COLIN (France/Burgundy)
Chassagne-Montrachet Clos Devant 1988 $26 (5/15/90) **83**
Puligny-Montrachet Les Demoiselles 1988 $47 (6/30/90) **89**

MICHEL COLIN-DELEGER (France/Burgundy)
Chassagne-Montrachet 1989 $32 (8/31/91) **86**
Chassagne-Montrachet 1988 $40 (2/28/91) **86**
Chassagne-Montrachet Les Chaumées 1989 $38 (8/31/91) **91**
Chassagne-Montrachet Les Chaumées 1988 $48 (2/28/91) **90**
Chassagne-Montrachet Les Chenevottes 1989 $66 (8/31/91) **89**
Chassagne-Montrachet Morgeot 1989 $40 (8/31/91) **79**
Chassagne-Montrachet Morgeot 1987 $43 (5/31/89) **88**
Chassagne-Montrachet Les Remilly 1989 $38 (8/31/91) **91**
Chassagne-Montrachet Les Remilly 1988 $30 (5/15/90) **90**
Chassagne-Montrachet Les Remilly 1986 $38 (10/31/88) **93**
Chassagne-Montrachet Les Vergers 1989 $57 (8/31/91) **93**
Chassagne-Montrachet Les Vergers 1988 $33 (5/15/90) **88**
Chassagne-Montrachet Les Vergers 1987 $42 (11/15/89) **90**

COLLAVINI (Italy/North)
Brut Spumante il Grigio NV $11 (5/15/92) **83**
Cabernet Sauvignon Grave del Friuli 1984 $8 (4/15/90) BB **85**

IL COLLE (Italy/Tuscany)
Rosso delle Colline Lucchesi 1986 $7.50 (3/31/90) **81**

COLLE DEI BARDELLINI (Italy/Other)
Vermentino Riviera Ligure di Ponent Vigna U Munte 1989 $18 (1/31/91) **89**

COLLECTION FOLLE EPOQUE (France)
Blanc de Blancs NV $5.50 (6/30/92) **78**

LE COLLINE (Italy/Piedmont)
Barbaresco Riserva Spéciale 1979 $15 (7/31/87) **79**

CHATEAU COLOMBIER-MONPELOU (France/Bordeaux)
Pauillac 1988 $15 (10/31/91) **75**

JEAN-LUC COLOMBO (France/Rhône)
Cornas Les Ruchets 1989 $45 (11/15/91) **89**
Cornas Les Ruchets 1988 $45 (10/15/91) **87**
Cornas Les Ruchets 1987 $45 (11/15/91) **75**

COLONY (United States/California)
Cabernet Sauvignon Sonoma County 1982 $7 (3/16/86) BB **89**

COLORADO CELLARS (United States/Colorado)
Alpenglo Riesling Turley Vineyards Colorado 1990 $8.50 (2/29/92) **77**

Key to Symbols

The scores reported here are the results of blind tastings conducted by our panel of senior editors. Wines that carry the initials below are results of individual tastings.

THE WINE SPECTATOR 100-POINT SCALE 95-100—Classic, a great wine; ***90-94***—Outstanding, superior character and style; ***80-89***—Good to very good, a wine with special qualities; ***70-79***—Average, drinkable wine that may have minor flaws; ***60-69***—Below average, drinkable but not recommended; ***50-59***—Poor, undrinkable, not recommended. "+"—With a score indicates a range; used primarily with barrel tastings to indicate a preliminary score.

SPECIAL DESIGNATIONS SS—Spectator Selection, CS—Cellar Selection, BB—Best Buy, ($NA)—Price not available, (NR)—Not released.

TASTER'S INITIALS (JG)—Jim Gordon, (HS)—Harvey Steiman, (JL)—James Laube, (JS)—James Suckling, (TM)—Thomas Matthews, (TR)—Terry Robards, (PM)—Per-Henrik Mansson, (BT)—Barrel Tasting (these wines were tasted blind from barrel samples), (CA-date)—*California's Great Cabernets* by James Laube, (CH-date)—*California's Great Chardonnays* by James Laube, (VP-date)—*Vintage Port* by James Suckling.

DATE TASTED Dates in parentheses represent the issue in which the rating was published.

Cherry Wine Colorado 1990 $5 (2/29/92) **73**
Grand Gamé Rocky Mountain 1988 $8.50 (2/29/92) **79**

COLOSI (Italy/Dessert)
Malvasia delle Lipari Passito di Salina 1989 $20/375ml (3/31/92) **81**

COLTERENZIO (Italy/North)
Chardonnay Alto Adige 1989 $8 (1/31/91) BB **84**
Pinot Grigio Alto Adige 1989 $10 (3/31/91) **79**

COLUMBIA (United States/Washington)
Cabernet Sauvignon Columbia Valley 1988 $10 (3/31/91) **86**
Cabernet Sauvignon Columbia Valley 1987 $9.50 (6/15/90) **87**
Cabernet Sauvignon Columbia Valley 1986 $10 (10/15/89) **85**
Cabernet Sauvignon Columbia Valley 1985 $9.50 (7/15/88) **79**
Cabernet Sauvignon Columbia Valley David Lake Sagemoor Vineyards 1986 $16 (5/15/91) **85**
Cabernet Sauvignon Columbia Valley Sagemoor Vineyards 1985 $15 (10/15/89) **85**
Cabernet Sauvignon Columbia Valley Signature Series Otis Vineyard 1988 $20 (4/15/92) **89**
Cabernet Sauvignon Columbia Valley Signature Series Red Willow Vineyard 1988 $20 (4/15/92) **86**
Cabernet Sauvignon Columbia Valley Signature Series Sagemoor Vineyards 1988 $20 (4/30/92) **81**
Cabernet Sauvignon Washington Bacchus Vineyard 1981 $12 (8/01/84) **86**
Cabernet Sauvignon Yakima Valley 1981 $8 (8/01/84) **76**
Cabernet Sauvignon Yakima Valley Otis Vineyard 1985 $15 (10/15/89) **91**
Cabernet Sauvignon Yakima Valley Otis Vineyard 1981 $13 (8/01/84) **83**
Cabernet Sauvignon Yakima Valley Red Willow Vineyard 1985 $15 (10/15/89) **82**
Cabernet Sauvignon Yakima Valley Red Willow Vineyard 1981 $35 (10/15/89) **84**
Chardonnay Columbia Valley 1989 $7 (5/31/91) **78**
Chardonnay Columbia Valley 1988 $8.50 (9/30/90) **79**
Chardonnay Columbia Valley Sagemoor Vineyards Barrel Fermented The Woodburne Collection 1989 $10 (3/31/91) **89**
Chardonnay Columbia Valley Woodburne Cuvée 1990 $12 (11/30/91) **84**
Chardonnay Washington 1985 $8 (7/31/87) **79**
Chardonnay Washington Barrel Fermented The Woodburne Collection 1987 $10 (3/31/91) **83**
Chardonnay Washington Jolona Vineyard 1982 $12 (9/01/84) **80**
Chardonnay Yakima Valley Brookside Vineyards 1987 $15 (10/15/89) **80**
Chardonnay Yakima Valley Wyckoff Vineyard 1983 $8.50 (4/16/86) **46**
Johannisberg Riesling Columbia Valley Cellarmaster's Reserve 1990 $7 (6/15/92) **77**
Johannisberg Riesling Late Harvest Columbia Valley Cellarmaster's Reserve 1988 $7 (10/15/89) BB **85**
Merlot Columbia Valley 1989 $12 (3/31/92) **80**
Merlot Columbia Valley 1988 $10 (3/31/91) **81**
Merlot Columbia Valley 1986 $10 (10/15/89) **84**
Merlot Columbia Valley 1985 $9.50 (5/31/88) **86**
Merlot Washington 1984 $9 (5/15/87) **75**
Merlot Washington 1981 $25 (10/15/89) **87**
Merlot Yakima Valley Red Willow Vineyard Milestone 1987 $15 (10/15/89) **80**
Merlot Yakima Valley Red Willow Vineyard Milestone David Lake 1989 $18 (6/15/92) **88**
Merlot Yakima Valley Red Willow Vineyard Milestone David Lake 1988 $16 (3/31/91) **82**
Merlot Yakima Valley Red Willow Vineyard 1989 $20 (11/15/91) **89**
Pinot Noir Washington The Woodburne Collection 1987 $10 (3/31/91) **88**
Pinot Noir Washington Woodburne Cuvée 1990 $12 (3/31/92) **77**
Pinot Noir Washington Woodburne Cuvée 1989 $12 (6/15/92) **84**
Sémillon Columbia Valley 1988 $6 (10/15/89) BB **84**
Sémillon Columbia Valley Sur Lie Chevrier 1990 $12 (1/31/92) **84**
Syrah Yakima Valley Red Willow Vineyard 1988 $25 (5/15/91) **90**

COLUMBIA CREST (United States/Washington)
Cabernet Sauvignon Columbia Valley 1987 $10 (8/31/91) **85**
Cabernet Sauvignon Columbia Valley 1986 $8 (1/31/91) BB **88**
Cabernet Sauvignon Columbia Valley 1985 $8 (10/15/89) **81**
Cabernet Sauvignon Columbia Valley 1984 $7.50 (7/15/88) **79**
Chardonnay Columbia Valley 1989 $7 (9/30/90) BB **86**
Chardonnay Columbia Valley 1987 $7 (12/31/88) **80**
Chardonnay Columbia Valley 1986 $8 (12/31/87) **79**
Chardonnay Columbia Valley Barrel Select 1989 $15 (5/31/91) **86**
Chardonnay Columbia Valley Vintage Select 1987 $7 (10/15/89) **77**
Chenin Blanc Columbia Valley 1986 $5.25 (10/15/89) **77**
Gewürztraminer Columbia Valley 1990 $6 (8/31/91) **76**
Gewürztraminer Columbia Valley 1987 $6 (10/15/89) **81**
Johannisberg Riesling Columbia Valley 1990 $6 (8/31/91) BB **81**
Johannisberg Riesling Columbia Valley 1986 $6 (10/15/89) **70**
Merlot Columbia Valley 1989 $10 (2/29/92) SS **88**
Merlot Columbia Valley 1987 $8 (9/30/90) BB **86**
Merlot Columbia Valley 1985 $8 (10/15/89) **85**
Merlot Columbia Valley 1984 $7.50 (5/31/88) **78**
Merlot Columbia Valley Barrel Select 1987 $15 (5/31/91) **84**
Riesling Columbia Valley Dry 1990 $6 (8/31/91) **77**
Sauvignon Blanc Columbia Valley 1986 $7 (10/15/89) **82**
Sémillon Columbia Valley 1990 $6 (7/15/91) BB **86**
Sémillon Columbia Valley 1986 $5.75 (10/15/89) **78**
Semillon-Chardonnay Columbia Valley 1989 $7 (7/15/91) **73**

PIERRE COMBE (France/Rhône)
Côtes du Rhône-Villages Domaine des Richards 1990 $7.50 (10/15/91) BB **89**
Côtes du Rhône-Villages Domaine des Richards 1987 $4 (1/31/89) **78**
Vacqueyras Domaine des Richards 1989 $9.50 (10/15/91) **86**

LA COMBE DES DAMES (France/Bordeaux)
Bordeaux 1985 $6.50 (3/15/88) **74**

CHATEAU LA COMMANDERIE (France/Bordeaux)
St.-Emilion 1991 (NR) (5/15/92) (BT) **70+**
St.-Emilion 1990 (NR) (5/15/92) (BT) **90+**
St.-Emilion 1989 $19 (3/15/92) **92**
St.-Emilion 1988 $15 (10/31/91) **79**
St.-Emilion 1983 $10.50 (1/01/86) **79**
St.-Estèphe 1988 ($NA) (6/30/89) (BT) **75+**

COMPTE LAFOND (France/Loire)
Sancerre Omina Pro Petri Sede 1988 $16 (11/15/90) **84**

CONCANNON (United States/California)
Assemblage Livermore Valley 1986 $20 (3/15/92) **80**
Cabernet Sauvignon Livermore Valley 1983 $11.50 (6/15/87) **77**
Cabernet Sauvignon Livermore Valley 1981 $12 (12/16/84) **82**
Cabernet Sauvignon Livermore Valley Reserve 1987 $16 (7/15/91) **83**
Cabernet Sauvignon Livermore Valley Reserve 1985 $13.50 (2/15/89) **87**
Chardonnay California Selected Vineyards 1985 $10.50 (6/30/87) **81**
Chardonnay California Selected Vineyards 1984 $9 (4/16/86) **88**
Chardonnay Santa Clara Valley Mistral Vineyard 1988 $12 (7/15/91) **83**
Fumé Blanc California Selected Vineyards 1987 $9.50 (4/30/91) **73**

Petite Sirah Livermore Valley 1987 $11 (8/31/91) **77**
Petite Sirah Livermore Valley Reserve 1985 $15 (8/31/91) **83**
Sauvignon Blanc Livermore Valley 1990 $8 (2/15/92) BB **85**
Sauvignon Blanc Livermore Valley Reserve 1988 $10 (4/15/92) **79**
Sauvignon Blanc Santa Clara County Mistral Vineyard 1989 $7.50 (11/15/91) **79**

CONCHA Y TORO (Chile)
Cabernet Sauvignon Maipo 1985 $5 (3/15/90) **75**
Cabernet Sauvignon Maipo 1984 $5.50 (4/30/88) BB **89**
Cabernet Sauvignon Maipo Casillero del Diablo Pirque Vineyard 1984 $9 (6/15/92) **74**
Cabernet Sauvignon Maipo Marqués de Casa Concha Puente Alto Vineyard 1987 $9.50 (6/15/92) **67**
Cabernet Sauvignon Maipo Puente Alto Vineyard Private Reserve Don Melchor 1988 $14 (5/15/92) SS **91**
Cabernet Sauvignon Maipo Puente Alto Vineyard Private Reserve Don Melchor 1987 $13 (6/30/90) **85**
Cabernet Sauvignon Maipo Puente Alto Vineyard Special Reserve 1983 $8 (9/15/90) **75**
Cabernet Sauvignon Maipo Reserva Special Casillero del Diablo 1984 $7 (11/15/87) **85**
Cabernet Sauvignon Maipo Special Reserve 1981 $6.75 (4/30/88) **80**
Cabernet Sauvignon Merlot Rapel 1986 $4.25 (9/15/90) BB **80**
Chardonnay Maipo 1987 $5 (4/30/90) **67**
Chardonnay Maipo Casillero del Diablo Santa Isabel Vineyard 1989 $7.50 (6/15/92) **78**
Chardonnay Maipo Marqués de Casa Concha Santa Isabel Vineyard 1990 $9.50 (6/15/92) **86**
Merlot Rapel 1986 $4.50 (3/15/90) **76**
Merlot Rapel Marqués de Casa Concha Peumo Vineyard 1989 $9.50 (5/15/92) **85**
Sauvignon Blanc Maipo Casillero del Diablo Santa Isabel Vineyard Special Reserve 1989 $7.50 (5/15/92) **80**

CHATEAU LES CONFRERIES (France/Bordeaux)
Bordeaux 1985 $3.50 (2/15/88) **75**

CONGRESS SPRINGS (United States/California)
Brut Santa Clara County Brut de Pinot 1986 $8 (3/31/88) **77**
Cabernet Franc Santa Cruz Mountains 1986 $18 (7/31/89) **88**
Chardonnay Santa Clara County Barrel Fermented 1989 $12 (7/15/91) **85**
Chardonnay Santa Clara County Barrel Fermented 1988 $14 (2/15/90) **68**
Chardonnay Santa Clara County 1987 Rel: $12 Cur: $19 (CH-4/90) **84**
Chardonnay Santa Clara County 1986 Rel: $12 Cur: $18 (CH-4/90) **83**
Chardonnay Santa Clara County 1985 Rel: $12 Cur: $20 (CH-4/90) **87**
Chardonnay Santa Clara County 1984 Rel: $11 Cur: $25 (CH-4/90) **90**
Chardonnay Santa Clara County Barrel Fermented 1983 Rel: $10 Cur: $25 (CH-4/90) **85**
Chardonnay Santa Clara County 1982 Rel: $10 Cur: $20 (CH-4/90) **79**
Chardonnay Santa Cruz Mountains Monmartre 1988 $30 (CH-4/90) **88**
Chardonnay Santa Cruz Mountains Monmartre 1987 Rel: $28 Cur: $32 (CH-4/90) **87**
Chardonnay Santa Cruz Mountains Private Reserve 1986 Rel: $20 Cur: $23 (CH-4/90) **85**
Chardonnay Santa Cruz Mountains Private Reserve 1985 Rel: $16 Cur: $27 (CH-4/90) **84**
Chardonnay Santa Cruz Mountains Private Reserve 1984 Rel: $16 Cur: $27 (CH-4/90) **80**
Chardonnay Santa Cruz Mountains Private Reserve 1983 Rel: $15 Cur: $28 (CH-4/90) **74**
Chardonnay Santa Cruz Mountains Private Reserve 1982 Rel: $15 Cur: $28 (CH-4/90) **87**
Chardonnay Santa Clara County San Ysidro Reserve 1989 $15 (7/15/91) **88**
Chardonnay Santa Clara County San Ysidro Reserve 1988 $20 (CH-4/90) **86**
Chardonnay Santa Clara County San Ysidro Reserve 1987 Rel: $16 Cur: $22 (CH-4/90) **90**
Chardonnay Santa Clara County San Ysidro Reserve 1986 Rel: $15 Cur: $20 (CH-4/90) **85**
Merlot Santa Clara County 1988 $14 (3/31/91) **74**
Pinot Blanc Santa Clara County 1989 $9 (4/30/91) **78**
Pinot Blanc Santa Clara County San Ysidro Vineyard 1988 $9.50 (8/31/89) **84**
Pinot Noir Santa Clara County 1989 $10 (4/30/91) **84**
Pinot Noir Santa Clara County San Ysidro Vineyard 1988 $9 (3/31/90) **87**
Zinfandel Santa Cruz Mountains 1987 $12 (3/15/90) **83**

CONN CREEK (United States/California)
Cabernet Sauvignon Napa Valley Barrel Select 1987 $17 (7/15/91) **87**
Cabernet Sauvignon Napa Valley Barrel Select 1986 Rel: $15 Cur: $18 (2/28/91) **55**
Cabernet Sauvignon Napa Valley Barrel Select 1985 Rel: $15 Cur: $18 (9/15/90) **90**
Cabernet Sauvignon Napa Valley Barrel Select Lot 79 1984 Rel: $13 Cur: $22 (CA-3/89) **86**
Cabernet Sauvignon Napa Valley Barrel Select 1983 Rel: $13 Cur: $25 (CA-3/89) **82**
Cabernet Sauvignon Napa Valley Barrel Select 1982 Rel: $12 Cur: $22 (CA-3/89) **85**
Cabernet Sauvignon Napa Valley 1981 Rel: $14 Cur: $19 (CA-3/89) **85**
Cabernet Sauvignon Napa Valley 1980 Rel: $13 Cur: $35 (CA-3/89) **88**
Cabernet Sauvignon Napa Valley 1979 Rel: $13 Cur: $60 (CA-3/89) **77**
Cabernet Sauvignon Napa Valley 1977 Rel: $12 Cur: $27 (CA-3/89) **90**
Cabernet Sauvignon Napa Valley 1976 Rel: $12 Cur: $26 (CA-3/89) **86**
Cabernet Sauvignon Napa Valley 1974 Rel: $9 Cur: $210 (CA-3/89) **94**
Cabernet Sauvignon Stags Leap District 1973 Rel: $9 Cur: $70 (CA-3/89) **92**
Cabernet Sauvignon Napa Valley Barrel Select Private Reserve 1987 $19 (4/15/89) (BT) **90+**
Cabernet Sauvignon Napa Valley Barrel Select Private Reserve 1986 Rel: $37 Cur: $41 (12/15/90) **91**
Cabernet Sauvignon Napa Valley Barrel Select Private Reserve 1985 Rel: $30 Cur: $33 (9/15/90) **91**
Cabernet Sauvignon Napa Valley Collins Vineyard Private Reserve 1984 Rel: $23 Cur: $37 (3/31/89) **94**
Cabernet Sauvignon Napa Valley Collins Vineyard Proprietor's Special Selection 1983 $7 (CA-3/89) **87**
Cabernet Sauvignon Napa Valley Collins Vineyard Proprietor's Special Selection 1982 $70 (CA-3/89) **85**
Cabernet Sauvignon Napa Valley Collins Vineyard Proprietor's Special Selection 1981 $70 (CA-3/89) **86**
Cabernet Sauvignon Napa Valley Collins Vineyard Proprietor's Special Selection 1980 $70 (CA-3/89) **93**
Cabernet Sauvignon Napa Valley Lot 1 1978 Rel: $12 Cur: $55 (CA-3/89) **86**
Cabernet Sauvignon Napa Valley Lot 2 1978 Rel: $12 Cur: $55 (CA-3/89) **92**
Chardonnay Carneros Barrel Select 1988 $13 (7/15/91) **80**
Chardonnay Napa Valley Barrel Select 1988 $13 (7/15/91) **86**
Chardonnay Napa Valley Barrel Select 1987 $12 (9/15/90) **88**
Chardonnay Napa Valley Barrel Select Lot No. 32 1985 $12 (2/15/88) **80**
Chardonnay Napa Valley Barrel Select Lot No. 139 1985 $12.50 (12/31/88) **78**
Chardonnay Napa Valley Barrel Select 1983 $14 (6/30/87) **83**
Chardonnay Napa Valley 1982 $12.50 (11/01/85) **81**
Chardonnay Napa Valley Château Maja 1984 $6.50 (4/16/86) BB **84**
Merlot Napa Valley Barrel Select 1988 $22 (11/15/91) **86**
Merlot Napa Valley Collins Vineyard 1985 $14 (3/31/88) **84**
Merlot Napa Valley Collins Vineyard Barrel Select Limited Bottling 1987 $22 (12/31/90) **87**
Sauvignon Blanc Napa Valley Barrel Select 1987 $10 (4/30/89) **83**
Zinfandel Napa Valley 1979 $7.50 (3/16/84) **60**
Zinfandel Napa Valley Barrel Select 1987 $10 (11/15/91) **80**
Zinfandel Napa Valley Barrel Select 1986 $9 (10/15/90) **86**
Zinfandel Napa Valley Collins Vineyard 1983 $10 (12/15/88) **84**

CHATEAU LA CONSEILLANTE (France/Bordeaux)
Pomerol 1991 (NR) (5/15/92) (BT) **80+**
Pomerol 1990 (NR) (5/15/92) (BT) **90+**
Pomerol 1989 $107 (3/15/92) **92**
Pomerol 1988 $56 (3/31/91) **90**
Pomerol 1987 $35 (5/15/90) **86**
Pomerol 1986 Rel: $40 Cur: $54 (6/15/89) **93**
Pomerol 1985 Rel: $50 Cur: $60 (2/29/88) **93**
Pomerol 1984 Rel: $26 Cur: $37 (3/31/87) **93**
Pomerol 1983 Rel: $33 Cur: $40 (11/15/86) **84**
Pomerol 1982 Rel: $29 Cur: $72 (5/15/89) (TR) **96**
Pomerol 1962 $55 (11/30/87) (JS) **60**
Pomerol 1959 $150 (10/15/90) (JS) **88**

ALDO CONTERNO (Italy/Piedmont)
Barolo Bricco Bussia Vigna Cicala 1985 $40 (6/15/90) **90**
Barolo Bricco Bussia Vigna Cicala 1982 $20 (9/15/87) **86**
Barolo Bricco Bussia Vigna Colonnello 1985 $40 (6/15/90) **84**
Barolo Bussia Soprana 1985 $40 (9/15/90) **87**
Barolo Bussia Soprana 1983 $25 (9/15/88) (HS) **85**
Barolo Bussia Soprana 1982 Rel: $17.50 Cur: $30 (9/15/87) **85**
Barolo Bussia Soprana 1980 $35 (9/15/88) (HS) **86**
Barolo Bussia Soprana 1978 $70 (9/15/88) (HS) **92**
Barolo Bussia Soprana 1974 $60 (9/15/88) (HS) **90**
Barolo Bussia Soprana 1971 $50 (9/15/88) (HS) **87**
Barolo Granbussia 1982 ($NA) (9/15/88) (HS) **93**
Dolcetto d'Alba 1987 $12 (9/15/90) **84**
Nebbiolo Il Favot Monforte Bussia 1983 $12.50 (5/31/90) **84**
Nebbiolo Il Favot Monforte Bussia NV $10 (5/31/90) **83**
Nebbiolo delle Langhe Bussia Conca Tre Pile 1985 $13 (11/15/88) **85**

GIACOMO CONTERNO (Italy/Piedmont)
Barolo 1985 $23 (4/15/90) **87**
Barolo 1983 $23 (9/15/88) (HS) **88**
Barolo 1982 $25 (9/15/88) (HS) **90**
Barolo Monfortino Reserva 1982 $57 (6/30/87) **91**
Barolo Riserva Spéciale 1978 $40 (9/15/88) (HS) **83**
Barolo Riserva Spéciale 1970 ($NA) (9/15/88) (HS) **88**

CONTERNO FANTINO (Italy/Piedmont)
Barbera d'Alba Vignota 1989 $20 (3/15/91) **86**
Barolo Sorì Ginestra Riserva 1982 $24 (1/31/90) **84**
Monprá 1988 $27 (3/15/91) **91**

CONTI D'ATTIMIS (Italy/Tuscany)
Brunello di Montalcino Ferrante 1983 $35 (9/30/90) **88**
Chianti Classico Ermanno 1987 $11 (9/15/90) **82**
Chianti Classico Ermanno Riserva 1985 $13 (9/15/90) **84**
Chianti Classico Odorico 1988 $10 (11/30/90) **78**
Vino Nobile di Montepulciano Varnero 1987 $14 (9/15/90) **75**

CONTRATTO (Italy/Piedmont)
Barolo 1983 $10 (3/31/90) **75**
Barolo 1979 $9 (9/30/86) **76**
Barolo del Centenario Riserva 1978 $18 (5/16/86) **86**
Brut Classico Winter Disgorged 1989 NV $10 (6/15/90) **82**

BORGO CONVENTI (Italy/North)
Merlot Collio 1987 $15 (3/31/89) **84**

COOK'S (United States/Other US)
Brut American Champagne NV $4 (3/31/92) **74**
Chardonnay California Captain's Reserve 1990 $5.50 (3/31/92) **77**
Extra Dry American NV $4 (3/31/92) **76**
Extremely Dry American Grand Reserve NV $4 (3/31/92) **70**
Merlot California Captain's Reserve 1989 $5.50 (5/31/92) **77**

R. & J. COOK (United States/California)
Chenin Blanc Clarksburg 1988 $5.50 (7/31/89) **83**
Merlot Clarksburg 1989 $9.50 (5/31/92) **82**

COOPER MOUNTAIN (United States/Oregon)
Pinot Noir Willamette Valley 1988 $13 (4/15/91) **83**
Pinot Noir Willamette Valley 1987 $13 (2/15/90) **87**
Pinot Noir Willamette Valley Reserve 1988 $20 (4/15/91) **83**

COOPERS CREEK (New Zealand)
Cabernet Sauvignon Huapai Valley 1989 $10 (4/15/92) **79**

LUIGI COPPO (Italy/Piedmont)
Barbera d'Asti Camp du Rouss 1988 $21 (3/15/91) **88**
Barbera d'Asti Camp du Rouss 1986 $19 (3/31/90) **87**
Barbera d'Asti Pomorosso 1987 $41 (3/15/91) **90**
Barbera d'Asti Pomorosso 1986 $41 (3/15/91) **84**
Dolcetto d'Alba 1989 $10.50 (7/15/91) **81**
Mondaccione 1988 $34 (1/31/92) **73**
Mondaccione 1987 $13 (3/31/90) **87**

CORBANS (New Zealand)
Chardonnay Marlborough 1986 $10 (5/15/88) **92**

CORBETT CANYON (United States/California)
Cabernet Sauvignon California Coastal Classic 1989 $7 (11/15/91) **76**
Cabernet Sauvignon Central Coast Coastal Classic 1986 $6.50/1L (12/15/89) **80**
Cabernet Sauvignon Central Coast 1983 $7 (5/16/86) BB **80**
Cabernet Sauvignon Central Coast Reserve 1987 $9.50 (11/15/91) **82**
Cabernet Sauvignon Central Coast Select 1984 $8 (2/15/87) **82**
Cabernet Sauvignon Santa Barbara-San Luis Obispo Counties Select 1985 $10 (5/31/88) **79**
Chardonnay Central Coast 1984 $8 (3/01/86) BB **84**
Chardonnay Central Coast Coastal Classic 1990 $6 (7/15/92) **74**
Chardonnay Central Coast Coastal Classic 1989 $7/1L (7/15/91) BB **84**
Chardonnay Central Coast Coastal Classic 1988 $6.50/1L (12/15/89) **75**
Chardonnay Central Coast Coastal Classic 1987 $7/1L (7/15/88) **79**
Chardonnay Central Coast Coastal Classic 1986 $6.50/1L (11/15/87) **68**
Chardonnay Central Coast Reserve 1988 $9.50 (7/15/91) **78**
Chardonnay Central Coast Reserve 1987 $8 (12/15/89) **80**
Chardonnay Central Coast Select 1986 $8.75 (3/15/89) **66**
Chardonnay Central Coast Select 1985 $9 (1/31/87) **83**
Chardonnay Edna Valley Winemaker's Reserve 1984 $10 (7/01/86) **67**
Chardonnay Santa Barbara County Reserve 1990 $9.50 (7/15/92) **77**
Merlot California Coastal Classic 1989 $7 (11/15/91) BB **81**
Pinot Noir Central Coast Reserve 1989 $9.50 (11/15/91) **81**
Pinot Noir Central Coast Reserve 1986 $8 (12/15/89) **83**
Pinot Noir Santa Maria Valley Sierra Madre Vineyard Reserve 1985 $12 (2/15/88) **81**
Sauvignon Blanc Central Coast Coastal Classic 1988 $5.50/1L (12/15/89) **78**
Sauvignon Blanc Central Coast Reserve 1988 $6 (12/15/89) **77**
Zinfandel San Luis Obispo County Select 1984 $7.50 (5/15/88) **87**

CHATEAU CORBIN (France/Bordeaux)
St.-Emilion 1986 $15 (6/30/89) **88**
St.-Emilion 1985 $15 (5/31/88) **86**

CHATEAU CORBIN-MICHOTTE (France/Bordeaux)
St.-Emilion 1988 $15 (7/15/91) **72**

CHATEAU CORDEILLAN-BAGES (France/Bordeaux)
Pauillac 1991 (NR) (5/15/92) (BT) **85+**
Pauillac 1990 (NR) (5/15/92) (BT) **90+**
Pauillac 1989 $24 (3/15/92) **96**

PAOLO CORDERO DI MONTEZEMOLO (Italy/Piedmont)
Barolo 1980 Rel: $16 Cur: $20 (12/15/87) CS **91**
Barolo Enrico VI 1983 $20 (9/15/88) (HS) **86**
Barolo Enrico VI 1982 $20 (9/15/88) (HS) **88**
Barolo Enrico VI 1981 $25 (9/15/88) (HS) **88**
Barolo Enrico VI 1980 ($NA) (9/15/88) (HS) **85**
Barolo Monfalletto 1984 ($NA) (9/15/88) (HS) **88**
Barolo Monfalletto 1983 $17 (2/28/89) **85**
Barolo Monfalletto 1980 Rel: $11 Cur: $20 (1/31/87) **91**
Barolo Monfalletto 1979 $35 (9/15/88) (HS) **82**
Barolo Monfalletto 1978 $25 (9/15/88) (HS) **84**
Barolo Monfalletto 1977 ($NA) (9/15/88) (HS) **69**
Barolo Monfalletto 1975 ($NA) (9/15/88) (HS) **77**
Barolo Monfalletto 1973 ($NA) (9/15/88) (HS) **65**
Barolo Monfalletto 1971 ($NA) (9/15/88) (HS) **85**

JEAN CORDIER (France/Other)
Rouge NV $3 (12/31/90) **75**
Vin de Table Blanc Français NV $3 (12/31/90) **72**

CORINO (Italy/Piedmont)
Barbera d'Alba Vigna Giachini 1989 $14 (11/30/91) **91**

CORISON (United States/California)
Cabernet Sauvignon Napa Valley 1990 (NR) (5/15/91) (BT) **90+**
Cabernet Sauvignon Napa Valley 1989 (NR) (5/15/91) (BT) **85+**
Cabernet Sauvignon Napa Valley 1988 Rel: $22 Cur: $24 (11/15/91) **89**
Cabernet Sauvignon Napa Valley 1987 $20 (11/15/90) **92**

CHATEAU CORMEIL-FIGEAC (France/Bordeaux)
St.-Emilion 1988 $20 (4/30/91) **85**
St.-Emilion 1986 $12 (6/30/89) **75**

BARONE CORNACCHIA (Italy/Other)
Montepulciano d'Abruzzo 1988 $5 (12/31/90) **78**

EDMOND CORNU (France/Burgundy)
Aloxe-Corton Les Moutottes 1987 $35 (12/31/90) **83**
Corton Les Bressandes 1987 $53 (12/31/90) **90**
Ladoix 1987 $18 (2/28/91) **78**

CORON PERE (France/Burgundy)
Chassagne-Montrachet 1985 $20 (8/31/87) **83**
Meursault 1985 $18 (8/31/87) **64**

BODEGAS CORRAL (Spain)
Rioja Don Jacobo 1985 $8 (3/31/90) **79**
Rioja Don Jacobo 1982 $7 (11/15/87) (JL) **79**
Rioja Don Jacobo Reserva 1981 $10.50 (3/31/90) **86**

CORTE VECCHIA (Italy/Piedmont)
Bianco di Custoza 1989 $7 (7/15/91) **77**

JACQUES CORTENAY (France/Rhône)
Châteauneuf-du-Pape 1985 $8 (9/30/87) BB **85**

GIUSEPPE CORTESE (Italy/Piedmont)
Barbaresco 1982 $19 (12/15/88) **85**
Barbaresco Rabajà 1986 $19 (9/15/90) **89**
Barbaresco Rabajà 1983 $18 (1/31/90) **75**
Barbaresco Rabajà 1981 $12 (8/31/89) **72**
Barbaresco Spéciale 1983 $13 (8/31/89) **79**
Barbera d'Alba 1990 $12 (2/15/92) **71**
Barbera d'Alba 1989 $11 (7/15/91) **86**
Barbera d'Alba 1988 $9 (3/15/91) **86**
Dolcetto d'Alba 1990 $13 (1/31/92) **79**
Dolcetto d'Alba 1989 $9.75 (12/31/90) **83**
Dolcetto d'Alba 1988 $8 (3/31/90) **78**
Nebbiolo delle Langhe Vigna in Rabajà 1988 $12.50 (2/28/91) **80**

FATTORIA LE CORTI (Italy/Tuscany)
Masso Tondo 1985 $20 (4/30/89) **86**

CORVO (Italy/Other)
Duca di Salaparuta Bianca di Valguarnera 1987 $34 (12/31/90) **81**
Duca di Salaparuta Duca Enrico 1984 $27 (9/15/89) **92**

CHATEAU COS D'ESTOURNEL (France/Bordeaux)
St.-Estèphe 1991 (NR) (5/15/92) (BT) **90+**
St.-Estèphe 1989 $60 (3/15/92) **95**
St.-Estèphe 1988 Rel: $30 Cur: $36 (7/15/91) CS **95**
St.-Estèphe 1987 $30 (5/15/90) **81**
St.-Estèphe 1986 Rel: $40 Cur: $45 (5/15/90) (HS) **92**
St.-Estèphe 1985 Rel: $33 Cur: $54 (5/15/90) (HS) **95**
St.-Estèphe 1984 $29 (5/15/90) (HS) **81**
St.-Estèphe 1983 Rel: $29 Cur: $61 (5/15/90) (HS) **85**
St.-Estèphe 1983 Rel: $29 Cur: $61 (5/16/86) SS **95**
St.-Estèphe 1982 Rel: $23 Cur: $95 (5/15/90) (HS) **92**
St.-Estèphe 1982 Rel: $23 Cur: $95 (7/16/85) CS **93**
St.-Estèphe 1981 Rel: $23 Cur: $41 (5/15/90) (HS) **87**
St.-Estèphe 1980 $38 (5/15/90) (HS) **83**
St.-Estèphe 1979 $45 (5/15/90) (HS) **92**
St.-Estèphe 1978 $54 (5/15/90) (HS) **93**
St.-Estèphe 1977 $30 (5/15/90) (HS) **85**
St.-Estèphe 1976 $46 (5/15/90) (HS) **84**
St.-Estèphe 1975 $69 (5/15/90) (HS) **88**
St.-Estèphe 1973 $31 (5/15/90) (HS) **82**
St.-Estèphe 1971 $50 (5/15/90) (HS) **91**
St.-Estèphe 1970 $95 (5/15/90) (HS) **89**
St.-Estèphe 1969 $21 (5/15/90) (HS) **58**
St.-Estèphe 1967 $34 (5/15/90) (HS) **82**
St.-Estèphe 1966 $120 (5/15/90) (HS) **74**
St.-Estèphe 1964 $75 (5/15/90) (HS) **84**
St.-Estèphe 1962 $124 (5/15/90) (HS) **79**
St.-Estèphe 1961 $190 (5/15/90) (HS) **87**
St.-Estèphe 1960 $85 (5/15/90) (HS) **79**
St.-Estèphe 1959 $200 (10/15/90) (JS) **90**
St.-Estèphe 1958 $95 (5/15/90) (HS) **89**
St.-Estèphe 1956 $60 (5/15/90) (HS) **79**
St.-Estèphe 1955 $140 (5/15/90) (HS) **90**
St.-Estèphe 1954 $80 (5/15/90) (HS) **81**
St.-Estèphe 1953 $240 (5/15/90) (HS) **91**
St.-Estèphe 1952 $100 (5/15/90) (HS) **95**
St.-Estèphe 1950 $100 (5/15/90) (HS) **86**
St.-Estèphe 1949 $195 (5/15/90) (HS) **80**
St.-Estèphe 1947 $220 (5/15/90) (HS) **91**
St.-Estèphe 1945 $300 (5/15/90) (HS) **77**
St.-Estèphe 1943 $220 (5/15/90) (HS) **85**
St.-Estèphe 1942 $110 (5/15/90) (HS) **78**
St.-Estèphe 1937 $260 (5/15/90) (HS) **64**
St.-Estèphe 1934 $220 (5/15/90) (HS) **88**
St.-Estèphe 1929 $450 (5/15/90) (HS) **92**
St.-Estèphe 1928 $500 (5/15/90) (HS) **90**
St.-Estèphe 1926 $300 (5/15/90) (HS) **77**
St.-Estèphe 1924 $300 (5/15/90) (HS) **82**
St.-Estèphe 1921 $200 (5/15/90) (HS) **65**
St.-Estèphe 1920 $350 (5/15/90) (HS) **93**
St.-Estèphe 1917 $250 (5/15/90) (HS) **73**
St.-Estèphe 1905 $250 (5/15/90) (HS) **65**
St.-Estèphe 1904 $210 (5/15/90) (HS) **63**
St.-Estèphe 1899 $850 (5/15/90) (HS) **87**
St.-Estèphe 1898 $500 (5/15/90) (HS) **72**
St.-Estèphe 1890 $330 (5/15/90) (HS) **69**
St.-Estèphe 1870 $1,240 (5/15/90) (HS) **90**
St.-Estèphe 1869 $1,200 (5/15/90) (HS) **82**

CHATEAU COS-LABORY (France/Bordeaux)
St.-Estèphe 1991 (NR) (5/15/92) (BT) **75+**
St.-Estèphe 1990 (NR) (5/15/92) (BT) **90+**
St.-Estèphe 1989 $18 (3/15/92) **93**
St.-Estèphe 1988 $20 (4/30/91) **85**
St.-Estèphe 1987 $15 (6/30/88) (BT) **65+**
St.-Estèphe 1986 $16 (6/30/88) (BT) **75+**
St.-Estèphe 1985 $16 (4/30/88) **87**
St.-Estèphe 1984 $12 (6/15/87) **73**
St.-Estèphe 1983 Rel: $9.50 Cur: $20 (5/16/86) **86**

COSENTINO (United States/California)
Cabernet Franc Napa County 1987 $12.50 (9/30/89) **75**
Cabernet Franc North Coast 1988 $16 (11/15/91) **80**
Cabernet Franc North Coast 1986 $14 (7/31/88) **92**
Cabernet Sauvignon Napa County 1989 $15 (3/31/92) **86**
Cabernet Sauvignon North Coast 1988 $15 (5/31/91) **88**
Cabernet Sauvignon North Coast 1987 $16 (6/30/90) **80**
Cabernet Sauvignon North Coast 1985 $10.50 (9/15/88) **84**
Cabernet Sauvignon North Coast Reserve 1987 $28 (2/28/91) **86**
Cabernet Sauvignon North Coast Reserve 1986 $18 (5/15/90) **90**
Cabernet Sauvignon North Coast Reserve 1985 $18 (4/30/89) **81**
Cabernet Sauvignon North Coast Reserve Edition 1984 $14 (3/31/88) **78**
Chardonnay Napa County 1990 $14 (3/31/92) **83**
Chardonnay Napa County 1989 $13 (4/15/91) **81**
Chardonnay Napa Valley 1987 $11.50 (3/15/89) **91**
Chardonnay Napa County The Sculptor 1990 $18 (7/15/92) **83**
Chardonnay Napa Valley The Sculptor 1989 $18 (7/15/91) **80**
Chardonnay Napa Valley The Sculptor 1988 $18 (6/15/90) **86**
Chardonnay Napa Valley The Sculptor 1987 $18 (7/15/89) **84**
Chardonnay Napa Valley The Sculptor 1986 $17 (9/15/88) **80**
Cos Meritage Napa Valley 1988 $45 (11/15/91) **89**
Merlot Napa Valley 1989 $18 (5/31/92) **85**
Merlot Napa County 1988 $18 (4/15/91) **82**
Merlot Napa County 1986 $14 (9/30/88) **85**
Merlot Napa County Reserve 1987 $18 (7/31/90) **80**
Pinot Noir Sonoma County 1989 $13 (6/30/91) **82**
The Poet California 1989 (NR) (5/15/91) (BT) **85+**
The Poet California 1988 $27 (5/31/91) **85**
The Poet California 1987 $25 (9/15/90) **85**
The Poet California 1986 $22 (7/31/89) **86**
The Poet California 1985 $18 (8/31/88) **79**

EMILIO COSTANTI (Italy/Tuscany)
Brunello di Montalcino 1982 $32 (7/31/88) **81**
Brunello di Montalcino 1981 $20 (9/15/86) **80**
Brunello di Montalcino 1980 $17 (9/15/86) **89**
Vermiglio 1981 $7.50 (10/31/86) **79**

DOMAINE COSTE-CAUMARTIN (France/Burgundy)
Bourgogne 1989 $15 (1/31/92) **87**
Pommard 1987 $21 (11/15/90) **76**
Pommard Clos de Boucherottes 1989 $38 (1/31/92) **92**
Pommard Les Fremiers 1989 $35 (1/31/92) **92**
Pommard Les Fremiers 1987 $26 (11/15/90) **79**

PAUL COTAT (France/Loire)
Sancerre Chavignol Les Culs de Beaujeu 1989 $22 (2/28/91) **85**
Sancerre Chavignol Les Culs de Beaujeu 1988 $15 (4/15/90) **77**

Key to Symbols

The scores reported here are the results of blind tastings conducted by our panel of senior editors. Wines that carry the initials below are results of individual tastings.

THE WINE SPECTATOR 100-POINT SCALE ***95-100***—Classic, a great wine; ***90-94***—Outstanding, superior character and style; ***80-89***—Good to very good, a wine with special qualities; ***70-79***—Average, drinkable wine that may have minor flaws; ***60-69***—Below average, drinkable but not recommended; ***50-59***—Poor, undrinkable, not recommended. "+"—With a score indicates a range; used primarily with barrel tastings to indicate a preliminary score.

SPECIAL DESIGNATIONS SS—Spectator Selection, CS—Cellar Selection, BB—Best Buy, ($NA)—Price not available, (NR)—Not released.

TASTER'S INITIALS (JG)—Jim Gordon, (HS)—Harvey Steiman, (JL)—James Laube, (JS)—James Suckling, (TM)—Thomas Matthews, (TR)—Terry Robards, (PM)—Per-Henrik Mansson, (BT)—Barrel Tasting (these wines were tasted blind from barrel samples), (CA-date)—*California's Great Cabernets* by James Laube, (CH-date)—*California's Great Chardonnays* by James Laube, (VP-date)—*Vintage Port* by James Suckling.

DATE TASTED Dates in parentheses represent the issue in which the rating was published.

Sancerre Chavignol La Grande Côte 1989 $25 (2/28/91) **86**
Sancerre Chavignol La Grande Côte 1988 $18 (4/15/90) **85**
Sancerre Chavignol Réserve des Monts Damnés 1989 $19 (2/28/91) **82**

CHATEAU COTE DE BALEAU (France/Bordeaux)
St.-Emilion 1991 (NR) (5/15/92) (BT) **80+**
St.-Emilion 1989 (NR) (3/15/92) **81**

COTES DE SONOMA (United States/California)
Cabernet Sauvignon Sonoma County 1989 $7 (11/15/91) BB **83**
Deux Cépages Sonoma County 1990 $6 (11/15/91) **73**

CHATEAU COTES DES CHARIS (France/Bordeaux)
Bordeaux Blanc Sauvignon Blanc Sec 1990 $10 (6/15/91) **70**

BODEGAS EL COTO (Spain)
Rioja Coto de Imaz Gran Reserva 1982 ($NA) (11/30/91) (TM) **85**
Rioja Coto de Imaz Reserva 1981 $9 (3/31/90) **81**
Rioja Crianza 1987 $11 (9/30/91) **79**
Rioja Crianza 1985 $5 (3/31/90) BB **81**
Rioja Crianza 1984 $7 (3/31/90) BB **81**

COTTONWOOD CANYON (United States/California)
Chardonnay Central Coast 1989 $14 (7/15/91) **85**
Chardonnay Santa Barbara County Barrel Select 1989 $19/500ml (3/31/92) **90**

CHATEAU COUCHEROY (France/Bordeaux)
Pessac-Léognan Blanc 1990 $8 (3/31/92) BB **81**

CHATEAU COUFRAN (France/Bordeaux)
Haut-Médoc 1990 (NR) (4/30/91) (BT) **85+**
Haut-Médoc 1989 $14 (3/15/92) **89**
Haut-Médoc 1988 $15 (4/30/91) **84**
Haut-Médoc 1987 $12 (11/30/89) (JS) **81**
Haut-Médoc 1986 Rel: $13 Cur: $15 (11/30/89) (JS) **82**
Haut-Médoc 1985 Rel: $11 Cur: $17 (6/30/88) **85**
Haut-Médoc 1982 Rel: $9 Cur: $18 (11/30/89) (JS) **83**

CHATEAU COUHINS-LURTON (France/Bordeaux)
Pessac-Léognan Blanc 1990 (NR) (9/30/91) (BT) **90+**
Pessac-Léognan Blanc 1989 $25 (9/30/91) **88**
Pessac-Léognan Blanc 1988 $28 (5/31/90) **83**
Pessac-Léognan Blanc 1987 $25 (6/30/89) (BT) **90+**
Pessac-Léognan Blanc 1986 $22 (8/31/88) **88**
Graves Blanc 1983 $12 (7/16/86) **74**

LA COUR PAVILLON (France/Bordeaux)
Bordeaux 1986 $7.25 (2/28/91) **77**
Bordeaux 1985 $6.75 (7/15/88) **67**
Bordeaux 1983 $7 (8/31/87) **68**
Bordeaux Blanc Sec 1989 $7.25 (3/31/91) **78**
Bordeaux Blanc Sec 1986 $7 (3/31/89) **71**
Bordeaux Blanc Sec 1984 $7 (7/15/87) **63**

DOMAINE DE COURCEL (France/Burgundy)
Pommard Clos des Epeneaux 1985 $37 (4/30/88) **89**
Pommard Rugiens 1985 $40 (4/30/88) **92**

DOMAINE LE COUROULU (France/Rhône)
Vacqueyras 1985 $8 (1/31/89) BB **83**

COUSINO-MACUL (Chile)
Cabernet Sauvignon Maipo 1988 $8 (5/15/92) **81**
Cabernet Sauvignon Maipo 1987 $6 (9/15/90) **71**
Cabernet Sauvignon Maipo 1986 $8 (9/15/90) **72**
Cabernet Sauvignon Maipo 1984 $5.50 (2/15/89) BB **86**
Cabernet Sauvignon Maipo 1983 $6 (5/15/88) BB **85**
Cabernet Sauvignon Maipo Antiguas Reservas 1987 $10 (6/15/92) **82**
Cabernet Sauvignon Maipo Antiguas Reservas 1986 $10 (5/31/92) **83**
Cabernet Sauvignon Maipo Antiguas Reservas 1985 $10.50 (10/15/91) **81**
Cabernet Sauvignon Maipo Antiguas Reservas 1984 $9 (9/15/90) **77**
Cabernet Sauvignon Maipo Antiguas Reservas 1981 $9 (2/15/89) **80**
Cabernet Sauvignon Maipo Antiguas Reservas 1980 $8 (5/15/88) **80**
Chardonnay Maipo 1989 $7 (9/15/90) **76**
Chardonnay Maipo 1987 $6 (3/31/90) BB **85**
Chardonnay Maipo Reserva 1989 $10.50 (5/15/92) **84**
Chardonnay Maipo Reserva 1988 $7.75 (4/30/90) BB **82**
Merlot Maipo Limited Release 1989 $11 (5/31/92) **85**
Merlot Maipo Limited Release 1988 $11 (5/31/92) **84**
Sauvignon Blanc Maipo 1991 $7 (6/15/92) **70**

CHATEAU COUTET (France/Sauternes)
Barsac 1989 ($NA) (6/15/90) (BT) **95+**
Barsac 1988 $47 (6/15/90) (BT) **90+**
Barsac 1987 $27 (6/15/90) **80**
Barsac 1986 $32 (6/30/88) (BT) **80+**
Barsac 1983 $30 (1/31/88) **86**

CHATEAU LE COUVENT (France/Bordeaux)
St.-Emilion 1982 $13 (6/16/86) **78**

COUVENT DES JACOBINS (France/Bordeaux)
St.-Emilion 1989 $28 (4/30/92) **89**
St.-Emilion 1988 $28 (3/31/91) **81**
St.-Emilion 1985 $27 (3/31/88) **84**
St.-Emilion 1983 Rel: $18 Cur: $27 (3/16/86) **95**

COVEY RUN (United States/Washington)
Cabernet Sauvignon Yakima Valley 1988 $11 (4/30/92) **85**
Cabernet Sauvignon Yakima Valley 1986 $10 (10/15/89) **80**
Chardonnay Yakima Valley 1990 $10 (4/30/92) **84**
Chardonnay Yakima Valley 1989 $10 (3/31/91) **86**
Chardonnay Yakima Valley 1987 $9 (10/15/89) **82**
Chardonnay Yakima Valley Reserve 1989 $15 (7/15/91) **89**
Fumé Blanc Washington 1988 $8 (10/15/89) **80**
Gewürztraminer Yakima Valley 1989 $7 (6/15/91) **76**
Gewürztraminer Yakima Valley 1988 $5.50 (10/15/89) **77**
Johannisberg Riesling Washington 1988 $5.50 (10/15/89) **79**
Johannisberg Riesling Yakima Valley 1989 $7 (8/31/90) BB **88**
Merlot Yakima Valley 1989 $11 (6/15/92) **79**
Merlot Yakima Valley 1988 $10 (3/31/91) **87**
Merlot Yakima Valley 1986 $9 (10/15/89) **82**
Merlot Yakima Valley 1985 $9 (4/15/89) **85**
Merlot Yakima Valley 1984 $8.50 (11/15/87) **82**
Merlot Yakima Valley Reserve 1989 $17 (3/31/92) **83**
Riesling Yakima Valley Dry 1990 $8 (6/15/92) **74**
White Riesling Late Harvest Yakima Valley Ice Wine 1987 $24/375ml (10/15/89) **87**
White Riesling Late Harvest Yakima Valley Mahre Vineyards Botrytis 1986 $7 (10/15/89) **83**

CRESTON (United States/California)
Cabernet Sauvignon Central Coast Winemaker's Selection 1985 $16.50 (12/15/89) **75**
Cabernet Sauvignon Central Coast Winemaker's Selection 1984 $16 (12/15/87) **71**
Cabernet Sauvignon Paso Robles 1987 $10 (11/15/91) **79**
Cabernet Sauvignon Paso Robles Winemaker's Selection 1987 $16 (11/15/91) **82**
Cabernet Sauvignon San Luis Obispo County 1985 $12 (12/15/89) **68**
Chardonnay Central Coast 1985 $10 (11/15/87) **81**
Chardonnay Paso Robles Barrel Fermented 1989 $10 (12/31/91) **83**
Chardonnay San Luis Obispo County 1987 $12 (12/15/89) **80**
Pinot Noir Paso Robles 1990 $8 (11/15/91) **70**
Pinot Noir San Luis Obispo County Petit d'Noir 1987 $8 (8/31/88) **80**
Pinot Noir San Luis Obispo County Petit d'Noir Maceration Carbonique 1988 $8 (12/15/89) **74**
Sauvignon Blanc San Luis Obispo County 1987 $8.25 (12/15/89) **72**
White Zinfandel San Luis Obispo 1988 $7 (6/15/89) **86**

CRICHTON HALL (United States/California)
Chardonnay Napa Valley 1990 $18 (7/15/92) **84**
Chardonnay Napa Valley 1989 $16.50 (7/15/91) **82**
Chardonnay Napa Valley 1988 $16 (12/31/90) **82**
Chardonnay Napa Valley 1987 $16 (11/15/89) **75**

CHATEAU LE CROCK (France/Bordeaux)
St.-Estèphe 1987 $16 (11/30/89) (JS) **79**
St.-Estèphe 1986 Rel: $18 Cur: $21 (11/30/89) (JS) **92**
St.-Estèphe 1985 Rel: $16 Cur: $18 (2/15/88) **79**
St.-Estèphe 1983 $9.50 (12/16/85) **81**
St.-Estèphe 1982 $20 (11/30/89) (JS) **80**

CROFT (Portugal)
Tawny Port 20 Year Old NV $38 (2/28/90) (JS) **76**
Vintage Port 1985 Rel: $30 Cur: $43 (VP-6/90) **81**
Vintage Port 1982 Rel: $22 Cur: $42 (VP-4/90) **69**
Vintage Port 1977 Rel: $14 Cur: $53 (VP-4/90) **85**
Vintage Port 1975 $38 (10/31/88) **80**
Vintage Port 1970 $69 (VP-12/89) **89**
Vintage Port 1966 $91 (VP-12/89) **90**
Vintage Port 1963 $116 (VP-12/89) **91**
Vintage Port 1960 $94 (VP-9/89) **90**
Vintage Port 1955 $170 (VP-11/89) **84**
Vintage Port 1950 $145 (VP-4/90) **77**
Vintage Port 1945 $410 (VP-11/89) **99**
Vintage Port 1935 $270 (VP-2/90) **93**
Vintage Port 1927 $420 (VP-12/89) **87**
Vintage Port Quinta da Roêda 1987 ($NA) (VP-2/90) **79**
Vintage Port Quinta da Roêda 1983 $22 (VP-2/90) **85**
Vintage Port Quinta da Roêda 1980 Rel: $25 Cur: $30 (VP-2/90) **75**
Vintage Port Quinta da Roêda 1978 Rel: $22 Cur: $27 (VP-2/90) **83**
Vintage Port Quinta da Roêda 1967 $50 (VP-1/90) **85**

CHATEAU LA CROIX (France/Bordeaux)
Pomerol 1990 (NR) (4/30/91) (BT) **90+**
Pomerol 1989 (NR) (4/30/91) (BT) **90+**
Pomerol 1988 $19 (7/31/91) **82**
Pomerol 1987 $15 (6/30/89) (BT) **75+**
Pomerol 1986 $25 (6/30/88) (BT) **80+**
Pomerol 1985 $25 (5/15/88) **93**
Pomerol 1983 Rel: $14 Cur: $20 (11/30/86) **84**
Pomerol 1982 $23 (5/15/89) (TR) **89**
Pomerol 1981 $14 (5/01/89) **72**
Pomerol 1979 Rel: $11 Cur: $22 (4/01/84) **60**

CHATEAU LA CROIX DU CASSE (France/Bordeaux)
Pomerol 1991 (NR) (5/15/92) (BT) **65+**
Pomerol 1989 (NR) (4/30/91) (BT) **90+**
Pomerol 1988 $20 (6/30/89) (BT) **85+**
Pomerol 1987 $17 (6/30/88) (BT) **75+**
Pomerol 1985 $25 (5/15/88) **82**

CHATEAU LA CROIX DE GAY (France/Bordeaux)
Pomerol 1991 (NR) (5/15/92) (BT) **85+**
Pomerol 1990 (NR) (5/15/92) (BT) **90+**
Pomerol 1989 Rel: $19 Cur: $25 (3/15/92) **88**
Pomerol 1988 $26 (6/30/91) **89**
Pomerol 1987 $20 (6/30/89) (BT) **80+**
Pomerol 1986 Rel: $20 Cur: $25 (6/30/88) (BT) **90+**
Pomerol 1985 $33 (3/15/88) CS **91**
Pomerol 1983 Rel: $16 Cur: $23 (7/01/86) CS **94**
Pomerol 1982 Rel: $16 Cur: $23 (5/15/89) (TR) **91**
Pomerol 1945 $360 (3/16/86) (JL) **70**

CHATEAU LA CROIX DE GIRON (France/Bordeaux)
Bordeaux Supérieur 1986 $5.25 (5/15/89) **76**

CHATEAU LA CROIX-LANDON (France/Bordeaux)
Médoc 1988 ($NA) (6/30/89) (BT) **75+**

CHATEAU LA CROIX DE MILLORIT (France/Bordeaux)
Côtes de Bourg 1986 $9/375ml (5/15/91) **79**

CHATEAU LA CROIX-ST.-JEAN (France/Bordeaux)
Bordeaux Supérieur 1986 $6 (11/30/88) BB **81**

CHATEAU LA CROIX-TOULIFAUT (France/Bordeaux)
Pomerol 1982 ($NA) (5/15/89) (TR) **80**

CHATEAU CROIZET-BAGES (France/Bordeaux)
Pauillac 1991 (NR) (5/15/92) (BT) **80+**
Pauillac 1990 (NR) (4/30/91) (BT) **85+**
Pauillac 1989 $17 (4/30/91) (BT) **80+**
Pauillac 1988 $28 (8/31/91) **73**
Pauillac 1987 $15 (6/30/88) (BT) **60+**
Pauillac 1986 $15 (6/30/89) **78**
Pauillac 1962 $60 (11/30/87) (JS) **83**

CRONIN (United States/California)
Cabernet Sauvignon Merlot Robinson Vineyard Stags Leap District 1988 $17 (3/31/92) **88**
Cabernet Sauvignon Merlot Robinson Vineyard 1987 $17 (2/28/91) **89**
Cabernet Sauvignon Merlot Robinson Vineyard 1986 $16 (2/15/90) **88**
Cabernet Sauvingon Merlot Santa Cruz Mountains 1987 $17 (3/31/92) **84**
Cabernet Sauvignon Merlot Shaw-Cronin Cuvée San Mateo County 1986 $15 (2/28/91) **88**

Chardonnay Alexander Valley 1989 $14 (8/31/91) **86**
Chardonnay Alexander Valley Stuhlmuller Vineyard 1990 $16 (7/15/92) **88**
Chardonnay Alexander Valley Stuhlmuller Vineyard 1988 $18 (6/30/90) **87**
Chardonnay Monterey County Ventana Vineyard 1990 $14 (7/15/92) **88**
Chardonnay Monterey County Ventana Vineyard 1988 $18 (6/30/90) **84**
Chardonnay Napa Valley 1990 $18 (7/15/92) **90**
Chardonnay Napa Valley 1989 $18 (8/31/91) **87**
Chardonnay Napa Valley 1988 $18 (5/31/90) **78**
Chardonnay Santa Cruz Mountains 1989 $20 (3/31/92) **74**
Chardonnay Santa Cruz Mountains 1988 $20 (4/30/91) **85**
Chardonnay Santa Cruz Mountains 1987 $18 (2/15/90) **90**
Pinot Noir Santa Cruz Mountains Peter Martin Ray Vineyard 1988 $27 (3/31/92) **81**
Sauvignon Blanc Sémillon Robison Vineyard Stags Leap District 1989 $8 (4/30/92) **79**

CHATEAU CROQUE-MICHOTTE (France/Bordeaux)
St.-Emilion 1982 $25 (5/15/89) (TR) **83**

CROSSWOODS (United States/New York)
Chardonnay North Fork of Long Island Ressler Vineyards 1988 $10 (2/29/92) **75**
Chardonnay Southeastern New England 1986 $15 (10/31/89) **77**
Merlot North Fork of Long Island Ressler Vineyards 1987 $10 (2/29/92) **84**
Scrimshaw White Connecticut NV $5 (2/29/92) **75**

CRU DE COUDELET (France/Rhône)
Côtes du Rhône 1987 $12 (12/15/89) **76**
Côtes du Rhône 1986 $15 (9/30/88) **84**
Côtes du Rhône 1985 $12 (4/30/88) **85**

HANS CRUSIUS & SOHN (Germany)
Riesling Auslese Halbtrocken Nahe Schlossböckelheimer Felsenberg 1990 $25 (12/15/91) **89**
Riesling Auslese Nahe Niederhäusener Felsensteyer 1990 $26/375ml (12/15/91) **87**
Riesling Auslese Nahe Schlossböckelheimer Felsenberg Gold Cap 1989 $35 (12/15/90) **91**
Riesling Auslese Nahe Traisener Rotenfels 1989 $24 (12/15/90) **88**
Riesling Kabinett Nahe Traisener Rotenfels 1989 $14 (12/15/90) **85**
Riesling Kabinett Nahe Traiser Rotenfels 1990 $15 (12/15/91) **86**
Riesling Qualitätswein Halbtrocken Nahe 1989 $11 (12/15/90) **82**
Riesling Qualitätswein Halbtrocken Nahe Crusius Riesling 1990 $12 (12/15/91) **80**
Riesling Spätlese Halbtrocken Nahe Schlossböckelheimer Felsenberg 1990 (NR) (12/15/91) **88**
Riesling Spätlese Nahe Traisener Rotenfels 1990 $18 (12/15/91) **84**
Riesling Spätlese Nahe Traisener Rotenfels 1989 $17 (12/15/90) **78**

CRUVINET (United States/California)
Cabernet Sauvignon Alexander Valley 1985 $7 (9/15/88) BB **85**
Chardonnay California 1984 $4.50 (9/15/86) **90**

CHATEAU DE CRUZEAU (France/Bordeaux)
Pessac-Léognan 1990 (NR) (5/15/92) (BT) **90+**
Pessac-Léognan 1989 $14 (3/15/92) **86**
Pessac-Léognan 1988 $14 (2/28/91) **87**
Pessac-Léognan 1987 $12 (6/30/89) (BT) **75+**
Pessac-Léognan 1986 $10 (6/30/89) **87**
Graves 1985 $9 (6/15/88) BB **85**
Graves 1982 $7 (12/16/85) **84**
Pessac-Léognan Blanc 1990 $14 (3/31/92) **83**
Pessac-Léognan Blanc 1989 $16 (6/15/91) **90**
Pessac-Léognan Blanc 1988 $13 (5/31/90) **82**
Pessac-Léognan Blanc 1987 $9 (7/31/89) **82**
Pessac-Léognan Blanc 1986 $8 (4/30/88) **82**

CRYSTAL VALLEY (United States/California)
Cabernet Sauvignon North Coast 1983 $8.50 (8/31/86) BB **89**
Cabernet Sauvignon North Coast Reserve Edition 1984 $14 (10/15/87) **75**
Chardonnay North Coast 1986 $8.50 (11/15/87) **70**
Pinot Noir North Coast Reserve Edition 1986 $10.50 (6/15/88) **74**

CUILLERON (France/Rhône)
Condrieu 1988 $34 (12/31/90) **91**
St.-Joseph 1983 $12.50 (2/16/86) **76**
St.-Joseph Blanc Blanc 1988 $17 (12/31/90) **81**
St.-Joseph Cuvée de la Côte 1987 $16 (11/30/90) **80**

CULBERTSON (United States/California)
Blanc de Noir California 1983 $14 (5/16/86) **68**
Blanc de Noir California NV $14 (12/31/90) **77**
Brut California 1985 $14 (5/31/89) **83**
Brut California 1983 $14 (5/16/86) **66**
Brut California NV $12 (5/15/92) **80**
Brut Rosé California 1986 $17.50 (5/31/89) **80**
Cuvée Rouge California NV $14 (12/31/90) **79**
Demi-Sec California Cuvée de Frontignan NV $12 (5/15/92) **81**
Natural California 1986 $18.50 (12/31/90) **74**
Natural California 1985 $17.50 (5/31/89) **81**
Natural California 1983 $16.50 (5/16/86) **72**

CULLENS (Australia)
Cabernet Merlot Margaret River 1985 $15 (11/15/87) **87**
Chardonnay Western Australia Margaret River 1985 $18 (11/15/87) **83**

CUNE (Spain)
Rioja Clarete 1987 $7 (11/15/91) **78**
Rioja Clarete 1986 $7 (3/31/92) BB **84**
Rioja Clarete 1985 $7 (3/31/90) (TM) **88**
Rioja Clarete 1984 $6 (10/15/88) BB **80**
Rioja Clarete 1982 $4.50 (6/01/85) **83**
Rioja Clarete 1978 $5.50 (6/16/85) **78**
Rioja Contino Reserva 1985 $14 (12/15/90) **88**
Rioja Contino Reserva 1984 $12 (3/31/90) **84**
Rioja Contino Reserva 1983 $13 (3/31/92) **89**
Rioja Contino Reserva 1982 $12 (3/31/92) **92**
Rioja Contino Reserva 1980 $10.75 (1/31/87) **83**
Rioja Crianza 1989 (NR) (3/31/92) (BT) **80+**
Rioja Imperial Gran Reserva 1982 $22 (3/31/92) **86**
Rioja Imperial Gran Reserva 1981 $26 (3/31/92) **82**
Rioja Imperial Gran Reserva 1978 $15 (3/31/90) **70**
Rioja Imperial Gran Reserva 1975 $24 (3/31/92) **84**
Rioja Imperial Gran Reserva 1973 ($NA) (3/31/90) (TM) **85**
Rioja Imperial Reserva 1986 ($NA) (3/31/92) **87**
Rioja Reserva 1985 $8.50 (3/31/90) **85**
Rioja Viña Real 1988 $10 (3/31/92) **87**
Rioja Viña Real 1987 $10 (3/31/92) **86**
Rioja Viña Real 1986 $8 (3/31/90) **81**
Rioja Viña Real 1985 $7 (3/31/90) (TM) **85**
Rioja Viña Real 1980 $5.50 (6/01/85) **75**
Rioja Viña Real Gran Reserva 1981 $17 (3/31/90) **88**
Rioja Viña Real Gran Reserva 1973 ($NA) (3/31/92) **84**
Rioja Viña Real Gran Reserva 1970 ($NA) (3/31/92) **85**
Rioja White Monopole Crianza 1988 ($NA) (5/31/92) **78**

RICHARD CUNEO (United States/California)
Blanc de Blancs Sonoma County Cuvée de Chardonnay 1987 $14 (11/15/91) **84**

CHATEAU CURE-BON-LA-MADELAINE (France/Bordeaux)
St.-Emilion 1982 $30 (5/15/89) (TR) **84**

CHATEAU CURSON (France/Rhône)
Crozes-Hermitage 1989 $17 (7/15/91) **89**
Crozes-Hermitage Blanc 1990 $18 (10/15/91) **82**

LOUIS CURVEUX (France/Burgundy)
Pouilly-Fuissé Les Menestrières 1988 $23 (7/31/90) **86**

CUTLER (United States/California)
Cabernet Sauvignon Sonoma Valley Batto Ranch 1987 $17 (3/31/92) **90**
Cabernet Sauvignon Sonoma Valley Batto Ranch 1986 $17 (11/15/90) **86**
Cabernet Sauvignon Sonoma Valley Batto Ranch 1985 $20 (7/31/89) **91**
Satyre Sonoma Valley 1986 $20 (2/28/91) **85**

CUVAISON (United States/California)
Cabernet Sauvignon Napa Valley 1988 $18 (11/15/91) **82**
Cabernet Sauvignon Napa Valley 1987 Rel: $17.50 Cur: $21 (10/31/90) **92**
Cabernet Sauvignon Napa Valley 1986 Rel: $15 Cur: $20 (7/15/89) **94**
Cabernet Sauvignon Napa Valley 1985 Rel: $14 Cur: $25 (3/31/89) **91**
Cabernet Sauvignon Napa Valley 1984 Rel: $14 Cur: $18 (CA-3/89) **89**
Cabernet Sauvignon Napa Valley 1983 Rel: $12 Cur: $15 (CA-3/89) **75**
Cabernet Sauvignon Napa Valley 1982 Rel: $11 Cur: $18 (CA-3/89) **82**
Cabernet Sauvignon Napa Valley 1981 Rel: $11 Cur: $18 (CA-3/89) **74**
Cabernet Sauvignon Napa Valley 1980 Rel: $11 Cur: $19 (CA-3/89) **77**
Cabernet Sauvignon Napa Valley 1979 Rel: $11 Cur: $20 (CA-3/89) **75**
Cabernet Sauvignon Napa Valley 1978 Rel: $10 Cur: $30 (CA-3/89) **72**
Cabernet Sauvignon Napa Valley 1977 Rel: $10 Cur: $30 (CA-3/89) **79**
Cabernet Sauvignon Napa Valley 1976 Rel: $10 Cur: $30 (CA-3/89) **79**
Cabernet Sauvignon Napa Valley 1975 Rel: $10 Cur: $33 (CA-3/89) **79**
Cabernet Sauvignon Napa Valley Philip Togni Signature 1975 Rel: $40 Cur: $60 (CA-3/89) **88**
Chardonnay Carneros Napa Valley 1990 $16 (3/31/92) **81**
Chardonnay Carneros Napa Valley 1989 $14 (7/15/91) **82**
Chardonnay Carneros Napa Valley 1988 Rel: $15 Cur: $17 (2/28/90) SS **91**
Chardonnay Napa Valley 1987 Rel: $13.50 Cur: $17 (CH-4/90) **90**
Chardonnay Napa Valley 1986 Rel: $12.75 Cur: $18 (CH-4/90) **89**
Chardonnay Napa Valley 1985 Rel: $12 Cur: $20 (CH-4/90) **93**
Chardonnay Napa Valley 1984 Rel: $12 Cur: $20 (CH-4/90) **82**
Chardonnay Napa Valley 1983 Rel: $12 Cur: $17 (CH-4/90) **62**
Chardonnay Napa Valley 1982 Rel: $12 Cur: $17 (CH-4/90) **61**
Chardonnay Napa Valley 1981 Rel: $12 Cur: $18 (CH-4/90) **75**
Chardonnay Napa Valley 1980 Rel: $11 Cur: $26 (CH-4/90) **87**
Chardonnay Napa Valley 1979 Rel: $10 Cur: $26 (CH-4/90) **84**
Chardonnay Napa Valley 1978 Rel: $10 Cur: $28 (CH-4/90) **81**
Chardonnay Carneros Napa Valley Reserve 1988 $25 (CH-6/90) **92**
Chardonnay Carneros Napa Valley Reserve 1987 $22 (CH-7/90) **91**
Chardonnay Carneros Napa Valley Reserve 1986 Rel: $20 Cur: $28 (CH-6/90) **94**
Merlot Napa Valley 1989 $23 (5/31/92) **89**
Merlot Napa Valley 1988 $24 (4/15/91) **86**
Merlot Napa Valley 1985 $19 (6/30/88) **89**
Merlot Napa Valley Anniversary Release 1984 $13.50 (8/31/87) **90**
Zinfandel Napa Valley 1986 $10 (3/15/89) **85**
Zinfandel Napa Valley 1983 $8.50 (9/15/87) **75**

CUVEE DU BELVEDERE (France/Rhône)
Châteauneuf-du-Pape Le Boucou 1986 $16 (1/31/89) **86**
Châteauneuf-du-Pape Le Boucou 1985 $18 (2/15/88) **93**
Châteauneuf-du-Pape Le Boucou 1983 $16 (11/15/87) **62**

CUVEE DES ERMITES (France/Other)
NV $7.50 (1/31/92) **78**

CUVEE PIERRE ROUGE (France/Other)
1990 $7 (6/30/92) **78**

CYPRESS LANE (United States/California)
Chardonnay California 1986 $6 (12/31/87) **71**
Chardonnay California 1985 $6 (1/31/87) **72**

C. DA SILVA (Portugal)
Vintage Port Presidential 1987 ($NA) (VP-2/90) **80**
Vintage Port Presidential 1985 $30 (VP-2/90) **78**
Vintage Port Presidential 1978 $37 (VP-2/90) **77**
Vintage Port Presidential 1977 $39 (VP-2/90) **72**
Vintage Port Presidential 1970 $54 (VP-2/90) **75**
White Port Presidential NV $9 (4/15/92) **80**

DAL FORNO ROMANO (Italy/North)
Valpolicella Superiore 1986 $20 (4/30/92) **84**

CHATEAU DALEM (France/Bordeaux)
Fronsac 1990 (NR) (5/15/92) (BT) **90+**

DALLA VALLE (United States/California)
Cabernet Sauvignon Napa Valley 1988 $25 (11/15/91) **85**
Cabernet Sauvignon Napa Valley 1986 $20 (6/30/90) **85**

Key to Symbols

The scores reported here are the results of blind tastings conducted by our panel of senior editors. Wines that carry the initials below are results of individual tastings.

THE WINE SPECTATOR 100-POINT SCALE ***95-100***—Classic, a great wine; ***90-94***—Outstanding, superior character and style; ***80-89***—Good to very good, a wine with special qualities; ***70-79***—Average, drinkable wine that may have minor flaws; ***60-69***—Below average, drinkable but not recommended; ***50-59***—Poor, undrinkable, not recommended. "+"—With a score indicates a range; used primarily with barrel tastings to indicate a preliminary score.

SPECIAL DESIGNATIONS SS—Spectator Selection, CS—Cellar Selection, BB—Best Buy, ($NA)—Price not available, (NR)—Not released.

TASTER'S INITIALS (JG)—Jim Gordon, (HS)—Harvey Steiman, (JL)—James Laube, (JS)—James Suckling, (TM)—Thomas Matthews, (TR)—Terry Robards, (PM)—Per-Henrik Mansson, (BT)—Barrel Tasting (these wines were tasted blind from barrel samples), (CA-date)—*California's Great Cabernets* by James Laube, (CH-date)—*California's Great Chardonnays* by James Laube, (VP-date)—*Vintage Port* by James Suckling.

DATE TASTED Dates in parentheses represent the issue in which the rating was published.

Maya Napa Valley 1988 $45 (11/15/91) **86**
Zinfandel Napa Valley 1986 $25 (2/15/91) **84**

CHATEAU DE LA DAME (France/Bordeaux)
Margaux 1988 $15 (2/15/91) **86**

CHATEAU LA DAME DE MALESCOT (France/Bordeaux)
Margaux 1989 (NR) (3/15/92) **86**

COMTE AUDOIN DE DAMPIERRE (France/Champagne)
Brut Champagne Grande Année 1983 $32 (12/31/90) **89**

DANIEL (United States/California)
Cabernet Sauvignon Napa Valley 1984 $21 (7/15/88) **89**
Cabernet Sauvignon Napa Valley 1983 $20 (4/30/89) **79**

DARGENT (France/Other)
Brut Blanc de Blancs Côtes du Jura Chardonnay 1988 $10.50 (6/15/90) **83**

VINCENT L. DARNAT (France/Rhône)
Côtes du Rhône Blanc 1985 $5.50 (2/29/88) BB **81**

CHATEAU DASSAULT (France/Bordeaux)
St.-Emilion 1989 (NR) (4/30/91) (BT) **85+**
St.-Emilion 1988 $16 (7/15/91) **83**
St.-Emilion 1987 $14 (6/30/89) (BT) **75+**
St.-Emilion 1982 $20 (5/15/89) (TR) **90**

CHATEAU DE LA DAUPHINE (France/Bordeaux)
Fronsac 1990 (NR) (5/15/92) (BT) **80+**
Fronsac 1989 $20 (3/15/92) **80**
Fronsac 1988 $12 (8/31/90) (BT) **80+**
Fronsac 1987 $17 (6/30/89) (BT) **75+**
Fronsac 1986 $20 (6/30/88) (BT) **75+**
Fronsac 1985 $20 (9/30/88) **84**

JEAN DAUVISSAT (France/Chablis)
Chablis Les Preuses 1986 $30 (7/15/90) **82**
Chablis Les Vaillons 1987 $22 (1/31/91) **91**
Chablis Les Vaillons 1986 $19 (7/15/90) **82**
Chablis Les Vaillons Vieilles Vignes 1986 $24 (7/15/90) **85**

RENE DAUVISSAT (France/Chablis)
Chablis Les Clos 1987 $40 (3/31/89) **95**
Chablis La Forêt 1987 $25 (3/31/89) **92**
Chablis Premier Cru La Forêt 1986 $25 (3/31/89) **91**
Chablis Les Preuses 1987 $43 (3/31/89) **97**
Chablis Séchet 1987 $24 (3/31/89) **90**
Chablis Tribaut 1987 $24 (3/31/89) **88**
Chablis Les Vaillons 1987 $24 (3/31/89) **92**

DOMAINE DAUVISSAT-CAMUS (France/Chablis)
Chablis Les Clos 1988 $41 (7/31/90) **92**
Chablis Les Clos 1987 $37 (10/15/89) **88**
Chablis Les Clos 1986 $40 (9/15/88) **95**
Chablis La Forest 1989 $24 (12/15/91) **87**
Chablis La Forest 1988 $25 (7/31/90) **74**
Chablis La Forest 1987 $22 (10/15/89) **83**
Chablis La Forest 1986 $25 (9/15/88) **85**
Chablis La Forest 1985 $28 (11/15/87) **74**
Chablis Les Preuses 1988 $41 (7/31/90) **86**
Chablis Les Preuses 1987 $37 (10/15/89) **87**
Chablis Les Preuses 1986 $40 (9/15/88) **94**
Chablis Les Vaillons 1989 $24 (12/15/91) **80**
Chablis Les Vaillons 1988 $25 (7/15/90) **91**
Chablis Les Vaillons 1987 $22 (10/15/89) **78**
Chablis Les Vaillons 1986 $25 (9/15/88) **84**
Chablis Les Vaillons 1985 $28 (11/15/87) **88**

CHATEAU DAUZAC (France/Bordeaux)
Margaux 1989 $26 (3/15/92) **90**
Margaux 1988 $20 (6/30/91) **90**
Margaux 1987 $15 (6/30/89) (BT) **70+**
Margaux 1986 $20 (6/30/88) (BT) **70+**
Margaux 1985 $21 (9/30/88) **87**

CHATEAU DAVRIL (France/Bordeaux)
Bordeaux 1987 $5 (9/30/89) **79**

DE LOACH (United States/California)
Cabernet Sauvignon Dry Creek Valley 1984 $11 (12/15/87) **89**
Cabernet Sauvignon Dry Creek Valley 1983 $11 (9/30/86) **85**
Cabernet Sauvignon Dry Creek Valley 1981 $11 (4/01/85) **80**
Cabernet Sauvignon Russian River Valley 1989 $16 (11/15/91) **86**
Cabernet Sauvignon Russian River Valley O.F.S. 1987 $22 (10/15/90) **85**
Chardonnay Russian River Valley 1990 $15 (5/15/92) **85**
Chardonnay Russian River Valley 1989 Rel: $15 Cur: $18 (3/31/91) **87**
Chardonnay Russian River Valley 1988 Rel: $15 Cur: $19 (11/15/89) **86**
Chardonnay Russian River Valley 1987 Rel: $15 Cur: $22 (CH-2/90) **87**
Chardonnay Russian River Valley 1986 Rel: $14 Cur: $25 (CH-2/90) **89**
Chardonnay Russian River Valley 1985 Rel: $14 Cur: $33 (CH-2/90) **90**
Chardonnay Russian River Valley 1984 Rel: $12.50 Cur: $30 (CH-2/90) **88**
Chardonnay Russian River Valley 1983 Rel: $12 Cur: $22 (CH-2/90) **83**
Chardonnay Russian River Valley 1982 Rel: $12 Cur: $20 (CH-2/90) **74**
Chardonnay Russian River Valley 1981 Rel: $10 Cur: $18 (CH-2/90) **72**
Chardonnay Russian River Valley 1980 Rel: $10 Cur: $18 (CH-2/90) **62**
Chardonnay Russian River Valley O.F.S 1990 $25 (5/15/92) **90**
Chardonnay Russian River Valley O.F.S. 1989 Rel: $22 Cur: $24 (3/31/91) **89**
Chardonnay Russian River Valley O.F.S. 1988 Rel: $22 Cur: $25 (2/15/90) **88**
Chardonnay Russian River Valley O.F.S. 1987 Rel: $22 Cur: $40 (CH-5/90) **92**
Chardonnay Russian River Valley O.F.S. 1986 Rel: $22 Cur: $28 (CH-2/90) **86**
Chardonnay Russian River Valley O.F.S. 1985 Rel: $20 Cur: $47 (CH-2/90) **79**
Chardonnay Russian River Valley O.F.S. 1984 $20 (CH-2/90) **90**
Fumé Blanc Russian River Valley 1990 $9 (11/15/91) **84**
Fumé Blanc Russian River Valley 1988 $9 (7/31/89) **86**
Gewürztraminer Early Harvest Russian River Valley 1990 $8 (4/30/91) **81**
Gewürztraminer Early Harvest Russian River Valley 1989 $7.50 (6/30/90) **83**
Gewürztraminer Late Harvest Russian River Valley 1989 $10/375ml (4/30/91) **88**
Gewürztraminer Late Harvest Russian River Valley 1987 $10/375ml (12/31/88) **93**
Gewürztraminer Late Harvest Russian River Valley 1984 $10 (10/01/85) BB **92**
Merlot Russian River Valley 1991 (NR) (5/15/92) (BT) **78+**
Pinot Noir Russian River Valley 1986 $12 (5/31/90) **87**
Pinot Noir Russian River Valley 1985 $12 (6/15/88) **72**
Pinot Noir Russian River Valley 1983 $10 (3/01/86) **75**
Pinot Noir Russian River Valley 1982 $10 (8/31/86) **76**
Pinot Noir Russian River Valley O.F.S. 1987 $25 (10/31/90) **82**
Sauvignon Blanc Russian River Valley 1989 $9 (5/15/90) **84**
Sauvignon Blanc Russian River Valley 1988 $9 (7/31/89) **81**
White Zinfandel Russian River Valley 1990 $7.50 (3/31/91) **77**
White Zinfandel Russian River Valley 1988 $7.50 (6/15/89) **82**
Zinfandel Russian River Valley 1990 $11.50 (5/15/92) **89**
Zinfandel Russian River Valley 1989 $11 (9/30/91) **82**
Zinfandel Russian River Valley 1988 $11 (9/15/90) **78**
Zinfandel Russian River Valley 1987 $10 (9/15/89) **90**
Zinfandel Russian River Valley 1986 $9 (10/15/88) **88**
Zinfandel Russian River Valley 1984 $8.50 (7/31/87) **84**
Zinfandel Russian River Valley 1983 $8 (10/15/86) **69**
Zinfandel Russian River Valley 1982 $8 (11/01/85) **77**
Zinfandel Russian River Valley 1981 $7.50 (6/01/85) **89**
Zinfandel Russian River Valley Barbieri Ranch 1990 $14 (5/15/92) **82**
Zinfandel Russian River Valley Papera Ranch 1990 $14 (5/15/92) **81**
Zinfandel Russian River Valley Pelletti Ranch 1990 $14 (5/15/92) **87**

DE LORIMIER (United States/California)
Mosaic Alexander Valley 1987 $18 (3/31/92) **81**
Mosaic Alexander Valley 1986 $16 (10/31/89) **84**
Chardonnay Alexander Valley Prism 1989 $13.50 (3/31/92) **76**
Chardonnay Alexander Valley Prism 1988 $13.50 (9/30/90) **90**
Chardonnay Alexander Valley Prism 1987 $13.50 (4/15/89) **86**
Sauvignon Blanc Late Harvest Alexander Valley Lace 1986 $11/375ml (2/29/88) **82**
Spectrum Alexander Valley 1989 $10 (10/31/91) **86**
Spectrum Alexander Valley 1988 $8.50 (9/30/90) **83**
Spectrum Alexander Valley 1987 $8.50 (3/31/89) **81**

DE MOOR (United States/California)
Cabernet Sauvignon Napa Valley 1987 $16 (11/15/91) **76**
Cabernet Sauvignon Napa Valley 1985 $14 (CA-3/89) **79**
Cabernet Sauvignon Napa Valley 1984 Rel: $14 Cur: $16 (CA-3/89) **88**
Cabernet Sauvignon Napa Valley 1983 Rel: $12 Cur: $16 (CA-3/89) **86**
Cabernet Sauvignon Napa Valley 1982 Rel: $12 Cur: $18 (CA-3/89) **86**
Cabernet Sauvignon Napa Valley Napa Cellars 1981 Rel: $12 Cur: $25 (CA-3/89) **86**
Cabernet Sauvignon Napa Valley Napa Cellars 1980 Rel: $12 Cur: $20 (CA-3/89) **80**
Cabernet Sauvignon Napa Valley Napa Cellars 1979 Rel: $10 Cur: $25 (CA-3/89) **85**
Cabernet Sauvignon Napa Valley Napa Cellars 1978 Rel: $10 Cur: $28 (CA-3/89) **89**
Cabernet Sauvignon Napa Valley Owners Select 1986 $16 (2/28/91) **78**
Cabernet Sauvignon Napa Valley Owners Select 1982 Rel: $12 Cur: $19 (CA-3/89) **88**
Chardonnay Alexander Valley Napa Cellars Black Mountain Vineyard 1981 $11 (4/16/84) **86**
Chardonnay Napa Valley 1990 $14 (6/30/92) **76**
Chardonnay Napa Valley 1989 $13 (3/15/92) **85**
Chardonnay Napa Valley Napa Cellars 1990 $7 (3/15/92) **80**
Chardonnay Napa Valley Napa Cellars 1989 $7 (4/15/91) BB **85**
Chardonnay Napa Valley Owners Select 1988 $14 (7/15/91) **87**
Merlot California Napa Cellars 1990 $7 (5/31/92) **79**
Merlot California Napa Cellars 1989 $7 (5/31/91) **70**
Sauvignon Blanc Late Harvest Napa Valley Fie Doux 1989 $12/375ml (3/15/92) **84**
Zinfandel Napa Valley 1988 $10 (4/30/91) **72**

DEBONNE (United States/Ohio)
Chambourcin Ohio Lake Erie 1989 $6 (2/29/92) **79**
Chardonnay Ohio Lake Erie Proprietor's Reserve 1989 $12 (2/29/92) **70**
Johannisberg Riesling Grand River Valley 1990 $7.50 (2/29/92) **76**

CHATEAU LA DECELLE (France/Other)
Côteaux du Tricastin 1989 $7.50 (7/15/91) BB **82**

CHATEAU DECORDE (France/Bordeaux)
Haut-Médoc 1989 (NR) (3/15/92) **83**

DEER PARK (United States/California)
Chardonnay Napa Valley 1989 $14 (7/15/91) **67**
Petite Sirah Howell Mountain Parks-Muscatine Vineyards 1987 $14 (10/31/91) **82**
Zinfandel Howell Mountain Beatty Ranch 1987 $14 (8/31/91) **79**
Zinfandel Howell Mountain Beatty Ranch Reserve 1987 $18 (8/31/91) **85**

DEER VALLEY (United States/California)
Cabernet Sauvignon Monterey 1985 $5.50 (12/31/87) **72**
Chardonnay California 1989 $7 (7/15/91) **74**
Merlot California 1990 $6 (5/31/92) **77**

DEHLINGER (United States/California)
Cabernet Franc Russian River Valley 1989 $12 (3/31/92) **75**
Cabernet Franc Russian River Valley 1988 $13 (4/30/91) **84**
Cabernet Sauvignon Russian River Valley 1988 $15 (3/31/92) **83**
Cabernet Sauvignon Russian River Valley 1987 $13 (2/28/91) **88**
Cabernet Sauvignon Russian River Valley 1986 $13 (3/15/90) **90**
Cabernet Sauvignon Russian River Valley 1985 $13 (5/31/89) **74**
Cabernet Sauvignon Russian River Valley 1984 $12 (2/15/88) **76**
Cabernet Sauvignon Russian River Valley 1983 $11 (6/15/87) **85**
Cabernet Sauvignon Russian River Valley 1982 $11 (8/31/86) **73**
Cabernet Sauvignon Sonoma County 1981 $9 (5/16/85) **87**
Chardonnay Russian River Valley 1990 $13.50 (4/15/92) **88**
Chardonnay Russian River Valley 1989 Rel: $13 Cur: $16 (2/28/91) **89**
Chardonnay Russian River Valley 1988 Rel: $12 Cur: $15 (2/15/90) **85**
Chardonnay Russian River Valley 1987 Rel: $11.50 Cur: $16 (CH-4/90) **90**
Chardonnay Russian River Valley 1986 Rel: $11 Cur: $16 (CH-4/90) **87**
Chardonnay Russian River Valley 1985 Rel: $10 Cur: $19 (CH-5/90) **86**
Chardonnay Russian River Valley 1984 Rel: $10 Cur: $17 (CH-4/90) **86**
Chardonnay Russian River Valley 1983 Rel: $10 Cur: $17 (CH-4/90) **85**
Chardonnay Russian River Valley 1982 $10 (9/01/85) **55**
Chardonnay Russian River Valley The Montrachet Cuvée 1990 $18 (4/15/92) **87**
Merlot Sonoma County 1986 $13 (7/31/89) **83**
Merlot Sonoma County 1985 $10.50 (4/30/88) **89**
Merlot Sonoma County 1984 Rel: $12 Cur: $18 (6/15/87) SS **94**
Pinot Noir Russian River Valley 1989 $16.50 (3/31/92) **80**
Pinot Noir Russian River Valley 1987 $14 (2/15/90) **91**
Pinot Noir Russian River Valley 1986 $13 (5/31/89) **88**
Pinot Noir Russian River Valley 1985 $12 (2/15/88) **85**
Pinot Noir Russian River Valley 1984 $11 (6/30/87) **89**
Pinot Noir Russian River Valley 1983 $10 (8/31/86) **89**
Pinot Noir Russian River Valley 1982 $10 (10/01/85) **86**
Russian River Valley Young Vines1985 $9 (4/15/89) **68**
Zinfandel Sonoma County 1983 $8 (7/31/87) **73**

DEHOURS (France/Champagne)
Brut Champagne Reserve NV (NR) (12/31/91) **87**
Demi-Sec Champagne NV $30 (12/31/91) **84**

DEI (Italy/Tuscany)
Vino Nobile di Montepulciano Riserva 1985 $13 (4/15/90) **85**

DEINHARD (Germany)
Sparkling Riesling Lila Imperial NV $7 (8/31/89) BB **81**

DOMAINE MARCEL DEISS (France/Alsace)
Gewürztraminer Alsace Altenberg de Bergheim Vendange Tardive 1990 (NR) (2/15/92) (BT) **90+**
Gewürztraminer Alsace Bergheim 1990 $12 (2/15/92) **87**
Gewürztraminer Alsace St.-Hippolyte 1990 (NR) (2/15/92) **85**
Pinot Blanc Alsace Bennwihr 1990 $13 (2/15/92) **89**
Pinot Blanc Alsace Bergheim 1990 (NR) (2/15/92) **87**
Riesling Alsace Altenberg de Bergheim Vendange Tardive 1990 (NR) (2/15/92) (BT) **90+**
Riesling Alsace Bennwihr 1990 (NR) (2/15/92) **88**
Riesling Alsace Bergheim Engelgarten 1990 (NR) (2/15/92) **90**
Riesling Alsace Bergheim Engelgarten Vieilles Vignes 1990 (NR) (2/15/92) **93**
Riesling Alsace Graberg 1990 (NR) (2/15/92) **90**
Riesling Alsace St.-Hippolyte 1990 (NR) (2/15/92) **92**
Riesling Alsace Schoenenbourg Vendange Tardive 1990 (NR) (2/15/92) (BT) **85+**
Tokay Pinot Gris Alsace Bergheim 1990 $23 (2/15/92) **90**

DOMAINE DELACOUR (France/Burgundy)
Pouilly-Fuissé 1984 $18 (3/31/87) **84**

DELAFORCE (Portugal)
Vintage Port 1985 Rel: $24 Cur: $35 (VP-6/90) **81**
Vintage Port 1982 Rel: $20 Cur: $27 (VP-6/90) **69**
Vintage Port 1977 Rel: $11 Cur: $54 (VP-2/90) **80**
Vintage Port 1975 $43 (VP-2/90) **76**
Vintage Port 1970 $53 (VP-2/90) **89**
Vintage Port 1966 $75 (VP-2/90) **85**
Vintage Port 1963 $90 (VP-2/90) **93**
Vintage Port Quinta da Corte 1987 ($NA) (VP-2/90) **87**
Vintage Port Quinta da Corte 1984 ($NA) (VP-2/90) **84**
Vintage Port Quinta da Corte 1980 ($NA) (VP-2/90) **81**
Vintage Port Quinta da Corte 1978 $24 (VP-2/90) **80**

DELAMOTTE (France/Champagne)
Blanc de Blancs Champagne 1985 $43 (12/31/91) **87**
Blanc de Blancs Champagne 1982 $28 (4/15/88) **84**
Blanc de Blancs Champagne NV $24 (12/31/87) **79**
Brut Champagne NV $30 (12/31/91) **85**
Brut Rosé Champagne NV $38 (12/31/91) **88**
Rosé Champagne Spécial NV $28 (12/31/87) **91**

DOMAINE DELARCHE (France/Burgundy)
Corton-Charlemagne 1986 $65 (9/30/88) **85**
Pernand-Vergelesses 1989 $15/375ml (4/30/91) **82**
Pernand-Vergelesses Ile des Vergelesses 1985 $23 (10/15/88) **89**

MARIUS DELARCHE PERE & FILS (France/Burgundy)
Corton-Charlemagne 1989 $60 (8/31/91) **89**
Corton-Charlemagne 1988 $60 (7/31/90) **94**
Pernand-Vergelesses Blanc Ile des Vergelesses 1989 ($NA) (8/31/91) **80**

DELAS (France/Rhône)
Châteauneuf-du-Pape 1985 $17 (10/31/87) **91**
Châteauneuf-du-Pape 1983 $18 (10/15/91) **72**
Châteauneuf-du-Pape Blanc 1985 $18 (11/15/87) **73**
Châteauneuf-du-Pape Blanc Cuvée de Haute Pierre 1990 $21 (10/15/91) **80**
Châteauneuf-du-Pape Blanc Cuvée de Haute Pierre 1989 $20 (10/15/91) **79**
Châteauneuf-du-Pape Cuvée de Haute Pierre 1989 $16 (10/15/91) **90**
Châteauneuf-du-Pape Cuvée de Haute Pierre 1988 $17 (10/15/91) **86**
Châteauneuf-du-Pape Cuvée de Haute Pierre 1986 $20 (10/15/91) **86**
Châteauneuf-du-Pape Cuvée de Haute Pierre 1985 $20 (10/15/91) **86**
Côtes du Rhône St.-Esprit 1988 $6.75 (12/15/90) BB **84**
Côtes du Rhône St.-Esprit 1985 $5.50 (12/15/87) BB **80**
Crozes-Hermitage 1985 $7.50 (12/15/87) **78**

DELBECK (France/Champagne)
Brut Champagne Heritage NV (NR) (12/31/91) **84**

GEORGES DELEGER (France/Burgundy)
Chassagne-Montrachet 1986 $82 (12/15/88) **89**

DELICATO (United States/California)
Cabernet Sauvignon California 1985 $6 (6/30/88) **66**
Cabernet Sauvignon Carneros Napa Valley 1983 $10 (6/15/87) **72**
Chardonnay Napa Valley Barrel Fermented Golden Anniversary 1984 $10 (4/30/87) **87**
White Zinfandel California 1988 $5.25 (6/15/89) **73**

BERNARD DELMAS (France/Other)
Brut Blanquette de Limoux NV $14 (3/31/90) **79**

CHATEAU DEMERAULMONT (France/Bordeaux)
St.-Estèphe 1988 $10 (8/31/91) BB **82**

JAKOB DEMMER (Germany)
Riesling Spätlese Rheinpfalz Weingartener Trappenberg 1986 $5 (11/30/88) BB **88**

DEMOISELLE DE SOCIANDO-MALLET (France/Bordeaux)
Haut-Médoc 1989 $21 (3/15/92) **84**

DENMAN (Australia)
Cabernet Sauvignon Hunter Valley 1983 $5 (11/15/87) **76**
Chardonnay Hunter Valley Private Bin 1985 $6 (12/31/87) **80**

Key to Symbols

The scores reported here are the results of blind tastings conducted by our panel of senior editors. Wines that carry the initials below are results of individual tastings.

THE WINE SPECTATOR 100-POINT SCALE 95-100—Classic, a great wine; ***90-94***—Outstanding, superior character and style; ***80-89***—Good to very good, a wine with special qualities; ***70-79***—Average, drinkable wine that may have minor flaws; ***60-69***—Below average, drinkable but not recommended; ***50-59***—Poor, undrinkable, not recommended. "+"—With a score indicates a range; used primarily with barrel tastings to indicate a preliminary score.

SPECIAL DESIGNATIONS SS—Spectator Selection, CS—Cellar Selection, BB—Best Buy, ($NA)—Price not available, (NR)—Not released.

TASTER'S INITIALS (JG)—Jim Gordon, (HS)—Harvey Steiman, (JL)—James Laube, (JS)—James Suckling, (TM)—Thomas Matthews, (TR)—Terry Robards, (PM)—Per-Henrik Mansson, (BT)—Barrel Tasting (these wines were tasted blind from barrel samples), (CA-date)—*California's Great Cabernets* by James Laube, (CH-date)—*California's Great Chardonnays* by James Laube, (VP-date)—*Vintage Port* by James Suckling.

DATE TASTED Dates in parentheses represent the issue in which the rating was published.

M. DEOLIVEIRA (France/Chablis)
Chablis Les Clos 1985 $34 (8/31/87) **67**

A. DERVIEUX-THAIZE (France/Rhône)
Côte-Rôtie Côte Blonde la Garde Cuvée Réserve 1988 $42 (8/31/91) **79**

DOMAINE CLAUDINE DESCHAMPS (France/Burgundy)
Côte de Beaune Blanc 1989 ($NA) (8/31/91) **78**
Gevrey-Chambertin Bel-Air 1985 $28 (3/31/88) **87**

LUCIEN DESCHAUX (France/Bordeaux)
Bordeaux Rouge 1990 $6 (1/31/92) **75**
Châteauneuf-du-Pape Le Vieux Abbe 1987 $10 (12/31/91) **82**
Côtes du Ventoux La Cuvée du Chanoine 1990 $5.50 (1/31/92) **75**
Côtes du Ventoux Le Vieux Presbytere 1989 $6 (12/31/91) BB **80**
Médoc 1990 $8 (1/31/92) BB **80**
Pouilly-Fuissé La Cuvée du Maitre 1990 $14 (3/31/92) **64**

DESMEURE (France/Rhône)
Crozes-Hermitage Domaine des Remizières Cuvée Particulaire 1986 $8 (5/31/89) BB **84**
Hermitage Domaine des Remizières 1986 $19 (4/15/89) **68**

CHATEAU DESMIRAIL (France/Bordeaux)
Margaux 1989 $27 (3/15/92) **86**
Margaux 1988 $25 (6/30/89) (BT) **80+**
Margaux 1987 $18 (6/30/89) (BT) **70+**
Margaux 1986 $22 (6/30/89) **90**
Margaux 1985 $20 (5/15/87) (BT) **80+**

DESSILANI (Italy/Piedmont)
Barbera del Piemonte 1986 $7 (3/15/91) BB **87**
Caramino Riserva 1985 $13 (9/15/90) **79**

CHATEAU DESTIEUX (France/Bordeaux)
St.-Emilion 1988 $19 (6/30/91) **81**
St.-Emilion 1985 $14 (3/31/88) **84**

DEUTZ (France/Champagne)
Brut Blanc de Blancs Champagne 1985 $42 (12/31/90) **83**
Brut Blanc de Blancs Champagne 1982 $39 (5/31/87) **90**
Brut Champagne 1985 $40 (12/31/90) **83**
Brut Champagne NV $25 (12/31/91) **82**
Brut Champagne 150 Anniversaire NV $50 (12/31/88) **89**
Brut Champagne Cuvée Lallier Gold Lack NV $33 (12/31/90) **80**
Brut Champagne Cuvée William Deutz 1982 Rel: $61 Cur: $72 (12/31/89) **85**
Brut Champagne Cuvée William Deutz 1979 Rel: $35 Cur: $47 (7/16/85) **90**
Brut Champagne Georges Mathieu 1982 $40 (12/31/89) **89**
Brut Champagne Georges Mathieu Réserve 1985 $46 (12/31/90) **86**
Brut Rosé Champagne 1985 $46 (12/31/90) **88**
Brut Rosé Champagne 1982 $35 (12/31/87) **86**
Brut Rosé Champagne 1981 $27 (12/16/85) **67**

DEUX AMIS (United States/California)
Cabernet Sauvignon Dry Creek Valley 1987 $14 (11/15/91) **83**

VVE. A. DEVAUX (France/Champagne)
Brut Champagne Grande Réserve NV (NR) (12/31/91) **88**

DEVLIN (United States/California)
Cabernet Sauvignon Sonoma County 1981 $6 (8/01/85) **83**
Chardonnay Santa Cruz Mountains Meyley Vineyard 1989 $10 (7/15/91) **70**
Merlot Central Coast 1982 $8 (7/16/85) **80**

DOMAINE JEAN DEYDIER & FILS (France/Rhône)
Châteauneuf-du-Pape Blanc Les Clefs d'Or 1986 $17 (11/15/87) **74**
Châteauneuf-du-Pape Les Clefs d'Or 1983 $16 (10/31/87) **78**

DEZORMEAUX (France/Rhône)
Condrieu Viognier Côteaux du Colombier 1987 $37 (3/15/89) **87**

DIABLO VISTA (United States/California)
Merlot Dry Creek Valley 1981 $7.50 (5/01/84) **79**

DIAMOND CREEK (United States/California)
Cabernet Sauvignon Napa Valley Gravelly Meadow 1991 (NR) (5/15/92) (BT) **91+**
Cabernet Sauvignon Napa Valley Gravelly Meadow 1990 (NR) (5/15/91) (BT) **85+**
Cabernet Sauvignon Napa Valley Gravelly Meadow 1989 $50 (1/31/92) **83**
Cabernet Sauvignon Napa Valley Gravelly Meadow 1988 Rel: $40 Cur: $45 (11/15/90) **87**
Cabernet Sauvignon Napa Valley Gravelly Meadow 1987 Rel: $40 Cur: $45 (12/15/89) **90**
Cabernet Sauvignon Napa Valley Gravelly Meadow 1986 Rel: $30 Cur: $52 (CA-3/89) **94**
Cabernet Sauvignon Napa Valley Gravelly Meadow 1985 Rel: $30 Cur: $55 (CA-3/89) **92**
Cabernet Sauvignon Napa Valley Gravelly Meadow 1984 Rel: $25 Cur: $62 (CA-3/89) **94**
Cabernet Sauvignon Napa Valley Gravelly Meadow 1983 Rel: $20 Cur: $47 (CA-3/89) **89**
Cabernet Sauvignon Napa Valley Gravelly Meadow 1983 Rel: $20 Cur: $47 (2/01/86) CS **93**
Cabernet Sauvignon Napa Valley Gravelly Meadow 1982 Rel: $20 Cur: $66 (CA-3/89) **89**
Cabernet Sauvignon Napa Valley Gravelly Meadow 1981 Rel: $20 Cur: $67 (CA-3/89) **89**
Cabernet Sauvignon Napa Valley Gravelly Meadow 1980 Rel: $20 Cur: $60 (CA-3/89) **92**
Cabernet Sauvignon Napa Valley Gravelly Meadow 1979 Rel: $15 Cur: $100 (CA-3/89) **91**
Cabernet Sauvignon Napa Valley Gravelly Meadow 1978 Rel: $12.50 Cur: $115 (CA-3/89) **93**
Cabernet Sauvignon Napa Valley Gravelly Meadow 1977 Rel: $10 Cur: $61 (CA-3/89) **89**
Cabernet Sauvignon Napa Valley Gravelly Meadow 1976 Rel: $9 Cur: $90 (CA-3/89) **85**
Cabernet Sauvignon Napa Valley Gravelly Meadow 1975 Rel: $7.50 Cur: $80 (CA-3/89) **85**
Cabernet Sauvignon Napa Valley Gravelly Meadow 1974 Rel: $7.50 Cur: $144 (CA-3/89) **88**
Cabernet Sauvignon Napa Valley Gravelly Meadow Special Selection 1982 Rel: $20 Cur: $45 (CA-3/89) **84**
Cabernet Sauvignon Napa Valley Lake 1987 Rel: $100 Cur: $230 (11/15/90) **91**
Cabernet Sauvignon Napa Valley Lake 1984 Rel: $50 Cur: $250 (CA-3/89) **92**
Cabernet Sauvignon Napa Valley Lake 1978 Rel: $25 Cur: $480 (CA-3/89) **99**
Cabernet Sauvignon Napa Valley Red Rock Terrace 1991 (NR) (5/15/92) (BT) **87+**
Cabernet Sauvignon Napa Valley Red Rock Terrace 1990 (NR) (5/15/91) (BT) **85+**
Cabernet Sauvignon Napa Valley Red Rock Terrace 1989 $50 (1/31/92) **89**
Cabernet Sauvignon Napa Valley Red Rock Terrace 1988 Rel: $40 Cur: $45 (11/15/90) **89**
Cabernet Sauvignon Napa Valley Red Rock Terrace 1987 Rel: $40 Cur: $46 (12/15/89) **94**
Cabernet Sauvignon Napa Valley Red Rock Terrace 1986 Rel: $30 Cur: $48 (CA-3/89) **96**
Cabernet Sauvignon Napa Valley Red Rock Terrace 1985 Rel: $30 Cur: $55 (CA-3/89) **93**
Cabernet Sauvignon Napa Valley Red Rock Terrace 1984 Rel: $25 Cur: $65 (CA-3/89) **96**
Cabernet Sauvignon Napa Valley Red Rock Terrace 1984 Rel: $25 Cur: $65 (9/30/86) CS **95**
Cabernet Sauvignon Napa Valley Red Rock Terrace 1983 Rel: $20 Cur: $42 (CA-3/89) **88**
Cabernet Sauvignon Napa Valley Red Rock Terrace 1982 Rel: $20 Cur: $67 (CA-3/89) **87**
Cabernet Sauvignon Napa Valley Red Rock Terrace 1981 Rel: $20 Cur: $66 (CA-3/89) **91**
Cabernet Sauvignon Napa Valley Red Rock Terrace 1980 Rel: $20 Cur: $59 (CA-3/89) **86**
Cabernet Sauvignon Napa Valley Red Rock Terrace 1979 Rel: $15 Cur: $100 (CA-3/89) **92**
Cabernet Sauvignon Napa Valley Red Rock Terrace 1978 Rel: $12.50 Cur: $110 (CA-3/89) **92**
Cabernet Sauvignon Napa Valley Red Rock Terrace First Pick 1977 Rel: $10 Cur: $72 (CA-3/89) **88**

Cabernet Sauvignon Napa Valley Red Rock Terrace Second Pick 1977 Rel: $10 Cur: $45 (CA-3/89) **75**
Cabernet Sauvignon Napa Valley Red Rock Terrace 1976 Rel: $9 Cur: $95 (CA-3/89) **85**
Cabernet Sauvignon Napa Valley Red Rock Terrace 1975 Rel: $7.50 Cur: $87.5 (CA-3/89) **88**
Cabernet Sauvignon Napa Valley Red Rock Terrace 1972 Rel: $7.50 Cur: $200 (CA-3/89) **74**
Cabernet Sauvignon Napa Valley Red Rock Terrace Special Selection 1982 Rel: $20 Cur: $40 (CA-3/89) **80**
Cabernet Sauvignon Napa Valley Three Vineyard Blend 1985 Rel: $50 Cur: $100 (CA-3/89) **89**
Cabernet Sauvignon Napa Valley Three Vineyard Blend 1984 Rel: $50 Cur: $100 (CA-3/89) **89**
Cabernet Sauvignon Napa Valley Three Vineyard Blend 1981 Rel: $20 Cur: $100 (CA-3/89) **90**
Cabernet Sauvignon Napa Valley Volcanic Hill 1991 (NR) (5/15/92) (BT) **86+**
Cabernet Sauvignon Napa Valley Volcanic Hill 1990 (NR) (5/15/91) (BT) **85+**
Cabernet Sauvignon Napa Valley Volcanic Hill 1989 $50 (1/31/92) **86**
Cabernet Sauvignon Napa Valley Volcanic Hill 1988 Rel: $40 Cur: $44 (11/15/90) **88**
Cabernet Sauvignon Napa Valley Volcanic Hill 1987 Rel: $40 Cur: $44 (12/15/89) **95**
Cabernet Sauvignon Napa Valley Volcanic Hill 1986 Rel: $30 Cur: $63 (CA-3/89) **96**
Cabernet Sauvignon Napa Valley Volcanic Hill 1985 Rel: $30 Cur: $55 (CA-3/89) **93**
Cabernet Sauvignon Napa Valley Volcanic Hill 1984 Rel: $25 Cur: $60 (CA-3/89) **94**
Cabernet Sauvignon Napa Valley Volcanic Hill 1983 Rel: $20 Cur: $46 (CA-3/89) **89**
Cabernet Sauvignon Napa Valley Volcanic Hill 1982 Rel: $20 Cur: $69 (CA-3/89) **89**
Cabernet Sauvignon Napa Valley Volcanic Hill 1982 Rel: $20 Cur: $69 (12/16/84) CS **92**
Cabernet Sauvignon Napa Valley Volcanic Hill 1981 Rel: $20 Cur: $72 (CA-3/89) **92**
Cabernet Sauvignon Napa Valley Volcanic Hill 1980 Rel: $20 Cur: $67 (CA-3/89) **90**
Cabernet Sauvignon Napa Valley Volcanic Hill First Pick 1979 Rel: $15 Cur: $95 (CA-3/89) **95**
Cabernet Sauvignon Napa Valley Volcanic Hill Second Pick 1979 Rel: $15 Cur: $45 (CA-3/89) **82**
Cabernet Sauvignon Napa Valley Volcanic Hill 1978 Rel: $12.50 Cur: $110 (CA-3/89) **95**
Cabernet Sauvignon Napa Valley Volcanic Hill 1977 Rel: $10 Cur: $63 (CA-3/89) **84**
Cabernet Sauvignon Napa Valley Volcanic Hill 1976 Rel: $9 Cur: $47 (CA-3/89) **87**
Cabernet Sauvignon Napa Valley Volcanic Hill 1975 Rel: $7.50 Cur: $81 (CA-3/89) **93**
Cabernet Sauvignon Napa Valley Volcanic Hill 1974 Rel: $7.50 Cur: $138 (CA-3/89) **87**
Cabernet Sauvignon Napa Valley Volcanic Hill 1973 Rel: $7.50 Cur: $200 (CA-3/89) **80**
Cabernet Sauvignon Napa Valley Volcanic Hill 1972 Rel: $7.50 Cur: $200 (CA-3/89) **85**
Cabernet Sauvignon Napa Valley Volcanic Hill Special Selection 1982 Rel: $20 Cur: $40 (CA-3/89) **79**

J. DIAZ (Spain)
Madrid 1985 $5.75 (3/31/90) BB **85**

DICKERSON (United States/California)
Ruby Cabernet Napa Valley 1988 $9 (2/28/91) **79**

JEAN-PIERRE DICONNE (France/Burgundy)
Auxey-Duresses 1989 ($NA) (8/31/91) **84**
Meursault Clos des Luchets 1989 ($NA) (8/31/91) **87**
Meursault Les Narvaux 1989 ($NA) (8/31/91) **89**

DIEBOLT-VALLOIS (France/Champagne)
Brut Rosé Champagne Cramant NV $21 (10/31/87) **89**

SCHLOSSGUT DIEL (Germany)
Grauburgunder Tafelwein Nahe 1990 (NR) (12/15/91) **85**
Nahe Victor 1990 $33 (12/15/91) **88**
Riesling Auslese Nahe Dorsheimer Goldloch 1990 $33 (12/15/91) **88**
Riesling Auslese Nahe Gold Cap 1990 $52 (12/15/91) **91**
Riesling Eiswein Nahe 1990 (NR) (12/15/91) **94**
Riesling Kabinett Nahe 1990 $17 (12/15/91) **85**
Riesling Spätlese Nahe 1990 $18 (12/15/91) **86**
Riesling Spätlese Nahe Dorsheimer Pittersmännchen 1990 $24 (12/15/91) **89**

DIEVOLE (Italy/Tuscany)
Broccato 1987 $19 (12/15/91) **86**
Chianti Classico 1988 $13 (9/15/91) **85**
Chianti Classico Dieulele 1988 $22 (4/15/91) **91**
Chianti Classico Vigna Campi Nuovi 1988 $15 (4/15/91) **82**
Chianti Classico Vigna Campi Nuovi 1987 $10 (11/30/90) **84**
Chianti Classico Vigna Petrignano 1988 $12 (1/31/92) **84**
Chianti Classico Vigna Sessina 1988 $12 (1/31/92) **84**
Chianti Classico Villa Dievole 1987 $8 (12/15/90) **83**

DIEZ HERMANOS (Portugal)
Vintage Port 1977 ($NA) (VP-4/90) **82**

FRANCOIS DILIGENT (France/Champagne)
Brut Champagne Carte Blanche NV (NR) (12/31/91) **83**

DION (United States/California)
Chardonnay Sonoma Valley 1986 $10 (12/31/88) **78**

CHATEAU DOISY-DAENE (France/Sauternes)
Sauternes 1989 $27 (6/15/90) (BT) **85+**
Sauternes 1988 $34/375ml (11/15/91) **87**
Sauternes 1986 $35 (12/31/89) **68**
Sauternes 1985 $24 (5/31/88) **73**
Sauternes 1983 Rel: $21 Cur: $30 (1/31/88) **87**

CHATEAU DOISY-DUBROCA (France/Sauternes)
Barsac 1989 ($NA) (6/15/90) (BT) **90+**
Barsac 1988 $30 (6/15/90) (BT) **85+**

CHATEAU DOISY-VEDRINES (France/Sauternes)
Sauternes 1989 $46 (6/15/90) (BT) **90+**
Sauternes 1988 $31 (6/15/90) (BT) **90+**
Sauternes 1986 $19 (12/31/89) **86**
Sauternes 1983 Rel: $18 Cur: $29 (1/31/88) **73**

DOLAN (United States/California)
Cabernet Sauvignon Mendocino 1984 $12 (5/31/88) **88**
Cabernet Sauvignon Mendocino 1983 $12 (2/29/88) **86**
Chardonnay Mendocino 1987 $15 (12/31/88) **88**

R.W. DOLAN (United States/California)
Merlot California 1986 $8 (1/31/89) **88**

DOLCE (United States/California)
Late Harvest California 1989 $50/375ml (6/15/92) **91**

DOMAINE BRETON (United States/California)
Zinfandel Lake County 1989 $8 (2/29/92) **79**
Zinfandel Lake County 1988 $8 (2/15/91) **82**

DOMAINE CARNEROS (United States/California)
Brut Carneros NV $14 (11/15/90) **88**

DOMAINE CHANDON (United States/California)
Blanc de Noirs Napa-Sonoma Counties NV $15 (12/31/89) **80**
Blanc de Noirs Napa Valley NV $14 (5/31/89) **84**
Brut Napa-Sonoma Counties NV $15 (12/31/89) **80**
Brut Napa County Etoile NV $23 (12/31/91) **85**
Brut Napa Valley Club Cuvée NV $17 (6/15/91) **77**
Brut Napa Valley Reserve NV $19 (12/31/89) **81**
Brut Napa Valley Reserve NV $38/1.5L (5/31/89) **89**

DOMAINE CHARBAY (United States/California)
Dessert Chardonnay Sonoma County NV $5/Q (3/31/92) **71**

DOMAINE CHEURLIN (United States/New Mexico)
Brut New Mexico NV $12 (2/29/92) **82**
Extra Dry New Mexico NV $12 (2/29/92) **77**

DOMAINE DE CLARCK (United States/California)
Chardonnay Monterey County 1990 $14 (3/31/92) **86**
Chardonnay Monterey County Première 1989 $14 (4/15/91) **89**
Chardonnay Monterey County Première Réserve Unfiltered 1990 $20 (3/31/92) **86**
Pinot Noir Monterey County Villages 1990 $10 (3/31/92) **82**
Pinot Noir Monterey Première 1989 $15 (4/30/91) **77**
Pinot Noir Sonoma County Villages 1989 $10 (3/31/92) **72**

DOMAINE DE LA TERRE ROUGE (United States/California)
Sierra Foothills 1986 $12 (4/15/89) **89**

DOMAINE DROUHIN (United States/Oregon)
Pinot Noir Oregon 1989 $32 (1/31/92) **87**
Pinot Noir Oregon 1988 $32 (5/31/91) **89**

DOMAINE MICHEL (United States/California)
Cabernet Sauvignon Sonoma County 1989 (NR) (5/15/91) (BT) **85+**
Cabernet Sauvignon Sonoma County 1987 $19.50 (3/31/91) **84**
Cabernet Sauvignon Sonoma County 1986 $19 (6/30/90) **75**
Cabernet Sauvignon Sonoma County 1984 $19 (9/15/87) **86**
Cabernet Sauvignon Sonoma County Reserve 1989 (NR) (5/15/91) (BT) **85+**
Chardonnay Sonoma County 1989 $15 (6/15/92) **82**
Chardonnay Sonoma County 1988 $16 (3/31/91) **83**
Chardonnay Sonoma County 1987 $16 (6/30/90) **76**
Chardonnay Sonoma County 1986 $16 (12/31/88) **76**

DOMAINE NAPA (United States/California)
Cabernet Sauvignon Napa Valley 1985 $12 (12/15/88) **81**
Chardonnay California 1989 $8 (2/28/91) BB **82**
Chardonnay Napa Valley 1990 $14 (7/15/92) **82**
Chardonnay Napa Valley 1989 $12.50 (7/15/91) **77**
Chardonnay Napa Valley 1988 $12.50 (6/30/90) **81**
Chardonnay Napa Valley 1987 $12 (7/15/89) **80**
Chardonnay Napa Valley 1986 $9.50 (10/15/88) **82**
Chardonnay Napa Valley Barrel Fermented 1986 $14.50 (12/31/88) **73**
Merlot Napa Valley 1990 $14.50 (5/31/92) **84**

DOMAINE PHILIPPE (United States/California)
Cabernet Sauvignon Napa Valley Select Cuvée 1984 $6.50 (5/15/88) BB **87**

DOMAINE POTELLE (United States/California)
Chardonnay California 1987 $7 (4/15/89) **71**
Chardonnay California 1986 $6 (4/15/88) BB **80**

DOMAINE ST. GEORGE (United States/California)
Cabernet Sauvignon Russian River Valley Select Reserve 1986 $9 (5/31/90) **79**
Cabernet Sauvignon Sonoma County 1988 $6 (11/15/90) BB **83**
Chardonnay Sonoma County 1986 $4.50 (12/31/87) **77**
Chardonnay Sonoma County 1984 $5 (12/16/85) BB **91**
Chardonnay Sonoma County Select Reserve 1988 $9 (6/30/90) **79**
Chardonnay Sonoma County Select Reserve Barrel Fermented Barrel Aged 1987 $8 (12/31/88) BB **86**
Zinfandel California 1989 $5 (2/15/91) **77**

DOMAINE STE. MICHELLE (United States/Washington)
Blanc de Blancs Columbia Valley 1986 $15 (12/31/90) **85**
Blanc de Noirs Columbia Valley 1986 $17 (1/31/92) **80**
Blanc de Noirs Columbia Valley 1985 $20 (12/31/90) **86**
Brut Columbia Valley NV $10 (12/31/90) **78**
Brut Columbia Valley Champagne NV $9 (1/31/92) BB **84**

DOMAINE SAN MARTIN (United States/California)
Cabernet Sauvignon Central Coast 1981 $7.75 (10/01/85) **76**
Chardonnay Central Coast 1984 $7 (4/16/86) **66**
Chardonnay Central Coast 1983 $7 (8/01/85) **85**

LE DOMAINE (United States/California)
Brut California NV $5 (2/28/89) **67**

CHATEAU LA DOMINIQUE (France/Bordeaux)
St.-Emilion 1990 (NR) (4/30/91) (BT) **90+**
St.-Emilion 1989 $32 (3/15/92) **91**
St.-Emilion 1988 $25 (6/30/91) **86**
St.-Emilion 1987 $20 (6/30/89) (BT) **80+**
St.-Emilion 1986 $29 (6/30/89) **95**
St.-Emilion 1985 $30 (3/31/88) **83**
St.-Emilion 1983 Rel: $18 Cur: $32 (5/16/86) **88**
St.-Emilion 1979 $27 (10/15/89) (JS) **81**

EL DOMINO (Spain)
Jumilla 1990 $7 (4/15/92) BB **80**

DOMINUS (United States/California)
Napa Valley 1987 $45 (11/15/91) **89**
Napa Valley 1986 $45 (2/28/91) **91**
Napa Valley 1985 Rel: $45 Cur: $55 (2/15/90) **84**
Napa Valley 1984 Rel: $40 Cur: $55 (5/15/88) CS **90**
Napa Valley 1983 Rel: $43 Cur: $52 (4/15/89) **86**

CHATEAU DOMS (France/Bordeaux)
Graves Blanc 1985 $7 (4/30/87) **70**

CHATEAU DONA BAISSAS (France/Other)
Côtes du Roussillon-Villages 1990 $8 (3/31/92) **79**
Côtes du Roussillon-Villages 1988 $7 (10/15/90) **77**

DONNA MARIA (United States/California)
Pinot Noir Chalk Hill 1981 $6 (9/16/84) **79**

DOPFF & IRION (France/Alsace)
Gewürztraminer Alsace 1989 ($NA) (11/15/90) **81**
Gewürztraminer Alsace 1988 $11 (10/15/89) **82**
Gewürztraminer Alsace Cuvée René Dopff 1990 (NR) (2/15/92) **84**
Gewürztraminer Alsace Cuvée René Dopff 1989 ($NA) (11/15/90) **80**

Gewürztraminer Alsace Les Sorcières 1990 (NR) (2/15/92) **85**
Gewürztraminer Alsace Sporen 1990 (NR) (2/15/92) **86**
Gewürztraminer Alsace Vendange Tardive 1990 (NR) (2/15/92) (BT) **90+**
Muscat Alsace Les Amandiers 1990 (NR) (2/15/92) **73**
Pinot Blanc Alsace 1989 ($NA) (11/15/90) **84**
Pinot Blanc Alsace Cuvée René Dopff 1990 (NR) (2/15/92) **85**
Pinot Blanc Alsace Cuvée René Dopff 1988 ($NA) (10/15/89) **82**
Riesling Alsace 1989 ($NA) (11/15/90) **81**
Riesling Alsace Cuvée René Dopff 1990 (NR) (2/15/92) **82**
Riesling Alsace Cuvée René Dopff 1988 $9.25 (10/15/89) **85**
Riesling Alsace Les Murailles 1990 (NR) (2/15/92) **83**
Riesling Alsace Les Murailles 1989 ($NA) (11/15/90) **80**
Riesling Alsace Les Murailles 1988 ($NA) (10/15/89) **79**
Riesling Alsace Schoenenbourg 1990 (NR) (2/15/92) **87**
Riesling Alsace Schoenenbourg 1989 ($NA) (11/15/90) **81**
Riesling Alsace Vendange Tardive 1990 (NR) (2/15/92) (BT) **90+**
Riesling Alsace Vendange Tardive 1988 ($NA) (10/15/89) **87**
Tokay Pinot Gris Alsace Cuvée René Dopff 1990 (NR) (2/15/92) **91**
Tokay Pinot Gris Alsace Cuvée René Dopff 1989 ($NA) (11/15/90) **85**
Tokay Pinot Gris Alsace Cuvée René Dopff 1988 $10 (10/15/89) **79**
Tokay Pinot Gris Alsace Les Maquisards 1990 (NR) (2/15/92) **86**
Tokay Pinot Gris Alsace Les Maquisards 1989 ($NA) (11/15/90) **87**
Tokay Pinot Gris Alsace Sporen 1990 (NR) (2/15/92) **86**
Tokay Pinot Gris Alsace Vendange Tardive 1990 (NR) (2/15/92) (BT) **85+**

DOPFF AU MOULIN (France/Alsace)
Gewürztraminer Alsace 1989 $14 (11/15/90) **82**
Gewürztraminer Alsace 1988 ($NA) (10/15/89) **84**
Gewürztraminer Alsace Brand 1988 ($NA) (10/15/89) **82**
Gewürztraminer Alsace Brand de Turckheim 1990 (NR) (2/15/92) **87**
Gewürztraminer Alsace Réserve 1990 (NR) (2/15/92) **84**
Gewürztraminer Alsace Réserve 1989 $13 (11/15/90) **87**
Gewürztraminer Alsace de Riquewihr 1990 (NR) (2/15/92) **84**
Gewürztraminer Alsace Sélection de Grains Nobles 1990 (NR) (2/15/92) (BT) **90+**
Gewürztraminer Alsace Sélection de Grains Nobles 1989 ($NA) (11/15/90) **94**
Gewürztraminer Alsace Vendange Tardive 1989 ($NA) (11/15/90) **81**
Gewürztraminer Alsace Vendange Tardive 1988 ($NA) (10/15/89) **90**
Riesling Alsace 1988 ($NA) (10/15/89) **84**
Riesling Alsace Propre Récolte 1989 ($NA) (11/15/90) **79**
Riesling Alsace Réserve 1990 (NR) (2/15/92) **85**
Riesling Alsace Réserve 1989 $12 (9/15/91) **82**
Riesling Alsace de Riquewihr 1990 (NR) (2/15/92) **87**
Riesling Alsace Schoenenbourg 1990 (NR) (2/15/92) **90**
Riesling Alsace Schoenenbourg 1989 ($NA) (11/15/90) **78**
Riesling Alsace Sélection de Grains Nobles 1989 ($NA) (11/15/90) **95**
Riesling Alsace Vendange Tardive 1989 ($NA) (11/15/90) **86**
Riesling Alsace Vendange Tardive 1988 ($NA) (10/15/89) **83**
Tokay Pinot Gris Alsace 1988 ($NA) (10/15/89) **86**
Tokay Pinot Gris Alsace Sélection de Grains Nobles 1989 ($NA) (11/15/90) **87**
Tokay Pinot Gris Alsace Sélection de Grains Nobles 1988 ($NA) (10/15/89) **87**

DORE (United States/California)
Cabernet Sauvignon California 1984 $5 (12/31/87) **64**
Cabernet Sauvignon California Limited Release Lot 102 1987 $8.50 (11/15/91) **80**
Chardonnay California Limited Release Lot 101 1989 $8.50 (7/15/91) **74**
Chardonnay Santa Maria Valley Signature Selections 1984 $5 (4/16/86) **85**

GIROLAMO DORIGO (Italy/North)
Montsclapade 1987 $25 (2/15/91) **84**

DOUDET-NAUDIN (France/Burgundy)
Corton Renardes 1945 ($NA) (8/31/90) (TR) **86**

LES DOUELLES (France/Bordeaux)
Bordeaux 1982 $3 (10/01/85) BB **79**

PIERRE DOURTHE (France/Bordeaux)
Bordeaux Blanc 1987 $10 (9/30/88) **83**
Bordeaux Blanc Sémillon 1990 $4 (6/15/91) **75**

DOW (Portugal)
Tawny Port 20 Year Old NV $23 (2/28/90) (JS) **82**
Vintage Port 1985 Rel: $30 Cur: $36 (VP-6/90) **89**
Vintage Port 1983 Rel: $20 Cur: $34 (VP-6/90) **94**
Vintage Port 1980 Rel: $15 Cur: $41 (VP-6/90) **90**
Vintage Port 1977 Rel: $12 Cur: $57 (VP-4/90) **94**
Vintage Port 1975 $44 (VP-4/89) **80**
Vintage Port 1972 $36 (VP-1/90) **79**
Vintage Port 1970 $70 (VP-12/89) **94**
Vintage Port 1966 $85 (VP-12/89) **94**
Vintage Port 1963 $112 (VP-2/90) **92**
Vintage Port 1960 $96 (VP-2/90) **88**
Vintage Port 1955 $190 (VP-4/90) **91**
Vintage Port 1950 $110 (VP-11/89) **86**
Vintage Port 1947 $340 (VP-11/89) **88**
Vintage Port 1945 $340 (VP-11/89) **89**
Vintage Port 1935 $330 (VP-6/90) **79**
Vintage Port 1934 $260 (VP-6/90) **84**
Vintage Port 1927 $480 (VP-4/90) **87**
Vintage Port Quinta do Bomfim 1989 Rel: $24 Cur: $29 (11/30/91) CS **90**
Vintage Port Quinta do Bomfim 1987 ($NA) (VP-2/90) **86**
Vintage Port Quinta do Bomfim 1986 ($NA) (VP-2/90) **82**
Vintage Port Quinta do Bomfim 1984 ($NA) (VP-2/90) **86**
Vintage Port Quinta do Bomfim 1982 ($NA) (VP-2/90) **82**
Vintage Port Quinta do Bomfim 1979 $28 (VP-2/90) **81**
Vintage Port Quinta do Bomfim 1978 Rel: $27 Cur: $33 (VP-2/90) **85**
Vintage Port Quinta do Bomfim 1965 ($NA) (VP-6/90) **87**

CHATEAU DE DRACY (France/Burgundy)
Bourgogne Pinot Noir 1988 $8 (2/28/90) **68**

CASCINO DRAGO (Italy/Piedmont)
Bricco del Drago Vigna delle Mace 1987 $17 (1/31/92) **75**
Bricco del Drago Vigna delle Mace 1986 $22 (1/31/92) **81**
Bricco del Drago Vigna delle Mace 1985 $22 (1/31/89) **79**
Bricco del Drago Vigna delle Mace 1982 $14 (11/30/87) **84**
Campo Romano 1990 $14 (1/31/92) **73**

ANDRE DRAPPIER (France/Champagne)
Brut Blanc de Blancs Champagne NV $30 (5/31/87) **76**
Brut Blanc de Blancs Champagne Signature NV $23 (2/01/86) **86**
Brut Champagne Carte d'Or NV $39 (12/31/91) **89**
Brut Rosé Champagne Val des Demoiselles 1981 $23 (12/16/85) **72**

DREYER SONOMA (United States/California)
Chardonnay Carneros 1990 $15 (6/30/92) **85**

GIOVANNI DRI (Italy/North)
Refosco Colli Orientali del Friuli 1986 $11 (9/15/89) **82**

JEAN-PAUL DROIN (France/Chablis)
Chablis 1987 ($NA) (3/31/89) **80**
Chablis Les Clos 1987 $38 (3/31/89) **93**
Chablis Les Clos 1986 $32 (5/15/88) **87**
Chablis Fourchaume 1987 $24 (3/31/89) **87**
Chablis Fourchaume 1986 $17 (7/15/88) **85**
Chablis Les Grenouilles 1987 $40 (3/31/89) **82**
Chablis Les Montains 1987 $24 (3/31/89) **89**
Chablis Montée de Tonnerre 1987 $24 (3/31/89) **90**
Chablis Montée de Tonnerre 1986 $21 (5/15/88) **90**
Chablis Les Vaillons 1987 $24 (3/31/89) **91**
Chablis Valmur 1987 $38 (3/31/89) **86**
Chablis Vaudésir 1987 $38 (3/31/89) **90**
Chablis Vosgros 1987 $24 (3/31/89) **81**

JOSEPH DROUHIN (France/Burgundy)
Aloxe-Corton 1989 $27 (1/31/92) **89**
Aloxe-Corton 1988 $37 (7/15/90) (BT) **75+**
Aloxe-Corton 1986 $25 (4/30/89) **83**
Aloxe-Corton 1985 $23 (11/15/87) **90**
Auxey-Duresses 1989 $22 (8/31/91) **84**
Bâtard-Montrachet 1990 $128 (5/15/92) **90**
Bâtard-Montrachet 1989 $155 (8/31/91) **90**
Bâtard-Montrachet 1987 $98 (3/31/89) **90**
Bâtard-Montrachet 1986 $113 (12/31/88) **94**
Bâtard-Montrachet 1985 $95 (2/29/88) **95**
Bâtard-Montrachet 1984 $65 (2/29/88) **92**
Beaune Blanc Clos des Mouches 1990 $64 (5/15/92) CS **92**
Beaune Blanc Clos des Mouches 1988 $64 (7/31/90) **90**
Beaune Blanc Clos des Mouches 1987 Rel: $48 Cur: $53 (4/30/89) **81**
Beaune Blanc Clos des Mouches 1986 $56 (12/15/88) **87**
Beaune Clos des Mouches 1989 Rel: $40 Cur: $46 (2/29/92) **92**
Beaune Clos des Mouches 1988 $50 (2/15/91) **88**
Beaune Clos des Mouches 1987 $47 (6/15/90) **83**
Beaune Clos des Mouches 1986 $38 (11/15/87) (BT) **7894+**
Beaune Les Grèves 1989 $47 (1/31/92) **88**
Beaune Les Grèves 1959 $90 (8/31/90) (TR) **80**
Bonnes Mares 1989 $99 (1/31/92) **93**
Bourgogne Blanc Chardonnay Laforêt 1989 $9 (4/30/91) BB **82**
Bourgogne Blanc Chardonnay Laforêt 1988 $8.75 (9/30/89) **79**
Bourgogne Blanc Chardonnay Laforêt 1986 $8.50 (1/31/88) **81**
Bourgogne Blanc Chardonnay Laforêt 1985 $8.25 (3/31/87) **85**
Bourgogne Blanc Chardonnay Laforêt 1983 $7.50 (6/01/86) **61**
Bourgogne Pinot Noir Laforêt 1989 $9 (4/30/91) BB **85**
Bourgogne Pinot Noir Laforêt 1988 $10 (3/31/91) BB **84**
Bourgogne Pinot Noir Laforêt 1987 $8.75 (6/15/89) **78**
Bourgogne Pinot Noir Laforêt 1985 $8.50 (11/15/87) **78**
Bourgogne Pinot Noir Laforêt 1983 $7.50 (11/01/85) **71**
Chablis 1988 $18 (3/31/90) **72**
Chablis 1987 $14 (3/31/89) **84**
Chablis 1986 $14 (5/15/88) **83**
Chablis Bougros 1986 $33 (5/15/88) **87**
Chablis Les Clos 1986 $31 (3/31/89) **95**
Chablis Les Montmains 1989 $23 (2/28/91) **86**
Chablis Les Montmains 1987 $22 (3/31/89) **83**
Chablis Premier Cru 1987 $20 (3/31/89) **87**
Chablis Premier Cru 1986 $20 (5/15/88) **85**
Chablis Les Roncières 1987 $23 (3/31/89) **91**
Chablis Les Suchots 1987 $20 (3/31/89) **89**
Chablis Vaudésir 1989 $54 (2/28/91) **89**
Chablis Vaudésir 1988 $38 (3/31/90) **87**
Chablis Vaudésir 1986 $34 (3/31/89) **92**
Chablis Domaine de Vaudon 1989 $30 (8/31/91) **84**
Chambertin 1989 $114 (1/31/92) **90**
Chambertin 1988 $112 (2/15/91) **94**
Chambertin 1986 $80 (2/28/89) **90**
Chambertin 1985 Rel: $75 Cur: $102 (11/15/87) **95**
Chambolle-Musigny 1989 $41 (1/31/92) **91**
Chambolle-Musigny 1988 $38 (7/15/90) (BT) **85+**
Chambolle-Musigny 1986 $27 (7/31/88) **88**
Chambolle-Musigny 1985 $33 (11/15/87) **93**
Chambolle-Musigny Les Amoureuses 1988 $76 (12/31/90) **87**
Chambolle-Musigny Les Amoureuses 1955 $250 (8/31/90) (TR) **65**
Chambolle-Musigny Les Baudes 1989 $52 (1/31/92) **89**
Chambolle-Musigny Feusselottes 1989 (NR) (1/31/92) **92**
Chambolle-Musigny Premier Cru 1989 (NR) (1/31/92) **89**
Chambolle-Musigny Les Sentiers 1989 (NR) (1/31/92) **92**
Charmes-Chambertin 1989 $80 (1/31/92) **92**
Charmes-Chambertin 1988 $65 (11/15/90) **93**
Charmes-Chambertin 1986 Rel: $56 Cur: $60 (2/28/89) CS **91**
Charmes-Chambertin 1985 $60 (11/15/87) **89**
Chassagne-Montrachet 1990 $36 (5/15/92) **85**

Key to Symbols

The scores reported here are the results of blind tastings conducted by our panel of senior editors. Wines that carry the initials below are results of individual tastings.

THE WINE SPECTATOR 100-POINT SCALE 95-100—Classic, a great wine; ***90-94***—Outstanding, superior character and style; ***80-89***—Good to very good, a wine with special qualities; ***70-79***—Average, drinkable wine that may have minor flaws; ***60-69***—Below average, drinkable but not recommended; ***50-59***—Poor, undrinkable, not recommended. "+"—With a score indicates a range; used primarily with barrel tastings to indicate a preliminary score.

SPECIAL DESIGNATIONS SS—Spectator Selection, CS—Cellar Selection, BB—Best Buy, ($NA)—Price not available, (NR)—Not released.

TASTER'S INITIALS (JG)—Jim Gordon, (HS)—Harvey Steiman, (JL)—James Laube, (JS)—James Suckling, (TM)—Thomas Matthews, (TR)—Terry Robards, (PM)—Per-Henrik Mansson, (BT)—Barrel Tasting (these wines were tasted blind from barrel samples), (CA-date)—*California's Great Cabernets* by James Laube, (CH-date)—*California's Great Chardonnays* by James Laube, (VP-date)—*Vintage Port* by James Suckling.

DATE TASTED Dates in parentheses represent the issue in which the rating was published.

Chassagne-Montrachet 1989 $50 (8/31/91) **88**
Chassagne-Montrachet 1988 $39 (3/31/90) **87**
Chassagne-Montrachet 1987 $39 (3/15/89) **82**
Chassagne-Montrachet 1986 $35 (6/30/88) **84**
Chassagne-Montrachet 1982 $22 (10/01/84) **87**
Chassagne-Montrachet Clos St.-Jean 1989 ($NA) (8/31/91) **88**
Chassagne-Montrachet Marquis de Laguiche 1989 $58 (2/15/91) **90**
Chassagne-Montrachet Marquis de Laguiche 1987 Rel: $48 Cur: $61 (3/15/89) **84**
Chassagne-Montrachet Marquis de Laguiche 1986 $43 (5/31/88) **91**
Chassagne-Montrachet Marquis de Laguiche 1985 $40 (2/29/88) **93**
Chassagne-Montrachet Marquis de Laguiche 1983 $35 (2/29/88) **91**
Chassagne-Montrachet Rouge 1989 $23 (1/31/92) **87**
Chevalier-Montrachet 1989 $110 (8/31/91) **95**
Chevalier-Montrachet 1985 $100 (4/30/87) **84**
Clos de la Roche 1989 $77 (1/31/92) **88**
Clos de la Roche 1988 $73 (2/15/91) **93**
Clos de la Roche 1986 $53 (7/31/88) **85**
Clos de la Roche 1985 $60 (11/15/87) **97**
Clos St.-Denis 1989 $76 (1/31/92) **91**
Clos de Vougeot 1988 $85 (2/15/91) **90**
Clos de Vougeot 1986 $55 (4/15/89) **86**
Clos de Vougeot 1985 $57 (11/15/87) **94**
Corton 1988 $64 (7/15/90) (BT) **85+**
Corton 1985 $48 (11/15/87) **92**
Corton-Bressandes 1988 $60 (11/15/90) **92**
Corton-Bressandes 1986 $45 (4/30/89) **90**
Corton-Charlemagne 1990 $75 (5/15/92) **92**
Corton-Charlemagne 1989 $92 (8/31/91) **97**
Corton-Charlemagne 1987 $90 (3/31/89) **90**
Corton-Charlemagne 1986 $98 (12/15/88) **90**
Corton-Charlemagne 1985 $78 (4/30/87) **94**
Côte de Beaune-Villages 1986 $13 (6/15/89) **78**
Côte de Beaune-Villages 1985 $14 (11/15/87) **85**
Côte de Nuits-Villages 1985 $19 (11/15/87) **86**
Echézeaux 1988 $60 (11/15/90) **93**
Echézeaux 1986 $60 (7/31/88) **92**
Gevrey-Chambertin 1988 $41 (7/15/90) (BT) **75+**
Gevrey-Chambertin 1986 $27 (2/28/89) **83**
Gevrey-Chambertin 1985 $33 (11/15/87) **91**
Gevrey-Chambertin Les Cazetiers 1989 $70 (1/31/92) **91**
Gevrey-Chambertin Lavaux St.-Jacques 1989 $70 (1/31/92) **86**
Grands Echézeaux 1989 $114 (1/31/92) **91**
Grands Echézeaux 1985 $75 (11/15/87) **93**
Griotte-Chambertin 1989 $90 (1/31/92) **91**
Griotte-Chambertin 1988 $81 (11/15/90) **91**
Griotte-Chambertin 1986 $81 (7/31/88) **92**
Griotte-Chambertin 1985 $68 (11/15/87) **95**
Latricières-Chambertin 1988 $72 (2/15/91) **87**
Maranges Première Cru 1989 $20 (1/31/92) **85**
Mazis-Chambertin 1989 $86 (1/31/92) **92**
Mercurey 1985 $17 (11/15/87) **83**
Meursault 1990 $32 (5/15/92) **91**
Meursault 1989 $45 (8/31/91) **90**
Meursault 1988 $34 (3/31/90) **89**
Meursault 1986 $29 (5/31/88) **83**
Meursault Les Charmes 1990 $48 (5/15/92) **90**
Meursault Les Charmes 1989 $65 (8/31/91) **91**
Meursault Les Genevrières 1989 $60 (8/31/91) **86**
Meursault Les Perrières 1990 $48 (5/15/92) **87**
Meursault Les Perrières 1989 $60 (8/31/91) **87**
Meursault Les Perrières 1988 $48 (3/31/90) **88**
Meursault Les Perrières 1987 $44 (4/30/89) **80**
Meursault Les Perrières 1986 $41 (5/31/88) **88**
Meursault Les Perrières 1985 $40 (4/30/87) **87**
Montagny 1986 $15 (6/15/88) **83**
Montrachet Marquis de Laguiche 1989 $360 (8/31/91) **98**
Montrachet Marquis de Laguiche 1988 Rel: $180 Cur: $230 (2/28/91) **95**
Montrachet Marquis de Laguiche 1987 Rel: $180 Cur: $200 (10/15/90) **95**
Montrachet Marquis de Laguiche 1986 Rel: $200 Cur: $240 (10/31/88) CS **97**
Montrachet Marquis de Laguiche 1985 Rel: $142 Cur: $300 (2/29/88) **100**
Montrachet Marquis de Laguiche 1979 $250 (2/29/88) **97**
Morey-St.-Denis Clos Sorbé 1989 (NR) (1/31/92) **86**
Morey-St.-Denis Monts-Luisants 1988 $38 (2/28/91) **92**
Nuits-St.-Georges 1989 $43 (7/15/90) (BT) **85+**
Nuits-St.-Georges 1986 $25 (4/30/89) **86**
Nuits-St.-Georges 1985 $29 (11/15/87) **92**
Nuits-St.-Georges Les Boudots 1989 $70 (1/31/92) **80**
Nuits-St.-Georges Les Roncières 1986 $38 (4/30/89) **85**
Nuits-St.-Georges Les Roncières 1985 $38 (11/15/87) **93**
Pernand-Vergelesses 1985 $17 (11/15/87) **91**
Pernand-Vergelesses Blanc 1989 $23 (8/31/91) **86**
Pommard 1989 $43 (1/31/92) **85**
Pommard 1988 $40 (7/15/90) (BT) **85+**
Pommard 1986 $27 (4/30/89) **87**
Pommard 1985 $33 (11/15/87) **93**
Pommard 1981 $28 (9/01/84) **83**
Pommard Epenottes 1989 $56 (1/31/92) **89**
Pommard Epenottes 1988 $55 (7/15/90) (BT) **85+**
Pommard Epenottes 1986 $40 (7/31/88) **83**
Pommard Epenottes 1985 $41 (11/15/87) **95**
Pommard Rugiens 1989 $56 (1/31/92) **87**
Pouilly-Fuissé 1987 $18 (4/30/89) **83**
Pouilly-Fuissé 1986 $18 (6/30/88) **76**
Puligny-Montrachet 1990 $36 (5/15/92) **81**
Puligny-Montrachet 1989 $50 (8/31/91) **83**
Puligny-Montrachet 1988 $39 (3/15/90) **78**
Puligny-Montrachet 1987 $38 (4/15/89) **87**
Puligny-Montrachet 1986 $34 (2/29/88) **88**
Puligny-Montrachet 1984 $27 (2/29/88) **83**
Puligny-Montrachet Clos de la Garenne 1989 $67 (8/31/91) **90**
Puligny-Montrachet Clos de la Garenne 1987 $44 (4/15/89) **81**
Puligny-Montrachet Clos de la Garenne 1986 $40 (6/15/88) **89**
Puligny-Montrachet Les Folatières 1990 $60 (5/15/92) **85**
Puligny-Montrachet Les Folatières 1989 $67 (8/31/91) **94**
Puligny-Montrachet Les Folatières 1987 $44 (4/15/89) **78**
Puligny-Montrachet Les Folatières 1986 Rel: $40 Cur: $48 (5/31/88) **91**
Puligny-Montrachet Les Folatières 1985 $35 (2/29/88) **88**
Puligny-Montrachet Les Pucelles 1990 $64 (5/15/92) **86**
Puligny-Montrachet Les Pucelles 1989 $68 (8/31/91) **84**
Puligny-Montrachet Les Pucelles 1986 $50 (2/29/88) **90**
Puligny-Montrachet Les Pucelles 1985 $50 (4/30/87) **92**
Romanée-St.-Vivant 1989 (NR) (1/31/92) **92**
Rully Blanc 1989 $18 (2/28/91) **86**
Rully Blanc 1987 $15 (4/30/89) **81**
Rully Blanc 1986 $14 (6/15/88) **88**
St.-Aubin 1987 $21 (4/15/89) **81**
St.-Aubin 1986 $20 (10/15/88) **82**
St.-Romain 1989 $22 (8/31/91) **84**
St.-Véran 1989 $16 (2/28/91) **85**
Santenay 1989 $44 (1/31/92) **87**
Santenay 1985 $17 (11/15/87) **88**
Savigny-lès-Beaune 1989 $23 (1/31/92) **87**
Savigny-lès-Beaune 1988 $22 (7/15/90) (BT) **80+**
Savigny-lès-Beaune 1985 Rel: $21 Cur: $25 (11/15/87) SS **91**
Savigny-lès-Beaune 1981 $16 (9/01/84) **79**
Volnay 1989 $43 (7/15/90) (BT) **80+**
Volnay 1988 $36 (7/15/90) (BT) **80+**
Volnay 1985 $29 (11/15/87) **88**
Volnay Chevret 1989 (NR) (1/31/92) **90**
Volnay Clos des Chênes 1989 $50 (1/31/92) **91**
Volnay Clos des Chênes 1988 $45 (2/15/91) **85**
Volnay Clos des Chênes 1987 $30 (6/15/90) **85**
Volnay Clos des Chênes 1986 $31 (4/30/89) **80**
Vosne-Romanée Les Beaumonts 1989 $70 (1/31/92) **91**
Vosne-Romanée Les Beaumonts 1988 $56 (3/31/91) **80**
Vosne-Romanée Les Beaumonts 1985 Rel: $42 Cur: $53 (11/15/87) **93**
Vosne-Romanée Les Suchots 1989 $70 (1/31/92) **89**
Vosne-Romanée Les Suchots 1988 $57 (2/28/91) **90**
Vosne-Romanée Les Suchots 1985 $42 (11/15/87) **94**

ROBERT DROUHIN (France/Burgundy)
Clos de Vougeot 1989 $88 (1/31/92) **89**

DROUHIN-LAROZE (France/Burgundy)
Bonnes Mares 1988 $81 (12/31/90) **93**
Bonnes Mares 1987 $38 (3/31/90) **89**
Chambertin Clos de Bèze 1988 $88 (12/31/90) **92**
Chambertin Clos de Bèze 1987 $40 (3/31/90) **90**
Chambertin Clos de Bèze 1985 Rel: $70 Cur: $110 (10/15/88) **92**
Chapelle-Chambertin 1988 $68 (12/31/90) **88**
Clos de Vougeot 1988 $81 (12/31/90) **89**
Clos de Vougeot 1987 $38 (3/31/90) **79**
Clos de Vougeot 1985 $60 (10/15/88) **88**
Gevrey-Chambertin Clos Prieur 1988 $44 (12/31/90) **88**
Gevrey-Chambertin Lavaux-St.-Jacques 1988 $44 (12/31/90) **80**
Latricières-Chambertin 1988 $68 (12/31/90) **91**
Latricières-Chambertin 1987 $36 (3/31/90) **88**
Mazis-Chambertin 1985 $47 (10/15/88) **90**

DRY CREEK (United States/California)
Cabernet Sauvignon Sonoma County 1989 $14 (3/31/92) **86**
Cabernet Sauvignon Sonoma County 1988 $14 (5/31/91) **81**
Cabernet Sauvignon Sonoma County 1987 $12.50 (4/15/90) **84**
Cabernet Sauvignon Sonoma County 1986 $11 (3/31/89) **88**
Cabernet Sauvignon Sonoma County 1985 Rel: $11 Cur: $16 (5/31/88) SS **91**
Cabernet Sauvignon Sonoma County 1984 $10 (5/15/87) **85**
Cabernet Sauvignon Sonoma County 1982 $9.50 (2/01/85) **81**
Cabernet Sauvignon Sonoma County 1980 $9.50 (4/16/84) **78**
Cabernet Sauvignon Sonoma County Special Reserve 1980 $13 (5/01/86) **78**
Chardonnay Dry Creek Valley Reserve 1990 $20 (7/15/92) **83**
Chardonnay Sonoma County Reserve 1988 $20 (7/15/91) **85**
Chardonnay Dry Creek Valley Reserve 1987 $18 (4/15/90) **91**
Chardonnay Dry Creek Valley Reserve 1986 $18 (11/30/89) **86**
Chardonnay Dry Creek Valley Reserve David S. Stare 1985 $15 (10/15/88) **82**
Chardonnay Dry Creek Valley Reserve David S. Stare 1984 $15 (12/31/86) **75**
Chardonnay Dry Creek Valley David S. Stare 1982 $15 (11/01/85) **75**
Chardonnay Sonoma County Vintners Reserve 1980 $14 (7/16/84) **67**
Chardonnay Sonoma County 1990 $13 (4/30/92) **82**
Chardonnay Sonoma County 1989 $12.50 (12/31/90) **87**
Chardonnay Sonoma County 1988 $12.50 (5/31/90) **85**
Chardonnay Sonoma County 1987 $9.75 (2/15/89) **82**
Chardonnay Sonoma County 1986 $11 (5/31/88) **88**
Chardonnay Sonoma County 1985 $10 (3/15/87) **92**
Chardonnay Sonoma County 1984 $10 (8/31/86) **88**
Chardonnay Sonoma County 1983 $10 (2/16/85) **87**
Chardonnay Sonoma County 1982 $10 (1/01/84) **87**
Chardonnay Sonoma County 1978 $8 (7/16/84) **60**
Chardonnay Sonoma County 1976 $7 (7/16/84) **73**
Chenin Blanc Yolo-Napa Counties 1988 $6.50 (7/31/89) **86**
Fumé Blanc Sonoma County 1990 $9 (11/15/91) **82**
Johannisberg Riesling Sonoma County 1988 $7 (7/31/89) **86**
Meritage Dry Creek Valley 1987 $24 (1/31/92) **87**
Meritage Dry Creek Valley 1986 $22 (9/15/90) **80**
Meritage Dry Creek Valley 1985 $22 (11/15/89) **89**
Merlot Dry Creek Valley 1989 $14 (4/15/92) **86**
Merlot Dry Creek Valley 1988 $15 (3/31/91) **83**
Merlot Dry Creek Valley 1985 $7.50 (2/15/88) **80**
Merlot Sonoma County 1986 $15 (3/31/89) **78**
Sauvignon Blanc Late Harvest Dry Creek Valley Soleil David S. Stare Vintner's Reserve 1986 $15/375ml (6/15/89) **90**
Sauvignon Blanc Sonoma County 1989 $9 (12/31/90) **87**
David S. Stare Vintner's Reserve Sonoma County 1984 $18 (5/31/88) **88**
David S. Stare Vintner's Selection Dry Creek Valley 1983 $15 (12/31/86) **74**
Zinfandel Dry Creek Valley 1986 $9 (4/15/89) **85**
Zinfandel Dry Creek Valley Old Vines 1989 $11 (5/15/92) **85**
Zinfandel Dry Creek Valley Old Vines 1988 $11 (2/15/91) **86**

GEORGES DUBOEUF (France/Beaujolais)
Beaujolais 1990 $6.50 (9/30/91) BB **84**
Beaujolais 1989 $7 (11/15/90) BB **86**
Beaujolais Blanc 1989 $9 (11/30/90) **80**
Beaujolais Château de la Plume 1990 $6.50 (10/31/91) BB **84**
Beaujolais-Villages 1990 $7 (9/15/91) BB **87**
Beaujolais-Villages 1989 $8 (11/15/90) BB **87**

Beaujolais-Villages 1988 $8 (5/31/89) (TM) **83**
Beaujolais-Villages Château de la Grande Grange 1990 $7 (9/15/91) BB **82**
Beaujolais-Villages Château des Vierres 1990 $7 (11/15/91) **79**
Brouilly 1990 $9.50 (9/15/91) **81**
Brouilly 1988 $11 (5/31/89) (TM) **83**
Brouilly Domaine des Nazins 1990 $9.50 (9/15/91) **87**
Brouilly Château de Nervers 1990 $9.50 (9/15/91) **82**
Brouilly Château de Nervers 1988 $11 (5/31/89) (TM) **89**
Chardonnay Vin de Pays d'Oc 1989 $6.50 (11/15/90) BB **80**
Châteauneuf-du-Pape 1989 $14 (5/31/92) **83**
Chénas 1990 $8.50 (9/15/91) **88**
Chénas 1988 $10 (5/31/89) (TM) **85**
Chiroubles 1990 $9.50 (9/15/91) **88**
Chiroubles 1988 $11 (5/31/89) (TM) **84**
Chiroubles Domaine Desmures Père et Fils 1990 $9.50 (10/31/91) **79**
Côte-de-Brouilly 1990 $9.50 (11/15/91) **76**
Côte-de-Brouilly Domaine de la Madone 1990 $9.50 (9/15/91) **77**
Côte-Rôtie Domaine de la Rousse 1988 $18 (7/31/91) **87**
Côtes du Rhône 1990 $8 (12/31/91) BB **84**
Côtes du Rhône 1989 $6 (10/15/90) BB **80**
Crozes-Hermitage 1989 $10 (6/15/92) **87**
Crozes-Hermitage 1988 $9 (1/31/91) **85**
Fleurie 1990 $11 (9/15/91) **89**
Fleurie 1988 $14.50 (5/31/89) (TM) **89**
Fleurie Château des Déduits 1990 $11 (10/31/91) **87**
Gigondas 1989 $12 (1/31/92) **84**
Gigondas 1988 $10 (9/30/90) **79**
Juliénas 1990 $9.50 (9/15/91) **86**
Juliénas Domaine de la Seigneurie 1990 $9.50 (10/31/91) **84**
Mâcon-Lugny Fête des Fleurs 1989 $9 (10/31/90) **84**
Mâcon-Villages 1989 $8.50 (10/31/90) **81**
Mâcon-Villages 1988 $8 (9/30/89) **79**
Mâcon-Villages La Coupe Perration 1988 $8 (9/30/89) **77**
Morgon 1990 $9 (9/15/91) **80**
Morgon 1988 $10.75 (5/31/89) (TM) **87**
Morgon Jean Descombes 1990 $9 (9/30/91) BB **87**
Morgon Jean Descombes 1988 $11.25 (5/31/89) (TM) **90**
Moulin-à-Vent 1990 $11 (9/15/91) **84**
Moulin-à-Vent 1988 $12.25 (5/31/89) (TM) **87**
Moulin-à-Vent New Barrel Aged 1988 $12.25 (5/31/89) (TM) **93**
Moulin-à-Vent Domaine des Rosiers 1990 $11 (9/15/91) **85**
Pouilly-Fuissé 1989 $15 (10/31/90) **86**
Pouilly-Fuissé 1988 $12 (9/30/89) **84**
Pouilly-Fuissé 1987 $12 (6/15/88) **81**
Pouilly-Fuissé 1986 $14 (7/31/87) **82**
Pouilly-Fuissé 1985 $15 (3/31/87) **80**
Régnié 1990 $8 (9/15/91) **81**
Régnié 1988 $8 (5/31/89) (TM) **83**
Régnié Domaine du Potet 1990 $8 (9/30/91) BB **85**
St.-Amour 1990 $11 (9/15/91) **87**
St.-Amour Domaine des Pins 1990 $11 (9/15/91) **82**
St.-Joseph 1988 $11 (11/30/90) **76**
St.-Véran 1989 $10 (10/31/90) **85**
St.-Véran 1988 $9 (9/30/89) **82**
St.-Véran 1987 $9 (10/15/88) **77**
St.-Véran 1986 $9 (7/31/87) **79**
St.-Véran 1985 $10 (3/31/87) **87**
St.-Véran Coupe Louis Dailly 1988 $9 (9/30/89) **80**
St.-Véran Coupe Louis Dailly 1987 $9 (10/15/88) **80**

DUBREUIL-FONTAINE (France/Burgundy)
Aloxe-Corton 1988 ($NA) (7/15/90) (BT) **75+**
Corton-Bressandes 1989 (NR) (7/15/90) (BT) **85+**
Corton-Bressandes 1985 $50 (1/31/89) **86**
Corton-Bressandes 1982 $24 (10/16/85) **85**
Corton-Charlemagne 1989 $71 (3/31/92) **84**
Corton Clos du Roi 1989 (NR) (1/31/92) **92**
Corton Clos du Roi 1987 Rel: $34 Cur: $55 (12/31/90) **85**
Corton Clos du Roi 1985 Rel: $49 Cur: $63 (7/15/88) **90**
Corton Clos du Roi 1982 $25 (9/16/85) **86**
Pernand-Vergelesses Blanc Ile des Vergelesses 1985 $22 (2/28/89) **73**
Pernand-Vergelesses Ile des Vergelesses 1989 (NR) (1/31/92) **84**
Pernand-Vergelesses Ile des Vergelesses 1982 $18 (10/16/85) **78**
Savigny-lès-Beaune Les Vergelesses 1989 (NR) (7/15/90) (BT) **80+**
Savigny-lès-Beaune Les Vergelesses 1988 ($NA) (7/15/90) (BT) **75+**
Savigny-lès-Beaune Les Vergelesses 1985 $24 (1/31/89) **88**

DOMAINE DUCHET (France/Burgundy)
Beaune Cent-Vignes 1985 $27 (3/15/88) **85**

DUCKHORN (United States/California)
Cabernet Sauvignon Napa Valley 1988 Rel: $20 Cur: $27 (7/31/91) **85**
Cabernet Sauvignon Napa Valley 1987 Rel: $20 Cur: $31 (6/30/90) CS **95**
Cabernet Sauvignon Napa Valley 1986 Rel: $18 Cur: $30 (7/31/89) SS **94**
Cabernet Sauvignon Napa Valley 1985 Rel: $17.50 Cur: $39 (CA-3/89) **92**
Cabernet Sauvignon Napa Valley 1985 Rel: $17.50 Cur: $39 (6/15/88) CS **91**
Cabernet Sauvignon Napa Valley 1984 Rel: $17 Cur: $32 (CA-3/89) **92**
Cabernet Sauvignon Napa Valley 1983 Rel: $16 Cur: $45 (CA-3/89) **88**
Cabernet Sauvignon Napa Valley 1982 Rel: $15 Cur: $53 (CA-3/89) **90**
Cabernet Sauvignon Napa Valley 1981 Rel: $15 Cur: $68 (CA-3/89) **87**

Key to Symbols

The scores reported here are the results of blind tastings conducted by our panel of senior editors. Wines that carry the initials below are results of individual tastings.

THE WINE SPECTATOR 100-POINT SCALE 95-100—Classic, a great wine; ***90-94***—Outstanding, superior character and style; ***80-89***—Good to very good, a wine with special qualities; ***70-79***—Average, drinkable wine that may have minor flaws; ***60-69***—Below average, drinkable but not recommended; ***50-59***—Poor, undrinkable, not recommended. "+"—With a score indicates a range; used primarily with barrel tastings to indicate a preliminary score.

SPECIAL DESIGNATIONS SS—Spectator Selection, CS—Cellar Selection, BB—Best Buy, ($NA)—Price not available, (NR)—Not released.

TASTER'S INITIALS (JG)—Jim Gordon, (HS)—Harvey Steiman, (JL)—James Laube, (JS)—James Suckling, (TM)—Thomas Matthews, (TR)—Terry Robards, (PM)—Per-Henrik Mansson, (BT)—Barrel Tasting (these wines were tasted blind from barrel samples), (CA-date)—*California's Great Cabernets* by James Laube, (CH-date)—*California's Great Chardonnays* by James Laube, (VP-date)—*Vintage Port* by James Suckling.

DATE TASTED Dates in parentheses represent the issue in which the rating was published.

Cabernet Sauvignon Napa Valley 1980 Rel: $14 Cur: $70 (CA-3/89) **91**
Cabernet Sauvignon Napa Valley 1978 Rel: $10.50 Cur: $82 (CA-3/89) **92**
Merlot Napa Valley 1990 (NR) (5/15/91) (BT) **85+**
Merlot Napa Valley 1989 Rel: $20 Cur: $25 (4/15/92) **82**
Merlot Napa Valley 1988 Rel: $19 Cur: $28 (12/31/90) **86**
Merlot Napa Valley 1987 Rel: $18 Cur: $25 (12/31/89) **91**
Merlot Napa Valley 1986 Rel: $17 Cur: $30 (1/31/89) **86**
Merlot Napa Valley 1985 Rel: $16 Cur: $35 (12/31/87) CS **93**
Merlot Napa Valley 1984 Rel: $15 Cur: $40 (12/31/86) SS **94**
Merlot Napa Valley 1983 Rel: $15 Cur: $28 (11/01/85) CS **94**
Merlot Napa Valley 1982 Rel: $13 Cur: $56 (12/16/84) SS **92**
Merlot Napa Valley Three Palms Vineyard 1989 Rel: $25 Cur: $29 (5/31/92) **89**
Merlot Napa Valley Three Palms Vineyard 1988 Rel: $25 Cur: $46 (11/15/91) **84**
Merlot Napa Valley Three Palms Vineyard 1987 Rel: $25 Cur: $55 (7/31/90) **92**
Merlot Napa Valley Three Palms Vineyard 1986 Rel: $20 Cur: $58 (7/31/89) **88**
Merlot Napa Valley Three Palms Vineyard 1985 Rel: $20 Cur: $63 (6/30/88) **91**
Merlot Napa Valley Three Palms Vineyard 1984 Rel: $18 Cur: $50 (7/31/87) **89**
Merlot Napa Valley Vine Hill Ranch 1987 $18 (7/31/90) **87**
Merlot Napa Valley Vine Hill Ranch 1986 $18 (7/31/89) **80**
Merlot Napa Valley Vine Hill Ranch 1985 $16 (6/30/88) **91**
Sauvignon Blanc Napa Valley 1990 $10 (2/15/92) **89**
Sauvignon Blanc Napa Valley 1989 $10 (12/31/90) **87**
Sauvignon Blanc Napa Valley 1988 $10 (2/15/90) **86**
Sémillon Napa Valley Decoy 1990 $7.25 (12/31/91) BB **80**

CHATEAU DUCLA (France/Bordeaux)
Bordeaux 1988 $7 (8/31/91) **74**
Entre-Deux-Mers 1990 $7 (6/15/91) BB **84**
Entre-Deux-Mers 1987 $5 (9/30/88) BB **81**

CHATEAU DUCLUZEAU (France/Bordeaux)
Listrac 1987 $7 (11/30/89) (JS) **79**
Listrac 1986 $11 (11/30/89) (JS) **83**
Listrac 1982 $12 (11/30/89) (JS) **80**

CHATEAU DUCRU-BEAUCAILLOU (France/Bordeaux)
St.-Julien 1991 (NR) (5/15/92) (BT) **85+**
St.-Julien 1990 (NR) (5/15/92) (BT) **85+**
St.-Julien 1989 $65 (3/15/92) **91**
St.-Julien 1988 $48 (4/30/91) **92**
St.-Julien 1987 $35 (5/15/90) **86**
St.-Julien 1986 $52 (6/30/89) **91**
St.-Julien 1985 $50 (6/15/88) **95**
St.-Julien 1984 Rel: $24 Cur: $31 (8/31/87) **87**
St.-Julien 1983 Rel: $27 Cur: $43 (6/16/86) **90**
St.-Julien 1982 Rel: $28 Cur: $74 (5/01/85) **92**
St.-Julien 1981 Rel: $25 Cur: $45 (5/01/85) **93**
St.-Julien 1980 Rel: $13 Cur: $25 (5/01/84) CS **88**
St.-Julien 1979 $51 (10/15/89) (JS) **87**
St.-Julien 1978 $74 (5/01/85) **91**
St.-Julien 1962 $120 (11/30/87) (JS) **80**
St.-Julien 1961 $290 (3/16/86) (TR) **94**
St.-Julien 1959 $220 (10/15/90) (JS) **90**
St.-Julien 1945 $540 (3/16/86) (JL) **79**

CHATEAU DUDON (France/Sauternes)
Barsac 1989 ($NA) (6/15/90) (BT) **60+**

CHATEAU DUHART-MILON (France/Bordeaux)
Pauillac 1991 (NR) (5/15/92) (BT) **85+**
Pauillac 1990 (NR) (5/15/92) (BT) **90+**
Pauillac 1989 $30 (3/15/92) **90**
Pauillac 1988 Rel: $20 Cur: $29 (8/31/91) **88**
Pauillac 1987 $22 (5/15/90) **79**
Pauillac 1986 $30 (5/31/89) **90**
Pauillac 1985 $34 (6/30/88) **87**
Pauillac 1979 $31 (10/15/89) (JS) **86**

DOMAINE DUJAC (France/Burgundy)
Bonnes Mares 1989 $80 (7/15/90) (BT) **75+**
Bonnes Mares 1988 $86 (7/15/90) (BT) **90+**
Bonnes Mares 1987 $62 (3/31/90) **91**
Bonnes Mares 1986 $60 (4/15/89) **85**
Chambolle-Musigny Les Gruenchers 1987 $47 (3/31/90) **93**
Chambolle-Musigny Les Gruenchers 1986 $48 (7/31/88) **76**
Chambolle-Musigny Les Gruenchers 1985 $43 (3/31/88) **74**
Charmes-Chambertin 1989 $72 (1/31/92) **90**
Charmes-Chambertin 1988 $60 (3/31/91) **85**
Charmes-Chambertin 1986 $50 (7/31/88) **85**
Charmes-Chambertin 1985 $100 (3/15/88) **95**
Clos de la Roche Clos la Roche 1989 $80 (1/31/92) **89**
Clos de la Roche Clos la Roche 1988 $75 (3/31/91) **90**
Clos de la Roche Clos la Roche 1987 $53 (3/31/90) **86**
Clos de la Roche Clos la Roche 1986 $56 (7/31/88) **79**
Clos de la Roche Clos la Roche 1985 $85 (3/15/88) **95**
Clos St.-Denis 1989 $80 (1/31/92) **91**
Clos St.-Denis 1987 $58 (3/31/90) **85**
Clos St.-Denis 1986 $56 (7/31/88) **89**
Clos St.-Denis 1985 $89 (3/15/88) **91**
Echézeaux 1988 $70 (3/31/91) **90**
Echézeaux 1987 $56 (5/15/90) **82**
Echézeaux 1986 $52 (4/30/89) **89**
Gevrey-Chambertin Aux Combottes 1989 $65 (1/31/92) **86**
Gevrey-Chambertin Aux Combottes 1988 $54 (3/31/91) **86**
Gevrey-Chambertin Aux Combottes 1987 $42 (5/31/90) **80**
Morey-St.-Denis 1989 $40 (1/31/92) **84**
Morey-St.-Denis Blanc Vin Gris de Pinot Noir 1986 $13 (4/15/89) **80**

CHATEAU DULUC (France/Bordeaux)
St.-Julien 1989 (NR) (3/15/92) **84**

DUNN (United States/California)
Cabernet Sauvignon Howell Mountain 1990 (NR) (5/15/91) (BT) **90+**
Cabernet Sauvignon Howell Mountain 1989 (NR) (5/15/91) (BT) **90+**
Cabernet Sauvignon Howell Mountain 1988 Rel: $39 Cur: $56 (2/29/92) **86**
Cabernet Sauvignon Howell Mountain 1987 Rel: $36 Cur: $70 (4/15/91) **94**
Cabernet Sauvignon Howell Mountain 1986 Rel: $30 Cur: $100 (7/31/90) CS **95**
Cabernet Sauvignon Howell Mountain 1985 Rel: $30 Cur: $125 (11/30/91) (JL) **88**
Cabernet Sauvignon Howell Mountain 1984 Rel: $25 Cur: $145 (11/30/91) (JL) **96**
Cabernet Sauvignon Howell Mountain 1983 Rel: $18 Cur: $115 (11/30/91) (JL) **91**
Cabernet Sauvignon Howell Mountain 1982 Rel: $15 Cur: $160 (11/30/91) (JL) **94**

Cabernet Sauvignon Howell Mountain 1981 Rel: $14 Cur: $160 (11/30/91) (JL) **93**
Cabernet Sauvignon Howell Mountain 1980 Rel: $13 Cur: $170 (11/30/91) (JL) **95**
Cabernet Sauvignon Howell Mountain 1979 Rel: $12.50 Cur: $210 (11/30/91) (JL) **94**
Cabernet Sauvignon Napa Valley 1990 (NR) (5/15/91) (BT) **90+**
Cabernet Sauvignon Napa Valley 1989 (NR) (5/15/91) (BT) **85+**
Cabernet Sauvignon Napa Valley 1988 Rel: $33 Cur: $43 (11/15/91) **87**
Cabernet Sauvignon Napa Valley 1987 Rel: $33 Cur: $52 (11/15/90) **93**
Cabernet Sauvignon Napa Valley 1986 Rel: $27 Cur: $62 (10/15/89) CS **95**
Cabernet Sauvignon Napa Valley 1985 Rel: $20 Cur: $70 (11/30/91) (JL) **93**
Cabernet Sauvignon Napa Valley 1985 Rel: $20 Cur: $70 (9/15/88) CS **94**
Cabernet Sauvignon Napa Valley 1984 Rel: $18 Cur: $65 (11/30/91) (JL) **97**
Cabernet Sauvignon Napa Valley 1983 Rel: $15 Cur: $90 (11/30/91) (JL) **91**
Cabernet Sauvignon Napa Valley 1983 Rel: $15 Cur: $90 (10/31/86) SS **95**
Cabernet Sauvignon Napa Valley 1982 Rel: $13 Cur: $95 (11/30/91) (JL) **91**
Cabernet Sauvignon Napa Valley 1982 Rel: $13 Cur: $95 (11/01/85) SS **97**

DUNNEWOOD (United States/California)
Cabernet Sauvignon California 1986 $7 (6/15/90) **73**
Cabernet Sauvignon Napa Valley Reserve 1986 $10.50 (6/15/90) **82**
Cabernet Sauvignon Napa Valley Reserve 1984 $10.50 (12/31/88) **85**
Chardonnay Napa Valley Reserve 1987 $10.50 (12/31/88) **78**
Chardonnay North Coast 1989 $7 (3/31/91) **78**
Reserve Red California NV $3.75 (2/28/89) **76**

CHATEAU DUPLESSIS-FABRE (France/Bordeaux)
Moulis 1989 $9 (3/15/92) **88**
Moulis 1987 $7 (11/30/89) (JS) **71**
Moulis 1986 $7 (11/30/89) (JS) **74**
Moulis 1982 $10 (11/30/89) (JS) **79**

CHATEAU DUPLESSY (France/Bordeaux)
Premières Côtes de Bordeaux 1985 $6 (5/31/88) **75**

CHATEAU DURAND-LAPLAGNE (France/Bordeaux)
St.-Emilion 1982 $7.50 (9/16/85) **79**

DOMAINE DE DURBAN (France/Other)
Muscat de Beaumes-de-Venise 1988 $15 (3/31/91) **86**

PIERRE & PAUL DURDILLY (France/Beaujolais)
Beaujolais Les Grandes Coasses 1990 $7 (9/30/91) **74**

CHATEAU DURFORT-VIVENS (France/Bordeaux)
Margaux 1989 $28 (3/15/92) **92**
Margaux 1988 $40 (8/31/91) **73**
Margaux 1987 $24 (6/30/89) (BT) **75+**
Margaux 1986 $25 (6/15/89) **90**
Margaux 1985 $20 (5/15/87) (BT) **80+**

DOMAINE DURIEU (France/Rhône)
Châteauneuf-du-Pape 1989 $17 (10/15/91) **85**
Châteauneuf-du-Pape 1988 $16 (10/15/91) **86**
Châteauneuf-du-Pape 1986 $16 (10/15/91) **89**
Châteauneuf-du-Pape 1985 $14 (10/15/91) **79**
Châteauneuf-du-Pape 1984 $13 (11/15/87) **78**
Châteauneuf-du-Pape 1983 $14 (10/15/91) **82**
Châteauneuf-du-Pape 1981 $25 (10/15/91) **90**
Côtes du Rhône-Villages 1988 $6 (3/15/91) **78**

DURNEY (United States/California)
Cabernet Sauvignon Carmel Valley 1981 $12.50 (9/01/84) **82**
Cabernet Sauvignon Carmel Valley Private Reserve 1983 $20 (4/30/91) **86**
Chardonnay Carmel Valley 1988 $18 (9/30/90) **88**
Chenin Blanc Carmel Valley 1986 $7 (7/31/89) **72**
Pinot Noir Carmel Valley 1988 $16 (4/30/91) **80**

JEAN DURUP (France/Chablis)
Chablis 1987 ($NA) (3/31/89) **86**
Chablis Fourchaume 1987 ($NA) (3/31/89) **88**
Chablis Vaudevey 1987 ($NA) (3/31/89) **90**

DUVAL-LEROY (France/Champagne)
Brut Blanc de Blancs Champagne Chardonnay NV $30 (12/31/91) **88**
Brut Champagne NV (NR) (12/31/91) **89**
Brut Champagne Fleur de Champagne NV $25 (12/31/91) **87**
Cuvée des Roys Champagne 1985 ($NA) (12/31/90) **84**

DUVERNAY (France/Burgundy)
Mercurey Blanc La Chiquette 1988 $17 (4/30/91) **87**
Rully Les Cloux 1988 $18 (12/31/90) **82**

DUXOUP (United States/California)
Charbono Napa Valley 1987 $9.50 (6/15/89) **88**
Napa Gamay Dry Creek Valley 1988 $7.50 (2/28/90) **76**
Napa Gamay Dry Creek Valley 1987 $7 (2/28/89) BB **86**
Syrah Dry Creek Valley 1987 $12 (4/15/89) **87**
Syrah Dry Creek Valley 1986 $9 (4/15/89) **85**
Syrah Sonoma County 1982 $9 (3/16/84) **78**

EBERLE (United States/California)
Cabernet Sauvignon Paso Robles 1988 ($NA) (5/15/90) (BT) **80+**
Cabernet Sauvignon Paso Robles 1987 $16 (11/15/91) **76**
Cabernet Sauvignon Paso Robles 1986 Rel: $12 Cur: $15 (11/15/89) **85**
Cabernet Sauvignon Paso Robles 1985 Rel: $12 Cur: $17 (2/15/89) **82**
Cabernet Sauvignon Paso Robles 1984 Rel: $12 Cur: $17 (CA-3/89) **86**
Cabernet Sauvignon Paso Robles 1983 Rel: $10 Cur: $18 (CA-3/89) **84**
Cabernet Sauvignon Paso Robles 1982 Rel: $10 Cur: $24 (CA-3/89) **72**
Cabernet Sauvignon Paso Robles 1981 Rel: $10 Cur: $24 (CA-3/89) **85**
Cabernet Sauvignon Paso Robles 1980 Rel: $10 Cur: $24 (CA-3/89) **78**
Cabernet Sauvignon San Luis Obispo 1979 Rel: $10 Cur: $25 (CA-3/89) **82**
Cabernet Sauvignon Paso Robles Reserve 1982 Rel: $25 Cur: $30 (CA-3/89) **71**
Cabernet Sauvignon Paso Robles Reserve 1981 Rel: $25 Cur: $35 (CA-3/89) **80**
Chardonnay Paso Robles 1990 $12 (7/15/92) **72**
Chardonnay Paso Robles 1989 $12 (7/15/91) **86**
Chardonnay Paso Robles 1988 $12 (6/30/90) **76**
Chardonnay Paso Robles 1987 $12 (6/30/90) **74**
Chardonnay Paso Robles 1986 $10 (12/31/88) **85**
Chardonnay Paso Robles 1982 $10 (4/16/85) **79**
Muscat Canelli Paso Robles 1990 $8.50 (8/31/91) **83**
Muscat Canelli Paso Robles 1988 $7.50 (12/15/89) **76**

MAURICE ECARD (France/Burgundy)
Savigny-lès-Beaune Les Peuillets 1989 $25 (11/15/91) **87**
Savigny-lès-Beaune Les Serpentières 1989 $25 (11/15/91) **88**
Savigny-lès-Beaune Les Serpentières 1987 $17 (10/15/89) **80**

EDEN ROC (United States/California)
Brut California NV $4 (5/15/92) **76**
Extra Dry California NV $4 (5/15/92) **78**

EDMEADES (United States/California)
Pinot Noir Anderson Valley 1982 $10 (2/16/85) **89**
Zinfandel Mendocino Ciapusci Vineyard 1981 $9 (3/01/85) **87**

EDMUNDS ST. JOHN (United States/California)
Les Fleurs du Chaparral Napa Valley 1987 $15 (8/31/90) **91**
Les Côtes Sauvages California 1989 $19 (7/15/91) **79**
Les Côtes Sauvages California 1986 $13.50 (4/15/89) **88**
Mourvèdre Napa Valley 1986 $15 (4/15/89) **87**
Port o'Call New World Red California 1989 $9.50 (8/31/91) **84**
Syrah California 1987 $18 (12/15/89) **81**
Syrah Sonoma County 1986 $12 (4/15/89) **91**
Syrah Sonoma Valley 1988 $19 (8/31/91) **85**

EDNA VALLEY (United States/California)
Chardonnay Edna Valley 1990 $15 (2/15/92) **74**
Chardonnay Edna Valley 1989 $15 (12/31/90) **88**
Chardonnay Edna Valley 1988 $14.75 (12/15/89) **85**
Chardonnay Edna Valley 1987 Rel: $14 Cur: $20 (CH-3/90) **91**
Chardonnay Edna Valley 1986 Rel: $13.50 Cur: $20 (CH-3/90) **88**
Chardonnay Edna Valley 1985 Rel: $13 Cur: $30 (CH-3/90) **85**
Chardonnay Edna Valley 1984 Rel: $12.50 Cur: $29 (CH-6/90) **86**
Chardonnay Edna Valley 1983 Rel: $12.50 Cur: $20 (CH-3/90) **76**
Chardonnay Edna Valley 1982 Rel: $12 Cur: $32 (CH-3/90) **70**
Chardonnay Edna Valley 1981 Rel: $12 Cur: $25 (CH-3/90) **94**
Chardonnay Edna Valley 1980 Rel: $12 Cur: $44 (CH-3/90) **87**
Pinot Noir Edna Valley 1986 $15 (12/15/89) **76**
Pinot Noir Edna Valley 1985 $15 (6/15/88) **78**
Pinot Noir Edna Valley 1984 $10 (12/15/87) **85**
Pinot Noir Edna Valley 1983 $10 (4/15/87) **57**
Pinot Noir Edna Valley 1982 $11.50 (8/31/86) **80**

DOMAINE DE L'EGLANTIERE (France/Chablis)
Chablis 1985 $14 (1/31/87) **88**

BODEGAS C. AUGUSTO EGLI (Spain)
Utiel-Requena Casa lo Alto 1983 $9 (7/31/89) **82**

DOMAINE DE L'EGLISE (France/Bordeaux)
Pomerol 1990 (NR) (4/30/91) (BT) **90+**
Pomerol 1989 $33 (3/15/92) **93**

CHATEAU L'EGLISE-CLINET (France/Bordeaux)
Pomerol 1988 $47 (12/31/90) **91**
Pomerol 1987 $22 (2/15/90) **83**
Pomerol 1986 Rel: $29 Cur: $44 (6/15/89) **91**
Pomerol 1985 Rel: $30 Cur: $57 (2/29/88) **93**
Pomerol 1983 Rel: $19 Cur: $24 (3/16/86) **88**
Pomerol 1982 Rel: $18 Cur: $42 (5/15/89) (TR) **87**

EHLERS LANE (United States/California)
Cabernet Sauvignon Napa Valley 1983 $12 (6/15/87) **79**

LUIGI EINAUDI (Italy/Piedmont)
Barolo 1982 $23 (6/30/87) **81**
Nebbiolo delle Langhe 1983 $8 (7/01/86) **70**

EL MOLINO (United States/California)
Chardonnay Napa Valley 1989 $30 (3/31/92) **86**
Pinot Noir Napa County 1988 $30 (11/15/91) **82**
Pinot Noir Napa County 1987 $29 (10/31/91) **85**

ELDERTON (Australia)
Cabernet Sauvignon Merlot Barossa Valley 1984 $11 (4/30/88) **86**

ELIZABETH (United States/California)
Chardonnay Mendocino 1989 $12.50 (7/15/91) **85**
Chardonnay Mendocino 1988 $11.50 (7/15/91) **84**

ELK COVE (United States/Oregon)
Cabernet Sauvignon Willamette Valley Dundee Hills Vineyard Commander's Cabernet 1987 $15 (3/31/91) **80**
Chardonnay Willamette Valley 1989 $12 (3/31/92) **74**
Chardonnay Willamette Valley 1988 $12 (3/31/91) **75**
Pinot Noir Willamette Valley 1989 $10 (3/31/92) **88**
Pinot Noir Willamette Valley 1988 $15 (1/31/91) **78**
Pinot Noir Willamette Valley Dundee Hills Vineyards 1989 $18 (3/31/92) **84**
Pinot Noir Willamette Valley Dundee Hills Vineyards 1987 $15 (2/15/90) **81**
Pinot Noir Willamette Valley Dundee Hills Vineyards 1986 $15 (6/15/88) **78**
Pinot Noir Willamette Valley Dundee Hills Vineyards 1985 $15 (6/15/87) **85**
Pinot Noir Willamette Valley Estate Bottled 1987 $15 (2/15/90) **78**
Pinot Noir Willamette Valley Estate Bottled 1986 $15 (2/15/90) **65**
Pinot Noir Willamette Valley Reserve 1987 $15 (12/15/90) **85**
Pinot Noir Willamette Valley Reserve 1985 $15 (2/15/90) **79**
Pinot Noir Willamette Valley Reserve 1983 $20 (2/15/90) **79**
Pinot Noir Willamette Valley Wind Hill Vineyards 1989 $25 (3/31/92) **82**
Pinot Noir Willamette Valley Wind Hills Vineyard 1988 $18 (1/31/91) **80**
Pinot Noir Willamette Valley Wind Hills Vineyard 1987 $15 (2/15/90) **75**
Pinot Noir Willamette Valley Wind Hills Vineyard 1986 $15 (6/15/88) **85**
Pinot Noir Willamette Valley Wind Hills Vineyard 1985 $15 (6/15/87) **91**

ELLENDALE (United States/Oregon)
Pinot Noir Willamette Valley Estate Bottled 1986 $12 (6/15/88) **71**
Pinot Noir Willamette Valley Estate Bottled 1985 $15 (6/15/88) **78**

ELLISTON (United States/California)
Cabernet Sauvignon Central Coast Sunol Valley Vineyard 1985 $16 (11/15/91) **74**
Chardonnay Central Coast Elliston Vineyard 1990 $16 (4/30/92) **72**
Chardonnay Central Coast Elliston Vineyard 1989 $12 (12/31/91) **74**
Chardonnay Central Coast Elliston Vineyard 1987 $18 (7/15/91) **84**
Chardonnay Central Coast Sunol Valley Vineyard 1990 $12 (4/30/92) **84**
Chardonnay Central Coast Sunol Valley Vineyard 1989 $14 (7/15/91) **80**
Pinot Blanc Central Coast Sunol Valley Vineyard 1989 $10 (11/15/91) **75**
Pinot Blanc Central Coast Sunol Valley Vineyard 1987 $10 (5/31/91) **82**

ELLNER (France/Champagne)
Brut Blanc de Blancs Champagne NV $32 (7/31/89) **90**
Brut Champagne 1982 $38 (7/31/89) **91**
Brut Champagne Réserve NV $30 (7/31/89) **87**

ELYSE (United States/California)
Nero Misto Napa Valley 1990 $15 (6/30/92) **86**
Zinfandel Napa Valley Rutherford Bench Morisoli Ranch 1989 $12.50 (8/31/91) **85**

DOMAINE EMILIAN GILLET (France/Burgundy)
Mâcon-Clessé Quintaine 1988 $17 (8/31/90) **80**

CHATEAU L'ENCLOS (France/Bordeaux)
Pomerol 1989 $30 (4/30/92) **82**
Pomerol 1988 $17 (3/15/91) **85**
Pomerol 1987 $15 (6/30/89) (BT) **80+**
Pomerol 1986 $20 (6/15/89) **92**
Pomerol 1984 Rel: $16 Cur: $20 (3/31/87) **83**
Pomerol 1982 Rel: $20 Cur: $32 (5/15/89) (TR) **86**
Pomerol 1945 $100 (3/16/86) (JL) **78**

CHATEAU ENCLOS-HAUT-MAZEYRES (France/Bordeaux)
Pomerol 1982 ($NA) (5/15/89) (TR) **84**

RENE ENGEL (France/Burgundy)
Clos Vougeot 1989 $66 (11/15/91) **85**
Clos Vougeot 1988 $75 (3/15/91) **91**
Clos Vougeot 1986 $50 (11/30/88) **81**
Clos Vougeot 1985 $43 (10/15/87) **85**
Clos Vougeot 1983 $30 (2/16/86) **80**
Echézeaux 1989 $47 (11/15/91) **89**
Echézeaux 1988 $56 (3/31/91) **92**
Echézeaux 1986 $38 (11/30/88) **78**
Echézeaux 1985 $32 (10/15/87) **90**
Grands Echézeaux 1989 $75 (11/15/91) **90**
Grands Echézeaux 1986 $50 (11/30/88) **71**
Grands Echézeaux 1985 $43 (10/15/87) **86**
Vosne-Romanée 1989 $34 (11/15/91) **85**
Vosne-Romanée 1988 $30 (7/15/90) **81**
Vosne-Romanée 1986 $29 (2/28/89) **75**
Vosne-Romanée 1985 $24 (10/15/87) **77**
Vosne-Romanée 1983 $19 (2/16/86) **67**
Vosne-Romanée Les Brûlées 1989 $35 (11/15/91) **87**
Vosne-Romanée Les Brûlées 1988 $45 (2/28/91) **89**
Vosne-Romanée Les Brûlées 1986 $32 (10/31/88) **68**
Vosne-Romanée Les Brûlées 1985 $28 (10/15/87) **85**
Vosne-Romanée Les Brûlées 1983 $22 (3/16/86) **78**

ENO-FRIULIA (Italy/North)
Cabernet Sauvignon Collio 1988 $12 (7/15/91) **76**
Chardonnay 1989 $12 (3/31/91) **80**
Merlot Collio 1988 $12 (4/30/91) **82**
Pinot Bianco Collio 1990 $14 (1/31/92) **78**
Pinot Grigio Collio 1990 $14 (1/31/92) **77**
Pinot Grigio Collio 1989 $12 (3/31/91) **80**
Tocai Friulano Collio 1990 $14 (1/31/92) **80**

EOLA HILLS (United States/Oregon)
Pinot Noir Oregon 1987 $12 (2/15/90) **76**
Pinot Noir Oregon 1986 $12 (2/15/90) **77**

ERRAZURIZ (Chile)
Cabernet Sauvignon Aconcagua Valley 1987 $9 (9/15/90) **82**
Cabernet Sauvignon Aconcagua Valley 1985 $5.50 (9/15/88) **82**
Cabernet Sauvignon Aconcagua Valley Antigua Reserva Don Maximiano 1984 $7.50 (9/15/88) BB **87**
Cabernet Sauvignon Aconcagua Valley Antigua Reserva Don Maximiano 1980 $6 (11/15/87) **68**
Cabernet Sauvignon Aconcagua Valley Don Maximo Estate Reserva 1989 $10 (6/15/92) **87**
Cabernet Sauvignon Aconcagua Valley Don Maximo Estate Reserva 1988 $9 (6/15/92) **85**
Chardonnay Maule Valley 1991 $11 (6/15/92) **84**
Chardonnay Maule Valley Reserva 1989 $7 (9/15/90) BB **83**
Sauvignon Blanc Maule Valley Reserva 1991 $7 (6/15/92) BB **87**

FREDERIC ESMONIN (France/Burgundy)
Gevrey-Chambertin Les Corbeaux 1989 $42 (3/31/92) **88**
Gevrey-Chambertin Estournelles St.-Jacques 1989 $42 (3/31/92) **86**
Gevrey-Chambertin Lavaux St.-Jacques 1989 $42 (3/31/92) **88**
Griotte-Chambertin 1989 $80 (3/31/92) **92**
Mazis-Chambertin Mazy-Chambertin 1989 $80 (3/31/92) **89**
Ruchottes-Chambertin 1989 $80 (3/31/92) **91**

DOMAINE MICHEL ESMONIN (France/Burgundy)
Gevrey-Chambertin Clos-St.-Jacques 1987 $44 (3/31/90) **87**
Gevrey-Chambertin Estournelles St.-Jacques 1988 $40 (3/31/91) **84**

CHATEAU L'ESPERANCE (France/Bordeaux)
Bordeaux 1986 $7 (9/30/89) **77**

ESTANCIA (United States/California)
Cabernet Sauvignon Alexander Valley 1988 $9 (5/31/91) **81**
Cabernet Sauvignon Alexander Valley 1987 $7 (7/15/90) BB **80**
Cabernet Sauvignon Alexander Valley 1986 $8 (4/15/89) BB **85**
Cabernet Sauvignon Alexander Valley 1985 $6.50 (6/15/88) BB **87**
Cabernet Sauvignon Alexander Valley 1984 $6.50 (12/31/87) **79**
Cabernet Sauvignon Alexander Valley 1982 $6 (4/15/87) BB **87**
Meritage Alexander Valley 1988 $14 (11/15/91) **83**
Meritage Alexander Valley 1987 $12 (1/31/91) **88**
Chardonnay Alexander Valley 1988 $8 (4/30/90) BB **83**
Chardonnay Alexander Valley 1987 $7 (6/30/89) **85**

Key to Symbols

The scores reported here are the results of blind tastings conducted by our panel of senior editors. Wines that carry the initials below are results of individual tastings.

THE WINE SPECTATOR 100-POINT SCALE 95-100— Classic, a great wine; ***90-94***— Outstanding, superior character and style; ***80-89***—Good to very good, a wine with special qualities; ***70-79*** —Average, drinkable wine that may have minor flaws; ***60-69*** —Below average, drinkable but not recommended; ***50-59*** —Poor, undrinkable, not recommended. "+"— With a score indicates a range; used primarily with barrel tastings to indicate a preliminary score.

SPECIAL DESIGNATIONS SS—Spectator Selection, CS—Cellar Selection, BB—Best Buy, ($NA)—Price not available, (NR)—Not released.

TASTER'S INITIALS (JG)—Jim Gordon, (HS)—Harvey Steiman, (JL)—James Laube, (JS)—James Suckling, (TM)—Thomas Matthews, (TR)—Terry Robards, (PM)—Per-Henrik Mansson, (BT)—Barrel Tasting (these wines were tasted blind from barrel samples), (CA-date)—*California's Great Cabernets* by James Laube, (CH-date)—*California's Great Chardonnays* by James Laube, (VP-date)—*Vintage Port* by James Suckling.

DATE TASTED Dates in parentheses represent the issue in which the rating was published.

Chardonnay Alexander Valley 1986 $6.50 (1/31/88) BB **84**
Chardonnay Alexander Valley 1983 $7 (4/16/86) **89**
Chardonnay Monterey 1990 $9 (2/15/92) BB **88**
Chardonnay Monterey 1989 $8 (3/31/91) BB **85**
Chardonnay Monterey 1988 $8 (4/30/90) BB **82**
Sauvignon Blanc Alexander Valley 1989 $7 (3/15/91) **79**
Sauvignon Blanc Alexander Valley 1988 $6 (5/15/90) BB **82**
Sauvignon Blanc Monterey 1990 $7.50 (6/15/92) BB **81**

ESTOLA (Spain)
La Mancha Reserva 1985 $10 (2/15/92) **80**
La Mancha Reserva 1982 $6 (11/15/89) BB **87**

ESTRELLA RIVER (United States/California)
Blanc de Blancs Paso Robles Star Cuvée 1983 $13 (2/29/88) **81**
Cabernet Sauvignon Paso Robles 1985 $9 (11/15/89) **67**
Cabernet Sauvignon Paso Robles 1983 $8 (4/15/88) **80**
Cabernet Sauvignon Paso Robles 1982 $10 (6/15/87) **85**
Cabernet Sauvignon Paso Robles 1981 $9 (5/01/85) **88**
Cabernet Sauvignon Paso Robles Founders Epic Collection 1983 $12 (12/15/89) **65**
Cabernet Sauvignon San Luis Obispo County 1980 $10 (3/16/85) **77**
Cabernet Sauvignon San Luis Obispo County 1979 $6 (3/01/84) BB **84**
Chardonnay Paso Robles 1987 $8.50 (12/15/89) **74**
Chardonnay Paso Robles 1986 $8 (4/30/88) **82**
Chardonnay Paso Robles 1985 $8 (12/31/87) **65**
Johannisberg Riesling Paso Robles 1988 $6 (12/15/89) **71**
Sauvignon Blanc Paso Robles 1987 $6 (12/15/89) **81**
Syrah Paso Robles 1986 $8 (9/30/89) **82**
Syrah Paso Robles 1985 $6.50 (3/31/88) **79**
Syrah Paso Robles 1983 $6.50 (1/31/88) BB **80**
Zinfandel Paso Robles 1987 $8 (12/15/89) **72**
Zinfandel San Luis Obispo County 1980 $6 (12/01/84) **77**

CHATEAU ETANG DES COLOMBES (France/Other)
Corbières Cuvée du Bicentenaire 1986 $9 (3/31/91) **77**

ETIENNE HENRI (France/Loire)
Sancerre 1988 $35 (2/28/91) **75**

ETUDE (United States/California)
Cabernet Sauvignon California 1985 $16 (12/15/88) **92**
Cabernet Sauvignon Napa Valley 1987 $24 (10/31/90) **85**
Cabernet Sauvignon Napa Valley 1986 $20 (9/30/89) **92**
Pinot Noir Carneros 1989 $20 (11/15/91) **85**
Pinot Noir Napa Valley 1988 $20 (12/15/90) **86**
Pinot Noir Napa Valley 1985 $16 (6/15/88) **83**

CHATEAU L'EVANGILE (France/Bordeaux)
Pomerol 1991 (NR) (5/15/92) (BT) **75+**
Pomerol 1990 (NR) (5/15/92) (BT) **90+**
Pomerol 1989 $70 (3/15/92) **92**
Pomerol 1988 Rel: $38 Cur: $48 (6/30/91) **87**
Pomerol 1987 Rel: $25 Cur: $31 (6/30/89) (BT) **80+**
Pomerol 1986 $62 (9/15/89) **88**
Pomerol 1985 Rel: $55 Cur: $78 (2/29/88) **92**
Pomerol 1984 Rel: $31 Cur: $40 (2/15/87) **79**
Pomerol 1983 Rel: $42 Cur: $52 (3/16/86) **92**
Pomerol 1982 Rel: $55 Cur: $105 (5/01/89) **90**
Pomerol 1961 $260 (3/16/86) (TR) **77**

EVANS FAMILY (Australia)
Chardonnay Hunter Valley 1985 $13 (4/15/87) **78**
Chardonnay Hunter Valley Vintage Selection 1986 $14 (2/15/88) **88**

EVESHAM WOOD (United States/Oregon)
Pinot Noir Willamette Valley 1986 $12 (2/15/90) **68**

EYE OF THE SWAN (United States/California)
Cabernet Sauvignon California Limited Edition NV $7 (3/31/92) **77**
Chardonnay California 1990 $7 (3/31/92) **74**
Pinot Noir California 1989 $6 (4/30/92) **77**

EYRIE (United States/Oregon)
Pinot Noir Willamette Valley 1987 $20 (2/15/90) **80**
Pinot Noir Willamette Valley 1986 $19.50 (6/15/88) **83**
Pinot Noir Willamette Valley 1985 $19 (2/15/90) **91**
Pinot Noir Willamette Valley 1984 $15 (8/31/86) **84**
Pinot Noir Willamette Valley 1983 $30 (2/15/90) **87**
Pinot Noir Willamette Valley Reserve 1987 $25 (2/15/90) **86**

CHATEAU FABAS (France/Other)
Minervois 1986 $5.50 (9/15/89) **72**

FACELLI (United States/Washington)
Johannisberg Riesling Washington Dry 1988 $7.50 (10/15/89) **78**
Sémillon Washington 1988 $8 (10/15/89) **82**

FAIVELEY (France/Burgundy)
Beaune Champs-Pimont 1989 $34 (1/31/92) **90**
Beaune Champs-Pimont 1985 $36 (3/15/88) **86**
Bourgogne Blanc Chardonnay 1988 $14 (7/31/90) **74**
Bourgogne Blanc Chardonnay Cuvée Joseph Faiveley 1989 $21 (8/31/91) **85**
Bourgogne Blanc Chardonnay Cuvée Joseph Faiveley 1985 $14 (3/31/87) **71**
Bourgogne Blanc Chardonnay Cuvée Joseph Faiveley 1983 $7.50 (5/01/86) **61**
Bourgogne Joseph Faiveley 1989 $12 (1/31/92) **84**
Bourgogne Joseph Faiveley 1979 $8 (4/16/86) BB **75**
Chambertin Clos de Bèze 1989 $99 (1/31/92) **90**
Chambertin Clos de Bèze 1988 $114 (7/15/90) (BT) **95+**
Chambertin Clos de Bèze 1987 $70 (3/31/90) **83**
Chambertin Clos de Bèze 1986 $66 (7/15/89) **88**
Chambertin Clos de Bèze 1985 $105 (3/15/88) **96**
Chambolle-Musigny 1989 $34 (1/31/92) **85**
Chambolle-Musigny 1985 $45 (5/15/88) **89**
Chambolle-Musigny 1981 $24 (5/01/86) **88**
Chassagne-Montrachet 1989 $70 (8/31/91) **83**
Chassagne-Montrachet Les Vergers 1989 $83 (8/31/91) **90**
Clos de la Roche 1986 $55 (7/15/89) **82**
Clos de la Roche 1985 $88 (3/15/88) **78**
Clos de Vougeot 1989 $78 (1/31/92) **85**
Clos de Vougeot 1988 $92 (7/15/90) (BT) **90+**
Corton Clos des Cortons 1989 Rel: $68 Cur: $74 (1/31/92) **91**
Corton Clos des Cortons 1988 $120 (3/31/91) **90**
Corton Clos des Cortons 1987 $50 (3/31/90) **92**

Corton Clos des Cortons 1985 $80 (3/15/88) **79**
Corton-Charlemagne 1989 ($NA) (8/31/91) **98**
Echézeaux 1989 $68 (1/31/92) **89**
Echézeaux 1987 $53 (3/31/90) **80**
Echézeaux 1985 $74 (3/31/88) **89**
Echézeaux 1981 $40 (5/01/86) **68**
Fixin 1989 $21 (1/31/92) **85**
Gevrey-Chambertin 1989 $34 (1/31/92) **87**
Gevrey-Chambertin 1985 $38 (4/15/88) **90**
Gevrey-Chambertin Les Cazetiers 1989 $47 (1/31/92) **89**
Gevrey-Chambertin Les Cazetiers 1988 $57 (3/31/91) **89**
Gevrey-Chambertin Les Cazetiers 1985 $53 (3/31/88) **92**
Gevrey-Chambertin La Combe aux Moines 1989 $47 (1/31/92) **87**
Latricières-Chambertin 1989 $81 (1/31/92) **89**
Latricières-Chambertin 1985 $77 (3/15/88) **88**
Mazis-Chambertin 1989 $79 (1/31/92) **95**
Mazis-Chambertin 1985 $81 (3/15/88) **92**
Mercurey Blanc Clos de la Rochette 1988 $22 (4/30/91) **86**
Mercurey Blanc Clos de la Rochette 1983 $14 (3/31/87) **62**
Mercurey Clos des Myglands 1985 $20 (4/30/88) **75**
Mercurey Clos des Myglands 1981 $11 (6/16/86) **68**
Mercurey Clos du Roy 1988 $22 (3/31/91) **84**
Mercurey Clos du Roy 1985 $23 (4/30/88) **81**
Mercurey Domaine de la Croix Jacquelet 1988 $18 (3/31/91) **81**
Meursault 1989 $68 (8/31/91) **87**
Meursault Les Bouchères 1989 $82 (8/31/91) **88**
Morey-St.-Denis Clos des Ormes 1989 $44 (1/31/92) **88**
Musigny Le Musigny 1949 $250 (8/31/90) (TR) **92**
Nuits-St.-Georges 1989 $33 (1/31/92) **83**
Nuits-St.-Georges 1985 $40 (3/15/88) **90**
Nuits-St.-Georges Clos de la Maréchale 1989 $42 (1/31/92) **85**
Nuits-St.-Georges Clos de la Maréchale 1988 $50 (3/15/91) **76**
Nuits-St.-Georges Clos de la Maréchale 1985 $51 (3/15/88) **85**
Nuits-St.-Georges Clos de la Maréchale 1982 $20 (5/01/86) **84**
Nuits-St.-Georges Les Damodes 1989 $45 (1/31/92) **90**
Nuits-St.-Georges Les Damodes 1988 $52 (3/31/91) **85**
Nuits-St.-Georges Les Porêts St.-Georges 1989 $42 (1/31/92) **84**
Nuits-St.-Georges Les Porêts St.-Georges 1988 $54 (7/15/90) (BT) **90+**
Nuits-St.-Georges Les Porêts St.-Georges 1985 $47 (3/15/88) **76**
Nuits-St.-Georges Les St.-Georges 1989 $54 (1/31/92) **92**
Pommard Les Chaponnières 1989 $50 (1/31/92) **90**
Puligny-Montrachet 1989 $72 (8/31/91) **88**
Puligny-Montrachet Les Combettes 1989 $89 (8/31/91) **87**
Rully 1986 $18 (6/15/89) **83**
Rully Blanc 1983 $10 (8/31/86) **74**
Vosne-Romanée 1989 $35 (1/31/92) **88**

CHATEAU FAIZEAU (France/Bordeaux)
Montagne-St.-Emilion 1983 $9 (11/15/87) **75**

RICCARDO FALCHINI (Italy/Tuscany)
Vernaccia di San Gimignano 1990 $9 (5/15/92) **84**

FALCONER (United States/California)
Brut Blanc de Blancs Russian River Valley 1984 $15 (3/15/91) **89**
Chardonnay California 1989 $12 (2/28/91) **70**

FALESCO (Italy/Other)
Est! Est!! Est!!! di Montefiascone 1989 $5.75 (8/31/91) **74**
Est! Est!! Est!!! di Montefiascone Poggio dei Gelsi 1989 $12 (7/15/91) **77**

FALL CREEK (United States/Texas)
Cabernet Sauvignon Texas 1989 $13 (2/29/92) **75**
Cabernet Sauvignon Texas 1988 $13 (7/15/91) **78**
Carnelian Llano County 1988 $13 (7/15/91) **73**
Chardonnay Texas Grand Reserve 1990 $16 (2/29/92) **88**
Sauvignon Blanc Llano County 1991 $9 (2/29/92) **81**
Sauvignon Blanc Llano County 1990 $9 (2/29/92) **79**
Sauvignon Blanc Texas 1989 $8.50 (7/15/91) **83**

FALLENLEAF (United States/California)
Chardonnay Sonoma Valley 1989 $12 (3/31/91) **85**
Chardonnay Sonoma Valley Carneros Special Reserve 1989 $15 (12/31/91) **78**
Sauvignon Blanc Sonoma Valley 1990 $9 (6/15/92) **73**

FAR NIENTE (United States/California)
Cabernet Sauvignon Napa Valley 1991 (NR) (5/15/92) (BT) **87+**
Cabernet Sauvignon Napa Valley 1988 $36 (11/15/91) **85**
Cabernet Sauvignon Napa Valley 1987 $33 (11/15/90) **88**
Cabernet Sauvignon Napa Valley 1986 $30 (9/30/89) **91**
Cabernet Sauvignon Napa Valley 1985 Rel: $28 Cur: $31 (CA-3/89) **92**
Cabernet Sauvignon Napa Valley 1984 Rel: $25 Cur: $30 (CA-3/89) **92**
Cabernet Sauvignon Napa Valley 1983 Rel: $25 Cur: $31 (CA-3/89) **87**
Cabernet Sauvignon Napa Valley 1982 Rel: $25 Cur: $36 (CA-3/89) **82**
Chardonnay Napa Valley 1990 $30 (6/15/92) CS **90**
Chardonnay Napa Valley 1989 Rel: $28 Cur: $30 (2/28/91) **89**
Chardonnay Napa Valley 1988 Rel: $26 Cur: $29 (2/15/90) **91**
Chardonnay Napa Valley 1987 Rel: $26 Cur: $30 (CH-2/90) **91**
Chardonnay Napa Valley 1986 Rel: $24 Cur: $31 (CH-2/90) **88**
Chardonnay Napa Valley 1985 Rel: $24 Cur: $33 (CH-2/90) **90**
Chardonnay Napa Valley 1984 Rel: $22 Cur: $31 (CH-2/90) **86**
Chardonnay Napa Valley 1983 Rel: $22 Cur: $35 (CH-2/90) **87**
Chardonnay Napa Valley 1983 Rel: $22 Cur: $35 (4/01/85) SS **92**
Chardonnay Napa Valley 1982 Rel: $18 Cur: $38 (CH-2/90) **86**
Chardonnay Napa Valley 1981 Rel: $16.50 Cur: $40 (CH-2/90) **88**
Chardonnay Napa Valley 1980 Rel: $16.50 Cur: $45 (CH-2/90) **93**
Chardonnay Napa Valley 1979 Rel: $15 Cur: $45 (CH-2/90) **92**
Chardonnay Napa Valley Estate 1983 Rel: $22 Cur: $38 (CH-2/90) **89**
Chardonnay Napa Valley Estate 1982 Rel: $18 Cur: $38 (CH-2/90) **91**

FARALTA (Italy/North)
Rosso del Friuli-Venezia Giulia 1986 $12.50 (4/15/90) **74**

MICHEL FARAUD (France/Rhône)
Gigondas Domaine du Cayron 1988 $14 (10/15/91) **89**
Gigondas Domaine du Cayron 1985 $16 (11/30/88) **93**

FARINA (Spain)
Tinto Crianzano Tierra del Vino 1986 $7 (11/30/89) **79**

REMO FARINA (Italy/North)
Recioto della Valpolicella Amarone Classico 1983 $12.50 (3/31/90) **70**

CHATEAU FARLURET (France/Sauternes)
Barsac 1988 ($NA) (6/15/90) (BT) **85+**

TENUTA FARNETA (Italy/Tuscany)
Bongoverno 1986 $30 (9/30/91) **87**
Chianti di Collalto 1989 $7.50 (10/31/91) BB **81**
Chianti di Collalto 1988 $6 (12/15/90) BB **88**
Chianti Villa Farneta 1988 $13.50 (10/31/91) **79**

GARY FARRELL (United States/California)
Cabernet Sauvignon Sonoma County Ladi's Vineyard 1988 $18 (8/31/91) **86**
Cabernet Sauvignon Sonoma County 1987 $16 (10/31/90) **87**
Chardonnay Russian River Valley Aquarius Ranch 1987 $13.50 (12/31/88) **70**
Chardonnay Sonoma County 1989 $16 (7/15/91) **85**
Chardonnay Sonoma County 1986 $12 (8/31/88) **82**
Pinot Noir Russian River Valley 1989 $16 (7/31/91) **88**
Pinot Noir Russian River Valley 1988 $16 (10/31/90) **88**
Pinot Noir Russian River Valley 1986 $15 (6/15/88) **90**
Pinot Noir Russian River Valley 1985 $13.50 (6/15/88) **62**
Pinot Noir Russian River Valley 1984 $12 (4/15/87) **79**
Pinot Noir Russian River Valley 1983 $12 (8/31/86) **88**
Pinot Noir Russian River Valley Allen Vineyard 1988 $25 (10/31/90) **87**
Pinot Noir Sonoma County Howard Allen Vineyard 1987 $20 (2/15/90) **84**
Zinfandel Sonoma County 1985 $10 (4/30/88) **91**

FARVIEW FARM (United States/California)
Merlot California Templeton 1980 $6.50 (3/16/84) **78**
Zinfandel San Luis Obispo Reserve 1980 $7 (3/16/84) **62**

FASSATI (Italy/Tuscany)
Vino Nobile di Montepulciano Riserva 1985 $22 (11/30/89) **86**
Vino Nobile di Montepulciano Riserva 1978 $8.50 (7/01/86) **73**

CHATEAU JEAN FAURE (France/Bordeaux)
St.-Emilion 1983 $17 (3/31/87) **87**
St.-Emilion 1982 $14 (11/16/85) **85**

CHATEAU FAURIE-PASCAUD (France/Bordeaux)
Bordeaux 1986 $5 (6/30/88) **79**

CHATEAU FAURIE-DE-SOUCHARD (France/Bordeaux)
St.-Emilion 1989 (NR) (4/30/91) (BT) **80+**
St.-Emilion 1988 $22 (6/30/89) (BT) **75+**
St.-Emilion 1987 $19 (6/30/89) (BT) **70+**

SERGE FAUST (France/Champagne)
Brut Champagne Cuvée de Réserve à Vandières NV $33 (12/31/90) **86**

BODEGAS FAUSTINO MARTINEZ (Spain)
Rioja Faustino I Gran Reserva 1982 $25 (3/31/92) **82**
Rioja Faustino I Gran Reserva 1981 $12 (10/31/88) **88**
Rioja Faustino I Gran Reserva 1978 ($NA) (3/31/92) **76**
Rioja Faustino I Gran Reserva 1973 ($NA) (3/31/92) **82**
Rioja Faustino I Gran Reserva 1970 ($NA) (3/31/92) **89**
Rioja Faustino V 1985 $7.50 (10/15/88) **83**
Rioja Faustino V Reserva 1987 $13 (1/31/92) **81**
Rioja Faustino V Reserva 1986 ($NA) (3/31/92) **86**
Rioja Faustino V Reserva 1985 $18 (3/31/92) **82**
Rioja Faustino VII 1988 $8.50 (1/31/92) BB **85**

YVONNE FEBVRE (France/Chablis)
Chablis Blanchot 1988 $23 (1/31/91) **85**
Chablis Montée de Tonnerre 1984 $15 (1/31/87) **73**

FEIST (Portugal)
Vintage Port 1985 Rel: $20 Cur: $28 (VP-1/90) **72**
Vintage Port 1982 ($NA) (VP-1/90) **78**
Vintage Port 1978 ($NA) (VP-1/90) **78**

LIVIO FELLUGA (Italy/North)
Cabernet Collio Franc 1988 $15 (6/30/91) **84**
Merlot Collio 1988 $16 (7/15/91) **84**
Pinot Grigio Colli Orientali del Friuli 1989 $18 (3/31/91) **78**
Tocai Friulano Colli Orientali del Friuli 1989 $16 (4/15/91) **81**

MARCO FELLUGA (Italy/North)
Carantan 1988 $36 (4/30/92) **88**
Chardonnay 1988 $9 (9/15/89) **82**
Chardonnay 1987 $9 (9/15/89) **80**
Sauvignon Collio 1990 $21 (5/15/92) **73**

FATTORIA DI FELSINA (Italy/Tuscany)
Berardenga I Sistri 1988 $24 (3/31/90) **86**
Chianti Classico 1988 $13 (11/30/89) BT (HS) **86**
Chianti Classico 1987 $10 (11/30/89) (HS) **83**
Chianti Classico 1986 $7.50 (11/30/89) (HS) **78**
Chianti Classico Berardenga 1988 $13 (9/15/91) **89**
Chianti Classico Berardenga 1987 $8 (5/15/90) **83**
Chianti Classico Berardenga 1986 $7.50 (12/15/88) **72**
Chianti Classico Berardenga Riserva 1985 $15 (9/15/91) **86**
Chianti Classico Berardenga Riserva 1983 $12 (11/30/89) (HS) **87**
Chianti Classico Berardenga Vigneto Rancia Riserva 1985 $23 (4/30/90) CS **93**
Chianti Classico Berardenga Vigneto Rancia Riserva 1983 $17 (12/15/88) **91**
Fontalloro 1986 $25 (8/31/91) **84**
Fontalloro 1985 $24 (9/15/88) **91**

FELTA SPRINGS (United States/California)
Cabernet Sauvignon Sonoma County 1983 $5 (3/31/87) **78**
Chardonnay Sonoma County 1986 $6 (6/15/88) BB **80**

FELTON EMPIRE (United States/California)
Chardonnay Monterey County 1990 $13 (4/30/92) **87**
Chardonnay Monterey County 1988 $12 (4/15/90) **84**
Chardonnay Monterey County Reserve 1990 $16 (4/30/92) **80**
Chardonnay Monterey County Reserve 1988 $15 (4/15/90) **86**
Pinot Noir California Tonneaux Français 1984 $12 (5/15/87) **77**

FENESTRA (United States/California)
Cabernet Sauvignon Livermore Valley 1988 $12 (11/15/91) **85**
Cabernet Sauvignon Monterey Smith & Hook Vineyard 1987 $14 (11/15/91) **75**
Merlot Livermore Valley 1989 $13 (5/31/92) **87**
Merlot Livermore Valley Special Reserve 1989 $40/1.5L (5/31/92) **89**
Merlot Sonoma County 1986 $11 (10/15/89) **83**
White Zinfandel Livermore Valley 1987 $5 (6/15/89) **80**

FENN VALLEY (United States/Michigan)
Chancellor Lake Michigan Shore 1989 $9.50 (2/29/92) **81**
Johannisberg Riesling Lake Michigan Shore 1989 $8 (2/29/92) **85**

RICCARDO FENOCCHIO (Italy/Piedmont)
Barbera d'Alba Pianpolvere Soprano 1988 $10 (3/15/91) **84**
Barbera d'Alba Pianpolvere Soprano 1987 $10 (3/15/91) **75**
Barbera d'Alba Pianpolvere Soprano 1986 $8.50 (3/15/89) **83**
Barbera d'Alba Pianpolvere Soprano 1985 $15 (3/15/91) **86**
Barolo Pianpolvere Soprano 1984 $15 (7/31/89) **62**
Barolo Pianpolvero Soprano 1982 $26 (7/31/89) **74**

FENSALIR (United States/California)
Cabernet Sauvignon Napa Valley 1988 $14 (11/15/91) **85**

CHARLES DE FERE (France/Other)
Brut Blanc de Blancs NV $10 (1/31/92) **79**
Brut Blanc de Blancs Réserve NV $10 (6/15/90) **77**
Brut Rosé NV $10 (6/15/90) **70**
Brut Tradition NV $12 (11/30/91) **82**

CHATEAU FERRANDE (France/Bordeaux)
Graves 1981 $7.50 (3/16/85) **75**

FERRARI (Italy/Sparkling)
Brut NV $20 (12/31/90) **88**
Brut Perlè 1985 $30 (12/31/90) **88**

GIULIO FERRARI (Italy/Sparkling)
Riserva del Fondatore 1982 $50 (12/31/90) **86**

FERRARI-CARANO (United States/California)
Cabernet Sauvignon Alexander Valley 1987 $17.50 (7/15/91) **84**
Cabernet Sauvignon Alexander Valley 1986 $17.50 (9/15/90) **80**
Chardonnay Alexander Valley 1990 $20 (7/15/92) **90**
Chardonnay Alexander Valley 1989 $19.50 (6/15/91) **91**
Chardonnay Alexander Valley 1988 Rel: $18 Cur: $29 (5/31/90) SS **93**
Chardonnay Alexander Valley 1987 Rel: $16 Cur: $27 (CH-5/90) **94**
Chardonnay Alexander Valley 1986 Rel: $16 Cur: $31 (CH-5/90) **92**
Chardonnay Alexander Valley 1985 Rel: $14 Cur: $45 (9/15/87) SS **93**
Chardonnay California Reserve 1989 $32 (7/15/92) **87**
Chardonnay California Reserve 1988 $30 (6/15/91) **90**
Chardonnay California Reserve 1987 Rel: $28 Cur: $35 (5/31/90) **87**
Chardonnay California Reserve 1986 Rel: $28 Cur: $42 (CH-5/90) **93**
Fumé Blanc Sonoma County 1990 $10 (7/15/91) **87**
Fumé Blanc Sonoma County 1989 $10 (10/15/90) **80**
Fumé Blanc Sonoma County 1988 $9 (9/15/89) **88**
Fumé Blanc Sonoma County 1987 $9 (3/15/89) **89**
Merlot Alexander Valley 1987 $16.50 (7/31/90) **84**
Merlot Alexander Valley 1986 $15 (6/30/89) **87**
Merlot Sonoma County 1989 $15 (5/31/92) **86**
Merlot Sonoma County 1988 $17.50 (8/31/91) **85**
Sauvignon Blanc Late Harvest Alexander Valley Eldorado Gold 1989 $16.50/375ml (9/15/91) **88**

FERRATON PERE (France/Rhône)
Crozes-Hermitage La Matinière 1988 $14 (6/30/90) **85**

PIERRE FERRAUD & FILS (France/Beaujolais)
Beaujolais-Villages Cuvée Ensorceleuse 1988 $10 (5/31/89) (TM) **81**
Brouilly Domaine Rolland 1988 $16 (5/31/89) (TM) **84**
Chénas Cuvée Jean-Michel 1988 $10 (5/31/89) (TM) **89**
Chiroubles Domaine de la Chapelle du Bois 1988 $12 (5/31/89) (TM) **79**
Côte-de-Brouilly 1988 $16 (5/31/89) (TM) **83**
Fleurie 1988 $15 (5/31/89) (TM) **87**
Fleurie Château de Grand Pre 1988 $16 (5/31/89) (TM) **86**
Juliénas 1988 $12 (5/31/89) (TM) **73**
Morgon Domaine de l'Eveque 1988 $16 (5/31/89) (TM) **89**
Moulin-à-Vent 1988 $16 (5/31/89) (TM) **83**
Régnié 1988 $10 (5/31/89) (TM) **81**
St.-Amour 1988 $12 (5/31/89) (TM) **85**

FERREIRA (Portugal)
Tawny Port 20 Year Old Duque de Beaganca NV $38 (2/28/90) (JS) **80**
Vintage Port 1987 ($NA) (VP-11/89) **88**
Vintage Port 1985 Rel: $20 Cur: $30 (VP-11/89) **87**
Vintage Port 1982 Rel: $14 Cur: $28 (VP-11/89) **81**
Vintage Port 1980 Rel: $13 Cur: $27 (VP-11/89) **80**
Vintage Port 1978 Rel: $11 Cur: $33 (VP-11/89) **89**
Vintage Port 1977 Rel: $11 Cur: $45 (VP-11/89) **86**
Vintage Port 1975 $47 (VP-11/89) **81**
Vintage Port 1970 $50 (VP-4/89) **86**
Vintage Port 1966 $81 (VP-11/89) **85**
Vintage Port 1963 $105 (10/31/88) **90**
Vintage Port 1960 $83 (10/31/88) **86**
Vintage Port 1955 $120 (VP-11/89) **85**
Vintage Port 1950 $85 (VP-11/89) **79**
Vintage Port 1945 $250 (VP-11/89) **81**
Vintage Port 1935 $200 (VP-2/90) **93**
Vintage Port Quinta do Seixo 1983 Rel: $14 Cur: $26 (VP-11/89) **91**

GLORIA FERRER (United States/California)
Brut Carneros Cuvée 1985 $20 (5/15/92) **81**
Brut Carneros Royal Cuvée 1987 $17 (5/15/92) **84**
Brut Carneros Royal Cuvée 1986 $17 (12/31/91) **84**
Brut Sonoma County NV $14 (5/15/92) **84**
Brut Sonoma County Royal Cuvée 1986 $16 (4/30/91) **84**
Brut Sonoma County Royal Cuvée 1985 $16 (3/15/91) **83**
Brut Sonoma County Royal Cuvée 1984 $15 (4/15/88) **89**
Natural Sonoma County Cuvée Emerald NV $11 (5/16/86) **89**

EREDI VIRGINIA FERRERO (Italy/Piedmont)
Barolo S. Rocco 1982 $22 (7/15/88) **92**
Barolo S. Rocco Riserva 1979 $19 (7/31/89) **67**

J.A. FERRET (France/Burgundy)
Pouilly-Fuissé Les Perrières Cuvée Spéciale 1986 $30 (7/31/90) **82**

HENRY FESSY (France/Burgundy)
Pouilly-Fuissé 1986 $10 (10/15/88) **82**

SYLVAIN FESSY (France/Burgundy)
Pouilly-Fuissé Cuvée Gilles Guérrin 1986 $12 (12/31/87) **86**
St.-Véran Cuvée Prissé 1986 $8 (2/15/88) **75**

FETZER (United States/California)
Cabernet Sauvignon California 1988 $8 (1/31/91) BB **81**
Cabernet Sauvignon California Reserve 1985 $17 (11/15/89) **87**
Cabernet Sauvignon California Valley Oaks 1988 $8 (11/15/91) **82**
Cabernet Sauvignon Lake County 1985 $6.50 (8/31/87) BB **82**
Cabernet Sauvignon Lake County 1984 $8 (5/15/87) **74**
Cabernet Sauvignon Lake County 1983 $5.50 (5/01/86) **83**
Cabernet Sauvignon Lake County 1982 $5.50 (5/16/84) **78**
Cabernet Sauvignon Mendocino County 1981 $7 (12/16/84) **86**
Cabernet Sauvignon Mendocino Barrel Select 1986 $11 (4/15/90) **90**
Cabernet Sauvignon Mendocino Barrel Select 1985 $10 (12/15/88) **85**
Cabernet Sauvignon Mendocino Barrel Select 1984 $9 (11/30/87) **82**
Cabernet Sauvignon California Barrel Select 1983 $8 (6/15/87) **70**
Cabernet Sauvignon Mendocino Barrel Select 1982 $7 (2/01/85) **73**
Cabernet Sauvignon Mendocino Special Reserve 1987 ($NA) (4/15/89) (BT) **85+**
Cabernet Sauvignon Sonoma County Reserve 1986 $24 (9/30/91) **88**
Cabernet Sauvignon Sonoma County Reserve 1985 $24 (8/31/90) **86**
Cabernet Sauvignon Mendocino Special Reserve 1984 $14 (12/31/88) **85**
Chardonnay Mendocino County Barrel Select 1990 $11 (7/15/92) **89**
Chardonnay Mendocino County Barrel Select 1989 $11 (7/15/91) **84**
Chardonnay Mendocino County Barrel Select 1988 $12 (3/15/90) **82**
Chardonnay Mendocino County Barrel Select 1987 $10 (3/15/89) **88**
Chardonnay Mendocino County Barrel Select 1986 $10 (8/31/88) **73**
Chardonnay California Barrel Select 1985 $8.50 (4/30/87) **79**
Chardonnay California Barrel Select 1984 $8.50 (3/01/86) **72**
Chardonnay Mendocino Barrel Select 1981 $8.50 (6/01/86) **93**
Chardonnay Mendocino County Reserve 1990 $18.50 (7/15/92) **87**
Chardonnay Mendocino County Reserve 1989 $18 (7/15/91) **87**
Chardonnay Mendocino County Reserve 1988 $17.50 (5/31/90) **82**
Chardonnay Mendocino County Reserve 1987 $15 (7/15/89) **82**
Chardonnay Mendocino County Special Reserve 1986 $14 (12/31/88) **88**
Chardonnay California Special Reserve 1985 $13 (11/15/87) **86**
Chardonnay California Special Reserve 1984 $13 (6/01/86) **84**
Chardonnay California Special Reserve 1982 $10 (4/01/84) **78**
Chardonnay California Special Reserve 1981 $11 (6/01/86) **88**
Chardonnay California Sundial 1990 $8 (9/15/91) **79**
Chardonnay California Sundial 1989 $8 (4/30/90) BB **82**
Chardonnay California Sundial 1988 $7 (5/15/89) **78**
Chardonnay California Sundial 1987 $6.50 (7/31/88) **76**
Chardonnay California Sundial 1986 $6.50 (9/15/87) BB **86**
Chardonnay Mendocino County Sundial 1985 $6.50 (9/15/86) BB **84**
Chardonnay Mendocino County 1984 $6.50 (4/16/86) **86**
Chenin Blanc California 1988 $6 (7/31/89) **88**
Chenin Blanc Mendocino County 1990 $6.75 (11/15/91) **77**
Fumé Blanc California Valley Oaks Fumé 1989 $6.50 (12/31/90) **76**
Fumé Blanc California Valley Oaks Fumé 1988 $6.50 (7/31/89) **79**
Gamay Beaujolais Mendocino County 1988 $5 (7/15/89) **74**
Gewürztraminer California 1990 $6.75 (4/30/91) **75**
Gewürztraminer California 1989 $6 (6/30/90) **79**
Gewürztraminer California 1988 $6.50 (2/28/89) BB **88**
Johannisberg Riesling California 1990 $6.75 (5/15/91) BB **85**
Johannisberg Riesling California 1988 $6 (7/31/89) BB **81**
Johannisberg Riesling Late Harvest Sonoma County Reserve 1988 $10/375ml (3/31/91) **91**
Petite Sirah California Reserve 1986 $14 (8/31/90) **74**
Pinot Noir California Special Reserve 1980 $13 (8/31/86) **65**
Pinot Noir Mendocino 1981 $5.50 (4/01/84) **80**
Pinot Noir Mendocino County Reserve 1986 $17.50 (10/31/90) **87**
Pinot Noir Mendocino County Special Reserve 1985 $13 (6/15/88) **78**
Sauvignon Blanc California Barrel Select 1990 $9 (2/15/92) **80**
White Zinfandel California 1988 $7 (6/15/89) **85**
Zinfandel California 1989 $6.50 (11/30/90) **76**
Zinfandel California 1986 $6 (9/15/88) **78**
Zinfandel Lake County 1986 $6 (2/15/88) BB **83**
Zinfandel Lake County 1984 $5 (4/15/87) **81**
Zinfandel Lake County 1983 $4.50 (7/16/86) BB **83**
Zinfandel Mendocino 1982 $5.50 (4/01/85) **81**
Zinfandel Mendocino 1980 $5.50 (4/01/84) **78**
Zinfandel Mendocino County Reserve 1986 $14 (7/31/90) **83**
Zinfandel Mendocino Home Vineyard 1982 $8 (11/01/84) **77**
Zinfandel Mendocino Lolonis Vineyards 1982 $8 (11/01/84) **79**
Zinfandel Mendocino Ricetti Vineyard 1985 $14 (10/15/88) **79**
Zinfandel Mendocino Ricetti Vineyard 1983 $8.50 (2/16/86) **82**
Zinfandel Mendocino Ricetti Vineyard 1982 $8 (10/16/84) **79**
Zinfandel Mendocino Ricetti Vineyard Reserve 1986 $14 (7/31/90) **74**
Zinfandel Mendocino Scharffenberger Vineyard 1982 $8 (10/16/84) **85**
Zinfandel Mendocino Special Reserve 1985 $14 (12/15/88) **81**
Zinfandel Mendocino Special Reserve 1983 $8.50 (5/01/86) **63**

FEUERHEERD (Portugal)
Vintage Port 1985 ($NA) (VP-1/90) **72**
Vintage Port 1980 ($NA) (VP-1/90) **76**
Vintage Port 1977 $17 (VP-1/90) **69**
Vintage Port 1970 $45 (VP-1/90) **80**

NICHOLAS FEUILLATTE (France/Champagne)
Brut Champagne Réserve Particulière NV $22 (12/31/91) **82**

CHATEAU FEYTIT-CLINET (France/Bordeaux)
Pomerol 1990 (NR) (5/15/92) (BT) **90+**
Pomerol 1989 (NR) (4/30/91) (BT) **90+**
Pomerol 1985 $30 (4/30/88) **88**

Key to Symbols

The scores reported here are the results of blind tastings conducted by our panel of senior editors. Wines that carry the initials below are results of individual tastings.

THE WINE SPECTATOR 100-POINT SCALE ***95-100***—Classic, a great wine; ***90-94***—Outstanding, superior character and style; ***80-89***—Good to very good, a wine with special qualities; ***70-79***—Average, drinkable wine that may have minor flaws; ***60-69***—Below average, drinkable but not recommended; ***50-59***—Poor, undrinkable, not recommended. "+"—With a score indicates a range; used primarily with barrel tastings to indicate a preliminary score.

SPECIAL DESIGNATIONS SS—Spectator Selection, CS—Cellar Selection, BB—Best Buy, ($NA)—Price not available, (NR)—Not released.

TASTER'S INITIALS (JG)—Jim Gordon, (HS)—Harvey Steiman, (JL)—James Laube, (JS)—James Suckling, (TM)—Thomas Matthews, (TR)—Terry Robards, (PM)—Per-Henrik Mansson, (BT)—Barrel Tasting (these wines were tasted blind from barrel samples), (CA-date)—*California's Great Cabernets* by James Laube, (CH-date)—*California's Great Chardonnays* by James Laube, (VP-date)—*Vintage Port* by James Suckling.

DATE TASTED Dates in parentheses represent the issue in which the rating was published.

Pomerol 1983 Rel: $13 Cur: $19 (7/16/86) **70**
Pomerol 1982 Rel: $15 Cur: $20 (5/15/89) (TR) **91**

JEAN-PHILIPPE FICHET (France/Burgundy)
Meursault 1989 $28 (8/31/91) **88**
Meursault Perrières 1989 $43 (8/31/91) **91**

MARSILIO FICINO (Italy/Tuscany)
Poggio Il Pino 1986 $6 (7/31/89) **70**

FICKLIN (United States/California)
Port California Special Bottling No. 5 1980 $19 (4/30/91) **84**
Port California Special Bottling No. 6 1983 $25 (11/30/91) **87**
Port California Tinta NV $10 (4/30/91) **78**

LES FIEFS DE LAGRANGE (France/Bordeaux)
St.-Julien 1991 (NR) (5/15/92) (BT) **85+**
St.-Julien 1990 (NR) (5/15/92) (BT) **90+**
St.-Julien 1989 (NR) (4/30/91) (BT) **85+**
St.-Julien 1988 $17 (4/30/91) **92**
St.-Julien 1987 $14 (6/30/88) (BT) **70+**
St.-Julien 1986 Rel: $17 Cur: $19 (6/30/88) (BT) **80+**
St.-Julien 1985 Rel: $17 Cur: $20 (5/15/87) (BT) **70+**
St.-Julien 1983 Rel: $10 Cur: $13 (5/01/86) **85**

FIELD STONE (United States/California)
Cabernet Sauvignon Alexander Valley 1987 $14 (2/28/91) **85**
Cabernet Sauvignon Alexander Valley 1983 $11 (10/15/88) **74**
Cabernet Sauvignon Alexander Valley Home Ranch Vineyard 1985 $14 (4/15/89) **70**
Cabernet Sauvignon Alexander Valley Hoot Owl Reserve 1986 $20 (12/15/90) **85**
Cabernet Sauvignon Alexander Valley Hoot Owl Creek Vineyards 1985 $20 (3/31/89) **87**
Cabernet Sauvignon Alexander Valley Hoot Owl Creek Vineyards 1984 $14 (10/15/88) **82**
Cabernet Sauvignon Alexander Valley Staten Family Reserve 1987 $25 (11/15/91) **72**
Cabernet Sauvignon Alexander Valley Turkey Hill Vineyard 1985 $18 (2/28/91) **84**
Cabernet Sauvignon Alexander Valley Turkey Hill Vineyard 1984 $16 (12/31/88) **88**
Cabernet Sauvignon Alexander Valley Turkey Hill Vineyard 1982 $12 (3/16/86) **78**
Chardonnay Sonoma County 1989 $14 (3/31/91) **87**
Chardonnay Sonoma County 1988 $14 (4/15/91) **85**
Gewürztraminer Alexander Valley 1987 $7 (2/28/89) **69**
Petite Sirah Alexander Valley 1988 $15 (12/31/90) **85**
Petite Sirah Alexander Valley 1987 $15 (12/31/90) **84**
Petite Sirah Alexander Valley 1986 $15 (9/30/89) **79**
Petite Sirah Alexander Valley 1985 $11 (2/15/89) **83**

FIELDS OF FAIR (United States/Kansas)
Concord Kansas 1991 $5 (2/29/92) **70**
Flint Hills Red Proprietor's Reserve Kansas 1990 $6.50 (2/29/92) **70**
Vintage One Proprietor's Reserve Kansas 1991 $7 (2/29/92) **70**

CHATEAU DE FIEUZAL (France/Bordeaux)
Pessac-Léognan 1991 (NR) (5/15/92) (BT) **80+**
Pessac-Léognan 1990 (NR) (5/15/92) (BT) **90+**
Pessac-Léognan 1989 $32 (3/15/92) **95**
Pessac-Léognan 1988 $32 (4/30/91) **91**
Pessac-Léognan 1987 $18 (5/15/90) **81**
Pessac-Léognan 1986 Rel: $21 Cur: $25 (6/30/89) **90**
Graves 1985 $24 (6/15/88) **90**
Graves 1982 Rel: $12 Cur: $22 (5/01/85) **81**
Graves 1982 Rel: $12 Cur: $22 (2/01/85) **81**
Graves 1979 $25 (10/15/89) (JS) **83**
Graves Blanc 1985 $39 (11/15/87) **90**
Pessac-Léognan Blanc 1990 (NR) (9/30/91) (BT) **90+**
Pessac-Léognan Blanc 1988 $45 (6/30/89) (BT) **95+**
Pessac-Léognan Blanc 1987 $40 (6/30/89) (BT) **90+**

CHATEAU FIGEAC (France/Bordeaux)
St.-Emilion 1990 (NR) (5/15/92) (BT) **90+**
St.-Emilion 1989 $69 (3/15/92) **93**
St.-Emilion 1988 $45 (6/30/91) **93**
St.-Emilion 1987 $35 (10/31/91) (JS) **83**
St.-Emilion 1986 Rel: $45 Cur: $49 (10/31/91) (JS) **87**
St.-Emilion 1985 Rel: $37 Cur: $50 (10/31/91) (JS) **95**
St.-Emilion 1984 Rel: $26 Cur: $29 (3/31/87) **83**
St.-Emilion 1983 Rel: $37 Cur: $42 (10/31/91) (JS) **85**
St.-Emilion 1982 $67 (10/31/91) (JS) **93**
St.-Emilion 1981 $39 (10/31/91) (JS) **73**
St.-Emilion 1980 $30 (5/01/85) **90**
St.-Emilion 1979 $43 (10/31/91) (JS) **88**
St.-Emilion 1978 $51 (10/31/91) (JS) **89**
St.-Emilion 1976 ($NA) (10/31/91) (JS) **87**
St.-Emilion 1975 $60 (10/31/91) (JS) **78**
St.-Emilion 1971 $75 (10/31/91) (JS) **84**
St.-Emilion 1970 $75 (10/31/91) (JS) **92**
St.-Emilion 1966 $125 (10/31/91) (JS) **85**
St.-Emilion 1964 $110 (10/31/91) (JS) **93**
St.-Emilion 1962 $66 (10/31/91) (JS) **85**
St.-Emilion 1961 $139 (10/31/91) (JS) **97**
St.-Emilion 1955 $250 (10/31/91) (JS) **96**
St.-Emilion 1953 $150 (10/31/91) (JS) **86**
St.-Emilion 1952 $100 (10/31/91) (JS) **85**
St.-Emilion 1950 ($NA) (10/31/91) (JS) **91**
St.-Emilion 1949 $220 (10/31/91) (JS) **99**
St.-Emilion 1947 $620 (10/31/91) (JS) **93**
St.-Emilion 1945 $300 (10/31/91) (JS) **96**
St.-Emilion 1943 $150 (10/31/91) (JS) **90**
St.-Emilion 1942 $125 (10/31/91) (JS) **85**
St.-Emilion 1939 $125 (10/31/91) (JS) **83**
St.-Emilion 1937 $125 (10/31/91) (JS) **69**
St.-Emilion 1934 $160 (10/31/91) (JS) **79**
St.-Emilion 1929 $400 (10/31/91) (JS) **98**
St.-Emilion 1926 $300 (10/31/91) (JS) **87**
St.-Emilion 1924 $350 (10/31/91) (JS) **88**
St.-Emilion 1911 $400 (10/31/91) (JS) **78**
St.-Emilion 1906 $350 (10/31/91) (JS) **78**
St.-Emilion 1905 $430 (10/31/91) (JS) **95**

PAUL FIGEAT (France/Loire)
Pouilly-Fumé 1989 $20 (11/15/91) **74**
Pouilly-Fumé 1988 $14 (4/15/90) **88**

CHATEAU FILHOT (France/Sauternes)
Sauternes 1989 ($NA) (6/15/90) (BT) **85+**
Sauternes 1988 $25 (6/15/90) (BT) **85+**
Sauternes 1987 $19 (6/15/90) **68**
Sauternes 1986 $19 (12/31/89) **83**
Sauternes 1983 Rel: $21 Cur: $34 (1/31/88) **86**
Sauternes 1980 Rel: $11.50 Cur: $25 (5/01/84) **80**

FATTORIA LE FILIGARE (Italy/Tuscany)
Chianti Classico 1988 ($NA) (9/15/91) **91**

CHATEAU DES FINES ROCHES (France/Rhône)
Châteauneuf-du-Pape 1989 $20 (5/31/92) **81**
Châteauneuf-du-Pape 1986 $14 (9/30/90) **85**
Châteauneuf-du-Pape 1985 $12 (10/31/87) **80**
Châteauneuf-du-Pape 1984 $12 (9/30/87) **89**

BARONE FINI (Italy/North)
Cabernet Sauvignon Cabernello 1988 $10 (7/15/91) **76**

FIRELANDS (United States/Ohio)
Brut American Champagne NV $12 (2/29/92) **73**
Cabernet Sauvignon Ohio Lake Erie 1988 $10 (2/29/92) **82**
Chardonnay Ohio Lake Erie Barrel Select 1990 $10 (2/29/92) **86**

FIRESTONE (United States/California)
Blanc de Noirs Santa Ynez Valley 1985 $15 (12/31/88) **79**
Cabernet Sauvignon Santa Ynez Valley 1988 $12 (11/15/91) **75**
Cabernet Sauvignon Santa Ynez Valley 1987 $11 (5/31/90) **82**
Cabernet Sauvignon Santa Ynez Valley 1986 $10 (12/15/89) **81**
Cabernet Sauvignon Santa Ynez Valley 1985 $9.50 (8/31/88) **72**
Cabernet Sauvignon Santa Ynez Valley 1984 $9.50 (3/31/88) **72**
Cabernet Sauvignon Santa Ynez Valley 1983 $9 (6/15/87) **77**
Cabernet Sauvignon Santa Ynez Valley 1981 $8 (3/01/85) **89**
Cabernet Sauvignon Santa Ynez Valley Reserve 1988 $18 (2/28/91) **84**
Cabernet Sauvignon Santa Ynez Valley Special Release 1977 $9.50 (4/16/85) **77**
Cabernet Sauvignon Santa Ynez Valley Vintage Reserve 1985 $25 (12/15/89) **67**
Cabernet Sauvignon Santa Ynez Valley Vintage Reserve 1979 $12 (3/16/86) **73**
Chardonnay Santa Ynez Valley 1987 $10 (12/15/89) **72**
Chardonnay Santa Ynez Valley 1986 $10 (12/31/88) **83**
Chardonnay Santa Ynez Valley 10th Anniversary 1985 $10 (4/15/88) **63**
Chardonnay Santa Ynez Valley 1984 $10 (5/31/87) **76**
Chardonnay Santa Ynez Valley 1983 $10 (3/01/86) **63**
Chardonnay Santa Ynez Valley Barrel Fermented 1990 $13 (1/31/92) **78**
Chardonnay Santa Ynez Valley Barrel Fermented 1989 $12 (4/30/91) **87**
Gewürztraminer Santa Ynez Valley 1990 $8 (11/15/91) **73**
Johannisberg Riesling Late Harvest Santa Barbara County Selected Harvest 1989 $12/375ml (4/30/91) **84**
Johannisberg Riesling Late Harvest Santa Ynez Valley Ambassador's Vineyard Selected Harvest 1988 $9.50/375ml (12/15/89) **79**
Johannisberg Riesling Late Harvest Santa Ynez Valley Ambassador's Vineyard Selected Harvest 1986 $9.50/375ml (2/28/89) **89**
Johannisberg Riesling Santa Barbara County Dry 1990 $9 (7/15/91) **82**
Johannisberg Riesling Santa Ynez Valley 1990 $7.50 (7/15/91) **84**
Johannisberg Riesling Santa Ynez Valley 1989 $7.50 (12/31/90) **84**
Johannisberg Riesling Santa Ynez Valley 1988 $7 (12/15/89) **82**
Johannisberg Riesling Santa Ynez Valley 1987 $6.50 (2/28/89) **74**
Merlot Santa Ynez Valley 1989 $12 (8/31/91) **86**
Merlot Santa Ynez Valley 1988 $11 (3/31/91) **82**
Merlot Santa Ynez Valley 1987 $9 (12/15/89) **83**
Merlot Santa Ynez Valley 1986 $9 (9/30/88) **83**
Merlot Santa Ynez Valley 1985 $9 (4/30/88) **78**
Merlot Santa Ynez Valley 1981 $6.50 (5/16/86) **50**
Pinot Noir Santa Ynez Valley 1986 $10 (12/15/89) **77**
Pinot Noir Santa Ynez Valley 1983 $9 (11/15/87) **71**
Pinot Noir Santa Ynez Valley 1981 $8.25 (5/16/86) **73**
Red Table Wine Santa Ynez Valley 1990 $6 (4/30/92) **74**
Sauvignon Blanc Santa Ynez Valley 1987 $7.50 (12/15/89) **77**

DR. FISCHER (Germany)
Riesling Auslese Mosel-Saar-Ruwer Gold Cap Wawerner Herrenberg 1990 $65/375ml (12/15/91) **88**
Riesling Auslese Mosel-Saar-Ruwer Ockfener Bockstein 1990 $29 (12/15/91) **92**
Riesling Auslese Mosel-Saar-Ruwer Ockfener Bockstein 1983 $12 (3/16/85) **90**
Riesling Auslese Mosel-Saar-Ruwer Wawerner Herrenberg 1990 $21 (12/15/91) **91**
Riesling Auslese Mosel-Saar-Ruwer Wawerner Herrenberg 1988 ($NA) (9/30/89) **94**
Riesling Beerenauslese Mosel-Saar-Ruwer Ockfener Bockstein 1990 (NR) (12/15/91) **88**
Riesling Eiswein Mosel-Saar-Ruwer Wawerner Herrenberg 1990 (NR) (12/15/91) **88**
Riesling Kabinett Mosel-Saar-Ruwer Ockfener Bockstein 1990 $16 (12/15/91) **82**
Riesling Kabinett Mosel-Saar-Ruwer Ockfener Bockstein 1988 $13 (9/30/89) **85**
Riesling Qualitätswein Mosel-Saar-Ruwer Ockfener Bockstein 1990 $14 (12/15/91) **74**
Riesling Qualitätswein Mosel-Saar-Ruwer Ockfener Bockstein 1988 $6 (9/30/89) **81**
Riesling Spätlese Mosel-Saar-Ruwer Ockfener Bockstein 1990 $20 (12/15/91) **90**
Riesling Spätlese Mosel-Saar-Ruwer Ockfener Bockstein 1988 $15 (9/30/89) **83**
Riesling Spätlese Mosel-Saar-Ruwer Ockfener Bockstein 1985 $13 (5/15/87) **88**

FISHER (United States/California)
Cabernet Sauvignon Napa-Sonoma Counties Coach Insignia 1991 (NR) (5/15/92) (BT) **85+**
Cabernet Sauvignon Napa-Sonoma Counties Coach Insignia 1990 (NR) (5/15/91) (BT) **90+**
Cabernet Sauvignon Napa-Sonoma Counties Coach Insignia 1989 $18 (3/31/92) **82**
Cabernet Sauvignon Napa-Sonoma Counties Coach Insignia 1988 $15 (5/15/90) (BT) **85+**
Cabernet Sauvignon Napa-Sonoma Counties Coach Insignia 1987 Rel: $20 Cur: $23 (11/15/91) **84**
Cabernet Sauvignon Sonoma County 1983 $12.50 (6/15/87) **73**
Cabernet Sauvignon Sonoma County 1982 $12.50 (11/01/85) **88**
Cabernet Sauvignon Sonoma County 1981 $12 (12/01/84) **85**
Cabernet Sauvignon Sonoma County Coach Insignia 1986 $20 (1/31/90) **87**
Cabernet Sauvignon Sonoma County Coach Insignia 1985 Rel: $18 Cur: $22 (CA-3/89) **90**
Cabernet Sauvignon Sonoma County Coach Insignia 1984 Rel: $18 Cur: $25 (CA-3/89) **89**
Chardonnay Napa-Sonoma Counties 1989 $12 (9/30/90) **74**
Chardonnay Napa-Sonoma Counties 1988 $11 (9/15/89) **88**
Chardonnay Napa-Sonoma Counties 1987 $11 (4/15/89) **85**
Chardonnay Napa-Sonoma Counties 1986 $11 (7/15/88) **86**
Chardonnay Napa-Sonoma Counties 1985 $11 (7/15/87) **82**
Chardonnay Napa-Sonoma Counties 1983 Rel: $14 Cur: $18 (CH-6/90) **82**
Chardonnay Sonoma County 1982 Rel: $14 Cur: $22 (CH-2/90) **81**
Chardonnay Sonoma County 1981 Rel: $14 Cur: $25 (CH-2/90) **88**
Chardonnay Sonoma County 1980 Rel: $14 Cur: $22 (CH-2/90) **85**
Chardonnay Sonoma County Coach Insignia 1989 $15 (3/31/92) **85**
Chardonnay Sonoma County Coach Insignia 1988 Rel: $18 Cur: $20 (6/30/90) **90**
Chardonnay Sonoma County Coach Insignia 1987 Rel: $18 Cur: $22 (1/31/90) **84**
Chardonnay Sonoma County Coach Insignia 1986 Rel: $17 Cur: $20 (CH-2/90) **90**
Chardonnay Sonoma County Coach Insignia 1985 Rel: $16 Cur: $20 (CH-2/90) **84**
Chardonnay Sonoma County Coach Insignia 1984 Rel: $15 Cur: $20 (CH-2/90) **82**

Chardonnay Sonoma County Whitney's Vineyard 1988 $24 (CH-2/90) **88**
Chardonnay Sonoma County Whitney's Vineyard 1987 $24 (CH-2/90) **86**
Chardonnay Sonoma County Whitney's Vineyard 1985 Rel: $24 Cur: $30 (CH-2/90) **84**
Chardonnay Sonoma County Whitney's Vineyard 1984 Rel: $20 Cur: $30 (CH-2/90) **90**
Chardonnay Sonoma County Whitney's Vineyard 1983 Rel: $20 Cur: $30 (CH-2/90) **78**
Chardonnay Sonoma County Whitney's Vineyard 1982 Rel: $20 Cur: $25 (CH-6/90) **78**
Chardonnay Sonoma County Whitney's Vineyard 1981 Rel: $20 Cur: $25 (CH-2/90) **85**
Chardonnay Sonoma County Whitney's Vineyard 1980 Rel: $20 Cur: $30 (CH-2/90) **92**

FITCH MOUNTAIN (United States/California)
Cabernet Sauvignon Napa Valley 1985 $9 (4/15/89) **74**
Chardonnay Napa Valley 1986 $8 (11/15/88) **81**
Merlot Napa Valley 1986 $9 (9/30/88) **84**
Merlot Napa Valley 1985 $9 (12/15/87) **89**
Zinfandel Dry Creek Valley 1989 $10 (3/31/92) **86**

FIVE PALMS (United States/California)
Cabernet Sauvignon Napa Valley 1984 $6 (3/31/87) BB **87**
Chardonnay Napa Valley 1985 $8 (4/30/87) **87**

FLAX (United States/California)
Chardonnay Sonoma County 1986 $14 (12/31/88) **77**
Chardonnay Sonoma County 1985 $12 (10/15/87) **82**

CHATEAU LA FLEUR (France/Bordeaux)
St.-Emilion 1990 (NR) (5/15/92) (BT) **85+**
St.-Emilion 1989 $18 (3/15/92) **84**
St.-Emilion 1986 $13.50 (2/15/90) **82**

CHATEAU LA FLEUR BECADE (France/Bordeaux)
Haut-Médoc 1988 ($NA) (6/30/89) (BT) **70+**

CHATEAU LA FLEUR DE GAY (France/Bordeaux)
Pomerol 1991 (NR) (5/15/92) (BT) **90+**
Pomerol 1990 (NR) (5/15/92) (BT) **95+**
Pomerol 1989 $88 (3/15/92) **98**
Pomerol 1988 $57 (6/30/91) **94**
Pomerol 1987 $38 (6/30/89) (BT) **85+**
Pomerol 1986 Rel: $43 Cur: $63 (10/31/89) CS **95**
Pomerol 1982 $45 (5/15/89) (TR) **88**

CHATEAU LA FLEUR-PETRUS (France/Bordeaux)
Pomerol 1990 (NR) (5/15/92) (BT) **90+**
Pomerol 1989 Rel: $57 Cur: $66 (3/15/92) **88**
Pomerol 1988 $63 (6/30/89) (BT) **85+**
Pomerol 1987 $36 (6/30/89) (BT) **80+**
Pomerol 1986 Rel: $52 Cur: $57 (2/15/90) CS **93**
Pomerol 1985 Rel: $50 Cur: $62 (6/30/88) **86**
Pomerol 1982 $85 (5/15/89) (TR) **88**
Pomerol 1945 $300 (3/16/86) (JL) **63**
Pomerol (English Bottled) 1959 $150 (10/15/90) (JS) **92**

CHATEAU LA FLEUR-POURRET (France/Bordeaux)
St.-Emilion 1991 (NR) (5/15/92) (BT) **65+**
St.-Emilion 1990 (NR) (5/15/92) (BT) **85+**
St.-Emilion 1989 (NR) (3/15/92) **82**
St.-Emilion 1988 ($NA) (8/31/90) (BT) **75+**
St.-Emilion 1987 ($NA) (6/30/88) (BT) **75+**

FINCA FLICHMAN (Other/Argentina)
Argenta Mendoza 1988 $4 (3/15/91) BB **84**
Cabernet Sauvignon Mendoza Caballero de la Cepa 1985 $8 (3/15/91) **68**
Cabernet Sauvignon Mendoza Proprietor's Private Reserve 1987 $6 (3/15/91) BB **81**
Chardonnay Mendoza Caballero de la Cepa 1990 $8 (7/15/91) **78**
Chardonnay Mendoza Proprietor's Private Reserve 1990 $6 (4/30/91) BB **83**
Mendoza 1990 $4 (7/15/91) **76**
Merlot Proprietor's Private Reserve Mendoza 1988 $6 (3/15/91) **66**
Selection Flichman Mendoza 1990 $4.50 (7/15/91) **79**
Selection Mendoza 1988 $4.50 (3/15/91) BB **79**

FLORA SPRINGS (United States/California)
Cabernet Sauvignon Napa Valley Reserve 1991 (NR) (5/15/92) (BT) **86+**
Cabernet Sauvignon Napa Valley 1990 (NR) (5/15/91) (BT) **90+**
Cabernet Sauvignon Napa Valley 1989 (NR) (5/15/91) (BT) **85+**
Cabernet Sauvignon Napa Valley Cellar Select 1988 $24 (2/29/92) **85**
Cabernet Sauvignon Napa Valley Cellar Select 1987 $25 (11/15/90) **91**
Cabernet Sauvignon Napa Valley 1986 Rel: $15 Cur: $18 (3/15/90) **85**
Cabernet Sauvignon Napa Valley 1985 Rel: $15 Cur: $18 (7/31/89) **90**
Cabernet Sauvignon Napa Valley 1984 Rel: $13 Cur: $18 (CA-3/89) **85**
Cabernet Sauvignon Napa Valley 1983 Rel: $13 Cur: $17 (12/15/86) **79**
Cabernet Sauvignon Napa Valley 1982 $9 (10/15/86) **78**
Cabernet Sauvignon Napa Valley 1981 $12 (12/16/84) **82**
Cabernet Sauvignon Napa Valley 1980 Rel: $12 Cur: $28 (CA-3/89) **85**
Chardonnay Napa Valley 1990 $15 (1/31/92) **89**
Chardonnay Napa Valley 1989 $15 (7/15/91) **87**
Chardonnay Napa Valley 1988 $15 (3/15/90) **87**
Chardonnay Napa Valley 1987 $15 (6/15/89) **87**
Chardonnay Napa Valley 1986 $13 (7/15/88) **77**
Chardonnay Napa Valley 1985 $14 (2/28/87) **85**
Chardonnay Napa Valley 1984 $13.50 (10/31/86) **88**
Chardonnay Napa Valley 1983 $13 (10/01/85) **77**
Chardonnay Napa Valley 1982 $12 (5/16/84) **59**
Chardonnay Napa Valley Barrel Fermented 1990 $24 (4/15/92) **92**
Chardonnay Napa Valley Barrel Fermented 1989 $23 (5/15/91) **91**
Chardonnay Napa Valley Barrel Fermented 1988 Rel: $24 Cur: $27 (6/30/90) **91**
Chardonnay Napa Valley Barrel Fermented 1987 Rel: $20 Cur: $27 (CH-1/90) **95**
Chardonnay Napa Valley Barrel Fermented 1986 Rel: $20 Cur: $27 (CH-1/90) **87**
Chardonnay Napa Valley Barrel Fermented 1985 Rel: $18 Cur: $22 (CH-1/90) **85**
Chardonnay Napa Valley Barrel Fermented 1984 Rel: $18 Cur: $28 (CH-1/90) **88**
Chardonnay Napa Valley Barrel Fermented 1983 Rel: $18 Cur: $28 (CH-1/90) **94**
Chardonnay Napa Valley Barrel Fermented 1982 $15 (CH-6/88) **70**
Chardonnay Napa Valley Special Selection 1981 Rel: $12 Cur: $25 (CH-1/90) **89**
Chardonnay Napa Valley Special Selection 1980 Rel: $12 Cur: $25 (CH-1/90) **88**
Chardonnay Napa Valley 1979 Rel: $9 Cur: $25 (CH-1/90) **91**
Chardonnay Napa Valley Floréal 1990 $12.50 (4/15/92) **85**
Merlot Napa Valley 1990 (NR) (5/15/91) (BT) **85+**
Merlot Napa Valley 1988 $15 (8/31/91) **83**
Merlot Napa Valley 1987 $16.50 (7/31/90) **87**
Merlot Napa Valley 1985 $15 (6/30/88) **82**
Merlot Napa Valley Floréal 1989 $12.50 (5/31/92) **84**
Sauvignon Blanc Napa Valley 1990 $9.25 (11/30/91) SS **90**
Sauvignon Blanc Napa Valley 1988 $8.50 (3/31/90) **67**
Sauvignon Blanc Napa Valley Soliloquy Special Select 1990 $20 (6/15/92) **88**
Sauvignon Blanc Napa Valley Soliloquy Special Select 1989 $20 (3/15/91) **88**
Trilogy Napa Valley 1991 (NR) (5/15/92) (BT) **85+**
Trilogy Napa Valley 1990 (NR) (5/15/91) (BT) **90+**
Trilogy Napa Valley 1989 (NR) (5/15/91) (BT) **90+**
Trilogy Napa Valley 1988 $33 (2/29/92) **86**
Trilogy Napa Valley 1987 $35 (5/15/91) **90**
Trilogy Napa Valley 1986 Rel: $33 Cur: $36 (2/15/90) **94**
Trilogy Napa Valley 1985 Rel: $30 Cur: $38 (CA-3/89) **88**
Trilogy Napa Valley 1984 Rel: $30 Cur: $33 (CA-3/89) **84**

FLYNN (United States/Oregon)
Brut Willamette Valley Première Cuvée 1987 $14 (5/15/92) **81**

THOMAS FOGARTY (United States/California)
Cabernet Sauvignon Napa Valley 1985 $15 (7/15/91) **70**
Chardonnay Carneros Napa Valley 1986 $15 (12/31/88) **83**
Chardonnay Carneros Napa Valley Winery Lake Vineyard 1985 $15 (2/15/88) **73**
Chardonnay Edna Valley 1987 $13.50 (12/15/89) **81**
Chardonnay Edna Valley Paragon Vineyards 1989 $15 (7/15/91) **88**
Chardonnay Monterey 1985 $15 (2/15/88) **88**
Chardonnay Monterey Ventana Vineyards 1986 $15 (5/31/88) **68**
Chardonnay Monterey Ventana Vineyards 1984 $13.50 (2/28/87) **84**
Chardonnay Santa Cruz Mountains 1988 $18 (7/15/91) **87**
Chardonnay Santa Cruz Mountains 1985 $16.50 (2/15/88) **69**
Gewürztraminer Monterey Ventana Vineyards 1990 $9 (3/31/92) **73**
Pinot Noir Carneros Napa Valley 1985 $15 (6/15/88) **73**
Pinot Noir Napa Valley 1988 $15 (2/28/91) **86**
Pinot Noir Santa Cruz Mountains Estate 1988 $15 (2/28/91) **83**
Pinot Noir Santa Cruz Mountains Estate 1986 $20 (6/15/88) **64**
Pinot Noir Santa Cruz Mountains Estate 1985 $20 (6/15/88) **58**

FATTORIA DI FOGNANO (Italy/Tuscany)
Chianti Colli Senesi 1985 $6.50 (5/15/89) **67**
Vino Nobile di Montepulciano Riserva Talosa 1983 $7 (5/15/89) BB **85**
Vino Nobile di Montepulciano Riserva Talosa 1981 $8.50 (5/15/89) **76**

FOLIE A DEUX (United States/California)
Brut Napa Valley Fantasie 1989 $18 (6/15/91) **81**
Cabernet Sauvignon Napa Valley 1987 $18 (11/15/90) **92**
Cabernet Sauvignon Napa Valley 1986 $16.50 (4/15/90) **85**
Cabernet Sauvignon Napa Valley 1984 $14.50 (5/31/88) **88**
Chardonnay Napa Valley 1990 $16 (7/15/92) **87**
Chardonnay Napa Valley 1989 $16 (7/15/91) **80**
Chardonnay Napa Valley 1988 Rel: $16 Cur: $18 (5/31/90) **85**
Chardonnay Napa Valley 1987 Rel: $15 Cur: $18 (CH-6/90) **90**
Chardonnay Napa Valley 1986 Rel: $15 Cur: $18 (CH-6/90) **88**
Chardonnay Napa Valley 1985 Rel: $14.50 Cur: $18 (CH-6/90) **88**
Chardonnay Napa Valley 1984 Rel: $14 Cur: $18 (CH-6/90) **87**
Chardonnay Napa Valley 1983 $12 (9/16/85) **76**
Chardonnay Napa Valley 1982 $12.50 (CH-7/90) **78**
Chardonnay Napa Valley Pas de Deux 1989 $10 (7/15/91) **83**
Chenin Blanc Napa Valley 1988 $7 (7/31/89) **88**
Merlot Napa Valley 1988 $18 (3/31/91) **82**
Muscat Canelli Napa Valley Muscat à Deux 1990 $8.50 (8/31/91) **80**
Muscat Canelli Napa Valley Muscat à Deux 1988 $7.50 (8/31/89) **83**

LA FOLIE (France/Other)
Brut Blanc de Blancs Réserve NV $5.50 (6/15/90) **63**

FOLONARI (Italy/Other)
Chardonnay 1987 $5 (9/15/89) **76**

CHATEAU FOMBRAUGE (France/Bordeaux)
St.-Emilion 1986 $19 (6/30/89) **86**
St.-Emilion 1985 Rel: $15 Cur: $22 (5/15/88) **87**

CHATEAU FONBADET (France/Bordeaux)
Pauillac 1988 $16 (8/31/91) **89**
Pauillac 1987 $15 (6/30/89) (BT) **75+**
Pauillac 1982 $16 (8/01/85) **86**

FOND DE CAVE (Other/Argentina)
Cabernet Sauvignon Mendoza 1982 $7 (2/15/89) **76**

CHATEAU FONPLEGADE (France/Bordeaux)
St.-Emilion 1989 (NR) (4/30/91) (BT) **85+**
St.-Emilion 1988 $18 (6/30/91) **85**
St.-Emilion 1987 $15 (6/30/89) (BT) **70+**
St.-Emilion 1986 $15 (6/30/88) (BT) **80+**
St.-Emilion 1985 $15 (5/15/87) (BT) **70+**
St.-Emilion 1982 $25 (5/15/89) (TR) **77**

CHATEAU FONREAUD (France/Bordeaux)
Listrac 1991 (NR) (5/15/92) (BT) **75+**
Listrac 1989 (NR) (4/30/91) (BT) **85+**
Listrac 1988 $15 (4/30/91) **82**
Listrac 1987 $10 (6/30/89) (BT) **65+**
Listrac 1986 $10 (6/30/88) (BT) **70+**

CHATEAU FONROQUE (France/Bordeaux)
St.-Emilion 1990 (NR) (5/15/92) (BT) **85+**
St.-Emilion 1989 $24 (3/15/92) **88**
St.-Emilion 1988 $18 (8/31/90) (BT) **90+**
St.-Emilion 1987 $15 (6/30/89) (BT) **75+**

Key to Symbols

The scores reported here are the results of blind tastings conducted by our panel of senior editors. Wines that carry the initials below are results of individual tastings.

THE WINE SPECTATOR 100-POINT SCALE ***95-100***—Classic, a great wine; ***90-94***—Outstanding, superior character and style; ***80-89***—Good to very good, a wine with special qualities; ***70-79***—Average, drinkable wine that may have minor flaws; ***60-69***—Below average, drinkable but not recommended; ***50-59***—Poor, undrinkable, not recommended. "+"—With a score indicates a range; used primarily with barrel tastings to indicate a preliminary score.

SPECIAL DESIGNATIONS SS—Spectator Selection, CS—Cellar Selection, BB—Best Buy, ($NA)—Price not available, (NR)—Not released.

TASTER'S INITIALS (JG)—Jim Gordon, (HS)—Harvey Steiman, (JL)—James Laube, (JS)—James Suckling, (TM)—Thomas Matthews, (TR)—Terry Robards, (PM)—Per-Henrik Mansson, (BT)—Barrel Tasting (these wines were tasted blind from barrel samples), (CA-date)—*California's Great Cabernets* by James Laube, (CH-date)—*California's Great Chardonnays* by James Laube, (VP-date)—*Vintage Port* by James Suckling.

DATE TASTED Dates in parentheses represent the issue in which the rating was published.

St.-Emilion 1986 $19 (6/30/88) (BT) **80+**
St.-Emilion 1985 $23 (5/15/87) (BT) **80+**
St.-Emilion 1982 $21 (5/15/89) (TR) **78**

CHATEAU DE FONSALETTE (France/Rhône)
Côtes du Rhône Blanc 1986 $18.50 (3/15/89) **80**
Côtes du Rhône Réserve 1985 $15.50 (9/30/88) **87**

FONSECA (Portugal)
Tawny Port 20 Year Old NV $40 (2/28/90) (JS) **90**
Vintage Port 1985 Rel: $32 Cur: $39 (VP-6/90) **95**
Vintage Port 1983 Rel: $24 Cur: $38 (VP-6/90) **90**
Vintage Port 1983 Rel: $24 Cur: $38 (3/31/87) **89**
Vintage Port 1980 Rel: $22 Cur: $40 (VP-6/90) **74**
Vintage Port 1977 Rel: $16 Cur: $62 (VP-4/90) **100**
Vintage Port 1975 $47 (10/31/88) **81**
Vintage Port 1970 $68 (VP-12/89) **96**
Vintage Port 1966 $80 (VP-2/90) **97**
Vintage Port 1963 $164 (VP-12/89) **98**
Vintage Port 1960 $88 (10/31/88) **81**
Vintage Port 1955 $210 (VP-8/88) **96**
Vintage Port 1948 $310 (VP-11/89) **100**
Vintage Port 1945 $580 (VP-11/89) **91**
Vintage Port 1934 $350 (VP-2/90) **91**
Vintage Port 1927 $500 (VP-12/89) **100**
Vintage Port Guimaraens 1987 ($NA) (VP-2/90) **90**
Vintage Port Guimaraens 1986 ($NA) (VP-2/90) **86**
Vintage Port Guimaraens 1984 ($NA) (VP-2/90) **85**
Vintage Port Guimaraens 1982 ($NA) (VP-2/90) **82**
Vintage Port Guimaraens 1978 Rel: $32 Cur: $35 (VP-2/90) **80**
Vintage Port Guimaraens 1976 Rel: $32 Cur: $38 (VP-2/90) **89**
Vintage Port Guimaraens 1974 $42 (VP-1/90) **84**
Vintage Port Guimaraens 1972 $37 (VP-2/90) **75**
Vintage Port Guimaraens 1968 $44 (VP-2/90) **84**
Vintage Port Guimaraens 1967 $55 (VP-2/90) **90**
Vintage Port Guimaraens 1965 $54 (VP-2/90) **89**
Vintage Port Guimaraens 1964 $85 (VP-2/90) **90**
Vintage Port Guimaraens 1962 $70 (VP-2/90) **88**
Vintage Port Guimaraens 1961 $70 (VP-2/90) **85**
Vintage Port Guimaraens 1958 $90 (VP-2/90) **88**
Vintage Port Quinta do Panascal 1987 ($NA) (VP-2/90) **82**
Vintage Port Quinta do Panascal 1986 ($NA) (VP-2/90) **79**
Vintage Port Quinta do Panascal 1985 ($NA) (VP-2/90) **78**
Vintage Port Quinta do Panascal 1984 ($NA) (VP-2/90) **70**
Vintage Port Quinta do Panascal 1983 ($NA) (VP-2/90) **79**

JOSE MARIA DA FONSECA (Portugal)
Dão Terras Altas 1987 $7 (11/15/91) **69**
Garrafeira CO 1982 $13.50 (12/31/90) **83**
Garrafeira RA 1982 $13.50 (12/31/90) **88**
Pasmados 1984 $7.25 (4/30/91) BB **83**
Periquita 1987 $5.75 (12/31/90) BB **84**
Periquita Vintage Selection Unfiltered 1987 $7.25 (11/15/91) **80**
Portalegre Morgado do Reguengo 1987 $8.75 (11/15/91) **86**
Tinto Velho Requengos de Monsarax Colheita 1986 $9.75 (12/31/90) **82**

DOMAINE FONT DE MICHELLE (France/Rhône)
Châteauneuf-du-Pape 1989 $18 (10/15/91) **83**
Châteauneuf-du-Pape 1988 $21 (10/15/91) **86**
Châteauneuf-du-Pape 1986 $20 (10/15/91) **89**
Châteauneuf-du-Pape 1985 Rel: $13 Cur: $20 (10/15/91) **84**
Châteauneuf-du-Pape 1983 $25 (10/15/91) **85**
Châteauneuf-du-Pape 1981 $20 (10/15/91) **88**
Châteauneuf-du-Pape Blanc 1990 $20 (10/15/91) **89**
Châteauneuf-du-Pape Blanc 1985 $15 (11/15/87) **81**

DOMAINE DE FONT-SANE (France/Rhône)
Gigondas 1985 $13 (1/31/89) **86**

FONTAINE-GAGNARD (France/Burgundy)
Chassagne-Montrachet Morgeot 1985 $45 (5/31/88) **71**
Chassagne-Montrachet Rouge 1985 $16 (12/31/88) **85**

FONTANAFREDDA (Italy/Piedmont)
Barbaresco 1983 $11.50 (9/15/88) (HS) **80**
Barbaresco 1982 ($NA) (9/15/88) (HS) **81**
Barbaresco 1978 ($NA) (9/15/88) (HS) **86**
Barolo 1983 $16 (9/15/88) (HS) **83**
Barolo 1982 $16 (9/15/88) (HS) **84**
Barolo 1978 $13 (2/15/84) **80**
Barolo Lazarito 1982 $42 (9/15/88) (HS) **90**
Barolo San Pietro 1982 $42 (9/15/88) (HS) **85**
Barolo Vigna la Rosa 1982 Rel: $40 Cur: $45 (2/15/88) CS **90**

CHATEAU FONTENIL (France/Bordeaux)
Fronsac 1990 (NR) (5/15/92) (BT) **90+**
Fronsac 1989 (NR) (4/30/91) (BT) **85+**
Fronsac 1986 $14 (2/15/90) **76**
Fronsac 1985 Rel: $14 Cur: $17 (9/30/88) **87**

CASTELLO DI FONTERUTOLI (Italy/Tuscany)
Chianti Classico 1988 $14 (11/30/90) **85**
Chianti Classico 1987 $11 (11/30/89) **90**
Chianti Classico 1986 $11 (1/31/89) **85**
Chianti Classico 1985 $11 (11/30/89) (HS) **88**
Chianti Classico Riserva 1983 $15 (11/30/89) (HS) **88**
Chianti Classico Ser Lapo Riserva 1986 $25 (11/30/90) **88**
Chianti Classico Ser Lapo Riserva 1985 $18 (9/15/91) **87**
Chianti Classico Ser Lapo Riserva 1983 $15 (1/31/89) **88**
Concerto di Fonterutoli 1986 $35 (3/15/91) **87**
Concerto di Fonterutoli 1985 $25 (2/15/89) **84**
Concerto di Fonterutoli 1983 $15 (11/30/89) (HS) **86**

CHATEAU FONTESTEAU (France/Bordeaux)
Haut-Médoc 1988 ($NA) (6/30/89) (BT) **70+**
Haut-Médoc 1987 ($NA) (6/30/89) (BT) **70+**

FONTODI (Italy/Tuscany)
Chianti Classico 1989 $13 (11/30/91) **89**
Chianti Classico 1988 $13 (9/15/91) SS **91**
Chianti Classico 1987 $8 (11/30/89) **81**
Chianti Classico 1986 $9 (1/31/89) **74**
Chianti Classico Riserva 1985 $16 (9/15/91) **93**
Chianti Classico Riserva 1983 $8.75 (9/15/87) **87**
Chianti Classico Riserva 1982 $7.50 (9/15/87) **87**
Chianti Classico Vigna del Sorbo Riserva 1985 $25 (9/15/91) **88**
Flaccianello 1987 $35 (12/15/91) **83**
Flaccianello 1986 $29 (1/31/90) **88**
Flaccianello 1985 Rel: $23 Cur: $35 (1/31/89) **91**
Flaccianello 1983 $18 (7/15/87) **95**
Meriggio 1987 $17 (3/31/90) **82**

DOMAINE DE FONTSAINTE (France/Other)
Corbières Réserve la Demoiselle 1986 $7 (8/31/89) **77**

FOPPIANO (United States/California)
Cabernet Sauvignon Russian River Valley 1985 $9 (6/30/89) **71**
Cabernet Sauvignon Russian River Valley 1984 $8.50 (4/30/88) **77**
Cabernet Sauvignon Russian River Valley 1981 $7.75 (4/16/85) **81**
Cabernet Sauvignon Sonoma County 1989 $9.50 (3/15/92) **82**
Cabernet Sauvignon Sonoma County 1986 $9 (11/15/90) **79**
Chardonnay Russian River Valley 1987 $9 (7/15/89) **72**
Chardonnay Sonoma County 1989 $10 (7/15/92) **80**
Chardonnay Sonoma County 1986 $9 (5/31/88) **75**
Chardonnay Sonoma County 1983 $10 (10/01/85) **78**
Petite Sirah Russian River Valley 1988 $8.25 (8/31/90) **86**
Petite Sirah Russian River Valley 1986 $8 (6/15/89) **83**
Petite Sirah Russian River Valley Reserve Le Grande Petite 1987 $20 (8/31/90) **79**
Petite Sirah Sonoma County 1990 $10 (6/30/92) **87**
Zinfandel Dry Creek Valley Proprietor's Reserve 1987 $12 (12/31/90) **86**

FORADORI (Italy/North)
Granato di Mezzolombardo 1988 $33 (1/31/92) **86**
Teroldego Rotaliano Vigneto Morei 1988 $16 (1/31/92) **69**

FOREST HILL (United States/California)
Chardonnay Napa Valley Private Reserve 1990 $24 (3/31/92) **90**
Chardonnay Napa Valley Private Reserve 1989 $24 (7/15/91) **83**

FOREST LAKE (United States/California)
Cabernet Sauvignon California 1988 $6.50 (11/15/91) **81**

DOMAINE FOREY PERE & FILS (France/Burgundy)
Echézeaux 1989 (NR) (1/31/92) **90**
Nuits-St.-Georges Les Perrières 1989 (NR) (1/31/92) **89**
Vosne-Romanée 1989 (NR) (1/31/92) **85**

LA FORGE (France/Rhône)
Côtes du Lubéron 1989 $7 (11/15/91) **79**
Côtes du Lubéron Blanc 1990 $7 (11/15/91) BB **81**

FORGERON (United States/Oregon)
Chenin Blanc Oregon 1987 $7.50 (7/31/89) **69**
Pinot Noir Oregon 1985 $19 (2/15/90) **89**
Pinot Noir Oregon Vinters Reserve 1987 $12 (2/15/90) **76**

FORMAN (United States/California)
Cabernet Sauvignon Napa Valley 1988 Rel: $32 Cur: $45 (8/31/91) **88**
Cabernet Sauvignon Napa Valley 1987 Rel: $26 Cur: $44 (9/30/90) **93**
Cabernet Sauvignon Napa Valley 1986 Rel: $20 Cur: $51 (6/15/89) **93**
Cabernet Sauvignon Napa Valley 1985 Rel: $18 Cur: $76 (CA-3/89) **93**
Cabernet Sauvignon Napa Valley 1984 Rel: $18 Cur: $70 (CA-3/89) **92**
Cabernet Sauvignon Napa Valley 1983 Rel: $15.50 Cur: $70 (CA-3/89) **90**
Chardonnay Napa Valley 1990 $22 (6/30/92) **90**
Chardonnay Napa Valley 1989 Rel: $22 Cur: $25 (2/15/91) **88**
Chardonnay Napa Valley 1988 Rel: $20 Cur: $40 (6/30/90) **92**
Chardonnay Napa Valley 1987 Rel: $18 Cur: $33 (CH-2/90) **89**
Chardonnay Napa Valley 1986 Rel: $18 Cur: $45 (CH-2/90) **92**
Chardonnay Napa Valley 1985 Rel: $15 Cur: $60 (CH-2/90) **93**
Chardonnay Napa Valley 1984 Rel: $15 Cur: $45 (CH-2/90) **86**

JEAN-CHARLES FORNEROT (France/Burgundy)
Chassagne-Montrachet Rouge Les Champs-Gains 1985 $19 (7/31/89) **83**
Chassagne-Montrachet Rouge La Maltroie 1985 $19 (7/31/89) **86**
St.-Aubin Rouge Les Perrières 1985 $15 (7/31/89) **82**

FORTANT (France/Other)
Cabernet Sauvignon Vin de Pays d'Oc 1988 $6 (4/30/91) **70**
Chardonnay Vin de Pays d'Oc 1989 $6 (5/31/91) **69**
Merlot Vin de Pays d'Oc 1988 $6 (5/31/91) **70**

CHATEAU FORTIA (France/Rhône)
Châteauneuf-du-Pape 1983 Rel: $14 Cur: $24 (12/31/87) **87**
Châteauneuf-du-Pape Tête de Cru 1985 $22 (5/31/92) **81**

FORTINO (United States/California)
Johannisberg Riesling Santa Clara County 1988 $5.50 (7/31/89) **77**

FORTNUM & MASON (France/Burgundy)
Charmes-Chambertin (English Bottled) 1947 ($NA) (8/31/90) (TR) **94**

LES FORTS DE LATOUR (France/Bordeaux)
Pauillac 1991 (NR) (5/15/92) (BT) **85+**
Pauillac 1990 (NR) (5/15/92) (BT) **90+**
Pauillac 1989 (NR) (3/15/92) **91**
Pauillac 1987 ($NA) (6/30/89) (BT) **75+**
Pauillac 1986 $38 (5/15/87) (BT) **70+**
Pauillac 1985 Rel: $40 Cur: $51 (8/31/91) **87**
Pauillac 1983 $32 (10/15/90) **85**
Pauillac 1982 $55 (10/15/90) **86**
Pauillac 1979 $33 (10/15/89) (JS) **87**

DE FORVILLE (Italy/Piedmont)
Barbaresco 1981 $14 (2/16/86) **63**
Chardonnay 1989 $12 (2/15/91) **75**
Dolcetto d'Alba Vigneto Loreto 1989 $12 (2/28/91) **81**

FOSSI (Italy/North)
Chardonnay dell' Alto Adige 1988 $11.50 (7/15/91) **82**
Chianti 1990 $8.50 (4/30/92) **83**
Chianti 1988 $8 (10/31/91) BB **84**
Chianti Classico Riserva 1985 $18 (9/15/91) **82**

CHATEAU FOURCAS-DUPRE (France/Bordeaux)
Listrac 1991 (NR) (5/15/92) (BT) **70+**
Listrac 1989 $25 (3/15/92) **86**
Listrac 1988 $22 (4/30/91) **83**
Listrac 1987 $15 (6/30/89) (BT) **75+**

Listrac 1986 $15 (6/30/88) (BT) **75+**
Listrac 1983 Rel: $9 Cur: $15 (10/31/86) **89**

CHATEAU FOURCAS-HOSTEN (France/Bordeaux)
Listrac 1990 (NR) (4/30/91) (BT) **85+**
Listrac 1989 $19 (3/15/92) **87**
Listrac 1988 $13 (7/15/91) **82**
Listrac 1987 $11 (6/30/89) (BT) **70+**
Listrac 1986 $13 (11/15/89) **79**
Listrac 1983 Rel: $11 Cur: $16 (10/15/86) **83**

CHATEAU FOURCAS-LOUBANEY (France/Bordeaux)
Listrac 1988 $17 (2/28/91) **83**

CHATEAU FOURNAS BERNADOTTE (France/Bordeaux)
Haut-Médoc 1988 $18 (6/15/91) **76**
Haut-Médoc 1987 $13 (6/30/89) (BT) **65+**

FOX MOUNTAIN (United States/California)
Cabernet Sauvignon Russian River Valley Reserve 1985 $19 (9/15/89) **75**
Cabernet Sauvignon Russian River Valley Reserve 1984 $18 (3/15/89) **85**
Cabernet Sauvignon Russian River Valley Reserve 1982 $18 (12/31/87) **77**
Cabernet Sauvignon Russian River Valley Reserve 1981 $16 (12/15/86) **79**
Chardonnay Sonoma County Reserve 1986 $15 (4/15/91) **85**
Chardonnay Sonoma County Reserve 1985 $14 (12/31/88) **70**
Chardonnay Sonoma County Reserve 1984 $14.50 (12/31/87) **80**

FOXEN (United States/California)
Cabernet Sauvignon Santa Barbara County 1989 $20 (11/15/91) **91**
Cabernet Sauvignon Santa Barbara County 1988 $18 (11/15/91) **89**
Chardonnay Santa Maria Valley 1987 $18 (12/15/89) **90**
Pinot Noir Santa Maria Valley 1987 $16 (12/15/89) **78**

CHATEAU FRANC BIGAROUX (France/Bordeaux)
St.-Emilion 1988 $24 (7/31/91) **91**

CHATEAU DE FRANC-MAYNE (France/Bordeaux)
St.-Emilion 1991 (NR) (5/15/92) (BT) **80+**
St.-Emilion 1990 (NR) (5/15/92) (BT) **90+**
St.-Emilion 1989 $28 (3/15/92) **94**
St.-Emilion 1988 Rel: $15 Cur: $20 (7/15/91) **83**
St.-Emilion 1987 ($NA) (6/30/88) (BT) **75+**
St.-Emilion 1986 $16 (6/30/88) (BT) **65+**

CHATEAU DE FRANCE (France/Bordeaux)
Pessac-Léognan 1991 (NR) (5/15/92) (BT) **80+**
Pessac-Léognan 1989 $22 (3/15/92) **89**
Pessac-Léognan 1988 $18 (2/28/91) SS **92**
Pessac-Léognan 1987 $15 (6/30/89) (BT) **80+**
Pessac-Léognan 1986 $15 (6/30/88) (BT) **80+**

CASA FRANCESCO (Italy/Tuscany)
Chianti Riserva 1985 $8.50 (9/15/91) **88**

FRANCISCAN (United States/California)
Cabernet Sauvignon Alexander Valley 1980 $7.50 (10/16/84) **86**
Cabernet Sauvignon Napa Valley Library Selection 1985 Rel: $17.50 Cur: $20 (CA-3/89) **88**
Cabernet Sauvignon Napa Valley Oakville Estate 1988 $12 (11/15/91) **81**
Cabernet Sauvignon Napa Valley Oakville Estate 1987 $12 (2/15/91) **89**
Cabernet Sauvignon Napa Valley Oakville Estate 1986 $11 (7/15/90) **84**
Cabernet Sauvignon Napa Valley Oakville Estate 1985 $11 (5/15/89) **86**
Cabernet Sauvignon Napa Valley Oakville Estate 1984 $9.50 (9/15/88) **84**
Cabernet Sauvignon Napa Valley Oakville Estate 1983 $9 (4/30/87) **75**
Cabernet Sauvignon Napa Valley 1979 Rel: $8.50 Cur: $18 (CA-3/89) **79**
Cabernet Sauvignon Napa Valley Oakville Estate Reserve 1987 $16 (11/15/91) SS **91**
Cabernet Sauvignon Napa Valley Oakville Estate Reserve 1985 Rel: $17.50 Cur: $20 (5/31/90) **88**
Cabernet Sauvignon Napa Valley Private Reserve 1984 Rel: $9 Cur: $15 (CA-3/89) **87**
Cabernet Sauvignon Napa Valley Private Reserve 1983 Rel: $8.50 Cur: $16 (CA-3/89) **85**
Cabernet Sauvignon Napa Valley Reserve 1978 Rel: $15 Cur: $23 (CA-3/89) **78**
Cabernet Sauvignon Napa Valley Reserve 1975 Rel: $12 Cur: $28 (CA-3/89) **82**
Chardonnay Alexander Valley 1983 $10.50 (2/01/85) **87**
Chardonnay Alexander Valley 1982 $10 (4/16/84) **83**
Chardonnay Napa Valley Oakville Estate 1990 $12 (7/15/92) **87**
Chardonnay Napa Valley Oakville Estate 1989 $12 (7/15/91) **83**
Chardonnay Napa Valley Oakville Estate 1988 $11 (6/30/90) **82**
Chardonnay Napa Valley Oakville Estate 1987 $11 (2/15/89) **81**
Chardonnay Napa Valley Oakville Estate 1986 $9.25 (5/31/88) **87**
Chardonnay Napa Valley Oakville Estate 1984 $8.50 (3/15/87) BB **90**
Chardonnay Napa Valley Estate Bottled 1982 $9.50 (8/01/85) **84**
Chardonnay Napa Valley Oakville Estate Reserve 1990 $16 (7/15/92) **85**
Chardonnay Napa Valley Oakville Estate Reserve 1987 $20 (6/15/90) **92**
Chardonnay Napa Valley Oakville Estate Reserve 1986 $14 (CH-4/90) **91**
Chardonnay Napa Valley Oakville Estate Reserve 1984 Rel: $12 Cur: $23 (CH-4/90) **86**
Chardonnay Napa Valley Oakville Estate Reserve 1983 $12 (CH-4/90) **82**
Chardonnay Carneros Reserve 1982 Rel: $9.50 Cur: $17 (CH-4/90) **84**
Chardonnay Napa Valley Oakville Estate Cuvée Sauvage 1990 $25 (7/15/92) **88**
Chardonnay Napa Valley Oakville Estate Cuvée Sauvage 1989 Rel: $24 Cur: $28 (7/15/91) **90**
Chardonnay Napa Valley Oakville Estate Cuvée Sauvage 1988 Rel: $20 Cur: $25 (6/30/90) **93**
Chardonnay Napa Valley Oakville Estate Cuvée Sauvage 1987 Rel: $20 Cur: $30 (6/15/90) **90**
Johannisberg Riesling Late Harvest Napa Valley Select 1983 $10/375ml (1/31/88) **88**
Meritage Napa Valley 1988 Rel: $16 Cur: $20 (11/15/91) **83**
Meritage Napa Valley 1987 Rel: $17 Cur: $21 (4/30/91) **87**
Meritage Napa Valley 1986 Rel: $15 Cur: $23 (7/31/90) **79**
Meritage Napa Valley 1985 Rel: $20 Cur: $28 (3/31/90) **90**

Merlot Napa Valley 1981 $8.50 (10/01/85) **91**
Merlot Napa Valley Oakville Estate 1989 $12 (5/31/92) **79**
Merlot Napa Valley Oakville Estate 1988 ($NA) (4/30/90) (BT) **80+**
Merlot Napa Valley Oakville Estate 1987 $12.50 (6/15/90) **88**
Merlot Napa Valley Oakville Estate 1986 $12 (7/31/89) **80**
Merlot Napa Valley Oakville Estate 1985 Rel: $9.25 Cur: $15 (5/31/88) **89**
Merlot Napa Valley Oakville Estate 1984 Rel: $8.50 Cur: $15 (6/30/87) SS **90**
Merlot Napa Valley Oakville Estate 1983 $8.50 (2/28/87) **88**
Zinfandel Napa Valley Oakville Estate 1989 $10 (7/31/91) **88**
Zinfandel Napa Valley Oakville Estate 1988 $9 (5/31/90) **87**

NINO FRANCO (Italy/Sparkling)
Prosecco di Valdobbiadene Rustico 1987 $12 (12/31/91) **79**

FRANCO-ESPANOLAS (Spain)
Rioja White Viña Soledad Gran Reserva 1978 ($NA) (5/31/92) **86**

FRANCO-FIORINA (Italy/Piedmont)
Barolo 1982 $22 (5/31/88) **79**
Chardonnay 1989 $21 (3/31/91) **83**
Dolcetto d'Alba 1989 $13 (4/30/91) **83**
Dolcetto d'Alba 1987 $8.75 (7/31/89) **76**
Favorita delle Langhe 1988 $12 (4/30/90) **75**
Freisa delle Langhe 1989 $16 (7/15/91) **78**
Freisa delle Langhe 1989 $15 (4/15/91) **70**

CHATEAU DE FRANCS (France/Bordeaux)
Côtes de Francs 1989 (NR) (4/30/90) (BT) **75+**
Côtes de Francs 1988 ($NA) (8/31/90) (BT) **80+**
Côtes de Francs Blanc 1990 (NR) (9/30/91) (BT) **80+**

FREEMARK ABBEY (United States/California)
Cabernet Sauvignon Napa Valley Bosché 1987 $25 (11/15/91) **87**
Cabernet Sauvignon Napa Valley Bosché 1986 $24 (7/31/90) **76**
Cabernet Sauvignon Napa Valley Bosché 1985 Rel: $24 Cur: $33 (7/31/89) **90**
Cabernet Sauvignon Napa Valley Bosché 1984 Rel: $20 Cur: $24 (CA-3/89) **88**
Cabernet Sauvignon Napa Valley Bosché 1983 Rel: $18 Cur: $33 (CA-3/89) **86**
Cabernet Sauvignon Napa Valley Bosché 1982 Rel: $15 Cur: $41 (CA-3/89) **88**
Cabernet Sauvignon Napa Valley Bosché 1982 Rel: $15 Cur: $41 (5/16/86) CS **93**
Cabernet Sauvignon Napa Valley Bosché 1981 Rel: $14 Cur: $33 (CA-3/89) **86**
Cabernet Sauvignon Napa Valley Bosché 1980 Rel: $14.50 Cur: $35 (CA-3/89) **88**
Cabernet Sauvignon Napa Valley Bosché 1979 Rel: $12 Cur: $25 (CA-3/89) **93**
Cabernet Sauvignon Napa Valley Bosché 1978 Rel: $12.50 Cur: $56 (CA-3/89) **93**
Cabernet Sauvignon Napa Valley Bosché 1977 Rel: $12.50 Cur: $25 (CA-3/89) **88**
Cabernet Sauvignon Napa Valley Bosché 1976 Rel: $12.50 Cur: $32 (CA-3/89) **85**
Cabernet Sauvignon Napa Valley Bosché 1975 Rel: $10 Cur: $57 (CA-3/89) **90**
Cabernet Sauvignon Napa Valley Bosché 1974 Rel: $7.75 Cur: $70 (CA-3/89) **91**
Cabernet Sauvignon Napa Valley Bosché 1973 Rel: $8 Cur: $70 (CA-3/89) **88**
Cabernet Sauvignon Napa Valley Bosché 1972 Rel: $6 Cur: $30 (CA-3/89) **80**
Cabernet Sauvignon Napa Valley Bosché 1971 Rel: $6.75 Cur: $45 (CA-3/89) **86**
Cabernet Sauvignon Napa Valley Bosché 1970 Rel: $8.75 Cur: $125 (CA-3/89) **91**
Cabernet Sauvignon Napa Valley 1987 $16 (7/31/91) **86**
Cabernet Sauvignon Napa Valley 1986 $15 (11/15/90) **83**
Cabernet Sauvignon Napa Valley 1985 $15 (10/31/89) **79**
Cabernet Sauvignon Napa Valley 1984 $14 (2/15/89) **84**
Cabernet Sauvignon Napa Valley 1983 $12 (2/15/88) **68**
Cabernet Sauvignon Napa Valley 1982 Rel: $12 Cur: $17 (2/15/87) **84**
Cabernet Sauvignon Napa Valley 1981 $10.50 (10/01/85) **79**
Cabernet Sauvignon Napa Valley 1980 Rel: $14.50 Cur: $22 (5/16/84) **84**
Cabernet Sauvignon Napa Valley 1979 Rel: $10.50 Cur: $25 (1/01/84) **89**
Cabernet Sauvignon Napa Valley 1969 $52 (4/01/86) **68**
Cabernet Sauvignon Napa Valley Sycamore Vineyards 1986 $25 (11/15/91) **91**
Cabernet Sauvignon Napa Valley Sycamore Vineyards 1985 $25 (10/31/89) **88**
Cabernet Sauvignon Napa Valley Sycamore Vineyards 1984 Rel: $20 Cur: $23 (12/15/88) **91**
Chardonnay Napa Valley 1989 $15 (7/15/91) **75**
Chardonnay Napa Valley 1988 $15 (6/30/90) **91**
Chardonnay Napa Valley 1987 Rel: $15 Cur: $17 (CH-2/90) **84**
Chardonnay Napa Valley 1986 Rel: $15 Cur: $18 (CH-2/90) **86**
Chardonnay Napa Valley 1985 Rel: $14 Cur: $25 (CH-2/90) **80**
Chardonnay Napa Valley 1984 Rel: $14 Cur: $20 (CH-2/90) **87**
Chardonnay Napa Valley 1983 Rel: $14 Cur: $20 (CH-2/90) **85**
Chardonnay Napa Valley 1982 Rel: $12.75 Cur: $18 (CH-2/90) **72**
Chardonnay Napa Valley 1981 Rel: $13.50 Cur: $20 (CH-2/90) **81**
Chardonnay Napa Valley 1980 Rel: $13.50 Cur: $38 (CH-2/90) **84**
Chardonnay Napa Valley 1979 Rel: $13.25 Cur: $25 (CH-2/90) **76**
Chardonnay Napa Valley 1978 Rel: $10 Cur: $26 (CH-2/90) **70**
Chardonnay Napa Valley 1977 Rel: $10 Cur: $36 (CH-2/90) **58**
Chardonnay Napa Valley 1976 Rel: $9.75 Cur: $26 (CH-2/90) **62**
Chardonnay Napa Valley 1975 Rel: $9 Cur: $45 (CH-2/90) **82**
Chardonnay Napa Valley 1974 Rel: $7.95 Cur: $42 (CH-2/90) **74**
Chardonnay Napa Valley 1973 Rel: $6.50 Cur: $32 (CH-2/90) **77**
Chardonnay Napa Valley 1972 Rel: $6.50 Cur: $48 (CH-2/90) **77**
Chardonnay Napa Valley 1971 Rel: $7 Cur: $40 (CH-2/90) **70**
Chardonnay Napa Valley 1970 Rel: $7 Cur: $35 (CH-2/90) **55**
Chardonnay Napa Valley 1969 Rel: $6 Cur: $37 (CH-2/90) **60**
Chardonnay Napa Valley 1968 Rel: $5 Cur: $35 (CH-2/90) **73**
Chardonnay Napa Valley Carpy Ranch 1990 $22 (7/15/92) **85**
Chardonnay Napa Valley Carpy Ranch 1989 $22 (7/15/91) **84**
Chardonnay Napa Valley Carpy Ranch 1988 Rel: $22 Cur: $25 (4/30/90) **84**
Johannisberg Riesling Late Harvest Napa Valley Edelwein Gold 1989 $22/375ml (7/15/90) **92**
Johannisberg Riesling Late Harvest Napa Valley Edelwein Gold 1988 $18/375ml (6/15/89) **87**
Johannisberg Riesling Late Harvest Napa Valley Edelwein Gold 1986 $18.50/375ml (6/15/87) **87**
Johannisberg Riesling Late Harvest Napa Valley Edelwein Gold 1973 ($NA) (2/28/87) **91**
Johannisberg Riesling Napa Valley 1990 $8 (4/30/91) BB **85**
Johannisberg Riesling Napa Valley 1988 $8 (8/31/89) **90**
Merlot Napa Valley 1985 $10 (12/31/88) **90**

FREIHERR ZU KNYPHAUSEN (Germany)
Riesling Kabinett Halbtrocken Rheingau Erbacher Marcobrunn Charta 1988 ($NA) (9/30/89) **82**
Riesling Kabinett Halbtrocken Rheingau Erbacher Steinmorgen 1988 ($NA) (9/30/89) **86**
Riesling Kabinett Rheingau Erbacher Steinmorgen 1988 ($NA) (9/30/89) **87**
Riesling Kabinett Rheingau Kiedricher Sandgrub 1988 ($NA) (9/30/89) **84**

FREIXENET (Spain)
Brut Cava Carta Nevada NV $7 (12/31/90) **78**
Brut Cava Cordon Negro NV $9 (2/29/92) **80**
Brut Cava Nature 1987 $10 (5/15/92) **80**
Brut Cava Nature 1985 $10 (12/31/90) **81**
Extra Dry Cava Cordon Negro NV $9 (2/29/92) **80**

Key to Symbols

The scores reported here are the results of blind tastings conducted by our panel of senior editors. Wines that carry the initials below are results of individual tastings.

THE WINE SPECTATOR 100-POINT SCALE ***95-100***—Classic, a great wine; ***90-94***—Outstanding, superior character and style; ***80-89***—Good to very good, a wine with special qualities; ***70-79***—Average, drinkable wine that may have minor flaws; ***60-69***—Below average, drinkable but not recommended; ***50-59***—Poor, undrinkable, not recommended. "+"—With a score indicates a range; used primarily with barrel tastings to indicate a preliminary score.

SPECIAL DESIGNATIONS SS—Spectator Selection, CS—Cellar Selection, BB—Best Buy, ($NA)—Price not available, (NR)—Not released.

TASTER'S INITIALS (JG)—Jim Gordon, (HS)—Harvey Steiman, (JL)—James Laube, (JS)—James Suckling, (TM)—Thomas Matthews, (TR)—Terry Robards, (PM)—Per-Henrik Mansson, (BT)—Barrel Tasting (these wines were tasted blind from barrel samples), (CA-date)—*California's Great Cabernets* by James Laube, (CH-date)—*California's Great Chardonnays* by James Laube, (VP-date)—*Vintage Port* by James Suckling.

DATE TASTED Dates in parentheses represent the issue in which the rating was published.

DOMAINE LOU FREJAU (France/Rhône)
Châteauneuf-du-Pape 1988 $17 (3/31/91) **82**
Châteauneuf-du-Pape 1986 $15.50 (1/31/89) **87**
Côtes du Rhône 1986 $8 (5/31/89) **73**

FREMONT CREEK (United States/California)
Cabernet Sauvignon Mendocino-Napa Counties 1986 $8 (4/30/91) BB **85**
Cabernet Sauvignon Mendocino-Napa Counties 1985 $9.50 (3/31/88) **78**
Chardonnay Mendocino County 1988 $9.50 (6/30/90) **75**
Chardonnay Mendocino-Napa Counties 1987 $9.50 (7/15/89) **76**
Chardonnay Mendocino-Napa Counties 1986 $9.50 (4/30/88) **87**
Sauvignon Blanc Mendocino-Napa Counties 1989 $5.50 (10/15/91) BB **82**

FRENCH CREEK (United States/Washington)
Cabernet Sauvignon Washington 1988 $9.50 (4/15/92) **73**
Cabernet Sauvignon Washington 1985 $8 (10/15/88) **82**
Chardonnay Washington 1989 $9.50 (4/30/92) **66**
Merlot Washington 1985 $11.50 (12/31/88) **83**
Riesling Washington Dry 1990 $4 (11/15/91) **80**

LES FRERES COUILLAUD (France/Loire)
Muscadet de Sèvre et Maine Château de la Ragotière Sur Lie 1987 $10 (7/15/89) **77**

FRESCOBALDI (Italy/Tuscany)
Brut 1985 $12 (12/31/90) **86**
Chianti 1989 $5.50 (4/15/91) **70**
Chianti 1988 $5 (11/30/89) BB **85**
Chianti 1987 $4.50 (5/15/89) **75**
Chianti 1986 $3.50 (12/15/87) **75**
Chianti Rufina Castello di Nipozzano Riserva 1988 ($NA) (11/30/89) BT (HS) **90**
Chianti Rufina Castello di Nipozzano Riserva 1986 $11 (9/15/90) **82**
Chianti Rufina Castello di Nipozzano Riserva 1985 $11 (11/30/89) **88**
Chianti Rufina Castello di Nipozzano Riserva 1983 $10 (11/30/89) (HS) **89**
Chianti Rufina Montesodi 1988 $19 (11/30/89) BT (HS) **87**
Chianti Rufina Montesodi 1985 $35 (9/15/91) **90**
Chianti Rufina Montesodi 1982 Rel: $28 Cur: $34 (12/15/88) **86**
Mormoreto Predicato di Bitùrica 1983 $34 (2/15/89) **88**
Mormoreto Predicato de Bitùrica 1988 $30 (9/15/91) **91**
Pomino Tenuta di Pomino 1986 $14 (1/31/90) **87**
Pomino Tenuta di Pomino 1985 Rel: $12 Cur: $17 (9/15/88) SS **93**
Pomino Tenuta di Pomino Il Benefizio 1986 $20 (3/31/90) **85**
Pomino Tenuta di Pomino Vin Santo 1981 $20 (10/15/88) **87**

FREY (United States/California)
Syrah Mendocino Bulow Vineyard 1986 $10 (4/15/89) **82**

FRICK (United States/California)
Grenache Napa County 1985 $7.50 (4/15/89) **86**
Petite Sirah Monterey County 1985 $8 (2/15/89) **87**
Pinot Noir California 1981 $12 (8/31/86) **89**
Pinot Noir Santa Maria Valley 1984 $12 (2/28/89) **75**

FRIEDRICH-WILHELM-GYMNASIUM (Germany)
Riesling Auslese Mosel-Saar-Ruwer Graacher Domprobst 1990 $20 (12/15/91) **89**
Riesling Auslese Mosel-Saar-Ruwer Graacher Himmelreich 1988 ($NA) (9/30/89) **81**
Riesling Auslese Mosel-Saar-Ruwer Mehringer Blattenberg 1989 ($NA) (12/15/90) **82**
Riesling Auslese Mosel-Saar-Ruwer Mehringer Goldkupp 1988 $30 (9/30/89) **95**
Riesling Auslese Mosel-Saar-Ruwer Neumagener Rosengärtchen 1990 $20 (12/15/91) **85**
Riesling Auslese Mosel-Saar-Ruwer Trittenheimer Apotheke 1990 $20 (12/15/91) **89**
Riesling Auslese Mosel-Saar-Ruwer Trittenheimer Apotheke 1989 $19 (12/15/90) **82**
Riesling Beerenauslese Mosel-Saar-Ruwer Graacher Himmelreich 1989 $150 (12/15/90) **90**
Riesling Kabinett Mosel-Saar-Ruwer Falkensteiner Hofberg 1990 $11 (12/15/91) **84**
Riesling Kabinett Mosel-Saar-Ruwer Graacher Himmelreich 1989 $10 (12/15/90) **84**
Riesling Kabinett Mosel-Saar-Ruwer Mehringer Zellerberg 1990 $10 (12/15/91) **87**
Riesling Spätlese Mosel-Saar-Ruwer Falkensteiner Hofberg 1989 ($NA) (12/15/90) **83**
Riesling Spätlese Mosel-Saar-Ruwer Graacher Himmelreich 1990 $12 (12/15/91) **86**
Riesling Spätlese Mosel-Saar-Ruwer Oberemmeler Raul 1990 $11 (12/15/91) **91**
Riesling Spätlese Mosel-Saar-Ruwer Oberemmeler Rosenberg 1989 ($NA) (12/15/90) **80**
Riesling Spätlese Mosel-Saar-Ruwer Trittenheimer Apotheke 1990 $12 (12/15/91) **86**

J. FRITZ (United States/California)
Cabernet Sauvignon Alexander Valley 1985 $10 (12/31/88) **57**
Chardonnay Alexander Valley Gauer Ranch 1981 $10 (4/16/84) **80**
Chardonnay Dry Creek Valley 1990 $9.50 (3/31/92) **85**
Chardonnay Russian River Valley 1990 $12.50 (4/30/92) **77**
Chardonnay Russian River Valley 1989 $12.50 (7/15/91) **86**
Chardonnay Russian River Valley 1986 $9 (2/29/88) **81**
Chardonnay Russian River Valley 1985 $8.50 (11/30/87) **81**
Chardonnay Sonoma County 1982 $9 (5/16/84) **72**
Sauvignon Blanc Dry Creek Valley 1989 $8 (10/15/91) **72**
Zinfandel Dry Creek Valley 1986 $9 (3/15/89) **86**
Zinfandel Dry Creek Valley 1984 $7 (2/15/88) **84**
Zinfandel Dry Creek Valley 80-Year-Old Vines 1989 $10 (3/31/92) **84**
Zinfandel Dry Creek Valley 80-Year-Old Vines 1988 $10 (7/31/91) **79**

FROG'S LEAP (United States/California)
Cabernet Sauvignon Napa Valley 1991 (NR) (5/15/92) (BT) **85+**
Cabernet Sauvignon Napa Valley 1988 Rel: $17 Cur: $19 (12/15/90) **88**
Cabernet Sauvignon Napa Valley 1987 Rel: $15 Cur: $25 (12/31/89) SS **94**
Cabernet Sauvignon Napa Valley 1986 Rel: $14 Cur: $41 (CA-3/89) **94**
Cabernet Sauvignon Napa Valley 1985 Rel: $12 Cur: $20 (CA-3/89) **85**
Cabernet Sauvignon Napa Valley 1984 Rel: $10 Cur: $30 (3/31/87) SS **95**
Cabernet Sauvignon Napa Valley 1983 Rel: $10 Cur: $22 (CA-3/89) **80**
Cabernet Sauvignon Napa Valley 1982 Rel: $9 Cur: $25 (CA-3/89) **87**
Chardonnay Carneros 1990 $16 (4/15/92) **90**
Chardonnay Carneros 1989 Rel: $16 Cur: $18 (7/15/91) **83**
Chardonnay Carneros 1988 Rel: $16 Cur: $19 (4/30/90) **87**
Chardonnay Carneros 1987 Rel: $15 Cur: $19 (CH-3/90) **86**
Chardonnay Carneros 1986 Rel: $14 Cur: $18 (CH-6/90) **87**
Chardonnay Napa Valley 1988 Rel: $15 Cur: $18 (6/30/90) **85**
Chardonnay Napa Valley 1987 Rel: $14 Cur: $18 (CH-3/90) **88**
Chardonnay Napa Valley 1986 Rel: $12 Cur: $18 (CH-3/90) **90**
Chardonnay Napa Valley 1985 Rel: $12 Cur: $16 (CH-6/90) **84**
Chardonnay Napa Valley 1984 Rel: $12 Cur: $23 (CH-3/90) **91**
Sauvignon Blanc Late Harvest Napa Valley Late Leap 1989 $14/375ml (10/31/91) **84**
Sauvignon Blanc Late Harvest Napa Valley Late Leap 1986 $9.50/375ml (9/30/88) **85**
Sauvignon Blanc Napa Valley 1990 $10 (10/15/91) **85**
Sauvignon Blanc Napa Valley 1989 $9.50 (10/31/90) **87**
Sauvignon Blanc Napa Valley 1988 $9.50 (11/30/89) **76**
Zinfandel Napa Valley 1989 $12 (11/15/91) **83**
Zinfandel Napa Valley 1988 $11.50 (12/15/90) **88**
Zinfandel Napa Valley 1987 $10.50 (3/15/90) **86**
Zinfandel Napa Valley 1986 $10 (12/15/88) **85**
Zinfandel Napa Valley 1985 $9 (11/15/87) **79**

CHATEAU FUMET-PEYROUTAS (France/Bordeaux)
St.-Emilion 1985 $7.25 (7/31/88) BB **84**

FRANCO FURLAN (Italy/North)
Tai di Castelcosa NV $16 (4/30/90) **81**

FURST LOWENSTEIN (Germany)
Riesling Kabinett Halbtrocken Rheingau Blausilber 1990 (NR) (12/15/91) **81**
Riesling Kabinett Rheingau Charta 1990 (NR) (12/15/91) **82**
Riesling Spätlese Halbtrocken Rheingau Rosasilber 1990 (NR) (12/15/91) **85**
Riesling Spätlese Rheingau Charta 1990 (NR) (12/15/91) **83**

FURST VON METTERNICH (Germany)
Riesling Kabinett Halbtrocken Rheingau Schloss Johannisberg 1988 $15 (9/30/89) **85**
Riesling Qualitätswein Rheingau Schloss Johannisberg 1988 $15 (9/30/89) **75**

CASTELLO DI GABBIANO (Italy/Tuscany)
Ania 1985 $30 (1/31/90) **93**
Ania 1983 $25 (7/15/87) **83**
Bianco del Castello 1987 $8 (12/31/90) **78**
Chardonnay Ariella 1988 $23 (1/31/91) **83**
Chardonnay Ariella 1987 $23 (3/31/90) **87**
Chianti Classico 1987 $7 (11/30/89) **81**
Chianti Classico 1986 $7.75 (5/31/89) BB **82**
Chianti Classico 1985 $7 (2/15/88) **72**
Chianti Classico 1983 $6 (5/31/87) BB **85**
Chianti Classico 1982 $6.25 (1/01/86) **68**
Chianti Classico Riserva 1982 $10.50 (7/31/88) **84**
Chianti Classico Riserva Gold Label 1982 $21 (11/30/89) **79**
Chianti Classico Riserva Gold Label 1981 $18 (2/15/88) **81**
Merlot 1988 $55 (7/15/91) **86**
R & R 1986 $38 (1/31/91) **90**
R & R 1985 $30 (3/31/90) **91**
Vin Santo 1985 $20 (3/15/91) **78**

GABRIELLI (United States/California)
Chardonnay Mendocino 1990 $16 (5/31/92) **83**

CHATEAU LA GAFFELIERE (France/Bordeaux)
St.-Emilion 1990 (NR) (4/30/91) (BT) **60+**
St.-Emilion 1989 $33 (4/30/91) (BT) **90+**
St.-Emilion 1988 $36 (4/30/91) **84**
St.-Emilion 1987 Rel: $20 Cur: $22 (6/30/89) (BT) **75+**
St.-Emilion 1986 $28 (5/15/87) (BT) **80+**
St.-Emilion 1985 $31 (5/15/87) (BT) **80+**
St.-Emilion 1982 $29 (5/15/89) (TR) **88**
St.-Emilion 1979 $28 (10/15/89) (JS) **81**
St.-Emilion 1962 $60 (11/30/87) (JS) **88**
St.-Emilion 1961 $102 (3/16/86) (TR) **76**
St.-Emilion 1959 $93 (10/15/90) (JS) **82**
St.-Emilion 1945 $140 (3/16/86) (JL) **85**

JEAN-NOEL GAGNARD (France/Burgundy)
Bâtard-Montrachet 1989 $140 (8/31/91) **97**
Bâtard-Montrachet 1986 $93 (12/31/88) **95**
Chassagne-Montrachet 1989 $55 (8/31/91) **88**
Chassagne-Montrachet 1986 $36 (3/15/89) **83**
Chassagne-Montrachet 1985 $40 (9/15/87) **92**
Chassagne-Montrachet 1984 $32 (4/30/87) **96**
Chassagne-Montrachet 1983 $25 (10/01/85) **87**
Chassagne-Montrachet Les Caillerets 1989 $64 (8/31/91) **91**
Chassagne-Montrachet Les Caillerets 1985 $45 (9/15/87) **94**
Chassagne-Montrachet Morgeot 1989 $63 (8/31/91) **90**
Chassagne-Montrachet Morgeot 1988 $54 (11/15/90) **80**
Chassagne-Montrachet Morgeot 1986 $54 (11/15/88) **89**
Chassagne-Montrachet Morgeot 1985 $45 (9/15/87) **86**
Chassagne-Montrachet Première Cru 1989 $60 (8/31/91) **89**
Chassagne-Montrachet Première Cru 1988 $50 (10/15/90) **91**
Chassagne-Montrachet Première Cru 1986 $47 (12/15/88) **74**
Chassagne-Montrachet Rouge Morgeot 1989 $25 (11/15/91) **87**
Chassagne-Montrachet Rouge Morgeot 1988 $20 (12/31/90) **86**
Chassagne-Montrachet Rouge Morgeot 1985 $18 (11/30/87) **79**
Santenay Clos de Tavannes 1989 $25 (11/15/91) **85**
Santenay Clos de Tavannes 1988 $25 (11/15/90) **84**

GAIERHOF (Italy/North)
Pinot Grigio Trentino 1990 $11 (1/31/92) **75**
Teroldego Rotaliano 1988 $11 (9/30/91) **75**

PIERRE GAILLARD (France/Rhône)
Côte-Rôtie Côte Brune et Blonde 1989 $28 (10/15/91) **89**
Côte-Rôtie Côte Brune et Blonde 1988 $30 (11/30/90) **90**
Côte-Rôtie Côte Brune et Blonde 1987 $24 (8/31/89) **82**
Côte-Rôtie Côte Brune et Blonde 1986 $25 (11/30/88) **86**
Côtes du Rhône Blanc Viognier Clos de Cuminaille 1990 $30 (10/15/91) **92**
Côtes du Rhône Blanc Viognier Clos de Cuminaille 1986 $25 (3/15/89) **87**
St.-Joseph Clos de Cuminaille 1988 $15 (12/31/90) **87**
St.-Joseph Clos de Cuminaille 1987 $14 (3/15/90) **87**

GAINEY (United States/California)
Cabernet Sauvignon Santa Maria Valley 1988 $13 (3/15/92) **77**
Cabernet Sauvignon Santa Barbara County 1987 $13 (11/15/90) **82**
Cabernet Sauvignon Santa Barbara County Limited Selection 1986 $15 (12/15/89) **89**
Chardonnay Santa Barbara County 1990 $14 (6/30/92) **83**
Chardonnay Santa Barbara County 1989 $13 (5/31/91) **86**
Chardonnay Santa Barbara County 1988 $12.50 (2/28/91) **81**
Chardonnay Santa Barbara County 1987 $12 (12/15/89) **85**
Chardonnay Santa Barbara County Limited Selection 1987 $16 (12/15/89) **89**
Johannisberg Riesling Santa Barbara County 1989 $7.75 (9/15/90) **76**
Johannisberg Riesling Santa Barbara County 1988 $7.50 (12/15/89) **84**
Johannisberg Riesling Santa Ynez Valley 1990 $8 (6/15/91) **82**
Merlot Santa Barbara County 1989 $14 (5/31/92) **70**
Merlot Santa Barbara County 1988 $13 (4/15/91) **82**
Merlot Santa Ynez Valley Limited Selection 1988 $20 (2/29/92) **89**
Pinot Noir Santa Barbara County 1986 $15 (12/15/89) **88**
Pinot Noir Santa Ynez Valley Limited Selection 1988 $25 (11/15/91) **86**
Sauvignon Blanc Santa Barbara County 1987 $8.50 (12/15/89) **82**

GAJA (Italy/Piedmont)
Barbaresco 1988 $65 (4/30/92) **91**
Barbaresco 1986 Rel: $47 Cur: $54 (1/31/90) CS **92**
Barbaresco 1985 Rel: $45 Cur: $77 (12/15/88) CS **95**
Barbaresco 1983 Rel: $35 Cur: $50 (9/15/89) (HS) **93**
Barbaresco 1982 $95 (9/15/89) (HS) **93**
Barbaresco 1981 $95 (9/15/89) (HS) **90**
Barbaresco 1980 Rel: $14 Cur: $75 (7/01/85) **88**
Barbaresco 1979 $110 (9/15/89) (HS) **89**
Barbaresco 1978 $130 (9/15/89) (HS) **93**
Barbaresco 1976 $115 (9/15/89) (HS) **91**
Barbaresco 1974 $125 (9/15/89) (HS) **89**
Barbaresco 1971 $135 (9/15/89) (HS) **86**
Barbaresco 1967 $88 (9/15/89) (HS) **83**
Barbaresco 1964 $100 (9/15/89) (HS) **87**
Barbaresco 1961 $210 (9/15/89) (HS) **92**
Barbaresco Costa Russi 1988 $100 (4/30/92) **92**
Barbaresco Costa Russi 1986 Rel: $85 Cur: $109 (1/31/90) **89**
Barbaresco Costa Russi 1985 Rel: $83 Cur: $108 (12/15/88) **96**
Barbaresco Costa Russi 1982 $95 (9/15/88) (HS) **91**
Barbaresco Sorì San Lorenzo 1988 $125 (4/30/92) CS **96**
Barbaresco Sorì San Lorenzo 1986 Rel: $89 Cur: $109 (1/31/90) **91**
Barbaresco Sorì San Lorenzo 1985 Rel: $88 Cur: $150 (12/15/88) **96**
Barbaresco Sorì San Lorenzo 1983 $95 (9/15/88) (HS) **90**
Barbaresco Sorì Tildìn 1988 $125 (4/30/92) **92**
Barbaresco Sorì Tildìn 1986 Rel: $94 Cur: $105 (1/31/90) **93**
Barbaresco Sorì Tildìn 1985 Rel: $94 Cur: $120 (9/15/89) (HS) **98**
Barbaresco Sorì Tildìn 1985 Rel: $94 Cur: $120 (12/15/88) **97**
Barbaresco Sorì Tildìn 1983 $95 (9/15/89) (HS) **88**
Barbaresco Sorì Tildìn 1982 $130 (9/15/89) (HS) **94**
Barbaresco Sorì Tildìn 1981 $140 (9/15/89) (HS) **87**
Barbaresco Sorì Tildìn 1979 $195 (9/15/89) (HS) **89**
Barbaresco Sorì Tildìn 1978 $200 (9/15/89) (HS) **90**
Barbaresco Sorì Tildìn 1973 $150 (9/15/89) (HS) **88**
Barbaresco Sorì Tildìn 1971 $180 (9/15/89) (HS) **91**
Barbaresco Sorì Tildìn 1970 $220 (9/15/89) (HS) **78**
Barbera d'Alba Vignarey 1987 $35 (4/15/91) **88**
Barbera d'Alba Vignarey 1986 $27 (3/15/91) **88**
Barbera d'Alba Vignarey 1984 $13 (2/15/87) **82**
Cabernet Sauvignon Darmagi 1986 $76 (1/31/90) **94**
Cabernet Sauvignon Darmagi 1985 Rel: $70 Cur: $75 (3/15/89) CS **94**
Cabernet Sauvignon Darmagi 1983 $51 (7/15/88) **91**
Chardonnay Gaia & Rey 1988 $68 (12/31/90) **86**
Chardonnay Gaia & Rey 1987 $43 (9/15/89) **95**
Chardonnay Gaia & Rey 1985 Rel: $45 Cur: $58 (9/15/89) **98**
Chardonnay Rossj-Bass 1988 $45 (3/31/90) **85**
Nebbiolo d'Alba Vignaveja 1985 $30 (2/15/89) **87**
Nebbiolo d'Alba Vignaveja 1983 Rel: $16 Cur: $28 (2/15/87) SS **94**

E. & J. GALLO (United States/California)
Cabernet Sauvignon California Reserve NV $6 (11/15/91) **84**
Cabernet Sauvignon California Limited Release Reserve 1980 $8 (11/15/86) **78**
Cabernet Sauvignon Limited Release 1981 $5 (12/31/88) **75**
Cabernet Sauvignon Northern Sonoma Reserve 1984 $7 (10/15/91) **80**
Cabernet Sauvignon Northern Sonoma Reserve 1982 $6 (5/31/91) BB **82**
Chardonnay California Limited Release NV $6 (4/16/86) **58**
Chardonnay California Reserve NV $5 (7/15/92) **77**
Chardonnay North Coast 1990 $7 (7/15/92) **77**
Chardonnay North Coast Reserve 1989 $6.50 (7/15/91) BB **81**
Chardonnay North Coast Reserve 1987 $6 (11/30/90) **78**
Chardonnay North Coast 1985 $5 (12/31/88) **79**
Chenin Blanc California 1987 $3.50/1.5L (7/31/89) **77**
Chenin Blanc California Chablis Blanc NV $2.50 (7/31/89) **83**
Chenin Blanc North Coast Dry Chablis 1987 $4 (7/31/89) **73**
Sauvignon Blanc California Reserve 1989 $4 (7/31/91) BB **82**
White Grenache California 1987 $3.50 (4/15/89) **72**
White Zinfandel California 1988 $5 (6/15/89) **79**

STELIO GALLO (Italy/North)
Chardonnay 1987 ($NA) (9/15/89) **83**
Chardonnay 1986 ($NA) (9/15/89) **81**

GAMLA (Other/Israel)
Cabernet Sauvignon Galil 1987 $9.50 (3/31/91) **75**
Cabernet Sauvignon Galil Special Reserve 1986 $12 (3/31/91) **83**
Chardonnay Galil Special Reserve 1988 $11 (3/31/91) **66**
Sauvignon Blanc Galil 1988 $9 (3/31/91) **75**
Sauvignon Blanc Galil Special Reserve 1988 $10 (3/31/91) **74**
Sauvignon Blanc Late Harvest Galil 1988 $14 (3/31/91) **75**

GAN EDEN (United States/California)
Cabernet Sauvignon Alexander Valley 1987 $18 (3/31/91) **90**
Cabernet Sauvignon Alexander Valley 1986 $15 (2/15/89) **86**
Chardonnay Alexander Valley 1987 $9.50 (3/15/89) **89**
Chardonnay Sonoma County 1988 $12 (3/31/91) **87**
Sauvignon Blanc Sonoma County 1988 $9 (3/31/91) **72**

GANCIA (Italy/Sparkling)
Asti Spumante NV $12.50 (8/31/90) **84**
Brut Chardonnay NV $11 (12/31/90) **82**
Brut Chardonnay NV $7 (12/31/89) BB **86**

Key to Symbols

The scores reported here are the results of blind tastings conducted by our panel of senior editors. Wines that carry the initials below are results of individual tastings.

THE WINE SPECTATOR 100-POINT SCALE ***95-100****—Classic, a great wine;* ***90-94****—* Outstanding, superior character and style; ***80-89****—*Good to very good, a wine with special qualities; ***70-79****—*Average, drinkable wine that may have minor flaws; ***60-69*** —Below average, drinkable but not recommended; ***50-59*** —Poor, undrinkable, not recommended. "+"—With a score indicates a range; used primarily with barrel tastings to indicate a preliminary score.

SPECIAL DESIGNATIONS SS—Spectator Selection, CS—Cellar Selection, BB—Best Buy, ($NA)—Price not available, (NR)—Not released.

TASTER'S INITIALS (JG)—Jim Gordon, (HS)—Harvey Steiman, (JL)—James Laube, (JS)—James Suckling, (TM)—Thomas Matthews, (TR)—Terry Robards, (PM)—Per-Henrik Mansson, (BT)—Barrel Tasting (these wines were tasted blind from barrel samples), (CA-date)—*California's Great Cabernets* by James Laube, (CH-date)—*California's Great Chardonnays* by James Laube, (VP-date)—*Vintage Port* by James Suckling.

DATE TASTED Dates in parentheses represent the issue in which the rating was published.

JEAN GARAUDET (France/Burgundy)
Beaune Clos des Mouches 1989 $32 (11/15/91) **91**
Beaune Clos des Mouches 1988 $40 (11/15/90) **86**
Bourgogne Passetoutgrains 1990 $10 (6/15/92) **84**
Monthélie 1989 $22 (11/15/91) **86**
Monthélie 1988 $23 (11/15/90) **88**
Pommard 1988 $37 (11/15/90) **88**
Pommard 1987 $25 (9/15/89) **88**
Pommard Les Charmots 1988 $46 (11/15/90) **90**
Pommard Les Charmots 1987 $30 (9/15/89) **88**
Pommard Noizons 1989 $34 (11/15/91) **91**

CHATEAU LA GARDE (France/Bordeaux)
Pessac-Léognan 1988 $15 (6/30/89) (BT) **75+**
Pessac-Léognan 1987 $13 (6/30/89) (BT) **70+**
Pessac-Léognan 1986 $14 (5/15/87) (BT) **70+**
Pessac-Léognan Blanc 1988 $15 (6/30/89) (BT) **85+**
Pessac-Léognan Blanc 1987 $13 (6/30/89) (BT) **80+**

CHATEAU DE LA GARDINE (France/Rhône)
Châteauneuf-du-Pape 1989 $25 (10/15/91) **95**
Châteauneuf-du-Pape 1988 $33 (10/15/91) **85**
Châteauneuf-du-Pape 1986 Rel: $17 Cur: $23 (10/15/91) **90**
Châteauneuf-du-Pape 1985 Rel: $15 Cur: $18 (12/31/87) **87**
Châteauneuf-du-Pape 1984 $15 (12/31/87) **78**
Châteauneuf-du-Pape 1983 Rel: $12 Cur: $20 (10/15/91) **89**
Châteauneuf-du-Pape 1981 $30 (10/15/91) **86**
Châteauneuf-du-Pape Blanc 1990 $20 (10/15/91) **86**
Châteauneuf-du-Pape Blanc Vieilles Vignes 1989 $25 (10/15/91) **90**
Châteauneuf-du-Pape Cuvée des Générations 1985 $25 (10/15/91) **92**

GARLAND RANCH (United States/California)
Cabernet Sauvignon Central Coast 1986 $6.75 (10/31/89) **70**
Cabernet Sauvignon Monterey County 1984 $6.75 (8/31/88) BB **84**
Chardonnay California 1991 $6 (7/15/92) **72**
Chardonnay Central Coast 1989 $5 (8/31/90) **76**
Merlot California 1986 $6 (5/31/92) **76**
White Zinfandel Monterey 1987 $6 (6/15/89) **75**

ANDREW GARRETT (Australia)
Chardonnay South Australia 1986 $9.75 (12/31/87) **80**
Shiraz South Australia Clarendon Estate 1982 $8.75 (11/15/87) **80**

CANTINA GATTAVECCHI (Italy/Tuscany)
Chianti Colli Senesi 1990 $7.75 (4/30/92) **80**
Vino Nobile di Montepulciano Riserva 1985 $11 (11/30/89) **81**

DOMAINE JEAN GAUDET (France/Beaujolais)
Morgon 1988 $10 (5/31/89) (TM) **87**

DOMAINE DENIS GAUDRY (France/Loire)
Pouilly-Fumé Côteaux du Petit Boisgibault 1989 $15 (3/31/91) **85**

GAUER ESTATE (United States/California)
Chardonnay Alexander Valley 1988 $16 (12/31/90) **85**
Chardonnay Alexander Valley 1987 $16 (11/30/90) **84**
Chardonnay Alexander Valley Library Edition 1987 $18 (7/15/92) **86**

REMY GAUTHIER (France/Burgundy)
Volnay Santenots 1985 $27 (3/15/88) **87**

DOMAINES GAVOTY (France/Other)
Côtes de Provence Cuvée Clarendon 1987 $8.50 (3/31/90) **72**

CHATEAU LE GAY (France/Bordeaux)
Pomerol 1990 (NR) (5/15/92) (BT) **95+**
Pomerol 1989 Rel: $70 Cur: $110 (3/15/92) **91**
Pomerol 1988 $30 (4/30/91) **83**
Pomerol 1985 $25 (4/16/86) (BT) **60+**
Pomerol 1982 $44 (5/15/89) (TR) **89**

CHATEAU GAZIN (France/Bordeaux)
Pomerol 1991 (NR) (5/15/92) (BT) **85+**
Pomerol 1990 (NR) (5/15/92) (BT) **95+**
Pomerol 1989 $45 (3/15/92) **91**
Pomerol 1988 $30 (6/30/91) **87**
Pomerol 1987 $22 (6/30/89) (BT) **80+**
Pomerol 1986 Rel: $21 Cur: $23 (5/15/87) (BT) **80+**
Pomerol 1985 Rel: $21 Cur: $31 (9/30/88) **90**
Pomerol 1982 $30 (5/15/89) (TR) **88**
Pomerol 1961 $120 (3/16/86) (TR) **83**

GEBERT (Germany)
Riesling Qualitätswein Mosel-Saar-Ruwer Ockfener Bockstein 1986 $6 (11/30/87) **74**
Riesling Qualitätswein Mosel-Saar-Ruwer Ockfener Bockstein 1985 $6.50 (5/15/87) **82**

GERARD GELIN (France/Beaujolais)
Beaujolais-Villages Domaine des Nugues 1989 $8 (11/15/90) BB **86**

PIERRE GELIN (France/Burgundy)
Chambertin Clos de Bèze 1985 $77 (3/15/88) **84**
Fixin Clos Napolèon 1985 $25 (4/30/88) **76**
Gevrey-Chambertin 1985 $25 (4/15/88) **93**
Gevrey-Chambertin 1982 $19 (3/16/85) **80**
Mazis-Chambertin 1985 $25 (3/15/88) **90**

GELIN & MOLIN (France/Burgundy)
Fixin Clos du Châpitre Domaine Marion 1985 $25 (4/30/88) **82**

GENTAZ-DERVIEUX (France/Rhône)
Côte-Rôtie Côte Brune Cuvée Réserve 1987 $40 (6/30/90) **73**

DOMAINE GEOFFROY (France/Burgundy)
Gevrey-Chambertin Les Champeaux 1986 $36 (7/15/89) **85**
Gevrey-Chambertin Clos Prieur 1987 $29 (3/31/90) **93**
Gevrey-Chambertin Clos Prieur 1986 $29 (7/15/89) **89**
Gevrey-Chambertin Les Escorvées 1986 $26 (7/15/89) **79**
Mazis-Chambertin 1987 $48 (3/31/90) **92**

GEOGRAFICO (Italy/Tuscany)
Brunello di Montalcino 1985 $30 (7/15/91) **80**
Chianti Classico 1988 $9.75 (11/30/91) **78**
Chianti Classico Castello di Fagnano 1989 $9.75 (1/31/92) **70**
Chianti Classico Castello di Fagnano 1988 $9.75 (10/31/91) **86**
Chianti Classico Contessa di Radda 1987 $11 (10/31/91) **80**
Chianti Classico Tenuta Montegiachi Riserva 1986 $14.50 (10/31/91) **79**
Predicato di Bitùrica 1986 $21 (8/31/91) **85**

Vino Nobile di Montepulciano Vigneti alla Cerraia 1986 $15 (7/15/91) **85**

GEORGES BLANC (France/Burgundy)
St.-Véran 1986 $10 (12/31/87) **72**

GEORIS (United States/California)
Merlot Carmel Valley 1987 $27 (3/31/91) **89**
Merlot Carmel Valley 1986 $25 (12/31/90) **77**
Merlot Carmel Valley 1985 $20 (4/15/89) **83**

FRANCOIS GERARD (France/Rhône)
Côte-Rôtie 1988 $36 (7/31/91) **70**
Côte-Rôtie 1987 $30 (10/15/90) **77**

HENRI GERMAIN (France/Burgundy)
Chassagne-Montrachet Morgeot 1989 ($NA) (8/31/91) **91**
Chassagne-Montrachet Morgeot 1988 $43 (4/30/91) **83**
Chassagne-Montrachet Morgeot 1986 $39 (3/15/89) **86**
Meursault 1988 $35 (2/28/91) **91**
Meursault 1986 $27 (4/30/89) **88**
Meursault Les Charmes 1989 $55 (8/31/91) **93**
Meursault Les Charmes 1988 $42 (5/15/90) **89**
Meursault Les Charmes 1986 $39 (4/30/89) **86**
Meursault Clos du Cromin 1989 $55 (8/31/91) **88**
Meursault Limozin 1989 $50 (8/31/91) **88**

JACQUES GERMAIN (France/Burgundy)
Beaune Les Boucherottes 1989 $45 (7/15/90) (BT) **85+**
Beaune Cent Vignes 1989 $45 (7/15/90) (BT) **85+**
Beaune Cent Vignes 1988 $45 (7/15/90) (BT) **90+**
Beaune Les Crâs 1989 (NR) (1/31/92) **90**
Beaune Les Crâs 1988 ($NA) (7/15/90) (BT) **90+**
Beaune Les Teurons 1989 $50 (1/31/92) **92**
Beaune Les Teurons 1988 $42 (2/15/91) **90**
Beaune Les Teurons 1986 $33 (7/31/88) **70**
Beaune Vignes-Franches 1989 $45 (1/31/92) **91**
Beaune Vignes-Franches 1988 $42 (7/15/90) (BT) **90+**
Chorey-lès-Beaune Château de Chorey-lès-Beaune 1986 $16 (7/31/89) **80**
Chorey-Côte-de-Beaune Château de Chorey-lès-Beaune 1989 $24 (1/31/92) **84**
Pernand-Vergelesses Blanc 1989 ($NA) (8/31/91) **84**

JEAN GERMAIN (France/Burgundy)
Bourgogne Blanc Clos de la Fortune 1989 ($NA) (8/31/91) **81**
Chassagne-Montrachet 1985 $35 (9/15/87) **89**
Chassagne-Montrachet 1983 $18 (9/01/85) **93**
Meursault 1989 $40 (8/31/91) **86**
Meursault Bouchères 1989 ($NA) (8/31/91) **87**
Meursault Clos des Meix-Chavaux 1989 ($NA) (8/31/91) **89**
Meursault Goutte d'Or 1989 ($NA) (8/31/91) **91**
Meursault Meix-Chavaux 1989 $38 (8/31/91) **89**
Puligny-Montrachet 1989 ($NA) (8/31/91) **86**
Puligny-Montrachet 1983 $12 (9/01/85) **90**
Puligny-Montrachet Les Champs-Gains 1989 $54 (8/31/91) **91**
Puligny-Montrachet Les Champs-Gains 1983 $27 (3/01/86) **96**
Puligny-Montrachet Les Grands Champs 1989 $48 (8/31/91) **85**
St.-Romain Clos Sous le Château 1989 $24 (8/31/91) **85**
St.-Romain Clos Sous le Château 1984 $15 (7/16/86) **77**
St.-Romain Clos Sous le Château 1983 $12 (9/16/85) **83**

MARIE-PIERRE GERMAIN (France/Burgundy)
Aloxe-Corton Les Vercots 1989 (NR) (1/31/92) **88**

H. GERMAINE (France/Champagne)
Blanc de Blancs Crémant Champagne 1983 $24 (12/31/90) **89**
Blanc de Blancs Crémant Champagne 1982 $53 (5/31/87) **77**
Brut Champagne NV $28 (12/31/91) **88**

GEYSER PEAK (United States/California)
Cabernet Sauvignon Alexander Valley 1984 $7.50 (3/15/88) **77**
Cabernet Sauvignon Alexander Valley 1983 $7 (3/15/87) BB **87**
Cabernet Sauvignon Alexander Valley 1982 $7 (9/15/86) **68**
Cabernet Sauvignon Alexander Valley 1980 $6.50 (1/01/85) **57**
Cabernet Sauvignon Alexander Valley Estate Reserve 1987 $14 (6/15/91) **89**
Cabernet Sauvignon Alexander Valley Estate Reserve 1986 $15 (9/30/90) **85**
Cabernet Sauvignon Alexander Valley Estate Reserve 1985 $15 (5/15/89) **77**
Cabernet Sauvignon Sonoma County 1987 $8.50 (11/30/90) BB **88**
Cabernet Sauvignon Sonoma County 1981 $7 (6/16/85) **83**
Chardonnay Alexander Valley Barrel Fermented Estate Reserve 1989 $13 (6/15/91) **89**
Chardonnay Alexander Valley Estate Reserve 1987 $12 (6/30/89) **80**
Chardonnay Sonoma County 1990 $8 (3/15/92) BB **83**
Chardonnay Sonoma County Carneros 1985 $7 (2/28/87) BB **84**
Chardonnay Sonoma County Carneros 1984 $8 (4/16/86) **76**
Chardonnay Sonoma County Carneros 1982 $6.75 (12/16/84) **68**
Château Alexandre Meritage Alexander Valley 1990 $13 (4/30/92) **86**
Johannisberg Riesling California Soft 1989 $6 (7/31/90) **71**
Johannisberg Riesling Late Harvest Mendocino County Selected Dried Berry 1990 $13/375ml (8/31/91) **93**
Merlot Alexander Valley 1989 $9 (5/31/92) **79**
Merlot Alexander Valley 1987 $8 (7/15/90) **82**
Merlot Alexander Valley 1985 $7.75 (10/15/88) **77**
Merlot Alexander Valley 1984 $7 (2/29/88) **69**
Merlot Alexander Valley 1983 $7 (12/31/86) **80**
Opulence California NV $7.50 (1/31/87) **80**
Petite Sirah Alexander Valley 1989 $15 (6/30/92) **79**
Pinot Noir Sonoma County Carneros 1985 $6 (6/15/88) **82**
Pinot Noir Sonoma County Carneros 1981 $5.75 (8/31/86) **82**
Réserve Alexandre Alexander Valley 1987 $18 (6/15/91) **90**
Réserve Alexandre Alexander Valley 1986 $20 (9/30/90) **89**
Réserve Alexandre Alexander Valley 1985 $19 (9/30/89) **88**
Réserve Alexandre Alexander Valley 1984 $19 (8/31/88) **89**
Réserve Alexandre Alexander Valley 1983 $15 (4/30/87) **80**
Sauvignon Blanc Sonoma County 1990 $6.50 (4/15/92) BB **85**
Semchard California 1990 $8 (9/15/91) BB **88**
Semchard California 1989 $8 (2/15/91) BB **87**
Trione Vineyards California 1987 $3.25 (2/28/90) **77**
Zinfandel Alexander Valley 1984 $7.75 (7/31/88) **79**

BRUNO GIACOSA (Italy/Piedmont)
Barbaresco 1985 $42 (8/31/89) **84**
Barbaresco 1983 $24 (7/31/87) **88**
Barbaresco Gallina di Neive 1986 $40 (8/31/91) **88**
Barbaresco Santo Stefano 1982 $57 (9/15/88) **92**
Barbaresco Santo Stefano di Neive 1986 $62 (8/31/91) **83**
Barbaresco Santo Stefano di Neive Riserva 1985 $60 (8/31/91) **77**
Barbaresco Santo Stefano di Neive Riserva 1982 $60 (9/15/88) (HS) **90**
Barbera d'Alba Altavilla d'Alba 1987 $12 (3/15/91) **73**
Barbera d'Alba Altavilla d'Alba 1986 $12 (3/15/91) **77**
Barolo 1980 $19 (9/15/87) **78**
Barolo 1978 $31 (9/16/84) **88**
Barolo Collina Rionda di Serralunga 1985 $50 (4/30/91) **86**
Barolo Le Rocche di Castiglione Falletto 1982 $38 (7/31/89) **80**
Barolo Riserva 1982 $65 (1/31/90) **72**
Barolo Rocche 1982 $41 (9/15/88) **90**
Barolo Villero di Castiglione 1983 $29 (1/31/89) **85**
Dolcetto d'Alba 1989 $12 (2/28/91) **88**

GIACOSA FRATELLI (Italy/Piedmont)
Barbaresco 1986 $17 (7/15/91) **87**
Barbaresco Suri Secondine 1986 $11.50 (10/31/90) **72**
Barbera d'Alba Maria Gioana 1986 $22 (3/15/91) **86**
Barolo 1985 $20 (8/31/91) **59**
Gavi 1989 $14 (7/15/91) **71**
Roero Arneis 1989 $17 (7/15/91) **77**

GIRARD (United States/California)
Cabernet Sauvignon Napa Valley 1991 (NR) (5/15/92) (BT) **87+**
Cabernet Sauvignon Napa Valley 1990 (NR) (5/15/91) (BT) **90+**
Cabernet Sauvignon Napa Valley 1989 (NR) (5/15/91) (BT) **85+**
Cabernet Sauvignon Napa Valley 1988 $16 (11/15/91) **85**
Cabernet Sauvignon Napa Valley 1987 Rel: $16 Cur: $20 (11/15/90) **86**
Cabernet Sauvignon Napa Valley 1986 Rel: $16 Cur: $19 (11/15/89) **89**
Cabernet Sauvignon Napa Valley 1985 Rel: $15 Cur: $18 (9/15/88) **88**
Cabernet Sauvignon Napa Valley 1984 Rel: $11 Cur: $18 (11/30/87) **88**
Cabernet Sauvignon Napa Valley 1983 Rel: $12 Cur: $15 (12/15/86) **71**
Cabernet Sauvignon Napa Valley 1982 Rel: $12.50 Cur: $32 (CA-3/89) **87**
Cabernet Sauvignon Napa Valley 1981 Rel: $12.50 Cur: $20 (CA-3/89) **86**
Cabernet Sauvignon Napa Valley 1980 Rel: $11 Cur: $25 (CA-3/89) **92**
Cabernet Sauvignon Napa Valley Reserve 1991 (NR) (5/15/92) (BT) **87+**
Cabernet Sauvignon Napa Valley Reserve 1990 (NR) (5/15/91) (BT) **90+**
Cabernet Sauvignon Napa Valley Reserve 1989 (NR) (5/15/91) (BT) **90+**
Cabernet Sauvignon Napa Valley Reserve 1988 ($NA) (5/15/90) (BT) **85+**
Cabernet Sauvignon Napa Valley Reserve 1987 Rel: $25 Cur: $29 (11/15/91) **88**
Cabernet Sauvignon Napa Valley Reserve 1986 Rel: $25 Cur: $39 (11/15/90) **87**
Cabernet Sauvignon Napa Valley Reserve 1985 Rel: $25 Cur: $35 (2/15/90) **86**
Cabernet Sauvignon Napa Valley Reserve 1984 Rel: $25 Cur: $37 (CA-3/89) **92**
Cabernet Sauvignon Napa Valley Reserve 1983 Rel: $18 Cur: $23 (CA-3/89) **87**
Chardonnay Napa Valley 1990 $16 (7/31/92) **90**
Chardonnay Napa Valley 1989 $16 (11/30/91) **85**
Chardonnay Napa Valley 1988 $16 (11/15/90) **90**
Chardonnay Napa Valley 1987 Rel: $14.50 Cur: $19 (CH-3/90) **81**
Chardonnay Napa Valley 1986 Rel: $13.50 Cur: $28 (8/31/88) SS **93**
Chardonnay Napa Valley 1985 Rel: $13.50 Cur: $25 (CH-3/90) **90**
Chardonnay Napa Valley 1984 Rel: $13.50 Cur: $22 (CH-3/90) **80**
Chardonnay Napa Valley 1983 Rel: $12.50 Cur: $20 (CH-3/90) **76**
Chardonnay Napa Valley 1982 Rel: $12.50 Cur: $21 (CH-3/90) **76**
Chardonnay Napa Valley 1981 Rel: $12.50 Cur: $35 (CH-3/90) **90**
Chardonnay Napa Valley 1980 Rel: $11 Cur: $25 (CH-3/90) **85**
Chardonnay Napa Valley Reserve 1988 ($NA) (CH-6/90) **91**
Chardonnay Napa Valley Reserve 1987 Rel: $25 Cur: $29 (11/15/90) **90**
Chardonnay Napa Valley Reserve 1986 Rel: $25 Cur: $35 (CH-3/90) **92**
Chardonnay Napa Valley Reserve 1985 Rel: $25 Cur: $30 (CH-3/90) **91**
Chenin Blanc Napa Valley Dry 1988 $7 (7/31/89) **82**
Pinot Noir Oregon 1987 $12 (2/15/90) **67**
Sémillon Napa Valley Estate Grown 1989 $11 (11/15/91) **80**

GIRARDET (United States/Oregon)
Pinot Noir Umpqua Valley 1987 $12 (2/15/90) **75**

DOMAINE ALETH GIRARDIN (France/Burgundy)
Beaune Clos des Mouches 1988 $36 (7/15/91) **71**
Pommard Charmots 1988 $44 (7/15/91) **87**

DOMAINE JEAN GIRARDIN (France/Burgundy)
Santenay Clos Rousseau Château de la Charrière 1987 $25 (2/28/91) **87**
Santenay Comme Château de la Charrière 1987 $25 (2/28/91) **83**
Santenay Comme Château de la Charrière 1986 $23 (10/15/89) **80**

CASA GIRELLI (Italy/North)
Chardonnay Trentino i Mesi 1989 $8 (2/15/91) BB **81**
Pinot Nero Trentino i Mesi 1988 $10 (2/15/91) **81**

CHATEAU GISCOURS (France/Bordeaux)
Margaux 1991 (NR) (5/15/92) (BT) **85+**
Margaux 1990 (NR) (5/15/92) (BT) **90+**
Margaux 1989 $41 (3/15/92) **92**
Margaux 1988 $30 (4/30/91) **89**
Margaux 1987 $20 (6/30/89) (BT) **75+**
Margaux 1986 $30 (6/15/89) **83**
Margaux 1985 $35 (9/30/88) **86**
Margaux 1983 $30 (5/01/89) **78**
Margaux 1982 Rel: $26 Cur: $34 (12/01/85) **88**
Margaux 1981 Rel: $12 Cur: $44 (6/01/84) **82**
Margaux 1980 $23 (2/16/84) **80**
Margaux 1979 $36 (10/15/89) (JS) **87**
Margaux 1978 $46 (2/16/84) **87**
Margaux 1976 $45 (2/16/84) **83**
Margaux 1970 $90 (2/16/84) **81**
Margaux 1964 $121/1.5L (2/16/84) **89**
Margaux 1962 $33 (11/30/87) (JS) **68**
Margaux 1961 $125 (3/16/86) (TR) **78**

CHATEAU DU GLANA (France/Bordeaux)
St.-Julien 1989 (NR) (3/15/92) **87**
St.-Julien 1988 ($NA) (6/30/89) (BT) **75+**
St.-Julien 1987 ($NA) (11/30/89) (JS) **81**
St.-Julien 1986 $17 (11/30/89) (JS) **84**
St.-Julien 1982 $12 (11/30/89) (JS) **85**

GLASS MOUNTAIN QUARRY (United States/California)
Cabernet Sauvignon Napa Valley 1988 $8 (10/15/91) BB **85**
Chardonnay Napa Valley 1989 $8 (9/15/91) BB **86**
Petite Sirah Napa Valley 1988 $8 (10/31/91) BB **81**
Rubis du Val Napa Valley 1988 $8 (10/31/91) BB **82**

GLEN ELLEN (United States/California)
Aleatico California Blanc de Noirs Barrel Fermented Imagery Series 1990 $12 (3/31/92) **87**
Cabernet Franc Alexander Valley Imagery Series 1988 $16 (3/31/92) **86**
Cabernet Sauvignon California Proprietor's Reserve 1988 $6 (11/15/91) BB **79**
Cabernet Sauvignon California Proprietor's Reserve 1987 $6 (1/31/91) **79**
Cabernet Sauvignon California Proprietor's Reserve 1986 $4.50 (7/15/88) BB **82**
Cabernet Sauvignon Sonoma Valley Benziger Family Selection 1984 $14 (10/15/87) **82**
Cabernet Sauvignon Sonoma Valley Benziger Family Selection 1983 $9.75 (5/15/87) **91**
Cabernet Sauvignon Sonoma Valley Glen Ellen Estate 1982 $9.75 (2/01/85) **85**
Cabernet Sauvignon Sonoma Valley Imagery Series 1985 $12.50 (2/15/89) **86**
Chardonnay California Proprietor's Reserve 1990 $7 (7/15/91) **78**
Chardonnay California Proprietor's Reserve 1989 $6 (12/31/90) **79**
Chardonnay California Proprietor's Reserve 1984 $3.50 (10/16/85) BB **85**
Chardonnay Sonoma Valley 1984 $9 (3/16/86) **60**
Chardonnay Sonoma Valley 1983 $10 (2/01/85) **80**
Chenin Blanc California Proprietor's Reserve 1988 $6 (7/31/89) **79**
Merlot California Proprietor's Reserve 1990 $6 (5/31/92) **79**
Merlot California Proprietor's Reserve 1986 $6 (1/31/89) BB **84**
Petite Verdot Alexander Valley Imagery Series 1988 $16 (3/31/92) **88**
Riesling Late Harvest Santa Maria Valley Imagery Series 1989 $10/375ml (3/31/92) **79**
Sauvignon Blanc California Proprietor's Reserve 1990 $6 (7/31/91) BB **80**
Sauvignon Blanc California Proprietor's Reserve 1989 $5 (8/31/90) **77**
White Zinfandel California Proprietor's Reserve 1989 $5 (12/31/90) **80**
White Zinfandel California Proprietor's Reserve 1988 $5.75 (6/15/89) **84**

GLENORA (United States/New York)
Blanc de Blancs Finger Lakes 1987 $12 (12/31/90) **85**
Brut New York 1987 $12 (12/31/90) **81**

CHATEAU GLORIA (France/Bordeaux)
St.-Julien 1991 (NR) (5/15/92) (BT) **80+**
St.-Julien 1990 (NR) (5/15/92) (BT) **90+**
St.-Julien 1989 $29 (3/15/92) **92**
St.-Julien 1988 $23 (3/31/91) **90**
St.-Julien 1987 $14 (5/15/90) **80**
St.-Julien 1986 $18 (11/30/89) (JS) **89**
St.-Julien 1985 Rel: $14 Cur: $22 (4/15/88) **89**
St.-Julien 1984 Rel: $8 Cur: $15 (3/15/87) BB **87**
St.-Julien 1983 Rel: $10 Cur: $20 (10/15/86) **83**
St.-Julien 1982 Rel: $15 Cur: $34 (11/30/89) (JS) **83**
St.-Julien 1981 Rel: $10 Cur: $24 (6/01/84) **82**
St.-Julien 1979 $18 (10/15/89) (JS) **83**

CHATEAU GODARD (France/Bordeaux)
Côtes de Francs Blanc Les Charmes 1990 (NR) (9/30/91) (BT) **80+**

CHATEAU GOFFRETEAU (France/Bordeaux)
Bordeaux Rouge 1989 $8 (5/15/91) BB **84**
Bordeaux Supérieur 1988 $6 (2/28/91) BB **81**
Bordeaux Supérieur 1986 $6 (6/15/89) BB **82**

GOLAN (Other/Israel)
Cabernet Sauvignon Galil 1987 $11.50 (4/15/92) **83**
Cabernet Sauvignon Galil 1986 $11 (3/31/91) **85**
Chardonnay Galil 1990 $11.50 (4/15/92) **81**
Sauvignon Blanc Galil 1988 $8 (3/31/91) **72**

GOLD SEAL (United States/Other US)
Blanc de Blancs American Charles Fournier Special Selection NV $10 (6/30/90) **77**
Brut New York Bottle Fermented NV $7 (12/31/90) **69**

GOLDEN CREEK (United States/California)
Merlot Sonoma County 1989 $12.50 (5/31/92) **81**
Merlot Sonoma County Reserve 1989 $16 (5/31/92) **87**

GOLDENER OKTOBER (Germany)
Riesling Qualitätswein Mosel-Saar-Ruwer Piesporter Michelsberg 1987 $7 (11/30/88) **85**

CHATEAU GOMBAUDE-GUILLOT (France/Bordeaux)
Pomerol 1987 $17 (6/30/89) (BT) **70+**
Pomerol 1982 $28 (5/15/89) (TR) **83**

MICHEL GONET (France/Champagne)
Brut Rosé Champagne NV $21 (12/16/85) **89**

GOOSECROSS (United States/California)
Chardonnay Napa Valley 1988 $14 (8/31/90) **81**
Chardonnay Napa Valley 1987 $15 (1/31/90) **82**
Chardonnay Napa Valley 1986 $15 (5/31/88) **71**
Chardonnay Napa Valley 1985 $14 (8/31/87) **90**
Chardonnay Napa Valley Reserve 1988 $18 (8/31/90) **77**

GORDON BROTHERS (United States/Washington)
Cabernet Sauvignon Washington 1988 $19 (11/15/91) **89**

CHATEAU LE GORRE (France/Bordeaux)
Bordeaux Blanc Sec 1988 $9 (3/31/90) **72**

GOSSET (France/Champagne)
Brut Champagne Grande Millésime 1985 $72 (4/30/91) **89**
Brut Champagne Grande Millésime 1983 $75 (5/15/92) **90**
Brut Champagne Grande Millésime 1982 Rel: $60 Cur: $70 (12/31/90) **90**
Brut Champagne Grande Millésime 1979 Rel: $45 Cur: $112 (7/15/87) **96**
Brut Champagne Grande Réserve NV $35 (12/31/91) **91**
Brut Champagne Réserve NV $27 (12/31/91) **88**
Brut Rosé Champagne 1982 $75 (12/31/88) **88**
Brut Rosé Champagne NV $37 (12/31/90) **85**

DOMAINE LES GOUBERT (France/Rhône)
Côtes du Rhône 1986 $6.75 (3/31/88) **78**
Côtes du Rhône-Villages Beaumes de Venise 1987 $9 (7/31/89) **81**
Côtes du Rhône-Villages Beaumes de Venise 1985 $9.25 (4/30/88) **80**
Côtes du Rhône-Villages Blanc Sablet 1986 $7 (3/31/88) **68**
Côtes du Rhône-Villages Sablet 1985 $8.25 (4/30/88) **76**
Gigondas 1986 $13 (3/15/90) **81**
Gigondas 1985 $11 (4/30/88) **89**
Gigondas Cuvée Florence 1986 $24 (4/30/88) **92**

DOMAINE HENRI GOUGES (France/Burgundy)
Nuits-St.-Georges 1986 $30 (7/31/88) **84**
Nuits-St.-Georges Les Chaignots 1986 $40 (7/31/88) **90**
Nuits-St.-Georges Clos des Porrets-St.-Georges 1989 $45 (1/31/92) **87**
Nuits-St.-Georges Clos des Porrets-St.-Georges 1988 $50 (7/15/90) (BT) **80+**
Nuits-St.-Georges Les Pruliers 1989 $45 (1/31/92) **86**
Nuits-St.-Georges Les St.-Georges 1989 $49 (1/31/92) **89**
Nuits-St.-Georges Les St.-Georges 1988 $54 (7/15/90) (BT) **75+**
Nuits-St.-Georges Les St.-Georges 1985 $45 (2/15/88) **68**
Nuits-St.-Georges Les Vaucrains 1989 $49 (1/31/92) **90**

GOULD CAMPBELL (Portugal)
Late Bottled Port 1985 Rel: $23 Cur: $32 (4/15/92) **86**
Vintage Port 1985 Rel: $23 Cur: $32 (VP-6/90) **85**
Vintage Port 1983 Rel: $22 Cur: $38 (VP-6/90) **90**
Vintage Port 1980 Rel: $15 Cur: $42 (VP-2/90) **86**
Vintage Port 1977 Rel: $11 Cur: $54 (VP-2/90) **93**
Vintage Port 1975 Rel: $44 Cur: $51 (VP-2/90) **76**
Vintage Port 1970 $65 (VP-2/90) **88**
Vintage Port 1966 $75 (VP-2/90) **84**

GEORGE GOULET (France/Champagne)
Blanc de Blancs Crémant Champagne 1982 $30 (7/31/88) **86**
Brut Blanc de Blancs Champagne Cuvée G NV $26 (7/31/88) **74**
Brut Champagne 1982 $30 (7/31/88) **90**
Brut Champagne NV $21 (7/31/88) **83**
Brut Champagne Cuvée du Centenaire 1982 $47 (7/31/88) **87**
Brut Rosé Champagne 1982 $31 (7/31/88) **85**

DOMAINE DU GOUR DE CHAULE (France/Rhône)
Gigondas 1986 $13 (9/15/90) **90**

GOVERNOR PHILLIP (Australia)
Cabernet Sauvignon Shiraz Barossa Valley 1986 $6 (7/31/89) BB **83**
Classic Australian Red Australia NV $5 (7/31/89) BB **82**

GRACE FAMILY (United States/California)
Cabernet Sauvignon Napa Valley 1991 (NR) (5/15/92) (BT) **90+**
Cabernet Sauvignon Napa Valley 1990 (NR) (5/15/91) (BT) **90+**
Cabernet Sauvignon Napa Valley 1989 (NR) (5/15/91) (BT) **85+**
Cabernet Sauvignon Napa Valley 1988 Rel: $63 Cur: $160 (6/30/91) **92**
Cabernet Sauvignon Napa Valley 1987 Rel: $56 Cur: $200 (6/30/90) **97**
Cabernet Sauvignon Napa Valley 1986 Rel: $40 Cur: $230 (CA-3/89) **93**
Cabernet Sauvignon Napa Valley 1985 Rel: $50 Cur: $290 (CA-3/89) **95**
Cabernet Sauvignon Napa Valley 1984 Rel: $38 Cur: $280 (CA-3/89) **92**
Cabernet Sauvignon Napa Valley 1983 Rel: $38 Cur: $300 (CA-3/89) **91**
Cabernet Sauvignon Napa Valley 1982 Rel: $31 Cur: $250 (CA-3/89) **89**
Cabernet Sauvignon Napa Valley 1981 Rel: $28 Cur: $260 (CA-3/89) **88**
Cabernet Sauvignon Napa Valley 1980 Rel: $25 Cur: $330 (CA-3/89) **92**
Cabernet Sauvignon Napa Valley 1979 Rel: $20 Cur: $380 (CA-3/89) **92**
Cabernet Sauvignon Napa Valley 1978 Rel: $20 Cur: $500 (CA-3/89) **86**

WEINGUT GRAFSCHAFT LEININGEN (Germany)
Gewürztraminer Spätlese Rheinpfalz Kirchheimer Geibkopf 1989 $14 (1/31/92) **90**
Riesling Auslese Rheinpfalz Kirchheimer Römerstrabe 1989 $15 (1/31/92) **83**
Riesling Kabinett Halbtrocken Rheinpfalz Kirchheimer Römerstrabe Renommée 1989 $10 (1/31/92) **80**
Riesling Kabinett Rheinpfalz Kirchheimer Schwarzerde 1990 $9 (12/15/91) BB **88**
Ruländer Auslese Trocken Rheinpfalz Kirchheimer Kreuz 1989 $14 (1/31/92) **80**
Ruländer Beerenauslese Rheinpfalz Kircheimer Kreuz Secundus 1989 $45 (1/31/92) **84**
Ruländer Trockenbeerenauslese Rheinpfalz Kircheimer Kreuz Primus 1989 $60 (1/31/92) **85**
Scheurebe Auslese Rheinpfalz Bissersheimer Goldberg 1989 $13 (1/31/92) **84**
Spätburgunder Rotwein Trocken Rheinpfalz Kleinkarlbacher Herrenberg 1989 $10/500ml (1/31/92) **82**

GRAHAM (Portugal)
Tawny Port 20 Year Old NV $36 (2/28/90) (JS) **84**
Vintage Port 1985 Rel: $31 Cur: $48 (VP-6/90) **96**
Vintage Port 1985 Rel: $31 Cur: $48 (9/30/87) CS **91**
Vintage Port 1983 Rel: $30 Cur: $43 (VP-6/90) **93**
Vintage Port 1980 Rel: $18 Cur: $42 (VP-6/90) **90**
Vintage Port 1980 Rel: $18 Cur: $42 (4/16/85) CS **88**
Vintage Port 1977 Rel: $15 Cur: $66 (VP-4/90) **90**
Vintage Port 1977 Rel: $15 Cur: $66 (3/16/84) CS **91**
Vintage Port 1975 $51 (VP-2/89) **78**
Vintage Port 1970 $76 (VP-12/89) **94**
Vintage Port 1966 $75 (VP-12/89) **93**
Vintage Port 1963 $145 (VP-12/89) **97**
Vintage Port 1960 $92 (10/31/88) **88**
Vintage Port 1955 $210 (VP-11/89) **94**
Vintage Port 1954 $155 (VP-2/90) **91**
Vintage Port 1948 $300 (VP-11/89) **95**
Vintage Port 1945 $480 (VP-11/89) **95**
Vintage Port 1942 $420 (VP-4/90) **89**
Vintage Port 1935 $350 (VP-4/90) **94**
Vintage Port 1927 $510 (VP-2/90) **94**
Vintage Port Malvedos 1988 Rel: $26 Cur: $29 (1/31/91) **93**
Vintage Port Malvedos 1987 ($NA) (VP-2/90) **91**
Vintage Port Malvedos 1986 $35 (VP-2/90) **85**
Vintage Port Malvedos 1984 ($NA) (VP-2/90) **83**
Vintage Port Malvedos 1982 ($NA) (VP-2/90) **90**
Vintage Port Malvedos 1979 $34 (VP-2/90) **74**
Vintage Port Malvedos 1978 Rel: $30 Cur: $35 (VP-2/90) **82**
Vintage Port Malvedos 1976 Rel: $17 Cur: $28 (VP-2/90) **74**
Vintage Port Malvedos 1968 $50 (VP-2/90) **70**
Vintage Port Malvedos 1965 $58 (VP-2/90) **79**
Vintage Port Malvedos 1964 $54 (VP-2/90) **82**
Vintage Port Malvedos 1962 $52 (VP-2/90) **89**

Key to Symbols

The scores reported here are the results of blind tastings conducted by our panel of senior editors. Wines that carry the initials below are results of individual tastings.

THE WINE SPECTATOR 100-POINT SCALE 95-100—Classic, a great wine; ***90-94***—Outstanding, superior character and style; ***80-89***—Good to very good, a wine with special qualities; ***70-79***—Average, drinkable wine that may have minor flaws; ***60-69***—Below average, drinkable but not recommended; ***50-59***—Poor, undrinkable, not recommended. "+"—With a score indicates a range; used primarily with barrel tastings to indicate a preliminary score.

SPECIAL DESIGNATIONS SS—Spectator Selection, CS—Cellar Selection, BB—Best Buy, ($NA)—Price not available, (NR)—Not released.

TASTER'S INITIALS (JG)—Jim Gordon, (HS)—Harvey Steiman, (JL)—James Laube, (JS)—James Suckling, (TM)—Thomas Matthews, (TR)—Terry Robards, (PM)—Per-Henrik Mansson, (BT)—Barrel Tasting (these wines were tasted blind from barrel samples), (CA-date)—*California's Great Cabernets* by James Laube, (CH-date)—*California's Great Chardonnays* by James Laube, (VP-date)—*Vintage Port* by James Suckling.

DATE TASTED Dates in parentheses represent the issue in which the rating was published.

Vintage Port Malvedos 1961 $65 (VP-2/90) **87**
Vintage Port Malvedos 1958 $65 (VP-2/90) **79**
Vintage Port Malvedos 1957 $70 (VP-2/90) **84**
Vintage Port Malvedos 1952 $125 (VP-11/89) **85**

ALAIN GRAILLOT (France/Rhône)
Crozes-Hermitage 1989 $14 (3/31/91) **88**
Crozes-Hermitage 1986 $9.75 (4/15/89) **88**

MACHARD DE GRAMONT (France/Burgundy)
Aloxe-Corton Les Morais 1985 $34 (7/15/88) **80**
Beaune Les Chouacheux 1985 $34 (5/31/88) **89**
Bourgogne Pinot Noir Domaine de la Vierge Romaine 1985 $13 (6/30/88) **81**
Chorey-lès-Beaune Les Beaumonts 1985 $22 (7/31/88) **84**
Nuits-St.-Georges Les Allots 1985 $35 (5/31/88) **86**
Nuits-St.-Georges Les Hauts Poirets 1985 $41 (6/15/88) **84**
Nuits-St.-Georges Les Hauts Pruliers 1985 $36 (2/15/88) **90**
Nuits-St.-Georges en la Perrière Noblot 1985 $41 (5/31/88) **89**
Nuits-St.-Georges Les Vallerots 1985 $47 (5/31/88) **78**
Puligny-Montrachet Les Houillères 1985 $47 (5/31/88) **73**
Savigny-lès-Beaune Les Guettes 1985 $25 (7/31/88) **89**

GRAN CAUS (Spain)
Cabernet Sauvignon-Cabernet Franc-Merlot Penedès 1986 $12 (4/30/89) **77**
Cabernet Sauvignon-Cabernet Franc-Merlot Penedès 1985 $12 (10/15/88) **77**
Chardonnay Penedès Chenin Blanc Xarel-lo 1987 $10 (5/15/89) **81**
Penedès 1984 $12 (9/15/88) **68**
Penedès Can Ràfols dels Caus 1987 $11 (10/15/90) **78**

GRAN CONDAL (Spain)
Rioja 1987 $6.50 (3/31/90) **80**
Rioja Gran Reserva 1982 $10 (11/15/87) (JL) **79**
Rioja Gran Reserva 1981 $8 (11/30/87) **80**
Rioja Reserva 1980 $7 (11/30/87) BB **82**

CHATEAU DU GRAND ABORD (France/Bordeaux)
Graves Blanc 1984 $4 (6/01/86) **57**

CHATEAU GRAND-BARRAIL-LAMARZELLE-FIGEAC (France/Bordeaux)
St.-Emilion 1986 $15 (6/30/89) **72**
St.-Emilion 1982 ($NA) (5/15/89) (TR) **85**

CHATEAU GRAND CHEMIN (France/Bordeaux)
Côtes de Bourg 1985 $8 (6/15/89) **76**

CHATEAU GRAND CLARET (France/Bordeaux)
Premières Côtes de Bordeaux 1988 $7 (7/31/91) **78**

CHATEAU GRAND-CORBIN-DESPAGNE (France/Bordeaux)
St.-Emilion 1945 $100 (3/16/86) (JL) **70**

GRAND CRU (United States/California)
Cabernet Sauvignon Alexander Valley Collector's Reserve 1986 $22 (5/15/90) **85**
Cabernet Sauvignon Alexander Valley Collector's Reserve 1985 $18 (7/15/89) **81**
Cabernet Sauvignon Alexander Valley Collector's Reserve 1982 $15 (9/30/87) **70**
Cabernet Sauvignon Alexander Valley Collector's Reserve 1980 $14.50 (11/01/84) **85**
Cabernet Sauvignon Sonoma County Premium Selection 1988 $12 (3/15/92) **84**
Cabernet Sauvignon Sonoma County Premium Selection 1987 $12 (11/15/91) **85**
Cabernet Sauvignon Sonoma County Premium Selection 1986 $12 (4/30/90) **79**
Cabernet Sauvignon Sonoma County Premium Selection 1985 $9 (6/15/89) **79**
Cabernet Sauvignon Sonoma County 1984 $8.50 (12/31/87) **75**
Cabernet Sauvignon Sonoma County 1983 $8.50 (11/16/85) **68**
Chardonnay Carneros Premium Selection 1989 $14 (3/31/92) **84**
Chardonnay Carneros Premium Selection 1988 $13.50 (6/15/90) **84**
Chardonnay Carneros Premium Selection 1987 $12 (3/15/89) **88**
Chenin Blanc Clarksburg Dry 1989 $6.50 (6/30/90) **83**
Chenin Blanc Clarksburg Dry Premium Selection 1990 $6.50 (11/15/91) BB **85**
Chenin Blanc Clarksburg Dry Premium Selection 1988 $7 (7/31/89) **85**
Gewürztraminer Alexander Valley 1990 $9.50 (9/30/91) **75**
Gewürztraminer Late Harvest Sonoma County Select 1987 $10/375ml (3/31/90) **72**
White Zinfandel California 1988 $5 (6/15/89) **73**

GRAND IMPERIAL (France/Other)
Brut NV $4.50 (6/15/90) **76**

DOMAINE DE GRAND MAISON (France/Bordeaux)
Pessac-Léognan 1986 $8.50 (4/15/90) **80**

CHATEAU GRAND-MAYNE (France/Bordeaux)
St.-Emilion 1989 $22 (3/15/92) **93**
St.-Emilion 1988 Rel: $15 Cur: $19 (7/15/91) **87**
St.-Emilion 1986 $16 (6/30/89) **87**

CHATEAU GRAND MOULIN (France/Bordeaux)
Haut-Médoc 1983 $6.75 (4/16/86) **63**

CHATEAU GRAND ORMEAU (France/Bordeaux)
Lalande-de-Pomerol 1985 $16 (5/31/88) **88**

CHATEAU GRAND PONTET (France/Bordeaux)
St.-Emilion 1988 $21 (7/15/91) **86**
St.-Emilion 1982 $26 (5/15/89) (TR) **83**

CHATEAU GRAND-PUY-DUCASSE (France/Bordeaux)
Pauillac 1989 $23 (4/30/92) **86**
Pauillac 1988 $21 (4/30/91) **89**
Pauillac 1987 $18 (6/30/89) (BT) **75+**
Pauillac 1986 Rel: $22 Cur: $26 (6/30/89) **85**
Pauillac 1985 Rel: $19 Cur: $24 (2/29/88) **90**

CHATEAU GRAND-PUY-LACOSTE (France/Bordeaux)
Pauillac 1991 (NR) (5/15/92) (BT) **80+**
Pauillac 1990 (NR) (5/15/92) (BT) **90+**
Pauillac 1989 $36 (3/15/92) **91**
Pauillac 1988 $33 (4/30/91) **90**
Pauillac 1987 $22 (5/15/90) **77**
Pauillac 1986 $25 (5/31/89) **88**
Pauillac 1985 Rel: $23 Cur: $30 (6/30/88) **91**
Pauillac 1984 $24 (10/15/87) **83**
Pauillac 1979 $37 (10/15/89) (JS) **88**
Pauillac 1961 $150 (3/16/86) (TR) **96**
Pauillac 1945 $380 (3/16/86) (JL) **80**

DOMAINE GRAND-ROMAINE (France/Rhône)
Gigondas 1989 $16 (8/31/91) **87**
Gigondas Medaille d'Argent 1990 $16 (1/31/92) **85**
Gigondas Medaille d'Or 1990 $16 (1/31/92) **87**

DOMAINE DU GRAND TINEL (France/Rhône)
Châteauneuf-du-Pape 1989 $15 (10/15/91) **88**
Châteauneuf-du-Pape 1988 $17 (10/15/91) **87**
Châteauneuf-du-Pape 1986 $20 (10/15/91) **86**
Châteauneuf-du-Pape 1985 $23 (10/15/91) **75**
Châteauneuf-du-Pape 1983 $25 (10/15/91) **87**
Châteauneuf-du-Pape 1981 $27 (10/15/91) **89**
Châteauneuf-du-Pape Blanc 1990 $18 (10/15/91) **81**

CHATEAU LE GRAND VERDUS (France/Bordeaux)
Bordeaux Supérieur 1988 $7.50 (10/31/91) BB **80**

CHATEAU GRANDES-MURAILLES (France/Bordeaux)
St.-Emilion 1989 (NR) (3/15/92) **88**
St.-Emilion 1982 ($NA) (5/15/89) (TR) **81**

GRANDIN (France/Other)
Brut Ingrandes-Sur-Loire NV $10 (6/15/90) **82**

CHATEAU LES GRANDS JAYS (France/Bordeaux)
Bordeaux Supérieur 1986 $6 (5/15/89) **77**

DOMAINE ALAIN GRANGEON (France/Rhône)
Châteauneuf-du-Pape 1986 $16 (1/31/89) **77**

GRANITE SPRINGS (United States/California)
Chenin Blanc El Dorado 1988 $5.50 (7/31/89) **85**

GRANTS (Australia)
Cabernet Sauvignon Barossa Valley 1984 $8 (11/15/87) **73**
Chardonnay McLaren Vale 1986 $8 (12/15/87) **77**

ALAIN GRAS (France/Burgundy)
St.-Romain 1989 $20 (8/31/91) **84**

ELIO GRASSO (Italy/Piedmont)
Barolo Gavarini Vigna Rüncot 1985 $42 (8/31/91) **59**
Dolcetto d'Alba Gavarini Vigna dei Grassi 1989 $18 (7/15/91) **76**
Gavarini 1989 $20 (7/15/91) **83**

GRATEFUL RED (United States/Oregon)
Pinot Noir Willamette Valley 1990 $10 (6/15/92) **84**

GRATIEN (France/Other)
Brut Saumur NV $9.25 (6/15/90) **83**

ALFRED GRATIEN (France/Champagne)
Brut Champagne 1979 $28 (9/16/85) **92**
Brut Champagne NV $23 (11/01/85) **93**
Rosé Champagne NV $24 (10/01/85) **81**

GRATTAMACCO (Italy/Tuscany)
1988 ($NA) (9/15/91) **87**

CHATEAU DE LA GRAVE (France/Bordeaux)
Bordeaux Supérieur 1988 $8 (7/15/90) BB **82**
Côtes de Bourg 1982 $5.25 (2/16/85) **70**
Côtes de Bourg 1981 $4.99 (2/16/85) **74**

CHATEAU LA GRAVE TRIGANT DE BOISSET (France/Bordeaux)
Pomerol 1990 (NR) (5/15/92) (BT) **90+**
Pomerol 1989 $35 (3/15/92) **88**
Pomerol 1988 Rel: $24 Cur: $26 (8/31/90) (BT) **90+**
Pomerol 1987 $21 (6/30/89) (BT) **80+**
Pomerol 1986 $35 (3/31/90) **89**
Pomerol 1985 $24 (5/15/87) (BT) **80+**
Pomerol 1982 $43 (5/15/89) (TR) **91**
Pomerol 1979 $23 (10/15/89) (JS) **90**

CHATEAU GRAVES (France/Sauternes)
Barsac 1989 ($NA) (6/15/90) (BT) **90+**

CHATEAU GRAVILLE-LACOSTE (France/Bordeaux)
Graves Blanc Dry 1990 $13 (9/15/91) **75**

GRAYSON (United States/Other US)
White Zinfandel American NV $4 (6/15/89) **82**

GREAT WESTERN (United States/New York)
Blanc de Blancs New York NV $14 (6/30/90) **76**
Blanc de Noirs American NV $14 (3/31/90) **70**
Brut Very Dry New York NV $9.75 (12/31/90) **69**
Extra Dry New York NV $9.75 (12/31/90) **68**
Natural New York NV $14 (6/30/90) **74**
Rosé New York NV $9.75 (12/31/90) **71**

GREEN & RED (United States/California)
Chardonnay Napa Valley 1989 $14 (3/31/91) **86**
Chardonnay Napa Valley 1988 $12 (4/30/90) **72**
Chardonnay Napa Valley 1987 $11 (7/15/89) **78**
Zinfandel Napa Valley 1987 $9.50 (2/15/91) **77**
Zinfandel Napa Valley 1986 $9 (3/15/90) **76**
Zinfandel Napa Valley 1985 $8.50 (6/15/89) **73**
Zinfandel Napa Valley 1984 $7.75 (11/15/87) **82**
Zinfandel Napa Valley 1983 $7.25 (7/31/87) **64**
Zinfandel Napa Valley 1982 $7.50 (12/16/85) **82**

GREENWOOD RIDGE (United States/California)
Cabernet Sauvignon Mendocino 1988 $15 (2/29/92) **83**
Chardonnay Mendocino 1990 $16 (2/15/92) **85**
Merlot Anderson Valley 1989 $16 (11/15/91) **85**
Pinot Noir Anderson Valley 1989 $13.50 (6/30/91) **87**
Sauvignon Blanc Anderson Valley 1989 $8 (10/15/91) **78**
White Riesling Anderson Valley 1991 $8.50 (5/31/92) **82**
White Riesling Late Harvest Mendocino 1989 $18/375ml (8/31/91) **89**
White Riesling Mendocino 1987 $8 (7/31/89) **77**
Zinfandel Sonoma County 1988 $11 (5/15/91) **86**

CHATEAU GRENOUILLES (France/Chablis)
Chablis Grenouille 1985 $34 (8/31/87) **89**

GREPPONE MAZZI (Italy/Tuscany)
Brunello di Montalcino 1982 ($NA) (9/15/86) **90**
Brunello di Montalcino 1981 ($NA) (9/15/86) **70**

MARCHESI DI GRESY (Italy/Piedmont)
Barbaresco Camp Gros Martinenga 1985 Rel: $58 Cur: $70 (1/31/89) **92**
Barbaresco Camp Gros Martinenga 1983 Rel: $30 Cur: $76 (9/15/88) (HS) **88**
Barbaresco Camp Gros Martinenga 1982 $26 (9/15/88) (HS) **89**
Barbaresco Camp Gros Martinenga 1979 $40 (9/15/88) (HS) **88**

Barbaresco Gaiun Martinenga 1986 $64 (9/15/90) **90**
Barbaresco Gaiun Martinenga 1985 Rel: $55 Cur: $72 (1/31/89) CS **95**
Barbaresco Gaiun Martinenga 1983 Rel: $30 Cur: $76 (9/15/88) (HS) **84**
Barbaresco Gaiun Martinenga 1982 $26 (9/15/88) (HS) **87**
Barbaresco Martinenga 1986 $56 (9/15/90) **88**
Barbaresco Martinenga 1985 Rel: $39 Cur: $52 (1/31/89) **90**
Barbaresco Martinenga 1984 Rel: $20 Cur: $38 (9/15/88) (HS) **84**
Barbaresco Martinenga 1983 Rel: $20 Cur: $62 (9/15/88) (HS) **87**
Barbaresco Martinenga 1982 Rel: $20 Cur: $70 (9/15/88) (HS) **86**
Barbaresco Martinenga 1979 $30 (9/15/88) (HS) **81**
Barbaresco Martinenga 1978 $40 (9/15/88) (HS) **89**
Chardonnay 1987 $37 (9/15/89) (HS) **85**
Nebbiolo Martinenga 1986 $11 (10/15/88) **82**

PODERI DI GRETOLE (Italy/Tuscany)
Chianti Classico 1988 $8 (10/31/91) BB **82**
Chianti Classico Riserva 1986 $11 (10/31/91) **83**

CASTELLI DEL GREVEPESA (Italy/Tuscany)
Chianti Classico Sant'Angiolo Vico Labate 1988 ($NA) (9/15/91) **88**

CHATEAU GREYSAC (France/Bordeaux)
Médoc 1991 (NR) (5/15/92) (BT) **75+**
Médoc 1990 (NR) (4/30/91) (BT) **80+**
Médoc 1989 $12 (3/15/92) **79**
Médoc 1988 $15 (4/30/91) **87**
Médoc 1987 $9 (6/30/89) (BT) **75+**
Médoc 1986 $10 (11/30/89) (JS) **85**
Médoc 1985 $9 (12/31/88) **77**
Médoc 1983 Rel: $8.50 Cur: $12 (7/31/87) **65**
Médoc 1982 Rel: $8 Cur: $16 (11/30/89) (JS) **80**
Médoc 1981 $8 (6/01/84) **77**

GRGICH HILLS (United States/California)
Cabernet Sauvignon Napa Valley 1987 ($NA) (4/15/89) (BT) **95+**
Cabernet Sauvignon Napa Valley 1986 Rel: $20 Cur: $26 (11/15/91) **88**
Cabernet Sauvignon Napa Valley 1985 Rel: $20 Cur: $25 (10/31/90) **90**
Cabernet Sauvignon Napa Valley 1984 Rel: $17 Cur: $37 (4/30/89) **87**
Cabernet Sauvignon Napa Valley 1983 Rel: $17 Cur: $33 (CA-3/89) **88**
Cabernet Sauvignon Napa Valley 1982 Rel: $17 Cur: $29 (CA-3/89) **87**
Cabernet Sauvignon Napa Valley 1981 Rel: $17 Cur: $42 (CA-3/89) **86**
Cabernet Sauvignon Napa-Sonoma Counties 1980 Rel: $16 Cur: $34 (CA-3/89) **90**
Chardonnay Napa Valley 1989 Rel: $22 Cur: $28 (7/15/91) **88**
Chardonnay Napa Valley 1988 Rel: $22 Cur: $29 (11/15/90) **89**
Chardonnay Napa Valley 1987 Rel: $22 Cur: $31 (CH-6/90) **90**
Chardonnay Napa Valley 1986 Rel: $22 Cur: $44 (CH-3/90) **91**
Chardonnay Napa Valley 1985 Rel: $22 Cur: $41 (CH-3/90) **92**
Chardonnay Napa Valley 1984 Rel: $18 Cur: $33 (CH-3/90) **90**
Chardonnay Napa Valley 1983 Rel: $17 Cur: $33 (CH-3/90) **92**
Chardonnay Napa Valley 1983 Rel: $17 Cur: $33 (10/01/85) SS **96**
Chardonnay Napa Valley 1982 Rel: $17 Cur: $48 (CH-3/90) **87**
Chardonnay Napa Valley 1981 Rel: $17 Cur: $60 (CH-3/90) **88**
Chardonnay Napa Valley 1980 Rel: $17 Cur: $51 (CH-3/90) **88**
Chardonnay Napa Valley 1979 Rel: $16 Cur: $63 (CH-3/90) **95**
Chardonnay Napa Valley 1978 Rel: $13.75 Cur: $60 (CH-3/90) **92**
Chardonnay Sonoma County 1977 Rel: $11 Cur: $105 (CH-3/90) **89**
Chardonnay Napa Valley Hill's Cellars 1976 Rel: $8 Cur: $50 (CH-3/90) **85**
Fumé Blanc Napa Valley 1990 $12 (2/15/92) **90**
Fumé Blanc Napa Valley 1989 $11 (3/15/91) **85**
Fumé Blanc Napa Valley 1988 $10 (3/31/90) **90**
Fumé Blanc Napa Valley 1987 $10 (7/31/89) **89**
Johannisberg Riesling Napa Valley 1987 $7.75 (8/31/89) **90**
Zinfandel Alexander Valley 1986 Rel: $12 Cur: $16 (5/15/90) **85**
Zinfandel Alexander Valley 1985 Rel: $12 Cur: $16 (7/31/89) **84**
Zinfandel Alexander Valley 1984 Rel: $10 Cur: $18 (3/15/87) **90**
Zinfandel Alexander Valley 1983 Rel: $10 Cur: $18 (5/01/86) **85**
Zinfandel Alexander Valley 1982 Rel: $10 Cur: $18 (5/16/85) SS **91**
Zinfandel Sonoma County 1988 $12 (3/31/92) **85**
Zinfandel Sonoma County 1987 Rel: $12 Cur: $17 (10/15/90) **84**
Zinfandel Sonoma County 1984 $11 (10/31/88) **86**
Zinfandel Sonoma County 1981 $10 (4/01/84) **80**

CHATEAU DE LA GRILLE (France/Loire)
Chinon 1987 $18 (8/31/91) **77**

CHATEAU GRILLET (France/Rhône)
Château-Grillet 1986 $75 (11/30/90) **80**

MARQUES DE GRINON (Spain)
Tinto do Toledo 1985 $12 (2/28/90) **86**

GRISTINA (United States/New York)
Cabernet Sauvignon North Fork of Long Island 1988 $14 (6/30/91) (TM) **90**
Chardonnay North Fork of Long Island 1989 $13 (6/30/91) (TM) **90**
Merlot North Fork of Long Island 1988 $13 (6/30/91) (TM) **81**

ALBERT GRIVAULT (France/Burgundy)
Meursault 1989 $48 (8/31/91) **88**
Meursault Clos des Perrières 1989 $80 (8/31/91) **87**
Meursault Clos des Perrières 1984 $50 (8/31/87) **90**

JEAN GRIVOT (France/Burgundy)
Chambolle-Musigny La Combe d'Orvaux 1987 $47 (6/15/90) **85**
Clos de Vougeot 1988 $70 (4/30/91) **85**
Clos de Vougeot 1985 $62 (4/30/88) **81**
Nuits-St.-Georges Les Boudots 1989 (NR) (1/31/92) **77**
Nuits-St.-Georges Les Boudots 1988 $54 (4/30/91) **87**
Nuits-St.-Georges Les Charmois 1987 $47 (7/15/90) **81**
Nuits-St.-Georges Les Pruliers 1988 Rel: $53 Cur: $57 (4/30/91) **89**
Nuits-St.-Georges Les Pruliers 1987 $55 (7/15/90) **71**
Nuits-St.-Georges Les Roncières 1987 $55 (7/15/90) **88**
Richebourg 1989 (NR) (1/31/92) **93**
Vosne-Romanée 1985 $31 (4/30/88) **87**
Vosne-Romanée Les Beaumonts 1989 (NR) (1/31/92) **75**

SCHLOSS GROENESTEYN (Germany)
Riesling Auslese Rheingau Rüdesheimer Berg Rottland 1989 $40 (12/15/90) **85**
Riesling Kabinett Halbtrocken Rheingau Kiedricher Wasseros 1990 $12 (12/15/91) **85**
Riesling Kabinett Rheingau Kiedricher Gräfenberg 1989 $12 (12/15/90) **83**
Riesling Kabinett Rheingau Kiedricher Gräfenberg 1988 ($NA) (9/30/89) **91**
Riesling Kabinett Rheingau Kiedricher Sandgrub 1990 $12 (12/15/91) **80**
Riesling Kabinett Rheingau Kiedricher Sandgrub 1989 $12 (12/15/90) **81**
Riesling Kabinett Rheingau Kiedricher Sandgrub 1988 ($NA) (9/30/89) **89**
Riesling Kabinett Rheingau Rüdesheimer Berg Rottland 1990 $12 (12/15/91) **79**
Riesling Kabinett Rheingau Rüdesheimer Berg Rottland 1988 ($NA) (9/30/89) **74**
Riesling Kabinett Rheingau Rüdesheimer Berg Rottland 1985 $9 (10/15/87) **78**
Riesling Kabinett Rheingau Rüdesheimer Berg Rottland 1983 $5.75 (1/01/85) BB **86**
Riesling Kabinett Rheingau Rüdesheimer Klosterlay 1988 ($NA) (9/30/89) **82**
Riesling Spätlese Rheingau Kiedricher Gräfenberg 1989 $16 (12/15/90) **78**
Riesling Spätlese Rheingau Kiedricher Sandgrub 1989 $16 (12/15/90) **83**
Riesling Spätlese Rheingau Rüdesheimer Berg Rottland 1990 $18 (12/15/91) **75**
Riesling Spätlese Rheingau Rüdesheimer Berg Rottland 1989 $15 (12/15/90) **80**
Riesling Spätlese Rheingau Rüdesheimer Berg Schlossberg 1990 $18 (12/15/91) **82**

DOMAINE ROBERT GROFFIER (France/Burgundy)
Bonnes Mares 1989 $79 (1/31/92) **81**
Bonnes Mares 1988 $80 (11/15/90) **90**
Bonnes Mares 1987 $67 (7/31/89) **89**
Bourgogne 1989 $14 (1/31/92) **78**
Chambertin Clos de Bèze 1987 $45 (7/31/89) **88**
Chambolle-Musigny Amoureuses 1988 $66 (11/15/90) **93**
Chambolle-Musigny Amoureuses 1987 $51 (8/31/89) **86**
Chambolle-Musigny Amoureuses 1986 $50 (2/28/89) **84**
Chambolle-Musigny Les Sentiers 1988 $45 (11/15/90) **89**
Chambolle-Musigny Les Sentiers 1987 $37 (8/31/89) **87**
Chambolle-Musigny Les Sentiers 1986 $36 (2/28/89) **90**
Gevrey-Chambertin 1986 $27 (2/28/89) **85**

CHATEAU LA GROLET (France/Bordeaux)
Côtes de Bourg 1989 $9 (8/31/91) BB **82**
Côtes de Bourg 1985 $5 (5/15/88) **69**

A.-F. GROS (France/Burgundy)
Bourgogne Hautes Côtes de Nuits 1988 $22 (3/31/91) **80**
Clos Vougeot Le Grand Maupertuis 1989 (NR) (1/31/92) **90**
Echézeaux 1988 $84 (2/15/91) **91**
Hautes Côtes de Nuits 1989 $19 (6/15/92) **78**
Richebourg 1989 $130 (1/31/92) **97**
Richebourg 1988 $190 (2/15/91) **97**
Vosne-Romanée Aux Réas 1988 $41 (2/28/91) **71**

JEAN GROS (France/Burgundy)
Nuits-St.-Georges 1989 $39 (1/31/92) **87**
Nuits-St.-Georges 1988 $42 (2/28/91) **81**
Nuits-St.-Georges 1985 $36 (7/31/88) **85**
Richebourg 1989 $180 (1/31/92) **98**
Richebourg 1988 $190 (2/28/91) **98**
Richebourg 1987 Rel: $99 Cur: $175 (3/31/90) **95**
Vosne-Romanée 1989 $39 (1/31/92) **90**
Vosne-Romanée 1988 $38 (2/28/91) **90**
Vosne-Romanée 1987 $32 (4/30/90) **89**
Vosne-Romanée Clos des Réas 1989 $70 (1/31/92) **92**
Vosne-Romanée Clos des Réas 1988 $50 (2/28/91) **94**
Vosne-Romanée Clos des Réas 1987 Rel: $37 Cur: $50 (4/30/90) **93**
Vosne-Romanée Clos des Réas 1986 $36 (2/28/89) **90**
Vosne-Romanée Clos des Réas 1985 Rel: $55 Cur: $58 (7/31/88) **87**

MICHEL GROS (France/Burgundy)
Bourgogne Hautes Côtes de Nuits 1989 (NR) (1/31/92) **82**
Hautes Côtes de Nuits 1987 $14 (2/28/90) **78**

DOMAINE GROS FRERE & SOEUR (France/Burgundy)
Bourgogne Hautes Côtes de Nuits 1989 (NR) (1/31/92) **82**
Clos de Vougeot Musigny 1989 $60 (1/31/92) **91**
Clos de Vougeot Musigny 1988 $95 (3/31/91) **92**
Clos de Vougeot Musigny 1985 $70 (3/31/88) **75**
Grands Echézeaux 1989 $80 (1/31/92) **92**
Grands Echézeaux 1988 $110 (3/15/91) **94**
Grands Echézeaux 1985 $75 (3/31/88) **71**
Richebourg 1989 $130 (1/31/92) **95**
Richebourg 1988 $192 (2/28/91) **91**
Vosne-Romanée 1989 $39 (1/31/92) **91**
Vosne-Romanée 1988 $46 (3/31/91) **89**
Vosne-Romanée 1985 $35 (4/15/88) **70**

GROTH (United States/California)
Cabernet Sauvignon Napa Valley 1991 (NR) (5/15/92) (BT) **89+**
Cabernet Sauvignon Napa Valley 1990 (NR) (5/15/91) (BT) **90+**
Cabernet Sauvignon Napa Valley 1989 (NR) (5/15/91) (BT) **90+**
Cabernet Sauvignon Napa Valley 1988 $20 (11/15/91) **75**
Cabernet Sauvignon Napa Valley 1987 Rel: $20 Cur: $23 (10/31/90) **81**
Cabernet Sauvignon Napa Valley 1986 Rel: $18 Cur: $25 (11/15/89) **92**
Cabernet Sauvignon Napa Valley 1985 Rel: $16 Cur: $50 (CA-3/89) **91**
Cabernet Sauvignon Napa Valley 1984 Rel: $14 Cur: $41 (CA-3/89) **92**
Cabernet Sauvignon Napa Valley 1983 Rel: $13 Cur: $23 (CA-3/89) **88**
Cabernet Sauvignon Napa Valley 1982 Rel: $13 Cur: $40 (CA-3/89) **88**
Cabernet Sauvignon Napa Valley Reserve 1987 $40 (3/31/92) **88**
Cabernet Sauvignon Napa Valley Reserve 1986 Rel: $40 Cur: $78 (4/30/91) **91**
Cabernet Sauvignon Napa Valley Reserve 1985 Rel: $30 Cur: $260 (4/15/90) **95**
Cabernet Sauvignon Napa Valley Reserve 1984 Rel: $25 Cur: $120 (CA-3/89) **94**
Cabernet Sauvignon Napa Valley Reserve 1983 Rel: $25 Cur: $90 (CA-3/89) **92**
Chardonnay Napa Valley 1990 $13.50 (6/30/92) **84**
Chardonnay Napa Valley 1989 $13.50 (7/15/91) **89**
Chardonnay Napa Valley 1988 $13 (6/30/90) **83**
Chardonnay Napa Valley 1987 $13 (7/15/89) **79**

Key to Symbols

The scores reported here are the results of blind tastings conducted by our panel of senior editors. Wines that carry the initials below are results of individual tastings.

THE WINE SPECTATOR 100-POINT SCALE ***95-100***—Classic, a great wine; ***90-94***—Outstanding, superior character and style; ***80-89***—Good to very good, a wine with special qualities; ***70-79***—Average, drinkable wine that may have minor flaws; ***60-69***—Below average, drinkable but not recommended; ***50-59***—Poor, undrinkable, not recommended. "+"—With a score indicates a range; used primarily with barrel tastings to indicate a preliminary score.

SPECIAL DESIGNATIONS SS—Spectator Selection, CS—Cellar Selection, BB—Best Buy, ($NA)—Price not available, (NR)—Not released.

TASTER'S INITIALS (JG)—Jim Gordon, (HS)—Harvey Steiman, (JL)—James Laube, (JS)—James Suckling, (TM)—Thomas Matthews, (TR)—Terry Robards, (PM)—Per-Henrik Mansson, (BT)—Barrel Tasting (these wines were tasted blind from barrel samples), (CA-date)—*California's Great Cabernets* by James Laube, (CH-date)—*California's Great Chardonnays* by James Laube, (VP-date)—*Vintage Port* by James Suckling.

DATE TASTED Dates in parentheses represent the issue in which the rating was published.

Chardonnay Napa Valley 1986 $12.50 (1/31/89) **87**
Chardonnay Napa Valley 1985 $11 (2/15/88) **85**
Chardonnay Napa Valley 1984 $12 (7/31/87) **90**
Chardonnay Napa Valley 1982 $13 (4/16/84) **82**
Sauvignon Blanc Napa Valley 1990 $8.50 (11/30/91) **87**
Sauvignon Blanc Napa Valley 1989 $8.50 (10/31/90) **81**
Sauvignon Blanc Napa Valley 1988 $8 (2/15/90) **85**

CHATEAU GRUAUD LAROSE (France/Bordeaux)
St.-Julien 1991 (NR) (5/15/92) (BT) **85+**
St.-Julien 1990 (NR) (5/15/92) (BT) **90+**
St.-Julien 1989 $49 (3/15/92) **93**
St.-Julien 1988 $31 (3/31/91) **84**
St.-Julien 1987 $22 (2/28/91) (TR) **83**
St.-Julien 1986 Rel: $34 Cur: $38 (2/28/91) (TR) **89**
St.-Julien 1985 Rel: $31 Cur: $35 (2/28/91) (TR) **93**
St.-Julien 1984 Rel: $21 Cur: $23 (2/28/91) (TR) **83**
St.-Julien 1983 Rel: $19 Cur: $41 (2/28/91) (TR) **85**
St.-Julien 1982 Rel: $40 Cur: $55 (2/28/91) (TR) **89**
St.-Julien 1981 Rel: $18 Cur: $36 (2/28/91) (TR) **90**
St.-Julien 1980 $25 (2/28/91) (TR) **83**
St.-Julien 1979 $34 (2/28/91) (TR) **89**
St.-Julien 1978 $47 (2/28/91) (TR) **91**
St.-Julien 1977 $33 (2/28/91) (TR) **71**
St.-Julien 1976 $30 (2/28/91) (TR) **85**
St.-Julien 1975 $55 (2/28/91) (TR) **89**
St.-Julien 1974 $28 (2/28/91) (TR) **63**
St.-Julien 1973 $28 (2/28/91) (TR) **76**
St.-Julien 1971 $31 (2/28/91) (TR) **85**
St.-Julien 1970 $70 (2/28/91) (TR) **89**
St.-Julien 1969 $15 (2/28/91) (TR) **50**
St.-Julien 1968 $15 (2/28/91) (TR) **65**
St.-Julien 1967 $33 (2/28/91) (TR) **78**
St.-Julien 1966 $115 (2/28/91) (TR) **87**
St.-Julien 1964 $70 (2/28/91) (TR) **88**
St.-Julien 1962 $90 (2/28/91) (TR) **94**
St.-Julien 1961 $240 (2/28/91) (TR) **95**
St.-Julien 1959 $140 (2/28/91) (TR) **85**
St.-Julien 1957 $65 (2/28/91) (TR) **78**
St.-Julien 1955 $150 (2/28/91) (TR) **87**
St.-Julien 1953 $150 (2/28/91) (TR) **88**
St.-Julien 1952 $185 (2/28/91) (TR) **85**
St.-Julien 1950 $250 (2/28/91) (TR) **83**
St.-Julien 1949 $270 (2/28/91) (TR) **85**
St.-Julien 1947 $400 (2/28/91) (TR) **88**
St.-Julien 1945 $300 (2/28/91) (TR) **96**
St.-Julien 1943 $200 (2/28/91) (TR) **83**
St.-Julien 1937 $150 (2/28/91) (TR) **87**
St.-Julien 1934 $182 (2/28/91) (TR) **83**
St.-Julien 1929 $550 (2/28/91) (TR) **85**
St.-Julien 1928 $500 (2/28/91) (TR) **94**
St.-Julien 1926 $230 (2/28/91) (TR) **95**
St.-Julien 1924 $400 (2/28/91) (TR) **89**
St.-Julien 1921 $250 (2/28/91) (TR) **87**
St.-Julien 1920 $300 (2/28/91) (TR) **85**
St.-Julien 1918 $300 (2/28/91) (TR) **78**
St.-Julien 1907 $260 (2/28/91) (TR) **72**
St.-Julien 1906 $300 (2/28/91) (TR) **85**
St.-Julien 1899 $600 (2/28/91) (TR) **83**
St.-Julien 1893 $500 (2/28/91) (TR) **78**
St.-Julien 1887 $400 (2/28/91) (TR) **71**
St.-Julien 1878 $500 (2/28/91) (TR) **83**
St.-Julien 1870 $2,300 (2/28/91) (TR) **87**
St.-Julien 1865 $1,800 (2/28/91) (TR) **65**
St.-Julien 1844 ($NA) (2/28/91) (TR) **85**
St.-Julien 1834 ($NA) (2/28/91) (TR) **83**
St.-Julien 1819 ($NA) (2/28/91) (TR) **89**

GRUET (United States/New Mexico)
Brut Blanc de Noirs New Mexico NV $13 (3/31/90) **80**
Brut New Mexico NV $13 (3/31/90) **79**

CHATEAU GUADET-ST.-JULIEN (France/Bordeaux)
St.-Emilion 1989 (NR) (4/30/91) (BT) **75+**
St.-Emilion 1988 ($NA) (6/30/89) (BT) **75+**
St.-Emilion 1987 ($NA) (6/30/89) (BT) **70+**

BODEGAS GUELBENZU (Spain)
Navarra 1989 $11 (4/15/92) **87**
Navarra Evo 1989 $20 (4/15/92) **85**

GUENOC (United States/California)
Cabernet Franc Lake County 1985 $12 (2/15/89) **70**
Cabernet Sauvignon Guenoc Valley Première Cuvée 1985 $17 (10/15/90) **84**
Cabernet Sauvignon Lake County 1987 $12 (7/15/91) **89**
Cabernet Sauvignon Lake County 1986 $12.50 (4/30/91) **78**
Cabernet Sauvignon Lake County 1983 $9.75 (9/30/86) **89**
Cabernet Sauvignon Lake County 1981 $8.50 (12/16/84) **78**
Cabernet Sauvignon Napa Valley Beckstoffer Reserve 1987 $24 (6/30/91) **92**
Chardonnay Guenoc Valley 1989 $14 (3/31/91) **88**
Chardonnay Guenoc Valley 1987 $10 (2/15/90) **73**
Chardonnay Guenoc Valley Estate Barrel Fermented 1990 $14 (3/31/92) **80**
Chardonnay Guenoc Valley Genevieve Magoon Vineyard Reserve 1990 $23 (6/30/92) **91**
Chardonnay Guenoc Valley Genevieve Magoon Vineyard Reserve 1989 $23 (12/31/91) **86**
Chardonnay Guenoc Valley Genevieve Magoon Vineyard Reserve 1988 $17 (12/31/90) **81**
Chardonnay Guenoc Valley Première Cuvée 1986 $17.50 (12/31/88) **70**
Chardonnay North Coast 1986 $9.75 (12/31/88) **88**
Chardonnay North Coast 1985 $9.75 (11/15/87) **80**
Chardonnay North Coast 1984 $10 (9/15/86) **83**
Chenin Blanc Guenoc Valley 1987 $5.50 (7/31/89) **82**
Langtry Meritage Lake-Napa Counties 1988 $35 (11/15/91) **86**
Langtry Meritage Lake-Napa Counties 1987 $35 (4/15/91) **88**
Merlot Guenoc Valley 1985 $15 (3/31/89) **85**
Merlot Lake-Napa Counties 1987 $14 (11/15/91) **86**
Merlot Lake-Napa Counties 1986 $12 (6/15/90) **80**
Petite Sirah Guenoc Valley 1988 $10 (8/31/91) **86**
Petite Sirah Guenoc Valley 1985 $7 (2/15/89) **83**
Petite Sirah North Coast 1989 $14 (6/30/92) **82**
Sauvignon Blanc Guenoc Valley 1989 $10 (4/30/91) **77**
Sauvignon Blanc Guenoc Valley Estate 1990 $10 (4/15/92) **82**
Zinfandel California 1989 $9.50 (5/15/92) **85**
Zinfandel California 1988 $7.50 (9/15/90) **76**
Zinfandel Guenoc Valley 1987 $8 (5/15/90) **84**
Zinfandel Guenoc Valley 1984 $5.50 (9/15/87) **67**
Zinfandel Lake County 1985 $5.50 (3/31/89) **79**
Zinfandel Lake County 1981 $5 (5/16/84) **78**

RENE GUERIN (France/Burgundy)
Pouilly-Fuissé La Roche 1988 $22 (9/30/91) **84**

THIERRY GUERIN (France/Burgundy)
Pouilly-Fuissé 1985 $19 (3/31/87) **81**
Pouilly-Fuissé Clos de France 1988 $23 (7/31/90) **89**
St.-Véran 1989 $9 (3/31/91) **79**
St.-Véran La Côte Rôtie 1987 $8.50 (4/30/89) **80**
St.-Véran La Côte Rôtie 1986 $11 (10/15/88) **79**
St.-Véran La Côte Rôtie 1985 $10 (3/31/87) **72**

GUERRIERI-RIZZARDI (Italy)
Chardonnay 1988 ($NA) (9/15/89) **80**
Valpolicella Classico Superiore 1987 $6.50 (3/31/90) **79**
Valpolicella Poiega Classico 1988 $9 (12/15/89) **82**

CHATEAU GUIBON (France/Bordeaux)
Entre-Deux-Mers 1990 $5.50 (3/31/92) BB **82**

DOMAINE DE LA GUICHARDE (France/Rhône)
Côtes du Rhône 1988 $7 (3/15/91) BB **84**

E. GUIGAL (France/Rhône)
Châteauneuf-du-Pape 1988 Rel: $20 Cur: $23 (11/30/90) **90**
Châteauneuf-du-Pape 1986 $19 (3/15/90) **87**
Châteauneuf-du-Pape 1985 Rel: $18 Cur: $24 (10/15/88) **87**
Châteauneuf-du-Pape 1983 Rel: $18 Cur: $30 (11/30/87) **87**
Condrieu Viognier 1990 Rel: $40 Cur: $45 (12/31/91) **90**
Condrieu Viognier 1987 $48 (3/15/89) **89**
Côte-Rôtie Côtes Brune et Blonde 1987 Rel: $25 Cur: $34 (1/31/91) **90**
Côte-Rôtie Côtes Brune et Blonde 1986 Rel: $28 Cur: $36 (2/28/90) **90**
Côte-Rôtie Côtes Brune et Blonde 1985 Rel: $30 Cur: $34 (1/31/89) **92**
Côte-Rôtie Côtes Brune et Blonde 1984 Rel: $25 Cur: $28 (11/30/87) **83**
Côte-Rôtie Côtes Brune et Blonde 1983 Rel: $21 Cur: $34 (4/30/87) CS **92**
Côte-Rôtie Côtes Brune et Blonde 1982 $40 (3/15/90) (HS) **89**
Côte-Rôtie Côtes Brune et Blonde 1980 Rel: $13 Cur: $30 (9/16/84) **89**
Côte-Rôtie Côtes Brune et Blonde 1978 $83 (3/15/90) (HS) **95**
Côte-Rôtie Côtes Brune et Blonde 1976 $55 (3/15/90) (HS) **88**
Côte-Rôtie Côtes Brune et Blonde 1969 $100 (3/15/90) (HS) **93**
Côte-Rôtie Côtes Brune et Blonde 1966 $125 (3/15/90) (HS) **88**
Côte-Rôtie Côtes Brune et Blonde 1964 $100 (3/15/90) (HS) **92**
Côte-Rôtie Côtes Brune et Blonde 1962 $85 (3/15/90) (HS) **89**
Côte-Rôtie Côtes Brune et Blonde 1961 $100 (3/15/90) (HS) **82**
Côte-Rôtie La Landonne 1987 Rel: $125 Cur: $135 (7/31/91) CS **93**
Côte-Rôtie La Landonne 1986 Rel: $99 Cur: $135 (10/15/90) **91**
Côte-Rôtie La Landonne 1985 $350 (3/15/90) (HS) **90**
Côte-Rôtie La Landonne 1984 $100 (3/15/90) (HS) **86**
Côte-Rôtie La Landonne 1983 $290 (3/15/90) (HS) **94**
Côte-Rôtie La Landonne 1982 $180 (3/15/90) (HS) **90**
Côte-Rôtie La Landonne 1981 $150 (3/15/90) (HS) **82**
Côte-Rôtie La Landonne 1980 $150 (3/15/90) (HS) **84**
Côte-Rôtie La Landonne 1979 $195 (3/15/90) (HS) **91**
Côte-Rôtie La Landonne 1978 $430 (3/15/90) (HS) **95**
Côte-Rôtie La Mouline 1987 Rel: $115 Cur: $125 (7/31/91) **92**
Côte-Rôtie La Mouline 1986 Rel: $99 Cur: $150 (10/15/90) **93**
Côte-Rôtie La Mouline 1985 $350 (3/15/90) (HS) **98**
Côte-Rôtie La Mouline 1983 $310 (3/15/90) (HS) **94**
Côte-Rôtie La Mouline 1982 $200 (3/15/90) (HS) **92**
Côte-Rôtie La Mouline 1981 $150 (3/15/90) (HS) **90**
Côte-Rôtie La Mouline 1979 $185 (3/15/90) (HS) **85**
Côte-Rôtie La Mouline 1978 $450 (3/15/90) (HS) **96**
Côte-Rôtie La Mouline 1977 $250 (3/15/90) (HS) **75**
Côte-Rôtie La Mouline 1976 $350 (3/15/90) (HS) **87**
Côte-Rôtie La Mouline 1975 $110 (3/15/90) (HS) **75**
Côte-Rôtie La Mouline 1974 $300 (3/15/90) (HS) **89**
Côte-Rôtie La Mouline 1973 $130 (3/15/90) (HS) **84**
Côte-Rôtie La Mouline 1971 $300 (3/15/90) (HS) **88**
Côte-Rôtie La Mouline 1970 $300 (3/15/90) (HS) **74**
Côte-Rôtie La Mouline 1969 $900 (3/15/90) (HS) **90**
Côte-Rôtie La Mouline 1968 $300 (3/15/90) (HS) **82**
Côte-Rôtie La Mouline 1967 $510 (3/15/90) (HS) **86**
Côte-Rôtie La Mouline 1966 $370 (3/15/90) (HS) **88**
Côte-Rôtie La Turque 1987 Rel: $145 Cur: $165 (7/31/91) **95**
Côte-Rôtie La Turque 1986 Rel: $99 Cur: $350 (10/15/90) CS **95**
Côte-Rôtie La Turque 1985 $570 (3/15/90) (HS) **98**
Côtes du Rhône 1988 $11.50 (7/15/91) **81**
Côtes du Rhône 1986 $9 (2/28/90) **84**
Côtes du Rhône 1985 $8 (9/30/88) **85**
Côtes du Rhône 1984 $7 (12/15/87) BB **84**
Côtes du Rhône 1982 $6 (5/01/86) BB **85**
Côtes du Rhône 1981 $5 (5/01/84) BB **86**
Côtes du Rhône 1980 $4.50 (5/01/84) BB **85**
Côtes du Rhône Blanc 1990 $9 (12/31/91) **81**
Côtes du Rhône Blanc 1989 $10 (3/31/91) **83**
Côtes du Rhône Blanc 1988 $9 (3/15/90) **83**
Gigondas 1988 Rel: $13 Cur: $16 (3/31/91) **85**
Gigondas 1986 Rel: $15 Cur: $18 (11/30/90) **87**
Gigondas 1985 Rel: $12 Cur: $17 (9/30/88) SS **91**
Gigondas 1984 Rel: $12 Cur: $15 (11/30/87) **86**
Gigondas 1983 Rel: $12 Cur: $19 (7/31/87) **91**
Hermitage 1988 Rel: $30 Cur: $35 (12/31/91) **83**
Hermitage 1987 Rel: $29 Cur: $36 (1/31/91) **86**
Hermitage 1986 Rel: $32 Cur: $41 (2/28/90) CS **92**
Hermitage 1985 Rel: $33 Cur: $39 (4/15/89) CS **92**
Hermitage 1983 Rel: $21 Cur: $33 (4/30/87) **87**
Hermitage 1982 Rel: $18 Cur: $27 (5/01/86) **91**
Hermitage 1980 Rel: $13 Cur: $42 (9/01/84) CS **91**
Hermitage 1978 $65 (3/15/90) (HS) **91**
Hermitage 1976 $75 (3/15/90) (HS) **80**
Hermitage 1969 $100 (3/15/90) (HS) **84**
Hermitage 1966 $100 (3/15/90) (HS) **90**
Hermitage 1964 $100 (3/15/90) (HS) **93**

Hermitage Blanc 1989 Rel: $25 Cur: $31 (1/31/92) **81**
Hermitage Blanc 1988 Rel: $23 Cur: $30 (3/31/91) **87**
Hermitage Blanc 1986 $27 (3/15/90) (HS) **88**
Hermitage Blanc 1985 $23 (12/15/87) **76**
Hermitage Blanc 1981 $15 (5/01/86) **64**
Tavel 1989 $15 (3/31/91) **80**

CHATEAU GUIRAUD (France/Sauternes)
Sauternes 1989 ($NA) (6/15/90) (BT) **85+**
Sauternes 1988 $38 (6/15/90) (BT) **85+**
Sauternes 1987 ($NA) (6/15/90) **72**
Sauternes 1986 $48 (12/31/89) **89**
Sauternes 1983 $30 (1/31/88) **76**
Sauternes Le Dauphin 1987 $11 (12/31/89) **72**

DOMAINE JEAN GUITTON (France/Burgundy)
Beaune Les Sizies 1986 $19 (5/31/89) **69**

GUNDERLOCH (Germany)
Riesling Auslese Rheinhessen Gold Cap Nackenheimer Rothenberg 1990 $40 (12/15/91) **93**
Riesling Auslese Rheinhessen Nackenheimer Rothenberg 1990 $26 (12/15/91) **91**
Riesling Kabinett Rheinhessen Semi-Dry Nackenheimer Rothenberg 1990 $11 (12/15/91) **89**
Riesling Qualitätswein Trocken Rheinhessen 1990 $10 (12/15/91) **82**
Riesling Spätlese Rheinhessen Nackenheimer Rothenberg 1990 $16 (12/15/91) **87**
Riesling Spätlese Trocken Rheinhessen Nackenheimer Rothenberg 1990 $21 (12/15/91) **86**

GUNDLACH BUNDSCHU (United States/California)
#2 Sonoma Red Sonoma Valley NV $5 (11/15/89) **77**
Cabernet Franc Sonoma Valley Rhinefarm Vineyards 1989 $12 (2/29/92) **87**
Cabernet Franc Sonoma Valley Rhinefarm Vineyards 1987 $12 (9/15/90) **89**
Cabernet Sauvignon Sonoma Valley 1986 $9.50 (11/15/89) **87**
Cabernet Sauvignon Sonoma Valley 1981 Rel: $7 Cur: $20 (CA-3/89) **84**
Cabernet Sauvignon Sonoma Valley Batto Ranch 1984 Rel: $14 Cur: $17 (CA-3/89) **79**
Cabernet Sauvignon Sonoma Valley Batto Ranch 1983 Rel: $10 Cur: $15 (CA-3/89) **77**
Cabernet Sauvignon Sonoma Valley Batto Ranch 1982 Rel: $10 Cur: $17 (CA-3/89) **70**
Cabernet Sauvignon Sonoma Valley Batto Ranch 1981 Rel: $10 Cur: $18 (CA-3/89) **88**
Cabernet Sauvignon Sonoma Valley Batto Ranch 1980 Rel: $8 Cur: $20 (CA-3/89) **80**
Cabernet Sauvignon Sonoma Valley Batto Ranch 1979 Rel: $8 Cur: $20 (CA-3/89) **80**
Cabernet Sauvignon Sonoma Valley Batto Ranch 1977 Rel: $8 Cur: $20 (CA-3/89) **89**
Cabernet Sauvignon Sonoma Valley Rhinefarm Vineyards 1988 ($NA) (5/15/90) (BT) **90+**
Cabernet Sauvignon Sonoma Valley Rhinefarm Vineyards 1987 $15 (5/15/91) **85**
Cabernet Sauvignon Sonoma Valley Rhinefarm Vineyards 1986 Rel: $12 Cur: $17 (CA-3/89) **89**
Cabernet Sauvignon Sonoma Valley Rhinefarm Vineyards 1985 Rel: $9 Cur: $14 (CA-3/89) **91**
Cabernet Sauvignon Sonoma Valley Rhinefarm Vineyards 1984 Rel: $9 Cur: $15 (CA-3/89) **85**
Cabernet Sauvignon Sonoma Valley Rhinefarm Vineyards 1983 Rel: $9 Cur: $14 (CA-3/89) **73**
Cabernet Sauvignon Sonoma Valley Rhinefarm Vineyards 1982 Rel: $9 Cur: $13 (CA-3/89) **65**
Cabernet Sauvignon Sonoma Valley Rhinefarm Vineyards Reserve 1986 $25 (8/31/91) **83**
Cabernet Sauvignon Sonoma Valley Rhinefarm Vineyards Reserve 1982 $20 (9/15/87) **71**
Cabernet Sauvignon Sonoma Valley Rhinefarm Vineyards Reserve 1981 Rel: $20 Cur: $26 (CA-3/89) **90**
Chardonnay Sonoma Valley 1990 $11 (3/31/92) **86**
Chardonnay Sonoma Valley 1989 $12 (7/15/91) **78**
Chardonnay Sonoma Valley 1988 $10 (4/30/90) **76**
Chardonnay Sonoma Valley 1987 $11 (3/15/89) **79**
Chardonnay Sonoma Valley 1986 $9 (2/15/88) **87**
Chardonnay Sonoma Valley 1985 $10 (7/31/87) **80**
Chardonnay Sonoma Valley 1984 $10 (5/31/87) **84**
Chardonnay Sonoma Valley 1983 $9.75 (5/01/85) **83**
Chardonnay Sonoma Valley Sangiacomo Ranch Special Selection 1990 $15 (12/31/91) **84**
Chardonnay Sonoma Valley Sangiacomo Ranch Special Selection 1989 $15 (7/15/91) **75**
Chardonnay Sonoma Valley Sangiacomo Ranch Special Selection 1988 $14 (6/30/90) **79**
Chardonnay Sonoma Valley Sangiacomo Ranch Special Selection 1987 $12 (7/15/89) **77**
Chardonnay Sonoma Valley Sangiacomo Ranch Special Selection 1986 $12 (9/30/88) **89**
Chardonnay Sonoma Valley Sangiacomo Ranch Special Selection 1984 $11.50 (5/31/87) **88**
Chardonnay Sonoma Valley Sangiacomo Ranch Special Selection 1983 $12 (12/01/85) **74**
Merlot Sonoma Valley Rhinefarm Vineyards 1989 $16 (5/31/92) **80**
Merlot Sonoma Valley Rhinefarm Vineyards 1988 Rel: $16 Cur: $20 (5/31/91) **81**
Merlot Sonoma Valley Rhinefarm Vineyards 1987 Rel: $13 Cur: $16 (10/31/89) SS **93**
Merlot Sonoma Valley Rhinefarm Vineyards 1986 Rel: $12 Cur: $18 (12/31/88) **91**
Merlot Sonoma Valley Rhinefarm Vineyards 1985 Rel: $12 Cur: $20 (2/29/88) SS **92**
Merlot Sonoma Valley Rhinefarm Vineyards 1984 Rel: $12 Cur: $20 (2/28/87) **88**
Merlot Sonoma Valley Rhinefarm Vineyards 1983 Rel: $12 Cur: $20 (5/01/86) **92**
Merlot Sonoma Valley Rhinefarm Vineyards 1982 $8.50 (10/01/85) **88**
Pinot Noir Sonoma Valley Rhinefarm Vineyards 1989 $14 (10/31/91) **83**
Pinot Noir Sonoma Valley Rhinefarm Vineyards 1988 $12 (2/28/91) **88**
Pinot Noir Sonoma Valley Rhinefarm Vineyards 1986 Rel: $10 Cur: $14 (6/15/88) **89**
Pinot Noir Sonoma Valley Rhinefarm Vineyards 1985 $10 (2/29/88) **81**
Pinot Noir Sonoma Valley Rhinefarm Vineyards 1984 $10 (6/30/87) **53**
Pinot Noir Sonoma Valley Rhinefarm Vineyards 1982 $9.25 (5/01/84) **75**
Zinfandel Sonoma Valley 1989 $7.50 (7/31/91) **84**
Zinfandel Sonoma Valley 1988 $7 (5/31/90) BB **88**
Zinfandel Sonoma Valley 1987 $7.75 (3/31/89) **87**
Zinfandel Sonoma Valley Rhinefarm Vineyards 1989 $12 (7/31/91) **87**
Zinfandel Sonoma Valley Rhinefarm Vineyards 1988 $10 (12/15/90) **88**
Zinfandel Sonoma Valley Rhinefarm Vineyards 1987 $8.50 (9/15/89) **71**
Zinfandel Sonoma Valley Rhinefarm Vineyards 1986 $8 (9/15/88) **90**
Zinfandel Sonoma Valley Rhinefarm Vineyards 1985 $8.50 (2/29/88) **84**
Zinfandel Sonoma Valley Rhinefarm Vineyards 1984 $7 (4/30/87) BB **87**
Zinfandel Sonoma Valley Rhinefarm Vineyards 1982 $7 (2/16/86) **87**

Key to Symbols

The scores reported here are the results of blind tastings conducted by our panel of senior editors. Wines that carry the initials below are results of individual tastings.

THE WINE SPECTATOR 100-POINT SCALE ***95-100***—Classic, a great wine; ***90-94***—Outstanding, superior character and style; ***80-89***—Good to very good, a wine with special qualities; ***70-79***—Average, drinkable wine that may have minor flaws; ***60-69*** —Below average, drinkable but not recommended; ***50-59*** —Poor, undrinkable, not recommended. "+"—With a score indicates a range; used primarily with barrel tastings to indicate a preliminary score.

SPECIAL DESIGNATIONS SS—Spectator Selection, CS—Cellar Selection, BB—Best Buy, ($NA)—Price not available, (NR)—Not released.

TASTER'S INITIALS (JG)—Jim Gordon, (HS)—Harvey Steiman, (JL)—James Laube, (JS)—James Suckling, (TM)—Thomas Matthews, (TR)—Terry Robards, (PM)—Per-Henrik Mansson, (BT)—Barrel Tasting (these wines were tasted blind from barrel samples), (CA-date)—*California's Great Cabernets* by James Laube, (CH-date)—*California's Great Chardonnays* by James Laube, (VP-date)—*Vintage Port* by James Suckling.

DATE TASTED Dates in parentheses represent the issue in which the rating was published.

LOUIS GUNTRUM (Germany)
Riesling Auslese Rheinhessen Oppenheimer Schützenhütte 1989 ($NA) (12/15/90) **91**
Riesling Auslese Trocken Rheinhessen Niersteiner Pettenthal 1989 ($NA) (12/15/90) **84**
Riesling Beerenauslese Rheinhessen Niersteiner Pettenthal 1989 ($NA) (12/15/90) **86**
Riesling Kabinett Halbtrocken Rheinhessen Oppenheimer Herrenberg 1988 ($NA) (9/30/89) **88**
Riesling Kabinett Rheinhessen Niersteiner Bergkirche 1989 ($NA) (12/15/90) **84**
Riesling Kabinett Trocken Rheinhessen Classic Niersteiner Olberg 1989 ($NA) (12/15/90) **86**
Riesling Kabinett Trocken Rheinhessen Classic Oppenheimer Sackträger 1989 ($NA) (12/15/90) **86**
Riesling Spätlese Rheinhessen Heiligenbaum 1988 ($NA) (9/30/89) **91**
Riesling Spätlese Rheinhessen Oppenheimer Herrenberg 1989 ($NA) (12/15/90) **74**
Riesling Spätlese Trocken Rheinhessen Niersteiner Pettenthal 1989 ($NA) (12/15/90) **82**
Riesling Spätlese Trocken Rheinhessen Oppenheimer Kreuz 1989 ($NA) (12/15/90) **79**
Riesling Trockenbeerenauslese Rheinhessen Oppenheimer Sackträger 1989 ($NA) (12/15/90) **85**

CHATEAU LA GURGUE (France/Bordeaux)
Margaux 1991 (NR) (5/15/92) (BT) **85+**
Margaux 1989 $30 (3/15/92) **92**
Margaux 1988 Rel: $29 Cur: $32 (4/30/91) **90**
Margaux 1987 $13 (5/15/90) **81**
Margaux 1986 $22 (11/30/89) (JS) **85**
Margaux 1985 Rel: $17 Cur: $19 (2/15/88) **90**
Margaux 1983 $9.75 (1/01/86) **90**
Margaux 1982 $24 (11/30/89) (JS) **85**

BERNARD GUY (France/Rhône)
Côte-Rôtie 1987 $25 (8/31/89) **87**
Côte-Rôtie 1986 $29 (9/30/88) **89**

ALAIN GUYARD (France/Burgundy)
Vosne-Romanée Aux Réas 1987 $29 (7/15/90) **71**

JEAN-CLAUDE GUYOT (France/Loire)
Pouilly-Fumé Les Loges 1988 $11 (3/31/91) **84**

FRITZ HAAG (Germany)
Riesling Auslese Mosel-Saar-Ruwer Brauneberger Juffer-Sonnenuhr 1990 $37 (12/15/91) **89**
Riesling Auslese Mosel-Saar-Ruwer Brauneberger Juffer-Sonnenuhr 1989 $32 (12/15/90) **81**
Riesling Auslese Mosel-Saar-Ruwer Brauneberger Juffer-Sonnenuhr 1988 (NR) (9/30/89) **86**
Riesling Auslese Mosel-Saar-Ruwer Brauneberger Juffer-Sonnenuhr (AP16) 1988 (NR) (9/30/89) **85**
Riesling Auslese Mosel-Saar-Ruwer Brauneberger Juffer-Sonnenuhr Gold Cap 1990 $104 (12/15/91) **92**
Riesling Auslese Mosel-Saar-Ruwer Brauneberger Juffer-Sonnenuhr Gold Cap 1989 $60 (12/15/90) **90**
Riesling Auslese Mosel-Saar-Ruwer Brauneberger Juffer-Sonnenuhr Long Gold Cap 1990 $113/375ml (12/15/91) **94**
Riesling Auslese Mosel-Saar-Ruwer Brauneberger Juffer-Sonnenuhr Long Gold Cap 1989 $150 (12/15/90) **92**
Riesling Kabinett Mosel-Saar-Ruwer Brauneberger Juffer-Sonnenuhr 1990 $16 (12/15/91) **87**
Riesling Kabinett Mosel-Saar-Ruwer Brauneberger Juffer-Sonnenuhr 1989 $18 (12/15/90) **85**
Riesling Kabinett Mosel-Saar-Ruwer Brauneberger Juffer-Sonnenuhr 1988 (NR) (9/30/89) **83**
Riesling Kabinett Mosel-Saar-Ruwer Brauneberger Juffer-Sonnenuhr 1985 $9 (6/30/87) **70**
Riesling Spätlese Mosel-Saar-Ruwer Brauneberger Juffer-Sonnenuhr 1990 $23 (12/15/91) **91**
Riesling Spätlese Mosel-Saar-Ruwer Brauneberger Juffer-Sonnenuhr 1989 $27 (12/15/90) **86**
Riesling Spätlese Mosel-Saar-Ruwer Brauneberger Juffer-Sonnenuhr 1988 (NR) (9/30/89) **86**
Riesling Spätlese Mosel-Saar-Ruwer Brauneberger Juffer-Sonnenuhr 1986 (NR) (4/15/89) **91**
Riesling Spätlese Mosel-Saar-Ruwer Brauneberger Juffer-Sonnenuhr 1985 (NR) (4/15/89) **97**

REINHOLD HAART (Germany)
Riesling Auslese Mosel-Saar-Ruwer Piesporter Goldtröpfchen 1988 (NR) (9/30/89) **88**
Riesling Kabinett Mosel-Saar-Ruwer Piesporter Goldtröpfchen 1988 (NR) (9/30/89) **88**
Riesling Spätlese Mosel-Saar-Ruwer Piesporter Goldtröpfchen 1988 (NR) (9/30/89) **92**
Riesling Spätlese Mosel-Saar-Ruwer Piesporter Goldtröpfchen 1985 (NR) (4/15/89) **78**
Riesling Spätlese Mosel-Saar-Ruwer Piesporter Goldtröpfchen (AP6) 1988 (NR) (9/30/89) **91**

HACIENDA (United States/California)
Antares Sonoma County 1987 $28 (11/15/90) **91**
Antares Sonoma County 1986 $28 (7/31/89) **91**
Cabernet Sauvignon Sonoma County 1986 $15 (11/15/91) **87**
Cabernet Sauvignon Sonoma County 1985 $15 (9/30/90) **83**
Cabernet Sauvignon Sonoma Valley Estate Reserve 1984 $18 (5/31/91) **87**
Cabernet Sauvignon Sonoma Valley 1983 $11 (5/31/88) **86**
Cabernet Sauvignon Sonoma Valley Selected Reserve 1982 $18 (3/31/87) **86**
Cabernet Sauvignon Sonoma Valley 1982 $11 (9/01/85) **63**
Chardonnay Sonoma County Clair de Lune 1989 $15 (8/31/91) **86**
Chardonnay Sonoma County Clair de Lune 1988 $15 (6/30/90) **83**
Chardonnay Sonoma County Clair de Lune 1987 Rel: $12 Cur: $15 (7/15/89) **73**
Chardonnay Sonoma County Clair de Lune 1986 Rel: $12 Cur: $18 (7/15/88) SS **92**
Chardonnay Sonoma County Clair de Lune 1985 Rel: $11 Cur: $20 (CH-4/90) **87**
Chardonnay Sonoma County Clair de Lune 1984 Rel: $10 Cur: $18 (CH-4/90) **88**
Chardonnay Sonoma County Clair de Lune 1983 Rel: $10 Cur: $22 (CH-4/90) **83**
Chardonnay Sonoma County Clair de Lune 1982 Rel: $9 Cur: $20 (CH-4/90) **78**
Chardonnay Sonoma County Clair de Lune 1981 Rel: $12 Cur: $20 (CH-4/90) **74**
Chardonnay Sonoma County Clair de Lune 1980 Rel: $10.50 Cur: $22 (CH-4/90) **80**
Chardonnay Sonoma County Clair de Lune 1979 Rel: $9 Cur: $25 (CH-4/90) **86**
Chardonnay Sonoma County Clair de Lune 1978 Rel: $9 Cur: $25 (CH-4/90) **73**
Chardonnay Sonoma County Clair de Lune 1977 Rel: $8 Cur: $23 (CH-4/90) **76**
Chardonnay Sonoma County Clair de Lune 1976 Rel: $7 Cur: $40 (CH-4/90) **85**
Chardonnay Sonoma County Clair de Lune 1974 Rel: $5 Cur: $40 (CH-4/90) **80**
Chardonnay Sonoma County Clair de Lune 1973 Rel: $5 Cur: $50 (CH-4/90) **91**
Chenin Blanc Clarksburg Dry 1988 $5.50 (7/31/89) **84**
Pinot Noir Sonoma Valley 1982 $12 (12/16/84) **85**
Pinot Noir Sonoma Valley Estate Reserve 1987 $15 (10/31/90) **78**
Pinot Noir Sonoma Valley Estate Reserve 1986 $15 (6/15/88) **80**
Pinot Noir Sonoma Valley Estate Reserve 1985 $15 (6/15/88) **86**

HAEGELEN-JAYER (France/Burgundy)
Chambolle-Musigny 1988 $39 (5/15/91) **73**
Clos de Vougeot 1985 $64 (4/15/88) **90**
Clos de Vougeot 1988 $69 (5/15/91) **73**
Echézeaux 1988 $61 (8/31/91) **67**
Nuits-St.-Georges Les Damodes 1988 $39 (5/15/91) **89**

HAGAFEN (United States/California)
Cabernet Sauvignon Napa Valley 1988 $20 (3/31/91) **88**
Cabernet Sauvignon Napa Valley 1987 $20 (4/30/90) **88**
Chardonnay Napa Valley 1990 $14 (7/15/92) **83**
Chardonnay Napa Valley 1989 $12.50 (3/31/91) **85**
Chardonnay Napa Valley Reserve 1990 $17 (6/30/92) **86**
Johannisberg Riesling Napa Valley 1991 $9 (5/31/92) **84**
Johannisberg Riesling Napa Valley 1989 $8.75 (3/31/91) **81**
Johannisberg Riesling Napa Valley 1988 $8.75 (7/31/89) **74**

Pinot Noir Blanc California 1989 $6 (3/31/91) **74**
Red Table Wine Napa Valley NV $7.50 (6/30/92) **75**

HAHN (United States/California)
Merlot Monterey 1990 $10 (5/31/92) **83**
Merlot Monterey 1989 $10 (5/31/92) **86**

HALLCREST (United States/California)
Cabernet Sauvignon El Dorado County De Cascabel Vineyard 1987 $13 (11/15/91) **83**
Chardonnay California Fortuyn Cuvée 1990 $9.50 (7/15/92) **71**
Chardonnay California Fortuyn Cuvée 1989 $9 (4/30/91) **82**
Chardonnay California Fortuyn Cuvée 1988 $9 (6/30/90) **85**
Chardonnay El Dorado County Hillside Cuvée 1988 $11 (6/30/90) **88**
Chardonnay Santa Cruz Mountains Meylay Vineyard 1989 $16.50 (4/30/91) **91**
Clos de Jeannine California 1989 $8.50 (10/31/91) **82**
Gewürztraminer Mendocino County Dry Talmage Town 1989 $8.50 (9/30/91) **78**
Merlot El Dorado County De Cascabel Vineyard 1989 $14.50 (5/31/92) **74**
Merlot El Dorado County De Cascabel Vineyard 1988 $14.50 (5/31/92) **78**
Syrah California Doe Mill Cuvée 1989 $7 (4/30/91) **86**

MAISON HAMM (France/Champagne)
Brut Champagne Réserve Premier Cru NV $22 (12/31/91) **90**

HANDLEY (United States/California)
Brut Anderson Valley 1984 $15 (10/15/88) **81**
Brut Rosé Anderson Valley 1984 $16.75 (12/31/88) **75**
Chardonnay Anderson Valley 1988 $12.50 (7/15/91) **87**
Chardonnay Dry Creek Valley 1989 $14.50 (7/15/91) **87**
Chardonnay Dry Creek Valley 1987 $14 (7/15/89) **86**
Chardonnay Dry Creek Valley 1986 $15 (10/31/88) **81**
Gewürztraminer Anderson Valley 1988 $7 (1/31/90) BB **89**
Gewürztraminer Anderson Valley 1987 $7 (2/28/89) **86**
Sauvignon Blanc Dry Creek Valley 1988 $8 (8/31/90) **84**

HANNA (United States/California)
Cabernet Sauvignon Sonoma County 1988 $16 (11/15/91) **86**
Cabernet Sauvignon Sonoma County 1987 $16 (8/31/90) **80**
Cabernet Sauvignon Sonoma County 1986 $16 (7/31/89) **87**
Cabernet Sauvignon Sonoma Valley 1985 $14 (6/30/88) **86**
Chardonnay Sonoma County 1990 $13.50 (7/15/92) **82**
Chardonnay Sonoma County 1989 $13.50 (12/31/91) **85**
Chardonnay Sonoma County 1988 $13.50 (9/30/90) **89**
Chardonnay Sonoma County 1987 $14.50 (7/15/89) **73**
Chardonnay Sonoma County 1986 $13.50 (9/30/88) **81**
Chardonnay Sonoma County 1985 $13.50 (8/31/87) **83**
Sauvignon Blanc Sonoma County 1989 $8.50 (7/15/91) **87**
Sauvignon Blanc Sonoma County 1988 $8.75 (8/31/90) **71**

CHATEAU HANTEILLAN (France/Bordeaux)
Haut-Médoc 1991 (NR) (5/15/92) (BT) **80+**
Haut-Médoc 1989 $14 (3/15/92) **77**
Haut-Médoc 1988 $17 (6/30/89) (BT) **75+**
Haut-Médoc 1987 $13 (11/30/89) (JS) **75**
Haut-Médoc 1986 $15 (11/30/89) (JS) **81**
Haut-Médoc 1982 $18 (11/30/89) (JS) **81**

HANZELL (United States/California)
Cabernet Sauvignon Sonoma Valley 1987 Rel: $22 Cur: $32 (11/15/91) **84**
Cabernet Sauvignon Sonoma Valley 1986 Rel: $22 Cur: $29 (10/31/90) **90**
Cabernet Sauvignon Sonoma Valley 1982 Rel: $20 Cur: $27 (3/31/87) **76**
Chardonnay Sonoma Valley 1988 Rel: $24 Cur: $34 (CH-5/90) **90**
Chardonnay Sonoma Valley 1987 Rel: $24 Cur: $33 (2/28/90) **89**
Chardonnay Sonoma Valley 1986 Rel: $22 Cur: $38 (CH-1/90) **87**
Chardonnay Sonoma Valley 1985 Rel: $22 Cur: $46 (CH-1/90) **90**
Chardonnay Sonoma Valley 1984 Rel: $20 Cur: $45 (CH-1/90) **84**
Chardonnay Sonoma Valley 1983 Rel: $20 Cur: $47 (CH-1/90) **84**
Chardonnay Sonoma Valley 1982 Rel: $19 Cur: $45 (CH-1/90) **89**
Chardonnay Sonoma Valley 1981 Rel: $18 Cur: $50 (CH-1/90) **86**
Chardonnay Sonoma Valley 1980 Rel: $17 Cur: $60 (CH-1/90) **90**
Chardonnay Sonoma Valley 1979 Rel: $16 Cur: $70 (CH-1/90) **85**
Chardonnay Sonoma Valley 1978 Rel: $13 Cur: $68 (CH-1/90) **95**
Chardonnay Sonoma Valley 1977 Rel: $12 Cur: $85 (CH-1/90) **88**
Chardonnay Sonoma Valley 1976 Rel: $12 Cur: $90 (CH-1/90) **91**
Chardonnay Sonoma Valley 1975 Rel: $10 Cur: $70 (CH-1/90) **86**
Chardonnay Sonoma Valley 1974 Rel: $9 Cur: $70 (CH-1/90) **88**
Chardonnay Sonoma Valley 1973 Rel: $8 Cur: $100 (CH-1/90) **85**
Chardonnay Sonoma Valley 1972 Rel: $7 Cur: $75 (CH-1/90) **90**
Chardonnay Sonoma Valley 1971 Rel: $7 Cur: $120 (CH-1/90) **85**
Chardonnay Sonoma Valley 1970 Rel: $7 Cur: $110 (CH-1/90) **84**
Chardonnay Sonoma Valley 1969 Rel: $6 Cur: $140 (CH-1/90) **90**
Chardonnay Sonoma Valley 1968 Rel: $6 Cur: $140 (CH-1/90) **91**
Chardonnay Sonoma Valley 1967 Rel: $6 Cur: $125 (CH-1/90) **89**
Chardonnay Sonoma Valley 1966 Rel: $6 Cur: $170 (CH-1/90) **94**
Chardonnay Sonoma Valley 1965 Rel: $6 Cur: $180 (CH-1/90) **84**
Chardonnay California 1959 Rel: $4 Cur: $200 (CH-12/89) **88**
Chardonnay California 1957 Rel: $4 Cur: $240 (CH-12/89) **90**
Pinot Noir Sonoma Valley 1987 $19 (2/15/92) **84**
Pinot Noir Sonoma Valley 1986 $19 (10/31/90) **84**
Pinot Noir Sonoma Valley 1985 Rel: $19 Cur: $29 (3/31/90) **82**
Pinot Noir Sonoma Valley 1984 Rel: $17 Cur: $32 (5/31/89) **78**
Pinot Noir Sonoma Valley 1983 Rel: $17 Cur: $38 (4/15/88) **70**
Pinot Noir Sonoma Valley 1981 Rel: $17 Cur: $21 (8/31/86) **93**

HARDY'S (Australia)
Brut Australia Grand Reserve NV $8 (2/29/92) BB **83**
Cabernet Malbec Reynella McLaren Vale Hardy Collection No. 9 1984 $6.50 (7/15/88) **76**
Cabernet Sauvignon Coonawarra 1987 $10.50 (7/15/90) **81**
Cabernet Sauvignon Keppoch 1986 $7.50 (7/15/90) **79**
Cabernet Sauvignon Keppoch 1985 $7.25 (10/31/88) **80**
Cabernet Sauvignon Keppoch Bird Series 1985 $6 (9/30/88) BB **81**
Cabernet Sauvignon McLaren Vale Captain's Selection 1985 $4.50 (7/15/88) **75**
Cabernet Sauvignon McLaren Vale The Hardy Collection No. Eight 1986 $10.50 (1/31/89) **76**
Cabernet Sauvignon South Australia Bird Series 1988 $8 (3/15/92) BB **83**
Cabernet Sauvignon South Australia The Hardy Collection 1988 $10 (2/15/91) **83**
Chardonnay Australia NV $10 (5/31/87) **86**
Chardonnay Padthaway Hardy Collection No. 1 1987 $11.50 (2/15/89) **69**
Chardonnay Padthaway Hardy Collection No. 1 1987 $7 (5/31/88) **72**
Chardonnay Padthaway Clare Valley The Hardy Collection 1988 $10.50 (7/15/90) **80**
Chardonnay South Australia Eileen Hardy 1989 $19 (2/15/92) **91**
Chardonnay South Australia Nottage Hill 1991 $8 (5/31/92) BB **87**
Chardonnay South Eastern Australia 1987 $7.50 (7/15/90) **69**
Chardonnay South Eastern Australia Bird Series 1991 $7.50 (6/30/92) BB **85**
Chardonnay South Eastern Australia Bird Series 1990 $7.50 (9/15/91) BB **84**
Chardonnay South Eastern Australia Bird Series 1987 $6 (5/31/88) **75**
Chardonnay Sunraysia 1988 $7 (7/31/90) BB **82**
Port Australia 1982 $15 (7/31/90) **72**
Premium Classic Dry Red McLaren Vale 1986 $6 (5/15/89) **75**
Premium Classic Dry Red South Australia 1988 $5.25 (7/31/90) BB **78**
Premium Classic Dry White South Australia 1988 $5.25 (6/15/90) BB **79**
Sémillon Chardonnay South Eastern Australia Captain's Selection 1991 $6 (6/30/92) BB **83**
Shiraz McLaren Vale 1989 $7.50 (5/31/92) BB **85**
Shiraz McLaren Vale 1987 $7.50 (7/15/90) BB **87**
Shiraz McLaren Vale 1986 $7.50 (12/31/88) BB **89**
Shiraz McLaren Vale Bird Series 1988 $7.50 (9/30/91) BB **84**
Shiraz McLaren Vale Padthaway Bird Series 1984 $5.50 (7/15/88) **79**
Shiraz South Australia Eileen Hardy 1988 $19 (2/15/92) **91**
Shiraz Cabernet South Eastern Australia Captain's Selection 1990 $6 (6/30/92) BB **82**
Tawny Port Australia Tall Ships NV $11 (7/31/90) **83**

HARGRAVE (United States/New York)
Cabernet Franc North Fork of Long Island 1988 $14 (6/30/91) (TM) **81**
Chardonnay North Fork of Long Island 1988 $15 (6/30/91) (TM) **82**
Merlot North Fork of Long Island 1988 $17.50 (6/30/91) (TM) **81**
Pinot Blanc North Fork of Long Island 1989 $10 (6/30/91) (TM) **83**

HARRISON (United States/California)
Cabernet Sauvignon Napa Valley 1991 (NR) (5/15/92) (BT) **86+**
Cabernet Sauvignon Napa Valley 1989 $30 (4/15/92) **91**
Chardonnay Napa Valley 1990 $24 (1/31/92) **84**
Chardonnay Napa Valley 1989 $24 (7/15/91) **87**

HART (United States/California)
Merlot Temecula 1989 $15 (5/31/92) **80**

CARLO HAUNER (Italy/Other)
Salina Bianco 1989 $11.50 (7/15/91) **81**

CHATEAU HAUT-BAGES-AVEROUS (France/Bordeaux)
Pauillac 1991 (NR) (5/15/92) (BT) **75+**
Pauillac 1990 (NR) (5/15/92) (BT) **90+**
Pauillac 1989 $26 (3/15/92) **90**
Pauillac 1988 $23 (4/30/91) **93**
Pauillac 1987 $15 (11/30/89) (JS) **85**
Pauillac 1986 Rel: $15 Cur: $19 (11/30/89) (JS) **90**
Pauillac 1985 $17 (4/30/88) **82**
Pauillac 1982 $25 (11/30/89) (JS) **89**
Pauillac 1979 $18 (10/15/89) (JS) **84**

CHATEAU HAUT-BAGES-LIBERAL (France/Bordeaux)
Pauillac 1991 (NR) (5/15/92) (BT) **85+**
Pauillac 1990 (NR) (5/15/92) (BT) **85+**
Pauillac 1989 $24 (3/15/92) **89**
Pauillac 1988 $17 (3/15/91) **88**
Pauillac 1987 $14 (6/30/89) (BT) **75+**
Pauillac 1986 Rel: $17 Cur: $21 (5/31/89) **91**
Pauillac 1985 Rel: $16 Cur: $24 (4/30/88) **88**
Pauillac 1984 $19 (6/15/87) **67**
Pauillac 1983 $18 (5/01/86) **67**
Pauillac 1959 $55 (10/15/90) (JS) **85**

CHATEAU HAUT-BAGES-MONPELOU (France/Bordeaux)
Pauillac 1989 (NR) (4/30/90) (BT) **85+**

CHATEAU HAUT-BAILLY (France/Bordeaux)
Pessac-Léognan 1990 (NR) (4/30/91) (BT) **85+**
Pessac-Léognan 1989 $32 (3/15/92) **92**
Pessac-Léognan 1988 $30 (4/30/91) **94**
Pessac-Léognan 1987 $20 (6/30/88) (BT) **85+**
Pessac-Léognan 1986 Rel: $23 Cur: $25 (6/15/89) **91**
Graves 1985 $28 (6/15/88) **89**
Graves 1984 $15 (6/15/87) **87**
Graves 1983 $21 (4/16/86) **86**
Graves 1981 Rel: $13 Cur: $21 (6/01/84) **87**
Graves 1979 $28 (10/15/89) (JS) **84**
Graves 1945 $200 (3/16/86) (JL) **94**

CHATEAU HAUT-BATAILLEY (France/Bordeaux)
Pauillac 1991 (NR) (5/15/92) (BT) **85+**
Pauillac 1990 (NR) (5/15/92) (BT) **80+**
Pauillac 1989 $30 (3/15/92) **87**
Pauillac 1988 $26 (8/31/91) **87**
Pauillac 1987 $17 (5/15/90) **86**
Pauillac 1986 $23 (5/31/89) **85**
Pauillac 1985 Rel: $17 Cur: $21 (11/30/88) **81**
Pauillac 1979 $30 (10/15/89) (JS) **82**
Pauillac 1961 $95 (3/16/86) (TR) **91**

CHATEAU HAUT-BERGERON (France/Sauternes)
Sauternes 1989 (NR) (6/15/90) (BT) **90+**
Sauternes 1988 (NR) (6/15/90) (BT) **90+**
Sauternes 1987 (NR) (6/15/90) **81**

CHATEAU HAUT-BERGEY (France/Bordeaux)
Pessac-Léognan 1989 (NR) (4/30/91) (BT) **85+**
Pessac-Léognan 1988 $12 (6/30/89) (BT) **80+**
Pessac-Léognan 1987 (NR) (6/30/89) (BT) **65+**
Pessac-Léognan 1986 (NR) (6/30/88) (BT) **80+**

CHATEAU HAUT-BOMMES (France/Sauternes)
Sauternes 1989 (NR) (6/15/90) (BT) **85+**
Sauternes 1988 (NR) (6/15/90) (BT) **75+**
Sauternes 1987 (NR) (6/15/90) **74**

CHATEAU HAUT-BRETON-LARIGAUDIERE (France/Bordeaux)
Margaux 1985 $16 (2/15/88) **82**

CHATEAU HAUT-BRION (France/Bordeaux)
Pessac-Léognan 1991 (NR) (5/15/92) (BT) **85+**
Pessac-Léognan 1990 (NR) (5/15/92) (BT) **95+**
Pessac-Léognan 1989 $150 (3/15/92) **97**
Pessac-Léognan 1988 $95 (4/30/91) **98**
Pessac-Léognan 1987 $70 (10/15/90) **90**
Pessac-Léognan 1986 $88 (6/30/89) **92**
Graves 1985 Rel: $70 Cur: $83 (4/30/88) **96**
Graves 1984 Rel: $36 Cur: $44 (7/31/87) **80**

Graves 1983 $86 (9/30/86) SS **95**
Graves 1982 Rel: $60 Cur: $120 (7/01/85) **92**
Graves 1981 Rel: $56 Cur: $73 (5/01/89) **92**
Graves 1979 $90 (11/15/91) (JS) **92**
Graves 1978 $105 (11/15/91) (JS) **96**
Graves 1975 $125 (11/15/91) (JS) **92**
Graves 1974 $33 (11/15/91) (JS) **74**
Graves 1971 $110 (11/15/91) (JS) **85**
Graves 1970 $140 (11/15/91) (JS) **94**
Graves 1966 $310 (11/15/91) (JS) **94**
Graves 1962 $170 (11/15/91) (JS) **93**
Graves 1961 $430 (11/15/91) (JS) **100**
Graves 1959 $340 (11/15/91) (JS) **98**
Graves 1949 $370 (11/15/91) (JS) **95**
Graves 1945 $840 (11/15/91) (JS) **99**
Pessac-Léognan Blanc 1990 (NR) (9/30/91) (BT) **90+**
Pessac-Léognan Blanc 1989 $90 (9/30/91) **94**
Pessac-Léognan Blanc 1988 $84 (12/15/90) **87**
Pessac-Léognan Blanc 1987 Rel: $70 Cur: $75 (1/31/90) **78**
Graves Blanc 1985 Rel: $81 Cur: $105 (11/15/87) **79**

CHATEAU HAUT-CADET (France/Bordeaux)
St.-Emilion 1981 $6.50 (4/01/85) **73**

CHATEAU HAUT-CANON-LA TRUFFIERE (France/Bordeaux)
Canon Fronsac 1991 (NR) (5/15/92) (BT) **75+**

CHATEAU HAUT-CLAVERIE (France/Sauternes)
Sauternes 1988 (NR) (6/15/90) (BT) **85+**

CHATEAU HAUT-COLAS NOUET (France/Bordeaux)
Bordeaux Supérieur 1985 $4 (11/15/87) **71**

CHATEAU HAUT-CORBIN (France/Bordeaux)
St.-Emilion 1991 (NR) (5/15/92) (BT) **85+**
St.-Emilion 1990 (NR) (5/15/92) (BT) **85+**
St.-Emilion 1989 $26 (3/15/92) **89**
St.-Emilion 1986 $14 (5/15/87) (BT) **70+**

CHATEAU HAUT-COUTELIN (France/Bordeaux)
St.-Estèphe 1982 $13 (2/15/88) **81**

CHATEAU HAUT-FAUGERES (France/Bordeaux)
St.-Emilion 1988 $17 (4/30/92) **84**

CHATEAU HAUT-GARDERE (France/Bordeaux)
Pessac-Léognan 1986 $11 (9/30/89) **81**
Graves 1985 $15 (7/31/88) **77**

CHATEAU HAUT-LAGRANGE (France/Bordeaux)
Pessac-Léognan 1991 (NR) (5/15/92) (BT) **85+**

CHATEAU HAUT-MAILLET (France/Bordeaux)
Pomerol 1989 (NR) (4/30/91) (BT) **85+**

CHATEAU HAUT-MALLET (France/Bordeaux)
Bordeaux Supérieur 1987 $7.50 (4/15/90) **76**

CHATEAU HAUT-MARBUZET (France/Bordeaux)
St.-Estèphe 1991 (NR) (5/15/92) (BT) **85+**
St.-Estèphe 1990 (NR) (5/15/92) (BT) **95+**
St.-Estèphe 1989 $32 (3/15/92) **90**
St.-Estèphe 1988 Rel: $25 Cur: $28 (12/31/90) SS **91**
St.-Estèphe 1987 $20 (5/15/90) **85**
St.-Estèphe 1986 $30 (11/30/89) (JS) **92**
St.-Estèphe 1985 Rel: $25 Cur: $47 (6/30/88) **91**
St.-Estèphe 1982 $57 (11/30/89) (JS) **92**
St.-Estèphe 1979 $30 (10/15/89) (JS) **85**
St.-Estèphe 1962 $50 (11/30/87) (JS) **70**
St.-Estèphe (English Bottled) 1959 $60 (10/15/90) (JS) **83**

CHATEAU HAUT-RIAN (France/Bordeaux)
Premières Côtes de Bordeaux 1988 $7 (5/15/90) BB **81**

CHATEAU HAUT-SARPE (France/Bordeaux)
St.-Emilion 1989 (NR) (4/30/91) (BT) **85+**
St.-Emilion 1988 $16 (6/30/91) **83**
St.-Emilion 1987 $14 (6/30/89) (BT) **75+**
St.-Emilion 1982 $20 (5/15/89) (TR) **87**
St.-Emilion 1979 Rel: $11 Cur: $14 (4/01/84) **78**

DOMAINE DU HAUT DES TERRES BLANCHES (France/Rhône)
Châteauneuf-du-Pape 1989 $16 (5/31/92) **84**
Châteauneuf-du-Pape 1988 $16 (7/15/91) **85**
Châteauneuf-du-Pape Réserve du Vatican 1983 $12 (9/30/87) **88**

CHATEAU LES HAUTS DE BRAME (France/Bordeaux)
St.-Estèphe 1986 $18.50 (10/31/89) **82**

CHATEAU LES HAUTS DE SMITH (France/Bordeaux)
Pessac-Léognan 1988 (NR) (6/30/89) (BT) **75+**
Pessac-Léognan 1987 (NR) (6/30/89) (BT) **70+**

HAVEMEYER (Germany)
Riesling Spätlese Mosel-Saar-Ruwer Piesporter Goldtröpfchen 1985 $17 (11/30/87) **68**

HAVENS (United States/California)
Chardonnay Carneros Napa Valley 1989 $14 (7/15/91) **87**
Chardonnay Carneros Napa Valley 1988 $14 (4/30/90) **89**

Key to Symbols

The scores reported here are the results of blind tastings conducted by our panel of senior editors. Wines that carry the initials below are results of individual tastings.

THE WINE SPECTATOR 100-POINT SCALE ***95-100***—Classic, a great wine; ***90-94***—Outstanding, superior character and style; ***80-89***—Good to very good, a wine with special qualities; ***70-79***—Average, drinkable wine that may have minor flaws; ***60-69***—Below average, drinkable but not recommended; ***50-59***—Poor, undrinkable, not recommended. "+"—With a score indicates a range; used primarily with barrel tastings to indicate a preliminary score.

SPECIAL DESIGNATIONS SS—Spectator Selection, CS—Cellar Selection, BB—Best Buy, ($NA)—Price not available, (NR)—Not released.

TASTER'S INITIALS (JG)—Jim Gordon, (HS)—Harvey Steiman, (JL)—James Laube, (JS)—James Suckling, (TM)—Thomas Matthews, (TR)—Terry Robards, (PM)—Per-Henrik Mansson, (BT)—Barrel Tasting (these wines were tasted blind from barrel samples), (CA-date)—*California's Great Cabernets* by James Laube, (CH-date)—*California's Great Chardonnays* by James Laube, (VP-date)—*Vintage Port* by James Suckling.

DATE TASTED Dates in parentheses represent the issue in which the rating was published.

Merlot Carneros Napa Valley Truchard Vineyard 1988 $20 (8/31/91) **76**
Merlot Carneros Napa Valley Truchard Vineyard Reserve 1989 $20 (5/31/92) **82**
Merlot Napa Valley 1989 $14 (5/31/92) **84**
Merlot Napa Valley 1988 $14 (3/31/91) **82**
Merlot Napa Valley 1987 $14 (7/15/90) **89**
Merlot Napa Valley 1986 $13.50 (3/31/90) **72**
Merlot Napa Valley 1985 $12.50 (5/31/88) **84**

HAVILAND (United States/Washington)
Merlot Washington 1982 $8 (10/01/84) **76**

HAWK CREST (United States/California)
Cabernet Sauvignon California 1989 $9 (3/15/92) **77**
Cabernet Sauvignon Mendocino 1981 $5 (3/16/85) BB **84**
Cabernet Sauvignon North Coast 1987 $8 (3/31/90) **79**
Cabernet Sauvignon North Coast 1986 $7.50 (10/15/88) BB **82**
Cabernet Sauvignon North Coast 1985 $6.50 (7/31/88) **75**
Cabernet Sauvignon North Coast 1984 $7 (10/15/87) **76**
Cabernet Sauvignon North Coast 1981 $5 (2/01/86) **65**
Chardonnay California 1990 $9 (3/15/92) **81**
Chardonnay California 1989 $9 (7/15/91) **72**
Chardonnay California 1988 $9 (12/15/89) **74**
Chardonnay California 1987 $7.50 (10/15/88) **71**
Chardonnay California 1984 $6 (4/16/86) **67**
Chardonnay Sonoma County 1987 $9 (7/15/89) **86**
Sauvignon Blanc California 1989 $6 (8/31/90) BB **80**
Sauvignon Blanc California 1988 $6 (5/15/90) **76**
Sauvignon Blanc California 1987 $6 (10/31/89) BB **83**

HAYWOOD (United States/California)
Cabernet Sauvignon California Vintner's Select 1989 $8 (3/15/92) **80**
Cabernet Sauvignon Sonoma Valley Los Chamizal Vineyards 1988 $16 (11/15/91) **85**
Cabernet Sauvignon Sonoma Valley Los Chamizal Vineyards 1987 $16 (4/15/89) (BT) **80+**
Cabernet Sauvignon Sonoma Valley 1986 Rel: $16 Cur: $20 (11/15/89) **92**
Cabernet Sauvignon Sonoma Valley 1985 Rel: $14.50 Cur: $20 (CA-3/89) **89**
Cabernet Sauvignon Sonoma Valley 1984 Rel: $12.50 Cur: $20 (CA-3/89) **88**
Cabernet Sauvignon Sonoma Valley 1983 Rel: $12.50 Cur: $20 (CA-3/89) **77**
Cabernet Sauvignon Sonoma Valley 1982 Rel: $11 Cur: $20 (CA-3/89) **79**
Cabernet Sauvignon Sonoma Valley 1981 Rel: $11 Cur: $20 (CA-3/89) **85**
Cabernet Sauvignon Sonoma Valley 1980 Rel: $9.75 Cur: $15 (CA-3/89) **86**
Chardonnay California Vintner's Select 1990 $8 (11/15/91) BB **83**
Chardonnay Sonoma Valley Los Chamizal Vineyards 1989 $13.50 (3/31/91) **81**
Chardonnay Sonoma Valley Los Chamizal Vineyards 1988 $13.50 (11/30/90) **76**
Chardonnay Sonoma Valley Los Chamizal Vineyards 1987 $12.50 (6/30/90) **74**
Chardonnay Sonoma Valley 1986 $9.50 (10/15/88) **82**
Chardonnay Sonoma Valley 1982 $10 (5/16/84) **80**
Chardonnay Sonoma Valley Reserve 1985 $14.50 (12/31/87) **77**
Fumé Blanc Sonoma Valley 1988 $9.50 (11/30/89) **88**
Fumé Blanc Sonoma Valley Los Chamizal Vineyards 1990 $9.50 (6/15/92) **81**
Zinfandel Sonoma Valley 1986 $11 (9/15/88) **89**
Zinfandel Sonoma Valley 1985 $9.50 (11/15/87) **85**
Zinfandel Sonoma Valley 1984 $9 (5/31/87) **92**
Zinfandel Sonoma Valley 1983 $8 (1/01/86) **85**
Zinfandel Sonoma Valley 1982 $8 (11/01/84) **89**
Zinfandel Sonoma Valley Los Chamizal Vineyards 1989 $14 (11/15/91) **85**
Zinfandel Sonoma Valley Los Chamizal Vineyards 1988 $12.50 (11/30/90) **89**
Spaghetti Red California NV $6 (2/15/90) **74**

HEDGES (United States/Washington)
Cabernet Merlot Columbia Valley 1990 $9 (6/15/92) BB **88**
Cabernet Merlot Columbia Valley 1989 $7 (9/30/91) BB **89**

HEGGIES (Australia)
Chardonnay Barossa Valley 1987 $14 (1/31/90) **83**
Chardonnay Barossa Valley 1985 $13 (12/15/87) **69**
Rhine Riesling Late Harvest Barossa Valley Botrytis Affected 1986 $8/375ml (2/15/88) **92**

DR. HEIDEMANNS-BERGWEILER (Germany)
Riesling Auslese Mosel-Saar-Ruwer Bernkasteler Alte Badstube am Doctorberg 1988 (NR) (9/30/89) **81**
Riesling Auslese Mosel-Saar-Ruwer Graacher Himmelreich 1988 (NR) (9/30/89) **79**
Riesling Spätlese Mosel-Saar-Ruwer Bernkasteler Badstube 1988 (NR) (9/30/89) **85**
Riesling Spätlese Mosel-Saar-Ruwer Bernkasteler Doctor 1986 (NR) (4/15/89) **85**
Riesling Spätlese Mosel-Saar-Ruwer Wehlener Sonnenuhr 1988 (NR) (9/30/89) **88**

CHARLES HEIDSIECK (France/Champagne)
Brut Champagne 1985 $50 (12/31/90) **93**
Brut Champagne 1983 $41 (3/31/91) **90**
Brut Champagne 1982 Rel: $33 Cur: $40 (12/31/88) SS **93**
Brut Champagne Blanc des Millénaires 1983 $65 (3/31/92) **90**
Brut Champagne Millésime 1983 $38 (12/31/89) **87**
Brut Champagne Réserve NV $34 (12/31/91) **90**
Brut Blanc de Blancs Champagne NV $33 (12/31/90) **84**
Brut Blanc de Blancs Champagne Brut de Chardonnay 1981 $30 (5/31/87) **78**
Brut Rosé Champagne 1983 $49 (3/31/91) **89**
Brut Rosé Champagne 1982 $40 (12/31/88) **91**
Brut Rosé Champagne 1976 $25 (12/16/85) **61**

HEIDSIECK MONOPOLE (France/Champagne)
Brut Champagne Diamant Bleu 1982 Rel: $40 Cur: $56 (11/30/87) **89**
Brut Champagne Diamant Bleu 1979 $39 (5/16/86) **93**
Brut Champagne Diamant Rosé 1982 Rel: $55 Cur: $68 (11/30/87) **90**
Brut Champagne Dry Monopole 1985 (NR) (12/31/90) **90**
Brut Champagne Dry Monopole 1982 $37.50 (12/31/88) **88**
Brut Champagne Dry Monopole NV $31 (12/31/91) **82**
Brut Rosé Champagne 1983 $40 (12/31/89) **75**
Brut Rosé Champagne 1982 $43 (12/31/88) **84**
Brut Rosé Champagne 1979 $27 (12/16/85) **72**
Extra Dry Champagne NV $35 (12/31/88) **86**

HEITZ (United States/California)
Cabernet Sauvignon Napa Valley 1987 Rel: $20 Cur: $22 (4/15/92) SS **90**
Cabernet Sauvignon Napa Valley 1986 Rel: $18 Cur: $21 (4/15/91) **88**
Cabernet Sauvignon Napa Valley 1985 Rel: $18 Cur: $25 (5/15/90) **80**
Cabernet Sauvignon Napa Valley 1984 Rel: $15 Cur: $30 (1/31/90) (JL) **89**
Cabernet Sauvignon Napa Valley 1983 Rel: $13 Cur: $20 (1/31/90) (JL) **85**
Cabernet Sauvignon Napa Valley 1982 Rel: $13.50 Cur: $26 (1/31/90) (JL) **80**
Cabernet Sauvignon Napa Valley 1981 Rel: $13.25 Cur: $27 (1/31/90) (JL) **86**
Cabernet Sauvignon Napa Valley 1980 Rel: $12 Cur: $24 (1/31/90) (JL) **88**
Cabernet Sauvignon Napa Valley 1979 Rel: $11.25 Cur: $45 (1/31/90) (JL) **86**
Cabernet Sauvignon Napa Valley 1978 Rel: $11 Cur: $30 (1/31/90) (JL) **90**

Cabernet Sauvignon Napa Valley 1977 Rel: $11 Cur: $48 (1/31/90) (JL) **83**
Cabernet Sauvignon Napa Valley 1973 $38 (1/31/90) (JL) **78**
Cabernet Sauvignon Napa Valley 1970 $75 (1/31/90) (JL) **74**
Cabernet Sauvignon Napa Valley NV (NR) (1/31/90) (JL) **68**
Cabernet Sauvignon Napa Valley MZ-1 NV (NR) (1/31/90) (JL) **75**
Cabernet Sauvignon Napa Valley Z-91 NV (NR) (1/31/90) (JL) **90**
Cabernet Sauvignon Napa Valley Bella Oaks Vineyard 1987 Rel: $27 Cur: $31 (6/30/92) **85**
Cabernet Sauvignon Napa Valley Bella Oaks Vineyard 1986 Rel: $21.50 Cur: $28 (4/15/91) **89**
Cabernet Sauvignon Napa Valley Bella Oaks Vineyard 1985 Rel: $25 Cur: $55 (5/15/90) CS **92**
Cabernet Sauvignon Napa Valley Bella Oaks Vineyard 1984 Rel: $25 Cur: $39 (5/15/89) **86**
Cabernet Sauvignon Napa Valley Bella Oaks Vineyard 1983 Rel: $15 Cur: $33 (CA-3/89) **86**
Cabernet Sauvignon Napa Valley Bella Oaks Vineyard 1982 Rel: $16 Cur: $42 (CA-3/89) **85**
Cabernet Sauvignon Napa Valley Bella Oaks Vineyard 1981 Rel: $16 Cur: $50 (CA-3/89) **90**
Cabernet Sauvignon Napa Valley Bella Oaks Vineyard 1980 Rel: $20 Cur: $47 (CA-3/89) **93**
Cabernet Sauvignon Napa Valley Bella Oaks Vineyard 1978 Rel: $15 Cur: $60 (CA-3/89) **89**
Cabernet Sauvignon Napa Valley Bella Oaks Vineyard 1977 Rel: $30 Cur: $65 (CA-3/89) **91**
Cabernet Sauvignon Napa Valley Bella Oaks Vineyard 1976 Rel: $30 Cur: $46 (CA-3/89) **85**
Cabernet Sauvignon Napa Valley Fay Vineyard 1978 Rel: $12.75 Cur: $32 (2/16/84) (HS) **80**
Cabernet Sauvignon Napa Valley Fay Vineyard 1977 Rel: $17.50 Cur: $32 (2/16/84) (HS) **78**
Cabernet Sauvignon Napa Valley Martha's Vineyard 1987 Rel: $65 Cur: $75 (3/31/92) CS **95**
Cabernet Sauvignon Napa Valley Martha's Vineyard 1986 Rel: $60 Cur: $70 (4/15/91) CS **95**
Cabernet Sauvignon Napa Valley Martha's Vineyard 1985 Rel: $60 Cur: $140 (4/30/90) **98**
Cabernet Sauvignon Napa Valley Martha's Vineyard 1984 Rel: $40 Cur: $95 (3/15/89) SS **97**
Cabernet Sauvignon Napa Valley Martha's Vineyard 1983 Rel: $32.50 Cur: $61 (CA-3/89) **89**
Cabernet Sauvignon Napa Valley Martha's Vineyard 1982 Rel: $30 Cur: $68 (CA-3/89) **88**
Cabernet Sauvignon Napa Valley Martha's Vineyard 1982 Rel: $30 Cur: $68 (4/15/87) CS **94**
Cabernet Sauvignon Napa Valley Martha's Vineyard 1981 Rel: $30 Cur: $62 (CA-3/89) **89**
Cabernet Sauvignon Napa Valley Martha's Vineyard 1981 Rel: $30 Cur: $62 (4/16/86) CS **91**
Cabernet Sauvignon Napa Valley Martha's Vineyard 1980 Rel: $30 Cur: $68 (CA-3/89) **89**
Cabernet Sauvignon Napa Valley Martha's Vineyard 1980 Rel: $30 Cur: $68 (7/01/85) CS **93**
Cabernet Sauvignon Napa Valley Martha's Vineyard 1979 Rel: $25 Cur: $85 (CA-3/89) **93**
Cabernet Sauvignon Napa Valley Martha's Vineyard 1979 Rel: $25 Cur: $85 (2/15/84) SS **94**
Cabernet Sauvignon Napa Valley Martha's Vineyard 1978 Rel: $22 Cur: $110 (CA-3/89) **91**
Cabernet Sauvignon Napa Valley Martha's Vineyard 1977 Rel: $30 Cur: $81 (1/31/90) (JL) **90**
Cabernet Sauvignon Napa Valley Martha's Vineyard 1976 Rel: $30 Cur: $88 (CA-3/89) **85**
Cabernet Sauvignon Napa Valley Martha's Vineyard 1975 Rel: $25 Cur: $95 (CA-3/89) **92**
Cabernet Sauvignon Napa Valley Martha's Vineyard 1974 Rel: $25 Cur: $290 (CA-3/89) **99**
Cabernet Sauvignon Napa Valley Martha's Vineyard 1973 Rel: $11 Cur: $120 (CA-3/89) **92**
Cabernet Sauvignon Napa Valley Martha's Vineyard 1972 Rel: $12.75 Cur: $140 (CA-3/89) **79**
Cabernet Sauvignon Napa Valley Martha's Vineyard 1970 Rel: $12.75 Cur: $320 (CA-3/89) **98**
Cabernet Sauvignon Napa Valley Martha's Vineyard 1969 Rel: $12.75 Cur: $280 (CA-3/89) **93**
Cabernet Sauvignon Napa Valley Martha's Vineyard 1968 Rel: $9.50 Cur: $430 (CA-3/89) **99**
Cabernet Sauvignon Napa Valley Martha's Vineyard 1967 Rel: $7.50 Cur: $280 (CA-3/89) **86**
Cabernet Sauvignon Napa Valley Martha's Vineyard 1966 Rel: $8 Cur: $440 (CA-3/89) **92**
Joe's White Napa Valley NV $5 (4/30/89) BB **83**
Ryan's Red Napa Valley NV $6 (2/28/89) **74**

HENRIOT (France/Champagne)
Brut Champagne NV $21 (7/01/86) **86**
Brut Champagne Cuvée du Soleil NV $27 (12/31/87) **70**
Brut Champagne Souverain NV $40 (12/31/91) **86**
Brut Blanc de Blancs Champagne de Chardonnay NV (NR) (12/31/90) **85**
Brut Rosé Champagne 1981 $28 (7/01/86) **93**

HENRY (United States/Oregon)
Pinot Noir Umpqua Valley 1986 $10 (4/15/91) **81**
Pinot Noir Umpqua Valley 1985 $15 (2/15/90) **85**

HENSCHKE (Australia)
Cabernet Sauvignon Barossa Ranges Keyneton Cyril Henschke 1988 $23 (6/30/92) **85**
Cabernet Sauvignon Barossa Valley Cyril Henschke 1986 $23 (9/15/89) **91**
Cabernet Sauvignon Barossa Valley Cyril Henschke 1985 $21 (1/31/89) **90**
Cabernet Sauvignon Barossa Valley Cyril Henschke 1984 $18.50 (12/15/87) **94**
Keyneton Estate Barossa Ranges Keyneton 1988 $14 (6/30/92) **82**
Keyneton Estate Barossa Valley 1985 $11.50 (3/31/89) **79**
Keyneton Estate Barossa Valley 1984 $12 (2/15/88) **85**
Shiraz Australia Keyneton Mount Edelstone 1987 $16.50 (5/31/91) **86**
Shiraz Barossa Ranges Keyneton Hill of Grace 1988 $27 (5/31/92) **88**
Shiraz Barossa Ranges Keyneton Hill of Grace 1987 $27 (5/31/92) CS **91**
Shiraz Barossa Ranges Keyneton Mount Edelstone 1989 $17 (5/31/92) **88**
Shiraz Barossa Ranges Keyneton Mount Edelstone 1988 $17 (5/31/92) **90**
Shiraz Barossa Valley Hill of Grace 1986 $26 (9/30/89) **87**
Shiraz Barossa Valley Mount Edelstone 1986 $17 (10/31/89) HR **90**
Shiraz Barossa Valley Mount Edelstone 1985 $14.50 (3/31/89) **81**
Shiraz Barossa Valley Mount Edelstone 1984 $14 (2/15/88) **90**

PHILIPPE HERARD (France/Other)
Brut Blanc de Blancs NV $9.50 (6/15/90) **74**

CHATEAU DES HERBEUX (France/Burgundy)
Chambertin 1988 $75 (12/31/90) **87**
Chevalier-Montrachet 1988 $100 (7/31/90) **90**
Clos Vougeot 1988 $65 (11/30/90) **86**
Meursault Perrières 1988 $42 (7/15/90) **92**
Montrachet 1988 $165 (7/31/90) **78**
Musigny 1988 $75 (12/31/90) **83**
Puligny-Montrachet Les Combettes 1986 $21 (2/28/89) **89**
Volnay Santenots 1988 $36 (11/30/90) **88**

BERNARD HERESZTYN (France/Burgundy)
Gevrey-Chambertin Les Goulots 1988 $44 (7/15/91) **90**

STANISLAS HERESZTYN (France/Burgundy)
Gevrey-Chambertin 1987 $25 (3/31/90) **83**
Gevrey-Chambertin Les Champonnets 1988 $37 (12/31/90) **82**

R. HERESZTYN-BAILLY (France/Burgundy)
Gevrey-Chambertin 1986 $20 (7/15/89) **86**
Gevrey-Chambertin Les Goulots 1986 $28 (10/15/89) **82**

L'HERITIER-GUYOT (France/Burgundy)
Vougeot Blanc Clos Blanc de Vougeot 1988 $52 (4/15/92) **68**

DOMAINE DE L'HERMITE (France/Rhône)
Hermitage 1983 $9.50 (5/01/86) **88**
Hermitage 1980 $12.25 (5/01/86) **84**

CHATEAU HERMITAGE (France/Bordeaux)
Pomerol 1982 (NR) (5/15/89) (TR) **83**

HERZOG (France/Other)
Cabernet Sauvignon Vin de Pays d'Oc 1988 $6 (3/15/90) **67**
Cabernet Sauvignon Vin de Pays d'Oc NV $7 (3/31/91) BB **88**
Chardonnay Vin de Pays d'Oc 1989 $9 (3/31/91) **76**
Merlot Vin de Pays d'Oc NV $7 (3/31/91) **75**

THE HESS COLLECTION (United States/California)
Cabernet Sauvignon Napa Valley 1991 (NR) (5/15/92) (BT) **85+**
Cabernet Sauvignon Napa Valley 1990 (NR) (5/15/91) (BT) **85+**
Cabernet Sauvignon Napa Valley 1989 (NR) (5/15/91) (BT) **90+**
Cabernet Sauvignon Napa Valley 1988 Rel: $17.50 Cur: $20 (1/31/92) CS **90**
Cabernet Sauvignon Napa Valley 1987 Rel: $17 Cur: $22 (4/15/91) SS **94**
Cabernet Sauvignon Napa Valley 1986 Rel: $14 Cur: $24 (11/15/89) **90**
Cabernet Sauvignon Napa Valley 1985 Rel: $13 Cur: $50 (CA-3/89) **96**
Cabernet Sauvignon Napa Valley 1983 Rel: $13 Cur: $25 (CA-3/89) **84**
Cabernet Sauvignon Napa Valley Reserve 1987 Rel: $34 Cur: $55 (10/15/91) **96**
Cabernet Sauvignon Napa Valley Reserve 1986 Rel: $33 Cur: $44 (9/15/90) **93**
Cabernet Sauvignon Napa Valley Reserve 1984 Rel: $22 Cur: $100 (CA-3/89) **93**
Cabernet Sauvignon Napa Valley Reserve 1983 Rel: $22 Cur: $75 (CA-3/89) **88**
Chardonnay Napa Valley 1989 $14.50 (7/15/91) **86**
Chardonnay Napa Valley 1988 Rel: $13.75 Cur: $17 (4/15/90) **85**
Chardonnay Napa Valley 1987 Rel: $13.25 Cur: $19 (7/15/89) **90**
Chardonnay Napa Valley 1986 Rel: $12.75 Cur: $18 (CH-4/90) **88**
Merlot Napa Valley 1989 $25 (5/31/92) **86**

HESS SELECT (United States/California)
Cabernet Sauvignon California 1988 $9.50 (3/31/91) **86**
Chardonnay California 1990 $9.50 (12/15/91) BB **86**
Chardonnay Napa Valley 1989 $9.50 (12/31/90) **86**
Chardonnay California 1988 $9 (11/30/89) SS **90**

HEYL ZU HERRNSHEIM (Germany)
Riesling Auslese Rheinhessen Niersteiner Olberg 1990 $24 (12/15/91) **91**
Riesling Auslese Rheinhessen Niersteiner Olberg 1989 $25 (12/15/90) **88**
Riesling Kabinett Rheinhessen Niersteiner Olberg 1989 $12 (12/15/90) **85**
Riesling Kabinett Rheinhessen Niersteiner Olberg 1988 (NR) (9/30/89) **90**
Riesling Kabinett Rheinhessen Niersteiner Pettenthal 1990 $9 (12/15/91) **85**
Riesling Kabinett Rheinhessen Niersteiner Pettenthal 1989 $11 (12/15/90) **85**
Riesling Kabinett Halbtrocken Rheinhessen Niersteiner Pettenthal 1988 (NR) (9/30/89) **91**
Riesling Spätlese Rheinhessen Niersteiner Brudersberg 1990 $15 (12/15/91) **90**
Riesling Spätlese Rheinhessen Niersteiner Brudersberg 1989 $15 (12/15/90) **86**
Riesling Spätlese Rheinhessen Niersteiner Olberg 1990 $15 (12/15/91) **85**
Riesling Spätlese Rheinhessen Niersteiner Olberg 1989 $15 (12/15/90) **84**
Riesling Spätlese Rheinhessen Niersteiner Olberg 1988 (NR) (9/30/89) **89**
Riesling Spätlese Rheinhessen Niersteiner Pettenthal 1989 $15 (12/15/90) **84**
Riesling Spätlese Halbtrocken Rheinhessen Niersteiner Pettenthal 1990 $14 (12/15/91) **86**
Riesling Spätlese Halbtrocken Rheinhessen Niersteiner Pettenthal 1988 (NR) (9/30/89) **95**
Riesling Spätlese Trocken Rheinhessen Niersteiner Brudersberg 1990 $15 (12/15/91) **85**
Riesling Trockenbeerenauslese Rheinhessen Niersteiner Olberg 1989 $50 (12/15/90) **90**

HIDDEN CELLARS (United States/California)
Cabernet Sauvignon Mendocino County Mountanos Vineyard 1984 $12 (8/31/88) **88**
Chardonnay Mendocino County 1990 $12 (4/30/92) **85**
Chardonnay Mendocino County 1989 $12 (3/31/91) **83**
Chardonnay Mendocino County 1987 $12 (7/15/89) **89**
Chardonnay Mendocino County 1986 $10.50 (5/31/88) **78**
Chardonnay Mendocino County Grasso Vineyard 1985 $9.75 (7/31/87) **78**
Chardonnay Mendocino County Reserve 1990 $16 (12/15/91) **86**
Chardonnay Mendocino County Reserve Barrel Fermented 1989 $16 (7/15/91) **91**
Chanson d'Or Bailey J. Lovin Vineyard Mendocino County 1989 $15/375ml (9/15/91) **84**
Gewürztraminer Mendocino County 1987 $7 (2/28/89) **83**
Johannisberg Riesling Potter Valley 1990 $7.50 (6/30/91) BB **85**
Johannisberg Riesling Potter Valley 1989 $8 (9/15/90) **83**
Riesling Late Harvest Mendocino Bailey Lovin Vineyard 1984 $10 (10/16/85) **94**
Sauvignon Blanc Mendocino County 1990 $9 (4/15/92) **88**
Sauvignon Blanc Mendocino County 1989 $9 (11/15/91) **87**
Sauvignon Blanc Mendocino County White Table Wine Alchemy 1989 $18 (7/31/91) **90**
Zinfandel Mendocino County Pacini Vineyard 1989 $10 (2/29/92) **81**
Zinfandel Mendocino County Pacini Vineyard 1988 $10 (12/31/90) **85**
Zinfandel Mendocino County Pacini Vineyard 1986 $7.50 (10/31/88) **86**
Zinfandel Mendocino County Pacini Vineyard 1984 $7.50 (4/15/87) **88**

HIDDEN SPRINGS (United States/Oregon)
Pinot Noir Oregon 1985 $12 (6/15/88) **78**

WILLIAM HILL (United States/California)
Cabernet Sauvignon Napa Valley Silver Label 1987 $14 (11/15/90) **85**
Cabernet Sauvignon Napa Valley Silver Label 1986 $13 (4/15/88) (BT) **85+**
Cabernet Sauvignon Napa Valley Silver Label 1985 $12 (4/30/88) **90**
Cabernet Sauvignon Napa Valley Reserve 1990 (NR) (5/15/91) (BT) **80+**
Cabernet Sauvignon Napa Valley Reserve 1989 (NR) (5/15/91) (BT) **85+**
Cabernet Sauvignon Napa Valley Reserve 1988 $24 (11/15/91) **84**
Cabernet Sauvignon Napa Valley Reserve 1987 Rel: $24 Cur: $27 (11/15/90) SS **95**
Cabernet Sauvignon Napa Valley Reserve 1986 Rel: $24.50 Cur: $29 (11/15/89) **91**
Cabernet Sauvignon Napa Valley Reserve 1986 Rel: $24.50 Cur: $29 (CA-3/89) **95**
Cabernet Sauvignon Napa Valley Reserve 1985 Rel: $22.50 Cur: $30 (CA-3/89) **94**
Cabernet Sauvignon Napa Valley Reserve 1984 Rel: $18.25 Cur: $28 (4/15/88) CS **91**
Cabernet Sauvignon Napa Valley Gold Label 1983 Rel: $18.25 Cur: $25 (CA-3/89) **85**
Cabernet Sauvignon Napa Valley Gold Label 1982 Rel: $18 Cur: $36 (CA-3/89) **90**
Cabernet Sauvignon Napa Valley Gold Label 1982 Rel: $18 Cur: $36 (6/16/86) SS **94**
Cabernet Sauvignon Napa Valley Gold Label 1981 Rel: $16.25 Cur: $33 (CA-3/89) **85**
Cabernet Sauvignon Napa Valley Gold Label 1980 Rel: $18.25 Cur: $32 (CA-3/89) **87**
Cabernet Sauvignon Napa Valley Gold Label 1979 Rel: $18 Cur: $45 (CA-3/89) **93**
Cabernet Sauvignon Napa Valley Gold Label 1978 Rel: $16.25 Cur: $50 (CA-3/89) **95**
Cabernet Sauvignon Sonoma County Silver Label 1988 $14 (11/15/91) **82**
Chardonnay Napa Valley Reserve 1990 $18 (7/15/92) **87**
Chardonnay Napa Valley Reserve 1989 $18 (6/30/91) **90**
Chardonnay Napa Valley Reserve 1988 $18 (4/30/90) **90**
Chardonnay Napa Valley Reserve 1987 Rel: $18 Cur: $20 (CH-3/90) **91**
Chardonnay Napa Valley Reserve 1986 Rel: $17 Cur: $20 (CH-3/90) **91**
Chardonnay Napa Valley Reserve 1985 Rel: $16 Cur: $24 (CH-3/90) **90**
Chardonnay Napa Valley Reserve 1984 Rel: $20 Cur: $24 (CH-3/90) **88**
Chardonnay Napa Valley Reserve 1983 Rel: $22 Cur: $28 (CH-3/90) **85**
Chardonnay Napa Valley Reserve 1982 Rel: $24 Cur: $28 (CH-3/90) **86**
Chardonnay Napa Valley Reserve 1980 Rel: $16 Cur: $30 (CH-3/90) **70**
Chardonnay Napa Valley Silver Label 1989 $12 (1/31/91) **81**
Chardonnay Napa Valley Silver Label 1988 $11.50 (6/30/90) **85**
Chardonnay Napa Valley Silver Label 1987 $13 (6/15/89) **73**
Chardonnay Napa Valley Silver Label 1986 $10 (4/30/88) **80**

HILL-SMITH (Australia)
Cabernet Sauvignon Barossa Valley 1984 $9.50 (8/31/87) **75**
Cabernet Sauvignon Barossa Valley 1981 $9.50 (7/16/86) **82**

Chardonnay Barossa Valley 1986 $8 (11/15/87) **73**
Chardonnay Barossa Valley 1985 $9.50 (5/15/87) **72**
Sémillon Late Harvest Barossa Valley Autumn Harvest Botrytis Affected 1986 $10/375ml (3/15/89) **84**
Sémillon Late Harvest Barossa Valley Autumn Harvest Botrytis 1985 $8/375ml (2/15/88) **88**
Sémillon Late Harvest Barossa Valley Autumn Harvest Botrytis 1983 $8/375ml (8/31/86) **84**
Shiraz Barossa Valley 1986 $9 (2/28/91) BB **86**
Shiraz Barossa Valley 1984 $6.25 (5/15/87) **82**

HINZERLING (United States/Washington)
Gewüztraminer Late Harvest Yakima Valley Selected Cluster Die Sonne 1985 $12/375ml (10/15/89) **82**

HMR (United States/California)
Pinot Noir Paso Robles 1979 $6.50 (2/01/85) **72**

HOGUE (United States/Washington)
Blush Washington 1988 $6 (10/15/89) **82**
Brut Yakima Valley NV $12 (10/15/89) **82**
Cabernet Sauvignon Washington 1989 $12 (11/15/91) **84**
Cabernet Sauvignon Washington 1988 $12 (3/31/92) **88**
Cabernet Sauvignon Washington Reserve 1988 $18 (11/15/91) **89**
Cabernet Sauvignon Washington Reserve 1987 $19 (3/31/91) **88**
Cabernet Sauvignon Washington Reserve 1985 $18 (10/15/89) **81**
Chardonnay Washington 1990 $9 (4/30/92) **89**
Chardonnay Washington 1988 $8 (6/15/90) **80**
Chardonnay Washington 1987 $8 (10/15/89) **83**
Chardonnay Washington 1986 $8 (12/31/87) **81**
Chardonnay Washington Reserve 1989 $13 (5/31/91) **86**
Chardonnay Yakima Valley Reserve 1987 $10 (10/15/89) **88**
Chenin Blanc Washington 1988 $6 (10/15/89) **74**
Fumé Blanc Washington 1988 $8 (10/15/89) **88**
Johannisberg Riesling Yakima Valley 1988 $6 (10/15/89) BB **90**
Johannisberg Riesling Yakima Valley Dry Schwartzman Vineyard 1988 $6.50 (10/15/89) **84**
Merlot Washington 1989 $12 (10/15/91) SS **92**
Merlot Washington 1986 $12 (4/15/89) **85**
Merlot Washington 1985 $12 (11/15/87) **80**
Merlot Washington Reserve 1988 $18 (11/15/91) **90**
Merlot Washington Reserve 1987 $19 (3/31/91) **89**
Riesling Washington Dry Schwartzman Vineyard Reserve 1989 $8.50 (6/15/91) **80**
Sémillon Washington 1990 $7 (6/15/92) **83**
Sémillon Washington 1989 $6.50 (11/30/91) BB **84**
Sémillon Washington Reserve 1986 $8 (10/15/89) **72**
White Riesling Late Harvest Yakima Valley Markin Vineyard 1987 $7.50 (10/15/89) **79**

HOLLICK (Australia)
Cabernet Merlot Coonawarra 1985 $16 (5/31/88) **72**
Cabernet Sauvignon Coonawarra 1988 $14 (3/15/92) **74**
Chardonnay Coonawarra 1986 $16 (5/15/88) **86**

HONEYWOOD (United States/Oregon)
Pinot Noir Willamette Valley 1986 $9 (6/15/88) **86**

HONIG (United States/California)
Sauvignon Blanc Napa Valley 1990 $9.25 (6/15/92) **85**
Sauvignon Blanc Napa Valley 1989 $9 (11/15/91) **84**
Sauvignon Blanc Napa Valley 1988 $8.75 (5/15/90) **78**
Sauvignon Blanc Napa Valley 1987 $8.75 (7/31/89) **84**

HOODSPORT (United States/Washington)
Gewürztraminer Washington 1988 $6 (10/15/89) BB **85**
Johannisberg Riesling Washington 1988 $6 (10/15/89) BB **87**

HOOPER (Portugal)
Tawny Port 20 Year Old NV $35 (2/28/90) (JS) **78**
Vintage Port 1985 Rel: $15 Cur: $19 (VP-6/90) **80**
Vintage Port 1983 $20 (VP-3/90) **60**
Vintage Port 1982 $18 (VP-5/90) **68**
Vintage Port 1980 $22 (VP-5/90) **67**

HOP KILN (United States/California)
Cabernet Sauvignon Alexander Valley 1984 $10 (3/31/88) **77**
Cabernet Sauvignon Dry Creek Valley 1986 $12 (6/15/89) **69**
Cabernet Sauvignon Dry Creek Valley 1985 $10 (10/15/88) **75**
Chardonnay Alexander Valley 10th Anniversary Reserve 1983 $10 (10/01/85) **86**
Chardonnay Russian River Valley Marty Griffin Vineyards 1990 $12 (2/29/92) **86**
Gewürztraminer Russian River Valley 1988 $7.50 (1/31/90) **72**
Johannisberg Riesling Russian River Valley Marty Griffin Vineyards 1990 $7.50 (12/31/91) BB **87**
Marty Griffin's Big Red Russian River Valley 1988 $7.50 (11/30/90) BB **85**
Marty Griffin's Big Red Russian River Valley 1987 $7.50 (12/15/89) BB **89**
Marty Griffin's Big Red Russian River Valley 1986 $6.50 (6/15/89) BB **85**
Petite Sirah Russian River Valley Marty Griffin Vineyards 1987 $11 (2/28/90) **82**
Valdiguié Russian River Valley Marty Griffin Vineyards 1990 $15 (6/30/92) **77**
White Zinfandel Russian River Valley 1988 $6.75 (6/15/89) **88**
Zinfandel Russian River Valley 1988 $12 (12/15/90) **88**
Zinfandel Russian River Valley 1986 $10 (6/15/89) **85**
Zinfandel Russian River Valley 1982 $8.50 (11/01/85) **85**
Zinfandel Russian River Valley Primitivo 1985 $12 (3/15/88) **80**
Zinfandel Russian River Valley Primitivo Reserve 1985 $12 (6/15/89) **90**
Zinfandel Sonoma County Primitivo 1988 $14 (12/31/90) **89**

HOSTATTER (Italy/North)
Chardonnay Alto Adige 1988 (NR) (9/15/89) **83**

Key to Symbols

The scores reported here are the results of blind tastings conducted by our panel of senior editors. Wines that carry the initials below are results of individual tastings.

THE WINE SPECTATOR 100-POINT SCALE 95-100—Classic, a great wine; ***90-94***—Outstanding, superior character and style; ***80-89***—Good to very good, a wine with special qualities; ***70-79***—Average, drinkable wine that may have minor flaws; ***60-69***—Below average, drinkable but not recommended; ***50-59***—Poor, undrinkable, not recommended. "+"—With a score indicates a range; used primarily with barrel tastings to indicate a preliminary score.

SPECIAL DESIGNATIONS SS—Spectator Selection, CS—Cellar Selection, BB—Best Buy, ($NA)—Price not available, (NR)—Not released.

TASTER'S INITIALS (JG)—Jim Gordon, (HS)—Harvey Steiman, (JL)—James Laube, (JS)—James Suckling, (TM)—Thomas Matthews, (TR)—Terry Robards, (PM)—Per-Henrik Mansson, (BT)—Barrel Tasting (these wines were tasted blind from barrel samples), (CA-date)—*California's Great Cabernets* by James Laube, (CH-date)—*California's Great Chardonnays* by James Laube, (VP-date)—*Vintage Port* by James Suckling.

DATE TASTED Dates in parentheses represent the issue in which the rating was published.

HOUGHTON (Australia)
Cabernet Sauvignon Frankland River Wildflower Ridge 1988 $9 (7/15/91) **78**
Cabernet Shiraz McLaren Vale Wildflower Ridge 1985 $9 (12/31/88) **88**
Chardonnay Western Australia Gold Reserve 1987 $10 (10/31/90) **69**
Chardonnay Western Australia Wildflower Ridge 1990 $9 (11/30/91) BB **84**
Chardonnay Western Australia Wildflower Ridge 1989 $9 (9/15/91) **76**
Shiraz McLaren Vale Wildflower Ridge 1985 $9 (12/31/88) **88**
White Burgundy Swan Valley 1988 $7.50 (9/30/91) BB **84**

HOUTZ (United States/California)
Cabernet Sauvignon Santa Ynez Valley 1985 $8 (12/15/89) **63**
Chardonnay Santa Ynez Valley 1986 $11 (12/15/89) **83**
Chenin Blanc Santa Ynez Valley 1987 $6 (7/31/89) **62**

HUGEL (France/Alsace)
Gewürztraminer Alsace 1990 (NR) (2/15/92) **84**
Gewürztraminer Alsace 1989 $16 (11/15/90) **85**
Gewürztraminer Alsace 1988 $14.25 (10/15/89) **83**
Gewürztraminer Alsace "R" Sélection de Grains Nobles 1989 (NR) (11/15/90) **89**
Gewürztraminer Alsace "S" Sélection de Grains Nobles 1989 (NR) (11/15/90) **96**
Gewürztraminer Alsace "T" Sélection de Grains Nobles 1989 (NR) (11/15/90) **91**
Gewürztraminer Alsace Personnelle Jubilée Réserve 1990 (NR) (2/15/92) **92**
Gewürztraminer Alsace Vendange Tardive 1990 (NR) (2/15/92) (BT) **90+**
Gewürztraminer Alsace Vendange Tardive 1989 (NR) (11/15/90) **90**
Muscat Alsace Cuvée Tradition 1990 (NR) (2/15/92) **80**
Pinot Blanc Alsace 1990 (NR) (2/15/92) **85**
Pinot Blanc Alsace 1989 (NR) (11/15/90) **86**
Pinot Blanc Alsace 1988 $9 (10/15/89) **83**
Riesling Alsace 1990 $14 (2/15/92) **91**
Riesling Alsace 1989 (NR) (11/15/90) **87**
Riesling Alsace 1988 $12.50 (10/15/89) **87**
Riesling Alsace Cuvée Tradition 1989 (NR) (11/15/90) **86**
Riesling Alsace Cuvée Tradition 1988 (NR) (10/15/89) **89**
Riesling Alsace Personnelle Jubilée Réserve 1989 (NR) (11/15/90) **90**
Riesling Alsace Personnelle Jubilée Réserve 1990 (NR) (2/15/92) **91**
Riesling Alsace Vendange Tardive 1990 (NR) (2/15/92) (BT) **90+**
Riesling Alsace Vendange Tardive 1989 (NR) (11/15/90) **90**
Tokay Pinot Gris Alsace Cuvée Tradition 1990 (NR) (2/15/92) **88**
Tokay Pinot Gris Alsace Jubilée 1990 (NR) (2/15/92) **92**
Tokay Pinot Gris Alsace Sélection de Grains Nobles 1990 (NR) (2/15/92) (BT) **90+**
Tokay Pinot Gris Alsace Sélection de Grains Nobles 1989 (NR) (11/15/90) **94**
Tokay Pinot Gris Alsace Tradition 1988 (NR) (10/15/89) **86**
Tokay Pinot Gris Alsace Vendange Tardive 1990 (NR) (2/15/92) (BT) **90+**
Tokay Pinot Gris Alsace Vendange Tardive 1989 (NR) (11/15/90) **90**

HULTGREN & SAMPERTON (United States/California)
Pinot Noir Sonoma County 1980 $5.75 (9/01/84) **55**

HUNGERFORD HILL (Australia)
Cabernet Merlot Hunter Valley 1985 $10 (2/28/90) **80**
Cabernet Sauvignon Coonawarra 1984 $11 (3/15/88) **79**
Chardonnay Hunter Valley 1986 $12 (2/15/88) **86**
Pinot Noir Hunter Valley 1986 $12 (2/28/90) **74**
Pinot Noir Hunter Valley 1984 $11 (3/15/88) **70**
Shiraz Hunter Valley 1988 $10 (2/28/90) **80**

ROBERT HUNTER (United States/California)
Blanc de Noirs Sonoma Valley Brut de Noirs 1984 $15 (10/15/88) **84**
Blanc de Noirs Sonoma Valley Brut de Noirs 1983 $15 (1/31/88) **84**
Blanc de Noirs Sonoma Valley Brut de Noirs 1982 $14 (12/31/86) **90**
Blanc de Noirs Sonoma Valley Brut de Noirs 1981 $14 (12/16/84) **87**
Blanc de Noirs Sonoma Valley Brut de Noirs Later Disgorged 1981 $14 (2/01/86) **69**

HUNTER ASHBY (United States/California)
Merlot Napa Valley 1985 $9.75 (7/31/89) **84**

HUNTER'S (New Zealand)
Chardonnay Marlborough 1986 $13 (2/15/88) **87**

WEINGUT HUPFELD (Germany)
Riesling Kabinett Rheingau Hochheimer Königin Victoria Berg 1990 $13 (12/15/91) **84**
Riesling Spätlese Rheingau Hochheimer Königin Victoria Berg 1990 $17 (12/15/91) **85**

HUSCH (United States/California)
Cabernet Sauvignon Mendocino 1986 $12 (2/15/90) **84**
Cabernet Sauvignon Mendocino La Ribera Cabernet 1985 $5 (11/30/87) BB **84**
Cabernet Sauvignon Mendocino La Ribera Vineyards 1988 $12 (6/30/91) **86**
Cabernet Sauvignon Mendocino La Ribera Vineyards 1987 $12 (11/15/90) **90**
Cabernet Sauvignon Mendocino La Ribera Vineyards 1984 $10 (12/31/87) **73**
Cabernet Sauvignon Mendocino North Field Select 1987 $16 (11/15/90) **87**
Chardonnay Anderson Valley Special Reserve 1987 $16 (6/30/90) **82**
Chardonnay Mendocino 1990 $12 (11/15/91) **84**
Chardonnay Mendocino 1989 $11 (12/31/90) **88**
Chardonnay Mendocino 1988 $11 (2/28/90) **88**
Chardonnay Mendocino 1987 $10 (11/15/88) **88**
Chardonnay Mendocino 1986 $9.75 (11/30/87) **86**
Chardonnay Mendocino 1985 $9.75 (3/31/87) **88**
Chenin Blanc Mendocino 1988 $5.75 (7/31/89) **86**
Gewürztraminer Anderson Valley 1990 $8.50 (10/31/91) **84**
Gewürztraminer Anderson Valley 1989 $8 (6/30/90) **81**
Gewürztraminer Anderson Valley 1987 $7 (9/15/88) **90**
Pinot Noir Anderson Valley 1989 $14 (11/15/91) **87**
Pinot Noir Anderson Valley 1988 $13 (12/15/90) **84**
Pinot Noir Anderson Valley 1987 $13 (2/15/90) **80**
Pinot Noir Anderson Valley 1986 $13 (10/15/89) **81**
Pinot Noir Anderson Valley 1985 $10 (6/15/88) **84**
Pinot Noir Anderson Valley 1983 $9 (5/31/88) **74**
Pinot Noir Anderson Valley 1982 $9 (8/31/86) **88**
Sauvignon Blanc Mendocino 1990 $8.50 (11/15/91) **87**

HUTCHESON (Portugal)
Vintage Port 1979 $35 (VP-1/90) **69**
Vintage Port 1970 $50 (VP-1/90) **79**

HYATT (United States/Washington)
Riesling Late Harvest Yakima Valley 1987 $8 (10/15/89) **87**

VILLA IL POGGIOLO (Italy/Tuscany)
Carmignano Riserva 1985 $16 (5/15/90) **80**

IMMICH-BATTERIEBERG (Germany)
Riesling Auslese Halbtrocken Mosel-Saar-Ruwer Enkircher Batterieberg 1990 (NR) (12/15/91) **87**
Riesling Auslese Mosel-Saar-Ruwer 1988 ($NA) (9/30/89) **96**

Riesling Auslese Mosel-Saar-Ruwer Enkircher Batterieberg 1990 (NR) (12/15/91) **91**
Riesling Spätlese Halbtrocken Mosel-Saar-Ruwer Enkircher Batterieberg 1990 (NR) (12/15/91) **88**
Riesling Spätlese Mosel-Saar-Ruwer Enkircher Batterieberg 1990 (NR) (12/15/91) **90**
Riesling Spätlese Mosel-Saar-Ruwer Enkircher Batterieberg 1988 ($NA) (9/30/89) **96**

INGLENOOK (United States/California)
Cabernet Sauvignon Napa Valley 1987 $10 (11/15/91) **86**
Cabernet Sauvignon Napa Valley 1986 Rel: $7.50 Cur: $10 (2/28/91) BB **85**
Cabernet Sauvignon Napa Valley 1985 $9.50 (3/31/89) **83**
Cabernet Sauvignon Napa Valley 1983 $9.50 (3/15/88) **80**
Cabernet Sauvignon Napa Valley 1980 $8 (2/15/84) **87**
Cabernet Sauvignon Napa Valley 1960 $135 (6/01/85) (JL) **89**
Cabernet Sauvignon Napa Valley 1958 $140 (6/01/85) (JL) **88**
Cabernet Sauvignon Napa Valley Reserve Cask 1987 ($NA) (4/15/89) (BT) **90+**
Cabernet Sauvignon Napa Valley Reserve Cask 1986 $25 (10/31/91) **91**
Cabernet Sauvignon Napa Valley Reserve Cask 1985 Rel: $16 Cur: $22 (2/15/91) CS **90**
Cabernet Sauvignon Napa Valley Reserve Cask 1984 $22 (7/31/90) **90**
Cabernet Sauvignon Napa Valley Reserve Cask 1983 Rel: $15.50 Cur: $19 (9/15/87) **88**
Cabernet Sauvignon Napa Valley Reserve Cask 1982 Rel: $22 Cur: $28 (CA-3/89) **91**
Cabernet Sauvignon Napa Valley Reserve Cask 1981 Rel: $15.50 Cur: $25 (CA-3/89) **93**
Cabernet Sauvignon Napa Valley Cask 1980 Rel: $15.50 Cur: $22 (CA-3/89) **88**
Cabernet Sauvignon Napa Valley Cask 1979 Rel: $10.75 Cur: $23 (CA-3/89) **77**
Cabernet Sauvignon Napa Valley Cask 1978 Rel: $9.25 Cur: $23 (CA-3/89) **86**
Cabernet Sauvignon Napa Valley Cask 1977 Rel: $8.75 Cur: $25 (CA-3/89) **84**
Cabernet Sauvignon Napa Valley Cask 1976 Rel: $8.75 Cur: $19 (CA-3/89) **72**
Cabernet Sauvignon Napa Valley Cask A8 1974 Rel: $9 Cur: $47 (2/15/90) (JG) **79**
Cabernet Sauvignon Napa Valley Cask 1974 Rel: $9 Cur: $47 (CA-3/89) **86**
Cabernet Sauvignon Napa Valley Cask 1973 Rel: $8 Cur: $37 (CA-3/89) **67**
Cabernet Sauvignon Napa Valley Cask 1972 Rel: $7 Cur: $42 (CA-3/89) **67**
Cabernet Sauvignon Napa Valley Cask 1971 Rel: $6.50 Cur: $50 (CA-3/89) **73**
Cabernet Sauvignon Napa Valley Cask 1970 Rel: $6.50 Cur: $90 (CA-3/89) **85**
Cabernet Sauvignon Napa Valley Cask 1969 Rel: $6.50 Cur: $75 (CA-3/89) **80**
Cabernet Sauvignon Napa Valley Cask 1968 Rel: $6 Cur: $85 (CA-3/89) **85**
Cabernet Sauvignon Napa Valley Cask 1967 Rel: $6 Cur: $84 (CA-3/89) **73**
Cabernet Sauvignon Napa Valley Cask 1966 Rel: $5.75 Cur: $115 (CA-3/89) **73**
Cabernet Sauvignon Napa Valley Cask 1960 Rel: $2.75 Cur: $125 (CA-3/89) **80**
Cabernet Sauvignon Napa Valley Cask 1958 Rel: $2.50 Cur: $250 (CA-3/89) **94**
Cabernet Sauvignon Napa Valley Cask 1955 Rel: $1.85 Cur: $400 (CA-3/89) **93**
Cabernet Sauvignon Napa Valley Cask 1949 Rel: $1.49 Cur: $750 (CA-3/89) **92**
Cabernet Sauvignon Napa Valley 1946 Rel: $1.49 Cur: $900 (CA-3/89) **87**
Cabernet Sauvignon Napa Valley 1943 Rel: $1.49 Cur: $1,000 (CA-3/89) **91**
Cabernet Sauvignon Napa Valley 1941 Rel: $1.49 Cur: $1,800 (CA-3/89) **100**
Cabernet Sauvignon Napa Valley 1941 Rel: $1.49 Cur: $1,800 (6/01/85) (JL) **95**
Cabernet Sauvignon Napa Valley 1933 Rel: $1.30 Cur: $1,600 (CA-3/89) **95**
Cabernet Sauvignon California Claret-Médoc Type 1897 ($NA) (CA-3/89) **87**
Chardonnay Napa Valley 1990 $10.25 (7/15/92) **87**
Chardonnay Napa Valley 1989 $7.50 (2/28/91) BB **87**
Chardonnay Napa Valley 1986 $9.50 (3/15/88) **80**
Chardonnay Napa Valley 1983 $9.50 (10/01/84) **79**
Chardonnay Napa Valley Reserve 1988 ($NA) (CH-4/90) **88**
Chardonnay Napa Valley Reserve 1987 $14 (5/31/90) **89**
Chardonnay Napa Valley Reserve 1986 $14.50 (CH-4/90) **88**
Chardonnay Napa Valley Reserve 1985 $14.50 (CH-4/90) **78**
Chardonnay Napa Valley Reserve 1984 Rel: $12.50 Cur: $18 (CH-4/90) **86**
Chardonnay Napa Valley Reserve 1983 Rel: $16 Cur: $19 (CH-4/90) **82**
Gewürztraminer Late Harvest Napa Valley 1986 $9.50/375ml (5/15/88) **78**
Gravion Napa Valley 1987 $9.50 (2/28/89) **89**
Gravion Napa Valley 1986 $9.50 (4/30/88) SS **91**
Merlot Napa Valley 1981 $12 (10/01/85) **77**
Merlot Napa Valley Limited Bottling 1982 $8.50 (5/16/86) **67**
Merlot Napa Valley Limited Cask Reserve Selection 1981 $12 (2/16/85) **80**
Merlot Napa Valley Reserve 1988 $11.50 (5/31/92) **83**
Merlot Napa Valley Reserve 1986 $12 (10/31/89) **81**
Merlot Napa Valley Reserve 1985 Rel: $10.50 Cur: $14 (10/15/88) SS **91**
Merlot Napa Valley Reserve 1983 $9.50 (10/15/87) **85**
Niebaum Claret Napa Valley 1987 ($NA) (4/15/89) (BT) **85+**
Niebaum Claret Napa Valley 1986 $13 (6/30/91) **74**
Niebaum Claret Napa Valley 1985 $12 (3/15/89) **82**
Niebaum Claret Napa Valley 1983 $12 (11/30/87) **88**
Pinot Noir Napa Valley 1985 $9.50 (6/15/88) **82**
Pinot Noir Napa Valley 1982 $7.50 (12/31/86) **64**
Pinot Noir Napa Valley 1981 $7.50 (2/01/85) **62**
Pinot Noir Napa Valley 1980 $6 (3/01/84) **71**
Reunion Napa Valley 1985 Rel: $35 Cur: $38 (7/15/89) **91**
Reunion Napa Valley 1984 $35 (CA-3/89) **92**
Reunion Napa Valley 1983 Rel: $33 Cur: $38 (11/30/87) CS **95**
Zinfandel Napa Valley 1986 $8 (4/30/91) **73**
Zinfandel Napa Valley 1983 $7.50 (3/15/88) **81**
Zinfandel Napa Valley 1981 $7 (2/01/85) **79**

INGLENOOK-NAVALLE (United States/California)
Chenin Blanc California NV $3.75/1.5L (7/31/89) **76**
White Zinfandel California NV $7.50/1.5L (6/15/89) **69**

INNISFREE (United States/California)
Cabernet Sauvignon Napa Valley 1988 $11 (4/30/91) **84**
Cabernet Sauvignon Napa Valley 1986 $10.50 (6/30/90) **73**
Cabernet Sauvignon Napa Valley 1985 $9 (3/15/89) **86**
Cabernet Sauvignon Napa Valley 1984 $9 (12/15/87) **68**
Cabernet Sauvignon Napa Valley 1983 $9 (11/15/86) **82**
Cabernet Sauvignon Napa Valley 1982 $9 (12/16/85) **80**
Chardonnay Carneros 1988 $12 (5/31/90) **77**
Chardonnay Napa Valley 1989 $11 (4/30/91) **83**
Chardonnay Napa Valley 1988 $12 (6/15/90) **86**
Chardonnay Napa Valley 1987 $9 (2/15/89) **80**
Chardonnay Napa Valley 1986 $9 (12/31/87) **80**
Chardonnay Napa Valley 1985 $9 (12/31/86) **92**
Chardonnay Napa Valley 1984 $9 (11/16/85) **88**
Pinot Noir California 1989 $11 (4/30/91) **84**
Sauvignon Blanc Napa Valley 1989 $7.50 (4/30/91) **82**

INNISKILLIN NAPA (United States/California)
Chardonnay Napa Valley 1988 $14 (7/15/91) **81**

VITTORIO INNOCENTI (Italy/Tuscany)
Acerone 1988 $13 (7/15/91) **80**
Acerone 1985 $9 (9/15/89) **78**
Chianti 1987 $7 (5/15/90) BB **83**
Chianti 1986 $7 (3/31/90) **77**
Vino Nobile di Montepulciano 1985 $10 (3/31/90) **77**

DOMAINE DE L'INSTITUT PASTEUR (France/Beaujolais)
Côte-de-Brouilly 1988 $10 (5/31/89) (TM) **84**

BODEGAS IRACHE (Spain)
Navarra Castillo Irache Reserva 1978 $12 (3/31/90) **81**

IRON HORSE (United States/California)
Blanc de Blancs Sonoma County Green Valley 1987 $25 (12/31/91) **89**
Blanc de Blancs Sonoma County Green Valley 1986 $22 (12/31/90) **87**
Blanc de Blancs Sonoma County Green Valley 1985 $21 (12/31/89) **85**
Blanc de Blancs Sonoma County Green Valley 1982 $16.50 (5/16/86) **78**
Blanc de Blancs Sonoma County Green Valley 1981 $18 (11/01/84) **86**
Blanc de Blancs Sonoma County Green Valley Late Disgorged 1982 $24 (12/31/87) **85**
Blanc de Noirs Sonoma County Green Valley Wedding Cuvée 1988 $24 (10/31/91) **84**
Blanc de Noirs Sonoma County Green Valley Wedding Cuvée 1986 $19 (5/31/89) **90**
Blanc de Noirs Sonoma County Green Valley Wedding Cuvée 1985 $17 (12/31/88) **86**
Blanc de Noirs Sonoma County Green Valley Wedding Cuvée 1984 $16.50 (12/31/87) **85**
Blanc de Noirs Sonoma County Green Valley Wedding Cuvée 1983 $16.50 (12/31/86) **82**
Brut Rosé Sonoma County Green Valley 1988 $28 (12/15/91) **87**
Brut Rosé Sonoma County Green Valley 1987 $28 (12/31/90) **84**
Brut Rosé Sonoma County Green Valley 1986 $23 (12/31/89) **80**
Brut Rosé Sonoma County Green Valley 1985 $20 (12/31/88) **88**
Brut Sonoma County Green Valley 1987 $21 (11/15/90) **89**
Brut Sonoma County Green Valley 1986 $20 (12/31/89) **82**
Brut Sonoma County Green Valley 1985 $17.50 (12/31/88) **83**
Brut Sonoma County Green Valley 1984 $16.50 (12/31/87) **79**
Brut Sonoma County Green Valley 1983 $16.50 (12/31/86) **87**
Brut Sonoma County Green Valley 1982 $16.50 (5/16/86) **80**
Brut Sonoma County Green Valley Late Disgorged 1986 $24 (11/30/91) **91**
Brut Sonoma County Green Valley Late Disgorged 1984 $23 (12/31/89) **80**
Brut Sonoma County Green Valley Late Disgorged Vrais Amis 1986 $25 (12/15/91) **90**
Cabernets Alexander Valley 1988 $18.50 (3/31/92) **85**
Cabernets Alexander Valley 1987 $18.50 (3/15/91) **86**
Cabernets Alexander Valley 1986 Rel: $17.50 Cur: $22 (4/15/90) **90**
Cabernets Alexander Valley 1985 Rel: $16 Cur: $21 (CA-3/89) **87**
Cabernet Sauvignon Alexander Valley 1984 Rel: $14 Cur: $20 (CA-3/89) **86**
Cabernet Sauvignon Alexander Valley 1983 Rel: $12 Cur: $18 (CA-3/89) **82**
Cabernet Sauvignon Alexander Valley 1982 Rel: $12 Cur: $18 (CA-3/89) **83**
Cabernet Sauvignon Alexander Valley 1981 Rel: $12 Cur: $18 (CA-3/89) **79**
Cabernet Sauvignon Alexander Valley 1980 Rel: $12 Cur: $22 (CA-3/89) **86**
Cabernet Sauvignon Alexander Valley 1979 Rel: $12 Cur: $25 (CA-3/89) **91**
Cabernet Sauvignon Alexander Valley 1978 Rel: $12 Cur: $32 (CA-3/89) **80**
Chardonnay Sonoma County Green Valley 1990 $18 (4/30/92) **88**
Chardonnay Sonoma County Green Valley 1989 $18 (3/31/91) **86**
Chardonnay Sonoma County Green Valley 1988 $18 (2/15/90) **81**
Chardonnay Sonoma County Green Valley 1987 $17 (1/31/89) **76**
Chardonnay Sonoma County Green Valley 1986 $12 (3/31/88) **83**
Chardonnay Sonoma County Green Valley 1985 $12.50 (7/31/87) **75**
Chardonnay Sonoma County Green Valley 1984 $12 (6/16/86) **88**
Chardonnay Sonoma County Green Valley 1983 $12 (11/16/85) **76**
Fumé Blanc Alexander Valley Barrel Fermented 1989 $11 (8/31/90) **77**
Fumé Blanc Alexander Valley Barrel Fermented 1988 $11 (11/30/89) **84**
Fumé Blanc Alexander Valley T-T Vineyards Barrel Fermented 1990 $15 (10/15/91) **89**
Pinot Noir Sonoma County Green Valley 1987 $19 (10/31/90) **72**
Pinot Noir Sonoma County Green Valley 1986 $18 (6/15/88) **92**
Pinot Noir Sonoma County Green Valley 1985 $18 (6/15/88) **77**
Pinot Noir Sonoma County Green Valley 1982 $10 (10/01/85) **76**
Zinfandel Alexander Valley 1982 $7 (10/16/84) **81**

ISOLE E OLENA (Italy/Tuscany)
Antiche Tenute 1989 $6 (10/31/90) BB **82**
Antiche Tenute 1988 $6 (9/15/89) BB **83**
Antiche Tenute 1987 $4.50 (1/31/89) BB **81**
Antiche Tenute 1986 $5 (11/15/88) **78**
Cabernet Sauvignon Collezióne de Marchi 1988 ($NA) (9/15/91) **94**
Cepparello 1988 $32 (9/15/91) **93**
Cepparello 1986 $20 (9/30/89) **86**
Cepparello 1985 $15 (11/15/88) **87**
Chardonnay Collezióne de Marchi 1989 $23 (7/15/91) **87**
Chardonnay Collezióne de Marchi 1988 $16 (9/15/89) **87**
Chianti Classico 1988 $9 (11/30/90) BB **89**
Chianti Classico 1987 Rel: $9 Cur: $12 (9/15/89) **88**
Chianti Classico 1986 $7.50 (7/31/88) **86**
Chianti Classico 1985 Rel: $7.50 Cur: $14 (5/31/88) BB **89**
Chianti Classico 1983 Rel: $5 Cur: $9 (12/15/86) BB **85**
Collezióne de Marchi l'Ermo 1988 ($NA) (9/15/91) **90**
Vin Santo NV $17/375ml (3/31/90) **93**

CHATEAU D'ISSAN (France/Bordeaux)
Margaux 1991 (NR) (5/15/92) (BT) **85+**
Margaux 1990 (NR) (5/15/92) (BT) **85+**
Margaux 1989 $27 (3/15/92) **84**
Margaux 1988 $30 (4/30/91) **88**
Margaux 1987 $20 (5/15/90) **76**
Margaux 1986 Rel: $22 Cur: $27 (6/15/89) **83**
Margaux 1985 Rel: $23 Cur: $26 (4/15/88) **88**
Margaux 1984 Rel: $10 Cur: $19 (3/31/87) **86**
Margaux 1983 Rel: $24 Cur: $32 (4/16/86) **91**

ISTITUTO AGRARIO PROVINCIALE (Italy/North)
Chardonnay Trentino 1987 $10 (9/15/89) **80**
Chardonnay Trentino 1982 $10.50 (9/15/89) **80**

PAUL JABOULET AINE (France/Rhône)
Châteauneuf-du-Pape 1983 Rel: $10 Cur: $20 (10/15/91) **85**
Châteauneuf-du-Pape Blanc Les Cèdres 1989 $22 (10/15/91) **80**
Châteauneuf-du-Pape Les Cèdres 1989 $23 (10/15/91) **88**
Châteauneuf-du-Pape Les Cèdres 1988 $23 (10/15/91) **86**
Châteauneuf-du-Pape Les Cèdres 1986 $20 (10/15/91) **87**
Châteauneuf-du-Pape Les Cèdres 1985 Rel: $20 Cur: $23 (10/15/91) **88**
Châteauneuf-du-Pape Les Cèdres 1981 $30 (10/15/91) **86**
Côte-Rôtie Les Jumelles 1985 $35 (9/30/88) **93**
Côtes du Rhône Parallele 45 1988 $6.50 (12/15/89) BB **84**
Côtes du Rhône Parallele 45 1985 $6.50 (4/30/88) **73**
Crozes-Hermitage Blanc Moute Blanche 1987 $11.50 (10/15/88) **70**
Crozes-Hermitage Domaine de Thalabert 1989 $18 (7/15/91) **90**
Crozes-Hermitage Domaine de Thalabert 1988 Rel: $13 Cur: $15 (10/15/90) **83**
Crozes-Hermitage Domaine de Thalabert 1987 $10 (3/31/90) **83**

Crozes-Hermitage Domaine de Thalabert 1986 Rel: $13.50 Cur: $16 (9/30/88) **88**
Crozes-Hermitage Domaine de Thalabert 1985 Rel: $13 Cur: $20 (9/30/88) **85**
Gigondas 1989 $18 (7/15/91) **84**
Hermitage Blanc Le Chevalier de Sterimberg 1983 $11 (5/01/86) **78**
Hermitage La Chapelle 1989 $45 (8/31/91) CS **93**
Hermitage La Chapelle 1988 $40 (3/31/91) **92**
Hermitage La Chapelle 1986 $35 (11/15/89) (JS) **89**
Hermitage La Chapelle 1985 $50 (11/15/89) (JS) **93**
Hermitage La Chapelle 1984 $25 (11/15/89) (JS) **80**
Hermitage La Chapelle 1983 $72 (11/15/89) (JS) **94**
Hermitage La Chapelle 1982 Rel: $17 Cur: $55 (11/15/89) (JS) **89**
Hermitage La Chapelle 1982 Rel: $17 Cur: $55 (11/01/84) CS **93**
Hermitage La Chapelle 1981 $40 (11/15/89) (JS) **83**
Hermitage La Chapelle 1980 $38 (11/15/89) (JS) **79**
Hermitage La Chapelle 1979 $50 (11/15/89) (JS) **86**
Hermitage La Chapelle 1978 $180 (11/15/89) (JS) **98**
Hermitage La Chapelle 1976 $100 (11/15/89) (JS) **87**
Hermitage La Chapelle 1975 $45 (11/15/89) (JS) **81**
Hermitage La Chapelle 1974 $105 (11/15/89) (JS) **85**
Hermitage La Chapelle 1973 $70 (11/15/89) (JS) **89**
Hermitage La Chapelle 1972 $125 (11/15/89) (JS) **90**
Hermitage La Chapelle 1971 $155 (11/15/89) (JS) **85**
Hermitage La Chapelle 1970 $155 (11/15/89) (JS) **93**
Hermitage La Chapelle 1969 $210 (11/15/89) (JS) **92**
Hermitage La Chapelle 1967 $71 (11/15/89) (JS) **83**
Hermitage La Chapelle 1966 $270 (11/15/89) (JS) **95**
Hermitage La Chapelle 1964 $250 (11/15/89) (JS) **93**
Hermitage La Chapelle 1962 $250 (11/15/89) (JS) **91**
Hermitage La Chapelle 1961 $600 (11/15/89) (JS) **100**
Hermitage La Chapelle 1959 $500 (11/15/89) (JS) **77**
Hermitage La Chapelle 1955 $330 (11/15/89) (JS) **88**
Hermitage La Chapelle 1953 $550 (11/15/89) (JS) **90**
Hermitage La Chapelle 1952 $480 (11/15/89) (JS) **77**
Hermitage La Chapelle 1949 $680 (11/15/89) (JS) **77**
Hermitage La Chapelle 1944 $800 (11/15/89) (JS) **93**
Hermitage La Chapelle 1937 $800 (11/15/89) (JS) **50**
St.-Joseph Le Grand Pompée 1985 $11.25 (10/15/88) **86**

JACQUART (France/Champagne)
Brut Blanc de Blancs Champagne NV $25 (12/31/90) **85**
Brut Champagne 1983 $43 (4/15/90) **88**
Brut Champagne 1982 $39 (12/31/88) **90**
Brut Champagne NV $24 (12/31/88) **83**
Brut Champagne La Cuvée Renommée 1982 $64 (12/31/88) **90**
Brut Rosé Champagne NV $38 (12/31/88) **90**
Brut Rosé Champagne La Cuvée Renommée 1982 $74 (12/31/88) **88**
Extra Dry Champagne NV $23 (12/31/88) **89**

CHATEAU JACQUES-BLANC (France/Bordeaux)
St.-Emilion Cuvée du Maitre 1988 $23 (4/30/91) **78**

JACQUESSON (France/Champagne)
Blanc de Blancs Champagne NV $45 (12/31/91) **87**
Brut Champagne Perfection 1985 ($NA) (12/31/90) **84**
Brut Champagne Perfection NV $28 (12/31/91) **87**
Brut Champagne Signature 1979 $34 (7/31/87) **93**
Brut Rosé Champagne Perfection NV $27 (12/31/88) **84**

JADE MOUNTAIN (United States/California)
Cabernet Sauvignon Alexander Valley Icaria Creek Vineyard deCarteret 1984 $8.75 (6/30/88) **75**
Grenache American NV $8.50 (3/31/92) **82**
La Provençale California 1990 $12 (3/15/92) **80**
Mourvèdre California 1990 $15 (3/15/92) **81**
Mourvèdre California Unfiltered 1990 $15 (3/15/92) **83**

LOUIS JADOT (France/Burgundy)
Auxey-Duresses Domaine du Duc de Magenta 1989 $25 (8/31/91) **88**
Auxey-Duresses Domaine du Duc de Magenta 1988 $23 (4/30/91) **88**
Bâtard-Montrachet 1989 Rel: $110 Cur: $135 (8/31/91) **93**
Bâtard-Montrachet 1986 $99 (5/31/89) **93**
Bâtard-Montrachet 1985 $88 (2/29/88) **94**
Bâtard-Montrachet 1983 $80 (2/29/88) **92**
Beaujolais Jadot 1990 $9.25 (9/30/91) BB **85**
Beaujolais Jadot 1989 $6 (11/15/90) **79**
Beaune Boucherottes 1989 $38 (1/31/92) **90**
Beaune Boucherottes 1988 $33 (3/31/91) **92**
Beaune Boucherottes 1985 $30 (3/15/88) **91**
Beaune Bressandes 1989 $42 (7/15/90) (BT) **80+**
Beaune Bressandes 1988 Rel: $26 Cur: $30 (7/15/90) (BT) **80+**
Beaune Bressandes 1986 Rel: $24 Cur: $28 (5/31/89) **90**
Beaune Bressandes 1985 $30 (3/15/88) **87**
Beaune Les Chouacheux 1989 $42 (7/15/90) (BT) **85+**
Beaune Les Chouacheux 1988 $25 (7/15/90) (BT) **90+**
Beaune Les Chouacheux 1986 $24 (5/31/89) **85**
Beaune Les Chouacheux 1985 $30 (3/15/88) **91**
Beaune Clos des Couchereaux 1989 $42 (7/15/90) (BT) **85+**
Beaune Clos des Couchereaux 1988 $33 (3/31/91) **90**
Beaune Clos des Couchereaux 1985 Rel: $30 Cur: $39 (3/15/88) **91**
Beaune Clos des Ursules 1989 $43 (2/29/92) **91**
Beaune Clos des Ursules 1988 $40 (3/31/91) **91**
Beaune Clos des Ursules 1987 Rel: $27 Cur: $29 (6/15/90) **81**
Beaune Clos des Ursules 1986 Rel: $27 Cur: $33 (3/15/89) (JS) **88**
Beaune Clos des Ursules 1985 Rel: $30 Cur: $48 (3/15/89) (JS) **91**
Beaune Clos des Ursules 1985 Rel: $30 Cur: $48 (3/15/88) SS **95**
Beaune Clos des Ursules 1983 $25 (3/15/89) (JS) **93**
Beaune Clos des Ursules 1980 $26 (3/15/89) (JS) **83**
Beaune Clos des Ursules 1978 $47 (3/15/89) (JS) **89**
Beaune Clos des Ursules 1976 $40 (3/15/89) (JS) **85**
Beaune Clos des Ursules 1973 ($NA) (3/15/89) (JS) **86**
Beaune Clos des Ursules 1971 $60 (3/15/89) (JS) **78**
Beaune Clos des Ursules 1969 $120 (3/15/89) (JS) **90**
Beaune Clos des Ursules 1966 $130 (3/15/89) (JS) **90**
Beaune Clos des Ursules 1964 ($NA) (3/15/89) (JS) **86**
Beaune Clos des Ursules 1962 ($NA) (3/15/89) (JS) **79**
Beaune Clos des Ursules 1961 ($NA) (3/15/89) (JS) **88**
Beaune Clos des Ursules 1959 ($NA) (3/15/89) (JS) **98**
Beaune Clos des Ursules 1957 ($NA) (3/15/89) (JS) **89**
Beaune Clos des Ursules 1954 ($NA) (3/15/89) (JS) **81**
Beaune Clos des Ursules 1952 ($NA) (3/15/89) (JS) **87**
Beaune Clos des Ursules 1949 ($NA) (3/15/89) (JS) **86**
Beaune Clos des Ursules 1947 ($NA) (3/15/89) (JS) **95**
Beaune Clos des Ursules 1945 ($NA) (3/15/89) (JS) **84**
Beaune Clos des Ursules 1937 ($NA) (3/15/89) (JS) **92**
Beaune Clos des Ursules 1933 ($NA) (3/15/89) (JS) **80**
Beaune Clos des Ursules 1928 ($NA) (3/15/89) (JS) **97**
Beaune Clos des Ursules 1926 ($NA) (3/15/89) (JS) **88**
Beaune Clos des Ursules 1923 ($NA) (3/15/89) (JS) **78**
Beaune Clos des Ursules 1919 ($NA) (3/15/89) (JS) **90**
Beaune Clos des Ursules 1915 ($NA) (3/15/89) (JS) **95**
Beaune Clos des Ursules 1911 ($NA) (3/15/89) (JS) **81**
Beaune Clos des Ursules 1906 ($NA) (3/15/89) (JS) **92**
Beaune Clos des Ursules 1904 ($NA) (3/15/89) (JS) **88**
Beaune Clos des Ursules 1895 ($NA) (3/15/89) (JS) **80**
Beaune Clos des Ursules 1887 ($NA) (3/15/89) (JS) **90**
Beaune Hospices de Beaune Cuvée Dames-Hospitalier 1985 $85 (3/15/88) **90**
Beaune Hospices de Beaune Cuvée Nicolas-Rolin 1985 $85 (3/15/88) **92**
Bonnes Mares 1988 $65 (3/15/91) **88**
Bonnes Mares 1987 $52 (6/15/90) **91**
Bonnes Mares 1986 $57 (4/15/89) **89**
Bonnes Mares 1985 Rel: $48 Cur: $68 (3/15/88) **95**
Bourgogne 1989 (NR) (7/15/90) (BT) **70+**
Bourgogne Blanc Chardonnay 1988 $9.50 (9/30/89) **81**
Bourgogne Blanc Chardonnay 1986 $10 (10/15/88) **78**
Bourgogne Blanc Chardonnay 1985 $9 (3/31/87) **65**
Bourgogne Pinot Noir 1989 (NR) (1/31/92) **83**
Bourgogne Pinot Noir 1988 ($NA) (7/15/90) (BT) **70+**
Bourgogne Pinot Noir Jadot 1985 $11 (4/30/88) **78**
Chambertin Clos de Bèze 1989 $105 (1/31/92) **93**
Chambertin Clos de Bèze 1988 $97 (3/15/91) **96**
Chambertin Clos de Bèze 1987 $65 (7/15/90) **89**
Chambertin Clos de Bèze 1986 $63 (7/15/89) **90**
Chambertin Clos de Bèze 1985 Rel: $66 Cur: $79 (3/15/88) **89**
Chambolle-Musigny 1986 $30 (7/15/89) **78**
Chambolle-Musigny 1985 Rel: $33 Cur: $39 (5/15/88) **91**
Chapelle-Chambertin 1989 (NR) (7/15/90) (BT) **85+**
Chapelle-Chambertin 1988 $75 (3/15/91) **93**
Chapelle-Chambertin 1985 $54 (3/15/88) **90**
Chassagne-Montrachet 1989 $39 (8/31/91) **89**
Chassagne-Montrachet 1986 $32 (5/31/89) **91**
Chassagne-Montrachet 1985 $32 (2/29/88) **91**
Chassagne-Montrachet 1984 $30 (2/29/88) **81**
Chassagne-Montrachet 1983 $28 (2/29/88) **89**
Chassagne-Montrachet Morgeot 1984 $38 (2/29/88) **88**
Chassagne-Montrachet Morgeot 1983 $34 (2/29/88) **86**
Chassagne-Montrachet Morgeot Clos de la Chapelle Domaine du Duc de Magenta 1989 $50 (8/31/91) **90**
Chassagne-Montrachet Morgeot Clos de la Chapelle Domaine du Duc de Magenta 1988 $43 (4/30/91) **89**
Chassagne-Montrachet Morgeot Clos de la Chapelle Domaine du Duc de Magenta 1986 $41 (5/31/89) **85**
Chassagne-Montrachet Morgeot Clos de la Chapelle Domaine du Duc de Magenta 1985 $38 (2/29/88) **89**
Chassagne-Montrachet Rouge Morgeot Clos de la Chapelle Domaine du Duc de Magenta 1989 (NR) (7/15/90) (BT) **80+**
Chassagne-Montrachet Rouge Morgeot Clos de la Chapelle Domaine du Duc de Magenta 1988 $20 (3/31/91) **85**
Chassagne-Montrachet Rouge Morgeot Clos de la Chapelle Domaine du Duc de Magenta 1986 $18 (10/31/89) **77**
Chassagne-Montrachet Rouge Morgeot Clos de la Chapelle Domaine du Duc de Magenta 1985 $19 (4/15/88) **83**
Chevalier-Montrachet Les Demoiselles 1988 $127 (5/31/91) **92**
Chevalier-Montrachet Les Demoiselles 1985 Rel: $150 Cur: $168 (2/29/88) **94**
Chevalier-Montrachet Les Demoiselles 1984 $95 (2/29/88) **92**
Clos Vougeot 1989 $74 (1/31/92) **87**
Clos Vougeot 1988 $68 (11/15/91) **73**
Clos Vougeot 1986 $50 (4/15/89) **87**
Clos Vougeot 1985 Rel: $53 Cur: $85 (3/31/88) **82**
Corton Pougets 1989 $64 (1/31/92) **93**
Corton Pougets 1988 $61 (3/31/91) **93**
Corton Pougets 1987 Rel: $39 Cur: $45 (6/15/90) **87**
Corton Pougets 1986 $42 (4/30/89) **86**
Corton Pougets 1985 $47 (3/15/88) **89**
Corton-Charlemagne 1989 $114 (8/31/91) **89**
Corton-Charlemagne 1988 $98 (4/30/91) **93**
Corton-Charlemagne 1986 $92 (5/31/89) **92**
Côte de Beaune-Villages 1989 $18 (1/31/92) **84**
Côte de Beaune-Villages 1988 $14 (7/15/90) (BT) **75+**
Côte de Beaune-Villages 1986 $15 (6/15/89) **78**
Côte de Beaune-Villages 1985 $17 (4/15/88) **79**
Fixin 1989 $21 (1/31/92) **88**
Gevrey-Chambertin 1986 $25 (7/15/89) **77**
Gevrey-Chambertin Clos St.-Jacques 1989 $65 (1/31/92) **90**
Gevrey-Chambertin Clos St.-Jacques 1988 $52 (3/15/91) **88**
Gevrey-Chambertin Clos St.-Jacques 1986 $44 (7/15/89) **84**
Gevrey-Chambertin Clos St.-Jacques 1985 $45 (3/31/88) **94**
Gevrey-Chambertin Estournelles St.-Jacques 1988 $50 (3/15/91) **91**
Gevrey-Chambertin Estournelles St.-Jacques 1986 $40 (7/15/89) **87**

Key to Symbols

The scores reported here are the results of blind tastings conducted by our panel of senior editors. Wines that carry the initials below are results of individual tastings.

THE WINE SPECTATOR 100-POINT SCALE 95-100—Classic, a great wine; *90-94*—Outstanding, superior character and style; *80-89*—Good to very good, a wine with special qualities; *70-79*—Average, drinkable wine that may have minor flaws; *60-69*—Below average, drinkable but not recommended; *50-59*—Poor, undrinkable, not recommended. "+"—With a score indicates a range; used primarily with barrel tastings to indicate a preliminary score.

SPECIAL DESIGNATIONS SS—Spectator Selection, CS—Cellar Selection, BB—Best Buy, ($NA)—Price not available, (NR)—Not released.

TASTER'S INITIALS (JG)—Jim Gordon, (HS)—Harvey Steiman, (JL)—James Laube, (JS)—James Suckling, (TM)—Thomas Matthews, (TR)—Terry Robards, (PM)—Per-Henrik Mansson, (BT)—Barrel Tasting (these wines were tasted blind from barrel samples), (CA-date)—*California's Great Cabernets* by James Laube, (CH-date)—*California's Great Chardonnays* by James Laube, (VP-date)—*Vintage Port* by James Suckling.

DATE TASTED Dates in parentheses represent the issue in which the rating was published.

Gevrey-Chambertin Estournelles St.-Jacques 1985 $41 (3/31/88) **86**
Griotte-Chambertin 1988 $75 (3/15/91) **94**
Griotte-Chambertin 1987 $50 (7/15/90) **80**
Mâcon-Villages La Fontaine 1988 $9 (9/15/89) **84**
Marsannay 1986 $11 (6/15/89) **77**
Mazis-Chambertin 1987 $50 (5/31/90) **92**
Meursault 1989 $35 (8/31/91) **89**
Meursault Les Perrières 1989 ($NA) (8/31/91) **91**
Meursault Les Perrières 1988 $57 (4/30/91) **90**
Monthélie 1989 $21 (1/31/92) **87**
Montrachet 1973 $300 (2/29/88) **98**
Morgon 1990 $12 (9/30/91) **83**
Moulin-à-Vent 1990 $15 (9/30/91) **79**
Musigny Le Musigny 1989 $100 (7/15/90) (BT) **85+**
Musigny Le Musigny 1988 Rel: $82 Cur: $100 (7/15/90) (BT) **85+**
Musigny Le Musigny 1986 $70 (4/15/89) **77**
Musigny Le Musigny 1985 $74 (3/31/88) **88**
Nuits-St.-Georges 1989 (NR) (7/15/90) (BT) **80+**
Nuits-St.-Georges 1988 $27 (7/15/90) (BT) **75+**
Nuits-St.-Georges 1985 $30 (4/15/88) **91**
Nuits-St.-Georges Les Boudots 1988 $49 (2/28/91) **88**
Nuits-St.-Georges Les Boudots 1986 $38 (4/30/89) **85**
Nuits-St.-Georges Les Boudots 1985 $42 (3/15/88) **75**
Nuits-St.-Georges Clos des Corvées 1989 $56 (1/31/92) **85**
Nuits-St.-Georges Clos des Corvées 1988 $49 (2/28/91) **89**
Nuits-St.-Georges Clos des Corvées 1987 $35 (4/30/90) **84**
Nuits-St.-Georges Clos des Corvées 1986 $37 (4/30/89) **83**
Nuits-St.-Georges Clos des Corvées 1985 $44 (3/15/88) **96**
Pernand-Vergelesses 1989 (NR) (7/15/90) (BT) **80+**
Pernand-Vergelesses 1988 $16 (7/15/90) (BT) **80+**
Pernand-Vergelesses 1985 $18 (4/15/88) **85**
Pernand-Vergelesses Blanc 1989 ($NA) (8/31/91) **87**
Pernand-Vergelesses Blanc 1988 $21 (4/30/91) **85**
Pernand-Vergelesses Clos de la Croix de Pierre 1989 $21 (1/31/92) **86**
Pernand-Vergelesses Clos de la Croix de Pierre 1988 $17 (3/31/91) **86**
Pernand-Vergelesses Clos de la Croix de Pierre 1987 $15 (11/15/90) **79**
Pernand-Vergelesses Clos de la Croix de Pierre 1986 $17 (7/31/89) **85**
Pernand-Vergelesses Clos de la Croix de Pierre 1985 $18 (4/15/88) **83**
Pommard 1988 $36 (3/31/91) **83**
Pommard Chaponnières 1985 $39 (3/15/88) **91**
Pommard Grands Epenottes 1989 $50 (1/31/92) **88**
Pommard Grands Epenottes 1988 $38 (3/31/91) **86**
Pouilly-Fuissé 1988 $16 (9/30/89) **85**
Pouilly-Fuissé 1985 $19 (3/31/87) **90**
Pouilly-Fuissé Cuvée Réserve Spéciale 1989 $21 (7/31/91) **87**
Puligny-Montrachet 1989 $36 (1/31/92) **86**
Puligny-Montrachet 1988 $36 (5/31/91) **87**
Puligny-Montrachet 1985 $33 (2/29/88) **90**
Puligny-Montrachet 1984 $30 (2/29/88) **89**
Puligny-Montrachet 1983 $25 (2/29/88) **66**
Puligny-Montrachet Clos de la Garenne Domaine du Duc de Magenta 1989 $61 (8/31/91) **93**
Puligny-Montrachet Clos de la Garenne Domaine du Duc de Magenta 1988 $52 (4/30/91) **91**
Puligny-Montrachet Clos de la Garenne Domaine du Duc de Magenta 1986 $57 (5/31/89) **91**
Puligny-Montrachet Clos de la Garenne Domaine du Duc de Magenta 1985 $50 (2/29/88) **92**
Puligny-Montrachet Les Combettes 1989 $67 (8/31/91) **90**
Puligny-Montrachet Les Combettes 1985 $45 (2/29/88) **93**
Puligny-Montrachet Les Combettes 1984 $37 (2/29/88) **89**
Puligny-Montrachet Les Combettes 1983 $34 (2/29/88) **87**
Ruchottes-Chambertin 1988 $75 (3/15/91) **91**
St.-Véran 1984 $9 (3/31/87) **81**
St.-Véran La Chapelle 1989 $14 (8/31/91) **78**
Santenay Clos de Malte 1989 (NR) (7/15/90) (BT) **80+**
Savigny-lès-Beaune Blanc 1988 $24 (4/30/91) **80**
Vosne-Romanée 1989 $40 (1/31/92) **89**
Vosne-Romanée 1985 $33 (3/31/88) **86**
Vosne-Romanée Les Suchots 1988 $63 (8/31/91) **82**

JAEGER (United States/California)
Merlot Napa Valley Inglewood Vineyard 1987 $15 (5/31/92) **81**
Merlot Napa Valley Inglewood Vineyard 1986 $15 (5/31/92) **88**
Merlot Napa Valley Inglewood Vineyard 1985 $16 (2/15/90) **89**
Merlot Napa Valley Inglewood Vineyard 1983 $14 (2/29/88) **87**

JAFFELIN (France/Burgundy)
Aloxe-Corton 1989 $27 (1/31/92) **89**
Auxey-Duresses 1989 $16 (8/31/91) **85**
Auxey-Duresses 1985 $13 (3/31/87) **79**
Auxey-Duresses 1983 $11 (11/01/85) **79**
Auxey-Duresses Rouge 1989 $16 (1/31/92) **85**
Bâtard-Montrachet 1990 $75 (4/15/92) **85**
Bâtard-Montrachet 1989 $110 (8/31/91) **90**
Bâtard-Montrachet 1984 $77 (6/01/86) **84**
Beaujolais-Villages Domaine de Riberolles 1987 $7 (4/15/89) **79**
Beaune Les Bressandes 1989 $28 (1/31/92) **85**
Beaune Les Champimonts 1989 $27 (1/31/92) **89**
Beaune Les Champimonts 1988 $30 (7/15/90) (BT) **75+**
Beaune Les Champimonts 1983 $18 (9/15/86) **68**
Beaune du Châpitre 1986 $18 (12/31/88) **77**
Beaune Hospices de Beaune Cuvée Clos des Avaux 1986 $65 (12/31/88) **85**
Bienvenues-Bâtard-Montrachet 1989 $75 (8/31/91) **91**
Bourgogne Blanc 1988 $9 (3/31/90) **85**
Bourgogne Blanc Chardonnay 1990 $9 (7/31/91) BB **81**
Bourgogne Blanc Chardonnay du Châpitre 1989 $9 (8/31/91) **80**
Bourgogne Blanc Chardonnay du Châpitre 1987 $9.50 (3/15/89) **76**
Bourgogne Blanc Chardonnay du Châpitre 1985 $9.50 (3/31/87) **80**
Bourgogne Blanc Chardonnay du Châpitre 1983 $6.25 (1/01/85) **74**
Bourgogne Pinot Noir 1989 $10 (1/31/92) **83**
Chablis Fourchaume 1983 $14 (10/16/85) **86**
Chambertin Le Chambertin 1986 $65 (12/31/88) **89**
Chambertin Le Chambertin 1983 $48 (4/16/86) **93**
Chambolle-Musigny 1989 $28 (1/31/92) **89**
Chambolle-Musigny 1988 $32 (12/31/90) **88**
Chambolle-Musigny 1983 $21 (3/16/86) **81**
Charmes-Chambertin 1989 $66 (1/31/92) **87**
Charmes-Chambertin 1988 $68 (7/15/90) (BT) **90+**
Charmes-Chambertin 1986 $45 (12/31/88) **77**
Chassagne-Montrachet 1990 $28 (4/15/92) **81**
Chassagne-Montrachet 1989 $40 (8/31/91) **87**
Chassagne-Montrachet 1987 $30 (3/15/89) **83**
Chassagne-Montrachet Les Caillerets 1989 $30 (8/31/91) **86**
Chassagne-Montrachet Les Caillerets 1983 $20 (6/01/85) **91**
Chassagne-Montrachet Rouge 1989 $18 (1/31/92) **86**
Chassagne-Montrachet Rouge 1988 $20 (7/15/90) (BT) **80+**
Chassagne-Montrachet Les Vergers 1990 $32 (4/15/92) **85**
Chassagne-Montrachet Les Vergers 1989 $30 (8/31/91) **87**
Chorey-Côte-de-Beaune 1989 $13 (1/31/92) **75**
Clos St.-Denis 1989 $53 (1/31/92) **94**
Clos de Vougeot 1989 $60 (1/31/92) **89**
Clos de Vougeot 1986 $45 (12/31/88) **77**
Clos de Vougeot 1985 $49 (6/15/88) **96**
Corton 1989 $54 (1/31/92) **91**
Corton 1986 $45 (12/31/88) **87**
Corton 1983 Rel: $33 Cur: $45 (4/01/86) CS **91**
Corton-Charlemagne 1990 $55 (4/15/92) **84**
Corton-Charlemagne 1989 $75 (8/31/91) **94**
Corton-Charlemagne 1984 $60 (5/01/86) **86**
Côte de Beaune-Villages 1989 $14 (1/31/92) **82**
Côte de Nuits-Villages 1989 $15 (1/31/92) **84**
Echézeaux 1989 $60 (1/31/92) **91**
Echézeaux 1986 $45 (12/31/88) **86**
Echézeaux 1983 $30 (5/01/86) **90**
Fixin 1989 $18 (1/31/92) **85**
Gevrey-Chambertin 1989 $30 (1/31/92) **88**
Gevrey-Chambertin 1988 $25 (8/31/91) **88**
Gevrey-Chambertin 1986 $49 (2/28/89) **85**
Gevrey-Chambertin 1983 $17 (10/01/85) **77**
Gevrey-Chambertin Lavaux St.-Jacques 1989 $40 (1/31/92) **81**
Ladoix Côte de Beaune 1989 $13 (1/31/92) **85**
Meursault 1990 $24 (5/15/92) **84**
Meursault 1989 $25 (8/31/91) **85**
Meursault 1987 $25 (3/15/89) **83**
Meursault 1983 $17 (6/01/85) **86**
Meursault Les Bouchères 1989 $27 (8/31/91) **81**
Monthélie 1989 $19 (1/31/92) **87**
Monthélie 1988 $21 (7/15/90) (BT) **80+**
Monthélie 1986 $15 (6/15/89) **79**
Montrachet Le Montrachet 1989 $150 (8/31/91) **96**
Morey-St.-Denis Les Ruchots 1989 $30 (1/31/92) **86**
Morey-St.-Denis Les Ruchots 1988 $31 (7/15/90) (BT) **80+**
Nuits-St.-Georges 1989 $27 (1/31/92) **83**
Nuits-St.-Georges 1986 $28 (2/28/89) **80**
Nuits-St.-Georges 1983 $19 (9/15/86) **72**
Nuits-St.-Georges Les Damodes 1989 $36 (1/31/92) **90**
Pernand-Vergelesses 1989 $19 (1/31/92) **86**
Pommard 1989 $33 (1/31/92) **85**
Pommard 1986 $26 (4/30/89) **79**
Pommard 1985 $38 (3/15/88) **89**
Pommard 1983 $19 (9/15/86) **81**
Pouilly-Fuissé 1990 $18 (7/31/91) **83**
Pouilly-Fuissé 1985 $19 (4/15/87) **89**
Pouilly-Fuissé 1984 $19 (3/31/87) **89**
Puligny-Montrachet 1990 $28 (5/15/92) **87**
Puligny-Montrachet 1989 $42 (8/31/91) **83**
Puligny-Montrachet 1985 $33 (4/15/87) **92**
Puligny-Montrachet 1983 $21 (2/01/86) **92**
Puligny-Montrachet Champ Canet 1986 $40 (12/15/88) **85**
Puligny-Montrachet Les Folatières 1983 $20 (6/16/85) **90**
Puligny-Montrachet La Garenne 1990 $34 (4/15/92) **85**
Puligny-Montrachet La Garenne 1989 $30 (8/31/91) **91**
Romanée-St.-Vivant 1989 $80 (1/31/92) **91**
Rully 1986 $13 (6/15/89) **77**
Rully Blanc 1987 $13 (3/15/89) **82**
Rully Blanc 1986 $12 (2/15/88) **87**
Rully Blanc 1985 $11 (3/31/87) **88**
Rully Blanc Barrel Fermented 1989 $16 (8/31/91) **82**
Rully Blanc Barrel Fermented 1988 $13 (3/15/90) **86**
St.-Aubin 1989 $16 (8/31/91) **83**
St.-Aubin 1985 $13 (3/31/87) **84**
St.-Aubin Rouge 1989 $14 (1/31/92) **84**
St.-Romain 1989 $18 (8/31/91) **82**
St.-Véran 1989 $14 (7/31/91) **80**
St.-Véran 1985 $9.25 (3/31/87) **88**
Santenay 1989 $17 (1/31/92) **85**
Santenay Blanc Les Gravières 1989 $25 (8/31/91) **88**
Santenay La Maladière 1989 $20 (1/31/92) **82**
Santenay La Maladière 1988 $21 (8/31/91) **84**
Santenay La Maladière 1985 $22 (3/15/88) **84**
Savigny-lès-Beaune 1989 $18 (1/31/92) **85**
Volnay 1989 $29 (1/31/92) **89**
Volnay 1988 $30 (8/31/91) **88**
Volnay 1986 $27 (4/30/89) **86**
Volnay 1985 $30 (3/15/88) **88**
Volnay 1983 $17 (10/16/85) **92**
Vosne-Romanée 1989 $29 (1/31/92) **86**
Vosne-Romanée 1986 $30 (2/28/89) **79**

CHATEAU JALOUSIE-BEAULIEU (France/Bordeaux)
Bordeaux Supérieur 1985 $7 (12/31/88) **70**

MARCUS JAMES (Other/Brazil)
White Zinfandel Aurora Valley 1987 $4 (6/15/89) **78**

JAMESPORT (United States/New York)
Cabernet Sauvignon North Fork of Long Island North House 1987 $10 (6/30/91) (TM) **78**
Merlot North Fork of Long Island 1986 $9 (6/30/91) (TM) **72**

JOSEPH JAMET (France/Rhône)
Côte-Rôtie 1985 $33 (4/15/89) **88**

DOMAINE DE LA JANASSE (France/Rhône)
Châteauneuf-du-Pape Blanc 1989 $20 (11/15/91) **85**

PIERRE JANNY (France/Burgundy)
Mâcon-Villages Domaine du Prieuré 1987 $7 (1/31/89) **74**

JASMIN (France/Rhône)
Côte-Rôtie 1988 $32 (12/31/90) **89**

Côte-Rôtie 1987 $30 (6/30/90) **90**

CHATEAU DE JAU (France/Other)
Côtes du Roussillon 1988 $6 (8/31/91) **75**

HENRI JAYER (France/Burgundy)
Echézeaux 1988 $140 (5/15/91) (HS) **94**
Echézeaux 1987 ($NA) (5/15/91) (HS) **87**
Echézeaux 1986 $120 (5/15/91) (HS) **88**
Echézeaux 1985 $330 (5/15/91) (HS) **96**
Echézeaux 1982 Rel: $41 Cur: $160 (6/16/86) CS **94**
Echézeaux 1981 $130 (5/15/91) (HS) **82**
Echézeaux 1980 $220 (5/15/91) (HS) **89**
Echézeaux 1979 $200 (5/15/91) (HS) **92**
Echézeaux 1978 $380 (5/15/91) (HS) **91**
Echézeaux 1976 ($NA) (5/15/91) (HS) **90**
Echézeaux 1972 ($NA) (5/15/91) (HS) **81**
Echézeaux 1970 ($NA) (5/15/91) (HS) **80**
Echézeaux 1969 ($NA) (5/15/91) (HS) **91**
Richebourg 1987 ($NA) (5/15/91) (HS) **87**
Richebourg 1986 $330 (5/15/91) (HS) **93**
Richebourg 1985 $510 (5/15/91) (HS) **99**
Richebourg 1980 $290 (5/15/91) (HS) **88**
Richebourg 1979 $300 (5/15/91) (HS) **93**
Vosne-Romanée Les Beaumonts 1988 ($NA) (5/15/91) (HS) **89**
Vosne-Romanée Les Brûlées 1987 ($NA) (5/15/91) (HS) **85**
Vosne-Romanée Les Brûlées 1986 $105 (5/15/91) (HS) **90**
Vosne-Romanée Les Brûlées 1985 $240 (5/15/91) (HS) **93**
Vosne-Romanée Les Brûlées 1980 $185 (5/15/91) (HS) **88**
Vosne-Romanée Les Brûlées 1979 $150 (5/15/91) (HS) **88**
Vosne-Romanée Les Brûlées 1978 $280 (5/15/91) (HS) **92**
Vosne-Romanée Les Brûlées 1976 ($NA) (5/15/91) (HS) **81**
Vosne-Romanée Les Brûlées 1972 ($NA) (5/15/91) (HS) **87**
Vosne-Romanée Cros Parantoux 1988 ($NA) (5/15/91) (HS) **93**
Vosne-Romanée Cros Parantoux 1987 ($NA) (5/15/91) (HS) **86**
Vosne-Romanée Cros Parantoux 1986 $100 (5/15/91) (HS) **87**
Vosne-Romanée Cros Parantoux 1985 $240 (5/15/91) (HS) **95**
Vosne-Romanée Cros Parantoux 1980 $175 (5/15/91) (HS) **89**
Vosne-Romanée Cros Parantoux 1978 $200 (5/15/91) (HS) **94**

J. JAYER (France/Burgundy)
Echézeaux 1988 $100 (3/15/91) **91**
Nuits-St.-Georges Les Lavières 1985 $38 (3/15/88) **88**
Vosne-Romanée Les Rouges 1985 $44 (3/15/88) **80**

JAYER-GILLES (France/Burgundy)
Bourgogne Hautes Côtes de Beaune 1989 $24 (8/31/91) **86**
Bourgogne Hautes Côtes de Beaune 1988 $22 (6/15/91) **84**
Bourgogne Hautes Côtes de Beaune Rouge 1989 $24 (1/31/92) **84**
Bourgogne Hautes Côtes de Beaune Rouge 1988 $26 (5/15/91) **88**
Bourgogne Hautes Côtes de Nuits 1989 $24 (1/31/92) **86**
Bourgogne Hautes Côtes de Nuits Blanc 1989 $18 (8/31/91) **85**
Côte de Nuits-Villages 1989 $32 (1/31/92) **87**
Echézeaux 1989 $101 (1/31/92) **94**
Echézeaux 1982 $23 (11/01/85) **58**

PIERRE JEAN (France/Bordeaux)
Bordeaux Blanc Blanc de Blancs 1990 $7 (6/15/91) BB **81**
St.-Emilion 1988 $10 (6/30/91) BB **85**

JEAN-MARIE (France/Champagne)
Brut Blanc de Blancs Champagne NV (NR) (12/31/90) **77**
Brut Champagne 1985 ($NA) (12/31/90) **75**
Brut Champagne NV (NR) (12/31/91) **83**

JEKEL (United States/California)
Cabernet Sauvignon Arroyo Seco 1986 $13 (11/15/90) **83**
Cabernet Sauvignon Arroyo Seco Home Vineyard 1980 $25 (2/01/86) **63**
Cabernet Sauvignon Monterey 1984 $12 (7/31/89) **63**
Cabernet Sauvignon Monterey 1983 $8 (2/15/89) **67**
Cabernet Sauvignon Monterey 1982 $11 (1/31/87) **71**
Cabernet Sauvignon Monterey Home Vineyard Private Reserve 1982 $20 (2/01/86) **69**
Cabernet Sauvignon Monterey Home Vineyard Private Reserve 1981 $20 (2/01/86) **76**
Cabernet Sauvignon Monterey Home Vineyard Private Reserve 1979 $18 (2/01/86) **77**
Cabernet Sauvignon Monterey Home Vineyard Private Reserve 1978 $16 (2/01/86) **70**
Chardonnay Arroyo Seco 1989 $12 (6/30/92) **80**
Chardonnay Arroyo Seco 1988 $11 (4/15/90) **87**
Chardonnay Arroyo Seco 1986 $11 (4/30/89) **76**
Chardonnay Arroyo Seco 1985 $10.50 (12/31/88) **71**
Chardonnay Arroyo Seco 1984 $10.50 (5/31/87) **83**
Chardonnay Arroyo Seco 1983 $10 (4/01/86) **66**
Chardonnay Arroyo Seco 1982 $10 (1/01/84) **88**
Chardonnay Arroyo Seco 1981 $11 (6/01/86) **86**
Chardonnay Arroyo Seco Home Vineyard Private Reserve 1985 $18 (4/15/89) **91**
Chardonnay Arroyo Seco Home Vineyard Private Reserve 1984 $16 (11/30/87) **79**
Chardonnay Arroyo Seco Home Vineyard Private Reserve 1982 $14 (10/01/85) **93**
Chardonnay Arroyo Seco Home Vineyard Private Reserve 1981 $15 (6/01/86) **84**
Pinot Blanc Arroyo Seco Arroyo Blanc 1985 $6 (6/15/89) BB **83**
Pinot Blanc Arroyo Seco Home Vineyard 1984 $8 (3/31/89) **81**
Pinot Noir Arroyo Seco Home Vineyard 1982 Rel: $9 Cur: $20 (6/30/87) **57**
Riesling Late Harvest Arroyo Seco Gravelstone Vineyard 1987 $13.50/375ml (2/28/89) **77**
White Riesling Arroyo Seco 1987 $6.75 (2/28/89) **75**
White Riesling Arroyo Seco Gravelstone Vineyard Dry Styled 1987 $11.50 (2/28/89) **85**
White Riesling Arroyo Seco Gravelstone Vineyard Sweet Styled 1987 $11.50 (2/28/89) **90**

JEPSON (United States/California)
Blanc de Blancs Mendocino 1986 $16 (4/30/91) **86**
Brut Mendocino 1985 $16 (12/31/88) **82**
Chardonnay Mendocino 1989 $14 (7/15/91) **79**
Chardonnay Mendocino 1988 $12.50 (4/30/91) **85**
Chardonnay Mendocino 1986 $12 (11/15/88) **89**
Chardonnay Mendocino 1985 $12 (1/31/88) **92**
Chardonnay Mendocino Estate Reserve 1988 $21 (11/30/91) **91**
Chardonnay Mendocino Vintage Reserve 1986 $15 (5/31/89) **80**
Sauvignon Blanc Mendocino 1987 $7 (7/31/89) **66**

JERMANN (Italy/North)
Chardonnay 1989 $18 (3/31/91) **80**
Chardonnay 1987 $15 (9/15/89) **85**
Chardonnay 1985 $12 (9/15/89) **91**
Chardonnay Dreams 1988 $40 (4/30/90) **86**
Chardonnay Dreams NV $34 (3/31/90) **92**
Moscato Rosa del FVG Vigna Bellina 1989 $26 (3/15/91) **81**
Pinot Bianco 1989 $18 (4/15/91) **87**
Pinot Grigio 1989 $18 (3/31/91) **82**
Sauvignon 1989 $18 (4/15/91) **84**
Vinnae da Vinnaioli 1989 $18 (4/15/91) **84**
Vintage Tunina 1989 $35 (4/15/91) **88**

JESSIAUME PERE & FILS (France/Burgundy)
Santenay Les Gravières 1988 $21 (3/31/91) **86**

DE JESSY (France/Other)
Extra Dry NV $9 (6/15/90) **81**

FRANCOIS JOBARD (France/Burgundy)
Meursault 1987 $25 (7/15/90) **76**
Meursault 1986 $30 (9/30/89) **82**
Meursault Blagny 1987 $37 (7/15/90) **85**
Meursault Les Charmes 1987 $34 (8/31/90) **80**
Meursault Les Genevrières 1987 $34 (8/31/90) **75**
Meursault Poruzot 1987 $40 (7/15/90) **76**
Meursault Poruzot 1985 $28 (11/15/87) **73**

DOMAINE JOBLOT (France/Burgundy)
Givry Clos du Cellier aux Moines 1989 $25 (1/31/92) **90**
Givry Clos du Cellier aux Moines 1988 $19 (12/31/90) **84**
Givry Clos de la Servoisine 1989 $25 (1/31/92) **88**

SCHLOSS JOHANNISBERG (Germany)
Riesling Auslese Rheingau 1990 $40 (12/15/91) **90**
Riesling Kabinett Rheingau 1990 $18 (12/15/91) **83**
Riesling Kabinett Rheingau 1989 ($NA) (12/15/90) **86**
Riesling Kabinett Rheingau Rotlack 1983 $12 (8/01/85) **88**
Riesling Qualitätswein Rheingau 1990 $12 (12/15/91) **86**
Riesling Qualitätswein Rheingau 1989 ($NA) (12/15/90) **84**
Riesling Spätlese Rheingau 1990 $25 (12/15/91) **88**
Riesling Spätlese Rheingau Grunlack 1983 $20 (8/01/85) **90**
Riesling Spätlese Trocken Rheingau 1990 $25 (12/15/91) **83**

JOHNSON TURNBULL (United States/California)
Cabernet Sauvignon Napa Valley 1988 $16 (11/15/91) **84**
Cabernet Sauvignon Napa Valley 1987 $16 (11/15/90) **80**
Cabernet Sauvignon Napa Valley Vineyard Selection 82 1986 Rel: $14.50 Cur: $25 (8/31/89) **95**
Cabernet Sauvignon Napa Valley 1985 Rel: $14.50 Cur: $22 (CA-3/89) **83**
Cabernet Sauvignon Napa Valley 1984 Rel: $14.50 Cur: $23 (CA-3/89) **90**
Cabernet Sauvignon Napa Valley 1983 Rel: $12.50 Cur: $21 (CA-3/89) **88**
Cabernet Sauvignon Napa Valley 1982 Rel: $12.50 Cur: $20 (CA-3/89) **82**
Cabernet Sauvignon Napa Valley 1981 Rel: $12 Cur: $31 (CA-3/89) **87**
Cabernet Sauvignon Napa Valley 1980 Rel: $12 Cur: $29 (CA-3/89) **87**
Cabernet Sauvignon Napa Valley 1979 Rel: $10.50 Cur: $31 (CA-3/89) **85**
Cabernet Sauvignon Napa Valley Vineyard Selection 67 1991 (NR) (5/15/92) (BT) **85+**
Cabernet Sauvignon Napa Valley Vineyard Selection 67 1990 (NR) (5/15/91) (BT) **90+**
Cabernet Sauvignon Napa Valley Vineyard Selection 67 1989 (NR) (5/15/91) (BT) **85+**
Cabernet Sauvignon Napa Valley Vineyard Selection 67 1988 $15 (5/15/90) (BT) **85+**
Cabernet Sauvignon Napa Valley Vineyard Selection 67 1987 $22 (6/30/91) **89**
Cabernet Sauvignon Napa Valley Vineyard Selection 67 1986 Rel: $20 Cur: $35 (4/15/90) **86**
Chardonnay Knights Valley Teviot Springs Vineyard 1987 $12.50 (9/15/89) **70**

JOHNSTONE (Australia)
Cabernet Shiraz Hunter Valley 1988 $6.50 (7/15/91) **75**
Chardonnay Hunter River Valley 1989 $7 (5/31/92) BB **84**

JEAN-LUC JOILLOT (France/Burgundy)
Bourgogne Tastevinage 1985 $15 (6/30/88) **84**

JEHAN JOLIET (France/Burgundy)
Fixin Clos de la Perrière 1985 $25 (7/31/88) **90**

PASCAL JOLIVET (France/Loire)
Pouilly-Fumé Cuvée Pascal Jolivet 1987 $29 (9/15/90) **88**
Sancerre 1988 $15.50 (9/15/90) **84**
Sancerre Domaine du Colombier 1988 $18 (9/15/90) **82**

A. JOLY (France/Loire)
Savennières Clos de la Coulée de Serrant 1987 $36 (2/15/89) (TM) **86**
Savennières Clos de la Coulée de Serrant 1986 $38 (7/15/89) **87**
Savennières Clos de la Coulée de Serrant 1982 ($NA) (2/15/89) (TM) **87**
Savennières Clos de la Coulée de Serrant 1976 ($NA) (2/15/89) (TM) **93**

N. JOLY (France/Loire)
Savennières Clos de la Coulée de Serrant 1989 $33 (11/30/90) **91**

CHATEAU JONQUEYRES (France/Bordeaux)
Bordeaux Supérieur Cuvée Vieilles Vignes 1988 $12 (3/31/91) **65**

JORDAN (United States/California)
Cabernet Sauvignon Alexander Valley 1988 ($NA) (5/15/90) (BT) **85+**
Cabernet Sauvignon Alexander Valley 1987 Rel: $20 Cur: $24 (11/15/91) **90**
Cabernet Sauvignon Alexander Valley 1986 Rel: $22 Cur: $25 (11/15/90) **88**
Cabernet Sauvignon Alexander Valley 1985 Rel: $19.50 Cur: $35 (9/15/89) **88**
Cabernet Sauvignon Alexander Valley 1984 Rel: $19 Cur: $45 (CA-3/89) **86**
Cabernet Sauvignon Alexander Valley 1983 Rel: $18 Cur: $31 (CA-3/89) **78**
Cabernet Sauvignon Alexander Valley 1982 Rel: $18 Cur: $39 (CA-3/89) **73**
Cabernet Sauvignon Alexander Valley 1981 Rel: $17 Cur: $46 (CA-3/89) **84**
Cabernet Sauvignon Alexander Valley 1981 Rel: $17 Cur: $46 (5/01/85) CS **90**
Cabernet Sauvignon Alexander Valley 1980 Rel: $17 Cur: $50 (CA-3/89) **80**

Key to Symbols

The scores reported here are the results of blind tastings conducted by our panel of senior editors. Wines that carry the initials below are results of individual tastings.

THE WINE SPECTATOR 100-POINT SCALE 95-100—Classic, a great wine; ***90-94***—Outstanding, superior character and style; ***80-89***—Good to very good, a wine with special qualities; ***70-79***—Average, drinkable wine that may have minor flaws; ***60-69***—Below average, drinkable but not recommended; ***50-59***—Poor, undrinkable, not recommended. "+"—With a score indicates a range; used primarily with barrel tastings to indicate a preliminary score.

SPECIAL DESIGNATIONS SS—Spectator Selection, CS—Cellar Selection, BB—Best Buy, ($NA)—Price not available, (NR)—Not released.

TASTER'S INITIALS (JG)—Jim Gordon, (HS)—Harvey Steiman, (JL)—James Laube, (JS)—James Suckling, (TM)—Thomas Matthews, (TR)—Terry Robards, (PM)—Per-Henrik Mansson, (BT)—Barrel Tasting (these wines were tasted blind from barrel samples), (CA-date)—*California's Great Cabernets* by James Laube, (CH-date)—*California's Great Chardonnays* by James Laube, (VP-date)—*Vintage Port* by James Suckling.

DATE TASTED Dates in parentheses represent the issue in which the rating was published.

Cabernet Sauvignon Alexander Valley 1979 Rel: $16 Cur: $53 (CA-3/89) **79**
Cabernet Sauvignon Alexander Valley 1978 Rel: $16 Cur: $66 (CA-3/89) **81**
Cabernet Sauvignon Alexander Valley 1977 Rel: $14 Cur: $46 (CA-3/89) **77**
Cabernet Sauvignon Alexander Valley 1976 Rel: $10 Cur: $82 (CA-3/89) **79**
Chardonnay Alexander Valley 1988 $20 (11/30/91) **86**
Chardonnay Alexander Valley 1987 $20 (6/30/90) **88**
Chardonnay Alexander Valley 1986 $20 (4/15/89) **82**
Chardonnay Alexander Valley 1985 $17 (3/15/88) **87**
Chardonnay Alexander Valley 1983 $16 (7/16/86) **67**
Chardonnay Alexander Valley 1982 $15.75 (5/16/85) **85**
Chardonnay Alexander Valley 1981 $15.75 (4/16/84) **77**
J Sonoma County 1987 $22 (5/15/91) **88**

JORY (United States/California)
Chardonnay California 1990 $20 (4/30/92) **78**
Chardonnay Santa Clara County San Ysidro Vineyard 1989 $17 (4/30/91) **82**
Chardonnay Santa Clara County San Ysidro Vineyard 1987 $16.50 (10/31/88) **89**
Pinot Noir Santa Clara County 1986 $19 (6/15/88) **76**

JOSMEYER (France/Alsace)
Gewürztraminer Alsace Les Archenets 1990 $28 (2/15/92) **85**
Gewürztraminer Alsace Cuvée des Folastries 1989 $16 (11/15/90) **83**
Gewürztraminer Alsace Les Folastries 1990 $20 (2/15/92) **89**
Gewürztraminer Alsace Hengst 1989 ($NA) (11/15/90) **90**
Gewürztraminer Alsace Sélection de Grains Nobles 1990 (NR) (2/15/92) (BT) **90+**
Gewürztraminer Alsace Sélection de Grains Nobles 1989 ($NA) (11/15/90) **85**
Gewürztraminer Alsace Vendange Tardive 1990 (NR) (2/15/92) (BT) **85+**
Gewürztraminer Alsace Vendange Tardive 1989 ($NA) (11/15/90) **88**
Muscat Alsace 1990 $28 (2/15/92) **89**
Pinot Blanc Alsace Les Lutines 1990 $16 (2/15/92) **86**
Pinot Blanc Alsace Les Lutins 1989 $15 (11/15/90) **85**
Pinot Blanc Alsace Pinot Auxerrois "H" Vieilles Vignes 1990 $24 (2/15/92) **91**
Pinot Blanc Alsace Pinot Auxerrois "H" Vieilles Vignes 1989 ($NA) (11/15/90) **89**
Riesling Alsace Brand Vendange Tardive 1990 (NR) (2/15/92) (BT) **85+**
Riesling Alsace Hengst 1990 (NR) (2/15/92) **89**
Riesling Alsace Hengst 1989 ($NA) (11/15/90) **90**
Riesling Alsace Hengst Cuvée de la St.-Martin 1990 $45 (2/15/92) **88**
Riesling Alsace Hengst Vendange Tardive 1990 (NR) (2/15/92) (BT) **90+**
Riesling Alsace Le Kottabe 1990 $17 (2/15/92) **86**
Riesling Alsace La Kottabe 1989 ($NA) (11/15/90) **86**
Riesling Alsace Les Pierrets 1990 (NR) (2/15/92) **89**
Tokay Pinot Gris Alsace 1990 $18 (2/15/92) **86**
Tokay Pinot Gris Alsace 1989 ($NA) (11/15/90) **86**
Tokay Pinot Gris Alsace Cuvée de Centennaire 1990 $30 (2/15/92) **91**
Tokay Pinot Gris Alsace Hengst Sélection de Grains Nobles 1989 ($NA) (11/15/90) **86**
Tokay Pinot Gris Alsace Vendange Tardive 1990 (NR) (2/15/92) (BT) **90+**

MAURICE JOSSERAND (France/Burgundy)
Mâcon-Péronne Domaine du Mortier 1988 $8 (12/31/90) BB **84**

KARL JOSTOCK-THUL (Germany)
Riesling Kabinett Mosel-Saar-Ruwer Piesporter Treppchen 1983 $4.75 (11/01/84) **79**

DOMAINE DES JOUGLA (France/Other)
Limoux 1988 $8 (3/31/90) **80**
St.-Chinian 1986 $6.75 (5/15/89) **76**

JOULLIAN (United States/California)
Cabernet Sauvignon Carmel Valley 1987 $14 (7/31/91) **81**
Chardonnay Carmel Valley 1989 $12 (7/15/91) **73**

JUD'S HILL (Australia)
Cabernet Merlot Australia 1985 $13 (4/30/88) **80**

JUDD'S HILL (United States/California)
Cabernet Sauvignon Napa Valley 1991 (NR) (5/15/92) (BT) **91+**
Cabernet Sauvignon Napa Valley 1989 $20 (4/15/92) **89**

MARCEL JUGE (France/Rhône)
Cornas 1986 $23 (11/30/90) **83**
Cornas Cuvée C 1986 $25 (6/15/89) **85**
Cornas Cuvée S C 1986 $30 (6/15/89) **87**

MICHEL JUILLOT (France/Burgundy)
Corton-Charlemagne 1987 $77 (2/28/90) **84**

CASTILLO JUMILLA (Spain)
Jumilla 1985 $5 (7/31/89) **75**

CHATEAU LE JURAT (France/Bordeaux)
St.-Emilion 1986 ($NA) (5/15/87) (BT) **70+**

CHATEAU LES JUSTICES (France/Sauternes)
Sauternes 1989 ($NA) (6/15/90) (BT) **85+**
Sauternes 1988 $38 (11/15/91) **87**
Sauternes 1987 ($NA) (6/15/90) **75**
Sauternes 1986 $16 (12/31/89) **85**
Sauternes 1983 $15 (1/31/88) **67**

JUSTIN (United States/California)
Blanc de Noir Paso Robles 1985 $23 (12/31/91) **84**
Cabernet Sauvignon Paso Robles 1988 $19 (11/15/91) **72**
Chardonnay Paso Robles 1990 $16.50 (7/15/92) **74**
Chardonnay Paso Robles 1989 $16.50 (7/15/91) **85**
Chardonnay Paso Robles 1988 $14 (2/15/91) **92**
Reserve Paso Robles 1988 $23 (11/15/91) **75**
Reserve Paso Robles 1987 $20 (2/15/91) **90**

JUVE Y CAMPS (Spain)
Brut Cava Extra Reserva de la Familia 1986 $16 (11/15/91) **82**

KALIN (United States/California)
Cabernet Sauvignon Sonoma County Reserve 1985 $23 (4/15/91) **83**
Chardonnay Potter Valley Cuvée BL 1988 $25 (3/31/91) **86**
Chardonnay Sonoma County Cuvée DD 1989 $22 (7/15/92) **74**
Chardonnay Sonoma County Cuvée DD 1988 $23 (3/31/91) **87**
Chardonnay Sonoma County Cuvée LD 1988 $23 (3/15/91) **88**
Chardonnay Sonoma County Cuvée LD 1987 $25 (3/15/91) **79**
Chardonnay Sonoma County Cuvée LR 1989 $22 (7/15/92) **80**
Chardonnay Sonoma County Cuvée LV 1989 $22 (7/15/92) **70**
Pinot Noir Sonoma County Cuvée DD 1986 $20 (4/30/91) **80**

KALINDA (United States/California)
Chardonnay Knights Valley 1989 $7 (7/15/91) **81**
KARLY (United States/California)
Chardonnay California 1986 $12.50 (4/15/88) **54**

Chardonnay Santa Maria Valley 1985 $12 (8/31/87) **81**
Petite Sirah Amador County 1989 $11.50 (3/15/92) **65**
Petite Sirah Amador County Not So Petite Sirah 1988 $14 (12/31/90) **81**
White Zinfandel Amador County 1988 $7 (6/15/89) **76**
Zinfandel Amador County 1988 $9.50 (12/31/90) **83**
Zinfandel Amador County 1987 $9.50 (3/31/90) **83**
Zinfandel Amador County 1986 $9 (3/31/89) **79**
Zinfandel Amador County 1985 $8.50 (12/31/87) **72**
Zinfandel Amador County Sadie Upton 1989 $15 (3/31/92) **81**

KEDEM (United States/New York)
Charmat Kosher New York NV $6 (12/31/90) **72**

ROBERT KEEBLE (United States/California)
Cabernet Franc Sonoma County 1988 $12 (11/15/91) **79**
Cabernet Sauvignon Napa Valley 1987 $14 (10/15/91) **89**

KEENAN (United States/California)
Cabernet Sauvignon Napa Valley 1988 $18 (3/31/92) **85**
Cabernet Sauvignon Napa Valley 1987 Rel: $18 Cur: $20 (5/31/90) **86**
Cabernet Sauvignon Napa Valley 1986 Rel: $16.50 Cur: $22 (8/31/89) **93**
Cabernet Sauvignon Napa Valley 1985 Rel: $15 Cur: $21 (CA-3/89) **86**
Cabernet Sauvignon Napa Valley 1984 Rel: $13.50 Cur: $27 (CA-3/89) **92**
Cabernet Sauvignon Napa Valley 1984 Rel: $13.50 Cur: $27 (10/15/87) SS **94**
Cabernet Sauvignon Napa Valley 1983 Rel: $11 Cur: $18 (CA-3/89) **87**
Cabernet Sauvignon Napa Valley 1982 Rel: $10 Cur: $28 (CA-3/89) **88**
Cabernet Sauvignon Napa Valley 1981 Rel: $13.50 Cur: $22 (CA-3/89) **84**
Cabernet Sauvignon Napa Valley 1980 Rel: $13.50 Cur: $40 (CA-3/89) **80**
Cabernet Sauvignon Napa Valley 1979 Rel: $12 Cur: $45 (CA-3/89) **74**
Cabernet Sauvignon Napa Valley 1978 Rel: $12 Cur: $35 (CA-3/89) **74**
Cabernet Sauvignon Napa Valley 1977 Rel: $12 Cur: $15 (CA-3/89) **69**
Chardonnay Napa Valley 1990 $15 (4/15/92) **87**
Chardonnay Napa Valley 1989 $15 (7/15/91) **84**
Chardonnay Napa Valley 1988 $15 (6/30/90) SS **91**
Chardonnay Napa Valley 1987 $12.50 (6/15/89) **82**
Chardonnay Napa Valley 1986 $12 (7/15/88) **85**
Chardonnay Napa Valley 1985 $11 (7/31/87) **81**
Chardonnay Napa Valley 1983 $12.50 (9/16/85) **74**
Chardonnay Napa Valley Ann's Vineyard 1987 $13.50 (6/30/90) **59**
Chardonnay Napa Valley Ann's Vineyard 1986 $14 (4/15/89) **77**
Chardonnay Napa Valley Estate 1985 $13.50 (2/15/88) **80**
Chardonnay Napa Valley Estate 1983 $12.50 (8/31/86) **70**
Merlot Napa Valley 1989 $18 (5/31/92) **82**
Merlot Napa Valley 1988 Rel: $18 Cur: $21 (5/31/92) **84**
Merlot Napa Valley 1987 Rel: $18 Cur: $20 (3/31/90) **88**
Merlot Napa Valley 1986 Rel: $18 Cur: $20 (6/30/89) **90**
Merlot Napa Valley 1985 $18 (5/31/88) **83**
Merlot Napa Valley 1984 Rel: $16.50 Cur: $20 (7/31/87) CS **94**

KENDALL-JACKSON (United States/California)
Cardinale Meritage California 1987 $50 (3/31/92) **95**
Cabernet Sauvignon California Cardinale 1986 $65 (11/15/90) **91**
Cabernet Sauvignon California Cardinale 1985 Rel: $45 Cur: $80 (11/15/89) **97**
Cardinale California 1984 $12 (7/31/87) **84**
Cardinale California 1983 $9 (10/16/85) **82**
Cabernet Sauvignon California Proprietor's Grand Reserve 1987 $16 (3/31/92) **87**
Cabernet Sauvignon California The Proprietor's 1986 $24 (3/15/90) **85**
Cabernet Sauvignon California Proprietor's Reserve 1985 $20 (12/15/88) **95**
Cabernet Sauvignon California Vintner's Reserve 1987 $14 (11/15/91) **82**
Cabernet Sauvignon California Vintner's Reserve 1986 $11 (12/31/88) **85**
Cabernet Sauvignon Lake County 1986 $7.75 (7/31/88) **74**
Cabernet Sauvignon Lake County 1984 $7.50 (11/15/87) BB **81**
Cabernet Sauvignon Lake County 1983 $7 (5/01/86) **69**
Chardonnay Anderson Valley Dennison Vineyard 1987 Rel: $14 Cur: $16 (CH-4/90) **82**
Chardonnay Anderson Valley Dennison Vineyard 1985 Rel: $14 Cur: $20 (CH-4/90) **85**
Chardonnay Santa Maria Valley Camelot Vineyard 1990 $14 (7/15/92) **84**
Chardonnay Anderson Valley DuPratt Vineyard 1988 Rel: $14 Cur: $17 (CH-4/90) **85**
Chardonnay Anderson Valley DePatie Vineyard 1987 Rel: $14 Cur: $17 (7/15/89) **91**
Chardonnay Redwood Valley Lolonis Vineyard 1988 $14 (CH-4/90) **85**
Chardonnay Sonoma Valley Durell Vineyard 1990 $16 (7/15/92) **87**
Chardonnay Sonoma Valley Durell Vineyard 1989 $16 (7/15/91) **86**
Chardonnay Sonoma Valley Durell Vineyard 1987 Rel: $14 Cur: $18 (CH-4/90) **86**
Chardonnay Sonoma Valley Durell Vineyard 1986 Rel: $14 Cur: $20 (CH-6/90) **91**
Chardonnay Sonoma Valley Durell Vineyard 1985 Rel: $14 Cur: $20 (CH-4/90) **87**
Chardonnay California Proprietor's Grand Reserve 1990 $23 (7/15/92) **86**
Chardonnay California Proprietor's Grand Reserve 1989 $23 (5/31/91) **90**
Chardonnay California The Proprietor's 1988 $24.50 (2/28/90) **88**
Chardonnay California The Proprietor's 1987 Rel: $20 Cur: $25 (CH-4/90) **92**
Chardonnay California The Proprietor's 1986 Rel: $17 Cur: $20 (CH-4/90) **86**
Chardonnay California The Proprieter's 1985 $18 (9/15/87) **79**
Chardonnay California Proprietor's Reserve 1983 $13.50 (8/01/85) **86**
Chardonnay California Vintner's Reserve 1991 $13 (7/15/92) **84**
Chardonnay California Vintner's Reserve 1989 $13 (7/15/91) **84**
Chardonnay California Vintner's Reserve 1988 $12.50 (10/31/89) **89**
Chardonnay California Vintner's Reserve 1987 $12 (9/30/88) **85**
Chardonnay California Vintner's Reserve 1985 $9.50 (3/15/87) **84**
Chardonnay California Vintner's Reserve 1984 $7 (4/16/86) **59**
Johannisberg Riesling Clear Lake Vintner's Reserve 1989 $9 (12/31/90) **80**
Merlot Alexander Valley 1986 $16 (12/31/88) **93**
Merlot California Vintner's Reserve 1989 $14 (5/31/92) **75**
Merlot California Vintner's Reserve 1988 $13.50 (11/15/91) **84**
Merlot Sonoma County The Proprietor's 1987 $20 (12/31/90) **87**
Pinot Noir Santa Maria Valley Julia's Vineyard 1988 $14 (11/15/91) **82**
Sauvignon Blanc Lake County Vintner's Reserve 1989 $9 (10/31/90) **90**
Sauvignon Blanc Lake County Vintner's Reserve 1988 $9 (3/31/90) **89**
Syrah Sonoma Valley Durell Vineyard 1988 $24 (8/31/91) **89**
Syrah Sonoma Valley Durell Vineyard 1987 $17 (12/15/89) **90**
Syrah Sonoma Valley Durell Vineyard 1986 $14 (11/30/88) **92**
Zinfandel Anderson Valley DuPratt Vineyard 1987 $20 (7/31/91) **90**
Zinfandel Anderson Valley DuPratt-DePatie Vineyard 1986 $16 (12/15/89) **85**
Zinfandel Anderson Valley DuPratt-DePatie Vineyard 1983 $10 (11/01/85) **76**
Zinfandel California Vintner's Reserve 1989 $11 (9/30/91) **84**
Zinfandel Clear Lake Viña Las Lomas Vineyard 1983 $7 (6/01/85) **80**
Zinfandel Mendocino 1987 $9 (3/15/90) **88**
Zinfandel Mendocino 1986 $9 (9/15/88) **86**
Zinfandel Mendocino Ciapusci Vineyard 1984 $16 (12/15/89) **86**

KATHRYN KENNEDY (United States/California)
Cabernet Sauvignon Santa Cruz Mountains 1988 $45 (11/15/91) **88**

Cabernet Sauvignon Santa Cruz Mountains 1987 $45 (1/31/91) **89**
Cabernet Sauvignon Santa Cruz Mountains 1986 $30 (3/15/90) **81**
Cabernet Sauvignon Santa Cruz Mountains 1985 $25 (12/15/88) **93**
Lateral California 1989 $16.50 (11/15/91) **86**
Lateral California 1988 $14.50 (10/15/90) **87**

KENWOOD (United States/California)
Cabernet Sauvignon Sonoma Valley 1987 $15 (7/15/91) **90**
Cabernet Sauvignon Sonoma Valley 1986 $15 (9/30/89) **86**
Cabernet Sauvignon Sonoma Valley 1985 $14.50 (2/15/89) **91**
Cabernet Sauvignon Sonoma Valley 1984 $12 (5/31/88) **83**
Cabernet Sauvignon Sonoma Valley 1983 $10 (2/15/88) **85**
Cabernet Sauvignon Sonoma Valley Artist Series 1988 $35 (3/15/92) **83**
Cabernet Sauvignon Sonoma Valley Artist Series 1987 $35 (11/15/90) **88**
Cabernet Sauvignon Sonoma Valley Artist Series 1986 Rel: $30 Cur: $34 (11/30/89) CS **95**
Cabernet Sauvignon Sonoma Valley Artist Series 1985 Rel: $30 Cur: $35 (CA-3/89) **91**
Cabernet Sauvignon Sonoma Valley Artist Series 1984 Rel: $30 Cur: $39 (CA-3/89) **93**
Cabernet Sauvignon Sonoma Valley Artist Series 1983 Rel: $30 Cur: $38 (CA-3/89) **87**
Cabernet Sauvignon Sonoma Valley Artist Series 1983 Rel: $30 Cur: $38 (11/15/86) CS **92**
Cabernet Sauvignon Sonoma Valley Artist Series 1982 Rel: $25 Cur: $40 (CA-3/89) **87**
Cabernet Sauvignon Sonoma Valley Artist Series 1981 Rel: $25 Cur: $52 (CA-3/89) **89**
Cabernet Sauvignon Sonoma Valley Artist Series 1981 Rel: $25 Cur: $52 (9/16/84) SS **89**
Cabernet Sauvignon Sonoma Valley Artist Series 1980 Rel: $20 Cur: $55 (CA-3/89) **80**
Cabernet Sauvignon Sonoma Valley Artist Series 1979 Rel: $20 Cur: $64 (CA-3/89) **91**
Cabernet Sauvignon Sonoma Valley Artist Series 1978 Rel: $20 Cur: $95 (CA-3/89) **90**
Cabernet Sauvignon Sonoma Valley Artist Series 1977 Rel: $15 Cur: $175 (CA-3/89) **82**
Cabernet Sauvignon Sonoma County Artist Series 1976 Rel: $10 Cur: $95 (CA-3/89) **77**
Cabernet Sauvignon Sonoma County Artist Series 1975 Rel: $6.50 Cur: $320 (CA-3/89) **73**
Cabernet Sauvignon Sonoma Valley Jack London Vineyard 1987 Rel: $18 Cur: $21 (1/31/91) **92**
Cabernet Sauvignon Sonoma Valley Jack London Vineyard 1986 $18 (9/15/89) **90**
Cabernet Sauvignon Sonoma Valley Jack London Vineyard 1985 Rel: $18 Cur: $21 (10/15/88) **89**
Cabernet Sauvignon Sonoma Valley Jack London Vineyard 1984 Rel: $16 Cur: $21 (11/30/87) **91**
Cabernet Sauvignon Sonoma Valley Jack London Vineyard 1983 Rel: $15 Cur: $21 (2/15/87) **86**
Cabernet Sauvignon Sonoma Valley Jack London Vineyard 1980 Rel: $12.50 Cur: $25 (5/16/84) **80**
Chardonnay Sonoma Valley 1988 $14 (5/31/90) **82**
Chardonnay Sonoma Valley 1987 $13 (7/15/89) **86**
Chardonnay Sonoma Valley 1986 $12 (2/15/89) **85**
Chardonnay Sonoma Valley Beltane Ranch 1990 $16 (1/31/92) **83**
Chardonnay Sonoma Valley Beltane Ranch 1989 Rel: $16 Cur: $19 (7/15/91) **83**
Chardonnay Sonoma Valley Beltane Ranch 1988 Rel: $15 Cur: $17 (11/30/90) **88**
Chardonnay Sonoma Valley Beltane Ranch 1987 Rel: $15 Cur: $17 (CH-7/90) **87**
Chardonnay Sonoma Valley Beltane Ranch 1986 Rel: $14 Cur: $18 (CH-7/90) **85**
Chardonnay Sonoma Valley Beltane Ranch 1985 Rel: $14 Cur: $18 (CH-7/90) **84**
Chardonnay Sonoma Valley Yulupa Vineyard 1988 Rel: $14 Cur: $17 (5/31/90) **87**
Chardonnay Sonoma Valley Yulupa Vineyard 1987 Rel: $14 Cur: $16 (CH-7/90) **85**
Chardonnay Sonoma Valley Yulupa Vineyard 1986 Rel: $12 Cur: $17 (CH-7/90) **82**
Chardonnay Sonoma Valley Yulupa Vineyard 1985 Rel: $12 Cur: $17 (CH-7/90) **84**
Chardonnay Sonoma Valley Yulupa Vineyard 1983 Rel: $11 Cur: $18 (CH-7/90) **85**
Johannisberg Riesling Late Harvest Sonoma Valley 1985 $10/375ml (2/28/87) BB **89**
Johannisberg Riesling Late Harvest Sonoma Valley 1984 $8.50/375ml (9/16/85) **79**
Pinot Noir Sonoma Valley Jack London Vineyard 1989 $15 (10/31/91) **80**
Pinot Noir Sonoma Valley Jack London Vineyard 1984 $15 (5/31/89) **77**
Sauvignon Blanc Sonoma County 1990 $9.50 (11/15/91) **78**
Sauvignon Blanc Sonoma County 1988 $9 (11/30/89) **85**
Vintage Red California 1988 $5 (12/31/90) **77**
White Zinfandel Sonoma Valley 1988 $6.75 (6/15/89) **86**
Zinfandel Sonoma Valley 1988 $11 (12/31/90) **82**
Zinfandel Sonoma Valley 1987 $11 (10/31/89) **90**
Zinfandel Sonoma Valley 1985 $9.50 (5/15/88) **89**
Zinfandel Sonoma Valley 1984 $8.50 (9/15/87) **90**
Zinfandel Sonoma Valley 1983 $7.50 (11/15/86) **88**
Zinfandel Sonoma Valley 1982 $7.50 (7/16/86) **90**
Zinfandel Sonoma Valley Jack London Vineyard 1989 $14 (9/30/91) **83**
Zinfandel Sonoma Valley Jack London Vineyard 1987 $12 (12/15/89) **88**

HERIBERT KERPEN (Germany)
Riesling Auslese Mosel-Saar-Ruwer Wehlener Sonnenuhr ** 1990 $22 (12/15/91) **90**
Riesling Auslese Mosel-Saar-Ruwer Wehlener Sonnenuhr *** 1990 $18/375ml (12/15/91) **90**
Riesling Auslese Mosel-Saar-Ruwer Bernkasteler Badstube 1990 $17 (12/15/91) **89**
Riesling Auslese Mosel-Saar-Ruwer Graacher Himmelreich 1990 $17 (12/15/91) **88**
Riesling Auslese Mosel-Saar-Ruwer Kollektion Kerpen Wehlener Sonnenuhr 1990 (NR) (12/15/91) **88**
Riesling Auslese Mosel-Saar-Ruwer Wehlener Sonnenuhr 1990 $17 (12/15/91) **87**
Riesling Auslese Mosel-Saar-Ruwer Wehlener Sonnenuhr (AP12) 1988 $15 (9/30/89) **84**
Riesling Beerenauslese Mosel-Saar-Ruwer Wehlener Sonnenuhr 1990 $66/375ml (12/15/91) **91**
Riesling Eiswein Mosel-Saar-Ruwer Wehlener Sonnenuhr 1990 $75/375ml (12/15/91) **89**
Riesling Spätlese Mosel-Saar-Ruwer Wehlener Sonnenuhr 1988 $12 (9/30/89) **90**

KESSELSTATT (Germany)
Riesling Auslese Mosel-Saar-Ruwer Bernkasteler Doctor 1990 $50 (12/15/91) **90**
Riesling Auslese Mosel-Saar-Ruwer Josephshöfer 1989 $39 (12/15/90) **86**
Riesling Auslese Mosel-Saar-Ruwer Oberemmeler Karlsberg 1989 $32 (12/15/90) **92**
Riesling Auslese Mosel-Saar-Ruwer Scharzhofberger 1989 $25 (12/15/90) **87**
Riesling Auslese Mosel-Saar-Ruwer Scharzhofberger Gold Cap 1989 $48 (12/15/90) **92**
Riesling Beerenauslese Mosel-Saar-Ruwer Scharzhofberger 1989 $220 (12/15/90) **94**
Riesling Eiswein Mosel-Saar-Ruwer Oberemmeler Karlsberg 1983 $150 (4/30/89) **90**
Riesling Kabinett Mosel-Saar-Ruwer Graacher Himmelreich 1989 $10 (12/15/90) **77**
Riesling Kabinett Mosel-Saar-Ruwer Josephshöfer 1990 $11 (12/15/91) **84**
Riesling Kabinett Mosel-Saar-Ruwer Josephshöfer 1989 $8.50 (12/15/90) **87**
Riesling Kabinett Mosel-Saar-Ruwer Josephshöfer 1988 $14 (9/30/89) **90**
Riesling Kabinett Mosel-Saar-Ruwer Piesporter Goldtröpfchen 1990 $14 (12/15/91) **86**
Riesling Kabinett Mosel-Saar-Ruwer Piesporter Goldtröpfchen 1988 ($NA) (9/30/89) **84**
Riesling Kabinett Mosel-Saar-Ruwer Scharzhofberger 1990 $11 (12/15/91) **84**
Riesling Kabinett Mosel-Saar-Ruwer Scharzhofberger 1989 $11 (12/15/90) **84**
Riesling Qualitätswein Mosel-Saar-Ruwer 1990 $10 (12/15/91) **83**
Riesling Qualitätswein Mosel-Saar-Ruwer Berkastler Badstube 1989 $8 (12/15/90) **82**
Riesling Qualitätswein Mosel-Saar-Ruwer Josephshöfer 1989 $7 (12/15/90) **83**
Riesling Spätlese Mosel-Saar-Ruwer Bernkastler Lay 1989 $13 (12/15/90) **85**
Riesling Spätlese Mosel-Saar-Ruwer Josephshöfer 1990 $17 (12/15/91) **90**
Riesling Spätlese Mosel-Saar-Ruwer Josephshöfer 1989 $14 (12/15/90) **84**
Riesling Spätlese Mosel-Saar-Ruwer Kaseler Nies'chen 1990 $16 (12/15/91) **88**
Riesling Spätlese Mosel-Saar-Ruwer Kaseler Nies'chen 1988 $20 (9/30/89) **94**
Riesling Spätlese Mosel-Saar-Ruwer Ockfener Bockstein 1989 $16 (12/15/90) **82**
Riesling Spätlese Mosel-Saar-Ruwer Piesporter Goldtröpfchen 1990 $15 (12/15/91) **90**
Riesling Spätlese Mosel-Saar-Ruwer Piesporter Goldtröpfchen 1989 $15 (12/15/90) **86**
Riesling Spätlese Mosel-Saar-Ruwer Scharzhofberger 1989 $13 (12/15/90) **90**
Riesling Trockenbeerenauslese Mosel-Saar-Ruwer Scharzhofberger 1989 $150 (12/15/90) **94**

KETTMEIR (Italy/North)
Chardonnay Alto Adige 1988 $11 (9/15/89) **84**

KIENTZHEIM-KAYSERBERG (France/Alsace)
Gewürztraminer Alsace 1990 (NR) (2/15/92) **84**
Gewürztraminer Alsace Altenberg 1990 (NR) (2/15/92) **87**
Gewürztraminer Alsace Furstentum 1990 (NR) (2/15/92) **87**
Pinot Blanc Alsace 1990 (NR) (2/15/92) **86**
Riesling Alsace 1990 (NR) (2/15/92) **85**
Riesling Alsace Schlossberg 1990 (NR) (2/15/92) **86**
Tokay Pinot Gris Alsace 1990 (NR) (2/15/92) **85**

KIONA (United States/Washington)
Cabernet Sauvignon Yakima Valley Estate Bottled 1986 $14 (10/15/89) **89**
Cabernet Sauvignon Yakima Valley Tapteil Vineyard 1988 $12 (3/31/92) **85**
Chardonnay Yakima Valley Barrel Fermented 1987 $10 (10/15/89) **91**
Chenin Blanc Yakima Valley Estate Bottled 1988 $5.75 (10/15/89) **76**
Ice Wine Yakima Valley 1989 $15/375ml (6/15/91) **75**
Lemberger Columbia Valley 1989 $9 (5/15/92) **76**
Merlot Columbia Valley 1989 $12 (3/31/92) **86**
Merlot Columbia Valley 1988 $12 (5/31/91) **84**
White Riesling Columbia Valley 1988 $6 (10/15/89) **74**

CHATEAU KIRWAN (France/Bordeaux)
Margaux 1991 (NR) (5/15/92) (BT) **75+**
Margaux 1990 (NR) (5/15/92) (BT) **85+**
Margaux 1989 $32 (3/15/92) **87**
Margaux 1988 $28 (4/30/91) **87**
Margaux 1987 $22 (6/30/89) (BT) **70+**
Margaux 1986 $25 (6/30/89) **82**
Margaux 1985 Rel: $29 Cur: $33 (2/15/89) **90**
Margaux 1983 Rel: $16 Cur: $22 (7/16/86) **86**
Margaux 1945 $150 (3/16/86) (JL) **88**

KISTLER (United States/California)
Cabernet Sauvignon Sonoma Valley Kistler Estate Vineyard 1987 $25 (2/28/91) **83**
Cabernet Sauvignon Sonoma Valley Kistler Estate Vineyard 1986 Rel: $20 Cur: $28 (9/30/89) **84**
Cabernet Sauvignon Sonoma Valley Kistler Estate Vineyard 1985 Rel: $16 Cur: $28 (CA-3/89) **93**
Cabernet Sauvignon Napa Valley Veeder Hills Vineyard 1983 Rel: $13.50 Cur: $25 (CA-3/89) **78**
Cabernet Sauvignon Napa Valley Veeder Hills Vineyard 1982 Rel: $12 Cur: $26 (CA-3/89) **86**
Cabernet Sauvignon Napa Valley Veeder Hills-Veeder Peak 1981 Rel: $12 Cur: $32 (CA-3/89) **87**
Cabernet Sauvignon Napa Valley Veeder Hills-Veeder Peak 1980 Rel: $16 Cur: $42 (CA-3/89) **85**
Cabernet Sauvignon Sonoma Valley Glen Ellen Vineyard 1980 Rel: $16 Cur: $42 (CA-3/89) **84**
Chardonnay Russian River Valley Dutton Ranch 1990 $28 (1/31/92) **88**
Chardonnay Russian River Valley Dutton Ranch 1989 Rel: $24 Cur: $31 (2/15/91) **89**
Chardonnay Russian River Valley Dutton Ranch 1988 Rel: $22 Cur: $40 (2/15/90) **90**
Chardonnay Russian River Valley Dutton Ranch 1987 Rel: $18 Cur: $35 (CH-2/90) **93**
Chardonnay Russian River Valley Dutton Ranch 1986 Rel: $16.50 Cur: $28 (CH-2/90) **90**
Chardonnay Russian River Valley Dutton Ranch 1985 Rel: $15 Cur: $30 (CH-2/90) **88**
Chardonnay Russian River Valley Dutton Ranch 1984 Rel: $15 Cur: $30 (CH-2/90) **89**
Chardonnay Russian River Valley Vine Hill Road Vineyard 1990 $25 (1/31/92) **90**
Chardonnay Sonoma Mountain McCrea Vineyard 1990 $28 (5/31/92) **90**
Chardonnay Sonoma Mountain McCrea Vineyard 1989 Rel: $28 Cur: $33 (6/15/91) **88**
Chardonnay Sonoma Mountain McCrea Vineyard 1988 Rel: $24 Cur: $32 (4/30/90) **92**
Chardonnay Sonoma Valley 1989 Rel: $18 Cur: $25 (2/15/91) **88**
Chardonnay Sonoma Valley Durell Vineyard Sand Hill 1990 $28 (5/31/92) **93**
Chardonnay Sonoma Valley Durell Vineyard 1989 Rel: $24 Cur: $27 (5/15/91) **90**
Chardonnay Sonoma Valley Durell Vineyard 1988 Rel: $17 Cur: $29 (2/28/90) **90**
Chardonnay Sonoma Valley Durell Vineyard 1988 Rel: $17 Cur: $29 (CH-2/90) **91**
Chardonnay Sonoma Valley Durell Vineyard 1987 Rel: $16 Cur: $30 (CH-2/90) **93**
Chardonnay Sonoma Valley Durell Vineyard 1986 Rel: $16 Cur: $30 (CH-2/90) **89**
Chardonnay Sonoma Valley Kistler Estate Vineyard 1990 $32 (6/15/92) **92**
Chardonnay Sonoma Valley Kistler Estate Vineyard 1989 Rel: $32 Cur: $36 (6/15/91) **91**
Chardonnay Sonoma Valley Kistler Estate Vineyard 1988 Rel: $26 Cur: $35 (4/30/90) **94**
Chardonnay Sonoma Valley Kistler Estate Vineyard 1987 Rel: $22 Cur: $45 (CH-2/90) **90**
Chardonnay Sonoma Valley Kistler Estate Vineyard 1986 Rel: $18 Cur: $40 (CH-2/90) **92**
Pinot Noir Russian River Valley Dutton Ranch 1987 $15 (3/31/90) **85**
Pinot Noir Russian River Valley Dutton Ranch 1986 $13.50 (6/15/88) **89**

KLEIN (United States/California)
Cabernet Sauvignon Santa Cruz Mountains 1988 $25 (1/31/92) **83**
Cabernet Sauvignon Santa Cruz Mountains 1987 $19 (10/15/90) **87**
Cabernet Sauvignon Santa Cruz Mountains 1986 $22 (9/30/89) **89**

KNUDSEN ERATH (United States/Oregon)
Chardonnay Willamette Valley 1988 $11 (8/31/91) **67**
Gewürztraminer Willamette Valley Dry 1989 $7 (6/30/91) **81**
Pinot Noir Willamette Valley 1988 $11 (5/31/91) **82**
Pinot Noir Willamette Valley 1987 $11 (2/15/90) **65**
Pinot Noir Willamette Valley 1986 $9 (2/15/90) **64**
Pinot Noir Willamette Valley NV $6 (6/16/86) BB **81**
Pinot Noir Willamette Valley Leland Vineyards Reserve 1987 $24 (2/15/90) **89**
Pinot Noir Willamette Valley Vintage Select 1986 $15 (6/15/88) **87**
Pinot Noir Willamette Valley Vintage Select 1985 ($NA) (9/30/87) **90**
Pinot Noir Yamhill County Vintage Select 1985 $20 (2/15/90) **75**
Pinot Noir Yamhill County Vintage Select 1983 $35 (2/15/90) **81**
Riesling Willamette Valley Dry 1989 $7 (8/31/91) **79**

KOALA RIDGE (Australia)
Cabernet Sauvignon Barossa Valley 1988 $10 (3/15/92) **83**
Cabernet Sauvignon Barossa Valley 1985 $9 (1/31/89) **84**
Chardonnay Barossa Valley 1990 $10 (11/30/91) **80**
Chardonnay Barossa Valley 1989 $9 (5/31/91) **85**

Key to Symbols

The scores reported here are the results of blind tastings conducted by our panel of senior editors. Wines that carry the initials below are results of individual tastings.

THE WINE SPECTATOR 100-POINT SCALE ***95-100***—Classic, a great wine; ***90-94***—Outstanding, superior character and style; ***80-89***—Good to very good, a wine with special qualities; ***70-79***—Average, drinkable wine that may have minor flaws; ***60-69*** —Below average, drinkable but not recommended; ***50-59*** —Poor, undrinkable, not recommended. "+"—With a score indicates a range; used primarily with barrel tastings to indicate a preliminary score.

SPECIAL DESIGNATIONS SS—Spectator Selection, CS—Cellar Selection, BB—Best Buy, ($NA)—Price not available, (NR)—Not released.

TASTER'S INITIALS (JG)—Jim Gordon, (HS)—Harvey Steiman, (JL)—James Laube, (JS)—James Suckling, (TM)—Thomas Matthews, (TR)—Terry Robards, (PM)—Per-Henrik Mansson, (BT)—Barrel Tasting (these wines were tasted blind from barrel samples), (CA-date)—*California's Great Cabernets* by James Laube, (CH-date)—*California's Great Chardonnays* by James Laube, (VP-date)—*Vintage Port* by James Suckling.

DATE TASTED Dates in parentheses represent the issue in which the rating was published.

Chardonnay Barossa Valley 1987 $7 (3/15/90) **80**
Chardonnay Barossa Valley 1986 $8 (2/15/89) **84**
Hermitage Barossa Valley 1985 $9 (1/31/90) **80**
Sauvignon Blanc Barossa Valley 1987 $8 (10/31/89) **68**

KONOCTI (United States/California)
Cabernet Franc Lake County 1988 $9.50 (2/28/91) **83**
Cabernet Sauvignon Lake County 1986 $9 (4/30/90) **80**
Cabernet Sauvignon Lake County 1985 $7.50 (11/15/89) BB **89**
Cabernet Sauvignon Lake County 1984 $7.50 (2/15/89) **76**
Cabernet Sauvignon Lake County 1983 $6 (6/15/87) BB **84**
Cabernet Sauvignon Lake County 1982 $7 (11/15/86) **78**
Meritage Red Clear Lake 1987 $17 (4/15/91) **85**
Chardonnay Lake County 1990 $10 (3/15/92) **87**
Chardonnay Lake County 1989 $9.50 (4/30/91) **74**
Chardonnay Lake County 1988 $9 (4/15/90) **83**
Chardonnay Lake County 1987 $9 (11/15/89) **73**
Chardonnay Lake County 1986 $8 (12/31/88) **80**
Fumé Blanc Lake County 1990 $7.50 (2/15/92) BB **87**
Meritage Clear Lake 1989 $14 (2/15/92) **75**
Meritage Clear Lake 1988 $14 (4/30/91) **89**
Merlot Lake County 1989 $10 (2/29/92) **85**
Merlot Lake County 1988 $9.50 (3/31/91) BB **83**
Merlot Lake County 1987 $9.50 (12/31/90) **73**
Merlot Lake County 1985 $8 (12/31/88) **83**

KONRAD (United States/California)
Chardonnay Mendocino County 1990 $14 (3/31/92) **84**
Chardonnay Mendocino County Estate 1989 $12 (7/15/91) **85**
Zinfandel Mendocino County 1989 $10 (3/31/92) **84**

KOPKE (Portugal)
Tawny Port 20 Year Old NV $30 (2/28/90) (JS) **88**
Vintage Port 1987 $24 (VP-1/90) **86**
Vintage Port 1985 Rel: $18 Cur: $20 (VP-1/90) **90**
Vintage Port 1983 Rel: $18 Cur: $23 (VP-1/90) **85**
Vintage Port 1982 Rel: $16 Cur: $26 (VP-1/90) **83**
Vintage Port 1980 Rel: $16 Cur: $29 (VP-1/90) **71**
Vintage Port 1979 ($NA) (VP-1/90) **69**
Vintage Port 1978 $29 (VP-1/90) **70**
Vintage Port 1977 ($NA) (VP-1/90) **68**
Vintage Port 1975 $28 (VP-1/90) **82**
Vintage Port 1974 ($NA) (VP-1/90) **74**
Vintage Port 1970 $41 (VP-1/90) **82**
Vintage Port 1966 $65 (VP-1/90) **81**
Vintage Port 1960 $65 (VP-1/90) **87**

KORBEL (United States/California)
Blanc de Blancs California NV $14 (5/15/92) **72**
Blanc de Blancs California Private Reserve 1981 $34/1.5L (2/29/88) **69**
Blanc de Noirs California NV $14 (5/15/92) **80**
Brut California NV $10 (5/15/92) **80**
Brut Rosé California NV $11 (5/15/92) **82**
Extra Dry California NV $11 (5/15/92) **78**
Natural California NV $14 (5/15/92) **83**
Sec California NV $10 (8/31/89) **73**

HANNS KORNELL (United States/California)
Blanc de Blancs California 1982 $14.75 (11/30/86) **77**
Blanc de Noirs California 1987 $15 (6/15/91) **87**
Blanc de Noirs California 1986 $15 (5/31/89) **69**
Brut California NV $11.50 (6/15/91) **79**
Extra Dry California NV $11 (5/31/89) **73**
Sehr Trocken California 1984 $14.50 (6/15/91) **74**

LEONARD KREUSCH (Germany)
Riesling Kabinett Mosel-Saar-Ruwer Bereich Bernkastel 1986 $6 (11/30/88) **84**
Riesling Kabinett Mosel-Saar-Ruwer Zeltinger Himmelreich 1986 $5.75 (11/30/88) **84**

MARC KREYDENWEISS (France/Alsace)
Gewürztraminer Alsace Kritt 1990 $20 (2/15/92) **85**
Gewürztraminer Alsace Kritt 1989 $19 (11/15/90) **79**
Gewürztraminer Alsace Kritt 1988 $19 (10/15/89) **86**
Gewürztraminer Alsace Kritt Sélection de Grains Nobles 1990 (NR) (2/15/92) (BT) **90+**
Gewürztraminer Alsace Vendange Tardive Kritt 1989 ($NA) (11/15/90) **83**
Pinot Blanc Alsace Kritt 1989 $14 (11/15/90) **83**
Pinot Blanc Alsace Kritt 1988 $13 (10/15/89) **87**
Pinot Blanc Alsace Kritt Klevner 1990 (NR) (2/15/92) **89**
Pinot Blanc Alsace Kritt Klevner 1989 $17 (11/15/90) **86**
Riesling Alsace 1988 $15.50 (10/15/89) **86**
Riesling Alsace Andlau 1990 (NR) (2/15/92) **88**
Riesling Alsace Andlau 1989 $18 (11/15/90) **83**
Riesling Alsace Grand Cru Weibelsberg 1990 (NR) (2/15/92) **93**
Riesling Alsace Grand Cru Weibelsberg 1988 $23 (10/15/89) **84**
Riesling Alsace Kastelberg 1990 (NR) (2/15/92) **91**
Riesling Alsace Kastelberg 1989 ($NA) (11/15/90) **82**
Riesling Alsace Vendange Tardive Kastelberg 1988 $26 (10/15/89) **90**
Riesling Alsace Vendange Tardive Weibelsberg 1989 ($NA) (11/15/90) **79**
Riesling Alsace Weibelsberg 1989 ($NA) (11/15/90) **84**
Riesling Alsace Weibelsberg Sélection de Grains Nobles 1988 ($NA) (10/15/89) **95**
Tokay Pinot Gris Alsace 1988 $23 (10/15/89) **86**
Tokay Pinot Gris Alsace Grand Cru Moenchberg 1990 (NR) (2/15/92) **87**
Tokay Pinot Gris Alsace Grand Cru Moenchberg Sélection de Grains Nobles 1990 (NR) (2/15/92) (BT) **90+**
Tokay Pinot Gris Alsace Moenchberg Sélection de Grains Nobles 1989 ($NA) (11/15/90) **90**
Tokay Pinot Gris Alsace Vendange Tardive Grand Cru Moenchberg 1989 ($NA) (11/15/90) **88**

KRITER (France/Other)
Blanc de Blancs Brut de Brut 1985 $9 (6/15/90) **57**
Brut Blanc de Blancs Imperial 1983 $12 (6/15/90) **57**
Brut Rosé NV $9 (6/15/90) **71**
Demi-Sec NV $9 (6/15/90) **71**
Demi-Sec Délicatesse NV $12 (6/15/90) **83**

KRONDORF (Australia)
Cabernet Sauvignon Franc McLaren Vale 1984 $9 (4/15/87) BB **89**
Chardonnay Australia 1985 $13 (4/15/87) **85**
Chardonnay Barossa Valley 1986 $8 (3/31/87) BB **87**

KRUG (France/Champagne)
Brut Blanc de Blancs Champagne Clos du Mesnil 1982 Rel: $120 Cur: $195 (12/31/90) **84**
Brut Blanc de Blancs Champagne Clos du Mesnil 1981 Rel: $120 Cur: $155 (12/31/90) **87**
Brut Blanc de Blancs Champagne Clos du Mesnil 1980 Rel: $100 Cur: $160 (5/31/87) **80**
Brut Champagne 1982 $135 (12/31/89) **92**
Brut Champagne 1981 Rel: $85 Cur: $103 (12/31/88) **91**
Brut Champagne 1976 Rel: $70 Cur: $132 (5/16/86) **93**
Brut Champagne Grande Cuvée NV $80 (12/31/91) **90**
Brut Rosé Champagne NV $115 (12/31/89) **93**

CHARLES KRUG (United States/California)
Cabernet Sauvignon Napa Valley 1988 $12 (3/15/92) **73**
Cabernet Sauvignon Napa Valley 1987 $10.50 (11/15/91) **79**
Cabernet Sauvignon Napa Valley 1986 $10.50 (2/28/91) **87**
Cabernet Sauvignon Napa Valley 1985 $10.50 (1/31/90) **77**
Cabernet Sauvignon Napa Valley 1982 $7 (10/31/87) **79**
Cabernet Sauvignon Napa Valley 1965 $35 (7/16/85) (JL) **74**
Cabernet Sauvignon Napa Valley 1962 $55 (7/16/85) (JL) **84**
Cabernet Sauvignon Napa Valley 1961 $105 (7/16/85) (JL) **84**
Cabernet Sauvignon Napa Valley 1952 $250 (7/16/85) (JL) **86**
Cabernet Sauvignon Napa Valley 1951 $250 (7/16/85) (JL) **80**
Cabernet Sauvignon Napa Valley 1947 $300 (7/16/85) (JL) **89**
Cabernet Sauvignon Napa Valley Vintage Select 1986 ($NA) (CA-3/89) **87**
Cabernet Sauvignon Napa Valley Vintage Select 1985 Rel: $28 Cur: $30 (3/15/92) **89**
Cabernet Sauvignon Napa Valley Vintage Select 1984 Rel: $20 Cur: $28 (6/30/90) **87**
Cabernet Sauvignon Napa Valley Vintage Select 1983 Rel: $20 Cur: $26 (6/30/90) **81**
Cabernet Sauvignon Napa Valley Vintage Select 1981 Rel: $20 Cur: $24 (9/30/90) **90**
Cabernet Sauvignon Napa Valley Vintage Select 1980 Rel: $15 Cur: $22 (CA-3/89) **79**
Cabernet Sauvignon Napa Valley Vintage Select 1979 Rel: $12.50 Cur: $26 (CA-3/89) **82**
Cabernet Sauvignon Napa Valley Vintage Select 1978 Rel: $11 Cur: $26 (CA-3/89) **78**
Cabernet Sauvignon Napa Valley Vintage Select 1977 Rel: $10 Cur: $30 (CA-3/89) **74**
Cabernet Sauvignon Napa Valley Vintage Select 1974 Rel: $9 Cur: $50 (2/15/90) (JG) **87**
Cabernet Sauvignon Napa Valley Vintage Select Lot F-1 1974 Rel: $9 Cur: $50 (CA-3/89) **88**
Cabernet Sauvignon Napa Valley Vintage Select 1973 Rel: $9 Cur: $40 (CA-3/89) **73**
Cabernet Sauvignon Napa Valley Vintage Select 1972 Rel: $9 Cur: $37 (CA-3/89) **77**
Cabernet Sauvignon Napa Valley Vintage Select 1971 Rel: $7.50 Cur: $41 (CA-3/89) **79**
Cabernet Sauvignon Napa Valley Vintage Select 1970 Rel: $7.50 Cur: $60 (CA-3/89) **75**
Cabernet Sauvignon Napa Valley Vintage Select 1969 Rel: $6.50 Cur: $55 (CA-3/89) **81**
Cabernet Sauvignon Napa Valley Vintage Select 1968 Rel: $6.50 Cur: $80 (CA-3/89) **80**
Cabernet Sauvignon Napa Valley Vintage Select 1966 Rel: $6 Cur: $82 (6/01/85) (JL) **87**
Cabernet Sauvignon Napa Valley Vintage Select 1965 Rel: $5 Cur: $70 (CA-3/89) **87**
Cabernet Sauvignon Napa Valley Vintage Select 1964 Rel: $4 Cur: $68 (CA-3/89) **86**
Cabernet Sauvignon Napa Valley Vintage Select 1963 Rel: $3.50 Cur: $70 (CA-3/89) **74**
Cabernet Sauvignon Napa Valley Vintage Select 1962 Rel: $3.50 Cur: $100 (CA-3/89) **78**
Cabernet Sauvignon Napa Valley Vintage Select 1961 Rel: $3.50 Cur: $140 (CA-3/89) **89**
Cabernet Sauvignon Napa Valley Vintage Select 1960 Rel: $2.25 Cur: $45 (CA-3/89) **79**
Cabernet Sauvignon Napa Valley Vintage Select 1959 Rel: $2.25 Cur: $140 (CA-3/89) **85**
Cabernet Sauvignon Napa Valley Vintage Select 1958 Rel: $2 Cur: $280 (CA-3/89) **88**
Cabernet Sauvignon Napa Valley Vintage Select 1957 Rel: $2 Cur: $240 (7/16/85) (JL) **81**
Cabernet Sauvignon Napa Valley Vintage Select 1956 Rel: $1.40 Cur: $350 (CA-3/89) **90**
Cabernet Sauvignon Napa Valley Vintage Select 1952 Rel: $1.26 Cur: $530 (CA-3/89) **92**
Cabernet Sauvignon Napa Valley Vintage Select 1951 Rel: $1.25 Cur: $400 (CA-3/89) **85**
Cabernet Sauvignon Napa Valley Vintage Select 1950 Rel: $1.25 Cur: $500 (CA-3/89) **79**
Cabernet Sauvignon Napa Valley Vintage Select 1946 Rel: $1 Cur: $750 (CA-3/89) **88**
Cabernet Sauvignon Napa Valley 1944 Rel: $0.95 Cur: $420 (CA-3/89) **88**
Chardonnay Carneros Napa Valley Reserve 1990 $16 (7/15/92) **90**
Chardonnay Napa Valley 1990 $12 (1/31/92) **76**
Chardonnay Napa Valley 1989 $10 (9/15/91) **82**
Chardonnay Carneros Napa Valley 1988 $11.50 (1/31/90) **80**
Chenin Blanc Napa Valley 1987 $5.50 (7/31/89) **82**
Gewürztraminer Napa Valley 1988 $7.25 (1/31/90) **78**
Merlot Napa Valley 1989 $13 (5/31/92) **84**
Pinot Noir Carneros 1987 $8.50 (2/28/91) BB **87**
Pinot Noir Carneros Napa Valley 1989 $10 (2/15/92) **82**
Pinot Noir Carneros Napa Valley 1985 $8.50 (2/15/90) **81**
White Zinfandel North Coast 1988 $6 (6/15/89) **72**
Zinfandel Napa Valley 1989 $6 (12/15/90) BB **83**

KUENTZ-BAS (France/Alsace)
Gewürztraminer Alsace 1989 ($NA) (11/15/90) **86**
Gewürztraminer Alsace Cuvée Tradition 1988 ($NA) (10/15/89) **84**
Gewürztraminer Alsace Eichberg 1990 $30 (2/15/92) (BT) **80+**
Gewürztraminer Alsace Eichberg 1989 ($NA) (11/15/90) **93**
Gewürztraminer Alsace Eichberg (Cask 2) 1990 $30 (2/15/92) **83**
Gewürztraminer Alsace Eichberg Vendange Tardive 1989 ($NA) (11/15/90) **86**
Gewürztraminer Alsace Pfersigberg Vendange Tardive 1990 $45 (2/15/92) (BT) **85+**
Gewürztraminer Alsace Réserve Personnelle 1990 $22 (2/15/92) **84**
Gewürztraminer Alsace Réserve Personnelle 1989 ($NA) (11/15/90) **84**
Pinot Blanc Alsace 1989 ($NA) (11/15/90) **73**
Pinot Blanc Alsace Cuvée Tradition 1990 $12.50 (2/15/92) **84**
Pinot Blanc Alsace Cuvée Tradition 1989 $14 (9/15/91) **79**
Pinot Blanc Alsace Cuvée Tradition 1988 ($NA) (10/15/89) **84**
Riesling Alsace 1989 ($NA) (11/15/90) **69**
Riesling Alsace Cuvée Tradition 1988 ($NA) (10/15/89) **84**
Riesling Alsace Eichberg 1990 $25 (2/15/92) **87**
Riesling Alsace Pfersigberg 1989 ($NA) (11/15/90) **83**
Riesling Alsace Pfersigberg Vendange Tardive 1990 $45 (2/15/92) (BT) **85+**
Riesling Alsace Réserve Personnelle 1989 ($NA) (11/15/90) **79**
Riesling Alsace Réserve Personnelle 1988 ($NA) (10/15/89) **84**
Riesling Alsace Réserve Personnelle (Cask 1) 1990 $20 (2/15/92) **88**
Riesling Alsace Réserve Personnelle (Cask 2) 1990 $20 (2/15/92) **83**
Sylvaner Alsace Cuvée Tradition 1990 $11 (2/15/92) **81**
Tokay Pinot Gris Alsace Cuvée Jeremy Sélection de Grains Nobles 1989 ($NA) (11/15/90) **90**
Tokay Pinot Gris Alsace Cuvée Tradition 1989 ($NA) (11/15/90) **86**
Tokay Pinot Gris Alsace Cuvée Tradition 1988 ($NA) (10/15/89) **81**
Tokay Pinot Gris Alsace Pfersigberg Vendange Tardive 1990 $60 (2/15/92) (BT) **90+**
Tokay Pinot Gris Alsace Réserve Personnelle 1990 $22 (2/15/92) **84**
Tokay Pinot Gris Alsace Réserve Personnelle 1989 ($NA) (11/15/90) **81**
Tokay Pinot Gris Alsace Réserve Personnelle 1988 ($NA) (10/15/89) **86**
Tokay Pinot Gris Alsace Vendange Tardive 1990 $45 (2/15/92) (BT) **85+**

KUMEU RIVER (New Zealand)
Chardonnay Kumeu 1990 $28 (4/15/92) **88**
Chardonnay Kumeu 1989 $27 (12/31/90) **91**
Chardonnay Kumeu 1987 $29 (3/31/89) **93**
Merlot Cabernet Kumeu 1987 $18 (12/31/90) **87**

KUNDE (United States/California)
Chardonnay Sonoma Valley Estate Reserve 1990 $19 (4/30/92) **92**
Chardonnay Sonoma Valley 1990 $12 (12/15/91) SS **91**
Sauvignon Blanc Sonoma Valley 1990 $9 (6/15/92) **81**

FRANZ KUNSTLER (Germany)
Riesling Auslese Rheingau Hochheimer Herrenberg 1990 $25 (12/15/91) **94**
Riesling Auslese Rheingau Hochheimer Hölle 1990 $30 (12/15/91) **92**
Riesling Kabinett Rheingau Hochheimer Kirchenstück Charta 1990 $14 (12/15/91) **89**
Riesling Spätlese Rheingau Hochheimer Herrenberg 1990 $15 (12/15/91) **92**
Riesling Spätlese Rheingau Hochheimer Hölle Charta 1990 $20 (12/15/91) **91**

KURFURSTENHOF (Germany)
Riesling Spätlese Rheinhessen Bornheimer Adelberg 1983 $4.50 (12/01/85) **51**

L DE LA LOUVIERE (France/Bordeaux)
Pessac-Léognan 1990 (NR) (5/15/92) (BT) **85+**
Sémillon Washington 1989 $10 (1/31/92) **72**

LA CREMA (United States/California)
Chardonnay California 1989 $12 (7/15/91) **85**
Chardonnay California 1988 $13.50 (6/30/90) **82**
Chardonnay California 1987 $12 (12/31/88) **88**
Chardonnay California 1986 $11.50 (7/15/88) **78**
Chardonnay California 1985 $11 (2/28/87) **93**
Chardonnay California Reserve 1989 $22 (7/15/91) **88**
Chardonnay California Reserve 1988 $22 (5/31/90) **91**
Chardonnay California Reserve 1987 $22 (5/15/89) **84**
Chardonnay California Reserve 1986 Rel: $18 Cur: $22 (CH-6/90) **85**
Chardonnay California Reserve 1985 Rel: $18 Cur: $22 (CH-6/90) **86**
Chardonnay Monterey Ventana Vineyard 1984 Rel: $18 Cur: $24 (CH-6/90) **88**
Crème de Tête Select White California 1988 $5.50 (12/15/89) BB **83**
Pinot Noir California 1986 $11.75 (12/31/88) **89**
Pinot Noir California 1985 $11 (9/30/87) **90**
Pinot Noir California 1984 $11 (3/15/87) **89**
Pinot Noir California Reserve 1986 $22 (5/31/89) **85**
Pinot Noir California Reserve 1985 $17.50 (12/31/87) **82**

LA FERRONNIERE (United States/California)
Cabernet Sauvignon Napa Valley 1985 $14 (1/31/90) **80**

LA JOTA (United States/California)
Cabernet Franc Howell Mountain 1988 $28 (8/31/91) **89**
Cabernet Franc Howell Mountain 1986 $25 (10/15/89) **81**
Cabernet Sauvignon Howell Mountain 1991 (NR) (5/15/92) (BT) **90+**
Cabernet Sauvignon Howell Mountain 1990 (NR) (5/15/91) (BT) **90+**
Cabernet Sauvignon Howell Mountain 1989 $24 (5/15/91) (BT) **90+**
Cabernet Sauvignon Howell Mountain 1988 Rel: $28 Cur: $32 (8/31/91) **85**
Cabernet Sauvignon Howell Mountain 1987 Rel: $25 Cur: $30 (7/31/90) SS **95**
Cabernet Sauvignon Howell Mountain 1986 Rel: $21 Cur: $30 (10/15/89) **85**
Cabernet Sauvignon Howell Mountain 1985 Rel: $18 Cur: $40 (CA-3/89) **88**
Cabernet Sauvignon Howell Mountain 1984 Rel: $15 Cur: $34 (CA-3/89) **88**
Cabernet Sauvignon Howell Mountain 1983 Rel: $15 Cur: $28 (CA-3/89) **84**
Cabernet Sauvignon Howell Mountain 1982 Rel: $13.50 Cur: $35 (CA-3/89) **84**
Viognier Howell Mountain 1989 $25 (1/31/91) **88**
Viognier Howell Mountain 1987 $18 (4/15/89) **84**
Zinfandel Howell Mountain 1987 $12 (10/31/89) **83**
Zinfandel Howell Mountain 1986 $10 (10/31/88) **89**
Zinfandel Howell Mountain 1985 $10 (4/30/88) **85**
Zinfandel Howell Mountain 1984 $10 (11/15/87) **88**

LA REINA (United States/California)
Chardonnay Monterey County 1987 $13.50 (3/31/89) **85**
Chardonnay Monterey County 1986 $13 (12/31/88) **75**
Chardonnay Monterey 1984 $12 (2/01/86) **86**

LA VIEILLE MONTAGNE (United States/California)
Cabernet Sauvignon Napa Valley 1987 $14 (6/15/91) **81**
Cabernet Sauvignon Napa Valley 1986 $14 (6/30/90) **84**

CHATEAU LABAT (France/Bordeaux)
Haut-Médoc 1981 $7 (4/01/85) **72**

CHATEAU LABEGORCE (France/Bordeaux)
Margaux 1991 (NR) (5/15/92) (BT) **75+**
Margaux 1987 $30 (3/31/91) **77**
Margaux 1986 $15 (2/15/90) **86**

CHATEAU LABEGORCE-ZEDE (France/Bordeaux)
Margaux 1991 (NR) (5/15/92) (BT) **80+**
Margaux 1990 (NR) (5/15/92) (BT) **90+**
Margaux 1989 $24 (3/15/92) **86**
Margaux 1988 $20 (4/30/91) **83**
Margaux 1987 $16 (11/30/89) (JS) **84**
Margaux 1986 Rel: $18 Cur: $22 (11/30/89) (JS) **91**
Margaux 1985 $13 (2/29/88) **84**
Margaux 1983 $15 (10/15/86) **88**
Margaux 1982 $21 (11/30/89) (JS) **87**

DOMAINE PIERRE LABET (France/Burgundy)
Beaune Coucherias 1989 (NR) (7/15/90) (BT) **90+**

J. LABET & N. DECHELETTE (France/Burgundy)
Clos Vougeot Château de la Tour 1989 $77 (7/15/90) (BT) **85+**
Clos Vougeot Château de la Tour 1988 $50 (11/30/90) **91**
Clos Vougeot Château de la Tour 1987 $50 (2/15/91) **84**
Clos Vougeot Château de la Tour 1985 $53 (6/15/88) **90**
Clos Vougeot Château de la Tour 1979 $40 (9/01/84) **66**

LABOURE-ROI (France/Burgundy)
Bourgogne 1988 $12 (3/31/91) **83**

Key to Symbols

The scores reported here are the results of blind tastings conducted by our panel of senior editors. Wines that carry the initials below are results of individual tastings.

THE WINE SPECTATOR 100-POINT SCALE ***95-100***—Classic, a great wine; ***90-94***—Outstanding, superior character and style; ***80-89***—Good to very good, a wine with special qualities; ***70-79***—Average, drinkable wine that may have minor flaws; ***60-69***—Below average, drinkable but not recommended; ***50-59***—Poor, undrinkable, not recommended. "+"—With a score indicates a range; used primarily with barrel tastings to indicate a preliminary score.

SPECIAL DESIGNATIONS SS—Spectator Selection, CS—Cellar Selection, BB—Best Buy, ($NA)—Price not available, (NR)—Not released.

TASTER'S INITIALS (JG)—Jim Gordon, (HS)—Harvey Steiman, (JL)—James Laube, (JS)—James Suckling, (TM)—Thomas Matthews, (TR)—Terry Robards, (PM)—Per-Henrik Mansson, (BT)—Barrel Tasting (these wines were tasted blind from barrel samples), (CA-date)—*California's Great Cabernets* by James Laube, (CH-date)—*California's Great Chardonnays* by James Laube, (VP-date)—*Vintage Port* by James Suckling.

DATE TASTED Dates in parentheses represent the issue in which the rating was published.

Chablis Les Fourchaumes 1988 $22 (7/31/90) **70**
Chambolle-Musigny 1988 $35 (2/28/91) **86**
Chambolle-Musigny Domaine Cottin 1989 $30 (3/31/92) **76**
Chardonnay Vin de Pays d'Oc 1989 $6 (6/30/92) BB **81**
Chassagne-Montrachet 1989 $42 (8/31/91) **88**
Chassagne-Montrachet 1985 $32 (8/31/87) **91**
Corton-Charlemagne 1989 $59 (4/15/92) **88**
Corton-Charlemagne 1988 $50 (10/15/90) **90**
Gevrey-Chambertin 1988 $35 (12/31/90) **81**
Mâcon-Villages 1989 $10 (4/30/91) **80**
Meursault 1989 $38 (8/31/91) **89**
Meursault 1988 $35 (8/31/90) **87**
Meursault 1986 $28 (4/30/88) **86**
Meursault 1985 $32 (11/15/86) **70**
Pommard Les Bertins 1985 $29 (3/15/88) **79**
Pouilly-Fuissé 1988 $18 (10/31/90) **89**
Pouilly-Fuissé 1985 $18 (3/31/87) **92**
Puligny-Montrachet 1989 $45 (8/31/91) **80**
Puligny-Montrachet 1985 $23 (11/15/86) **81**

CHATEAU LACHESNAYE (France/Bordeaux)
Haut-Médoc 1991 (NR) (5/15/92) (BT) **75+**
Haut-Médoc 1988 $24 (6/30/89) (BT) **75+**
Haut-Médoc 1987 $19 (6/30/89) (BT) **75+**

CHATEAU LACOSTE-BORIE (France/Bordeaux)
Pauillac 1989 $18 (3/15/92) **89**
Pauillac 1988 $19 (4/30/91) **89**
Pauillac 1986 $15 (6/30/89) **84**
Pauillac 1983 $7.50 (6/15/87) **75**

DE LADOUCETTE (France/Loire)
Pouilly-Fumé 1989 $22 (4/30/91) **86**
Pouilly-Fumé Baron de L 1988 $49 (5/31/91) **88**
Pouilly-Fumé Baron de L 1985 $40 (7/15/89) **90**
Pouilly-Fumé La Ladoucette 1988 $18 (9/15/90) **82**

DOMAINE MICHEL LAFARGE (France/Burgundy)
Bourgogne 1989 $19 (1/31/92) **85**
Volnay 1989 $41 (1/31/92) **88**
Volnay Clos des Chênes 1989 $67 (1/31/92) **95**
Volnay Clos des Chênes 1988 $65 (7/15/91) **90**
Volnay Clos du Château des Ducs 1989 $67 (1/31/92) **94**
Volnay Clos du Château des Ducs 1988 $65 (7/15/91) **90**
Volnay Premier Cru 1988 $44 (7/15/91) **87**

CHATEAU LAFAURIE-PEYRAGUEY (France/Sauternes)
Sauternes 1989 ($NA) (6/15/90) (BT) **95+**
Sauternes 1988 Rel: $35 Cur: $40 (4/30/91) **85**
Sauternes 1987 $27 (6/15/90) **87**
Sauternes 1986 Rel: $27 Cur: $38 (12/31/89) **86**
Sauternes 1985 Rel: $32 Cur: $38 (9/30/88) **92**
Sauternes 1983 Rel: $24 Cur: $70 (1/31/88) **91**

LAFAYETTE (United States/Florida)
Blanc de Fleur Florida NV $11 (2/29/92) **73**
Stover Special Reserve Florida 1988 $9 (2/29/92) **74**
Sunblush Florida NV $7 (2/29/92) **75**

CHATEAU LAFFITTE-CARCASSET (France/Bordeaux)
St.-Estèphe 1981 $7 (3/16/85) **74**

CHATEAU LAFITE-ROTHSCHILD (France/Bordeaux)
Pauillac 1991 (NR) (5/15/92) (BT) **85+**
Pauillac 1990 (NR) (5/15/92) (BT) **95+**
Pauillac 1989 $145 (3/15/92) **95**
Pauillac 1988 $100 (4/30/91) CS **96**
Pauillac 1987 $60 (11/30/91) (JG) **88**
Pauillac 1986 $102 (11/30/91) (JG) **96**
Pauillac 1985 Rel: $80 Cur: $101 (11/30/91) (JG) **95**
Pauillac 1985 Rel: $80 Cur: $101 (5/31/88) CS **97**
Pauillac 1984 Rel: $51 Cur: $62 (11/30/91) (JG) **87**
Pauillac 1983 Rel: $60 Cur: $100 (11/30/91) (JG) **90**
Pauillac 1982 Rel: $85 Cur: $180 (11/30/91) (JG) **96**
Pauillac 1981 Rel: $70 Cur: $150 (11/30/91) (JG) **91**
Pauillac 1980 $60 (11/30/91) (JG) **86**
Pauillac 1979 $115 (11/30/91) (JG) **92**
Pauillac 1978 $155 (11/30/91) (JG) **94**
Pauillac 1977 $40 (11/30/91) (JG) **87**
Pauillac 1976 $150 (11/30/91) (JG) **88**
Pauillac 1975 $190 (11/30/91) (JG) **71**
Pauillac 1974 $62 (11/30/91) (JG) **89**
Pauillac 1973 $55 (11/30/91) (JG) **87**
Pauillac 1972 $47 (11/30/91) (JG) **82**
Pauillac 1971 $105 (11/30/91) (JG) **87**
Pauillac 1970 $210 (11/30/91) (JG) **92**
Pauillac 1969 $45 (11/30/91) (JG) **80**
Pauillac 1968 $125 (11/30/91) (JG) **61**
Pauillac 1967 $80 (11/30/91) (JG) **80**
Pauillac 1966 $180 (11/30/91) (JG) **84**
Pauillac 1965 $120 (11/30/91) (JG) **73**
Pauillac 1964 $90 (11/30/91) (JG) **87**
Pauillac 1963 $200 (11/30/91) (JG) **69**
Pauillac 1962 $190 (11/30/91) (JG) **93**
Pauillac 1961 $520 (11/30/91) (JG) **91**
Pauillac 1961 $1,150/1.5L (11/30/91) (JG) **93**
Pauillac 1960 $105 (11/30/91) (JG) **92**
Pauillac 1959 $580 (11/30/91) (JG) **94**
Pauillac 1959 $1,270/1.5L (11/30/91) (JG) **98**
Pauillac 1958 $100 (11/30/91) (JG) **77**
Pauillac 1957 $110 (11/30/91) (JG) **87**
Pauillac 1956 $230 (11/30/91) (JG) **85**
Pauillac 1955 $350 (11/30/91) (JG) **94**
Pauillac 1954 $290 (11/30/91) (JG) **82**
Pauillac 1953 $500 (11/30/91) (JG) **94**
Pauillac 1953 $1,100/1.5L (11/30/91) (JG) **96**
Pauillac 1952 $240 (11/30/91) (JG) **90**
Pauillac 1951 $150 (11/30/91) (JG) **78**
Pauillac 1950 $300 (11/30/91) (JG) **91**
Pauillac 1949 $750 (11/30/91) (JG) **87**
Pauillac 1949 $1,650/1.5L (11/30/91) (JG) **90**

Pauillac 1948 $680 (11/30/91) (JG) **61**
Pauillac 1947 $450 (11/30/91) (JG) **74**
Pauillac 1946 $450 (11/30/91) (JG) **79**
Pauillac 1945 $950 (11/30/91) (JG) **96**
Pauillac 1944 $380 (11/30/91) (JG) **63**
Pauillac 1943 $290 (11/30/91) (JG) **87**
Pauillac 1943 $630/1.5L (11/30/91) (JG) **85**
Pauillac 1942 $320 (11/30/91) (JG) **80**
Pauillac 1941 $500 (11/30/91) (JG) **69**
Pauillac 1940 $700 (11/30/91) (JG) **85**
Pauillac 1939 $320 (12/15/88) (TR) **78**
Pauillac 1938 $230 (11/30/91) (JG) **83**
Pauillac 1937 $250 (11/30/91) (JG) **81**
Pauillac 1934 $450 (11/30/91) (JG) **90**
Pauillac 1933 $200 (11/30/91) (JG) **80**
Pauillac 1931 $550 (11/30/91) (JG) **77**
Pauillac 1929 $950 (11/30/91) (JG) **87**
Pauillac 1929 $2,090/1.5L (11/30/91) (JG) **88**
Pauillac 1928 $700 (11/30/91) (JG) **66**
Pauillac 1926 $550 (11/30/91) (JG) **89**
Pauillac 1926 $1,210/1.5L (11/30/91) (JG) **69**
Pauillac 1925 $195 (11/30/91) (JG) **56**
Pauillac 1924 $450 (11/30/91) (JG) **88**
Pauillac 1923 $300 (11/30/91) (JG) **75**
Pauillac 1922 $330 (11/30/91) (JG) **64**
Pauillac 1921 $500 (12/15/88) (TR) **77**
Pauillac 1920 $580 (11/30/91) (JG) **94**
Pauillac 1919 $600 (11/30/91) (JG) **76**
Pauillac 1918 $530 (11/30/91) (JG) **80**
Pauillac 1917 ($NA) (11/30/91) (JG) **75**
Pauillac 1916 $380 (11/30/91) (JG) **71**
Pauillac 1916 $830/1.5L (11/30/91) (JG) **89**
Pauillac 1914 $550 (11/30/91) (JG) **58**
Pauillac 1913 $500 (11/30/91) (JG) **82**
Pauillac 1912 $680 (11/30/91) (JG) **69**
Pauillac 1911 $400 (11/30/91) (JG) **83**
Pauillac 1910 $580 (11/30/91) (JG) **69**
Pauillac 1909 $500 (11/30/91) (JG) **73**
Pauillac 1908 ($NA) (11/30/91) (JG) **86**
Pauillac 1907 $700 (11/30/91) (JG) **64**
Pauillac 1906 $350 (11/30/91) (JG) **90**
Pauillac 1905 $550 (11/30/91) (JG) **88**
Pauillac 1904 $650 (11/30/91) (JG) **84**
Pauillac 1903 ($NA) (11/30/91) (JG) **68**
Pauillac 1902 $850 (11/30/91) (JG) **80**
Pauillac 1901 $700 (11/30/91) (JG) **74**
Pauillac 1900 $1,900 (11/30/91) (JG) **79**
Pauillac 1900 $4,180/1.5L (11/30/91) (JG) **70**
Pauillac 1898 $1,000 (12/15/88) (TR) **79**
Pauillac 1897 $1,200 (12/15/88) (TR) **81**
Pauillac 1896 $1,100 (12/15/88) (TR) **79**
Pauillac 1895 $2,100 (12/15/88) (TR) **89**
Pauillac 1894 $1,000 (11/30/91) (JG) **71**
Pauillac 1893 $1,200 (12/15/88) (TR) **84**
Pauillac 1892 $1,200 (11/30/91) (JG) **72**
Pauillac 1891 $1,100 (11/30/91) (JG) **70**
Pauillac 1890 $1,100 (12/15/88) (TR) **83**
Pauillac 1889 $850 (12/15/88) (TR) **85**
Pauillac 1888 $900 (12/15/88) (TR) **82**
Pauillac 1887 $1,000 (11/30/91) (JG) **67**
Pauillac 1886 $1,100 (12/15/88) (TR) **88**
Pauillac 1882 $800 (12/15/88) (TR) **82**
Pauillac 1881 $750 (11/30/91) (JG) **66**
Pauillac 1880 $1,400 (12/15/88) (TR) **82**
Pauillac 1879 $2,800 (12/15/88) (TR) **83**
Pauillac 1878 $2,200 (12/15/88) (TR) **83**
Pauillac 1877 $2,500 (12/15/88) (TR) **88**
Pauillac 1876 $1,800 (12/15/88) (TR) **84**
Pauillac 1875 $3,000 (12/15/88) (TR) **91**
Pauillac 1875 $6,600/1.5L (12/15/88) (TR) **97**
Pauillac 1874 $2,200 (12/15/88) (TR) **84**
Pauillac 1870 $3,500 (11/30/91) (JG) **92**
Pauillac 1870 $7,700/1.5L (11/30/91) (JG) **62**
Pauillac 1869 $4,000 (11/30/91) (JG) **87**
Pauillac 1868 $4,000 (11/30/91) (JG) **91**
Pauillac 1865 $6,500 (11/30/91) (JG) **50**
Pauillac 1864 $5,000 (12/15/88) (TR) **84**
Pauillac 1858 $4,000 (12/15/88) (TR) **96**
Pauillac 1848 ($NA) (12/15/88) (TR) **92**
Pauillac 1846 $8,000 (12/15/88) (TR) **83**
Pauillac 1844 $6,000 (12/15/88) (TR) **84**
Pauillac 1832 $9,000 (11/30/91) (JG) **78**
Pauillac 1806 $5,000 (12/15/88) (TR) **83**

CHARLES LAFITTE (France/Champagne)
Brut Champagne Tête de Cuvée NV (NR) (12/31/91) **84**

CHATEAU LAFLEUR (France/Bordeaux)
Pomerol 1990 (NR) (5/15/92) (BT) **95+**
Pomerol 1989 $225 (3/15/92) **96**
Pomerol 1988 Rel: $95 Cur: $125 (10/31/91) **90**
Pomerol 1986 Rel: $100 Cur: $160 (10/31/89) **90**
Pomerol 1985 $170 (5/01/89) **95**
Pomerol 1982 $250 (5/01/89) **91**
Pomerol 1981 Rel: $22 Cur: $100 (6/01/84) **80**
Pomerol 1979 $220 (10/15/89) (JS) **96**
Pomerol 1945 $400 (3/16/86) (JL) **64**

PENSEES DE LAFLEUR (France/Bordeaux)
Pomerol 1990 (NR) (5/15/92) (BT) **95+**

CHATEAU LAFLEUR-GAZIN (France/Bordeaux)
Pomerol 1989 (NR) (3/15/92) **87**
Pomerol 1945 ($NA) (3/16/86) (JL) **58**

CHATEAU LAFLEUR-POURRET (France/Bordeaux)
St.-Emilion 1989 (NR) (4/30/91) (BT) **70+**

CHATEAU LAFLEUR DU ROY (France/Bordeaux)
Pomerol 1982 ($NA) (5/15/89) (TR) **83**

CHATEAU LAFLEUR-ST.-EMILION (France/Bordeaux)
St.-Emilion 1990 (NR) (4/30/91) (BT) **95+**
St.-Emilion 1989 (NR) (4/30/91) (BT) **85+**

CHATEAU LAFON-ROCHET (France/Bordeaux)
St.-Estèphe 1991 (NR) (5/15/92) (BT) **80+**
St.-Estèphe 1990 (NR) (5/15/92) (BT) **90+**
St.-Estèphe 1989 $18 (3/15/92) **92**
St.-Estèphe 1988 $17 (6/30/89) (BT) **85+**
St.-Estèphe 1987 $14 (6/30/89) (BT) **80+**
St.-Estèphe 1986 $20 (6/30/88) (BT) **85+**
St.-Estèphe 1985 $16 (5/15/87) (BT) **70+**
St.-Estèphe 1961 $80 (3/16/86) (TR) **58**
St.-Estèphe 1945 $100 (3/16/86) (JL) **75**

COMTE LAFOND (France/Loire)
Sancerre 1989 $21 (4/30/91) **88**

JEAN LAFOUGE (France/Burgundy)
Auxey-Duresses 1985 $19 (6/15/87) **75**

CHATEAU LAGARENNE (France/Bordeaux)
Bordeaux Supérieur 1988 $8 (7/31/90) BB **82**

ALOIS LAGEDER (Italy/North)
Chardonnay Alto Adige Buchhoiz 1988 $13 (9/15/89) **88**
Chardonnay Alto Adige Loewengang 1986 $19 (9/15/89) **82**
Chardonnay Alto Adige Loewengang 1985 $19 (9/15/89) **90**

DOMAINE FRANCOIS LAGET (France/Rhône)
Châteauneuf-du-Pape 1985 $14 (9/30/87) **71**
Châteauneuf-du-Pape 1984 $14 (12/31/87) **76**
Châteauneuf-du-Pape 1983 $12 (9/30/87) **89**

CHATEAU LAGRANGE (France/Bordeaux)
Pomerol 1990 (NR) (4/30/91) (BT) **90+**
Pomerol 1988 $25 (6/30/89) (BT) **85+**
Pomerol 1985 $21 (4/16/86) (BT) **80+**
Pomerol 1982 $30 (5/15/89) (TR) **84**

CHATEAU LAGRANGE (France/Bordeaux)
Pomerol 1990 (NR) (5/15/92) (BT) **90+**
Pomerol 1989 $29 (3/15/92) **87**
St.-Julien 1991 (NR) (5/15/92) (BT) **85+**
St.-Julien 1990 (NR) (5/15/92) (BT) **95+**
St.-Julien 1989 $29 (3/15/92) **95**
St.-Julien 1988 $26 (4/30/91) **96**
St.-Julien 1987 $25 (6/30/88) (BT) **75+**
St.-Julien 1986 Rel: $20 Cur: $28 (2/15/90) **86**
St.-Julien 1985 Rel: $23 Cur: $25 (9/30/88) **83**
St.-Julien 1961 $90 (3/16/86) (TR) **67**

CHATEAU LAGRAVE PARAN (France/Bordeaux)
Bordeaux 1989 $8 (2/28/91) **79**
Bordeaux 1988 $6 (7/15/90) BB **82**
Bordeaux 1987 $7 (5/15/90) BB **80**

CHATEAU LA LAGUNE (France/Bordeaux)
Haut-Médoc 1989 $35 (3/15/92) **86**
Haut-Médoc 1988 $24 (4/30/91) **91**
Haut-Médoc 1987 $20 (5/15/90) **89**
Haut-Médoc 1986 Rel: $22 Cur: $26 (6/30/89) **89**
Haut-Médoc 1985 Rel: $22 Cur: $29 (5/15/88) **89**
Haut-Médoc 1984 Rel: $13 Cur: $16 (3/31/87) **86**
Haut-Médoc 1983 Rel: $20 Cur: $30 (4/16/86) **85**
Haut-Médoc 1982 Rel: $28 Cur: $46 (5/01/89) **97**
Haut-Médoc 1981 Rel: $25 Cur: $30 (5/01/89) **82**
Haut-Médoc 1979 $29 (10/15/89) (JS) **86**
Haut-Médoc 1962 $65 (11/30/87) (JS) **80**
Haut-Médoc 1945 $200 (3/16/86) (JL) **87**

LAKE SONOMA (United States/California)
Merlot Dry Creek Valley Yoakim Bridge Ranch 1990 $13.50 (5/31/92) **86**

LAKE'S FOLLY (Australia)
Cabernet Hunter Valley 1985 $15.50 (3/31/89) **80**

LAKERIDGE (United States/Florida)
Crescendo Florida NV $12 (2/29/92) **79**
Cuvée Blanc Florida NV $9 (2/29/92) **73**
Southern White Wine Florida NV $7 (2/29/92) **77**

LAKESIDE (United States/Washington)
Chenin Blanc Washington NV $6 (7/31/89) **68**

LAKESPRING (United States/California)
Cabernet Sauvignon Napa Valley 1987 Rel: $14 Cur: $18 (10/15/91) **84**
Cabernet Sauvignon Napa Valley 1986 Rel: $14 Cur: $18 (CA-3/89) **88**
Cabernet Sauvignon Napa Valley 1985 Rel: $12 Cur: $19 (CA-3/89) **88**
Cabernet Sauvignon Napa Valley Reserve Selection 1984 Rel: $15 Cur: $21 (10/31/88) SS **92**
Cabernet Sauvignon Napa Valley 1983 Rel: $11 Cur: $14 (CA-3/89) **85**
Cabernet Sauvignon Napa Valley Vintage Selection 1982 Rel: $14 Cur: $32 (CA-3/89) **88**
Cabernet Sauvignon Napa Valley 1981 Rel: $11 Cur: $22 (CA-3/89) **86**
Cabernet Sauvignon Napa Valley 1980 Rel: $10 Cur: $21 (CA-3/89) **88**
Chardonnay Alexander Valley 1981 $10 (4/16/84) **78**
Chardonnay Napa Valley 1989 $13.50 (1/31/92) **79**
Chardonnay Napa Valley 1988 $13 (5/15/91) **88**
Chardonnay Napa Valley 1987 $12 (10/31/89) **72**
Chardonnay Napa Valley 1986 $11 (12/31/88) **90**
Chardonnay Napa Valley 1985 $11 (11/15/87) **71**
Chardonnay Napa Valley 1984 $12 (10/31/86) **70**
Merlot Napa Valley 1987 $14 (6/15/90) **85**
Merlot Napa Valley 1986 $14 (3/31/89) **79**
Merlot Napa Valley 1985 Rel: $12 Cur: $15 (3/31/88) SS **91**
Merlot Napa Valley 1984 $12 (5/15/87) **88**
Merlot Napa Valley 1983 $11 (5/16/86) **87**
Merlot Napa Valley 1982 $10 (10/01/85) **78**
Merlot Napa Valley Yountmill Vineyard 1988 $15 (2/29/92) **85**
Sauvignon Blanc Napa Valley 1988 $8.50 (11/30/89) **76**
Sauvignon Blanc Napa Valley Yountmill Vineyard 1990 $8.50 (10/15/91) **83**

CHATEAU LALANDE-BORIE (France/Bordeaux)
St.-Julien 1989 $22 (3/15/92) **88**
St.-Julien 1988 $17 (4/30/91) **87**
St.-Julien 1987 $15 (11/30/89) (JS) **81**

St.-Julien 1986 $17 (11/30/89) (JS) **91**
St.-Julien 1982 Rel: $15 Cur: $17 (11/30/89) (JS) **92**

DOMAINE FRANCOIS LAMARCHE (France/Burgundy)
Clos de Vougeot 1987 $55 (9/30/90) **86**
Clos de Vougeot 1985 $48 (10/15/88) **90**
Echézeaux 1987 $48 (9/30/90) **87**
Vosne-Romanée La Grande Rue 1987 $68 (9/30/90) **91**
Vosne-Romanée La Grande Rue 1985 $60 (10/15/88) **89**
Vosne-Romanée Malconsorts 1985 $44 (10/15/88) **84**
Vosne-Romanée Suchots 1985 $36 (10/15/88) **91**

CHATEAU DE LAMARQUE (France/Bordeaux)
Haut-Médoc 1991 (NR) (5/15/92) (BT) **85+**
Haut-Médoc 1989 $26 (3/15/92) **89**
Haut-Médoc 1988 $20 (4/30/91) **86**
Haut-Médoc 1987 $10 (11/30/89) (JS) **74**
Haut-Médoc 1986 $12 (11/30/89) (JS) **75**
Haut-Médoc 1982 $14 (11/30/89) (JS) **79**

CHATEAU LAMARTINE (France/Bordeaux)
Bordeaux 1989 (NR) (4/30/91) (BT) **75+**
Bordeaux Supérieur 1991 (NR) (5/15/92) (BT) **80+**
Bordeaux Supérieur 1984 $9 (5/15/87) **76**

LAMBERT BRIDGE (United States/California)
Cabernet Sauvignon Sonoma County 1984 $10 (4/15/87) **80**
Cabernet Sauvignon Sonoma County 1981 $12 (1/01/85) **75**
Chardonnay Sonoma County 1985 $10 (2/15/88) **73**
Chardonnay Sonoma County 1982 $13.50 (12/16/84) **83**
Merlot Sonoma County 1985 $10 (12/15/87) **69**
Merlot Sonoma County 1982 $11.50 (12/16/84) **79**

LAMBORN FAMILY (United States/California)
Zinfandel Howell Mountain 1988 $11 (2/15/91) **89**
Zinfandel Howell Mountain 1987 $10 (3/15/90) **84**

LAMOLE DI LAMOLE (Italy/Tuscany)
Chianti Classico 1988 $12 (9/15/91) **90**
Chianti Classico Vigneto di Campolungo 1985 $20 (4/30/90) **90**

CHATEAU LAMOTHE (France/Bordeaux)
Bordeaux Blanc 1985 $5 (10/15/87) **71**
Sauternes 1988 $16/375ml (3/31/91) **84**
Sauternes 1986 $29 (12/31/89) **85**

CHATEAU LAMOTHE-BERGERON (France/Bordeaux)
Haut-Médoc 1988 $15 (6/30/89) (BT) **80+**
Haut-Médoc 1987 $10 (6/30/89) (BT) **70+**

CHATEAU LAMOTHE-CISSAC (France/Bordeaux)
Haut-Médoc 1987 $10 (11/30/89) (JS) **74**
Haut-Médoc 1986 $12 (11/30/89) (JS) **69**

CHATEAU LAMOTHE-DESPUJOLS (France/Sauternes)
Sauternes 1989 ($NA) (6/15/90) (BT) **85+**
Sauternes 1987 ($NA) (6/15/90) **84**

CHATEAU LAMOTHE-GUIGNARD (France/Sauternes)
Sauternes 1989 ($NA) (6/15/90) (BT) **85+**
Sauternes 1988 $35 (6/15/90) (BT) **85+**
Sauternes 1987 ($NA) (6/15/90) **77**
Sauternes 1986 $30 (6/30/88) (BT) **75+**

CHATEAU LAMOUROUX (France/Bordeaux)
Margaux 1988 ($NA) (6/30/89) (BT) **75+**
Margaux 1987 ($NA) (6/30/89) (BT) **70+**

LANCIOLA II (Italy/Tuscany)
Chianti Colli Fiorentini 1987 $7.75 (5/15/89) **68**

LANCON PERE & FILS (France/Rhône)
Châteauneuf-du-Pape Domaine de la Solitude 1983 $14 (12/31/87) **58**

CHATEAU LANDAT (France/Bordeaux)
Haut-Médoc 1987 $7 (11/30/89) (JS) **73**

CHATEAU LANDAY (France/Bordeaux)
Haut-Médoc 1982 $6.75 (2/16/85) **77**
Haut-Médoc 1981 $6.50 (2/16/85) **72**

CHATEAU LANDEREAU (France/Bordeaux)
Bordeaux Supérieur 1985 $6.75 (2/15/88) BB **81**

LANDGRAF VON HESSEN (Germany)
Riesling Kabinett Halbtrocken Rheingau Winkeler Jesuitengarten 1988 ($NA) (9/30/89) **80**
Riesling Kabinett Rheingau Johannisberger Klaus 1988 ($NA) (9/30/89) **81**
Riesling Kabinett Rheingau Prinz von Hessen 1988 ($NA) (9/30/89) **80**
Riesling Spätlese Rheingau Eltville Sonnenberg 1988 ($NA) (9/30/89) **89**

LANDMARK (United States/California)
Chardonnay Alexander Valley Proprietor's Grown 1982 $10 (5/01/84) **76**
Chardonnay Sonoma County 1990 $12 (7/15/92) **84**
Chardonnay Sonoma County 1989 $12 (11/30/91) **62**
Chardonnay Sonoma County 1988 $10 (4/15/91) **87**
Chardonnay Sonoma County 1985 $10 (2/15/88) **71**
Chardonnay Sonoma County 1983 $9 (1/01/86) **80**
Chardonnay Sonoma Valley 1982 $9 (5/01/84) **78**
Chardonnay Alexander Valley Damaris Reserve 1990 $16 (7/15/92) **83**

Key to Symbols

The scores reported here are the results of blind tastings conducted by our panel of senior editors. Wines that carry the initials below are results of individual tastings.

THE WINE SPECTATOR 100-POINT SCALE 95-100—Classic, a great wine; ***90-94***—Outstanding, superior character and style; ***80-89***—Good to very good, a wine with special qualities; ***70-79***—Average, drinkable wine that may have minor flaws; ***60-69***—Below average, drinkable but not recommended; ***50-59***—Poor, undrinkable, not recommended. "+"—With a score indicates a range; used primarily with barrel tastings to indicate a preliminary score.

SPECIAL DESIGNATIONS SS—Spectator Selection, CS—Cellar Selection, BB—Best Buy, ($NA)—Price not available, (NR)—Not released.

TASTER'S INITIALS (JG)—Jim Gordon, (HS)—Harvey Steiman, (JL)—James Laube, (JS)—James Suckling, (TM)—Thomas Matthews, (TR)—Terry Robards, (PM)—Per-Henrik Mansson, (BT)—Barrel Tasting (these wines were tasted blind from barrel samples), (CA-date)—*California's Great Cabernets* by James Laube, (CH-date)—*California's Great Chardonnays* by James Laube, (VP-date)—*Vintage Port* by James Suckling.

DATE TASTED Dates in parentheses represent the issue in which the rating was published.

Chardonnay Sonoma Valley Damaris Vineyard 1989 $16 (6/30/91) **87**
Chardonnay Sonoma Valley Two Williams 1990 $16 (7/15/92) **69**
Chardonnay Sonoma Valley Two Williams Vineyard 1989 $16 (7/15/91) **78**

LANE TANNER (United States/California)
Pinot Noir Santa Barbara County Benedict Vineyard 1989 $25 (11/15/91) **85**

CHATEAU LANESSAN (France/Bordeaux)
Haut-Médoc 1991 (NR) (5/15/92) (BT) **85+**
Haut-Médoc 1990 (NR) (4/30/91) (BT) **80+**
Haut-Médoc 1989 $29 (3/15/92) **85**
Haut-Médoc 1988 $25 (7/31/91) **80**
Haut-Médoc 1987 $14 (6/30/89) (BT) **70+**
Haut-Médoc 1986 $16 (6/30/88) (BT) **80+**
Haut-Médoc 1985 $16 (4/30/88) **87**

CHATEAU LANGE (France/Sauternes)
Sauternes 1988 ($NA) (6/15/90) (BT) **80+**
Sauternes 1987 ($NA) (6/15/90) **78**

LADY LANGOA (France/Bordeaux)
St.-Julien 1989 (NR) (4/30/91) (BT) **80+**

CHATEAU LANGOA BARTON (France/Bordeaux)
St.-Julien 1991 (NR) (5/15/92) (BT) **80+**
St.-Julien 1990 (NR) (5/15/92) (BT) **90+**
St.-Julien 1989 $28 (3/15/92) **94**
St.-Julien 1988 $25 (7/15/91) **86**
St.-Julien 1987 $17 (6/30/89) (BT) **75+**
St.-Julien 1986 Rel: $22 Cur: $26 (6/30/88) (BT) **85+**
St.-Julien 1985 $20 (6/15/88) **91**
St.-Julien 1961 $113 (3/16/86) (TR) **63**
St.-Julien 1945 $250 (3/16/86) (JL) **71**

LANGWERTH VON SIMMERN (Germany)
Riesling Auslese Rheingau Hattenheimer Mannberg 1989 $50 (12/15/90) **94**
Riesling Auslese Rheingau Hattenheimer Nussbrunnen 1990 $30 (12/15/91) **87**
Riesling Auslese Rheingau Hattenheimer Nussbrunnen 1989 $57 (12/15/90) **91**
Riesling Beerenauslese Rheingau Erbacher Marcobrunn 1990 $300 (12/15/91) **91**
Riesling Beerenauslese Rheingau Hattenheimer Nussbrunnen 1990 $300 (12/15/91) **90**
Riesling Kabinett Rheingau Eltviller Sonnenberg 1990 $10 (12/15/91) **84**
Riesling Kabinett Rheingau Eltviller Sonnenberg 1989 $11 (12/15/90) **80**
Riesling Kabinett Rheingau Erbacher Marcobrunn 1989 $16 (12/15/90) **83**
Riesling Kabinett Rheingau Hattenheimer Mannberg 1989 $25 (12/15/90) **84**
Riesling Kabinett Rheingau Hattenheimer Mannberg 1985 $8.50 (1/31/87) **83**
Riesling Kabinett Rheingau Hattenheimer Nussbrunnen 1990 $10 (12/15/91) **86**
Riesling Kabinett Rheingau Hattenheimer Nussbrunnen 1989 $13.50 (12/15/90) **88**
Riesling Kabinett Rheingau Kiedricher Sandgrub 1990 $13 (12/15/91) **86**
Riesling Kabinett Rheingau Kiedricher Sandgrub 1988 ($NA) (9/30/89) **80**
Riesling Spätlese Rheingau Erbacher Marcobrunn 1989 $25 (12/15/90) **87**
Riesling Spätlese Rheingau Hattenheimer Nussbrunnen 1990 $22 (12/15/91) **89**
Riesling Spätlese Rheingau Hattenheimer Nussbrunnen 1989 $25 (12/15/90) **84**
Riesling Spätlese Rheingau Hattenheimer Nussbrunnen 1988 ($NA) (9/30/89) **84**
Riesling Spätlese Rheingau Hattenheimer Nussbrunnen 1983 $12 (4/01/85) **76**
Riesling Spätlese Rheingau Rauenthaler Baiken 1989 $25 (12/15/90) **87**
Riesling Spätlese Rheingau Rauenthaler Baiken 1988 ($NA) (9/30/89) **90**
Riesling Trockenbeerenauslese Rheingau Erbacher Marcobrunn 1989 ($NA) (12/15/90) **99**
Riesling Trockenbeerenauslese Rheingau Hattenheimer Nussbrunnen 1990 $500 (12/15/91) **94**

LANSON (France/Champagne)
225th Anniversary Cuvée Champagne 1981 $43 (10/15/88) **89**
225th Anniversary Spécial Cuvée Champagne 1980 $43 (11/30/86) **95**
Brut Champagne 1985 $37 (12/31/90) **93**
Brut Champagne 1983 $30 (12/31/89) **85**
Brut Champagne 1982 $27 (10/15/88) **92**
Brut Champagne Black Label NV $35 (12/31/91) **87**
Brut Rosé Champagne 1982 $35 (12/31/88) **88**
Brut Rosé Champagne NV $24 (12/31/86) **73**
Extra Dry Champagne Ivory Label NV $19 (12/31/88) **86**
Extra Dry Champagne White Label NV $19 (12/31/88) **70**

DOMAINE LAPIERRE (France/Burgundy)
Pouilly-Fuissé 1985 $13 (3/31/87) **90**

DOMAINE LAPORTE (France/Loire)
Sancerre Domaine du Rochoy 1988 $16 (4/15/90) **76**
Sancerre Domaine du Rochoy 1987 $14 (2/28/89) **85**

LAR DE BARROS (Spain)
Tierra de Barros Tinto Reserva 1988 $10 (4/15/92) **79**
Tierra de Barros Tinto Reserva 1986 $8 (10/15/90) SS **91**

LAR DE LARES (Spain)
Tierra de Barros Gran Reserva 1982 $14 (6/15/91) **90**

CHATEAU LARCIS-DUCASSE (France/Bordeaux)
St.-Emilion 1991 (NR) (5/15/92) (BT) **80+**
St.-Emilion 1989 $28 (3/15/92) **91**
St.-Emilion 1988 $20 (4/30/91) **82**
St.-Emilion 1987 $17 (6/30/89) (BT) **75+**
St.-Emilion 1986 Rel: $20 Cur: $25 (6/30/88) (BT) **80+**
St.-Emilion 1982 $25 (5/15/89) (TR) **85**

CHATEAU LARMANDE (France/Bordeaux)
St.-Emilion 1991 (NR) (5/15/92) (BT) **75+**
St.-Emilion 1990 (NR) (4/30/91) (BT) **85+**
St.-Emilion 1989 $26 (3/15/92) **95**
St.-Emilion 1988 $23 (4/30/91) **86**
St.-Emilion 1987 $17 (6/30/89) (BT) **80+**
St.-Emilion 1986 Rel: $19 Cur: $24 (6/30/89) **91**
St.-Emilion 1985 $23 (5/15/88) **93**
St.-Emilion 1983 Rel: $13 Cur: $16 (3/16/86) **87**
St.-Emilion 1982 $28 (5/15/89) (TR) **91**
St.-Emilion 1981 $10 (8/01/84) **76**

GUY LARMANDIER (France/Champagne)
Brut Blanc de Blancs Champagne Cramant NV $27 (5/31/87) **92**
Brut Rosé Champagne NV $20 (12/31/89) **84**

LAROCHE (France/Burgundy)
Chablis 1986 $12 (5/15/88) **88**
Chablis Fourchaume 1988 $23 (7/31/90) **80**
Chardonnay 1987 $7 (10/31/89) **73**
Chassagne-Montrachet 1989 $45 (2/28/91) **90**
Chassagne-Montrachet 1988 $33 (2/15/91) **83**

Chassagne-Montrachet Première Cru 1988 $39 (2/15/91) **90**
Criots-Bâtard-Montrachet 1986 $63 (10/31/88) **87**
Mâcon-Villages 1988 $8.50 (7/15/90) **79**
Meursault 1988 $28 (8/31/90) **82**
Meursault Les Perrières 1986 $20 (10/31/88) **82**
Nuits-St.-Georges 1988 $28 (11/15/90) **87**
Puligny-Montrachet 1989 $47 (2/28/91) **80**
St.-Véran 1988 $10 (7/31/90) **81**

DOMAINE LAROCHE (France/Burgundy)
Bourgogne Blanc Clos du Château 1986 $16 (1/31/89) **80**
Chablis 1990 $16 (11/30/91) **90**
Chablis 1988 $16 (7/31/90) **87**
Chablis 1987 $26 (3/31/91) **74**
Chablis 1983 $13 (11/15/86) **91**
Chablis Les Beauroys 1984 $19 (10/31/87) **79**
Chablis Les Blanchots 1989 $47 (8/31/91) **89**
Chablis Les Blanchots 1987 $40 (3/31/89) **95**
Chablis Les Blanchots 1984 $27 (2/28/87) **93**
Chablis Les Blanchots Vieilles Vignes 1989 $72 (1/31/91) **88**
Chablis Les Blanchots Vieilles Vignes 1988 $58 (7/31/90) **86**
Chablis Les Blanchots Vieilles Vignes 1987 $50 (3/31/89) **94**
Chablis Les Bouguerots 1985 $33 (6/15/87) **86**
Chablis Les Clos 1988 $49 (12/15/89) **83**
Chablis Les Clos 1987 $50 (3/31/89) **90**
Chablis Les Clos 1986 $50 (12/31/88) **89**
Chablis Cuvée Première 1989 $25 (1/31/91) **87**
Chablis Les Fourchaumes 1988 $23 (12/15/89) **88**
Chablis Les Fourchaumes 1987 $26 (3/31/89) **90**
Chablis Les Fourchaumes 1986 $29 (5/15/88) **86**
Chablis Les Fourchaumes 1984 $18 (1/31/87) **85**
Chablis Les Fourchaumes Vieilles Vignes 1987 $45 (3/31/89) **93**
Chablis Laroche Cuvée Première 1988 $16 (12/15/89) **83**
Chablis Les Montmains 1988 $25 (7/31/90) **84**
Chablis St.-Martin 1990 $18 (11/30/91) **90**
Chablis St.-Martin 1989 $21 (2/28/91) **82**
Chablis St.-Martin 1988 $15 (12/15/89) **90**
Chablis St.-Martin 1987 $17 (3/31/89) **82**
Chablis St.-Martin 1986 $16 (12/31/88) **86**
Chablis St.-Martin 1985 $16 (6/30/87) **83**
Chablis Les Vaillons 1989 $33 (1/31/91) **86**
Chablis Les Vaillons 1988 $22 (12/15/89) **88**
Chablis Les Vaillons 1987 $25 (3/31/89) **87**
Chablis Les Vaillons 1986 $23 (12/31/88) **86**
Chablis Les Vaillons 1983 $15 (2/16/86) **66**
Chablis Les Vaudevey 1990 $25 (11/30/91) **87**
Chablis Les Vaudevey 1988 $24 (7/31/90) **87**
Chablis Les Vaudevey 1987 $23 (3/31/89) **85**
Chablis Les Vaudevey 1985 $19 (6/15/87) **80**
Chablis Les Vaudevey 1984 $17 (1/31/87) **75**
Chablis Les Vaudevey 1983 $15 (12/01/85) **77**
Meursault Porusot 1986 $27 (10/31/88) **89**
Puligny-Montrachet Les Folatières 1988 $39 (6/30/90) **84**
Puligny-Montrachet Château de Puligny-Montrachet 1986 $60 (9/30/88) **92**

CHATEAU LAROQUE (France/Bordeaux)
St.-Emilion 1983 $13 (2/15/88) **64**

CHATEAU LAROSE-TRINTAUDON (France/Bordeaux)
Haut-Médoc 1991 (NR) (5/15/92) (BT) **75+**
Haut-Médoc 1990 (NR) (5/15/92) (BT) **85+**
Haut-Médoc 1989 $12 (3/15/92) **87**
Haut-Médoc 1988 $12 (4/30/91) **84**
Haut-Médoc 1987 $9 (11/30/89) (JS) **71**
Haut-Médoc 1986 $10 (11/30/89) (JS) **78**
Haut-Médoc 1985 $8.50 (11/30/88) BB **84**
Haut-Médoc 1983 Rel: $7 Cur: $13 (10/15/86) **73**
Haut-Médoc 1982 Rel: $6 Cur: $15 (11/30/89) (JS) **79**
Haut-Médoc 1979 Rel: $5 Cur: $15 (10/15/89) (JS) **76**

CHATEAU LARRIVET-HAUT-BRION (France/Bordeaux)
Pessac-Léognan 1991 (NR) (5/15/92) (BT) **75+**
Pessac-Léognan 1990 (NR) (5/15/92) (BT) **90+**
Pessac-Léognan 1989 $33 (3/15/92) **89**
Pessac-Léognan 1988 $25 (4/30/91) **94**
Pessac-Léognan 1987 $17 (6/30/89) (BT) **75+**
Pessac-Léognan 1986 $17 (6/15/89) **82**
Pessac-Léognan Blanc 1990 (NR) (9/30/91) (BT) **85+**
Pessac-Léognan Blanc 1989 ($NA) (9/30/91) **82**
Pessac-Léognan Blanc 1987 ($NA) (7/15/88) (BT) **80+**

CHATEAU LARROQUE (France/Bordeaux)
Bordeaux Blanc 1985 $3.75 (10/15/87) BB **79**
Bordeaux Blanc 1984 $3.75 (12/15/86) BB **85**
Bordeaux Blanc Sec 1987 $5 (3/31/89) **78**

CHATEAU LASCOMBES (France/Bordeaux)
Margaux 1989 $23 (4/30/90) (BT) **80+**
Margaux 1988 $25 (8/31/91) **82**
Margaux 1987 $24 (6/30/89) (BT) **80+**
Margaux 1986 $24 (6/30/88) (BT) **80+**
Margaux 1985 Rel: $20 Cur: $31 (5/15/87) (BT) **80+**
Margaux 1983 $32 (2/15/88) **84**
Margaux 1981 Rel: $19 Cur: $31 (5/16/85) **85**
Margaux 1979 $15 (10/15/89) (JS) **84**

ROGER LASSARAT (France/Burgundy)
Pouilly-Fuissé Clos de France 1986 $26 (4/30/88) **90**
Pouilly-Fuissé Clos de France 1985 $23 (12/31/87) **88**
St.-Véran La Côte-Rôtie 1986 $13 (4/30/88) **73**
St.-Véran Cuvée Prestige 1988 $15 (8/31/90) **77**

LASSETER (Australia)
Brut Australia 1985 $17 (10/31/89) **87**
Brut Australia NV $10 (12/31/88) **84**

LATAH CREEK (United States/Washington)
Cabernet Sauvignon Washington 1986 $13 (10/15/88) **80**
Cabernet Sauvignon Washington Limited Bottling 1988 $12.50 (10/15/91) **91**
Cabernet Sauvignon Washington Limited Bottling 1987 $13 (7/31/89) **83**
Chardonnay Washington 1990 $8.50 (1/31/92) **86**
Chardonnay Washington 1987 $9 (10/15/89) **82**
Chardonnay Washington 1986 $8.50 (12/31/87) **70**
Chardonnay Washington Feather 1988 $6 (10/15/89) **80**
Johannisberg Riesling Washington 1990 $7 (1/31/92) **79**
Johannisberg Riesling Washington 1987 $5.50 (4/15/89) BB **82**
Merlot Washington 1986 $10 (5/31/88) **89**
Merlot Washington Limited Bottling 1989 $11 (9/30/91) **91**
Merlot Washington Limited Bottling 1987 $10 (10/15/89) **90**
Muscat Canelli Washington 1987 $6 (10/15/89) **81**
Red Table Wine Washington Lemberger 1990 $8.50 (1/31/92) **85**
Sémillon Washington 1986 $6 (10/15/89) **79**

CHATEAU LATOUR (France/Bordeaux)
Pauillac 1991 (NR) (5/15/92) (BT) **90+**
Pauillac 1990 (NR) (5/15/92) (BT) **95+**
Pauillac 1989 $145 (3/15/92) **97**
Pauillac 1988 $90 (4/30/91) **93**
Pauillac 1987 $60 (10/15/90) **80**
Pauillac 1986 $90 (3/31/90) (HS) **93**
Pauillac 1985 Rel: $82 Cur: $91 (3/31/90) (HS) **96**
Pauillac 1984 Rel: $40 Cur: $56 (3/31/87) **92**
Pauillac 1983 Rel: $72 Cur: $85 (3/31/90) (HS) **93**
Pauillac 1982 $151 (3/31/90) (HS) **99**
Pauillac 1981 $90 (3/31/90) (HS) **90**
Pauillac 1979 $100 (3/31/90) (HS) **90**
Pauillac 1978 $145 (3/31/90) (HS) **94**
Pauillac 1976 $90 (3/31/90) (HS) **87**
Pauillac 1975 $150 (3/31/90) (HS) **93**
Pauillac 1971 $120 (3/31/90) (HS) **84**
Pauillac 1970 $220 (3/31/90) (HS) **97**
Pauillac 1967 $110 (3/31/90) (HS) **79**
Pauillac 1966 $210 (3/31/90) (HS) **93**
Pauillac 1965 $135 (3/31/90) (HS) **74**
Pauillac 1964 $190 (3/31/90) (HS) **86**
Pauillac 1964 $420/1.5L (3/31/90) (HS) **88**
Pauillac 1963 $100 (3/31/90) (HS) **77**
Pauillac 1962 $550/1.5L (3/31/90) (HS) **92**
Pauillac 1961 $700 (3/31/90) (HS) **99**
Pauillac 1960 $200 (3/31/90) (HS) **88**
Pauillac 1959 $450 (10/15/90) (JS) **98**
Pauillac 1959 $990/1.5L (3/31/90) (HS) **95**
Pauillac 1958 $130 (3/31/90) (HS) **81**
Pauillac 1956 $250 (3/31/90) (HS) **62**
Pauillac 1955 $320 (3/31/90) (HS) **90**
Pauillac 1953 $290 (3/31/90) (HS) **80**
Pauillac 1952 $250 (3/31/90) (HS) **91**
Pauillac 1950 $330 (3/31/90) (HS) **79**
Pauillac 1949 $630 (3/31/90) (HS) **94**
Pauillac 1948 $380 (3/31/90) (HS) **84**
Pauillac 1947 $400 (3/31/90) (HS) **91**
Pauillac 1945 $1,200 (3/31/90) (HS) **98**
Pauillac 1944 $500 (3/31/90) (HS) **70**
Pauillac 1943 $330 (3/31/90) (HS) **67**
Pauillac 1942 $330 (3/31/90) (HS) **59**
Pauillac 1940 $370 (3/31/90) (HS) **64**
Pauillac 1937 $430 (3/31/90) (HS) **89**
Pauillac 1936 $400 (3/31/90) (HS) **75**
Pauillac 1934 $410 (3/31/90) (HS) **83**
Pauillac 1929 $2,310/1.5L (3/31/90) (HS) **95**
Pauillac 1928 $2,560/1.5L (3/31/90) (HS) **91**
Pauillac 1926 $780 (3/31/90) (HS) **87**
Pauillac 1924 $700 (3/31/90) (HS) **91**
Pauillac 1920 $550 (3/31/90) (HS) **50**
Pauillac 1918 $580 (3/31/90) (HS) **75**
Pauillac 1900 $1,900 (3/31/90) (HS) **90**
Pauillac 1899 $1,900 (3/31/90) (HS) **94**
Pauillac 1899 $4,180/1.5L (3/31/90) (HS) **50**
Pauillac 1893 $4,500 (3/31/90) (HS) **67**
Pauillac 1892 $1,200 (3/31/90) (HS) **63**
Pauillac 1875 $1,800 (3/31/90) (HS) **77**
Pauillac 1875 $3,960/1.5L (12/15/88) **95**
Pauillac 1874 $3,200 (3/31/90) (HS) **97**
Pauillac 1870 $4,000 (3/31/90) (HS) **94**
Pauillac 1865 $15,400/1.5L (3/31/90) (HS) **94**
Pauillac 1864 $22,000/1.5L (3/31/90) (HS) **59**
Pauillac 1847 $39,600/1.5L (3/31/90) (HS) **93**

LOUIS LATOUR (France/Burgundy)
Aloxe-Corton 1955 ($NA) (8/31/90) (TR) **85**
Aloxe-Corton Les Chaillots 1985 $37 (4/15/88) **76**
Aloxe-Corton Domaine Latour 1989 (NR) (1/31/92) **84**
Bâtard-Montrachet 1987 $82 (2/28/90) **89**
Bâtard-Montrachet 1985 $93 (11/15/87) **93**
Beaune Domaine Latour 1989 (NR) (1/31/92) **91**
Beaune Vignes Franches 1985 Rel: $31 Cur: $42 (3/15/88) **90**
Bonnes Mares 1989 (NR) (1/31/92) **93**
Bourgogne Blanc Chardonnay Latour 1985 $11 (3/31/87) **79**
Bourgogne Cuvée Latour 1989 (NR) (1/31/92) **80**
Chambertin Cuvée Hèritiers Latour 1989 (NR) (1/31/92) **78**
Chambertin Cuvée Hèritiers Latour 1985 Rel: $76 Cur: $90 (3/15/88) **95**
Charmes-Chambertin 1985 Rel: $50 Cur: $68 (3/15/88) **85**
Chassagne-Montrachet 1989 $42 (8/31/91) **88**
Chassagne-Montrachet 1986 $38 (9/30/88) **90**
Chassagne-Montrachet 1985 $33 (2/29/88) **88**
Chassagne-Montrachet 1984 $33 (2/29/88) **78**
Chassagne-Montrachet 1982 $33 (2/29/88) **88**
Chassagne-Montrachet Première Cru 1986 $43 (2/29/88) **92**
Chevalier-Montrachet Les Demoiselles 1989 $122 (8/31/91) **90**
Chevalier-Montrachet Les Demoiselles 1986 Rel: $150 Cur: $170 (10/31/88) **94**
Corton Clos de la Vigne au Saint 1985 $43 (3/15/88) **89**
Corton Château Corton Grancey 1989 (NR) (1/31/92) **89**
Corton Château Corton Grancey 1985 Rel: $46 Cur: $60 (3/15/88) **89**
Corton Château Corton Grancey 1959 $130 (8/31/90) (TR) **89**
Corton Château Corton Grancey 1953 $195 (8/31/90) (TR) **91**
Corton Château Corton Grancey 1947 $96 (8/31/90) (TR) **85**
Corton Domaine Latour 1985 $38 (3/15/88) **90**
Corton-Charlemagne 1989 $93 (8/31/91) **93**

Corton-Charlemagne 1988 $85 (10/15/90) **95**
Corton-Charlemagne 1985 Rel: $88 Cur: $95 (11/15/87) **96**
Corton-Charlemagne 1982 Rel: $65 Cur: $78 (12/01/85) **82**
Echézeaux 1985 $49 (3/15/88) **87**
Gevrey-Chambertin 1989 (NR) (1/31/92) **87**
Gevrey-Chambertin 1985 $36 (10/15/88) **77**
Meursault 1989 $38 (8/31/91) **89**
Meursault 1985 $25 (11/15/87) **86**
Meursault 1984 $28 (4/30/87) **83**
Meursault Château de Blagny 1989 $93 (8/31/91) **86**
Meursault Première Cru 1983 $24 (11/16/85) **83**
Montrachet 1988 $200 (10/15/90) **93**
Montrachet 1986 Rel: $125 Cur: $188 (10/31/88) **95**
Montrachet 1979 $176 (2/29/88) **88**
Pommard Epenottes 1985 $46 (3/15/88) **89**
Pouilly-Fuissé Latour 1984 $25 (4/30/87) **68**
Puligny-Montrachet 1989 $43 (8/31/91) **87**
Puligny-Montrachet 1986 $41 (9/30/88) **82**
Puligny-Montrachet 1985 $30 (2/29/88) **89**
Puligny-Montrachet 1983 $35 (2/29/88) **90**
Puligny-Montrachet Les Folatières 1989 $52 (8/31/91) **90**
Puligny-Montrachet Les Folatières 1982 $38 (2/29/88) **86**
Romanée-St.-Vivant Les Quatre Journaux 1989 (NR) (1/31/92) **93**
Romanée-St.-Vivant Les Quatre Journaux 1985 $99 (3/15/88) **98**
Romanée-St.-Vivant Les Quatre Journaux 1953 ($NA) (8/31/90) (TR) **94**
Santenay 1989 (NR) (1/31/92) **80**
Savigny-lès-Beaune 1989 (NR) (1/31/92) **84**
Vosne-Romanée Beaumonts 1985 $36 (3/15/88) **86**

PIERRE LATOUR (France/Burgundy)
Volnay Les Caillerets 1953 ($NA) (8/31/90) (TR) **86**
Volnay Les Caillerets 1952 ($NA) (8/31/90) (TR) **90**

CHATEAU LATOUR A POMEROL (France/Bordeaux)
Pomerol 1990 (NR) (5/15/92) (BT) **85+**
Pomerol 1989 $39 (3/15/92) **90**
Pomerol 1988 $55 (6/30/89) (BT) **95+**
Pomerol 1987 $35 (6/30/89) (BT) **80+**
Pomerol 1986 $35 (5/15/87) (BT) **90+**
Pomerol 1985 $50 (5/15/87) (BT) **90+**
Pomerol 1982 $77 (5/15/89) (TR) **92**
Pomerol 1961 $1,700 (3/16/86) (TR) **94**
Pomerol 1959 $580 (10/15/90) (JS) **90**

DOMAINE LATOUR GIRAUD (France/Burgundy)
Bourgogne Blanc Chardonnay 1985 $11 (3/31/87) **79**

J. LAUERBURG (Germany)
Riesling Spätlese Mosel-Saar-Ruwer Bernkasteler Doctor 1986 ($NA) (4/15/89) **83**
Riesling Spätlese Mosel-Saar-Ruwer Bernkasteler Doctor 1985 ($NA) (4/15/89) **82**
Riesling Spätlese Mosel-Saar-Ruwer Bernkasteler Lay 1985 ($NA) (4/15/89) **78**

CHATEAU LAUNAY (France/Bordeaux)
Bordeaux Blanc Sec 1990 $9 (9/15/91) **84**

LAURA'S (United States/California)
Cabernet Sauvignon Paso Robles 1985 $12 (12/15/89) **71**
Cabernet Sauvignon Paso Robles 1983 $8.50 (12/31/87) **80**
Chardonnay Paso Robles 1987 $12 (12/15/89) **79**
Chardonnay San Luis Obispo 1985 $7 (12/31/87) **73**

LAURENS (France/Other)
Blanc de Blancs Blanquette de Limoux Clos des Demoiselles 1986 $11 (12/31/90) **81**

LAUREL GLEN (United States/California)
Cabernet Sauvignon Sonoma Mountain 1991 (NR) (5/15/92) (BT) **94+**
Cabernet Sauvignon Sonoma Mountain 1990 (NR) (5/15/91) (BT) **90+**
Cabernet Sauvignon Sonoma Mountain 1989 (NR) (5/15/91) (BT) **90+**
Cabernet Sauvignon Sonoma Mountain 1988 $30 (5/15/91) CS **90**
Cabernet Sauvignon Sonoma Mountain 1987 Rel: $22 Cur: $26 (9/15/90) **90**
Cabernet Sauvignon Sonoma Mountain 1986 Rel: $20 Cur: $30 (5/15/89) **87**
Cabernet Sauvignon Sonoma Mountain 1985 Rel: $18 Cur: $40 (CA-3/89) **93**
Cabernet Sauvignon Sonoma Mountain 1984 Rel: $15 Cur: $45 (CA-3/89) **89**
Cabernet Sauvignon Sonoma Mountain 1983 Rel: $11 Cur: $20 (CA-3/89) **59**
Cabernet Sauvignon Sonoma Mountain 1982 Rel: $12.50 Cur: $35 (CA-3/89) **85**
Cabernet Sauvignon Sonoma Mountain 1981 Rel: $12.50 Cur: $44 (CA-3/89) **92**
Cabernet Sauvignon Sonoma Mountain 1981 Rel: $12.50 Cur: $44 (2/16/85) SS **93**
Cabernet Sauvignon Sonoma Mountain Counterpoint 1989 $15 (1/31/92) **85**
Cabernet Sauvignon Sonoma County Counterpoint 1988 $13 (7/15/91) **83**
Cabernet Sauvignon Sonoma Mountain Counterpoint 1987 $13 (10/31/89) **94**
Cabernet Sauvignon Sonoma Mountain Counterpoint Cuvée 85-86 NV $11 (5/31/88) **89**
Terra Rosa Napa Valley 1988 $12 (11/15/90) **85**
Terra Rosa Napa Valley 1987 $14 (7/31/90) **86**

LAURENT-PERRIER (France/Champagne)
Brut Champagne 1985 $40 (12/31/90) **87**
Brut Champagne 1982 Rel: $36 Cur: $95 (12/31/88) **93**
Brut Champagne NV $23 (12/31/87) **90**
Brut Champagne Cuvée Grand Siècle 1982 $70 (12/31/88) **92**
Brut Champagne Cuvée Grand Siècle 1979 Rel: $45 Cur: $87 (2/15/88) **90**
Brut Champagne L.P. NV $36 (12/31/91) **87**
Brut Champagne Ultra Cuvée Sans Dosage NV $27 (1/31/88) **73**
Brut Rosé Champagne Cuvée NV $28 (3/15/88) **92**

Key to Symbols

The scores reported here are the results of blind tastings conducted by our panel of senior editors. Wines that carry the initials below are results of individual tastings.

THE WINE SPECTATOR 100-POINT SCALE ***95-100***—Classic, a great wine; ***90-94***—Outstanding, superior character and style; ***80-89***—Good to very good, a wine with special qualities; ***70-79***—Average, drinkable wine that may have minor flaws; ***60-69***—Below average, drinkable but not recommended; ***50-59***—Poor, undrinkable, not recommended. "+"—With a score indicates a range; used primarily with barrel tastings to indicate a preliminary score.

SPECIAL DESIGNATIONS SS—Spectator Selection, CS—Cellar Selection, BB—Best Buy, ($NA)—Price not available, (NR)—Not released.

TASTER'S INITIALS (JG)—Jim Gordon, (HS)—Harvey Steiman, (JL)—James Laube, (JS)—James Suckling, (TM)—Thomas Matthews, (TR)—Terry Robards, (PM)—Per-Henrik Mansson, (BT)—Barrel Tasting (these wines were tasted blind from barrel samples), (CA-date)—*California's Great Cabernets* by James Laube, (CH-date)—*California's Great Chardonnays* by James Laube, (VP-date)—*Vintage Port* by James Suckling.

DATE TASTED Dates in parentheses represent the issue in which the rating was published.

Brut Rosé Champagne Grand Siècle Cuvée Alexandra 1982 $125 (12/31/89) **91**

CHATEAU LAURETAN (France/Bordeaux)
Bordeaux 1986 $5 (5/15/89) **79**
Bordeaux Blanc 1986 $5.50 (8/31/88) **78**

LAURIER (United States/California)
Cabernet Sauvignon Sonoma County Green Valley 1982 $12 (2/16/85) **82**
Chardonnay Sonoma County 1989 $16 (4/30/91) **88**
Chardonnay Sonoma County 1986 $13.50 (12/31/88) **83**
Chardonnay Sonoma County 1985 $13 (10/31/87) **71**
Chardonnay Sonoma County 1984 $13 (6/16/86) **74**
Chardonnay Sonoma County 1982 $13 (4/01/85) **89**
Pinot Noir Sonoma County Green Valley 1986 $10 (6/15/88) **90**
Pinot Noir Sonoma County Green Valley 1982 $10 (11/15/87) **63**
Pinot Noir Sonoma County Green Valley 1981 $10 (2/16/85) **78**

LAURIOL (France/Bordeaux)
Côtes de Francs 1986 $8 (6/15/89) **73**
Côtes de Francs 1985 $6.50 (6/30/88) **78**

LAVA CAP (United States/California)
Chardonnay El Dorado Reserve 1989 $14 (5/31/92) **79**

ROLAND LAVANTUREUX (France/Chablis)
Chablis 1986 $16 (1/31/89) **68**
Chablis 1985 $17 (5/15/88) **80**
Petit Chablis 1986 $11 (5/15/88) **75**

CHATEAU LAVILLE BERTROU (France/Other)
Minervois 1988 $8 (8/31/91) **76**

CHATEAU LAVILLE HAUT-BRION (France/Bordeaux)
Pessac-Léognan Blanc 1990 (NR) (9/30/91) (BT) **90+**
Pessac-Léognan Blanc 1989 Rel: $70 Cur: $109 (9/30/91) **94**
Pessac-Léognan Blanc 1988 $64 (12/15/90) **85**
Pessac-Léognan Blanc 1987 $50 (11/15/91) (JS) **93**
Graves Blanc 1985 $66 (11/15/91) (JS) **95**
Graves Blanc 1983 Rel: $57 Cur: $72 (11/15/91) (JS) **89**
Graves Blanc 1982 $99 (11/15/91) (JS) **83**
Graves Blanc 1981 $87 (11/15/91) (JS) **83**
Graves Blanc 1980 $61 (11/15/91) (JS) **65**
Graves Blanc 1979 $56 (11/15/91) (JS) **87**
Graves Blanc 1975 $130 (11/15/91) (JS) **89**
Graves Blanc 1972 $90 (11/15/91) (JS) **86**
Graves Blanc 1971 $151 (11/15/91) (JS) **91**
Graves Blanc 1970 $137 (11/15/91) (JS) **88**
Graves Blanc 1969 $125 (11/15/91) (JS) **86**
Graves Blanc 1968 $80 (11/15/91) (JS) **78**
Graves Blanc 1967 $135 (11/15/91) (JS) **90**
Graves Blanc 1966 $135 (11/15/91) (JS) **73**
Graves Blanc 1965 $70 (11/15/91) (JS) **78**
Graves Blanc 1962 $135 (11/15/91) (JS) **89**
Graves Blanc 1961 $230 (11/15/91) (JS) **77**
Graves Blanc 1960 $125 (11/15/91) (JS) **50**
Graves Blanc 1959 $300 (11/15/91) (JS) **96**
Graves Blanc 1958 $190 (11/15/91) (JS) **85**
Graves Blanc 1957 $125 (11/15/91) (JS) **83**
Graves Blanc 1955 $300 (11/15/91) (JS) **65**
Graves Blanc 1954 $240 (11/15/91) (JS) **78**
Graves Blanc 1953 $380 (11/15/91) (JS) **69**
Graves Blanc 1952 $250 (11/15/91) (JS) **84**
Graves Blanc 1950 $350 (11/15/91) (JS) **92**
Graves Blanc 1949 $350 (11/15/91) (JS) **99**
Graves Blanc 1948 $300 (11/15/91) (JS) **94**
Graves Blanc 1947 $300 (11/15/91) (JS) **95**
Graves Blanc 1946 $200 (11/15/91) (JS) **84**
Graves Blanc 1945 $580 (11/15/91) (JS) **98**
Graves Blanc 1943 $280 (11/15/91) (JS) **87**
Graves Blanc 1942 $250 (11/15/91) (JS) **85**
Graves Blanc 1941 $175 (11/15/91) (JS) **78**
Graves Blanc 1940 $175 (11/15/91) (JS) **83**
Graves Blanc 1939 $330 (11/15/91) (JS) **84**
Graves Blanc 1938 $200 (11/15/91) (JS) **77**
Graves Blanc 1936 $200 (11/15/91) (JS) **80**
Graves Blanc 1935 $200 (11/15/91) (JS) **79**
Graves Blanc 1934 $300 (11/15/91) (JS) **87**
Graves Blanc 1933 $200 (11/15/91) (JS) **76**
Graves Blanc 1929 $750 (11/15/91) (JS) **94**
Graves Blanc 1928 $500 (11/15/91) (JS) **83**
Graves Blanc Crème de Tête 1964 $200 (11/15/91) (JS) **93**

CHATEAU DE LAYE (France/Burgundy)
Pouilly-Vinzelles 1983 $8 (12/01/85) **55**

LAZY CREEK (United States/California)
Chardonnay Anderson Valley 1989 $8.50 (7/15/91) **86**
Chardonnay Anderson Valley 1987 $10 (5/15/89) **90**

LEASINGHAM (Australia)
Cabernet Malbec Australia Bin 56 Winemakers Selection 1984 $7.25 (11/15/87) **84**
Cabernet Sauvignon Australia Bin 49 Winemakers Selection 1982 $7.25 (11/15/87) **83**
Cabernet Shiraz Australia Bin 68 1983 $5.25 (11/15/87) **79**
Chardonnay Clare Valley Domaine 1989 $8.50 (10/15/90) **83**
Shiraz Australia Bin 61 1982 $4.25 (12/15/87) **79**
Shiraz Cabernet Malbec Australia Hutt Creek Claret 1984 $4 (9/30/87) BB **81**

L'ECOLE NO. 41 (United States/Washington)
Merlot Washington 1987 $13 (11/30/91) **90**

LEBEGUE-BICHOT (France/Burgundy)
Chambertin Clos de Bèze 1945 $310 (8/31/90) (TR) **96**

LECHERE (France/Champagne)
Brut Blanc de Blancs Champagne 1985 $44 (5/15/92) **78**
Brut Blanc de Blancs Champagne NV $25 (12/31/87) **89**
Brut Blanc de Blancs Champagne Cuvée Orient Express NV $45 (12/31/90) **86**
Brut Blanc de Blancs Champagne Grand Cru 1983 $90 (5/15/92) **92**
Brut Blanc de Blancs Champagne Première Cru NV $42 (12/31/91) **91**
Brut Champagne Première Cru NV $37 (12/31/91) **90**
Brut Champagne Première Cru Orient Express NV $49 (3/31/92) **88**
Brut Rosé Champagne Première Cru Orient Express NV $54 (3/31/92) **90**

PHILIPPE LECLERC (France/Burgundy)
Bourgogne Les Bons Bâtons 1988 $22 (8/31/91) **64**
Gevrey-Chambertin 1984 $26 (7/15/87) **90**
Gevrey-Chambertin Les Cazetiers 1988 $80 (7/15/91) **82**
Gevrey-Chambertin Les Cazetiers 1987 $63 (5/31/90) **85**
Gevrey-Chambertin Les Cazetiers 1985 Rel: $64 Cur: $70 (10/15/88) **89**
Gevrey-Chambertin Les Cazetiers 1984 $38 (8/31/87) **83**
Gevrey-Chambertin Les Cazetiers 1982 Rel: $21 Cur: $45 (11/16/85) **68**
Gevrey-Chambertin Les Champeaux 1985 $55 (10/31/88) **79**
Gevrey-Chambertin La Combe aux Moines 1988 $80 (7/15/91) **82**
Gevrey-Chambertin La Combe aux Moines 1987 $68 (5/31/90) **76**
Gevrey-Chambertin La Combe aux Moines 1985 $70 (10/15/88) **92**
Gevrey-Chambertin La Combe aux Moines 1984 $42 (8/31/87) **82**
Gevrey-Chambertin Les Platières 1988 $45 (7/15/91) **74**
Gevrey-Chambertin Les Platières 1987 $35 (5/31/90) **81**
Gevrey-Chambertin Les Platières 1985 Rel: $38 Cur: $45 (10/15/88) **90**

DOMAINE RENE LECLERC (France/Burgundy)
Gevrey-Chambertin Combes aux Moines 1985 Rel: $55 Cur: $61 (10/31/88) **82**

LECLERC-BRIANT (France/Champagne)
Brut Champagne 1979 $31 (3/15/88) **85**
Brut Champagne Cuvée Wolfgang Mozart 1983 $60 (12/31/91) **85**
Brut Champagne Divine 1985 $45 (12/31/91) **89**
Brut Champagne Réserve NV $23 (3/15/88) **80**
Brut Champagne Spécial Club 1983 $35 (12/31/89) **83**
Brut Rosé Champagne NV $28 (3/15/88) **84**

LEEUWIN (Australia)
Cabernet Sauvignon Margaret River 1983 $18 (5/31/88) **86**
Cabernet Sauvignon Margaret River 1979 $20 (9/15/89) **79**
Chardonnay Margaret River Second Release 1983 $24 (5/31/88) **84**

LEEWARD (United States/California)
Cabernet Sauvignon Alexander Valley 1987 $13 (11/15/90) **84**
Cabernet Sauvignon Alexander Valley 1986 $12 (10/15/89) **79**
Cabernet Sauvignon Alexander Valley 1985 $12 (10/31/87) **83**
Chardonnay Central Coast 1990 $11 (1/31/92) **89**
Chardonnay Central Coast 1989 $11 (8/31/90) **83**
Chardonnay Central Coast 1988 $10.50 (12/15/89) **89**
Chardonnay Central Coast 1987 $9 (10/31/88) **81**
Chardonnay Central Coast 1986 $8.50 (10/31/87) **86**
Chardonnay Central Coast 1984 $8 (6/16/86) **78**
Chardonnay Edna Valley 1989 $15 (11/30/91) **87**
Chardonnay Edna Valley MacGregor Vineyard 1988 $16 (4/30/90) **86**
Chardonnay Edna Valley MacGregor Vineyard 1987 $16 (12/15/89) **90**
Chardonnay Edna Valley MacGregor Vineyard 1986 $14 (2/29/88) **85**
Chardonnay Edna Valley MacGregor Vineyard 1985 $14 (5/31/87) **70**
Chardonnay Edna Valley MacGregor Vineyard 1984 $12 (6/16/86) **93**
Chardonnay Edna Valley MacGregor Vineyard 1983 $14 (11/01/84) **80**
Chardonnay Monterey County 1989 $14 (11/30/90) **74**
Chardonnay Monterey County Ventana Vineyards 1983 $8 (10/16/84) **78**
Chardonnay Santa Maria Valley Bien Nacido Vineyard 1984 $12 (12/01/85) **64**
Merlot Napa Valley 1989 $14 (11/15/91) **83**
Merlot Napa Valley 1985 $10 (5/15/87) **88**
Pinot Noir Santa Barbara County 1989 $16 (2/15/92) **59**

DOMAINE LEFLAIVE (France/Burgundy)
Bâtard-Montrachet 1989 $119 (8/31/91) **93**
Bienvenues-Bâtard-Montrachet 1987 $79 (12/31/90) **83**
Bienvenues-Bâtard-Montrachet 1979 $130 (2/29/88) **95**
Chevalier-Montrachet 1989 $132 (8/31/91) **96**
Chevalier-Montrachet 1987 $99 (12/31/90) **94**
Chevalier-Montrachet 1983 $175 (2/29/88) **97**
Puligny-Montrachet 1989 $49 (8/31/91) **86**
Puligny-Montrachet 1985 Rel: $40 Cur: $43 (2/29/88) **88**
Puligny-Montrachet Clavoillon 1989 $62 (8/31/91) **94**
Puligny-Montrachet Clavoillon 1985 $65 (2/29/88) **90**
Puligny-Montrachet Les Folatières 1985 $49 (2/29/88) **91**
Puligny-Montrachet Les Pucelles 1989 $79 (8/31/91) **88**
Puligny-Montrachet Les Pucelles 1986 Rel: $65 Cur: $77 (9/30/88) **93**
Puligny-Montrachet Les Pucelles 1985 $80 (2/29/88) **92**
Puligny-Montrachet Les Pucelles 1982 $71 (2/29/88) **94**
Puligny-Montrachet Les Pucelles 1979 $100 (2/29/88) **95**

OLIVIER LEFLAIVE FRERES (France/Burgundy)
Bâtard-Montrachet 1989 $137 (8/31/91) **91**
Bonnes Mares 1987 $50 (9/30/90) **88**
Bourgogne Blanc Les Sétilles 1989 $15 (8/31/91) **81**
Bourgogne Blanc Les Sétilles 1987 $8.50 (3/31/90) **79**
Bourgogne Blanc Les Sétilles 1985 $12 (3/31/87) **87**
Charmes-Chambertin 1989 $60 (1/31/92) **88**
Charmes-Chambertin 1986 $50 (7/31/88) **88**
Chassagne-Montrachet 1989 $41 (8/31/91) **85**
Chassagne-Montrachet 1988 $37 (8/31/91) **86**
Chassagne-Montrachet Les Baudines 1986 $38 (10/15/90) **85**
Chassagne-Montrachet Les Chaumées 1989 ($NA) (8/31/91) **90**
Chassagne-Montrachet Rouge 1989 (NR) (7/15/90) (BT) **80+**
Chassagne-Montrachet Rouge 1986 $26 (2/29/88) **89**
Chassagne-Montrachet Rouge 1985 $32 (10/31/88) **83**
Clos de la Roche 1988 $60 (7/15/90) (BT) **90+**
Clos St.-Denis 1989 $56 (1/31/92) **93**
Corton Bressandes 1986 $45 (7/31/88) **88**
Corton-Charlemagne 1989 ($NA) (8/31/91) **92**
Corton-Charlemagne 1988 $78 (8/31/91) **91**
Corton-Charlemagne 1986 $67 (7/31/90) **83**
Gevrey-Chambertin 1989 (NR) (7/15/90) (BT) **75+**
Gevrey-Chambertin 1988 $35 (7/15/90) (BT) **80+**
Meursault 1989 $39 (8/31/91) **88**
Meursault 1988 $37 (8/31/91) **86**
Meursault 1984 $22 (7/16/86) **80**
Meursault Les Charmes 1989 ($NA) (8/31/91) **90**
Meursault Les Genevrières 1988 $40 (8/31/91) **90**
Meursault Les Poruzots 1989 ($NA) (8/31/91) **86**
Montagny Premier Cru 1987 $16 (8/31/90) **80**
Morey-St.-Denis 1989 $30 (1/31/92) **87**
Pommard 1989 $32 (1/31/92) **84**
Pommard 1988 $31 (7/15/90) (BT) **75+**
Pommard Epenottes 1989 $40 (1/31/92) **88**
Puligny-Montrachet 1989 $43 (8/31/91) **90**
Puligny-Montrachet 1988 $38 (8/31/91) **83**
Puligny-Montrachet 1987 $33 (6/30/90) **93**
Puligny-Montrachet 1986 $30 (7/31/89) **88**
Puligny-Montrachet 1984 $25 (6/01/86) **83**
Puligny-Montrachet Les Chalumeaux 1986 $36 (4/15/89) **93**
Puligny-Montrachet Les Champs-Gains 1989 $53 (8/31/91) **91**
Puligny-Montrachet Les Champs-Gains 1986 $36 (2/29/88) **87**
Puligny-Montrachet Les Combettes 1986 $46 (2/29/88) **90**
Puligny-Montrachet Les Folatières 1986 $36 (2/29/88) **91**
Puligny-Montrachet Les Garennes 1989 ($NA) (8/31/91) **86**
Rully Blanc Premier Cru 1989 $20 (7/31/91) **81**
St.-Aubin Premier Cru 1989 $31 (8/31/91) **84**
Santenay 1986 $17 (7/31/88) **81**
Volnay 1987 $27 (8/31/90) **78**
Volnay Clos de la Barre 1989 $38 (1/31/92) **92**
Volnay Clos de la Barre 1988 $40 (7/15/90) (BT) **85+**
Volnay Clos de la Barre 1986 $28 (7/31/88) **89**

CHARLES LEFRANC (United States/California)
Cabernet Sauvignon Monterey County 1981 $8.50 (9/16/85) **76**
Cabernet Sauvignon Napa County 1984 $12 (10/15/87) **80**
Gewürztraminer Late Harvest San Benito County Selected 1984 $11 (3/16/86) **75**
Merlot Monterey County San Lucas Ranch 1984 $8.50 (12/15/87) **70**

R. & L. LEGRAS (France/Champagne)
Brut Blanc de Blancs Champagne NV $32 (12/31/91) **85**
Brut Blanc de Blancs Champagne Cuvée St.-Vincent 1976 $33 (5/31/87) **85**
Brut Blanc de Blancs Champagne Présidence 1982 $29 (5/31/87) **85**

DOMAINE FRANCOIS LEGROS (France/Burgundy)
Chambolle-Musigny Les Noirots 1989 $30 (11/15/91) **92**
Nuits-St.-Georges Les Perrières 1989 $29 (11/15/91) **87**

PETER LEHMANN (Australia)
Barossa Valley 1986 $8 (2/28/91) **78**
Cabernet Sauvignon Barossa Valley 1987 $8 (3/31/91) **80**
Cabernet Sauvignon Barossa Valley 1986 $9 (1/31/90) **85**
Cabernet Sauvignon Barossa Valley 1983 $9 (7/01/87) **81**
Chardonnay Barossa Valley 1988 $11 (7/31/89) **81**
Sémillon Late Harvest Barossa Valley Botrytis Sauternes 1988 $6/375ml (4/15/91) BB **83**
Sémillon Late Harvest Barossa Valley Botrytis Sauternes 1987 $8/375ml (10/31/89) **89**
Sémillon Late Harvest Barossa Valley Botrytis Sauternes 1984 $15 (7/01/87) **89**
Shiraz Barossa Valley 1987 $8 (4/15/91) BB **84**
Shiraz Barossa Valley 1983 $7 (7/01/87) **81**
Shiraz Barossa Valley Dry Red 1985 $7.25 (7/31/89) BB **84**
Shiraz Barossa Valley Dry Red 1983 $5 (4/30/87) **79**
Shiraz Cabernet Sauvignon Barossa Valley 1985 $7 (1/31/90) **83**

JOSEFINENGRUND LEIWEN (Germany)
Riesling Auslese Mosel-Saar-Ruwer Leiwener Laurentiuslay 1985 $11 (1/31/87) **83**
Riesling Kabinett Mosel-Saar-Ruwer Leiwener Klostergarten 1985 $6 (1/31/87) **82**

LEMBEY (Spain)
Brut Cava 1988 $6 (5/15/92) BB **83**
Brut Cava Pedro Domecq 1986 $7.25 (7/15/90) **79**
Sparkling Cava Première Cuvée 1985 $12 (7/15/91) **85**

LENZ (United States/New York)
Chardonnay North Fork of Long Island 1989 $10 (6/30/91) (TM) **81**
Chardonnay North Fork of Long Island Barrel Fermented 1989 $15 (6/30/91) (TM) **84**
Merlot North Fork of Long Island 1987 $12 (6/30/91) (TM) **80**
North Fork North Fork of Long Island 1986 $17.50 (12/31/90) **68**

CHATEAU LEON (France/Bordeaux)
Côtes de Bordeaux 1983 $5.50 (11/15/86) **79**

CUVEE LEON (France/Alsace)
Gewürztraminer Alsace 1988 $11 (3/31/91) **80**
Pinot Blanc Alsace 1988 $10 (3/31/91) **83**

JEAN LEON (Spain)
Cabernet Sauvignon Penedès 1984 $12 (3/31/91) **77**
Cabernet Sauvignon Penedès 1983 $8.50 (3/31/90) **85**
Cabernet Sauvignon Penedès 1978 $6.50 (4/16/84) **66**
Chardonnay Penedès 1989 $35 (5/31/92) **84**
Chardonnay Penedès 1988 $34 (1/31/91) **88**

LEONARDINI (Italy/North)
Valpolicella 1990 $5 (4/30/92) BB **81**

LEONETTI (United States/Washington)
Cabernet Sauvignon Columbia Valley 1986 $20 (10/15/89) **81**
Cabernet Sauvignon Walla Walla Valley Seven Hills Vineyard 1988 $25 (8/31/91) **91**
Cabernet Sauvignon Walla Walla Valley Seven Hills Vineyard 1985 $22 (10/15/89) **85**
Cabernet Sauvignon Washington 1988 $22 (8/31/91) **87**
Cabernet Sauvignon Washington 1987 $22 (6/15/90) **91**
Cabernet Sauvignon Washington Reserve 1985 $40 (6/15/91) **84**
Merlot Columbia Valley 1987 $16 (10/15/89) **88**
Merlot Washington 1990 $22 (6/15/92) **92**
Merlot Washington 1989 $18 (5/31/91) **93**
Merlot Washington 1988 $17 (4/15/90) **90**

CHATEAU LEOVILLE-BARTON (France/Bordeaux)
St.-Julien 1991 (NR) (5/15/92) (BT) **80+**
St.-Julien 1990 (NR) (5/15/92) (BT) **90+**
St.-Julien 1989 $41 (3/15/92) **94**
St.-Julien 1988 Rel: $20 Cur: $24 (3/31/91) **91**
St.-Julien 1987 $20 (5/15/90) **80**
St.-Julien 1986 Rel: $24 Cur: $28 (5/31/89) **90**
St.-Julien 1985 Rel: $24 Cur: $33 (4/15/88) **92**
St.-Julien 1983 Rel: $24 Cur: $27 (3/01/86) **92**
St.-Julien 1962 $80 (11/30/87) (JS) **70**
St.-Julien 1961 $100 (3/16/86) (TR) **76**
St.-Julien 1959 $125 (10/15/90) (JS) **85**
St.-Julien 1945 $340 (3/16/86) (JL) **73**

CHATEAU LEOVILLE-LAS CASES (France/Bordeaux)
St.-Julien 1988 $45 (2/15/92) (HS) **95**
St.-Julien 1987 $32 (2/15/92) (HS) **88**
St.-Julien 1986 Rel: $44 Cur: $61 (2/15/92) (HS) **95**
St.-Julien 1985 Rel: $45 Cur: $56 (2/15/92) (HS) **92**
St.-Julien 1985 Rel: $45 Cur: $56 (8/31/88) **90**
St.-Julien 1984 $33 (2/15/92) (HS) **85**
St.-Julien 1983 Rel: $26 Cur: $45 (2/15/92) (HS) **88**

St.-Julien 1982 Rel: $30 Cur: $120 (2/15/92) (HS) **95**
St.-Julien 1981 Rel: $23 Cur: $45 (2/15/92) (HS) **90**
St.-Julien 1980 $29 (2/15/92) (HS) **82**
St.-Julien 1979 $53 (2/15/92) (HS) **89**
St.-Julien 1978 $75 (2/15/92) (HS) **87**
St.-Julien 1977 ($NA) (2/15/92) (HS) **78**
St.-Julien 1976 $64 (2/15/92) (HS) **83**
St.-Julien 1975 $75 (2/15/92) (HS) **88**
St.-Julien 1971 $75 (4/01/86) **76**
St.-Julien 1970 $90 (2/15/92) (HS) **77**
St.-Julien 1966 $110 (2/15/92) (HS) **86**
St.-Julien 1964 $71 (2/15/92) (HS) **88**
St.-Julien 1962 $93 (2/15/92) (HS) **81**
St.-Julien 1961 $200 (2/15/92) (HS) **92**
St.-Julien 1959 $210 (2/15/92) (HS) **80**
St.-Julien 1955 $125 (2/15/92) (HS) **81**
St.-Julien 1953 $300 (2/15/92) (HS) **87**
St.-Julien 1952 ($NA) (2/15/92) (HS) **73**
St.-Julien 1950 $230 (2/15/92) (HS) **73**
St.-Julien 1949 $195 (2/15/92) (HS) **89**
St.-Julien 1948 $150 (2/15/92) (HS) **65**
St.-Julien 1947 ($NA) (2/15/92) (HS) **86**
St.-Julien 1945 $430 (2/15/92) (HS) **94**
St.-Julien 1928 $600 (2/15/92) (HS) **90**

CHATEAU LEOVILLE-POYFERRE (France/Bordeaux)
St.-Julien 1991 (NR) (5/15/92) (BT) **80+**
St.-Julien 1990 (NR) (5/15/92) (BT) **95+**
St.-Julien 1989 $42 (3/15/92) **90**
St.-Julien 1988 Rel: $23 Cur: $25 (7/15/91) **81**
St.-Julien 1987 $24 (5/15/90) **86**
St.-Julien 1986 $24 (5/31/89) **86**
St.-Julien 1985 Rel: $19 Cur: $29 (4/30/88) **92**
St.-Julien 1984 $24 (10/15/87) **85**
St.-Julien 1983 Rel: $20 Cur: $28 (3/01/86) **83**
St.-Julien 1982 Rel: $20 Cur: $40 (6/01/85) **89**
St.-Julien 1981 Rel: $12 Cur: $20 (6/01/84) **88**
St.-Julien 1961 $97 (3/16/86) (TR) **77**
St.-Julien 1945 $210 (3/16/86) (JL) **80**

DOMAINE LEQUIN-ROUSSOT (France/Burgundy)
Bâtard-Montrachet 1987 $79 (7/31/90) **85**
Chassagne-Montrachet Rouge Morgeot 1985 $24 (5/31/88) **86**
Corton Les Languettes 1985 $39 (7/15/88) **86**
Nuits-St.-Georges 1985 $39 (4/15/88) **75**
Santenay 1987 $15 (11/15/90) **76**
Santenay 1985 $18 (5/31/88) **78**
Santenay La Comme 1985 $24 (5/31/88) **85**

LEROY (France/Burgundy)
Auxey-Duresses 1989 $37 (8/31/91) **89**
Auxey-Duresses Rouge Les Clous 1988 $52 (5/15/91) **85**
Bourgogne 1989 $18 (1/31/92) **85**
Bourgogne d'Auvenay 1988 $15 (4/30/91) **87**
Bourgogne d'Auvenay 1985 $12 (3/31/88) **73**
Bourgogne Blanc d'Auvenay 1988 $15 (4/30/91) **76**
Bourgogne Blanc d'Auvenay 1986 $17 (9/15/89) **84**
Bourgogne Blanc d'Auvenay 1983 $15 (12/31/87) **79**
Chassagne-Montrachet Les Chenevottes 1988 $116 (4/30/91) **86**
Chassagne-Montrachet Les Ruchottes 1988 $116 (4/30/91) **90**
Clos de Vougeot 1988 $260 (4/30/91) **89**
Meursault Les Narvaux 1988 $100 (4/30/91) **87**
Meursault Les Perrières 1988 $150 (4/30/91) **89**
Richebourg 1988 $325 (4/30/91) **96**
Romanée-St.-Vivant 1988 $325 (4/30/91) **95**
Vosne-Romanée Les Beaux Monts 1988 $180 (4/30/91) **93**

DOMAINE LEROY (France/Burgundy)
Chambertin 1989 $306 (1/31/92) **93**
Chambolle-Musigny Les Fremières 1989 $80 (1/31/92) **94**
Clos de la Roche 1989 $230 (1/31/92) **94**
Clos de Vougeot 1989 $193 (1/31/92) **95**
Corton Renardes 1989 $117 (1/31/92) **95**
Gevrey-Chambertin Les Combottes 1989 $117 (1/31/92) **93**
Latricières-Chambertin 1989 $250 (1/31/92) **93**
Nuits-St.-Georges Aux Allots 1989 $75 (1/31/92) **92**
Nuits-St.-Georges Aux Allots 1988 $84 (4/30/91) **89**
Nuits-St.-Georges Aux Boudots 1989 $117 (1/31/92) **95**
Nuits-St.-Georges Aux Boudots 1988 $230 (4/30/91) **93**
Nuits-St.-Georges Aux Lavières 1989 $75 (1/31/92) **89**
Nuits-St.-Georges Aux Lavières 1988 $84 (4/30/91) **82**
Nuits-St.-Georges Les Vignerondes 1989 $117 (1/31/92) **92**
Pommard Les Vignots 1989 $75 (1/31/92) **96**
Pommard Les Vignots 1988 $84 (4/30/91) **88**
Richebourg 1989 $306 (1/31/92) **96**
Romanée-St.-Vivant 1989 $306 (1/31/92) **95**
Savigny-lès-Beaune Les Narbantons 1989 $65 (1/31/92) **91**
Vosne-Romanée Les Beaux-Monts 1989 $117 (1/31/92) **92**
Vosne-Romanée Les Brûlées 1989 $117 (1/31/92) **94**
Vosne-Romanée Les Genevrières 1989 $75 (1/31/92) **91**

Key to Symbols

The scores reported here are the results of blind tastings conducted by our panel of senior editors. Wines that carry the initials below are results of individual tastings.

THE WINE SPECTATOR 100-POINT SCALE 95-100—Classic, a great wine; ***90-94***—Outstanding, superior character and style; ***80-89***—Good to very good, a wine with special qualities; ***70-79***—Average, drinkable wine that may have minor flaws; ***60-69***—Below average, drinkable but not recommended; ***50-59***—Poor, undrinkable, not recommended. "+"—With a score indicates a range; used primarily with barrel tastings to indicate a preliminary score.

SPECIAL DESIGNATIONS SS—Spectator Selection, CS—Cellar Selection, BB—Best Buy, ($NA)—Price not available, (NR)—Not released.

TASTER'S INITIALS (JG)—Jim Gordon, (HS)—Harvey Steiman, (JL)—James Laube, (JS)—James Suckling, (TM)—Thomas Matthews, (TR)—Terry Robards, (PM)—Per-Henrik Mansson, (BT)—Barrel Tasting (these wines were tasted blind from barrel samples), (CA-date)—*California's Great Cabernets* by James Laube, (CH-date)—*California's Great Chardonnays* by James Laube, (VP-date)—*Vintage Port* by James Suckling.

DATE TASTED Dates in parentheses represent the issue in which the rating was published.

CHATEAU LESCALLE (France/Bordeaux)
Bordeaux Supérieur 1986 $8 (6/30/89) **81**

DOMAINE CHANTAL LESCURE (France/Burgundy)
Pommard Les Bertins 1988 $40 (11/30/90) **88**

CHATEAU LESTAGE (France/Bordeaux)
Listrac 1988 $20 (8/31/91) **82**

CHATEAU LESTAGE-SIMON (France/Bordeaux)
Haut-Médoc 1991 (NR) (5/15/92) (BT) **80+**
Haut-Médoc 1990 (NR) (5/15/92) (BT) **85+**
Haut-Médoc 1987 $13 (11/30/89) (JS) **74**
Haut-Médoc 1986 $13 (11/30/89) (JS) **85**
Haut-Médoc 1982 Rel: $10 Cur: $15 (11/30/89) (JS) **84**

CHATEAU LEYDET-FIGEAC (France/Bordeaux)
St.-Emilion 1985 $18 (9/30/88) **84**

LEYRAT (France/Other)
Pineau des Charentes Grande Réserve Sélection Robert Haas NV $23 (3/31/91) **82**

CHATEAU LEZONGARS (France/Bordeaux)
Premières Côtes de Bordeaux 1985 $7 (11/15/87) **72**

LIBERTY SCHOOL (United States/California)
Cabernet Sauvignon Alexander Valley Lot 13 NV $6 (1/01/86) **64**
Cabernet Sauvignon California Vintner Select Series Two NV $7.50 (11/15/91) BB **82**
Cabernet Sauvignon California Lot 17 NV $6 (2/29/88) **73**
Cabernet Sauvignon California Lot 18 NV $7.50 (4/30/89) BB **81**
Cabernet Sauvignon California Lot 19 NV $7.50 (11/15/89) **77**
Cabernet Sauvignon Lontue NV $6 (9/15/88) BB **80**
Chardonnay Santa Barbara County Sierra Madre Vineyard Vintner Select Barrel Fermented Series T 1990 $12 (1/31/92) **79**
Chardonnay California Vintner Select Series Two 1990 $7.50 (11/15/91) **78**
Chardonnay California Vintner Select Series One 1989 $7.50 (2/28/91) **80**
Chardonnay Napa Valley 1989 $7.50 (11/15/90) **72**
Chardonnay California Lot 17 NV $7.50 (2/28/90) **77**
Chardonnay Napa Valley Lot 15 1987 $7.50 (3/31/89) BB **83**
Chardonnay California Lot 11 1986 $6 (2/29/88) **74**
Three Valley Select Series One California 1989 $4.50 (6/15/91) BB **83**

ALEXIS LICHINE (France/Bordeaux)
Bordeaux Blanc 1986 $4.50 (3/31/89) **70**

LIGER-BELAIR (France/Burgundy)
Beaune Les Avaux 1947 ($NA) (8/31/90) (TR) **87**

A. LIGERET (France/Burgundy)
Chassagne-Montrachet Réserve Antonin Toursier 1988 $45 (2/15/91) **84**
Corton-Charlemagne 1987 $83 (10/15/90) **90**
Meursault Les Narvaux 1988 $45 (10/15/90) **83**
Pouilly-Fuissé 1988 $21 (2/15/91) **70**
Puligny-Montrachet Les Referts 1988 $51 (12/31/90) **92**

GEORGES LIGNIER (France/Burgundy)
Bonnes Mares 1987 $75 (3/31/90) **92**
Chambolle-Musigny 1987 $32 (6/15/90) **77**
Clos de la Roche 1987 $55 (3/31/90) **90**
Clos de la Roche 1985 $63 (3/15/88) **85**
Clos St.-Denis 1987 $49 (5/15/90) **89**
Clos St.-Denis 1985 $54 (3/15/88) **91**
Gevrey-Chambertin 1987 $29 (5/31/90) **84**
Gevrey-Chambertin Les Combottes 1987 $34 (5/31/90) **87**
Morey-St.-Denis 1987 $25 (5/15/90) **82**
Morey-St.-Denis 1985 $23 (3/15/88) **82**
Morey-St.-Denis Clos des Ormes 1987 $32 (5/15/90) **88**
Morey-St.-Denis Clos des Ormes 1985 $28 (3/15/88) **86**

CHATEAU LILIAN-LADOUYS (France/Bordeaux)
St.-Estèphe 1991 (NR) (5/15/92) (BT) **80+**
St.-Estèphe 1990 (NR) (5/15/92) (BT) **90+**
St.-Estèphe 1989 (NR) (4/30/91) (BT) **85+**

LILLIANO (Italy/Tuscany)
Anagallis 1985 $34 (3/31/90) **86**
Chianti Classico 1988 $10 (11/30/90) **81**
Chianti Classico 1987 $8.50 (11/30/89) **86**
Chianti Classico 1986 $7.75 (5/15/89) **70**
Chianti Classico 1985 $6 (10/31/87) **74**
Chianti Classico Riserva 1985 $14 (11/30/89) **89**

LIMUR (United States/California)
Chardonnay Napa Valley 1989 $19 (7/15/91) **88**

LINDEMANS (Australia)
Cabernet Sauvignon Coonawarra 1986 $14 (10/31/90) **83**
Cabernet Sauvignon Coonawarra 1985 $14 (4/30/89) **86**
Cabernet Sauvignon Coonawarra 1984 $12 (2/15/88) **84**
Cabernet Sauvignon Coonawarra 1982 $8 (9/30/86) **79**
Cabernet Sauvignon Coonawarra St. George Vineyard 1986 $25 (6/30/92) **82**
Cabernet Sauvignon Coonawarra St.-George Vineyard 1985 $21 (4/30/89) **80**
Cabernet Sauvignon Coonawarra St.-George Vineyard 1984 $15 (1/31/88) **88**
Cabernet Sauvignon Coonawarra St.-George Vineyard NV $15 (5/31/87) **88**
Cabernet Sauvignon South Australia Bin 45 1985 $6 (1/31/88) **79**
Cabernet Shiraz Coonawarra Limestone Ridge Vineyard 1984 $15 (7/01/87) **87**
Chardonnay Padthaway 1989 $12 (5/31/92) **88**
Chardonnay Padthaway 1988 $15 (7/31/90) **81**
Chardonnay Padthaway 1986 $12 (12/31/87) **87**
Chardonnay Padthaway 1985 $9 (2/28/87) **81**
Chardonnay South Australia Bin 65 1985 $6 (2/28/87) **77**
Chardonnay South Eastern Australia Bin 65 1991 $7 (5/31/92) BB **87**
Chardonnay South Eastern Australia Bin 65 1990 $7 (2/28/91) BB **85**
Chardonnay South Eastern Australia Bin 65 1989 $6 (4/30/90) BB **85**
Chardonnay South Eastern Australia Bin 65 1988 $6 (5/15/89) BB **87**
Chardonnay Victoria Bin 65 1987 $6 (2/15/88) BB **83**
Pinot Noir Padthaway 1986 $12 (9/15/89) **73**
Pinot Noir Padthaway 1984 $12 (2/15/88) **82**
Pyrus Coonawarra 1986 $25 (6/30/92) **77**
Pyrus Coonawarra 1985 $20 (5/31/88) **87**
Sauvignon Blanc South Eastern Australia Bin 95 1990 $6 (6/30/92) **79**
Sémillon Chardonnay Bin 77 South Eastern Australia 1990 $6 (6/30/92) BB **81**
Sémillon Chardonnay Bin 77 South Eastern Australia 1988 $6 (4/15/91) BB **81**
Sémillon Late Harvest Padthaway Botrytis Griffith 1988 $12/375ml (7/31/90) **83**
Sémillon Late Harvest Padthaway Botrytis Griffith 1987 $12/375ml (10/31/89) **91**

Shiraz Barossa Valley 1986 $12 (5/15/89) **83**
Shiraz Cabernet Coonawarra Limestone Ridge Vineyard 1986 $25 (6/30/92) **86**
Shiraz Cabernet Coonawarra Limestone Ridge Vineyard 1986 $24 (7/31/90) **84**
Shiraz Cabernet Coonawarra Limestone Ridge Vineyard 1985 $21 (7/31/89) **68**
Shiraz Cabernet Coonawarra Limestone Ridge Vineyard Lindemans Classic 1982 $38 (7/31/90) **70**
Shiraz Hunter Valley 1987 $10 (2/15/91) **81**
Shiraz Hunter Valley Bin 3110 Lindemans Classic 1965 $95 (9/15/89) **96**
Shiraz Hunter Valley Bin 4110 Lindemans Classic 1970 $60 (9/15/89) **89**
Shiraz Hunter Valley Bin 5910 Lindemans Classic 1980 $30 (7/31/90) **73**
Shiraz South Australia Bin 50 1986 $5.50 (5/15/89) **78**
Shiraz South Eastern Australia Bin 50 1989 $6 (5/31/92) **80**
Shiraz South Eastern Australia Bin 50 1987 $5.50 (7/15/90) BB **84**
Tawny Port Australia Macquarie Very Special Wood Matured NV $11 (7/31/90) **84**

LINDEN (United States/Virginia)
Cabernet Virginia 1988 $15 (2/29/92) **84**
Chardonnay Virginia 1990 $12 (2/29/92) **79**
Chardonnay Virginia 1989 $12 (2/29/92) **80**
Seyval Blanc Virginia 1990 $9 (2/29/92) **78**

LINGENFELDER (Germany)
Riesling Spätlese Halbtrocken Rheinpfalz Freinsheimer Goldberg 1990 $13 (12/15/91) **91**
Riesling Spätlese Rheinpfalz Freinsheimer Goldberg 1990 $13 (12/15/91) **92**
Riesling Spätlese Rheinpfalz Freinsheimer Goldberg 1989 $15 (12/15/90) **90**
Riesling Spätlese Rheinpfalz Freinsheimer Goldberg 1988 $12 (9/30/89) **89**
Riesling Spätlese Trocken Rheinpfalz Freinsheimer Goldberg 1989 $15 (12/15/90) **88**
Riesling Spätlese Trocken Rheinpfalz Freinsheimer Goldberg 1988 $12 (9/30/89) **91**
Riesling Trockenbeerenauslese Rheinpfalz Freinsheimer Goldberg 1989 $100/375ml (12/15/90) **96**
Riesling Trockenbeerenauslese Rheinpfalz Grosskarlbacher Osterberg 1989 $85/375ml (12/15/90) **92**
Scheurebe Auslese Mosel-Saar-Ruwer Grosskarlbacher Burgweg 1989 $20/375ml (12/15/90) **88**
Scheurebe Auslese Rheinpfalz Grosskarlbacher Burgweg 1990 $15 (12/15/91) **91**
Scheurebe Beerenauslese Mosel-Saar-Ruwer Grosskarlbacher Burgweg 1989 $65/375ml (12/15/90) **88**
Scheurebe Spätlese Mosel-Saar-Ruwer Grosskarlbacher Burgweg 1989 $14 (12/15/90) **90**
Scheurebe Spätlese Rheinpfalz Freinsheimer Goldberg 1990 (NR) (12/15/91) **92**
Scheurebe Spätlese Trocken Rheinpfalz Grosskarlbacher Burgweg 1990 $14 (12/15/91) **88**
Scheurebe Trockenbeerenauslese Rheinpfalz Grosskarlbacher Burgweg 1990 $150 (12/15/91) **96**

JEAN LIONNET (France/Rhône)
Cornas 1987 $23 (3/31/90) **90**
Cornas 1986 $23 (1/31/89) **87**
Cornas Cuvée Rochepertuis 1988 $28 (1/31/91) **83**
Côtes du Rhône Cépage Syrah 1986 $10 (9/30/88) **79**

CHATEAU LIOT (France/Sauternes)
Barsac 1989 $28 (6/15/90) (BT) **85+**
Barsac 1988 $25/375ml (11/15/91) **84**
Barsac 1986 $22 (12/31/89) **87**
Barsac 1985 $9.25 (5/31/88) **84**
Barsac 1983 Rel: $11 Cur: $17 (4/01/86) **56**

LISINI (Italy/Tuscany)
Brunello di Montalcino 1985 $33 (8/31/91) **81**
Brunello di Montalcino 1983 $22 (7/31/89) **73**
Brunello di Montalcino 1982 $25 (1/31/89) **84**
Brunello di Montalcino 1975 $30 (9/15/86) **78**
Rosso di Montalcino 1988 $14 (4/30/91) **79**

CHATEAU LIVERSAN (France/Bordeaux)
Haut-Médoc 1990 (NR) (5/15/92) (BT) **85+**
Haut-Médoc 1989 $18 (3/15/92) **87**
Haut-Médoc 1988 $14 (7/31/91) **87**
Haut-Médoc 1987 $13 (6/30/89) (BT) **75+**
Haut-Médoc 1985 $16 (4/30/88) **90**

LIVINGSTON (United States/California)
Cabernet Sauvignon Napa Valley Moffett Vineyard 1991 (NR) (5/15/92) (BT) **88+**
Cabernet Sauvignon Napa Valley Moffett Vineyard 1990 (NR) (5/15/91) (BT) **90+**
Cabernet Sauvignon Napa Valley Moffett Vineyard 1989 (NR) (5/15/91) (BT) **85+**
Cabernet Sauvignon Napa Valley Moffett Vineyard 1988 $30 (11/15/91) **85**
Cabernet Sauvignon Napa Valley Moffett Vineyard 1987 Rel: $24 Cur: $28 (11/15/90) **94**
Cabernet Sauvignon Napa Valley Moffett Vineyard 1986 Rel: $24 Cur: $29 (11/30/89) **88**
Cabernet Sauvignon Napa Valley Moffett Vineyard 1985 Rel: $18 Cur: $33 (CA-3/89) **86**
Cabernet Sauvignon Napa Valley Moffett Vineyard 1984 Rel: $18 Cur: $35 (CA-3/89) **87**
Cabernet Sauvignon Napa Valley Stanley's Selection 1990 (NR) (5/15/91) (BT) **85+**
Cabernet Sauvignon Napa Valley Stanley's Selection 1989 $20 (5/15/91) (BT) **85+**

STEVEN THOMAS LIVINGSTONE (United States/Washington)
Chardonnay Columbia Valley 1990 $10 (11/30/91) **80**
Johannisberg Riesling Columbia Valley 1990 $6 (8/31/91) **85**
Merlot Columbia Valley 1989 $11 (8/31/91) **84**
Riesling Columbia Valley Dry 1990 $7 (8/31/91) **87**

LIVON (Italy/North)
Chardonnay Grave del Friuli Vigneto Medeuzza 1988 $14 (12/31/90) **82**
Pinot Grigio Grave del Friuli Braide Grande 1989 $11 (1/31/92) **81**
Refosco Colli Orientali del Friuli dal Peduncolo Rosso Riul 1988 $11 (1/31/92) **79**
Schioppettino 1988 $13 (1/31/92) **86**
Schioppettino 1987 $18 (4/15/90) **81**
Tocai Friulano Collio Vigneto di Ruttars 1988 $15 (12/31/90) **82**

LLANO ESTACADO (United States/Texas)
Cabernet Sauvignon Texas 1988 $12 (2/29/92) **81**
Chardonnay Texas 1990 $12 (2/29/92) **83**
Chenin Blanc Texas 1988 $6.50 (7/31/89) **82**
Johannisberg Riesling Texas 1990 $9 (2/29/92) **84**
Sauvignon Blanc Lubbock County 1990 $8 (2/29/92) **85**

LLORDS & ELWOOD (United States/California)
Cabernet Sauvignon Napa Valley 1982 $8 (12/15/87) **79**

LOCKWOOD (United States/California)
Chardonnay Monterey County 1990 $8 (7/15/92) BB **86**
Chardonnay Monterey County 1989 $14 (7/15/91) **79**
Chardonnay Monterey Partners Reserve 1990 $14 (7/15/92) **84**

LOGAN (United States/California)
Chardonnay Monterey 1990 $12 (1/31/92) **88**
Chardonnay Monterey 1989 $12 (6/30/91) **88**
Chardonnay Monterey 1988 $12 (6/30/90) **84**

LOGIS DE LA GIRAUDIERE (France/Loire)
Anjou Rouge de Cépage Cabernet 1989 $8.50 (8/31/91) **80**

J. LOHR (United States/California)
Cabernet Sauvignon California Cypress 1988 $7 (11/15/91) **80**
Cabernet Sauvignon California 1987 $7 (2/15/90) BB **84**
Cabernet Sauvignon California 1986 $6.50 (4/15/89) BB **84**
Cabernet Sauvignon California 1984 $5 (11/30/86) BB **82**
Cabernet Sauvignon Napa Valley Carol's Vineyard Reserve 1985 $14.50 (12/15/88) **89**
Cabernet Sauvignon Napa Valley Carol's Vineyard Reserve Lot 2 1985 $17.50 (9/30/90) **88**
Cabernet Sauvignon Paso Robles Seven Oaks 1988 $13 (3/15/92) **83**
Cabernet Sauvignon Paso Robles Seven Oaks 1987 $12 (4/30/91) **86**
Chardonnay California Cypress 1990 $8.50 (3/31/92) **70**
Chardonnay California Cypress 1989 $7 (7/15/91) **76**
Chardonnay Monterey Riverstone 1990 $13 (2/15/92) **87**
Chardonnay Monterey Riverstone 1989 $12 (3/15/91) SS **90**
Chardonnay Monterey Riverstone 1988 $12 (4/30/90) **90**
Chardonnay Monterey Riverstone 1987 $12 (11/15/89) **90**
Chardonnay Monterey County 1987 $10 (4/15/89) **78**
Chardonnay Monterey County Cypress Vineyard Reserve 1986 $13.50 (12/31/88) **87**
Chardonnay Monterey County Greenfield Vineyards 1986 $10 (4/15/88) **89**
Chardonnay Monterey County Greenfield Vineyards 1985 $9 (6/30/87) **80**
Chardonnay Monterey County Greenfield Vineyards 1984 $9 (4/16/86) **69**
Chardonnay Monterey County Greenfield Vineyards 1983 $9 (7/01/85) **75**
Chenin Blanc Clarksburg Pheasant's Call Vineyard 1988 $4.50 (7/31/89) **58**
Johannisberg Riesling California Bay Mist 1990 $7.75 (12/31/91) **77**
Johannisberg Riesling Monterey County Greenfield Vineyards 1989 $6.50 (12/31/90) **82**
Merlot California Cypress 1989 $8.50 (2/29/92) BB **85**

LOLONIS (United States/California)
Cabernet Sauvignon Mendocino County Lolonis Vineyard Private Reserve 1989 $15 (11/15/91) **86**
Cabernet Sauvignon Mendocino County Private Reserve 1986 $15 (5/15/90) **83**
Chardonnay Mendocino County 1990 $10 (5/31/92) **82**
Chardonnay Mendocino County Lolonis Vineyards 1989 $12 (7/15/91) **86**
Chardonnay Mendocino County Lolonis Vineyards 1984 $14 (6/30/87) **74**
Chardonnay Mendocino County Private Reserve 1990 $15 (6/30/92) **85**
Chardonnay Mendocino County Private Reserve 1988 $19 (4/30/90) **91**
Chardonnay Mendocino County Private Reserve Lolonis Vineyards 1989 $19 (7/15/91) **88**
Zinfandel Mendocino County Lolonis Vineyards Private Reserve 1989 $12 (8/31/91) **83**

DOMAINE DES LONES (France/Rhône)
Côteaux du Tricastin 1988 $11 (5/31/91) **84**
Côteaux du Tricastin 1988 $7.50 (10/15/90) **78**
Côteaux du Tricastin 1986 $7.25 (10/15/88) **82**

LONG (United States/California)
Cabernet Sauvignon Napa Valley 1990 (NR) (5/15/91) (BT) **90+**
Cabernet Sauvignon Napa Valley 1989 (NR) (5/15/91) (BT) **90+**
Cabernet Sauvignon Napa Valley 1986 Rel: $40 Cur: $48 (CA-3/89) **86**
Cabernet Sauvignon Napa Valley 1985 Rel: $36 Cur: $46 (CA-3/89) **92**
Cabernet Sauvignon Napa Valley 1984 Rel: $32 Cur: $46 (CA-3/89) **88**
Cabernet Sauvignon Napa Valley 1983 Rel: $32 Cur: $41 (CA-3/89) **78**
Cabernet Sauvignon Napa Valley 1980 Rel: $32 Cur: $46 (CA-3/89) **91**
Cabernet Sauvignon Napa Valley 1979 Rel: $32 Cur: $50 (CA-3/89) **90**
Chardonnay Napa Valley 1990 $29 (6/30/92) CS **90**
Chardonnay Napa Valley 1989 Rel: $30 Cur: $33 (7/15/91) **91**
Chardonnay Napa Valley 1988 Rel: $27.50 Cur: $33 (5/15/91) **89**
Chardonnay Napa Valley 1987 Rel: $27.50 Cur: $35 (CH-4/90) **90**
Chardonnay Napa Valley 1986 Rel: $27.50 Cur: $48 (CH-4/90) **92**
Chardonnay Napa Valley 1985 Rel: $27.50 Cur: $60 (CH-4/90) **91**
Chardonnay Napa Valley 1984 Rel: $27.50 Cur: $65 (CH-4/90) **88**
Johannisberg Riesling Late Harvest Napa Valley Botrytis 1990 $18 (9/15/91) **86**
Sauvignon Blanc Napa Valley 1989 $12 (7/15/91) **78**
Sauvignon Blanc Sonoma County 1987 $11 (1/31/89) **87**

DOMAINE LONG DEPAQUIT (France/Chablis)
Chablis 1990 $14 (1/31/92) **79**
Chablis 1987 $12 (3/31/89) **83**
Chablis 1986 $15 (5/15/88) **71**
Chablis 1985 $14 (11/15/87) **80**
Chablis Les Beugnons 1984 $12 (7/16/86) **67**
Chablis Les Blanchots 1989 $36 (1/31/92) **83**
Chablis Les Blanchots 1988 $38 (1/31/91) **88**
Chablis Les Blanchots 1987 $29 (3/31/89) **88**
Chablis Les Blanchots 1986 $28 (3/31/88) **87**
Chablis Les Blanchots 1984 $20 (9/15/86) **76**
Chablis Les Clos 1988 $42 (7/15/90) **90**
Chablis Les Clos 1986 $32 (3/31/88) **90**
Chablis Les Clos 1985 $32 (8/31/87) **88**
Chablis Les Lys 1987 $15 (12/31/88) **85**
Chablis Moutonne 1989 $40 (3/31/92) **85**
Chablis Moutonne 1988 $47 (7/31/90) **92**
Chablis Moutonne 1987 $36 (3/31/89) **85**
Chablis Moutonne 1986 $35 (3/31/88) **88**
Chablis Moutonne 1985 $35 (11/15/87) **87**
Chablis Moutonne 1983 $20 (12/16/85) **87**
Chablis Les Preuses 1987 $30 (3/31/89) **90**
Chablis Les Vaillons 1988 $20 (7/31/90) **87**
Chablis Les Vaillons 1987 $15 (12/31/88) **86**
Chablis Les Vaillons 1986 $18 (5/15/88) **77**
Chablis Les Vaillons 1985 $21 (6/30/87) **80**
Chablis Les Vaucopins 1989 $18 (3/31/92) **66**
Chablis Les Vaucopins 1986 $18 (5/15/88) **67**
Chablis Les Vaudésirs 1988 $40 (7/31/90) **87**
Chablis Les Vaudésirs 1987 $30 (3/31/89) **86**
Chablis Les Vaudésirs 1986 $28 (3/31/88) **85**
Chablis Les Vaudésirs 1985 $30 (6/30/87) **86**
Chablis Les Vaudésirs 1984 Rel: $20 Cur: $30 (10/15/86) CS **91**

LONGLEAT (Australia)
Cabernet Sauvignon Goulburn Valley Revi Resco 1986 $9 (9/30/89) **73**

LONGRIDGE (New Zealand)
Cabernet Sauvignon Hawke's Bay 1987 $10 (9/15/91) **68**
Chardonnay Hawke's Bay 1989 $10 (7/15/91) **82**

DR. LOOSEN (Germany)
Riesling Auslese Mosel-Saar-Ruwer Erdener Prälat 1990 $31 (12/15/91) **91**
Riesling Auslese Mosel-Saar-Ruwer Erdener Prälat Gold Cap 1990 $46 (12/15/91) **95**
Riesling Auslese Mosel-Saar-Ruwer Urziger Würzgarten 1990 $27 (12/15/91) **92**
Riesling Auslese Mosel-Saar-Ruwer Urziger Würzgarten Gold Cap 1990 $46 (12/15/91) **94**
Riesling Auslese Mosel-Saar-Ruwer Wehlener Sonnenuhr Gold Cap 1990 $34 (12/15/91) **93**
Riesling Kabinett Mosel-Saar-Ruwer Bernkasteler Lay 1990 $13 (12/15/91) **90**

Riesling Kabinett Mosel-Saar-Ruwer Erdener Treppchen 1990 $16 (12/15/91) **93**
Riesling Spätlese Mosel-Saar-Ruwer Erdener Treppchen 1990 $20 (12/15/91) **93**

R. LOPEZ DE HEREDIA VINA TONDONIA (Spain)
Rioja Bosconia 1982 $6 (12/31/87) **70**
Rioja Bosconia Gran Reserva 1976 $14 (3/31/90) **72**
Rioja Bosconia Gran Reserva 1973 $14 (3/31/90) **80**
Rioja Bosconia Reserva 1986 $13 (3/31/92) **79**
Rioja Bosconia Reserva 1983 $13 (3/31/92) **78**
Rioja Bosconia Reserva 1982 $5.50 (11/15/87) (JL) **84**
Rioja Cubillo 1987 $9.50 (3/31/92) **84**
Rioja Cubillo 1984 $5.50 (3/31/90) **70**
Rioja Tondonia 1981 $6 (12/31/87) **78**
Rioja Tondonia Gran Reserva 1981 ($NA) (3/31/92) **79**
Rioja Tondonia Gran Reserva 1976 $37 (3/31/92) **85**
Rioja Tondonia Gran Reserva 1973 $44 (3/31/92) **87**
Rioja Tondonia Gran Reserva 1970 $44 (3/31/92) **75**
Rioja Tondonia Reserva 1985 $13 (3/31/92) **86**
Rioja Tondonia Reserva 1983 $5.50 (3/31/90) **79**
Rioja White Gravonia 1987 ($NA) (5/31/92) **80**
Rioja White Tondonia Gran Reserva 1985 ($NA) (5/31/92) **90**
Rioja White Tondonia Gran Reserva 1976 ($NA) (5/31/92) **85**

GUSTAVE LORENTZ (France/Alsace)
Gewürztraminer Alsace 1989 ($NA) (11/15/90) **85**
Gewürztraminer Alsace 1988 ($NA) (10/15/89) **89**
Gewürztraminer Alsace 1986 $11 (7/31/89) **86**
Gewürztraminer Alsace Altenberg 1990 $39 (2/15/92) **86**
Gewürztraminer Alsace Altenberg 1989 ($NA) (11/15/90) **85**
Gewürztraminer Alsace du Domaine 1990 $20 (2/15/92) **76**
Gewürztraminer Alsace Réserve 1990 (NR) (2/15/92) **87**
Gewürztraminer Alsace Réserve 1989 ($NA) (11/15/90) **79**
Gewürztraminer Alsace Sélection de Grains Nobles 1988 ($NA) (10/15/89) **91**
Gewürztraminer Alsace Vendange Tardive 1990 $49 (2/15/92) (BT) **75+**
Pinot Blanc Alsace 1990 (NR) (2/15/92) **85**
Pinot Blanc Alsace 1989 $11 (11/15/90) **83**
Pinot Blanc Alsace 1988 $12 (10/15/89) **79**
Pinot Blanc Alsace Réserve 1986 $7 (7/31/89) **78**
Riesling Alsace 1990 $11 (2/15/92) **84**
Riesling Alsace 1989 $15 (11/15/90) **74**
Riesling Alsace 1988 $15 (10/15/89) **85**
Riesling Alsace Altenberg 1990 $35 (2/15/92) **88**
Riesling Alsace Altenberg 1989 ($NA) (11/15/90) **88**
Riesling Alsace Altenberg de Bergheim 1988 ($NA) (10/15/89) **84**
Riesling Alsace du Domaine 1990 $15 (2/15/92) **82**
Riesling Alsace Réserve 1990 $13 (2/15/92) **89**
Riesling Alsace Réserve 1989 ($NA) (11/15/90) **75**
Riesling Alsace Réserve 1986 $9.50 (7/31/89) **79**
Riesling Alsace Vendange Tardive 1990 $59 (2/15/92) (BT) **90+**
Tokay Pinot Gris Alsace 1989 $15 (11/15/90) **82**
Tokay Pinot Gris Alsace 1988 $14 (10/15/89) **87**
Tokay Pinot Gris Alsace Altenberg 1990 $39 (2/15/92) **79**
Tokay Pinot Gris Alsace Altenberg de Bergheim 1988 ($NA) (10/15/89) **83**
Tokay Pinot Gris Alsace Réserve 1989 ($NA) (11/15/90) **82**
Tokay Pinot Gris Alsace Sélection de Grains Nobles 1989 ($NA) (11/15/90) **86**
Tokay Pinot Gris Alsace Vendange Tardive 1990 $59 (2/15/92) (BT) **90+**

LORINON (Spain)
Rioja Crianza 1988 $10 (1/31/92) **83**

LOS HERMANOS (United States/California)
Chenin Blanc California NV $4/1.5L (7/31/89) **74**
White Zinfandel California 1988 $8/1.5L (6/15/89) **61**

CHATEAU LA LOUBIERE (France/Bordeaux)
Pomerol 1983 $15 (6/16/86) **77**
Pomerol 1982 $13 (5/15/89) (TR) **88**

CHATEAU LOUDENNE (France/Bordeaux)
Bordeaux Blanc 1986 $12 (3/31/89) **72**
Bordeaux Blanc 1985 $10.50 (7/15/87) **73**
Médoc 1989 $13 (3/15/92) **81**
Médoc 1988 $10 (8/31/91) **82**
Médoc 1987 $10 (11/30/89) (JS) **75**
Médoc 1986 $12 (11/30/89) (JS) **74**
Médoc 1985 $13 (11/30/88) **75**
Médoc 1982 Rel: $10 Cur: $17 (11/30/89) (JS) **74**
Médoc 1981 $11 (9/01/84) **84**

CHATEAU LA LOUVIERE (France/Bordeaux)
Pessac-Léognan 1990 (NR) (5/15/92) (BT) **90+**
Pessac-Léognan 1989 $22 (3/15/92) **91**
Pessac-Léognan 1988 $20 (8/31/91) SS **92**
Pessac-Léognan 1987 $20 (6/30/89) (BT) **80+**
Pessac-Léognan 1986 Rel: $15 Cur: $25 (6/15/89) **91**
Graves 1985 $16 (6/30/88) **87**
Graves 1983 Rel: $11 Cur: $17 (11/30/86) **78**
Graves 1982 Rel: $11 Cur: $25 (10/16/85) SS **94**
Pessac-Léognan Blanc 1990 $25 (3/31/92) **89**
Pessac-Léognan Blanc 1989 $30 (9/30/91) **87**
Pessac-Léognan Blanc 1988 Rel: $15 Cur: $22 (5/31/90) **83**
Pessac-Léognan Blanc 1987 $15 (7/31/89) **85**
Pessac-Léognan Blanc 1986 $20 (8/31/88) **87**
Graves Blanc 1983 $9.75 (9/16/85) **88**

CHATEAU DE LUCAT (France/Bordeaux)
Bordeaux Supérieur 1982 $4 (10/01/85) **71**

FATTORIA DI LUCIGNANO (Italy/Tuscany)
Chianti Colli Fiorentini 1990 $7.50 (4/30/92) BB **85**
Chianti Colli Fiorentini 1987 $6 (6/30/89) **76**

LUIANO (Italy/Tuscany)
Chianti Classico Riserva 1978 $6 (8/31/86) **71**

LUNGAROTTI (Italy/Other)
Brut NV $23 (3/15/89) **82**
Cabernet Sauvignon 1983 $18 (5/15/91) **85**
Chardonnay 1989 $11 (3/31/91) **77**
Chardonnay 1988 $10 (9/15/89) **82**
Chardonnay 1987 $10.50 (9/15/89) **83**
Chardonnay I Palazzi 1985 $16 (9/15/89) **87**
Pinot Grigio 1989 $11 (3/31/91) **81**
San Giorgio 1982 $34 (7/15/91) **77**
Torgiano Rubesco 1987 $11 (5/15/91) **83**
Torgiano Rubesco 1985 $11 (9/15/89) **74**
Torgiano Rubesco Monticchio Riserva 1980 $27 (7/15/91) **84**
Torgiano Rubesco Monticchio Riserva 1978 $23 (9/15/89) **82**
Torgiano Torre di Giano 1989 $11 (7/15/91) **83**
Vin Santo 1985 $7/375ml (3/15/91) **79**
Vin Santo 1983 $9.50 (3/15/89) **81**

LUPE-CHOLET (France/Burgundy)
Aloxe-Corton 1985 $18 (3/15/88) **84**
Beaune Avaux 1986 ($NA) (7/31/88) **89**
Bonnes Mares 1988 ($NA) (7/15/90) (BT) **90+**
Bourgogne Blanc Chardonnay Comtesse de Lupé 1988 $9 (4/30/90) BB **84**
Bourgogne Blanc Chardonnay Comtesse de Lupé 1987 $8.25 (3/15/89) BB **80**
Bourgogne Clos de Lupé 1985 $15 (3/31/88) **79**
Bourgogne Clos de la Roche 1986 $10 (7/31/88) **78**
Bourgogne Hautes Côtes de Beaune 1988 $10 (4/30/90) **80**
Bourgogne Hautes Côtes de Beaune Rouge 1987 $10 (4/15/90) **78**
Bourgogne Pinot Noir Comte de Lupé 1989 $7.50 (1/31/92) **86**
Bourgogne Pinot Noir Comte de Lupé 1988 $9 (2/28/90) BB **83**
Chablis Château de Viviers 1988 $15 (3/31/90) **82**
Chambolle-Musigny 1986 $20 (7/31/88) **81**
Chassagne-Montrachet Morgeot Vignes Blanches 1987 $45 (11/15/89) **73**
Chassagne-Montrachet La Romanée 1986 $26 (2/29/88) **85**
Crozes-Hermitage 1987 $8 (3/31/90) BB **83**
Gevrey-Chambertin Lavaux St.-Jacques 1983 $27 (11/30/86) **59**
Meursault 1986 $26 (2/15/88) **80**
Meursault 1984 $20 (10/31/86) **90**
Meursault Les Charmes 1988 $40 (2/28/90) **69**
Meursault Hospices de Beaune Cuvée Goureau 1986 $45 (2/15/88) **89**
Monthélie 1983 $9 (9/15/86) **69**
Nuits-St.-Georges Château Gris 1989 $48 (7/15/90) (BT) **85+**
Nuits-St.-Georges Château Gris 1988 $50 (7/15/90) (BT) **90+**
Nuits-St.-Georges Château Gris 1987 $38 (3/31/90) **84**
Nuits-St.-Georges Château Gris 1986 $33 (7/31/88) **86**
Nuits-St.-Georges Château Gris 1985 $39 (2/15/88) **88**
Nuits-St.-Georges Château Gris 1983 $24 (6/16/86) **77**
Nuits-St.-Georges Les Vignes Rondex Hospice de Nuits 1986 ($NA) (7/31/88) **91**
Pernand-Vergelesses Blanc 1988 $15 (3/15/90) **83**
Pommard Les Boucherottes 1983 $19 (6/16/86) **86**
Pouilly-Fuissé 1987 $13 (4/30/89) **70**
Pouilly-Fuissé 1984 $19 (8/31/86) **64**
Puligny-Montrachet Les Chalumeaux 1987 $46 (11/15/89) **82**
Rully Blanc Marissou 1988 $16 (3/15/90) **80**
Savigny-lès-Beaune Blanc 1985 $10 (11/15/86) **78**
Savigny-lès-Beaune Les Serpentières 1985 $17 (3/15/88) **83**
Volnay Hospices de Beaune Cuvée Blondeau 1986 ($NA) (7/31/88) **91**

CHATEAU DE LUSSAC (France/Bordeaux)
Lussac-St.-Emilion 1982 $6.75 (5/01/84) **73**

LYETH (United States/California)
Red Alexander Valley 1988 ($NA) (5/15/90) (BT) **85+**
Red Alexander Valley 1986 $23 (11/15/90) **88**
Red Alexander Valley 1985 $22 (5/31/89) **86**
Red Alexander Valley 1984 Rel: $18 Cur: $24 (CA-3/89) **90**
Red Alexander Valley 1983 Rel: $17 Cur: $23 (CA-3/89) **78**
Red Alexander Valley 1982 Rel: $16 Cur: $30 (CA-3/89) **85**
Red Alexander Valley 1981 Rel: $15 Cur: $35 (CA-3/89) **77**
White Alexander Valley 1988 $12 (10/31/90) **89**
White Alexander Valley 1986 $12 (9/15/89) **78**

KERMIT LYNCH (France/Beaujolais)
Beaujolais 1990 $10 (9/15/91) **83**
Côtes du Rhône 1985 $9 (1/31/89) **83**

MICHEL LYNCH (France/Bordeaux)
Bordeaux 1988 $8 (10/31/91) **76**
Bordeaux 1983 $6.75 (10/15/87) **75**
Bordeaux Blanc 1990 $8 (10/15/91) BB **85**
Bordeaux Blanc 1986 $6 (10/15/87) **77**

BLANC DE LYNCH-BAGES (France/Bordeaux)
Bordeaux Blanc 1990 $29 (5/15/92) **92**

CHATEAU LYNCH-BAGES (France/Bordeaux)
Pauillac 1991 (NR) (5/15/92) (BT) **85+**
Pauillac 1990 (NR) (5/15/92) (BT) **95+**
Pauillac 1989 $53 (3/15/92) **98**
Pauillac 1988 $35 (3/15/91) CS **95**
Pauillac 1987 $27 (2/15/90) **86**
Pauillac 1986 $37 (10/31/89) (JS) **94**
Pauillac 1985 Rel: $37 Cur: $50 (10/31/89) (JS) **93**
Pauillac 1985 Rel: $37 Cur: $50 (4/30/88) CS **97**
Pauillac 1984 Rel: $19 Cur: $22 (10/31/89) (JS) **87**
Pauillac 1983 Rel: $25 Cur: $45 (10/31/89) (JS) **88**
Pauillac 1982 Rel: $27 Cur: $70 (10/31/89) (JS) **90**
Pauillac 1982 Rel: $27 Cur: $70 (3/01/85) CS **94**
Pauillac 1981 Rel: $15 Cur: $40 (10/31/89) (JS) **90**
Pauillac 1980 $24 (10/31/89) (JS) **88**

Key to Symbols

The scores reported here are the results of blind tastings conducted by our panel of senior editors. Wines that carry the initials below are results of individual tastings.

THE WINE SPECTATOR 100-POINT SCALE ***95-100***—Classic, a great wine; ***90-94***—Outstanding, superior character and style; ***80-89***—Good to very good, a wine with special qualities; ***70-79***—Average, drinkable wine that may have minor flaws; ***60-69***—Below average, drinkable but not recommended; ***50-59***—Poor, undrinkable, not recommended. "+"—With a score indicates a range; used primarily with barrel tastings to indicate a preliminary score.

SPECIAL DESIGNATIONS SS—Spectator Selection, CS—Cellar Selection, BB—Best Buy, ($NA)—Price not available, (NR)—Not released.

TASTER'S INITIALS (JG)—Jim Gordon, (HS)—Harvey Steiman, (JL)—James Laube, (JS)—James Suckling, (TM)—Thomas Matthews, (TR)—Terry Robards, (PM)—Per-Henrik Mansson, (BT)—Barrel Tasting (these wines were tasted blind from barrel samples), (CA-date)—*California's Great Cabernets* by James Laube, (CH-date)—*California's Great Chardonnays* by James Laube, (VP-date)—*Vintage Port* by James Suckling.

DATE TASTED Dates in parentheses represent the issue in which the rating was published.

Pauillac 1979 $38 (10/31/89) (JS) **87**
Pauillac 1978 $53 (10/31/89) (JS) **92**
Pauillac 1977 $25 (10/31/89) (JS) **78**
Pauillac 1976 $52 (10/31/89) (JS) **70**
Pauillac 1975 $65 (10/31/89) (JS) **90**
Pauillac 1973 $30 (10/31/89) (JS) **82**
Pauillac 1971 $65 (10/31/89) (JS) **67**
Pauillac 1970 $125 (10/31/89) (JS) **90**
Pauillac 1967 $45 (10/31/89) (JS) **79**
Pauillac 1966 $102 (10/31/89) (JS) **90**
Pauillac 1964 $90 (10/31/89) (JS) **76**
Pauillac 1962 $139 (10/31/89) (JS) **94**
Pauillac 1961 $220 (10/31/89) (JS) **86**
Pauillac 1960 $55 (10/31/89) (JS) **76**
Pauillac 1959 $250 (10/15/90) (JS) **95**
Pauillac 1958 $60 (10/31/89) (JS) **79**
Pauillac 1957 $85 (10/31/89) (JS) **88**
Pauillac 1955 $250 (10/31/89) (JS) **92**
Pauillac 1954 $75 (10/31/89) (JS) **74**
Pauillac 1953 $320 (10/31/89) (JS) **77**
Pauillac 1952 $100 (10/31/89) (JS) **83**
Pauillac 1949 $175 (10/31/89) (JS) **84**
Pauillac 1947 $350 (10/31/89) (JS) **90**
Pauillac 1945 $350 (3/16/86) (JL) **65**
Pauillac (Danish Bottled) 1945 $350 (10/31/89) (JS) **80**

CHATEAU LYNCH-MOUSSAS (France/Bordeaux)
Pauillac 1991 (NR) (5/15/92) (BT) **75+**
Pauillac 1990 (NR) (4/30/91) (BT) **85+**
Pauillac 1989 $21 (3/15/92) **90**
Pauillac 1988 $25 (8/31/91) **85**
Pauillac 1987 $17 (6/30/89) (BT) **70+**
Pauillac 1986 $18 (6/30/89) **86**
Pauillac 1959 $115 (10/15/90) (JS) **86**

LYTTON SPRINGS (United States/California)
Cabernet Sauvignon Mendocino County Private Reserve 1988 $18 (11/15/91) **80**
Cabernet Sauvignon Mendocino County Private Reserve 1987 $18 (9/15/90) **88**
Palette Sonoma-Mendocino Counties NV $10 (11/15/91) **83**
Zinfandel Sonoma County 1989 $15 (8/31/91) **84**
Zinfandel Sonoma County 1988 $12 (7/31/90) **90**
Zinfandel Sonoma County 1987 $12 (5/31/89) **88**
Zinfandel Sonoma County 1986 $10 (10/15/88) **87**
Zinfandel Sonoma County 1985 $8 (8/31/87) **90**
Zinfandel Sonoma County 1984 $8 (10/31/86) **70**
Zinfandel Sonoma County Valley Vista Vineyard Private Reserve 1981 $12 (1/01/85) **85**

M & G (France/Burgundy)
Côte de Beaune-Villages 1987 $20 (3/31/91) **73**
Gevrey-Chambertin 1987 $40 (3/31/91) **73**
Mâcon-Villages 1988 $14 (3/31/91) **78**
Meursault Les Forges 1987 $42 (3/31/91) **75**
Vouvray Moelleux 1988 $10 (3/31/91) **81**

MAACAMA CREEK (United States/California)
Cabernet Sauvignon Sonoma County Melim Vineyard 1989 $8 (11/15/91) BB **86**

BERTRAND MACHARD DE GRAMONT (France/Burgundy)
Nuits-St.-Georges Les Allots 1987 $30 (7/15/90) **82**
Nuits-St.-Georges Les Hauts Pruliers 1988 $37 (7/15/91) **88**
Nuits-St.-Georges Les Hauts Pruliers 1987 $32 (4/30/90) **85**
Nuits-St.-Georges Les Hauts Pruliers 1986 $22 (12/15/89) **77**
Vosne-Romanée Les Réas 1988 $32 (7/15/91) **89**

MACHIAVELLI (Italy/Tuscany)
Chianti Classico Riserva 1986 $16 (10/31/91) **84**
Chianti Classico Vigna di Fontalle Riserva 1985 ($NA) (9/15/91) **91**

MACROSTIE (United States/California)
Chardonnay Carneros 1990 $16 (12/15/91) **90**
Chardonnay Carneros 1989 $14 (12/31/90) **87**
Chardonnay Carneros 1988 $14 (2/28/90) **90**
Chardonnay Carneros 1987 $14.50 (11/30/88) **89**

MACULAN (Italy/North)
Breganze Bianco Breganze di Breganze 1987 $7.50 (5/15/89) BB **85**
Breganze Cabernet Fratta 1986 $29 (3/31/89) **92**
Breganze Rosso Brentino 1986 $9.50 (3/31/89) **85**
Cabernet Sauvignon Palazzotto 1987 $30 (1/31/92) **82**
Cabernet Sauvignon Palazzotto 1986 $19 (3/31/89) **71**
Chardonnay 1985 $22 (9/15/89) **87**
Chardonnay Ferrata 1987 $22 (9/15/89) **90**
Chardonnay Ferrata 1986 $18 (9/15/89) **87**
Chardonnay Ferrata 1984 $25 (9/15/89) **87**
Dindarello 1989 $24 (7/15/91) **84**
Prato di Canzio 1987 $17 (10/15/89) **83**
Torcolato 1988 $35 (4/15/91) **91**
Torcolato 1985 $15/375ml (3/31/89) **84**
Torcolato 1983 $29 (11/15/87) **82**

MADDALENA (United States/California)
Cabernet Sauvignon Alexander Valley Reserve 1986 $10 (3/31/90) **77**
Cabernet Sauvignon Alexander Valley Reserve 1985 $11 (6/30/89) **78**
Cabernet Sauvignon Sonoma County 1988 $7.50 (3/31/92) **79**
Cabernet Sauvignon Sonoma County 1985 $6 (5/31/88) **74**
Cabernet Sauvignon Sonoma County Vintner's Reserve 1984 $9 (3/31/87) **82**
Chardonnay Central Coast 1990 $7.50 (3/31/92) **80**
Chardonnay Central Coast 1989 $8 (4/30/91) BB **83**
Chardonnay Central Coast San Simeon Collection 1990 $14 (3/31/92) **77**
Chardonnay Central Coast San Simeon Collection 1989 $14 (11/30/91) **88**
Chardonnay Napa Valley 1989 $10 (7/15/91) **80**
Chardonnay San Luis Obispo County 1982 $6 (5/16/84) **70**
Chardonnay Santa Barbara County 1984 $5 (4/16/86) **72**
Gewürztraminer Central Coast 1990 $6 (9/30/91) **78**
Merlot Central Coast San Simeon Collection 1989 $12 (5/31/92) **73**

CHATEAU LA MADELEINE (France/Bordeaux)
Pomerol 1985 $10 (3/15/88) **56**

MADER (France/Alsace)
Gewürztraminer Alsace 1990 $14 (2/15/92) **85**
Gewürztraminer Alsace Vendange Tardive 1990 $48 (2/15/92) (BT) **80+**
Muscat d'Alsace Alsace 1990 $11 (2/15/92) **89**
Pinot Blanc Alsace 1990 $9 (2/15/92) **85**
Riesling Alsace 1990 $12 (2/15/92) **90**
Riesling Alsace Rosacker 1990 $22 (2/15/92) **94**
Riesling Alsace Vendange Tardive 1990 $48 (2/15/92) (BT) **90+**
Tokay Pinot Gris Alsace 1990 $14 (2/15/92) **85**
Tokay Pinot Gris Alsace Vendange Tardive 1990 $48 (2/15/92) (BT) **85+**

LA MADONNINA (Italy/Tuscany)
Chianti Classico 1988 ($NA) (9/15/91) **84**

MADRON LAKE HILLS (United States/Michigan)
Chardonnay Michigan Lake Erie Heartland Vineyards 1990 $13.50 (2/29/92) **79**
White Riesling Late Harvest Michigan Lake Erie Semi-Dry Heartland Vineyards 1990 $10 (2/29/92) **74**

MADRONA (United States/California)
Cabernet Franc El Dorado 1986 $11 (3/31/92) **73**
Cabernet Sauvignon El Dorado 1985 $12 (4/15/92) **82**
Chardonnay El Dorado 1989 $10 (7/15/92) **80**
Chardonnay El Dorado 1987 $12 (3/31/92) **82**
Johannisberg Riesling El Dorado 1987 $6 (7/31/89) **79**
White Zinfandel El Dorado 1988 $5.25 (6/15/89) **76**

BODEGAS MAGANA (Spain)
Navarra 1982 $14 (3/31/90) **73**

CHATEAU MAGDELAINE (France/Bordeaux)
St.-Emilion 1990 (NR) (5/15/92) (BT) **90+**
St.-Emilion 1989 $44 (3/15/92) **88**
St.-Emilion 1988 $50 (10/31/91) **81**
St.-Emilion 1987 $34 (6/30/89) (BT) **80+**
St.-Emilion 1986 $48 (2/15/90) **94**
St.-Emilion 1985 Rel: $40 Cur: $44 (6/30/88) **90**
St.-Emilion 1982 $51 (5/15/89) (TR) **95**
St.-Emilion 1979 $38 (10/15/89) (JS) **89**
St.-Emilion 1961 $250 (3/16/86) (TR) **86**
St.-Emilion 1959 $125 (10/15/90) (JS) **89**

CHATEAU MAGNEAU (France/Bordeaux)
Graves 1987 $12 (5/15/90) **78**

HENRI MAGNIEN (France/Burgundy)
Gevrey-Chambertin 1985 $25 (10/15/87) **81**
Gevrey-Chambertin 1983 $13 (2/01/86) **68**
Gevrey-Chambertin 1982 $12 (7/01/85) **89**
Gevrey-Chambertin Les Cazetiers 1985 $35 (10/15/87) **88**
Gevrey-Chambertin Les Cazetiers 1983 $18 (12/16/85) **72**
Gevrey-Chambertin Les Cazetiers 1982 $16 (5/01/84) **80**
Gevrey-Chambertin Premier Cru 1985 $29 (10/15/87) **80**

CHATEAU MAGNOL (France/Bordeaux)
Haut-Médoc 1988 ($NA) (6/30/89) (BT) **80+**
Haut-Médoc 1987 ($NA) (6/30/89) (BT) **75+**
Haut-Médoc 1983 $9.50 (7/31/87) **77**
Haut-Médoc 1981 $8.75 (8/31/87) **69**

CHATEAU MAISON-BLANCHE (France/Bordeaux)
Montagne-St.-Emilion 1985 $13 (2/15/89) **80**

MAISON DEUTZ (United States/California)
Brut Rosé Santa Barbara County NV $24 (5/15/92) **85**
Brut San Luis Obispo County Reserve 1987 $22 (10/31/91) **88**
Brut San Luis Obispo County Reserve 1986 $22 (4/30/91) **77**
Brut Santa Barbara County Cuvée NV $15 (1/31/88) **85**
Brut Santa Barbara County Cuvée 3 NV $17 (5/31/89) **89**

CHATEAU MAISON-NEUVE (France/Bordeaux)
Montagne-St.-Emilion 1985 $7 (3/15/88) **78**

MAITRE D'ESTOURNEL (France/Bordeaux)
Bordeaux 1985 $7.25 (5/31/88) **84**
Bordeaux Blanc 1987 $7 (8/31/88) BB **83**
Bordeaux Blanc 1985 $5 (12/31/86) BB **84**

DOMAINE DE LA MALADIERE (France/Chablis)
Chablis 1988 $13 (2/28/91) **81**

CHATEAU MALARTIC-LAGRAVIERE (France/Bordeaux)
Pessac-Léognan 1989 $24 (3/15/92) **85**
Pessac-Léognan 1988 $20 (7/15/91) **84**
Pessac-Léognan 1987 $18 (6/30/89) (BT) **80+**
Pessac-Léognan 1986 Rel: $18 Cur: $27 (6/15/89) **90**
Graves 1985 $22 (5/15/87) (BT) **90+**
Pessac-Léognan Blanc 1988 $31 (7/31/91) **79**
Pessac-Léognan Blanc 1987 $30 (6/30/89) (BT) **90+**
Graves Blanc 1985 $23 (11/15/87) **84**

CHATEAU MALESCASSE (France/Bordeaux)
Haut-Médoc 1991 (NR) (5/15/92) (BT) **75+**
Haut-Médoc 1990 (NR) (5/15/92) (BT) **80+**
Haut-Médoc 1989 $16 (3/15/92) **84**
Haut-Médoc 1988 Rel: $14 Cur: $22 (6/30/89) (BT) **85+**
Haut-Médoc 1987 $9 (11/30/89) (JS) **74**
Haut-Médoc 1986 $9 (11/30/89) (JS) **88**
Haut-Médoc 1982 Rel: $7 Cur: $18 (11/30/89) (JS) **82**

CHATEAU MALESCOT-ST.-EXUPERY (France/Bordeaux)
Margaux 1989 $28 (3/15/92) **87**
Margaux 1988 $23 (4/30/91) **89**
Margaux 1987 $20 (6/30/89) (BT) **70+**
Margaux 1986 Rel: $26 Cur: $29 (6/15/89) **88**
Margaux 1985 Rel: $24 Cur: $27 (9/30/88) **87**
Margaux 1983 Rel: $16 Cur: $22 (9/30/86) **82**
Margaux 1981 Rel: $13 Cur: $22 (5/01/89) **87**
Margaux 1962 $80 (11/30/87) (JS) **65**
Margaux 1961 $105 (3/16/86) (TR) **66**
Margaux 1959 $150 (10/15/90) (JS) **87**
Margaux 1945 $200 (3/16/86) (JL) **81**

CHATEAU DE MALIGNY (France/Chablis)
Chablis 1988 $15 (7/31/90) **76**
Chablis Fourchaume 1990 $20 (8/31/91) **84**
Chablis Fourchaume 1988 $22 (7/31/90) **71**
Chablis Fourchaume 1986 $18 (3/31/89) **85**

CHATEAU DE MALLE (France/Sauternes)
Sauternes 1989 ($NA) (6/15/90) (BT) **85+**
Sauternes 1988 $15 (6/15/90) (BT) **85+**
Sauternes 1987 $15 (6/15/90) **81**
Sauternes 1986 $15 (6/30/88) (BT) **85+**
Sauternes 1981 $13 (8/31/86) **84**

M. DE MALLE (France/Bordeaux)
Bordeaux Blanc 1983 $6.25 (7/01/86) **54**

CHATEAU DE MALLERET (France/Bordeaux)
Haut-Médoc 1989 (NR) (3/15/92) **90**
Haut-Médoc 1981 $5.99 (3/01/85) **77**

CHATEAU MALMAISON (France/Bordeaux)
Moulis 1991 (NR) (5/15/92) (BT) **80+**
Moulis 1989 (NR) (3/15/92) **85**

MALPAGA (Italy/North)
Chardonnay Trentino 1988 $8 (9/15/89) **85**
Chardonnay Trentino 1987 $8 (9/15/89) **75**

CHATEAU DE LA MALTROYE (France/Burgundy)
Chassagne-Montrachet Clos de la Maltroye 1983 $21 (6/01/86) **80**
Chassagne-Montrachet Grandes Ruchottes 1989 $40 (2/28/91) **86**
Chassagne-Montrachet Maltroie-Crets 1986 $27 (10/31/88) **74**
Chassagne-Montrachet Morgeot-Fairendes 1986 $26 (9/30/88) **86**
Chassagne-Montrachet Morgeot-Fairendes 1983 $19 (11/16/85) **79**
Chassagne-Montrachet Morgeot Vigne Blanche 1989 $40 (2/28/91) **87**
Chassagne-Montrachet Morgeot Vigne Blanche 1986 $29 (9/30/88) **90**
Chassagne-Montrachet Morgeot Vigne Blanche 1983 $17 (6/16/85) **88**
Chassagne-Montrachet La Romanée Première Cuvée 1988 $31 (8/31/91) **83**
Chassagne-Montrachet Rouge Boudriottes 1985 $17 (10/15/88) **86**
Chassagne-Montrachet Rouge Clos St.-Jean 1985 $19 (10/15/88) **89**
Chassagne-Montrachet Rouge Clos St.-Jean 1983 $12.50 (11/16/85) **65**

MANCIAT-PONCET (France/Burgundy)
Pouilly-Fuissé La Roche 1985 $20 (2/15/88) **88**

MANISCHEWITZ (United States/California)
Chardonnay Alexander Valley 1988 $7 (3/31/91) **87**
Pinot Noir Russian River Valley 1989 $9 (3/31/91) **74**
White Zinfandel Sonoma County 1989 $6 (3/31/91) **77**

ALBERT MANN (France/Alsace)
Gewürztraminer Alsace Furstentum Vendange Tardive 1990 (NR) (2/15/92) (BT) **85+**
Gewürztraminer Alsace Hengst Vendange Tardive 1990 (NR) (2/15/92) (BT) **90+**
Gewürztraminer Alsace Steingrubler Vendange Tardive 1990 (NR) (2/15/92) (BT) **85+**
Gewürztraminer Alsace Steingrubler Vieilles Vignes 1990 (NR) (2/15/92) **87**
Pinot Blanc Alsace Pinot Auxerrois Non Filtré 1990 $9.50 (2/15/92) **84**
Riesling Alsace Grand Cru Schlossberg 1990 $16 (2/15/92) **90**
Riesling Alsace Hardt 1990 $12 (2/15/92) **90**
Riesling Alsace Pfleck Vendange Tardive 1990 (NR) (2/15/92) (BT) **90+**
Tokay Pinot Gris Alsace 1990 $11 (2/15/92) **84**
Tokay Pinot Gris Alsace Grand Cru Hengst Vendange Tardive 1990 (NR) (2/15/92) (BT) **85+**
Tokay Pinot Gris Alsace Sélection de Grains Nobles 1990 (NR) (2/15/92) (BT) **90+**
Tokay Pinot Gris Alsace Vieilles Vignes 1990 $15 (2/15/92) **86**

DOMAINE RENE MANUEL (France/Burgundy)
Bourgogne Blanc Blanc 1989 ($NA) (8/31/91) **80**
Meursault Clos de la Baronne 1989 $29 (1/31/92) **89**
Meursault Clos des Bouches Chères 1989 $68 (8/31/91) **84**
Meursault Clos des Bouches Chères 1988 $50 (8/31/90) **86**
Meursault Clos des Bouches Chères 1985 $39 (8/31/87) **93**
Meursault Poruzot 1985 $37 (8/31/87) **85**
Meursault Rouge Clos de la Baronne 1988 $18 (3/31/91) **79**

MANZANITA (United States/California)
Chardonnay Napa Valley 1984 $12.50 (10/31/86) **71**
Chardonnay Napa Valley 1983 $12.50 (1/01/86) SS **93**
Chardonnay Napa Valley 1982 $14 (4/01/84) **84**

MANZANITA RIDGE (United States/California)
Chardonnay Sonoma County Barrel Fermented 1989 $8 (6/30/91) BB **86**

FOSS MARAI (Italy/North)
Brut Chardonnay NV $8 (3/15/89) BB **84**
Cabernet Piave 1990 $8.75 (1/31/92) **76**
Prosecco di Valdobbiadene 1989 $7.50 (12/31/90) **78**
Prosecco di Valdobbiadene NV $11 (12/31/90) **78**

CHATEAU DE MARBUZET (France/Bordeaux)
St.-Estèphe 1991 (NR) (5/15/92) (BT) **80+**
St.-Estèphe 1989 $21 (3/15/92) **89**
St.-Estèphe 1988 Rel: $15 Cur: $17 (7/15/91) SS **92**
St.-Estèphe 1987 $14 (11/30/89) (JS) **80**
St.-Estèphe 1986 $15 (11/30/89) (JS) **86**
St.-Estèphe 1985 Rel: $11 Cur: $21 (6/30/88) **87**
St.-Estèphe 1983 Rel: $9 Cur: $22 (10/15/86) **91**
St.-Estèphe 1982 $19 (11/30/89) (JS) **86**

MARCARINI (Italy/Piedmont)
Barbera d'Alba Ciabot Camerano 1988 $18 (3/15/91) **90**
Barolo Brunate 1985 $35 (3/31/90) **90**
Barolo Brunate 1983 $23 (9/15/88) (HS) **89**
Barolo Brunate 1982 $18 (9/15/88) (HS) **90**
Barolo Brunate 1979 $29 (9/15/88) (HS) **88**
Barolo Brunate 1978 $50 (9/15/88) (HS) **80**
Barolo Brunate 1971 $60 (9/15/88) (HS) **89**
Barolo Brunate 1964 ($NA) (9/15/88) (HS) **96**
Barolo La Serra 1983 $17 (9/15/88) (HS) **87**
Barolo La Serra 1982 $18 (9/15/88) (HS) **91**
Barolo La Serra 1980 $9.50 (4/16/86) **89**
Barolo La Serra 1978 $18 (9/16/84) **79**
Dolcetto d'Alba Boschi di Berri 1989 $23 (4/30/91) **89**
Dolcetto d'Alba Boschi di Berri 1988 $17 (3/31/90) **86**
Dolcetto d'Alba Boschi di Berri 1987 $13 (3/15/89) **89**
Dolcetto d'Alba Fontanazza 1989 $13 (4/30/91) **84**
Dolcetto d'Alba Fontanazza 1988 $11 (3/31/90) **87**
Dolcetto d'Alba Fontanazza 1987 $9.75 (3/15/89) **78**
Lasarin Nebbiolo delle Langhe 1989 $9.50 (4/30/91) **84**
Nebbiolo delle Langhe 1988 $10 (3/31/90) **84**

CLAUDE MARCHAND (France/Burgundy)
Chambolle-Musigny 1986 $32 (7/15/89) **85**
Charmes-Chambertin 1986 $50 (7/15/89) **92**
Gevrey-Chambertin 1987 $22 (7/15/90) **81**
Gevrey-Chambertin 1986 $28 (7/15/89) **89**
Morey-St.-Denis 1987 $30 (9/30/90) **80**
Morey-St.-Denis Clos des Ormes 1987 $30 (9/30/90) **69**
Morey-St.-Denis Clos des Ormes 1986 $33 (7/15/89) **85**

DOMAINE JEAN-PHILIPPE MARCHAND (France/Burgundy)
Charmes-Chambertin 1987 $60 (12/31/90) **76**
Gevrey-Chambertin Les Combottes 1987 $30 (7/15/90) **82**

DOMAINE MARCHAND-GRILLOT (France/Burgundy)
Gevrey-Chambertin Petite Chapelle 1986 $30 (10/15/89) **76**

MARCHESI DI BAROLO (Italy/Piedmont)
Barbaresco Rio Sordo 1988 $18 (1/31/92) **86**
Barbera del Monferrato 1985 $5 (9/15/87) BB **82**
Barbera del Monferrato Le Lune 1988 $6 (7/15/91) **78**
Barolo Brunate 1985 $29 (10/15/90) **85**
Barolo Brunate 1982 $14 (2/15/89) **89**
Barolo Cannubi 1985 $29 (10/15/90) **88**
Barolo Castel la Volta 1987 Rel: $20 Cur: $22 (1/31/92) **89**
Barolo Coste di Rosé 1985 $29 (10/15/90) **86**
Barolo Riserva 1982 $14 (2/15/89) **87**
Barolo Riserva 1978 $20 (2/28/89) **86**
Barolo Valletta 1985 $29 (10/15/90) **88**
Dolcetto d'Alba Madonna di Como 1990 $10 (1/31/92) **77**
Dolcetto d'Alba Madonna di Como 1989 $9 (12/31/90) BB **88**
Dolcetto d'Alba Madonna di Como 1987 $8 (2/15/89) **87**

MARCHISIO (Italy/Piedmont)
Roero Vigneti Mongalletto 1987 $10 (3/31/90) **78**

VILLA MARCIALLA (Italy/Tuscany)
Chianti Colli Fiorentini 1986 $6 (10/15/89) **79**

DOMAINE DE MARCOUX (France/Rhône)
Châteauneuf-du-Pape 1988 $24 (10/15/91) **82**
Châteauneuf-du-Pape 1986 $20 (10/15/91) **84**
Châteauneuf-du-Pape 1983 $25 (10/15/91) **87**
Châteauneuf-du-Pape 1981 $30 (10/15/91) **85**
Châteauneuf-du-Pape Blanc 1990 $20 (10/15/91) **88**
Châteauneuf-du-Pape Vieilles Vignes 1989 $30 (10/15/91) **95**

PODERI E MARENGO-MARENDA (Italy/Piedmont)
Dolcetto d'Alba Le Terre Forti 1990 $12 (1/31/92) **84**

ROGER MARES (France/Other)
Cabernet Syrah Mas des Bressades 1988 $10.50 (10/31/90) **81**

CHATEAU MARGAUX (France/Bordeaux)
Margaux 1991 (NR) (5/15/92) (BT) **90+**
Margaux 1990 (NR) (5/15/92) (BT) **95+**
Margaux 1989 $145 (3/15/92) CS **99**
Margaux 1988 Rel: $75 Cur: $80 (3/31/91) CS **97**
Margaux 1987 $55 (5/15/90) **87**
Margaux 1986 Rel: $80 Cur: $110 (12/15/89) (JS) **98**
Margaux 1986 Rel: $80 Cur: $110 (6/15/89) CS **98**
Margaux 1985 Rel: $76 Cur: $98 (12/15/89) (JS) **97**
Margaux 1984 Rel: $35 Cur: $60 (2/28/87) CS **93**
Margaux 1983 Rel: $70 Cur: $103 (12/15/89) (JS) **92**
Margaux 1983 Rel: $70 Cur: $103 (4/16/86) SS **99**
Margaux 1982 Rel: $60 Cur: $135 (12/15/89) (JS) **98**
Margaux 1982 Rel: $60 Cur: $135 (6/16/85) CS **96**
Margaux 1981 $95 (7/15/87) (HS) **97**
Margaux 1980 Rel: $30 Cur: $66 (7/15/87) (HS) **80**
Margaux 1980 Rel: $30 Cur: $66 (5/01/84) CS **90**
Margaux 1979 $116 (12/15/89) (JS) **91**
Margaux 1978 $165 (12/15/89) (JS) **92**
Margaux 1977 $40 (7/15/87) (HS) **75**
Margaux 1976 $89 (7/15/87) (HS) **81**
Margaux 1975 $110 (7/15/87) (HS) **88**
Margaux 1971 $88 (7/15/87) (HS) **77**
Margaux 1970 $135 (7/15/87) (HS) **70**
Margaux 1967 $60 (7/15/87) (HS) **84**
Margaux 1966 $170 (7/15/87) (HS) **90**
Margaux 1964 $85 (7/15/87) (HS) **86**
Margaux 1962 $250/1.5L (12/15/89) (JS) **86**
Margaux 1961 $1,060/1.5L (12/15/89) (JS) **98**
Margaux 1959 $330 (10/15/90) (JS) **93**
Margaux 1957 $150 (7/15/87) (HS) **90**
Margaux 1955 $150 (7/15/87) (HS) **79**
Margaux 1953 $430 (12/15/89) (JS) **84**
Margaux 1952 $550/1.5L (7/15/87) (HS) **85**
Margaux 1950 $1,320/1.5L (7/15/87) (HS) **89**
Margaux 1949 $300 (7/15/87) (HS) **95**
Margaux 1947 $380 (7/15/87) (HS) **96**
Margaux 1945 $700 (3/16/86) (JL) **90**
Margaux 1943 $320 (7/15/87) (HS) **78**
Margaux 1937 $400 (7/15/87) (HS) **82**
Margaux 1934 $300 (7/15/87) (HS) **88**
Margaux 1929 $750 (7/15/87) (HS) **83**
Margaux 1928 $1,300 (7/15/87) (HS) **73**

Key to Symbols

The scores reported here are the results of blind tastings conducted by our panel of senior editors. Wines that carry the initials below are results of individual tastings.

THE WINE SPECTATOR 100-POINT SCALE ***95-100***—Classic, a great wine; ***90-94***—Outstanding, superior character and style; ***80-89***—Good to very good, a wine with special qualities; ***70-79***—Average, drinkable wine that may have minor flaws; ***60-69***—Below average, drinkable but not recommended; ***50-59***—Poor, undrinkable, not recommended. "+"—With a score indicates a range; used primarily with barrel tastings to indicate a preliminary score.

SPECIAL DESIGNATIONS SS—Spectator Selection, CS—Cellar Selection, BB—Best Buy, ($NA)—Price not available, (NR)—Not released.

TASTER'S INITIALS (JG)—Jim Gordon, (HS)—Harvey Steiman, (JL)—James Laube, (JS)—James Suckling, (TM)—Thomas Matthews, (TR)—Terry Robards, (PM)—Per-Henrik Mansson, (BT)—Barrel Tasting (these wines were tasted blind from barrel samples), (CA-date)—*California's Great Cabernets* by James Laube, (CH-date)—*California's Great Chardonnays* by James Laube, (VP-date)—*Vintage Port* by James Suckling.

DATE TASTED Dates in parentheses represent the issue in which the rating was published.

Margaux 1928 $2,860/1.5L (7/15/87) (HS) **84**
Margaux 1926 $450 (7/15/87) (HS) **77**
Margaux 1924 $173 (7/15/87) (HS) **73**
Margaux 1923 $300 (7/15/87) (HS) **81**
Margaux 1920 $420 (7/15/87) (HS) **79**
Margaux 1918 $440 (7/15/87) (HS) **80**
Margaux 1917 $300 (7/15/87) (HS) **62**
Margaux 1909 $480 (7/15/87) (HS) **65**
Margaux 1908 $530 (7/15/87) (HS) **85**
Margaux 1905 $800 (7/15/87) (HS) **64**
Margaux 1900 $2,400 (7/15/87) (HS) **93**
Margaux 1899 $1,700 (7/15/87) (HS) **94**
Margaux 1898 $2,000 (7/15/87) (HS) **75**
Margaux 1893 $1,500 (7/15/87) (HS) **95**
Margaux 1892 $1,000 (7/15/87) (HS) **80**
Margaux 1887 $850 (7/15/87) (HS) **81**
Margaux 1875 $15,000/D (12/15/88) (JS) **100**
Margaux 1870 $3,300 (7/15/87) (HS) **89**
Margaux 1868 $1,900 (7/15/87) (HS) **69**
Margaux 1865 $5,000 (7/15/87) (HS) **97**
Margaux 1864 $3,500 (7/15/87) (HS) **98**
Margaux 1848 ($NA) (7/15/87) (HS) **95**
Margaux 1847 $11,000/1.5L (7/15/87) (HS) **96**
Margaux 1791 ($NA) (7/15/87) (HS) **97**
Margaux 1771 ($NA) (7/15/87) (HS) **99**

MARIETTA (United States/California)
Cabernet Sauvignon Sonoma County 1987 $10 (2/28/91) **87**
Cabernet Sauvignon Sonoma County 1985 $10 (6/30/90) **83**
Cabernet Sauvignon Sonoma County 1984 $10 (12/31/87) **78**
Cabernet Sauvignon Sonoma County 1981 $9 (6/16/84) **78**
Old Vine Red Lot No. 7 Sonoma County NV $6 (11/15/89) BB **82**
Old Vine Red Lot No. 8 Sonoma County NV $5.50 (5/31/90) BB **81**
Old Vine Red Lot No. 10 Sonoma County NV $6 (4/30/92) **79**
Petite Sirah Sonoma County 1988 $10 (3/15/92) **84**
Zinfandel Sonoma County 1988 $8 (12/31/91) BB **87**
Zinfandel Sonoma County 1987 $8 (11/30/90) **79**
Zinfandel Sonoma County 1985 $7.50 (12/31/87) **87**
Zinfandel Sonoma County 1984 $7.50 (1/31/87) **90**
Zinfandel Sonoma County 1982 $6.50 (6/16/84) **73**
Zinfandel Sonoma County Reserve 1985 $10 (12/31/87) **88**

MARILYN MERLOT (United States/California)
Merlot Napa Valley 1989 $13.50 (5/31/92) **87**
Merlot Napa Valley 1988 $12.50 (5/31/91) **85**
Merlot Napa Valley 1986 $13 (12/31/88) **85**
Merlot France Vin de Pays de l'Aude 1987 $6 (3/15/90) **77**

MARION (United States/California)
Cabernet Sauvignon California 1989 $9 (11/15/91) **83**
Cabernet Sauvignon California 1985 $5.50 (12/31/87) **62**
Chardonnay California 1989 $8 (7/15/91) **70**
Chardonnay California 1986 $5.50 (2/15/88) BB **81**
Johannisberg Riesling California 1987 $4.50 (2/28/89) **74**

MARK WEST (United States/California)
Blanc de Noirs Russian River Valley 1984 $16.50 (12/31/88) **71**
Chardonnay Russian River Valley 1982 $10.50 (10/16/85) **80**
Chardonnay Russian River Valley Le Beau Vineyards 1990 $14 (3/31/92) **80**
Chardonnay Russian River Valley Le Beau Vineyards 1987 $12 (6/30/90) **73**
Chardonnay Russian River Valley Le Beau Vineyards 1986 $12 (9/15/88) **77**
Chardonnay Russian River Valley Le Beau Vineyards Reserve 1987 $17 (4/15/91) **88**
Chardonnay Russian River Valley Le Beau Vineyards Reserve 1985 $16 (10/31/87) **88**
Chardonnay Russian River Valley Vintner's Library Selection 1980 $14 (10/01/85) **88**
Chardonnay Sonoma Valley 1987 $8 (12/31/88) **78**
Johannisberg Riesling Late Harvest Russian River Valley 1983 $10/375ml (3/16/86) **79**
Pinot Noir Russian River Valley 1983 $10 (5/16/86) **67**
Pinot Noir Russian River Valley Ellis Vineyard 1986 $14 (3/31/90) **81**
Pinot Noir Russian River Valley Ellis Vineyard 1984 $10 (3/15/87) **84**
Pinot Noir Sonoma County 1986 $8 (2/28/89) **80**
Zinfandel Sonoma County Robert Rue Vineyard 1986 $14 (3/15/90) **83**
Zinfandel Sonoma County Robert Rue Vineyard 1985 $14 (7/31/88) **85**
Zinfandel Sonoma County Robert Rue Vineyards 1987 $16.50 (5/15/92) **86**

MARKHAM (United States/California)
Cabernet Sauvignon Napa Valley 1990 (NR) (5/15/91) (BT) **85+**
Cabernet Sauvignon Napa Valley 1989 (NR) (5/15/91) (BT) **85+**
Cabernet Sauvignon Napa Valley 1988 $18 (5/15/90) (BT) **85+**
Cabernet Sauvignon Napa Valley 1987 $15 (8/31/91) **87**
Cabernet Sauvignon Napa Valley 1986 Rel: $13 Cur: $16 (4/30/91) **87**
Cabernet Sauvignon Napa Valley 1985 Rel: $13 Cur: $17 (4/15/90) **91**
Cabernet Sauvignon Napa Valley 1984 Rel: $12 Cur: $18 (CA-3/89) **91**
Cabernet Sauvignon Napa Valley 1983 Rel: $13 Cur: $17 (7/31/89) **90**
Cabernet Sauvignon Napa Valley 1982 Rel: $13 Cur: $20 (CA-3/89) **90**
Cabernet Sauvignon Napa Valley 1981 Rel: $13 Cur: $20 (CA-3/89) **86**
Cabernet Sauvignon Napa Valley 1980 Rel: $13 Cur: $26 (CA-3/89) **89**
Cabernet Sauvignon Napa Valley 1979 Rel: $13 Cur: $31 (CA-3/89) **88**
Cabernet Sauvignon Napa Valley 1978 Rel: $13 Cur: $32 (CA-3/89) **85**
Chardonnay Napa Valley Barrel Fermented 1990 $14 (7/15/92) **85**
Chardonnay Napa Valley 1989 $12 (6/15/91) SS **92**
Chardonnay Napa Valley 1988 Rel: $12 Cur: $19 (5/31/90) **82**
Chardonnay Napa Valley 1987 Rel: $12 Cur: $16 (CH-2/90) **87**
Chardonnay Napa Valley Estate 1986 Rel: $12 Cur: $15 (CH-2/90) **84**
Chardonnay Napa Valley Estate 1983 Rel: $11.50 Cur: $18 (CH-2/90) **81**
Chardonnay Napa Valley Estate 1982 Rel: $12 Cur: $17 (CH-2/90) **83**
Merlot Napa Valley 1990 (NR) (5/15/91) (BT) **85+**
Merlot Napa Valley 1989 $15 (5/31/92) **85**
Merlot Napa Valley 1988 $13.50 (4/15/91) **90**
Merlot Napa Valley 1987 $13.50 (10/15/89) **91**
Merlot Napa Valley 1985 $11 (4/30/88) **88**
Merlot Napa Valley 1981 $8.75 (8/01/84) **86**
Muscat Napa Valley Blanc 1989 $9 (7/15/90) **79**
Muscat Napa Valley Blanc Markham Vineyard 1988 $9 (4/30/89) **84**
Sauvignon Blanc Napa Valley 1990 $8 (10/15/91) **87**
Sauvignon Blanc Napa Valley 1989 $7 (10/31/90) BB **87**
Sauvignon Blanc Napa Valley 1988 $7 (9/15/89) **82**
Sauvignon Blanc Napa Valley 1987 $7 (4/15/89) **86**

MARKKO (United States/Ohio)
Cabernet Sauvignon Conneaut 1988 $10 (2/29/92) **76**
Pinot Noir Conneaut 1989 $15 (2/29/92) **76**

DOMAINE MAROSLAVAC (France/Burgundy)
Puligny-Montrachet Clos du Vieux Château 1988 $40 (7/31/90) **83**

CHATEAU MAROT (France/Other)
Bergerac 1988 $7 (8/31/91) **79**

CHATEAU MAROTTE (France/Bordeaux)
Bordeaux 1986 $3.50 (4/30/88) **70**
Bordeaux Blanc 1986 $3.50 (3/31/88) **73**

CHATEAU MARQUERITE DE BOURGOGNE (France/Burgundy)
Bourgogne Blanc Chardonnay 1985 $14 (6/30/87) **72**

CHATEAU MARQUIS-D'ALESME-BECKER (France/Bordeaux)
Margaux 1988 $20 (6/30/89) (BT) **75+**
Margaux 1987 $15 (6/30/89) (BT) **70+**
Margaux 1985 Rel: $19 Cur: $30 (6/30/88) **84**
Margaux 1984 $16 (6/15/87) **69**
Margaux 1983 $15 (12/31/86) **84**

MARQUIS D'ANGERVILLE (France/Burgundy)
Volnay Clos des Ducs 1985 $35 (3/15/88) **80**

MARQUIS DE SADE (France/Champagne)
Brut Blanc de Blancs Champagne Grand Cru NV $35 (3/31/92) **85**
Brut Champagne Private Reserve 1985 $48 (3/31/92) **79**
Brut Champagne Private Reserve 1981 $56 (12/31/90) **89**

CHATEAU MARQUIS DE TERME (France/Bordeaux)
Margaux 1988 Rel: $23 Cur: $30 (4/30/91) **92**
Margaux 1987 $20 (6/30/89) (BT) **75+**
Margaux 1986 Rel: $23 Cur: $30 (6/30/89) **79**

MARQUIS DES TOURS (France/Bordeaux)
Bordeaux 1988 $5 (2/28/91) **78**

CHATEAU MARSAC-SEGUINEAU (France/Bordeaux)
Margaux 1988 ($NA) (6/30/89) (BT) **75+**
Margaux 1987 $10 (6/30/89) (BT) **65+**
Margaux 1983 $9 (9/30/86) **68**

MARTIN BROTHERS (United States/California)
Aleatico California 1990 $10/375ml (3/15/92) **78**
Cabernet Sauvignon Paso Robles 1989 $12 (11/15/91) **77**
Chardonnay Paso Robles 1988 $10 (12/15/89) **81**
Chenin Blanc Paso Robles 1988 $6 (7/31/89) **85**
Moscato Frizzante California 1991 $9 (3/31/92) **88**
Nebbiolo California 1989 $9 (11/15/91) **76**
Nebbiolo California 1987 $12 (12/15/89) **75**
Nebbiolo California 1986 $12 (12/15/89) **75**
Nebbiolo Paso Robles 1987 $12 (12/15/89) **85**
Vin Santo Sweet Malvasia Bianca California 1990 $15/500ml (3/15/92) **81**
Zinfandel Paso Robles 1986 $8 (12/15/89) **78**
Zinfandel Paso Robles 1985 $6.50 (2/15/88) **83**
Zinfandel Port Paso Robles Primitivo Appassito 1990 $12 (3/15/92) **83**

MARTINELLI (United States/California)
Chardonnay Russian River Valley 1989 $9 (7/15/91) **82**
Zinfandel Russian River Valley 1988 $11 (4/30/91) **85**

MARTINEZ (Portugal)
Tawny Port 20-Year-Old Directors NV $25 (2/28/90) (JS) **93**
Vintage Port 1987 ($NA) (VP-5/90) **84**
Vintage Port 1985 Rel: $21 Cur: $27 (VP-6/90) **89**
Vintage Port 1982 Rel: $17 Cur: $28 (VP-6/90) **82**
Vintage Port 1975 $40 (VP-2/90) **75**
Vintage Port 1970 $30 (VP-2/90) **89**
Vintage Port 1967 $56 (VP-2/90) **93**
Vintage Port 1963 $108 (VP-2/90) **82**
Vintage Port 1955 $110 (VP-11/89) **86**

LOUIS M. MARTINI (United States/California)
Barbera California 1987 $6 (12/31/90) BB **83**
Barbera California 1984 $7 (11/15/89) **80**
Cabernet Sauvignon Sonoma County 1988 $9 (4/30/91) BB **81**
Cabernet Sauvignon North Coast 1986 $9.25 (9/15/89) **80**
Cabernet Sauvignon North Coast 1985 $8.25 (10/31/88) **76**
Cabernet Sauvignon North Coast 1983 $7 (3/31/87) **69**
Cabernet Sauvignon North Coast 1981 $6.50 (3/01/85) **83**
Cabernet Sauvignon Napa Valley Reserve 1987 $14 (10/15/90) **87**
Cabernet Sauvignon Sonoma Valley Monte Rosso 1989 (NR) (5/15/91) (BT) **85+**
Cabernet Sauvignon Sonoma Valley Monte Rosso 1988 $25 (11/15/91) **81**
Cabernet Sauvignon Sonoma Valley Monte Rosso 1987 Rel: $20 Cur: $23 (11/15/90) **93**
Cabernet Sauvignon Sonoma Valley Monte Rosso 1986 $20 (CA-3/89) **86**
Cabernet Sauvignon Sonoma Valley Monte Rosso 1985 $22 (CA-3/89) **80**
Cabernet Sauvignon Sonoma Valley Monte Rosso 1984 $22 (CA-3/89) **89**
Cabernet Sauvignon Sonoma Valley Monte Rosso 1983 $22 (CA-3/89) **86**
Cabernet Sauvignon Sonoma Valley Monte Rosso 1982 $22 (CA-3/89) **85**
Cabernet Sauvignon Sonoma Valley Monte Rosso 1981 $25 (12/15/86) **90**
Cabernet Sauvignon Sonoma Valley Monte Rosso Los Niños 1983 $25 (CA-3/89) **83**
Cabernet Sauvignon Sonoma Valley Monte Rosso Los Niños 1982 $25 (CA-3/89) **82**
Cabernet Sauvignon Sonoma Valley Monte Rosso Los Niños 1981 $25 (CA-3/89) **85**
Cabernet Sauvignon Sonoma Valley Monte Rosso Lot 2 1979 Rel: $10 Cur: $19 (CA-3/89) **84**
Cabernet Sauvignon North Coast Special Selection 1984 ($NA) (CA-3/89) **85**
Cabernet Sauvignon North Coast Special Selection 1980 Rel: $12 Cur: $17 (CA-3/89) **84**
Cabernet Sauvignon California Special Selection 1978 Rel: $9 Cur: $25 (CA-3/89) **86**
Cabernet Sauvignon California Special Selection 1977 Rel: $9 Cur: $16 (CA-3/89) **70**
Cabernet Sauvignon California Special Selection 1976 Rel: $9 Cur: $25 (CA-3/89) **86**
Cabernet Sauvignon California Special Selection 1974 Rel: $10 Cur: $40 (CA-3/89) **77**
Cabernet Sauvignon California Special Selection 1972 Rel: $5 Cur: $50 (CA-3/89) **63**
Cabernet Sauvignon California Special Selection 1970 Rel: $6 Cur: $60 (CA-3/89) **88**
Cabernet Sauvignon California Special Selection 1968 Rel: $6 Cur: $70 (CA-3/89) **90**
Cabernet Sauvignon California Special Selection 1966 Rel: $6 Cur: $135 (CA-3/89) **87**
Cabernet Sauvignon California Special Selection 1964 Rel: $6 Cur: $95 (CA-3/89) **85**
Cabernet Sauvignon California Private Reserve 1962 Rel: $3.50 Cur: $80 (CA-3/89) **73**
Cabernet Sauvignon California Special Selection 1961 Rel: $4 Cur: $160 (CA-3/89) **80**
Cabernet Sauvignon California Special Selection 1959 Rel: $4.50 Cur: $140 (CA-3/89) **87**
Cabernet Sauvignon California Special Selection 1958 Rel: $4.50 Cur: $185 (CA-3/89) **88**
Cabernet Sauvignon California Special Selection 1957 Rel: $3.50 Cur: $160 (CA-3/89) **91**
Cabernet Sauvignon California Private Reserve 1956 Rel: $2.50 Cur: $80 (CA-3/89) **77**
Cabernet Sauvignon California Special Selection 1955 Rel: $2.50 Cur: $180 (CA-3/89) **87**
Cabernet Sauvignon California Special Selection 1952 Rel: $2.50 Cur: $300 (CA-3/89) **93**

Cabernet Sauvignon California Special Selection 1951 Rel: $2 Cur: $300 (CA-3/89) **87**
Cabernet Sauvignon California Special Selection 1947 Rel: $1.50 Cur: $550 (CA-3/89) **90**
Cabernet Sauvignon California Special Selection 1945 Rel: $1.50 Cur: $400 (CA-3/89) **75**
Cabernet Sauvignon California Private Reserve Villa del Rey 1943 Rel: $1.50 Cur: $400 (CA-3/89) **70**
Cabernet Sauvignon California Special Reserve 1939 Rel: $1.25 Cur: $1,000 (CA-3/89) **90**
Chardonnay California 1982 $7 (3/16/84) **71**
Chardonnay Los Carneros Las Amigas Vineyard Vineyard Selection 1989 $20 (7/15/91) **83**
Chardonnay Napa-Sonoma Counties 1990 $9 (3/15/92) BB **89**
Chardonnay Napa-Sonoma Counties 1989 $9 (4/30/91) **75**
Chardonnay Napa Valley Reserve 1989 $14 (12/31/90) **87**
Chardonnay North Coast 1986 $9.50 (5/31/88) **74**
Chardonnay North Coast 1984 $8 (4/16/86) **70**
Chenin Blanc Napa Valley 1987 $5 (7/31/89) **70**
Gewürztraminer Russian River Valley Los Vinedos del Rio 1987 $7 (1/31/90) **71**
Merlot North Coast 1989 $9 (5/31/92) **74**
Merlot North Coast 1988 $10 (8/31/91) **85**
Merlot North Coast 1986 $12 (10/31/89) **79**
Merlot North Coast 1984 $6.75 (2/15/88) **79**
Merlot North Coast 1982 $5.85 (2/16/86) **71**
Merlot Russian River Valley Los Vinedos del Rio 1988 $22 (5/31/92) **74**
Merlot Russian River Valley Los Vinedos del Rio 1986 $20 (3/31/90) **79**
Merlot Russian River Valley Los Vinedos del Rio 1984 $12 (2/15/88) **82**
Merlot Russian River Valley Los Vinedos del Rio 1981 $10 (10/01/85) **81**
Petite Sirah Napa Valley 1985 $7 (10/31/89) BB **85**
Petite Sirah Napa Valley Reserve 1987 $11 (11/30/91) **85**
Petite Sirah Napa Valley Reserve 1986 $12 (10/31/90) **81**
Pinot Noir Carneros 1987 $7 (2/28/91) BB **82**
Pinot Noir Carneros Napa Valley La Loma Vineyard 1988 $18 (3/31/92) **75**
Pinot Noir Carneros Napa Valley Las Amigas 1982 $12 (3/31/90) **85**
Pinot Noir Los Carneros 1988 $8 (7/15/91) BB **85**
Pinot Noir Napa Valley 1986 $8 (12/31/89) BB **85**
Pinot Noir Napa Valley Las Amigas Vineyard Selection 1980 $10 (3/15/87) **68**
Sauvignon Blanc Napa Valley 1989 $8 (4/30/91) **80**
White Zinfandel Napa Valley 1988 $5.50 (6/15/89) **81**
Zinfandel California 1974 $22 (6/16/85) **78**
Zinfandel California 1973 $25 (6/16/85) **87**
Zinfandel North Coast 1985 $6.25 (3/31/89) **80**
Zinfandel North Coast 1984 $6 (2/15/88) BB **84**
Zinfandel North Coast 1983 $7.75 (10/15/86) **87**
Zinfandel Paso Robles 1989 $8 (8/31/91) **83**
Zinfandel Sonoma County 1986 $7 (10/31/89) **79**

MARTINI DI CIGALA (Italy/Tuscany)
Chianti Classico San Giusto a Rentennano 1987 $9 (3/31/90) **74**
Chianti Classico San Giusto a Rentennano 1986 $8 (1/31/89) **79**
Chianti Classico San Giusto a Rentennano 1985 $8 (11/30/87) **87**
Chianti Classico San Giusto a Rentennano 1983 $6.25 (9/15/87) **80**
Chianti Classico San Giusto a Rentennano Riserva 1985 $17 (11/30/89) **91**
Chianti Classico San Giusto a Rentennano Riserva 1983 $11 (11/15/87) **87**
San Giusto a Rentennano Percarlo 1986 $24 (11/30/89) **88**
San Giusto a Rentennano Percarlo 1985 $25 (2/15/89) **92**
San Giusto a Rentennano Percarlo 1983 $13 (9/15/87) **77**
San Giusto a Rentennano Vin Santo 1982 $18/375ml (12/31/88) **96**
San Giusto a Rentennano Vin Santo 1981 $25 (12/31/87) **89**

MARTINI & ROSSI (Italy/Sparkling)
Brut Riserva Montelera NV $15 (12/31/90) **72**

DOMAINE DE MARTINOLLES (France/Other)
Brut Blanquette de Limoux 1990 $10 (3/31/92) **84**
Brut Blanquette de Limoux 1989 $9 (3/31/92) BB **83**
Brut Blanquette de Limoux 1986 $11 (3/31/92) **78**
Brut Blanquette de Limoux NV $8 (4/15/90) BB **84**
Chardonnay Vin de Pays de l'Aude 1990 $7 (6/30/92) **77**

DOMAINE DU MAS BLANC (France/Other)
Banyuls Vendanges Tardives 1982 $26 (2/28/91) **80**
Banyuls Vieilles Vignes 1982 $27 (2/28/91) **82**
Banyuls Vieilles Vignes 1976 $40 (2/28/91) **85**
Collioure Cuvée Cosprons Levants 1988 $21 (3/31/91) **82**

MAS DE DAUMAS GASSAC (France/Other)
Vin de Pays de l'Herault 1989 $25 (12/15/91) **83**
Vin de Pays de l'Herault 1987 $23 (10/31/89) **85**
Vin de Pays de l'Herault 1986 $25 (12/15/88) **81**
Vin de Pays de l'Herault Blanc NV $37 (3/31/90) **85**

MAS DE GOURGONNIER (France/Other)
Côteaux des Baux en Provence Les Baux de Provence 1988 $8.50 (4/30/91) **79**

BARTOLO MASCARELLO (Italy/Piedmont)
Barolo 1983 $27 (5/31/88) **88**

GIUSEPPE MASCARELLO & FIGLIO (Italy/Piedmont)
Barbaresco Marcarini 1985 $30 (8/31/89) **85**
Barbera d'Alba Fasana 1987 $10 (3/15/91) **80**
Barbera d'Alba Fasana 1985 $9 (11/30/87) **85**
Barbera d'Alba Superiore Ginestra 1987 $11 (3/15/91) **85**
Barbera d'Alba Superiore Santo Stefano di Perno 1987 $13 (9/15/90) **83**
Barolo 1982 $28 (6/30/87) **81**
Barolo 1978 $19 (9/16/84) **91**
Barolo Belvedere 1985 Rel: $35 Cur: $42 (6/15/90) CS **93**

Key to Symbols

The scores reported here are the results of blind tastings conducted by our panel of senior editors. Wines that carry the initials below are results of individual tastings.

THE WINE SPECTATOR 100-POINT SCALE 95-100—Classic, a great wine; ***90-94***—Outstanding, superior character and style; ***80-89***—Good to very good, a wine with special qualities; ***70-79***—Average, drinkable wine that may have minor flaws; ***60-69***—Below average, drinkable but not recommended; ***50-59***—Poor, undrinkable, not recommended. "+"—With a score indicates a range; used primarily with barrel tastings to indicate a preliminary score.

SPECIAL DESIGNATIONS SS—Spectator Selection, CS—Cellar Selection, BB—Best Buy, ($NA)—Price not available, (NR)—Not released.

TASTER'S INITIALS (JG)—Jim Gordon, (HS)—Harvey Steiman, (JL)—James Laube, (JS)—James Suckling, (TM)—Thomas Matthews, (TR)—Terry Robards, (PM)—Per-Henrik Mansson, (BT)—Barrel Tasting (these wines were tasted blind from barrel samples), (CA-date)—*California's Great Cabernets* by James Laube, (CH-date)—*California's Great Chardonnays* by James Laube, (VP-date)—*Vintage Port* by James Suckling.

DATE TASTED Dates in parentheses represent the issue in which the rating was published.

Barolo Dardi 1982 $18 (9/15/87) **87**
Barolo Monprivato 1986 $47 (7/15/91) **88**
Barolo Monprivato 1985 $53 (6/15/90) **86**
Barolo Monprivato 1983 Rel: $28 Cur: $40 (9/15/88) (HS) **86**
Barolo Monprivato 1982 Rel: $22 Cur: $30 (9/15/88) (HS) **89**
Barolo Monprivato 1981 $23 (9/15/88) (HS) **84**
Barolo Monprivato 1980 $23 (9/15/88) (HS) **76**
Barolo Monprivato 1979 $23 (9/15/88) (HS) **83**
Barolo Monprivato 1978 $42 (9/15/88) (HS) **86**
Barolo Monprivato 1974 $80 (9/15/88) (HS) **91**
Barolo Monprivato 1971 $73 (9/15/88) (HS) **81**
Barolo Monprivato 1970 $60 (9/15/88) (HS) **80**
Barolo Monprivato Falletto 1983 $23 (7/31/89) **80**
Barolo Santo Stefano di Perno 1985 $35 (10/15/90) **94**
Barolo Villero 1983 $17 (10/15/88) **77**
Dolcetto d'Alba Bricco Falletto 1987 $9 (3/15/89) **88**
Dolcetto d'Alba Bricco Ravera 1988 $10 (9/15/90) **82**
Dolcetto d'Alba Gagliassi 1989 $13 (7/15/91) **85**
Dolcetto d'Alba Gagliassi 1987 $10 (3/31/90) **80**
Dolcetto d'Alba Gagliassi Monforte 1987 $9 (3/15/89) **82**
Grignolino del Monferrato Casalese Besso 1988 $9.50 (1/31/90) **75**
Nebbiolo d'Alba San Rocco 1986 $15 (9/15/90) **85**

MASI (Italy/North)
Bardolino Classico Superiore 1988 $9 (5/15/91) BB **82**
Campo Fiorin 1985 $11.50 (9/15/90) **77**
Campo Fiorin 1983 $7.50 (5/15/89) BB **81**
Chardonnay Trentino Rosabel 1987 ($NA) (9/15/89) **79**
Masianco 1987 $6.75 (5/15/89) **78**
Valpolicella Classico Superiore 1987 $7.25 (12/31/90) **78**

MASO CANTANGHEL (Italy/North)
Chardonnay Altesino Vigna Piccola 1989 $25 (1/31/91) **89**
Pinot Nero Altesino Riserva 1988 $33 (2/15/91) **84**

FATTORIA MASSARA (Italy/Piedmont)
Barbera d'Alba 1987 $7.75 (9/15/90) **74**
Barolo 1985 $20 (6/15/90) **80**
Dolcetto d'Alba 1990 $9.50 (1/31/92) **86**

LE MASSE (Italy/Tuscany)
Chianti Classico 1988 $12.50 (4/30/91) **87**
Chianti Classico 1985 $12 (7/15/89) **92**
Chianti Classico Riserva 1985 $20 (9/15/91) **89**

PAUL MASSON (United States/California)
Blanc de Noirs Monterey Centennial Cuvée 1984 $9 (12/31/87) **83**
Cabernet Sauvignon California Vintners Selection 1986 $6 (6/30/89) **84**
Cabernet Sauvignon Monterey County Vintage Selection Masson 1986 $9 (11/15/89) **79**
Cabernet Sauvignon Monterey County Vintage Selection Masson 1985 $8 (9/15/88) **78**
Chardonnay Monterey 1981 $8.50 (4/16/84) **77**
Chardonnay Monterey County Masson 1987 $8 (11/15/88) **82**
Chenin Blanc California 1988 $5/1.5L (7/31/89) **65**
Merlot California Vintners Selection 1989 $4.50/1.5L (4/15/92) BB **80**
Merlot Monterey County Masson 1988 $8 (5/31/92) **79**
Merlot Monterey County Vintage Selection Masson 1987 $8.50 (7/15/90) **83**
White Zinfandel California 1988 $7/1.5L (6/15/89) **74**

DOMAINE J.-M. MASSON-BLONDELET (France/Loire)
Pouilly-Fumé Les Angelots 1989 $20 (3/31/91) **84**
Pouilly-Fumé Les Bascoins 1989 $20 (3/31/91) **90**

MASTANTUONO (United States/California)
Carminello California 1988 $7 (7/15/91) **79**
Zinfandel San Luis Obispo County Dante Dusi Vineyards 1986 $9 (8/31/91) **84**
Zinfandel San Luis Obispo County Dante Dusi Vineyards Unfined & Unfiltered 1984 $18 (7/31/91) **73**

MASTROBERARDINO (Italy/Other)
Avellanio 1989 $10.50 (7/15/91) **87**
Fiano di Avellino Apianum Vigna d'Oro 1988 $25 (4/30/90) **79**
Fiano di Avellino Vignadora 1989 $30 (7/15/91) **84**
Fiano di Avellino Vignadora 1986 $22.50 (10/15/89) **78**
Greco di Tufo Vignadangelo 1986 $15 (10/15/89) **79**
Lacryma Christi del Vesùvio 1989 $14 (7/15/91) **89**
Lacryma Christi del Vesùvio White 1989 $13 (7/15/91) **76**
Lacryma Christi del Vesùvio White 1987 $9 (3/31/89) **89**
Plinius 1990 $19 (5/15/92) **88**
Plinius d'Irpinia Bianco 1989 $17 (7/15/91) **84**
Taurasi 1986 $18 (7/15/91) **87**
Taurasi Riserva 1985 $22 (6/30/91) **84**
Taurasi Riserva 1981 Rel: $21 Cur: $30 (2/15/89) **78**
Taurasi Riserva 1980 Rel: $15 Cur: $24 (9/15/89) **75**
Taurasi Riserva 1977 Rel: $28 Cur: $54 (10/16/84) CS **92**

MASTROIANNI (Italy/Tuscany)
Brunello di Montalcino 1982 $17 (6/15/90) **87**
Brunello di Montalcino 1979 $17 (9/15/86) **72**
Rosso di Montalcino 1987 $10 (7/15/91) **79**

MATANZAS CREEK (United States/California)
Cabernet Sauvignon Sonoma Valley 1983 Rel: $14 Cur: $17.5 (7/16/86) **75**
Cabernet Sauvignon Sonoma Valley 1982 $14 (8/01/85) **88**
Cabernet Sauvignon Sonoma Valley 1981 $16 (4/16/84) **84**
Chardonnay Sonoma Valley 1989 $19 (5/15/92) **85**
Chardonnay Sonoma County 1988 $18.75 (4/30/90) **91**
Chardonnay Sonoma County 1987 Rel: $18 Cur: $22 (CH-2/90) **90**
Chardonnay Sonoma County 1986 Rel: $17.50 Cur: $24 (CH-2/90) **89**
Chardonnay Sonoma County 1985 Rel: $16.50 Cur: $28 (CH-2/90) **88**
Chardonnay Sonoma County 1984 Rel: $15 Cur: $28 (CH-2/90) **89**
Chardonnay Sonoma County 1983 Rel: $15 Cur: $25 (CH-2/90) **85**
Chardonnay Sonoma County 1982 Rel: $15 Cur: $25 (CH-2/90) **78**
Chardonnay Sonoma County 1981 Rel: $15 Cur: $28 (CH-2/90) **85**
Chardonnay Sonoma County 1980 Rel: $15 Cur: $23 (CH-2/90) **82**
Chardonnay Napa-Sonoma Counties 1979 Rel: $14.50 Cur: $40 (CH-2/90) **80**
Chardonnay Sonoma County 1978 Rel: $12.50 Cur: $50 (CH-2/90) **79**
Chardonnay Sonoma Valley Estate 1985 Rel: $18 Cur: $39 (CH-2/90) **86**
Chardonnay Sonoma Valley Estate 1984 Rel: $18 Cur: $30 (CH-2/90) **80**
Chardonnay Sonoma Valley Estate 1983 $18 (CH-2/90) **68**
Chardonnay Sonoma Valley Estate 1982 Rel: $18 Cur: $25 (7/16/84) SS **88**
Chardonnay Sonoma County Estate 1980 Rel: $18 Cur: $25 (CH-2/90) **70**
Merlot Sonoma County 1987 Rel: $25 Cur: $29 (6/15/90) SS **92**

Merlot Sonoma County 1986 $20 (6/30/89) **92**
Merlot Sonoma Valley 1989 $28 (4/15/92) **90**
Merlot Sonoma Valley 1988 $28 (8/31/91) **88**
Merlot Sonoma Valley 1985 Rel: $18 Cur: $40 (5/31/88) **88**
Merlot Sonoma Valley 1984 Rel: $14.50 Cur: $25 (6/30/87) **91**
Merlot Sonoma Valley 1982 Rel: $13.50 Cur: $28 (10/01/85) **88**
Merlot Sonoma Valley 1981 Rel: $12.50 Cur: $30 (4/16/84) **80**
Sauvignon Blanc Sonoma County 1990 $12 (4/15/92) **87**
Sauvignon Blanc Sonoma County 1989 $12 (7/15/91) **85**
Sauvignon Blanc Sonoma County 1988 $12 (2/15/90) **86**
Sauvignon Blanc Sonoma County 1987 $12 (3/15/89) **85**

CHATEAU MATRAS (France/Bordeaux)
St.-Emilion 1982 ($NA) (5/15/89) (TR) **80**

DOMAINE JOSEPH MATROT (France/Burgundy)
Bourgogne Blanc Chardonnay 1989 $15 (8/31/91) **81**
Bourgogne Blanc Chardonnay 1988 $15 (4/30/91) **76**
Bourgogne Blanc Chardonnay 1987 $14 (4/15/90) **78**
Meursault 1989 $42 (8/31/91) **82**
Meursault 1987 $25 (5/15/90) **81**
Meursault Blagny 1989 $63 (8/31/91) **93**
Meursault Les Charmes 1989 $65 (8/31/91) **89**
Meursault Les Chevalières 1989 $48 (8/31/91) **87**
Meursault Les Chevalières 1986 $36 (12/15/88) **65**
Puligny-Montrachet Les Chalumeaux 1989 $66 (8/31/91) **89**

PIERRE MATROT (France/Burgundy)
Meursault 1985 $28 (12/31/87) **75**
Meursault Perrières 1989 ($NA) (8/31/91) **91**
Puligny-Montrachet Les Combettes 1989 $45 (8/31/91) **93**
Puligny-Montrachet Les Combettes 1986 $37 (12/15/88) **88**

MATTITUCK HILLS (United States/New York)
Cabernet Sauvignon North Fork of Long Island 1987 $9 (6/30/91) (TM) **82**
Chardonnay North Fork of Long Island 1988 $11 (6/30/91) (TM) **77**

YVON MAU (France/Bordeaux)
Bordeaux Blanc Officiel du Bicentenaire de la Revolution Française 1988 $4.50 (7/31/89) **77**
Bordeaux Officiel du Bicentenaire de la Revolution Française 1986 $4.50 (6/30/89) **72**

CHATEAU MAUCAILLOU (France/Bordeaux)
Moulis 1988 $14 (7/31/91) **82**
Moulis 1987 $14 (6/30/89) (BT) **70+**
Moulis 1986 $18 (6/30/88) (BT) **85+**
Moulis 1985 $18 (8/31/88) **88**
Moulis 1983 $16 (3/15/87) **87**
Moulis 1982 Rel: $15 Cur: $25 (11/30/89) (JS) **90**
Moulis 1981 Rel: $12 Cur: $14 (10/01/85) **88**

CHATEAU MAUCOIL (France/Rhône)
Châteauneuf-du-Pape Réserve Suzeraine 1985 $13 (11/15/87) **86**

PROSPER MAUFOUX (France/Burgundy)
Aloxe-Corton 1982 $27 (6/15/92) **79**
Auxey-Duresses 1988 $18 (4/30/91) **75**
Bâtard-Montrachet 1989 $88 (8/31/91) **91**
Bourgogne Aligoté 1989 $12 (7/31/91) **78**
Bourgogne Blanc Chardonnay 1989 $12 (8/31/91) **81**
Chablis Mont de Milieu 1989 $24 (8/31/91) **84**
Chassagne-Montrachet 1985 $31 (4/30/88) **89**
Chassagne-Montrachet Les Chenevottes 1989 $37 (8/31/91) **88**
Chassagne-Montrachet Les Chenevottes 1987 $37 (2/28/91) **71**
Châteauneuf-du-Pape 1988 $16 (5/31/92) **81**
Corton-Charlemagne 1989 $70 (8/31/91) **88**
Côtes du Rhône 1990 $8 (6/15/92) BB **84**
Côtes du Rhône 1989 $9 (5/31/91) **84**
Côtes du Rhône 1988 $6.50 (6/30/90) **79**
Côtes du Rhône 1987 $6.25 (6/15/89) **74**
Côtes du Rhône Blanc 1989 $8 (3/31/91) **67**
Côtes du Rhône Blanc 1987 $6 (7/15/89) **81**
Criots-Bâtard-Montrachet 1989 $87 (8/31/91) **91**
Gigondas 1985 $11 (4/30/88) **65**
Mâcon-Villages 1989 $11 (8/31/91) **81**
Mâcon-Villages 1988 $10.50 (7/15/90) **82**
Meursault 1989 $32 (4/15/92) **77**
Meursault 1987 $27 (5/15/90) **86**
Montagny 1984 $11 (3/31/87) **56**
Montagny Première Cru 1989 $20 (8/31/91) **84**
Montrachet 1989 $172 (8/31/91) **89**
Muscat de Beaumes-de-Venise NV $18 (7/15/91) **85**
Pouilly-Fuissé 1989 $23 (8/31/91) **83**
Pouilly-Fuissé 1984 $17 (3/31/87) **78**
Puligny-Montrachet 1989 $36 (8/31/91) **87**
Puligny-Montrachet 1988 $31 (4/30/90) **90**
Puligny-Montrachet 1986 $36 (5/31/89) **68**
Puligny-Montrachet Folatières 1989 $43 (8/31/91) **85**
Puligny-Montrachet Hameau de Blagny 1989 $39 (8/31/91) **81**
St.-Véran 1989 $14 (8/31/91) **82**
St.-Véran 1988 $12 (7/31/90) **82**
St.-Véran 1985 $12 (3/31/87) **67**
Sancerre 1989 $19 (11/15/91) **78**
Sancerre 1988 $15 (4/15/90) **76**
Santenay Les Gravières 1985 $17 (10/15/89) **85**

DOMAINE MAUME (France/Burgundy)
Charmes-Chambertin 1988 $60 (7/15/91) **86**
Gevrey-Chambertin 1987 $25 (3/31/90) **77**
Gevrey-Chambertin en Pallud 1987 $36 (3/31/90) **80**
Mazis-Chambertin 1987 $56 (3/31/90) **74**

BODEGAS MAURO (Spain)
Ribera del Duero 1987 $17 (10/15/90) **82**
Ribera del Duero 1986 $17 (3/31/90) **76**
Ribera del Duero 1985 $15 (3/31/90) **88**
Ribera del Duero 1984 $16 (3/31/90) (TM) **78**
Ribera del Duero 1983 $15 (10/15/87) **82**

PAOLA DI MAURO (Italy/Other)
Colle Picchioni 1986 $15 (3/31/90) **80**
Vigna del Vassalle 1986 $12 (3/31/90) **83**

CHATEAU MAUVINON (France/Bordeaux)
St.-Emilion 1983 $10 (11/30/86) **87**

ROBERT MAX (France/Burgundy)
Pommard 1982 $16 (12/16/84) **82**

MAXIM'S (France/Champagne)
Brut Champagne NV (NR) (12/31/91) **85**

MAYACAMAS (United States/California)
Cabernet Sauvignon Napa Valley 1986 Rel: $20 Cur: $38 (11/15/91) **82**
Cabernet Sauvignon Napa Valley 1985 Rel: $25 Cur: $38 (1/31/90) **92**
Cabernet Sauvignon Napa Valley 1984 Rel: $20 Cur: $28 (CA-3/89) **90**
Cabernet Sauvignon Napa Valley 1983 Rel: $20 Cur: $25 (CA-3/89) **90**
Cabernet Sauvignon Napa Valley 1982 Rel: $20 Cur: $29 (CA-3/89) **77**
Cabernet Sauvignon Napa Valley 1981 Rel: $18 Cur: $41 (CA-3/89) **91**
Cabernet Sauvignon Napa Valley 1980 Rel: $18 Cur: $45 (CA-3/89) **92**
Cabernet Sauvignon Napa Valley 1979 Rel: $18 Cur: $54 (CA-3/89) **95**
Cabernet Sauvignon Napa Valley 1978 Rel: $18 Cur: $80 (CA-3/89) **94**
Cabernet Sauvignon Napa Valley 1977 Rel: $15 Cur: $60 (CA-3/89) **92**
Cabernet Sauvignon Napa Valley 1976 Rel: $15 Cur: $38 (CA-3/89) **84**
Cabernet Sauvignon Napa Valley 1975 Rel: $12 Cur: $63 (CA-3/89) **89**
Cabernet Sauvignon Napa Valley 1974 Rel: $9.50 Cur: $120 (CA-3/89) **95**
Cabernet Sauvignon Napa Valley 1973 Rel: $9 Cur: $80 (CA-3/89) **87**
Cabernet Sauvignon Napa Valley 1972 Rel: $8 Cur: $63 (CA-3/89) **82**
Cabernet Sauvignon Napa Valley 1971 Rel: $8 Cur: $65 (CA-3/89) **86**
Cabernet Sauvignon Napa Valley 1970 Rel: $8 Cur: $110 (CA-3/89) **96**
Cabernet Sauvignon California 1969 Rel: $6.50 Cur: $90 (CA-3/89) **89**
Cabernet Sauvignon California 1968 Rel: $4.50 Cur: $135 (CA-3/89) **88**
Cabernet Sauvignon California 1967 Rel: $4 Cur: $125 (CA-3/89) **65**
Cabernet Sauvignon California 1966 Rel: $3.50 Cur: $125 (CA-3/89) **75**
Cabernet Sauvignon California 1965 Rel: $2.75 Cur: $200 (CA-3/89) **65**
Cabernet Sauvignon California 1963 Rel: $2 Cur: $150 (CA-3/89) **69**
Cabernet Sauvignon California 1962 Rel: $2 Cur: $150 (CA-3/89) **68**
Chardonnay Napa Valley 1989 $20 (7/15/92) **83**
Chardonnay Napa Valley 1988 $20 (7/15/91) **86**
Chardonnay Napa Valley 1987 Rel: $20 Cur: $30 (9/15/90) **86**
Chardonnay Napa Valley 1986 Rel: $20 Cur: $32 (7/15/92) **86**
Chardonnay Napa Valley 1985 Rel: $20 Cur: $29 (CH-1/90) **90**
Chardonnay Napa Valley 1984 Rel: $18 Cur: $28 (CH-3/90) **88**
Chardonnay Napa Valley 1983 Rel: $16 Cur: $25 (CH-1/90) **86**
Chardonnay Napa Valley 1982 Rel: $16 Cur: $29 (CH-1/90) **85**
Chardonnay Napa Valley 1981 Rel: $16 Cur: $35 (CH-1/90) **78**
Chardonnay Napa Valley 1980 Rel: $16 Cur: $35 (CH-1/90) **74**
Chardonnay Napa Valley 1979 Rel: $15 Cur: $28 (CH-1/90) **70**
Chardonnay Napa Valley 1978 Rel: $13 Cur: $30 (CH-1/90) **75**
Chardonnay Napa Valley 1977 Rel: $12 Cur: $35 (CH-1/90) **70**
Chardonnay Napa Valley 1976 Rel: $11 Cur: $45 (CH-1/90) **81**
Chardonnay Napa Valley 1975 Rel: $9 Cur: $50 (CH-1/90) **78**
Chardonnay Napa Valley 1974 Rel: $7.50 Cur: $50 (CH-1/90) **70**
Chardonnay Napa Valley 1973 Rel: $7 Cur: $50 (CH-1/90) **60**
Chardonnay Napa Valley 1972 Rel: $7 Cur: $60 (CH-1/90) **59**
Chardonnay Napa Valley 1965 Rel: $2.50 Cur: $125 (CH-1/90) **58**
Chardonnay Napa Valley 1964 Rel: $1.75 Cur: $200 (CH-1/90) **92**
Chardonnay Napa Valley 1963 Rel: $1.75 Cur: $150 (CH-1/90) **58**
Chardonnay Napa Valley 1962 Rel: $1.75 Cur: $150 (CH-1/90) **58**
Chardonnay Napa Valley 1958 Rel: $1 Cur: $200 (CH-1/90) **60**
Chardonnay Napa Valley 1955 Rel: $1 Cur: $330 (CH-1/90) **88**
Pinot Noir Napa Valley 1987 $14 (4/30/91) **80**
Pinot Noir Napa Valley 1986 $14 (3/31/90) **67**
Pinot Noir Napa Valley 1985 $12 (6/15/88) **72**
Pinot Noir Napa Valley 1984 $12 (12/31/88) **71**
Sauvignon Blanc Napa Valley 1989 $11 (10/15/91) **75**
Sauvignon Blanc Napa Valley 1988 $11 (8/31/90) **66**
Sauvignon Blanc Napa Valley 1987 $11 (9/15/89) **87**
Zinfandel Late Harvest Napa Valley 1984 $18 (11/15/89) **84**

CHATEAU DU MAYNE (France/Bordeaux)
Graves Blanc 1983 $6 (9/16/85) **78**

CHATEAU LE MAYNE (France/Bordeaux)
Puisseguin-St.-Emilion 1982 $7.50 (12/01/85) **64**

CHATEAU MAYNE DES CARMES (France/Sauternes)
Sauternes 1989 $20 (6/30/92) **83**

CHATEAU MAYNE-DAVID (France/Bordeaux)
Côtes de Castillon 1985 $6 (2/28/87) BB **81**

VINA MAYOR (Spain)
Ribera del Duero Crianza 1990 $7 (2/15/92) BB **83**
Ribera del Duero Crianza 1989 $7 (3/31/91) BB **85**
Ribera del Duero Crianza 1987 $9 (2/15/92) **82**

CHATEAU MAZERIS (France/Bordeaux)
Canon-Fronsac 1990 (NR) (5/15/92) (BT) **85+**
Canon-Fronsac 1989 (NR) (4/30/91) (BT) **85+**
Canon-Fronsac 1988 $18 (6/30/89) (BT) **75+**
Canon-Fronsac 1987 $12 (6/30/89) (BT) **75+**
Canon-Fronsac 1986 $12 (6/30/88) (BT) **80+**
Canon-Fronsac 1985 Rel: $12 Cur: $16 (5/15/87) (BT) **80+**

CHATEAU MAZERIS-BELLEVUE (France/Bordeaux)
Canon-Fronsac 1991 (NR) (5/15/92) (BT) **80+**

CHATEAU MAZEYRES (France/Bordeaux)
Pomerol 1989 (NR) (4/30/91) (BT) **90+**
Pomerol 1986 ($NA) (6/30/88) (BT) **70+**

MAZILLY PERE (France/Burgundy)
Meursault 1984 $18 (4/30/87) **64**

MAZZOCCO (United States/California)
Cabernet Sauvignon Alexander Valley Claret Style 1988 $18 (3/15/92) **85**
Cabernet Sauvignon Alexander Valley Claret Style 1987 $20 (8/31/90) **93**
Cabernet Sauvignon Alexander Valley Claret Style 1986 $20 (7/31/89) **78**
Chardonnay Alexander Valley River Lane Vineyard 1989 $16.50 (4/30/92) **82**
Chardonnay Alexander Valley River Lane Vineyard 1988 $16.50 (6/30/90) **84**
Chardonnay Alexander Valley River Lane Vineyard 1987 $16.50 (4/15/89) **88**
Chardonnay Alexander Valley River Lane Vineyard Barrel Fermented 1986 $16.50 (2/15/88) **86**
Chardonnay Sonoma County Barrel Fermented 1989 $11 (7/15/91) **85**
Chardonnay Sonoma County Barrel Fermented 1988 $12 (11/30/89) **78**
Chardonnay Sonoma County Barrel Fermented 1987 $11 (11/15/88) **83**

Chardonnay Sonoma County Winemaster's Cuvée 1986 $10 (2/15/88) **85**
Matrix Sonoma County 1987 $28 (1/31/92) **91**
Merlot Dry Creek Valley Estate Unfiltered 1989 $14 (5/31/92) **89**
Zinfandel Sonoma County Traditional Style 1988 $13 (10/15/90) **89**
Zinfandel Sonoma County Traditional Style 1986 $10 (12/15/88) **90**

TENUTA MAZZOLINO (Italy/North)
Noir 1987 $45 (9/30/91) **86**
Oltrepò Pavese 1990 $14 (1/31/92) **77**
Oltrepò Pavese Barbera 1990 $10.50 (4/30/92) **82**
Oltrepò Pavese Barbera 1989 $10 (4/15/91) **82**
Oltrepò Pavese Pinot Guarnazzola 1990 $15 (1/31/92) **77**

MCDOWELL VALLEY (United States/California)
Bistro Red Les Vieux Cépages Mendocino NV $7 (6/30/92) **79**
Cabernet Sauvignon California 1988 $10 (11/15/91) **78**
Cabernet Sauvignon California 1987 $9 (11/15/90) **78**
Cabernet Sauvignon McDowell Valley 1986 $8 (4/30/90) **70**
Cabernet Sauvignon McDowell Valley 1983 $11 (4/15/88) **76**
Cabernet Sauvignon McDowell Valley 1982 $11 (12/15/86) **89**
Cabernet Sauvignon McDowell Valley 1981 $11 (12/16/84) **78**
Chardonnay Mendocino 1990 $9 (7/15/92) **83**
Chardonnay California 1989 $10 (7/15/91) **72**
Chardonnay California 1988 $8.50 (12/15/89) **78**
Chardonnay California 1987 $8 (7/15/89) **86**
Chardonnay McDowell Valley Estate Reserve 1988 $13 (7/15/91) **75**
Chardonnay McDowell Valley 1987 $12 (12/15/89) **59**
Chardonnay McDowell Valley 1986 $11 (5/31/88) **76**
Chardonnay McDowell Valley 1984 $11 (2/28/87) **85**
Fumé Blanc Mendocino 1989 $8.50 (11/15/91) **73**
Fumé Blanc Mendocino 1988 $7.50 (3/31/90) **79**
Grenache Rosé McDowell Valley Les Vieux Cépages 1990 $7.50 (6/15/91) BB **82**
Grenache Rosé McDowell Valley Les Vieux Cépages 1989 $6.50 (10/31/90) BB **82**
Grenache Rosé McDowell Valley Les Vieux Cépages 1988 $6.50 (11/15/89) BB **80**
Les Trésor McDowell Valley Les Vieux Cépages 1988 $12 (6/30/92) **75**
Les Trésor McDowell Valley Les Vieux Cépages 1987 $14 (8/31/90) **82**
Les Trésor McDowell Valley Les Vieux Cépages 1986 $13 (9/30/89) **86**
Syrah McDowell Valley 1985 $12 (9/30/89) **90**
Syrah McDowell Valley 1984 $9.50 (2/15/89) **86**
Syrah McDowell Valley 1983 $10 (5/31/88) **69**
Syrah McDowell Valley 1982 $10 (1/31/87) **75**
Syrah McDowell Valley 1981 $10 (12/16/84) **90**
Syrah McDowell Valley Bistro Syrah Les Vieux Cépages 1990 $9 (6/30/92) **76**
Syrah McDowell Valley Les Vieux Cépages 1987 $16 (3/31/91) **74**
Syrah McDowell Valley Les Vieux Cépages 1986 $14 (8/31/90) **80**
Zinfandel McDowell Valley 1988 $9.50 (12/31/90) **80**
Zinfandel McDowell Valley 1987 $8 (12/15/89) BB **87**

MCGREGOR (United States/New York)
Blanc de Blancs Finger Lakes 1985 $15 (12/31/90) **64**

MCHENRY (United States/California)
Pinot Noir Santa Cruz Mountains 1985 $13 (6/15/88) **75**

MCKINLAY (United States/Oregon)
Pinot Noir Willamette Valley 1988 $13 (4/15/91) **90**

MEADOW GLEN (United States/California)
Chardonnay Sonoma County Barrel Fermented 1989 $8.50 (4/30/91) **81**
Merlot Napa Valley 1989 $8 (5/31/92) **81**

MEEKER (United States/California)
Cabernet Sauvignon Dry Creek Valley 1987 $14 (10/15/91) **87**
Cabernet Sauvignon Dry Creek Valley 1986 $18.50 (2/15/90) **72**
Cabernet Sauvignon Dry Creek Valley 1985 $18 (4/30/89) **76**
Cabernet Sauvignon Dry Creek Valley 1984 $18 (6/15/88) **78**
Chardonnay Dry Creek Valley 1990 $11.50 (4/30/92) **78**
Chardonnay Dry Creek Valley 1989 $12 (7/15/91) **85**
Chardonnay Dry Creek Valley 1988 $13.50 (2/15/90) **75**
Chardonnay Dry Creek Valley 1987 $12 (2/15/89) **79**
Chardonnay Dry Creek Valley 1986 $11 (5/31/88) **91**
Zinfandel Dry Creek Valley 1988 $10 (8/31/91) **82**
Zinfandel Dry Creek Valley 1987 $10 (3/31/90) **85**
Zinfandel Dry Creek Valley 1986 $9 (3/15/89) **83**
Zinfandel Dry Creek Valley 1985 $8 (5/15/88) **90**

MELINI (Italy/Tuscany)
Chianti Borghi d'Elsa 1989 $6.50 (10/31/91) **81**
Chianti Classico 1987 $7 (4/30/90) **80**
Chianti Classico 1986 $6 (10/31/88) BB **83**
Chianti Classico 1985 $5 (7/31/88) BB **82**
Chianti Classico Isassi 1988 $8.50 (9/15/91) **89**
Chianti Classico Laborel Riserva 1986 $10 (10/31/91) **83**
Chianti Classico Vigneti la Selvanella Riserva 1985 $7 (9/15/91) BB **87**
Chianti Classico Vigneti la Selvanella Riserva 1982 $6 (6/30/88) BB **85**
Vernaccia di San Gimignano Lydia 1989 $8 (7/15/91) **78**
Vino Nobile di Montepulciano 1985 $10 (4/15/90) **82**
Vino Nobile di Montepulciano Riserva 1983 $7.50 (6/30/88) **74**

DOMAINE ALPHONSE MELLOT (France/Loire)
Sancerre 1987 $16 (3/31/91) **68**

DOMAINE DE LA MELOTERIE (France/Other)
Vouvray Demi-Sec 1989 $9 (6/15/91) **87**

Key to Symbols

The scores reported here are the results of blind tastings conducted by our panel of senior editors. Wines that carry the initials below are results of individual tastings.

THE WINE SPECTATOR 100-POINT SCALE *95-100*—Classic, a great wine; *90-94*—Outstanding, superior character and style; *80-89*—Good to very good, a wine with special qualities; *70-79*—Average, drinkable wine that may have minor flaws; *60-69*—Below average, drinkable but not recommended; *50-59*—Poor, undrinkable, not recommended. "+"—With a score indicates a range; used primarily with barrel tastings to indicate a preliminary score.

SPECIAL DESIGNATIONS SS—Spectator Selection, CS—Cellar Selection, BB—Best Buy, ($NA)—Price not available, (NR)—Not released.

TASTER'S INITIALS (JG)—Jim Gordon, (HS)—Harvey Steiman, (JL)—James Laube, (JS)—James Suckling, (TM)—Thomas Matthews, (TR)—Terry Robards, (PM)—Per-Henrik Mansson, (BT)—Barrel Tasting (these wines were tasted blind from barrel samples), (CA-date)—*California's Great Cabernets* by James Laube, (CH-date)—*California's Great Chardonnays* by James Laube, (VP-date)—*Vintage Port* by James Suckling.

DATE TASTED Dates in parentheses represent the issue in which the rating was published.

MENDIANI (Spain)
Navarra 1990 $4 (4/15/92) **72**

MENDOCINO ESTATE (United States/California)
Cabernet Sauvignon Mendocino 1985 $5.50 (2/15/88) **61**
Cabernet Sauvignon Mendocino 1984 $4.75 (6/15/87) **78**
Cabernet Sauvignon Mendocino 1982 $4.25 (10/15/86) BB **87**
Chardonnay Mendocino 1989 $6.50 (7/15/91) **79**
Chardonnay Mendocino 1988 $6.25 (12/15/89) **73**
Chardonnay Mendocino 1986 $5.50 (12/31/87) **65**
Chardonnay Mendocino 1985 $5 (12/15/86) BB **89**
Zinfandel Mendocino 1985 $4.75 (2/15/88) **79**
Zinfandel Mendocino 1984 $4.25 (5/31/87) **68**

MENDOCINO VINEYARDS (United States/California)
Cabernet Sauvignon Mendocino County NV $6 (4/15/89) **73**

CHATEAU MENOTA (France/Sauternes)
Barsac 1988 ($NA) (6/15/90) (BT) **80+**
Barsac 1987 ($NA) (6/15/90) **78**

DOMAINE MEO-CAMUZET (France/Burgundy)
Bourgogne 1989 $23 (11/15/91) **83**
Bourgogne Passetoutgrains 1990 $17 (3/31/92) **86**
Bourgogne Passetoutgrains 1989 $17 (7/15/91) **84**
Clos de Vougeot 1989 $91 (11/15/91) CS **94**
Clos de Vougeot 1988 $95 (11/30/90) **92**
Clos de Vougeot 1986 $55 (11/30/88) **91**
Clos de Vougeot 1985 Rel: $65 Cur: $101 (3/31/88) **93**
Corton 1989 $76 (11/15/91) **93**
Corton 1986 $50 (10/31/88) **89**
Nuits-St.-Georges 1989 $52 (11/15/91) **92**
Nuits-St.-Georges 1988 $50 (11/30/90) **91**
Nuits-St.-Georges 1987 $42 (12/15/89) **86**
Nuits-St.-Georges 1986 $32 (11/15/88) **90**
Nuits-St.-Georges Aux Boudots 1989 $81 (11/15/91) **90**
Nuits-St.-Georges Aux Boudots 1988 $80 (11/30/90) **92**
Nuits-St.-Georges Aux Boudots 1987 $56 (12/15/89) **88**
Nuits-St.-Georges Aux Boudots 1986 $46 (11/15/88) **92**
Nuits-St.-Georges Aux Murgers 1989 $81 (11/15/91) **94**
Nuits-St.-Georges Aux Murgers 1988 $80 (11/30/90) **91**
Nuits-St.-Georges Aux Murgers 1987 $56 (12/15/89) **93**
Nuits-St.-Georges Aux Murgers 1986 $48 (11/15/88) **90**
Nuits-St.-Georges Aux Murgers 1985 $50 (4/15/88) **90**
Richebourg 1989 $270 (11/15/91) **97**
Richebourg 1988 $253 (11/30/90) **96**
Richebourg 1987 $165 (12/15/89) **96**
Richebourg 1986 $160 (7/31/88) **97**
Richebourg 1985 Rel: $150 Cur: $280 (3/31/88) **97**
Vosne-Romanée 1989 $47 (11/15/91) **91**
Vosne-Romanée 1988 $50 (12/31/90) **87**
Vosne-Romanée 1987 $35 (12/15/89) **90**
Vosne-Romanée 1986 $30 (10/31/88) **88**
Vosne-Romanée Au Cros-Parantoux 1989 $91 (11/15/91) **95**
Vosne-Romanée Au Cros-Parantoux 1988 $84 (11/30/90) **94**
Vosne-Romanée Au Cros-Parantoux 1987 $63 (12/15/89) **95**
Vosne-Romanée Au Cros-Parantoux 1986 $60 (7/31/88) **93**
Vosne-Romanée Aux Brûlées 1989 $91 (11/15/91) **94**
Vosne-Romanée Aux Brûlées 1988 $84 (11/30/90) **89**
Vosne-Romanée Aux Brûlées 1987 $63 (12/15/89) **95**
Vosne-Romanée Les Chaumes 1989 $62 (1/31/92) **91**
Vosne-Romanée Les Chaumes 1988 $60 (11/30/90) **88**
Vosne-Romanée Les Chaumes 1986 $38 (12/31/88) **83**
Vosne-Romanée Les Chaumes 1985 $80 (3/31/88) **92**

MERCER RANCH (United States/Washington)
Cabernet Sauvignon Columbia Valley Mercer Ranch Vineyard Block 1 1985 $13 (10/15/89) **81**

DOMAINE DU CHATEAU DE MERCEY (France/Burgundy)
Bourgogne Blanc Côtes de Beaune 1985 $8.50 (3/31/87) **71**
Mercurey 1983 $10 (5/01/86) **56**

MEREDYTH (United States/Virginia)
Cabernet Sauvignon Virginia 1989 $11 (2/29/92) **79**
Merlot Virginia 1989 $25 (2/29/92) **81**
Seyval Blanc Virginia 1989 $7.50 (2/29/92) **80**

CHATEAU MERIC (France/Bordeaux)
Graves 1988 $17 (4/30/91) **76**

MERIDIAN (United States/California)
Cabernet Sauvignon Paso Robles 1988 $12 (9/30/91) SS **92**
Chardonnay Edna Valley 1990 $15 (7/15/92) **89**
Chardonnay Edna Valley 1989 $14 (7/15/91) **82**
Chardonnay Edna Valley 1988 $9.75 (9/30/90) **80**
Chardonnay Edna Valley 1987 $12 (12/15/89) **78**
Chardonnay Napa Valley 1986 $12 (5/31/88) **85**
Chardonnay Napa Valley 1985 $11 (4/30/87) **88**
Chardonnay Santa Barbara County 1990 $9.75 (1/31/92) BB **87**
Chardonnay Santa Barbara County 1989 $10 (2/28/91) **87**
Chardonnay Santa Barbara County 1988 $10 (4/15/90) **89**
Pinot Noir Santa Barbara County Riverbench Vineyard 1988 $14 (2/28/91) **86**
Syrah Paso Robles 1988 $14 (3/31/91) **91**

CHATEAU LE MERLE (France/Bordeaux)
Graves Blanc 1984 $6 (12/01/85) **74**

MERLION (United States/California)
Cabernet Sauvignon Napa Valley 1986 $16.50 (11/15/90) **84**
Cabernet Sauvignon Napa Valley 1985 $13.50 (8/31/88) **85**
Chardonnay Napa Valley 1987 $9 (12/31/90) **63**
Chardonnay Napa Valley 1985 $15 (2/15/88) **84**
Chevrier Hyde Vineyards Los Carneros 1987 $10 (8/31/90) **70**
Pinot Blanc Napa Valley Coeur de Melon 1987 $9 (11/30/90) **82**
Pinot Noir Los Carneros Hyde Vineyards 1986 $13.50 (2/28/89) **66**

PRINCE FLORENT DE MERODE (France/Burgundy)
Aloxe-Corton 1987 $30 (2/28/91) **87**
Corton-Bressandes 1987 $42 (3/31/91) **92**
Corton-Bressandes 1986 $38 (8/31/89) **84**
Corton-Bressandes 1985 $52 (2/15/88) **93**
Corton Clos du Roi 1987 $44 (3/31/90) **87**
Corton Clos du Roi 1986 $49 (8/31/89) **80**

Corton-Maréchaudes 1987 $36 (8/31/90) **88**
Corton-Maréchaudes 1986 $33 (8/31/89) **82**
Corton-Maréchaudes 1985 $49 (3/15/88) **81**
Corton-Renardes 1987 $36 (3/31/90) **92**
Corton-Renardes 1986 $38 (8/31/89) **76**
Ladoix Les Chaillots 1987 $18 (11/15/90) **77**
Ladoix Les Chaillots 1986 $18 (8/31/89) **74**
Pommard Clos de la Platière 1987 $36 (8/31/90) **76**
Pommard Clos de la Platière 1986 $35 (7/31/89) **86**
Pommard Clos de la Platière 1985 $45 (3/15/88) **94**
Pommard Clos de la Platière 1984 $23 (2/15/88) **71**

MERRY VINTNERS (United States/California)
Chardonnay Sonoma County 1989 $12 (3/15/92) **86**
Chardonnay Sonoma County 1988 $12 (1/31/91) **89**
Chardonnay Sonoma County 1987 $12 (7/15/89) **84**
Chardonnay Sonoma County 1984 $13.75 (6/16/86) **88**
Chardonnay Sonoma County Reserve 1987 $15 (9/15/89) **86**
Chardonnay Sonoma County Reserve 1986 $14.75 (11/30/88) **85**
Chardonnay Sonoma County Reserve 1985 $15 (9/15/87) **81**
Chardonnay Sonoma County Signature Reserve 1989 $15 (3/15/92) **86**
Chardonnay Sonoma County Signature Reserve 1988 $15 (1/31/91) **90**
Chardonnay Sonoma County Sylvan Hills Vineyard 1987 $11 (7/15/89) **85**
Chardonnay Sonoma County Vintage Preview 1986 $9.75 (7/15/88) **85**
Chardonnay Sonoma County Vintage Preview 1985 $9.75 (12/15/86) **83**

MERRYVALE (United States/California)
Cabernet Sauvignon Napa Valley 1988 $18 (7/15/91) **86**
Cabernet Sauvignon Napa Valley Profile 1987 $25 (11/15/91) **83**
Chardonnay Napa Valley 1988 $23 (6/30/90) **91**
Chardonnay Napa Valley 1987 $19 (2/15/90) **93**
Chardonnay Napa Valley 1986 $20 (10/31/88) **72**
Chardonnay Napa Valley 1985 $16.50 (10/31/87) **90**
Chardonnay Napa Valley Reserve 1990 $23 (6/30/92) **91**
Chardonnay Napa Valley Reserve 1989 $23 (11/30/91) **90**
Chardonnay Napa Valley Starmont 1990 $16 (11/30/91) **90**
Chardonnay Napa Valley Starmont 1989 $16 (12/31/90) **89**
Chardonnay Stags Leap District 1990 $18 (11/30/91) **91**
Chardonnay Stags Leap District 1989 $19 (12/31/90) **90**
Meritage Napa Valley 1990 $12 (7/15/91) **89**
Merlot Napa Valley 1989 $16 (5/31/92) **84**
Muscat de Frontignan Napa Valley Antigua NV $12 (11/30/91) **86**
Profile Napa Valley 1990 (NR) (5/15/91) (BT) **90+**
Profile Napa Valley 1989 (NR) (5/15/91) (BT) **85+**
Profile Napa Valley 1988 ($NA) (5/15/90) (BT) **85+**
Red Table Wine Napa Valley 1986 $25 (10/15/90) **86**
Red Table Wine Napa Valley 1985 Rel: $24 Cur: $27 (CA-3/89) **91**
Red Table Wine Napa Valley 1984 Rel: $24 Cur: $28 (CA-3/89) **86**
Red Table Wine Napa Valley 1983 Rel: $18 Cur: $33 (CA-3/89) **88**
Sauvignon Blanc Napa Valley Meritage 1989 $12 (4/30/91) **80**

MESSIAS (Portugal)
Vintage Port 1985 Rel: $12 Cur: $16 (VP-2/90) **67**
Vintage Port 1984 Rel: $11 Cur: $15 (VP-2/90) **78**
Vintage Port 1982 Rel: $7 Cur: $13 (VP-2/90) **72**
Vintage Port 1963 $40 (VP-2/90) **71**
Vintage Port Quinta do Cachão 1983 Rel: $8 Cur: $11 (VP-2/90) **77**
Vintage Port Quinta do Cachão 1977 Rel: $7 Cur: $22 (VP-2/90) **60**
Vintage Port Quinta do Cachão 1970 $55 (VP-2/90) **87**
Vintage Port Quinta do Cachão 1966 $30 (VP-2/90) **84**

MESSINA HOF (United States/Texas)
Chardonnay Texas Bell Brothers Vineyard Private Reserve 1989 $15 (2/29/92) **76**
Chenin Blanc Brazos Valley 1988 $7 (7/31/89) **86**
Johannisberg Riesling Late Harvest Texas Angel 1990 $15 (2/29/92) **90**
Reflections Texas 1988 $15 (2/29/92) **77**

MESTRE-MICHELOT (France/Burgundy)
Meursault Les Charmes 1987 $50 (8/31/90) **79**
Meursault Le Limozin 1986 $39 (3/15/89) **86**
Meursault Sous la Velle 1988 $40 (2/28/91) **83**

LOUIS METAIREAU (France/Loire)
Muscadet de Sèvre et Maine Sur Lie Carte Noire 1989 $13 (9/30/91) **80**
Muscadet de Sèvre et Maine Sur Lie Carte Noire 1988 $8 (11/30/90) BB **85**
Muscadet de Sèvre et Maine Sur Lie Carte Noire 1986 $8.75 (2/28/89) **80**
Muscadet de Sèvre et Maine Sur Lie Cuvée One 1989 $18 (9/30/91) **82**
Muscadet de Sèvre et Maine Sur Lie Cuvée One 1987 $11 (7/15/89) **81**

LA METAIRIE (France/Other)
Corbières 1989 $7 (12/15/91) **78**

CHATEAU DE LA MEULIERE (France/Bordeaux)
Premières Côtes de Bordeaux 1988 $9 (2/28/91) **76**

HENRI MEURGEY (France/Burgundy)
Chassagne-Montrachet Rouge Clos de la Boudriotte 1985 $40 (10/31/88) **88**

CHATEAU DE MEURSAULT (France/Burgundy)
Beaune Cent-Vignes 1985 $31 (2/28/90) **87**
Bourgogne Blanc Chardonnay Clos du Château 1988 $23 (4/30/91) **83**
Bourgogne Blanc Chardonnay Clos du Château 1985 $20 (3/31/90) **82**
Bourgogne Pinot Noir du Château 1988 $16 (1/31/92) **82**
Meursault 1986 $55 (7/31/91) **94**
Meursault 1985 $50 (12/31/87) **95**
Volnay Clos des Chênes 1988 $47 (7/15/91) **87**

DR. MEYER (Germany)
Riesling Kabinett Rheinhessen Bereich Nierstein 1987 $4 (10/15/88) BB **81**
Riesling Qualitätswein Mosel-Saar-Ruwer Piesporter Michelsberg 1987 $4 (10/15/88) BB **88**
Riesling Qualitätswein Rheinhessen Zeller Schwarze Katz 1987 $4 (11/30/88) **75**
Riesling Spätlese Rheinhessen Mainzer Domherr 1986 $5 (11/30/88) BB **82**

CHATEAU MEYNEY (France/Bordeaux)
St.-Estèphe 1991 (NR) (5/15/92) (BT) **80+**
St.-Estèphe 1990 (NR) (5/15/92) (BT) **85+**
St.-Estèphe 1989 $22 (3/15/92) **93**
St.-Estèphe 1988 $17 (3/15/91) **88**
St.-Estèphe 1987 $14 (5/15/90) **87**
St.-Estèphe 1986 $19 (11/30/89) (JS) **88**
St.-Estèphe 1985 Rel: $16 Cur: $20 (8/31/88) **92**
St.-Estèphe 1984 Rel: $10 Cur: $14 (5/15/87) **79**
St.-Estèphe 1983 Rel: $11 Cur: $21 (10/15/86) **92**
St.-Estèphe 1982 $25 (11/30/89) (JS) **86**
St.-Estèphe 1979 $18 (10/15/89) (JS) **87**

PETER MICHAEL (United States/California)
Cabernet Sauvignon Knights Valley Les Pavots 1988 $25 (11/15/91) **90**
Chardonnay Howell Mountain 1990 $22 (6/30/92) **91**
Chardonnay Sonoma County Mon Plaisir 1989 $28 (7/15/91) **88**

MICHAEL'S (United States/California)
Cabernet Sauvignon Napa Valley Summit Vineyard Reserve 1984 $15 (3/31/88) **75**

RICHARD MICHAELS (United States/California)
Cabernet Sauvignon California 1985 $10 (9/30/88) **78**

LOUIS MICHEL & FILS (France/Chablis)
Chablis 1989 $22 (8/31/91) **86**
Chablis 1988 $17 (7/15/90) **77**
Chablis Montée de Tonnerre 1988 $26 (7/31/90) **86**
Chablis Montée de Tonnerre 1987 $20 (7/15/90) **87**
Chablis Montmain 1987 $20 (7/15/90) **80**
Chablis Vaudésir 1987 $31 (7/15/90) **89**

ROBERT MICHELE (France/Loire)
Vouvray Les Trois Fils 1989 $9 (4/30/91) **77**

ALAIN MICHELOT (France/Burgundy)
Nuits-St.-Georges 1988 $39 (7/15/91) **91**
Nuits-St.-Georges 1982 $17 (5/01/84) **86**
Nuits-St.-Georges Les Cailles 1988 $54 (5/15/91) **83**
Nuits-St.-Georges Les Cailles 1982 $19 (7/16/85) **90**
Nuits-St.-Georges Les Chaignots 1988 $56 (5/15/91) **90**
Nuits-St.-Georges Les Champs-Perdrix 1986 $30 (12/15/89) **81**
Nuits-St.-Georges Les Porets-St.-Georges 1988 $56 (5/15/91) **83**
Nuits-St.-Georges Les Richemone 1988 $54 (5/15/91) **89**
Nuits-St.-Georges Les Vaucrains 1988 $56 (5/15/91) **87**
Nuits-St.-Georges Les Vaucrains 1986 $30 (12/15/89) **88**

C. MICHELOT (France/Burgundy)
Meursault Les Charmes 1988 $55 (2/28/91) **84**
Meursault Grands Charrons 1987 $41 (8/31/90) **82**
Meursault Les Tillets 1987 $32 (8/31/90) **78**
Puligny-Montrachet 1987 $41 (6/30/90) **80**

G. MICHELOT (France/Bordeaux)
Bordeaux Supérieur 1982 $5 (1/01/86) BB **74**
Meursault Clos du Cromin 1986 $39 (3/15/89) **91**

JEAN MICHELOT (France/Burgundy)
Bourgogne Aligoté 1988 $12 (7/31/90) **84**
Meursault 1988 $33 (5/15/90) **88**
Meursault 1986 $27 (12/15/88) **90**
Pommard 1987 $33 (8/31/90) **78**
Pommard 1985 $29 (4/30/88) **87**
Pommard 1983 $21 (6/16/86) **78**

MICHELOT-BUISSON (France/Burgundy)
Meursault 1987 $37 (8/31/90) **81**
Meursault Les Charmes 1986 $50 (3/15/89) **85**
Meursault Les Genevrières 1988 $55 (2/28/91) **93**
Meursault Les Genevrières 1987 $50 (8/31/90) **78**
Meursault Les Genevrières 1986 $50 (3/15/89) **72**
Meursault Le Limozin 1985 $37 (8/31/87) **93**

MICHTOM (United States/California)
Chardonnay Alexander Valley 1983 $8 (10/16/85) **71**

MIETZ (United States/California)
Merlot Sonoma County 1989 $13.50 (4/15/92) **91**

MILANO (United States/California)
Cabernet Sauvignon Mendocino County Sanel Valley Vineyard 1985 $18 (9/30/89) **80**
Cabernet Sauvignon Mendocino County Sanel Valley Vineyard 1982 $12.50 (12/15/87) **83**
Chardonnay California 1985 $10 (4/15/88) **79**
Chardonnay Mendocino County Sanel Valley Vineyard 1988 $18 (7/15/91) **88**
Chardonnay Sonoma County Vine Hill Ranch 1985 $14 (12/31/88) **71**
Zinfandel Mendocino County 1981 $6 (10/01/84) **80**
Zinfandel Mendocino County Sanel Valley Vineyard 1988 $8 (4/30/91) **85**

MILDARA (Australia)
Cabernet Merlot Murray River Valley 1986 $7.50 (3/31/89) **80**
Cabernet Sauvignon Coonawarra 1986 $10 (1/31/89) **90**
Cabernet Sauvignon Coonawarra 1985 $8 (4/15/88) BB **89**
Cabernet Sauvignon Coonawarra 1984 $6.50 (4/30/87) **77**
Cabernet Sauvignon McLaren Vale Private Reserve 1985 $13 (1/31/89) **85**
Cabernet Sauvignon Merlot Coonawarra 1985 $5.50 (1/31/88) BB **80**
Cabernet Sauvignon Merlot Coonawarra 1984 $5 (6/15/87) BB **82**
Cabernet Sauvignon Murray River Valley 1986 $8 (1/31/89) **80**
Chardonnay Barossa Valley 1989 $7.50 (2/28/91) **75**
Chardonnay Barossa Valley 1987 $12 (12/31/88) **88**
Chardonnay Coonawarra 1985 $7.50 (4/15/87) **84**
Chardonnay Merbian Church Hill 1987 $5.50 (2/15/88) **79**
Chardonnay Merbian Church Hill 1986 $5 (6/15/87) BB **82**
Chardonnay Murray River Valley 1987 $8 (2/15/89) **70**
Shiraz Coonawarra 1986 $9 (12/31/88) **89**

MILL CREEK (United States/California)
Cabernet Sauvignon Dry Creek Valley 1988 $12 (11/15/91) **78**
Cabernet Sauvignon Dry Creek Valley 1982 $8.50 (12/31/87) **81**
Chardonnay Dry Creek Valley 1985 $10 (12/31/87) **75**
Merlot Dry Creek Valley 1988 $12 (5/31/92) **77**
Merlot Dry Creek Valley 1987 $12 (11/15/91) **84**
Merlot Dry Creek Valley 1984 $8.50 (2/15/88) **68**
Merlot Dry Creek Valley 1983 $9 (10/01/85) **80**
Merlot Dry Creek Valley 1982 $8.50 (4/01/85) **85**

CHATEAU DE MILLE (France/Rhône)
Côtes du Lubéron 1985 $8.50 (12/15/88) **83**

CHATEAU MILLEGRAND (France/Other)
Minervois 1988 $5 (4/30/90) **77**

MILZ (Germany)
Riesling Auslese Mosel-Saar-Ruwer Dhroner Hofberger 1988 ($NA) (9/30/89) **91**
Riesling Auslese Mosel-Saar-Ruwer Piesporter Hofberger 1990 $20 (12/15/91) **86**
Riesling Auslese Mosel-Saar-Ruwer Trittenheimer Altärchen 1990 $20 (12/15/91) **90**
Riesling Auslese Mosel-Saar-Ruwer Trittenheimer Felsenkopf 1988 ($NA) (9/30/89) **78**

Riesling Auslese Mosel-Saar-Ruwer Trittenheimer Felsenkopf Gold Cap 1990 $23 (12/15/91) **87**
Riesling Auslese Mosel-Saar-Ruwer Trittenheimer Leiterchen Gold Cap 1990 $23 (12/15/91) **88**
Riesling Eiswein Mosel-Saar-Ruwer Trittenheimer Apotheke 1990 $42/375ml (12/15/91) **91**
Riesling Spätlese Mosel-Saar-Ruwer 1990 $9.25 (12/15/91) **78**
Riesling Spätlese Mosel-Saar-Ruwer Piesporter Hofberg 1988 ($NA) (9/30/89) **83**
Riesling Spätlese Mosel-Saar-Ruwer Trittenheimer Altärchen 1990 $14 (12/15/91) **81**
Riesling Spätlese Mosel-Saar-Ruwer Trittenheimer Altärchen 1988 ($NA) (9/30/89) **83**
Riesling Spätlese Mosel-Saar-Ruwer Trittenheimer Apotheke 1990 $14 (12/15/91) **84**

ROGER MINET (France/Loire)
Pouilly-Fumé Cuvée Spéciale Vieilles Vignes 1989 $18 (9/30/91) **88**

MIRABELLE (United States/California)
Brut North Coast NV $12 (5/15/92) **84**

MIRAFIORE (Italy/Piedmont)
Barbera d'Alba 1987 $12 (4/15/91) **83**

MIRASSOU (United States/California)
Blanc de Noirs Monterey 1983 $11 (12/31/88) **69**
Blanc de Noirs Monterey 1982 $10 (8/31/87) **66**
Blanc de Noirs Monterey Fifth Generation Cuvée 1989 $13 (5/15/92) **82**
Blanc de Noirs Monterey Fifth Generation Cuvée 1987 $12 (11/15/91) **77**
Brut Monterey 1983 $10 (7/31/88) **66**
Brut Monterey 1982 $12 (9/16/85) **78**
Brut Monterey County 1987 $13 (12/31/91) **76**
Brut Monterey Cuvée 1984 $12 (6/15/91) **84**
Brut Monterey Fifth Generation Cuvée 1988 $13 (5/15/92) **78**
Brut Monterey Fifth Generation Cuvée Reserve 1984 $15 (12/31/91) **85**
Brut Monterey Reserve 1983 $15 (12/31/89) **76**
Cabernet Sauvignon Monterey County Fifth Generation Harvest Reserve Limited Bottling 1987 $12.50 (11/15/91) **86**
Cabernet Sauvignon Monterey County Fifth Generation Harvest Reserve 1986 $12.50 (7/31/91) **60**
Cabernet Sauvignon California Fifth Generation Family Selection 1986 $9.75 (5/31/91) **83**
Cabernet Sauvignon Napa Valley Fifth Generation Harvest Reserve 1985 $12 (11/15/89) **81**
Cabernet Sauvignon Napa Valley Fifth Generation Harvest Reserve 1983 $12 (12/15/86) **67**
Cabernet Sauvignon Napa Valley Harvest Reserve 1982 $12 (4/16/86) **82**
Cabernet Sauvignon North Coast 1982 $7 (10/16/85) BB **82**
Chardonnay Monterey County Family Selection 1990 $10 (6/30/92) **86**
Chardonnay Monterey County Family Selection 1989 $9.75 (7/15/91) **74**
Chardonnay Monterey County Family Selection 1986 $8 (11/15/87) **77**
Chardonnay Monterey County Family Selection 1985 $8 (12/31/86) **86**
Chardonnay Monterey County Harvest Reserve 1990 $12.50 (3/31/92) **86**
Chardonnay Monterey County Harvest Reserve 1989 $12.50 (5/15/91) **87**
Chardonnay Monterey County Harvest Reserve 1984 $12 (4/01/86) **68**
Chardonnay Monterey County Harvest Reserve 1983 $11 (1/01/85) **74**
Chenin Blanc Monterey 1987 $5.50 (7/31/89) **75**
Johannisberg Riesling Late Harvest Monterey Select Harvest Reserve 1987 $12.50/375ml (8/31/91) **87**
Natural Monterey Au Naturel 1988 $15 (5/15/92) **85**
Natural Monterey Cuvée au Naturel 1984 $15 (6/15/91) **83**
Natural Monterey Fifth Generation Cuvée au Naturel 1987 $15 (11/15/91) **85**
Petite Sirah Monterey County Fifth Generation Family Selection 1989 $7.50 (3/15/92) **79**
Pinot Blanc Monterey County Limited Bottling Fifth Generation Harvest Reserve 1989 $12.50 (5/31/91) **86**
Pinot Blanc Monterey County White Burgundy 1989 $7 (12/31/91) BB **83**
Pinot Noir Monterey County Fifth Generation Family Selection 1988 $7.50 (4/30/91) BB **81**
Pinot Noir Monterey County Harvest Reserve 1988 $13 (4/30/92) **84**
Pinot Noir Monterey Harvest Reserve 1986 $12 (4/30/91) **78**
Riesling Monterey County Monterey Riesling 1988 $6.75 (7/31/89) **79**
White Zinfandel California 1988 $6.50 (6/15/89) **75**
Zinfandel California Dry Red Lot No. 3 NV $5 (7/31/91) **73**
Zinfandel California Lot No. 4 NV $5.50 (7/31/91) BB **81**

MIRO (Spain)
Brut Cava NV $9 (2/29/92) **78**

CHATEAU LA MISSION-HAUT-BRION (France/Bordeaux)
Pessac-Léognan 1991 (NR) (5/15/92) (BT) **85+**
Pessac-Léognan 1990 (NR) (5/15/92) (BT) **95+**
Pessac-Léognan 1989 $120 (3/15/92) **96**
Pessac-Léognan 1988 $90 (11/15/91) (JS) **90**
Pessac-Léognan 1987 $39 (11/15/91) (JS) **84**
Pessac-Léognan 1986 Rel: $50 Cur: $60 (11/15/91) (JS) **97**
Graves 1985 $70 (11/15/91) (JS) **95**
Graves 1984 $55 (11/15/91) (JS) **85**
Graves 1983 $63 (11/15/91) (JS) **87**
Graves 1982 $110 (11/15/91) (JS) **93**
Graves 1981 $60 (11/15/91) (JS) **87**
Graves 1980 $35 (11/15/91) (JS) **86**
Graves 1979 Rel: $48 Cur: $75 (11/15/91) (JS) **86**
Graves 1978 $135 (11/15/91) (JS) **94**
Graves 1975 $280 (11/15/91) (JS) **90**
Graves 1974 $60 (11/15/91) (JS) **87**
Graves 1973 $36 (11/15/91) (JS) **80**
Graves 1972 $50 (11/15/91) (JS) **77**
Graves 1971 $90 (11/15/91) (JS) **91**
Graves 1970 $145 (11/15/91) (JS) **83**
Graves 1969 $38 (11/15/91) (JS) **84**
Graves 1968 ($NA) (11/15/91) (JS) **67**
Graves 1967 $85 (11/15/91) (JS) **89**
Graves 1966 $185 (11/15/91) (JS) **93**
Graves 1965 ($NA) (11/15/91) (JS) **76**
Graves 1964 $200 (11/15/91) (JS) **91**
Graves 1963 ($NA) (11/15/91) (JS) **78**
Graves 1962 $161 (11/15/91) (JS) **90**
Graves 1961 $520 (11/15/91) (JS) **98**
Graves 1960 $200 (11/15/91) (JS) **84**
Graves 1959 $310 (11/15/91) (JS) **94**
Graves 1958 ($NA) (11/15/91) (JS) **83**
Graves 1957 ($NA) (11/15/91) (JS) **85**
Graves 1956 $210 (11/15/91) (JS) **87**
Graves 1955 $400 (11/15/91) (JS) **89**
Graves 1954 $380 (11/15/91) (JS) **86**
Graves 1953 $400 (11/15/91) (JS) **93**
Graves 1952 $190 (11/15/91) (JS) **98**
Graves 1950 $350 (11/15/91) (JS) **79**
Graves 1949 $600 (11/15/91) (JS) **95**
Graves 1948 $600 (11/15/91) (JS) **98**
Graves 1947 $680 (11/15/91) (JS) **100**
Graves 1946 $700 (11/15/91) (JS) **85**
Graves 1945 $800 (11/15/91) (JS) **94**
Graves 1944 ($NA) (11/15/91) (JS) **78**
Graves 1943 ($NA) (11/15/91) (JS) **88**
Graves 1942 $260 (11/15/91) (JS) **83**
Graves 1941 ($NA) (11/15/91) (JS) **81**
Graves 1940 $330 (11/15/91) (JS) **82**
Graves 1939 ($NA) (11/15/91) (JS) **87**
Graves 1938 $128 (11/15/91) (JS) **81**
Graves 1937 $195 (11/15/91) (JS) **88**
Graves 1936 ($NA) (11/15/91) (JS) **62**
Graves 1935 $580 (11/15/91) (JS) **85**
Graves 1934 $350 (11/15/91) (JS) **86**
Graves 1933 $480 (11/15/91) (JS) **74**
Graves 1931 ($NA) (11/15/91) (JS) **70**
Graves 1929 $780 (11/15/91) (JS) **100**
Graves 1928 $470 (11/15/91) (JS) **84**
Graves 1926 ($NA) (11/15/91) (JS) **59**
Graves 1924 ($NA) (11/15/91) (JS) **89**
Graves 1921 $650 (11/15/91) (JS) **85**
Graves 1919 ($NA) (11/15/91) (JS) **85**
Graves 1918 ($NA) (11/15/91) (JS) **83**
Graves 1916 ($NA) (11/15/91) (JS) **82**
Graves 1914 $780 (11/15/91) (JS) **65**
Graves 1904 ($NA) (11/15/91) (JS) **85**
Graves 1899 $850 (11/15/91) (JS) **92**
Graves 1895 $750 (11/15/91) (JS) **99**
Graves 1888 $1,000 (11/15/91) (JS) **95**
Graves 1877 $1,000 (11/15/91) (JS) **93**

MISSION VIEW (United States/California)
Cabernet Sauvignon Paso Robles 1986 $12 (12/15/89) **72**
Muscat Canelli Paso Robles 1988 $7 (12/15/89) **68**

MISTY MOUNTAIN (United States/Virginia)
Cabernet Sauvignon Virginia 1988 $18 (2/29/92) **82**
Chardonnay Virginia Barrel Fermented Vintners Reserve 1989 $16 (2/29/92) **80**
Merlot Virginia 1988 $18 (2/29/92) **77**

MITCHELL (Australia)
Shiraz Clare Valley Peppertree Vineyard 1989 $10.50 (2/15/92) **76**

MITCHELTON (Australia)
Cabernet Sauvignon Goulburn Valley 1988 $13 (4/15/91) **86**
Cabernet Sauvignon Goulburn Valley 1986 $13 (1/31/90) **73**
Cabernet Sauvignon Merlot Australia Print Label 1985 $17 (1/31/90) **78**
Cabernet-Shiraz-Merlot Victoria 1987 $9 (1/31/90) **86**
Chardonnay Goulburn Valley Reserve 1988 $14 (3/15/90) **90**
Chardonnay Goulburn Valley Wood Matured 1990 $15 (2/15/92) **82**
Chardonnay Goulburn Valley Wood Matured Reserve 1989 $15 (6/30/92) **86**
Chardonnay Victoria 1991 $8 (2/29/92) **77**
Chardonnay Victoria 1989 $8 (4/15/91) **80**
Chardonnay Victoria 1988 $10 (3/15/90) **79**
Marsanne Goulburn Valley 1990 $8 (6/30/92) BB **84**
Shiraz Goulburn Valley 1989 $8 (2/15/92) **80**
Shiraz Goulburn Valley 1988 $8 (3/15/91) BB **86**

MOCCAGATTA (Italy/Piedmont)
Barbaresco Bric Balin 1987 $28 (7/15/91) **89**
Barbaresco Vigneto Basarin 1987 $23 (7/15/91) **86**
Barbera d'Alba 1989 $14 (3/15/91) **89**
Chardonnay Bric Buschet 1987 ($NA) (9/15/89) **75**
Chardonnay Vigneto Buschet 1988 ($NA) (9/15/89) **74**

MOCERI (France/Other)
Cabernet Sauvignon Vin de Pays de l'Aude 1987 $4 (6/30/90) BB **77**
Chardonnay Monterey County San Bernabe Vineyard 1984 $5 (7/01/86) BB **87**
Merlot Vin de Pays de l'Aude 1987 $4 (6/30/90) BB **78**

MOET & CHANDON (France/Champagne)
Brut Champagne Impériale 1986 $40 (3/31/92) **77**
Brut Champagne Impériale 1985 $57 (12/31/90) **87**
Brut Champagne Impériale 1983 Rel: $40 Cur: $43 (12/31/89) **69**
Brut Champagne Impériale 1982 Rel: $33 Cur: $39 (4/15/88) **84**
Brut Champagne Impériale 1980 Rel: $30 Cur: $58 (3/16/85) **91**
Brut Champagne Impériale NV $35 (12/31/91) **85**
Brut Rosé Champagne Impériale 1986 $43 (3/31/92) **83**
Brut Rosé Champagne Impériale 1983 $40 (12/31/89) **88**
Brut Rosé Champagne Impériale 1982 $36 (4/15/88) **90**
Brut Rosé Champagne Impériale 1978 $55 (12/16/85) **70**
Extra Dry Champagne White Star NV $33 (5/15/92) **85**

MOILLARD (France/Burgundy)
Aloxe-Corton Les Affouages 1989 (NR) (1/31/92) **83**
Bâtard-Montrachet 1986 $70 (5/31/88) **94**
Beaune 1983 $10 (10/16/85) **68**
Beaune Grèves 1985 $25 (3/15/87) **89**
Beaune Grèves 1984 $11.50 (2/15/87) **87**
Beaune Grèves Domaine Thomas-Moillard 1989 $28 (1/31/92) **89**
Beaune Grèves Domaine Thomas-Moillard 1986 $14 (12/31/88) **80**
Beaune Hospices de Beaune Cuvée Clos des Avaux 1988 $80 (8/31/91) **88**
Bonnes Mares 1984 $35 (5/31/87) **92**
Bonnes Mares Domaine Thomas-Moillard 1986 $45 (11/15/88) **86**

Key to Symbols

The scores reported here are the results of blind tastings conducted by our panel of senior editors. Wines that carry the initials below are results of individual tastings.

THE WINE SPECTATOR 100-POINT SCALE 95-100—Classic, a great wine; ***90-94***— Outstanding, superior character and style; ***80-89***—Good to very good, a wine with special qualities; ***70-79***—Average, drinkable wine that may have minor flaws; ***60-69***—Below average, drinkable but not recommended; ***50-59***—Poor, undrinkable, not recommended. "+"—With a score indicates a range; used primarily with barrel tastings to indicate a preliminary score.

SPECIAL DESIGNATIONS SS—Spectator Selection, CS—Cellar Selection, BB—Best Buy, ($NA)—Price not available, (NR)—Not released.

TASTER'S INITIALS (JG)—Jim Gordon, (HS)—Harvey Steiman, (JL)—James Laube, (JS)—James Suckling, (TM)—Thomas Matthews, (TR)—Terry Robards, (PM)—Per-Henrik Mansson, (BT)—Barrel Tasting (these wines were tasted blind from barrel samples), (CA-date)—*California's Great Cabernets* by James Laube, (CH-date)—*California's Great Chardonnays* by James Laube, (VP-date)—*Vintage Port* by James Suckling.

DATE TASTED Dates in parentheses represent the issue in which the rating was published.

Bourgogne Aligoté Long du Bois 1990 $12 (8/31/91) **74**
Bourgogne Blanc Chante Fluté 1988 $13 (8/31/91) **79**
Bourgogne Hautes Côtes de Beaune Les Alouettes 1989 $15 (6/15/91) **78**
Bourgogne Hautes Côtes de Beaune Rouge Les Alouettes 1989 $17 (1/31/92) **83**
Bourgogne Hautes Côtes de Beaune Rouge Les Alouettes 1988 $15 (7/15/91) **83**
Bourgogne Hautes Côtes de Nuits Les Hameaux 1986 $11 (12/31/88) **81**
Bourgogne Hautes Côtes de Nuits Les Vignes Hautes 1989 (NR) (1/31/92) **84**
Bourgogne Passetoutgrains Notre Dame des Ceps 1990 $9.50 (8/31/91) **75**
Bourgogne Pinot Noir 1985 $7 (3/31/88) **78**
Brouilly Château Belliard 1990 $13 (9/15/91) **82**
Chablis 1989 $26 (2/28/91) **81**
Chablis 1987 $17 (10/15/89) **86**
Chablis 1985 $14 (5/31/87) **68**
Chablis Les Vaillons 1985 $16 (5/31/87) **89**
Chambertin 1984 $42 (5/31/87) **76**
Chambertin Clos de Bèze 1984 $42 (5/31/87) **80**
Chambertin Clos de Bèze 1983 Rel: $37 Cur: $60 (9/16/85) CS **93**
Chambolle-Musigny 1984 $15 (11/30/86) **89**
Charmes-Chambertin 1985 $55 (5/31/88) **94**
Chassagne-Montrachet La Romanée 1987 $31 (11/15/89) **74**
Chassagne-Montrachet La Romanée 1986 $40 (4/30/88) **88**
Chassagne-Montrachet Rouge Morgeot 1985 $15 (5/31/87) **84**
Chiroubles 1990 $13 (9/15/91) **84**
Clos de Vougeot 1984 $32 (5/31/87) **90**
Clos de Vougeot 1983 Rel: $26 Cur: $45 (10/16/85) CS **95**
Corton Clos du Roi 1984 $24 (5/31/87) **87**
Corton Clos du Roi Domaine Thomas-Moillard 1989 $41 (1/31/92) **85**
Corton Clos des Vergennes 1989 $40 (1/31/92) **89**
Corton Clos des Vergennes 1985 $36 (5/31/87) **92**
Corton Clos des Vergennes 1983 $19 (10/01/85) **88**
Corton-Charlemagne 1986 $70 (5/31/88) **90**
Corton-Charlemagne 1984 $51 (5/31/87) **90**
Corton-Charlemagne 1983 $34 (10/01/85) **92**
Côtes du Rhône Les Violettes 1990 $7 (10/15/91) BB **82**
Côtes du Rhône Les Violettes 1989 $7.50 (5/31/91) BB **85**
Côtes du Rhône Les Violettes 1988 $6 (8/31/89) BB **84**
Côtes du Rhône Les Violettes 1985 $4.50 (11/15/86) BB **85**
Echézeaux 1985 $47 (4/15/88) **94**
Echézeaux 1984 Rel: $22 Cur: $30 (11/15/86) SS **96**
Fixin 1989 (NR) (1/31/92) **88**
Fixin Clos d'Entre Deux Velles 1989 (NR) (1/31/92) **86**
Fixin Clos d'Entre Deux Velles 1985 $16 (5/31/87) **79**
Fixin Clos d'Entre Deux Velles 1984 $11 (11/30/86) **78**
Fixin Clos de la Perrière 1986 $18 (2/28/89) **85**
Fixin Clos de la Perrière 1983 $12 (10/16/85) **78**
Fixin Confrérie des Chevaliers du Tastevin 1988 $19 (8/31/91) **84**
Fleurie Château du Vivier 1990 $17 (9/15/91) **91**
Gevrey-Chambertin 1987 $20 (3/31/90) **66**
Grands Echézeaux 1984 $39 (5/31/87) **90**
Hautes Côtes de Nuits 1983 $6.50 (11/01/85) **76**
Hautes Côtes de Nuits Blanc 1986 $12 (1/31/89) **78**
Juliénas Bois de la Salle 1990 $13 (9/15/91) **81**
Ladoix Côte de Beaune 1989 (NR) (1/31/92) **85**
Mâcon-Villages Domaine de Montbellet 1989 $10.50 (4/30/91) **77**
Meursault 1987 $24 (11/15/89) **63**
Meursault Les Charmes 1987 $33 (9/30/89) **74**
Meursault Les Charmes 1986 $37 (5/31/88) **74**
Meursault Les Charmes 1985 $30 (11/30/86) **95**
Meursault Clos du Cromin 1986 $28 (10/15/88) **88**
Meursault Poruzots 1986 $37 (5/31/88) **82**
Morey-St.-Denis Monts Luisants 1989 $28 (1/31/92) **89**
Morey-St.-Denis Monts Luisants 1988 $30 (12/15/90) **91**
Morey-St.-Denis Monts Luisants 1985 $21 (5/31/87) **87**
Morgon Domaine du Crêt de Ruyère 1990 $13 (9/15/91) **86**
Moulin-à-Vent Château du Vivier 1990 $16 (9/30/91) **82**
Musigny 1984 $38 (5/31/87) **92**
Nuits-St.-Georges Clos de Thorey 1985 $38 (5/31/87) **89**
Nuits-St.-Georges Clos de Thorey 1984 $24 (5/31/87) **84**
Nuits-St.-Georges Clos de Thorey 1983 $19 (9/16/85) **84**
Nuits-St.-Georges Clos de Thorey Domaine Thomas-Moillard 1989 $35 (1/31/92) **89**
Nuits-St.-Georges Clos de Thorey Domaine Thomas-Moillard 1988 $50 (12/31/90) **89**
Nuits-St.-Georges Clos de Thorey Domaine Thomas-Moillard 1987 $27 (12/15/89) **88**
Nuits-St.-Georges Clos de Thorey Domaine Thomas-Moillard 1986 $28 (11/15/88) **78**
Nuits-St.-Georges Hospices de Nuits Cuvée Jacques Duret 1988 $68 (8/31/91) **89**
Pommard Clos des Epeneaux 1985 Rel: $40 Cur: $45 (6/30/88) CS **92**
Pommard Rugiens 1985 $40 (6/30/88) **85**
Puligny-Montrachet 1986 $33 (5/31/88) **88**
Régnié Domaine de Reyssiers 1990 $12 (9/30/91) **66**
Romanée-St.-Vivant 1984 $42 (5/31/87) **87**
Rully 1989 $14 (8/31/91) **82**
St.-Amour Domaine des Pins 1990 $16 (9/15/91) **86**
St.-Joseph 1988 $15 (8/31/91) **85**
Vacqueyras 1989 $9.50 (10/15/91) **77**
Volnay Clos des Chênes 1985 $32 (7/15/88) **89**
Volnay Clos des Chênes 1983 $15 (12/01/85) **75**
Vosne-Romanée Malconsorts 1984 Rel: $21 Cur: $28 (12/15/86) CS **95**
Vosne-Romanée Malconsorts Domaine Thomas-Moillard 1989 (NR) (1/31/92) **93**
Vosne-Romanée Malconsorts Domaine Thomas-Moillard 1988 $50 (3/31/91) **88**
Vosne-Romanée Malconsorts Domaine Thomas-Moillard 1987 $30 (8/31/89) **91**
Vosne-Romanée Malconsorts Domaine Thomas-Moillard 1986 $29 (10/31/88) **88**
Vosne-Romanée Malconsorts Domaine Thomas-Moillard 1985 $38 (7/31/88) **95**

MAURO MOLINO (Italy/Piedmont)
Acanzio 1989 $15 (1/31/92) **85**
Barolo Vigna Conca 1986 $29 (2/28/91) **87**
Barolo Vigna Conca 1985 $25 (3/31/90) **82**
Dolcetto d'Alba 1989 $14 (2/28/91) **87**
Dolcetto d'Alba 1988 $12 (3/31/90) **82**
Nebbiolo delle Langhe 1989 $14 (2/28/91) **86**
Nebbiolo delle Langhe 1988 $12 (3/31/90) **84**
Pinotu 1989 $20 (8/31/91) **84**

MOMMESSIN (France/Burgundy)
Aloxe-Corton Les Valzoières 1989 $28 (1/31/92) **88**
Auxey-Duresses Rouge 1989 $13 (1/31/92) **82**
Beaujolais-Villages Château de Montmelas 1988 $9.50 (5/31/89) (TM) **78**
Beaune 1989 $18 (1/31/92) **90**
Beaune Les Cent Vignes 1989 $23 (1/31/92) **86**
Beaune Les Epenottes 1989 $23 (7/15/90) (BT) **90+**
Bourgogne Pinot Noir 1983 $5 (2/16/86) **61**
Brouilly Château de Briante 1988 $11.50 (5/31/89) (TM) **81**
Chambolle-Musigny Les Charmes 1988 $42 (7/15/90) (BT) **90+**
Charmes-Chambertin 1985 $45 (2/15/88) **83**
Chassagne-Montrachet 1989 ($NA) (8/31/91) **83**
Chassagne-Montrachet Première Cru 1989 ($NA) (8/31/91) **85**
Chassagne-Montrachet Rouge 1989 (NR) (7/15/90) (BT) **75+**
Chiroubles Château de Raosset 1988 $11.25 (5/31/89) (TM) **83**
Clos de Tart 1989 $52 (1/31/92) **92**
Clos de Tart 1988 $112 (7/15/90) (BT) **95+**
Clos de Tart 1985 $95 (2/15/88) **91**
Clos de Tart 1950 $125 (8/31/90) (TR) **78**
Corton 1985 $28 (2/15/88) **91**
Corton-Bressandes 1988 $30 (7/15/90) (BT) **90+**
Corton Les Grèves 1989 $45 (1/31/92) **91**
Côte de Beaune-Villages 1985 $13 (2/15/88) **85**
Côte de Nuits-Villages 1985 $17 (7/31/88) **85**
Côtes du Rhône 1986 $4.75 (4/30/88) BB **82**
Echézeaux 1989 (NR) (7/15/90) (BT) **80+**
Echézeaux 1979 $18 (2/16/86) **86**
Fixin 1989 $15 (1/31/92) **87**
Fixin 1988 $19 (7/15/90) (BT) **75+**
Fleurie 1988 $13.50 (5/31/89) (TM) **87**
Gevrey-Chambertin 1985 $25 (2/15/88) **90**
Gevrey-Chambertin Estournelles St.-Jacques 1989 (NR) (7/15/90) (BT) **80+**
Gevrey-Chambertin Lavaux St.-Jacques 1989 $45 (1/31/92) **85**
Juliénas Domaine de la Conseillere 1988 $10.50 (5/31/89) (TM) **81**
Maranges 1989 $13 (1/31/92) **87**
Meursault 1989 ($NA) (8/31/91) **84**
Meursault Premier Cru 1989 ($NA) (8/31/91) **86**
Morgon 1988 $10 (5/31/89) (TM) **86**
Morgon Domaine de Lathevalle 1988 $10 (5/31/89) (TM) **88**
Moulin-à-Vent Domaine de Champ de Cour 1988 $12.50 (5/31/89) (TM) **91**
Nuits-St.-Georges Les Vaucrains 1989 $45 (1/31/92) **90**
Pommard 1989 $28 (1/31/92) **88**
Puligny-Montrachet 1989 ($NA) (8/31/91) **84**
Régnié 1988 $10.50 (5/31/89) (TM) **85**
St.-Amour Domaine de Monreve 1988 $12 (5/31/89) (TM) **84**
St.-Véran Domaine de l'Evèque 1985 $11 (3/31/87) **76**
Santenay Grand Clos Rousseau 1989 (NR) (7/15/90) (BT) **80+**
Santenay Grand Clos Rousseau 1988 $23 (7/15/90) (BT) **75+**
Savigny-lès-Beaune 1985 $17 (7/31/88) **80**
Volnay Le Clos des Chênes 1988 $38 (7/15/90) (BT) **85+**
Volnay Hospices de Beaune Cuvée General-Muteau 1985 $80 (3/15/88) **91**
Vosne-Romanée Aux Brûlées 1989 $38 (1/31/92) **89**

CHATEAU MONBRISON (France/Bordeaux)
Margaux 1990 (NR) (5/15/92) (BT) **90+**
Margaux 1989 $40 (3/15/92) **93**
Margaux 1988 $20 (2/28/91) **92**
Margaux 1987 $20 (5/15/90) **85**
Margaux 1986 $20 (11/30/89) (JS) **92**
Margaux 1984 $15 (5/15/87) **78**
Margaux 1982 Rel: $14 Cur: $22 (11/30/89) (JS) **90**

CHARLES MONCAUT (France/Burgundy)
Meursault 1983 $16 (6/01/86) **66**
Nuits-St.-Georges Les Argillières 1984 $32 (6/15/87) **90**
Pouilly-Fuissé 1985 $18 (6/15/87) **62**
St.-Véran 1985 $10 (6/15/87) **75**
Vosne-Romanée Cuvée Particulière 1983 $16 (9/15/86) **62**

MONCHHOF (Germany)
Riesling Kabinett Mosel-Saar-Ruwer Urziger Würzgarten 1988 $15 (9/30/89) **90**
Riesling Spätlese Mosel-Saar-Ruwer Erdener Treppchen 1988 ($NA) (9/30/89) **86**
Riesling Spätlese Mosel-Saar-Ruwer Urziger Würzgarten 1988 ($NA) (9/30/89) **84**
Riesling Spätlese Mosel-Saar-Ruwer Wehlener Klosterberg 1988 ($NA) (9/30/89) **83**

CK MONDAVI (United States/California)
Cabernet Sauvignon Napa Valley 1983 $4.50 (10/15/87) **65**
Chardonnay California 1986 $4.50 (8/31/87) **70**
White Zinfandel California 1988 $5.25 (6/15/89) **85**

ROBERT MONDAVI (United States/California)
Brut Napa Valley Chardonnay Reserve 1985 $35 (12/31/91) **85**
Brut Napa Valley Reserve 1985 $35 (12/31/91) **90**
Cabernet Sauvignon California Woodbridge 1988 $6 (2/28/91) BB **81**
Cabernet Sauvignon California Woodbridge 1987 $6 (9/15/89) **74**
Cabernet Sauvignon California Cabernet 1986 $5.50 (12/15/88) BB **80**
Cabernet Sauvignon California Cabernet 1985 $4.25 (10/31/87) BB **78**
Cabernet Sauvignon Napa Valley 1990 (NR) (5/15/91) (BT) **90+**
Cabernet Sauvignon Napa Valley Unfiltered 1988 $18 (11/15/91) **83**
Cabernet Sauvignon Napa Valley 1987 $20 (5/31/90) **87**
Cabernet Sauvignon Napa Valley 1986 Rel: $18 Cur: $21 (7/31/89) **93**
Cabernet Sauvignon Napa Valley 1985 Rel: $15 Cur: $30 (12/15/88) SS **94**
Cabernet Sauvignon Napa Valley 1984 Rel: $13 Cur: $34 (12/31/87) **80**
Cabernet Sauvignon Napa Valley 1983 Rel: $12 Cur: $26 (4/15/87) **94**
Cabernet Sauvignon Napa Valley 1982 Rel: $11 Cur: $24 (7/01/85) **90**
Cabernet Sauvignon Napa Valley 1981 Rel: $11 Cur: $29 (12/16/84) **90**
Cabernet Sauvignon Napa Valley 1979 $25 (7/16/85) (JL) **85**
Cabernet Sauvignon Napa Valley 1978 $34 (6/01/86) **88**
Cabernet Sauvignon Napa Valley 1977 $30 (7/16/85) (JL) **89**
Cabernet Sauvignon Napa Valley 1976 $69 (7/16/85) (JL) **84**
Cabernet Sauvignon Napa Valley 1975 $56 (11/30/91) (JL) **85**
Cabernet Sauvignon Napa Valley 1974 $59 (2/15/90) (JG) **79**
Cabernet Sauvignon Napa Valley 1973 $35 (7/16/85) (JL) **86**
Cabernet Sauvignon Napa Valley 1972 Rel: $6 Cur: $42 (CA-3/89) **75**
Cabernet Sauvignon Napa Valley 1971 Rel: $6 Cur: $60 (7/16/85) (JL) **87**
Cabernet Sauvignon Napa Valley 1970 $93 (11/30/91) (JL) **92**
Cabernet Sauvignon Napa Valley 1969 $80 (11/30/91) (JL) **91**
Cabernet Sauvignon Napa Valley 1968 $100 (11/30/91) (JL) **88**
Cabernet Sauvignon Napa Valley 1967 Rel: $5 Cur: $95 (11/30/91) (JL) **79**
Cabernet Sauvignon Napa Valley 1967 Rel: $5 Cur: $210/1.5L (7/16/85) (JL) **83**
Cabernet Sauvignon Napa Valley 1966 Rel: $5 Cur: $165 (11/30/91) (JL) **88**
Cabernet Sauvignon Napa Valley 1966 Rel: $10/1.5L Cur: $370/1.5L (7/16/85) (JL) **79**
Cabernet Sauvignon Napa Valley Reserve 1991 (NR) (5/15/92) (BT) **87+**
Cabernet Sauvignon Napa Valley Reserve 1990 (NR) (11/30/91) (BT) **92+**

Cabernet Sauvignon Napa Valley Reserve 1989 $18 (11/30/91) (JL) **90**
Cabernet Sauvignon Napa Valley Reserve 1988 $45 (5/31/91) CS **91**
Cabernet Sauvignon Napa Valley Reserve 1987 Rel: $43 Cur: $51 (8/31/90) **90**
Cabernet Sauvignon Napa Valley Reserve 1986 Rel: $35 Cur: $42 (11/15/89) **95**
Cabernet Sauvignon Napa Valley Reserve 1985 Rel: $40 Cur: $50 (11/30/91) (JL) **94**
Cabernet Sauvignon Napa Valley Reserve 1985 Rel: $40 Cur: $50 (11/15/89) SS **95**
Cabernet Sauvignon Napa Valley Reserve 1984 Rel: $37 Cur: $42 (11/30/91) (JL) **90**
Cabernet Sauvignon Napa Valley Reserve 1983 Rel: $30 Cur: $37 (11/30/91) (JL) **82**
Cabernet Sauvignon Napa Valley Reserve 1982 Rel: $30 Cur: $43 (11/30/91) (JL) **82**
Cabernet Sauvignon Napa Valley Reserve 1981 Rel: $30 Cur: $36 (11/30/91) (JL) **85**
Cabernet Sauvignon Napa Valley Reserve 1981 Rel: $30 Cur: $36 (2/16/86) CS **94**
Cabernet Sauvignon Napa Valley Reserve 1980 Rel: $30 Cur: $42 (11/30/91) (JL) **86**
Cabernet Sauvignon Napa Valley Reserve 1979 Rel: $25 Cur: $48 (11/30/91) (JL) **91**
Cabernet Sauvignon Napa Valley Reserve 1978 Rel: $40 Cur: $70 (11/30/91) (JL) **91**
Cabernet Sauvignon Napa Valley Reserve 1978 Rel: $40 Cur: $70 (8/01/83) CS **92**
Cabernet Sauvignon Napa Valley Reserve 1977 Rel: $35 Cur: $47 (11/30/91) (JL) **89**
Cabernet Sauvignon Napa Valley Reserve 1976 Rel: $25 Cur: $47 (11/30/91) (JL) **84**
Cabernet Sauvignon Napa Valley Reserve 1975 Rel: $30 Cur: $50 (CA-3/89) **86**
Cabernet Sauvignon Napa Valley Reserve 1974 Rel: $30 Cur: $101 (11/30/91) (JL) **89**
Cabernet Sauvignon Napa Valley Reserve 1973 Rel: $12 Cur: $80 (11/30/91) (JL) **92**
Cabernet Sauvignon Napa Valley Reserve 1972 ($NA) (11/30/91) (JL) **78**
Cabernet Sauvignon Napa Valley Reserve 1971 Rel: $12 Cur: $130 (11/30/91) (JL) **91**
Cabernet Sauvignon Napa Valley Unfined 1970 Rel: $12 Cur: $115 (CA-3/89) **89**
Cabernet Sauvignon Napa Valley Unfiltered 1970 Rel: $12 Cur: $115 (7/16/85) () **93**
Cabernet Sauvignon Napa Valley Unfined 1969 Rel: $12 Cur: $135 (CA-3/89) **86**
Cabernet Sauvignon Napa Valley Unfined 1968 Rel: $8.50 Cur: $135 (CA-3/89) **83**
Chardonnay California Woodbridge 1990 $6.50 (7/15/92) **79**
Chardonnay California Woodbridge 1989 $7.25 (4/30/91) **74**
Chardonnay Napa Valley 1990 $15 (12/31/91) **83**
Chardonnay Napa Valley 1989 $16 (4/15/91) **87**
Chardonnay Napa Valley 1988 Rel: $16 Cur: $19 (11/30/89) **86**
Chardonnay Napa Valley 1987 Rel: $17 Cur: $21 (4/30/89) **83**
Chardonnay Napa Valley 1986 $15 (7/15/88) **88**
Chardonnay Napa Valley 1985 Rel: $12 Cur: $20 (7/15/87) **79**
Chardonnay Napa Valley 1984 Rel: $10 Cur: $16 (9/15/86) **83**
Chardonnay Napa Valley 1983 Rel: $14 Cur: $17 (8/01/85) **90**
Chardonnay Napa Valley 1982 $10 (8/01/84) **82**
Chardonnay Napa Valley 1981 $15 (6/01/86) **94**
Chardonnay Napa Valley Reserve 1990 $28 (12/31/91) **88**
Chardonnay Napa Valley Reserve Barrel Fermented 1989 $28 (7/15/91) **87**
Chardonnay Napa Valley Reserve 1988 Rel: $26 Cur: $29 (CH-6/90) **91**
Chardonnay Napa Valley Reserve 1987 Rel: $26 Cur: $34 (CH-6/90) **92**
Chardonnay Napa Valley Reserve 1986 Rel: $25 Cur: $30 (CH-3/90) **89**
Chardonnay Napa Valley Reserve 1985 Rel: $25 Cur: $30 (CH-3/90) **88**
Chardonnay Napa Valley Reserve 1984 Rel: $22 Cur: $41 (CH-3/90) **87**
Chardonnay Napa Valley Reserve 1983 Rel: $20 Cur: $28 (CH-3/90) **88**
Chardonnay Napa Valley Reserve 1982 Rel: $20 Cur: $25 (CH-3/90) **81**
Chardonnay Napa Valley Reserve 1981 Rel: $20 Cur: $24 (CH-3/90) **86**
Chardonnay Napa Valley Reserve 1980 Rel: $20 Cur: $30 (CH-3/90) **69**
Chardonnay Napa Valley Reserve 1979 Rel: $20 Cur: $27 (CH-3/90) **79**
Chardonnay Napa Valley Reserve 1978 Rel: $20 Cur: $24 (CH-3/90) **69**
Chardonnay Napa Valley Reserve 1977 Rel: $14 Cur: $32 (CH-3/90) **68**
Chardonnay Napa Valley Reserve 1976 Rel: $12 Cur: $32 (CH-3/90) **78**
Chardonnay Napa Valley Reserve 1975 Rel: $10 Cur: $35 (CH-3/90) **75**
Chardonnay Napa Valley Reserve 1974 Rel: $10 Cur: $45 (CH-3/90) **88**
Chenin Blanc Napa Valley 1989 $8 (11/15/91) **82**
Chenin Blanc Napa Valley 1988 $8 (6/30/90) **69**
Chenin Blanc Napa Valley 1987 $8 (7/31/89) **78**
Fumé Blanc Napa Valley 1989 $9.50 (11/15/91) **87**
Fumé Blanc Napa Valley 1988 $9.50 (5/15/90) **74**
Fumé Blanc Napa Valley 1987 $9.50 (7/31/89) **87**
Fumé Blanc Napa Valley To-Kalon Vineyard Reserve 1990 $17.50 (2/15/92) **82**
Fumé Blanc Napa Valley To-Kalon Vineyard Reserve 1989 $15 (7/15/91) **83**
Fumé Blanc Napa Valley To-Kalon Vineyard Reserve 1988 $15 (8/31/90) **84**
Fumé Blanc Napa Valley To-Kalon Vineyard Reserve 1987 $15 (3/31/90) **80**
Fumé Blanc Napa Valley To-Kalon Vineyard Reserve 1986 $15 (7/31/89) **77**
Johannisberg Riesling Napa Valley 1989 $8.25 (5/15/91) **69**
Johannisberg Riesling Napa Valley 1988 $8 (9/15/90) **55**
Merlot Napa Valley 1989 $21 (5/31/92) **87**
Muscat Napa Valley Moscoto d'Oro 1990 $12 (11/30/91) **72**
Muscat Napa Valley Moscoto d'Oro 1988 $10 (4/30/90) **78**
Muscat Napa Valley Moscoto d'Oro 1987 $11 (11/15/89) **79**
Pinot Noir Napa Valley 1990 Rel: $15 Cur: $18 (3/31/92) **86**
Pinot Noir Napa Valley 1989 $15 (4/30/91) **86**
Pinot Noir Napa Valley 1988 $13 (2/15/90) **89**
Pinot Noir Napa Valley 1987 $12 (7/31/89) **88**
Pinot Noir Napa Valley 1985 $10.50 (6/15/88) **79**
Pinot Noir Napa Valley 1984 $8.25 (11/15/87) **75**
Pinot Noir Napa Valley 1982 $9.50 (8/31/86) **79**
Pinot Noir Napa Valley 1981 $7.50 (11/01/84) **80**
Pinot Noir Napa Valley Reserve 1990 $28 (3/31/92) **92**
Pinot Noir Napa Valley Reserve 1988 Rel: $23 Cur: $26 (10/31/90) **82**
Pinot Noir Napa Valley Reserve 1986 $22 (10/15/89) **91**
Pinot Noir Napa Valley Reserve 1985 Rel: $19 Cur: $31 (4/15/89) SS **92**
Pinot Noir Napa Valley Reserve 1983 Rel: $16 Cur: $25 (11/15/87) **80**
Pinot Noir Napa Valley Reserve 1982 Rel: $15 Cur: $25 (8/31/86) **78**
Pinot Noir Napa Valley Reserve 1981 Rel: $14 Cur: $17 (8/31/86) **86**
Pinot Noir Napa Valley Reserve 1980 $13.25 (8/01/84) **81**

Key to Symbols

The scores reported here are the results of blind tastings conducted by our panel of senior editors. Wines that carry the initials below are results of individual tastings.

THE WINE SPECTATOR 100-POINT SCALE 95-100—Classic, a great wine; ***90-94***—Outstanding, superior character and style; ***80-89***—Good to very good, a wine with special qualities; ***70-79***—Average, drinkable wine that may have minor flaws; ***60-69***—Below average, drinkable but not recommended; ***50-59***—Poor, undrinkable, not recommended. "+"—With a score indicates a range; used primarily with barrel tastings to indicate a preliminary score.

SPECIAL DESIGNATIONS SS—Spectator Selection, CS—Cellar Selection, BB—Best Buy, ($NA)—Price not available, (NR)—Not released.

TASTER'S INITIALS (JG)—Jim Gordon, (HS)—Harvey Steiman, (JL)—James Laube, (JS)—James Suckling, (TM)—Thomas Matthews, (TR)—Terry Robards, (PM)—Per-Henrik Mansson, (BT)—Barrel Tasting (these wines were tasted blind from barrel samples), (CA-date)—*California's Great Cabernets* by James Laube, (CH-date)—*California's Great Chardonnays* by James Laube, (VP-date)—*Vintage Port* by James Suckling.

DATE TASTED Dates in parentheses represent the issue in which the rating was published.

Sauvignon Blanc California $5 (3/15/89) BB **81**
Sauvignon Blanc California Woodbridge 1990 $5.50 (6/15/92) BB **83**
Sauvignon Blanc California Woodbridge 1989 $5 (4/30/91) BB **80**
Sauvignon Blanc California Woodbridge 1988 $5 (10/31/89) **78**
White Zinfandel California 1988 $5.50 (6/15/89) **80**

COLLI MONFORTESI (Italy/Piedmont)
Barolo 1982 $15 (4/30/87) SS **92**

MONGEARD-MUGNERET (France/Burgundy)
Bourgogne 1989 $9.50 (1/31/92) **85**
Bourgogne Hautes Côtes de Nuits 1989 $16 (1/31/92) **77**
Clos de Vougeot 1989 $77 (1/31/92) **87**
Clos de Vougeot 1987 $53 (5/15/90) **81**
Clos de Vougeot 1986 $56 (7/31/89) **87**
Echézeaux 1984 $28 (2/15/88) **68**
Echézeaux Vieilles Vignes 1989 $59 (1/31/92) **93**
Echézeaux Vieilles Vignes 1988 $61 (2/15/91) **88**
Echézeaux Vieilles Vignes 1987 $42 (5/15/90) **86**
Echézeaux Vieilles Vignes 1986 $44 (8/31/89) **90**
Fixin 1989 $25 (1/31/92) **83**
Fixin 1986 $19 (10/15/89) **84**
Grands Echézeaux 1989 $95 (1/31/92) **93**
Grands Echézeaux 1987 $65 (5/15/90) **85**
Grands Echézeaux 1986 $73 (8/31/89) **92**
Nuits-St.-Georges Les Boudots 1989 $49 (1/31/92) **84**
Nuits-St.-Georges Les Boudots 1987 $32 (4/30/90) **81**
Nuits-St.-Georges Les Boudots 1984 $23 (2/15/88) **78**
Richebourg 1989 $95 (1/31/92) **92**
Richebourg 1985 $123 (3/15/88) **92**
Savigny-lès-Beaune Les Narbantons 1989 $28 (1/31/92) **78**
Vosne-Romanée 1989 $34 (1/31/92) **85**
Vosne-Romanée 1986 $26 (8/31/89) **79**
Vosne-Romanée Les Orveaux 1989 $43 (1/31/92) **94**
Vosne-Romanée Les Orveaux 1987 $35 (7/15/90) **62**
Vosne-Romanée Les Orveaux 1986 $34 (8/31/89) **82**
Vosne-Romanée Les Orveaux 1985 $32 (3/15/88) **82**
Vosne-Romanée Les Orveaux 1984 $18 (2/15/88) **68**
Vosne-Romanée Les Petits Monts 1987 $35 (4/30/90) **74**
Vosne-Romanée Les Suchots 1987 $35 (6/15/90) **82**
Vougeot Les Cras 1989 (NR) (1/31/92) **93**

MONMOUSSIN (France/Other)
Brut Touraine Etoile 1986 $13 (12/31/90) **82**
Extra Dry Vouvray 1985 $13 (12/31/90) **81**

DOMAINE RENE MONNIER (France/Burgundy)
Beaune Cent Vignes 1985 $25 (10/31/87) **89**
Meursault Les Charmes 1985 $39 (12/15/88) **87**
Meursault Les Chevalires 1986 $34 (10/15/88) **89**
Meursault Le Limozin 1986 $32 (12/15/88) **89**
Pommard Les Vignots 1985 $30 (11/15/88) **89**
Pommard Les Vignots 1982 $17 (7/01/85) **81**
Puligny-Montrachet Les Folatières 1986 $44 (11/15/88) **81**

DOMAINE DE MONPERTUIS (France/Rhône)
Châteauneuf-du-Pape 1987 $14 (6/30/90) **83**
Châteauneuf-du-Pape 1986 $18 (9/30/89) **73**
Châteauneuf-du-Pape Blanc 1988 $29 (3/31/91) **87**

CASTELLO DI MONSANTO (Italy/Tuscany)
Chianti Classico Il Poggio Vineyard Riserva 1985 Rel: $25 Cur: $30 (3/31/90) **80**
Chianti Classico Il Poggio Vineyard Riserva 1983 Rel: $23 Cur: $25 (11/30/89) (HS) **86**
Chianti Classico Il Poggio Vineyard Riserva 1982 Rel: $23 Cur: $25 (11/30/89) (HS) **93**
Chianti Classico Il Poggio Vineyard Riserva 1981 Rel: $17 Cur: $19 (11/30/89) (HS) **82**
Chianti Classico Il Poggio Vineyard Riserva 1979 $16 (9/15/87) **93**
Chianti Classico Riserva 1986 $15 (4/15/91) **85**
Chianti Classico Riserva 1985 $10 (11/30/89) (HS) **89**
Chianti Classico Riserva 1982 $10 (2/15/88) **72**
Chianti Classico Riserva 1981 $10 (12/15/87) **67**
Chianti Classico Riserva 1979 $9.50 (11/01/84) **83**
Fabrizio Bianchi Vigneto Scanni 1988 $30 (9/15/91) **82**
Nemo 1988 $30 (9/15/91) **91**
Nemo 1983 $28 (9/15/90) **87**
Tinscvil 1985 $22 (9/15/90) **88**

CHATEAU MONT BELAIR (France/Bordeaux)
St.-Emilion 1989 $12 (11/15/91) **81**

CHATEAU MONT-JOYE (France/Sauternes)
Barsac 1989 ($NA) (6/15/90) (BT) **75+**
Barsac 1987 ($NA) (6/15/90) **63**

MONT-MARCAL (Spain)
Brut Cava NV $8 (7/15/90) **78**
Penedès Tinto 1988 $8 (3/31/91) **83**

CHATEAU MONT-REDON (France/Rhône)
Châteauneuf-du-Pape 1989 $21 (10/15/91) **91**
Châteauneuf-du-Pape 1988 Rel: $21 Cur: $25 (10/15/91) **83**
Châteauneuf-du-Pape 1986 $17 (10/15/91) **85**
Châteauneuf-du-Pape 1985 Rel: $12 Cur: $25 (10/15/91) **90**
Châteauneuf-du-Pape 1984 $11 (9/30/87) **92**
Châteauneuf-du-Pape 1983 $25 (10/15/91) **88**
Châteauneuf-du-Pape 1981 $30 (10/15/91) **90**
Châteauneuf-du-Pape Blanc 1990 $20 (10/15/91) **85**
Châteauneuf-du-Pape Blanc 1987 $20 (10/31/89) **79**
Côtes du Rhône Blanc 1987 $8 (10/31/89) BB **86**

MONT ST. JOHN (United States/California)
Cabernet Sauvignon Napa Valley 1986 $14 (4/30/91) **87**
Cabernet Sauvignon Napa Valley 1983 $15 (7/31/89) **78**
Cabernet Sauvignon Napa Valley 1982 $15 (3/15/89) **82**
Cabernet Sauvignon Napa Valley Private Reserve 1980 $11.50 (5/16/84) **75**
Chardonnay Carneros Napa Valley 1987 $15 (7/15/89) **81**
Pinot Noir Carneros Napa Valley 1988 $14 (4/30/91) **81**
Pinot Noir Carneros Napa Valley 1987 $15 (3/31/90) **76**
Pinot Noir Carneros Napa Valley 1985 $15 (10/15/89) **82**
Pinot Noir Carneros Napa Valley 1981 $9.75 (5/16/84) **73**
Pinot Noir Carneros Napa Valley Madonna Vineyard 1985 $11 (6/15/88) **78**

LES PRODUCTEURS DU MONT TAUCH (France/Other)
Corbières 1987 $5 (2/15/89) **68**

Fitou 1985 $6 (4/15/89) **79**

DOMAINE DU MONT VERRIER (France/Beaujolais)
Beaujolais-Villages 1988 $10 (5/31/89) (TM) **76**

FATTORIA DI MONTAGLIARI (Italy/Tuscany)
Chianti Classico Riserva 1985 ($NA) (9/15/91) **83**

MONTAUDON (France/Champagne)
Brut Champagne M NV $25 (12/31/91) **90**

MONTDOMAINE (United States/Virginia)
Heritage Monticello 1988 $14 (2/29/92) **82**
Merlot Monticello Reserve 1987 $15 (2/29/92) **86**

VILLA DE MONTE (Italy/Tuscany)
Chianti Rufina Riserva 1985 $13 (4/30/92) **80**
Chianti Rufina Riserva 1979 $16 (4/30/92) **81**

CASTELLO DI MONTE ANTICO (Italy/Tuscany)
1985 $6.75 (6/30/88) **85**
1982 $3.75 (4/01/86) BB **82**

MONTE DUCAY (Spain)
Cariñena Gran Reserva 1982 $8 (11/30/89) **85**

MONTE VELAZ (Spain)
Rioja 1981 $4 (10/15/87) **73**

MONTE VERDE (United States/California)
Cabernet Sauvignon California Proprietor's Reserve 1987 $6.50/L (12/15/89) **80**
Chardonnay California 1988 $9 (12/15/89) **71**
Chardonnay California Proprietor's Reserve 1989 $5.50 (3/31/91) **78**
Chardonnay California Proprietor's Reserve 1987 $6.50 (12/15/89) **76**

MONTE VERTINE (Italy/Tuscany)
1983 Rel: $15 Cur: $18 (2/15/87) **85**
Le Pergole Torte 1988 $44 (9/15/91) **93**
Le Pergole Torte 1987 Rel: $41 Cur: $45 (1/31/91) **90**
Le Pergole Torte 1986 Rel: $36 Cur: $42 (9/30/89) **90**
Le Pergole Torte 1985 Rel: $33 Cur: $42 (4/30/89) **88**
Le Pergole Torte 1983 $24.50 (2/15/87) **90**
Le Pergole Torte 1982 $16.50 (7/16/86) **90**
Le Pergole Torte 1981 $11.25 (7/16/85) **87**
Riserva 1988 $30 (9/15/91) **90**
Riserva 1987 Rel: $30 Cur: $36 (3/15/91) **91**
Riserva 1986 Rel: $26 Cur: $35 (9/30/89) **86**
Riserva 1982 $18 (2/15/87) **84**
Riserva 1981 $15 (8/31/86) **90**
Sangioveto 1985 $17 (8/31/88) **89**
Il Sodaccio 1988 $35 (9/15/91) **91**
Il Sodaccio 1987 $32 (1/31/91) **87**
Il Sodaccio 1986 Rel: $30 Cur: $35 (9/30/89) **90**
Il Sodaccio 1985 $25 (3/15/89) **91**
Il Sodaccio 1983 Rel: $19.50 Cur: $23 (2/15/87) **93**

BODEGAS MONTECILLO (Spain)
Rioja Crianza 1989 (NR) (3/31/92) (BT) **85+**
Rioja Crianza 1988 ($NA) (3/31/92) **89**
Rioja Crianza 1987 $6 (3/31/92) **79**
Rioja Especial Gran Reserva 1978 $30 (3/31/90) **85**
Rioja Gran Reserva 1975 $29 (12/15/88) **85**
Rioja Viña Cumbrero 1987 $6 (8/31/91) BB **85**
Rioja Viña Cumbrero 1985 $5 (11/15/88) BB **80**
Rioja Viña Cumbrero 1984 $4 (11/30/87) **69**
Rioja Viña Cumbrero 1982 $4 (12/31/86) BB **89**
Rioja Viña Cumbrero 1981 $4 (6/01/86) BB **73**
Rioja Viña Monty 1978 $7 (9/30/86) **81**
Rioja Viña Monty 1976 $6 (5/16/86) **70**
Rioja Viña Monty Gran Reserva 1982 $14 (3/31/92) **87**
Rioja Viña Monty Gran Reserva 1981 $13 (3/31/92) **88**
Rioja Viña Monty Gran Reserva 1980 $7 (11/30/87) **79**
Rioja Viña Monty Gran Reserva 1978 $28 (3/31/92) **82**
Rioja Viña Monty Gran Reserva 1975 $28 (3/31/92) **86**
Rioja Viña Monty Gran Reserva 1973 ($NA) (3/31/92) **85**
Rioja Viña Monty Gran Reserva 1970 ($NA) (3/31/92) **87**
Rioja White Viña Cumbrero 1989 $6 (7/15/91) BB **80**
Rioja White Viña Cumbrero 1988 $5 (3/31/90) **72**

CASTELLO DI MONTEGROSSI (Italy/Tuscany)
Chianti Classico 1988 $15 (9/15/91) **91**
Chianti Classico 1986 $8 (7/15/89) **89**
Chianti Classico 1985 $5.50 (9/15/88) **86**
Vin Santo 1982 $19/375ml (3/31/90) **92**

DOMAINE DE MONTEILS (France/Sauternes)
Sauternes 1988 ($NA) (6/15/90) (BT) **80+**
Sauternes 1987 ($NA) (6/15/90) **72**

FATTORIA MONTELLORI (Italy/Tuscany)
Chianti Putto 1988 $6 (11/30/89) **83**

MONTEREY PENINSULA (United States/California)
Cabernet Sauvignon Monterey County 1982 $11 (3/31/87) **74**
Cabernet Sauvignon Monterey Doctors' Reserve 1984 $16 (2/28/91) **81**
Cabernet Sauvignon Monterey Doctors' Reserve Lot II 1982 $14 (6/15/87) **83**
California NV $6.50 (7/15/91) BB **82**
Chardonnay Monterey Sleepy Hollow 1989 $12 (5/31/91) **83**
Merlot Monterey Doctors' Reserve 1986 $16 (5/31/92) **83**
Merlot Monterey Doctors' Reserve 1985 $14 (1/31/89) **83**
Merlot Monterey Doctors' Reserve 1984 $12 (12/15/87) **74**
Pinot Blanc Monterey Doctor's Reserve 1988 $12 (4/30/91) **87**
Pinot Noir Monterey Sleepy Hollow 1987 $18 (2/28/91) **86**
Zinfandel Amador County Ferrero Ranch Doctors' Reserve 1987 $15 (5/15/91) **83**
Zinfandel Amador County Ferrero Ranch Doctors' Reserve 1982 $10 (2/29/88) **83**

MONTEREY VINEYARD (United States/California)
Cabernet Sauvignon Monterey Classic 1989 $6 (3/15/92) BB **83**
Cabernet Sauvignon Monterey County Classic 1987 $6 (1/31/91) BB **83**
Cabernet Sauvignon Monterey County Classic 1986 $5.50 (10/31/89) **76**
Cabernet Sauvignon Monterey County Limited Release 1986 $10 (11/15/89) **83**
Cabernet Sauvignon Monterey County Limited Release 1985 $10 (8/31/88) **75**
Cabernet Sauvignon Monterey-Sonoma-San Luis Obispo Counties Classic 1985 $5 (2/15/89) **73**
Chardonnay Monterey Classic 1990 $6 (2/29/92) **76**
Chardonnay Central Coast Classic 1989 $6 (12/31/90) **77**
Chardonnay Monterey County 1985 $7 (10/15/87) **70**
Chardonnay Monterey County Classic 1987 $5 (2/15/89) BB **83**
Chardonnay Monterey County Limited Release 1988 $12 (2/28/91) **80**
Chardonnay Monterey County Limited Release 1986 $10 (8/31/88) **89**
Chenin Blanc Monterey Classic 1988 $6.50 (7/31/89) **88**
Merlot Monterey Classic 1989 $6 (2/29/92) BB **84**
Merlot Monterey County Classic 1988 $6 (12/31/90) **76**
Pinot Noir Monterey County 1987 $8.50 (3/31/90) **84**
Pinot Noir Monterey County 1986 $7 (6/15/88) **83**
Pinot Noir Monterey County Limited Release 1988 $9 (2/28/91) **80**
Sauvignon Blanc Monterey County Classic 1989 $5.50 (3/31/91) **79**

MONTES (Chile)
Cabernet Sauvignon Curicó 1988 $8 (6/15/92) **84**
Cabernet Sauvignon Curicó Montes Alpha Private Selection 1988 $14 (5/15/92) **87**
Cabernet Sauvignon Curicó Villa Montes 1989 $6 (6/15/92) BB **84**
Cabernet Sauvignon Curicó Villa Montes 1988 $4.50 (2/15/90) **73**
Cabernet Sauvignon Curicó Villa Montes 1987 $7 (2/15/90) BB **84**
Cabernet Sauvignon Curicó Villa Montes Special Selection 1987 $12 (9/15/90) **84**
Chardonnay Curicó Oak Barrel Fermented 1991 $9 (6/15/92) **78**
Merlot Curicó Valley Villa Montes 1989 $7 (9/15/90) **79**
Sauvignon Blanc Curicó Villa Montes 1991 $6 (6/15/92) BB **80**
Sauvignon Blanc Curicó Villa Montes 1990 $4.50 (10/15/91) **78**

MONTESIERRA (Spain)
Somontano 1988 $6 (3/31/90) **81**

MONTEVINA (United States/California)
Cabernet Sauvignon California 1988 $8.50 (2/15/90) **77**
Cabernet Sauvignon Shenandoah Valley Limited Release 1984 $7.50 (8/31/88) BB **86**
Zinfandel Amador County 1987 $7.50 (3/31/90) **75**
Zinfandel Shenandoah Valley Montino 1985 $5.50 (10/15/88) **75**
Zinfandel Shenandoah Valley Winemaker's Choice 1984 $9 (8/31/87) **75**
Zinfandel Shenandoah Valley Winemaker's Choice 1980 $9 (4/16/84) **78**

MONTEVINO (Italy/North)
Pinot Grigio del Veneto 1989 $6.50 (7/15/91) **74**

DOMAINE MONTHELIE-DOUHAIRET (France/Burgundy)
Meursault 1989 $25 (8/31/91) **85**
Meursault Les Santenots 1989 ($NA) (8/31/91) **87**
Monthélie 1985 $16 (6/30/88) **81**
Monthélie Blanc 1989 ($NA) (8/31/91) **71**
Monthélie Blanc Premier Cru 1989 ($NA) (8/31/91) **82**
Volnay Champans 1985 $25 (7/15/88) **87**

ANTONIO & ELIO MONTI (Italy/Other)
Montepulciano d'Abruzzo 1989 $7 (9/30/91) **75**
Montepulciano d'Abruzzo 1988 $6.25 (2/15/91) BB **83**

MONTICELLO (United States/California)
Cabernet Sauvignon Napa Valley Corley Reserve 1991 (NR) (5/15/92) (BT) **87+**
Cabernet Sauvignon Napa Valley Corley Reserve 1990 (NR) (5/15/91) (BT) **85+**
Cabernet Sauvignon Napa Valley Corley Reserve 1989 (NR) (5/15/91) (BT) **90+**
Cabernet Sauvignon Napa Valley Corley Reserve 1987 $25 (11/15/90) **90**
Cabernet Sauvignon Napa Valley Corley Reserve 1986 Rel: $24 Cur: $28 (3/15/90) **92**
Cabernet Sauvignon Napa Valley Corley Reserve 1985 Rel: $22.50 Cur: $35 (7/31/89) **92**
Cabernet Sauvignon Napa Valley Corley Reserve 1984 Rel: $18.50 Cur: $30 (CA-3/89) **91**
Cabernet Sauvignon Napa Valley Corley Reserve 1983 Rel: $24 Cur: $27 (CA-3/89) **88**
Cabernet Sauvignon Napa Valley Corley Reserve 1982 Rel: $15 Cur: $32 (CA-3/89) **90**
Cabernet Sauvignon Napa Valley Jefferson Cuvée 1988 $16 (11/15/91) **85**
Cabernet Sauvignon Napa Valley Jefferson Cuvée 1987 $14 (9/30/90) **90**
Cabernet Sauvignon Napa Valley Jefferson Cuvée 1986 $14 (4/15/89) **89**
Cabernet Sauvignon Napa Valley Jefferson Cuvée 1985 $12 (2/29/88) **87**
Cabernet Sauvignon Napa Valley Jefferson Cuvée 1984 $11 (11/30/87) **90**
Cabernet Sauvignon Napa Valley Jefferson Cuvée 1983 $10 (11/30/86) **77**
Cabernet Sauvignon Napa Valley Jefferson Cuvée 1982 $10 (2/01/86) **91**
Cabernet Sauvignon Napa Valley 1981 $13.50 (7/16/84) **74**
Chardonnay Napa Valley Corley Reserve 1990 $17 (7/15/92) **87**
Chardonnay Napa Valley Corley Reserve 1989 $18 (7/15/91) **89**
Chardonnay Napa Valley Corley Reserve 1988 Rel: $17.25 Cur: $20 (1/31/91) SS **92**
Chardonnay Napa Valley Corley Reserve 1987 Rel: $17.25 Cur: $20 (CH-6/90) **86**
Chardonnay Napa Valley Corley Reserve 1986 Rel: $16.50 Cur: $20 (CH-2/90) **89**
Chardonnay Napa Valley Corley Reserve 1985 Rel: $14 Cur: $20 (CH-2/90) **85**
Chardonnay Napa Valley Corley Reserve 1984 Rel: $12.50 Cur: $25 (CH-2/90) **94**
Chardonnay Napa Valley Barrel Fermented 1983 Rel: $12.50 Cur: $20 (CH-2/90) **80**
Chardonnay Napa Valley Barrel Fermented 1982 Rel: $14 Cur: $20 (CH-2/90) **84**
Chardonnay Napa Valley Jefferson Ranch 1989 $12.50 (7/15/91) **74**
Chardonnay Napa Valley Jefferson Ranch 1988 $12.25 (6/30/90) **81**
Chardonnay Napa Valley Jefferson Ranch 1987 Rel: $12.25 Cur: $16 (4/30/89) **77**
Chardonnay Napa Valley Jefferson Ranch 1986 Rel: $11 Cur: $18 (CH-2/90) **86**
Chardonnay Napa Valley Jefferson Ranch 1985 Rel: $11 Cur: $18 (CH-2/90) **82**
Chardonnay Napa Valley Jefferson Ranch 1984 Rel: $10 Cur: $18 (CH-2/90) **86**
Chardonnay Napa Valley Jefferson Ranch 1983 Rel: $10 Cur: $20 (CH-2/90) **93**
Chardonnay Napa Valley 1982 Rel: $13.50 Cur: $20 (CH-2/90) **82**
Chardonnay Napa Valley 1981 Rel: $12 Cur: $20 (CH-2/90) **76**
Chardonnay Napa Valley 1980 Rel: $12 Cur: $20 (CH-2/90) **86**
Gewürztraminer Napa Valley 1986 $7.50 (2/28/89) **76**
Merlot Napa Valley 1991 (NR) (5/15/92) (BT) **85+**
Pinot Noir Napa Valley 1987 $14.50 (10/15/89) **85**
Pinot Noir Napa Valley 1986 $12 (6/15/88) **89**
Pinot Noir Napa Valley 1985 $12 (12/15/87) **89**
Sémillon Napa Valley Chevrier Blanc 1986 $7.50 (1/31/89) **77**

MONTINORE (United States/Oregon)
Chardonnay Washington County 1988 $11 (3/31/91) **77**
Pinot Noir Washington County 1988 Rel: $13.50 Cur: $35 (4/15/91) **88**
Pinot Noir Washington County 1987 $12.50 (2/15/90) **81**
White Riesling Late Harvest Yamhill County 1989 $7 (3/31/91) **84**
White Riesling Ultra Late Harvest Oregon 1987 $22/375ml (3/31/91) **83**

DOMAINE DU MONTMARIN (France/Other)
Vin de Pays des Côtes de Thongue Cépage Marsanne 1987 $5 (2/15/89) **74**

CHATEAU DE MONTMIRAIL (France/Rhône)
Gigondas Cuvée de Beauchamp 1985 $14 (9/30/88) **78**
Gigondas Cuvée de Beauchamp 1983 $11 (11/30/86) **90**

CAMILLO MONTORI (Italy/Other)
Montepulciano d'Abruzzo 1987 $8 (3/31/90) **80**

MONTPELLIER (United States/California)
Cabernet Sauvignon California 1988 $7 (7/31/91) BB **83**

Chardonnay California 1990 $6 (7/15/92) **78**
Chardonnay California 1989 $7 (9/15/91) **76**
Chardonnay California 1988 $7 (3/31/90) **73**

MONTREAUX (United States/California)
Brut Napa Valley 1986 $26 (12/15/91) **88**
Brut Napa Valley 1985 $32 (12/31/90) **79**

MONTROSE (Australia)
Cabernet Sauvignon Mudgee 1987 $10 (2/28/91) **81**
Cabernet Sauvignon Mudgee 1986 $8 (7/31/89) **86**
Cabernet Sauvignon Mudgee 1984 $10 (4/30/88) **88**
Cabernet Sauvignon Mudgee Special Reserve 1985 $16 (1/31/90) **80**
Chardonnay Australia Show Reserve 1986 $14 (5/31/87) **91**
Chardonnay Mudgee 1989 $10 (2/28/91) **85**
Chardonnay Mudgee 1988 $9 (6/15/90) **84**
Chardonnay Mudgee 1987 $8 (7/31/89) **78**
Chardonnay Mudgee 1986 $10 (2/15/88) **81**
Chardonnay Mudgee Special Reserve 1984 $15 (5/15/87) **89**
Chardonnay Mudgee Stoney Creek Vineyard Special Reserve 1986 $13 (3/15/90) **87**
Chardonnay South Eastern Australia Bin 747 1989 $8 (2/28/91) BB **83**
Shiraz Mudgee 1988 $9 (3/15/91) **78**
Shiraz Mudgee 1984 $10 (7/01/87) **87**
Shiraz Mudgee 1983 $7 (3/15/88) **86**

CHATEAU MONTROSE (France/Bordeaux)
St.-Estèphe 1991 (NR) (5/15/92) (BT) **80+**
St.-Estèphe 1990 (NR) (5/15/92) (BT) **90+**
St.-Estèphe 1989 $47 (3/15/92) **95**
St.-Estèphe 1988 $41 (3/31/91) **87**
St.-Estèphe 1987 Rel: $17 Cur: $19 (2/15/90) **80**
St.-Estèphe 1986 Rel: $31 Cur: $35 (5/15/89) SS **96**
St.-Estèphe 1985 $33 (4/30/88) **90**
St.-Estèphe 1984 Rel: $14 Cur: $19 (3/31/87) **88**
St.-Estèphe 1983 Rel: $18.50 Cur: $35 (5/16/86) **87**
St.-Estèphe 1982 Rel: $18 Cur: $42 (5/01/85) **92**
St.-Estèphe 1981 Rel: $14 Cur: $32 (12/01/84) **90**
St.-Estèphe 1979 $30 (10/15/89) (JS) **81**
St.-Estèphe 1970 $102 (4/01/86) **80**
St.-Estèphe 1962 $98 (11/30/87) (JS) **90**
St.-Estèphe 1961 $185 (3/16/86) (TR) **87**
St.-Estèphe 1959 $125 (10/15/90) (JS) **90**
St.-Estèphe 1945 $300 (3/16/86) (JL) **88**

CHATEAU MONTUS (France/Other)
Madiran 1985 $10 (4/15/89) **79**

CHATEAU MONTVIEL (France/Bordeaux)
Pomerol 1989 (NR) (4/30/91) (BT) **85+**
Pomerol 1987 $20 (6/30/89) (BT) **80+**
Pomerol 1986 $29 (6/30/88) (BT) **80+**

Z. MOORE (United States/California)
Gewürztraminer Russian River Valley 1987 $8.50 (2/28/89) **86**

MORBELLI (Italy/Tuscany)
Carema 1982 $21 (11/30/89) **87**

DOMAINE DE LA MORDOREE (France/Rhône)
Côtes du Rhône 1988 $5.50 (2/28/90) **68**
Lirac 1986 $11 (9/30/88) **88**

MOREAU (France/Burgundy)
Bourgogne Blanc Chardonnay 1988 $8 (4/30/91) BB **84**
Bourgogne Blanc Chardonnay 1983 $6.50 (6/01/86) **64**
Chablis 1987 ($NA) (3/31/89) **83**
Chablis 1986 ($NA) (3/31/89) **85**
Chablis 1983 $9.50 (12/01/85) **62**
Chablis Beauroy 1986 ($NA) (3/31/89) **90**
Chablis Domaine de Bieville 1988 $15 (2/28/91) **88**
Chablis Domaine de Bieville 1985 $14 (4/15/87) **84**
Chablis Bougros 1987 ($NA) (3/31/89) **89**
Chablis Bougros 1986 ($NA) (3/31/89) **89**
Chablis Les Clos 1987 $38 (2/28/91) **84**
Chablis Les Clos 1986 $36 (3/31/89) **96**
Chablis Les Clos Clos des Hospices 1987 $60 (2/28/91) **89**
Chablis Les Clos Clos des Hospices 1986 $35 (10/15/88) **78**
Chablis Clos des Hospices 1987 ($NA) (3/31/89) **95**
Chablis Côte de Lechet 1987 $11 (3/31/89) **85**
Chablis Côte de Lechet 1986 $11 (3/31/89) **85**
Chablis Fourchaume 1987 $24 (3/31/89) **90**
Chablis Fourchaume 1986 $21 (3/31/89) **81**
Chablis Mont de Milieu 1986 $30 (3/31/89) **90**
Chablis Montmain 1987 $21 (3/31/89) **87**
Chablis Montmain 1986 $21 (2/28/91) **87**
Chablis Les Preuses 1987 ($NA) (3/31/89) **90**
Chablis Les Preuses 1986 ($NA) (3/31/89) **95**
Chablis Vaillon 1989 $20 (2/28/91) **87**
Chablis Vaillon 1987 $20 (3/31/89) **91**
Chablis Vaillon 1986 $21 (3/31/89) **92**
Chablis Valmur 1987 ($NA) (3/31/89) **91**
Chablis Valmur 1986 $38 (2/28/91) **90**
Chablis Vaudésir 1987 ($NA) (3/31/89) **90**

Key to Symbols

The scores reported here are the results of blind tastings conducted by our panel of senior editors. Wines that carry the initials below are results of individual tastings.

THE WINE SPECTATOR 100-POINT SCALE ***95-100***—Classic, a great wine; ***90-94***—Outstanding, superior character and style; ***80-89***—Good to very good, a wine with special qualities; ***70-79***—Average, drinkable wine that may have minor flaws; ***60-69***—Below average, drinkable but not recommended; ***50-59***—Poor, undrinkable, not recommended. "+"—With a score indicates a range; used primarily with barrel tastings to indicate a preliminary score.

SPECIAL DESIGNATIONS SS—Spectator Selection, CS—Cellar Selection, BB—Best Buy, ($NA)—Price not available, (NR)—Not released.

TASTER'S INITIALS (JG)—Jim Gordon, (HS)—Harvey Steiman, (JL)—James Laube, (JS)—James Suckling, (TM)—Thomas Matthews, (TR)—Terry Robards, (PM)—Per-Henrik Mansson, (BT)—Barrel Tasting (these wines were tasted blind from barrel samples), (CA-date)—*California's Great Cabernets* by James Laube, (CH-date)—*California's Great Chardonnays* by James Laube, (VP-date)—*Vintage Port* by James Suckling.

DATE TASTED Dates in parentheses represent the issue in which the rating was published.

Chablis Vaudésir 1986 $36 (3/31/89) **91**
Chablis Vaudevey 1987 ($NA) (3/31/89) **88**
Chablis Vaudevey 1986 ($NA) (3/31/89) **87**
Chablis Voucoupin 1987 ($NA) (3/31/89) **84**
Chablis Voucoupin 1986 ($NA) (3/31/89) **86**
Mâcon-Villages 1990 $9 (3/31/92) **68**

BERNARD MOREAU (France/Burgundy)
Chassagne-Montrachet Grandes Ruchottes 1986 $38 (9/30/88) **91**
Chassagne-Montrachet Rouge Morgeot La Cardeuse 1986 $16 (12/31/88) **61**

DOMAINE JEAN MORETEAUX (France/Burgundy)
Bourgogne Pinot Noir Les Clous 1985 $9 (11/15/87) **77**
Côte de Beaune-Villages 1983 $8.50 (3/16/86) **63**

BERNARD MOREY (France/Burgundy)
Chassagne-Montrachet 1982 $11 (3/01/85) **86**
Chassagne-Montrachet Les Baudines 1986 $38 (12/15/88) **88**
Chassagne-Montrachet Les Embrazées 1986 $40 (12/15/88) **91**
Chassagne-Montrachet Morgeot 1987 $42 (5/31/89) **88**
Chassagne-Montrachet Morgeot 1986 $35 (12/15/88) **88**
Chassagne-Montrachet Rouge 1987 $20 (10/31/89) **75**
Santenay Grand Clos Rousseau 1987 $24 (10/15/89) **87**

JEAN-MARC MOREY (France/Burgundy)
Chassagne-Montrachet Les Caillerets 1989 $54 (3/31/92) **88**
Chassagne-Montrachet Les Caillerets 1986 $39 (12/15/88) **85**
Chassagne-Montrachet Les Champs-Gains 1989 $54 (3/31/92) **90**
Chassagne-Montrachet Les Champs-Gains 1986 $38 (12/15/88) **88**
Chassagne-Montrachet Les Champs-Gains 1985 $30 (10/31/87) **75**
Chassagne-Montrachet Les Chaumées 1986 $38 (12/15/88) **90**
Chassagne-Montrachet Les Chênevottes 1989 $54 (3/31/92) **91**
Chassagne-Montrachet Les Chênevottes 1986 $34 (12/15/88) **86**

DOMAINE MARC MOREY (France/Burgundy)
Beaune Les Paules 1988 $24 (8/31/90) **85**
Beaune Les Paules 1985 $15 (12/31/88) **84**
Chassagne-Montrachet 1986 $34 (9/30/88) **83**
Chassagne-Montrachet Morgeot 1986 $37 (9/30/88) **94**
Chassagne-Montrachet Virondot 1986 $42 (12/15/88) **91**

PIERRE MOREY (France/Burgundy)
Bourgogne Blanc Aligoté 1985 $9.75 (2/15/88) **74**
Bourgogne Blanc Chardonnay 1989 $20 (8/31/91) **81**
Meursault Les Charmes 1989 $64 (11/30/91) **84**
Meursault Les Charmes 1987 $41 (2/28/90) **87**
Meursault Les Charmes 1986 $47 (12/15/88) **89**
Meursault Les Genevrières 1987 $41 (11/15/89) **91**
Meursault Les Perrières 1989 $64 (8/31/91) **94**
Meursault Les Perrières 1986 $47 (12/15/88) **92**
Meursault Les Tessons 1989 $44 (3/31/92) **82**
Meursault Les Tessons 1986 $35 (12/15/88) **90**
Meursault Les Tessons 1983 $17 (10/16/85) **76**

MORGADIO ALBARINO (Spain)
Rias Baixas 1990 $22 (7/15/91) **85**
Rias Baixas Albariño 1991 $20 (5/31/92) **82**

MORGAN (United States/California)
Cabernet Sauvignon Carmel Valley 1988 $19 (11/15/91) **81**
Cabernet Sauvignon Carmel Valley 1987 $16 (9/30/90) **92**
Cabernet Sauvignon Carmel Valley 1986 $16 (9/15/89) **90**
Chardonnay Edna Valley MacGregor Vineyard 1989 $16.50 (7/15/91) **86**
Chardonnay Monterey 1990 $16.50 (4/30/92) **82**
Chardonnay Monterey 1989 Rel: $16 Cur: $18 (3/31/91) **84**
Chardonnay Monterey 1988 Rel: $15 Cur: $18 (2/28/90) **88**
Chardonnay Monterey 1987 Rel: $15 Cur: $18 (CH-5/90) **84**
Chardonnay Monterey 1986 Rel: $14 Cur: $20 (CH-5/90) **89**
Chardonnay Monterey County 1985 Rel: $14 Cur: $23 (CH-7/90) **86**
Chardonnay Monterey County 1984 Rel: $12.75 Cur: $23 (CH-5/90) **86**
Chardonnay Monterey County 1983 Rel: $12.50 Cur: $23 (CH-5/90) **80**
Chardonnay Monterey County 1982 Rel: $12 Cur: $28 (CH-5/90) **89**
Chardonnay Monterey Reserve 1989 $23 (12/31/91) **87**
Chardonnay Monterey Reserve 1988 Rel: $20 Cur: $23 (5/31/90) **89**
Chardonnay Monterey Reserve 1987 Rel: $19 Cur: $23 (7/15/89) **84**
Pinot Noir California 1989 $14 (3/31/92) **85**
Pinot Noir California 1988 $14 (4/30/91) **75**
Pinot Noir California 1987 $15 (7/31/89) **81**
Pinot Noir California 1986 $14 (6/15/88) **84**
Sauvignon Blanc Alexander Valley 1988 $8.50 (11/30/89) **83**

MORGAN (Portugal)
Vintage Port 1985 ($NA) (VP-2/90) **85**
Vintage Port 1977 ($NA) (VP-1/90) **78**
Vintage Port 1970 ($NA) (VP-2/90) **88**
Vintage Port 1966 ($NA) (VP-2/90) **80**
Vintage Port 1963 ($NA) (VP-2/90) **86**

ALBERT MOROT (France/Burgundy)
Beaune Bressandes 1988 $30 (3/31/91) **87**
Beaune Cent-Vignes 1988 $30 (4/30/91) **91**
Beaune Grèves 1988 $32 (7/15/91) **86**
Beaune Les Teurons 1988 $33 (7/15/91) **80**
Savigny-lès-Beaune Vergelesses La Bataillère 1988 $26 (3/31/91) **86**

MORRIS (Australia)
Tokay Australia Show Reserve NV $15 (7/01/87) **92**

J.W. MORRIS (United States/California)
Cabernet Sauvignon Alexander Valley 1985 $8 (2/15/89) **74**
Cabernet Sauvignon California Private Reserve 1988 $7 (11/15/91) **74**
Cabernet Sauvignon California Private Reserve 1987 $8 (3/31/90) **83**
Chardonnay California Private Reserve 1989 $8 (7/15/91) **79**
Chardonnay California Private Reserve 1988 $8 (5/15/90) **66**
Private Reserve California 1987 $3.50 (6/30/90) **70**
White Zinfandel California 1988 $5 (6/15/89) **73**

CHARLES MORTET (France/Burgundy)
Bourgogne 1989 $14 (1/31/92) **87**
Bourgogne 1986 $15 (6/15/89) **79**
Chambertin 1989 $68 (1/31/92) **94**
Chambertin 1987 $69 (3/31/90) **87**
Chambertin 1986 $62 (2/28/89) **91**

Chambertin 1985 $64 (6/15/88) **90**
Chambolle-Musigny Les Beaux Bruns 1989 $34 (1/31/92) **89**
Clos de Vougeot 1989 $47 (1/31/92) **86**
Clos de Vougeot 1986 $43 (4/15/89) **84**
Gevrey-Chambertin 1989 $25 (1/31/92) **88**
Gevrey-Chambertin 1988 $35 (2/15/91) **89**
Gevrey-Chambertin 1987 $28 (3/31/90) **86**
Gevrey-Chambertin 1986 $24 (2/28/89) **87**
Gevrey-Chambertin Les Champeaux 1989 $34 (1/31/92) **90**
Gevrey-Chambertin Les Champeaux 1988 $46 (3/15/91) **87**
Gevrey-Chambertin Les Champeaux 1987 $36 (3/31/90) **81**
Gevrey-Chambertin Les Champeaux 1986 $33 (2/28/89) **86**
Gevrey-Chambertin Clos Prieur 1989 $30 (1/31/92) **88**
Gevrey-Chambertin Clos Prieur 1988 $41 (2/15/91) **91**
Gevrey-Chambertin Clos Prieur 1987 $32 (3/31/90) **83**
Gevrey-Chambertin Clos Prieur 1986 $30 (2/28/89) **84**
Gevrey-Chambertin Clos Prieur 1985 $29 (7/31/88) **92**

MORTON (New Zealand)
Chardonnay Hawke's Bay 1990 $10 (7/15/91) **83**
Chardonnay Hawke's Bay White Label 1989 $17 (4/15/92) **76**
Chardonnay Hawke's Bay Winemakers Selection 1988 $13 (7/15/91) **78**
Chardonnay Hawke's Bay Winemakers Selection 1986 $12 (2/15/88) **90**
Chardonnay New Zealand Winery Reserve 1986 $38 (5/15/88) **90**

A. MOUEIX (France/Bordeaux)
Bordeaux Blanc 1984 $2.50 (4/16/86) BB **86**
Fronsac 1985 $9.50 (9/30/88) **83**
St.-Emilion 1981 $7.50 (9/01/85) **78**

JEAN-PIERRE MOUEIX (France/Bordeaux)
St.-Emilion 1988 $12.50 (4/30/92) **82**

MAISON MOUEIX (France/Bordeaux)
Bordeaux Rouge 1988 $6 (1/31/92) BB **81**

CHATEAUX DE MOUJAN (France/Other)
Côteaux du Languedoc 1987 $4 (8/31/89) **80**

DOMAINE DU MOULIN AUX MOINES (France/Burgundy)
Auxey-Duresses Rouge 1983 $10 (3/15/87) **76**

CHATEAU MOULIN DE BEL-AIR (France/Bordeaux)
Médoc 1989 (NR) (3/15/92) **77**

CHATEAU DU MOULIN DE LA BRIDAN (France/Bordeaux)
St.-Julien 1983 $11 (4/01/86) **76**

CHATEAU MOULIN DU CADET (France/Bordeaux)
St.-Emilion 1990 (NR) (5/15/92) (BT) **85+**
St.-Emilion 1989 (NR) (3/15/92) **86**
St.-Emilion 1988 ($NA) (6/30/89) (BT) **80+**
St.-Emilion 1987 ($NA) (6/30/89) (BT) **75+**

MOULIN DES CARRUADES (France/Bordeaux)
Pauillac 1983 $14 (10/31/86) **88**

CHATEAU MOULIN DE CITRAN (France/Bordeaux)
Haut-Médoc 1989 $14 (3/15/92) **80**

MOULIN DE DUHART (France/Bordeaux)
Pauillac 1989 (NR) (4/30/90) (BT) **80+**
Pauillac 1987 ($NA) (6/30/89) (BT) **70+**

CHATEAU MOULIN HAUT-LAROQUE (France/Bordeaux)
Fronsac 1991 (NR) (5/15/92) (BT) **80+**
Fronsac 1986 $11 (11/15/89) **78**

CHATEAU MOULIN-PEY LABRIE (France/Bordeaux)
Canon-Fronsac 1991 (NR) (5/15/92) (BT) **80+**

CHATEAU DU MOULIN DE PEYRONIN (France/Bordeaux)
Bordeaux 1986 $10 (3/31/90) **73**

CHATEAU MOULIN RICHE (France/Bordeaux)
St.-Julien 1987 $18 (11/30/89) (JS) **79**
St.-Julien 1986 $20 (11/30/89) (JS) **88**
St.-Julien 1985 $20 (6/15/88) **83**
St.-Julien 1982 $22 (11/30/89) (JS) **90**

CHATEAU MOULIN ROUGE (France/Bordeaux)
Haut-Médoc 1987 $12 (11/30/89) (JS) **74**
Haut-Médoc 1986 $14 (11/30/89) (JS) **87**
Haut-Médoc 1983 $10 (7/31/87) **83**
Haut-Médoc 1982 $13 (11/30/89) (JS) **80**

CHATEAU LA MOULINE (France/Bordeaux)
Moulis 1988 $20 (2/15/91) **81**

CHATEAU MOULINET (France/Bordeaux)
Pomerol 1989 (NR) (4/30/91) (BT) **90+**
Pomerol 1988 $17 (7/31/91) **88**
Pomerol 1987 $15 (6/30/89) (BT) **75+**
Pomerol 1986 $15 (6/30/88) (BT) **80+**
Pomerol 1982 $9.75 (5/15/89) (TR) **87**

MOUNT BAKER (United States/Washington)
Cabernet Sauvignon Washington 1988 $16 (3/31/92) **84**
Müller-Thurgau Washington 1988 $6 (10/15/89) **63**

MOUNT EDEN (United States/California)
Cabernet Sauvignon Santa Cruz Mountains 1988 $21 (5/15/90) (BT) **85+**
Cabernet Sauvignon Santa Cruz Mountains 1987 $28 (4/30/91) **65**
Cabernet Sauvignon Santa Cruz Mountains 1986 Rel: $28 Cur: $32 (8/31/90) **83**
Cabernet Sauvignon Santa Cruz Mountains 1985 Rel: $28 Cur: $37 (11/15/89) **81**
Cabernet Sauvignon Santa Cruz Mountains 1984 Rel: $22 Cur: $35 (CA-3/89) **84**
Cabernet Sauvignon Santa Cruz Mountains 1983 Rel: $20 Cur: $22 (CA-3/89) **79**
Cabernet Sauvignon Santa Cruz Mountains 1982 Rel: $18 Cur: $27 (CA-3/89) **70**
Cabernet Sauvignon Santa Cruz Mountains 1981 Rel: $18 Cur: $23 (CA-3/89) **86**
Cabernet Sauvignon Santa Cruz Mountains 1980 Rel: $30 Cur: $33 (CA-3/89) **85**
Cabernet Sauvignon Santa Cruz Mountains 1979 Rel: $25 Cur: $35 (CA-3/89) **69**
Cabernet Sauvignon Santa Cruz Mountains 1978 Rel: $25 Cur: $48 (CA-3/89) **88**
Cabernet Sauvignon Santa Cruz Mountains 1977 Rel: $20 Cur: $41 (CA-3/89) **91**
Cabernet Sauvignon Santa Cruz Mountains 1976 Rel: $20 Cur: $81 (CA-3/89) **83**
Cabernet Sauvignon Santa Cruz Mountains 1975 Rel: $20 Cur: $30 (CA-3/89) **90**
Cabernet Sauvignon Santa Cruz Mountains 1974 Rel: $20 Cur: $105 (2/15/90) (JG) **87**
Cabernet Sauvignon Santa Cruz Mountains 1973 Rel: $14 Cur: $110 (CA-3/89) **91**
Cabernet Sauvignon Santa Cruz Mountains 1972 Rel: $20 Cur: $60 (CA-3/89) **84**
Cabernet Sauvignon Santa Cruz Mountains Lathweisen Ridge 1988 $12 (4/30/91) **87**
Cabernet Sauvignon Santa Cruz Mountains Young Vines Cuvée 1987 $12 (4/15/90) **85**
Chardonnay Santa Cruz Mountains 1988 $30 (11/30/90) **88**
Chardonnay Santa Cruz Mountains 1987 Rel: $28 Cur: $39 (11/15/89) **88**
Chardonnay Santa Cruz Mountains 1986 Rel: $25 Cur: $37 (CH-3/90) **88**
Chardonnay Santa Cruz Mountains 1985 Rel: $25 Cur: $57 (CH-3/90) **87**
Chardonnay Santa Cruz Mountains 1984 Rel: $23 Cur: $56 (CH-3/90) **85**
Chardonnay Santa Cruz Mountains 1983 Rel: $20 Cur: $48 (CH-3/90) **84**
Chardonnay Santa Cruz Mountains 1982 Rel: $18 Cur: $43 (CH-3/90) **76**
Chardonnay Santa Cruz Mountains 1981 Rel: $18 Cur: $50 (CH-3/90) **89**
Chardonnay Santa Cruz Mountains 1980 Rel: $30 Cur: $52 (CH-3/90) **87**
Chardonnay Santa Cruz Mountains 1979 Rel: $16 Cur: $52 (CH-3/90) **90**
Chardonnay Santa Cruz Mountains 1978 Rel: $16 Cur: $50 (CH-3/90) **66**
Chardonnay Santa Cruz Mountains 1977 Rel: $16 Cur: $70 (CH-8/90) **85**
Chardonnay Santa Cruz Mountains 1976 Rel: $16 Cur: $50 (CH-3/90) **78**
Chardonnay Santa Cruz Mountains 1975 Rel: $14 Cur: $45 (CH-3/90) **60**
Chardonnay Santa Cruz Mountains 1974 Rel: $14 Cur: $50 (CH-3/90) **59**
Chardonnay Santa Cruz Mountains 1973 Rel: $12 Cur: $55 (CH-3/90) **82**
Chardonnay Santa Cruz Mountains 1972 Rel: $20 Cur: $50 (CH-3/90) **80**
Chardonnay Edna Valley MacGregor Vineyard 1989 Rel: $14.50 Cur: $23 (11/30/90) **89**
Chardonnay Edna Valley MacGregor Vineyard 1988 $14 (6/30/90) **83**
Chardonnay Edna Valley M.E.V. MacGregor Vineyard 1987 Rel: $14 Cur: $20 (CH-3/90) **94**
Chardonnay Edna Valley M.E.V. MacGregor Vineyard 1987 Rel: $14 Cur: $20 (4/30/89) SS **93**
Chardonnay Edna Valley M.E.V. MacGregor Vineyard 1986 Rel: $13 Cur: $16 (CH-3/90) **81**
Chardonnay Edna Valley M.E.V. MacGregor Vineyard 1985 $12.50 (CH-3/90) **87**
Chardonnay Monterey County 1982 $12.50 (4/01/84) **76**
Chardonnay Santa Barbara County 1990 $14.50 (6/15/92) **89**
Pinot Noir Santa Cruz Mountains 1987 Rel: $20 Cur: $25 (4/15/90) **79**
Pinot Noir Santa Cruz Mountains 1985 Rel: $25 Cur: $30 (6/15/88) **90**
Pinot Noir Santa Cruz Mountains 1984 Rel: $20 Cur: $30 (4/15/88) **86**
Pinot Noir Santa Cruz Mountains 1983 Rel: $18 Cur: $28 (8/31/86) **77**

MT. MADONNA (United States/California)
Chardonnay San Luis Obispo County 1987 $7.50 (3/31/89) **70**
Merlot San Luis Obispo County 1987 $8 (5/31/92) **69**

MOUNT PLEASANT (United States/Missouri)
Chardonnay Augusta Estate Limited Bottling 1989 $18 (2/29/92) **75**
Port Augusta 1988 $19 (2/29/92) **80**
Vidal Blanc Missouri Parkers' Point 1989 $12 (2/29/92) **77**
Vidal Late Harvest Augusta Ice Wine 1989 $20 (2/29/92) **78**

MOUNT VEEDER (United States/California)
Cabernet Sauvignon Napa Valley 1987 $20 (4/30/91) **85**
Cabernet Sauvignon Napa Valley 1986 Rel: $18 Cur: $21 (11/15/90) **83**
Cabernet Sauvignon Napa Valley 1985 Rel: $18 Cur: $22 (CA-3/89) **87**
Cabernet Sauvignon Napa Valley 1984 Rel: $14 Cur: $21 (CA-3/89) **88**
Cabernet Sauvignon Napa Valley 1983 Rel: $14 Cur: $23 (CA-3/89) **84**
Cabernet Sauvignon Napa Valley 1982 Rel: $12.50 Cur: $17 (CA-3/89) **68**
Cabernet Sauvignon Napa Valley 1981 Rel: $12.50 Cur: $21 (CA-3/89) **77**
Cabernet Sauvignon Napa Valley Bernstein Vineyards 1980 Rel: $13.50 Cur: $31 (CA-3/89) **87**
Cabernet Sauvignon Napa Valley Bernstein Vineyards 1979 Rel: $13.50 Cur: $42 (CA-3/89) **92**
Cabernet Sauvignon Napa Valley Bernstein Vineyards 1978 Rel: $12.75 Cur: $31 (CA-3/89) **89**
Cabernet Sauvignon Napa Valley Bernstein Vineyards 1977 Rel: $11 Cur: $32 (CA-3/89) **85**
Cabernet Sauvignon Napa Valley Bernstein Vineyards 1976 Rel: $11 Cur: $16 (CA-3/89) **77**
Cabernet Sauvignon Napa Valley Bernstein Vineyards 1975 Rel: $11 Cur: $22 (CA-3/89) **83**
Cabernet Sauvignon Napa Valley 1974 Rel: $8 Cur: $64 (CA-3/89) **80**
Cabernet Sauvignon Napa Valley 1973 Rel: $8 Cur: $65 (CA-3/89) **90**
Cabernet Sauvignon Napa Valley Sidehill Ranch 1978 Rel: $13.50 Cur: $40 (CA-3/89) **86**
Cabernet Sauvignon Napa Valley Niebaum-Coppola 1977 Rel: $9.75 Cur: $60 (CA-3/89) **88**
Chardonnay Napa Valley 1990 $14 (6/30/92) **88**
Chardonnay Napa Valley 1989 $18 (4/30/91) **83**
Chardonnay Napa Valley 1988 $15 (6/30/90) **91**
Chardonnay Napa Valley 1987 $14 (6/15/89) **83**
Chardonnay Napa County 1986 $14 (2/29/88) **86**
Chardonnay Napa County 1985 $13.50 (5/31/87) **89**
Meritage Napa Valley 1988 Rel: $18 Cur: $24 (11/15/91) **88**
Meritage Napa Valley 1986 Rel: $18 Cur: $24 (CA-3/89) **93**
Zinfandel Napa County 1982 $8.50 (3/16/85) **86**

MOUNTADAM (Australia)
Chardonnay Eden Valley 1990 $20 (2/29/92) **90**
Chardonnay Eden Valley 1989 $25 (3/31/91) **90**
Chardonnay Eden Valley High Eden Ridge 1986 $17 (5/15/88) **77**
Pinot Noir Eden Valley 1988 $25 (3/31/91) **86**

MOUNTAIN HOUSE (United States/California)
Chardonnay Sonoma County 1981 $11 (2/15/84) **90**

MOUNTAIN VALLEY (United States/Tennessee)
Blackberry Table Wine Tennessee 1991 $8 (2/29/92) **75**
Mountain Valley White Tennessee 1990 $8 (2/29/92) **74**

MOUNTAIN VIEW (United States/California)
Cabernet Sauvignon Mendocino County 1986 $6.50 (3/31/90) **79**
Cabernet Sauvignon Mendocino County 1985 $6 (2/15/89) **77**
Cabernet Sauvignon North Coast 1988 $6 (4/30/91) BB **80**
Cabernet Sauvignon North Coast 1980 $5 (4/16/84) **62**
Chardonnay Monterey County 1990 $6 (3/15/92) BB **80**
Chardonnay Monterey County 1989 $6 (4/15/91) BB **84**
Chardonnay Monterey County 1988 $6.50 (4/30/90) BB **81**
Chardonnay Monterey County 1987 $6 (4/30/89) **79**
Chardonnay Monterey County 1985 $5 (2/15/87) BB **89**
Merlot Napa County 1989 $6 (5/31/91) **72**
Pinot Noir Carneros 1986 $6 (2/28/89) BB **80**
Pinot Noir Monterey-Napa Counties 1990 $6 (4/30/92) BB **82**
Pinot Noir Monterey-Napa Counties 1989 $6 (2/28/91) BB **82**
Pinot Noir Monterey-Napa Counties 1988 $6.50 (3/31/90) **72**

LOUIS MOUSSET (France/Rhône)
Châteauneuf-du-Pape 1982 $6 (12/16/84) **75**
Côtes du Rhône 1983 $2.50 (12/16/84) BB **81**
Gigondas 1983 $6 (12/01/84) **75**

CHATEAU MOUTON-BARONNE-PHILIPPE (France/Bordeaux)
Pauillac 1990 (NR) (4/30/91) (BT) **85+**
Pauillac 1988 $25 (4/30/91) **90**
Pauillac 1987 Rel: $16 Cur: $20 (6/30/89) (BT) **80+**
Pauillac 1986 Rel: $23 Cur: $25 (5/31/89) **93**
Pauillac 1985 Rel: $18 Cur: $29 (5/15/88) SS **91**
Pauillac 1984 $17 (6/15/87) **64**

Pauillac 1983 $16 (3/01/86) **88**
Pauillac 1982 Rel: $15 Cur: $28 (4/01/85) **86**
Pauillac 1981 Rel: $12 Cur: $16 (6/01/84) **81**
Pauillac 1961 $123 (3/16/86) (TR) **62**
Pauillac 1945 $390 (3/16/86) (JL) **80**

MOUTON-CADET (France/Bordeaux)
Bordeaux 1988 $9 (4/30/91) BB **81**
Bordeaux 1987 $7.50 (4/15/90) **79**
Bordeaux 1986 $7.25 (2/15/89) BB **81**
Bordeaux 1985 $6.50 (5/15/88) BB **80**
Bordeaux Blanc 1987 $7.25 (7/31/89) **70**
Bordeaux Blanc 1986 $5.50 (5/31/88) **75**

CHATEAU MOUTON-ROTHSCHILD (France/Bordeaux)
Pauillac 1991 (NR) (5/15/92) (BT) **90+**
Pauillac 1990 (NR) (5/15/92) (BT) **95+**
Pauillac 1989 $150 (3/15/92) **99**
Pauillac 1988 $105 (4/30/91) **100**
Pauillac 1987 Rel: $56 Cur: $78 (5/15/90) **89**
Pauillac 1986 Rel: $102 Cur: $140 (5/15/91) (PM) **97**
Pauillac 1986 Rel: $102 Cur: $140 (5/31/89) CS **98**
Pauillac 1985 Rel: $90 Cur: $96 (4/30/88) **94**
Pauillac 1984 Rel: $40 Cur: $59 (3/31/87) **92**
Pauillac 1983 Rel: $57 Cur: $90 (3/01/86) **96**
Pauillac 1982 $210 (5/15/91) (PM) **93**
Pauillac 1981 Rel: $40 Cur: $100 (6/16/86) (TR) **86**
Pauillac 1980 $85 (6/16/86) (TR) **67**
Pauillac 1979 $110 (10/15/89) (JS) **96**
Pauillac 1978 $140 (5/15/91) (PM) **92**
Pauillac 1977 $78 (6/16/86) (TR) **68**
Pauillac 1976 $88 (6/16/86) (TR) **85**
Pauillac 1975 $160 (5/15/91) (PM) **89**
Pauillac 1974 $145 (6/16/86) (TR) **67**
Pauillac 1973 $120 (6/16/86) (TR) **75**
Pauillac 1972 $100 (6/16/86) (TR) **55**
Pauillac 1971 $95 (6/16/86) (TR) **78**
Pauillac 1970 $195 (5/15/91) (PM) **84**
Pauillac 1969 $220 (6/16/86) (TR) **78**
Pauillac 1968 $420 (6/16/86) (TR) **64**
Pauillac 1967 $90 (6/16/86) (TR) **87**
Pauillac 1966 $220 (5/15/91) (PM) **88**
Pauillac 1965 $850 (6/16/86) (TR) **61**
Pauillac 1964 $120 (6/16/86) (TR) **84**
Pauillac 1963 $1,150 (6/16/86) (TR) **77**
Pauillac 1962 $230 (5/15/91) (PM) **93**
Pauillac 1961 $620 (5/15/91) (PM) **90**
Pauillac 1960 $550 (6/16/86) (TR) **84**
Pauillac 1959 $500 (5/15/91) (PM) **98**
Pauillac 1958 $850 (6/16/86) (TR) **68**
Pauillac 1957 $580 (6/16/86) (TR) **86**
Pauillac 1956 $2,500 (6/16/86) (TR) **85**
Pauillac 1955 $400 (5/15/91) (PM) **95**
Pauillac 1954 $3,000 (6/16/86) (TR) **81**
Pauillac 1953 $680 (5/15/91) (PM) **94**
Pauillac 1952 $400 (6/16/86) (TR) **90**
Pauillac 1951 $1,600 (6/16/86) (TR) **84**
Pauillac 1950 $800 (6/16/86) (TR) **83**
Pauillac 1949 $1,250 (5/15/91) (PM) **87**
Pauillac 1948 $1,650 (6/16/86) (TR) **87**
Pauillac 1947 $1,350 (5/15/91) (PM) **75**
Pauillac 1946 $7,000 (6/16/86) (TR) **77**
Pauillac 1945 $2,000 (5/15/91) (PM) **100**
Pauillac 1944 $950 (6/16/86) (TR) **86**
Pauillac 1943 $500 (6/16/86) (TR) **78**
Pauillac 1940 $530 (6/16/86) (TR) **77**
Pauillac 1939 $500 (6/16/86) (TR) **55**
Pauillac 1938 $500 (6/16/86) (TR) **73**
Pauillac 1937 $440 (5/15/91) (PM) **91**
Pauillac 1936 $250 (6/16/86) (TR) **63**
Pauillac 1934 $450 (5/15/91) (PM) **90**
Pauillac 1933 $280/375ml (6/16/86) (TR) **78**
Pauillac 1929 $1,000 (5/15/91) (PM) **75**
Pauillac 1928 $950 (5/15/91) (PM) **89**
Pauillac 1926 $800 (6/16/86) (TR) **65**
Pauillac 1925 $1,100 (6/16/86) (TR) **40**
Pauillac 1924 $1,900 (6/16/86) (TR) **69**
Pauillac 1921 $500 (5/15/91) (PM) **80**
Pauillac 1920 $700 (6/16/86) (TR) **75**
Pauillac 1919 $600 (5/15/91) (PM) **79**
Pauillac 1918 $1,600 (5/15/91) (PM) **83**
Pauillac 1916 $400 (6/16/86) (TR) **67**
Pauillac 1914 $400 (6/16/86) (TR) **65**
Pauillac 1912 $400 (6/16/86) (TR) **62**
Pauillac 1910 $400 (5/15/91) (PM) **76**
Pauillac 1909 $750 (6/16/86) (TR) **65**
Pauillac 1908 $700 (6/16/86) (TR) **50**
Pauillac 1907 $600 (6/16/86) (TR) **50**
Pauillac 1906 $800 (6/16/86) (TR) **66**
Pauillac 1905 $950 (5/15/91) (PM) **88**
Pauillac 1900 $1,800 (5/15/91) (PM) **90**
Pauillac 1899 $1,800 (6/16/86) (TR) **82**
Pauillac 1888 $1,100 (6/16/86) (TR) **60**
Pauillac 1886 $1,200 (6/16/86) (TR) **60**
Pauillac 1881 $1,400 (6/16/86) (TR) **74**
Pauillac 1878 $3,200 (5/15/91) (PM) **99**
Pauillac 1874 $2,100 (5/15/91) (PM) **95**
Pauillac 1870 $3,500 (5/15/91) (PM) **87**
Pauillac 1869 $1,700 (6/16/86) (TR) **40**
Pauillac 1867 $2,100 (6/16/86) (TR) **40**

MOYER (United States/Texas)
Brut Texas NV $13 (2/29/92) **80**
Brut Texas Especial NV $9 (2/29/92) **78**
Brut Texas Natural NV $11 (7/31/89) **79**
Extra Dry Texas NV $9 (2/29/92) **81**

BODEGAS MUERZA (Spain)
Rioja Vega 1989 $7 (3/31/91) **77**
Rioja Vega Crianza 1986 $10 (3/31/91) **75**

BODEGAS MUGA-VILLFRANCA (Spain)
Navarra Mendiani 1989 $4 (6/15/91) BB **82**

BODEGAS MUGA (Spain)
Rioja 1986 $12 (5/31/91) **81**
Rioja 1985 $12 (3/31/90) (TM) **83**
Rioja 1984 $8.50 (4/30/89) **82**
Rioja 1982 $7 (11/15/87) (JL) **77**
Rioja Gran Reserva 1976 $20 (3/31/90) (TM) **77**
Rioja Prado Enea Gran Reserva 1982 $40 (11/30/91) (TM) **84**
Rioja Prado Enea Gran Reserva 1981 $35 (3/31/90) (TM) **79**
Rioja Prado Enea Gran Reserva 1976 $24 (3/31/90) (TM) **84**
Rioja Prado Enea Reserva 1981 $20 (4/30/89) **80**
Rioja Prado Enea Reserva 1978 $18 (3/31/90) **79**
Rioja White Crianza 1988 ($NA) (5/31/92) **91**

GEORGES MUGNERET (France/Burgundy)
Chambolle-Musigny Les Feusselottes 1989 $47 (4/30/92) **87**
Chambolle-Musigny Les Feusselottes 1988 $54 (11/15/90) **86**
Chambolle-Musigny Les Feusselottes 1987 $41 (10/15/89) **92**
Chambolle-Musigny Les Feusselottes 1986 $45 (11/15/88) **90**
Clos Vougeot 1988 $90 (11/15/90) **84**
Clos Vougeot 1987 $68 (10/15/89) **91**
Clos Vougeot 1986 $73 (11/30/88) **90**
Nuits-St.-Georges Les Chaignots 1989 $43 (4/30/92) **86**
Nuits-St.-Georges Les Chaignots 1988 $47 (11/15/90) **80**
Nuits-St.-Georges Les Chaignots 1987 $41 (10/15/89) **87**
Nuits-St.-Georges Les Chaignots 1986 $40 (11/15/88) **89**
Nuits-St.-Georges Les Chaignots 1984 $26 (3/15/87) **89**
Ruchottes-Chambertin 1989 $66 (4/30/92) **91**
Ruchottes-Chambertin 1988 $80 (11/15/90) **92**
Ruchottes-Chambertin 1987 $56 (10/15/89) **93**
Ruchottes-Chambertin 1986 $55 (11/15/88) **91**
Ruchottes-Chambertin 1985 $63 (2/15/88) **92**
Ruchottes-Chambertin 1984 $34 (3/15/87) **83**
Ruchottes-Chambertin 1982 $26 (9/01/85) SS **92**

GERARD MUGNERET (France/Burgundy)
Nuits-St.-Georges Les Boudots 1988 $48 (2/28/91) **76**
Nuits-St.-Georges Les Boudots 1987 $40 (7/15/90) **88**
Vosne-Romanée 1988 $37 (2/28/91) **86**
Vosne-Romanée 1987 $32 (7/15/90) **79**
Vosne-Romanée Les Suchots 1988 $57 (2/28/91) **84**
Vosne-Romanée Les Suchots 1987 $42 (7/15/90) **82**

RENE MUGNERET (France/Burgundy)
Vosne-Romanée 1985 $27 (4/30/88) **90**
Vosne-Romanée 1983 $16 (11/16/85) **73**
Vosne-Romanée 1982 $17 (7/16/85) **86**

MUGNERET-GIBOURG (France/Burgundy)
Bourgogne 1989 $17 (6/15/92) **82**
Echézeaux 1989 $62 (4/30/92) **88**
Echézeaux 1988 $70 (11/15/90) **89**
Echézeaux 1987 $50 (10/15/89) **93**
Echézeaux 1986 $55 (11/30/88) **83**
Echézeaux 1985 $57 (2/29/88) **93**
Echézeaux 1984 $32 (3/15/87) **85**
Vosne-Romanée 1989 $34 (4/30/92) **81**
Vosne-Romanée 1988 $34 (12/31/90) **64**
Vosne-Romanée 1987 $30 (10/15/89) **90**
Vosne-Romanée 1986 $33 (12/31/88) **81**
Vosne-Romanée 1985 $33 (2/29/88) **85**

B. MUGNERET-GOUACHON (France/Burgundy)
Echézeaux 1985 $29 (12/31/88) **91**

JACQUES-FREDERIC MUGNIER (France/Burgundy)
Chambolle-Musigny 1989 $41 (1/31/92) **91**
Chambolle-Musigny 1988 $48 (5/15/91) **86**
Chambolle-Musigny Les Amoureuses 1989 $62 (1/31/92) **90**
Chambolle-Musigny Les Amoureuses 1988 $80 (5/15/91) **86**
Chambolle-Musigny Les Fuées 1988 $60 (5/15/91) **89**
Musigny 1989 $125 (1/31/92) **88**

EGON MULLER (Germany)
Riesling Auslese Mosel-Saar-Ruwer Le Gallais Wiltingener Braune Kupp 1989 ($NA) (12/15/90) **89**
Riesling Auslese Mosel-Saar-Ruwer Scharzhofberger 1990 (NR) (12/15/91) **90**
Riesling Auslese Mosel-Saar-Ruwer Scharzhofberger 1989 ($NA) (12/15/90) **93**
Riesling Auslese Mosel-Saar-Ruwer Scharzhofberger Gold Cap 1990 (NR) (12/15/91) **95**
Riesling Auslese Mosel-Saar-Ruwer Scharzhofberger Gold Cap 1989 $385 (12/15/90) **97**
Riesling Beerenauslese Mosel-Saar-Ruwer Le Gallais Wiltingener Braune Kupp 1990 (NR) (12/15/91) **96**
Riesling Beerenauslese Mosel-Saar-Ruwer Le Gallais Wiltingener Braune Kupp 1989 ($NA) (12/15/90) **91**
Riesling Beerenauslese Mosel-Saar-Ruwer Scharzhofberger 1990 (NR) (12/15/91) **97**
Riesling Beerenauslese Mosel-Saar-Ruwer Scharzhofberger 1989 ($NA) (12/15/90) **95**
Riesling Beerenauslese Mosel-Saar-Ruwer Scharzhofberger 1988 $70 (9/30/89) **99**
Riesling Eiswein Mosel-Saar-Ruwer Scharzhofberger 1989 ($NA) (12/15/90) **97**
Riesling Eiswein Mosel-Saar-Ruwer Scharzhofberger 1988 ($NA) (9/30/89) **92**

Key to Symbols

The scores reported here are the results of blind tastings conducted by our panel of senior editors. Wines that carry the initials below are results of individual tastings.

THE WINE SPECTATOR 100-POINT SCALE ***95-100***—Classic, a great wine; ***90-94***—Outstanding, superior character and style; ***80-89***—Good to very good, a wine with special qualities; ***70-79***—Average, drinkable wine that may have minor flaws; ***60-69***—Below average, drinkable but not recommended; ***50-59***—Poor, undrinkable, not recommended. "+"—With a score indicates a range; used primarily with barrel tastings to indicate a preliminary score.

SPECIAL DESIGNATIONS SS—Spectator Selection, CS—Cellar Selection, BB—Best Buy, ($NA)—Price not available, (NR)—Not released.

TASTER'S INITIALS (JG)—Jim Gordon, (HS)—Harvey Steiman, (JL)—James Laube, (JS)—James Suckling, (TM)—Thomas Matthews, (TR)—Terry Robards, (PM)—Per-Henrik Mansson, (BT)—Barrel Tasting (these wines were tasted blind from barrel samples); (CA-date)—*California's Great Cabernets* by James Laube, (CH-date)—*California's Great Chardonnays* by James Laube, (VP-date)—*Vintage Port* by James Suckling.

DATE TASTED Dates in parentheses represent the issue in which the rating was published.

Riesling Kabinett Mosel-Saar-Ruwer Le Gallais Wiltingener Braune Kupp 1990 $17 (12/15/91) **85**
Riesling Kabinett Mosel-Saar-Ruwer Scharzhofberger 1990 $22 (12/15/91) **84**
Riesling Kabinett Mosel-Saar-Ruwer Scharzhofberger 1989 $25 (12/15/90) **86**
Riesling Kabinett Mosel-Saar-Ruwer Scharzhofberger 1988 $13 (9/30/89) **92**
Riesling Spätlese Mosel-Saar-Ruwer Le Gallais Wiltingener Braune Kupp 1989 $29 (12/15/90) **85**
Riesling Spätlese Mosel-Saar-Ruwer Scharzhofberger 1990 $29 (12/15/91) **88**
Riesling Spätlese Mosel-Saar-Ruwer Scharzhofberger 1989 $31 (12/15/90) **94**
Riesling Trockenbeerenauslese Mosel-Saar-Ruwer Le Gallais Wiltingener Braune Kupp 1989 ($NA) (12/15/90) **95**
Riesling Trockenbeerenauslese Mosel-Saar-Ruwer Scharzhofberger 1990 (NR) (12/15/91) **99**
Riesling Trockenbeerenauslese Mosel-Saar-Ruwer Scharzhofberger 1989 ($NA) (12/15/90) **100**

RUDOLF MULLER (Germany)
Riesling Kabinett Mosel-Saar-Ruwer Ockfener Bockstein 1985 $7 (4/15/87) **83**
Riesling Kabinett Mosel-Saar-Ruwer Piesporter Goldtröpfchen 1985 $9.50 (4/15/87) **90**
Riesling Kabinett Mosel-Saar-Ruwer Piesporter Goldtröpfchen 1983 $7.50 (6/16/85) **90**
Riesling Kabinett Mosel-Saar-Ruwer Piesporter Treppchen 1986 $6.75 (1/31/88) **78**
Riesling Kabinett Mosel-Saar-Ruwer Piesporter Treppchen 1985 $6 (4/15/87) **79**
Riesling Kabinett Mosel-Saar-Ruwer Reiler Mullay-Hofberg 1986 $7.25 (1/31/88) **76**
Riesling Kabinett Mosel-Saar-Ruwer Scharzhofberger 1985 $8 (4/15/87) **74**
Riesling Kabinett Rheinhessen Niersteiner Spiegelberg 1986 $5.75 (11/30/87) **64**
Riesling Qualitätswein Mosel-Saar-Ruwer Scharzhofberger 1985 $6.50 (5/15/87) **84**
Riesling Spätlese Mosel-Saar-Ruwer Ockfener Bockstein 1983 $9.25 (5/15/87) **72**
Riesling Spätlese Mosel-Saar-Ruwer Piesporter Treppchen 1986 $8.25 (11/30/87) **80**
Riesling Spätlese Mosel-Saar-Ruwer Wehlener Sonnenuhr 1986 $8.25 (11/30/87) **83**
Riesling Spätlese Mosel-Saar-Ruwer Wehlener Sonnenuhr 1985 $7.50 (3/31/87) **92**

MULLER-BURGGRAEF (Germany)
Riesling Auslese Mosel-Saar-Ruwer Kanzemer Sonnenberg 1990 (NR) (12/15/91) **84**
Riesling Auslese Mosel-Saar-Ruwer Ockfener Bockstein 1990 (NR) (12/15/91) **86**
Riesling Auslese Mosel-Saar-Ruwer Ockfener Geisberg 1990 (NR) (12/15/91) **85**
Riesling Auslese Mosel-Saar-Ruwer Reiler Mullay-Hofberg 1990 (NR) (12/15/91) **81**
Riesling Kabinett Mosel-Saar-Ruwer Ockfener Bockstein 1990 (NR) (12/15/91) **84**
Riesling Kabinett Mosel-Saar-Ruwer Scharzhofberger 1990 (NR) (12/15/91) **83**
Riesling Spätlese Mosel-Saar-Ruwer Kanzemer Sonnenberg 1990 (NR) (12/15/91) **80**
Riesling Spätlese Mosel-Saar-Ruwer Reiler Mullay-Hofberg 1990 (NR) (12/15/91) **85**

MULLER-CATOIR (Germany)
Muscateller Spätlese Rheinpfalz Haardter Bürgergarten 1990 (NR) (12/15/91) **92**
Rieslaner Auslese Rheinpfalz Mussbacher Eselshaut 1990 $23 (12/15/91) **93**
Rieslaner Beerenauslese Rheinpfalz Mussbacher Eselshaut 1990 $39/375ml (12/15/91) **96**
Rieslaner Trockenbeerenauslese Rheinpfalz Mussbacher Eselshaut 1990 $53/375ml (12/15/91) **97**
Riesling Kabinett Halbtrocken Rheinpfalz Haardter Bürgergarten 1990 $13 (12/15/91) **89**
Riesling Kabinett Halbtrocken Rheinpfalz Haardter Bürgergarten 1988 $9 (9/30/89) **92**
Riesling Spätlese Rheinpfalz Haardter Herrenletten 1990 $16 (12/15/91) **95**
Riesling Spätlese Trocken Rheinpfalz Mussbacher Eselshaut 1988 $14 (9/30/89) **92**
Scheurebe Eiswein Rheinpfalz Haardter Mandelring 1990 (NR) (12/15/91) **94**
Scheurebe Spätlese Rheinpfalz Haardter Mandelring 1990 $15 (12/15/91) **91**

J.Y. MULTIER (France/Rhône)
Côtes du Rhône Cépage Syrah 1990 $15 (6/15/92) **85**
Côtes du Rhône Cépage Syrah 1988 $10 (12/15/90) **74**

G.H. MUMM (France/Champagne)
Brut Blanc de Blancs Champagne Mumm de Cramant NV $43 (12/31/90) **91**
Brut Champagne Cordon Rouge 1985 $34 (12/31/90) **86**
Brut Champagne Cordon Rouge 1982 Rel: $37 Cur: $42 (12/31/88) **85**
Brut Champagne Cordon Rouge 1979 Rel: $24 Cur: $40 (2/16/86) **93**
Brut Champagne Cordon Rouge NV $25 (12/31/91) **88**
Brut Champagne Grand Cordon 1985 $100 (11/15/91) **85**
Brut Champagne René Lalou 1985 Rel: $58 Cur: $70 (12/31/90) **86**
Brut Champagne René Lalou 1982 Rel: $55 Cur: $61 (9/30/88) **90**
Brut Champagne René Lalou 1979 Rel: $56 Cur: $68 (5/16/86) **95**
Brut Rosé Champagne Cordon Rosé 1985 $45 (1/31/92) **86**
Brut Rosé Champagne Cordon Rosé 1983 $30 (12/31/89) **81**
Brut Rosé Champagne Cordon Rosé 1982 $30 (12/31/88) **83**
Extra Dry Champagne NV $20 (12/31/91) **84**
Extra Dry Champagne Cordon Vert NV $31 (1/31/92) **86**

MUMM NAPA VALLEY (United States/California)
Blanc de Noirs Napa Valley Cuvée Napa NV $15 (11/15/90) **83**
Brut Carneros Napa Valley Winery Lake Cuvée Napa 1988 $22 (11/15/91) **89**
Brut Carneros Napa Valley Winery Lake Cuvée Napa 1987 $22 (11/15/90) **91**
Brut Carneros Napa Valley Winery Lake Cuvée Napa 1986 $23 (5/31/89) **87**
Brut Napa Valley Cuvée Napa NV $14 (12/31/87) **89**
Brut Napa Valley Prestige Cuvée Napa NV $15 (12/31/90) **82**
Brut Napa Valley Reserve Cuvée Napa 1987 $22 (12/31/90) **87**
Brut Napa Valley Reserve Cuvée Napa 1985 $21 (5/31/89) **86**

ALEJANDRO HERNANDEZ MUNOZ (Chile)
Cabernet Sauvignon Maipo Cabernet Viña Portal del Alto Gran Vino 1984 $3.50 (3/15/90) **77**
Cabernet Sauvignon Maipo Viña Portal del Alto Gran Reserva Tinto 1983 $4 (9/15/90) BB **82**
Pinot Noir Maipo Viña Portal del Alto Gran Vino 1984 $3.50 (3/15/90) **74**

MURE (France/Alsace)
Brut Crémant d'Alsace Réserve NV $7 (6/15/90) **79**
Gewürztraminer Alsace Vorbourg Clos St.-Landelin Sélection de Grains Nobles 1989 $56 (9/15/91) **93**
Gewürztraminer Alsace Vorbourg Clos St.-Landelin Vendanges Tardives 1990 $28 (2/15/92) (BT) **85+**
Gewürztraminer Alsace Vorbourg Clos St.-Landelin Vendanges Tardives 1989 $29 (9/15/91) **90**
Gewürztraminer Alsace Zinnkoepflé 1990 $15 (2/15/92) **86**
Gewürztraminer Alsace Zinnkoepflé 1989 ($NA) (11/15/90) **84**
Muscat Alsace Vorbourg Clos St.-Landelin Vendanges Tardives 1989 $29 (9/15/91) **87**
Riesling Alsace Vorbourg Clos St.-Landelin 1990 (NR) (2/15/92) **85**
Riesling Alsace Vorbourg Clos St.-Landelin 1989 ($NA) (11/15/90) **87**
Riesling Alsace Vorbourg Clos St.-Landelin Sélection de Grains Nobles 1990 $67 (2/15/92) (BT) **85+**
Riesling Alsace Vorbourg Clos St.-Landelin Sélection de Grains Nobles 1989 $69 (9/15/91) **87**
Riesling Alsace Vorbourg Clos St.-Landelin Sélection de Grains Nobles 1989 ($NA) (11/15/90) **89**
Riesling Alsace Vorbourg Clos St.-Landelin Vendanges Tardives 1990 (NR) (2/15/92) (BT) **85+**
Riesling Alsace Vorbourg Clos St.-Landelin Vendanges Tardives 1989 $37 (9/15/91) **80**
Riesling Alsace Vorbourg Clos St.-Landelin Vendanges Tardives 1989 ($NA) (11/15/90) **78**
Tokay Pinot Gris Alsace Vorbourg Clos St.-Landelin 1990 $57 (2/15/92) **88**
Tokay Pinot Gris Alsace Vorbourg Clos St.-Landelin 1989 ($NA) (11/15/90) **82**
Tokay Pinot Gris Alsace Vorbourg Clos St.-Landelin Sélection de Grains Nobles 1989 $60 (9/15/91) **85**
Tokay Pinot Gris Alsace Vorbourg Clos St.-Landelin Sélection de Grains Nobles 1989 ($NA) (11/15/90) **86**
Tokay Pinot Gris Alsace Vorbourg Clos St.-Landelin Sélection de Grains Nobles 1990 (NR) (2/15/92) (BT) **90+**
Tokay Pinot Gris Alsace Vorbourg Clos St.-Landelin Vendanges Tardives 1989 $33 (9/15/91) **81**
Tokay Pinot Gris Alsace Vorbourg Clos St.-Landelin Vendanges Tardives 1989 ($NA) (11/15/90) **90**

MURPHY-GOODE (United States/California)
Cabernet Sauvignon Alexander Valley Estate Vineyard 1988 $16 (11/15/91) **87**
Cabernet Sauvignon Alexander Valley 1987 $16.50 (5/31/90) **89**
Cabernet Sauvignon Alexander Valley Premier Vineyard 1986 $16 (11/15/89) **90**
Cabernet Sauvignon Alexander Valley Goode-Ready The Second Cabernet 1989 $10 (6/15/91) **80**
Chardonnay Alexander Valley Estate Vineyard 1990 $12.50 (12/31/91) **89**
Chardonnay Alexander Valley Estate Vineyard 1989 Rel: $12 Cur: $14 (6/30/91) **82**
Chardonnay Alexander Valley Estate Vineyard 1988 Rel: $11.50 Cur: $15 (11/30/89) **91**
Chardonnay Alexander Valley Premier Vineyard 1987 Rel: $11 Cur: $14 (CH-4/90) **87**
Chardonnay Alexander Valley Estate Vineyard 1986 Rel: $10 Cur: $15 (CH-4/90) **86**
Chardonnay Alexander Valley Estate Vineyard 1985 Rel: $9 Cur: $14 (CH-4/90) **85**
Fumé Blanc Alexander Valley 1987 $7.50 (3/15/89) **76**
Fumé Blanc Alexander Valley Barrel Fermented Reserve 1990 $12.50 (2/15/92) **90**
Fumé Blanc Alexander Valley Estate Vineyard 1990 $9 (7/15/91) **87**
Fumé Blanc Alexander Valley Estate Vineyard 1988 $8 (11/30/89) **89**
Merlot Alexander Valley Murphy Ranch 1989 $15 (5/31/92) **82**
Merlot Alexander Valley Premier Vineyard 1986 $14 (1/31/89) **90**

MARQUES DE MURRIETA (Spain)
Rioja 1985 $17 (2/28/90) **87**
Rioja Gran Reserva 1978 $30 (3/31/92) **87**
Rioja Gran Reserva 1975 $35 (3/31/92) **93**
Rioja Gran Reserva 1973 ($NA) (3/31/92) **89**
Rioja Gran Reserva 1970 ($NA) (3/31/92) **83**
Rioja Reserva 1986 $20 (3/31/92) **88**
Rioja Reserva 1985 $20 (3/31/92) **90**
Rioja Reserva 1983 $13 (3/31/92) **85**
Rioja Reserva 1982 $39 (3/31/92) **84**
Rioja Reserva 1981 $39 (3/31/92) **88**
Rioja Reserva 1980 $27 (3/31/90) **83**
Rioja White 1985 $14 (3/31/90) **88**
Rioja White 1984 $13 (3/31/90) **85**
Rioja White Gran Reserva 1978 $29 (3/31/90) **91**
Rioja White Reserva 1986 $20 (5/31/92) **92**
Rioja Castillo Ygay Gran Reserva 1968 Rel: $85 Cur: $96 (3/31/90) **92**
Rioja Castillo Ygay Gran Reserva 1952 $150 (3/31/90) **94**

CHATEAU MUSAR (Other/Lebanon)
Lebanon 1983 Rel: $17 Cur: $20 (7/15/91) **86**
Lebanon 1982 Rel: $15 Cur: $18 (7/15/91) **87**
Lebanon 1981 Rel: $18 Cur: $21 (7/15/91) **84**
Lebanon 1980 Rel: $11 Cur: $24 (7/31/88) **91**

DOMAINE MUSSY (France/Burgundy)
Beaune Epenottes 1986 $28 (5/31/89) **86**
Beaune Montremenots 1986 $28 (5/31/89) **86**
Pommard 1986 $32 (4/30/89) **66**
Pommard 1985 $35 (10/15/88) **86**
Pommard Premier Cru 1986 $35 (4/30/89) **86**

PHILIPPE NADDEF (France/Burgundy)
Gevrey-Chambertin 1988 $25 (7/15/91) **80**
Gevrey-Chambertin 1987 $19 (3/31/90) **86**
Gevrey-Chambertin 1985 $25 (4/15/88) **94**
Gevrey-Chambertin Les Cazetiers 1987 $35 (3/31/90) **88**
Gevrey-Chambertin Les Champeaux 1987 $28 (3/31/90) **90**
Gevrey-Chambertin Les Champeaux 1985 $29 (3/31/88) **80**
Mazis-Chambertin 1988 $60 (7/15/91) **69**
Mazis-Chambertin 1987 $50 (3/31/90) **89**

CHATEAU NAIRAC (France/Sauternes)
Barsac 1989 ($NA) (6/15/90) (BT) **85+**
Barsac 1988 $30 (6/15/90) (BT) **85+**
Barsac 1987 $31 (6/15/90) **81**
Barsac 1986 $31 (12/31/89) **77**
Barsac 1983 Rel: $15 Cur: $29 (4/15/87) **92**

NALLE (United States/California)
Cabernet Sauvignon Dry Creek Valley 1987 $18 (1/31/91) **89**
Zinfandel Dry Creek Valley 1989 $13.50 (7/31/91) **85**
Zinfandel Dry Creek Valley 1988 Rel: $12.50 Cur: $15 (7/31/90) **89**
Zinfandel Dry Creek Valley 1987 $10 (5/31/89) SS **92**
Zinfandel Dry Creek Valley 1986 $9 (6/30/88) **90**
Zinfandel Dry Creek Valley 1985 $8 (9/15/87) **91**
Zinfandel Dry Creek Valley 1984 $7.50 (10/15/86) **91**

NAPA CREEK (United States/California)
Chardonnay Napa Valley 1989 $13 (4/30/91) **77**
Chardonnay Napa Valley 1988 $13.50 (4/15/90) **86**
Chardonnay Napa Valley 1986 $12 (5/31/88) **86**
Merlot Napa Valley 1988 $13 (3/31/91) **75**
Merlot Napa Valley 1987 $13.50 (6/15/90) **83**

NAPA RIDGE (United States/California)
Cabernet Sauvignon North Coast Coastal 1989 $6 (11/15/91) **79**
Cabernet Sauvignon North Coast 1987 $7 (11/15/90) **74**
Cabernet Sauvignon North Coast 1982 $5.75 (3/31/87) **72**
Chardonnay California 1984 $5.75 (1/31/87) BB **85**
Chardonnay Central Coast 1989 $7 (11/15/90) BB **83**
Chardonnay Central Coast 1988 $7 (6/30/90) **77**
Chardonnay North Coast 1987 $6.50 (7/15/88) **77**
Chardonnay North Coast Coastal 1989 $7 (6/30/91) BB **88**
Pinot Noir North Coast Coastal 1989 $7.50 (7/31/91) BB **82**
White Zinfandel Lodi 1988 $6 (6/15/89) **75**

NAVARRO (United States/California)
Brut Anderson Valley Gewürztraminer 1989 $8.50 (5/15/92) **82**
Cabernet Sauvignon Mendocino 1986 $16 (10/15/91) **87**
Cabernet Sauvignon Mendocino 1985 $14 (11/15/90) **87**
Chardonnay Anderson Valley 1989 $11 (11/15/91) **86**
Chardonnay Anderson Valley 1987 $9.75 (9/30/89) **89**
Chardonnay Anderson Valley Table Wine 1989 $7.50 (11/15/91) BB **81**
Chardonnay Anderson Valley Première Reserve 1988 Rel: $14 Cur: $18 (12/31/90) **89**
Chardonnay Anderson Valley Première Reserve 1987 Rel: $14 Cur: $17 (9/30/89) **84**
Chardonnay Anderson Valley Première Reserve 1986 Rel: $14 Cur: $18 (CH-3/90) **87**
Chardonnay Anderson Valley Première Reserve 1985 Rel: $12 Cur: $18 (CH-3/90) **89**
Chardonnay Anderson Valley Première Reserve 1984 Rel: $12 Cur: $22 (CH-3/90) **91**
Chardonnay Mendocino 1988 $9.75 (11/30/90) **87**
Chardonnay Mendocino 1986 $9.75 (9/30/88) **88**
Chardonnay Mendocino 1985 $8.50 (10/31/87) **88**

Chardonnay Mendocino Première Reserve 1989 $14 (12/31/91) **88**
Chardonnay Mendocino Table Wine 1987 $7 (9/30/89) BB **85**
Gewürztraminer Anderson Valley 1989 $8.50 (4/30/91) BB **89**
Gewürztraminer Anderson Valley 1988 $8.50 (1/31/90) **79**
Gewürztraminer Anderson Valley 1987 $7.50 (2/28/89) **89**
Gewürztraminer Late Harvest Anderson Valley Sweet Cluster Selected 1989 $12 (4/30/91) **86**
Gewürztraminer Late Harvest Anderson Valley Sweet Cluster Selected 1989 $15/375ml (3/15/92) **86**
Gewürztraminer Late Harvest Anderson Valley Vineyard Selection 1986 $18.50 (2/28/89) **93**
Pinot Noir Anderson Valley 1984 $12 (1/31/88) **91**
Pinot Noir Anderson Valley 1982 $9.75 (4/15/87) **82**
Pinot Noir Anderson Valley Méthode à l'Ancienne 1988 $14 (3/31/92) **89**
Pinot Noir Anderson Valley Méthode à l'Ancienne 1987 $14 (4/30/91) **85**
Pinot Noir Anderson Valley Méthode à l'Ancienne 1986 $14 (3/31/90) **87**
Pinot Noir Anderson Valley Méthode à l'Ancienne 1985 $14 (2/28/89) **85**
Pinot Noir Anderson Valley Whole Berry Fermentation 1987 $9.75 (2/28/89) **81**
Sauvignon Blanc Anderson Valley Cuvée 128 1990 $9.75 (6/15/92) **88**
White Riesling Anderson Valley 1989 $8.50 (4/30/91) **83**
White Riesling Anderson Valley 1986 $7.50 (4/30/88) **90**
White Riesling Late Harvest Anderson Valley Cluster Selected 1985 $10/375ml (5/15/87) **81**
White Riesling Late Harvest Anderson Valley Sweet Cluster Selected 1989 $15 (3/31/92) **83**
White Riesling Late Harvest Anderson Valley Sweet Cluster Selected 1986 $25 (3/31/90) **85**

NAVARRO CORREAS (Other/Argentina)
Cabernet Sauvignon Mendoza 1981 $8.50 (2/15/89) **79**

NAYLOR (United States/Pennsylvania)
Chambourcin York County 1986 $10 (2/29/92) **70**
Chardonnay York County 1990 $10 (2/29/92) **80**
Ekem York County 1990 $9 (2/29/92) **77**

K. NECKERAUER (Germany)
Riesling Kabinett Halbtrocken Rheinpfalz Weisenheimer Hasenzeile 1988 $7 (9/30/89) **72**
Riesling Spätlese Trocken Rheinpfalz Weisenheimer Altenberg 1988 $8 (9/30/89) **81**
Riesling Spätlese Trocken Rheinpfalz Weisenheimer Hahnen 1988 $8 (9/30/89) **82**

NEGRO (Italy/Piedmont)
Barbera d'Alba Nicolon 1989 $11.50 (3/15/91) **88**

CASTELLO DI NEIVE (Italy/Piedmont)
Barbaresco Vigneto Santo Stefano 1987 $20 (12/31/90) **79**
Barbaresco Vigneto Santo Stefano 1982 $27 (9/15/88) (HS) **86**
Barbera d'Alba Vigneto Messoirano 1988 $11 (7/15/91) **83**
Barbera d'Alba Vigneto Messoirano 1987 $11 (4/15/91) **69**
Dolcetto d'Alba Vigneto Basarin 1989 $12 (2/28/91) **80**
Dolcetto d'Alba Vigneto Basarin 1987 $11 (3/15/89) **80**
Dolcetto d'Alba Vigneto Valtorta 1986 $12 (3/15/89) **73**

NELSON ESTATE (United States/California)
Cabernet Franc Sonoma County 1987 $16 (4/30/91) **82**

CHATEAU NENIN (France/Bordeaux)
Pomerol 1987 $20 (6/30/88) (BT) **75+**
Pomerol 1986 $22 (6/30/89) **84**
Pomerol 1982 $26 (5/15/89) (TR) **89**
Pomerol 1959 $100 (10/15/90) (JS) **88**
Pomerol 1945 $250 (3/16/86) (JL) **74**

CHATEAU DE LA NERTHE (France/Rhône)
Châteauneuf-du-Pape 1989 $25 (10/15/91) **87**
Châteauneuf-du-Pape 1988 $25 (10/15/91) **88**
Châteauneuf-du-Pape 1986 $18 (10/15/91) **87**
Châteauneuf-du-Pape 1985 $17 (10/15/91) **86**
Châteauneuf-du-Pape 1983 $25 (10/15/91) **88**
Châteauneuf-du-Pape 1981 $30 (10/15/91) **94**
Châteauneuf-du-Pape Blanc 1990 $30 (10/15/91) **87**
Châteauneuf-du-Pape Blanc 1989 $20 (10/15/91) **87**
Châteauneuf-du-Pape Blanc Clos de Beavenir 1990 $30 (10/15/91) **87**
Châteauneuf-du-Pape Cuvée des Cadettes 1989 $30 (10/15/91) **88**
Châteauneuf-du-Pape Cuvée des Cadettes 1988 $30 (10/15/91) **89**

LUIGI & ITALO NERVI (Italy/Piedmont)
Gattinara 1983 $11 (5/31/90) **63**
Gattinara Vigneto Molsino 1983 $15 (5/31/90) **68**
Gattinara Vigneto Valferana 1983 $15 (5/31/90) **77**
Spanna 1988 $9 (7/15/91) **80**

NEUHARTH (United States/Washington)
Johannisberg Riesling Washington 1987 $8.75 (10/15/89) **65**

NEVADA CITY (United States/California)
Claret The Director's Reserve Nevada County 1989 $15 (5/31/92) **83**
Merlot Nevada County 1989 $14 (5/31/92) **80**

NEWLAN (United States/California)
Cabernet Sauvignon Napa Valley 1986 $15 (4/30/91) **89**
Cabernet Sauvignon Napa Valley 1985 $15 (3/31/90) **87**
Chardonnay Napa Valley 1990 $14 (3/31/92) **86**
Chardonnay Napa Valley 1989 $14 (7/15/91) **90**
Chardonnay Napa Valley 1988 $13 (6/15/90) **91**
Chardonnay Napa Valley 1987 $13 (6/30/90) **86**
Pinot Noir Napa Valley 1988 $18 (11/15/91) **81**
Pinot Noir Napa Valley 1987 $16 (3/31/90) **81**
Pinot Noir Napa Valley 1985 $12 (6/15/88) **88**
Pinot Noir Napa Valley Vieilles Vignes 1986 $19 (3/31/90) **76**
Pinot Noir Napa Valley Vieilles Vignes 1985 $16 (6/15/88) **80**

Key to Symbols

The scores reported here are the results of blind tastings conducted by our panel of senior editors. Wines that carry the initials below are results of individual tastings.

THE WINE SPECTATOR 100-POINT SCALE 95-100—Classic, a great wine; ***90-94***—Outstanding, superior character and style; ***80-89***—Good to very good, a wine with special qualities; ***70-79***—Average, drinkable wine that may have minor flaws; ***60-69***—Below average, drinkable but not recommended; ***50-59***—Poor, undrinkable, not recommended. "+"—With a score indicates a range; used primarily with barrel tastings to indicate a preliminary score.

SPECIAL DESIGNATIONS SS—Spectator Selection, CS—Cellar Selection, BB—Best Buy, ($NA)—Price not available, (NR)—Not released.

TASTER'S INITIALS (JG)—Jim Gordon, (HS)—Harvey Steiman, (JL)—James Laube, (JS)—James Suckling, (TM)—Thomas Matthews, (TR)—Terry Robards, (PM)—Per-Henrik Mansson, (BT)—Barrel Tasting (these wines were tasted blind from barrel samples), (CA-date)—*California's Great Cabernets* by James Laube, (CH-date)—*California's Great Chardonnays* by James Laube, (VP-date)—*Vintage Port* by James Suckling.

DATE TASTED Dates in parentheses represent the issue in which the rating was published.

NEWTON (United States/California)
Cabernet Sauvignon Napa Valley 1988 ($NA) (5/15/90) (BT) **85+**
Cabernet Sauvignon Napa Valley 1987 $17 (11/15/91) **87**
Cabernet Sauvignon Napa Valley 1986 Rel: $16 Cur: $19 (5/31/90) **91**
Cabernet Sauvignon Napa Valley 1985 Rel: $15.25 Cur: $20 (1/31/89) **89**
Cabernet Sauvignon Napa Valley 1984 Rel: $13.50 Cur: $22 (CA-3/89) **87**
Cabernet Sauvignon Napa Valley 1983 Rel: $12.50 Cur: $36 (CA-3/89) **92**
Cabernet Sauvignon Napa Valley 1983 Rel: $12.50 Cur: $36 (4/15/87) SS **96**
Cabernet Sauvignon Napa Valley 1982 Rel: $12.50 Cur: $21 (CA-3/89) **66**
Cabernet Sauvignon Napa Valley 1981 Rel: $12.50 Cur: $21 (CA-3/89) **83**
Cabernet Sauvignon Napa Valley 1980 Rel: $12 Cur: $30 (CA-3/89) **55**
Cabernet Sauvignon Napa Valley 1979 Rel: $12 Cur: $30 (CA-3/89) **85**
Claret Napa Valley 1988 $11 (3/15/91) **89**
Chardonnay Napa Valley 1989 $15 (5/15/92) **86**
Chardonnay Napa Valley 1988 $14.50 (6/30/90) **90**
Chardonnay Napa Valley 1987 $14 (3/15/90) **84**
Chardonnay Napa Valley 1986 $14 (CH-3/90) **85**
Chardonnay Napa Valley 1985 Rel: $12.75 Cur: $19 (CH-3/90) **85**
Chardonnay Napa Valley 1984 Rel: $11.50 Cur: $18 (CH-5/90) **86**
Chardonnay Napa Valley 1983 Rel: $12 Cur: $19 (CH-5/90) **89**
Chardonnay Napa Valley 1982 $16 (9/01/84) **82**
Merlot Napa Valley 1989 $20 (5/31/92) **88**
Merlot Napa Valley 1987 $17 (7/31/90) **81**
Merlot Napa Valley 1986 $15 (12/31/88) **83**
Merlot Napa Valley 1985 $14 (3/31/88) **93**
Merlot Napa Valley 1983 $11.50 (2/28/87) **90**
Merlot Napa Valley 1982 $12.50 (2/16/86) **83**
Merlot Napa Valley 1981 $12.50 (12/16/84) **91**
Merlot Napa Valley Reserve 1987 Rel: $17 Cur: $20 (4/15/89) (BT) **85+**

NEYERS (United States/California)
Cabernet Franc Napa Valley 1987 $16 (11/15/90) **79**
Cabernet Sauvignon Napa Valley 1988 $15 (11/15/91) **82**
Cabernet Sauvignon Napa Valley 1987 $15 (4/15/89) (BT) **85+**
Cabernet Sauvignon Napa Valley 1986 $15.50 (4/15/88) (BT) **85+**
Cabernet Sauvignon Napa Valley 1985 $14 (7/15/89) **83**
Cabernet Sauvignon Napa Valley 1984 $12.50 (4/30/88) **75**
Cabernet Sauvignon Napa Valley 1983 $12 (8/31/87) **79**
Chardonnay California 1987 $14 (7/15/89) **77**
Chardonnay Carneros District 1989 $17 (7/15/92) **75**
Chardonnay Carneros 1988 $17 (7/15/91) **81**
Chardonnay Napa Valley 1990 $15 (7/15/92) **82**
Chardonnay Napa Valley 1989 $15 (7/15/91) **78**
Chardonnay Napa Valley 1988 $15 (5/15/90) **79**
Chardonnay Napa Valley 1986 $12.50 (4/30/88) **81**
Chardonnay Napa Valley 1985 $12 (8/31/87) **90**

NICCOLINI (Italy/Tuscany)
Chianti 1990 $6 (4/30/92) BB **84**

VILLA NICOLA (Italy/Tuscany)
Brunello di Montalcino 1985 $32 (11/30/90) **91**
Brunello di Montalcino Riserva 1981 $14 (9/15/88) **75**
Rosso di Montalcino 1988 $15 (1/31/91) **89**

NICOLAS (France/Beaujolais)
Beaujolais-Villages 1989 $8 (11/15/90) BB **82**
Bonnes Mares 1959 ($NA) (8/31/90) (TR) **75**

PETER NICOLAY (Germany)
Riesling Auslese Mosel-Saar-Ruwer Erdeener Treppchen 1990 $22 (1/31/92) **91**
Riesling Auslese Mosel-Saar-Ruwer Erdener Prälat 1986 $21 (1/31/88) **83**
Riesling Auslese Mosel-Saar-Ruwer Urziger Goldwingert 1990 $35 (1/31/92) **88**
Riesling Auslese Mosel-Saar-Ruwer Urziger Goldwingert 1989 $30 (12/15/90) **89**
Riesling Auslese Mosel-Saar-Ruwer Urziger Goldwingert 1985 $10 (1/31/87) **79**
Riesling Auslese Mosel-Saar-Ruwer Urziger Würzgarten 1989 $30 (12/15/90) **83**
Riesling Auslese Trocken Mosel-Saar-Ruwer Urziger Würzgarten 1990 $35 (1/31/92) **65**
Riesling Beerenauslese Mosel-Saar-Ruwer Erdener Prälat 1990 $90 (1/31/92) **92**
Riesling Eiswein Mosel-Saar-Ruwer Urziger Würzgarten 1985 $66 (11/30/87) **94**
Riesling Kabinett Mosel-Saar-Ruwer Erdener Treppchen Artist 1986 $40/1.5L (9/15/88) **77**
Riesling Kabinett Mosel-Saar-Ruwer Urziger Goldwinger 1988 ($NA) (9/30/89) **85**
Riesling Kabinett Mosel-Saar-Ruwer Urziger Würzgarten 1986 $10 (11/30/87) **90**
Riesling Kabinett Mosel-Saar-Ruwer Urziger Würzgarten 1985 $7 (11/15/86) **85**
Riesling Spätlese Mosel-Saar-Ruwer Erdener Treppchen 1985 $8 (11/15/86) **68**
Riesling Spätlese Mosel-Saar-Ruwer Urziger Goldwingert 1990 $22 (1/31/92) **87**
Riesling Spätlese Mosel-Saar-Ruwer Urziger Goldwingert 1986 ($NA) (4/15/89) **86**
Riesling Spätlese Mosel-Saar-Ruwer Urziger Goldwingert 1985 ($NA) (4/15/89) **84**
Riesling Trockenbeerenauslese Mosel-Saar-Ruwer Urziger Goldwingert 1990 $350 (1/31/92) **94**
Riesling Trockenbeerenauslese Mosel-Saar-Ruwer Urziger Würzgarten 1989 $325 (12/15/90) **91**

CHATEAU NICOT (France/Bordeaux)
Haut-Benauge Blanc 1984 $4 (11/16/85) **69**

GUSTAVE NIEBAUM (United States/California)
Cabernet Sauvignon Napa Valley Reference 1985 $13.50 (10/31/89) **89**
Cabernet Sauvignon Napa Valley Tench Vineyard 1986 $16 (10/15/89) **93**
Chardonnay Carneros Napa Valley Bayview Vineyard 1988 $14.50 (10/31/89) **91**
Chardonnay Carneros Napa Valley Bayview Vineyard Barrel Fermented 1989 $15 (6/30/92) **86**
Chardonnay Carneros Napa Valley Bayview Vineyard Special Reserve 1988 $18 (5/31/90) **90**
Chardonnay Carneros Napa Valley Laird Vineyards 1989 $13.50 (1/31/91) **82**
Chardonnay Carneros Napa Valley Laird Vineyards 1988 $13.50 (10/31/89) **90**
Chardonnay Napa Valley Reference 1990 $11 (7/15/92) **85**
Chardonnay Napa Valley Reference 1989 $11 (6/15/91) **86**
Chevrier Herrick Vineyard Napa Valley 1988 $11.50 (12/15/89) **88**

NIEBAUM-COPPOLA (United States/California)
Rubicon Napa Valley 1991 (NR) (5/15/92) (BT) **87+**
Rubicon Napa Valley 1989 (NR) (5/15/91) (BT) **85+**
Rubicon Napa Valley 1988 ($NA) (5/15/90) (BT) **85+**
Rubicon Napa Valley 1986 ($NA) (CA-3/89) **92**
Rubicon Napa Valley 1985 Rel: $25 Cur: $35 (11/15/90) **87**
Rubicon Napa Valley 1984 Rel: $30 Cur: $35 (CA-3/89) **85**
Rubicon Napa Valley 1982 $40 (10/15/89) **88**
Rubicon Napa Valley 1981 Rel: $35 Cur: $42 (CA-3/89) **87**
Rubicon Napa Valley 1980 Rel: $30 Cur: $35 (CA-3/89) **87**
Rubicon Napa Valley 1979 Rel: $25 Cur: $44 (CA-3/89) **75**
Rubicon Napa Valley 1978 Rel: $25 Cur: $50 (CA-3/89) **88**
Rubicon Napa Valley 1977 ($NA) (2/28/87) (JG) **93**

MICHEL NIELLON (France/Burgundy)
Chassagne-Montrachet Les Vergers 1988 $38 (8/31/91) **87**

Chevalier-Montrachet 1988 $92 (8/31/91) **86**

NIEPOORT (Portugal)
Vintage Port 1987 Rel: $27 Cur: $29 (VP-11/89) **91**
Vintage Port 1985 Rel: $25 Cur: $39 (VP-6/90) **92**
Vintage Port 1983 Rel: $14 Cur: $41 (VP-6/90) **84**
Vintage Port 1982 Rel: $13 Cur: $39 (VP-6/90) **90**
Vintage Port 1980 Rel: $12 Cur: $41 (VP-6/90) **87**
Vintage Port 1978 Rel: $11 Cur: $32 (VP-11/89) **81**
Vintage Port 1977 Rel: $11 Cur: $50 (VP-4/90) **89**
Vintage Port 1975 $37 (VP-11/89) **79**
Vintage Port 1970 $55 (VP-1/90) **93**
Vintage Port 1966 $70 (VP-11/89) **89**
Vintage Port 1963 $90 (VP-11/89) **90**
Vintage Port 1955 $175 (VP-8/90) **98**
Vintage Port 1945 $250 (VP-2/90) **97**
Vintage Port 1942 $240 (VP-4/90) **93**
Vintage Port 1927 $300 (VP-4/90) **97**

HOUSE OF NOBILO (New Zealand)
Chardonnay Gisborne 1990 $15 (9/15/91) **91**
Chardonnay Gisborne Tietjen Vineyard Reserve 1989 $18 (9/15/91) **93**
Pinotage Huapai Valley 1988 $15 (7/15/91) **82**

DOMAINE LA NOBLE (France/Other)
Merlot Vin de Pays de l'Aude 1990 $7 (3/31/92) **73**

NOIROT-CARRIERE (France/Burgundy)
Meursault Les Perrières 1986 $39 (2/28/90) **77**

NORMANS (Australia)
Chardonnay South Australia Chais Clarendon 1989 $14 (2/15/92) **78**
Chardonnay South Australia Chandlers Hill 1991 $7 (2/29/92) BB **86**

NORTH COAST CELLARS (United States/California)
White Zinfandel North Coast 1987 $6 (6/15/89) **68**

NOZZOLE (Italy/Tuscany)
Chardonnay Vigneto le Bruniche 1988 $9.25 (3/31/90) **86**
Chianti Classico Riserva 1986 $9.50 (10/31/91) **83**
Chianti Classico Riserva 1985 $13 (9/15/91) **88**
Chianti Classico Riserva 1981 $7 (10/31/87) **72**
Chianti Classico Vigneto la Forra 1982 $20 (10/31/91) **77**
Il Pareto 1988 ($NA) (9/15/91) **89**

NUESTRA SENORA DE LA ANTIGUA (Spain)
Rioja 1982 ($NA) (11/15/87) (JL) **84**

OAK BLUFFS (Chile)
Cabernet Sauvignon Colchagua 1990 $6 (6/15/92) BB **85**
Sauvignon Blanc Colchagua 1990 $6 (6/15/92) **70**

OAK KNOLL (United States/Oregon)
Chardonnay Willamette Valley 1988 $11 (3/31/91) **83**
Pinot Noir Oregon Vintage Select 1983 $20 (2/15/90) **78**
Pinot Noir Oregon Vintage Select 1982 $25 (2/15/90) **77**
Pinot Noir Willamette Valley 1988 $11 (4/15/91) **81**
Pinot Noir Willamette Valley 1985 $10 (6/15/87) **65**
Pinot Noir Willamette Valley Vintage Select 1988 $18 (5/31/91) **81**
Pinot Noir Willamette Valley Vintage Select 1987 $17.50 (2/15/90) **77**
Pinot Noir Willamette Valley Vintage Select 1985 $17.50 (2/15/90) **59**

OAKFORD (United States/California)
Cabernet Sauvignon Napa Valley 1987 $25 (11/15/90) **91**

OAKVILLE BENCH (United States/California)
Cabernet Sauvignon Napa Valley 1989 $12 (3/15/92) **87**
Chardonnay Napa Valley 1989 $12 (7/15/92) **85**

LUIGI OBERTO (Italy/Piedmont)
Dolcetto d'Alba 1990 $14 (3/31/92) **87**

OBESTER (United States/California)
Chardonnay Mendocino County 1988 $13 (7/15/91) **83**
Chardonnay Mendocino County Barrel Fermented 1989 $13 (7/15/91) **71**

OCHOA (Spain)
Cabernet Sauvignon Navarra 1987 $14 (9/30/91) **77**
Navarra 1988 $8 (9/30/91) BB **83**
Navarra 1987 $14 (9/30/91) **79**
Navarra 1986 $5.50 (4/15/89) **73**
Navarra Crianza 1986 $10 (11/15/91) **73**
Navarra Crianza 1984 $7.50 (4/15/89) **82**
Navarra Reserva 1982 $14 (9/30/91) **73**
Navarra Reserva 1980 $10.50 (4/15/89) **85**
Navarra White 1989 $8 (11/15/91) **74**

OCTOPUS MOUNTAIN (United States/California)
Cabernet Sauvignon Anderson Valley Dennison Vineyards 1989 $12.50 (7/31/91) **83**
Pinot Noir Anderson Valley 1989 $12.50 (10/31/91) **86**
Sauvignon Blanc Anderson Valley 1989 $9 (10/15/91) **87**

ODDERO (Italy/Piedmont)
Barbaresco 1982 $15 (9/15/88) **84**
Barbera d'Alba 1985 $9 (7/15/88) **77**
Barolo 1983 $15 (9/15/88) (HS) **85**
Barolo 1982 $14 (9/15/88) (HS) **92**
Barolo 1980 $7 (5/16/86) **73**
Barolo Rocche di Bussia 1985 $21 (8/31/91) **65**
Chardonnay delle Langhe 1990 $11 (1/31/92) **77**
Dolcetto d'Alba 1989 $8.75 (4/30/91) **78**
Dolcetto d'Alba 1987 $9.50 (3/15/89) **78**
Dolcetto d'Alba 1986 $9.50 (3/15/89) **85**

OFFLEY (Portugal)
Tawny Port 20-Year-Old Baron Forrester NV $35 (2/28/90) (JS) **89**
Vintage Port 1987 ($NA) (VP-1/90) **84**
Vintage Port Boa Vista 1987 ($NA) (VP-1/90) **88**
Vintage Port Boa Vista 1985 Rel: $22 Cur: $35 (VP-6/90) **89**
Vintage Port Boa Vista 1983 Rel: $22 Cur: $33 (VP-1/90) **91**
Vintage Port Boa Vista 1982 Rel: $18 Cur: $29 (VP-6/90) **84**
Vintage Port Boa Vista 1980 Rel: $14 Cur: $29 (VP-6/90) **90**
Vintage Port Boa Vista 1977 Rel: $11 Cur: $40 (VP-1/90) **88**
Vintage Port Boa Vista 1975 $27 (VP-2/89) **75**
Vintage Port Boa Vista 1972 $30 (VP-2/89) **79**
Vintage Port Boa Vista 1970 $56 (VP-2/89) **81**
Vintage Port Boa Vista 1966 $80 (VP-2/89) **90**
Vintage Port Boa Vista 1963 $106 (VP-2/89) **80**
Vintage Port Boa Vista 1960 $60 (VP-2/89) **78**

MICHEL OGIER (France/Rhône)
Côte-Rôtie 1988 $38 (11/15/91) **87**

OJAI (United States/California)
Cabernet Syrah California Red 1986 $7.50 (4/15/89) **74**
Chardonnay Santa Barbara County 1990 $15 (7/15/92) **81**
Cuvée Spéciale Sainte Hélène California 1989 $12.50 (9/15/91) **76**
Syrah California 1986 $7.50 (4/15/89) **77**

BODEGAS OLARRA (Spain)
Rioja 1982 ($NA) (11/15/87) (JL) **86**
Rioja Añares 1987 $6.50 (3/31/92) **79**
Rioja Añares 1985 $6 (2/28/89) BB **82**
Rioja Añares 1983 $6.50 (2/28/90) **76**
Rioja Añares Gran Reserva 1983 $19 (3/31/92) **75**
Rioja Añares Gran Reserva 1982 $27 (11/30/91) (TM) **75**
Rioja Añares Gran Reserva 1981 $25 (3/31/92) **76**
Rioja Añares Reserva 1985 $25 (3/31/92) **83**
Rioja Añares Reserva 1983 $12 (2/28/90) **73**
Rioja Añares Reserva 1981 $8 (9/30/86) **88**
Rioja Cerro Añon 1984 $4.50 (12/01/85) **70**
Rioja Cerro Añon 1980 $4.50 (4/01/85) **75**
Rioja Cerro Añon Gran Reserva 1983 $19 (3/31/92) **83**
Rioja Cerro Añon Gran Reserva 1982 $27 (11/30/91) (TM) **71**
Rioja Cerro Añon Gran Reserva 1981 $25 (3/31/92) **87**
Rioja Cerro Añon Gran Reserva 1973 ($NA) (3/31/92) **81**
Rioja Cerro Añon Gran Reserva 1970 ($NA) (3/31/92) **75**
Rioja Cerro Añon Reserva 1985 ($NA) (3/31/92) **73**
Rioja Cerro Añon Reserva 1983 $10.50 (3/31/90) **61**
Rioja Cerro Añon Reserva 1981 $8 (9/30/86) **78**
Rioja Cerro Añon Reserva 1978 $8 (3/01/85) **83**
Rioja Reserva 1978 $7.50 (3/16/85) **82**
Rioja Tinto 1983 $5 (9/30/86) BB **87**
Rioja Tinto 1980 $4.50 (3/16/85) BB **87**
Rioja White Añares Blanco Seco 1988 $7 (3/31/90) BB **82**

OLIVER (United States/Indiana)
Gewürztraminer Indiana 1989 $8.75 (2/29/92) **73**
Merlot Indiana 1988 $15 (2/29/92) **82**
Sauvignon Blanc Indiana 1990 $10 (2/29/92) **84**

OLIVET LANE (United States/California)
Chardonnay Russian River Valley 1989 $12 (7/15/91) **80**
Pinot Noir Russian River Valley 1988 $9 (6/30/91) BB **85**

CHATEAU OLIVIER (France/Bordeaux)
Pessac-Léognan 1991 (NR) (5/15/92) (BT) **80+**
Pessac-Léognan 1990 (NR) (5/15/92) (BT) **90+**
Pessac-Léognan 1989 Rel: $19 Cur: $21 (3/15/92) SS **95**
Pessac-Léognan 1988 Rel: $23 Cur: $31 (2/15/91) **91**
Pessac-Léognan 1987 Rel: $20 Cur: $24 (6/30/89) (BT) **80+**
Pessac-Léognan 1986 Rel: $16 Cur: $20 (6/30/88) (BT) **85+**
Graves 1985 Rel: $15 Cur: $25 (2/15/89) SS **93**
Graves 1983 Rel: $15 Cur: $23 (5/01/89) **92**
Graves 1982 Rel: $17 Cur: $26 (3/15/87) **89**
Graves 1981 $14 (10/16/85) **86**
Pessac-Léognan Blanc 1990 (NR) (9/30/91) (BT) **80+**
Pessac-Léognan Blanc 1989 $27 (5/15/92) **79**
Pessac-Léognan Blanc 1988 $23 (3/31/91) **82**
Pessac-Léognan Blanc 1987 Rel: $20 Cur: $25 (6/30/89) (BT) **75+**
Pessac-Léognan Blanc 1986 Rel: $16 Cur: $19 (3/31/89) **88**
Graves Blanc 1984 $15 (3/31/87) **73**

CHATEAU LES OLLIEUX (France/Other)
Corbières 1988 $5.25 (11/30/90) BB **80**

OLSON (United States/California)
Chardonnay Mendocino County 1984 $9 (4/16/86) **57**
Merlot California 1989 $11 (5/31/92) **76**

BODEGAS ONDARRE (Spain)
Rioja Ondarre 1984 $5 (11/15/88) BB **80**
Rioja Reserva 1981 $7 (12/15/88) BB **84**
Rioja Tidon 1986 $4.50 (12/15/88) **78**

OPTIMA (United States/California)
Cabernet Sauvignon Sonoma County 1987 $22 (12/15/90) **92**
Cabernet Sauvignon Sonoma County 1986 $22 (2/15/90) **91**
Cabernet Sauvignon Sonoma County 1985 $18.50 (12/15/88) **93**
Cabernet Sauvignon Sonoma County 1984 $16.50 (2/29/88) **90**
Chardonnay Sonoma County 1990 $25 (2/29/92) **87**
Chardonnay Sonoma County 1989 $25 (7/15/91) **86**

OPUS ONE (United States/California)
Napa Valley 1988 $62 (10/31/91) **92**
Napa Valley 1987 Rel: $68 Cur: $74 (11/15/90) CS **97**
Napa Valley 1986 Rel: $55 Cur: $85 (11/30/89) **95**
Napa Valley 1985 Rel: $55 Cur: $100 (6/15/89) **95**
Napa Valley 1984 Rel: $50 Cur: $82 (CA-3/89) **94**
Napa Valley 1983 Rel: $50 Cur: $78 (CA-3/89) **89**
Napa Valley 1982 Rel: $50 Cur: $84 (CA-3/89) **90**
Napa Valley 1982 Rel: $50 Cur: $84 (5/01/86) CS **93**
Napa Valley 1981 Rel: $50 Cur: $95 (CA-3/89) **88**
Napa Valley 1981 Rel: $50 Cur: $95 (5/16/85) CS **94**
Napa Valley 1980 Rel: $50 Cur: $135 (CA-3/89) **93**
Napa Valley 1980 Rel: $50 Cur: $135 (4/01/84) CS **91**
Napa Valley 1979 Rel: $50 Cur: $220 (CA-3/89) **90**

ORGANIC WINE WORKS (United States/California)
Chardonnay Sonoma County Freiberg Vinyard 1991 $9.50 (7/15/92) **72**
Merlot Napa Valley Thompson Ranch 1991 $12.50 (5/31/92) **84**

ORLANDO (Australia)
Cabernet Sauvignon Coonawarra St.-Hugo 1987 $15 (5/31/91) **78**
Cabernet Sauvignon Coonawarra St.-Hugo 1986 $8 (2/28/91) **81**
Cabernet Sauvignon Coonawarra St.-Hugo 1985 $15 (4/30/89) **90**
Cabernet Sauvignon South Eastern Australia Jacob's Creek 1989 $7 (6/30/92) **77**
Cabernet Sauvignon South Eastern Australia Jacob's Creek 1988 $7 (7/15/91) BB **83**
Cabernet Sauvignon South Eastern Australia Jacob's Creek 1987 $7 (7/31/90) BB **85**

Cabernet Sauvignon South Eastern Australia Jacob's Creek 1986 $7 (5/15/89) BB **87**
Chardonnay McLaren Vale St.-Hugo 1986 $15 (7/31/90) **68**
Chardonnay McLaren Vale St.-Hugo 1985 $15 (7/31/89) **91**
Chardonnay South Australia St.-Hugo 1988 $15 (9/15/91) **89**
Chardonnay South Eastern Australia Jacob's Creek 1991 $7 (5/31/92) BB **86**
Chardonnay South Eastern Australia Jacob's Creek 1990 $7 (5/15/91) BB **84**
Chardonnay South Eastern Australia Jacob's Creek 1989 $7 (6/15/90) **76**
Chardonnay South Eastern Australia Jacob's Creek 1988 $7 (1/31/90) **80**
Chardonnay South Eastern Australia Jacob's Creek 1987 $6.50 (3/15/89) BB **83**
Merlot South Eastern Australia Jacob's Creek 1990 $7 (6/30/92) **79**
Merlot South Eastern Australia Jacob's Creek 1989 $7 (9/30/91) **82**
Sauvignon Blanc South Eastern Australia Jacob's Creek 1990 $7 (6/30/92) **79**

CHATEAU LES ORMES DE PEZ (France/Bordeaux)
St.-Estèphe 1991 (NR) (5/15/92) (BT) **80+**
St.-Estèphe 1990 (NR) (5/15/92) (BT) **85+**
St.-Estèphe 1989 $24 (3/15/92) **86**
St.-Estèphe 1988 $21 (4/30/91) **88**
St.-Estèphe 1987 $15 (5/15/90) **83**
St.-Estèphe 1986 $21 (11/30/89) (JS) **87**
St.-Estèphe 1985 $16 (4/30/88) **89**
St.-Estèphe 1983 $17 (10/15/86) **86**
St.-Estèphe 1982 $25 (11/30/89) (JS) **87**

CHATEAU LES ORMES-SORBET (France/Bordeaux)
Médoc 1988 $20 (4/30/91) **84**
Médoc 1987 $14 (6/30/89) (BT) **75+**

DOMAINE D'ORMESSON (France/Other)
Vin de Pays d'Oc 1985 $4 (4/15/89) **77**

ORNELLAIA (Italy/Tuscany)
1988 $49 (9/15/91) **94**
1987 $46 (11/30/90) **89**
1986 Rel: $25 Cur: $44 (12/15/89) CS **93**
Masseto 1988 $49 (9/15/91) **90**

CHATEAU D'ORSAN (France/Rhône)
Côtes du Rhône 1987 $4 (11/15/88) **77**
Côtes du Rhône 1986 $4 (2/29/88) BB **81**
Côtes du Rhône 1985 $6.75 (12/15/87) **79**

OSBORNE (Portugal)
Vintage Port 1985 Rel: $20 Cur: $26 (VP-2/89) **76**
Vintage Port 1982 Rel: $13 Cur: $26 (VP-1/90) **72**
Vintage Port 1970 $50 (VP-1/90) **77**
Vintage Port 1960 $60 (VP-1/90) **82**

DOMAINE OSTERTAG (France/Alsace)
Gewürztraminer Alsace 1988 ($NA) (10/15/89) **86**
Gewürztraminer Alsace Fronholz Sélection de Grains Nobles 1990 (NR) (2/15/92) (BT) **90+**
Gewürztraminer Alsace Vignoble d'Epfig 1989 $14 (11/15/90) **90**
Gewürztraminer Alsace Vignoble d'Epfig Vendange Tardive 1990 $50 (2/15/92) (BT) **85+**
Muscat Alsace Fronholz 1990 $18 (2/15/92) **87**
Pinot Blanc Alsace Barriques 1990 $15 (2/15/92) **89**
Pinot Blanc Alsace Barriques 1989 $14 (7/31/91) **81**
Pinot Gris Alsace Barriques 1989 $24 (7/31/91) **84**
Pinot Gris Alsace Muenchberg Sélection de Grains Nobles 1990 (NR) (2/15/92) (BT) **90+**
Riesling Alsace 1988 ($NA) (10/15/89) **89**
Riesling Alsace en Barriques Heissenberg 1989 $24 (7/31/91) **85**
Riesling Alsace Fronholz 1989 $24 (7/31/91) **87**
Riesling Alsace Fronholz Elevée en Barriques Vendange Tardive 1990 (NR) (2/15/92) (BT) **85+**
Riesling Alsace Fronholz Sélection de Grains Nobles 1990 (NR) (2/15/92) (BT) **90+**
Riesling Alsace Heissenberg Elevée en Barriques Vendange Tardive 1990 $50 (2/15/92) (BT) **85+**
Riesling Alsace Muenchberg 1989 $33 (7/31/91) **88**
Riesling Alsace Muenchberg 1988 ($NA) (10/15/89) **81**
Riesling Alsace Muenchberg Sélection de Grains Nobles 1990 (NR) (2/15/92) (BT) **90+**
Riesling Alsace Muenchberg Vendange Tardive 1990 $50 (2/15/92) (BT) **90+**
Riesling Alsace Vignoble d'Epfig 1990 $16 (2/15/92) **85**
Riesling Alsace Vignoble d'Epfig 1989 $14 (7/31/91) **87**
Sylvaner Alsace Vieilles Vignes 1990 $13 (2/15/92) **83**
Sylvaner Alsace Vieilles Vignes 1989 $12 (7/31/91) **77**
Tokay Pinot Gris Alsace Barriques 1990 $26 (2/15/92) **91**
Tokay Pinot Gris Alsace Muenchberg 1988 $28 (10/15/89) **84**
Tokay Pinot Gris Alsace Muenchberg Vendange Tardive 1990 $50 (2/15/92) (BT) **85+**

DOMAINES OTT (France/Other)
Bandol Blanc 1989 $22 (6/30/92) **76**
Bandol Rosé Cuvée Marine 1989 $19 (7/15/91) **79**
Côtes de Provence Rosé Clair de Noirs 1990 $20 (6/30/92) **73**
Côtes de Provence Rosé Clair de Noirs 1987 $18.50 (7/15/89) **83**
Côtes de Provence Rosé Clair de Noirs 1986 $17.50 (7/31/88) **80**
Côtes de Provence Société Civile des Domaines Ott Frères 1987 $22 (5/31/91) **78**

OUDINOT (France/Champagne)
Brut Blanc de Blancs Champagne NV $25 (12/31/90) **74**
Brut Champagne 1985 $28 (12/31/90) **90**
Brut Rosé Champagne 1983 $25 (12/31/89) **88**

OXFORD LANDING (Australia)
Cabernet Sauvignon Shiraz South Australia 1988 $7 (9/15/90) **73**
Chardonnay South Australia 1990 $7 (2/28/91) BB **85**
Chardonnay South Australia 1989 $7 (10/15/90) BB **82**

Key to Symbols

The scores reported here are the results of blind tastings conducted by our panel of senior editors. Wines that carry the initials below are results of individual tastings.

THE WINE SPECTATOR 100-POINT SCALE ***95-100***—Classic, a great wine; ***90-94***—Outstanding, superior character and style; ***80-89***—Good to very good, a wine with special qualities; ***70-79***—Average, drinkable wine that may have minor flaws; ***60-69***—Below average, drinkable but not recommended; ***50-59***—Poor, undrinkable, not recommended. "+"—With a score indicates a range; used primarily with barrel tastings to indicate a preliminary score.

SPECIAL DESIGNATIONS SS—Spectator Selection, CS—Cellar Selection, BB—Best Buy, ($NA)—Price not available, (NR)—Not released.

TASTER'S INITIALS (JG)—Jim Gordon, (HS)—Harvey Steiman, (JL)—James Laube, (JS)—James Suckling, (TM)—Thomas Matthews, (TR)—Terry Robards, (PM)—Per-Henrik Mansson, (BT)—Barrel Tasting (these wines were tasted blind from barrel samples), (CA-date)—*California's Great Cabernets* by James Laube, (CH-date)—*California's Great Chardonnays* by James Laube, (VP-date)—*Vintage Port* by James Suckling.

DATE TASTED Dates in parentheses represent the issue in which the rating was published.

VIGNETI PACENTI SIRO (Italy/Tuscany)
Rosso di Montalcino 1989 $14 (4/30/92) **87**

PACHECO RANCH (United States/California)
Cabernet Sauvignon Marin County 1985 $10 (11/15/91) **76**

PADORNINA (Spain)
El Bierzo 1987 $8 (3/31/90) **81**
El Bierzo 1985 $7 (6/30/90) **74**

PAGE MILL (United States/California)
Pinot Noir Santa Barbara County Bien Nacido Vineyard 1985 $12.50 (6/15/88) **87**

PAGLIARESE (Italy/Tuscany)
Chianti Classico 1985 $6 (3/31/88) **76**
Chianti Classico Boscardini Riserva 1981 $9.25 (5/31/88) **82**
Chianti Classico Boscardini Riserva 1980 $9.50 (3/15/87) **85**

PAGOR (United States/California)
Merlot Santa Maria Valley 1984 $10.25 (4/30/88) **70**
Pinot Noir Santa Barbara County 1987 $10.50 (12/15/89) **85**

PAHLMEYER (United States/California)
Caldwell Vineyard Napa Valley 1990 (NR) (5/15/91) (BT) **95+**
Caldwell Vineyard Napa Valley 1989 (NR) (5/15/91) (BT) **85+**
Caldwell Vineyard Napa Valley 1988 $32 (11/15/91) **89**
Caldwell Vineyard Napa Valley 1987 $28 (11/15/90) **91**
Caldwell Vineyard Napa Valley 1986 $25 (11/15/89) **89**
Chardonnay Napa Valley Caldwell Vineyard 1989 $20 (4/30/91) **86**

BRUNO PAILLARD (France/Champagne)
Blanc de Blancs Crémant Champagne NV $36 (12/31/90) **85**
Brut Blanc de Blancs Champagne 1983 $40 (5/31/87) **94**
Brut Blanc de Blancs Champagne 1975 $42 (5/31/87) **70**
Brut Champagne 1985 $40 (12/31/90) **90**
Brut Champagne Premiére Cuvée NV $40 (12/31/91) **85**

CHATEAU PAJOT (France/Sauternes)
Sauternes 1983 $8 (1/31/88) **62**

BODEGAS PALACIO (Spain)
Rioja Cosme Palacio y Hermanos 1987 ($NA) (3/31/90) (TM) **83**
Rioja Cosme Palacio y Hermanos 1986 $9 (2/28/89) **88**
Rioja Glorioso 1986 $8 (3/31/90) (TM) **80**
Rioja Glorioso 1985 $7 (2/28/89) BB **85**
Rioja Glorioso Gran Reserva 1982 $19 (11/30/91) (TM) **84**
Rioja Glorioso Gran Reserva 1981 ($NA) (3/31/90) (TM) **75**
Rioja Glorioso Gran Reserva 1978 $15 (2/28/89) **88**
Rioja Glorioso Reserva 1982 $18 (3/31/90) (TM) **79**
Rioja Glorioso Reserva 1981 $10 (2/28/89) **83**

BODEGAS PALACIOS REMONDO (Spain)
Rioja Herencia Remondo 1987 $6 (3/31/92) **84**
Rioja Herencia Remondo 1986 $6 (3/31/92) **76**
Rioja Herencia Remondo 1985 ($NA) (3/31/90) (TM) **81**
Rioja Herencia Remondo 1982 ($NA) (11/15/87) (JL) **90**
Rioja Herencia Remondo Gran Reserva 1982 $13 (3/31/92) **75**
Rioja Herencia Remondo Gran Reserva 1981 ($NA) (3/31/92) **59**
Rioja Herencia Remondo Gran Reserva 1975 ($NA) (3/31/92) **79**
Rioja Herencia Remondo Gran Reserva 1973 ($NA) (3/31/92) **77**
Rioja Herencia Remondo Gran Reserva 1970 ($NA) (3/31/92) **59**
Rioja Herencia Remondo Reserva 1986 $9.50 (3/31/92) **79**
Rioja Herencia Remondo Reserva 1985 ($NA) (3/31/92) **71**

PODERE IL PALAZZINO (Italy/Tuscany)
Chianti Classico 1988 $16 (9/15/91) **90**
Chianti Classico 1987 $12 (3/31/90) **67**
Chianti Classico 1986 $9 (1/31/89) **86**
Chianti Classico 1985 $11 (11/30/87) SS **93**
Chianti Classico 1983 $5 (9/16/85) **78**
Chianti Classico Riserva 1985 $22 (9/15/91) **88**
Chianti Classico Riserva 1983 $21 (11/15/87) **80**
Chianti Classico Riserva 1981 $6.25 (4/16/86) **69**
Grosso Sanese 1988 $29 (3/15/91) **88**
Grosso Sanese 1987 $25 (11/30/89) (HS) **90**
Grosso Sanese 1986 $22 (2/15/89) **87**
Grosso Sanese 1985 $13 (12/15/87) **94**

DOMAINE LES PALLIERES (France/Rhône)
Gigondas 1986 $21 (11/15/91) **79**
Gigondas 1984 $14 (9/30/89) **86**
Gigondas 1983 $15 (1/31/89) **88**
Gigondas 1982 $11 (5/31/87) **89**
Gigondas 1981 $10.25 (3/15/87) **90**

CHATEAU LA PALME (France/Other)
Côtes du Frontonnais 1988 $7 (7/31/91) **63**

PALMER (United States/New York)
Cabernet Franc North Fork of Long Island Proprietor's Reserve 1989 $13 (11/15/91) **76**
Cabernet Sauvignon North Fork of Long Island 1988 $13.50 (6/30/91) (TM) **83**
Chardonnay North Fork of Long Island 1989 $11.50 (6/30/91) (TM) **84**
Chardonnay North Fork of Long Island Barrel Fermented 1989 $15 (6/30/91) (TM) **82**
Merlot North Fork of Long Island 1988 $13 (6/30/91) (TM) **86**

CHATEAU PALMER (France/Bordeaux)
Margaux 1991 (NR) (5/15/92) (BT) **85+**
Margaux 1990 (NR) (5/15/92) (BT) **90+**
Margaux 1989 $60 (3/15/92) **95**
Margaux 1988 $65 (2/28/91) CS **96**
Margaux 1987 Rel: $28 Cur: $32 (5/15/90) **84**
Margaux 1986 Rel: $40 Cur: $54 (6/15/89) **94**
Margaux 1985 Rel: $40 Cur: $50 (4/15/88) **90**
Margaux 1984 $41 (10/15/87) **84**
Margaux 1983 Rel: $45 Cur: $81 (7/16/86) CS **90**
Margaux 1982 $78 (5/01/85) **95**
Margaux 1981 Rel: $24 Cur: $52 (5/01/85) **90**
Margaux 1980 $28 (5/01/85) **86**
Margaux 1979 $67 (10/15/89) (JS) **90**
Margaux 1978 Rel: $35 Cur: $92 (5/01/85) **81**
Margaux 1962 $190 (11/30/87) (JS) **80**
Margaux 1961 $500 (3/16/86) (TR) **93**
Margaux 1959 $300 (10/15/90) (JS) **98**
Margaux 1945 $430 (3/16/86) (JL) **90**

CASTELLO DELLA PANERETTA (Italy/Tuscany)
Chianti Classico 1988 ($NA) (9/15/91) **79**
Chianti Classico Riserva 1985 ($NA) (9/15/91) **92**

PANTHER CREEK (United States/Oregon)
Pinot Noir Willamette Valley 1988 $15 (4/15/91) **75**
Pinot Noir Willamette Valley 1987 $17 (4/15/90) **74**
Pinot Noir Willamette Valley Oak Grove and Abbey Ridge Vineyards 1986 $15 (6/15/88) **69**
Pinot Noir Willamette Valley Oak Knoll and Freedom Hill Vineyards 1987 $17 (2/15/90) **58**

PANZANO (Italy/Tuscany)
Chianti Classico Riserva 1985 ($NA) (9/15/91) **86**

TONI PAOLA (Italy/Tuscany)
Vernaccia di San Gimignano Ambra delle Torri 1989 $9.75 (7/15/91) **75**

CHATEAU LE PAPE (France/Bordeaux)
Pessac-Léognan 1988 ($NA) (6/30/89) (BT) **60+**
Pessac-Léognan 1987 ($NA) (6/30/89) (BT) **75+**

CHATEAU PAPE-CLEMENT (France/Bordeaux)
Pessac-Léognan 1990 (NR) (5/15/92) (BT) **85+**
Pessac-Léognan 1989 $43 (3/15/92) **88**
Pessac-Léognan 1988 $40 (12/31/90) **93**
Pessac-Léognan 1987 Rel: $24 Cur: $27 (5/15/90) **84**
Pessac-Léognan 1986 $36 (6/30/89) **92**
Graves 1985 $44 (6/30/88) **83**
Graves 1983 Rel: $20 Cur: $30 (3/31/87) **89**
Graves 1982 Rel: $24 Cur: $34 (2/01/85) **84**
Graves 1981 Rel: $17 Cur: $20 (6/01/84) **77**
Graves 1979 $40 (10/15/89) (JS) **84**
Graves 1962 $120 (11/30/87) (JS) **90**
Graves 1961 $140 (3/16/86) (TR) **77**
Graves 1959 $100 (10/15/90) (JS) **80**

FATTORIA PARADISO (Italy/Other)
Albana di Romagna Secco Vigna dell'Olivo 1989 $13 (7/15/91) **81**
Barbarossa 1983 $13.50 (3/15/89) **80**
Chardonnay 1988 $10 (9/15/89) **83**
Pagadebit di Romagna Secco Vigna dello Spungone 1989 $13 (7/15/91) **79**
Sangiovese di Romagna Riserva Superiore Vigna delle Lepri 1987 $16 (7/15/91) **85**

PARAISO SPRINGS (United States/California)
Pinot Blanc Monterey County 1990 $8 (2/29/92) **82**

CHATEAU DE PARAZA (France/Other)
Minervois Cuvée Spéciale 1988 $7 (5/31/91) **67**

PARDUCCI (United States/California)
Cabernet Franc Mendocino County 1989 $10 (11/15/91) **85**
Cabernet Merlot Cellarmaster Selection Mendocino County 1986 $15 (4/30/91) **79**
Cabernet Merlot Cellarmaster Selection Mendocino County 1978 $12 (2/01/86) **75**
Cabernet Sauvignon Mendocino County 1984 $8.50 (7/31/88) **74**
Cabernet Sauvignon Mendocino County 1981 $6.50 (2/01/86) **73**
Cabernet Sauvignon Mendocino County 1980 $6.25 (2/01/86) **79**
Cabernet Sauvignon Mendocino County 1979 $8 (2/01/86) **69**
Cabernet Sauvignon Mendocino County 1978 $5.50 (2/01/86) **75**
Cabernet Sauvignon North Coast 1987 $9.50 (4/30/91) **80**
Chardonnay Mendocino County 1990 $10 (1/31/92) **81**
Chardonnay Mendocino County 1989 $9.50 (7/15/91) BB **83**
Chardonnay Mendocino County 1988 $9.75 (4/30/90) **83**
Chardonnay Mendocino County 1987 $7 (10/31/88) BB **85**
Chardonnay Mendocino County 1986 $8 (12/31/87) **68**
Chardonnay Mendocino County 1984 $6 (4/16/86) **55**
Chardonnay Mendocino County Cellarmaster Selection 1988 $16 (6/30/90) **91**
Chenin Blanc Mendocino 1987 $5.75 (7/31/89) **87**
Fumé Blanc Mendocino County Cellarmaster Selection 1988 $12 (4/30/91) **82**
Gewürztraminer Mendocino County 1990 $8 (3/31/92) BB **84**
Johannisberg Riesling North Coast 1990 $7 (5/31/92) **80**
Merlot Mendocino County 1983 $8 (12/15/87) **75**
Merlot North Coast 1989 $10 (11/15/91) **85**
Merlot North Coast 1988 $9.50 (4/30/91) **78**
Pinot Noir Mendocino County 1988 $7.50 (4/15/90) BB **85**
Pinot Noir Mendocino County 1986 $7 (6/15/88) **70**
Pinot Noir Mendocino County 1985 $5.50 (11/15/87) **76**
Pinot Noir Mendocino County 1983 $6 (8/31/86) **65**
Pinot Noir Mendocino County 1980 $5.65 (8/01/84) **56**
Pinot Noir Mendocino County Cellarmaster Selection 1987 $15 (4/30/91) **84**
Sauvignon Blanc Mendocino County 1988 $7.50 (5/15/90) **78**
Zinfandel Mendocino County 1986 $5.75 (7/15/88) **80**

CHATEAU DE PARENCHERE (France/Bordeaux)
Bordeaux Supérieur 1986 $9 (6/30/89) **81**

DOMAINE PARENT (France/Burgundy)
Pommard 1982 $18 (11/01/85) **83**
Pommard Les Epenottes 1959 ($NA) (8/31/90) (TR) **94**

PARIGOT PERE & FILS (France/Burgundy)
Beaune Grèves 1987 $26 (2/28/90) **88**
Pommard Les Charmots 1987 $28 (7/31/89) **87**
Pommard Les Charmots 1985 Rel: $24 Cur: $34 (6/15/87) CS **93**

PARKER (United States/California)
Chardonnay Santa Barbara County 1989 $15 (8/31/91) **87**
Johannisberg Riesling Santa Barbara County 1989 $7.50 (9/15/91) **74**

PARSONS CREEK (United States/California)
Brut Mendocino County Reserve NV $15 (5/31/89) **79**
Cabernet Sauvignon Sonoma County 1986 $13 (11/15/89) **75**
Cabernet Sauvignon Sonoma County 1985 $13 (6/30/89) **76**
Chardonnay Sonoma County Winemaker's Select 1988 $10 (2/28/91) **86**

PARUSSO (Italy/Piedmont)
Barbera d'Alba 1988 $12 (3/15/91) **85**
Barolo 1985 $27 (4/30/91) **84**
Barolo Mariondino 1986 $23 (4/30/91) **83**

PARXET (Spain)
Brut Nature Chardonnay NV $22 (5/15/92) **76**

DOMAINE JEAN PASCAL (France/Burgundy)
Pommard La Chanière 1986 $30 (10/15/88) **78**
Puligny-Montrachet Les Chalumeaux 1986 $40 (6/15/88) **91**
Puligny-Montrachet Les Champs-Gains 1985 $31 (9/15/87) **92**
Puligny-Montrachet Hameau de Blagny 1986 $40 (6/15/88) **93**

CHATEAU PASCAUD-VILLEFRANCHE (France/Sauternes)
Sauternes 1986 $24 (12/31/89) **78**
Sauternes 1983 $10 (1/31/88) **65**

BODEGA HNOS. PEREZ PASCUAS (Spain)
Ribera del Duero Viña Pedrosa 1989 $18 (4/15/92) **86**
Ribera del Duero Viña Pedrosa 1988 $16 (5/31/91) **82**
Ribera del Duero Viña Pedrosa 1987 $15 (9/30/90) **77**
Ribera del Duero Viña Pedrosa 1986 $14 (3/31/90) **88**
Ribera del Duero Viña Pedrosa 1985 $16 (9/15/88) **83**

VOLPE PASINI (Italy/North)
Chardonnay 1987 ($NA) (9/15/89) **82**

PASOLINI (Italy/Tuscany)
Chianti 1986 $6.50 (12/15/90) **78**
Chianti 1985 $5 (9/15/88) **79**

ELIA PASQUERO (Italy/Piedmont)
Barbaresco Sorì Paitin 1985 $14 (3/31/90) **88**
Barbera d'Alba Sorì Paitin 1989 $10 (11/30/91) BB **88**
Barbera d'Alba Sorì Paitin 1988 $8 (3/15/91) **83**

ANDRE PASSAT (France/Rhône)
Côte-Rôtie 1985 $25 (10/15/87) **88**

CHATEAU PATACHE D'AUX (France/Bordeaux)
Médoc 1988 Rel: $10 Cur: $17 (4/30/91) **80**
Médoc 1982 Rel: $5 Cur: $18 (5/01/85) **83**

FREDERICO PATERNINA (Spain)
Rioja Banda Azul 1985 $5 (3/15/90) BB **80**
Rioja White Banda Dorada 1987 $5 (3/31/90) **69**
Rioja White Reserva 1981 ($NA) (5/31/92) **83**

PATERNOSTER (Italy/Other)
Aglianico del Vulture 1987 $16 (1/31/92) **82**

PATRIARCHE (France/Burgundy)
Chablis Cuvée des Quatre Vents 1986 $13 (10/15/89) **79**
Côtes du Rhône-Villages Cuvée Leblanc-Vatel 1985 $5.50 (8/31/89) **77**
Hautes Côtes de Nuits Cuvée Varache 1989 $11 (1/31/92) **81**
Meursault Réserve Ste.-Anne 1986 $29 (12/15/91) **85**
Meursault Réserve Ste.-Anne 1985 $23 (9/30/89) **88**
Puligny-Montrachet 1985 $30 (9/30/89) **90**
Vin de Pays du Jardin de la France Chardonnay Patriarche 1989 $7 (8/31/91) **78**

BARON PATRICK (France/Chablis)
Chablis 1987 $17 (3/31/89) **82**
Chablis 1986 $17 (3/31/89) **84**
Chablis 1979 $13 (6/16/84) **87**
Chablis Clos 1987 $30 (3/31/89) **86**
Chablis Clos 1986 $30 (3/31/89) **89**
Chablis Premier Cru 1987 $22 (3/31/89) **85**
Chablis Premier Cru 1986 $22 (3/31/89) **85**
Chablis Valmur 1987 $30 (3/31/89) **88**
Chablis Valmur 1986 $30 (3/31/89) **91**

PATZ & HALL (United States/California)
Chardonnay Napa Valley 1990 $23 (1/31/92) **87**
Chardonnay Napa Valley 1989 $25 (7/15/91) **86**
Chardonnay Napa Valley 1988 $24 (6/30/90) **77**

PAUILLAC DE LATOUR (France/Bordeaux)
Pauillac 1991 (NR) (5/15/92) (BT) **80+**
Pauillac 1990 (NR) (5/15/92) (BT) **85+**

PATRICK M. PAUL (United States/Washington)
Cabernet Franc Walla Walla Valley 1988 $12 (2/29/92) **84**

PAT PAULSEN (United States/California)
Cabernet Sauvignon Alexander Valley 1984 $11 (4/30/87) **70**
Cabernet Sauvignon Alexander Valley 1983 $11 (7/01/86) **84**
Cabernet Sauvignon Alexander Valley 1982 $10 (3/01/85) BB **85**
Cabernet Sauvignon Sonoma County 1985 $11 (12/31/87) **78**
Cabernet Sauvignon Sonoma County 1981 $8 (1/01/84) **78**
Chardonnay Sonoma County 1983 $11 (2/16/85) **75**

DR. PAULY-BERGWEILER (Germany)
Riesling Auslese Mosel-Saar-Ruwer Bernkasteler Alte Badstube am Doctorberg 1990 $45 (1/31/92) **90**
Riesling Auslese Mosel-Saar-Ruwer Bernkasteler Alte Badstube am Doctorberg 1989 $45 (12/15/90) **80**
Riesling Auslese Mosel-Saar-Ruwer Bernkasteler Alte Badstube am Doctorberg 1985 $30 (1/31/88) **91**
Riesling Auslese Mosel-Saar-Ruwer Bernkasteler Lay 1985 $14 (1/31/87) **85**
Riesling Auslese Mosel-Saar-Ruwer Graacher Himmelreich 1988 ($NA) (9/30/89) **80**
Riesling Auslese Mosel-Saar-Ruwer Wehlener Sonnenuhr 1990 $35 (1/31/92) **87**
Riesling Auslese Mosel-Saar-Ruwer Wehlener Sonnenuhr 1983 $15.50 (9/01/85) **82**
Riesling Beerenauslese Mosel-Saar-Ruwer Bernkasteler Alte Badstube am Doctorberg 1990 $86 (1/31/92) **95**
Riesling Beerenauslese Mosel-Saar-Ruwer Bernkasteler Badstube 1989 $60 (12/15/90) **86**
Riesling Beerenauslese Mosel-Saar-Ruwer Wehlener Sonnenuhr 1989 $70 (12/15/90) **83**
Riesling Eiswein Mosel-Saar-Ruwer Bernkasteler Badstube 1985 $100 (9/15/88) **87**
Riesling Eiswein Mosel-Saar-Ruwer Graacher Himmelreich 1990 $90 (1/31/92) **96**
Riesling Eiswein Mosel-Saar-Ruwer Graacher Himmelreich 1989 $100 (12/15/90) **81**
Riesling Eiswein Mosel-Saar-Ruwer Graacher Himmelreich 1983 $90 (9/16/85) **87**
Riesling Kabinett Mosel-Saar-Ruwer Bernkasteler Alte Badstube am Doctorberg 1988 ($NA) (9/30/89) **76**
Riesling Kabinett Mosel-Saar-Ruwer Graacher Himmelreich 1985 $8 (11/15/86) **82**
Riesling Kabinett Mosel-Saar-Ruwer Wehlener Sonnenuhr 1989 $18 (12/15/90) **84**
Riesling Spätlese Mosel-Saar-Ruwer Bernkasteler Alte Badstube am Doctorberg 1990 $35 (1/31/92) **89**
Riesling Spätlese Mosel-Saar-Ruwer Bernkasteler Alte Badstube am Doctorberg 1989 $30 (12/15/90) **80**
Riesling Spätlese Mosel-Saar-Ruwer Bernkasteler Alte Badstube am Doctorberg 1986 $24 (4/15/89) **82**
Riesling Spätlese Mosel-Saar-Ruwer Bernkasteler Alte Badstube am Doctorberg 1985 ($NA) (4/15/89) **86**
Riesling Spätlese Mosel-Saar-Ruwer Bernkasteler Badstube 1985 $10 (9/30/86) **90**
Riesling Spätlese Mosel-Saar-Ruwer Bernkasteler Badstube 1983 $9.50 (10/01/85) **78**
Riesling Spätlese Mosel-Saar-Ruwer Bernkasteler Lay 1988 ($NA) (9/30/89) **86**
Riesling Spätlese Mosel-Saar-Ruwer Brauneberger Juffer 1983 $9.50 (10/01/85) **70**
Riesling Spätlese Mosel-Saar-Ruwer Wehlener Sonnenuhr 1986 $13 (11/30/87) **86**

Riesling Trockenbeerenauslese Mosel-Saar-Ruwer Bernkasteler Alte Badstube am Doctorberg 1990 $350 (1/31/92) **98**

PAUMANOK (United States/New York)
Chardonnay North Fork of Long Island 1989 $10 (6/30/91) (TM) **80**

JEAN-MARC PAVELOT (France/Burgundy)
Savigny-lès-Beaune 1986 $18 (10/15/89) **84**
Savigny-lès-Beaune Les Guettes 1985 $20 (2/15/88) **89**

LIVIO PAVESE (Italy/Piedmont)
Barbera d'Asti Superiore 1986 $9 (3/15/91) **76**
Barolo Riserva Spéciale 1978 $12 (9/16/84) **90**

CHATEAU PAVIE (France/Bordeaux)
St.-Emilion 1991 (NR) (5/15/92) (BT) **80+**
St.-Emilion 1990 (NR) (5/15/92) (BT) **85+**
St.-Emilion 1989 $45 (3/15/92) **90**
St.-Emilion 1988 $46 (3/31/91) **89**
St.-Emilion 1987 $30 (5/15/90) **82**
St.-Emilion 1986 $35 (6/30/89) **93**
St.-Emilion 1985 $38 (5/15/88) **92**
St.-Emilion 1983 Rel: $23 Cur: $28 (3/16/86) **92**
St.-Emilion 1982 Rel: $23 Cur: $45 (5/15/89) (TR) **89**
St.-Emilion 1981 Rel: $15 Cur: $21 (6/01/84) **84**
St.-Emilion 1979 $34 (10/15/89) (JS) **86**
St.-Emilion 1961 $125 (3/16/86) (TR) **62**

CHATEAU PAVIE-DECESSE (France/Bordeaux)
St.-Emilion 1991 (NR) (5/15/92) (BT) **80+**
St.-Emilion 1990 (NR) (5/15/92) (BT) **90+**
St.-Emilion 1989 $29 (3/15/92) **90**
St.-Emilion 1988 $27 (3/31/91) **94**
St.-Emilion 1987 $21 (6/30/89) (BT) **75+**
St.-Emilion 1986 $33 (6/30/89) **93**
St.-Emilion 1985 $27 (3/31/88) **89**
St.-Emilion 1983 Rel: $17 Cur: $25 (3/16/86) **92**
St.-Emilion 1982 $30 (5/15/89) (TR) **89**

CHATEAU PAVIE-MACQUIN (France/Bordeaux)
St.-Emilion 1982 ($NA) (5/15/89) (TR) **89**

PAVILLON BLANC DU CHATEAU MARGAUX (France/Bordeaux)
Bordeaux Blanc 1983 $93 (7/15/87) (HS) **86**
Bordeaux Blanc 1979 $49 (7/15/87) (HS) **91**
Bordeaux Blanc 1978 $50 (7/15/87) (HS) **80**
Bordeaux Blanc 1961 ($NA) (7/15/87) (HS) **84**
Bordeaux Blanc 1928 $300 (7/15/87) (HS) **86**
Bordeaux Blanc 1926 $300 (7/15/87) (HS) **92**

PAVILLON ROUGE DU CHATEAU MARGAUX (France/Bordeaux)
Margaux 1991 (NR) (5/15/92) (BT) **85+**
Margaux 1990 (NR) (5/15/92) (BT) **90+**
Margaux 1989 $32 (4/30/92) **87**
Margaux 1988 $30 (4/30/91) **88**
Margaux 1987 Rel: $19 Cur: $23 (5/15/90) **79**
Margaux 1986 Rel: $24 Cur: $29 (6/30/89) **84**
Margaux 1985 Rel: $23 Cur: $35 (4/15/88) SS **93**
Margaux 1983 Rel: $25 Cur: $34 (6/30/87) **80**
Margaux 1982 $38 (7/15/87) (HS) **85**
Margaux 1981 $26 (7/15/87) (HS) **87**
Margaux 1980 $20 (7/15/87) (HS) **76**
Margaux 1979 $33 (7/15/87) (HS) **78**
Margaux 1916 ($NA) (7/15/87) (HS) **63**

WEINGUT HERBERT PAZEN (Germany)
Riesling Spätlese Mosel-Saar-Ruwer Zeltinger Himmelreich 1990 $11.50 (12/15/91) **87**
Scheurebe Hochgewächs Mosel-Saar-Ruwer 1990 $9 (12/15/91) **79**

PEACHY CANYON (United States/California)
Zinfandel Paso Robles 1989 $10 (12/31/91) **82**
Zinfandel Paso Robles Especial Reserve 1989 $12 (12/31/91) **89**

PEACOCK HILL (Australia)
Chardonnay Hunter Valley 1987 $11 (5/31/88) **73**

PEBBLEWOOD (United States/California)
Merlot Alexander Valley Limited Release 1987 $9 (5/31/92) **76**

CHATEAU PECH DE JAMMES (France/Other)
Cahors 1987 $9 (6/30/90) **78**

PECONIC BAY (United States/New York)
Cabernet Sauvignon North Fork of Long Island 1988 $13 (6/30/91) (TM) **81**
Cabernet Sauvignon North Fork of Long Island 1987 $13 (6/30/91) (TM) **78**
Chardonnay North Fork of Long Island 1989 $11 (6/30/91) (TM) **80**
Chardonnay North Fork of Long Island Reserve 1989 $15 (6/30/91) (TM) **79**
Merlot North Fork of Long Island 1989 $13 (6/30/91) (TM) **78**

ROBERT PECOTA (United States/California)
Cabernet Sauvignon Napa Valley Kara's Vineyard 1991 (NR) (5/15/92) (BT) **88+**
Cabernet Sauvignon Napa Valley Kara's Vineyard 1990 (NR) (5/15/91) (BT) **90+**
Cabernet Sauvignon Napa Valley Kara's Vineyard 1989 (NR) (5/15/91) (BT) **90+**
Cabernet Sauvignon Napa Valley Kara's Vineyard 1988 Rel: $16 Cur: $20 (11/15/91) **89**
Cabernet Sauvignon Napa Valley Kara's Vineyard 1987 Rel: $16 Cur: $19 (10/15/90) **90**
Cabernet Sauvignon Napa Valley Kara's Vineyard 1986 Rel: $16 Cur: $19 (9/15/89) **86**
Cabernet Sauvignon Napa Valley Kara's Vineyard 1985 Rel: $16 Cur: $20 (CA-3/89) **86**
Cabernet Sauvignon Napa Valley Kara's Vineyard 1984 Rel: $14 Cur: $20 (CA-3/89) **85**
Cabernet Sauvignon Napa Valley 1982 Rel: $12 Cur: $20 (CA-3/89) **85**
Chardonnay Alexander Valley Canepa Vineyard 1988 $16 (5/15/90) **80**
Chardonnay Alexander Valley Canepa Vineyard 1987 Rel: $16 Cur: $20 (CH-4/90) **91**
Chardonnay Alexander Valley Canepa Vineyard 1986 Rel: $16 Cur: $19 (CH-4/90) **85**
Chardonnay Alexander Valley Canepa Vineyard 1985 Rel: $16 Cur: $18 (CH-7/90) **89**
Chardonnay Alexander Valley Canepa Vineyard 1984 Rel: $14 Cur: $18 (CH-4/90) **83**
Chardonnay Alexander Valley Canepa Vineyard 1983 Rel: $14 Cur: $18 (CH-4/90) **79**
Chardonnay Alexander Valley Canepa Vineyard 1981 Rel: $12 Cur: $20 (CH-4/90) **75**
Chardonnay Alexander Valley Canepa Vineyard 1980 Rel: $12 Cur: $20 (CH-4/90) **89**
Merlot Napa Valley Steven André 1991 (NR) (5/15/92) (BT) **86+**
Merlot Napa Valley Steven André 1990 $16.50 (5/31/92) **86**
Merlot Napa Valley Steven André 1989 $16.50 (11/15/91) **86**
Muscato di Andrea Napa Valley 1990 $9.75 (9/15/91) **87**
Muscato di Andrea Napa Valley 1989 $9.25 (7/15/90) **86**
Sauvignon Blanc Napa Valley 1989 $9.25 (8/31/90) **78**
Sauvignon Blanc Napa Valley 1985 $9.25 (10/15/86) SS **94**

REINE PEDAUQUE (France/Burgundy)
Auxey-Duresses 1989 $22 (8/31/91) **79**
Bâtard-Montrachet 1989 $100 (8/31/91) **86**
Bourgogne Blanc Chardonnay Buchère 1989 $12 (8/31/91) **81**
Chassagne-Montrachet 1989 $35 (8/31/91) **88**
Corton-Charlemagne 1989 $78 (8/31/91) **85**
Corton-Charlemagne 1985 $60 (11/15/89) **92**
Corton-Charlemagne 1982 $33 (8/01/85) **73**
Mâcon-Villages Coupées 1988 $9.50 (9/30/89) **76**
Meursault Les Genevrières 1989 $48 (8/31/91) **91**
Pouilly-Fuissé Griselles 1988 $16 (9/30/89) **76**
Puligny-Montrachet Les Folatières 1989 $42 (8/31/91) **90**
St.-Aubin 1989 $18 (8/31/91) **82**
Savigny-lès-Beaune Blanc 1989 $22 (8/31/91) **71**

CHATEAU PEDESCLAUX (France/Bordeaux)
Pauillac 1988 $20 (6/30/89) (BT) **80+**
Pauillac 1986 $18 (2/15/90) **79**

J. PEDRONCELLI (United States/California)
Brut Rosé Sonoma County 1986 $10 (7/31/89) **84**
Cabernet Sauvignon Sonoma County 1988 $9.50 (10/15/91) **83**
Cabernet Sauvignon Dry Creek Valley 1987 $8.50 (11/15/90) BB **85**
Cabernet Sauvignon Dry Creek Valley 1986 $7 (9/15/89) BB **83**
Cabernet Sauvignon Dry Creek Valley 1985 $7 (10/15/88) **79**
Cabernet Sauvignon Dry Creek Valley 1983 $6.50 (8/31/87) **75**
Cabernet Sauvignon Dry Creek Valley 1981 $6 (12/01/84) BB **80**
Cabernet Sauvignon Dry Creek Valley Reserve 1985 $14 (3/31/90) **85**
Cabernet Sauvignon Dry Creek Valley Reserve 1982 $13 (10/15/89) **73**
Chardonnay Dry Creek Valley 1990 $10 (3/31/92) **80**
Chardonnay Dry Creek Valley 1989 $9.50 (12/31/90) **77**
Chardonnay Dry Creek Valley 1988 $9 (12/15/89) **79**
Chardonnay Dry Creek Valley 1987 $8 (12/31/88) BB **85**
Chardonnay Dry Creek Valley 1986 $8 (6/15/88) **83**
Chardonnay Sonoma County 1985 $7.75 (7/31/87) **83**
Chardonnay Sonoma County 1984 $7.75 (3/01/86) **81**
Chardonnay Sonoma County 1983 $7.75 (6/01/85) **66**
Fumé Blanc Dry Creek Valley 1989 $7 (4/30/91) BB **84**
Fumé Blanc Dry Creek Valley 1988 $6 (9/15/89) BB **83**
Fumé Blanc Dry Creek Valley 1987 $6 (4/30/89) **79**
Fumé Blanc Sonoma County 1990 $8 (10/15/91) **85**
Gewürztraminer Sonoma County 1987 $5.50 (2/28/89) **71**
Merlot Sonoma County 1989 $12.50 (2/29/92) **76**
Pinot Noir Dry Creek Valley 1989 $8.50 (3/31/92) **75**
Pinot Noir Dry Creek Valley 1988 $8 (2/28/91) BB **84**
Pinot Noir Dry Creek Valley 1986 $7 (5/31/90) **70**
Pinot Noir Dry Creek Valley 1985 $7.50 (6/15/88) **76**
Pinot Noir Sonoma County 1983 $6 (4/15/88) **67**
Pinot Noir Sonoma County 1982 $5.50 (6/30/87) **68**
White Riesling Dry Creek Valley 1989 $5.50 (9/30/90) BB **81**
White Riesling Dry Creek Valley 1988 $5.50 (8/31/89) BB **87**
White Zinfandel Sonoma County 1988 $6 (6/15/89) **87**
Zinfandel Dry Creek Valley 1988 $7 (11/30/90) BB **84**
Zinfandel Dry Creek Valley 1987 $7 (7/31/90) **65**
Zinfandel Dry Creek Valley 1986 $6 (3/31/89) BB **86**
Zinfandel Dry Creek Valley 1984 $5.50 (7/15/88) BB **88**
Zinfandel Sonoma County 1983 $4.50 (9/15/87) **77**
Zinfandel Sonoma County 1982 $4.50 (10/31/86) BB **79**
Zinfandel Sonoma County 1981 $4.50 (1/01/85) **78**
Zinfandel Sonoma County Reserve 1981 $8 (11/15/87) **82**

DOMAINE DU PEGAU (France/Rhône)
Châteauneuf-du-Pape Cuvée Réserve 1988 $17 (11/15/91) **88**

PEJU (United States/California)
Cabernet Sauvignon Napa Valley HB Vineyard 1988 $30 (8/31/91) **82**
Cabernet Sauvignon Napa Valley HB Vineyard 1987 $20 (11/15/90) **87**
Cabernet Sauvignon Napa Valley HB Vineyard 1986 $20 (11/15/89) **92**
Chardonnay Late Harvest Napa Valley Select 1989 $12.50/375ml (3/15/92) **88**

DOMAINE HENRY PELLE (France/Loire)
Menetou-Salon Morogues 1987 $11 (7/15/89) **85**

PELLEGRINI FAMILY (United States/California)
Cabernet Sauvignon Alexander Valley Cloverdale Ranch Estate Cuvée 1988 $12 (6/15/91) **82**

PELLERIN (France/Beaujolais)
Brouilly 1987 $8.50 (4/15/89) **83**
Pouilly-Fuissé 1987 $12 (4/30/89) **75**

PELLIER (United States/Oregon)
Pinot Noir Willamette Valley 1985 $8 (6/15/88) **73**

PELLIGRINI (United States/California)
Chenin Blanc North Coast Vintage White 1988 $4.50 (7/31/89) **79**

DU PELOUX (France/Rhône)
Châteauneuf-du-Pape 1986 $12 (4/15/89) **85**
Côtes du Rhône 1986 $4.50 (5/15/89) **75**
Côtes du Rhône-Villages 1986 $5.50 (5/15/89) **78**

PENALBA (Spain)
Ribera del Duero 1983 $12 (2/28/90) **86**
Ribera del Duero Crianza 1985 $9 (2/28/90) **87**
Ribera del Duero Gran Reserva 1980 ($NA) (3/31/90) (TM) **73**

Key to Symbols

The scores reported here are the results of blind tastings conducted by our panel of senior editors. Wines that carry the initials below are results of individual tastings.

THE WINE SPECTATOR 100-POINT SCALE 95-100—Classic, a great wine; *90-94*—Outstanding, superior character and style; *80-89*—Good to very good, a wine with special qualities; *70-79*—Average, drinkable wine that may have minor flaws; *60-69*—Below average, drinkable but not recommended; *50-59*—Poor, undrinkable, not recommended. "+"—With a score indicates a range; used primarily with barrel tastings to indicate a preliminary score.

SPECIAL DESIGNATIONS SS—Spectator Selection, CS—Cellar Selection, BB—Best Buy, ($NA)—Price not available, (NR)—Not released.

TASTER'S INITIALS (JG)—Jim Gordon, (HS)—Harvey Steiman, (JL)—James Laube, (JS)—James Suckling, (TM)—Thomas Matthews, (TR)—Terry Robards, (PM)—Per-Henrik Mansson, (BT)—Barrel Tasting (these wines were tasted blind from barrel samples), (CA-date)—*California's Great Cabernets* by James Laube, (CH-date)—*California's Great Chardonnays* by James Laube, (VP-date)—*Vintage Port* by James Suckling.

DATE TASTED Dates in parentheses represent the issue in which the rating was published.

Ribera del Duero Reserva 1982 ($NA) (3/31/90) (TM) **70**

PENFOLDS (Australia)
Cabernet Sauvignon Shiraz South Australia Koonunga Hill 1987 $7.50 (2/28/91) BB **86**
Cabernet Sauvignon Shiraz South Australia Koonunga Hill 1986 $7.50 (5/15/89) **78**
Cabernet Sauvignon South Australia Bin 707 1987 $38 (5/31/91) **83**
Cabernet Sauvignon South Australia Bin 707 1986 $28 (9/30/89) **90**
Cabernet Sauvignon South Australia Bin 707 1981 $18 (7/01/87) **90**
Cabernet Shiraz South Australia Bin 389 1987 $14 (2/28/91) **88**
Cabernet Shiraz South Australia Bin 389 1986 $15 (1/31/90) **83**
Cabernet Shiraz South Australia Bin 389 1985 $14 (12/31/88) **86**
Cabernet Shiraz South Australia Bin 389 1983 $15 (7/01/87) **91**
Cabernet Shiraz South Australia Koonunga Hill 1984 $7 (7/01/87) **89**
Chardonnay South Australia 1988 $9.50 (1/31/90) **83**
Chardonnay South Australia 1987 $8 (2/15/89) **80**
Rhine Riesling Late Harvest South Australia 1987 $5.50/375ml (3/15/89) BB **88**
Sémillon Chardonnay Koonunga Hill South Australia 1989 $6 (9/15/90) BB **86**
Sémillon Late Harvest South Australia 1987 $6.50/375ml (3/15/89) **84**
Shiraz South Australia Grange Hermitage Bin 95 1985 $80 (2/29/92) **88**
Shiraz South Australia Grange Hermitage Bin 95 1984 $80 (4/15/91) (TM) **89**
Shiraz South Australia Grange Hermitage Bin 95 1983 $80 (3/15/91) **92**
Shiraz South Australia Grange Hermitage Bin 95 1982 Rel: $60 Cur: $80 (4/15/91) (TM) **94**
Shiraz South Australia Grange Hermitage Bin 95 1982 Rel: $60 Cur: $80 (9/30/89) CS **96**
Shiraz South Australia Grange Hermitage Bin 95 1981 Rel: $49 Cur: $70 (4/15/91) (TM) **89**
Shiraz South Australia Grange Hermitage Bin 95 1981 Rel: $49 Cur: $70 (12/31/88) CS **93**
Shiraz South Australia Grange Hermitage Bin 95 1980 $112 (4/15/91) (TM) **88**
Shiraz South Australia Grange Hermitage Bin 95 1979 $125 (4/15/91) (TM) **89**
Shiraz South Australia Grange Hermitage Bin 95 1978 $129 (4/15/91) (TM) **85**
Shiraz South Australia Grange Hermitage Bin 95 1977 $155 (4/15/91) (TM) **82**
Shiraz South Australia Grange Hermitage Bin 95 1976 $125 (4/15/91) (TM) **86**
Shiraz South Australia Grange Hermitage Bin 95 1974 $45 (4/15/91) (TM) **79**
Shiraz South Australia Grange Hermitage Bin 95 1971 $230 (4/15/91) (TM) **95**
Shiraz South Australia Grange Hermitage Bin 95 1970 $75 (4/15/91) (TM) **85**
Shiraz South Australia Grange Hermitage Bin 95 1968 $55 (4/15/91) (TM) **87**
Shiraz South Australia Grange Hermitage Bin 95 1967 $67 (4/15/91) (TM) **91**
Shiraz South Australia Grange Hermitage Bin 95 1966 $110 (4/15/91) (TM) **96**
Shiraz South Australia Grange Hermitage Bin 95 1965 $120 (4/15/91) (TM) **84**
Shiraz South Australia Grange Hermitage Bin 95 1955 $350 (4/15/91) (TM) **93**
Shiraz South Australia Magill Estate Vineyard 1985 $45 (7/31/89) **87**

CHATEAU DE PENNAUTIER (France/Other)
Cabardès 1989 $7 (12/15/91) **75**

ROBERT PEPI (United States/California)
Cabernet Sauvignon Napa Valley Vine Hill Ranch 1988 ($NA) (5/15/90) (BT) **85+**
Cabernet Sauvignon Napa Valley Vine Hill Ranch 1987 $20 (4/30/91) **90**
Cabernet Sauvignon Napa Valley Vine Hill Ranch 1986 Rel: $18 Cur: $24 (10/31/90) **88**
Cabernet Sauvignon Napa Valley Vine Hill Ranch 1985 Rel: $18 Cur: $23 (7/31/90) **85**
Cabernet Sauvignon Napa Valley Vine Hill Ranch 1984 Rel: $16 Cur: $22 (8/31/89) **80**
Cabernet Sauvignon Napa Valley Vine Hill Ranch 1983 Rel: $16 Cur: $24 (CA-3/89) **80**
Cabernet Sauvignon Napa Valley Vine Hill Ranch 1982 Rel: $14 Cur: $24 (CA-3/89) **88**
Cabernet Sauvignon Napa Valley Vine Hill Ranch 1981 Rel: $14 Cur: $25 (CA-3/89) **86**
Cabernet Sauvignon Napa Valley Vine Hill Ranch 1981 Rel: $14 Cur: $25 (1/01/86) CS **93**
Chardonnay Napa Valley Puncheon Fermented 1990 $15 (7/15/92) **82**
Chardonnay Napa Valley Puncheon Fermented 1989 $12 (12/31/91) **84**
Chardonnay Napa Valley Puncheon Fermented Reserve 1989 $20 (2/28/91) **81**
Chardonnay Napa Valley Puncheon Fermented 1988 $14 (5/31/90) **88**
Chardonnay Napa Valley 1987 $13.50 (2/15/90) **84**
Chardonnay Napa Valley 1986 $12 (10/31/88) **80**
Chardonnay Napa Valley 1985 $12 (11/15/87) **81**
Chardonnay Napa Valley 1983 $11 (3/01/86) **70**
Chardonnay Napa Valley 1982 $11 (5/01/84) **72**
Sangiovese Napa Valley Colline di Sassi Sangiovese Grosso 1989 $25 (10/31/91) **83**
Sauvignon Blanc Napa Valley 1987 $8.50 (11/30/89) **76**
Sauvignon Blanc Napa Valley Two-Heart Canopy 1990 $9.50 (11/15/91) **81**
Sauvignon Blanc Napa Valley Two-Heart Canopy 1989 $9.50 (3/31/91) **88**
Sauvignon Blanc Napa Valley Two-Heart Canopy 1988 $9.50 (2/15/90) **87**

MARIO PERELLI-MINETTI (United States/California)
Cabernet Sauvignon Napa Valley 1987 $12 (4/30/91) **83**
Chardonnay Napa Valley 1990 $12.50 (5/31/92) **81**
Chardonnay Napa Valley 1989 $12.50 (4/30/91) **83**
Chardonnay Napa Valley 1988 $11.50 (6/30/90) **80**

CHATEAU PERENNE (France/Bordeaux)
Premières Côtes de Blaye 1989 $9 (3/31/91) **78**
Premières Côtes de Blaye 1986 $7 (6/30/89) **82**
Premières Côtes de Blaye 1985 $7 (2/15/88) **80**
Premières Côtes de Blaye 1982 $5 (11/16/85) BB **79**

PEREZ-LLANO (Chile)
Cabernet Sauvignon Rancagua Gran Vino 1988 $5 (6/15/92) **76**

DOM PERIGNON (France/Champagne)
Brut Champagne 1983 $97 (5/15/92) **95**
Brut Champagne 1982 Rel: $75 Cur: $91 (10/15/88) **93**
Brut Champagne 1980 Rel: $60 Cur: $95 (9/15/86) SS **94**
Brut Champagne 1978 Rel: $61 Cur: $149 (5/16/86) **88**
Brut Rosé Champagne 1978 Rel: $89 Cur: $200 (10/15/86) **90**
Brut Rosé Champagne 1975 Rel: $85 Cur: $290 (12/16/85) **93**

A. PERNIN-ROSSIN (France/Burgundy)
Vosne-Romanée 1986 $31 (2/28/89) **61**

PAUL PERNOT (France/Burgundy)
Bâtard-Montrachet 1989 $160 (2/28/91) **93**
Beaune Les Teurons 1990 $33 (4/30/92) **90**
Beaune Les Teurons 1988 $33 (3/31/91) **86**
Blagny Rouge La Pièce Sous le Bois 1990 $33 (4/30/92) **79**
Bourgogne Blanc Chardonnay Champerrier 1989 $16 (4/30/91) **83**
Puligny-Montrachet 1990 $45 (4/15/92) **81**
Puligny-Montrachet 1989 $52 (2/28/91) **80**
Puligny-Montrachet 1988 $40 (2/28/91) **72**
Puligny-Montrachet Les Folatières 1990 $60 (4/15/92) **91**
Puligny-Montrachet Les Folatières 1989 $70 (2/28/91) **89**
Puligny-Montrachet Les Folatières 1988 $74 (12/31/90) **93**
Puligny-Montrachet Les Folatières 1986 $50 (2/28/89) **89**
Puligny-Montrachet Les Pucelles 1988 $60 (12/31/90) **90**

PERRET (United States/California)
Chardonnay Carneros Napa Valley Perret Vineyard 1985 $14 (12/31/88) **78**
Chardonnay Carneros Napa Valley Perret Vineyard 1984 $14.50 (10/15/87) **91**
Chardonnay Carneros Napa Valley Perret Vineyard 1982 $14.50 (11/01/84) **81**
Chardonnay Carneros Napa Valley Winery Lake Vineyard 1985 $14.50 (12/31/88) **84**

JOSEPH PERRIER (France/Champagne)
Brut Blanc de Blancs Champagne Cuvée Royale NV $37 (12/31/90) **88**
Brut Champagne 1985 $37 (12/31/90) **82**
Brut Champagne 1979 $22 (10/01/85) **87**
Brut Champagne NV $19 (11/16/85) **92**
Brut Champagne Cuvée Josephine 1982 $100 (12/31/90) **93**
Brut Champagne Cuvée Royale 1985 $37 (12/31/90) **82**
Brut Champagne Cuvée Royale 1982 $35 (12/31/89) **89**
Brut Champagne Cuvée Royale NV $32 (12/31/91) **84**
Brut Rosé Champagne Cuvée Royale NV $40 (12/31/90) **86**

PERRIER-JOUET (France/Champagne)
Brut Champagne 1955 ($NA)/1.5L (10/15/87) (JS) **90**
Brut Champagne 1947 ($NA)/1.5L (10/15/87) (JS) **85**
Brut Champagne 1928 ($NA) (10/15/87) (JS) **97**
Brut Champagne 1914 ($NA) (10/15/87) (JS) **55**
Brut Champagne 1911 ($NA) (10/15/87) (JS) **95**
Brut Champagne 1900 ($NA) (10/15/87) (JS) **97**
Brut Champagne 1893 ($NA) (10/15/87) (JS) **80**
Brut Champagne 1825 ($NA) (10/15/87) (JS) **95**
Brut Champagne Fleur de Champagne 1985 $75 (12/31/90) **86**
Brut Champagne Fleur de Champagne 1983 $65 (12/31/89) **88**
Brut Champagne Fleur de Champagne 1982 Rel: $65 Cur: $87 (12/31/88) **88**
Brut Champagne Fleur de Champagne 1979 Rel: $50 Cur: $90 (2/01/86) **93**
Brut Champagne Grand Brut NV $25 (12/31/91) **88**
Brut Rosé Champagne Fleur de Champagne 1978 Rel: $55 Cur: $100 (12/16/85) **90**

DOMAINE PERRIERE (France/Other)
Vin de Pays de l'Aude Les Amandiers 1988 $4.50 (4/15/90) **77**

PERTIMALI (Italy/Tuscany)
Brunello di Montalcino 1982 $25 (1/31/88) **77**
Brunello di Montalcino Riserva 1985 $41 (11/30/90) **83**
Rosso di Montalcino 1987 $12.50 (1/31/91) **84**

BATISTE PERTOIS (France/Champagne)
Brut Blanc de Blancs Champagne Cramant Cuvée de Réserve NV $24 (12/31/89) **88**

PESENTI (United States/California)
Cabernet Sauvignon San Luis Obispo County Family Reserve 1987 $8 (12/15/89) **84**
Cabernet Sauvignon San Luis Obispo County Family Reserve 1985 $13 (12/15/89) **77**
Zinfandel San Luis Obispo County Family Reserve 1984 $6 (12/15/89) **79**

PESQUERA (Spain)
Ribera del Duero 1989 $20 (4/15/92) CS **91**
Ribera del Duero 1988 $17 (9/30/91) **89**
Ribera del Duero 1987 $17 (9/30/90) **84**
Ribera del Duero 1986 Rel: $16 Cur: $20 (4/30/89) **91**
Ribera del Duero 1985 Rel: $16 Cur: $21 (4/30/88) **89**
Ribera del Duero 1984 $14 (10/15/87) **86**
Ribera del Duero 1983 $12 (11/15/87) (JL) **94**
Ribera del Duero 1982 $26 (11/15/87) (JL) **89**
Ribera del Duero 1979 $45 (11/15/87) (JL) **90**
Ribera del Duero 1978 $55 (11/15/87) (JL) **89**
Ribera del Duero 1975 $50 (11/15/87) (JL) **88**
Ribera del Duero Janus Reserva Especial 1982 Rel: $75 Cur: $95 (3/31/90) **92**
Ribera del Duero Reserva 1986 $26 (9/30/90) **92**
Ribera del Duero Reserva 1985 $30 (3/31/90) (TM) **89**

PETALUMA (Australia)
Cabernet Merlot Coonawarra 1986 $25 (5/31/91) **87**
Cabernet Merlot Coonawarra 1984 $18 (5/31/87) **92**
Cabernet Sauvignon Coonawarra 1984 $18 (5/31/87) **91**
Cabernet Shiraz Coonawarra 1982 $16 (7/01/87) **89**
Chardonnay Australia 1989 $18 (11/30/91) **91**
Chardonnay Australia 1987 $21 (5/31/91) **88**
Chardonnay Australia 1986 $18 (5/31/87) **90**

LE PETIT CHEVAL (France/Bordeaux)
St.-Emilion 1988 $35 (3/31/91) **89**

CHATEAU PETIT-FIGEAC (France/Bordeaux)
St.-Emilion 1990 (NR) (5/15/92) (BT) **90+**
St.-Emilion 1989 $21 (3/15/92) **90**
St.-Emilion 1988 $17 (8/31/90) (BT) **85+**

DOMAINE DE PETIT ROUBIE (France/Other)
Sauvignon Blanc Côteaux du Languedoc Picpoul de Pinet 1988 $7 (3/31/90) **74**

CHATEAU PETIT-VILLAGE (France/Bordeaux)
Pomerol 1991 (NR) (5/15/92) (BT) **80+**
Pomerol 1990 (NR) (5/15/92) (BT) **85+**
Pomerol 1989 Rel: $46 Cur: $52 (3/15/92) **88**
Pomerol 1988 Rel: $26 Cur: $33 (8/31/90) (BT) **90+**
Pomerol 1987 $22 (6/30/89) (BT) **80+**
Pomerol 1986 $24 (6/30/88) (BT) **90+**
Pomerol 1982 $58 (5/15/89) (TR) **92**
Pomerol 1959 $90 (10/15/90) (JS) **86**

DOMAINE DE PETIT-CHENE (France/Beaujolais)
Moulin-à-Vent 1988 $10 (5/31/89) (TM) **88**

CHATEAU PETIT-FAURIE-DE-SOUTARD (France/Bordeaux)
St.-Emilion 1989 (NR) (4/30/91) (BT) **75+**
St.-Emilion 1988 $20 (4/30/91) **82**
St.-Emilion 1987 $15 (6/30/89) (BT) **75+**
St.-Emilion 1986 $15 (6/30/89) **80**

PETITE CHATEAU (United States/New York)
Cabernet Sauvignon North Fork of Long Island NV $10 (6/30/91) (TM) **79**

LA PETITE EGLISE (France/Bordeaux)
Pomerol 1986 $15 (9/15/89) **78**

CHATEAU PETITE FIGEAC (France/Bordeaux)
St.-Emilion 1991 (NR) (5/15/92) (BT) **70+**

FATTORIA PETRIOLO (Italy/Tuscany)
Merlot 1988 $24 (8/31/91) **83**

PODERE PETROIO (Italy/Tuscany)
Chianti Classico 1988 ($NA) (9/15/91) **83**
Chianti Classico Cru Montetondo 1988 ($NA) (9/15/91) **90**

CHATEAU PETRUS (France/Bordeaux)
Pomerol 1990 (NR) (5/15/92) (BT) **95+**
Pomerol 1989 $390 (3/15/92) **100**
Pomerol 1988 Rel: $221 Cur: $300 (8/31/91) **94**
Pomerol 1987 $175 (2/15/91) (JS) **85**
Pomerol 1986 Rel: $200 Cur: $350 (2/15/91) (JS) **96**
Pomerol 1985 Rel: $160 Cur: $390 (2/15/91) (JS) **97**
Pomerol 1984 Rel: $125 Cur: $250 (2/15/91) (JS) **83**
Pomerol 1983 Rel: $125 Cur: $300 (2/15/91) (JS) **91**
Pomerol 1982 $550 (2/15/91) (JS) **96**
Pomerol 1981 $290 (2/15/91) (JS) **90**
Pomerol 1980 $180 (2/15/91) (JS) **86**
Pomerol 1979 $310 (2/15/91) (JS) **90**
Pomerol 1978 $350 (2/15/91) (JS) **89**
Pomerol 1976 $280 (2/15/91) (JS) **86**
Pomerol 1975 $500 (2/15/91) (JS) **93**
Pomerol 1973 $290 (2/15/91) (JS) **78**
Pomerol 1971 $470 (2/15/91) (JS) **94**
Pomerol 1970 $510 (2/15/91) (JS) **92**
Pomerol 1968 $200 (2/15/91) (JS) **79**
Pomerol 1967 $360 (2/15/91) (JS) **87**
Pomerol 1966 $450 (2/15/91) (JS) **93**
Pomerol 1964 $580 (2/15/91) (JS) **94**
Pomerol 1962 $470 (2/15/91) (JS) **94**
Pomerol 1961 $2,100 (2/15/91) (JS) **100**
Pomerol 1959 $820 (2/15/91) (JS) **96**
Pomerol 1958 $420 (2/15/91) (JS) **85**
Pomerol 1955 $580 (2/15/91) (JS) **91**
Pomerol 1953 $740 (2/15/91) (JS) **92**
Pomerol 1952 $650 (2/15/91) (JS) **89**
Pomerol 1950 $1,100 (2/15/91) (JS) **99**
Pomerol 1949 $1,550 (2/15/91) (JS) **98**
Pomerol 1948 $1,200 (2/15/91) (JS) **91**
Pomerol 1947 $1,900 (2/15/91) (JS) **97**
Pomerol 1945 $2,700 (2/15/91) (JS) **100**

DOMAINE LE PEU DE LA MORIETTE (France/Loire)
Vouvray 1989 $12 (4/30/91) **90**
Vouvray 1987 $10 (2/28/89) **69**
Vouvray Moelleux Cuvée Exceptionelle 1989 $19 (6/15/91) **80**

PEWSEY VALE (Australia)
Rhine Riesling Adelaide Hills Individual Vineyard Selection 1990 $9.50 (7/15/91) **76**
Rhine Riesling Barossa Valley Individual Vineyard Selection 1987 $5.50 (3/15/89) **79**
Rhine Riesling Late Harvest Barossa Valley Botrytis 1986 $8/375ml (2/15/88) **90**
Rhine Riesling Late Harvest Barossa Valley Botrytis Individual Vineyard Selection 1987 $9/375ml (10/31/89) **71**

CHATEAU PEYRAUD (France/Bordeaux)
Premières Côtes de Blaye 1989 $8 (3/31/91) **80**

CHATEAU DE PEZ (France/Bordeaux)
St.-Estèphe 1989 $21 (3/15/92) **89**
St.-Estèphe 1988 $19 (6/15/91) **83**
St.-Estèphe 1986 $17 (6/30/89) **90**
St.-Estèphe 1985 Rel: $15 Cur: $20 (6/30/88) **90**
St.-Estèphe 1982 Rel: $12 Cur: $21 (4/01/86) **90**

PFEFFINGEN (Germany)
Riesling Auslese Rheinpfalz Ungsteiner Herrenberg 1989 $25 (12/15/90) **85**
Riesling Auslese Rheinpfalz Ungsteiner Weilberg 1989 $25 (12/15/90) **85**
Riesling Kabinett Halbtrocken Rheinpfalz Ungsteiner Hönigsäckel 1990 $12 (12/15/91) **89**
Riesling Kabinett Halbtrocken Rheinpfalz Ungsteiner Hönigsäckel 1988 ($NA) (9/30/89) **92**
Riesling Kabinett Rheinpfalz Ungsteiner Hönigsäckel 1990 $12 (12/15/91) **87**
Riesling Kabinett Rheinpfalz Ungsteiner Hönigsäckel 1989 $16 (12/15/90) **81**
Riesling Kabinett Rheinpfalz Ungsteiner Hönigsäckel 1988 $15 (9/30/89) **88**
Riesling Spätlese Halbtrocken Rheinpfalz Ungsteiner Herrenberg 1990 $16 (12/15/91) **91**
Riesling Spätlese Halbtrocken Rheinpfalz Ungsteiner Herrenberg 1989 $16 (12/15/90) **85**
Riesling Spätlese Halbtrocken Rheinpfalz Ungsteiner Herrenberg 1988 $16 (9/30/89) **90**
Riesling Spätlese Rheinpfalz Ungsteiner Herrenberg 1990 $16 (12/15/91) **87**
Riesling Spätlese Rheinpfalz Ungsteiner Herrenberg 1989 $16 (12/15/90) **90**
Riesling Spätlese Rheinpfalz Ungsteiner Herrenberg 1988 $16 (9/30/89) **94**
Riesling Spätlese Trocken Rheinpfalz Ungsteiner Weilberg 1990 $17 (12/15/91) **87**
Riesling Spätlese Trocken Rheinpfalz Ungsteiner Weilberg 1989 $16 (12/15/90) **84**
Scheurebe Auslese Rheinpfalz Ungsteiner Herrenberg 1990 $28 (12/15/91) **92**
Scheurebe Auslese Trocken Rheinpfalz Ungsteiner Herrenberg 1989 $25 (12/15/90) **85**
Scheurebe Beerenauslese Rheinpfalz Ungsteiner Herrenberg 1990 $30/375ml (12/15/91) **93**
Scheurebe Spätlese Halbtrocken Rheinpfalz Ungsteiner Herrenberg 1989 $16 (12/15/90) **84**
Scheurebe Spätlese Rheinpfalz Ungsteiner Herrenberg 1990 $16 (12/15/91) **88**
Scheurebe Spätlese Rheinpfalz Ungsteiner Herrenberg 1989 $16 (12/15/90) **81**

PHEASANT RIDGE (United States/Texas)
Cabernet Franc Lubbock County Cox Family Vineyards 1988 $12 (2/29/92) **79**
Cabernet Sauvignon Lubbock County 1988 $13 (2/29/92) **83**
Chardonnay Lubbock County 1989 $13 (2/29/92) **83**
Chenin Blanc Lubbock County 1989 $6 (2/29/92) **79**

CHATEAU PHELAN-SEGUR (France/Bordeaux)
St.-Estèphe 1991 (NR) (5/15/92) (BT) **80+**
St.-Estèphe 1990 (NR) (5/15/92) (BT) **85+**
St.-Estèphe 1989 $23 (3/15/92) **85**
St.-Estèphe 1988 $20 (7/15/91) **87**
St.-Estèphe 1987 $16 (11/30/89) (JS) **82**
St.-Estèphe 1986 $19 (11/30/89) (JS) **86**
St.-Estèphe 1982 $26 (11/30/89) (JS) **88**
St.-Estèphe 1961 $43 (3/16/86) (TR) **67**

JOSEPH PHELPS (United States/California)
Cabernet Sauvignon Napa Valley 1990 (NR) (5/15/91) (BT) **85+**
Cabernet Sauvignon Napa Valley 1989 $17.50 (4/15/92) **78**
Cabernet Sauvignon Napa Valley 1988 Rel: $17.50 Cur: $20 (11/15/91) **86**
Cabernet Sauvignon Napa Valley 1987 $14.50 (7/15/91) **75**
Cabernet Sauvignon Napa Valley 1986 Rel: $15 Cur: $27 (4/15/88) (BT) **85+**
Cabernet Sauvignon Napa Valley 1985 Rel: $14 Cur: $27 (5/15/89) **84**
Cabernet Sauvignon Napa Valley 1984 Rel: $14 Cur: $31 (10/31/88) **91**
Cabernet Sauvignon Napa Valley 1983 Rel: $13 Cur: $31 (8/31/87) **84**
Cabernet Sauvignon Napa Valley 1982 Rel: $12 Cur: $17 (12/15/86) **82**
Cabernet Sauvignon Napa Valley 1981 Rel: $11 Cur: $25 (9/01/85) **86**
Cabernet Sauvignon Napa Valley 1980 Rel: $10.75 Cur: $38 (7/01/84) **89**
Cabernet Sauvignon Napa Valley Backus Vineyard 1991 (NR) (5/15/92) (BT) **89+**
Cabernet Sauvignon Napa Valley Backus Vineyard 1990 (NR) (5/15/91) (BT) **90+**
Cabernet Sauvignon Napa Valley Backus Vineyard 1989 (NR) (5/15/91) (BT) **90+**
Cabernet Sauvignon Napa Valley Backus Vineyard 1987 $30 (7/15/91) **88**
Cabernet Sauvignon Napa Valley Backus Vineyard 1986 Rel: $22 Cur: $37 (1/31/90) **83**
Cabernet Sauvignon Napa Valley Backus Vineyard 1985 Rel: $27.50 Cur: $45 (12/31/88) **91**
Cabernet Sauvignon Napa Valley Backus Vineyard 1984 Rel: $20 Cur: $42 (CA-3/89) **86**
Cabernet Sauvignon Napa Valley Backus Vineyard 1983 Rel: $16.50 Cur: $28 (CA-3/89) **85**
Cabernet Sauvignon Napa Valley Backus Vineyard 1981 Rel: $15 Cur: $48 (CA-3/89) **91**
Cabernet Sauvignon Napa Valley Backus Vineyard 1978 Rel: $16.50 Cur: $56 (CA-3/89) **89**
Cabernet Sauvignon Napa Valley Backus Vineyard 1977 Rel: $15 Cur: $46 (CA-3/89) **86**
Cabernet Sauvignon Napa Valley Eisele Vineyard 1991 (NR) (5/15/92) (BT) **85+**
Cabernet Sauvignon Napa Valley Eisele Vineyard 1989 (NR) (5/15/91) (BT) **90+**
Cabernet Sauvignon Napa Valley Eisele Vineyard 1987 $40 (4/15/89) (BT) **75+**
Cabernet Sauvignon Napa Valley Eisele Vineyard 1986 Rel: $40 Cur: $45 (8/31/90) **77**
Cabernet Sauvignon Napa Valley Eisele Vineyard 1985 Rel: $40 Cur: $52 (5/31/89) **81**
Cabernet Sauvignon Napa Valley Eisele Vineyard 1984 Rel: $35 Cur: $40 (CA-3/89) **87**
Cabernet Sauvignon Napa Valley Eisele Vineyard 1983 Rel: $25 Cur: $37 (CA-3/89) **86**
Cabernet Sauvignon Napa Valley Eisele Vineyard 1982 Rel: $30 Cur: $47 (CA-3/89) **85**
Cabernet Sauvignon Napa Valley Eisele Vineyard 1981 Rel: $30 Cur: $47 (CA-3/89) **89**
Cabernet Sauvignon Napa Valley Eisele Vineyard 1979 Rel: $30 Cur: $64 (CA-3/89) **92**
Cabernet Sauvignon Napa Valley Eisele Vineyard 1978 Rel: $30 Cur: $106 (CA-3/89) **97**
Cabernet Sauvignon Napa Valley Eisele Vineyard 1977 Rel: $25 Cur: $61 (CA-3/89) **82**
Cabernet Sauvignon Napa Valley Eisele Vineyard 1975 Rel: $15 Cur: $145 (CA-3/89) **97**
Chardonnay Napa Valley 1990 $16 (12/15/91) **90**
Chardonnay Napa Valley 1989 $16 (7/15/91) **81**
Chardonnay Napa Valley 1988 $16 (6/30/90) **86**
Chardonnay Napa Valley 1987 $15 (3/15/89) **81**
Chardonnay Napa Valley 1984 $13 (6/30/87) **75**
Chardonnay Napa Valley 1983 $12.75 (12/15/86) **68**
Chardonnay Napa Valley 1982 $12.50 (4/16/85) **85**
Chardonnay Carneros Sangiacomo Vineyard 1989 $20 (7/15/91) **85**
Chardonnay Carneros Sangiacomo Vineyard 1988 $16 (6/30/90) **89**
Chardonnay Carneros Sangiacomo Vineyard 1987 $18 (5/15/89) **68**
Chardonnay Carneros Sangiacomo Vineyard 1986 $16 (7/15/88) **93**
Chardonnay Carneros Sangiacomo Vineyard 1985 $14 (11/15/87) **84**
Chardonnay Carneros Sangiacomo Vineyard 1982 $14 (4/01/84) **79**
Gewürztraminer Napa Valley 1988 $8.50 (6/30/90) **81**
Grenache Rosé California Vin du Mistral 1990 $9 (6/15/91) BB **87**
Grenache Rosé California Vin du Mistral 1989 $9 (11/30/90) **84**
Insignia Napa Valley 1991 (NR) (5/15/92) (BT) **87+**
Insignia Napa Valley 1990 (NR) (5/15/91) (BT) **90+**
Insignia Napa Valley 1989 (NR) (5/15/91) (BT) **85+**
Insignia Napa Valley 1988 $35 (11/15/91) **86**
Insignia Napa Valley 1986 Rel: $40 Cur: $44 (8/31/90) CS **93**
Insignia Napa Valley 1985 Rel: $40 Cur: $58 (7/31/89) CS **93**
Insignia Napa Valley 1984 Rel: $30 Cur: $39 (CA-3/89) **89**
Insignia Napa Valley 1983 Rel: $25 Cur: $38 (CA-3/89) **89**
Insignia Napa Valley 1982 Rel: $25 Cur: $36 (CA-3/89) **85**
Insignia Napa Valley 1981 Rel: $25 Cur: $53 (CA-3/89) **92**
Insignia Napa Valley 1980 Rel: $25 Cur: $52 (CA-3/89) **90**
Insignia Napa Valley 1980 Rel: $25 Cur: $52 (7/01/84) CS **90**
Insignia Napa Valley 1979 Rel: $25 Cur: $53 (CA-3/89) **90**
Insignia Napa Valley 1978 Rel: $25 Cur: $77 (CA-3/89) **87**
Insignia Napa Valley 1977 Rel: $25 Cur: $72 (CA-3/89) **91**
Insignia Napa Valley 1976 Rel: $20 Cur: $110 (CA-3/89) **93**
Insignia Napa Valley 1975 Rel: $15 Cur: $110 (CA-3/89) **85**
Insignia Napa Valley 1974 Rel: $12 Cur: $180 (CA-3/89) **90**
Johannisberg Riesling Late Harvest Napa Valley 1985 $11.75 (12/15/86) **93**
Johannisberg Riesling Late Harvest Napa Valley Special Select 1983 $25 (3/16/86) H **75**
Johannisberg Riesling Late Harvest Napa Valley Special Select 1982 $22.50/375ml (4/16/84) **92**
Johannisberg Riesling Napa Valley 1987 $8.50 (2/28/89) **86**
Johannisberg Riesling Napa Valley Early Harvest 1987 $8 (8/31/89) **85**
Merlot Napa Valley 1989 $15 (5/31/92) **88**
Merlot Napa Valley 1987 $18 (7/31/90) **80**
Merlot Napa Valley 1986 $15 (6/30/88) **84**
Rouge California Vin du Mistral 1989 $14 (7/15/91) **85**
Sauvignon Blanc Napa Valley 1990 $10 (4/15/92) **82**
Sauvignon Blanc Napa Valley 1988 $9.50 (6/30/90) **55**
Scheurebe Late Harvest Napa Valley 1990 $12.50/375ml (6/15/92) **81**
Scheurebe Late Harvest Napa Valley 1985 Rel: $15 Cur: $21 (8/31/86) SS **94**
Scheurebe Late Harvest Napa Valley 1983 $15 (9/16/84) **87**
Scheurebe Late Harvest Napa Valley 1982 Rel: $15 Cur: $21 (4/16/84) CS **90**
Scheurebe Late Harvest Napa Valley Special Select 1989 $18/375ml (4/30/91) **88**
Scheurebe Late Harvest Napa Valley Special Select 1982 $25/375ml (5/16/85) **88**
Sémillon Late Harvest Napa Valley Délice du Sémillon 1989 $12.50/375ml (4/30/91) **89**
Sémillon Late Harvest Napa Valley Délice du Sémillon 1985 $8.75/375ml (8/31/87) **91**
Sémillon Late Harvest Napa Valley Délice du Sémillon 1983 $15 (1/31/87) **61**
Syrah Napa Valley 1984 $8.50 (11/15/88) **89**
Syrah Napa Valley 1983 $8.50 (11/15/87) **71**
Syrah Napa Valley 1979 $7.50 (9/16/84) **78**
Syrah Napa Valley Vin du Mistral 1988 $16 (6/30/92) **87**
Syrah Napa Valley Vin du Mistral 1987 $14 (8/31/91) **81**
Syrah Napa Valley Vin du Mistral 1986 $14 (10/31/90) **88**
Viognier Napa Valley Vin du Mistral 1990 $20 (6/15/91) **89**
Zinfandel Alexander Valley 1985 $10 (7/31/87) **74**
Zinfandel Alexander Valley 1981 $6.75 (4/16/85) **80**
Zinfandel Alexander Valley 1980 $6.75 (7/16/84) **85**
Zinfandel Napa Valley 1985 $6 (12/31/86) **82**
Zinfandel Napa Valley 1980 $6.75 (1/01/86) **60**

Key to Symbols

The scores reported here are the results of blind tastings conducted by our panel of senior editors. Wines that carry the initials below are results of individual tastings.

THE WINE SPECTATOR 100-POINT SCALE *95-100*—Classic, a great wine; *90-94*—Outstanding, superior character and style; *80-89*—Good to very good, a wine with special qualities; *70-79*—Average, drinkable wine that may have minor flaws; *60-69*—Below average, drinkable but not recommended; *50-59*—Poor, undrinkable, not recommended. "+"—With a score indicates a range; used primarily with barrel tastings to indicate a preliminary score.

SPECIAL DESIGNATIONS SS—Spectator Selection, CS—Cellar Selection, BB—Best Buy, ($NA)—Price not available, (NR)—Not released.

TASTER'S INITIALS (JG)—Jim Gordon, (HS)—Harvey Steiman, (JL)—James Laube, (JS)—James Suckling, (TM)—Thomas Matthews, (TR)—Terry Robards, (PM)—Per-Henrik Mansson, (BT)—Barrel Tasting (these wines were tasted blind from barrel samples), (CA-date)—*California's Great Cabernets* by James Laube, (CH-date)—*California's Great Chardonnays* by James Laube, (VP-date)—*Vintage Port* by James Suckling.

DATE TASTED Dates in parentheses represent the issue in which the rating was published.

Zinfandel Napa Valley 1979 $6.75 (4/16/84) **60**

JEAN PHILIPPE (France/Other)
Brut Blanquette de Limoux 1986 $11 (6/15/90) **80**

PHILIPPE-LORRAINE (United States/California)
Chardonnay Napa Valley 1990 $10 (5/15/92) **83**
Merlot Napa Valley 1989 $15 (5/31/92) **89**

PHILIPPONNAT (France/Champagne)
Brut Blanc de Blancs Champagne 1980 $26 (5/31/87) **92**
Brut Blanc de Blancs Champagne Cuvée Première 1980 $39 (12/31/88) **89**
Brut Blanc de Blancs Champagne Grand Blanc 1985 $40 (12/31/90) **87**
Brut Champagne Clos des Goisses 1985 $118 (12/31/90) **85**
Brut Champagne Clos des Goisses 1982 $89 (12/31/88) **84**
Brut Champagne Grand Blanc 1982 $38 (12/31/88) **84**
Brut Champagne Royale Réserve NV $32 (12/31/91) **85**
Brut Rosé Champagne NV $26 (12/16/85) **72**

R.H. PHILLIPS (United States/California)
Alliance California 1989 $10 (11/30/91) **88**
Cabernet Sauvignon California 1989 $8 (7/31/91) BB **82**
Cabernet Sauvignon California 1985 $6 (11/30/88) **80**
Cabernet Sauvignon California Night Harvest NV $4 (11/30/88) BB **83**
Chardonnay California 1990 $8 (7/15/91) BB **83**
Chardonnay California 1989 $7 (4/30/91) BB **83**
Chardonnay California 1987 $6 (2/15/89) **77**
Chenin Blanc Yolo County Dunnigan Hills 1987 $4.50 (7/31/89) **82**
Cuvée California Night Harvest NV $5 (5/15/89) BB **86**
Cuvée Rouge California Night Harvest NV $6 (5/31/91) BB **84**
Mourvèdre California EXP 1988 $13/375ml (4/30/91) **74**
Sauvignon Blanc California Night Harvest 1991 $3.50/500ml (6/15/92) BB **86**
Sauvignon Blanc Yolo County Dunnigan Hills Night Harvest 1987 $4 (3/15/89) **67**
Syrah California EXP 1988 $15 (11/15/91) **91**
Syrah California Reserve 1987 $13 (12/31/90) **80**

CHATEAU PIADA (France/Sauternes)
Barsac 1989 ($NA) (6/15/90) (BT) **85+**
Barsac 1988 ($NA) (6/15/90) (BT) **90+**
Barsac 1983 $11 (1/31/88) **70**
Sauternes 1987 $35 (3/31/91) **86**

PIAN DI CONTE (Italy/Tuscany)
Brunello di Montalcino 1982 ($NA) (9/15/86) **90**
Brunello di Montalcino 1981 ($NA) (9/15/86) **88**

CHATEAU DE PIBARNON (France/Other)
Bandol 1987 $17 (3/15/90) **75**

CHATEAU PIBRAN (France/Bordeaux)
Pauillac 1991 (NR) (5/15/92) (BT) **75+**
Pauillac 1990 (NR) (5/15/92) (BT) **90+**
Pauillac 1989 $25 (3/15/92) **95**
Pauillac 1988 $27 (8/31/90) (BT) **85+**
Pauillac 1987 $20 (11/30/89) (JS) **85**
Pauillac 1986 $18 (11/30/89) (JS) **88**
Pauillac 1982 $18 (11/30/89) (JS) **90**

ALBERT PIC & FILS (France/Chablis)
Chablis 1987 $16 (3/31/89) **82**
Chablis 1986 $16 (3/31/89) **83**
Chablis Les Blanchots 1987 $40 (3/31/89) **87**
Chablis Les Blanchots 1986 $40 (3/31/89) **87**
Chablis Bougros 1987 $38 (3/31/89) **85**
Chablis Bougros 1986 $38 (3/31/89) **85**
Chablis Les Clos 1987 $40 (3/31/89) **91**
Chablis Les Clos 1986 $40 (3/31/89) **92**
Chablis Les Grenouilles 1987 $40 (3/31/89) **89**
Chablis Les Grenouilles 1986 $40 (3/31/89) **92**
Chablis Les Preuses 1987 $38 (3/31/89) **84**
Chablis Les Preuses 1986 $37 (9/15/88) **88**
Chablis Valmur 1987 $40 (3/31/89) **86**
Chablis Valmur 1986 $40 (3/31/89) **93**
Chablis Vaudésir 1987 $40 (3/31/89) **89**
Chablis Vaudésir 1986 $40 (3/31/89) **91**

JEAN PAUL PICARD (France/Loire)
Sancerre 1989 $14.50 (4/30/91) **82**

PHILIPPE PICHON (France/Rhône)
Condrieu 1989 $45 (11/15/91) **94**
St.-Joseph 1988 $21.50 (11/15/91) **76**

CHATEAU PICHON (France/Bordeaux)
Haut-Médoc 1985 $13 (8/31/88) **85**

CHATEAU PICHON-BARON (France/Bordeaux)
Pauillac 1991 (NR) (5/15/92) (BT) **90+**
Pauillac 1990 (NR) (5/15/92) (BT) **95+**
Pauillac 1989 $60 (3/15/92) **98**
Pauillac 1988 Rel: $30 Cur: $33 (3/31/91) SS **95**
Pauillac 1987 Rel: $20 Cur: $25 (10/15/90) **88**
Pauillac 1986 Rel: $31 Cur: $41 (5/31/89) **97**
Pauillac 1985 Rel: $32 Cur: $36 (4/30/88) **94**
Pauillac 1984 $23 (9/30/88) **78**
Pauillac 1983 Rel: $18 Cur: $36 (3/01/86) **94**
Pauillac 1982 Rel: $12 Cur: $43 (9/30/88) **78**
Pauillac 1981 Rel: $13 Cur: $32 (9/30/88) **84**
Pauillac 1980 $17 (9/30/88) **79**
Pauillac 1979 $38 (10/15/89) (JS) **88**
Pauillac 1978 $51 (9/30/88) **80**
Pauillac 1977 $13 (9/30/88) **76**
Pauillac 1976 $30 (9/30/88) **73**
Pauillac 1975 $46 (9/30/88) **74**
Pauillac 1974 $4 (9/30/88) **78**
Pauillac 1973 $13 (9/30/88) **78**
Pauillac 1972 $13 (9/30/88) **68**
Pauillac 1971 $31 (9/30/88) **71**
Pauillac 1970 $70 (9/30/88) **83**
Pauillac 1969 $21 (9/30/88) **78**
Pauillac 1967 $65 (9/30/88) **80**
Pauillac 1966 $62 (9/30/88) **80**
Pauillac 1964 $85 (9/30/88) **88**
Pauillac 1962 $85 (9/30/88) **88**
Pauillac 1961 $165 (9/30/88) **84**
Pauillac 1960 $50 (9/30/88) **81**
Pauillac 1959 $135 (10/15/90) (JS) **94**
Pauillac 1958 $95 (9/30/88) **79**
Pauillac 1957 $110 (9/30/88) **76**
Pauillac 1955 $100 (9/30/88) **81**
Pauillac 1954 $95 (9/30/88) **80**
Pauillac 1953 $150 (9/30/88) **80**
Pauillac 1952 $105 (9/30/88) **84**
Pauillac 1950 $150 (9/30/88) **83**
Pauillac 1949 $175 (9/30/88) **87**
Pauillac 1947 $175 (9/30/88) **80**
Pauillac 1945 $290 (9/30/88) **75**

CHATEAU PICHON-LALANDE (France/Bordeaux)
Pauillac 1991 (NR) (5/15/92) (BT) **85+**
Pauillac 1990 (NR) (5/15/92) (BT) **85+**
Pauillac 1989 $71 (3/15/92) **92**
Pauillac 1988 $50 (4/30/91) **91**
Pauillac 1987 $30 (2/15/90) **87**
Pauillac 1986 Rel: $50 Cur: $59 (5/31/89) **97**
Pauillac 1985 Rel: $40 Cur: $52 (2/29/88) CS **95**
Pauillac 1984 $27 (1/31/87) CS **94**
Pauillac 1983 Rel: $44 Cur: $54 (3/01/86) SS **97**
Pauillac 1982 Rel: $29 Cur: $115 (2/01/85) SS **94**
Pauillac 1981 Rel: $21 Cur: $56 (5/01/85) **93**
Pauillac 1980 Rel: $14 Cur: $33 (5/01/85) **92**
Pauillac 1980 Rel: $14 Cur: $33 (3/01/84) CS **90**
Pauillac 1979 $65 (5/01/85) **90**
Pauillac 1978 $90 (5/01/85) **91**
Pauillac 1962 $138 (11/30/87) (JS) **85**
Pauillac 1961 $230 (3/16/86) (TR) **79**
Pauillac 1959 $200 (10/15/90) (JS) **97**
Pauillac 1945 $400 (3/16/86) (JL) **80**

CHATEAU PICQUE CAILLOU (France/Bordeaux)
Pessac-Léognan 1991 (NR) (5/15/92) (BT) **65+**

PIEDMONT (United States/Virginia)
Chardonnay Virginia Barrel Fermented Special Reserve 1990 $12 (2/29/92) **83**
Sémillon Virginia 1989 $15 (2/29/92) **74**

PIERRE JEAN (France/Bordeaux)
Bordeaux Supérieur 1988 $8 (7/31/91) **75**

CHATEAU LA PIERRIERE (France/Bordeaux)
Côtes de Castillon 1986 $6 (12/31/88) **77**

PIGHIN (Italy/North)
Chardonnay Grave del Friuli 1990 $12 (1/31/92) **77**
Chardonnay Grave del Friuli 1988 $8 (9/15/89) **85**
Chardonnay Grave del Friuli Pighin di Capriva 1988 $9.25 (9/15/89) **80**

PIGNAN (France/Rhône)
Châteauneuf-du-Pape Réserve 1988 Rel: $25 Cur: $30 (10/15/91) **82**
Châteauneuf-du-Pape Réserve 1986 $23 (10/15/91) **83**
Châteauneuf-du-Pape Réserve 1985 Rel: $14 Cur: $38 (8/31/87) SS **95**
Châteauneuf-du-Pape Réserve 1983 $38 (10/15/91) **85**
Châteauneuf-du-Pape Réserve 1981 $35 (10/15/91) **94**
Châteauneuf-du-Pape Réserve 1980 Rel: $13 Cur: $30 (10/15/86) **87**

FERNAND PILLOT (France/Burgundy)
Chassagne-Montrachet Grandes Ruchottes 1988 $43 (5/15/90) **90**
Chassagne-Montrachet Morgeot 1988 $35 (5/15/90) **91**
Chassagne-Montrachet Les Vergers 1988 $35 (5/15/90) **87**
Chassagne-Montrachet Les Vergers 1985 $28 (5/31/89) **85**

JEAN PILLOT (France/Burgundy)
Chassagne-Montrachet Les Caillerets 1988 $39 (2/28/91) **88**
Puligny-Montrachet 1989 $42 (4/30/91) **76**

PAUL PILLOT (France/Burgundy)
Chassagne-Montrachet Les Caillerets 1985 $30 (10/31/87) **84**
Chassagne-Montrachet Les Grandes Ruchottes 1987 $38 (2/28/90) **91**
Chassagne-Montrachet Les Grandes Ruchottes 1986 $30 (11/15/88) **91**
Chassagne-Montrachet Les Grandes Ruchottes 1985 $30 (10/31/87) **88**
Chassagne-Montrachet La Romanée 1987 $48 (2/28/90) **91**
Chassagne-Montrachet Rouge Clos St.-Jean 1986 $23 (2/28/90) **84**
Chassagne-Montrachet Rouge Clos St.-Jean 1985 $24 (11/15/88) **86**

CHATEAU LE PIN (France/Bordeaux)
Pomerol 1989 $163 (4/30/90) (BT) **95+**
Pomerol 1988 $65 (6/30/91) CS **95**
Pomerol 1987 Rel: $45 Cur: $90 (6/30/89) (BT) **85+**
Pomerol 1986 Rel: $55 Cur: $140 (6/15/89) **95**
Pomerol 1982 $280 (5/15/89) (TR) **95**

PINDAR (United States/New York)
Brut Premier Cuvée North Fork of Long Island 1986 $13 (12/31/90) **80**
Cabernet Sauvignon North Fork of Long Island Reserve 1988 $14 (6/30/91) (TM) **85**
Chardonnay North Fork of Long Island 1988 $9 (6/30/91) (TM) **86**
Chardonnay North Fork of Long Island 1988 $9 (12/15/90) **87**
Chardonnay North Fork of Long Island Reserve 1988 $12 (6/30/91) (TM) **82**
Merlot North Fork of Long Island 1987 $13 (12/15/90) **80**
Merlot North Fork of Long Island Reserve 1988 $14 (6/30/91) (TM) **83**
Mythology North Fork of Long Island 1988 $20 (6/30/91) (TM) **83**
Mythology North Fork of Long Island 1987 $20 (3/31/90) **86**
Pinot Meunier New York 1987 $25 (12/31/90) **80**

PINE RIDGE (United States/California)
Cabernet Sauvignon Napa Valley Andrus Reserve 1990 (NR) (5/15/91) (BT) **80+**
Cabernet Sauvignon Napa Valley Andrus Reserve 1987 ($NA) (4/15/89) (BT) **85+**
Cabernet Sauvignon Napa Valley Andrus Reserve 1986 Rel: $40 Cur: $44 (5/15/90) **80**
Cabernet Sauvignon Napa Valley Andrus Reserve Cuvée Duet 1985 Rel: $40 Cur: $45 (CA-3/89) **92**
Cabernet Sauvignon Napa Valley Andrus Reserve 1984 Rel: $37 Cur: $40 (CA-3/89) **93**
Cabernet Sauvignon Napa Valley Andrus Reserve 1983 Rel: $35 Cur: $40 (CA-3/89) **88**
Cabernet Sauvignon Napa Valley Andrus Reserve 1980 Rel: $30 Cur: $60 (CA-3/89) **96**
Cabernet Sauvignon Napa Valley Andrus Reserve 1980 Rel: $30 Cur: $60 (12/01/84) CS **93**
Cabernet Sauvignon Napa Valley Diamond Mountain 1989 (NR) (5/15/91) (BT) **85+**
Cabernet Sauvignon Napa Valley Rutherford Cuvée 1987 $16.50 (3/15/92) **77**
Cabernet Sauvignon Napa Valley Rutherford Cuvée 1986 Rel: $16 Cur: $19 (5/31/90) **90**
Cabernet Sauvignon Napa Valley Rutherford Cuvée 1985 Rel: $16 Cur: $20 (CA-3/89) **93**

Cabernet Sauvignon Napa Valley Rutherford Cuvée 1984 Rel: $14 Cur: $29 (CA-3/89) **90**
Cabernet Sauvignon Napa Valley Rutherford Cuvée 1983 Rel: $14 Cur: $18 (CA-3/89) **84**
Cabernet Sauvignon Napa Valley Rutherford Cuvée 1982 Rel: $13 Cur: $24 (CA-3/89) **90**
Cabernet Sauvignon Napa Valley Rutherford Cuvée 1981 Rel: $13 Cur: $28 (CA-3/89) **88**
Cabernet Sauvignon Napa Valley Rutherford District 1980 Rel: $12 Cur: $32 (CA-3/89) **91**
Cabernet Sauvignon Napa Valley Rutherford District 1979 Rel: $9 Cur: $45 (CA-3/89) **85**
Cabernet Sauvignon Napa Valley Rutherford District 1978 Rel: $7.50 Cur: $46 (CA-3/89) **89**
Cabernet Sauvignon Stags Leap District Pine Ridge Stags Leap Vineyard 1990 (NR) (5/15/91) (BT) **85+**
Cabernet Sauvignon Stags Leap District Pine Ridge Stags Leap Vineyard 1989 (NR) (5/15/91) (BT) **80+**
Andrus Reserve Stags Leap District 1988 $15 (11/15/91) **82**
Cabernet Sauvignon Stags Leap District 1987 Rel: $28 Cur: $32 (1/31/92) **85**
Cabernet Sauvignon Stags Leap District Pine Ridge Stags Leap Vineyard 1986 $29 (CA-3/89) **91**
Cabernet Sauvignon Stags Leap District Pine Ridge Stags Leap Vineyard 1985 Rel: $26 Cur: $29 (CA-3/89) **94**
Cabernet Sauvignon Stags Leap District Pine Ridge Stags Leap Vineyard 1984 Rel: $25 Cur: $33 (CA-3/89) **93**
Cabernet Sauvignon Stags Leap District Pine Ridge Stags Leap Vineyard 1983 Rel: $20 Cur: $34 (CA-3/89) **85**
Cabernet Sauvignon Stags Leap District Pine Ridge Stags Leap Vineyard 1982 Rel: $20 Cur: $34 (CA-3/89) **90**
Cabernet Sauvignon Stags Leap District Pine Ridge Stags Leap Vineyard 1982 Rel: $20 Cur: $34 (10/31/86) CS **91**
Cabernet Sauvignon Stags Leap District Pine Ridge Stags Leap Vineyard 1981 Rel: $20 Cur: $46 (CA-3/89) **92**
Chardonnay Napa Valley Knollside Cuvée 1990 $14 (7/15/92) **79**
Chardonnay Napa Valley Knollside Cuvée 1989 $16 (7/15/91) **67**
Chardonnay Napa Valley Knollside Cuvée 1988 Rel: $15 Cur: $17 (5/15/90) **85**
Chardonnay Napa Valley Knollside Cuvée 1987 Rel: $15 Cur: $17 (CH-4/90) **90**
Chardonnay Napa Valley Knollside Cuvée 1986 Rel: $14 Cur: $17 (CH-4/90) **88**
Chardonnay Napa Valley Knollside Cuvée 1985 Rel: $14 Cur: $16 (CH-4/90) **87**
Chardonnay Napa Valley Knollside Cuvée 1984 Rel: $14 Cur: $17 (CH-4/90) **85**
Chardonnay Napa Valley Oak Knoll Cuvée 1983 Rel: $13 Cur: $18 (CH-4/90) **88**
Chardonnay Napa Valley Oak Knoll Cuvée 1982 Rel: $13 Cur: $19 (3/16/84) SS **89**
Chardonnay Napa Valley Oak Knoll Cuvée 1981 Rel: $13 Cur: $20 (CH-4/90) **84**
Chardonnay Napa Valley Stags Leap District 1988 $20 (11/30/90) **78**
Chardonnay Stags Leap District Pine Ridge Stags Leap Vineyard 1988 $20 (CH-7/90) **88**
Chardonnay Stags Leap District Pine Ridge Stags Leap Vineyard 1987 Rel: $20 Cur: $23 (4/30/89) **82**
Chardonnay Stags Leap District Pine Ridge Stags Leap Vineyard 1986 Rel: $19 Cur: $23 (CH-4/90) **88**
Chardonnay Stags Leap District Pine Ridge Stags Leap Vineyard 1985 Rel: $18 Cur: $23 (CH-4/90) **85**
Chardonnay Stags Leap District Pine Ridge Stags Leap Vineyard 1984 Rel: $18 Cur: $25 (CH-4/90) **84**
Chardonnay Stags Leap District Pine Ridge Stags Leap Vineyard 1983 Rel: $16 Cur: $25 (12/16/85) SS **94**
Chardonnay Stags Leap District Stags Leap Vineyard 1982 Rel: $15 Cur: $27 (CH-4/90) **82**
Chardonnay Stags Leap District Stags Leap Vineyard 1981 Rel: $15 Cur: $31 (CH-4/90) **86**
Chardonnay Stags Leap District Stags Leap Vineyard 1979 Rel: $9.50 Cur: $32 (CH-4/90) **82**
Chenin Blanc Napa Valley Yountville Cuvée 1989 $7 (4/30/90) **81**
Chenin Blanc Napa Valley Yountville Cuvée 1988 $7 (7/31/89) **83**
Howell Mountain Andrus Reserve 1988 $15 (11/15/91) **82**
Merlot Napa Valley Selected Cuvée 1990 (NR) (5/15/91) (BT) **85+**
Merlot Napa Valley Selected Cuvée 1989 $16.50 (5/31/92) **73**
Merlot Napa Valley Selected Cuvée 1988 $17 (8/31/91) **80**
Merlot Napa Valley Selected Cuvée 1987 $15 (4/15/90) **88**
Merlot Napa Valley Selected Cuvée 1986 $15 (6/30/89) **80**
Merlot Napa Valley Selected Cuvée 1985 Rel: $13 Cur: $18 (2/15/88) SS **91**
Merlot Napa Valley Selected Cuvée 1984 $13 (5/15/87) **80**
Merlot Napa Valley Selected Cuvée 1983 $13 (12/16/85) **83**
Merlot Napa Valley Selected Cuvée 1982 $13 (10/01/85) **90**
Merlot Napa Valley Selected Cuvée 1981 $12.50 (3/16/84) **82**
Cabernet Sauvignon Napa Valley Diamond Mountain 1987 $35 (11/15/90) **84**
Cabernet Sauvignon Napa Valley Diamond Mountain 1986 Rel: $30 Cur: $33 (11/30/89) **92**
Cabernet Sauvignon Napa Valley Rutherford Cuvée 1990 (NR) (5/15/91) (BT) **85+**
Cabernet Sauvignon Napa Valley Rutherford Cuvée 1989 (NR) (5/15/91) (BT) **90+**
Napa Valley Diamond Mountain Andrus Reserve 1988 $15 (11/15/91) **82**
Napa Valley Rutherford Cuvée Andrus Reserve 1988 $15 (11/15/91) **65**

PINNACLES (United States/California)
Chardonnay Monterey 1990 $16 (7/15/92) **85**
Pinot Noir Monterey Pinnacles Vineyard 1988 $16 (10/31/91) **74**

PINSON (Other/Mexico)
Chardonnay Mexico 1987 $4.50 (6/30/90) **73**

CHATEAU DU PINTEY (France/Bordeaux)
Bordeaux Supérieur 1988 $11 (8/31/91) **75**

PINTLER (United States/Idaho)
Cabernet Sauvignon Idaho 1988 $16 (2/29/92) **81**
Chardonnay Idaho Vickers Vineyard Barrel Fermented 1990 $11 (2/29/92) **84**
White Riesling Idaho Dry 1989 $6.25 (2/29/92) **82**

A. PINTOS DOS SANTOS (Portugal)
Vintage Port 1985 ($NA) (VP-1/90) **69**
Vintage Port 1982 ($NA) (VP-1/90) **70**
Vintage Port 1980 ($NA) (VP-1/90) **70**
Vintage Port 1970 ($NA) (VP-1/90) **70**

Key to Symbols

The scores reported here are the results of blind tastings conducted by our panel of senior editors. Wines that carry the initials below are results of individual tastings.

THE WINE SPECTATOR 100-POINT SCALE 95-100—Classic, a great wine; ***90-94***—Outstanding, superior character and style; ***80-89***—Good to very good, a wine with special qualities; ***70-79***—Average, drinkable wine that may have minor flaws; ***60-69***—Below average, drinkable but not recommended; ***50-59***—Poor, undrinkable, not recommended. "+"—With a score indicates a range; used primarily with barrel tastings to indicate a preliminary score.

SPECIAL DESIGNATIONS SS—Spectator Selection, CS—Cellar Selection, BB—Best Buy, ($NA)—Price not available, (NR)—Not released.

TASTER'S INITIALS (JG)—Jim Gordon, (HS)—Harvey Steiman, (JL)—James Laube, (JS)—James Suckling, (TM)—Thomas Matthews, (TR)—Terry Robards, (PM)—Per-Henrik Mansson, (BT)—Barrel Tasting (these wines were tasted blind from barrel samples), (CA-date)—*California's Great Cabernets* by James Laube, (CH-date)—*California's Great Chardonnays* by James Laube, (VP-date)—*Vintage Port* by James Suckling.

DATE TASTED Dates in parentheses represent the issue in which the rating was published.

CHATEAU PIOT-DAVID (France/Sauternes)
Barsac 1989 ($NA) (6/15/90) (BT) **85+**

PIPER-HEIDSIECK (France/Champagne)
Brut Champagne 1985 $43 (12/31/90) **88**
Brut Champagne 1982 $32 (12/31/88) **86**
Brut Champagne Cuvée Brut NV $28 (12/31/91) **88**
Brut Champagne Extra NV $26 (12/31/87) **78**
Brut Champagne Sauvage 1982 $30 (12/31/89) **89**
Extra Dry Champagne NV $24 (12/31/91) **85**
Rare Champagne 1985 ($NA) (12/31/90) **80**
Rare Champagne 1979 $65 (3/15/87) **89**
Rare Champagne 1976 $66 (8/01/85) **88**

PIPER SONOMA (United States/California)
Blanc de Noirs Sonoma County 1988 $13.50 (1/31/92) **86**
Blanc de Noirs Sonoma County 1987 $16 (6/15/91) **83**
Blanc de Noirs Sonoma County 1986 $15 (5/31/89) **87**
Blanc de Noirs Sonoma County 1983 $15 (12/31/86) **88**
Blanc de Noirs Sonoma County 1982 $15 (4/01/86) **86**
Brut Sonoma County 1988 $13.50 (1/31/92) **88**
Brut Sonoma County 1987 $16 (6/15/91) **87**
Brut Sonoma County 1986 $14 (5/31/89) **82**
Brut Sonoma County 1985 $14 (7/15/88) **79**
Brut Sonoma County 1983 $13 (12/31/86) **79**
Brut Sonoma County 1982 $13 (5/01/86) **62**
Brut Sonoma County Reserve 1982 $20 (12/31/89) **93**
Brut Sonoma County Tête de Cuvée 1981 $29 (5/31/89) **88**

PIPERS BROOK (Australia)
Chardonnay Tasmania 1990 $25 (2/15/92) **87**
Chardonnay Tasmania 1989 $25 (3/31/91) **86**
Chardonnay Tasmania 1988 $25 (3/31/91) **86**
Pinot Noir Tasmania 1990 $25 (2/29/92) **81**

CHATEAU PIQUE-CAILLOU (France/Bordeaux)
Pessac-Léognan 1988 ($NA) (6/30/89) (BT) **75+**
Pessac-Léognan 1987 ($NA) (6/30/89) (BT) **70+**
Pessac-Léognan 1986 ($NA) (6/30/88) (BT) **80+**

BODEGAS PIQUERAS (Spain)
Almansa Castillo de Almansa Vino de Crianza 1986 $8.50 (4/15/92) BB **83**
Almansa Castillo de Almansa Vino de Crianza 1985 $8 (9/30/91) BB **85**
Almansa Castillo de Almansa Vino de Crianza 1983 $6.50 (7/31/89) BB **88**

CHATEAU PIRON (France/Bordeaux)
Graves Blanc 1984 $7.50 (7/16/86) **80**
Graves Blanc 1983 $6.50 (5/16/85) **73**
Graves Blanc 1982 $6.75 (3/01/84) **71**

CHATEAU PITRAY (France/Bordeaux)
Côtes de Castillon 1988 $7 (2/28/91) BB **83**
Côtes de Castillon 1986 $6 (9/30/89) BB **81**

PLACE D'ARGENT (France/Other)
Cabernet Sauvignon Vin de Pays de l'Aude 1985 $5.50 (4/15/89) **78**
Merlot Vin de Pays de l'Aude 1987 $5 (4/30/90) **77**

PLACIDO (Italy/Tuscany)
1989 $6 (7/15/91) **74**
Chianti 1989 $6 (7/15/91) **76**

CHATEAU PLAGNAC (France/Bordeaux)
Médoc 1991 (NR) (5/15/92) (BT) **75+**
Médoc 1990 (NR) (5/15/92) (BT) **80+**
Médoc 1989 $11.50 (3/15/92) **88**
Médoc 1988 $8.50 (4/30/91) **79**
Médoc 1987 $8 (11/30/89) (JS) **77**
Médoc 1986 $9 (11/30/89) (JS) **82**
Médoc 1985 $9 (8/31/88) **68**

CHATEAU PLAISANCE (France/Bordeaux)
Premières Côtes de Blaye Cuvée Spéciale 1989 $9 (2/28/91) BB **85**
Premières Côtes de Bordeaux Cuvée Spéciale 1989 $13 (1/31/92) **86**

PLAM (United States/California)
Cabernet Sauvignon Napa Valley 1988 $28 (9/30/91) **79**
Cabernet Sauvignon Napa Valley 1986 $24 (9/15/89) **92**
Cabernet Sauvignon Napa Valley 1985 $24 (6/30/88) **91**
Chardonnay Napa Valley 1989 $16 (7/15/91) **85**
Chardonnay Napa Valley 1988 $16 (6/30/90) **85**
Chardonnay Napa Valley 1986 $18 (4/15/89) **84**
Chardonnay Napa Valley 1985 $12 (7/15/88) **79**
Fumé Blanc Napa Valley 1989 $9 (11/15/91) **80**

CHATEAU PLANTEY (France/Bordeaux)
Pauillac 1989 (NR) (3/15/92) **78**

LES PLANTIERS DU HAUT-BRION (France/Bordeaux)
Graves Blanc 1974 $24 (3/31/89) **80**

LA PLAYA (Chile)
Cabernet Sauvignon Maipo Valley 1988 $5 (6/15/92) BB **83**
Cabernet Sauvignon Maipo Valley 1986 $4.50 (3/15/90) **74**
Merlot Maipo Valley 1988 $5 (6/16/92) BB **82**
Merlot Maipo Valley 1988 $5 (10/15/91) BB **81**
Merlot Maipo Valley 1987 $4.50 (3/15/90) **75**
Sauvignon Blanc Maipo Valley 1990 $5 (10/15/91) **71**

CHATEAU PLINCE (France/Bordeaux)
Pomerol 1990 (NR) (5/15/92) (BT) **85+**
Pomerol 1989 $15 (4/30/91) (BT) **80+**
Pomerol 1987 Rel: $16 Cur: $19 (6/30/89) (BT) **75+**
Pomerol 1985 $17 (5/15/87) (BT) **70+**

PLOZNER (Italy/North)
Chardonnay Grave del Friuli 1988 $6 (9/15/89) **78**

POCAS JUNIOR (Portugal)
Tawny Port 20 Year Old NV $35 (2/28/90) (JS) **89**
Vintage Port 1985 Rel: $17 Cur: $19 (VP-2/90) **85**
Vintage Port 1975 $38 (VP-2/90) **74**
Vintage Port 1970 $52 (VP-2/90) **84**
Vintage Port 1963 $100 (VP-2/90) **82**
Vintage Port 1960 $80 (VP-2/90) **82**

PODERE IL POGGIOLO (Italy/Tuscany)
Brunello di Montalcino 1985 $34 (11/30/90) **93**

LA PODERINA (Italy/Tuscany)
Brunello di Montalcino 1979 $13 (2/16/86) **69**

IL PODERUCCIO (Italy/Tuscany)
Brunello di Montalcino 1986 $21 (3/31/92) **83**
Brunello di Montalcino I Due Cipressi 1985 $22 (4/15/91) **91**
Rosso di Montalcino 1989 $9 (4/30/92) **83**
Rosso di Montalcino I Due Cipressi 1988 $9.50 (4/30/91) **83**

POGGERINO (Italy/Tuscany)
Chianti Classico 1988 $12.50 (11/30/91) **78**

POGGIARELLO (Italy/Tuscany)
Chianti Classico De Rham i Riservati 4 1985 $6 (10/31/88) BB **83**

POGGIO ANTICO (Italy/Tuscany)
Brunello di Montalcino 1986 $40 (8/31/91) **91**
Brunello di Montalcino 1985 Rel: $36 Cur: $42 (11/30/90) CS **95**
Brunello di Montalcino 1982 $25 (11/30/89) **92**
Brunello di Montalcino 1979 $12.50 (9/15/86) **72**
Brunello di Montalcino Riserva 1985 $55 (8/31/91) **93**
Rosso di Montalcino 1989 $21 (8/31/91) **85**

POGGIO A 'FRATI (Italy/Tuscany)
Chianti Classico Riserva 1985 ($NA) (9/15/91) **84**

CASTELLO POGGIO (Italy/Piedmont)
Barbera d'Asti 1988 $9 (10/31/91) BB **85**

GIUSEPPE POGGIO (Italy/Piedmont)
Bricco Trionzo 1985 $10 (3/15/89) **72**

POGGIO AL SOLE (Italy/Tuscany)
Chianti Classico 1988 ($NA) (9/15/91) **91**
Chianti Classico Riserva 1985 ($NA) (9/15/91) **88**

POGGIO ALLE GAZZE (Italy/Tuscany)
1989 $18 (9/15/91) **79**

TENUTA POGGIO DEL LUPO (Italy/Other)
Orvieto 1989 $9 (8/31/91) **80**

POGGIO SALVI (Italy/Tuscany)
Brunello di Montalcino 1981 $20 (10/15/88) **88**

IL POGGIOLINO (Italy/Tuscany)
Chianti Classico Riserva 1985 ($NA) (9/15/91) **84**

IL POGGIONE (Italy/Tuscany)
Brunello di Montalcino 1982 $30 (9/15/88) **88**
Brunello di Montalcino 1981 $28 (9/15/86) **93**
Brunello di Montalcino Riserva 1979 $35 (9/15/86) **79**
Brunello di Montalcino Riserva 1978 $35 (7/01/84) SS **92**

CHATEAU LA POINTE (France/Bordeaux)
Pomerol 1990 (NR) (5/15/92) (BT) **85+**
Pomerol 1989 $28 (3/15/92) **95**
Pomerol 1988 $35 (7/31/91) **83**
Pomerol 1987 $21 (6/30/88) (BT) **70+**
Pomerol 1986 $21 (6/15/89) **90**
Pomerol 1982 $22 (5/15/89) (TR) **85**
Pomerol 1962 $35 (11/30/87) (JS) **80**
Pomerol 1945 $250 (3/16/86) (JL) **78**

POJER E SANDRI (Italy/North)
Chardonnay Trentino 1987 $8 (9/15/89) **84**
Chardonnay Trentino 1985 $7.50 (9/15/89) **82**

POLIZIANO (Italy/Tuscany)
Vino Nobile di Montepulciano 1988 $12 (12/15/91) **81**
Vino Nobile di Montepulciano 1987 $12 (3/15/91) **84**
Vino Nobile di Montepulciano 1985 $13 (9/15/88) **89**

CHATEAU DE POMMARD (France/Burgundy)
Pommard 1989 (NR) (1/31/92) **86**
Pommard 1979 $33 (9/01/85) **88**

POMMERY (France/Champagne)
Brut Champagne 1985 $40 (12/31/90) **87**
Brut Champagne 1982 $24 (2/15/88) **93**
Brut Champagne NV $23 (12/31/87) **79**
Brut Champagne Royal NV $30 (12/31/91) **87**
Brut Rosé Champagne NV $27 (12/16/85) **86**

DOMAINE PONAVOY (France/Burgundy)
Chassagne-Montrachet 1988 $40 (2/15/91) **86**

DOMAINE PONNELLE (France/Burgundy)
Côte de Beaune Blanc Les Pierres Blanches 1988 $18 (2/28/91) **68**
Côte de Beaune Les Pierres Blanches 1987 $14 (3/31/91) **83**

PIERRE PONNELLE (France/Burgundy)
Bourgogne Hautes Côtes de Nuits Blanc 1989 $15 (8/31/91) **69**
Corton-Charlemagne 1989 $85 (8/31/91) **88**
Fixin Hervelets 1959 ($NA) (8/31/90) (TR) **94**
Vougeot Blanc Le Village 1989 $32 (8/31/91) **82**

DOMAINE PONSOT (France/Burgundy)
Chambolle-Musigny Les Charmes 1988 $58 (4/30/91) **92**
Chambolle-Musigny Les Charmes 1985 $75 (6/15/88) **94**
Clos de la Roche 1984 Rel: $29 Cur: $48 (2/15/88) **73**
Clos de la Roche Cuvée Vieilles Vignes 1988 $185 (5/15/91) **88**
Clos de la Roche Cuvée Vieilles Vignes 1985 $200 (6/15/88) **90**
Clos de la Roche Cuvée William 1988 $150 (5/15/91) **89**
Clos St.-Denis Cuvée Vieilles Vignes 1988 $165 (7/15/91) **85**
Griotte-Chambertin 1988 $150 (5/15/91) **89**
Latricières-Chambertin 1988 $150 (5/15/91) **91**
Morey-St.-Denis Blanc Monts-Luisants 1988 $50 (5/31/91) **87**
Morey-St.-Denis Monts-Luisants 1988 $40 (4/30/91) **85**

PONTALLIER JOHNSON (France/Bordeaux)
Bordeaux Merlot 1982 $8 (10/15/87) **77**

CHATEAU PONTET-CANET (France/Bordeaux)
Pauillac 1991 (NR) (5/15/92) (BT) **85+**
Pauillac 1990 (NR) (5/15/92) (BT) **90+**
Pauillac 1989 $27 (3/15/92) **89**
Pauillac 1988 $24 (6/30/89) (BT) **80+**
Pauillac 1987 $14 (6/30/89) (BT) **75+**
Pauillac 1986 $21 (5/31/89) **89**
Pauillac 1985 $22 (5/15/87) (BT) **80+**
Pauillac 1961 $95 (3/16/86) (TR) **66**
Pauillac 1945 $250 (3/16/86) (JL) **60**

LANZA GINORI PONTI (Italy/Tuscany)
Vigna di Bugialla Poggerino 1988 $17 (1/31/92) **84**

PONTIN DEL ROZA (United States/Washington)
Roza Sunset Yakima Valley 1988 $6 (10/15/89) **80**

PONZI (United States/Oregon)
Pinot Noir Willamette Valley 1988 $16 (5/31/91) **76**
Pinot Noir Willamette Valley 1987 $15 (2/15/90) **88**
Pinot Noir Willamette Valley 1985 $20 (2/15/90) **84**
Pinot Noir Willamette Valley Reserve 1988 $25 (4/15/91) **86**
Pinot Noir Willamette Valley Reserve 1987 $20 (2/15/90) **91**
Pinot Noir Willamette Valley Reserve 1986 $15 (6/15/88) **81**

POPPY HILL (United States/California)
Cabernet Sauvignon California 1987 $7.50 (5/31/91) **78**

CANTINA DELLA PORTA ROSSA (Italy/Piedmont)
Barolo Riserva 1985 $26 (1/31/92) **87**
Barolo Vigna Delizia Riserva 1982 $25 (8/31/91) **87**
Diano d'Alba Vigna Bruni 1990 $14 (3/31/92) **84**
Roero Arneis 1990 $17 (1/31/92) **78**

PORTAL DEL ALTO (Chile)
Cabernet Sauvignon Maipo Valley 1987 $3.50 (6/15/92) BB **83**
Cabernet Sauvignon Maipo Valley Gran Reserva 1986 $3.75 (6/15/92) BB **79**
Sauvignon Blanc Maipo Valley 1991 $3.50 (6/16/92) **76**

PORTTEUS (United States/Washington)
Cabernet Sauvignon Yakima Valley 1987 $18 (3/31/92) **86**
Sémillon Yakima Valley 1987 $7 (10/15/89) **67**

CHATEAU POTENSAC (France/Bordeaux)
Médoc 1988 $14 (10/31/91) **80**
Médoc 1987 Rel: $9.50 Cur: $12 (5/15/90) **72**
Médoc 1986 $15 (11/30/89) (JS) **86**
Médoc 1985 Rel: $11 Cur: $21 (5/15/87) (BT) **80+**
Médoc 1983 Rel: $9 Cur: $28 (10/15/86) **75**

POTHIER-EMONIN (France/Burgundy)
Volnay 1986 $24 (4/30/89) **85**

POTHIER-RIEUSSET (France/Burgundy)
Beaune Boucherottes 1988 $35 (11/30/90) **88**
Beaune Boucherottes 1986 $19 (5/31/89) **88**
Bourgogne Rouge 1986 $10 (6/15/89) **79**
Bourgogne Rouge 1985 $7.50 (6/30/88) BB **83**
Pommard 1986 $25 (9/15/89) **76**
Pommard Clos de Verger 1986 $33 (9/15/89) **87**
Pommard Rugiens 1986 $35 (9/15/89) **72**
Volnay 1985 $21 (2/15/88) **93**

CHATEAU POUGET (France/Bordeaux)
Margaux 1988 $18 (6/30/89) (BT) **85+**
Margaux 1987 $15 (6/30/89) (BT) **70+**
Margaux 1986 $16 (5/15/87) (BT) **70+**
Margaux 1985 Rel: $14 Cur: $16 (5/15/87) (BT) **70+**
Margaux 1983 Rel: $11 Cur: $19 (2/15/87) **86**

MICHEL POUHIN-SEURRE (France/Burgundy)
Meursault Le Limosin 1989 $44 (11/15/91) **89**
Meursault Le Limosin 1986 $25 (2/15/88) **88**
Meursault Les Poruzots 1989 $64 (11/15/91) **90**
Puligny-Montrachet 1989 $52 (11/15/91) **78**

CHATEAU POUJEAUX (France/Bordeaux)
Moulis 1991 (NR) (5/15/92) (BT) **80+**
Moulis 1990 (NR) (5/15/92) (BT) **85+**
Moulis 1989 $21 (3/15/92) **90**
Moulis 1988 $15 (2/28/91) **88**
Moulis 1987 $15 (5/15/90) **74**
Moulis 1986 $22 (11/30/89) (JS) **88**
Moulis 1985 $18 (9/30/88) **87**
Moulis 1983 Rel: $13 Cur: $19 (10/31/86) **79**
Moulis 1982 $27 (11/30/89) (JS) **88**

LA POUSSE D'OR (France/Burgundy)
Pommard Les Jarollières 1988 $57 (8/31/91) **88**
Pommard Les Jarollières 1986 $45 (4/30/89) **70**
Pommard Les Jarollières 1985 $39 (3/15/88) **87**
Santenay Clos Tavannes 1989 $29 (1/31/92) **91**
Santenay Clos Tavannes 1988 $28 (8/31/91) **83**
Santenay Clos Tavannes 1986 $27 (6/15/89) **78**
Santenay Clos Tavannes 1985 $22 (3/15/88) **67**
Volnay Les Caillerets 1988 $49 (8/31/91) **85**
Volnay Les Caillerets 1985 $35 (3/15/88) **90**
Volnay Les Caillerets Clos des 60 Ouvrées 1988 $53 (8/31/91) **82**
Volnay Les Caillerets Clos des 60 Ouvrées 1987 $29 (6/15/90) **82**
Volnay Les Caillerets Clos des 60 Ouvrées 1986 $41 (4/30/89) **83**
Volnay Les Caillerets Clos des 60 Ouvrées 1985 $39 (3/15/88) **86**
Volnay Clos d'Audignac 1989 $45 (1/31/92) **92**
Volnay Clos de la Bousse d'Or 1989 $60 (1/31/92) **90**
Volnay Clos de la Bousse d'Or 1986 $46 (4/30/89) **75**

DOMAINE DE POUY (France/Other)
Vin de Pays des Côtes de Gascogne Cépage Ugni Blanc 1989 $5 (11/30/90) BB **80**

SALVADOR POVEDA (Spain)
Tinto Gran Reserva Alicante No. 1 1985 $9 (11/15/91) **79**

CHATEAU LA PRADE (France/Bordeaux)
Côtes de Francs 1988 ($NA) (6/30/89) (BT) **70+**

CHATEAU PRADEAUX (France/Other)
Bandol 1986 $18 (10/31/90) **83**

BERNARD PRADEL (United States/California)
Cabernet Sauvignon Napa Valley Limited Barrel Selection 1988 $20 (11/15/91) **80**
Cabernet Sauvignon Napa Valley 1987 $20 (10/15/90) **86**
Cabernet Sauvignon Napa Valley 1986 $12 (1/31/90) **82**

Cabernet Sauvignon Napa Valley 1985 $12 (4/30/89) **91**
Cabernet Sauvignon Napa Valley 1984 $11 (2/29/88) **88**
Chardonnay Napa Valley 1986 $9.50 (2/29/88) **82**
Sauvignon Blanc Late Harvest Napa Valley Allais Vineyard Botrytis 1985 $9/375ml (5/31/88) **75**

PRATOSCURO (Italy/Other)
1989 $18 (12/31/90) **79**

PREECE (Australia)
Cabernet Sauvignon Goulburn Valley 1989 $13 (3/15/92) **84**
Chardonnay Goulburn Valley 1990 $13 (2/15/92) **83**
Chardonnay Goulburn Valley 1989 $14 (9/15/91) **86**

PREISS-HENNY (France/Alsace)
Gewürztraminer Alsace 1990 (NR) (2/15/92) **86**
Gewürztraminer Alsace Cuvée Marcel Preiss Vendange Tardive 1990 (NR) (2/15/92) (BT) **85+**
Pinot Blanc Alsace 1990 (NR) (2/15/92) **86**
Riesling Alsace 1990 $11 (2/15/92) **80**
Riesling Alsace Cuvée Marcel Preiss 1990 (NR) (2/15/92) **85**
Riesling Alsace Château de Mittelwihr 1989 $13 (10/31/91) **78**
Sylvaner Alsace Château de Mittelwihr 1989 $10 (10/31/91) **68**

PRESTON (United States/California)
Barbera Dry Creek Valley 1989 $12.50 (3/15/92) **86**
Cabernet Sauvignon Dry Creek Valley 1988 Rel: $14 Cur: $16 (3/15/92) **80**
Cabernet Sauvignon Dry Creek Valley 1987 Rel: $14 Cur: $17 (10/31/90) **88**
Cabernet Sauvignon Dry Creek Valley 1986 Rel: $11 Cur: $17 (3/15/90) **87**
Cabernet Sauvignon Dry Creek Valley 1985 Rel: $11 Cur: $18 (CA-3/89) **89**
Cabernet Sauvignon Dry Creek Valley 1984 Rel: $11 Cur: $17 (CA-3/89) **87**
Cabernet Sauvignon Dry Creek Valley 1983 Rel: $11 Cur: $15 (CA-3/89) **86**
Cabernet Sauvignon Dry Creek Valley 1982 Rel: $11 Cur: $18 (CA-3/89) **87**
Chenin Blanc Dry Creek Valley 1988 $7.50 (7/31/89) **82**
Estate Red Dry Creek Valley 1989 $5.50 (6/30/90) **77**
Estate Red Dry Creek Valley 1988 $5 (8/31/89) BB **82**
Estate White Dry Creek Valley 1988 $5 (9/15/89) BB **83**
Faux-Castel Rouge Dry Creek Valley 1990 $9 (6/30/92) **82**
Gamay Beaujolais Dry Creek Valley 1988 $7 (2/15/89) **85**
Muscat Canelli Dry Creek Valley 1987 $7 (8/31/89) **78**
Muscat Canelli Late Harvest Dry Creek Valley Muscat Brûlée 1989 $12/375ml (3/15/92) **82**
Muscat Canelli Late Harvest Dry Creek Valley Muscat Brûlée 1987 $12/375ml (8/31/89) **91**
Sauvignon Blanc Dry Creek Valley Cuvée de Fumé 1990 $9.50 (7/15/91) **87**
Sauvignon Blanc Dry Creek Valley Cuvée de Fumé 1989 $8 (5/15/90) **86**
Sauvignon Blanc Dry Creek Valley Cuvée de Fumé 1988 $8 (9/15/89) **86**
Sauvignon Blanc Dry Creek Valley Estate Reserve 1989 $12 (12/31/90) **82**
Sauvignon Blanc Dry Creek Valley Estate Reserve 1988 $10 (11/30/89) **87**
Syrah-Sirah Dry Creek Valley 1989 $18 (3/15/92) **78**
Syrah-Sirah Dry Creek Valley 1986 $11 (2/15/89) **90**
Syrah-Sirah Dry Creek Valley 1985 $9.50 (1/31/88) **91**
Zinfandel Dry Creek Valley 1988 $10 (10/15/90) **86**
Zinfandel Dry Creek Valley 1987 $10 (3/15/90) **83**
Zinfandel Dry Creek Valley 1986 $8.50 (12/15/88) **84**
Zinfandel Dry Creek Valley 1985 $8.50 (11/15/87) **91**
Zinfandel Dry Creek Valley 1984 $8 (12/31/86) **80**

PRESTON WINE CELLARS (United States/Washington)
Cabernet Sauvignon Washington 1982 $8 (5/31/88) **84**
Cabernet Sauvignon Washington Oak Aged 1989 $10 (5/15/91) **85**
Cabernet Sauvignon Washington Preston Vineyard Oak Aged 1990 $12 (4/30/92) **76**
Cabernet Sauvignon Washington Preston Vineyard Reserve 1990 $21 (3/31/92) **91**
Cabernet Sauvignon Washington Preston Vineyard Selected Reserve 1987 $13.50 (10/15/89) **62**
Cabernet Sauvignon Washington Reserve 1989 $24 (8/31/91) **90**
Chardonnay Washington Barrel Fermented 1990 $12 (11/30/91) **81**
Chardonnay Washington Barrel Fermented 1989 $12 (5/31/91) **91**
Chardonnay Washington Preston Vineyard Hand Harvested 1987 $10 (10/15/89) **82**
Fumé Blanc Washington Oak Aged 1989 $7 (7/15/91) **78**
Johannisberg Riesling Washington Preston Vineyard 1989 $6 (6/15/92) **78**
Johannisberg Riesling Washington Preston Vineyard Hand Harvested 1987 $5.75 (10/15/89) **71**
Merlot Washington Oak Aged 1988 $7 (8/31/91) **77**
White Riesling Late Harvest Washington Ice Wine 1986 $38 (10/15/89) **80**

PREYS (France/Loire)
Touraine Côte Cuvée Prestige 1989 $9 (1/31/92) **75**

DOMAINE JACQUES PRIEUR (France/Burgundy)
Meursault Clos de Mazeray 1989 $25 (8/31/91) **86**
Meursault Les Perrières 1989 $30 (8/31/91) **89**
Montrachet 1989 $100 (8/31/91) **92**
Montrachet 1986 $165 (2/28/89) **92**
Puligny-Montrachet Les Combettes 1989 $33 (8/31/91) **90**

DOMAINE PRIEUR-BRUNET (France/Burgundy)
Bâtard-Montrachet 1988 $75 (7/31/90) **87**
Beaune Clos du Roy 1988 $30 (12/31/90) **82**
Bourgogne Blanc Chardonnay Prieur 1989 ($NA) (8/31/91) **83**
Chassagne-Montrachet Les Embazées 1989 $54 (8/31/91) **88**
Chassagne-Montrachet Rouge Morgeot 1988 $17 (11/15/90) **83**
Meursault 1989 ($NA) (8/31/91) **88**
Meursault Les Charmes 1989 $54 (8/31/91) **89**
Meursault Les Charmes 1988 $35 (8/31/90) **85**
Meursault Les Charmes 1986 $30 (4/30/89) **90**
Meursault Les Chevalières 1989 $45 (8/31/91) **90**
Meursault Les Chevalières 1988 $30 (2/28/91) **89**
Meursault Les Forges Dessus 1989 ($NA) (8/31/91) **89**

Key to Symbols

The scores reported here are the results of blind tastings conducted by our panel of senior editors. Wines that carry the initials below are results of individual tastings.

THE WINE SPECTATOR 100-POINT SCALE 95-100—Classic, a great wine; ***90-94***—Outstanding, superior character and style; ***80-89***—Good to very good, a wine with special qualities; ***70-79***—Average, drinkable wine that may have minor flaws; ***60-69***—Below average, drinkable but not recommended; ***50-59***—Poor, undrinkable, not recommended. "+"—With a score indicates a range; used primarily with barrel tastings to indicate a preliminary score.

SPECIAL DESIGNATIONS SS—Spectator Selection, CS—Cellar Selection, BB—Best Buy, ($NA)—Price not available, (NR)—Not released.

TASTER'S INITIALS (JG)—Jim Gordon, (HS)—Harvey Steiman, (JL)—James Laube, (JS)—James Suckling, (TM)—Thomas Matthews, (TR)—Terry Robards, (PM)—Per-Henrik Mansson, (BT)—Barrel Tasting (these wines were tasted blind from barrel samples), (CA-date)—*California's Great Cabernets* by James Laube, (CH-date)—*California's Great Chardonnays* by James Laube, (VP-date)—*Vintage Port* by James Suckling.

DATE TASTED Dates in parentheses represent the issue in which the rating was published.

Santenay Maladière 1988 $20 (11/15/90) **80**
Volnay-Santenots 1988 $35 (11/30/90) **85**

CHATEAU DE PRIEURE (France/Bordeaux)
Premières Côtes de Bordeaux 1985 $4.50 (5/31/88) **71**

PRIEURE DE ST.-JEAN DE BEBIAN (France/Other)
Côteaux du Languedoc 1989 $23 (6/30/92) **77**

CHATEAU PRIEURE-LICHINE (France/Bordeaux)
Margaux 1991 (NR) (5/15/92) (BT) **80+**
Margaux 1990 (NR) (5/15/92) (BT) **90+**
Margaux 1989 $31 (3/15/92) **86**
Margaux 1988 $30 (4/30/91) **90**
Margaux 1987 Rel: $13 Cur: $16 (2/15/90) **78**
Margaux 1986 Rel: $21 Cur: $25 (6/15/89) **92**
Margaux 1985 $24 (2/15/88) **82**
Margaux 1984 $14 (11/30/86) **80**
Margaux 1983 Rel: $18 Cur: $30 (4/16/86) **96**
Margaux 1982 Rel: $15 Cur: $32 (5/01/85) **89**
Margaux 1981 Rel: $12 Cur: $22 (11/01/84) **86**
Margaux 1959 $50 (10/15/90) (JS) **80**

CHATEAU PRIEURS DE LA COMMANDERIE (France/Bordeaux)
Pomerol 1989 (NR) (4/30/91) (BT) **90+**
Pomerol 1987 ($NA) (6/30/88) (BT) **70+**
Pomerol 1986 ($NA) (6/30/88) (BT) **75+**
Pomerol 1985 $27 (9/30/88) **93**
Pomerol 1983 $25 (9/30/86) **79**

PRINCE MICHEL (United States/Virginia)
Chardonnay Virginia 1990 $13 (2/29/92) **75**
Chardonnay Virginia 1989 $9 (8/31/91) **79**
Chardonnay Virginia Barrel Select 1990 $15 (2/29/92) **76**
Chardonnay Virginia Barrel Select 1988 $15 (6/30/90) **87**
Le Ducq Lot 87 NV $50 (2/29/92) **79**

DORO PRINCIC (Italy/North)
Pinot Bianco Collio 1989 $14 (7/15/91) **78**
Tocai Friulano Collio 1989 $14 (8/31/91) **82**

BODEGAS PRINCIPE DE VIANA (Spain)
Cabernet Sauvignon Navarra 1989 $8 (3/31/91) BB **83**

CAVE DE PRISSE (France/Burgundy)
Mâcon-Prissé Les Clochettes 1986 $8.50 (1/31/89) **84**
St.-Véran Les Blanchettes 1985 $10 (3/31/87) **92**

PRIVILEGIO DEL RAY SANCHO (Spain)
Rioja 1978 $3 (4/01/84) **76**

CHATEAU PROCHE PONTET (France/Bordeaux)
Haut-Médoc 1988 ($NA) (6/30/89) (BT) **60+**

PRODUTTORI DEL BARBARESCO (Italy/Piedmont)
Barbaresco 1988 $16 (4/30/92) **86**
Barbaresco 1986 $12 (10/31/90) **90**
Barbaresco 1984 $12 (9/15/88) (HS) **80**
Barbaresco 1983 $17 (9/15/88) (HS) **85**
Barbaresco 1982 $16 (9/15/88) (HS) **87**
Barbaresco 1979 $17 (9/15/88) (HS) **90**
Barbaresco Asili Riserva 1985 $27 (10/31/90) **92**
Barbaresco Asili Riserva 1982 $22 (9/15/88) (HS) **89**
Barbaresco Moccagatta Riserva 1982 $22 (9/15/88) (HS) **89**
Barbaresco Montefico Riserva 1982 $22 (9/15/88) (HS) **85**
Barbaresco Montefico Riserva 1978 $22 (9/15/88) (HS) **92**
Barbaresco Montestefano Riserva 1985 $25 (10/31/90) **82**
Barbaresco Montestefano Riserva 1982 Rel: $18 Cur: $22 (9/15/88) (HS) **88**
Barbaresco Ovello Riserva 1985 $25 (10/31/90) **86**
Barbaresco Ovello Riserva 1982 $22 (9/15/88) (HS) **86**
Barbaresco Paje Riserva 1982 $22 (9/15/88) (HS) **91**
Barbaresco Pora Riserva 1982 $18 (9/15/88) (HS) **91**
Barbaresco Pora Riserva 1979 $24 (9/15/88) (HS) **91**
Barbaresco Rabajà Riserva 1982 $22 (9/15/88) (HS) **89**
Barbaresco Rio Sordo Riserva 1982 $22 (9/15/88) (HS) **87**
Barbaresco Selezióne del Trentennio 30 1988 $28 (4/30/92) **91**
Nebbioio delle Langhe 1988 $9 (2/28/91) **82**

CHATEAU PROST (France/Sauternes)
Barsac 1989 ($NA) (6/15/90) (BT) **70+**

ZACH. BERGWEILER PRUM-ERBEN (Germany)
Riesling Qualitätswein Mosel-Saar-Ruwer Bernkasteler Badstube Dr. Heidemanns 1987 $11 (4/30/89) **81**

DR. F. PRUM (Germany)
Riesling Spätlese Mosel-Saar-Ruwer Graacher Domprobst 1985 $12 (10/15/87) **74**

JOH. JOS. PRUM (Germany)
Riesling Auslese Mosel-Saar-Ruwer Graacher Himmelreich 1990 $24 (12/15/91) **92**
Riesling Auslese Mosel-Saar-Ruwer Wehlener Sonnenuhr 1989 $35 (12/15/90) **92**
Riesling Auslese Mosel-Saar-Ruwer Wehlener Sonnenuhr 1988 $33 (9/30/89) **90**
Riesling Auslese Mosel-Saar-Ruwer Wehlener Sonnenuhr 1985 $20 (5/31/87) **90**
Riesling Auslese Mosel-Saar-Ruwer Wehlener Sonnenuhr (Cask 27) 1990 (NR) (12/15/91) (BT) **86+**
Riesling Auslese Mosel-Saar-Ruwer Wehlener Sonnenuhr (AP1191) 1990 $29 (12/15/91) **93**
Riesling Auslese Mosel-Saar-Ruwer Wehlener Sonnenuhr Gold Cap 1990 $62 (12/15/91) (BT) **96+**
Riesling Auslese Mosel-Saar-Ruwer Wehlener Sonnenuhr Gold Cap 1988 $80 (9/30/89) **98**
Riesling Auslese Mosel-Saar-Ruwer Wehlener Sonnenuhr Long Gold Cap 1990 $250 (12/15/91) (BT) **96+**
Riesling Auslese Mosel-Saar-Ruwer Wehlener Sonnenuhr Long Gold Cap 1989 $249 (12/15/90) **94**
Riesling Beerenauslese Mosel-Saar-Ruwer Wehlener Sonnenuhr 1989 ($NA) (12/15/90) **95**
Riesling Eiswein Mosel-Saar-Ruwer Bernkasteler Johannisbrünchen 1990 (NR) (12/15/91) **96**
Riesling Kabinett Mosel-Saar-Ruwer Wehlener Klosterberg 1990 $15 (12/15/91) **91**
Riesling Kabinett Mosel-Saar-Ruwer Wehlener Klosterberg 1983 $9 (11/16/84) SS **91**
Riesling Kabinett Mosel-Saar-Ruwer Wehlener Nonnenberg 1983 $9 (5/01/85) **87**
Riesling Kabinett Mosel-Saar-Ruwer Wehlener Sonnenuhr 1989 $21 (12/15/90) **91**
Riesling Kabinett Mosel-Saar-Ruwer Wehlener Sonnenuhr 1985 $11.50 (4/15/87) **76**
Riesling Spätlese Mosel-Saar-Ruwer Bernkasteler Badstube 1983 $11 (11/16/85) **50**
Riesling Spätlese Mosel-Saar-Ruwer Graacher Himmelreich 1985 $15.50 (4/15/89) **91**
Riesling Spätlese Mosel-Saar-Ruwer Graacher Himmelreich 1985 $15.50 (5/15/87) **77**
Riesling Spätlese Mosel-Saar-Ruwer Wehlener Sonnenuhr 1990 $24 (12/15/91) **93**
Riesling Spätlese Mosel-Saar-Ruwer Wehlener Sonnenuhr 1989 $29 (12/15/90) **91**
Riesling Spätlese Mosel-Saar-Ruwer Wehlener Sonnenuhr 1986 ($NA) (4/15/89) **92**
Riesling Spätlese Mosel-Saar-Ruwer Wehlener Sonnenuhr 1985 ($NA) (4/15/89) **88**
Riesling Spätlese Mosel-Saar-Ruwer Wehlener Sonnenuhr 1983 $13 (5/01/85) SS **91**

Riesling Spätlese Mosel-Saar-Ruwer Wehlener Sonnenuhr (Cask 1) 1988 $20 (9/30/89) **97**
Riesling Spätlese Mosel-Saar-Ruwer Wehlener Sonnenuhr (Cask 2) 1988 $24 (9/30/89) **98**
Scheurebe Kabinett Mosel-Saar-Ruwer Wehlener Klosterberg 1990 $15 (1/31/92) **91**

S.A. PRUM (Germany)
Riesling Auslese Mosel-Saar-Ruwer Graacher Himmelreich 1988 $25 (9/30/89) **94**
Riesling Auslese Mosel-Saar-Ruwer Wehlener Sonnenuhr 1988 $25 (9/30/89) **85**
Riesling Kabinett Mosel-Saar-Ruwer Graacher Himmelreich 1988 ($NA) (9/30/89) **81**
Riesling Spätlese Mosel-Saar-Ruwer Bernkasteler Graben 1988 $17.50 (9/30/89) **88**
Riesling Spätlese Mosel-Saar-Ruwer Graacher Himmelreich 1988 $18 (9/30/89) **81**
Riesling Spätlese Mosel-Saar-Ruwer Wehlener Sonnenuhr 1988 $18 (9/30/89) **83**

PRUNIER (France/Burgundy)
Auxey-Duresses 1986 $25 (11/15/89) **84**
Auxey-Duresses Rouge Clos du Val 1987 $25 (11/15/89) **84**

PRUNOTTO (Italy/Piedmont)
Barbaresco 1987 $27 (3/31/92) **70**
Barbaresco Montestefano 1987 $37 (3/31/92) **76**
Barbaresco Montestefano 1986 $37 (12/31/90) **86**
Barbaresco Montestefano 1985 $29 (3/31/90) **87**
Barbaresco Rabajà Riserva 1982 $19 (7/31/87) **81**
Barbera d'Alba 1989 $11 (2/15/92) **83**
Barbera d'Alba 1987 $9.50 (3/31/90) **85**
Barbera d'Alba 1985 $8 (7/15/88) **81**
Barbera d'Alba 1983 $6 (7/15/87) BB **89**
Barbera d'Alba Pian Romualdo 1987 $14 (9/15/90) **81**
Barolo 1987 $27 (3/31/92) **85**
Barolo 1985 $31 (3/31/90) **82**
Barolo Bussia 1986 Rel: $39 Cur: $44 (3/31/92) **78**
Barolo Bussia 1985 $38 (9/15/90) **92**
Barolo Bussia 1983 $23 (9/15/88) (HS) **88**
Barolo Bussia 1982 Rel: $25 Cur: $30 (9/15/88) (HS) **91**
Barolo Bussia 1978 $50 (9/15/88) (HS) **86**
Barolo Bussia 1974 $65 (9/15/88) (HS) **80**
Barolo Bussia 1971 $75 (9/15/88) (HS) **90**
Barolo Bussia 1967 $49 (9/15/88) (HS) **82**
Barolo Bussia 1964 $85 (9/15/88) (HS) **80**
Barolo Bussia 1961 $110 (9/15/88) (HS) **91**
Barolo Cannubi 1985 $32 (3/31/90) **85**
Barolo Cannubi 1983 $26 (9/15/88) (HS) **85**
Barolo Cannubi 1982 $25 (9/15/88) (HS) **75**
Barolo Cannubi 1978 $21 (9/15/88) (HS) **78**
Barolo Ginestra di Monforte d'Alba Riserva 1980 $13 (6/30/87) **78**
Barolo Riserva 1980 $12 (6/30/87) **65**
Dolcetto d'Alba 1985 $10 (3/15/89) **84**
Dolcetto d'Alba Gagliassi di Monforte Riserva 1985 $11.50 (3/15/89) **88**

MARQUES DEL PUERTO (Spain)
Rioja 1984 $7 (2/28/90) **78**
Rioja 1982 $6 (11/15/87) (JL) **78**
Rioja Gran Reserva 1978 $20 (3/31/90) **85**

DOMAINE DU PUGET (France/Other)
Cabernet Sauvignon Vin de Pays de l'Aude 1989 $5 (6/30/92) **72**
Merlot Vin de Pays de l'Aude 1989 $5 (6/30/92) **77**
Merlot Vin de Pays de l'Aude 1988 $4 (6/30/90) **76**

PUGLIESE (United States/New York)
Chardonnay North Fork of Long Island 1988 $10 (6/30/91) (TM) **78**

PUIATTI (Italy/North)
Chardonnay 1989 $17 (3/31/91) **84**
Chardonnay Collio 1990 $19 (1/31/92) **81**
Merlot Collio 1989 $26 (1/31/92) **78**
Pinot Bianco Collio 1989 $17 (4/15/91) **85**
Pinot Grigio Collio 1990 $19 (1/31/92) **82**
Pinot Grigio Collio 1989 $17 (3/31/91) **85**

CHATEAU DE PULIGNY-MONTRACHET (France/Burgundy)
Bourgogne Blanc Clos du Château 1988 $19 (7/31/90) **81**
Côte de Nuits-Villages 1988 $17 (3/31/91) **82**
Côte de Nuits-Villages Blanc 1989 $27 (2/28/91) **83**
Meursault 1989 $42 (2/28/91) **82**
Meursault Les Perrières 1989 $57 (2/28/91) **91**
Meursault Les Poruzots 1989 $55 (2/28/91) **90**
Meursault Les Poruzots 1988 $52 (7/15/90) **79**
Monthélie 1988 $16 (11/15/90) **77**
Monthélie Blanc Chardonnay 1989 $26 (2/28/91) **82**
Pommard 1988 $34 (8/31/90) **83**
Puligny-Montrachet 1989 $66 (2/28/91) **74**
Puligny-Montrachet 1986 $60 (2/29/88) **81**
Puligny-Montrachet 1985 $55 (2/29/88) **79**

LOS PUMAS (Chile)
Cabernet Sauvignon Curicó Valley 1988 $4 (9/15/90) **69**

LE PUPILLE (Italy/Tuscany)
Morellino di Scansano Riserva 1986 $16 (6/30/91) **86**

CHATEAU PUY-BLANQUET (France/Bordeaux)
St.-Emilion 1990 (NR) (5/15/92) (BT) **85+**
St.-Emilion 1989 $16 (3/15/92) **90**
St.-Emilion 1988 $15 (6/30/89) (BT) **75+**
St.-Emilion 1987 $14 (6/30/88) (BT) **75+**
St.-Emilion 1986 $16 (6/30/88) (BT) **80+**
St.-Emilion 1985 $13 (4/16/86) (BT) **60+**
St.-Emilion 1983 Rel: $9.50 Cur: $12 (12/31/86) **76**

CHATEAU PUYGUERAUD (France/Bordeaux)
Côtes de Francs 1989 $18 (3/15/92) **83**
Côtes de Francs 1988 $15 (8/31/90) (BT) **80+**
Côtes de Francs 1986 $12 (6/15/89) **84**
Côtes de Francs 1985 $9 (6/30/88) **83**
Côtes de Francs 1983 $7.50 (10/16/85) **82**

QUADY (United States/California)
Black Muscat California Elysium 1990 $12 (11/30/91) **86**
Black Muscat California Elysium 1989 $12 (10/15/90) **85**
Black Muscat California Elysium 1988 $11 (8/31/89) **90**
Black Muscat California Elysium 1987 $6.50/375ml (9/30/88) **82**
Black Muscat California Elysium 1985 $11 (9/15/86) **85**
Black Muscat California Elysium 1984 $11 (8/01/85) **87**
Orange Muscat California Electra 1991 $9.50 (6/15/92) **84**
Orange Muscat California Essensia 1990 $12 (11/30/91) **83**
Orange Muscat California Essensia 1989 $12 (10/15/90) **89**
Orange Muscat California Essensia 1987 $11 (8/31/89) **78**
Orange Muscat California Essensia 1985 $11 (9/30/86) **79**
Orange Muscat California Essensia 1984 $11 (7/01/85) **88**
Port Amador County 1984 $9 (10/01/85) **82**
Port Amador County Frank's Vineyard 1986 $12 (10/15/90) **75**
Port Amador County Frank's Vineyard 1985 $16 (8/31/89) **65**
Port California 1985 $9.50 (8/31/89) **73**
Starboard Amador County 1987 $25 (3/31/91) **81**
Starboard Amador County Batch 88 Rich Ruby 1988 $15 (11/30/91) **87**

QUAFF (United States/California)
Gewürztraminer Sonoma County 1990 $6.25 (4/30/91) **78**
Gewürztraminer Sonoma County 1987 $6.50 (2/28/89) **78**

QUAIL RIDGE (United States/California)
Cabernet Sauvignon Napa Valley 1987 $16 (9/30/91) **93**
Cabernet Sauvignon Napa Valley 1986 $15 (11/15/90) **89**
Cabernet Sauvignon Napa Valley 1985 $15 (7/31/89) **82**
Cabernet Sauvignon Napa Valley 1984 $15 (3/31/89) **88**
Cabernet Sauvignon Napa Valley 1982 $13 (9/16/85) **86**
Chardonnay Napa Valley 1989 $15 (4/30/92) **78**
Chardonnay Napa Valley 1988 $14 (2/15/90) **89**
Chardonnay Napa Valley 1987 $15 (7/15/89) **68**
Chardonnay Napa Valley 1986 $15 (10/31/88) **81**
Chardonnay Napa Valley 1983 $14 (9/01/85) **80**
Chardonnay Napa Valley 1982 $14 (5/16/84) **85**
Chardonnay Napa Valley Winemakers' Selection 1984 $17 (12/15/87) **80**
Chardonnay Sonoma County 1982 $9 (3/16/84) **84**
Merlot Napa Valley 1988 $15 (5/31/92) **84**
Merlot Napa Valley 1987 $15 (6/15/90) **86**
Merlot Napa Valley 1985 $13.50 (3/31/89) **90**
Sauvignon Blanc Napa Valley 1990 $8 (4/15/92) **84**
Sauvignon Blanc Napa Valley 1989 $8 (12/31/90) **80**
Sauvignon Blanc Napa Valley 1988 $8 (11/30/89) **85**
Sauvignon Blanc Napa Valley 1987 $7.50 (3/15/89) **89**

QUARLES HARRIS (Portugal)
Vintage Port 1985 Rel: $21 Cur: $29 (VP-6/90) **85**
Vintage Port 1983 Rel: $18 Cur: $33 (VP-2/90) **89**
Vintage Port 1980 Rel: $13 Cur: $29 (VP-2/90) **83**
Vintage Port 1977 Rel: $11 Cur: $41 (VP-2/90) **89**
Vintage Port 1975 $38 (VP-4/90) **73**
Vintage Port 1970 $52 (VP-2/90) **89**
Vintage Port 1966 $78 (VP-2/90) **74**
Vintage Port 1963 $110 (VP-2/90) **85**

QUARRY LAKE (United States/Washington)
Cabernet Sauvignon Washington 1986 $10 (10/15/89) **78**
Chardonnay Washington 1987 $10 (10/15/89) **74**
Chenin Blanc Washington 1987 $5.50 (10/15/89) **83**
Merlot Washington 1986 $10 (10/15/89) **81**
Sauvignon Blanc Washington 1987 $7.50 (10/15/89) **68**

FATTORIA LA QUERCE (Italy/Tuscany)
Chianti 1985 $9.50 (11/30/87) **83**
Chianti Classico 1988 $9 (11/30/89) BT (HS) **86**
Chianti Classico 1987 $7 (11/30/89) (HS) **80**
Chianti Classico 1986 $7 (11/30/89) (HS) **81**

LA QUERCIA (Italy/Tuscany)
Chianti Classico 1988 ($NA) (9/15/91) **86**

CASTELLO DI QUERCETO (Italy/Tuscany)
Chianti Classico 1988 $14 (9/15/91) **86**
Chianti Classico Riserva 1985 $16 (11/30/89) **91**
La Corte 1988 $35 (9/15/91) **87**
La Corte 1985 $20 (11/30/89) **93**
La Corte 1983 $17 (11/30/89) (HS) **83**
Il Querciolaia 1988 $40 (9/15/91) **88**
Il Querciolaia 1986 $35 (11/30/89) (HS) **85**
Il Querciolaia 1985 $30 (2/15/89) **85**

FATTORIA QUERCIABELLA (Italy/Tuscany)
Chianti Classico 1988 $13 (9/15/91) **90**
Chianti Classico Riserva 1985 $17 (9/15/91) **89**

QUILCEDA CREEK (United States/Washington)
Cabernet Sauvignon Washington 1985 $16.50 (10/15/89) **74**

DOMAINE DE LA QUILLA (France/Loire)
Muscadet de Sèvre et Maine Sur Lie 1989 $7 (11/30/90) BB **88**

QUINTA DO CARDO (Portugal)
Douro Castelo Rodrigo 1989 $7 (12/31/90) BB **84**

QUINTA DO COTTO (Portugal)
Douro Grande Escolha 1987 $18 (12/31/90) **81**
Douro Vinho Tinto 1987 $9 (4/30/91) **74**

QUINTA DO CRASTO (Portugal)
Vintage Port 1987 ($NA) (VP-1/90) **80**
Vintage Port 1985 $24 (VP-1/90) **71**
Vintage Port 1978 ($NA) (VP-1/90) **70**
Vintage Port 1958 ($NA) (VP-8/90) **79**

QUINTA DA EIRA VELHA (Portugal)
Vintage Port 1987 ($NA) (VP-5/90) **86**
Vintage Port 1982 ($NA) (VP-3/90) **81**
Vintage Port 1978 Rel: $22 Cur: $30 (VP-3/90) **85**

QUINTA DO INFANTADO (Portugal)
Vintage Port 1985 $33 (VP-7/90) **76**
Vintage Port 1982 $35 (VP-7/90) **70**
Vintage Port 1978 ($NA) (VP-7/90) **75**

QUINTA DO NOVAL (Portugal)
Late Bottled Port LB NV $14 (11/30/91) **83**
Tawny Port 20 Year Old NV $32 (2/28/90) (JS) **82**
Vintage Port 1987 ($NA) (VP-1/90) **89**
Vintage Port 1985 Rel: $22 Cur: $36 (VP-6/90) **86**
Vintage Port 1982 Rel: $23 Cur: $42 (VP-6/90) **78**
Vintage Port 1978 Rel: $18 Cur: $39 (VP-11/89) **72**

Vintage Port 1977 $50 (10/31/88) **78**
Vintage Port 1975 $50 (VP-11/89) **81**
Vintage Port 1970 $65 (VP-11/89) **89**
Vintage Port 1967 $75 (VP-12/89) **88**
Vintage Port 1966 $87 (VP-12/89) **91**
Vintage Port 1963 $100 (VP-12/89) **84**
Vintage Port 1960 $86 (VP-11/89) **82**
Vintage Port 1958 $85 (VP-11/89) **82**
Vintage Port 1955 $135 (VP-8/90) **88**
Vintage Port 1950 $230 (VP-11/89) **85**
Vintage Port 1947 $210 (VP-11/89) **93**
Vintage Port 1945 $430 (VP-11/89) **92**
Vintage Port 1942 $200 (VP-4/90) **86**
Vintage Port 1941 $70 (VP-9/85) **50**
Vintage Port 1938 $110 (VP-9/85) **71**
Vintage Port 1934 $310 (VP-2/90) **98**
Vintage Port 1931 $900 (VP-11/89) **99**
Vintage Port 1927 $390 (VP-12/89) **93**
Vintage Port Nacional 1987 ($NA) (VP-1/90) **94**
Vintage Port Nacional 1985 $200 (VP-11/89) **95**
Vintage Port Nacional 1982 $165 (VP-11/89) **86**
Vintage Port Nacional 1980 $250 (VP-2/90) **80**
Vintage Port Nacional 1978 $250 (VP-11/89) **77**
Vintage Port Nacional 1975 $240 (VP-11/89) **86**
Vintage Port Nacional 1970 $310 (VP-11/89) **98**
Vintage Port Nacional 1967 $400 (VP-11/89) **95**
Vintage Port Nacional 1966 $300 (VP-11/89) **98**
Vintage Port Nacional 1964 $350 (VP-11/89) **84**
Vintage Port Nacional 1963 $780 (VP-11/89) **100**
Vintage Port Nacional 1962 $280 (VP-11/89) **86**
Vintage Port Nacional 1960 $500 (VP-11/89) **84**
Vintage Port Nacional 1950 $800 (VP-11/89) **90**
Vintage Port Nacional 1931 $3,200 (VP-11/89) **100**

QUINTA DA ROMANEIRA (Portugal)
Vintage Port 1987 ($NA) (VP-1/90) **81**
Vintage Port 1985 $29 (VP-1/90) **78**
Vintage Port 1935 ($NA) (VP-2/90) **90**

QUINTA DE LA ROSA (Portugal)
Vintage Port 1988 $18 (4/15/92) **85**
Vintage Port 1972 ($NA) (VP-10/89) **76**
Vintage Port 1966 ($NA) (VP-10/89) **82**
Vintage Port 1963 ($NA) (VP-10/89) **85**
Vintage Port 1960 ($NA) (VP-10/89) **88**
Vintage Port Feuerheerd Quinta de la Rosa 1927 ($NA) (VP-12/89) **87**

QUINTA DE VAL DA FIGUEIRA (Portugal)
Vintage Port 1987 ($NA) (VP-2/90) **83**

QUIVIRA (United States/California)
Cabernet Sauvignon Dry Creek Valley 1988 $17.50 (11/15/91) **84**
Cabernet Sauvignon Dry Creek Valley 1987 $15 (11/15/90) **87**
Sauvignon Blanc Dry Creek Valley 1990 $10 (11/15/91) **84**
Sauvignon Blanc Dry Creek Valley 1989 $9.25 (10/31/90) **83**
Sauvignon Blanc Dry Creek Valley 1988 $9.50 (11/30/89) **88**
Zinfandel Dry Creek Valley 1989 $13 (7/31/91) **84**
Zinfandel Dry Creek Valley 1988 $12 (5/31/90) **88**
Zinfandel Dry Creek Valley 1987 $11 (7/31/89) **88**
Zinfandel Dry Creek Valley 1986 $9.75 (12/15/88) **88**
Zinfandel Dry Creek Valley 1984 $7 (4/15/87) **88**
Zinfandel Dry Creek Valley 1983 $7 (1/01/86) **75**

QUPE (United States/California)
Chardonnay Santa Barbara County Sierra Madre Reserve 1990 $22 (7/15/92) **86**
Chardonnay Santa Barbara County Sierra Madre Reserve 1989 $25 (7/15/91) **91**
Chardonnay Santa Barbara County Sierra Madre Reserve 1988 $12.50 (12/15/89) **81**
Los Olivos Cuvée Santa Barbara County 1989 $15 (8/31/91) **85**
Marsanne Santa Barbara County 1988 $12.50 (12/15/89) **87**
Syrah Central Coast 1989 $12.50 (8/31/91) **87**
Syrah Central Coast 1988 $10.25 (12/15/89) **90**
Syrah Central Coast 1987 $9 (4/15/89) **88**
Syrah Central Coast 1986 $9.50 (4/15/89) **79**
Syrah Central Coast 1985 $5.75 (4/15/88) **78**
Syrah Santa Barbara County Bien Nacido Vineyard 1989 $20 (8/31/91) **89**
Syrah Santa Barbara County Bien Nacido Vineyard 1987 $20 (2/28/90) **81**

CHATEAU R (France/Bordeaux)
Graves Blanc Dry 1983 $6 (2/01/85) **78**

DOMAINE RABASSE CHARAVIN (France/Rhône)
Côtes du Rhône 1985 $6 (8/31/87) BB **81**

CHATEAU RABAUD-PROMIS (France/Sauternes)
Sauternes 1989 ($NA) (6/15/90) (BT) **85+**
Sauternes 1988 $35 (6/15/90) (BT) **95+**
Sauternes 1987 ($NA) (6/15/90) **83**
Sauternes 1986 $28 (6/30/88) (BT) **95+**
Sauternes 1983 $54 (1/31/88) **90**

RABBIT RIDGE (United States/California)
Cabernet Sauvignon Sonoma County 1988 $12 (8/31/91) **89**
Chardonnay Sonoma County 1990 $12.50 (3/31/92) **76**
Chardonnay Sonoma County 1989 $12 (4/30/91) **85**
Mystique Sonoma County 1989 $7 (6/30/91) BB **82**
Zinfandel Russian River Valley Rabbit Ridge Ranch 1988 $8 (4/30/91) **86**
Zinfandel Sonoma County 1989 $9.50 (8/31/91) **86**

A. RAFANELLI (United States/California)
Cabernet Sauvignon Dry Creek Valley 1988 $12.50 (8/31/91) **90**
Cabernet Sauvignon Dry Creek Valley 1987 $12 (8/31/90) **91**
Cabernet Sauvignon Dry Creek Valley 1986 $9.50 (9/30/89) **91**
Cabernet Sauvignon Dry Creek Valley 1985 $8 (9/15/88) **78**
Zinfandel Dry Creek Valley 1989 $11 (9/30/91) **85**
Zinfandel Dry Creek Valley 1988 $9.75 (9/15/90) **90**
Zinfandel Dry Creek Valley 1987 $9 (12/15/89) **84**
Zinfandel Dry Creek Valley 1986 $7 (9/15/88) **91**
Zinfandel Dry Creek Valley 1985 $6.25 (12/31/87) **77**
Zinfandel Dry Creek Valley 1983 $6.50 (3/01/86) BB **91**

CHATEAU DE LA RAGOTIERE (France/Loire)
Muscadet de Sèvre et Maine Sur Lie 1990 $14.50 (6/15/91) **84**
Muscadet de Sèvre et Maine Sur Lie 1988 $10 (4/15/90) **78**

CHATEAU RAHOUL (France/Bordeaux)
Graves 1988 $18 (8/31/91) **80**
Graves 1986 $18 (12/31/90) **83**
Graves Blanc 1988 $20 (3/31/91) **84**

RAIMAT (Spain)
Abadia Costers del Segre 1987 $9 (3/31/90) **84**
Cabernet Sauvignon Costers del Segre 1986 $10 (3/31/90) **81**
Chardonnay Costers del Segre 1989 $10 (12/15/90) **82**

CHATEAU RAMAGE LA BATISSE (France/Bordeaux)
Haut-Médoc 1991 (NR) (5/15/92) (BT) **75+**
Haut-Médoc 1989 $15 (3/15/92) **88**
Haut-Médoc 1987 $12 (11/30/89) (JS) **82**
Haut-Médoc 1986 $14 (11/30/89) (JS) **82**
Haut-Médoc 1982 $11 (11/30/89) (JS) **68**

LA RAMILLADE (France/Rhône)
Côtes du Rhône 1982 $5 (11/01/85) BB **84**

DOMAINE RAMONET (France/Burgundy)
Bâtard-Montrachet 1988 $190 (2/28/91) **95**
Bâtard-Montrachet 1987 Rel: $119 Cur: $280 (2/28/90) **87**
Bâtard-Montrachet 1986 $154 (9/30/91) (HS) **94**
Bâtard-Montrachet 1985 $141 (9/30/91) (HS) **92**
Bâtard-Montrachet 1984 $95 (9/30/91) (HS) **84**
Bâtard-Montrachet 1983 $150 (9/30/91) (HS) **93**
Bâtard-Montrachet 1982 $140 (9/30/91) (HS) **92**
Bâtard-Montrachet 1979 $150 (9/30/91) (HS) **88**
Bâtard-Montrachet 1978 $230 (9/30/91) (HS) **95**
Bâtard-Montrachet 1976 $165 (9/30/91) (HS) **85**
Bâtard-Montrachet 1974 ($NA) (9/30/91) (HS) **86**
Bâtard-Montrachet 1973 $160 (9/30/91) (HS) **94**
Bâtard-Montrachet 1971 $300 (9/30/91) (HS) **94**
Bâtard-Montrachet 1970 $250 (9/30/91) (HS) **87**
Bâtard-Montrachet 1969 $300 (9/30/91) (HS) **96**
Bâtard-Montrachet 1966 $300 (9/30/91) (HS) **91**
Bâtard-Montrachet 1964 $300 (9/30/91) (HS) **88**
Bienvenues-Bâtard-Montrachet 1988 $100 (9/30/91) (HS) **95**
Bienvenues-Bâtard-Montrachet 1987 $91 (9/30/91) (HS) **91**
Bienvenues-Bâtard-Montrachet 1986 $123 (9/30/91) (HS) **93**
Bienvenues-Bâtard-Montrachet 1985 $137 (9/30/91) (HS) **92**
Bienvenues-Bâtard-Montrachet 1984 $90 (9/30/91) (HS) **87**
Bienvenues-Bâtard-Montrachet 1983 $135 (9/30/91) (HS) **88**
Bienvenues-Bâtard-Montrachet 1982 $130 (9/30/91) (HS) **93**
Bienvenues-Bâtard-Montrachet 1979 $100 (9/30/91) (HS) **92**
Bienvenues-Bâtard-Montrachet 1978 $150 (9/30/91) (HS) **90**
Chassagne-Montrachet 1989 $45 (9/30/91) (HS) **87**
Chassagne-Montrachet 1988 $43 (2/28/91) **86**
Chassagne-Montrachet Les Caillerets 1989 $60 (9/30/91) (HS) **92**
Chassagne-Montrachet Les Caillerets 1988 $61 (9/30/91) (HS) **93**
Chassagne-Montrachet Les Caillerets 1987 $40 (9/30/91) (HS) **88**
Chassagne-Montrachet Les Caillerets 1985 $70 (9/30/91) (HS) **90**
Chassagne-Montrachet Morgeot 1988 $59 (2/28/91) **92**
Chassagne-Montrachet Morgeot 1987 $49 (2/28/90) **79**
Chassagne-Montrachet Morgeot 1986 ($NA) (9/30/91) (HS) **90**
Chassagne-Montrachet Morgeot 1985 ($NA) (9/30/91) (HS) **88**
Chassagne-Montrachet Morgeot 1983 ($NA) (9/30/91) (HS) **87**
Chassagne-Montrachet Morgeot 1970 ($NA) (9/30/91) (HS) **92**
Chassagne-Montrachet Les Ruchottes 1988 $45 (9/30/91) (HS) **92**
Chassagne-Montrachet Les Ruchottes 1987 $52 (2/28/90) **86**
Chassagne-Montrachet Les Ruchottes 1986 $83 (9/30/91) (HS) **90**
Chassagne-Montrachet Les Ruchottes 1985 $70 (9/30/91) (HS) **87**
Chassagne-Montrachet Les Ruchottes 1984 ($NA) (9/30/91) (HS) **86**
Chassagne-Montrachet Les Ruchottes 1983 $70 (9/30/91) (HS) **89**
Chassagne-Montrachet Les Ruchottes 1982 ($NA) (9/30/91) (HS) **91**
Chassagne-Montrachet Les Ruchottes 1981 ($NA) (9/30/91) (HS) **87**
Chassagne-Montrachet Les Ruchottes 1978 ($NA) (9/30/91) (HS) **86**
Chassagne-Montrachet Les Ruchottes 1974 ($NA) (9/30/91) (HS) **81**
Chassagne-Montrachet Les Ruchottes 1973 ($NA) (9/30/91) (HS) **89**
Chassagne-Montrachet Les Ruchottes 1972 ($NA) (9/30/91) (HS) **93**
Chassagne-Montrachet Les Ruchottes 1969 ($NA) (9/30/91) (HS) **89**
Chassagne-Montrachet Les Ruchottes 1966 ($NA) (9/30/91) (HS) **86**
Chassagne-Montrachet Les Ruchottes 1959 ($NA) (9/30/91) (HS) **84**
Montrachet 1988 Rel: $590 Cur: $680 (2/28/91) **96**
Montrachet 1987 $330 (9/30/91) (HS) **93**
Montrachet 1986 $710 (9/30/91) (HS) **93**
Montrachet 1985 $720 (9/30/91) (HS) **96**
Montrachet 1984 $330 (9/30/91) (HS) **89**
Montrachet 1983 $550 (9/30/91) (HS) **94**
Montrachet 1982 $680 (9/30/91) (HS) **96**
Montrachet 1981 $320 (9/30/91) (HS) **92**
Montrachet 1980 $250 (9/30/91) (HS) **90**
Montrachet 1979 $460 (9/30/91) (HS) **93**
Montrachet 1978 $820 (9/30/91) (HS) **97**

RAMOS-PINTO (Portugal)
Tawny Port 20 Year Old Quinta Bom-Retiro NV $39 (2/28/90) (JS) **84**
Vintage Port 1985 Rel: $21 Cur: $36 (VP-11/89) **85**
Vintage Port 1983 Rel: $17 Cur: $33 (VP-11/89) **89**

Key to Symbols

The scores reported here are the results of blind tastings conducted by our panel of senior editors. Wines that carry the initials below are results of individual tastings.

THE WINE SPECTATOR 100-POINT SCALE ***95-100***—Classic, a great wine; ***90-94***—Outstanding, superior character and style; ***80-89***—Good to very good, a wine with special qualities; ***70-79***—Average, drinkable wine that may have minor flaws; ***60-69***—Below average, drinkable but not recommended; ***50-59***—Poor, undrinkable, not recommended. "+"—With a score indicates a range; used primarily with barrel tastings to indicate a preliminary score.

SPECIAL DESIGNATIONS SS—Spectator Selection, CS—Cellar Selection, BB—Best Buy, ($NA)—Price not available, (NR)—Not released.

TASTER'S INITIALS (JG)—Jim Gordon, (HS)—Harvey Steiman, (JL)—James Laube, (JS)—James Suckling, (TM)—Thomas Matthews, (TR)—Terry Robards, (PM)—Per-Henrik Mansson, (BT)—Barrel Tasting (these wines were tasted blind from barrel samples), (CA-date)—*California's Great Cabernets* by James Laube, (CH-date)—*California's Great Chardonnays* by James Laube, (VP-date)—*Vintage Port* by James Suckling.

DATE TASTED Dates in parentheses represent the issue in which the rating was published.

Vintage Port 1982 Rel: $12 Cur: $35 (VP-11/89) **79**
Vintage Port 1980 Rel: $11 Cur: $25 (VP-11/89) **74**
Vintage Port 1970 $100 (VP-11/89) **81**
Vintage Port 1963 $80 (VP-11/89) **83**

CASTELLO DEI RAMPOLLA (Italy/Tuscany)
Chianti Classico 1987 $15 (4/15/91) **84**
Chianti Classico 1985 $8 (9/15/88) **90**
Chianti Classico 1983 $6.50 (7/31/87) BB **84**
Chianti Classico 1982 $6 (10/16/85) **64**
Chianti Classico Riserva 1985 $16 (4/30/90) **81**
Sammarco 1986 $46 (3/15/91) **76**
Sammarco 1985 $42 (11/30/89) (HS) **90**
Sammarco 1983 $28 (9/15/88) **88**

RAMSAY (United States/California)
Merlot Napa Valley 1989 $12 (4/15/92) **86**

RANCHO SISQUOC (United States/California)
Cabernet Sauvignon Santa Maria Valley 1986 $10 (12/15/89) **73**
Chardonnay Santa Maria Valley 1987 $10 (12/15/89) **76**
Johannisberg Riesling Late Harvest Santa Maria Valley Special Select 1986 $18/375ml (12/15/89) **68**
Johannisberg Riesling Santa Maria Valley 1988 $6.50 (12/15/89) **78**
Merlot Santa Maria Valley 1989 $12 (5/31/92) **81**
Merlot Santa Maria Valley 1986 $9 (12/15/89) **77**
Riesling Sylvaner Santa Maria Valley Franken 1988 $7 (12/15/89) **81**

DOMAINE RAPET (France/Burgundy)
Bourgogne en Bully 1988 $19 (3/31/91) **80**
Pernand-Vergelesses 1988 $31 (2/28/91) **79**

RAPIDAN RIVER (United States/Virginia)
Gewürztraminer Virginia 1990 $13 (2/29/92) **83**

KENT RASMUSSEN (United States/California)
Cabernet Sauvignon Napa Valley 1988 $20 (11/15/91) **83**
Cabernet Sauvignon Napa Valley 1987 $20 (4/15/89) (BT) **90+**
Chardonnay Carneros 1989 $20 (1/31/91) **79**
Chardonnay Carneros 1988 $19 (9/15/90) **90**
Chardonnay Carneros Napa Valley 1989 $19 (3/15/91) **87**
Dolcetto Napa Valley 1990 $20 (3/15/92) **85**
Pinot Noir Carneros 1988 $22 (10/31/90) **84**

CHATEAU RASPAIL-AY (France/Rhône)
Gigondas 1988 $19 (11/15/91) **79**
Gigondas 1986 $15 (1/31/89) **92**

PIERRETTE & JEAN-CLAUDE RATEAU (France/Bordeaux)
Beaune Clos des Mariages 1988 $25 (1/31/92) **77**

RENATO RATTI (Italy/Piedmont)
Barolo 1985 Rel: $23 Cur: $26 (9/15/90) **85**
Barolo 1983 Rel: $20 Cur: $22 (10/15/88) **87**
Barolo 1982 Rel: $17 Cur: $27 (6/30/87) CS **93**
Barolo 1980 Rel: $10 Cur: $13 (2/15/87) **83**
Barolo 1979 $8.50 (1/01/86) **89**
Barolo Marcenasco 1985 Rel: $37 Cur: $43 (10/15/90) **82**
Barolo Marcenasco 1982 Rel: $23 Cur: $36 (6/30/87) **90**
Barolo Marcenasco 1981 $15 (6/30/87) **84**
Barolo Marcenasco Rocche 1983 $30 (1/31/89) **86**
Barolo Marcenasco Rocche 1981 $19 (6/30/87) **88**

CHATEAU RAUSAN-SEGLA (France/Bordeaux)
Margaux 1991 (NR) (5/15/92) (BT) **80+**
Margaux 1990 (NR) (5/15/92) (BT) **85+**
Margaux 1989 $44 (3/15/92) **88**
Margaux 1988 $40 (3/15/91) **92**
Margaux 1986 Rel: $28 Cur: $40 (9/15/89) **87**
Margaux 1985 Rel: $24 Cur: $33 (5/31/88) **92**
Margaux 1981 Rel: $16 Cur: $23 (10/16/84) **86**
Margaux 1979 $34 (10/15/89) (JS) **69**
Margaux 1961 $125 (3/16/86) (TR) **63**
Margaux 1945 $150 (3/16/86) (JL) **73**

CHATEAU RAUZAN-DESPAGNE (France/Bordeaux)
Bordeaux 1985 $5.75 (2/15/88) **72**

CHATEAU RAUZAN-GASSIES (France/Bordeaux)
Margaux 1991 (NR) (5/15/92) (BT) **75+**
Margaux 1990 (NR) (4/30/91) (BT) **80+**
Margaux 1989 $24 (4/30/91) (BT) **80+**
Margaux 1988 $35 (8/31/91) **85**
Margaux 1987 $20 (6/30/88) (BT) **70+**
Margaux 1986 $24 (6/30/89) **88**
Margaux 1959 $93 (10/15/90) (JS) **73**
Margaux 1945 $300 (3/16/86) (JL) **91**

CHATEAU DES RAVATYS (France/Beaujolais)
Brouilly 1988 $10 (5/31/89) (TM) **78**

GASTON & PIERRE RAVAUT (France/Burgundy)
Aloxe-Corton 1985 $35 (7/31/88) **88**
Corton Hautes-Mourottes 1985 $46 (7/31/88) **92**
Ladoix Les Corvées 1985 $26 (7/31/88) **88**

FRANCOIS RAVENEAU (France/Chablis)
Chablis Blanchot 1987 $40 (3/31/90) **92**
Chablis Clos 1987 $50 (3/31/90) **90**
Chablis Montée de Tonnerre 1987 $35 (3/31/90) **90**
Chablis Valmur 1986 $35 (3/31/89) **93**

JEAN-MARIE RAVENEAU (France/Chablis)
Chablis Chapelot 1987 $25 (3/31/90) **90**
Chablis Les Vaillons 1987 $25 (3/31/90) **88**
Chablis Valmur 1987 $40 (3/31/90) **92**

RAVENSWOOD (United States/California)
Cabernet Sauvignon Sonoma Valley 1988 Rel: $14 Cur: $17 (3/15/91) **89**
Cabernet Sauvignon Sonoma Valley 1987 Rel: $11 Cur: $20 (5/31/90) **84**
Cabernet Sauvignon Sonoma County 1986 Rel: $12 Cur: $18 (CA-3/89) **86**
Cabernet Sauvignon Sonoma County 1985 Rel: $12 Cur: $20 (CA-3/89) **85**
Cabernet Sauvignon Sonoma County 1984 Rel: $12 Cur: $25 (CA-3/89) **80**
Cabernet Sauvignon Sonoma County 1983 Rel: $9.50 Cur: $19 (CA-3/89) **76**
Cabernet Sauvignon Sonoma County 1982 Rel: $11 Cur: $24 (CA-3/89) **84**
Cabernet Sauvignon Sonoma County 1982 Rel: $11 Cur: $24 (4/01/86) SS **95**
Cabernet Sauvignon Sonoma County 1980 Rel: $10.50 Cur: $16 (CA-3/89) **79**
Cabernet Sauvignon Sonoma Valley Olive Hill 1978 Rel: $10.50 Cur: $26 (CA-3/89) **83**
Cabernet Sauvignon California 1979 $8 (CA-3/89) **59**
Cabernet Sauvignon California 1978 Rel: $10.50 Cur: $20 (CA-3/89) **81**
Cabernet Sauvignon El Dorado County Madrona Vineyards 1977 $8.50 (CA-3/89) **82**
Cabernet Sauvignon Sonoma Valley Gregory 1988 $18 (11/15/91) **80**
Chardonnay Sonoma Valley Sangiacomo 1990 $18 (5/31/92) **83**
Chardonnay Sonoma Valley Sangiacomo 1989 $18 (7/15/91) **65**
Chardonnay Sonoma Valley Sangiacomo 1988 $18 (2/28/90) **80**
Chardonnay Sonoma Valley Sangiacomo 1987 $15 (7/15/89) **87**
Chardonnay Sonoma Valley Sangiacomo 1986 $15 (3/15/88) **71**
Chardonnay Sonoma Valley Sangiacomo 1985 $15 (3/31/87) **91**
Merlot Carneros Sangiacomo 1989 $20 (11/15/91) **90**
Merlot North Coast Vintners Blend 1990 $9.50 (5/31/92) BB **84**
Merlot Sonoma County 1989 $15 (5/31/92) **86**
Merlot Sonoma County 1987 $18 (1/31/90) **87**
Merlot Sonoma County 1986 $18 (12/31/88) **80**
Merlot Sonoma County 1984 $11 (2/28/87) **85**
Merlot Sonoma County 1983 $11 (5/16/86) **61**
Merlot Sonoma County Vintners Blend 1989 $9 (3/31/91) BB **84**
Pickberry Vineyards Sonoma Mountain 1991 (NR) (5/15/92) (BT) **83+**
Pickberry Vineyards Sonoma Mountain 1989 (NR) (5/15/91) (BT) **80+**
Pickberry Vineyards Sonoma Mountain 1988 $27 (4/30/91) **82**
Pickberry Vineyards Sonoma Mountain 1986 Rel: $25 Cur: $32 (CA-3/89) **89**
Zinfandel Napa Valley Canard 1988 $11.50 (8/31/91) **75**
Zinfandel Napa Valley Canard 1986 $11 (3/15/90) **81**
Zinfandel Napa Valley Canard 1985 $10 (3/15/89) **85**
Zinfandel Napa Valley Dickerson 1987 $13 (3/15/90) **86**
Zinfandel Napa Valley Dickerson 1986 $12 (12/15/88) **88**
Zinfandel Napa Valley Dickerson 1985 $10.50 (12/31/87) **80**
Zinfandel Napa Valley Dickerson Vineyard 1989 $13 (11/15/91) **87**
Zinfandel Napa Valley Dickerson Vineyard 1988 $13 (8/31/91) **84**
Zinfandel Napa Valley Vintners Blend 1985 $6.25 (5/31/87) **80**
Zinfandel North Coast Vintners Blend 1989 $7.50 (7/31/91) BB **83**
Zinfandel North Coast Vintners Blend 1988 $7.25 (10/15/90) BB **81**
Zinfandel Sonoma County 1987 $11 (3/15/90) **88**
Zinfandel Sonoma County 1986 $9 (12/15/88) **90**
Zinfandel Sonoma County 1985 $8.25 (12/31/87) **80**
Zinfandel Sonoma County 1983 $8 (5/01/86) **57**
Zinfandel Sonoma County Dry Creek Benchland 1981 $6.50 (4/01/84) **81**
Zinfandel Sonoma County Old Vine 1989 $11 (12/31/91) **82**
Zinfandel Sonoma County Old Vine 1988 $11 (11/30/90) **87**
Zinfandel Sonoma County Vintners Blend 1987 $6 (6/15/89) BB **88**
Zinfandel Sonoma County Vogensen Vineyard 1981 $8 (4/16/84) **68**
Zinfandel Sonoma-Napa Counties Vintners Blend 1986 $5.75 (6/30/88) BB **85**
Zinfandel Sonoma Valley Cooke 1987 $13 (3/15/90) **84**
Zinfandel Sonoma Valley Old Hill Vineyard 1987 $15 (3/15/90) **87**
Zinfandel Sonoma Valley Old Hill Vineyard 1986 $13 (12/15/88) **92**
Zinfandel Sonoma Valley Old Hill Vineyard 1985 $12 (12/31/87) **87**

CHATEAU RAYAS (France/Rhône)
Châteauneuf-du-Pape Blanc Réserve 1989 Rel: $30 Cur: $59 (10/15/91) **90**
Châteauneuf-du-Pape Blanc Réserve 1986 $44 (3/15/89) **85**
Châteauneuf-du-Pape Réserve 1988 $71 (10/15/91) **90**
Châteauneuf-du-Pape Réserve 1986 $48 (12/15/89) **88**
Châteauneuf-du-Pape Réserve 1985 $41 (7/31/88) **93**
Châteauneuf-du-Pape Réserve 1983 Rel: $30 Cur: $43 (10/15/91) **89**

RAYMOND (United States/California)
Cabernet Sauvignon Napa Valley 1988 $17 (5/15/90) (BT) **85+**
Cabernet Sauvignon Napa Valley 1987 $17 (2/28/91) **83**
Cabernet Sauvignon Napa Valley 1986 $16 (5/31/90) **90**
Cabernet Sauvignon Napa Valley 1985 $15 (12/15/89) **84**
Cabernet Sauvignon Napa Valley 1984 Rel: $13 Cur: $17 (2/15/89) **90**
Cabernet Sauvignon Napa Valley 1983 Rel: $13 Cur: $20 (2/15/88) **89**
Cabernet Sauvignon Napa Valley 1982 Rel: $12 Cur: $18 (11/15/86) **91**
Cabernet Sauvignon Napa Valley 1981 Rel: $11 Cur: $16.5 (CA-3/89) **85**
Cabernet Sauvignon Napa Valley 1980 Rel: $12 Cur: $25 (CA-3/89) **82**
Cabernet Sauvignon Napa Valley 1979 Rel: $12 Cur: $20 (CA-3/89) **85**
Cabernet Sauvignon Napa Valley 1978 Rel: $10 Cur: $31 (CA-3/89) **82**
Cabernet Sauvignon Napa Valley 1977 Rel: $8.50 Cur: $25 (CA-3/89) **84**
Cabernet Sauvignon Napa Valley 1976 Rel: $6 Cur: $35 (CA-3/89) **78**
Cabernet Sauvignon Napa Valley 1974 Rel: $5.50 Cur: $60 (CA-3/89) **78**
Cabernet Sauvignon Napa Valley Private Reserve 1988 ($NA) (5/15/90) (BT) **90+**
Cabernet Sauvignon Napa Valley Private Reserve 1986 Rel: $26 Cur: $29 (11/15/91) **88**
Cabernet Sauvignon Napa Valley Private Reserve 1985 Rel: $24 Cur: $28 (7/15/90) CS **91**
Cabernet Sauvignon Napa Valley Private Reserve 1984 Rel: $20 Cur: $25 (7/15/89) **87**
Cabernet Sauvignon Napa Valley Private Reserve 1983 Rel: $18 Cur: $30 (CA-3/89) **84**
Cabernet Sauvignon Napa Valley Private Reserve 1982 Rel: $16 Cur: $27 (CA-3/89) **85**
Cabernet Sauvignon Napa Valley Private Reserve 1981 Rel: $16 Cur: $35 (CA-3/89) **87**
Cabernet Sauvignon Napa Valley Private Reserve 1980 $34 (CA-3/89) **85**
Chardonnay California Selection 1990 $11.50 (11/15/91) **83**
Chardonnay California Selection 1989 $11.50 (2/28/91) **83**
Chardonnay California Selection 1988 $11 (10/31/89) **82**
Chardonnay California Selection 1987 $9 (12/31/88) **84**
Chardonnay California Selection 1986 $8.50 (11/15/87) **82**
Chardonnay California Selection 1985 $8.50 (2/28/87) **83**
Chardonnay California Selection 1984 $8.50 (3/01/86) **93**
Chardonnay California Selection 1983 $8.50 (12/01/84) **82**
Chardonnay Napa Valley 1990 $13.50 (5/31/92) **82**
Chardonnay Napa Valley 1989 Rel: $15 Cur: $17 (7/15/91) **80**
Chardonnay Napa Valley 1988 $15 (6/15/90) **85**
Chardonnay Napa Valley 1987 $13 (12/31/88) **85**
Chardonnay Napa Valley 1986 Rel: $13 Cur: $19 (2/15/88) **80**
Chardonnay Napa Valley 1985 $12 (9/15/87) **92**
Chardonnay Napa Valley 1983 $12 (11/01/85) **94**
Chardonnay Napa Valley 1982 Rel: $13 Cur: $15 (5/16/84) **83**
Chardonnay Napa Valley Private Reserve 1990 $18 (5/31/92) **87**
Chardonnay Napa Valley Private Reserve 1989 $18 (3/31/92) **89**
Chardonnay Napa Valley Private Reserve 1988 $22 (7/15/91) **85**
Chardonnay Napa Valley Private Reserve 1987 Rel: $22 Cur: $24 (5/15/90) **90**
Chardonnay Napa Valley Private Reserve 1986 Rel: $18 Cur: $21 (CH-5/90) **87**
Chardonnay Napa Valley Private Reserve 1985 Rel: $18 Cur: $21 (CH-5/90) **91**
Chardonnay Napa Valley Private Reserve 1984 $16 (7/15/87) **86**
Chardonnay Napa Valley Private Reserve 1983 $16 (9/15/86) **73**
Chardonnay Napa Valley Private Reserve 1981 Rel: $15 Cur: $25 (CH-6/90) **70**
Johannisberg Riesling Late Harvest Napa Valley 1985 $8.50 (9/15/86) **91**
Sauvignon Blanc Napa Valley 1989 $10 (4/30/91) **80**

Sauvignon Blanc Napa Valley 1988 $8.50 (11/30/89) **88**
Sauvignon Blanc Napa Valley 1987 $8 (1/31/89) **85**
Vintage Select White California 1987 $4.25 (2/28/89) **76**

CHATEAU RAYMOND-LAFON (France/Sauternes)
Sauternes 1983 Rel: $38 Cur: $54 (1/31/88) **93**

CHATEAU DE RAYNE VIGNEAU (France/Sauternes)
Sauternes 1989 $41 (6/15/90) (BT) **80+**
Sauternes 1988 $24/375ml (11/15/91) **86**
Sauternes 1987 ($NA) (6/15/90) **77**
Sauternes 1986 $49 (12/31/89) **86**
Sauternes 1983 Rel: $17 Cur: $20 (1/31/88) **77**

REBELLO-VALENTE (Portugal)
Vintage Port 1985 Rel: $23 Cur: $39 (VP-6/90) **81**
Vintage Port 1983 Rel: $23 Cur: $33 (VP-6/90) **78**
Vintage Port 1980 Rel: $16 Cur: $41 (VP-2/90) **80**
Vintage Port 1977 Rel: $12 Cur: $42 (VP-2/90) **89**
Vintage Port 1975 $55 (VP-2/90) **75**
Vintage Port 1972 $55 (VP-1/90) **83**
Vintage Port 1970 $59 (VP-2/90) **92**
Vintage Port 1967 $82 (VP-2/90) **91**
Vintage Port 1966 $70 (VP-2/90) **82**
Vintage Port 1963 $92 (VP-2/90) **85**
Vintage Port 1960 $55 (VP-11/88) **85**
Vintage Port 1945 $200 (VP-5/90) **92**
Vintage Port 1942 $140 (VP-2/85) **75**

HENRI REBOURSEAU (France/Burgundy)
Clos de Vougeot 1983 $25 (11/16/85) **49**

REDBANK (Australia)
Cabernet Sauvignon South Eastern Australia Long Paddock 1986 $13 (1/31/90) **74**
Cabernet Sauvignon South Eastern Australia Long Paddock 1985 $7 (7/15/91) **74**
Cabernet Sauvignon South Eastern Australia Redbank Cabernet 1986 $54 (1/31/90) **89**
Sally's Paddock South Eastern Australia 1986 $32 (1/31/90) **86**
Shiraz Victoria Mountain Creek 1985 $9 (9/30/91) **84**

REDWOOD VALLEY (United States/California)
White Zinfandel California 1987 $6/1.5L (6/15/89) **66**

REGALEALI (Italy/Other)
Chardonnay 1989 $45 (1/31/92) **86**
Nozze d'Oro 1989 $20 (7/15/91) **82**
Rosso 1987 $11 (12/15/89) **77**
Rosso del Conte 1984 $19 (7/31/89) **84**

A. REGNARD & FILS (France/Chablis)
Chablis Fourchaume 1987 $22 (3/31/89) **89**
Chablis Fourchaume 1986 $22 (3/31/89) **90**
Chablis Fourchaume 1983 $11 (11/01/84) **79**
Chablis Mont de Milieu 1987 $20 (3/31/89) **85**
Chablis Mont de Milieu 1986 $20 (3/31/89) **85**
Chablis Montée de Tonnerre 1987 $20 (3/31/89) **83**
Chablis Montée de Tonnerre 1986 $20 (3/31/89) **90**
Chablis Les Montmains 1987 $20 (3/31/89) **84**
Chablis Les Montmains 1986 $20 (9/15/88) **70**
Chablis Les Vaillons 1987 $20 (3/31/89) **88**
Chablis Les Vaillons 1986 $20 (3/31/89) **87**

REICHSRAT VON BUHL (Germany)
Riesling Auslese Rheinpfalz Forster Freundstück 1990 $14 (12/15/91) **90**
Riesling Auslese Rheinpfalz Forster Ungeheuer 1990 $28 (12/15/91) **91**
Riesling Beerenauslese Rheinpfalz Forster Pechstein 1990 $75 (12/15/91) **78**
Riesling Kabinett Halbtrocken Rheinpfalz Deidesheimer Nonnenstück 1990 $14 (12/15/91) **83**
Riesling Kabinett Rheinpfalz Forster Freundstück 1990 $14 (12/15/91) **87**
Riesling Spätlese Rheinpfalz Forster Jesuitengarten 1990 $22 (12/15/91) **89**
Riesling Spätlese Trocken Rheinpfalz Forster Ungeheuer 1990 $22 (12/15/91) **83**

SCHLOSS REINHARTSHAUSEN (Germany)
Riesling Auslese Rheingau Erbacher Schlossberg 1990 $25 (12/15/91) **90**
Riesling Auslese Rheingau Erbacher Siegelsberg 1989 ($NA) (12/15/90) **92**
Riesling Beerenauslese Rheingau Hattenheimer Wisselbrunnen 1990 $100 (12/15/91) **87**
Riesling Kabinett Halbtrocken Rheingau Rüdesheimer Bischofsberg 1990 $18 (12/15/91) **85**
Riesling Qualitätswein Rheingau Erbacher Schlossberg 1989 ($NA) (12/15/90) **86**
Riesling Spätlese Rheingau Erbacher Marcobrunn 1990 $25 (12/15/91) **91**
Riesling Spätlese Rheingau Erbacher Siegelsberg 1989 ($NA) (12/15/90) **89**
Riesling Spätlese Rheingau Hattenheimer Nussbrunnen 1990 $25 (12/15/91) **89**
Riesling Trockenbeerenauslese Rheingau Erbacher Marcobrunn 1937 ($NA) (12/15/88) **95**

REMELLURI (Spain)
Rioja 1990 (NR) (3/31/92) (BT) **80+**
Rioja 1989 (NR) (3/31/92) **82**
Rioja 1988 ($NA) (3/31/92) **75**
Rioja 1986 $11 (12/15/90) **87**
Rioja 1985 $10 (3/31/90) (TM) **88**
Rioja 1984 $9 (3/31/90) (TM) **77**
Rioja 1983 $11.50 (3/31/90) **77**
Rioja 1982 $12 (3/31/90) (TM) **82**
Rioja Alavesa Labastida 1982 $8 (9/30/86) **84**
Rioja Gran Reserva 1985 $40 (3/31/92) **84**
Rioja Gran Reserva 1982 ($NA) (11/30/91) (TM) **87**
Rioja Reserva 1987 $14 (3/31/92) **76**
Rioja Reserva 1986 ($NA) (3/31/92) **78**

REMOISSENET (France/Burgundy)
Bâtard-Montrachet 1986 $87 (2/29/88) **81**
Beaune Grèves 1988 Rel: $30 Cur: $38 (11/30/90) **90**
Bienvenues-Bâtard-Montrachet 1986 $100 (11/15/88) **95**
Bonnes Mares 1988 $80 (12/31/90) **84**
Bonnes Mares 1985 $88 (3/15/88) **82**
Chambertin 1985 $100 (3/15/88) **91**
Chassagne-Montrachet Les Caillerets 1985 $63 (2/29/88) **90**
Clos de la Roche 1985 $72 (3/15/88) **91**
Corton-Charlemagne Diamond Jubilee 1986 $82 (12/15/88) **82**
Corton-Charlemagne Diamond Jubilee 1985 Rel: $100 Cur: $110 (3/15/88) **90**
Echézeaux 1985 $73 (3/15/88) **75**
Givry du Domaine Thénard 1988 $19 (3/31/91) **68**
Givry du Domaine Thénard 1985 $18 (4/30/88) **77**
Mercurey Clos Fortoul 1988 $17 (3/31/91) **83**
Meursault Les Charmes 1986 $49 (12/15/88) **68**
Meursault Cuvée Maurice Chevalier 1986 $35 (3/15/89) **65**
Meursault Cuvée Maurice Chevalier 1985 $42 (3/15/88) **75**
Meursault Les Genevrières 1986 $49 (12/15/88) **91**
Meursault Les Genevrières 1985 $60 (3/15/88) **89**
Montrachet Le Montrachet du Domaine Thénard 1986 Rel: $125 Cur: $137 (12/31/88) **85**
Montrachet Le Montrachet du Domaine Thénard 1985 $145 (2/29/88) **91**
Nuits-St.-Georges Aux Argillats 1985 $34 (10/15/88) **87**
Puligny-Montrachet Les Combettes 1986 $57 (11/15/88) **92**
Puligny-Montrachet Les Folatières 1986 $50 (11/15/88) **85**
Puligny-Montrachet Les Folatières 1985 $56 (2/29/88) **79**
Richebourg 1985 $138 (3/15/88) **91**
Vosne-Romanée Clos de Réas 1949 $138 (8/31/90) (TR) **95**
Vosne-Romanée Les Suchots 1985 $75 (3/15/88) **91**

GILLES REMORIQUET (France/Burgundy)
Nuits-St.-Georges 1982 $19 (7/16/85) **84**

HENRI & GILLES REMORIQUET (France/Burgundy)
Nuits-St.-Georges Rue de Chaux 1985 $22 (7/31/88) **81**

RENAISSANCE (United States/California)
Cabernet Sauvignon North Yuba 1986 $15 (7/15/91) **83**
Riesling North Yuba Dry 1989 $8 (5/15/91) **83**
Sauvignon Blanc North Yuba 1988 $10 (11/15/91) **75**

DOMAINE DE LA RENJARDIERE (France/Rhône)
Côtes du Rhône 1983 $4.50 (3/16/86) BB **84**

RESERVE DE LA COMTESSE (France/Bordeaux)
Pauillac 1988 $23 (3/15/91) **88**
Pauillac 1987 $14 (5/15/90) **82**
Pauillac 1986 Rel: $20 Cur: $22 (5/31/89) **90**
Pauillac 1983 Rel: $18 Cur: $21 (3/01/86) **82**

RESERVE ST.-MARTIN (France/Other)
Corbières Marsanne 1991 $7 (6/30/92) **75**
Minervois Mourvèdre 1989 $8 (12/31/91) BB **80**

CHATEAU RESPIDE-MEDEVILLE (France/Bordeaux)
Graves 1985 $12 (2/29/88) **85**
Graves Blanc 1984 $7.50 (7/16/86) **84**

RESPLANDY (France/Other)
Merlot Vin de Pays d'Oc 1989 $6 (6/30/92) **79**
Marsanne Vin de Pays d'Oc 1990 $8 (6/30/92) **80**

BALTHASAR RESS (Germany)
Riesling Auslese Rheingau Rüdesheimer Berg Rottland 1990 $33 (12/15/91) **90**
Riesling Kabinett Halbtrocken Rheingau Geisenheimer Kläuserweg Charta 1988 $9.50 (9/30/89) **89**
Riesling Kabinett Halbtrocken Rheingau Hattenheimer Nussbrunnen Charta 1988 $9.50 (9/30/89) **78**
Riesling Kabinett Rheingau Hattenheimer Charta 1990 $14 (12/15/91) **86**
Riesling Kabinett Rheingau Johannisberger Erntebringer 1990 $12 (12/15/91) **84**
Riesling Spätlese Halbtrocken Rheingau Rüdesheimer Berg Rottland 1988 $14 (9/30/89) **89**
Riesling Spätlese Rheingau Charta Hochheimer 1990 $19 (12/15/91) **85**
Riesling Spätlese Rheingau Rüdesheimer Berg Schlossberg 1990 $20 (12/15/91) **80**
Riesling Spätlese Rheingau Rüdesheimer Berg Schlossberg 1988 $13.50 (9/30/89) **84**
Riesling Spätlese Rheingau Rüdesheimer Klosterlay 1990 $19 (12/15/91) **81**
Riesling Spätlese Rheingau Schloss Reichartshausen 1990 $18 (12/15/91) **84**

HIPPOLYTE REVERDY (France/Loire)
Sancerre Les Perriers 1987 $13 (2/28/89) **88**

REVERE (United States/California)
Chardonnay Napa Valley 1989 $13 (7/15/91) **79**
Chardonnay Napa Valley 1988 Rel: $14 Cur: $22 (2/28/91) **84**
Chardonnay Napa Valley 1987 Rel: $14 Cur: $22 (9/15/90) **76**
Chardonnay Napa Valley 1986 $15 (CH-4/90) **85**
Chardonnay Napa Valley 1985 Rel: $15 Cur: $20 (CH-4/90) **85**
Chardonnay Napa Valley Berlenbach Vineyards 1989 $15 (7/15/91) **89**
Chardonnay Napa Valley Reserve 1989 $18 (7/15/91) **77**
Chardonnay Napa Valley Reserve 1988 Rel: $18 Cur: $26 (5/15/91) **93**
Chardonnay Napa Valley Reserve 1987 $25 (9/15/90) **81**
Chardonnay Napa Valley Reserve 1986 Rel: $22 Cur: $30 (CH-4/90) **87**

REX HILL (United States/Oregon)
Pinot Noir Oregon 1985 $15 (2/15/90) **81**
Pinot Noir Oregon Archibald Vineyards 1985 $30 (2/15/90) **84**
Pinot Noir Oregon Dundee Hills Vineyards 1985 $25 (2/15/90) **74**
Pinot Noir Oregon Dundee Hills Vineyards 1983 $35 (2/15/90) **77**
Pinot Noir Oregon Maresh Vineyards 1985 $40 (2/15/90) **66**
Pinot Noir Oregon Maresh Vineyards 1983 $40 (2/15/90) **64**
Pinot Noir Oregon Medici Vineyard 1985 $28 (2/15/90) **77**
Pinot Noir Oregon Wirtz Vineyards 1985 $18 (6/15/88) **82**
Pinot Noir Willamette Valley 1988 $18 (4/15/91) **88**
Pinot Noir Willamette Valley 1985 $15 (6/15/88) **79**

CHATEAU LE REY (France/Bordeaux)
Bordeaux Blanc 1986 $4 (9/30/88) **76**

PAR E. REYNAUD (France/Rhône)
Côtes du Rhône Château des Tours 1989 $12 (3/15/91) **80**
Vacqueyras Château des Tours Réserve 1989 $14.50 (10/15/91) **85**
Vin de Pays de Vaucluse Domaine des Tours 1989 $8 (3/31/91) **78**

CHATEAU REYNIER (France/Bordeaux)
Bordeaux Supérieur 1983 $3.50 (10/16/85) BB **83**
Entre-Deux-Mers 1984 $3.25 (12/16/85) **62**

Key to Symbols

The scores reported here are the results of blind tastings conducted by our panel of senior editors. Wines that carry the initials below are results of individual tastings.

THE WINE SPECTATOR 100-POINT SCALE ***95-100***—Classic, a great wine; ***90-94***—Outstanding, superior character and style; ***80-89***—Good to very good, a wine with special qualities; ***70-79***—Average, drinkable wine that may have minor flaws; ***60-69***—Below average, drinkable but not recommended; ***50-59***—Poor, undrinkable, not recommended. "+"—With a score indicates a range; used primarily with barrel tastings to indicate a preliminary score.

SPECIAL DESIGNATIONS SS—Spectator Selection, CS—Cellar Selection, BB—Best Buy, ($NA)—Price not available, (NR)—Not released.

TASTER'S INITIALS (JG)—Jim Gordon, (HS)—Harvey Steiman, (JL)—James Laube, (JS)—James Suckling, (TM)—Thomas Matthews, (TR)—Terry Robards, (PM)—Per-Henrik Mansson, (BT)—Barrel Tasting (these wines were tasted blind from barrel samples), (CA-date)—*California's Great Cabernets* by James Laube, (CH-date)—*California's Great Chardonnays* by James Laube, (VP-date)—*Vintage Port* by James Suckling.

DATE TASTED Dates in parentheses represent the issue in which the rating was published.

BARONE RICASOLI (Italy/Tuscany)
Brolio Vin Santo 1981 $25 (9/15/91) **90**
Brolio Vin Santo 1977 $13 (3/31/90) **85**
Chianti 1989 $7 (4/15/91) BB **83**
Chianti Classico Brolio 1988 $9.50 (9/15/91) **84**
Chianti Classico Brolio 1987 $12 (10/31/91) **84**
Chianti Classico Brolio 1986 $8 (11/30/90) **77**
Chianti Classico Brolio 1985 $7 (11/30/89) (HS) **85**
Chianti Classico Brolio 1984 $4 (9/15/87) **73**
Chianti Classico Brolio Riserva 1985 $12 (9/15/91) **86**
Chianti Classico Brolio Riserva 1983 $10 (5/15/90) **80**
Chianti Classico Brolio Riserva del Barone 1983 $11 (11/30/89) (HS) **85**
Chianti Classico Brolio Riserva del Barone 1978 $10.50 (6/01/85) **90**
Chianti Classico Ricasoli 1987 $6 (11/30/89) (HS) **79**
Chianti Classico Ricasoli Riserva 1983 $8 (11/30/89) (HS) **83**
Chianti Classico San Ripolo 1988 $9.50 (10/31/91) BB **84**
Chianti Classico San Ripolo 1987 $10 (4/15/91) **79**
Chianti Ricasoli 1990 $6 (11/30/91) BB **81**
Chianti Ricasoli 1986 $5.50 (5/15/89) BB **84**
Orvieto Classico Secco 1990 $8 (3/31/92) BB **82**
Orvieto Classico Secco 1989 $8 (4/15/91) BB **81**
Tremalvo 1987 $18 (12/15/91) **87**
Vernaccia di San Gimignano 1990 $9 (5/15/92) **79**
Vernaccia di San Gimignano 1989 $9 (4/15/91) **82**

CHATEAU DE RICAUD (France/Other)
Loupiac 1986 $17/375ml (12/31/89) **80**

RICHARDSON (United States/California)
Cabernet Sauvignon Sonoma Valley Horne 1989 $14 (11/15/91) **78**
Cabernet Sauvignon Sonoma Valley 1985 $12 (11/30/88) **78**
Synergy California 1989 $15 (11/15/91) **83**
Synergy Los Carneros 1989 $15 (5/31/92) **84**
Merlot Sonoma Valley Carneros Gregory 1990 $14.50 (5/31/92) **89**
Merlot Sonoma Valley Carneros Gregory 1989 $14 (3/31/91) **83**
Merlot Sonoma Valley Carneros Sangiacomo 1990 $14.50 (5/31/92) **87**
Pinot Noir Sonoma Valley Carneros Sangiacomo 1989 $14 (4/30/91) **86**
Pinot Noir Sonoma Valley Carneros Sangiacomo 1987 $12 (10/15/89) **88**
Pinot Noir Sonoma Valley Carneros Sangiacomo 1986 $12 (6/15/88) **87**
Zinfandel Sonoma Valley NV $9 (7/31/89) **76**

DOMAINE RICHEAUME (France/Other)
Cabernet Sauvignon Côtes de Provence 1988 $15 (10/31/90) **75**
Syrah Côtes de Provence 1988 $15 (10/31/90) **73**

CHATEAU RICHETERRE (France/Bordeaux)
Margaux 1986 $12.50 (2/15/89) **78**

RICHMOND GROVE (Australia)
Chardonnay Hunter Valley French Cask 1989 $7 (5/15/91) BB **83**

MAX FERD. RICHTER (Germany)
Riesling Auslese Mosel-Saar-Ruwer Brauneberger Juffer 1989 $17 (12/15/90) **80**
Riesling Auslese Mosel-Saar-Ruwer Brauneberger Juffer-Sonnenuhr 1990 $25 (12/15/91) **90**
Riesling Auslese Mosel-Saar-Ruwer Brauneberger Juffer-Sonnenuhr 1988 ($NA) (9/30/89) **87**
Riesling Auslese Mosel-Saar-Ruwer Graacher Himmelreich 1990 $25 (12/15/91) **87**
Riesling Auslese Mosel-Saar-Ruwer Mülheimer Helenenkloster 1990 $22 (12/15/91) **90**
Riesling Auslese Mosel-Saar-Ruwer Mülheimer Helenenkloster 1989 $20 (12/15/90) **87**
Riesling Auslese Mosel-Saar-Ruwer Veldenzer Elisenberg 1989 $16 (12/15/90) **80**
Riesling Eiswein Mosel-Saar-Ruwer Mülheimer Helenenkloster 1990 $100 (12/15/91) **93**
Riesling Eiswein Mosel-Saar-Ruwer Mülheimer Helenenkloster 1989 $50/375ml (12/15/90) **82**
Riesling Kabinett Mosel-Saar-Ruwer Brauneberger Juffer 1989 $11 (12/15/90) **84**
Riesling Kabinett Mosel-Saar-Ruwer Graacher Himmelreich 1989 $11 (12/15/90) **85**
Riesling Kabinett Mosel-Saar-Ruwer Wehlener Sonnenuhr 1990 $12 (12/15/91) **84**
Riesling Kabinett Mosel-Saar-Ruwer Wehlener Sonnenuhr 1989 $11 (12/15/90) **85**
Riesling Qualitätswein Halbtrocken Mosel-Saar-Ruwer Dr. Richter's Riesling 1990 $9 (12/15/91) **84**
Riesling Qualitätswein Halbtrocken Mosel-Saar-Ruwer Dr. Richter's Riesling 1989 $8 (12/15/90) **83**
Riesling Spätlese Mosel-Saar-Ruwer Brauneberger Juffer 1989 $13 (12/15/90) **84**
Riesling Spätlese Mosel-Saar-Ruwer Brauneberger Juffer-Sonnenuhr 1990 $15 (12/15/91) **90**
Riesling Spätlese Mosel-Saar-Ruwer Brauneberger Juffer-Sonnenuhr 1988 ($NA) (9/30/89) **94**
Riesling Spätlese Mosel-Saar-Ruwer Veldenzer Elisenberg 1990 $14 (12/15/91) **90**
Riesling Spätlese Mosel-Saar-Ruwer Veldenzer Elisenberg 1988 ($NA) (9/30/89) **94**
Riesling Spätlese Mosel-Saar-Ruwer Wehlener Sonnenuhr 1989 $13 (12/15/90) **81**
Riesling Spätlese Mosel-Saar-Ruwer Wehlener Sonnenuhr 1988 ($NA) (9/30/89) **88**
Riesling Trockenbeerenauslese Mosel-Saar-Ruwer Mülheimer Sonnenlay 1989 $100/375ml (12/15/90) **92**

RIDDOCH (Australia)
Chardonnay Victoria 1987 $9 (10/15/90) **88**
Chardonnay Victoria 1986 $9 (5/31/88) **69**

RIDGE (United States/California)
Cabernet Sauvignon Howell Mountain 1983 $12 (3/16/86) **83**
Cabernet Sauvignon Howell Mountain 1982 $12 (6/01/85) **88**
Cabernet Sauvignon Napa County 1981 $12 (2/15/84) **63**
Cabernet Sauvignon Napa County York Creek 1986 $18 (CA-3/89) **88**
Cabernet Sauvignon Napa County York Creek 1985 Rel: $16 Cur: $20 (CA-3/89) **92**
Cabernet Sauvignon Napa County York Creek 1984 Rel: $14 Cur: $19 (CA-3/89) **88**
Cabernet Sauvignon Napa County York Creek 1983 Rel: $12 Cur: $20 (CA-3/89) **73**
Cabernet Sauvignon Napa County York Creek 1982 Rel: $12 Cur: $25 (CA-3/89) **73**
Cabernet Sauvignon Napa County York Creek 1981 Rel: $12 Cur: $23 (CA-3/89) **76**
Cabernet Sauvignon Napa County York Creek 1980 Rel: $12 Cur: $30 (CA-3/89) **88**
Cabernet Sauvignon Napa County York Creek 1979 Rel: $12 Cur: $27 (CA-3/89) **88**
Cabernet Sauvignon Napa County York Creek 1978 Rel: $12 Cur: $30 (CA-3/89) **87**
Cabernet Sauvignon Napa County York Creek 1977 Rel: $12 Cur: $35 (CA-3/89) **88**
Cabernet Sauvignon Napa County York Creek 1976 Rel: $10 Cur: $27 (CA-3/89) **68**
Cabernet Sauvignon Napa County York Creek 1975 Rel: $10 Cur: $60 (CA-3/89) **87**
Cabernet Sauvignon Napa County York Creek 1974 Rel: $6.75 Cur: $87 (CA-3/89) **87**
Cabernet Sauvignon Santa Barbara County Tepusquet Vineyard 1981 $9 (4/16/84) **83**
Cabernet Sauvignon Santa Cruz Mountains 1989 $12 (3/31/92) **82**
Cabernet Sauvignon Santa Cruz Mountains 1986 $15 (10/31/89) **68**
Cabernet Sauvignon Santa Cruz Mountains 1985 $12 (6/15/89) **64**
Cabernet Sauvignon Santa Cruz Mountains 1984 $12 (6/15/87) **64**
Cabernet Sauvignon Santa Cruz Mountains 1983 Rel: $12 Cur: $20 (CA-3/89) **84**
Cabernet Sauvignon Santa Cruz Mountains Jimsomare 1985 $16 (2/15/89) **87**
Cabernet Sauvignon Santa Cruz Mountains Jimsomare 1984 $16 (10/31/87) **69**
Cabernet Sauvignon Santa Cruz Mountains Jimsomare 1983 $10 (11/30/86) **78**
Cabernet Sauvignon Santa Cruz Mountains Jimsomare-Monte Bello 1981 $12 (1/01/85) **87**
Cabernet Sauvignon Santa Cruz Mountains Monte Bello 1991 (NR) (5/15/92) (BT) **90+**
Cabernet Sauvignon Santa Cruz Mountains Monte Bello 1990 (NR) (5/15/91) (BT) **90+**
Cabernet Sauvignon Santa Cruz Mountains Monte Bello 1988 $60 (1/31/92) **84**
Cabernet Sauvignon Santa Cruz Mountains Monte Bello 1987 Rel: $45 Cur: $52 (11/15/90) **88**
Cabernet Sauvignon Santa Cruz Mountains Monte Bello 1986 Rel: $35 Cur: $40 (9/15/89) **82**
Cabernet Sauvignon Santa Cruz Mountains Monte Bello 1985 Rel: $40 Cur: $89 (7/15/88) CS **95**
Cabernet Sauvignon Santa Cruz Mountains Monte Bello 1984 Rel: $35 Cur: $83 (CA-3/89) **97**
Cabernet Sauvignon Santa Cruz Mountains Monte Bello 1984 Rel: $35 Cur: $83 (9/15/87) CS **95**
Cabernet Sauvignon Santa Cruz Mountains Monte Bello 1982 Rel: $18 Cur: $30 (CA-3/89) **75**
Cabernet Sauvignon Santa Cruz Mountains Monte Bello 1981 Rel: $25 Cur: $64 (CA-3/89) **92**
Cabernet Sauvignon Santa Cruz Mountains Monte Bello 1980 Rel: $30 Cur: $57 (CA-3/89) **80**
Cabernet Sauvignon Santa Cruz Mountains Monte Bello 1978 Rel: $30 Cur: $100 (CA-3/89) **91**
Cabernet Sauvignon Santa Cruz Mountains Monte Bello 1978 Rel: $30 Cur: $100 (10/16/83) CS **91**
Cabernet Sauvignon Santa Cruz Mountains Monte Bello 1977 Rel: $40 Cur: $86 (CA-3/89) **94**
Cabernet Sauvignon Santa Cruz Mountains Monte Bello 1976 Rel: $15 Cur: $57 (CA-3/89) **83**
Cabernet Sauvignon Santa Cruz Mountains Monte Bello 1975 Rel: $10 Cur: $41 (CA-3/89) **88**
Cabernet Sauvignon Santa Cruz Mountains Monte Bello 1974 Rel: $12 Cur: $160 (CA-3/89) **93**
Cabernet Sauvignon Santa Cruz Mountains Monte Bello 1973 Rel: $10 Cur: $110 (CA-3/89) **87**
Cabernet Sauvignon Santa Cruz Mountains Monte Bello 1972 Rel: $10 Cur: $90 (CA-3/89) **84**
Cabernet Sauvignon Santa Cruz Mountains Monte Bello 1971 Rel: $10 Cur: $135 (CA-3/89) **85**
Cabernet Sauvignon Santa Cruz Mountains Monte Bello 1970 Rel: $10 Cur: $220 (CA-3/89) **96**
Cabernet Sauvignon Santa Cruz Mountains Monte Bello 1969 Rel: $7.50 Cur: $200 (CA-3/89) **92**
Cabernet Sauvignon Santa Cruz Mountains Monte Bello 1968 Rel: $7.50 Cur: $200 (CA-3/89) **87**
Cabernet Sauvignon Santa Cruz Mountains Monte Bello 1965 Rel: $6.50 Cur: $260 (CA-3/89) **86**
Cabernet Sauvignon Santa Cruz Mountains Monte Bello 1964 Rel: $6.50 Cur: $300 (CA-3/89) **90**
Cabernet Sauvignon Santa Cruz Mountains Monte Bello 1963 Rel: $5 Cur: $490 (CA-3/89) **70**
Chardonnay Howell Mountain 1990 $12 (3/15/92) **85**
Chardonnay Howell Mountain 1989 $14 (7/15/91) **81**
Chardonnay Howell Mountain 1988 $14 (7/15/91) **85**
Chardonnay Howell Mountain 1987 $14 (4/30/89) **87**
Chardonnay Santa Cruz Mountains 1989 $14 (7/15/91) **84**
Chardonnay Santa Cruz Mountains 1988 $14 (7/15/91) **89**
Merlot Sonoma County Bradford Mountain 1987 $17 (7/15/90) **75**
Merlot Sonoma County Bradford Mountain 1986 $16 (7/31/89) **64**
Mourvèdre California Evangelo Vineyards Mataro 1990 $14 (3/15/92) **73**
Petite Sirah Napa County York Creek 1987 $11.50 (8/31/91) **76**
Petite Sirah Napa County York Creek 1985 $9 (10/31/89) **87**
Petite Sirah Napa Valley 1988 $16 (3/15/92) **80**
Zinfandel Blend Geyserville Sonoma County 1989 $14 (11/15/91) **84**
Zinfandel Howell Mountain 1989 $12 (3/31/92) **87**
Zinfandel Howell Mountain 1988 $12 (7/31/91) **82**
Zinfandel Howell Mountain 1987 $10 (5/31/90) **83**
Zinfandel Howell Mountain 1985 $9 (5/15/88) **73**
Zinfandel Howell Mountain 1984 $9 (6/30/87) **81**
Zinfandel Howell Mountain 1983 $9 (5/01/86) **89**
Zinfandel Howell Mountain 1982 $9 (6/01/85) **85**
Zinfandel Napa County York Creek 1985 $10.50 (12/31/87) **82**
Zinfandel Napa County York Creek 1984 $10.50 (3/15/87) **86**
Zinfandel Napa County York Creek 1982 $10.50 (7/16/85) SS **91**
Zinfandel Napa County York Creek 1981 $9.50 (1/01/84) **89**
Zinfandel Paso Robles 1989 $10 (11/15/91) **84**
Zinfandel Paso Robles 1987 $10 (3/15/90) **85**
Zinfandel Paso Robles 1986 $7.25 (10/31/88) **81**
Zinfandel Paso Robles 1982 $8.50 (1/01/85) **90**
Zinfandel Sonoma County 1989 $8.50 (3/31/92) **80**
Zinfandel Sonoma County 1988 $8.50 (2/15/91) BB **88**
Zinfandel Sonoma County Geyserville 1988 $14 (11/30/90) SS **90**
Zinfandel Sonoma County Geyserville 1987 $14 (10/31/89) **90**
Zinfandel Sonoma County Geyserville 1986 Rel: $12 Cur: $30 (10/31/88) **79**
Zinfandel Sonoma County Geyserville 1985 Rel: $10.50 Cur: $15 (9/15/87) **83**
Zinfandel Sonoma County Geyserville 1984 $10.50 (12/31/86) **79**
Zinfandel Sonoma County Geyserville 1982 Rel: $9.50 Cur: $32 (9/16/84) **90**
Zinfandel Sonoma County Geyserville 1975 $28 (6/16/85) **67**
Zinfandel Sonoma County Geyserville 1974 $44 (6/16/85) **79**
Zinfandel Sonoma County Geyserville 1973 $55 (6/16/85) **80**
Zinfandel Sonoma County Lytton Springs 1989 $13 (11/15/91) **82**
Zinfandel Sonoma County Lytton Springs 1988 $12 (11/30/90) **82**
Zinfandel Sonoma County Lytton Springs 1987 $11 (10/31/89) **91**
Zinfandel Sonoma County Lytton Springs 1986 Rel: $10 Cur: $14 (10/15/88) **88**
Zinfandel Sonoma County Lytton Springs 1985 $9 (9/15/87) **81**
Zinfandel Sonoma County Lytton Springs 1984 Rel: $9 Cur: $17 (11/15/86) **79**

RIECINE (Italy/Tuscany)
Chianti Classico 1988 $22 (4/30/91) **89**
Chianti Classico 1987 $20 (4/30/91) **83**
Chianti Classico Riserva 1985 $19 (9/15/91) **87**
La Gioia di Riecine 1988 $65 (9/15/91) **91**
La Gioia di Riecine 1987 $45 (4/30/91) **82**

CHATEAU RIEUSSEC (France/Sauternes)
Sauternes 1989 $66 (6/15/90) (BT) **90+**
Sauternes 1988 Rel: $45 Cur: $55 (11/15/91) **84**
Sauternes 1987 $31 (6/15/90) **89**
Sauternes 1986 Rel: $50 Cur: $55 (12/31/89) **80**
Sauternes 1985 $38 (5/31/88) **86**
Sauternes 1983 Rel: $52 Cur: $60 (1/31/88) **94**
Sauternes 1983 Rel: $52 Cur: $60 (3/16/86) CS **93**
Sauternes 1982 Rel: $13 Cur: $45 (2/01/85) **86**
Sauternes 1981 Rel: $14 Cur: $32 (12/01/84) **90**

J. RIGER-BRISET (France/Burgundy)
Puligny-Montrachet 1987 $35 (3/15/90) **82**

LUIGI RIGHETTI (Italy/North)
Recioto della Valpolicella Amarone Capitel de' Roari 1983 $16 (2/15/89) **90**

GIOVANNI & BATTISTA RINALDI (Italy/Piedmont)
Barolo 1983 ($NA) (9/15/88) (HS) **86**
Barolo 1982 ($NA) (9/15/88) (HS) **84**

FRANCESCO RINALDI & FIGLI (Italy/Piedmont)
Barbaresco 1985 $23 (9/15/90) **87**
Barbaresco 1983 $16 (1/31/89) **79**
Barbera d'Alba 1987 $10 (3/15/91) **87**
Barbera d'Alba 1986 $9 (2/15/89) **88**
Barolo 1986 Rel: $22 Cur: $30 (7/15/91) **83**
Barolo 1983 $20 (9/15/88) (HS) **84**
Barolo 1982 Rel: $16 Cur: $50 (9/15/88) (HS) **83**
Barolo 1978 Rel: $12 Cur: $70 (9/16/84) **89**
Barolo La Brunata Riserva 1985 $24 (7/15/91) **89**
Barolo La Brunata Riserva 1982 $27 (6/30/87) **79**
Barolo Cannubbio 1985 $25 (6/15/90) **78**
Barolo Cannubbio 1982 $16 (10/31/87) **75**

Dolcetto d'Alba 1989 $12 (7/15/91) **80**
Dolcetto d'Alba Roussot 1988 $10 (7/15/91) **78**
Dolcetto d'Alba Roussot Alto 1987 $9 (3/31/90) **86**

LA RIOJA ALTA (Spain)
Rioja Reserva 890 Gran Reserva 1973 $55 (3/31/92) **77**
Rioja Reserva 904 Gran Reserva 1982 ($NA) (3/31/92) **84**
Rioja Reserva 904 Gran Reserva 1981 $29 (3/31/92) **82**
Rioja Reserva 904 Gran Reserva 1976 $26 (3/31/90) (TM) **90**
Rioja Reserva 904 Gran Reserva 1975 ($NA) (3/31/92) **82**
Rioja Reserva 904 Gran Reserva 1973 $10 (9/30/86) **84**
Rioja Reserva 904 Gran Reserva 1970 ($NA) (3/31/92) **75**
Rioja Viña Alberdi 1987 $11.50 (3/31/92) **79**
Rioja Viña Alberdi 1986 $11.50 (3/31/92) **83**
Rioja Viña Alberdi 1985 $8 (3/15/90) BB **85**
Rioja Viña Ardanza Reserva 1985 $18 (3/31/92) **85**
Rioja Viña Ardanza Reserva 1983 $18 (3/31/92) **81**
Rioja Viña Ardanza Reserva 1982 $17 (3/31/92) **84**
Rioja Viña Ardanza Reserva 1978 $6 (9/30/86) **65**
Rioja White Viña Ardanza Reserva 1988 ($NA) (5/31/92) **77**
Rioja White Viña Ardanza Reserva 1985 ($NA) (5/31/92) **82**

BODEGAS RIOJANAS (Spain)
Rioja Canchales 1987 $4 (3/15/90) **75**
Rioja Monte Real Gran Reserva 1982 $19 (3/31/92) **82**
Rioja Monte Real Gran Reserva 1981 $19 (3/31/92) **89**
Rioja Monte Real Gran Reserva 1975 ($NA) (3/31/92) **78**
Rioja Monte Real Gran Reserva 1973 ($NA) (3/31/92) **85**
Rioja Monte Real Gran Reserva 1970 ($NA) (3/31/92) **72**
Rioja Monte Real Reserva 1985 ($NA) (3/31/92) **87**
Rioja Monte Real Reserva 1983 $7.50 (3/31/90) BB **83**
Rioja Puerta Vieja Crianza 1988 ($NA) (3/31/92) **86**
Rioja Viña Albina 1983 $7.50 (3/31/90) **68**
Rioja Viña Albina Gran Reserva 1982 $19 (3/31/92) **87**
Rioja Viña Albina Gran Reserva 1981 $19 (3/31/92) **86**
Rioja Viña Albina Gran Reserva 1975 ($NA) (3/31/92) **85**
Rioja Viña Albina Gran Reserva 1973 ($NA) (3/31/92) **81**
Rioja Viña Albina Gran Reserva 1970 ($NA) (3/31/92) **70**
Rioja Viña Albina Reserva 1985 ($NA) (3/31/92) **78**
Rioja White Monte Real 1991 $6 (5/31/92) **83**
Rioja White Monte Real Crianza 1987 ($NA) (5/31/92) **89**
Rioja White Viña Albina Gran Reserva 1983 ($NA) (5/31/92) **87**

DOMAINE DANIEL RION (France/Burgundy)
Chambolle-Musigny Les Beaux Bruns 1989 $45 (1/31/92) **89**
Chambolle-Musigny Les Beaux Bruns 1988 $37 (1/31/91) **87**
Chambolle-Musigny Les Beaux Bruns 1986 $39 (4/15/89) **86**
Chambolle-Musigny Les Beaux Bruns 1985 $33 (3/31/88) **88**
Clos Vougeot 1989 $94 (1/31/92) **92**
Clos Vougeot 1988 $75 (1/31/91) **92**
Clos Vougeot 1986 $70 (4/15/89) **90**
Côte de Nuits-Villages 1986 $15 (7/31/88) **81**
Nuits-St.-Georges 1986 $31 (4/30/89) **85**
Nuits-St.-Georges 1985 $28 (3/15/88) **85**
Nuits-St.-Georges Clos des Argillières 1989 $63 (1/31/92) **91**
Nuits-St.-Georges Clos des Argillières 1988 $54 (1/31/91) **91**
Nuits-St.-Georges Clos des Argillières 1987 Rel: $30 Cur: $36 (4/30/90) **92**
Nuits-St.-Georges Clos des Argillières 1986 $47 (4/30/89) **90**
Nuits-St.-Georges Clos des Argillières 1985 Rel: $44 Cur: $55 (3/15/88) **94**
Nuits-St.-Georges Grandes Vignes 1989 $38 (1/31/92) **88**
Nuits-St.-Georges Grandes Vignes 1988 $33 (7/15/90) (BT) **85+**
Nuits-St.-Georges Hauts Pruliers 1989 $63 (1/31/92) **92**
Nuits-St.-Georges Hauts Pruliers 1988 $54 (1/31/91) **91**
Nuits-St.-Georges Hauts Pruliers 1987 $35 (4/30/90) **91**
Nuits-St.-Georges Hauts Pruliers 1986 $45 (4/30/89) **91**
Nuits-St.-Georges Hauts Pruliers 1985 Rel: $43 Cur: $50 (3/15/88) **88**
Nuits-St.-Georges Les Lavières 1988 $33 (2/15/91) **93**
Nuits-St.-Georges Les Lavières 1987 $21 (4/30/90) **87**
Nuits-St.-Georges Les Vignes Rondes 1989 $63 (1/31/92) **93**
Nuits-St.-Georges Les Vignes Rondes 1988 $54 (1/31/91) **92**
Nuits-St.-Georges Les Vignes Rondes 1987 $35 (4/30/90) **95**
Nuits-St.-Georges Les Vignes Rondes 1986 $43 (4/30/89) **88**
Nuits-St.-Georges Les Vignes Rondes 1985 $40 (3/15/88) **91**
Vosne-Romanée 1989 $37 (1/31/92) **89**
Vosne-Romanée 1987 $21 (4/30/90) **89**
Vosne-Romanée 1986 $31 (4/30/89) **87**
Vosne-Romanée 1985 $28 (2/29/88) **78**
Vosne-Romanée 1983 $19 (2/01/86) **63**
Vosne-Romanée Beaux-Monts 1989 $63 (1/31/92) **90**
Vosne-Romanée Beaux-Monts 1988 $53 (2/15/91) **92**
Vosne-Romanée Beaux-Monts 1986 $43 (4/30/89) **91**
Vosne-Romanée Beaux-Monts 1985 Rel: $38 Cur: $55 (2/29/88) **95**
Vosne-Romanée Les Chaumes 1989 $63 (1/31/92) **92**
Vosne-Romanée Les Chaumes 1988 $54 (1/31/91) **93**
Vosne-Romanée Les Chaumes 1987 $35 (4/30/90) **88**
Vosne-Romanée Les Chaumes 1986 Rel: $47 Cur: $54 (4/30/89) CS **93**

RION PERE & FILS (France/Burgundy)
Clos Vougeot 1987 $48 (11/15/90) **86**
Nuits-St.-Georges Les Murgers 1987 $31 (3/31/90) **79**

Key to Symbols

The scores reported here are the results of blind tastings conducted by our panel of senior editors. Wines that carry the initials below are results of individual tastings.

THE WINE SPECTATOR 100-POINT SCALE 95-100—Classic, a great wine; ***90-94***—Outstanding, superior character and style; ***80-89***—Good to very good, a wine with special qualities; ***70-79***—Average, drinkable wine that may have minor flaws; ***60-69***—Below average, drinkable but not recommended; ***50-59***—Poor, undrinkable, not recommended. "+"—With a score indicates a range; used primarily with barrel tastings to indicate a preliminary score.

SPECIAL DESIGNATIONS SS—Spectator Selection, CS—Cellar Selection, BB—Best Buy, ($NA)—Price not available, (NR)—Not released.

TASTER'S INITIALS (JG)—Jim Gordon, (HS)—Harvey Steiman, (JL)—James Laube, (JS)—James Suckling, (TM)—Thomas Matthews, (TR)—Terry Robards, (PM)—Per-Henrik Mansson, (BT)—Barrel Tasting (these wines were tasted blind from barrel samples), (CA-date)—*California's Great Cabernets* by James Laube, (CH-date)—*California's Great Chardonnays* by James Laube, (VP-date)—*Vintage Port* by James Suckling.

DATE TASTED Dates in parentheses represent the issue in which the rating was published.

CHATEAU RIPEAU (France/Bordeaux)
St.-Emilion 1982 $18 (5/15/89) (TR) **88**

MARQUES DE RISCAL (Spain)
Rioja 1984 $9 (3/31/90) **58**
Rioja 1982 $7 (11/15/87) (JL) **84**
Rioja Gran Reserva 1982 ($NA) (11/30/91) (TM) **84**
Rioja Reserva 1985 $9.50 (3/31/90) **62**
Sauvignon Blanc Rueda 1988 $7.50 (3/31/90) **81**

RITCHIE CREEK (United States/California)
Chardonnay Napa Valley 1989 $15 (7/15/91) **88**
Viognier Napa Valley 1987 $13 (4/15/89) **89**

RIUNITE (Italy/Other)
Lambrusco Reggiano NV $4.50 (9/30/91) BB **81**

RIVENDELL (United States/New York)
Chardonnay New York 1989 $12 (6/30/91) **80**
Chardonnay New York Barrel Selection 1989 $14 (6/30/91) (TM) **85**
Chardonnay New York Reserve 1989 $17 (6/30/91) **86**
Chardonnay North Fork of Long Island Cuvée 1988 $12 (6/30/91) (TM) **87**
Sarabande Sur Lie New York 1989 $7.50 (6/30/91) **84**

RIVER OAKS (United States/California)
Cabernet Sauvignon North Coast 1984 $6 (10/15/87) **75**
Cabernet Sauvignon Sonoma County 1983 $6 (12/15/86) **75**
Cabernet Sauvignon Sonoma County 1982 $6 (4/01/85) BB **82**
Cabernet Sauvignon Sonoma County 1981 $6 (7/01/84) **76**
Chardonnay Alexander Valley 1984 $6 (4/01/85) **79**
Chardonnay Sonoma County 1985 $6 (4/16/86) **77**

RIVERA (Italy/Other)
Castel del Monte Il Falcone Riserva 1985 $16.50 (12/31/90) **83**

RIVERSIDE FARM (United States/California)
Cabernet Sauvignon California 1985 $4.50 (5/31/88) **72**
Cabernet Sauvignon North Coast 1983 $3.75 (9/15/86) **77**
Chardonnay California 1991 $7 (7/15/92) BB **82**
Chardonnay California 1989 $6.75 (12/31/90) **79**
White Zinfandel California 1988 $5.25 (6/15/89) **80**

ALFREDO & GIOVANNI ROAGNA (Italy/Piedmont)
Barbaresco 1986 $26 (7/15/91) **86**
Barbaresco 1985 $27 (2/28/89) **89**
Chardonnay 1987 $20 (9/15/89) **89**
Opera Prima Imbottigliato il 15 Novembre 1986 NV $17 (12/31/87) **82**
Opera Prima IV NV $23 (7/31/89) **76**

DOMAINE ROBERT (France/Other)
Brut Blanc de Blancs Blanquette de Limoux 1986 $8.75 (6/15/90) **78**

ROBERTSON (Portugal)
Tawny Port 20 Year Old Imperial NV $33 (2/28/90) (JS) **81**

GUY ROBIN (France/Chablis)
Chablis Vaudésir 1986 $37 (2/28/91) **83**

DOMAINE MICHEL ROBIN (France/Chablis)
Chablis Les Blanchots 1985 $34 (8/31/87) **74**
Chablis Les Vaillons 1985 $22 (8/31/87) **79**

CHATEAU ROC DE CAMBES (France/Bordeaux)
Côtes de Bourg 1991 (NR) (5/15/92) (BT) **75+**
Côtes de Bourg 1990 (NR) (5/15/92) (BT) **90+**

CHATEAU ROC MIGNON D'ADRIEN (France/Bordeaux)
Bordeaux Supérieur 1989 $6 (2/28/91) BB **82**

LA ROCCA (Italy/Piedmont)
Gavi 1989 $19.50 (8/31/91) **70**

ROCCA DELLE MACIE (Italy/Tuscany)
Chianti Classico 1987 ($NA) (11/30/89) (HS) **82**
Chianti Classico 1986 ($NA) (11/30/89) (HS) **80**
Chianti Classico Riserva 1985 $14 (9/15/91) **77**
Chianti Classico Riserva di Fizzano 1987 ($NA) (11/30/89) (HS) **89**
Chianti Classico Riserva di Fizzano 1985 ($NA) (11/30/89) (HS) **88**
Chianti Classico Riserva di Fizzano 1982 $15.50 (3/31/89) **87**
Chianti Classico Tenuta Sant'Alfonso 1988 ($NA) (9/15/91) **89**
Roccato 1988 ($NA) (9/15/91) **90**
Ser Gioveto 1987 ($NA) (11/30/89) (HS) **90**
Ser Gioveto 1986 $15 (2/15/89) **84**
Ser Gioveto 1985 $15 (11/30/89) (HS) **88**

ROCCHE COSTAMAGNA (Italy/Piedmont)
Barbera d'Alba 1988 $11.50 (3/15/91) **90**
Barolo Rocche di la Morra 1985 $25 (2/28/91) **72**
Dolcetto d'Alba 1989 $12 (4/30/91) **83**
Roccardo Nebbiolo delle Langhe 1989 $13 (4/30/91) **85**

ROCHA (Portugal)
Vintage Port 1985 $32 (4/15/91) **88**
Vintage Port 1977 $19 (4/30/91) **81**

ROCHE (United States/California)
Chardonnay Carneros 1990 $13 (3/15/92) **89**
Chardonnay Carneros 1989 $13 (3/31/91) **81**
Chardonnay Carneros 1988 $11 (10/31/89) **90**
Pinot Noir Carneros 1989 $15 (4/30/91) **81**
Pinot Noir Carneros 1988 $14 (12/31/89) **89**
Pinot Noir Carneros Unfiltered 1989 $19 (4/30/91) **78**

DOMAINE DE LA ROCHELLE (France/Beaujolais)
Moulin-à-Vent 1988 $10 (5/31/89) (TM) **91**

CHATEAU DE ROCHEMORIN (France/Bordeaux)
Pessac-Léognan 1990 (NR) (5/15/92) (BT) **90+**
Pessac-Léognan 1989 $14 (3/15/92) **88**
Pessac-Léognan 1988 $15 (6/30/89) (BT) **75+**
Pessac-Léognan 1987 ($NA) (6/30/89) (BT) **75+**
Pessac-Léognan 1986 Rel: $10 Cur: $15 (6/15/89) **84**
Graves 1985 Rel: $9 Cur: $14 (6/15/88) **85**
Pessac-Léognan Blanc 1990 $16 (5/15/92) **80**
Pessac-Léognan Blanc 1989 $17 (6/15/91) **90**
Pessac-Léognan Blanc 1988 $15 (5/31/90) **82**
Pessac-Léognan Blanc 1987 $9 (7/31/89) **80**
Pessac-Léognan Blanc 1986 $10 (8/31/88) **86**

CHATEAU DU ROCHER (France/Bordeaux)
St.-Emilion 1983 $11 (5/15/87) **73**

CHATEAU DU ROCHER-BELLEVUE-FIGEAC (France/Bordeaux)
St.-Emilion 1991 (NR) (5/15/92) (BT) **80+**
St.-Emilion 1990 (NR) (5/15/92) (BT) **80+**
St.-Emilion 1989 $15 (4/30/90) (BT) **80+**
St.-Emilion 1988 $13 (4/30/91) **87**
St.-Emilion 1986 Rel: $12 Cur: $17 (5/15/87) (BT) **80+**

DOMAINE DES ROCHES (France/Burgundy)
Mâcon-Igé 1989 $9 (10/31/90) **76**
Mâcon-Igé 1987 $7 (5/15/89) BB **84**

ROCHIOLI (United States/California)
Chardonnay Russian River Valley 1990 $15 (6/30/92) **90**
Chardonnay Russian River Valley 1989 $14 (12/15/91) **85**
Chardonnay Russian River Valley 1988 $15 (4/15/90) **81**
Chardonnay Russian River Valley 1987 $14 (5/31/89) **83**
Chardonnay Russian River Valley 1986 $12 (1/31/88) **72**
Chardonnay Russian River Valley J. Rochioli Reserve 1990 $24 (6/30/92) **91**
Pinot Noir Russian River Valley 1989 $16 (11/15/91) **84**
Pinot Noir Russian River Valley 1988 $15 (10/31/90) **85**
Pinot Noir Russian River Valley 1987 $15 (5/31/90) **89**
Pinot Noir Russian River Valley 1986 $14.25 (10/15/89) **87**
Pinot Noir Russian River Valley 1985 $12.50 (6/15/88) **92**
Pinot Noir Russian River Valley 1984 $12 (11/15/87) **84**
Pinot Noir Russian River Valley 1982 $12.50 (8/31/86) **89**
Sauvignon Blanc Russian River Valley 1990 $9 (11/15/91) **87**

ROCKING HORSE (United States/California)
Cabernet Sauvignon Napa Valley Hillside Cuvée 1989 $17 (3/31/92) **85**

ANTONIN RODET (France/Burgundy)
Bâtard-Montrachet 1989 ($NA) (8/31/91) **92**
Beaujolais-Villages Rodet 1988 $8 (11/15/90) **75**
Chablis Les Montmains 1985 $20 (4/15/87) **88**
Chassagne-Montrachet 1981 $14 (12/01/84) **58**
Chassagne-Montrachet Morgeot 1989 $40 (8/31/91) **91**
Corton-Charlemagne 1989 $65 (8/31/91) **92**
Gevrey-Chambertin 1986 $25 (7/15/90) **86**
Gevrey-Chambertin Lavaux St.-Jacques 1982 $35 (6/30/87) **92**
Meursault Les Perrières 1989 ($NA) (8/31/91) **88**
Montagny Les Chagnots 1985 $10 (11/15/86) **65**
Montrachet 1989 $195 (8/31/91) **89**
Pouilly-Fuissé Rodet 1985 $19 (10/15/87) **80**
Puligny-Montrachet Les Clavoillons 1989 $43 (8/31/91) **82**

LOUIS ROEDERER (France/Champagne)
Brut Blanc de Blancs Champagne 1983 $45 (12/31/90) **83**
Brut Blanc de Blancs Champagne 1979 $39 (5/31/87) **94**
Brut Champagne 1985 $50 (12/31/90) **85**
Brut Champagne 1982 $45 (12/31/88) **93**
Brut Champagne NV $25 (5/16/86) **82**
Brut Champagne Cristal 1985 $132 (5/15/92) **85**
Brut Champagne Cristal 1983 $120 (12/31/89) **88**
Brut Champagne Cristal 1982 Rel: $106 Cur: $119 (9/30/87) **92**
Brut Champagne Cristal 1981 Rel: $85 Cur: $100 (5/16/86) **91**
Brut Champagne Premier NV $30 (12/31/91) **88**
Brut Rosé Champagne NV $37 (12/16/85) **79**
Brut Rosé Champagne Cristal 1979 $87 (12/16/85) **69**

ROEDERER ESTATE (United States/California)
Brut Anderson Valley NV $16 (5/31/89) **88**

DOMAINE JEAN-MAX ROGER (France/Loire)
Sancerre Le Chêne Marchand 1988 $17.50 (9/15/90) **85**

POL ROGER (France/Champagne)
Brut Blanc de Blancs Champagne Blanc de Chardonnay 1985 $62 (1/31/92) **89**
Brut Blanc de Blancs Champagne Blanc de Chardonnay 1982 $50 (12/31/90) **91**
Brut Blanc de Blancs Champagne Blanc de Chardonnay 1979 $41 (12/31/90) **84**
Brut Champagne 1979 $41 (9/01/85) **90**
Brut Champagne NV $37 (12/31/91) **92**
Brut Champagne Cuvée Sir Winston Churchill 1982 $50 (4/15/90) **92**
Brut Champagne Extra Cuvée de Réserve 1982 $50 (12/31/90) **82**
Brut Champagne Réserve 1985 $62 (12/31/90) **86**
Brut Champagne Réserve NV $32 (11/15/91) **87**
Brut Rosé Champagne 1985 $62 (1/31/92) **89**
Rosé Champagne 1982 $50 (12/31/88) **80**
Rosé Champagne 1979 $41 (12/16/85) **88**
Rosé Champagne 1975 Rel: $33 Cur: $95 (12/16/85) **67**

LA ROGUE (France/Other)
Bandol 1987 $10.50 (11/30/90) **83**

CHATEAU ROLAND (France/Bordeaux)
St.-Emilion 1986 $11.25 (6/30/89) **79**

CHATEAU ROLLAND (France/Sauternes)
Barsac 1988 ($NA) (6/15/90) (BT) **80+**
Barsac 1987 ($NA) (6/15/90) **77**

ROLLING HILLS (United States/California)
Cabernet Sauvignon California 1987 $7 (12/15/89) BB **86**
Pinot Noir Santa Maria Valley 1985 $6 (6/15/88) **77**

ROMANEE-CONTI (France/Burgundy)
Echézeaux 1988 $225 (4/30/91) **92**
Echézeaux 1987 $98 (9/30/90) **92**
Echézeaux 1986 Rel: $110 Cur: $171 (8/31/89) **92**
Echézeaux 1985 Rel: $95 Cur: $140 (2/29/88) **96**
Echézeaux 1984 Rel: $52 Cur: $82 (2/28/87) **90**
Echézeaux 1983 Rel: $75 Cur: $88 (11/30/86) **63**
Echézeaux 1952 $125 (8/31/90) (TR) **97**
Grands Echézeaux 1988 $315 (4/30/91) **92**
Grands Echézeaux 1987 $145 (9/30/90) **89**
Grands Echézeaux 1986 $160 (8/31/89) **94**
Grands Echézeaux 1985 Rel: $140 Cur: $183 (2/29/88) **94**
Grands Echézeaux 1984 Rel: $64 Cur: $85 (2/28/87) **88**
Grands Echézeaux 1983 $100 (11/30/86) **64**
Grands Echézeaux 1942 $230 (8/31/90) (TR) **93**
Montrachet 1988 Rel: $600 Cur: $640 (4/30/91) **94**
Montrachet 1987 Rel: $525 Cur: $700 (12/31/90) **94**
Montrachet 1985 $720 (2/28/87) (HS) **96**
Montrachet 1984 $450 (2/28/87) (HS) **93**
Montrachet 1983 $690 (2/28/87) (HS) **95**
Montrachet 1982 $560 (2/28/87) (HS) **93**
Montrachet 1981 $470 (2/28/87) (HS) **91**
Montrachet 1980 $400 (2/28/87) (HS) **88**
Montrachet 1979 $500 (2/28/87) (HS) **89**
Montrachet 1978 $730 (2/28/87) (HS) **98**
Montrachet 1977 $300 (2/28/87) (HS) **90**
Montrachet 1976 $510 (2/28/87) (HS) **94**
Montrachet 1975 $430 (2/28/87) (HS) **89**
Montrachet 1974 $430 (2/28/87) (HS) **87**
Montrachet 1973 $560 (2/28/87) (HS) **99**
Montrachet 1972 $600 () (HS) **92**
Montrachet 1971 $750 () (HS) **94**
Montrachet 1970 $680 () (HS) **86**
Montrachet 1969 $990 () (HS) **88**
Montrachet 1968 $830 () (HS) **85**
Montrachet 1967 $1,280 () (HS) **85**
Montrachet 1966 $1,200 () (HS) **95**
Montrachet 1964 $800 () (HS) **82**
Richebourg 1988 $400 (4/30/91) **94**
Richebourg 1987 $190 (9/30/90) **93**
Richebourg 1986 $230 (8/31/89) **94**
Richebourg 1985 Rel: $210 Cur: $320 (2/29/88) **100**
Richebourg 1984 $102 (2/28/87) **91**
Richebourg 1983 $150 (11/30/86) **52**
Richebourg 1954 ($NA) (8/31/90) (TR) **88**
Richebourg 1947 $750 (8/31/90) (TR) **65**
Romanée-Conti 1988 $600 (4/30/91) **98**
Romanée-Conti 1987 Rel: $350 Cur: $580 (9/30/90) **89**
Romanée-Conti 1986 Rel: $400 Cur: $600 (8/31/89) **95**
Romanée-Conti 1985 Rel: $375 Cur: $1,100 (1/31/90) (JS) **99**
Romanée-Conti 1984 $640 (1/31/90) (JS) **94**
Romanée-Conti 1983 Rel: $250 Cur: $650 (1/31/90) (JS) **78**
Romanée-Conti 1982 $450 (1/31/90) (JS) **85**
Romanée-Conti 1979 $790 (1/31/90) (JS) **90**
Romanée-Conti 1978 $1,330 (1/31/90) (JS) **95**
Romanée-Conti 1975 $680 (1/31/90) (JS) **82**
Romanée-Conti 1964 $950 (1/31/90) (JS) **98**
Romanée-Conti 1963 $1,100 (1/31/90) (JS) **50**
Romanée-Conti 1959 $1,600 (1/31/90) (JS) **68**
Romanée-Conti 1953 $2,000 (1/31/90) (JS) **93**
Romanée-Conti 1937 $1,950 (12/15/88) **94**
Romanée-Conti 1935 $700 (1/31/90) (JS) **50**
Romanée-Conti 1934 $1,800 (1/31/90) (JS) **66**
Romanée-Conti 1929 $2,100 (1/31/90) (JS) **50**
Romanée-St.-Vivant 1988 $360 (4/30/91) **97**
Romanée-St.-Vivant 1987 $175 (9/30/90) **89**
Romanée-St.-Vivant 1986 $195 (8/31/89) **98**
Romanée-St.-Vivant 1985 $175 (2/29/88) **88**
Romanée-St.-Vivant 1984 Rel: $70 Cur: $89 (2/28/87) **96**
Romanée-St.-Vivant 1983 $125 (11/30/86) **66**
La Tâche 1988 $450 (4/30/91) **98**
La Tâche 1987 $225 (9/30/90) **92**
La Tâche 1986 $250 (8/31/89) CS **98**
La Tâche 1985 Rel: $225 Cur: $360 (2/29/88) **98**
La Tâche 1984 Rel: $105 Cur: $160 (2/28/87) **95**
La Tâche 1983 Rel: $150 Cur: $195 (11/30/86) **61**

ROMBAUER (United States/California)
Cabernet Sauvignon Napa Valley 1987 $16 (11/15/91) **87**
Cabernet Sauvignon Napa Valley 1986 Rel: $15 Cur: $18 (4/15/90) **88**
Cabernet Sauvignon Napa Valley 1985 Rel: $14.75 Cur: $20 (4/30/89) **85**
Cabernet Sauvignon Napa Valley 1984 Rel: $13.50 Cur: $21 (CA-3/89) **84**
Cabernet Sauvignon Napa Valley 1983 Rel: $13.50 Cur: $19 (CA-3/89) **73**
Cabernet Sauvignon Napa Valley 1982 Rel: $12 Cur: $35 (CA-3/89) **83**
Cabernet Sauvignon Napa Valley 1981 Rel: $12 Cur: $24 (CA-3/89) **82**
Cabernet Sauvignon Napa Valley 1980 Rel: $10 Cur: $25 (CA-3/89) **86**
Chardonnay Napa Valley 1989 $14 (3/15/92) **84**
Chardonnay Napa Valley 1988 $15 (12/31/90) **86**
Chardonnay Napa Valley 1987 Rel: $14.50 Cur: $17 (1/31/90) **88**
Chardonnay Napa Valley 1986 Rel: $14.50 Cur: $17 (CH-6/90) **85**
Chardonnay Napa Valley 1985 Rel: $14.50 Cur: $18 (CH-6/90) **84**
Chardonnay Napa Valley 1984 Rel: $14.50 Cur: $20 (CH-6/90) **78**
Chardonnay Napa Valley 1983 Rel: $14.50 Cur: $25 (CH-7/90) **87**
Chardonnay Napa Valley 1982 Rel: $14.50 Cur: $25 (CH-6/90) **84**
Chardonnay Napa Valley French Vineyard 1984 $13.50 (4/01/86) **71**
Chardonnay Napa Valley Private Reserve 1988 $20 (12/31/91) **85**
Chardonnay Napa Valley Reserve 1988 $20 (CH-6/90) **89**
Chardonnay Napa Valley Reserve 1987 $25 (CH-6/90) **87**
Chardonnay Napa Valley Reserve 1986 $24 (CH-6/90) **86**
Le Meilleur du Chai Napa Valley 1986 $35 (5/15/91) **84**
Le Meilleur du Chai Napa Valley 1985 Rel: $37.50 Cur: $43 (10/31/89) **90**
Le Meilleur du Chai Napa Valley 1984 Rel: $32.50 Cur: $40 (3/31/89) **94**
Le Meilleur du Chai Napa Valley 1983 Rel: $30 Cur: $43 (CA-3/89) **90**
Merlot Napa Valley 1989 $16 (11/15/91) **84**
Merlot Napa Valley 1987 $14 (2/15/90) **87**
Merlot Napa Valley 1986 $14 (7/31/89) **78**

CHATEAU ROMER DU HAYOT (France/Sauternes)
Sauternes 1989 ($NA) (6/15/90) (BT) **80+**
Sauternes 1988 $17/375ml (4/30/91) **72**
Sauternes 1986 $22 (12/31/89) **78**
Sauternes 1983 $19 (1/31/88) **72**
Sauternes 1982 $13 (10/16/85) **82**

UMANI RONCHI (Italy/Other)
Montepulciano d'Abruzzo 1989 $5 (2/15/91) **75**

RONCHI DI CIALLA (Italy/North)
Refosco Colli Orientali del Friuli dal Peduncolo Rosso di Cialla 1983 $23 (3/31/89) **79**
Schiopettino di Cialla 1983 $25 (3/31/89) **84**

MARIN RONCO FORNAZ (Italy/North)
Chardonnay 1988 ($NA) (9/15/89) **84**

RONCO DEL GNEMIZ (Italy/North)
Chardonnay 1989 $27 (7/15/91) **88**

Chardonnay 1987 $18 (9/15/89) **90**
Müller Thurgau 1989 $18 (7/15/91) **82**
Rosso 1986 $15 (3/31/89) **80**
Tocai Friulano Colli Orientali del Friuli 1989 $18 (8/31/91) **83**

CA' RONESCA (Italy/North)
Pinot Grigio Colli Orientali del Friuli 1989 $19 (3/31/91) **81**
Sauvignon Colli Orientali del Friuli del Podere 1989 $19 (4/15/91) **84**

ROO'S LEAP (Australia)
Cabernet Sauvignon McLaren Vale 1985 $10 (11/30/88) **89**
Cabernet Sauvignon McLaren Vale Limited Edition 1986 $9.50 (1/31/90) **85**
Chardonnay Coonawarra Barrel Fermented 1991 $10 (6/30/92) **83**
Chardonnay Coonawarra Barrel Fermented 1990 $10 (9/15/91) **82**
Chardonnay Hunter Valley Barrel Fermented 1987 $10 (2/15/89) **88**
Fumé Blanc Barossa Valley 1991 $8 (6/30/92) **83**
Pinot Noir McLaren Vale 1988 $8 (2/28/91) **86**

ROOIBERG (Other/South Africa)
Sauvignon Blanc Robertson 1991 $8 (4/15/92) **84**
Syrah Goree 1989 $11 (4/15/92) **82**

CHATEAU ROQUEGRAVE (France/Bordeaux)
Médoc 1983 $6 (4/01/86) **63**

CHATEAU DES ROQUES (France/Rhône)
Côtes du Rhône-Villages Blanc Cuvée Bethleem 1988 $7.50 (3/31/90) **68**
Vacqueyras Cuvée de Noe 1986 $7.50 (12/15/89) BB **88**

DOMAINE DE LA ROQUETTE (France/Rhône)
Châteauneuf-du-Pape 1989 $17 (10/15/91) **86**
Châteauneuf-du-Pape 1988 $17 (10/15/91) **86**
Châteauneuf-du-Pape 1986 $18 (10/15/91) **85**
Châteauneuf-du-Pape 1985 $13 (7/31/88) SS **90**
Châteauneuf-du-Pape Blanc 1990 $25 (10/15/91) **84**

ROSE CREEK (United States/Idaho)
Chardonnay Idaho 1990 $13 (2/29/92) **72**
Johannisberg Riesling Idaho 1990 $6 (2/29/92) **83**

CHATEAU LA ROSE-FIGEAC (France/Bordeaux)
Pomerol 1982 $25 (5/15/89) (TR) **85**

ROSEMOUNT (Australia)
Cabernet Sauvignon Coonawarra Kirri Billi Vineyard 1986 $19.50 (10/31/90) **88**
Cabernet Sauvignon Coonawarra Show Reserve 1988 $16 (5/31/91) **89**
Cabernet Sauvignon Coonawarra Show Reserve 1987 $15 (2/28/91) **88**
Cabernet Sauvignon Coonawarra Show Reserve 1985 $14 (1/31/89) **82**
Cabernet Sauvignon Coonawarra Show Reserve 1984 $13.50 (2/28/87) **86**
Cabernet Sauvignon Hunter Valley 1989 $10 (9/30/91) **82**
Cabernet Sauvignon Hunter Valley 1988 $10 (1/31/90) **76**
Cabernet Sauvignon Hunter Valley 1987 $10 (7/31/89) **83**
Cabernet Sauvignon Hunter Valley 1986 $11 (1/31/89) SS **93**
Cabernet Sauvignon Hunter Valley 1985 $9 (1/31/88) **85**
Cabernet Sauvignon Hunter Valley 1984 $9.50 (4/30/87) **78**
Cabernet Shiraz South Eastern Australia 1990 $7 (7/15/91) BB **84**
Cabernet Shiraz South Eastern Australia 1989 $6 (7/31/90) BB **81**
Chardonnay Hunter Valley Giants Creek Vineyard 1987 $20 (3/15/90) **80**
Chardonnay Hunter Valley Matured in Oak Casks 1990 $9 (5/15/91) **88**
Chardonnay Hunter Valley Matured in Oak Casks 1989 $9 (4/30/90) **80**
Chardonnay Hunter Valley Matured in Oak Casks 1988 $10 (3/15/90) **82**
Chardonnay Hunter Valley Matured in Oak Casks 1987 $10.50 (3/15/89) **87**
Chardonnay Hunter Valley Matured in Oak Casks 1986 $9 (5/31/88) **87**
Chardonnay Hunter Valley Matured in Oak Casks 1985 $10 (4/15/87) **83**
Chardonnay Hunter Valley Roxburgh 1986 $25 (5/31/87) **91**
Chardonnay Hunter Valley Roxburgh 1985 $25 (8/31/87) **88**
Chardonnay Hunter Valley Show Reserve 1989 $16 (5/31/91) **92**
Chardonnay Hunter Valley Show Reserve 1988 $16 (3/15/90) **85**
Chardonnay Hunter Valley Show Reserve 1987 $16.50 (2/15/89) **92**
Chardonnay Hunter Valley Show Reserve 1986 $16 (12/31/87) **90**
Chardonnay Hunter Valley Show Reserve 1985 $15 (4/15/87) **88**
Dry Red Diamond Reserve Hunter Valley 1988 $6.50 (2/28/90) BB **83**
Dry White Diamond Reserve Hunter Valley 1987 $6.50 (7/31/89) **68**
Pinot Noir Hunter Valley 1989 $10 (9/30/91) **81**
Pinot Noir Hunter Valley 1985 $9.50 (4/30/87) **84**
Pinot Noir Hunter Valley NV $9 (7/01/87) **80**
Pinot Noir Hunter Valley Giants Creek Vineyard 1987 $20 (2/28/90) **84**
Sémillon Chardonnay Hunter Valley 1987 $9 (7/31/89) **82**
Sémillon Chardonnay South Eastern Australia 1990 $7 (5/31/91) BB **84**
Sémillon Chardonnay South Eastern Australia 1988 $6 (6/15/90) BB **78**
Sémillon Hunter Valley Wood Matured 1987 $9 (10/31/89) **84**
Shiraz Hunter Valley 1989 $8 (2/15/91) SS **91**
Shiraz Hunter Valley 1988 $8 (1/31/90) SS **90**
Shiraz Hunter Valley 1987 $9 (7/31/89) **87**
Shiraz Hunter Valley 1986 $9 (4/15/89) **92**
Shiraz Hunter Valley 1985 $8 (2/15/88) **80**
Shiraz Hunter Valley 1984 $7.50 (4/30/87) **83**
Shiraz McLaren Vale Show Reserve 1989 $15 (2/29/92) **89**
Shiraz South Eastern Australia 1990 $8.50 (2/15/92) SS **92**
Traminer Riesling South Eastern Australia 1991 $7 (2/29/92) BB **83**

ROSENBLUM (United States/California)
Merlot Napa Valley Holbrook Mitchell Vineyard 1989 $20 (5/31/92) **80**
Merlot Russian River Valley 1989 $14 (5/31/92) **85**

Key to Symbols

The scores reported here are the results of blind tastings conducted by our panel of senior editors. Wines that carry the initials below are results of individual tastings.

THE WINE SPECTATOR 100-POINT SCALE 95-100—Classic, a great wine; ***90-94***—Outstanding, superior character and style; ***80-89***—Good to very good, a wine with special qualities; ***70-79***—Average, drinkable wine that may have minor flaws; ***60-69***—Below average, drinkable but not recommended; ***50-59***—Poor, undrinkable, not recommended. "+"—With a score indicates a range; used primarily with barrel tastings to indicate a preliminary score.

SPECIAL DESIGNATIONS SS—Spectator Selection, CS—Cellar Selection, BB—Best Buy, ($NA)—Price not available, (NR)—Not released.

TASTER'S INITIALS (JG)—Jim Gordon, (HS)—Harvey Steiman, (JL)—James Laube, (JS)—James Suckling, (TM)— … Matthews, (TR)—Terry Robards, (PM)—Per-Henrik Mansson, (BT)—Barrel Tasting (these wines were tasted … mples), (CA-date)—*California's Great Cabernets* by James Laube, (CH-date)—*California's Great* … (VP-date)—*Vintage Port* by James Suckling.

… nt the issue in which the rating was published.

Zinfandel Napa Valley 1987 $9 (10/31/89) 77

Zinfandel Napa Valley 1987 $9 (10/31/89) **77**
Zinfandel Napa Valley Hendry Vineyard Reserve 1988 $14 (4/30/91) **84**

DEI ROSETI (Italy/Tuscany)
Belconvento 1987 $24 (3/15/91) **85**
Belconvento 1985 $23 (7/15/89) **86**
Brunello di Montalcino 1982 $20 (7/31/89) **89**
Brunello di Montalcino 1979 $10 (8/31/86) **88**
Rosso di Montalcino 1988 $13 (1/31/91) **87**
Rosso di Montalcino 1985 $9 (7/15/89) **78**

ROSEWOOD (Australia)
Muscat Australia Liqueur NV $50 (7/01/87) **91**
Muscat Rutherglen Old Liqueur NV $40 (7/01/87) **90**
Muscat Rutherglen Special Liqueur NV $30 (7/01/87) **91**

DOMAINE LA ROSIERE (France/Other)
Syrah Côteaux des Baronnies 1988 $6.50 (2/28/90) **78**

ROSS VALLEY (United States/California)
Zinfandel Sonoma County Tom and Kelley Parsons' Vineyard 1988 $11 (8/31/91) **83**

PHILIPPE ROSSIGNOL (France/Burgundy)
Côte de Nuits-Villages 1985 $24 (7/31/88) **89**
Gevrey-Chambertin 1987 $23 (5/31/90) **69**

ROSSIGNOL-FEVRIER (France/Burgundy)
Volnay 1988 $32 (3/31/91) **92**

R. ROSTAING (France/Rhône)
Côte-Rôtie Côte Blonde 1987 $40 (6/30/90) **86**

ROTHBURY (Australia)
Chardonnay Hunter Valley 1991 $9.50 (2/29/92) **83**
Chardonnay Hunter Valley 1984 $8 (7/01/86) **69**
Chardonnay Hunter Valley Brokenback Vineyard 1989 $9 (10/15/90) **84**
Chardonnay Hunter Valley Brokenback Vineyard 1988 $10 (3/15/89) **89**
Chardonnay Hunter Valley Brokenback Vineyard 1987 $7.50 (2/15/88) **88**
Chardonnay Hunter Valley Brokenback Vineyard 1986 $9.50 (5/31/87) **90**
Chardonnay Hunter Valley Brokenback Vineyard Barrel Fermented 1990 $15 (5/31/92) **89**
Chardonnay Hunter Valley Reserve 1988 $18.50 (10/15/90) **85**
Chardonnay Hunter Valley Reserve 1987 $19 (2/15/89) **89**
Chardonnay Hunter Valley Reserve 1986 $15 (2/15/88) **83**
Chardonnay Hunter Valley Reserve 1985 $25 (5/31/87) **92**
Pinot Noir Hunter Valley 1983 $10 (7/01/87) **87**
Pinot Noir Hunter Valley Director's Reserve 1983 $15 (7/01/87) **89**
Shiraz Hunter Valley Herlstone Vineyard 1987 $9.50 (5/31/91) **85**
Shiraz Hunter Valley Herlstone Vineyard 1986 $10.50 (7/31/89) **76**
Shiraz Hunter Valley Herlstone Vineyard 1985 $10.50 (3/31/89) **78**
Shiraz Hunter Valley Herlstone Vineyard 1984 $9.50 (5/15/87) **90**
Shiraz Hunter Valley Syrah 1989 $9.50 (2/29/92) **80**

BARONS EDMOND & BENJAMIN ROTHSCHILD (France/Bordeaux)
Haut-Médoc 1987 $24 (3/31/91) **75**
Haut-Médoc 1986 $48 (3/31/91) **76**

BARON PHILIPPE DE ROTHSCHILD (France/Bordeaux)
St.-Emilion 1985 $10.50 (9/30/88) **85**

ROUDON-SMITH (United States/California)
Cabernet Sauvignon Santa Cruz Mountains 1986 $12 (3/15/91) **81**
Cabernet Sauvignon Santa Cruz Mountains 1984 $12 (6/30/88) **78**
Chardonnay Mendocino Nelson Ranch 1986 $12 (9/15/88) **85**
Chardonnay Santa Cruz Mountains 1985 $15 (3/31/89) **70**
Claret California Cuvée Five NV $4.50 (3/31/89) **78**
Pinot Noir Santa Cruz Mountains 1985 $15 (6/15/88) **86**
Pinot Noir Santa Cruz Mountains Cox Vineyard 1987 $15 (2/28/91) **84**
Zinfandel Sonoma County 1988 $12 (2/15/91) **87**
Zinfandel Sonoma Valley Chauvet Vineyard 1985 $8.50 (3/31/89) **80**

CHATEAU DE ROUFFLIAC (France/Bordeaux)
St.-Emilion 1985 $15 (9/30/88) **89**

ROUGE HOMME (Australia)
Cabernet Sauvignon Coonawarra 1984 $12 (2/15/88) **84**

CHATEAU ROUGET (France/Bordeaux)
Pomerol 1990 (NR) (5/15/92) (BT) **85+**
Pomerol 1989 $21 (4/30/91) (BT) **85+**
Pomerol 1982 $21 (5/15/89) (TR) **86**

EMMANUEL ROUGET (France/Burgundy)
Echézeaux 1989 $98 (11/15/91) **93**
Echézeaux 1988 $81 (11/15/90) **96**
Echézeaux 1987 $55 (3/31/90) **88**
Echézeaux 1986 $55 (12/31/88) **87**
Nuits-St.-Georges 1989 $48 (11/15/91) **86**
Nuits-St.-Georges 1987 $32 (3/31/90) **86**
Vosne-Romanée 1989 $48 (11/15/91) **91**
Vosne-Romanée 1987 $32 (3/31/90) **91**
Vosne-Romanée Les Beaumonts 1986 $40 (12/31/88) **89**
Vosne-Romanée Cros Parantoux 1989 $83 (11/15/91) **94**

DOMAINE ROUGEOT-LATOUR (France/Burgundy)
Bourgogne Blanc Chardonnay Clos des Six Ouvrées 1986 $15 (10/15/88) **80**
Meursault Les Charmes 1986 $38 (6/30/88) **90**
Meursault Les Pellans 1986 $25 (10/15/88) **69**

DOMAINE GUY ROULOT (France/Burgundy)
Meursault Les Charmes 1989 $65 (8/31/91) **91**
Meursault Les Luchets 1989 $39 (8/31/91) **91**
Meursault Les Meix Chavaux 1988 $33 (5/15/90) **87**
Meursault Perrières 1989 $65 (8/31/91) **90**
Meursault Les Tessons Clos de Mon Plaisir 1989 $50 (8/31/91) **93**
Meursault Les Tessons Clos de Mon Plaisir 1988 $35 (5/15/90) **91**

CHRISTOPHE ROUMIER (France/Burgundy)
Ruchottes-Chambertin 1989 $70 (1/31/92) **94**

DOMAINE G. ROUMIER (France/Burgundy)
Bonnes Mares 1989 $70 (1/31/92) **93**
Chambolle-Musigny 1989 $38 (1/31/92) **90**
Chambolle-Musigny 1988 $30 (7/15/91) **89**
Chambolle-Musigny 1985 $26 (2/15/88) **87**
Chambolle-Musigny Amoureuses 1989 $62 (1/31/92) **88**
Clos Vougeot 1989 $62 (1/31/92) **87**
Morey-St.-Denis Clos de la Bussière 1989 $38 (1/31/92) **85**

Morey-St.-Denis Clos de la Bussière 1988 $30 (7/15/91) **83**
Morey-St.-Denis Clos de la Bussière 1985 $27 (4/30/88) **92**
Musigny 1989 $95 (1/31/92) **96**

HERVE ROUMIER (France/Burgundy)
Chambolle-Musigny 1986 $29 (8/31/89) **82**
Chambolle-Musigny Les Amoureuses 1985 $65 (3/31/88) **89**

CHATEAU ROUMIEU-LACOSTE (France/Sauternes)
Barsac 1989 ($NA) (6/15/90) (BT) **85+**

ROUND HILL (United States/California)
Cabernet Sauvignon California House Lot 5 NV $5 (9/30/86) BB **76**
Cabernet Sauvignon California House Lot 6 NV $5 (10/15/87) **72**
Cabernet Sauvignon California House Lot 7 NV $6.25 (2/15/89) **78**
Cabernet Sauvignon California House Lot 8 NV $6.25 (7/31/91) **79**
Cabernet Sauvignon California Lot 7 NV $6 (10/31/90) **79**
Cabernet Sauvignon Napa Valley 1988 $9 (11/15/91) **81**
Cabernet Sauvignon Napa Valley 1986 $8 (10/15/88) **82**
Cabernet Sauvignon Napa Valley 1984 $8.50 (5/31/88) **84**
Cabernet Sauvignon Napa Valley 1982 $9 (5/16/86) **88**
Cabernet Sauvignon Napa Valley 1981 $9 (3/16/85) **86**
Cabernet Sauvignon Napa Valley 1980 $7.50 (4/16/84) **81**
Cabernet Sauvignon Napa Valley Reserve 1987 $11 (11/15/91) **77**
Cabernet Sauvignon Napa Valley Reserve 1986 $9 (6/30/90) **80**
Cabernet Sauvignon Napa Valley Reserve 1985 $10.50 (5/31/88) **86**
Cabernet Sauvignon Napa Valley Reserve 1984 $10 (10/31/87) **88**
Cabernet Sauvignon Napa Valley Reserve 1983 $9.50 (12/15/86) **92**
Chardonnay California 1990 $6 (2/29/92) BB **82**
Chardonnay California 1988 $7.50 (2/28/91) BB **81**
Chardonnay California House 1989 $6.50 (7/15/91) BB **83**
Chardonnay California House 1988 $5.50 (4/15/90) BB **83**
Chardonnay California House 1987 $6.25 (11/15/88) **79**
Chardonnay California House 1986 $5.25 (11/30/87) BB **83**
Chardonnay California House 1985 $5 (9/30/86) BB **81**
Chardonnay California House 1984 $4.75 (4/16/86) **79**
Chardonnay Napa Valley 1989 $9 (6/30/91) **84**
Chardonnay Napa Valley Reserve 1990 $11 (7/15/92) **85**
Chardonnay Napa Valley Reserve 1989 $11 (6/15/91) **89**
Chardonnay Napa Valley Reserve 1988 $11 (2/28/91) **82**
Chardonnay Napa Valley Reserve 1986 $9.50 (5/31/88) **75**
Chardonnay Napa Valley Reserve 1985 $9.50 (11/15/87) **82**
Chardonnay Napa Valley Reserve Van Asperen Selection 1990 $12 (7/15/92) **89**
Chardonnay Napa Valley Van Asperen Vineyard 1988 $11 (2/28/91) **74**
Chardonnay Napa Valley Van Asperen Vineyard 1987 $11 (7/15/89) **74**
Chardonnay Napa Valley Van Asperen Reserve 1986 $11 (5/31/88) **72**
Chardonnay North Coast 1986 $6.75 (12/15/87) **78**
Fumé Blanc Napa Valley House 1989 $5.75 (11/30/90) BB **83**
Gewürztraminer Napa Valley 1989 $6 (2/15/91) **79**
Gewürztraminer Napa Valley 1988 $6.25 (1/31/90) BB **84**
Merlot Napa Valley 1984 $9 (5/15/87) **87**
Merlot Napa Valley 1983 $7.50 (1/31/87) SS **92**
Merlot Napa Valley 1982 $7.50 (2/16/86) **65**
Merlot Napa Valley Reserve 1989 $11 (5/31/92) **78**
Merlot Napa Valley Reserve 1988 $11 (11/15/91) **80**
Merlot Napa Valley Reserve 1986 $10.75 (12/31/88) **82**
Merlot Napa Valley Reserve 1985 $10 (5/31/88) **84**
Zinfandel Napa Valley 1989 $6 (3/31/92) BB **81**
Zinfandel Napa Valley 1988 $6.50 (2/15/91) BB **89**
Zinfandel Napa Valley 1985 $5.50 (5/15/88) BB **82**
Zinfandel Napa Valley 1981 $5 (4/16/84) **84**
Zinfandel Napa Valley Select 1987 $6 (3/31/90) BB **84**

ARMAND ROUSSEAU (France/Burgundy)
Chambertin 1988 $201 (5/15/91) **93**
Chambertin 1985 Rel: $100 Cur: $120 (3/15/88) **97**
Chambertin Clos de Bèze 1989 $135 (1/31/92) **93**
Chambertin Clos de Bèze 1988 $188 (5/15/91) **95**
Charmes-Chambertin 1985 $63 (10/15/88) **86**
Clos de la Roche 1988 $75 (5/15/91) **91**
Gevrey-Chambertin 1989 (NR) (1/31/92) **88**
Gevrey-Chambertin Clos St.-Jacques 1989 $93 (1/31/92) **90**
Gevrey-Chambertin Clos St.-Jacques 1985 $80 (10/15/88) **92**
Mazis-Chambertin Mazy-Chambertin 1989 (NR) (1/31/92) **90**
Mazis-Chambertin Mazy-Chambertin 1985 $61 (10/15/88) **85**
Ruchottes-Chambertin Clos des Ruchottes 1989 (NR) (1/31/92) **90**

CHATEAU ROUSSELLE (France/Bordeaux)
Fronsac 1991 (NR) (5/15/92) (BT) **75+**

ARMAND ROUX (France/Bordeaux)
Bordeaux Verdillac 1989 $7 (1/31/92) **71**
Bordeaux Verdillac 1988 $6.25 (7/15/90) BB **79**
Côtes du Rhône La Berberine 1988 $7.50 (10/31/90) BB **81**
Echézeaux 1959 $110 (8/31/90) (TR) **94**
Richebourg 1959 $130 (8/31/90) (TR) **91**
Volnay Hospices de Beaune Général Muteau 1959 $115 (8/31/90) (TR) **91**

CHARLES ROUX (France/Rhône)
Côtes du Rhône-Villages Rasteau 1985 $10 (2/28/90) **89**

DOMAINE ROUX PERE & FILS (France/Burgundy)
Bourgogne Blanc Chardonnay 1989 $18 (8/31/91) **74**
Chassagne-Montrachet 1989 $45 (8/31/91) **89**
Chassagne-Montrachet 1988 $35 (2/28/90) **88**
Chassagne-Montrachet 1986 $34 (2/29/88) **90**
Chassagne-Montrachet 1985 $32 (8/31/87) **86**
Chassagne-Montrachet Morgeot 1989 $55 (8/31/91) **92**
Chassagne-Montrachet Morgeot 1988 $39 (2/28/90) **86**
Chassagne-Montrachet Morgeot 1987 $43 (5/31/89) **79**
Chassagne-Montrachet Morgeot 1986 $36 (2/29/88) **91**
Chassagne-Montrachet Rouge Clos St.-Jean 1983 $13 (9/16/85) **86**
Meursault 1985 $27.50 (2/28/87) **82**
Meursault Clos des Poruzots 1989 $45 (8/31/91) **89**
Puligny-Montrachet Les Champs-Gains 1989 $55 (2/28/91) **83**
Puligny-Montrachet Les Champs-Gains 1988 $40 (3/15/90) **92**
Puligny-Montrachet Les Enseignères 1989 $45 (8/31/91) **89**
Puligny-Montrachet Les Enseignères 1986 $36 (2/29/88) **92**
Puligny-Montrachet Les Enseignères 1985 $34 (9/15/87) **88**
Puligny-Montrachet La Garenne 1989 $55 (8/31/91) **90**
Puligny-Montrachet La Garenne 1987 $44 (4/15/89) **83**
Puligny-Montrachet La Garenne 1986 $38 (12/31/87) **89**
Puligny-Montrachet La Garenne 1985 $30 (4/15/87) **92**
St.-Aubin La Chatenière 1989 $26 (8/31/91) **81**
St.-Aubin La Pucelle 1989 $26 (8/31/91) **80**
Santenay 1985 $21 (10/31/87) **83**
Volnay en Champans 1988 $35 (3/31/90) **86**
Volnay en Champans 1985 $25 (3/15/87) **92**

ROVELLATS (Spain)
Brut Cava Imperial NV $13 (12/31/90) **83**
Brut Cava Nature Gran Reserva NV $17 (12/31/90) **78**

DOMAINE ROY PERE & FILS (France/Burgundy)
Gevrey-Chambertin Clos Prieur 1988 $35 (12/31/90) **68**
Gevrey-Chambertin Vieilles Vignes 1988 $30 (12/31/90) **72**

ALAIN ROY-THEVENIN (France/Burgundy)
Montagny Château de la Saule 1988 $12 (8/31/90) **83**

ROYAL OPORTO (Portugal)
Tawny Port 20 Year Old NV $25 (2/28/90) (JS) **77**
Vintage Port 1987 Rel: $12 Cur: $15 (11/30/91) **81**
Vintage Port 1985 Rel: $12 Cur: $24 (VP-6/90) **71**
Vintage Port 1984 Rel: $11 Cur: $16 (VP-11/89) **65**
Vintage Port 1983 Rel: $9 Cur: $17 (VP-6/90) **76**
Vintage Port 1982 Rel: $9 Cur: $17 (VP-6/90) **60**
Vintage Port 1980 Rel: $8 Cur: $19 (VP-6/90) **60**
Vintage Port 1978 Rel: $8 Cur: $24 (VP-11/89) **68**
Vintage Port 1977 Rel: $8 Cur: $30 (VP-11/89) **74**
Vintage Port 1970 $28 (VP-11/89) **75**
Vintage Port 1967 $30 (VP-11/89) **72**
Vintage Port 1963 $83 (VP-11/89) **73**
Vintage Port 1871 ($NA) (VP-11/89) **98**

CHARLES ROYER (France/Champagne)
Brut Champagne Sélections de Proprietaires NV (NR) (12/31/91) **84**

ROZES (Portugal)
Vintage Port 1987 ($NA) (VP-6/90) **86**
Vintage Port 1985 Rel: $16 Cur: $21 (VP-5/90) **81**
Vintage Port 1982 ($NA) (VP-6/90) **75**

RUBENTINO (Italy/Tuscany)
Chianti 1990 $6.50 (4/30/92) **78**
Chianti Classico 1989 $8.50 (4/30/92) **81**

RUBISSOW-SARGENT (United States/California)
Cabernet Sauvignon Mt. Veeder 1988 $16 (4/15/92) **87**
Merlot Mt. Veeder 1988 $15 (5/31/92) **84**

RUFFINO (Italy/Tuscany)
Cabreo Il Borgo Predicato di Bitùrica 1988 ($NA) (9/15/91) **90**
Cabreo Il Borgo Predicato di Bitùrica 1985 $21 (9/30/89) **90**
Cabreo la Pietra Predicato del Muschio 1986 $18 (9/15/89) **90**
Cabreo la Pietra Predicato del Muschio 1985 $17 (9/15/89) **83**
Cabreo la Pietra Predicato del Muschio 1983 $17 (3/31/87) **90**
Chianti 1990 $8 (1/31/92) **77**
Chianti Classico 1987 $7 (4/30/90) BB **83**
Chianti Classico 1984 $5 (11/30/86) **78**
Chianti Classico Aziano 1989 $10 (4/30/92) **79**
Chianti Classico Aziano 1988 $11 (9/15/91) **83**
Chianti Classico Aziano 1986 $8 (5/31/89) BB **85**
Chianti Classico Aziano 1985 $8.75 (8/31/88) **80**
Chianti Classico Ducale Riserva 1986 $16 (10/31/91) **89**
Chianti Classico Ducale Riserva 1985 Rel: $13 Cur: $22 (9/15/91) **90**
Chianti Classico Ducale Riserva 1983 Rel: $17 Cur: $21 (11/30/89) (HS) **84**
Chianti Classico Ducale Riserva 1982 Rel: $20 Cur: $24 (5/31/89) **80**
Chianti Classico Ducale Riserva 1981 $9 (10/31/86) **66**
Chianti Classico Ducale Riserva 1979 Rel: $16 Cur: $23 (9/16/85) **80**
Chianti Classico Ducale Riserva 1978 $16 (11/30/89) (HS) **82**
Chianti Classico Ducale Riserva 1977 $28 (9/16/85) (JS) **89**
Chianti Classico Ducale Riserva 1975 $57 (9/16/85) (JS) **86**
Chianti Classico Ducale Riserva 1971 $61 (9/16/85) (JS) **85**
Chianti Classico Ducale Riserva 1962 $45 (9/16/85) (JS) **68**
Chianti Classico Ducale Riserva 1958 $144 (9/16/85) (JS) **82**
Chianti Classico Nozzole Vigneto la Forra 1985 ($NA) (11/30/89) (HS) **90**
Chianti Classico Tenuta Santedame 1988 ($NA) (9/15/91) **88**
Libaio 1990 $10 (1/31/92) **81**
Libaio 1987 $8.50 (9/15/89) **78**
Nero del Tondo 1988 $18 (9/15/91) **88**
Orvieto Classico 1990 $8.50 (3/31/92) **82**
Orvieto Classico 1987 $6.25 (5/15/89) **78**

CASTEL RUGGERO (Italy/Tuscany)
Chianti Classico 1988 ($NA) (9/15/91) **86**

DOM RUINART (France/Champagne)
Brut Blanc de Blancs Champagne 1985 $88 (12/31/91) **87**
Brut Blanc de Blancs Champagne 1983 $60 (12/31/90) **87**
Brut Blanc de Blancs Champagne 1982 Rel: $61 Cur: $70 (12/31/90) **90**
Brut Blanc de Blancs Champagne 1982 Rel: $61 Cur: $70 (12/31/89) CS **94**
Brut Blanc de Blancs Champagne 1981 $61 (12/31/89) **90**
Brut Blanc de Blancs Champagne 1979 Rel: $39 Cur: $52 (10/31/86) **91**
Brut Blanc de Blancs Champagne 1978 Rel: $40 Cur: $50 (5/16/86) **87**
Brut Blanc de Blancs Champagne 1976 Rel: $30 Cur: $45 (10/01/84) **84**
Brut Champagne Ruinart NV $26 (12/31/91) **89**
Brut Rosé Champagne 1979 Rel: $55 Cur: $80 (9/30/88) **92**
Brut Rosé Champagne 1978 Rel: $40 Cur: $52 (9/30/86) **91**
Brut Rosé Champagne 1976 Rel: $35 Cur: $60 (12/16/85) **61**

RUSSIZ SUPERIORE (Italy/North)
Merlot Collio 1989 $27 (4/30/92) **86**
Sauvignon Collio 1990 $27 (5/15/92) **80**

RUTHERFORD ESTATE (United States/California)
Cabernet Sauvignon Napa Valley 1986 $7 (11/15/91) **80**
Cabernet Sauvignon Napa Valley 1984 $5 (11/15/87) **72**
Chardonnay Napa Valley 1990 $6.50 (7/15/92) BB **81**
Chardonnay Napa Valley 1989 $8.50 (7/15/91) **77**
Chardonnay Napa Valley 1985 $5 (11/15/87) **70**

RUTHERFORD HILL (United States/California)
Cabernet Sauvignon Napa Valley 1986 Rel: $14 Cur: $17 (2/28/91) **68**
Cabernet Sauvignon Napa Valley 1985 Rel: $14 Cur: $17 (4/30/90) **82**

Cabernet Sauvignon Napa Valley 1984 Rel: $12.50 Cur: $17 (CA-3/89) **88**
Cabernet Sauvignon Napa Valley 1983 Rel: $12.50 Cur: $22 (CA-3/89) **83**
Cabernet Sauvignon Napa Valley 1982 Rel: $12.50 Cur: $25 (CA-3/89) **83**
Cabernet Sauvignon Napa Valley 1981 Rel: $11.50 Cur: $22 (CA-3/89) **85**
Cabernet Sauvignon Napa Valley 1980 Rel: $11.50 Cur: $21 (CA-3/89) **82**
Cabernet Sauvignon Napa Valley 1979 Rel: $11.50 Cur: $22 (CA-3/89) **87**
Cabernet Sauvignon Napa Valley 1978 Rel: $12 Cur: $25 (CA-3/89) **82**
Cabernet Sauvignon Napa Valley 1977 Rel: $10 Cur: $18 (CA-3/89) **72**
Cabernet Sauvignon Napa Valley 1976 Rel: $9 Cur: $17 (CA-3/89) **73**
Cabernet Sauvignon Napa Valley 1975 Rel: $9 Cur: $18 (CA-3/89) **69**
Cabernet Sauvignon Napa Valley Cask Lot 2 Limited Edition 1980 Rel: $11.50 Cur: $21 (CA-3/89) **88**
Cabernet Sauvignon Napa Valley XVS 1986 $32 (CA-3/89) **88**
Cabernet Sauvignon Napa Valley XVS 1985 Rel: $25 Cur: $29 (4/30/89) **88**
Chardonnay Napa Valley Cellar Reserve 1987 $18 (2/15/91) **90**
Chardonnay Napa Valley Cellar Reserve 1986 $18 (5/31/90) **87**
Chardonnay Napa Valley Cellar Reserve 1985 $15 (5/31/88) **87**
Chardonnay Napa Valley Jaeger Vineyards 1983 $10.75 (5/16/85) **77**
Chardonnay Napa Valley Jaeger Vineyards Cellar Reserve 1981 $14 (3/16/86) **89**
Chardonnay Napa Valley Jaeger Vineyards 1988 $13 (2/15/91) **83**
Chardonnay Napa Valley Jaeger Vineyards 1986 $12 (12/31/88) **87**
Chardonnay Napa Valley Jaeger Vineyards 1985 $11 (5/31/88) **80**
Chardonnay Napa Valley Partners Chardonnay 1984 $7 (4/16/86) **57**
Chardonnay Napa Valley Rutherford Knoll Special Cuvée 1987 $11 (4/30/89) **86**
Chardonnay Napa Valley Rutherford Knoll Special Cuvée 1986 $11 (1/31/88) **83**
Chardonnay Napa Valley XVS 1988 $18 (7/15/91) **87**
Merlot Napa Valley 1989 $14 (5/31/92) **70**
Merlot Napa Valley 1988 $14.50 (5/31/92) **82**
Merlot Napa Valley 1987 $14 (3/31/91) **74**
Merlot Napa Valley 1986 $13 (6/15/90) **68**
Merlot Napa Valley 1985 $12 (1/31/89) **92**
Merlot Napa Valley 1984 $11 (4/30/88) **84**
Merlot Napa Valley 1983 $10 (8/31/87) **87**
Merlot Napa Valley 1982 $10.50 (5/16/86) **79**
Merlot Napa Valley 1981 $10 (10/01/85) **78**
Port Napa Valley Vintage 1983 $18 (11/15/87) **66**
Sauvignon Blanc Napa Valley 1987 $8 (7/31/89) **75**

RUTHERFORD RANCH (United States/California)
Cabernet Sauvignon Napa Valley 1987 $13 (4/30/91) **83**
Cabernet Sauvignon Napa Valley 1985 Rel: $11 Cur: $15 (5/15/90) SS **92**
Cabernet Sauvignon Napa Valley 1984 $12.50 (5/31/89) **85**
Cabernet Sauvignon Napa Valley 1983 $10.25 (12/31/87) **83**
Cabernet Sauvignon Napa Valley 1982 $9 (6/15/87) **84**
Chardonnay Napa Valley 1987 $11 (5/15/90) **83**
Chardonnay Napa Valley Reese Vineyard 1985 $10 (11/15/87) **72**
Merlot Napa Valley 1988 $12 (8/31/91) **80**
Merlot Napa Valley 1986 $11.75 (12/31/88) **87**
Merlot Napa Valley 1985 $10.50 (4/30/88) **92**
Merlot Napa Valley 1984 $9.75 (10/15/87) **83**
Zinfandel Napa Valley 1986 $7.75 (10/31/88) **62**
Zinfandel Napa Valley 1985 $7.75 (3/15/88) **89**
Zinfandel Napa Valley 1982 $6 (9/16/85) **80**

SCHLOSS SAARSTEIN (EBERT) (Germany)
Riesling Auslese Mosel-Saar-Ruwer Serriger Schloss Saarstein 1990 $23 (12/15/91) **85**
Riesling Auslese Mosel-Saar-Ruwer Serriger Schloss Saarsteiner Gold Cup 1988 $25 (9/30/89) **88**
Riesling Beerenauslese Mosel-Saar-Ruwer Serriger Schloss Saarstein 1990 (NR) (12/15/91) **94**
Riesling Beerenauslese Mosel-Saar-Ruwer Serriger Schloss Saarstein Gold Cap 1990 $47 (12/15/91) **93**
Riesling Eiswein Mosel-Saar-Ruwer Serriger Schloss Saarstein 1990 (NR) (12/15/91) **92**
Riesling Kabinett Mosel-Saar-Ruwer Serriger Schloss Saarstein 1990 $11 (12/15/91) **86**
Riesling Kabinett Mosel-Saar-Ruwer Serriger Schloss Saarstein (AP15) 1988 ($NA) (9/30/89) **90**
Riesling Kabinett Mosel-Saar-Ruwer Serriger Schloss Saarstein (AP10) 1988 ($NA) (9/30/89) **83**
Riesling Qualitätswein Mosel-Saar-Ruwer 1990 $9 (12/15/91) **82**
Riesling Spätlese Mosel-Saar-Ruwer Serriger Schloss Saarstein 1990 $15 (12/15/91) **90**
Riesling Spätlese Mosel-Saar-Ruwer Serriger Schloss Saarstein 1988 ($NA) (9/30/89) **85**

LE SABLE (Other/Yugoslavia)
Cabernet Sauvignon Primorski 1986 $4.50 (3/31/91) **64**
Pinot Noir Oplenac 1987 $4.50 (3/31/91) **70**

DOMAINE ROGER SABON & FILS (France/Rhône)
Châteauneuf-du-Pape 1988 $20 (9/30/90) **88**
Châteauneuf-du-Pape Cuvée Prestige 1988 $23 (9/30/90) **85**
Châteauneuf-du-Pape Cuvée Réserve 1988 $20 (9/30/90) **80**
Côtes du Rhône 1989 $12 (11/15/91) **70**
Côtes du Rhône 1988 $11 (10/31/90) **79**

SACCARDI (Italy/Tuscany)
Chianti Classico 1987 $10 (5/15/90) **75**
Chianti Classico 1985 $6 (11/30/87) BB **89**
Chianti Classico Riserva 1983 $12 (5/15/90) **87**
Chianti Classico Riserva 1981 $9 (11/30/87) **81**

SADDLE MOUNTAIN (United States/Washington)
Chenin Blanc Columbia Valley 1988 $5 (10/15/89) **76**
Fumé Blanc Columbia Valley 1988 $5 (10/15/89) BB **86**

SADDLEBACK (United States/California)
Chardonnay Napa Valley 1990 $12 (7/15/92) **72**

Key to Symbols

The scores reported here are the results of blind tastings conducted by our panel of senior editors. Wines that carry the initials below are results of individual tastings.

THE WINE SPECTATOR 100-POINT SCALE ***95-100***—Classic, a great wine; ***90-94***—Outstanding, superior character and style; ***80-89***—Good to very good, a wine with special qualities; ***70-79***—Average, drinkable wine that may have minor flaws; ***60-69***—Below average, drinkable but not recommended; ***50-59***—Poor, undrinkable, not recommended. "+"—With a score indicates a range; used primarily with barrel tastings to indicate a preliminary score.

SPECIAL DESIGNATIONS SS—Spectator Selection, CS—Cellar Selection, BB—Best Buy, ($NA)—Price not available, (NR)—Not released.

TASTER'S INITIALS (JG)—Jim Gordon, (HS)—Harvey Steiman, (JL)—James Laube, (JS)—James Suckling, (TM)—Thomas Matthews, (TR)—Terry Robards, (PM)—Per-Henrik Mansson, (BT)—Barrel Tasting (these wines were tasted blind from barrel samples), (CA-date)—*California's Great Cabernets* by James Laube, (CH-date)—*California's Great Chardonnays* by James Laube, (VP-date)—*Vintage Port* by James Suckling.

DATE TASTED Dates in parentheses represent the issue in which the rating was published.

DOMAINE F. & L. SAIER (France/Burgundy)
Clos des Lambrays 1989 $68 (11/15/91) **85**
Clos des Lambrays 1988 $75 (3/31/91) **91**
Clos des Lambrays Domaine des Lambrays 1985 $55 (2/15/88) **78**
Mercurey Blanc Les Chenelots 1988 $17 (4/30/91) **83**
Mercurey Les Champs-Martins 1988 $17 (8/31/91) **80**
Mercurey Les Champs-Martins 1985 $20 (3/31/88) **83**
Mercurey Les Chenelots 1988 $17 (4/30/91) **67**

CHATEAU ST.-ANDRE (France/Rhône)
Châteauneuf-du-Pape 1988 $16 (11/30/90) **87**

CHATEAU ST.-ANDRE-CORBIN (France/Bordeaux)
St.-Georges-St.-Emilion 1990 (NR) (5/15/92) (BT) **80+**
St.-Georges-St.-Emilion 1989 $15 (4/30/92) **91**
St.-Georges-St.-Emilion 1988 ($NA) (6/30/89) (BT) **80+**
St.-Georges-St.-Emilion 1987 ($NA) (6/30/89) (BT) **75+**
St.-Georges-St.-Emilion 1986 $22 (3/31/90) **77**
St.-Georges-St.-Emilion 1985 ($NA) (5/15/87) (BT) **80+**

ST. ANDREW'S VINEYARD (United States/California)
Chardonnay Napa Valley 1989 $14 (9/15/91) **87**
Chardonnay Napa Valley 1988 $13 (12/31/90) **89**
Chardonnay Napa Valley 1987 $14 (1/31/90) **85**
Chardonnay Napa Valley 1986 $13 (4/30/88) **90**
Chardonnay Napa Valley 1985 $13 (6/30/87) **87**
Chardonnay Napa Valley 1984 $13 (1/01/86) **92**
Chardonnay Napa Valley 1982 $12.50 (10/01/84) **89**
Chardonnay Napa Valley Limited Bottling 1989 $17 (7/15/92) **77**

ST. ANDREW'S WINERY (United States/California)
Cabernet Sauvignon Napa Valley 1986 $14.50 (4/30/90) **87**
Cabernet Sauvignon Napa Valley 1985 $10.50 (5/15/88) **89**
Chardonnay Napa Valley 1990 $10 (2/15/92) **83**
Chardonnay Napa Valley 1989 $10 (7/15/91) **80**
Chardonnay Napa Valley 1988 $10.50 (4/15/90) **84**
Chardonnay Napa Valley 1987 $6.50 (7/15/88) **80**
Chardonnay Napa Valley 1986 $8 (8/31/87) **80**
Chardonnay Napa Valley 1985 $7.50 (11/30/86) SS **93**
Chardonnay Napa Valley 1984 $7 (2/01/86) BB **91**
Chardonnay Napa Valley House 1982 $7 (10/16/84) **79**

LEONARD DE ST.-AUBIN (France/Burgundy)
Chassagne-Montrachet 1986 $25 (12/31/87) **76**
Gevrey-Chambertin 1985 $25 (11/30/87) **66**
Nuits-St.-Georges 1985 $25 (11/30/87) **71**
Pouilly-Fuissé 1990 $15 (8/31/91) **75**
Puligny-Montrachet 1989 $28 (8/31/91) **73**
Puligny-Montrachet 1986 $25 (11/15/87) **87**

CHATEAU ST.-BONNET (France/Bordeaux)
Médoc 1985 $6 (4/15/88) **79**

ST.-CESAIRE (France/Other)
Vin de Pays des Bouches du Rhône NV $4.25 (6/30/90) **72**

DOMAINE ST.-CHARLES (France/Beaujolais)
Beaujolais-Villages Château du Bluizard 1988 $8 (11/15/90) BB **82**

CHATEAU ST.-CHRISTOPHE (France/Bordeaux)
Médoc 1985 $6.50 (7/31/88) BB **82**

ST. CLEMENT (United States/California)
Cabernet Sauvignon Napa Valley 1988 $20 (3/31/92) **86**
Cabernet Sauvignon Napa Valley 1987 Rel: $20 Cur: $23 (9/30/91) CS **90**
Cabernet Sauvignon Napa Valley 1986 Rel: $18 Cur: $21 (9/30/90) **90**
Cabernet Sauvignon Napa Valley 1985 Rel: $17 Cur: $25 (3/15/90) **90**
Cabernet Sauvignon Napa Valley 1984 Rel: $15 Cur: $22 (CA-3/89) **89**
Cabernet Sauvignon Napa Valley 1983 Rel: $14.50 Cur: $20 (CA-3/89) **91**
Cabernet Sauvignon Napa Valley 1982 Rel: $13.50 Cur: $25 (CA-3/89) **91**
Cabernet Sauvignon Napa Valley 1982 Rel: $13.50 Cur: $25 (3/16/85) CS **92**
Cabernet Sauvignon Napa Valley 1981 Rel: $12.50 Cur: $24 (CA-3/89) **85**
Cabernet Sauvignon Napa Valley 1981 Rel: $12.50 Cur: $24 (6/01/84) SS **89**
Cabernet Sauvignon Napa Valley 1980 Rel: $12.50 Cur: $26 (CA-3/89) **82**
Cabernet Sauvignon Napa Valley 1979 Rel: $11 Cur: $38 (CA-3/89) **90**
Cabernet Sauvignon Napa Valley 1978 Rel: $10 Cur: $36 (CA-3/89) **88**
Cabernet Sauvignon Napa Valley 1977 Rel: $10 Cur: $45 (CA-3/89) **90**
Cabernet Sauvignon Napa Valley 1975-76 Rel: $8 Cur: $50 (CA-3/89) **87**
Chardonnay Carneros Abbott's Vineyard 1989 $18 (2/28/91) **85**
Chardonnay Carneros Abbott's Vineyard 1987 $17 (10/31/89) **89**
Chardonnay Napa Valley 1990 Rel: $16 Cur: $18 (1/31/92) **90**
Chardonnay Napa Valley 1989 $16 (5/31/91) SS **90**
Chardonnay Napa Valley 1988 $15 (6/15/90) **88**
Chardonnay Napa Valley 1987 $15 (CH-3/90) **86**
Chardonnay Napa Valley 1986 Rel: $15 Cur: $18 (CH-3/90) **89**
Chardonnay Napa Valley 1985 Rel: $14.50 Cur: $18 (CH-3/90) **85**
Chardonnay Napa Valley 1984 Rel: $14.50 Cur: $18 (CH-3/90) **88**
Chardonnay Napa Valley 1983 Rel: $14.50 Cur: $18 (CH-3/90) **76**
Chardonnay Napa Valley 1982 Rel: $14.50 Cur: $20 (CH-3/90) **73**
Chardonnay Napa Valley 1981 Rel: $13.50 Cur: $25 (CH-3/90) **75**
Chardonnay Napa Valley 1980 Rel: $12 Cur: $35 (CH-3/90) **83**
Chardonnay Napa Valley 1979 Rel: $12 Cur: $27 (CH-3/90) **93**
Merlot Napa Valley 1989 $18 (5/31/92) **87**
Merlot Napa Valley 1987 $16 (12/31/90) **85**
Merlot Napa Valley 1986 $15 (10/31/89) **74**
Merlot Napa Valley 1985 $15 (3/31/89) **91**
Merlot Napa Valley 1983 $14.50 (5/31/88) **81**
Sauvignon Blanc Napa Valley 1990 $9.75 (10/15/91) **88**
Sauvignon Blanc Napa Valley 1989 $9.50 (8/31/90) **81**
Sauvignon Blanc Napa Valley 1988 $9.50 (3/31/90) **78**
Sauvignon Blanc Napa Valley 1987 $9.50 (7/31/89) **68**

CHATEAU SAINT ESTEVE D'UCHAUX (France/Rhône)
Côtes du Rhône 1989 $9 (11/15/91) **80**
Côtes du Rhône Blanc de Viognier 1990 $24 (11/15/91) **87**
Côtes du Rhône Grand Réserve 1989 $11.50 (11/15/91) **83**
Côtes du Rhône-Villages 1989 $10 (11/15/91) **84**

ST. FRANCIS (United States/California)
Brut Sonoma Valley 1984 $9.50 (12/16/85) **82**
Cabernet Sauvignon California 1985 $9 (11/30/87) **88**
Cabernet Sauvignon Sonoma County 1988 $14 (8/31/91) **90**
Cabernet Sauvignon Sonoma County 1986 $12 (1/31/90) **89**

Cabernet Sauvignon Sonoma Valley Reserve 1988 $24 (8/31/91) **87**
Cabernet Sauvignon Sonoma Valley Reserve Black Label 1986 $20 (11/30/89) **94**
Chardonnay California 1989 $10 (7/15/91) **70**
Chardonnay California 1988 $10 (3/31/90) **82**
Chardonnay California 1987 $9.50 (10/15/88) **79**
Chardonnay California 1986 $9 (11/15/87) **83**
Chardonnay Sonoma County 1990 $10 (1/31/92) SS **89**
Chardonnay Sonoma Valley 1983 $10.75 (12/01/84) **89**
Chardonnay Sonoma Valley Barrel Select 1989 $15 (7/15/91) **84**
Chardonnay Sonoma Valley Barrel Select 1988 $15 (11/30/89) **79**
Chardonnay Sonoma Valley Barrel Select 1987 $14.50 (12/31/88) **82**
Chardonnay Sonoma Valley Barrel Select 1986 $12.50 (7/15/88) **91**
Chardonnay Sonoma Valley Barrel Select 1984 $12 (10/31/86) **69**
Chardonnay Sonoma Valley Poverello 1984 $6.75 (3/16/86) **75**
Gewürztraminer Sonoma County 1990 $10 (3/31/92) **75**
Gewürztraminer Sonoma Valley 1988 $7.50 (1/31/90) **80**
Johannisberg Riesling Sonoma Valley 1988 $7.50 (7/31/90) **80**
Merlot Sonoma Valley 1989 $14 (5/31/92) **79**
Merlot Sonoma Valley 1988 $16 (11/15/91) **82**
Merlot Sonoma Valley 1987 $14 (6/15/90) **80**
Merlot Sonoma Valley 1986 $14 (6/30/89) **85**
Merlot Sonoma Valley 1985 $12 (10/15/88) **66**
Merlot Sonoma Valley 1984 $12 (10/31/87) **88**
Merlot Sonoma Valley 1983 $11 (7/31/87) **80**
Merlot Sonoma Valley 1982 $10.75 (10/01/85) **78**
Merlot Sonoma Valley Reserve 1989 $24 (5/31/92) **90**
Merlot Sonoma Valley Reserve 1988 $24 (11/15/91) **82**
Merlot Sonoma Valley Reserve 1986 $20 (1/31/90) **94**
Merlot Sonoma Valley Reserve 1985 $14.50 (12/31/88) **81**
Merlot Sonoma Valley Reserve 1984 $16 (2/15/88) **74**
Muscat Canelli Sonoma County 1990 $10 (11/30/91) **80**
Pinot Noir Sonoma Valley 1986 $14 (6/15/88) **74**
Zinfandel Sonoma Valley Old Vines 1989 $12 (3/31/92) **76**

DOMAINE ST.-GAYAN (France/Rhône)
Côtes du Rhône 1988 $8 (10/31/90) **75**
Côtes du Rhône 1985 $6 (4/30/88) **75**

CHATEAU ST.-GEORGES (France/Bordeaux)
St.-Georges-St.-Emilion 1988 $18 (4/30/92) **73**
St.-Georges-St.-Emilion 1986 $14 (7/15/90) **87**
St.-Georges-St.-Emilion 1985 $11 (7/31/89) **87**

SAINT GREGORY (United States/California)
Chardonnay Mendocino 1990 $14 (7/15/92) **84**
Chardonnay Mendocino 1989 $15 (7/15/91) **87**

ST.-HUBERTS (Australia)
Cabernet Sauvignon Yarra Valley 1984 $13 (11/15/87) **84**
Chardonnay Yarra Valley 1985 $13.25 (12/31/87) **66**
Pinot Noir Yarra Valley 1985 $11.50 (11/15/87) **80**

DR. LOOSEN ST. JOHANNISHOF (Germany)
Riesling Auslese Mosel-Saar-Ruwer Erdener Prälat 1985 $20 (11/15/86) **92**
Riesling Auslese Mosel-Saar-Ruwer Erdener Prälat Gold Cap 1988 ($NA) (9/30/89) **90**
Riesling Auslese Mosel-Saar-Ruwer Wehlener Sonnenuhr Gold Cap 1988 ($NA) (9/30/89) **93**
Riesling Kabinett Mosel-Saar-Ruwer Bernkasteler Badstube 1983 $6.50 (4/01/85) **78**
Riesling Kabinett Mosel-Saar-Ruwer Erdener Treppchen 1983 $7 (3/16/85) **85**
Riesling Kabinett Mosel-Saar-Ruwer Wehlener Sonnenuhr 1988 ($NA) (9/30/89) **84**
Riesling Kabinett Mosel-Saar-Ruwer Wehlener Sonnenuhr 1985 $8 (1/31/87) **81**
Riesling Kabinett Mosel-Saar-Ruwer Wehlener Sonnenuhr 1983 $6 (4/01/85) **78**
Riesling Spätlese Mosel-Saar-Ruwer Bernkasteler Doctor 1986 ($NA) (4/15/89) **82**
Riesling Spätlese Mosel-Saar-Ruwer Erdener Prälat 1988 ($NA) (9/30/89) **90**
Riesling Spätlese Mosel-Saar-Ruwer Erdener Prälat 1986 ($NA) (4/15/89) **85**
Riesling Spätlese Mosel-Saar-Ruwer Erdener Treppchen 1985 $11 (1/31/87) **85**
Riesling Spätlese Mosel-Saar-Ruwer Erdener Treppchen 1983 $9 (3/01/85) **87**

ST. JOSEF'S (United States/Oregon)
Cabernet Sauvignon Oregon 1986 $12 (8/31/91) **68**
Cabernet Sauvignon Oregon 1985 $15 (3/31/91) **87**
Chardonnay Oregon 1987 $11.50 (8/31/91) **68**
Gewürztraminer Oregon L'Esprit NV $7 (8/31/91) **65**
Pinot Noir Oregon 1987 $8 (4/15/91) **76**
Pinot Noir Oregon 1985 $16 (2/15/90) **89**
White Riesling Oregon 1989 $6.25 (8/31/91) **80**

ST.-JOVIAN (France/Bordeaux)
Bordeaux 1985 $4.50 (5/15/88) **75**
Bordeaux Blanc Premium 1990 $5.50 (6/15/91) **76**
Bordeaux Blanc Sauvignon Blanc 1987 $4 (8/31/88) **69**
Bordeaux Cabernet Sauvignon 1986 $4.50 (7/31/88) **78**
Bordeaux Merlot 1986 $5 (5/15/89) **76**
Bordeaux Supérieur Premium 1988 $5.50 (7/31/91) BB **80**

ST. JULIAN (United States/Michigan)
Chambourcin Lake Michigan Shore 1989 $8.50 (2/29/92) **76**
Chardonnay Lake Michigan Shore Barrel Fermented 1990 $12 (2/29/92) **78**
Solera Light Cream Sherry Michigan NV $12 (2/29/92) **88**

DOMAINE DE ST.-LUC (France/Other)
Côteaux du Tricastin 1989 $7 (12/31/91) BB **83**
Côteaux du Tricastin 1988 $11 (8/31/91) **77**

CHATEAU ST.-MARC (France/Sauternes)
Barsac 1989 ($NA) (6/15/90) (BT) **85+**
Barsac 1987 ($NA) (6/15/90) **69**

DOMAINE ST. MARTIN DE LA GARRIGUE (France/Other)
Chardonnay Vin de Pays des Côteaux de Bessilles 1989 $12 (4/30/91) **82**

ST.-MORILLON (Chile)
Cabernet Sauvignon Lontue 1986 $5.50 (10/15/91) BB **83**
Cabernet Sauvignon Lontue 1985 $4 (9/15/90) **75**
Sauvignon Blanc Lontue 1991 $5.50 (6/15/92) **79**

CHATEAU ST.-PIERRE (France/Bordeaux)
St.-Julien 1991 (NR) (5/15/92) (BT) **80+**
St.-Julien 1990 (NR) (5/15/92) (BT) **90+**
St.-Julien 1989 $39 (3/15/92) **94**
St.-Julien 1988 $32 (4/30/91) **85**
St.-Julien 1987 $17 (5/15/90) **89**
St.-Julien 1986 Rel: $17 Cur: $22 (9/15/89) SS **92**
St.-Julien 1985 $19 (4/16/86) (BT) **70+**
St.-Julien 1982 Rel: $15 Cur: $22 (12/16/85) CS **93**
St.-Julien 1979 $24 (10/15/89) (JS) **84**
St.-Julien 1962 $55 (11/30/87) (JS) **68**

DOMAINE ST.-SAUVEUR (France/Rhône)
Côtes du Ventoux 1988 $4.50 (10/15/91) BB **83**
Muscat de Beaumes-de-Venise Vin Doux Naturel 1988 $17 (3/31/91) **80**

CHATEAU ST.-SEVE (France/Bordeaux)
Médoc 1985 $6 (11/15/87) **70**

CHATEAU ST.-SULPICE (France/Bordeaux)
Bordeaux 1988 $7.50 (8/31/91) BB **81**
Bordeaux 1982 $6 (5/15/87) **73**

ST. SUPERY (United States/California)
Cabernet Sauvignon Napa Valley Dollarhide Ranch 1988 $13.50 (9/30/91) **85**
Cabernet Sauvignon Napa Valley Dollarhide Ranch 1987 $13 (7/15/90) **85**
Chardonnay Napa Valley Dollarhide Ranch 1990 $13 (4/30/92) **86**
Chardonnay Napa Valley 1989 $12 (3/31/91) **81**
Chardonnay Napa Valley St.-Supery Vineyards 1988 $11 (11/15/89) **83**
Merlot Napa Valley Dollarhide Ranch 1989 $13.50 (5/31/92) **89**
Sauvignon Blanc Napa Valley Dollarhide Ranch 1989 $8 (3/15/91) **82**
Sauvignon Blanc Napa Valley Dollarhide Ranch 1988 $7.50 (10/31/89) **87**

DOMAINE SAINTE-ANNE (France/Bordeaux)
Bordeaux 1987 $5 (5/15/90) **77**

DOMAINE STE.-ANNE (France/Rhône)
Côtes du Rhône-Villages Cuvée Notre-Dame des Cellettes 1987 $7.50 (1/31/89) **80**

STE. CHAPELLE (United States/Idaho)
Cabernet Sauvignon Idaho Reserve 1988 $20 (2/29/92) **74**
Cabernet Sauvignon Washington 1988 $10 (2/29/92) **84**
Cabernet Sauvignon Washington 1986 $10 (8/31/91) **83**
Cabernet Sauvignon Washington 1983 $9 (4/30/88) **77**
Cabernet Sauvignon Washington 1981 $9 (5/15/87) **80**
Cabernet Sauvignon Washington Collectors' Series 1981 $18 (10/15/89) **81**
Chardonnay Idaho 1988 $10 (12/15/90) **83**
Chardonnay Idaho Reserve 1988 $15 (2/29/92) **84**
Fumé Blanc Idaho Dry 1989 $8 (8/31/91) **81**
Johannisberg Riesling Idaho 1990 $6 (11/15/91) BB **84**
Johannisberg Riesling Idaho 1989 $6 (12/15/90) BB **81**
Johannisberg Riesling Idaho 1988 $6 (7/31/89) BB **88**
Johannisberg Riesling Idaho Dry Vineyard Select 1990 $6 (2/29/92) **85**
Johannisberg Riesling Idaho Dry Vineyard Select 1989 $6 (8/31/91) BB **84**
Merlot Washington 1987 $10 (9/30/90) **73**
Merlot Washington Dionysus Vineyard 1986 $12 (5/31/88) **81**
Pinot Noir Idaho 1988 $8 (2/29/92) **74**

STE. GENEVIEVE (United States/Texas)
Chardonnay Texas Grand Reserve 1989 $8 (2/29/92) **79**
Fumé Blanc Texas NV $6/1.5L (2/29/92) **82**
Fumé Blanc Texas Grand Reserve 1989 $6 (2/29/92) **78**
Sauvignon Blanc Texas 1990 $6 (2/29/92) **81**

SAINTSBURY (United States/California)
Chardonnay Carneros 1990 Rel: $15 Cur: $17 (12/31/91) SS **90**
Chardonnay Carneros 1989 $14 (11/15/90) **91**
Chardonnay Carneros 1988 Rel: $14 Cur: $16 (3/15/90) **90**
Chardonnay Carneros 1987 Rel: $13 Cur: $18 (CH-2/90) **90**
Chardonnay Carneros 1986 Rel: $12 Cur: $19 (CH-2/90) **88**
Chardonnay Carneros 1985 Rel: $11 Cur: $19 (CH-2/90) **90**
Chardonnay Carneros 1984 Rel: $11 Cur: $25 (CH-2/90) **92**
Chardonnay Carneros 1983 Rel: $11 Cur: $20 (CH-2/90) **80**
Chardonnay Carneros Reserve 1990 $25 (7/15/92) **80**
Chardonnay Carneros Reserve 1988 Rel: $20 Cur: $22 (5/31/90) **92**
Chardonnay Carneros Reserve 1987 Rel: $20 Cur: $22 (CH-2/90) **89**
Chardonnay Carneros Reserve 1986 Rel: $20 Cur: $25 (CH-2/90) **84**
Chardonnay Sonoma County 1982 Rel: $11 Cur: $14 (CH-2/90) **65**
Chardonnay Sonoma County 1981 Rel: $10 Cur: $25 (CH-2/90) **87**
Pinot Noir Carneros 1989 $16.50 (2/15/92) **85**
Pinot Noir Carneros 1988 Rel: $15 Cur: $17 (12/15/90) SS **91**
Pinot Noir Carneros 1987 $15 (7/31/89) **86**
Pinot Noir Carneros 1986 $14 (6/15/88) **92**
Pinot Noir Carneros 1985 $13 (9/15/87) **92**
Pinot Noir Carneros 1984 $12 (12/15/86) **93**
Pinot Noir Carneros 1983 $12 (12/01/85) **93**
Pinot Noir Carneros 1982 $8 (11/30/87) (JL) **86**
Pinot Noir Carneros Garnet 1990 $10 (2/15/92) **86**
Pinot Noir Carneros Garnet 1989 $9 (12/15/90) **88**
Pinot Noir Carneros Garnet 1988 $9 (3/31/90) **84**
Pinot Noir Carneros Garnet 1987 $9 (12/31/88) **91**
Pinot Noir Carneros Garnet 1986 $8 (12/15/87) **87**
Pinot Noir Carneros Garnet 1985 $9 (3/15/87) **86**
Pinot Noir Carneros Garnet 1984 $8 (8/31/86) **76**
Pinot Noir Carneros Garnet 1983 $8 (11/30/87) (JL) **73**
Pinot Noir Carneros Rancho 1981 ($NA) (11/30/87) (JL) **80**

SAKONNET (United States/New England)
Chardonnay Southeastern New England Barrel Select 1989 $14 (2/29/92) **87**
Gewürztraminer Southeastern New England Apponagansett Bay Vineyards 1990 $11 (2/29/92) **75**
Vidal Blanc Southeastern New England 1990 $8 (2/29/92) **78**

CHATEAU DE SALES (France/Bordeaux)
Pomerol 1990 (NR) (5/15/92) (BT) **85+**
Pomerol 1989 $18 (4/30/91) (BT) **90+**
Pomerol 1988 $17 (6/30/89) (BT) **70+**
Pomerol 1986 $20 (6/30/89) **86**
Pomerol 1985 Rel: $14 Cur: $18 (6/30/88) **87**
Pomerol 1982 $32 (5/15/89) (TR) **88**

SALISHAN (United States/Washington)
Chenin Blanc Washington Dry 1988 $6.25 (10/15/89) **71**
White Riesling Washington Dry 1988 $5 (10/15/89) **79**

CASTELLO DI SALLE (Italy/Other)
Montepulciano d'Abruzzo 1985 $15 (6/15/90) BB **84**

CHATEAU LA SALLE DE POUJEAUX (France/Bordeaux)
Moulis 1989 $15 (3/15/92) **85**

SALON (France/Champagne)
Brut Blanc de Blancs Champagne Disgorged Summer 1988 Le Mesnil 1979 $119 (12/31/89) **93**
Brut Blanc de Blancs Champagne Le Mesnil 1982 $119 (12/31/91) CS **91**

Brut Blanc de Blancs Champagne Le Mesnil 1979 $119 (12/31/88) **92**
Brut Blanc de Blancs Champagne Le Mesnil 1976 $225/1.5L (12/31/88) **91**

SALTRAM (Australia)
Cabernet Sauvignon Hazelwood 1985 $8.50 (7/31/89) **79**
Cabernet Sauvignon Shiraz Barossa Valley 1984 $12 (1/31/90) **89**
Chardonnay Hazelwood 1987 $8.50 (7/31/89) **82**
Chardonnay McLaren Vale Hunter Valley Mamre Brook 1987 $12 (7/31/89) **82**
Shiraz Hazelwood 1984 $8.50 (7/31/89) **81**

POGGIO SALVI (Italy/Tuscany)
Brunello di Montalcino 1985 $30 (11/30/90) **83**
Brunello di Montalcino 1979 $15 (3/15/87) **88**
Brunello di Montalcino Riserva 1981 $35 (11/30/90) **85**

SALVUCCI (Italy/Tuscany)
Vernaccia di San Gimignano 1987 $5.50 (5/15/89) **77**

SAN FABIANO (Italy/Tuscany)
Chianti Classico 1988 $11.25 (9/15/91) **84**
Chianti Classico Cellole 1988 $14.25 (9/15/91) **83**
Chianti Classico Cellole Riserva 1985 $13 (11/30/89) **91**

SAN FELICE (Italy/Tuscany)
Belcaro 1990 $10 (1/31/92) **83**
Brunello di Montalcino Campogiovanni 1986 $28 (11/30/91) **92**
Brunello di Montalcino Campogiovanni 1985 $24 (9/30/90) **85**
Brunello di Montalcino Campogiovanni 1982 Rel: $22 Cur: $27 (7/31/88) CS **92**
Chianti Classico Campo del Civettino 1988 ($NA) (9/15/91) **84**
Chianti Classico Il Grigio Riserva 1987 $13 (1/31/92) **83**
Chianti Classico Il Grigio Riserva 1985 $10 (9/15/90) **86**
Chianti Classico Il Grigio Riserva 1982 $11 (11/30/89) (HS) **90**
Chianti Classico Il Grigio Riserva 1983 $12 (11/30/89) (HS) **85**
Chianti Classico Poggio Rosso Riserva 1986 $24 (1/31/92) **86**
Chianti Classico Poggio Rosso Riserva 1985 ($NA) (9/15/91) **85**
Chianti Classico Poggio Rosso Riserva 1983 ($NA) (11/30/89) (HS) **87**
Chianti Classico Poggio Rosso Riserva 1982 $15 (9/15/90) **81**
Chianti Classico Poggio Rosso Riserva 1981 $15 (11/30/89) (HS) **87**
Chianti Classico Poggio Rosso Riserva 1978 $14 (3/15/87) **73**
Predicato di Bitùrica 1985 $28 (12/15/91) **82**
Predicato di Bitùrica 1983 ($NA) (11/30/89) (HS) **87**
Predicato di Bitùrica 1982 Rel: $19 Cur: $25 (1/31/88) SS **92**
Vigorello 1986 $19 (12/15/91) **84**
Vigorello 1985 $18 (9/15/90) **89**
Vigorello 1983 $17 (11/30/89) (HS) **90**
Vigorello 1982 $15 (11/30/89) (HS) **87**
Vigorello 1981 Rel: $13 Cur: $18 (1/31/88) **84**
Vigorello 1980 Rel: $12 Cur: $18 (2/28/87) SS **95**

VALLE DE SAN FERNANDO (Chile)
Cabernet Sauvignon San Fernando 1988 $5 (6/15/92) BB **83**
Cabernet Sauvignon San Fernando 1985 $7 (7/31/89) **79**
Cabernet Sauvignon San Fernando 1983 $4 (11/15/88) **77**
Cabernet Sauvignon San Fernando Gran Reserva 1986 $5 (6/15/92) BB **84**
Cabernet Sauvignon San Fernando Gran Reserva 1984 $6 (9/15/90) BB **81**
Cabernet Sauvignon San Fernando Gran Reserva 1982 $6 (11/15/88) BB **81**
Cabernet Sauvignon San Fernando Valley 1988 $6 (9/15/90) BB **84**
Merlot San Fernando 1990 $5 (6/15/92) **75**
Sauvignon Blanc San Fernando 1990 $4 (6/15/92) **77**

SAN FILIPPO (Italy/Tuscany)
Rosso di Montalcino 1987 $11 (4/30/91) **68**

SAN JOSE DE SANTIAGO (Chile)
Cabernet Sauvignon Colchagua Valley 1990 $5 (5/15/92) BB **85**
Sauvignon Blanc Colchagua Valley 1990 $3 (10/15/91) **75**

SAN LEONINO (Italy/Tuscany)
Chianti Classico 1988 $10 (12/15/90) **87**

SAN MARTIN (Chile)
Cabernet Sauvignon Maipo Valley International Series 1987 $4.50 (6/15/90) BB **78**
Chardonnay Maipo Valley International Series 1988 $4.50 (4/30/90) BB **81**
Petite Sirah Baja California International Series 1987 $4 (8/31/90) BB **82**

SAN PEDRO (Chile)
Cabernet Sauvignon Las Encinas Vino Tinto Seco 1987 ($NA) (6/15/92) **80**
Cabernet Sauvignon Lontue Castillo de Molina 1982 $7.50 (2/15/89) **78**
Cabernet Sauvignon Lontue Castillo de Molina 1981 $7.50 (11/15/87) BB **83**
Cabernet Sauvignon Lontue Castillo de Molina 1979 $7.50 (3/15/87) **81**
Cabernet Sauvignon Lontue Gato de Oro 1986 $4.50 (2/15/90) BB **85**
Cabernet Sauvignon Lontue Gato Negro 1989 $4.75 (6/15/92) **75**
Cabernet Sauvignon Lontue Gato Negro 1985 $4.50 (11/15/88) BB **80**
Cabernet Sauvignon Lontue Gato Negro 1984 $4.50 (5/15/88) BB **83**
Cabernet Sauvignon Lontue Gato Negro 1983 $4.50 (3/15/87) **76**
Chardonnay Lontue 1990 $7 (6/15/92) **76**
Merlot Lontue 1989 $7 (5/31/92) BB **89**
Merlot Lontue 1988 $5 (12/31/90) BB **84**
Merlot Lontue Gato de Oro 1987 $6 (2/15/89) BB **81**
Sauvignon Blanc Lontue 1991 $7 (6/15/92) **79**
Sauvignon Blanc Lontue Gato Blanco 1991 $4.75 (6/15/92) **75**

CASTELLO DI SAN POLO IN ROSSO (Italy/Tuscany)
Chianti Classico 1985 $10 (11/30/89) **67**
Chianti Classico Riserva 1985 $14 (11/30/89) **78**

Key to Symbols

The scores reported here are the results of blind tastings conducted by our panel of senior editors. Wines that carry the initials below are results of individual tastings.

THE WINE SPECTATOR 100-POINT SCALE ***95-100***—Classic, a great wine; ***90-94***—Outstanding, superior character and style; ***80-89***—Good to very good, a wine with special qualities; ***70-79***—Average, drinkable wine that may have minor flaws; ***60-69***—Below average, drinkable but not recommended; ***50-59***—Poor, undrinkable, not recommended. "+"—With a score indicates a range; used primarily with barrel tastings to indicate a preliminary score.

SPECIAL DESIGNATIONS SS—Spectator Selection, CS—Cellar Selection, BB—Best Buy, ($NA)—Price not available, (NR)—Not released.

TASTER'S INITIALS (JG)—Jim Gordon, (HS)—Harvey Steiman, (JL)—James Laube, (JS)—James Suckling, (TM)—Thomas Matthews, (TR)—Terry Robards, (PM)—Per-Henrik Mansson, (BT)—Barrel Tasting (these wines were tasted blind from barrel samples), (CA-date)—*California's Great Cabernets* by James Laube, (CH-date)—*California's Great Chardonnays* by James Laube, (VP-date)—*Vintage Port* by James Suckling.

DATE TASTED Dates in parentheses represent the issue in which the rating was published.

SAN QUIRICO (Italy/Tuscany)
Chianti Vecchione 1988 $9 (1/31/92) **79**
Vernaccia di San Gimignano 1989 $8.50 (7/15/91) **78**

SAN STEFANO (Italy/Piedmont)
1990 $17 (1/31/92) **88**

BODEGA SAN VALERO (Spain)
Cariñena Don Mendo Tinto Especial 1987 $5 (11/30/89) BB **81**

SANDEMAN (Portugal)
Tawny Port 20-Year-Old Imperial NV $29 (2/28/90) (JS) **87**
Vintage Port 1985 Rel: $22 Cur: $38 (VP-6/90) **83**
Vintage Port 1982 Rel: $19 Cur: $41 (VP-6/90) **82**
Vintage Port 1980 Rel: $19 Cur: $43 (VP-6/90) **85**
Vintage Port 1977 Rel: $15 Cur: $64 (VP-6/90) **85**
Vintage Port 1975 $55 (VP-3/90) **78**
Vintage Port 1970 $74 (VP-3/90) **83**
Vintage Port 1967 $58 (VP-3/90) **90**
Vintage Port 1966 $89 (7/15/90) (JS) **90**
Vintage Port 1963 $125 (7/15/90) (JS) **96**
Vintage Port 1960 $66 (7/15/90) (JS) **79**
Vintage Port 1958 $75 (VP-3/90) **82**
Vintage Port 1957 ($NA) (VP-10/88) **85**
Vintage Port 1955 $135 (VP-3/90) **94**
Vintage Port 1950 $155 (VP-3/90) **87**
Vintage Port 1947 $150 (VP-3/90) **90**
Vintage Port 1945 $280 (VP-3/90) **95**
Vintage Port 1942 $200 (VP-3/90) **88**
Vintage Port 1935 $360 (VP-3/90) **92**
Vintage Port 1934 $240 (VP-3/90) **94**
Vintage Port 1927 $360 (VP-3/90) **92**
Vintage Port 1920 $310 (VP-3/90) **78**
Vintage Port 1917 $250 (VP-3/90) **88**
Vintage Port 1911 $280 (VP-6/90) **82**
Vintage Port 1908 $320 (VP-3/90) **75**
Vintage Port 1904 $420 (VP-3/90) **88**
Vintage Port 1896 $480 (VP-3/90) **81**
Vintage Port 1887 $600 (VP-3/90) **74**
Vintage Port 1870 $700 (VP-3/90) **98**

SANDERLING (United States/California)
Zinfandel Amador County 1984 $6 (5/01/86) **70**

LUCIANO SANDRONE (Italy/Piedmont)
Barolo 1984 $13.50 (8/31/88) **82**
Barolo 1983 $20 (12/15/87) **90**
Barolo 1982 $15 (6/30/87) **94**
Barolo Cannubi Boschis 1986 $34 (12/31/90) **89**
Barolo Cannubi Boschis 1985 $30 (1/31/90) **92**
Dolcetto d'Alba 1990 $14 (3/31/92) **87**
Dolcetto d'Alba 1989 $12 (7/15/91) **87**

SANFORD (United States/California)
Chardonnay Santa Barbara County 1990 $16.50 (3/15/92) **78**
Chardonnay Santa Barbara County 1989 Rel: $16 Cur: $18 (4/30/91) **87**
Chardonnay Santa Barbara County 1988 Rel: $16 Cur: $18 (5/15/90) **91**
Chardonnay Santa Barbara County 1987 Rel: $15 Cur: $18 (CH-2/90) **92**
Chardonnay Santa Barbara County 1986 Rel: $14 Cur: $18 (CH-2/90) **88**
Chardonnay Santa Barbara County 1985 Rel: $13.50 Cur: $20 (CH-2/90) **90**
Chardonnay Central Coast 1984 Rel: $12.50 Cur: $17 (CH-2/90) **78**
Chardonnay Central Coast 1983 Rel: $12 Cur: $17 (CH-2/90) **88**
Chardonnay Santa Maria Valley 1982 Rel: $12 Cur: $20 (CH-2/90) **68**
Chardonnay Santa Maria Valley 1981 Rel: $11 Cur: $20 (CH-2/90) **74**
Chardonnay Santa Barbara County Barrel Select 1990 $30 (6/30/92) **91**
Chardonnay Santa Barbara County Barrel Select 1989 Rel: $28 Cur: $30 (7/15/91) **90**
Chardonnay Santa Barbara County Barrel Select 1988 Rel: $25 Cur: $28 (8/31/90) **94**
Chardonnay Santa Barbara County Barrel Select 1987 Rel: $24 Cur: $30 (12/15/89) **91**
Chardonnay Santa Barbara County Barrel Select 1985 Rel: $20 Cur: $30 (CH-2/90) **92**
Merlot Santa Barbara County 1984 $18 (12/31/87) **66**
Pinot Noir Central Coast 1984 $12 (5/15/87) **85**
Pinot Noir Santa Barbara County 1989 $15 (3/31/92) **85**
Pinot Noir Santa Barbara County 1988 $15 (6/30/91) **78**
Pinot Noir Santa Barbara County 1987 $14 (2/28/91) **76**
Pinot Noir Santa Barbara County 1986 $14 (12/15/89) **75**
Pinot Noir Santa Barbara County 1985 $14 (6/15/88) **74**
Pinot Noir Santa Barbara County Barrel Select 1986 $20 (12/15/89) **78**
Pinot Noir Santa Barbara County Barrel Select 1985 $20 (6/15/88) **75**
Pinot Noir Santa Maria Valley 1982 $11 (12/01/84) **63**
Sauvignon Blanc Santa Barbara County 1989 $9 (7/31/91) **65**
Sauvignon Blanc Santa Barbara County 1987 $8.50 (12/15/89) **85**

SANGUINETO (Italy/Tuscany)
Vino Nobile di Montepulciano Riserva 1980 $9 (10/31/86) **86**

SANTA BARBARA (United States/California)
Cabernet Sauvignon Santa Ynez Valley 1988 $12 (11/15/91) **83**
Cabernet Sauvignon Santa Ynez Valley Reserve 1988 $18 (11/15/91) **83**
Cabernet Sauvignon Santa Ynez Valley Reserve 1987 $18 (11/15/90) **77**
Cabernet Sauvignon Santa Ynez Valley Reserve 1984 $13.50 (10/31/87) **81**
Cabernet Sauvignon Santa Ynez Valley Reserve 1974 $16 (12/15/89) **81**
Chardonnay Santa Barbara County 1990 $12 (6/15/92) **80**
Chardonnay Santa Barbara County 1989 $12 (1/31/91) **80**
Chardonnay Santa Ynez Valley 1988 $12 (4/15/90) **74**
Chardonnay Santa Ynez Valley 1987 $10 (12/15/89) **83**
Chardonnay Santa Ynez Valley 1986 $8.50 (2/29/88) **67**
Chardonnay Santa Ynez Valley Reserve 1989 $18 (5/15/91) **87**
Chardonnay Santa Ynez Valley Reserve 1988 $18 (9/30/90) **86**
Chardonnay Santa Ynez Valley Reserve 1987 $16 (12/15/89) **84**
Chardonnay Santa Ynez Valley Reserve 1986 $14 (10/15/88) **84**
Chenin Blanc Santa Ynez Valley 1987 $7 (7/31/89) **77**
Johannisberg Riesling Late Harvest Santa Ynez Valley Botrytised Grapes 1986 $15/375ml (10/15/87) **88**
Johannisberg Riesling Santa Ynez Valley 1988 $7.50 (12/15/89) **76**
Johannisberg Riesling Santa Ynez Valley 1987 $7 (12/15/89) **84**
Pinot Noir Santa Barbara County 1989 $11 (7/31/91) **84**
Pinot Noir Santa Barbara County 1986 $11 (6/15/88) **80**
Pinot Noir Santa Barbara County Reserve 1989 $20 (11/15/91) **87**
Pinot Noir Santa Ynez Valley Reserve 1987 $20 (12/15/89) **89**
Sauvignon Blanc Santa Ynez Valley Reserve 1987 $11 (12/15/89) **68**
Sauvignon Blanc Santa Ynez Valley Valley View Vineyards 1987 $8.50 (12/15/89) **72**

Zinfandel Late Harvest Santa Ynez Valley Essence 1987 $15/375ml (12/15/89) **74**
Zinfandel Santa Ynez Valley 1987 $8.50 (12/15/89) **82**
Zinfandel Santa Ynez Valley Beaujour 1988 $7 (12/15/89) **80**

SANTA CAROLINA (Chile)
Cabernet Sauvignon Maipo Valley Estrella de Oro 1982 $8 (3/15/90) **76**
Cabernet Sauvignon Maipo Valley Los Toros Vineyard Reserva 1985 $8 (5/15/92) **77**
Cabernet Sauvignon Maipo Valley Santa Rosa Vineyard 1986 $4 (4/30/88) **78**
Chardonnay Maipo Valley Santa Rosa Vineyard Reserva 1990 $8 (6/15/92) BB **89**
Chardonnay Maipo Valley Valle del Maipo NV $5 (3/31/90) **71**
Merlot Maipo Valley Santa Rosa Vineyard Reserva Especial 1989 $8 (6/15/92) BB **83**
Sauvignon Blanc Maipo Valley Santa Rosa Vineyard Reserva 1990 $8 (6/15/92) **73**

SANTA CRUZ MOUNTAIN (United States/California)
Cabernet Sauvignon Santa Cruz Mountains Bates Ranch 1989 (NR) (5/15/91) (BT) **85+**
Cabernet Sauvignon Santa Cruz Mountains Bates Ranch 1988 (NR) (5/15/90) (BT) **85+**
Cabernet Sauvignon Santa Cruz Mountains Bates Ranch 1987 ($NA) (4/15/89) (BT) **90+**
Cabernet Sauvignon Santa Cruz Mountains Bates Ranch 1986 Rel: $15 Cur: $18 (11/15/91) **89**
Cabernet Sauvignon Santa Cruz Mountains Bates Ranch 1985 Rel: $15 Cur: $18 (CA-3/89) **92**
Cabernet Sauvignon Santa Cruz Mountains Bates Ranch 1984 Rel: $14 Cur: $18 (CA-3/89) **87**
Cabernet Sauvignon Santa Cruz Mountains Bates Ranch 1983 Rel: $12 Cur: $17 (6/15/89) **80**
Cabernet Sauvignon Santa Cruz Mountains Bates Ranch 1982 Rel: $12 Cur: $17 (CA-3/89) **72**
Cabernet Sauvignon Santa Cruz Mountains Bates Ranch 1981 Rel: $12 Cur: $20 (CA-3/89) **79**
Cabernet Sauvignon Santa Cruz Mountains Bates Ranch 1980 Rel: $12 Cur: $27 (CA-3/89) **86**
Cabernet Sauvignon Santa Cruz Mountains Bates Ranch 1979 Rel: $12 Cur: $35 (CA-3/89) **79**
Cabernet Sauvignon Santa Cruz Mountains Bates Ranch 1978 Rel: $12 Cur: $30 (CA-3/89) **90**
Merlot California 1983 $10 (10/01/85) **82**
Merlot Central Coast 1988 (NR) (4/30/90) (BT) **90+**
Merlot Central Coast 1987 ($NA) (4/15/89) (BT) **80+**
Pinot Noir Santa Cruz Mountains 1985 $15 (6/15/88) **89**
Pinot Noir Santa Cruz Mountains Jarvis Vineyard 1981 $15 (8/31/86) **89**

SANTA MARGHERITA (Italy/North)
Chardonnay Alto Adige 1989 $13 (12/31/90) **75**
Cuvée Margherita del Veneto Orientale 1988 $11 (12/31/90) **73**

SANTA MONICA (Chile)
Cabernet Sauvignon Rancagua 1989 $5 (10/15/91) BB **85**
Cabernet Sauvignon Rancagua 1988 $6 (3/15/90) BB **86**
Cabernet Sauvignon Rancagua Tierra de Sol 1985 ($NA) (6/15/92) **74**
Chardonnay Rancagua 1989 $6 (6/15/92) BB **80**
Chardonnay Rancagua 1988 $6 (3/31/90) **70**
Chardonnay Rancagua Tierra de Sol 1991 (NR) (6/15/92) **85**
Sauvignon Blanc Rancagua 1991 $6 (5/15/92) BB **85**
Sauvignon Blanc Rancagua 1989 $5 (10/15/91) BB **80**
Sauvignon Blanc Rancagua 1988 $6 (3/31/90) BB **85**
Sémillon Rancagua Seaborne 1989 $4 (10/15/91) BB **84**
Sémillon Rancagua Seaborne 1988 $5 (3/31/90) BB **81**

SANTA RITA (Chile)
Cabernet Sauvignon Maipo Valley 120 1988 $6 (5/31/92) BB **86**
Cabernet Sauvignon Maipo Valley 120 1986 $5 (5/15/89) BB **83**
Cabernet Sauvignon Maipo Valley 120 Medalla Real 1987 $11 (6/15/90) **78**
Cabernet Sauvignon Maipo Valley 120 Medalla Real 1984 $9 (11/15/87) **85**
Cabernet Sauvignon Maipo Valley 120 Medalla Real 1984 $9 (7/15/87) **87**
Cabernet Sauvignon Maipo Valley Casa Real 1989 (NR) (6/15/92) **81**
Cabernet Sauvignon Maipo Valley Medalla Real 1988 $11 (5/15/92) **88**
Cabernet Sauvignon Maipo Valley Medalla Real 1987 $12 (6/15/91) **82**
Cabernet Sauvignon Maipo Valley Medalla Real 1986 $5 (3/15/90) **78**
Cabernet Sauvignon Maipo Valley Medalla Real 1985 $8 (3/31/88) **75**
Cabernet Sauvignon Maipo Valley Reserva 1988 $8.50 (6/15/92) **86**
Cabernet Sauvignon Maipo Valley Reserva 1987 $11.50 (9/15/90) **85**
Cabernet Sauvignon Maipo Valley Reserva 1986 $6.25 (5/15/89) BB **87**
Chardonnay Maipo Valley 120 1991 $7 (5/15/92) BB **89**
Chardonnay Maipo Valley Casa Blanca 1991 (NR) (6/15/92) **78**
Chardonnay Maipo Valley Medalla Real 1991 $11 (5/15/92) **83**
Chardonnay Maipo Valley Medalla Real 1990 $11.50 (6/15/91) **82**
Chardonnay Maipo Valley Reserva 1991 (NR) (6/15/92) **90**
Chardonnay Maipo Valley Reserva 1989 $9.50 (6/30/90) **78**
Chardonnay Maipo Valley Reserva 1987 $7.50 (3/31/90) **79**
Merlot Maipo Valley 120 1989 $6 (6/15/92) BB **85**
Sauvignon Blanc Maipo Valley 120 1991 $6 (6/15/92) BB **84**
Sauvignon Blanc Maipo Valley 120 1990 $7 (10/15/91) BB **86**
Sauvignon Blanc Maipo Valley Medalla Real 1991 (NR) (6/15/92) **84**
Sauvignon Blanc Maipo Valley Reserva 1991 $7.50 (6/15/92) BB **88**
Sauvignon Blanc Maipo Valley Reserva 1990 $8.50 (10/15/91) BB **85**

SANTA SOFIA (Italy/North)
Soave Classico Superiore 1990 $8.75 (5/15/92) **83**

SANTA TRINITA (Italy/Tuscany)
Chianti Classico 1988 ($NA) (9/15/91) **86**

SANTA YNEZ VALLEY (United States/California)
Cabernet Merlot Santa Barbara County 1987 $13 (3/31/90) **72**
Chardonnay Santa Barbara County 1988 $13 (2/28/90) **88**
Pinot Noir Santa Maria Valley 1987 $13 (3/31/90) **62**
Zinfandel Paso Robles 1987 $8 (3/31/90) **84**

SANTI (Italy/North)
Bianco di Custoza I Frari 1990 $10 (9/15/91) **83**
Recioto della Valpolicella 1985 $20 (6/30/91) **83**

VILLA SANTINA (Italy/Tuscany)
Chianti 1987 $5 (11/30/89) BB **80**
Chianti Classico 1984 $5 (11/15/87) **72**

SANTINO (United States/California)
Alfresco Amador County NV $6 (8/31/91) BB **83**
Barbera Amador County Aged Release 1988 $12 (10/31/91) **85**
Johannisberg Riesling Late Harvest Sonoma County Dry Berry Select 1989 $18/375ml (11/30/91) **92**
Satyricon California 1988 $14 (10/31/91) **83**
White Zinfandel Amador County 1988 $5 (6/15/89) **87**
Zinfandel Amador County Aged Release 1988 $7 (2/29/92) **75**
Zinfandel Amador County Aged Release 1984 $7 (3/31/89) **67**
Zinfandel Fiddletown Eschen Vineyards 1983 $7.50 (4/15/87) **84**
Zinfandel Shenandoah Valley Grandpère Vineyards 1988 $12 (8/31/91) **79**

SARAFORNIA (United States/California)
Zinfandel Napa Valley 1988 $8 (2/15/91) **81**
Zinfandel Napa Valley 1987 $7 (3/15/90) **78**

SARAH'S (United States/California)
Chardonnay Central Coast Estate 1988 $45 (5/31/91) **77**
Chardonnay Monterey County Ventana Vineyard 1989 $22 (5/31/91) **82**
Grenache California Cadenza 1988 ($NA) (4/15/89) **80**
Merlot San Luis Obispo County John Radike Vineyard 1987 $30 (5/31/92) **65**

DOMAINE SARDA-MALET (France/Other)
Côtes du Roussillon 1986 $7.50 (10/15/90) **60**

A. SARDELLI (Italy/Tuscany)
Chianti Classico Bartenura 1987 $9 (3/31/91) **70**

ROBERT SARRAU (France/Burgundy)
Mâcon-Villages 1989 $8 (10/31/90) **81**

SENORIO DE SARRIA (Spain)
Navarra 1984 $5 (2/28/90) BB **83**
Navarra Gran Reserva 1981 $11 (3/31/90) **65**

SARTORI (Italy/North)
Pinot Grigio Grave del Friuli 1990 $8 (1/31/92) **78**

CHATEAU LE SARTRE (France/Bordeaux)
Pessac-Léognan 1991 (NR) (5/15/92) (BT) **75+**
Pessac-Léognan 1990 (NR) (5/15/92) (BT) **80+**
Pessac-Léognan 1987 ($NA) (6/30/89) (BT) **75+**
Pessac-Léognan Blanc 1990 (NR) (9/30/91) (BT) **80+**
Pessac-Léognan Blanc 1989 $13.50 (3/31/91) **88**
Pessac-Léognan Blanc 1988 $12 (6/30/89) (BT) **80+**

SASSICAIA (Italy/Tuscany)
1988 Rel: $60 Cur: $66 (9/15/91) **98**
1987 $45 (3/15/91) **82**
1986 $50 (12/15/89) **95**
1985 Rel: $48 Cur: $120 (5/15/89) CS **92**
1984 $57 (3/15/89) **85**
1982 Rel: $45 Cur: $110 (7/31/87) **84**

SASSO (Italy/Other)
Aglianico del Vulture 1985 $11 (3/15/89) **83**

V. SATTUI (United States/California)
Cabernet Sauvignon Napa Valley Preston Vineyard 1988 $20 (11/15/91) **86**
Cabernet Sauvignon Napa Valley Preston Vineyard 1986 Rel: $16.75 Cur: $20 (CA-3/89) **88**
Cabernet Sauvignon Napa Valley Preston Vineyard 1985 Rel: $15.75 Cur: $25 (CA-3/89) **87**
Cabernet Sauvignon Napa Valley Preston Vineyard 1984 Rel: $13.75 Cur: $25 (CA-3/89) **86**
Cabernet Sauvignon Napa Valley Preston Vineyard 1983 Rel: $13.75 Cur: $20 (CA-3/89) **81**
Cabernet Sauvignon Napa Valley Preston Vineyard Reserve 1982 Rel: $22.50 Cur: $45 (CA-3/89) **78**
Cabernet Sauvignon Napa Valley Preston Vineyard Reserve 1980 Rel: $30 Cur: $85 (CA-3/89) **85**

SAUCELITO CANYON (United States/California)
Zinfandel San Luis Obispo County 1986 $9.50 (12/15/89) **87**

DOMAINE DU SAULT (France/Other)
Corbières 1988 $5 (6/30/90) **74**

ROGER SAUMAIZE (France/Burgundy)
Pouilly-Fuissé Clos de la Roche 1989 $28 (7/31/91) **91**
Pouilly-Fuissé Les Ronchevats 1989 $31 (7/31/91) **89**

SAUSAL (United States/California)
Cabernet Sauvignon Alexander Valley 1985 $12 (7/31/89) **74**
Chardonnay Alexander Valley 1990 $11 (7/15/92) **84**
White Zinfandel Alexander Valley 1988 $6 (6/15/89) **70**
Zinfandel Alexander Valley 1989 $8.50 (3/31/92) **79**
Zinfandel Alexander Valley 1988 $8.50 (4/30/91) **82**
Zinfandel Alexander Valley 1987 $7.75 (9/15/89) **83**
Zinfandel Alexander Valley 1986 $6.75 (3/31/89) SS **90**
Zinfandel Alexander Valley 1985 $6.25 (10/15/88) **72**
Zinfandel Alexander Valley 1984 $6.75 (5/31/88) **78**
Zinfandel Alexander Valley 1983 $5.75 (9/15/87) BB **82**
Zinfandel Alexander Valley Private Reserve 1988 $14 (4/30/91) **88**
Zinfandel Alexander Valley Private Reserve 1984 $10 (2/15/88) **86**

CHATEAU SAUVAGE (France/Bordeaux)
Premières Côtes de Bordeaux 1986 $9 (4/15/90) **81**

DOMAINE ETIENNE SAUZET (France/Burgundy)
Bâtard-Montrachet 1989 $156 (8/31/91) **97**
Bâtard-Montrachet 1988 Rel: $92 Cur: $195 (2/28/91) **93**
Bâtard-Montrachet 1986 $85 (2/29/88) **90**
Bourgogne Blanc Chardonnay Blanc 1989 $31 (8/31/91) **86**
Chassagne-Montrachet 1989 $60 (8/31/91) **90**
Chassagne-Montrachet 1988 $38 (2/15/91) **91**
Puligny-Montrachet 1989 $63 (8/31/91) **90**
Puligny-Montrachet 1986 $40 (4/30/88) **92**
Puligny-Montrachet Champ Canet 1989 $85 (8/31/91) **87**
Puligny-Montrachet Champ Canet 1988 $50 (12/31/90) **91**
Puligny-Montrachet Champ Canet 1986 $48 (4/30/88) **91**
Puligny-Montrachet Champ Canet 1985 $37 (10/15/87) **90**
Puligny-Montrachet Les Combettes 1989 $84 (8/31/91) **90**
Puligny-Montrachet Les Combettes 1988 Rel: $56 Cur: $61 (12/31/90) **93**
Puligny-Montrachet Les Combettes 1986 $50 (4/30/88) **93**
Puligny-Montrachet Les Combettes 1985 $50 (2/29/88) **90**
Puligny-Montrachet Les Perrières 1989 $84 (8/31/91) **88**
Puligny-Montrachet Les Perrières 1988 $70 (2/28/91) **90**
Puligny-Montrachet Les Perrières 1985 $39 (10/15/87) **93**
Puligny-Montrachet Les Referts 1989 Rel: $81 Cur: $87 (8/31/91) **91**
Puligny-Montrachet Les Referts 1988 $47 (12/31/90) **92**
Puligny-Montrachet Les Referts 1986 $45 (2/29/88) **87**
Puligny-Montrachet Les Truffières 1986 $45 (2/29/88) **93**
Puligny-Montrachet Les Truffières 1985 $42 (2/29/88) **91**

SBARBORO (United States/California)
Cabernet Sauvignon Sonoma County 1983 $10 (11/15/87) **71**
Chardonnay Alexander Valley Gauer Ranch 1985 $10 (8/31/87) **64**

SCARPA (Italy/Piedmont)
Barbaresco 1981 $20 (9/15/88) (HS) **84**
Barbaresco 1979 $20 (9/15/88) (HS) **90**
Barbaresco 1978 $27 (9/15/88) (HS) **90**
Barbaresco 1974 $30 (9/15/88) (HS) **89**
Barbaresco I Tetti di Neive 1978 $27 (3/15/87) **83**
Barbera d'Asti 1985 $12 (8/31/89) **88**
Barolo 1985 ($NA) (9/15/88) (HS) **90**
Barolo 1982 ($NA) (9/15/88) (HS) **88**

Barolo 1978 $27 (9/15/88) (HS) **89**
Barolo Le Coste di Monforte 1978 $27 (3/15/87) **81**

PAOLO SCAVINO (Italy/Piedmont)
Barolo 1985 $21 (10/15/90) **88**
Barolo 1983 ($NA) (9/15/88) (HS) **85**
Barolo 1982 ($NA) (9/15/88) (HS) **88**
Barolo Brico dell Fiasco 1985 $39 (6/15/90) **90**
Barolo Cannubi 1985 $30 (1/31/90) **74**

WILLI SCHAEFER (Germany)
Riesling Auslese Mosel-Saar-Ruwer Graacher Domprobst 1988 $13 (9/30/89) **80**
Riesling Kabinett Mosel-Saar-Ruwer Graacher Himmelreich 1988 $8 (9/30/89) **81**
Riesling Spätlese Mosel-Saar-Ruwer Graacher Domprobst 1988 $10 (9/30/89) **80**
Riesling Spätlese Mosel-Saar-Ruwer Wehlener Sonnenuhr 1988 $10 (9/30/89) **87**

SCHARFFENBERGER (United States/California)
Blanc de Blancs Mendocino County 1987 $20 (12/31/91) **83**
Blanc de Blancs Mendocino County 1986 $20 (3/15/91) **91**
Blanc de Blancs Mendocino County 1985 $18 (12/31/88) **85**
Blanc de Blancs Mendocino County 1984 $17.50 (12/31/87) **78**
Brut Mendocino County 1983 $13 (9/30/87) **84**
Brut Mendocino County 1982 $12.50 (2/01/86) **85**
Brut Mendocino County NV $16.50 (12/31/91) **90**
Brut Rosé Mendocino County NV $18 (12/31/91) **82**
Crémant Mendocino County NV $18 (12/31/91) **83**

DOMAINES SCHLUMBERGER (France/Alsace)
Gewürztraminer Alsace 1989 ($NA) (11/15/90) **73**
Gewürztraminer Alsace 1988 ($NA) (10/15/89) **78**
Gewürztraminer Alsace Fleur de Guebwiller 1990 (NR) (2/15/92) **81**
Gewürztraminer Alsace Kessler 1989 ($NA) (11/15/90) **90**
Gewürztraminer Alsace Kitterlé 1989 ($NA) (11/15/90) **78**
Gewürztraminer Alsace Sélection de Grains Nobles 1989 ($NA) (11/15/90) **79**
Gewürztraminer Alsace Sélection de Grains Nobles 1988 ($NA) (10/15/89) **78**
Muscat Alsace 1990 (NR) (2/15/92) **86**
Pinot Blanc Alsace 1990 (NR) (2/15/92) **89**
Pinot Blanc Alsace 1988 ($NA) (10/15/89) **84**
Riesling Alsace 1989 ($NA) (11/15/90) **86**
Riesling Alsace 1988 ($NA) (10/15/89) **85**
Riesling Alsace Kitterlé 1989 ($NA) (11/15/90) **89**
Riesling Alsace Kitterlé 1988 $14 (10/15/89) **90**
Riesling Alsace des Prince Abbés 1990 (NR) (2/15/92) **87**
Riesling Alsace Saering 1988 ($NA) (10/15/89) **82**
Sylvaner Alsace 1990 (NR) (2/15/92) **79**
Tokay Pinot Gris Alsace 1988 ($NA) (10/15/89) **81**
Tokay Pinot Gris Alsace Vendange Tardive 1989 ($NA) (11/15/90) **78**

SCHLOSS SCHONBORN (Germany)
Riesling Auslese Rheingau 1990 (NR) (12/15/91) **91**
Riesling Auslese Rheingau Hattenheimer Nussbrunnen 1989 ($NA) (12/15/90) **87**
Riesling Auslese Rheingau Rüdeshemier Berg Schlossberg 1989 ($NA) (12/15/90) **90**
Riesling Kabinett Halbtrocken Rheingau Geisenheimer Schlossberg 1988 ($NA) (9/30/89) **81**
Riesling Kabinett Rheingau Bereich Johannisberg 1985 $10.50 (1/31/88) **81**
Riesling Kabinett Rheingau Johannisberger Klaus 1989 $10 (12/15/90) **83**
Riesling Kabinett Rheingau Winkeler Gutenberg 1989 ($NA) (12/15/90) **92**
Riesling Spätlese Halbtrocken Rheingau Hochheimer Hölle 1988 ($NA) (9/30/89) **89**
Riesling Spätlese Halbtrocken Rheingau Hochheimer Kirchenstück 1989 ($NA) (12/15/90) **87**
Riesling Spätlese Halbtrocken Rheingau Johannisberger Klaus 1990 (NR) (12/15/91) **90**
Riesling Spätlese Halbtrocken Rheingau Rüdesheimer Bischofsberg 1988 ($NA) (9/30/89) **88**
Riesling Spätlese Rheingau 1989 ($NA) (12/15/90) **86**
Riesling Spätlese Rheingau Erbacher Marcobrunn 1990 $41 (12/15/91) **91**
Riesling Spätlese Rheingau Erbacher Marcobrunn 1989 ($NA) (12/15/90) **93**
Riesling Spätlese Rheingau Hattenheimer Nussbrunnen 1989 ($NA) (12/15/90) **90**
Riesling Spätlese Rheingau Hattenheimer Nussbrunnen 1988 $21 (9/30/89) **86**
Riesling Spätlese Rheingau Hattenheimer Pfaffenberg 1990 (NR) (12/15/91) **87**
Riesling Spätlese Rheingau Hattenheimer Pfaffenberg 1989 ($NA) (12/15/90) **91**
Riesling Spätlese Rheingau Hochheimer Kirchenstück 1990 (NR) (12/15/91) **87**
Riesling Spätlese Rheingau Hochheimer Kirchenstück 1989 ($NA) (12/15/90) **84**
Riesling Spätlese Trocken Rheingau Hattenheimer Pfaffenberg 1990 (NR) (12/15/91) **81**
Riesling Trockenbeerenauslese Rheingau Hochheimer 1990 (NR) (12/15/91) **92**

SCHOPPAUL HILL (United States/Texas)
Chenin Blanc Texas 1990 $7 (2/29/92) **82**
Muscat Canelli Texas 1990 $8 (2/29/92) **81**
Sauvignon Blanc Texas 1989 $7 (2/29/92) **81**

SCHRAMSBERG (United States/California)
Blanc de Blancs Napa Valley 1987 $21 (12/15/91) **87**
Blanc de Blancs Napa Valley 1986 $20 (12/31/90) **89**
Blanc de Blancs Napa Valley 1985 $20 (5/31/89) **84**
Blanc de Blancs Napa Valley 1983 $17.50 (5/16/86) **82**
Blanc de Noirs Napa Valley 1985 $22 (12/31/91) **83**
Blanc de Noirs Napa Valley 1984 $22 (12/31/90) **82**
Blanc de Noirs Napa Valley 1983 $21 (5/31/89) **90**
Blanc de Noirs Napa Valley 1981 $20 (5/16/86) **91**
Blanc de Blancs Napa Valley Late Disgorged 1985 $27 (6/15/91) **87**
Blanc de Noirs Napa Valley Late Disgorged 1983 $28 (6/15/91) **87**
Brut Napa Valley Reserve 1983 $29 (12/31/90) **82**
Brut Napa Valley Reserve 1982 $28 (5/31/89) **85**
Brut Napa Valley Reserve 1981 $27 (7/31/87) **78**
Brut Napa Valley Reserve 1980 $30 (5/16/86) **61**

Key to Symbols

The scores reported here are the results of blind tastings conducted by our panel of senior editors. Wines that carry the initials below are results of individual tastings.

THE WINE SPECTATOR 100-POINT SCALE ***95-100***—Classic, a great wine; ***90-94***—Outstanding, superior character and style; ***80-89***—Good to very good, a wine with special qualities; ***70-79***—Average, drinkable wine that may have minor flaws; ***60-69***—Below average, drinkable but not recommended; ***50-59***—Poor, undrinkable, not recommended. "+"—With a score indicates a range; used primarily with barrel tastings to indicate a preliminary score.

SPECIAL DESIGNATIONS SS—Spectator Selection, CS—Cellar Selection, BB—Best Buy, ($NA)—Price not available, (NR)—Not released.

TASTER'S INITIALS (JG)—Jim Gordon, (HS)—Harvey Steiman, (JL)—James Laube, (JS)—James Suckling, (TM)—Thomas Matthews, (TR)—Terry Robards, (PM)—Per-Henrik Mansson, (BT)—Barrel Tasting (these wines were tasted blind from barrel samples), (CA-date)—*California's Great Cabernets* by James Laube, (CH-date)—*California's Great Chardonnays* by James Laube, (VP-date)—*Vintage Port* by James Suckling.

DATE TASTED Dates in parentheses represent the issue in which the rating was published.

Brut Rosé Napa Valley Cuvée de Pinot 1987 $20 (12/31/90) **81**
Brut Rosé Napa Valley Cuvée de Pinot 1986 $19 (5/31/89) **76**
Brut Rosé Napa Valley Cuvée de Pinot 1985 $17 (4/30/88) **80**
Brut Rosé Napa Valley Cuvée de Pinot 1984 $17 (5/31/87) **83**
Demi-Sec Crémant Napa Valley 1987 $20 (12/31/91) **80**
Demi-Sec Crémant Napa Valley 1986 $20 (12/31/90) **77**
Demi-Sec Crémant Napa Valley 1985 $19 (5/31/89) **85**

C. VON SCHUBERT MAXIMIN GRUNHAUSER (Germany)
Riesling Auslese Mosel-Saar-Ruwer Abtsberg 1990 $48 (12/15/91) **90**
Riesling Auslese Mosel-Saar-Ruwer Herrenberg 1990 $55 (12/15/91) **90**
Riesling Auslese Mosel-Saar-Ruwer Herrenberg (Cask 92) 1990 (NR) (12/15/91) **90**
Riesling Auslese Mosel-Saar-Ruwer Abtsberg 1989 $40 (12/15/90) **85**
Riesling Auslese Mosel-Saar-Ruwer Abtsberg (Cask 133) 1989 $70 (12/15/90) **90**
Riesling Auslese Mosel-Saar-Ruwer Abtsberg (Cask 96) 1989 ($NA) (12/15/90) **95**
Riesling Auslese Mosel-Saar-Ruwer Abtsberg (Cask 98) 1989 $45 (12/15/90) **90**
Riesling Auslese Mosel-Saar-Ruwer Herrenberg 1989 $40 (12/15/90) **86**
Riesling Auslese Mosel-Saar-Ruwer Herrenberg (Cask 93) 1989 $80 (12/15/90) **91**
Riesling Auslese Mosel-Saar-Ruwer Herrenberg (AP153) 1988 $30 (9/30/89) **95**
Riesling Beerenauslese Mosel-Saar-Ruwer Abtsberg 1989 ($NA) (12/15/90) **99**
Riesling Eiswein Mosel-Saar-Ruwer Abtsberg 1990 (NR) (12/15/91) **96**
Riesling Kabinett Mosel-Saar-Ruwer Abtsberg 1990 $25 (12/15/91) **91**
Riesling Kabinett Mosel-Saar-Ruwer Brüderberg 1989 $9.50 (12/15/90) **78**
Riesling Kabinett Mosel-Saar-Ruwer Herrenberg 1990 $23 (12/15/91) **90**
Riesling Kabinett Mosel-Saar-Ruwer Abtsberg 1989 $20 (12/15/90) **90**
Riesling Kabinett Mosel-Saar-Ruwer Herrenberg 1988 $10 (9/30/89) **89**
Riesling Kabinett Mosel-Saar-Ruwer Herrenberg 1987 $12 (4/30/89) **82**
Riesling Qualitätswein Mosel-Saar-Ruwer Abtsberg 1988 $10 (9/30/89) **80**
Riesling Qualitätswein Mosel-Saar-Ruwer Abtsberg 1987 $13 (4/30/89) **87**
Riesling Qualitätswein Mosel-Saar-Ruwer Herrenberg 1989 $13 (12/15/90) **80**
Riesling Spätlese Mosel-Saar-Ruwer Abtsberg 1990 $30 (12/15/91) **92**
Riesling Spätlese Mosel-Saar-Ruwer Abtsberg (Cask 96) 1990 (NR) (12/15/91) **91**
Riesling Spätlese Mosel-Saar-Ruwer Abtsberg 1989 $28 (12/15/90) **90**
Riesling Spätlese Mosel-Saar-Ruwer Abtsberg 1988 $18 (9/30/89) **96**
Riesling Trockenbeerenauslese Mosel-Saar-Ruwer Herrenberg 1989 ($NA) (12/15/90) **96**

SCHUG (United States/California)
Chardonnay Carneros Barrel Fermented 1989 $12 (3/31/92) **80**
Chardonnay Carneros Beckstoffer Vineyard 1988 $15 (2/28/91) **75**
Chardonnay Carneros Beckstoffer Vineyard 1987 $15 (5/31/90) **79**
Chardonnay Carneros Napa Valley Ahollinger Vineyard 1985 $9.75 (4/30/87) **63**
Pinot Noir Carneros Beckstoffer Vineyard 1987 $13 (2/28/91) **81**
Pinot Noir Carneros Beckstoffer Vineyard 1986 $13 (10/31/90) **87**
Pinot Noir Carneros Rouge de Noir 1987 $18 (12/15/91) **85**
Pinot Noir Napa Valley Heinemann Vineyard Reserve 1985 $15 (11/15/91) **83**

SCHWARZENBERG (United States/Oregon)
Pinot Noir Oregon 1987 $13.50 (2/15/90) **70**

ALFRED SCHYLER (France/Bordeaux)
Médoc 1985 $8.50 (6/30/88) **72**

SEA RIDGE (United States/California)
Chardonnay Sonoma Coast Mill Station Vineyard 1989 $14 (4/30/92) **76**
Merlot Sonoma Coast Occidental Vineyards 1989 $15 (5/31/92) **86**
Pinot Noir Sonoma Coast Hirsch Vinyard 1990 $20 (3/31/92) **82**
Pinot Noir Sonoma Coast Hirsch Vinyard 1989 $18 (3/31/92) **81**
Pinot Noir Sonoma County 1982 $10.50 (8/31/86) **72**

SEAVIEW (Australia)
Brut South Australia 1988 $9.75 (11/15/91) BB **83**
Cabernet Sauvignon South Australia 1986 $10 (7/31/90) **88**
Cabernet Shiraz South Australia 1987 $8 (9/30/91) BB **82**
Chardonnay South Australia 1989 $10 (9/15/91) **82**
Chardonnay South Australia 1988 $10 (7/15/90) **71**
Port Australia Flagship NV $9 (11/15/91) **79**
Shiraz South Australia 1987 $10 (9/30/91) **86**
South Australia 1989 $8 (9/30/91) **83**

SEBASTE (Italy/Piedmont)
Barolo 1985 ($NA) (9/15/88) (HS) **90**
Barolo 1984 ($NA) (9/15/88) (HS) **85**
Barolo 1983 ($NA) (9/15/88) (HS) **86**
Barolo 1982 ($NA) (9/15/88) (HS) **91**
Barolo 1979 ($NA) (9/15/88) (HS) **85**
Barolo Bussia Riserva 1984 $17 (7/31/89) **84**
Barolo Bussia Riserva 1982 $15 (11/15/87) **90**
Bricco Viole 1986 $16 (1/31/89) **89**
Bricco Viole 1985 $13 (10/31/87) **91**

SEBASTIANI (United States/California)
Barbera Sonoma Valley 1987 $11 (4/30/91) **86**
Blanc de Noirs Sonoma County Five Star NV $11 (4/30/90) **77**
Brut Sonoma County Five Star NV $11 (4/30/90) **72**
Cabernet Franc California 1988 $8.50 (7/15/91) **77**
Cabernet Sauvignon North Coast Emilia 1986 $12.50 (3/31/92) **71**
Cabernet Sauvignon North Coast Proprietor's Reserve 1979 $11 (8/01/84) **58**
Cabernet Sauvignon Sonoma County Family Selection 1985 $8 (10/15/88) **80**
Cabernet Sauvignon Sonoma County Reserve 1986 $13 (1/31/91) **86**
Cabernet Sauvignon Sonoma County Reserve 1985 $12.50 (11/15/90) **86**
Cabernet Sauvignon Sonoma Valley Cherry Block 1985 $16.50 (3/31/90) **89**
Cabernet Sauvignon Sonoma Valley Eagle Vineyards 1982 $26.50 (9/15/86) **75**
Cabernet Sauvignon Sonoma Valley Eagle Vineyards 1981 $25 (8/01/85) **91**
Cabernet Sauvignon Sonoma Valley Reserve 1982 $11 (12/31/87) **74**
Chardonnay Sonoma County 1989 $10 (7/15/91) **81**
Chardonnay Sonoma County Reserve 1990 $12 (5/31/92) **88**
Chardonnay Sonoma County Reserve 1988 $15 (6/30/91) **89**
Chardonnay Sonoma County Reserve 1986 $10 (10/31/88) **79**
Chardonnay Sonoma Valley Reserve 1985 $10 (2/15/88) **74**
Chardonnay Sonoma County Wildwood Hill 1987 $14 (6/30/90) **90**
Chardonnay Sonoma County Wilson Ranch 1987 $14 (6/30/90) **77**
Chardonnay Sonoma Valley Clark Ranch 1987 $14 (6/30/90) **83**
Chardonnay Sonoma Valley Clark Ranch 1986 $14 (3/15/88) **88**
Chardonnay Sonoma Valley Kinneybrook 1987 $14 (6/30/90) **80**
Chardonnay Sonoma Valley Kinneybrook 1986 $14 (3/15/88) **74**
Chardonnay Sonoma Valley Niles 1986 $17 (3/15/88) **82**
Chenin Blanc California 1987 $5.25 (7/31/89) **65**
La Sorella California 1988 $4 (3/31/90) **79**
Merlot Sonoma County 1989 $9 (5/31/92) **85**
Merlot Sonoma County Family Selection 1985 $7 (9/30/88) **85**
White Zinfandel California 1988 $5 (6/15/89) **69**

Wildwood Sonoma Valley 1987 $15 (8/31/91) **86**
Zinfandel Sonoma County Family Selection 1985 $5 (9/15/88) BB **88**
Zinfandel Sonoma Valley Proprietor's Reserve Black Beauty 1980 $9 (12/16/85) **76**

AUGUST SEBASTIANI (United States/California)
Merlot California Country NV $4.50 (5/31/92) **72**
White Zinfandel California 1988 $7.50/1.5L (6/15/89) **65**

SEGHESIO (United States/California)
Cabernet Sauvignon Northern Sonoma 1986 $8 (6/30/90) **76**
Cabernet Sauvignon Northern Sonoma 1985 $5.50 (4/15/89) BB **84**
Cabernet Sauvignon Northern Sonoma 1983 $6.75 (7/15/88) **69**
Cabernet Sauvignon Northern Sonoma 1982 $5 (4/30/87) **77**
Cabernet Sauvignon Sonoma County 1987 $9 (4/30/91) **85**
Chardonnay Mendocino-Sonoma Counties 1990 $9 (3/31/92) **80**
Chardonnay Mendocino-Sonoma Counties 1989 $9 (4/30/91) **86**
Chardonnay Sonoma County 1988 $12 (4/30/91) **84**
Chardonnay Sonoma County 1987 $7 (12/31/88) **79**
Chardonnay Sonoma County Reserve 1988 $12 (2/28/91) **71**
Pinot Noir Northern Sonoma 1983 $5 (4/15/87) **72**
Pinot Noir Russian River Valley 1988 $9 (10/31/91) **83**
Pinot Noir Russian River Valley 1987 $8 (4/15/90) **84**
Pinot Noir Russian River Valley Reserve 1987 $13 (4/15/90) **83**
Pinot Noir Sonoma County 1989 $9 (4/30/92) **79**
Pinot Noir Sonoma-Mendocino Counties 1984 $6.75 (5/31/88) **84**
Sonoma Red Lot 4 Sonoma County NV $5 (6/30/90) **75**
White Zinfandel Northern Sonoma 1988 $5.50 (6/15/89) **84**
Zinfandel Alexander Valley Reserve 1988 $12 (8/31/91) **88**
Zinfandel Alexander Valley Reserve 1986 $9 (10/31/89) **80**
Zinfandel Northern Sonoma 1987 $6.50 (7/31/90) BB **85**
Zinfandel Northern Sonoma 1986 $6.50 (5/15/90) BB **80**
Zinfandel Northern Sonoma 1985 $5.50 (3/15/89) BB **80**
Zinfandel Northern Sonoma 1984 $5.50 (6/30/88) **76**
Zinfandel Sonoma County 1988 $6.50 (9/30/91) BB **86**

RENZO SEGHESIO (Italy/Piedmont)
Barbera d'Alba 1989 $12 (11/30/91) **81**
Barolo Bussia-Pianpolvere 1986 $28 (1/31/92) **84**
Dolcetto d'Alba 1989 $12 (11/30/91) **77**
Ruri Nebbiolo 1989 $14 (1/31/92) **84**

CHATEAU SEGONNES (France/Bordeaux)
Margaux 1988 $18 (6/30/89) (BT) **75+**
Margaux 1987 $15 (6/30/89) (BT) **70+**

CHATEAU SEGONZAC (France/Bordeaux)
Premières Côtes de Blaye 1986 $9.75 (6/30/89) **79**
Premières Côtes de Blaye 1985 $9 (2/15/88) **85**

CHATEAU DE SEGRIES (France/Rhône)
Lirac 1985 $10 (12/15/89) **81**

DOMAINE SEGUINOT (France/Chablis)
Chablis 1988 $16 (2/28/91) **79**

CHATEAU SEGUR (France/Bordeaux)
Haut-Médoc 1988 $15 (12/31/90) **82**
Haut-Médoc 1982 $6 (4/16/85) **75**

SEGURA VIUDAS (Spain)
Brut Cava Aria Estate NV $10 (11/15/91) **87**
Extra Dry Cava Aria Estate NV $10 (11/15/91) **85**

J. & H. SELBACH (Germany)
Riesling Hochgewächs Mosel-Saar-Ruwer 1987 $7 (10/15/88) **78**
Riesling Kabinett Mosel-Saar-Ruwer Brauneberger Mandelgraben 1983 $4.50 (11/16/84) BB **84**
Riesling Kabinett Mosel-Saar-Ruwer Zeltinger Himmelreich 1985 $7.50 (10/15/88) **86**
Riesling Spätlese Mosel-Saar-Ruwer Bernkasteler Kurfürstlay 1990 $9 (12/15/91) **78**
Riesling Spätlese Mosel-Saar-Ruwer Piesporter Goldtröpfchen 1985 $14 (9/15/88) **89**
Scheurebe Hochgewächs Mosel-Saar-Ruwer 1989 $8 (12/15/91) **70**
Scheurebe Qualitätswein Halbtrocken Mosel-Saar-Ruwer Brauneberger Klostergarten 1990 $8.50 (12/15/91) BB **85**

SELBACH-OSTER (Germany)
Riesling Auslese Mosel-Saar-Ruwer Zeltinger Sonnenuhr *** 1990 $21/375ml (12/15/91) **90**
Riesling Auslese Mosel-Saar-Ruwer Bernkasteler Badstube 1989 ($NA) (12/15/90) **87**
Riesling Auslese Mosel-Saar-Ruwer Zeltingen-Rachtiger Sonnenuhr 1989 $18/375ml (12/15/90) **86**
Riesling Auslese Mosel-Saar-Ruwer Zeltinger Himmelreich 1990 (NR) (12/15/91) **90**
Riesling Auslese Mosel-Saar-Ruwer Zeltinger Sonnenuhr 1990 (NR) (12/15/91) **91**
Riesling Auslese Mosel-Saar-Ruwer Zeltinger Sonnenuhr (AP5) 1988 $22 (9/30/89) **91**
Riesling Beerenauslese Mosel-Saar-Ruwer Zeltingen-Rachtiger Sonnenuhr 1989 $56/375ml (12/15/90) **91**
Riesling Beerenauslese Mosel-Saar-Ruwer Zeltinger Sonnenuhr 1990 $75/375ml (12/15/91) **91**
Riesling Eiswein Mosel-Saar-Ruwer Bernkasteler Badstube 1990 $87/375ml (12/15/91) **95**
Riesling Eiswein Mosel-Saar-Ruwer Zeltinger Himmelreich 1986 $40/375ml (4/30/89) **76**
Riesling Eiswein Mosel-Saar-Ruwer Zeltinger Himmelreich 1985 $35/375ml (4/30/89) **83**
Riesling Hochgewächs Mosel-Saar-Ruwer Graacher Himmelreich 1986 $6 (10/15/88) **81**
Riesling Kabinett Mosel-Saar-Ruwer Bernkasteler Badstube 1989 $10 (12/15/90) **84**
Riesling Kabinett Mosel-Saar-Ruwer Graacher Himmelreich 1985 $10 (10/15/88) **80**
Riesling Kabinett Mosel-Saar-Ruwer Wehlener Klosterberg 1986 $8 (11/30/88) **86**
Riesling Kabinett Mosel-Saar-Ruwer Wehlener Sonnenuhr 1989 $10 (12/15/90) **81**
Riesling Kabinett Mosel-Saar-Ruwer Zeltingen-Rachtiger Sonnenuhr 1989 $10.50 (12/15/90) **85**
Riesling Kabinett Mosel-Saar-Ruwer Zeltinger Himmelreich 1988 $8.50 (9/30/89) **81**
Riesling Spätlese Mosel-Saar-Ruwer Bernkasteler Badstube 1989 $11.50 (12/15/90) **87**
Riesling Spätlese Mosel-Saar-Ruwer Bernkasteler Badstube 1985 $9.50 (9/15/88) **90**
Riesling Spätlese Mosel-Saar-Ruwer Graacher Himmelreich 1985 $8 (9/15/88) **82**
Riesling Spätlese Mosel-Saar-Ruwer Wehlener Klosterberg 1988 $11 (9/30/89) **84**
Riesling Spätlese Mosel-Saar-Ruwer Wehlener Sonnenuhr 1989 ($NA) (12/15/90) **87**
Riesling Spätlese Mosel-Saar-Ruwer Zeltingen-Rachtiger Himmelreich 1989 $11.50 (12/15/90) **86**
Riesling Spätlese Mosel-Saar-Ruwer Zeltinger Schlossberg 1990 $13 (12/15/91) **89**
Riesling Spätlese Mosel-Saar-Ruwer Zeltinger Sonnenuhr 1990 (NR) (12/15/91) **88**
Riesling Spätlese Mosel-Saar-Ruwer Zeltinger Sonnenuhr 1988 $12.50 (9/30/89) **93**
Riesling Trockenbeerenauslese Mosel-Saar-Ruwer Zeltingen-Rachtiger Sonnenuhr 1989 $100/375ml (12/15/90) **97**
Riesling Trockenbeerenauslese Mosel-Saar-Ruwer Zeltinger Sonnenuhr 1990 (NR) (12/15/91) **93**

SELVAPIANA (Italy/Tuscany)
Chianti Classico 1986 $5 (11/30/89) (HS) **82**
Chianti Classico Riserva 1985 $11 (11/30/89) (HS) **89**
Chianti Classico Riserva 1983 $10 (11/30/89) (HS) **86**
Chianti Classico Riserva 1982 $10 (11/30/89) (HS) **87**
Chianti Rufina Bucerchiale Riserva 1985 $19 (9/15/90) **91**

I SELVATICI (Italy/Tuscany)
Claresco 1990 $6 (9/30/91) **79**
Predicato di Cardisco 1985 $25 (8/31/91) **81**
Vin Santo 1984 $16/375ml (4/30/91) **89**

FATTORIA DI SELVOLE (Italy/Tuscany)
Chianti Classico 1988 ($NA) (9/15/91) **78**
Chianti Classico Lanfredini Riserva 1985 ($NA) (9/15/91) **77**

DOMAINE DES SENECHAUX (France/Rhône)
Châteauneuf-du-Pape 1985 $17 (10/15/88) **85**

CHATEAU SENEJAC (France/Bordeaux)
Haut-Médoc 1989 $11 (4/30/91) (BT) **85+**
Haut-Médoc 1988 Rel: $11 Cur: $14 (4/30/91) **78**
Haut-Médoc 1987 $9 (6/30/89) (BT) **70+**

REINHOLD SENFTER (Germany)
Riesling Kabinett Rheinhessen Niersteiner Oelberg 1986 $8.25 (1/31/88) **85**

SENORIO DE NAVA (Spain)
Ribera del Duero 1986 $8 (11/15/89) **81**

SENORIO DE SARRIA (Spain)
Navarra 1985 $5 (7/31/89) **77**

SENORIO DEL MAR (Spain)
Vino Tinto Seco 1987 $4 (10/31/91) BB **81**

EL SENORIO DE TORO (Spain)
Tarragona Vino Blanco Seco 1988 $4 (5/31/92) **76**
Toro Etiqueta Blanca 1989 $10 (4/15/92) **82**

SEPPELT (Australia)
Brut Australia Fleur de Lys 1985 $18 (12/31/88) **85**
Brut South Eastern Australia Imperial NV $10 (1/31/90) **82**
Cabernet Sauvignon Padthaway Black Label 1988 $12 (3/31/91) **81**
Cabernet Sauvignon South Eastern Australia Black Label 1985 $11 (4/30/88) **64**
Cabernet Sauvignon South Eastern Australia Black Label 1982 $12.50 (4/01/86) **78**
Cabernet Sauvignon South Eastern Australia Murray River 1987 $5 (4/15/88) **77**
Cabernet Sauvignon South Eastern Australia Reserve Bin 1988 $9 (7/15/91) **82**
Cabernet Shiraz South Eastern Australia 1986 $8 (1/31/90) **82**
Chardonnay Barooga Padthaway Black Label 1989 $12 (9/15/91) **82**
Chardonnay Barooga Padthaway Black Label 1989 $14 (3/31/91) **89**
Chardonnay Barooga Padthaway Black Label Great Western Vineyards 1987 $15 (7/31/89) **79**
Chardonnay South Eastern Australia Reserve Bin 1990 $9 (9/15/91) **78**
Chardonnay South Eastern Australia Reserve Bin 1989 $10 (7/31/90) **88**
Chardonnay South Eastern Australia Reserve Bin 1987 $9 (5/31/88) **80**
Chardonnay South Eastern Australia Reserve Bin 1986 $8 (2/15/88) **87**
Chardonnay South Eastern Australia Reserve Bin 1985 $8 (9/30/86) **74**
Chardonnay South Eastern Australia Reserve Bin 1984 $8.50 (2/01/86) **84**
Port Australia Para No. 113 NV $25 (11/15/91) **83**
Port Barossa Valley Para Port Bin 109 NV $25 (2/15/88) **92**
Port Barossa Valley Para Port No. 110 NV $25 (3/15/89) **79**
Port McLaren Flat Barossa 1978 $15 (2/15/88) **70**
Sémillon Chardonnay Moyston South Australia 1991 $7 (6/30/92) **81**
Shiraz South Eastern Australia Black Label 1984 $12 (12/31/88) **87**
Shiraz South Eastern Australia Black Label 1983 $10 (2/15/88) **74**
Tawny Port Australia Old Trafford NV $15 (3/15/89) **95**
Tawny Port Barossa Valley Mt. Rufus NV $12 (2/15/88) **78**

SEQUOIA GROVE (United States/California)
Cabernet Sauvignon Napa Valley 1987 $18 (11/15/91) **70**
Cabernet Sauvignon Napa County 1986 $16 (CA-3/89) **88**
Cabernet Sauvignon Napa County 1985 Rel: $16 Cur: $21 (CA-3/89) **86**
Cabernet Sauvignon Napa Valley 1984 Rel: $12 Cur: $20 (CA-3/89) **85**
Cabernet Sauvignon Napa-Alexander Valleys 1983 Rel: $12.50 Cur: $18 (CA-3/89) **77**
Cabernet Sauvignon Napa-Alexander Valleys 1982 Rel: $12 Cur: $22 (CA-3/89) **78**
Cabernet Sauvignon Alexander Valley 1981 Rel: $12 Cur: $25 (CA-3/89) **84**
Cabernet Sauvignon Napa Valley 1981 Rel: $12 Cur: $25 (CA-3/89) **80**
Cabernet Sauvignon Napa Valley Cask One 1980 Rel: $12 Cur: $27 (CA-3/89) **85**
Cabernet Sauvignon Napa Valley Cask Two 1980 Rel: $12 Cur: $27 (CA-3/89) **87**
Cabernet Sauvignon Napa Valley Estate 1988 ($NA) (5/15/90) (BT) **90+**
Cabernet Sauvignon Napa Valley Estate 1987 $26 (11/15/91) **87**
Cabernet Sauvignon Napa Valley Estate 1986 Rel: $22 Cur: $25 (9/30/89) **84**
Cabernet Sauvignon Napa Valley Estate 1985 Rel: $28 Cur: $34 (CA-3/89) **92**
Cabernet Sauvignon Napa Valley Estate 1982 Rel: $14 Cur: $28 (CA-3/89) **82**
Chardonnay Carneros 1989 Rel: $14 Cur: $18 (7/15/91) **86**
Chardonnay Carneros 1988 Rel: $14 Cur: $17 (4/30/90) **89**
Chardonnay Carneros 1987 $14 (6/15/89) **79**
Chardonnay Carneros 1986 Rel: $13 Cur: $16 (CH-5/90) **78**
Chardonnay Carneros 1985 Rel: $12 Cur: $16 (CH-5/90) **88**
Chardonnay Napa Valley Estate 1989 $16 (7/15/91) **85**
Chardonnay Napa Valley Estate 1988 $16 (4/30/90) **91**
Chardonnay Napa Valley Estate 1987 $16 (CH-5/90) **88**
Chardonnay Napa Valley Estate 1986 $15 (CH-5/90) **88**
Chardonnay Napa Valley Estate 1985 $16 (CH-5/90) **89**
Chardonnay Napa Valley Estate 1984 $14 (CH-5/90) **89**
Chardonnay Napa Valley Estate 1983 $12 (CH-5/90) **87**
Chardonnay Napa Valley Estate 1982 $12 (CH-5/90) **72**
Chardonnay Napa Valley Estate 1981 $12 (CH-7/90) **88**
Chardonnay Napa Valley Estate 1980 $10 (CH-5/90) **87**
Chardonnay Sonoma County 1982 $10.50 (11/01/84) **86**

SERAFIN PERE & FILS (France/Burgundy)
Charmes-Chambertin 1989 $65 (1/31/92) **92**
Gevrey-Chambertin 1988 $35 (3/31/91) **92**
Gevrey-Chambertin Les Cazetiers 1989 $54 (1/31/92) **89**
Gevrey-Chambertin Les Cazetiers 1988 $53 (5/15/91) **91**
Gevrey-Chambertin Le Fonteny 1989 $50 (1/31/92) **86**
Gevrey-Chambertin Le Fonteny 1988 $50 (5/15/91) **92**
Gevrey-Chambertin Vieilles Vignes 1989 $45 (1/31/92) **92**
Gevrey-Chambertin Vieilles Vignes 1987 $35 (3/31/90) **91**

BODEGAS JAUME SERRA (Spain)
Brut Cava Cristalino NV $8 (2/29/92) **75**
Penedès 1985 $7.50 (4/15/92) BB **80**
Penedès Tempranillo 1988 $6 (4/15/92) BB **80**
Seco Cava Dry Cristalino NV $8 (2/29/92) BB **82**

CHATEAU LA SERRE (France/Bordeaux)
St.-Emilion 1989 $17 (4/30/91) (BT) **85+**
St.-Emilion 1988 $18 (6/15/91) **80**

St.-Emilion 1987 $15 (6/30/89) (BT) **75+**
St.-Emilion 1985 $15 (5/15/88) **91**

SERRE DE LAUZIERE (France/Rhône)
Côtes du Rhône-Villages 1988 $7 (10/31/90) **78**

DOMAINE B. SERVEAU (France/Burgundy)
Bourgogne 1989 $10 (1/31/92) **83**
Bourgogne Blanc Chardonnay 1989 $16 (4/30/91) **73**
Bourgogne Rouge 1985 $13 (11/15/87) **76**
Chambolle-Musigny 1989 (NR) (1/31/92) **83**
Chambolle-Musigny Les Amoureuses 1989 $50 (1/31/92) **85**
Chambolle-Musigny Les Amoureuses 1988 $66 (2/28/91) **84**
Chambolle-Musigny Les Amoureuses 1985 $75 (6/15/88) **91**
Chambolle-Musigny Les Chabiots 1989 $30 (1/31/92) **79**
Chambolle-Musigny Les Chabiots 1988 $39 (2/28/91) **86**
Chambolle-Musigny Les Chabiots 1987 $30 (6/15/90) **78**
Chambolle-Musigny Les Chabiots 1985 $39 (6/15/88) **90**
Chambolle-Musigny Les Chabiots 1984 $23 (4/15/87) **91**
Chambolle-Musigny Les Sentiers 1989 $30 (1/31/92) **93**
Chambolle-Musigny Les Sentiers 1988 $39 (2/28/91) **79**
Morey-St.-Denis Les Sorbets 1989 $30 (1/31/92) **86**
Morey-St.-Denis Les Sorbets 1988 $35 (2/28/91) **88**
Morey-St.-Denis Les Sorbets 1987 $30 (5/15/90) **83**
Morey-St.-Denis Les Sorbets 1985 $39 (6/15/88) **88**
Morey-St.-Denis Les Sorbets 1984 $22 (3/15/87) **87**
Nuits-St.-Georges Chaines Carteaux 1988 $39 (3/31/91) **84**
Nuits-St.-Georges Chaines Carteaux 1985 $39 (6/15/88) **86**

SETTESOLI (Italy/Other)
Bianco 1990 $7 (7/15/91) **79**
Bianco Feudo dei Fiori 1990 $9 (6/30/91) **80**

AURELIO SETTIMO (Italy/Piedmont)
Barolo Vigna Rocche 1982 $19 (5/31/88) **83**
Barolo Vigna Rocche 1980 $17 (5/31/88) **73**
Barolo Vigna Rocche 1979 $25 (5/31/88) **67**

SEVEN HILLS (United States/Washington)
Cabernet Sauvignon Walla Walla Valley 1989 $20 (3/31/92) **85**
White Riesling Columbia Valley 1990 $6 (6/15/92) BB **84**

SHADOW CREEK (United States/California)
Blanc de Blancs California 1984 $14.50 (1/31/88) **77**
Blanc de Blancs Sonoma County 1983 $15 (5/16/86) **88**
Blanc de Blancs Sonoma County 1982 $15 (10/16/85) **89**
Blanc de Noirs California 1984 $12.50 (5/31/87) **86**
Blanc de Noirs California NV $11 (6/15/91) **80**
Blanc de Noirs Sonoma County 1982 $13 (5/16/86) **79**
Brut California NV $11 (6/15/91) **76**
Brut California Reserve Cuvée 1983 $20 (5/31/89) **87**

SHADOWBROOK (United States/California)
Cabernet Sauvignon Napa Valley 1985 $9.50 (7/15/91) **84**
Chardonnay Napa Valley 1989 $9.50 (7/15/91) **76**

SHAFER (United States/California)
Cabernet Sauvignon Stags Leap District 1988 $19 (8/31/91) **88**
Cabernet Sauvignon Stags Leap District 1987 Rel: $18 Cur: $21 (7/31/90) **92**
Cabernet Sauvignon Stags Leap District 1986 Rel: $16 Cur: $21 (9/30/89) SS **93**
Cabernet Sauvignon Stags Leap District 1985 Rel: $15.50 Cur: $22 (CA-3/89) **91**
Cabernet Sauvignon Stags Leap District 1984 Rel: $14 Cur: $24 (CA-3/89) **91**
Cabernet Sauvignon Stags Leap District 1984 Rel: $14 Cur: $24 (12/15/87) SS **93**
Cabernet Sauvignon Stags Leap District 1983 Rel: $13 Cur: $20 (CA-3/89) **87**
Cabernet Sauvignon Stags Leap District 1982 Rel: $13 Cur: $21 (CA-3/89) **88**
Cabernet Sauvignon Stags Leap District 1980 Rel: $12 Cur: $27 (CA-3/89) **77**
Cabernet Sauvignon Stags Leap District 1979 Rel: $12 Cur: $35 (CA-3/89) **89**
Cabernet Sauvignon Stags Leap District 1978 Rel: $11 Cur: $40 (CA-3/89) **85**
Cabernet Sauvignon Stags Leap District Hillside Select 1991 (NR) (5/15/92) (BT) **88+**
Cabernet Sauvignon Stags Leap District Hillside Select 1990 (NR) (5/15/91) (BT) **90+**
Cabernet Sauvignon Stags Leap District Hillside Select 1989 (NR) (5/15/91) (BT) **85+**
Cabernet Sauvignon Stags Leap District Hillside Select 1987 $38 (4/15/89) (BT) **85+**
Cabernet Sauvignon Stags Leap District Hillside Select 1986 Rel: $32 Cur: $35 (3/15/91) **91**
Cabernet Sauvignon Stags Leap District Hillside Select 1985 Rel: $24.50 Cur: $30 (5/31/90) CS **91**
Cabernet Sauvignon Stags Leap District Hillside Select 1984 Rel: $24.50 Cur: $32.33 (4/30/89) **89**
Cabernet Sauvignon Stags Leap District Hillside Select 1983 Rel: $22 Cur: $24 (CA-3/89) **89**
Cabernet Sauvignon Stags Leap District Reserve 1982 Rel: $18 Cur: $35 (CA-3/89) **89**
Chardonnay Napa Valley 1990 $15 (3/15/92) **87**
Chardonnay Napa Valley 1989 $15 (4/30/91) **84**
Chardonnay Napa Valley 1988 $13.50 (5/31/90) **83**
Chardonnay Napa Valley 1987 $13.50 (4/15/89) **79**
Chardonnay Napa Valley 1986 $12 (7/15/88) **89**
Chardonnay Napa Valley 1985 $11.50 (1/31/88) **67**
Chardonnay Napa Valley 1984 $12 (10/31/86) **66**
Chardonnay Napa Valley 1983 $12 (9/01/85) **80**
Chardonnay Napa Valley 1982 $11 (10/01/84) **79**
Chardonnay Napa Valley 1981 $11 (3/16/84) **64**
Merlot Napa Valley 1991 (NR) (5/15/92) (BT) **90+**
Merlot Napa Valley 1990 $18 (5/31/92) **91**
Merlot Napa Valley 1989 $18 (8/31/91) **87**
Merlot Napa Valley 1988 $16.50 (12/31/90) **83**
Merlot Napa Valley 1987 $15 (10/15/89) **92**
Merlot Napa Valley 1986 $13 (12/31/88) **91**
Merlot Napa Valley 1985 $12.50 (12/15/87) **90**
Merlot Napa Valley 1984 $12.50 (2/28/87) **87**
Merlot Napa Valley 1983 $10 (2/16/86) **93**
Zinfandel Napa Valley Last Chance 1983 $7 (2/16/86) **73**

CHARLES SHAW (United States/California)
Chardonnay Napa Valley 1989 $12 (2/15/92) **84**
Chardonnay Napa Valley 1988 $11 (8/31/90) **85**
Chardonnay Napa Valley 1987 $11 (CH-5/90) **85**
Chardonnay Napa Valley 1986 $11 (CH-5/90) **85**
Chardonnay Napa Valley 1985 Rel: $12 Cur: $15 (CH-5/90) **87**
Chardonnay Napa Valley 1984 Rel: $12 Cur: $15 (CH-5/90) **82**
Chardonnay Napa Valley 1983 Rel: $12 Cur: $16 (CH-5/90) **84**
Gamay Beaujolais Napa Valley 1988 $6.50 (7/15/89) **78**

SHENANDOAH (United States/California)
Amador County Serene Varietal Adventure Series 1989 $8 (3/31/91) **74**
Cabernet Franc Amador County Varietal Adventure Series 1989 $10 (8/31/91) **87**
Cabernet Sauvignon Amador County Artist Series 1987 $10 (2/28/91) **80**
Cabernet Sauvignon Amador County Artist Series 1986 $12 (10/31/88) **86**
Cabernet Sauvignon Amador County Artist Series 1984 $9 (8/31/87) **89**
Orange Muscat Amador County 1990 $10 (6/15/92) **84**
Sauvignon Blanc Amador County 1990 $7.50 (10/15/91) **84**
White Zinfandel Amador County 1988 $6 (6/15/89) **81**
Zinfandel Amador County Classico Varietal Adventure Series 1989 $6 (4/30/91) BB **82**
Zinfandel Amador County Special Reserve 1989 $8.50 (2/29/92) **84**
Zinfandel Amador County Special Reserve 1987 $8.50 (7/31/89) **81**
Zinfandel Amador County Special Reserve 1986 $7.50 (7/15/88) **86**
Zinfandel Amador County Special Reserve 1985 $7.50 (2/15/88) **85**
Zinfandel Fiddletown Special Reserve 1983 $7 (10/15/86) **74**

SHOWN AND SONS (United States/California)
Cabernet Sauvignon Napa Valley Rutherford 1979 $15 (4/01/84) **63**
Zinfandel Napa Valley 1981 $7.50 (4/16/84) **85**

CHATEAU SIAURAC (France/Bordeaux)
Lalande-de-Pomerol 1990 (NR) (5/15/92) (BT) **85+**
Lalande-de-Pomerol 1989 (NR) (4/30/91) (BT) **80+**
Lalande-de-Pomerol 1988 $20 (6/30/89) (BT) **75+**
Lalande-de-Pomerol 1987 $17 (6/30/89) (BT) **75+**

SICHEL (Germany)
Novum 1987 $7.50 (10/15/88) **85**
Riesling Beerenauslese Rheinpfalz Deidesheimer Hofstuck 1988 $9.75/375ml (3/15/90) **92**

BODEGAS SIERRA CANTABRIA (Spain)
Rioja Codice 1989 $6 (4/15/92) **77**

SIERRA VISTA (United States/California)
Cabernet Sauvignon El Dorado 1988 $11 (4/15/92) **84**
Cabernet Sauvignon El Dorado 1984 $9 (3/31/88) **86**
Chardonnay El Dorado 1989 $12 (3/31/92) **80**
Syrah El Dorado Sierra 1985 $9.75 (4/15/89) **82**
Syrah El Dorado Sierra 1983 $9 (4/15/89) **89**
Zinfandel El Dorado 1989 $9 (3/31/92) **78**
Zinfandel El Dorado Herbert Vineyards 1986 $8 (3/31/89) **84**
Zinfandel El Dorado Reeves Vineyard Special Reserve 1985 $12 (4/30/88) **73**

CHATEAU SIGALAS RABAUD (France/Sauternes)
Sauternes 1989 ($NA) (6/15/90) (BT) **90+**
Sauternes 1986 $42 (12/31/89) **77**
Sauternes 1985 $41 (7/15/88) **82**
Sauternes 1983 $24 (1/31/88) **88**

SIGNORELLO (United States/California)
Cabernet Sauvignon Napa Valley Founder's Reserve 1988 $25 (5/15/91) **92**
Chardonnay Napa Valley 1990 $15 (6/30/92) **88**
Chardonnay Napa Valley 1989 $15 (7/15/91) **85**
Chardonnay Napa Valley 1988 $14.50 (2/28/91) **87**
Chardonnay Napa Valley Founder's Reserve 1990 $25 (5/31/92) **82**
Chardonnay Napa Valley Founder's Reserve 1989 $25 (7/15/91) **78**
Chardonnay Napa Valley Founder's Reserve 1986 $13 (7/15/89) **77**
Chardonnay Napa Valley Founder's Reserve 1985 $12 (2/15/88) **82**
Pinot Noir Napa Valley 1988 $25 (2/28/91) **85**
Pinot Noir Napa Valley Founder's Reserve 1989 $25 (11/15/91) **78**
Sauvignon Blanc Napa Valley 1987 $8.25 (4/30/89) **78**

SILVER CLOUD (France/Other)
Brut Blanc de Blancs Blanquette de Limoux 1985 $9 (4/15/90) **85**

SILVER FALLS (United States/Oregon)
Pinot Noir Willamette Valley 1987 $10 (2/15/90) **75**

SILVER LAKE (United States/Washington)
Chardonnay Columbia Valley Reserve 1989 $16 (5/31/91) **88**
Ice Wine Columbia Valley 1989 $25/375ml (6/15/91) **85**
Riesling Columbia Valley Dry 1989 $6 (6/15/91) BB **87**

SILVER OAK (United States/California)
Cabernet Sauvignon Alexander Valley 1987 Rel: $29 Cur: $31 (10/15/91) **89**
Cabernet Sauvignon Alexander Valley 1986 Rel: $26 Cur: $37 (10/31/90) SS **93**
Cabernet Sauvignon Alexander Valley 1985 Rel: $24 Cur: $61 (10/31/89) **86**
Cabernet Sauvignon Alexander Valley 1984 Rel: $22 Cur: $62 (CA-3/89) **89**
Cabernet Sauvignon Alexander Valley 1983 Rel: $20 Cur: $39 (CA-3/89) **86**
Cabernet Sauvignon Alexander Valley 1982 Rel: $19 Cur: $83 (CA-3/89) **90**
Cabernet Sauvignon Alexander Valley 1981 Rel: $19 Cur: $69 (CA-3/89) **86**
Cabernet Sauvignon Alexander Valley 1980 Rel: $18 Cur: $69 (CA-3/89) **88**
Cabernet Sauvignon Alexander Valley 1979 Rel: $16 Cur: $70 (CA-3/89) **85**
Cabernet Sauvignon Alexander Valley 1978 Rel: $16 Cur: $110 (CA-3/89) **93**
Cabernet Sauvignon Alexander Valley 1977 Rel: $14 Cur: $85 (CA-3/89) **88**
Cabernet Sauvignon Alexander Valley 1976 Rel: $12 Cur: $65 (CA-3/89) **86**
Cabernet Sauvignon Alexander Valley 1975 Rel: $10 Cur: $60 (CA-3/89) **88**
Cabernet Sauvignon Napa Valley 1987 Rel: $29 Cur: $34 (10/15/91) **89**
Cabernet Sauvignon Napa Valley 1986 Rel: $26 Cur: $49 (10/31/90) CS **94**
Cabernet Sauvignon Napa Valley 1985 Rel: $24 Cur: $68 (10/31/89) **88**
Cabernet Sauvignon Napa Valley 1984 Rel: $22 Cur: $55 (CA-3/89) **86**
Cabernet Sauvignon Napa Valley 1983 Rel: $20 Cur: $37 (CA-3/89) **74**
Cabernet Sauvignon Napa Valley 1982 Rel: $19 Cur: $61 (2/15/87) CS **96**
Cabernet Sauvignon Napa Valley 1981 Rel: $19 Cur: $58 (CA-3/89) **79**
Cabernet Sauvignon Napa Valley 1980 Rel: $18 Cur: $80 (CA-3/89) **73**
Cabernet Sauvignon Napa Valley 1979 Rel: $18 Cur: $75 (CA-3/89) **82**
Cabernet Sauvignon Napa Valley Bonny's Vineyard 1986 Rel: $50 Cur: $60 (10/15/91) **88**
Cabernet Sauvignon Napa Valley Bonny's Vineyard 1985 Rel: $50 Cur: $74 (11/15/90) **83**

Key to Symbols

The scores reported here are the results of blind tastings conducted by our panel of senior editors. Wines that carry the initials below are results of individual tastings.

THE WINE SPECTATOR 100-POINT SCALE ***95-100***—Classic, a great wine; ***90-94***—Outstanding, superior character and style; ***80-89***—Good to very good, a wine with special qualities; ***70-79***—Average, drinkable wine that may have minor flaws; ***60-69***—Below average, drinkable but not recommended; ***50-59***—Poor, undrinkable, not recommended. "+"—With a score indicates a range; used primarily with barrel tastings to indicate a preliminary score.

SPECIAL DESIGNATIONS SS—Spectator Selection, CS—Cellar Selection, BB—Best Buy, ($NA)—Price not available, (NR)—Not released.

TASTER'S INITIALS (JG)—Jim Gordon, (HS)—Harvey Steiman, (JL)—James Laube, (JS)—James Suckling, (TM)—Thomas Matthews, (TR)—Terry Robards, (PM)—Per-Henrik Mansson, (BT)—Barrel Tasting (these wines were tasted blind from barrel samples), (CA-date)—*California's Great Cabernets* by James Laube, (CH-date)—*California's Great Chardonnays* by James Laube, (VP-date)—*Vintage Port* by James Suckling.

DATE TASTED Dates in parentheses represent the issue in which the rating was published.

Cabernet Sauvignon Napa Valley Bonny's Vineyard 1984 Rel: $45 Cur: $80 (10/15/89) **84**
Cabernet Sauvignon Napa Valley Bonny's Vineyard 1983 Rel: $40 Cur: $55 (CA-3/89) **82**
Cabernet Sauvignon Napa Valley Bonny's Vineyard 1982 Rel: $35 Cur: $57 (CA-3/89) **78**
Cabernet Sauvignon Napa Valley Bonny's Vineyard 1981 Rel: $35 Cur: $58 (CA-3/89) **77**
Cabernet Sauvignon Napa Valley Bonny's Vineyard 1980 Rel: $30 Cur: $60 (CA-3/89) **70**
Cabernet Sauvignon Napa Valley Bonny's Vineyard 1979 Rel: $30 Cur: $60 (CA-3/89) **72**
Cabernet Sauvignon North Coast 1974 Rel: $8 Cur: $115 (CA-3/89) **93**
Cabernet Sauvignon North Coast 1973 Rel: $7 Cur: $130 (CA-3/89) **81**
Cabernet Sauvignon North Coast 1972 Rel: $6 Cur: $135 (CA-3/89) **86**

SILVERADO (United States/California)
Cabernet Sauvignon Stags Leap District 1988 $16 (3/31/91) **86**
Cabernet Sauvignon Stags Leap District 1987 Rel: $14 Cur: $21 (4/15/90) SS **92**
Cabernet Sauvignon Stags Leap District 1986 Rel: $13.50 Cur: $25 (8/31/89) SS **94**
Cabernet Sauvignon Stags Leap District 1985 Rel: $12.50 Cur: $36 (11/15/88) SS **91**
Cabernet Sauvignon Stags Leap District 1984 Rel: $11.50 Cur: $26 (CA-3/89) **91**
Cabernet Sauvignon Stags Leap District 1983 Rel: $11 Cur: $22 (CA-3/89) **88**
Cabernet Sauvignon Stags Leap District 1982 Rel: $11 Cur: $25 (CA-3/89) **88**
Cabernet Sauvignon Stags Leap District 1981 Rel: $11 Cur: $30 (CA-3/89) **90**
Cabernet Sauvignon Stags Leap District Limited Reserve 1987 Rel: $38 Cur: $43 (10/31/91) **93**
Cabernet Sauvignon Stags Leap District Limited Reserve 1986 Rel: $35 Cur: $39 (12/15/90) CS **96**
Chardonnay Napa Valley 1990 $14.50 (4/15/92) **81**
Chardonnay Napa Valley 1989 $14.50 (3/31/91) **86**
Chardonnay Napa Valley 1988 Rel: $14 Cur: $17 (11/30/89) **88**
Chardonnay Napa Valley 1987 Rel: $13.50 Cur: $17 (CH-3/90) **88**
Chardonnay Napa Valley 1986 Rel: $12 Cur: $20 (CH-3/90) **90**
Chardonnay Napa Valley 1985 Rel: $11.50 Cur: $17 (CH-3/90) **87**
Chardonnay Napa Valley 1984 Rel: $11 Cur: $20 (CH-3/90) **81**
Chardonnay Napa Valley 1983 Rel: $11 Cur: $20 (CH-3/90) **84**
Chardonnay Napa Valley 1982 Rel: $10 Cur: $20 (CH-3/90) **73**
Chardonnay Napa Valley 1981 Rel: $10 Cur: $20 (CH-3/90) **70**
Chardonnay Napa Valley Limited Reserve 1987 Rel: $30 Cur: $33 (8/31/91) **92**
Chardonnay Napa Valley Limited Reserve 1986 Rel: $25 Cur: $35 (11/15/90) **93**
Merlot Stags Leap District 1989 $16 (4/15/92) **87**
Merlot Stags Leap District 1988 $15.50 (5/31/91) **86**
Merlot Stags Leap District 1987 $14 (4/15/90) **92**
Merlot Stags Leap District 1986 $12 (8/31/89) **91**
Merlot Stags Leap District 1984 $12.50 (12/15/87) **78**
Sauvignon Blanc Napa Valley 1990 $9 (11/30/91) **84**
Sauvignon Blanc Napa Valley 1989 $9 (10/31/90) **83**
Sauvignon Blanc Napa Valley 1988 $8.50 (2/15/90) SS **90**

SILVERADO CELLARS (United States/California)
Chardonnay California 1988 $11 (6/30/90) **90**

SILVERADO HILL CELLARS (United States/California)
Chardonnay Napa Valley 1990 $10 (6/30/92) **86**
Chardonnay Napa Valley 1989 $10 (7/15/91) **82**
Chardonnay Napa Valley Winemaker's Traditional Méthode 1988 $10 (7/15/91) **73**

SIMI (United States/California)
Cabernet Sauvignon Alexander Valley 1986 $15.50 (9/30/90) **88**
Cabernet Sauvignon Alexander Valley 1981 Rel: $11 Cur: $20 (11/01/85) **79**
Cabernet Sauvignon Alexander Valley 1980 Rel: $10 Cur: $28 (7/01/84) **81**
Cabernet Sauvignon Alexander Valley 1979 Rel: $9 Cur: $28 (4/01/84) SS **91**
Cabernet Sauvignon Alexander Valley 1975 Rel: $6 Cur: $32 (CA-3/89) **85**
Cabernet Sauvignon Alexander Valley 1973 Rel: $6 Cur: $25 (CA-3/89) **72**
Cabernet Sauvignon Alexander Valley 1972 Rel: $5 Cur: $25 (CA-3/89) **80**
Cabernet Sauvignon Alexander Valley 1971 Rel: $5 Cur: $30 (CA-3/89) **75**
Cabernet Sauvignon Alexander Valley 1970 Rel: $4.50 Cur: $48 (CA-3/89) **73'**
Cabernet Sauvignon Alexander Valley Reserve 1987 $28 (4/15/89) (BT) **90+**
Cabernet Sauvignon Alexander Valley Reserve 1986 Rel: $30 Cur: $34 (7/31/91) **89**
Cabernet Sauvignon Alexander Valley Reserve 1985 Rel: $25 Cur: $29 (8/31/90) SS **94**
Cabernet Sauvignon Alexander Valley Reserve 1985 Rel: $25 Cur: $29 (CA-3/89) **94**
Cabernet Sauvignon Alexander Valley Reserve 1984 Rel: $22.50 Cur: $26 (CA-3/89) **92**
Cabernet Sauvignon Alexander Valley Reserve 1981 Rel: $25 Cur: $30 (12/15/88) **86**
Cabernet Sauvignon Alexander Valley Reserve 1980 Rel: $20 Cur: $25 (CA-3/89) **84**
Cabernet Sauvignon Alexander Valley Reserve 1979 Rel: $20 Cur: $36 (CA-3/89) **87**
Cabernet Sauvignon Alexander Valley Reserve 1978 Rel: $17 Cur: $42 (CA-3/89) **72**
Cabernet Sauvignon Alexander Valley Special Selection 1977 Rel: $20 Cur: $23 (CA-3/89) **70**
Cabernet Sauvignon Alexander Valley Reserve 1974 Rel: $20 Cur: $62 (2/15/90) (JG) **85**
Cabernet Sauvignon Alexander Valley Reserve Vintage 1974 Rel: $20 Cur: $62 (CA-3/89) **87**
Cabernet Sauvignon Alexander Valley Special Reserve 1974 Rel: $20 Cur: $62 (CA-3/89) **83**
Cabernet Sauvignon Sonoma County 1987 $16.50 (5/15/91) **89**
Cabernet Sauvignon Sonoma County 1985 Rel: $13 Cur: $21 (9/30/89) **91**
Cabernet Sauvignon Sonoma County 1984 Rel: $11 Cur: $20 (10/31/88) **86**
Cabernet Sauvignon Sonoma County 1982 Rel: $12 Cur: $15 (11/15/86) **90**
Cabernet Sauvignon Sonoma-Napa Counties Reserve 1982 Rel: $20 Cur: $28 (4/15/89) **90**
Chardonnay Mendocino-Sonoma-Napa Counties 1990 $12 (7/15/92) **81**
Chardonnay Mendocino-Sonoma-Napa Counties 1989 $15.50 (5/31/91) **88**
Chardonnay Mendocino-Sonoma-Napa Counties 1987 $14 (11/30/89) **91**
Chardonnay Mendocino-Sonoma-Napa Counties 1986 $12 (2/15/89) **84**
Chardonnay Mendocino-Sonoma Counties 1985 $11 (3/15/88) **89**
Chardonnay Mendocino-Sonoma Counties 1984 $13 (10/31/86) **77**
Chardonnay Mendocino-Sonoma Counties 1983 $12 (10/01/85) **87**
Chardonnay Mendocino County 1981 $11 (6/01/86) **86**
Chardonnay Sonoma County 1988 $16 (6/15/90) **87**
Chardonnay Sonoma County 1982 $11 (10/16/84) **90**
Chardonnay Sonoma County Reserve 1988 $32 (5/31/92) **89**
Chardonnay Sonoma County Reserve 1987 $32 (7/15/91) **92**
Chardonnay Sonoma County Reserve 1986 Rel: $28 Cur: $35 (9/15/90) **92**
Chardonnay Sonoma County Reserve 1985 Rel: $28 Cur: $32 (CH-4/90) **91**
Chardonnay Sonoma County Reserve 1984 Rel: $28 Cur: $32 (CH-4/90) **89**
Chardonnay Sonoma County Reserve 1983 Rel: $22 Cur: $32 (CH-4/90) **88**
Chardonnay Sonoma County Reserve 1982 Rel: $22 Cur: $60 (CH-4/90) **94**
Chardonnay Sonoma County Reserve 1982 Rel: $22 Cur: $60 (5/01/86) SS **96**
Chardonnay Sonoma County Reserve 1981 Rel: $20 Cur: $40 (CH-4/90) **91**
Chardonnay Sonoma County Reserve 1980 Rel: $20 Cur: $40 (CH-4/90) **94**
Chardonnay Mendocino County Reserve 1980 Rel: $20 Cur: $40 (4/16/84) **93**
Chenin Blanc Mendocino 1987 $6.50 (7/31/89) **83**
Pinot Noir North Coast 1981 $7 (9/16/85) **64**
Rosé of Cabernet Sauvignon Sonoma County 1990 $7 (4/30/92) **77**
Rosé of Cabernet Sauvignon Sonoma County 1988 $7 (11/15/89) **81**
Sauvignon Blanc Mendocino-Sonoma-Napa Counties 1990 $9 (2/15/92) **83**
Sauvignon Blanc Sonoma County 1989 $9.50 (4/30/91) **84**
Sauvignon Blanc Sonoma County 1988 $8 (10/31/90) **90**
Sauvignon Blanc Sonoma County 1987 $9.50 (7/31/89) **72**
Zinfandel Sonoma County 1982 $6.25 (5/01/86) **60**

CHATEAU SIMIAN (France/Rhône)
Châteauneuf-du-Pape 1988 $20 (7/15/91) **86**

BERT SIMON (Germany)
Riesling Auslese Mosel-Saar-Ruwer Gold Cap Serriger Würtzberg 1990 $30 (12/15/91) **91**
Riesling Auslese Mosel-Saar-Ruwer Kaseler Gold Cap 1989 $32 (12/15/90) **84**
Riesling Auslese Mosel-Saar-Ruwer Patheiger Kaseler Kehrnagel Long Gold Cap 1989 $24/375ml (12/15/90) **86**
Riesling Auslese Mosel-Saar-Ruwer Serriger Herrenberg 1990 $21 (12/15/91) **84**
Riesling Auslese Mosel-Saar-Ruwer Serriger Würtzberg 1990 $21 (12/15/91) **88**
Riesling Auslese Mosel-Saar-Ruwer Serriger Würtzberg 1988 ($NA) (9/30/89) **87**
Riesling Auslese Mosel-Saar-Ruwer Serriger Würtzberg Gold Cap 1989 $31 (12/15/90) **86**
Riesling Auslese Mosel-Saar-Ruwer Serringer Herrenberg 1989 $21 (12/15/90) **85**
Riesling Beerenauslese Mosel-Saar-Ruwer Serriger Würtzberg 1989 $53/375ml (12/15/90) **93**
Riesling Kabinett Halbtrocken Mosel-Saar-Ruwer Mertesdorfer Herrenberg 1989 $13 (12/15/90) **79**
Riesling Kabinett Mosel-Saar-Ruwer Eitelsbacher Marienholz 1990 $11 (12/15/91) **85**
Riesling Kabinett Mosel-Saar-Ruwer Eitelsbacher Marienholz 1989 $13 (12/15/90) **87**
Riesling Kabinett Mosel-Saar-Ruwer Serriger Herrenberg 1990 $11 (12/15/91) **84**
Riesling Kabinett Mosel-Saar-Ruwer Serriger Würtzberg 1990 $11 (12/15/91) **84**
Riesling Kabinett Mosel-Saar-Ruwer Serriger Würtzberg 1989 $13 (12/15/90) **84**
Riesling Kabinett Mosel-Saar-Ruwer Serriger Würtzberg 1988 ($NA) (9/30/89) **82**
Riesling Kabinett Mosel-Saar-Ruwer Serringer Herrenberg 1989 $11.50 (12/15/90) **85**
Riesling Qualitätswein Mosel-Saar-Ruwer 1988 $6 (9/30/89) **84**
Riesling Spätlese Mosel-Saar-Ruwer Kastel-Staadt Maximiner Prälat 1989 $13 (12/15/90) **85**
Riesling Spätlese Mosel-Saar-Ruwer Patheiger Kaseler Kehrnagel 1990 $13 (12/15/91) **86**
Riesling Spätlese Mosel-Saar-Ruwer Patheiger Kaseler Kehrnagel 1989 $15 (12/15/90) **78**
Riesling Spätlese Mosel-Saar-Ruwer Serriger Würtzberg 1990 $13 (12/15/91) **87**
Riesling Spätlese Mosel-Saar-Ruwer Serriger Würtzberg 1989 $15 (12/15/90) **87**
Riesling Spätlese Mosel-Saar-Ruwer Serriger Würtzberg 1988 ($NA) (9/30/89) **90**
Riesling Trockenbeerenauslese Mosel-Saar-Ruwer Serriger Würtzberg 1989 $96/375ml (12/15/90) **95**

SIMONNET-FEBVRE (France/Chablis)
Chablis 1986 $12 (5/15/88) **68**
Chablis Les Clos 1986 $29 (7/15/88) **55**
Chablis Les Vaillons 1986 $17 (5/15/88) **76**

ROBERT SINSKEY (United States/California)
Claret RSV Carneros Carneros 1988 $28 (11/15/91) **89**
Chardonnay Carneros 1988 $16 (2/28/91) **87**
Chardonnay Carneros Napa Valley 1987 $16 (10/31/89) **88**
Chardonnay Carneros Napa Valley 1986 $16.50 (7/31/88) **75**
Chardonnay Carneros Napa Valley Selected Cuvée 1989 $16 (7/15/91) **84**
Merlot Napa Valley 1987 $18 (3/31/91) **88**
Merlot Napa Valley 1986 $17 (10/15/89) **83**
Merlot Napa Valley Los Carneros 1989 $18 (5/31/92) **83**
Merlot Napa Valley Los Carneros Aries 1989 $18 (5/31/92) **86**
Pinot Noir Carneros 1988 $18 (2/28/91) **81**
Pinot Noir Carneros Napa Valley 1987 $14 (3/31/90) **86**
Pinot Noir Carneros Napa Valley 1986 $12 (6/15/88) **79**

LOUIS SIPP (France/Alsace)
Gewürztraminer Alsace 1990 (NR) (2/15/92) **87**
Gewürztraminer Alsace Osterberg Cuvée Particulière de Nos Vignobles 1990 (NR) (2/15/92) **92**
Gewürztraminer Alsace Sélection de Grains Nobles 1990 (NR) (2/15/92) (BT) **90+**
Gewürztraminer Alsace Vendange Tardive 1990 (NR) (2/15/92) (BT) **90+**
Pinot Blanc Alsace 1990 (NR) (2/15/92) **85**
Riesling Alsace 1990 (NR) (2/15/92) **87**
Riesling Alsace Kirchberg de Barr Cuvée Particulière de Nos Vignobles 1990 (NR) (2/15/92) **89**
Tokay Pinot Gris Alsace Barrique 1990 (NR) (2/15/92) **85**
Tokay Pinot Gris Alsace Vendange Tardive 1990 (NR) (2/15/92) (BT) **85+**

CHATEAU SIRAN (France/Bordeaux)
Margaux 1991 (NR) (5/15/92) (BT) **80+**
Margaux 1990 (NR) (4/30/91) (BT) **85+**
Margaux 1989 $25 (3/15/92) **88**
Margaux 1988 Rel: $19 Cur: $22 (6/30/91) **88**
Margaux 1987 $14 (6/30/89) (BT) **75+**
Margaux 1985 $15 (9/30/88) **90**

SIRIUS (France/Bordeaux)
Bordeaux 1988 $15 (8/31/91) **77**
Bordeaux Blanc 1988 $15 (9/15/91) **79**

DOMAINE SIRUGUE (France/Burgundy)
Côte de Nuits-Villages Clos de la Belle Marguerite 1988 $16 (3/31/91) **83**

SISKIYOU (United States/Oregon)
Pinot Noir Oregon Estate 1987 $13 (2/15/90) **80**

SKY (United States/California)
Zinfandel Napa Valley 1988 $12 (8/31/91) **78**
Zinfandel Napa Valley 1987 Rel: $12 Cur: $17 (10/15/90) **90**
Zinfandel Napa Valley 1985 $9 (10/31/88) **88**

SLAUGHTER LEFTWICH (United States/Texas)
Cabernet Sauvignon Texas 1989 $9 (2/29/92) **76**
Sauvignon Blanc Texas 1990 $7 (2/29/92) **80**

CHATEAU SMITH-HAUT-LAFITTE (France/Bordeaux)
Pessac-Léognan 1991 (NR) (5/15/92) (BT) **85+**
Pessac-Léognan 1990 (NR) (4/30/91) (BT) **85+**
Pessac-Léognan 1989 $19 (3/15/92) **91**
Pessac-Léognan 1988 $15 (6/30/89) (BT) **80+**
Pessac-Léognan 1987 $15 (5/15/90) **84**
Pessac-Léognan 1986 $15 (6/30/88) (BT) **85+**
Graves 1985 Rel: $15 Cur: $23 (11/30/88) **89**
Graves 1981 Rel: $12 Cur: $18 (6/01/84) **79**
Graves 1979 $20 (10/15/89) (JS) **69**
Pessac-Léognan Blanc 1990 (NR) (9/30/91) (BT) **80+**
Pessac-Léognan Blanc 1989 $30 (9/30/91) **88**
Pessac-Léognan Blanc 1988 $30 (6/30/89) (BT) **80+**
Pessac-Léognan Blanc 1987 $17 (6/30/89) (BT) **85+**

SMITH & HOOK (United States/California)
Cabernet Sauvignon Monterey Santa Lucia Highlands 1988 $15 (11/15/91) **80**
Cabernet Sauvignon Monterey 1983 $13.50 (11/15/87) **78**
Cabernet Sauvignon Monterey County 1981 $13.50 (12/16/84) **90**
Cabernet Sauvignon Napa County 1985 $12 (9/30/89) **88**
Cabernet Sauvignon Napa County 1982 $17 (6/15/87) **79**
Merlot Monterey Santa Lucia Highlands 1989 $15 (5/31/92) **70**
Merlot Monterey Santa Lucia Highlands 1988 $15 (5/31/92) **80**

Merlot Napa County 1987 $15 (12/31/90) **83**
Merlot Napa County 1986 $20 (8/31/89) **86**

SMITH-MADRONE (United States/California)
Cabernet Sauvignon Napa Valley 1985 Rel: $14 Cur: $19 (4/15/90) **74**
Cabernet Sauvignon Napa Valley 1984 Rel: $14 Cur: $25 (CA-3/89) **91**
Cabernet Sauvignon Napa Valley 1983 Rel: $12.50 Cur: $16 (CA-3/89) **84**
Cabernet Sauvignon Napa Valley 1982 Rel: $12.50 Cur: $16 (CA-3/89) **79**
Cabernet Sauvignon Napa Valley 1981 Rel: $12.50 Cur: $16 (CA-3/89) **78**
Cabernet Sauvignon Napa Valley 1980 Rel: $12.50 Cur: $18 (CA-3/89) **79**
Cabernet Sauvignon Napa Valley 1979 Rel: $14 Cur: $25 (CA-3/89) **86**
Cabernet Sauvignon Napa Valley 1978 Rel: $14 Cur: $25 (CA-3/89) **84**
Chardonnay Napa Valley 1988 $13 (CH-5/90) **88**
Chardonnay Napa Valley 1987 $13 (CH-5/90) **91**
Chardonnay Napa Valley 1986 Rel: $12.50 Cur: $16 (CH-5/90) **89**
Chardonnay Napa Valley 1985 Rel: $12.50 Cur: $16 (CH-5/90) **87**
Chardonnay Napa Valley 1984 Rel: $12 Cur: $16 (CH-5/90) **80**
Chardonnay Napa Valley 1983 Rel: $12 Cur: $15 (CH-5/90) **71**
Chardonnay Napa Valley 1982 Rel: $12 Cur: $18 (CH-5/90) **86**
Chardonnay Napa Valley 1981 Rel: $12 Cur: $18 (CH-5/90) **81**
Chardonnay Napa Valley 1980 Rel: $11 Cur: $20 (CH-5/90) **85**
Chardonnay Napa Valley 1979 Rel: $10 Cur: $28 (CH-5/90) **92**
Chardonnay Napa Valley 1978 Rel: $10 Cur: $30 (CH-5/90) **86**
Pinot Noir Napa Valley 1984 $10 (12/15/87) **65**
Riesling Napa Valley 1988 $8.50 (9/15/90) **76**

SMITH WOODHOUSE (Portugal)
Vintage Port 1985 Rel: $22 Cur: $37 (VP-6/90) **89**
Vintage Port 1983 Rel: $22 Cur: $37 (VP-6/90) **92**
Vintage Port 1980 Rel: $15 Cur: $36 (VP-6/90) **90**
Vintage Port 1977 Rel: $11 Cur: $50 (VP-2/90) **89**
Vintage Port 1975 $40 (VP-2/90) **80**
Vintage Port 1970 $51 (VP-2/90) **86**
Vintage Port 1966 $88 (VP-2/90) **83**
Vintage Port 1963 $100 (VP-2/90) **89**

SNOQUALMIE (United States/Washington)
Cabernet Sauvignon Columbia Valley 1987 $10 (9/30/90) **90**
Chardonnay Columbia Valley 1987 $8 (10/15/89) **83**
Chardonnay Columbia Valley Reserve 1987 $13 (10/15/89) **85**
Chardonnay Yakima Valley 1984 $9 (4/16/86) **53**
Chardonnay Yakima Valley Early Release 1984 $7 (4/16/86) **70**
Chenin Blanc Columbia Valley 1988 $6 (10/15/89) **80**
Fumé Blanc Columbia Valley 1987 $7 (10/15/89) BB **88**
Gewürztraminer Columbia Valley 1988 $6 (10/15/89) **79**
Johannisberg Riesling Columbia Valley 1988 $6 (10/15/89) **80**
Johannisberg Riesling Columbia Valley RS 1.9% 1988 $6 (10/15/89) **81**
Merlot Columbia Valley Reserve 1987 $12 (9/30/90) **91**
Sémillon Columbia Valley 1988 $6 (10/15/89) **74**
White Riesling Late Harvest Columbia Valley 1988 $7 (10/15/89) **84**

SOBON ESTATE (United States/California)
Cabernet Sauvignon Shenandoah Valley 1987 $15 (11/30/90) **83**
Zinfandel Shenandoah Valley 1988 $10 (11/30/90) **88**

CHATEAU SOCIANDO-MALLET (France/Bordeaux)
Haut-Médoc 1991 (NR) (5/15/92) (BT) **85+**
Haut-Médoc 1990 (NR) (4/30/91) (BT) **85+**
Haut-Médoc 1989 $32 (3/15/92) **90**
Haut-Médoc 1988 $26 (3/31/91) **87**
Haut-Médoc 1987 $15 (5/15/90) **88**
Haut-Médoc 1986 $25 (11/30/89) (JS) **94**
Haut-Médoc 1985 Rel: $17 Cur: $24 (4/30/88) **85**
Haut-Médoc 1984 Rel: $11 Cur: $17 (3/31/87) **84**
Haut-Médoc 1983 Rel: $15 Cur: $26 (4/16/86) **77**
Haut-Médoc 1982 $43 (11/30/89) (JS) **92**

SODA CANYON (United States/California)
Chardonnay Napa Valley 8th Leaf 1986 $11 (10/15/88) **78**
Chardonnay Napa Valley 12th Leaf 1990 $10 (3/31/92) **88**

SOKOL BLOSSER (United States/Oregon)
Chardonnay Yamhill County Redland 1988 $12 (3/31/91) **87**
Pinot Noir Willamette Valley Red Hills Vineyard 1985 ($NA) (9/30/87) **92**
Pinot Noir Yamhill County 1986 $10 (6/15/88) **59**
Pinot Noir Yamhill County 1982 $8.95 (2/16/85) **63**
Pinot Noir Yamhill County Hyland Vineyards 1986 $15 (6/15/88) **79**
Pinot Noir Yamhill County Hyland Vineyards 1985 $15 (6/15/87) **86**
Pinot Noir Yamhill County Hyland Vineyards 1983 $14 (8/31/86) **82**
Pinot Noir Yamhill County Hyland Vineyards Reserve 1985 $18 (6/15/88) **86**
Pinot Noir Yamhill County Hyland Vineyards Reserve 1983 $30 (2/15/90) **67**
Pinot Noir Yamhill County Red Hills 1986 $15 (6/15/88) **77**
Pinot Noir Yamhill County Red Hills 1985 $15 (6/15/87) **80**
Pinot Noir Yamhill County Red Hills Reserve 1985 $30 (2/15/90) **74**
Pinot Noir Yamhill County Redland 1988 $13 (4/15/91) **82**
Pinot Noir Yamhill County Redland 1987 $13 (2/15/90) **66**

SOLARI (United States/California)
Cabernet Sauvignon Napa Valley Larkmead Vineyards 1985 $10 (3/15/90) **80**
Cabernet Sauvignon Napa Valley Larkmead Vineyards 1984 $12 (4/15/88) **80**

SOLDERA (Italy/Tuscany)
Brunello di Montalcino 1985 $90 (7/15/91) **89**

Key to Symbols

The scores reported here are the results of blind tastings conducted by our panel of senior editors. Wines that carry the initials below are results of individual tastings.

THE WINE SPECTATOR 100-POINT SCALE ***95-100***—Classic, a great wine; ***90-94***—Outstanding, superior character and style; ***80-89***—Good to very good, a wine with special qualities; ***70-79***—Average, drinkable wine that may have minor flaws; ***60-69***—Below average, drinkable but not recommended; ***50-59***—Poor, undrinkable, not recommended. "+"—With a score indicates a range; used primarily with barrel tastings to indicate a preliminary score.

SPECIAL DESIGNATIONS SS—Spectator Selection, CS—Cellar Selection, BB—Best Buy, ($NA)—Price not available, (NR)—Not released.

TASTER'S INITIALS (JG)—Jim Gordon, (HS)—Harvey Steiman, (JL)—James Laube, (JS)—James Suckling, (TM)—Thomas Matthews, (TR)—Terry Robards, (PM)—Per-Henrik Mansson, (BT)—Barrel Tasting (these wines were tasted blind from barrel samples), (CA-date)—*California's Great Cabernets* by James Laube, (CH-date)—*California's Great Chardonnays* by James Laube, (VP-date)—*Vintage Port* by James Suckling.

DATE TASTED Dates in parentheses represent the issue in which the rating was published.

SOLETERRA (United States/California)
Pinot Noir Napa Valley Three Palms Vineyard 1982 $12 (10/16/84) **80**

SOLICHIATA (Italy/Other)
Torrepalino 1987 $5.75 (4/15/90) **73**

SOLIS (United States/California)
Chardonnay Santa Clara County 1989 $12.50 (7/15/91) **76**
Merlot Monterey County 1988 $10.50 (5/31/92) **73**
Pinot Noir Santa Clara County 1988 $9 (4/30/91) **78**

DOMAINE DE LA SOLITUDE (France/Rhône)
Châteauneuf-du-Pape 1989 $19 (5/31/92) **86**

SONOITA (United States/Arizona)
Cabernet Sauvignon Soñoita Private Reserve 1987 $15 (2/29/92) **79**
Cabernet Sauvignon Soñoita Private Reserve 1985 $22 (2/29/92) **71**
Pinot Noir Soñoita 1989 $30 (2/29/92) **75**

SONOMA CREEK (United States/California)
Cabernet Sauvignon Sonoma Valley 1988 $12 (11/15/91) **74**
Chardonnay Carneros Barrel Fermented 1989 $10 (11/30/91) **89**

SONOMA-CUTRER (United States/California)
Chardonnay Sonoma Coast Cutrer Vineyard 1990 $18 (5/31/92) **87**
Chardonnay Sonoma Coast Cutrer Vineyard 1988 Rel: $17.50 Cur: $20 (12/31/90) **89**
Chardonnay Russian River Valley Cutrer Vineyard 1987 Rel: $17.50 Cur: $24 (CH-3/90) **91**
Chardonnay Russian River Valley Cutrer Vineyard 1986 Rel: $16 Cur: $24 (CH-3/90) **89**
Chardonnay Russian River Valley Cutrer Vineyard 1985 Rel: $14.75 Cur: $29 (CH-3/90) **87**
Chardonnay Russian River Valley Cutrer Vineyard 1984 Rel: $14.25 Cur: $25 (CH-3/90) **87**
Chardonnay Russian River Valley Cutrer Vineyard 1983 Rel: $13.75 Cur: $25 (CH-3/90) **86**
Chardonnay Russian River Valley Cutrer Vineyard 1982 Rel: $13 Cur: $25 (CH-3/90) **87**
Chardonnay Russian River Valley Cutrer Vineyard 1981 Rel: $12.50 Cur: $30 (CH-3/90) **91**
Chardonnay Sonoma Coast Les Pierres 1989 $23 (1/31/91) **86**
Chardonnay Sonoma Coast Russian River Ranches 1990 $13.50 (5/31/92) **86**
Chardonnay Sonoma Coast Russian River Ranches 1989 $14 (7/15/91) **82**
Chardonnay Sonoma Valley Les Pierres 1988 Rel: $22.50 Cur: $25 (CH-7/90) **93**
Chardonnay Sonoma Valley Les Pierres 1987 Rel: $22.50 Cur: $27 (CH-3/90) **92**
Chardonnay Sonoma Valley Les Pierres 1986 Rel: $19.50 Cur: $34 (CH-3/90) **88**
Chardonnay Sonoma Valley Les Pierres 1985 Rel: $17.50 Cur: $47 (9/30/87) SS **93**
Chardonnay Sonoma Valley Les Pierres 1984 Rel: $16.50 Cur: $75 (CH-3/90) **89**
Chardonnay Sonoma Valley Les Pierres 1983 Rel: $15.50 Cur: $50 (CH-3/90) **86**
Chardonnay Sonoma Valley Les Pierres 1982 Rel: $15 Cur: $35 (CH-3/90) **88**
Chardonnay Sonoma Valley Les Pierres 1981 Rel: $14.50 Cur: $53 (CH-3/90) **94**
Chardonnay Russian River Valley Russian River Ranches 1988 Rel: $13.25 Cur: $20 (6/30/90) **88**
Chardonnay Russian River Valley Russian River Ranches 1987 Rel: $12 Cur: $16 (CH-3/90) **88**
Chardonnay Russian River Valley Russian River Ranches 1986 Rel: $12 Cur: $20 (CH-3/90) **86**
Chardonnay Russian River Valley Russian River Ranches 1985 Rel: $11.50 Cur: $25 (CH-3/90) **88**
Chardonnay Russian River Valley Russian River Ranches 1984 $11.25 (6/01/86) **88**
Chardonnay Russian River Valley Russian River Ranches 1983 Rel: $10.50 Cur: $25 (CH-3/90) **85**
Chardonnay Russian River Valley Russian River Ranches 1983 Rel: $10.50 Cur: $25 (11/16/85) SS **95**
Chardonnay Russian River Valley Russian River Ranches 1982 Rel: $10 Cur: $24 (CH-3/90) **87**
Chardonnay Russian River Valley Russian River Ranches 1982 Rel: $10 Cur: $24 (10/16/84) SS **92**
Chardonnay Russian River Valley Russian River Ranches 1981 Rel: $9.35 Cur: $40 (CH-3/90) **82**

SONOMA-LOEB (United States/California)
Cabernet Sauvignon Alexander Valley 1988 $10 (2/29/92) **82**
Chardonnay Alexander Valley 1990 $18 (2/29/92) **86**
Chardonnay Sonoma County Private Reserve 1990 $27 (2/29/92) **90**

SOQUEL (United States/California)
Chardonnay Santa Cruz Mountains 1990 $16 (7/15/92) **74**

SORBAIANO (Italy/Tuscany)
Montescudaio Rosso delle Minière 1988 $24 (8/31/91) **86**

H. SORREL (France/Rhône)
Hermitage 1985 $29 (7/31/88) **87**
Hermitage Blanc Les Rocoules 1984 $20 (5/01/86) **83**
Hermitage Le Gréal 1988 $49 (11/15/91) **88**
Hermitage Le Gréal 1983 $19 (5/01/86) **84**
Hermitage Le Gréal 1980 $25 (5/01/86) **74**
Hermitage Le Vignon 1988 $36 (8/31/91) **77**

SOTOYOME (United States/California)
Syrah Russian River Valley 1986 $7 (4/15/89) **85**
Syrah Russian River Valley 1985 $7 (4/15/89) **77**

CHATEAU SOUDARS (France/Bordeaux)
Haut-Médoc 1991 (NR) (5/15/92) (BT) **80+**
Haut-Médoc 1990 (NR) (4/30/91) (BT) **85+**
Haut-Médoc 1989 $18 (3/15/92) **85**
Haut-Médoc 1988 $15 (4/30/91) **88**
Haut-Médoc 1987 $12 (11/30/89) (JS) **77**
Haut-Médoc 1986 $13 (11/30/89) (JS) **79**

PIERRE & YVES SOULEZ (France/Loire)
Quarts de Chaume L'Amandier 1988 $28 (11/30/90) **84**
Savennières Château de Chamboureau 1986 $12 (2/28/89) **83**
Savennières Clos du Papillon 1989 $22.50 (9/30/91) **85**
Savennières Clos du Papillon 1986 $15 (2/28/89) **84**
Savennières Roche aux Moines Château de Chamboureau 1986 $19 (2/28/89) **77**

DOMAINE LA SOUMADE (France/Rhône)
Côtes du Rhône-Villages Rasteau 1986 $11 (2/28/90) **82**
Côtes du Rhône-Villages Rasteau Cuvée Réserve 1982 $5.50 (10/31/87) **69**

CHATEAU DE SOURS (France/Bordeaux)
Bordeaux Supérieur 1986 $7 (9/30/89) **78**

CHATEAU SOUTARD (France/Bordeaux)
St.-Emilion 1985 Rel: $20 Cur: $22 (5/15/88) **85**
St.-Emilion 1982 $30 (5/15/89) (TR) **84**

PIERRE SPARR (France/Alsace)
Gewürztraminer Alsace 1989 ($NA) (11/15/90) **79**
Gewürztraminer Alsace Brand 1990 $22 (2/15/92) **87**
Gewürztraminer Alsace Brand 1989 ($NA) (11/15/90) **88**
Gewürztraminer Alsace Carte d'Or 1990 $10 (2/15/92) **82**
Gewürztraminer Alsace Cuvée Centenaire Mambo Sélection de Grains Nobles 1989 ($NA) (11/15/90) **87**
Gewürztraminer Alsace Mambourg Cuvée Centenaire 1990 $18 (2/15/92) **86**
Gewürztraminer Alsace Mambourg Cuvée Centenaire Vendange Tardive 1989 ($NA) (11/15/90) **68**
Gewürztraminer Alsace Mambourg Vendange Tardive 1990 $37 (2/15/92) (BT) **70+**
Gewürztraminer Alsace Réserve 1990 $14 (2/15/92) **89**

Pinot Blanc Alsace Diamant d'Alsace 1990 $10 (2/15/92) **87**
Riesling Alsace Altenbourg Cuvée Centenaire 1989 ($NA) (11/15/90) **79**
Riesling Alsace Carte d'Or 1990 $10 (2/15/92) **81**
Riesling Alsace Carte d'Or Réserve 1990 $12 (2/15/92) **90**
Riesling Alsace Schlossberg Cuvée Réserve 1989 ($NA) (11/15/90) **86**
Tokay Pinot Gris Alsace Carte d'Or 1990 $9.50 (2/15/92) **85**
Tokay Pinot Gris Alsace Carte d'Or 1989 ($NA) (11/15/90) **88**
Tokay Pinot Gris Alsace Cuvée Centenaire Vendange Tardive 1989 ($NA) (11/15/90) **78**
Tokay Pinot Gris Alsace Cuvée Réserve 1990 $11 (2/15/92) **92**
Tokay Pinot Gris Alsace Prestige Tête de Cuvée 1989 ($NA) (11/15/90) **89**

SPOTTSWOODE (United States/California)
Cabernet Sauvignon Napa Valley 1990 (NR) (5/15/91) (BT) **90+**
Cabernet Sauvignon Napa Valley 1989 (NR) (5/15/91) (BT) **90+**
Cabernet Sauvignon Napa Valley 1988 Rel: $36 Cur: $42 (11/15/91) **90**
Cabernet Sauvignon Napa Valley 1987 Rel: $36 Cur: $60 (9/15/90) SS **96**
Cabernet Sauvignon Napa Valley 1986 Rel: $30 Cur: $100 (9/15/89) **95**
Cabernet Sauvignon Napa Valley 1985 Rel: $25 Cur: $122 (11/15/88) CS **95**
Cabernet Sauvignon Napa Valley 1984 Rel: $25 Cur: $75 (CA-3/89) **90**
Cabernet Sauvignon Napa Valley 1983 Rel: $25 Cur: $95 (CA-3/89) **89**
Cabernet Sauvignon Napa Valley 1982 Rel: $18 Cur: $110 (CA-3/89) **90**
Sauvignon Blanc Napa Valley 1989 $11 (8/31/90) **81**

SPRING MOUNTAIN (United States/California)
Cabernet Sauvignon Napa Valley 1988 ($NA) (5/15/90) (BT) **85+**
Cabernet Sauvignon Napa Valley 1986 ($NA) (CA-3/89) **90**
Cabernet Sauvignon Napa Valley 1985 $20 (10/15/89) **85**
Cabernet Sauvignon Napa Valley 1984 Rel: $15 Cur: $18 (3/15/89) **89**
Cabernet Sauvignon Napa Valley 1983 Rel: $15 Cur: $19 (CA-3/89) **79**
Cabernet Sauvignon Napa Valley 1982 Rel: $15 Cur: $18 (CA-3/89) **66**
Cabernet Sauvignon Napa Valley 1981 Rel: $14 Cur: $16 (CA-3/89) **78**
Cabernet Sauvignon Napa Valley 1980 Rel: $13 Cur: $19 (CA-3/89) **86**
Cabernet Sauvignon Napa Valley 1979 Rel: $13 Cur: $27 (CA-3/89) **87**
Cabernet Sauvignon Napa Valley 1978 Rel: $12 Cur: $25 (CA-3/89) **83**
Cabernet Sauvignon Napa Valley 1977 Rel: $9.50 Cur: $39 (CA-3/89) **85**
Chardonnay Napa Valley 1987 $15 (11/15/89) **81**
Chardonnay Napa Valley 1985 $15 (11/15/87) **82**
Chardonnay Napa Valley 1984 $15 (12/31/86) **58**

STAATLICHEN WEINBAUDOMANEN (Germany)
Riesling Auslese Nahe Münsterer Dautenpflänzer 1989 $14 (12/15/90) **86**
Riesling Auslese Nahe Niederhausener Hermannshöhle 1989 $25 (12/15/90) **86**
Riesling Auslese Nahe Schlossböckelheimer Kupfergrube 1989 $19 (12/15/90) **90**
Riesling Beerenauslese Nahe Münsterer Pittersberg 1989 $41 (12/15/90) **91**
Riesling Beerenauslese Nahe Niederhausener Hermannsberg 1989 $65 (12/15/90) **87**
Riesling Kabinett Nahe Altenbamberger Rothenberg 1989 $10 (12/15/90) **78**
Riesling Kabinett Nahe Niederhausener Steinberg 1989 $9 (12/15/90) **80**
Riesling Kabinett Nahe Schlossböckelheimer Kupfergrube 1990 $10 (12/15/91) **87**
Riesling Qualitätswein Nahe Münsterer Pittersberg 1990 $7 (12/15/91) **84**
Riesling Qualitätswein Nahe Niederhäusener Steinberg 1990 $8 (12/15/91) **79**
Riesling Qualitätswein Nahe Schlossböckelheimer Kupfergrube 1990 $8 (12/15/91) **87**
Riesling Qualitätswein Nahe Schlossböckelheimer Kupfergrube 1989 $9 (12/15/90) **85**
Riesling Spätlese Halbtrocken Nahe Niederhäusener Hermannshöhle 1990 $14 (12/15/91) **79**
Riesling Spätlese Nahe Niederhäusener Hermannsberg 1990 $14 (12/15/91) **89**
Riesling Spätlese Nahe Niederhausener Kertz 1989 $14 (12/15/90) **86**
Riesling Spätlese Nahe Schlossböckelheimer Kupfergrube 1989 ($NA) (12/15/90) **90**
Riesling Spätlese Nahe Serriger Vogelsang 1983 $7 (11/01/84) **80**
Riesling Trockenbeerenauslese Nahe Schlossböckelheimer Kupfergrube 1990 $250 (12/15/91) **92**
Riesling Trockenbeerenauslese Nahe Schlossböckelheimer Kupfergrube 1989 $150 (12/15/90) **88**

STAATSWEINGUTER (Germany)
Riesling Kabinett Halbtrocken Rheingau Eltville Hochheimer Kirchenstück 1988 $8 (9/30/89) **88**
Riesling Kabinett Rheingau Eltville Rauenthaler Baiken 1988 $7.50 (9/30/89) **79**
Riesling Kabinett Rheingau Eltville Rauenthaler Gehrn 1988 $8 (9/30/89) **78**
Riesling Spätlese Rheingau Eltville Rauenthaler Baiken 1988 $25 (9/30/89) **89**

STAGLIN FAMILY (United States/California)
Chardonnay Napa Valley 1989 $20 (1/31/92) **86**

STAG'S LEAP WINE CELLARS (United States/California)
Cabernet Sauvignon Napa Valley 1988 $18 (6/15/91) **90**
Cabernet Sauvignon Napa Valley 1987 $18 (8/31/90) **75**
Cabernet Sauvignon Napa Valley 1986 $18 (6/15/89) **82**
Cabernet Sauvignon Napa Valley 1985 $16 (9/15/88) **90**
Cabernet Sauvignon Napa Valley 1984 $15 (7/15/87) **83**
Cabernet Sauvignon Napa Valley 1981 $15 (12/16/84) **82**
Cabernet Sauvignon Stags Leap District Stag's Leap Vineyards Cask 23 1984 Rel: $40 Cur: $88 (12/31/88) **90**
Cabernet Sauvignon Stags Leap District Stag's Leap Vineyards Cask 23 1983 Rel: $35 Cur: $60 (CA-3/89) **88**
Cabernet Sauvignon Stags Leap District Stag's Leap Vineyards Cask 23 1979 Rel: $35 Cur: $85 (CA-3/89) **88**
Cabernet Sauvignon Stags Leap District Stag's Leap Vineyards Cask 23 1978 Rel: $35 Cur: $150 (CA-3/89) **92**
Cabernet Sauvignon Stags Leap District Stag's Leap Vineyards Cask 23 1977 Rel: $30 Cur: $73 (CA-3/89) **91**
Cabernet Sauvignon Stags Leap District Stag's Leap Vineyards Cask 23 1977 Rel: $30 Cur: $73 (12/01/83) CS **91**
Cabernet Sauvignon Stags Leap District Stag's Leap Vineyards Cask 23 1974 Rel: $12 Cur: $135 (CA-3/89) **88**
Cabernet Sauvignon Stags Leap District SLV-Fay Vineyard Blend 1989 (NR) (5/15/91) (BT) **85+**
Cabernet Sauvignon Stags Leap District SLV 1988 $32 (11/15/91) **85**
Cabernet Sauvignon Stags Leap District SLV 1987 $28 (11/15/90) **77**
Cabernet Sauvignon Stags Leap District SLV 1986 Rel: $28 Cur: $30 (11/30/89) **91**
Cabernet Sauvignon Stags Leap District SLV 1985 Rel: $26 Cur: $42 (CA-3/89) **94**
Cabernet Sauvignon Stags Leap District SLV 1984 Rel: $21 Cur: $28 (CA-3/89) **92**
Cabernet Sauvignon Stags Leap District Stag's Leap Vineyards 1983 Rel: $18 Cur: $33 (CA-3/89) **73**
Cabernet Sauvignon Stags Leap District Stag's Leap Vineyards 1982 Rel: $16.50 Cur: $28 (CA-3/89) **75**
Cabernet Sauvignon Stags Leap District Stag's Leap Vineyards 1981 Rel: $15 Cur: $35 (CA-3/89) **91**
Cabernet Sauvignon Stags Leap District Stag's Leap Vineyards 1981 Rel: $15 Cur: $35 (9/16/84) CS **90**
Cabernet Sauvignon Stags Leap District Stag's Leap Vineyards 1979 Rel: $15 Cur: $40 (CA-3/89) **68**
Cabernet Sauvignon Stags Leap District Stag's Leap Vineyards 1978 Rel: $13.50 Cur: $42 (CA-3/89) **89**
Cabernet Sauvignon Stags Leap District Stag's Leap Vineyards 1977 Rel: $9 Cur: $29 (CA-3/89) **85**
Cabernet Sauvignon Stags Leap District Stag's Leap Vineyards 1976 Rel: $10 Cur: $75 (CA-3/89) **73**
Cabernet Sauvignon Stags Leap District Stag's Leap Vineyards 1975 Rel: $8.50 Cur: $67 (CA-3/89) **74**
Cabernet Sauvignon Stags Leap District Stag's Leap Vineyards 1974 Rel: $8 Cur: $101 (2/15/90) **83**
Cabernet Sauvignon Stags Leap District Stag's Leap Vineyards 1973 Rel: $6 Cur: $150 (CA-3/89) **86**
Cabernet Sauvignon Stags Leap District Stag's Leap Vineyards 1972 Rel: $5.50 Cur: $90 (CA-3/89) **70**
Cabernet Sauvignon Stags Leap District Stag's Leap Vineyards Lot 2 1977 Rel: $10 Cur: $40 (CA-3/89) **90**
Cabernet Sauvignon Stags Leap District Stag's Leap Vineyards Lot 2 1976 Rel: $11 Cur: $23 (CA-3/89) **80**
Chardonnay Napa Valley 1990 $19 (3/15/92) **89**
Chardonnay Napa Valley 1989 Rel: $18 Cur: $22 (1/31/91) **88**
Chardonnay Napa Valley 1988 $18 (2/15/90) **87**
Chardonnay Napa Valley 1987 Rel: $18 Cur: $25 (CH-3/90) **89**
Chardonnay Napa Valley 1986 Rel: $17 Cur: $20 (CH-3/90) **86**
Chardonnay Napa Valley 1985 Rel: $16 Cur: $25 (CH-3/90) **83**
Chardonnay Napa Valley 1984 Rel: $14 Cur: $17 (CH-6/90) **77**
Chardonnay Napa Valley 1983 Rel: $13.50 Cur: $17 (CH-3/90) **62**
Chardonnay Napa Valley 1982 Rel: $13.50 Cur: $17 (CH-3/90) **70**
Chardonnay Napa Valley 1981 Rel: $13.50 Cur: $60 (CH-3/90) **79**
Chardonnay Napa Valley 1980 Rel: $10.50 Cur: $17 (CH-3/90) **78**
Chardonnay Napa Valley 1977 Rel: $8 Cur: $17 (CH-3/90) **59**
Chardonnay Napa Valley 1976 Rel: $8 Cur: $17 (CH-3/90) **58**
Chardonnay Napa Valley Beckstoffer Ranch 1987 $19 (9/15/89) **91**
Chardonnay Napa Valley Haynes 1979 Rel: $12.50 Cur: $20 (CH-3/90) **82**
Chardonnay Napa Valley Haynes 1978 Rel: $10 Cur: $20 (CH-3/90) **74**
Chardonnay Napa Valley Haynes 1977 Rel: $9 Cur: $20 (CH-3/90) **67**
Chardonnay Napa Valley Mirage 1982 Rel: $11.50 Cur: $18 (CH-3/90) **70**
Chardonnay Napa Valley Reserve 1990 $28 (7/15/92) **90**
Chardonnay Napa Valley Reserve 1988 $28 (1/31/91) **90**
Chardonnay Napa Valley Reserve 1987 $28 (5/31/90) **88**
Chardonnay Napa Valley Reserve 1986 $26 (CH-6/90) **88**
Chardonnay Napa Valley Reserve 1985 Rel: $22 Cur: $26 (CH-3/90) **85**
Merlot Napa Valley 1985 $16 (5/31/88) **86**
Merlot Napa Valley 1984 $15 (5/15/87) **78**
Merlot Napa Valley 1982 $13.50 (10/01/85) **78**
Merlot Napa Valley 1981 $13.50 (4/16/84) **82**
Petite Sirah Napa Valley 1987 $12 (8/31/90) **87**
Sauvignon Blanc Napa Valley Rancho Chimiles 1990 $10 (11/15/91) **78**
Sauvignon Blanc Napa Valley Rancho Chimiles 1988 $9 (11/30/89) **76**
Sauvignon Blanc Napa Valley Rancho Chimiles 1987 $9 (1/31/89) **80**
SLV Cask 23 Stags Leap District 1987 Rel: $55 Cur: $60 (11/15/91) **87**
Stag's Leap Vineyards Cask 23 Stags Leap District 1986 Rel: $55 Cur: $73 (11/15/90) **93**
Stag's Leap Vineyards Cask 23 Stags Leap District 1986 Rel: $55 Cur: $73 (CA-3/89) **92**
Stag's Leap Vineyards Cask 23 Stags Leap District 1985 Rel: $75 Cur: $165 (11/30/89) **96**
White Riesling Late Harvest Napa Valley Birkmyer Vineyards Selected Bunches 1983 $13.50/375ml (10/01/84) **85**

STAGS' LEAP WINERY (United States/California)
Cabernet Sauvignon Stags Leap District 1987 $18 (6/30/91) **89**
Cabernet Sauvignon Stags Leap District 1986 $17 (10/31/90) **89**
Cabernet Sauvignon Stags Leap District 1985 Rel: $15 Cur: $18 (CA-3/89) **85**
Cabernet Sauvignon Stags Leap District 1984 Rel: $13.50 Cur: $25 (CA-3/89) **87**
Cabernet Sauvignon Stags Leap District 1983 Rel: $12.75 Cur: $20 (CA-3/89) **80**
Cabernet Sauvignon Stags Leap District 1982 Rel: $12 Cur: $20 (CA-3/89) **71**
Cabernet Sauvignon Stags Leap District 1981 Rel: $11 Cur: $22 (CA-3/89) **85**
Chardonnay Napa Valley 1989 $14.50 (12/15/91) **81**
Merlot Napa Valley 1989 $17 (5/31/92) **88**
Merlot Napa Valley 1987 $17 (11/15/91) **85**
Merlot Napa Valley 1986 $17 (12/31/90) **84**
Merlot Napa Valley 1981 $12 (2/16/85) **83**
Petite Sirah Napa Valley 1987 $13.50 (10/31/91) **82**

STANFORD (United States/California)
Brut California Governor's Cuvée NV $5 (12/31/90) **76**
Extra Dry California Governor's Cuvée NV $5 (12/31/90) **73**

STANLEY (Australia)
Shiraz Cabernet Sauvignon Coonawarra Private Reserve 1985 $4 (12/15/87) **78**

STAR HILL (United States/California)
Cabernet Sauvignon Napa Valley Doc's Reserve 1987 $24 (11/15/91) **88**
Chardonnay Napa Valley Barrel Fermented 1989 $19 (7/15/91) **78**
Chardonnay Napa Valley Doc's Reserve Barrel Fermented 1988 $19 (6/30/90) **84**
Pinot Noir Napa Valley Doc's Reserve 1988 $19 (2/15/92) **82**
Pinot Noir Napa Valley Doc's Reserve 1987 $19 (5/31/90) **87**

STATON HILLS (United States/Washington)
Blanc de Noir Washington NV $16 (10/15/89) **77**
Brut Rosé Washington NV $16 (4/30/92) **84**
Cabernet Sauvignon Washington 1988 $15 (3/31/92) **81**
Cabernet Sauvignon Washington 1987 $13 (3/31/91) **86**
Cabernet Sauvignon Washington 1986 $12 (10/15/89) **80**
Cabernet Sauvignon Washington Estate 1987 $20 (2/29/92) **79**
Cabernet Sauvignon Washington Estate 1986 $20 (3/31/91) **83**
Cabernet Sauvignon Washington Reserve 1987 $22 (3/31/92) **85**
Cabernet Sauvignon Washington Reserve 1986 $22 (8/31/91) **83**
Chardonnay Washington 1989 $10 (7/15/91) **82**
Chardonnay Washington 1988 $10 (5/31/91) **79**
Chardonnay Washington 1987 $10 (10/15/89) **81**
Gewürztraminer Washington 1990 $7 (10/15/91) **66**
Johannisberg Riesling Washington 1990 $6 (11/15/91) BB **86**
Merlot Washington 1988 $15 (3/31/92) **82**
Merlot Washington 1987 $14 (8/31/91) **79**
Muscat Canelli Washington 1990 $8 (11/15/91) **78**
Oregon 1988 $15 (3/31/92) **85**
Pinot Noir Oregon 1987 $13 (4/15/91) **84**
Pinot Noir Oregon 1986 $13 (2/15/90) **64**
Riesling Late Harvest Washington 1987 $10/375ml (3/31/92) **82**
Sauvignon Blanc Washington 1987 $8 (10/15/89) **71**

STELTZNER (United States/California)
Cabernet Sauvignon Stags Leap District 1990 (NR) (5/15/91) (BT) **90+**
Cabernet Sauvignon Stags Leap District 1989 (NR) (5/15/91) (BT) **85+**
Cabernet Sauvignon Stags Leap District 1988 $16 (5/15/90) (BT) **85+**
Cabernet Sauvignon Stags Leap District 1987 Rel: $16 Cur: $20 (11/15/91) **86**
Cabernet Sauvignon Stags Leap District 1986 Rel: $16 Cur: $19 (12/31/89) **91**
Cabernet Sauvignon Stags Leap District 1985 Rel: $16 Cur: $20 (CA-3/89) **93**
Cabernet Sauvignon Stags Leap District 1984 Rel: $15 Cur: $19 (CA-3/89) **91**
Cabernet Sauvignon Stags Leap District 1983 Rel: $14 Cur: $18 (CA-3/89) **90**
Cabernet Sauvignon Stags Leap District 1982 Rel: $14 Cur: $27 (CA-3/89) **90**
Cabernet Sauvignon Stags Leap District 1982 Rel: $14 Cur: $27 (9/01/85) CS **91**
Cabernet Sauvignon Stags Leap District 1981 Rel: $14 Cur: $33 (CA-3/89) **89**

Cabernet Sauvignon Stags Leap District 1980 Rel: $14 Cur: $30 (CA-3/89) **88**
Cabernet Sauvignon Stags Leap District 1979 Rel: $14 Cur: $42 (CA-3/89) **89**
Cabernet Sauvignon Stags Leap District 1978 Rel: $14 Cur: $45 (CA-3/89) **87**
Cabernet Sauvignon Stags Leap District 1977 Rel: $14 Cur: $45 (CA-3/89) **85**
Merlot Stags Leap District 1990 (NR) (5/15/91) (BT) **85+**
Merlot Stags Leap District 1989 $15 (11/15/91) **85**

ROBERT STEMMLER (United States/California)
Cabernet Sauvignon Sonoma County 1982 $15 (4/01/85) **66**
Pinot Noir Sonoma County 1987 $19 (10/31/90) **82**
Pinot Noir Sonoma County 1986 $18 (6/15/88) **84**
Pinot Noir Sonoma County 1985 $18 (9/30/87) **79**
Pinot Noir Sonoma County 1984 $16 (8/31/86) **90**
Pinot Noir Sonoma County 1983 $15 (3/16/85) SS **93**
Sauvignon Blanc Late Harvest Sonoma County 1985 $10/375ml (9/30/88) **68**

STEPHENS (United States/California)
Cabernet Sauvignon Napa Valley 1981 $8 (2/15/84) **74**

STERLING (United States/California)
Cabernet Sauvignon Napa Valley 1991 (NR) (5/15/92) (BT) **88+**
Cabernet Sauvignon Napa Valley 1990 (NR) (5/15/91) (BT) **85+**
Cabernet Sauvignon Napa Valley 1989 (NR) (5/15/91) (BT) **80+**
Cabernet Sauvignon Napa Valley 1988 Rel: $15 Cur: $17 (11/15/91) **80**
Cabernet Sauvignon Napa Valley 1987 Rel: $13 Cur: $16 (5/15/90) **91**
Cabernet Sauvignon Napa Valley 1986 Rel: $14.50 Cur: $18 (3/31/89) **91**
Cabernet Sauvignon Napa Valley 1985 Rel: $13 Cur: $17 (5/15/88) **89**
Cabernet Sauvignon Napa Valley 1983 Rel: $12.50 Cur: $21 (2/15/87) **81**
Cabernet Sauvignon Napa Valley 1982 Rel: $12.50 Cur: $19 (5/16/86) **66**
Cabernet Sauvignon Napa Valley 1981 Rel: $12 Cur: $16 (8/01/85) **88**
Cabernet Sauvignon Napa Valley 1980 Rel: $12.50 Cur: $35 (2/15/84) **84**
Cabernet Sauvignon Napa Valley 1978 $26 (6/01/86) **95**
Cabernet Sauvignon Napa Valley 1974 $50 (2/15/90) (JG) **90**
Cabernet Sauvignon Napa Valley Diamond Mountain Ranch 1991 (NR) (5/15/92) (BT) **91+**
Cabernet Sauvignon Napa Valley Diamond Mountain Ranch 1990 (NR) (5/15/91) (BT) **85+**
Cabernet Sauvignon Napa Valley Diamond Mountain Ranch 1989 (NR) (5/15/91) (BT) **85+**
Cabernet Sauvignon Napa Valley Diamond Mountain Ranch 1988 ($NA) (5/15/90) (BT) **85+**
Cabernet Sauvignon Napa Valley Diamond Mountain Ranch 1987 Rel: $16 Cur: $19 (11/15/90) **91**
Cabernet Sauvignon Napa Valley Diamond Mountain Ranch 1986 Rel: $14.50 Cur: $18 (3/15/90) **91**
Cabernet Sauvignon Napa Valley Diamond Mountain Ranch 1985 Rel: $16 Cur: $21 (5/31/89) **88**
Cabernet Sauvignon Napa Valley Diamond Mountain Ranch 1984 Rel: $15 Cur: $18 (CA-3/89) **85**
Cabernet Sauvignon Napa Valley Diamond Mountain Ranch 1983 Rel: $15 Cur: $22 (CA-3/89) **87**
Cabernet Sauvignon Napa Valley Diamond Mountain Ranch 1982 Rel: $15 Cur: $37 (CA-3/89) **82**
Cabernet Sauvignon Napa Valley Diamond Mountain Ranch 1982 Rel: $15 Cur: $37 (11/16/85) CS **94**
Cabernet Sauvignon Napa Valley Reserve 1984 Rel: $25 Cur: $40 (3/31/89) CS **92**
Cabernet Sauvignon Napa Valley Reserve 1983 Rel: $22.50 Cur: $34 (CA-3/89) **82**
Cabernet Sauvignon Napa Valley Reserve 1982 Rel: $22.50 Cur: $36 (CA-3/89) **75**
Cabernet Sauvignon Napa Valley Reserve 1981 Rel: $22.50 Cur: $29 (CA-3/89) **85**
Cabernet Sauvignon Napa Valley Reserve 1980 Rel: $27.50 Cur: $44 (CA-3/89) **91**
Cabernet Sauvignon Napa Valley Reserve 1980 Rel: $27.50 Cur: $44 (11/01/84) CS **90**
Cabernet Sauvignon Napa Valley Reserve 1979 Rel: $27.50 Cur: $50 (CA-3/89) **85**
Cabernet Sauvignon Napa Valley Reserve 1978 Rel: $27.50 Cur: $45 (CA-3/89) **90**
Cabernet Sauvignon Napa Valley Reserve 1977 Rel: $27.50 Cur: $48 (CA-3/89) **93**
Cabernet Sauvignon Napa Valley Reserve 1976 Rel: $25 Cur: $34 (CA-3/89) **76**
Cabernet Sauvignon Napa Valley Reserve 1975 Rel: $20 Cur: $49 (CA-3/89) **78**
Cabernet Sauvignon Napa Valley Reserve 1974 Rel: $20 Cur: $80 (CA-3/89) **90**
Cabernet Sauvignon Napa Valley Reserve 1973 Rel: $10 Cur: $70 (CA-3/89) **89**
Chardonnay Carneros Winery Lake 1989 $18 (7/15/91) **83**
Chardonnay Carneros Winery Lake 1988 $20 (7/15/91) **87**
Chardonnay Carneros Winery Lake 1987 $20 (CH-4/90) **89**
Chardonnay Carneros Winery Lake 1986 Rel: $20 Cur: $23 (CH-4/90) **89**
Chardonnay Napa Valley Diamond Mountain Ranch 1988 $16 (7/15/92) **88**
Chardonnay Napa Valley Diamond Mountain Ranch 1987 Rel: $16 Cur: $21 (2/28/91) **84**
Chardonnay Napa Valley Diamond Mountain Ranch 1986 Rel: $15 Cur: $20 (CH-4/90) **86**
Chardonnay Napa Valley Diamond Mountain Ranch 1985 Rel: $15 Cur: $17 (CH-7/90) **87**
Chardonnay Napa Valley Diamond Mountain Ranch 1984 Rel: $15 Cur: $17 (CH-4/90) **86**
Chardonnay Napa Valley Diamond Mountain Ranch 1983 Rel: $15 Cur: $18 (CH-4/90) **86**
Chardonnay Napa Valley Estate 1990 $15 (7/15/92) **84**
Chardonnay Napa Valley Estate 1989 $15 (4/30/91) **88**
Chardonnay Napa Valley Estate 1988 Rel: $13 Cur: $19 (3/15/90) **90**
Chardonnay Napa Valley Estate 1987 Rel: $14.50 Cur: $19 (4/15/89) **89**
Chardonnay Napa Valley Estate 1986 Rel: $14.50 Cur: $19 (3/15/88) **83**
Chardonnay Napa Valley Estate 1985 $14 (7/31/87) **69**
Chardonnay Napa Valley Estate 1984 $14 (6/16/86) **77**
Chardonnay Napa Valley Estate 1983 $14 (10/01/85) **86**
Chardonnay Napa Valley Estate 1982 Rel: $14 Cur: $17 (CH-4/90) **73**
Chardonnay Napa Valley Estate 1981 Rel: $14 Cur: $17 (CH-4/90) **71**
Chardonnay Napa Valley Estate 1980 Rel: $13 Cur: $17 (CH-4/90) **70**
Chardonnay Napa Valley Estate 1979 Rel: $13 Cur: $38 (CH-4/90) **73**
Chardonnay Napa Valley Estate 1977 Rel: $10 Cur: $31 (CH-4/90) **70**
Chardonnay Napa Valley Estate 1976 Rel: $5.25 Cur: $18 (CH-4/90) **59**
Chardonnay Napa Valley Estate 1974 Rel: $4.75 Cur: $35 (CH-4/90) **78**
Merlot Carneros Winery Lake 1987 $25 (12/31/90) **90**
Merlot Napa Valley 1991 (NR) (5/15/92) (BT) **88+**
Merlot Napa Valley 1990 (NR) (5/15/91) (BT) **85+**
Merlot Napa Valley 1989 $15 (5/31/92) **82**
Merlot Napa Valley 1988 $15 (4/15/91) **83**
Merlot Napa Valley 1987 $13 (6/15/90) **83**
Merlot Napa Valley 1986 $14 (3/31/89) **85**
Merlot Napa Valley 1985 $14 (3/31/88) **87**
Merlot Napa Valley 1984 $11.50 (4/30/87) **93**
Merlot Napa Valley 1983 $11 (6/01/86) **91**
Merlot Napa Valley 1982 $12 (10/01/85) **83**
Merlot Napa Valley 1981 $11 (3/01/84) **83**
Pinot Noir Carneros Napa Valley Winery Lake 1989 $14 (3/31/92) **87**
Pinot Noir Carneros Napa Valley Winery Lake 1988 $14 (4/30/91) **87**
Pinot Noir Carneros Napa Valley Winery Lake 1987 $18 (12/31/89) **86**
Pinot Noir Carneros Napa Valley Winery Lake 1986 $18 (2/28/89) **89**
Reserve Napa Valley 1991 (NR) (5/15/92) (BT) **88+**
Reserve Napa Valley 1990 (NR) (5/15/91) (BT) **85+**
Reserve Napa Valley 1989 (NR) (5/15/91) (BT) **90+**
Reserve Napa Valley 1988 $40 (3/31/92) **85**
Reserve Napa Valley 1987 Rel: $43 Cur: $48 (11/15/90) **93**
Reserve Napa Valley 1986 Rel: $35 Cur: $44 (3/15/90) CS **95**
Reserve Napa Valley 1985 Rel: $30 Cur: $46 (7/15/89) SS **96**
Sauvignon Blanc Napa Valley 1990 $8.50 (11/30/91) **80**
Sauvignon Blanc Napa Valley 1989 $9 (3/15/91) **79**
Sauvignon Blanc Napa Valley 1988 $9 (11/30/89) **84**
Three Palms Vineyard Napa Valley 1991 (NR) (5/15/92) (BT) **86+**
Three Palms Vineyard Napa Valley 1989 (NR) (5/15/91) (BT) **85+**
Three Palms Vineyard Napa Valley 1988 $23 (11/15/91) **79**
Three Palms Vineyard Napa Valley 1987 $23 (11/15/90) **87**
Three Palms Vineyard Napa Valley 1986 $19 (12/31/89) **86**
Three Palms Vineyard Napa Valley 1985 Rel: $20 Cur: $22 (12/31/88) **93**

STEVENOT (United States/California)
Cabernet Sauvignon Calaveras County 1985 $7.50 (6/30/89) **76**
Cabernet Sauvignon Calaveras County Grand Reserve 1987 $9 (3/31/92) **82**
Cabernet Sauvignon Calaveras County Grand Reserve 1984 $15 (12/31/87) **75**
Chardonnay Calaveras County Grand Reserve 1989 $9 (2/29/92) **78**
Chardonnay California 1990 $7.50 (7/15/92) BB **80**
Chardonnay California 1987 $7.50 (6/30/89) **83**
Chardonnay California 1986 $6 (11/15/87) **79**
Chenin Blanc Calaveras County 1987 $5.50 (7/31/89) **69**
Merlot North Coast Reserve 1989 $10 (5/31/92) **83**
White Zinfandel Amador County 1989 $5 (12/31/90) BB **84**
Zinfandel Amador County Grand Reserve 1985 $7.50 (12/31/87) **72**
Zinfandel Calaveras County 1986 $7.50 (7/31/89) BB **84**
Zinfandel Calaveras County 1984 $6 (6/30/87) **73**

STEWART (United States/Washington)
Cabernet Sauvignon Columbia Valley 1988 $11 (8/31/91) **79**
Chardonnay Columbia Valley 1988 $10 (3/31/91) **85**
Chardonnay Columbia Valley Reserve 1988 $17 (5/31/91) **78**
Chardonnay Columbia Valley Reserve 1987 $15 (3/31/90) **90**
Gewürztraminer Yakima Valley 1988 $5.50 (10/15/89) **69**
Johannisberg Riesling Columbia Valley 1988 $6.50 (10/15/89) **72**
Johannisberg Riesling Columbia Valley 1987 $6 (4/15/89) **80**
Sauvignon Blanc Yakima Valley 1988 $8 (10/15/89) **78**
White Riesling Columbia Valley 1988 $15/375ml (10/15/89) **68**
White Riesling Late Harvest Columbia Valley 1987 $8/375ml (7/31/89) **83**
White Riesling Late Harvest Columbia Valley Select 1986 $6.50/375ml (10/15/89) **80**

STONE CREEK (United States/California)
Cabernet Sauvignon Napa Valley Limited Bottling 1986 $10 (6/15/90) **85**
Cabernet Sauvignon Napa Valley Special Selection 1986 $10 (11/15/91) **80**
Cabernet Sauvignon Napa Valley Special Selection 1983 $8.75 (5/31/87) BB **91**
Chardonnay Alexander Valley 1989 $10 (7/15/91) **86**
Chardonnay Napa Valley Special Selection 1989 $10 (7/15/91) **78**
Chardonnay North Coast 1988 $7 (6/30/90) **68**
Merlot California Special Selection 1989 $6 (5/31/92) **79**
Merlot Columbia Valley 1989 $7 (5/31/91) BB **86**
Merlot Columbia Valley 1988 $6 (9/30/90) **78**

STONEGATE (United States/California)
Cabernet Sauvignon Napa Valley 1991 (NR) (5/15/92) (BT) **83+**
Cabernet Sauvignon Napa Valley 1990 (NR) (5/15/91) (BT) **85+**
Cabernet Sauvignon Napa Valley 1989 (NR) (5/15/91) (BT) **80+**
Cabernet Sauvignon Napa Valley 1987 $14 (3/31/92) **82**
Cabernet Sauvignon Napa Valley 1986 Rel: $15 Cur: $17 (2/28/91) **86**
Cabernet Sauvignon Napa Valley 1985 Rel: $16 Cur: $19 (8/31/90) **86**
Cabernet Sauvignon Napa Valley 1984 Rel: $14 Cur: $17 (CA-3/89) **88**
Cabernet Sauvignon Napa Valley 1982 Rel: $12 Cur: $18 (CA-3/89) **80**
Cabernet Sauvignon Napa Valley 1981 Rel: $12 Cur: $17 (CA-3/89) **79**
Cabernet Sauvignon Napa Valley 1980 Rel: $12 Cur: $22 (CA-3/89) **86**
Cabernet Sauvignon Napa Valley 1979 Rel: $12 Cur: $25 (CA-3/89) **84**
Cabernet Sauvignon Napa Valley 1978 Rel: $12 Cur: $27 (CA-3/89) **91**
Cabernet Sauvignon Napa Valley 1977 Rel: $10 Cur: $25 (CA-3/89) **81**
Chardonnay Napa Valley 1988 $15 (4/15/91) **83**
Chardonnay Napa Valley 1987 $13 (6/30/90) **78**
Chardonnay Napa Valley 1986 $13 (12/31/88) **89**
Chardonnay Napa Valley 1982 $10 (3/01/85) **83**
Chardonnay Napa Valley Spaulding Vineyard 1983 $14 (2/15/87) **86**
Chardonnay Napa Valley Spaulding Vineyard 1982 $14 (12/01/85) **53**
Chardonnay Napa Valley Reserve 1988 $20 (2/15/91) **90**
Late Harvest Napa Valley 1990 $9.50/375ml (3/31/92) **83**
Late Harvest Napa Valley 1989 $13/375ml (4/30/91) **87**
Merlot Napa Valley 1991 (NR) (5/15/92) (BT) **80+**
Merlot Napa Valley 1988 $16.50 (5/31/92) **81**
Merlot Napa Valley 1986 $15 (4/15/90) **84**
Merlot Napa Valley Pershing Vineyard 1990 (NR) (5/15/91) (BT) **85+**
Merlot Napa Valley Pershing Vineyard 1987 $16.50 (3/31/91) **83**
Merlot Napa Valley Spaulding Vineyard 1987 $16.50 (3/31/91) **86**
Merlot Napa Valley Spaulding Vineyard 1982 $14 (2/28/87) **84**
Merlot Napa Valley Spaulding Vineyard Proprietor's Reserve 1984 $15 (12/31/88) **85**
Sauvignon Blanc Napa Valley 1990 $9.50 (11/15/91) **87**
Sauvignon Blanc Napa Valley 1988 $8.50 (6/30/90) **87**

STONELEIGH (New Zealand)
Chardonnay Marlborough 1989 $11 (7/15/91) **86**

STONESTREET (United States/California)
Chardonnay Sonoma County 1990 $20 (6/15/92) **91**
Merlot Alexander Valley 1989 $24 (5/31/92) **88**

STONY HILL (United States/California)
Chardonnay Napa Valley 1988 Rel: $18 Cur: $82 (CH-6/90) **90**
Chardonnay Napa Valley 1987 Rel: $18 Cur: $65 (CH-5/90) **87**
Chardonnay Napa Valley 1986 Rel: $16 Cur: $64 (CH-7/90) **87**

Key to Symbols

The scores reported here are the results of blind tastings conducted by our panel of senior editors. Wines that carry the initials below are results of individual tastings.

THE WINE SPECTATOR 100-POINT SCALE 95-100—Classic, a great wine; ***90-94***—Outstanding, superior character and style; ***80-89***—Good to very good, a wine with special qualities; ***70-79***—Average, drinkable wine that may have minor flaws; ***60-69***—Below average, drinkable but not recommended; ***50-59***—Poor, undrinkable, not recommended. "+"—With a score indicates a range; used primarily with barrel tastings to indicate a preliminary score.

SPECIAL DESIGNATIONS SS—Spectator Selection, CS—Cellar Selection, BB—Best Buy, ($NA)—Price not available, (NR)—Not released.

TASTER'S INITIALS (JG)—Jim Gordon, (HS)—Harvey Steiman, (JL)—James Laube, (JS)—James Suckling, (TM)—Thomas Matthews, (TR)—Terry Robards, (PM)—Per-Henrik Mansson, (BT)—Barrel Tasting (these wines were tasted blind from barrel samples), (CA-date)—*California's Great Cabernets* by James Laube, (CH-date)—*California's Great Chardonnays* by James Laube, (VP-date)—*Vintage Port* by James Suckling.

DATE TASTED Dates in parentheses represent the issue in which the rating was published.

Chardonnay Napa Valley 1985 Rel: $16 Cur: $76 (CH-5/90) **92**
Chardonnay Napa Valley 1984 Rel: $13 Cur: $75 (CH-5/90) **90**
Chardonnay Napa Valley 1983 Rel: $13 Cur: $70 (CH-5/90) **85**
Chardonnay Napa Valley 1982 Rel: $12 Cur: $65 (CH-5/90) **85**
Chardonnay Napa Valley 1981 Rel: $12 Cur: $68 (CH-5/90) **86**
Chardonnay Napa Valley 1980 Rel: $12 Cur: $75 (CH-5/90) **86**
Chardonnay Napa Valley 1979 Rel: $12 Cur: $92 (CH-5/90) **81**
Chardonnay Napa Valley 1978 Rel: $10 Cur: $100 (CH-5/90) **85**
Chardonnay Napa Valley 1977 Rel: $9 Cur: $95 (CH-6/90) **91**
Chardonnay Napa Valley 1976 Rel: $9 Cur: $105 (CH-6/90) **88**
Chardonnay Napa Valley 1975 Rel: $9 Cur: $150 (CH-5/90) **75**
Chardonnay Napa Valley 1974 Rel: $7 Cur: $125 (CH-5/90) **73**
Chardonnay Napa Valley 1973 Rel: $7 Cur: $120 (CH-5/90) **79**
Chardonnay Napa Valley 1972 Rel: $7 Cur: $110 (CH-5/90) **83**
Chardonnay Napa Valley 1971 Rel: $6 Cur: $110 (CH-5/90) **80**
Chardonnay Napa Valley 1970 Rel: $6 Cur: $175 (CH-5/90) **92**
Chardonnay Napa Valley 1969 Rel: $5 Cur: $175 (CH-5/90) **85**
Chardonnay Napa Valley 1968 Rel: $5 Cur: $250 (CH-5/90) **93**
Chardonnay Napa Valley 1967 Rel: $4.50 Cur: $310 (CH-5/90) **83**
Chardonnay Napa Valley 1966 Rel: $4.50 Cur: $300 (CH-5/90) **91**
Chardonnay Napa Valley 1965 Rel: $4 Cur: $420 (CH-5/90) **90**
Chardonnay Napa Valley 1964 Rel: $4 Cur: $450 (CH-5/90) **98**
Chardonnay Napa Valley 1963 Rel: $4 Cur: $450 (CH-5/90) **87**
Chardonnay Napa Valley 1962 Rel: $3.25 Cur: $470 (CH-5/90) **96**
Chardonnay Napa Valley 1960 Rel: $3 Cur: $430 (CH-5/90) **88**
Chardonnay Napa Valley SHV 1988 Rel: $20 Cur: $90 (6/30/90) **81**
Chardonnay Napa Valley SHV 1987 Rel: $9 Cur: $62 (4/15/89) **84**

STONY HOLLOW (Chile)
Cabernet Sauvignon San Fernando 1988 $6 (6/15/92) BB **84**
Chardonnay San Fernando 1990 $6 (6/15/92) BB **81**

STONY RIDGE (United States/California)
Zinfandel Livermore Valley 1980 $7 (6/16/84) **75**

STORRS (United States/California)
Chardonnay Santa Cruz Mountains 1989 $11.50 (7/15/91) **76**
Chardonnay Santa Cruz Mountains Gaspar Vineyard 1989 $16 (7/15/91) **86**
Chardonnay Santa Cruz Mountains Meyley Vineyard 1989 $16 (7/15/91) **83**
Chardonnay Santa Cruz Mountains Vanumanutagi Vineyards 1989 $14 (7/15/91) **71**

STORY (United States/California)
Zinfandel Amador County 1987 $8.50 (4/30/91) **84**
Zinfandel Amador County 1986 $8.50 (8/31/91) **80**
Zinfandel Amador County 1980 $6 (4/01/84) **73**
Zinfandel Amador County Shenandoah Valley Private Reserve 1984 $14 (4/30/91) **79**

STORYBOOK MOUNTAIN (United States/California)
Zinfandel Napa Valley 1989 Rel: $13 Cur: $18 (3/31/92) **80**
Zinfandel Napa Valley 1988 $12.50 (12/31/90) **75**
Zinfandel Napa Valley 1987 $11.50 (12/15/89) **88**
Zinfandel Napa Valley 1986 $10.50 (12/15/88) **88**
Zinfandel Napa Valley 1985 $10 (12/31/87) **90**
Zinfandel Napa Valley 1984 $9.50 (3/15/87) **80**
Zinfandel Napa Valley 1983 $8.75 (4/16/86) **90**
Zinfandel Napa Valley 1982 $8.50 (12/01/84) **86**
Zinfandel Napa Valley Reserve 1988 Rel: $20 Cur: $22 (3/31/92) **84**
Zinfandel Napa Valley Reserve 1987 Rel: $17.50 Cur: $27 (12/31/90) **89**
Zinfandel Napa Valley Reserve 1986 Rel: $17.50 Cur: $24 (5/15/90) **82**
Zinfandel Napa Valley Reserve 1985 Rel: $16.50 Cur: $22 (5/31/89) **88**
Zinfandel Napa Valley Reserve 1984 Rel: $14.50 Cur: $24 (4/30/88) **92**
Zinfandel Napa Valley Reserve 1983 Rel: $12.50 Cur: $22 (7/31/87) **81**
Zinfandel Napa Valley Reserve 1981 $9.50 (4/16/84) **86**
Zinfandel Sonoma County 1986 $8.50 (10/15/88) **87**
Zinfandel Sonoma County 1982 $7.50 (9/16/85) **81**

STRATFORD (United States/California)
Cabernet Sauvignon California 1985 $10 (11/30/88) **83**
Cabernet Sauvignon California 1983 $8.50 (2/15/87) **86**
Cabernet Sauvignon Napa Valley 1987 $11.50 (4/30/90) **85**
Cabernet Sauvignon Napa Valley Partners' Reserve 1988 $16 (3/15/92) **68**
Cabernet Sauvignon Napa Valley Partners' Reserve 1987 $15.50 (4/30/91) **90**
Chardonnay California 1989 $10 (7/15/91) BB **87**
Chardonnay California 1987 $10 (7/15/89) **75**
Chardonnay California 1986 $9.50 (2/29/88) **89**
Chardonnay California 1985 $9 (2/28/87) **80**
Chardonnay California 1984 $8.50 (2/01/86) **71**
Chardonnay California 1983 $8.50 (11/01/84) **80**
Chardonnay California Partners' Reserve 1990 $12 (6/15/92) **81**
Chardonnay California Partners' Reserve 1988 $14.50 (6/30/90) **88**
Chardonnay California Partners' Reserve 1987 $15 (7/15/89) **82**
Chardonnay California Partners' Reserve 1986 $14.50 (12/31/88) **76**
Merlot California 1990 $9.75 (5/31/92) BB **85**
Merlot California 1987 $13 (10/31/89) **83**
Merlot California 1986 $10 (1/31/89) **78**
Merlot California 1983 $8.50 (9/30/86) **79**
Sauvignon Blanc California 1988 $8 (5/15/90) **83**
Sauvignon Blanc California Partners' Reserve 1989 $9.50 (11/15/91) **85**

STRAUSS (United States/California)
Merlot Napa Valley 1989 $15 (11/15/91) **81**
Merlot Napa Valley 1988 $14 (12/31/90) **82**
Merlot Napa Valley 1987 $12 (2/15/90) **90**
Merlot Napa Valley 1986 $11 (2/28/89) **93**
Merlot Napa Valley 1985 $10 (2/15/88) **81**

STREBLOW (United States/California)
Cabernet Sauvignon Napa Valley 1987 $16 (10/15/90) **79**
Cabernet Sauvignon Napa Valley 1986 $16 (7/31/89) **87**
Cabernet Sauvignon Napa Valley 1985 $14.50 (6/15/88) **89**
Merlot Napa Valley 1989 $20 (5/31/92) **89**

RODNEY STRONG (United States/California)
Cabernet Sauvignon Alexander Valley Alexander's Crown Vineyard 1987 $17 (7/15/91) **89**
Cabernet Sauvignon Alexander Valley Alexander's Crown Vineyard 1985 $17 (5/31/91) **87**
Cabernet Sauvignon Alexander Valley Alexander's Crown Vineyard 1984 $12 (4/30/89) **80**
Cabernet Sauvignon Alexander Valley Alexander's Crown Vineyard 1982 $12 (10/31/88) **80**
Cabernet Sauvignon Alexander Valley Alexander's Crown Vineyard 1981 $12 (11/30/87) **77**
Cabernet Sauvignon Alexander Valley Alexander's Crown Vineyard 1980 $11 (4/16/85) **86**
Cabernet Sauvignon Alexander Valley Alexander's Crown Vineyard 1979 $12 (4/16/84) **79**
Cabernet Sauvignon Alexander Valley Alexander's Crown Vineyard 1978 $12 (1/01/84) **80**
Cabernet Sauvignon Alexander Valley Reserve 1987 $28 (9/30/91) **92**
Cabernet Sauvignon Sonoma County 1988 $10 (11/15/91) **80**
Cabernet Sauvignon Sonoma County 1987 $10 (6/30/91) **85**
Cabernet Sauvignon Sonoma County 1982 $7 (12/15/86) **69**
Cabernet Sauvignon Sonoma Valley 1981 $7.50 (12/16/84) **86**
Chardonnay Chalk Hill Chalk Hill Vineyard 1990 $13 (5/31/92) **89**
Chardonnay Chalk Hill Chalk Hill Vineyard 1988 $12 (3/31/91) **79**
Chardonnay Chalk Hill Chalk Hill Vineyard 1987 $12 (2/15/91) **90**
Chardonnay Chalk Hill Chalk Hill Vineyard 1985 $10 (12/31/87) **72**
Chardonnay Chalk Hill Chalk Hill Vineyard 1983 $10 (1/31/87) **73**
Chardonnay Chalk Hill Chalk Hill Vineyard 1982 $9.95 (7/01/84) **79**
Chardonnay Russian River Valley River West Vineyard 1984 $10 (3/15/87) **68**
Chardonnay Sonoma County 1990 $9 (7/15/92) **82**
Chardonnay Sonoma County 1989 $9 (7/15/91) BB **86**
Chardonnay Sonoma County 1987 $6.50 (10/15/88) **80**
Chardonnay Sonoma County 1986 $7 (12/15/87) BB **85**
Chardonnay Sonoma County 1983 $8 (11/01/84) **78**
Gewürztraminer Sonoma County 1990 $7 (9/30/91) BB **83**
Gewürztraminer Sonoma County 1987 $5.50 (2/28/89) **75**
Merlot Russian River Valley River West Vineyard 1985 $12 (2/28/89) **79**
Pinot Noir Russian River Valley River East Vineyard 1985 $10 (2/28/91) **83**
Pinot Noir Russian River Valley River East Vineyard 1984 $8 (11/15/87) **78**
Pinot Noir Russian River Valley River East Vineyard 1981 $8.50 (8/31/86) **63**
Pinot Noir Russian River Valley River East Vineyard 1980 $10 (7/01/84) **78**
Sauvignon Blanc Alexander Valley Charlotte's Home Vineyard 1989 $9 (11/15/91) **75**
Zinfandel Russian River Valley Old Vines River West Vineyard 1987 $14 (8/31/91) **82**
Zinfandel Russian River Valley Old Vines River West Vineyard 1980 $12 (11/15/87) **68**
Zinfandel Russian River Valley Old Vines River West Vineyard 1979 $10 (3/15/87) **71**
Zinfandel Sonoma County 1986 $5.50 (3/31/89) **79**
Zinfandel Sonoma County 1982 $5.50 (12/31/87) **70**

STRUZZIERO (Italy/Other)
Taurasi Riserva 1977 Rel: $22 Cur: $26 (8/31/86) CS **93**

MARIE STUART (France/Champagne)
Brut Blanc de Blancs Champagne 1979 $25 (12/31/87) **87**
Brut Blanc de Blancs Champagne NV $19 (12/31/87) **85**
Brut Champagne NV $22 (12/31/87) **82**
Brut Champagne Cuvée de la Reine NV $26 (12/31/87) **84**
Brut Rosé Champagne NV $23 (12/31/87) **80**
Extra Dry Champagne NV $19 (12/31/87) **74**

STUDERT-PRUM (Germany)
Riesling Auslese Mosel-Saar-Ruwer Wehlener Sonnenuhr 1988 ($NA) (9/30/89) **86**

STUERMER (United States/California)
Cabernet Sauvignon Lake County 1984 $15 (9/30/89) **66**

CHATEAU SUAU (France/Sauternes)
Barsac 1989 ($NA) (6/15/90) (BT) **85+**
Barsac 1988 ($NA) (6/15/90) (BT) **80+**
Barsac 1986 ($NA) (6/30/88) (BT) **85+**

SUBIDA DI MONTE (Italy/North)
Pinot Grigio Collio 1989 $10.50 (7/15/91) **79**
Sauvignon Collio 1989 $11 (7/15/91) **87**

CHATEAU SUDUIRAUT (France/Sauternes)
Sauternes 1989 $60 (6/15/90) (BT) **90+**
Sauternes 1988 $45 (6/15/90) (BT) **85+**
Sauternes 1986 $35 (12/31/89) **85**
Sauternes 1985 $30 (11/30/88) (JS) **81**
Sauternes 1984 $22 (11/30/88) (JS) **81**
Sauternes 1983 Rel: $30 Cur: $40 (11/30/88) (JS) **85**
Sauternes 1982 $42 (11/30/88) (JS) **83**
Sauternes 1979 Rel: $19 Cur: $40 (11/30/88) (JS) **86**
Sauternes 1979 Rel: $19 Cur: $40 (2/16/84) CS **92**
Sauternes 1978 $35 (11/30/88) (JS) **78**
Sauternes 1976 $65 (11/30/88) (JS) **77**
Sauternes 1975 $66 (11/30/88) (JS) **84**
Sauternes 1972 $25 (11/30/88) (JS) **77**
Sauternes 1970 $52 (11/30/88) (JS) **81**
Sauternes 1969 $70 (11/30/88) (JS) **88**
Sauternes 1959 $240 (11/30/88) (JS) **93**
Sauternes 1928 $300 (11/30/88) (JS) **90**
Sauternes Cuvée Madame 1982 $150 (11/30/88) (JS) **90**

SUGARLOAF RIDGE (United States/California)
Cabernet Sauvignon Sonoma Valley 1986 $13 (3/31/90) **82**

SULLIVAN (United States/California)
Merlot Napa Valley 1989 $20 (4/15/92) **92**

SUMMIT LAKE (United States/California)
Zinfandel Howell Mountain 1987 $11 (2/15/91) **87**
Zinfandel Howell Mountain 1986 $11 (3/15/90) **84**
Zinfandel Howell Mountain 1985 $9.50 (12/15/88) **88**
Zinfandel Howell Mountain 1984 $8.50 (4/30/88) **90**

SUNNY ST. HELENA (United States/California)
Cabernet Sauvignon California 1989 $10 (11/15/91) **86**
Cabernet Sauvignon Napa Valley 1985 $9 (10/31/87) **81**
Cabernet Sauvignon North Coast 1988 $13 (4/30/91) **85**
Chardonnay California 1989 $12 (4/30/91) **78**
Chardonnay Napa Valley 1986 $9 (10/31/87) **65**
Sauvignon Blanc Napa Valley 1989 $9 (4/30/91) **79**

SUNRISE (United States/California)
Pinot Noir Santa Clara County San Ysidro Vineyard 1985 $12 (6/15/88) **71**
Pinot Noir Sonoma County Green Valley Dutton Ranch Vineyard 1986 $10 (6/15/88) **60**

SUTTER HOME (United States/California)
Cabernet Sauvignon California 1989 $5.50 (10/15/91) BB **83**
Cabernet Sauvignon California 1988 $5 (11/15/90) BB **81**
Cabernet Sauvignon California 1987 $5.50 (6/30/89) **77**
Cabernet Sauvignon California 1986 $5 (11/30/88) **79**
Chardonnay California 1990 $6 (9/15/91) BB **84**
Chardonnay California 1989 $5 (11/15/90) BB **80**
Chenin Blanc California 1988 $4 (7/31/89) **66**
Muscat Alexandria California 1990 $5 (11/30/91) **77**
Sauvignon Blanc California 1989 $4.50 (4/30/91) **79**
White Zinfandel California 1990 $5.50 (3/31/91) **77**
White Zinfandel California 1989 $4.50 (12/31/90) **68**

White Zinfandel California 1988 $5.25 (6/15/89) **77**
Zinfandel Amador County 1981 $6.25 (5/16/84) **80**
Zinfandel Amador County 1973 $30 (6/16/85) **86**
Zinfandel Amador County 1972 $8 (6/16/85) **85**
Zinfandel Amador County 1970 $25 (6/16/85) **80**
Zinfandel Amador County Reserve 1988 $10 (3/31/92) **84**
Zinfandel Amador County Reserve 1987 $9.50 (5/15/91) **79**
Zinfandel Amador County Reserve 1985 $8.75 (11/30/90) **81**
Zinfandel Amador County Reserve 1984 $9.50 (7/31/89) **82**
Zinfandel Amador County Reserve 1984 $9 (7/31/88) **79**
Zinfandel California 1989 $5 (5/15/91) BB **85**
Zinfandel California 1988 $5 (3/31/91) **72**
Zinfandel California 1987 $5.50 (7/31/89) **78**
Zinfandel California 1986 $7 (10/15/88) **76**
Zinfandel California 1984 $6 (12/31/86) **77**

JOSEPH SWAN (United States/California)
Chardonnay Sonoma Coast 1986 $18 (7/15/88) **73**
Chardonnay Sonoma Coast Russian River Valley 1989 $20 (5/31/91) **77**
Pinot Noir 1982 $17 (8/31/86) **82**
Pinot Noir Sonoma Coast 1985 $18 (6/15/88) **89**
Pinot Noir Sonoma Coast Russian River Valley 1988 $20 (6/30/91) **79**
Zinfandel California 1973 $55 (6/16/85) **84**
Zinfandel California 1969 $80 (6/16/85) **83**
Zinfandel Sonoma Coast 1986 Rel: $12.50 Cur: $17 (3/15/90) **89**
Zinfandel Sonoma Coast 1985 Rel: $12 Cur: $17 (3/15/89) **82**
Zinfandel Sonoma Coast Ziegler Vineyard 1987 $12.50 (9/15/90) **86**
Zinfandel Sonoma County 1988 $12.50 (8/31/91) **82**
Zinfandel Sonoma County 1987 $12.50 (7/31/90) **86**
Zinfandel Sonoma Valley Stellwagen Vineyard 1987 $12.50 (9/15/90) **86**

MARK SWANN (Australia)
Cabernet Sauvignon Coonawarra 1987 $7 (2/28/91) BB **84**
Cabernet Sauvignon Coonawarra 1985 $7 (10/31/88) BB **88**
Cabernet Sauvignon Coonawarra 1984 $8 (8/31/87) **77**
Cabernet Sauvignon Coonawarra 1982 $7.50 (3/16/84) **78**
Cabernet Sauvignon South Australia 1989 $8 (3/15/92) **81**
Cabernet Sauvignon South Australia Proprietor's Reserve 1988 $5.50 (2/28/91) BB **86**
Cabernet Sauvignon South Australia Proprietor's Reserve 1987 $5.50 (7/31/89) BB **81**
Cabernet Sauvignon South Australia Proprietor's Reserve 1986 $5 (10/31/88) **78**
Chardonnay Barossa Valley 1989 $7 (2/28/91) **79**
Chardonnay McLaren Vale 1983 $11 (9/16/84) **81**
Chardonnay South Australia Proprietor's Reserve 1987 $5 (2/15/89) **79**
Chardonnay Victoria 1990 $8 (11/30/91) BB **84**
Chardonnay Victoria Proprietor's Reserve 1989 $7 (5/31/91) **78**
Gold Vintner's Select Rutherglen NV $10/375ml (12/31/88) **92**
Port Australia Vintage 1980 $10 (4/16/84) **78**
Shiraz Eden Valley 1980 $6.50 (3/16/84) **80**

SWANSON (United States/California)
Cabernet Sauvignon Napa Valley 1987 $25 (10/15/91) **92**
Chardonnay Napa Valley 1989 $15 (7/15/91) **84**
Chardonnay Napa Valley 1988 $14.50 (6/30/90) **79**
Chardonnay Napa Valley Reserve 1988 $19 (7/15/91) **90**
Merlot Napa Valley 1990 $16 (5/31/92) **82**

SYCAMORE CREEK (United States/California)
Zinfandel California 1982 $9 (6/16/84) **87**

SYLVAN SPRINGS (United States/California)
Cabernet Sauvignon California Vintner's Reserve 1985 $5 (9/30/88) BB **80**

TAFT STREET (United States/California)
Cabernet Sauvignon California 1985 $7.50 (10/15/88) **78**
Cabernet Sauvignon Napa Valley 1983 $9 (1/31/87) **84**
Chardonnay Russian River Valley 1989 $12 (3/31/92) **74**
Chardonnay Russian River Valley 1988 $12 (7/15/91) **83**
Chardonnay Russian River Valley 1986 $10 (12/31/88) **86**
Chardonnay Sonoma County 1990 $8.50 (3/31/92) BB **82**
Chardonnay Sonoma County 1989 $8.50 (7/15/91) BB **86**
Chardonnay Sonoma County 1988 $8 (1/31/90) **79**
Chardonnay Sonoma County 1987 $7.50 (10/15/88) **84**
Chardonnay Sonoma County 1986 $7 (11/15/87) **78**
Merlot Sonoma County 1990 $11.50 (5/31/92) **89**
Merlot Sonoma County 1989 $12 (5/31/92) **85**
Merlot Sonoma County 1985 $10 (5/31/88) **83**
Pinot Noir Monterey County 1982 $7.50 (5/01/84) **76**
Pinot Noir Santa Maria Valley 1983 $9 (4/15/87) **76**
Sauvignon Blanc Sonoma County 1990 $6.50 (6/15/92) BB **83**
Sauvignon Blanc Sonoma County 1989 $8 (10/15/91) **68**

TAGARIS (United States/Washington)
Fumé Blanc Washington 1988 $8 (10/15/89) **76**

CHATEAU TAILHAS (France/Bordeaux)
Pomerol 1988 $20 (4/30/91) **91**
Pomerol 1982 $15 (5/15/89) (TR) **82**

CHATEAU TAILLEFER (France/Bordeaux)
Pomerol 1989 (NR) (4/30/91) (BT) **90+**
Pomerol 1988 $22 (6/30/91) **87**
Pomerol 1987 $18 (6/30/89) (BT) **75+**
Pomerol 1986 $20 (6/30/88) (BT) **80+**

Key to Symbols

The scores reported here are the results of blind tastings conducted by our panel of senior editors. Wines that carry the initials below are results of individual tastings.

THE WINE SPECTATOR 100-POINT SCALE 95-100—Classic, a great wine; ***90-94***—Outstanding, superior character and style; ***80-89***—Good to very good, a wine with special qualities; ***70-79***—Average, drinkable wine that may have minor flaws; ***60-69***—Below average, drinkable but not recommended; ***50-59***—Poor, undrinkable, not recommended. "+"—With a score indicates a range; used primarily with barrel tastings to indicate a preliminary score.

SPECIAL DESIGNATIONS SS—Spectator Selection, CS—Cellar Selection, BB—Best Buy, ($NA)—Price not available, (NR)—Not released.

TASTER'S INITIALS (JG)—Jim Gordon, (HS)—Harvey Steiman, (JL)—James Laube, (JS)—James Suckling, (TM)—Thomas Matthews, (TR)—Terry Robards, (PM)—Per-Henrik Mansson, (BT)—Barrel Tasting (these wines were tasted blind from barrel samples), (CA-date)—*California's Great Cabernets* by James Laube, (CH-date)—*California's Great Chardonnays* by James Laube, (VP-date)—*Vintage Port* by James Suckling.

DATE TASTED Dates in parentheses represent the issue in which the rating was published.

Pomerol 1985 Rel: $19 Cur: $24 (6/30/88) **81**
Pomerol 1982 ($NA) (5/15/89) (TR) **85**

TAILLEVENT (France/Champagne)
Brut Blanc de Blancs Champagne 1985 $49 (11/15/91) **84**
Brut Blanc de Blancs Champagne 1983 $33 (12/31/89) **82**
Brut Champagne Grande Réserve NV $43 (11/15/91) **88**
Brut Rosé Champagne Phantom of the Opera NV $32 (12/31/89) **82**
Rosé Champagne Grande Réserve NV $56 (11/15/91) **88**

CAVE DE TAIN L'HERMITAGE (France/Rhône)
Cornas Michel Courtial 1986 $11 (7/31/89) **89**
Crozes-Hermitage Blanc Michel Courtial 1986 $8.50 (3/15/90) **84**
Crozes-Hermitage Michel Courtial 1986 $6 (5/15/89) **77**
Hermitage 1986 $15 (7/15/89) **82**
Hermitage Michel Courtial 1986 $15 (3/31/90) **89**
St.-Joseph Michel Courtial 1986 $8 (7/31/89) **79**

TAITTINGER (France/Champagne)
Brut Blanc de Blancs Champagne Comtes de Champagne 1985 $96 (12/31/90) **92**
Brut Blanc de Blancs Champagne Comtes de Champagne 1983 $92 (12/31/90) **93**
Brut Blanc de Blancs Champagne Comtes de Champagne 1982 Rel: $83 Cur: $99 (12/31/89) **95**
Brut Blanc de Blancs Champagne Comtes de Champagne 1981 Rel: $69 Cur: $75 (4/15/88) **93**
Brut Blanc de Blancs Champagne Comtes de Champagne 1979 Rel: $65 Cur: $110 (5/31/87) **92**
Brut Blanc de Blancs Champagne Comtes de Champagne 1976 Rel: $66 Cur: $121 (5/16/86) **83**
Brut Champagne 1985 $50 (12/31/90) **89**
Brut Champagne 1983 $35 (12/31/89) **84**
Brut Champagne NV $26 (12/31/87) **89**
Brut Champagne Collection Arman 1981 Rel: $80 Cur: $85 (5/31/87) CS **92**
Brut Champagne Collection Lichtenstein 1985 $150 (5/15/92) **89**
Brut Champagne Collection Masson 1982 $96 (5/15/92) **94**
Brut Champagne Collection Vieira da Silva 1983 $95 (5/15/92) **94**
Brut Champagne La Française NV $35 (12/31/91) **86**
Brut Champagne Millésime 1982 $38 (12/31/88) **89**
Brut Champagne Réserve NV $24 (5/16/86) **73**
Brut Rosé Champagne Comtes de Champagne 1985 $110 (5/15/92) **88**
Brut Rosé Champagne Comtes de Champagne 1982 Rel: $100 Cur: $120 (12/31/89) **92**
Brut Rosé Champagne Comtes de Champagne 1981 Rel: $88 Cur: $100 (4/15/88) **94**
Brut Rosé Champagne Comtes de Champagne 1976 Rel: $70 Cur: $112 (12/16/85) **90**

TAJA (Spain)
Jumilla 1987 $6 (3/31/90) BB **80**

CHATEAU TALBOT (France/Bordeaux)
Bordeaux Blanc 1985 $9 (4/30/87) **75**
St.-Julien 1991 (NR) (5/15/92) (BT) **85+**
St.-Julien 1990 (NR) (5/15/92) (BT) **90+**
St.-Julien 1989 $43 (3/15/92) **90**
St.-Julien 1988 $25 (3/15/91) **90**
St.-Julien 1987 $23 (5/15/90) **85**
St.-Julien 1986 $32 (5/31/89) **91**
St.-Julien 1985 $26 (4/30/88) **87**
St.-Julien 1984 $19 (5/15/87) **80**
St.-Julien 1983 Rel: $22 Cur: $28 (9/30/86) **89**
St.-Julien 1982 Rel: $26 Cur: $45 (5/01/89) **88**
St.-Julien 1981 Rel: $17 Cur: $34 (6/01/84) **83**
St.-Julien 1979 $31 (10/15/89) (JS) **84**
St.-Julien 1962 $55 (11/30/87) (JS) **55**
St.-Julien 1959 $100 (10/15/90) (JS) **86**
St.-Julien 1945 $310 (3/16/86) (JL) **81**

TALBOTT (United States/California)
Chardonnay Carmel Valley Diamond T Estate 1989 $28 (4/30/92) **87**
Chardonnay Monterey 1989 $24 (12/15/91) **89**

TALLEY (United States/California)
Chardonnay Arroyo Grande Valley 1990 $15 (3/31/92) **85**
Chardonnay Arroyo Grande Valley 1989 $14.50 (7/15/91) **84**
Chardonnay San Luis Obispo County 1987 $12 (12/15/89) **78**
Pinot Noir Arroyo Grande Valley 1989 $17 (10/31/91) **75**

DOMAINE TALMARD (France/Burgundy)
Mâcon-Chardonnay 1989 $10 (10/31/90) **78**
Mâcon-Chardonnay 1988 $9 (7/15/90) **80**

CHATEAU TALMONT (France/Bordeaux)
Bordeaux 1989 $8 (2/28/91) **74**

TALOSA (Italy/Tuscany)
Chianti Colli Senesi 1988 $8 (11/30/90) BB **88**
Rosso di Montepulciano 1989 $11 (1/31/92) **79**
Vino Nobile di Montepulciano Riserva 1986 $15 (7/15/91) **84**
Vino Nobile di Montepulciano Riserva 1982 $8.50 (4/15/88) **72**

TALTARNI (Australia)
Brut Australia Taché NV $16 (6/30/92) **83**
Cabernet Sauvignon Victoria 1986 $10 (9/30/91) **81**
Cabernet Sauvignon Victoria 1984 $9.25 (11/15/87) **85**
Cabernet Sauvignon Victoria 1982 $9.25 (4/30/87) **84**
Cabernet Sauvignon Victoria 1981 $7.50 (5/16/85) **80**
Cabernet Sauvignon Victoria 1980 $6.75 (3/01/84) **81**
Sauvignon Blanc Victoria 1989 $10 (10/31/90) **76**
Sauvignon Blanc Victoria 1988 $15 (9/15/89) **89**
Sauvignon Blanc Victoria Frenchmans Vineyard 1991 $11.50 (6/30/92) **84**
Shiraz Victoria 1988 $14 (5/31/92) **89**
Shiraz Victoria 1987 $10 (9/30/91) **82**
Shiraz Victoria 1986 $10 (10/31/90) **84**
Shiraz Victoria 1985 $10 (11/30/88) SS **91**
Shiraz Victoria 1984 $9.25 (2/15/88) **75**
Shiraz Victoria 1982 $9.25 (4/30/87) **86**
Shiraz Victoria 1980 $6.75 (3/16/84) **77**

IVAN TAMAS (United States/California)
Cabernet Sauvignon Mendocino McNab Ranch 1984 $6 (2/15/87) BB **84**
Cabernet Sauvignon North Coast 1985 $7 (12/31/87) **79**
Chardonnay Livermore Valley 1988 $7.50 (4/30/90) **75**
Chardonnay Napa Valley Reserve 1986 $15 (9/30/88) **86**
Chardonnay Napa Valley-Central Coast 1986 $7 (12/31/87) **77**
Trebbiano Livermore Valley 1990 $8 (9/15/91) **81**
White Zinfandel Mendocino 1988 $5.75 (6/15/89) **85**

TARARA (United States/Virginia)
Cabernet Frederick County 1989 $12 (2/29/92) **82**

Chardonnay Virginia 1990 $11 (2/29/92) **85**
Charval Virginia 1990 $8 (2/29/92) **79**

JEAN TARDY (France/Burgundy)
Clos de Vougeot 1987 $49 (3/31/90) **70**

CHATEAU TAREY DU CASTEL (France/Bordeaux)
Bordeaux Blanc NV $3.25 (5/31/88) **77**

JULIEN TARIN (France/Champagne)
Brut Champagne NV $25 (2/15/87) **78**

DOMAINE DU TARIQUET (France/Other)
Vin de Pays des Côtes de Gascogne 1989 $5.75 (11/15/90) BB **86**

TARRA WARRA (Australia)
Chardonnay Yarra Glen 1989 $28 (2/29/92) **88**
Chardonnay Yarra Glen 1988 $25 (12/31/90) **92**
Pinot Noir Yarra Glen 1989 $28 (4/15/92) **80**
Pinot Noir Yarra Glen 1988 $25 (12/31/90) **86**

DR. COSIMO TAURINO (Italy/Other)
Brindisi Patriglione 1981 $14 (12/31/90) **85**
Brindisi Patriglione Riserva 1979 $12 (3/31/89) **82**
Chardonnay 1990 $7 (5/15/92) **75**
Notarpanaro 1981 $9 (5/15/91) **86**
Notarpanaro 1978 $8 (3/31/89) **80**
Salice Salentino Riserva 1986 $8 (1/31/92) BB **84**
Salice Salentino Riserva 1985 $8 (2/15/91) BB **85**
Salice Salentino Riserva 1983 $6.50 (12/15/89) BB **81**
Salice Salentino Riserva 1982 $6 (3/31/89) BB **82**
Salice Salentino Riserva 1980 $5 (12/15/87) BB **84**
Salice Salentino Rosato 1989 $9 (3/31/92) **82**
Salice Salentino Rosato 1988 $7.25 (3/15/91) BB **84**
Salice Salentino Rosato 1987 $6.50 (12/31/89) BB **84**

CHATEAU TAYAC (France/Bordeaux)
Côtes de Bourg 1988 $10 (1/31/92) **78**

TAYLOR (United States/New York)
Brut Bottle Fermented New York NV $6.50 (12/31/90) **61**
Chenin Blanc California NV $3/1.5L (7/31/89) **71**

TAYLOR FLADGATE (Portugal)
First Estate Port NV $13.50 (4/15/92) **81**
Late Bottled Port 1985 $16 (4/15/92) **87**
Tawny Port 20 Year Old NV $38 (2/28/90) (JS) **85**
Vintage Port 1985 Rel: $32 Cur: $45 (VP-6/90) **90**
Vintage Port 1983 Rel: $25 Cur: $42 (VP-6/90) **89**
Vintage Port 1980 Rel: $21 Cur: $37 (VP-6/90) **88**
Vintage Port 1977 Rel: $17 Cur: $75 (VP-4/90) **98**
Vintage Port 1977 Rel: $17 Cur: $75 (12/16/83) CS **98**
Vintage Port 1975 $46 (VP-12/89) **78**
Vintage Port 1970 $75 (VP-12/89) **98**
Vintage Port 1966 $86 (VP-12/89) **89**
Vintage Port 1963 $152 (VP-12/89) **97**
Vintage Port 1960 $96 (10/31/88) **84**
Vintage Port 1955 $200 (VP-11/89) **88**
Vintage Port 1948 $290 (VP-11/89) **99**
Vintage Port 1945 $590 (VP-11/89) **97**
Vintage Port 1942 $280 (VP-4/90) **78**
Vintage Port 1938 $270 (VP-4/90) **79**
Vintage Port 1935 $400 (VP-2/90) **88**
Vintage Port 1927 $450 (VP-12/89) **95**
Vintage Port Quinta de Vargellas 1987 ($NA) (VP-2/90) **93**
Vintage Port Quinta de Vargellas 1986 ($NA) (VP-2/90) **88**
Vintage Port Quinta de Vargellas 1984 ($NA) (VP-2/90) **87**
Vintage Port Quinta de Vargellas 1982 ($NA) (VP-2/90) **81**
Vintage Port Quinta de Vargellas 1978 Rel: $29 Cur: $36 (VP-2/90) **85**
Vintage Port Quinta de Vargellas 1976 Rel: $29 Cur: $42 (VP-2/90) **81**
Vintage Port Quinta de Vargellas 1974 Rel: $27 Cur: $37 (VP-2/90) **78**
Vintage Port Quinta de Vargellas 1972 $48 (VP-2/90) **84**
Vintage Port Quinta de Vargellas 1969 $50 (VP-2/90) **85**
Vintage Port Quinta de Vargellas 1968 $57 (VP-2/90) **82**
Vintage Port Quinta de Vargellas 1967 $52 (VP-2/90) **82**
Vintage Port Quinta de Vargellas 1965 $53 (VP-2/90) **80**
Vintage Port Quinta de Vargellas 1964 $50 (VP-7/90) **75**
Vintage Port Quinta de Vargellas 1961 $45 (VP-2/90) **68**
Vintage Port Quinta de Vargellas 1958 $55 (VP-2/90) **68**

TEDESCHI (Italy/North)
Capitel San Rocco 1983 $11 (2/15/89) **84**

TEDESCHI VINEYARDS (United States/Hawaii)
Blanc Pineapple Wine Maui NV $6.75 (2/29/92) **80**
Brut Blanc de Noirs Maui 1984 $19 (2/29/92) **79**
Nouveau Maui 1991 $15 (2/29/92) **78**
Rosé Hawaii Ranch Cuvée 1984 $20 (2/29/92) **79**

DOMAINE TEMPIER (France/Other)
Bandol Cuvée Spéciale Cabassaou 1987 $23 (10/31/90) **88**
Bandol Cuvée Spéciale La Migoua 1987 $22 (10/31/90) **86**
Bandol Cuvée Spéciale La Tourtine 1987 $22 (10/31/90) **82**

TENNESSEE VALLEY (United States/Tennessee)
Cabernet Sauvignon Tennessee 1988 $14 (2/29/92) **72**

TENREBAC (United States/Washington)
Port Washington 1989 $24 (11/30/91) **74**

TERRA (United States/California)
Chardonnay Napa Valley 1987 $12 (7/15/91) **87**
Merlot Napa Valley 1988 $14 (5/31/92) **84**

TERRABIANCA (Italy/Tuscany)
Campaccio Barriques 1988 $31 (9/15/91) **87**
Chianti Classico Vigna della Croce Riserva 1985 ($NA) (9/15/91) **87**
Piano del Cipresso 1988 $29 (9/15/91) **83**

TERRACE VALE (Australia)
Pinot Noir Hunter Valley 1986 $9.25 (3/15/88) **81**
Shiraz Hunter Valley Bin 6 1986 $9.50 (3/15/88) **73**

TERRACES (United States/California)
Cabernet Sauvignon Napa Valley 1987 $38 (2/29/92) **92**
Cabernet Sauvignon Napa Valley 1986 $23 (1/31/91) **96**
Zinfandel Napa Valley 1988 $12.50 (2/29/92) **86**
Zinfandel Napa Valley 1987 $12.50 (2/15/91) **89**
Zinfandel Napa Valley Hogue Vineyard 1985 $12.50 (10/31/88) **87**

CHATEAU LA TERRASSE (France/Bordeaux)
Bordeaux Supérieur 1989 $8 (3/31/91) **79**
Bordeaux Supérieur 1986 $8 (6/30/89) **76**
Bordeaux Supérieur 1985 $6 (11/15/87) **78**
Bordeaux Supérieur 1982 $4.50 (11/16/85) **74**

LE TERRE FORTI (Italy/Piedmont)
Barbaresco 1982 $19 (9/15/90) **77**

CHATEAU TERREY-GROS-CAILLOUX (France/Bordeaux)
St.-Julien 1991 (NR) (5/15/92) (BT) **65+**
St.-Julien 1989 $16 (4/30/91) (BT) **85+**
St.-Julien 1988 $14 (6/30/89) (BT) **80+**
St.-Julien 1987 $12 (11/30/89) (JS) **85**
St.-Julien 1986 $12 (11/30/89) (JS) **87**

TERRICCI (Italy/Tuscany)
Antiche Terre de'Ricci 1986 $23 (5/15/90) **83**
Antiche Terre de'Ricci 1985 $22 (3/15/89) **91**
Terricci 1986 $20 (9/30/91) **67**

CHATEAU DU TERTRE (France/Bordeaux)
Margaux 1991 (NR) (5/15/92) (BT) **80+**
Margaux 1990 (NR) (4/30/91) (BT) **85+**
Margaux 1989 $29 (3/15/92) **90**
Margaux 1988 $40 (6/30/91) **86**
Margaux 1987 $18 (6/30/89) (BT) **70+**
Margaux 1986 $22 (6/15/89) **89**
Margaux 1985 Rel: $14 Cur: $29 (6/30/88) SS **93**
Margaux 1983 Rel: $14 Cur: $30 (7/16/86) **91**

CHATEAU TERTRE-DAUGAY (France/Bordeaux)
St.-Emilion 1989 $29 (4/30/92) **83**
St.-Emilion 1988 $20 (4/30/91) **85**
St.-Emilion 1985 Rel: $15 Cur: $18 (5/15/87) (BT) **80+**

CHATEAU TERTRE-ROTEBOEUF (France/Bordeaux)
St.-Emilion 1991 (NR) (5/15/92) (BT) **85+**
St.-Emilion 1990 (NR) (5/15/92) (BT) **90+**
St.-Emilion 1989 $45 (3/15/92) **93**
St.-Emilion 1988 $40 (6/15/91) **90**
St.-Emilion 1987 Rel: $15 Cur: $22 (2/15/90) **83**
St.-Emilion 1986 Rel: $25 Cur: $34 (6/30/89) **90**
St.-Emilion 1985 Rel: $23 Cur: $27 (6/30/88) **89**
St.-Emilion 1983 Rel: $11 Cur: $20 (5/16/86) **81**
St.-Emilion 1982 Rel: $10 Cur: $25 (9/16/85) **85**

TERUZZI & PUTHOD (Italy/Tuscany)
Vernaccia di San Gimignano Terre di Tufo 1989 $20 (12/31/90) **84**
Vigna Peperino 1986 $11 (1/31/90) **68**
Vigna Peperino 1985 $10.50 (10/31/88) **92**

PHILIPPE TESTUT (France/Chablis)
Chablis 1984 $12 (4/15/87) **90**

TEWKSBURY (United States/New Jersey)
Cherry Wine New Jersey NV $6.25 (2/29/92) **78**
Sunset New Jersey 1990 $7 (2/29/92) **78**
Vidal Blanc New Jersey 1990 $8 (2/29/92) **73**

TEYSHA (United States/Texas)
Cabernet Sauvignon Texas Late Harvest 1990 $10 (2/29/92) **78**
Gewürztraminer Texas Casa Nueva Vineyards 1989 $10 (2/29/92) **84**
Rosé of Cabernet Sauvignon Texas Cabernet Royale 1990 $9 (2/29/92) **77**

SEAN H. THACKREY (United States/California)
Mourvèdre California Taurus 1989 $24 (8/31/91) **86**
Mourvèdre California Taurus 1988 $24 (9/30/90) **86**
Petite Sirah Napa Valley Sirius Marston Vineyard Old Vines 1989 $24 (8/31/91) **87**
Pleiades California NV $15 (6/30/92) **83**
Syrah Napa Valley Orion 1989 $45 (12/31/91) **90**
Syrah Napa Valley Orion 1988 $30 (9/30/90) **89**
Syrah Napa Valley Orion 1987 $30 (9/30/89) **92**
Syrah Napa Valley Orion 1986 $26 (4/15/89) **83**

THANISCH (KNABBEN-SPIER) (Germany)
Riesling Auslese Mosel-Saar-Ruwer Bernkasteler Badstube 1988 $25 (9/30/89) **82**
Riesling Auslese Mosel-Saar-Ruwer Bernkasteler Lay 1988 ($NA) (9/30/89) **92**
Riesling Spätlese Mosel-Saar-Ruwer Bernkasteler Doctor 1988 $15 (9/30/89) **90**
Riesling Spätlese Mosel-Saar-Ruwer Bernkasteler Doctor 1986 ($NA) (4/15/89) **79**
Riesling Spätlese Mosel-Saar-Ruwer Bernkasteler Lay 1988 $12 (9/30/89) **89**
Riesling Spätlese Mosel-Saar-Ruwer Bernkasteler Lay 1985 ($NA) (4/15/89) **82**
Riesling Spätlese Mosel-Saar-Ruwer Graacher Himmelreich 1985 ($NA) (4/15/89) **85**

DR. H. THANISCH (MULLER-BURGGRAEFF) (Germany)
Riesling Auslese Mosel-Saar-Ruwer Bernkasteler Doctor 1990 $55 (12/15/91) **86**
Riesling Auslese Mosel-Saar-Ruwer Bernkasteler Doctor 1988 ($NA) (9/30/89) **90**
Riesling Auslese Mosel-Saar-Ruwer Brauneberger Juffer-Sonnenuhr 1989 $25 (12/15/90) **85**
Riesling Auslese Mosel-Saar-Ruwer Brauneberger Juffer-Sonnenuhr 1988 ($NA) (9/30/89) **85**
Riesling Beerenauslese Mosel-Saar-Ruwer Bernkasteler Doctor 1989 $240 (12/15/90) **91**
Riesling Eiswein Mosel-Saar-Ruwer Bernkasteler Doctor 1989 $190 (12/15/90) **88**
Riesling Kabinett Halbtrocken Mosel-Saar-Ruwer Bernkasteler Doctor 1989 ($NA) (12/15/90) **74**
Riesling Kabinett Mosel-Saar-Ruwer Bernkasteler Badstube 1990 $17 (12/15/91) **87**
Riesling Kabinett Mosel-Saar-Ruwer Bernkasteler Badstube 1986 $11 (11/30/87) **72**
Riesling Kabinett Mosel-Saar-Ruwer Bernkasteler Badstube 1985 $11 (4/15/87) **88**
Riesling Kabinett Mosel-Saar-Ruwer Bernkasteler Doctor 1986 $29 (11/30/87) **84**
Riesling Kabinett Mosel-Saar-Ruwer Bernkastler Lay 1989 $13.50 (12/15/90) **81**
Riesling Kabinett Mosel-Saar-Ruwer Graacher Himmelreich 1989 $14 (12/15/90) **79**
Riesling Kabinett Mosel-Saar-Ruwer Lieserer Niederberg-Helden 1990 $10 (12/15/91) **81**
Riesling Kabinett Mosel-Saar-Ruwer Lieserer Niederberg-Heldenberg 1989 $14 (12/15/90) **87**
Riesling Kabinett Mosel-Saar-Ruwer Lieserer Niederberg-Heldenberg 1988 ($NA) (9/30/89) **86**
Riesling Spätlese Mosel-Saar-Ruwer Bernkasteler Doctor 1990 $43 (12/15/91) **87**
Riesling Spätlese Mosel-Saar-Ruwer Bernkasteler Doctor 1989 ($NA) (12/15/90) **71**
Riesling Spätlese Mosel-Saar-Ruwer Bernkasteler Doctor 1986 ($NA) (4/15/89) **64**
Riesling Spätlese Mosel-Saar-Ruwer Bernkasteler Doctor 1985 ($NA) (4/15/89) **77**
Riesling Spätlese Mosel-Saar-Ruwer Bernkasteler Graben 1990 $16 (12/15/91) **82**
Riesling Spätlese Mosel-Saar-Ruwer Bernkasteler Kurfurstlay 1986 $12 (11/30/87) **88**
Riesling Spätlese Mosel-Saar-Ruwer Bernkasteler Kurfurstlay 1985 $9.50 (4/15/89) **72**
Riesling Spätlese Mosel-Saar-Ruwer Brauneberger-Juffer-Sonnenuhr 1990 $20 (12/15/91) **86**
Riesling Spätlese Mosel-Saar-Ruwer Brauneberger-Juffer-Sonnenuhr 1989 $19 (12/15/90) **78**

Riesling Spätlese Mosel-Saar-Ruwer Graacher Himmelreich 1990 (NR) (12/15/91) **87**
Riesling Spätlese Mosel-Saar-Ruwer Lieserer Niederberg-Helden 1990 $13 (12/15/91) **85**
Riesling Spätlese Mosel-Saar-Ruwer Lieserer Niederberg-Helden 1989 $15 (12/15/90) **81**
Riesling Spätlese Mosel-Saar-Ruwer Lieserer Niederberg-Helden 1988 ($NA) (9/30/89) **70**

DR. H. THANISCH (VDP) (Germany)
Riesling Beerenauslese Mosel-Saar-Ruwer Bernkasteler Doctor 1990 (NR) (12/15/91) **95**
Riesling Qualitätswein Mosel-Saar-Ruwer 1990 $11 (12/15/91) (BT) **80+**
Riesling Spätlese Mosel-Saar-Ruwer Bernkasteler Doctor 1990 $51 (12/15/91) **87**
Riesling Spätlese Mosel-Saar-Ruwer Bernkasteler Lay 1990 $22 (12/15/91) **88**
Riesling Spätlese Mosel-Saar-Ruwer Bernkasteler Schlossberg 1990 $20 (12/15/91) **90**

H. THAPRICH (Germany)
Riesling Spätlese Mosel-Saar-Ruwer Bernkasteler Badstube 1983 $8.50 (4/01/85) **80**
Riesling Spätlese Mosel-Saar-Ruwer Bernkasteler Lay 1983 $8.25 (3/16/85) **78**

DOMAINE BARON THENARD (France/Burgundy)
Montrachet 1988 $180 (12/31/90) **93**

JEAN-CLAUDE THEVENET (France/Burgundy)
Mâcon-Pierreclos 1988 $6.25 (7/15/90) BB **84**

ROLAND THEVENIN (France/Burgundy)
Auxey-Duresses Chanterelle 1984 $10 (3/31/87) **69**
Bourgogne Blanc Chardonnay Réserve Roland Thévenin 1985 $8 (3/31/87) **76**
Meursault Les Casse Têtes 1985 $20 (4/30/87) **87**
Pouilly-Fuissé Les Moulins 1985 $19 (3/31/87) **84**

BERNARD THEVENOT (France/Burgundy)
Puligny-Montrachet 1982 $15 (10/16/84) **84**

THEVENOT-LE-BRUN (France/Burgundy)
Bourgogne Aligoté 1988 $12 (7/31/90) **72**

JACQUES THEVENOT-MACHAL (France/Burgundy)
Meursault Porusot 1987 $38 (7/31/89) **81**
Meursault Porusot 1986 $38 (3/15/88) **86**
Puligny-Montrachet Les Charmes 1986 $35 (2/29/88) **82**
Puligny-Montrachet Les Folatières au Chaniot 1988 $40 (12/31/90) **88**
Puligny-Montrachet Les Folatières au Chaniot 1987 $43 (4/15/89) **78**
Puligny-Montrachet Les Folatières au Chaniot 1986 $38 (2/29/88) **81**
Volnay-Santenots 1988 $36 (11/15/90) **89**

ALAIN THIENOT (France/Champagne)
Brut Champagne NV (NR) (12/31/91) **89**

CHATEAU THIEULEY (France/Bordeaux)
Bordeaux Blanc 1985 $4 (5/31/88) **78**

GERARD THOMAS (France/Burgundy)
St.-Aubin La Chatenière 1989 $28 (8/31/91) **87**
St.-Aubin Murgers des Dents Chien 1989 $25 (8/31/91) **83**

PAUL THOMAS (United States/Washington)
Cabernet Sauvignon Washington 1989 $12 (3/31/92) **80**
Cabernet Sauvignon Washington 1986 $14 (9/30/90) **84**
Cabernet Sauvignon Washington 1985 $20 (10/15/89) **88**
Cabernet Sauvignon Washington Reserve 1987 $16 (3/31/92) **86**
Chardonnay Washington 1990 $12 (3/31/92) **89**
Chardonnay Washington 1988 $11 (10/15/89) **89**
Chardonnay Washington 1987 $10 (10/15/89) **81**
Chardonnay Washington Private Reserve 1987 $18 (10/15/89) **85**
Chardonnay Washington Reserve 1989 $18 (3/31/92) **76**
Chenin Blanc Washington 1988 $7 (10/15/89) **84**
Johannisberg Riesling Washington 1988 $7 (10/15/89) **85**
Merlot Washington 1987 $16 (9/30/90) **89**
Merlot Washington Reserve 1989 $15 (3/31/92) **79**
Riesling Washington Dry 1988 $7 (10/15/89) **85**
Riesling Washington Dry 1987 $7 (7/31/89) **77**
Sauvignon Blanc Washington 1987 $9 (10/15/89) **85**

THOMAS-HSI (United States/California)
Chardonnay Napa Valley 1988 $18 (6/30/91) **89**
Chardonnay Napa Valley 1987 $18 (6/30/90) **82**

THORIN (France)
Beaujolais-Villages 1988 $7 (5/31/89) (TM) **79**
Chablis Fourchaume 1987 $24 (10/15/89) **91**
Chablis Fourchaume 1986 $23 (2/15/89) **86**
Châteauneuf-du-Pape 1986 $13 (11/30/88) **87**
Côtes du Rhône L'Escalou 1987 $6 (1/31/89) **67**
Mâcon-Villages 1987 $8.50 (1/31/89) **74**
Meursault 1987 $25 (12/15/88) **84**
Moulin-à-Vent Château des Jacques 1988 $16 (5/31/89) (TM) **88**
Pommard 1986 $24 (2/28/90) **75**
Puligny-Montrachet 1987 $32 (11/15/89) **87**

THURSTON WOLFE (United States/Washington)
Black Muscat Washington 1987 $9 (10/15/89) **85**
Sauvignon Blanc Late Harvest Washington Sweet Rebecca 1987 $9 (10/15/89) **83**

TIEFENBRUNNER (Italy/North)
Cabernet Alto Adige 1987 $9 (3/31/89) **84**
Chardonnay Alto Adige 1990 $10 (1/31/92) **83**
Chardonnay Alto Adige 1989 $10 (7/15/91) **82**
Chardonnay Alto Adige Linticlarus 1989 $10.50 (1/31/92) **81**
Pinot Bianco Alto Adige 1989 $9 (8/31/91) **78**
Pinot Grigio Alto Adige 1990 $11 (1/31/92) **80**
Pinot Grigio Alto Adige 1989 $10 (6/30/91) **83**

TIFFANY HILL (United States/California)
Chardonnay Edna Valley 1989 $18 (7/15/91) **73**
Chardonnay Edna Valley 1987 $19 (3/31/89) **85**
Chardonnay Edna Valley 1986 $19 (6/15/88) **90**

TIJSSELING (United States/California)
Blanc de Blancs Mendocino 1986 $13 (12/31/91) **72**
Blanc de Blancs Mendocino Cuvée de Chardonnay 1985 $13 (12/31/89) **80**
Brut Mendocino 1987 $11.50 (12/31/91) **81**
Brut Mendocino 1986 $11.50 (12/31/89) **89**
Cabernet Sauvignon Mendocino 1986 $8 (1/31/90) BB **85**
Chardonnay Mendocino 1989 $10 (7/15/91) **69**
Chardonnay Mendocino 1988 $10 (2/28/90) **70**

TIN PONY (United States/California)
Chardonnay Sonoma County Green Valley 1986 $8 (9/30/88) **71**

F. TINEL-BLONDELET (France/Loire)
Pouilly-Fumé 1987 $12 (2/28/89) **78**
Pouilly-Fumé L'Arret Buffatte 1987 $15 (2/28/89) **86**

CASTELLO DI TIZZANO (Italy/Tuscany)
Chianti Classico Riserva 1982 $18 (7/15/89) **78**

PHILIP TOGNI (United States/California)
Cabernet Sauvignon Napa Valley 1991 (NR) (5/15/92) (BT) **87+**
Cabernet Sauvignon Napa Valley 1990 $24 (5/15/91) (BT) **90+**
Cabernet Sauvignon Napa Valley 1988 Rel: $26 Cur: $28 (7/15/91) **92**
Cabernet Sauvignon Napa Valley 1987 Rel: $24 Cur: $32 (8/31/90) **94**
Cabernet Sauvignon Napa Valley 1986 Rel: $22 Cur: $30 (CA-3/89) **93**
Cabernet Sauvignon Napa Valley 1985 Rel: $20 Cur: $25 (CA-3/89) **89**
Cabernet Sauvignon Napa Valley 1984 Rel: $18 Cur: $33 (CA-3/89) **86**
Cabernet Sauvignon Napa Valley 1983 Rel: $18 Cur: $40 (CA-3/89) **87**
Cabernet Sauvignon Napa Valley Tanbark Hill Vineyard 1988 $24 (6/30/91) **87**
Sauvignon Blanc Napa Valley 1989 $12.50 (7/15/91) **82**

TOLLEY'S (Australia)
Pinot Noir Barossa Valley Selected Harvest 1983 $5 (11/15/87) **76**

TOLLOT-BEAUT (France/Burgundy)
Aloxe-Corton 1989 (NR) (1/31/92) **90**
Aloxe-Corton 1988 $35 (7/15/90) (BT) **85+**
Aloxe-Corton 1985 $35 (3/15/88) **89**
Beaune Clos du Roi 1988 $53 (2/28/91) **86**
Beaune Clos du Roi Premier Cru 1989 (NR) (1/31/92) **91**
Beaune Grèves 1989 (NR) (1/31/92) **90**
Beaune Grèves 1988 $35 (7/15/90) (BT) **85+**
Bourgogne Blanc Chardonnay 1989 ($NA) (8/31/91) **87**
Chorey-Côte-de-Beaune 1989 (NR) (1/31/92) **87**
Chorey-Côte-de-Beaune 1985 $18 (4/15/88) **83**
Chorey-lès-Beaune 1988 $25 (12/31/90) **88**
Corton 1989 $67 (1/31/92) **90**
Corton 1988 $55 (7/15/90) (BT) **80+**
Corton 1986 $45 (8/31/89) **87**
Corton 1985 $49 (3/15/88) **97**
Corton-Bressandes 1989 $67 (1/31/92) **92**
Corton-Bressandes 1988 $55 (7/15/90) (BT) **90+**
Savigny-lès-Beaune Lavières 1989 (NR) (1/31/92) **90**
Savigny-lès-Beaune Lavières 1988 $28 (7/15/90) (BT) **85+**

CHATEAU LA TONNELLE (France/Bordeaux)
Haut-Médoc 1987 ($NA) (11/30/89) (JS) **76**
Haut-Médoc 1986 $11 (11/30/89) (JS) **70**
Haut-Médoc 1985 $10 (2/15/89) **77**

TOPAZ (United States/California)
Rouge de Trois Napa Valley 1988 $14.50 (11/15/91) **87**
Sauvignon Blanc Sémillon Late Harvest Napa Valley Special Select 1989 $19/375ml (8/31/91) **90**

TOPOLOS (United States/California)
Zinfandel Sonoma County Ultimo 1988 $12 (5/15/92) **77**

LA TORRE (Italy/Tuscany)
Brunello di Montalcino 1985 $30 (4/15/91) **78**

TORREBIANCO (Italy/Other)
Chardonnay 1987 $11 (12/31/90) **78**

TORRE ROSAZZA (Italy/North)
Chardonnay 1989 $15 (2/15/91) **78**
Chardonnay 1988 $14 (9/15/89) **81**

TORRES (Spain)
Merlot Penedès Viña Las Torres 1990 $12 (11/15/91) **86**
Merlot Penedès Viña Las Torres 1989 $13 (10/15/90) **82**
Merlot Penedès Viña Las Torres 1988 $10 (3/31/90) **83**
Penedès Coronas 1989 $8 (4/15/92) **81**
Penedès Coronas 1988 $7 (6/15/91) BB **81**
Penedès Coronas 1987 $6.50 (10/15/90) BB **80**
Penedès Coronas 1986 $6.25 (11/30/89) **78**
Penedès Coronas 1985 $5.50 (11/30/88) BB **86**
Penedès Coronas 1983 $4.50 (6/30/87) BB **84**
Penedès Coronas 1982 $4.50 (2/16/86) (JS) **76**
Penedès De Casta 1990 $6 (7/15/91) **78**
Penedès Fransola 1988 $14.50 (3/31/90) **79**
Penedès Fransola Green Label 1990 $16 (7/15/91) **81**
Penedès Gran Coronas 1985 $11 (11/30/88) **89**
Penedès Gran Coronas 1979 $9 (2/16/86) (JS) **75**
Penedès Gran Coronas Black Label Reserva 1982 Rel: $27 Cur: $33 (6/15/88) **85**
Penedès Gran Coronas Black Label Reserva 1981 Rel: $18 Cur: $21 (10/15/87) **83**
Penedès Gran Coronas Black Label Reserva 1978 $45 (2/16/86) **85**
Penedès Gran Coronas Más la Plana Reserva 1985 $32 (10/15/90) **85**
Penedès Gran Coronas Más la Plana Reserva 1983 Rel: $26 Cur: $30 (3/31/90) **85**
Penedès Gran Coronas Reserva 1987 $15 (4/15/92) **84**
Penedès Gran Coronas Reserva 1986 $12 (11/30/89) **86**
Penedès Gran Coronas Reserva 1985 $12 (3/31/90) **77**
Penedès Gran Sangre de Toro 1984 $9 (9/15/88) **78**
Penedès Gran Sangre de Toro 1979 $9 (2/16/86) (JS) **79**
Penedès Gran Sangre de Toro Reserva 1987 $10 (11/15/91) **83**
Penedès Gran Sangre de Toro Reserva 1986 $10 (10/15/90) **83**
Penedès Gran Sangre de Toro Reserva 1985 $9 (11/30/89) **87**
Penedès Gran Sangre de Toro Reserva 1983 $9.50 (6/15/88) SS **91**

Key to Symbols

The scores reported here are the results of blind tastings conducted by our panel of senior editors. Wines that carry the initials below are results of individual tastings.

THE WINE SPECTATOR 100-POINT SCALE ***95-100***—Classic, a great wine; ***90-94***—Outstanding, superior character and style; ***80-89***—Good to very good, a wine with special qualities; ***70-79***—Average, drinkable wine that may have minor flaws; ***60-69***—Below average, drinkable but not recommended; ***50-59***—Poor, undrinkable, not recommended. "+"—With a score indicates a range; used primarily with barrel tastings to indicate a preliminary score.

SPECIAL DESIGNATIONS SS—Spectator Selection, CS—Cellar Selection, BB—Best Buy, ($NA)—Price not available, (NR)—Not released.

TASTER'S INITIALS (JG)—Jim Gordon, (HS)—Harvey Steiman, (JL)—James Laube, (JS)—James Suckling, (TM)—Thomas Matthews, (TR)—Terry Robards, (PM)—Per-Henrik Mansson, (BT)—Barrel Tasting (these wines were tasted blind from barrel samples), (CA-date)—*California's Great Cabernets* by James Laube, (CH-date)—*California's Great Chardonnays* by James Laube, (VP-date)—*Vintage Port* by James Suckling.

DATE TASTED Dates in parentheses represent the issue in which the rating was published.

Penedès Gran Sangre de Toro Reserva 1981 $5.50 (6/15/87) **80**
Penedès Gran Viña Sol 1989 $10 (12/15/90) **80**
Penedès Gran Viña Sol 1988 $14 (3/31/90) **83**
Penedès Más Borras 1989 $20 (11/15/91) **79**
Penedès Más Borras 1988 $18 (10/15/90) **79**
Penedès Milmanda 1990 $35 (10/31/91) **91**
Penedès Milmanda 1989 $40 (12/15/90) **93**
Penedès Milmanda 1988 $35 (3/31/90) **80**
Penedès Milmanda 1987 $35 (12/15/88) **94**
Penedès Sangre de Toro 1989 $7 (4/15/92) BB **82**
Penedès Sangre de Toro 1988 $6.50 (3/31/91) BB **82**
Penedès Sangre de Toro 1987 $5.25 (11/30/89) BB **82**
Penedès Sangre de Toro 1986 $4.75 (12/15/88) BB **80**
Penedès Sangre de Toro 1985 $5.50 (6/15/88) BB **81**
Penedès Sangre de Toro 1983 $4 (6/15/87) **79**
Penedès Sangre de Toro 1982 ($NA) (2/16/86) (JS) **83**
Penedès Viña Esmeralda 1991 $10 (5/31/92) **80**
Penedès Viña Esmeralda 1990 $10.50 (7/15/91) **84**
Penedès Viña Esmeralda 1989 $9 (3/31/90) **84**
Penedès Viña Magdala 1986 $13.50 (11/15/91) **82**
Penedès Viña Magdala 1984 $11 (7/31/89) **76**
Penedès Viña Magdala 1983 $9.50 (6/15/88) **74**
Penedès Viña Magdala 1979 ($NA) (2/16/86) (JS) **72**
Penedès Viña Sol 1990 $6 (11/15/91) BB **80**
Penedès Viña Sol 1989 $7 (7/15/91) **73**
Penedès Viña Sol 1988 $5.25 (3/31/90) **72**

MIGUEL TORRES (Chile)
Cabernet Sauvignon Curicó District 1990 $7 (6/15/92) BB **85**
Cabernet Sauvignon Curicó District 1989 $7 (6/15/91) BB **82**
Cabernet Sauvignon Curicó District 1988 $4.50 (9/15/90) BB **87**
Cabernet Sauvignon Curicó District 1985 $5 (3/31/88) **73**
Cabernet Sauvignon Curicó District 1984 $4.50 (1/31/87) **79**
Chardonnay Curicó District 1991 $8 (6/15/92) **74**
Chardonnay Curicó District 1989 $7.50 (3/31/90) **75**
Sauvignon Blanc Curicó District 1991 $7 (4/15/92) BB **84**
Sauvignon Blanc Curicó District 1990 $7 (10/15/91) **74**
Sauvignon Blanc Curicó District Bellaterra 1990 (NR) (6/15/92) **77**

MARIMAR TORRES (United States/California)
Chardonnay Sonoma County Green Valley Don Miguel Vineyard 1990 $24 (7/15/92) **87**
Chardonnay Sonoma County Green Valley Don Miguel Vineyard 1989 $20 (5/15/91) **90**

BODEGAS TORRES FILOSO (Spain)
La Mancha Cosecha Arboles de Castillejo 1986 $7 (4/15/92) **79**

TORRESELLA (Italy/North)
Chardonnay 1988 $6 (9/15/89) **83**
Chardonnay 1986 $5.75 (3/31/89) **79**

DOMAINE TORTOCHOT (France/Burgundy)
Chambertin 1985 $90 (12/31/88) **94**

VIGNE TOSCANE (Italy/Tuscany)
Chianti Terre Toscane 1989 $5 (11/30/90) BB **80**

TOSCOLO (Italy/Tuscany)
Red Tuscan Table Wine 1986 $4.25 (1/31/89) **79**

PASCUAL TOSO (Other/Argentina)
Cabernet Sauvignon Mendoza 1988 $7 (3/15/91) **79**

TOTT'S (United States/California)
Brut California NV $8 (5/15/92) **77**
Brut California Reserve Cuvée NV $8 (5/31/89) **80**
Extra Dry California NV $8 (5/15/92) **75**
Extra Dry California Reserve Cuvée NV $8 (2/28/89) **75**

J. TOUCHAIS (France/Loire)
Anjou Blanc Moulin Doué la Fontaine 1979 $28 (11/15/91) **90**

CHATEAU DE LA TOUR DE L'ANGE (France/Burgundy)
Mâcon-Villages Chardonnay 1989 $9 (8/31/91) **72**

CHATEAU TOUR-BALADOZ (France/Bordeaux)
St.-Emilion 1985 $11.50 (2/29/88) **82**

CHATEAU TOUR DE BELLEGARDE (France/Bordeaux)
Bordeaux Supérieur 1986 $4.75 (5/15/89) **77**

CHATEAU LA TOUR-DE-BESSAN (France/Bordeaux)
Margaux 1989 (NR) (3/15/92) **87**

CHATEAU LA TOUR-BLANCHE (France/Sauternes)
Sauternes 1989 ($NA) (6/15/90) (BT) **85+**
Sauternes 1988 Rel: $29 Cur: $33 (6/15/90) (BT) **85+**
Sauternes 1987 $23 (6/15/90) **82**
Sauternes 1986 $26 (12/31/89) **79**
Sauternes 1985 Rel: $25 Cur: $29 (7/15/88) **85**
Sauternes 1983 $32 (1/31/88) **87**

LE SEC DE LA TOUR-BLANCHE (France/Bordeaux)
Bordeaux Blanc Sauvignon 1989 $9 (3/31/91) **78**

CHATEAU LA TOUR DE BY (France/Bordeaux)
Médoc 1991 (NR) (5/15/92) (BT) **75+**
Médoc 1989 $15 (3/15/92) **85**
Médoc 1988 $12.50 (6/15/91) **86**
Médoc 1987 $10 (11/30/89) (JS) **79**
Médoc 1986 $12 (11/30/89) (JS) **80**
Médoc 1983 $7 (10/16/85) **78**
Médoc 1982 Rel: $5.50 Cur: $15 (11/30/89) (JS) **80**

CHATEAU TOUR-CALON (France/Bordeaux)
Montagne-St.-Emilion 1986 $10 (9/30/89) **81**

CHATEAU LA TOUR-FIGEAC (France/Bordeaux)
St.-Emilion 1989 (NR) (4/30/91) (BT) **85+**
St.-Emilion 1988 $17 (6/30/89) (BT) **70+**
St.-Emilion 1987 $14 (6/30/89) (BT) **75+**
St.-Emilion 1982 $22 (5/15/89) (TR) **89**

CHATEAU LA TOUR-CARNET (France/Bordeaux)
Haut-Médoc 1991 (NR) (5/15/92) (BT) **75+**
Haut-Médoc 1990 (NR) (4/30/91) (BT) **75+**
Haut-Médoc 1989 $24 (3/15/92) **92**
Haut-Médoc 1988 $15 (8/31/91) **82**
Haut-Médoc 1986 $22 (5/15/87) (BT) **80+**
Haut-Médoc 1985 $22 (12/31/88) **71**
Haut-Médoc 1983 $13 (2/29/88) **69**
Haut-Médoc 1945 $130 (3/16/86) (JL) **88**

CHATEAU TOUR-GRAND-FAURIE (France/Bordeaux)
St.-Emilion 1985 $9.75 (2/15/89) **79**

CHATEAU LA TOUR-HAUT-BRION (France/Bordeaux)
Pessac-Léognan 1991 (NR) (5/15/92) (BT) **80+**
Pessac-Léognan 1990 (NR) (5/15/92) (BT) **85+**
Pessac-Léognan 1989 $52 (3/15/92) **95**
Pessac-Léognan 1988 $37 (6/15/91) CS **91**
Pessac-Léognan 1987 $22 (5/15/90) **87**
Pessac-Léognan 1986 $33 (6/30/88) (BT) **85+**
Graves 1985 $42 (2/15/89) **86**
Graves 1983 Rel: $25 Cur: $31 (3/15/87) **90**
Graves 1979 $30 (11/15/91) (JS) **85**
Graves 1975 $115 (11/15/91) (JS) **84**
Graves 1970 $150 (11/15/91) (JS) **84**
Graves 1966 $175 (11/15/91) (JS) **84**
Graves 1964 $110 (11/15/91) (JS) **83**
Graves 1962 $40 (11/30/87) (JS) **85**
Graves 1961 $200 (11/15/91) (JS) **89**
Graves 1959 $190 (11/15/91) (JS) **84**
Graves 1958 ($NA) (11/15/91) (JS) **85**
Graves 1957 $125 (11/15/91) (JS) **86**
Graves 1955 $300 (11/15/91) (JS) **87**
Graves 1953 $290 (11/15/91) (JS) **86**
Graves 1950 $200 (11/15/91) (JS) **50**
Graves 1947 ($NA) (11/15/91) (JS) **91**
Graves 1945 $520 (11/15/91) (JS) **87**
Graves 1943 $230 (11/15/91) (JS) **85**
Graves 1940 $190 (11/15/91) (JS) **83**
Graves 1929 ($NA) (11/15/91) (JS) **85**
Graves 1928 $300 (11/15/91) (JS) **68**

CHATEAU LA TOUR-HAUT-CAUSSAN (France/Bordeaux)
Médoc 1991 (NR) (5/15/92) (BT) **80+**
Médoc 1989 $15 (3/15/92) **87**
Médoc 1988 $12.50 (7/15/91) **79**
Médoc 1987 $11 (11/30/89) (JS) **80**
Médoc 1986 $14 (11/30/89) (JS) **88**
Médoc 1984 $10 (2/15/88) **80**
Médoc 1982 $10 (11/30/89) (JS) **83**

CHATEAU TOUR DU HAUT-MOULIN (France/Bordeaux)
Haut-Médoc 1988 $20 (4/30/91) **88**
Haut-Médoc 1987 $15 (11/30/89) (JS) **80**
Haut-Médoc 1986 $16 (11/30/89) (JS) **90**
Haut-Médoc 1985 $15 (2/15/89) **84**
Haut-Médoc 1982 $16 (11/30/89) (JS) **84**

CHATEAU LA TOUR-LEOGNAN (France/Bordeaux)
Pessac-Léognan 1987 ($NA) (6/30/89) (BT) **70+**
Pessac-Léognan 1986 $11 (2/15/89) **85**
Pessac-Léognan Blanc 1990 $19 (6/30/92) **86**
Pessac-Léognan Blanc 1988 ($NA) (6/30/89) (BT) **80+**

CHATEAU LA TOUR-MARTILLAC (France/Bordeaux)
Pessac-Léognan 1991 (NR) (5/15/92) (BT) **85+**
Pessac-Léognan 1990 (NR) (5/15/92) (BT) **90+**
Pessac-Léognan 1989 $28 (4/30/91) (BT) **85+**
Pessac-Léognan 1988 $24 (2/28/91) **88**
Pessac-Léognan 1987 $15 (6/30/88) (BT) **75+**
Pessac-Léognan 1986 $15 (2/15/90) **90**
Graves 1985 $19 (8/31/88) **87**
Pessac-Léognan Blanc 1990 (NR) (9/30/91) (BT) **90+**
Pessac-Léognan Blanc 1989 $28 (2/28/91) **86**
Pessac-Léognan Blanc 1987 $15 (1/31/90) **93**

CHATEAU TOUR-DU-MIRAIL (France/Bordeaux)
Haut-Médoc 1987 $10 (11/30/89) (JS) **83**
Haut-Médoc 1986 $12 (11/30/89) (JS) **79**
Haut-Médoc 1982 $9 (11/30/89) (JS) **79**

CHATEAU LA TOUR-DE-MONS (France/Bordeaux)
Margaux 1991 (NR) (5/15/92) (BT) **85+**
Margaux 1989 $25 (3/15/92) **88**
Margaux 1986 $19 (11/30/89) (JS) **90**
Margaux 1986 $17 (6/15/89) **90**
Margaux 1982 $17 (11/30/89) (JS) **90**
Margaux 1945 $200 (3/16/86) (JL) **89**

CHATEAU LA TOUR DU PIN (France/Bordeaux)
St.-Emilion 1982 $12 (5/01/85) **81**

CHATEAU LA TOUR-DU-PIN-FIGEAC (France/Bordeaux)
St.-Emilion 1988 $24 (7/15/91) **77**
St.-Emilion 1987 $17 (6/30/89) (BT) **80+**
St.-Emilion 1982 $21 (5/15/89) (TR) **88**

CHATEAU LA TOUR-DU-PIN-FIGEAC-BELIEVIER (France/Bordeaux)
St.-Emilion 1989 $24 (4/30/92) **83**
St.-Emilion 1982 ($NA) (5/15/89) (TR) **82**

CHATEAU TOUR-DU-ROC (France/Bordeaux)
Haut-Médoc 1987 $10 (11/30/89) (JS) **74**
Haut-Médoc 1986 $11 (11/30/89) (JS) **76**
Haut-Médoc 1982 $12 (11/30/89) (JS) **84**

CHATEAU LA TOUR-ST.-BONNET (France/Bordeaux)
Médoc 1985 $9 (6/30/88) **83**

LES TOURELLES DE LONGUEVILLE (France/Bordeaux)
Pauillac 1991 (NR) (5/15/92) (BT) **85+**
Pauillac 1990 (NR) (5/15/92) (BT) **90+**
Pauillac 1989 $27 (3/15/92) **94**
Pauillac 1988 $25 (8/31/90) (BT) **85+**
Pauillac 1987 $17 (6/30/89) (BT) **75+**

TOYON (United States/California)
Cabernet Sauvignon Alexander Valley 1982 $10 (11/15/86) **83**

TRACOLLE (Italy/Tuscany)
Chianti Classico 1988 ($NA) (9/15/91) **69**

LOUIS TRAPET (France/Burgundy)
Chambertin 1988 $133 (7/15/91) **92**
Chambertin 1987 $75 (5/31/90) **91**
Chambertin 1985 $80 (3/15/88) **88**
Chambertin Cuvée Vieilles Vignes 1988 $133 (7/15/91) **89**
Chapelle-Chambertin 1988 $84 (7/15/91) **89**
Chapelle-Chambertin 1985 Rel: $64 Cur: $73 (3/15/88) **84**
Chapelle-Chambertin Réserve Jean Trapet 1987 $62 (3/15/91) **79**
Gevrey-Chambertin 1988 $40 (7/15/91) **81**
Gevrey-Chambertin 1987 $30 (7/15/90) **74**
Gevrey-Chambertin 1985 $40 (5/31/88) **79**
Latricières-Chambertin 1988 $84 (7/15/91) **84**
Latricières-Chambertin 1987 $62 (5/31/90) **88**
Marsannay 1987 $17 (3/31/91) **78**

TRAPICHE (Other/Argentina)
Cabernet Sauvignon Mendoza 1982 $4 (2/15/89) BB **81**
Cabernet Sauvignon Mendoza Oak Cask Reserve Vintner's Selection 1986 $9.75 (10/15/91) **82**
Cabernet Sauvignon Mendoza Reserve 1986 $5.50 (9/15/90) **77**
Cabernet Sauvignon Mendoza Vintner's Selection Oak Cask Reserve 1986 $8 (7/15/91) **69**
Chardonnay Mendoza Oak Cask Reserve Vintners Selection 1990 $8 (11/15/91) **81**
Chardonnay Mendoza Reserve 1989 $5.50 (9/15/90) **78**
Malbec Mendoza Oak Cask Reserve Vintner's Selection 1988 $6.50 (10/15/91) **81**
Malbec Mendoza Reserve 1987 $5 (9/15/90) BB **83**

TRAVAGLINI (Italy/Piedmont)
Gattinara 1986 $18 (1/31/92) **82**
Gattinara Numerata 1985 $26 (1/31/92) **84**
Spanna 1988 $10 (7/15/91) **83**

TRAVERSA (Italy/Piedmont)
Barbaresco Sorì Ciabot 1985 $23 (9/15/90) **86**

TREFETHEN (United States/California)
Cabernet Sauvignon Napa Valley 1987 Rel: $16 Cur: $19 (11/15/90) **86**
Cabernet Sauvignon Napa Valley 1986 Rel: $15.25 Cur: $19 (10/31/89) **84**
Cabernet Sauvignon Napa Valley 1985 Rel: $15 Cur: $19 (CA-3/89) **80**
Cabernet Sauvignon Napa Valley 1984 Rel: $14 Cur: $17 (CA-3/89) **84**
Cabernet Sauvignon Napa Valley 1983 Rel: $11.75 Cur: $36 (CA-3/89) **84**
Cabernet Sauvignon Napa Valley 1982 Rel: $11 Cur: $22 (CA-3/89) **58**
Cabernet Sauvignon Napa Valley 1981 Rel: $11 Cur: $36 (CA-3/89) **87**
Cabernet Sauvignon Napa Valley 1981 Rel: $11 Cur: $36 (12/16/84) SS **88**
Cabernet Sauvignon Napa Valley 1980 Rel: $11 Cur: $35 (CA-3/89) **68**
Cabernet Sauvignon Napa Valley 1979 Rel: $11 Cur: $28 (CA-3/89) **86**
Cabernet Sauvignon Napa Valley 1978 Rel: $10 Cur: $38 (CA-3/89) **81**
Cabernet Sauvignon Napa Valley 1977 Rel: $8.50 Cur: $28 (CA-3/89) **86**
Cabernet Sauvignon Napa Valley 1976 Rel: $7.50 Cur: $22 (CA-3/89) **76**
Cabernet Sauvignon Napa Valley 1975 Rel: $7.50 Cur: $55 (CA-3/89) **83**
Cabernet Sauvignon Napa Valley 1974 Rel: $8 Cur: $75 (CA-3/89) **84**
Cabernet Sauvignon Napa Valley Hillside Selection 1987 ($NA) (4/15/89) (BT) **90+**
Cabernet Sauvignon Napa Valley Hillside Selection 1986 ($NA) (CA-3/89) **90**
Cabernet Sauvignon Napa Valley Hillside Selection 1985 $30 (11/15/90) **80**
Chardonnay Napa Valley Library Selection 1985 $30 (3/15/92) **92**
Chardonnay Napa Valley 1990 $18 (7/15/92) **83**
Chardonnay Napa Valley 1988 Rel: $17.50 Cur: $20 (12/31/90) **85**
Chardonnay Napa Valley 1987 Rel: $16.75 Cur: $20 (CH-3/90) **88**
Chardonnay Napa Valley 1986 Rel: $16.25 Cur: $22 (CH-3/90) **87**
Chardonnay Napa Valley 1985 Rel: $15.25 Cur: $34 (CH-3/90) **88**
Chardonnay Napa Valley 1984 Rel: $14.25 Cur: $40 (CH-3/90) **86**
Chardonnay Napa Valley 1983 Rel: $13.75 Cur: $35 (CH-3/90) **77**
Chardonnay Napa Valley 1982 Rel: $13.50 Cur: $30 (CH-3/90) **73**
Chardonnay Napa Valley 1981 Rel: $13 Cur: $30 (CH-3/90) **83**
Chardonnay Napa Valley 1980 Rel: $13 Cur: $40 (CH-3/90) **86**
Chardonnay Napa Valley 1979 Rel: $12 Cur: $30 (CH-3/90) **73**
Chardonnay Napa Valley 1978 Rel: $10 Cur: $35 (CH-3/90) **90**
Chardonnay Napa Valley 1977 Rel: $8.50 Cur: $35 (CH-3/90) **81**
Chardonnay Napa Valley 1976 Rel: $7 Cur: $40 (CH-3/90) **74**
Chardonnay Napa Valley 1975 Rel: $6.50 Cur: $45 (CH-3/90) **73**
Chardonnay Napa Valley 1974 Rel: $5.75 Cur: $50 (CH-3/90) **80**
Chardonnay Napa Valley 1973 Rel: $6.50 Cur: $50 (CH-3/90) **85**
Eschol Red Napa Valley NV $6 (2/15/91) **79**
Eshcol Red #3 Napa Valley NV $6.25 (11/15/89) BB **80**
Eschol White Napa Valley NV $6.50 (1/31/91) BB **81**
Pinot Noir Napa Valley 1986 $13 (7/31/89) **68**
Pinot Noir Napa Valley 1985 $12 (6/15/88) **74**
Pinot Noir Napa Valley 1984 $9.25 (5/31/88) **80**
White Riesling Napa Valley 1988 $8.25 (7/31/89) **87**

JACQUES TREMBLAY (France/Chablis)
Chablis Fourchaume 1986 ($NA) (3/31/89) **88**

TRENEL & FILS (France/Beaujolais)
Beaujolais-Villages 1990 $10 (9/15/91) **81**
Beaujolais-Villages 1988 $9 (5/31/89) (TM) **78**
Chénas 1988 $14 (5/31/89) (TM) **86**
Chiroubles 1988 $12 (5/31/89) (TM) **83**
Côte-de-Brouilly 1990 $15 (9/15/91) **82**
Fleurie 1988 $14 (5/31/89) (TM) **86**
Morgon Côte de Py 1988 $17 (5/31/89) (TM) **92**
Moulin-à-Vent La Rochelle 1988 $17 (5/31/89) (TM) **90**
Régnié 1988 $12 (5/31/89) (TM) **83**
St.-Amour 1988 $15 (5/31/89) (TM) **87**

TENUTA TREROSE (Italy/Tuscany)
Vino Nobile di Montepulciano 1986 $16 (7/15/91) **80**
Vino Nobile di Montepulciano 1985 $11 (11/15/88) **90**
Vino Nobile di Montepulciano Riserva 1985 $19 (7/15/91) **85**

DOMAINE DE TREVALLON (France/Other)
Côteaux d'Aix en Provence Les Baux 1987 $18 (3/31/90) **78**
Côteaux d'Aix en Provence Les Baux 1986 $21 (4/15/89) **87**

M. TRIBAUT (United States/California)
Blanc de Noirs Monterey County NV $10 (1/31/92) **82**
Brut Monterey County 1985 $13 (5/31/89) **91**
Brut Monterey County 1984 $14 (12/31/87) **85**
Brut Monterey County 1983 $14 (2/15/87) **81**
Rosé Monterey County 1984 $14 (12/31/87) **80**
Rosé Monterey County NV $13 (1/31/92) **77**

LAURENT TRIBUT (France/Chablis)
Chablis 1988 $17 (7/31/90) **87**
Chablis Beauroy 1988 $17 (7/15/90) **89**

DOMAINE TRIBUT-DAUVISSAT (France/Chablis)
Chablis 1988 $18 (1/31/91) **84**
Chablis 1987 $15 (10/15/89) **68**

CHATEAU DU TRIGNON (France/Rhône)
Côtes du Rhône-Villages Rasteau 1986 $9 (12/15/90) **80**

TRIMBACH (France/Alsace)
Gewürztraminer Alsace 1990 $13 (2/15/92) **86**
Gewürztraminer Alsace 1989 $11 (11/15/90) **86**
Gewürztraminer Alsace 1988 $8.50 (10/15/89) **83**
Gewürztraminer Alsace Carte d'Or 1989 ($NA) (11/15/90) **85**
Gewürztraminer Alsace Cuvée des Seigneurs de Ribeauvillé 1990 (NR) (2/15/92) **90**
Gewürztraminer Alsace Hors Choix Sélection de Grains Nobles 1989 ($NA) (11/15/90) **97**
Gewürztraminer Alsace Réserve 1989 ($NA) (11/15/90) **92**
Gewürztraminer Alsace Vendange Tardive 1990 $77 (2/15/92) (BT) **90+**
Gewürztraminer Alsace Vendange Tardive 1989 ($NA) (11/15/90) **97**
Gewürztraminer Alsace Vendange Tardive 1988 ($NA) (10/15/89) **87**
Pinot Blanc Alsace 1990 $9 (2/15/92) **84**
Pinot Blanc Alsace 1989 $9.50 (11/15/90) **86**
Pinot Blanc Alsace 1988 $8 (11/15/90) BB **87**
Pinot Blanc Alsace Sélection 1989 ($NA) (11/15/90) **86**
Riesling Alsace 1990 $14 (2/15/92) **87**
Riesling Alsace 1989 $10 (11/15/90) **86**
Riesling Alsace 1988 $7.50 (10/15/89) **86**
Riesling Alsace Clos Ste.-Hune 1986 ($NA) (5/15/89) (JS) **91**
Riesling Alsace Clos Ste.-Hune 1985 $50 (5/15/89) (JS) **90**
Riesling Alsace Clos Ste.-Hune 1983 ($NA) (5/15/89) (JS) **95**
Riesling Alsace Clos Ste.-Hune 1982 $24 (5/15/89) (JS) **85**
Riesling Alsace Clos Ste.-Hune 1981 ($NA) (5/15/89) (JS) **91**
Riesling Alsace Clos Ste.-Hune 1979 ($NA) (5/15/89) (JS) **87**
Riesling Alsace Clos Ste.-Hune 1976 ($NA) (5/15/89) (JS) **91**
Riesling Alsace Clos Ste.-Hune 1975 ($NA) (5/15/89) (JS) **95**
Riesling Alsace Clos Ste.-Hune 1973 ($NA) (5/15/89) (JS) **82**
Riesling Alsace Clos Ste.-Hune 1971 ($NA) (5/15/89) (JS) **94**
Riesling Alsace Clos Ste.-Hune 1967 ($NA) (5/15/89) (JS) **85**
Riesling Alsace Clos Ste.-Hune 1966 ($NA) (5/15/89) (JS) **94**
Riesling Alsace Clos Ste.-Hune Hors Choix Vendange Tardive 1989 ($NA) (11/15/90) **97**
Riesling Alsace Clos Ste.-Hune Vendange Tardive 1989 ($NA) (11/15/90) **96**
Riesling Alsace Cuvée Frédéric Emile 1990 (NR) (2/15/92) **91**
Riesling Alsace Cuvée Frédéric Emile 1989 ($NA) (11/15/90) **92**
Riesling Alsace Cuvée Frédéric Emile 1988 $15 (10/15/89) **91**
Riesling Alsace Cuvée Frédéric Emile Sélection de Grains Nobles 1990 $100 (2/15/92) (BT) **85+**
Riesling Alsace Cuvée Frédéric Emile Vendange Tardive 1990 $75 (2/15/92) (BT) **95+**
Riesling Alsace Cuvée Frédéric Emile Vendange Tardive 1989 ($NA) (11/15/90) **95**
Riesling Alsace Frédéric Emile Sélection de Grains Nobles 1989 ($NA) (11/15/90) **90**
Riesling Alsace Réserve 1989 ($NA) (11/15/90) **90**
Sylvaner Alsace Sélection 1989 ($NA) (11/15/90) **81**
Tokay Pinot Gris Alsace 1988 $9 (10/15/89) **83**
Tokay Pinot Gris Alsace Hors Choix Sélection de Grains Nobles 1989 ($NA) (11/15/90) **99**
Tokay Pinot Gris Alsace Réserve 1990 $16 (2/15/92) **88**
Tokay Pinot Gris Alsace Réserve Sélection de Grains Nobles 1989 ($NA) (11/15/90) **90**
Tokay Pinot Gris Alsace Réserve Tradition 1989 ($NA) (11/15/90) **85**
Tokay Pinot Gris Alsace Réserve Tradition 1988 ($NA) (10/15/89) **86**
Tokay Pinot Gris Alsace Sélection de Grains Nobles 1990 (NR) (2/15/92) (BT) **90+**
Tokay Pinot Gris Alsace Vendange Tardive 1990 (NR) (2/15/92) (BT) **90+**

CHATEAU TRIMOULET (France/Bordeaux)
St.-Emilion 1988 $16 (6/15/91) **91**
St.-Emilion 1982 $15 (5/15/89) (TR) **81**

CHATEAU TRINITE VALROSE (France/Bordeaux)
Bordeaux Supérieur Ile de Patiras 1988 $7 (8/31/91) **78**

TRIONE (United States/California)
Cabernet Sauvignon Alexander Valley 1984 $10 (12/31/87) **74**

CHATEAU TROCARD (France/Bordeaux)
Bordeaux Supérieur 1988 $8.50 (1/31/92) BB **83**

CHATEAU TRONQUOY-LALANDE (France/Bordeaux)
St.-Estèphe 1991 (NR) (5/15/92) (BT) **65+**
St.-Estèphe 1989 $14 (4/30/90) (BT) **90+**
St.-Estèphe 1988 $14 (7/15/91) **84**
St.-Estèphe 1987 $13 (11/30/89) (JS) **84**
St.-Estèphe 1986 $15 (11/30/89) (JS) **92**
St.-Estèphe 1982 $18 (11/30/89) (JS) **86**

CHATEAU TROPLONG-MONDOT (France/Bordeaux)
St.-Emilion 1991 (NR) (5/15/92) (BT) **80+**
St.-Emilion 1990 (NR) (5/15/92) (BT) **90+**
St.-Emilion 1989 $26 (3/15/92) **89**
St.-Emilion 1988 Rel: $21 Cur: $23 (7/15/91) **85**
St.-Emilion 1987 $16 (6/30/89) (BT) **80+**
St.-Emilion 1986 Rel: $20 Cur: $23 (6/30/89) **88**
St.-Emilion 1985 $21 (6/30/88) **88**

CHATEAU TROTANOY (France/Bordeaux)
Pomerol 1990 (NR) (5/15/92) (BT) **95+**

Key to Symbols

The scores reported here are the results of blind tastings conducted by our panel of senior editors. Wines that carry the initials below are results of individual tastings.

THE WINE SPECTATOR 100-POINT SCALE ***95-100***—Classic, a great wine; ***90-94***—Outstanding, superior character and style; ***80-89***—Good to very good, a wine with special qualities; ***70-79***—Average, drinkable wine that may have minor flaws; ***60-69***—Below average, drinkable but not recommended; ***50-59***—Poor, undrinkable, not recommended. "+"—With a score indicates a range; used primarily with barrel tastings to indicate a preliminary score.

SPECIAL DESIGNATIONS SS—Spectator Selection, CS—Cellar Selection, BB—Best Buy, ($NA)—Price not available, (NR)—Not released.

TASTER'S INITIALS (JG)—Jim Gordon, (HS)—Harvey Steiman, (JL)—James Laube, (JS)—James Suckling, (TM)—Thomas Matthews, (TR)—Terry Robards, (PM)—Per-Henrik Mansson, (BT)—Barrel Tasting (these wines were tasted blind from barrel samples), (CA-date)—*California's Great Cabernets* by James Laube, (CH-date)—*California's Great Chardonnays* by James Laube, (VP-date)—*Vintage Port* by James Suckling.

DATE TASTED Dates in parentheses represent the issue in which the rating was published.

Pomerol 1989 $87 (3/15/92) **90**
Pomerol 1988 Rel: $48 Cur: $59 (8/31/91) **89**
Pomerol 1987 $45 (6/30/89) (BT) **85+**
Pomerol 1986 $68 (10/31/89) **83**
Pomerol 1985 Rel: $70 Cur: $76 (4/30/88) **93**
Pomerol 1983 $54 (10/15/88) (JS) **88**
Pomerol 1982 $155 (5/15/89) (TR) **90**
Pomerol 1981 $64 (10/15/88) (JS) **95**
Pomerol 1980 $42 (10/15/88) (JS) **83**
Pomerol 1979 $62 (10/15/89) (JS) **88**
Pomerol 1978 $89 (10/15/88) (JS) **83**
Pomerol 1976 $71 (10/15/88) (JS) **86**
Pomerol 1975 $130 (10/15/88) (JS) **84**
Pomerol 1971 $195 (10/15/88) (JS) **90**
Pomerol 1970 $175 (10/15/88) (JS) **95**
Pomerol 1967 $95 (10/15/88) (JS) **84**
Pomerol 1966 $140 (10/15/88) (JS) **92**
Pomerol 1962 $139 (10/15/88) (JS) **88**
Pomerol 1961 $610 (10/15/88) (JS) **96**
Pomerol 1959 $360 (10/15/90) (JS) **90**
Pomerol 1955 $200 (10/15/88) (JS) **94**
Pomerol 1953 $300 (10/15/88) (JS) **86**
Pomerol 1952 $140 (10/15/88) (JS) **83**
Pomerol 1947 $550 (10/15/88) (JS) **80**
Pomerol 1945 $1,050 (10/15/88) (JS) **98**
Pomerol 1934 $350 (10/15/88) (JS) **60**
Pomerol 1928 $600 (10/15/88) (JS) **95**
Pomerol 1924 $650 (10/15/88) (JS) **89**

CHATEAU TROTTE VIEILLE (France/Bordeaux)
St.-Emilion 1990 (NR) (4/30/91) (BT) **90+**
St.-Emilion 1989 Rel: $32 Cur: $46 (3/15/92) **90**
St.-Emilion 1988 Rel: $20 Cur: $36 (4/30/91) **85**
St.-Emilion 1987 $15 (6/30/89) (BT) **80+**
St.-Emilion 1982 $35 (5/15/89) (TR) **87**
St.-Emilion 1962 $30 (11/30/87) (JS) **75**

TROUBADOUR (France/Other)
Merlot Vin de Pays de l'Aude 1987 $5 (8/31/89) **76**

CHATEAU TROUPIAN (France/Bordeaux)
Haut-Médoc 1991 (NR) (5/15/92) (BT) **75+**
Haut-Médoc 1990 (NR) (5/15/92) (BT) **80+**

TRUCHARD (United States/California)
Chardonnay Carneros Napa Valley 1990 $16 (3/31/92) **82**
Chardonnay Carneros 1989 $16 (11/30/91) **87**
Merlot Carneros Napa Valley 1989 $18 (5/31/92) **81**
Pinot Noir Carneros 1989 $18 (10/31/91) **90**

TRUMPETVINE (United States/California)
Syrah California Berkeley Red NV $5 (4/15/89) **79**

TUALATIN (United States/Oregon)
Chardonnay Willamette Valley 1989 $14 (6/15/92) **88**
Chardonnay Willamette Valley Barrel Fermented 1988 $14 (3/31/91) **86**
Chardonnay Willamette Valley Barrel Fermented Private Reserve 1988 $20 (3/31/91) **91**
Chardonnay Willamette Valley Selected Private Reserve 1989 $20 (6/15/92) **91**
Pinot Noir Willamette Valley 1983 $10 (8/31/86) **64**
Pinot Noir Willamette Valley Estate Bottled 1987 $14 (2/15/90) **79**
Pinot Noir Willamette Valley Estate Bottled 1986 $13.50 (6/15/88) **85**
Pinot Noir Willamette Valley Private Reserve 1985 $14 (2/15/90) **84**
White Riesling Willamette Valley 1989 $6.50 (6/30/91) **80**
White Riesling Willamette Valley 1988 $6 (7/31/89) BB **89**

TUDAL (United States/California)
Cabernet Sauvignon Napa Valley 1986 Rel: $14.50 Cur: $18 (12/15/89) **91**
Cabernet Sauvignon Napa Valley 1985 Rel: $14.50 Cur: $20 (CA-3/89) **89**
Cabernet Sauvignon Napa Valley 1984 Rel: $12.50 Cur: $27 (CA-3/89) **91**
Cabernet Sauvignon Napa Valley 1983 Rel: $12.50 Cur: $38 (CA-3/89) **86**
Cabernet Sauvignon Napa Valley 1982 Rel: $12 Cur: $39 (CA-3/89) **72**
Cabernet Sauvignon Napa Valley 1981 Rel: $12 Cur: $40 (CA-3/89) **88**
Cabernet Sauvignon Napa Valley 1980 Rel: $11.50 Cur: $55 (CA-3/89) **85**
Cabernet Sauvignon Napa Valley 1979 Rel: $10.75 Cur: $50 (CA-3/89) **90**

ANGELO DEL TUFO (Italy/Tuscany)
Vernaccia di San Gimignano 1988 $7.50 (4/30/90) **81**

TULOCAY (United States/California)
Cabernet Sauvignon Napa Valley 1986 $12 (6/30/90) **70**
Cabernet Sauvignon Napa Valley Egan Vineyard 1988 $15 (11/15/91) **86**
Cabernet Sauvignon Napa Valley Egan Vineyard 1987 $16.50 (2/15/91) **74**
Chardonnay Napa Valley De Celles Vineyard 1989 $13 (4/30/92) **84**
Chardonnay Napa Valley De Celles Vineyard 1988 $14 (4/30/91) **80**
Pinot Noir Napa Valley Haynes Vineyard 1989 $16 (3/31/92) **76**
Pinot Noir Napa Valley Haynes Vineyard 1988 $15 (3/31/92) **75**
Pinot Noir Napa Valley Haynes Vineyard 1985 $18 (2/28/91) **83**

TUNNEL HILL (Australia)
Chardonnay Yarra Valley 1990 $16 (2/15/92) **83**
Pinot Noir Yarra Valley 1990 $16 (2/29/92) **84**

DOMAINE LA TUQUE BEL-AIR (France/Bordeaux)
Côtes de Castillon 1985 $8.50 (9/30/88) **72**

TURCKHEIM (France/Alsace)
Chasselas Alsace 1989 $11.50 (10/31/91) **75**
Gewürztraminer Alsace Cuvée Réserve 1989 $16.50 (10/31/91) **87**
Pinot Noir Alsace Cuvée à l'Ancienne 1988 $25 (10/31/91) **82**
Pinot Noir Alsace Cuvée Réserve 1989 $15 (10/31/91) **80**
Pinot Noir Alsace Rouge de Turckheim (100% Pinot Noir) 1988 $40 (10/31/91) **77**
Riesling Alsace Cuvée Réserve 1989 $14 (10/31/91) **84**
Sylvaner Alsace Cuvée Réserve 1989 $11.50 (10/31/91) **77**
Tokay Pinot Gris Alsace Cuvée Réserve 1989 $15 (10/31/91) **79**

TYRELL (Germany)
Riesling Auslese Mosel-Saar-Ruwer Eitelsbacher Karthäuserhofberg 1990 $21 (12/15/91) **90**
Riesling Auslese Mosel-Saar-Ruwer Eitelsbacher Karthäuserhofberg (Cask 4) 1990 (NR) (12/15/91) **88**
Riesling Auslese Mosel-Saar-Ruwer Eitelsbacher Karthäuserhofberg (Cask 6) 1990 (NR) (12/15/91) **91**
Riesling Auslese Mosel-Saar-Ruwer Eitelsbacher Karthäuserhofberg (Cask 16) 1990 (NR) (12/15/91) **88**
Riesling Kabinett Mosel-Saar-Ruwer Eitelsbacher Karthäuserhofberg 1990 $16 (12/15/91) **88**
Riesling Kabinett Mosel-Saar-Ruwer Karthäuserhofberg (AP3) 1988 ($NA) (9/30/89) **85**
Riesling Kabinett Mosel-Saar-Ruwer Karthäuserhofberg (AP9) 1988 ($NA) (9/30/89) **85**
Riesling Qualitätswein Mosel-Saar-Ruwer Eitelsbacher Karthäuserhofberg 1990 $14 (12/15/91) **88**
Riesling Spätlese Mosel-Saar-Ruwer Eitelsbacher Karthäuserhofberg 1990 (NR) (12/15/91) **90**
Riesling Spätlese Mosel-Saar-Ruwer Karthäuserhofberg 1988 ($NA) (9/30/89) **86**
Riesling Spätlese Mosel-Saar-Ruwer Karthäuserhofberg (AP10) 1988 ($NA) (9/30/89) **95**
Riesling Spätlese Mosel-Saar-Ruwer Karthäuserhofberg (AP8) 1988 ($NA) (9/30/89) **85**

TYRRELL'S (Australia)
Brut Pinot Noir Hunter Valley 1983 $19 (9/30/88) **82**
Cabernet Merlot Australia Old Winery 1988 $7.50 (3/31/91) BB **84**
Cabernet Merlot Hunter Valley 1985 $9 (7/31/89) **84**
Cabernet Merlot New South Wales Victoria 1983 $8 (3/15/88) **84**
Cabernet Sauvignon Hunter Valley Classic 1984 $7 (9/15/90) BB **88**
Cabernet Sauvignon Hunter Valley Premier Selection 1983 $8 (4/30/88) BB **87**
Cabernet Sauvignon Merlot Hunter Valley 1987 $7 (9/15/90) **79**
Cabernet Sauvignon Merlot Hunter Valley 1986 $8 (1/31/90) BB **88**
Cabernet Sauvignon Merlot Hunter Valley 1984 $9 (7/15/88) **82**
Cabernet Sauvignon South Eastern Australia Old Winery 1986 $9 (3/15/92) **84**
Chardonnay Hunter Valley 1989 $7 (10/15/90) BB **84**
Chardonnay Hunter Valley 1988 $9 (7/31/89) **68**
Chardonnay Hunter Valley 1986 $7.50 (5/15/88) **82**
Chardonnay Hunter Valley Vat 47 Pinot Chardonnay 1989 $16 (11/30/91) **88**
Chardonnay Hunter Valley Vat 47 Pinot Chardonnay 1988 $16 (7/31/89) **77**
Chardonnay Hunter Valley Vat 47 Pinot Chardonnay 1986 $12 (5/15/88) **85**
Chardonnay South Eastern Australia Old Winery 1990 $8 (11/30/91) **77**
Dry Red Winemaker's Selection Vat 9 Hunter River 1984 $14.50 (2/15/92) **83**
Long Flat Red Hunter Valley 1986 $6 (1/31/90) **79**
Long Flat Red Hunter Valley 1985 $5.25 (7/31/89) BB **81**
Long Flat Red South Eastern Australia 1988 $7 (2/15/92) BB **84**
Long Flat White Hunter Valley 1989 $5 (10/31/90) BB **86**
Pinot Noir Hunter River 1988 $14 (1/31/90) **68**
Pinot Noir Hunter River 1985 $10 (7/01/87) **87**
Sémillon Hunter Valley Classic 1988 $7 (4/15/91) **80**
Shiraz Hunter Valley 1982 $7 (7/15/88) **75**
Shiraz Hunter Valley Classic 1986 $8 (1/31/90) BB **84**

ULTRAVINO (United States/California)
Chardonnay Napa Valley 1984 $8.50 (2/15/87) **82**

UNDURRAGA (Chile)
Cabernet Sauvignon Maipo Valley 1989 $6 (6/15/92) **74**
Cabernet Sauvignon Maipo Valley 1988 $5.25 (9/15/90) BB **83**
Cabernet Sauvignon Maipo Valley 1987 $5.25 (2/15/90) BB **87**
Cabernet Sauvignon Maipo Valley Reserve Selection 1987 $8 (6/15/92) BB **87**
Cabernet Sauvignon Maipo Valley Reserve Selection 1986 $8 (6/15/91) BB **83**
Cabernet Sauvignon Maipo Valley Reserve Selection 1985 $7.75 (3/15/90) BB **85**
Cabernet Sauvignon Maipo Valley Santa Ana 1985 $5 (11/15/87) **78**
Chardonnay Maipo Valley 1991 $7 (6/15/92) **78**
Sauvignon Blanc Maipo Valley 1991 $6 (5/15/92) **79**
Sauvignon Blanc Maipo Valley 1989 $5.25 (3/31/90) **75**

UNISSENT (United States/California)
Cabernet Sauvignon California 1988 $15 (11/15/91) **83**

JEAN VACHET (France/Burgundy)
Montagny Les Coeres 1986 $16 (1/31/89) **83**

G. VACHET-ROUSSEAU (France/Burgundy)
Gevrey-Chambertin 1988 $30 (12/31/90) **85**
Gevrey-Chambertin 1983 $16 (5/01/86) **64**

G.D. VAJRA (Italy/Piedmont)
Barbera d'Alba Bricco delle Viole Riserva 1985 $22 (7/31/89) **83**
Barolo 1982 $14 (3/15/87) **91**
Barolo Bricco delle Viole 1982 $19 (8/31/88) **91**
Barolo Fossati Vineyard 1985 $34 (12/31/90) **91**

CHATEAU VAL JOANIS (France/Rhône)
Côtes du Lubéron 1988 $7 (6/30/90) BB **82**

VAL DI SUGA (Italy/Tuscany)
Brunello di Montalcino 1985 $23 (9/30/90) **88**
Brunello di Montalcino Riserva 1982 $20 (11/30/89) **89**
Brunello di Montalcino Riserva 1978 $13.50 (3/15/87) **67**
Brunello di Montalcino Vigna del Lago 1985 $52 (7/15/91) **90**
Rosso di Montalcino 1988 $10 (4/30/91) **87**
Rosso di Montalcino 1986 $9 (11/30/89) **81**

CHATEAU LA VALADE (France/Bordeaux)
Fronsac 1986 $5.25 (5/15/89) BB **81**

VALDEOBISPO (Spain)
Bierzo Tinto 1990 $7 (4/15/92) **80**
Bierzo Unfiltered 1989 $10 (4/15/92) **87**

VALDIVIESO (Chile)
Cabernet Sauvignon Maipo Valley 1984 $8 (6/15/92) **71**
Merlot Maipo Valley 1989 $8 (6/15/92) **79**

VALDUMIA (Spain)
Rias Baixas Albariño 1990 $17.50 (11/15/91) **82**

VALENTINI (Italy/Other)
Montepulciano d'Abruzzo 1979 $28 (2/15/89) **80**
Trebbiano d'Abruzzo 1984 $20 (3/31/89) **80**

S. VALERIA (Italy/Tuscany)
Chianti Classico Riserva 1985 ($NA) (9/15/91) **78**

VALFIERI (Italy/Piedmont)
Barbaresco 1986 $12 (9/15/90) **82**
Barbaresco 1985 $8.25 (7/31/89) **70**
Barbera d'Alba 1987 $7 (9/15/90) **69**
Barolo 1985 $13 (10/15/90) **90**
Dolcetto d'Alba 1988 $8.50 (12/31/90) **81**
Dolcetto d'Alba 1987 $5.75 (3/15/89) **78**
Gavi 1987 $5.75 (7/31/89) **79**
Gavi Villa Montersino Vigneti Borghero 1989 $16 (7/15/91) **83**

VALLANA (Italy/Piedmont)
Barbera 1988 $7 (3/31/90) **80**
Barbera 1986 $6 (2/15/89) BB **90**
Barbera del Piemonte 1988 $8 (3/15/91) **88**
Gattinara 1983 $10 (1/31/90) **76**

VALLANIA (Italy/Other)
Cabernet Sauvignon Colli Bolognesi Terre Rosse Monte San Pietro 1986 $18 (9/30/91) **66**
Chardonnay 1989 $16.50 (1/31/92) **73**
Chardonnay Cuvée Terre Rosse 1985 $20 (8/31/91) **85**
Terre Rosse 1985 $9 (3/31/90) **70**

VALLE SELEZIONE ARALDICA (Italy/North)
L'Araldo Collina Friulana 1985 $20 (5/15/91) **84**

M.G. VALLEJO (United States/California)
Cabernet Sauvignon California 1986 $5 (6/15/90) BB **82**
Cabernet Sauvignon California 1985 $4 (2/15/89) **78**
Cabernet Sauvignon California 1983 $4.50 (8/31/87) **67**
Chardonnay California 1989 $6.50 (7/15/91) **74**
Chardonnay California 1988 $5 (4/30/90) **78**
Chardonnay California 1987 $5 (2/15/89) **74**
Fumé Blanc California 1988 $4 (5/15/90) BB **81**
Merlot California 1990 $6 (5/31/92) BB **80**
Merlot California 1987 $5 (6/15/90) **77**
M.G.V. Red California NV $3 (5/31/90) **74**

VALLEY OF THE MOON (United States/California)
Zinfandel Sonoma Valley 1984 $9 (3/15/90) **76**

VALLEY RIDGE (United States/California)
Cabernet Sauvignon Sonoma County 1989 $9 (11/15/91) **83**
Zinfandel Sonoma County 1988 $9 (11/15/91) **86**

VALLEY VIEW (United States/Oregon)
Cabernet Sauvignon Rogue Valley Barrel Select 1989 $12.50 (6/15/92) **83**
Chardonnay Oregon Barrel Select 1988 $12 (3/31/91) **81**
Chardonnay Rogue Valley 1990 $7.50 (6/15/92) **78**
Chardonnay Rogue Valley Barrel Select 1989 $12.50 (6/15/92) **83**
Pinot Noir Oregon 1982 $8.50 (3/01/86) **73**
Pinot Noir Oregon 1980 $7.50 (9/16/84) **76**

VALLFORMOSA (Spain)
Brut Cava NV $7 (12/31/90) BB **80**
Brut Nature Cava NV $9 (12/31/90) **79**
Penedès Vall Fort 1986 $7 (5/31/91) **76**
Penedès Vall Fort 1984 $7 (3/31/91) BB **84**
Penedès Vall Reserva Tinto Propia 1980 $10 (3/31/91) **84**

CHATEAU DE VALLONGUE (France/Other)
Côteaux d'Aix en Provence Les Baux 1988 $11 (12/15/91) **73**

CHATEAU DES VALLONNIERES (France/Rhône)
Côtes du Rhône 1990 $8.75 (6/15/92) **83**

L. DE VALLOUIT (France/Rhône)
Châteauneuf-du-Pape 1989 $16 (12/31/91) **77**
Côte-Rôtie 1989 $30 (1/31/92) **89**
Côte-Rôtie 1985 $20 (10/15/87) **75**
Côtes du Rhône St.-Vincent 1990 $7 (6/15/92) BB **82**
Crozes-Hermitage Blanc 1990 $11 (12/31/91) **81**
Gigondas 1989 $13 (1/31/92) **89**
Hermitage 1983 $12 (5/01/86) **79**
St.-Joseph Blanc 1990 $15 (12/31/91) **85**
St.-Joseph Rouge 1989 $13 (1/31/92) **76**
Vin de Pays des Collines Rhodanienn les Sables 1989 $6.25 (12/31/91) BB **81**
Vin de Pays des Collines Rhodanienn les Sables 1988 $4.75 (6/30/90) BB **78**

VALMAISON (France/Bordeaux)
Bordeaux Blanc 1986 $4 (11/15/87) BB **78**

FATTORIA VALTELLINA (Italy/Tuscany)
Chianti Classico Giorgio Regni 1988 $19 (9/15/91) **83**
Chianti Classico Giorgio Regni Riserva 1985 $20 (9/15/91) **92**

VAN DER HAYDEN (United States/California)
Chardonnay Napa Valley Private Reserve 1989 $18 (7/15/92) **78**

VAN DER KAMP (United States/California)
Brut Rosé Sonoma Valley Midnight Cuvée 1988 $12 (5/15/92) **75**
Brut Rosé Sonoma Valley Midnight Cuvée 1987 $15 (11/15/90) **81**
Brut Rosé Sonoma Valley Midnight Cuvée 1986 $15 (5/31/89) **83**
Brut Rosé Sonoma Valley Midnight Cuvée 1985 $17.50 (12/31/87) **84**
Brut Sonoma Valley 1985 $15 (12/15/91) **84**
Brut Sonoma Valley 1984 $15 (5/31/89) **86**
Brut Sonoma Valley 1983 $17.50 (12/31/87) **86**

VAN DUZER (United States/Oregon)
Chardonnay Oregon Reserve 1990 $16 (6/15/92) **82**
Chardonnay Oregon Reserve 1989 $16 (11/15/91) **86**
Pinot Noir Willamette Valley Reserve 1989 $16 (6/15/92) **87**
Riesling Oregon Dry 1990 $8 (6/15/92) **87**

VAN ZELLER (Portugal)
Vintage Port 1985 ($NA) (VP-1/90) **80**
Vintage Port 1983 Rel: $22 Cur: $36 (VP-1/90) **84**
Vintage Port Quinta do Roriz 1985 ($NA) (VP-7/90) **87**
Vintage Port Quinta do Roriz 1983 $22 (VP-7/90) **84**
Vintage Port Quinta do Roriz 1970 ($NA) (VP-7/90) **86**
Vintage Port Quinta do Roriz 1960 ($NA) (VP-7/90) **83**

VANINO (United States/California)
Cabernet Sauvignon Sonoma County 1985 $11 (9/30/88) **80**

Key to Symbols

The scores reported here are the results of blind tastings conducted by our panel of senior editors. Wines that carry the initials below are results of individual tastings.

THE WINE SPECTATOR 100-POINT SCALE ***95-100***—Classic, a great wine; ***90-94***—Outstanding, superior character and style; ***80-89***—Good to very good, a wine with special qualities; ***70-79***—Average, drinkable wine that may have minor flaws; ***60-69***—Below average, drinkable but not recommended; ***50-59***—Poor, undrinkable, not recommended. "+"—With a score indicates a range; used primarily with barrel tastings to indicate a preliminary score.

SPECIAL DESIGNATIONS SS—Spectator Selection, CS—Cellar Selection, BB—Best Buy, ($NA)—Price not available, (NR)—Not released.

TASTER'S INITIALS (JG)—Jim Gordon, (HS)—Harvey Steiman, (JL)—James Laube, (JS)—James Suckling, (TM)—Thomas Matthews, (TR)—Terry Robards, (PM)—Per-Henrik Mansson, (BT)—Barrel Tasting (these wines were tasted blind from barrel samples), (CA-date)—*California's Great Cabernets* by James Laube, (CH-date)—*California's Great Chardonnays* by James Laube, (VP-date)—*Vintage Port* by James Suckling.

DATE TASTED Dates in parentheses represent the issue in which the rating was published.

ANDRE VANNIER (France/Chablis)
Chablis Les Clos 1986 $32 (9/15/88) **62**
Chablis Les Clos 1983 $18 (3/16/85) **63**
Chablis Les Preuses 1986 $33 (5/15/88) **87**
Chablis Les Preuses 1983 $18 (3/01/85) **90**

CHATEAU VANNIERES (France/Other)
Bandol 1986 $15 (9/15/89) **67**
Côtes de Provence La Provence de Vannières 1986 $15 (8/31/89) **80**

VARICHON & CLERC (France/Other)
Blanc de Blancs 1989 $9 (3/31/92) BB **87**
Brut Blanc de Blancs NV $7 (12/31/89) BB **87**
Brut Blanc de Blancs Black Orchid Cuvée Spéciale NV $8 (3/31/92) **77**
Demi-Sec NV $7 (1/31/90) BB **82**

VASCONCELLOS (Portugal)
Vintage Port Butler & Nephew 1975 $30 (VP-7/90) **74**
Vintage Port Butler & Nephew 1970 $45 (VP-7/90) **76**
Vintage Port Gonzalez Byass 1970 $50 (VP-6/90) **81**
Vintage Port Gonzalez Byass 1963 $82 (VP-7/90) **87**

LOS VASCOS (Chile)
Cabernet Sauvignon Colchagua 1990 $7 (5/31/92) BB **88**
Cabernet Sauvignon Colchagua 1989 $7 (6/15/92) BB **83**
Cabernet Sauvignon Colchagua 1988 $7 (6/15/91) BB **82**
Cabernet Sauvignon Colchagua 1987 $5 (9/15/90) BB **86**
Cabernet Sauvignon Colchagua 1985 $5 (11/15/87) **84**
Cabernet Sauvignon Colchagua 1984 $4.50 (4/30/88) BB **88**
Cabernet Sauvignon Colchagua Reserve 1989 $11 (6/15/92) **84**
Chardonnay Colchagua 1990 $9 (6/15/92) **78**
Sauvignon Blanc Colchagua 1990 $7 (10/15/91) BB **86**
Sauvignon Blanc Colchagua 1988 $4.75 (3/31/90) BB **83**

VASELLI (Italy/Other)
Orvieto Classico Secco 1989 $7.75 (7/15/91) **75**
Orvieto Classico Torre Sant' Andrea 1989 $11 (12/31/90) **83**
Santa Giulia 1988 $10 (1/31/92) **83**
Santa Giulia Rosso NV $19 (1/31/92) **80**

CHATEAU DE VAUDIEU (France/Rhône)
Châteauneuf-du-Pape 1984 $13 (11/15/87) **72**

VIGNA VECCHIA (Italy/Tuscany)
Chianti Classico 1988 $10.50 (10/31/91) **83**

VECCHIE TERRE DI MONTEFILI (Italy/Tuscany)
Chianti Classico 1988 $20 (9/15/91) **90**
Chianti Classico 1986 $14 (4/30/90) **85**
Chianti Classico Riserva 1985 ($NA) (9/15/91) **90**

VEGA (United States/California)
Chardonnay Santa Barbara County 1986 $14 (12/15/89) **89**
Johannisberg Riesling Late Harvest Santa Barbara County Special Selection 1987 $10.50/375ml (12/15/89) **78**

VEGA DE MORIZ (Spain)
Valdepeñas Cencibel 1989 $5.50 (6/15/91) BB **81**

BODEGAS VEGA SICILIA (Spain)
Ribera del Duero Unico 1979 Rel: $75 Cur: $100 (3/31/90) **95**
Ribera del Duero Unico 1976 Rel: $60 Cur: $90 (4/30/89) **91**
Ribera del Duero Unico 1973 $97 (3/31/90) (TM) **90**
Ribera del Duero Unico 1962 Rel: $106 Cur: $145 (3/31/90) **89**
Ribera del Duero Unico Reserva Especial NV $156 (3/31/90) **79**
Ribera del Duero Valbuena 3 Años 1986 $47 (12/15/90) **90**
Ribera del Duero Valbuena 3 Años 1985 Rel: $40 Cur: $55 (3/31/90) CS **92**
Ribera del Duero Valbuena 3 Años 1984 $28 (4/30/89) **79**
Ribera del Duero Valbuena 3 Años 1983 $22 (10/15/88) **88**
Ribera del Duero Valbuena 3 Años 1982 $25 (10/15/88) **90**
Ribera del Duero Valbuena 5 Años 1984 $49 (3/31/90) **90**
Ribera del Duero Valbuena 5 Años 1982 $37 (3/31/90) **91**

VENDANGE (United States/California)
Chardonnay California 1990 $6 (7/15/92) **79**
Merlot California 1990 $6 (5/31/92) BB **80**
Zinfandel California 1987 $5.50 (9/15/90) **78**

VENEGAZZU (Italy/North)
Della Casa 1985 $25 (3/31/90) **91**
Della Casa 1983 $25 (2/15/89) **86**
Chardonnay 1988 $8.50 (9/15/89) **77**

VENICA (Italy/North)
Chardonnay Dolegna del Collio 1989 $17 (1/31/91) **84**
Tocai Friulano Collio 1989 $15 (2/15/91) **82**

DE VENOGE (France/Champagne)
Brut Blanc de Blancs Champagne NV $38 (12/31/90) **86**
Brut Champagne 1985 $38 (12/31/90) **86**
Brut Champagne Cordon Bleu NV $22 (12/31/91) **84**
Rosé Champagne Crémant NV $26 (12/31/88) **88**

VENTANA (United States/California)
Chardonnay Monterey Barrel Fermented 1987 $16 (10/31/89) **76**
Chardonnay Monterey Crystal Ventana Vineyards 1986 $16 (10/31/89) **79**
Chardonnay Monterey Gold Stripe Selection 1989 $10 (7/15/91) **87**
Chardonnay Monterey Gold Stripe Selection 1988 $10 (9/30/89) **81**
Chardonnay Monterey Gold Stripe Selection 1985 $7.50 (9/15/87) BB **87**
Chardonnay Monterey Gold Stripe Selection 1984 $8 (4/16/86) **69**
Chardonnay Monterey Ventana Vineyards Gold Stripe Selection 1987 $10 (6/30/89) **88**
Chenin Blanc Monterey 1988 $5.50 (7/31/89) **78**
Magnus Meritage Monterey 1986 $20 (10/31/89) **79**
Sauvignon Blanc Monterey 1988 $8 (3/31/90) **81**
Sauvignon Blanc Monterey 1987 $8 (10/31/89) **85**
White Riesling Late Harvest Monterey Ventana Vineyards Hand-Selected Clusters 1987 $14/375ml (8/31/89) **70**

CHATEAU VERDIGNAN (France/Bordeaux)
Haut-Médoc 1991 (NR) (5/15/92) (BT) **80+**
Haut-Médoc 1990 (NR) (4/30/91) (BT) **85+**
Haut-Médoc 1989 $17 (3/15/92) **90**
Haut-Médoc 1988 $15 (4/30/91) **86**
Haut-Médoc 1987 $15 (11/30/89) (JS) **78**
Haut-Médoc 1986 $15 (11/30/89) (JS) **76**
Haut-Médoc 1985 $13 (2/15/88) **81**

Haut-Médoc 1983 Rel: $8 Cur: $18 (4/01/86) **69**
Haut-Médoc 1982 Rel: $7.50 Cur: $16 (11/30/89) (JS) **76**

VEREINIGTE HOSPITIEN (Germany)
Riesling Auslese Mosel-Saar-Ruwer Piesporter Schubertslay 1988 ($NA) (9/30/89) **90**
Riesling Auslese Mosel-Saar-Ruwer Wehlener Sonnenuhr 1988 ($NA) (9/30/89) **90**
Riesling Kabinett Mosel-Saar-Ruwer Serriger Schloss Saarfelser Schlossberger 1988 ($NA) (9/30/89) **79**
Riesling Spätlese Mosel-Saar-Ruwer Wiltinger Hölle 1988 ($NA) (9/30/89) **83**

ROGER VERGE (France/Beaujolais)
Pouilly-Fuissé 1986 $15 (3/15/88) **79**

VERITAS (United States/Oregon)
Chardonnay Willamette Valley 1988 $12 (3/31/91) **83**
Pinot Noir Oregon 1985 $15 (6/15/87) **88**
Pinot Noir Willamette Valley 1988 $15 (5/31/91) **87**
Pinot Noir Willamette Valley 1987 $15 (2/15/90) **77**

VINA VERMETA (Spain)
Tinto 1987 $6 (11/15/91) **76**

GEORGES VERNAY (France/Rhône)
Condrieu 1990 $43 (10/15/91) **88**
Condrieu 1988 $40 (10/31/89) **81**
Condrieu 1987 $36 (3/15/89) **85**
Condrieu Côteau de Vernon 1987 $43 (10/31/89) **77**

VEUVE CLICQUOT (France/Champagne)
Brut Champagne 1982 Rel: $32 Cur: $40 (5/31/87) SS **93**
Brut Champagne 1979 Rel: $50 Cur: $75 (12/16/85) **88**
Brut Champagne NV $40 (12/31/91) **91**
Brut Champagne Gold Label 1983 $42 (12/31/90) **90**
Brut Champagne Gold Label 1982 $37 (12/31/88) **85**
Brut Champagne La Grande Dame 1985 Rel: $72 Cur: $80 (12/31/90) **91**
Brut Champagne La Grande Dame 1983 $79 (12/31/89) **92**
Brut Champagne La Grande Dame 1979 Rel: $61 Cur: $74 (5/16/86) **96**
Brut Rosé Champagne 1983 $47 (12/31/89) **86**
Brut Rosé Champagne 1979 $35 (7/16/86) **89**
Brut Rosé Champagne 1978 $60 (12/16/85) **82**

VEUVE DU VERNAY (France/Other)
Brut Blanc de Blancs NV $7 (11/30/91) BB **82**

CASTELLO DI VERRAZZANO (Italy/Tuscany)
Chianti Classico 1988 $8 (9/15/91) **85**
Chianti Classico Cinquecentenario di Verrazzano Riserva 1985 ($NA) (9/15/91) **83**

NOEL VERSET (France/Rhône)
Cornas 1987 $23 (3/31/90) **88**
Cornas 1986 $25 (1/31/89) **86**

VESCOVADO DI MURLO (Italy/Tuscany)
Chianti 1990 $6 (10/31/91) BB **83**

CA' VESCOVO (Italy/North)
Aquileia 1989 $9 (1/31/92) **75**
Chardonnay Aquileia 1989 $8 (7/15/91) **76**

GEORGES VESSELLE (France/Champagne)
Brut Champagne Grand Cru NV (NR) (12/31/91) **86**
Brut Rosé Champagne de Noirs NV $30 (12/16/85) **53**

VEUVE AMIOT (France/Other)
Brut Saumur Cuvée Haute Tradition NV $13 (3/31/90) **78**

VINCENT VIAL (France/Burgundy)
Meursault 1947 ($NA) (8/31/90) (TR) **90**

VIANSA (United States/California)
Cabernet Sauvignon Napa-Alexander Valleys 1986 ($NA) (4/15/88) (BT) **85+**
Cabernet Sauvignon Napa-Sonoma Counties 1984 $13 (7/31/88) **85**
Cabernet Sauvignon Napa-Sonoma Counties Sam J. Sebastiani 1983 $15 (11/30/86) **88**
Cabernet Sauvignon Sonoma Valley Grand Reserve 1983 $35 (10/15/88) **88**
Cabernet Sauvignon Sonoma Valley Reserve 1983 $18 (10/15/88) **88**
Cabernet Sauvignon Napa-Sonoma Counties 1986 $15 (7/31/90) **77**
Cabernet Sauvignon Napa-Sonoma Counties 1985 $13 (9/15/89) **72**
Chardonnay Napa-Sonoma Counties 1988 $15 (9/15/90) **85**
Chardonnay Napa-Sonoma Counties 1987 $13 (4/15/89) **84**
Chardonnay Napa-Sonoma Counties 1986 $12.50 (3/31/88) **87**
Chardonnay Napa-Sonoma Counties Sam J. Sebastiani 1985 $12.50 (6/30/87) **68**
Chardonnay Napa-Sonoma Counties Reserve 1988 $18 (11/30/90) **84**
Obsidian Napa-Sonoma Counties 1987 $65 (7/15/91) **85**
Sauvignon Blanc Napa-Sonoma Counties 1988 $10 (10/31/90) **73**
Sauvignon Blanc Napa-Sonoma Counties 1987 $9.50 (4/30/89) **81**

LA VIARTE (Italy/North)
Colli Orientali del Friuli Ribolla 1988 $18 (12/31/90) **85**
Liende 1989 $22 (8/31/91) **79**
Roi 1986 $24 (1/31/92) **78**
Sauvignon Colli Orientali del Friuli 1989 $19 (7/15/91) **83**

CASTELLO VICCHIOMAGGIO (Italy/Tuscany)
Chianti Classico Prima Vigna Riserva 1985 $20 (9/15/91) **86**

VICHON (United States/California)
Cabernet Sauvignon Napa Valley 1988 $16 (5/15/91) **84**
Cabernet Sauvignon Napa Valley 1985 Rel: $13 Cur: $19 (CA-3/89) **88**
Cabernet Sauvignon Napa Valley 1984 Rel: $11.25 Cur: $15 (CA-3/89) **88**
Cabernet Sauvignon Napa Valley 1983 Rel: $10 Cur: $14 (CA-3/89) **80**
Cabernet Sauvignon Napa Valley 1982 Rel: $13 Cur: $19 (CA-3/89) **76**
Cabernet Sauvignon Napa Valley 1981 Rel: $13 Cur: $22 (CA-3/89) **80**
Cabernet Sauvignon Stags Leap District SLD 1988 $24 (11/15/91) **90**
Cabernet Sauvignon Stags Leap District SLD 1987 Rel: $17 Cur: $22 (7/31/90) **87**
Cabernet Sauvignon Stags Leap District SLD 1986 Rel: $21 Cur: $25 (10/31/89) **91**
Cabernet Sauvignon Stags Leap District SLD 1986 Rel: $21 Cur: $25 (CA-3/89) **90**
Cabernet Sauvignon Stags Leap District SLD 1985 Rel: $18 Cur: $29 (CA-3/89) **92**
Cabernet Sauvignon Stags Leap District Fay Vineyard 1984 Rel: $14 Cur: $28 (CA-3/89) **85**
Cabernet Sauvignon Napa Valley Volker Eisele Vineyard 1982 Rel: $16 Cur: $19 (CA-3/89) **78**
Cabernet Sauvignon Napa Valley Volker Eisele Vineyard 1980 Rel: $16 Cur: $25 (CA-3/89) **83**
Cabernet Sauvignon Stags Leap District Fay Vineyard 1982 Rel: $14 Cur: $23 (CA-3/89) **79**
Cabernet Sauvignon Stags Leap District Fay Vineyard 1980 Rel: $16 Cur: $25 (CA-3/89) **85**
Chardonnay Napa Valley 1990 $15 (3/31/92) **81**
Chardonnay Napa Valley Tenth Harvest 1989 Rel: $16 Cur: $18 (3/31/91) **86**
Chardonnay Napa Valley 1988 Rel: $17 Cur: $19 (11/15/89) **89**
Chardonnay Napa Valley 1987 Rel: $16 Cur: $18 (CH-3/90) **87**
Chardonnay Napa Valley 1986 Rel: $15 Cur: $17 (CH-3/90) **90**
Chardonnay Napa Valley 1985 Rel: $15 Cur: $17 (CH-3/90) **88**
Chardonnay Napa Valley 1984 Rel: $15 Cur: $17 (CH-3/90) **86**
Chardonnay Napa Valley 1983 Rel: $15 Cur: $18 (CH-3/90) **71**
Chardonnay Napa Valley 1982 Rel: $15 Cur: $20 (CH-3/90) **66**
Chardonnay Napa Valley 1981 Rel: $15 Cur: $25 (CH-3/90) **76**
Chardonnay Napa Valley 1980 Rel: $15 Cur: $25 (CH-3/90) **87**
Chevrignon Napa Valley 1990 $9.75 (3/15/92) **85**
Chevrignon Napa Valley 1989 $9.75 (5/31/91) **81**
Chevrignon Napa Valley 1988 $9.75 (1/31/91) **86**
Chevrignon Napa Valley 1986 $9.75 (1/31/89) **74**
Merlot Napa Valley 1988 $16 (12/31/90) **81**
Merlot Napa Valley 1987 $16 (2/15/90) **91**
Merlot Napa Valley 1986 $16 (8/31/89) **86**
Merlot Napa Valley 1985 $14 (12/15/87) **88**
Merlot Napa Valley Tenth Harvest 1989 $17 (4/15/92) **88**
Sémillon Late Harvest Napa Valley Botrytis 1986 $15/375ml (12/31/88) **86**
Sémillon Late Harvest Napa Valley Botrytis 1985 $15/375ml (7/15/88) **88**

ANGEL RODRIGUEZ VIDAL (Spain)
Rueda Martinsancho Verdejo 1990 $10 (5/31/92) **78**
Rueda Martinsancho Verdejo 1988 $9 (3/31/90) **77**

J. VIDAL-FLEURY (France/Rhône)
Cornas 1988 $20 (1/31/91) **85**
Côte-Rôtie Côte Blonde la Chatillonne 1984 $26 (10/31/87) **73**
Côte-Rôtie Côtes Brune et Blonde 1988 $30 (10/15/90) **88**
Côte-Rôtie Côtes Brune et Blonde 1985 $25 (3/15/90) (HS) **90**
Côte-Rôtie Côtes Brune et Blonde 1945 $175 (3/15/90) (HS) **85**
Côte-Rôtie Côtes Brune et Blonde 1934 $280 (3/15/90) (HS) **85**
Côtes du Rhône 1989 $10 (6/15/92) **81**
Côtes du Rhône 1988 $9 (12/15/90) **85**
Côtes du Rhône 1985 $7.50 (10/31/87) BB **88**
Crozes-Hermitage 1988 $13 (12/31/90) **86**
Crozes-Hermitage 1986 $10 (5/31/88) **78**
Crozes-Hermitage 1985 Rel: $11 Cur: $15 (10/31/87) CS **92**
Gigondas 1985 $13 (10/31/87) **86**
Hermitage 1985 $22 (10/31/87) **89**
Hermitage 1945 $175 (3/15/90) (HS) **80**
Hermitage 1937 $135 (3/15/90) (HS) **91**
St.-Joseph 1988 $14 (1/31/91) **84**
Vacqueyras 1988 $13.50 (12/15/90) **89**

CHATEAU LA VIEILLE CURE (France/Bordeaux)
Fronsac 1990 (NR) (5/15/92) (BT) **85+**
Fronsac 1989 $16 (3/15/92) **88**
Fronsac 1988 $19 (10/31/91) **81**
Fronsac 1987 $14 (5/15/90) **82**
Fronsac 1986 $15 (5/15/91) **81**
Fronsac 1985 $15 (12/31/88) **88**

LA VIEILLE FERME (France/Rhône)
Côtes du Lubéron Blanc 1989 $7 (4/30/91) BB **80**
Côtes du Lubéron Blanc 1988 $6.50 (3/15/90) **78**
Côtes du Lubéron Blanc 1986 $6 (4/15/88) **71**
Côtes du Rhône Blanc Réserve 1988 $8 (10/31/89) **85**
Côtes du Rhône Réserve 1989 $9 (3/15/91) BB **87**
Côtes du Rhône Réserve 1988 $7.50 (12/15/90) BB **84**
Côtes du Rhône Réserve 1987 $6.50 (6/15/89) BB **80**
Côtes du Rhône Réserve 1985 $7 (11/15/88) BB **85**
Côtes du Ventoux 1988 $8 (6/30/90) **78**
Côtes du Ventoux 1987 $5.75 (6/15/89) BB **81**
Côtes du Ventoux 1986 $6 (10/15/88) BB **83**

DOMAINE DE LA VIEILLE JULIENNE (France/Rhône)
Châteauneuf-du-Pape 1978 $20 (11/15/87) **67**
Châteauneuf-du-Pape 1972 $20 (11/15/87) **73**

VIEIRA DE SOUSA (Portugal)
Vintage Port 1985 ($NA) (VP-1/90) **70**
Vintage Port 1980 ($NA) (VP-1/90) **70**
Vintage Port 1978 ($NA) (VP-1/90) **74**
Vintage Port 1970 ($NA) (VP-1/90) **71**

CHARLES VIENOT (France/Burgundy)
Bourgogne 1985 $9 (6/15/89) **78**
Bourgogne 1983 $6.50 (12/16/85) **75**
Bourgogne 1982 $6 (11/01/85) **52**
Chablis Vauignot 1987 $20 (3/31/89) **89**
Corton-Maréchaude 1985 $57 (7/15/88) **84**
Gevrey-Chambertin 1985 $32 (4/30/88) **87**
Mercurey 1985 $12 (4/30/88) **85**
Meursault 1989 $35 (8/31/91) **84**
Pommard 1985 $33 (4/30/88) **81**
Pouilly-Fuissé 1987 $14 (4/30/89) **75**
Pouilly-Fuissé 1984 $19 (3/31/87) **80**
Pouilly-Vinzelles 1985 $16 (3/31/87) **70**
Puligny-Montrachet 1984 $31 (2/28/87) **63**
Puligny-Montrachet Les Champs-Gains 1989 $42 (8/31/91) **83**
Puligny-Montrachet Les Champs-Gains 1987 $38 (7/31/89) **79**
St.-Aubin 1984 $13 (3/31/87) **78**
Savigny-lès-Beaune Blanc 1989 $24 (8/31/91) **82**

VIETTI (Italy/Piedmont)
Arneis 1990 $17 (9/15/91) **85**
Barbaresco 1985 $28 (7/31/89) **81**
Barbaresco 1982 $15 (7/31/87) **84**
Barbaresco della Località Rabajà 1986 $18 (10/31/90) **87**
Barbera d'Alba della Località Scarrone 1987 $11 (8/31/89) **86**
Barbera d'Alba Pian Romualdo 1989 $19 (11/30/91) **83**
Barbera d'Alba Pianromualdo 1988 $15 (3/15/91) **79**
Barbera d'Alba Scarrone 1989 $13 (3/15/91) **85**
Barolo 1978 $12 (9/16/84) **84**
Barolo Bussia 1982 $20 (9/15/87) **89**
Barolo Rocche 1982 Rel: $45 Cur: $60 (7/31/89) **85**
Barolo Rocche 1980 $30 (9/15/88) (HS) **87**
Barolo Rocche 1979 ($NA) (9/15/88) (HS) **79**
Barolo Rocche 1978 $75 (9/15/88) (HS) **92**
Barolo Rocche 1971 $70 (9/15/88) (HS) **86**
Barolo Rocche 1961 $100 (9/15/88) (HS) **93**
Barolo Villero Riserva 1982 $45 (9/15/88) (HS) **89**

Dolcetto d'Alba Bussia 1990 $11 (11/30/91) **85**
Dolcetto d'Alba Bussia 1989 $12 (2/28/91) **85**
Dolcetto d'Alba della Località Disa 1988 $12 (9/15/90) **87**
Fioretto 1987 $17 (6/15/90) **85**

VIEUX CHATEAU CERTAN (France/Bordeaux)
Pomerol 1989 $89 (3/15/92) **91**
Pomerol 1988 $60 (3/31/91) **91**
Pomerol 1987 $30 (5/15/90) **84**
Pomerol 1986 Rel: $40 Cur: $55 (6/15/89) **93**
Pomerol 1985 Rel: $38 Cur: $49 (6/30/88) **90**
Pomerol 1983 Rel: $33 Cur: $42 (3/16/86) **83**
Pomerol 1982 Rel: $29 Cur: $59 (5/15/89) (TR) **89**
Pomerol 1979 $40 (10/15/89) (JS) **87**
Pomerol 1962 $65 (11/30/87) (JS) **60**
Pomerol 1961 $180 (3/16/86) (TR) **90**
Pomerol 1959 $165 (10/15/90) (JS) **91**
Pomerol 1945 $700 (3/16/86) (JL) **50**

DOMAINE DU VIEUX CHENE (France/Rhône)
Vin de Pays de Vaucluse 1990 $7 (1/31/92) **77**

LE VIEUX DONJON (France/Rhône)
Châteauneuf-du-Pape 1989 $17 (10/15/91) **85**
Châteauneuf-du-Pape 1988 $16 (10/15/91) **85**
Châteauneuf-du-Pape 1986 $15 (10/15/91) **88**
Châteauneuf-du-Pape 1985 $16 (2/15/88) **79**
Châteauneuf-du-Pape 1984 $14 (10/31/87) **79**
Châteauneuf-du-Pape 1981 $30 (10/15/91) **89**

CHATEAU VIEUX-FERRAND (France/Bordeaux)
Pomerol 1982 ($NA) (5/15/89) (TR) **82**

CHATEAU VIEUX GABRIAN (France/Bordeaux)
Bordeaux Supérieur 1988 $11 (4/30/91) **84**

VIEUX CHATEAU GUIBEAU (France/Bordeaux)
St.-Emilion 1982 $8 (9/16/85) **80**

DOMAINE DU VIEUX LAZARET (France/Rhône)
Châteauneuf-du-Pape 1989 $16 (10/15/91) **85**
Châteauneuf-du-Pape 1986 $14 (1/31/89) **89**
Châteauneuf-du-Pape 1985 Rel: $12 Cur: $20 (10/15/91) **82**
Châteauneuf-du-Pape Blanc 1990 $16 (10/15/91) **81**
Châteauneuf-du-Pape Blanc 1986 $14.50 (3/15/89) **81**

DOMAINE DU VIEUX ST.-SORLIN (France/Burgundy)
Mâcon-la-Roche Vineuse 1989 $13.50 (2/28/91) **82**
Mâcon-la-Roche Vineuse Eleve en futs de Chêne 1988 $11 (7/15/90) **86**

CHATEAU VIEUX SARPE (France/Bordeaux)
St.-Emilion 1982 ($NA) (5/15/89) (TR) **83**

DOMAINE DU VIEUX TELEGRAPHE (France/Rhône)
Châteauneuf-du-Pape 1989 $24 (10/15/91) **87**
Châteauneuf-du-Pape 1988 Rel: $20 Cur: $23 (10/15/91) **85**
Châteauneuf-du-Pape 1987 $17 (9/30/90) **81**
Châteauneuf-du-Pape 1986 Rel: $17 Cur: $20 (10/15/91) **90**
Châteauneuf-du-Pape 1986 $17 (11/30/88) CS **91**
Châteauneuf-du-Pape 1985 Rel: $17 Cur: $34 (10/15/91) **82**
Châteauneuf-du-Pape 1984 Rel: $12 Cur: $25 (9/30/87) **89**
Châteauneuf-du-Pape 1983 Rel: $17 Cur: $35 (10/15/91) **85**
Châteauneuf-du-Pape 1981 Rel: $35 Cur: $40 (10/15/91) **80**
Châteauneuf-du-Pape Blanc 1990 $20 (10/15/91) **86**
Châteauneuf-du-Pape Blanc 1986 $15 (11/15/87) **77**

FATTORIA VIGNALE (Italy/Tuscany)
Chianti Classico 1988 ($NA) (9/15/91) **85**
Chianti Classico Riserva 1985 ($NA) (9/15/91) **88**

VIGNALTA (Italy/North)
Chardonnay 1989 $18 (8/31/91) **84**
Chardonnay Selezióne Vendemmia 1988 $18 (2/15/91) **80**
Gemola 1988 $22 (9/30/91) **81**
Merlot 1988 $18 (4/15/91) **80**

VIGNAMAGGIO (Italy/Tuscany)
Chianti Classico 1988 $16.50 (9/15/91) **85**
Chianti Classico 1986 $12 (5/15/90) **85**
Chianti Classico 1985 $11 (8/31/88) **86**
Chianti Classico Mona Lisa Riserva 1986 ($20) (10/31/91) **88**
Chianti Classico Mona Lisa Riserva 1985 $17 (9/15/91) **89**
Chianti Classico Riserva 1985 $17 (9/15/91) **81**
Chianti Classico Riserva 1983 $14 (5/15/90) **85**
Gerardino 1987 ($NA) (11/30/89) (HS) **92**
Gerardino 1986 ($NA) (11/30/89) (HS) **91**
Gerardino 1985 $18 (1/31/92) **87**

VIGNE DAL LEON (Italy/North)
Chardonnay Tullio Zamò 1989 $27 (7/15/91) **84**
Tocai Friulano Colli Orientali del Friuli 1989 $18 (7/15/91) **77**

VIGNERONS (France/Burgundy)
St.-Véran 1983 $7 (10/16/85) BB **82**

VIGNOLE (Italy/Tuscany)
Chianti Classico 1988 ($NA) (9/15/91) **90**

Key to Symbols

The scores reported here are the results of blind tastings conducted by our panel of senior editors. Wines that carry the initials below are results of individual tastings.

THE WINE SPECTATOR 100-POINT SCALE ***95-100***—Classic, a great wine; ***90-94***—Outstanding, superior character and style; ***80-89***—Good to very good, a wine with special qualities; ***70-79***—Average, drinkable wine that may have minor flaws; ***60-69***—Below average, drinkable but not recommended; ***50-59***—Poor, undrinkable, not recommended. "+"—With a score indicates a range; used primarily with barrel tastings to indicate a preliminary score.

SPECIAL DESIGNATIONS SS—Spectator Selection, CS—Cellar Selection, BB—Best Buy, ($NA)—Price not available, (NR)—Not released.

TASTER'S INITIALS (JG)—Jim Gordon, (HS)—Harvey Steiman, (JL)—James Laube, (JS)—James Suckling, (TM)—Thomas Matthews, (TR)—Terry Robards, (PM)—Per-Henrik Mansson, (BT)—Barrel Tasting (these wines were tasted blind from barrel samples), (CA-date)—*California's Great Cabernets* by James Laube, (CH-date)—*California's Great Chardonnays* by James Laube, (VP-date)—*Vintage Port* by James Suckling.

DATE TASTED Dates in parentheses represent the issue in which the rating was published.

VIGNOBLE DE LA JASSE (France/Rhône)
Côtes du Rhône 1986 $8 (12/15/89) **79**

VILLA MT. EDEN (United States/California)
Cabernet Sauvignon Napa Valley 1988 ($NA) (5/15/90) (BT) **80+**
Cabernet Sauvignon Napa Valley 1987 Rel: $13 Cur: $15 (2/15/91) **88**
Cabernet Sauvignon Napa Valley 1986 Rel: $13 Cur: $15 (2/15/91) **84**
Cabernet Sauvignon Napa Valley 1985 $13 (CA-3/89) **82**
Cabernet Sauvignon Napa Valley 1984 ($NA) (CA-3/89) **80**
Cabernet Sauvignon Napa Valley 1983 $10 (CA-3/89) **72**
Cabernet Sauvignon Napa Valley 1982 Rel: $9 Cur: $13 (CA-3/89) **70**
Cabernet Sauvignon Napa Valley 1980 Rel: $11.70 Cur: $16 (CA-3/89) **62**
Cabernet Sauvignon Napa Valley 1979 Rel: $12 Cur: $27 (CA-3/89) **78**
Cabernet Sauvignon Napa Valley 1978 Rel: $8 Cur: $42 (CA-3/89) **78**
Cabernet Sauvignon Napa Valley 1977 Rel: $8 Cur: $22 (CA-3/89) **86**
Cabernet Sauvignon Napa Valley 1976 Rel: $7 Cur: $21 (CA-3/89) **70**
Cabernet Sauvignon Napa Valley 1975 Rel: $7 Cur: $22 (CA-3/89) **89**
Cabernet Sauvignon Napa Valley 1974 Rel: $7 Cur: $95 (CA-3/89) **90**
Cabernet Sauvignon Napa Valley Reserve 1988 $20 (5/15/90) (BT) **85+**
Cabernet Sauvignon Napa Valley Reserve 1982 Rel: $16.70 Cur: $20 (CA-3/89) **84**
Cabernet Sauvignon Napa Valley Reserve 1981 Rel: $16.70 Cur: $20 (CA-3/89) **85**
Cabernet Sauvignon Napa Valley Reserve 1980 Rel: $20 Cur: $22 (CA-3/89) **70**
Cabernet Sauvignon Napa Valley Reserve 1979 Rel: $20 Cur: $30 (CA-3/89) **75**
Cabernet Sauvignon Napa Valley Reserve 1978 Rel: $20 Cur: $50 (CA-3/89) **88**
Chardonnay California Cellar Select 1990 $8 (6/15/92) BB **82**
Chardonnay Carneros 1989 $12 (2/28/91) **79**
Chardonnay Carneros 1988 $13.50 (9/30/90) **87**
Chardonnay Napa Valley 1989 $12 (2/28/91) **82**
Chardonnay Napa Valley 1986 $12 (7/31/88) **86**
Chardonnay Napa Valley 1984 $9 (4/30/87) **84**
Chardonnay Napa Valley 1983 $10 (4/16/85) **75**
Chardonnay Napa Valley Grand Reserve 1990 $12 (6/30/92) **89**
Chenin Blanc Napa Valley Dry 1987 $6 (7/31/89) **81**
Pinot Noir Napa Valley 1988 $12 (2/28/91) **82**
Pinot Noir Napa Valley Tres Niños Vineyard 1981 $5 (4/16/85) BB **86**
Sauvignon Blanc Late Harvest Napa Valley 1989 $13/375ml (4/30/91) **83**
Sauvignon Blanc Late Harvest Napa Valley 1986 $10/375ml (5/15/88) **89**
Zinfandel Napa Valley 1986 $8.50 (12/15/88) **90**

VILLA ZAPU (United States/California)
Cabernet Sauvignon Napa Valley 1988 $20 (11/15/91) **86**
Cabernet Sauvignon Napa Valley 1986 $16 (10/31/89) **79**
Chardonnay Napa Valley 1990 $11 (7/31/92) **87**
Chardonnay Napa Valley 1988 $14 (6/30/90) **88**
Chardonnay Napa Valley 1987 $14 (5/31/89) **73**
Chardonnay Napa Valley 1986 $13.75 (12/31/88) **77**

CHATEAU VILLADIERE (France/Bordeaux)
St.-Emilion 1982 $8 (9/01/85) **75**

VILLADORIA (Italy/Piedmont)
Barolo Riserva Spéciale 1978 $14 (8/31/86) **73**
Dolcetto d'Alba 1987 $6 (3/15/89) **65**

A. & P. DE VILLAINE (France/Burgundy)
Bourgogne Blanc Les Clous Bouzeron 1986 $16 (1/31/89) **65**
Bourgogne La Digoine Bouzeron 1989 $17 (11/15/91) **84**

HENRI DE VILLAMONT (France/Burgundy)
Bourgogne Pinot Noir 1989 $11 (3/31/91) **78**
Chambolle-Musigny 1988 $39 (2/15/91) **83**
Chassagne-Montrachet Les Vergers 1986 $29 (12/15/88) **81**
Meursault Les Genevrières 1986 $29 (12/15/88) **71**
Puligny-Montrachet Les Folatières 1986 $30 (12/15/88) **85**
Savigny-lès-Beaune Le Village 1988 $18 (3/31/91) **80**

CHATEAU VILLARS (France/Bordeaux)
Fronsac 1991 (NR) (5/15/92) (BT) **75+**

CHATEAU VILLEGEORGE (France/Bordeaux)
Haut-Médoc 1989 $14 (3/15/92) **79**
Haut-Médoc 1988 $15 (6/30/89) (BT) **80+**
Haut-Médoc 1987 $12 (6/30/89) (BT) **75+**
Haut-Médoc 1986 $13 (5/15/87) (BT) **70+**
Haut-Médoc 1985 $13 (5/15/87) (BT) **80+**

CLOS DE VILLEMAJOU (France/Other)
Corbières 1988 $6 (4/30/90) **78**
Corbières 1985 $7.50 (5/31/90) **71**

CHATEAU VILLEMAURINE (France/Bordeaux)
St.-Emilion 1991 (NR) (5/15/92) (BT) **85+**
St.-Emilion 1989 (NR) (3/15/92) **93**
St.-Emilion 1987 ($NA) (6/30/88) (BT) **75+**
St.-Emilion 1986 $39 (6/30/88) (BT) **80+**
St.-Emilion 1982 $40 (5/15/89) (TR) **83**

CHATEAU JULIEN VILLERAMBERT (France/Other)
Minervois Cuvée Trianon 1989 $15 (12/15/91) **73**

VINA DEL MAR (Chile)
Cabernet Sauvignon Curicó Selección Especial 35 1988 $6 (6/15/91) BB **81**
Cabernet Sauvignon Curicó Selección Especial 35 1987 $6 (9/15/90) BB **83**
Cabernet Sauvignon Lontue 1988 $6 (6/15/92) **79**
Cabernet Sauvignon Lontue 1985 $6 (4/30/88) BB **86**
Cabernet Sauvignon Lontue Selección Especial 17 1986 $6 (2/15/90) BB **80**
Cabernet Sauvignon Maipo Reserve 1986 $9 (6/15/92) **78**
Chardonnay Lontue Reserve 1991 $9 (6/15/92) **83**
Fumé Blanc Lontue 1991 $6 (6/15/92) BB **85**
Merlot Curicó Selección Especial 12 1989 $6 (6/15/91) BB **80**
Merlot Curicó Selección Especial 12 1988 $6 (9/15/90) BB **82**
Merlot Lontue 1990 $6 (6/15/92) BB **83**
Merlot Lontue 1988 $6 (7/31/89) BB **80**
Merlot Maipo Reserve 1989 $9 (5/15/92) **78**

VINA VISTA (United States/California)
Merlot Alexander Valley 1988 $12 (5/31/92) **86**
Merlot Alexander Valley 1985 $8 (10/31/87) **90**

VINATTIERRI (Italy/North)
Chardonnay Alto Adige Atesino Vinattieri Bianco 1989 $18 (8/31/91) **80**
Rosso 1986 $18 (8/31/91) **83**
Rosso 1985 ($NA) (9/15/87) (HS) **91**
Rosso 1983 $14 (9/15/87) (HS) **84**
Rosso II 1986 $18 (8/31/91) **84**

J.J. VINCENT (France/Burgundy)
Mâcon-Villages 1988 $7 (10/31/90) **79**
Mâcon-Villages Pièce d'Or 1990 $9.50 (8/31/91) **81**
Mâcon-Villages Pièce d'Or 1987 $7 (5/15/89) **77**
Pouilly-Fuissé 1990 $18 (8/31/91) **82**
Pouilly-Fuissé 1989 $15 (4/30/91) **79**
Pouilly-Fuissé 1988 $15 (10/31/90) **90**
Pouilly-Fuissé 1984 $17 (2/16/86) **71**
St.-Véran 1988 $10 (10/31/90) **85**
St.-Véran 1985 $12 (3/31/87) **87**

M. VINCENT (France/Burgundy)
Pouilly-Fuissé Château Fuissé 1989 $38 (8/31/91) **85**
Pouilly-Fuissé Château Fuissé 1987 $23 (11/30/90) **77**
Pouilly-Fuissé Château Fuissé 1986 $29 (10/31/90) **89**

VINOS EXPOSICION (Chile)
Cabernet Sauvignon Talca Conde del Maule 1988 $6 (6/15/92) **79**
Cabernet Sauvignon Talca Escudo de Talca 1990 $5 (6/15/92) BB **82**
Cabernet Sauvignon Talca Molino Viejo 1990 $5 (6/15/92) BB **82**
Cabernet Sauvignon Talca Reserva de Talca 1989 $6 (6/15/92) **77**
Sauvignon Blanc Talca Conde del Maule 1991 $6 (6/15/92) **75**

VINOS DE LEON (Spain)
Tinto Palacio de Leon 1985 $4.50 (11/15/89) BB **85**

VINTERRA (Chile)
Cabernet Sauvignon Maipo-Napa Valleys NV $7 (2/15/90) BB **86**
Chardonnay Maipo-Napa Valleys NV $7 (3/31/90) BB **84**

CHATEAU VIOLET (France/Sauternes)
Sauternes 1987 ($NA) (6/15/90) **79**

CHATEAU LA VIOLETTE (France/Bordeaux)
Pomerol 1982 $25 (5/15/89) (TR) **88**
Pomerol 1979 $35 (10/15/89) (JS) **79**

GEORGES VIORNERY (France/Beaujolais)
Côte-de-Brouilly 1990 $13 (10/31/91) **88**

VIRGIN HILLS (Australia)
Cabernet Sauvignon Bendigo 1984 $17 (4/30/88) **68**

VISTARENNI (Italy/Tuscany)
Chianti Classico 1988 $11 (9/15/91) **86**
Chianti Classico 1987 $10 (10/15/89) **89**
Chianti Classico 1986 $18 (7/31/89) **78**
Chianti Classico Riserva 1985 ($NA) (9/15/91) **81**
Chianti Classico Vigneto Assòlo 1988 $16 (9/15/91) **78**
Codirosso 1986 $22 (11/30/89) **90**

VITA NOVA (United States/California)
Chardonnay Santa Barbara County 1989 $18 (7/15/91) **86**
Chardonnay Santa Barbara County 1988 $13.50 (2/15/90) **91**
Chardonnay Santa Barbara County Rancho Vinedo Vineyards 1990 $18 (7/15/92) **83**
Reservatum Santa Barbara County 1986 $20 (12/15/89) **87**

VITICCIO (Italy/Tuscany)
Chianti Classico 1988 $10 (9/15/91) **87**
Chianti Classico 1987 $9 (4/30/90) **78**
Chianti Classico 1986 $8 (3/31/89) BB **88**
Chianti Classico 1984 $5.75 (11/15/87) **74**
Chianti Classico Riserva 1985 $11 (11/30/89) **85**
Chianti Classico Riserva 1983 $12 (11/30/89) **80**
Chianti Classico Viticcio Riserva 1983 $8 (11/15/87) **77**
Chianti Classico Viticcio Riserva 1982 $8.75 (11/15/87) **84**
Chianti Classico Viticcio Riserva 1978 $12.50 (11/30/87) **78**
Chianti Classico Viticcio Riserva 1975 $13.50 (11/15/87) **71**
Prunaio 1988 $28 (3/31/92) **88**
Prunaio 1986 $19 (3/31/90) SS **92**
Prunaio 1985 $18 (4/30/89) **88**

CHATEAU DE VIVIERS (France/Chablis)
Chablis 1984 $12 (7/16/86) **72**

ROBERTO VOERZIO (Italy/Piedmont)
Barolo 1985 $18 (1/31/90) **87**
Barolo 1983 $15 (9/15/88) (HS) **88**
Barolo 1982 $12 (9/15/88) (HS) **90**
Barolo La Serra di la Morra 1982 $12 (7/31/87) **91**
Dolcetto d'Alba 1990 $12 (1/31/92) **82**
Dolcetto d'Alba Priavino 1988 $11 (12/31/90) **87**
Piccoli Vigneti di Langhe 1990 $16 (5/15/92) **74**
Vignaserra 1988 $24 (3/31/92) **85**
Vignaserra 1987 $18 (8/31/91) **85**

COMTE DE VOGUE (France/Burgundy)
Bonnes Mares 1989 $93 (1/31/92) **94**
Bonnes Mares 1988 $93 (3/31/91) **89**
Bonnes Mares 1987 $69 (7/15/90) **87**
Bonnes Mares 1979 $60 (11/16/84) (HS) **88**
Bonnes Mares 1976 $55 (11/16/84) (HS) **90**
Bonnes Mares 1972 $115 (11/16/84) (HS) **79**
Bonnes Mares 1971 $175 (11/16/84) (HS) **88**
Bonnes Mares 1959 $172 (11/16/84) (HS) **83**
Bonnes Mares 1955 ($NA) (11/16/84) (HS) **91**
Bonnes Mares 1949 ($NA)/1.5L (11/16/84) (HS) **90**
Bonnes Mares Avery Bottling 1959 $172 (11/16/84) (HS) **87**
Bonnes Mares Grivolet 1934 ($NA) (11/16/84) (HS) **82**
Chambolle-Musigny 1989 $44 (1/31/92) **89**
Chambolle-Musigny Les Amoureuses 1989 $93 (1/31/92) **93**
Chambolle-Musigny Les Amoureuses 1988 $93 (2/28/91) **89**
Chambolle-Musigny Les Amoureuses 1987 $74 (3/31/90) **87**
Chambolle-Musigny Les Amoureuses 1971 $95 (11/16/84) (HS) **86**
Chambolle-Musigny Les Amoureuses 1970 ($NA) (11/16/84) (HS) **78**
Musigny 1953 $200 (11/16/84) (HS) **81**
Musigny 1952 ($NA) (11/16/84) (HS) **85**
Musigny 1949 $480 (11/16/84) (HS) **98**
Musigny 1945 $1,210/1.5L (11/16/84) (HS) **96**
Musigny 1937 $650 (11/16/84) (HS) **93**
Musigny 1934 ($NA) (11/16/84) (HS) **95**
Musigny Cuvée Vieilles Vignes 1989 $134 (1/31/92) **96**
Musigny Cuvée Vieilles Vignes 1988 Rel: $134 Cur: $149 (2/28/91) **90**
Musigny Cuvée Vieilles Vignes 1987 $100 (3/31/90) **87**
Musigny Cuvée Vieilles Vignes 1985 Rel: $125 Cur: $150 (3/31/88) **92**
Musigny Cuvée Vieilles Vignes 1979 $114 (11/16/84) (HS) **87**
Musigny Cuvée Vieilles Vignes 1976 $87 (11/16/84) (HS) **86**
Musigny Cuvée Vieilles Vignes 1972 $130 (11/16/84) (HS) **80**
Musigny Cuvée Vieilles Vignes 1971 $240 (11/16/84) (HS) **90**
Musigny Cuvée Vieilles Vignes 1969 $210 (11/16/84) (HS) **65**
Musigny Cuvée Vieilles Vignes 1966 $210 (11/16/84) (HS) **92**
Musigny Cuvée Vieilles Vignes 1962 $500/1.5L (11/16/84) (HS) **90**
Musigny Cuvée Vieilles Vignes 1961 $300 (11/16/84) (HS) **93**
Musigny Cuvée Vieilles Vignes 1959 $350 (11/16/84) (HS) **89**
Musigny Cuvée Vieilles Vignes 1957 $160 (8/31/90) (HS) **95**

LEON VOILLAND (France/Burgundy)
Beaune Clos du Roy 1945 ($NA) (8/31/90) (TR) **90**

HEINRICH VOLLMER (Germany)
Pinot Blanc Kabinett Trocken Rheinpfalz Weisser Burgunder Ellerstadter Kirchenstück 1990 $9 (1/31/92) **85**

SCHLOSS VOLLRADS (Germany)
Riesling Kabinett Halbtrocken Rheingau Blausilber 1990 (NR) (12/15/91) **86**
Riesling Kabinett Rheingau 1983 $8 (3/01/85) **80**
Riesling Kabinett Rheingau Blaugold 1985 $12 (5/15/87) **78**
Riesling Kabinett Rheingau Charta 1990 (NR) (12/15/91) **85**
Riesling Qualitätswein Rheingau Grungold 1985 $8.50 (5/15/87) **89**
Riesling Spätlese Halbtrocken Rheingau Rosasilber 1990 (NR) (12/15/91) **86**
Riesling Spätlese Rheingau Charta 1990 (NR) (12/15/91) **83**

CASTELLO DI VOLPAIA (Italy/Tuscany)
Balifico 1987 ($NA) (11/30/89) (HS) **89**
Balifico 1986 $19 (4/30/89) **83**
Balifico 1985 $21 (11/30/89) (HS) **91**
Chianti Classico 1988 $13.50 (9/15/91) **85**
Chianti Classico 1987 $16 (11/30/89) (HS) **85**
Chianti Classico 1986 $10 (3/31/90) **75**
Chianti Classico 1985 $10 (6/30/89) SS **90**
Chianti Classico 1983 $8 (9/15/87) (HS) **88**
Chianti Classico Riserva 1985 $13 (9/15/91) **84**
Chianti Classico Riserva 1983 $11.50 (5/31/89) **87**
Chianti Classico Riserva 1982 $11 (9/15/87) (HS) **84**
Chianti Classico Riserva 1981 ($NA) (9/15/87) (HS) **86**
Chianti Classico Riserva 1977 ($NA) (9/15/87) (HS) **81**
Chianti Classico Riserva 1970 ($NA) (9/15/87) (HS) **85**
Coltassala 1986 ($NA) (11/30/89) (HS) **86**
Coltassala 1985 $19 (11/30/89) (HS) **88**
Coltassala 1983 $22 (9/15/88) **86**
Coltassala 1982 ($NA) (9/15/87) (HS) **87**
Coltassala 1981 ($NA) (9/15/87) (HS) **90**

JEAN-CLAUDE VOLPATO (France/Burgundy)
Bourgogne Passetoutgrain 1988 $13 (3/31/91) **73**

VOLPATO-COSTAILLE (France/Burgundy)
Chambolle-Musigny 1988 $34 (2/28/91) **78**

DEMOISELLE VRANKEN (France/Champagne)
Brut Champagne Grande Cuvée NV (NR) (12/31/91) **86**

WAGNER (United States/New York)
Chardonnay Finger Lakes Barrel Fermented 1988 $13 (8/31/91) **76**
Chardonnay Finger Lakes Reserve 1988 $17 (8/31/91) **77**
Gewürztraminer Finger Lakes 1987 $8 (1/31/92) **80**
Johannisberg Riesling Late Harvest Finger Lakes Ice Wine 1989 $14/375ml (1/31/92) **85**
Seyval Blanc Finger Lakes Barrel Fermented 1988 $6 (3/31/92) **75**

WALNUT CREST (Chile)
Cabernet Sauvignon Maipo 1985 $4 (6/30/90) BB **80**
Chardonnay Maipo 1988 $4 (4/30/90) **74**
Merlot Rapel 1989 $4.50 (5/15/92) BB **83**
Merlot Rapel 1987 $4 (6/30/90) BB **85**

WARRE (Portugal)
10 Year Old Sir William Port NV $20 (4/30/91) **83**
Tawny Port 20 Year Old Nimrod NV $38 (2/28/90) (JS) **84**
Tawny Port Very Finest Rare Nimrod NV $24 (4/15/91) **85**
Vintage Port 1985 Rel: $28 Cur: $40 (VP-6/90) **91**
Vintage Port 1983 Rel: $28 Cur: $38 (VP-6/90) **88**
Vintage Port 1983 Rel: $28 Cur: $38 (12/31/86) CS **94**
Vintage Port 1980 Rel: $16 Cur: $40 (VP-6/90) **88**
Vintage Port 1980 Rel: $16 Cur: $40 (10/01/84) CS **92**
Vintage Port 1977 Rel: $15 Cur: $61 (VP-4/90) **92**
Vintage Port 1975 $44 (10/31/88) **74**
Vintage Port 1970 $59 (VP-12/89) **88**
Vintage Port 1966 $84 (VP-6/89) **91**
Vintage Port 1963 $121 (VP-12/89) **92**
Vintage Port 1960 $71 (VP-8/88) **82**
Vintage Port 1958 $110 (VP-11/89) **81**
Vintage Port 1955 $185 (VP-11/89) **86**
Vintage Port 1947 $162 (VP-11/89) **88**
Vintage Port 1945 $310 (VP-11/89) **87**
Vintage Port 1934 $250 (VP-2/90) **87**
Vintage Port 1927 $350 (VP-12/89) **93**
Vintage Port 1900 $410 (VP-11/89) **79**
Vintage Port Quinta da Cavadinha 1987 ($NA) (VP-2/90) **86**
Vintage Port Quinta da Cavadinha 1986 ($NA) (VP-2/90) **85**
Vintage Port Quinta da Cavadinha 1984 ($NA) (VP-2/90) **81**
Vintage Port Quinta da Cavadinha 1982 ($NA) (VP-2/90) **86**
Vintage Port Quinta da Cavadinha 1979 Rel: $25 Cur: $31 (7/31/90) **82**
Vintage Port Quinta da Cavadinha 1978 $28 (VP-2/90) **83**

WASSON BROS (United States/Oregon)
Pinot Noir Oregon 1985 ($NA) (9/30/87) **93**

WATERBROOK (United States/Washington)
Cabernet Sauvignon Columbia Valley 1988 $14 (4/15/92) **85**
Chardonnay Columbia Valley 1990 $8 (4/30/92) BB **87**
Chardonnay Columbia Valley 1989 $6.50 (11/30/91) **84**
Chardonnay Columbia Valley Barrel Fermented Reserve 1990 $13 (4/30/92) **87**
Merlot Columbia Valley 1989 $14 (4/30/92) **94**
Sauvignon Blanc Washington 1987 $9 (10/15/89) **85**

WATSON (United States/California)
Pinot Noir Santa Maria Valley Bien Nacido Vineyard 1986 $9 (12/15/89) **77**

WEGELER-DEINHARD (Germany)
Riesling Auslese Mosel-Saar-Ruwer Bernkasteler Graben 1989 $22 (12/15/90) **85**
Riesling Auslese Mosel-Saar-Ruwer Wehlener Sonnenuhr 1990 $18 (12/15/91) **85**
Riesling Auslese Mosel-Saar-Ruwer Wehlener Sonnenuhr 1988 $17.50 (9/30/89) **85**
Riesling Auslese Rheingau Rüdesheimer Berg Rottland 1990 $25 (12/15/91) **85**
Riesling Auslese Rheingau Winkler Hasensprung 1990 $23 (12/15/91) **83**
Riesling Auslese Rheinpfalz Deidesheimer Herrgottsacker 1989 $17 (12/15/90) **85**
Riesling Kabinett Halbtrocken Rheingau Winkeler Hasensprung Charta 1988 $15 (9/30/89) **92**
Riesling Kabinett Mosel-Saar-Ruwer 1990 (NR) (12/15/91) **86**
Riesling Kabinett Mosel-Saar-Ruwer Bernkasteler Badstube 1989 $10.50 (12/15/90) **83**
Riesling Kabinett Mosel-Saar-Ruwer Bernkasteler Badstube 1988 $9 (9/30/89) **79**
Riesling Kabinett Mosel-Saar-Ruwer Wehlener Sonnenuhr 1989 $13.50 (12/15/90) **86**
Riesling Kabinett Mosel-Saar-Ruwer Wehlener Sonnenuhr 1985 $10 (10/15/87) **73**
Riesling Kabinett Rheingau 1990 (NR) (12/15/91) **85**
Riesling Kabinett Rheingau Rüdesheimer Berg Rottland 1990 $12 (12/15/91) **85**
Riesling Kabinett Rheingau Rüdesheimer Berg Rottland 1988 ($NA) (9/30/89) **88**
Riesling Kabinett Rheinpfalz 1990 $11 (12/15/91) **89**
Riesling Kabinett Rheinpfalz Deidesheimer Herrgottsacker 1989 $10 (12/15/90) **82**
Riesling Spätlese Mosel-Saar-Ruwer 1990 $16 (12/15/91) **85**
Riesling Spätlese Mosel-Saar-Ruwer Bernkasteler Doctor 1990 $46 (12/15/91) **86**
Riesling Spätlese Mosel-Saar-Ruwer Bernkasteler Doctor 1986 ($NA) (4/15/89) **91**
Riesling Spätlese Mosel-Saar-Ruwer Bernkasteler Graben 1989 $17 (12/15/90) **81**
Riesling Spätlese Mosel-Saar-Ruwer Bernkasteler Graben 1988 $14.50 (9/30/89) **84**
Riesling Spätlese Mosel-Saar-Ruwer Graacher Himmelreich 1989 $17 (12/15/90) **83**
Riesling Spätlese Mosel-Saar-Ruwer Wehlener Sonnenuhr 1990 $18 (12/15/91) **87**
Riesling Spätlese Mosel-Saar-Ruwer Wehlener Sonnenuhr 1989 $17 (12/15/90) **87**
Riesling Spätlese Mosel-Saar-Ruwer Wehlener Sonnenuhr 1988 $15 (9/30/89) **88**
Riesling Spätlese Mosel-Saar-Ruwer Wehlener Sonnenuhr 1986 ($NA) (4/15/89) **88**
Riesling Spätlese Mosel-Saar-Ruwer Wehlener Sonnenuhr 1985 ($NA) (4/15/89) **84**
Riesling Spätlese Rheingau 1990 (NR) (12/15/91) **85**
Riesling Spätlese Rheingau Mittelheimer St. Nikolaus 1988 ($NA) (9/30/89) **89**
Riesling Spätlese Rheingau Rüdesheimer Berg Rottland 1988 ($NA) (9/30/89) **81**
Riesling Spätlese Rheinpfalz 1990 $15 (12/15/91) **86**
Riesling Spätlese Rheinpfalz Deidesheimer Herrgottsacker 1989 $13 (12/15/90) **87**
Riesling Spätlese Rheinpfalz Deidesheimer Herrgottsacker 1988 $11 (9/30/89) **84**
Riesling Spätlese Rheinpfalz Forster Ungeheuer 1990 $15 (12/15/91) **78**
Riesling Spätlese Rheinpfalz Forster Ungeheuer 1988 $12 (9/30/89) **86**
Riesling Spätlese Trocken Rheinpfalz Deidesheimer Herrgottsacker 1988 ($NA) (9/30/89) **85**
Riesling Trockenbeerenauslese Rheinpfalz Deidesheimer Herrgottsacker 1989 ($NA) (12/15/90) **93**

WEIBEL (United States/California)
Brut Mendocino County 1982 $13 (9/15/86) **77**
Cabernet Sauvignon Mendocino County 1988 $8 (3/15/92) BB **81**
Cabernet Sauvignon Mendocino County 1987 $8 (2/28/91) BB **84**
Chardonnay Mendocino County 1989 $8 (3/31/91) BB **82**
Chenin Blanc Mendocino 1988 $5 (7/31/89) **83**
Pinot Noir Mendocino County 1988 $6 (2/28/91) **74**
White Zinfandel Mendocino 1988 $5 (6/15/89) **65**

DR. WEIL (Germany)
Riesling Auslese Rheingau Kiedricher Gräfenberg 1989 ($NA) (12/15/90) **83**
Riesling Beerenauslese Rheingau 1989 ($NA) (12/15/90) **98**
Riesling Kabinett Halbtrocken Rheingau Kiedricher Wasseros Charta 1988 ($NA) (9/30/89) **84**
Riesling Kabinett Rheingau Kiedricher Gräfenberg 1989 ($NA) (12/15/90) **83**
Riesling Spätlese Halbtrocken Rheingau 1989 ($NA) (12/15/90) **91**
Riesling Spätlese Rheingau 1989 ($NA) (12/15/90) **78**
Riesling Spätlese Rheingau Kiedricher Gräfenberg 1988 ($NA) (9/30/89) **84**
Riesling Trockenbeerenauslese Rheingau 1989 ($NA) (12/15/90) **93**

DOMAINE WEINBACH (France/Alsace)
Gewürztraminer Alsace Clos des Capucins (Cask 21) 1989 ($NA) (11/15/90) **79**
Gewürztraminer Alsace Clos des Capucins Cuvée Laurence (Cask 8) 1989 $50 (11/15/90) **79**
Gewürztraminer Alsace Clos des Capucins Cuvée Laurence (Cask 17) 1989 $50 (11/15/90) **80**
Gewürztraminer Alsace Clos des Capucins Quintes Sélection de Grains Nobles 1989 $275 (11/15/90) **87**
Gewürztraminer Alsace Clos des Capucins Réserve Personnelle 1988 $21 (6/30/91) **84**
Gewürztraminer Alsace Cuvée Laurence 1990 $29 (2/15/92) **87**
Gewürztraminer Alsace Cuvée Laurence 1988 $34 (10/15/89) **83**
Gewürztraminer Alsace Cuvée Théo 1990 $20 (2/15/92) **85**
Gewürztraminer Alsace Cuvée Théo 1988 ($NA) (10/15/89) **85**
Gewürztraminer Alsace Vendange Tardive 1990 $57 (2/15/92) (BT) **90+**
Gewürztraminer Alsace Vendange Tardive 1988 $67.50 (10/15/89) **92**
Muscat Alsace Clos des Capucins 1988 $23 (7/31/91) **78**
Pinot Blanc Alsace 1989 $18 (11/15/90) **88**
Pinot Blanc Alsace Clos des Capucins 1988 ($NA) (10/15/89) **80**
Pinot Blanc Alsace Clos des Capucins Réserve Particulière 1988 $19 (10/15/89) **74**
Pinot Blanc Alsace Réserve 1990 $11 (2/15/92) **88**
Riesling Alsace Clos des Capucins Cuvée Ste.-Catherine 1989 $43 (11/15/90) **80**
Riesling Alsace Clos des Capucins Cuvée Théo 1989 $31 (11/15/90) **88**
Riesling Alsace Clos des Capucins Réserve Personnelle 1989 $23 (7/31/91) **81**
Riesling Alsace Clos des Capucins Réserve Personnelle 1988 $18 (7/31/91) **78**
Riesling Alsace Clos des Capucins Schlossberg 1989 $31 (11/15/90) **84**
Riesling Alsace Clos des Capucins Sélection de Grains Nobles 1990 (NR) (2/15/92) (BT) **95+**
Riesling Alsace Clos des Capucins Sélection de Grains Nobles 1989 ($NA) (11/15/90) **96**
Riesling Alsace Cuvée Ste.-Catherine 1988 $30 (10/15/89) **87**
Riesling Alsace Cuvée Ste.-Catherine (Cask 1) 1990 $25 (2/15/92) **88**
Riesling Alsace Cuvée Ste.-Catherine (Cask 2) 1990 $25 (2/15/92) **91**
Riesling Alsace Cuvée Ste.-Catherine (Cask 3) 1990 $25 (2/15/92) **87**
Riesling Alsace Cuvée Ste.-Catherine (Cask 17) 1990 $25 (2/15/92) **88**
Riesling Alsace Cuvée Théo 1990 $18 (2/15/92) **88**
Riesling Alsace Cuvée Théo 1988 ($NA) (10/15/89) **80**
Riesling Alsace Schlossberg 1990 $18 (2/15/92) **90**
Riesling Alsace Vendange Tardive 1990 $57 (2/15/92) (BT) **90+**
Sylvaner Alsace Réserve 1990 $9.50 (2/15/92) **83**
Tokay Pinot Gris Alsace Clos des Capucins Cuvée Ste.-Catherine 1989 $43 (11/15/90) **90**
Tokay Pinot Gris Alsace Clos des Capucins Cuvée Ste.-Catherine 1988 $35 (7/31/91) **79**
Tokay Pinot Gris Alsace Clos des Capucins Sélection de Grains Nobles 1990 (NR) (2/15/92) (BT) **90+**
Tokay Pinot Gris Alsace Clos des Capucins Sélection de Grains Nobles 1989 ($NA) (11/15/90) **95**
Tokay Pinot Gris Alsace Clos des Capucins Vendange Tardive 1989 ($NA) (11/15/90) **86**
Tokay Pinot Gris Alsace Cuvée Ste.-Catherine 1990 $25 (2/15/92) **83**
Tokay Pinot Gris Alsace Vendange Tardive 1990 $57 (2/15/92) (BT) **85+**

DR. WEINS-PRUM (Germany)
Riesling Auslese Mosel-Saar-Ruwer Erdener Prälat 1988 ($NA) (9/30/89) **86**
Riesling Auslese Mosel-Saar-Ruwer Graacher Domprobst 1990 $22 (12/15/91) **90**
Riesling Auslese Mosel-Saar-Ruwer Urziger Würzgarten 1990 $22 (12/15/91) **88**
Riesling Auslese Mosel-Saar-Ruwer Wehlener Sonnenuhr Gold Cap 1990 $34 (12/15/91) **89**
Riesling Kabinett Mosel-Saar-Ruwer Bernkasteler Badstube 1990 $11 (12/15/91) **90**
Riesling Kabinett Mosel-Saar-Ruwer Wehlener Sonnenuhr 1988 ($NA) (9/30/89) **84**
Riesling Spätlese Mosel-Saar-Ruwer Urziger Würzgarten 1988 ($NA) (9/30/89) **82**
Riesling Spätlese Mosel-Saar-Ruwer Waldracher Sonnenberg 1990 $15 (12/15/91) **86**
Riesling Spätlese Mosel-Saar-Ruwer Wehlener Sonnenuhr 1990 $16 (12/15/91) **89**
Riesling Spätlese Mosel-Saar-Ruwer Wehlener Sonnenuhr 1988 ($NA) (9/30/89) **84**

WEINSTOCK (United States/California)
Chardonnay Alexander Valley Winemaker Selection Reserve 1989 $10 (1/31/92) **79**
Chardonnay Alexander Valley 1989 $11 (3/31/91) **87**
Gamay Sonoma County 1989 $8 (3/31/91) **75**
Pinot Noir Sonoma County Winemaker Selection Reserve 1989 $12.50 (11/15/91) **79**
White Zinfandel Sonoma County 1989 $8 (3/31/91) **75**

WELLER-LEHNERT (Germany)
Riesling Auslese Mosel-Saar-Ruwer Piesporter Goldtröpfchen 1988 ($NA) (9/30/89) **86**

WELLINGTON (United States/California)
Chardonnay Sonoma Valley Barrel Fermented 1990 $12.50 (4/30/92) **74**
Criolla Old Vines Sonoma Valley 1990 $7 (3/31/92) **85**

WENTE BROS. (United States/California)
Blanc de Noir Arroyo Seco 1983 $15 (3/31/89) **78**
Brut Arroyo Seco 1983 $10 (8/31/88) **79**
Brut Arroyo Seco 1982 $8 (12/31/86) **84**
Brut Arroyo Seco 1981 $8 (4/01/86) **78**
Cabernet Sauvignon California 1981 $7 (12/16/85) **65**
Cabernet Sauvignon Central Coast 1985 $8 (11/15/89) **78**
Cabernet Sauvignon Livermore Valley Charles Wetmore Vineyard Estate Reserve 1987 $18 (4/30/91) **86**
Cabernet Sauvignon Livermore Valley Estate Reserve 1986 $12 (10/15/90) **82**
Chardonnay Arroyo Seco Reserve Arroyo Seco Vineyards 1988 $12 (4/15/90) **90**
Chardonnay Arroyo Seco Reserve Arroyo Seco Vineyards 1987 $14 (10/31/89) **77**
Chardonnay Arroyo Seco Reserve Arroyo Seco Vineyards 1985 $10 (10/15/87) **84**
Chardonnay Arroyo Seco Reserve Arroyo Seco Vineyards 1984 $9 (6/01/86) **90**
Chardonnay Arroyo Seco Riva Ranch 1990 $12 (6/30/92) SS **90**
Chardonnay Arroyo Seco Vineyard Reserve 1985 $30/1.5L (3/31/90) **79**
Chardonnay Central Coast Estate Grown 1991 $8 (7/15/92) SS **91**
Chardonnay Central Coast Estate Grown 1989 $10.50 (7/15/91) **83**
Chardonnay Livermore Valley Herman Wente Vineyard Reserve 1990 $18 (7/15/92) **88**
Chardonnay Livermore Valley Herman Wente Vineyard Reserve 1989 $18 (4/30/91) **88**
Chardonnay Livermore Valley Herman Wente Vineyard Reserve 1986 $11 (5/31/88) **80**
Gewürztraminer Arroyo Seco Vintner Grown Arroyo Seco Vineyards 1987 $9 (12/15/89) **64**
Riesling Late Harvest Arroyo Seco Auslese 1973 ($NA) (2/28/87) **95**
Riesling Late Harvest Arroyo Seco Reserve Arroyo Seco Vineyard 1987 $12 (7/15/90) **76**
Zinfandel Livermore Valley Special Selection Raboli Vineyards 1985 $10 (12/15/89) **77**

DOMDECHANT WERNER'SCHES (Germany)
Riesling Auslese Rheingau Hochheimer 1989 ($NA) (12/15/90) **88**
Riesling Auslese Rheingau Hochheimer Domdechaney 1990 (NR) (12/15/91) **85**
Riesling Beerenauslese Rheingau Hochheimer 1989 ($NA) (12/15/90) **79**
Riesling Eiswein Rheingau Hochheimer Domdechaney 1990 (NR) (12/15/91) **93**
Riesling Kabinett Halbtrocken Rheingau Hochheimer Stein 1989 ($NA) (12/15/90) **84**
Riesling Kabinett Halbtrocken Rheingau Werner Hochheimer Stein 1988 $10.50 (9/30/89) **87**
Riesling Kabinett Rheingau Hochheimer Domdechaney 1989 ($NA) (12/15/90) **79**
Riesling Kabinett Rheingau Hochheimer Domdechaney 1989 ($NA) (12/15/90) **88**
Riesling Kabinett Rheingau Hochheimer Hölle 1990 (NR) (12/15/91) **88**
Riesling Kabinett Rheingau Hochheimer Hölle 1988 $10.50 (9/30/89) **87**
Riesling Kabinett Rheingau Hochheimer Hölle (AP1490) 1989 ($NA) (12/15/90) **83**
Riesling Kabinett Rheingau Hochheimer Hölle (AP989) 1989 ($NA) (12/15/90) **86**
Riesling Qualitätswein Rheingau Hochheimer 1989 ($NA) (12/15/90) **77**
Riesling Spätlese Halbtrocken Rheingau Hochheimer Hölle 1990 (NR) (12/15/91) **84**
Riesling Spätlese Halbtrocken Rheingau Hochheimer Hölle 1988 $12.50 (9/30/89) **93**
Riesling Spätlese Rheingau Hochheimer Domdechaney 1990 (NR) (12/15/91) **85**
Riesling Spätlese Rheingau Hochheimer Domdechaney 1989 $16 (12/15/90) **83**
Riesling Spätlese Rheingau Hochheimer Domdechaney 1988 $12.50 (9/30/89) **93**
Riesling Spätlese Rheingau Hochheimer Hölle 1990 (NR) (12/15/91) **84**
Riesling Spätlese Trocken Rheingau Hochheimer Kirchenstück 1990 (NR) (12/15/91) **78**
Riesling Trockenbeerenauslese Rheingau Hochheimer 1989 ($NA) (12/15/90) **84**

WESTWOOD (United States/California)
Chardonnay El Dorado 1989 $10 (7/15/91) **75**
Pinot Noir California 1989 $9.75 (4/30/91) **75**

WILLIAM WHEELER (United States/California)
Cabernet Sauvignon Dry Creek Valley 1987 $14 (11/15/91) **84**
Cabernet Sauvignon Dry Creek Valley 1986 $12 (8/31/90) **83**
Cabernet Sauvignon Dry Creek Valley 1985 $12 (7/15/89) **76**
Cabernet Sauvignon Dry Creek Valley 1984 $11 (4/15/88) **75**
Cabernet Sauvignon Dry Creek Valley Norse Vineyard Private Reserve 1985 $18 (11/15/90) **83**
Cabernet Sauvignon Dry Creek Valley Norse Vineyard Private Reserve 1984 $15 (7/31/89) **60**
Chardonnay Sonoma County 1990 $13 (3/31/92) **83**
Chardonnay Sonoma County 1989 $13 (12/31/91) **88**
Chardonnay Sonoma County 1988 $12 (6/30/90) **85**
Chardonnay Sonoma County 1987 $12 (7/15/89) **88**
Chardonnay Sonoma County 1986 $11.50 (1/31/88) **79**
Chardonnay Sonoma County 1984 $11 (1/31/87) **88**
Chardonnay Sonoma County 1983 $11 (6/01/85) **82**
RS Reserve California 1989 $10.50 (10/31/91) **77**
RS Reserve California 1988 $10 (8/31/90) **83**
White Zinfandel Sonoma County Young Vines 1988 $6 (6/15/89) **84**

WHITE HERON (United States/Washington)
Chantepierre Washington 1988 $11 (4/15/92) **80**
Johannisberg Riesling Washington 1987 $5 (7/31/89) **68**

Key to Symbols

The scores reported here are the results of blind tastings conducted by our panel of senior editors. Wines that carry the initials below are results of individual tastings.

THE WINE SPECTATOR 100-POINT SCALE ***95-100***—Classic, a great wine; ***90-94***—Outstanding, superior character and style; ***80-89***—Good to very good, a wine with special qualities; ***70-79***—Average, drinkable wine that may have minor flaws; ***60-69***—Below average, drinkable but not recommended; ***50-59***—Poor, undrinkable, not recommended. "+"—With a score indicates a range; used primarily with barrel tastings to indicate a preliminary score.

SPECIAL DESIGNATIONS SS—Spectator Selection, CS—Cellar Selection, BB—Best Buy, ($NA)—Price not available, (NR)—Not released.

TASTER'S INITIALS (JG)—Jim Gordon, (HS)—Harvey Steiman, (JL)—James Laube, (JS)—James Suckling, (TM)—Thomas Matthews, (TR)—Terry Robards, (PM)—Per-Henrik Mansson, (BT)—Barrel Tasting (these wines were tasted blind from barrel samples), (CA-date)—*California's Great Cabernets* by James Laube, (CH-date)—*California's Great Chardonnays* by James Laube, (VP-date)—*Vintage Port* by James Suckling.

DATE TASTED Dates in parentheses represent the issue in which the rating was published.

WHITE OAK (United States/California)
Cabernet Sauvignon Sonoma County 1987 $14 (2/29/92) **85**
Cabernet Sauvignon Alexander Valley Myers Limited Reserve 1985 $18 (7/31/89) **85**
Chardonnay Sonoma County 1989 $12 (3/31/91) **85**
Chardonnay Sonoma County 1990 Rel: $13 Cur: $15 (12/31/91) **81**
Chardonnay Sonoma County 1988 Rel: $12 Cur: $16 (4/30/90) **88**
Chardonnay Sonoma County 1987 Rel: $11 Cur: $16 (CH-5/90) **85**
Chardonnay Sonoma County 1986 Rel: $11 Cur: $17 (CH-5/90) **86**
Chardonnay Sonoma County 1985 Rel: $10.50 Cur: $18 (CH-5/90) **89**
Chardonnay Sonoma County 1984 Rel: $10 Cur: $18 (CH-5/90) **86**
Chardonnay Sonoma County Myers Limited Reserve 1990 $20 (2/29/92) **86**
Chardonnay Sonoma County Myers Limited Reserve 1989 $20 (3/31/91) **80**
Chardonnay Sonoma County Myers Limited Release 1988 Rel: $18 Cur: $20 (CH-5/90) **88**
Chardonnay Sonoma County Myers Limited Release 1987 Rel: $18 Cur: $20 (CH-5/90) **81**
Chardonnay Sonoma County Myers Limited Release 1986 Rel: $16 Cur: $20 (CH-5/90) **87**
Chardonnay Alexander Valley Myers Limited Release 1985 Rel: $14.50 Cur: $22 (CH-5/90) **90**
Chenin Blanc Alexander Valley 1990 $7 (11/15/91) BB **87**
Chenin Blanc Dry Creek Valley 1988 $6.50 (7/31/89) **84**
Sauvignon Blanc Sonoma County 1990 $9 (11/15/91) **81**
Zinfandel Sonoma County 1989 $10 (2/29/92) **87**

WHITE ROCK (United States/California)
Claret Napa Valley 1986 $18 (10/31/89) **80**
Chardonnay Napa Valley 1990 $15 (7/15/92) **89**
Chardonnay Napa Valley Barrel Fermented 1989 $16 (7/15/91) **87**

WHITEHALL LANE (United States/California)
Cabernet Franc Napa Valley 1988 $18.50 (11/15/90) **88**
Cabernet Sauvignon California NV $7 (10/15/88) **70**
Cabernet Sauvignon California Le Petit NV $8.50 (3/31/90) **81**
Cabernet Sauvignon Napa Valley 1989 (NR) (5/15/91) (BT) **85+**
Cabernet Sauvignon Napa Valley 1988 $18 (11/15/91) **87**
Cabernet Sauvignon Napa Valley 1987 $18 (9/15/90) **84**
Cabernet Sauvignon Napa Valley 1986 $16 (8/31/89) **89**
Cabernet Sauvignon Napa Valley 1985 $16 (11/15/88) **93**
Cabernet Sauvignon Napa Valley 1984 $14 (12/31/87) **84**
Cabernet Sauvignon Napa Valley 1983 $14 (11/30/86) **77**
Cabernet Sauvignon Napa Valley 1982 $12 (2/16/85) **86**
Cabernet Sauvignon Napa Valley NV $6 (12/31/87) **77**
Cabernet Sauvignon Napa Valley Morisoli Vineyard 1991 (NR) (5/15/92) (BT) **83+**
Cabernet Sauvignon Napa Valley Morisoli Vineyard 1990 (NR) (5/15/91) (BT) **95+**
Cabernet Sauvignon Napa Valley Reserve 1987 $28 (11/15/91) **90**
Cabernet Sauvignon Napa Valley Reserve 1986 $30 (11/15/90) **77**
Cabernet Sauvignon Napa Valley Reserve 1985 $30 (11/30/89) **88**
Chardonnay Napa Valley Cerro Vista Vineyard 1982 $12 (9/01/84) **74**
Chardonnay Napa Valley Estate Bottled 1988 $15 (6/30/90) **78**
Chardonnay Napa Valley Le Petit 1990 $8 (3/15/92) **82**
Chardonnay Napa Valley Le Petit 1989 $9 (2/28/91) **77**
Chardonnay Napa Valley Le Petit 1988 $8 (4/30/90) BB **84**
Chardonnay Napa Valley Reserve 1990 $16 (7/15/92) **87**
Merlot Knights Valley 1987 $16 (7/15/90) **77**
Merlot Knights Valley 1986 ($NA) (4/15/88) (BT) **90+**
Merlot Knights Valley 1984 $14 (12/31/87) **87**
Merlot Knights Valley 1983 $12 (10/01/85) **85**
Merlot Knights Valley 1982 Rel: $10 Cur: $19 (6/01/85) CS **92**
Merlot Knights Valley Reserve 1986 $15 (7/31/89) **72**
Merlot Knights Valley Summers Ranch 1989 $18 (4/15/92) **84**
Merlot Knights Valley Summers Ranch 1988 $18 (3/31/91) **82**
Pinot Noir Alexander Valley 1988 $13.50 (10/31/90) **82**
Pinot Noir Napa Valley 1987 $12 (10/15/89) **88**
Pinot Noir Napa Valley 1985 $7.50 (6/15/88) **82**
Pinot Noir Napa Valley 1984 $7.50 (3/01/86) **86**

WHITTLESEY MARK (United States/Oregon)
Brut de Noir Willamette Valley Sans Année NV $16.50 (5/15/92) **74**
Brut Oregon 1987 $16.50 (5/15/92) **78**

WIEDERKEHR (United States/Arkansas)
Altus Spumante Arkansas NV $6.50 (2/29/92) **80**
Cabernet Sauvignon Arkansas Mountain 1978 $35 (2/29/92) **70**
Muscat di Tanta Maria Altus Arkansas 1990 $9 (2/29/92) **71**

WIESE & KROHN (Portugal)
Tawny Port 20 Year Old NV $33 (2/28/90) (JS) **88**
Vintage Port 1985 Rel: $21 Cur: $34 (VP-1/90) **81**
Vintage Port 1984 Rel: $13 Cur: $24 (VP-1/90) **86**
Vintage Port 1982 Rel: $23 Cur: $33 (VP-1/90) **83**
Vintage Port 1978 Rel: $11 Cur: $37 (VP-1/90) **84**
Vintage Port 1975 $55 (VP-1/90) **80**
Vintage Port 1970 $62 (VP-1/90) **74**
Vintage Port 1967 $65 (VP-1/90) **75**
Vintage Port 1965 $100 (VP-1/90) **85**
Vintage Port 1963 $140 (VP-1/90) **87**
Vintage Port 1961 $115 (VP-1/90) **85**
Vintage Port 1960 $115 (VP-1/90) **89**
Vintage Port 1958 $170 (VP-1/90) **87**

WILD HORSE (United States/California)
Cabernet Sauvignon Paso Robles 1987 $13 (4/30/91) **88**
Cabernet Sauvignon Paso Robles Wild Horse Vineyards 1985 $10.50 (6/30/88) **70**
Chardonnay Central Coast 1990 $13 (12/31/91) **88**
Chardonnay Central Coast 1989 $13 (4/30/91) **86**
Chardonnay San Luis Obispo County 1988 $12 (4/15/90) **90**
Chardonnay San Luis Obispo County Wild Horse Vineyards 1987 $12 (6/15/89) **81**
Chardonnay San Luis Obispo County Wild Horse Vineyards 1986 $9.75 (5/31/88) **79**
Merlot Central Coast 1989 $15 (5/31/92) **76**
Merlot Central Coast 1986 $11 (7/31/89) **77**
Pinot Noir Paso Robles 1987 $14 (10/15/89) **90**
Pinot Noir Santa Barbara County 1988 $14 (4/30/91) **79**
Pinot Noir Santa Barbara County 1987 $13.50 (3/31/90) **82**
Pinot Noir Santa Barbara County 1986 $13.50 (6/15/88) **85**
Pinot Noir Santa Barbara County 1985 $12.50 (6/15/88) **86**

WILDCAT (United States/California)
Merlot Sonoma Valley 1989 $20 (5/31/92) **74**
Merlot Sonoma Valley 1988 $18 (5/31/92) **78**

WILDHURST (United States/California)
Chardonnay Napa Valley 1990 $10 (6/15/92) **85**

J. WILE & SONS (United States/California)
Cabernet Sauvignon Napa Valley 1987 $10 (5/31/91) **78**
Cabernet Sauvignon Napa Valley 1986 $7 (9/15/88) **75**
Cabernet Sauvignon Napa Valley 1985 $7 (11/15/87) **78**
Chardonnay Napa Valley 1990 $10 (7/15/92) **69**
Chardonnay Napa Valley 1987 $7 (2/15/89) **79**
Chardonnay Napa Valley 1986 $7 (9/15/87) **77**
Merlot Napa Valley 1989 $10 (5/31/92) **77**

AUDREY WILKINSON (Australia)
Cabernet Sauvignon Hunter Valley 1986 $13.50 (9/30/91) **87**
Chardonnay Hunter Valley 1987 $14 (9/15/91) **78**
Shiraz Hunter Valley Hermitage 1985 $13 (9/30/91) **79**

WILLI'S WINE BAR (France/Rhône)
Crozes-Hermitage Cuvée Anniversaire 1980-1990 1988 $11 (3/31/91) **70**

WILLIAMS SELYEM (United States/California)
Pinot Noir Russian River Valley Allen Vineyard 1988 $40 (5/31/90) **88**
Pinot Noir Russian River Valley Allen Vineyard 1987 $20 (5/31/89) **92**
Pinot Noir Russian River Valley Olivet Lane Vineyard 1989 $25 (11/15/91) **90**
Pinot Noir Russian River Valley Rochioli Vineyard 1988 $40 (2/28/91) **92**
Pinot Noir Sonoma Coast 1988 $40 (5/31/90) **92**
Pinot Noir Sonoma Coast Summa Vineyard 1988 $40 (5/31/90) **88**
Pinot Noir Sonoma County 1987 $16 (5/31/89) **88**
Pinot Noir Sonoma County 1986 $16 (6/15/88) **91**
Zinfandel Russian River Valley Leno Martinelli Vineyard 1985 $10 (7/31/88) **79**

WILLIAMSBURG (United States/Virginia)
Chardonnay Virginia Acte 12 of 1619 1990 $12 (2/29/92) **88**
Chardonnay Virginia Barrel Fermented Vintage Reserve 1990 $16 (2/29/92) **87**

ALSACE WILLM (France/Alsace)
Brut Crémant d'Alsace NV $10.50 (4/15/90) **83**
Gewürztraminer Alsace 1990 $13 (2/15/92) **85**
Gewürztraminer Alsace 1989 $12.50 (9/15/91) **86**
Gewürztraminer Alsace 1985 $11 (7/15/88) **91**
Gewürztraminer Alsace Clos Gaensbroennel 1990 $24 (2/15/92) **89**
Gewürztraminer Alsace Clos Gaensbroennel Kirchberg de Barr 1989 ($NA) (11/15/90) **83**
Gewürztraminer Alsace Clos Gaensbroennel Vendange Tardive 1990 $50 (2/15/92) (BT) **85+**
Gewürztraminer Alsace Gaensbroennel Vendange Tardive 1989 ($NA) (11/15/90) **80**
Gewürztraminer Alsace Sélection de Grains Nobles 1990 (NR) (2/15/92) (BT) **80+**
Gewürztraminer Alsace Sélection de Grains Nobles 1989 ($NA) (11/15/90) **86**
Pinot Blanc Alsace 1990 $9 (2/15/92) **84**
Pinot Blanc Alsace 1989 ($NA) (11/15/90) **83**
Riesling Alsace 1990 $11 (2/15/92) **87**
Riesling Alsace 1989 $12.50 (11/15/90) **85**
Riesling Alsace Cuvée Emile Willm 1990 $23 (2/15/92) **90**
Riesling Alsace Cuvée Emile Willm 1989 ($NA) (11/15/90) **80**
Riesling Alsace Kirchberg de Barr 1990 $23 (2/15/92) **89**
Riesling Alsace Kirchberg de Barr 1989 ($NA) (11/15/90) **82**
Tokay Pinot Gris Alsace 1990 $13 (2/15/92) **84**
Tokay Pinot Gris Alsace 1989 ($NA) (11/15/90) **87**
Tokay Pinot Gris Alsace Cuvée Emile Willm 1990 $25 (2/15/92) **89**
Tokay Pinot Gris Alsace Cuvée Emile Willm Vendange Tardive 1990 $51 (2/15/92) (BT) **85+**
Tokay Pinot Gris Alsace Sélection de Grains Nobles 1990 (NR) (2/15/92) (BT) **85+**
Tokay Pinot Gris Alsace Sélection de Grains Nobles 1989 ($NA) (11/15/90) **90**

WILLOW CREEK (United States/California)
Cabernet Sauvignon Napa Valley 1984 $8.50 (3/31/88) **73**
Cabernet Sauvignon Napa-Alexander Valleys 1986 $9.50 (7/31/89) **82**
Chardonnay Sonoma County 1989 $11 (9/30/90) **84**
Chardonnay Sonoma County 1988 $10 (2/28/90) **87**

WINDEMERE (United States/California)
Chardonnay Edna Valley MacGregor Vineyard 1989 $13 (12/15/91) **83**
Chardonnay Edna Valley MacGregor Vineyard 1988 $13 (4/30/91) **83**
Chardonnay Edna Valley MacGregor Vineyard 1987 $12 (7/15/89) **88**

WINDSOR (United States/California)
Merlot Russian River Valley Signature Series 1987 $25 (5/31/92) **84**
Pinot Noir Russian River Valley Winemaster's Private Reserve 1985 $8 (6/15/88) **83**

WINZERGENOSSENSCHAFT (Germany)
Riesling Auslese Mosel-Saar-Ruwer Piesporter Goldtröpfchen 1990 $14.50 (1/31/92) **80**
Riesling Auslese Mosel-Saar-Ruwer Piesporter Michelsberg 1990 $11 (1/31/92) **87**
Riesling Spätlese Mosel-Saar-Ruwer Graacher Himmelreich 1990 $9 (12/15/91) **80**
Riesling Spätlese Mosel-Saar-Ruwer Piesporter Goldtröpfchen 1990 $11.50 (1/31/92) **88**
Riesling Spätlese Mosel-Saar-Ruwer Piesporter Michelsberg 1990 $9.50 (12/15/91) **80**
Riesling Spätlese Mosel-Saar-Ruwer Zeltinger Himmelreich 1990 $9 (12/15/91) **85**

WIRRA WIRRA (Australia)
Cabernet Sauvignon McLaren Vale 1984 $14 (1/31/88) **84**
Cabernet Shiraz Merlot McLaren Vale Church Block 1985 $11 (3/15/88) **89**
Chardonnay McLaren Vale David Paxton's Hillstowe Vineyard 1985 $14 (12/31/87) **64**

WOLFBERGER (France/Alsace)
Crémant d'Alsace NV $12 (7/31/89) **83**
Riesling Alsace 1987 $8 (7/31/89) **71**

WOLLERSHEIM (United States/Wisconsin)
Dry Red Wine Wisconsin Domaine du Sac 1990 $8 (2/29/92) **81**
Domaine Reserve Wisconsin 1989 $12 (2/29/92) **73**
Pinot Noir Wisconsin Sugarloaf Hill 1989 (NR) (2/29/92) **75**
Seyval Blanc American Prairie Fumé 1990 $6 (2/29/92) **78**

WOLTNER (United States/California)
Cabernet Sauvignon North Coast 1979 $3.50 (3/16/84) **76**
Merlot Alexander Valley Cask 465 1982 $4.75 (4/16/85) **60**

WOODBURY (CALIFORNIA) (United States/California)
Port Alexander Valley Old Vines 1981 $10 (1/01/86) **91**

WOODBURY (NEW YORK) (United States/New York)
Blanc de Noirs New York 1987 $12 (12/31/90) **70**
Brut Blanc de Blancs New York 1987 $12 (12/31/90) **82**

WOODLEY (Australia)
Chardonnay South Eastern Australia Queen Adelaide 1990 $7 (9/15/91) **74**
Chardonnay South Eastern Australia Queen Adelaide 1987 $8 (5/31/88) **78**
Shiraz Cabernet Sauvignon South Eastern Australia Queen Adelaide 1988 $7 (2/29/92) BB **82**

WOODSTOCK (Australia)
Sémillon McLaren Vale 1989 $8 (2/29/92) **83**

WOODWARD CANYON (United States/Washington)
Cabernet Sauvignon Columbia Valley 1989 $27 (5/15/92) **92**
Cabernet Sauvignon Columbia Valley 1988 $24 (10/15/91) **93**
Cabernet Sauvignon Columbia Valley 1987 Rel: $18.50 Cur: $24 (12/31/90) **95**
Cabernet Sauvignon Columbia Valley 1986 Rel: $18.50 Cur: $24 (10/15/89) **93**
Cabernet Sauvignon Columbia Valley 1985 ($NA) (4/15/92) (JL) **86**
Cabernet Sauvignon Columbia Valley 1984 ($NA) (4/15/92) (JL) **81**
Cabernet Sauvignon Columbia Valley 1983 ($NA) (4/15/92) (JL) **88**
Cabernet Sauvignon Columbia Valley 1982 ($NA) (4/15/92) (JL) **83**
Cabernet Sauvignon Columbia Valley 1981 ($NA) (4/15/92) (JL) **85**
Charbonneau Walla Walla County 1989 $30 (5/15/92) **88**
Charbonneau Walla Walla County 1988 $26 (10/15/91) **95**
Charbonneau Walla Walla County 1987 $20 (12/31/90) **89**
Charbonneau Walla Walla County 1985 $30 (4/15/92) (JL) **86**
Chardonnay Columbia Valley 1990 $18.50 (11/15/91) **93**
Chardonnay Columbia Valley 1987 $18 (10/15/89) **81**
Chardonnay Walla Walla Valley Reserve 1990 $25 (11/15/91) **90**
Chardonnay Washington 1986 $16 (4/30/88) **85**
Chardonnay Washington 1984 $21 (5/15/87) **81**
Chardonnay Washington Roza Berge' Vineyard 1990 $23 (11/15/91) **87**

WORDEN (United States/Washington)
Cabernet Merlot Washington 1989 $10 (2/29/92) **86**
Chenin Blanc Washington 1988 $6 (10/15/89) **81**
Fumé Blanc Washington 1987 $7 (10/15/89) **73**
Gewürztraminer Washington 1990 $6.50 (10/15/91) BB **83**
Johannisberg Riesling Washington Charbonneau Vineyards 1988 $6 (10/15/89) **85**

WYNDHAM (Australia)
Cabernet Sauvignon Hunter Valley Bin 444 1983 $6.50 (7/15/88) BB **82**
Cabernet Sauvignon South Eastern Australia Bin 444 1988 $7.50 (6/30/92) **80**
Cabernet Shiraz Hunter Valley 1987 $7 (1/31/90) BB **91**
Cabernet Shiraz Hunter Valley 1986 $6.50 (12/31/88) BB **87**
Cabernet Shiraz Hunter Valley 1985 $6.50 (3/15/88) BB **87**
Cabernet Shiraz South Eastern Australia 1989 $7.50 (6/30/92) **76**
Chardonnay Hunter Valley 1989 $11.50 (5/15/91) **85**
Chardonnay Hunter Valley 1987 $7.75 (1/31/90) **71**
Chardonnay Hunter Valley Bin 222 1988 $7 (1/31/90) **83**
Chardonnay South Eastern Australia Bin 222 1990 $7.25 (5/31/92) **75**
Chardonnay South Eastern Australia Bin 222 1989 $6.50 (9/15/91) BB **86**
Merlot Hunter Valley 1986 $8 (1/31/90) BB **85**
Shiraz Hunter Valley Bin 555 1986 $7 (1/31/90) BB **85**
Shiraz South Eastern Australia Bin 555 1988 $7.50 (6/30/92) **83**

DAVID WYNN (Australia)
Chardonnay South Eastern Australia 1990 $11 (11/30/91) **79**

WYNNS (Australia)
Cabernet Hermitage Coonawarra 1984 $10 (12/31/88) **79**
Cabernet Sauvignon Coonawarra 1982 $15 (11/30/88) **90**
Chardonnay Coonawarra 1987 $16 (12/31/88) **84**

XENIUS (Spain)
Sparkling Cava NV $7.50 (7/15/90) BB **82**

XIPELLA (Spain)
Blanc de Blancs Conca de Barberá 1988 $6 (3/31/90) **74**

YAKIMA RIVER (United States/Washington)
Cabernet Sauvignon Columbia Valley 1988 $15 (3/31/92) **74**
Merlot Columbia Valley 1988 $15 (4/15/92) **83**
Lemberger Rendezvous Yakima Valley 1989 $7.50 (3/31/92) **81**

YALUMBA (Australia)
Brut de Brut Australia 1984 $8.25 (3/15/88) **84**
Brut South Australia Angas NV $9 (12/31/90) **78**
Brut Rosé South Australia Angas NV $9 (12/31/90) **84**
Cabernet Sauvignon Shiraz Coonawarra 1984 $6 (1/31/88) **78**
Cabernet Sauvignon Shiraz South Eastern Australia Oxford Landing 1989 $7 (2/29/92) BB **82**
Cabernet Shiraz Coonawarra 1985 $6.50 (9/30/89) **67**
Chardonnay Barossa Valley 1987 $8 (3/15/89) **85**
Chardonnay Eden Valley 1986 $7 (12/31/87) **78**
Chardonnay South Eastern Australia Oxford Landing 1991 $7 (2/29/92) BB **83**
Muscat Rutherglen Museum Show Reserve NV $10/375ml (4/15/91) **91**
Port Barossa Valley Galway Pipe NV $18 (4/15/91) **91**
Sémillon Chardonnay Eden Valley 1987 $7.50 (4/15/89) **79**
Sémillon Late Harvest Barossa Valley Botrytis Affected 1984 $5.50/375ml (3/15/89) **83**
Tawny Port South Australia Clocktower NV $8.50 (4/15/91) BB **84**

YAMHILL VALLEY (United States/Oregon)
Chardonnay Willamette Valley 1988 $12 (3/31/91) **84**
Pinot Noir Oregon 1985 $16 (6/15/87) **86**
Pinot Noir Oregon 1983 $17 (8/31/86) **92**
Pinot Noir Willamette Valley 1988 $12 (1/31/91) **76**
Pinot Noir Willamette Valley 1983 $35 (2/15/90) **87**
Pinot Noir Willamette Valley Estate Reserve 1988 $18 (11/15/91) **78**
Pinot Gris Willamette Valley 1990 $10 (6/30/91) **85**

YARDEN (Other/Israel)
Cabernet Sauvignon Galil 1986 $14 (6/30/90) **79**
Cabernet Sauvignon Galil 1985 $14 (6/30/90) **82**
Chardonnay Galil 1989 $10 (3/31/91) **84**
Merlot Galil Special Reserve 1988 $14 (3/31/91) **77**
Merlot Galil Special Reserve 1986 $12 (6/30/90) **79**
Mt. Hermon Red Galil 1989 $7 (3/31/91) **70**
Mt. Hermon White Galil 1989 $6 (3/31/91) **77**
Sauvignon Blanc Galil 1989 $9 (3/31/91) **79**

YARRA YERING (Australia)
Cabernet Sauvignon Coldstream Dry Red Wine No. 1 1984 $14 (5/31/88) **73**

CHATEAU YON-FIGEAC (France/Bordeaux)
St.-Emilion 1982 (NR) (5/15/89) (TR) **87**

YORK MOUNTAIN (United States/California)
Cabernet Sauvignon San Luis Obispo 1986 $15 (11/15/90) **84**
Cabernet Sauvignon San Luis Obispo 1985 $15 (12/15/89) **83**
Chardonnay San Luis Obispo 1987 $9 (12/15/89) **77**
Merlot San Luis Obispo County 1989 $13 (5/31/92) **84**
Merlot San Luis Obispo County 1986 $10 (12/15/89) **80**
Pinot Noir Central Coast 1986 $6 (6/15/88) **81**
Pinot Noir San Luis Obispo County 1985 $9 (6/15/88) **80**
Zinfandel San Luis Obispo County 1986 $8 (12/15/89) **85**

CHATEAU D'YQUEM (France/Sauternes)
Sauternes 1986 $310 (2/28/91) **87**
Sauternes 1985 $225 (3/31/90) **94**
Sauternes 1984 Rel: $149 Cur: $175 (3/31/90) **96**
Sauternes 1983 Rel: $180 Cur: $240 (1/31/88) **97**
Sauternes 1983 Rel: $180 Cur: $240 (10/15/87) CS **95**
Sauternes 1976 $370 (12/15/88) **94**
Sauternes 1937 $2,640/1.5L (12/15/88) **93**

ZACA MESA (United States/California)
Cabernet Sauvignon Central Coast 1988 $12 (11/15/91) **58**
Cabernet Sauvignon Central Coast Reserve 1987 $25 (11/15/91) **83**
Cabernet Sauvignon Santa Barbara County 1986 $9.50 (12/15/89) **78**
Cabernet Sauvignon Santa Barbara County 1984 $8.50 (10/31/88) **79**
Cabernet Sauvignon Santa Barbara County 1981 $8 (4/01/84) **76**
Cabernet Sauvignon Santa Barbara County American Reserve 1983 $13 (3/31/87) **87**
Cabernet Sauvignon Santa Barbara County Reserve 1986 $15 (12/15/88) **80**
Cabernet Sauvignon Santa Barbara County Reserve 1985 $15 (10/15/88) **79**
Chardonnay Santa Barbara County 1990 $9.75 (6/15/92) **85**
Chardonnay Santa Barbara County 1989 $11 (11/15/90) **85**
Chardonnay Santa Barbara County 1988 $10 (2/15/90) **84**
Chardonnay Santa Barbara County 1987 $10 (3/31/89) **87**
Chardonnay Santa Barbara County 1986 $9.75 (10/15/88) **74**
Chardonnay Santa Barbara County 1985 $8 (10/31/87) **77**
Chardonnay Santa Barbara County 1983 $9.75 (4/16/86) **58**
Chardonnay Santa Barbara County American Reserve 1984 $13 (2/28/87) **85**
Chardonnay Santa Barbara County Barrel Select 1985 $9.75 (10/15/88) **84**
Chardonnay Santa Barbara County Reserve 1989 $16.50 (7/15/91) **86**
Chardonnay Santa Barbara County Reserve 1988 $15.50 (9/15/90) **87**
Chardonnay Santa Barbara County Reserve 1987 $15 (12/15/89) **80**
Chardonnay Santa Barbara County Reserve 1986 $15 (10/15/88) **81**
Johannisberg Riesling Santa Barbara County 1987 $6 (12/15/89) BB **85**
Pinot Noir Santa Barbara County American Reserve 1984 $12.75 (2/15/87) **93**
Pinot Noir Santa Barbara County American Reserve 1983 $13 (8/31/86) **60**
Pinot Noir Santa Barbara County Reserve 1988 $15.50 (10/31/90) **86**
Pinot Noir Santa Barbara County Reserve 1987 $15 (12/15/89) **82**
Pinot Noir Santa Barbara County Reserve 1986 $15 (6/15/88) **91**
Pinot Noir Santa Ynez Valley 1981 $12 (4/01/84) **59**
Sauvignon Blanc Santa Barbara County 1988 $8 (12/15/89) **71**
Syrah Santa Barbara County 1989 $12 (8/31/91) **83**

WOLFGANG ZAHN (Germany)
Riesling Spätlese Mosel-Saar-Ruwer Piesporter Goldtröpfchen 1983 $10 (5/16/85) **86**

ZD (United States/California)
Cabernet Sauvignon Napa Valley 1991 (NR) (5/15/92) (BT) **84+**
Cabernet Sauvignon Napa Valley 1990 (NR) (5/15/91) (BT) **85+**
Cabernet Sauvignon Napa Valley 1989 (NR) (5/15/91) (BT) **80+**
Cabernet Sauvignon Napa Valley 1988 $20 (4/30/91) **86**
Cabernet Sauvignon Napa Valley 1987 $16 (2/15/91) **78**
Cabernet Sauvignon Napa Valley 1985 $14 (5/15/89) **81**
Cabernet Sauvignon California 1982 $12 (7/16/86) **66**
Cabernet Sauvignon Napa Valley Estate Bottled 1987 $40 (1/31/91) **90**
Chardonnay California 1989 $21 (2/28/91) **87**
Chardonnay California 1988 $20 (CH-3/90) **89**
Chardonnay California 1987 $18.50 (CH-3/90) **85**
Chardonnay California 1986 Rel: $18 Cur: $22 (CH-6/90) **85**
Chardonnay California 1985 Rel: $16 Cur: $28 (CH-3/90) **90**
Chardonnay California 1984 Rel: $15 Cur: $30 (CH-3/90) **90**
Chardonnay California 1983 Rel: $14 Cur: $25 (CH-3/90) **74**
Chardonnay California 1982 Rel: $14 Cur: $30 (CH-3/90) **76**
Chardonnay California 1981 Rel: $13 Cur: $28 (CH-3/90) **87**
Chardonnay California 1980 Rel: $13 Cur: $28 (CH-3/90) **81**
Pinot Noir Carneros Napa Valley 1989 $16 (11/15/91) **82**
Pinot Noir Carneros Napa Valley 1988 $17 (6/30/91) **82**
Pinot Noir Carneros Napa Valley 1985 $14 (7/31/89) **79**
Pinot Noir Napa Valley 1982 $12.50 (8/31/86) **75**

STEPHEN ZELLERBACH (United States/California)
Cabernet Sauvignon Alexander Valley 1988 $10 (10/31/90) **82**
Cabernet Sauvignon Alexander Valley 1984 $8 (11/30/88) **86**
Cabernet Sauvignon Alexander Valley 1982 $6 (11/30/86) **80**
Cabernet Sauvignon Alexander Valley 1980 $8 (4/01/85) **77**
Chardonnay Alexander Valley 1984 $6 (2/15/87) **79**
Chardonnay Alexander Valley 1983 $9.95 (1/01/85) **84**
Chardonnay Alexander Valley Warnecke Sonoma Vineyard 1982 $10 (4/16/84) **75**
Chardonnay California 1987 $7 (10/15/88) BB **82**
Chardonnay Sonoma County 1990 $9 (3/15/92) BB **86**
Chardonnay Sonoma County 1989 $8.50 (11/30/90) BB **85**
Chardonnay Sonoma County 1988 $8 (4/15/90) BB **88**
Chardonnay Sonoma County Reserve 1989 $13 (7/15/91) **87**
Merlot Alexander Valley 1982 $8.50 (10/01/85) **84**
Merlot Alexander Valley 1980 $8.50 (5/01/84) **68**
Sauvignon Blanc Sonoma County 1989 $5.50 (12/31/90) BB **82**

PETER ZEMMER (Italy/North)
Chardonnay Alto Adige 1990 $10 (1/31/92) **78**
Pinot Grigio Alto Adige 1990 $10 (1/31/92) **76**

ZENATO (Italy/North)
Bardolino Classico Superiore 1989 $7.75 (7/15/91) **78**
Bianco di Custoza Sole del Benaco 1989 $9 (6/30/91) **80**

Key to Symbols

The scores reported here are the results of blind tastings conducted by our panel of senior editors. Wines that carry the initials below are results of individual tastings.

THE WINE SPECTATOR 100-POINT SCALE 95-100—Classic, a great wine; ***90-94***—Outstanding, superior character and style; ***80-89***—Good to very good, a wine with special qualities; ***70-79***—Average, drinkable wine that may have minor flaws; ***60-69***—Below average, drinkable but not recommended; ***50-59***—Poor, undrinkable, not recommended. "+"—With a score indicates a range; used primarily with barrel tastings to indicate a preliminary score.

SPECIAL DESIGNATIONS SS—Spectator Selection, CS—Cellar Selection, BB—Best Buy, ($NA)—Price not available, (NR)—Not released.

TASTER'S INITIALS (JG)—Jim Gordon, (HS)—Harvey Steiman, (JL)—James Laube, (JS)—James Suckling, (TM)—Thomas Matthews, (TR)—Terry Robards, (PM)—Per-Henrik Mansson, (BT)—Barrel Tasting (these wines were tasted blind from barrel samples), (CA-date)—*California's Great Cabernets* by James Laube, (CH-date)—*California's Great Chardonnays* by James Laube, (VP-date)—*Vintage Port* by James Suckling.

DATE TASTED Dates in parentheses represent the issue in which the rating was published.

Lugana San Benedetto 1989 $9.25 (7/15/91) **77**
Recioto della Valpolicella Amarone Classico 1981 $11 (3/15/89) **81**
Valpolicella Classico Superiore 1988 $8 (4/30/92) BB **83**

ZENI (Italy/North)
Chardonnay Trentino 1988 $12 (9/15/89) **85**

DR. ZENZEN (Germany)
Riesling Beerenauslese Mosel-Saar-Ruwer Erdener Treppchen 1976 $90 (2/01/86) **90**
Riesling Kabinett Mosel-Saar-Ruwer Erdener Treppchen 1981 $8 (4/01/86) **70**
Riesling Spätlese Mosel-Saar-Ruwer Valwiger Herrenberg 1982 $12 (2/01/86) **74**

ZILLIKEN (Germany)
Riesling Auslese Mosel-Saar-Ruwer Ockfener Bockstein 1990 $25 (12/15/91) **89**
Riesling Auslese Mosel-Saar-Ruwer Saarburger Rausch 1990 $31 (12/15/91) **89**
Riesling Auslese Mosel-Saar-Ruwer Saarburger Rausch 1989 $35 (12/15/90) **88**
Riesling Auslese Mosel-Saar-Ruwer Saarburger Rausch Gold Cap 1990 $110 (12/15/91) **93**
Riesling Auslese Mosel-Saar-Ruwer Saarburger Rausch Long Gold Cap 1989 $64 (12/15/90) **95**
Riesling Eiswein Mosel-Saar-Ruwer Saarburger Rausch 1990 (NR) (12/15/91) **91**
Riesling Eiswein Mosel-Saar-Ruwer Saarburger Rausch 1989 (NR) (12/15/90) **96**
Riesling Eiswein Mosel-Saar-Ruwer Saarburger Rausch 1988 (NR) (9/30/89) **97**
Riesling Kabinett Mosel-Saar-Ruwer Ockfener Bockstein 1990 $12 (12/15/91) **86**
Riesling Kabinett Mosel-Saar-Ruwer Ockfener Bockstein 1989 $14 (12/15/90) **81**
Riesling Kabinett Mosel-Saar-Ruwer Saarburger Rausch 1990 $13 (12/15/91) **86**
Riesling Kabinett Mosel-Saar-Ruwer Saarburger Rausch (AP5) 1989 $14 (12/15/90) **77**
Riesling Kabinett Mosel-Saar-Ruwer Saarburger Rausch (AP5) 1988 $9 (9/30/89) **78**
Riesling Kabinett Mosel-Saar-Ruwer Saarburger Rausch (AP7) 1988 $9 (9/30/89) **79**
Riesling Kabinett Mosel-Saar-Ruwer Saarburger Rausch (AP12) 1989 $14 (12/15/90) **85**
Riesling Qualitätswein Mosel-Saar-Ruwer Zilliken 1990 $9.25 (12/15/91) **84**
Riesling Spätlese Mosel-Saar-Ruwer Ockfener Bockstein 1989 $18 (12/15/90) **79**
Riesling Spätlese Mosel-Saar-Ruwer Saarburger Rausch 1990 $17 (12/15/91) **85**
Riesling Spätlese Mosel-Saar-Ruwer Saarburger Rausch 1989 $19 (12/15/90) **85**
Riesling Spätlese Mosel-Saar-Ruwer Saarburger Rausch 1988 $17 (9/30/89) **95**
Riesling Spätlese Mosel-Saar-Ruwer Saarburger Rausch 1985 $9.25 (5/15/87) **78**
Riesling Spätlese Mosel-Saar-Ruwer Saarburger Rausch (AP6) 1989 $19 (12/15/90) **84**

DOMAINE ZIND-HUMBRECHT (France/Alsace)
Gewürztraminer Alsace 1988 (NR) (10/15/89) **83**
Gewürztraminer Alsace Clos Windsbuhl 1989 $36 (11/15/90) **83**
Gewürztraminer Alsace Clos Windsbuhl Vendange Tardive 1990 $70 (2/15/92) (BT) **90+**
Gewürztraminer Alsace Goldert Vendange Tardive 1990 $60 (2/15/92) (BT) **90+**
Gewürztraminer Alsace Heimbourg Vendange Tardive 1990 $45 (2/15/92) (BT) **85+**
Gewürztraminer Alsace Hengst Vendange Tardive 1990 $65 (2/15/92) (BT) **95+**
Gewürztraminer Alsace Herrenweg 1990 $23 (2/15/92) **82**
Gewürztraminer Alsace Herrenweg Turckheim 1989 $25 (11/15/90) **84**
Gewürztraminer Alsace Rangen de Thann Clos St.-Urbain 1990 $50 (2/15/92) **91**
Gewürztraminer Alsace Rangen Vendange Tardive 1988 (NR) (10/15/89) **85**
Muscat d'Alsace 1990 $14 (2/15/92) **83**
Pinot d'Alsace Alsace 1990 $15 (2/15/92) **86**
Pinot Blanc Alsace 1989 (NR) (11/15/90) **76**
Pinot Blanc Alsace 1988 (NR) (10/15/89) **87**
Riesling Alsace 1988 (NR) (10/15/89) **87**
Riesling Alsace Brand 1990 $35 (2/15/92) **93**
Riesling Alsace Brand Vendange Tardive 1990 $55 (2/15/92) (BT) **90+**
Riesling Alsace Brand Vendange Tardive 1989 (NR) (11/15/90) **87**
Riesling Alsace Clos St.-Urbain Rangen 1989 $45 (11/15/90) **86**
Riesling Alsace Clos Windsbuhl Vendange Tardive 1990 $75 (2/15/92) (BT) **90+**
Riesling Alsace Herrenweg 1990 $25 (2/15/92) **90**
Riesling Alsace Herrenweg 1989 $24 (11/15/90) **89**
Riesling Alsace Herrenweg Vendange Tardive 1990 $40 (2/15/92) (BT) **95+**
Riesling Alsace Rangen 1988 (NR) (10/15/89) **86**
Riesling Alsace Turckheim 1990 $20 (2/15/92) **90**
Riesling Alsace Wintzenheim 1989 $21 (10/31/91) **87**
Sylvaner Alsace 1990 $12.50 (2/15/92) **92**
Tokay Pinot Gris Alsace 1988 (NR) (10/15/89) **82**
Tokay Pinot Gris Alsace Clos Jebsal 1988 (NR) (10/15/89) **90**
Tokay Pinot Gris Alsace Clos Jebsal Vendange Tardive 1990 $70 (2/15/92) (BT) **90+**
Tokay Pinot Gris Alsace Clos St.-Urbain Rangen Sélection de Grains Nobles 1989 (NR) (11/15/90) **85**
Tokay Pinot Gris Alsace Clos Windsbuhl Vendange Tardive 1990 $75 (2/15/92) (BT) **85+**
Tokay Pinot Gris Alsace Clos Windsbuhl Vendange Tardive 1989 (NR) (11/15/90) **91**
Tokay Pinot Gris Alsace Rangen de Thann Clos St.-Urbain 1990 $50 (2/15/92) **87**
Tokay Pinot Gris Alsace Vieilles Vignes 1990 $30 (2/15/92) **90**

VILLA ZINGALE (Italy/Tuscany)
Chianti Riserva 1988 $8.50 (4/30/92) **77**

ZONIN (Italy/North)
1989 $7 (7/15/91) **75**
Berengario Barrel Aged 1988 $30 (1/31/92) **84**
Brut Blanc de Blancs Chardonnay NV $12 (12/31/91) **88**
Merlot Cabernet del Friuli Le Vendemmie 1989 $6 (1/31/92) **78**
Montepulciano d'Abruzzo 1988 $6 (6/30/91) BB **80**
Montepulciano d'Abruzzo 1987 $4.50 (3/31/90) **78**
Pinot Grigio 1990 $7 (1/31/92) **79**

SECTION D: SELECTED RED WINES BY VINTAGE/SCORE/PRODUCER

FRANCE

BORDEAUX RED

1989

100 CHATEAU PETRUS Pomerol 1989 $390 (3/15/92)
99 CHATEAU MARGAUX Margaux 1989 $145 (3/15/92) CS
99 CHATEAU MOUTON-ROTHSCHILD Pauillac 1989 $150 (3/15/92)
98 CHATEAU LA FLEUR DE GAY Pomerol 1989 $88 (3/15/92)
98 CHATEAU LYNCH-BAGES Pauillac 1989 $53 (3/15/92)
98 CHATEAU PICHON-BARON Pauillac 1989 $60 (3/15/92)
97 CHATEAU HAUT-BRION Pessac-Léognan 1989 $150 (3/15/92)
97 CHATEAU LATOUR Pauillac 1989 $145 (3/15/92)
96 DOMAINE DE CHEVALIER Pessac-Léognan 1989 $59 (3/15/92)
96 CHATEAU CLERC-MILON Pauillac 1989 $32 (3/15/92)

96 CHATEAU CORDEILLAN-BAGES Pauillac 1989 $24 (3/15/92)
96 CHATEAU LAFLEUR Pomerol 1989 $225 (3/15/92)
96 CHATEAU LA MISSION-HAUT-BRION Pessac-Léognan 1989 $120 (3/15/92)
95 CHATEAU BEYCHEVELLE St.-Julien 1989 $48 (3/15/92)
95 CHATEAU CALON-SEGUR St.-Estèphe 1989 $41 (3/15/92)
95 CHATEAU CHASSE-SPLEEN Moulis 1989 $35 (3/15/92)
95 CHATEAU COS D'ESTOURNEL St.-Estèphe 1989 $60 (3/15/92)
95 CHATEAU DE FIEUZAL Pessac-Léognan 1989 $32 (3/15/92)
95 CHATEAU LAFITE-ROTHSCHILD Pauillac 1989 $145 (3/15/92)
95 CHATEAU LAGRANGE St.-Julien 1989 $29 (3/15/92)

95 CHATEAU LARMANDE St.-Emilion 1989 $26 (3/15/92)
95 CHATEAU MONTROSE St.-Estèphe 1989 $47 (3/15/92)
95 CHATEAU OLIVIER Pessac-Léognan 1989 Rel: $19 Cur: $21 (3/15/92) SS
95 CHATEAU PALMER Margaux 1989 $60 (3/15/92)
95 CHATEAU PIBRAN Pauillac 1989 $25 (3/15/92)
95 CHATEAU LA POINTE Pomerol 1989 $28 (3/15/92)
95 CHATEAU LA TOUR-HAUT-BRION Pessac-Léognan 1989 $52 (3/15/92)
95+ CLOS L'EGLISE Pomerol 1989 $24 (4/30/91) (BT)
95+ CHATEAU LE PIN Pomerol 1989 $163 (4/30/90) (BT)
94 CHATEAU L'ANGELUS St.-Emilion 1989 $53 (3/15/92)

94 CHATEAU ARMAILHAC Pauillac 1989 $26 (3/15/92)
94 CHATEAU BRANE-CANTENAC Margaux 1989 $42 (3/15/92)
94 CHATEAU DE FRANC-MAYNE St.-Emilion 1989 $28 (3/15/92)
94 CHATEAU LANGOA BARTON St.-Julien 1989 $28 (3/15/92)
94 CHATEAU LEOVILLE-BARTON St.-Julien 1989 $41 (3/15/92)
94 CHATEAU ST.-PIERRE St.-Julien 1989 $39 (3/15/92)
94 LES TOURELLES DE LONGUEVILLE Pauillac 1989 $27 (3/15/92)
93 CHATEAU L'ARROSEE St.-Emilion 1989 $40 (4/30/92)
93 CHATEAU AUSONE St.-Emilion 1989 $180 (3/15/92)
93 CHATEAU BARET Pessac-Léognan 1989 $18 (3/15/92)

93 CHATEAU BOUSCAUT Pessac-Léognan 1989 $22 (3/15/92)
93 CHATEAU CITRAN Haut-Médoc 1989 $20 (3/15/92)
93 CHATEAU COS-LABORY St.-Estèphe 1989 $18 (3/15/92)
93 DOMAINE DE L'EGLISE Pomerol 1989 $33 (3/15/92)
93 CHATEAU FIGEAC St.-Emilion 1989 $69 (3/15/92)
93 CHATEAU GRAND-MAYNE St.-Emilion 1989 $22 (3/15/92)
93 CHATEAU GRUAUD LAROSE St.-Julien 1989 $49 (3/15/92)
93 CHATEAU MEYNEY St.-Estèphe 1989 $22 (3/15/92)
93 CHATEAU MONBRISON Margaux 1989 $40 (3/15/92)
93 CHATEAU TERTRE-ROTEBOEUF St.-Emilion 1989 $45 (3/15/92)

93 CHATEAU VILLEMAURINE St.-Emilion 1989 (NR) (3/15/92)
92 CHATEAU LA CABANNE Pomerol 1989 $30 (3/15/92)
92 CLOS LARCIS St.-Emilion 1989 $28 (3/15/92)
92 CHATEAU LA COMMANDERIE St.-Emilion 1989 $19 (3/15/92)
92 CHATEAU LA CONSEILLANTE Pomerol 1989 $107 (3/15/92)
92 CHATEAU DURFORT-VIVENS Margaux 1989 $28 (3/15/92)
92 CHATEAU L'EVANGILE Pomerol 1989 $70 (3/15/92)
92 CHATEAU GISCOURS Margaux 1989 $41 (3/15/92)
92 CHATEAU GLORIA St.-Julien 1989 $29 (3/15/92)
92 CHATEAU LA GURGUE Margaux 1989 $30 (3/15/92)

92 CHATEAU HAUT-BAILLY Pessac-Léognan 1989 $32 (3/15/92)
92 CHATEAU LAFON-ROCHET St.-Estèphe 1989 $18 (3/15/92)
92 CHATEAU PICHON-LALANDE Pauillac 1989 $71 (3/15/92)
92 CHATEAU LA TOUR CARNET Haut-Médoc 1989 $24 (3/15/92)
91 CHATEAU BEAUSEJOUR-DUFFAU-LAGARROSSE St.-Emilion 1989 $44 (3/15/92)
91 CHATEAU CANTEMERLE Haut-Médoc 1989 $35 (3/15/92)
91 CHATEAU LA DOMINIQUE St.-Emilion 1989 $32 (3/15/92)
91 CHATEAU DUCRU-BEAUCAILLOU St.-Julien 1989 $65 (3/15/92)
91 LES FORTS DE LATOUR Pauillac 1989 (NR) (3/15/92)
91 CHATEAU LE GAY Pomerol 1989 Rel: $70 Cur: $110 (3/15/92)

91 CHATEAU GAZIN Pomerol 1989 $45 (3/15/92)
91 CHATEAU GRAND-PUY-LACOSTE Pauillac 1989 $36 (3/15/92)
91 CHATEAU LARCIS-DUCASSE St.-Emilion 1989 $28 (3/15/92)
91 CHATEAU LA LOUVIERE Pessac-Léognan 1989 $22 (3/15/92)
91 CHATEAU ST.-ANDRE-CORBIN St.-Georges-St.-Emilion 1989 $15 (4/30/92)
91 CHATEAU SMITH-HAUT-LAFITTE Pessac-Léognan 1989 $19 (3/15/92)

Key to Symbols

The scores reported here are the results of blind tastings conducted by our panel of senior editors. Wines that carry the initials below are results of individual tastings.

THE WINE SPECTATOR 100-POINT SCALE 95-100—Classic, a great wine; ***90-94***—Outstanding, superior character and style; ***80-89***—Good to very good, a wine with special qualities; ***70-79***—Average, drinkable wine that may have minor flaws; ***60-69***—Below average, drinkable but not recommended; ***50-59***—Poor, undrinkable, not recommended. "+"—With a score indicates a range; used primarily with barrel tastings to indicate a preliminary score.

SPECIAL DESIGNATIONS SS—Spectator Selection, CS—Cellar Selection, BB—Best Buy, ($NA)—Price not available, (NR)—Not released.

TASTER'S INITIALS (JG)—Jim Gordon, (HS)—Harvey Steiman, (JL)—James Laube, (JS)—James Suckling, (TM)—Thomas Matthews, (TR)—Terry Robards, (PM)—Per-Henrik Mansson, (BT)—Barrel Tasting (these wines were tasted blind from barrel samples), (CA- date)—*California's Great Cabernets* by James Laube, (CH-date)—*California's Great Chardonnays* by James Laube, (VP -date)—*Vintage Port* by James Suckling.

DATE TASTED Dates in parentheses represent the issue in which the rating was published.

91 VIEUX CHATEAU CERTAN Pomerol 1989 $89 (3/15/92)
90 CHATEAU BAHANS-HAUT-BRION Pessac-Léognan 1989 $32 (3/15/92)
90 CHATEAU BEAU-SITE St.-Estèphe 1989 Rel: $17 Cur: $20 (3/15/92)
90 CHATEAU BOURGNEUF-VAYRON Pomerol 1989 $32 (3/15/92)

90 CHATEAU BRANAIRE-DUCRU St.-Julien 1989 $35 (3/15/92)
90 CHATEAU CANON St.-Emilion 1989 $53 (3/15/92)
90 CHATEAU CHEVAL BLANC St.-Emilion 1989 $150 (3/15/92)
90 CHATEAU DAUZAC Margaux 1989 $26 (3/15/92)
90 CHATEAU DUHART-MILON Pauillac 1989 $30 (3/15/92)
90 CHATEAU HAUT-BAGES-AVEROUS Pauillac 1989 $26 (3/15/92)
90 CHATEAU HAUT-MARBUZET St.-Estèphe 1989 $32 (3/15/92)
90 CHATEAU LATOUR A POMEROL Pomerol 1989 $39 (3/15/92)
90 CHATEAU LEOVILLE-POYFERRE St.-Julien 1989 $42 (3/15/92)
90 CHATEAU LYNCH-MOUSSAS Pauillac 1989 $21 (3/15/92)

90 CHATEAU DE MALLERET Haut-Médoc 1989 (NR) (3/15/92)
90 CHATEAU PAVIE St.-Emilion 1989 $45 (3/15/92)
90 CHATEAU PAVIE-DECESSE St.-Emilion 1989 $29 (3/15/92)
90 CHATEAU PETIT-FIGEAC St.-Emilion 1989 $21 (3/15/92)
90 CHATEAU POUJEAUX Moulis 1989 $21 (3/15/92)
90 CHATEAU PUY-BLANQUET St.-Emilion 1989 $16 (3/15/92)
90 CHATEAU SOCIANDO-MALLET Haut-Médoc 1989 $32 (3/15/92)
90 CHATEAU TALBOT St.-Julien 1989 $43 (3/15/92)
90 CHATEAU DU TERTRE Margaux 1989 $29 (3/15/92)
90 CHATEAU TROTANOY Pomerol 1989 $87 (3/15/92)

90 CHATEAU TROTTE VIEILLE St.-Emilion 1989 Rel: $32 Cur: $46 (3/15/92)
90 CHATEAU VERDIGNAN Haut-Médoc 1989 $17 (3/15/92)
90+ CHATEAU CERTAN DE MAY Pomerol 1989 $75 (4/30/91) (BT)
90+ CHATEAU CLINET Pomerol 1989 $56 (4/30/91) (BT)
90+ CHATEAU LA CROIX Pomerol 1989 (NR) (4/30/91) (BT)
90+ CHATEAU LA CROIX DU CASSE Pomerol 1989 (NR) (4/30/91) (BT)
90+ CHATEAU FEYTIT-CLINET Pomerol 1989 (NR) (4/30/91) (BT)
90+ CHATEAU LA GAFFELIERE St.-Emilion 1989 $33 (4/30/91) (BT)
90+ CHATEAU MAZEYRES Pomerol 1989 (NR) (4/30/91) (BT)
90+ CHATEAU MOULINET Pomerol 1989 (NR) (4/30/91) (BT)

90+ CHATEAU PRIEURS DE LA COMMANDERIE Pomerol 1989 (NR) (4/30/91) (BT)
90+ CHATEAU DE SALES Pomerol 1989 $18 (4/30/91) (BT)
90+ CHATEAU TAILLEFER Pomerol 1989 (NR) (4/30/91) (BT)
90+ CHATEAU TRONQUOY-LALANDE St.-Estèphe 1989 $14 (4/30/90) (BT)
89 CHATEAU BARON DE BRANE Margaux 1989 (NR) (3/15/92)
89 CHATEAU BELAIR St.-Emilion 1989 $34 (3/15/92)
89 CHATEAU CANTENAC-BROWN Margaux 1989 $32 (3/15/92)
89 CARRUADES DE LAFITE Pauillac 1989 Rel: $24 Cur: $27 (3/15/92)
89 CLOS FOURTET St.-Emilion 1989 Rel: $26 Cur: $31 (3/15/92)
89 CHATEAU COUFRAN Haut-Médoc 1989 $14 (3/15/92)

89 COUVENT DES JACOBINS St.-Emilion 1989 $28 (4/30/92)
89 CHATEAU DE FRANCE Pessac-Léognan 1989 $22 (3/15/92)
89 CHATEAU HAUT-BAGES-LIBERAL Pauillac 1989 $24 (3/15/92)
89 CHATEAU HAUT-CORBIN St.-Emilion 1989 $26 (3/15/92)
89 CHATEAU LACOSTE-BORIE Pauillac 1989 $18 (3/15/92)
89 CHATEAU DE LAMARQUE Haut-Médoc 1989 $26 (3/15/92)
89 CHATEAU LARRIVET-HAUT-BRION Pessac-Léognan 1989 $33 (3/15/92)
89 CHATEAU DE MARBUZET St.-Estèphe 1989 $21 (3/15/92)
89 CHATEAU DE PEZ St.-Estèphe 1989 $21 (3/15/92)
89 CHATEAU PONTET-CANET Pauillac 1989 $27 (3/15/92)

89 CHATEAU TROPLONG-MONDOT St.-Emilion 1989 $26 (3/15/92)
88 CHATEAU D'AGASSAC Haut-Médoc 1989 (NR) (3/15/92)
88 CHATEAU ARNAULD Haut-Médoc 1989 $14 (3/15/92)
88 CHATEAU LE BON-PASTEUR Pomerol 1989 $35 (4/30/92)
88 CHATEAU CANON-LA-GAFFELIERE St.-Emilion 1989 $29 (3/15/92)
88 CHATEAU DE CHANTEGRIVE Pessac-Léognan 1989 (NR) (3/15/92)
88 CHATEAU LA CLAVERIE Côtes de Francs 1989 $21 (3/15/92)
88 CHATEAU LA CROIX DE GAY Pomerol 1989 Rel: $19 Cur: $25 (3/15/92)
88 CHATEAU DUPLESSIS-FABRE Moulis 1989 $9 (3/15/92)
88 CHATEAU LA FLEUR-PETRUS Pomerol 1989 Rel: $57 Cur: $66 (3/15/92)

88 CHATEAU FONROQUE St.-Emilion 1989 $24 (3/15/92)
88 CHATEAU GRANDES-MURAILLES St.-Emilion 1989 (NR) (3/15/92)
88 CHATEAU LA GRAVE TRIGANT DE BOISSET Pomerol 1989 $35 (3/15/92)
88 CHATEAU LALANDE-BORIE St.-Julien 1989 $22 (3/15/92)
88 CHATEAU MAGDELAINE St.-Emilion 1989 $44 (3/15/92)
88 CHATEAU PAPE-CLEMENT Pessac-Léognan 1989 $43 (3/15/92)
88 CHATEAU PETIT-VILLAGE Pomerol 1989 Rel: $46 Cur: $52 (3/15/92)
88 CHATEAU PLAGNAC Médoc 1989 $11.50 (3/15/92)
88 CHATEAU RAMAGE LA BATISSE Haut-Médoc 1989 $15 (3/15/92)
88 CHATEAU RAUSAN-SEGLA Margaux 1989 $44 (3/15/92)

88 CHATEAU DE ROCHEMORIN Pessac-Léognan 1989 $14 (3/15/92)
88 CHATEAU SIRAN Margaux 1989 $25 (3/15/92)
88 CHATEAU LA TOUR-DE-MONS Margaux 1989 $25 (3/15/92)
88 CHATEAU LA VIEILLE CURE Fronsac 1989 $16 (3/15/92)
87 CHATEAU D'ANGLUDET Margaux 1989 $33 (3/15/92)
87 CHATEAU CAP DE MOURLIN St.-Emilion 1989 $23 (3/15/92)
87 CHATEAU FOURCAS-HOSTEN Listrac 1989 $19 (3/15/92)
87 CHATEAU DU GLANA St.-Julien 1989 (NR) (3/15/92)
87 CHATEAU HAUT-BATAILLEY Pauillac 1989 $30 (3/15/92)
87 CHATEAU KIRWAN Margaux 1989 $32 (3/15/92)

87 CHATEAU LAFLEUR-GAZIN Pomerol 1989 (NR) (3/15/92)
87 CHATEAU LAGRANGE Pomerol 1989 $29 (3/15/92)
87 CHATEAU LAROSE-TRINTAUDON Haut-Médoc 1989 $12 (3/15/92)
87 CHATEAU LIVERSAN Haut-Médoc 1989 $18 (3/15/92)
87 CHATEAU MALESCOT-ST.-EXUPERY Margaux 1989 $28 (3/15/92)
87 PAVILLON ROUGE DU CHATEAU MARGAUX Margaux 1989 $32 (4/30/92)
87 CHATEAU LA TOUR-DE-BESSAN Margaux 1989 (NR) (3/15/92)
87 CHATEAU LA TOUR-HAUT-CAUSSAN Médoc 1989 $15 (3/15/92)
86 CHATEAU BRILLETTE Moulis 1989 $17 (3/15/92)
86 CHATEAU DE CAMENSAC Haut-Médoc 1989 $22 (3/15/92)
86 CHATEAU CANON MOUEIX Canon-Fronsac 1989 $22 (3/15/92)

86 CHATEAU LES CHARMES-GODARD Côtes de Francs 1989 (NR) (3/15/92)
86 CHATEAU CLOS ST.-MARTIN St.-Emilion 1989 (NR) (3/15/92)
86 CHATEAU DE CRUZEAU Pessac-Léognan 1989 $14 (3/15/92)
86 CHATEAU LA DAME DE MALESCOT Margaux 1989 (NR) (3/15/92)
86 CHATEAU DESMIRAIL Margaux 1989 $27 (3/15/92)
86 CHATEAU FOURCAS-DUPRE Listrac 1989 $25 (3/15/92)
86 CHATEAU GRAND-PUY-DUCASSE Pauillac 1989 $23 (4/30/92)
86 CHATEAU LABEGORCE-ZEDE Margaux 1989 $24 (3/15/92)
86 CHATEAU LA LAGUNE Haut-Médoc 1989 $35 (3/15/92)
86 CHATEAU MOULIN DU CADET St.-Emilion 1989 (NR) (3/15/92)

86 CHATEAU LES ORMES DE PEZ St.-Estèphe 1989 $24 (3/15/92)
86 CHATEAU PLAISANCE Premières Côtes de Bordeaux Cuvée Spéciale 1989 $13 (1/31/92)
86 CHATEAU PRIEURE-LICHINE Margaux 1989 $31 (3/15/92)
85 CHATEAU BALESTARD LA TONNELLE St.-Emilion 1989 $28 (3/15/92)
85 CHATEAU CARBONNIEUX Pessac-Léognan 1989 $22 (3/15/92)
85 CHATEAU DE CHANTEGRIVE Pessac-Léognan Cuvée Edouard 1989 (NR) (3/15/92)
85 CHATEAU CISSAC Haut-Médoc 1989 $19 (3/15/92)
85 CHATEAU CLARKE Listrac 1989 $16 (3/15/92)
85 CHATEAU CLOS DES JACOBINS St.-Emilion 1989 $45 (3/15/92)
85 CHATEAU LANESSAN Haut-Médoc 1989 $29 (3/15/92)

85 CHATEAU MALARTIC-LAGRAVIERE Pessac-Léognan 1989 $24 (3/15/92)
85 CHATEAU MALMAISON Moulis 1989 (NR) (3/15/92)
85 CHATEAU PHELAN-SEGUR St.-Estèphe 1989 $23 (3/15/92)
85 CHATEAU PLAISANCE Premières Côtes de Blaye Cuvée Spéciale 1989 $9 (2/28/91) BB
85 CHATEAU LA SALLE DE POUJEAUX Moulis 1989 $15 (3/15/92)
85 CHATEAU SOUDARS Haut-Médoc 1989 $18 (3/15/92)
85 CHATEAU LA TOUR DE BY Médoc 1989 $15 (3/15/92)
85+ CHATEAU BONALGUE Pomerol 1989 (NR) (4/30/91) (BT)
85+ CHATEAU CHAMBERT-MARBUZET St.-Estèphe 1989 $21 (4/30/91) (BT)
85+ CLOS DU CLOCHER Pomerol 1989 (NR) (4/30/91) (BT)

85+ CHATEAU DASSAULT St.-Emilion 1989 (NR) (4/30/91) (BT)
85+ LES FIEFS DE LAGRANGE St.-Julien 1989 (NR) (4/30/91) (BT)
85+ CHATEAU FONPLEGADE St.-Emilion 1989 (NR) (4/30/91) (BT)
85+ CHATEAU FONREAUD Listrac 1989 (NR) (4/30/91) (BT)
85+ CHATEAU FONTENIL Fronsac 1989 (NR) (4/30/91) (BT)
85+ CHATEAU HAUT-BAGES-MONPELOU Pauillac 1989 (NR) (4/30/90) (BT)
85+ CHATEAU HAUT-BERGEY Pessac-Léognan 1989 (NR) (4/30/91) (BT)
85+ CHATEAU HAUT-MAILLET Pomerol 1989 (NR) (4/30/91) (BT)
85+ CHATEAU HAUT-SARPE St.-Emilion 1989 (NR) (4/30/91) (BT)
85+ CHATEAU LAFLEUR-ST.-EMILION St.-Emilion 1989 (NR) (4/30/91) (BT)

85+ CHATEAU LILIAN-LADOUYS St.-Estèphe 1989 (NR) (4/30/91) (BT)
85+ CHATEAU MAZERIS Canon-Fronsac 1989 (NR) (4/30/91) (BT)
85+ CHATEAU MONTVIEL Pomerol 1989 (NR) (4/30/91) (BT)
85+ CHATEAU ROUGET Pomerol 1989 $21 (4/30/91) (BT)
85+ CHATEAU SENEJAC Haut-Médoc 1989 $11 (4/30/91) (BT)
85+ CHATEAU LA SERRE St.-Emilion 1989 $17 (4/30/91) (BT)
85+ CHATEAU TERREY-GROS-CAILLOUX St.-Julien 1989 $16 (4/30/91) (BT)
85+ CHATEAU LA TOUR-FIGEAC St.-Emilion 1989 (NR) (4/30/91) (BT)
85+ CHATEAU LA TOUR-MARTILLAC Pessac-Léognan 1989 $28 (4/30/91) (BT)
84 CHATEAU CANON DE BREM Canon-Fronsac 1989 $23 (3/15/92)

84 CHATEAU CAPBERN-GASQUETON St.-Estèphe 1989 $27 (3/15/92)
84 DEMOISELLE DE SOCIANDO-MALLET Haut-Médoc 1989 $21 (3/15/92)
84 CHATEAU DULUC St.-Julien 1989 (NR) (3/15/92)
84 CHATEAU LA FLEUR St.-Emilion 1989 $18 (3/15/92)
84 CHATEAU GOFFRETEAU Bordeaux Rouge 1989 $8 (5/15/91) BB
84 CHATEAU D'ISSAN Margaux 1989 $27 (3/15/92)
84 CHATEAU MALESCASSE Haut-Médoc 1989 $16 (3/15/92)
83 CHATEAU DECORDE Haut-Médoc 1989 (NR) (3/15/92)
83 CHATEAU PUYGUERAUD Côtes de Francs 1989 $18 (3/15/92)
83 CHATEAU TERTRE-DAUGAY St.-Emilion 1989 $29 (4/30/92)

83 CHATEAU LA TOUR-DU-PIN-FIGEAC-BELIEVIER St.-Emilion 1989 $24 (4/30/92)
82 CHATEAU D'ARSAC Haut-Médoc 1989 $9 (3/15/92)
82 CHATEAU BEAUMONT Haut-Médoc 1989 $14 (3/15/92)
82 CHATEAU CANON-FRONSAC Canon-Fronsac 1989 (NR) (3/15/92)
82 CHATEAU CANUET Margaux 1989 $18 (3/15/92)
82 LA CAVE TROISGROS Bordeaux Rouge 1989 $9.50 (5/15/91)
82 CHATEAU L'ENCLOS Pomerol 1989 $30 (4/30/92)
82 CHATEAU LA FLEUR-POURRET St.-Emilion 1989 (NR) (3/15/92)
82 CHATEAU LA GROLET Côtes de Bourg 1989 $9 (8/31/91) BB
82 CHATEAU ROC MIGNON D'ADRIEN Bordeaux Supérieur 1989 $6 (2/28/91) BB

81 CHATEAU BATAILLEY Pauillac 1989 $28 (3/15/92)
81 CHATEAU LE BONNAT Graves 1989 $18 (4/30/92)
81 CHATEAU COTE DE BALEAU St.-Emilion 1989 (NR) (3/15/92)
81 CHATEAU LOUDENNE Médoc 1989 $13 (3/15/92)
81 CHATEAU MONT BELAIR St.-Emilion 1989 $12 (11/15/91)
80 CHATEAU DE LA DAUPHINE Fronsac 1989 $20 (3/15/92)
80 CHATEAU MOULIN DE CITRAN Haut-Médoc 1989 $14 (3/15/92)
80 CHATEAU PEYRAUD Premières Côtes de Blaye 1989 $8 (3/31/91)
80+ CHATEAU BERGAT St.-Emilion 1989 (NR) (4/30/90) (BT)
80+ CHATEAU BONNET Bordeaux 1989 (NR) (4/30/91) (BT)

80+ CHATEAU CADET-PIOLA St.-Emilion 1989 $24 (4/30/91) (BT)
80+ CHATEAU LA CARDONNE Médoc 1989 $11 (4/30/91) (BT)
80+ CHATEAU DE CARLES Fronsac 1989 (NR) (4/30/91) (BT)
80+ CHATEAU CARONNE STE.-GEMME Haut-Médoc 1989 (NR) (4/30/91) (BT)

Key to Symbols

The scores reported here are the results of blind tastings conducted by our panel of senior editors. Wines that carry the initials below are results of individual tastings.

THE WINE SPECTATOR 100-POINT SCALE ***95-100***—Classic, a great wine; ***90-94***—Outstanding, superior character and style; ***80-89***—Good to very good, a wine with special qualities; ***70-79***—Average, drinkable wine that may have minor flaws; ***60-69***—Below average, drinkable but not recommended; ***50-59***—Poor, undrinkable, not recommended. "+"—With a score indicates a range; used primarily with barrel tastings to indicate a preliminary score.

SPECIAL DESIGNATIONS SS—Spectator Selection, CS—Cellar Selection, BB—Best Buy, ($NA)—Price not available, (NR)—Not released.

TASTER'S INITIALS (JG)—Jim Gordon, (HS)—Harvey Steiman, (JL)—James Laube, (JS)—James Suckling, (TM)—Thomas Matthews, (TR)—Terry Robards, (PM)—Per-Henrik Mansson, (BT)—Barrel Tasting (these wines were tasted blind from barrel samples), (CA-date)—*California's Great Cabernets* by James Laube, (CH-date)—*California's Great Chardonnays* by James Laube, (VP-date)—*Vintage Port* by James Suckling.

DATE TASTED Dates in parentheses represent the issue in which the rating was published.

80+ CLOS DE L'ORATOIRE St.-Emilion 1989 (NR) (4/30/91) (BT)
80+ CHATEAU LA CLUSIERE St.-Emilion 1989 (NR) (4/30/91) (BT)
80+ CHATEAU CROIZET-BAGES Pauillac 1989 $17 (4/30/91) (BT)
80+ CHATEAU FAURIE-DE-SOUCHARD St.-Emilion 1989 (NR) (4/30/91) (BT)
80+ LADY LANGOA St.-Julien 1989 (NR) (4/30/91) (BT)
80+ CHATEAU LASCOMBES Margaux 1989 $23 (4/30/90) (BT)

80+ MOULIN DE DUHART Pauillac 1989 (NR) (4/30/90) (BT)
80+ CHATEAU PLINCE Pomerol 1989 $15 (4/30/91) (BT)
80+ CHATEAU RAUZAN-GASSIES Margaux 1989 $24 (4/30/91) (BT)
80+ CHATEAU DU ROCHER-BELLEVUE-FIGEAC St.-Emilion 1989 $15 (4/30/90) (BT)
80+ CHATEAU SIAURAC Lalande-de-Pomerol 1989 (NR) (4/30/91) (BT)
79 CHATEAU GREYSAC Médoc 1989 $12 (3/15/92)
79 CHATEAU LAGRAVE PARAN Bordeaux 1989 $8 (2/28/91)
79 CHATEAU LA TERRASSE Bordeaux Supérieur 1989 $8 (3/31/91)
79 CHATEAU VILLEGEORGE Haut-Médoc 1989 $14 (3/15/92)
78 CHATEAU PERENNE Premières Côtes de Blaye 1989 $9 (3/31/91)

78 CHATEAU PLANTEY Pauillac 1989 (NR) (3/15/92)
77 CHATEAU HANTEILLAN Haut-Médoc 1989 $14 (3/15/92)
77 CHATEAU MOULIN DE BEL-AIR Médoc 1989 (NR) (3/15/92)
75 BARTON & GUESTIER Bordeaux Fondation Rouge 1989 $9 (7/31/91)
75+ CHATEAU DE FRANCS Côtes de Francs 1989 (NR) (4/30/90) (BT)
75+ CHATEAU GUADET-ST.-JULIEN St.-Emilion 1989 (NR) (4/30/91) (BT)
75+ CHATEAU LAFLEUR-ST.-EMILION St.-Emilion 1989 (NR) (4/30/90) (BT)
75+ CHATEAU LAMARTINE Bordeaux 1989 (NR) (4/30/91) (BT)
75+ CHATEAU PETIT-FAURIE-DE-SOUTARD St.-Emilion 1989 (NR) (4/30/91) (BT)
74 CHATEAU TALMONT Bordeaux 1989 $8 (2/28/91)

71 ARMAND ROUX Bordeaux Verdillac 1989 $7 (1/31/92)
70+ CHATEAU LAFLEUR-POURRET St.-Emilion 1989 (NR) (4/30/91) (BT)

1988

100 CHATEAU MOUTON-ROTHSCHILD Pauillac 1988 $105 (4/30/91)
98 CHATEAU HAUT-BRION Pessac-Léognan 1988 $95 (4/30/91)
97 CHATEAU MARGAUX Margaux 1988 Rel: $75 Cur: $80 (3/31/91) CS
96 CHATEAU LAFITE-ROTHSCHILD Pauillac 1988 $100 (4/30/91) CS
96 CHATEAU LAGRANGE St.-Julien 1988 $26 (4/30/91)
96 CHATEAU PALMER Margaux 1988 $65 (2/28/91) CS
95 CHATEAU COS D'ESTOURNEL St.-Estèphe 1988 Rel: $30 Cur: $36 (7/15/91) CS
95 CHATEAU LEOVILLE-LAS CASES St.-Julien 1988 $45 (2/15/92) (HS)
95 CHATEAU LYNCH-BAGES Pauillac 1988 $35 (3/15/91) CS
95 CHATEAU PICHON-BARON Pauillac 1988 Rel: $30 Cur: $33 (3/31/91) SS

95 CHATEAU LE PIN Pomerol 1988 $65 (6/30/91) CS
95+ CHATEAU AUSONE St.-Emilion 1988 Rel: $76 Cur: $98 (8/31/90) (BT)
95+ CHATEAU LATOUR A POMEROL Pomerol 1988 $55 (6/30/89) (BT)
94 CHATEAU L'ARROSEE St.-Emilion 1988 $34 (3/15/91)
94 CHATEAU CLERC-MILON Pauillac 1988 $26 (4/30/91) SS
94 CHATEAU LA FLEUR DE GAY Pomerol 1988 $57 (6/30/91)
94 CHATEAU HAUT-BAILLY Pessac-Léognan 1988 $30 (4/30/91)
94 CHATEAU LARRIVET-HAUT-BRION Pessac-Léognan 1988 $25 (4/30/91)
94 CHATEAU PAVIE-DECESSE St.-Emilion 1988 $27 (3/31/91)
94 CHATEAU PETRUS Pomerol 1988 Rel: $221 Cur: $300 (8/31/91)

93 CHATEAU L'ANGELUS St.-Emilion 1988 $41 (3/31/91)
93 CHATEAU BEYCHEVELLE St.-Julien 1988 $40 (4/30/91)
93 CHATEAU CHEVAL BLANC St.-Emilion 1988 $105 (12/31/90) CS
93 CHATEAU FIGEAC St.-Emilion 1988 $45 (6/30/91)
93 CHATEAU HAUT-BAGES-AVEROUS Pauillac 1988 $23 (4/30/91)
93 CHATEAU LATOUR Pauillac 1988 $90 (4/30/91)
93 CHATEAU PAPE-CLEMENT Pessac-Léognan 1988 $40 (12/31/90)
92 CHATEAU CLINET Pomerol 1988 $31 (2/28/91)
92 CHATEAU DUCRU-BEAUCAILLOU St.-Julien 1988 $48 (4/30/91)
92 LES FIEFS DE LAGRANGE St.-Julien 1988 $17 (4/30/91)

92 CHATEAU DE FRANCE Pessac-Léognan 1988 $18 (2/28/91) SS
92 CHATEAU LA LOUVIERE Pessac-Léognan 1988 $20 (8/31/91) SS
92 CHATEAU DE MARBUZET St.-Estèphe 1988 Rel: $15 Cur: $17 (7/15/91) SS
92 CHATEAU MARQUIS DE TERME Margaux 1988 Rel: $23 Cur: $30 (4/30/91)
92 CHATEAU MONBRISON Margaux 1988 $20 (2/28/91)
92 CHATEAU RAUSAN-SEGLA Margaux 1988 $40 (3/15/91)
91 CHATEAU BALESTARD LA TONNELLE St.-Emilion 1988 $25 (4/30/91)
91 DOMAINE DE CHEVALIER Pessac-Léognan 1988 $37 (7/15/91)
91 CHATEAU CITRAN Haut-Médoc 1988 Rel: $15 Cur: $20 (4/30/91)
91 CHATEAU L'EGLISE-CLINET Pomerol 1988 $47 (12/31/90)

91 CHATEAU DE FIEUZAL Pessac-Léognan 1988 $32 (4/30/91)
91 CHATEAU FRANC BIGAROUX St.-Emilion 1988 $24 (7/31/91)
91 CHATEAU HAUT-MARBUZET St.-Estèphe 1988 Rel: $25 Cur: $28 (12/31/90) SS
91 CHATEAU LA LAGUNE Haut-Médoc 1988 $24 (4/30/91)
91 CHATEAU LEOVILLE-BARTON St.-Julien 1988 Rel: $20 Cur: $24 (3/31/91)
91 CHATEAU OLIVIER Pessac-Léognan 1988 Rel: $23 Cur: $31 (2/15/91)
91 CHATEAU PICHON-LALANDE Pauillac 1988 $50 (4/30/91)
91 CHATEAU TAILHAS Pomerol 1988 $20 (4/30/91)
91 CHATEAU LA TOUR-HAUT-BRION Pessac-Léognan 1988 $37 (6/15/91) CS
91 CHATEAU TRIMOULET St.-Emilion 1988 $16 (6/15/91)

91 VIEUX CHATEAU CERTAN Pomerol 1988 $60 (3/31/91)
90 CHATEAU BATAILLEY Pauillac 1988 Rel: $23 Cur: $27 (4/30/91)
90 CHATEAU BEAUREGARD Pomerol 1988 $36 (7/31/91)
90 CHATEAU BOURGNEUF-VAYRON Pomerol 1988 $19 (6/30/91)
90 CHATEAU CANON St.-Emilion 1988 $40 (6/30/91)
90 CHATEAU CERTAN DE MAY Pomerol 1988 $66 (6/30/91)
90 CHATEAU CLOS DES JACOBINS St.-Emilion 1988 $26 (4/15/91)
90 CHATEAU LA CONSEILLANTE Pomerol 1988 $56 (3/31/91)
90 CHATEAU DAUZAC Margaux 1988 $20 (6/30/91)
90 CHATEAU GLORIA St.-Julien 1988 $23 (3/31/91)

90 CHATEAU GRAND-PUY-LACOSTE Pauillac 1988 $33 (4/30/91)
90 CHATEAU LA GURGUE Margaux 1988 Rel: $29 Cur: $32 (4/30/91)
90 CHATEAU LAFLEUR Pomerol 1988 Rel: $95 Cur: $125 (10/31/91)
90 CHATEAU LA MISSION-HAUT-BRION Pessac-Léognan 1988 $90 (11/15/91) (JS)
90 CHATEAU MOUTON-BARONNE-PHILIPPE Pauillac 1988 $25 (4/30/91)
90 CHATEAU PRIEURE-LICHINE Margaux 1988 $30 (4/30/91)
90 CHATEAU TALBOT St.-Julien 1988 $25 (3/15/91)
90 CHATEAU TERTRE-ROTEBOEUF St.-Emilion 1988 $40 (6/15/91)
90+ CHATEAU CLOS ST.-MARTIN St.-Emilion 1988 ($NA) (6/30/89) (BT)
90+ CHATEAU FONROQUE St.-Emilion 1988 $18 (8/31/90) (BT)

90+ CHATEAU LA GRAVE TRIGANT DE BOISSET Pomerol 1988 Rel: $24 Cur: $26 (8/31/90) (BT)
90+ CHATEAU PETIT-VILLAGE Pomerol 1988 Rel: $26 Cur: $33 (8/31/90) (BT)
89 CHATEAU CADET-PIOLA St.-Emilion 1988 $20 (7/15/91)
89 CHATEAU CANTENAC-BROWN Margaux 1988 $25 (4/30/91)
89 CHATEAU CERTAN-GIRAUD Pomerol 1988 $23 (2/28/91)
89 CHATEAU CHASSE-SPLEEN Moulis 1988 $26 (3/31/91)
89 CHATEAU LA CROIX DE GAY Pomerol 1988 $26 (6/30/91)
89 CHATEAU FONBADET Pauillac 1988 $16 (8/31/91)
89 CHATEAU GISCOURS Margaux 1988 $30 (4/30/91)
89 CHATEAU GRAND-PUY-DUCASSE Pauillac 1988 $21 (4/30/91)
89 CHATEAU LACOSTE-BORIE Pauillac 1988 $19 (4/30/91)
89 CHATEAU MALESCOT-ST.-EXUPERY Margaux 1988 $23 (4/30/91)
89 CHATEAU PAVIE St.-Emilion 1988 $46 (3/31/91)
89 LE PETIT CHEVAL St.-Emilion 1988 $35 (3/31/91)
89 CHATEAU TROTANOY Pomerol 1988 Rel: $48 Cur: $59 (8/31/91)
88 CLOS RENE Pomerol 1988 $24 (4/30/91)
88 CHATEAU DUHART-MILON Pauillac 1988 Rel: $20 Cur: $29 (8/31/91)
88 CHATEAU HAUT-BAGES-LIBERAL Pauillac 1988 $17 (3/15/91)
88 CHATEAU D'ISSAN Margaux 1988 $30 (4/30/91)
88 CHATEAU MEYNEY St.-Estèphe 1988 $17 (3/15/91)
88 CHATEAU MOULINET Pomerol 1988 $17 (7/31/91)
88 CHATEAU LES ORMES DE PEZ St.-Estèphe 1988 $21 (4/30/91)
88 PAVILLON ROUGE DU CHATEAU MARGAUX Margaux 1988 $30 (4/30/91)
88 CHATEAU POUJEAUX Moulis 1988 $15 (2/28/91)
88 RESERVE DE LA COMTESSE Pauillac 1988 $23 (3/15/91)
88 CHATEAU SIRAN Margaux 1988 Rel: $19 Cur: $22 (6/30/91)
88 CHATEAU SOUDARS Haut-Médoc 1988 $15 (4/30/91)
88 CHATEAU TOUR DU HAUT-MOULIN Haut-Médoc 1988 $20 (4/30/91)
88 CHATEAU LA TOUR-MARTILLAC Pessac-Léognan 1988 $24 (2/28/91)
87 CHATEAU BEAU-SEJOUR BECOT St.-Emilion 1988 $21 (6/30/91)
87 CHATEAU BEAUSEJOUR-DUFFAU-LAGARROSSE St.-Emilion 1988 $32 (4/30/91)
87 CHATEAU LE BONNAT Graves 1988 $18 (12/31/90)
87 CHATEAU BOUSCAUT Pessac-Léognan 1988 $20 (4/30/91)
87 CHATEAU DE CRUZEAU Pessac-Léognan 1988 $14 (2/28/91)
87 CHATEAU L'EVANGILE Pomerol 1988 Rel: $38 Cur: $48 (6/30/91)
87 CHATEAU GAZIN Pomerol 1988 $30 (6/30/91)
87 CHATEAU GRAND-MAYNE St.-Emilion 1988 Rel: $15 Cur: $19 (7/15/91)
87 CHATEAU GREYSAC Médoc 1988 $15 (4/30/91)
87 CHATEAU HAUT-BATAILLEY Pauillac 1988 $26 (8/31/91)
87 CHATEAU KIRWAN Margaux 1988 $28 (4/30/91)
87 CHATEAU LALANDE-BORIE St.-Julien 1988 $17 (4/30/91)
87 CHATEAU LIVERSAN Haut-Médoc 1988 $14 (7/31/91)
87 CHATEAU MONTROSE St.-Estèphe 1988 $41 (3/31/91)
87 CHATEAU PHELAN-SEGUR St.-Estèphe 1988 $20 (7/15/91)
87 CHATEAU DU ROCHER-BELLEVUE-FIGEAC St.-Emilion 1988 $13 (4/30/91)
87 CHATEAU SOCIANDO-MALLET Haut-Médoc 1988 $26 (3/31/91)
87 CHATEAU TAILLEFER Pomerol 1988 $22 (6/30/91)
86 CHATEAU CANON-LA-GAFFELIERE St.-Emilion 1988 $30 (6/30/91)
86 CHATEAU CARBONNIEUX Pessac-Léognan 1988 $20 (2/28/91)
86 CLOS FOURTET St.-Emilion 1988 $23 (10/31/91)
86 CHATEAU DE LA DAME Margaux 1988 $15 (2/15/91)
86 CHATEAU LA DOMINIQUE St.-Emilion 1988 $25 (6/30/91)
86 CHATEAU GRAND PONTET St.-Emilion 1988 $21 (7/15/91)
86 CHATEAU DE LAMARQUE Haut-Médoc 1988 $20 (4/30/91)
86 CHATEAU LANGOA BARTON St.-Julien 1988 $25 (7/15/91)
86 CHATEAU LARMANDE St.-Emilion 1988 $23 (4/30/91)
86 CHATEAU DU TERTRE Margaux 1988 $40 (6/30/91)
86 CHATEAU LA TOUR DE BY Médoc 1988 $12.50 (6/15/91)
86 CHATEAU VERDIGNAN Haut-Médoc 1988 $15 (4/30/91)
85 CHATEAU D'ANGLUDET Margaux 1988 $22 (2/28/91)
85 CHATEAU BEL AIR Haut-Médoc 1988 $15 (4/30/91)
85 CHATEAU BERTINERIE Premières Côtes de Blaye 1988 $10 (7/15/90)
85 CHATEAU LE BON-PASTEUR Pomerol 1988 $23 (2/28/91)
85 CHATEAU CALON-SEGUR St.-Estèphe 1988 $30 (7/15/91)
85 CHATEAU CANTEMERLE Haut-Médoc 1988 $25 (3/15/91)
85 CHATEAU CORMEIL-FIGEAC St.-Emilion 1988 $20 (4/30/91)
85 CHATEAU COS-LABORY St.-Estèphe 1988 $20 (4/30/91)
85 CHATEAU L'ENCLOS Pomerol 1988 $17 (3/15/91)
85 CHATEAU FONPLEGADE St.-Emilion 1988 $18 (6/30/91)
85 PIERRE JEAN St.-Emilion 1988 $10 (6/30/91) BB
85 CHATEAU LYNCH-MOUSSAS Pauillac 1988 $25 (8/31/91)
85 CHATEAU RAUZAN-GASSIES Margaux 1988 $35 (8/31/91)
85 CHATEAU ST.-PIERRE St.-Julien 1988 $32 (4/30/91)
85 CHATEAU TERTRE-DAUGAY St.-Emilion 1988 $20 (4/30/91)
85 CHATEAU TROPLONG-MONDOT St.-Emilion 1988 Rel: $21 Cur: $23 (7/15/91)
85 CHATEAU TROTTE VIEILLE St.-Emilion 1988 Rel: $20 Cur: $36 (4/30/91)
85+ CHATEAU BONALGUE Pomerol 1988 ($NA) (6/30/89) (BT)
85+ CHATEAU BOYD-CANTENAC Margaux 1988 $20 (6/30/89) (BT)
85+ CHATEAU BRANAIRE-DUCRU St.-Julien 1988 Rel: $16 Cur: $22 (8/31/90) (BT)
85+ CHATEAU CANON MOUEIX Canon-Fronsac 1988 $16 (8/31/90) (BT)
85+ CHATEAU CANUET Margaux 1988 $15 (8/31/90) (BT)
85+ CHATEAU LA CROIX DU CASSE Pomerol 1988 $20 (6/30/89) (BT)
85+ CHATEAU LA FLEUR-PETRUS Pomerol 1988 $63 (6/30/89) (BT)
85+ CHATEAU LAFON-ROCHET St.-Estèphe 1988 $17 (6/30/89) (BT)
85+ CHATEAU LAGRANGE Pomerol 1988 $25 (6/30/89) (BT)
85+ CHATEAU MALESCASSE Haut-Médoc 1988 Rel: $14 Cur: $22 (6/30/89) (BT)
85+ CHATEAU PETIT-FIGEAC St.-Emilion 1988 $17 (8/31/90) (BT)
85+ CHATEAU PIBRAN Pauillac 1988 $27 (8/31/90) (BT)
85+ CHATEAU POUGET Margaux 1988 $18 (6/30/89) (BT)
85+ LES TOURELLES DE LONGUEVILLE Pauillac 1988 $25 (8/31/90) (BT)
84 CHATEAU ARNAULD Haut-Médoc 1988 $15 (4/30/91)
84 BARTON & GUESTIER Bordeaux Merlot 1988 $6 (2/15/90) BB
84 CHATEAU LE BOSCQ Médoc 1988 $20 (4/30/91)
84 CHATEAU CAP DE MOURLIN St.-Emilion 1988 $20 (4/30/91)
84 CHATEAU CHAUVIN St.-Emilion 1988 $20 (6/30/91)
84 CHATEAU COUFRAN Haut-Médoc 1988 $15 (4/30/91)
84 CHATEAU LA GAFFELIERE St.-Emilion 1988 $36 (4/30/91)
84 CHATEAU GRUAUD LAROSE St.-Julien 1988 $31 (3/31/91)
84 CHATEAU HAUT-FAUGERES St.-Emilion 1988 $17 (4/30/92)
84 CHATEAU LAROSE-TRINTAUDON Haut-Médoc 1988 $12 (4/30/91)
84 CHATEAU MALARTIC-LAGRAVIERE Pessac-Léognan 1988 $20 (7/15/91)
84 CHATEAU LES ORMES-SORBET Médoc 1988 $20 (4/30/91)
84 CHATEAU TRONQUOY-LALANDE St.-Estèphe 1988 $14 (7/15/91)
84 CHATEAU VIEUX GABRIAN Bordeaux Supérieur 1988 $11 (4/30/91)
83 CHATEAU BELLEGRAVE-VAN DER VOORT Pauillac 1988 $20 (8/31/91)
83 CLOS L'EGLISE Pomerol 1988 Rel: $24 Cur: $26 (6/30/91)
83 CHATEAU DASSAULT St.-Emilion 1988 $16 (7/15/91)
83 CHATEAU FOURCAS-DUPRE Listrac 1988 $22 (4/30/91)
83 CHATEAU FOURCAS-LOUBANEY Listrac 1988 $17 (2/28/91)
83 CHATEAU DE FRANC-MAYNE St.-Emilion 1988 Rel: $15 Cur: $20 (7/15/91)
83 CHATEAU LE GAY Pomerol 1988 $30 (4/30/91)
83 CHATEAU HAUT-SARPE St.-Emilion 1988 $16 (6/30/91)
83 CHATEAU LABEGORCE-ZEDE Margaux 1988 $20 (4/30/91)
83 CHATEAU DE PEZ St.-Estèphe 1988 $19 (6/15/91)
83 CHATEAU PITRAY Côtes de Castillon 1988 $7 (2/28/91) BB
83 CHATEAU LA POINTE Pomerol 1988 $35 (7/31/91)
83 CHATEAU TROCARD Bordeaux Supérieur 1988 $8.50 (1/31/92) BB
82 CHATEAU BEAUMONT Haut-Médoc 1988 $15 (7/15/91)
82 CHATEAU LA CROIX Pomerol 1988 $19 (7/31/91)
82 CHATEAU DEMERAULMONT St.-Estèphe 1988 $10 (8/31/91) BB
82 CHATEAU FONREAUD Listrac 1988 $15 (4/30/91)
82 CHATEAU FOURCAS-HOSTEN Listrac 1988 $13 (7/15/91)
82 CHATEAU DE LA GRAVE Bordeaux Supérieur 1988 $8 (7/15/90) BB
82 CHATEAU LAGARENNE Bordeaux Supérieur 1988 $8 (7/31/90) BB
82 CHATEAU LAGRAVE PARAN Bordeaux 1988 $6 (7/15/90) BB
82 CHATEAU LARCIS-DUCASSE St.-Emilion 1988 $20 (4/30/91)
82 CHATEAU LASCOMBES Margaux 1988 $25 (8/31/91)
82 CHATEAU LESTAGE Listrac 1988 $20 (8/31/91)
82 CHATEAU LOUDENNE Médoc 1988 $10 (8/31/91)
82 CHATEAU MAUCAILLOU Moulis 1988 $14 (7/31/91)
82 JEAN-PIERRE MOUEIX St.-Emilion 1988 $12.50 (4/30/92)
82 CHATEAU PETIT-FAURIE-DE-SOUTARD St.-Emilion 1988 $20 (4/30/91)
82 CHATEAU SEGUR Haut-Médoc 1988 $15 (12/31/90)
82 CHATEAU LA TOUR CARNET Haut-Médoc 1988 $15 (8/31/91)
81 CHATEAU BRILLETTE Moulis 1988 $15 (8/31/91)
81 CHATEAU CLARKE Listrac 1988 $18 (4/30/91)
81 COUVENT DES JACOBINS St.-Emilion 1988 $28 (3/31/91)
81 CHATEAU DESTIEUX St.-Emilion 1988 $19 (6/30/91)
81 CHATEAU GOFFRETEAU Bordeaux Supérieur 1988 $6 (2/28/91) BB
81 CHATEAU HAUT RIAN Premières Côtes de Bordeaux 1988 $7 (5/15/90) BB
81 CHATEAU LEOVILLE-POYFERRE St.-Julien 1988 Rel: $23 Cur: $25 (7/15/91)
81 CHATEAU MAGDELAINE St.-Emilion 1988 $50 (10/31/91)
81 MAISON MOUEIX Bordeaux Rouge 1988 $6 (1/31/92) BB
81 CHATEAU LA MOULINE Moulis 1988 $20 (2/15/91)
81 MOUTON-CADET Bordeaux 1988 $9 (4/30/91) BB
81 CHATEAU ST.-SULPICE Bordeaux 1988 $7.50 (8/31/91) BB
81 CHATEAU LA VIEILLE CURE Fronsac 1988 $19 (10/31/91)
80 CLOS DU MARQUIS St.-Julien 1988 $19 (10/31/91)
80 CHATEAU LE GRAND VERDUS Bordeaux Supérieur 1988 $7.50 (10/31/91) BB
80 CHATEAU LANESSAN Haut-Médoc 1988 $25 (7/31/91)
80 CHATEAU PATACHE D'AUX Médoc 1988 Rel: $10 Cur: $17 (4/30/91)
80 CHATEAU POTENSAC Médoc 1988 $14 (10/31/91)
80 CHATEAU RAHOUL Graves 1988 $18 (8/31/91)
80 ST.-JOVIAN Bordeaux Supérieur Premium 1988 $5.50 (7/31/91) BB
80 CHATEAU LA SERRE St.-Emilion 1988 $18 (6/15/91)
80+ CHATEAU BAHANS-HAUT-BRION Pessac-Léognan 1988 $20 (8/31/90) (BT)
80+ CHATEAU BEAU-SITE St.-Estèphe 1988 $14 (6/30/89) (BT)
80+ CHATEAU BELAIR St.-Emilion 1988 $28 (8/31/90) (BT)
80+ CHATEAU BERNADOTTE Pauillac 1988 $20 (6/30/89) (BT)
80+ CHATEAU BROWN Pessac-Léognan 1988 $17 (6/30/89) (BT)
80+ CHATEAU CANON DE BREM Canon-Fronsac 1988 $13 (6/30/89) (BT)
80+ CARRUADES DE LAFITE Pauillac 1988 Rel: $19 Cur: $25 (8/31/90) (BT)
80+ CHATEAU LA CLAVERIE Côtes de Francs 1988 $18 (8/31/90) (BT)
80+ CLOS DU CLOCHER Pomerol 1988 $22 (6/30/89) (BT)
80+ CHATEAU DE LA DAUPHINE Fronsac 1988 $12 (8/31/90) (BT)
80+ CHATEAU DESMIRAIL Margaux 1988 $25 (6/30/89) (BT)
80+ CHATEAU DE FRANCS Côtes de Francs 1988 ($NA) (8/31/90) (BT)
80+ CHATEAU HAUT-BERGEY Pessac-Léognan 1988 $12 (6/30/89) (BT)
80+ CHATEAU LAMOTHE-BERGERON Haut-Médoc 1988 $15 (6/30/89) (BT)
80+ CHATEAU MAGNOL Haut-Médoc 1988 ($NA) (6/30/89) (BT)
80+ CHATEAU MOULIN DU CADET St.-Emilion 1988 ($NA) (6/30/89) (BT)
80+ CHATEAU PEDESCLAUX Pauillac 1988 $20 (6/30/89) (BT)
80+ CHATEAU PONTET-CANET Pauillac 1988 $24 (6/30/89) (BT)
80+ CHATEAU PUYGUERAUD Côtes de Francs 1988 $15 (8/31/90) (BT)
80+ CHATEAU ST.-ANDRE-CORBIN St.-Georges-St.-Emilion 1988 ($NA) (6/30/89) (BT)
80+ CHATEAU SMITH-HAUT-LAFITTE Pessac-Léognan 1988 $15 (6/30/89) (BT)
80+ CHATEAU TERREY-GROS-CAILLOUX St.-Julien 1988 $14 (6/30/89) (BT)
80+ CHATEAU VILLEGEORGE Haut-Médoc 1988 $15 (6/30/89) (BT)
79 BEAUCLAIRE Bordeaux Supérieur 1988 $6 (12/31/90)
79 CHATEAU BELGRAVE Haut-Médoc 1988 $28 (7/31/91)
79 CHATEAU LA COMMANDERIE St.-Emilion 1988 $15 (10/31/91)
79 CHATEAU PLAGNAC Médoc 1988 $8.50 (4/30/91)
79 ARMAND ROUX Bordeaux Verdillac 1988 $6.25 (7/15/90) BB
79 CHATEAU LA TOUR-HAUT-CAUSSAN Médoc 1988 $12.50 (7/15/91)
78 CHATEAU BONNET Bordeaux Reserve 1988 $11 (7/15/91)
78 CHATEAU CLEMENT-PICHON Haut-Médoc 1988 $15 (8/31/91)
78 CHATEAU GRAND CLARET Premières Côtes de Bordeaux 1988 $7 (7/31/91)
78 CHATEAU JACQUES-BLANC St.-Emilion Cuvée du Maitre 1988 $23 (4/30/91)
78 MARQUIS DES TOURS Bordeaux 1988 $5 (2/28/91)
78 CHATEAU SENEJAC Haut-Médoc 1988 Rel: $11 Cur: $14 (4/30/91)
78 CHATEAU TAYAC Côtes de Bourg 1988 $10 (1/31/92)
78 CHATEAU TRINITE VALROSE Bordeaux Supérieur Ile de Patiras 1988 $7 (8/31/91)
77 CHATEAU BONNET Bordeaux 1988 $7.50 (4/30/91)
77 SIRIUS Bordeaux 1988 $15 (8/31/91)
77 CHATEAU LA TOUR-DU-PIN-FIGEAC St.-Emilion 1988 $24 (7/15/91)
76 CHATEAU BRANE-CANTENAC Margaux 1988 $42 (8/31/91)
76 CHATEAU FOURNAS BERNADOTTE Haut-Médoc 1988 $18 (6/15/91)
76 MICHEL LYNCH Bordeaux 1988 $8 (10/31/91)
76 CHATEAU MERIC Graves 1988 $17 (4/30/91)
76 CHATEAU DE LA MEULIERE Premières Côtes de Bordeaux 1988 $9 (2/28/91)
75 CHATEAU COLOMBIER-MONPELOU Pauillac 1988 $15 (10/31/91)

FRANCE
Bordeaux Red

75 PIERRE JEAN Bordeaux Supérieur 1988 $8 (7/31/91)
75 CHATEAU DU PINTEY Bordeaux Supérieur 1988 $11 (8/31/91)
75+ CHATEAU CAPBERN-GASQUETON St.-Estèphe 1988 ($NA) (6/30/89) (BT)
75+ CHATEAU CARMES-HAUT-BRION Pessac-Léognan 1988 $22 (6/30/89) (BT)
75+ CHATEAU CARONNE STE.-GEMME Haut-Médoc 1988 ($NA) (6/30/89) (BT)
75+ CHATEAU CHAMBERT-MARBUZET St.-Estèphe 1988 $26 (8/31/90) (BT)
75+ CLOS DE L'ORATOIRE St.-Emilion 1988 ($NA) (6/30/89) (BT)
75+ CHATEAU LA COMMANDERIE St.-Estèphe 1988 ($NA) (6/30/89) (BT)
75+ CHATEAU LA CROIX LANDON Médoc 1988 ($NA) (6/30/89) (BT)
75+ CHATEAU FAURIE-DE-SOUCHARD St.-Emilion 1988 $22 (6/30/89) (BT)
75+ CHATEAU LA FLEUR-POURRET St.-Emilion 1988 ($NA) (8/31/90) (BT)
75+ CHATEAU LA GARDE Pessac-Léognan 1988 $15 (6/30/89) (BT)
75+ CHATEAU DU GLANA St.-Julien 1988 ($NA) (6/30/89) (BT)
75+ CHATEAU GUADET-ST.-JULIEN St.-Emilion 1988 ($NA) (6/30/89) (BT)
75+ CHATEAU HANTEILLAN Haut-Médoc 1988 $17 (6/30/89) (BT)
75+ CHATEAU LES HAUTS DE SMITH Pessac-Léognan 1988 ($NA) (6/30/89) (BT)
75+ CHATEAU LACHESNAYE Haut-Médoc 1988 $24 (6/30/89) (BT)
75+ CHATEAU LAMOUROUX Margaux 1988 ($NA) (6/30/89) (BT)
75+ CHATEAU MARQUIS-D'ALESME-BECKER Margaux 1988 $20 (6/30/89) (BT)
75+ CHATEAU MARSAC-SEGUINEAU Margaux 1988 ($NA) (6/30/89) (BT)
75+ CHATEAU MAZERIS Canon-Fronsac 1988 $18 (6/30/89) (BT)
75+ CHATEAU PIQUE-CAILLOU Pessac-Léognan 1988 ($NA) (6/30/89) (BT)
75+ CHATEAU PUY-BLANQUET St.-Emilion 1988 $15 (6/30/89) (BT)
75+ CHATEAU DE ROCHEMORIN Pessac-Léognan 1988 $15 (6/30/89) (BT)
75+ CHATEAU SEGONNES Margaux 1988 $18 (6/30/89) (BT)
75+ CHATEAU SIAURAC Lalande-de-Pomerol 1988 $20 (6/30/89) (BT)
74 CHATEAU DUCLA Bordeaux 1988 $7 (8/31/91)
73 BARTON & GUESTIER Bordeaux Cabernet Sauvignon 1988 $6 (2/15/90)
73 CHATEAU CROIZET-BAGES Pauillac 1988 $28 (8/31/91)
73 CHATEAU DURFORT-VIVENS Margaux 1988 $40 (8/31/91)
73 CHATEAU ST.-GEORGES St.-Georges-St.-Emilion 1988 $18 (4/30/92)
72 CHATEAU CORBIN-MICHOTTE St.-Emilion 1988 $15 (7/15/91)
70+ CHATEAU D'ARSAC Haut-Médoc 1988 $7 (6/30/89) (BT)
70+ CHATEAU BARET Pessac-Léognan 1988 $15 (6/30/89) (BT)
70+ CHATEAU LA FLEUR BECADE Haut-Médoc 1988 ($NA) (6/30/89) (BT)
70+ CHATEAU FONTESTEAU Haut-Médoc 1988 ($NA) (6/30/89) (BT)
70+ CHATEAU LA PRADE Côtes de Francs 1988 ($NA) (6/30/89) (BT)
70+ CHATEAU DE SALES Pomerol 1988 $17 (6/30/89) (BT)
70+ CHATEAU LA TOUR-FIGEAC St.-Emilion 1988 $17 (6/30/89) (BT)
69 CHATEAU BAULOS Bordeaux Prince Albert Poniatowski 1988 $8.75 (8/31/91)
65 CHATEAU JONQUEYRES Bordeaux Supérieur Cuvée Vieilles Vignes 1988 $12 (3/31/91)
65+ CHATEAU LA CLUSIERE St.-Emilion 1988 $20 (6/30/89) (BT)
60+ CHATEAU LE PAPE Pessac-Léognan 1988 ($NA) (6/30/89) (BT)
60+ CHATEAU PROCHE PONTET Haut-Médoc 1988 ($NA) (6/30/89) (BT)
55 CHATEAU DE CAMENSAC Haut-Médoc 1988 $16 (7/15/91)

1986

98 CHATEAU CHEVAL BLANC St.-Emilion 1986 Rel: $80 Cur: $85 (6/30/89) CS
98 CHATEAU MARGAUX Margaux 1986 Rel: $80 Cur: $110 (6/15/89) CS
98 CHATEAU MOUTON-ROTHSCHILD Pauillac 1986 Rel: $102 Cur: $140 (5/31/89) CS
97 CHATEAU CLERC-MILON Pauillac 1986 Rel: $23 Cur: $37 (5/31/89)
97 CHATEAU LA MISSION-HAUT-BRION Pessac-Léognan 1986 Rel: $50 Cur: $60 (11/15/91) (JS)
97 CHATEAU MOUTON-ROTHSCHILD Pauillac 1986 Rel: $102 Cur: $140 (5/15/91) (PM)
97 CHATEAU PICHON-BARON Pauillac 1986 Rel: $31 Cur: $41 (5/31/89)
97 CHATEAU PICHON-LALANDE Pauillac 1986 Rel: $50 Cur: $59 (5/31/89)
96 CHATEAU LAFITE-ROTHSCHILD Pauillac 1986 $102 (11/30/91) (JG)
96 CHATEAU LEOVILLE-LAS CASES St.-Julien 1986 Rel: $44 Cur: $61 (9/15/89) CS
96 CHATEAU MONTROSE St.-Estèphe 1986 Rel: $31 Cur: $35 (5/15/89) SS
96 CHATEAU PETRUS Pomerol 1986 Rel: $200 Cur: $350 (2/15/91) (JS)
95 CHATEAU LA DOMINIQUE St.-Emilion 1986 $29 (6/30/89)
95 CHATEAU LA FLEUR DE GAY Pomerol 1986 Rel: $43 Cur: $63 (10/31/89) CS
95 CHATEAU LEOVILLE-LAS CASES St.-Julien 1986 Rel: $44 Cur: $61 (2/15/92) (HS)
95 CHATEAU LE PIN Pomerol 1986 Rel: $55 Cur: $140 (6/15/89)
94 CHATEAU L'ANGELUS St.-Emilion 1986 Rel: $26 Cur: $30 (6/30/89)
94 CHATEAU CLOS DES JACOBINS St.-Emilion 1986 $34 (6/30/89)
94 CLOS RENE Pomerol 1986 Rel: $19 Cur: $24 (6/15/89) SS
94 CHATEAU LYNCH-BAGES Pauillac 1986 $37 (10/31/89) (JS)
94 CHATEAU MAGDELAINE St.-Emilion 1986 $48 (2/15/90)
94 CHATEAU PALMER Margaux 1986 Rel: $40 Cur: $54 (6/15/89)
94 CHATEAU SOCIANDO-MALLET Haut-Médoc 1986 $25 (11/30/89) (JS)
93 CHATEAU BEYCHEVELLE St.-Julien 1986 $37 (5/31/89)
93 CHATEAU CANON St.-Emilion 1986 $45 (6/30/89)
93 CHATEAU CERTAN DE MAY Pomerol 1986 Rel: $53 Cur: $71 (9/15/89)
93 CHATEAU CHEVAL BLANC St.-Emilion 1986 Rel: $80 Cur: $85 (2/15/91) (JS)
93 CHATEAU LA CONSEILLANTE Pomerol 1986 Rel: $40 Cur: $54 (6/15/89)
93 CHATEAU LA FLEUR-PETRUS Pomerol 1986 Rel: $52 Cur: $57 (2/15/90) CS
93 CHATEAU LATOUR Pauillac 1986 $90 (3/31/90) (HS)
93 CHATEAU MOUTON-BARONNE-PHILIPPE Pauillac 1986 Rel: $23 Cur: $25 (5/31/89)
93 CHATEAU PAVIE St.-Emilion 1986 $35 (6/30/89)
93 CHATEAU PAVIE-DECESSE St.-Emilion 1986 $33 (6/30/89)
93 VIEUX CHATEAU CERTAN Pomerol 1986 Rel: $40 Cur: $55 (6/15/89)
92 CHATEAU BERNADOTTE Pauillac 1986 Rel: $20 Cur: $22 (11/30/89) (JS)
92 CHATEAU LE BON-PASTEUR Pomerol 1986 Rel: $22 Cur: $25 (6/15/89)

Key to Symbols

The scores reported here are the results of blind tastings conducted by our panel of senior editors. Wines that carry the initials below are results of individual tastings.

THE WINE SPECTATOR 100-POINT SCALE 95-100—Classic, a great wine; ***90-94***—Outstanding, superior character and style; ***80-89***—Good to very good, a wine with special qualities; ***70-79***—Average, drinkable wine that may have minor flaws; ***60-69***—Below average, drinkable but not recommended; ***50-59***—Poor, undrinkable, not recommended. "+"—With a score indicates a range; used primarily with barrel tastings to indicate a preliminary score.

SPECIAL DESIGNATIONS SS—Spectator Selection, CS—Cellar Selection, BB—Best Buy, ($NA)—Price not available, (NR)—Not released.

TASTER'S INITIALS (JG)—Jim Gordon, (HS)—Harvey Steiman, (JL)—James Laube, (JS)—James Suckling, (TM)—Thomas Matthews, (TR)—Terry Robards, (PM)—Per-Henrik Mansson, (BT)—Barrel Tasting (these wines were tasted blind from barrel samples), (CA-date)—*California's Great Cabernets* by James Laube, (CH-date)—*California's Great Chardonnays* by James Laube, (VP-date)—*Vintage Port* by James Suckling.

DATE TASTED Dates in parentheses represent the issue in which the rating was published.

92 CHATEAU COS D'ESTOURNEL St.-Estèphe 1986 Rel: $40 Cur: $45 (5/15/90) (HS)
92 CHATEAU LE CROCK St.-Estèphe 1986 Rel: $18 Cur: $21 (11/30/89) (JS)
92 CHATEAU L'ENCLOS Pomerol 1986 $20 (6/15/89)
92 CHATEAU HAUT-BRION Pessac-Léognan 1986 $88 (6/30/89)
92 CHATEAU HAUT-MARBUZET St.-Estèphe 1986 $30 (11/30/89) (JS)
92 CHATEAU DE MARBUZET St.-Estèphe 1986 $15 (6/30/89)
92 CHATEAU MONBRISON Margaux 1986 $20 (11/30/89) (JS)
92 CHATEAU PAPE-CLEMENT Pessac-Léognan 1986 $36 (6/30/89)
92 CHATEAU PRIEURE-LICHINE Margaux 1986 Rel: $21 Cur: $25 (6/15/89)
92 CHATEAU ST.-PIERRE St.-Julien 1986 Rel: $17 Cur: $22 (9/15/89) SS
92 CHATEAU TRONQUOY-LALANDE St.-Estèphe 1986 $15 (11/30/89) (JS)
91 CHATEAU BEAUSEJOUR-DUFFAU-LAGARROSSE St.-Emilion 1986 Rel: $27 Cur: $34 (6/30/89)
91 CHATEAU CANON-LA-GAFFELIERE St.-Emilion 1986 Rel: $21 Cur: $28 (6/30/89)
91 CLOS J. KANON St.-Emilion 1986 $17 (11/15/89)
91 CHATEAU DUCRU-BEAUCAILLOU St.-Julien 1986 $52 (6/30/89)
91 CHATEAU L'EGLISE-CLINET Pomerol 1986 Rel: $29 Cur: $44 (6/15/89)
91 CHATEAU HAUT-BAGES-LIBERAL Pauillac 1986 Rel: $17 Cur: $21 (5/31/89)
91 CHATEAU HAUT-BAILLY Pessac-Léognan 1986 Rel: $23 Cur: $25 (6/15/89)
91 CHATEAU LABEGORCE-ZEDE Margaux 1986 Rel: $18 Cur: $22 (11/30/89) (JS)
91 CHATEAU LALANDE-BORIE St.-Julien 1986 $17 (11/30/89) (JS)
91 CHATEAU LARMANDE St.-Emilion 1986 Rel: $19 Cur: $24 (6/30/89)
91 CHATEAU LA LOUVIERE Pessac-Léognan 1986 Rel: $15 Cur: $25 (6/15/89)
91 CHATEAU TALBOT St.-Julien 1986 $32 (5/31/89)
90 CHATEAU D'ANGLUDET Margaux 1986 Rel: $17 Cur: $25 (11/30/89) (JS)
90 CHATEAU CHASSE-SPLEEN Moulis 1986 $26 (11/30/89) (JS)
90 CHATEAU CLARKE Listrac 1986 $17 (11/15/89)
90 CHATEAU DESMIRAIL Margaux 1986 $22 (6/30/89)
90 CHATEAU DUHART-MILON Pauillac 1986 $30 (5/31/89)
90 CHATEAU DURFORT-VIVENS Margaux 1986 $25 (6/15/89)
90 CHATEAU DE FIEUZAL Pessac-Léognan 1986 Rel: $21 Cur: $25 (6/30/89)
90 CHATEAU HAUT-BAGES-AVEROUS Pauillac 1986 Rel: $15 Cur: $19 (11/30/89) (JS)
90 CHATEAU LAFLEUR Pomerol 1986 Rel: $100 Cur: $160 (10/31/89)
90 CHATEAU LEOVILLE-BARTON St.-Julien 1986 Rel: $24 Cur: $28 (5/31/89)
90 CHATEAU MALARTIC-LAGRAVIERE Pessac-Léognan 1986 Rel: $18 Cur: $27 (6/15/89)
90 CHATEAU DE PEZ St.-Estèphe 1986 $17 (6/30/89)
90 CHATEAU LA POINTE Pomerol 1986 $21 (6/15/89)
90 RESERVE DE LA COMTESSE Pauillac 1986 Rel: $20 Cur: $22 (5/31/89)
90 CHATEAU TERTRE-ROTEBOEUF St.-Emilion 1986 Rel: $25 Cur: $34 (6/30/89)
90 CHATEAU TOUR DU HAUT-MOULIN Haut-Médoc 1986 $16 (11/30/89) (JS)
90 CHATEAU LA TOUR-MARTILLAC Pessac-Léognan 1986 $15 (2/15/90)
90 CHATEAU LA TOUR-DE-MONS Margaux 1986 $19 (11/30/89) (JS)
90+ CHATEAU LA CROIX DE GAY Pomerol 1986 Rel: $20 Cur: $25 (6/30/88)
90+ CHATEAU LATOUR A POMEROL Pomerol 1986 $35 (5/15/87) (BT)
90+ CHATEAU PETIT-VILLAGE Pomerol 1986 $24 (6/30/88) (BT)
89 CHATEAU CANTEMERLE Haut-Médoc 1986 $30 (6/30/89)
89 CHATEAU CHAMBERT-MARBUZET St.-Estèphe 1986 Rel: $25 Cur: $28 (11/30/89) (JS)
89 DOMAINE DE CHEVALIER Pessac-Léognan 1986 Rel: $33 Cur: $38 (6/15/89)
89 CHATEAU GLORIA St.-Julien 1986 $18 (11/30/89) (JS)
89 CHATEAU LA GRAVE TRIGANT DE BOISSET Pomerol 1986 $35 (3/31/90)
89 CHATEAU GRUAUD LAROSE St.-Julien 1986 Rel: $34 Cur: $38 (2/28/91) (TR)
89 CHATEAU LA LAGUNE Haut-Médoc 1986 Rel: $22 Cur: $26 (6/30/89)
89 CHATEAU PONTET-CANET Pauillac 1986 $21 (5/31/89)
89 CHATEAU DU TERTRE Margaux 1986 $22 (6/15/89)
88 CHATEAU BEL-AIR Haut-Médoc 1986 $9 (11/15/89) BB
88 CHATEAU CANUET Margaux 1986 $15 (11/30/89) (JS)
88 CHATEAU CORBIN St.-Emilion 1986 $15 (6/30/89)
88 CHATEAU L'EVANGILE Pomerol 1986 $62 (9/15/89)
88 CHATEAU GRAND-PUY-LACOSTE Pauillac 1986 $25 (5/31/89)
88 CHATEAU MALESCASSE Haut-Médoc 1986 $9 (11/30/89) (JS)
88 CHATEAU MALESCOT-ST.-EXUPERY Margaux 1986 Rel: $26 Cur: $29 (6/15/89)
88 CHATEAU MEYNEY St.-Estèphe 1986 $19 (11/30/89) (JS)
88 CHATEAU MOULIN RICHE St.-Julien 1986 $20 (11/30/89) (JS)
88 CHATEAU PIBRAN Pauillac 1986 $18 (11/30/89) (JS)
88 CHATEAU POUJEAUX Moulis 1986 $22 (11/30/89) (JS)
88 CHATEAU RAUZAN-GASSIES Margaux 1986 $24 (6/30/89)
88 CHATEAU LA TOUR-HAUT-CAUSSAN Médoc 1986 $14 (11/30/89) (JS)
88 CHATEAU TROPLONG-MONDOT St.-Emilion 1986 Rel: $20 Cur: $23 (6/30/89)
87 CHATEAU L'ARROSEE St.-Emilion 1986 Rel: $31 Cur: $36 (2/15/89)
87 CHATEAU BEAUREGARD Pomerol 1986 Rel: $22 Cur: $24 (6/15/89)
87 CHATEAU BRANE-CANTENAC Margaux 1986 Rel: $26 Cur: $30 (6/15/89)
87 CHATEAU CAP DE MOURLIN St.-Emilion 1986 $18 (6/30/89)
87 CHATEAU CARBONNIEUX Pessac-Léognan 1986 $18 (9/15/89)
87 CHATEAU DE CRUZEAU Pessac-Léognan 1986 $10 (6/30/89)
87 CHATEAU FIGEAC St.-Emilion 1986 Rel: $45 Cur: $49 (10/31/91) (JS)
87 CHATEAU GRAND-MAYNE St.-Emilion 1986 $16 (6/30/89)
87 CHATEAU MOULIN ROUGE Haut-Médoc 1986 $14 (11/30/89) (JS)
87 CHATEAU LES ORMES DE PEZ St.-Estèphe 1986 $21 (11/30/89) (JS)
87 CHATEAU RAUSAN-SEGLA Margaux 1986 Rel: $28 Cur: $40 (9/15/89)
87 CHATEAU ST.-GEORGES St.-Georges-St.-Emilion 1986 $14 (7/15/90)
87 CHATEAU TERREY-GROS-CAILLOUX St.-Julien 1986 $12 (11/30/89) (JS)
86 CHATEAU BAHANS-HAUT-BRION Pessac-Léognan 1986 Rel: $22 Cur: $26 (9/15/89)
86 CHATEAU BEAU-SITE St.-Estèphe 1986 Rel: $15 Cur: $18 (11/30/89) (JS)
86 CHATEAU CALON-SEGUR St.-Estèphe 1986 $32 (5/31/89)
86 CHATEAU CANON DE BREM Canon-Fronsac 1986 $15 (3/31/90)
86 CHATEAU CERTAN-GIRAUD Pomerol 1986 $22 (6/30/89)
86 CLOS L'EGLISE Pomerol 1986 $28 (2/15/90)
86 CHATEAU FOMBRAUGE St.-Emilion 1986 $19 (6/30/89)
86 CHATEAU LABEGORCE Margaux 1986 $15 (2/15/90)
86 CHATEAU LAGRANGE St.-Julien 1986 Rel: $20 Cur: $28 (2/15/90)
86 CHATEAU LEOVILLE-POYFERRE St.-Julien 1986 $24 (5/31/89)
86 CHATEAU LYNCH-MOUSSAS Pauillac 1986 $18 (6/30/89)
86 CHATEAU DE MARBUZET St.-Estèphe 1986 $15 (11/30/89) (JS)
86 CHATEAU PHELAN-SEGUR St.-Estèphe 1986 $19 (11/30/89) (JS)
86 CHATEAU POTENSAC Médoc 1986 $15 (11/30/89) (JS)
86 CHATEAU DE SALES Pomerol 1986 $20 (6/30/89)
85 CHATEAU AUSONE St.-Emilion 1986 Rel: $90 Cur: $115 (6/30/89)
85 CHATEAU GRAND-PUY-DUCASSE Pauillac 1986 Rel: $22 Cur: $26 (6/30/89)
85 CHATEAU GREYSAC Médoc 1986 $10 (11/30/89) (JS)
85 CHATEAU LA GURGUE Margaux 1986 $22 (11/30/89) (JS)
85 CHATEAU HAUT-BATAILLEY Pauillac 1986 $23 (5/31/89)

85 CHATEAU LESTAGE-SIMON Haut-Médoc 1986 $13 (11/30/89) (JS)
85 CHATEAU LA TOUR-LEOGNAN Pessac-Léognan 1986 $11 (2/15/89)
85+ CHATEAU BONALGUE Pomerol 1986 $27 (6/30/88) (BT)
85+ CHATEAU BRANAIRE-DUCRU St.-Julien 1986 Rel: $16 Cur: $27 (6/30/88) (BT)
85+ CHATEAU LA CABANNE Pomerol 1986 $30 (6/30/88) (BT)
85+ CHATEAU CANTENAC-BROWN Margaux 1986 Rel: $24 Cur: $26 (6/30/88) (BT)
85+ CHATEAU LAFON-ROCHET St.-Estèphe 1986 $20 (6/30/88) (BT)
85+ CHATEAU LANGOA BARTON St.-Julien 1986 Rel: $22 Cur: $26 (6/30/88) (BT)
85+ CHATEAU MAUCAILLOU Moulis 1986 $18 (6/30/88) (BT)
85+ CHATEAU OLIVIER Pessac-Léognan 1986 Rel: $16 Cur: $20 (6/30/88) (BT)
85+ CHATEAU SMITH-HAUT-LAFITTE Pessac-Léognan 1986 $15 (6/30/88) (BT)
85+ CHATEAU LA TOUR-HAUT-BRION Pessac-Léognan 1986 $33 (6/30/88) (BT)
84 CHATEAU DU BEAU-VALLON St.-Emilion 1986 $10 (9/30/89)
84 CHATEAU BEAUMONT Haut-Médoc 1986 $9 (6/30/89)
84 CHATEAU LA CARDONNE Médoc 1986 $10 (2/15/90)
84 CHATEAU DU CAUZE St.-Emilion 1986 $15 (6/30/89)
84 CLOS DU MARQUIS St.-Julien 1986 Rel: $17 Cur: $20 (9/15/89)
84 CHATEAU DU GLANA St.-Julien 1986 $17 (11/30/89) (JS)
84 CHATEAU LACOSTE-BORIE Pauillac 1986 $15 (6/30/89)
84 CHATEAU NENIN Pomerol 1986 $22 (6/30/89)
84 PAVILLON ROUGE DU CHATEAU MARGAUX Margaux 1986 Rel: $24 Cur: $29 (6/30/89)
84 CHATEAU PUYGUERAUD Côtes de Francs 1986 $12 (6/15/89)
84 CHATEAU DE ROCHEMORIN Pessac-Léognan 1986 Rel: $10 Cur: $15 (6/15/89)
83 CHATEAU DE CAMENSAC Haut-Médoc 1986 $14 (6/30/89)
83 CHATEAU DUCLUZEAU Listrac 1986 $11 (11/30/89) (JS)
83 CHATEAU GISCOURS Margaux 1986 $30 (6/15/89)
83 CHATEAU D'ISSAN Margaux 1986 Rel: $22 Cur: $27 (6/15/89)
83 CHATEAU RAHOUL Graves 1986 $18 (12/31/90)
83 CHATEAU TROTANOY Pomerol 1986 $68 (10/31/89)
82 CHATEAU ARNAULD Haut-Médoc 1986 $18 (11/30/89) (JS)
82 CHATEAU BELAIR St.-Emilion 1986 Rel: $26 Cur: $35 (3/31/90)
82 CLOS LABARDE St.-Emilion 1986 $15 (6/30/89)
82 CHATEAU COUFRAN Haut-Médoc 1986 Rel: $13 Cur: $15 (11/30/89) (JS)
82 CHATEAU LA FLEUR St.-Emilion 1986 $13.50 (2/15/90)
82 CHATEAU GOFFRETEAU Bordeaux Supérieur 1986 $6 (6/15/89) BB
82 CHATEAU LES HAUTS DE BRAME St.-Estèphe 1986 $18.50 (10/31/89)
82 CHATEAU KIRWAN Margaux 1986 $25 (6/30/89)
82 CHATEAU LARRIVET-HAUT-BRION Pessac-Léognan 1986 $17 (6/15/89)
82 CHATEAU PERENNE Premières Côtes de Blaye 1986 $7 (6/30/89)
82 CHATEAU PLAGNAC Médoc 1986 $9 (11/30/89) (JS)
82 CHATEAU RAMAGE LA BATISSE Haut-Médoc 1986 $14 (11/30/89) (JS)
81 CHATEAU BELGRAVE Haut-Médoc 1986 $16 (3/31/90)
81 CHATEAU LA CROIX ST.-JEAN Bordeaux Supérieur 1986 $6 (11/30/88) BB
81 CHATEAU HANTEILLAN Haut-Médoc 1986 $15 (11/30/89) (JS)
81 CHATEAU HAUT-GARDERE Pessac-Léognan 1986 $11 (9/30/89)
81 CHATEAU LESCALLE Bordeaux Supérieur 1986 $8 (6/30/89)
81 MOUTON-CADET Bordeaux 1986 $7.25 (2/15/89) BB
81 CHATEAU DE PARENCHERE Bordeaux Supérieur 1986 $9 (6/30/89)
81 CHATEAU PITRAY Côtes de Castillon 1986 $6 (9/30/89) BB
81 CHATEAU SAUVAGE Premières Côtes de Bordeaux 1986 $9 (4/15/90)
81 CHATEAU TOUR CALON Montagne-St.-Emilion 1986 $10 (9/30/89)
81 CHATEAU LA VALADE Fronsac 1986 $5.25 (5/15/89) BB
81 CHATEAU LA VIEILLE CURE Fronsac 1986 $15 (5/15/91)
80 CHATEAU BEAUSEJOUR Côtes de Castillon 1986 $5 (6/15/89) BB
80 CHATEAU BELLEGRAVE-VAN DER VOORT Pauillac 1986 $19 (10/31/91)
80 CHATEAU BRASSAC Bordeaux Supérieur 1986 $5.50 (8/31/88) BB
80 CHEVALIER DUCLA Bordeaux 1986 $5.50 (5/15/89) BB
80 CLOS FOURTET St.-Emilion 1986 Rel: $29 Cur: $41 (6/30/89)
80 DOMAINE DE GRAND MAISON Pessac-Léognan 1986 $8.50 (4/15/90)
80 CHATEAU PETIT-FAURIE-DE-SOUTARD St.-Emilion 1986 $15 (6/30/89)
80 CHATEAU LA TOUR DE BY Médoc 1986 $12 (11/30/89) (JS)
80+ CHATEAU BALESTARD LA TONNELLE St.-Emilion 1986 $22 (6/30/88) (BT)
80+ CHATEAU BATAILLEY Pauillac 1986 $34 (6/30/88) (BT)
80+ CHATEAU BOURGNEUF-VAYRON Pomerol 1986 Rel: $22 Cur: $26 (6/30/88) (BT)
80+ CHATEAU BOYD-CANTENAC Margaux 1986 $15 (5/15/87) (BT)
80+ CHATEAU BROWN Pessac-Léognan 1986 $19 (5/15/87) (BT)
80+ CHATEAU CANON MOUEIX Canon-Fronsac 1986 Rel: $15 Cur: $18 (6/30/88) (BT)
80+ CHATEAU CARMES-HAUT-BRION Pessac-Léognan 1986 $26 (6/30/88) (BT)
80+ CLOS DU CLOCHER Pomerol 1986 $20 (6/30/88) (BT)
80+ CHATEAU LA CROIX Pomerol 1986 $25 (6/30/88) (BT)
80+ LES FIEFS DE LAGRANGE St.-Julien 1986 Rel: $17 Cur: $19 (6/30/88) (BT)
80+ CHATEAU FONPLEGADE St.-Emilion 1986 $15 (6/30/88) (BT)
80+ CHATEAU FONROQUE St.-Emilion 1986 $19 (6/30/88) (BT)
80+ CHATEAU DE FRANCE Pessac-Léognan 1986 $15 (6/30/88) (BT)
80+ CHATEAU LA GAFFELIERE St.-Emilion 1986 $28 (5/15/87) (BT)
80+ CHATEAU GAZIN Pomerol 1986 Rel: $21 Cur: $23 (5/15/87) (BT)
80+ CHATEAU HAUT-BERGEY Pessac-Léognan 1986 ($NA) (6/30/88) (BT)
80+ CHATEAU LANESSAN Haut-Médoc 1986 $16 (6/30/88) (BT)
80+ CHATEAU LARCIS-DUCASSE St.-Emilion 1986 Rel: $20 Cur: $25 (6/30/88) (BT)
80+ CHATEAU LASCOMBES Margaux 1986 $24 (6/30/88) (BT)
80+ CHATEAU MAZERIS Canon-Fronsac 1986 $12 (6/30/88) (BT)
80+ CHATEAU MONTVIEL Pomerol 1986 $29 (6/30/88) (BT)
80+ CHATEAU MOULINET Pomerol 1986 $15 (6/30/88) (BT)
80+ CHATEAU PIQUE-CAILLOU Pessac-Léognan 1986 ($NA) (6/30/88) (BT)
80+ CHATEAU PUY-BLANQUET St.-Emilion 1986 $16 (6/30/88) (BT)
80+ CHATEAU DU ROCHER-BELLEVUE-FIGEAC St.-Emilion 1986 Rel: $12 Cur: $17 (5/15/87) (BT)
80+ CHATEAU TAILLEFER Pomerol 1986 $20 (6/30/88) (BT)
80+ CHATEAU LA TOUR CARNET Haut-Médoc 1986 $22 (5/15/87) (BT)
80+ CHATEAU VILLEMAURINE St.-Emilion 1986 $39 (6/30/88) (BT)
79 CHATEAU BEAU-SEJOUR BECOT St.-Emilion 1986 $22 (7/31/89)
79 CHATEAU BELLERIVE Médoc 1986 $4.50 (2/15/89)
79 CHATEAU CISSAC Haut-Médoc 1986 $20 (11/30/89) (JS)
79 CHATEAU LA CROIX DE MILLORIT Côtes de Bourg 1986 $9/375ml (5/15/91)
79 CHATEAU FAURIE-PASCAUD Bordeaux 1986 $5 (6/30/88)
79 CHATEAU FOURCAS-HOSTEN Listrac 1986 $13 (11/15/89)
79 CHATEAU LAURETAN Bordeaux 1986 $5 (5/15/89)
79 CHATEAU MARQUIS DE TERME Margaux 1986 Rel: $23 Cur: $30 (6/30/89)
79 CHATEAU PEDESCLAUX Pauillac 1986 $18 (2/15/90)
79 CHATEAU ROLAND St.-Emilion 1986 $11.25 (6/30/89)
79 CHATEAU SEGONZAC Premières Côtes de Blaye 1986 $9.75 (6/30/89)
79 CHATEAU SOUDARS Haut-Médoc 1986 $13 (11/30/89) (JS)
79 CHATEAU TOUR-DU-MIRAIL Haut-Médoc 1986 $12 (11/30/89) (JS)
78 CHATEAU BARREYRES Haut-Médoc 1986 $8.25 (6/30/89)
78 CHATEAU BOUSCAUT Pessac-Léognan 1986 Rel: $9 Cur: $14 (2/15/89)
78 CHATEAU BRILLETTE Moulis 1986 $14 (11/30/89) (JS)
78 CHATEAU CANDELAY Bordeaux Supérieur 1986 $5 (6/15/89)
78 CHATEAU CANTELAUDE Haut-Médoc 1986 $17 (6/30/89)
78 CHATEAU CLINET Pomerol 1986 Rel: $25 Cur: $29 (9/15/89)
78 CHATEAU CROIZET-BAGES Pauillac 1986 $15 (6/30/89)
78 CHATEAU LAROSE-TRINTAUDON Haut-Médoc 1986 $10 (11/30/89) (JS)
78 CHATEAU MOULIN HAUT-LAROQUE Fronsac 1986 $11 (11/15/89)
78 LA PETITE EGLISE Pomerol 1986 $15 (9/15/89)
78 CHATEAU RICHETERRE Margaux 1986 $12.50 (2/15/89)
78 ST.-JOVIAN Bordeaux Cabernet Sauvignon 1986 $4.50 (7/31/88)
78 CHATEAU DE SOURS Bordeaux Supérieur 1986 $7 (9/30/89)
77 LA COUR PAVILLON Bordeaux 1986 $7.25 (2/28/91)
77 CHATEAU L'ESPERANCE Bordeaux 1986 $7 (9/30/89)
77 CHATEAU LES GRANDS JAYS Bordeaux Supérieur 1986 $6 (5/15/89)
77 CHATEAU LA PIERRIERE Côtes de Castillon 1986 $6 (12/31/88)
77 CHATEAU ST.-ANDRE-CORBIN St.-Georges-St.-Emilion 1986 $22 (3/31/90)
77 CHATEAU TOUR DE BELLEGARDE Bordeaux Supérieur 1986 $4.75 (5/15/89)
76 CHATEAU CAPBERN-GASQUETON St.-Estèphe 1986 $20 (11/30/89) (JS)
76 CHATEAU CAYLA Premières Côtes de Bordeaux 1986 $7 (6/30/89)
76 CHATEAU LA CROIX DE GIRON Bordeaux Supérieur 1986 $5.25 (5/15/89)
76 CHATEAU FONTENIL Fronsac 1986 $14 (2/15/90)
76 BARONS EDMOND & BENJAMIN ROTHSCHILD Haut-Médoc 1986 $48 (3/31/91)
76 ST.-JOVIAN Bordeaux Merlot 1986 $5 (5/15/89)
76 CHATEAU LA TERRASSE Bordeaux Supérieur 1986 $8 (6/30/89)
76 CHATEAU TOUR-DU-ROC Haut-Médoc 1986 $11 (11/30/89) (JS)
76 CHATEAU VERDIGNAN Haut-Médoc 1986 $15 (11/30/89) (JS)
75 CHATEAU LE BOSCQ Médoc 1986 $10 (6/30/89)
75 CHATEAU CHAUVIN St.-Emilion 1986 $15 (6/30/89)
75 CHATEAU CORMEIL-FIGEAC St.-Emilion 1986 $12 (6/30/89)
75 CHATEAU DE LAMARQUE Haut-Médoc 1986 $12 (11/30/89) (JS)
75+ CHATEAU COS-LABORY St.-Estèphe 1986 $16 (6/30/88) (BT)
75+ CHATEAU DE LA DAUPHINE Fronsac 1986 $20 (6/30/88) (BT)
75+ CHATEAU FOURCAS-DUPRE Listrac 1986 $15 (6/30/88) (BT)
75+ CHATEAU PRIEURS DE LA COMMANDERIE Pomerol 1986 ($NA) (6/30/88) (BT)
74 CHARTRON LA FLEUR Bordeaux 1986 $4.50 (5/15/89)
74 CHATEAU DUPLESSIS-FABRE Moulis 1986 $7 (11/30/89) (JS)
74 CHATEAU LOUDENNE Médoc 1986 $12 (11/30/89) (JS)
73 CHATEAU BONNET Bordeaux 1986 $6 (5/15/89)
73 LAURIOL Côtes de Francs 1986 $8 (6/15/89)
73 CHATEAU DU MOULIN DE PEYRONIN Bordeaux 1986 $10 (3/31/90)
72 CHATEAU GRAND-BARRAIL-LAMARZELLE-FIGEAC St.-Emilion 1986 $15 (6/30/89)
72 YVON MAU Bordeaux Officiel du Bicentenaire de la Revolution Française 1986 $4.50 (6/30/89)
71 CHATEAU DU CHEVALIER Montagne-St.-Emilion 1986 $19 (3/31/91)
70 CHATEAU LES ALOUETTES Bordeaux Kosher 1986 $10 (3/31/90)
70 CHATEAU MAROTTE Bordeaux 1986 $3.50 (4/30/88)
70 CHATEAU LA TONNELLE Haut-Médoc 1986 $11 (11/30/89) (JS)
70+ CHATEAU BARET Pessac-Léognan 1986 $16 (5/15/87) (BT)
70+ CARRUADES DE LAFITE Pauillac 1986 $30 (5/15/87) (BT)
70+ CHATEAU DAUZAC Margaux 1986 $20 (6/30/88) (BT)
70+ CHATEAU FONREAUD Listrac 1986 $10 (6/30/88) (BT)
70+ LES FORTS DE LATOUR Pauillac 1986 $38 (5/15/87) (BT)
70+ CHATEAU LA GARDE Pessac-Léognan 1986 $14 (5/15/87) (BT)
70+ CHATEAU HAUT-CORBIN St.-Emilion 1986 $14 (5/15/87) (BT)
70+ CHATEAU LE JURAT St.-Emilion 1986 ($NA) (5/15/87) (BT)
70+ CHATEAU MAZEYRES Pomerol 1986 ($NA) (6/30/88) (BT)
70+ CHATEAU POUGET Margaux 1986 $16 (5/15/87) (BT)
70+ CHATEAU VILLEGEORGE Haut-Médoc 1986 $13 (5/15/87) (BT)
69 CHATEAU LAMOTHE-CISSAC Haut-Médoc 1986 $12 (11/30/89) (JS)
65+ CHATEAU DE FRANC-MAYNE St.-Emilion 1986 $16 (6/30/88) (BT)

1985

99 CHATEAU MARGAUX Margaux 1985 Rel: $76 Cur: $98 (4/30/88)
98 CHATEAU CHEVAL BLANC St.-Emilion 1985 Rel: $80 Cur: $91 (2/15/91) (JS)
98 CHATEAU PETRUS Pomerol 1985 Rel: $160 Cur: $390 (5/31/88)
97 CHATEAU LAFITE-ROTHSCHILD Pauillac 1985 Rel: $80 Cur: $101 (5/31/88) CS
97 CHATEAU LATOUR Pauillac 1985 Rel: $82 Cur: $91 (4/30/88)
97 CHATEAU LYNCH-BAGES Pauillac 1985 Rel: $37 Cur: $50 (4/30/88) CS
97 CHATEAU MARGAUX Margaux 1985 Rel: $76 Cur: $98 (12/15/89) (JS)
97 CHATEAU PETRUS Pomerol 1985 Rel: $160 Cur: $390 (2/15/91) (JS)
96 CHATEAU HAUT-BRION Graves 1985 Rel: $70 Cur: $83 (4/30/88)
96 CHATEAU LATOUR Pauillac 1985 Rel: $82 Cur: $91 (3/31/90) (HS)
95 CHATEAU BEYCHEVELLE St.-Julien 1985 Rel: $35 Cur: $39 (8/31/88) CS
95 CHATEAU COS D'ESTOURNEL St.-Estèphe 1985 Rel: $33 Cur: $54 (5/15/90) (HS)
95 CHATEAU DUCRU-BEAUCAILLOU St.-Julien 1985 $50 (6/15/88)
95 CHATEAU FIGEAC St.-Emilion 1985 Rel: $37 Cur: $50 (10/31/91) (JS)
95 CHATEAU LAFITE-ROTHSCHILD Pauillac 1985 Rel: $80 Cur: $101 (11/30/91) (JG)
95 CHATEAU LAFLEUR Pomerol 1985 $170 (5/01/89)
95 CHATEAU LA MISSION-HAUT-BRION Graves 1985 $70 (11/15/91) (JS)
95 CHATEAU PICHON-LALANDE Pauillac 1985 Rel: $40 Cur: $52 (2/29/88) CS
94 CHATEAU L'ANGELUS St.-Emilion 1985 Rel: $26 Cur: $32 (3/31/88) CS
94 CHATEAU MOUTON-ROTHSCHILD Pauillac 1985 Rel: $90 Cur: $96 (4/30/88)
94 CHATEAU PICHON-BARON Pauillac 1985 Rel: $32 Cur: $36 (4/30/88)
93 CHATEAU LA CONSEILLANTE Pomerol 1985 Rel: $50 Cur: $60 (2/29/88)
93 CHATEAU LA CROIX Pomerol 1985 $25 (5/15/88)
93 CHATEAU L'EGLISE-CLINET Pomerol 1985 Rel: $30 Cur: $57 (2/29/88)
93 CHATEAU GRUAUD LAROSE St.-Julien 1985 Rel: $31 Cur: $35 (2/28/91) (TR)
93 CHATEAU LARMANDE St.-Emilion 1985 $23 (5/15/88)
93 CHATEAU LYNCH-BAGES Pauillac 1985 Rel: $37 Cur: $50 (10/31/89) (JS)
93 CHATEAU OLIVIER Graves 1985 Rel: $15 Cur: $25 (2/15/89) SS
93 PAVILLON ROUGE DU CHATEAU MARGAUX Margaux 1985 Rel: $23 Cur: $35 (4/15/88) SS
93 CHATEAU PRIEURS DE LA COMMANDERIE Pomerol 1985 $27 (9/30/88)
93 CHATEAU DU TERTRE Margaux 1985 Rel: $14 Cur: $29 (6/30/88) SS
93 CHATEAU TROTANOY Pomerol 1985 Rel: $70 Cur: $76 (4/30/88)
92 CHATEAU LE BON-PASTEUR Pomerol 1985 Rel: $20 Cur: $29 (5/15/88)
92 DOMAINE DE CHEVALIER Graves 1985 Rel: $43 Cur: $62 (9/30/88) CS

FRANCE

Bordeaux Red

92 CLOS RENE Pomerol 1985 Rel: $17 Cur: $20 (3/15/88)
92 CHATEAU L'EVANGILE Pomerol 1985 Rel: $55 Cur: $78 (2/29/88)
92 CHATEAU LEOVILLE-BARTON St.-Julien 1985 Rel: $24 Cur: $33 (4/15/88)
92 CHATEAU LEOVILLE-LAS CASES St.-Julien 1985 Rel: $45 Cur: $56 (2/15/92) (HS)
92 CHATEAU LEOVILLE-POYFERRE St.-Julien 1985 Rel: $19 Cur: $29 (4/30/88)

92 CHATEAU MEYNEY St.-Estèphe 1985 Rel: $16 Cur: $20 (8/31/88)
92 CHATEAU PAVIE St.-Emilion 1985 $38 (5/15/88)
92 CHATEAU RAUSAN-SEGLA Margaux 1985 Rel: $24 Cur: $33 (5/31/88)
91 CHATEAU CANON St.-Emilion 1985 Rel: $34 Cur: $47 (5/15/89) (TM)
91 CHATEAU CLERC-MILON Pauillac 1985 Rel: $18 Cur: $28 (5/15/88)
91 CHATEAU CLINET Pomerol 1985 $34 (4/30/88)
91 CHATEAU LA CROIX DE GAY Pomerol 1985 $33 (3/15/88) CS
91 CHATEAU GRAND-PUY-LACOSTE Pauillac 1985 Rel: $23 Cur: $30 (6/30/88)
91 CHATEAU HAUT-MARBUZET St.-Estèphe 1985 Rel: $25 Cur: $47 (6/30/88)
91 CHATEAU LANGOA BARTON St.-Julien 1985 $20 (6/15/88)

91 CHATEAU MOUTON-BARONNE-PHILIPPE Pauillac 1985 Rel: $18 Cur: $29 (5/15/88) SS
91 CHATEAU LA SERRE St.-Emilion 1985 $15 (5/15/88)
90 CHATEAU D'ANGLUDET Margaux 1985 Rel: $17 Cur: $23 (4/15/88)
90 CHATEAU BOUSCAUT Graves 1985 $15 (12/31/88)
90 CHATEAU BOYD-CANTENAC Margaux 1985 Rel: $22 Cur: $24 (4/15/88)
90 CHATEAU DE FIEUZAL Graves 1985 $24 (6/15/88)
90 CHATEAU GAZIN Pomerol 1985 Rel: $21 Cur: $31 (9/30/88)
90 CHATEAU GRAND-PUY-DUCASSE Pauillac 1985 Rel: $19 Cur: $24 (2/29/88)
90 CHATEAU LA GURGUE Margaux 1985 Rel: $17 Cur: $19 (2/15/88)
90 CHATEAU KIRWAN Margaux 1985 Rel: $29 Cur: $33 (2/15/89)

90 CHATEAU LEOVILLE-LAS CASES St.-Julien 1985 Rel: $45 Cur: $56 (8/31/88)
90 CHATEAU LIVERSAN Haut-Médoc 1985 $16 (4/30/88)
90 CHATEAU MAGDELAINE St.-Emilion 1985 Rel: $40 Cur: $44 (6/30/88)
90 CHATEAU MONTROSE St.-Estèphe 1985 $33 (4/30/88)
90 CHATEAU PALMER Margaux 1985 Rel: $40 Cur: $50 (4/15/88)
90 CHATEAU DE PEZ St.-Estèphe 1985 Rel: $15 Cur: $20 (6/30/88)
90 CHATEAU SIRAN Margaux 1985 $15 (9/30/88)
90 VIEUX CHATEAU CERTAN Pomerol 1985 Rel: $38 Cur: $49 (6/30/88)
90+ CHATEAU DE CAMENSAC Haut-Médoc 1985 $16 (5/15/87) (BT)
90+ CHATEAU CANON-LA-GAFFELIERE St.-Emilion 1985 Rel: $20 Cur: $37 (5/15/87) (BT)

90+ CHATEAU LATOUR A POMEROL Pomerol 1985 $50 (5/15/87) (BT)
90+ CHATEAU MALARTIC-LAGRAVIERE Graves 1985 $22 (5/15/87) (BT)
89 CHATEAU BERNADOTTE Pauillac 1985 $19 (3/31/88)
89 CHATEAU BRANAIRE-DUCRU St.-Julien 1985 Rel: $25 Cur: $29 (6/30/88)
89 CHATEAU BRANE-CANTENAC Margaux 1985 Rel: $24 Cur: $30 (6/30/88)
89 CHATEAU CLOS DES JACOBINS St.-Emilion 1985 $31 (9/30/88)
89 CHATEAU GLORIA St.-Julien 1985 Rel: $14 Cur: $22 (4/15/88)
89 CHATEAU HAUT-BAILLY Graves 1985 $28 (6/15/88)
89 CHATEAU LA LAGUNE Haut-Médoc 1985 Rel: $22 Cur: $29 (5/15/88)
89 CHATEAU LES ORMES DE PEZ St.-Estèphe 1985 $16 (4/30/88)

89 CHATEAU PAVIE-DECESSE St.-Emilion 1985 $27 (3/31/88)
89 CHATEAU DE ROUFFLIAC St.-Emilion 1985 $15 (9/30/88)
89 CHATEAU SMITH-HAUT-LAFITTE Graves 1985 Rel: $15 Cur: $23 (11/30/88)
89 CHATEAU TERTRE-ROTEBOEUF St.-Emilion 1985 Rel: $23 Cur: $27 (6/30/88)
88 CHATEAU CALON-SEGUR St.-Estèphe 1985 $30 (5/31/88)
88 CHATEAU CANTEMERLE Haut-Médoc 1985 $30 (8/31/88)
88 CLOS DU CLOCHER Pomerol 1985 Rel: $17 Cur: $20 (2/29/88)
88 CHATEAU FEYTIT-CLINET Pomerol 1985 $30 (4/30/88)
88 CHATEAU GRAND ORMEAU Lalande-de-Pomerol 1985 $16 (5/31/88)
88 CHATEAU HAUT-BAGES-LIBERAL Pauillac 1985 Rel: $16 Cur: $24 (4/30/88)

88 CHATEAU D'ISSAN Margaux 1985 Rel: $23 Cur: $26 (4/15/88)
88 CHATEAU MAUCAILLOU Moulis 1985 $18 (8/31/88)
88 CHATEAU TROPLONG-MONDOT St.-Emilion 1985 $21 (6/30/88)
88 CHATEAU LA VIEILLE CURE Fronsac 1985 $15 (12/31/88)
87 CHATEAU AUSONE St.-Emilion 1985 $100 (5/31/88)
87 CHATEAU CARBONNIEUX Graves 1985 Rel: $16 Cur: $18 (11/30/88)
87 CHATEAU CHAMBERT-MARBUZET St.-Estèphe 1985 Rel: $28 Cur: $32 (6/30/88)
87 CHATEAU LA CLOTTE St.-Emilion 1985 Rel: $27 Cur: $32 (5/15/88)
87 CHATEAU COS-LABORY St.-Estèphe 1985 $16 (4/30/88)
87 CHATEAU DAUZAC Margaux 1985 $21 (9/30/88)

87 CHATEAU DUHART-MILON Pauillac 1985 $34 (6/30/88)
87 CHATEAU FOMBRAUGE St.-Emilion 1985 Rel: $15 Cur: $22 (5/15/88)
87 CHATEAU FONTENIL Fronsac 1985 Rel: $14 Cur: $17 (9/30/88)
87 LES FORTS DE LATOUR Pauillac 1985 Rel: $40 Cur: $51 (8/31/91)
87 CHATEAU LANESSAN Haut-Médoc 1985 $16 (4/30/88)
87 CHATEAU LA LOUVIERE Graves 1985 $16 (6/30/88)
87 CHATEAU MALESCOT-ST.-EXUPERY Margaux 1985 Rel: $24 Cur: $27 (9/30/88)
87 CHATEAU DE MARBUZET St.-Estèphe 1985 Rel: $11 Cur: $21 (6/30/88)
87 CHATEAU POUJEAUX Moulis 1985 $18 (9/30/88)
87 CHATEAU ST.-GEORGES St.-Georges-St.-Emilion 1985 $11 (7/31/89)

87 CHATEAU DE SALES Pomerol 1985 Rel: $14 Cur: $18 (6/30/88)
87 CHATEAU TALBOT St.-Julien 1985 $26 (4/30/88)
87 CHATEAU LA TOUR-MARTILLAC Graves 1985 $19 (8/31/88)
86 CHATEAU BOURGNEUF-VAYRON Pomerol 1985 $28 (11/30/88)
86 CHATEAU CERTAN DE MAY Pomerol 1985 Rel: $70 Cur: $84 (4/30/88)
86 CHATEAU CHASSE-SPLEEN Moulis 1985 Rel: $22 Cur: $30 (5/15/88)
86 CHATEAU CORBIN St.-Emilion 1985 $15 (5/31/88)
86 CHATEAU LA FLEUR-PETRUS Pomerol 1985 Rel: $50 Cur: $62 (6/30/88)
86 CHATEAU GISCOURS Margaux 1985 $35 (9/30/88)

86 CHATEAU LA TOUR-HAUT-BRION Graves 1985 $42 (2/15/89)
85 CHATEAU L'ARROSEE St.-Emilion 1985 Rel: $24 Cur: $47 (2/29/88)
85 CHATEAU DE BEL-AIR Lalande-de-Pomerol 1985 $18 (9/30/88)
85 CHATEAU CAPBERN-GASQUETON St.-Estèphe 1985 Rel: $18 Cur: $23 (8/31/88)
85 CHATEAU CERTAN-GIRAUD Pomerol 1985 $25 (4/30/88)
85 CHATEAU COUFRAN Haut-Médoc 1985 Rel: $11 Cur: $17 (6/30/88)
85 CHATEAU DE CRUZEAU Graves 1985 $9 (6/15/88) BB
85 CHATEAU PICHON Haut-Médoc 1985 $13 (8/31/88)
85 CHATEAU RESPIDE-MEDEVILLE Graves 1985 $12 (2/29/88)
85 CHATEAU DE ROCHEMORIN Graves 1985 Rel: $9 Cur: $14 (6/15/88)
85 BARON PHILIPPE DE ROTHSCHILD St.-Emilion 1985 $10.50 (9/30/88)

85 CHATEAU SEGONZAC Premières Côtes de Blaye 1985 $9 (2/15/88)
85 CHATEAU SOCIANDO-MALLET Haut-Médoc 1985 Rel: $17 Cur: $24 (4/30/88)
85 CHATEAU SOUTARD St.-Emilion 1985 Rel: $20 Cur: $22 (5/15/88)
84 CHATEAU BONNET Graves 1985 $5.50 (4/15/88) BB
84 CLOS DU MARQUIS St.-Julien 1985 Rel: $14 Cur: $20 (9/30/88)
84 COUVENT DES JACOBINS St.-Emilion 1985 $27 (3/31/88)
84 CHATEAU DE LA DAUPHINE Fronsac 1985 $20 (9/30/88)
84 CHATEAU DESTIEUX St.-Emilion 1985 $14 (3/31/88)
84 CHATEAU FUMET-PEYROUTAS St.-Emilion 1985 $7.25 (7/31/88) BB
84 CHATEAU LABEGORCE-ZEDE Margaux 1985 $13 (2/29/88)

84 CHATEAU LAROSE-TRINTAUDON Haut-Médoc 1985 $8.50 (11/30/88) BB
84 CHATEAU LEYDET-FIGEAC St.-Emilion 1985 $18 (9/30/88)
84 MAITRE D'ESTOURNEL Bordeaux 1985 $7.25 (5/31/88)
84 CHATEAU MARQUIS-D'ALESME-BECKER Margaux 1985 Rel: $19 Cur: $30 (6/30/88)
84 CHATEAU TOUR DU HAUT-MOULIN Haut-Médoc 1985 $15 (2/15/89)
83 BARTON & GUESTIER St.-Julien 1985 $13 (2/15/88)
83 CHATEAU LA CARDONNE Médoc 1985 Rel: $9 Cur: $11 (12/31/88)
83 CHATEAU LA DOMINIQUE St.-Emilion 1985 $30 (3/31/88)
83 CHATEAU LAGRANGE St.-Julien 1985 Rel: $23 Cur: $25 (9/30/88)
83 A. MOUEIX Fronsac 1985 $9.50 (9/30/88)

83 CHATEAU MOULIN RICHE St.-Julien 1985 $20 (6/15/88)
83 CHATEAU PAPE-CLEMENT Graves 1985 $44 (6/30/88)
83 CHATEAU PUYGUERAUD Côtes de Francs 1985 $9 (6/30/88)
83 CHATEAU LA TOUR-ST.-BONNET Médoc 1985 $9 (6/30/88)
82 CHATEAU ARNAULD Haut-Médoc 1985 $15 (2/15/88)
82 CHATEAU LA BATISSE Haut-Médoc 1985 $10 (6/30/88)
82 CHATEAU DU BEAU-VALLON St.-Emilion 1985 $8.50 (9/30/88)
82 CHATEAU LA CROIX DU CASSE Pomerol 1985 $25 (5/15/88)
82 CHATEAU HAUT-BAGES-AVEROUS Pauillac 1985 $17 (4/30/88)
82 CHATEAU HAUT-BRETON-LARIGAUDIERE Margaux 1985 $16 (2/15/88)

82 CHATEAU PRIEURE-LICHINE Margaux 1985 $24 (2/15/88)
82 CHATEAU ST.-CHRISTOPHE Médoc 1985 $6.50 (7/31/88) BB
82 CHATEAU TOUR-BALADOZ St.-Emilion 1985 $11.50 (2/29/88)
81 CHATEAU HAUT-BATAILLEY Pauillac 1985 Rel: $17 Cur: $21 (11/30/88)
81 CHATEAU LANDEREAU Bordeaux Supérieur 1985 $6.75 (2/15/88) BB
81 CHATEAU MAYNE-DAVID Côtes de Castillon 1985 $6 (2/28/87) BB
81 CHATEAU TAILLEFER Pomerol 1985 Rel: $19 Cur: $24 (6/30/88)
81 CHATEAU VERDIGNAN Haut-Médoc 1985 $13 (2/15/88)
80 CHATEAU BEL-AIR Haut-Médoc 1985 $5 (3/15/88) BB
80 LE BORDEAUX PRESTIGE Bordeaux 1985 $9.50 (9/30/88)

80 CHATEAU MAISON-BLANCHE Montagne-St.-Emilion 1985 $13 (2/15/89)
80 MOUTON-CADET Bordeaux 1985 $6.50 (5/15/88) BB
80 CHATEAU PERENNE Premières Côtes de Blaye 1985 $7 (2/15/88)
80+ CHATEAU BAHANS-HAUT-BRION Graves 1985 $20 (5/15/87) (BT)
80+ CHATEAU BELAIR St.-Emilion 1985 $29 (4/16/86) (BT)
80+ CHATEAU LA CABANNE Pomerol 1985 $30 (5/15/87) (BT)
80+ CHATEAU CANON DE BREM Canon-Fronsac 1985 $19 (5/15/87) (BT)
80+ CHATEAU CANON MOUEIX Canon-Fronsac 1985 Rel: $15 Cur: $19 (5/15/87) (BT)
80+ CHATEAU CAP DE MOURLIN St.-Emilion 1985 $15 (5/15/87) (BT)
80+ CLOS L'EGLISE Pomerol 1985 Rel: $21 Cur: $25 (5/15/87) (BT)

80+ CHATEAU DESMIRAIL Margaux 1985 $20 (5/15/87) (BT)
80+ CHATEAU DURFORT-VIVENS Margaux 1985 $20 (5/15/87) (BT)
80+ CHATEAU FONROQUE St.-Emilion 1985 $23 (5/15/87) (BT)
80+ CHATEAU LA GAFFELIERE St.-Emilion 1985 $31 (5/15/87) (BT)
80+ CHATEAU LA GRAVE TRIGANT DE BOISSET Pomerol 1985 $24 (5/15/87) (BT)
80+ CHATEAU LAGRANGE Pomerol 1985 $21 (4/16/86) (BT)
80+ CHATEAU LASCOMBES Margaux 1985 Rel: $20 Cur: $31 (5/15/87) (BT)
80+ CHATEAU MAZERIS Canon-Fronsac 1985 Rel: $12 Cur: $16 (5/15/87) (BT)
80+ CHATEAU PONTET-CANET Pauillac 1985 $22 (5/15/87) (BT)
80+ CHATEAU POTENSAC Médoc 1985 Rel: $11 Cur: $21 (5/15/87) (BT)

80+ CHATEAU ST.-ANDRE-CORBIN St.-Georges-St.-Emilion 1985 ($NA) (5/15/87) (BT)
80+ CHATEAU TERTRE-DAUGAY St.-Emilion 1985 Rel: $15 Cur: $18 (5/15/87) (BT)
80+ CHATEAU VILLEGEORGE Haut-Médoc 1985 $13 (5/15/87) (BT)
79 CHATEAU CISSAC Haut-Médoc 1985 $16 (7/31/88)
79 CHATEAU DE CLAIREFONT Margaux 1985 $9.25 (4/30/88)
79 CHATEAU LE CROCK St.-Estèphe 1985 Rel: $16 Cur: $18 (2/15/88)
79 CHATEAU ST.-BONNET Médoc 1985 $6 (4/15/88)
79 CHATEAU TOUR-GRAND-FAURIE St.-Emilion 1985 $9.75 (2/15/89)
78 DOMAINE DE CHEVAL BLANC Bordeaux 1985 $5 (5/15/88)
78 LAURIOL Côtes de Francs 1985 $6.50 (6/30/88)

78 CHATEAU MAISON-NEUVE Montagne-St.-Emilion 1985 $7 (3/15/88)
78 CHATEAU LA TERRASSE Bordeaux Supérieur 1985 $6 (11/15/87)
77 CHEVALIER VEDRINES Bordeaux 1985 $6 (6/30/88)
77 CHATEAU GREYSAC Médoc 1985 $9 (12/31/88)
77 CHATEAU HAUT-GARDERE Graves 1985 $15 (7/31/88)
77 CHATEAU LA TONNELLE Haut-Médoc 1985 $10 (2/15/89)
76 CHATEAU DE BELCIER Côtes de Castillon 1985 $5 (6/30/88)
76 CHATEAU CLAIRAC Premières Côtes de Blaye 1985 $4.50 (4/15/88)
76 CHATEAU GRAND CHEMIN Côtes de Bourg 1985 $8 (6/15/89)
75 CHATEAU D'ARSAC Haut-Médoc 1985 $5.75 (2/15/89)

75 BARTON & GUESTIER Margaux 1985 $12 (4/30/88)
75 CHATEAU BRIOT Bordeaux 1985 $4 (5/15/87)
75 CHATEAU LES CONFRERIES Bordeaux 1985 $3.50 (2/15/88)
75 CHATEAU DUPLESSY Premières Côtes de Bordeaux 1985 $6 (5/31/88)
75 CHATEAU LOUDENNE Médoc 1985 $13 (11/30/88)
75 ST.-JOVIAN Bordeaux 1985 $4.50 (5/15/88)
74 CHATEAU BEAUMONT Haut-Médoc 1985 $8.50 (4/30/88)
74 LA COMBE DES DAMES Bordeaux 1985 $6.50 (3/15/88)
73 CHATEAU CAYLA Premières Côtes de Bordeaux 1985 $4 (5/31/88)
72 CHATEAU LEZONGARS Premières Côtes de Bordeaux 1985 $7 (11/15/87)

Key to Symbols

The scores reported here are the results of blind tastings conducted by our panel of senior editors. Wines that carry the initials below are results of individual tastings.

THE WINE SPECTATOR 100-POINT SCALE 95-100— Classic, a great wine; ***90-94***— Outstanding, superior character and style; ***80-89***—Good to very good, a wine with special qualities; ***70-79*** —Average, drinkable wine that may have minor flaws; ***60-69*** —Below average, drinkable but not recommended; ***50-59*** —Poor, undrinkable, not recommended. "+"— With a score indicates a range; used primarily with barrel tastings to indicate a preliminary score.

SPECIAL DESIGNATIONS SS—Spectator Selection, CS—Cellar Selection, BB—Best Buy, ($NA)—Price not available, (NR)—Not released.

TASTER'S INITIALS (JG)—Jim Gordon, (HS)—Harvey Steiman, (JL)—James Laube, (JS)—James Suckling, (TM)—Thomas Matthews, (TR)—Terry Robards, (PM)—Per-Henrik Mansson, (BT)—Barrel Tasting (these wines were tasted blind from barrel samples), (CA-date)—*California's Great Cabernets* by James Laube, (CH-date)—*California's Great Chardonnays* by James Laube, (VP-date)—*Vintage Port* by James Suckling.

DATE TASTED Dates in parentheses represent the issue in which the rating was published.

72 CHATEAU RAUZAN DESPAGNE Bordeaux 1985 $5.75 (2/15/88)
72 ALFRED SCHYLER Médoc 1985 $8.50 (6/30/88)
72 DOMAINE LA TUQUE BEL-AIR Côtes de Castillon 1985 $8.50 (9/30/88)
71 CHATEAU LES CHARMILLES Bordeaux Supérieur 1985 $8 (2/15/88)
71 CHATEAU HAUT-COLAS NOUET Bordeaux Supérieur 1985 $4 (11/15/87)
71 CHATEAU DE PRIEURE Premières Côtes de Bordeaux 1985 $4.50 (5/31/88)
71 CHATEAU LA TOUR CARNET Haut-Médoc 1985 $22 (12/31/88)
70 CHATEAU BELLERIVE Bordeaux Supérieur 1985 $7 (11/15/87)
70 CHATEAU JALOUSIE-BEAULIEU Bordeaux Supérieur 1985 $7 (12/31/88)
70 CHATEAU ST.-SEVE Médoc 1985 $6 (11/15/87)

70+ LES FIEFS DE LAGRANGE St.-Julien 1985 Rel: $17 Cur: $20 (5/15/87) (BT)
70+ CHATEAU FONPLEGADE St.-Emilion 1985 $15 (5/15/87) (BT)
70+ CHATEAU LAFON-ROCHET St.-Estèphe 1985 $16 (5/15/87) (BT)
70+ CHATEAU PLINCE Pomerol 1985 $17 (5/15/87) (BT)
70+ CHATEAU POUGET Margaux 1985 Rel: $14 Cur: $16 (5/15/87) (BT)
70+ CHATEAU ST.-PIERRE St.-Julien 1985 $19 (4/16/86) (BT)
69 CHATEAU LA GROLET Côtes de Bourg 1985 $5 (5/15/88)
68 CHATEAU PLAGNAC Médoc 1985 $9 (8/31/88)
67 LA COUR PAVILLON Bordeaux 1985 $6.75 (7/15/88)
60+ CHATEAU LE GAY Pomerol 1985 $25 (4/16/86) (BT)
60+ CHATEAU PUY-BLANQUET St.-Emilion 1985 $13 (4/16/86) (BT)
56 CHATEAU LA MADELEINE Pomerol 1985 $10 (3/15/88)

BURGUNDY RED

1989

98 JEAN GROS Richebourg 1989 $180 (1/31/92)
97 A.-F. GROS Richebourg 1989 $130 (1/31/92)
97 DOMAINE MEO-CAMUZET Richebourg 1989 $270 (11/15/91)
96 DOMAINE LEROY Pommard Les Vignots 1989 $75 (1/31/92)
96 DOMAINE LEROY Richebourg 1989 $306 (1/31/92)
96 DOMAINE G. ROUMIER Musigny 1989 $95 (1/31/92)
96 COMTE DE VOGUE Musigny Cuvée Vieilles Vignes 1989 $134 (1/31/92)
95 DOMAINE DU CLOS FRANTIN Richebourg 1989 $117 (1/31/92)
95 FAIVELEY Mazis-Chambertin 1989 $79 (1/31/92)

95 DOMAINE GROS FRERE & SOEUR Richebourg 1989 $130 (1/31/92)
95 DOMAINE MICHEL LAFARGE Volnay Clos des Chênes 1989 $67 (1/31/92)
95 DOMAINE LEROY Clos de Vougeot 1989 $193 (1/31/92)
95 DOMAINE LEROY Corton Renardes 1989 $117 (1/31/92)
95 DOMAINE LEROY Nuits-St.-Georges Aux Boudots 1989 $117 (1/31/92)
95 DOMAINE LEROY Romanée-St.-Vivant 1989 $306 (1/31/92)
95 DOMAINE MEO-CAMUZET Vosne-Romanée Au Cros-Parantoux 1989 $91 (11/15/91)
95+ BOUCHARD PERE & FILS Beaune Grèves Vigne de l'Enfant Jésus 1989 $59 (7/15/90) (BT)
94 BERTRAND AMBROISE Nuits-St.-Georges Les Vaucrains 1989 $38 (1/31/92)
94 BOUCHARD PERE & FILS Volnay Caillerets Ancienne Cuvée Carnot Château de Beaune 1989 $52 (2/29/92) CS

94 PIERRE BOUREE FILS Clos de la Roche 1989 $65 (1/31/92)
94 F. CHAUVENET Pommard Epenottes 1989 $45 (1/31/92)
94 CHOPIN-GROFFIER Clos de Vougeot 1989 $72 (1/31/92)
94 JAFFELIN Clos St.-Denis 1989 $53 (1/31/92)
94 JAYER-GILLES Echézeaux 1989 $101 (1/31/92)
94 DOMAINE MICHEL LAFARGE Volnay Clos du Château des Ducs 1989 $67 (1/31/92)
94 DOMAINE LEROY Chambolle-Musigny Les Fremières 1989 $80 (1/31/92)
94 DOMAINE LEROY Clos de la Roche 1989 $230 (1/31/92)
94 DOMAINE LEROY Vosne-Romanée Les Brûlées 1989 $117 (1/31/92)
94 DOMAINE MEO-CAMUZET Clos de Vougeot 1989 $91 (11/15/91) CS

94 DOMAINE MEO-CAMUZET Nuits-St.-Georges Aux Murgers 1989 $81 (11/15/91)
94 DOMAINE MEO-CAMUZET Vosne-Romanée Aux Brûlées 1989 $91 (11/15/91)
94 MONGEARD-MUGNERET Vosne-Romanée Les Orveaux 1989 $43 (1/31/92)
94 CHARLES MORTET Chambertin 1989 $68 (1/31/92)
94 EMMANUEL ROUGET Vosne-Romanée Cros-Parantoux 1989 $83 (11/15/91)
94 CHRISTOPHE ROUMIER Ruchottes-Chambertin 1989 $70 (1/31/92)
94 COMTE DE VOGUE Bonnes Mares 1989 $93 (1/31/92)
93 BERTRAND AMBROISE Corton Le Rognet 1989 $45 (1/31/92)
93 BOUCHARD PERE & FILS Vosne-Romanée Aux Reignots Château de Vosne-Romanée 1989 (NR) (1/31/92)
93 GUY CASTAGNIER Latricières-Chambertin 1989 $62 (1/31/92)

93 GUY CASTAGNIER Mazis-Chambertin Mazy-Chambertin 1989 $62 (1/31/92)
93 F. CHAUVENET Corton 1989 $50 (1/31/92)
93 CHOPIN-GROFFIER Nuits-St.-Georges Les Chaignots 1989 $40 (1/31/92)
93 CHOPIN-GROFFIER Vougeot 1989 $32 (1/31/92)
93 DOMAINE DU CLOS FRANTIN Echézeaux 1989 $45 (1/31/92)
93 JOSEPH DROUHIN Bonnes Mares 1989 $99 (1/31/92)
93 JEAN GRIVOT Richebourg 1989 (NR) (1/31/92)
93 LOUIS JADOT Chambertin Clos de Bèze 1989 $105 (1/31/92)
93 LOUIS JADOT Corton Pougets 1989 $64 (1/31/92)
93 LOUIS LATOUR Bonnes Mares 1989 (NR) (1/31/92)

93 LOUIS LATOUR Romanée-St.-Vivant Les Quatre Journaux 1989 (NR) (1/31/92)
93 OLIVIER LEFLAIVE FRERES Clos St.-Denis 1989 $56 (1/31/92)
93 DOMAINE LEROY Chambertin 1989 $306 (1/31/92)
93 DOMAINE LEROY Gevrey-Chambertin Les Combottes 1989 $117 (1/31/92)
93 DOMAINE LEROY Latricières-Chambertin 1989 $250 (1/31/92)
93 DOMAINE MEO-CAMUZET Corton 1989 $76 (11/15/91)
93 MOILLARD Vosne-Romanée Malconsorts Domaine Thomas-Moillard 1989 (NR) (1/31/92)
93 MONGEARD-MUGNERET Echézeaux Vieille Vigne 1989 $59 (1/31/92)
93 MONGEARD-MUGNERET Grands Echézeaux 1989 $95 (1/31/92)
93 MONGEARD-MUGNERET Vougeot Les Crâs 1989 (NR) (1/31/92)

93 DOMAINE DANIEL RION Nuits-St.-Georges Les Vignes Rondes 1989 $63 (1/31/92)
93 EMMANUEL ROUGET Echézeaux 1989 $98 (11/15/91)
93 DOMAINE G. ROUMIER Bonnes Mares 1989 $70 (1/31/92)
93 ARMAND ROUSSEAU Chambertin Clos de Bèze 1989 $135 (1/31/92)
93 DOMAINE B. SERVEAU Chambolle-Musigny Les Sentiers 1989 $30 (1/31/92)
93 COMTE DE VOGUE Chambolle-Musigny Les Amoureuses 1989 $93 (1/31/92)
92 BOUCHARD PERE & FILS Chambertin Clos de Bèze 1989 $92 (1/31/92)
92 BOUCHARD PERE & FILS Corton Le Corton Domaines du Château de Beaune 1989 $79 (1/31/92)
92 BOUCHARD PERE & FILS Pommard Clos du Pavillon 1989 (NR) (1/31/92)
92 F. CHAUVENET Echézeaux 1989 $56 (1/31/92)

92 DOMAINE COSTE-CAUMARTIN Pommard Clos de Boucherottes 1989 $38 (1/31/92)
92 DOMAINE COSTE-CAUMARTIN Pommard Les Fremiers 1989 $35 (1/31/92)

92 JOSEPH DROUHIN Beaune Clos des Mouches 1989 Rel: $40 Cur: $46 (2/29/92)
92 JOSEPH DROUHIN Chambolle-Musigny Feusselottes 1989 (NR) (1/31/92)
92 JOSEPH DROUHIN Chambolle-Musigny Les Sentiers 1989 (NR) (1/31/92)
92 JOSEPH DROUHIN Charmes-Chambertin 1989 $80 (1/31/92)
92 JOSEPH DROUHIN Mazis-Chambertin 1989 $86 (1/31/92)
92 JOSEPH DROUHIN Romanée-St.-Vivant 1989 (NR) (1/31/92)
92 DUBREUIL-FONTAINE Corton Clos du Roi 1989 (NR) (1/31/92)
92 FREDERIC ESMONIN Griotte-Chambertin 1989 $80 (3/31/92)

92 FAIVELEY Nuits-St.-Georges Les St.-Georges 1989 $54 (1/31/92)
92 JACQUES GERMAIN Beaune-Teurons 1989 $50 (1/31/92)
92 JEAN GROS Vosne-Romanée Clos des Réas 1989 $70 (1/31/92)
92 DOMAINE GROS FRERE & SOEUR Grands Echézeaux 1989 $80 (1/31/92)
92 OLIVIER LEFLAIVE FRERES Volnay Clos de la Barre 1989 $38 (1/31/92)
92 DOMAINE FRANCOIS LEGROS Chambolle-Musigny Les Noirots 1989 $30 (11/15/91)
92 DOMAINE LEROY Nuits-St.-Georges Aux Allots 1989 $75 (1/31/92)
92 DOMAINE LEROY Nuits-St.-Georges Les Vignerondes 1989 $117 (1/31/92)
92 DOMAINE LEROY Vosne-Romanée Les Beaux-Monts 1989 $117 (1/31/92)
92 DOMAINE MEO-CAMUZET Nuits-St.-Georges 1989 $52 (11/15/91)

92 MOMMESSIN Clos de Tart 1989 $52 (1/31/92)
92 MONGEARD-MUGNERET Richebourg 1989 $95 (1/31/92)
92 LA POUSSE D'OR Volnay Clos d'Audignac 1989 $45 (1/31/92)
92 DOMAINE DANIEL RION Clos de Vougeot 1989 $94 (1/31/92)
92 DOMAINE DANIEL RION Nuits-St.-Georges Hauts Pruliers 1989 $63 (1/31/92)
92 DOMAINE DANIEL RION Vosne-Romanée Les Chaumes 1989 $63 (1/31/92)
92 SERAFIN PERE & FILS Charmes-Chambertin 1989 $65 (1/31/92)
92 SERAFIN PERE & FILS Gevrey-Chambertin Vieilles Vignes 1989 $45 (1/31/92)
92 TOLLOT-BEAUT Corton-Bressandes 1989 $67 (1/31/92)
91 BERTRAND AMBROISE Nuits-St.-Georges en rue de Chaux 1989 $38 (1/31/92)

91 PIERRE BOUREE FILS Beaune Epenottes 1989 $30 (1/31/92)
91 GUY CASTAGNIER Bonnes Mares 1989 $67 (1/31/92)
91 GUY CASTAGNIER Clos St.-Denis 1989 $62 (1/31/92)
91 PHILLIPE CHARLOPIN Chambertin 1989 $35 (11/15/91)
91 F. CHAUVENET Beaune Grèves 1989 $30 (1/31/92)
91 F. CHAUVENET Gevrey-Chambertin Estournelles St.-Jacques 1989 $40 (1/31/92)
91 F. CHAUVENET Nuits-St.-Georges Les Chaignots 1989 $45 (1/31/92)
91 CHOPIN-GROFFIER Nuits-St.-Georges 1989 $32 (1/31/92)
91 DOMAINE BRUNO CLAIR Vosne-Romanée Les Champs Pedrix 1989 (NR) (1/31/92)
91 DOMAINE DU CLOS FRANTIN Clos de Vougeot 1989 $56 (1/31/92)

91 DOMAINE DU CLOS FRANTIN Nuits-St.-Georges 1989 $29 (2/29/92)
91 JOSEPH DROUHIN Chambolle-Musigny 1989 $41 (1/31/92)
91 JOSEPH DROUHIN Clos St.-Denis 1989 $76 (1/31/92)
91 JOSEPH DROUHIN Gevrey-Chambertin Les Cazetiers 1989 $70 (1/31/92)
91 JOSEPH DROUHIN Grands Echézeaux 1989 $114 (1/31/92)
91 JOSEPH DROUHIN Griotte-Chambertin 1989 $90 (1/31/92)
91 JOSEPH DROUHIN Volnay Clos des Chênes 1989 $50 (1/31/92)
91 JOSEPH DROUHIN Vosne-Romanée Les Beaumonts 1989 $70 (1/31/92)
91 DOMAINE DUJAC Clos St.-Denis 1989 $80 (1/31/92)
91 FREDERIC ESMONIN Ruchottes-Chambertin 1989 $80 (3/31/92)

91 FAIVELEY Corton Clos des Cortons 1989 Rel: $68 Cur: $74 (1/31/92)
91 JEAN GARAUDET Beaune Clos des Mouches 1989 $32 (11/15/91)
91 JEAN GARAUDET Pommard Noizons 1989 $34 (11/15/91)
91 JACQUES GERMAIN Beaune Vignes-Franches 1989 $45 (1/31/92)
91 DOMAINE GROS FRERE & SOEUR Clos de Vougeot Musigny 1989 $60 (1/31/92)
91 DOMAINE GROS FRERE & SOEUR Vosne-Romanée 1989 $39 (1/31/92)
91 LOUIS JADOT Beaune Clos des Ursules 1989 $43 (2/29/92)
91 JAFFELIN Corton 1989 $54 (1/31/92)
91 JAFFELIN Echézeaux 1989 $60 (1/31/92)
91 JAFFELIN Romanée-St.-Vivant 1989 $80 (1/31/92)

91 LOUIS LATOUR Beaune Domaine Latour 1989 (NR) (1/31/92)
91 DOMAINE LEROY Savigny-lès-Beaune Les Narbantons 1989 $65 (1/31/92)
91 DOMAINE LEROY Vosne-Romanée Les Genevrières 1989 $75 (1/31/92)
91 DOMAINE MEO-CAMUZET Vosne-Romanée 1989 $47 (11/15/91)
91 DOMAINE MEO-CAMUZET Vosne-Romanée Les Chaumes 1989 $62 (1/31/92)
91 MOMMESSIN Corton Les Grèves 1989 $45 (1/31/92)
91 GEORGES MUGNERET Ruchottes-Chambertin 1989 $66 (4/30/92)
91 JACQUES-FREDERIC MUGNIER Chambolle-Musigny 1989 $41 (1/31/92)
91 LA POUSSE D'OR Santenay Clos Tavannes 1989 $29 (1/31/92)
91 DOMAINE DANIEL RION Nuits-St.-Georges Clos des Argillières 1989 $63 (1/31/92)

91 EMMANUEL ROUGET Vosne-Romanée 1989 $48 (11/15/91)
91 TOLLOT-BEAUT Beaune Clos du Roi Premier Cru 1989 (NR) (1/31/92)
90 BERTRAND AMBROISE Nuits-St.-Georges 1989 $30 (1/31/92)
90 DOMAINE DE L'ARLOT Nuits-St.-Georges Clos des Forêts St.-Georges 1989 (NR) (1/31/92)
90 BOUCHARD PERE & FILS Beaune Marconnets Domaines du Château de Beaune 1989 $39 (1/31/92)
90 GUY CASTAGNIER Charmes-Chambertin 1989 $62 (1/31/92)
90 GUY CASTAGNIER Clos de la Roche 1989 $62 (1/31/92)
90 F. CHAUVENET Clos de Vougeot 1989 $60 (1/31/92)
90 F. CHAUVENET Volnay Clos des Chênes 1989 $40 (1/31/92)
90 CHOPIN-GROFFIER Chambolle-Musigny 1989 $32 (1/31/92)

90 DOMAINE BRUNO CLAIR Morey-St.-Denis en la rue de Vergy 1989 $36 (1/31/92)
90 DOMAINE DU CLOS FRANTIN Grands Echézeaux 1989 $56 (1/31/92)
90 JOSEPH DROUHIN Chambertin 1989 $114 (1/31/92)
90 JOSEPH DROUHIN Volnay Chevret 1989 (NR) (1/31/92)
90 DOMAINE DUJAC Charmes-Chambertin 1989 $72 (1/31/92)
90 RENE ENGEL Grands Echézeaux 1989 $75 (11/15/91)
90 FAIVELEY Beaune Champs-Pimont 1989 $34 (1/31/92)
90 FAIVELEY Chambertin Clos de Bèze 1989 $99 (1/31/92)
90 FAIVELEY Nuits-St.-Georges Les Damodes 1989 $45 (1/31/92)
90 FAIVELEY Pommard Les Chaponnières 1989 $50 (1/31/92)

90 DOMAINE FOREY PERE & FILS Echézeaux 1989 (NR) (1/31/92)
90 JACQUES GERMAIN Beaune Les Crâs 1989 (NR) (1/31/92)
90 DOMAINE HENRI GOUGES Nuits-St.-Georges Les Vaucrains 1989 $49 (1/31/92)
90 A.-F. GROS Clos Vougeot Le Grand Maupertuis 1989 (NR) (1/31/92)
90 JEAN GROS Vosne-Romanée 1989 $39 (1/31/92)
90 LOUIS JADOT Beaune Boucherottes 1989 $38 (1/31/92)
90 LOUIS JADOT Gevrey-Chambertin Clos St.-Jacques 1989 $65 (1/31/92)
90 JAFFELIN Nuits-St.-Georges Les Damodes 1989 $36 (1/31/92)
90 DOMAINE JOBLOT Givry Clos du Cellier aux Moines 1989 $25 (1/31/92)
90 DOMAINE MEO-CAMUZET Nuits-St.-Georges Aux Boudots 1989 $81 (11/15/91)

90 MOMMESSIN Beaune 1989 $18 (1/31/92)
90 MOMMESSIN Nuits-St.-Georges Les Vaucrains 1989 $45 (1/31/92)

FRANCE
Burgundy Red

90 CHARLES MORTET Gevrey-Chambertin Les Champeaux 1989 $34 (1/31/92)
90 JACQUES-FREDERIC MUGNIER Chambolle-Musigny Les Amoureuses 1989 $62 (1/31/92)
90 LA POUSSE D'OR Volnay Clos de la Bousse d'Or 1989 $60 (1/31/92)
90 DOMAINE DANIEL RION Vosne-Romanée Beaux-Monts 1989 $63 (1/31/92)
90 DOMAINE G. ROUMIER Chambolle-Musigny 1989 $38 (1/31/92)
90 ARMAND ROUSSEAU Gevrey-Chambertin Clos St.-Jacques 1989 $93 (1/31/92)
90 ARMAND ROUSSEAU Mazis-Chambertin Mazy-Chambertin 1989 (NR) (1/31/92)
90 ARMAND ROUSSEAU Ruchottes-Chambertin Clos des Ruchottes 1989 (NR) (1/31/92)

90 TOLLOT-BEAUT Aloxe-Corton 1989 (NR) (1/31/92)
90 TOLLOT-BEAUT Beaune Grèves 1989 (NR) (1/31/92)
90 TOLLOT-BEAUT Corton 1989 $67 (1/31/92)
90 TOLLOT-BEAUT Savigny-lès-Beaune Lavières 1989 (NR) (1/31/92)
90+ BOUCHARD PERE & FILS Chambertin 1989 (NR) (7/15/90) (BT)
90+ BOUCHARD PERE & FILS La Romanée Château de Vosne-Romanée 1989 $298 (7/15/90) (BT)
85+ LOUIS JADOT Chapelle-Chambertin 1989 (NR) (7/15/90) (BT)
90+ DOMAINE PIERRE LABET Beaune Coucherias 1989 (NR) (7/15/90) (BT)
90+ MOMMESSIN Beaune Les Epenottes 1989 $23 (7/15/90) (BT)
89 BOUCHARD PERE & FILS Clos de la Roche 1989 (NR) (1/31/92)

89 BOUCHARD PERE & FILS Nuits-St.-Georges Clos-St.-Marc 1989 $59 (1/31/92)
89 BOUCHARD PERE & FILS Nuits-St.-Georges La Richemone 1989 (NR) (1/31/92)
89 F. CHAUVENET Gevrey-Chambertin Clos St.-Jacques 1989 $45 (1/31/92)
89 ROBERT CHEVILLON Nuits-St.-Georges 1989 $36 (1/31/92)
89 ROBERT CHEVILLON Nuits-St.-Georges Les Vaucrains 1989 $65 (1/31/92)
89 DOMAINE BRUNO CLAIR Gevrey-Chambertin Les Cazetiers 1989 $61 (1/31/92)
89 DOMAINE BRUNO CLAIR Savigny-lès-Beaune La Dominode 1989 (NR) (1/31/92)
89 DOMAINE DU CLOS FRANTIN Vosne-Romanée 1989 $30 (1/31/92)
89 JOSEPH DROUHIN Aloxe-Corton 1989 $27 (1/31/92)
89 JOSEPH DROUHIN Chambolle-Musigny Les Baudes 1989 $52 (1/31/92)

89 JOSEPH DROUHIN Chambolle-Musigny Premier Cru 1989 (NR) (1/31/92)
89 JOSEPH DROUHIN Pommard Epenottes 1989 $56 (1/31/92)
89 JOSEPH DROUHIN Vosne-Romanée Les Suchots 1989 $70 (1/31/92)
89 ROBERT DROUHIN Clos de Vougeot 1989 $88 (1/31/92)
89 DOMAINE DUJAC Clos de la Roche Clos la Roche 1989 $80 (1/31/92)
89 RENE ENGEL Echézeaux 1989 $47 (11/15/91)
89 FREDERIC ESMONIN Mazis-Chambertin Mazy-Chambertin 1989 $80 (3/31/92)
89 FAIVELEY Echézeaux 1989 $68 (1/31/92)
89 FAIVELEY Gevrey-Chambertin Les Cazetiers 1989 $47 (1/31/92)
89 FAIVELEY Latricières-Chambertin 1989 $81 (1/31/92)

89 DOMAINE FOREY PERE & FILS Nuits-St.-Georges Les Perrières 1989 (NR) (1/31/92)
89 DOMAINE HENRI GOUGES Nuits-St.-Georges Les St.-Georges 1989 $49 (1/31/92)
89 LOUIS JADOT Vosne-Romanée 1989 $40 (1/31/92)
89 JAFFELIN Aloxe-Corton 1989 $27 (1/31/92)
89 JAFFELIN Beaune Les Champimonts 1989 $27 (1/31/92)
89 JAFFELIN Chambolle-Musigny 1989 $28 (1/31/92)
89 JAFFELIN Clos de Vougeot 1989 $60 (1/31/92)
89 JAFFELIN Volnay 1989 $29 (1/31/92)
89 LOUIS LATOUR Corton Château Corton Grancey 1989 (NR) (1/31/92)
89 DOMAINE LEROY Nuits-St.-Georges Aux Lavières 1989 $75 (1/31/92)

89 MOILLARD Beaune Grèves Domaine Thomas-Moillard 1989 $28 (1/31/92)
89 MOILLARD Corton Clos des Vergennes 1989 $40 (1/31/92)
89 MOILLARD Morey-St.-Denis Monts Luisants 1989 $28 (1/31/92)
89 MOILLARD Nuits-St.-Georges Clos de Thorey Domaine Thomas-Moillard 1989 $35 (1/31/92)
89 MOMMESSIN Vosne-Romanée Aux Brûlées 1989 $38 (1/31/92)
89 CHARLES MORTET Chambolle-Musigny Les Beaux Bruns 1989 $34 (1/31/92)
89 DOMAINE DANIEL RION Chambolle-Musigny Les Beaux Bruns 1989 $45 (1/31/92)
89 DOMAINE DANIEL RION Vosne-Romanée 1989 $37 (1/31/92)
89 SERAFIN PERE & FILS Gevrey-Chambertin Les Cazetiers 1989 $54 (1/31/92)
89 COMTE DE VOGUE Chambolle-Musigny 1989 $44 (1/31/92)

88 DOMAINE D'AUVENAY Auxey-Duresses Rouge 1989 $42 (1/31/92)
88 BICHOT Corton Hospices de Beaune Cuvée Docteur-Peste 1989 $100 (1/31/92)
88 BOUCHARD AINE Chambertin Clos de Bèze Domaine Marion 1989 (NR) (1/31/92)
88 BOUCHARD PERE & FILS Echézeaux 1989 $62 (1/31/92)
88 BOUCHARD PERE & FILS Volnay Taillepieds Domaines du Château de Beaune 1989 $48 (1/31/92)
88 GUY CASTAGNIER Chambolle-Musigny 1989 $39 (1/31/92)
88 CHARLOPIN-PARIZOT Gevrey-Chambertin Cuvée Vieilles Vignes 1989 $75 (11/15/91)
88 F. CHAUVENET Gevrey-Chambertin Lavaux St.-Jacques 1989 $45 (1/31/92)
88 F. CHAUVENET Nuits-St.-Georges Les Pruliers 1989 $45 (1/31/92)
88 F. CHAUVENET Volnay Premier Cru 1989 $36 (1/31/92)

88 DOMAINE DU CLOS FRANTIN Chambertin 1989 $73 (1/31/92)
88 JOSEPH DROUHIN Beaune Grèves 1989 $47 (1/31/92)
88 JOSEPH DROUHIN Clos de la Roche 1989 $77 (1/31/92)
88 MAURICE ECARD Savigny-lès-Beaune Les Serpentières 1989 $25 (11/15/91)
88 FREDERIC ESMONIN Gevrey-Chambertin Les Corbeaux 1989 $42 (3/31/92)
88 FREDERIC ESMONIN Gevrey-Chambertin Lavaux St.-Jacques 1989 $42 (3/31/92)
88 FAIVELEY Morey-St.-Denis Clos des Ormes 1989 $44 (1/31/92)
88 FAIVELEY Vosne-Romanée 1989 $35 (1/31/92)
88 MARIE-PIERRE GERMAIN Aloxe-Corton Les Vercots 1989 (NR) (1/31/92)
88 LOUIS JADOT Fixin 1989 $21 (1/31/92)

88 LOUIS JADOT Pommard Grands Epenottes 1989 $50 (1/31/92)
88 JAFFELIN Gevrey-Chambertin 1989 $30 (1/31/92)
88 DOMAINE JOBLOT Givry Clos de la Servoisine 1989 $25 (1/31/92)
88 DOMAINE MICHEL LAFARGE Volnay 1989 $41 (1/31/92)

Key to Symbols

The scores reported here are the results of blind tastings conducted by our panel of senior editors. Wines that carry the initials below are results of individual tastings.

THE WINE SPECTATOR 100-POINT SCALE 95-100—Classic, a great wine; ***90-94***—Outstanding, superior character and style; ***80-89***—Good to very good, a wine with special qualities; ***70-79***—Average, drinkable wine that may have minor flaws; ***60-69***—Below average, drinkable but not recommended; ***50-59***—Poor, undrinkable, not recommended. "+"—With a score indicates a range; used primarily with barrel tastings to indicate a preliminary score.

SPECIAL DESIGNATIONS SS—Spectator Selection, CS—Cellar Selection, BB—Best Buy, (\$NA)—Price not available, (NR)—Not released.

TASTER'S INITIALS (JG)—Jim Gordon, (HS)—Harvey Steiman, (JL)—James Laube, (JS)—James Suckling, (TM)—Thomas Matthews, (TR)—Terry Robards, (PM)—Per-Henrik Mansson, (BT)—Barrel Tasting (these wines were tasted blind from barrel samples), (CA-date)—*California's Great Cabernets* by James Laube, (CH-date)—*California's Great Chardonnays* by James Laube, (VP-date)—*Vintage Port* by James Suckling.

DATE TASTED Dates in parentheses represent the issue in which the rating was published.

88 OLIVIER LEFLAIVE FRERES Charmes-Chambertin 1989 $60 (1/31/92)
88 OLIVIER LEFLAIVE FRERES Pommard Epenottes 1989 $40 (1/31/92)
88 MOILLARD Fixin 1989 (NR) (1/31/92)
88 MOMMESSIN Aloxe-Corton Les Valzoières 1989 $28 (1/31/92)
88 MOMMESSIN Pommard 1989 $28 (1/31/92)
88 CHARLES MORTET Gevrey-Chambertin 1989 $25 (1/31/92)

88 CHARLES MORTET Gevrey-Chambertin Clos Prieur 1989 $30 (1/31/92)
88 MUGNERET-GIBOURG Echézeaux 1989 $62 (4/30/92)
88 JACQUES-FREDERIC MUGNIER Musigny 1989 $125 (1/31/92)
88 DOMAINE DANIEL RION Nuits-St.-Georges Grandes Vignes 1989 $38 (1/31/92)
88 DOMAINE G. ROUMIER Chambolle-Musigny Amoureuses 1989 $62 (1/31/92)
88 ARMAND ROUSSEAU Gevrey-Chambertin 1989 (NR) (1/31/92)
87 SIMON BIZE & FILS Savigny-lès-Beaune Aux Vergelesses 1989 $27 (1/31/92)
87 BOUCHARD PERE & FILS Aloxe-Corton 1989 $36 (1/31/92)
87 F. CHAUVENET Clos St.-Denis 1989 $60 (1/31/92)
87 DOMAINE BRUNO CLAIR Marsannay Les Longeroies 1989 $18 (1/31/92)

87 DOMAINE COSTE-CAUMARTIN Bourgogne 1989 $15 (1/31/92)
87 JOSEPH DROUHIN Chassagne-Montrachet Rouge 1989 $23 (1/31/92)
87 JOSEPH DROUHIN Pommard Rugiens 1989 $56 (1/31/92)
87 JOSEPH DROUHIN Santenay 1989 $44 (1/31/92)
87 JOSEPH DROUHIN Savigny-lès-Beaune 1989 $23 (1/31/92)
87 MAURICE ECARD Savigny-lès-Beaune Les Peuillets 1989 $25 (11/15/91)
87 RENE ENGEL Vosne-Romanée Les Brûlées 1989 $35 (11/15/91)
87 FAIVELEY Gevrey-Chambertin 1989 $34 (1/31/92)
87 FAIVELEY Gevrey-Chambertin La Combe aux Moines 1989 $47 (1/31/92)
87 JEAN-NOEL GAGNARD Chassagne-Montrachet Rouge Morgeot 1989 $25 (11/15/91)

87 DOMAINE HENRI GOUGES Nuits-St.-Georges Clos des Porrets-St.-Georges 1989 $45 (1/31/92)
87 JEAN GROS Nuits-St.-Georges 1989 $39 (1/31/92)
87 LOUIS JADOT Clos de Vougeot 1989 $74 (1/31/92)
87 LOUIS JADOT Monthélie 1989 $21 (1/31/92)
87 JAFFELIN Charmes-Chambertin 1989 $66 (1/31/92)
87 JAFFELIN Monthélie 1989 $19 (1/31/92)
87 JAYER-GILLES Côte de Nuits-Villages 1989 $32 (1/31/92)
87 LOUIS LATOUR Gevrey-Chambertin 1989 (NR) (1/31/92)
87 OLIVIER LEFLAIVE FRERES Morey-St.-Denis 1989 $30 (1/31/92)
87 DOMAINE FRANCOIS LEGROS Nuits-St.-Georges Les Perrières 1989 $29 (11/15/91)

87 MOMMESSIN Fixin 1989 $15 (1/31/92)
87 MOMMESSIN Maranges 1989 $13 (1/31/92)
87 MONGEARD-MUGNERET Clos de Vougeot 1989 $77 (1/31/92)
87 CHARLES MORTET Bourgogne 1989 $14 (1/31/92)
87 GEORGES MUGNERET Chambolle-Musigny Les Feusselottes 1989 $47 (4/30/92)
87 DOMAINE G. ROUMIER Clos de Vougeot 1989 $62 (1/31/92)
87 TOLLOT-BEAUT Chorey-Côte-de-Beaune 1989 (NR) (1/31/92)
86 BERTRAND AMBROISE Côte de Nuits-Villages 1989 $20 (1/31/92)
86 BICHOT Pommard Hospices de Beaune Cuvée Cyrot-Chaudron 1989 $70 (1/31/92)
86 GUY CASTAGNIER Morey-St.-Denis 1989 (NR) (1/31/92)

86 F. CHAUVENET Pommard Chanlins 1989 $45 (1/31/92)
86 DOMAINE DU CLOS FRANTIN Corton 1989 (NR) (1/31/92)
86 JOSEPH DROUHIN Gevrey-Chambertin Lavaux St.-Jacques 1989 $70 (1/31/92)
86 JOSEPH DROUHIN Morey-St.-Denis Clos Sorbé 1989 (NR) (1/31/92)
86 DOMAINE DUJAC Gevrey-Chambertin Aux Combottes 1989 $65 (1/31/92)
86 FREDERIC ESMONIN Gevrey-Chambertin Estournelles St.-Jacques 1989 $42 (3/31/92)
86 JEAN GARAUDET Monthélie 1989 $22 (11/15/91)
86 DOMAINE HENRI GOUGES Nuits-St.-Georges Les Pruliers 1989 $45 (1/31/92)
86 LOUIS JADOT Pernand-Vergelesses Clos de la Croix de Pierre 1989 $21 (1/31/92)
86 JAFFELIN Chassagne-Montrachet Rouge 1989 $18 (1/31/92)

86 JAFFELIN Morey-St.-Denis Les Ruchots 1989 $30 (1/31/92)
86 JAFFELIN Pernand-Vergelesses 1989 $19 (1/31/92)
86 JAFFELIN Vosne-Romanée 1989 $29 (1/31/92)
86 JAYER-GILLES Bourgogne Hautes Côtes de Nuits 1989 $24 (1/31/92)
86 LUPE-CHOLET Bourgogne Pinot Noir Comte de Lupé 1989 $7.50 (1/31/92)
86 MOILLARD Fixin Clos d'Entre Deux Velles 1989 (NR) (1/31/92)
86 MOMMESSIN Beaune Les Cent Vignes 1989 $23 (1/31/92)
86 CHARLES MORTET Clos de Vougeot 1989 $47 (1/31/92)
86 GEORGES MUGNERET Nuits-St.-Georges Les Chaignots 1989 $43 (4/30/92)
86 CHATEAU DE POMMARD Pommard 1989 (NR) (1/31/92)

86 EMMANUEL ROUGET Nuits-St.-Georges 1989 $48 (11/15/91)
86 SERAFIN PERE & FILS Gevrey-Chambertin Le Fonteny 1989 $50 (1/31/92)
86 DOMAINE B. SERVEAU Morey-St.-Denis Les Sorbets 1989 $30 (1/31/92)
85 BICHOT Bourgogne Château de Montpatey Pinot Noir 1989 $10 (6/15/92) BB
85 SIMON BIZE & FILS Savigny-lès-Beaune Les Bourgeots 1989 $19 (1/31/92)
85 PIERRE BOUREE FILS Gevrey-Chambertin 1989 $35 (1/31/92)
85 GUY CASTAGNIER Clos de Vougeot 1989 $64 (1/31/92)
85 JOSEPH DROUHIN Bourgogne Pinot Noir Laforêt 1989 $9 (4/30/91) BB
85 JOSEPH DROUHIN Maranges Première Cru 1989 $20 (1/31/92)
85 JOSEPH DROUHIN Pommard 1989 $43 (1/31/92)

85 RENE ENGEL Clos de Vougeot 1989 $66 (11/15/91)
85 RENE ENGEL Vosne-Romanée 1989 $34 (11/15/91)
85 FAIVELEY Chambolle-Musigny 1989 $34 (1/31/92)
85 FAIVELEY Clos de Vougeot 1989 $78 (1/31/92)
85 FAIVELEY Fixin 1989 $21 (1/31/92)
85 FAIVELEY Nuits-St.-Georges Clos de la Maréchale 1989 $42 (1/31/92)
85 DOMAINE FOREY PERE & FILS Vosne-Romanée 1989 (NR) (1/31/92)
85 JEAN-NOEL GAGNARD Santenay Clos de Tavannes 1989 $25 (11/15/91)
85 LOUIS JADOT Nuits-St.-Georges Clos des Corvées 1989 $56 (1/31/92)
85 JAFFELIN Auxey-Duresses Rouge 1989 $16 (1/31/92)

85 JAFFELIN Beaune Les Bressandes 1989 $28 (1/31/92)
85 JAFFELIN Fixin 1989 $18 (1/31/92)
85 JAFFELIN Ladoix Côte de Beaune 1989 $13 (1/31/92)
85 JAFFELIN Pommard 1989 $33 (1/31/92)
85 JAFFELIN Santenay 1989 $17 (1/31/92)
85 JAFFELIN Savigny-lès-Beaune 1989 $18 (1/31/92)
85 DOMAINE MICHEL LAFARGE Bourgogne 1989 $19 (1/31/92)
85 LEROY Bourgogne 1989 $18 (1/31/92)
85 MOILLARD Corton Clos du Roi Domaine Thomas-Moillard 1989 $41 (1/31/92)
85 MOILLARD Ladoix Côte de Beaune 1989 (NR) (1/31/92)

85 MOMMESSIN Gevrey-Chambertin Lavaux St.-Jacques 1989 $45 (1/31/92)
85 MONGEARD-MUGNERET Bourgogne 1989 $9.50 (1/31/92)
85 MONGEARD-MUGNERET Vosne-Romanée 1989 $34 (1/31/92)
85 DOMAINE G. ROUMIER Morey-St.-Denis Clos de la Bussière 1989 $38 (1/31/92)

85 DOMAINE F. & L. SAIER Clos des Lambrays 1989 $68 (11/15/91)
85 DOMAINE B. SERVEAU Chambolle-Musigny Les Amoureuses 1989 $50 (1/31/92)
85+ BOUCHARD PERE & FILS Beaune Clos de la Mousse Domaines du Château de Beaune 1989 $36 (7/15/90) (BT)
85+ BOUCHARD PERE & FILS Chambolle-Musigny 1989 (NR) (7/15/90) (BT)
85+ DOMAINE JEAN CHARTRON Puligny-Montrachet Rouge Clos du Caillerets 1989 (NR) (7/15/90) (BT)
85+ MAURICE CHENU Côte de Beaune-Villages 1989 (NR) (7/15/90) (BT)
85+ DOMAINE DU CLOS FRANTIN Vosne-Romanée Les Malconsorts 1989 $32 (7/15/90) (BT)
85+ JOSEPH DROUHIN Nuits-St.-Georges 1989 $43 (7/15/90) (BT)
85+ DUBREUIL-FONTAINE Corton-Bressandes 1989 (NR) (7/15/90) (BT)
85+ JACQUES GERMAIN Beaune Les Boucherottes 1989 $45 (7/15/90) (BT)
85+ JACQUES GERMAIN Beaune Cent Vignes 1989 $45 (7/15/90) (BT)
85+ LOUIS JADOT Beaune Les Chouacheux 1989 $42 (7/15/90) (BT)
85+ LOUIS JADOT Beaune Clos des Couchereaux 1989 $42 (7/15/90) (BT)
85+ LOUIS JADOT Musigny Le Musigny 1989 $100 (7/15/90) (BT)
85+ J. LABET & N. DECHELETTE Clos Vougeot Château de la Tour 1989 $77 (7/15/90) (BT)
85+ LUPE-CHOLET Nuits-St.-Georges Château Gris 1989 $48 (7/15/90) (BT)
84 DOMAINE DU CLOS FRANTIN Gevrey-Chambertin 1989 $29 (1/31/92)
84 DUBREUIL-FONTAINE Pernand-Vergelesses Ile des Vergelesses 1989 (NR) (1/31/92)
84 DOMAINE DUJAC Morey-St.-Denis 1989 $40 (1/31/92)
84 FAIVELEY Bourgogne Joseph Faiveley 1989 $12 (1/31/92)
84 FAIVELEY Nuits-St.-Georges Les Porêts St.-Georges 1989 $42 (1/31/92)
84 JACQUES GERMAIN Chorey-Côte-de-Beaune Château de Chorey-lès-Beaune 1989 $24 (1/31/92)
84 LOUIS JADOT Côte de Beaune-Villages 1989 $18 (1/31/92)
84 JAFFELIN Côte de Nuits-Villages 1989 $15 (1/31/92)
84 JAFFELIN St.-Aubin Rouge 1989 $14 (1/31/92)
84 JAYER-GILLES Bourgogne Hautes Côtes de Beaune Rouge 1989 $24 (1/31/92)
84 LOUIS LATOUR Aloxe-Corton Domaine Latour 1989 (NR) (1/31/92)
84 LOUIS LATOUR Savigny-lès-Beaune 1989 (NR) (1/31/92)
84 OLIVIER LEFLAIVE FRERES Pommard 1989 $32 (1/31/92)
84 DOMAINE MEO-CAMUZET Bourgogne Passetoutgrains 1989 $17 (7/15/91)
84 MOILLARD Bourgogne Hautes Côtes de Nuits Les Vignes Hautes 1989 (NR) (1/31/92)
84 MONGEARD-MUGNERET Nuits-St.-Georges Les Boudots 1989 $49 (1/31/92)
84 A. & P. DE VILLAINE Bourgogne La Digoine Bouzeron 1989 $17 (11/15/91)
83 DOMAINE DE L'ARLOT Côte de Nuits-Villages Clos du Châpeau 1989 (NR) (1/31/92)
83 BICHOT Beaune Hospices de Beaune Cuvée Guigone-de-Salins 1989 $68 (1/31/92)
83 BICHOT Bourgogne Croix St.-Louis Pinot Noir 1989 $9 (6/15/92) BB
83 FAIVELEY Nuits-St.-Georges 1989 $33 (1/31/92)
83 LOUIS JADOT Bourgogne Pinot Noir 1989 (NR) (1/31/92)
83 JAFFELIN Bourgogne Pinot Noir 1989 $10 (1/31/92)
83 JAFFELIN Nuits-St.-Georges 1989 $27 (1/31/92)
83 DOMAINE MEO-CAMUZET Bourgogne 1989 $23 (11/15/91)
83 MOILLARD Aloxe-Corton Les Affouages 1989 (NR) (1/31/92)
83 MOILLARD Bourgogne Hautes Côtes de Beaune Rouge Les Alouettes 1989 $17 (1/31/92)
83 MONGEARD-MUGNERET Fixin 1989 $25 (1/31/92)
83 DOMAINE B. SERVEAU Bourgogne 1989 $10 (1/31/92)
83 DOMAINE B. SERVEAU Chambolle-Musigny 1989 (NR) (1/31/92)
82 BICHOT Bourgogne Pinot Noir Château de Dracy 1989 $9 (6/15/92)
82 BOUCHARD PERE & FILS Savigny-lès-Beaune 1989 $29 (1/31/92)
82 DOMAINE DELARCHE Pernand-Vergelesses 1989 $15/375ml (4/30/91)
82 MICHEL GROS Bourgogne Hautes Côtes de Nuits 1989 (NR) (1/31/92)
82 DOMAINE GROS FRERE & SOEUR Bourgogne Hautes Côtes de Nuits 1989 (NR) (1/31/92)
82 JAFFELIN Côte de Beaune-Villages 1989 $14 (1/31/92)
82 JAFFELIN Santenay La Maladière 1989 $20 (1/31/92)
82 MOILLARD Rully 1989 $14 (8/31/91)
82 MOMMESSIN Auxey-Duresses Rouge 1989 $13 (1/31/92)
82 MUGNERET-GIBOURG Bourgogne 1989 $17 (6/15/92)
81 F. CHAUVENET Monthélie Champs-Fulliot 1989 $20 (1/31/92)
81 DOMAINE BRUNO CLAIR Marsannay Les Vaudenelles 1989 $18 (1/31/92)
81 DOMAINE ROBERT GROFFIER Bonnes Mares 1989 $79 (1/31/92)
81 JAFFELIN Gevrey-Chambertin Lavaux St.-Jacques 1989 $40 (1/31/92)
81 MUGNERET-GIBOURG Vosne-Romanée 1989 $34 (4/30/92)
81 PATRIARCHE Hautes Côtes de Nuits Cuvée Varache 1989 $11 (1/31/92)
80 JOSEPH DROUHIN Nuits-St.-Georges Les Boudots 1989 $70 (1/31/92)
80 LOUIS LATOUR Bourgogne Cuvée Latour 1989 (NR) (1/31/92)
80 LOUIS LATOUR Santenay 1989 (NR) (1/31/92)
80+ BOUCHARD PERE & FILS Pommard 1989 $38 (7/15/90) (BT)
80+ BOUCHARD PERE & FILS Savigny-lès-Beaune Les Lavières Domaines du Château de Beaune 1989 $29 (7/15/90) (BT)
80+ JOSEPH DROUHIN Volnay 1989 $43 (7/15/90) (BT)
80+ DUBREUIL-FONTAINE Savigny-lès-Beaune Les Vergelesses 1989 (NR) (7/15/90) (BT)
80+ LOUIS JADOT Beaune Bressandes 1989 $42 (7/15/90) (BT)
80+ LOUIS JADOT Chassagne-Montrachet Rouge Morgeot Clos de la Chapelle Domaine du Duc de Magenta 1989 (NR) (7/15/90) (BT)
80+ LOUIS JADOT Nuits-St.-Georges 1989 (NR) (7/15/90) (BT)
80+ LOUIS JADOT Pernand-Vergelesses 1989 (NR) (7/15/90) (BT)
80+ LOUIS JADOT Santenay Clos de Malte 1989 (NR) (7/15/90) (BT)
80+ OLIVIER LEFLAIVE FRERES Chassagne-Montrachet Rouge 1989 (NR) (7/15/90) (BT)
80+ MOMMESSIN Echézeaux 1989 (NR) (7/15/90) (BT)
80+ MOMMESSIN Gevrey-Chambertin Estournelles St.-Jacques 1989 (NR) (7/15/90) (BT)
80+ MOMMESSIN Santenay Grand Clos Rousseau 1989 (NR) (7/15/90) (BT)
79 F. CHAUVENET Auxey-Duresses Rouge Le Val 1989 (NR) (1/31/92)
79 DOMAINE B. SERVEAU Chambolle-Musigny Les Chabiots 1989 $30 (1/31/92)
78 DOMAINE DE L'ARLOT Nuits-St.-Georges Clos de l'Arlot 1989 (NR) (1/31/92)
78 DOMAINE ROBERT GROFFIER Bourgogne 1989 $14 (1/31/92)
78 A.-F. GROS Hautes Côtes de Nuits 1989 $19 (6/15/92)
78 LOUIS LATOUR Chambertin Cuvée Hèritiers Latour 1989 (NR) (1/31/92)
78 MONGEARD-MUGNERET Savigny-lès-Beaune Les Narbantons 1989 $28 (1/31/92)
78 HENRI DE VILLAMONT Bourgogne Pinot Noir 1989 $11 (3/31/91)
77 ROBERT CHEVILLON Bourgogne 1989 $16 (1/31/92)
77 JEAN GRIVOT Nuits-St.-Georges Les Boudots 1989 (NR) (1/31/92)
77 MONGEARD-MUGNERET Bourgogne Hautes Côtes de Nuits 1989 $16 (1/31/92)
76 JEAN CLAUDE BOISSET Bourgogne Confërie des Chevaliers du Tastevin 1989 $7 (6/15/92)
76 LABOURE-ROI Chambolle-Musigny Domaine Cottin 1989 $30 (3/31/92)
75 JEAN GRIVOT Vosne-Romanée Les Beaumonts 1989 (NR) (1/31/92)
75 JAFFELIN Chorey-Côte-de-Beaune 1989 $13 (1/31/92)
75+ CHARTRON & TREBUCHET Bourgogne 1989 (NR) (7/15/90) (BT)
75+ MAURICE CHENU Savigny-lès-Beaune 1989 (NR) (7/15/90) (BT)
75+ DOMAINE DUJAC Bonnes Mares 1989 $80 (7/15/90) (BT)
75+ OLIVIER LEFLAIVE FRERES Gevrey-Chambertin 1989 (NR) (7/15/90) (BT)
75+ MOMMESSIN Chassagne-Montrachet Rouge 1989 (NR) (7/15/90) (BT)
70+ MAURICE CHENU Pommard 1989 (NR) (7/15/90) (BT)
70+ LOUIS JADOT Bourgogne 1989 (NR) (7/15/90) (BT)

1988

98 JEAN GROS Richebourg 1988 $190 (2/28/91)
98 ROMANEE-CONTI Romanée-Conti 1988 $600 (4/30/91)
98 ROMANEE-CONTI La Tâche 1988 $450 (4/30/91)
97 A.-F. GROS Richebourg 1988 $190 (2/15/91)
97 ROMANEE-CONTI Romanée-St.-Vivant 1988 $360 (4/30/91)
96 LOUIS JADOT Chambertin Clos de Bèze 1988 $97 (3/15/91)
96 LEROY Richebourg 1988 $325 (4/30/91)
96 DOMAINE MEO-CAMUZET Richebourg 1988 $253 (11/30/90)
96 EMMANUEL ROUGET Echézeaux 1988 $81 (11/15/90)
95 LEROY Romanée-St.-Vivant 1988 $325 (4/30/91)
95 ARMAND ROUSSEAU Chambertin Clos de Bèze 1988 $188 (5/15/91)
95+ DOMAINE DU CLOS FRANTIN Echézeaux 1988 $56 (7/15/90) (BT)
95+ FAIVELEY Chambertin Clos de Bèze 1988 $114 (7/15/90) (BT)
95+ MOMMESSIN Clos de Tart 1988 $112 (7/15/90) (BT)
94 JOSEPH DROUHIN Chambertin 1988 $112 (2/15/91)
94 JEAN GROS Vosne-Romanée Clos des Réas 1988 $50 (2/28/91)
94 DOMAINE GROS FRERE & SOEUR Grands Echézeaux 1988 $110 (3/15/91)
94 LOUIS JADOT Griotte-Chambertin 1988 $75 (3/15/91)
94 HENRI JAYER Echézeaux 1988 $140 (5/15/91) (HS)
94 DOMAINE MEO-CAMUZET Vosne-Romanée Au Cros-Parantoux 1988 $84 (11/30/90)
94 ROMANEE-CONTI Richebourg 1988 $400 (4/30/91)
93 BERTRAND AMBROISE Nuits-St.-Georges en rue de Chaux 1988 $40 (5/15/91)
93 GUY CASTAGNIER Latricières-Chambertin 1988 $63 (7/15/91)
93 DOMAINE CECI Clos de Vougeot 1988 $48 (7/15/91)
93 JOSEPH DROUHIN Charmes-Chambertin 1988 $65 (11/15/90)
93 JOSEPH DROUHIN Clos de la Roche 1988 $73 (2/15/91)
93 JOSEPH DROUHIN Echézeaux 1988 $60 (11/15/90)
93 DROUHIN-LAROZE Bonnes Mares 1988 $81 (12/31/90)
93 DOMAINE ROBERT GROFFIER Chambolle-Musigny Amoureuses 1988 $66 (11/15/90)
93 LOUIS JADOT Chapelle-Chambertin 1988 $75 (3/15/91)
93 LOUIS JADOT Corton Pougets 1988 $61 (3/31/91)
93 HENRI JAYER Vosne-Romanée Cros-Parantoux 1988 ($NA) (5/15/91) (HS)
93 LEROY Vosne-Romanée Les Beaux Monts 1988 $180 (4/30/91)
93 DOMAINE LEROY Nuits-St.-Georges Aux Boudots 1988 $230 (4/30/91)
93 DOMAINE DANIEL RION Nuits-St.-Georges Les Lavières 1988 $33 (2/15/91)
93 DOMAINE DANIEL RION Vosne-Romanée Les Chaumes 1988 $54 (1/31/91)
93 ARMAND ROUSSEAU Chambertin 1988 $201 (5/15/91)
93 COMTE DE VOGUE Musigny Cuvée Vieilles Vignes 1988 Rel: $134 Cur: $149 (12/31/90)
92 MAISON AMBROISE Corton Le Rognet 1988 $43 (11/30/90)
92 CHOPIN-GROFFIER Vougeot 1988 $32 (5/15/91)
92 JOSEPH DROUHIN Corton-Bressandes 1988 $60 (11/15/90)
92 JOSEPH DROUHIN Morey-St.-Denis Monts-Luisants 1988 $38 (2/28/91)
92 DROUHIN-LAROZE Chambertin Clos de Bèze 1988 $88 (12/31/90)
92 RENE ENGEL Echézeaux 1988 $56 (3/31/91)
92 DOMAINE GROS FRERE & SOEUR Clos de Vougeot Musigny 1988 $95 (3/31/91)
92 LOUIS JADOT Beaune Boucherottes 1988 $33 (3/31/91)
92 DOMAINE MEO-CAMUZET Clos de Vougeot 1988 $95 (11/30/90)
92 DOMAINE MEO-CAMUZET Nuits-St.-Georges Aux Boudots 1988 $80 (11/30/90)
92 GEORGES MUGNERET Ruchottes-Chambertin 1988 $80 (11/15/90)
92 DOMAINE PONSOT Chambolle-Musigny Les Charmes 1988 $58 (4/30/91)
92 DOMAINE DANIEL RION Clos de Vougeot 1988 $75 (1/31/91)
92 DOMAINE DANIEL RION Nuits-St.-Georges Les Vignes Rondes 1988 $54 (1/31/91)
92 DOMAINE DANIEL RION Vosne-Romanée Beaux-Monts 1988 $53 (2/15/91)
92 ROMANEE-CONTI Echézeaux 1988 $225 (4/30/91)
92 ROMANEE-CONTI Grands Echézeaux 1988 $315 (4/30/91)
92 ROSSIGNOL-FEVRIER Volnay 1988 $32 (3/31/91)
92 SERAFIN PERE & FILS Gevrey-Chambertin 1988 $35 (3/31/91)
92 SERAFIN PERE & FILS Gevrey-Chambertin Le Fonteny 1988 $50 (5/15/91)
92 LOUIS TRAPET Chambertin 1988 $133 (7/15/91)
91 ROBERT ARNOUX Romanée-St.-Vivant 1988 $250 (11/15/90)
91 BOUCHARD PERE & FILS Beaune Grèves Vigne de l'Enfant Jésus 1988 $59 (4/30/91)
91 BOUCHARD PERE & FILS Corton Le Corton Domaines du Château de Beaune 1988 $77 (3/31/91)
91 PIERRE BOUREE FILS Clos de la Roche 1988 $85 (3/31/91)
91 GUY CASTAGNIER Clos de la Roche 1988 $63 (7/15/91)
91 GUY CASTAGNIER Mazis-Chambertin Mazy-Chambertin 1988 $63 (7/15/91)
91 DOMAINE CECI Chambolle-Musigny Aux Echanges 1988 $33 (7/15/91)
91 A. CHOPIN Nuits-St.-Georges Aux Murgers 1988 $28 (7/15/90)
91 JOSEPH DROUHIN Griotte-Chambertin 1988 $81 (11/15/90)
91 DROUHIN-LAROZE Latricières-Chambertin 1988 $68 (12/31/90)
91 RENE ENGEL Clos de Vougeot 1988 $75 (3/15/91)
91 A.-F. GROS Echézeaux 1988 $84 (2/15/91)
91 DOMAINE GROS FRERE & SOEUR Richebourg 1988 $192 (2/28/91)
91 LOUIS JADOT Beaune Clos des Ursules 1988 $40 (3/31/91)
91 LOUIS JADOT Gevrey-Chambertin Estournelles St.-Jacques 1988 $50 (3/15/91)
91 LOUIS JADOT Ruchottes-Chambertin 1988 $75 (3/15/91)
91 J. JAYER Echézeaux 1988 $100 (3/15/91)
91 J. LABET & N. DECHELETTE Clos Vougeot Château de la Tour 1988 $50 (11/30/90)
91 DOMAINE MEO-CAMUZET Nuits-St.-Georges 1988 $50 (11/30/90)
91 DOMAINE MEO-CAMUZET Nuits-St.-Georges Aux Murgers 1988 $80 (11/30/90)
91 ALAIN MICHELOT Nuits-St.-Georges 1988 $39 (7/15/91)
91 MOILLARD Morey-St.-Denis Monts Luisants 1988 $30 (12/15/90)
91 ALBERT MOROT Beaune Cent-Vignes 1988 $30 (4/30/91)
91 CHARLES MORTET Gevrey-Chambertin Clos Prieur 1988 $41 (2/15/91)
91 DOMAINE PONSOT Latricières-Chambertin 1988 $150 (5/15/91)
91 DOMAINE DANIEL RION Nuits-St.-Georges Clos des Argillières 1988 $54 (1/31/91)
91 DOMAINE DANIEL RION Nuits-St.-Georges Hauts Pruliers 1988 $54 (1/31/91)
91 ARMAND ROUSSEAU Clos de la Roche 1988 $75 (5/15/91)
91 DOMAINE F. & L. SAIER Clos des Lambrays 1988 $75 (3/31/91)
91 SERAFIN PERE & FILS Gevrey-Chambertin Les Cazetiers 1988 $53 (5/15/91)
90 COMTE ARMAND Pommard Clos des Epeneaux 1988 $46 (2/28/91)
90 BOUCHARD PERE & FILS Pommard 1988 $37 (4/30/91)
90 JEANNE-MARIE DE CHAMPS Nuits-St.-Georges Les Terres Blanches 1988 $39 (7/15/91)
90 DOMAINE DES CHEZEAUX Griotte-Chambertin 1988 $110 (5/15/91)
90 JOSEPH DROUHIN Clos de Vougeot 1988 $85 (2/15/91)

FRANCE

Burgundy Red

90 JOSEPH DROUHIN Vosne-Romanée Les Suchots 1988 $57 (2/28/91)
90 DOMAINE DUJAC Clos de la Roche Clos la Roche 1988 $75 (3/31/91)
90 DOMAINE DUJAC Echézeaux 1988 $70 (3/31/91)
90 FAIVELEY Corton Clos des Cortons 1988 $120 (3/31/91)
90 JEAN GARAUDET Pommard Les Charmots 1988 $46 (11/15/90)
90 JACQUES GERMAIN Beaune-Teurons 1988 $42 (2/15/91)
90 DOMAINE ROBERT GROFFIER Bonnes Mares 1988 $80 (11/15/90)
90 JEAN GROS Vosne-Romanée 1988 $38 (2/28/91)
90 BERNARD HERESZTYN Gevrey-Chambertin Les Goulots 1988 $44 (7/15/91)
90 LOUIS JADOT Beaune Clos des Couchereaux 1988 $33 (3/31/91)
90 DOMAINE MICHEL LAFARGE Volnay Clos des Chênes 1988 $65 (7/15/91)
90 DOMAINE MICHEL LAFARGE Volnay Clos du Château des Ducs 1988 $65 (7/15/91)
90 ALAIN MICHELOT Nuits-St.-Georges Les Chaignots 1988 $56 (5/15/91)
90 REMOISSENET Beaune Grèves 1988 Rel: $30 Cur: $38 (11/30/90)
90 COMTE DE VOGUE Musigny Cuvée Vieilles Vignes 1988 Rel: $134 Cur: $149 (2/28/91)
90+ BOUCHARD PERE & FILS La Romanée Château de Vosne-Romanée 1988 $238 (7/15/90) (BT)
90+ F. CHAUVENET Charmes-Chambertin 1988 $78 (7/15/90) (BT)
90+ F. CHAUVENET Corton-Bressandes 1988 $58 (7/15/90) (BT)
90+ F. CHAUVENET Echézeaux 1988 $50 (7/15/90) (BT)
90+ DOMAINE DUJAC Bonnes Mares 1988 $86 (7/15/90) (BT)
90+ FAIVELEY Clos de Vougeot 1988 $92 (7/15/90) (BT)
90+ FAIVELEY Nuits-St.-Georges Les Porêts St.-Georges 1988 $54 (7/15/90) (BT)
90+ JACQUES GERMAIN Beaune Cent Vignes 1988 $45 (7/15/90) (BT)
90+ JACQUES GERMAIN Beaune Les Crâs 1988 ($NA) (7/15/90) (BT)
90+ JACQUES GERMAIN Beaune Vignes-Franches 1988 $42 (7/15/90) (BT)
90+ LOUIS JADOT Beaune Les Chouacheux 1988 $25 (7/15/90) (BT)
90+ JAFFELIN Charmes-Chambertin 1988 $68 (7/15/90) (BT)
90+ OLIVIER LEFLAIVE FRERES Clos de la Roche 1988 $60 (7/15/90) (BT)
90+ LUPE-CHOLET Bonnes Mares 1988 ($NA) (7/15/90) (BT)
90+ LUPE-CHOLET Nuits-St.-Georges Château Gris 1988 $50 (7/15/90) (BT)
90+ MOMMESSIN Chambolle-Musigny Les Charmes 1988 $42 (7/15/90) (BT)
90+ MOMMESSIN Corton-Bressandes 1988 $30 (7/15/90) (BT)
90+ TOLLOT-BEAUT Corton-Bressandes 1988 $55 (7/15/90) (BT)
89 DOMAINE PIERRE AMIOT Gevrey-Chambertin Les Combottes 1988 $64 (3/15/91)
89 BOUCHARD PERE & FILS Chambertin Clos de Bèze 1988 $82 (4/30/91)
89 BOUCHARD PERE & FILS Pommard Premier Cru Domaines du Château de Beaune 1988 $53 (3/31/91)
89 PIERRE BOUREE FILS Charmes-Chambertin 1988 $75 (3/31/91)
89 GUY CASTAGNIER Clos St.-Denis 1988 $63 (7/15/91)
89 JEANNE-MARIE DE CHAMPS Nuits-St.-Georges Les Didiers Hospices de Nuits Cuvée Jacques Duret 1988 $49 (9/30/90)
89 DOMAINE CHANDON DE BRIAILLES Corton-Bressandes 1988 $75 (2/28/91)
89 DROUHIN-LAROZE Clos de Vougeot 1988 $81 (12/31/90)
89 RENE ENGEL Vosne-Romanée Les Brûlées 1988 $45 (2/28/91)
89 FAIVELEY Gevrey-Chambertin Les Cazetiers 1988 $57 (3/31/91)
89 JEAN GRIVOT Nuits-St.-Georges Les Pruliers 1988 Rel: $53 Cur: $57 (4/30/91)
89 DOMAINE ROBERT GROFFIER Chambolle-Musigny Les Sentiers 1988 $45 (11/15/90)
89 DOMAINE GROS FRERE & SOEUR Vosne-Romanée 1988 $46 (3/31/91)
89 HAEGELEN-JAYER Nuits-St.-Georges Les Damodes 1988 $39 (5/15/91)
89 LOUIS JADOT Nuits-St.-Georges Clos des Corvées 1988 $49 (2/28/91)
89 HENRI JAYER Vosne-Romanée Les Beaumonts 1988 ($NA) (5/15/91) (HS)
89 LEROY Clos de Vougeot 1988 $260 (4/30/91)
89 DOMAINE LEROY Nuits-St.-Georges Aux Allots 1988 $84 (4/30/91)
89 BERTRAND MACHARD DE GRAMONT Vosne-Romanée Les Réas 1988 $32 (7/15/91)
89 DOMAINE MEO-CAMUZET Vosne-Romanée Aux Brûlées 1988 $84 (11/30/90)
89 ALAIN MICHELOT Nuits-St.-Georges Les Richemone 1988 $54 (5/15/91)
89 MOILLARD Nuits-St.-Georges Clos de Thorey Domaine Thomas-Moillard 1988 $50 (12/31/90)
89 MOILLARD Nuits-St.-Georges Hospices de Nuits Cuvée Jacques Duret 1988 $68 (8/31/91)
89 CHARLES MORTET Gevrey-Chambertin 1988 $35 (2/15/91)
89 MUGNERET-GIBOURG Echézeaux 1988 $70 (11/15/90)
89 JACQUES-FREDERIC MUGNIER Chambolle-Musigny Les Fuées 1988 $60 (5/15/91)
89 DOMAINE PONSOT Clos de la Roche Cuvée William 1988 $150 (5/15/91)
89 DOMAINE PONSOT Griotte-Chambertin 1988 $150 (5/15/91)
89 DOMAINE G. ROUMIER Chambolle-Musigny 1988 $30 (7/15/91)
89 JACQUES THEVENOT-MACHAL Volnay-Santenots 1988 $36 (11/15/90)
89 LOUIS TRAPET Chambertin Cuvée Vieilles Vignes 1988 $133 (7/15/91)
89 LOUIS TRAPET Chapelle-Chambertin 1988 $84 (7/15/91)
89 COMTE DE VOGUE Bonnes Mares 1988 $93 (3/31/91)
89 COMTE DE VOGUE Chambolle-Musigny Les Amoureuses 1988 $93 (2/28/91)
88 GHISLAINE BARTHOD Chambolle-Musigny 1988 $50 (3/15/91)
88 JEAN-MARC BOILLOT Beaune Montrevenots 1988 $37 (5/15/91)
88 BOUCHARD PERE & FILS Volnay Taillepieds Domaines du Château de Beaune 1988 $50 (3/31/91)
88 ALAIN BURGUET Gevrey-Chambertin Vieilles Vignes 1988 $45 (12/31/90)
88 DOMAINE CHANTEL-LESCURE Pommard Les Bertins 1988 $40 (11/30/90)
88 DOMAINE JEAN CHARTRON Beaune Hospices de Beaune Cuvée Cyrot-Chaudron 1988 $40 (2/15/91)
88 JOSEPH DROUHIN Beaune Clos des Mouches 1988 $50 (2/15/91)
88 DROUHIN-LAROZE Chapelle-Chambertin 1988 $68 (12/31/90)
88 DROUHIN-LAROZE Gevrey-Chambertin Clos Prieur 1988 $44 (12/31/90)
88 JEAN GARAUDET Monthélie 1988 $23 (11/15/90)
88 JEAN GARAUDET Pommard 1988 $37 (11/15/90)
88 CHATEAU DES HERBEUX Volnay Santenots 1988 $36 (11/30/90)
88 LOUIS JADOT Bonnes Mares 1988 $65 (3/15/91)
88 LOUIS JADOT Gevrey-Chambertin Clos St.-Jacques 1988 $52 (3/15/91)
88 LOUIS JADOT Nuits-St.-Georges Les Boudots 1988 $49 (2/28/91)
88 JAFFELIN Chambolle-Musigny 1988 $32 (12/31/90)
88 JAFFELIN Gevrey-Chambertin 1988 $25 (8/31/91)
88 JAFFELIN Volnay 1988 $30 (8/31/91)
88 JAYER-GILLES Bourgogne Hautes Côtes de Beaune Rouge 1988 $26 (5/15/91)
88 DOMAINE LEROY Pommard Les Vignots 1988 $84 (4/30/91)
88 BERTRAND MACHARD DE GRAMONT Nuits-St.-Georges Les Hauts Pruliers 1988 $37 (7/15/91)
88 DOMAINE MEO-CAMUZET Vosne-Romanée Les Chaumes 1988 $60 (11/30/90)
88 MOILLARD Beaune Hospices de Beaune Cuvée Clos des Avaux 1988 $80 (8/31/91)
88 MOILLARD Vosne-Romanée Malconsorts Domaine Thomas-Moillard 1988 $50 (3/31/91)
88 MONGEARD-MUGNERET Echézeaux Vieille Vigne 1988 $61 (2/15/91)
88 DOMAINE PONSOT Clos de la Roche Cuvée Vieilles Vignes 1988 $185 (5/15/91)
88 POTHIER-RIEUSSET Beaune Boucherottes 1988 $35 (11/30/90)
88 LA POUSSE D'OR Pommard Les Jarollières 1988 $57 (8/31/91)
88 DOMAINE B. SERVEAU Morey-St.-Denis Les Sorbets 1988 $35 (2/28/91)
88 TOLLOT-BEAUT Chorey-lès-Beaune 1988 $25 (12/31/90)
87 DOMAINE DE L'ARLOT Nuits-St.-Georges Clos de l'Arlot 1988 $43 (3/31/91)
87 GHISLAINE BARTHOD Chambolle-Musigny Les Crâs 1988 $45 (2/28/91)
87 BICHOT Pommard 1988 $25 (8/31/91)
87 BICHOT Volnay Hospices de Beaune Cuvée Blondeau 1988 $60 (6/15/92)
87 BICHOT Vosne-Romanée Les Beaux Monts 1988 $34 (7/15/90)
87 BOUCHARD PERE & FILS Volnay Caillerets Ancienne Cuvée Carnot Château de Beaune 1988 $47 (3/31/91)
87 GUY CASTAGNIER Bonnes Mares 1988 $67 (7/15/91)
87 CHANSON PERE & FILS Vosne-Romanée Suchots 1988 $55 (9/30/90)
87 CHARTRON & TREBUCHET Pommard Les Epenottes 1988 $45 (2/28/91)
87 CHOPIN-GROFFIER Clos de Vougeot 1988 $70 (5/15/91)
87 DOMAINE DU CLOS FRANTIN Gevrey-Chambertin 1988 $37 (7/15/90)
87 JOSEPH DROUHIN Chambolle-Musigny Les Amoureuses 1988 $76 (12/31/90)
87 JOSEPH DROUHIN Latricières-Chambertin 1988 $72 (2/15/91)
87 DOMAINE ALETH GIRARDIN Pommard Charmots 1988 $44 (7/15/91)
87 JEAN GRIVOT Nuits-St.-Georges Les Boudots 1988 $54 (4/30/91)
87 CHATEAU DES HERBEUX Chambertin 1988 $75 (12/31/90)
87 DOMAINE MICHEL LAFARGE Volnay Premier Cru 1988 $44 (7/15/91)
87 LAROCHE Nuits-St.-Georges 1988 $28 (11/15/90)
87 LEROY Bourgogne d'Auvenay 1988 $15 (4/30/91)
87 DOMAINE MEO-CAMUZET Vosne-Romanée 1988 $50 (12/31/90)
87 CHATEAU DE MEURSAULT Volnay Clos des Chênes 1988 $47 (7/15/91)
87 ALAIN MICHELOT Nuits-St.-Georges Les Vaucrains 1988 $56 (5/15/91)
87 ALBERT MOROT Beaune Bressandes 1988 $30 (3/31/91)
87 CHARLES MORTET Gevrey-Chambertin Les Champeaux 1988 $46 (3/15/91)
87 DOMAINE DANIEL RION Chambolle-Musigny Les Beaux Bruns 1988 $37 (1/31/91)
86 DOMAINE PIERRE AMIOT Clos de la Roche 1988 $75 (3/15/91)
86 ROBERT ARNOUX Vosne-Romanée Les Suchots 1988 $60 (2/28/91)
86 GUY CASTAGNIER Clos de Vougeot 1988 $65 (8/31/91)
86 DOMAINE CHANDON DE BRIAILLES Savigny-lès-Beaune Les Lavières 1988 $31 (2/28/91)
86 DOMAINE DUJAC Gevrey-Chambertin Aux Combottes 1988 $54 (3/31/91)
86 JEAN-NOEL GAGNARD Chassagne-Montrachet Rouge Morgeot 1988 $20 (12/31/90)
86 JEAN GARAUDET Beaune Clos des Mouches 1988 $40 (11/15/90)
86 CHATEAU DES HERBEUX Clos de Vougeot 1988 $65 (11/30/90)
86 LOUIS JADOT Pernand-Vergelesses Clos de la Croix de Pierre 1988 $17 (3/31/91)
86 LOUIS JADOT Pommard Grands Epenottes 1988 $38 (3/31/91)
86 JESSIAUME PERE & FILS Santenay Gravières 1988 $21 (3/31/91)
86 LABOURE-ROI Chambolle-Musigny 1988 $35 (2/28/91)
86 DOMAINE MAUME Charmes-Chambertin 1988 $60 (7/15/91)
86 ALBERT MOROT Beaune Grèves 1988 $32 (7/15/91)
86 ALBERT MOROT Savigny-lès-Beaune Vergelesses La Bataillère 1988 $26 (3/31/91)
86 GEORGES MUGNERET Chambolle-Musigny Les Feusselottes 1988 $54 (11/15/90)
86 GERARD MUGNERET Vosne-Romanée 1988 $37 (2/28/91)
86 JACQUES-FREDERIC MUGNIER Chambolle-Musigny 1988 $48 (5/15/91)
86 JACQUES-FREDERIC MUGNIER Chambolle-Musigny Les Amoureuses 1988 $80 (5/15/91)
86 PAUL PERNOT Beaune-Teurons 1988 $33 (3/31/91)
86 DOMAINE ROUX PERE & FILS Volnay en Champans 1988 $35 (3/31/90)
86 DOMAINE B. SERVEAU Chambolle-Musigny Les Chabiots 1988 $39 (2/28/91)
86 TOLLOT-BEAUT Beaune Clos du Roi 1988 $53 (2/28/91)
85 DOMAINE DE L'ARLOT Nuits-St.-Georges Clos des Forêts St.-Georges 1988 $53 (3/31/91)
85 PIERRE BOILLOT Volnay-Santenots 1988 $37 (8/31/90)
85 BOUCHARD PERE & FILS Chassagne-Montrachet Rouge 1988 $22 (4/30/91)
85 CHANSON PERE & FILS Pernand-Vergelesses Les Vergelesses 1988 $24 (8/31/90)
85 FRANCOISE & DENIS CLAIR Santenay Clos de la Comme 1988 $25 (6/15/92)
85 JOSEPH DROUHIN Volnay Clos des Chênes 1988 $45 (2/15/91)
85 DOMAINE DUJAC Charmes-Chambertin 1988 $60 (3/31/91)
85 FAIVELEY Nuits-St.-Georges Les Damodes 1988 $52 (3/31/91)
85 JEAN GRIVOT Clos de Vougeot 1988 $70 (4/30/91)
85 LOUIS JADOT Chassagne-Montrachet Rouge Morgeot Clos de la Chapelle Domaine du Duc de Magenta 1988 $20 (3/31/91)
85 LEROY Auxey-Duresses Rouge Les Clous 1988 $52 (5/15/91)
85 DOMAINE MARC MOREY Beaune Les Paules 1988 $24 (8/31/90)
85 DOMAINE PONSOT Clos St.-Denis Cuvée Vieilles Vignes 1988 $165 (7/15/91)
85 DOMAINE PONSOT Morey-St.-Denis Monts-Luisants 1988 $40 (4/30/91)
85 LA POUSSE D'OR Volnay Les Caillerets 1988 $49 (8/31/91)
85 DOMAINE PRIEUR-BRUNET Volnay-Santenots 1988 $35 (11/30/90)
85 G. VACHET-ROUSSEAU Gevrey-Chambertin 1988 $30 (12/31/90)
85+ DOMAINE JEAN CHARTRON Puligny-Montrachet Rouge Clos du Cailleret 1988 ($NA) (7/15/90) (BT)
85+ F. CHAUVENET Beaune Grèves 1988 $25 (7/15/90) (BT)
85+ F. CHAUVENET Clos St.-Denis 1988 $48 (7/15/90) (BT)
85+ F. CHAUVENET Pommard Chanlins 1988 $55 (7/15/90) (BT)
85+ DOMAINE DU CLOS FRANTIN Vosne-Romanée Les Malconsorts 1988 $58 (7/15/90) (BT)
85+ JOSEPH DROUHIN Chambolle-Musigny 1988 $38 (7/15/90) (BT)
85+ JOSEPH DROUHIN Corton 1988 $64 (7/15/90) (BT)
85+ JOSEPH DROUHIN Pommard 1988 $40 (7/15/90) (BT)
85+ JOSEPH DROUHIN Pommard Epenottes 1988 $55 (7/15/90) (BT)
85+ LOUIS JADOT Musigny Le Musigny 1988 Rel: $82 Cur: $100 (7/15/90) (BT)
85+ OLIVIER LEFLAIVE FRERES Volnay Clos de la Barre 1988 $40 (7/15/90) (BT)
85+ MOMMESSIN Volnay Le Clos des Chênes 1988 $38 (7/15/90) (BT)
85+ DOMAINE DANIEL RION Nuits-St.-Georges Grandes Vignes 1988 $33 (7/15/90) (BT)
85+ TOLLOT-BEAUT Aloxe-Corton 1988 $35 (7/15/90) (BT)

Key to Symbols

The scores reported here are the results of blind tastings conducted by our panel of senior editors. Wines that carry the initials below are results of individual tastings.

THE WINE SPECTATOR 100-POINT SCALE 95-100—Classic, a great wine; ***90-94***—Outstanding, superior character and style; ***80-89***—Good to very good, a wine with special qualities; ***70-79***—Average, drinkable wine that may have minor flaws; ***60-69***—Below average, drinkable but not recommended; ***50-59***—Poor, undrinkable, not recommended. "+"—With a score indicates a range; used primarily with barrel tastings to indicate a preliminary score.

SPECIAL DESIGNATIONS SS—Spectator Selection, CS—Cellar Selection, BB—Best Buy, ($NA)—Price not available, (NR)—Not released.

TASTER'S INITIALS (JG)—Jim Gordon, (HS)—Harvey Steiman, (JL)—James Laube, (JS)—James Suckling, (TM)—Thomas Matthews, (TR)—Terry Robards, (PM)—Per-Henrik Mansson, (BT)—Barrel Tasting (these wines were tasted blind from barrel samples), (CA-date)—*California's Great Cabernets* by James Laube, (CH-date)—*California's Great Chardonnays* by James Laube, (VP-date)—*Vintage Port* by James Suckling.

DATE TASTED Dates in parentheses represent the issue in which the rating was published.

85+ TOLLOT-BEAUT Beaune Grèves 1988 $35 (7/15/90) (BT)
85+ TOLLOT-BEAUT Savigny-lès-Beaune Lavières 1988 $28 (7/15/90) (BT)
84 BICHOT Volnay 1988 $25 (8/31/90)
84 CHANSON PERE & FILS Beaune Clos des Fèves 1988 $35 (8/31/90)
84 JOSEPH DROUHIN Bourgogne Pinot Noir Laforêt 1988 $10 (3/31/91) BB
84 DOMAINE MICHEL ESMONIN Gevrey-Chambertin Estournelles St.-Jacques 1988 $40 (3/31/91)
84 FAIVELEY Mercurey Clos du Roy 1988 $22 (3/31/91)
84 JEAN-NOEL GAGNARD Santenay Clos de Tavannes 1988 $25 (11/15/90)
84 JAFFELIN Santenay La Maladière 1988 $21 (8/31/91)
84 DOMAINE JOBLOT Givry Clos du Cellier aux Moines 1988 $19 (12/31/90)
84 MOILLARD Fixin Confrérie des Chevaliers du Tastevin 1988 $19 (8/31/91)
84 GEORGES MUGNERET Clos de Vougeot 1988 $90 (11/15/90)
84 GERARD MUGNERET Vosne-Romanée Les Suchots 1988 $57 (2/28/91)
84 REMOISSENET Bonnes Mares 1988 $80 (12/31/90)
84 DOMAINE B. SERVEAU Chambolle-Musigny Les Amoureuses 1988 $66 (2/28/91)
84 DOMAINE B. SERVEAU Nuits-St.-Georges Chaines Carteaux 1988 $39 (3/31/91)
84 LOUIS TRAPET Latricières-Chambertin 1988 $84 (7/15/91)
83 GHISLAINE BARTHOD Chambolle-Musigny Les Beaux-Bruns 1988 $45 (2/28/91)
83 BOUCHARD PERE & FILS Savigny-lès-Beaune Les Lavières Domaines du Château de Beaune 1988 $29 (4/30/91)
83 VALENTIN BOUCHOTTE Savigny-lès-Beaune Hauts-Jarrons 1988 $31 (2/28/91)
83 JEANNE-MARIE DE CHAMPS Nuits-St.-Georges Les Didiers Hospices de Nuits Cuvée Cabet 1988 $49 (9/30/90)
83 DOMAINE CHANDON DE BRIAILLES Pernand-Vergelesses Ile des Vergelesses 1988 $35 (2/28/91)
83 CHATEAU DES HERBEUX Musigny 1988 $75 (12/31/90)
83 LOUIS JADOT Pommard 1988 $36 (3/31/91)
83 LABOURE-ROI Bourgogne 1988 $12 (3/31/91)
83 LUPE-CHOLET Bourgogne Pinot Noir Comte de Lupé 1988 $9 (2/28/90) BB
83 ALAIN MICHELOT Nuits-St.-Georges Les Cailles 1988 $54 (5/15/91)
83 ALAIN MICHELOT Nuits-St.-Georges Les Porêts-St.-Georges 1988 $56 (5/15/91)
83 MOILLARD Bourgogne Hautes Côtes de Beaune Rouge Les Alouettes 1988 $15 (7/15/91)
83 LA POUSSE D'OR Santenay Clos Tavannes 1988 $28 (8/31/91)
83 DOMAINE PRIEUR-BRUNET Chassagne-Montrachet Rouge Morgeot 1988 $17 (11/15/90)
83 CHATEAU DE PULIGNY-MONTRACHET Pommard 1988 $34 (8/31/90)
83 REMOISSENET Mercurey Clos Fortoul 1988 $17 (3/31/91)
83 DOMAINE G. ROUMIER Morey-St.-Denis Clos de la Bussière 1988 $30 (7/15/91)
83 DOMAINE SIRUGUE Côte de Nuits-Villages Clos de la Belle Marguerite 1988 $16 (3/31/91)
83 HENRI DE VILLAMONT Chambolle-Musigny 1988 $39 (2/15/91)
82 GHISLAINE BARTHOD Bourgogne 1988 $20 (3/31/91)
82 BICHOT Beaune 1988 $15 (8/31/90)
82 DUVERNAY Rully Les Cloux 1988 $18 (12/31/90)
82 STANISLAS HERESZTYN Gevrey-Chambertin Les Champonnets 1988 $37 (12/31/90)
82 LOUIS JADOT Vosne-Romanée Les Suchots 1988 $63 (8/31/91)
82 PHILIPPE LECLERC Gevrey-Chambertin Les Cazetiers 1988 $80 (7/15/91)
82 PHILIPPE LECLERC Gevrey-Chambertin La Combe aux Moines 1988 $80 (7/15/91)
82 DOMAINE LEROY Nuits-St.-Georges Aux Lavières 1988 $84 (4/30/91)
82 CHATEAU DE MEURSAULT Bourgogne Pinot Noir du Chateau 1988 $16 (1/31/92)
82 LA POUSSE D'OR Volnay Les Caillerets Clos des 60 Ouvrées 1988 $53 (8/31/91)
82 DOMAINE PRIEUR-BRUNET Beaune Clos du Roy 1988 $30 (12/31/90)
82 CHATEAU DE PULIGNY-MONTRACHET Côte de Nuits-Villages 1988 $17 (3/31/91)
81 GHISLAINE BARTHOD Chambolle-Musigny Les Véroilles 1988 $45 (2/28/91)
81 RENE ENGEL Vosne-Romanée 1988 $30 (7/15/90)
81 FAIVELEY Mercurey Domaine de la Croix Jacquelet 1988 $18 (3/31/91)
81 JEAN GROS Nuits-St.-Georges 1988 $42 (2/28/91)
81 LABOURE-ROI Gevrey-Chambertin 1988 $35 (12/31/90)
81 LOUIS TRAPET Gevrey-Chambertin 1988 $40 (7/15/91)
80 DOMAINE PIERRE AMIOT Morey-St.-Denis Les Ruchots 1988 $57 (2/28/91)
80 DOMAINE DE L'ARLOT Côte de Nuits-Villages Clos du Châpeau 1988 $21 (3/31/91)
80 ROBERT ARNOUX Vosne-Romanée Les Chaumes 1988 $45 (2/28/91)
80 DOMAINE BRUNO CLAIR Marsannay 1988 $16 (11/15/91)
80 JOSEPH DROUHIN Vosne-Romanée Les Beaumonts 1988 $56 (3/31/91)
80 DROUHIN-LAROZE Gevrey-Chambertin Lavaux-St.-Jacques 1988 $44 (12/31/90)
80 A.-F. GROS Bourgogne Hautes Côtes de Nuits 1988 $22 (3/31/91)
80 ALBERT MOROT Beaune-Teurons 1988 $33 (7/15/91)
80 GEORGES MUGNERET Nuits-St.-Georges Les Chaignots 1988 $47 (11/15/90)
80 PHILIPPE NADDEF Gevrey-Chambertin 1988 $25 (7/15/91)
80 DOMAINE PRIEUR-BRUNET Santenay Maladière 1988 $20 (11/15/90)
80 DOMAINE RAPET Bourgogne en Bully 1988 $19 (3/31/91)
80 DOMAINE F. & L. SAIER Mercurey Les Champs-Martins 1988 $17 (8/31/91)
80 HENRI DE VILLAMONT Savigny-lès-Beaune Le Village 1988 $18 (3/31/91)
80+ BICHOT Pommard Rugiens 1988 $40 (7/15/90) (BT)
80+ BICHOT Savigny-lès-Beaune 1988 $17 (7/15/90) (BT)
80+ F. CHAUVENET Nuits-St.-Georges Les Chaignots 1988 $38 (7/15/90) (BT)
80+ MAURICE CHENU Côte de Beaune-Villages 1988 ($NA) (7/15/90) (BT)
80+ DOMAINE DU CLOS FRANTIN Nuits-St.-Georges 1988 $37 (7/15/90) (BT)
80+ JOSEPH DROUHIN Savigny-lès-Beaune 1988 $22 (7/15/90) (BT)
80+ JOSEPH DROUHIN Volnay 1988 $36 (7/15/90) (BT)
80+ DOMAINE HENRI GOUGES Nuits-St.-Georges Clos des Porrets-St.-Georges 1988 $50 (7/15/90) (BT)
80+ LOUIS JADOT Beaune Bressandes 1988 Rel: $26 Cur: $30 (7/15/90) (BT)
80+ LOUIS JADOT Pernand-Vergelesses 1988 $16 (7/15/90) (BT)
80+ JAFFELIN Chassagne-Montrachet Rouge 1988 $20 (7/15/90) (BT)
80+ JAFFELIN Monthélie 1988 $21 (7/15/90) (BT)
80+ JAFFELIN Morey-St.-Denis Les Ruchots 1988 $31 (7/15/90) (BT)
80+ OLIVIER LEFLAIVE FRERES Gevrey-Chambertin 1988 $35 (7/15/90) (BT)
80+ TOLLOT-BEAUT Corton 1988 $55 (7/15/90) (BT)
79 CHARLOPIN-PARIZOT Gevrey-Chambertin Cuvée Vieilles Vignes 1988 $31 (12/31/90)
79 CHARTRON & TREBUCHET Côte de Beaune-Villages 1988 $16 (2/28/91)
79 DOMAINE RENE MANUEL Meursault Rouge Clos de La Baronne 1988 $18 (3/31/91)
79 DOMAINE RAPET Pernand-Vergelesses 1988 $31 (2/28/91)
79 DOMAINE B. SERVEAU Chambolle-Musigny Les Sentiers 1988 $39 (2/28/91)
78 ROBERT ARNOUX Clos de Vougeot 1988 $70 (3/15/91)
78 BICHOT Savigny-lès-Beaune Hospices de Beaune Cuvée Fouquerand 1988 $39 (1/31/92)
78 PIERRE BOUREE FILS Gevrey-Chambertin Clos de la Justice 1988 $54 (3/31/92)
78 CHANSON PERE & FILS Givry 1988 $13 (12/31/90)
78 VOLPATO-COSTAILLE Chambolle-Musigny 1988 $34 (2/28/91)
77 JEAN-MARC BOILLOT Pommard Saucilles 1988 $47 (5/15/91)
77 CHATEAU DE PULIGNY-MONTRACHET Monthélie 1988 $16 (11/15/90)
77 PIERRETTE & JEAN-CLAUDE RATEAU Beaune Clos des Mariages 1988 $25 (1/31/92)
76 FAIVELEY Nuits-St.-Georges Clos de la Maréchale 1988 $50 (3/15/91)
76 GERARD MUGNERET Nuits-St.-Georges Les Boudots 1988 $48 (2/28/91)
75+ BOUCHARD PERE & FILS Nuits-St.-Georges Clos-St.-Marc 1988 $52 (7/15/90) (BT)
75+ DOMAINE JEAN CHARTRON Bourgogne Pinot Noir L'Orme 1988 ($NA) (7/15/90) (BT)
75+ MAURICE CHENU Pommard 1988 ($NA) (7/15/90) (BT)
75+ MAURICE CHENU Savigny-lès-Beaune 1988 ($NA) (7/15/90) (BT)
75+ DOMAINE DU CLOS FRANTIN Corton 1988 $52 (7/15/90) (BT)
75+ JOSEPH DROUHIN Aloxe-Corton 1988 $37 (7/15/90) (BT)
75+ JOSEPH DROUHIN Gevrey-Chambertin 1988 $41 (7/15/90) (BT)
75+ DUBREUIL-FONTAINE Aloxe-Corton 1988 ($NA) (7/15/90) (BT)
75+ DUBREUIL-FONTAINE Savigny-lès-Beaune Les Vergelesses 1988 ($NA) (7/15/90) (BT)
75+ DOMAINE HENRI GOUGES Nuits-St.-Georges Les St.-Georges 1988 $54 (7/15/90) (BT)
75+ LOUIS JADOT Côte de Beaune-Villages 1988 $14 (7/15/90) (BT)
75+ LOUIS JADOT Nuits-St.-Georges 1988 $27 (7/15/90) (BT)
75+ JAFFELIN Beaune Les Champimonts 1988 $30 (7/15/90) (BT)
75+ OLIVIER LEFLAIVE FRERES Pommard 1988 $31 (7/15/90) (BT)
75+ MOMMESSIN Fixin 1988 $19 (7/15/90) (BT)
75+ MOMMESSIN Santenay Grand Clos Rousseau 1988 $23 (7/15/90) (BT)
74 PHILIPPE LECLERC Gevrey-Chambertin Les Platières 1988 $45 (7/15/91)
73 PIERRE BOUREE FILS Bourgogne 1988 $15 (3/31/92)
73 HAEGELEN-JAYER Chambolle-Musigny 1988 $39 (5/15/91)
73 HAEGELEN-JAYER Clos de Vougeot 1988 $69 (5/15/91)
73 LOUIS JADOT Clos de Vougeot 1988 $68 (11/15/91)
73 JEAN-CLAUDE VOLPATO Bourgogne Passetoutgrain 1988 $13 (3/31/91)
72 JEAN CLAUDE BOISSET Bourgogne Rouge Tastevinage 1988 $11 (8/31/91)
72 DOMAINE ROY PERE & FILS Gevrey-Chambertin Vieilles Vignes 1988 $30 (12/31/90)
71 DOMAINE ALETH GIRARDIN Beaune Clos des Mouches 1988 $36 (7/15/91)
71 A.-F. GROS Vosne-Romanée aux Réas 1988 $41 (2/28/91)
70+ BICHOT Santenay Clos Rousseau 1988 $20 (7/15/90) (BT)
70+ BOUCHARD PERE & FILS Beaune-Teurons Domaines du Château de Beaune 1988 $36 (7/15/90) (BT)
70+ BOUCHARD PERE & FILS Vosne-Romanée Aux Reignots Château de Vosne-Romanée 1988 $50 (7/15/90) (BT)
70+ F. CHAUVENET Beaune Les Theurons 1988 $25 (7/15/90) (BT)
70+ F. CHAUVENET Gevrey-Chambertin Lavaux St.-Jacques 1988 $48 (7/15/90) (BT)
70+ F. CHAUVENET Gevrey-Chambertin Petite Chapelle 1988 $40 (7/15/90) (BT)
70+ LOUIS JADOT Bourgogne Pinot Noir 1988 ($NA) (7/15/90) (BT)
69 PHILIPPE NADDEF Mazis-Chambertin 1988 $60 (7/15/91)
68 CHATEAU DE DRACY Bourgogne Pinot Noir 1988 $8 (2/28/90)
68 REMOISSENET Givry du Domaine Thénard 1988 $19 (3/31/91)
68 DOMAINE ROY PERE & FILS Gevrey-Chambertin Clos Prieur 1988 $35 (12/31/90)
67 HAEGELEN-JAYER Echézeaux 1988 $61 (8/31/91)
67 DOMAINE F. & L. SAIER Mercurey Les Chenelots 1988 $17 (4/30/91)
64 PHILIPPE LECLERC Bourgogne Les Bons Bâtons 1988 $22 (8/31/91)
64 MUGNERET-GIBOURG Vosne-Romanée 1988 $34 (12/31/90)

1985

100 ROMANEE-CONTI Richebourg 1985 Rel: $210 Cur: $320 (2/29/88)
99 HENRI JAYER Richebourg 1985 $510 (5/15/91) (HS)
99 ROMANEE-CONTI Romanée-Conti 1985 Rel: $375 Cur: $1,100 (1/31/90) (JS)
98 LOUIS LATOUR Romanée-St.-Vivant Les Quatre Journaux 1985 $99 (3/15/88)
98 ROMANEE-CONTI La Tâche 1985 Rel: $225 Cur: $360 (2/29/88)
97 F. CHAUVENET Charmes-Chambertin 1985 $72 (7/31/87)
97 F. CHAUVENET Corton Hospices de Beaune Docteur-Peste 1985 $133 (7/15/88)
97 JOSEPH DROUHIN Clos de la Roche 1985 $60 (11/15/87)
97 DOMAINE MEO-CAMUZET Richebourg 1985 Rel: $150 Cur: $280 (3/31/88)
97 ARMAND ROUSSEAU Chambertin 1985 Rel: $100 Cur: $120 (3/15/88)
97 TOLLOT-BEAUT Corton 1985 $49 (3/15/88)
96 JEANNE-MARIE DE CHAMPS Nuits-St.-Georges Les Didiers Hospices de Nuits Cuvée Cabet 1985 $53 (3/15/88)
96 F. CHAUVENET Corton 1985 $53 (7/31/87)
96 DOMAINE DU CLOS FRANTIN Echézeaux 1985 $37 (9/15/87)
96 FAIVELEY Chambertin Clos de Bèze 1985 $105 (3/15/88)
96 LOUIS JADOT Nuits-St.-Georges Clos des Corvées 1985 $44 (3/15/88)
96 JAFFELIN Clos de Vougeot 1985 $49 (6/15/88)
96 HENRI JAYER Echézeaux 1985 $330 (5/15/91) (HS)
96 ROMANEE-CONTI Echézeaux 1985 Rel: $95 Cur: $140 (2/29/88)
95 F. CHAUVENET Pommard Epenottes 1985 $48 (7/31/87)
95 DOMAINE DU CLOS FRANTIN Vosne-Romanée Les Malconsorts 1985 $40 (9/30/87)
95 JOSEPH DROUHIN Chambertin 1985 Rel: $75 Cur: $102 (11/15/87)
95 JOSEPH DROUHIN Griotte-Chambertin 1985 $68 (11/15/87)
95 JOSEPH DROUHIN Pommard Epenottes 1985 $41 (11/15/87)
95 DOMAINE DUJAC Charmes-Chambertin 1985 $100 (3/15/88)
95 DOMAINE DUJAC Clos de la Roche Clos la Roche 1985 $85 (3/15/88)
95 LOUIS JADOT Beaune Clos des Ursules 1985 Rel: $30 Cur: $48 (3/15/88) SS
95 LOUIS JADOT Bonnes Mares 1985 Rel: $48 Cur: $68 (3/15/88)
95 HENRI JAYER Vosne-Romanée Cros-Parantoux 1985 $240 (5/15/91) (HS)
95 LOUIS LATOUR Chambertin Cuvée Hèritiers Latour 1985 Rel: $76 Cur: $90 (3/15/88)
95 MOILLARD Vosne-Romanée Malconsorts Domaine Thomas-Moillard 1985 $38 (7/31/88)
95 DOMAINE DANIEL RION Vosne-Romanée Beaux-Monts 1985 Rel: $38 Cur: $55 (2/29/88)
94 F. CHAUVENET Clos St.-Denis 1985 $67 (7/31/87)
94 JOSEPH DROUHIN Clos de Vougeot 1985 $57 (11/15/87)
94 JOSEPH DROUHIN Vosne-Romanée Les Suchots 1985 $42 (11/15/87)
94 LOUIS JADOT Gevrey-Chambertin Clos St.-Jacques 1985 $45 (3/31/88)
94 PRINCE FLORENT DE MERODE Pommard Clos de la Platière 1985 $45 (3/15/88)
94 MOILLARD Charmes-Chambertin 1985 $55 (5/31/88)
94 MOILLARD Echézeaux 1985 $47 (4/15/88)
94 PHILIPPE NADDEF Gevrey-Chambertin 1985 $25 (4/15/88)
94 DOMAINE PONSOT Chambolle-Musigny Les Charmes 1985 $75 (6/15/88)
94 DOMAINE DANIEL RION Nuits-St.-Georges Clos des Argillières 1985 Rel: $44 Cur: $55 (3/15/88)
94 ROMANEE-CONTI Grands Echézeaux 1985 Rel: $140 Cur: $183 (2/29/88)
94 DOMAINE TORTOCHOT Chambertin 1985 $90 (12/31/88)
93 PIERRE BOUREE FILS Nuits-St.-Georges Les Vaucrains 1985 $68 (5/31/88)
93 JOSEPH DROUHIN Chambolle-Musigny 1985 $33 (11/15/87)
93 JOSEPH DROUHIN Grands Echézeaux 1985 $75 (11/15/87)
93 JOSEPH DROUHIN Nuits-St.-Georges Les Roncières 1985 $38 (11/15/87)
93 JOSEPH DROUHIN Pommard 1985 $33 (11/15/87)
93 JOSEPH DROUHIN Vosne-Romanée Les Beaumonts 1985 Rel: $42 Cur: $53 (11/15/87)
93 PIERRE GELIN Gevrey-Chambertin 1985 $25 (4/15/88)
93 HENRI JAYER Vosne-Romanée Les Brûlées 1985 $240 (5/15/91) (HS)

93 DOMAINE MEO-CAMUZET Clos de Vougeot 1985 Rel: $65 Cur: $101 (3/31/88)
93 PRINCE FLORENT DE MERODE Corton-Bressandes 1985 $52 (2/15/88)
93 MUGNERET-GIBOURG Echézeaux 1985 $57 (2/29/88)
93 PARIGOT PERE & FILS Pommard Les Charmots 1985 Rel: $24 Cur: $34 (6/15/87) CS
93 POTHIER-RIEUSSET Volnay 1985 $21 (2/15/88)
92 DOMAINE JEAN-MARC BOULEY Pommard Les Rugiens 1985 $30 (10/31/88)
92 PIERRE BOUREE FILS Chambertin 1985 $113 (5/31/88)

92 CAPTAIN-GAGNEROT Corton Les Renardes 1985 $70 (12/31/88)
92 CHANSON PERE & FILS Beaune Clos des Fèves 1985 Rel: $25 Cur: $33 (1/31/89)
92 F. CHAUVENET Vosne-Romanée Les Suchots 1985 $46 (7/31/87)
92 DOMAINE DE COURCEL Pommard Rugiens 1985 $40 (4/30/88)
92 JOSEPH DROUHIN Corton 1985 $48 (11/15/87)
92 JOSEPH DROUHIN Nuits-St.-Georges 1985 $29 (11/15/87)
92 DROUHIN-LAROZE Chambertin Clos de Bèze 1985 Rel: $70 Cur: $110 (10/15/88)
92 FAIVELEY Gevrey-Chambertin Les Cazetiers 1985 $53 (3/31/88)
92 FAIVELEY Mazis-Chambertin 1985 $81 (3/15/88)
92 LOUIS JADOT Beaune Hospices de Beaune Cuvée Nicolas-Rolin 1985 $85 (3/15/88)

92 PHILIPPE LECLERC Gevrey-Chambertin Combe aux Moines 1985 $70 (10/15/88)
92 DOMAINE MEO-CAMUZET Vosne-Romanée Les Chaumes 1985 $80 (3/31/88)
92 MOILLARD Corton Clos des Vergennes 1985 $36 (5/31/87)
92 MOILLARD Pommard Clos des Epeneaux 1985 Rel: $40 Cur: $45 (6/30/88) CS
92 MONGEARD-MUGNERET Richebourg 1985 $123 (3/15/88)
92 CHARLES MORTET Gevrey-Chambertin Clos Prieur 1985 $29 (7/31/88)
92 GEORGES MUGNERET Ruchottes-Chambertin 1985 $63 (2/15/88)
92 GASTON & PIERRE RAVAUT Corton Hautes-Mourottes 1985 $46 (7/31/88)
92 DOMAINE G. ROUMIER Morey-St.-Denis Clos de la Bussière 1985 $27 (4/30/88)
92 ARMAND ROUSSEAU Gevrey-Chambertin Clos St.-Jacques 1985 $80 (10/15/88)

92 DOMAINE ROUX PERE & FILS Volnay en Champans 1985 $25 (3/15/87)
92 COMTE DE VOGUE Musigny Cuvée Vieilles Vignes 1985 Rel: $125 Cur: $150 (3/31/88)
91 COMTE ARMAND Pommard Clos des Epeneaux 1985 $44 (3/15/88)
91 BICHOT Pommard Hospices de Beaune Cuvée Cyrot-Chaudron 1985 $60 (10/31/88)
91 BITOUZET-PRIEUR Volnay Pitures 1985 $36 (7/31/88)
91 BONNEAU DU MARTRAY Corton 1985 $62 (10/15/88)
91 BOUCHARD PERE & FILS Beaune Grèves Vigne de l'Enfant Jésus 1985 $61 (1/31/89)
91 PIERRE BOUREE FILS Bonnes Mares 1985 $85 (5/31/88)
91 PIERRE BOUREE FILS Gevrey-Chambertin Les Cazetiers 1985 $67 (5/31/88)
91 DOMAINE F. BUFFET Volnay en Champans 1985 $35 (10/15/88)

91 DOMAINE F. BUFFET Volnay Clos de la Rougeotte 1985 $35 (10/15/88)
91 DOMAINE DES CHEZEAUX Chambolle-Musigny Les Charmes 1985 $75 (6/15/88)
91 DOMAINE DES CHEZEAUX Griotte-Chambertin 1985 $100 (6/15/88)
91 DOMAINE DU CLOS FRANTIN Vosne-Romanée 1985 $29 (10/15/87)
91 JOSEPH DROUHIN Gevrey-Chambertin 1985 $33 (11/15/87)
91 JOSEPH DROUHIN Pernand-Vergelesses 1985 $17 (11/15/87)
91 JOSEPH DROUHIN Savigny-lès-Beaune 1985 Rel: $21 Cur: $25 (11/15/87) SS
91 DOMAINE DUJAC Clos St.-Denis 1985 $89 (3/15/88)
91 LOUIS JADOT Beaune Boucherottes 1985 $30 (3/15/88)
91 LOUIS JADOT Beaune Les Chouacheux 1985 $30 (3/15/88)

91 LOUIS JADOT Beaune Clos des Couchereaux 1985 Rel: $30 Cur: $39 (3/15/88)
91 LOUIS JADOT Beaune Clos des Ursules 1985 Rel: $30 Cur: $48 (3/15/89) (JS)
91 LOUIS JADOT Chambolle-Musigny 1985 Rel: $33 Cur: $39 (5/15/88)
91 LOUIS JADOT Nuits-St.-Georges 1985 $30 (4/15/88)
91 LOUIS JADOT Pommard Chaponnières 1985 $39 (3/15/88)
91 DOMAINE FRANCOIS LAMARCHE Vosne-Romanée Les Suchots 1985 $36 (10/15/88)
91 GEORGES LIGNIER Clos St.-Denis 1985 $54 (3/15/88)
91 MOMMESSIN Clos de Tart 1985 $95 (2/15/88)
91 MOMMESSIN Corton 1985 $28 (2/15/88)
91 MOMMESSIN Volnay Hospices de Beaune Cuvée General-Muteau 1985 $80 (3/15/88)

91 B. MUGNERET-GOUACHON Echézeaux 1985 $29 (12/31/88)
91 REMOISSENET Chambertin 1985 $100 (3/15/88)
91 REMOISSENET Clos de la Roche 1985 $72 (3/15/88)
91 REMOISSENET Richebourg 1985 $138 (3/15/88)
91 REMOISSENET Vosne-Romanée Les Suchots 1985 $75 (3/15/88)
91 DOMAINE DANIEL RION Nuits-St.-Georges Les Vignes Rondes 1985 $40 (3/15/88)
91 DOMAINE B. SERVEAU Chambolle-Musigny Les Amoureuses 1985 $75 (6/15/88)
90 PIERRE ANDRE Corton Pougets 1985 $45 (7/15/88)
90 ROBERT ARNOUX Vosne-Romanée Les Suchots 1985 $52 (7/31/88)
90 BOUCHARD PERE & FILS Vosne-Romanée Aux Reignots Château de Vosne-Romanée 1985 $51 (2/28/89)

90 DOMAINE JEAN-MARC BOULEY Volnay Les Caillerets 1985 $27 (10/15/88)
90 A.R. CHOPPIN Beaune Bressandes 1985 $32 (9/30/87)
90 JOSEPH DROUHIN Aloxe-Corton 1985 $23 (11/15/87)
90 DROUHIN-LAROZE Mazis-Chambertin 1985 $47 (10/15/88)
90 DUBREUIL-FONTAINE Corton Clos du Roi 1985 Rel: $49 Cur: $63 (7/15/88)
90 RENE ENGEL Echézeaux 1985 $32 (10/15/87)
90 FAIVELEY Gevrey-Chambertin 1985 $38 (4/15/88)
90 FAIVELEY Nuits-St.-Georges 1985 $40 (3/15/88)
90 PIERRE GELIN Mazis-Chambertin 1985 $25 (3/15/88)
90 MACHARD DE GRAMONT Nuits-St.-Georges Les Hauts Pruliers 1985 $36 (2/15/88)

90 HAEGELEN-JAYER Clos de Vougeot 1985 $64 (4/15/88)
90 LOUIS JADOT Beaune Hospices de Beaune Cuvée Dames-Hospitalier 1985 $85 (3/15/88)
90 LOUIS JADOT Chapelle-Chambertin 1985 $54 (3/15/88)
90 JEHAN JOLIET Fixin Clos de la Perrière 1985 $25 (7/31/88)
90 J. LABET & N. DECHELETTE Clos Vougeot Château de la Tour 1985 $53 (6/15/88)
90 DOMAINE FRANCOIS LAMARCHE Clos de Vougeot 1985 $48 (10/15/88)

Key to Symbols

The scores reported here are the results of blind tastings conducted by our panel of senior editors. Wines that carry the initials below are results of individual tastings.

THE WINE SPECTATOR 100-POINT SCALE 95-100— Classic, a great wine; ***90-94***— Outstanding, superior character and style; ***80-89***—Good to very good, a wine with special qualities; ***70-79***—Average, drinkable wine that may have minor flaws; ***60-69*** —Below average, drinkable but not recommended; ***50-59*** —Poor, undrinkable, not recommended. "+"—With a score indicates a range; used primarily with barrel tastings to indicate a preliminary score.

SPECIAL DESIGNATIONS SS—Spectator Selection, CS—Cellar Selection, BB—Best Buy, ($NA)—Price not available, (NR)—Not released.

TASTER'S INITIALS (JG)—Jim Gordon, (HS)—Harvey Steiman, (JL)—James Laube, (JS)—James Suckling, (TM)—Thomas Matthews, (TR)—Terry Robards, (PM)—Per-Henrik Mansson, (BT)—Barrel Tasting (these wines were tasted blind from barrel samples), (CA-date)—*California's Great Cabernets* by James Laube, (CH-date)—*California's Great Chardonnays* by James Laube, (VP-date)—*Vintage Port* by James Suckling.

DATE TASTED Dates in parentheses represent the issue in which the rating was published.

90 LOUIS LATOUR Beaune Vignes Franches 1985 Rel: $31 Cur: $42 (3/15/88)
90 LOUIS LATOUR Corton Domaine Latour 1985 $38 (3/15/88)
90 PHILIPPE LECLERC Gevrey-Chambertin Les Platières 1985 Rel: $38 Cur: $45 (10/15/88)
90 DOMAINE MEO-CAMUZET Nuits-St.-Georges Aux Murgers 1985 $50 (4/15/88)

90 MOMMESSIN Gevrey-Chambertin 1985 $25 (2/15/88)
90 CHARLES MORTET Chambertin 1985 $64 (6/15/88)
90 RENE MUGNERET Vosne-Romanée 1985 $27 (4/30/88)
90 DOMAINE PONSOT Clos de la Roche Cuvée Vieilles Vignes 1985 $200 (6/15/88)
90 LA POUSSE D'OR Volnay Les Caillerets 1985 $35 (3/15/88)
90 DOMAINE B. SERVEAU Chambolle-Musigny Les Chabiots 1985 $39 (6/15/88)
89 BARTON & GUESTIER Gevrey-Chambertin 1985 $21 (4/30/88)
89 BOUCHARD PERE & FILS Beaune Marconnets Domaines du Château de Beaune 1985 $35 (1/31/89)
89 F. CHAUVENET Echézeaux 1985 $47 (7/31/87)
89 DOMAINE DE COURCEL Pommard Clos des Epeneaux 1985 $37 (4/30/88)

89 DOMAINE DELARCHE Pernand-Vergelesses Ile des Vergelesses 1985 $23 (10/15/88)
89 JOSEPH DROUHIN Charmes-Chambertin 1985 $60 (11/15/87)
89 FAIVELEY Chambolle-Musigny 1985 $45 (5/15/88)
89 FAIVELEY Echézeaux 1985 $74 (3/31/88)
89 MACHARD DE GRAMONT Beaune Les Chouacheux 1985 $34 (5/31/88)
89 MACHARD DE GRAMONT Nuits-St.-Georges en la Perrière Noblot 1985 $41 (5/31/88)
89 MACHARD DE GRAMONT Savigny-lès-Beaune Les Guettes 1985 $25 (7/31/88)
89 LOUIS JADOT Chambertin Clos de Bèze 1985 Rel: $66 Cur: $79 (3/15/88)
89 LOUIS JADOT Corton Pougets 1985 $47 (3/15/88)
89 JAFFELIN Pommard 1985 $38 (3/15/88)

89 DOMAINE FRANCOIS LAMARCHE Vosne-Romanée La Grande Rue 1985 $60 (10/15/88)
89 LOUIS LATOUR Corton Clos de la Vigne au Saint 1985 $43 (3/15/88)
89 LOUIS LATOUR Corton Château Corton Grancey 1985 Rel: $46 Cur: $60 (3/15/88)
89 LOUIS LATOUR Pommard Epenottes 1985 $46 (3/15/88)
89 PHILIPPE LECLERC Gevrey-Chambertin Les Cazetiers 1985 Rel: $64 Cur: $70 (10/15/88)
89 CHATEAU DE LA MALTROYE Chassagne-Montrachet Rouge Clos St.-Jean 1985 $19 (10/15/88)
89 MOILLARD Beaune Grèves 1985 $25 (3/15/87)
89 MOILLARD Nuits-St.-Georges Clos de Thorey 1985 $38 (5/31/87)
89 MOILLARD Volnay Clos des Chênes 1985 $32 (7/15/88)
89 DOMAINE RENE MONNIER Beaune Cent Vignes 1985 $25 (10/31/87)

89 DOMAINE RENE MONNIER Pommard Les Vignots 1985 $30 (11/15/88)
89 JEAN-MARC PAVELOT Savigny-lès-Beaune Les Guettes 1985 $20 (2/15/88)
89 PHILIPPE ROSSIGNOL Côte de Nuits-Villages 1985 $24 (7/31/88)
89 HERVE ROUMIER Chambolle-Musigny Les Amoureuses 1985 $65 (3/31/88)
89 TOLLOT-BEAUT Aloxe-Corton 1985 $35 (3/15/88)
88 PIERRE ANDRE Corton Clos du Roi 1985 $45 (7/15/88)
88 G. BARTHOD-NOELLAT Chambolle-Musigny Les Crâs 1985 $37 (7/31/88)
88 BICHOT Volnay Hospices de Beaune Cuvée Blondeau 1985 $53 (4/30/89)
88 BOUCHARD PERE & FILS Volnay Frémiets Clos de la Rougeotte Domaines du Château 1985 $35 (1/31/89)
88 PIERRE BOUREE FILS Charmes-Chambertin 1985 Rel: $68 Cur: $85 (5/31/88)

88 PIERRE BOUREE FILS Santenay Les Gravières 1985 $30 (5/31/88)
88 DOMAINE F. BUFFET Pommard Rugiens 1985 $40 (10/15/88)
88 F. CHAUVENET Beaune-Teurons 1985 $23 (7/31/87)
88 F. CHAUVENET Gevrey-Chambertin Charreux 1985 $33 (10/15/87)
88 JEAN CHAUVENET Nuits-St.-Georges Les Bousselots 1985 $49 (5/31/88)
88 LOUIS CLAIR Santenay Gravières Domaine de l'Abbaye 1985 $17 (10/15/87)
88 JOSEPH DROUHIN Santenay 1985 $17 (11/15/87)
88 JOSEPH DROUHIN Volnay 1985 $29 (11/15/87)
88 DROUHIN-LAROZE Clos de Vougeot 1985 $60 (10/15/88)
88 DUBREUIL-FONTAINE Savigny-lès-Beaune Les Vergelesses 1985 $24 (1/31/89)

88 FAIVELEY Latricières-Chambertin 1985 $77 (3/15/88)
88 LOUIS JADOT Musigny Le Musigny 1985 $74 (3/31/88)
88 JAFFELIN Volnay 1985 $30 (3/15/88)
88 J. JAYER Nuits-St.-Georges Les Lavières 1985 $38 (3/15/88)
88 LUPE-CHOLET Nuits-St.-Georges Château Gris 1985 $39 (2/15/88)
88 HENRI MAGNIEN Gevrey-Chambertin Les Cazetiers 1985 $35 (10/15/87)
88 HENRI MEURGEY Chassagne-Montrachet Rouge Clos de la Boudriotte 1985 $40 (10/31/88)
88 GASTON & PIERRE RAVAUT Aloxe-Corton 1985 $35 (7/31/88)
88 GASTON & PIERRE RAVAUT Ladoix Les Corvées 1985 $26 (7/31/88)
88 DOMAINE DANIEL RION Chambolle-Musigny Les Beaux Bruns 1985 $33 (3/31/88)

88 DOMAINE DANIEL RION Nuits-St.-Georges Hauts Pruliers 1985 Rel: $43 Cur: $50 (3/15/88)
88 ROMANEE-CONTI Romanée-St.-Vivant 1985 $175 (2/29/88)
88 DOMAINE B. SERVEAU Morey-St.-Denis Les Sorbets 1985 $39 (6/15/88)
88 LOUIS TRAPET Chambertin 1985 $80 (3/15/88)
87 DOMAINE BERTAGNA Vougeot Clos de la Perrière 1985 $40 (4/15/89)
87 BOUCHARD PERE & FILS Nuits-St.-Georges Clos-St.-Marc 1985 $53 (2/28/89)
87 BOUCHARD PERE & FILS Volnay Caillerets Ancienne Cuvée Carnot Château de Beaune 1985 $44 (1/31/89)
87 DOMAINE JEAN-MARC BOULEY Volnay Clos des Chênes 1985 $27 (10/15/88)
87 JEANNE-MARIE DE CHAMPS Corton Hospices de Beaune Cuvée Charlotte-Dumay 1985 $76 (10/15/88)
87 A.R. CHOPPIN Beaune-Teurons 1985 $32 (10/31/87)

87 A.R. CHOPPIN Savigny-lès-Beaune Vergelesses 1985 $25 (10/31/87)
87 DOMAINE CLAUDINE DESCHAMPS Gevrey-Chambertin Bel-Air 1985 $28 (3/31/88)
87 REMY GAUTHIER Volnay Santenots 1985 $27 (3/15/88)
87 JEAN GRIVOT Vosne-Romanée 1985 $31 (4/30/88)
87 JEAN GROS Vosne-Romanée Clos des Réas 1985 Rel: $55 Cur: $58 (7/31/88)
87 LOUIS JADOT Beaune Bressandes 1985 $30 (3/15/88)
87 LOUIS LATOUR Echézeaux 1985 $49 (3/15/88)
87 CHATEAU DE MEURSAULT Beaune Cent-Vignes 1985 $31 (2/28/90)
87 JEAN MICHELOT Pommard 1985 $29 (4/30/88)
87 MOILLARD Morey-St.-Denis Monts Luisants 1985 $21 (5/31/87)

87 DOMAINE MONTHELIE-DOUHAIRET Volnay en Champans 1985 $25 (7/15/88)
87 LA POUSSE D'OR Pommard Les Jarollières 1985 $39 (3/15/88)
87 REMOISSENET Nuits-St.-Georges Aux Argillats 1985 $34 (10/15/88)
87 DOMAINE G. ROUMIER Chambolle-Musigny 1985 $26 (2/15/88)
87 CHARLES VIENOT Gevrey-Chambertin 1985 $32 (4/30/88)
86 BICHOT Monthélie Hospices de Beaune Cuvée Lebelin 1985 $52 (10/15/87)
86 DOMAINE LUCIEN BOILLOT Volnay Les Angles 1985 $33 (7/15/88)
86 JEAN CLAUDE BOISSET Volnay Clos des Chênes 1985 $28 (4/15/88)
86 CAPTAIN-GAGNEROT Clos de Vougeot 1985 $67 (12/31/88)
86 JOSEPH DROUHIN Côte de Nuits-Villages 1985 $19 (11/15/87)

86 DUBREUIL-FONTAINE Corton-Bressandes 1985 $50 (1/31/89)
86 RENE ENGEL Grands Echézeaux 1985 $43 (10/15/87)

86 FAIVELEY Beaune Champs-Pimont 1985 $36 (3/15/88)
86 JEAN-CHARLES FORNEROT Chassagne-Montrachet Rouge La Maltroie 1985 $19 (7/31/89)
86 MACHARD DE GRAMONT Nuits-St.-Georges Les Allots 1985 $35 (5/31/88)
86 LOUIS JADOT Gevrey-Chambertin Estournelles St.-Jacques 1985 $41 (3/31/88)
86 LOUIS JADOT Vosne-Romanée 1985 $33 (3/31/88)
86 LOUIS LATOUR Vosne-Romanée Beaumonts 1985 $36 (3/15/88)
86 DOMAINE LEQUIN-ROUSSOT Chassagne-Montrachet Rouge Morgeot 1985 $24 (5/31/88)
86 DOMAINE LEQUIN-ROUSSOT Corton Les Languettes 1985 $39 (7/15/88)
86 GEORGES LIGNIER Morey-St.-Denis Clos des Ormes 1985 $28 (3/15/88)
86 CHATEAU DE LA MALTROYE Chassagne-Montrachet Rouge Boudriottes 1985 $17 (10/15/88)
86 DOMAINE MUSSY Pommard 1985 $35 (10/15/88)
86 PAUL PILLOT Chassagne-Montrachet Rouge Clos St.-Jean 1985 $24 (11/15/88)
86 LA POUSSE D'OR Volnay Les Caillerets Clos des 60 Ouvrées 1985 $39 (3/15/88)
86 ARMAND ROUSSEAU Charmes-Chambertin 1985 $63 (10/15/88)
86 DOMAINE B. SERVEAU Nuits-St.-Georges Chaines Carteaux 1985 $39 (6/15/88)
85 PIERRE ANDRE Savigny-lès-Beaune Clos des Guettes 1985 $20 (7/31/88)
85 DOMAINE BERTAGNA Nuits-St.-Georges Aux Murgers 1985 $41 (2/28/89)
85 DOMAINE BERTAGNA Vougeot Les Crâs 1985 $30 (3/31/88)
85 BOUCHARD PERE & FILS Beaune-Teurons Domaines du Château de Beaune 1985 $35 (1/31/89)
85 PIERRE BOUREE FILS Gevrey-Chambertin Clos de la Justice 1985 $51 (5/31/88)
85 ROBERT CHEVILLON Nuits-St.-Georges 1985 $40 (4/30/88)
85 JOSEPH DROUHIN Côte de Beaune-Villages 1985 $14 (11/15/87)
85 DOMAINE DUCHET Beaune Cent-Vignes 1985 $27 (3/15/88)
85 RENE ENGEL Clos de Vougeot 1985 $43 (10/15/87)
85 RENE ENGEL Vosne-Romanée Les Brûlées 1985 $28 (10/15/87)
85 FAIVELEY Nuits-St.-Georges Clos de la Maréchale 1985 $51 (3/15/88)
85 FONTAINE-GAGNARD Chassagne-Montrachet Rouge 1985 $16 (12/31/88)
85 JEAN GROS Nuits-St.-Georges 1985 $36 (7/31/88)
85 LOUIS JADOT Pernand-Vergelesses 1985 $18 (4/15/88)
85 LOUIS LATOUR Charmes-Chambertin 1985 Rel: $50 Cur: $68 (3/15/88)
85 DOMAINE LEQUIN-ROUSSOT Santenay La Comme 1985 $24 (5/31/88)
85 GEORGES LIGNIER Clos de la Roche 1985 $63 (3/15/88)
85 PROSPER MAUFOUX Santenay Les Gravières 1985 $17 (10/15/89)
85 MOILLARD Pommard Rugiens 1985 $40 (6/30/88)
85 MOMMESSIN Côte de Beaune-Villages 1985 $13 (2/15/88)
85 MOMMESSIN Côte de Nuits-Villages 1985 $17 (7/31/88)
85 MUGNERET-GIBOURG Vosne-Romanée 1985 $33 (2/29/88)
85 DOMAINE DANIEL RION Nuits-St.-Georges 1985 $28 (3/15/88)
85 ARMAND ROUSSEAU Mazis-Chambertin Mazy-Chambertin 1985 $61 (10/15/88)
85 CHARLES VIENOT Mercurey 1985 $12 (4/30/88)
84 F. CHAUVENET Côte de Beaune-Villages 1985 $16 (7/31/87)
84 F. CHAUVENET Nuits-St.-Georges Les Plateaux 1985 $34 (7/31/87)
84 F. CHAUVENET Santenay 1985 $18 (7/31/87)
84 CHEVALIER DE BEAUBASSIN Nuits-St.-Georges 1985 $31 (4/30/88)
84 PIERRE GELIN Chambertin Clos de Bèze 1985 $77 (3/15/88)
84 MACHARD DE GRAMONT Chorey-lès-Beaune Les Beaumonts 1985 $22 (7/31/88)
84 MACHARD DE GRAMONT Nuits-St.-Georges Les Hauts Poirets 1985 $41 (6/15/88)
84 JAFFELIN Santenay La Maladière 1985 $22 (3/15/88)
84 JEAN-LUC JOILLOT Bourgogne Tastevinage 1985 $15 (6/30/88)
84 DOMAINE FRANCOIS LAMARCHE Vosne-Romanée Malconsorts 1985 $44 (10/15/88)
84 LUPE-CHOLET Aloxe-Corton 1985 $18 (3/15/88)
84 MOILLARD Chassagne-Montrachet Rouge Morgeot 1985 $15 (5/31/87)
84 DOMAINE MARC MOREY Beaune Les Paules 1985 $15 (12/31/88)
84 LOUIS TRAPET Chapelle-Chambertin 1985 Rel: $64 Cur: $73 (3/15/88)
84 CHARLES VIENOT Corton Maréchaude 1985 $57 (7/15/88)
83 A. CHOPIN Côte de Nuits-Villages 1985 $9 (10/31/87) BB
83 MICHEL CLERGET Chambolle-Musigny Les Charmes 1985 $56 (5/15/88)
83 JOSEPH DROUHIN Mercurey 1985 $17 (11/15/87)
83 JEAN-CHARLES FORNEROT Chassagne-Montrachet Rouge Les Champs-Gains 1985 $19 (7/31/89)
83 LOUIS JADOT Chassagne-Montrachet Rouge Morgeot Clos de la Chapelle Domaine du Duc de Magenta 1985 $19 (4/15/88)
83 LOUIS JADOT Pernand-Vergelesses Clos de la Croix de Pierre 1985 $18 (4/15/88)
83 OLIVIER LEFLAIVE FRERES Chassagne-Montrachet Rouge 1985 $32 (10/31/88)
83 LUPE-CHOLET Savigny-lès-Beaune Les Serpentières 1985 $17 (3/15/88)
83 MOMMESSIN Charmes-Chambertin 1985 $45 (2/15/88)
83 POTHIER-RIEUSSET Bourgogne Rouge 1985 $7.50 (6/30/88) BB
83 DOMAINE ROUX PERE & FILS Santenay 1985 $21 (10/31/87)
83 DOMAINE F. & L. SAIER Mercurey Les Champs-Martins 1985 $20 (3/31/88)
83 TOLLOT-BEAUT Chorey-Côte-de-Beaune 1985 $18 (4/15/88)
82 DOMAINE BERTAGNA Vosne-Romanée Les Beaux Monts Bas 1985 $35 (10/15/88)
82 MICHEL CLERGET Echézeaux 1985 $51 (7/31/88)
82 JEAN-CHARLES FORNEROT St.-Aubin Rouge Les Perrières 1985 $15 (7/31/89)
82 GELIN & MOLIN Fixin Clos du Châpitre Domaine Marion 1985 $25 (4/30/88)
82 LOUIS JADOT Clos de Vougeot 1985 Rel: $53 Cur: $85 (3/31/88)
82 DOMAINE RENE LECLERC Gevrey-Chambertin Combes aux Moines 1985 Rel: $55 Cur: $61 (10/31/88)
82 GEORGES LIGNIER Morey-St.-Denis 1985 $23 (3/15/88)
82 MONGEARD-MUGNERET Vosne-Romanée Les Orveaux 1985 $32 (3/15/88)
82 REMOISSENET Bonnes Mares 1985 $88 (3/15/88)
81 BARTON & GUESTIER Pommard 1985 $21 (11/30/87)
81 BICHOT Bourgogne Le Bourgogne Bichot Pinot Noir 1985 $8 (11/15/87)
81 F. CHAUVENET Puligny-Montrachet Rouge 1985 $16 (6/15/87)
81 A.R. CHOPPIN Beaune Cent Vignes 1985 $32 (10/31/87)
81 DOMAINE HENRI CLERC & FILS Beaune Chaume Gaufriot 1985 $29 (11/15/88)
81 FAIVELEY Mercurey Clos du Roy 1985 $23 (4/30/88)
81 MACHARD DE GRAMONT Bourgogne Pinot Noir Domaine de la Vierge Romaine 1985 $13 (6/30/88)
81 JEAN GRIVOT Clos de Vougeot 1985 $62 (4/30/88)
81 HENRI MAGNIEN Gevrey-Chambertin 1985 $25 (10/15/87)
81 PRINCE FLORENT DE MERODE Corton Maréchaudes 1985 $49 (3/15/88)
81 DOMAINE MONTHELIE-DOUHAIRET Monthélie 1985 $16 (6/30/88)
81 HENRI & GILLES REMORIQUET Nuits-St.-Georges Rue de Chaux 1985 $22 (7/31/88)
81 CHARLES VIENOT Pommard 1985 $33 (4/30/88)
80 F. CHAUVENET Bourgogne Pinot Noir Château Marguerite de Bourgogne 1985 $10 (6/30/88)
80 F. CHAUVENET Nuits-St.-Georges Les Perrières 1985 $48 (7/31/87)
80 DOMAINE BRUNO CLAIR Savigny-lès-Beaune La Dominode 1985 $24 (3/15/88)
80 MACHARD DE GRAMONT Aloxe-Corton Les Morais 1985 $34 (7/15/88)
80 J. JAYER Vosne-Romanée Les Rouges 1985 $44 (3/15/88)
80 HENRI MAGNIEN Gevrey-Chambertin Premier Cru 1985 $29 (10/15/87)
80 MARQUIS D'ANGERVILLE Volnay Clos des Ducs 1985 $35 (3/15/88)
80 MOMMESSIN Savigny-lès-Beaune 1985 $17 (7/31/88)
80 PHILIPPE NADDEF Gevrey-Chambertin Les Champeaux 1985 $29 (3/31/88)
79 JEAN CLAUDE BOISSET Nuits-St.-Georges 1985 $25 (4/30/88)
79 A.R. CHOPPIN Beaune Grèves 1985 $32 (9/30/87)
79 FAIVELEY Corton Clos des Cortons 1985 $80 (3/15/88)
79 JEAN-NOEL GAGNARD Chassagne-Montrachet Rouge Morgeot 1985 $18 (11/30/87)
79 LOUIS JADOT Côte de Beaune-Villages 1985 $17 (4/15/88)
79 LABOURE-ROI Pommard Les Bertins 1985 $29 (3/15/88)
79 PHILIPPE LECLERC Gevrey-Chambertin Les Champeaux 1985 $55 (10/31/88)
79 LUPE-CHOLET Bourgogne Clos de Lupé 1985 $15 (3/31/88)
79 MOILLARD Fixin Clos d'Entre Deux Velles 1985 $16 (5/31/87)
79 LOUIS TRAPET Gevrey-Chambertin 1985 $40 (5/31/88)
78 JEAN CLAUDE BOISSET Pommard 1985 $28 (4/30/88)
78 JOSEPH DROUHIN Bourgogne Pinot Noir Laforêt 1985 $8.50 (11/15/87)
78 FAIVELEY Clos de la Roche 1985 $88 (3/15/88)
78 MACHARD DE GRAMONT Nuits-St.-Georges Les Vallerots 1985 $47 (5/31/88)
78 LOUIS JADOT Bourgogne Pinot Noir Jadot 1985 $11 (4/30/88)
78 DOMAINE LEQUIN-ROUSSOT Santenay 1985 $18 (5/31/88)
78 MOILLARD Bourgogne Pinot Noir 1985 $7 (3/31/88)
78 DOMAINE DANIEL RION Vosne-Romanée 1985 $28 (2/29/88)
78 DOMAINE F. & L. SAIER Clos des Lambrays Domaine des Lambrays 1985 $55 (2/15/88)
78 CHARLES VIENOT Bourgogne 1985 $9 (6/15/89)
77 RENE ENGEL Vosne-Romanée 1985 $24 (10/15/87)
77 LOUIS LATOUR Gevrey-Chambertin 1985 $36 (10/15/88)
77 DOMAINE JEAN MORETEAUX Bourgogne Pinot Noir Les Clous 1985 $9 (11/15/87)
77 REMOISSENET Givry du Domaine Thénard 1985 $18 (4/30/88)
76 HENRI BOILLOT Bourgogne 1985 $13 (12/31/88)
76 JEAN CLAUDE BOISSET Pommard Rugiens 1985 $33 (3/15/88)
76 FAIVELEY Nuits-St.-Georges Les Porêts St.-Georges 1985 $47 (3/15/88)
76 PIERRE GELIN Fixin Clos Napolèon 1985 $25 (4/30/88)
76 LOUIS LATOUR Aloxe-Corton Les Chaillots 1985 $37 (4/15/88)
76 DOMAINE B. SERVEAU Bourgogne Rouge 1985 $13 (11/15/87)
75 CAVE DES VIGNERONS DE BUXY Bourgogne Pinot Noir Grande Réserve 1985 $7 (6/30/88)
75 FAIVELEY Mercurey Clos des Myglands 1985 $20 (4/30/88)
75 DOMAINE GROS FRERE & SOEUR Clos de Vougeot Musigny 1985 $70 (3/31/88)
75 LOUIS JADOT Nuits-St.-Georges Les Boudots 1985 $42 (3/15/88)
75 DOMAINE LEQUIN-ROUSSOT Nuits-St.-Georges 1985 $39 (4/15/88)
75 REMOISSENET Echézeaux 1985 $73 (3/15/88)
74 DOMAINE DUJAC Chambolle-Musigny Les Gruenchers 1985 $43 (3/31/88)
73 DOMAINE BRUNO CLAIR Morey-St.-Denis 1985 $20 (5/15/88)
73 MICHEL CLERGET Chambolle-Musigny 1985 $38 (5/15/88)
73 LEROY Bourgogne d'Auvenay 1985 $12 (3/31/88)
71 CLEMANCEY FRERES Fixin Les-Hervelets 1985 $21 (4/30/88)
71 DOMAINE GROS FRERE & SOEUR Grands Echézeaux 1985 $75 (3/31/88)
71 LEONARD DE ST.-AUBIN Nuits-St.-Georges 1985 $25 (11/30/87)
70 JEAN CHOFFLET Givry 1985 $12 (11/15/87)
70 DOMAINE GROS FRERE & SOEUR Vosne-Romanée 1985 $35 (4/15/88)
68 DOMAINE HENRI GOUGES Nuits-St.-Georges Les St.-Georges 1985 $45 (2/15/88)
67 PIERRE BITOUZET Savigny-lès-Beaune Lavières 1985 $19 (3/15/88)
67 LA POUSSE D'OR Santenay Clos Tavannes 1985 $22 (3/15/88)
66 BICHOT Santenay Les Gravières 1985 $15 (3/15/88)
66 LEONARD DE ST.-AUBIN Gevrey-Chambertin 1985 $25 (11/30/87)
64 CHARLOPIN-PARIZOT Gevrey-Chambertin 1985 $22 (11/30/87)

PORTUGAL

Vintage Port

1985

96 GRAHAM Vintage Port 1985 Rel: $31 Cur: $48 (VP-6/90)
95 FONSECA Vintage Port 1985 Rel: $32 Cur: $39 (VP-6/90)
95 QUINTA DO NOVAL Vintage Port Nacional 1985 $200 (VP-11/89)
93 BURMESTER Vintage Port 1985 $25 (VP-1/90)
92 NIEPOORT Vintage Port 1985 Rel: $25 Cur: $39 (VP-6/90)
91 GRAHAM Vintage Port 1985 Rel: $31 Cur: $48 (9/30/87) CS
91 WARRE Vintage Port 1985 Rel: $28 Cur: $40 (VP-6/90)
90 COCKBURN Vintage Port 1985 Rel: $33 Cur: $45 (VP-6/90)
90 KOPKE Vintage Port 1985 Rel: $18 Cur: $20 (VP-1/90)
90 TAYLOR FLADGATE Vintage Port 1985 Rel: $32 Cur: $45 (VP-6/90)
89 DOW Vintage Port 1985 Rel: $30 Cur: $36 (VP-6/90)
89 MARTINEZ Vintage Port 1985 Rel: $21 Cur: $27 (VP-6/90)
89 OFFLEY Vintage Port Boa Vista 1985 Rel: $22 Cur: $35 (VP-6/90)
89 SMITH WOODHOUSE Vintage Port 1985 Rel: $22 Cur: $37 (VP-6/90)
88 CALEM Vintage Port 1985 Rel: $25 Cur: $40 (VP-6/90)
88 ROCHA Vintage Port 1985 $32 (4/15/91)
87 FERREIRA Vintage Port 1985 Rel: $20 Cur: $30 (VP-11/89)
87 VAN ZELLER Vintage Port Quinta do Roriz 1985 ($NA) (VP-7/90)
86 QUINTA DO NOVAL Vintage Port 1985 Rel: $22 Cur: $36 (VP-6/90)
85 GOULD CAMPBELL Vintage Port 1985 Rel: $23 Cur: $32 (VP-6/90)
85 MORGAN Vintage Port 1985 ($NA) (VP-2/90)
85 POCAS JUNIOR Vintage Port 1985 Rel: $17 Cur: $19 (VP-2/90)
85 QUARLES HARRIS Vintage Port 1985 Rel: $21 Cur: $29 (VP-6/90)
85 RAMOS-PINTO Vintage Port 1985 Rel: $21 Cur: $36 (VP-11/89)
83 SANDEMAN Vintage Port 1985 Rel: $22 Cur: $38 (VP-6/90)
81 CHURCHILL Vintage Port 1985 Rel: $22 Cur: $51 (VP-2/90)
81 CROFT Vintage Port 1985 Rel: $30 Cur: $43 (VP-6/90)
81 DELAFORCE Vintage Port 1985 Rel: $24 Cur: $35 (VP-6/90)
81 REBELLO-VALENTE Vintage Port 1985 Rel: $23 Cur: $39 (VP-6/90)
81 ROZES Vintage Port 1985 Rel: $16 Cur: $21 (VP-5/90)
81 WIESE & KROHN Vintage Port 1985 Rel: $21 Cur: $34 (VP-1/90)
80 BARROS Vintage Port 1985 Rel: $24 Cur: $29 (VP-1/90)
80 HOOPER Vintage Port 1985 Rel: $15 Cur: $19 (VP-6/90)
80 VAN ZELLER Vintage Port 1985 ($NA) (VP-1/90)
78 C. DA SILVA Vintage Port Presidential 1985 $30 (VP-2/90)
78 FONSECA Vintage Port Quinta do Panascal 1985 ($NA) (VP-2/90)
78 QUINTA DA ROMANEIRA Vintage Port 1985 $29 (VP-1/90)
76 OSBORNE Vintage Port 1985 Rel: $20 Cur: $26 (VP-2/89)

PORTUGAL
Vintage Port

76 QUINTA DO INFANTADO Vintage Port 1985 $33 (VP-7/90)
72 FEIST Vintage Port 1985 Rel: $20 Cur: $28 (VP-1/90)
72 FEUERHEERD Vintage Port 1985 ($NA) (VP-1/90)
71 QUINTA DO CRASTO Vintage Port 1985 $24 (VP-1/90)
71 ROYAL OPORTO Vintage Port 1985 Rel: $12 Cur: $24 (VP-6/90)
70 BORGES Vintage Port 1985 $15 (VP-5/90)
70 VIEIRA DE SOUSA Vintage Port 1985 ($NA) (VP-1/90)
69 A. PINTOS DOS SANTOS Vintage Port 1985 ($NA) (VP-1/90)
67 MESSIAS Vintage Port 1985 Rel: $12 Cur: $16 (VP-2/90)

1983

94 DOW Vintage Port 1983 Rel: $20 Cur: $34 (VP-6/90)
94 WARRE Vintage Port 1983 Rel: $28 Cur: $38 (12/31/86) CS
93 GRAHAM Vintage Port 1983 Rel: $30 Cur: $43 (VP-6/90)
92 COCKBURN Vintage Port 1983 Rel: $22 Cur: $45 (8/31/87) CS
92 SMITH WOODHOUSE Vintage Port 1983 Rel: $22 Cur: $37 (VP-6/90)
91 FERREIRA Vintage Port Quinta do Seixo 1983 Rel: $14 Cur: $26 (VP-11/89)
91 OFFLEY Vintage Port Boa Vista 1983 Rel: $22 Cur: $33 (VP-1/90)
90 FONSECA Vintage Port 1983 Rel: $24 Cur: $38 (VP-6/90)
90 GOULD CAMPBELL Vintage Port 1983 Rel: $22 Cur: $38 (VP-6/90)

89 FONSECA Vintage Port 1983 Rel: $24 Cur: $38 (3/31/87)
89 QUARLES HARRIS Vintage Port 1983 Rel: $18 Cur: $33 (VP-2/90)
89 RAMOS-PINTO Vintage Port 1983 Rel: $17 Cur: $33 (VP-11/89)
89 TAYLOR FLADGATE Vintage Port 1983 Rel: $25 Cur: $42 (VP-6/90)
88 WARRE Vintage Port 1983 Rel: $28 Cur: $38 (VP-6/90)
85 CROFT Vintage Port Quinta da Roêda 1983 $22 (VP-2/90)
85 KOPKE Vintage Port 1983 Rel: $18 Cur: $23 (VP-1/90)
84 CALEM Vintage Port 1983 Rel: $18 Cur: $44 (VP-6/90)
84 NIEPOORT Vintage Port 1983 Rel: $14 Cur: $41 (VP-6/90)
84 VAN ZELLER Vintage Port 1983 Rel: $22 Cur: $36 (VP-1/90)

84 VAN ZELLER Vintage Port Quinta do Roriz 1983 $22 (VP-7/90)
79 FONSECA Vintage Port Quinta do Panascal 1983 ($NA) (VP-2/90)
78 REBELLO-VALENTE Vintage Port 1983 Rel: $23 Cur: $33 (VP-6/90)
77 MESSIAS Vintage Port Quinta do Cachão 1983 Rel: $8 Cur: $11 (VP-2/90)
76 BARROS Vintage Port 1983 Rel: $8 Cur: $30 (VP-1/90)
76 ROYAL OPORTO Vintage Port 1983 Rel: $9 Cur: $17 (VP-6/90)
70 BORGES Vintage Port 1983 Rel: $12 Cur: $26 (VP-5/90)
69 CHURCHILL Vintage Port Agua Alta 1983 Rel: $22 Cur: $40 (VP-7/90)
60 HOOPER Vintage Port 1983 $20 (VP-3/90)

1977

100 FONSECA Vintage Port 1977 Rel: $16 Cur: $62 (VP-4/90)
98 TAYLOR FLADGATE Vintage Port 1977 Rel: $17 Cur: $75 (VP-4/90)
94 DOW Vintage Port 1977 Rel: $12 Cur: $57 (VP-4/90)
93 GOULD CAMPBELL Vintage Port 1977 Rel: $11 Cur: $54 (VP-2/90)
92 WARRE Vintage Port 1977 Rel: $15 Cur: $61 (VP-4/90)
91 GRAHAM Vintage Port 1977 Rel: $15 Cur: $66 (3/16/84) CS
90 GRAHAM Vintage Port 1977 Rel: $15 Cur: $66 (VP-4/90)
89 NIEPOORT Vintage Port 1977 Rel: $11 Cur: $50 (VP-4/90)
89 QUARLES HARRIS Vintage Port 1977 Rel: $11 Cur: $41 (VP-2/90)

89 REBELLO-VALENTE Vintage Port 1977 Rel: $12 Cur: $42 (VP-2/90)
89 SMITH WOODHOUSE Vintage Port 1977 Rel: $11 Cur: $50 (VP-2/90)
88 OFFLEY Vintage Port Boa Vista 1977 Rel: $11 Cur: $40 (VP-1/90)
86 FERREIRA Vintage Port 1977 Rel: $11 Cur: $45 (VP-11/89)
85 CROFT Vintage Port 1977 Rel: $14 Cur: $53 (VP-4/90)
85 SANDEMAN Vintage Port 1977 Rel: $15 Cur: $64 (VP-6/90)
82 BURMESTER Vintage Port 1977 Rel: $11 Cur: $35 (VP-1/90)
82 DIEZ HERMANOS Vintage Port 1977 ($NA) (VP-4/90)
81 ROCHA Vintage Port 1977 $19 (4/30/91)
80 DELAFORCE Vintage Port 1977 Rel: $11 Cur: $54 (VP-2/90)

78 MORGAN Vintage Port 1977 ($NA) (VP-1/90)
78 QUINTA DO NOVAL Vintage Port 1977 $50 (10/31/88)
74 ROYAL OPORTO Vintage Port 1977 Rel: $8 Cur: $30 (VP-11/89)
72 C. DA SILVA Vintage Port Presidential 1977 $39 (VP-2/90)
70 CALEM Vintage Port 1977 Rel: $11 Cur: $58 (VP-11/89)
69 FEUERHEERD Vintage Port 1977 $17 (VP-1/90)
68 KOPKE Vintage Port 1977 ($NA) (VP-1/90)
60 MESSIAS Vintage Port Quinta do Cachão 1977 Rel: $7 Cur: $22 (VP-2/90)

UNITED STATES
California/*Cabernet Sauvignon & Blends*

1987

98 CAYMUS Cabernet Sauvignon Napa Valley Special Selection 1987 Rel: $60 Cur: $82 (10/31/91) CS
97 GRACE FAMILY Cabernet Sauvignon Napa Valley 1987 Rel: $56 Cur: $200 (6/30/90)
97 OPUS ONE Napa Valley 1987 Rel: $68 Cur: $74 (11/15/90) CS
96 THE HESS COLLECTION Cabernet Sauvignon Napa Valley Reserve 1987 Rel: $34 Cur: $55 (10/15/91)
96 SPOTTSWOODE Cabernet Sauvignon Napa Valley 1987 Rel: $36 Cur: $60 (9/15/90) SS
95 CHATEAU MONTELENA Cabernet Sauvignon Napa Valley 1987 Rel: $30 Cur: $37 (10/31/91) SS
95 DIAMOND CREEK Cabernet Sauvignon Napa Valley Volcanic Hill 1987 Rel: $40 Cur: $44 (12/15/89)
95 DUCKHORN Cabernet Sauvignon Napa Valley 1987 Rel: $20 Cur: $31 (6/30/90) CS
95 HEITZ Cabernet Sauvignon Napa Valley Martha's Vineyard 1987 Rel: $65 Cur: $75 (3/31/92) CS

95 WILLIAM HILL Cabernet Sauvignon Napa Valley Reserve 1987 Rel: $24 Cur: $27 (11/15/90) SS
95 KENDALL-JACKSON Cardinale Meritage California 1987 $50 (3/31/92)
95 LA JOTA Cabernet Sauvignon Howell Mountain 1987 Rel: $25 Cur: $30 (7/31/90) SS
95+ GRGICH HILLS Cabernet Sauvignon Napa Valley 1987 (NR) (4/15/89) (BT)
94 BERINGER Cabernet Sauvignon Napa Valley Private Reserve 1987 Rel: $40 Cur: $47 (10/31/91)
94 CHAPPELLET Cabernet Sauvignon Napa Valley Reserve 1987 Rel: $18 Cur: $21 (10/15/91)
94 DIAMOND CREEK Cabernet Sauvignon Napa Valley Red Rock Terrace 1987 Rel: $40 Cur: $46 (12/15/89)
94 DUNN Cabernet Sauvignon Howell Mountain 1987 Rel: $36 Cur: $70 (4/15/91)
94 FROG'S LEAP Cabernet Sauvignon Napa Valley 1987 Rel: $15 Cur: $25 (12/31/89) SS
94 THE HESS COLLECTION Cabernet Sauvignon Napa Valley 1987 Rel: $17 Cur: $22 (4/15/91) SS

94 LAUREL GLEN Cabernet Sauvignon Sonoma Mountain Counterpoint 1987 $13 (10/31/89)
94 LIVINGSTON Cabernet Sauvignon Napa Valley Moffett Vineyard 1987 Rel: $24 Cur: $28 (11/15/90)
94 PHILIP TOGNI Cabernet Sauvignon Napa Valley 1987 Rel: $24 Cur: $32 (8/31/90)
93 BENZIGER Cabernet Sauvignon Sonoma County 1987 Rel: $10 Cur: $20 (9/30/90) SS
93 CAYMUS Cabernet Sauvignon Napa Valley 1987 Rel: $16 Cur: $23 (9/15/90)
93 DUNN Cabernet Sauvignon Napa Valley 1987 Rel: $33 Cur: $52 (11/15/90)
93 FORMAN Cabernet Sauvignon Napa Valley 1987 Rel: $26 Cur: $44 (9/30/90)
93 LOUIS M. MARTINI Cabernet Sauvignon Sonoma Valley Monte Rosso 1987 Rel: $20 Cur: $23 (11/15/90)
93 MAZZOCCO Cabernet Sauvignon Alexander Valley Claret Style 1987 $20 (8/31/90)
93 QUAIL RIDGE Cabernet Sauvignon Napa Valley 1987 $16 (9/30/91)

93 SILVERADO Cabernet Sauvignon Stags Leap District Limited Reserve 1987 Rel: $38 Cur: $43 (10/31/91)
93 STERLING Reserve Napa Valley 1987 Rel: $43 Cur: $48 (11/15/90)
92 BEAULIEU Cabernet Sauvignon Napa Valley Georges de Latour Private Reserve 1987 Rel: $35 Cur: $39 (11/15/91)
92 CAIN Cabernet Sauvignon Napa Valley Estate 1987 $25 (10/15/90)
92 CHATEAU ST. JEAN Cabernet Sauvignon Alexander Valley 1987 $16 (6/30/91) SS
92 CLOS DU VAL Cabernet Sauvignon Stags Leap District 1987 Rel: $18.50 Cur: $22 (6/30/91)
92 B.R. COHN Cabernet Sauvignon Sonoma Valley Olive Hill Vineyard 1987 Rel: $25 Cur: $28 (6/30/90)
92 CORISON Cabernet Sauvignon Napa Valley 1987 $20 (11/15/90)
92 CUVAISON Cabernet Sauvignon Napa Valley 1987 Rel: $17.50 Cur: $21 (10/31/90)
92 FOLIE A DEUX Cabernet Sauvignon Napa Valley 1987 $18 (11/15/90)

92 GUENOC Cabernet Sauvignon Napa Valley Beckstoffer Reserve 1987 $24 (6/30/91)
92 KENWOOD Cabernet Sauvignon Sonoma Valley Jack London Vineyard 1987 Rel: $18 Cur: $21 (1/31/91)
92 MORGAN Cabernet Sauvignon Carmel Valley 1987 $16 (9/30/90)
92 OPTIMA Cabernet Sauvignon Sonoma County 1987 $22 (12/15/90)
92 SHAFER Cabernet Sauvignon Stags Leap District 1987 Rel: $18 Cur: $21 (7/31/90)
92 SILVERADO Cabernet Sauvignon Stags Leap District 1987 Rel: $14 Cur: $21 (4/15/90) SS
92 RODNEY STRONG Cabernet Sauvignon Alexander Valley Reserve 1987 $28 (9/30/91)
92 SWANSON Cabernet Sauvignon Napa Valley 1987 $25 (10/15/91)
92 TERRACES Cabernet Sauvignon Napa Valley 1987 $38 (2/29/92)
91 VINCENT ARROYO Cabernet Sauvignon Napa Valley 1987 $12 (11/15/90)

91 CAIN Five Napa Valley 1987 $30 (4/30/91)
91 DIAMOND CREEK Cabernet Sauvignon Napa Valley Lake 1987 Rel: $100 Cur: $230 (11/15/90)
91 EDMUNDS ST. JOHN Les Fleurs du Chaparral Napa Valley 1987 $15 (8/31/90)
91 FLORA SPRINGS Cabernet Sauvignon Napa Valley Cellar Select 1987 $25 (11/15/90)
91 FRANCISCAN Cabernet Sauvignon Napa Valley Oakville Estate Reserve 1987 $16 (11/15/91) SS
91 HACIENDA Antares Sonoma County 1987 $28 (11/15/90)
91 MAZZOCCO Matrix Sonoma County 1987 $28 (1/31/92)
91 OAKFORD Cabernet Sauvignon Napa Valley 1987 $25 (11/15/90)
91 PAHLMEYER Caldwell Vineyard Napa Valley 1987 $28 (11/15/90)
91 A. RAFANELLI Cabernet Sauvignon Dry Creek Valley 1987 $12 (8/31/90)

91 STERLING Cabernet Sauvignon Napa Valley 1987 Rel: $13 Cur: $16 (5/15/90)
91 STERLING Cabernet Sauvignon Napa Valley Diamond Mountain Ranch 1987 Rel: $16 Cur: $19 (11/15/90)
90 BERINGER Cabernet Sauvignon Knights Valley 1987 $15.50 (11/15/90)
90 CAKEBREAD Cabernet Sauvignon Napa Valley 1987 Rel: $18 Cur: $23 (10/15/90)
90 CHIMNEY ROCK Cabernet Sauvignon Stags Leap District 1987 $18 (7/31/91) SS
90 CLOS DU BOIS Marlstone Vineyard Alexander Valley 1987 $20 (7/31/91)
90 CLOS PEGASE Hommage California 1987 $20 (8/31/91)
90 CUTLER Cabernet Sauvignon Sonoma Valley Batto Ranch 1987 $17 (3/31/92)
90 DIAMOND CREEK Cabernet Sauvignon Napa Valley Gravelly Meadow 1987 Rel: $40 Cur: $45 (12/15/89)
90 FLORA SPRINGS Trilogy Napa Valley 1987 $35 (5/15/91)

90 GAN EDEN Cabernet Sauvignon Alexander Valley 1987 $18 (3/31/91)
90 GEYSER PEAK Réserve Alexandre Alexander Valley 1987 $18 (6/15/91)
90 HEITZ Cabernet Sauvignon Napa Valley 1987 Rel: $20 Cur: $22 (4/15/92) SS
90 HUSCH Cabernet Sauvignon Mendocino La Ribera Vineyards 1987 $12 (11/15/90)
90 JORDAN Cabernet Sauvignon Alexander Valley 1987 Rel: $20 Cur: $24 (11/15/91)
90 JUSTIN Reserve Paso Robles 1987 $20 (2/15/91)
90 KENWOOD Cabernet Sauvignon Sonoma Valley 1987 $15 (7/15/91)
90 LAUREL GLEN Cabernet Sauvignon Sonoma Mountain 1987 Rel: $22 Cur: $26 (9/15/90)
90 ROBERT MONDAVI Cabernet Sauvignon Napa Valley Reserve 1987 Rel: $43 Cur: $51 (8/31/90)
90 MONTICELLO Cabernet Sauvignon Napa Valley Corley Reserve 1987 $25 (11/15/90)

90 MONTICELLO Cabernet Sauvignon Napa Valley Jefferson Cuvée 1987 $14 (9/30/90)
90 ROBERT PECOTA Cabernet Sauvignon Napa Valley Kara's Vineyard 1987 Rel: $16 Cur: $19 (10/15/90)
90 ROBERT PEPI Cabernet Sauvignon Napa Valley Vine Hill Ranch 1987 $20 (4/30/91)
90 ST. CLEMENT Cabernet Sauvignon Napa Valley 1987 Rel: $20 Cur: $23 (9/30/91) CS
90 STRATFORD Cabernet Sauvignon Napa Valley Partners' Reserve 1987 $15.50 (4/30/91)
90 WHITEHALL LANE Cabernet Sauvignon Napa Valley Reserve 1987 $28 (11/15/91)
90 ZD Cabernet Sauvignon Napa Valley Estate Bottled 1987 $40 (1/31/91)
90+ BERINGER Cabernet Sauvignon Napa Valley Chabot Vineyard 1987 (NR) (4/15/89) (BT)
90+ CONN CREEK Cabernet Sauvignon Napa Valley Barrel Select Private Reserve 1987 $19 (4/15/89) (BT)
90+ INGLENOOK Cabernet Sauvignon Napa Valley Reserve Cask 1987 (NR) (4/15/89) (BT)

Key to Symbols

The scores reported here are the results of blind tastings conducted by our panel of senior editors. Wines that carry the initials below are results of individual tastings.

THE WINE SPECTATOR 100-POINT SCALE ***95-100***—Classic, a great wine; ***90-94***—Outstanding, superior character and style; ***80-89***—Good to very good, a wine with special qualities; ***70-79***—Average, drinkable wine that may have minor flaws; ***60-69***—Below average, drinkable but not recommended; ***50-59***—Poor, undrinkable, not recommended. "+"—With a score indicates a range; used primarily with barrel tastings to indicate a preliminary score.

SPECIAL DESIGNATIONS SS—Spectator Selection, CS—Cellar Selection, BB—Best Buy, ($NA)—Price not available, (NR)—Not released.

TASTER'S INITIALS (JG)—Jim Gordon, (HS)—Harvey Steiman, (JL)—James Laube, (JS)—James Suckling, (TM)—Thomas Matthews, (TR)—Terry Robards, (PM)—Per-Henrik Mansson, (BT)—Barrel Tasting (these wines were tasted blind from barrel samples), (CA-date)—*California's Great Cabernets* by James Laube, (CH-date)—*California's Great Chardonnays* by James Laube, (VP-date)—*Vintage Port* by James Suckling.

DATE TASTED Dates in parentheses represent the issue in which the rating was published.

90+ KENT RASMUSSEN Cabernet Sauvignon Napa Valley 1987 $20 (4/15/89) (BT)
90+ SANTA CRUZ MOUNTAIN Cabernet Sauvignon Santa Cruz Mountains Bates Ranch 1987 (NR) (4/15/89) (BT)
90+ SIMI Cabernet Sauvignon Alexander Valley Reserve 1987 $28 (4/15/89) (BT)
90+ TREFETHEN Cabernet Sauvignon Napa Valley Hillside Selection 1987 (NR) (4/15/89) (BT)
89 ABREU Cabernet Sauvignon Napa Valley Madrona Ranch 1987 $25 (7/31/91)
89 ADELAIDA Cabernet Sauvignon Paso Robles 1987 $14 (2/28/91)
89 BANDIERA Cabernet Sauvignon Napa Valley 1987 $7 (11/15/91) BB
89 CARMENET Red Sonoma Valley 1987 Rel: $20 Cur: $24 (11/15/90)
89 CRONIN Cabernet Sauvignon Merlot Robinson Vineyard 1987 $17 (2/28/91)
89 DOMINUS Napa Valley 1987 $45 (11/15/91)
89 FRANCISCAN Cabernet Sauvignon Napa Valley Oakville Estate 1987 $12 (2/15/91)
89 GEYSER PEAK Cabernet Sauvignon Alexander Valley Estate Reserve 1987 $14 (6/15/91)
89 GUENOC Cabernet Sauvignon Lake County 1987 $12 (7/15/91)
89 JOHNSON TURNBULL Cabernet Sauvignon Napa Valley Vineyard Selection 67 1987 $22 (6/30/91)
89 ROBERT KEEBLE Cabernet Sauvignon Napa Valley 1987 $14 (10/15/91)
89 KATHRYN KENNEDY Cabernet Sauvignon Santa Cruz Mountains 1987 $45 (1/31/91)
89 MURPHY-GOODE Cabernet Sauvignon Alexander Valley 1987 $16.50 (5/31/90)
89 NALLE Cabernet Sauvignon Dry Creek Valley 1987 $18 (1/31/91)
89 SILVER OAK Cabernet Sauvignon Alexander Valley 1987 Rel: $29 Cur: $31 (10/15/91)
89 SILVER OAK Cabernet Sauvignon Napa Valley 1987 Rel: $29 Cur: $34 (10/15/91)
89 SIMI Cabernet Sauvignon Sonoma County 1987 $16.50 (5/15/91)
89 STAGS' LEAP WINERY Cabernet Sauvignon Stags Leap District 1987 $18 (6/30/91)
89 RODNEY STRONG Cabernet Sauvignon Alexander Valley Alexander's Crown Vineyard 1987 $17 (7/15/91)
88 CLOS DU BOIS Cabernet Sauvignon Alexander Valley Briarcrest Vineyard 1987 Rel: $18 Cur: $20 (11/15/91)
88 DEHLINGER Cabernet Sauvignon Russian River Valley 1987 $13 (2/28/91)
88 ESTANCIA Meritage Alexander Valley 1987 $12 (1/31/91)
88 FAR NIENTE Cabernet Sauvignon Napa Valley 1987 $33 (11/15/90)
88 GEYSER PEAK Cabernet Sauvignon Sonoma County 1987 $8.50 (11/30/90) BB
88 GIRARD Cabernet Sauvignon Napa Valley Reserve 1987 Rel: $25 Cur: $29 (11/15/91)
88 GROTH Cabernet Sauvignon Napa Valley Reserve 1987 $40 (3/31/92)
88 GUENOC Langtry Meritage Lake-Napa Counties 1987 $35 (4/15/91)
88 HAGAFEN Cabernet Sauvignon Napa Valley 1987 $20 (4/30/90)
88 KENWOOD Cabernet Sauvignon Sonoma Valley Artist Series 1987 $35 (11/15/90)
88 LYTTON SPRINGS Cabernet Sauvignon Mendocino County Private Reserve 1987 $18 (9/15/90)
88 JOSEPH PHELPS Cabernet Sauvignon Napa Valley Backus Vineyard 1987 $30 (7/15/91)
88 PRESTON Cabernet Sauvignon Dry Creek Valley 1987 Rel: $14 Cur: $17 (10/31/90)
88 RIDGE Cabernet Sauvignon Santa Cruz Mountains Monte Bello 1987 Rel: $45 Cur: $52 (11/15/90)
88 STAR HILL Cabernet Sauvignon Napa Valley Doc's Reserve 1987 $24 (11/15/91)
88 VILLA MT. EDEN Cabernet Sauvignon Napa Valley 1987 Rel: $13 Cur: $15 (2/15/91)
88 WILD HORSE Cabernet Sauvignon Paso Robles 1987 $13 (4/30/91)
87 ALEXANDER VALLEY VINEYARDS Cabernet Sauvignon Alexander Valley 1987 Rel: $12 Cur: $15 (5/31/90)
87 ARROWOOD Cabernet Sauvignon Sonoma County 1987 Rel: $22 Cur: $25 (11/15/90)
87 CHATEAU SOUVERAIN Cabernet Sauvignon Alexander Valley 1987 $9.50 (11/15/90)
87 CONN CREEK Cabernet Sauvignon Napa Valley Barrel Select 1987 $17 (7/15/91)
87 DRY CREEK Meritage Dry Creek Valley 1987 $24 (1/31/92)
87 GARY FARRELL Cabernet Sauvignon Sonoma County 1987 $16 (10/31/90)
87 FRANCISCAN Meritage Napa Valley 1987 Rel: $17 Cur: $21 (4/30/91)
87 FREEMARK ABBEY Cabernet Sauvignon Napa Valley Bosché 1987 $25 (11/15/91)
87 HUSCH Cabernet Sauvignon Mendocino North Field Select 1987 $16 (11/15/90)
87 KENDALL-JACKSON Cabernet Sauvignon California Proprietor's Grand Reserve 1987 $16 (3/31/92)
87 KLEIN Cabernet Sauvignon Santa Cruz Mountains 1987 $19 (10/15/90)
87 MARIETTA Cabernet Sauvignon Sonoma County 1987 $10 (2/28/91)
87 MARKHAM Cabernet Sauvignon Napa Valley 1987 $15 (8/31/91)
87 LOUIS M. MARTINI Cabernet Sauvignon Napa Valley Reserve 1987 $14 (10/15/90)
87 MEEKER Cabernet Sauvignon Dry Creek Valley 1987 $14 (10/15/91)
87 ROBERT MONDAVI Cabernet Sauvignon Napa Valley 1987 $20 (5/31/90)
87 NEWTON Cabernet Sauvignon Napa Valley 1987 $17 (11/15/91)
87 PEJU Cabernet Sauvignon Napa Valley HB Vineyard 1987 $20 (11/15/90)
87 QUIVIRA Cabernet Sauvignon Dry Creek Valley 1987 $15 (11/15/90)
87 ROMBAUER Cabernet Sauvignon Napa Valley 1987 $16 (11/15/91)
87 SEQUOIA GROVE Cabernet Sauvignon Napa Valley Estate 1987 $26 (11/15/91)
87 STAG'S LEAP WINE CELLARS SLV Cask 23 Stags Leap District 1987 Rel: $55 Cur: $60 (11/15/91)
87 STERLING Three Palms Vineyard Napa Valley 1987 $23 (11/15/90)
87 VICHON Cabernet Sauvignon Stags Leap District SLD 1987 Rel: $17 Cur: $22 (7/31/90)
86 BYINGTON Cabernet Sauvignon Napa Valley 1987 $16 (11/15/91)
86 CLOS DU BOIS Cabernet Sauvignon Alexander Valley 1987 $11 (2/15/90)
86 COSENTINO Cabernet Sauvignon North Coast Reserve 1987 $28 (2/28/91)
86 FREEMARK ABBEY Cabernet Sauvignon Napa Valley 1987 $16 (7/31/91)
86 GIRARD Cabernet Sauvignon Napa Valley 1987 Rel: $16 Cur: $20 (11/15/90)
86 INGLENOOK Cabernet Sauvignon Napa Valley 1987 $10 (11/15/91)
86 IRON HORSE Cabernets Alexander Valley 1987 $18.50 (3/15/91)
86 KEENAN Cabernet Sauvignon Napa Valley 1987 Rel: $18 Cur: $20 (5/31/90)
86 LAUREL GLEN Terra Rosa Napa Valley 1987 $14 (7/31/90)
86 J. LOHR Cabernet Sauvignon Paso Robles Seven Oaks 1987 $12 (4/30/91)
86 MIRASSOU Cabernet Sauvignon Monterey County Fifth Generation Harvest Reserve Limited Bottling 1987 $12.50 (11/15/91)
86 BERNARD PRADEL Cabernet Sauvignon Napa Valley 1987 $20 (10/15/90)
86 ROLLING HILLS Cabernet Sauvignon California 1987 $7 (12/15/89) BB
86 SEBASTIANI Wildwood Sonoma Valley 1987 $15 (8/31/91)
86 STELTZNER Cabernet Sauvignon Stags Leap District 1987 Rel: $16 Cur: $20 (11/15/91)
86 TREFETHEN Cabernet Sauvignon Napa Valley 1987 Rel: $16 Cur: $19 (11/15/90)
86 WENTE BROS. Cabernet Sauvignon Livermore Valley Charles Wetmore Vineyard Estate Reserve 1987 $18 (4/30/91)
85 BEAULIEU Cabernet Sauvignon Napa Valley Rutherford 1987 Rel: $10 Cur: $13 (12/15/90)
85 BENZIGER Cabernet Sauvignon Sonoma Valley Estate Bottled 1987 $12 (11/15/90)
85 BENZIGER A Tribute Sonoma Mountain 1987 $20 (12/31/90)
85 BOEGER Cabernet Sauvignon El Dorado 1987 $11 (3/15/91)
85 BUEHLER Cabernet Sauvignon Napa Valley 1987 Rel: $16 Cur: $19 (7/31/90)
85 BURGESS Cabernet Sauvignon Napa Valley Vintage Selection 1987 Rel: $20 Cur: $23 (10/15/91)
85 COSENTINO The Poet California 1987 $25 (9/15/90)
85 DE LOACH Cabernet Sauvignon Russian River Valley O.F.S. 1987 $22 (10/15/90)
85 ETUDE Cabernet Sauvignon Napa Valley 1987 $24 (10/31/90)
85 FIELD STONE Cabernet Sauvignon Alexander Valley 1987 $14 (2/28/91)
85 GRAND CRU Cabernet Sauvignon Sonoma County Premium Selection 1987 $12 (11/15/91)
85 GUNDLACH BUNDSCHU Cabernet Sauvignon Sonoma Valley Rhinefarm Vineyards 1987 $15 (5/15/91)
85 HEITZ Cabernet Sauvignon Napa Valley Bella Oaks Vineyard 1987 Rel: $27 Cur: $31 (6/30/92)
85 WILLIAM HILL Cabernet Sauvignon Napa Valley Silver Label 1987 $14 (11/15/90)
85 KONOCTI Meritage Red Clear Lake 1987 $17 (4/15/91)
85 MOUNT EDEN Cabernet Sauvignon Santa Cruz Mountains Young Vine Cuvée 1987 $12 (4/15/90)
85 MOUNT VEEDER Cabernet Sauvignon Napa Valley 1987 $20 (4/30/91)
85 J. PEDRONCELLI Cabernet Sauvignon Dry Creek Valley 1987 $8.50 (11/15/90) BB
85 PINE RIDGE Cabernet Sauvignon Stags Leap District 1987 Rel: $28 Cur: $32 (1/31/92)
85 ST. SUPERY Cabernet Sauvignon Napa Valley Dollarhide Ranch 1987 $13 (7/15/90)
85 SEGHESIO Cabernet Sauvignon Sonoma County 1987 $9 (4/30/91)
85 STRATFORD Cabernet Sauvignon Napa Valley 1987 $11.50 (4/30/90)
85 RODNEY STRONG Cabernet Sauvignon Sonoma County 1987 $10 (6/30/91)
85 VIANSA Obsidian Sonoma-Napa Counties 1987 $65 (7/15/91)
85 WHITE OAK Cabernet Sauvignon Sonoma County 1987 $14 (2/29/92)
85+ FETZER Cabernet Sauvignon Mendocino Special Reserve 1987 (NR) (4/15/89) (BT)
85+ INGLENOOK Niebaum Claret Napa Valley 1987 (NR) (4/15/89) (BT)
85+ NEYERS Cabernet Sauvignon Napa Valley 1987 $15 (4/15/89) (BT)
85+ PINE RIDGE Cabernet Sauvignon Napa Valley Andrus Reserve 1987 (NR) (4/15/89) (BT)
85+ SHAFER Cabernet Sauvignon Stags Leap District Hillside Select 1987 $38 (4/15/89) (BT)
84 BRAREN PAULI Cabernet Sauvignon Mendocino 1987 $8.50 (3/31/91) BB
84 CAFARO Cabernet Sauvignon Napa Valley 1987 $20 (11/15/90)
84 CINNABAR Cabernet Sauvignon Santa Cruz Mountains 1987 $18 (3/31/91)
84 CRONIN Cabernet Sauvignon Merlot Santa Cruz Mountains 1987 $17 (3/31/92)
84 DOMAINE MICHEL Cabernet Sauvignon Sonoma County 1987 $19.50 (3/31/91)
84 DRY CREEK Cabernet Sauvignon Sonoma County 1987 $12.50 (4/15/90)
84 FERRARI-CARANO Cabernet Sauvignon Alexander Valley 1987 $17.50 (7/15/91)
84 FISHER Cabernet Sauvignon Napa-Sonoma Counties Coach Insignia 1987 Rel: $20 Cur: $23 (11/15/91)
84 HANZELL Cabernet Sauvignon Sonoma Valley 1987 Rel: $22 Cur: $32 (11/15/91)
84 LAKESPRING Cabernet Sauvignon Napa Valley 1987 Rel: $14 Cur: $18 (10/15/91)
84 LEEWARD Cabernet Sauvignon Alexander Valley 1987 $13 (11/15/90)
84 J. LOHR Cabernet Sauvignon California 1987 $7 (2/15/90) BB
84 PESENTI Cabernet Sauvignon San Luis Obispo County Family Reserve 1987 $8 (12/15/89)
84 PINE RIDGE Cabernet Sauvignon Napa Valley Diamond Mountain 1987 $35 (11/15/90)
84 RAVENSWOOD Cabernet Sauvignon Sonoma Valley 1987 Rel: $11 Cur: $20 (5/31/90)
84 WEIBEL Cabernet Sauvignon Mendocino County 1987 $8 (2/28/91) BB
84 WILLIAM WHEELER Cabernet Sauvignon Dry Creek Valley 1987 $14 (11/15/91)
84 WHITEHALL LANE Cabernet Sauvignon Napa Valley 1987 $18 (9/15/90)
83 BELLEROSE Cabernet Sauvignon Dry Creek Valley Reserve Cuvée 1987 $18 (11/15/91)
83 BUENA VISTA Cabernet Sauvignon Carneros 1987 $11 (10/15/90)
83 CHATEAU POTELLE Cabernet Sauvignon Alexander Valley 1987 $16 (8/31/91)
83 CHATEAU SOUVERAIN Cabernet Sauvignon Alexander Valley Private Reserve 1987 $15 (5/15/91)
83 CHRISTOPHE Cabernet Sauvignon Napa Valley Reserve 1987 $12 (11/15/91)
83 CONCANNON Cabernet Sauvignon Livermore Valley Reserve 1987 $16 (7/15/91)
83 DEUX AMIS Cabernet Sauvignon Dry Creek Valley 1987 $14 (11/15/91)
83 HALLCREST Cabernet Sauvignon El Dorado County De Cascabel Vineyard 1987 $13 (11/15/91)
83 KISTLER Cabernet Sauvignon Sonoma Valley Kistler Estate Vineyard 1987 $25 (2/28/91)
83 MERRYVALE Cabernet Sauvignon Napa Valley Profile 1987 $25 (11/15/91)
83 MONTEREY VINEYARD Cabernet Sauvignon Monterey County Classic 1987 $6 (1/31/91) BB
83 J.W. MORRIS Cabernet Sauvignon California Private Reserve 1987 $8 (3/31/90)
83 MARIO PERELLI-MINETTI Cabernet Sauvignon Napa Valley 1987 $12 (4/30/91)
83 RAYMOND Cabernet Sauvignon Napa Valley 1987 $17 (2/28/91)
83 RUTHERFORD RANCH Cabernet Sauvignon Napa Valley 1987 $13 (4/30/91)
83 SOBON ESTATE Cabernet Sauvignon Shenandoah Valley 1987 $15 (11/30/90)
83 ZACA MESA Cabernet Sauvignon Central Coast Reserve 1987 $25 (11/15/91)
82 CORBETT CANYON Cabernet Sauvignon Central Coast Reserve 1987 $9.50 (11/15/91)
82 CRESTON Cabernet Sauvignon Paso Robles Winemaker's Selection 1987 $16 (11/15/91)
82 FIRESTONE Cabernet Sauvignon Santa Ynez Valley 1987 $11 (5/31/90)
82 GAINEY Cabernet Sauvignon Santa Barbara County 1987 $13 (11/15/90)
82 KENDALL-JACKSON Cabernet Sauvignon California Vintner's Reserve 1987 $14 (11/15/91)
82 STEVENOT Cabernet Sauvignon Calaveras County Grand Reserve 1987 $9 (3/31/92)
82 STONEGATE Cabernet Sauvignon Napa Valley 1987 $14 (3/31/92)
81 BEAULIEU Cabernet Sauvignon Napa Valley Beau Tour 1987 $8 (5/31/89) BB
81 CAREY Cabernet Sauvignon Santa Ynez Valley La Cuesta Vineyard Reserve 1987 $16 (5/31/91)
81 DE LORIMIER Mosaic Alexander Valley 1987 $18 (3/31/92)
81 GROTH Cabernet Sauvignon Napa Valley 1987 Rel: $20 Cur: $23 (10/31/90)
81 JOULLIAN Cabernet Sauvignon Carmel Valley 1987 $14 (7/31/91)
81 LA VIEILLE MONTAGNE Cabernet Sauvignon Napa Valley 1987 $14 (6/15/91)
80 CHESTNUT HILL Cabernet Sauvignon Sonoma County 1987 $9 (3/31/90)
80 COSENTINO Cabernet Sauvignon North Coast 1987 $16 (6/30/90)
80 DORE Cabernet Sauvignon California Limited Release Lot 102 1987 $8.50 (11/15/91)
80 ESTANCIA Cabernet Sauvignon Alexander Valley 1987 $7 (7/15/90) BB
80 HANNA Cabernet Sauvignon Sonoma County 1987 $16 (8/31/90)
80 JOHNSON TURNBULL Cabernet Sauvignon Napa Valley 1987 $16 (11/15/90)
80 MONTE VERDE Cabernet Sauvignon California Proprietor's Reserve 1987 $6.50/L (12/15/89)
80 PARDUCCI Cabernet Sauvignon North Coast 1987 $9.50 (4/30/91)
80 SHENANDOAH Cabernet Sauvignon Amador County Artist Series 1987 $10 (2/28/91)
80+ HAYWOOD Cabernet Sauvignon Sonoma Valley Los Chamizal Vineyards 1987 $16 (4/15/89) (BT)
79 DAVIS BYNUM Cabernet Sauvignon Sonoma County 1987 $10.50 (11/15/90)
79 CHRISTIAN BROTHERS Cabernet Sauvignon Napa Valley 1987 $7.50 (10/15/91)
79 CRESTON Cabernet Sauvignon Paso Robles 1987 $10 (11/15/91)
79 GLEN ELLEN Cabernet Sauvignon California Proprietor's Reserve 1987 $6 (1/31/91)
79 HAWK CREST Cabernet Sauvignon North Coast 1987 $8 (3/31/90)
79 CHARLES KRUG Cabernet Sauvignon Napa Valley 1987 $10.50 (11/15/91)
79 STREBLOW Cabernet Sauvignon Napa Valley 1987 $16 (10/15/90)
78 MCDOWELL VALLEY Cabernet Sauvignon California 1987 $9 (11/15/90)
78 POPPY HILL Cabernet Sauvignon California 1987 $7.50 (5/31/91)
78 J. WILE & SONS Cabernet Sauvignon Napa Valley 1987 $10 (5/31/91)
78 ZD Cabernet Sauvignon Napa Valley 1987 $16 (2/15/91)
77 PINE RIDGE Cabernet Sauvignon Napa Valley Rutherford Cuvée 1987 $16.50 (3/15/92)
77 ROUND HILL Cabernet Sauvignon Napa Valley Reserve 1987 $11 (11/15/91)

77 SANTA BARBARA Cabernet Sauvignon Santa Ynez Valley Reserve 1987 $18 (11/15/90)
77 STAG'S LEAP WINE CELLARS Cabernet Sauvignon Stags Leap District SLV 1987 $28 (11/15/90)
77 SUTTER HOME Cabernet Sauvignon California 1987 $5.50 (6/30/89)
76 DE MOOR Cabernet Sauvignon Napa Valley 1987 $16 (11/15/91)
76 EBERLE Cabernet Sauvignon Paso Robles 1987 $16 (11/15/91)
75 BELVEDERE Cabernet Sauvignon Sonoma County Discovery Series 1987 $6 (6/15/90)
75 FENESTRA Cabernet Sauvignon Monterey Smith & Hook Vineyard 1987 $14 (11/15/91)
75 JOSEPH PHELPS Cabernet Sauvignon Napa Valley 1987 $14.50 (7/15/91)
75 STAG'S LEAP WINE CELLARS Cabernet Sauvignon Napa Valley 1987 $18 (8/31/90)
75+ JOSEPH PHELPS Cabernet Sauvignon Napa Valley Eisele Vineyard 1987 $40 (4/15/89) (BT)
74 ROBERT MONDAVI Cabernet Sauvignon California Woodbridge 1987 $6 (9/15/89)
74 NAPA RIDGE Cabernet Sauvignon North Coast 1987 $7 (11/15/90)
74 TULOCAY Cabernet Sauvignon Napa Valley Egan Vineyard 1987 $16.50 (2/15/91)
72 FIELD STONE Cabernet Sauvignon Alexander Valley Staten Family Reserve 1987 $25 (11/15/91)
72 SANTA YNEZ VALLEY Cabernet-Merlot Santa Barbara County 1987 $13 (3/31/90)
70 SEQUOIA GROVE Cabernet Sauvignon Napa Valley 1987 $18 (11/15/91)
65 MOUNT EDEN Cabernet Sauvignon Santa Cruz Mountains 1987 $28 (4/30/91)

1986

98 CAYMUS Cabernet Sauvignon Napa Valley Special Selection 1986 Rel: $50 Cur: $122 (CA-3/89)
96 DIAMOND CREEK Cabernet Sauvignon Napa Valley Red Rock Terrace 1986 Rel: $30 Cur: $48 (CA-3/89)
96 DIAMOND CREEK Cabernet Sauvignon Napa Valley Volcanic Hill 1986 Rel: $30 Cur: $63 (CA-3/89)
96 SILVERADO Cabernet Sauvignon Stags Leap District Limited Reserve 1986 Rel: $35 Cur: $39 (12/15/90) CS
96 TERRACES Cabernet Sauvignon Napa Valley 1986 $23 (1/31/91)
95 BERINGER Cabernet Sauvignon Napa Valley Private Reserve 1986 Rel: $35 Cur: $49 (9/15/90) CS
95 DUNN Cabernet Sauvignon Howell Mountain 1986 Rel: $30 Cur: $100 (7/31/90) CS
95 DUNN Cabernet Sauvignon Napa Valley 1986 Rel: $27 Cur: $62 (10/15/89) CS
95 HEITZ Cabernet Sauvignon Napa Valley Martha's Vineyard 1986 Rel: $60 Cur: $70 (4/15/91) CS
95 WILLIAM HILL Cabernet Sauvignon Napa Valley Reserve 1986 Rel: $24.50 Cur: $29 (CA-3/89)
95 JOHNSON TURNBULL Cabernet Sauvignon Napa Valley Vineyard Selection 82 1986 Rel: $14.50 Cur: $25 (8/31/89)
95 KENWOOD Cabernet Sauvignon Sonoma Valley Artist Series 1986 Rel: $30 Cur: $34 (11/30/89) CS
95 ROBERT MONDAVI Cabernet Sauvignon Napa Valley Reserve 1986 Rel: $35 Cur: $42 (11/15/89)
95 OPUS ONE Napa Valley 1986 Rel: $55 Cur: $85 (11/30/89)
95 SPOTTSWOODE Cabernet Sauvignon Napa Valley 1986 Rel: $30 Cur: $100 (9/15/89)
95 STERLING Reserve Napa Valley 1986 Rel: $35 Cur: $44 (3/15/90) CS
94 CAYMUS Cabernet Sauvignon Napa Valley 1986 Rel: $22 Cur: $33 (3/15/90) SS
94 B.R. COHN Cabernet Sauvignon Sonoma Valley Olive Hill Vineyard 1986 Rel: $18 Cur: $26 (5/31/89)
94 CUVAISON Cabernet Sauvignon Napa Valley 1986 Rel: $15 Cur: $20 (7/15/89)
94 DIAMOND CREEK Cabernet Sauvignon Napa Valley Gravelly Meadow 1986 Rel: $30 Cur: $52 (CA-3/89)
94 DUCKHORN Cabernet Sauvignon Napa Valley 1986 Rel: $18 Cur: $30 (7/31/89) SS
94 FLORA SPRINGS Trilogy Napa Valley 1986 Rel: $33 Cur: $36 (2/15/90)
94 FROG'S LEAP Cabernet Sauvignon Napa Valley 1986 Rel: $14 Cur: $41 (CA-3/89)
94 FROG'S LEAP Cabernet Sauvignon Napa Valley 1986 Rel: $14 Cur: $41 (12/31/88)
94 ST. FRANCIS Cabernet Sauvignon Sonoma Valley Reserve Black Label 1986 $20 (11/30/89)
94 SILVER OAK Cabernet Sauvignon Napa Valley 1986 Rel: $26 Cur: $49 (10/31/90) CS
94 SILVERADO Cabernet Sauvignon Stags Leap District 1986 Rel: $13.50 Cur: $25 (8/31/89) SS
93 BEAULIEU Cabernet Sauvignon Napa Valley Georges de Latour Private Reserve 1986 Rel: $31 Cur: $40 (3/31/91) (JL)
93 BERINGER Cabernet Sauvignon Napa Valley Chabot Vineyard 1986 $30 (CA-3/89)
93 BUENA VISTA Cabernet Sauvignon Carneros Private Reserve 1986 Rel: $25 Cur: $28 (10/15/90)
93 CAFARO Cabernet Sauvignon Napa Valley 1986 $18 (11/15/89)
93 CHATEAU MONTELENA Cabernet Sauvignon Napa Valley 1986 Rel: $25 Cur: $35 (10/15/90)
93 CINNABAR Cabernet Sauvignon Santa Cruz Mountains 1986 $15 (11/15/89)
93 DOMINUS Napa Valley 1986 $45 (CA-3/89)
93 FORMAN Cabernet Sauvignon Napa Valley 1986 Rel: $20 Cur: $51 (6/15/89)
93 GRACE FAMILY Cabernet Sauvignon Napa Valley 1986 Rel: $40 Cur: $230 (CA-3/89)
93 THE HESS COLLECTION Cabernet Sauvignon Napa Valley Reserve 1986 Rel: $33 Cur: $44 (9/15/90)
93 KEENAN Cabernet Sauvignon Napa Valley 1986 Rel: $16.50 Cur: $22 (8/31/89)
93 ROBERT MONDAVI Cabernet Sauvignon Napa Valley 1986 Rel: $18 Cur: $21 (7/31/89)
93 MOUNT VEEDER Meritage Napa Valley 1986 Rel: $18 Cur: $24 (CA-3/89)
93 GUSTAVE NIEBAUM Cabernet Sauvignon Napa Valley Tench Vineyard 1986 $16 (10/15/89)
93 JOSEPH PHELPS Insignia Napa Valley 1986 Rel: $40 Cur: $44 (8/31/90) CS
93 SHAFER Cabernet Sauvignon Stags Leap District 1986 Rel: $16 Cur: $21 (9/30/89) SS
93 SILVER OAK Cabernet Sauvignon Alexander Valley 1986 Rel: $26 Cur: $37 (10/31/90) SS
93 STAG'S LEAP WINE CELLARS Stags Leap District Stag's Leap Vineyards Cask 23 1986 Rel: $55 Cur: $73 (11/15/90)
93 PHILIP TOGNI Cabernet Sauvignon Napa Valley 1986 Rel: $22 Cur: $30 (CA-3/89)
92 ARROWOOD Cabernet Sauvignon Sonoma County 1986 Rel: $20 Cur: $25 (10/15/89)

Key to Symbols

The scores reported here are the results of blind tastings conducted by our panel of senior editors. Wines that carry the initials below are results of individual tastings.

THE WINE SPECTATOR 100-POINT SCALE ***95-100***—Classic, a great wine; ***90-94***—Outstanding, superior character and style; ***80-89***—Good to very good, a wine with special qualities; ***70-79***—Average, drinkable wine that may have minor flaws; ***60-69***—Below average, drinkable but not recommended; ***50-59***—Poor, undrinkable, not recommended. "+"—With a score indicates a range; used primarily with barrel tastings to indicate a preliminary score.

SPECIAL DESIGNATIONS SS—Spectator Selection, CS—Cellar Selection, BB—Best Buy, ($NA)—Price not available, (NR)—Not released.

TASTER'S INITIALS (JG)—Jim Gordon, (HS)—Harvey Steiman, (JL)—James Laube, (JS)—James Suckling, (TM)—Thomas Matthews, (TR)—Terry Robards, (PM)—Per-Henrik Mansson, (BT)—Barrel Tasting (these wines were tasted blind from barrel samples), (CA-date)—*California's Great Cabernets* by James Laube, (CH-date)—*California's Great Chardonnays* by James Laube, (VP-date)—*Vintage Port* by James Suckling.

DATE TASTED Dates in parentheses represent the issue in which the rating was published.

92 CHAPPELLET Cabernet Sauvignon Napa Valley Reserve 1986 Rel: $18 Cur: $21 (CA-3/89)
92 ETUDE Cabernet Sauvignon Napa Valley 1986 $20 (9/30/89)
92 GROTH Cabernet Sauvignon Napa Valley 1986 Rel: $18 Cur: $25 (11/15/89)
92 HAYWOOD Cabernet Sauvignon Sonoma Valley 1986 Rel: $16 Cur: $20 (11/15/89)
92 MONTICELLO Cabernet Sauvignon Napa Valley Corley Reserve 1986 Rel: $24 Cur: $28 (3/15/90)
92 NIEBAUM-COPPOLA Rubicon Napa Valley 1986 ($NA) (CA-3/89)
92 PEJU Cabernet Sauvignon Napa Valley HB Vineyard 1986 $20 (11/15/89)
92 PINE RIDGE Cabernet Sauvignon Napa Valley Diamond Mountain 1986 Rel: $30 Cur: $33 (11/30/89)
92 PLAM Cabernet Sauvignon Napa Valley 1986 $24 (9/15/89)
92 SIMI Cabernet Sauvignon Alexander Valley Reserve 1986 Rel: $30 Cur: $34 (CA-3/89)
92 STAG'S LEAP WINE CELLARS Stag's Leap Vineyards Cask 23 Stags Leap District 1986 Rel: $55 Cur: $73 (CA-3/89)
91 BUENA VISTA Cabernet Sauvignon Carneros 1986 $11 (10/15/89)
91 CAIN Five Napa Valley 1986 $30 (2/15/90)
91 CARMENET Red Sonoma Valley 1986 Rel: $20 Cur: $27 (7/31/89)
91 CLOS DU VAL Cabernet Sauvignon Stags Leap District 1986 Rel: $17.50 Cur: $21 (5/31/90)
91 CONN CREEK Cabernet Sauvignon Napa Valley Barrel Select Private Reserve 1986 Rel: $37 Cur: $41 (12/15/90)
91 DOMINUS Napa Valley 1986 $45 (2/28/91)
91 FAR NIENTE Cabernet Sauvignon Napa Valley 1986 $30 (9/30/89)
91 FREEMARK ABBEY Cabernet Sauvignon Napa Valley Sycamore Vineyards 1986 $25 (11/15/91)
91 GRGICH HILLS Cabernet Sauvignon Napa Valley 1986 Rel: $20 Cur: $26 (CA-3/89)
91 GROTH Cabernet Sauvignon Napa Valley Reserve 1986 Rel: $40 Cur: $78 (4/30/91)
91 HACIENDA Antares Sonoma County 1986 $28 (7/31/89)
91 WILLIAM HILL Cabernet Sauvignon Napa Valley Reserve 1986 Rel: $24.50 Cur: $29 (11/15/89)
91 INGLENOOK Cabernet Sauvignon Napa Valley Reserve Cask 1986 $25 (10/31/91)
91 KENDALL-JACKSON Cabernet Sauvignon California Cardinale 1986 $65 (11/15/90)
91 NEWTON Cabernet Sauvignon Napa Valley 1986 Rel: $16 Cur: $19 (5/31/90)
91 OPTIMA Cabernet Sauvignon Sonoma County 1986 $22 (2/15/90)
91 PINE RIDGE Cabernet Sauvignon Stags Leap District Pine Ridge Stags Leap Vineyard 1986 $29 (CA-3/89)
91 A. RAFANELLI Cabernet Sauvignon Dry Creek Valley 1986 $9.50 (9/30/89)
91 SHAFER Cabernet Sauvignon Stags Leap District Hillside Select 1986 Rel: $32 Cur: $35 (3/15/91)
91 STAG'S LEAP WINE CELLARS Cabernet Sauvignon Stags Leap District SLV 1986 Rel: $28 Cur: $30 (11/30/89)
91 STELTZNER Cabernet Sauvignon Stags Leap District 1986 Rel: $16 Cur: $19 (12/31/89)
91 STERLING Cabernet Sauvignon Napa Valley 1986 Rel: $14.50 Cur: $18 (3/31/89)
91 STERLING Cabernet Sauvignon Napa Valley Diamond Mountain Ranch 1986 Rel: $14.50 Cur: $18 (3/15/90)
91 TUDAL Cabernet Sauvignon Napa Valley 1986 Rel: $14.50 Cur: $18 (12/15/89)
91 VICHON Cabernet Sauvignon Stags Leap District SLD 1986 Rel: $21 Cur: $25 (10/31/89)
90 BUENA VISTA Cabernet Sauvignon Sonoma County 1986 $11 (11/15/89)
90 CAKEBREAD Cabernet Sauvignon Napa Valley 1986 Rel: $18 Cur: $21 (8/31/89)
90 CAYMUS Cabernet Sauvignon Napa Valley Cuvée 1986 $15 (8/31/89)
90 CHATEAU ST. JEAN Cabernet Sauvignon Alexander Valley 1986 $19 (10/15/89)
90 COSENTINO Cabernet Sauvignon North Coast Reserve 1986 $18 (5/15/90)
90 DEHLINGER Cabernet Sauvignon Russian River Valley 1986 $13 (3/15/90)
90 FETZER Cabernet Sauvignon Mendocino Barrel Select 1986 $11 (4/15/90)
90 HANZELL Cabernet Sauvignon Sonoma Valley 1986 Rel: $22 Cur: $29 (10/31/90)
90 THE HESS COLLECTION Cabernet Sauvignon Napa Valley 1986 Rel: $14 Cur: $24 (11/15/89)
90 IRON HORSE Cabernets Alexander Valley 1986 Rel: $17.50 Cur: $22 (4/15/90)
90 KENWOOD Cabernet Sauvignon Sonoma Valley Jack London Vineyard 1986 $18 (9/15/89)
90 MORGAN Cabernet Sauvignon Carmel Valley 1986 $16 (9/15/89)
90 MURPHY-GOODE Cabernet Sauvignon Alexander Valley Premier Vineyard 1986 $16 (11/15/89)
90 PINE RIDGE Cabernet Sauvignon Napa Valley Rutherford Cuvée 1986 Rel: $16 Cur: $19 (5/31/90)
90 RAYMOND Cabernet Sauvignon Napa Valley 1986 $16 (5/31/90)
90 ST. CLEMENT Cabernet Sauvignon Napa Valley 1986 Rel: $18 Cur: $21 (9/30/90)
90 SPRING MOUNTAIN Cabernet Sauvignon Napa Valley 1986 ($NA) (CA-3/89)
90 TREFETHEN Cabernet Sauvignon Napa Valley Hillside Selection 1986 ($NA) (CA-3/89)
90 VICHON Cabernet Sauvignon Stags Leap District SLD 1986 Rel: $21 Cur: $25 (CA-3/89)
89 CAKEBREAD Cabernet Sauvignon Napa Valley Rutherford Reserve 1986 $43 (11/15/91)
89 GAINEY Cabernet Sauvignon Santa Barbara County Limited Selection 1986 $15 (12/15/89)
89 GEYSER PEAK Réserve Alexandre Alexander Valley 1986 $20 (9/30/90)
89 GIRARD Cabernet Sauvignon Napa Valley 1986 Rel: $16 Cur: $19 (11/15/89)
89 GUNDLACH BUNDSCHU Cabernet Sauvignon Sonoma Valley Rhinefarm Vineyards 1986 Rel: $12 Cur: $17 (CA-3/89)
89 HEITZ Cabernet Sauvignon Napa Valley Bella Oaks Vineyard 1986 Rel: $21.50 Cur: $28 (4/15/91)
89 KLEIN Cabernet Sauvignon Santa Cruz Mountains 1986 $22 (9/30/89)
89 MERRYVALE Red Table Wine Napa Valley 1986 $25 (CA-3/89)
89 MONTICELLO Cabernet Sauvignon Napa Valley Jefferson Cuvée 1986 $14 (4/15/89)
89 NEWLAN Cabernet Sauvignon Napa Valley 1986 $15 (4/30/91)
89 PAHLMEYER Caldwell Vineyard Napa Valley 1986 $25 (11/15/89)
89 QUAIL RIDGE Cabernet Sauvignon Napa Valley 1986 $15 (11/15/90)
89 RAVENSWOOD Pickberry Vineyards Sonoma Mountain 1986 Rel: $25 Cur: $32 (CA-3/89)
89 ST. FRANCIS Cabernet Sauvignon Sonoma County 1986 $12 (1/31/90)
89 SANTA CRUZ MOUNTAIN Cabernet Sauvignon Santa Cruz Mountains Bates Ranch 1986 Rel: $15 Cur: $18 (11/15/91)
89 SIMI Cabernet Sauvignon Alexander Valley Reserve 1986 Rel: $30 Cur: $34 (7/31/91)
89 STAGS' LEAP WINERY Cabernet Sauvignon Stags Leap District 1986 $17 (10/31/90)
89 WHITEHALL LANE Cabernet Sauvignon Napa Valley 1986 $16 (8/31/89)
88 ALEXANDER VALLEY VINEYARDS Cabernet Sauvignon Alexander Valley 1986 Rel: $11.50 Cur: $16 (CA-3/89)
88 BURGESS Cabernet Sauvignon Napa Valley Vintage Selection 1986 Rel: $20 Cur: $23 (7/15/90)
88 CHATEAU CHEVRE Chev Reserve Napa Valley 1986 $25 (7/31/89)
88 CHRISTIAN BROTHERS Cabernet Sauvignon Napa Valley 1986 Rel: $9.50 Cur: $12 (11/15/90)
88 CLOS PEGASE Cabernet Sauvignon Napa Valley 1986 $16.50 (9/30/90)
88 CRONIN Cabernet Merlot Robinson Vineyard 1986 $16 (2/15/90)
88 CRONIN Cabernet Merlot Shaw-Cronin Cuvée San Mateo County 1986 $15 (2/28/91)
88 DRY CREEK Cabernet Sauvignon Sonoma County 1986 $11 (3/31/89)
88 FETZER Cabernet Sauvignon Sonoma County Reserve 1986 $24 (9/30/91)
88 GRGICH HILLS Cabernet Sauvignon Napa Valley 1986 Rel: $20 Cur: $26 (11/15/91)

88 HEITZ Cabernet Sauvignon Napa Valley 1986 Rel: $18 Cur: $21 (4/15/91)
88 JORDAN Cabernet Sauvignon Alexander Valley 1986 Rel: $22 Cur: $25 (11/15/90)
88 LAKESPRING Cabernet Sauvignon Napa Valley 1986 Rel: $14 Cur: $18 (CA-3/89)
88 LIVINGSTON Cabernet Sauvignon Napa Valley Moffett Vineyard 1986 Rel: $24 Cur: $29 (11/30/89)
88 LYETH Red Alexander Valley 1986 $23 (11/15/90)
88 ROBERT PEPI Cabernet Sauvignon Napa Valley Vine Hill Ranch 1986 Rel: $18 Cur: $24 (10/31/90)
88 RAYMOND Cabernet Sauvignon Napa Valley Private Reserve 1986 Rel: $26 Cur: $29 (11/15/91)
88 RIDGE Cabernet Sauvignon Napa County York Creek 1986 $18 (CA-3/89)
88 ROMBAUER Cabernet Sauvignon Napa Valley 1986 Rel: $15 Cur: $18 (4/15/90)
88 RUTHERFORD HILL Cabernet Sauvignon Napa Valley XVS 1986 $32 (CA-3/89)
88 V. SATTUI Cabernet Sauvignon Napa Valley Preston Vineyard 1986 Rel: $16.75 Cur: $20 (CA-3/89)
88 SEQUOIA GROVE Cabernet Sauvignon Napa County 1986 $16 (CA-3/89)
88 SILVER OAK Cabernet Sauvignon Napa Valley Bonny's Vineyard 1986 Rel: $50 Cur: $60 (10/15/91)
88 SIMI Cabernet Sauvignon Alexander Valley 1986 $15.50 (9/30/90)
87 BUENA VISTA L'Année Carneros 1986 $35 (2/28/91)
87 CHIMNEY ROCK Cabernet Sauvignon Stags Leap District 1986 Rel: $15 Cur: $19 (9/30/89)
87 CLOS DU BOIS Cabernet Sauvignon Alexander Valley Briarcrest Vineyard 1986 Rel: $17 Cur: $20 (8/31/90)
87 CLOS DU VAL Cabernet Sauvignon Napa Valley Joli Val 1986 $12.50 (12/15/89)
87 FISHER Cabernet Sauvignon Sonoma County Coach Insignia 1986 $20 (1/31/90)
87 GIRARD Cabernet Sauvignon Napa Valley Reserve 1986 Rel: $25 Cur: $39 (11/15/90)
87 GUNDLACH BUNDSCHU Cabernet Sauvignon Sonoma Valley 1986 $9.50 (11/15/89)
87 HACIENDA Cabernet Sauvignon Sonoma County 1986 $15 (11/15/91)
87 HANNA Cabernet Sauvignon Sonoma County 1986 $16 (7/31/89)
87 CHARLES KRUG Cabernet Sauvignon Napa Valley 1986 $10.50 (2/28/91)
87 CHARLES KRUG Cabernet Sauvignon Napa Valley Vintage Select 1986 ($NA) (CA-3/89)
87 LAUREL GLEN Cabernet Sauvignon Sonoma Mountain 1986 Rel: $20 Cur: $30 (5/15/89)
87 MARKHAM Cabernet Sauvignon Napa Valley 1986 Rel: $13 Cur: $16 (4/30/91)
87 MONT ST. JOHN Cabernet Sauvignon Napa Valley 1986 $14 (4/30/91)
87 NAVARRO Cabernet Sauvignon Mendocino 1986 $16 (10/15/91)
87 PRESTON Cabernet Sauvignon Dry Creek Valley 1986 Rel: $11 Cur: $17 (3/15/90)
87 ST. ANDREW'S WINERY Cabernet Sauvignon Napa Valley 1986 $14.50 (4/30/90)
87 STREBLOW Cabernet Sauvignon Napa Valley 1986 $16 (7/31/89)
87 VITA NOVA Reservatum Santa Barbara County 1986 $20 (12/15/89)
86 BLACK MOUNTAIN Cabernet Sauvignon Alexander Valley Fat Cat 1986 $20 (11/15/91)
86 CLOS DU BOIS Cabernet Sauvignon Alexander Valley 1986 $12 (5/31/89)
86 COSENTINO The Poet California 1986 $22 (7/31/89)
86 CUTLER Cabernet Sauvignon Sonoma Valley Batto Ranch 1986 $17 (11/15/90)
86 GAN EDEN Cabernet Sauvignon Alexander Valley 1986 $15 (2/15/89)
86 JOHNSON TURNBULL Cabernet Sauvignon Napa Valley Vineyard Selection 67 1986 Rel: $20 Cur: $35 (4/15/90)
86 KENWOOD Cabernet Sauvignon Sonoma Valley 1986 $15 (9/30/89)
86 LONG Cabernet Sauvignon Napa Valley 1986 Rel: $40 Cur: $48 (CA-3/89)
86 LOUIS M. MARTINI Cabernet Sauvignon Sonoma Valley Monte Rosso 1986 $20 (CA-3/89)
86 MERRYVALE Red Table Wine Napa Valley 1986 $25 (10/15/90)
86 ROBERT PECOTA Cabernet Sauvignon Napa Valley Kara's Vineyard 1986 Rel: $16 Cur: $19 (9/15/89)
86 RAVENSWOOD Cabernet Sauvignon Sonoma County 1986 Rel: $12 Cur: $18 (CA-3/89)
86 SEBASTIANI Cabernet Sauvignon Sonoma County Reserve 1986 $13 (1/31/91)
86 SHENANDOAH Cabernet Sauvignon Amador County Artist Series 1986 $12 (10/31/88)
86 STERLING Three Palms Vineyard Napa Valley 1986 $19 (12/31/89)
86 STONEGATE Cabernet Sauvignon Napa Valley 1986 Rel: $15 Cur: $17 (2/28/91)
85 BANDIERA Cabernet Sauvignon Napa Valley 1986 $6.50 (10/31/89) BB
85 BEAUCANON Cabernet Sauvignon Napa Valley 1986 $15 (12/31/88)
85 BEAULIEU Cabernet Sauvignon Napa Valley Rutherford 1986 $11.25 (9/15/89)
85 BUEHLER Cabernet Sauvignon Napa Valley 1986 Rel: $15 Cur: $18 (4/30/89)
85 CAIN Cabernet Sauvignon Napa Valley 1986 $16 (8/31/90)
85 CHATEAU SOUVERAIN Cabernet Sauvignon Alexander Valley 1986 $8.50 (11/15/89) BB
85 CLOS DU BOIS Marlstone Vineyard Alexander Valley 1986 Rel: $20 Cur: $23 (8/31/90)
85 CUTLER Satyre Sonoma Valley 1986 $20 (2/28/91)
85 DALLA VALLE Cabernet Sauvignon Napa Valley 1986 $20 (6/30/90)
85 EBERLE Cabernet Sauvignon Paso Robles 1986 Rel: $12 Cur: $15 (11/15/89)
85 ESTANCIA Cabernet Sauvignon Alexander Valley 1986 $8 (4/15/89) BB
85 FIELD STONE Cabernet Sauvignon Alexander Valley Hoot Owl Reserve 1986 $20 (12/15/90)
85 FLORA SPRINGS Cabernet Sauvignon Napa Valley 1986 Rel: $15 Cur: $18 (3/15/90)
85 FOLIE A DEUX Cabernet Sauvignon Napa Valley 1986 $16.50 (4/15/90)
85 FREMONT CREEK Cabernet Sauvignon Mendocino-Napa Counties 1986 $8 (4/30/91) BB
85 GEYSER PEAK Cabernet Sauvignon Alexander Valley Estate Reserve 1986 $15 (9/30/90)
85 GRAND CRU Cabernet Sauvignon Alexander Valley Collector's Reserve 1986 $22 (5/15/90)
85 INGLENOOK Cabernet Sauvignon Napa Valley 1986 Rel: $7.50 Cur: $10 (2/28/91) BB
85 KENDALL-JACKSON Cabernet Sauvignon California The Proprietor's 1986 $24 (3/15/90)
85 KENDALL-JACKSON Cabernet Sauvignon California Vintner's Reserve 1986 $11 (12/31/88)
85 LA JOTA Cabernet Sauvignon Howell Mountain 1986 Rel: $21 Cur: $30 (10/15/89)
85 STONE CREEK Cabernet Sauvignon Napa Valley Limited Bottling 1986 $10 (6/15/90)
85 TIJSSELING Cabernet Sauvignon Mendocino 1986 $8 (1/31/90) BB
85+ WILLIAM HILL Cabernet Sauvignon Napa Valley Silver Label 1986 $13 (4/15/88) (BT)
85+ NEYERS Cabernet Sauvignon Napa Valley 1986 $15.50 (4/15/88) (BT)
85+ JOSEPH PHELPS Cabernet Sauvignon Napa Valley 1986 Rel: $15 Cur: $27 (4/15/88) (BT)
85+ VIANSA Cabernet Sauvignon Napa-Alexander Valleys 1986 ($NA) (4/15/88) (BT)
84 DAVIS BYNUM Cabernet Sauvignon Sonoma County 1986 $10 (11/15/89)
84 CHATEAU POTELLE Cabernet Sauvignon Alexander Valley 1986 $14.50 (10/31/90)
84 DE LORIMIER Mosaic Alexander Valley 1986 $16 (10/31/89)
84 FRANCISCAN Cabernet Sauvignon Napa Valley Oakville Estate 1986 $11 (7/15/90)
84 HUSCH Cabernet Sauvignon Mendocino 1986 $12 (2/15/90)
84 KISTLER Cabernet Sauvignon Sonoma Valley Kistler Estate Vineyard 1986 Rel: $20 Cur: $28 (9/30/89)
84 LA VIEILLE MONTAGNE Cabernet Sauvignon Napa Valley 1986 $14 (6/30/90)
84 J. LOHR Cabernet Sauvignon California 1986 $6.50 (4/15/89) BB
84 PAUL MASSON Cabernet Sauvignon California Vintners Selection 1986 $6 (6/30/89)
84 MERLION Cabernet Sauvignon Napa Valley 1986 $16.50 (11/15/90)
84 ROMBAUER Le Meilleur du Chai Napa Valley 1986 $35 (5/15/91)
84 SEQUOIA GROVE Cabernet Sauvignon Napa Valley Estate 1986 Rel: $22 Cur: $25 (9/30/89)
84 TREFETHEN Cabernet Sauvignon Napa Valley 1986 Rel: $15.25 Cur: $19 (10/31/89)
84 VILLA MT. EDEN Cabernet Sauvignon Napa Valley 1986 Rel: $13 Cur: $15 (2/15/91)
84 YORK MOUNTAIN Cabernet Sauvignon San Luis Obispo 1986 $15 (11/15/90)
83 BEAULIEU Cabernet Sauvignon Napa Valley Beau Tour 1986 $7 (10/31/88)
83 BELLEROSE Cuvée Bellerose Sonoma County 1986 $18 (1/31/90)
83 CECCHETTI SEBASTIANI Cabernet Sauvignon Alexander Valley 1986 $8.50 (4/15/89)
83 FREEMARK ABBEY Cabernet Sauvignon Napa Valley 1986 $15 (11/15/90)
83 GUNDLACH BUNDSCHU Cabernet Sauvignon Sonoma Valley Rhinefarm Vineyards Reserve 1986 $25 (8/31/91)
83 JEKEL Cabernet Sauvignon Arroyo Seco 1986 $13 (11/15/90)
83 LOLONIS Cabernet Sauvignon Mendocino County Private Reserve 1986 $15 (5/15/90)
83 MIRASSOU Cabernet Sauvignon California Fifth Generation Family Selection 1986 $9.75 (5/31/91)
83 MONTEREY VINEYARD Cabernet Sauvignon Monterey County Limited Release 1986 $10 (11/15/89)
83 MOUNT EDEN Cabernet Sauvignon Santa Cruz Mountains 1986 Rel: $28 Cur: $32 (8/31/90)
83 MOUNT VEEDER Cabernet Sauvignon Napa Valley 1986 Rel: $18 Cur: $21 (11/15/90)
83 J. PEDRONCELLI Cabernet Sauvignon Dry Creek Valley 1986 $7 (9/15/89) BB
83 JOSEPH PHELPS Cabernet Sauvignon Napa Valley Backus Vineyard 1986 Rel: $22 Cur: $37 (1/31/90)
83 RENAISSANCE Cabernet Sauvignon North Yuba 1986 $15 (7/15/91)
83 WILLIAM WHEELER Cabernet Sauvignon Dry Creek Valley 1986 $12 (8/31/90)
82 BENZIGER Cabernet Sauvignon Sonoma County 1986 $10 (7/31/89)
82 BRUTOCAO Cabernet Sauvignon Mendocino 1986 $12.50 (3/31/92)
82 CHATEAU DIANA Cabernet Sauvignon California Limited Edition 1986 $5 (10/15/91) BB
82 DUNNEWOOD Cabernet Sauvignon Napa Valley Napa Reserve 1986 $10.50 (6/15/90)
82 GLEN ELLEN Cabernet Sauvignon California Proprietor's Reserve 1986 $4.50 (7/15/88) BB
82 HAWK CREST Cabernet Sauvignon North Coast 1986 $7.50 (10/15/88) BB
82 MAYACAMAS Cabernet Sauvignon Napa Valley 1986 Rel: $20 Cur: $38 (11/15/91)
82 BERNARD PRADEL Cabernet Sauvignon Napa Valley 1986 $12 (1/31/90)
82 RIDGE Cabernet Sauvignon Santa Cruz Mountains Monte Bello 1986 Rel: $35 Cur: $40 (9/15/89)
82 ROUND HILL Cabernet Sauvignon Napa Valley 1986 $8 (10/15/88)
82 STAG'S LEAP WINE CELLARS Cabernet Sauvignon Napa Valley 1986 $18 (6/15/89)
82 SUGARLOAF RIDGE Cabernet Sauvignon Sonoma Valley 1986 $13 (3/31/90)
82 M.G. VALLEJO Cabernet Sauvignon California 1986 $5 (6/15/90) BB
82 WENTE BROS. Cabernet Sauvignon Livermore Valley Estate Reserve 1986 $12 (10/15/90)
82 WILLOW CREEK Cabernet Sauvignon Napa-Alexander Valleys 1986 $9.50 (7/31/89)
81 FIRESTONE Cabernet Sauvignon Santa Ynez Valley 1986 $10 (12/15/89)
81 KATHRYN KENNEDY Cabernet Sauvignon Santa Cruz Mountains 1986 $30 (3/15/90)
81 ROUDON-SMITH Cabernet Sauvignon Santa Cruz Mountains 1986 $12 (3/15/91)
80 ARCIERO Cabernet Sauvignon Paso Robles 1986 $8.50 (11/15/90)
80 CASTORO Cabernet Sauvignon Paso Robles Hope Farms 1986 $8.50 (12/15/89)
80 CORBETT CANYON Cabernet Sauvignon Central Coast Coastal Classic 1986 $6.50/L (12/15/89)
80 DRY CREEK Meritage Dry Creek Valley 1986 $22 (9/15/90)
80 FERRARI-CARANO Cabernet Sauvignon Alexander Valley 1986 $17.50 (9/15/90)
80 KONOCTI Cabernet Sauvignon Lake County 1986 $9 (4/30/90)
80 LOUIS M. MARTINI Cabernet Sauvignon North Coast 1986 $9.25 (9/15/89)
80 ROBERT MONDAVI Cabernet Sauvignon California Cabernet 1986 $5.50 (12/15/88) BB
80 PINE RIDGE Cabernet Sauvignon Napa Valley Andrus Reserve 1986 Rel: $40 Cur: $44 (5/15/90)
80 ROUND HILL Cabernet Sauvignon Napa Valley Reserve 1986 $9 (6/30/90)
80 RUTHERFORD ESTATE Cabernet Sauvignon Napa Valley 1986 $7 (11/15/91)
80 STONE CREEK Cabernet Sauvignon Napa Valley Special Selection 1986 $10 (11/15/91)
80 WHITE ROCK Claret Napa Valley 1986 $18 (10/31/89)
80 ZACA MESA Cabernet Sauvignon Santa Barbara County Reserve 1986 $15 (12/15/88)
79 DOMAINE ST. GEORGE Cabernet Sauvignon Russian River Valley Select Reserve 1986 $9 (5/31/90)
79 FOPPIANO Cabernet Sauvignon Sonoma County 1986 $9 (11/15/90)
79 FRANCISCAN Meritage Napa Valley 1986 Rel: $15 Cur: $23 (7/31/90)
79 GRAND CRU Cabernet Sauvignon Sonoma County Premium Selection 1986 $12 (4/30/90)
79 LEEWARD Cabernet Sauvignon Alexander Valley 1986 $12 (10/15/89)
79 MASSON Cabernet Sauvignon Monterey County Vintage Selection 1986 $9 (11/15/89)
79 MOUNTAIN VIEW Cabernet Sauvignon Mendocino County 1986 $6.50 (3/31/90)
79 PARDUCCI Cabernet Merlot Cellarmaster Selection Mendocino County 1986 $15 (4/30/91)
79 SUTTER HOME Cabernet Sauvignon California 1986 $5 (11/30/88)
79 VENTANA Magnus Meritage Monterey 1986 $20 (10/31/89)
79 VILLA ZAPU Cabernet Sauvignon Napa Valley 1986 $16 (10/31/89)
78 BENZIGER Cabernet Sauvignon Sonoma Valley 1986 $17 (4/30/90)
78 CHARTRONS Claret California 1986 $14.50 (11/15/91)
78 CHRISTOPHE Cabernet Sauvignon Napa Valley Reserve 1986 $12 (11/15/90)
78 DE MOOR Cabernet Sauvignon Napa Valley Owners Select 1986 $16 (2/28/91)
78 GUENOC Cabernet Sauvignon Lake County 1986 $12.50 (4/30/91)
78 MAZZOCCO Cabernet Sauvignon Alexander Valley Claret Style 1986 $20 (7/31/89)
78 ZACA MESA Cabernet Sauvignon Santa Barbara County 1986 $9.50 (12/15/89)
77 MADDALENA Cabernet Sauvignon Alexander Valley Reserve 1986 $10 (3/31/90)
77 JOSEPH PHELPS Cabernet Sauvignon Napa Valley Eisele Vineyard 1986 Rel: $40 Cur: $45 (8/31/90)
77 VIANSA Cabernet Sauvignon Sonoma-Napa Counties 1986 $15 (7/31/90)
77 WHITEHALL LANE Cabernet Sauvignon Napa Valley Reserve 1986 $30 (11/15/90)
76 FREEMARK ABBEY Cabernet Sauvignon Napa Valley Bosché 1986 $24 (7/31/90)
76 MONTEREY VINEYARD Cabernet Sauvignon Monterey County Classic 1986 $5.50 (10/31/89)
76 SEGHESIO Cabernet Sauvignon Northern Sonoma 1986 $8 (6/30/90)
75 DOMAINE MICHEL Cabernet Sauvignon Sonoma County 1986 $19 (6/30/90)
75 PARSONS CREEK Cabernet Sauvignon Sonoma County 1986 $13 (11/15/89)
75 J. WILE & SONS Cabernet Sauvignon Napa Valley 1986 $7 (9/15/88)
74 AUSTIN A Genoux Santa Barbara County 1986 $15 (12/15/89)
74 BARON HERZOG Cabernet Sauvignon Sonoma County Special Reserve 1986 $16 (3/31/91)
74 INGLENOOK Niebaum Claret Napa Valley 1986 $13 (6/30/91)
74 KENDALL-JACKSON Cabernet Sauvignon Lake County 1986 $7.75 (7/31/88)
73 DUNNEWOOD Cabernet Sauvignon California 1986 $7 (6/15/90)
73 INNISFREE Cabernet Sauvignon Napa Valley 1986 $10.50 (6/30/90)
73 RANCHO SISQUOC Cabernet Sauvignon Santa Maria Valley 1986 $10 (12/15/89)
72 MEEKER Cabernet Sauvignon Dry Creek Valley 1986 $18.50 (2/15/90)
72 MISSION VIEW Cabernet Sauvignon Paso Robles 1986 $12 (12/15/89)
71 SEBASTIANI ESTATES Cabernet Sauvignon North Coast Emilia 1986 $12.50 (3/31/92)
70 GARLAND RANCH Cabernet Sauvignon Central Coast 1986 $6.75 (10/31/89)
70 MCDOWELL VALLEY Cabernet Sauvignon McDowell Valley 1986 $8 (4/30/90)
70 TULOCAY Cabernet Sauvignon Napa Valley 1986 $12 (6/30/90)
69 HOP KILN Cabernet Sauvignon Dry Creek Valley 1986 $12 (6/15/89)
68 RIDGE Cabernet Sauvignon Santa Cruz Mountains 1986 $15 (10/31/89)
68 RUTHERFORD HILL Cabernet Sauvignon Napa Valley 1986 Rel: $14 Cur: $17 (2/28/91)

60 MIRASSOU Cabernet Sauvignon Monterey County Fifth Generation Harvest Reserve 1986 $12.50 (7/31/91)
55 CONN CREEK Cabernet Sauvignon Napa Valley Barrel Select 1986 Rel: $15 Cur: $18 (2/28/91)

1985

99 CAYMUS Cabernet Sauvignon Napa Valley Special Selection 1985 Rel: $50 Cur: $190 (4/30/90)
98 HEITZ Cabernet Sauvignon Napa Valley Martha's Vineyard 1985 Rel: $60 Cur: $140 (4/30/90)
97 KENDALL-JACKSON Cabernet Sauvignon California Cardinale 1985 Rel: $45 Cur: $80 (11/15/89)
96 THE HESS COLLECTION Cabernet Sauvignon Napa Valley 1985 Rel: $13 Cur: $50 (CA-3/89)
96 STAG'S LEAP WINE CELLARS Stags Leap District Stag's Leap Vineyards Cask 23 1985 Rel: $75 Cur: $165 (11/30/89)
96 STERLING Reserve Napa Valley 1985 Rel: $30 Cur: $46 (7/15/89) SS
95 BEAULIEU Cabernet Sauvignon Napa Valley Georges de Latour Private Reserve 1985 Rel: $25 Cur: $46 (3/31/91) (JL)
95 BERINGER Cabernet Sauvignon Napa Valley Private Reserve 1985 Rel: $30 Cur: $75 (12/15/89) SS
95 GRACE FAMILY Cabernet Sauvignon Napa Valley 1985 Rel: $50 Cur: $290 (CA-3/89)
95 GROTH Cabernet Sauvignon Napa Valley Reserve 1985 Rel: $30 Cur: $260 (4/15/90)
95 KENDALL-JACKSON Cabernet Sauvignon California Proprietor's Reserve 1985 $20 (12/15/88)
95 ROBERT MONDAVI Cabernet Sauvignon Napa Valley Reserve 1985 Rel: $40 Cur: $50 (11/15/89) SS
95 OPUS ONE Napa Valley 1985 Rel: $55 Cur: $100 (6/15/89)
95 RIDGE Cabernet Sauvignon Santa Cruz Mountains Monte Bello 1985 Rel: $40 Cur: $89 (7/15/88) CS
95 SPOTTSWOODE Cabernet Sauvignon Napa Valley 1985 Rel: $25 Cur: $122 (11/15/88) CS
94 ARROWOOD Cabernet Sauvignon Sonoma County 1985 Rel: $19 Cur: $35 (12/15/88)
94 BUENA VISTA Cabernet Sauvignon Carneros Private Reserve 1985 Rel: $18 Cur: $26 (10/15/89) SS
94 CLOS DU VAL Reserve Stags Leap District 1985 Rel: $45 Cur: $53 (11/15/90)
94 B.R. COHN Cabernet Sauvignon Sonoma Valley Olive Hill Vineyard 1985 Rel: $16 Cur: $50 (CA-3/89)
94 DUNN Cabernet Sauvignon Napa Valley 1985 Rel: $20 Cur: $70 (9/15/88) CS
94 WILLIAM HILL Cabernet Sauvignon Napa Valley Reserve 1985 Rel: $22.50 Cur: $30 (CA-3/89)
94 ROBERT MONDAVI Cabernet Sauvignon Napa Valley 1985 Rel: $15 Cur: $30 (12/15/88) SS
94 ROBERT MONDAVI Cabernet Sauvignon Napa Valley Reserve 1985 Rel: $40 Cur: $50 (11/30/91) (JL)
94 PINE RIDGE Cabernet Sauvignon Stags Leap District Pine Ridge Stags Leap Vineyard 1985 Rel: $26 Cur: $29 (CA-3/89)
94 SIMI Cabernet Sauvignon Alexander Valley Reserve 1985 Rel: $25 Cur: $29 (8/31/90) SS
94 STAG'S LEAP WINE CELLARS Cabernet Sauvignon Stags Leap District SLV 1985 Rel: $26 Cur: $42 (CA-3/89)
93 BUEHLER Cabernet Sauvignon Napa Valley 1985 Rel: $14 Cur: $18 (CA-3/89)
93 DIAMOND CREEK Cabernet Sauvignon Napa Valley Red Rock Terrace 1985 Rel: $30 Cur: $55 (CA-3/89)
93 DIAMOND CREEK Cabernet Sauvignon Napa Valley Volcanic Hill 1985 Rel: $30 Cur: $55 (CA-3/89)
93 DUNN Cabernet Sauvignon Napa Valley 1985 Rel: $20 Cur: $70 (11/30/91) (JL)
93 FORMAN Cabernet Sauvignon Napa Valley 1985 Rel: $18 Cur: $76 (CA-3/89)
93 KATHRYN KENNEDY Cabernet Sauvignon Santa Cruz Mountains 1985 $25 (12/15/88)
93 KISTLER Cabernet Sauvignon Sonoma Valley Kistler Estate Vineyard 1985 Rel: $16 Cur: $28 (CA-3/89)
93 LAUREL GLEN Cabernet Sauvignon Sonoma Mountain 1985 Rel: $18 Cur: $40 (CA-3/89)
93 OPTIMA Cabernet Sauvignon Sonoma County 1985 $18.50 (12/15/88)
93 JOSEPH PHELPS Insignia Napa Valley 1985 Rel: $40 Cur: $58 (7/31/89) CS
93 PINE RIDGE Cabernet Sauvignon Napa Valley Rutherford Cuvée 1985 Rel: $16 Cur: $20 (CA-3/89)
93 STELTZNER Cabernet Sauvignon Stags Leap District 1985 Rel: $16 Cur: $20 (CA-3/89)
93 STERLING Three Palms Vineyard Napa Valley 1985 Rel: $20 Cur: $22 (12/31/88)
93 WHITEHALL LANE Cabernet Sauvignon Napa Valley 1985 $16 (11/15/88)
92 BURGESS Cabernet Sauvignon Napa Valley Vintage Selection 1985 Rel: $18 Cur: $22 (7/15/89)
92 CAYMUS Cabernet Sauvignon Napa Valley 1985 Rel: $18 Cur: $55 (CA-3/89)
92 CAYMUS Cabernet Sauvignon Napa Valley Cuvée 1985 $12 (7/15/88)
92 CHATEAU MONTELENA Cabernet Sauvignon Napa Valley 1985 Rel: $25 Cur: $57 (11/15/89) CS
92 DIAMOND CREEK Cabernet Sauvignon Napa Valley Gravelly Meadow 1985 Rel: $30 Cur: $55 (CA-3/89)
92 DUCKHORN Cabernet Sauvignon Napa Valley 1985 Rel: $17.50 Cur: $39 (CA-3/89)
92 ETUDE Cabernet Sauvignon California 1985 $16 (12/15/88)
92 FAR NIENTE Cabernet Sauvignon Napa Valley 1985 Rel: $28 Cur: $31 (CA-3/89)
92 HEITZ Cabernet Sauvignon Napa Valley Bella Oaks Vineyard 1985 Rel: $25 Cur: $55 (5/15/90) CS
92 LONG Cabernet Sauvignon Napa Valley 1985 Rel: $36 Cur: $46 (CA-3/89)
92 MAYACAMAS Cabernet Sauvignon Napa Valley 1985 Rel: $25 Cur: $38 (1/31/90)
92 MONTICELLO Cabernet Sauvignon Napa Valley Corley Reserve 1985 Rel: $22.50 Cur: $35 (7/31/89)
92 PINE RIDGE Cabernet Sauvignon Napa Valley Andrus Reserve Cuvée Duet 1985 Rel: $40 Cur: $45 (CA-3/89)
92 RIDGE Cabernet Sauvignon Napa County York Creek 1985 Rel: $16 Cur: $20 (CA-3/89)
92 RUTHERFORD RANCH Cabernet Sauvignon Napa Valley 1985 Rel: $11 Cur: $15 (5/15/90) SS
92 SANTA CRUZ MOUNTAIN Cabernet Sauvignon Santa Cruz Mountains Bates Ranch 1985 Rel: $15 Cur: $18 (CA-3/89)
92 SEQUOIA GROVE Cabernet Sauvignon Napa Valley Estate 1985 Rel: $28 Cur: $34 (CA-3/89)
92 VICHON Cabernet Sauvignon Stags Leap District SLD 1985 Rel: $18 Cur: $29 (CA-3/89)
91 CARMENET Red Sonoma Valley 1985 Rel: $18.50 Cur: $28 (CA-3/89)
91 CONN CREEK Cabernet Sauvignon Napa Valley Barrel Select Private Reserve 1985 Rel: $30 Cur: $33 (9/15/90)
91 CUTLER Cabernet Sauvignon Sonoma Valley Batto Ranch 1985 $20 (7/31/89)
91 CUVAISON Cabernet Sauvignon Napa Valley 1985 Rel: $14 Cur: $25 (3/31/89)
91 DRY CREEK Cabernet Sauvignon Sonoma County 1985 Rel: $11 Cur: $16 (5/31/88) SS
91 DUCKHORN Cabernet Sauvignon Napa Valley 1985 Rel: $17.50 Cur: $39 (6/15/88) CS
91 GROTH Cabernet Sauvignon Napa Valley 1985 Rel: $16 Cur: $50 (CA-3/89)
91 GUNDLACH BUNDSCHU Cabernet Sauvignon Sonoma Valley Rhinefarm Vineyards 1985 Rel: $9 Cur: $14 (CA-3/89)
91 INGLENOOK Reunion Napa Valley 1985 Rel: $35 Cur: $38 (7/15/89)
91 KENWOOD Cabernet Sauvignon Sonoma Valley 1985 $14.50 (2/15/89)
91 KENWOOD Cabernet Sauvignon Sonoma Valley Artist Series 1985 Rel: $30 Cur: $35 (CA-3/89)
91 MARKHAM Cabernet Sauvignon Napa Valley 1985 Rel: $13 Cur: $17 (4/15/90)
91 MERRYVALE Red Table Wine Napa Valley 1985 Rel: $24 Cur: $27 (CA-3/89)
91 JOSEPH PHELPS Cabernet Sauvignon Napa Valley Backus Vineyard 1985 Rel: $27.50 Cur: $45 (12/31/88)
91 PLAM Cabernet Sauvignon Napa Valley 1985 $24 (6/30/88)
91 BERNARD PRADEL Cabernet Sauvignon Napa Valley 1985 $12 (4/30/89)
91 RAYMOND Cabernet Sauvignon Napa Valley Private Reserve 1985 Rel: $24 Cur: $28 (7/15/90) CS
91 SHAFER Cabernet Sauvignon Stags Leap District Hillside Select 1985 Rel: $24.50 Cur: $30 (5/31/90) CS
91 SHAFER Cabernet Sauvignon Stags Leap District 1985 Rel: $15.50 Cur: $22 (CA-3/89)
91 SILVERADO Cabernet Sauvignon Stags Leap District 1985 Rel: $12.50 Cur: $36 (11/15/88) SS
91 SIMI Cabernet Sauvignon Sonoma County 1985 Rel: $13 Cur: $21 (9/30/89)
90 BERINGER Cabernet Sauvignon Napa Valley Chabot Vineyard 1985 $30 (11/15/91)
90 CARNEROS CREEK Cabernet Sauvignon Los Carneros 1985 $15 (10/31/89)
90 CHRISTIAN BROTHERS Cabernet Sauvignon Napa Valley 1985 $8 (6/15/88)
90 CLOS DU VAL Cabernet Sauvignon Stags Leap District 1985 Rel: $16 Cur: $28 (6/15/89)
90 CONN CREEK Cabernet Sauvignon Napa Valley Barrel Select 1985 Rel: $15 Cur: $18 (9/15/90)
90 FISHER Cabernet Sauvignon Sonoma County Coach Insignia 1985 Rel: $18 Cur: $22 (CA-3/89)
90 FLORA SPRINGS Cabernet Sauvignon Napa Valley 1985 Rel: $15 Cur: $18 (7/31/89)
90 FRANCISCAN Meritage Napa Valley 1985 Rel: $20 Cur: $28 (3/31/90)
90 FREEMARK ABBEY Cabernet Sauvignon Napa Valley Bosché 1985 Rel: $24 Cur: $33 (7/31/89)
90 GRGICH HILLS Cabernet Sauvignon Napa Valley 1985 Rel: $20 Cur: $25 (10/31/90)
90 WILLIAM HILL Cabernet Sauvignon Napa Valley Silver Label 1985 $12 (4/30/88)
90 INGLENOOK Cabernet Sauvignon Napa Valley Reserve Cask 1985 Rel: $16 Cur: $22 (2/15/91) CS
90 ROMBAUER Le Meilleur du Chai Napa Valley 1985 Rel: $37.50 Cur: $43 (10/31/89)
90 ST. CLEMENT Cabernet Sauvignon Napa Valley 1985 Rel: $17 Cur: $25 (3/15/90)
90 SMITH-MADRONE Cabernet Sauvignon Napa Valley 1985 Rel: $14 Cur: $19 (CA-3/89)
90 STAG'S LEAP WINE CELLARS Cabernet Sauvignon Napa Valley 1985 $16 (9/15/88)
89 DIAMOND CREEK Cabernet Sauvignon Napa Valley Three Vineyard Blend 1985 Rel: $50 Cur: $100 (CA-3/89)
89 DRY CREEK Meritage Dry Creek Valley 1985 $22 (11/15/89)
89 HAYWOOD Cabernet Sauvignon Sonoma Valley 1985 Rel: $14.50 Cur: $20 (CA-3/89)
89 KENWOOD Cabernet Sauvignon Sonoma Valley Jack London Vineyard 1985 Rel: $18 Cur: $21 (10/15/88)
89 KONOCTI Cabernet Sauvignon Lake County 1985 $7.50 (11/15/89) BB
89 CHARLES KRUG Cabernet Sauvignon Napa Valley Vintage Select 1985 Rel: $28 Cur: $30 (3/15/92)
89 J. LOHR Cabernet Sauvignon Napa Valley Carol's Vineyard Reserve 1985 $14.50 (12/15/88)
89 NEWTON Cabernet Sauvignon Napa Valley 1985 Rel: $15.25 Cur: $20 (1/31/89)
89 GUSTAVE NIEBAUM Cabernet Sauvignon Napa Valley Reference 1985 $13.50 (10/31/89)
89 PRESTON Cabernet Sauvignon Dry Creek Valley 1985 Rel: $11 Cur: $18 (CA-3/89)
89 ST. ANDREW'S WINERY Cabernet Sauvignon Napa Valley 1985 $10.50 (5/15/88)
89 SEBASTIANI ESTATES Cabernet Sauvignon Sonoma Valley Cherry Block 1985 $16.50 (3/31/90)
89 STERLING Cabernet Sauvignon Napa Valley 1985 Rel: $13 Cur: $17 (5/15/88)
89 STREBLOW Cabernet Sauvignon Napa Valley 1985 $14.50 (6/15/88)
89 PHILIP TOGNI Cabernet Sauvignon Napa Valley 1985 Rel: $20 Cur: $25 (CA-3/89)
89 TUDAL Cabernet Sauvignon Napa Valley 1985 Rel: $14.50 Cur: $20 (CA-3/89)
88 ALEXANDER VALLEY VINEYARDS Cabernet Sauvignon Alexander Valley 1985 Rel: $11 Cur: $18 (CA-3/89)
88 CLOS DU VAL Cabernet Sauvignon Napa Valley Gran Val 1985 $8.50 (5/31/88)
88 DUNN Cabernet Sauvignon Howell Mountain 1985 Rel: $30 Cur: $125 (11/30/91) (JL)
88 FLORA SPRINGS Trilogy Napa Valley 1985 Rel: $30 Cur: $38 (CA-3/89)
88 FRANCISCAN Cabernet Sauvignon Napa Valley Library Selection 1985 Rel: $17.50 Cur: $20 (CA-3/89)
88 FRANCISCAN Cabernet Sauvignon Napa Valley Oakville Estate Reserve 1985 Rel: $17.50 Cur: $20 (5/31/90)
88 FREEMARK ABBEY Cabernet Sauvignon Napa Valley Sycamore Vineyards 1985 $25 (10/31/89)
88 GEYSER PEAK Réserve Alexandre Alexander Valley 1985 $19 (9/30/89)
88 GIRARD Cabernet Sauvignon Napa Valley 1985 Rel: $15 Cur: $18 (9/15/88)
88 JORDAN Cabernet Sauvignon Alexander Valley 1985 Rel: $19.50 Cur: $35 (9/15/89)
88 LA JOTA Cabernet Sauvignon Howell Mountain 1985 Rel: $18 Cur: $40 (CA-3/89)
88 LAKESPRING Cabernet Sauvignon Napa Valley 1985 Rel: $12 Cur: $19 (CA-3/89)
88 J. LOHR Cabernet Sauvignon Napa Valley Carol's Vineyard Reserve Lot 2 1985 $17.50 (9/30/90)
88 RUTHERFORD HILL Cabernet Sauvignon Napa Valley XVS 1985 Rel: $25 Cur: $29 (4/30/89)
88 ST. FRANCIS Cabernet Sauvignon California 1985 $9 (11/30/87)
88 SILVER OAK Cabernet Sauvignon Napa Valley 1985 Rel: $24 Cur: $68 (10/31/89)
88 SMITH & HOOK Cabernet Sauvignon Napa County 1985 $12 (9/30/89)
88 STERLING Cabernet Sauvignon Napa Valley Diamond Mountain Ranch 1985 Rel: $16 Cur: $21 (5/31/89)
88 VICHON Cabernet Sauvignon Napa Valley 1985 Rel: $13 Cur: $19 (CA-3/89)
88 WHITEHALL LANE Cabernet Sauvignon Napa Valley Reserve 1985 $30 (11/30/89)
87 BERINGER Cabernet Sauvignon Knights Valley 1985 $12 (5/31/88)

Key to Symbols

The scores reported here are the results of blind tastings conducted by our panel of senior editors. Wines that carry the initials below are results of individual tastings.

THE WINE SPECTATOR 100-POINT SCALE ***95-100***—Classic, a great wine; ***90-94***—Outstanding, superior character and style; ***80-89***—Good to very good, a wine with special qualities; ***70-79***—Average, drinkable wine that may have minor flaws; ***60-69***—Below average, drinkable but not recommended; ***50-59***—Poor, undrinkable, not recommended. "+"—With a score indicates a range; used primarily with barrel tastings to indicate a preliminary score.

SPECIAL DESIGNATIONS SS—Spectator Selection, CS—Cellar Selection, BB—Best Buy, ($NA)—Price not available, (NR)—Not released.

TASTER'S INITIALS (JG)—Jim Gordon, (HS)—Harvey Steiman, (JL)—James Laube, (JS)—James Suckling, (TM)—Thomas Matthews, (TR)—Terry Robards, (PM)—Per-Henrik Mansson, (BT)—Barrel Tasting (these wines were tasted blind from barrel samples), (CA-date)—*California's Great Cabernets* by James Laube, (CH-date)—*California's Great Chardonnays* by James Laube, (VP-date)—*Vintage Port* by James Suckling.

DATE TASTED Dates in parentheses represent the issue in which the rating was published.

87 BLACK MOUNTAIN Cabernet Sauvignon Alexander Valley Fat Cat 1985 $18 (4/30/90)
87 CAIN Five Napa Valley 1985 $26 (6/15/89)
87 CHATEAU SOUVERAIN Cabernet Sauvignon Sonoma County 1985 $8 (11/30/88)
87 CHIMNEY ROCK Cabernet Sauvignon Stags Leap District 1985 Rel: $15 Cur: $19 (CA-3/89)
87 CLOS DU BOIS Cabernet Sauvignon Alexander Valley 1985 $10.50 (4/15/88)
87 CONCANNON Cabernet Sauvignon Livermore Valley Reserve 1985 $13.50 (2/15/89)
87 ESTANCIA Cabernet Sauvignon Alexander Valley 1985 $6.50 (6/15/88) BB
87 FETZER Cabernet Sauvignon California Reserve 1985 $17 (11/15/89)
87 FIELD STONE Cabernet Sauvignon Alexander Valley Hoot Owl Creek Vineyards 1985 $20 (3/31/89)
87 IRON HORSE Cabernets Alexander Valley 1985 Rel: $16 Cur: $21 (CA-3/89)
87 MONTICELLO Cabernet Sauvignon Napa Valley Jefferson Cuvée 1985 $12 (2/29/88)
87 MOUNT VEEDER Cabernet Sauvignon Napa Valley 1985 Rel: $18 Cur: $22 (CA-3/89)
87 NAVARRO Cabernet Sauvignon Mendocino 1985 $14 (11/15/90)
87 NEWLAN Cabernet Sauvignon Napa Valley 1985 $15 (3/31/90)
87 NIEBAUM-COPPOLA Rubicon Napa Valley 1985 Rel: $25 Cur: $35 (11/15/90)
87 RIDGE Cabernet Sauvignon Santa Cruz Mountains Jimsomare 1985 $16 (2/15/89)
87 V. SATTUI Cabernet Sauvignon Napa Valley Preston Vineyard 1985 Rel: $15.75 Cur: $25 (CA-3/89)
87 RODNEY STRONG Cabernet Sauvignon Alexander Valley Alexander's Crown Vineyard 1985 $17 (5/31/91)
86 CHATEAU ST. JEAN Cabernet Sauvignon Alexander Valley 1985 Rel: $19 Cur: $22 (11/15/88)
86 CLOS DU BOIS Cabernet Sauvignon Alexander Valley Briarcrest Vineyard 1985 Rel: $16 Cur: $24 (6/15/89)
86 CLOS PEGASE Cabernet Sauvignon Napa Valley 1985 $17 (5/31/88)
86 FETZER Cabernet Sauvignon Sonoma County Reserve 1985 $24 (8/31/90)
86 FRANCISCAN Cabernet Sauvignon Napa Valley Oakville Estate 1985 $11 (5/15/89)
86 GIRARD Cabernet Sauvignon Napa Valley Reserve 1985 Rel: $25 Cur: $35 (2/15/90)
86 GLEN ELLEN Cabernet Sauvignon Sonoma Valley Imagery Series 1985 $12.50 (2/15/89)
86 HANNA Cabernet Sauvignon Sonoma Valley 1985 $14 (6/30/88)
86 INNISFREE Cabernet Sauvignon Napa Valley 1985 $9 (3/15/89)
86 KEENAN Cabernet Sauvignon Napa Valley 1985 Rel: $15 Cur: $21 (CA-3/89)
86 LIVINGSTON Cabernet Sauvignon Napa Valley Moffett Vineyard 1985 Rel: $18 Cur: $33 (CA-3/89)
86 LYETH Red Alexander Valley 1985 $22 (5/31/89)
86 ROBERT PECOTA Cabernet Sauvignon Napa Valley Kara's Vineyard 1985 Rel: $16 Cur: $20 (CA-3/89)
86 ROUND HILL Cabernet Sauvignon Napa Valley Reserve 1985 $10.50 (5/31/88)
86 SEBASTIANI Cabernet Sauvignon Sonoma County Reserve 1985 $12.50 (11/15/90)
86 SEQUOIA GROVE Cabernet Sauvignon Napa County 1985 Rel: $16 Cur: $21 (CA-3/89)
86 SILVER OAK Cabernet Sauvignon Alexander Valley 1985 Rel: $24 Cur: $61 (10/31/89)
86 STONEGATE Cabernet Sauvignon Napa Valley 1985 Rel: $16 Cur: $19 (8/31/90)
85 BEAULIEU Cabernet Sauvignon Napa Valley Rutherford 1985 Rel: $9.50 Cur: $13 (6/15/88)
85 CAKEBREAD Cabernet Sauvignon Napa Valley Rutherford Reserve 1985 $40 (CA-3/89)
85 CRUVINET Cabernet Sauvignon Alexander Valley 1985 $7 (9/15/88) BB
85 FETZER Cabernet Sauvignon Mendocino Barrel Select 1985 $10 (12/15/88)
85 FROG'S LEAP Cabernet Sauvignon Napa Valley 1985 Rel: $12 Cur: $20 (CA-3/89)
85 MERLION Cabernet Sauvignon Napa Valley 1985 $13.50 (8/31/88)
85 J. PEDRONCELLI Cabernet Sauvignon Dry Creek Valley Reserve 1985 $14 (3/31/90)
85 ROBERT PEPI Cabernet Sauvignon Napa Valley Vine Hill Ranch 1985 Rel: $18 Cur: $23 (7/31/90)
85 RAVENSWOOD Cabernet Sauvignon Sonoma County 1985 Rel: $12 Cur: $20 (CA-3/89)
85 ROMBAUER Cabernet Sauvignon Napa Valley 1985 Rel: $14.75 Cur: $20 (4/30/89)
85 SPRING MOUNTAIN Cabernet Sauvignon Napa Valley 1985 $20 (10/15/89)
85 STAGS' LEAP WINERY Cabernet Sauvignon Stags Leap District 1985 Rel: $15 Cur: $18 (CA-3/89)
85 WHITE OAK Cabernet Sauvignon Alexander Valley Myers Limited Reserve 1985 $18 (7/31/89)
84 BUENA VISTA Cabernet Sauvignon Carneros 1985 $10 (11/15/88)
84 CAKEBREAD Cabernet Sauvignon Napa Valley 1985 Rel: $17 Cur: $20 (CA-3/89)
84 CHAPPELLET Cabernet Sauvignon Napa Valley Reserve 1985 Rel: $20 Cur: $25 (2/15/90)
84 COSENTINO Cabernet Sauvignon North Coast 1985 $10.50 (9/15/88)
84 DOMINUS Napa Valley 1985 Rel: $45 Cur: $55 (2/15/90)
84 FIELD STONE Cabernet Sauvignon Alexander Valley Turkey Hill Vineyard 1985 $18 (2/28/91)
84 GUENOC Cabernet Sauvignon Guenoc Valley Premier Cuvée 1985 $17 (10/15/90)
84 HUSCH Cabernet Sauvignon Mendocino La Ribera Cabernet 1985 $5 (11/30/87) BB
84 JOSEPH PHELPS Cabernet Sauvignon Napa Valley 1985 Rel: $14 Cur: $27 (5/15/89)
84 RAYMOND Cabernet Sauvignon Napa Valley 1985 $15 (12/15/89)
84 SEGHESIO Cabernet Sauvignon Northern Sonoma 1985 $5.50 (4/15/89) BB
84 SHADOWBROOK Cabernet Sauvignon Napa Valley 1985 $9.50 (7/15/91)
83 BEAULIEU Cabernet Sauvignon Napa Valley Beau Tour 1985 $7 (6/15/88)
83 BENZIGER Cabernet Sauvignon Sonoma Valley 1985 $16 (12/15/88)
83 CAREY Cabernet Sauvignon Santa Ynez Valley 1985 $10 (11/15/89)
83 HACIENDA Cabernet Sauvignon Sonoma County 1985 $15 (9/30/90)
83 INGLENOOK Cabernet Sauvignon Napa Valley 1985 $9.50 (3/31/89)
83 JOHNSON TURNBULL Cabernet Sauvignon Napa Valley 1985 Rel: $14.50 Cur: $22 (CA-3/89)
83 KALIN Cabernet Sauvignon Sonoma County Reserve 1985 $23 (4/15/91)
83 LEEWARD Cabernet Sauvignon Alexander Valley 1985 $12 (10/31/87)
83 MARIETTA Cabernet Sauvignon Sonoma County 1985 $10 (6/30/90)
83 NEYERS Cabernet Sauvignon Napa Valley 1985 $14 (7/15/89)
83 SILVER OAK Cabernet Sauvignon Napa Valley Bonny's Vineyard 1985 Rel: $50 Cur: $74 (11/15/90)
83 STRATFORD Cabernet Sauvignon California 1985 $10 (11/30/88)
83 WILLIAM WHEELER Cabernet Sauvignon Dry Creek Valley Norse Vineyard Private Reserve 1985 $18 (11/15/90)
83 YORK MOUNTAIN Cabernet Sauvignon San Luis Obispo 1985 $15 (12/15/89)
82 BELLEROSE Cuvée Bellerose Sonoma County 1985 $16 (12/15/88)
82 EBERLE Cabernet Sauvignon Paso Robles 1985 Rel: $12 Cur: $17 (2/15/89)
82 FETZER Cabernet Sauvignon Lake County 1985 $6.50 (8/31/87) BB
82 INGLENOOK Niebaum Claret Napa Valley 1985 $12 (3/15/89)
82 MADRONA Cabernet Sauvignon El Dorado 1985 $12 (4/15/92)
82 QUAIL RIDGE Cabernet Sauvignon Napa Valley 1985 $15 (7/31/89)
82 RUTHERFORD HILL Cabernet Sauvignon Napa Valley 1985 Rel: $14 Cur: $17 (4/30/90)
82 VILLA MT. EDEN Cabernet Sauvignon Napa Valley 1985 $13 (CA-3/89)
81 BELVEDERE Cabernet Sauvignon Alexander Valley Robert Young Vineyard Gifts of the Land 1985 $16 (1/31/91)
81 CAIN Cabernet Sauvignon Napa Valley 1985 $16 (4/15/89)
81 CLOS DU BOIS Marlstone Vineyard Alexander Valley 1985 Rel: $19.50 Cur: $23 (6/15/89)
81 COSENTINO Cabernet Sauvignon North Coast Reserve 1985 $18 (4/30/89)
81 DOMAINE DE NAPA Cabernet Sauvignon Napa Valley 1985 $12 (12/15/88)
81 GRAND CRU Cabernet Sauvignon Alexander Valley Collector's Reserve 1985 $18 (7/15/89)
81 MIRASSOU Cabernet Sauvignon Napa Valley Fifth Generation Harvest Reserve 1985 $12 (11/15/89)
81 MOUNT EDEN Cabernet Sauvignon Santa Cruz Mountains 1985 Rel: $28 Cur: $37 (11/15/89)
81 JOSEPH PHELPS Cabernet Sauvignon Napa Valley Eisele Vineyard 1985 Rel: $40 Cur: $52 (5/31/89)
81 SUNNY ST. HELENA Cabernet Sauvignon Napa Valley 1985 $9 (10/31/87)
81 ZD Cabernet Sauvignon Napa Valley 1985 $14 (5/15/89)
80 HEITZ Cabernet Sauvignon Napa Valley 1985 Rel: $18 Cur: $25 (5/15/90)
80 LA FERRONNIERE Cabernet Sauvignon Napa Valley 1985 $14 (1/31/90)
80 LOUIS M. MARTINI Cabernet Sauvignon Sonoma Valley Monte Rosso 1985 $22 (CA-3/89)
80 MILANO Cabernet Sauvignon Mendocino County Sanel Valley Vineyard 1985 $18 (9/30/89)
80 R.H. PHILLIPS Cabernet Sauvignon California 1985 $6 (11/30/88)
80 SEBASTIANI Cabernet Sauvignon Sonoma County Family Selection 1985 $8 (10/15/88)
80 SOLARI Cabernet Sauvignon Napa Valley Larkmead Vineyards 1985 $10 (3/15/90)
80 SYLVAN SPRINGS Cabernet Sauvignon California Vintner's Reserve 1985 $5 (9/30/88) BB
80 TREFETHEN Cabernet Sauvignon Napa Valley 1985 Rel: $15 Cur: $19 (CA-3/89)
80 TREFETHEN Cabernet Sauvignon Napa Valley Hillside Selection 1985 $30 (11/15/90)
80 VANINO Cabernet Sauvignon Sonoma County 1985 $11 (9/30/88)
79 LAWRENCE J. BARGETTO Cabernet Sauvignon Sonoma County Cypress 1985 $8.50 (11/15/89)
79 CORBETT CANYON Cabernet Sauvignon Santa Barbara-San Luis Obispo Counties Select 1985 $10 (5/31/88)
79 COSENTINO The Poet California 1985 $18 (8/31/88)
79 DE MOOR Cabernet Sauvignon Napa Valley 1985 $14 (CA-3/89)
79 FREEMARK ABBEY Cabernet Sauvignon Napa Valley 1985 $15 (10/31/89)
79 GRAND CRU Cabernet Sauvignon Sonoma County Premium Selection 1985 $9 (6/15/89)
79 J. PEDRONCELLI Cabernet Sauvignon Dry Creek Valley 1985 $7 (10/15/88)
79 IVAN TAMAS Cabernet Sauvignon North Coast 1985 $7 (12/31/87)
79 ZACA MESA Cabernet Sauvignon Santa Barbara County Reserve 1985 $15 (10/15/88)
78 FREMONT CREEK Cabernet Sauvignon Mendocino-Napa Counties 1985 $9.50 (3/31/88)
78 MADDALENA Cabernet Sauvignon Alexander Valley Reserve 1985 $11 (6/30/89)
78 MASSON Cabernet Sauvignon Monterey County Vintage Selection 1985 $8 (9/15/88)
78 RICHARD MICHAELS Cabernet Sauvignon California 1985 $10 (9/30/88)
78 ROBERT MONDAVI Cabernet Sauvignon California Cabernet 1985 $4.25 (10/31/87) BB
78 PAT PAULSEN Cabernet Sauvignon Sonoma County 1985 $11 (12/31/87)
78 A. RAFANELLI Cabernet Sauvignon Dry Creek Valley 1985 $8 (9/15/88)
78 RICHARDSON Cabernet Sauvignon Sonoma Valley 1985 $12 (11/30/88)
78 TAFT STREET Cabernet Sauvignon California 1985 $7.50 (10/15/88)
78 M.G. VALLEJO Cabernet Sauvignon California 1985 $4 (2/15/89)
78 WENTE BROS. Cabernet Sauvignon Central Coast 1985 $8 (11/15/89)
78 J. WILE & SONS Cabernet Sauvignon Napa Valley 1985 $7 (11/15/87)
77 ARCIERO Cabernet Sauvignon Paso Robles 1985 $6 (12/31/87)
77 AUDUBON Cabernet Sauvignon Napa Valley 1985 $11 (6/15/88)
77 BOEGER Cabernet Sauvignon El Dorado 1985 $11 (2/15/89)
77 CHESTNUT HILL Cabernet Sauvignon Sonoma County 1985 $7.75 (10/15/88)
77 GEYSER PEAK Cabernet Sauvignon Alexander Valley Estate Reserve 1985 $15 (5/15/89)
77 CHARLES KRUG Cabernet Sauvignon Napa Valley 1985 $10.50 (1/31/90)
77 MOUNTAIN VIEW Cabernet Sauvignon Mendocino County 1985 $6 (2/15/89)
77 PESENTI Cabernet Sauvignon San Luis Obispo County Family Reserve 1985 $13 (12/15/89)
76 BYRON Cabernet Sauvignon Central Coast 1985 $14 (12/15/89)
76 LOUIS M. MARTINI Cabernet Sauvignon North Coast 1985 $8.25 (10/31/88)
76 MEEKER Cabernet Sauvignon Dry Creek Valley 1985 $18 (4/30/89)
76 PACHECO RANCH Cabernet Sauvignon Marin County 1985 $10 (11/15/91)
76 PARSONS CREEK Cabernet Sauvignon Sonoma County 1985 $13 (6/30/89)
76 STEVENOT Cabernet Sauvignon Calaveras County 1985 $7.50 (6/30/89)
76 WILLIAM WHEELER Cabernet Sauvignon Dry Creek Valley 1985 $12 (7/15/89)
75 CRESTON Cabernet Sauvignon Central Coast Winemaker's Selection 1985 $16.50 (12/15/89)
75 FOX MOUNTAIN Cabernet Sauvignon Russian River Valley Reserve 1985 $19 (9/15/89)
75 HAWK CREST Cabernet Sauvignon North Coast 1985 $6.50 (7/31/88)
75 HOP KILN Cabernet Sauvignon Dry Creek Valley 1985 $10 (10/15/88)
75 MONTEREY VINEYARD Cabernet Sauvignon Monterey County Limited Release 1985 $10 (8/31/88)
74 CHRISTOPHE Cabernet Sauvignon Napa Valley Reserve 1985 $12.50 (11/15/89)
74 DEHLINGER Cabernet Sauvignon Russian River Valley 1985 $13 (5/31/89)
74 ELLISTON Cabernet Sauvignon Central Coast Sunol Valley Vineyard 1985 $16 (11/15/91)
74 FITCH MOUNTAIN Cabernet Sauvignon Napa Valley 1985 $9 (4/15/89)
74 MADDALENA Cabernet Sauvignon Sonoma County 1985 $6 (5/31/88)
74 J.W. MORRIS Cabernet Sauvignon Alexander Valley 1985 $8 (2/15/89)
74 SAUSAL Cabernet Sauvignon Alexander Valley 1985 $12 (7/31/89)
74 SMITH-MADRONE Cabernet Sauvignon Napa Valley 1985 Rel: $14 Cur: $19 (4/15/90)
73 MONTEREY VINEYARD Cabernet Sauvignon Monterey-Sonoma-San Luis Obispo Counties Classic 1985 $5 (2/15/89)
72 DEER VALLEY Cabernet Sauvignon Monterey 1985 $5.50 (12/31/87)
72 FIRESTONE Cabernet Sauvignon Santa Ynez Valley 1985 $9.50 (8/31/88)
72 RIVERSIDE FARM Cabernet Sauvignon California 1985 $4.50 (5/31/88)
72 VIANSA Cabernet Sauvignon Sonoma-Napa Counties 1985 $13 (9/15/89)
71 FOPPIANO Cabernet Sauvignon Russian River Valley 1985 $9 (6/30/89)
71 LAURA'S Cabernet Sauvignon Paso Robles 1985 $12 (12/15/89)
70 AMIZETTA Cabernet Sauvignon Napa Valley 1985 $16 (5/31/88)
70 FIELD STONE Cabernet Sauvignon Alexander Valley Home Ranch Vineyard 1985 $14 (4/15/89)
70 THOMAS FOGARTY Cabernet Sauvignon Napa Valley 1985 $15 (7/15/91)
70 WILD HORSE Cabernet Sauvignon Paso Robles Wild Horse Vineyards 1985 $10.50 (6/30/88)
68 CRESTON Cabernet Sauvignon San Luis Obispo County 1985 $12 (12/15/89)
67 ESTRELLA RIVER Cabernet Sauvignon Paso Robles 1985 $9 (11/15/89)
67 FIRESTONE Cabernet Sauvignon Santa Ynez Valley Vintage Reserve 1985 $25 (12/15/89)
66 DELICATO Cabernet Sauvignon California 1985 $6 (6/30/88)
64 RIDGE Cabernet Sauvignon Santa Cruz Mountains 1985 $12 (6/15/89)
63 HOUTZ Cabernet Sauvignon Santa Ynez Valley 1985 $8 (12/15/89)
62 MARION Cabernet Sauvignon California 1985 $5.50 (12/31/87)
61 MENDOCINO ESTATE Cabernet Sauvignon Mendocino 1985 $5.50 (2/15/88)
57 J. FRITZ Cabernet Sauvignon Alexander Valley 1985 $10 (12/31/88)

1984

98 CAYMUS Cabernet Sauvignon Napa Valley Special Selection 1984 Rel: $35 Cur: $185 (7/15/89) CS
97 DUNN Cabernet Sauvignon Napa Valley 1984 Rel: $18 Cur: $65 (11/30/91) (JL)
97 HEITZ Cabernet Sauvignon Napa Valley Martha's Vineyard 1984 Rel: $40 Cur: $95 (3/15/89) SS

97 RIDGE Cabernet Sauvignon Santa Cruz Mountains Monte Bello 1984 Rel: $35 Cur: $83 (CA-3/89)
96 DIAMOND CREEK Cabernet Sauvignon Napa Valley Red Rock Terrace 1984 Rel: $25 Cur: $65 (CA-3/89)
96 DUNN Cabernet Sauvignon Howell Mountain 1984 Rel: $25 Cur: $145 (11/30/91) (JL)
95 DIAMOND CREEK Cabernet Sauvignon Napa Valley Red Rock Terrace 1984 Rel: $25 Cur: $65 (9/30/86) CS
95 FROG'S LEAP Cabernet Sauvignon Napa Valley 1984 Rel: $10 Cur: $30 (3/31/87) SS
95 RIDGE Cabernet Sauvignon Santa Cruz Mountains Monte Bello 1984 Rel: $35 Cur: $83 (9/15/87) CS

94 BERINGER Cabernet Sauvignon Napa Valley Private Reserve 1984 Rel: $25 Cur: $45 (2/15/89) CS
94 BUENA VISTA Cabernet Sauvignon Carneros 1984 $10 (8/31/87)
94 CHATEAU MONTELENA Cabernet Sauvignon Napa Valley 1984 Rel: $20 Cur: $55 (CA-3/89)
94 CONN CREEK Cabernet Sauvignon Napa Valley Collins Vineyard Private Reserve 1984 Rel: $23 Cur: $37 (3/31/89)
94 DIAMOND CREEK Cabernet Sauvignon Napa Valley Gravelly Meadow 1984 Rel: $25 Cur: $62 (CA-3/89)
94 DIAMOND CREEK Cabernet Sauvignon Napa Valley Volcanic Hill 1984 Rel: $25 Cur: $60 (CA-3/89)
94 GROTH Cabernet Sauvignon Napa Valley Reserve 1984 Rel: $25 Cur: $120 (CA-3/89)
94 KEENAN Cabernet Sauvignon Napa Valley 1984 Rel: $13.50 Cur: $27 (10/15/87) SS
94 OPUS ONE Napa Valley 1984 Rel: $50 Cur: $82 (CA-3/89)
94 ROMBAUER Le Meilleur du Chai Napa Valley 1984 Rel: $32.50 Cur: $40 (3/31/89)

93 ALEXANDER VALLEY VINEYARDS Cabernet Sauvignon Alexander Valley 1984 Rel: $10.50 Cur: $18 (5/15/87) SS
93 BURGESS Cabernet Sauvignon Napa Valley Vintage Selection 1984 Rel: $17 Cur: $25 (CA-3/89)
93 B.R. COHN Cabernet Sauvignon Sonoma Valley Olive Hill Vineyard 1984 Rel: $15 Cur: $35 (CA-3/89)
93 THE HESS COLLECTION Cabernet Sauvignon Napa Valley Reserve 1984 Rel: $22 Cur: $100 (CA-3/89)
93 KENWOOD Cabernet Sauvignon Sonoma Valley Artist Series 1984 Rel: $30 Cur: $39 (CA-3/89)
93 PINE RIDGE Cabernet Sauvignon Napa Valley Andrus Reserve 1984 Rel: $37 Cur: $40 (CA-3/89)
93 PINE RIDGE Cabernet Sauvignon Stags Leap District Pine Ridge Stags Leap Vineyard 1984 Rel: $25 Cur: $33 (CA-3/89)
93 SHAFER Cabernet Sauvignon Stags Leap District 1984 Rel: $14 Cur: $24 (12/15/87) SS
92 ALEXANDER VALLEY VINEYARDS Cabernet Sauvignon Alexander Valley 1984 Rel: $10.50 Cur: $18 (CA-3/89)
92 BEAULIEU Cabernet Sauvignon Napa Valley Georges de Latour Private Reserve 1984 Rel: $25 Cur: $36 (3/31/91) (JL)

92 CARMENET Red Sonoma Valley 1984 Rel: $16 Cur: $30 (CA-3/89)
92 DIAMOND CREEK Cabernet Sauvignon Napa Valley Lake 1984 Rel: $50 Cur: $250 (CA-3/89)
92 DUCKHORN Cabernet Sauvignon Napa Valley 1984 Rel: $17 Cur: $32 (CA-3/89)
92 FAR NIENTE Cabernet Sauvignon Napa Valley 1984 Rel: $25 Cur: $30 (CA-3/89)
92 FORMAN Cabernet Sauvignon Napa Valley 1984 Rel: $18 Cur: $70 (CA-3/89)
92 GIRARD Cabernet Sauvignon Napa Valley Reserve 1984 Rel: $25 Cur: $37 (CA-3/89)
92 GRACE FAMILY Cabernet Sauvignon Napa Valley 1984 Rel: $38 Cur: $280 (CA-3/89)
92 GROTH Cabernet Sauvignon Napa Valley 1984 Rel: $14 Cur: $41 (CA-3/89)
92 INGLENOOK Reunion Napa Valley 1984 $35 (CA-3/89)
92 KEENAN Cabernet Sauvignon Napa Valley 1984 Rel: $13.50 Cur: $27 (CA-3/89)
92 LAKESPRING Cabernet Sauvignon Napa Valley Reserve Selection 1984 Rel: $15 Cur: $21 (10/31/88) SS

92 SIMI Cabernet Sauvignon Alexander Valley Reserve 1984 Rel: $22.50 Cur: $26 (CA-3/89)
92 SPOTTSWOODE Cabernet Sauvignon Napa Valley 1984 Rel: $25 Cur: $75 (11/30/87)
92 STAG'S LEAP WINE CELLARS Cabernet Sauvignon Stags Leap District SLV 1984 Rel: $21 Cur: $28 (CA-3/89)
92 STERLING Cabernet Sauvignon Napa Valley Reserve 1984 Rel: $25 Cur: $40 (3/31/89) CS
91 CAYMUS Cabernet Sauvignon Napa Valley 1984 Rel: $16 Cur: $50 (CA-3/89)
91 FREEMARK ABBEY Cabernet Sauvignon Napa Valley Sycamore Vineyards 1984 Rel: $20 Cur: $23 (12/15/88)
91 WILLIAM HILL Cabernet Sauvignon Napa Valley Reserve 1984 Rel: $18.25 Cur: $28 (4/15/88) CS
91 KENWOOD Cabernet Sauvignon Sonoma Valley Jack London Vineyard 1984 Rel: $16 Cur: $21 (11/30/87)
91 MARKHAM Cabernet Sauvignon Napa Valley 1984 Rel: $12 Cur: $18 (CA-3/89)
91 MONTICELLO Cabernet Sauvignon Napa Valley Corley Reserve 1984 Rel: $18.50 Cur: $30 (CA-3/89)

91 JOSEPH PHELPS Cabernet Sauvignon Napa Valley 1984 Rel: $14 Cur: $31 (10/31/88)
91 SHAFER Cabernet Sauvignon Stags Leap District 1984 Rel: $14 Cur: $24 (CA-3/89)
91 SILVERADO Cabernet Sauvignon Stags Leap District 1984 Rel: $11.50 Cur: $26 (CA-3/89)
91 SMITH-MADRONE Cabernet Sauvignon Napa Valley 1984 Rel: $14 Cur: $25 (CA-3/89)
91 STELTZNER Cabernet Sauvignon Stags Leap District 1984 Rel: $15 Cur: $19 (CA-3/89)
91 TUDAL Cabernet Sauvignon Napa Valley 1984 Rel: $12.50 Cur: $27 (CA-3/89)
90 BUENA VISTA Cabernet Sauvignon Carneros Private Reserve 1984 Rel: $18 Cur: $25 (CA-3/89)
90 DOMINUS Napa Valley 1984 Rel: $40 Cur: $55 (5/15/88) CS
90 INGLENOOK Cabernet Sauvignon Napa Valley Reserve Cask 1984 $22 (7/31/90)
90 JOHNSON TURNBULL Cabernet Sauvignon Napa Valley 1984 Rel: $14.50 Cur: $23 (CA-3/89)
90 LYETH Red Alexander Valley 1984 Rel: $18 Cur: $24 (CA-3/89)

Key to Symbols

The scores reported here are the results of blind tastings conducted by our panel of senior editors. Wines that carry the initials below are results of individual tastings.

THE WINE SPECTATOR 100-POINT SCALE 95-100—Classic, a great wine; ***90-94***—Outstanding, superior character and style; ***80-89***—Good to very good, a wine with special qualities; ***70-79***—Average, drinkable wine that may have minor flaws; ***60-69***—Below average, drinkable but not recommended; ***50-59***—Poor, undrinkable, not recommended. "+"—With a score indicates a range; used primarily with barrel tastings to indicate a preliminary score.

SPECIAL DESIGNATIONS SS—Spectator Selection, CS—Cellar Selection, BB—Best Buy, ($NA)—Price not available, (NR)—Not released.

TASTER'S INITIALS (JG)—Jim Gordon, (HS)—Harvey Steiman, (JL)—James Laube, (JS)—James Suckling, (TM)—Thomas Matthews, (TR)—Terry Robards, (PM)—Per-Henrik Mansson, (BT)—Barrel Tasting (these wines were tasted blind from barrel samples), (CA-date)—*California's Great Cabernets* by James Laube, (CH-date)—*California's Great Chardonnays* by James Laube, (VP-date)—*Vintage Port* by James Suckling.

DATE TASTED Dates in parentheses represent the issue in which the rating was published.

90 MAYACAMAS Cabernet Sauvignon Napa Valley 1984 Rel: $20 Cur: $28 (CA-3/89)
90 ROBERT MONDAVI Cabernet Sauvignon Napa Valley Reserve 1984 Rel: $37 Cur: $42 (11/30/91) (JL)
90 MONTICELLO Cabernet Sauvignon Napa Valley Jefferson Cuvée 1984 $11 (11/30/87)
90 OPTIMA Cabernet Sauvignon Sonoma County 1984 $16.50 (2/29/88)
90 PINE RIDGE Cabernet Sauvignon Napa Valley Rutherford Cuvée 1984 Rel: $14 Cur: $29 (CA-3/89)
90 RAYMOND Cabernet Sauvignon Napa Valley 1984 Rel: $13 Cur: $17 (2/15/89)
90 SPOTTSWOODE Cabernet Sauvignon Napa Valley 1984 Rel: $25 Cur: $75 (CA-3/89)
90 STAG'S LEAP WINE CELLARS Cabernet Sauvignon Stags Leap District Stag's Leap Vineyards Cask 23 1984 Rel: $40 Cur: $88 (12/31/88)
89 CAKEBREAD Cabernet Sauvignon Napa Valley 1984 Rel: $16 Cur: $25 (CA-3/89)

89 CLOS DU BOIS Marlstone Vineyard Alexander Valley 1984 Rel: $19.50 Cur: $30 (CA-3/89)
89 CUVAISON Cabernet Sauvignon Napa Valley 1984 Rel: $14 Cur: $18 (CA-3/89)
89 DANIEL Cabernet Sauvignon Napa Valley 1984 $21 (7/15/88)
89 DE LOACH Cabernet Sauvignon Dry Creek Valley 1984 $11 (12/15/87)
89 DIAMOND CREEK Cabernet Sauvignon Napa Valley Three Vineyard Blend 1984 Rel: $50 Cur: $100 (CA-3/89)
89 FISHER Cabernet Sauvignon Sonoma County Coach Insignia 1984 Rel: $18 Cur: $25 (CA-3/89)
89 GEYSER PEAK Réserve Alexandre Alexander Valley 1984 $19 (8/31/88)
89 HEITZ Cabernet Sauvignon Napa Valley 1984 Rel: $15 Cur: $30 (1/31/90) (JL)
89 LAUREL GLEN Cabernet Sauvignon Sonoma Mountain 1984 Rel: $15 Cur: $45 (CA-3/89)
89 LOUIS M. MARTINI Cabernet Sauvignon Sonoma Valley Monte Rosso 1984 $22 (CA-3/89)

89 JOSEPH PHELPS Insignia Napa Valley 1984 Rel: $30 Cur: $39 (CA-3/89)
89 ST. CLEMENT Cabernet Sauvignon Napa Valley 1984 Rel: $15 Cur: $22 (CA-3/89)
89 SHAFER Cabernet Sauvignon Stags Leap District Hillside Select 1984 Rel: $24.50 Cur: $32.33 (4/30/89)
89 SHENANDOAH Cabernet Sauvignon Amador County Artist Series 1984 $9 (8/31/87)
89 SILVER OAK Cabernet Sauvignon Alexander Valley 1984 Rel: $22 Cur: $62 (CA-3/89)
89 SPRING MOUNTAIN Cabernet Sauvignon Napa Valley 1984 Rel: $15 Cur: $18 (3/15/89)
88 BELVEDERE Cabernet Sauvignon Alexander Valley Robert Young Vineyards 1984 $13 (7/15/88)
88 BUENA VISTA L'Année Carneros 1984 $32/1.5L (2/15/88)
88 CAYMUS Cabernet Sauvignon Napa Valley Cuvée 1984 $12 (8/31/87)
88 DE MOOR Cabernet Sauvignon Napa Valley 1984 Rel: $14 Cur: $16 (CA-3/89)

88 DOLAN Cabernet Sauvignon Mendocino 1984 $12 (5/31/88)
88 DRY CREEK Sonoma County David S. Stare Vintner's Reserve 1984 $18 (5/31/88)
88 FIELD STONE Cabernet Sauvignon Alexander Valley Turkey Hill Vineyard 1984 $16 (12/31/88)
88 FOLIE A DEUX Cabernet Sauvignon Napa Valley 1984 $14.50 (5/31/88)
88 FREEMARK ABBEY Cabernet Sauvignon Napa Valley Bosché 1984 Rel: $20 Cur: $24 (CA-3/89)
88 GIRARD Cabernet Sauvignon Napa Valley 1984 Rel: $11 Cur: $18 (11/30/87)
88 HAYWOOD Cabernet Sauvignon Sonoma Valley 1984 Rel: $12.50 Cur: $20 (CA-3/89)
88 HIDDEN CELLARS Cabernet Sauvignon Mendocino County Mountanos Vineyard 1984 $12 (8/31/88)
88 LA JOTA Cabernet Sauvignon Howell Mountain 1984 Rel: $15 Cur: $34 (CA-3/89)
88 LONG Cabernet Sauvignon Napa Valley 1984 Rel: $32 Cur: $46 (CA-3/89)

88 MOUNT VEEDER Cabernet Sauvignon Napa Valley 1984 Rel: $14 Cur: $21 (CA-3/89)
88 BERNARD PRADEL Cabernet Sauvignon Napa Valley 1984 $11 (2/29/88)
88 QUAIL RIDGE Cabernet Sauvignon Napa Valley 1984 $15 (3/31/89)
88 RIDGE Cabernet Sauvignon Napa County York Creek 1984 Rel: $14 Cur: $19 (CA-3/89)
88 ROUND HILL Cabernet Sauvignon Napa Valley Reserve 1984 $10 (10/31/87)
88 RUTHERFORD HILL Cabernet Sauvignon Napa Valley 1984 Rel: $12.50 Cur: $17 (CA-3/89)
88 STONEGATE Cabernet Sauvignon Napa Valley 1984 Rel: $14 Cur: $17 (CA-3/89)
88 VICHON Cabernet Sauvignon Napa Valley 1984 Rel: $11.25 Cur: $15 (CA-3/89)
87 BUEHLER Cabernet Sauvignon Napa Valley 1984 Rel: $13 Cur: $23 (CA-3/89)
87 CHAPPELLET Cabernet Sauvignon Napa Valley Reserve 1984 Rel: $18 Cur: $21 (CA-3/89)

87 CHRISTIAN BROTHERS Cabernet Sauvignon Napa Valley 1984 $7 (10/15/87) BB
87 CLOS DU BOIS Cabernet Sauvignon Alexander Valley 1984 $10 (6/15/87)
87 CLOS DU BOIS Cabernet Sauvignon Alexander Valley Briarcrest Vineyard 1984 Rel: $16 Cur: $24 (CA-3/89)
87 DOMAINE PHILIPPE Cabernet Sauvignon Napa Valley Select Cuvée 1984 $6.50 (5/15/88) BB
87 FIVE PALMS Cabernet Sauvignon Napa Valley 1984 $6 (3/31/87) BB
87 FRANCISCAN Cabernet Sauvignon Napa Valley Private Reserve 1984 Rel: $9 Cur: $15 (CA-3/89)
87 GRGICH HILLS Cabernet Sauvignon Napa Valley 1984 Rel: $17 Cur: $37 (4/30/89)
87 HACIENDA Cabernet Sauvignon Sonoma Valley Estate Reserve 1984 $18 (5/31/91)
87 CHARLES KRUG Cabernet Sauvignon Napa Valley Vintage Select 1984 Rel: $20 Cur: $28 (6/30/90)
87 LIVINGSTON Cabernet Sauvignon Napa Valley Moffett Vineyard 1984 Rel: $18 Cur: $35 (CA-3/89)

87 NEWTON Cabernet Sauvignon Napa Valley 1984 Rel: $13.50 Cur: $22 (CA-3/89)
87 JOSEPH PHELPS Cabernet Sauvignon Napa Valley Eisele Vineyard 1984 Rel: $35 Cur: $40 (CA-3/89)
87 PRESTON Cabernet Sauvignon Dry Creek Valley 1984 Rel: $11 Cur: $17 (CA-3/89)
87 RAYMOND Cabernet Sauvignon Napa Valley Private Reserve 1984 Rel: $20 Cur: $25 (7/15/89)
87 SANTA CRUZ MOUNTAIN Cabernet Sauvignon Santa Cruz Mountains Bates Ranch 1984 Rel: $14 Cur: $18 (CA-3/89)
87 STAGS' LEAP WINERY Cabernet Sauvignon Stags Leap District 1984 Rel: $13.50 Cur: $25 (CA-3/89)
86 CONN CREEK Cabernet Sauvignon Napa Valley Barrel Select Lot 79 1984 Rel: $13 Cur: $22 (CA-3/89)
86 DOMAINE MICHEL Cabernet Sauvignon Sonoma County 1984 $19 (9/15/87)
86 EBERLE Cabernet Sauvignon Paso Robles 1984 Rel: $12 Cur: $17 (CA-3/89)
86 GROTH Cabernet Sauvignon Napa Valley 1984 Rel: $14 Cur: $41 (2/15/88)

86 HEITZ Cabernet Sauvignon Napa Valley Bella Oaks Vineyard 1984 Rel: $25 Cur: $39 (5/15/89)
86 IRON HORSE Cabernet Sauvignon Alexander Valley 1984 Rel: $14 Cur: $20 (CA-3/89)
86 JORDAN Cabernet Sauvignon Alexander Valley 1984 Rel: $19 Cur: $45 (CA-3/89)
86 MERRYVALE Red Table Wine Napa Valley 1984 Rel: $24 Cur: $28 (CA-3/89)
86 MONTEVINA Cabernet Sauvignon Shenandoah Valley Limited Release 1984 $7.50 (8/31/88) BB
86 JOSEPH PHELPS Cabernet Sauvignon Napa Valley Backus Vineyard 1984 Rel: $20 Cur: $42 (CA-3/89)
86 V. SATTUI Cabernet Sauvignon Napa Valley Preston Vineyard 1984 Rel: $13.75 Cur: $25 (CA-3/89)
86 SIERRA VISTA Cabernet Sauvignon El Dorado 1984 $9 (3/31/88)
86 SILVER OAK Cabernet Sauvignon Napa Valley 1984 Rel: $22 Cur: $55 (CA-3/89)
86 SIMI Cabernet Sauvignon Sonoma County 1984 Rel: $11 Cur: $20 (10/31/88)

86 PHILIP TOGNI Cabernet Sauvignon Napa Valley 1984 Rel: $18 Cur: $33 (CA-3/89)
86 STEPHEN ZELLERBACH Cabernet Sauvignon Alexander Valley 1984 $8 (11/30/88)
85 BERINGER Cabernet Sauvignon Napa Valley Chabot Vineyard 1984 Rel: $30 Cur: $34 (9/15/90)
85 CAKEBREAD Cabernet Sauvignon Napa Valley Rutherford Reserve 1984 $35 (2/15/90)
85 CLOS DU VAL Cabernet Sauvignon Napa Valley Gran Val 1984 $8.50 (2/15/87) BB
85 DRY CREEK Cabernet Sauvignon Sonoma County 1984 $10 (5/15/87)
85 DUNNEWOOD Cabernet Sauvignon Napa Valley Reserve 1984 $10.50 (12/31/88)
85 FETZER Cabernet Sauvignon Mendocino Special Reserve 1984 $14 (12/31/88)
85 FLORA SPRINGS Cabernet Sauvignon Napa Valley 1984 Rel: $13 Cur: $18 (CA-3/89)
85 FOX MOUNTAIN Cabernet Sauvignon Russian River Valley Reserve 1984 $18 (3/15/89)

85 GUNDLACH BUNDSCHU Cabernet Sauvignon Sonoma Valley Rhinefarm Vineyards 1984 Rel: $9 Cur: $15 (CA-3/89)
85 LOUIS M. MARTINI Cabernet Sauvignon North Coast Special Selection 1984 ($NA) (CA-3/89)
85 NIEBAUM-COPPOLA Rubicon Napa Valley 1984 Rel: $30 Cur: $35 (CA-3/89)
85 ROBERT PECOTA Cabernet Sauvignon Napa Valley Kara's Vineyard 1984 Rel: $14 Cur: $20 (CA-3/89)
85 RUTHERFORD RANCH Cabernet Sauvignon Napa Valley 1984 $12.50 (5/31/89)
85 SEQUOIA GROVE Cabernet Sauvignon Napa Valley 1984 Rel: $12 Cur: $20 (CA-3/89)
85 STERLING Cabernet Sauvignon Napa Valley Diamond Mountain Ranch 1984 Rel: $15 Cur: $18 (CA-3/89)
85 VIANSA Cabernet Sauvignon Napa-Sonoma Counties 1984 $13 (7/31/88)
85 VICHON Cabernet Sauvignon Stags Leap District Fay Vineyard 1984 Rel: $14 Cur: $28 (CA-3/89)
84 FLORA SPRINGS Trilogy Napa Valley 1984 Rel: $30 Cur: $33 (CA-3/89)

84 FRANCISCAN Cabernet Sauvignon Napa Valley Oakville Estate 1984 $9.50 (9/15/88)
84 FREEMARK ABBEY Cabernet Sauvignon Napa Valley 1984 $14 (2/15/89)
84 GARLAND RANCH Cabernet Sauvignon Monterey County 1984 $6.75 (8/31/88) BB
84 GUNDLACH BUNDSCHU Cabernet Sauvignon Sonoma Valley Rhinefarm Vineyards 1984 Rel: $9 Cur: $15 (9/30/88)
84 KENDALL-JACKSON Cardinale California 1984 $12 (7/31/87)
84 MOUNT EDEN Cabernet Sauvignon Santa Cruz Mountains 1984 Rel: $22 Cur: $35 (CA-3/89)
84 ROMBAUER Cabernet Sauvignon Napa Valley 1984 Rel: $13.50 Cur: $21 (CA-3/89)
84 ROUND HILL Cabernet Sauvignon Napa Valley 1984 $8.50 (5/31/88)
84 SILVER OAK Cabernet Sauvignon Napa Valley Bonny's Vineyard 1984 Rel: $45 Cur: $80 (10/15/89)
84 IVAN TAMAS Cabernet Sauvignon Mendocino McNab Ranch 1984 $6 (2/15/87) BB

84 TREFETHEN Cabernet Sauvignon Napa Valley 1984 Rel: $14 Cur: $17 (CA-3/89)
84 WHITEHALL LANE Cabernet Sauvignon Napa Valley 1984 $14 (12/31/87)
83 CHATEAU POTELLE Cabernet Sauvignon Alexander Valley 1984 $13 (12/31/88)
83 CHATEAU SOUVERAIN Cabernet Sauvignon Sonoma County 1984 $8.50 (8/31/87)
83 KENWOOD Cabernet Sauvignon Sonoma Valley 1984 $12 (5/31/88)
83 STAG'S LEAP WINE CELLARS Cabernet Sauvignon Napa Valley 1984 $15 (7/15/87)
82 CHATEAU DIANA Cabernet Sauvignon Central Coast Limited Edition 1984 $6 (11/30/88) BB
82 CHIMNEY ROCK Cabernet Sauvignon Stags Leap District 1984 Rel: $15 Cur: $19 (CA-3/89)
82 CORBETT CANYON Cabernet Sauvignon Central Coast Select 1984 $8 (2/15/87)
82 FETZER Cabernet Sauvignon Mendocino Barrel Select 1984 $9 (11/30/87)

82 FIELD STONE Cabernet Sauvignon Alexander Valley Hoot Owl Creek Vineyards 1984 $14 (10/15/88)
82 GLEN ELLEN Cabernet Sauvignon Sonoma Valley Benziger Family Selection 1984 $14 (10/15/87)
82 J. LOHR Cabernet Sauvignon California 1984 $5 (11/30/86) BB
82 MADDALENA Cabernet Sauvignon Sonoma County Vintner's Reserve 1984 $9 (3/31/87)
81 BOEGER Cabernet Sauvignon El Dorado 1984 $11 (5/31/88)
81 KENDALL-JACKSON Cabernet Sauvignon Lake County 1984 $7.50 (11/15/87) BB
81 MONTEREY PENINSULA Cabernet Sauvignon Monterey Doctors' Reserve 1984 $16 (2/28/91)
81 SANTA BARBARA Cabernet Sauvignon Santa Ynez Valley Reserve 1984 $13.50 (10/31/87)
80 E. & J.GALLO Cabernet Sauvignon Northern Sonoma Reserve 1984 $7 (10/15/91)
80 LAMBERT BRIDGE Cabernet Sauvignon Sonoma County 1984 $10 (4/15/87)

80 CHARLES LEFRANC Cabernet Sauvignon Napa County 1984 $12 (10/15/87)
80 ROBERT MONDAVI Cabernet Sauvignon Napa Valley 1984 Rel: $13 Cur: $34 (12/31/87)
80 ROBERT PEPI Cabernet Sauvignon Napa Valley Vine Hill Ranch 1984 Rel: $16 Cur: $22 (8/31/89)
80 RAVENSWOOD Cabernet Sauvignon Sonoma County 1984 Rel: $12 Cur: $25 (CA-3/89)
80 SOLARI Cabernet Sauvignon Napa Valley Larkmead Vineyards 1984 $12 (4/15/88)
80 RODNEY STRONG Cabernet Sauvignon Alexander Valley Alexander's Crown Vineyard 1984 $12 (4/30/89)
80 VILLA MT. EDEN Cabernet Sauvignon Napa Valley 1984 ($NA) (CA-3/89)
79 CAIN Cabernet Sauvignon Napa Valley 1984 $14 (5/31/88)
79 ESTANCIA Cabernet Sauvignon Alexander Valley 1984 $6.50 (12/31/87)
79 GUNDLACH BUNDSCHU Cabernet Sauvignon Sonoma Valley Batto Ranch 1984 Rel: $14 Cur: $17 (CA-3/89)

79 ZACA MESA Cabernet Sauvignon Santa Barbara County 1984 $8.50 (10/31/88)
78 BEAULIEU Cabernet Sauvignon Napa Valley Rutherford 1984 Rel: $9.50 Cur: $15 (8/31/87)
78 COSENTINO Cabernet Sauvignon North Coast Reserve Edition 1984 $14 (3/31/88)
78 MARIETTA Cabernet Sauvignon Sonoma County 1984 $10 (12/31/87)
78 MEEKER Cabernet Sauvignon Dry Creek Valley 1984 $18 (6/15/88)
78 MENDOCINO ESTATE Cabernet Sauvignon Mendocino 1984 $4.75 (6/15/87)
78 ROUDON-SMITH Cabernet Sauvignon Santa Cruz Mountains 1984 $12 (6/30/88)
77 BELLEROSE Cuvée Bellerose Sonoma County 1984 $14 (11/15/87)
77 FOPPIANO Cabernet Sauvignon Russian River Valley 1984 $8.50 (4/30/88)
77 GEYSER PEAK Cabernet Sauvignon Alexander Valley 1984 $7.50 (3/15/88)

77 HOP KILN Cabernet Sauvignon Alexander Valley 1984 $10 (3/31/88)
76 DEHLINGER Cabernet Sauvignon Russian River Valley 1984 $12 (2/15/88)
76 HAWK CREST Cabernet Sauvignon North Coast 1984 $7 (10/15/87)
76 KONOCTI Cabernet Sauvignon Lake County 1984 $7.50 (2/15/89)
75 ACACIA Cabernet Sauvignon Napa Valley 1984 $15 (12/15/86)
75 CRYSTAL VALLEY Cabernet Sauvignon North Coast Reserve Edition 1984 $14 (10/15/87)
75 GRAND CRU Cabernet Sauvignon Sonoma County 1984 $8.50 (12/31/87)
75 JADE MOUNTAIN Cabernet Sauvignon Alexander Valley Icaria Creek Vineyard deCarteret 1984 $8.75 (6/30/88)
75 MICHAEL'S Cabernet Sauvignon Napa Valley Summit Vineyard Reserve 1984 $15 (3/31/88)
75 NEYERS Cabernet Sauvignon Napa Valley 1984 $12.50 (4/30/88)

75 RIVER OAKS Cabernet Sauvignon North Coast 1984 $6 (10/15/87)
75 STEVENOT Cabernet Sauvignon Calaveras County Grand Reserve 1984 $15 (12/31/87)
75 WILLIAM WHEELER Cabernet Sauvignon Dry Creek Valley 1984 $11 (4/15/88)
74 FETZER Cabernet Sauvignon Lake County 1984 $8 (5/15/87)
74 PARDUCCI Cabernet Sauvignon Mendocino County 1984 $8.50 (7/31/88)
74 TRIONE Cabernet Sauvignon Alexander Valley 1984 $10 (12/31/87)
73 HUSCH Cabernet Sauvignon Mendocino La Ribera Vineyards 1984 $10 (12/31/87)
73 WILLOW CREEK Cabernet Sauvignon Napa Valley 1984 $8.50 (3/31/88)

72 JEAN CLAUDE BOISSET Cabernet Sauvignon Napa Valley 1984 $7 (12/31/87)
72 CAREY Cabernet Sauvignon Santa Ynez Valley 1984 $9 (3/31/88)

72 FIRESTONE Cabernet Sauvignon Santa Ynez Valley 1984 $9.50 (3/31/88)
72 RUTHERFORD ESTATE Cabernet Sauvignon Napa Valley 1984 $5 (11/15/87)
71 DAVIS BYNUM Cabernet Sauvignon Napa Valley Reserve Bottling 1984 $7 (12/15/87)
71 CLOS ROBERT Cabernet Sauvignon Napa Valley Proprietor's Reserve 1984 $7 (12/31/87)
71 CRESTON Cabernet Sauvignon Central Coast Winemaker's Selection 1984 $16 (12/15/87)
70 PAT PAULSEN Cabernet Sauvignon Alexander Valley 1984 $11 (4/30/87)
69 RIDGE Cabernet Sauvignon Santa Cruz Mountains Jimsomare 1984 $16 (10/31/87)
68 INNISFREE Cabernet Sauvignon Napa Valley 1984 $9 (12/15/87)
66 STUERMER Cabernet Sauvignon Lake County 1984 $15 (9/30/89)
64 DORE Cabernet Sauvignon California 1984 $5 (12/31/87)

64 RIDGE Cabernet Sauvignon Santa Cruz Mountains 1984 $12 (6/15/87)
63 JEKEL Cabernet Sauvignon Monterey 1984 $12 (7/31/89)
60 WILLIAM WHEELER Cabernet Sauvignon Dry Creek Valley Norse Vineyard Private Reserve 1984 $15 (7/31/89)

SECTION E: Special Ratings

The editors of *The Wine Spectator* meet twice a week to taste and evaluate wines for each issue of the magazine. While the Buying Guide in each issue contains reviews and ratings of more than 100 wines, the editors always find several wines they believe deserve special recognition.

Typically, the reviews of these wines are placed on the opening page of the Buying Guide and are given one of four special designations: Spectator Selection, Cellar Selection or Best Buy. Here are the criteria for these special designations:

Spectator Selection

Our highest recommendation in each issue. Although it is not necessarily the highest-scoring wine, it is the wine we think would make the most outstanding purchase. High quality balanced against value is the key to this rating. More expensive wines must be especially good to earn this distinction. Our top-scoring Spectator Selection is the 1983 Château Margaux (99, $70).

Cellar Selection

This, as the name implies, is the wine we believe is the best candidate for addition to your cellar. We believe this wine will improve most with additional bottle age and shows the greatest potential as a collectible. Our top-scoring Cellar Selection is the 1989 Châteaux Margaux (99, $145).

Best Buy

Wines carrying this designation are chosen because the editors feel they show outstanding quality at modest prices. Because of their extremely attractive prices, these wines tend to disappear from retail shelves very quickly. Our top-scoring Best Buy is the 1991 Canepa Sauvignon Blanc Maipo Valley (88, $5).

In this section, we present the cumulative lists of three of these special designations: Spectator Selection, Cellar Selection and Best Buy. They are listed on the following pages by score. First are lists of wines receiving our Spectator Selection designation. Next are those earning our Cellar Selection designation. Since the lists of Spectator and Cellar Selections date back as far as 1984, we have provided a release price and, where available, a verified current price. Finally, we list the Best Buys from 1990 through 1992.

Spectator Selections by Score

Score	Winery	Type/Appellation/Vineyard/Vintage	Release Price	Current Price	Percent Change	Issue Published
99	CHATEAU MARGAUX	Margaux 1983	$70	$103	47%	4/16/86
97	A. CHARBAUT	Brut Blanc de Blancs Champagne Certificate 1976	63	82	30	2/01/86
97	DUNN	Cabernet Sauvignon Napa Valley 1982	13	95	631	11/01/85
97	HEITZ	Cabernet Sauvignon Napa Valley Martha's Vineyard 1984	40	95	138	3/15/89
97	CHATEAU PICHON-LALANDE	Pauillac 1983	44	54	23	3/01/86
96	CAYMUS	Cabernet Sauvignon Napa Valley Special Selection 1980	$30	$145	383%	3/16/86
96	CERETTO	Barolo Zonchera 1980	10	16	68	2/16/86
96	F. CHAUVENET	Chassagne-Montrachet 1985	35	43	23	3/15/87
96	GRGICH HILLS	Chardonnay Napa Valley 1983	17	33	94	10/01/85
96	MOILLARD	Echézeaux 1984	22	30	36	11/15/86
96	CHATEAU MONTROSE	St.-Estèphe 1986	$31	$ 35	13%	5/15/89
96	NEWTON	Cabernet Sauvignon Napa Valley 1983	13	36	188	4/15/87
96	SIMI	Chardonnay Sonoma County Reserve 1982	22	60	173	5/01/86
96	SPOTTSWOODE	Cabernet Sauvignon Napa Valley 1987	36	60	67	9/15/90
96	STERLING	Reserve Napa Valley 1985	30	46	53	7/15/89
95	ACACIA	Pinot Noir Carneros Napa Valley 1984	$11	$ —	—%	12/15/86
95	BELVEDERE	Cabernet Sauvignon Alexander Valley Robert Young Vineyards 1982	12	17	42	12/01/85
95	BERINGER	Cabernet Sauvignon Napa Valley Private Reserve 1985	30	75	150	12/15/89
95	CHATEAU COS D'ESTOURNEL	St.-Estèphe 1983	29	61	110	5/16/86
95	CHATEAU MONTELENA	Cabernet Sauvignon Napa Valley 1987	30	37	23	10/31/91
95	DUNN	Cabernet Sauvignon Napa Valley 1983	$15	$ 90	500%	10/31/86
95	FROG'S LEAP	Cabernet Sauvignon Napa Valley 1984	10	30	200	3/31/87
95	CHATEAU HAUT-BRION	Graves 1983	86	—	—	9/30/86
95	WILLIAM HILL	Cabernet Sauvignon Napa Valley Reserve 1987	24	27	13	11/15/90
95	LOUIS JADOT	Beaune Clos des Ursules 1985	30	48	60	3/15/88
95	LA JOTA	Cabernet Sauvignon Howell Mountain 1987	$25	$ 30	20%	7/31/90
95	ROBERT MONDAVI	Cabernet Sauvignon Napa Valley Reserve 1985	40	50	25	11/15/89
95	CHATEAU OLIVIER	Pessac-Léognan 1989	19	21	11	3/15/92
95	CHATEAU PICHON-BARON	Pauillac 1988	30	33	10	3/31/91
95	PIGNAN	Châteauneuf-du-Pape Réserve 1985	14	38	171	8/31/87
95	RAVENSWOOD	Cabernet Sauvignon Sonoma County 1982	$11	$ 24	118%	4/01/86
95	SAN FELICE	Vigorello 1980	12	18	50	2/28/87
95	SONOMA-CUTRER	Chardonnay Russian River Valley Russian River Ranches 1983	11	25	138	11/16/85
94	BUENA VISTA	Cabernet Sauvignon Carneros Private Reserve 1985	18	26	44	10/15/89
94	CAYMUS	Cabernet Sauvignon Napa Valley 1986	22	33	50	3/15/90
94	CHATEAU CLERC-MILON	Pauillac 1988	$26	$ —	—%	4/30/91
94	CLOS RENE	Pomerol 1986	19	24	26	6/15/89
94	DEHLINGER	Merlot Sonoma County 1984	12	18	50	6/15/87
94	DUCKHORN	Cabernet Sauvignon Napa Valley 1986	18	30	67	7/31/89
94	DUCKHORN	Merlot Napa Valley 1984	15	40	167	12/31/86
94	FROG'S LEAP	Cabernet Sauvignon Napa Valley 1987	$15	$ 25	67%	12/31/89
94	GAJA	Nebbiolo d'Alba Vignaveja 1983	16	28	75	2/15/87
94	HEITZ	Cabernet Sauvignon Napa Valley Martha's Vineyard 1979	25	85	240	2/15/84
94	THE HESS COLLECTION	Cabernet Sauvignon Napa Valley 1987	17	22	29	4/15/91
94	WILLIAM HILL	Cabernet Sauvignon Napa Valley Gold Label 1982	18	36	100	6/16/86
94	KEENAN	Cabernet Sauvignon Napa Valley 1984	$14	$ 27	100%	10/15/87
94	KNUDSEN ERATH	Pinot Noir Yamhill County Vintage Select 1983	12	19	58	7/01/86
94	CHATEAU LA LOUVIERE	Graves 1982	11	25	127	10/16/85
94	ROBERT MONDAVI	Cabernet Sauvignon Napa Valley 1985	15	30	100	12/15/88
94	ROBERT PECOTA	Sauvignon Blanc Napa Valley 1985	9	—	—	10/15/86
94	DOM PERIGNON	Brut Champagne 1980	$60	$ 95	58%	9/15/86
94	JOSEPH PHELPS	Scheurebe Late Harvest Napa Valley 1985	15	21	40	8/31/86
94	CHATEAU PICHON-LALANDE	Pauillac 1982	29	115	297	2/01/85
94	PINE RIDGE	Chardonnay Stags Leap District Pine Ridge Stags Leap Vineyard 1983	16	25	56	12/16/85
94	SILVERADO	Cabernet Sauvignon Stags Leap District 1986	14	25	85	8/31/89
94	SIMI	Cabernet Sauvignon Alexander Valley Reserve 1985	$25	$ 29	16%	8/31/90
93	ALEXANDER VALLEY VINEYARDS	Cabernet Sauvignon Alexander Valley 1984	11	18	71	5/15/87
93	DOMAINE PIERRE AMIOT	Clos de la Roche 1982	28	—	—	6/16/85
93	BEAULIEU	Cabernet Sauvignon Napa Valley Georges de Latour Private Reserve 1980	24	49	104	9/16/85
93	BEAULIEU	Cabernet Sauvignon Napa Valley Georges de Latour Private Reserve 1979	21	55	162	3/01/84
93	BENZIGER	Cabernet Sauvignon Sonoma County 1987	$10	$ 20	100%	9/30/90
93	BUEHLER	Cabernet Sauvignon Napa Valley 1983	12	23	92	7/16/86
93	CAYMUS	Cabernet Sauvignon Napa Valley Special Selection 1979	30	220	633	6/01/85
93	CLOS DU BOIS	Chardonnay Alexander Valley Calcaire Vineyard 1984	12	30	150	6/01/86
93	FERRARI-CARANO	Chardonnay Alexander Valley 1988	18	29	61	5/31/90
93	FERRARI-CARANO	Chardonnay Alexander Valley 1985	$14	$ 45	221%	9/15/87
93	FRESCOBALDI	Pomino Tenuta di Pomino 1985	12	17	42	9/15/88
93	GIRARD	Chardonnay Napa Valley 1986	14	28	107	8/31/88
93	GUNDLACH BUNDSCHU	Merlot Sonoma Valley Rhinefarm Vineyards 1987	13	16	23	10/31/89
93	CHARLES HEIDSIECK	Brut Champagne 1982	33	40	21	12/31/88
93	LAUREL GLEN	Cabernet Sauvignon Sonoma Mountain 1981	$13	$ 44	252%	2/16/85
93	MANZANITA	Chardonnay Napa Valley 1983	13	—	—	1/01/86
93	MOUNT EDEN	Chardonnay Edna Valley M.E.V. MacGregor Vineyard 1987	14	20	43	4/30/89
93	CHATEAU OLIVIER	Graves 1985	15	25	67	2/15/89
93	PODERE IL PALAZZINO	Chianti Classico 1985	11	—	—	11/30/87
93	PAVILLON ROUGE DU CHATEAU MARGAUX	Margaux 1985	$23	$ 35	52%	4/15/88
93	ROSEMOUNT	Cabernet Sauvignon Hunter Valley 1986	11	—	—	1/31/89
93	ST. ANDREW'S WINERY	Chardonnay Napa Valley 1985	8	—	—	11/30/86
93	SHAFER	Cabernet Sauvignon Stags Leap District 1986	16	21	31	9/30/89
93	SHAFER	Cabernet Sauvignon Stags Leap District 1984	14	24	71	12/15/87
93	SILVER OAK	Cabernet Sauvignon Alexander Valley 1986	$26	$ 37	42%	10/31/90
93	SONOMA-CUTRER	Chardonnay Sonoma Valley Les Pierres 1985	18	47	169	9/30/87
93	ROBERT STEMMLER	Pinot Noir Sonoma County 1983	15	—	—	3/16/85
93	CHATEAU DU TERTRE	Margaux 1985	14	29	107	6/30/88
93	VEUVE CLICQUOT	Brut Champagne 1982	32	40	25	5/31/87

Score	Winery	Type/Appellation/Vineyard/Vintage	Release Price	Current Price	Percent Change	Issue Published
92	ALEXANDER VALLEY VINEYARDS	Cabernet Sauvignon Alexander Valley 1982	$ 10	$ 16	60%	11/01/84
92	BICHOT	Volnay Hospices de Beaune Cuvée Blondeau 1982	26	38	46	8/01/84
92	BOLLINGER	Brut Champagne Spécial Cuvée NV	25	—	—	12/31/87
92	BYRON	Chardonnay Santa Barbara County 1988	12	—	—	4/30/90
92	CARNEROS CREEK	Pinot Noir Carneros Fleur de Carneros 1987	9	—	—	2/28/89
92	CHATEAU ST. JEAN	Cabernet Sauvignon Alexander Valley 1987	$ 16	$ —	—%	6/30/91
92	CHATEAU ST. JEAN	Johannisberg Riesling Late Harvest Alexander Valley Robert Young Vineyards 1983	25	—	—	8/01/85
92	CLOS DU BOIS	Chardonnay Dry Creek Valley Flintwood Vineyard 1983	11	37	252	7/01/85
92	CLOS DU BOIS	Merlot Sonoma County 1985	10	16	60	10/31/87
92	DUCKHORN	Merlot Napa Valley 1982	13	56	331	12/16/84
92	FAR NIENTE	Chardonnay Napa Valley 1983	$ 22	$ 35	59%	4/01/85
92	CHATEAU DE FRANCE	Pessac-Léognan 1988	18	—	—	2/28/91
92	GUNDLACH BUNDSCHU	Merlot Sonoma Valley Rhinefarm Vineyards 1985	12	20	67	2/29/88
92	HACIENDA	Chardonnay Sonoma County Clair de Lune 1986	12	18	50	7/15/88
92	HOGUE	Merlot Washington 1989	12	—	—	10/15/91
92	LAKESPRING	Cabernet Sauvignon Napa Valley Reserve Selection 1984	$ 15	$ 21	40%	10/31/88
92	CHATEAU LA LOUVIERE	Pessac-Léognan 1988	20	—	—	8/31/91
92	CHATEAU DE MARBUZET	St.-Estèphe 1988	15	17	13	7/15/91
92	MARKHAM	Chardonnay Napa Valley 1989	12	—	—	6/15/91
92	MATANZAS CREEK	Merlot Sonoma County 1987	25	29	16	6/15/90
92	MERIDIAN	Cabernet Sauvignon Paso Robles 1988	$ 12	$ —	—%	9/30/91
92	ROBERT MONDAVI	Pinot Noir Napa Valley Reserve 1985	19	31	63	4/15/89
92	COLLI MONFORTESI	Barolo 1982	15	—	—	4/30/87
92	MONTICELLO	Chardonnay Napa Valley Corley Reserve 1988	17	20	16	1/31/91
92	GEORGES MUGNERET	Ruchottes-Chambertin 1982	26	—	—	9/01/85
92	NALLE	Zinfandel Dry Creek Valley 1987	$ 10	$ —	—%	5/31/89
92	IL POGGIONE	Brunello di Montalcino Riserva 1978	35	—	—	7/01/84
92	ROSEMOUNT	Shiraz South Eastern Australia 1990	9	—	—	2/15/92
92	ROUND HILL	Merlot Napa Valley 1983	8	—	—	1/31/87
92	RUTHERFORD RANCH	Cabernet Sauvignon Napa Valley 1985	11	15	36	5/15/90
92	CHATEAU ST.-PIERRE	St.-Julien 1986	$ 17	$ 22	29%	9/15/89
92	SAN FELICE	Predicato di Bitùrica 1982	19	25	32	1/31/88
92	SILVERADO	Cabernet Sauvignon Stags Leap District 1987	14	21	50	4/15/90
92	SONOMA-CUTRER	Chardonnay Russian River Valley Russian River Ranches 1982	10	24	140	10/16/84
92	VITICCIO	Prunaio 1986	19	—	—	3/31/90
91	BROWN BROTHERS	Chardonnay King Valley Family Reserve 1987	$ 16	$ —	—%	7/15/90
91	BUENA VISTA	Sauvignon Blanc Lake County 1986	7	—	—	7/15/87
91	BURGESS	Chardonnay Napa Valley Triere Vineyard 1990	15	17	13	5/31/92
91	CHALK HILL	Chardonnay Chalk Hill 1990	15	—	—	6/15/92
91	CHATEAU STE. MICHELLE	Sauvignon Blanc Columbia Valley 1990	9	—	—	4/30/92
91	CLOS DU VAL	Cabernet Sauvignon Stags Leap District Reserve 1979	$ 25	$ 55	120%	9/01/84
91	CONCHA Y TORO	Cabernet Sauvignon Maipo Puente Alto Vineyard Private Reserve Don Melchor 1988	14	—	—	5/15/92
91	CUVAISON	Chardonnay Napa Valley Carneros 1988	15	17	13	2/28/90
91	JOSEPH DROUHIN	Savigny-lès-Beaune 1985	21	25	19	11/15/87
91	DRY CREEK	Cabernet Sauvignon Sonoma County 1985	11	16	45	5/31/88
91	FONTODI	Chianti Classico 1988	$ 13	$ —	—%	9/15/91
91	FRANCISCAN	Cabernet Sauvignon Napa Valley Oakville Estate Reserve 1987	16	—	—	11/15/91
91	GRGICH HILLS	Zinfandel Alexander Valley 1982	10	18	80	5/16/85
91	E. GUIGAL	Gigondas 1985	12	17	42	9/30/88
91	CHATEAU HAUT-MARBUZET	St.-Estèphe 1988	25	28	12	12/31/90
91	INGLENOOK	Merlot Napa Valley Reserve 1985	$ 11	$ 14	33%	10/15/88
91	INGLENOOK	Gravion Napa Valley 1986	10	—	—	4/30/88
91	KEENAN	Chardonnay Napa Valley 1988	15	—	—	6/30/90
91	KUNDE	Chardonnay Sonoma Valley 1990	12	—	—	12/15/91
91	LAKESPRING	Merlot Napa Valley 1985	12	15	25	3/31/88
91	LAR DE BARROS	Tierra de Barros Tinto Reserva 1986	$ 8	$ —	—%	10/15/90
91	CHATEAU MOUTON-BARONNE-PHILIPPE	Pauillac 1985	18	29	61	5/15/88
91	PINE RIDGE	Merlot Napa Valley Selected Cuvée 1985	13	18	38	2/15/88
91	JOH. JOS. PRUM	Riesling Kabinett Mosel-Saar-Ruwer Wehlener Klosterberg 1983	9	—	—	11/16/84
91	JOH. JOS. PRUM	Riesling Spätlese Mosel-Saar-Ruwer Wehlener Sonnenuhr 1983	13	—	—	5/01/85
91	RIDGE	Zinfandel Napa County York Creek 1982	$ 11	$ —	—%	7/16/85
91	ROSEMOUNT	Shiraz Hunter Valley 1989	8	—	—	2/15/91
91	SAINTSBURY	Pinot Noir Carneros 1988	15	17	13	12/15/90
91	SILVERADO	Cabernet Sauvignon Stags Leap District 1985	13	36	188	11/15/88
91	SIMI	Cabernet Sauvignon Alexander Valley 1979	9	28	211	4/01/84
91	TALTARNI	Shiraz Victoria 1985	$ 10	$ —	—%	11/30/88
91	TORRES	Penedès Gran Sangre de Toro Reserva 1983	10	—	—	6/15/88
90	CASTELLO BANFI	Brunello di Montalcino 1979	18	—	—	4/16/85
90	BOUCHAINE	Chardonnay Napa Valley 1982	150	18	24	6/16/84
90	BURGESS	Cabernet Sauvignon Napa Valley Vintage Selection 1980	16	46	188	5/01/84
90	CARNEROS CREEK	Chardonnay Los Carneros 1990	$ 13	$ —	—%	3/31/92
90	CHALK HILL	Chardonnay Chalk Hill 1989	14	—	—	5/15/91
90	CHIMNEY ROCK	Cabernet Sauvignon Stags Leap District 1987	18	—	—	7/31/91
90	FLORA SPRINGS	Sauvignon Blanc Napa Valley 1990	9	—	—	11/30/91
90	FRANCISCAN	Merlot Napa Valley Oakville Estate 1984	9	15	76	6/30/87
90	HEITZ	Cabernet Sauvignon Napa Valley 1987	$ 20	$ 22	10%	4/15/92
90	HESS SELECT	Chardonnay California 1988	9	—	—	11/30/89
90	J. LOHR	Chardonnay Monterey Riverstone 1989	12	—	—	3/15/91
90	RIDGE	Zinfandel Sonoma County Geyserville 1988	14	—	—	11/30/90
90	DOMAINE DE LA ROQUETTE	Châteauneuf-du-Pape 1985	13	—	—	7/31/88
90	ROSEMOUNT	Shiraz Hunter Valley 1988	$ 8	$ —	—%	1/31/90
90	ST. CLEMENT	Chardonnay Napa Valley 1989	16	—	—	5/31/91
90	SAINTSBURY	Chardonnay Carneros 1990	15	17	13	12/31/91
90	SAUSAL	Zinfandel Alexander Valley 1986	7	—	—	3/31/89
90	SILVERADO	Sauvignon Blanc Napa Valley 1988	9	—	—	2/15/90
90	CASTELLO DI VOLPAIA	Chianti Classico 1985	$ 10	$ —	—%	6/30/89
90	WENTE BROS.	Chardonnay Arroyo Seco Riva Ranch 1990	12	—	—	6/30/92
89	PIO CESARE	Barolo Riserva 1978	19	28	47	10/01/84
89	KENWOOD	Cabernet Sauvignon Sonoma Valley Artist Series 1981	25	52	108	9/16/84
89	PINE RIDGE	Chardonnay Napa Valley Oak Knoll Cuvée 1982	13	19	46	3/16/84
89	ST. CLEMENT	Cabernet Sauvignon Napa Valley 1981	$ 13	$ 24	92%	6/01/84
89	ST. FRANCIS	Chardonnay Sonoma County 1990	10	—	—	1/31/92
88	BOUCHARD PERE & FILS	Côte de Beaune-Villages 1982	19	—	—	5/16/84
88	COLUMBIA CREST	Merlot Columbia Valley 1989	10	—	—	2/29/92
88	MATANZAS CREEK	Chardonnay Sonoma Valley Estate 1982	18	25	39	7/16/84
88	TREFETHEN	Cabernet Sauvignon Napa Valley 1981	$ 11	$ 36	223%	12/16/84

Cellar Selections by Score

Score	Winery	Type/Appellation/Vineyard/Vintage	Release Price	Current Price	Percent Change	Issue Published
99	CHATEAU MARGAUX	Margaux 1989	$145	$ —	—%	3/15/92
98	CAYMUS	Cabernet Sauvignon Napa Valley Special Selection 1987	60	82	37	10/31/91
98	CAYMUS	Cabernet Sauvignon Napa Valley Special Selection 1986	50	122	144	1/31/91
98	CAYMUS	Cabernet Sauvignon Napa Valley Special Selection 1984	35	185	429	7/15/89
98	CHATEAU CHEVAL BLANC	St.-Emilion 1986	80	85	6	6/30/89
98	CHATEAU MARGAUX	Margaux 1986	$ 80	$110	38%	6/15/89
98	CHATEAU MOUTON-ROTHSCHILD	Pauillac 1986	102	140	37	5/31/89
98	ROMANEE-CONTI	La Tâche 1986	250	—	—	8/31/89
97	CHATEAU DE BEAUCASTEL	Châteauneuf-du-Pape 1989	35	—	—	10/15/91
97	JOSEPH DROUHIN	Montrachet Marquis de Laguiche 1986	200	240	20	10/31/88
97	CHATEAU LAFITE-ROTHSCHILD	Pauillac 1985	$ 80	$101	26%	5/31/88
97	CHATEAU LYNCH-BAGES	Pauillac 1985	37	50	35	4/30/88
97	CHATEAU MARGAUX	Margaux 1988	75	80	7	3/31/91
97	OPUS ONE	Napa Valley 1987	68	74	9	11/15/90
96	F. CHAUVENET	Chassagne-Montrachet Morgeot 1985	37	52	41	5/15/87
96	CHATEAU CHEVAL BLANC	St.-Emilion 1982	$ 69	$150	117%	2/16/85
96	GAJA	Barbaresco Sorì San Lorenzo 1988	125	—	—	4/30/92
96	CHATEAU LAFITE-ROTHSCHILD	Pauillac 1988	100	—	—	4/30/91
96	CHATEAU LEOVILLE-LAS CASES	St.-Julien 1986	44	61	39	9/15/89
96	CHATEAU MARGAUX	Margaux 1982	60	135	125	6/16/85
96	CHATEAU PALMER	Margaux 1988	$ 65	$ —	—%	2/28/91
96	PENFOLDS	Shiraz South Australia Grange Hermitage Bin 95 1982	60	80	33	9/30/89
96	SILVER OAK	Cabernet Sauvignon Napa Valley 1982	19	61	221	2/15/87
96	SILVERADO	Cabernet Sauvignon Stags Leap District Limited Reserve 1986	35	39	11	12/15/90
95	ACACIA	Pinot Noir Carneros Napa Valley St. Clair Vineyard 1983	15	30	100	10/01/85
95	CHATEAU D'ANGLUDET	Margaux 1982	$ 15	$ 25	67%	12/01/85
95	BERINGER	Cabernet Sauvignon Napa Valley Private Reserve 1986	35	49	40	9/15/90
95	CHATEAU BEYCHEVELLE	St.-Julien 1985	35	39	11	8/31/88
95	CAYMUS	Cabernet Sauvignon Napa Valley Special Selection 1978	30	230	667	6/16/84
95	CHATEAU CLIMENS	Barsac 1983	50	55	10	1/31/88
95	CHATEAU COS D'ESTOURNEL	St.-Estèphe 1988	$ 30	$ 36	20%	7/15/91
95	DIAMOND CREEK	Cabernet Sauvignon Napa Valley Red Rock Terrace 1984	25	65	160	9/30/86
95	DUCKHORN	Cabernet Sauvignon Napa Valley 1987	20	31	55	6/30/90
95	DUNN	Cabernet Sauvignon Howell Mountain 1986	30	100	233	7/31/90
95	DUNN	Cabernet Sauvignon Napa Valley 1986	27	62	130	10/15/89
95	CHATEAU LA FLEUR DE GAY	Pomerol 1986	$ 43	$ 63	47%	10/31/89
95	GAJA	Barbaresco 1985	45	77	71	12/15/88
95	MARCHESI DI GRESY	Barbaresco Gaiun Martinenga 1985	55	72	31	1/31/89
95	E. GUIGAL	Côte-Rôtie La Turque 1986	99	350	254	10/15/90
95	HEITZ	Cabernet Sauvignon Napa Valley Martha's Vineyard 1987	65	75	15	3/31/92
95	HEITZ	Cabernet Sauvignon Napa Valley Martha's Vineyard 1986	$ 60	$ 70	17%	4/15/91
95	INGLENOOK	Reunion Napa Valley 1983	33	38	15	11/30/87
95	KENWOOD	Cabernet Sauvignon Sonoma Valley Artist Series 1986	30	34	13	11/30/89
95	CHATEAU LYNCH-BAGES	Pauillac 1988	35	—	—	3/15/91
95	MOILLARD	Clos de Vougeot 1983	26	45	73	10/16/85
95	MOILLARD	Vosne-Romanée Malconsorts 1984	$ 21	$ 28	33%	12/15/86
95	CHATEAU PICHON-LALANDE	Pauillac 1985	40	52	30	2/29/88
95	CHATEAU LE PIN	Pomerol 1988	65	—	—	6/30/91
95	POGGIO ANTICO	Brunello di Montalcino 1985	36	42	17	11/30/90
95	RIDGE	Cabernet Sauvignon Santa Cruz Mountains Monte Bello 1985	40	89	123	7/15/88
95	RIDGE	Cabernet Sauvignon Santa Cruz Mountains Monte Bello 1984	$ 35	$ 83	137%	9/15/87
95	SPOTTSWOODE	Cabernet Sauvignon Napa Valley 1985	25	122	388	11/15/88
95	STERLING	Reserve Napa Valley 1986	35	44	26	3/15/90
95	CHATEAU D'YQUEM	Sauternes 1983	180	240	33	10/15/87
94	CHATEAU L'ANGELUS	St.-Emilion 1985	26	32	23	3/31/88
94	BERINGER	Cabernet Sauvignon Napa Valley Private Reserve 1984	$ 25	$ 45	80%	2/15/89
94	BIONDI-SANTI	Brunello di Montalcino Riserva 1982	80	97	21	10/15/88
94	BOUCHARD PERE & FILS	Volnay Caillerets Ancienne Cuvée Carnot Château de Beaune 1989	52	—	—	2/29/92
94	CAYMUS	Cabernet Sauvignon Napa Valley 1983	15	54	260	11/30/86
94	COL D'ORCIA	Brunello di Montalcino 1979	15	24	60	9/15/86
94	CHATEAU LA CROIX DE GAY	Pomerol 1983	$ 16	$ 23	44%	7/01/86
94	DUCKHORN	Merlot Napa Valley 1983	15	28	87	11/01/85
94	DUNN	Cabernet Sauvignon Napa Valley 1985	20	70	250	9/15/88
94	GAJA	Cabernet Sauvignon Darmagi 1985	70	75	7	3/15/89
94	HEITZ	Cabernet Sauvignon Napa Valley Martha's Vineyard 1982	30	68	127	4/15/87
94	HENRI JAYER	Echézeaux 1982	$ 41	$160	290%	6/16/86
94	KEENAN	Merlot Napa Valley 1984	17	20	21	7/31/87
94	CHATEAU LYNCH-BAGES	Pauillac 1982	27	70	159	3/01/85
94	DOMAINE MEO-CAMUZET	Clos de Vougeot 1989	91	—	—	11/15/91
94	ROBERT MONDAVI	Cabernet Sauvignon Napa Valley Reserve 1981	30	36	20	2/16/86
94	OPUS ONE	Napa Valley 1981	$ 50	$ 95	90%	5/16/85
94	CHATEAU PICHON-LALANDE	Pauillac 1984	27	—	—	1/31/87
94	DOM RUINART	Brut Blanc de Blancs Champagne 1982	61	70	15	12/31/89
94	SILVER OAK	Cabernet Sauvignon Napa Valley 1986	26	49	88	10/31/90
94	STERLING	Cabernet Sauvignon Napa Valley Diamond Mountain Ranch 1982	15	37	147	11/16/85
94	WARRE	Vintage Port 1983	$ 28	$ 38	36%	12/31/86
93	BEAULIEU	Cabernet Sauvignon Napa Valley Georges de Latour Private Reserve 1982	24	40	67	3/15/87
93	BERINGER	Cabernet Sauvignon Napa Valley Private Reserve Lemmon-Chabot Vineyard 1980	20	42	110	8/01/84
93	CHATEAU MONTELENA	Cabernet Sauvignon Napa Valley 1983	18	34	89	11/15/87
93	CHATEAU CHEVAL BLANC	St.-Emilion 1988	105	—	—	12/31/90
93	CHATEAU COS D'ESTOURNEL	St.-Estèphe 1982	$ 23	$ 95	313%	7/16/85
93	DIAMOND CREEK	Cabernet Sauvignon Napa Valley Gravelly Meadow 1983	20	47	135	2/01/86
93	DUCKHORN	Merlot Napa Valley 1985	16	35	119	12/31/87
93	FATTORIA DI FELSINA	Chianti Classico Berardenga Vigneto Rancia Riserva 1985	23	—	—	4/30/90
93	CHATEAU LA FLEUR-PETRUS	Pomerol 1986	52	57	10	2/15/90

Score	Winery	Type/Appellation/Vineyard/Vintage	Release Price	Current Price	Percent Change	Issue Published
93	FREEMARK ABBEY	Cabernet Sauvignon Napa Valley Bosché 1982	$ 15	$ 41	173%	5/16/86
93	E. GUIGAL	Côte-Rôtie La Landonne 1987	125	135	8	7/31/91
93	HEITZ	Cabernet Sauvignon Napa Valley Martha's Vineyard 1980	30	68	127	7/01/85
90	FERRARI-CARANO	Chardonnay Alexander Valley 1990	20	—	—	7/15/92
93	PAUL JABOULET AINE	Hermitage La Chapelle 1989	45	—	—	8/31/91
93	PAUL JABOULET AINE	Hermitage La Chapelle 1982	$ 17	$ 55	224%	11/01/84
93	CHATEAU MARGAUX	Margaux 1984	35	60	71	2/28/87
93	GIUSEPPE MASCARELLO & FIGLIO	Barolo Belvedere 1985	35	42	20	6/15/90
93	MOILLARD	Chambertin Clos de Bèze 1983	37	60	62	9/16/85
93	OPUS ONE	Napa Valley 1982	50	84	68	5/01/86
93	ORNELLAIA	1986	$ 25	$ 44	76%	12/15/89
93	PARIGOT PERE & FILS	Pommard Les Charmots 1985	24	34	42	6/15/87
93	PENFOLDS	Shiraz South Australia Grange Hermitage Bin 95 1981	49	70	43	12/31/88
93	ROBERT PEPI	Cabernet Sauvignon Napa Valley Vine Hill Ranch 1981	14	25	79	1/01/86
93	JOSEPH PHELPS	Insignia Napa Valley 1986	40	44	10	8/31/90
93	JOSEPH PHELPS	Insignia Napa Valley 1985	$ 40	$ 58	45%	7/31/89
93	PINE RIDGE	Cabernet Sauvignon Napa Valley Andrus Reserve 1980	30	60	100	12/01/84
93	RENATO RATTI	Barolo 1982	17	27	59	6/30/87
93	CHATEAU RIEUSSEC	Sauternes 1983	52	60	15	3/16/86
93	DOMAINE DANIEL RION	Vosne-Romanée Les Chaumes 1986	47	54	15	4/30/89
93	CHATEAU ST.-PIERRE	St.-Julien 1982	$ 15	$ 22	47%	12/16/85
93	STRUZZIERO	Taurasi Riserva 1977	22	26	18	8/31/86
92	CASTELLO BANFI	Brunello di Montalcino 1981	23	32	39	3/31/87
92	CASTELLO BANFI	Brunello di Montalcino Poggio all'Oro 1985	30	—	—	12/15/91
92	BERINGER	Cabernet Sauvignon Napa Valley Private Reserve 1981	18	31	72	6/01/86
92	CHATEAU MONTELENA	Cabernet Sauvignon Napa Valley 1985	$ 25	$ 57	128%	11/15/89
92	F. CHAUVENET	Meursault Hospices de Beaune Cuvée Loppin 1982	33	65	97	1/01/85
92	DOMAINE DE CHEVALIER	Graves 1985	43	62	44	9/30/88
92	CLERICO	Barolo Ciabot Mentin Ginestra 1985	27	40	48	4/15/90
92	COCKBURN	Vintage Port 1983	22	45	105	8/31/87
92	DIAMOND CREEK	Cabernet Sauvignon Napa Valley Volcanic Hill 1982	$ 20	$ 69	245%	12/16/84
92	JOSEPH DROUHIN	Beaune Blanc Clos des Mouches 1990	64	—	—	5/15/92
92	GAJA	Barbaresco 1986	47	54	15	1/31/90
92	E. GUIGAL	Côte-Rôtie Côtes Brune et Blonde 1983	21	34	62	4/30/87
92	E. GUIGAL	Hermitage 1986	32	41	28	2/28/90
92	E. GUIGAL	Hermitage 1985	$ 33	$ 39	18%	4/15/89
92	HEITZ	Cabernet Sauvignon Napa Valley Bella Oaks Vineyard 1985	25	55	120	5/15/90
92	KENWOOD	Cabernet Sauvignon Sonoma Valley Artist Series 1983	30	38	27	11/15/86
92	MASTROBERARDINO	Taurasi Riserva 1977	28	54	93	10/16/84
92	MOILLARD	Pommard Clos des Epeneaux 1985	40	45	13	6/30/88
92	ST. CLEMENT	Cabernet Sauvignon Napa Valley 1982	$ 14	$ 25	85%	3/16/85
92	SAN FELICE	Brunello di Montalcino Campogiovanni 1982	22	27	23	7/31/88
92	SASSICAIA	1985	48	120	150	5/15/89
92	STERLING	Cabernet Sauvignon Napa Valley Reserve 1984	25	40	60	3/31/89
92	CHATEAU SUDUIRAUT	Sauternes 1979	19	40	111	2/16/84
92	TAITTINGER	Brut Champagne Collection Arman 1981	$ 80	$ 85	6%	5/31/87
92	BODEGAS VEGA SICILIA	Ribera del Duero Valbuena 3 Años 1985	40	55	38	3/31/90
92	J. VIDAL-FLEURY	Crozes-Hermitage 1985	11	15	36	10/31/87
92	WARRE	Vintage Port 1980	16	40	150	10/01/84
92	WHITEHALL LANE	Merlot Knights Valley 1982	10	19	90	6/01/85
91	ACACIA	Pinot Noir Carneros Napa Valley Iund Vineyard 1982	$ 15	$ 31	107%	7/16/84
91	ANTINORI	Tignanello 1982	37	43	16	7/15/87
91	ADRIEN BELLAND	Santenay Comme 1982	12	25	108	8/01/85
91	BOUCHAINE	Pinot Noir Napa Valley Los Carneros Winery Lake Vineyard 1982	15	18	20	3/01/86
91	F. CHAUVENET	Pommard Hospices de Beaune Cuvée Dames-de-la-Charite 1982	36	55	53	2/01/85
91	PAOLO CORDERO DI MONTEZEMOLO	Barolo 1980	$ 16	$ 20	25%	12/15/87
91	CHATEAU LA CROIX DE GAY	Pomerol 1985	33	—	—	3/15/88
91	JOSEPH DROUHIN	Charmes-Chambertin 1986	56	60	7	2/28/89
91	DUCKHORN	Cabernet Sauvignon Napa Valley 1985	18	39	123	6/15/88
91	GRAHAM	Vintage Port 1985	31	48	55	9/30/87
91	GRAHAM	Vintage Port 1977	$ 15	$ 66	340%	3/16/84
91	E. GUIGAL	Hermitage 1980	13	42	223	9/01/84
91	HEITZ	Cabernet Sauvignon Napa Valley Martha's Vineyard 1981	30	62	107	4/16/86
91	HENSCHKE	Shiraz Barossa Ranges Keyneton Hill of Grace 1987	27	—	—	5/31/92
91	WILLIAM HILL	Cabernet Sauvignon Napa Valley Reserve 1984	18	28	53	4/15/88
91	JAFFELIN	Corton 1983	$ 33	$ 45	36%	4/01/86
91	DOMAINE LONG DEPAQUIT	Chablis Les Vaudésirs 1984	20	30	50	10/15/86
91	ROBERT MONDAVI	Cabernet Sauvignon Napa Valley Reserve 1988	45	—	—	5/31/91
91	OPUS ONE	Napa Valley 1980	50	135	170	4/01/84
91	PESQUERA	Ribera del Duero 1989	20	—	—	4/15/92
91	PINE RIDGE	Cabernet Sauvignon Stags Leap District Pine Ridge Stags Leap Vineyard 1982	$ 20	$ 34	70%	10/31/86
91	RAYMOND	Cabernet Sauvignon Napa Valley Private Reserve 1985	24	28	17	7/15/90
91	SALON	Brut Blanc de Blancs Champagne Le Mesnil 1982	119	—	—	12/31/91
91	SHAFER	Cabernet Sauvignon Stags Leap District Hillside Select 1985	25	30	22	5/31/90
91	STELTZNER	Cabernet Sauvignon Stags Leap District 1982	14	27	93	9/01/85
91	CHATEAU LA TOUR-HAUT-BRION	Pessac-Léognan 1988	$ 37	$ —	—%	6/15/91
91	DOMAINE DU VIEUX TELEGRAPHE	Châteauneuf-du-Pape 1986	17	—	—	11/30/88
90	CLOS DU VAL	Zinfandel Napa Valley 1981	9	18	100	5/16/84
90	DOMINUS	Napa Valley 1984	40	55	38	5/15/88
90	DOW	Vintage Port Quinta do Bomfim 1989	24	29	21	11/30/91
90	FAR NIENTE	Chardonnay Napa Valley 1990	$ 30	$ —	—%	6/15/92
90	FONTANAFREDDA	Barolo Vigna la Rosa 1982	40	45	13	2/15/88
90	THE HESS COLLECTION	Cabernet Sauvignon Napa Valley 1988	18	20	14	1/31/92
90	INGLENOOK	Cabernet Sauvignon Napa Valley Reserve Cask 1985	16	22	38	2/15/91
90	JORDAN	Cabernet Sauvignon Alexander Valley 1981	17	46	171	5/01/85
90	LAUREL GLEN	Cabernet Sauvignon Sonoma Mountain 1988	$ 30	$ —	—%	5/15/91
90	LONG	Chardonnay Napa Valley 1990	29	—	—	6/30/92
90	CHATEAU MARGAUX	Margaux 1980	30	66	120	5/01/84
90	CHATEAU PALMER	Margaux 1983	45	81	80	7/16/86
90	JOSEPH PHELPS	Insignia Napa Valley 1980	25	52	108	7/01/84
90	JOSEPH PHELPS	Scheurebe Late Harvest Napa Valley 1982	$ 15	$ 21	40%	4/16/84
90	CHATEAU PICHON-LALANDE	Pauillac 1980	14	33	136	3/01/84
90	ST. CLEMENT	Cabernet Sauvignon Napa Valley 1987	20	23	15	9/30/91
90	STAG'S LEAP WINE CELLARS	Cabernet Sauvignon Stags Leap District Stag's Leap Vineyards 1981	15	35	133	9/16/84
90	STERLING	Cabernet Sauvignon Napa Valley Reserve 1980	28	44	60	11/01/84
88	CHATEAU DUCRU-BEAUCAILLOU	St.-Julien 1980	$ 13	$ 25	92%	5/01/84
88	GRAHAM	Vintage Port 1980	18	42	133	4/16/85

Best Buys 1990-1992

UNDER $6

88 CANEPA Sauvignon Blanc Maipo Valley 1991 $5 (5/15/92)
87 MIGUEL TORRES Cabernet Sauvignon Curicó District 1988 $4.50 (9/15/90)
87 UNDURRAGA Cabernet Sauvignon Maipo Valley 1987 $5.25 (2/15/90)
86 R.H. PHILLIPS Sauvignon Blanc California Night Harvest 1991 $3.50/500ml (6/15/92)
86 MARK SWANN Cabernet Sauvignon South Australia Proprietor's Reserve 1988 $5.50 (2/28/91)
86 DOMAINE DU TARIQUET Vin de Pays des Côtes de Gascogne 1989 $5.75 (11/15/90)
86 TYRRELL'S Long Flat White Hunter Valley 1989 $5 (10/31/90)
86 LOS VASCOS Cabernet Sauvignon Colchagua 1987 $5 (9/15/90)
85 CLOS DU VAL Le Clos Napa Valley NV $5.50 (8/31/90)
85 J. DIAZ Madrid 1985 $5.75 (3/31/90)
85 SAN JOSE DE SANTIAGO Cabernet Sauvignon Colchagua Valley 1990 $5 (5/15/92)
85 SAN PEDRO Cabernet Sauvignon Lontue Gato de Oro 1986 $4.50 (2/15/90)
85 SANTA MONICA Cabernet Sauvignon Rancagua 1989 $5 (10/15/91)
85 SUTTER HOME Zinfandel California 1989 $5 (5/15/91)
85 WALNUT CREST Merlot Rapel 1987 $4 (6/30/90)
84 ALAMEDA Cabernet Sauvignon Maipo Valley 1988 $5.50 (6/15/92)
84 LOS CATADORES Cabernet Sauvignon Lontue Selección Especial 1986 $5 (6/15/92)
84 FINCA FLICHMAN Argenta Mendoza 1988 $4 (3/15/91)
84 JOSE MARIA DA FONSECA Periquita 1987 $5.75 (12/31/90)
84 LINDEMANS Shiraz South Eastern Australia Bin 50 1987 $5.50 (7/15/90)
84 VALLE DE SAN FERNANDO Cabernet Sauvignon San Fernando Gran Reserva 1986 $5 (6/15/92)
84 SAN PEDRO Merlot Lontue 1988 $5 (12/31/90)
84 SANTA MONICA Sémillon Rancagua Seaborne 1989 $4 (10/15/91)
84 STEVENOT White Zinfandel Amador County 1989 $5 (12/31/90)
83 BEAUCLAIRE Vin de Pays des Côtes de Gascogne 1990 $5 (6/30/92)
83 LIBERTY SCHOOL Three Valley Select Series One California 1989 $4.50 (6/15/91)
83 ROBERT MONDAVI Sauvignon Blanc California Woodbridge 1990 $5.50 (6/15/92)
83 LA PLAYA Cabernet Sauvignon Maipo Valley 1988 $5 (6/15/92)
83 PORTAL DEL ALTO Cabernet Sauvignon Maipo Valley 1987 $3.50 (6/15/92)
83 ROUND HILL Fumé Blanc Napa Valley House 1989 $5.75 (11/30/90)
83 ROUND HILL Chardonnay California House 1988 $5.50 (4/15/90)
83 ST.-MORILLON Cabernet Sauvignon Lontue 1986 $5.50 (10/15/91)
83 DOMAINE ST.-SAUVEUR Côtes du Ventoux 1988 $4.50 (10/15/91)
83 VALLE DE SAN FERNANDO Cabernet Sauvignon San Fernando 1988 $5 (6/15/92)
83 SENORIO DE SARRIA Navarra 1984 $5 (2/28/90)
83 SUTTER HOME Cabernet Sauvignon California 1989 $5.50 (10/15/91)
83 TRAPICHE Malbec Mendoza Reserve 1987 $5 (9/15/90)
83 UNDURRAGA Cabernet Sauvignon Maipo Valley 1988 $5.25 (9/15/90)
83 LOS VASCOS Sauvignon Blanc Colchagua 1988 $4.75 (3/31/90)
83 WALNUT CREST Merlot Rapel 1989 $4.50 (5/15/92)
82 ALAMEDA Merlot Maipo Valley Santa Maria Vineyard 1987 $5.50 (6/15/92)
82 BOEGER Hangtown Red California 1987 $5.25 (2/28/90)
82 CHATEAU DE BAUN Château Blanc Reserve Sonoma County 1989 $5 (6/15/91)
82 CHATEAU DIANA Cabernet Sauvignon California Limited Edition 1986 $5 (10/15/91)
82 FREMONT CREEK Sauvignon Blanc Mendocino-Napa Counties 1989 $5.50 (10/15/91)
82 E. & J. GALLO Sauvignon Blanc California Reserve 1989 $4 (7/31/91)
82 CHATEAU GUIBON Entre-Deux-Mers 1990 $5.50 (3/31/92)
82 BODEGAS MUGA-VILLFRANCA Navarra Mendiani 1989 $4 (6/15/91)
82 ALEJANDRO HERNANDEZ MUNOZ Cabernet Sauvignon Maipo Viña Portal del Alto Gran Reserva Tinto 1983 $4 (9/15/90)
82 LA PLAYA Merlot Maipo Valley 1988 $5 (6/16/92)
82 SAN MARTIN Petite Sirah Baja California International Series 1987 $4 (8/31/90)
82 M.G. VALLEJO Cabernet Sauvignon California 1986 $5 (6/15/90)
82 VINOS EXPOSICION Cabernet Sauvignon Talca Escudo de Talca 1990 $5 (6/15/92)
82 VINOS EXPOSICION Cabernet Sauvignon Talca Molino Viejo 1990 $5 (6/15/92)
82 STEPHEN ZELLERBACH Sauvignon Blanc Sonoma County 1989 $5.50 (12/31/90)
81 CHATEAU DE BEAUREGARD Côteaux du Languedoc 1989 $5 (12/15/91)
81 BODEGAS EL COTO Rioja Crianza 1985 $5 (3/31/90)
81 LEONARDINI Valpolicella 1990 $5 (4/30/92)
81 MARIETTA Old Vine Red Lot No. 8 Sonoma County NV $5.50 (5/31/90)
81 MIRASSOU Zinfandel California Lot No. 4 NV $5.50 (7/31/91)
81 J. PEDRONCELLI White Riesling Dry Creek Valley 1989 $5.50 (9/30/90)
81 LA PLAYA Merlot Maipo Valley 1988 $5 (10/15/91)
81 RIUNITE Lambrusco Reggiano NV $4.50 (9/30/91)
81 SAN MARTIN Chardonnay Maipo Valley International Series 1988 $4.50 (4/30/90)
81 SANTA MONICA Sémillon Rancagua Seaborne 1988 $5 (3/31/90)
81 SENORIO DEL MAR Vino Tinto Seco 1987 $4 (10/31/91)
81 SUTTER HOME Cabernet Sauvignon California 1988 $5 (11/15/90)
81 M.G. VALLEJO Fumé Blanc California 1988 $4 (5/15/90)
81 VEGA DE MORIZ Valdepeñas Cencibel 1989 $5.50 (6/15/91)
80 RENE BARBIER Red Table Wine 1983 $3 (3/31/90)
80 BEAULIEU Burgundy Napa Valley 1987 $5 (1/31/91)
80 BOEGER Hangtown Red Lot No. 16 California NV $5.75 (10/31/91)
80 LE CARDINALE Brut NV $5.25 (6/15/90)
80 BODEGAS JAIME CARRERAS Valencia 1985 $4 (3/31/90)
80 CASAL THAULERO Montepulciano d'Abruzzo 1988 $5 (5/31/90)
80 CHATEAU ST. JEAN Vin Blanc Sonoma County 1989 $5 (2/15/91)
80 CONCHA Y TORO Cabernet Sauvignon Merlot Rapel 1986 $4.25 (9/15/90)
80 PAUL MASSON Merlot California Vintners Selection 1989 $4.50/1.5L (4/15/92)
80 ROBERT MONDAVI Sauvignon Blanc California Woodbridge 1989 $5 (4/30/91)
80 CHATEAU LES OLLIEUX Corbières 1988 $5.25 (11/30/90)
80 FREDERICO PATERNINA Rioja Banda Azul 1985 $5 (3/15/90)
80 DOMAINE DE POUY Vin de Pays des Côtes de Gascogne Cépage Ugni Blanc 1989 $5 (11/30/90)
80 ST.-JOVIAN Bordeaux Supérieur Premium 1988 $5.50 (7/31/91)
80 SANTA MONICA Sauvignon Blanc Rancagua 1989 $5 (10/15/91)
80 SUTTER HOME Chardonnay California 1989 $5 (11/15/90)
80 VIGNE TOSCANE Chianti Terre Toscane 1989 $5 (11/30/90)
80 WALNUT CREST Cabernet Sauvignon Maipo 1985 $4 (6/30/90)
79 VIGNERONS ARDECHOIS Vin de Pays des Côteaux de l'Ardeche 1988 $4.50 (4/30/90)
79 FINCA FLICHMAN Selection Mendoza 1988 $4.50 (3/15/91)
79 HARDY'S Premium Classic Dry White South Australia 1988 $5.25 (6/15/90)
79 PORTAL DEL ALTO Cabernet Sauvignon Maipo Valley Gran Reserva 1986 $3.75 (6/15/92)
78 HARDY'S Premium Classic Dry Red South Australia 1988 $5.25 (7/31/90)
78 MOCERI Merlot Vin de Pays de l'Aude 1987 $4 (6/30/90)
78 SAN MARTIN Cabernet Sauvignon Maipo Valley International Series 1987 $4.50 (6/15/90)
78 L. DE VALLOUIT Vin de Pays des Collines Rhodaniенn Les Sables 1988 $4.75 (6/30/90)
77 MOCERI Cabernet Sauvignon Vin de Pays de l'Aude 1987 $4 (6/30/90)

$6-$6.99

89 ROUND HILL Zinfandel Napa Valley 1988 $6.50 (2/15/91)
88 TENUTA FARNETA Chianti di Collalto 1988 $6 (12/15/90)
87 CALITERRA Cabernet Sauvignon Maipo 1989 $6 (6/15/92)
87 SILVER LAKE Riesling Columbia Valley Dry 1989 $6 (6/15/91)
86 CALITERRA Cabernet Sauvignon Maipo 1987 $6 (9/15/90)
86 CALITERRA Chardonnay Curicó 1991 $6 (6/15/92)
86 LAS CAMPANAS Navarra 1984 $6 (3/31/90)
86 CHESTNUT HILL Zinfandel San Luis Obispo 1988 $6 (8/31/91)
86 COLUMBIA CREST Sémillon Columbia Valley 1990 $6 (7/15/91)
86 PENFOLDS Sémillon Chardonnay Koonunga Hill South Australia 1989 $6 (9/15/90)
86 SANTA MONICA Cabernet Sauvignon Rancagua 1988 $6 (3/15/90)
86 SANTA RITA Cabernet Sauvignon Maipo Valley 120 1988 $6 (5/31/92)
86 SEGHESIO Zinfandel Sonoma County 1988 $6.50 (9/30/91)
86 STATON HILLS Johannisberg Riesling Washington 1990 $6 (11/15/91)
86 WYNDHAM Chardonnay South Eastern Australia Bin 222 1989 $6.50 (9/15/91)
85 ANTINORI Santa Cristina 1988 $6.50 (1/31/91)
85 BODEGAS BRANAVIEJA Navarra Pleno 1988 $6 (12/15/90)
85 CEDAR CREEK Chardonnay South Eastern Australia Bin 33 1990 $6 (5/31/92)
85 COUSINO-MACUL Chardonnay Maipo 1987 $6 (3/31/90)
85 FETZER Johannisberg Riesling California 1990 $6.75 (5/15/91)
85 GEYSER PEAK Sauvignon Blanc Sonoma County 1990 $6.50 (4/15/92)
85 GRAND CRU Chenin Blanc Clarksburg Dry Premium Selection 1990 $6.50 (11/15/91)
85 LINDEMANS Chardonnay South Eastern Australia Bin 65 1989 $6 (4/30/90)
85 BODEGAS MONTECILLO Rioja Viña Cumbrero 1987 $6 (8/31/91)
85 OAK BLUFFS Cabernet Sauvignon Colchagua 1990 $6 (6/15/92)
85 SANTA MONICA Sauvignon Blanc Rancagua 1991 $6 (5/15/92)
85 SANTA MONICA Sauvignon Blanc Rancagua 1988 $6 (3/31/90)
85 SANTA RITA Merlot Maipo Valley 120 1989 $6 (6/15/92)
85 SEGHESIO Zinfandel Northern Sonoma 1987 $6.50 (7/31/90)
85 VINA DEL MAR Fumé Blanc Lontue 1991 $6 (6/15/92)
84 BARTON & GUESTIER Bordeaux Merlot 1988 $6 (2/15/90)
84 BUENA VISTA Sauvignon Blanc Lake County 1990 $6.50 (10/31/91)
84 CANEPA Cabernet Sauvignon Maipo Valley Reserva 1988 $6.50 (6/15/90)
84 CANEPA Merlot Maipo Valley 1990 $6 (6/15/92)
84 CHATEAU STE. MICHELLE Gewürztraminer Columbia Valley 1990 $6.50 (8/31/91)
84 CHATEAU STE. MICHELLE Sémillon Columbia Valley 1990 $6 (7/15/91)
84 CLOS DE BEAUREGARD Muscadet de Sèvre et Maine Sur Lie 1988 $6.75 (4/15/90)
84 DELAS Côtes du Rhône St.-Esprit 1988 $6.75 (12/15/90)
84 GEORGES DUBOEUF Beaujolais 1990 $6.50 (9/30/91)
84 GEORGES DUBOEUF Beaujolais Château de la Plume 1990 $6.50 (10/31/91)
84 HOGUE Sémillon Washington 1989 $6.50 (11/30/91)
84 MONTEREY VINEYARD Merlot Monterey Classic 1989 $6 (2/29/92)
84 MONTES Cabernet Sauvignon Curicó Villa Montes 1989 $6 (6/15/92)
84 MOUNTAIN VIEW Chardonnay Monterey County 1989 $6 (4/15/91)
84 NICCOLINI Chianti 1990 $6 (4/30/92)
84 R.H. PHILLIPS Cuvée Rouge Night Harvest California NV $6 (5/31/91)
84 ROUND HILL Gewürztraminer Napa Valley 1988 $6.25 (1/31/90)
84 ROUND HILL Zinfandel Napa Valley Select 1987 $6 (3/31/90)
84 STE. CHAPELLE Johannisberg Riesling Idaho 1990 $6 (11/15/91)
84 STE. CHAPELLE Johannisberg Riesling Idaho Dry Vineyard Select 1989 $6 (8/31/91)
84 VALLE DE SAN FERNANDO Cabernet Sauvignon San Fernando Valley 1988 $6 (9/15/90)
84 SANTA RITA Sauvignon Blanc Maipo Valley 120 1991 $6 (6/15/92)
84 SEVEN HILLS White Riesling Columbia Valley 1990 $6 (6/15/92)
84 STONY HOLLOW Cabernet Sauvignon San Fernando 1988 $6 (6/15/92)
84 SUTTER HOME Chardonnay California 1990 $6 (9/15/91)
84 JEAN-CLAUDE THEVENET Mâcon-Pierreclos 1988 $6.25 (7/15/90)
83 BRIDGEVIEW Chardonnay Oregon 1990 $6.50 (11/15/91)
83 BRIDGEVIEW Riesling Oregon Dry Vintage Select 1990 $6 (6/15/92)
83 CALLAWAY Fumé Blanc Temecula 1989 $6.50 (2/15/92)
83 BODEGAS CAMPO VIEJO Rioja 1985 $6.50 (3/15/90)
83 CHATEAU STE. MICHELLE Muscat Canelli Columbia Valley 1990 $6.50 (11/30/91)
83 DOMAINE ST. GEORGE Cabernet Sauvignon Sonoma County 1988 $6 (11/15/90)
83 FINCA FLICHMAN Chardonnay Mendoza Proprietors Private Reserve 1990 $6 (4/30/91)
83 HARDY'S Sémillon Chardonnay Captain's Selection South Eastern Australia 1991 $6 (6/30/92)
83 CHARLES KRUG Zinfandel Napa Valley 1989 $6 (12/15/90)
83 PETER LEHMANN Sémillon Late Harvest Barossa Valley Botrytis Sauternes 1988 $6/375ml (4/15/91)
83 LEMBEY Brut Cava 1988 $6 (5/15/92)
83 LOUIS M. MARTINI Barbera California 1987 $6 (12/31/90)
83 MONTEREY VINEYARD Cabernet Sauvignon Monterey Classic 1989 $6 (3/15/92)
83 MONTEREY VINEYARD Cabernet Sauvignon Monterey County Classic 1987 $6 (1/31/91)
83 ANTONIO & ELIO MONTI Montepulciano d'Abruzzo 1988 $6.25 (2/15/91)
83 BODEGAS OLARRA Rioja Añares 1987 $6.50 (3/31/90)
83 ROSEMOUNT Dry Red Diamond Reserve Hunter Valley 1988 $6.50 (2/28/90)
83 ROUND HILL Chardonnay California House 1989 $6.50 (7/15/91)
83 SANTINO Alfresco Amador County NV $6 (8/31/91)
83 TAFT STREET Sauvignon Blanc Sonoma County 1990 $6.50 (6/15/92)
83 VESCOVADO DI MURLO Chianti 1990 $6 (10/31/91)
83 VINA DEL MAR Cabernet Sauvignon Curicó Selección Especial 35 1987 $6 (9/15/90)
83 VINA DEL MAR Merlot Lontue 1990 $6 (6/15/92)
83 WORDEN Gewürztraminer Washington 1990 $6.50 (10/15/91)

82 CHATEAU BERGEY Entre-Deux-Mers 1990 $6 (11/15/91)
82 CHATEAU DE BLOMAC Minervois Cuvée Tradition 1988 $6 (12/31/91)
82 CASTELLBLANCH Brut Cava Extra NV $6 (2/29/92)
82 CLOS DU VAL Le Clos Napa Valley 1989 $6 (3/15/92)
82 COLDRIDGE Sémillon Chardonnay Victoria 1990 $6 (4/15/91)
82 ESTANCIA Sauvignon Blanc Alexander Valley 1988 $6 (5/15/90)
82 E. & J. GALLO Cabernet Sauvignon Northern Sonoma Reserve 1982 $6 (5/31/91)
82 HARDY'S Shiraz Cabernet South Eastern Australia Captain's Selection 1990 $6 (6/30/92)
82 ISOLE E OLENA Antiche Tenute 1989 $6 (10/31/90)
82 CHATEAU LAGRAVE PARAN Bordeaux 1988 $6 (7/15/90)
82 MCDOWELL VALLEY Grenache Rosé McDowell Valley Les Vieux Cépages 1989 $6.50 (10/31/90)
82 MONTEREY PENINSULA California NV $6.50 (7/15/91)
82 MOUNTAIN VIEW Pinot Noir Monterey-Napa Counties 1990 $6 (4/30/92)
82 MOUNTAIN VIEW Pinot Noir Monterey-Napa Counties 1989 $6 (2/28/91)
82 CHATEAU ROC MIGNON D'ADRIEN Bordeaux Supérieur 1989 $6 (2/28/91)
82 ROUND HILL Chardonnay California 1990 $6 (2/29/92)
82 SHENANDOAH Zinfandel Amador County Classico Varietal Adventure Series 1989 $6 (4/30/91)
82 TORRES Penedès Sangre de Toro 1988 $6.50 (3/31/91)
82 VINA DEL MAR Merlot Curicó Selección Especial 12 1988 $6 (9/15/90)
81 BEL ARBORS Merlot American Cask 89 NV $6 (11/15/91)
81 BICHOT Côtes de Duras 1989 $6 (3/31/92)
81 CAVE DES COTEAUX CAIRANNE Côtes du Rhône-Villages 1988 $6.50 (2/28/90)
81 BODEGAS CAMPO VIEJO Rioja 1987 $6.50 (9/30/90)
81 CANEPA Cabernet Sauvignon Maipo Valley 1990 $6 (6/15/92)
81 CASAL THAULERO Montepulciano d'Abruzzo 1989 $6 (6/30/91)
81 CHANTOVENT Cabernet Sauvignon Vin de Pays d'Oc Prestige 1988 $6 (3/15/90)
81 COLUMBIA CREST Johannisberg Riesling Columbia Valley 1990 $6 (8/31/91)
81 FINCA FLICHMAN Cabernet Sauvignon Mendoza Proprietor's Private Reserve 1987 $6 (3/15/91)
81 E. & J. GALLO Chardonnay North Coast Reserve 1989 $6.50 (7/15/91)
81 CHATEAU GOFFRETEAU Bordeaux Supérieur 1988 $6 (2/28/91)
81 LABOURE-ROI Chardonnay Vin de Pays d'Oc 1989 $6 (6/30/92)
81 LINDEMANS Sémillon Chardonnay Bin 77 South Eastern Australia 1990 $6 (6/30/92)
81 LINDEMANS Sémillon Chardonnay Bin 77 South Eastern Australia 1988 $6 (4/15/91)
81 ROBERT MONDAVI Cabernet Sauvignon California Woodbridge 1988 $6 (2/28/91)
81 MAISON MOUEIX Bordeaux Rouge 1988 $6 (1/31/92)
81 MOUNTAIN VIEW Chardonnay Monterey County 1988 $6.50 (4/30/90)
81 BARONE RICASOLI Chianti Ricasoli 1990 $6 (11/30/91)
81 ROSEMOUNT Cabernet Shiraz South Eastern Australia 1989 $6 (7/31/90)
81 ROUND HILL Zinfandel Napa Valley 1989 $6 (3/31/92)
81 STE. CHAPELLE Johannisberg Riesling Idaho 1989 $6 (12/15/90)
81 VALLE DE SAN FERNANDO Cabernet Sauvignon San Fernando Gran Reserva 1984 $6 (9/15/90)
81 STONY HOLLOW Chardonnay San Fernando 1990 $6 (6/15/92)
81 TREFETHEN Eschol White Napa Valley NV $6.50 (1/31/91)
81 L. DE VALLOUIT Vin de Pays des Collines Rhodanienn Les Sables 1989 $6.25 (12/31/91)
81 VINA DEL MAR Cabernet Sauvignon Curicó Selección Especial 35 1988 $6 (6/15/91)
80 BANDIERA Chardonnay Napa County 1990 $6.50 (3/15/92)
80 BANDIERA Cabernet Sauvignon Napa Valley 1988 $6.50 (4/15/92)
80 BELVEDERE Chardonnay Sonoma County Discovery Series 1989 $6 (12/31/90)
80 CANTERBURY Cabernet Sauvignon California 1989 $6 (11/15/91)
80 CHANTEFLEUR Cabernet Sauvignon Vin de Pays de l'Ardèche 1988 $6 (5/31/90)
80 ABEL CLEMENT Côtes du Rhône 1988 $6 (2/28/90)
80 LUCIEN DESCHAUX Côtes du Ventoux Le Vieux Presbytere 1989 $6 (12/31/91)
80 GEORGES DUBOEUF Côtes du Rhône 1989 $6 (10/15/90)
80 GEORGES DUBOEUF Chardonnay Vin de Pays d'Oc 1989 $6.50 (11/15/90)
80 GLEN ELLEN Sauvignon Blanc California Proprietor's Reserve 1990 $6 (7/31/91)
80 HAWK CREST Sauvignon Blanc California 1989 $6 (8/31/90)
80 BODEGAS MONTECILLO Rioja White Viña Cumbrero 1989 $6 (7/15/91)
80 MONTES Sauvignon Blanc Curicó Villa Montes 1991 $6 (6/15/92)
80 MOUNTAIN VIEW Cabernet Sauvignon North Coast 1988 $6 (4/30/91)
80 MOUNTAIN VIEW Chardonnay Monterey County 1990 $6 (3/15/92)
80 SANTA MONICA Chardonnay Rancagua 1989 $6 (6/15/92)
80 SEGHESIO Zinfandel Northern Sonoma 1986 $6.50 (5/15/90)
80 BODEGAS JAUME SERRA Penedès Tempranillo 1988 $6 (4/15/92)
80 TAJA Jumilla 1987 $6 (3/31/90)
80 TORRES Penedès Coronas 1987 $6.50 (10/15/90)
80 TORRES Penedès Viña Sol 1990 $6 (11/15/91)
80 M.G. VALLEJO Merlot California 1990 $6 (5/31/92)
80 VENDANGE Merlot California 1990 $6 (5/31/92)
80 VINA DEL MAR Cabernet Sauvignon Lontue Selección Especial 17 1986 $6 (2/15/90)
80 VINA DEL MAR Merlot Curicó Selección Especial 12 1989 $6 (6/15/91)
80 ZONIN Montepulciano d'Abruzzo 1988 $6 (6/30/91)
79 CANEPA Merlot Maipo Valley 1988 $6 (6/30/90)
79 GLEN ELLEN Cabernet Sauvignon California Proprietor's Reserve 1988 $6 (11/15/91)
79 ARMAND ROUX Bordeaux Verdillac 1988 $6.25 (7/15/90)
78 ROSEMOUNT Sémillon Chardonnay South Eastern Australia 1988 $6 (6/15/90)

$7-$7.99

91 WYNDHAM Cabernet Shiraz Hunter Valley 1987 $7 (1/31/90)
89 BANDIERA Cabernet Sauvignon Napa Valley 1987 $7 (11/15/91)
89 PIERRE COMBE Côtes du Rhône-Villages Domaine des Richards 1990 $7.50 (10/15/91)
89 HANDLEY Gewürztraminer Anderson Valley 1988 $7 (1/31/90)
89 HEDGES Cabernet Merlot Columbia Valley 1989 $7 (9/30/91)
89 SAN PEDRO Merlot Lontue 1989 $7 (5/31/92)
89 SANTA RITA Chardonnay Maipo Valley 120 1991 $7 (5/15/92)
88 BONNY DOON Grenache California Clos de Gilroy Cuvée Tremblement de Terre 1989 $7.50 (2/15/90)
88 COVEY RUN Johannisberg Riesling Yakima Valley 1989 $7 (8/31/90)
88 GUNDLACH BUNDSCHU Zinfandel Sonoma Valley 1988 $7 (5/31/90)
88 HERZOG Cabernet Sauvignon Vin de Pays d'Oc NV $7 (3/31/91)
88 NAPA RIDGE Chardonnay North Coast Coastal 1989 $7 (6/30/91)
88 DOMAINE DE LA QUILLA Muscadet de Sèvre et Maine Sur Lie 1989 $7 (11/30/90)
88 SANTA RITA Sauvignon Blanc Maipo Valley Reserva 1991 $7.50 (6/15/92)
88 TYRRELL'S Cabernet Sauvignon Hunter Valley Classic 1984 $7 (9/15/90)
88 LOS VASCOS Cabernet Sauvignon Colchagua 1990 $7 (5/31/92)
87 VINA BERCEO Rioja Crianza 1986 $7 (9/30/90)
87 DESSILANI Barbera del Piemonte 1986 $7 (3/15/91)
87 GEORGES DUBOEUF Beaujolais-Villages 1990 $7 (9/15/91)
87 ERRAZURIZ Sauvignon Blanc Maule Valley Reserva 1991 $7 (6/15/92)
87 HARDY'S Shiraz McLaren Vale 1987 $7.50 (7/15/90)
87 HOP KILN Johannisberg Riesling Russian River Valley Marty Griffin Vineyards 1990 $7.50 (12/31/91)
87 INGLENOOK Chardonnay Napa Valley 1989 $7.50 (2/28/91)
87 KONOCTI Fumé Blanc Lake County 1990 $7.50 (2/15/92)
87 LINDEMANS Chardonnay South Eastern Australia Bin 65 1991 $7 (5/31/92)
87 MARKHAM Sauvignon Blanc Napa Valley 1989 $7 (10/31/90)
87 WHITE OAK Chenin Blanc Alexander Valley 1990 $7 (11/15/91)
86 DOMAINE BRUSSET Côtes du Rhône-Villages Côteaux des Trabers 1988 $7.75 (12/15/90)
86 COLUMBIA CREST Chardonnay Columbia Valley 1989 $7 (9/30/90)
86 GEORGES DUBOEUF Beaujolais 1989 $7 (11/15/90)
86 NORMANS Chardonnay South Australia Chandlers Hill 1991 $7 (2/29/92)
86 ORLANDO Chardonnay South Eastern Australia Jacob's Creek 1991 $7 (5/31/92)
86 PENFOLDS Cabernet Sauvignon Shiraz South Australia Koonunga Hill 1987 $7.50 (2/28/91)
86 SANTA RITA Sauvignon Blanc Maipo Valley 120 1990 $7 (10/15/91)
86 STONE CREEK Merlot Columbia Valley 1989 $7 (5/31/91)
86 LOS VASCOS Sauvignon Blanc Colchagua 1990 $7 (10/15/91)
86 VINTERRA Cabernet Sauvignon Maipo-Napa Valleys NV $7 (2/15/90)
85 BONNY DOON Ca' del Solo Big House Red California 1990 $7.50 (6/30/92)
85 CHATEAU STE. MICHELLE Riesling Columbia Valley Dry River Ridge Vineyard 1990 $7 (6/15/91)
85 HARDY'S Chardonnay South Eastern Australia Bird Series 1991 $7.50 (6/30/92)
85 HARDY'S Shiraz McLaren Vale 1989 $7.50 (5/31/92)
85 HIDDEN CELLARS Johannisberg Riesling Potter Valley 1990 $7.50 (6/30/91)
85 HOP KILN Marty Griffin's Big Red Russian River Valley 1988 $7.50 (11/30/90)
85 INGLENOOK Cabernet Sauvignon Napa Valley 1986 Rel: $7.50 Cur: $10 (2/28/91)
85 LINDEMANS Chardonnay South Eastern Australia Bin 65 1990 $7 (2/28/91)
85 FATTORIA DI LUCIGNANO Chianti Colli Fiorentini 1990 $7.50 (4/30/92)
85 VINA MAYOR Ribera del Duero Crianza 1989 $7 (3/31/91)
85 MOILLARD Côtes du Rhône Les Violettes 1989 $7.50 (5/31/91)
85 NAPA CELLARS Chardonnay Napa Valley 1989 $7 (4/15/91)
85 ORLANDO Cabernet Sauvignon South Eastern Australia Jacob's Creek 1987 $7 (7/31/90)
85 OXFORD LANDING Chardonnay South Australia 1990 $7 (2/28/91)
85 PARDUCCI Pinot Noir Mendocino County 1988 $7.50 (4/15/90)
85 MIGUEL TORRES Cabernet Sauvignon Curicó District 1990 $7 (6/15/92)
85 UNDURRAGA Cabernet Sauvignon Maipo Valley Reserve Selection 1985 $7.75 (3/15/90)
85 WYNDHAM Shiraz Hunter Valley Bin 555 1986 $7 (1/31/90)
84 BODEGAS BERBERANA Rioja Carta de Plata 1987 $7.50 (12/15/90)
84 BONNY DOON California Vin Gris de Cigare 1990 $7 (7/15/91)
84 CALERA Pinot Noir Blanc California 1990 $7 (10/31/91)
84 LES CAVES ST.-PIERRE Côtes du Rhône-Villages Les Lissandres 1988 $7.25 (12/15/90)
84 CHATEAU STE. MICHELLE Sémillon Columbia Valley 1990 $7 (4/15/92)
84 CORBETT CANYON Chardonnay Central Coast Coastal Classic 1989 $7/1L (7/15/91)
84 CHATEAU DUCLA Entre-Deux-Mers 1990 $7 (6/15/91)
84 DOMAINE DE LA GUICHARDE Côtes du Rhône 1988 $7 (3/15/91)
84 HARDY'S Chardonnay South Eastern Australia Bird Series 1990 $7.50 (9/15/91)
84 HARDY'S Shiraz McLaren Vale Bird Series 1988 $7.50 (9/30/91)
84 HOUGHTON White Burgundy Swan Valley 1988 $7.50 (9/30/91)
84 JOHNSTONE Chardonnay Hunter River Valley 1989 $7 (5/31/92)
84 J. LOHR Cabernet Sauvignon California 1987 $7 (2/15/90)
84 MONTES Cabernet Sauvignon Curicó Villa Montes 1987 $7 (2/15/90)
84 ORLANDO Chardonnay South Eastern Australia Jacob's Creek 1990 $7 (5/15/91)
84 J. PEDRONCELLI Fumé Blanc Dry Creek Valley 1989 $7 (4/30/91)
84 J. PEDRONCELLI Zinfandel Dry Creek Valley 1988 $7 (11/30/90)
84 QUINTA DO CARDO Douro Castelo Rodrigo 1989 $7 (12/31/90)
84 ROSEMOUNT Shiraz Cabernet Sauvignon South Eastern Australia 1990 $7 (7/15/91)
84 ROSEMOUNT Sémillon Chardonnay South Eastern Australia 1990 $7 (5/31/91)
84 MARK SWANN Cabernet Sauvignon Coonawarra 1987 $7 (2/28/91)
84 DR. COSIMO TAURINO Salice Salentino Rosato 1988 $7.25 (3/15/91)
84 MIGUEL TORRES Sauvignon Blanc Curicó District 1991 $7 (4/15/92)
84 TYRRELL'S Cabernet Merlot Australia Old Winery 1988 $7.50 (3/31/91)
84 TYRRELL'S Chardonnay Hunter Valley 1989 $7 (10/15/90)
84 TYRRELL'S Long Flat Red South Eastern Australia 1988 $7 (2/15/92)
84 VALLFORMOSA Penedès Vall Fort 1984 $7 (3/31/91)
84 LA VIEILLE FERME Côtes du Rhône Réserve 1988 $7.50 (12/15/90)
84 VINTERRA Chardonnay Maipo-Napa Valleys NV $7 (3/31/90)
83 BODEGAS BERBERANA Rioja Carta de Plata 1988 $7.50 (9/30/91)
83 VILLA BIANCHI Verdicchio dei Castelli di Jesi Classico 1989 $7 (6/30/91)
83 BODEGAS MARTINEZ BUJANDA Rioja Valdemar Vino Tinto 1989 $7 (6/30/92)
83 CHRISTOPHE Chardonnay California 1988 $7.50 (4/30/90)
83 CLAIRVAUX Grenache California 1989 $7 (3/31/92)
83 COTES DE SONOMA Cabernet Sauvignon Sonoma County 1989 $7 (11/15/91)
83 ERRAZURIZ Chardonnay Maule Valley Reserva 1989 $7 (9/15/90)
83 JOSE MARIA DA FONSECA Pasmados 1984 $7.25 (4/30/91)
83 VITTORIO INNOCENTI Chianti 1987 $7 (5/15/90)
83 VINA MAYOR Ribera del Duero Crianza 1990 $7 (2/15/92)
83 MIRASSOU Pinot Blanc Monterey County White Burgundy 1989 $7 (12/31/91)
83 MONTPELLIER Cabernet Sauvignon California 1988 $7 (7/31/91)
83 NAPA RIDGE Chardonnay Central Coast 1989 $7 (11/15/90)
83 ORLANDO Cabernet Sauvignon South Eastern Australia Jacob's Creek 1988 $7 (7/15/91)
83 R.H. PHILLIPS Chardonnay California 1989 $7 (4/30/91)
83 CHATEAU PITRAY Côtes de Castillon 1988 $7 (2/28/91)
83 RAVENSWOOD Zinfandel North Coast Vintners Blend 1989 $7.50 (7/31/91)
83 BARONE RICASOLI Chianti 1989 $7 (4/15/91)
83 RICHMOND GROVE Chardonnay Hunter Valley French Cask 1989 $7 (5/15/91)
83 BODEGAS RIOJANAS Rioja Monte Real Reserva 1983 $7.50 (3/31/90)
83 ROSEMOUNT Traminer Riesling South Eastern Australia 1991 $7 (2/29/92)
83 RUFFINO Chianti Classico 1987 $7 (4/30/90)
83 DOMAINE DE ST.-LUC Côteaux du Tricastin 1989 $7 (12/31/91)
83 RODNEY STRONG Gewürztraminer Sonoma County 1990 $7 (9/30/91)
83 LOS VASCOS Cabernet Sauvignon Colchagua 1989 $7 (6/15/92)
83 YALUMBA Chardonnay South Eastern Australia Oxford Landing 1991 $7 (2/29/92)
82 BADIA A COLTIBUONO Chianti Cetamura 1988 $7 (12/15/90)
82 CHATEAU DU BOIS DE LA GARDE Côtes du Rhône 1988 $7 (10/31/90)
82 BONNY DOON Grahm Crew Vin Rouge California 1989 $7.50 (10/31/90)
82 CANTERBURY Chardonnay California 1989 $7.50 (7/15/91)
82 CHATEAU SOUVERAIN Sauvignon Blanc Alexander Valley Barrel Fermented 1990 $7.50 (6/15/92)
82 CHATEAU SOUVERAIN Zinfandel Dry Creek Valley 1989 $7.50 (5/15/92)
82 COCKATOO RIDGE Cabernet Merlot South Eastern Australia 1990 $7 (6/30/92)
82 COUSINO-MACUL Chardonnay Maipo Reserva 1988 $7.75 (4/30/90)
82 CUNE Rioja Clarete 1986 $7 (2/28/90)

82 CHATEAU LA DECELLE Côteaux du Tricastin 1989 $7.50 (7/15/91)
82 GEORGES DUBOEUF Beaujolais-Villages Château de la Grande Grange 1990 $7 (9/15/91)
82 HARDY'S Chardonnay Sunraysia 1988 $7 (7/31/90)
82 LIBERTY SCHOOL Cabernet Sauvignon California Vintner Select Series Two NV $7.50 (11/15/91)
82 LOUIS M. MARTINI Pinot Noir Carneros 1987 $7 (2/28/91)
82 MCDOWELL VALLEY Grenache Rosé McDowell Valley Les Vieux Cépages 1990 $7.50 (6/15/91)
82 MOILLARD Côtes du Rhône Les Violettes 1990 $7 (10/15/91)
82 NAPA RIDGE Pinot Noir North Coast Coastal 1989 $7.50 (7/31/91)
82 BODEGAS OLARRA Rioja White Añares Blanco Seco 1988 $7 (3/31/90)
82 OXFORD LANDING Chardonnay South Australia 1989 $7 (10/15/90)
82 RABBIT RIDGE Mystique Sonoma County 1989 $7 (6/30/91)
82 TORRES Penedès Sangre de Toro 1989 $7 (4/15/92)
82 MIGUEL TORRES Cabernet Sauvignon Curicó District 1989 $7 (6/15/91)
82 CHATEAU VAL JOANIS Côtes du Lubéron 1988 $7 (6/30/90)
82 L. DE VALLOUIT Côtes du Rhône St.-Vincent 1990 $7 (6/15/92)
82 VARICHON & CLERC Demi-Sec NV $7 (1/31/90)
82 LOS VASCOS Cabernet Sauvignon Colchagua 1988 $7 (6/15/91)
82 VEUVE DU VERNAY Brut Blanc de Blancs NV $7 (11/30/91)
82 WOODLEY Shiraz Cabernet Sauvignon South Eastern Australia Queen Adelaide 1988 $7 (2/29/92)
82 XENIUS Sparkling Cava NV $7.50 (7/15/90)
82 YALUMBA Cabernet Sauvignon Shiraz South Eastern Australia Oxford Landing 1989 $7 (2/29/92)
81 CHESTNUT HILL Cabernet Sauvignon California 1988 $7.50 (10/15/91)
81 CORBETT CANYON Merlot California Coastal Classic 1989 $7 (11/15/91)
81 BODEGAS EL COTO Rioja Crianza 1984 $7 (3/31/90)
81 ESTANCIA Sauvignon Blanc Monterey 1990 $7.50 (6/15/92)
81 TENUTA FARNETA Chianti di Collalto 1989 $7.50 (10/31/91)
81 LA FORGE Côtes du Lubéron Blanc 1990 $7 (11/15/91)
81 CHATEAU HAUT RIAN Premières Côtes de Bordeaux 1988 $7 (5/15/90)
81 PIERRE JEAN Bordeaux Blanc Blanc de Blancs 1990 $7 (6/15/91)
81 MIRASSOU Pinot Noir Monterey County Fifth Generation Family Selection 1988 $7.50 (4/30/91)
81 NAVARRO Chardonnay Anderson Valley Table Wine 1989 $7.50 (11/15/91)
81 RAVENSWOOD Zinfandel North Coast Vintners Blend 1988 $7.25 (10/15/90)
81 ROUND HILL Chardonnay California 1988 $7.50 (2/28/91)
81 ARMAND ROUX Côtes du Rhône La Berberine 1988 $7.50 (10/31/90)
81 CHATEAU ST.-SULPICE Bordeaux 1988 $7.50 (8/31/91)
81 TORRES Penedès Coronas 1988 $7 (6/15/91)
80 CHATEAU BONNET Entre-Deux-Mers 1988 $7 (5/31/90)
80 BODEGAS MARTINEZ BUJANDA Rioja Conde de Valdemar 1986 $7 (6/30/90)
80 EL DOMINO Jumilla 1990 $7 (4/15/92)
80 DUCKHORN Sémillon Napa Valley Decoy 1990 $7.25 (12/31/91)
80 ESTANCIA Cabernet Sauvignon Alexander Valley 1987 $7 (7/15/90)
80 CHATEAU LE GRAND VERDUS Bordeaux Supérieur 1988 $7.50 (10/31/91)
80 CHATEAU LAGRAVE PARAN Bordeaux 1987 $7 (5/15/90)
80 SANTA RITA Merlot Maipo Valley 120 1989 $7 (6/15/91)
80 BODEGAS JAUME SERRA Penedès 1985 $7.50 (4/15/92)
80 VALLFORMOSA Brut Cava NV $7 (12/31/90)
80 LA VIEILLE FERME Côtes du Lubéron Blanc 1989 $7 (4/30/91)

$8 & Over

89 CASETTA Barbera d'Alba Vigna Lazaretto 1987 $9 (3/15/91)
89 CHATEAU ST. JEAN Pinot Blanc Alexander Valley Robert Young Vineyards 1988 $9 (5/31/91)
89 ISOLE E OLENA Chianti Classico 1988 $9 (11/30/90)
89 LOUIS M. MARTINI Chardonnay Napa-Sonoma Counties 1990 $9 (3/15/92)
89 NAVARRO Gewürztraminer Anderson Valley 1989 $8.50 (4/30/91)
89 SANTA CAROLINA Chardonnay Maipo Valley Santa Rosa Vineyard Reserva 1990 $8 (6/15/92)
88 BON MARCHE Chardonnay Alexander Valley 1989 $8 (3/31/91)
88 CHATEAU SOUVERAIN Chardonnay Sonoma County Barrel Fermented 1990 $10 (12/31/91)
88 COLUMBIA CREST Cabernet Sauvignon Columbia Valley 1986 $8 (1/31/91)
88 ESTANCIA Chardonnay Monterey 1990 $9 (2/15/92)
88 GEYSER PEAK Semchard California 1990 $8 (9/15/91)
88 GEYSER PEAK Cabernet Sauvignon Sonoma County 1987 $8.50 (11/30/90)
88 WEINGUT GRAFSCHAFT LEININGEN Riesling Kabinett Rheinpfalz Kirchheimer Schwarzerde 1990 $9 (12/15/91)
88 HEDGES Cabernet Merlot Columbia Valley 1990 $9 (6/15/92)
88 MARCHESI DI BAROLO Dolcetto d'Alba Madonna di Como 1989 $9 (12/31/90)
88 ELIA PASQUERO Barbera d'Alba Sorì Paitin 1989 $10 (11/30/91)
88 RIDGE Zinfandel Sonoma County 1988 $8.50 (2/15/91)
88 TALOSA Chianti Colli Senesi 1988 $8 (11/30/90)
88 TYRRELL'S Cabernet Sauvignon Merlot Hunter Valley 1986 $8 (1/31/90)
88 STEPHEN ZELLERBACH Chardonnay Sonoma County 1988 $8 (4/15/90)
87 BLACK MOUNTAIN Petite Sirah Alexander Valley Bosun Crest 1987 $8.50 (10/31/91)
87 BON MARCHE Cabernet Sauvignon Alexander Valley 1989 $8 (2/28/91)
87 BONNY DOON Grenache California Clos de Gilroy 1990 $8 (2/15/91)
87 GEORGES DUBOEUF Morgon Jean Descombes 1990 $9 (9/30/91)
87 GEORGES DUBOEUF Beaujolais-Villages 1989 $8 (11/15/90)
87 GEYSER PEAK Semchard California 1989 $8 (2/15/91)
87 HARDY'S Chardonnay South Australia Nottage Hill 1991 $8 (5/31/92)
87 CHARLES KRUG Pinot Noir Carneros 1987 $8.50 (2/28/91)
87 MARIETTA Zinfandel Sonoma County 1988 $8 (12/31/91)
87 MERIDIAN Chardonnay Santa Barbara County 1990 $9.75 (1/31/92)
87 JOSEPH PHELPS Grenache Rosé California Vin du Mistral 1990 $9 (6/15/91)
87 STRATFORD Chardonnay California 1989 $10 (7/15/91)
87 TRIMBACH Pinot Blanc Alsace 1988 $8 (11/15/90)
87 UNDURRAGA Cabernet Sauvignon Maipo Valley Reserve Selection 1987 $8 (6/15/92)
87 VARICHON & CLERC Blanc de Blancs 1989 $9 (3/31/92)
87 LA VIEILLE FERME Côtes du Rhône Réserve 1989 $9 (3/15/91)
87 WATERBROOK Chardonnay Columbia Valley 1990 $8 (4/30/92)
86 ALTESINO Rosso di Altesino 1989 $8 (1/31/92)
86 CARNEROS CREEK Chardonnay Carneros Fleur de Carneros 1989 $9 (6/30/91)
86 CLINE Sémillon California Barrel Fermented 1990 $9 (12/31/91)
86 COLUMBIA CREST Merlot Columbia Valley 1987 $8 (9/30/90)
86 GERARD GELIN Beaujolais-Villages Domaine des Nugues 1989 $8 (11/15/90)
86 GLASS MOUNTAIN QUARRY Chardonnay Napa Valley 1989 $8 (9/15/91)
86 HESS SELECT Chardonnay California 1990 $9.50 (12/15/91)
86 HILL-SMITH Shiraz Barossa Valley 1986 $9 (2/28/91)
86 MAACAMA CREEK Cabernet Sauvignon Sonoma County Melim Vineyard 1989 $8 (11/15/91)
86 MANZANITA RIDGE Chardonnay Sonoma County Barrel Fermented 1989 $8 (6/30/91)
86 MITCHELTON Shiraz Goulburn Valley 1988 $8 (3/15/91)
86 RODNEY STRONG Chardonnay Sonoma County 1989 $9 (7/15/91)
86 TAFT STREET Chardonnay Sonoma County 1989 $8.50 (7/15/91)
86 STEPHEN ZELLERBACH Chardonnay Sonoma County 1990 $9 (3/15/92)
85 CASTELLO BANFI Rosso di Montalcino Centine 1987 $8 (6/15/90)
85 BELVEDERE Zinfandel Dry Creek Valley 1989 $9 (5/15/92)
85 BERINGER Zinfandel North Coast 1988 $8.50 (2/29/92)
85 BICHOT Bourgogne Château de Montpatey Pinot Noir 1989 $10 (6/15/92)
85 BLACK OPAL Cabernet Sauvignon South Eastern Australia 1987 $8 (2/28/90)
85 CHATEAU BONNET Entre-Deux-Mers 1990 $9 (7/31/91)
85 BODEGAS MARTINEZ BUJANDA Rioja Conde de Valdemar 1987 $8 (9/30/91)
85 CELLIER DE LA DONA Côtes du Roussillon-Villages 1988 $8.50 (10/15/90)
85 COLLAVINI Cabernet Sauvignon Grave del Friuli 1984 $8 (4/15/90)
85 CONCANNON Sauvignon Blanc Livermore Valley 1990 $8 (2/15/92)
85 JOSEPH DROUHIN Bourgogne Pinot Noir Laforêt 1989 $9 (4/30/91)
85 GEORGES DUBOEUF Régnié Domaine du Potet 1990 $8 (9/30/91)
85 ESTANCIA Chardonnay Monterey 1989 $8 (3/31/91)
85 BODEGAS FAUSTINO MARTINEZ Rioja Faustino VII 1988 $8.50 (1/31/92)
85 FREEMARK ABBEY Johannisberg Riesling Napa Valley 1990 $8 (4/30/91)
85 FREMONT CREEK Cabernet Sauvignon Mendocino-Napa Counties 1986 $8 (4/30/91)
85 GLASS MOUNTAIN QUARRY Cabernet Sauvignon Napa Valley 1988 $8 (10/15/91)
85 LOUIS JADOT Beaujolais Jadot 1990 $9.25 (9/30/91)
85 PIERRE JEAN St.-Emilion 1988 $10 (6/30/91)
85 J. LOHR Merlot California Cypress 1989 $8.50 (2/29/92)
85 MICHEL LYNCH Bordeaux Blanc 1990 $8 (10/15/91)
85 LOUIS M. MARTINI Pinot Noir Los Carneros 1988 $8 (7/15/91)
85 LOUIS METAIREAU Muscadet de Sèvre et Maine Sur Lie Carte Noire 1988 $8 (11/30/90)
85 OLIVET LANE Pinot Noir Russian River Valley 1988 $9 (6/30/91)
85 J. PEDRONCELLI Cabernet Sauvignon Dry Creek Valley 1987 $8.50 (11/15/90)
85 BODEGAS PIQUERAS Almansa Castillo de Almansa Vino de Crianza 1985 $8 (9/30/91)
85 CHATEAU PLAISANCE Premières Côtes de Blaye Cuvée Spéciale 1989 $9 (2/28/91)
85 CASTELLO POGGIO Barbera d'Asti 1988 $9 (10/31/91)
85 LA RIOJA ALTA Rioja Viña Alberdi 1985 $8 (3/15/90)
85 SANTA RITA Sauvignon Blanc Maipo Valley Reserva 1990 $8.50 (10/15/91)
85 J. & H. SELBACH Scheurebe Qualitätswein Halbtrocken Mosel-Saar-Ruwer Brauneberger Klostergarten 1990 $8.50 (12/15/91)
85 STRATFORD Merlot California 1990 $9.75 (5/31/92)
85 DR. COSIMO TAURINO Salice Salentino Riserva 1985 $8 (2/15/91)
85 TIJSSELING Cabernet Sauvignon Mendocino 1986 $8 (1/31/90)
85 WYNDHAM Merlot Hunter Valley 1986 $8 (1/31/90)
85 STEPHEN ZELLERBACH Chardonnay Sonoma County 1989 $8.50 (11/30/90)
84 LAWRENCE J. BARGETTO Gewürztraminer Monterey County 1990 $8 (9/30/91)
84 BONNY DOON Malvasia Bianca Ca' del Solo Monterey 1990 $8 (6/15/91)
84 BONNY DOON Chardonnay California Grahm Crew 1989 $9 (9/30/90)
84 BRAREN PAULI Cabernet Sauvignon Mendocino 1987 $8.50 (3/31/91)
84 CODORNIU Brut Blanc de Blancs Cava 1988 $9 (12/31/90)
84 COLTERENZIO Chardonnay Alto Adige 1989 $8 (1/31/91)
84 DOMAINE STE. MICHELLE Brut Columbia Valley Champagne NV $9 (1/31/92)
84 JOSEPH DROUHIN Bourgogne Pinot Noir Laforêt 1988 $10 (3/31/91)
84 GEORGES DUBOEUF Côtes du Rhône 1990 $8 (12/31/91)
84 FOSSI Chianti 1988 $8 (10/31/91)
84 CHATEAU GOFFRETEAU Bordeaux Rouge 1989 $8 (5/15/91)
84 HOUGHTON Chardonnay Western Australia Wildflower Ridge 1990 $9 (11/30/91)
84 MAURICE JOSSERAND Mâcon-Péronne Domaine du Mortier 1988 $8 (12/31/90)
84 PETER LEHMANN Shiraz Barossa Valley 1987 $8 (4/15/91)
84 LUPE-CHOLET Bourgogne Blanc Chardonnay Comtesse de Lupé 1988 $9 (4/30/90)
84 DOMAINE DE MARTINOLLES Brut Blanquette de Limoux NV $8 (4/15/90)
84 PROSPER MAUFOUX Côtes du Rhône 1990 $8 (6/15/92)
84 MITCHELTON Marsanne Goulburn Valley 1990 $8 (6/30/92)
84 MOREAU Bourgogne Blanc Chardonnay 1988 $8 (4/30/91)
84 PARDUCCI Gewürztraminer Mendocino County 1990 $8 (3/31/92)
84 J. PEDRONCELLI Pinot Noir Dry Creek Valley 1988 $8 (2/28/91)
84 RAVENSWOOD Merlot North Coast Vintners Blend 1990 $9.50 (5/31/92)
84 RAVENSWOOD Merlot Sonoma County Vintners Blend 1989 $9 (3/31/91)
84 BARONE RICASOLI Chianti Classico San Ripolo 1988 $9.50 (10/31/91)
84 CASTELLO DI SALLE Montepulciano d'Abruzzo 1985 $15 (6/15/90)
84 MARK SWANN Chardonnay Victoria 1990 $8 (11/30/91)
84 DR. COSIMO TAURINO Salice Salentino Riserva 1986 $8 (1/31/92)
84 TYRRELL'S Shiraz Hunter Valley Classic 1986 $8 (1/31/90)
84 WEIBEL Cabernet Sauvignon Mendocino County 1987 $8 (2/28/91)
84 WHITEHALL LANE Chardonnay Napa Valley Le Petit 1988 $8 (4/30/90)
84 YALUMBA Tawny Port South Australia Clocktower NV $8.50 (4/15/91)
83 LAWRENCE J. BARGETTO Gewürztraminer Monterey County Dry Pinnacles Vineyard 1990 $8 (9/30/91)
83 BICHOT Bourgogne Croix St.-Louis Pinot Noir 1989 $9 (6/15/92)
83 ESTANCIA Chardonnay Alexander Valley 1988 $8 (4/30/90)
83 GEYSER PEAK Chardonnay Sonoma County 1990 $8 (3/15/92)
83 HARDY'S Cabernet Sauvignon South Australia Bird Series 1988 $8 (3/15/92)
83 HARDY'S Brut Australia Grand Reserve NV $8 (2/29/92)
83 HAYWOOD Chardonnay California Vintner's Select 1990 $8 (11/15/91)
83 INGLENOOK Chardonnay Napa Valley 1990 $8 (11/30/91)
83 KONOCTI Merlot Lake County 1988 $9.50 (3/31/91)
83 LUPE-CHOLET Bourgogne Pinot Noir Comte de Lupé 1988 $9 (2/28/90)
83 LUPE-CHOLET Crozes-Hermitage 1987 $8 (3/31/90)
83 MADDALENA Chardonnay Central Coast 1989 $8 (4/30/91)
83 DOMAINE DE MARTINOLLES Brut Blanquette de Limoux 1989 $9 (3/31/92)
83 MONTROSE Chardonnay South Eastern Australia Bin 747 1989 $8 (2/28/91)
83 OCHOA Navarra 1988 $8 (9/30/91)
83 PARDUCCI Chardonnay Mendocino County 1989 $9.50 (7/15/91)
83 R.H. PHILLIPS Chardonnay California 1990 $8 (7/15/91)
83 BODEGAS PIQUERAS Almansa Castillo de Almansa Vino de Crianza 1986 $8.50 (4/15/92)
83 BODEGAS PRINCIPE DE VIANA Cabernet Sauvignon Navarra 1989 $8 (3/31/91)
83 SANTA CAROLINA Merlot Maipo Valley Santa Rosa Vineyard Reserva Especial 1989 $8 (6/15/92)
83 SEAVIEW Brut South Australia 1988 $9.75 (11/15/91)
83 CHATEAU TROCARD Bordeaux Supérieur 1988 $8.50 (1/31/92)
83 UNDURRAGA Cabernet Sauvignon Maipo Valley Reserve Selection 1986 $8 (6/15/91)
83 ZENATO Valpolicella Classico Superiore 1988 $8 (4/30/92)
82 BOSCAINI Soave Classico Monteleone 1989 $8 (6/30/91)

82 BOUCHARD PERE & FILS Côtes du Rhône 1989 $8.50 (7/15/91)
82 CHATEAU DEMERAULMONT St.-Estèphe 1988 $10 (8/31/91)
82 DOMAINE NAPA Chardonnay California 1989 $8 (2/28/91)
82 JOSEPH DROUHIN Bourgogne Blanc Chardonnay Laforêt 1989 $9 (4/30/91)
82 ESTANCIA Chardonnay Monterey 1988 $8 (4/30/90)
82 FETZER Chardonnay California Sundial 1989 $8 (4/30/90)
82 GLASS MOUNTAIN QUARRY Rubis du Val Napa Valley 1988 $8 (10/31/91)
82 CHATEAU DE LA GRAVE Bordeaux Supérieur 1988 $8 (7/15/90)
82 PODERI DI GRETOLE Chianti Classico 1988 $8 (10/31/91)
82 CHATEAU LA GROLET Côtes de Bourg 1989 $9 (8/31/91)
82 CHATEAU LAGARENNE Bordeaux Supérieur 1988 $8 (7/31/90)
82 MASI Bardolino Classico Superiore 1988 $9 (5/15/91)
82 NICOLAS Beaujolais-Villages 1989 $8 (11/15/90)
82 R.H. PHILLIPS Cabernet Sauvignon California 1989 $8 (7/31/91)
82 BARONE RICASOLI Orvieto Classico Secco 1990 $8 (3/31/92)
82 DOMAINE ST.-CHARLES Beaujolais-Villages Château du Bluizard 1988 $8 (11/15/90)
82 SEAVIEW Cabernet Shiraz South Australia 1987 $8 (9/30/91)
82 BODEGAS JAUME SERRA Seco Cava Dry Cristalino NV $8 (2/29/92)
82 TAFT STREET Chardonnay Sonoma County 1990 $8.50 (3/31/92)
82 VILLA MT. EDEN Chardonnay California Cellar Select 1990 $8 (6/15/92)
82 WEIBEL Chardonnay Mendocino County 1989 $8 (3/31/91)
81 CASTELLO BANFI Rosso di Montalcino Centine 1988 $8 (12/15/91)
81 LAURENT CHARLES BROTTE Vin de Pays d'Oc Viognier 1991 $8 (6/30/92)
81 CAVE DE CHARDONNAY Mâcon-Chardonnay Chardonnay de Chardonnay 1988 $9 (7/15/90)
81 CHATEAU COUCHEROY Pessac-Léognan Blanc 1990 $8 (3/31/92)
81 FETZER Cabernet Sauvignon California 1988 $8 (1/31/91)
81 CASA GIRELLI Chardonnay Trentino i Mesi 1989 $8 (2/15/91)
81 GLASS MOUNTAIN QUARRY Petite Sirah Napa Valley 1988 $8 (10/31/91)
81 JAFFELIN Bourgogne Blanc Chardonnay 1990 $9 (7/31/91)
81 LOUIS M. MARTINI Cabernet Sauvignon Sonoma County 1988 $9 (4/30/91)
81 MOUTON-CADET Bordeaux 1988 $9 (4/30/91)
81 BARONE RICASOLI Orvieto Classico Secco 1989 $8 (4/15/91)
81 WEIBEL Cabernet Sauvignon Mendocino County 1988 $8 (3/15/92)
80 LUCIEN DESCHAUX Médoc 1990 $8 (1/31/92)
80 RESERVE ST.-MARTIN Minervois Mourvèdre 1989 $8 (12/31/91)

Tasting and Inventory Notes

WINE	VINTAGE	NOTES	RATING